ENCYCLOPEDIA OF
ASSOCIATIONS®

AN ASSOCIATIONS UNLIMITED REFERENCE

ISSN 0071-0202

ENCYCLOPEDIA OF ASSOCIATIONS®

AN ASSOCIATIONS UNLIMITED REFERENCE

A Guide to More Than 25,000 National and International Organizations, Including: Trade, Business, and Commercial; Environmental and Agricultural; Legal, Governmental, Public Administration, and Military; Engineering, Technological, and Natural and Social Sciences; Educational; Cultural; Social Welfare; Health and Medical; Public Affairs; Fraternal, Nationality, and Ethnic; Religious; Veterans', Hereditary, and Patriotic; Hobby and Avocational; Athletic and Sports; Labor Unions, Associations, and Federations; Chambers of Commerce and Trade and Tourism; Greek Letter and Related Organizations; Fan Clubs.

46th EDITION

VOLUME 1
NATIONAL ORGANIZATIONS OF THE U.S.

PART 3
NAME AND KEYWORD INDEX
Includes Association Addresses and Phone Numbers

Kristy A. Swartout, Project Editor

GALE
CENGAGE Learning

Detroit • New York • San Francisco • New Haven, Conn • Waterville, Maine • London

Encyclopedia of Associations, 46th Edition

Product Management: David Forman

Project Editor: Kristy Swartout

Editorial: Tara Atterberry, Verne Thompson

Composition and Electronic Capture: Gary Oudersluys

Manufacturing: Rita Wimberley

For product information and technology assistance, contact us at **Gale Customer Support, 1-800-877-4253.**
For permission to use material from this text or product, submit all requests online at **www.cengage.com/permissions.**
Further permissions questions can be emailed to **permissionrequest@cengage.com**

While every effort has been made to ensure the reliability of the information presented in this publication, Gale, a part of Cengage Learning, does not guarantee the accuracy of the data contained herein. Gale accepts no payment for listing; and inclusion in the publication of any organization, agency, institution, publication, service, or individual does not imply endorsement of the editors or publisher. Errors brought to the attention of the publisher and verified to the satisfaction of the publisher will be corrected in future editions.

EDITORIAL DATA PRIVACY POLICY: Does this product contain information about you as an individual? If so, for more information about our editorial data privacy policies, please see our Privacy Statement at www.gale.cengage.com.

Gale
27500 Drake Rd.
Farmington Hills, MI, 48331-3535

ISBN-13: 978-1-4144-2006-6 (vol. 1, 3-part set)
ISBN-10: 1-4144-2006-4 (vol. 1, 3-part set)
ISBN-13: 978-1-4144-2007-3 (vol. 1, part 1)
ISBN-10: 1-4144-2007-2 (vol. 1, part 1)
ISBN-13: 978-1-4144-2008-0 (vol. 1, part 2)
ISBN-10: 1-4144-2008-0 (vol. 1, part 2)
ISBN-13: 978-1-4144-2009-7 (vol. 1, part 3)
ISBN-10: 1-4144-2009-9 (vol. 1, part 3)
ISBN-13: 978-1-4144-2010-3 (vol. 2)
ISBN-10: 1-4144-2010-2 (vol. 2)

ISSN 0071-0202

Printed in the United States of America
1 2 3 4 5 6 7 12 11 10 09 08

Contents

Volume 1, Part 1: Sections 1-6

Foreword vii

Introduction ix

User's Guide xi

Abbreviations and Symbols xv

Keyword List xix

Descriptive Listings

  1. Trade, Business, and Commercial
     Organizations 1

  2. Environmental and Agricultural
     Organizations 483

  3. Legal, Governmental, Public
     Administration, and Military
     Organizations 629

  4. Engineering, Technological, and
     Natural and Social Sciences
     Organizations 749

  5. Educational Organizations 961

  6. Cultural Organizations 1159

Volume 1, Part 2: Sections 7-18

Introduction vii

User's Guide ix

Abbreviations and Symbols xiii

Keyword List xvii

Descriptive Listings

  7. Social Welfare Organizations 1393

  8. Health and Medical Organizations 1643

  9. Public Affairs Organizations 2057

  10. Fraternal, Nationality, and Ethnic
      Organizations 2271

  11. Religious Organizations 2331

  12. Veterans', Hereditary, and Patriotic
      Organizations 2461

  13. Hobby and Avocational Organizations 2537

  14. Athletic and Sports Organizations 2699

  15. Labor Unions, Associations, and
      Federations 2805

  16. Chambers of Commerce and Trade
      and Tourism Organizations 2829

  17. Greek and Non-Greek Letter Societies,
      Associations, and Federations 2849

  18. Fan Clubs 2885

Volume 1, Part 3: Name and Keyword Index

Introduction vii

User's Guide ix

Abbreviations and Symbols xiii

Keyword List xvii

Alphabetical Index to Organization Names
  and Keywords 2911

Volume 2: Geographic and Executive Indexes

Introduction vii

User's Guide ix

Abbreviations and Symbols xi

Geographic Index 4327

Executive Index 4765

The *Encyclopedia of Associations (EA),* Volume 1, is the only comprehensive source of detailed information concerning more than 25,000 nonprofit American membership organizations of national scope. For over fifty years and through 45 earlier editions, *EA's* listing of associations and professional societies is unsurpassed as a 'switchboard' connecting persons needing information to highly qualified sources.

Frequently, a phone call, fax, or email to one of the thousands of organizations formed around a specific interest or objective produces more information faster than research in books, periodicals, and other printed materials.

Organizations often operate with small, volunteer staffs. *Many such groups have requested that all written inquiries be accompanied by stamped, self-addressed envelopes.* Replies can then be expedited and costs to the organization kept to a minimum.

Preparation of This Edition

The editorial objective for each edition of *EA* is complete verification or updating of existing entries and the identification and description of new or previously unlisted organizations. This intensive effort includes direct contact by correspondence and telephone with non-responding groups.

Scope of the Encyclopedia

The organizations described in *EA* fall into the following seven general categories:

National, nonprofit membership associations, which represent the largest number of organizations listed;

International associations, which are generally North American in scope and membership or binational, representing a direct link between the United States and another country or region; also includes American or North American sections, chapters, or divisions of associations headquartered outside of the United States;

Local and regional associations, only if their subjects or objectives are national in interest;

Nonmembership organizations, if they disseminate information to the public as well as to the researcher;

For-profit associations, if their names suggest that they are nonprofit organizations;

Defunct associations, which appear only in the index with the appropriate 'defunct' annotation;

Untraceable associations, which are listed without address with the annotation 'address unknown since [edition year]' in place of contact information. (After requests for updated information have remained unanswered for two editions, these associations are listed in the index only, with the annotation 'address unknown.')

Available in Electronic Formats

Licensing. National Organizations of the U.S. is available for licensing. The complete database is provided in a fielded format and is deliverable on such media as disk or CD-ROM. For more information, contact Gale's Business Development Group at 1-800-877-GALE, or visit us on our web site at www.gale.com/bizdev.

Online. The complete *Encyclopedia of Associations (EA)* series (including associations listed in the international and regional, state and local editions) is available online as File 114 through The Dialog Corporation's DIALOG service and as File ENASSC through LexisNexis. For more information, contact The Dialog Corporation, 11000 Regency Parkway, Ste. 10, Cary, NC 27511, phone: (919) 462-8600; toll-free: 800-3-DIALOG; or LexisNexis, PO Box 933, Dayton, OH 45401-0933, phone: (937) 865-6800, toll-free: 800-227-4908.

Associations Unlimited. Associations Unlimited is a modular approach to the *Encyclopedia of Associations* database, allowing customers to select the pieces of the series that they want to purchase.

The four modules include each of the *EA* series (national, international, and regional) as well as one module featuring U.S. government data on more than 450,000 nonprofit organizations.

Associations Unlimited is available on a subscription basis through InfoTrac, Gale's online information resource that features an easy-to-use end-user interface, powerful search capabilities, and ease of access through the World-Wide Web. For more information, call 800-877-GALE.

The complete *EA* database is also available through InfoTrac as part of *Gale's Ready Reference Shelf.*

Acknowledgments

The editors are grateful to the large number of organization officials in the United States and abroad who generously responded to our requests for updated information, provided additional data by telephone, fax, email or website and helped in the shaping of this edition with their comments and suggestions throughout the year. Special thanks go to Jeannine M. James for her research contributions. Appreciation is also extended to the American Society of Association Executives for its ongoing support.

Comments and Suggestions Welcome

Matters pertaining to specific listings in *EA,* as well as suggestions for new listings, should be directed to Kristy Swartout, Editor, *Encyclopedia of Associations.*

Please write or call:
Encyclopedia of Associations
Gale
27500 Drake Rd.
Farmington Hills, MI 48331-3535

Phone: (248) 699-4253
Toll-free: 800-347-GALE
Fax: (248) 699-8075
Email: Kristy.Swartout@Cengage.com

Descriptive Listings

Entries in *EA* are arranged into 18 subject sections, as outlined on the Contents page. Within each section, organizations are arranged in alphabetical order, with numeric listings appearing first, according to the assigned principal subject keyword that appears as a subhead above the organization names. An alphabetical list of keywords used throughout *EA* follows the 'Abbreviations and Symbols' list. Within each keyword, entries are listed alphabetically by organization name.

Access to entries is facilitated by the alphabetical *Name and Keyword Index* found in Part 3 of this edition. An explanation of this index follows the discussion of the sample entry.

Sample Entry

The number preceding each portion of the sample entry designates an item of information that might be included in an entry. Each numbered item in the sample entry is explained in the paragraph of the same number following the diagram.

❙1❙ Storytelling

❙2❙ 3348 ■ **❙3❙** Association of Eclectic Storytellers **❙4❙** (AES)
❙5❙ 123 Amanda Ave.
PO Box 1992
Eldridge, NY 13201
❙6❙ Ph: (315)555-9500
❙7❙ Free: (800)555-2000
Fax: (315)555-9505
Telex: 123456
❙8❙ E-mail: harmersway@aes.org
❙9❙ Website: http://www.aes.org
❙10❙ Contact: Grant Smith, Pres.
❙11❙ Founded: 1950. **❙12❙ Members:** 150,000. **❙13❙ Membership Dues:** individual, $50 (annual). **❙14❙ Staff:** 15. **❙15❙ Budget:** $1,000,000. **❙16❙ Regional Groups:** 10. **Local Groups:** 20. **❙17❙ Languages:** English, Dutch. **❙18❙ Multinational. ❙19❙ Description:** Professional society of storytellers, focusing on storytellers that enjoy eclectic themes and others with an interest in this field. Promotes the study and tradition of storytelling. Conducts special programs for various types of audiences. Sponsors special seminars and courses on traditional forms of storytelling. **❙20❙ Libraries: Type:** lending. **Holdings:** 15,000; archival material, artwork, books, periodicals. **Subjects:** folktales, traditional stories, fairytales. **❙21❙ Awards:** Yaeko Abe Excellence Endowment. **Frequency:** annual. **Type:** monetary. • Michelle Eads's Founder Prize. **Frequency:** quarterly. **Type:** recognition. **❙22❙ Computer Services:** database on literature • publishing capabilities. **❙23❙ Telecommunication Services:** electronic bulletin board, (201)836-7569 • teleconference • teletype. **❙24❙ Committees:** Career Counseling; Cultural Studies; History of Stories. **Divisions:** Education; Literature. **❙25❙ Affiliated With:** Storytelling Institute. **❙26❙ Also Known As:** Story Time Society. **❙27❙ Formerly:** (1975) Storytelling Society of America. **❙28❙ Publications:** *AES News,* monthly. Newsletter. Contains happenings in the storytelling world, book reviews, and listing of seminars and courses offered. **❙29❙ Price:** $25. **❙30❙ ISSN:** 1234-5678. **❙31❙ Circulation:** 5000. **❙32❙ Advertising:** accepted. **❙33❙ Alternate Formats:** online. **❙34❙ Also Cited As:** *American Society of Eclectic Storytellers.* **❙35❙ Conventions/Meetings:** annual (with exhibits) - 2008 Sept. 14-16, Ypsilanti, MI; 2009 Nov. 1-9, Boulder, CO.

Description of Numbered Elements

❙1❙ Keyword. In each of the sections, keywords are given as subheadings and listed alphabetically. Organizations are listed in alphabetical order under their principal keyword subheading. Since the listings are arranged by keyword, the user will find organizations having similar interests grouped together within each keyword subheading.

❙2❙ Entry Number. Entries are numbered sequentially and the entry number (rather than the page number) is used in the Name and Keyword Index to refer to the organization. To facilitate location of the entries in the text, the first entry number on each left-hand page and the last entry number on each right-hand page are provided at the top outer corners of the pages.

❙3❙ Organization Name. The formal name is given; 'The' and 'Inc.' are omitted in most listings, unless they are an integral part of the acronym used by the association.

❙4❙ Acronym. Indicates the short form or abbreviation of the organization's name, usually composed of the initial letter or syllable of each word in it.

❙5❙ Address. The address is generally that of the permanent national headquarters, or of the chief official for groups that have no permanent office.

❙6❙ Telephone Numbers. These are listed when furnished by the organization.

▮7▮ **Toll-free, Fax, and Telex.** These are listed when furnished by the organization.

▮8▮ **E-mail.** This is listed when furnished by the organization.

▮9▮ **Website.** The primary web address for the organization or contact person listed.

▮10▮ **Chief Official and Title.** The name of a full-time executive, an elected officer, or other contact person designated by the association is provided.

▮11▮ **Founding Date.** Indicates the year in which the organization was formed. If the group has changed its name, the founding date is for the earliest name by which it was known. If, however, the group was formed by a merger or supersedes another group, the founding date refers to the year in which this action took place.

▮12▮ **Members.** The figure represents individuals, firms, institutions, other associations, or a combination of these categories. Since membership constantly fluctuates, the figure listed should be considered an approximation. If an organization describes itself as nonmembership, such notation is made in the entry preceding the descriptive text.

▮13▮ **Membership Dues.** Fees required of members as reported by the organization. Dues often vary according to membership category.

▮14▮ **Staff.** Many associations operate with a small paid or volunteer staff. The fact that an organization has no paid staff does not mean it has a limited program. Many groups carry on extensive activities through volunteer workers and committees.

▮15▮ **Budget.** The approximate annual budget for all activities is listed as reported by the organization.

▮16▮ **Regional, State, and Local Groups.** Indicates the number of regional, state, and local associations, chapters, clubs, councils, and posts affiliated with the national organization.

▮17▮ **Languages.** The official and/or working languages of the organization are listed, if other than English.

▮18▮ **Geographic Scope.** The boldface word **Multinational** indicates a multinational scope of the organization; otherwise, the geographic scope is assumed to be National.

▮19▮ **Description.** The description briefly outlines the membership, purpose, and activities of the association. Where no description is given, the title of the group usually is self-explanatory; in some cases, no summary of activities could be obtained.

▮20▮ **Libraries.** Provides information for organizations that maintain a library. Includes type of collection, holdings, and subject matter of collection, if available.

▮21▮ **Awards.** Provides information for organizations that offer awards. Includes name, frequency, type, and recipient of award.

▮22▮ **Computer Services.** Lists computer-based services offered by the organization, including online services and databases, bibliographic or other search services, automated mailing list services, and electronic publishing capabilities.

▮23▮ **Telecommunication Services.** Notes special communications services sponsored by the organization. Services included are hotlines, electronic mail/bulletin boards, and telephone referrals.

▮24▮ **Subgroups.** Lists those subgroups, including committees, sections, divisions, councils, departments, etc., that give an indication of the activities of the group, as distinguished from such administrative committees such as membership, finance, and convention. This information often supplements the description (see paragraph 19) by providing details about the organization's programs and fields of interest. Geographic divisions are omitted.

▮25▮ **Affiliated With.** Lists organizations sponsored by or directly related to the listed group. Organizations listed under this rubric can be found in *EA* or in *International Organizations*.

▮26▮ **Also Known As.** If the group is also known by another name, legally doing business under another name, or otherwise operates under a name different than its official title, that name is provided here.

▮27▮ **Supersessions, Mergers, and Former Names.** If the group superseded another organization or was formed by a merger, the original organizations are listed. Former names and the date of change to a new name, if available, are also listed.

▮28▮ **Publications.** The official publications are listed in alphabetical order with frequencies. When available, a brief description of the publication is provided. Additional publications, such as newspaper columns, are listed following the words 'Also publishes.' When provided, languages in which the publications are available are noted. If the group has indicated that no publications are issued, this is noted in the entry's main body.

▮29▮ **Price.** The figures are as provided by the organization.

▮30▮ **ISSN.** The International Standard Serial Number is a unique code for the purpose of identifying a specific serial publication. It is listed when provided by the organization; not all publications have been assigned an ISSN.

▮31▮ **Circulation.** This figure is as reported by the organization.

▮32▮ **Advertising.** Indicates whether or not the association accepts advertising in the publication.

▮33▮ **Alternate Formats.** Notes online, CD-ROM, diskette, and microform (includes microfiche and microfilm) availability.

▮34▮ **Also Cited As.** Lists any alternate or former names of the publication.

I35I Conventions/Meetings. The frequency of national or international sessions and the dates and locations (city, state, and country) of the association's conventions, meetings, or conferences are given, if available at the time of publication. Also noted is the inclusion of commercial exhibits. If the group has indicated that no conventions or meetings are held, this is noted in the entry's main body.

Name and Keyword Index

A comprehensive alphabetical Name and Keyword index is provided in Part 3 of this edition of the Encyclopedia. Note that *each reference refers to the entry number, rather than the page on which the entry is listed.* Alphabetization rules ignore articles, prepositions, and conjunctions. A collection of references in this index would appear this way:

I1I Amer. Soc. of Earth Sciences **[6359]**, 123 Salina St., Syracuse, NY 13201 (315)222-950
I2I Earth Sciences, Amer. Soc. of **[6359]**
I3I Earth Sciences Soc., USA **[★6359]**
I4I Geology
Amer. Soc. of Earth Sciences **[6359]**
I5I *Highways* Asphalt Recycling and Reclaiming Assn **[3728]**
I6I Natl. Soc. of Constitutional Training —Address unknown since 1988
I7I Soc. for the Advancement of Space Travel—Defunct
I8I Turkish Air Assn. **[IO]**

Description of Numbered Index References

I1I Each association's primary reference includes the mailing address and telephone number of the group.
I2I Associations are alphabetized by important words in the name. These references aid in locating organizations whose correct name is unknown to the user.
I3I Any reference with a ★ preceding the entry number indicates that the organization is not listed separately, but is mentioned within the description of another entry. These references would include the organization's former or alternate name as well as names of important committees, projects, or programs.
I4I Associations appear alphabetically by primary and added keywords (see keyword list in this volume). These references allow the user to access all organizations within a particular field of interest.
I5I Keywords that are italicized are added keywords and do not appear as subject headings within a section.
I6I Organizations that are untraceable are noted as 'address unknown.'
I7I Defunct associations are listed as such.
I8I This index includes references to associations listed in the *Encyclopedia of Associations: International Organizations.*

Geographic Index

Entries in *EA*'s Geographic Index are listed according to the state in which the organization's headquarters are located. They are then sub-arranged by city and listed alphabetically according to the names of the organizations within each city.

A sample entry is shown below.

I1I Amer. Soc. of Earth Sciences **I2I** [3348]
I3I 123 Salina St.
PO Box 1992
Allen Park, NY 13201
I4I Ph: (315)555-9500
I5I Patsy, Mrs. Rachel, Pres.

Description of Numbered Elements

I1I Organization Name. The formal name is given; 'The' and 'Inc.' are omitted in most listings, unless they are an integral part of the acronym used by the association.
I2I Entry Number. Refers to the sequential entry number (rather than the page number) assigned to the organization's main entry in Volume 1, where other details concerning membership, objectives and activities, and publications can be found.
I3I Address. The address is generally that of the permanent national headquarters, or of the chief official for groups that have no permanent offices. The city appears in **boldface.**
I4I Telephone Number. A telephone number is listed when furnished by the organization.
I5I Chief Official and Title. Lists the name of a full-time executive, an elected officer, or other contact person designated by the association.

Executive Index

Entries in *EA*'s Executive Index are listed alphabetically according to the surname of the chief executive of the organization. When an individual is listed as the chief executive of more than one organization, entries are arranged by organization name.

A sample entry is shown below.

I1I Patsy, Mrs. Rachel, Pres.
I2I Amer. Soc. of Earth Sciences **I3I** [3348]
I4I 123 Salina St.
PO Box 1992
Allen Park, NY 13201
I5I Ph: (315)555-9500

Description of Numbered Elements

I1I Chief Official and Title. Lists the name of a full-time executive, an elected officer, or other contact person designated by the association.
I2I Organization Name. The formal name is given; 'The' and 'Inc.' are omitted in most listings, unless they are an integral part of the acronym used by the association.
I3I Entry Number. Refers to the sequential entry number (rather than the page number) assigned to the organization's main entry in Volume 1, where other details concerning membership, objectives and activities, and publications can be found.
I4I Address. The address is generally that of the permanent national headquarters, or of the chief official for groups that have no permanent offices.
I5I Telephone Number. A telephone number is listed when furnished by the organization.

Geographic Abbreviations

United States and U.S. Territories

AK	Alaska
AL	Alabama
AR	Arkansas
AZ	Arizona
CA	California
CO	Colorado
CT	Connecticut
DC	District of Columbia
DE	Delaware
FL	Florida
GA	Georgia
GU	Guam
HI	Hawaii
IA	Iowa
ID	Idaho
IL	Illinois
IN	Indiana
KS	Kansas
KY	Kentucky
LA	Louisiana
MA	Massachusetts
MD	Maryland
ME	Maine
MI	Michigan
MN	Minnesota
MO	Missouri
MS	Mississippi
MT	Montana
NC	North Carolina
ND	North Dakota
NE	Nebraska
NH	New Hampshire
NJ	New Jersey
NM	New Mexico
NV	Nevada
NY	New York
OH	Ohio
OK	Oklahoma
OR	Oregon
PA	Pennsylvania
PR	Puerto Rico
RI	Rhode Island
SC	South Carolina
SD	South Dakota
TN	Tennessee
TX	Texas
UT	Utah
VA	Virginia
VI	Virgin Islands
VT	Vermont
WA	Washington
WI	Wisconsin
WV	West Virginia
WY	Wyoming

Table of Abbreviations Used in Addresses and the Index

Acad	Academy
AFB	Air Force Base
Amer	American
APO	Army Post Office
Apt	Apartment
Assn	Association
Ave	Avenue
Bd	Board
Bldg	Building
Blvd	Boulevard
Br	Branch
Bur	Bureau
c/o	Care of
Co	Company
Coll	College
Comm	Committee
Commn	Commission
Conf	Conference
Confed	Confederation
Cong	Congress
Corp	Corporation
Coun	Council
Ct	Court
Dept	Department
Div	Division
Dr	Drive
E	East
Expy	Expressway
Fed	Federation
Fl	Floor
Found	Foundation
FPO	Fleet Post Office
Ft	Fort
Fwy	Freeway
Govt	Government
GPO	General Post Office
Hwy	Highway
Inc	Incorporated
Inst	Institute
Intl	International
Ln	Lane
Ltd	Limited
Mfrs	Manufacturers
Mgt	Management
Mt	Mount
N	North
Natl	National
NE	Northeast
No	Number
NW	Northwest
Pkwy	Parkway
Pl	Place
PO	Post Office
Prof	Professor
Rd	Road
RD	Rural Delivery
RFD	Rural Free Delivery
Rm	Room
RR	Rural Route
Rte	Route
S	South
SE	Southeast
Sect	Section
Soc	Society

Sq	Square	Subcommn	Subcommission	UN	United Nations
St	Saint, Street	SW	Southwest	Univ	University
Sta	Station	Terr	Terrace, Territory	U.S.	United States
Ste	Sainte, Suite	Tpke	Turnpike	U.S.A.	United States of America
Subcomm	Subcommittee	T.V.	Television	W	West

Currency Abbreviations and Definitions

Arranged by Currency Abbreviation

Abbr.	Currency Unit	Country
$	U.S. dollar	American Samoa, British Virgin Islands, Guam, Marshall Islands, Federated States of Micronesia, U.S.
$A	Australian dollar	Australia, Kiribati, Nauru, Norfolk Island, Tuvalu
$B	Belizean dollar	Belize
$b	boliviano	Bolivia
$F	Fijian dollar	Fiji
œ	pound sterling	England, Northern Ireland, Scotland, Wales
œC	Cyprus pound	Cyprus
œE	Egyptian pound	Egypt
œG	Gibraltar pound	Gibraltar
œS	Sudanese pound	Sudan
Syr	Syrian pound	Syria
A	Argentinian austral	Argentina
Af	afghani	Afghanistan
AF	Aruban florin	Aruba
AS	Austrian Schilling	Austria
B	balboa	Panama
B$	Bahamian dollar	Bahamas
BD	Bahraini dinar	Bahrain
BD$	Barbados dollar	Barbados
BFr	Belgian franc	Belgium
Bht	baht	Thailand
Bm$	Bermuda dollar	Bermuda
Br$	Brunei dollar	Brunei Darussalam
Bs	bolivar	Venezuela
C	colon	Costa Rica, El Salvador
Cd	cedi	Ghana
C$	Canadian dollar	Canada
C$	new cordoba	Nicaragua
CFP	Colonial Francs Pacifique	New Caledonia
ChP	Chilean peso	Chile
CI$	Cayman Island dollar	Cayman Islands
CoP	Colombian peso	Colombia
Cr$	cruzado	Brazil
CRs	Ceylon rupee	Sri Lanka
CuP	Cuban peso	Cuba
D	dalasi	Gambia
DA	dinar	Algeria
Db	dobra	Sao Tome and Principe
DFr	Djibouti franc	Djibouti
Dg	dong	Vietnam
Dh	dirham	Morocco
Din	dinar	Bosnia-Hercegovina, Croatia, Macedonia, Slovenia, Yugoslavia
DKr	Danish krone	Denmark, Faroe Islands, Greenland
DM	Deutsche Mark	Germany
DP	Dominican peso	Dominican Republic
Dr	drachma	Greece
Ec	escudo	Cape Verde
EC$	East Caribbean dollar	Antigua-Barbuda, Dominica, Grenada, Montserrat, St.Christopher-Nevis, St. Lucia, St. Vincent and the Grenadines
ECU	European currency unit	European Economic Community
E$	Ethiopian birr	Ethiopia
Eg	emalangeni	Swaziland
Esc	escudo	Portugal
EUR	Euro	Austria, Belgium, Finland, France, Germany, Greece, Ireland, Italy, Luxembourg, Netherlands, Portugal, Spain
f	florin	Netherlands
FM	Finnish mark	Finland
Fr	franc	Andorra, France, French Guiana, Guadeloupe, Martinique, Monaco, Reunion Island, St. Pierre and Miquelon
FrB	Burundi franc	Burundi
Fr CFA	Communaute Financiere Africaine franc	Benin, Burkina Faso, Cameroon, Central African Republic, Chad, Comoros, Congo, Cote d'Ivoire, Equatorial Guinea, Gabon, Mali, Niger, Senegal, Togo
Ft	forint	Hungary
G	gourde	Haiti
GBP	Guinea-Bissau peso	Guinea-Bissau
G$	Guyana dollar	Guyana
GFr	Guinea franc	Guinea
Gs	guarani	Paraguay
HK$	Hong Kong dollar	Hong Kong
ID	Iraqi dinar	Iraq
IKr	Icelandic krona	Iceland
IRœ	Irish pound	Republic of Ireland
IS	Israel shekel	Israel
It	inti	Peru
J$	Jamaican dollar	Jamaica
JD	Jordanian dinar	Jordan
K	kina	Papua New Guinea
K	new kip	Laos
Kcs	koruna	Czech Republic, Slovakia
KD	Kuwaiti dinar	Kuwait
KSh	Kenyan shilling	Kenya
Ky	kyat	Myanmar (Burma)
Kz	kwanza	Angola
L	leu	Romania
L$	Liberian dollar	Liberia
LD	Libyan dinar	Libya
Le	leone	Sierra Leone
LFr	Luxembourg franc	Luxembourg
Lk	lek	Albania
Lp	lempira	Honduras
L£	Lebanese pound	Lebanon
Lr	lira	Italy, San Marino
Lv	leva	Bulgaria
M$	Malaysian dollar	Malaysia
MFr	Malagasy franc	Madagascar
MKw	Malawi kwacha	Malawi
Ml	maloti	Lesotho
ML	Maltese lira	Malta

MP	Mexican peso	Mexico
MRs	Mauritius rupee	Mauritius
MRu	Maldivian rufiya	Maldives
Mt	metical	Mozambique
N	naira	Nigeria
NAf	Antillean florin	Netherlands Antilles
Ng	ngultrum	Bhutan
NKr	Norwegian krone	Norway
NP	nuevo peso	Uruguay
NRs	Nepalese rupee	Nepal
NTs	New Taiwanese dollar	Taiwan
NZ$	New Zealand dollar	Cook Islands, New Zealand, Niue
Og	ouguiya	Mauritania
P	pula	Botswana
PP	Philippine peso	Philippines
PRs	Pakistan rupee	Pakistan
Ptas	peseta	Spain
Ptcs	pataca	Macao
Q	quetzal	Guatemala
QRl	riyal	Qatar
R	rand	South Africa, Namibia
Rb	ruble	Armenia, Azerbaijan, Belarus, Estonia, Georgia, Kazakhstan, Kirgizstan, Latvia, Lithuania, Moldova, Russia, Tajikstan, Turkmenistan, Ukraine, Uzbekistan
RFr	Rwandan franc	Rwanda
riel	riel	Cambodia
Rl	Iranian rial	Iran
Rlo	rial Omani	Oman
Rp	rupiah	Indonesia
Rs	rupee	India
S	sucre	Ecuador
S$	Singapore dollar	Singapore
Sf	Suriname florin	Suriname
SFr	Swiss franc	Switzerland, Liechtenstein
SI$	Solomon Island dollar	Soloman Islands
SKr	Swedish krona	Sweden
SRl	Saudi riyal	Saudi Arabia
SRs	Seychelles rupee	Seychelles
SSh	Somali shilling	Somalia
T$	pa'anga	Tonga
TD	Tunisian dinar	Tunisia
Tg	tugrik	Mongolia
Tk	taka	Bangladesh
TL	Turkish lira	Turkey
TSh	Tanzanian shilling	Tanzania
TT$	Trinidad and Tobagoan dollar	Trinidad and Tobago
USh	Ugandan shilling	Uganda
V	vatu	Vanuatu
W	won	Democratic People's Republic of Korea, Republic of Korea
Y	yen	Japan
YRl	Yemen rial	Yemen
Yu	yuan	People's Republic of China
Z	Zaire	Zaire
Z$	Zimbabwe dollar	Zimbabwe
ZKw	Zambian kwacha	Zambia
Zl	zloty	Poland

Following is a list of keywords used in EA. The section(s) in which each keyword appears are listed after each keyword. Within each keyword, entries are arranged alphabetically by organization name.

Abortion 7, 8, 9
Academic Freedom 5
Academic Placement 5
Accounting 1, 3, 8, 9, 17
Accreditation 5, 7, 8, 9
Acid Maltase Deficiency 8
Acoustics 4
Acquisitions 1
Acrobatics 14
Actors 1, 18
Acupuncture 8
Adhesives 1
Adirondacks 6
Administration 5
Administrative Services 1, 3, 15
Admissions 5
Adoption 7
Adult Education 5, 17
Adventist 7, 11
Advertising 1, 5, 13, 17
Advertising Auditors 1
Aerobics 14
Aerospace 1, 4, 5, 6, 12, 13, 14
Aerospace Medicine 8
Afghan 16
Afghanistan 6, 7, 9
Africa 1, 7, 9
African 5, 6, 10
African-American . . .1, 3, 4, 5, 6, 7, 9, 10
Agents 1
Aging 7, 8
Agribusiness 2
Agricultural Development 2
Agricultural Education 2, 5, 17
Agricultural Engineering 17
Agricultural Equipment 1, 2
Agricultural Law 3
Agricultural Science 2
Agriculture 1, 2, 3, 4, 9, 15, 17
Agroforestry 2
AIDS 7, 8, 9
Aikido 5, 14
Air Force 3, 12
Aircraft 1, 6, 15
Albanian 9, 10

Alcohol 8
Alcohol Abuse 7
Alcoholic Beverages 1, 3, 9, 13
Alleghenies 6
Allergy 8
Alpine 16
Alternative Education 5
Alternative Lifestyles 8
Alternative Medicine 8, 11
Alternative Technology 4
Alumni 10, 17
Alzheimer's Disease 8
Amateur Radio 13
Ambulatory Care 8
Amegroid 6
American 6, 9
American Indian 9, 10, 11
American Legion 12
American Revolution 6, 7, 12
American South 6
American West 6
Americans Overseas 10
Americas 9
Amish 11
Amusement Parks 1, 13
Amyotrophic Lateral Sclerosis 8
Anarchism 9
Anatomy 5, 8
Andean 6
Anesthesiology 8
Anglican 5, 11
Anglican Catholic 11
Anguilla 16
Animal Breeding 2, 13
Animal Research 4, 8
Animal Rights 7
Animal Science 1, 2, 4, 17
Animal Welfare 2, 7, 8, 9, 11
Animals 2, 7, 8, 13, 18
Animation 6
Anthropology 4, 5, 17
Anthroposophical 11
Anti-Communism 9
Anti-Poverty 7
Anti-Racism 7

Antiques 1, 13
Antiquities 6
Aphasia 8
Apheresis 8
Apiculture 2
Appalachian 6, 10
Apparel 1
Appliances 1, 13, 15
Appraisers 1
Appropriate Technology 9
Aquaculture 2
Aquatics 5
Arab 5, 9, 10, 16
Arabic 5, 6, 10
Arbitration and Mediation 3, 7
Archaeology 4
Archery 14
Architecture 1, 3, 4, 5, 17
Archives 1, 6
Argentina 16
Armed Forces 3, 7, 10, 12
Armenian 5, 6, 10, 11
Arms 13
Armwrestling 14
Army 3, 12
Art 1, 6, 8, 13, 15
Art History 5, 6
Art Therapy 8
Artifacts 6, 13
Artificial Intelligence 4
Artificial Organs 8
Artists 1, 6, 9, 13
Arts 1, 2, 5, 6, 7, 8, 13, 17
Arts and Crafts 1, 7, 13
Arts and Sciences 6, 17
Arumanian 10
Asatru 11
Asbestos 1
Ascended Masters 11
Asia 9
Asian 3, 5, 6, 10
Asian Studies 5
Asian-American 6, 10, 15
Asian-Indian 16
Assault 7

Associations 1
Assyrian 6, 7, 8
Astrology 4, 13
Astronomy 4, 13
Atheist 11
Athletes 11
Athletics 14, 17
Atlantic 9
Attorneys 1, 3
Auctions 1
Audiology 3, 8
Audiovisual 1
Audiovisual Communications 1, 4
Australia 16
Australian 10
Austria 16
Austrian 6, 10
Authors 6
Autism 8
Autoimmune Disorders 8
Automatic Control 4
Automatic Identification 1
Automation 1, 4
Automobile 3, 9, 13, 14
Automotive 4, 15
Automotive Education 1, 5
Automotive Industries 1
Automotive Manufacturers 1
Automotive Services 1
Aviation 1, 2, 3, 5, 8, 15
Awards 1, 9, 10, 12
Badminton 14
Baha'i 11
Bail 1, 3
Bakery 15
Baking 1
Ball Games 14
Ballooning 14
Baltic 6, 9, 10
Bangladeshi 5
Banking 1, 3, 9
Banks 13
Baptist 11
Barbados 16
Baseball 14, 15
Basketball 14
Basque 6
Baton Twirling 14
Batteries 1
Bay of Pigs 12
Beatles 18
Beekeeping 1
Beer 13
Behavioral Medicine 8
Behavioral Sciences 4, 5, 8
Behcet's Syndrome 8
Belarussian 6
Belgian 6, 10
Belgium 16
Bengal 6
Bereavement 7
Bermuda 16
Beverages 1, 4, 8, 15

Bible 11
Bicycle 1, 7, 9, 13
Bilingualism 5
Billiards 1, 14
Biochemistry 4, 8
Bioelectrics 4
Bioelectromagnetics 4
Bioethics 4
Biofeedback 8
Biological Weapons 9
Biology 4, 5, 17
Biomedical Engineering 4
Biophysics 4
Biotechnology 1, 4
Bird 2, 7, 13
Birth Defects 8
Bisexual 9
Blacksmiths 1, 15
Blind 1, 8, 11, 14
Blood 8, 10
Blues 13
Boating 1, 3, 13, 14
Bocce 14
Body Therapy 8
Bodybuilding 14
Bone 8
Book Clubs 6
Books 1, 6
Boomerangs 14
Botany 4
Bottles 13
Bowling 1, 14
Boxing 14
Brazil 16
Brazilian 6
Breast Diseases 8
Breastfeeding 8
Brethren 11
Breton 6
Bridal Services 1
Bridge 1, 13
British 6, 10, 16
Broadcasters 1, 18
Broadcasting 1, 5, 6, 9, 11, 15, 17
Bronchoesophagology 8
Buddhist 6, 11
Building Codes 3
Building Industries 1, 4, 5
Building Trades 15
Bulgaria 9
Bulgarian 16
Burns 8
Burro 7
Bus 13
Business 1, 5, 16, 17
Business Education 5, 17
Business Products 1
Business Studies 1
Business Tourism 16
Business and Commerce 1, 16
Business, Minority 16
Butterfly 2
Byzantine 6

Cable Television 1, 3
Cadets 12
Californian 10, 12
Camping 14
Camps 14
Canada 12
Canadian 5, 10
Canals 6
Cancer 7, 8
Canoeing 14
Capital Punishment 9
Cardio-Pulmonary 8
Cardiology 8
Cardiovascular Disease 8
Career Counseling 1, 7
Career Education 5
Caribbean 3, 5, 6, 10, 16
Carousels 13
Carriages 1
Cartography 4
Cartoons 18
Cat 2, 13
Catholic 5, 6, 10, 11
Cattle 2
Cayman Islands 16
Celtic 1, 6, 10
Censorship 9
Central America 9
Ceramics 1, 4, 5, 6, 13
Cerebral Palsy 8
Chambers of Commerce 1, 16
Chaplains 11
Chariot Racing 14
Chefs 1
Chemicals 1, 9, 15
Chemistry 4, 5, 8, 17
Chess 13
Child Abuse 7
Child Care 1, 7
Child Custody 7
Child Development 7, 8
Child Health 7, 8, 9
Child Welfare 7, 8, 9, 11
Childbirth 5, 7, 8
Childhood Education 5, 17
Children 5, 6, 7, 11
Chile 16
Chimpanzee 2
China 9, 16
Chinese 4, 5, 6, 8, 10, 17
Chiropractic 1, 5, 8, 14
Christian 5, 11, 14, 15, 16
Christian Reformed 11
Christianity 9, 11
Church and State 11
Church of God 11
Churches 1, 11
Churches of Christ--Christian
    Churches 11
Circumcision 7
Circus 6
Citizenship 9
Civics 5, 9

Civil Defense 3, 9
Civil Engineering. 4
Civil Rights and Liberties 5, 7, 9, 12
Civil Service 3
Civil War. 12
Classical Studies. 5, 6, 17
Cleaning Industry 1
Clergy 11
Climbing 13, 14
Clinical Studies 8
Clowns. 13
Clubs 1
Coaching 1, 7, 14
Coal 1, 2, 4
Coast Guard 12
Coatings 1, 4
Coins 13
Collectibles 1
Collective Bargaining 15
Collectors 1, 13
Colleges and Universities 2, 3, 5
Colombia .16
Colonial 12
Color 1, 4
Coma 8
Combustion. 4
Comedy 18
Comics 5, 13
Commercial Law. 3
Commodities 1, 2
Commodity Exchanges 2
Communications . .1, 3, 4, 5, 8, 9, 15, 17
Community 6, 7
Community Action 7, 9, 10
Community Colleges 5
Community Development . . .1, 2, 3, 7, 9
Community Education. 5
Community Improvement 9, 14
Community Organization 7
Community Service 7
Compensation Medicine. 4, 8
Composers 6
Computer Aided Design 1
Computer Science 1, 4, 5, 17
Computer Security. 4
Computer Software 1, 4, 5
Computer Users. 1, 4, 9
Computers 1, 4, 5, 7, 9
Concrete 1, 2, 15
Conflict. 5, 9
Conflict Resolution 5, 9
Congregational Christian 11
Congress 3, 9
Congressional. 3, 9
Consciousness Studies 5, 8
Conservation 1, 2, 4, 9
Conservationists 7
Conservative 3, 7, 9
Conservative Traditionalists 9
Constitution 3, 9
Constitutional Law 3, 9
Construction 1, 3, 4, 5, 15
Consulting 1, 3, 8

Consumers 1, 3, 7, 9
Contact Lenses 8
Containers 1, 2
Contests .13
Continuing Education 5
Contractors 1
Cooperative Education 5
Cooperative Extension 3, 17
Cooperatives 1, 2
Coptic 10
Copyright .3
Cordage. .1
Corporate Economics 9
Corporate Law 3
Corporate Responsibility 7, 9
Correctional 1
Correspondence 13
Corrosion .4
Cosmetic Surgery 8
Cosmetology 1, 3, 5
Cosmology 4, 5
Cossack .10
Cost Estimation 4
Costumes .6
Cotton 1
Counseling 1, 5, 7, 8, 11
Country Music 18
County Government. 3
Court Employees 3
Crafts. 1, 5, 6, 13
Craniofacial Abnormalities 8
Craniosacral Therapy 8
Creative Education. 5, 9
Credit 1, 7, 9
Credit Unions 1, 3
Cricket. .14
Crime. .3, 7
Criminal Justice 3, 7, 9
Criminal Law 3, 9
Criminology 3, 7
Critical Care 8
Croatian 6, 9, 10, 16
Croquet .14
Crosby, Bing 18
Cryogenics 4
Cryonics 1, 8
Cryptography 13
Cryptology 4
Crystallography 1, 4
Cuba 9
Cuban 6, 10
Culinary Arts 1, 5
Cults .9, 11
Cultural Centers 6
Cultural Exchange 5, 6, 9, 10
Cultural Resources. 6, 7
Curling 14
Curriculum 5
Customs .3
Cycling. .14
Cyprus 16
Cytology 4, 8
Czech 6, 10

Dairies 2
Dairy Products 1, 2
Dance 1, 5, 6, 11, 14
Danish 6, 10
Daoist 11
Darts 14
Data Processing 4, 8
Deaf 7
Death and Dying 7, 8
Debt Collection. 1
Defense. 1, 4, 9
Democracy 3, 7, 9
Democratic Party 3, 9
Democratic Socialism 3
Demography 4
Denmark 16
Dentistry 1, 5, 7, 8, 17
Dermatology 8
Design 1, 4, 6
Detergent .1
Developmental Education 5
Diabetes .8
Disabilities 8, 14
Disabled 1, 5, 7, 8, 9, 14
Disabled Veterans 12
Disarmament 9
Disaster Aid 7
Disc Sports 14
Discipline .5
Disease 8
Disposable Products 1
District Attorneys. 3
Divine Science 11
Diving 14
Divorce. 7, 9
Do It Yourself Aids. 1
Dog 1, 2, 7, 12, 13, 14
Dog Racing. 14
Dollhouses 1
Dolls 13
Domestic Service 15
Domestic Violence. 7
Donors 8
Door 1
Down's Syndrome 7
Draft 3, 9
Drag Racing 14
Dramatics 17
Driver Education. 5
Drug Abuse 3, 7
Drug Policy 3
Drug Rehabilitation 8
Drunk Driving 9
Dutch 6
Dyslexia. .8
E-Commerce 1, 9
Eagles 10
East Timor 9
Eastern Europe 9
Eastern Orthodox 11
Eating Disorders. 8
Ecology 2, 4
Economic Development 1, 4, 7, 9

Economics 1, 2, 3, 4, 5, 6, 7, 9, 17
Ecuador 16
Ecuadorean 10
Ecumenical 11
Editors .8, 17
Education 1, 2, 4, 5, 7, 9, 11, 15, 17
Education Law 3, 5
Education Youth 5
Education, Alternative 4
Educational Advocacy 5
Educational Facilities 5
Educational Freedom 5
Educational Funding 5, 7, 9
Educational Reform 5
Educators 1, 5, 7
Egypt 9
El Salvador .9
Elections 1, 9
Electrical 1
Electricity 4, 8, 13
Electroencephalography 8
Electrolysis 8
Electromedicine 8
Electronic Publishing 1, 7
Electronics 1, 4, 15
Elevators 1
Elks 10
Elvis Presley 18
Email 4
Emergency Aid 8
Emergency Medicine 8, 15
Emergency Services 7, 8
Employee Benefits 1
Employee Ownership 1
Employee Rights 7, 9
Employers .1
Employment 1, 3, 7, 9
Endocrinology 8
Energy 1, 2, 3, 4, 9
Engineering 1, 4, 5, 7, 15, 17
Engines 1, 4, 13
English 5, 6, 17
English-Speaking 10
Entertainers 7, 18
Entertainment 1, 9, 10
Entertainment Law 3
Entomology 4
Environment 2, 4, 5, 6, 7, 9, 11
Environmental Education 2, 5, 17
Environmental Health 2, 4, 8, 9
Environmental Law 3, 9
Environmental Quality 1, 2, 15
Ephemera 13
Epidemiology 7, 8
Epilepsy 8
Episcopal 5, 11
Equal Education 5
Esperanto 5, 6
Estonia 16
Estonian .10
Ethics 1, 4, 7, 9, 11
Ethiopian .10
Ethnic Studies 6, 10

Europe 9
European 5, 6
Euthanasia 7
Evaluation 4, 5
Evangelical 11
Evangelism 11
Evangelization 11
Evolution 4
Exhibitors .1
Experiential Education 5
Exploration 4, 6
Explosives 1, 4
Falconry .14
Families 5, 7, 9, 11
Family Law 3, 7
Family Medicine 8
Family Name Societies 10, 12
Family Planning 7
Fan Clubs 13, 18
Farm Management 2
Farming 2, 7
Farriers 1
Federal Government 3, 9
Feed 1, 2
Feminism 6, 9
Fencing 1, 13, 14
Ferret 13
Fertility 8
Fertilizer 1, 2
Fibers .1, 4
Fibromyalgia 8
Fiction 18
Field Hockey 14
Film 1, 5, 6, 13, 15, 18
Film Industry 1
Finance 1, 5, 9
Financial Aid 5, 9
Financial Planning 1, 5, 7
Finishing .1
Finland 16
Finnish 6, 10
Fire Fighting 3, 13, 15
Fire Protection 1, 4
Firearms 1, 3, 4, 5, 9, 13
Fish 13
Fishing 3, 9, 13, 14
Fishing Industries 1, 2
Flag 1, 12
Florists 1
Flowers 2, 13
Fluid Power 4
Folk 6
Folk Dance 6
Food 1, 2, 4, 6, 7, 8, 9, 15
Food Equipment 1
Food Service 1, 15
Food and Drugs 3, 4, 9
Footbag .14
Football .14
Footwear 1, 15
Foreign Policy 3, 9
Foreign Service 3, 17
Foreign Students 5

Forensic Medicine 8
Forensic Sciences 3, 4, 8
Forensics .5
Forest Industries 1, 15
Forest Products 1
Forestry 1, 2, 4
Foster Parents 7
Fragrances 1
France 9, 16
Franchising 1
Fraternities and Sororities 10, 17
Free Enterprise 7, 9
Free Methodist 5
Freedom 3, 9
Freelance .1
French 5, 6, 10, 17
Friedreich's Ataxia 8
Friends 5, 11
Fruits and Vegetables 1, 2
Fuel 1, 2
Fundraising 1, 3, 7, 9
Furniture 1, 6, 15
Future 4, 5, 9
Futures 1
Gambling 3, 7, 9
Games 1, 13
Gaming 1, 5, 13
Gardening 1, 2, 13
Gases 1, 4, 8
Gastroenterology 8
Gastronomy 6
Gay/Lesbian .1, 3, 5, 6, 7, 8, 9, 11, 14, 16
Genealogy 6, 10, 12
Genetic Disorders 8
Genetics 2, 4, 8
Genocide 7, 9
Geography 4, 5, 17
Geology 4, 5, 17
Georgian .10
Geoscience 4
German 5, 6, 10, 17
Germany 9, 16
Gerontology 5, 7, 8
Gifted .5, 6
Gifts 1
Glass 1, 4, 13, 15
Goats 2
Golf 14
Gone With the Wind 18
Good Templars 10
Gourmets 1, 13
Government 1, 3, 4, 9
Government Accountability 3, 9
Government Contracts 1
Government Employees 3, 10, 15
Government Relations 1, 9
Grain .1, 2
Grandparents 7
Graphic Arts 1, 5, 6, 15
Graphic Arts Products 1
Graphic Design 1
Graphics .4
Graphology 1

Grass 2	Horse Driving. 14	Intelligence 9, 10, 12
Great Plains 6	Horse Racing 7, 14	Intercultural Studies 5
Greece. 16	Horseback Riding 13, 14	Interdisciplinary Education 2
Greek. 6, 10	Horses 1, 2, 7, 9, 13, 14	Interdisciplinary Studies 5, 6
Greek Orthodox 11	Horseshoes 14	Interfaith 11
Greyhound 2, 9	Horticulture 2	Interior Design 1, 5
Grounds Management 2	Hospice 8	Internal Medicine 5, 8
Guardians 1, 7	Hospital 8	International Affairs 9, 11
Guatemala 9	Hospitality Industries 1, 15, 16	International Cooperation 6
Guitar 13	Hotel Management 5	International Development 7, 9
Gymnastics 14	Housewares 1, 13	International Exchange 5
Hair 8	Housing 1, 3, 7, 9	International Health 7, 8
Haiti 7, 9, 10	Hovercraft 13	International Law 3
Hand 8	Huguenot 12	International Relations 7, 9
Handball. 14	Human Development 1, 4, 6, 7	International Schools 5
Handguns. 9	Human Engineering 4	International Standards 1, 16
Hardware 1	Human Life Issues 8	International Studies 5, 6
Hazardous Material 2, 4	Human Potential 6	International Trade 1
Head Injury 8	Human Relations 6, 9	International Understanding. 5, 9
Headache. 8	Human Resources. 1	Internet 1, 4, 7, 9
Health 5, 7, 8, 9, 17	Human Rights 3, 6, 7, 9	Interspecies Communication 4
Health Care 1, 7, 8, 9, 11, 15	Human Services 1, 7	Inventors 4
Health Care Products 1, 8	Humanism. 6, 9, 11	Investigation. 1, 3
Health Education 5, 7, 8	Humanistic Education 5	Investments. 1, 3, 16
Health Law 3, 8	Humanities 3, 5, 6, 7	Iran 9
Health Plans 1, 8	Humor 6, 13, 18	Iranian 1, 6, 9, 10
Health Professionals 1, 8	Hungarian 5, 6, 10	Iraq 8, 9
Health Services. 1, 8	Hungary. 9	Ireland 9, 16
Health and Beauty Products 1	Hunger. 7, 9, 11	Irish 6, 10
Hearing Impaired 7, 8	Hunting 13, 14	Irrigation 4
Heart Disease 8	Hydroponics 1	Islam 10
Heating and Cooling 1, 15	Hypertension 8	Islamic 1, 5, 6, 11
Hematology. 8	Hypnosis 8	Israel 5, 7, 9, 10, 12, 16
Hemochromatosis 8	Hypoglycemia 8	Israeli 5, 6, 10
Hepatology 8	Ichthyology 2, 4	Italian 5, 6, 10, 16
Herbalism. 8	Iglesias, Julio. 18	Italy 16
Herbs 1	Imaging Media 4	Jamaica 16
Herpetology 4	Immigration 3, 6, 7, 9, 11	Japan 16
Higher Education 5	Immunology 8	Japanese 5, 6, 10, 16, 17
Hinduism 6	Implements 13	Jazz 6
Hispanic 1, 5, 6, 7, 8, 9, 10, 15, 16	Independent Schools 5	Jehovah's Witnesses 11
Historic	India 6, 7, 9, 11, 16	Jewelry 1, 6, 10
Preservation 1, 2, 3, 4, 6, 9, 12, 16	Indian 5, 6, 7, 10	Jewish 5, 6, 7, 9, 10, 11
Historical Revisionism. 9	Indigenous Peoples 6, 9	Jewish Science 11
History 5, 6, 11, 17	Indonesia 16	Jordan 16
Hobbies 13	Industrial Design. 4	Journalism 5, 17
Hobby Supplies 1	Industrial Development 3	Journalists 7
Hockey 14	Industrial Education 5	Jousting 14
Holistic Medicine. 8	Industrial Engineering. 4	Judicial Reform 9
Holocaust 9	Industrial Equipment 1	Judiciary 3
Home 9	Industrial Security 1	Judo 14
Home Based Business 1	Industrial Workers 15	Juggling 14
Home Care 7, 8	Infants 7, 8	Juvenile 1
Home Economics 5, 7, 17	Infectious Diseases 8	Juvenile Delinquency 3
Home Exchange 13	Informatics 1	Karate 14
Home Study 5, 14	Information Management . . .1, 3, 4, 8, 11	Kart Racing 14
Homeless. 7, 11	Innovation 1, 4	Kite Flying. 14
Homeopathy 8	Inspectors 1, 3	Knights of Pythias 10
Homiletics 11	Instructional Media 5	Knives 1, 13
Honduras 9	Instrumentation 1, 4	Korea 9, 16
Hong Kong 16	Insurance. 1, 3, 5, 8, 10, 17	Korean 6, 7, 8, 10
Honor Societies 17	Integration 9	Korean War. 12
Hoo-Hoo. 10	Intellectual Property 3	Krishna Consciousness 11

Kurdish 9, 10
Labor 3, 5, 6, 9, 15
Labor Reform 9
Labor Studies. 15
Labor Unions. 1
Laboratory 1, 4, 8
Lacrosse 14
Laity 11
Lakes 4
Lamps 1, 13
Land Control 3, 7, 9
Landscaping 1, 2, 5
Language 4, 5, 6, 7, 17
Laser Medicine. 8
Lasers 4
Latin America 9, 16
Latin American 6, 9, 10
Latter Day Saints. 11
Latvia 9
Latvian. 10
Laundry 1
Law 3, 9, 17
Law Enforcement 1, 3, 9, 10, 15
Leadership 1, 5, 9, 10, 11
Learning Disabled 7, 8
Leather 1
Lebanese 9, 10
Legal 3, 8
Legal Aid 3
Legal Education 3, 5, 17
Legal Services 3, 7, 9
Legislative Reform. 3
Lending 1, 3
Lepidopterology 4
Leprosy 8
Liability 3
Libel .3
Liberal Arts. 5, 17
Liberalism. 9
Libertarianism. 3, 9
Libraries 3, 5, 6
Library Science 5, 17
Licensing 8
Lifesaving. 14
Lighting 1, 4, 6
Linguistics 1, 6, 8
Literacy 5, 7, 9
Literature 5, 6, 17
Lithuania 9
Lithuanian 6, 10
Livestock 2
Lotteries. 3
Lubricants 4
Luge 14
Luggage 1
Lupus Erythematosus. 8
Lutheran 5, 10, 11
Lymphology. 8
Macedonian 6, 10, 11
Machinery 1
Magazines 1
Magic 13
Magicians. 7

Mail .1
Mail Order 1
Maintenance 1
Malacology. 4
Malaysia. 16
Maltese 10
Mammalogy 2, 4
Management 1, 5, 17
Managers 1
Manufactured Housing 1
Manufacturers Representatives 1
Manufacturing 1, 4, 5
Manx. 10
Maoism 3
Marbles 13
Marijuana 8, 9
Marine 1, 2, 3, 4, 5, 6, 14, 15
Marine Biology. 4
Marine Corps 1, 3, 10, 12
Marine Industries 1
Maritime. 5
Maritime Law 3
Marketing 1, 2, 4, 5, 17
Marriage 1, 5, 7, 9
Martial Arts 1, 5, 8, 14
Marxism. 6
Masons 10
Massage 8
Matchcover 13
Materials 4
Mathematics. 4, 5, 6, 17
Meat 1, 2
Mechanics. 4, 5
Media. 1, 2, 4, 5, 6, 7, 9
Medical 8, 11
Medical Accreditation 5
Medical Administration 8
Medical Aid 7, 8, 11
Medical Assistants. 8
Medical Education 5, 8, 17
Medical Examiners 5, 8
Medical Identification 8
Medical Records 1, 8
Medical Research 8
Medical Specialties 8
Medical Technology 4, 8
Medicine 8, 17
Medieval 6
Meditation 6
Meeting Places 1
Meeting Planners 1
Membrane Science 4
Men .7
Men's Rights 9
Mennonite 11
Mental Health. 5, 7, 8, 9
Mentally Disabled 7, 8
Merchant Marine 3, 4
Messianic Judaism. 11
Metabolic Disorders 8
Metal 1, 15
Metallurgy 4
Meteorology 4

Methodist 5, 6, 11
Mexican War 12
Mexico. 16
Microbiology 4
Microscopy 1, 4
Microwaves. 4
Middle East 9, 10, 16
Middle Schools. 5
Migrant Workers 7, 9
Migration. 6, 7
Military . . .1, 2, 3, 5, 8, 9, 10, 12, 13, 17
Military Families 5, 7, 12
Military History 3, 6, 12
Military Law. 3
Military Police. 12
Military Sports 14
Millers. 1
Mineralogy 4
Minerals 1, 8
Mining. 1, 3, 4, 7, 8, 9, 15
Ministry 11
Minorities 1, 3, 4, 5, 6, 9, 10
Minority Business 1
Minority Students 5
Missing Children. 7
Missing Persons 7
Missing-in-Action 9
Mission 11
Mobile Homes 13
Model Trains 13
Models. 13
Mollusks 2
Monarchy. 9
Mongolian 6
Montessori 5
Moravian. 11
Morocco 10
Mortuary Science. 3, 5
Mortuary Services 1
Mosaism. 11
Motion Picture 1
Motorcycle. 1, 13, 14
Mouse 13
Multiple Birth 7, 8
Municipal Employees 3
Municipal Government 3
Musculoskeletal Disorders 8
Museums 6
Mushrooms 2
Music 1, 5, 6, 7, 11, 13, 17, 18
Musicians 1, 7
Muslim 6, 9, 10, 11
Mutual Aid. 10
Mycology 4, 8
Mysticism 11
Mythology. 6
Naprapathy 8
National Sovereignty 9
National Spiritualist. 11
Nationalism. 9
Native American.1, 2, 5, 6, 7, 9, 10, 14, 16
Natural Disasters 1, 2, 4, 7
Natural Family Planning 7

Natural Hygiene 8
Natural Resources 2, 3, 9
Natural Sciences 4
Nature Religions. 6
Naturopathy 8
Naval Engineering. 4
Navigation 4
Navy. 1, 3, 12
Needlework 1, 13
Nematology. 4
Neo-American 11
Nepalese. 5, 10
Nephrology 8
Netball. 14
Netherlands. 16
Netherlands Antilles 16
Networking 1, 4
Neuro-Ophthalmology. 8
Neurological Disorders. 7, 8
Neurology. 8
Neuroscience 4, 8
Neurosurgery. 8
New Age 1
New Zealand 16
Newspapers 9, 15
Nicaragua. 9
Nigerian 10
Noise Control 4
Nonprofit Organizations. 7
Nonviolence 5, 7, 9
Norwegian 6, 10
Notaries Public. 3
Notions 1
Nuclear 4
Nuclear Energy. 4, 9
Nuclear Medicine 8
Nuclear War and Weapons 3, 9
Nudism 6
Numismatic 13
Nurseries 2
Nursing. 1, 5, 8, 17
Nursing Homes 8
Nutrition. 1, 5, 8
Nuts 1, 2
Obesity 7, 8, 9
Obstetrics and Gynecology 8
Occupational Medicine 8
Occupational Safety and Health. . .1, 5, 8
Oceanography 4
Odd Fellows 10
Office Equipment 1
Officers 12
Oils and Fats 1, 4
Olympic Games 14
Oncology 8
Onomatology. 6
Opera 6
Operations Research 4
Ophthalmology. 8
Optical Equipment 1
Opticianry. 8
Optics 1, 4
Optometry 8, 17

Oral and Maxillofacial Surgery. 8
Orchestras 6
Organic Farming 1, 2
Organization Development 1, 4
Organizations 7
Organizations Staff. 15
Orgonomy 8
Oriental Healing 8
Orienteering. 14
Origami 13
Orioles 10
Ornithology. 4, 13
Orthopedics 5, 8
Orthotics and Prosthetics 7, 8
Osteology. 8
Osteopathic Medicine 8
Osteopathy 17
Otorhinolaryngology 8
Outdoor Education 5
Outdoor Recreation 1, 13, 14
Outsourcing 1
Pacific 6, 9, 13
Packaging 1, 4, 5
Paganism. 6, 11
Pain 8
Paintball 14
Paints and Finishes. 1, 15
Pakistan 16
Paleontology 4
Palynology 4
Pancreatic Diseases 8
Paper. 1, 4
Paperweights 13
Papyrology 6
Parachuting 14
Paralegals 3
Paranormal 1, 4
Parapsychology 4
Parents 5, 7, 9
Parking 1
Parks and Recreation. 2, 3, 9
Parliaments. 6
Parole 3
Patent Law 3
Pathology. 8
Patriotism 9, 12
Patristics. 11
Pattern Recognition 4
Peace 4, 5, 7, 9, 10
Peace Corps 9
Peat 4
Pediatrics 8
Pennsylvania Dutch 6, 12
Pensions 3, 7, 11, 15
Pentecostal 11
Performing Arts. 6, 9, 15
Perinatology 8
Personal Computers 7
Personal Development 5, 7, 8
Personnel 1, 5
Pest Control 1, 2, 3
Petanque 14
Petroleum 1, 4, 15

Pets 1, 7, 13
Pharmaceuticals 1, 4
Pharmacy 1, 5, 8, 17
Phenomena 4
Philanthropy 6, 7, 8, 9, 12
Philatelic 6, 13
Philippine 6
Philippines 9, 12, 16
Philosophy. 4, 5, 6, 8, 9, 17
Phobias 7
Phonetics 6
Photogrammetry 4
Photography. 1, 2, 4, 5, 6, 13
Physical Education 5, 17
Physical Fitness 1, 8, 14
Physical Therapy 8
Physically Impaired 7
Physician Assistants 8
Physicians 1, 7, 8
Physics 4, 5, 8, 17
Physiology. 4, 8
Pigeons 13
Pilgrims 12
Pioneers. 12
Pipe Smoking. 13
Pipes 1
Pituitary. 8
Placement 5
Planning 1, 5, 9
Plaster 1
Plastics 1, 4
Play 1, 6, 7
Plumbing 1, 15
Podiatry 8
Poetry 6
Poker 13
Poland 16
Polar Studies. 4
Police. 1, 3, 7, 15
Policy 9
Polio. 8
Polish 6, 10, 12
Political Action 9
Political Education. 7
Political Federations. 9
Political Items. 13
Political Parties 9
Political Products 1
Political Reform. 3, 9
Political Science 4, 5, 17
Politics. 3, 9, 12
Polls. 9
Pollution Control 1, 2
Polo 14
Polynesian 6
Popular Culture 6
Population 7
Pornography 7, 9
Portugal 16
Portuguese 4, 6, 10
Post-Traumatic Stress 7
Postal Service 3, 9
Postal Workers 15

Postcards 1, 13	Radiology. 8	Rural Education 5
Poultry 2	Railroads 1, 6, 13, 15	Russian. 6, 7, 8, 9, 10, 16
Poverty 7, 9, 11	Rain Forests 2	Russian Orthodox 11
Power 1, 4	Rangeland. 1, 2	Sabbath 11
Powerlifting 14	Rape 7	Safety 1, 3, 4, 7, 8, 9
Presbyterian 5, 6, 11	Reading. 5	Sailboarding 14
Preschool Education 5	Real Estate 1, 3, 5, 9	Sales 1
Press 1, 3, 5, 6, 13	Recordings 1, 6	Sand Castles 13
Preventive Medicine. 8	Recreation 1, 2, 7, 13, 14	Sanitarians 8
Principals 5	Recreational Vehicles 1, 13, 14	Sanitation 4
Prisoners 11	Recycling 2, 7	Satellite Dishes 4
Prisoners of War 12	Red Men 10	Scalp 8
Private Schools 5	Reform. 11	Scandinavia. 16
Privatization 1	Reformation 6	Scandinavian 5, 6, 10
Pro-Life 7, 9, 11	Refugees 7, 9, 10	Scholarship 5, 17
Probate Law 3	Regional Government. 3	Scholarship Alumni 10
Process Serving 3	Rehabilitation 1, 7, 8	Scholarships 5
Proctology 8	Reiki 13	School Boards 5
Product Testing 1	Relief 7, 11	School Security 5
Professionals 1, 4	Religion 4, 5, 7, 8, 9, 11	School Services 1
Professions 6, 10, 15, 17	Religious Administration 8, 11	Schools 5
Professors 5	Religious Freedom 9, 11	Science 4, 5, 9, 11, 17
Programming Languages. 4	Religious Science 11	Science Fiction. 6
Property 1, 3	Religious Studies 5, 11, 17	Scientific Cooperation. 4
Property Management 1, 5	Religious Supplies. 1	Scientific Products. 1
Property Rights 3, 4, 9	Religious Understanding 11	Scientific Responsibility. 9
Prospectors. 13	Renaissance 6	Scleroderma 8
Prostitution 9	Renting and Leasing. 1, 9	Scoliosis 8
Protestant. 10, 11	Repair. 1	Scottish. 6, 10
Psychiatry 8	Reproductive Health 8	Scouting 7
Psychoanalysis 5, 8	Reproductive Medicine. 8	Scuba Diving 14
Psychology 4, 5, 8, 14, 17	Reproductive Rights. 9	Sculpture 6
Psychopathology 8	Reptiles 2	Seafood 1, 2
Psychosomatic Medicine 8	Republican Party 3, 9	Seamen. 7
Psychotherapy 8	Rescue. 7, 9	Secondary Education 5
Public Administration 3	Research 1, 2, 4, 5, 8, 9, 11	Securities 1, 3
Public Affairs 3, 9, 17	Respiratory Diseases 8	Security 1, 3, 4, 7, 9, 15
Public Finance 3, 9	Restaurant 1	Security Training. 5
Public Health 3, 7, 8, 17	Retailing 1, 15	Seed. 2
Public Information 6, 9	Reticuloendothelial System 8	Seismology 4
Public Interest Law 3	Retirees 10	Self Defense 1, 7, 14
Public Lands 1, 2	Retirement 5, 7, 9	Selfhelp 7
Public Policy 2, 3, 9	Reye's Syndrome 8	Semantics 6, 8
Public Relations 1, 3, 5, 9, 11	Rheology 4	Semiotics 4
Public Schools. 5	Rhetoric. 6	Serbia 16
Public Speaking 5, 6	Rheumatic Diseases 8	Serbian 10
Public Welfare 3, 9	Right to Life 7, 9	Service 1, 5, 15
Public Works 3	Rights of Way 3	Service Clubs 7
Publishing 1, 8, 13, 15	River Sports 14	Service Fraternities 17
Puerto Rican 10	Robotics 4	Service Sororities 17
Puerto Rico. 9	Rodeo 14	Seventh Day Adventist 11
Puppets 13	Roller Coasters. 13	Sex Addiction 7
Purchasing 1, 3	Romania 9, 16	Sexual Abuse 7
Pyramidology. 11	Romanian 6, 10	Sexual Freedom. 5, 7, 9
Pyrotechnics 1	Romanian Orthodox 11	Sexual Health 8
Quality Assurance 1, 8	Romany 6, 10	Sexuality 5, 11
Quality Control 4	Rope Jumping 14	Sexually Transmitted Diseases 8
Rabbits 2, 13	Rosicrucian 10, 11	Shakers 6
Racing 3, 6, 13, 14	Rowing 14	Sheep. 2
Racism 9	Rubber 1, 15	Sherlock Holmes 6
Racquetball 14	Rugby 14	Shipping 1
Radiation 1, 2, 3, 4, 8	Runaways 7	Shooting 1, 13, 14
Radio 1, 9, 13	Rural Development 3, 5, 7, 9	Shortness. 7

Shuffleboard 14	Sports Law 3	Technology Education 1, 4, 5, 7
Sicilian. 10	Sports Medicine 8	Telecommunications 1, 3, 4, 8
Sickle Cell Anemia 8	Sports Officials 14	Telegraphy 13
Sikh 8, 11	Squash 14	Telemetry 4
Sinatra, Frank 18	Sri Lanka 16	Telephone Service. 1
Singles 7	Sri Lankan 10	Telephones 13
Skating 14	Standards 3, 4, 5, 9	Television 9, 18
Skiing 6, 14	Star Trek 18	Temperance 7
Slavic 5, 6, 10	Star Wars 18	Tennis 14
Sleep. 8, 9	State Government 3	Terrorism 9
Slovak 6, 10	States Rights 9	Testing 4, 5
Slovenian 6, 10	Stationery. 1	Textbooks. 5
Small Business 1	Statistics 4	Textiles 1, 4, 13, 15
Smoking 8	Steam Engines 13	Thanatology 7
Snow Sports 14	Stoker, Bram 18	Theatre. 1, 5, 6, 17
Snowshoe Racing 14	Stone 1, 13	Theology 5, 11
Soap Box Derby 14	Storytelling 6	Theosophical 11
Soccer. 14	Strategic Defense Initiative 9	Therapy 7, 8
Social Action 9	Stress 8	Thermal Analysis 4, 8
Social Change 1, 7, 9	Stress Analysis. 4	Thoracic Medicine 8
Social Clubs 10	Stress Management 8	Thyroid 8
Social Fraternities 17	Stroke 8	Tibet 9
Social Issues 7, 9	Student Services 5, 7	Tibetan 6
Social Justice. 3, 5, 7, 9	Students 5	Time 6
Social Responsibility 9	Stuttering 8	Time Equipment 1
Social Sciences 4, 7, 17	Substance Abuse 3, 5, 7, 8, 9	Timepieces. 5, 13
Social Security 3, 9	Subterranean Construction. 4	Tires 1, 4
Social Service 7, 11	Subud 11	Tissue 8
Social Sororities 17	Sudden Infant Death Syndrome 8	Tithing 9, 11
Social Studies 5	Sugar. 1, 2	Tobacco 1, 2, 8, 9
Social Welfare 3, 5, 7, 9, 11	Suicide 7	Touch-Healing 8
Social Work 5, 7	Summer School 5	Tourism. 1, 16
Socialism 3, 9	Support Groups. 7, 8	Toxic Exposure 7, 8, 9
Sociology 4, 9, 17	Surfing 14	Toxicology 4, 8
Softball 14	Surgery 8	Toys 1, 13, 15
Soil 2, 4	Surplus 1	Track and Field. 14
Soil Conservation 2	Surrogate Parenthood 7	Tractor Pulling 14
Solar Energy 4, 9	Surveying 1, 4	Tractors 13
Somalia 10	Survival 5	Trade 1
Sonography 8	Swedish 6, 10	Traffic 3, 9
Sororities 17	Swimming 14	Trails 6, 14
South Africa 9, 16	Swine 2, 13	Trainers. 1, 14
Southern Africa 16	Swiss 6, 10	Transgender 7
Southern Asians 9	Switzerland 16	Translation 1, 4, 6
Space 1, 4, 5, 9	Systems Integrators 1	Transplantation. 8
Spain 16	T'ai Chi 8, 14	Transportation . . .1, 3, 4, 7, 9, 13, 15, 17
Spanish. 6, 9, 10, 17	Table Tennis 14	Trapping 2
Spanish American War 12	Tableware. 1	Trauma 8
Spanish Civil War 12	Taiwan 5, 9	Travel 1, 2, 3, 5, 7, 12, 13, 16
Special Days 9, 13	Taiwanese. 10	Travel Services 1
Special Education 5	Tallness 7	Trees 1
Special Forces 12	Tangible Assets 1	Trees and Shrubs 2
Spectroscopy. 4	Tarot 13	Trial Advocacy 3, 5
Speech 5, 9, 17	Tattooing 1, 6, 11	Tropical Medicine 8
Speech and Hearing 7, 8	Tax Reform 9	Tropical Studies 4
Speleology 4	Taxation. 1, 3, 9	Trucking 7, 11
Spina Bifida 8	Taxidermy. 1	Trucks. 13, 14
Spinal Injury 8	Tea 2	Tug of War 14
Spiritual Life 6, 11	Teacher Education. 5	Turkey 9, 16
Spiritual Understanding. 5, 11	Teachers 5	Turkish 5, 6, 10
Sporting Goods 1	Technical Consulting 1, 4	Tutoring 5
Sports. 1, 13, 14, 15, 18	Technical Education 5	Twins 8
Sports Facilities 1, 14	Technology 1, 4, 5, 7, 8, 17	Ukrainian 6, 9, 10

Ultimatism 11
Ultrasound 8
Undersea Medicine 8
Underwater Sports 14
Underwriters 1
Unemployment 7
Unions 1, 4, 15
Unitarian Universalist 11
United Church of Christ 11
United Kingdom 5
United Nations 9
United States 16
Urban Affairs 5, 6, 7, 9
Urban Education 5
Urology 8
Ushers 11
Utilities 1, 3, 4, 15
Vacuum Technology 4
Vascular System 8
Vaulting 14
Vedanta 11
Vegetables 1
Vegetarianism 6, 7, 11
Vending 1
Venezuela 16
Veterans 3, 5, 7, 12
Veterans of Foreign Wars 12
Veterinary Education 5
Veterinary Medicine 8, 17
Vexillology 6
Victims 3, 7, 9
Victorian 6
Vietnam 16

Vietnam Veterans 3, 9, 12
Vietnam War 12
Vietnamese 5, 10
Violence 7, 9
Virgin Islands 2
Visually Impaired 5, 7, 8
Vocational Education 5, 17
Volleyball 14
Voluntarism 3, 7, 9
Waldensian 11
Walking 14
War Resistance 9, 12
War of 1812 12
Warehousing 1
Waste 1, 2, 3, 9
Water 1, 2, 5, 7
Water Conservation 2
Water Pollution 2
Water Polo 14
Water Resources 2, 4
Water Skiing 14
Water Sports 14
Weather 1, 7
Weather Services 3
Weighing 1
Weightlifting 14
Welding 4
Welsh 6, 10
West Indian 10
Wetlands 2
White Supremacy 9
Wholesale Distribution 1
Wiccan 11

Widowhood 7, 12
Wildlife 1, 2
Wildlife Conservation 2
Wind Energy 4
Window 1
Wine 1, 2, 13
Witches 12
Women . . .1, 3, 4, 5, 6, 7, 8, 9, 10, 11, 16
Women's Rights 7
Women's Studies 5
Wood 1, 13
Wood Trades 1
Woodmen 10
Workers 3, 7, 9
Workmen's Compensation 1
World Affairs 9
World Notables 6
World War I 12
World War II 7, 12
World Wars 12
World's Fairs 13
Wrestling 14
Wristwrestling 14
Writers 1, 6, 11, 13, 15, 18
Writing 5, 6
YMCA 7
YWCA 7
Yoga 6, 11, 14
Youth 1, 3, 5, 7, 9, 11, 16
Zoological Gardens 4
Zoology 4

Association names are listed alphabetically by name and by keyword subheading (in bold). Index numbers refer to entry numbers, not to page numbers. A star ★ before an entry number signifies that the name is not listed separately, but is mentioned or described within the entry indicated by the entry number.

NUMERIC

1/77 Artillery Veterans Assn. [★21342]
1/77th Artillery Vietnam Veterans Assn. [★21342]
1/87 Vehicle Club [22641], PO Box 2701, Carlsbad, CA 92018-2701
1-800 Amer. Free Trade Assn. [3950], PO Box 1049, Burlington, VT 05402-1049, (802)383-0816
1% for Peace - Address unknown since 1999.
1st Fighter Assn. [21414], c/o Pete Marty, Sec.-Treas., 107 Bear Crossing, Hampton, VA 23669-2009
1st Fighter Gp. Assn. [★21414]
1st Marine Div. Assn. [21171], 410 Pier View Way, Oceanside, CA 92054, (760)967-8561
2-Lane America - Defunct.
2id, Korean War Veterans Alliance; 2nd Infantry Div. [21167]
2nd Chance 4 Pets [11481], 1484 Pollard Rd., No. 444, Los Gatos, CA 95032, (408)871-1133
2nd Infantry Div. (2id), Korean War Veterans Alliance [21167], c/o Ralph Hockley, Sec., 10027 Pine Forest Rd., Houston, TX 77042-1531, (713)334-0271
2nd Infantry Division (2id), Korean War Veterans Alliance [IO], Houston, TX, United States
3-A Sanitary Standards Committees, Inc. [1125], 6888 Elm St., Ste. 2D, McLean, VA 22101, (703)790-0295
3-Wheel Auto Club of America - Address unknown since 2002.
3AI, Affiliated Advertising Agencies Intl. - Defunct.
3HO Found. [20631], 6 Narayan Ct., Espanola, NM 87532, (505)367-1326
3rd Infantry Div; Soc. of the [21186]
4-Cam Register for Porsches - Defunct.
4-H Agents; Natl. Assn. of Extension [13495]
4-H Club Agents; Natl. Assn. of County [★13495]
4-H Coun; Natl. [13494]
4-H Found. of Am; Natl. [★13494]
4-H Ontario [IO], Guelph, ON, Canada
4-H Prog. and Youth Development [★13483]
4-H Ser. Comm; Natl. [★13494]
4Children [IO], London, United Kingdom
4H [IO], Arhus, Denmark
4th Class Cancellation Club - Defunct.
4th Field Artillery (Pack) Assn. - Address unknown since 1999.
4th Infantry (Ivy) Div. Assn; Natl. [20703]
4th Marine Div. Assn. WWII [21361], 337 Redwood Rd., Venice, FL 34293-1124
5/20 Kite Group - Defunct.
5P- Soc. [★16534]
5Star Assn; AFBA, The [18955]
6th Bomb Gp. Assn. [21362], c/o Warren Higgins, 29277 Garrard Ave., Frontenac, MN 55026
6th Defense Battalion USMC and Defenders of Midway Islands Reunion Assn. - Address unknown since 1999.
7th Infantry Div. Assn. - Address unknown since 2003.
7th Step Found. - Defunct.
8mm Video Coun. - Defunct.
9 to 5, Natl. Assn. of Working Women [17512], 207 E Buffalo St., No. 211, Milwaukee, WI 53202, (414)274-0925
9 to 5 Working Women Educ. Fund [17513], 207 E Buffalo St., No. 211, Milwaukee, WI 53202, (414)274-0925

9/11 CitizensWatch [18727], c/o Kyle F. Hence, PO Box 1255, Newport, RI 02840, (401)847-1963
9/11 Families for a Secure Am. [18728], PO Box 156, Hawley, PA 18428-0156, (860)927-3822
9P; Support Groups for Monosomy [★14443]
9th Infantry Division Assn. - Address unknown since 2001.
10 Gigabit Ethernet Alliance [7372]
10th Foot Royal Lincolnshire Regimental Assn. Amer. Contingent Br. [★9373]
11th Airborne Div. Assn. [20684], 4218 N Cris Hollow Rd., Fayetteville, AR 72704-7435, (479)442-2222
11th Armored Cavalry's Veterans of Vietnam and Cambodia [21341], PO Box 1948, Plainview, TX 79073-1948
11th Bombardment Group (H) Assn. - Address unknown since 2003.
13th Airborne Div. Assn. [20685], c/o Robert deLisle, Treas., PO Box 1332, Tualatin, OR 97062-1332, (913)722-1143
14th Air Force Assn; Flying Tigers of the [21393]
15 Assn; Coronado [★23164]
15 Natl. Assn; Coronado [23164]
17th Airborne Div. Assn. [21363], PO Box 4793, Dowling Park, FL 32064-1508, (386)658-1292
17th Bomb Gp. Reunion Assn. [20652], c/o Ted Baker, Mgr., 453 Hamilton Ave., Almont, MI 48003-8620, (810)798-8758
18 Square Meter Sailing Assn. - Address unknown since 1999.
18th St. Arts Center [★9408]
18th St. Arts Complex [9408], 1639 18th St., Santa Monica, CA 90404, (310)453-3711
19th Hole Intl. - Address unknown since 2002.
20/20 Vision Natl. Proj. [18277], 8403 Colesville Rd., Ste. 860, Silver Spring, MD 20910, (301)587-1782
20-30 Assn. of U.S./Canada; Active [13032]
20-30 Intl. [★13032]
21st Century Democrats [5665], 1731 Connecticut Ave. NW, 2nd Fl., Washington, DC 20009, (202)626-5620
21st Century Stud; Inst. for [★17647]
22nd Bomb Gp. Assn. [21364]
23rd Psalm Card Collectors and Traders - Defunct.
24th Infantry Div. Assn. [20686], c/o Billy Johnson, Ed., 2416 Kimberly Dr., Fayetteville, NC 28306-2345, (910)424-3840
25th Infantry Div. Assn. [20687], PO Box 7, Flourtown, PA 19031-0007
27th Troop Carrier Squadron Found. [21365], c/o Off. of the Secretary, 15003 SE 46th St., Bellevue, WA 98006, (425)641-9427
29th Infantry Div. Assn. [20679], PO Box 1546, Frederick, MD 21702-0546
30th Infantry Div. Assn. [21415], c/o Frank W. Towers, Pres./Historian, 2915 W SR, No. 235, Brooker, FL 32622-5167, (352)485-1173
32nd Infantry Div. Veterans Assn. [20688], c/o Pamela McVeigh, Sec., 1715 Nelson Ave. SE, Grand Rapids, MI 49507-2148, (616)452-6311
33rd Infantry Div. Assn. [20680], PO Box 13618, Mill Creek, WA 98082-1618, (425)741-3549
35th Div. Assn. [20681], PO Box 5004, Topeka, KS 66605, (915)598-0183
37th Div. Veterans Assn. - Defunct.

38th Bomb Wing France Assn. - Address unknown since 2007.
43rd Bomb Gp. Assn. [20653], PO Box 360, Snyder, TX 79550-0360, (602)840-7101
43rd Infantry Div. Assn. [★20689]
43rd Infantry Div. Veterans Assn. [20689], c/o Howard F. Brown, Asst. Sec.-Treas., 150 Lakedell Dr., East Greenwich, RI 02818-4716, (401)884-7052
50 Years is Enough: U.S. Network for Global Economic Justice [18829], 3628 12th St. NE, Washington, DC 20017, (202)463-2265
50 Years is Enough: U.S. Network for Global Economic Justice [IO], Washington, DC, United States
51st Medical Battalion Assn. - Defunct.
51st State Comm. - Defunct.
52 Assn. for the Handicapped - Defunct.
52 Plus Joker [21955], c/o Clarence Peterson, Sec.-Treas., 12290 W 18th Dr., Lakewood, CO 80215, (303)592-1227
56 Studebaker Golden Hawk Owners Register [★21555]
57 Oldsmobile Chap. - Address unknown since 1988.
60 Plus Assn. [11270], 1600 Wilson Blvd., Ste. 960, Arlington, VA 22209, (888)560-7587
63rd Infantry Div. Assn. [20690], c/o Donna LaCosse, Natl. Sec.-Treas., PO Box 86, Morocco, IN 47963, (219)285-2861
'65 Chevy Club - Defunct.
65th Infantry Div. Assn. - Address unknown since 1995.
70th Infantry Div. Assn. [21366], c/o Ms. Diane Kessler, Sec., PO Box 301, Atkinson, NH 03811, (603)362-9737
71 429 Mustang Registry [21551], c/o Mr. Marvin Scothorn, Dir., 6250 Germantown Pike, Dayton, OH 45418-1634
73rd Bomb Wing Assn. - Defunct.
74-75-76 Cadillac Talisman Registry - Defunct.
77th Artillery Assn. [21342], PO Box 141, Boonville, MO 65233-0141, (660)888-1129
78th Div. Veterans Assn. [21272], c/o Herman A. Gonzales, Membership Sec., 104 Oak Glen Rd., Pittsburgh, PA 15237, (412)364-1609
80th Fighter Squadron Headhunters' Assn. [5442], c/o Tom Reichert, 5263 Winchester Ln., Ogden, UT 84403-4329, (706)324-7360
82nd Airborne Div. Assn. [21273], PO Box 9308, Fayetteville, NC 28311-9308, (910)822-4534
84th Infantry Div., Railsplitter Soc. [21367], c/o Forrest T. Lothrop, Exec. Sec.-Treas., PO Box 827, Sioux Falls, SD 57101-0827, (605)334-8787
85th Infantry Div. [★21401]
86th Chem. Mortar Battalion Assn. [21368], c/o CSM George L. Murray, Adj., 818 W 62nd St., Anniston, AL 36206, (256)820-4415
90th Div. Assn. [21274], c/o James Reid, Exec. Sec.-Treas., 17 Lake Shore Dr., Willowbrook, IL 60527-2221, (630)789-0204
91st General Hospital Assn. - Address unknown since 2002.
92 Group - Address unknown since 1994.
94th Infantry Div. Assn. [21369], c/o Mr. Harry Helms, Sec.-Treas., 609 Dogwood Dr., Downingtown, PA 19335, (610)363-7826

95th Infantry Div. Assn. **[20691]**, PO Box 376, Willow Springs, IL 60480

96th Infantry Div. Assn. **[20692]**, PO Box 581254, Salt Lake City, UT 84158

99th Infantry Div. Assn. **[21370]**, PO Box 99, Marion, KS 66861

100 Black Men of Am. **[18865]**, 141 Auburn Ave., Atlanta, GA 30303, (404)688-5100

100% Recycled Paperboard Alliance **[2886]**, 1331 F St. NW, Ste. 800, Washington, DC 20004, (202)347-8000

100th Infantry Div. Assn. **[20693]**, c/o Patti Bonn, PO Box 629, Bedford, PA 15522, (814)632-8308

101st Airborne Div. Assn. **[20694]**, c/o Mr. Sam Bass, Exec. Sec.-Treas., PO Box 929, Fort Campbell, KY 42223-0929, (931)431-0199

104th Infantry Div. Natl. Timberwolf Assn. **[20695]**, c/o Glen E. Lytle, Sec.-Treas., 4002 Jasmine Dr., Wichita, KS 67226, (316)636-5334

106th Infantry Div. Assn. **[21371]**, c/o John Kline, 11 Harold Dr., Burnsville, MN 55337, (952)890-3155

106th Infantry Division Association **[IO]**, Burnsville, MN, United States

107th Engineer Assn. **[5467]**, 900 Palms Ave., Ishpeming, MI 49849-1064, (906)486-8741

127th Infantry Veterans Assn. - Address unknown since 2007.

135th Medical Regiment Assn. - Address unknown since 1999.

147th Engineers Veterans Assn. **[21372]**, 439 Greenlow Rd., Baltimore, MD 21228, (410)747-0291

150th Engineer Combat Battalion Assn. - Address unknown since 1988.

164th Infantry Assn. of the U.S. **[20696]**

187th Airborne Regimental Combat Team Assn. **[20697]**, 4015 Royal Arch Ct., Concord, CA 94519-1225, (510)686-0813

190SL Gp; Intl. **[21663]**

190SL Lone Gp., Inc; Intl. **[★21663]**

210 Assn; Intl. **[23179]**

210 Class **[★23179]**

210 Owners Assn; Natl. **[21463]**

303rd Bomb Gp. (H) Assn. **[21373]**, c/o William H. Cox, Pres., 441 Sandstone Dr., Vacaville, CA 95688-4225, (707)448-0571

304th Fighter Squadron Assn. - Address unknown since 2001.

325th Glider Infantry Assn. **[21374]**, c/o Jesse Oxendine, Chm., 1812 Woodberry Rd., Charlotte, NC 28212, (704)537-4912

339th Infantry Regiment **[★21401]**

359th Fighter Gp; 369th Fighter Squadron Assn., **[20654]**

361st Engineers Special Service Regiment Assn. - Address unknown since 1999.

369th Fighter Squadron Assn., 359th Fighter Gp. **[20654]**, 511 Crest Haven Dr., Pittsburgh, PA 15239, (412)793-7619

369th Veterans' Assn. **[21275]**, PO Box 91, New York, NY 10037-0091, (212)281-3308

381st Bomb Gp. Memorial Assn. **[20655]**, c/o Joseph K. Waddell, Jr., Sec.-Treas., PO Box 6064, Madison, WI 53716-0064, (608)222-4591

397th Bomb Gp. Assn. **[21375]**, PO Box 1786, Rockville, MD 20849-1786, (301)460-4488

401(k) Coun. of Am; Profit Sharing/ **[1279]**

401(k) Educ. Found; Profit Sharing/ **[1280]**

401(k)s for 501(c)s Coalition - Address unknown since 1999.

401st Bombardment Gp. (Heavy) Assn. **[20656]**, PO Box 15356, Savannah, GA 31416, (912)598-0276

401st Bombardment Group (Heavy) Association **[IO]**, Savannah, GA, United States

429 Owners Dir; Boss **[21596]**

452nd Bomb Wing/Group Assn. **[21376]**, c/o Ted Baker, 453 Hamilton Ave., Almont, MI 48003-8620

461st Bombardment Gp. Assn. **[20657]**, c/o Hughes Glantzberg, Webmaster/Ed., PO Box 926, Gunnison, CO 81230, (970)209-2788

483rd Bombardment Gp. (H) Assn. **[21377]**, c/o Sandee West Maeda, Sec., 1050 E 5th Ave., Escondido, CA 92025, (480)832-3567

494th Bombardment Gp. (H) Assn. 7th Air Force **[20658]**, 3160 E Main St., No. 103, Mesa, AZ 85213-9519, (480)924-6801

501 Soc. **[★9986]**

504th Parachute Infantry Regiment Assn. **[21378]**, c/o Ronald H. Rath, Treas., 1720 Nutley Dr., Fayetteville, NC 28303-3738, (910)822-4555

505 Yacht Racing Assn., Amer. Sect; Intl. **[23180]**

505th Ordnance Company - Address unknown since 2007.

505th Regimental Combat Team Assn. - Address unknown since 2002.

507th Parachute Infantry Assn. - Defunct.

508th Parachute Infantry Regiment Assn. **[21379]**, c/o Kenneth Merritt, 1517 Atwick Dr., Fayetteville, NC 28304-3901, (910)425-5818

509th Parachute Infantry Assn. **[21380]**

511 Engineer Light Ponton Company Veterans - Defunct.

511th Aircraft Control and Warning Gp. **[5443]**, c/o Don Simmons, Sec., 704 S Grove Rd., Richardson, TX 75081, (972)231-6518

517th Parachute Regimental Combat Team Assn. **[21381]**, c/o Leo P. Dean, 14 Stonehenge Ln., Albany, NY 12203

526th Armored Infantry Battalion Assn. **[21382]**, PO Box 456, Yolo, CA 95697, (530)662-8160

537th AAA (AW) Battalion Assn. - Address unknown since 2007.

542nd Parachute Infantry Assn. - Address unknown since 2003.

550th Airborne Infantry Assn. - Defunct.

605th Ordnance Battalion Assn. - Defunct.

606 Soc. **[★9986]**

704th Tank Destroyer Battalion Assn. **[21383]**

749th Bn Assn. **[★20698]**

749th Tank Battalion Assn. Friends **[20698]**

800-COCAINE - Defunct.

829-6662-3195th Assn. **[★21384]**

829th Signal Ser. Assn. **[21384]**, 700 Ocean Ave., Unit 426, Spring Lake, NJ 07762, (201)385-2246

906 Stamp Club - Address unknown since 1995.

911 Cyndi Lauper Fan Club **[IO]**, Frascati, Italy

911; Racial Justice **[18493]**

1099 Filers; Natl. Assn. of Form **[18711]**

1265 Soc. - Address unknown since 1995.

1334 North Beechwood Drive Irregulars - Address unknown since 1999.

1394 High Performance Serial Bus Trade Assn. **[3720]**, 1560 E Southlake Blvd., Ste. 242, Southlake, TX 76092, (817)416-2200

1812 in Connecticut; Soc. of the War of **[★21354]**

1812; Gen. Soc: of the War of **[21354]**

1812; Military Soc. War of **[★21204]**

1812; New England Assn. of Soldiers of the War of **[★21354]**

1812 in Pennsylvania; Soc. of the War of **[★21354]**

1812; Veteran Corps of Artillery, State of New York, Constituting the Military Soc. of the War of **[21204]**

1851-57 Unit; The Three Cent **[★22887]**

1869 Pictoral Res. Associates; U.S. **[★22887]**

1904 World's Fair Soc. **[23033]**, 2605 Causeway Dr., St. Louis, MO 63125

1929 Silver Anniversary Buick Club **[IO]**, Toronto, ON, Canada

1937-1938 Buick Club **[21552]**, PO Box 21000, Oakland, CA 94620

1948-50 Packard Convertible Roster **[21553]**, 84 Hoy Ave., Fords, NJ 08863, (732)738-7859

1948 Interim Period Study Group - Defunct.

1949-1959 Ford Products Club - Address unknown since 2001.

1950s Amer. Bandstand Fan Club **[★25024]**

1953-54 Buick Skylark Club **[21554]**, c/o Joanne De-Peppo, Treas., 51 Statesville Quarry Rd., Lafayette, NJ 07848, (973)383-6035

1956 Studebaker Golden Hawk Owners Register **[21555]**, c/o Frank Ambrogio, 31654 Wekiva River Rd., Sorrento, FL 32776-9233, (913)236-4029

1958 Cadillac Owners Association **[IO]**, Braintree, MA, United States

1958 Cadillac Owners Assn. **[21556]**, c/o David Becker, Dir, 54 Parkside Ave., Braintree, MA 02184, (781)843-4485

1958 Cadillac Owners Assn. of New England **[★IO]**

1958 Cadillac Owners Assn. of New England **[★21556]**

1963 Falcon Convertible Registry - Defunct.

1965-66 Full Size Chevrolet Club **[21557]**, c/o Harold J. Foos, Pres., 15615 State Rd. 23, Granger, IN 46530

1970 Dart Swinger 340s Registry **[21558]**, PO Box 9, Wethersfield, CT 06129-0009, (860)257-8434

1971 GTO and Judge Convertible Registry **[21559]**, 14906 Ferness Ln., Channelview, TX 77530, (281)452-0855

1980's Project - Defunct.

1995 Corvette Pace Car Registry **[21560]**, c/o T. Noel Osborn, Dir., 11825 IH-10 W, Ste. 213, San Antonio, TX 78230-1040, (210)641-7733

2030 Center - Address unknown since 2006.

70001—The Youth Employment Company **[12105]**

70001 Training and Employment Inst. **[★12105]**

66,67,68 High Country Special **[21561]**

66,67,68 High Country Special Mustang Registry **[21561]**, 6874 Benton Ct., Arvada, CO 80003-4244, (303)424-3866

A

A. C. Owners Club - Amer. Centre - Defunct.

A. J. Masters Fan Club - Defunct.

A. J. Muste Memorial Inst. **[IO]**, New York, NY, United States

A. Philip Randolph Educal. Fund **[17078]**

A. Philip Randolph Inst. **[18604]**, 815-16th St. NW, Washington, DC 20006, (202)508-3710

A-T Medical Res. Found. **[14436]**, 5241 Round Meadow Rd., Hidden Hills, CA 91302, (818)703-0151

AAA Found. for Traffic Safety **[12943]**, 607 14th St. NW, Ste. 201, Washington, DC 20005, (202)638-5944

AAAS Commn. on Science Education - Defunct.

AACC Intl. **[6660]**, 3340 Pilot Knob Rd., St. Paul, MN 55121, (651)454-7250

AACC Intl. **[IO]**, St. Paul, MN, United States

AACC Intl; Milling and Baking Division of **[7095]**

AACE Intl. **[6842]**, 209 Prairie Ave., Ste. 100, Morgantown, WV 26501, (304)296-8444

AACE Intl. **[IO]**, Morgantown, WV, United States

AACR-Women in Cancer Res. **[16893]**, 615 Chestnut St., 17th Fl., Philadelphia, PA 19106-4404, (215)440-9300

AACSB Intl. - Assn. to Advance Collegiate Schools of Bus. **[8010]**, 777 S Harbour Island Blvd., Ste. 750, Tampa, FL 33602-5730, (813)769-6500

AACSB Intl. - Assn. to Advance Collegiate Schools of Bus. **[IO]**, Tampa, FL, United States

AACSB-The Intl. Assn. for Mgt. Educ. **[★IO]**

AACSB-The Intl. Assn. for Mgt. Educ. **[★8010]**

AAEA Professional Improvement Foundation **[★3076]**

AAF/ADS **[★24393]**

AAF Coll. Chap. **[★24393]**

AAF Educ. Services **[★24393]**

AAFRC Trust for Philanthropy **[★12721]**

AAKSIS **[★14538]**

AAMED - The Amer. Assn. of Multiple Enchondroma Diseases **[15749]**, 357 Redwood Rd., Venice, FL 34293, (941)492-5117

AAMR - Natl. Assn. on Intellectual Disability **[★IO]**

AAP Political Action Comm. - Defunct.

Aaron Burr Accord **[11097]**, 8311 54th Ave. S, Seattle, WA 98118-4702, (206)725-0873

Aaron Burr Assn. **[11098]**, 1004 Butterworth Ln., Upper Marlboro, MD 20774-2205, (301)641-0494

Aaron Burr Commemorative Stamp Comm. **[★11097]**

AARP **[12895]**, 601 E St. NW, Washington, DC 20049, (888)OUR-AARP

AARP Grief and Loss Prog. **[13414]**, 601 E St. NW, Washington, DC 20049, (888)687-2277

AARP; Natl. Retired Teachers Assn., Division of **[9065]**

AARP Pharmacy Services **[2983]**, PO Box 1087, Bensalem, PA 19020-9956, (800)289-8849

AASK - Adopt a Special Kid **[11226]**, 8201 Edgewater Dr., Ste. 103, Oakland, CA 94621, (510)553-1748

AAU; Masters Swimming Comm. of the **[★23891]**

AAU Taekwondo Union of the U.S.A; Natl. **[★23610]**

AAU/U.S.A. Junior Olympics **[★23797]**

A star before a book entry number signifies that the name is not listed separately, but is mentioned within the entry.

AAU Youth Sports Prog. [★23797]
AAUW Educational Center [★9312]
AAUW Legal Advocacy Fund [5573], 1111 16th St. NW, Washington, DC 20036, (202)785-7700
ABA Center for Banking Information [★457]
ABA Comm. on Continuing Professional Educ; ALI-[8758]
ABA Educational Found. [★457]
ABA Marketing Network [2611], 1120 Connecticut Ave. NW, Washington, DC 20036, (800)BANKERS
Abandoned Infants Assistance Rsrc. Center; Natl. [12412]
ABANTU for Development [★IO]
ABANTU for Development - Regional Off. for Eastern and Southern Africa [IO], Nairobi, Kenya
ABANTU for Development - Regional Off. for West Africa [IO], London, United Kingdom
Abarth Register, U.S.A. [21562]
Abatement Worker and Training Prog; Asbestos [★620]
Abbott and Costello Fan Club [★24795]
Abbott and Costello Intl. Fan Club [24795], c/o Bill Honor, PO Box 5566, Fort Wayne, IN 46895-5566
Abbott and Costello Official Fan Club [24796], c/o Bill Honor, PO Box 5566, Fort Wayne, IN 46895-5566
Abbott Family - Address unknown since 2005.
ABC Quilts Projs. [11506]
ABCD: The Microcomputer Indus. Assn. [★898]
Abdominal Surgeons; Amer. Soc. of [16568]
Abdominal Surgery; Amer. Bd. of [16561]
ABDSA [★IO]
Abdus Salam Intl. Centre for Theoretical Physics [IO], Trieste, Italy
Aberdeen-Angus Breeder's Assn; Amer. [★4212]
Aberdeen-Angus Cattle Soc. [IO], Perth, United Kingdom
Aberdeen Formation Evaluation Soc. [IO], Aberdeen, United Kingdom
Aberdeen Geological Soc. [IO], Aberdeen, United Kingdom
Aberdeen and Grampian Chamber of Commerce [IO], Aberdeen, United Kingdom
Aberfeldie Bowls Club [IO], Essendon, Australia
ABET [6979], 111 Market Pl., Ste. 1050, Baltimore, MD 21202, (410)347-7700
ABET; Accreditation Bd. for Engg. and Tech. - [★6979]
ABET Inc. [★6979]
ABF Auxiliary - Defunct.
ABG Division United Steel Workers - Defunct.
Abhivyakti Media for Development [IO], Nashik, India
Abigail Adams Historical Soc. Inc. [11099]
ABIL - Agoraphobics Building Independent Lives [12546], 2501 Fox Harbor Ct., Richmond, VA 23235-2829, (804)353-3964
Abilities! [11913], 201 I.U. Willets Rd., Albertson, NY 11507-1599, (516)465-1400
Ability Center; Natl. [23347]
Ability Soc. [IO], Calgary, AB, Canada
Abingdon Pottery Club [21522], c/o Linda Thomas, 1544 180th St., Galesburg, IL 61401, (309)462-2951
ABJS [★15763]
ABLE: Assn. for Better Living and Educ. Intl. [11756], 7065 Hollywood Blvd., Los Angeles, CA 90028, (323)960-3530
ABLE: Association for Better Living and Education International [IO], Los Angeles, CA, United States
Abner Soc; Natl. Lum and [22925]
Abolafia's Assn. of Amer. Artists - Address unknown since 1995.
Abolish Corporal Punishment in Schools; Natl. Coalition to [8207]
Abolition 2000 [17421], 215 Lexington Ave., Ste. 1001, New York, NY 10016, (212)726-9161
Abolition 2000 [IO], New York, NY, United States
Abolitionist Party of Canada [IO], Brantford, ON, Canada
Aboriginal Evangelical Fellowship of Australia [IO], Doncaster, Australia
Aboriginal Nurses Assn. of Canada [IO], Ottawa, ON, Canada
Aboriginal Peoples Training and Employment Comm. [IO], Truro, NS, Canada

Aboriginal Res. Club - Address unknown since 1999.
Aboriginal Rights Coalition [IO], Ottawa, ON, Canada
Aboriginal Tourism Australia [IO], Melbourne, Australia
Aborigines' Protection Soc. [★IO]
Abortion
Abortion Access Proj. [11221]
Amer. Center for Law and Justice [12901]
Amer. Life League [12902]
Amer. Victims of Abortion [12903]
Assn. for Interdisciplinary Res. in Values and Social Change [12906]
Assn. of Reproductive Hea. Professionals [12177]
Black Americans for Life [12909]
Catholics United for Life [12910]
Center for Bio-Ethical Reform [18547]
Children of the Rosary [18548]
Clinicians for Choice [13528]
Dutch Assn. of Abortion Doctors [IO]
Elliot Inst. [16911]
EngenderHealth [12180]
Healthy Teen Network [12182]
Heartbeat Intl. [12912]
Intl. Planned Parenthood Fed., Western Hemisphere Region [12184]
Legal Action for Women [16912]
Liberty Godparent Home [12918]
Life Decisions Intl. [12920]
Life and Liberty for Women [11222]
Life Res. Inst. [14572]
Michael Fund/International Found. for Genetic Res. [14466]
NARAL Pro-Choice Am. [18518]
Natl. Abortion Fed. [11223]
Natl. Abortion Rights Action League [16913]
Natl. Assn. of Pro-Life Nurses [18378]
Natl. Coalition of Abortion Providers [13529]
Natl. Family Planning and Reproductive Hea. Assn. [12185]
Natl. Life Center [12922]
Natl. Network of Abortion Funds [16914]
Natl. Right to Life Comm. [12923]
Pathfinder Intl. [12186]
Planned Parenthood Fed. of Am. [12187]
Presbyterians Pro-Life [12926]
Pro-Choice Public Educ. Proj. [11224]
Pro-Life Alliance of Gays and Lesbians [12927]
Religious Coalition for Reproductive Choice [18519]
Republican Majority for Choice [18533]
Rock For Life [18567]
U.S. Coalition for Life [12929]
WISH List [5770]
Women Exploited by Abortion [12932]
Abortion Access Proj. [11221], 552 Massachusetts Ave., Ste. 215, Cambridge, MA 02139, (617)661-1161
Abortion; Alternatives to [★12912]
Abortion; Amer. Victims of [12903]
Abortion; Assn. for the Stud. of [★11223]
Abortion Coun; Natl. [★11223]
Abortion Facilities; Natl. Assn. of [★11223]
Abortion Fed; Natl. [11223]
Abortion Funds; Natl. Network of [16914]
Abortion Information Data Bank - Defunct.
Abortion Laws; Natl. Assn. for Repeal of [★18518]
Abortion League; Jewish Anti- [18555]
Abortion and Reproductive Action League; Natl. [★18518]
Abortion Rights [IO], London, United Kingdom
Abortion Rights Assn. [★18518]
Abortion Rights Mobilization - Address unknown since 2007.
Abortion Rights; Religious Coalition for [★18519]
Abortion; Women Exploited by [12932]
Abortion/Women's Hea. and Educ. Found; Alternatives to [★12912]
About Books, Inc. [3198], 1618 W Colorado Ave., Colorado Springs, CO 80904, (719)632-8226
About Buttonhooks, Spoons and Patents - Defunct.
About-Face [13415], PO Box 77665, San Francisco, CA 94107, (415)436-0212
AboutFace Intl. [IO], Toronto, ON, Canada
ABRADEMI - Brazilian Manga and Illustration Artists Assn. [IO], Sao Paulo, Brazil

Abraham Lincoln Assn. [11100], One Old State Capitol Plz., Springfield, IL 62701-1507, (866)865-8500
Abraham Lincoln Brigade; Veterans of the [21269]
Abraham Lincoln Natl. Cemetery Support Comm. [21160]
Abrams Peace Educ. Found; Grace Contrino [8139]
Abrasive Engg. Soc. [1989], 144 Moore Rd., Butler, PA 16001, (724)282-6210
Abrasive Engineering Society [IO], Butler, PA, United States
Abrasive Grain Assn. [★2567]
Abrasive Grain Assn. [★2074]
Abrasive Methods; Amer. Soc. for [★1989]
Abrasives; Amer. Soc. for [★1989]
Abrasives Mfrs'. Assn; Unified [2567]
Abri Intl. [★IO]
Absent-Minded Club - Defunct.
Absorbent Paper Mfrs. Assn. - Defunct.
Absorbents; Inst. for Polyacrylate [811]
Abstinence CH [16397], 801 E 41st St., Sioux Falls, SD 57105, (605)335-3643
Abstract Artists; Amer. [9488]
Absurd Special Interest Gp. [22590], c/o Hank Roll, Exec. Off., 1306 Lloyd St., Nanty Glo, PA 15943
Abundant Life Seed Found. [4338], PO Box 157, Saginaw, OR 97472-0157, (541)767-9606
Abundant Love Inst. [★13101]
Abundant Wildlife Soc. of North Am. [5287], PO Box 2, Beresford, SD 57004, (605)751-0979
Abundantly Yours - Address unknown since 1995.
Abuse Anonymous; Sexual [★13085]
Abuse of Children; Amer. Professional Soc. on the [11557]
Abuse Defense and Rsrc. Center; Natl. Child [13367]
Abuse for Everyone; Stop [12039]
Abuse and Family Violence; Natl. Coun. on Child [12035]
Abuse Finally Ends; SAFE - Self [★12557]
Abuse and Incest Natl. Network; Rape, [12791]
Abuse Listening and Mediation; Child [11565]
Abuse by Military Personnel; STAMP - Survivors Take Action Against [11507]
Abuse; Mothers Against Sexual [13078]
Abuse; Natl. Asian Pacific Amer. Families Against Substance [13258]
Abuse; Natl. Center on Elder [12033]
Abuse; Natl. Center for Prosecution of Child [11631]
Abuse; Natl. Comm. for the Prevention of Elder [11308]
Abuse; Natl. Exchange Club Found. for the Prevention of Child [★11637]
Abuse and Neglect Info; CH on Child [★11570]
Abuse and Neglect Info. and Natl. Adoption Info. CH; Natl. CH on Child [★11570]
Abuse and Neglect; Kempe Natl. Center for the Prevention and Treatment of Child [★11609]
Abuse; Prevent Child [★11647]
Abuse Prevention Research; National Center on Child [★11647]
Abuse Prevention Research; National Center on Child [★IO]
Abuse Prog. Coordinators; Natl. Assn. of State Drug [★13264]
Abuse and Retaliation; Natl. Org. of Fed. Employees Against [24078]
Abuse Services; Sect. for Psychiatric and Substance [16093]
Abused Deaf Women's Advocacy Services [11903], 8623 Roosevelt Way NE, Seattle, WA 98115, (206)726-0093
Abused by Priests; Survivors Network of Those [13372]
Abused Women's Aid in Crisis - Defunct.
Abusers; Assn. for the Behavioral Treatment of Sexual [★6529]
Abusive Men Exploring New Directions [★12020]
ABW Ministries [19468], PO Box 851, Valley Forge, PA 19482-0851, (800)ABC-3USA
Abwenzi African Stud. [18863], PO Box 1962, Basalt, CO 81621
Abyssinian Cat Club of Am. [21898], c/o Harford Gillaspie, Sec./Scorer, 23700 Stagecoach Rd., Volcano, CA 95689, (209)296-7390

Reference to "IO" in place of a book number signifies that the association may be found in the 45th edition of International Organizations.

A.C. Gilbert Heritage Soc. **[22992]**, 9 Bristol Knoll Rd., Newark, DE 19711

ACA Assurance **[19060]**, 1750 Elm St., Ste. 200, Manchester, NH 03104, (603)625-8577

ACA Intl. **[1144]**, PO Box 390106, Minneapolis, MN 55439, (952)926-6547

ACA Intl. **[IO]**, Minneapolis, MN, United States

Acacia **[24605]**, 8777 Purdue Rd., Ste. 225, Indianapolis, IN 46268, (317)872-8210

Acacia North Amer. User Group **[6759]**

Acadamh Rioga na hEireann **[★IO]**

Academi - Yr Academi Gymreig **[IO]**, Cardiff, United Kingdom

Academia; Accuracy in **[8352]**

Academia Argentina de Letras **[★IO]**

Academia Brasileira de Ciencias **[★IO]**

Academia Brasileira de Letras **[★IO]**

Academia Chilena de Bellas Artes **[IO]**, Santiago, Chile

Academia Chilena de la Historia **[★IO]**

Academia de Ciencias de Am. Latina **[★IO]**

Academia de Ciencias Fisicas, Matematicas y Naturales **[★IO]**

Academia das Ciencias de Lisboa **[★IO]**

Academia das Ciencias de Lisboa **[★IO]**

Academia de Ciencias Politicas y Sociales **[IO]**, Caracas, Venezuela

Academia Colombiana de Ciencias Exactas, Fisicas y Naturales **[★IO]**

Academia Colombiana de Ciencias Exactas, Fisicas y Naturales **[IO]**, Bogota, Colombia

Academia Europaea **[IO]**, London, United Kingdom

Academia Mexicana de Dermatologia **[★IO]**

Academia Musicale Chigiana **[IO]**, Siena, Italy

Academia Nacional de Agronomia y Veterinaria **[IO]**, Buenos Aires, Argentina

Academia Nacional de Ciencias de Bolivia **[★IO]**

Academia Nacional de Ciencias Exactas, Fisicas y Naturales **[★IO]**

Academia Nacional de Geografia **[★IO]**

Academia Nacional de la Historia **[★IO]**

Academia Nacional de la Historia de la Republica Argentina **[IO]**, Buenos Aires, Argentina

Academia Nacional de Medicina **[★IO]**

Academia Portuguesa da Historia **[★IO]**

Academia Romana **[★IO]**

Academia Scientiarum et Artium Croatian **[★IO]**

Academia Scientiarum Latviensis **[★IO]**

Academia Sinica **[IO]**, Taipei, Taiwan

Academia de Stiinte a Moldovei **[★IO]**

Academic Achievement; Soc. for **[9078]**

Academic Admin; Center for Leadership Development and **[★8745]**

Academic Admin. Internship Prog. **[★7881]**

Academic Advising Assn; Natl. **[8170]**

Academic Advisors for Athletics; Natl. Assn. of **[8171]**

Academic Advisors; Natl. Assn. of **[★8171]**

Academic Automotive Assn. **[IO]**, Minsk, Belarus

Academic Chairmen of Plastic Surgery; Assn. of **[14046]**

Academic Collective Bargaining Information Service - Defunct.

Academic Comm. on Soviet Jewry - Address unknown since 2006.

Academic Continuing Medical Educ; Soc. for **[8875]**

Academic Cooperation Assn. **[IO]**, Brussels, Belgium

Academic Coun. on the United Nations Sys. **[IO]**, Waterloo, ON, Canada

Academic Deans; Amer. Conf. of **[7885]**

Academic Emergency Medicine; Soc. for **[14344]**

Academic Freedom
Amer. Coun. of Trustees and Alumni **[7869]**
Coalition for Student and Academic Rights **[7870]**
Network for Educ. and Academic Rights **[IO]**

Academic Freedom Legal Defense Fund - Defunct.

Academic Hea. Centers; Assn. of **[14546]**

Academic Hea. Centers: Responses to the Malpractice Insurance Crisis **[★14546]**

Academic Language Therapy Assn. **[12488]**, 14070 Proton Rd., Ste. 100, LB 9, Dallas, TX 75244, (972)233-9107

Academic Medicine Club **[★8853]**

Academic Order; Univ. Professors for **[9026]**

Academic Orthopaedic Soc. **[15750]**, 6300 N River Rd., Ste. 505, Rosemont, IL 60018-4262, (847)823-7186

Academic Physiatrists; Assn. of **[16316]**

Academic Placement
Independent Educational Consultants Assn. **[7871]**

Academic Radiology Departments; Soc. of Chairmen of **[16296]**

Academic Resource Network - Defunct.

Academic Surgery; Assn. for **[16576]**

Academic Travel Abroad **[8588]**, 1920 N St. NW, Ste. 200, Washington, DC 20036, (202)785-9000

Academic Travel Abroad; Association for **[★8588]**

Academics for the Second Amendment **[17286]**, c/o Hamline Univ., School of Law, 1536 Hewitt Ave., St. Paul, MN 55104, (651)523-2142

Academie suisse des sciences naturelles **[★IO]**

Academie chretienne de dialogue europeen **[★IO]**

Academie internationale de droit et de sante mentale **[★IO]**

Academie internationale de droit compare **[★IO]**

Academie des Beaux-Arts **[IO]**, Paris, France

Academie Canadienne de Chirurgie Plastique et Reconstructive Faciale **[★IO]**

Academie Canadienne du Cinema et de la TV **[★IO]**

Academie Canadienne d'Endodontie **[★IO]**

Academie Canadienne du Genie **[★IO]**

Academie Canadienne de la Medcine de Sport **[★IO]**

Academie Canadienne de Parodontologie **[★IO]**

Academie des Chefs de Direction en Soins Infirmiers **[★IO]**

Academie nationale de Chirurgie **[★IO]**

Academie d'Agriculture de France **[IO]**, Paris, France

Academie Europeenne d'Allergologie et d'Immunologie Clinique **[★IO]**

Academie Francaise **[IO]**, Paris, France

Academie des Inscriptions et Belles-Lettres **[IO]**, Paris, France

Academie Internationale de la Ceramique **[★IO]**

Academie Internationale d'Astronautique **[★IO]**

L'Academie Internationale De Cytologie **[★IO]**

Academie Internationale de Droit Linguistique **[★IO]**

Academie Internationale de Medecine Aeronautique et Spatiale **[★IO]**

Academie Internationale de Medecine Legale **[★IO]**

Academie Mondiale de l'Art et de la Sci. **[★IO]**

Academie Mondiale de l'Art et de la Sci. **[★9612]**

Academie Royale de Medecine de Belgique **[★IO]**

Academie Royale des Sciences **[★IO]**

Academie Royale des Sciences d'Outre-Mer **[★IO]**

Academie Royale des Sciences, des Lettres et des Beaux-Arts de Belgique **[★IO]**

Academie Royale des Sciences, des Lettres, et des Beaux-Arts de Belgique **[★IO]**

Academie des Sciences **[IO]**, Paris, France

Academie des Sciences Morales et Politiques **[IO]**, Paris, France

Acad. of Accounting Historians **[10079]**, Univ. of Alabama, Culverhouse School of Accountancy, Box 870220, Tuscaloosa, AL 35487, (205)348-6131

Acad. of Ambulatory Care; Amer. **[★13662]**

Acad. of Ambulatory Foot and Ankle Surgery **[16023]**, 1601 Walnut, Ste. 1005, Philadelphia, PA 19102, (215)569-3303

Acad. of Ambulatory Foot and Ankle Surgery **[IO]**, Philadelphia, PA, United States

Acad. of Amer. Franciscan History **[19560]**, Proj. MUSE, 2715 N Charles St., Baltimore, MD 21218-4319, (410)516-6989

Acad. of Amer. Poets **[10859]**, 584 Broadway, Ste. 604, New York, NY 10012-5243, (212)274-0343

Acad. of Aphasia **[13704]**, c/o Executive Administrative Services, PO Box 26532, Minneapolis, MN 55426, (952)920-0484

Acad. of Applied Osteopathy **[★15790]**

Acad. of Applied Sci. **[7592]**, 24 Warren St., Concord, NH 03301, (603)228-4530

Acad. of Arts and Sciences of the Americas **[18830]**, 9450 Old Cutler Rd., Miami, FL 33156, (305)663-9897

Acad. of Arts and Sciences of the Americas **[IO]**, Miami, FL, United States

Acad. of Astrology - Defunct.

Acad. of Behavioral Medicine Res. **[13732]**, c/o Dr. Philip McCabe, Sec., Univ. of Miami, Dept. of Psychology, PO Box 248185, Coral Gables, FL 33124-0751, (305)284-5507

Acad. of Canadian Cinema and TV **[IO]**, Toronto, ON, Canada

Acad. of Canadian Executive Nurses **[IO]**, Ottawa, ON, Canada

Acad. for Catholic Healthcare Leadership - Defunct.

Acad. of Certified Archivists **[294]**, 90 State St., Ste. 1009, Albany, NY 12207, (518)463-8644

Acad. of Certified Hazardous Materials Managers **[4804]**, 9650 Rockville Pike, Bethesda, MD 20814, (301)634-7430

Acad. of Clinical Lab. Physicians and Scientists **[15981]**, c/o Elizabeth Frank, PhD, Sec.-Treas., 500 Chipeta Way, Salt Lake City, UT 84108, (801)583-2787

Academy of Clinical Laboratory Physicians and Scientists **[IO]**, Salt Lake City, UT, United States

Acad. of Clinical Mental Hea. Counselors **[★11828]**

Acad. of Comic Art Fans and Collectors - Defunct.

Acad. Conf. **[★7617]**

Acad. for Contemporary Problems **[★18417]**

Acad. of Counseling Psychology **[★16118]**

Acad. of Country Music **[10518]**, 5500 Balboa Blvd., Ste. 200, Encino, CA 91316, (818)788-8000

Acad. of Country and Western Music **[★10518]**

Acad. of Criminal Justice Sciences **[11850]**, PO Box 960, Greenbelt, MD 20768-0960, (301)446-6300

Acad. of Dental Materials **[14084]**, 21 Grouse Terr., Lake Oswego, OR 97035, (503)636-0861

Acad. of Dental Sleep Medicine **[16417]**, One Westbrook Corporate Center, Ste. 920, Westchester, IL 60154, (708)273-9366

Acad. of Dentistry Intl. **[14085]**, 3813 Gordon Creek Dr., Hicksville, OH 43526, (419)542-0101

Acad. of Dentistry Intl. **[IO]**, Hicksville, OH, United States

Acad. of Dentistry for Persons with Disabilities **[★14186]**

Acad. of Dispensing Audiologists **[★14733]**

Acad. of Doctors of Audiology **[14733]**, 401 N Michigan Ave., Ste. 2200, Chicago, IL 60611, (866)493-5544

Acad. for Eating Disorders **[14296]**, 60 Revere Dr., Ste. 500, Northbrook, IL 60062-1577, (847)498-4274

Acad. for Educational Development **[8219]**, c/o Stephen F. Moseley, Pres./CEO, 1825 Connecticut Ave. NW, Washington, DC 20009-5721, (202)884-8000

Acad. for Educational Development **[IO]**, Washington, DC, United States

Academy of Elecl. Contracting **[★1045]**

Acad. for Ethics in Medicine **[IO]**, Gottingen, Germany

Acad. of Experts **[IO]**, London, United Kingdom

Acad. of Family Films and Family TV - Address unknown since 2003.

Acad. of Family Mediators **[★5450]**

Acad. of Family Psychology **[★16125]**

Acad. of Forensic and Indus. Chiropractic Consultants **[830]**, c/o Thomas Bakman, DC, Pres., 18800 Delaware St., No. 150, Huntington Beach, CA 92648, (714)841-5333

Acad. for Friends of Secretarial Arts and Sciences - Defunct.

Acad. of Gen. Dentistry **[14086]**, 211 E Chicago Ave., Ste. 900, Chicago, IL 60611-1999, (312)440-4345

Acad. of Gen. Practice of Pharmacy **[★15918]**

Acad. of Hazard Control Mgt. - Defunct.

Acad. of Health Care Consultants - Defunct.

Acad. Hea. Sciences **[14534]**

Acad. for Health Services Marketing **[★2612]**

Acad. for Hea. Services Res. and Hea. Policy **[★14535]**

Acad. of Homiletics **[20081]**, c/o Dr. Jennifer Lord, Treas., 100 E 27th St., Austin, TX 78705

Acad. of Horror Films and Sci. Fiction Films **[★9925]**

Acad. of Human Service Sciences - Defunct.

Academy of Humanism **[★20085]**

Academy of Humanism **[★IO]**

Acad. for Implants and Transplants **[14087]**, 2250 Clarenden Blvd., Arlington, VA 22201, (703)841-0300

Acad. of Improbable Res. **[★7599]**

Acad. of Improbable Res. **[★IO]**

A star before a book entry number signifies that the name is not listed separately, but is mentioned within the entry.

Acad. of Independent Scholars - Defunct.

Acad. of Indus. Hygiene [★15627]

Acad. of Intl. Bus. [8011], The Eli Broad Coll. of Bus., Michigan State Univ., 7 Eppley Center, East Lansing, MI 48824-1121, (517)432-1452

Acad. of Intl. Bus. [IO], East Lansing, MI, United States

Acad. of Intl. Dental Studies - Defunct.

Acad. for Intl. Hea. Stud. [15044], 273 Hebron Ave., Glastonbury, CT 06033, (860)430-1388

Acad. for Intl. Hea. Stud. [IO], Glastonbury, CT, United States

Acad. for Interscience Methodology - Defunct.

Acad. of Laser Dentistry [14088], PO Box 8667, Coral Springs, FL 33075, (954)346-3776

Acad. of Learned Societies for the Social Sciences [IO], Reading, United Kingdom

Acad. of Learning and Developmental Disorders [12489]

Acad. of Legal Stud. in Bus. [8757], c/o Prof. Daniel J. Herron, Exec. Sec., 120 Upham Hall - Dept. of Finance, Miami Univ., Oxford, OH 45056

Academy of Legal Studies in Business [IO], Oxford, OH, United States

Acad. of Leisure Sciences [IO], Waterloo, ON, Canada

Academy Life Underwriting [★IO]

Academy Life Underwriting [★2148]

Acad. of Managed Care Pharmacy [15905], 100 N Pitt St., Ste. 400, Alexandria, VA 22314, (800)827-2627

Acad. of Managed Care Providers [14677], 1945 Palo Verde Ave., Ste. 202, Long Beach, CA 90815-3445, (562)682-3559

Acad. of Mgt. [8805], PO Box 3020, Briarcliff Manor, NY 10510-8020, (914)923-2607

Acad. of Marketing Sci. [8814], Univ. of Miami, School of Bus. Admin., PO Box 248012, Coral Gables, FL 33124-6536, (305)284-6673

Acad. of Master Wine Growers - Defunct.

Acad. of Medical Surgical Nurses [15426], PO Box 56, Pitman, NJ 08071, (866)877-2676

Acad. of Medicine, Singapore [IO], Singapore, Singapore

Acad. on Mental Retardation [15238], c/o Linda Hickson, PhD, Sec., Box 223, Teachers Coll., Columbia Univ., New York, NY 10027, (212)678-3854

Acad. of Model Aeronautics [21421], 5161 E Memorial Dr., Muncie, IN 47302, (765)287-1256

Acad. of Molecular Imaging [15150], PO Box 951735, Los Angeles, CA 90095-1735, (310)267-2614

Acad. of Motion Picture Arts and Sciences [1374], 8949 Wilshire Blvd., Beverly Hills, CA 90211-1907, (310)247-3000

Acad. of Natural Sciences [7356], 1900 Benjamin Franklin Pkwy., Philadelphia, PA 19103, (215)299-1000

Acad. of Natural Sciences [IO], Philadelphia, PA, United States

Acad. of Operative Dentistry [14089], c/o Dr. Gregory E. Smith, Sec., PO Box 14996, Gainesville, FL 32604-2996

Acad. of Oral Dynamics [14090], 134 E Church Rd., Elkins Park, PA 19027-2208, (215)635-2336

Acad. of Organizational and Occupational Psychiatry [15621], PO Box 343, Ridgefield Park, NJ 07660, (877)789-2667

Acad. of Organizational and Occupational Psychiatry [IO], Ridgefield Park, NJ, United States

Acad. of Osseointegration [14091], 85 W Algonquin Rd., Ste. 550, Arlington Heights, IL 60005, (847)439-1919

Acad. of Osteopathic Directors of Medical Education - Defunct.

Acad. of Parapsychology and Medicine - Defunct.

Acad. of Parish Clergy [20274], c/o Dr. Paul J. Binder, Admin. VP, 2249 Florinda St., Sarasota, FL 34231-4414, (941)922-8633

Acad. for Peace Res. [18187], PO Box 514, Soquel, CA 95073-0514, (831)425-3324

Acad. of Pharmaceutical Physicians and Investigators [8840], 500 Montgomery St., Ste. 800, Alexandria, VA 22314, (866)225-2779

Acad. of Pharmaceutical Res. and Sci. [15906], c/o Amer. Pharmacists Assn., 1100 15th St. NW, Ste. 400, Washington, DC 20005-1707, (202)628-4410

Acad. of Pharmaceutical Sciences [★15906]

Acad. of Pharmacy Practice [★15918]

Acad. of Pharmacy Practice and Mgt. [★15918]

Acad. of Pharmacy Practice and Mgt; Amer. Pharmacists Assn. - [15918]

Acad. of Physical, Mathematical and Natural Sciences [IO], Caracas, Venezuela

Acad. of Political Sci. [7519], 475 Riverside Dr., Ste. 1274, New York, NY 10115-1274, (212)870-2500

Acad. of Product Safety Mgt. - Defunct.

Acad. of Psychic Arts and Sciences [7439], 3523 McKinney Ave., No. 505, PO Box 191129, Dallas, TX 75219-8129, (214)219-2020

Acad. of Psychoanalysis [★16101]

Acad. of Psychosomatic Medicine [16195], 5272 River Rd., Ste. 630, Bethesda, MD 20816-1453, (301)718-6520

Acad. of Rehabilitative Audiology [14734], PO Box 952, DeSoto, TX 75123-0952

Acad. of Religion and Psychical Res. [★7440]

Acad. of Religion and Psychical Res. [★IO]

Acad. of Roofing Contractors - Defunct.

Acad. of Sci. Fiction, Fantasy, and Horror Films [9925], 334 W 54th St., Los Angeles, CA 90037-3806, (323)752-5811

Acad. of Sciences of Belarus [★IO]

Acad. of Sciences of Byelorussian SSR [★IO]

Acad. of Sciences of the Czech Republic [IO], Prague, Czech Republic

Acad. of Sciences for the Developing World [IO], Trieste, Italy

Acad. of Sciences - France [★IO]

Acad. of Sciences of Lisbon [IO], Lisbon, Portugal

Acad. of Sciences, Lithuania [IO], Vilnius, Lithuania

Acad. of Sciences of Moldova [IO], Chisinau, Moldova

Acad. of Sciences - Uzbekistan [IO], Tashkent, Uzbekistan

Acad. of Scientific Hypnotherapy [14913]

Acad. of Sci. Interrogation [★5753]

Acad. of Security Educators and Trainees [★9119]

Acad. of Security Educators and Trainees [★IO]

Academy of Security Educators and Trainers [IO], Berryville, VA, United States

Acad. of Security Educators and Trainers [9119], PO Box 802, Berryville, VA 22611-0802, (540)554-2540

Acad. of the Social Sciences in Australia [IO], Canberra, Australia

Acad. for Spatial Res. and Planning [IO], Hannover, Germany

Acad. of Spirituality and Paranormal Stud., Inc. [IO], Bloomfield, CT, United States

Acad. of Spirituality and Paranormal Stud., Inc. [7440], PO Box 614, Bloomfield, CT 06002-0614, (860)242-4593

Acad. of Sport Psychology Intl. - Address unknown since 1999.

Acad. for Sports Dentistry [★16481]

Acad. for Sports Dentistry [★IO]

Acad. for State and Local Govt. [18417]

Acad. of the Street of Puerto Rican Cong. - Address unknown since 1991.

Acad. of Stress and Chronic Disease - Address unknown since 1989.

Acad. of Student Pharmacists; Amer. Pharmacists Assn. [15919]

Acad. of Students of Pharmacy [★15919]

Acad. of Students of Pharmacy; Amer. Pharmaceutical Assn. [★15919]

Acad. of Surgical Res. [15099], 7500 Flying Cloud Dr., Ste. 900, Eden Prairie, MN 55344, (952)253-6240

Acad. of Teachers of Occupations - Defunct.

Acad. of TV Arts and Sciences [542], 5220 Lankershim Blvd., North Hollywood, CA 91601-3109, (818)754-2800

Acad. of Underwater Arts and Sciences - Defunct.

Acad. of Upper Cervical Chiropractic Organizations [13986], 1400 Court St., Clearwater, FL 33756

Acad. of Urban Leadership Training - Defunct.

Acad. of Veterinary Allergy and Clinical Immunology [16733], c/o Dr. Frederick Feibel, DVM, Membership Chm., 328 W Main St., Avon, CT 06001, (203)678-1122

Acad. of Veterinary Cardiology - Address unknown since 2004.

Acad. of Veterinary Emergency and Critical Care Technicians [16734], c/o Veterinary Emergency and Critical Care Soc., 6335 Camp Bullis Rd., Ste. 12, San Antonio, TX 78257, (210)698-5575

Acad. of Veterinary Homeopathy [16735], PO Box 9280, Wilmington, DE 19809, (866)652-1590

Academy of Wind and Percussion Arts [★10660]

AcademyHealth [14535], 1801 K St. NW, No. 701-L, Washington, DC 20006, (202)292-6700

Acadian
Savoie Acadian Cultural and Historical Soc. [21149]

Acadian Cultural Soc. [21096], PO Box 2304, Fitchburg, MA 01420-0015

Acadian Entomological Soc. [IO], Kentville, NS, Canada

Acadian Genealogical and Historical Assn. [★IO]

Acadian Genealogical and Historical Assn. [★21098]

Acadian Genealogical and Historical Assn. of New Hampshire [★21098]

Acadian Genealogical and Historical Assn. of New Hampshire [★IO]

Acarological Soc. of Am. [IO], Williamsburg, VA, United States

Acarological Soc. of Am. [7056], c/o Norman J. Fashing, Sec.-Treas., PO Box 8795, Williamsburg, VA 23185-8795, (757)221-2221

ACB Radio Amateurs [21492], c/o Mike Duke, Pres., 4911 Old Canton Rd., Apt. 239, Jackson, MS 39211, (601)432-6293

Accademia Agraria [IO], Pesaro, Italy

Accademia Americana in Rome [★IO]

Accademia d'Arte e Design - Leonetto Cappiello [IO], Florence, Italy

Accademia di Medicina di Torino [IO], Turin, Italy

Accademia delle Scienze di Torino [IO], Turin, Italy

ACCE Communications Coun. [24257], c/o ACCE, 4875 Eisenhower Ave., Ste. 250, Alexandria, VA 22304, (703)998-0072

Accelerated Cure Proj. for Multiple Sclerosis [15301], 300 Fifth Ave., Waltham, MA 02451, (781)487-0008

Accent on Information - Defunct.

Acceso - Address unknown since 2001.

Access America - Address unknown since 1994.

ACCESS: An International Affairs Information Service - Defunct.

access Cinema [IO], Dublin, Ireland

Access Copyright, The Canadian Copyright Licensing Agency [IO], Toronto, ON, Canada

ACCESS: Eurocities for a New Mobility Culture [★IO]

Access Floor Mfrs. Assn. - Defunct.

Access Flooring Assn. [IO], Hull, United Kingdom

Access Fund [23796], PO Box 17010, Boulder, CO 80308, (303)545-6772

Access for the Handicapped - Defunct.

Access to Justice Network [IO], Edmonton, AB, Canada

ACCESS: Networking in the Public Interest - Address unknown since 2006.

Access Point [11813], PO Box 6359, Los Osos, CA 93412, (805)534-1101

Access Professionals; Amer. Soc. of [5814]

Access Proj. [14605], 89 South St., Ste. 404, Lincoln Plz., Boston, MA 02111, (617)654-9911

Access Res. Network [9095], PO Box 38069, Colorado Springs, CO 80937-8069, (719)633-1772

Access Tech. Assn. - Defunct.

Accessibility Equip. Manufacturers Assn. [1156], PO Box 380, Metamora, IL 61548-0380, (800)514-1100

Accessible Apartment CH; Natl. [11963]

Accessible Golf; Natl. Alliance for [23348]

Accessible Housing Assn. [IO], Calgary, AB, Canada

Accessible Public Transit; Amer. Disabled for [★17413]

Accessories Assn; Natl. Fashion [250]

Accessories Coun. [220], 390 Fifth Ave., Ste. 710, New York, NY 10018, (212)947-1135

Accessories Distribution; Natl. Assn. of Hose and [2047]

Accessories Music Marketing Assn; Guitar and [★2805]

Accessories Shippers Assn; Fashion [★250]
Accessory Alliance - a SEMA Coun; Truck Cap and [★390]
Accessory Assn; Truck Cap and [★390]
Accessory Designers; Natl. Assn. of Fashion and [246]
Accessory Mfrs. Assn; Guitar and [★2805]
Accident Data Comm; Traffic [★12993]
Accident Data Proj. Comm; Traffic [★12993]
Accident and Hea. Counsels; Gen. Counsels' Assn. of [★5499]
Accident and Hea. Underwriters; Intl. Assn. of [★2208]
Accident and Hea. Underwriters; Natl. Assn. of [★2208]
Accident Reconstruction Specialists; Intl. Assn. of [2410]
Accident Reconstructionists and Investigators; Natl. Assn. of Traffic [5887]
Accident Reconstructionists; Natl. Assn. of Professional [6252]
Accident Statistics; Comm. on Uniform Traffic [★12993]
Accidental Nuclear War Prevention Proj. [★18229]
Accidental Nuclear War Prevention Proj. [18140], c/o Nuclear Age Peace Found., PMB 121, 1187 Coast Village Rd., Ste. 1, Santa Barbara, CA 93108-2794, (805)965-3443
Accidental Nuclear War Prevention Proj. [★IO]
Accidental War Info. Sharing Proj; Intl. [★18229]
Accidents Statistics; Natl. Comm. on Uniform Traffic [★12993]
Accio dels Cristians per l'Abolicio de la Tortura [IO], Barcelona, Spain
Accio Psoriasi [IO], Barcelona, Spain
Accion de los Cristianos para la Abolocion de la Tortura [★IO]
ACCION Intl. [IO], Boston, MA, United States
ACCION Intl. [17205], 56 Roland St., Ste. 300, Boston, MA 02129, (617)625-7080
Accion Intl. para la Salud [★IO]
Accion Permanente Por la Paz [★IO]
Accion Permanente Por la Paz [★18107]
Acclimatization Experiences Inst. [★8389]
Acclimatization Experiences Inst. [★IO]
Accokeek Found. [10006], 3400 Bryan Point Rd., Accokeek, MD 20607, (301)283-2113
Accommodators; Fed. of Exchange [3717]
Accordian Professionals Intl. [2826], 3964 Calculus, Dallas, TX 75244, (972)247-0071
Accordion Assn; New Zealand [IO]
Accordion Assn. of Southern California [★10519]
Accordion Fed. of North Am. [10519], 1101 W Orangethorpe Ave., Fullerton, CA 92833-4735, (714)447-9163
Accordion Musicological Soc; Amer. [10525]
Accordion Soc. of Australia [IO], Earlwood, Australia
Accordion Teachers' Guild [★IO]
Accordion Teachers' Guild [★8897]
Accordionists' Assn; Amer. [10526]
Accordionists and Teachers Guild, Intl. [8897], c/o Joan Cochran Sommers, Pres., 2312 W 71 Terr., Prairie Village, KS 66208-3322, (913)722-5625
Accordionists and Teachers Guild, Intl. [IO], Prairie Village, KS, United States
ACCOUNT (for the Prisoners and Missing in Lebanon) - Defunct.
Account Mgt. Assn; Natl. [★2650]
Account Mgt. Assn; Strategic [2650]
Account Managers; Amer. Guild of Patient [★15047]
Account Marketing Assn; Natl. [★2650]
Accountability; Evangelical Coun. for Financial [20002]
Accountability Proj; Govt. [17670]
Accountability Proj; Natl. Police [6174]
Accountancy; Accreditation Coun. for [★3]
Accountancy and Taxation; Accreditation Coun. for [3]
Accountant Examiners; Assn. of Certified Public [★5428]
Accountants
    Accountants Global Network [2]
    Alliance of Merger and Acquisition Advisors [54]
    Alliance of Practicing Certified Public Accountants [6]

Amer. Assn. of Medical Audit Specialists [15049]
Amer. Soc. of Tax Problem Solvers [6290]
Assn. of Public Pension Fund Auditors [24147]
Insurance Accounting and Systems Assn. [2172]
Leading Edge Alliance [39]
Medical Dental Hosp. Bus. Associates [40]
Natl. Assn. of State Boards of Accountancy [5428]
Professional Accounting Soc. of Am. [1]
Soc. of Professional Accountants [IO]
Accountants; Amer. Assn. of Hosp. [★15066]
Accountants Assn; Assn. of Casualty Accountants and Statisticians and Insurance [★53]
Accountants Assn; Fed. Govt. [★5426]
Accountants; Assn. of Insolvency [★15]
Accountants Assn; Natl. Machine [★8128]
Accountants and Auditors Assn. [IO], Sharjah, United Arab Emirates
Accountants Computer Users Technical Exchange - Address unknown since 2005.
Accountants Global Network [2], 2851 S Parker Rd., Ste. 850, Aurora, CO 80014, (303)743-7880
Accountants Global Network [IO], Aurora, CO, United States
Accountants in Insolvencies; Natl. Assn. of [★15]
Accountants; Natl. Assn. of [★34]
Accountants; Natl. Assn. of Cost [★34]
Accountants; Natl. Soc. of Public [★48]
Accountants for the Public Interest - Defunct.
Accountants and Statisticians and Insurance Accountants Assn; Assn. of Casualty [★53]
Accounting
    Acad. of Accounting Historians [10079]
    Accountants and Auditors Assn. [IO]
    Accountants Global Network [IO]
    Accountants Global Network [2]
    Accounting and Finance Assn. of Australia and New Zealand [IO]
    Accounting and Finance Benchmarking Consortium [690]
    Accreditation Coun. for Accountancy and Taxation [3]
    Affiliated Conf. of Practicing Accountants Intl. [4]
    Affiliated Conf. of Practicing Accountants Intl. [IO]
    African Org. of Supreme Audit Institutions [IO]
    AGN Intl. - North Am. [5]
    Alliance of Practicing Certified Public Accountants [6]
    Amer. Accounting Assn. [7]
    Amer. Assn. of Attorney-Certified Public Accountants [8]
    Amer. Assn. of Medical Audit Specialists [15049]
    Amer. Assn. of Medical Billers [15050]
    Amer. Cooperative Coun. on Compensation Tech. [4059]
    Amer. Inst. of Certified Public Accountants [9]
    Amer. Soc. of Tax Problem Solvers [6290]
    Amer. Soc. of Tax Professionals [10]
    Amer. Soc. of Women Accountants [11]
    Amer. Woman's Soc. of Certified Public Accountants [12]
    Asian Org. of Supreme Audit Institutions [IO]
    Asset Managers Forum [1401]
    Assn. for Accounting Admin. [13]
    Assn. of Accounting Companies in Bulgaria [IO]
    Assn. of Accounting Technicians [IO]
    Assn. of Authorised Public Accountants [IO]
    Assn. of Chartered Accountants in the U.S. [14]
    Assn. of Chartered Certified Accountants - Australia and New Zealand [IO]
    Assn. of Chartered Certified Accountants - Botswana [IO]
    Assn. of Chartered Certified Accountants - Cambodia [IO]
    Assn. of Chartered Certified Accountants Canada [IO]
    Assn. of Chartered Certified Accountants Caribbean [IO]
    Assn. of Chartered Certified Accountants - Central and Eastern Europe Off. [IO]
    Assn. of Chartered Certified Accountants - Cyprus [IO]
    Assn. of Chartered Certified Accountants - Ethiopia [IO]
    Assn. of Chartered Certified Accountants - Ghana [IO]

    Assn. of Chartered Certified Accountants - Gulf States [IO]
    Assn. of Chartered Certified Accountants - Hong Kong [IO]
    Assn. of Chartered Certified Accountants - Ireland [IO]
    Assn. of Chartered Certified Accountants - Kenya [IO]
    Assn. of Chartered Certified Accountants - Malaysia [IO]
    Assn. of Chartered Certified Accountants - Mauritius [IO]
    Assn. of Chartered Certified Accountants - Poland [IO]
    Assn. of Chartered Certified Accountants - Singapore [IO]
    Assn. of Chartered Certified Accountants - South Africa [IO]
    Assn. of Chartered Certified Accountants - Sri Lanka [IO]
    Assn. of Chartered Certified Accountants - Uganda [IO]
    Assn. of Chartered Certified Accountants - United Kingdom [IO]
    Assn. of Chartered Certified Accountants - Vietnam [IO]
    Assn. of Chartered Certified Accountants - Zambia [IO]
    Assn. of Chartered Certified Accountants - Zimbabwe [IO]
    Assn. of Cost Engineers [IO]
    Assn. of Govt. Accountants [5426]
    Assn. of Healthcare Internal Auditors [15061]
    Assn. of Insolvency and Restructuring Advisors [15]
    Assn. of Intl. Accountants [IO]
    Assn. of Latino Professionals in Finance and Accounting [16]
    Assn. of Practicing Certified Public Accountants [17]
    Assn. of Public Analysts [IO]
    Bahamas Inst. of Chartered Accountants [IO]
    Beta Alpha Psi [24391]
    BKR Intl. [18]
    BKR Intl. [IO]
    British Assn. of Hospitality Accountants [IO]
    Canadian Academic Accounting Assn. [IO]
    Canadian Assn. of Petroleum Production Accounting [IO]
    Canadian Environmental Auditing Assn. [IO]
    Canadian Inst. of Chartered Accountants [IO]
    Canadian Inst. of Quantity Surveyors [IO]
    Canadian Insurance Accountants Assn. [IO]
    Certified Practising Accountants Papua New Guinea [IO]
    Chamber of Tax Advisors of the Czech Republic [IO]
    Chartered Inst. of Mgt. Accountants [IO]
    Chartered Inst. of Mgt. Accountants - Australia [IO]
    Chartered Inst. of Mgt. Accountants - Hong Kong Div. [IO]
    Chartered Inst. of Mgt. Accountants - Ireland [IO]
    Chartered Inst. of Public Finance and Accountancy [IO]
    Chartered Inst. of Taxation [IO]
    Chinese Inst. of Certified Public Accountants [IO]
    CH for Volunteer Accounting Services [19]
    Community Banking Advisory Network [20]
    Confed. of Asian and Pacific Accountants [IO]
    Constr. Indus. CPAs/Consultants Assn. [21]
    Controllers Coun. [22]
    Cost Mgt. Gp. [2493]
    Coun. of Petroleum Accountants Societies [23]
    CPA Associates Intl. [24]
    CPA Associates Intl. [IO]
    CPA Associates Intl. Asia Pacific Region [IO]
    CPA Associates Intl. Latin Am. [IO]
    CPA Australia [IO]
    CPA Australia - Hong Kong China Div. [IO]
    CPA Auto Dealer Consultants Assn. [25]
    CPA Mfg. Services Assn. [26]
    CPAmerica Intl. [27]
    CPAmerica Intl. [IO]
    DFK International/USA [28]

A star before a book entry number signifies that the name is not listed separately, but is mentioned within the entry.

Educational Found. for Women in Accounting [9316]
European Accounting Assn. [IO]
European Fed. of Accountants [IO]
European Fed. of Accountants and Auditors for Small and Medium Sized Enterprises [IO]
Financial Accounting Standards Bd. [29]
Forensic Accountants Soc. of North Am. [30]
Found. for Accounting Educ. [31]
Governmental Accounting Standards Bd. [5427]
Healthcare Financial Mgt. Assn. [15066]
Healthcare Financial Mgt. Assn. [IO]
Hong Kong Inst. of Accredited Accounting Technicians [IO]
Hong Kong Inst. of Certified Public Accountants [IO]
Hospitality Financial and Tech. Professionals [IO]
Hospitality Financial and Tech. Professionals [32]
Institut des Reviseurs d'Entreprises - Luxembourg [IO]
Inst. of Accounting Technicians in Ireland [IO]
Inst. of Chartered Accountants in Australia [IO]
Inst. of Chartered Accountants of Bermuda [IO]
Inst. of Chartered Accountants in England and Wales [IO]
Inst. of Chartered Accountants of Guyana [IO]
Inst. of Chartered Accountants of India [IO]
Inst. of Chartered Accountants in Ireland [IO]
Inst. of Chartered Accountants of New Zealand [IO]
Inst. of Chartered Accountants of Nigeria [IO]
Inst. of Chartered Accountants of Scotland [IO]
Inst. of Chartered Accountants of Zimbabwe [IO]
Inst. of Financial Accountants [IO]
Inst. of Incorporated Public Accountants [IO]
Inst. of Internal Auditors [IO]
Inst. of Internal Auditors [33]
Inst. of Internal Auditors - Australia [IO]
Inst. of Internal Auditors - Hong Kong [IO]
Inst. of Internal Auditors - UK and Ireland [IO]
Inst. of Mgt. Accountants [34]
Inst. of Public Auditors in Germany [IO]
Insurance Accounting and Systems Assn. [2172]
Interamerican Accounting Assn. [35]
Interamerican Accounting Assn. [IO]
Intl. Accounting Standards Bd. [IO]
Intl. Assn. of Airline Internal Auditors [IO]
Intl. Assn. of Book-Keepers [IO]
Intl. Assn. of Financial Engineers [1424]
Intl. Assn. of Practising Accountants [IO]
Intl. Budget Proj. of the Center on Budget and Policy Priorities [IO]
Intl. Budget Proj. of the Center on Budget and Policy Priorities [16915]
Intl. Fed. of Accountants [36]
Intl. Fed. of Accountants [IO]
Intl. Gp. of Accounting Firms [IO]
Intl. Gp. of Accounting Firms [37]
Japanese Inst. of Certified Public Accountants [IO]
Law Firm Services Assn. [38]
Leading Edge Alliance [39]
Lebanese Assn. of Public Accountants [IO]
Leinster Soc. of Chartered Accountants [IO]
Malaysian Inst. of Certified Public Accountants [IO]
Medical Dental Hosp. Bus. Associates [40]
Moore Stephens North Am. [41]
Natl. Asian Amer. Soc. of Accountants [42]
Natl. Assoc. CPA Firms [43]
Natl. Assn. of Black Accountants [44]
Natl. Assn. of Certified Valuation Analysts [45]
National Association of Certified Valuation Analysts [IO]
Natl. Assn. of Forensic Accountants [46]
Natl. Assn. of Purchasing and Payables [3265]
Natl. Assn. of State Boards of Accountancy [5428]
Natl. Conf. of CPA Practitioners [47]
Natl. CPA Hea. Care Advisors Assn. [13530]
Natl. Litigation Support Services Assn. [IO]
Natl. Soc. of Accountants [48]
Natl. Soc. of Accountants for Cooperatives [49]
Norwegian Inst. of Public Accountants [IO]
Not-For-Profit Services Assn. [50]
Polaris Intl. North Amer. Network [51]

Polaris Intl. North Amer. Network [IO]
Production Guild of Great Britain [IO]
Professional Accounting Soc. of Am. [1]
Soc. of Depreciation Professionals [52]
Soc. of Insurance Financial Mgt. [53]
Soc. of Mgt. Accountants of Canada [IO]
Soc. of Professional Accountants of Canada [IO]
South African Inst. of Chartered Accountants [IO]
Swedish Assn. of Accounting Consultants [IO]
Vietnam Assn. of Certified Public Accountants [IO]
Accounting Administrators; Assn. of [★13]
Accounting; Amer. Assn. of Univ. Instructors in [★7]
Accounting Assn. of Australia and New Zealand [★IO]
Accounting; Assn. of Latino Professionals in Finance and [16]
Accounting and Bus. Officials of Public Schools; Natl. Assn. of School [★7892]
Accounting and Finance Assn. of Australia and New Zealand [IO], Carlton, Australia
Accounting and Finance Benchmarking Consortium [690], c/o The Benchmarking Network, 4606 FM 1960 W, Ste. 250, Houston, TX 77069-9949, (281)440-5044
Accounting and Finance Coun; Natl. [3876]
Accounting Historians; Acad. of [10079]
Accounting; Natl. Assn. for Bank, Cost, and Mgt. [★464]
Accounting; Natl. Comm. on [★3876]
Accounting Officers; Assn. of Comptrollers and [★6204]
Accounting Officers; Natl. Assn. of School [★7892]
Accounting Researchers Intl. Assn. - Defunct.
Accounting and Statistical Assn; Insurance [★2172]
Accounting and Systems Assn; Insurance [2172]
Accounting Technicians in Finance and Accounting [★IO]
ACCRA [★24272]
Accreditation
ABET [6979]
Accreditation Commn. for Acupuncture and Oriental Medicine [15739]
Accreditation Coun. for Accountancy and Taxation [3]
Accreditation Coun. for Graduate Medical Educ. [7872]
Accreditation Coun. on Optometric Educ. [15710]
Accreditation Rev. Commn. on Educ. for the Physician Asst. [15972]
Accreditation Rev. Comm. on Educ. in Surgical Tech. [15123]
Accrediting Commn. of Career Schools and Colleges of Tech. [7873]
Accrediting Coun. for Independent Colleges and Schools [7874]
Amer. Acad. of Optometry [15711]
Amer. Assn. of Christian Schools [7875]
Amer. Bd. of Opticiany [15704]
Amer. Optometric Assn. [15712]
Amer. Optometric Found. [15713]
Amer. Optometric Student Assn. [15714]
Assn. for the Accreditation of Human Res. Protection Programs [11225]
Assn. of Accredited Naturopathic Medical Colleges [8943]
Assn. of Regulatory Boards of Optometry [15716]
Assn. of Schools and Colleges of Optometry [15717]
Bd. of Registered Polysomnographic Technologists [15134]
Certification Bd. of Infection Control and Epidemiology [14702]
Certification of Disability Mgt. Specialists Commn. [13531]
Coll. of Optometrists in Vision Development [15718]
Commn. on Accreditation of Allied Hea. Educ. Programs [8832]
Commn. on Accreditation of Ambulance Services [13532]
Commn. on Accreditation of Rehabilitation Facilities Canada [IO]
Comm. on Accreditation for Opthalmic Medical Personnel [8834]
Continuing Care Accreditation Commn. [16318]

Healthcare Laundry Accreditation Coun. [2403]
Healthcare Quality Certification Bd. [13533]
IEEE Educ. Soc. [8262]
Intl. Assn. of Optometric Executives [15720]
Intl. Christian Accrediting Assn. [7876]
Intl. Christian Accrediting Assn. [IO]
Natl. Acad. of Opticianry [15707]
Natl. Accrediting Agency for Clinical Lab. Sciences [15141]
Natl. Accrediting Commn. of Cosmetology Arts and Sciences [7877]
Natl. Assn. of Optometrists and Opticians [15721]
Natl. Assn. of Private Catholic and Independent Schools [7878]
Natl. Assn. of Private, Nontraditional Schools and Colleges [7947]
Natl. Assn. for Regulatory Admin. [15011]
Natl. Assn. of Schools of Music [8921]
Natl. Bd. of Examiners in Optometry [15722]
Natl. Bd. of Surgical Tech. and Surgical Assisting [13534]
Natl. Comm. for Certifying Agencies [16916]
Natl. Coun. for Accreditation of Teacher Educ. [7879]
Natl. Coun. for Private School Accreditation [7880]
Natl. Credentialing Agency for Lab. Personnel [15145]
Natl. Examining Bd. of Ocularists [15694]
Natl. Fitness Therapy Assn. [15968]
Natl. Optometric Assn. [15725]
Opticians Assn. of Am. [15709]
Optometric Extension Prog. Found. [15727]
Optometric Historical Soc. [15728]
Oral Roberts Univ. Educational Fellowship [8089]
Social Accountability Intl. [18828]
Accreditation of Allied Hea. Educ. Programs; Commn. on [8832]
Accreditation of Ambulatory Plastic Surgery Facilities; Amer. Assn. for [★16557]
Accreditation of Ambulatory Surgery Facilities; Amer. Assn. for [16557]
Accreditation; Amer. Assn. for Lab. [7234]
Accreditation Assn. for Ambulatory Hea. Care [13661], 5200 Old Orchard Rd., Ste. 200, Skokie, IL 60077, (847)853-6060
Accreditation Bd. for Engg. and Tech. - ABET [★6979]
Accreditation Commn. for Acupuncture and Oriental Medicine [15739], 7501 Greenway Center Dr., Ste. 820, Greenbelt, MD 20770, (301)313-0855
Accreditation; Commission on Dental [★14121]
Accreditation; Commn. on Opticianry [15706]
Accreditation; Comm. on Allied Hea. Educ. and [★8832]
Accreditation Comm. on Educ. for Physicians Assistants [★15972]
Accreditation Coun. for Accountancy [★3]
Accreditation Coun. for Accountancy and Taxation [3], 1010 N Fairfax St., Alexandria, VA 22314-1574, (888)289-7763
Accreditation Coun. for Agencies Serving the Blind and Visually Handicapped; Natl. [★16870]
Accreditation Coun. for Agencies Serving the Blind and Visually Impaired; Natl. [16870]
Accreditation Coun; Certified Claims Professional [3865]
Accreditation Coun. for Continuing Medical Educ. [15151], 515 N State St., Ste. 2150, Chicago, IL 60610, (312)755-7401
Accreditation Coun; Diaper Ser. [2386]
Accreditation Coun. for Facilities for the Mentally Retarded [★12567]
Accreditation Coun. for Facilities for the Mentally Retarded [★IO]
Accreditation Coun. for Graduate Medical Educ. [7872], 515 N State St., Ste. 2000, Chicago, IL 60610-4322, (312)755-5000
Accreditation; Coun. for Higher Educ. [8247]
Accreditation Coun. on Optometric Educ. [15710], 243 N Lindbergh Blvd., 1st Fl., St. Louis, MO 63141-7881, (314)991-4100
Accreditation Coun. for Pharmacy Educ. [15907], 20 N Clark St., Ste. 2500, Chicago, IL 60602-5109, (312)664-3575

Reference to "IO" in place of a book number signifies that the association may be found in the 45th edition of International Organizations.

Accreditation Coun. for Services for Mentally Retarded and Other Developmentally Disabled Persons [★12567]

Accreditation Coun. for Services for Mentally Retarded and Other Developmentally Disabled Persons [★IO]

Accreditation Coun. on Services for People with Developmental Disabilities [★IO]

Accreditation Coun. on Services for People with Developmental Disabilities [★12567]

Accreditation Coun. on Services for People with Disabilities [★12567]

Accreditation Coun. on Services for People with Disabilities [★IO]

Accreditation of Counseling and Related Educational Programs; Coun. for [8168]

Accreditation for Educational Programs for the EMS Professions; Comm. on [8833]

Accreditation Healthcare Commn; Amer. [14679]

Accreditation of Healthcare Organizations; Joint Commn. on [14888]

Accreditation of Hospitals; Joint Commn on [★14888]

Accreditation of Lab. Animal Care; Amer. Assn. for [★13695]

Accreditation for Law Enforcement Agencies; Commn. on [5967]

Accreditation for Marriage and Family Therapy Educ; Commn. on [8819]

Accreditation of Medical Transport Systems; Comm. on [14347]

Accreditation of Nurse Anesthesia Educational Programs; Coun. on [8835]

Accreditation in Occupational Hearing Conservation; Coun. for [15632]

Accreditation in Psychoanalysis; Natl. Assn. for the Advancement of Psychoanalysis and the Amer. Bd. for [★16110]

Accreditation Rev. Commn. on Educ. for the Physician Asst. [15972], 12000 Findley Rd., Ste. 240, Duluth, GA 30097, (770)476-1224

Accreditation Rev. Comm. on Educ. for Physician Assistants [★15972]

Accreditation Rev. Comm. on Educ. in Surgical Tech. [15123], 6 W Dry Creek Cir., Ste. 210, Littleton, CO 80120, (303)694-9262

Accreditation Rev. Comm. for Educational Programs in Surgical Tech. [★15123]

Accreditation and School Improvement; North Central Assn. Commn. on [9093]

Accreditation of Vascular Labs; Intersocietal Commn. for the [★16726]

Accredited Chiropractic Educ; Found. for [★14004]

Accredited Cosmetology Schools; Teachers' Educational Coun. - Natl. Assn. of [★8160]

Accredited Gemologists Assn. [2354], c/o G-Force Services, 3315 Juanita St., San Diego, CA 92105, (619)501-5444

Accredited Home Newspapers of Am. [★3259]

Accredited Pet Cemetery Soc. [2953], c/o Angie Pavone, Pres., Paws Awhile Pet Memorial Park, 3426 Brush Rd., Richfield, OH 44286, (330)659-4270

Accredited Rev. Appraisers Coun. [269], 303 W Cypress St., San Antonio, TX 78212, (800)486-3676

Accredited Standards Comm. NCITS, Natl. Comm. for Info. Tech. Standards [★7738]

Accredited Standards Comm. X3, Info. Tech. [★7738]

Accrediting Agency for Clinical Lab. Sciences; Natl. [15141]

Accrediting Assn. of Bible Colleges [★8080]

Accrediting Assn. of Bible Colleges [★8080]

Accrediting Association; International Christian [★8089]

Accrediting Bd; Natl. Architectural [7962]

Accrediting Bur. of Hea. Educ. Schools [15124], 7777 Leesburg Pike, Ste. 314 N, Falls Church, VA 22043, (703)917-9503

Accrediting Bur. of Medical Lab. Schools [★15124]

Accrediting Commn. [★15126]

Accrediting Commn. of Career Schools and Colleges of Tech. [7873], 2101 Wilson Blvd., Ste. 302, Arlington, VA 22201, (703)247-4212

Accrediting Commn; Cosmetology [★7877]

Accrediting Commn. for Cosmetology Educ. [★7877]

Accrediting Commn. for Cosmetology Schools; Natl. [★7877]

Accrediting Commn. on Education for Health Services Administration - Address unknown since 2008.

Accrediting Commn. for Specialized Colls. - Defunct.

Accrediting Coun. for Continuing Educ. and Training [8145], 1722 N St. NW, Washington, DC 20036, (202)955-1113

Accrediting Coun. on Educ. in Journalism and Mass Communications [8703], Stauffer-Flint Hall, 1435 Jayhawk Blvd., Lawrence, KS 66045-7575, (785)864-3973

Accrediting Coun. for Independent Colleges and Schools [7874], 750 1st St. NE, Ste. 980, Washington, DC 20002-4241, (202)336-6780

Accrediting Coun. for Theological Educ. in Africa [IO], Jos, Nigeria

Accreditors; Assn. of Specialized and Professional [1174]

Accuracy in Academia [8352], 4455 Connecticut Ave. NW, Ste. 330, Washington, DC 20008, (202)364-3085

Accuracy in Financial Reporting; Center for Financial Freedom and [18404]

Accuracy in Media [17160], 4455 Connecticut Ave. NW, Ste. 330, Washington, DC 20008, (202)364-4401

ACDI/VOCA [4481], 50 F St. NW, Ste. 1075, Washington, DC 20001, (202)638-4661

ACDI/VOCA [IO], Washington, DC, United States

ACE Fellows Prog. [7881], c/o Amer. Coun. on Educ., 1 Dupont Cir. NW, Washington, DC 20036-1193, (202)939-9300

ACEC Res. and Mgt. Found. [6980], 1015 15th St. NW, 8th Fl., Washington, DC 20005-2605, (202)347-7474

Acetylene Assn; Intl. [★1721]

ACFO [IO], Petersfield, United Kingdom

Achievement; Soc. for Academic [9078]

Achievers Intl. [IO], London, United Kingdom

Achilles Track Club [23331], 42 W 38th St., Ste. 400, New York, NY 10018-6210, (212)354-0300

Achromatopsia Network [16820], PO Box 214, Berkeley, CA 94701-0214, (510)540-4700

ACI - Financial Markets Assn. [IO], Paris, France

Acid Maltase Deficiency
   Acid Maltase Deficiency Assn. [13535]
   Muscular Dystrophy Assn. [15339]

Acid Maltase Deficiency Assn. [13535], PO Box 700248, San Antonio, TX 78270-0248, (210)494-6144

Acid Producers Assn; Glycerine and Fatty [★822]

Acid Rain and Clean Air Policy Analyses; Center for [★5083]

The Acid Rain Found. - Defunct.

Acidemia Assn; Organic [14472]

Acidemia; Intl. Org. of Glutaric [15332]

Acidproof Cement Mfrs. Assn. - Defunct.

ACIL [★7236]

Acindar Found. [IO], Buenos Aires, Argentina

ACJ-YMCA Guatemala [IO], Guatemala City, Guatemala

Ackerman Family Inst; Nathan W. [★12134]

Ackerman Inst. for the Family [12134], 149 E 78th St., New York, NY 10021-0405, (212)879-4900

Ackerman Inst. for Family Therapy [★12134]

ACLU; Natl. Prison Proj. of the [11883]

ACLU; Roger Baldwin Found. of [★17085]

ACM Hong Kong Chap. [IO], Hong Kong, People's Republic of China

ACM Japan Chap. [IO], Tokyo, Japan

ACM SIGCHI [★6542]

ACM SIGGRAPH [894], PO Box 11414, New York, NY 10286-1414, (212)626-0500

ACM SIGGRAPH [IO], New York, NY, United States

ACM SIGGRAPH Kuala Lumpur Professional Chap. [IO], Kuala Lumpur, Malaysia

ACM - YMCA of Kuanza Sul [IO], Kuanza Sul, Angola

ACMC [★20293]

Acne Res. Inst. - Address unknown since 1995.

Acolytes; Intl. Guild of Lay Ministers and [★19963]

Acomb Reunion - Address unknown since 2006.

ACORD [2125], 2 Blue Hill Plz., 3rd Fl., PO Box 1529, Pearl River, NY 10965-8529, (845)620-1700

ACORD [IO], Pearl River, NY, United States

Acorn; Colonial Order of the [20735]

Acoustic Music in the U.S; Soc. for Electro- [10700]

Acoustic Neuroma Assn. [15816], 600 Peachtree Pkwy., Ste. 108, Cumming, GA 30041-6899, (770)205-8211

Acoustic Neuroma Assn. of Canada [IO], Edmonton, AB, Canada

Acoustical Consultants; Natl. Coun. of [646]

Acoustical Contractors Assn; Natl. [★1008]

Acoustical Door Inst. - Defunct.

Acoustical Soc. of Am. [6364], 2 Huntington Quadrangle, Ste. 1N01, Melville, NY 11747-4505, (516)576-2360

Acoustical Soc. of China [IO], Beijing, People's Republic of China

Acoustical Soc. of the Netherlands [IO], Maastricht, Netherlands

Acoustical Soc. of Scandinavia [IO], Lyngby, Denmark

Acoustics
   Acoustical Soc. of Am. [6364]
   Acoustical Soc. of China [IO]
   Acoustical Soc. of the Netherlands [IO]
   Acoustical Soc. of Scandinavia [IO]
   Australian Acoustical Soc. [IO]
   Canadian Acoustical Assn. [IO]
   Canadian Acoustical Assn. - Toronto [IO]
   Ibero-American Fed. of Acoustics [IO]
   IEEE Signal Processing Soc. [6365]
   IEEE Ultrasonics, Ferroelectrics, and Frequency Control Soc. [6366]
   Inst. of Acoustics [IO]
   Intl. Soc. of Acoustic Remote Sensing of the Atmosphere and Oceans [IO]
   New Violin Family Assn. [10672]
   Norwegian Signal Processing Soc. [IO]
   Soc. for Electro-Acoustic Music in the U.S. [10700]
   Southern African Acoustics Inst. [IO]

ACP-EU Joint Parliamentary Assembly [IO], Brussels, Belgium

ACP-UE Assembee Parlementaire Paritaire [★IO]

ACPA Intl. [★IO]

ACPA Intl. [★4]

Acquisition Inst. - Defunct.

Acquisitions
   Alliance of Merger and Acquisition Advisors [54]

Acquisitions of Lib. Materials - of ALA; Bd. of [★10333]

ACRES, Inc. [★4339]

Acres Land Trust [4339], 1802 Chapman Rd., Huntertown, IN 46748, (260)637-2273

Acrobatics
   U.S. Sports Acrobatics [23035]

ACROD, Natl. Indus. Assn. for Disability Services [★IO]

Acronym Inst. for Disarmament Diplomacy [IO], London, United Kingdom

Across [IO], Nairobi, Kenya

Acrylamide Producers Assn. - Address unknown since 1999.

Acrylic Coun. [3768], 1285 Ave. of the Americas, 35th Fl., New York, NY 10019, (212)554-4040

Acrylic Monomer Mfrs. Assn; Basic [★800]

Acrylic Monomer Mfrs; Basic [800]

Acrylic; Natl. Soc. of Painters in Casein and [9518]

Acrylic Painters' Soc; Natl. Oil and [9459]

Acrylonitrile Gp. [795], 1250 Connecticut Ave. NW, Ste. 700, Washington, DC 20036, (202)419-1500

ACSA [★6718]

ACT [9246], PO Box 168, Iowa City, IA 52244-0168, (319)337-1000

ACT Assn. for the Teaching of English [IO], Canberra, Australia

ACT Found. - Defunct.

ACT Hospice Palliative Care Soc. [IO], Civic Square, Australia

Act II Communities - Defunct.

ACT New Zealand [IO], Auckland, New Zealand

ACT and Region Chamber of Commerce and Indus. [IO], Deakin West, Australia

A star before a book entry number signifies that the name is not listed separately, but is mentioned within the entry.

ACT Right to Life Assn. [IO], Canberra, Australia
Act Together [IO], London, United Kingdom
Act Together - Defunct.
ACT UP [16961], 332 Bleecker St., Ste. G5, New York, NY 10014, (212)642-5499
ACTEC Foundation [★6183]
Acting
  Actors' Equity Assn. [24148]
  Actors' Fund of Am. [12112]
  Amer. Fed. of TV and Radio Artists [24022]
  Amer. Guild of Variety Artists [24151]
  Amer. Russian Theatrical Alliance [11001]
  Assoc. Actors and Artistes of Am. [24153]
  Assn. of Theatrical Press Agents and Managers [24154]
  Branscombe Richmond Fan Club [24779]
  Directors Guild of Am. [24055]
  Drama Assn. of Wales [IO]
  Friends of Dennis Lee Fan Club [24780]
  Golden Raspberry Award Found. [22419]
  Guild of Italian Amer. Actors [24155]
  Hispanic Org. of Latin Actors [10001]
  Intl. Alliance of Theatrical Stage Employees, Moving Picture Technicians, Artists and Allied Crafts of the U.S., Its Territories and Canada [24156]
  Intl. Guild of Symphony, Opera and Ballet Musicians [24157]
  Natl. Assn. Broadcast Employees and Technicians - Communications Workers of Am. [24024]
  Natl. Phyllis Diller Fan Club [24799]
  New York Coun. of Motion Picture and TV Unions [24056]
  Official Robert Newman Fan Club [24765]
  Oh Ji Ho Intl. Fan Club [24781]
  Org. of Professional Acting Coaches and Teachers [9267]
  Puerto Rican Traveling Theatre Company [11040]
  Richard Burgi Fan Club [24768]
  Screen Actors Guild [24158]
  Soc. of Amer. Fight Directors [9268]
  Soc. of Stage Directors and Choreographers [24159]
  United Scenic Artists [24160]
  Ziegfeld Club [11054]
  Zuzu News [24777]
Acting Coaches and Teachers; Org. of Professional [9267]
Action 81 - Defunct.
Action Against Allergy [IO], Twickenham, United Kingdom
Action Against Armageddon Project - Defunct.
Action Against Burns - Defunct.
Action Against Hunger [11999], 247 W 37th St., 10th Fl., New York, NY 10018, (212)967-7800
Action Against Hunger [IO], New York, NY, United States
Action Against Hunger - France [IO], Paris, France
Action Against Medical Accidents [IO], Croydon, United Kingdom
Action Aid - Nepal [IO], Kathmandu, Nepal
Action Amers. - Murder Must End Now - Address unknown since 2007.
Action for Autism [IO], New Delhi, India
Action for Better Living - Defunct.
Action for Blind People [IO], London, United Kingdom
Action for Brain-Handicapped Children - Defunct.
Action Canada for Population and Development [IO], Ottawa, ON, Canada
Action Canada pour la Population et le Developpement [★IO]
Action Cancer [IO], Belfast, United Kingdom
Action for Child Protection [11553], 2101 Sardis Rd. N, Ste. 204, Charlotte, NC 28227, (704)845-2121
Action for Child Transportation Safety - Defunct.
Action Children Aid [IO], Copenhagen, Denmark
Action for Children in Conflict [IO], Swindon, United Kingdom
Action for Children's TV - Defunct.
Action des Chretiens pour l'Abolition de la Torture - Belgium [IO], Brussels, Belgium
Action des Chretiens pour l'Abolition de la Torture - France [★IO]
Action des Chretiens pour L'Abolition de la Torture - Luxembourg [IO], Luxembourg, Luxembourg

Action des Chretiens pour l'Abolition de la Torture - Switzerland [IO], Bern, Switzerland
Action by Churches Together Intl. [IO], Geneva, Switzerland
Action Coalition for Media Educ. [18026], 2808 El Tesoro Escondido NW, Albuquerque, NM 87120, (505)893-9702
Action Comm. for Higher Education - Defunct.
Action Comm. for Rural Electrification [1177], c/o Pennsylvania Rural Elec. Assn., PO Box 1266, Harrisburg, PA 17108, (717)233-5704
Action Comm. Ser. for Peace [IO], Bonn, Germany
Action Consulting Assn. [★IO]
Action Consulting Assn. [★11757]
Action Contre la Faim [★IO]
Action for Corporate Accountability - Address unknown since 2001.
Action Coun; AIDS [18278]
Action for Development [IO], Kampala, Uganda
Action in Disabilities - India [IO], Chennai, India
Action on Disability and Development [IO], Frome, United Kingdom
Action for Dysphasic Adults [★IO]
Action Educ. Fund; Peace [18167]
Action on Elder Abuse [IO], London, United Kingdom
Action for Enterprise [IO], Arlington, VA, United States
Action for Enterprise [11757], 2009 N 14th St., Ste. 301, Arlington, VA 22201, (703)243-9172
Action for Food Production [IO], New Delhi, India
Action for Former Military Wives [★12012]
Action Gp; Treatment [13587]
Action Groups Against the Draft - Defunct.
Action Hea. - England [★IO]
Action Hea. - Nigeria [IO], Lagos, Nigeria
Action for Healthy Kids [13945], 4711 W Golf Rd., Ste. 625, Skokie, IL 60076, (800)416-5136
Action for Humanity - Uganda [IO], Kampala, Uganda
Action for Independent Maturity [★12895]
Action Intl. Ministries [19986], PO Box 398, Mountlake Terrace, WA 98043-0398, (425)775-4800
Action Intl. Ministries [IO], Mountlake Terrace, WA, United States
Action for Interracial Understanding - Defunct.
Action from Ireland [IO], Dublin, Ireland
Action Jeunesses pour la Paix [★IO]
Action League; Natl. Abortion and Reproductive [★18518]
Action League; Pro-Life [18565]
Action for Legal Rights - Defunct.
Action for Life - Defunct.
Action Linkage Network - Address unknown since 2003.
Action for Market Towns [IO], Bury St. Edmunds, United Kingdom
Action Now - Integration - Defunct.
Action Now - Political - Defunct.
Action; Peace [18166]
Action for Post-Soviet Jewry [17443], 24 Crescent St., Ste. 306, Waltham, MA 02453-4089, (781)893-2331
Action for Post-Soviet Jewry [IO], Waltham, MA, United States
Action Prog; United Auto Workers Community [★18298]
Action for Rational Drugs in Asia [★IO]
Action Reconciliation Ser. for Peace [IO], Berlin, Germany
Action for Relief and Rehabilitation in Kampuchea - Defunct.
Action for Sick Children [IO], Stockport, United Kingdom
Action for Singapore Dogs [IO], Singapore, Singapore
Action on Smoking and Hea. [16431], 2013 H St. NW, Washington, DC 20006, (202)659-4310
Action on Smoking and Hea. - England [IO], London, United Kingdom
Action on Smoking and Hea. - Ireland [IO], Dublin, Ireland
Action on Smoking and Hea. - Scotland [IO], Edinburgh, United Kingdom
Action; Socialist [18658]
Action for Solidarity, Equality, Env. and Development [IO], Tokyo, Japan

Action for Solidarity, Equality, Env. and Diversity - Europe [IO], Amsterdam, Netherlands
Action for Southern Africa [IO], London, United Kingdom
Action for Soviet Jewry [★IO]
Action for Soviet Jewry [★17443]
Action-Study Center for a Governed World - Defunct.
Action Through Creative Org., Res., and Discussion - Defunct.
Action Training Coalition - Defunct.
Action for Victims of Medical Accidents [★IO]
Action Volunteers for Animals [IO], Unionville, ON, Canada
Action Without Borders; Idealist and [★17640]
Action Without Borders/Idealist.org [17640], 360 W 31st St., Ste. 1510, New York, NY 10001, (212)843-3973
Action Without Borders/Idealist.org [IO], New York, NY, United States
Action for World Community: World Federalist Youth in the U.S.A. - Defunct.
Action for World Solidarity [IO], Berlin, Germany
ActionAid [IO], London, United Kingdom
Actionaid [★IO]
ActionAid - Brasil [IO], Rio de Janeiro, Brazil
ActionAid Intl. USA [IO], Washington, DC, United States
ActionAid Intl. USA [11758], 1420 K St. NW, Ste. 900, Washington, DC 20005, (202)835-1240
ActionAid Intl. - Vietnam [IO], Hanoi, Vietnam
ActionAid - Sierra Leone [IO], Nairobi, Kenya
ActionAid - United Kingdom [IO], London, United Kingdom
Actions for Intl. Solidarity - France [IO], Paris, France
Actions for Professional Excellence Recognition Prog. [★14865]
Actions de Solidarite Internationale - France [★IO]
ACTIS/ATIS [★13554]
Activ Found. [IO], Wembley, Australia
Active 20-30 Assn. of U.S./Canada [13032], 915 L St., Ste. 1000, Sacramento, CA 95814, (916)447-3217
Active 20-30 Intl. [★13032]
Active Intl. [★13032]
Active Learning Network for Accountability and Performance in Humanitarian Action [IO], London, United Kingdom
Active Living Alliance for Canadians with a Disability [IO], Ottawa, ON, Canada
Active Token Collectors Org. - Defunct.
Activism; Amer. Muslims Intent on Learning and [10728]
Activist Fund; The Woman [17574]
Activist; The Woman [17573]
Activists for Animal Rights; United [11469]
Activists for Protective Animal Legislation [11338], PO Box 11743, Costa Mesa, CA 92627, (714)540-0583
Acton Inst. for the Stud. of Religion and Liberty [20489], 161 Ottawa NW, Ste. 301, Grand Rapids, MI 49503, (616)454-3080
Actors
  Acad. of Motion Picture Arts and Sciences [1374]
  Actors' Equity Assn. [24148]
  Actors' Fund of Am. [12112]
  Actors and Others for Animals [11339]
  Aldo Ray Fan Club [24726]
  Amer. Conservatory Theater Found. [11000]
  Amer. Fed. of TV and Radio Artists [24022]
  Amer. Friends of Henry Irving [24727]
  Amer. Guild of Variety Artists [24151]
  Amer. Russian Theatrical Alliance [11001]
  America's Angel [12140]
  Andrea McArdle Fan Club [24728]
  Ann-Margret's Official Fan Club [24729]
  Asociacion Nacional de Actores [IO]
  Assoc. Actors and Artistes of Am. [24153]
  Assn. of Theatrical Press Agents and Managers [24154]
  Barbara Bain Intl. [24730]
  Barbara Bain Intl. [IO]
  Barbara Eden's Official Fan Club [24731]
  Betty White Fan Club [24732]
  Beyond the Rainbow [24733]

Reference to "IO" in place of a book number signifies that the association may be found in the 45th edition of International Organizations.

Branscombe Richmond Fan Club **[24779]**
British Actors' Equity Assn. **[IO]**
Bruce Boxleitner's Official Fan Club **[24734]**
Coalition of Asian Pacifics in Entertainment **[1300]**
Connie Stevens Fan Club **[24868]**
Conrad Veidt Soc. **[24735]**
Danny Cooksey Fan Club **[24736]**
David Birney Intl. Fan Club **[24737]**
David Birney International Fan Club **[IO]**
Dinah Shore Fan Club **[24876]**
Dinah Shore Memorial Fan Club **[24738]**
Directors Guild of Am. **[24055]**
Dollywood Found. **[24878]**
Dutch Don Johnson Fan Club **[IO]**
Episcopal Actors' Guild of Am. **[11013]**
Fanderson **[IO]**
Fans of Leonard Nimoy and DeForest Kelley **[24739]**
Far Beyond the Stars **[24740]**
Friends of Debbie Reynolds Fan Club **[24741]**
Friends of Dennis Lee Fan Club **[24780]**
Friends of Hopalong Cassidy Fan Club **[24742]**
Friends of Hopalong Cassidy Fan Club **[IO]**
Friends of Lainie Kazan **[24743]**
Gale Storm Appreciation Soc. **[24744]**
Gary Morris Fan Club **[24897]**
Gary's Web Intl. **[24745]**
Golden Raspberry Award Found. **[22419]**
Guiding Light Fan Club **[25031]**
Guild of Italian Amer. Actors **[24155]**
Hispanic Org. of Latin Actors **[10001]**
Intl. Alliance of Theatrical Stage Employees, Moving Picture Technicians, Artists and Allied Crafts of the U.S., Its Territories and Canada **[24156]**
Intl. Crosby Circle **[24804]**
Intl. Guild of Symphony, Opera and Ballet Musicians **[24157]**
Intl. Nick Tate Club **[IO]**
Intl. Sybil Jason Fan Club **[24746]**
Jane Powell Fan Club **[24747]**
Jeanette MacDonald Intl. Fan Club **[24748]**
Jeanette MacDonald Intl. Fan Club **[IO]**
Jon-Erik Hexum Fan Club **[24749]**
June Wilkinson Fan Club **[24750]**
Laura Hendler Fan Club **[24751]**
Leslie Charleson Fan Club **[24752]**
Linda Gray's Official Fan Club **[24753]**
Lindsay Wagner's Official Fan Club **[24754]**
Louise Brooks Soc. **[24755]**
Louise Brooks Soc. **[IO]**
Malcolm Wain Fan Club **[24756]**
Mamie Van Doren Fan Club **[24757]**
Mark Slade Fan Club **[24758]**
Marx Brotherhood **[24832]**
Mary Jo Cattlett Fan Club **[24759]**
Michael Crawford Intl. Fan Assn. **[24760]**
Michele Lee Fan Club/Michele Lee Online **[24761]**
Natl. Assn. Broadcast Employees and Technicians - Communications Workers of Am. **[24024]**
Natl. Theatre Workshop of the Handicapped **[11033]**
New York Coun. of Motion Picture and TV Unions **[24056]**
Nick Mancuso Fan Network **[24762]**
Nick Mancuso Fan Network **[IO]**
North Amer. Toyah Fan Club **[24951]**
The Official Austin Powers Collector's Club **[24826]**
Official Intl. Michael York Fan Club **[24763]**
Official Leonard Nimoy Fan Club **[IO]**
Official Michael Biehn Fan Club **[24764]**
Official Robert Newman Fan Club **[24765]**
Oh Ji Ho Intl. Fan Club **[24781]**
Peter Breck Fan Club **[24766]**
Peter Sellers Appreciation Soc. **[24767]**
Puerto Rican Traveling Theatre Company **[11040]**
Richard Burgi Fan Club **[24768]**
Rick's Loyal Supporters **[24967]**
Rita Hayworth Fan Club **[24769]**
Robert Redford Fan Club **[24770]**
Screen Actors Guild **[24158]**
Sharon Gless Fan Club (U.S.) **[24771]**
Shatner and Friends Intl. **[24772]**
Skidrow Joe Fan Club **[24773]**
Soc. of Stage Directors and Choreographers **[24159]**

Stars for Stripes **[20770]**
Stefanie Powers' Official Fan Club **[24774]**
Talent Managers Assn. **[1325]**
TV Audience Screen Extras Guild **[55]**
Theatre for Young Audiences/USA **[11051]**
Tom Mix Intl. Fan Club **[24775]**
United Scenic Artists **[24160]**
W.C. Fields Fan Club **[24801]**
We Love Lucy/International Lucille Ball Fan Club **[24776]**
We Love Lucy/International Lucille Ball Fan Club **[IO]**
Women's Interart Center **[11096]**
Young and the Restless Fan Club **[25047]**
Zuzu News **[24777]**
Actors and Athletes Against Drunk Driving; Recording Artists, **[12986]**
Actors' Equity Assn. **[24148]**, 165 W 46th St., New York, NY 10036, (212)869-8530
Actors' Equity Assn; Canadian **[IO]**
Actors' Fund of Am. **[12112]**, 729 Seventh Ave., 10th Fl., New York, NY 10019, (212)221-7300
Actors' Guild of Am; Episcopal **[11013]**
Actors; Guild of Italian Amer. **[24155]**
Actors Guild; Screen **[24158]**
Actors; Hispanic Org. of Latin **[10001]**
Actors and Others for Animals **[11339]**, 11523 Burbank Blvd., North Hollywood, CA 91601-2309, (818)755-6045
Actors Studio **[10995]**, 8341 Delongpre Ave., West Hollywood, CA 90069-2601, (323)654-7125
Actors Working for an Actors Guild - Defunct.
Acts for Peace **[★18259]**
Actualizations - Address unknown since 1988.
Actuarial Assn. **[IO]**, Woerden, Netherlands
Actuarial Assn; Crop-Hail Insurance **[★2223]**
Actuarial Soc. of Am. **[★2239]**
Actuarial Soc. of Australasia **[★IO]**
Actuarial Soc. of Australia and New Zealand **[★IO]**
Actuarial Soc; Casualty **[2153]**
Actuarial Soc. of Hong Kong **[IO]**, Hong Kong, People's Republic of China
Actuarial Soc. of New South Wales **[★IO]**
Actuarial Soc. of South Africa **[IO]**, Cape Town, Republic of South Africa
Actuarieel Genootschap **[★IO]**
Actuaries; Amer. Acad. of **[2127]**
Actuaries; Amer. Inst. of **[★2239]**
Actuaries; Amer. Soc. of Pension **[★1233]**
Actuaries; Assn. of Consulting **[IO]**
Actuaries; Conf. of Consulting **[2157]**
Actuaries; Faculty of **[IO]**
Actuaries in Public Practice; Conf. of **[★2157]**
Actuaries; Soc. of **[2239]**
ACU Educ. Res. Inst. **[★17634]**
ACUO **[8341]**, PO Box 65298, Washington, DC 20035, (202)659-2104
Acupressure; Jin Shin Do Found. for Bodymind **[15746]**

Acupuncture
  Accreditation Commn. for Acupuncture and Oriental Medicine **[15739]**
  Acupuncture and Oriental Medicine Alliance **[13607]**
  Acupuncturists Without Borders **[13536]**
  Acupuncturists Without Borders **[IO]**
  Amer. Acad. of Acupuncture and Oriental Medicine **[13611]**
  Amer. Acupuncture Assn. **[15741]**
  Amer. Assn. of Oriental Medicine **[15742]**
  Amer. Manual Medicine Assn. **[13618]**
  Amer. Org. for Bodywork Therapies of Asia **[15024]**
  Coun. of Colleges of Acupuncture and Oriental Medicine **[15743]**
  G-Jo Inst. **[15745]**
  Heart Disease Res. Found. **[13905]**
  Intl. Acupuncture Assn. of Physical Therapists **[IO]**
  Intl. Veterinary Acupuncture Soc. **[16796]**
  Jin Shin Do Found. for Bodymind Acupressure **[15746]**
  Natl. Certification Commn. for Acupuncture and Oriental Medicine **[15747]**
  Ohashi Inst. **[15748]**
  Soc. for Acupuncture Res. **[13537]**

  Soc. for Acupuncture Res. **[IO]**
Acupuncture; Amer. Acad. of Medical **[15740]**
Acupuncture Assn; Amer. **[15741]**
Acupuncture Assn. - Defunct.
Acupuncture Assn; Norwegian **[IO]**
Acupuncture; Austrian Soc. for **[IO]**
Acupuncture Coun; British **[IO]**
Acupuncture Detoxification Assn; Natl. **[16510]**
Acupuncture Found. of Canada Inst. **[IO]**, Scarborough, ON, Canada
Acupuncture and Oriental Medicine; Accreditation Commn. for **[15739]**
Acupuncture and Oriental Medicine Alliance **[13607]**, PO Box 738, Gig Harbor, WA 98335, (253)238-8134
Acupuncture and Oriental Medicine; Amer. Acad. of **[13611]**
Acupuncture and Oriental Medicine; Coun. of Colleges of **[15743]**
Acupuncture and Oriental Medicine; Natl. Accreditation Commn. for Schools and Colleges of **[★15739]**
Acupuncture and Oriental Medicine; Natl. Certification Commn. for **[15747]**
Acupuncture Res. Inst. - Defunct.
Acupuncture Soc; British Medical **[IO]**
Acupuncturists; Natl. Commn. for the Certification of **[★15747]**
Acupuncturists Without Borders **[13536]**, 37 Kelly Lynn Dr., Sandia Park, NM 87047, (505)991-0112
Acupuncturists Without Borders **[IO]**, Sandia Park, NM, United States
ACURIL **[★IO]**
ACURIL **[★10329]**
ACURP **[★16261]**
ACUTA: The Assn. of Coll. and Univ. Telecommunications Administrators Inc. **[★8548]**
ACUTA: The Assn. for Communications Tech. Professionals in Higher Educ. **[8548]**, 152 W Zandale Dr., Ste. 200, Lexington, KY 40503, (859)278-3338
ACUTA: The Assn. for Telecommunication Professionals in Higher Educ. **[★8548]**
Acute Idiopathic Polyneuritis
  Guillain-Barre Syndrome Found. Intl. **[15327]**
Acute Long Term Hosp. Assn. **[14852]**, c/o Jennifer Connors, Dir. of Communications, 625 Slaters Ln., Ste. 302, Alexandria, VA 22314, (703)518-9900
ACV - Bouw en Industrie **[IO]**, Brussels, Belgium
Ad Coun. **[18384]**, 261 Madison Ave., 11th Fl., New York, NY 10016, (212)922-1500
Ad Hoc Coalition Against Terrorism in America - Defunct.
Ad Hoc Coalition on Block Grants **[★13161]**
Ad Hoc Coalition of IMF Supporters - Defunct.
Ad Hoc Coalition for Women - Defunct.
Ad Hoc Comm. of Amer. Jews for Peace in the Middle East - Defunct.
Ad Hoc Comm. for Amer. Silver - Defunct.
Ad Hoc Comm. to Bring Nazi War Criminals to Justice **[★17719]**
Ad Hoc Comm. in Defense of Life - Address unknown since 2003.
Ad Hoc Comm. on the Drafting of an Intl. Convention Against Apartheid in Sports - Defunct.
Ad Hoc Comm. on Freedom of Scholarly Inquiry - Defunct.
Ad Hoc Comm. on the Human Rights and Genocide Treaties - Defunct.
Ad Hoc Comm. of Lead Consumers - Defunct.
Ad Hoc Comm. for Lebanese Freedom - Defunct.
Ad Hoc Comm. of Merchant Pig Iron Producers of America - Defunct.
Ad Hoc Comm. for Open Leetter on Vietnam - Defunct.
Ad Hoc Comm. of Scholars Opposed to U.S. Intervention in El Salvador - Defunct.
Ad Hoc Concerned Americans for Asia-Pacific Peace and Stability - Defunct.
Ad Hoc Congressional Comm. on the Baltic States and the Ukraine - Address unknown since 1994.
Ad Hoc Congressional Comm. for Irish Affairs - Address unknown since 2001.
Ad Hoc Foreign Passport Holders Comm. - Defunct.
Ad Hoc Gp. on Latin Amer. Anthropology **[★6431]**

A star before a book entry number signifies that the name is not listed separately, but is mentioned within the entry.

Ad Hoc Gp. on Latin Amer. Anthropology [★IO]

Ad Hoc Gp. for Medical Res. Funding [17686], c/o Assn. of Amer. Medical Colleges, 2450 N St. NW, Washington, DC 20037-1126, (202)828-0525

Ad Hoc Group on U.S. Policy Toward the U.N. - Defunct.

Ad Hoc Low Income Housing Coalition [★12330]

Ad Hoc Monitoring Group on Southern Africa - Defunct.

A.D. Johnson Family Assn. [20771], c/o John S. Walker, Family Historian/Pres., 930 W Long Ave., Du Bois, PA 15801-3512, (814)371-5149

Ada Cole Rescue Stables [IO], Waltham Abbey, United Kingdom

ADA Found. Res. Institute [★14131]

Ada; Special Interest Gp. on [7538]

ADABUSE - Defunct.

Adam Hawkes Family Assn. [20772], c/o Cynthia Hawkes Meehan, Pres., 65 Center St., Danvers, MA 01923

ADAM; Remembering [13280]

Adam Smith Inst. [IO], London, United Kingdom

Adam Wise Family Assn. [20773], 29801 Highview Cir., San Juan Capistrano, CA 92675, (949)661-4808

Adams Family Assn. - Address unknown since 2008.

Adams Historical Soc. Inc; Abigail [11099]

Adams Historical Soc; Mc [20995]

Adaptive Learning; Center for [★7104]

Adaptive Sports Assn. [23332], PO Box 1884, Durango, CO 81302, (970)259-0374

ADARA [★14735]

ADARA: Professionals Networking for Excellence in Ser. Delivery with Individuals who are Deaf or Hard of Hearing [14735], PO Box 480, Myersville, MD 21773, (301)293-8969

Adbusters Media Found. [IO], Vancouver, BC, Canada

ADC Res. Inst. [★17082]

Addict Care Today; Provide [★13262]

Addiction Coun.; Natl. Black Alcoholism and [13265]

Addiction Medicine; Amer. Osteopathic Acad. of [16500]

Addiction Medicine; Amer. Soc. of [16501]

Addiction to Narcotics; Natl. Assn. for the Prevention of [★13262]

Addiction Professionals; NAADAC The Assn. for [16509]

Addiction Professionals; Natl. Assn. of Lesbian/Gay [13263]

Addiction Psychiatry; Amer. Acad. of [16062]

Addiction Rehabilitation Assn; Christian [13229]

Addiction Res. and Treatment Corp. [13213], 22 Chapel St., Brooklyn, NY 11201, (718)260-2900

Addiction Treatment Administrators; Amer. Coll. of [13219]

Addictionology; Amer. Osteopathic Acad. [★16500]

Addictions; Natl. Nurses Soc. on [★15484]

Addictions and Offender Counselors; Intl. Assn. of [11824]

Addictions Ontario [IO], Kitchener, ON, Canada

Addicts Anonymous; Sex [13073]

Addicts Anonymous; Sex and Love [13074]

Addicts; Co-Dependents of Sex [★13072]

Addington Assn. [20774], 100 Oak Beech Ct., Holly Springs, NC 27540

Addington Bush Soc. [IO], Christchurch, New Zealand

Addis Ababa Chamber of Commerce [IO], Addis Ababa, Ethiopia

Addison's Disease Found; Natl. [★14358]

Addison's Disease Self Help Gp. [IO], Guildford, United Kingdom

Additive Mfg. Community; Rapid Technologies and [7267]

ADDult Support Network - Address unknown since 1999.

ADECOM Network [IO], Pondicherry, India

ADED: The Association for Driver Rehabilitation Specialists [IO], Ruston, LA, United States

ADED: The Assn. for Driver Rehabilitation Specialists [8209], 711 S Vienna St., Ruston, LA 71270, (318)257-5055

Adelaide Hosp. Soc. [IO], Dublin, Ireland

Adelantre - The Judezmo Soc. - Defunct.

Adelynrood Retreat Center [★19971]

ADHD-foreningen [IO], Lysaker, Norway

Adhesion Soc. [6661], 2 Davidson Hall - 0201, Blacksburg, VA 24061, (540)231-7257

Adhesions Soc; Intl. [15840]

Adhesive and Sealant Coun. [56], 7979 Old George-town Rd., Ste. 500, Bethesda, MD 20814, (301)986-9700

Adhesive and Sealant Manufacturers Coun; Rubber and Plastic [★56]

Adhesive Tape Mfrs'. Assn. [IO], Bromley, United Kingdom

Adhesives

Adhesive and Sealant Coun. [56]

Adhesive Tape Mfrs'. Assn. [IO]

Assn. of European Adhesives Mfrs. [IO]

British Adhesives and Sealants Assn. [IO]

European Assn. for the Self-Adhesive Tape Indus. [IO]

Fastener Engg. and Res. Assn. [IO]

Intl. Fed. of Mfrs. of Gummed Paper [IO]

Powder Actuated Systems Assn. [IO]

Pressure Sensitive Tape Coun. [57]

Sealant Waterproofing and Restoration Inst. [58]

Sealant Waterproofing and Restoration Institute [IO]

Taiwan Regional Assn. of Adhesive Tape Mfrs. [IO]

Worldwide Assn. of Self-Adhesive Labels and Related Products [IO]

Adhesives Mfrs. Assn. - Defunct.

The Adirondack Coun. [4340], 103 Hand Ave., Ste. 3, PO Box D-2, Elizabethtown, NY 12932, (518)873-2240

Adirondack Forty-Sixers [23930], PO Box 180, Cadyville, NY 12918-0180, (518)293-6401

Adirondack Historical Assn. [9340], c/o Adirondack Museum, PO Box 99, Blue Mountain Lake, NY 12812-0099, (518)352-7311

Adirondack Mountain Club [23931], 814 Goggins Rd., Lake George, NY 12845, (518)668-4447

Adirondack Trail Improvement Soc. [23932], PO Box 565, Keene Valley, NY 12943, (518)576-9949

Adirondacks

Adirondack Forty-Sixers [23930]

Adirondack Historical Assn. [9340]

Adirondack Mountain Club [23931]

Adirondack Trail Improvement Soc. [23932]

Adizes Network Intl. [★2483]

Adizes Network Intl. [★IO]

Adizes Practitioners Intl; Assn. of Certified [2483]

Adjudicator Assn; Natl. Fed. Music [★8928]

Adjusters' Assn; Canadian Independent [IO]

Adjusters; Natl. Assn. of Catastrophe [2205]

Adjusters; Organized Flying [2229]

Adjusters of the U.S; Assn. of Average [2145]

Adjustment Assn; Vocational Evaluation and Work [★16337]

Adjutants Gen. Assn. of the U.S. [6061], c/o Terri Kattes, Nebraska Military Dept., 1300 Military Rd., Lincoln, NE 68508-1090, (402)309-7107

Adlai Stevenson Inst. of Intl. Affairs - Defunct.

Adler Consultation Center; Alfred [★16117]

Adler Inst; Alfred [16117]

Adlerian Psychology; North Amer. Soc. of [16162]

Administration

ACE Fellows Prog. [7881]

Advt. Women of New York [81]

Amer. Assn. of Behavioral and Social Sciences [6522]

Amer. Assn. of Christian Schools [7875]

Amer. Assn. of Presidents of Independent Colleges and Universities [8534]

Amer. Assn. of School Administrators [7882]

Amer. Assn. of School Personnel Administrators [7883]

Amer. Assn. of School Personnel Administrators [IO]

Amer. Assn. of Univ. Administrators [7884]

Amer. Assn. for Women in Community Colleges [9313]

Amer. Coll. of Healthcare Info. Administrators [14611]

Amer. Collegiate Retailing Assn. [8815]

Amer. Conf. of Academic Deans [7885]

Amer. Coun. on Rural Special Educ. [9137]

Amer. Fed. of School Administrators [7886]

Assn. for the Advancement of Intl. Educ. [8640]

Assn. of Amer. Universities [8099]

Assn. of Arts Admin. Educators [7967]

Assn. for Career and Tech. Educ. [9300]

Assn. of Coll. Admin. Professionals [7887]

Assn. of Coll. and Univ. Auditors [7888]

Association of College and University Auditors [IO]

Assn. for Gender Equity Leadership in Educ. [8399]

Assn. of Governing Boards of Universities and Colleges [7889]

Assn. of Governing Bodies of Independent Schools [IO]

Assn. of Graduate Schools in Assn. of Amer. Universities [7890]

Assn. of Intl. Educ. Administrators [7891]

Assn. of Intl. Educ. Administrators [IO]

Assn. of Registrars of the Universities and Colleges of Canada [IO]

Assn. of School Bus. Officials Intl. [IO]

Assn. of School Bus. Officials Intl. [7892]

Assn. of School and Coll. Leaders [IO]

Assn. of Schools of Journalism and Mass Commun. [7893]

Assn. of Univ. Administrators [IO]

Australian Coun. for Educational Leaders [IO]

Australian Coun. for Educational Leaders - Newcastle [IO]

Australian Coun. for Educational Leaders - South Australia [IO]

Australian Coun. for Educational Leaders - Wagga Wagga [IO]

Bd. of Governors of the European Schools [IO]

British Educational Leadership, Mgt. and Admin. Soc. [IO]

Canadian Assn. of Principals [IO]

Canadian Assn. of Programs in Public Admin. [IO]

Canadian Assn. of School Administrators [IO]

Canadian Assn. of Univ. Bus. Officers [IO]

Canadian Fed. of Bus. School Deans [IO]

Center for Intl. Initiatives [8745]

Chaordic Commons [7409]

Coll. and Univ. Cmpt. Users Assn. [7894]

Coll. and Univ. Professional Assn. for Human Resources [8962]

Commonwealth Coun. for Educational Admin. and Mgt. [IO]

Cooperative Educ. and Internship Assn. [8157]

Coun. of Administrators of Special Educ. [9139]

Coun. of Chief State School Officers [8246]

Coun. for Elementary Sci. Intl. [9100]

Coun. on Governmental Relations [9058]

Coun. on Standards for Intl. Educational Travel [8610]

Educational Leadership Inst. [8746]

Educational Planning Inst. [8998]

Educational Res. Ser. [7895]

European School Heads Assn. [IO]

GuildHE [IO]

Headmasters' and Headmistresses' Conf. [IO]

HEATH Rsrc. Center [8203]

Intl. Assn. of French-Speaking Directors of Educational Institutions [IO]

Intl. Assn. of Jesuit Bus. Schools [8026]

Intl. Assn. of Schools and Institutes of Admin. [IO]

Intl. Assn. for Truancy and Dropout Prevention [8326]

Intl. Coun. on Educ. for Teaching [9216]

Intl. Coun. of Fine Arts Deans [7973]

Intl. Educator's Inst. [8645]

Intl. Reading Assn. [9043]

Jesuit Assn. of Student Personnel Administrators [7896]

Lutheran Educ. Assn. [8803]

MENC: The Natl. Assn. for Music Educ. [8913]

Metro Intl. Prog. Services of New York [8624]

Natl. Alliance for Safe Schools [9085]

Natl. Assn. of Coll. and Univ. Bus. Officers [7897]

Natl. Assn. of Educational Off. Professionals [7898]

Natl. Assn. of Educational Procurement [7899]

Natl. Assn. of Fed. Educ. Prog. Administrators [7900]

Reference to "IO" in place of a book number signifies that the association may be found in the 45th edition of International Organizations.

Natl. Assn. of Head Teachers [IO]
Natl. Assn. of Hebrew Day School Administrators [7901]
Natl. Assn. of Multicultural Engg. Prog. Advocates [8370]
Natl. Assn. of Pupil Services Administrators [7902]
Natl. Assn. of Scholars [8490]
Natl. Assn. of State Administrators and Supervisors of Private Schools [9021]
Natl. Assn. of State Boards of Educ. [9082]
Natl. Assn. of State Directors of Special Educ. [9149]
Natl. Assn. of State Directors of Vocational Tech. Educ. Consortium [9307]
Natl. Assn. of Student Affairs Professionals [7903]
Natl. Assn. of Student Personnel Administrators [7904]
Natl. Assn. of Supervisors and Administrators of Hea. Occupations Educ. [8870]
Natl. Assn. of Women Law Enforcement Executives [5989]
Natl. Center for Higher Educ. Mgt. Systems [7905]
Natl. Community Educ. Assn. [8126]
Natl. Conf. on Student Leadership [9188]
Natl. Coun. of State Educ. Associations [7906]
Natl. Coun. of Univ. Res. Administrators [9063]
Natl. Orientation Directors Assn. [7907]
Natl. PTA - Natl. Cong. of Parents and Teachers [8954]
Natl. Rsrc. Center for Paraprofessionals in Educ. and Related Services [9150]
Natl. Rural Educ. Assn. [9069]
Natl. School Boards Assn. [9083]
Natl. School Public Relations Assn. [9033]
Natl. Staff Development Coun. [7908]
Navajo Area School Bd. Assn. [8942]
New South Wales Secondary Principals Assn. [IO]
North Amer. Assn. of Commencement Officers [8492]
North Amer. Assn. of Summer Sessions [9200]
North Amer. Assn. of Synagogue Executives [20517]
Off. of Women in Higher Educ., Amer. Coun. on Educ. [9324]
Presbyterian Church Bus. Administrators' Assn. [20470]
Presidential Prayer Team [20210]
Queensland Secondary Principals Assn. [IO]
Secondary Principals Assn. of New Zealand [IO]
Soc. for the Advancement of Educ. [8305]
Soc. for Coll. and Univ. Planning [9000]
Soc. for Design Admin. [6481]
Soc. of Headmasters and Headmistresses of Independent Schools [IO]
Soc. of Schoolmasters and Schoolmistresses [IO]
Tasmanian Secondary Principals Assn. [IO]
Universities Australia [IO]
Universities UK [IO]
Univ. Coun. for Educational Admin. [7909]
Univ. Professors for Academic Order [9026]
Urban Superintendent's Assn. of Am. [9288]
Western Australian Secondary School Executives Assn. [IO]
Admin; Amer. Soc. for Public [6190]
Admin. Assn; Natl. Rehabilitation [★16325]
Admin. Assn; Property [★3190]
Admin; Center for Res. in Ambulatory Hea. Care [15064]
Admin. Educ. Found; Southern Public [6199]
Admin. and Gen. Ser. Officers; Natl. Assn. of State Directors of [★6278]
Admin. Inst; Bank [467]
Admin. Intl; Amer. Soc. for Personnel [★2907]
Admin. Internship Prog; Academic [★7881]
Admin. and Mgt. Assn; Lib. [10366]
Admin; Natl. Assn. of Church Bus. [20513]
Admin; Natl. Assn. for Regulatory [15011]
Admin; Natl. Assn. of Schools of Public Affairs and [6194]
Admin; Natl. Comm. for Women in Public [★6198]
Admin; Sect. for Women in Public [6198]
Admin; Soc. for Personnel [★1267]
Admin; Task Force for Women in Public [★6198]

Administrative Asst. Assn. [★73]
Administrative Assistants Assn. of the U.S. House of Representatives - Address unknown since 1999.
Administrative Assn; Plastic Surgery [14050]
Administrative Law Judges; Assn. of [5894]
Administrative Law Judges Conf; Fed. [5899]
Administrative Law Judges, Dept. of Hea. and Human Services; Assn. of [★5894]
Administrative Mgt. Soc. - Address unknown since 1994.
Administrative Professionals Assn. of Ghana [IO], Accra, Ghana

Administrative Services

Administrative Professionals Assn. of Ghana [IO]
Amer. Coll. of Healthcare Info. Administrators [14611]
Amer. Contract Compliance Assn. [17493]
Aruba Secretaries Assn. [IO]
Asian Development Bank Staff Assn. [IO]
Associatiacao Das Secretaries De Angola [IO]
Assn. of Administrative Assistants [IO]
Assn. of Administrative Professionals New Zealand [IO]
Assn. of Administrative Professionals New Zealand - Auckland Gp. [IO]
Assn. of Administrative Professionals New Zealand - Dunedin Gp. [IO]
Assn. of Administrative Professionals New Zealand - Manawatu Gp. [IO]
Assn. of Administrative Professionals New Zealand - Marlborough Gp. [IO]
Assn. of Administrative Professionals New Zealand - Porirua City Gp. [IO]
Assn. of Administrative Professionals New Zealand - Taranaki Gp. [IO]
Assn. of Celebrity Personal Assistants [59]
Assn. of Certified Professional Secretaries [60]
Assn. of Coun. Secretaries and Solicitors [IO]
Assn. for Financial Tech. [61]
Assn. of Local Govt. Auditors [5429]
Assn. of Medical Secretaries, Practice Managers, Administrators and Receptionists [IO]
Assn. of Secretaries and Administrative Professionals of Trinidad and Tobago [IO]
Assn. of Virtual Assistants of Ireland [IO]
Barbados Assn. of Off. Professionals [IO]
Black Data Processing Associates [62]
Canadian Assn. of Paralegals [IO]
Chartered Secretaries Australia [IO]
Chartered Secretaries Australia - Queensland Br. [IO]
Chartered Secretaries Australia - South Australia Br. [IO]
Chartered Secretaries Australia - Tasmania Br. [IO]
Chartered Secretaries Australia - Victoria Br. [IO]
Chartered Secretaries Australia - Western Australia Br. [IO]
Chartered Secretaries New Zealand [IO]
European Assn. of Professional Secretaries [IO]
Executive Women Intl. [IO]
Executive Women Intl. [63]
Executive Women Intl. - Calgary Chap. [IO]
GMB [IO]
Grand Bahamas Assn. of Administrative Professionals [IO]
Hea. Care Executive Assistants [64]
Hong Kong Assn. of Secretaries and Administrative Professionals [IO]
Hong Kong Inst. of Company Secretaries [IO]
Ikatan Sekretaris Indonesia [IO]
Incorporated Phonographic Soc. [IO]
Indian Assn. of Secretaries and Administrative Professionals [IO]
Info. Systems Audit and Control Assn. and Found. [IO]
Info. Systems Audit and Control Assn. and Found. [65]
Info. Systems Audit and Control Assn. and Found. Singapore [IO]
Inst. of Agricultural Secretaries and Administrators [IO]
Inst. of Chartered Secretaries and Administrators - Canada [IO]
Inst. of Chartered Secretaries and Administrators - United Kingdom [IO]

Inst. of Chartered Secretaries and Administrators - Zimbabwe [IO]
Inst. of Clerks of Works of Great Britain [IO]
Inst. of Legal Cashiers and Administrators [IO]
Inst. of Legal Executives [IO]
Inst. of Qualified Professional Secretaries [IO]
Intl. Assn. of Administrative Professionals [IO]
Intl. Assn. of Administrative Professionals [66]
Intl. Assn. for Human Rsrc. Info. Mgt. [67]
Intl. Assn. for Human Rsrc. Info. Mgt. [IO]
Intl. Virtual Assistants Assn. [68]
Jamaica Assn. of Secretaries and Administrative Professionals [IO]
Japan Secretaries Assn. [IO]
Legal Secretaries Intl. [IO]
Legal Secretaries Intl. [69]
Malaysian Assn. of Professional Secretaries and Administrators [IO]
Malaysian Inst. of Chartered Secretaries and Administrators [IO]
Mandate Trade Union [IO]
MEMA Info. Services Coun. [70]
NALS, the Assn. for Legal Professionals [71]
NALS, the Association for Legal Professionals [IO]
Natl. Assn. of Executive Secretaries and Administrative Assistants [72]
Natl. Contract Mgt. Assn. [1744]
Natl. Coun. of Youth Sports [23839]
Natl. Secretarial Assn. [73]
Non-Executive Directors Assn. [IO]
North Amer. Assn. of Synagogue Executives [20517]
Nursery and Landscape Assn. Executives of North Am. [5047]
Off. Bus. Center Assn. Intl. [74]
Off. and Professional Employees Intl. Union [23995]
Philippine Assn. of Secretaries and Administrative Professionals [IO]
SEIU, District 925, AFL-CIO [23996]
Singapore Assn. of Administrative Professionals [IO]
Singapore Assn. of the Inst. of Chartered Secretaries and Administrators [IO]
Soc. of Corporate Secretaries and Governance Professionals [75]
Soc. of Local Coun. Clerks [IO]
Special Interest Group for Business Data Processing and Mgt. [76]
Sri Lanka Assn. of Administrative and Professional Secretaries [IO]
Turks and Caicos Assn. of Off. Professionals [IO]
Union Network Intl. - Asian and Pacific Regional Off. [IO]
Women Secretaries' Assn. of Thailand [IO]
Worshipful Company of Scriveners of the City of London [IO]
Administrators; Amer. Acad. of Medical [15045]
Administrators; Amer. Assn. of Clinical Lab. Supervisors and [★14993]
Administrators; Amer. Assn. of Motor Vehicle [5535]
Administrators; Amer. Assn. of Psychiatric [14861]
Administrators; Amer. Coll. of Addiction Treatment [13219]
Administrators; Amer. Coll. of Cardiovascular [15052]
Administrators; Amer. Coll. of Hea. Care [15535]
Administrators; Amer. Coll. of Hosp. [★14862]
Administrators; Amer. Coll. of Medical Gp. [★15054]
Administrators; Amer. Coll. of Nursing Home [★15535]
Administrators; Amer. Coll. of Oncology [15055]
Administrators; Amer. Coll. of Osteopathic Hosp. [★14876]
Administrators; Amer. Healthcare Radiology [16275]
Administrators; Amer. Hosp. Radiology [★16275]
Administrators; Amer. Soc. for Healthcare Food Ser. [14867]
Administrators; Amer. Soc. for Hosp. Food Ser. [★14867]
Administrators; Amer. Soc. of Ophthalmic [15058]
Administrators; Assn. of Accounting [★13]
Administrators Assn. of Am; Correctional [★11858]
Administrators; Assn. of Family Practice [15060]

A star before a book entry number signifies that the name is not listed separately, but is mentioned within the entry.

Administrators; Assn. of Legal [5929]

Administrators and Assn. of Local Air Pollution Control Officials; State and Territorial Air Pollution Prog. [★5696]

Administrators Assn; Natl. Renal [15072]

Administrators Assn; Naval Civilian [★6094]

Administrators; Assn. of Problem Gambling Ser. [12208]

Administrators; Assn. of Small Loan [★5610]

Administrators; Canadian Assn. of Student Financial Aid [IO]

Administrators; Conf. on Jesuit Student Personnel [★7896]

Administrators; Conf. of Local Environmental Hea. [★16246]

Administrators; Conf. of State Court [5625]

Administrators of Educational Personnel; Amer. Assn. of Examiners and [★7883]

Administrators Guild; Sys. [★6806]

Administrators of Hea. Occupations Educ; Natl. Assn. for State [★8870]

Administrators of Hea. Occupations Educ; Natl. Assn. of Supervisors and [8870]

Administrators; Intl. Soc. of Performing Arts [★9575]

Administrators of the Interstate Compact on the Placement of Children; Assn. of [11559]

Administrators; Natl. Assn. of Church Personnel [20515]

Administrators; Natl. Assn. of Collegiate Women Athletics [8982]

Administrators; Natl. Assn. of Consumer Credit [5610]

Administrators; Natl. Assn. of County of Employment and Training [★5618]

Administrators; Natl. Assn. of County Hea. Fac. [15069]

Administrators; Natl. Assn. of Directors and [★14574]

Administrators; Natl. Assn. of Fleet [362]

Administrators; Natl. Assn. of Govt. Archives and Records [5820]

Administrators; Natl. Assn. of Govt. Deferred Compensation [★2340]

Administrators; Natl. Assn. of Govt. Defined Contribution [2340]

Administrators; Natl. Assn. of Pension Consultants and [★17350]

Administrators; Natl. Assn. of Professional Contracts [★1744]

Administrators; Natl. Assn. of Pupil Personnel [★7902]

Administrators; Natl. Assn. of Pupil Services [7902]

Administrators; Natl. Assn. of State Boating Law [5545]

Administrators; Natl. Assn. of State Chief [6278]

Administrators; Natl. Assn. of State Facilities [6195]

Administrators; Natl. Assn. of State Retirement [5569]

Administrators; Natl. Assn. of Student Financial Aid [8350]

Administrators; Natl. Assn. of Student Loan [8432]

Administrators; Natl. Assn. of Temple [20163]

Administrators; Natl. Conf. of Local Environmental Hea. [16246]

Administrators; Natl. Conf. of State Court [★5625]

Administrators; Natl. Conf. of State Liquor [5447]

Administrators; Natl. Coun. of Local Public Human Ser. [13178]

Administrators; Natl. Coun. of Local Public Welfare [★13178]

Administrators; Natl. Coun. of State Human Ser. [13179]

Administrators; Natl. Coun. of State Public Welfare [★13179]

Administrators for Native Amer. Rehabilitation; Consortia of [19270]

Administrators Res. and Educational Found; Amer. Acad. of Medical [15046]

Administrators; Soc. of Professional Benefit [1245]

Administrators; Soc. for Radiation Oncology [16302]

Administrators and Supervisors Organizing Comm; School [★7886]

Administrators and Supervisors of Private Schools; Natl. Assn. of State [9021]

Administrators of Vocational Rehabilitation; Coun. of State [16320]

Admission Assn; Natl. Catholic Coll. [19672]

Admissions
Amer. Assn. of Collegiate Registrars and Admissions Officers [7910]
Amer. Coll. and Career Counseling Center [7911]
Coll. Summit [8486]
Natl. Assn. for Coll. Admission Counseling [7912]
Natl. Assn. of Graduate Admissions Professionals [7913]
North Amer. Coalition for Christian Admissions Professionals [7914]
Pathways to Coll. Network [8493]

Admissions Advisory Center; Amer. Coll. [★7911]

Admissions Center; Amer. Coll. [★7911]

Admissions Professionals; Natl. Assn. of Graduate [7913]

Admissions Professionals; New England Assn. of Graduate [★7913]

Adolescence; Soc. for Res. on [13515]

Adolescent Development; Carnegie Coun. on [13477]

Adolescent Gastroesophageal Reflux Assn; Pediatric/ [14426]

Adolescent Medicine; Soc. for [13974]

Adolescent Pregnancy and Parenting; Natl. Org. of [★12182]

Adolescent Pregnancy, Parenting and Prevention; Natl. Org. on [★12182]

Adolescent Psychiatric Nurses; Assn. of Child and [★15487]

Adolescent Psychiatry; Amer. Acad. of Child and [16063]

Adolescent Psychiatry; Amer. Soc. for [16078]

Adolescent Psychiatry; European Soc. of Child and [IO]

Adolescent Psychiatry; Soc. of Professors of Child and [16096]

Adolescent Scoliosis Soc. of North Am. [16392], PO Box 1178, Rocky Mount, NC 27802-1178

Adolescents; Intl. Org. for [11606]

Adolph and Esther Gottlieb Found. [9486], 380 W Broadway, New York, NY 10012, (212)226-0581

Adopt-A-Church Intl. [19839], PO Box 510, Allendale, MI 49401, (616)892-4260

Adopt-A-Church Intl. [IO], Allendale, MI, United States

Adopt-A-Farm-Family of Am. [★4658]

Adopt-A-Hawk Prog. [★7419]

Adopt-A-Hawk Prog. [★IO]

Adopt-A-Horse Prog. [★4868]

Adopt A Husky [11340], PO Box 275, Salem, WI 53168-0275, (262)909-2244

Adopt-a-Manatee [★5378]

Adopt-A-Minefield [IO], London, United Kingdom

Adopt-A-Whale Program [★5363]

Adopt Am. Network [11227], 1025 N Reynolds Rd., Toledo, OH 43615, (419)534-3350

Adopt a Building Prog. [★11842]

Adopt a Dr. [12750], 150 Chestnut St., Providence, RI 02903, (401)421-0606

Adopt a Special Kid [★11226]

Adopt a Special Kid; AASK - [11226]

AdoptaPlatoon [11489], c/o Nanny Fran, PO Box 1457, Seabrook, NH 03874

Adopted Indians; Continental Confed. of [10737]

Adoptee-Birthparent Searches - Address unknown since 2001.

Adoptee-Birthparent Support Network [11228], 6439 Woodridge Rd., Alexandria, VA 22312-1336, (301)442-9106

Adoptee Rights Org; Bastard Nation: The [11237]

Adoptees' Birthparents' Assn. - Address unknown since 2001.

Adoptees' Liberty Movement Assn; ALMA Soc. - [11232]

Adoptees and Natural Parents Org. - Defunct.

Adoptees Registry - Defunct.

Adoptees in Search - Address unknown since 2006.

Adoption
AASK - Adopt a Special Kid [11226]
Action for Child Protection [11553]
Adopt Am. Network [11227]
Adoptee-Birthparent Support Network [11228]
Adoption Coun. of Canada [IO]
Adoption Identity Movement [11229]

Adoption Info. Services [11230]

AdoptionIreland: The Adopted People's Assn. [IO]

Adoptions Together [IO]

Adoptions Together [11231]

Alaskan Malamute Assistance League [11342]

Alliance for Animals [11344]

ALMA Soc. - Adoptees' Liberty Movement Assn. [11232]

Am. World Adoption Assn. [11233]

Amer. Adoption Cong. [11234]

Amer. Fertility Assn. [14388]

Amer. World War II Orphans Network [11235]

Amer. World War II Orphans Network [IO]

Assn. of Administrators of the Interstate Compact on Adoption and Medical Assistance [11236]

Assn. of Administrators of the Interstate Compact on the Placement of Children [11559]

Back in the Saddle Horse Adoption [4864]

Bastard Nation: The Adoptee Rights Org. [11237]

Bulldog Club of Am. Rescue Network [11372]

CARR Support Gp. [IO]

Catholic Guardian Soc. [11564]

Child Welfare Inst. [11571]

Children with AIDS Proj. of Am. [11238]

Children Awaiting Parents [11239]

Concerned Persons for Adoption [11240]

Concerned United Birthparents [11241]

Dogs Deserve Better [12017]

Echo Dogs White Shepherd Rescue [11388]

Families Adopting Children Everywhere [11242]

Families with Children from China [11243]

Families for Private Adoption [11244]

Friends in Adoption [11245]

Greyhound Adoption Center [11401]

Harmony House for Cats [11404]

Holt Intl. Children's Services [11698]

Independent Search Consultants [11246]

Independent Search Consultants [IO]

Inst. for Adoption Info. [11247]

Intl. Adoption Assn. - Ireland [IO]

Intl. Aid Serving Kids [11603]

Intl. Soundex Reunion Registry [11248]

International Soundex Reunion Registry [IO]

Interracial Family Circle [12161]

Jewish Children's Adoption Network [11249]

Joint Coun. on Intl. Children's Services [11250]

Joint Council on International Children's Services [IO]

Kidsave Intl. [IO]

Kidsave Intl. [11251]

Last Chance Corral [11425]

Latin Am. Parents Assn. [11252]

Liberal Educ. for Adoptive Families [11253]

Liberty Godparent Home [12918]

Little People of Am. [13105]

Mothers Without Borders [11624]

Natl. Adoption Center [11254]

Natl. Center for Lesbian Rights [12246]

Natl. Coun. for Adoption [11255]

Natl. Council for Single Adoptive Parents [11256]

Natl. Greyhound Adoption Prog. [11438]

North Amer. Coun. on Adoptable Children [11257]

The Nurturing Network [13434]

Off. of Population Affairs CH [12757]

One Child at a Time [11642]

Only a Child [11643]

Oper. Identity [11258]

Organized Adoption Search Info. Services [11259]

ORIGINS [11260]

Orphan Found. of Am. [11715]

Orphan Resources Intl. [11644]

Orphan Voyage [11261]

Parent Finders of Canada [IO]

Parents Network for the Post Institutionalized Child [16546]

People for Life [12925]

Proj. Cuddle [11648]

Single Mothers By Choice [12692]

Stars of David Intl. [11262]

Stars of David Intl. [IO]

World Assn. for Children and Parents [11666]

World Partners Adoption [11263]

World Partners Adoption [IO]

Adoption; Amerasians for Intl. Aid and [★11642]

Adoption; Celebrate [★11247]

Reference to "IO" in place of a book number signifies that the association may be found in the 45th edition of International Organizations.

Adoption Center; Greyhound [11401]
Adoption Coun. of Canada [IO], Ottawa, ON, Canada
Adoption and Family Reunion Center - Defunct.
Adoption and Fostering; British Assn. for [IO]
Adoption Identity Movement [11229]
Adoption Info. Services [11230], 558 Dovie Pl., Lawrenceville, GA 30045, (770)339-7236
Adoption Roots and Rights [IO], Dorchester, ON, Canada
Adoption Search Inst. - Defunct.
AdoptionIreland: The Adopted People's Assn. [IO], Dublin, Ireland
Adoptions Together [IO], Silver Spring, MD, United States
Adoptions Together [11231], 10230 New Hampshire Ave., Ste. 200, Silver Spring, MD 20903, (301)439-2900
Adoptive Families of America - Defunct.
Adoptive Parents; Comm. for Single [★11256]
Adoration in the Home; League of Night [★19695]
Adoration in the Home; Night [19695]
Adoration Soc; Nocturnal [19696]
ADOREMUS - Soc. for the Renewal of the Sacred Liturgy [19561], PO Box 300561, St. Louis, MO 63130, (314)863-8385
ADOREMUS - Society for the Renewal of the Sacred Liturgy [IO], St. Louis, MO, United States
ADR Inst. of Canada [IO], Toronto, ON, Canada
Adrenal Diseases Found; Natl. [14358]
Adrenal Metabolic Res. Soc. of the Hypoglycemia Found. - Defunct.
ADS, Natl. Professional Advt. Soc. [★24393]
ADSC: Intl. Assn. of Found. Drilling [2747], Pacific Center I, 14180 Dallas Pkwy., Ste. 510, Dallas, TX 75254, (214)343-2091
ADSC: Intl. Assn. of Found. Drilling [IO], Dallas, TX, United States
ADSC: The International Association of Foundation Drilling [IO], Dallas, TX, United States
ADSC: The Intl. Assn. of Found. Drilling [1000], Pacific Ctr. I, 14180 Dallas Pkwy., Ste. 510, Dallas, TX 75254, (214)343-2091
Adsum for Women and Children [IO], Halifax, NS, Canada
Adult Children of Alcoholics, Central Ser. Bd. [★IO]
Adult Children of Alcoholics, Central Ser. Bd. [★13012]
Adult Children of Alcoholics World Ser. Org. [13012], PO Box 3216, Torrance, CA 90510, (310)534-1815
Adult Children of Alcoholics World Service Organization [IO], Torrance, CA, United States
Adult Christian Educ. Found. [19913], 1410 Northport Dr., Madison, WI 53704-2041, (608)241-9220
Adult Congenital Heart Assn. [13884], 6757 Greene St., Ste. 335, Philadelphia, PA 19119, (215)849-1260
Adult and Continuing Educ; Amer. Assn. for [8146]
Adult Day Services Assn; Natl. [11298]
Adult Development Network; Career Planning and [12070]
Adult Education
  Accrediting Coun. for Continuing Educ. and Training [8145]
  Adult Higher Educ. Alliance [7915]
  Amer. Assn. for Adult and Continuing Educ. [8146]
  Assn. for Non-Traditional Students in Higher Educ. [7916]
  Assn. for Non-Traditional Students in Higher Educ. [IO]
  CAE [IO]
  Canadian Assn. for the Stud. of Adult Educ. [IO]
  Caribbean Regional Coun. for Adult Educ. [IO]
  Center for Consumer Affairs, Univ. of Wisconsin-Milwaukee [17313]
  Center for Lifelong Learning [8406]
  Center of Regional Cooperation for Adult Educ. in Latin Am. and the Caribbean [IO]
  Center for Stud. and Publications [IO]
  Christian Literacy Associates [8788]
  Elderhostel, Inc. [8149]
  European Assn. for the Educ. of Adults [IO]
  European Soc. for Res. on the Educ. of Adults [IO]

Fed. for Continuing Educ. in Tertiary Institutions [IO]
Finnish Folk High School Assn. [IO]
German Adult Educ. Assn. [IO]
HIMAL Assn. [IO]
Indian Adult Educ. Assn. [IO]
Inst. for People's Educ. and Action [8267]
Intl. Assn. for Continuing Educ. and Training [8150]
Intl. Coun. for Adult Educ. [IO]
Intl. Fed. of Workers' Educ. Associations [IO]
Intl. Soc. of Comparative Adult Educ. [IO]
Intl. Univ. Consortium [8566]
Loyola Extension Services [IO]
Natl. Adult Educ. Honor Soc. [24392]
Natl. Adult Educ. Professional Development Consortium [7917]
Natl. Adult School Org. [IO]
Natl. Assn. of Adult Educ. [IO]
Natl. Assn. for Educational Guidance for Adults [IO]
Natl. Assn. of Veterans Prog. Administrators [9292]
Natl. CH for English Language Acquisition and Language Instruction Educational Programs [8287]
Natl. Coalition for Literacy [8794]
Natl. Coun. for Continuing Educ. and Training [8152]
Natl. Inst. of Adult Continuing Educ. [IO]
Natl. Registration Center for Stud. Abroad [8626]
ORT Am. [12480]
ProLiteracy Worldwide [8797]
Routes to Learning Canada [IO]
School of Living [10178]
Senior Scholars [8153]
Swedish Natl. Coun. of Adult Educ. [IO]
Swiss Fed. for Adult Learning [IO]
Teachers of English to Speakers of Other Languages [8382]
Universities Assn. for Lifelong Learning [IO]
Univ. Continuing Educ. Assn. [8154]
WEA Scottish Assn. [IO]
Women in Adult and Vocational Educ. [IO]
Workers' Educational Assn. - East Midlands Region [IO]
Workers' Educational Assn. - Eastern Region [IO]
Workers' Educational Assn. - London Region [IO]
Workers' Educational Assn. - North East Region [IO]
Workers' Educational Assn. - North West Region [IO]
Workers' Educational Assn. - Northern Ireland [IO]
Workers' Educational Assn. - South Wales [IO]
Workers' Educational Assn. - South Western Region [IO]
Workers' Educational Assn. - Southern Region [IO]
Workers' Educational Assn. - United Kingdom [IO]
Workers' Educational Assn. - West Midlands Region [IO]
Workers' Educational Assn. - Yorkshire and Humber [IO]
World Educ. [IO]
World Educ. [7918]
Adult Educ. Assn. of the U.S.A. [★8146]
Adult and Experiential Learning; Coun. for [8412]
Adult Film Assn. of America - Address unknown since 1988.
Adult Higher Educ. Alliance [7915], c/o Sue Currey, Dir. of Membership, PACE Organizational Commun., St. Edward's Univ., 3001 S Cong. Ave., Austin, TX 78704, (512)428-1333
Adult Learning Australia [IO], Canberra, Australia
Adult Learning and Educational Credentials; Center for [★8406]
Adult Lib. Services Assn; Young [10395]
Adult Ministries; Bd. of Brethren Homes and Older [★11276]
Adult Ministries; Brethren Homes and Older [★11276]
Adult Performance Level Project - Defunct.
Adult Prog; Youth [★8808]
Adult Residential Colleges Assn. [IO], Felixstowe, United Kingdom

Adult Services Division of ALA [★10383]
Adult Soccer Assn; U.S. [23857]
Adult Stud; Hebrew Schools Prog. for [★20172]
Adult Video Assn. [17037], 8033 Sunset Blvd., No. 851, West Hollywood, CA 90046, (323)436-0060
Adult Welfare; Protecting [13028]
Adults with Autism; NSAC, The Natl. Soc. for Children and [★13723]
Adults; Children of Deaf [14747]
Adults; Helen Keller Natl. Center for Deaf-Blind Youths and [14760]
Adults with Learning Disabilities; Assn. for Children and [★12492]
Adults with Pseudo-Obstruction; Amer. Soc. of [★14410]
Adults Sect; Oral Deaf [★14775]
Adults with Special Learning Needs; Natl. Assn. for [8204]
Advanced Authoring Format Assn. [★3721]
Advanced Beef Breeds Fed. - Defunct.
Advanced Card Tech. Assn. of Canada [IO], Ajax, ON, Canada
Advanced Foods and Materials Network [IO], Guelph, ON, Canada
Advanced Intl. Studies Inst. - Address unknown since 1988.
Advanced Mfg; Natl. Coun. for [2563]
Advanced Media Workflow Assn. [3721], 436 N Westfield Rd., Madison, WI 53717, (770)414-9952
Advanced Medical Tech. Assn. [14669], 701 Pennsylvania Ave. NW, Ste. 800, Washington, DC 20004-2654, (202)783-8700
Advanced Particulate Materials Association [★2714]
Advanced Pastoral Stud; Inst. for [★19924]
Advanced Rabbinical and Talmudic Schools; Assn. of [8683]
Advanced Technologies; Natl. Center For [7751]
Advanced TV Systems Comm. [543], 1750 K St. NW, Ste. 1200, Washington, DC 20006, (202)872-9160
Advanced Training Projects - Defunct.
Advanced Transit Assn. [7808], c/o Stan Young, Sec., Box 220249, Boston, MA 02122-0013, (617)825-2318
Advancement of Black Chemists and Chem. Engineers; Natl. Org. for the Professional [6689]
Advancement of Criminology; Soc. for the [★11899]
Advancement in Higher Educ. Admin; Natl. Identification Prog. for the [★9324]
Advancement of Jewish Educ; Coalition for the [8689]
Advancement of Private Higher Educ; Consortium for the [★8535]
Advancement of Sports Potential; Assn. for the [★16480]
Advancement of Teaching; Carnegie Found. for the [9214]
Advancing Canadian Entrepreneurship [IO], Toronto, ON, Canada
Advancing Churches in Missions Commitment [20293], PO Box 5266, Fort Wayne, IN 46895-5266, (260)492-2262
Advancing Cmpt. Tech. Alumni Assn; Univ. of [18929]
Advancing the Ministries of the Gospel [★20298]
Advancing the Ministries of the Gospel [★IO]
Advancing Native Missions [IO], Charlottesville, VA, United States
Advancing Native Missions [19833], PO Box 5303, Charlottesville, VA 22905, (540)456-7111
Advent Christian Gen. Conf. of Am. [19442], PO Box 690848, Charlotte, NC 28227, (704)545-6161
Advent Christian Gen. Conf. of Am. [IO], Charlotte, NC, United States
Advent Mission Society; American [★IO]
Advent Mission Society; American [★19442]
Adventist
  Advent Christian Gen. Conf. of Am. [19442]
  Advent Christian Gen. Conf. of Am. [IO]
  Adventist World Aviation [IO]
  Adventist World Aviation [11264]
  Woman's Home and Foreign Mission Soc. [19443]
Adventist Community Services [20552], 12501 Old Columbia Pike, Silver Spring, MD 20904-6600, (301)680-6438

A star before a book entry number signifies that the name is not listed separately, but is mentioned within the entry.

Adventist Development and Relief Agency - Canada [IO], Oshawa, ON, Canada
Adventist Development and Relief Agency Intl. [IO], Silver Spring, MD, United States
Adventist Development and Relief Agency Intl. [12826], 12501 Old Columbia Pike, Silver Spring, MD 20904, (301)680-6380
Adventist Development and Relief Agency - Japan [IO], Tokyo, Japan
Adventist Development and Relief Agency - Togo [IO], Lome, Togo
Adventist Development and Relief Agency - Vietnam [IO], Hanoi, Vietnam
Adventist Dietetic Assn; Seventh-Day [15569]
Adventist Forums; Assn. of [20554]
Adventist Health Network of North America - Defunct.
Adventist Language Teachers Assn. - Defunct.
Adventist-Laymen's Services and Indus. [20553], c/o ASI Ministries, 12501 Old Columbia Pike, Silver Spring, MD 20904, (301)680-6450
Adventist Self-Supporting Institutions [★20553]
Adventist World Aviation [11264], PO Box 251, Berrien Springs, MI 49103-0251, (269)473-0135
Adventist World Aviation [IO], Berrien Springs, MI, United States
Adventure Cycling Assn. [23304], PO Box 8308, Missoula, MT 59802, (406)721-1776
Adventure Found. Pakistan [IO], Abbottabad, Pakistan
Adventure Tour Operators Assn. of India [IO], New Delhi, India
Adventure Travel Trade Assn. [3902], 601 Union St., 42nd Fl., Seattle, WA 98101, (360)805-3131
Adventurers Club of New York - Defunct.
Adventures in Movement for the Handicapped [16597], 945 Danbury Rd., Dayton, OH 45420, (937)294-4611
Advertisers; Amer. Coun. of Highway [85]
Advertisers' Assn. [IO], Istanbul, Turkey
Advertisers Assn; Financial [★2611]
Advertisers; Assn. of Natl. [91]
Advertisers; Constr. Equip. [★82]
Advertisers Coun; Automotive [★92]
Advertisers and Public Relations Coun; Constr. Equip. [★82]
Advertising
  ABA Marketing Network [2611]
  Advertisers' Assn. [IO]
  Advt. Agencies Assn. of Bangladesh [IO]
  Advt. Agencies Assn. of India [IO]
  Advt. Assn. of Thailand [IO]
  Advt. Assn. of the United Kingdom [IO]
  Advt. Bd. of the Philippines [IO]
  Advt. Club of New York [77]
  Advt. Coun. [78]
  Advt. Cup and Mug Collectors of Am. [21956]
  Advt. and Design Club of Canada [IO]
  Advt. Fed. of Australia [IO]
  Advt. and Marketing Intl. Network [IO]
  Advt. and Marketing Intl. Network [79]
  Advt. Producers Assn. [IO]
  Advt. Production Club of New York [1756]
  Advt. Specialty Assn. for Printers [80]
  Advt. Standards Authority [IO]
  Advt. Standards Canada [IO]
  Advt. Women of New York [81]
  AEM Marketing Coun. [82]
  Affiliated Warehouse Companies [3974]
  Amer. Acad. of Advt. [7919]
  Amer. Advt. Fed. [83]
  Amer. Advt. Fed. Educ. Services [24393]
  Amer. Assn. of Advt. Agencies [84]
  Amer. Coun. of Highway Advertisers [85]
  Amer. Marketing Assn. [2613]
  Amer. Soc. of Dermatological Retailers [86]
  Amer. Teleservices Assn. [2614]
  Antique Advt. Assn. of Am. [21420]
  ARF - Advt. Res. Found. [87]
  Argentine Advt. Agencies' Assn. [IO]
  Art Directors Club [9422]
  Asian Fed. of Advt. Associations [IO]
  Asociacion Espanola de Anunciantes [IO]
  Asociacion Nacional de Anunciantes Colombia [IO]

Asociacion Nacional de Anunciantes del Peru [IO]
Asociacion Nacional de Anunciantes - Venezuela [IO]
Asociacion Nacional de Avisadores [IO]
Associacao Portuguesa de Anunciantes [IO]
Assn. of Accredited Advt. Agents of Hong Kong [IO]
Assn. of Accredited Advt. Agents Singapore [IO]
Assn. of Advertisers in Ireland [IO]
Assn. of Advt. and Commun. Agencies [IO]
Assn. of Canadian Advertisers [IO]
Assn. of Czech Advt. Agencies and Marketing Commun. [IO]
Assn. of Danish Advertisers [IO]
Assn. of Finnish Advertisers [IO]
Association of Free Community Papers [IO]
Assn. of Free Community Papers [88]
Assn. of Hispanic Advt. Agencies [89]
Assn. of Independent Commercial Producers [90]
Assn. of Natl. Advertisers [91]
Assn. of New Zealand Advertisers [IO]
Assn. for Postal Commerce [2449]
Assn. of Swiss Advt. and Communications Agencies BSW [IO]
Assn. of Visual Merchandise Representatives [2535]
Assn. of Zimbabwe Advertisers [IO]
AssoComunicazione Associazione delle Imprese di Comunicazione [IO]
Audit Bur. of Circulations [126]
Australasian Promotional Products Assn. [IO]
Australian Assn. of Natl. Advertisers [IO]
Austrian Advt. Res. Assn. [IO]
Automotive Communications Coun. [92]
BBB Wise Giving Alliance [17309]
BPA Worldwide [93]
BPA Worldwide [IO]
Branded Goods Assn. Hungary [IO]
Brazilian Assn. of Advertisers [IO]
British Sign and Graphics Assn. [IO]
Business Marketing Association [IO]
Bus. Marketing Assn. [94]
Cabletelevision Advt. Bur. [95]
Camara de Anunciantes del Paraguay [IO]
Camara Anunciantes del Uruguay [IO]
Camara Argentina de Anunciantes [IO]
Canadian Advt. Res. Found. [IO]
Catalog and Multichannel Marketing Coun. [1763]
Children's Advt. Rev. Unit [96]
China Enterprise Confed. [IO]
City and Regional Magazine Assn. [3218]
Comm. of Advt. Practice [IO]
Commun. Agencies Assn. of New Zealand [IO]
Concerned Children's Advertisers [IO]
Cyprus Advertisers Assn. [IO]
Czech Assn. for Branded Products [IO]
Danish Assn. of Advt. and Relationship Agencies [IO]
Digital Distribution of Advt. for Publications [97]
Direct Marketing Assn. [2625]
Direct Marketing Assn. of Singapore [IO]
Doctors Ought to Care [14554]
Dutch Assn. of Commun. Agencies [IO]
eBusiness Assn. [98]
Eight Sheet Outdoor Advt. Assn. [99]
European Advt. Standards Alliance [IO]
European Assn. of Communications Agencies [IO]
European Fed. of Illuminated Signs [IO]
Finnish Assn. of Marketing Commun. Agencies [IO]
Graphic Arts Tech. Found. [1769]
Groupement des Annonceurs du Maroc [IO]
Healthcare Marketing and Communications Coun. [100]
Hellenic Advertisers Assn. [IO]
Hispanic Marketing and Commun. Assn. [2628]
Hollywood Radio and TV Soc. [559]
Hong Kong Advertisers Assn. [IO]
Hospitality Sales and Marketing Assn. [IO]
Hungarian Advt. Assn. [IO]
IDEAlliance - Intl. Digital Enterprise Alliance [1773]
Incorporated Soc. of British Advertisers [IO]
Indian Soc. of Advertisers [IO]
Indonesian Assn. of Advt. Agencies [IO]

Inflatable Advt. Dealers Assn. [101]
Inst. of Advt. Practitioners in Ireland [IO]
Inst. of Advt. Stud. and Res. [IO]
Inst. of Communications and Advt. [IO]
Inst. of Practitioners in Advt. [IO]
Insurance Marketing Communications Assn. [2179]
Interactive Advt. Bur. [102]
Interactive Advt. Bur. [IO]
Interactive Advt. Bur. - Europe [IO]
Intermarket Agency Network [IO]
Intermarket Agency Network [103]
Intl. Advt. Assn. [104]
Intl. Advt. Assn. [IO]
Intl. Advt. Festival [IO]
Intl. Classified Media Assn. [IO]
Intl. Communications Agency Network [IO]
Intl. Communications Agency Network [105]
Intl. Experiential Marketing Assn. [2631]
Intl. Labor Communications Assn., AFL-CIO/CLC [3229]
Intl. Vintage Poster Dealers Assn. [106]
International Vintage Poster Dealers Association [IO]
Internet Advt. Bur. [IO]
Japan Advertisers Assn. [IO]
Japan Advt. Agencies Assn. [IO]
Japan Magazine Advt. Assn. [IO]
Junior Hollywood Radio and TV Soc. [564]
Korea Fed. of Advt. Associations [IO]
Korean Advertisers Assn. [IO]
Los Angeles Advt. Agencies Assn. [107]
Mailing and Fulfillment Ser. Assn. [108]
Malaysian Advertisers Assn. [IO]
Marketing and Advt. Global Network [IO]
Marketing and Advt. Global Network [109]
Media Action Network for Asian Americans [18029]
Mexican Advt. Agencies' Assn. [IO]
Mobile Marketing Assn. [IO]
Mobile Marketing Assn. [110]
Mongolian Advt. Assn. [IO]
Natl. Advt. Assn. - Mexico [IO]
Natl. Advt. Assn. - Venezuela [IO]
Natl. Advt. Div. Coun. of Better Bus. Bureaus [111]
Natl. Advt. Golf Assn. [23456]
Natl. Advt. Rev. Bd. [112]
Natl. Agri-Marketing Assn. [2640]
Natl. Assn. of Display Indus. [2642]
Natl. Assn. of Paper and Advt. Collectors [22412]
Natl. Assn. of Publishers' Representatives [113]
Natl. Assn. of TV Prog. Executives [571]
Natl. Black Public Relations Soc. [3194]
Natl. Fed. of Advt. Agencies [IO]
Norwegian Assn. of Advertisers [IO]
Old Sleepy Eye Collectors' Club of Am. [21934]
Org. Werbungtreibende im Markenverband [IO]
Outdoor Advt. Assn. of Am. [114]
Outdoor Advt. Assn. of Great Britain [IO]
Pakistan Advertisers Soc. [IO]
Pakistan Advt. Assn. [IO]
Partnership for a Drug-Free Am. [13272]
Peanut Pals [22104]
Peruvian Assn. of Advt. Agencies [IO]
Point-of-Purchase Advt. Intl. [115]
PROMAX [577]
Promotion Marketing Assn. [2647]
Promotional Glass Collectors Assn. [22109]
Promotional Products Assn. of Canada [IO]
Promotional Products Assn. Intl. [IO]
Promotional Products Assn. Intl. [116]
Publishers Info. Bur. [128]
Radio Advt. Bur. [117]
Retail Advt. and Marketing Assn. [118]
The Rock Poster Soc. [9469]
Russian Advertisers Assn. [IO]
Sales and Marketing Executives Intl. [3473]
Scenic Am. [4606]
Schweizer Werbe-Auftraggeberverband [IO]
Screen Advt. World Assn. [IO]
Sign Assn. of Canada [IO]
Slovak Assn. for Branded Products [IO]
Slovenian Advt. Chamber [IO]
Soc. of Icelandic Advt. Agencies [IO]

Reference to "IO" in place of a book number signifies that the association may be found in the 45th edition of International Organizations.

Southern Classified Advt. Managers Assn. [119]
Spanish Advt. Agencies' Assn. [IO]
Swedish Advertisers' Assn. [IO]
Swedish Advt. Assn. [IO]
Syndicated Network TV Assn. [120]
Taipei Assn. of Advt. Agencies [IO]
TV Bur. of Advt. [121]
Trade Card Collectors Assn. [22124]
Trade Promotion Mgt. Associates [122]
Traffic Audit Bur. for Media Measurement [123]
Transworld Advt. Agency Network [124]
Transworld Advt. Agency Network [IO]
Union des Annnonceurs [IO]
Union Belge des Annonceurs [IO]
U.S. Tour Operators Assn. [3943]
Uruguayan Circle of Advt. Agencies [IO]
Utenti Pubblicita Associati [IO]
Utility Communicators Intl. [IO]
Utility Communicators Intl. [125]
Women in Direct Marketing Intl. [2652]
World Fed. of Advertisers [IO]
Yellow Pages Assn. [3261]
Advt. Agencies Assn. of Bangladesh [IO], Dhaka, Bangladesh
Advt. Agencies Assn. of India [IO], Bombay, India
Advt. Agencies Assn; Southern California [★107]
Advt. Agencies Assn; Western States [★107]
Advt. Agency Network; Transamerican [★124]
Advt. Agency Production Club of New York [★1756]
Advertising Agency Service Interchange - Defunct.
Advt. Assn. of Am; Premium [★2647]
Advt. Assn; Chicago Area Agricultural [★2640]
Advt. Assn; Direct Mail [★2625]
Advt. Assn. Intl; Specialty [★116]
Advt. Assn; Internet Marketing and [★98]
Advt. Assn; Junior Panel Outdoor [★99]
Advt. Assn; Shelter [★114]
Advt. Assn; Specialty [★116]
Advt. Assn. of Thailand [IO], Bangkok, Thailand
Advt. Assn. of the United Kingdom [IO], London, United Kingdom

Advertising Auditors

Audit Bur. of Circulations [126]
Certified Audit of Circulations [127]
Publishers Info. Bur. [128]
Advt. Bd. of the Philippines [IO], Makati City, Philippines
Advt. Bur; Broadcast [★117]
Advt. Bur; Newspaper [★3244]
Advt. Club of New York [77], 235 Park Ave. S, 6th Fl., New York, NY 10003-1405, (212)533-8080
Advt. Club; Pharmaceutical [★IO]
Advt. Co-Op Network; Newspaper [★3244]
Advt. Collectors; Natl. Assn. of Paper and [22412]
Advt. Conf; Insurance [★2179]
Advt. Coun. [78], 261 Madison Ave., 11th Fl., New York, NY 10016-2303, (212)922-1500
Advt. Coun; Pharmaceutical [★100]
Advt. Cup and Mug Collectors of Am. [21956]
Advt. and Design Club of Canada [IO], Toronto, ON, Canada
Advt. Fed. of Am. [★83]
Advt. Fed. of Australia [IO], Sydney, Australia
Advt. Film and Videotape Producers Assn. [★IO]
Advt. Funeral Directors of Am. [★IO]
Advt. Funeral Directors of Am. [★2790]
Advt. Golf Assn; Natl. [23456]
Advt. Guild Intl; Specialty [★116]
Advt. and Illustrative Photographers Assn. [IO], Auckland, New Zealand
Advt. Inst; Point-of-Purchase [★115]
Advt. Mail Marketing Assn. [★2449]
Advt. Managers; Assn. of Newspaper Classified [★3244]
Advertising and Marketing Assn. - Defunct.
Advt. and Marketing Assn., Intl; Retail [★118]
Advt. and Marketing Assn; Natl. Agricultural [★2640]
Advt. and Marketing Executives; Intl. Newspaper [★3244]
Advt. and Marketing Intl. Network [79], c/o B. Vaughn Sink, Exec. Dir., 12323 Nantucket, Wichita, KS 67235, (316)531-2342
Advt. and Marketing Intl. Network [IO], Wichita, KS, United States

Advt. and Marketing; Women in [★874]
Advt. Media Credit Executives Assn. [1397], 8840 Columbia 100 Pkwy., Columbia, MD 21045-2158, (410)992-7609
Advt. Men's League of New York [★77]
Advt. Natl. Assn. of Breweriana [22074]
Advt. Natl. Assn; Specialty [★116]
Advt. Newspaper Assn; Natl. [★3259]
Advertising Partnership for a Drug-Free Am; Media- [★13272]
Advt. Photographers of Am. [2989], PO Box 250, White Plains, NY 10605, (800)272-6264
Advt. Producers Assn. [IO], London, United Kingdom
Advt. Production Club of New York [1756], 428 E State St., Long Beach, NY 11561, (212)671-2975
Advt. Res. Found. [★87]
Advt. Res. Found; ARF - [87]
Advt. Rev. Coun; Natl. [★112]
Advt. Ser. Assn. Intl; Mail [★108]
Advt. Soc; ADS, Natl. Professional [★24393]
Advt. Specialty Assn. for Printers [80], 14015 Long Shadow, Houston, TX 77015, (713)330-1452
Advt. Standards Authority [IO], London, United Kingdom
Advt. Standards Canada [IO], Toronto, ON, Canada
Advt. Women of New York [81], 25 W 45th St., Ste. 403, New York, NY 10036, (212)221-7969
Advice UK [IO], London, United Kingdom
Advisers of Men; Natl. Assn. of Deans and [★7904]
Advising Assn; Natl. Academic [8170]
Advisors; Assn. of Fraternity [24475]
Advisors; Assn. of Insolvency and Restructuring [15]
Advisors for Athletics; Natl. Assn. of Academic [8171]
Advisors for the Hea. Professions; Natl. Assn. of [8866]
Advisors; Intl. Assn. for Professional Art [24002]
Advisors; Natl. Assn. of Academic [★8171]
Advisors; Natl. Assn. of Foreign Student [★8445]
Advisors; Pro Vita [20479]
Advisory Bd. for Medical Specialties [★15117]
Advisory Bd. on Veterinary Specialties [★16759]
Advisory Centre for Educ. [IO], London, United Kingdom
Advisory Comm. on Education of Spanish and Mexican Americans - Defunct.
Advisory Comm. on Equal Opportunities for Women and Men [IO], Brussels, Belgium
Advisory Comm. on Library Res. and Training Projects - Defunct.
Advisory Comm. to the OECD; U.S.A. - Bus. and Indus. [17466]
Advisory Comm. on Oil Pollution of the Sea [★IO]
Advisory Comm. on Pollution of the Sea [★IO]
Advisory Comm. on Problems of Census Enumeration - Defunct.
Advisory Comm. on Protection of the Sea [IO], London, United Kingdom
Advisory Comm. on Voter Education - Defunct.
Advisory Comm. on X-Ray and Radium Protection [★6242]
Advisory Coun. on Camps - Defunct.
Advisory Coun. for Children with Impaired Hearing [IO], Blackburn, Australia
Advisory Coun. on Coll. Library Resources - Defunct.
Advisory Coun. for the Educ. of Romany and Other Travellers [IO], Harlow, United Kingdom
Advisory Coun. on Historic Preservation [10007], 1100 Pennsylvania Ave. NW, Ste. 803, Old Post Off. Bldg., Washington, DC 20004, (202)606-8503
Advisory Coun. for Orthopedic Resident Educ. [★15752]
Advisory Coun. for Orthopedic Resident Educ. [★IO]
Advisory Coun. for Orthopedic Resident Education - Defunct.
Advisory Coun; Pet Indus. Joint [2965]
Advisory Coun. on Religious Rights in Eastern Europe and the Soviet Union - Defunct.
Advisory Councils; Natl. Assn. of Mental Hea. Planning and [15216]
Advisory Network; Community Banking [20]
Advocacy Center; Citizen [17695]
Advocacy Comm. for Human Experimentation Survivors and Mind Control [IO], Thunder Bay, ON, Canada

Advocacy Fund; AAUW Legal [5573]
Advocacy Fund; Amer. Assn. of Univ. Women Legal [6358]
Advocacy Inst. [12650], 1629 K St. NW, Ste. 200, Washington, DC 20006-1629, (202)777-7575
Advocacy Organizations; Natl. Assn. of State-Based Child [★11662]
Advocacy for the Rights and Interests of the Elderly; Center for [11279]
Advocacy Systems; Natl. Assn. of Protection and [★11970]
Advocacy Tasmania [IO], Sandy Bay, Australia
Advocate Assn; Natl. Court Appointed Special [11636]
Advocate Hea. Care [14821], 2025 Windsor Dr., Oak Brook, IL 60523, (630)572-9393
Advocate for Parents; Special Needs [11652]
Advocaten Zonder Grenzen [★IO]
Advocates Against Psychic Abuse - Defunct.
Advocates for the Amer. Osteopathic Assn. [15789], 142 E Ontario St., Chicago, IL 60611-2864, (312)202-8190
Advocates for Animals [IO], Edinburgh, United Kingdom
Advocates; Assn. of Child [★11662]
Advocates Assn; Judge [6078]
Advocates on Behalf of Jews in Russia, Ukraine, the Baltic States and Eurasia; NCSJ: [17448]
Advocates for Child Psychiatric Nursing [★15487]
Advocates for Child Psychiatric Nursing [★IO]
Advocates for Commun. Tech. for Deaf/Blind People - Defunct.
Advocates; Coun. of Parent Attorneys and [9142]
Advocates for Culture, Hea., Env. and Safety; Beach Educ. [10761]
Advocates and Defenders; Gay and Lesbian [17118]
Advocates for Fair Family Support [12135]
Advocates for Highway and Auto Safety [12944], 750 First St. NE, Ste. 901, Washington, DC 20002, (202)408-1711
Advocates; Inner Circle of [6043]
Advocates Intl. [17998], 8001 Braddock Rd., Ste. 300, Springfield, VA 22151-2110, (703)894-1084
Advocates Intl. [IO], Springfield, VA, United States
Advocates of Intl. Trade and Comity - Defunct.
Advocates; Natl. Assn. of Child [★11662]
Advocates; Natl. Assn. of Consumer [17334]
Advocates; National Assn. of Sentencing [★5645]
Advocates for a Safe Vaccine - Address unknown since 1995.
Advocates to Save Legal Services - Defunct.
Advocates for Self-Government [18012], Liberty Bldg., 213 S Erwin St., Cartersville, GA 30120, (770)386-8372
Advocates' Soc. [IO], Toronto, ON, Canada
Advocates for Students; Natl. Coalition of [8328]
Advocates for Survivors of Child Abuse [IO], Charlestown, Australia
Advocates; Tax Analysts and [★18718]
Advocates for Women - Defunct.
Advocates for Women in Sci., Engg., and Mathematics [7593], c/o Saturday Acad., PO Box 8728, Portland, OR 97207, (503)725-2330
Advocates for Youth [12173], 2000 M St. NW, Ste. 750, Washington, DC 20036, (202)419-3420
Advocates for Youth [IO], Washington, DC, United States
Advocates for Youth's Media Proj. [12174], 3940 Laurel Canyon Blvd., No. 237, Studio City, CA 91604, (323)318-0825
Advocating Change Together [11914], 1821 Univ. Ave. W, Ste. 306-S, St. Paul, MN 55104, (651)641-0297
Advocating Legislation for Adoption Reform Movement - Address unknown since 2001.
ADVOCIS [IO], Toronto, ON, Canada
AE-2/AE-23 Assn; USS Nitro [5468]
AE-23 Assn; USS Nitro AE-2/ [5468]
AE Sailors Assn. [6143], c/o Nicholas Nicolai, Treas., 26355 Grace Dr., Wind Lake, WI 53185
AeA - Advancing the Bus. of Tech. [1203], 601 Pennsylvania Ave. NW, North Bldg., Ste. 600, Washington, DC 20004, (202)682-9110
AeA - Advancing the Bus. of Tech. [IO], Washington, DC, United States

A star before a book entry number signifies that the name is not listed separately, but is mentioned within the entry.

AEC - TEA Volunteer Centre [IO], Capim Grosso, Brazil
AED Found. [★2000]
AEM Marketing Communications Coun. [★82]
AEM Marketing Coun. [82], 6737 W Washington St., Ste. 2400, Milwaukee, WI 53214-5647, (414)272-0943
Aer Lingus Volleyball Club [IO], Dublin, Ireland
Aeras Global TB Vaccine Foundation [IO], Rockville, MD, United States
Aeras Global TB Vaccine Found. [14372], 1405 Res. Blvd., Rockville, MD 20850, (301)547-2900
Aerial Agricultural Assn. of Australia [IO], Dickson, Australia
Aerial Applicators Assn; Natl. [★4188]
Aerial Biosensing Assn. - Defunct.
Aerial Devices and Digger-Derricks Coun; Mfrs. of [2038]
Aerial Firefighting Indus. Assn. - Defunct.
Aerial Phenomena; Natl. Investigation Comm. on [★7479]
Aerial Phenomena Res. Org. - Defunct.
Aerial Photographers Assn; Professional [3010]
Aerialift Industries Assn. - Defunct.
AERO [6935]
Aero Club of Am. [★158]
Aero Club of Canada [IO], Carleton Place, ON, Canada
Aero Club of Czech Republic [IO], Prague, Czech Republic
Aero Club d'Italia [IO], Rome, Italy
Aero Club of Egypt [IO], Cairo, Egypt
Aero Club de France [IO], Paris, France
Aero Club of India [IO], New Delhi, India
Aero Club of Israel [IO], Tel Aviv, Israel
Aero Club du Liban [IO], Beirut, Lebanon
Aero Club of Lithuania [IO], Vilnius, Lithuania
Aero Club de Monaco [IO], Monaco, Monaco
Aero Club of Poland [IO], Warsaw, Poland
Aero-club Royal de Belgique [★IO]
Aero Club of South Africa [IO], Germiston, Republic of South Africa
Aero Medical Assn. [★IO]
Aero Medical Assn. [★13538]
Aero Philatelic Soc. of Am. [★22780]
Aero Philatelists [★22780]
Aerobatic Club of America - Defunct.
Aerobatic Club of Canada [★IO]
Aerobatic Club; Intl. [23040]
Aerobatics Canada [IO], Toronto, ON, Canada
Aerobatics Model Pilots Assn; Precision [21473]
Aerobic Training Intl. [23036], Calle D F-14 El Dorado, Rio Piedras, PR 00926, (787)751-6665
Aerobic Training Intl. [IO], Rio Piedras, PR, United States
Aerobic Way Assn. - Defunct.
Aerobics
  Aerobic Training Intl. [23036]
  Aerobic Training Intl. [IO]
  Aerobics and Fitness Assn. of Am. [15956]
  African-Amer. Assn. of Fitness Professionals [15957]
  Amer. Nordic Walking Assn. [15960]
  Amer. Running Assn. [23651]
  Aquatic Exercise Assn. [23652]
  Cooper Inst. [15962]
  Exercise Safety Assn. [15963]
  IDEA Hea. and Fitness Assn. [15965]
  Natl. Hea. Club Assn. [3670]
  NETA - Natl. Exercise Trainers Assn. [23037]
  U.S. Competitive Aerobics Fed. [23038]
  U.S. Running Streak Assn. [23709]
  U.S. Water Fitness Assn. [23657]
Aerobics and Fitness Assn. of Am. [15956], 15250 Ventura Blvd., Ste. 200, Sherman Oaks, CA 91403-3297, (877)968-7263
Aerobics and Fitness Association of America [IO], Sherman Oaks, CA, United States
Aerobics Intl. Res. Soc. - Defunct.
Aerobics Res; Cooper Inst. for [★15962]
Aerobics Res; Inst. for [★15962]
Aeroclube do Brasil [IO], Rio de Janeiro, Brazil
Aeroclube de Mocambique [IO], Maputo, Mozambique
Aeroklub Ceske Republiky [★IO]

Aeroklub Polski [★IO]
Aeromedical Evacuation
  DUSTOFF Assn. [20700]
Aeronaut Soc. [23097]
Aeronautic Assn; Natl. [158]
Aeronautic Assn. of the U.S.A; Natl. [★158]
Aeronautica and Air Label Collectors Club [21422], c/o Basil S. Burrell, PO Box 1239, Elgin, IL 60121-1239
Aeronautical Chamber of Commerce of Am. [★130]
Aeronautical Engineers; Amer. Soc. of [★6520]
Aeronautical Repair Sta. Assn. [129], 121 N Henry St., Alexandria, VA 22314-2903, (703)739-9543
Aeronautical Soc. of India [IO], New Delhi, India
Aeronautical Weight Engineers, Inc; Soc. of [★7699]
Aeronautics; Acad. of Model [21421]
Aeronautics and Astronautics; Amer. Inst. of [6369]
Aeronautics; Radio Tech. Commn. for [★6308]
Aeronauts; Intl. Soc. of [★23097]
Aeronca Assn; Natl. [21464]
Aeronca Club [★21464]
Aeronca Lovers Club [21423]
Aeronca Sedan Club - Address unknown since 2001.
Aerophilatelic Fed. of the Americas [★22780]
Aerosmith's Official Fan Club [24836], Aero Force One, 4 Brussels St., Worcester, MA 01610, (508)791-3807
Aerosol Assn. of Australia [IO], Parramatta, Australia
Aerosol Assn. of Australia and New Zealand [★IO]
Aerosol Mfrs'. Assn; British [IO]
Aerosol Res; Israeli Assn. for [IO]
Aerosol Soc. [IO], Bristol, United Kingdom
Aerospace
  187th Airborne Regimental Combat Team Assn. [20697]
  508th Parachute Infantry Regiment Assn. [21379]
  Acad. of Model Aeronautics [21421]
  Aero Club of Canada [IO]
  Aero Club of Czech Republic [IO]
  Aero Club d'Italia [IO]
  Aero Club of Egypt [IO]
  Aero Club de France [IO]
  Aero Club of India [IO]
  Aero Club of Israel [IO]
  Aero Club du Liban [IO]
  Aero Club of Lithuania [IO]
  Aero Club de Monaco [IO]
  Aero Club of Poland [IO]
  Aero Club of South Africa [IO]
  Aerobatics Canada [IO]
  Aeroclube do Brasil [IO]
  Aeroclube de Mocambique [IO]
  Aeronaut Soc. [23097]
  Aeronautica and Air Label Collectors Club [21422]
  Aeronautical Repair Sta. Assn. [129]
  Aeronautical Soc. of India [IO]
  Aeronca Lovers Club [21423]
  Aerospace Dept. Chairman's Assn. [7920]
  Aerospace Elecl. Soc. [6367]
  Aerospace Indus. Assn. of Am. [130]
  Aerospace Indus. Assn. of Canada [IO]
  Aerospace Medical Assn. [13538]
  Aerostar Owners Assn. [21424]
  African Airlines Assn. [IO]
  Air Cadet League of Canada [IO]
  Air Force Assn. [6062]
  Air, Inc. - Aviation Info. Resources [131]
  Air Line Pilots Assn. Intl. - Canada [IO]
  Air Mail Pioneers [21425]
  Air Sailing Club [IO]
  Air and Surface Transport Nurses Assn. [15427]
  Air Traffic Control Assn. [132]
  Air Traffic Control Association [IO]
  Air Transport Action Gp. [IO]
  Air Transport Assn. of Am. [133]
  Air Transport Assn. of Canada [IO]
  Aircraft Electronics Assn. [IO]
  Aircraft Electronics Assn. [134]
  Aircraft Engine Historical Soc. [9364]
  Aircraft Locknut Mfrs. Assn. [1814]
  Aircraft Owners and Pilots Assn. [135]
  Aircraft Owners and Pilots Assn. - Australia [IO]
  Aircraft Owners and Pilots Assn. - Austria [IO]
  Aircraft Owners and Pilots Assn. - Belgium [IO]
  Aircraft Owners and Pilots Assn. - Brazil [IO]

  Aircraft Owners and Pilots Assn. - Colombia [IO]
  Aircraft Owners and Pilots Assn. - Cyprus [IO]
  Aircraft Owners and Pilots Assn. - Denmark [IO]
  Aircraft Owners and Pilots Assn. - Finland [IO]
  Aircraft Owners and Pilots Assn. - Hungary [IO]
  Aircraft Owners and Pilots Assn. - Iceland [IO]
  Aircraft Owners and Pilots Assn. - India [IO]
  Aircraft Owners and Pilots Assn. - Ireland [IO]
  Aircraft Owners and Pilots Assn. - Italy [IO]
  Aircraft Owners and Pilots Assn. - Jamaica [IO]
  Aircraft Owners and Pilots Assn. - Japan [IO]
  Aircraft Owners and Pilots Assn. - Liberia [IO]
  Aircraft Owners and Pilots Assn. - Lithuania [IO]
  Aircraft Owners and Pilots Assn. - Luxembourg [IO]
  Aircraft Owners and Pilots Assn. - Malta [IO]
  Aircraft Owners and Pilots Assn. - Monaco [IO]
  Aircraft Owners and Pilots Assn. - Netherlands [IO]
  Aircraft Owners and Pilots Assn. - New Zealand [IO]
  Aircraft Owners and Pilots Assn. - Norway [IO]
  Aircraft Owners and Pilots Assn. - Pakistan [IO]
  Aircraft Owners and Pilots Assn. - Philippines [IO]
  Aircraft Owners and Pilots Assn. - Poland [IO]
  Aircraft Owners and Pilots Assn. - Romania [IO]
  Aircraft Owners and Pilots Assn. - Russia [IO]
  Aircraft Owners and Pilots Assn. - Singapore [IO]
  Aircraft Owners and Pilots Assn. - Slovenia [IO]
  Aircraft Owners and Pilots Assn. - South Africa [IO]
  Aircraft Owners and Pilots Assn. - Spain [IO]
  Aircraft Owners and Pilots Assn. - Sweden [IO]
  Aircraft Owners and Pilots Assn. - Switzerland [IO]
  Aircraft Owners and Pilots Assn. - Turkey [IO]
  Aircraft Owners and Pilots Assn. of the United Kingdom [IO]
  Aircraft Owners and Pilots Assn. - Venezuela [IO]
  Aircraft Res. Assn. [IO]
  Airlift/Tanker Association [IO]
  Airlift/Tanker Assn. [20646]
  Airline Indus. Relations Conf. [136]
  Airlines Medical Directors Assn. [13539]
  Airport Consultants Coun. [951]
  Airport Ground Trans. Assn. [3858]
  Airport Operators Assn. [IO]
  Airports Coun. Intl. - Europe [IO]
  Airports Coun. Intl. - Latin America-Caribbean Off. [IO]
  Airports Coun. Intl. - North Am. [IO]
  Airports Coun. Intl. - North Am. [137]
  Airports Coun. Intl. - Pacific Region [IO]
  Airports Coun. Intl. - Switzerland [IO]
  Airship Assn. [IO]
  All Pakistan Aero Modelling and Ultralight Assn. [IO]
  Amer. Air Mail Soc. [22780]
  Amer. Assn. of Airport Executives [138]
  Amer. Astronautical Soc. [6368]
  Amer. Astronautical Soc. [IO]
  Amer. Aviation Historical Soc. [21426]
  Amer. Bonanza Soc. [21427]
  American Bonanza Society [IO]
  Amer. Fighter Aces Assn. [20647]
  Amer. Helicopter Soc. [139]
  Amer. Helicopter Soc. [IO]
  Amer. Inst. of Aeronautics and Astronautics [6369]
  Amer. Navion Soc. [21428]
  Amer. Osteopathic Coll. of Occupational and Preventive Medicine [15802]
  Amer. Yankee Assn. [21429]
  Antique Airplane Assn. [21430]
  Apollo Soc. [9341]
  Arab Air Carriers Org. [IO]
  Argentine Center of Agricultural Engineers [IO]
  ASD-STAN [IO]
  Asociacion Guatemalteca de Deportes Aereos [IO]
  Associacao Brasileira de Aviacao Geral [IO]
  Assn. of Asia Pacific Airlines [IO]
  Assn. for Aviation Psychology [6370]
  Assn. of European Airlines [IO]
  Assn. of the European Space Indus. [IO]
  Assn. of Intl. Airlines [IO]

Reference to "IO" in place of a book number signifies that the association may be found in the 45th edition of International Organizations.

Assn. of Light Aviation of Kazakhstan [IO]
Assn. in Scotland for Tech. and Res. Into Astronautics [IO]
Assn. of Space Explorers - U.S.A. [IO]
Assn. of Space Explorers - U.S.A. [6371]
Assn. of U.S. Members of the Intl. Inst. of Space Law [6372]
Astronaut Scholars Honor Soc. [24584]
Australian Capital Territory Aeromodellers Assn. [IO]
Australian Sport Aviation Confed. [IO]
Australian Women Pilots' Assn. [IO]
Austrian Cockpit Assn. [IO]
Aviation Development Coun. [140]
Aviation Distributors and Manufacturers Assn. [141]
Aviation Indus. CBT Comm. [142]
Aviation Maintenance Found. Intl. [143]
Aviation Technician Educ. Coun. [7921]
Avionics Maintenance Conf. [144]
Balloon Fed. of Am. [23098]
Baltic Air Charter Assn. [IO]
Belarusian Fed. of Air Sports [IO]
Belgian Aerospace Indus. Assn. [IO]
Bellanca-Champion Club [IO]
Bellanca-Champion Club [21431]
Bird Airplane Club [21432]
Bluenose Soaring Club [IO]
Bd. of Airline Representatives in the United Kingdom [IO]
Bonnechere Soaring [IO]
British Air Line Pilots Assn. [IO]
British Airports Gp. [IO]
British Assn. of Aviation Consultants [IO]
British Bus. and Gen. Aviation Assn. [IO]
British Gliding Assn. [IO]
British Hang Gliding and Paragliding Assn. [IO]
British Helicopter Advisory Bd. [IO]
British Microlight Aircraft Assn. [IO]
British Model Flying Assn. [IO]
British Parachute Assn. [IO]
British Women Pilots' Assn. [IO]
Canada's Aviation Hall of Fame [IO]
Canadian Aerial Applicators Assn. [IO]
Canadian Aeronautics and Space Inst. [IO]
Canadian Air Cushion Tech. Soc. [IO]
Canadian Airports Coun. [IO]
Canadian Aviation Maintenance Coun. [IO]
Canadian Bus. Aviation Assn. [IO]
Canadian Harvard Aircraft Assn. [IO]
Canadian Owners and Pilots Assn. [IO]
Canadian Soc. of Air Safety Investigators [IO]
Canadian Space Soc. [IO]
Cardinal Club [21433]
Cargo Airline Assn. [145]
Caterpillar Club [146]
Central States Assn. [21434]
Cessna 182 Assn. of Australia [IO]
Cessna Owner Org. [21435]
Cessna Pilots Assn. [21436]
Cherokee Pilots' Assn. [21437]
Chinese Soc. of Aeronautics and Astronautics [IO]
Chinese Taipei Aeromodelling Assn. [IO]
Chinese Taipei Microlight Assn. [IO]
Citizens Aviation Watch Assn. [11509]
Civil Air Operations Officers Assn. of Australia [IO]
Civil Aviation Medical Assn. [13540]
Club de Aviacion de Cuba [IO]
Collegiate Soaring Assn. [23039]
Combat Helicopter Pilots Assn. [20648]
Commemorative Air Force [21438]
Comm. on Earth Observation Satellites [IO]
Comm. on Space Res. [IO]
Confederacion Argentina de Entidades Aerodeportivas [IO]
Continental Luscombe Assn. [21439]
Corben Club [21440]
Coun. of Defense and Space Indus. Associations [147]
Croatian Aeronautical Fed. [IO]
Cyprus Airsports Fed. [IO]
Daedalian Found. [20649]
De Havilland Moth Club [IO]
Distinguished Flying Cross Soc. [20711]
EAA Ultralight Assn. [21441]

EAA Vintage Aircraft Assn. [21442]
EAA Warbirds of Am. [21443]
Eesti Lennuspordi Foderatsioon [IO]
Elliniki Aerathlitiki Omospondia [IO]
Ercoupe Owners Club [21444]
Europe Air Sports [IO]
European Acad. For Aviation Safety [IO]
European Bus. Aviation Assn. [IO]
European Helicopter Assn. [IO]
European Regions Airline Assn. [IO]
European Space Agency [IO]
Experimental Aircraft Assn. [6373]
F-4 Phantom II Soc. [21445]
F-4 Phantom II Society [IO]
Fairchild Club [21446]
Federacion Aerea de Chile [IO]
Federacion Colombiana de Deportes Aereos [IO]
Federacion Mexicana de Aeronautica [IO]
Federacion Salvadorena de Paracaidismo y Aerodeportes [IO]
Federasi Aero Sport Indonesia [IO]
Federatia de Aeromodelism din Republica Moldova [IO]
Fed. Aeronautique Internationale [IO]
Fed. Aeronautique Luxembourgeoise [IO]
Fed. of Aerospace Enterprises in Ireland [IO]
Fed. of Galaxy Explorers [9136]
Fed. of Korea Aeronautics [IO]
Fellowship of Christian Airline Personnel [20007]
Finnish Astronautical Soc. [IO]
First Flight Soc. [21447]
Flight Safety Found. [148]
Flight Safety Found. [IO]
Flugmalafelag Islands [IO]
Flying Apache Assn. [21448]
Flying Physicians Assn. [13731]
Funk Aircraft Owners Assn. [21449]
Gen. Aviation Manufacturers Assn. [149]
Georgian Aeronautical Fed. [IO]
German Aero Club [IO]
German Aerospace Center [IO]
German Aerospace Indus. Assn. [IO]
German Bus. Aviation Assn. [IO]
German Soc. for Aeronautics and Astronautics [IO]
Guild of Air Pilots and Air Navigators [IO]
Guild of Air Traffic Control Officers [IO]
Helicopter Assn. Intl. [IO]
Helicopter Assn. Intl. [150]
Helicopter Club of America [21450]
Helicopter Found. Intl. [151]
Helicopter Found. Intl. [IO]
Helicopter Safety Advisory Conf. [152]
High Frontier [6374]
Highamerica Balloon Club [23099]
Hong Kong Aviation Club [IO]
Hungarian Aeronautical Assn. [IO]
Ibero-American Inst. of Aeronautic and Space Law and Commercial Aviation [IO]
IEEE Aerospace and Electronics Systems Soc. [6912]
Intl. Acad. of Astronautics [IO]
Intl. Aerobatic Club [23040]
The Intl. Air Cargo Assn. [3873]
Intl. Air Carrier Assn. [IO]
Intl. Air Transport Assn. - Argentina [IO]
Intl. Air Transport Assn. - Australia [IO]
Intl. Air Transport Assn. - Austria [IO]
Intl. Air Transport Assn. - Bolivia [IO]
Intl. Air Transport Assn. - Brazil [IO]
Intl. Air Transport Assn. - Canada [IO]
Intl. Air Transport Assn. - Chile [IO]
Intl. Air Transport Assn. - Colombia [IO]
Intl. Air Transport Assn. - Costa Rica [IO]
Intl. Air Transport Assn. - Ecuador [IO]
Intl. Air Transport Assn. - Egypt [IO]
Intl. Air Transport Assn. - El Salvador [IO]
Intl. Air Transport Assn. - India [IO]
Intl. Air Transport Assn. - Indonesia [IO]
Intl. Air Transport Assn. - Israel [IO]
Intl. Air Transport Assn. - Japan [IO]
Intl. Air Transport Assn. - Jordan [IO]
Intl. Air Transport Assn. - Kenya [IO]
Intl. Air Transport Assn. - Korea [IO]
Intl. Air Transport Assn. - Malaysia [IO]

Intl. Air Transport Assn. - Mexico [IO]
Intl. Air Transport Assn. - New Zealand [IO]
Intl. Air Transport Assn. - Panama [IO]
Intl. Air Transport Assn. - Philippines [IO]
Intl. Air Transport Assn. - Poland [IO]
Intl. Air Transport Assn. - Portugal [IO]
Intl. Air Transport Assn. - Romania [IO]
Intl. Air Transport Assn. - Russia [IO]
Intl. Air Transport Assn. - Saudi Arabia [IO]
Intl. Air Transport Assn. - Singapore [IO]
Intl. Air Transport Assn. - Slovenia [IO]
Intl. Air Transport Assn. - South Africa [IO]
Intl. Air Transport Assn. - Spain [IO]
Intl. Air Transport Assn. - Sweden [IO]
Intl. Air Transport Assn. - Switzerland [IO]
Intl. Air Transport Assn. - Taiwan [IO]
Intl. Air Transport Assn. - Thailand [IO]
Intl. Air Transport Assn. - Trinidad and Tobago [IO]
Intl. Air Transport Assn. - Turkey [IO]
Intl. Air Transport Assn. - Uruguay [IO]
Intl. Air Transport Assn. - Venezuela [IO]
Intl. Airline Passengers Assn. [23015]
Intl. Assn. of Air Travel Couriers [153]
Intl. Assn. of Air Travel Couriers [IO]
Intl. Assn. of Air Travel Couriers - UK [IO]
Intl. Assn. of Machinists and Aerospace Workers [24012]
Intl. Assn. of Machinists and Aerospace Workers, Woodworkers District Lodge W1 [24026]
Intl. Assn. of Military Flight Surgeon-Pilots [13541]
Intl. Assn. of Natural Rsrc. Pilots [4187]
Intl. Astronautical Fed. [IO]
Intl. B and B Fly-Inn Club [21451]
Intl. Bird Dog Assn. [21452]
Intl. Bird Strike Comm. [IO]
Intl. Bus. Aviation Coun. [IO]
Intl. Cessna 120/140 Assn. [IO]
Intl. Cessna 120/140 Assn. [21453]
The Intl. Cessna 170 Assn. [21454]
The Intl. Cessna 170 Assn. [IO]
Intl. Coordinating Coun. of Aerospace Indus. Associations [IO]
Intl. Coordinating Coun. of Aerospace Indus. Associations [154]
Intl. Coun. of the Aeronautical Sciences [IO]
Intl. Coun. of Air Shows [IO]
Intl. Coun. of Air Shows [21455]
Intl. Coun. of Aircraft Owner and Pilot Associations [155]
Intl. Coun. of Aircraft Owner and Pilot Associations [IO]
Intl. Experimental Aerospace Soc. [IO]
Intl. Experimental Aerospace Soc. [6375]
Intl. Fed. of Air Line Pilots Associations [IO]
Intl. Fed. of Air Traffic Controllers' Associations [IO]
Intl. Fed. of Air Traffic Safety Electronics Assn. [IO]
Intl. Fed. of Airworthiness [IO]
International Flight Service Association [1583]
Intl. Inst. of Space Law [IO]
Intl. Pietenpol Assn. [IO]
Intl. Pietenpol Assn. [21456]
Intl. Scale Soaring Assn. [22648]
Intl. Soc. of Transport Aircraft Trading [156]
Intl. Soc. of Transport Aircraft Trading [IO]
Intl. Soc. of Women Airline Pilots [IO]
Intl. Soc. of Women Airline Pilots [157]
Intl. Space Exploration and Colonization Company [6376]
Intl. Space Exploration and Colonization Company [IO]
Intl. Union, United Auto., Aerospace and Agricultural Implement Workers of Am. [24004]
Intl. Wheelchair Aviators [21457]
Intl. Wheelchair Aviators [IO]
Interstate Club [21458]
Italian Indus. Assn. for Aerospace Systems and Defence [IO]
Jack Knight Air Mail Soc. [22834]
Japan Aeronautic Assn. [IO]
Japan Bus. Aviation Assn. [IO]
Kenya Air Sports Assn. [IO]
Koninklijke Nederlandse Vereniging Voor Luchtvaart [IO]

A star before a book entry number signifies that the name is not listed separately, but is mentioned within the entry.

Latin Amer. Aeronautical Assn. [438]
Latvijas Aeroklubs [IO]
League of World War I Aviation Historians [IO]
League of World War I Aviation Historians [21459]
Liechtensteinischer Hangegleiter Verband [IO]
Lighter-Than-Air Soc. [IO]
Lighter-Than-Air Soc. [21460]
Luscombe Endowment [21461]
Madagascar Aviation Assn. [IO]
MAPS Air Museum - Military Aviation Preservation Soc. [9342]
Metropolitan Air Post Soc. [22845]
Missile Defense Advocacy Alliance [17382]
Model Aeronautical Assn. of Queensland [IO]
Modellfluggruppe Liechtenstein [IO]
Monocoupe Club [21462]
Natl. 210 Owners Assn. [21463]
Natl. Aero Club of Bulgaria [IO]
Natl. Aero Club of Ireland [IO]
Natl. Aeronautic Assn. [158]
Natl. Aeronca Assn. [21464]
Natl. Air Carrier Assn. [159]
Natl. Air-Racing Gp. [23041]
Natl. Air Trans. Assn. [160]
Natl. Assn. of Flight Instructors [161]
Natl. Assn. of Rocketry [22650]
Natl. Assn. of Scale Aeromodelers [22651]
Natl. Assn. of Timetable Collectors [23008]
Natl. Aviation and Space Educ. Alliance [7994]
Natl. Biplane Assn. [21465]
Natl. Bus. Aviation Assn. [162]
Natl. Coalition for Aviation Educ. [7995]
Natl. Intercollegiate Flying Assn. [21466]
Natl. Soaring Found. [23042]
Natl. Space Club [6377]
Natl. Space Soc. [6378]
Natl. Stinson Club [21467]
Natl. World War II Glider Pilots Assn. [21468]
Natl. World War II Glider Pilots Assn. [IO]
Naval Airship Assn. [6379]
Negro Airmen Intl. [6380]
Nepal Airsport Assn. [IO]
Netherlands Aerospace Gp. [IO]
Ninety-Nines, Intl. Org. of Women Pilots [IO]
Ninety-Nines, Intl. Org. of Women Pilots [163]
Norwegian Aero Club [IO]
Norwegian Astronautical Soc. [IO]
Order of Daedalians [20650]
Org. of Black Airline Pilots [164]
Organized Flying Adjusters [2229]
Osterreichischer Aero Club [IO]
OX5 Aviation Pioneers [21469]
Pacific Rocket Soc. [6381]
Persekutuan Sukan Udara Malaysia [IO]
Pilots for Christ Intl. [20028]
Piper Owner Soc. [21470]
The Planetary Soc. [6382]
The Planetary Soc. [IO]
Popular Flying Assn. [IO]
Popular Flying Assn. [IO]
Popular Rotorcraft Assn. [21471]
Porterfield Airplane Club [21472]
Post Card Collectors Club [22908]
Precision Aerobatics Model Pilots Assn. [21473]
Professional Aviation Maintenance Assn. [165]
Rearwin Club [21474]
Regional Airline Assn. [166]
Royal Aeronautical Soc. - Australian Div. [IO]
Royal Aeronautical Soc., New Zealand Div. [IO]
Royal Aeronautical Soc. - United Kingdom [IO]
Royal Belgian Aero Club [IO]
Royal Danish Aeroclub [IO]
Royal Fed. of Aero Clubs of Australia [IO]
Royal New Zealand Aero Club [IO]
SAE Intl. - Soc. of Automotive Engineers [6520]
SAFE Assn. [6383]
Savez Aeroklubova Bosne I Hercegovine [IO]
Scottish Aeromodellers Assn. [IO]
Seaplane Pilots Assn. [167]
Short Wing Piper Club [21475]
Silver Wings Fraternity [21476]
Singapore Aircargo Agents Assn. [IO]
Soaring Assn. of Canada [IO]
Soaring Soc. of Am. [23043]
Sociedade de Aeroporto Internacional de Macau [IO]

Soc. of Antique Modelers [21477]
Soc. of British Aerospace Companies [IO]
Soc. of Experimental Test Pilots [6384]
Soc. of Flight Test Engineers [6385]
Soc. of Japanese Aerospace Companies [IO]
SOSA Gliding Club [IO]
Space Energy Assn. [6386]
Space Found. [7922]
Space Res. Org. Netherlands [IO]
Space Settlement Studies Program [6387]
Space Stud. Inst. [6388]
Space Topic Stud. Unit [22876]
Space Trans. Assn. [6389]
Sport Aircraft Assn. of Australia - Chap. 1 Sydney North [IO]
Sport Aircraft Assn. of Australia - Chap. 2 Camden [IO]
Sport Aircraft Assn. of Australia - Chap. 4 South Coast [IO]
Sport Aircraft Assn. of Australia - Chap. 5 Central Coast [IO]
Sport Aircraft Assn. of Australia - Chap. 6 Coffs Harbour [IO]
Sport Aircraft Assn. of Australia - Chap. 7 Mid North Coast [IO]
Sport Aircraft Assn. of Australia - Chap. 8 Manga-lore [IO]
Sport Aircraft Assn. of Australia - Chap. 10 South West, Western Australia [IO]
Sport Aircraft Assn. of Australia - Chap. 11 Hills District, New South Wales [IO]
Sport Aircraft Assn. of Australia - Chap. 12 Syd-ney Southern [IO]
Sport Aircraft Assn. of Australia - Chap. 13 Albany District, Western Australia [IO]
Sport Aircraft Assn. of Australia - Chap. 14 La-trobe Valley [IO]
Sport Aircraft Assn. of Australia - Chap. 15 Queensland [IO]
Sport Aircraft Assn. of Australia - Chap. 17 Pallamana-Murray Bridge [IO]
Sport Aircraft Assn. of Australia - Chap. 18 Mel-bourne [IO]
Sport Aircraft Assn. of Australia - Chap. 19 Gold Coast [IO]
Sport Aircraft Assn. of Australia - Chap. 20 Kyne-ton District [IO]
Sport Aircraft Assn. of Australia - Chap. 21 Moorabbin [IO]
Sport Aircraft Assn. of Australia - Chap. 22 Sunshine Coast, Queensland [IO]
Sport Aircraft Assn. of Australia - Chap. 23 Frogs Hollow, New South Wales [IO]
Sport Aircraft Assn. of Australia - Chap. 24 Janda-kot, Western Australia [IO]
Sport Aircraft Assn. of Australia - Chap. 25 Port Lincoln [IO]
Staggerwing Club [21478]
Stampe Club Intl. [21479]
Stampe Club Intl. [IO]
Stearman Restorers Assn. [21480]
Student Experimental Payload Prog. [6390]
Students for the Exploration and Development of Space [7923]
Swedish Soc. of Aeronautics and Astronautics [IO]
Swift Museum Found. [21481]
Trans Lunar Res. [6391]
Travel Air Club [21482]
Tuskegee Airmen, Inc. [20651]
Twin Bonanza Assn. [21483]
Twirly Birds [21484]
Union of French Aerospace and Space Indus. [IO]
United Flying Octogenarians [21485]
United Nations Comm. on the Peaceful Uses of Outer Space [IO]
U.S. Hang Gliding and Paragliding Assn. [23044]
U.S. Pilots Assn. [168]
U.S. Ultralight Assn. [21486]
Universities Space Res. Assn. [6392]
Univ. Aviation Assn. [7924]
Victorian Model Aeronautical Assn. [IO]
Vintage Sailplane Assn. [23045]
Western Assoc. Modelers [22661]
Whirly-Girls - Intl. Women Helicopter Pilots [21487]

Whirly-Girls - Intl. Women Helicopter Pilots [IO]
Women in Aerospace [6393]
World Airline Historical Soc. [21488]
World Airline Historical Soc. [IO]
World Airlines Clubs Assn. [IO]
World Beechcraft Soc. [IO]
World Beechcraft Soc. [21489]
World War I Aeroplanes [21490]
World War I Aeroplanes [IO]
Young Astronaut Coun. [7925]
Aerospace and Agricultural Implement Workers of Am; Intl. Union, United Auto., [24004]
Aerospace Companies; Society of Japanese [★154]
Aerospace Companies; Society of Japanese [★IO]
Aerospace Dept. Chairman's Assn. [7920], c/o Helen L. Reed, Chair, 710 H.R. Bright Bldg., Texas A&M Univ., 3141 TAMU, College Station, TX 77843, (979)458-2158
Aerospace Education Assn. - Address unknown since 1991.
Aerospace Educ. Found. [★6062]
Aerospace Elecl. Soc. [6367], 18231 Fernando Cir., Villa Park, CA 92861, (714)538-1002
Aerospace and Electronics Systems Soc; IEEE [6912]

Aerospace Engineering
High Frontier [6374]
Intl. Assn. of Machinists and Aerospace Workers [24012]
Intl. Experimental Aerospace Soc. [6375]
Intl. Miniature Aircraft Assn. [22938]
Natl. Safe Skies Alliance [18748]
Pheasants Forever [5366]
Sigma Gamma Tau [24466]
Soc. of Experimental Test Pilots [6384]
Soc. of Flight Test Engineers [6385]
Space Stud. Bd. [7687]
Student Experimental Payload Prog. [6390]
Aerospace Indus. Assn. of Am. [130], 1000 Wilson Blvd., Ste. 1700, Arlington, VA 22209-3928, (703)358-1000
Aerospace Indus. Assn. of Canada [★154]
Aerospace Indus. Assn. of Canada [IO], Ottawa, ON, Canada
Aerospace Indus. Assn. of Canada [★IO]
Aerospace Mfrs. Coun. - Defunct.
Aerospace Material and Process Engineers; Soc. of [★7285]
Aerospace Medical Assn. [13538], 320 S Henry St., Alexandria, VA 22314-3579, (703)739-2240
Aerospace Medical Assn. [IO], Alexandria, VA, United States

Aerospace Medicine
Aerospace Medical Assn. [IO]
Aerospace Medical Assn. [13538]
Airlines Medical Directors Assn. [13539]
Amer. Osteopathic Coll. of Occupational and Preventive Medicine [15802]
Assn. for the Development of Aerospace Medicine [IO]
Civil Aviation Medical Assn. [IO]
Civil Aviation Medical Assn. [13540]
German Soc. of Aviation and Space Medicine [IO]
Intl. Acad. of Aviation and Space Medicine [IO]
International Association of Military Flight Surgeon-Pilots [IO]
Intl. Assn. of Military Flight Surgeon-Pilots [13541]
Natl. Assn. of Air Medical Commun. Specialists [13542]
Soc. of U.S. Air Force Flight Surgeons [13543]
Soc. of U.S. Naval Flight Surgeons [13544]
Aerospace Primus Club - Defunct.
Aerospace Sciences; Inst. of the [★6369]
Aerospace Sys. Safety Soc. [★3457]
Aerospace Workers; Intl. Assn. of Machinists and [24012]
Aerospace Workers, Woodworkers District Lodge W1; Intl. Assn. of Machinists and [24026]
Aerospatial; Association Europeenne des Construc-teurs de Material [★154]
Aerospatial; Association Europeenne des Construc-teurs de Material [★IO]
Aerostar Owners Assn. [21424], 2608 W Kenosha St., No. 704, Broken Arrow, OK 74012, (918)258-2346

Reference to "IO" in place of a book number signifies that the association may be found in the 45th edition of International Organizations.

Aesculapian Club **[15982]**, Harvard Medical School, 25 Shattuck St., Bldg. A, Rm. 206, Boston, MA 02115, (617)432-1000

Aesculapius Intl. Medicine - Address unknown since 1999.

Aesthetic Plastic Surgeons; British Assn. of **[IO]**

Aesthetic Plastic Surgery; Amer. Soc. for **[14042]**

Aesthetic Realism Found. **[10781]**, 141 Greene St., New York, NY 10012, (212)777-4490

Aestheticians Intl. Assn. **[★1077]**

Aestheticians Intl. Assn. **[★IO]**

Aesthetics; Amer. Soc. for Dental **[14140]**

Aesthetics Intl. Assn. **[1077]**, 2611 N Beltline Rd., Ste. 140, Sunnyvale, TX 75182, (972)203-8530

Aesthetics Intl. Assn. **[IO]**, Sunnyvale, TX, United States

Aetherius Soc. **[IO]**, Los Angeles, CA, United States

Aetherius Soc. **[20568]**, 6202 Afton Pl., Los Angeles, CA 90028, (323)465-9652

Aetherius Soc. - United Kingdom **[IO]**, London, United Kingdom

af2 Natl. Fan Club **[24829]**, 2827 Greenway Dr., Bettendorf, IA 52722

AFAPAC Found. **[IO]**, Amsterdam, Netherlands

AFASIC - Overcoming Speech Impairments **[★IO]**

AFASIC - Unlocking Speech and Language **[IO]**, London, United Kingdom

AFBA, The 5Star Assn. **[18955]**, 909 N Washington St., Alexandria, VA 22314, (800)776-2322

AFCOM **[6781]**, 742 E Chapman Ave., Orange, CA 92866, (714)997-7966

AFEEC **[★IO]**

Affairs Coun. Found; State Govt. **[★1746]**

Affairs Exchange; Insurance Consumer **[2174]**

Affective Disorders Assn; Depression and Related **[15197]**

Affl. Artists - Address unknown since 2003.

Affiliated/Associated Drug Stores **[★2972]**

Affiliated/Associated Drug Stores **[★IO]**

Affiliated Boards of Officials **[★23875]**

Affiliated Conf. of Practicing Accountants Intl. **[4]**

Affiliated Conf. of Practicing Accountants Intl. **[IO]**, North Andover, MA, United States

Affiliated Dress Mfrs. - Defunct.

Affiliated Drug Stores **[★2972]**

Affiliated Drug Stores **[★IO]**

Affiliated Inventors Found. **[7224]**

Affiliated Leadership League of and for the Blind of America - Defunct.

Affiliated Nutritional Retailers Assn. - Address unknown since 1990.

Affiliated Tribes of Northwest Indians **[18948]**, 1827 NE 44th Ave., Ste. 130, Portland, OR 97213-1443, (503)249-5770

Affiliated Warehouse Companies **[3974]**, PO Box 295, Hazlet, NJ 07730-0295, (732)739-2323

Affiliated Woodcarvers **[9533]**, PO Box 104, Bettendorf, IA 52722, (563)359-9684

Affiliated Woodcarvers **[IO]**, Bettendorf, IA, United States

Affiliates of the Natl. Italian Amer. Foundation **[★IO]**

Affiliates of the Natl. Italian Amer. Foundation **[★19166]**

Affiliation of Honourable Photographers **[IO]**, Hailsham, United Kingdom

Affinity Gp. of Evolutionary Anarchists **[★IO]**

Affinity Gp. of Evolutionary Anarchists **[★16981]**

Affirm United **[IO]**, Ottawa, ON, Canada

Affirmation/Gay and Lesbian Mormons **[20046]**, PO Box 46022, Los Angeles, CA 90046-0022, (661)367-2421

Affirmation: United Methodists for Lesbian, Gay and Bisexual Concerns **[20047]**, PO Box 1021, Evanston, IL 60204

Affirmation: United Methodists for Lesbian/Gay Concerns **[★20047]**

Affirmative Action; Amer. Assn. for **[12066]**

Affirmative Action; Chinese for **[17101]**

Affirmative Action Coordinating Center - Address unknown since 2004.

Affirmative Action; Filipinos for **[18270]**

Affirmative/Gay Mormons United **[★20046]**

Affirmist Soc. - Defunct.

Affordable Hea. Insurance; Coun. for **[14686]**

Affordable Housing Lenders; Natl. Assn. of **[487]**

Affordable Housing Network; Natl. **[12318]**

Affordable Housing Tax Credit Coalition **[586]**, 1900 K St. NW, Ste. 1200, Washington, DC 20006, (202)419-2025

Affordable and Rural Housing; Coun. for **[12310]**

Afghan

Afghan-American Chamber of Commerce **[24222]**

Afghan Community in Am. **[12801]**

Afghan Hound Club of Am. **[22179]**

Afghan Women's Assn. Intl. **[13416]**

Kids 4 Afghan Kids **[11610]**

Soc. of Afghan Professionals **[9343]**

Solace Intl. **[13439]**

Afghan-American Chamber of Commerce **[24222]**, 8201 Greensboro Dr., Ste. 103, McLean, VA 22102, (703)442-5005

Afghan Amputee Bicyclist for Rehabilitation and Recreation **[IO]**, Kabul, Afghanistan

Afghan Canadian Youth Org. **[IO]**, Scarborough, ON, Canada

Afghan Community in Am. **[IO]**, Old Bethpage, NY, United States

Afghan Community in Am. **[12801]**, PO Box 73, Old Bethpage, NY 11804, (516)816-2525

Afghan Community Org. of London **[IO]**, London, United Kingdom

Afghan Cmpt. Sci. Assn. **[IO]**, Kabul, Afghanistan

Afghan Hea. and Development Services **[IO]**, Kabul, Afghanistan

Afghan Hound

Afghan Hound Club of Am. **[22179]**

Afghan Hound Club of Am. **[22179]**, c/o Donna Amos, Corresponding Sec., 10457 W Liberty Ct., Beach Park, IL 60099, (847)599-3505

Afghan Refugee Fund - Defunct.

Afghan Women Counselling and Integration Community Support Org. **[IO]**, Toronto, ON, Canada

Afghan Women; Women for **[12379]**

Afghan Women's Assn. Intl. **[13416]**, PO Box 637, Fremont, CA 94537-0637, (510)574-2182

Afghan Women's Assn. Intl. **[IO]**, Fremont, CA, United States

Afghan Women's Network **[IO]**, Kabul, Afghanistan

Afghan Youth Coun. in America - Address unknown since 1994.

Afghanaid **[IO]**, London, United Kingdom

Afghanerklubben **[★IO]**

Afghanistan

Afghan-American Chamber of Commerce **[24222]**

Afghan Community in Am. **[12801]**

Afghan Women's Assn. Intl. **[13416]**

Afghanaid **[IO]**

Afghanistan Peace Assn. **[IO]**

Afghanistan Peace Assn. **[16917]**

Afghans for Civil Soc. **[17079]**

AINA **[IO]**

America's Fund for Afghan Children **[11265]**

Direct Aid Intl. **[12849]**

Kids 4 Afghan Kids **[11610]**

Oper. Truth **[21317]**

Soc. of Afghan Professionals **[9343]**

Solace Intl. **[13439]**

Women's Alliance for Peace and Human Rights in Afghanistan **[12380]**

Afghanistan Athletic Fed. **[IO]**, Kabul, Afghanistan

Afghanistan Badminton Fed. **[IO]**, Kabul, Afghanistan

Afghanistan Cricket Fed. **[IO]**, Kabul, Afghanistan

Afghanistan Football Fed. **[IO]**, Kabul, Afghanistan

Afghanistan Handball Fed. **[IO]**, Kabul, Afghanistan

Afghanistan Paralympic Comm. **[IO]**, Kabul, Afghanistan

Afghanistan Peace Assn. **[IO]**, Flushing, NY, United States

Afghanistan Peace Assn. **[16917]**, 41-36 Coll. Point Blvd., Ste. 2A, Flushing, NY 11355, (718)461-6799

Afghanistan Relief Comm. - Defunct.

Afghanistan/Southwest Asia Resource Center - Defunct.

Afghanistan Studies Assn. - Defunct.

Afghanistan Tennis Fed. **[IO]**, Kabul, Afghanistan

Afghanistan Weightlifting Fed. **[IO]**, Kabul, Afghanistan

Afghans for Civil Soc. **[IO]**, Baltimore, MD, United States

Afghans for Civil Soc. **[17079]**, 806 N Charles St., Baltimore, MD 21201, (410)385-1445

AFL-CIO **[24096]**, 815 16th St. NW, Washington, DC 20006, (202)637-5000

AFL-CIO/ALA Joint Comm. on Lib. Ser. to Labor Groups **[10314]**, c/o Amer. Lib. Assn., 50 E Huron St., Chicago, IL 60611, (312)280-4395

AFL-CIO; Building and Constr. Trades Dept. - **[24025]**

AFL-CIO; Comm. on Political Educ., **[★18303]**

AFL-CIO Community Action Field Mobilization Dept. **[11801]**, 815 16th St. NW, Washington, DC 20006, (202)637-5309

AFL-CIO Community Services Activities **[★11801]**

AFL-CIO Demonstration Arts Project - Defunct.

AFL-CIO; Dept. of Civil, Human and Women's Rights, **[17110]**

AFL-CIO; Dept. of Civil Rights, **[★17110]**

AFL-CIO Dept. of Community Services **[★11801]**

AFL-CIO; Dept. for Professional Employees, **[24173]**

AFL-CIO; Intl. Org. of Masters, Mates and Pilots, ILA, **[24128]**

AFL-CIO; Intl. Woodworkers of Am., U.S. **[★24026]**

AFL-CIO; Maritime Trades Dept., **[24129]**

AFL-CIO; Metal Trades Dept., **[24135]**

AFL-CIO; Political Dept. of the **[18303]**

AFL-CIO; SEIU, District 925, **[23996]**

AFL-CIO; Union Label and Ser. Trades Dept., **[24213]**

AFL-CIO Unions for Professional Employees; Coun. of **[★24173]**

AFL-CIO Working for Am. Inst. **[12065]**, 815 16th St. NW, Washington, DC 20006, (202)508-3717

AFL Community Relations Comm. **[★11801]**

AFNA Natl. Educ. and Res. Fund **[8045]**, 117 S 17th St., Ste. 1200, Philadelphia, PA 19103, (215)854-1470

Afra-Span Network - Address unknown since 2001.

AFRC Babraham Inst. **[★IO]**

Afribike Assn. **[IO]**, Johannesburg, Republic of South Africa

Africa

Action for Southern Africa **[IO]**

Africa Action **[IO]**

Africa Action **[16918]**

Africa-America Inst. **[16919]**

Africa-American Friendship Soc. **[18862]**

Africa-Canada Development and Info. Services Assn. **[IO]**

Africa Faith and Justice Network **[16920]**

Africa Groups of Sweden **[IO]**

Africa Infrastructure Found. **[IO]**

Africa Inland Mission Intl. **[20294]**

Africa News Ser. **[16921]**

Africa Reconciliation Comm. **[IO]**

AFRICALINK **[16922]**

African Amer. Cultural Alliance **[9351]**

African Blackwood Conservation Proj. **[4342]**

African Conservation Trust **[IO]**

African Development Institute **[IO]**

African Development Inst. **[16923]**

African Medical and Res. Found. **[14971]**

African Stud. Assn. **[9348]**

African Youth For Transparency **[IO]**

Africare **[IO]**

Africare **[16924]**

Afro-American Historical Soc. Museum **[9354]**

Aid for Intl. Medicine **[14972]**

All-African People's Revolutionary Party **[16925]**

Amer. Mideast Bus. Associates **[24357]**

Amer.-Southern Africa Chamber of Trade and Indus. **[24375]**

Artists Against AIDS Worldwide **[11325]**

Assn. for Africanist Anthropology **[6408]**

Assn. of Concerned African Scholars **[16926]**

Assn. of Concerned African Scholars **[IO]**

Assn. for the Promotion of Tourism to Africa **[3826]**

Assn. for the Stud. of the Worldwide African Diaspora **[7929]**

Centre for Development and Population Activities **[12422]**

Constituency for Africa **[16927]**

Corporate Coun. on Africa **[169]**

Corporate Coun. on Africa **[IO]**

A star before a book entry number signifies that the name is not listed separately, but is mentioned within the entry.

Coun. for the Development of Social Sci. Res. in Africa [IO]
Debts AIDS Trade Africa [IO]
Debts AIDS Trade Africa [16928]
E-quip Africa [12704]
Empowerment Soc. Intl. [11775]
Friends of Animals [11397]
Friends of Malawi [9851]
Global Alliance for Africa [16929]
Global Coalition for Africa [16930]
Global Coalition for Africa [IO]
Guinea Development Foundation [IO]
Guinea Development Found. [16931]
Inst. of African Affairs [IO]
Intl. Bicycle Fund [13338]
Intl. Fed. of Ophthalmological Societies [15686]
Malawi Proj. [11266]
Mapendo Intl. [12868]
Natl. Org. for the Professional Advancement of Black Chemists and Chem. Engineers [6689]
Oper. Crossroads Africa [16932]
Operation Crossroads Africa [IO]
Org. for the Relief of Underprivileged Women and Children in Africa [12876]
Ozar Hatorah [20171]
People-to-People Hea. Found. [14984]
Reach the Children [11649]
Riders for Hea. [15271]
Saharan People's Support Comm. [16933]
Saharan People's Support Comm. [IO]
San Francisco African Amer. Historical and Cultural Soc. [9362]
Sierra Visions [12444]
Social Relief Intl. [12445]
Soc. of African Missions [19719]
Soc. of Missionaries of Africa [19721]
South African Tourism [24374]
Support A Child Intl. [11655]
Touching Hearts [11267]
TransAfrica Forum [16934]
TransAfrica Forum [IO]
U.S.A. for Africa [12882]
Washington Off. on Africa [16935]
Wimbum Cultural and Development Assn. in the U.S.A. [9344]
World Mercy Fund [12886]
Africa 2000Plus Network - Zimbabwe [IO], Harare, Zimbabwe
Africa Action [IO], Washington, DC, United States
Africa Action [16918], 1634 Eye St. NW, No. 810, Washington, DC 20006, (202)546-7961
Africa Action Alert; Trans [★16934]
Africa Action Alert; Trans [★IO]
Africa - Address unknown since 2001.
Africa Alliance of YMCAs [IO], Nairobi, Kenya
Africa-America Inst. [16919], Graybar Bldg., 420 Lexington Ave., Ste. 1706, New York, NY 10170, (212)949-5666
Africa-America Inst. - New York [11759], 420 Lexington Ave., Ste. 1706, New York, NY 10170-0002, (212)949-5666
Africa-America Inst. - New York [IO], New York, NY, United States
Africa; Amer. Comm. on [★16918]
Africa-American Friendship Soc. [18862], PO Box 1028, Maryland Heights, MO 63043, (417)255-1717
Africa-Canada Development and Info. Services Assn. [IO], Vancouver, BC, Canada
Africa Centre [IO], London, United Kingdom
Africa Chamber of Trade and Indus; Amer.-Southern [24375]
Africa; Church Proj. on U.S. Investments in Southern [★17353]
Africa Comm. [IO], Basel, Switzerland
Africa - Europe Faith and Justice Network [IO], Brussels, Belgium
Africa-Europe Gp. for Interdisciplinary Stud. [IO], London, United Kingdom
Africa Evangelical Fellowship - Defunct.
Africa Faith and Justice Network [16920], 125 Michigan Ave. NE, Ste. 481, Washington, DC 20017, (202)884-9780
The Africa Fund [★16918]
The Africa Fund [★IO]

Africa Groups of Sweden [IO], Stockholm, Sweden
Africa Guild - Defunct.
Africa Infrastructure Found. [IO], Lagos, Nigeria
Africa Inland Mission [★IO]
Africa Inland Mission [★20294]
Africa Inland Mission - Australia [★IO]
Africa Inland Mission Intl. [IO], Pearl River, NY, United States
Africa Inland Mission Intl. [20294], PO Box 178, Pearl River, NY 10965, (845)735-4014
Africa Inland Mission Intl. - Brazil [IO], Londrina, Brazil
Africa Inland Mission Intl. - Canada [IO], Scarborough, ON, Canada
Africa Inland Mission Intl. - France [IO], Le Breuil-Bernard, France
Africa Inland Mission Intl. Hong Kong Comm. [IO], Hong Kong, People's Republic of China
Africa Inland Mission Intl. - Netherlands [IO], Zeist, Netherlands
Africa Inland Mission Intl. - South Africa [IO], Plumstead, Republic of South Africa
Africa Inland Mission Intl. - United Kingdom [IO], Nottingham, United Kingdom
Africa Inland Mission New Zealand [IO], Auckland, New Zealand
Africa Leadership Forum [IO], Ota, Nigeria
Africa Mission; Heart of [★20034]
Africa Network [17740], c/o Dr. Cheryl Mwaria, Exec. Dir., Hofstra Univ., Dept. of Anthropology, Hempstead, NY 11549, (516)463-5589
Africa News Ser. [16921], 920 M St. SE, Washington, DC 20003, (202)546-0777
Africa; Project [★24603]
Africa Rainforest and River Conservation [4341], PO Box 2594, Jackson, WY 83001, (307)734-0077
Africa Rainforest and River Conservation [IO], Jackson, WY, United States
Africa Reconciliation Comm. [IO], Tokyo, Japan
Africa Rice Center [IO], Bouake, Cote d'Ivoire
Africa Service Inst. of New York - Defunct.
Africa; Soc. of Missionaries of [19721]
Africa - The African Travel Assn. [★3903]
Africa - The African Travel Assn. [★IO]
Africa Travel Assn. [IO], New York, NY, United States
Africa Travel Assn. [3903], 166 Madison Ave., 5th Fl., New York, NY 10016, (212)447-1357
Africa; United Support of Artists for [★12882]
Africa; U.S.A. for [12882]
Africa Youth Ministries [IO], Kampala, Uganda
AFRICALINK [16922], c/o USAID, 1325 G St. NW, Ste. 400, Washington, DC 20005, (202)712-0000
Africamix - Address unknown since 2008.

African
Abwenzi African Stud. [18863]
Africa Action [16918]
Africa-America Inst. [16919]
Africa-American Friendship Soc. [18862]
Africa Comm. [IO]
Africa Faith and Justice Network [16920]
Africa News Ser. [16921]
African Amer. Cultural Alliance [9351]
African Asian Latina Lesbians United [17649]
African Blackwood Conservation Proj. [4342]
African Children's Choir [9345]
African Children's Choir [IO]
African Dream Found. [IO]
African Family Film Found. [IO]
African Family Film Found. [9346]
African Heritage Center for African Dance and Music [9347]
African Heritage Center for African Dance and Music [IO]
African Info. and Documentation Center [IO]
African Language Teachers Assn. [9207]
African Peoples' Christian Org. [19759]
African Stud. Assn. [9348]
African Stud. Assn. [IO]
African Stud. Assn. of Australasia and the Pacific [IO]
African Stud. Centre [IO]
African Univ. Found. [IO]
African Univ. Found. [7926]
African Violet Soc. of Am. [22480]

African Wild Dog Conservancy [5288]
African Women Global Network [18808]
African Youth Development Found. [IO]
Africare [16924]
Afro-American Historical Soc. Museum [9354]
Amer. and African Bus. Women's Alliance [691]
Amer. Inst. for Maghrib Stud. [7927]
Amer. Inst. for Maghrib Stud. [IO]
Assn. of African Stud. Programs [7928]
Assn. for Africanist Anthropology [6408]
Assn. for the Stud. of Classical African Civilizations [9349]
Assn. for the Stud. of the Worldwide African Diaspora [7929]
Black World [IO]
Botswana Soc. [IO]
Constituency for Africa [16927]
Corporate Coun. on Africa [169]
Cross Cultural Collaborative [8177]
Egbe Omo Yoruba: Natl. Assn. of Yoruba Descendants in North America [19289]
Empowerment Soc. Intl. [11775]
Forum for African Women Educationalists [IO]
Friends of Animals [11397]
Homowo African Arts and Cultures [9350]
Info. Centre on Southern Africa [IO]
Inst. of African Stud. [IO]
Intl. African Inst. [IO]
Intl. People's Democratic Uhuru Movement [17395]
Intl. Possibilities Unlimited [18642]
Intl. Soc. of African Scientists [7611]
Japan Assn. for African Stud. [IO]
Kindness in Suffering [11616]
Leadership Enterprise for a Diverse Am. [9183]
Malawi Proj. [11266]
Malawi Proj. [IO]
Mapendo Intl. [12868]
Natl. Assn. of Black Storytellers [10981]
Natl. Black Child Development Inst. [11542]
Natl. Black Herstory Task Force [11089]
Natl. Black United Fund [12656]
Nordic Africa Inst. [IO]
North Amer. Tuli Assn. [4285]
Oper. Crossroads Africa [16932]
Org. for the Relief of Underprivileged Women and Children in Africa [12876]
Res. Action and Info. Network for the Bodily Integrity of Women [IO]
Riders for Hea. [15271]
Rites and Reason Theatre [11041]
Royal African Soc. [IO]
San Francisco African Amer. Historical and Cultural Soc. [9362]
Sierra Visions [12444]
Social Relief Intl. [12445]
Soc. of Africanists [IO]
South Africa Partners [18666]
Sudan-American Found. for Educ. [8073]
Sudan Stud. Assn. [7930]
Sudan Stud. Assn. [IO]
Sudan Stud. Soc. of the United Kingdom [IO]
Support A Child Intl. [11655]
Touching Hearts [11267]
TransAfrica Forum [16934]
Uganda Soc. [IO]
Washington Off. on Africa [16935]
Women's Africa Comm. of the African-American Inst. [18864]
African Acad. of Sciences [IO], Nairobi, Kenya
African Affairs Soc. of America - Defunct.
African AIDS Project - Address unknown since 1999.
African Airlines Assn. [IO], Nairobi, Kenya
African-American
100 Black Men of Am. [18865]
A. Philip Randolph Inst. [18604]
African Amer. Alliance for Homeownership [1975]
African Amer. Art Song Alliance [10520]
African-Amer. Assn. of Fitness Professionals [15957]
African Amer. Cinema Soc. [9926]
African Amer. Criminal Justice Soc. [17359]
African Amer. Cultural Alliance [9351]
African Amer. Environmentalist Assn. [4529]
African-American Female Entrepreneurs Alliance [4033]

Reference to "IO" in place of a book number signifies that the association may be found in the 45th edition of International Organizations.

African Amer. Holiday Assn. [22974]
African Amer. Life Alliance [11268]
African Amer. Literature and Culture Soc. [8798]
African Amer. Lutheran Assn. [20211]
African Amer. Museum [9352]
African Amer. Museum [IO]
African Amer. Museums Assn. [10488]
African-American Music Soc. [10521]
African Amer. Post Traumatic Stress Disorder
    Assn. [21276]
African Amer. Visual Arts Assn. [9409]
African Amer. Wine Tasting Soc. [190]
African-American Women in Tech. [6394]
African-Americans for Democracy [16936]
African Asian Latina Lesbians United [17649]
African Peoples' Christian Org. [19759]
Afro-American Historical and Genealogical Soc.
    [9353]
Afro-American Historical Soc. Museum [9354]
Amer. Assn. of Blacks in Energy [6936]
Amer. Bridge Assn. [21891]
Assn. of African Amer. Financial Advisors [1455]
Assn. of African Amer. Vintners [195]
Assn. of Black Anthropologists [6409]
Assn. of Black Nursing Faculty [8848]
Assn. of Black Psychologists [16138]
Assn. of Black Sociologists [7659]
Assn. of Minority Hea. Professions Schools [8850]
Assn. for the Preservation and Presentation of the
    Arts [9355]
Assn. for the Stud. of African-American Life and
    History [9356]
Assn. for the Stud. of the Worldwide African Di-
    aspora [7929]
Audience Development Comm. [11006]
Before Columbus Found. [10416]
Biblical Inst. for Social Change [20490]
The Black Agenda [16937]
Black Alliance for Educational Options [8322]
Black Americans for Life [12909]
Black Awareness in TV [17164]
Black Career Women [19323]
Black Caucus of the Amer. Lib. Assn. [10343]
Black Community Crusade for Children [11562]
Black Cops Against Police Brutality [5965]
Black Culinary Alliance [1122]
Black Farmers and Agriculturists Assn. [4111]
Black Filmmaker Found. [9933]
Black Flight Attendants of Am. [18866]
Black Flight Attendants of America [IO]
Black Gold Gp. [9501]
Black Holocaust Soc. [16938]
Black and Indian Mission Off. [19587]
Black Leadership Forum [18867]
Black Mental Hea. Alliance [15193]
Black Methodists for Church Renewal [20260]
Black Military History Inst. of Am. [10472]
Black Radical Cong. [18868]
Black Theatre Network [11008]
Black Veterans for Social Justice [21289]
Black Women in Church and Soc. [20617]
Black Women of Essence [11269]
Black Women in Sisterhood for Action [13422]
Black Women United for Action [13423]
Black Women's Agenda [13456]
Black World Found. [9357]
Catholic Negro-Amer. Mission Bd. [19601]
Charles H. Wright Museum of African Amer. His-
    tory [9358]
Charles H. Wright Museum of African Amer. His-
    tory [IO]
Charles W. Chesnutt Assn. [11166]
Coalition of Black Trade Unionists [24202]
Coalition on Urban Renewal and Educ. [18774]
Coll. Language Assn. [8729]
Conf. of Prince Hall Grand Masters [19230]
Cong. of Natl. Black Churches [19890]
Cong. of Racial Equality [16939]
Coun. on Career for Minorities [8047]
DIVAS of Lambda Fe Uson Sorority [24709]
Executive Leadership Coun. [2762]
Harriet Beecher Stowe Center [9655]
Helping Our Teen Girls in Real Life Situations
    [12261]
Hip-Hop Assn. [10887]

Homowo African Arts and Cultures [9350]
INROADS [8749]
Inst. for the Advanced Stud. of Black Family Life
    and Culture [9359]
InterAmerican Travel Agents Soc. [3920]
Intl. Assn. of African-American Music [10613]
Intl. Assn. of Black Actuaries [2186]
Intl. Black Women for Wages for Housework
    [18811]
Intl. Black Writers and Artists [11177]
Intl. Fed. of Black Prides [12238]
Intl. Org. of Black Security Executives [3533]
Intl. Possibilities Unlimited [18642]
Joint Center for Political and Economic Stud.
    [7526]
Land Loss Fund [12486]
Langston Hughes Soc. [9678]
Lawyers for One Am. [6028]
Lincoln Inst. for Res. and Educ. [16940]
Mgt. Educ. Alliance [8029]
Minority Hea. Professions Found. [18080]
Minority Peace Corps Assn. [18261]
Minority Student Achievement Network [8401]
Multicultural Golf Assn. of Am. [23455]
Museum of African Amer. History [9360]
Natl. African Amer. Drug Policy Coalition [17440]
Natl. African-American Insurance Assn. [2202]
Natl. African-American RV'ers Assn. [22958]
Natl. Alliance of Black Interpreters [3854]
Natl. Alliance of Black Salesmen and Black Sales-
    women [3469]
Natl. Alliance of Black School Educators [9217]
Natl. Assn. for the Advancement of Colored
    People [17129]
Natl. Assn. for the Advancement of Colored
    People Legal Defense and Educational Fund
    [17130]
Natl. Assn. of African Amer. Stud. [7931]
Natl. Assn. of African Americans for Positive
    Imagery [16941]
Natl. Assn. of Black Accountants [44]
Natl. Assn. of Black Citizens Action [16942]
Natl. Assn. of Black Female Executives in Music
    and Entertainment [12117]
Natl. Assn. of Black Hotel Owners, Operators and
    Developers [1950]
Natl. Assn. of Black Journalists [3129]
Natl. Assn. of Black Owned Broadcasters [568]
Natl. Assn. of Black Social Workers [13204]
Natl. Assn. of Black Telecommunications Profes-
    sionals [7778]
Natl. Assn. of Blacks in Criminal Justice [11877]
Natl. Assn. of Colored Women's Clubs [13051]
Natl. Assn. for Direct Care Workers of Color
    [14709]
Natl. Assn. for the Educ. of African Amer. Children
    with Learning Disabilities [12493]
Natl. Assn. for Equal Opportunity in Higher Educ.
    [8109]
Natl. Assn. of Fashion and Accessory Designers
    [246]
Natl. Assn. of Negro Bus. and Professional
    Women's Clubs [13053]
Natl. Assn. of Negro Musicians [10658]
Natl. Assn. of PreCollege Directors [8371]
Natl. Assn. for the Stud. and Performance of
    African-American Music [8922]
Natl. Assn. of Youth Clubs [13498]
Natl. Black Alcoholism and Addiction Coun.
    [13265]
Natl. Black Assn. for Speech-Language and Hear-
    ing [16448]
Natl. Black on Black Love Campaign [11842]
Natl. Black Bridal Assn. [535]
Natl. Black Bus. Coun. [170]
Natl. Black Catholic Clergy Caucus [19669]
Natl. Black Catholic Cong. [19670]
Natl. Black Child Development Inst. [11542]
Natl. Black Coll. Alumni Hall of Fame Found.
    [18911]
Natl. Black Deaf Advocates [17418]
Natl. Black Farmers Assn. [12189]
Natl. Black Graduate Student Assn. [18869]
Natl. Black Herstory Task Force [11089]
Natl. Black Home Educators [8519]

Natl. Black Justice Coalition [18643]
Natl. Black Law Students Assn. [8771]
Natl. Black Leadership Initiative on Cancer
    [13847]
Natl. Black MBA Assn. [8035]
Natl. Black McDonald's Operators Assn. [1955]
Natl. Black Nurses Assn. [15505]
Natl. Black Public Relations Soc. [3194]
Natl. Black Republican Assn. [18524]
Natl. Black Sisters' Conf. [19671]
Natl. Black State Troopers Coalition [5430]
Natl. Black United Fed. of Charities [16943]
Natl. Black United Fund [12656]
Natl. Center of Afro-American Artists [9361]
Natl. Coalition of Black Meeting Planners [2687]
Natl. Coalition of Blacks for Reparations in Am.
    [16944]
Natl. Community Development Org. [11798]
Natl. Conf. of Black Lawyers [5517]
Natl. Consortium of Arts and Letters for Histori-
    cally Black Colls. and Universities [8111]
Natl. Consortium for Black Professional Develop-
    ment [8049]
Natl. Economic Assn. [6888]
Natl. Juneteenth Observance Found. [16945]
Natl. Medical Assn. [15176]
Natl. Off. for Black Catholics [19691]
Natl. Org. of African Americans in Housing
    [12331]
Natl. Org. for People of Color Against Suicide
    [13289]
Natl. Org. for the Professional Advancement of
    Black Chemists and Chem. Engineers [6689]
Natl. Pan-Hellenic Coun. [24484]
Natl. Pinochle Bugs Social and Civic Club [13055]
Natl. Podiatric Medical Assn. [16047]
Natl. Religious Affairs Assn. [19872]
Natl. Soc. of Black Engineers [7034]
Natl. Soc. of Black Physicists [7504]
Natl. Trust for the Development of African Amer.
    Men [16946]
Natl. Urban League [17138]
Negro Airmen Intl. [6380]
Negro Leagues Baseball Museum [23123]
NIH Black Scientists Assn. [6395]
NuBian Exchange News [2770]
Off. for the Advancement of Public Black Colleges
    of the Natl. Assn. of State Universities and
    Land-Grant Colleges [8112]
Org. of Black Airline Pilots [164]
Org. of Black Designers [9907]
Org. of Black Screenwriters [1323]
Panamerican/PanAfrican Assn. [17371]
Praxis Proj. [17204]
Prog. for Res. on Black Americans [6396]
PUSH Commercial Div. [12098]
Quality Educ. for Minorities Network [8303]
Rainbow/PUSH Coalition [13185]
Richard Wright Circle [9707]
San Francisco African Amer. Historical and
    Cultural Soc. [9362]
Schomburg Center for Res. in Black Culture
    [9363]
Schomburg Center for Res. in Black Culture [IO]
Sickle Cell Disease Assn. of Am. [14797]
Soc. for the Anal. of African-American Public Hea.
    Issues [16253]
Southern Christian Leadership Conf. [17154]
Sphinx Org. [10710]
Student African Amer. Brotherhood [19444]
Thurgood Marshall Scholarship Fund [7932]
Twenty-First Century Found. [12740]
United Black Church Appeal [16947]
United Black Drag Racers Assn. [23397]
United Black Fund [12204]
United Black Republican Coalition [18538]
United Church of Christ Justice and Witness
    Ministries [20608]
United Negro Coll. Fund [8437]
UNITY: Journalists of Color [3172]
Women in Progress [13446]
Youth Organizations U.S.A. [13523]
African Amer. Alliance for Homeownership [1975],
    PO Box 11531, Portland, OR 97211, (503)595-
    3517

A star before a book entry number signifies that the name is not listed separately, but is mentioned within the entry.

African Amer. Art Song Alliance [10520], c/o Darryl Taylor, Founder, 15 Newton Ct., Irvine, CA 92604, (949)468-8031

African-Amer. Assn. for Dignity Unlimited - Address unknown since 1995.

African-Amer. Assn. of Fitness Professionals [15957]

African Amer. Breast Cancer Alliance [13786], PO Box 8981, Minneapolis, MN 55408, (612)825-3675

African Amer. Cinema Soc. [9926], 3617 Monclair St., Los Angeles, CA 90018, (626)794-4677

African Amer. Criminal Justice Soc. [17359]

African Amer. Cultural Alliance [9351], PO Box 22173, Nashville, TN 37202, (615)251-0007

African Amer. Environmentalist Assn. [4529], 9903 Caltor Ln., Fort Washington, MD 20744, (301)265-8185

African-American Female Entrepreneurs Alliance [4033], c/o Ms. Margo L. Davidson, Pres./Founder/ CEO, 333 Clearbrook Ave., Ste. 200, Lansdowne, PA 19050, (215)747-9282

African-Amer. History Assn. - Defunct.

African-Amer. History; Museum of [9360]

African Amer. Holiday Assn. [22974], 1855 Third St. NW, Washington, DC 20001, (202)667-2577

African-American Inst. [★16919]

African-Amer. Labor Center - Defunct.

African-American Lib. and Info. Sci. Assn. [IO], Los Angeles, CA, United States

African-American Lib. and Info. Sci. Assn. - Defunct.

African Amer. Life Alliance [11268], 1 Staton Dr., Upper Marlboro, MD 20774-1717, (301)249-2738

African-American Life and History; Assn. for the Stud. of [9356]

African Amer. Literature and Culture Soc. [8798], c/o Loretta G. Woodard PhD, Pres., Marygrove Coll., 8425 W McNichols Rd., Detroit, MI 48221-2599, (313)927-1452

African Amer. Lutheran Assn. [20211], c/o Rev. Gwendolyn Snell, Corresponding Sec., 11317 Parklawn Dr., Cleveland, OH 44108, (216)851-1528

African Amer. Museum [9352], 1765 Crawford Rd., Cleveland, OH 44106, (216)000-0000

African Amer. Museum [IO], Cleveland, OH, United States

African Amer. Museums Assn. [10488], PO Box 427, Wilberforce, OH 45384, (937)376-4944

African-American Music; Natl. Assn. for the Stud. and Performance of [8922]

African-American Music Soc. [10521], PO Box 2522, Springfield, MA 01101-2522, (413)734-2555

African-Amer. Natural Foods Assn. - Defunct.

African Amer. Post Traumatic Stress Disorder Assn. [21276], 9129 Veterans Dr. SW, Lakewood, WA 98498, (253)589-0766

African-Amer. Scholars Coun. - Defunct.

African-Amer. Solidarity Network - Defunct.

African-Amer. Trade and Development Assn. - Defunct.

African Amer. Visual Arts Assn. [9409], 3403 Milford Mill Rd., Baltimore, MD 21244, (410)521-0660

African Amer. Wine Tasting Soc. [190], PO Box 681, Powder Springs, GA 30127, (770)943-3649

African-American Women in Tech. [6394], 818-2 Twin Oaks Dr., Decatur, GA 30030

African-Amer. Women's Clergy Assn. [20615]

African Amers. Advocating Responsible Television - Address unknown since 2002.

African-Americans for Democracy [16936], PO Box 5423, West Lebanon, NH 03784, (832)567-8175

African-Americans for Humanism [★20085]

African-Americans for Humanism [★IO]

African Asian Latina Lesbians United [17649], PO Box 5412, Hillside, NJ 07205, (732)679-7687

African Assn. [★IO]

African Assn. for Lexicography [IO], Pretoria, Republic of South Africa

African Assn; Panamerican/Pan [17371]

African Assn. of Physiological Sciences [IO], Rabat, Morocco

African Assn. of Political Sci. [IO], Pretoria, Republic of South Africa

African Assn. for Public Admin. and Mgt. [IO], Nairobi, Kenya

African Assn. of Remote Sensing of the Env. [IO], Enschede, Netherlands

African Assn. for the Stud. of Liver Diseases [IO], Cairo, Egypt

African Assn. for the Study of Religions - Address unknown since 2002.

African Assn. of Zoos and Aquaria [IO], Pierre van Ryneveld, Republic of South Africa

African Bibliographic Center - Defunct.

African Bird Club [IO], Cambridge, United Kingdom

African Blackwood Conservation Proj. [IO], Red Rock, TX, United States

African Blackwood Conservation Proj. [4342], c/o James E. Harris, PO Box 26, Red Rock, TX 78662

African Books Collective [IO], Oxford, United Kingdom

African Bus. Roundtable [IO], Johannesburg, Republic of South Africa

African Capacity Building Found. [IO], Harare, Zimbabwe

African, Caribbean and Pacific Gp. of States [IO], Brussels, Belgium

African Centre for Democracy and Human Rights Stud. [IO], Serrekunda, Gambia

African Centre of Meteorological Applications for Development [IO], Niamey, Niger

African Centre for Tech. Stud. [IO], Nairobi, Kenya

African Chamber of Commerce - Address unknown since 2006.

African Chap. of Intl. Assn. of Agricultural Medicine and Rural Hea. - Egypt [IO], Cairo, Egypt

African Child Assn. [IO], London, United Kingdom

African Child Found. [IO], Kampala, Uganda

African Children's Choir [IO], Bellingham, WA, United States

African Children's Choir [9345], PO Box 29690, Bellingham, WA 98228-1690, (604)575-4500

African Children's Intl. Peace Forum and Ambassadors for Global Peace Intl. [IO], Lagos, Nigeria

African Christian Relief - Address unknown since 2006.

African Civil Aviation Commn. [IO], Dakar, Senegal

African Civil Ser. Observatory [IO], Cotonou, Benin

African Commn. on Human and Peoples' Rights [IO], Banjul, Gambia

African Communications Liaison Service - Defunct.

African Community Involvement Assn. [IO], Surrey, United Kingdom

African Conservation Trust [IO], Linkhills, Republic of South Africa

African Coun. of AIDS Ser. Organizations [IO], Dakar, Senegal

African Coun. for Commun. Educ. [IO], Nairobi, Kenya

African Cradle [11670], 1124 13th St., Modesto, CA 95354, (209)525-9377

African Cultural Found. - Address unknown since 2003.

African Development Bank [IO], Abidjan, Cote d'Ivoire

African Development Found. [IO], Washington, DC, United States

African Development Fund [IO], Abidjan, Cote d'Ivoire

African Development Institute [IO], New York, NY, United States

African Development Inst. [16923], PO Box 1644, New York, NY 10185, (888)619-7535

African Dream Found. [IO], Abeokuta, Nigeria

African Economic Community [IO], Addis Ababa, Ethiopia

African Economic Res. Consortium [IO], Nairobi, Kenya

African Educational Res. Network [IO], Albany, GA, United States

African Educational Res. Network [8220], c/o Dr. David Adewuyi, Managing Ed., Albany State Univ., Coll. of Educ., 504 Coll. Dr., Albany, GA 31705

African Energy Policy Res. Network/Foundation for Woodstove Dissemination [IO], Nairobi, Kenya

African Energy Policy Res. Network - Kenya [IO], Nairobi, Kenya

African Enterprise [IO], Kampala, Uganda

African Enterprise Canada [IO], Vancouver, BC, Canada

African Environmental Res. and Consulting Gp. [IO], Overland Park, KS, United States

African Environmental Res. and Consulting Gp. [4530], 14912 Walmer St., Overland Park, KS 66223, (913)897-6132

African Export-Import Bank [IO], Cairo, Egypt

African Fair - Defunct.

African Family Film Found. [9346], PO Box 630, Santa Cruz, CA 95061-0630

African Family Film Found. [IO], Santa Cruz, CA, United States

African Fed. of Gastroenterology [IO], Congella, Republic of South Africa

African Football Confed. [IO], 6th October City, Egypt

African Forum and Network on Debt and Development [IO], Harare, Zimbabwe

African Found. for Development [IO], London, United Kingdom

African Gender Inst. [IO], Rondebosch, Republic of South Africa

African Groundnut Coun. [IO], Lagos, Nigeria

African Hea. Educ. and Development; AHEAD-INC., [14536]

African Hea. For Empowerment and Development [IO], London, United Kingdom

African Heritage Center for African Dance and Music [IO], Washington, DC, United States

African Heritage Center for African Dance and Music [9347], 4018 Minnesota Ave. NE, Washington, DC 20019, (202)399-5252

African Heritage Fed. of the Americas - Defunct.

African Heritage Studies Assn. - Address unknown since 2002.

African Hockey Fed. [IO], Bulawayo, Zimbabwe

African Info. and Documentation Center [IO], Madrid, Spain

African Info. Soc. Initiative [IO], Addis Ababa, Ethiopia

African Inst. for Economic Development and Planning [IO], Dakar, Senegal

African Inst. of Private Intl. Law [IO], Rome, Italy

African Insurance Org. [IO], Douala, Cameroon

African Intellectual Property Org. [IO], Yaounde, Cameroon

African Jewish Bd. of Deputies; South [★IO]

African Jewish Bd. of Deputies; South [★20124]

African Language Assn. of Southern Africa [IO], Pretoria, Republic of South Africa

African Language Teachers Assn. [9207], Univ. of Wisconsin - Madison, 4231 Humanities Bldg., 455 N Park St., Madison, WI 53706, (608)265-7902

African Literature Assn. - Address unknown since 2002.

African Longhorn
World Watusi Assn. [4297]

African Love Bird Soc. [21832], PO Box 142, San Marcos, CA 92079-0142

African Medical and Res. Found. [14971], 4 W 43rd St., 2nd Fl., New York, NY 10036, (212)768-2440

African Medical and Res. Found. [★14971]

African Medical and Res. Found. [★IO]

African Medical and Res. Found. [IO], New York, NY, United States

African Medical and Res. Found. - Canada [IO], Toronto, ON, Canada

African Medical and Res. Found. - France [IO], Paris, France

African Medical and Res. Found. - Italy [IO], Rome, Italy

African Medical and Res. Found. - Kenya [IO], Nairobi, Kenya

African Medical and Res. Found. - Sweden [IO], Stockholm, Sweden

African Medical and Res. Found. - Tanzania [IO], Dar es Salaam, United Republic of Tanzania

African Medical and Res. Found. - Uganda [IO], Kampala, Uganda

African Natl. Network [★17740]

African Natl. People's Empire Re-Established - Address unknown since 1995.

African Nationalist Pioneer Movement - Defunct.

African Network for Agriculture, Agroforestry and Natural Resources Educ. [IO], Nairobi, Kenya

African Network for Agroforestry Educ. [★IO]

African Network for Prevention and Protection Against Child Abuse and Neglect [IO], Nairobi, Kenya

Reference to "IO" in place of a book number signifies that the association may be found in the 45th edition of International Organizations.

African Network for Rural Poultry Development [★IO]

African Network of Sci. and Technological Institutions [IO], Nairobi, Kenya

African Org. of Supreme Audit Institutions [IO], Tripoli, Libyan Arab Jamahiriya

African Parrot Soc. [21833], 301 E Garfield St., Clarinda, IA 51632

African Peace Support Trainers' Assn. [IO], Pretoria, Republic of South Africa

African Peoples' Christian Org. [19759]

African Progress; Alliance for Southern [12417]

African Publishers Network [IO], Abidjan, Cote d'Ivoire

African Refugees Found. [IO], Lagos, Nigeria

African Regional Coun. for Mental Hea. [IO], Harare, Zimbabwe

African Regional Indus. Property Org. [IO], Harare, Zimbabwe

African Regional Labour Admin. Centre - Zimbabwe [IO], Harare, Zimbabwe

African Regional Org. for Standardization - Kenya [IO], Nairobi, Kenya

African Regional Youth Initiative [IO], Dar es Salaam, United Republic of Tanzania

African Reinsurance Corp. [IO], Lagos, Nigeria

African Relief and Development Found. [★IO]

African Relief and Development Found. [★12882]

African Relief Fund [★7594]

African Res. Found. [★14971]

African Res. Found. [★IO]

African Rural and Agricultural Credit Assn. [IO], Nairobi, Kenya

African Safari Club of Philadelphia - Address unknown since 1987.

African Sci. Inst. [7594], PO Box 12153, Oakland, CA 94604, (510)653-7027

African Seed Trade Assn. [IO], Nairobi, Kenya

African Self-Help Program - Address unknown since 2003.

African Soc. for Bioinformatics and Computational Biology [IO], Pretoria, Republic of South Africa

African Soc. of Chemotherapy [IO], Casablanca, Morocco

African Soc. for Human Rights - Defunct.

African Sports Confed. of Disabled [IO], Giza, Egypt

African Starvation and Hunger Relief Fund - Address unknown since 1989.

African Student Aid Fund - Defunct.

African Student Service - Defunct.

African Stud. Assn. [9348], c/o Rutgers the State Univ., Douglass Campus, 132 George St., New Brunswick, NJ 08901-1400, (732)932-8173

African Stud. Assn. [IO], New Brunswick, NJ, United States

African Stud. Assn. of Australasia and the Pacific [IO], Adelaide, Australia

African Stud. Assn. of the United Kingdom [IO], London, United Kingdom

African Stud. Centre [IO], Leiden, Netherlands

African Succulent Plant Soc. - Defunct.

African Tourism Bd; South [★24374]

African Tourist Corp; South [★24374]

African Training and Res. Centre in Admin. for Development [IO], Tangiers, Morocco

African Union of the Blind - Kenya [IO], Nairobi, Kenya

African Univ. Found. [IO], Indianapolis, IN, United States

African Univ. Found. [7926], 3737 N Meridian St., Ste. 204, Indianapolis, IN 46208, (317)926-2175

African Venture Capital Assn. [IO], Yaounde, Cameroon

African Violet Soc. of Am. [22480], 2375 North St., Beaumont, TX 77702, (409)839-4725

African Violet Soc. of Canada [IO], Dollard-des-Ormeaux, QC, Canada

African Wild Dog Conservancy [IO], Tucson, AZ, United States

African Wild Dog Conservancy [5288], PO Box 30692, Tucson, AZ 85751

African Wildlife Found. [5289], 1400 16th St. NW, Ste. 120, Washington, DC 20036, (202)939-3333

African Wildlife Found. [IO], Washington, DC, United States

African Wildlife Leadership Found. [★IO]

African Wildlife Leadership Found. [★5289]

African Wind Energy Assn. [IO], Darling, Republic of South Africa

African Women Global Network [IO], Columbus, OH, United States

African Women Global Network [18808], c/o Center for African Stud., Ohio State Univ., 314 Oxley Hall, 1712 Neil Ave., Columbus, OH 43210-1219, (614)292-8169

African Women's Development and Commun. Network [IO], Nairobi, Kenya

African Women's Economic Policy Network [IO], Kampala, Uganda

African Youth Development Found. [IO], Owerri, Nigeria

African Youth For Transparency [IO], Lagos, Nigeria

African Youth Parliament [IO], Nairobi, Kenya

Africans; Christian Mission for Deaf [★20318]

Africans in Partnership Against AIDS [IO], Toronto, ON, Canada

Africare [IO], Washington, DC, United States

Africare [16924], 440 R St. NW, Washington, DC 20001, (202)462-3614

Africare - Angola [IO], Luanda, Angola

Africare - Benin [IO], Cotonou, Benin

Africare - Nigeria [IO], Abuja, Nigeria

Africare - Sierra Leone [IO], Freetown, Sierra Leone

Africare - Tanzania [IO], Dar es Salaam, United Republic of Tanzania

Afrika Komitee [★IO]

Afrika-Studiecentrum [★IO]

Afrikagrupperna [★IO]

Afrikanerbond [IO], Auckland Park, Republic of South Africa

Afro-Amer. Art Inst. - Address unknown since 1985.

Afro-American Artists; Natl. Center of [9361]

Afro-Amer. Cultural Found. - Address unknown since 1999.

Afro-American Cultural and Historical Soc. [★9352]

Afro-American Cultural and Historical Soc. [★IO]

Afro-American Historical and Genealogical Soc. [9353], PO Box 73067, Washington, DC 20056-3067

Afro-American Historical Soc. Museum [9354], c/o Neal E. Brunson, Esq., Dir., 1841 Kennedy Blvd., Jersey City, NJ 07305, (201)547-5262

Afro-American Museum of Detroit [★9358]

Afro-American Museum of Detroit [★IO]

Afro-Amer. Music Opportunities Assn. - Defunct.

Afro-Amer. Police League - Address unknown since 1999.

Afro-Amer. Soc. for Intl. Relations - Defunct.

Afro-Amer. Student Assn. - Address unknown since 1995.

Afro-American Women; Natl. Fed. of [★13051]

Afro-Asian Book Coun. [IO], New Delhi, India

Afro-Asian People's Solidarity Org. [IO], Cairo, Egypt

Afro-Asian Philosophy Assn. [IO], Cairo, Egypt

Afro-Asian Rural Development Org. [IO], New Delhi, India

Afro Asian Rural Reconstruction Org. [★IO]

Afro-Asian Soc. of Nematologists [IO], Luton, United Kingdom

Afro-Hispanic Inst. - Address unknown since 2001.

AFS Austauschprogramme fur interkulturelles Lernen [★IO]

AFS Del Peru Programas Interculturales [★IO]

AFS Egypt [★IO]

AFS Intercultura [★IO]

AFS Intercultura Brasil [★IO]

AFS Intercultura Portugal [★IO]

AFS Intercultural Programmes - New Zealand [IO], Wellington, New Zealand

AFS Intercultural Programs [IO], New York, NY, United States

AFS Intercultural Programs [8589], 71 W 23rd St., 17th Fl., New York, NY 10010-4102, (212)807-8686

AFS Intercultural Programs - Argentina [IO], Buenos Aires, Argentina

AFS Intercultural Programs - Australia [IO], Sydney, Australia

AFS Intercultural Programs - Austria [IO], Vienna, Austria

AFS Intercultural Programs - Brazil [IO], Rio de Janeiro, Brazil

AFS Intercultural Programs - Chile [IO], Santiago, Chile

AFS Intercultural Programs - China [IO], Beijing, People's Republic of China

AFS Intercultural Programs - Costa Rica [IO], San Jose, Costa Rica

AFS Intercultural Programs - Czech Republic [IO], Prague, Czech Republic

AFS Intercultural Programs - Denmark [IO], Frederiksberg, Denmark

AFS Intercultural Programs - Dominican Republic [IO], Santo Domingo, Dominican Republic

AFS Intercultural Programs - Ecuador [IO], Quito, Ecuador

AFS Intercultural Programs - Finland [IO], Helsinki, Finland

AFS Intercultural Programs - Germany [IO], Hamburg, Germany

AFS Intercultural Programs - Ghana [IO], Accra, Ghana

AFS Intercultural Programs - Guatemala [IO], Guatemala City, Guatemala

AFS Intercultural Programs - Honduras [IO], Tegucigalpa, Honduras

AFS Intercultural Programs - Hong Kong [IO], Hong Kong, People's Republic of China

AFS Intercultural Programs - Hungary [IO], Budapest, Hungary

AFS Intercultural Programs - Iceland [IO], Reykjavik, Iceland

AFS Intercultural Programs - India [IO], New Delhi, India

AFS Intercultural Programs - Italy [IO], Siena, Italy

AFS Intercultural Programs - Latvia [IO], Riga, Latvia

AFS Intercultural Programs - Malaysia [IO], Petaling Jaya, Malaysia

AFS Intercultural Programs - Panama [IO], Panama City, Panama

AFS Intercultural Programs - Peru [IO], Lima, Peru

AFS Intercultural Programs - Portugal [IO], Lisbon, Portugal

AFS Intercultural Programs - Slovakia [IO], Bratislava, Slovakia

AFS Intercultural Programs - Spain [IO], Madrid, Spain

AFS Intercultural Programs - Sweden [IO], Stockholm, Sweden

AFS Intercultural Programs - Thailand [IO], Bangkok, Thailand

AFS Intercultural Programs - Venezuela [IO], Caracas, Venezuela

AFS Interculture Canada [IO], Montreal, QC, Canada

AFS Interculture South Africa [IO], Rosebank, Republic of South Africa

AFS Interkultur [★IO]

AFS Interkulturell Utbildning [★IO]

AFS Interkulturelle Begegnungen e.V. [★IO]

AFS Intl. [IO], New York, NY, United States

AFS Intl. [8175], 71 W 23rd St., 17th Fl., New York, NY 10010, (212)807-8686

AFS a Islandi [★IO]

AFS Mezikulturni Programy - Ceska Republika [★IO]

AFS Norge [IO], Oslo, Norway

AFS Norge Internasjonal Utvekslings [★IO]

AFS Programas Interculturales - Argentina [★IO]

AFS Programas Interculturales - Costa Rica [★IO]

AFS Programas Interculturales - Ecuador [★IO]

AFS Programas Interculturales - Panama [★IO]

AFS Programas Interculturales - Venezuela [★IO]

AFSA Educ. Found. [17301], 919 18th St. NW, Washington, DC 20006, (202)296-5544

AFT Healthcare [24087], 555 New Jersey Ave. NW, Washington, DC 20001, (202)879-4400

After Death Commun. Res. Found. [14903], PO Box 23367, Federal Way, WA 98093

AFTER Rehabilitation and Training Center for Limb Birth Deficiencies/Amputations - Defunct.

Aftermarket Body Parts Assn. [★405]

Aftermarket Body Parts Assn. [★IO]

Aftermarket Body Parts Distributors Assn. [★IO]

A star before a book entry number signifies that the name is not listed separately, but is mentioned within the entry.

Aftermarket Body Parts Distributors Assn. [★405]
Aftermarket Coun. on Electronic Commerce [3835], c/o Alan Jones, Motor and Equip. Mfrs. Assn., 10 Lab. Dr., Research Triangle Park, NC 27709-3966, (919)549-4800
Aftermarket Indus. Assn; Automotive [374]
Afterschool Alliance [11524], 1616 H St. NW, Ste. 820, Washington, DC 20006, (202)347-2030
AG Communications in Educ. [★4098]
Ag Electronics Association - Address unknown since 2005.
Aga Khan Found. Canada [IO], Ottawa, ON, Canada
Aga Khan Found. - India [IO], New Delhi, India
Aga Khan Found. - Kyrgyz Republic [IO], Geneva, Switzerland
Aga Khan Found. - Switzerland [★IO]
Aga Khan Rural Support Programme - India [IO], Ahmedabad, India
Aga Khan Trust for Culture [IO], Geneva, Switzerland
Agac Mamuelleri ve Oman Ueruenleri Ikhracatcilari Biligi [★IO]
Against Child Abuse [IO], Hong Kong, People's Republic of China
Against Gun Violence; Women [18791]
Agajanian 98 Fan Club - Defunct.
AGAPE [★19562]
Agape Center [IO], Zama, Japan
Agape Force - Defunct.
Agape: Gospel of Life Disciples [19562], PO Box 192, Franklin, LA 70538, (337)828-2375
Agape Workshop for the Disabled [★IO]
Agassiz Assn; Chap. of [★7424]
Agatha Christie Appreciation Soc.: Partners in Crime - Defunct.
Agatha Christie Appreciation Soc.: Postern of Murder - Defunct.
Age Action Ireland [IO], Dublin, Ireland
Age Care [★IO]
Age Concern England [IO], London, United Kingdom
Age Concern Inst. of Gerontology [★IO]
Age Concern Scotland [IO], Edinburgh, United Kingdom
Age - The European Older People's Platform [IO], Brussels, Belgium
Aged Care Assn. Australia [IO], Curtin, Australia
Aged Care Assn. Australia - South Australia [IO], Frewville, Australia
Aged Care Assn. Australia - Tasmania [IO], Claremont, Australia
Aged Care Assn. Australia - Western Australia [IO], South Perth, Australia
Aged Care Assn. of Victoria [IO], Malvern, Australia
Aged Care Queensland [IO], Brisbane, Australia
Aged and Community Services Australia [IO], South Melbourne, Australia
Aged; Help the [★11274]
Aged; Natl. Assn. of Jewish Homes for the [★11277]
Aged; Natl. Caucus on the Black [★11306]
Aged; Natl. Center on Black [11306]
Aged Rights Advocacy Ser. [IO], Adelaide, Australia
Agence Canadienne des Droits de Reproduction Musicaux [★IO]
Agence de Consultation, de Commandement et de Conduite des Operations de l'OTAN [★IO]
Agence d'Aide a la Cooperation Technique Et au Developpement [★IO]
Agence de Developpement et de Secours Adventiste [★IO]
Agence islamique Intl. de Presse [★IO]
Agence Internationale ISBN [★IO]
Agence Internationale de l'Energie [★IO]
Agence Internationale de l'Energie Atomique [★IO]
Agence Latinoamericana de Informacion [★IO]
Agence de l'OCDE pour l'energie nucleaire [★IO]
Agence de Presse de l'OPEC [★IO]
Agence pour la Securite de la Navigation Aerienne en Afrique et Madagascar [★IO]
Agence Spatiale Europeene [★IO]
Agence Universitaire De La Francophonie [★IO]
Agence Universitaire de la Francophone, Bur. Afrique de l'Quest [IO], Dakar, Senegal
Agence Universitaire de la Francophonie [★IO]
Agence Universitaire de la Francophonie [★IO]

Agence Universitaire de la Francophonie [★IO]
Agence Universitaire de la Francophonie Antenne de Bruxelles [★IO]
Agencia de Informacao de Mocambique [★IO]
Agencies; Amer. Assn. of Grain Inspection and Weighing [1747]
Agencies and Bureaus; Intl. Gp. of [★10900]
Agencies; Natl. Assn. of State Contractors Licensing [1040]
Agency Broadcast Producers Workshop - Defunct.
Agency for Instructional Tech. [8549], Box A, 1800 N Stonelake Dr., Bloomington, IN 47402-0120, (812)339-2203
Agency for Instructional TV [★8549]
Agency Mgt. Assn; Life Insurance [★2195]
Agency for the Prohibition of Nuclear Weapons in Latin Am. and the Caribbean [IO], Mexico City, Mexico
Agency Risk Managers Assn; Public [5833]
Agency for the Safety of Air Navigation in Africa and Madagascar [IO], Dakar, Senegal
Agency for Tech. Cooperation and Development [IO], Paris, France
Agency; War Agencies Employee Protection [★5776]
Agenda Feminist Media [★IO]
AGENDA Feminist Media [IO], Durban, Republic of South Africa
Agenda; Public [18479]
Agent Coun; Real Estate Buyer's [3337]
Agent; Natl. Assn. Performing Arts Managers and [★175]

Agent Orange
Natl. Veterans Services Fund [13356]
Vietnam Veteran Wives [21332]
VietNow Natl. [13359]

Agent Orange Victims Intl. [★13356]
Agentia Nationala Romana de Energie Solara si Regenerabila [★IO]

Agents
Agents Assn. of Great Britain [IO]
Asian Amer. Real Estate Assn. [3299]
Assn. of Authors' Agents [IO]
Assn. of Authors' Representatives [171]
Assn. of Talent Agents [172]
Coalition of Exclusive Agent Associations [173]
Danish Assn. of Commercial Agents and Exclusive Distributors [IO]
Insurance Brokers and Agents of the West [2173]
Intl. Assn. of Speakers Bureaus [10900]
Mfrs'. Agents' Assn. of Great Britain and Ireland [IO]
Natl. Assn. of Estate Agents [IO]
Natl. Conf. of Personal Managers [174]
North Amer. Performing Arts Managers and Agents [175]
Personal Managers' Assn. [IO]
Sporting Goods Agents Assn. [IO]
Sporting Goods Agents Assn. [176]
Swedish Assn. of Agents [IO]

Agents; Amer. Assn. of Managing Gen. [2133]
Agents; Amer. Assn. of Premium Incentive, Travel Suppliers and [3904]
Agents Assn; Amer. [2128]
Agents; Assn. of Enrolled [★6299]
Agents Assn; Fed. Bur. of Investigation [5968]
Agents Assn. of Great Britain [IO], London, United Kingdom
Agents; Assn. of Talent [172]
Agents Assn; U.S. Treasury [★5653]
Agents of the Fed. Bur. of Investigation; Soc. of Former Special [19202]
Agents and Managers Conf. of NALU; Gen. [★2166]
Agents Mutagenes Presents dans l'Environnement; Assn. Internationale de Societes s'Occupant des [★6578]
Agents; Natl. Assn. of Enrolled [6299]
Agents; Natl. Assn. of Purchasing [★3263]
Agents; North Amer. Performing Arts Managers and [175]
Agents Soc; Certified Professional Insurance [★2140]
Agents of the U.S. Secret Ser; Assn. of Former [5877]
Agents - U.S.A; Assn. of Ship Brokers and [2603]

Agenturforetagen [★IO]
Aggregate and Concrete Executives - Defunct.
Aggregate and Sand Producers Assn. of South Africa [IO], Marshalltown, Republic of South Africa
Aggregates Assn; Natl. [★3699]
Aggregation of Congregation of Our Lady of Cenacle [19581]
Aggression; Assn. for the Behavioral Treatment of Sexual [★6529]
Aggression; Intl. Soc. for Res. on [6535]
Aggressive Aids Prevention [13546], PO Box 26227, San Francisco, CA 94126, (415)255-6022
Agile Mfg. Benchmarking Consortium [2545], 4606 FM 1960 W, Ste. 250, Houston, TX 77069, (281)440-5044
Agility Assn; U.S. Dog [23388]
Agility Dog Assn. of Australia [IO], Brisbane, Australia
Agility Dog Club of Queensland [IO], Brisbane, Australia

Aging
60 Plus Assn. [11270]
AARP [12895]
AARP Grief and Loss Prog. [13414]
Advocacy Tasmania [IO]
Age Action Ireland [IO]
Age Concern England [IO]
Age Concern Scotland [IO]
Age - The European Older People's Platform [IO]
Aged Care Assn. Australia [IO]
Aged Care Assn. Australia - South Australia [IO]
Aged Care Assn. Australia - Tasmania [IO]
Aged Care Assn. Australia - Western Australia [IO]
Aged Care Assn. of Victoria [IO]
Aged Care Queensland [IO]
Aged and Community Services Australia [IO]
Aged Rights Advocacy Ser. [IO]
Aging in Am. [11271]
Alliance for Aging Res. [11272]
Almshouse Assn. [IO]
Amer. Aging Assn. [14507]
Amer. Assisted Living Nurses Assn. [15432]
Amer. Assn. of Homes and Services for the Aging [11273]
American Association of Homes and Services for the Aging [IO]
Amer. Assn. for Intl. Aging [11274]
Amer. Assn. of Nurse Life Care Planners [15438]
Amer. Assn. of Retirement Communities [12896]
Amer. Assn. of Ser. Coordinators [1985]
Amer. Bd. of Psychiatry and Neurology [16071]
Amer. Coll. of Hea. Care Administrators [15535]
Amer. Disabled for Attendant Prog. Today [17413]
Amer. Fed. for Aging Res. [14508]
Amer. Found. for Aging Res. [14509]
Amer. Geriatrics Soc. [14510]
Amer. Hea. Care Assn. [14540]
Amer. Medical Directors Assn. [15536]
Amer. Podiatric Circulatory Soc. [16036]
Amer. Senior Fitness Assn. [15961]
Amer. Seniors Housing Assn. [12304]
Amer. Soc. on Aging [11275]
Asia Pacific Menopause Fed. [IO]
Asociacion Cosarricense de Climaterio y Menopausia [IO]
Assn. of Brethren Caregivers [11276]
Assn. of Jewish Aging Services [11277]
Assn. for the Planning and Development of Services for the Aged in Israel [IO]
Assn. of Retired Americans [12897]
Beverly Found. [11278]
B'nai B'rith Senior Citizens Housing Comm. [12469]
British Soc. of Gerontology [IO]
Brookdale Found. [12260]
Calgary Chinese Elderly Citizens' Assn. [IO]
Calgary Seniors Rsrc. Soc. [IO]
Canada's Assn. for the Fifty-Plus [IO]
Canadian Alliance of British Pensioners [IO]
Canadian Assn. of Pre-Retirement Planners [IO]
Catholic Golden Age [19597]
Center for Advocacy for the Rights and Interests of the Elderly [11279]
Center for Bio-Ethical Reform [18547]

Reference to "IO" in place of a book number signifies that the association may be found in the 45th edition of International Organizations.

Center for Medicare Advocacy [14684]
The Center for Social Gerontology [11280]
Center for the Stud. of Aging of Albany [11281]
Centre for Policy on Ageing [IO]
Children of Aging Parents [11282]
Christian Found. for Children and Aging [13159]
Coalition for Economic Survival [13160]
Coalition for Quality in Care [IO]
Consumer Consortium on Assisted Living [11283]
Dementia Advocacy and Support Network Intl.
   [12638]
Ebenezer Soc. [11284]
Elder Craftsmen [11285]
Elder Rights Advocacy [IO]
Energy Action [IO]
Environmental Alliance for Senior Involvement
   [11809]
European Fed. of Older Persons [IO]
Experience Works [12080]
Families U.S.A. Found. [11286]
Fed. of Active Retirement Assn. [IO]
French-speaking Intl. Assn. of Elder [IO]
Gerontological Soc. of Am. [14511]
Grace and Compassion Benedictines [IO]
Gray Panthers [11287]
Harvard Injury Control Res. Center [16690]
Hea. Promotion Inst. [11288]
Help the Aged [IO]
HelpAge Intl. [IO]
HelpAge Intl. - Africa Regional Development Cen-
   tre [IO]
HelpAge Intl. - Caribbean Regional Development
   Centre [IO]
HelpAge Intl. - EU Off. (Brussels) [IO]
HelpAge Intl. - Latin Am. Regional Development
   Centre [IO]
Intl. Assn. of Homes and Services for the Ageing
   [IO]
Intl. Assn. of Homes and Services for the Ageing
   [11289]
Intl. Fed. on Ageing [IO]
Intl. Fed. of the Little Bros. of the Poor [IO]
Intl. Senior Softball Assn. [23790]
Intl. Soc. for Aging and Physical Activity [13545]
Intl. Soc. for Aging and Physical Activity [IO]
ITEM Coalition [14690]
Jewish Assn. for Services for the Aged [11290]
John A. Hartford Found. [11291]
Latino Gerontological Center [11292]
Latino Gerontological Center [IO]
Leadership Coun. of Aging Organizations [11293]
Lewy Body Dementia Assn. [15335]
Life Acad. [IO]
Lifespan Resources [11294]
Little Bros. - Friends of the Elderly [11295]
Mature Market Rsrc. Center [11296]
Natl. Acad. of Elder Law Attorneys [6029]
Natl. Acad. for Teaching and Learning About Ag-
   ing [11297]
Natl. Adult Day Services Assn. [11298]
Natl. Alliance to Nurture the Aged and the Youth
   [12358]
Natl. Alliance of Senior Citizens [11299]
Natl. Asian Pacific Center on Aging [11300]
Natl. Assn. of Area Agencies on Aging [11301]
Natl. Assn. of County Aging Programs [11302]
Natl. Assn. of Geriatric Educ. Centers [14513]
Natl. Assn. of Hea. Care Assistants [14514]
Natl. Assn. for Hispanic Elderly [19100]
Natl. Assn. for Human Development [11303]
Natl. Assn. of Senior Companion Proj. Directors
   [11304]
Natl. Assn. of Senior Move Managers [2523]
Natl. Assn. of State Units on Aging [11305]
Natl. Assn. to Stop Guardian Abuse [12059]
Natl. Bd. for Certified Counselors and Affiliates
   [11828]
Natl. Caucus and Center on Black Aged [11306]
Natl. Coalition on Rural Aging [11307]
Natl. Comm. for the Prevention of Elder Abuse
   [11308]
Natl. Coun. on the Aging [11309]
Natl. Hispanic Coun. on Aging [11310]
Natl. Indian Coun. on Aging [11311]
Natl. Inst. on Community-Based Long-Term Care
   [11312]

Natl. Inst. of Senior Centers [11313]
Natl. Interfaith Coalition on Aging [11314]
Natl. Meals on Wheels Found. [11315]
Natl. Network for the Disabled [11973]
Natl. Pensioners and Senior Citizens Fed. [IO]
Natl. Reverse Mortgage Lenders Assn. [2430]
Natl. Senior Citizens Law Center [11316]
Natl. Senior Games Assn. [23655]
Natl. Soc. for Amer. Indian Elderly [19279]
North Amer. Squirrel Assn. [22773]
Ogden House Seniors 50 Club [IO]
Old Lesbians Organizing for Change [11317]
Older Women's League [13435]
Over the Hill Gang, Intl. [23846]
People-Animals-Love [16632]
P.R.I.D.E. Found. - Promote Real Independence
   for the Disabled and Elderly [11982]
Rebuilding Together [12337]
Retirement Res. Found. [11318]
Senior Action in a Gay Env. [12256]
Senior Companion Prog. [13405]
Senior Gleaners [12398]
Senior Roller Skaters of Am. [23739]
The Seniors Coalition [11319]
Seniors EyeCare Prog. [15701]
Significant Living [11320]
Sociedad Dominicana de Menopausia [IO]
Sociedad Venezolana de Menopausia y Os-
   teoporosis [IO]
Special Care Dentistry [14186]
Support Our Aging Religious [11321]
United Flying Octogenarians [21485]
United Seniors Assn. [11322]
Windward Found. [13195]
World Senior Golf Fed. [23472]
Aging in Am. [11271], 1000 Pelham Pkwy. S, Bronx,
   NY 10461, (718)409-8200
Aging; Amer. Assn. of Homes for the [★11273]
Aging Assn; Amer. [14507]
Aging; Center for Understanding [★11297]
Aging; Commn. on Law and [5935]
Aging and Human Development; Ebenezer Center
   for [★11284]
Aging Medicine; Amer. Acad. of Anti- [15125]
Aging; Natl. Center for Hea. Promotion and
   [★11288]
Aging; Natl. Center on Rural [★11307]
Aging; Natl. Pacific/Asian Rsrc. Center on [★11300]
Aging of Natl. Social Welfare Assembly; Natl. Comm.
   on [★11309]
Aging; North Amer. Assn. of Jewish Homes and
   Housing for the [★11277]
Aging Proj; Teaching and Learning About [★11297]
Aging Res; Amer. Fed. for [14508]
Aging Res; Amer. Found. for [14509]
Aging Res. Inst. - Defunct.
Aging Services Programs; Natl. Assn. of Nutrition
   and [15566]
AGIR Ici [IO], Paris, France
Aglow Intl. [IO], Edmonds, WA, United States
Aglow Intl. [20616], PO Box 1749, Edmonds, WA
   98020-1749, (425)775-7282
Aglow New Zealand [IO], Porirua, New Zealand
AGN Intl. - North Am. [5], 2851 S Parker Rd., Ste.
   850, Aurora, CO 80014, (303)743-7880
Agnes; Congregation of Sisters of Saint [19618]
Agnew Assn. of America - Address unknown since
   2008.
Agni Yoga Soc. [20632], 319 W 107th St., New
   York, NY 10025-2799, (212)864-7752
Agnostic Rights Found. - Address unknown since
   1999.

Agoraphobia

Pass-Gp. [12747]
Agoraphobics Building Independent Lives; ABIL -
   [12546]
Agoraphobics in Motion [12742], 1719 Crooks,
   Royal Oak, MI 48067, (248)547-0400
Agostiniani dell'Assunzione [★IO]
Agri-Club Natl. Togo [IO], Lome, Togo
Agri-Energy Roundtable [IO], Washington, DC,
   United States
Agri-Energy Roundtable [17826], 1312 18th St. NW,
   Ste. 300, Washington, DC 20036, (202)887-0528
Agri-Horticultural Soc. of India [IO], Calcutta, India

Agri-Marketing Assn; Natl. [2640]
Agri-Products Exporters Assn. - Defunct.
Agri-Service Ethiopia [IO], Addis Ababa, Ethiopia
Agri-Silviculture Inst. - Defunct.
Agri-Women; Amer. [16948]
Agri-Women Rsrc. Center; Amer. [16949]
Agribition Canadienne de l'Ouest [★IO]

Agribusiness

ACDI/VOCA [4481]
Agri-Energy Roundtable [17826]
Agribusiness Assn. of Australia [IO]
Agribusiness Coun. [4073]
Agribusiness Employers Fed. [IO]
Agricultural Economics Soc. [IO]
Amer. Agricultural Economics Assn. [6867]
Amer. Pheasant and Waterfowl Soc. [5292]
Amer. Soc. of Agricultural Consultants [4074]
Amer. Soc. of Agricultural Consultants [IO]
Assn. for the Development of Intl. Exchange of
   Food and Agricultural Productions and
   Techniques [IO]
Australian Inst. of Agricultural Sci. and Tech. [IO]
BCPC [IO]
Bio-Gro New Zealand [IO]
Canadian Agri-Marketing Assn. - Alberta [IO]
Canadian Agri-Marketing Assn. - Manitoba [IO]
Canadian Agri-Marketing Assn. - Ontario [IO]
Canadian Agri-Marketing Assn. - Saskatchewan
   [IO]
Canadian Western Agribition [IO]
Central Assn. of Agricultural Valuers [IO]
Coalition for a Competitive Food and Agricultural
   Sys. [4075]
Communicating for Am. [4076]
Coun. on Food, Agricultural and Rsrc. Economics
   [4524]
CropLife Australia [IO]
CUMELA Nederland [IO]
French Soc. of Agricultural Economics [IO]
Geode Rsrc., Conservation, and Development
   [4077]
German Agricultural Marketing Bd. - CMA [5020]
Independent Professional Seedsmen Assn. [187]
Indian Soc. of Agricultural Economics [IO]
Inst. of Agricultural Mgt. [IO]
Intl. Assn. of Agricultural Economists [6881]
Intl. Farm Mgt. Assn. [IO]
Intl. Food and Agribusiness Mgt. Assn. [1524]
IRI Res. Inst. [4103]
Member Insurance Assn. [1827]
Natl. Agri-Marketing Assn. [2640]
Natl. Alliance of Independent Crop Consultants
   [4078]
Natl. Assn. Agricultural Contractors [IO]
Natl. Coun. of Agricultural Employers [4079]
Natl. Sweet Sorghum Producers and Processors
   Assn. [871]
New Uses Coun. [4080]
New Uses Council [IO]
Northwest Farm Managers Assn. [4640]
Organic Consumers Assn. [5069]
Organic Exchange [2864]
Org. for Competitive Markets [4081]
Processors' and Growers' Res. Org. [IO]
Royal Agricultural Soc. of New Zealand [IO]
Samuel Roberts Noble Found. [4082]
Southern U.S. Trade Assn. [4083]
UNIMA [IO]
United Agribusiness League [4084]
Women in Agribusiness [4085]
Agribusiness Accountability Project - Defunct.
Agribusiness Assn. of Australia [IO], Adelaide,
   Australia
Agribusiness Coun. [4073], 1312 18th St. NW, Ste.
   300, Washington, DC 20036, (202)296-4563
Agribusiness Employers Fed. [IO], Adelaide,
   Australia
AgriChemical Retailers Assn; Natl. [★1363]
Agricultural Advt. Assn; Chicago Area [★2640]
Agricultural Advt. and Marketing Assn; Natl. [★2640]
Agricultural Aids Found. - Address unknown since
   1995.
Agricultural Appraisers; Amer. Soc. of [271]
Agricultural Aviation Assn. Intl. - Address unknown
   since 2003.

A star before a book entry number signifies that the name is not listed separately, but is mentioned within the entry.

Agricultural Aviation Assn; Natl. [4188]
Agricultural Aviation Assn; Women of the Natl. [4189]
Agricultural Bd. - Defunct.
Agricultural Chemicals Assn; Natl. [★807]
Agricultural Chemists; Assn. of Official [★6671]
Agricultural Coll. Editors; Amer. Assn. of [★4098]
Agricultural Coll. Magazines Assoc. [★8714]
Agricultural Communicators in Educ. [★4098]
Agricultural Communicators of Tomorrow; Amer. Assn. of [★8714]
Agricultural Communicators of Tomorrow; Natl. [8714]
Agricultural Computer Assn. - Defunct.
Agricultural Cooperative Development Intl. [★4481]
Agricultural Cooperative Development Intl. [★IO]
Agricultural Cooperative Development Intl. and Volunteers in Cooperative Assistance [★IO]
Agricultural Cooperative Development Intl. and Volunteers in Cooperative Assistance [★4481]
Agricultural Coun. of Denmark [★IO]
Agricultural Development
  Agri-Service Ethiopia [IO]
  Agricultural Development Found. [IO]
  Agricultural History Soc. [10080]
  Agriservices Found. [4094]
  Agromisa Found. [IO]
  Amer. Comm. for KEEP [12418]
  Amer. Rainwater Catchment Systems Assn. [7825]
  Arab Org. for Agricultural Development [IO]
  Armenian Tech. Gp. [IO]
  Armenian Tech. Gp. [4086]
  Asia Pacific Assn. of Agricultural Res. Institutions - India [IO]
  Assn. for the Advancement of Indus. Crops [4110]
  Assn. for Temperate Agroforestry [4119]
  Associazione Centro Aiuti Volontari Cooperazione Sviluppo Terzo Mondo [IO]
  Australian Agricultural and Rsrc. Economics Soc. [IO]
  Australian Women in Agriculture [IO]
  Brazilian Agroforestry Network [IO]
  Canadian Agricultural Economics Soc. [IO]
  Centre for Agricultural Strategy [IO]
  Comm. of Professional Agricultural Organisations in the EU [IO]
  Communicating for Am. [4076]
  Compatible Tech. Intl. [4087]
  Compatible Tech. Intl. [IO]
  Concern Am. [12845]
  Consultative Gp. on Intl. Agricultural Res. [12425]
  Cooperazione Padania-Mondo [IO]
  Coun. on Food, Agricultural and Rsrc. Economics [4524]
  Cover Crops Intl, CH [IO]
  Double Harvest [IO]
  Double Harvest [4088]
  Ecological Agriculture Projects [IO]
  Educational Concerns for Hunger Org. [12389]
  FARMS Intl. [12427]
  Food and Fertilizer Tech. Center for the Asian and Pacific Region [IO]
  Food for the Hungry [12391]
  French Agricultural Res. Centre for Intl. Development [IO]
  Future Harvest [IO]
  Future Harvest [4089]
  German Agricultural Soc. [IO]
  Heifer Proj. Intl. [12429]
  Inter-American Inst. for Cooperation on Agriculture - Costa Rica [IO]
  Inter-American Inst. for Cooperation on Agriculture - Dominican Republic [IO]
  Inter-American Inst. for Cooperation on Agriculture - Grenada [IO]
  Inter-American Inst. for Cooperation on Agriculture - Guyana [IO]
  Inter-American Inst. for Cooperation on Agriculture - Paraguay [IO]
  Inter-American Inst. for Cooperation on Agriculture - St. Lucia [IO]
  Intl. Assn. on Mechanization of Field Experiments [IO]
  Intl. Assn. for the Plant Protection Sciences [6397]

Intl. Food and Agribusiness Mgt. Assn. [1524]
The Intl. Found. [12434]
Intl. Fund for Agricultural Development - Italy [IO]
Intl. Inst. for Land Reclamation and Improvement [IO]
Intl. Inst. of Rural Reconstruction, U.S. Chap. [12938]
Intl. Rainwater Catchment Systems Assn. [7832]
Intl. Relief Friendship Found. [13171]
Intl. Ser. for the Acquisition of Agri-biotech Applications [6398]
Intl. Sprout Growers Assn. [4090]
Intl. Sprout Growers Assn. [IO]
Intl. Sunflower Assn. [IO]
IRI Res. Inst. [4103]
Jamaica Agricultural Soc. [IO]
Los Ninos [12589]
Macra Na Feirme [IO]
Natl. Hop Assn. of England [IO]
Organic Exchange [2864]
Palestinian Agricultural Relief Comm. [IO]
Plunkett Found. [IO]
Procicaribe - Caribbean Agricultural Sci. and Tech. Network Sys. [IO]
Red Sea Team Intl. [20385]
Royal Agricultural Soc. of the Commonwealth [IO]
Royal Agricultural Soc. of England [IO]
Royal Agricultural Soc. of NSW [IO]
Royal Highland and Agricultural Soc. of Scotland [IO]
Schweizerischer Verband fur Landtechnik [IO]
Soc. for the Responsible Use of Resources in Agriculture and on the Land [IO]
Sustainable Development Tech. Canada [IO]
Sustainable Harvest Intl. [4115]
Uganda IDEA Proj. [IO]
Wallace Genetic Found. [4117]
Wild Farm Alliance [4661]
Agricultural Development Coun. [★16959]
Agricultural Development Coun. [★IO]
Agricultural Development Found. [IO], Quito, Ecuador
Agricultural Development and Training Soc. [IO], Bagepalli, India
Agricultural Division of the Assn. for Career and Tech. Educ; Teacher Trainers Sect. of the [★7933]
Agricultural Economics Assn. of South Africa [IO], Matieland, Republic of South Africa
Agricultural Economics Soc. [IO], Whitchurch, United Kingdom
Agricultural Economists; Intl. Conf. of [★6881]
Agricultural Editors' Assn; Amer. [3076]
Agricultural Education
  Accokeek Found. [10006]
  Agriservices Found. [4094]
  Alpha Tau Alpha [24394]
  Amer. Assn. for Agricultural Educ. [7933]
  Amer. Comm. for KEEP [12418]
  Amer. Farm Bur. Found. for Agriculture [4095]
  Amer. Highland Cattle Assn. [4227]
  Amer. Junior Shorthorn Assn. [4233]
  Assn. for the Advancement of Indus. Crops [4110]
  Assn. for Agricultural Colleges in Denmark [IO]
  Assn. for Commun. Excellence in Agriculture, Natural Resources, and Life and Human Sciences [4098]
  Assn. for Intl. Agricultural and Extension Educ. [7934]
  Assn. for Intl. Agricultural and Extension Educ. [IO]
  Assn. for Intl. Agriculture and Rural Development [IO]
  Assn. for Intl. Agriculture and Rural Development [7935]
  Assn. of Rural Advisory Centres [IO]
  Center for Farm Hea. and Safety [12188]
  Coun. for Agricultural Sci. and Tech. [7936]
  Danish Fed. of Graduates in Agricultural Sci., Economics, Forestry, Horticulture and Landscape Architecture [IO]
  Educational Concerns for Hunger Org. [12389]
  Farm-Based Educ. Assn. [7937]
  The Gardeners of America/Men's Garden Clubs of Am. [4778]
  Intl. Agricultural Exchange Assn. - United Kingdom [IO]

Intl. Assn. of Students in Agriculture and Related Sciences [IO]
Intl. Assn. of Students in Agriculture and Related Sciences - Algarve [IO]
Intl. Assn. of Students in Agriculture and Related Sciences - Ancona [IO]
Intl. Assn. of Students in Agriculture and Related Sciences - Austria [IO]
Intl. Assn. of Students in Agriculture and Related Sciences - Bandung [IO]
Intl. Assn. of Students in Agriculture and Related Sciences - Belarus [IO]
Intl. Assn. of Students in Agriculture and Related Sciences - Berlin [IO]
Intl. Assn. of Students in Agriculture and Related Sciences - Bogor [IO]
Intl. Assn. of Students in Agriculture and Related Sciences - Bologna [IO]
Intl. Assn. of Students in Agriculture and Related Sciences - Bonn [IO]
Intl. Assn. of Students in Agriculture and Related Sciences - Brawijaya Univ. [IO]
Intl. Assn. of Students in Agriculture and Related Sciences - Bulgaria [IO]
Intl. Assn. of Students in Agriculture and Related Sciences - Cape Coast [IO]
Intl. Assn. of Students in Agriculture and Related Sciences - Coimbra [IO]
Intl. Assn. of Students in Agriculture and Related Sciences - Cordoba [IO]
Intl. Assn. of Students in Agriculture and Related Sciences - Croatia [IO]
Intl. Assn. of Students in Agriculture and Related Sciences - Czech Republic [IO]
Intl. Assn. of Students in Agriculture and Related Sciences - Denmark [IO]
Intl. Assn. of Students in Agriculture and Related Sciences - Finland [IO]
Intl. Assn. of Students in Agriculture and Related Sciences - France [IO]
Intl. Assn. of Students in Agriculture and Related Sciences - Gent [IO]
Intl. Assn. of Students in Agriculture and Related Sciences - Georgia [IO]
Intl. Assn. of Students in Agriculture and Related Sciences - Greece [IO]
Intl. Assn. of Students in Agriculture and Related Sciences - Hungary [IO]
Intl. Assn. of Students in Agriculture and Related Sciences - Ibadan [IO]
Intl. Assn. of Students in Agriculture and Related Sciences - Indonesia [IO]
Intl. Assn. of Students in Agriculture and Related Sciences - Italy [IO]
Intl. Assn. of Students in Agriculture and Related Sciences - Kendari [IO]
Intl. Assn. of Students in Agriculture and Related Sciences - Kenya [IO]
Intl. Assn. of Students in Agriculture and Related Sciences - Lautech [IO]
Intl. Assn. of Students in Agriculture and Related Sciences - Lisbon [IO]
Intl. Assn. of Students in Agriculture and Related Sciences - Ljubljana [IO]
Intl. Assn. of Students in Agriculture and Related Sciences - Macedonia [IO]
Intl. Assn. of Students in Agriculture and Related Sciences - Madrid [IO]
Intl. Assn. of Students in Agriculture and Related Sciences - Maribor [IO]
Intl. Assn. of Students in Agriculture and Related Sciences - Milan [IO]
Intl. Assn. of Students in Agriculture and Related Sciences - Monterrey [IO]
Intl. Assn. of Students in Agriculture and Related Sciences - Nepal [IO]
Intl. Assn. of Students in Agriculture and Related Sciences - Netherlands [IO]
Intl. Assn. of Students in Agriculture and Related Sciences - Niger [IO]
Intl. Assn. of Students in Agriculture and Related Sciences - Norway [IO]
Intl. Assn. of Students in Agriculture and Related Sciences - Osijek [IO]
Intl. Assn. of Students in Agriculture and Related Sciences - Piacenza [IO]

Reference to "IO" in place of a book number signifies that the association may be found in the 45th edition of International Organizations.

Intl. Assn. of Students in Agriculture and Related Sciences - Poland [IO]
Intl. Assn. of Students in Agriculture and Related Sciences - Ponte de Lima [IO]
Intl. Assn. of Students in Agriculture and Related Sciences - Porto [IO]
Intl. Assn. of Students in Agriculture and Related Sciences - Portugal [IO]
Intl. Assn. of Students in Agriculture and Related Sciences - Queretaro [IO]
Intl. Assn. of Students in Agriculture and Related Sciences - Russia [IO]
Intl. Assn. of Students in Agriculture and Related Sciences - St. Petersburg [IO]
Intl. Assn. of Students in Agriculture and Related Sciences - Santarem [IO]
Intl. Assn. of Students in Agriculture and Related Sciences - Sassari [IO]
Intl. Assn. of Students in Agriculture and Related Sciences - Switzerland [IO]
Intl. Assn. of Students in Agriculture and Related Sciences - Thailand [IO]
Intl. Assn. of Students in Agriculture and Related Sciences - Thessaloniki [IO]
Intl. Assn. of Students in Agriculture and Related Sciences - Togo [IO]
Intl. Assn. of Students in Agriculture and Related Sciences - Turin [IO]
Intl. Assn. of Students in Agriculture and Related Sciences - Uganda [IO]
Intl. Assn. of Students in Agriculture and Related Sciences - Ukraine [IO]
Intl. Assn. of Students in Agriculture and Related Sciences - Ultuna [IO]
Intl. Assn. of Students in Agriculture and Related Sciences - Uzbekistan [IO]
Intl. Assn. of Students in Agriculture and Related Sciences - Vila Real [IO]
Intl. Assn. of Students in Agriculture and Related Sciences - Viterbo [IO]
Intl. Assn. of Students in Agriculture and Related Sciences - Zambia [IO]
Intl. Assn. of Students in Agriculture and Related Sciences - Zimbabwe [IO]
Intl. Centre for Agricultural Educ. [IO]
Intl. Junior Brangus Breeders Assn. [4266]
Interstate Migrant Educ. Coun. [12588]
NAPAEO The Assn. for Land Based Colleges [IO]
Natl. Assn. of Agricultural Educators [7938]
Natl. Assn. of Supervisors of Agricultural Educ. [7939]
Natl. Coun. for Agricultural Educ. [4091]
Natl. FFA Org. [7940]
National FFA Organization [IO]
Natl. Inst. for Farm Safety [12976]
Natl. Junior Angus Assn. [4275]
Natl. Junior Hereford Assn. [4276]
Natl. Postsecondary Agricultural Student Org. [7941]
North Amer. Colleges and Teachers of Agriculture [7942]
North Amer. South Devon Assn. [4284]
Rural Advancement Found. Intl. - USA [4108]
Southeast Asian Regional Center for Graduate Stud. and Res. in Agriculture [IO]
Texas Longhorn Breeders Assn. of Am. [4294]
Village Educ. Rsrc. Center [IO]
Agricultural Educ; Assn. for Intl. [★7934]
Agricultural Educ; Dept. of Rural and [★9069]
Agricultural Educ. Fraternity; Natl. Professional Honorary [★24394]
Agricultural Educ. Natl. HQ [★4091]
Agricultural Employers; Natl. Coun. of [4079]

Agricultural Engineering
Alpha Epsilon [24395]
Amer. Soc. of Agricultural and Biological Engineers [6990]
Amer. Soc. for Plasticulture [4097]
Asian Assn. of Agricultural Engg. [IO]
Canadian Soc. for Bioengineering [IO]
Coachmakers' and Coach Harness Makers' Company [IO]
Intl. Network on Participatory Irrigation Mgt. [7233]
Italian Soc. of Agriculture Genetics [IO]

Soc. for Biological Engg. [6593]
Soc. for Engg. in Agriculture [IO]
Agricultural Engg. and Vocational Agriculture; Amer. Assn. for [★9298]
Agricultural Engineers; Amer. Soc. of [★6990]
Agricultural Engineers' Assn. [IO], Peterborough, United Kingdom

Agricultural Equipment
Agricultural Engineers' Assn. [IO]
Amer. Rainwater Catchment Systems Assn. [7825]
Assn. of Equip. Manufacturers [177]
Assn. of Equip. Manufacturers [IO]
British Agricultural and Garden Machinery Assn. [IO]
British Turf and Landscape Irrigation Assn. [IO]
Canada West Equip. Dealers Assn. [IO]
Equip. Mfrs. Coun. [178]
European Comm. of Associations of Mfrs. of Agricultural Machinery [IO]
Farm Equip. Manufacturers Assn. [179]
Farm Equip. Wholesalers Assn. [180]
Farm Equipment Wholesalers Association [IO]
Garden Centre Assn. [IO]
Garden Indus. Mfrs. Assn. [IO]
GARDENEX: Fed. of Garden and Leisure Mfrs. [IO]
Intl. Rainwater Catchment Systems Assn. [7832]
Intl. Silo Assn. [181]
Intl. Silo Assn. [IO]
Irrigation Assn. [IO]
Irrigation Assn. [182]
Irrigation Assn. of Australia [IO]
Midwest Equip. Dealers Assn. [4092]
Natl. Clay Pot Mfrs. [183]
Natl. Greenhouse Manufacturers Assn. [184]
North Amer. Equip. Dealers Assn. [185]
Saddle, Harness and Allied Trades Assn. [2419]
Spanish Assn. of Mfrs. of Irrigation Equip. [IO]
U.K. Irrigation Assn. [IO]
Wholesale Florist and Florist Supplier Assn. [1495]
Agricultural Film Mfrs. Assn; Construction and [1369]
Agricultural and Fishery Marketing Corp. [★IO]
Agricultural and Food Transporters Conf. [3856], c/o Russell Laird, Exec. Dir., 950 N Glebe Rd., Ste. 210, Arlington, VA 22203-4181, (703)838-7964
Agricultural and Forestry Machinery Assn. [IO], Brno, Czech Republic
Agricultural and Forestry Machinery Mfrs. Assn. [★IO]
Agricultural Groups Concerned About Resources and the Env. [IO], Guelph, ON, Canada

Agricultural History
Assn. for Living History, Farm and Agricultural Museums [10497]
Agricultural History Soc. [10080], c/o C. Fred Williams, Exec. Sec.-Treas., Univ. of Arkansas at Little Rock, Dept. of History, 2801 S Univ. Ave., Little Rock, AR 72204, (501)569-8782
Agricultural Implement Workers of Am; Intl. Union, United Auto., Aerospace and [24004]
Agricultural Implement Workers of Am; Intl. Union, United Auto., Aircraft, and [★24004]
Agricultural and Indus. Mfrs. Representatives Assn. [2533], c/o Jim Manke, Exec. Dir., 7500 Flying Cloud Dr., Ste. 900, Eden Prairie, MN 55344, (952)253-6230
Agricultural Indus. Confed. [IO], Peterborough, United Kingdom
Agricultural Insecticide and Fungicide Assn. [★807]
Agricultural Insecticides and Fungicide Manufacturers Assn. [★807]
Agricultural Inst. of Canada [IO], Ottawa, ON, Canada
Agricultural Journalists Assn. of Armenia [IO], Yerevan, Armenia

Agricultural Law
Agricultural Law Assn. [IO]
Amer. Agricultural Law Assn. [5431]
European Coun. for Agricultural Law [IO]
Farmers' Legal Action Gp. [6023]
Humane Farming Assn. [11411]
Org. for Competitive Markets [4081]
Agricultural Law Assn. [IO], Colchester, United Kingdom

Agricultural Libraries Network [IO], Rome, Italy
Agricultural Life and Labor Res. Fund; Natl. Coun. on [12322]
Agricultural Lime Assn. [IO], Peterborough, United Kingdom
Agricultural Marketing Bd. - CMA; German [5020]
Agricultural Marketing Officials; Natl. [★5025]
Agricultural Marketing Officials; North Amer. [5025]
Agricultural Marketing Project - Defunct.
Agricultural Missions [20295], 475 Riverside Dr., Rm. 725, New York, NY 10115, (212)870-2553
Agricultural Missions Found. [★20295]
Agricultural Movement; Amer. [★16950]
Agricultural Museums; Assn. for Living Historical Farms and [★10497]
Agricultural Museums; Assn. for Living History, Farm and [10497]
Agricultural Nitrogen Inst. [★1365]
Agricultural Personnel Mgt. Assn. [4638]
Agricultural Pilots Assn. - Defunct.
Agricultural Plastics Assn; Natl. [★4097]
Agricultural Policy Forum - Defunct.
Agricultural Producers Union [IO], Longueuil, QC, Canada
Agricultural Products Marketing Bd. [IO], St. John's, NL, Canada
Agricultural Publishers Assn. - Address unknown since 2002.
Agricultural Relations Coun. [3192], 62768 N Star Dr., Montrose, CO 81401, (970)249-1465
Agricultural Res. Coun. [IO], Pretoria, Republic of South Africa
Agricultural Res. Coun. - Biometry Unit [IO], Silverton, Republic of South Africa
Agricultural Res. Inst. - Defunct.
Agricultural Res. Trust [IO], Harare, Zimbabwe
Agricultural Retailers Assn. [1363], 1156 15th St. NW, Ste. 302, Washington, DC 20005, (202)457-0825
Agricultural and Rural Development Assn. in Ghana [IO], Accra, Ghana

Agricultural Science
Academie d'Agriculture de France [IO]
Agricultural Inst. of Canada [IO]
Agricultural Res. Coun. [IO]
Agricultural Res. Coun. - Biometry Unit [IO]
Agriculture, Food and Human Values [4093]
Agriservices Found. [4094]
Agronomy Soc. of New Zealand [IO]
Amer. Farm Bur. Found. for Agriculture [4095]
Amer. Soc. of Agronomy [4096]
Amer. Soc. for Plasticulture [4097]
ARC-Institute for Tropical and Subtropical Crops [IO]
Asia-Pacific Assn. of Agricultural Res. Institutions [IO]
Assn. of Agricultural Res. Institutions in the Near East and North Africa [IO]
Assn. for Commun. Excellence in Agriculture, Natural Resources, and Life and Human Sciences [4098]
Assn. of Fertilizer and Phosphate Chemists [6673]
Austrian Coun. for Agricultural Engg. and Rural Development [IO]
British Grassland Soc. [IO]
Canadian Consulting Agrologists Assn. [IO]
Canadian Soc. of Agronomy [IO]
Chinese Acad. of Agricultural Sciences [IO]
Coun. for Biotechnology Info. [6614]
Crop Sci. Soc. of Am. [4099]
Crop Science Society of America [IO]
Ecological Farming Assn. [4100]
European Assn. of Agricultural Economists [IO]
European Soc. for Agronomy [IO]
European Soc. of New Methods in Agricultural Res. [IO]
European Weed Res. Soc. [IO]
Farm Found. [4101]
Future Harvest [4089]
Grassland Soc. of Southern Africa [IO]
Honduran Agricultural Res. Found. [IO]
Indian Coun. of Agricultural Res. [IO]
Intl. Center for Agricultural Res. in the Dry Areas [IO]

A star before a book entry number signifies that the name is not listed separately, but is mentioned within the entry.

Intl. Centre for Advanced Mediterranean Agronomic Stud. [IO]
Intl. Crops Res. Inst. for the Semi-Arid Tropics - Bulawayo [IO]
Intl. Inst. of Tropical Agriculture [IO]
Intl. Maize and Wheat Improvement Center [IO]
Intl. Weed Sci. Soc. [IO]
Intl. Weed Sci. Soc. [4102]
IRI Res. Inst. [4103]
Josephine Porter Inst. for Applied Bio-Dynamics [4104]
Max-Eyth Soc. for Agricultural Engg. of the VDI [IO]
Minorities in Agriculture, Natural Resources and Related Sciences [10486]
Natl. Inst. for Sci., Law and Public Policy [4105]
Network of European Agricultural (Tropically and Sub-tropically Oriented) Universities and Sci. Complexes Related with Agricultural Development [IO]
New Zealand Inst. of Agricultural Sci. [IO]
Nordic Assn. of Agricultural Scientists [IO]
North American Weed Management Association [IO]
North Amer. Weed Mgt. Assn. [4106]
Potash and Phosphate Inst. [4107]
Rsrc. Efficient Agricultural Production - Canada [IO]
Royal Netherlands Soc. for Agricultural Sciences [IO]
Rural Advancement Found. Intl. - USA [IO]
Rural Advancement Found. Intl. - USA [4108]
Soc. of Dairy Tech. [IO]
Southern African Center for Cooperation in Agricultural and Natural Resources Res. and Training [IO]
Sugar Milling Res. Inst. [IO]
Swedish Res. Coun. for Env., Agricultural Sciences and Spatial Planning [IO]
Tropical Agricultural Res. and Higher Educ. Centre [IO]
Weed Sci. Soc. of Am. [4109]
Weed Soc. of Victoria [IO]
Agricultural Societies Coun. of New South Wales [IO], Hunters Hill, Australia
Agricultural Teachers Assn; Natl. Vocational [★7938]
Agricultural Technical Assistance Found. - Defunct.
Agricultural Trade Coun. [★2285]
Agricultural Transportation Alliance - Defunct.
Agricultural Transporters Conf. [★3856]
Agriculture
Accokeek Found. [10006]
ACDI/VOCA [4481]
Action for Food Production [IO]
Africare [16924]
Agricultural Development and Training Soc. [IO]
Agricultural History Soc. [10080]
Agricultural Personnel Mgt. Assn. [4638]
Agricultural Relations Coun. [3192]
Agricultural and Rural Development Assn. in Ghana [IO]
Agricultural Societies Coun. of New South Wales [IO]
Alliance for Sustainability [4641]
Alpha Epsilon [24395]
Alpha Gamma Rho [24396]
Alpha Zeta [24397]
Alternative Energy Resources Org. [6935]
Amer. Agri-Women [16948]
Amer. Agri-Women Rsrc. Center [16949]
Amer. Agricultural Economics Assn. [6867]
Amer. Agricultural Editors' Assn. [3076]
Amer. Agriculture Movement [16950]
Amer. Assn. of Bovine Practitioners [16741]
Amer. Comm. for KEEP [12418]
Amer. Farmland Trust [16951]
Amer. Feed Indus. Assn. [1357]
Amer. Forage and Grassland Coun. [5165]
Amer. Soc. of Agricultural Appraisers [271]
Amer. Soc. of Agricultural and Biological Engineers [6990]
Amer. Soc. of Agronomy [4096]
Amer. Soc. for Plasticulture [4097]
Amer. Soc. of Sugar Cane Technologists [3700]
Argentine Agricultural Assn. [IO]

Asia and Pacific Plant Protection Commn. [IO]
Associacion Comunitaria de Autosuficiencia [IO]
Assn. of Academic Agronomists [IO]
Assn. for the Advancement of Indus. Crops [4110]
Assn. of African Amer. Vintners [195]
Assn. of Amer. Feed Control Officials [5432]
Assn. of Amer. Plant Food Control Officials [5433]
Assn. of Amer. Seed Control Officials [5434]
Assn. of Amer. Seed Control Officials [IO]
Assn. of Farmworker Opportunity Programs [12585]
Assn. of Fruit and Vegetable Inspection and Standardization Agencies [1674]
Assn. for Living History, Farm and Agricultural Museums [10497]
Assn. of Official Seed Analysts [5435]
Assn. of Official Seed Analysts [IO]
Assn. of Official Seed Certifying Agencies [5436]
Assn. of Sugar Cane Growers of Colombia [IO]
Assn. for Temperate Agroforestry [4119]
Beyond Pesticides - Natl. Coalition Against the Misuse of Pesticides [13322]
Black Farmers and Agriculturists Assn. [4111]
Boerenbond [IO]
Brazilian Agricultural Assn. [IO]
Brazilian Agricultural Res. Corp. [IO]
Bugday Assn. for Supporting Ecological Living [IO]
Canadian Special Crops Assn. [IO]
Center for Rural Affairs [16952]
Central Union of Agricultural Producers and Forest Owners [IO]
Chem. Producers and Distributors Assn. [803]
Coalition for a Competitive Food and Agricultural Sys. [4075]
Colored Angora Goat Breeders Assn. [4782]
Commn. on Intl. Programs [17832]
Communicating for Am. [4076]
Compassion Over Killing [11382]
Compost Tea Indus. Assn. [186]
Concern Am. [12845]
Confed. of Portuguese Farmers [IO]
Consortium for Intl. Crop Protection [IO]
Consortium for Intl. Crop Protection [4112]
Construction and Agricultural Film Mfrs. Assn. [1369]
Controlled Release Soc. [6678]
Coun. for Biotechnology Info. [6614]
Coun. on Food, Agricultural and Rsrc. Economics [4524]
Crop Sci. Soc. of Am. [4099]
Danish Agricultural Coun. [IO]
Ecological Soc. of Am. [4506]
Educational Concerns for Hunger Org. [12389]
EnterpriseWorks/VITA [16996]
Epsilon Sigma Phi [24436]
European Conservation Agriculture Fed. [IO]
European Crop Protection Assn. [IO]
European Fed. for Info. Tech. in Agriculture [IO]
European and Mediterranean Plant Protection Org. [IO]
Farm Aid [16953]
Farm-Based Educ. Assn. [7937]
Farm Credit Coun. [474]
FARM (Farm Animal Reform Movement) [11394]
Farm Labor Organizing Comm. [23997]
Farm Labor Res. Proj. [23998]
Farm Sanctuary [11395]
Farm Worker Hea. Services [12586]
Farmers Assn. of Iceland [IO]
Farmers' Legal Action Gp. [6023]
FARMS Intl. [12427]
Fed. of Swedish Farmers [IO]
Fertilizer Indus. Round Table [1364]
Food Alliance [4676]
FOSFA Intl. [IO]
Fur Commn. U.S.A. [11399]
Future Harvest [4089]
Gamma Sigma Delta [24398]
Gamma Sigma Delta [IO]
The Gardeners of America/Men's Garden Clubs of Am. [4778]
German Agricultural Marketing Bd. - CMA [5020]
Groundswell Inc. of Minnesota [16954]
Hawaii Agriculture Res. Center [5228]

Heifer Proj. Intl. [12429]
Humane Farming Assn. [11411]
Independent Professional Seedsmen Assn. [187]
Inst. for Agriculture and Trade Policy [16955]
Intermediate Tech. Development Gp. of North Am. [16997]
Intl. Agricultural Centre [IO]
Intl. Assn. of Agricultural Economists [6881]
Intl. Assn. for Paratuberculosis [16793]
Intl. Assn. for the Plant Protection Sciences [6397]
International Association for the Plant Protection Sciences [IO]
Intl. Fed. of Agricultural Journalists [IO]
Intl. Flying Farmers [4646]
Intl. Food and Agribusiness Mgt. Assn. [1524]
The Intl. Found. [12434]
Intl. Network on Participatory Irrigation Mgt. [7233]
Intl. Pectin Producers Assn. [IO]
Intl. Ser. for the Acquisition of Agri-biotech Applications [IO]
Intl. Ser. for the Acquisition of Agri-biotech Applications [6398]
Intl. Union, United Auto., Aerospace and Agricultural Implement Workers of Am. [24004]
Intl. WWOOF Assn. [IO]
Interstate Migrant Educ. Coun. [12588]
IRI Res. Inst. [4103]
Japan Assn. for Intl. Collaboration of Agriculture and Forestry [IO]
Japanese Soc. of Agricultural Informatics [IO]
Japanese Soc. of Agricultural Machinery [IO]
Korea Agro-Fisheries Trade Corp. [IO]
Landscape Nursery Coun. [5045]
Malaysian Palm Oil Assn. [IO]
Merchants' Chamber of Agricultural Products [IO]
Midwest Old Settlers and Threshers Assn. [9483]
Migrant Hea. Promotion [12590]
Minorities in Agriculture, Natural Resources and Related Sciences [10486]
Namibia Agricultural Union [IO]
Natl. Agri-Marketing Assn. [2640]
Natl. Agricultural Aviation Assn. [4188]
Natl. Alliance for Food Safety and Security [1537]
Natl. Alliance for Migrant and Seasonal Farmworker Vocational Rehabilitation [12591]
Natl. Assn. of African Palm Growers [IO]
Natl. Assn. of Agricultural Produce Trading Companies [IO]
Natl. Assn. of Agriculture Employees [5437]
Natl. Assn. of County Agricultural Agents [5438]
Natl. Assn. of Farm Broadcasting [570]
Natl. Assn. of Farriers, Blacksmiths and Agricultural Engineers [IO]
Natl. Assn. of Produce Market Managers [5022]
Natl. Assn. of State Departments of Agriculture [5439]
Natl. Assn. of State Directors of Migrant Educ. [12592]
Natl. Barley Foods Coun. [1751]
Natl. Black Farmers Assn. [12189]
Natl. Catholic Rural Life Conf. [19677]
Natl. Center for Farmworker Hea. [14581]
Natl. Chamber of Agriculture and Agro-Industry [IO]
Natl. Comm. on the Educ. of Migrant Children (of the Natl. Child Labor Comm.) [12593]
Natl. Coun. on Agricultural Life and Labor Res. Fund [12322]
Natl. Family Farm Coalition [16956]
Natl. Farm Worker Ministry [12594]
Natl. Farmers' Fed. [IO]
Natl. Farmers Union [4651]
Natl. Farmers Union - Canada [IO]
Natl. Farmers' Union - England [IO]
Natl. Grain and Feed Assn. [1359]
Natl. Grange [4652]
Natl. Hay Assn. [1360]
Natl. Inst. for Farm Safety [12976]
Natl. Inst. for Sci., Law and Public Policy [4105]
Natl. Org. for Raw Materials [16957]
Natl. Palm Oil Growers' Fed. [IO]
Natl. Pesticide Info. Center [13327]
Natl. Plant Bd. [5440]

Reference to "IO" in place of a book number signifies that the association may be found in the 45th edition of International Organizations.

Natl. Sweet Sorghum Producers and Processors Assn. [871]
Natl. Urban Agriculture Coun. [4113]
New South Wales Farmers' Assn. [IO]
Nordic Joint Comm. for Agricultural Res. [IO]
North Amer. Agricultural Marketing Officials [5025]
North Amer. Farm Show Coun. [4114]
North Amer. Weed Mgt. Assn. [4106]
Northwest Coalition for Alternatives to Pesticides [13328]
Northwest Farm Managers Assn. [4640]
Norwegian Farmers' Union [IO]
Organic Agriculture Assn. [IO]
Organic Consumers Assn. [5069]
Organic Exchange [2864]
Org. of Professional Employees of the U.S. Dept. of Agriculture [5441]
Pear Bur. Northwest [4755]
People Food and Land Found. [4656]
Pesticide Action Network North Am. Regional Center [13329]
Proj. Food, Land and People [4525]
Raspberry Indus. Development Coun. [IO]
Royal Agricultural and Horticultural Soc. of South Australia [IO]
Royal Danish Agricultural Soc. [IO]
Royal Isle of Wight Agricultural Soc. [IO]
Royal Ulster Agricultural Soc. [IO]
Royal Welsh Agricultural Soc. [IO]
Rural Advancement Found. Intl. - USA [4108]
Samuel Roberts Noble Found. [4082]
Singles in Agriculture [22143]
Soc. of Agricultural Meteorology of Japan [IO]
Southern Alternative Agriculture Network [IO]
Student/Farmworker Alliance [24054]
Sun-Maid Growers of California [4762]
Sustainable Harvest Intl. [4115]
Tropical Grassland Soc. of Australia [IO]
True Food Network [4677]
Ulster Farmers' Union [IO]
Union of Agrarian Cooperators of Albania [IO]
United Farm Workers of Am. [23999]
U.S. Animal Hea. Assn. [16811]
U.S. Farmers Assn. [16958]
Universal Cooperatives [4484]
USA Dry Pea and Lentil Coun. [4116]
Wallace Genetic Found. [4117]
Western U.S. Agricultural Trade Assn. [4118]
Wild Farm Alliance [4661]
Willing Workers on Organic Farms - Australia [IO]
Willing Workers on Organic Farms - Austria [IO]
Willing Workers on Organic Farms - Denmark [IO]
Willing Workers on Organic Farms - Ghana [IO]
Willing Workers on Organic Farms - Japan [IO]
Willing Workers on Organic Farms - New Zealand [IO]
Willing Workers on Organic Farms - Norway [IO]
Winrock Intl. [IO]
Winrock Intl. [16959]
Women Involved in Farm Economics [16960]
World Fed. of Agriculture, Food, Hotel and Allied Workers [IO]
World Wide Opportunities on Organic Farms - Canada [IO]
World Wide Opportunities on Organic Farms - Czech Republic [IO]
World Wide Opportunities on Organic Farms - Italia [IO]
World Wide Opportunities on Organic Farms - Korea [IO]
World Wide Opportunities on Organic Farms - Nepal [IO]
World Wide Opportunities on Organic Farms - Slovenia [IO]
World Wide Opportunities on Organic Farms - Sweden [IO]
World Wide Opportunities on Organic Farms - Switzerland [IO]
World Wide Opportunities on Organic Farms - Uganda [IO]
Worldwide Opportunities on Organic Farms - Germany [IO]
Worldwide Opportunities on Organic Farms - UK [IO]
Zambia Natl. Farmers' Union [IO]

Agriculture Alliance; Animal [1501]
Agriculture; Amer. Assn. of Teacher Educators in [★7933]
Agriculture; Amer. Farm Bur. Found. for [4095]
Agriculture; Comm. for Sustainable [★4100]
Agriculture; Communicating for [★4076]
Agriculture Coun. of America - Defunct.
Agriculture Development Ser; Intl. [★16959]
Agriculture, Food and Human Values [4093], PO Box 118545, Gainesville, FL 32611, (352)392-0958
Agriculture and Livestock Professional Photographers Assn. - Defunct.
Agriculture Movements; Intl. Fed. of Organic [IO]
Agriculture; Natl. Assn. of Colleges and Teachers of [★7942]
Agriculture; Natl. Assn. of Commissioners, Secretaries and Directors of [★5439]
Agriculture; Natl. Inst. for Animal [5003]
Agriculture, Natural Resources, and Life and Human Sciences; Assn. for Commun. Excellence in [4098]
Agriculture; North Amer. Colleges and Teachers of [7942]
Agriculture Org. of the United Nations - Trinidad and Tobago; Food and [IO]
Agriculture Res. Center; Hawaii [5228]
Agriculture and the Self Employed; Communicating for [★4076]
Agriculture; Singles in [22143]
Agriculture; Steering Comm. for Sustainable [★4100]
Agrimetrics Inst. [★IO]
Agriservices Found. [4094]
Agroforestry
    Accademia Agraria [IO]
    Assn. for Temperate Agroforestry [4119]
Agroforestry and Natural Resources Educ; African Network for Agriculture, [IO]
Agroforestry Network; Brazilian [IO]
Agrologists Assn; Canadian Consulting [IO]
Agromisa Found. [IO], Wageningen, Netherlands
Agronomiliitto [★IO]
Agronomy; Amer. Soc. of [4096]'
Agronomy; Canadian Soc. of [IO]
Agronomy Soc. of New Zealand [IO], Palmerston North, New Zealand
Agronomy; Soils Sect. of Amer. Soc. of [★7674]
Agrupacion Espanola del Genero de Punto [★IO]
Aguda Leumit le Kimum Mefagrim Be'Israel [★IO]
Agudat Achsaniot Noar Beisrael [★IO]
Agudat Hacherehim Beisrael [★IO]
Agudat Hametargmim Beyisrael [★IO]
Agudath Harabonim [★20183]
Agudath Israel of Am. [20110]
Agudath Israel; Bnos [20127]
Agudath Israel; Pirchei [8699]
Agudath Israel; Young Men's Division-Zeirei [20199]
Agustinians of the Assumption [IO], Rome, Italy
ah Adurzia [★20095]
AHA [8590], 221 NW 2nd Ave., Ste. 200, Portland, OR 97209, (503)295-7730
AHA Intl. [IO], Portland, OR, United States
AHEAD [★IO]
AHEAD [★8201]
AHEAD-INC., African Hea. Educ. and Development [14536], PO Box 600379, Dallas, TX 75206, (214)823-0007
AHEPA; Order of [★19083]
Ahern Clan Assn. [19048], c/o Dennis J. Ahern, Sec., 298 Central St., Acton, MA 01720-2444
AHI Foundation [★2970]
Ahl-ul-Bait World Assembly [IO], Tehran, Iran
Ahmadiyya Anjuman Isha'at-e-Islam Lahore [★IO]
Ahmadiyya Anjuman Isha'at-e-Islam Lahore, Canada [★IO]
Ahmadiyya Movement in Islam, Canada [★IO]
Ahmadiyya Muslim Assn. [★IO]'
Ahmadiyya Muslim Community [IO], London, United Kingdom
Ahrens-Fox Fire Buffs Club - Defunct.
AI Foundation [★13033]
AI Foundation [★IO]
AIB Intl. [★445]
AIC Foundation [★6666]
AIC Intl. Christian Ministries - Address unknown since 1995.

Aicardi Syndrome Newsl. [14437], c/o Denise Park Parsons, 1510 Polo Fields Ct., Louisville, KY 40245, (502)244-9152
Aicardi Syndrome Newsl. [IO], Louisville, KY, United States
Aid for Afghan Refugees - Address unknown since 2003.
Aid for AIDS [13547], c/o Britanny Nuttal, 515 Greenwich St., Ste. No. 506, New York, NY 10013, (212)337-8043
Aid for AIDS [IO], New York, NY, United States
Aid; Americans for Intl. [★11642]
Aid to Artisans [12415], 331 Wethersfield Ave., Hartford, CT 06114, (860)947-3344
Aid Assn; Army and Air Force Mutual [18957]
Aid Assn; Army Mutual [★18957]
Aid Assn; Intl. Rescue and First [★14316]
Aid for Children; French-American [19064]
Aid to the Church in Need [19563], PO Box 220384, 725 Leonard St., Brooklyn, NY 11222, (800)628-6333
Aid to the Church in Need [IO], Konigstein, Germany
Aid Comm; Irish Northern [17934]
AID - Defunct.
Aid to Divorced and Separated Men [★18039]
Aid; Farm [16953]
Aid to Incarcerated Mothers [11851], 434 Massachusetts Ave., Boston, MA 02118, (617)536-0058
AID Intl. - Address unknown since 2000.
Aid for Intl. Medicine [14972], PO Box 119, Rockland, DE 19732, (302)655-8290
Aid for Intl. Medicine [IO], Rockland, DE, United States
Aid Refugee Chinese Intellectuals - Defunct.
Aid; Restoring Hope through Educational and Medical [★12881]
Aid for Romania; Christian [★18570]
Aid Societies; Natl. Org. of Travelers [★13191]
Aid Soc; Air Force [18956]
Aid Soc; Hebrew Sheltering and Immigrant [★12471]
Aid Soc; Mutual Benefit and [★19146]
Aid Soc. of U.S.A; Russian Orthodox Catholic Mutual [19341]
Aide et Action - France [IO], Paris, France
Aide aux Aines [★IO]
Aiding Leukemia Stricken Amer. Children [★13946]
Aiding Mothers and Fathers Experiencing Neonatal Death [11907], c/o Martha Eise, 1559 Ville Rosa, Hazelwood, MO 63042, (314)291-0892
AIDIS-USA Sect. [7589], PO Box 7737, McLean, VA 22106-7737, (703)734-0367
AIDIS-USA Sect. [IO], McLean, VA, United States
AIDS
    ACT UP [16961]
    Adventist Development and Relief Agency Intl. [12826]
    AFAPAC Found. [IO]
    African Community Involvement Assn. [IO]
    African Coun. of AIDS Ser. Organizations [IO]
    African Regional Youth Initiative [IO]
    Africans in Partnership Against AIDS [IO]
    Aggressive Aids Prevention [13546]
    Aid for AIDS [13547]
    Aid for AIDS [IO]
    AIDS Action [11323]
    AIDS Action Coun. [18278]
    AIDS Action Europe [IO]
    AIDS Alliance for Children, Youth and Families [13548]
    AIDS Calgary [IO]
    AIDS Clinical Trials Group [IO]
    AIDS Clinical Trials Gp. [13549]
    AIDS Empowerment and Treatment Intl. [13550]
    AIDS Empowerment and Treatment Intl. [IO]
    AIDS Evaluation [IO]
    AIDS, Medicine and Miracles [13551]
    AIDS Res. Alliance [13552]
    AIDS Rsrc. Found. for Children [13553]
    AIDS Soc. for Asia and the Pacific [IO]
    AIDS Treatment Activists Coalition [11324]
    AIDS Trust of Australia [IO]
    AIDSinfo [13554]
    Alliance for Microbicide Development [13555]

A star before a book entry number signifies that the name is not listed separately, but is mentioned within the entry.

Alliance for South Asian AIDS Prevention [IO]
Amer. Acad. of HIV Medicine [13556]
Amer. Found. for AIDS Res. [13557]
Amer. Found. for AIDS Res. [IO]
American Institute for Teen AIDS Prevention [13558]
Amer. Social Hea. Assn. [16410]
Artists Against AIDS Worldwide [11325]
Artists Against AIDS Worldwide [IO]
Artists for a New South Africa [11911]
Asia-Pacific Network of People Living with HIV/AIDS [IO]
Assn. Francois-Xavier Bagnoud [IO]
Assn. of Nurses in AIDS Care [13559]
Assn. of Nutrition Services Agencies [14720]
Assn. of Reproductive Hea. Professionals [12177]
Athletics and Entertainers for Kids [13560]
Australasian Soc. for HIV Medicine [IO]
Australian Fed. Of AIDS Organisations [IO]
AVERT [IO]
Awareness Gp. on AIDS Prevention [IO]
Balm in Gilead [IO]
Balm in Gilead [13561]
Black Coalition for AIDS Prevention [IO]
Body Positive Tayside [IO]
Brazilian Interdisciplinary AIDS Assn. [IO]
Bread and Roses [12113]
Brighton Body Positive [IO]
British HIV Assn. [IO]
Broadway Cares/Equity Fights AIDS [11326]
Cable Positive [11327]
Canadian AIDS Soc. [IO]
Canadian AIDS Treatment Info. Exchange [IO]
Canadian Found. for AIDS Res. [IO]
Canadian HIV/AIDS Legal Network [IO]
CAVDA-Citizens AIDS Proj. [13562]
CDC Natl. Prevention Info. Network [13563]
Children with AIDS Proj. of Am. [11238]
Children of the Dawn [IO]
Children's AIDS Fund [IO]
Children's AIDS Fund [16962]
Children's Blood Found. [14786]
Children's HIV Assn. of UK and Ireland [IO]
China AIDS Network [IO]
CHOICE [12178]
Citizens Alliance for VD Awareness [16411]
Community Youth HIV/AIDS Intervention Network [IO]
Consortium on AIDS and Intl. Development [IO]
Corporacion Chilena de Prevencion del SIDA [IO]
Damien Ministries [19866]
Dana-Farber Cancer Inst. [13820]
Debts AIDS Trade Africa [16928]
Design Indus. Found. Fighting AIDS [11328]
Do It Now Found. [13235]
Elton John AIDS Found. [16963]
EngenderHealth [12180]
Entertainment Indus. Found. [12114]
European AIDS Clinical Soc. [IO]
European AIDS Treatment Gp. [IO]
Family Hea. Intl. [12181]
Fenway Community Hea. [14430]
Freedom Found. [IO]
Gay and Lesbian Medical Assn. [14431]
Gay Men's Hea. Crisis [13564]
Global AIDS Alliance [13565]
Global Bus. Coalition on HIV/AIDS [11329]
Global Bus. Coalition on HIV/AIDS [IO]
Global Strategies for HIV Prevention [IO]
Global Strategies for HIV Prevention [13566]
God's Love We Deliver [12283]
Good Bears of the World [13041]
Grassroot Soccer [11330]
Haitian Coalition on AIDS [13567]
Hea. Educ. Rsrc. Org. [13568]
Hea. Global Access Proj. [11331]
Hea. Promotion Inst. [14565]
Healthy Teen Network [12182]
Herpes Rsrc. Center - Amer. Social Hea. Assn. [16412]
Hetrick-Martin Inst. [12234]
HIV/AIDS Assn. of Zambia [IO]
HIV/AIDS Prevention Grants Prog. [16964]
HIV Medicine Assn. [13569]
HivNorway [IO]

Hong Kong Coalition of AIDS Ser. Organizations [IO]
Hope for African Children Initiative [IO]
Human Rights Campaign [17653]
Immigration Equality [12237]
Infoshare Intl. [16965]
Infoshare Intl. [IO]
Inst. of HeartMath [10174]
Interagency Coalition on AIDS and Development [IO]
Intl. AIDS Soc. - USA [IO]
Intl. AIDS Soc. - USA [13570]
Intl. AIDS Vaccine Initiative [13571]
Intl. AIDS Vaccine Initiative [IO]
Intl. Gay and Lesbian Human Rights Commn. [12239]
Intl. Partnership for Microbicides [13572]
Intl. Partnership for Microbicides [IO]
Intl. Planned Parenthood Fed., Western Hemisphere Region [12184]
Intl. Treatment Preparedness Coalition [13573]
Intl. Treatment Preparedness Coalition [IO]
Intl. Union Against Sexually Transmitted Infections, Regional Off. for North Am. [16414]
Ittleson Found. [13122]
Jewish Guild for the Blind [16862]
Kenya AIDS Intervention/Prevention Proj. Gp. [IO]
Lambda Legal Defense and Educ. Fund [12241]
Magnus Hirschfeld Center for Human Rights [17773]
Malaysian AIDS Coun. [IO]
Maternal Life Intl. [16341]
Medical Found. for AIDS and Sexual Hea. [IO]
Minsaki Katende Found. [IO]
Mobilization Against AIDS [16966]
Mothers' Voices [13574]
Names Proj. Found. - AIDS Memorial Quilt [13575]
Natl. Abandoned Infants Assistance Rsrc. Center [12412]
Natl. Abortion Fed. [11223]
Natl. AIDS Comm. - Mexico [IO]
Natl. AIDS Control Org. [IO]
Natl. AIDS Fund [13576]
Natl. AIDS Housing Coalition [12319]
Natl. AIDS Treatment Advocacy Proj. [13577]
Natl. AIDS Treatment Advocacy Proj. [IO]
Natl. AIDS Trust [IO]
Natl. Alliance of State and Territorial AIDS Directors [16967]
Natl. Assn. on HIV Over Fifty [14952]
Natl. Assn. of People Living with HIV/AIDS [IO]
Natl. Assn. of People With AIDS [13578]
Natl. Assn. of State Alcohol and Drug Abuse Directors [13264]
Natl. Catholic AIDS Network [13579]
Natl. Episcopal AIDS Coalition [11332]
Natl. Family Planning and Reproductive Hea. Assn. [12185]
Natl. Gay and Lesbian Task Force [12249]
Natl. Minority AIDS Coun. [13580]
Natl. Native Amer. AIDS Prevention Center [16968]
Natl. Network for Youth [12935]
Natl. Pediatric and Family HIV Rsrc. Center [13581]
Native Amer. Community Bd. [12630]
North Yorkshire AIDS Action [IO]
Oasis [IO]
PACT [12439]
Pathfinder Intl. [12186]
Pediatric AIDS Found. [13582]
People Living with HIV/AIDS (SA) [IO]
Philippine Natl. AIDS Coun. [IO]
Planned Parenthood Fed. of Am. [12187]
Positively Women [IO]
Proj. Inform [13583]
Remedios AIDS Found. [IO]
River Fund [11333]
San Francisco AIDS Found. [13584]
Seva Found. [12443]
Seventh Day Adventist Kinship Intl. [20066]
Shanti [11831]
Soc. for Women and AIDS in Africa [IO]
Solidarity and Action Against the HIV Infection in India [IO]

Solidarity and Action Against the HIV Infection in India [16969]
Southern Africa HIV and AIDS Info. Dissemination Ser. [IO]
Southern African Network of AIDS Ser. Organizations [IO]
Student Global AIDS Campaign [13585]
Transatlantic Partners Against AIDS [13586]
Transatlantic Partners Against AIDS [IO]
Treatment Action Gp. [13587]
UK Coalition of People Living with HIV and AIDS [IO]
UNAIDS - Joint United Nations Programme on HIV/AIDS [IO]
Ursuline Companions in Mission [20408]
William Wendt Center for Loss and Healing [13317]
Women Alive Coalition [13588]
Women Organized to Respond to Life-Threatening Diseases [13589]
Women Organized to Respond to Life-Threatening Diseases [IO]
World Tech. Volunteers [13196]
Zimbabwe AIDS Network [IO]
AIDS Action [11323], 1730 M St. NW, Ste. 611, Washington, DC 20036, (202)530-8030
AIDS Action Coun. [18278], 1730 M St. NW, Ste. 611, Washington, DC 20036, (202)530-8030
AIDS Action Europe [IO], Amsterdam, Netherlands
AIDS Action Foundation [★18278]
AIDS Alliance for Children, Youth and Families [13548], 1600 K St. NW, Ste. 200, Washington, DC 20006, (202)785-3564
AIDS Calgary [IO], Calgary, AB, Canada
AIDS Care; Canadian Assn. of Nurses in [IO]
AIDS Care and Educ. Training [★IO]
AIDS CH; Natl. [★13563]
AIDS Clinical Trials Gp. [13549], c/o Dr. Yvette Delph, MD, Operations Center Dir., 8757 Georgia Ave., Ste. 1200, Silver Spring, MD 20910, (301)628-3338
AIDS Clinical Trials Group [IO], Silver Spring, MD, United States
AIDS Coalition to Unleash Power [★16961]
AIDS; Design Indus. Found. for [★11328]
AIDS Educ. and Res. Trust [★IO]
AIDS Empowerment and Treatment Intl. [IO], Washington, DC, United States
AIDS Empowerment and Treatment Intl. [13550], PO Box 27143, Washington, DC 20038-7143, (202)518-0402
AIDS Evaluation [IO], Bern, Switzerland
AIDS/HIV Policy; Americans for a Sound [★16962]
AIDS Hotline; Natl. Indian [★16968]
AIDS Info. CH; Natl. [★13563]
AIDS Intl. [★2475]
AIDS/Kaposi's Sarcoma Res. and Educ. Found. [★13584]
AIDS Law Project [★17118]
AIDS Leadership; Project Hea., Educ., and [★13580]
AIDS Medical Found. [★13557]
AIDS Medical Found. [★IO]
AIDS, Medicine and Miracles [13551], 3288 21st St., No. 201, San Francisco, CA 94110-2423, (415)252-7111
AIDS Memorial Quilt; Names Proj. Found. - [13575]
AIDS; Mobilization Against [★16966]
AIDS Natl. Interfaith Network - Defunct.
AIDS; Natl. Mobilization Against [★16966]
AIDS Policy; Americans for a Sound [★16962]
AIDS Prevention Grants Prog; HIV/ [16964]
AIDS Prevention League - Address unknown since 2003.
AIDS Prog; HIV/ [★16964]
AIDS Res. Alliance [13552], 621-A N San Vicente Blvd., West Hollywood, CA 90069, (310)358-2423
AIDS Res. Found; Natl. [★13557]
AIDS Rsrc. Found. for Children [13553], 77 Acad. St., Newark, NJ 07102, (973)643-0400
AIDS Ser. Prog. for the Elderly [★12256]
AIDS Soc. for Asia and the Pacific [IO], Randwick, Australia
AIDS Task Force for the Amer. Coll. Health Assn. - Defunct.

Reference to "IO" in place of a book number signifies that the association may be found in the 45th edition of International Organizations.

AIDS Treatment Activists Coalition [11324], 611
Broadway, No. 613, New York, NY 10112,
(617)267-0998
AIDS Treatment Info. Ser; HIV/ [★13554]
AIDS Trust of Australia [IO], Darlinghurst, Australia
AIDSinfo [13554], PO Box 6303, Rockville, MD
20849-6303, (301)519-0459
AIESEC Alumni Intl. [IO], Beringen, Belgium
AIESEC - Canada [IO], Toronto, ON, Canada
AIESEC China [IO], Beijing, People's Republic of
China
AIESEC Ireland [IO], Dublin, Ireland
AIESEC Kenya [IO], Nairobi, Kenya
AIESEC - U.S. [IO], New York, NY, United States
AIESEC - U.S. [8012], 127 W 26th St., 10th Fl.,
New York, NY 10001, (212)757-3774
AIIM - The Enterprise Content Mgt. Assn. [2095],
1100 Wayne Ave., Ste. 1100, Silver Spring, MD
20910, (301)587-8202
Aiki-Kai Australia Natl. Aikido Assn. [IO], Melbourne,
Australia
Aikido
Aiki-Kai Australia Natl. Aikido Assn. [IO]
Aikido Aikikai Fed. of Russia [IO]
Aikido Assn. of Am. [23046]
Aikido Assn. of North Am. [23047]
Aikido Assn. of North Am. [IO]
Aikido Assn. of Thailand [IO]
Aikido Fed. of Serbia and Montenegro - Aikikai
SCG [IO]
Aikido Fed. of South Africa [IO]
Aikido Yoshokai Assn. of North Am. [IO]
Aikido Yoshokai Assn. of North Am. [7943]
Aikikai Deutschland - Fachverband fur Aikido in
Deutschland [IO]
Aikikai Malaysia [IO]
Aikikai Singapore [IO]
All-Japan Aikido Fed. [IO]
Asociacion Argentina de Aikido [IO]
Asociacion Paraguaya de Aikido [IO]
Assn. Culturelle Suisse d'Aikido, Aikikai Suisse
[IO]
Assn. Sportive de Monaco - Aikido [IO]
Associazione di Cultura Tradizionale Giapponese
- Aikikai d'Italia [IO]
Belgian Aikikai [IO]
Bulgarian Aikido Fed. [IO]
Czech Aikido Assn. - Aikikai of Czech Republic
[IO]
Federacao Paulista de Aikido [IO]
Federacao Portuguesa de Aikido [IO]
Federacion Deportiva Chilena de Aikido - Aikikai
Chile [IO]
Federacion Mexicana de Aikido [IO]
Federacion Uruguaya de Aikido - Aikikai Uruguay
[IO]
Fed. Francaise d'Aikido, d'Aikibudo et Affinitaires
[IO]
Fed. Luxembourgeoise des Arts Martiaux-Aikido
[IO]
Fed. Royale Marocaine de Judo Aikido et AMA
[IO]
Finland Aikikai [IO]
Hong Kong Aikido Assn. [IO]
Intl. Aikido Assn. [IO]
Intl. Aikido Assn. [23048]
Irish Aikido Fed. [IO]
Japan Aikido Assn. U.S.A. [23595]
Lebanese Aikido Fed. [IO]
Nederlandse Culturele Aikikai Federatie [IO]
New Zealand Aikido Fed. [IO]
Norwegian Aikido Fed. [IO]
Pilipinas Aikido Propagation Assn. [IO]
Polska Federacja Aikido [IO]
Republic of China Aikido Assn. [IO]
Scottish Aikido Fed. [IO]
Slovak Aikido Assn. - Aikikai Slovakia [IO]
Svenska Budoforbundet Aikidosektionen [IO]
U.S. Aikido Fed. [23049]
U.S. Martial Arts Assn. [23607]
World Martial Arts Assn. [23616]
Yayasan Indonesia Aikikai [IO]
Aikido Aikikai Fed. of Russia [IO], Moscow, Russia
Aikido Assn. of Am. [23046], 1016 W Belmont Ave.,
Chicago, IL 60657, (773)525-3141

Aikido Assn; British [IO]
Aikido Assn. of North Am. [IO], Philadelphia, PA,
United States
Aikido Assn. of North Am. [23047], 5836-38 Henry
Ave., Philadelphia, PA 19128, (215)483-3000
Aikido Assn. of Thailand [IO], Bangkok, Thailand
Aikido Assn. U.S.A; Japan [23595]
Aikido Federacija Srbije i Crne Gore - Aikikai SCG
[★IO]
Aikido Fed. of Serbia and Montenegro - Aikikai SCG
[IO], Belgrade, Serbia
Aikido Fed. of South Africa [IO], Heidelberg,
Republic of South Africa
Aikido Yoshokai Assn. of North Am. [IO], Ann Arbor,
MI, United States
Aikido Yoshokai Assn. of North Am. [7943], Genyo-
kan Dojo, 749 Airport Blvd., Ste. 4, Ann Arbor, MI
48108, (734)662-4686
Aikikai Argentina [★IO]
Aikikai Deutschland - Fachverband fur Aikido in
Deutschland [IO], Viechtach, Germany
Aikikai Found. [★23049]
Aikikai Malaysia [IO], Kuching, Malaysia
Aikikai Singapore [IO], Singapore, Singapore
AIM [335], 125 Warrendale-Bayne Rd., Ste. 100,
Warrendale, PA 15086, (724)934-4470
AIM - European Brands Assn. [IO], Brussels,
Belgium
AIM Intl. [★IO]
AIM Intl. [★20294]
AIM Intl. - Australia [IO], Belmont, Australia
AIM U.S.A. [★335]
AIME; Iron and Steel Division of the Metallurgical
Soc. of [★7312]
AIME; Petroleum Br. of [★7464]
AINA [IO], Paris, France
AIPPI Gp. of Lithuania [IO], Vilnius, Lithuania
Air - Aviation Info. Resources [★131]
Air Balance Consultants - Defunct.
Air Balance Coun; Assoc. [598]
Air Barrier Assn. of Am. [587], 1600 Boston-
Providence Hwy., Walpole, MA 02081, (866)956-
5888
Air Brake Assn. [3274], c/o Joe Faust, Sec.-Treas.,
2098 E 10140 S, Sandy, UT 84092, (801)944-5270
Air-Britain Historians [IO], Suffolk, United Kingdom
Air Cadet Exchange; International [★5538]
Air Cadet League of Canada [IO], Ottawa, ON,
Canada
Air Care Alliance - Defunct.
Air Cargo Assn; The Intl. [3873]
Air Carrier Assn; Natl. [159]
Air Charity Network [14312], 4300 Westgrove Dr.,
Addison, TX 75001, (214)234-8458
Air Club; Travel [21482]
Air Commando Assn. [21277], PO Box 7, Mary Es-
ther, FL 32569, (850)581-0099
AIR Commercial Real Estate Assn. [3295], 800 W
6th St., Ste. 800, Los Angeles, CA 90017-2741,
(213)687-8777
Air Companies; Inst. of Clean [3071]
Air Compressor Res. Coun. - Defunct.
Air Conditioner Mfrs'. Assn. [★IO]
Air Conditioning Assn; Manufacturers Members of
the Natl. Warm Air Heating and [★1873]
Air Conditioning Assn; Natl. Warm Air Heating and
[★1872]
Air Conditioning Contractors of Am. [1872], 2800
Shirlington Rd., Ste. 300, Arlington, VA 22206,
(703)575-4477
Air Conditioning Contractors Natl. Assn; Heating and
Piping and [★1033]
Air Conditioning Contractors' Natl. Assn; Sheet Metal
and [1900]
Air-Conditioning Engineers; Amer. Soc. Heating and
[★6995]
Air-Conditioning Engineers; Amer. Soc. of Heating,
Refrigerating and [6995]
Air Conditioning Equip. Manufacturers' Assn. [IO],
Madrid, Spain
Air Conditioning and Mech. Contractors Assn. -
Australian Capital Territory [IO], Rosebery,
Australia
Air Conditioning and Mech. Contractors Assn. - New
South Wales [IO], Rosebery, Australia

Air Conditioning and Mech. Contractors Assn. -
Queensland [IO], Ashgrove, Australia
Air Conditioning and Mech. Contractors Assn. -
South Australia [IO], Mile End, Australia
Air Conditioning and Mech. Contractors Assn. -
Western Australia [IO], Victoria Park, Australia
Air Conditioning and Refrigeration Contractors of
Am. [★1872]
Air Conditioning and Refrigeration European Assn.
[IO], Uithoorn, Netherlands
Air-Conditioning and Refrigeration Inst. [1873], 4100
N Fairfax Dr., Ste. 200, Arlington, VA 22203,
(703)524-8800
Air-Conditioning and Refrigeration Machinery Assn.
[★1873]
Air-Conditioning and Refrigeration Mfrs'. Assn. [IO],
Istanbul, Turkey
Air-Conditioning and Refrigeration Wholesalers Intl.
[★IO]
Air-Conditioning and Refrigeration Wholesalers Intl.
[★1882]
Air Conditioning Soc; Mobile [★1893]
AIR Conf. [★136]
Air Cooled Heat Exchanger Mfrs. Assn. - Defunct.
Air Courier Assn. [3857], PO Box 2036, Cherry Hill,
NJ 08034, (877)303-4258
Air Courier Conf. of Am. [★3565]
Air Diffusion Coun. [1874], 1901 N Roselle Rd., Ste.
800, Schaumburg, IL 60195, (847)706-6750
Air Distribution Inst. [1875], 4415 W Harrison St.,
Ste. 322, Hillside, IL 60162, (708)449-2933
Air Div. Assn; Second [21403]
Air Duct Cleaners Assn; Natl. [2470]
Air and Expedited Motor Carriers Conf. - Address
unknown since 2001.
Air Filter Inst. [★1873]
Air Filtration Assn; Natl. [1894]
Air Force
17th Bomb Gp. Reunion Assn. [20652]
43rd Bomb Gp. Assn. [20653]
80th Fighter Squadron Headhunters' Assn. [5442]
187th Airborne Regimental Combat Team Assn.
[20697]
369th Fighter Squadron Assn., 359th Fighter Gp.
[20654]
381st Bomb Gp. Memorial Assn. [20655]
401st Bombardment Gp. (Heavy) Assn. [20656]
401st Bombardment Group (Heavy) Association
[IO]
461st Bombardment Gp. Assn. [20657]
494th Bombardment Gp. (H) Assn. 7th Air Force
[20658]
508th Parachute Infantry Regiment Assn. [21379]
511th Aircraft Control and Warning Gp. [5443]
AdoptaPlatoon [11489]
Air Force Assn. of Canada [IO]
Air Force Historical Found. [10470]
Air Force Navigators Observer Assn. [20659]
Air Force Public Affairs Alumni Assn. [6200]
Air Force Sergeants Assn. [6063]
Air Forces Escape and Evasion Soc. [20660]
Airman Memorial Assn. [20661]
Amer. Fighter Aces Assn. [20647]
Any Soldier [11490]
Arnold Air Soc. [24546]
Assn. of Air Force Missileers [20662]
Assn. of Military Surgeons of the U.S. [15263]
B-26 Marauder Historical Soc. [21389]
Beirut Veterans of Am. [21287]
Books For Soldiers [11491]
Combat Helicopter Pilots Assn. [20648]
Distinguished Flying Cross Soc. [20711]
Escort Carrier Sailors and Airmen Assn. [21185]
Hof Reunion Assn. [20682]
Intl. Military Community Executives Assn. [834]
Mosquito Assn. [20663]
Natl. Counter Intelligence Corps Assn. [21164]
Oper. AC [11492]
Oper. Homelink [11494]
Oper. Sandbox [11495]
Oper. ShoeBox [11496]
Oper. Soldier Support [11497]
Oper.: Take a Soldier to the Movies [11498]
Oper. We Do Care [11499]
Order of Daedalians [20650]

A star before a book entry number signifies that the name is not listed separately, but is mentioned within the entry.

P-51 Mustang Pilots Assn. [21398]
Reserve Officers Assn. of the U.S. [6103]
Royal Air Force Benevolent Fund [IO]
Royal Air Forces Assn. [IO]
Salute Our Services [11500]
Second Bombardment Assn. [20664]
Silver Wings [24549]
Soc. of Air Force Physician Assistants [20665]
Soc. of Air Force Physicians [15264]
Soc. of Medical Consultants to the Armed Forces [15265]
Soc. of Military Otolaryngologists - Head and Neck Surgeons [15267]
Support Our Soldiers Am. [11502]
Tragedy Assistance Prog. for Survivors [11503]
USAF Medical Ser. Corps Assn. [13590]
Vietnam Security Police Assn. [21340]
Air Force Acad; Assn. of Graduates of the U.S. [18875]
Air Force Aid Soc. [18956], 241 18th St. S, Ste. 202, Arlington, VA 22202, (703)607-3034
Air Force Anesthesiologists; Soc. of [★13683]
Air Force Assn. [6062], 1501 Lee Hwy., Arlington, VA 22209-1198, (703)247-5800
Air Force Assn. of Canada [IO], Ottawa, ON, Canada
Air Force Assn; Flying Tigers of the 14th [21393]
Air Force Clinical Surgeons; Soc. of [16587]
Air Force; Commemorative [21438]
Air Force; Confederate [★21438]
Air Force Flight Surgeons; Soc. of U.S. [13543]
Air Force Historical Found. [10470], 1535 Command Dr., Ste. A-122, Andrews AFB, MD 20762-7002, (301)736-1959
Air Force Historical Soc; Eighth [21392]
Air Force Missileers; Assn. of [20662]
Air Force Mutual Aid Assn; Army and [18957]
Air Force Navigators Observer Assn. [20659], c/o Clem Smith, Treas., 1095 Harriet, Canyon Lake, TX 78133-5244
Air Force Physicians; Soc. of [15264]
Air Force Public Affairs Alumni Assn. [6200], PO Box 447, Locust Grove, VA 22508-0447
Air Force Sergeants Assn. [6063], 5211 Auth Rd., Suitland, MD 20746, (301)899-3500
Air Forces Escape and Evasion Soc. [20660], c/o Larry Grauerholz, Ed., 19 Oak Ridge Pond, Hannibal, MO 63401-6539, (940)692-6700
Air Found. - Defunct.
Air Freight Assn. of Am. [★145]
Air Freight Forwarders Assn. of Am. [★145]
Air and Gas Inst; Compressed [2010]
Air Heating and Air Conditioning Assn; Manufacturers Members of the Natl. Warm [★1873]
Air Horn and Steam Whistle Enthusiasts [★22037]
Air, Inc. - Aviation Info. Resources [131], 1777 Phoenix Pkwy., Bldg. 100, Ste. 105, Atlanta, GA 30349, (404)592-6500
Air Label Collectors Club; Aeronautica and [21422]
Air League [IO], London, United Kingdom
Air Line Dispatchers Assn. - Defunct.
Air Line Employees Assn., Intl. - Address unknown since 2008.
Air Line Pilots Assn. [★24005]
Air Line Pilots Assn. [★IO]
Air Line Pilots Assn., Intl. [IO], Washington, DC, United States
Air Line Pilots Assn., Intl. [24005], 1625 Massachusetts Ave. NW, Washington, DC 20036, (703)689-2270
Air Line Pilots Assn. Intl. - Canada [IO], Ottawa, ON, Canada
Air Mail Pioneers [21425], c/o Ms. Nancy Allison Wright, Pres., PMB 504 C5, 26910 92nd Ave. NW, Stanwood, WA 98292-5437, (360)387-2009
Air Mail Soc; Amer. [22780]
Air Medical Commun. Specialists; Natl. Assn. of [13542]
Air Medical Physician Assn. [15983], c/o Pat Petersen, Exec. Dir., 951 E Montana Vista Ln., Salt Lake City, UT 84124, (801)263-2672
Air Medical Services; Amer. Soc. of Hospital-Based Emergency [★14314]
Air Movement and Control Assn. [★1876]
Air Movement and Control Assn. [★IO]

Air Movement Control Assn; Home Ventilating Inst. Division of the [★1883]
Air Movement and Control Assn. Intl. [1876], 30 W Univ. Dr., Arlington Heights, IL 60004-1806, (847)394-0150
Air Movement and Control Assn. Intl. [IO], Arlington Heights, IL, United States
Air Movement Inst. - Address unknown since 1988.
Air Moving and Conditioning Assn. [★1876]
Air Moving and Conditioning Assn. [★IO]
Air Natl. Guard Optometric Soc. - Address unknown since 1999.
Air Patrol; Civil [5538]
Air Policy; Center for Clean [5083]
Air Pollution Control Assn. [★5081]
Air Pollution Control Assn. [★IO]
Air Pollution Prog. Administrators and Assn. of Local Air Pollution Control Officials; State and Territorial [★5696]
Air Post Soc; Metropolitan [22845]
Air Quality Assn; Indoor [5093]
Air Quality Coun; Amer. Indoor [5082]
Air Racing Assn; U.S. [★23041]
Air-Racing Gp; Natl. [23041]
Air Reserve Assn. [★6062]
Air Safety Investigators; Soc. of [★12966]
Air Sailing Club [IO], Guelph, ON, Canada
Air, Sea, and Space Club [25023]
Air Serv Intl. [12827], 410 Rosedale Ct., Ste. 190, Warrenton, VA 20186, (540)428-2323
Air Serv Intl. [IO], Warrenton, VA, United States
Air Soc; Arnold [24546]
Air Stations Employee Organizations; Natl. Coun. of Naval [★6088]
Air Stations; Natl. Coun. of Indus. Naval [6088]
Air and Stream Improvement; Natl. Coun. for [4690]
Air Supply Fan Club [24837], c/o Julie Wolfe, PO Box 3367, Beverly Hills, CA 90212-0367, (310)535-6949
Air and Surface Transport Nurses Assn. [15427], 7995 E Prentice Ave., Ste. 100, Greenwood Village, CO 80111, (720)488-0492
Air Taxi and Commercial Pilots Assn. - Defunct.
Air Tour Assn; U.S. [3830]
Air Traffic Conf. of America - Defunct.
Air Traffic Control Assn. [132], 1101 King St., Ste. 300, Alexandria, VA 22314, (703)299-2430
Air Traffic Control Association [IO], Alexandria, VA, United States
Air Traffic Controllers Assn; Natl. [24013]
Air Traffic Specialists; Natl. Assn. of [24014]
Air Transport Action Gp. [IO], Geneva, Switzerland
Air Transport Assn. of Am. [133], 1301 Pennsylvania Ave. NW, Ste. 1100, Washington, DC 20004-7017, (202)626-4000
Air Transport Assn. of Canada [IO], Ottawa, ON, Canada
Air Transport Coordinating Comm; Natl. [★140]
Air Trans. Assn; Natl. [160]
Air Trans. Conferences; Natl. [★160]
Air and Waste Mgt. Assn. [5081], 1 Gateway Ctr., 3rd Fl., 420 Ft. Duquesne Blvd., Pittsburgh, PA 15222-1435, (412)232-3444
Air and Waste Mgt. Assn. [IO], Pittsburgh, PA, United States
Air Weather Assn. [21278], 1697 Capri Way, Charlottesville, VA 22911-3534, (434)296-2832
Air Weather Reconnaissance Assn. [21279], c/o Joseph Tabaco, Membership Chm., 59 3rd St., Ronkonkoma, NY 11779-5366, (800)697-5072
Airborne Assn. - Address unknown since 1995.
Airborne Assn; Amer. [20699]
Airborne Div. Assn; 11th [20684]
Airborne Div. Assn; 13th [20685]
Airborne Div. Assn; 17th [21363]
Airborne Div. Assn; 82nd [21273]
Airborne Div. Assn; 101st [20694]
Airborne Law Enforcement Assn. [5958], 411 Aviation Way, Ste. 200, Frederick, MD 21701, (301)631-2406
Airborne Regimental Combat Team Assn; 187th [20697]
Airconditioning Wholesalers Assn; Northamerican Heating, Refrigeration, and [★1882]

Aircraft
187th Airborne Regimental Combat Team Assn. [20697]

508th Parachute Infantry Regiment Assn. [21379]
Acad. of Model Aeronautics [21421]
Aeronaut Soc. [23097]
Aeronautica and Air Label Collectors Club [21422]
Aeronca Lovers Club [21423]
Aerospace Indus. Assn. of Am. [130]
Aerostar Owners Assn. [21424]
Air Charity Network [14312]
Air Courier Assn. [3857]
Air Line Pilots Assn., Intl. [24005]
Air Mail Pioneers [21425]
Air and Surface Transport Nurses Assn. [15427]
Air Traffic Control Assn. [132]
Airborne Law Enforcement Assn. [5958]
Aircraft Carrier Indus. Base Coalition [1148]
Aircraft Engine Historical Soc. [9364]
Aircraft Fleet Recycling Assn. [12800]
Aircraft Mechanics Fraternal Assn. [24006]
Aircraft Owners and Pilots Assn. [135]
Aircraft Recovery Assn. [12945]
Airlift/Tanker Assn. [20646]
Airlines Medical Directors Assn. [13539]
Airport Minority Advisory Coun. [2758]
Amer. Air Mail Soc. [22780]
Amer. Assn. of Airport Executives [138]
Amer. Aviation Historical Soc. [21426]
Amer. Bonanza Soc. [21427]
Amer. Fighter Aces Assn. [20647]
Amer. Helicopter Soc. [139]
Amer. Independent Cockpit Alliance [24008]
Amer. Navion Soc. [21428]
Amer. Pilots' Assn. [2571]
Amer. Yankee Assn. [21429]
Angel Flight West [12512]
Antique Airplane Assn. [21430]
Assn. of Air Medical Services [14314]
Assn. of Flight Attendants - CWA [24009]
Aviation Development Coun. [140]
Aviation Maintenance Found. Intl. [143]
Aviation Safety Inst. [12953]
Balloon Fed. of Am. [23098]
Bellanca-Champion Club [21431]
Bird Airplane Club [21432]
C.A.L./N-X-211 Collectors Soc. [11106]
Cardinal Club [21433]
Cessna Owner Org. [21435]
Cessna Pilots Assn. [21436]
Cherokee Pilots' Assn. [21437]
Citizens Aviation Watch Assn. [11509]
Civil Aviation Medical Assn. [13540]
Combat Helicopter Pilots Assn. [20648]
Continental Luscombe Assn. [21439]
Corben Club [21440]
Corporate Angel Network [13817]
Daedalian Found. [20649]
EAA Vintage Aircraft Assn. [21442]
EAA Warbirds of Am. [21443]
Ercoupe Owners Club [21444]
Experimental Aircraft Assn. [6373]
Express Delivery and Logistics Assn. [3565]
F-4 Phantom II Soc. [21445]
Fairchild Club [21446]
Fellowship of Christian Airline Personnel [20007]
First Flight Soc. [21447]
Flight Safety Found. [148]
Flying Apache Assn. [21448]
Flying Chiropractors Assn. [14002]
Flying Dentists Assn. [14153]
Flying Funeral Directors of America [2779]
Flying Physicians Assn. [13731]
Funk Aircraft Owners Assn. [21449]
Giant Scale Warbirds Assn. [22644]
Global MissionAir [20487]
Helicopter Club of America [21450]
Helicopter Found. Intl. [151]
High Frontier [6374]
Highamerica Balloon Club [23099]
Independent Pilots Assn. [24000]
Intl. Aerobatic Club [23040]
Intl. Airline Passengers Assn. [23015]
Intl. Assn. of Machinists [24011]
Intl. Assn. of Natural Rsrc. Pilots [4187]
Intl. B and B Fly-Inn Club [21451]
Intl. Bird Dog Assn. [21452]
Intl. Cessna 120/140 Assn. [21453]

Reference to "IO" in place of a book number signifies that the association may be found in the 45th edition of International Organizations.

The Intl. Cessna 170 Assn. [21454]
Intl. Comm. for the Rescue of KAL 007 Survivors [18541]
Intl. Coun. of Air Shows [21455]
Intl. Experimental Aerospace Soc. [6375]
Intl. Flying Farmers [4646]
Intl. Miniature Aircraft Assn. [22938]
Intl. Org. of Masters, Mates and Pilots, ILA, AFL-CIO [24128]
Intl. Pietenpol Assn. [21456]
Intl. Scale Soaring Assn. [22648]
Intl. Soc. of Air Safety Investigators [12966]
Intl. Soc. of Transport Aircraft Trading [156]
Interstate Club [21458]
Jack Knight Air Mail Soc. [22834]
Latin Amer. Aeronautical Assn. [438]
Lighter-Than-Air Soc. [21460]
Luscombe Endowment [21461]
Man Will Never Fly Memorial Soc. Internationale [22598]
MAPS Air Museum - Military Aviation Preservation Soc. [9342]
Metropolitan Air Post Soc. [22845]
Missile Defense Advocacy Alliance [17382]
Monocoupe Club [21462]
Natl. 210 Owners Assn. [21463]
Natl. Aeronca Assn. [21464]
Natl. Air Disaster Alliance [11510]
Natl. Air-Racing Gp. [23041]
Natl. Air Traffic Controllers Assn. [24013]
Natl. Aircraft Appraisers Assn. [188]
Natl. Aircraft Finance Assn. [2425]
Natl. Aircraft Resale Assn. [189]
Natl. Assn. of Air Traffic Specialists [24014]
Natl. Assn. of Priest Pilots [19667]
Natl. Assn. of Rocketry [22650]
Natl. Assn. of Scale Aeromodelers [22651]
Natl. Assn. of Timetable Collectors [23008]
Natl. Aviation and Space Educ. Alliance [7994]
Natl. Catholic Conf. of Airport Chaplains [19754]
Natl. Coalition for Aviation Educ. [7995]
Natl. Intercollegiate Flying Assn. [21466]
Natl. Safe Skies Alliance [18748]
Natl. Soaring Found. [23042]
Natl. Stinson Club [21467]
Natl. World War II Glider Pilots Assn. [21468]
Negro Airmen Intl. [6380]
Order of Daedalians [20650]
OX5 Aviation Pioneers [21469]
Pilots for Christ Intl. [20028]
Piper Owner Soc. [21470]
Popular Rotorcraft Assn. [21471]
Porterfield Airplane Club [21472]
Precision Aerobatics Model Pilots Assn. [21473]
Professional Airways Systems Specialists [24015]
Professional Aviation Maintenance Assn. [165]
Professional Pilots Fed. [24016]
Rearwin Club [21474]
Red River Valley Fighter Pilots Assn. [21318]
Scale Warbird Racing Assn. [22657]
Short Wing Piper Club [21475]
Silver Wings Fraternity [21476]
Soaring Soc. of Am. [23043]
Soc. of Antique Modelers [21477]
Soc. of Experimental Test Pilots [6384]
Stampe Club Intl. [21479]
Stearman Restorers Assn. [21480]
Swift Museum Found. [21481]
Travel Air Club [21482]
Twin Bonanza Assn. [21483]
United Flying Octogenarians [21485]
U.S. Hang Gliding and Paragliding Assn. [23044]
U.S. Powered Paragliding Assn. [23643]
U.S. Ultralight Assn. [21486]
US Scale Masters Assn. [22660]
Vintage Sailplane Assn. [23045]
Western Assoc. Modelers [22661]
Whirly-Girls - Intl. Women Helicopter Pilots [21487]
World Airline Historical Soc. [21488]
World Miniature Warbird Assn. [22662]
World War I Aeroplanes [21490]
Zeppelin Collectors Club [22892]
Aircraft, and Agricultural Implement Workers of Am; Intl. Union, United Auto., [★24004]

Aircraft Assn; EAA Vintage [21442]
Aircraft Assn; Experimental [6373]
Aircraft Assn; Natl. Bus. [★162]
Aircraft Assn; U.S. Anti [★6071]
Aircraft Carrier Indus. Base Coalition [1148], 700 13th St. NW, Ste. 1000, Washington, DC 20005, (202)585-2018
Aircraft Conf; Mutual [★2131]
Aircraft Control and Warning Gp; 511th [5443]
Aircraft Elecl. Soc. [★6367]
Aircraft Electronics Assn. [134], 4217 S Hocker, Independence, MO 64055-0963, (816)373-6565
Aircraft Electronics Assn. [IO], Independence, MO, United States
Aircraft Engine Historical Soc. [9364], 1019 Old Monrovia Rd. NW, Ste. 201, Huntsville, AL 35806, (256)683-1458
Aircraft Engineering Found. - Defunct.
Aircraft Finance Assn; Natl. [2425]
Aircraft Fleet Recycling Assn. [12800], 734 15th St. NW, Ste. 620, Washington, DC 20005
Aircraft Fleet Recycling Assn. [IO], Washington, DC, United States
Aircraft Indus. Assn. of Am. [★130]
Aircraft Locknut Mfrs. Assn. [1814], c/o Robert H. Ecker, Exec. Dir., 994 Old Eagle School Rd., Ste. 1019, Wayne, PA 19087-1802, (610)971-4850
Aircraft Maintenance Engineers Assn. [★IO]
Aircraft Material and Process Engineers; Soc. of [★7285]
Aircraft Mechanics Fraternal Assn. [24006], PO Box 51955, Indianapolis, IN 46251, (317)244-4413
Aircraft Owners Assn; Corp. [★162]
Aircraft Owners Assn; Funk [21449]
Aircraft Owners and Pilots Assn. [135], 421 Aviation Way, Frederick, MD 21701, (301)695-2000
Aircraft Owners and Pilots Assn. - Australia [IO], Georges Hall, Australia
Aircraft Owners and Pilots Assn. - Austria [IO], Vienna, Austria
Aircraft Owners and Pilots Assn. - Belgium [IO], Antwerp, Belgium
Aircraft Owners and Pilots Assn. - Brazil [IO], Sao Paulo, Brazil
Aircraft Owners and Pilots Assn. - Colombia [IO], Bogota, Colombia
Aircraft Owners and Pilots Assn. - Cyprus [IO], Nicosia, Cyprus
Aircraft Owners and Pilots Assn. - Denmark [IO], Roskilde, Denmark
Aircraft Owners and Pilots Assn. - Finland [IO], Helsinki, Finland
Aircraft Owners and Pilots Assn. - Hungary [IO], Budapest, Hungary
Aircraft Owners and Pilots Assn. - Iceland [IO], Reykjavik, Iceland
Aircraft Owners and Pilots Assn. - India [IO], Bombay, India
Aircraft Owners and Pilots Assn. - Ireland [IO], Dublin, Ireland
Aircraft Owners and Pilots Assn. - Italy [IO], Milan, Italy
Aircraft Owners and Pilots Assn. - Jamaica [IO], Kingston, Jamaica
Aircraft Owners and Pilots Assn. - Japan [IO], Tokyo, Japan
Aircraft Owners and Pilots Assn. - Liberia [IO], Monrovia, Liberia
Aircraft Owners and Pilots Assn. - Lithuania [IO], Vilnius, Lithuania
Aircraft Owners and Pilots Assn. - Luxembourg [IO], Luxembourg, Luxembourg
Aircraft Owners and Pilots Assn. - Malta [IO], Luqa, Malta
Aircraft Owners and Pilots Assn. - Monaco [IO], Monte Carlo, Monaco
Aircraft Owners and Pilots Assn. - Netherlands [IO], Amsterdam, Netherlands
Aircraft Owners and Pilots Assn. - New Zealand [IO], Dunedin, New Zealand
Aircraft Owners and Pilots Assn. - Norway [IO], Lysaker, Norway
Aircraft Owners and Pilots Assn. - Pakistan [IO], Lahore, Pakistan
Aircraft Owners and Pilots Assn. - Philippines [IO], Pasay City, Philippines

Aircraft Owners and Pilots Assn. - Poland [IO], Warsaw, Poland
Aircraft Owners and Pilots Assn. - Romania [IO], Bucharest, Romania
Aircraft Owners and Pilots Assn. - Russia [IO], Moscow, Russia
Aircraft Owners and Pilots Assn. - Singapore [IO], Singapore, Singapore
Aircraft Owners and Pilots Assn. - Slovenia [IO], Ljubljana, Slovenia
Aircraft Owners and Pilots Assn. - South Africa [IO], Pretoria, Republic of South Africa
Aircraft Owners and Pilots Assn. - Spain [IO], Barcelona, Spain
Aircraft Owners and Pilots Assn. - Sweden [IO], Bromma, Sweden
Aircraft Owners and Pilots Assn. - Switzerland [IO], Opfikon, Switzerland
Aircraft Owners and Pilots Assn. - Turkey [IO], Ankara, Turkey
Aircraft Owners and Pilots Assn. of the United Kingdom [IO], London, United Kingdom
Aircraft Owners and Pilots Assn. - Venezuela [IO], Caracas, Venezuela
Aircraft Recovery Assn. [12945]
Aircraft Res. Assn. [IO], Bedford, United Kingdom
Airedale Terrier Club of Am. [22180], c/o Shirley VanOver, Sec., 1897 S Tulane Rd., Hernando, MS 38632, (662)429-3815
Airfields Env. Fed. [★IO]
Airfields Env. Trust [IO], London, United Kingdom
Airflow Club of Am. [21563], c/o John Librenjak, Pres., 3595 McKinley St., Riverside, CA 92506, (951)788-4678
Airforce Ser. Pilots WWII; Women [21413]
Airforwarders Assn. [2444], 1156 15th St. NW, Ste. 900, Washington, DC 20005, (202)393-2818
Airgun Field Target Assn; Amer. [22976]
AirLifeLine [★14312]
Airlift Assn. [★20646]
Airlift Assn. [★IO]
Airlift Ser; Amer. Veterans Medical [6342]
Airlift/Tanker Assn. [20646], 9312 Convento Terr., Fairfax, VA 22031-3809, (703)385-2802
Airlift/Tanker Association [IO], Fairfax, VA, United States
Airline Ambassadors International [IO], Moss Beach, CA, United States
Airline Ambassadors Intl. [13147], PO Box 459, Moss Beach, CA 94038, (650)728-7844
Airline Assn. of Am; Commuter [★166]
Airline Assn; Cargo [145]
Airline Assn; Commuter [★166]
Airline Assn; Regional [166]
Airline Credit Union Assn. - Defunct.
Airline Entertainment Assn; World [440]
Airline Flight Attendants Assn. - Defunct.
Airline Ground Trans. Assn. [★3858]
Airline Hobby Club; World [★21488]
Airline Indus. Relations Conf. [136], 1300 19th St. NW, Ste. 750, Washington, DC 20036-1609, (202)861-7550
Airline Medical Examiners Assn. [★13540]
Airline Medical Examiners Assn. [★IO]
Airline Operational Control Soc. - Defunct.
Airline Passengers of America - Defunct.
Airline Passengers Assn. [★23015]
Airline Passengers Assn. [★IO]
Airline Personnel; Fellowship of Christian [20007]
Airline Pilots; Org. of Black [164]
Airline Pilots Security Alliance [432], 2526 Vineyard Ln., Crofton, MD 21114, (615)479-4140
Airline Services Assn. [★129]
Airline Sports and Cultural Assn. [IO], Vienna, Austria
Airline and Steamship Clerks, Freight Handlers, Express and Sta. Employees; Brotherhood of Railway, [★24180]
Airline and Steamship Clerks, Freight Handlers, Express and Sta. Employees; Carmen Division of the Brotherhood of Railway, [★24179]
Airline Stewards and Stewardesses Assn. [★24010]
Airline Supervisors Assn; Amer. Railway and [★24180]
Airline Suppliers Assn. [★2550]

A star before a book entry number signifies that the name is not listed separately, but is mentioned within the entry.

Airline Travel Clubs - Address unknown since 1997.
Airlines Electronic Engg. Comm. [6981], c/o ARINC Inc., 2551 Riva Rd., Annapolis, MD 21401-7435, (410)266-2982
Airlines Medical Directors Assn. [13539]
Airmail Cover Club; Metropolitan [★22845]
Airman Memorial Found. [20661], 5211 Auth Rd., Suitland, MD 20746, (301)899-3500
Airmen Assn; Escort Carrier Sailors and [21185]
Airmen, Inc; Tuskegee [20651]
Airmen Intl; Negro [6380]
Airmen; Union of Professional [★24005]
Airplane Assn; Antique [21430]
Airplane Club; Bird [21432]
Airplane Club; Porterfield [21472]
Airport Chaplains; Natl. Catholic Conf. of [19754]
Airport Consultants Coun. [951], 908 King St., Ste. 100, Alexandria, VA 22314, (703)683-5900
Airport Executives; Amer. Assn. of [138]
Airport Ground Trans. Assn. [3858], c/o USML Center for Trans. Stud., 154 Univ. Ctr., 8001 Natural Bridge Rd., St. Louis, MO 63121-4499, (314)516-7271
Airport Minority Advisory Coun. [2758], Ronald Reagan Washington Natl. Airport, Washington, DC 20001, (703)417-2622
Airport Operators Assn. [IO], London, United Kingdom
Airport Security Coun. - Address unknown since 1994.
Airports Coun. Intl. - Europe [IO], Brussels, Belgium
Airports Coun. Intl. - Latin America-Caribbean Off. [IO], Caracas, Venezuela
Airports Coun. Intl. - North Am. [IO], Washington, DC, United States
Airports Coun. Intl. - North Am. [137], 1775 K St. NW, Ste. 500, Washington, DC 20006, (202)293-8500
Airports Coun. Intl. - Pacific Region [IO], Hong Kong, People's Republic of China
Airports Coun. Intl. - Switzerland [IO], Geneva, Switzerland
Airship Assn. [IO], Folkestone, United Kingdom
Airship Assn; Naval [6379]
Airship Assn. - U.S. - Address unknown since 1999.
Airspace Action on Smoking and Hea. [IO], Burnaby, BC, Canada
Airts Cooncil o Norlin Airlann [★IO]
Airways Club [★IO]
Airways Club [★23015]
Airways Engineering Soc. - Defunct.
Airways Systems Specialists; Professional [24015]
Airwolf Recovery Team - Defunct.
AIVS Newsl. [★10539]
A.J. Muste Memorial Inst. [18188], 339 Lafayette St., New York, NY 10012, (212)533-4335
Akademie fur Ethik in der Medizin [★IO]
Akademie fur Raumforschung und Landesplanung [★IO]
Akademie Ved Ceske Republiky [★IO]
Akademiet for de Tekniske Videnskaber [★IO]
Akademikerforbundet SSR [IO], Stockholm, Sweden
Akademio Internacia de la Sciencoj [★IO]
Akademischer Arbeitskreis Japan [★IO]
Akerne Orchids [IO], Antwerp, Belgium
Akert Family Genealogy Res. Org. - Address unknown since 2001.
Akhal-Teke Assn. of Am. [4808], PO Box 1635, Rolla, MO 65402, (573)426-5207
Akhal-Teke Assn. of Am. [★4808]
Akhal-Teke Assn. of Am. - Inc. in Missouri [★4808]
Akhal-Teke Registry of Am. [★4808]
Akhal-Teke Sporthorse Registry of Am. [★4808]
Akina Mama wa Afrika [IO], London, United Kingdom
Akita Club of Am. [22181], 9337 B Katy Fwy., No. 150, Houston, TX 77024, (415)488-0886
Akita Kennel Club of Am. [★22181]
Akita Rescue Soc. of Am. [11341], 237 Venus St., Thousand Oaks, CA 91360-2958
Akiva; Hashomer Hadati, Bnei [★20178]
Akiva of North Am; Bnei [★20178]
Akiva of the U.S. and Canada; Religious Zionist Youth Movement - Bnei [20178]
Akro Agate Art Assn. - Defunct.

Aktion Boernehjaelp [★IO]
Aktion Gesunde Knochen [IO], Graz, Austria
Aktion Suehnezeichen Friedensdienste [★IO]
Aktionsgemeinschaft Dienst fuer den Frieden [★IO]
Aktionsgemeinschaft Solidarische Welt [★IO]
Al Alberts Archv; Original Four Aces and [24955]
Al Amel Iraqi Assn. [IO], Preston, Australia
Al-Anon Familjegrupper i Sverige [★IO]
Al-Anon Family Gp. HQ, World Ser. Off. [IO], Virginia Beach, VA; United States
Al-Anon Family Gp. HQ, World Ser. Off. [13214], 1600 Corporate Landing Pkwy., Virginia Beach, VA 23454-5617, (757)563-1600
Al-Anon Family Groups - United Kingdom and Eire [IO], London, United Kingdom
Al-Bakorah Adurzia [★20095]
Al-Haq [IO], Ramallah, Israel
Al-Itihad al-Arabi Linakl al-Jawi [★IO]
A.L. Mailman Family Found. [11671], 707 Westchester Ave., White Plains, NY 10604, (914)683-8089
Al-Mu'asasat al -Arabiyye I-Hoquq al-Insan [★IO]
Al-Rashid Islamic Inst. [IO], Cornwall, ON, Canada
ALA Joint Comm. on Lib. Ser. to Labor Groups; AFL-CIO/ [10314]
ALA Social Responsibilities Round Table Feminist Task Force [17514], c/o Amer. Lib. Assn., 50 E Huron St., Chicago, IL 60611, (800)545-2433
Alabama Fan Club [24838], PO Box 680529, Fort Payne, AL 35968-1606, (256)845-1646
Aladdin Knights of the Mystic Light [22617], c/o Dr. J.W. Courter, Bright Knight, 3935 Kelley Rd., Kevil, KY 42053, (270)488-2116
Alagille Syndrome Alliance [14438], c/o Cindy L. Hahn, Pres., 10500 SW Starr Dr., Tualatin, OR 97062, (503)885-0455
Alan Feinstein Fan Club - Defunct.
Alan Guttmacher Inst. [12175], 125 Maiden Ln., 7th Fl., New York, NY 10038, (212)248-1111
Alan Jackson Fan Club [24839], PO Box 440328, Nashville, TN 37244-0328, (615)321-5221
Alan Thicke Fan Club - Address unknown since 1999.
Alarm Assn. of Am; Natl. [3536]
Alarm Assn; Automatic Fire [3439]
Alarm Assn; Central Sta. [3442]
Alarm Assn; Natl. Burglar and Fire [3538]
Alarm Industry Comm. for Combating Crime - Defunct.
Alarm Industry Telecommunications Comm. - Defunct.
Alaska Coalition [4343], 122 C St. NW, Ste. 240, Washington, DC 20001, (202)544-5205
Alaska Collectors' Club [22779], c/o Jim Zuelow, Pres., 5300 N Paseo del Arenal, Tucson, AZ 85750
Alaska Conservation Soc. - Defunct.
Alaska Fairbanks Alumni Assn; Univ. of [18930]
Alaska Mission [★20348]
Alaska Mission [★IO]
Alaska Native Assn; Northwest [★12627]
Alaska Native Mental Hea. Res; Natl. Center for Amer. Indian and [15220]
Alaska Salmon Industry - Defunct.
Alaska Yukon Pioneers [21251]
Alaskan Malamute Assistance League [11342], PO Box 691, Mount Vernon, OH 43050, (419)512-2423
Alaskan Malamute Club of Am. [22182], c/o Leneia R. Rogowski, Corresponding Sec., 640 E 50 N, Hyrum, UT 84319, (435)245-3634
Alaskan Malamute Protection League [★11342]
Alateen [13215], 1600 Corporate Landing Pkwy., Virginia Beach, VA 23454-5617, (757)563-1600
Alateen [★13214]
Alateen [★IO]
Alateen [IO], Ottawa, ON, Canada
Alba Regia Chapel Memorial Park [★IO]
Alba Regia Chapel Memorial Park [★17791]
Albacore Assn. [★23226]
Albacore Assn; U.S. [23226]
Alban Inst. [19840], 2121 Cooperative Way, Ste. 100, Herndon, VA 20171, (703)964-2700
Albanian
  Albanian Amer. Civic League [16970]
  Albanian Amer. Civic League [IO]
  Assn. of Albanian Girls and Women [18382]
  Center for the Stud. of Aging of Albany [11281]

Natl. Albanian Amer. Coun. [18870]
Albanian Amateur Radio Assn. [IO], Tirana, Albania
Albanian Amer. Civic League [IO], Ossining, NY, United States
Albanian Amer. Civic League [16970], PO Box 70, Ossining, NY 10562, (914)762-5530
Albanian-American Trade and Development Assn. [24333], 159 E 4th St., Dunkirk, NY 14048
Albanian-American Trade and Development Assn. [IO], Dunkirk, NY, United States
Albanian Assn. of Consulting Engineers [IO], Tirana, Albania
Albanian Assn. of Gerontology and Geriatrics [IO], Tirana, Albania
Albanian Assn. in Support of Asthma and Allergy Patients [IO], Tirana, Albania
Albanian Catholic Charity; American- [★18506]
Albanian Catholic Info. Center [★18506]
Albanian Catholic Info. Center [★IO]
Albanian Catholic Inst. [IO], San Francisco, CA, United States
Albanian Catholic Inst. [18506], Univ. of San Francisco, 650 Parker Ave., San Francisco, CA 94118, (415)422-6966
Albanian Dance Sport Fed. [IO], Tirana, Albania
Albanian Dental Assn. [IO], Tirana, Albania
Albanian Kosovar Youth in the Free World - Address unknown since 1995.
Albanian League Against Epilepsy [IO], Tirana, Albania
Albanian Orthodontic Soc. [IO], Tirana, Albania
Albanian Pain Assn. [IO], Tirana, Albania
Albanian Political Sci. Assn. [IO], Tirana, Albania
Albanian Soc. of Cardiology [IO], Tirana, Albania
Albanian Soc. Jusuf Gervalla - Address unknown since 1990.
Albanian Soc. of Rheumatology [IO], Tirana, Albania
Albanian Taekwondo Fed. [IO], Tirana, Albania
Albanian Tennis Fed. [IO], Tirana, Albania
Albany Natural Trail Riders [IO], Albany, Australia
Alberg 37 Intl. Owners Assn. [21866], c/o Tom Assenmacher, PO Box 32, Kinsale, VA 22488, (804)472-3853
Albert A. List Found. - Defunct.
Albert Andrew Bahr Family Org. - Address unknown since 2003.
Albert Einstein Institution [18108], PO Box 455, East Boston, MA 02128, (617)247-4882
Albert Einstein Intl. Acad. Found. - Address unknown since 2000.
Albert Einstein Peace Prize Found. - Address unknown since 1999.
Albert Ellis Inst. [16197], 45 E 65th St., New York, NY 10021, (212)535-0822
Albert Schweitzer Coun. on Animals and the Environment - Defunct.
Albert Schweitzer Ecological Centre [IO], Neuchatel, Switzerland
Albert Schweitzer Fellowship [11101], 330 Brookline Ave., Boston, MA 02215, (617)667-5111
Alberta Amateur Boxing Assn. [IO], Edmonton, AB, Canada
Alberta Amateur Softball Assn. [IO], Edmonton, AB, Canada
Alberta Amputee Sport and Recreation Assn. [IO], Calgary, AB, Canada
Alberta Angus Assn. [IO], Edberg, AB, Canada
Alberta Arbitration and Mediation Soc. [IO], Edmonton, AB, Canada
Alberta Assn. for Community Living [IO], Edmonton, AB, Canada
Alberta Assn. on Gerontology [IO], Calgary, AB, Canada
Alberta Assn. of Landscape Architects [IO], Edmonton, AB, Canada
Alberta Assn. of Naturopathic Practitioners [IO], Calgary, AB, Canada
Alberta Assn. of Registered Nurses [★IO]
Alberta Ballet [IO], Calgary, AB, Canada
Alberta Bottle Depot Assn. [IO], Edmonton, AB, Canada
Alberta Community Crime Prevention Assn. [IO], Calgary, AB, Canada
Alberta Constr. Assn. [IO], Edmonton, AB, Canada
Alberta Constr. Safety Assn. [IO], Edmonton, AB, Canada

Reference to "IO" in place of a book number signifies that the association may be found in the 45th edition of International Organizations.

Alberta Equestrian Fed. [IO], Calgary, AB, Canada
Alberta Family Histories Soc. [IO], Calgary, AB, Canada
Alberta Ferret Soc. [IO], Edmonton, AB, Canada
Alberta Forest Products Assn. [IO], Edmonton, AB, Canada
Alberta Foster Parent Assn. [IO], Edmonton, AB, Canada
Alberta Funeral Ser. Assn. [IO], Red Deer, AB, Canada
Alberta Golf Assn. [IO], Calgary, AB, Canada
Alberta Lung Assn. [IO], Edmonton, AB, Canada
Alberta Magazine Publishers Assn. [IO], Calgary, AB, Canada
Alberta Motion Picture Industries Assn. [IO], Edmonton, AB, Canada
Alberta Motor Assn. [IO], Calgary, AB, Canada
Alberta Motor Transport Assn. [IO], Calgary, AB, Canada
Alberta New Media Assn. [★IO]
Alberta Occupational Hea. Nurses Assn. [IO], Edmonton, AB, Canada
Alberta Orienteering Assn. [IO], Calgary, AB, Canada
Alberta Real Estate Assn. [IO], Calgary, AB, Canada
Alberta Recreational Canoe Assn. [IO], Edmonton, AB, Canada
Alberta Rockies Gay Rodeo Assn. [IO], Calgary, AB, Canada
Alberta Senior Citizens' Housing Assn. [IO], Edmonton, AB, Canada
Alberta Snowboarding Assn. [IO], Calgary, AB, Canada
Alberta Standardbred Horse Assn. [IO], Calgary, AB, Canada
Alberta Table Tennis Assn. [IO], Edmonton, AB, Canada
Alberta Teachers' Assn. [IO], Edmonton, AB, Canada
Alberta Wilderness Assn. [IO], Calgary, AB, Canada
Alberta World Trade Center Edmonton [★IO]
Alberts Archv; Original Four Aces and Al [24955]
Albertus Magnus Guild - Defunct.
Albertus Magnus Lyceum - Defunct.
Albinism and Hypopigmentation; Natl. Org. for [15255]
Albinism World Alliance [15242], c/o Natl. Org. for Albinism and Hypopigmentation, PO Box 959, East Hampstead, NH 03826-0959, (603)887-2310
Albinism World Alliance [IO], East Hampstead, NH, United States
Albino Assn; Intl. Amer. [★4855]
Albison Family History Assn. - Address unknown since 2007.
Albrecht Duerer Study Unit - Address unknown since 1995.
Alcohol
Addiction Res. and Treatment Corp. [13213]
Adult Children of Alcoholics World Ser. Org. [13012]
Al-Anon Family Gp. HQ, World Ser. Off. [13214]
Alcohol Res. Info. Ser. [13217]
Alcoholics Anonymous World Services [13218]
Amer. Assn. of Medical Rev. Officers [14695]
Amer. Coun. on Alcohol Problems [13220]
Amer. Coun. on Alcoholism [13221]
Amer. Coun. for Drug Educ. [13222]
Amer. Hea. and Temperance Assn. [13303]
Amer. Outreach Assn. [13223]
Amer. Psychological Assn. - Addictions Div. [16123]
Amer. Soc. of Addiction Medicine [16501]
Amer. Sommelier Assn. [194]
Amer. Vineyard Found. [5408]
Amer. Wine Alliance for Res. and Educ. [5409]
Amer. Wine Soc. [5410]
Assn. of Halfway House Alcoholism Programs of North Am. [13224]
Assn. for Medical Educ. and Res. in Substance Abuse [8849]
Assn. of Recovering Motorcyclists [13225]
BACCHUS Network [13226]
Boaters Against Drunk Driving [12955]
Brotherhood of the Knights of the Vine [5411]
California Assn. of Winegrape Growers [5412]
Century Coun. [13591]

Children of Alcoholics Found. [13228]
Christian Addiction Rehabilitation Assn. [13229]
Do It Now Found. [13235]
Doctors Ought to Care [14554]
Eastern Coast Breweriana Assn. [21830]
Faces and Voices of Recovery [18688]
Families Worldwide [13241]
Finger Lakes Wine Growers Assn. [5413]
Free the Grapes! [16971]
Friendly Hand Found. [13243]
Hazelden Found. [13244]
Hea. Connection [13245]
Impaired Physician Prog. [13246]
Inst. for a Drug-Free Workplace [13247]
Inst. on Global Drug Policy [13248]
Inst. for Integral Development [13249]
Inter-Association Task Force on Alcohol and Other Substance Abuse Issues [13250]
Intl. Commn. for the Prevention of Alcoholism and Drug Dependency [13251]
Intl. Doctors in Alcoholics Anonymous [13252]
Intl. Hea. and Temperance Assn. [13304]
Monterey County Vintners and Growers Assn. [5414]
Mothers Against Drunk Driving [12969]
NAADAC The Assn. for Addiction Professionals [16509]
Napa Valley Grapegrowers [5415]
Napa Valley Vintners Assn. [5416]
Napa Valley Wine Lib. Assn. [23027]
Narcotic Educational Found. of Am. [13256]
Narcotics Anonymous [13257]
Natl. Alliance for Model State Drug Laws [5671]
Natl. Assn. of Addiction Treatment Providers [13259]
Natl. Assn. of Breweriana Advt. [22074]
Natl. Assn. for Children of Alcoholics [13261]
Natl. Assn. on Drug Abuse Problems [13262]
Natl. Assn. of Lesbian/Gay Addiction Professionals [13263]
Natl. Black Alcoholism and Addiction Coun. [13265]
Natl. Catholic Coun. on Alcoholism and Related Drug Problems [13266]
Natl. Commn. Against Drunk Driving [12973]
Natl. Comm. for the Prevention of Alcoholism and Drug Dependency [13267]
Natl. Conf. of State Liquor Administrators [5447]
Natl. Coun. on Alcoholism and Drug Dependence [13268]
Natl. Families in Action [13269]
Natl. Family Partnership [13270]
Natl. Latino Coun. on Alcohol and Tobacco Prevention [12269]
Natl. Liquor Law Enforcement Assn. [5996]
Natl. Temperance and Prohibition Coun. [13305]
Natl. Woman's Christian Temperance Union [13306]
New York Wine/Grape Found. [5417]
North Amer. Brewers' Assn. [208]
Organic Grapes Into Wine Alliance [5418]
Phoenix House [13273]
Pill Addicts Anonymous [13274]
Pills Anonymous [13275]
PRIDE Youth Programs [13276]
Recording Artists, Actors and Athletes Against Drunk Driving [12986]
San Joaquin Valley Wine Growers Assn. [5419]
Santa Cruz Mountains Winegrowers Assn. [5420]
Secular Organizations for Sobriety [13281]
Soc. of Medical Friends of Wine [23028]
Soc. of Wine Educators [23029]
Sonoma County Grape Growers Assn. [5421]
Sonoma County Vintners [5422]
Specialty Wine Retailers Assn. [4031]
Students Against Destructive Decisions, Students Against Drunk Driving [12992]
Vinifera Wine Growers Assn. [5423]
Wine Appreciation Guild [5424]
Wine Inst. [5425]
Women for Sobriety [13284]
Women for Winesense [23030]
Women's Drug Res. Project [13285]
Alcohol Abuse
Addiction Res. and Treatment Corp. [13213]

Adult Children of Alcoholics World Ser. Org. [13012]
African Amer. Wine Tasting Soc. [190]
Al-Anon Family Gp. HQ, World Ser. Off. [13214]
Alateen [13215]
Alcohol Res. Info. Ser. [13217]
Alcoholics Anonymous World Services [13218]
Allied Youth and Family Counseling Center [13465]
Amer. Assn. of Behavioral Therapists [13744]
Amer. Coll. of Addiction Treatment Administrators [13219]
Amer. Coun. on Alcohol Problems [13220]
Amer. Coun. on Alcoholism [13221]
Amer. Coun. for Drug Educ. [13222]
Amer. Hea. and Temperance Assn. [13303]
Amer. Osteopathic Acad. of Addiction Medicine [16500]
Amer. Outreach Assn. [13223]
Amer. Psychological Assn. - Addictions Div. [16123]
Amer. Soc. of Addiction Medicine [16501]
Assn. of Halfway House Alcoholism Programs of North Am. [13224]
Assn. for Medical Educ. and Res. in Substance Abuse [8849]
Assn. of Recovering Motorcyclists [13225]
BACCHUS Network [13226]
Because I Love You: The Parent Support Gp. [13293]
Boaters Against Drunk Driving [12955]
Center for Substance Abuse Prevention [16502]
Century Coun. [13591]
Children of Alcoholics Found. [13228]
Christian Addiction Rehabilitation Assn. [13229]
Do It Now Found. [13235]
Drug and Alcohol Testing Indus. Assn. [13236]
Ethos Found. [13239]
Eurocare: Advocacy for the Prevention of Alcohol Related Harm in Europe [IO]
European Soc. for Biomedical Res. on Alcoholism [IO]
Faces and Voices of Recovery [18688]
Families Worldwide [13241]
Friendly Hand Found. [13243]
Hazelden Found. [13244]
Hea. Connection [13245]
Hearts and Minds Network [18730]
Impaired Physician Prog. [13246]
Inst. for a Drug-Free Workplace [13247]
Inst. on Global Drug Policy [13248]
Inst. for Integral Development [13249]
Inter-Association Task Force on Alcohol and Other Substance Abuse Issues [13250]
Intl. Assn. of Addictions and Offender Counselors [11824]
Intl. Coalition for Addiction Stud. Educ. [9197]
Intl. Commn. for the Prevention of Alcoholism and Drug Dependency [13251]
Intl. Doctors in Alcoholics Anonymous [13252]
Intl. Hea. and Temperance Assn. [13304]
Join Together [18689]
Leadership to Keep Children Alcohol Free [11334]
Lifegain Inst. [14573]
Luz Social Services [13255]
Moderation Mgt. [16507]
Mothers Against Drunk Driving [12969]
Musicians' Assistance Prog. [12619]
Musicians' Assistance Prog. Alumni Assn. [12620]
NAADAC The Assn. for Addiction Professionals [16509]
Narcotic Educational Found. of Am. [13256]
Narcotics Anonymous [13257]
Natl. Assn. of Addiction Treatment Providers [13259]
Natl. Assn. for Children of Alcoholics [13261]
Natl. Assn. on Drug Abuse Problems [13262]
Natl. Assn. of Lesbian/Gay Addiction Professionals [13263]
Natl. Assn. for Regulatory Admin. [15011]
Natl. Black Alcoholism and Addiction Coun. [13265]
Natl. Catholic Coun. on Alcoholism and Related Drug Problems [13266]
Natl. Commn. Against Drunk Driving [12973]

A star before a book entry number signifies that the name is not listed separately, but is mentioned within the entry.

Natl. Comm. for the Prevention of Alcoholism and Drug Dependency [13267]
Natl. Coun. on Alcoholism and Drug Dependence [13268]
Natl. Families in Action [13269]
Natl. Family Partnership [13270]
Natl. Latino Coun. on Alcohol and Tobacco Prevention [12269]
Natl. Temperance and Prohibition Coun. [13305]
Natl. Woman's Christian Temperance Union [13306]
Partnership for a Drug-Free Am. [13272]
People Helping People [12385]
Phoenix House [13273]
Pill Addicts Anonymous [13274]
Pills Anonymous [13275]
PRIDE Youth Programs [13276]
Recording Artists, Actors and Athletes Against Drunk Driving [12986]
Res. Soc. on Alcoholism [16517]
Secular Organizations for Sobriety [13281]
SMART Recovery [16519]
Students Against Destructive Decisions, Students Against Drunk Driving [12992]
Substance Abuse Librarians and Info. Specialists [10390]
Substance Abuse Prog. Administrators Assn. [16521]
Women for Sobriety [13284]
Women in Transition [13447]
Women's Drug Res. Project [13285]
Alcohol Beverage Control Assn; Natl. [★5445]
Alcohol Beverage Control Assn; Natl. [5446]
Alcohol Beverage Laws; Joint Comm. of the States to Stud. [★5445]
Alcohol Beverage Legislative Coun. [5444], 5101 River Rd., Ste. 108, Bethesda, MD 20816-1560, (301)656-1494
Alcohol Concern [IO], London, United Kingdom
Alcohol and Drug Abuse Directors; Natl. Assn. of State [13264]
Alcohol and Drug Problems Assn. of North Am. [13216], 307 N Main, St. Charles, MO 63301, (314)589-6702
Alcohol and Drug Recovery Assn. of Ontario [★IO]
Alcohol and Drug Res; Nordic Coun. for [IO]
Alcohol, Drugs and Disability; Natl. Assn. on [16512]
Alcohol and Drugs; Natl. Episcopal Coalition on [★13279]
Alcohol Education for Youth and Community - Defunct.
Alcohol Focus Scotland [IO], Glasgow, United Kingdom
Alcohol Issues; Inter-Association Task Force on [★13250]
Alcohol and Other Drugs Coun. of Australia [IO], Woden, Australia
Alcohol and Other Substance Abuse Issues; Inter-Association Task Force on [13250]
Alcohol and Other Substance Abuse Issues; Inter-Association Task Force on Campus [★13250]
Alcohol Policies Proj; Center for Sci. in the Public Interest - [18703]
Alcohol Policy Coun. - Defunct.
Alcohol Problems; Amer. Coun. on [13220]
Alcohol Res. Info. Ser. [13217], 430 Lanthrop St., Lansing, MI 48912, (517)485-9900
Alcohol Tax Coalition; Natl. [★18703]
Alcohol Testing Indus. Assn; Drug and [13236]
Alcoholic Beverage Importers; Natl. Assn. of [★206]
Alcoholic Beverage Indus; Tax Council- [★199]
Alcoholic Beverages
Adult Children of Alcoholics World Ser. Org. [13012]
African Amer. Wine Tasting Soc. [190]
Al-Anon Family Gp. HQ, World Ser. Off. [13214]
Alcohol Beverage Legislative Coun. [5444]
Alcohol Res. Info. Ser. [13217]
Alcoholics Anonymous World Services [13218]
Am. Homebrewers Assn. [191]
Amer. Bartenders' Assn. [192]
Amer. Beverage Licensees [193]
Amer. Coun. on Alcohol Problems [13220]
Amer. Coun. on Alcoholism [13221]
Amer. Hea. and Temperance Assn. [13303]

Amer. Malting Barley Assn. [4303]
Amer. Outreach Assn. [13223]
Amer. Soc. of Brewing Chemists [6670]
Amer. Sommelier Assn. [194]
Amer. Vineyard Found. [5408]
Amer. Wine Alliance for Res. and Educ. [5409]
Amer. Wine Soc. [5410]
Assn. of African Amer. Vintners [195]
Assn. of Beer and Malt Mfrs. [IO]
Assn. of Bordeaux Wine and Alcohol Wholesalers [IO]
Assn. of Canadian Distillers [IO]
Assn. of German Wine Experts [IO]
Assn. of Halfway House Alcoholism Programs of North Am. [13224]
Assn. of Port Wine Companies [IO]
Assn. of Producers and Merchants of Wines and Spirits in Bulgaria [IO]
Assn. of Winery Suppliers [196]
Austrian Brewers' Assn. [IO]
BACCHUS Network [13226]
Beer Inst. [197]
Belgian Brewers [IO]
Brazilian Assn. of Drinks Producers [IO]
Breweries Central Off. [IO]
Brewers Assn. [198]
Brewers Assn. of Canada [IO]
Brewers Assn. of Japan [IO]
Brewers of Europe [IO]
Brewers of Spain [IO]
Brewery and Soft Drink Workers Conf. - U.S.A. and Canada [24020]
Brewing, Food and Beverage Indus. Suppliers Assn. [IO]
Brewing and Malting Barley Res. Inst. [IO]
Brewmeisters Anonymous [21829]
British Beer and Pub Assn. [IO]
Brotherhood of the Knights of the Vine [5411]
Caffeine Awareness Alliance [13747]
California Assn. of Winegrape Growers [5412]
Century Coun. [13591]
CEPS - The European Spirits Org. [IO]
Children of Alcoholics Found. [13228]
Danish Brewers' Assn. [IO]
Distilled Spirits Assn. of New Zealand [IO]
Distilled Spirits Coun. of the U.S. [199]
Distilled Spirits Indus. Coun. of Australia [IO]
Eastern Coast Breweriana Assn. [21830]
El Dorado Winery Assn. [200]
European Brewery Convention [IO]
Fed. Assn. of the German Spirits Indus. and Importers [IO]
Fed. des Brasseurs Luxembourgeois [IO]
Finger Lakes Wine Growers Assn. [5413]
Finnish Fed. of the Brewing and Soft Drink Indus. [IO]
Flair Bartenders' Assn. [201]
Free the Grapes! [16971]
French Fed. of Spirits [IO]
Friendly Hand Found. [13243]
Fruit Wine and Cider Makers of New Zealand [IO]
German Brewers Union [IO]
German Wine Inst. [IO]
German Winegrowers Assn. [IO]
Gin and Vodka Assn. of Great Britain [IO]
Hazelden Found. [13244]
Home Wine and Beer Trade Assn. [202]
Home Wine and Beer Trade Association [IO]
Inst. for a Drug-Free Workplace [13247]
Inst. on Global Drug Policy [13248]
Inst. of Masters of Wine [IO]
Inter-Association Task Force on Alcohol and Other Substance Abuse Issues [13250]
Intl. Beverage Packaging Assn. [508]
Intl. Bird Beer Label Assn. [21491]
Intl. Bird Beer Label Assn. [IO]
International Center for Alcohol Policies [IO]
Intl. Center for Alcohol Policies [203]
Intl. Commn. for the Prevention of Alcoholism and Drug Dependency [13251]
Intl. Doctors in Alcoholics Anonymous [13252]
Intl. Fed. of Wines and Spirits [IO]
Intl. Hea. and Temperance Assn. [13304]
Italian Wine and Food Inst. [1534]
Japan Craft Beer Assn. [IO]

Joint Comm. of the States [5445]
Latin Amer. Brewers Assn. [IO]
Liquor Merchants Assn. of Australia [IO]
Malt Distillers Assn. of Scotland [IO]
Maltsters' Assn. of Great Britain [IO]
Minnesota Beer Wholesalers Assn. [204]
Monterey County Vintners and Growers Assn. [5414]
Napa Valley Grapegrowers [5415]
Napa Valley Vintners Assn. [5416]
Napa Valley Wine Lib. Assn. [23027]
Natl. Alcohol Beverage Control Assn. [5446]
Natl. Assh. of Bar and Tavern Owners [205]
Natl. Assn. of Beverage Importers [206]
Natl. Assn. of Breweriana Advt. [22074]
Natl. Assn. for Children of Alcoholics [13261]
Natl. Assn. of Lesbian/Gay Addiction Professionals [13263]
Natl. Beer Wholesalers Assn. [207]
Natl. Catholic Coun. on Alcoholism and Related Drug Problems [13266]
Natl. Comm. for the Prevention of Alcoholism and Drug Dependency [13267]
Natl. Conf. of State Liquor Administrators [5447]
Natl. Coun. on Alcoholism and Drug Dependence [13268]
Natl. Interprofessional Off. of Cognac [IO]
Natl. Latino Coun. on Alcohol and Tobacco Prevention [12269]
Natl. Liquor Law Enforcement Assn. [5996]
Natl. Temperance and Prohibition Coun. [13305]
Natl. Woman's Christian Temperance Union [13306]
New York Wine/Grape Found. [5417]
North Amer. Brewers' Assn. [208]
North Amer. Shippers Assn. [3584]
Norwegian Brewers and Soft Drink Producers [IO]
Organic Grapes Into Wine Alliance [5418]
Royal Assn. of Dutch Wine Traders [IO]
San Joaquin Valley Wine Growers Assn. [5419]
Scotch Whisky Assn. [IO]
Secular Organizations for Sobriety [13281]
Soc. of Independent Brewers [IO]
Soc. of Medical Friends of Wine [23028]
Soc. of Wine Educators [23029]
Sommelier Soc. of Am. [209]
Sonoma County Grape Growers Assn. [5421]
Sonoma County Vintners [5422]
Spanish Assn. of Beer and Malt Technicians [IO]
Specialty Wine Retailers Assn. [4031]
Spirits Indus. Fed. [IO]
Swedish Brewers' Assn. [IO]
Swedish Spirits and Wine Suppliers [IO]
Swiss Brewers' Assn. [IO]
Swiss Spirits Producers' Assn. [IO]
Swiss Wine Exporters Assn. [IO]
Tasters Guild Intl. [210]
Union of Belgian Brewers [IO]
Union of Estonian Breweries [IO]
Union des Maisons de Bordeaux [IO]
Vinifera Wine Growers Assn. [5423]
Wine Inst. [5425]
Wine Inst. of New Zealand [IO]
Wine and Spirit Trade Assn. [IO]
Wine and Spirits Shippers Assn. [211]
Wine and Spirits Wholesalers of Am. [212]
WineAmerica Natl. Assn. of Amer. Wineries [4032]
Women for Winesense [23030]
World Assn. of the Alcohol Beverage Indus. [213]
World Assn. of the Alcohol Beverage Indus. [IO]
Worshipful Company of Vintners [IO]
Alcoholic Clergy Assn; Recovered [13278]
Alcoholic Rehabilitation Assn; Christian [★13229]
Alcoholic Res. Foundation; Parkside [★14821]
Alcoholics Anonymous - Australia [IO], Arncliffe, Australia
Alcoholics Anonymous - Brazil [IO], Sao Paulo, Brazil
Alcoholics Anonymous - England [IO], York, United Kingdom
Alcoholics Anonymous - French Gen. Services Off. [IO], Paris, France
Alcoholics Anonymous; Intl. Advisory Coun. for Homosexual Men and Women in [★13283]
Alcoholics Anonymous; Intl. Lawyers in [13253]

Reference to "IO" in place of a book number signifies that the association may be found in the 45th edition of International Organizations.

Alcoholics Anonymous World Services **[13218]**, PO Box 459, New York, NY 10163, (212)870-3400

Alcoholics Anonymous World Services **[IO]**, New York, NY, United States

Alcoholics Anonymous World Services - French Gen. Services Off. **[★IO]**

Alcoholics Anonymous World Services - Gen. Ser. Bd. for French-Speaking Belgium **[IO]**, Brussels, Belgium

Alcoholics Anonymous World Services - New Zealand Gen. Services Off. **[IO]**, Wellington, New Zealand

Alcoholics Anonymous World Services - Swedish Gen. Services Off. **[IO]**, Jarfalla, Sweden

Alcoholics Anonymous World Services - United Kingdom and Eire Gen. Services Off. **[★IO]**

Alcoholics Found; Children of **[13228]**

Alcoholics; Natl. Assn. for Children of **[13261]**

Alcoholics; Natl. Assn. for Native Amer. Children of **[11627]**

Alcoholism and Addiction Coun; Natl. Black **[13265]**

Alcoholism; Amer. Coun. on **[13221]**

Alcoholism; Baltimore Area Coun. on **[★13221]**

Alcoholism and Drug Abuse Counselors; Natl. Assn. of **[★16509]**

Alcoholism and Drug Dependence; Natl. Coun. on **[13268]**

Alcoholism and Drug Dependency; Natl. Comm. for the Prevention of **[13267]**

Alcoholism; Maryland Soc. on **[★13221]**

Alcoholism; Natl. Clergy Conf. on **[★13266]**

Alcoholism; Natl. Comm. on **[★13268]**

Alcoholism; Natl. Comm. for Educ. on **[★13268]**

Alcoholism; Natl. Comm. for the Prevention of **[★13267]**

Alcoholism; Natl. Coun. on **[★13268]**

Alcoholism; Natl. Nurses Soc. on **[★15484]**

Alcoholism; Natl. States Conf. on **[★13216]**

Alcoholism; New York City Medical Soc. on **[★16501]**

Alcoholism and Other Drug Dependencies; Amer. Medical Soc. on **[★16501]**

Alcoholism Professionals; Natl. Assn. of Gay **[★13263]**

Alcoholism Professionals; Natl. Assn. of Lesbian/Gay **[★13263]**

Alcoholism Programs of North Am; Assn. of Halfway House **[13224]**

Alcoholism Programs; North Amer. Assn. of **[★13216]**

Alcoholism and Related Drug Problems; Natl. Catholic Coun. on **[13266]**

Alcoholism and Related Drug Problems; Natl. Clergy Coun. on **[★13266]**

Alcoholism; Res. Soc. on **[16517]**

Alcoholism Treatment Programs; Natl. Assn. of **[★13259]**

Alcoolicos Anonimos no Brasil **[★IO]**

Alcooliques Anonymes France **[★IO]**

Alcor Found. **[★IO]**

Alcor Found. **[★14072]**

Alcor Life Extension Found. **[14072]**, 7895 E Acoma Dr., Ste. 110, Scottsdale, AZ 85260-6916, (480)905-1906

Alcor Life Extension Foundation **[IO]**, Scottsdale, AZ, United States

Alcort Sailfish-Sunfish Class **[★IO]**

Alcort Sailfish-Sunfish Class **[★23194]**

Alcort Sailfish-Sunfish Class; AMF **[★23194]**

Alcott Memorial Assn; Louisa May **[9682]**

Alcuin Club **[IO]**, Denbighs, United Kingdom

Alcuin Soc. **[IO]**, Vancouver, BC, Canada

Alden Kindred of Am. **[20775]**, PO Box 2754, Duxbury, MA 02331-2754, (781)934-9092

Alden Ocean Shell Assn. - Address unknown since 1990.

Alderian Psychology; Amer. Soc. of **[★16162]**

Alderson Cousins **[20776]**, c/o James A. Cross, Newsl. Ed., Box 2245, El Cajon, CA 92021

Aldo Ray Fan Club **[24726]**

Aldrich Family Assn; Natl. **[21006]**

Aldrig Mere Krig **[★IO]**

Aleksandr Solzhenitsyn Soc. for Freedom and Justice - Defunct.

ALEPH: Alliance for Jewish Renewal **[18141]**, 7000 Lincoln Dr., No. B2, Philadelphia, PA 19119-3046, (215)247-0210

ALEPH: Alliance for Jewish Renewal **[IO]**, Philadelphia, PA, United States

Alexander Graham Bell Assn. for the Deaf **[★IO]**

Alexander Graham Bell Assn. for the Deaf **[★14736]**

Alexander Graham Bell Assn. for the Deaf and Hard of Hearing **[14736]**, 3417 Volta Pl. NW, Washington, DC 20007, (202)337-5220

Alexander Graham Bell Assn. for the Deaf and Hard of Hearing **[IO]**, Washington, DC, United States

Alexander Graham Bell Assn. for the Deaf and Hard of Hearing; Parents' Sect. of the **[14776]**

Alexander Graham Bell Assn. for the Deaf; Parents' Sect. of the **[★14776]**

Alexander Hamilton Hutton, Sr., Family Org. - Address unknown since 2004.

Alexander Technique; Amer. Center for the **[13617]**

Alexander Technique; Amer. Soc. for the **[13623]**

Alexander Technique Intl. **[13608]**, c/o Linda Hein, Admin. Asst., 1692 Massachusetts Ave., 3rd Fl., Cambridge, MA 02138, (617)497-5151

Alexander Technique Intl. **[IO]**, Cambridge, MA, United States

Alexander Thomson Soc. **[IO]**, Glasgow, United Kingdom

Alexander Zonjic Fan Club - Address unknown since 2003.

Alexandra Writers' Centre Soc. **[IO]**, Calgary, AB, Canada

Alexandria Soc. and Educal. Found. **[8161]**

Alfa Romeo Assn. **[21564]**, PO Box 1458, Alameda, CA 94501

Alfa Romeo Club of Canada **[IO]**, Toronto, ON, Canada

Alfa Romeo Owners Club **[21565]**, PO Box 12340, Kansas City, MO 64116-0340, (816)459-7462

Alfalfa Alliance; Natl. **[★1358]**

Alfalfa Club - Address unknown since 1995.

Alfalfa Coun. **[★1358]**

Alfalfa and Forage Alliance; Natl. **[1358]**

Alfalfa Processors Assn; Amer. **[★1357]**

Alford Amer. Family Assn. **[20777]**, PO Box 1297, Florissant, MO 63031, (314)831-8648

Alfred Adler Consultation Center **[★16117]**

Alfred Adler Inst. **[16117]**, 594 Broadway, Ste. 1213, New York, NY 10012, (212)254-1048

Alfred Adler Inst. for Individual Psychology **[★16117]**

Alfred P. Sloan Found. **[18385]**, 630 5th Ave., Ste. 2550, New York, NY 10111, (212)649-1649

Algebraic Manipulation; Special Interest Gp. for Symbolic and **[7296]**

Algemeen Christelijk Vakverbond van Belgie **[IO]**, Brussels, Belgium

Algemene Centrale der Openbare Diensten Sector Onderwijs **[IO]**, Brussels, Belgium

Algemene Nederlandse Bond van Geitenhouders **[★IO]**

Algemene Nederlandse Branche Organisatie Schoonheidsverzorging **[★IO]**

Alger Assn. of Distinguished Americans; Horatio **[20712]**

Alger Awards Comm; Horatio **[★20712]**

Alger Soc; Horatio **[9659]**

Algerian Assn. of Medical Physicists **[IO]**, Geneva, Switzerland

Algerian Badminton Assn. **[IO]**, Algiers, Algeria

Algerian British Assn. **[IO]**, London, United Kingdom

Algerian League Against Epilepsy **[IO]**, Algiers, Algeria

Algerian Ostomy Assn. **[IO]**, Tizi Ouzou, Algeria

Algerian Soc. of Cardiology **[IO]**, Algiers, Algeria

Algerian Soc. of Dermatology **[IO]**, Algiers, Algeria

Algerian Soc. of Hypertension **[IO]**, Algiers, Algeria

Algerian Sports Fed. for Disabled **[IO]**, Algiers, Algeria

Algerian Taekwondo Fed. **[IO]**, Algiers, Algeria

Algerian Tennis Fed. **[IO]**, Algiers, Algeria

Algology; Amer. Acad. of **[★15832]**

Algonquin Arts Coun. **[IO]**, Bancroft, ON, Canada

Algorithms Computability Theory; Special Interest Gp. on **[★7539]**

Algorithms and Computation Theory; Special Interest Gp. on **[7539]**

Alhambra; Intl. Order of **[19001]**

Alhambra; Intl. Order of the **[★19001]**

Alhambra; Order of **[★19001]**

ALI-ABA Comm. on Continuing Professional Educ. **[8758]**, 4025 Chestnut St., Philadelphia, PA 19104-3099, (215)243-1600

ALI-ABA; Joint Comm. on Continuing Legal Educ. - of **[★8758]**

Ali Somon Cultural and Intellectual Found. **[IO]**, Dushanbe, Tajikistan

Alianza - Defunct.

Alianza Interamericana - Defunct.

Alice in Wonderland Collectors Network **[21957]**, 2765 Shellingham Dr., Lisle, IL 60532, (630)637-8530

Alien Nation Appreciation Soc. - The Tencton Planet - Defunct.

Alimentary Tract; Soc. for Surgery of the **[16590]**

Alimony Laws; Natl. Comm. for Fair Divorce and **[★18045]**

Aliran Kesedaran Negara **[★IO]**

Alisa Ann Ruch Burn Found. **[13780]**, Southern CA Off., 2501 W Burbank Blvd., Ste. 201, Burbank, CA 91505, (818)848-0223

Alive Alone **[11511]**, c/o Kay Bevington, Founder, 1112 Champaign Dr., Van Wert, OH 45891

Aliyah Center; Israel **[20146]**

Alkan Soc. **[IO]**, Hemel Hempstead, United Kingdom

Alkylphenols and Ethoxylates Res. Coun. **[796]**, 1250 Connecticut Ave., Ste. 700, Washington, DC 20036, (202)419-1506

All About Marilyn - Address unknown since 1999.

All Africa Baptist Fellowship **[IO]**, Kumasi, Ghana

All Africa Leprosy, Tuberculosis and Rehabilitation Training Centre **[IO]**, Addis Ababa, Ethiopia

All-African People's Revolutionary Party **[16925]**, PO Box 863, New York, NY 10116

All-America Camellias Selections - Defunct.

All-America Gladiolus Selections **[22481]**

All Am. Karate Fed. **[★23559]**

All-America Rose Selections **[4972]**, c/o Erin Walsh, Ruder Finn/San Francisco, 388 Market St., Ste. 1400, San Francisco, CA 94111, (415)348-2731

All-Amer. Amateur Baseball Assn. - Address unknown since 1999.

All-Amer. Bronze Club - Address unknown since 1995.

All-Amer. Collegiate Golf Found. **[23443]**

All-Amer. Conf. - Defunct.

All-American Indian Motorcycle Club **[22663]**, c/o Paul Clement, Treas., 4745 N Jerome Rd., Maumee, OH 43537, (440)647-3723

All-Amer. Intl. English Teachers Assn. - Address unknown since 1988.

All-American Judges Assn. of Michigan - Defunct.

All Amer. Premier Breeds Admin. **[22183]**, 2001 Delameter Rd., Castle Rock, WA 98611, (360)274-4209

All Breeds Cat Club **[IO]**, Cape Town, Republic of South Africa

All-Breeds Rescue Conservancy - Defunct.

All for the Children Found. - Defunct.

All China Fed. of Indus. and Commerce **[IO]**, Beijing, People's Republic of China

All China Fed. of Trade Unions **[IO]**, Beijing, People's Republic of China

All China Women's Fed. **[IO]**, Beijing, People's Republic of China

All Cossack Assn. New Kuban **[★19019]**

All-Craft Found. - Address unknown since 2001.

All Dressage Assn. - Defunct.

All England Lawn Tennis and Croquet Club **[IO]**, London, United Kingdom

All England Netball Assn. **[IO]**, Hitchin, United Kingdom

All European Academies **[IO]**, Amsterdam, Netherlands

All Food Importers Assn. **[IO]**, Istanbul, Turkey

All India Assn. of Indus. **[IO]**, Bombay, India

All India Biotech Assn. **[IO]**, New Delhi, India

All India Chess Fed. for the Blind **[IO]**, Bombay, India

All India Dance Sport Fed. **[IO]**, Bhubaneswar, India

All India Darts Assn. **[IO]**, Kolkata, India

All India Disaster Mitigation Inst. **[IO]**, Ahmedabad, India

All India Exporters' Assn. **[★IO]**

All India Exporters' Chamber **[IO]**, Bombay, India

A star before a book entry number signifies that the name is not listed separately, but is mentioned within the entry.

All-India Fine Arts and Crafts Soc. [IO], New Delhi, India
All India Indus. Gases Mfrs. Assn. [IO], New Delhi, India
All India Mgt. Assn. [IO], New Delhi, India
All India Manufacturer's Org. [IO], Chennai, India
All India Occupational Therapists Assn. [IO], Udupi, India
All India Ophthalmological Soc. [IO], New Delhi, India
All India Plastics Mfrs. Assn. [IO], Bombay, India
All India Plastics Mfrs. Assn. Ltd. [★IO]
All India Primary Teachers Fed. [IO], New Delhi, India
All India Railwaymen's Fed. [IO], New Delhi, India
All India Rubber Indus. Assn. [IO], Bombay, India
All India Skin and Hide Tanners' and Merchants' Assn. [IO], Chennai, India
All India Stainless Steel Indus. Assn. [IO], Bombay, India
All India Tennis Assn. [IO], New Delhi, India
All India Women's Conf. [IO], New Delhi, India
All India Women's Conf. - North Am. [IO], Jamaica, NY, United States
All India Women's Conf. - North Am. [13417], 86-42 Midland Pkwy., Jamaica Estate, Jamaica, NY 11432, (718)523-7668
All Indian Pueblo Coun. [18089]
All-Industry Res. Advisory Coun. [★2183]
All-Japan Aikido Fed. [IO], Tokyo, Japan
All Japan Cotton Spinners Assn. [★IO]
All Japan Dockworkers' Union [IO], Tokyo, Japan
All Japan Ju-Jitsu Intl. Fed. [IO], Glendale, CA, United States
All Japan Ju-Jitsu Intl. Fed. [23577], 622 W Colorado St., Glendale, CA 91204, (323)512-2538
All Japan Powder Indus. Assn. [★IO]
All-Japan Prefectural and Municipal Workers' Union [IO], Tokyo, Japan
All Japan Seamen's Union [IO], Tokyo, Japan
All Japan Taekwondo Fed. [IO], Tokyo, Japan
All Nations Women's League - Address unknown since 2004.
All Natural Healthcare Assn. - Address unknown since 2006.
All Navy Women's Natl. Alliance [6144], PO Box 147, Goldenrod, FL 32733-0147
All Nepal Tennis Assn. [IO], Kathmandu, Nepal
All Nippon Nonwovens Assn. [IO], Osaka, Japan
All One Heart [17080], 12190 Perris Blvd., Ste. F-141, Moreno Valley, CA 92557
All Out Arts [9534], c/o CSV Cultural Center, 107 Suffolk St., New York, NY 10002, (212)477-9945
All Pakistan Aero Modelling and Ultralight Assn. [IO], Karachi, Pakistan
All Pakistan Textile Mills Assn. [IO], Karachi, Pakistan
All Pakistan Women's Assn. [IO], Karachi, Pakistan
All-Peoples Cong. - Address unknown since 2001.
All-Poland Alliance of Trade Unions [IO], Warsaw, Poland
All Roads Ministry [19564], 55 Pallen Rd., No. 3, Hopewell Junction, NY 12533, (845)226-4172
All Russia Assn. of the Blind [IO], Moscow, Russia
All-Russia Athletic Fed. [IO], Moscow, Russia
All Russian Assn. of the Blind [★IO]
All-Russian Monarchist Front - Defunct.
All-Russian Soc. for Disabled [IO], Moscow, Russia
All Ser. Postal Chess Club [21941], c/o Mr. Steven Ledford, Sr., Dir., 2 Skiff St., No. 303, Hamden, CT 06514, (203)287-0349
All-Star Assn; Women's [23258]
All Star Dairy Assn. [1126], PO Box 911050, Lexington, KY 40591-1050, (859)255-3644
All Star Racing League - Defunct.
All-Terrain Vehicles
  ATV Safety Institute/Division of Specialty Vehicle Inst. of Am. [12952]
  Specialty Vehicle Inst. of Am. [398]
All Together - Address unknown since 2001.
All Trinidad Sugar and Gen. Workers' Trade Union [IO], Couva, Trinidad and Tobago
All-Ukrainian Evangelical Baptist Fellowship [19469]
All-Union Copyright Agency [★IO]
All of Us or None [17081], c/o Legal Services for Prisoners with Children, 1540 Market St., Ste. 490, San Francisco, CA 94102, (415)255-7036

All4Israel [12454], 53 Dewhurst St., Staten Island, NY 10314, (877)812-7162
All4Israel [IO], Staten Island, NY, United States
Allan Savory Center for Holistic Mgt. [★4408]
Allante Appreciation Group - Address unknown since 2008.
Allard Owners Club U.S.A. - Defunct.
Alleghenies
  Coun. of the Alleghenies [9365]
Allen Family Circle - Defunct.
Allen Hynek Center for UFO Stud; J. [7479]
Allen O. Whipple Surgical Soc. - Defunct.
Allergic Diseases; Amer. Found. for [★13598]
Allergists; Amer. Coll. of [★13596]
Allergology and Clinical Immunology; Intl. Assn. of [★13605]
Allergy
  Action Against Allergy [IO]
  Albanian Assn. in Support of Asthma and Allergy Patients [IO]
  Allergy/Asthma Info. Assn. [IO]
  Allergy and Asthma Network Mothers of Asthmatics [16352]
  Allergy Soc. of South Africa [IO]
  Amer. Acad. of Allergy, Asthma and Immunology [13592]
  Amer. Acad. of Otolaryngic Allergy and Found. [13593]
  Amer. Assn. of Certified Allergists [13594]
  Amer. Bd. of Allergy and Immunology [13595]
  Amer. Celiac Society/Dietary Support Coalition [15543]
  Amer. Coll. of Allergy, Asthma and Immunology [13596]
  Amer. Latex Allergy Assn. [13597]
  Amer. Partnership for Eosinophilic Disorders [14408]
  Anaphylaxis Australia Inc. [IO]
  Anaphylaxis Canada [IO]
  Asthma and Allergy Found. of Am. [13598]
  British Soc. for Allergy and Clinical Immunology [IO]
  British Soc. for Allergy, Environmental and Nutritional Medicine [IO]
  Churg Strauss Syndrome Assn. [13729]
  Environmental Res. Found. [13599]
  European Acad. of Allergology and Clinical Immunology [IO]
  European Soc. of Paediatric Allergy and Clinical Immunology [IO]
  Food Allergy and Anaphylaxis Network [13600]
  Gluten Intolerance Gp. [15559]
  Intl. Correspondence Soc. of Allergists and Clinical Immunologists [13601]
  Intl. Correspondence Soc. of Allergists and Clinical Immunologists [IO]
  Japanese Soc. of Allergology [IO]
  Joint Coun. of Allergy, Asthma and Immunology [13602]
  Kids With Food Allergies [13603]
  Malaysian Soc. of Allergy and Immunology [IO]
  MedicAlert Found. Intl. [14318]
  Natl. Soc. for Res. into Allergy [IO]
  Norwegian Asthma and Allergy Assn. [IO]
  Pan-American Allergy Soc. [13604]
  Pulmonary and Allergy Patients' Assn. of Slovenia [IO]
  U.S. Hereditary Angioedema Assn. [14487]
  World Allergy Org. [13605]
  World Allergy Org. [IO]
Allergy; Amer. Acad. of [★13592]
Allergy; Amer. Assn. for Clinical Immunology and [★13596]
Allergy; Amer. Assn. for the Stud. of [★13592]
Allergy; Amer. Soc. of Ophthalmologic and Otolaryngologic [★13593]
Allergy/Asthma Info. Assn. [IO], Vaughan, ON, Canada
Allergy and Asthma Network Mothers of Asthmatics [16352], 2751 Prosperity Ave., Ste. 150, Fairfax, VA 22031, (800)878-4403
Allergy and Asthma Network; Natl. [★16352]
Allergy and Clinical Immunology; Acad. of Veterinary [16733]
Allergy and Clinical Immunology; Canadian Soc. of [IO]

Allergy Found. of Am. [★13598]
Allergy and Immunology; Amer. Coll. of [★13596]
Allergy; Joint Coun. of Socio Economics of [★13602]
Allergy Soc. of South Africa [IO], Cape Town, Republic of South Africa
Alley Cat Allies [11343], 7920 Norfolk Ave., Ste. 600, Bethesda, MD 20814-2525, (240)482-1980
Alley Farming Network for Tropical Africa [IO], Ibadan, Nigeria
Allgemeiner Deutscher Automobil-Club [IO], Munich, Germany
Allgemeiner Deutscher Tanzlehrerverband [★IO]
Allgood Ancestry - Defunct.
The Alliance [★8591]
Alliance des manufacturiers de vitrage isolant [★IO]
L'alliance canadienne des associations etudiantes [★IO]
The Alliance [★IO]
L'Alliance 7 [★IO]
Alliance for Academic Internal Medicine [8586], 2501 M St. NW, Ste. 550, Washington, DC 20037-1325, (202)861-9351
Alliance for Acid Rain Control and Energy Policy - Defunct.
Alliance; Acupuncture and Oriental Medicine [13607]
Alliance for Advancing Nonprofit Hea. Care [14606], PO Box 41015, Washington, DC 20018, (877)299-6497
Alliance of African American Artists Found. - Address unknown since 2007.
Alliance Against Counterfeiting and Piracy [★IO]
Alliance Against Fraud in Telemarketing and Electronic Commerce [17302], c/o Natl. Consumers League, 1701 K St. NW, Ste. 1200, Washington, DC 20006, (202)835-3323
Alliance Against IP and Theft [IO], London, United Kingdom
Alliance Against Sexual Coercion - Defunct.
Alliance Against the Uniformed Services Former Spouses Protection Act (USFSPA) Law [6112]
Alliance for Aging Res. [11272], 2021 K St. NW, Ste. 305, Washington, DC 20006-1003, (202)293-2856
Alliance for Alternatives in Healthcare [13609], PO Box 730605, San Jose, CA 95119, (408)223-1787
Alliance for Am. [11807], PO Box 1018, Spearfish, SD 57783, (518)835-6702
Alliance of the Amer. Dental Assn. [14092], 211 E Chicago Ave., Ste. 730, Chicago, IL 60611, (312)440-2865
Alliance of Amer. Insurers [★2232]
Alliance of Amer. Insurers - Defunct.
Alliance for Amer. Quilts [9823], PO Box 6521, Louisville, KY 40206, (502)897-3819
Alliance of Amer. and Russian Women [13418]
Alliance for Animals [11344], 232 Silver St., South Boston, MA 02127-2206, (617)268-7800
Alliance of Area Bus. Publications [3199], c/o C. James Dowden, Exec. Dir., 4929 Wilshire Blvd., Ste. 428, Los Angeles, CA 90010, (323)937-5514
Alliance of Artists and Recording Companies [3346], 700 N Fairfax St., Ste. 601, Alexandria, VA 22314, (703)535-8101
Alliance for the Arts [9535], 330 W 42nd St., Ste. 1701, New York, NY 10036, (212)947-6340
Alliance for Arts and Culture [★IO]
Alliance for Arts Educ. [★7975]
Alliance for Asian Amer. Arts and Culture [★9552]
Alliance of Assns. for the Advancement of Education - Defunct.
Alliance of Atomic Veterans - Defunct.
Alliance of Auto. Mfrs. [368], 1401 Eye St. NW, Ste. 900, Washington, DC 20005, (202)326-5500
Alliance of Auto. Manufacturers [IO], Washington, DC, United States
Alliance for Balanced Environmental Solutions - Defunct.
Alliance for Better Foods [4674]
Alliance for Beverage Cartons and the Env. - Belgium [IO], Brussels, Belgium
Alliance for Beverage Cartons and the Env. - United Kingdom [IO], Wrexham, United Kingdom
Alliance Biblique du Togo [★IO]
Alliance Bielarusienne du Canada [★IO]
Alliance of Canadian Cinema, TV and Radio Artists [IO], Toronto, ON, Canada

Reference to "IO" in place of a book number signifies that the association may be found in the 45th edition of International Organizations.

Alliance for Canadian New Music Proj. [IO], Toronto, ON, Canada

Alliance Canadienne du Camionnage [★IO]

Alliance Canadienne Contre le vol de Logiciels [★IO]

Alliance Canadienne de Massotherapeutes [★IO]

Alliance Canadienne pour la Paix [★IO]

Alliance Canadienne des Responsables et Enseignants en Francais [★IO]

Alliance Canadienne des Victimes d'Accidents et de Maladies du Travail [★IO]

L'Alliance de vie active des Canadiens/Canadiennes ayant un handicap [★IO]

Alliance for Cannabis Therapeutics - Address unknown since 2000.

Alliance for Capital Access - Defunct.

Alliance of Cardiovascular Professionals [13885], PO Box 2007, Midlothian, VA 23113, (804)632-0078

Alliance Champlain [★IO]

Alliance for Child Survival - Defunct.

Alliance for Childhood Cancer [13787], c/o Jay Ingram, 1900 Duke St., Ste. 200, Alexandria, VA 22314, (703)299-1050

Alliance for Children and Families [12136], 11700 W Lake Park Dr., Milwaukee, WI 53224-3099, (414)359-1040

Alliance for Children and Families [IO], Milwaukee, WI, United States

Alliance for Children and TV [IO], Montreal, QC, Canada

Alliance of Claims Assistance Professionals [2126], c/o Lisa Norris, ACAP, Pres., 25500 Hawthorne Blvd., Ste. 1158, Torrance, CA 90505, (888)394-5163

Alliance for Clean Energy - Defunct.

Alliance for a Clean Rural Environment - Defunct.

Alliance for Communities in Action [12416]

Alliance of Community Hea. Plans [14678], 1729 H St. NW, Ste. 400, Washington, DC 20006, (202)785-2247

Alliance for Community Media [17161], 666 11th St. NW, Ste. 740, Washington, DC 20001, (202)393-2650

Alliance for Community Trees [4678], 4603 Calvert Rd., College Park, MD 20740-3421, (301)277-0040

Alliance for Consumer Rights [17303], c/o New York State Trial Lawyers Assn., 132 Nassau St., 2nd Fl., New York, NY 10038, (212)349-5890

Alliance for Continuing Medical Educ. [8841], 1025 Montgomery Hwy., Ste. 105, Southcrest Bldg., Birmingham, AL 35216, (205)824-1355

Alliance Cooperative Internationale [★IO]

Alliance Credit Counseling [11833], 15720 John J. Delaney Dr., Ste. 100, Charlotte, NC 28277, (704)341-1010

Alliance for Cultural Democracy [9536], PO Box 192244, San Francisco, CA 94119-2244, (415)821-9652

Alliance for Customers' Telecommunications Rights; TeleTruth: The [17346]

Alliance of the Danube Swabians of Canada [IO], Scarborough, ON, Canada

Alliance of Deep Found. Testing Professionals [6650], 5 del Valle, Orinda, CA 94563, (925)254-0460

Alliance Defense Fund [17372], 15333 N Pima Rd., Ste. 165, Scottsdale, AZ 85260, (800)835-5233

Alliance for Democracy [18386], PO Box 540115, Waltham, MA 02454-0115, (781)894-1179

Alliance for Democracy in Korea - Defunct.

Alliance Des Arts Mediatiques Independants [★IO]

Alliance for Eating Disorders Awareness [14297], PO Box 13155, North Palm Beach, FL 33408-3155, (561)841-0900

Alliance to End Childhood Lead Poisoning [★13320]

Alliance to End Hunger [12387], c/o Bread for the World Inst., 50 F St. NW, No. 500, Washington, DC 20001, (202)639-9400

Alliance to End Repression [★17128]

Alliance of Energy Suppliers [1284], c/o Edison Elec. Inst., 701 Pennsylvania Ave. NW, Washington, DC 20004-2696, (202)508-5000

Alliance for Engineering in Medicine and Biology - Defunct.

Alliance for Environmental Education - Address unknown since 2003.

Alliance for Environmental Tech. [1632], 1250 24th St. NW, Ste. 300, Washington, DC 20037, (800)999-PULP

Alliance of European Voluntary Ser. Organizations [IO], Copenhagen, Denmark

Alliance Europeenne pour l'Ethique en Publicite [★IO]

Alliance for Excellent Educ. [9118], 1201 Connecticut Ave. NW, Ste. 901, Washington, DC 20036, (202)828-0828

Alliance for Fair Competition [★3613]

Alliance for Fire and Emergency Mgt. [★5720]

Alliance for Fire and Emergency Mgt. [★IO]

Alliance of Foam Packaging Recyclers [5265], 1298 Cronson Blvd., Ste. 201, Crofton, MD 21114, (410)451-8340

Alliance de la Fonction Publique du Canada [★IO]

Alliance For Animal Rights [IO], Dublin, Ireland

Alliance Francaise [★IO]

Alliance Francaise; French Inst. [9968]

Alliance Francaise de New York [★9968]

Alliance of France [IO], Paris, France

Alliance of Free Democrats [IO], Budapest, Hungary

Alliance for Full Acceptance [12213], PO Box 22088, Charleston, SC 29413, (843)883-0343

Alliance for Gay and Lesbian Artists in the Entertainment Industry - Defunct.

Alliance of Genetic Support Groups [★15246]

Alliance of Genetic Support Groups [★16536]

Alliance of Girls' Schools Australasia [IO], Hobart, Australia

Alliance for Global Sustainability [IO], Zurich, Switzerland

Alliance Graphique Internationale [IO], Zurich, Switzerland

Alliance of Guardian Angels [★IO]

Alliance of Guardian Angels [IO], New York, NY, United States

Alliance of Guardian Angels [11834], 717 5th Ave., Ste. 401, New York, NY 10022, (212)860-5575

Alliance of Guardian Angels [★11834]

Alliance for Guidance of Rural Youth - Defunct.

Alliance for Hea. Reform [17687], 1444 Eye St. NW, Ste. 910, Washington, DC 20005-6573, (202)789-2300

Alliance for Healthcare Strategy and Marketing [2612]

Alliance for Healthy Homes [13320], PO Box 75941, Washington, DC 20013, (202)543-1147

Alliance for Higher Educ. [8477], 2602 Rutford Ave., Richardson, TX 75080, (972)713-8170

The Alliance for Human Empowerment [★18637]

Alliance for Human Res. Protection [17741], 142 W End Ave., Ste. 28P, New York, NY 10023

Alliance for Immigration Reform - Defunct.

Alliance for Inclusion in the Arts [10996], 1560 Broadway, Ste. 1600, New York, NY 10036, (212)730-4750

Alliance of Independent Academic Medical Centers [15085], 401 N Michigan Ave., Ste. 1200, Chicago, IL 60611, (312)836-3712

Alliance of Independent Retailers [IO], Worcester, United Kingdom

Alliance of Independent Retailers and Businesses [★IO]

Alliance of Independent Scholars - Address unknown since 2003.

Alliance of Info. and Referral Systems [7187], 11240 Waples Mill Rd., Ste. 200, Fairfax, VA 22030, (703)218-2477

Alliance of Information and Referral Systems [IO], Fairfax, VA, United States

Alliance for Intl. Conflict Prevention and Resolution [★IO]

Alliance for Intl. Conflict Prevention and Resolution [★17248]

Alliance for Intl. Educational and Cultural Exchange [8591], 1776 Massachusetts Ave. NW, Ste. 620, Washington, DC 20036-1912, (202)293-6141

Alliance for Intl. Educational and Cultural Exchange [IO], Washington, DC, United States

Alliance of Intl. Market Res. Institutes [IO], London, United Kingdom

Alliance for Intl. Monasticism [IO], Vanves, France

Alliance for Intl. Reforestation [4344], 421 N Woodland Blvd., Unit 8301, DeLand, FL 32723, (386)822-7575

Alliance Internationale des Femmes [★IO]

Alliance Internationale des Femmes - Droits Egaux - Responsabilites Egales [★IO]

Alliance Internationale Pour le Merite - Address unknown since 2004.

Alliance Internationale de Tourisme [★IO]

Alliance Israelite Universelle [★IO]

Alliance Israelite Universelle [★8675]

Alliance Israelite Universelle [★17947]

Alliance Israelite Universelle; Amer. Friends of the [8675]

Alliance Israelite Universelle; Canadian Friends of the [★17947]

Alliance Israelite Universelle; Canadian Friends of the [★IO]

Alliance for Jewish Renewal; ALEPH: [18141]

Alliance for Justice [6219], 11 Dupont Cir. NW, 2nd Fl., Washington, DC 20036, (202)822-6070

Alliance for Labor Action - Defunct.

Alliance of Latin Artistes Soc. - Defunct.

Alliance for Leadership Development - Defunct.

Alliance pour l'Enfant et la TV [★IO]

Alliance for Life Ministries [19760], PO Box 5468, Madison, WI 53705, (608)833-5569

Alliance of Light Artists - Defunct.

Alliance de L'Industrie Canadienne de L'Aquiculture [★IO]

Alliance of Literary Societies [IO], Havant, United Kingdom

Alliance for Lung Cancer Advocacy, Support and Educ. [13788]

Alliance for Lupus Res. [15013], 28 W 44th St., Ste. 1217, New York, NY 10036, (212)218-2840

Alliance for Lupus Res. [IO], New York, NY, United States

Alliance of Mfrs. and Exporters Canada [★IO]

Alliance of Marine Mammal Parks and Aquariums [IO], Brooklyn, NY, United States

Alliance of Marine Mammal Parks and Aquariums [5006], c/o Dave DeNardo, WCS/New York Aquarium, W 8th and Surf Ave., Coney Island, Brooklyn, NY 11224

Alliance for Maritime Heritage Conservation - Address unknown since 1995.

Alliance of Maritime Regional Interests in Europe [IO], Brussels, Belgium

Alliance for Marriage [12504], PO Box 2490, Merrifield, VA 22116-2490, (703)934-1212

Alliance for a Media Literate Am. [8830], 721 Glencoe St., Denver, CO 80220, (888)775-2652

Alliance of Merger and Acquisition Advisors [54], 150 N Michigan Ave., Ste. 2700, Chicago, IL 60601, (312)856-9590

Alliance of Metalworking Industries - Defunct.

Alliance of Microbicide Development [13555], 8484 Georgia Ave., Ste. 940, Silver Spring, MD 20910, (301)587-9690

Alliance of Minority Medical Associations [14607], 1200 New Hampshire Ave. NW, Ste. 575, Washington, DC 20036, (202)223-7560

Alliance of Minority Women for Bus. and Political Development [2759], c/o Brenda Alford, Pres., 1316 Fenwick, Ste. 908, Silver Spring, MD 20910, (301)585-8051

L'Alliance Monarchiste - Address unknown since 2000.

Alliance pour la Monde Responsable, Pluriel et Solidaire [★IO]

Alliance Mondiale des Unions Chretiennes Feminines [★IO]

Alliance des Moniteurs de Ski du Canada [★IO]

Alliance of Motion Picture and TV Producers [1375], 15503 Ventura Blvd., Encino, CA 91436, (818)995-3600

Alliance of Natl. Heritage Areas [9856], 221 Essex St., Ste. 41, Salem, MA 01970, (202)528-7549

Alliance for Natl. Renewal - Defunct.

Alliance Nationale des Unions Chretiennes de Jeunes Gens de France [★IO]

Alliance for Neighborhood Govt. [★11752]

Alliance for a New Trans. Charter [6311], c/o Surface Trans. Policy Proj., 1100 17th St. NW, 10th Fl., Washington, DC 20036, (202)466-2636

A star before a book entry number signifies that the name is not listed separately, but is mentioned within the entry.

Alliance New Zealand [IO], Glendene, New Zealand

Alliance of NGOs on Crime Prevention and Criminal Justice - Address unknown since 2002.

Alliance of Nonprofit Mailers [2445], 1211 Connecticut Ave. NW, Ste. 620, Washington, DC 20036-2701, (202)462-5132

Alliance for Nonprofit Mgt. [313], 1899 L St. NW, 6th Fl., Washington, DC 20036, (202)955-8406

Alliance for Nuclear Accountability [18125], 1914 N 34th St., Ste. 407, Seattle, WA 98103-9091, (206)547-3175

Alliance for Opportunity - Defunct.

Alliance of the Orders of St. John of Jerusalem [IO], Basel, Switzerland

Alliance of Organisations of Disabled People Slovakia [IO], Bratislava, Slovakia

Alliance of Pan Amer. Round Tables - Address unknown since 1995.

Alliance Party of Northern Ireland [IO], Belfast, United Kingdom

Alliance for a Paving Moratorium [17234], c/o Culture Change, PO Box 4347, Arcata, CA 95518, (215)243-3144

Alliance for Peacebuilding [17248], 11 Dupont Cir. NW, Ste. 200, Washington, DC 20036, (202)822-6135

Alliance for Peacebuilding [IO], Washington, DC, United States

Alliance for Perinatal Res. and Services - Address unknown since 1987.

Alliance for Philippine Concerns - Defunct.

Alliance of Pile Testing Lab. Engineers [★6650]

Alliance of Poles of Am. [19300]

Alliance for the Polyurethanes Indus. (A Bus. Unit of the Amer. Plastics Coun.) [★3047]

Alliance of Practicing Certified Public Accountants [6], 12149 Fremont St., Yucaipa, CA 92399, (909)705-7505

Alliance des Producteurs de Cacao [★IO]

Alliance of Professional Consultants [952], PO Box 441350, Aurora, CO 80044, (303)607-7566

Alliance of Professional Tattooists [3714], 9210 S Hwy. 17-92, Maitland, FL 32751, (407)831-5549

Alliance pour des Projets de Musique Canadienne Nouvelle [★IO]

Alliance for the Prudent Use of Antibiotics [15908], 75 Kneeland St., Boston, MA 02111-1901, (617)636-0966

Alliance for Public Tech. [7723], 919 18th St. NW, Ste. 900, Washington, DC 20006, (202)263-2970

Alliance for Rail Competition [3275], 101 Constitution Ave. NW, Ste. 800, Washington, DC 20001, (202)742-4435

Alliance Reformee Mondiale [★IO]

Alliance of Registered Homeopaths [IO], East Sussex, United Kingdom

Alliance of Religions and Conservation [IO], Bath, United Kingdom

Alliance of Resident Theatres/New York [10997], 575 8th Ave., Ste. 1720, New York, NY 10018-3054, (212)244-6667

Alliance for Responsible Atmospheric Policy [797], 2111 Wilson Blvd., Ste. 850, Arlington, VA 22201, (703)243-0344

Alliance for Responsible CFC Policy [★797]

Alliance for a Responsible, Plural and United World [IO], Paris, France

Alliance for Responsible Trade [IO], Hyattsville, MD, United States

Alliance for Responsible Trade [3836], PO Box 5206, Hyattsville, MD 20782, (301)699-0042

Alliance for Retired Americans [18543], 815 16th St. NW, 4th Fl., Washington, DC 20006, (202)637-5399

Alliance of Rhetoric Societies [10935], c/o David Henry, Exec. Sec., Univ. of Nevada, Greenspun School of Commun., Box 454052, Las Vegas, NV 89154-4052, (702)895-3030

Alliance for Safe Teenage Driving - Address unknown since 2006.

Alliance to Save Energy [6934], 1850 M St. NW, Ste. 600, Washington, DC 20036-5817, (202)857-0666

Alliance for Sci. and Tech. Res. in Am. [7595], Othmer Bldg., Rm. 320, 1155 16th St. NW, Washington, DC 20036, (202)872-6160

Alliance of Secular Humanist Societies [10193], c/o Coun. for Secular Humanism, PO Box 664, Amherst, NY 14226-0664, (716)636-7571

Alliance for the Separation of School and State [8221], 1071 N Fulton St., Fresno, CA 93728-3433, (559)499-1776

Alliance of Short Fiction Authors; Natl. [11182]

Alliance for Simple, Equitable and Rational Truck Taxation - Address unknown since 1999.

Alliance of Small Island States [17827], c/o Dr. E. Angus Friday, Chm., 800 Second Ave., Ste. 400k, New York, NY 10017, (212)599-0301

Alliance of Small Island States [IO], New York, NY, United States

Alliance for Social Security and Disability Recipients - Defunct.

Alliance de Societes Feminines Suisses [★IO]

Alliance for South Asian AIDS Prevention [IO], Toronto, ON, Canada

Alliance for Southern African Progress [IO], Astoria, NY, United States

Alliance for Southern African Progress [12417], 1424 31st Ave., Ste. 3R, Astoria, NY 11106, (877)375-5778

Alliance of State Car and Truck Renting and Leasing Assns. - Defunct.

Alliance of State Pain Initiatives [15830], 1300 Univ. Ave., Rm. 4720, Madison, WI 53706, (608)265-4013

Alliance in Support of Independent Res. [3390], c/o Lee A. Pickard, Counsel, 1990 M St. NW, Ste. 660, Washington, DC 20036, (202)223-4418

Alliance for Sustainability [4641], c/o Hillel Center, Univ. of Minnesota, 1521 Univ. Ave. SE, Minneapolis, MN 55414, (612)331-1099

Alliance for Sustainable Jobs and the Env. [24053], PO Box 1361, Eureka, CA 95502, (707)498-4481

Alliance for a Tax Free Am. - Address unknown since 2007.

Alliance for Tech. Access [11915], 1304 Southpoint Blvd., Ste. 240, Petaluma, CA 94954, (707)778-3011

Alliance for Telecommunications Indus. Solutions [3731], 1200 G St. NW, Ste. 500, Washington, DC 20005, (202)628-6380

Alliance for Telephone Progress - Defunct.

Alliance for Third-Class Nonprofit Mailers [★2445]

Alliance for Traffic Safety - Defunct.

Alliance for Transforming the Lives of Children [11554], 901 Preston Ave., Ste. 400, Charlottesville, VA 22903, (206)666-4301

Alliance of Transylvanian Saxons [19117], 5393 Pearl Rd., Cleveland, OH 44129-1597, (440)842-8442

Alliance of Tribal Tourism Advocates [19267], 522 7th St., Ste. 210, Rapid City, SD 57701, (605)545-3351

Alliance of Unitarian Women [★20604]

Alliance of Universities for Democracy [IO], Pecs, Hungary

Alliance of Veterinarians for the Env. [4626], c/o Gwen Griffith, DVM, 836 W Hillwood Dr., Nashville, TN 37205, (615)353-0272

Alliance for Volunteerism - Defunct.

Alliance of Warehouses and Feds. - Defunct.

Alliance of Women in Architecture - Address unknown since 1989.

Alliance of Women Bikers - Defunct.

Alliance of Women Road Riders and Associates - Address unknown since 1994.

Alliance for Women's Equality [13455], 25 Washington St., 4th Fl., Brooklyn, NY 11201, (718)237-8761

Alliance for Work-Life Progress [3179], 14040 N Northsight Blvd., Scottsdale, AZ 85260-3601, (480)922-2007

Alliance for Worker Freedom [24217], 1920 L St. NW, Ste. 200, Washington, DC 20036, (202)785-0266

Alliance for Worker Retirement Security [18544], c/o Derrick A. Max, Exec. Dir., 1331 Pennsylvania Ave. NW, Ste. 600, Washington, DC 20004-1751, (202)637-3453

Alliance for Youth; America's Promise - The [13470]

Allianz-China Mission [★IO]

Allied Airborne Assn. - Defunct.

Allied Artists of Am. [9487], 15 Gramercy Park S, New York, NY 10003, (212)582-6411

Allied Beauty Assn. [IO], Mississauga, ON, Canada

Allied Bd. of Trade [2249]

Allied Brewery Traders Assn. [★IO]

Allied Comm. of the Peoples of Eastern Turkmenistan, Inner Mongolia and Tibet - Address unknown since 2002.

Allied Craftsworkers; Intl. Coun. of Employers of Bricklayers and [★1029]

Allied Craftsworkers; Intl. Union of Bricklayers and [1029]

Allied Distribution, Inc. [3975], PO Box 607, Eagle River, WI 54521, (715)479-3530

Allied Exhibitors - Defunct.

Allied Farm Equip. Manufacturers Assn. [★179]

Allied Finance Adjusters Conf. - Defunct.

Allied Hea. Educ. and Accreditation; Comm. on [★8832]

Allied Hea. Educ. Programs; Commn. on Accreditation of [8832]

Allied Hea. Personnel in Ophthalmology; Joint Commn. on [15692]

Allied Linens and Domestics Assn. - Defunct.

Allied Lines [★21059]

Allied Pilots Assn. [24007], 14600 Trinity Blvd., Ste. 500, O'Connell Bldg., Fort Worth, TX 76155-2512, (817)302-2272

Allied Purchasing Company [1127], PO Box 1249, Mason City, IA 50402, (800)247-5956

Allied Social Sci. Associations [7645], 2014 Broadway, Ste. 305, Nashville, TN 37203, (615)322-2595

Allied States Assn. of Motion Picture Exhibitors [★1315]

Allied States Assn. of Motion Picture Exhibitors [★IO]

Allied Stone Indus. [3689], c/o Gary Weller, Pres., 40 Rolling Rock Rd., Boyertown, PA 19512, (610)987-6226

Allied Trades of the Baking Indus. [443], c/o Cereal Food Processors, Inc., 2001 Shawnee Mission Pkwy., Mission Woods, KS 66205, (913)890-6300

Allied Trades; Intl. Union of Painters and [24146]

Allied Underwear Assn. - Address unknown since 1994.

Allied Youth [★13465]

Allied Youth and Family Counseling Center [13465]

Allies Building Community [9613], PO Box 57250, Washington, DC 20037-0250, (202)496-1555

Allison Family Assn. [20778], c/o Sandra Allison, Chair, 10095 County Rd. 5120, Rolla, MO 65401-9717, (573)341-3549

Allison Smith Fan Club - Address unknown since 1999.

Alloway Family Assn. - Defunct.

Alloy Casting Inst. [★2070]

Alloy Casting Inst. [★IO]

Alloys Assn; The Ferro [★2734]

Allton, Alton, Aulton Family Assn. [20779], c/o Cecil C. Alton, Ed., 15510 Laurel Ridge Rd., Dumfries, VA 22026-1019, (703)670-4842

ALMA Soc. - Adoptees' Liberty Movement Assn. [11232], PO Box 85, Denville, NJ 07834

Alma Wesley Millet Family Org. - Defunct.

Almond Bd. of California [5048], 1150 9th St., Ste. 1500, Modesto, CA 95354, (209)549-8262

Almond Control Bd. [★5048]

Almond Growers Exchange; California [★5052]

Almshouse Assn. [IO], Wokingham, United Kingdom

Aloe Tech. Assn. - Defunct.

Aloha Intl. [12340], PO Box 426, Volcano, HI 96785, (808)826-1643

Aloha Intl. [IO], Volcano, HI, United States

Alopecia Areata Found; Natl. [16386]

Alpaca Assn. New Zealand [IO], Christchurch, New Zealand

Alpaca Assn; Rocky Mountain Llama and [4148]

Alpaca Breeders of the Rockies [4992], c/o Ron Hinds, Dir., 5704 Canyon Trail, Elizabeth, CO 80107, (303)646-1320

Alpaca Llama Show Assn. [21514], c/o Marilyn Nenni, Sec., 10912 E 166th St., Noblesville, IN 46060, (317)773-1201

Reference to "IO" in place of a book number signifies that the association may be found in the 45th edition of International Organizations.

Alpaca Owners and Breeders Assn. [4120], 5000 Linbar Dr., Ste. 297, Nashville, TN 37211, (615)834-4195

Alpenlite Travel Club [22940], PO Box 1726, Clackamas, OR 97015, (503)698-4461

Alpha 1 Antitrypsin Support Gp. [★16353]

Alpha-1 Assn. [16353], 2937 SW 27th Ave., Ste. 106, Miami, FL 33133, (305)648-0088

Alpha 1 Found. [14439], 2937 SW 27th Ave., Ste. 302, Miami, FL 33133, (305)567-9888

Alpha-66 [17363], PO Box 420067, Miami, FL 33142, (305)541-5433

Alpha-66 [IO], Miami, FL, United States

Alpha Alpha Gamma - Defunct.

Alpha Beta Chap; Rho Chi - [24571]

Alpha Beta Gamma [★24425]

Alpha Beta Gamma [★IO]

Alpha Beta Gamma Intl. [IO], Valhalla, NY, United States

Alpha Beta Gamma Intl. [24425], 75 Grasslands Rd., Valhalla, NY 10595, (914)606-6877

Alpha Center [★14535]

Alpha Chi [24498], Harding Univ., HU Box 12249, 900 E Center Ave., Searcy, AR 72149-0001, (501)279-4443

Alpha Chi Omega [24673], 5939 Castle Creek Pkwy., North Dr., Indianapolis, IN 46250-4343, (317)579-5050

Alpha Chi Omega Foundation [★24673]

Alpha Chi Rho [24606], 109 Oxford Way, Neptune, NJ 07753, (732)869-1895

Alpha Chi Sigma [24428], 2141 N Franklin Rd., Indianapolis, IN 46219-2497, (800)ALCHEMY

Alpha Delta Gamma [24607], 946 Sanders Dr., St. Louis, MO 63126

Alpha Delta Kappa [24449], 1615 W 92nd St., Kansas City, MO 64114, (816)363-5525

Alpha Delta Kappa [IO], Kansas City, MO, United States

Alpha Delta Phi [24608], 6126 Lincoln Ave., Morton Grove, IL 60053, (847)965-1832

Alpha Delta Pi [24609], 1386 Ponce de Leon Ave. NE, Atlanta, GA 30306, (404)378-3164

Alpha Delta Tau Fraternity [★24503]

Alpha Delta Theta - Defunct.

Alpha Development Gp. - Address unknown since 2004.

Alpha Epsilon [24395], c/o Dr. Joseph L. Purswell, Sec.-Treas., PO Box 5367, Mississippi State, MS 39762, (662)320-7480

Alpha Epsilon Delta [24541], c/o Natl. Off., James Madison Univ., MSC 9015, Harrisonburg, VA 22807, (540)568-2594

Alpha Epsilon; Kappa Sigma [★24463]

Alpha Epsilon Phi [24674], 11 Lake Ave. Extension, Ste. 1A, Danbury, CT 06811, (203)748-0029

Alpha Epsilon Pi [24610], 8815 Wesleyan Rd., Indianapolis, IN 46268-1171, (317)876-1913

Alpha Epsilon Pi Found. [★24610]

Alpha Epsilon Rho [★24411]

Alpha Epsilon Rho; Natl. Broadcasting Soc. - [24411]

Alpha Eta Rho - Address unknown since 1999.

Alpha Gamma Delta [24675], 8701 Founders Rd., Indianapolis, IN 46268, (317)872-2655

Alpha Gamma Rho [24396], 10101 N Ambassador Dr., Kansas City, MO 64153-1395, (816)891-9200

Alpha Gamma Upsilon [★24616]

Alpha Iota Delta [24412], c/o Ms. Shirley Groves, Admin. Coor., Georgia State Univ., J. Mack Robinson Coll. of Bus., 35 Broad St., Ste. 1022, Atlanta, GA 30303, (404)651-4056

Alpha Iota Omicron [24611], 1040 Hampton St., Atlanta, GA 30318, (850)832-8864

Alpha Iota Sorority [24413], PO Box 223223, Chantilly, VA 20153-3223, (703)378-8010

Alpha Iota Sorority [IO], Chantilly, VA, United States

Alpha Kappa Alpha [24595], 5656 S Stony Island Ave., Chicago, IL 60637, (773)684-1282

Alpha Kappa Delta [24701], c/o Marc Matre, Sec.-Treas., Box U-1147, Mobile, AL 36688, (251)460-7567

Alpha Kappa Delta [IO], Mobile, AL, United States

Alpha Kappa Kappa - Defunct.

Alpha Kappa Lambda [24612], 4735 Statesmen Dr., Ste. F, Indianapolis, IN 46250, (317)585-4911

Alpha Kappa Lambda Educational Foundation [★24612]

Alpha Kappa Mu [24499], 101 Longwood Ln., Greenwood, SC 29646, (864)229-1546

Alpha Kappa Phi [★24527]

Alpha Kappa Pi [★24616]

Alpha Kappa Psi [24414], 7801 E 88th St., Indianapolis, IN 46256-1233, (317)872-1553

Alpha Lambda Tau Intl. Social Fraternity [24613], 11003 Santorini Dr., Las Vegas, NV 89141-3938, (702)362-5276

Alpha Lambda Tau Intl. Social Fraternity [IO], Las Vegas, NV, United States

Alpha Micro Users Soc. - Defunct.

Alpha Mu Gamma [★24525]

Alpha Mu Gamma [24525], 855 N Vermont Ave., CMB 1009, Los Angeles, CA 90029, (323)644-9752

Alpha Mu Sigma - Defunct.

Alpha Omega Alpha [★24542]

Alpha Omega Alpha Honor Medical Soc. [24542], 525 Middlefield Rd., Ste. 130, Menlo Park, CA 94025, (650)329-0291

Alpha Omega Assn. [9537], c/o Harry W. Miller, 190 Peach Blossom Ln., Bowling Green, KY 42103, (270)843-2300

Alpha Omega Intl. Dental Fraternity [24437], 55 Harristown Rd., 2nd Fl., Glen Rock, NJ 07452, (201)447-0707

Alpha Omega Intl. Dental Fraternity [IO], Princeton Junction, NJ, United States

Alpha Omicron Pi [24676], 5390 Virginia Way, Brentwood, TN 37027, (615)370-0920

Alpha Phi Alpha Fraternity [24590], 2313 St. Paul St., Baltimore, MD 21218-5211, (410)554-0040

Alpha Phi Delta [24414], PO Box 200, Struthers, OH 44471, (330)755-1891

Alpha Phi Intl. Fraternity [24677], 1930 Sherman Ave., Evanston, IL 60201, (847)475-0663

Alpha Phi Intl. Fraternity [IO], Evanston, IL, United States

Alpha Phi Omega Natl. Ser. Fraternity [24591], 14901 E 42nd St., Independence, MO 64055-7347, (816)373-8667

Alpha Phi Sigma Honorary Scholastic Society [24450]

Alpha Pi Chi - Address unknown since 1999.

Alpha Pi Mu [24458], c/o Dr. Robert D. Dryden, Exec. Dir., PO Box 773, Portland, OR 97207-0773, (503)297-3604

Alpha Pi Omega - Address unknown since 2006.

Alpha Pi Sigma [24474], PO Box 3814, Torrance, CA 90510

Alpha Psi - Defunct.

Alpha Psi Lambda Natl. [24615], PO Box A3152, Chicago, IL 60690-3512

Alpha Psi Omega [24443], c/o Dr. Bret Jones, Natl. Bus. Mgr., East Central Univ., 1100 E 14th St., Ada, OK 74820, (580)310-5756

Alpha Rho Lambda Sorority [24703], 65 Hammell Pl., Maywood, NJ 07607

Alpha Sigma Alpha [24678], 9550 Zionsville Rd., Ste. 160, Indianapolis, IN 46268, (317)871-2920

Alpha Sigma Chi - Defunct.

Alpha Sigma Lambda - Address unknown since 1999.

Alpha Sigma Nu [24500], PO Box 1881, Milwaukee, WI 53201-1881, (414)288-0271

Alpha Sigma Nu [IO], Milwaukee, WI, United States

Alpha Sigma Phi [24616], 710 Adams St., Carmel, IN 46032, (317)843-1911

Alpha Sigma Tau [★24500]

Alpha Sigma Tau [24679], 1929 Canyon Rd., Birmingham, AL 35216, (205)978-2179

Alpha Sigma Tau [★IO]

Alpha Tau Alpha [24394], c/o Dr. Tim Buttles, Sec.-Treas., Univ. of Wisconsin - River Falls, Dept. of Agricultural Education, 410 S Third St., River Falls, WI 54022-5001, (715)425-3555

Alpha Tau Delta [24559], c/o Susan Carson, Pres., 11252 Camarillo St., Toluca Lake, CA 91602

Alpha Tau Omega [24617], One N Pennsylvania St., 12th Fl., Indianapolis, IN 46204, (317)684-1865

Alpha Xi Delta Women's Fraternity [24680], 8702 Founders Rd., Indianapolis, IN 46268, (317)872-3500

Alpha Zeta [24397], 16020 Swingley Ridge Rd., Ste. 300, Chesterfield, MO 63017, (636)449-5090

Alpha Zeta Beta - Address unknown since 1995.

Alpha Zeta Omega [24567], 4422 Porpoise Dr., Tampa, FL 33617-8316

Alpha Zeta Pi [★24526]

Alphabetisation mondiale Canada [★IO]

Alpine
    Alpine Tourist Commn. [24223]
    Amer. Alpine Club [7074]
    Working Group of Alpine Regions [IO]

Alpine Club; Amer. [7074]

Alpine Club of Canada [IO], Canmore, AB, Canada

Alpine Club - England [IO], London, United Kingdom

Alpine Coach Assn. [22941], 5808 A Summitview Ave., No. 337, Yakima, WA 98908, (509)853-2958

Alpine Garden Soc. [IO], Pershore, United Kingdom

Alpine and Schuhplattler Clubs in North Am; Fed. of [9627]

Alpine Tourist Commn. [24223], c/o Switzerland Tourism, PO Box 5513, 608 5th Ave., New York, NY 10020, (212)757-5944

Alpine Tourist Commn. [IO], Zurich, Switzerland

Alpines East; Tigers East/ [21796]

Alpines Intl. [4121], c/o Tina Antes, Sec.-Treas., 7195 City Rd. 315, Silt, CO 81652, (970)876-2738

Alpines Intl. [IO], Silt, CO, United States

ALS Assn. [★15306]

ALS Diagnostic Support Gp. [IO], Baarn, Netherlands

ALS Forbes Norris Res. Center [★15323]

ALS Found; Natl. [★15306]

ALS Liga Belgie [★IO]

ALS March of Faces [13666], 4594 Ashton Ct., Naples, FL 34112-8822, (239)404-9409

ALS and Neuromuscular Res. Found. [★15323]

ALS Res. Center [★15323]

ALS Res. Center; Forbes Norris MDA/ [15323]

ALS Res. Fund [IO], Baarn, Netherlands

ALS Support Gp. - Belgium [IO], Leuven, Belgium

ALSAC/Saint Jude Children's Res. Hosp. [13946], 332 N Lauderdale St., Memphis, TN 38105, (901)495-3300

Alston Wilkes Soc. [★11852]

Alston Wilkes Veterans Home [11852], c/o Palmetto State Base Camp, Inc., 3519 Medical Dr., Columbia, SC 29203, (803)748-7489

Alstrom Syndrome - Canada [IO], Finch, ON, Canada

Alstrom Syndrome Families; Intl. Soc. for [★14440]

Alstrom Syndrome Intl. [14440], 14 Whitney Farm Rd., Mount Desert, ME 04660, (207)288-6385

Alstrom Syndrome Intl. [IO], Mount Desert, ME, United States

Alstrom Syndrome Intl. - United Kingdom [IO], Paignton, United Kingdom

Alteraciones de Crecimiento/Desarrollo y Enfermedades Lisosomales [IO], Seville, Spain

Alternate Energy Inst. - Defunct.

Alternate Postal Systems; Assn. of [2447]

Alternating Hemiplegia of Childhood Vereniging Nederland [IO], Rhoon, Netherlands

Alternative Age of Healing Assn. - Address unknown since 2003.

Alternative Aquaculture Assn. [4167], 630 Independent Rd., Breinigsville, PA 18031, (610)398-1062

Alternative Birth Crisis Coalition - Defunct.

Alternative Broadcasting - Defunct.

Alternative Cancer Therapies; Found. for [★13824]

Alternative Education
    Adult Higher Educ. Alliance [7915]
    Amer. Assn. for Collegiate Independent Stud. [7944]
    Amer. Distance Educ. Consortium [8227]
    Assn. for Non-Traditional Students in Higher Educ. [7916]
    Assn. of Waldorf Schools of North Am. [8526]
    Australasian Assn. of Distance Educ. Schools [IO]
    Christian Home Educators Assn. of California [8516]
    Consciousness-Based Educ. Assn. [9029]
    Educational Center for Applied Ekistics [10228]
    Equine Guided Educ. Assn. [8524]
    Eta Sigma Alpha Natl. Home School Honor Soc. [8316]

A star before a book entry number signifies that the name is not listed separately, but is mentioned within the entry.

European Assn. of Distance Teaching Universities [IO]
Fed. Govt. Distance Learning Assn. [8256]
Inst. for Planetary Synthesis - Switzerland [IO]
Intl. Assn. for Learning Alternatives [7945]
Intl. Coun. for Open and Distance Educ. [IO]
Intl. Educ. and Rsrc. Network [8269]
Intl. Educ. and Rsrc. Network - Armenia [IO]
Intl. Educ. and Rsrc. Network - Canada [IO]
Intl. Educ. and Rsrc. Network - Egypt [IO]
Intl. Educ. and Rsrc. Network of Nepal [IO]
Intl. Educ. and Rsrc. Network of Sierra Leone [IO]
Intl. Educ. and Rsrc. Network - Trinidad and Tobago [IO]
Intl. Fed. of the Movements of Modern School [IO]
Intl. Fed. of Training Centers for the Promotion of Progressive Educ. [IO]
Natl. Assn. for Legal Support of Alternative Schools [7946]
Natl. Assn. of Private, Nontraditional Schools and Colleges [7947]
Natl. Black Home Educators [8519]
Natl. Coalition of Alternative Community Schools [7948]
North Amer. Coun. for Online Learning [7949]
North Amer. Coun. for Online Learning [IO]
Open and Distance Learning Assn. of Australia [IO]
Parents' Rights Org. [7950]
State Educational Tech. Directors Assn. [9244]
U.S. Distance Learning Assn. [8523]
Alternative Education Project - Address unknown since 2003.
Alternative Educ. Rsrc. Org. [8222], 417 Roslyn Rd., Roslyn Heights, NY 11577, (516)621-2195
Alternative Energy Assn. of America - Defunct.
Alternative Energy Resources Org. [6935], 432 N Last Chance Gulch St., Helena, MT 59601-5014, (406)443-7272
Alternative Energy Resources Org. [★6935]
Alternative Family Proj. [11814], Ctr. for Alternative Families, 425 Divisadero St., Ste. 203, San Francisco, CA 94117, (510)628-9065
Alternative Futures; Inst. for [7104]
Alternative Hea. and Fitness Assn. [10522], Lafferty Rd., Ste. 205, Pasadena, TX 77502, (713)378-9612
Alternative Hea. Insurance Services [★13609]
Alternative Hea. Professionals Assn. [13610], PO Box P, Aiken, SC 29802, (803)278-1002
Alternative Information Center - Defunct.
Alternative Information Network - Address unknown since 2004.
Alternative Investment Mgt. Assn. [IO], London, United Kingdom
Alternative Investment Mgt. Assn. - Australia [IO], Sydney, Australia
Alternative Investment Mgt. Assn. - Japan [IO], Tokyo, Japan

Alternative Lifestyles
Aloha Intl. [12340]
Alternatives to Marriage Proj. [18025]
Amer. Assn. for Nude Recreation [10760]
Amer. Vegan Soc. [11067]
BeachFront USA [10762]
Catholic Homesteading Movement [11742]
Center for Self-Sufficiency [11743]
Communal Stud. Assn. [10020]
Crossdressers Intl. [13089]
Earthstewards Network [12344]
Educational Center for Applied Ekistics [10228]
Everyday Ayurveda [13606]
Fed. of Egalitarian Communities [11746]
The FORUM [12346]
Hanuman Found. [12347]
HUNA Res. [12349]
Inst. for the Development of the Harmonious Human Being [12351]
Macro Soc. [10184]
The Naturist Soc. [10763]
North Amer. Man/Boy Love Assn. [13099]
Sacred Space Inst. [13101]
School of Living [10178]
Somatics Soc. [12363]

Vegan Action [11071]
Vegetarian Awareness Network [11072]
Wives of Older Men [12509]
Alternative Lifestyles; Soc. for the Stud. of [★13095]
Alternative Living Managers' Assn. - Defunct.
Alternative Medical Assn. - Address unknown since 2002.
Alternative Medicine
Acad. of Scientific Hypnotherapy [14913]
Accreditation Commn. for Acupuncture and Oriental Medicine [15739]
Acupuncture Found. of Canada Inst. [IO]
Acupuncture and Oriental Medicine Alliance [13607]
Acupuncturists Without Borders [13536]
Advocate Hea. Care [14821]
Alexander Technique Intl. [13608]
Alexander Technique Intl. [IO]
Alliance for Alternatives in Healthcare [13609]
Alternative Hea. Professionals Assn. [13610]
Amer. Acad. of Acupuncture and Oriental Medicine [13611]
Amer. Acad. of Alternative Medicine [13612]
Amer. Acupuncture Assn. [15741]
Amer. Alliance for Medical Cannabis [15020]
Amer. Alternative Medical Assn. [13613]
Amer. Apitherapy Soc. [13614]
Amer. Assn. of Drugless Practitioners [13615]
Amer. Assn. of Naturopathic Physicians [15280]
Amer. Assn. of Oriental Medicine [15742]
Amer. Assn. of Professional Hypnotherapists [14915]
Amer. Bd. of Alternative Medicine [13616]
Amer. Bd. of Alternative Medicine [IO]
Amer. Bd. of Psychological Hypnosis [14917]
Amer. Center for the Alexander Technique [13617]
Amer. Coll. of Nurse-Midwives [15447]
Amer. Guild of Hypnotherapists [14919]
Amer. Herbalists Guild [14817]
Amer. Holistic Hea. Assn. [14823]
Amer. Holistic Medical Assn. [14824]
Amer. Holistic Nurses' Assn. [14825]
Amer. Holistic Veterinary Medical Assn. [16773]
Amer. Inst. of Homeopathy [14845]
Amer. Integrative Medical Assn. [15034]
Amer. Manual Medicine Assn. [13618]
Amer. Massage Therapy Assn. [15022]
Amer. Naprapathic Assn. [15276]
Amer. Naturopathic Medical Assn. [15281]
Amer. Nutraceutical Assn. [14612]
Amer. Org. for Bodywork Therapies of Asia [15024]
Amer. Polarity Therapy Assn. [13619]
Amer. Qigong Assn. [13620]
Amer. Reflexology Certification Bd. [13621]
Amer. Reiki Master Assn. [13622]
Amer. Soc. for the Alexander Technique [13623]
Amer. Soc. of Alternative Therapists [13624]
Amer. Soc. of Clinical Hypnosis [14921]
Amer. Soc. of Clinical Hypnosis - Educ. and Res. Found. [14922]
Amer. Tai Chi Assn. [16593]
Archaeus Proj. [13625]
Assn. of Accredited Naturopathic Medical Colleges [8943]
Assn. for Applied Poetry [16211]
Assn. for Applied and Therapeutic Humor [16605]
Assn. for Childbirth at Home, Intl. [15591]
Assn. for Holotropic Breathwork Intl. [13626]
Assn. for Integrative Hea. Care Practitioners [15037]
Assn. of Reflexologists [IO]
Assn. for Therapeutic Eurythmy in North Am. [16608]
Australian Acupuncture and Chinese Medicine Assn. [IO]
Austrian Soc. for Acupuncture [IO]
Biofeedback Found. of Europe [IO]
Brazilian Medical Spiritist Assn. [IO]
British Acupuncture Coun. [IO]
British Holistic Medical Assn. [IO]
British Homeopathic Assn. [IO]
British Medical Acupuncture Soc. [IO]
Canadian Assn. of Naturopathic Doctors [IO]
Canadian Assn. of Specialized Kinesiology [IO]

Canadian Fed. of Aromatherapists [IO]
Canadian Reiki Assn. [IO]
Center for Humane Options in Childbirth Experiences [15594]
Central Inst. of Medical Medicinal and Aromatic Plants [IO]
Centre for Indian Medical Heritage [IO]
Certification Bd. for Music Therapists [16213]
Childbirth Connection [15595]
Chinese Medicine and Acupuncture Assn. of Canada [IO]
Citizens for Hea. [IO]
Citizens for Hea. [13627]
Commn. on Religious Counseling and Healing [19445]
Commission on Religious Counseling and Healing [IO]
Comm. for Freedom of Choice in Medicine [13628]
Complementary Alternative Medical Assn. [13629]
Complementary Medicine Assn. [13630]
Consciousness Res. and Training Project [12343]
Coun. of Colleges of Acupuncture and Oriental Medicine [15743]
Cross-Cultural Shamanism Network [20444]
Dinshah Hea. Soc. [13631]
Dinshah Health Society [IO]
European Herbal Practitioners Assn. [IO]
Everyday Ayurveda [13606]
Faculty of Homeopathy [IO]
Feldenkrais Guild of North Am. [10182]
Flower Essence Soc. [14818]
Found. for Advancement in Cancer Therapy [13824]
Found. for Revitalization of Local Hea. Traditions [IO]
Found. for Shamanic Stud. [20446]
Frontier Nursing Ser. [15479]
Gen. Coun. and Register of Naturopaths [IO]
Gerson Inst. [13632]
Guild for Structural Integration [13633]
Healers League of the Natl. Spiritualist Assn. of Churches [20449]
Healing Touch Assn. of Canada [IO]
Hea. Optimizing Inst. [14826]
Heart Disease Res. Found. [13905]
Herb Assn. of South Africa [IO]
Herbalists Without Borders [IO]
Herbalists Without Borders [13634]
Holistic Moms Network [12673]
Homeopathic Nurses Assn. [14846]
Hospital-Based Massage Network [15027]
Inst. for Complementary Medicine [IO]
Inst. for Female Alternative Medicine [16345]
Inst. for Traditional Medicine and Preventive Hea. Care [13635]
Institute for Traditional Medicine and Preventive Health Care [IO]
Intl. Aromatherapy and Herb Assn. [IO]
Intl. Aromatherapy and Herb Assn. [13636]
Intl. Assn. of Medical Intuitives [15040]
Intl. Assn. for Oxygen Therapy [16616]
Intl. Assn. of Reiki Professionals [13637]
Intl. Assn. of Reiki Professionals [IO]
Intl. Assn. of Structural Integrators [IO]
Intl. Assn. of Structural Integrators [13638]
Intl. Coun. of Reflexologists [IO]
Intl. EECP Therapists Assn. [16619]
Intl. Fed. of Aromatherapists (Australian Br.) [IO]
Intl. Fed. of Martial Arts and Oriental Medicine [15021]
Intl. Fed. of Professional Aromatherapists [IO]
Intl. Found. for Homeopathy [14849]
Intl. Inst. for Bioenergetic Anal. [IO]
Intl. Inst. of Reflexology [IO]
Intl. Medical and Dental Hypnotherapy Assn. [14924]
Intl. Soc. for Biological Therapy of Cancer [13835]
Intl. Soc. for Complementary Medicine Res. [13639]
Intl. Soc. for Complementary Medicine Res. [IO]
Intl. Thai Therapists Assn. [15031]
Intl. Veterinary Acupuncture Soc. [16796]
Intl. Yan Xin Qigong Assn. [13640]
Intl. Yan Xin Qigong Assn. [IO]

Reference to "IO" in place of a book number signifies that the association may be found in the 45th edition of International Organizations.

Jin Shin Do Found. for Bodymind Acupressure [15746]
Lamaze Birth Without Pain Educ. Assn. [15607]
Midwives Alliance of North Am. [15610]
Modernized Chinese Medicine Intl. Assn. [IO]
Natl. Acupuncture Detoxification Assn. [16510]
Natl. Alliance for Infusion Therapy [14839]
Natl. Assn. of Alternative Medicines [13641]
Natl. Ayurvedic Medical Assn. [13642]
Natl. Center for Complementary and Alternative Medicine [13643]
Natl. Center for Homeopathy [14850]
Natl. Certification Commn. for Acupuncture and Oriental Medicine [15747]
Natl. Fed. for Biblio/Poetry Therapy [16225]
Natl. Fed. of Spiritual Healers [IO]
Natl. Hea. Fed. [14587]
Natl. Inst. of Medical Herbalists [IO]
Natl. Qigong (Chi Kung) Assn. [13644]
New Zealand Natural Medicine Assn. [IO]
North Amer. Tang Shou Tao Assn. [13645]
Norwegian Acupuncture Assn. [IO]
Ohashi Inst. [15748]
Patience T'ai Chi Assn. [23897]
Physicians' Assn. for Anthroposophical Medicine [13646]
PROMETRA - France [IO]
PROMETRA - Spain [IO]
QiGong Res. Soc. [13647]
The Radiance Technique Intl. Assn. [13648]
The Radiance Technique Intl. Assn. [IO]
Radix Inst. [13649]
Reflexology Assn. of Am. [13650]
Reflexology Assn. of Am. [IO]
Reflexology Assn. of Australia [IO]
Reflexology Assn. of Canada [IO]
Reiki Alliance [IO]
Reiki Alliance [13651]
The Reiki Assn. [IO]
Rolf Inst. of Structural Integration [13652]
Scottish Inst. of Reflexology [IO]
Serendipity Assn. [14832]
Shiatsu Therapists Alliance [IO]
Soc. for Acupuncture Res. [13537]
Soc. for the Arts in Healthcare [13714]
Soc. for Clinical and Experimental Hypnosis [14927]
Soc. of Homeopaths [IO]
Somatics Soc. [12363]
Sound Healers Assn. [13653]
Touch for Hea. Kinesiology Assn. [13654]
United Plant Savers [13655]
United Plant Savers [IO]
U.S. Medical Massage Assn. [15033]
U.S. Trager Assn. [13656]
Upledger Inst. [13657]
Veterinary Botanical Medicine Assn. [16812]
World Wide Essence Soc. [14833]
Worldwide Aquatic Bodywork Assn. [13658]
Alternative to the New York Times Comm. - Address unknown since 2002.
Alternative Newsweeklies; Assn. of [3091]
Alternative Poland - Defunct.
Alternative Power Alliance - Defunct.
Alternative Press Center [10892], PO Box 33109, Baltimore, MD 21218, (410)243-2471
Alternative Press Syndicate - Defunct.
Alternative Religions Educational Network [20457], c/o William Kilborn, VP/Treas., PO Box 1893, Trenton, FL 32693, (321)243-2337
Alternative Sources of Energy - Defunct.
Alternative Technology
  Educational Center for Applied Ekistics [10228]
  Inst. for Local Self-Reliance [11747]
  Natl. Clean Cities [6399]
  School of Living [10178]
  TRANET [17002]
Alternative Tech. Assn. [IO], Melbourne, Australia
Alternative Wastewater Mgt. Assn. - Defunct.
Alternative World Org. [★18112]
Alternative World Org. [★IO]
Alternatives [★18605]
Alternatives to Abortion [★12912]
Alternatives to Abortion [★IO]
Alternatives to Abortion/Women's Hea. and Educ. Found. [★IO]

Alternatives to Abortion/Women's Hea. and Educ. Found. [★12912]
Alternatives, Action and Commun. Network for Intl. Development [IO], Montreal, QC, Canada
Alternatives to Fear; Feminist Karate Union/ [★23561]
Alternatives Found. - Defunct.
Alternatives to Marriage Proj. [18025], PO Box 320151, Brooklyn, NY 11232, (718)788-1911
Alternatives to Marriage Proj. [IO], Brooklyn, NY, United States
Alternatives in Print; Task Force on [★10315]
Alternatives in Publication Task Force [10315], c/o Amer. Lib. Assn., Social Responsibilities Round Table, 50 E Huron St., Chicago, IL 60611, (312)344-7072
Alternatives, Reseau d'Action et de Commun. pour le Developpement Intl. [★IO]
Alternatives for Simple Living [18605], 109 Gaul Dr., PO Box 340, Sergeant Bluff, IA 51054, (712)943-6153
ALTISA Intl. Network [IO], Prague, Czech Republic
Alton, Aulton Family Assn; Allton, [20779]
Altro Rehabilitation Agency Programs [★12075]
Altrusa Intl. [13033], 332 S Michigan Ave., Ste. 1123, Chicago, IL 60604, (312)427-4410
Altrusa Intl. [IO], Chicago, IL, United States
Alumina Ceramic Mfrs. Assn. - Defunct.
Aluminium Assn; European [IO]
Aluminium Assn. of India [IO], Bangalore, India
Aluminium in Building; Coun. for [IO]
Aluminium Extruders Assn. [IO], Birmingham, United Kingdom
Aluminium Fed. [IO], Birmingham, United Kingdom
Aluminium Fed; Japan [IO]
Aluminium Packaging Recycling Org. [IO], Redditch, United Kingdom
Aluminium Powder and Paste Assn. [IO], Birmingham, United Kingdom
Aluminium Primary Producers Assn. [IO], Birmingham, United Kingdom
Aluminium Rolled Products Mfrs. Assn. [IO], Birmingham, United Kingdom
Aluminium Stockholders Assn. [IO], Birmingham, United Kingdom
Aluminium Verband Schweiz [★IO]
Aluminum Anodizers Coun. [849], 1000 N Rand Rd., No. 214, Wauconda, IL 60084, (847)526-2010
Aluminum Assn. [2692], 1525 Wilson Blvd., Ste. 600, Arlington, VA 22209, (703)358-2960
Aluminum Building Products Credit Assn. - Defunct.
Aluminum Collectors Assn; Hammered [22033]
Aluminum Extruders Coun. [2693], 1000 N Rand Rd., Ste. 214, Wauconda, IL 60084, (847)526-2010
Aluminum Foil Container Manufacturers Assn. [971], 10 Vecilla Ln., Hot Springs Village, AR 71909, (501)922-7425
Aluminum Manufacturers Assn; Architectural [★588]
Aluminum Mfrs. Credit Bur. - Defunct.
Aluminum Recycling Assn. - Defunct.
Aluminum Siding Assn. [★588]
Aluminum Wares Assn. [★1970]
Aluminum Window Manufacturers Assn. [★588]
Aluminum Workers of Am. [★24137]
Alumnae; Assn. of Collegiate [★9311]
Alumnae Assn; Rockette [19386]
Alumni
  AIESEC Alumni Intl. [IO]
  AIESEC China [IO]
  AIESEC Ireland [IO]
  AIESEC Kenya [IO]
  Air Force Public Affairs Alumni Assn. [6200]
  Alumni Assn., Framingham State Coll. [18871]
  Alumni Assn. of the Universidad del Valle [18872]
  Alumni Assn. of the Univ. of Michigan [18873]
  Angelo State Univ. Alumni Assn. [18874]
  Asian Inst. of Tech. Alumni Assn. [IO]
  Assn. of Former Trainees of the European Union [IO]
  Assn. of Former UNESCO Staff Members [IO]
  Assn. of Former WHO Staff Members [IO]
  Assn. of Graduates of the School of Advanced Bus. Stud. [IO]
  Assn. of Graduates of the U.S. Air Force Acad. [18875]

  Assn. of Polytechnic Graduates [IO]
  Astronaut Scholars Honor Soc. [24584]
  Auburn Univ. Montgomery Alumni Assn. [18876]
  Benedict Coll. Natl. Alumni Soc. [18877]
  Bethune-Cookman Coll. Natl. Alumni Assn. [18878]
  Brandeis Univ. Alumni Assn. [18879]
  Brooklyn Coll. of the City Univ. of New York Alumni Assn. [18880]
  Cal State San Marcos Alumni Assn. [18881]
  California Coll. of Arts and Crafts Alumni Assn. [18882]
  California State Univ. - Northridge Alumni Assn. [18883]
  California State Univ. - Stanislaus Alumni Assn. [18884]
  Catholic Alumni Clubs, Intl. [18885]
  Catholic Alumni Clubs, Intl. [IO]
  Centenary Coll. of Louisiana Alumni Assn. [18886]
  Coastal Carolina Univ. Alumni Assn. [18887]
  Coll. for Creative Stud. Alumni Assn. [18888]
  Coll. of St. Scholastica Alumni Assn. [18889]
  Colorado Christian Univ. Alumni Assn. [18890]
  Columbia Coll. of Nursing Alumni Assn. [18891]
  Defense Intel Alumni Assn. [18892]
  D'Youville Coll. Alumni Assn. [18893]
  Emerson Coll. Alumni Assn. [18894]
  Erskine Alumni Assn. [18895]
  Excelsior Coll. Alumni Assn. [18896]
  Foster Care Alumni of Am. [11592]
  Gallaudet Univ. Alumni Assn. [18897]
  German PennState Alumni Chap. [IO]
  Hope Intl. Univ. Alumni Assn. [18898]
  Indiana State Univ. Alumni Assn. [18899]
  Intl. Alumni Assn. of Shri Mahavir Jain Vidyalaya [19346]
  Iowa Wesleyan Coll. Alumni Assn. [18900]
  Jackson State Univ. Natl. Alumni Assn. [18901]
  Kent State Univ. Alumni Assn. [18902]
  Keuka Coll. Alumni Assn. [18903]
  Lambda Pi Alumni Assn. [24481]
  Lawrence Technological Univ. Alumni Assn. [18904]
  LDS Bus. Coll. Alumni Assn. [18905]
  Lincoln Univ. Alumni Assn. [18906]
  Long Island Univ. - Southampton Coll. Alumni Assn. [18907]
  Major League Baseball Players Alumni Assn. [23114]
  Marquette Univ. Alumni Assn. [18908]
  Montreat Coll. Alumni Assn. [18909]
  Mt. Marty Coll. Alumni Assn. [24399]
  Musicians' Assistance Prog. Alumni Assn. [12620]
  Natl. Alumni Coun. of the United Negro Coll. Fund [18910]
  Natl. Black Coll. Alumni Hall of Fame Found. [18911]
  Nebraska Christian Coll. Alumni Assn. [18912]
  Network of Gay and Lesbian Alumni/ae Associations [18913]
  North Dakota State Univ. Alumni Assn. [18914]
  Northern Michigan Univ. Alumni Assn. [18915]
  Northwest Nazarene Univ. Alumni Assn. [18916]
  Oklahoma Baptist Univ. Alumni Assn. [18917]
  Oklahoma City Univ. Alumni Off. [18918]
  Oklahoma Univ. Alumni Assn. [18919]
  Ouachita Baptist Univ. Alumni Assn. [18920]
  Penn State Alumni Assn. - Austria [IO]
  Penn State Alumni Assn. - Brazil [IO]
  Penn State Alumni Assn. - Canada [IO]
  Penn State Alumni Assn. - Caracas [IO]
  Penn State Alumni Assn. - Chiba [IO]
  Penn State Alumni Assn. - Chile [18871]
  Penn State Alumni Assn. - China [IO]
  Penn State Alumni Assn. - Congo [IO]
  Penn State Alumni Assn. - Cyprus [IO]
  Penn State Alumni Assn. - Fiji [IO]
  Penn State Alumni Assn. - Greece [IO]
  Penn State Alumni Assn. - Hong Kong [IO]
  Penn State Alumni Assn. - India [IO]
  Penn State Alumni Assn. - Indonesia [IO]
  Penn State Alumni Assn. - Iran [IO]
  Penn State Alumni Assn. - Japan [IO]
  Penn State Alumni Assn. - Karachi [IO]
  Penn State Alumni Assn. - Kiev [IO]

A star before a book entry number signifies that the name is not listed separately, but is mentioned within the entry.

Penn State Alumni Assn. - Korea [IO]
Penn State Alumni Assn. - Lesotho [IO]
Penn State Alumni Assn. - Malaysia [IO]
Penn State Alumni Assn. - Morocco [IO]
Penn State Alumni Assn. - Moscow [IO]
Penn State Alumni Assn. - New Zealand [IO]
Penn State Alumni Assn. - Pakistan [IO]
Penn State Alumni Assn. - Philippines [IO]
Penn State Alumni Assn. - Russia [IO]
Penn State Alumni Assn. - St. Petersburg [IO]
Penn State Alumni Assn. - Saudi Arabia [IO]
Penn State Alumni Assn. - Slovakia [IO]
Penn State Alumni Assn. - Spain [IO]
Penn State Alumni Assn. - Sweden [IO]
Penn State Alumni Assn. - Taiwan [IO]
Penn State Alumni Assn. - Thailand [IO]
Penn State Alumni Assn. - Trinidad [IO]
Penn State Alumni Assn. - Turkey [IO]
Prescott Coll. Alumni Assn. [18921]
St. Mary's Coll. of California Alumni Assn. [18922]
Southern Connecticut State Univ. Alumni Assn. [18923]
Spalding Univ. Alumni Assn. [18924]
Stanford Chicano/Latino Alumni Assn. [18925]
Texas A&M Univ. - Commerce Alumni Assn. [18926]
Tufts Univ. Alumni Assn. [18927]
UCD Alumni Assn. [IO]
UERMMMC Nursing Alumni Assn. U.S.A. [18928]
Univ. of Advancing Cmpt. Tech. Alumni Assn. [18929]
Univ. of Alaska Fairbanks Alumni Assn. [18930]
Univ. of Colorado Medical Alumni Assn. [18931]
Univ. of Colorado School of Dentistry Alumni Assn. [18932]
Univ. of Iowa Alumni Assn. [18933]
Univ. of Louisville Alumni Assn. [18934]
Univ. of Mary Alumni Assn. [18935]
Univ. of Minnesota - Crookston Alumni Assn. [18936]
Univ. of South Dakota Alumni Assn. [18937]
Univ. of Texas at Brownsville and Texas Southmost Coll. Alumni Assn. [18938]
Univ. of Texas - Pan-American Alumni Assn. [18939]
Univ. of Wisconsin - Eau Claire Alumni Assn. [18940]
Univ. of Wisconsin - Platteville Alumni Assn. [18941]
Washburn Alumni Assn. [18942]
Wayland Baptist Univ. Assn. of Former Students [18943]
Wellesley Coll. Alumnae Assn. [24400]
Western New Mexico Univ. Alumni Assn. [18944]
William Penn Univ. Alumni Assn. [18945]
Wofford Coll. Natl. Alumni Assn. [18946]
Worcester Polytechnic Inst. Alumni Assn. [18947]
Zeta Beta Tau Fraternity [24489]
Alumni/ae Assn; Northeastern Gay and Lesbian [★18913]
Alumni Assn; California State Univ. of San Marcos [★18881]
Alumni Assn., Framingham State Coll. [18871], Development and Alumni Relations Off., Dwight Hall, PO Box 9101, Framingham, MA 01701-9101, (508)626-4035
Alumni Assn; Intl. Bobath [★15399]
Alumni Assn; Lambda Pi [24481]
Alumni Assn; Major League Baseball Players [23114]
Alumni Assn; Reagan [18365]
Alumni Assn; Reagan Appointees [★18365]
Alumni Assn. of Regents Coll. [★18896]
Alumni Assn. of Shriners Hospitals - Address unknown since 2003.
Alumni Assn. of the Universidad del Valle [18872], 4712 Richland Ave., Metairie, LA 70002, (504)842-3930
Alumni Assn; Univ. of Colorado Hea. Sciences Center [24494]
Alumni Assn; Univ. of Colorado School of Dentistry [18932]
Alumni Assn. of the Univ. of Michigan [18873], 200 Fletcher St., Ann Arbor, MI 48109-1007, (734)764-0384

Alumni Assn. Writers Workshop; Amer. Film Inst. [★11203]
Alumni Coun; Amer. [★8245]
Alumni, Inc; Natl. Football League [★23433]
Alumni of Intl. Educational and Cultural Exchange; Fulbright Assn. of [★8613]
Alumni; Natl. Football League [23433]
Alvis Owner Club [IO], Market Rasen, United Kingdom
Always Causing Legal Unrest - Address unknown since 2001.
Always Patsy Cline World Wide Fan Org. [24840], PO Box 2236, Winchester, VA 22604, (540)535-1148
ALYN Hosp; Amer. Friends of [12825]
Alzheimer Angehorige Austria [IO], Vienna, Austria
Alzheimer Europe [IO], Luxembourg, Luxembourg
Alzheimer Keskusliitto [IO], Helsinki, Finland
Alzheimer Nederland [IO], Bunnik, Netherlands
Alzheimer Scotland-Action on Dementia [IO], Edinburgh, United Kingdom
Alzheimer Soc. of Alberta and Northwest Territories [IO], Edmonton, AB, Canada
Alzheimer Soc. of Canada [IO], Toronto, ON, Canada
Alzheimer Soc. of Ireland [IO], Dublin, Ireland
Alzheimerforeningen [IO], Hellerup, Denmark
Alzheimerforeningen i Sverige [IO], Lund, Sweden
Alzheimer's Assn. [13659], 225 N Michigan Ave., 17th Fl., Chicago, IL 60601-7633, (312)335-8700
Alzheimer's Assn. of Australia [★IO]
Alzheimer's Assn. Japan [IO], Kyoto, Japan
Alzheimer's Australia [IO], Hawker, Australia
Alzheimer's Australia Australian Capital Territory [IO], Hawker, Australia
Alzheimer's Australia Central Queensland [IO], Rockhampton, Australia
Alzheimer's Australia Darling Downs and South West [IO], Toowoomba, Australia
Alzheimer's Australia Gold Coast [IO], Arundel, Australia
Alzheimer's Australia North Queensland [IO], Thuringowa, Australia
Alzheimer's Australia Northern Territory [IO], Darwin, Australia
Alzheimer's Australia NSW [IO], North Ryde, Australia
Alzheimer's Australia South Australia [IO], Glenside, Australia
Alzheimer's Australia Sunshine Coast [IO], Kuluin, Australia
Alzheimer's Australia Victoria [IO], Hawthorn, Australia
Alzheimer's Australia WA - Albany Regional Off. [IO], Albany, Australia
Alzheimer's Australia WA - Bunbury Br. [IO], Bunbury, Australia
Alzheimer's Australia WA - Kalgoorlie Regional Off. [IO], Kalgoorlie, Australia
Alzheimer's Australia WA - Mandurah Regional Off. [IO], Mandurah, Australia
Alzheimer's Australia WA - Rockingham Br. [IO], Rockingham, Australia
Alzheimer's Australia WA - York Regional Off. [IO], York, Australia
Alzheimer's Australia Western Australia [IO], Subiaco, Australia

Alzheimer's Disease
Alzheimer Angehorige Austria [IO]
Alzheimer Europe [IO]
Alzheimer Keskusliitto [IO]
Alzheimer Nederland [IO]
Alzheimer Scotland-Action on Dementia [IO]
Alzheimer Soc. of Alberta and Northwest Territories [IO]
Alzheimer Soc. of Canada [IO]
Alzheimer Soc. of Ireland [IO]
Alzheimerforeningen [IO]
Alzheimerforeningen i Sverige [IO]
Alzheimer's Assn. [13659]
Alzheimer's Assn. Japan [IO]
Alzheimer's Australia [IO]
Alzheimer's Australia Australian Capital Territory [IO]
Alzheimer's Australia Central Queensland [IO]

Alzheimer's Australia Darling Downs and South West [IO]
Alzheimer's Australia Gold Coast [IO]
Alzheimer's Australia North Queensland [IO]
Alzheimer's Australia Northern Territory [IO]
Alzheimer's Australia NSW [IO]
Alzheimer's Australia South Australia [IO]
Alzheimer's Australia Sunshine Coast [IO]
Alzheimer's Australia Victoria [IO]
Alzheimer's Australia WA - Albany Regional Off. [IO]
Alzheimer's Australia WA - Bunbury Br. [IO]
Alzheimer's Australia WA - Kalgoorlie Regional Off. [IO]
Alzheimer's Australia WA - Mandurah Regional Off. [IO]
Alzheimer's Australia WA - Rockingham Br. [IO]
Alzheimer's Australia WA - York Regional Off. [IO]
Alzheimer's Australia Western Australia [IO]
Alzheimer's Disease Assn. of Nigeria [IO]
Alzheimer's Disease Assn. of the Philippines [IO]
Alzheimer's Disease Assn. (Singapore) [IO]
Alzheimer's Disease Found. Malaysia [IO]
Alzheimer's Disease Intl. [IO]
Alzheimers Found. of Am. [13660]
Alzheimers NZ [IO]
Alzheimer's Pakistan [IO]
Alzheimer's and Related Disorders Soc. of India [IO]
Alzheimer's Soc. [IO]
Assn. Alzheimer Suisse [IO]
Assn. France Alzheimer [IO]
Assn. Luxembourg Alzheimer [IO]
Brookdale Found. [12260]
Dana Alliance for Brain Initiatives [15387]
Dementia Advocacy and Support Network Intl. [12638]
Dementia and Alzheimer's Assn. Tasmania - Hobart [IO]
Dementia and Alzheimer's Assn. Tasmania - Launceston [IO]
Deutsche Alzheimer Gesellschaft [IO]
Federazione Alzheimer Italia [IO]
Fundacion Alzheimer Espana [IO]
Greek Alzheimer's Assn. [IO]
Hong Kong Alzheimer's Disease Assn. [IO]
Polish Alzheimer's Assn. [IO]
Romanian Alzheimer Soc. [IO]
Spanish Confed. of Family Alzheimer Associations [IO]

Alzheimer's Disease Assn. of Nigeria [IO], Nnewi, Nigeria
Alzheimer's Disease Assn. of the Philippines [IO], Quezon City, Philippines
Alzheimer's Disease Assn. (Singapore) [IO], Singapore, Singapore
Alzheimer's Disease Found. Malaysia [IO], Kuala Lumpur, Malaysia
Alzheimer's Disease Intl. [IO], London, United Kingdom
Alzheimer's Disease and Related Disorders Assn. [★13659]
Alzheimer's Disease Soc. [★IO]
Alzheimer's Found. of Am. [13660], 322 Eighth Ave., 6th Fl., New York, NY 10001, (866)232-8484
Alzheimers NZ [IO], Wellington, New Zealand
Alzheimer's Pakistan [IO], Lahore, Pakistan
Alzheimer's and Related Disorders Soc. of India [IO], Kunnamkulam, India
Alzheimer's Soc. [IO], London, United Kingdom
Am Cham Cuba [★IO]
Am Cham Cuba [★24258]
AM/FM Intl. [★900]
Amalgamated Assn. of St., Elec. Railway and Motor Coach Employees of Am. [★24197]
Amalgamated Flying Saucer Clubs of America - Address unknown since 2004.
Amalgamated Footwear and Textile Workers' Union of Australia [★IO]
Amalgamated Lace Operatives of America - Defunct.
Amalgamated Meat Cutters and Bucher Workmen of North Am. [★24061]
Amalgamated Printers' Assn. [1805], c/o Mike O'Connor, Sec.-Treas., PO Box 18117, Fountain Hills, AZ 85269

Reference to "IO" in place of a book number signifies that the association may be found in the 45th edition of International Organizations.

Amalgamated Printers' Association [IO], Fountain Hills, AZ, United States

Amalgamated Transit Union [24197], 5025 Wisconsin Ave. NW, Washington, DC 20016-4121, (202)537-1645

Amandine Dupin
George Sand Soc. [9653]

Amaranth; Supreme Coun. Order of the [19254]

Amaryllis Res. Inst. [★6637]

Amaryllis Res. Inst. [★IO]

Amaryllis Soc. Gp; Amer. [★6637]

Amateur Artists Assn. of America - Defunct.

Amateur Astronomers Assn. [6496], PO Box 383, Gracie Sta., New York, NY 10028, (212)535-2922

Amateur Astronomers Assn. of New York City [★6496]

Amateur Astronomers, Inc. [21549], PO Box 111, Garwood, NJ 07027-0111, (908)276-2730

Amateur Athletes of Am; Intercollegiate Assn. of [23820]

Amateur Athletes Intl. - Defunct.

Amateur Athletic Assn. of Barbados [IO], Bridge-town, Barbados

Amateur Athletic Assn. of Cyprus [IO], Nicosia, Cyprus

Amateur Athletic Assn. of England [IO], Birmingham, United Kingdom

Amateur Athletic Assn. of Great Britain [★IO]

Amateur Athletic Assn. of Guyana [★IO]

Amateur Athletic Fed. of Iran [IO], Tehran, Iran

Amateur Athletic Fed. Turkmenistan [IO], Ashgabat, Turkmenistan

Amateur Athletic Union [23797], PO Box 22409, Lake Buena Vista, FL 32830-1000, (407)934-7200

Amateur Athletic Union of Australia [★IO]

Amateur Athletic Union; Competitive Swimming Comm. of the [★23893]

Amateur Athletic Union; Powerlifting Comm. of the [★23663]

Amateur Athletic Union; Senior Men's Boxing Comm. of the [★23267]

Amateur Athletic Union; Synchronized Swimming Division of the [★23889]

Amateur Athletic Union Taekwondo Comm; U.S. Natl. [★23610]

Amateur Athletic Union; Water Polo Comm. of the [★23973]

Amateur Ballroom Dancers Assn; U.S. [★9900]

Amateur Baseball Assn. of Thailand [IO], Ayutthaya, Thailand

Amateur Baseball Cong; Amer. [23100]

Amateur Baseball Fed; Natl. [23115]

Amateur Baseball Umpires' Assn. [23798], c/o Sports Mgt. Inc., 2537 Madison Ave., Kansas City, MO 64108, (816)474-8677

Amateur Basketball Assn. of the U.S.A. [★23138]

Amateur Bicycle League of Am. [★23320]

Amateur Boxing Assn. of England [★IO]

Amateur Boxing Assn. of England [IO], Sheffield, United Kingdom

Amateur Boxing Fed; U.S.A. [★23267]

Amateur Boxing Fed; U.S. of Amer. [★23267]

Amateur Chamber Music Players [10523], 1123 Broadway, Rm. 304, New York, NY 10010-2007, (212)645-7424

Amateur Chamber Music Players [IO], New York, NY, United States

Amateur Dodgeball Assn; Natl. [23091]

Amateur Entomologists' Soc. [IO], London, United Kingdom

Amateur Fencers League of Amer. [★23402]

Amateur Field Trial Clubs of Am. [22184], 1300 Tripp Rd., Somerville, TN 38068, (901)465-1556

Amateur Fisherman's Assn. of the Northern Territory [IO], Darwin, Australia

Amateur Golf Coun; World [★23453]

Amateur Golfers' Assn. of America - Defunct.

Amateur Hockey Assn. of the U.S. [★23488]

Amateur Horseman's Assn; Arabian Professional and [4862]

Amateur Karate Fed; Amer. [23559]

Amateur Motorcycle Assn. [IO], Cannock, United Kingdom

Amateur Movie Makers Assn. [22418], c/o Patricia K. Otto, Treas., 9839 Grackle Loop, Lakeland, FL 33810-2314, (863)858-2106

Amateur Organists and Keyboard Assn. Intl. - Defunct.

Amateur Press Alliance - Defunct.

Amateur Press Assn. of Am; United [22912]

Amateur Press Assn. of Am; United [★22912]

Amateur Press Assn; Amer. [22910]

Amateur Press Assn; Natl. [22911]

Amateur Press Assn; United [★22912]

Amateur Press; United [★22912]

Amateur-Professional Photoelectric Photometry; Intl. [6505]

Amateur Racquetball Assn; U.S. [★23678]

Amateur Radio
ACB Radio Amateurs [21492]
Albanian Amateur Radio Assn. [IO]
Amateur Radio Assn. of Bosnia and Hercegovina [IO]
Amateur Radio Soc. of India [IO]
Amateur Radio Soc. of Kenya [IO]
Amateur Radio Soc. of Moldova [IO]
Amer. CB Radio Assn. [21493]
Amer. Radio Relay League [21494]
Amer. Shortwave Listeners Club [21495]
Andorra Radioamateur Union [IO]
Antique Wireless Assn. [22923]
ARRL Found. [21496]
Aruba Amateur Radio Club [IO]
Assn. of Clandestine Radio Enthusiasts [21497]
Assn. of North Amer. Radio Clubs [21498]
Bangladesh Amateur Radio League [IO]
Calgary Amateur Radio Assn. [IO]
Canadian Intl. DX Club [IO]
Collins Collectors Assn. [21499]
Cyprus Amateur Radio Soc. [IO]
Czech Radio Club [IO]
Estonian Radio Amateurs Union [IO]
Finnish Amateur Radio League [IO]
Friends of Old-Time Radio [22924]
Friends of Radio for Peace Intl. [21500]
Friends of Radio for Peace Intl. [IO]
Hong Kong Amateur Radio Transmitting Soc. [IO]
Icelandic Radio Amateurs [IO]
Intl. Amateur Radio Union [IO]
Intl. Amateur Radio Union [21501]
Intl. Handicappers' Net [21502]
Intl. Radio Club of Am. [21503]
Iraqi Amateur Radio Soc. [IO]
Irish Radio Transmitters Soc. [IO]
Japan Amateur Radio League [IO]
Korean Amateur Radio League [IO]
Kuwait Amateur Radio Soc. [IO]
Lambda Amateur Radio Club [21504]
Lithuanian Amateur Radio Soc. [IO]
Longwave Club of Am. [21505]
Malaysian Amateur Radio Transmitter's Soc. [IO]
Malta Amateur Radio League [IO]
Mauritius Amateur Radio Soc. [IO]
Montserrat Amateur Radio Soc. [IO]
New Zealand Assn. of Radio Transmitters [IO]
No-Code Intl. [21506]
North Amer. Radio Archives [22926]
North Amer. Shortwave Assn. [21507]
Old Old Timers Club [21508]
Old Old Timers Club [IO]
Quarter Century Wireless Assn. [21509]
Radio Amateur Assn. of Greece [IO]
Radio Club of Am. [22928]
Radio Collectors of Am. [22929]
Radio Soc. of Bermuda [IO]
Radio Soc. of Great Britain [IO]
Soc. for Amateur Radio in The Netherlands [IO]
Vintage Radio and Phonograph Soc. [22931]
Wireless Inst. of Australia [IO]
World Assn. of Christian Radio Amateurs and Listeners [IO]
Worldwide Television-FM DX Assn. [IO]
Worldwide Television-FM DX Assn. [21510]

Amateur Radio Assn. of Bosnia and Hercegovina [IO], Sarajevo, Bosnia-Hercegovina

Amateur Radio Network - Address unknown since 2001.

Amateur Radio Service [★21504]

Amateur Radio Soc. of India [IO], Bombay, India

Amateur Radio Soc. of Kenya [IO], Nairobi, Kenya

Amateur Radio Soc. of Moldova [IO], Kishinev, Moldova

Amateur Retriever Club; Natl. [22309]

Amateur Roller Skaters; U.S. Fed. of [★23742]

Amateur Roller Skating Assn; U.S. [★23742]

Amateur Rose Breeders Assn. [IO], Fakenham, United Kingdom

Amateur Rowing Assn. [IO], London, United Kingdom

Amateur Scientist Res. Org. - Defunct.

Amateur Scientists; Soc. for [7631]

Amateur Ski Instructors Assn. [23748], 28 Park Dr., Woodstock, NY 12498-1726, (845)679-4609

Amateur Softball Assn. of Am. [23788], c/o Virgil Ackerson, Commissioner, 605 Rivera, Tonkawa, OK 74653, (580)628-2475

Amateur SpeedSkating Union of the U.S. [★23745]

Amateur SpeedSkating Union of the U.S. - Defunct.

Amateur Sports Fed. and Olympic Comm. of Hong Kong [★IO]

Amateur Swimming Assn. [IO], Loughborough, United Kingdom

Amateur Trapshooting Assn. [23713], 601 W Natl. Rd., Vandalia, OH 45377, (937)898-4638

Amateur TV Assn. - Address unknown since 1995.

Amateur Yacht Res. Soc. [IO], London, United Kingdom

AmateurJudo Assn. [★23556]

Amateurs; Intl. Order of Handicapped Radio [★21502]

Amatex Export Trade Assn. - Defunct.

Amatorteaterns Riksforbund [★IO]

Amaury Sport Org. [IO], Issy-les-Moulineaux, France

Amazon Alliance [IO], Washington, DC, United States

Amazon Alliance [4531], 1367 Connecticut Ave. NW, Ste. 400, Washington, DC 20036-1860, (202)785-3334

Amazona Guildingii
Center for Commun. Programs [12755]
Negative Population Growth [12756]
Population Action Intl. [12758]
Population Commun. [12759]
Population Connection [12761]
Population Coun. [12762]
Population-Environment Balance [12763]
Population Inst. [12764]
Population Rsrc. Center [12765]

The Amazona Soc. [7410], c/o Shari L. Beaudoin, Pres., 13000 Aldrich Ave. S, Burnsville, MN 55337, (952)928-9985

Amazone [IO], Brussels, Belgium

Amazonian Proj. [IO], Caracas, Venezuela

Ambassador Club; Beaver [22946]

Ambassador Prog; People to People Citizen [★17908]

Ambassador Programs [★17908]

Ambassador Programs [★IO]

Ambassadors for Friendship [★IO]

Ambassadors for Friendship [★17888]

Ambassadors Intl; Airline [13147]

Ambassadors of Mary [19565], 6003 W Diversey Ave., Chicago, IL 60639, (773)622-9542

Ambassadors; Sports [20400]

Ambedkar Center for Justice and Peace [IO], Toronto, ON, Canada

Amblyopia
Amer. Assn. of Certified Orthoptists [15657]

Ambroise Pare Soc. - Defunct.

Ambrose Monell Found. [13110], One Rockefeller Plz., Ste. 301, New York, NY 10020-2002, (212)586-0700

Ambrose Monell Foundation [IO], New York, NY, United States

AMBUCS [13034], PO Box 5127, High Point, NC 27262, (336)852-0052

Ambucs Rsrc. Center [14234], PO Box 5127, High Point, NC 27262, (336)852-0052

Ambulance Assn. of Am. [★14313]

Ambulance Assn; Amer. [14313]

Ambulance Mfrs. Div. [369], c/o Natl. Truck Equip. Assn., 37400 Hills Tech Dr., Farmington Hills, MI 48331-3414, (248)489-7090

Ambulance and Medical Ser. Assn. of Am. [★14313]

Ambulance and Medical Services Assn; Natl. [★14313]

Ambulance Ser. Assn. [IO], London, United Kingdom

A star before a book entry number signifies that the name is not listed separately, but is mentioned within the entry.

Ambulance Services; Commn. on Accreditation of [13532]

Ambulances for Nicaragua - Address unknown since 1990.

Ambulatory Behavioral Healthcare; Assn. for [16080]

Ambulatory Care
Accreditation Assn. for Ambulatory Hea. Care [13661]
Ambulatory Pediatric Assn. [15879]
Amer. Acad. of Ambulatory Care Nursing [15428]
Amer. Ambulance Assn. [14313]
Amer. Assn. for Accreditation of Ambulatory Surgery Facilities [16557]
Amer. Assn. of Ambulatory Surgery Centers [16558]
Amer. Bd. of Urgent Care Medicine [13662]
Assn. for Ambulatory Behavioral Healthcare [16080]
Federated Ambulatory Surgery Assn. [16582]
Natl. Assn. of Community Hea. Centers [14574]
North Amer. Assn. for Ambulatory Urgent Care [13663]
North Amer. Primary Care Res. Gp. [13664]
Soc. of Interventional Pain Mgt. Surgery Centers [16588]
Urgent Care Assn. of Am. [13665]

Ambulatory Care Medicine; Natl. Assn. for [★13663]

Ambulatory Care Nursing; Amer. Acad. of [15428]

Ambulatory Fracture Assn.; Amer. [★15756]

Ambulatory Hea. Care; Accreditation Assn. for [13661]

Ambulatory Hea. Care Admin; Center for Res. in [15064]

Ambulatory Nursing Admin; Amer. Acad. of [★15428]

Ambulatory Pediatric Assn. [15879], 6728 Old McLean Village Dr., McLean, VA 22101, (703)556-9222

Ambulatory Pediatric Services; Assn. for [★15879]

Ambulatory Plastic Surgery Facilities; Amer. Assn. for Accreditation of [★16557]

Ambulatory Surgery Assn; Federated [16582]

Ambulatory Surgery Assn; Freestanding [★16582]

Ambulatory Surgery Centers; Amer. Assn. of [16558]

Ambulatory Surgery Facilities; Amer. Assn. for Accreditation of [16557]

Ambulatory Surgical Care; Soc. for the Advancement of Freestanding [★16582]

Ambulatory Urgent Care; North Amer. Assn. for [13663]

AMC Institute [IO], Philadelphia, PA, United States

AMC Pacer Club [21566], c/o Frank E. Wrenick, Pres./Founder, 2628 Queenston Rd., Cleveland Heights, OH 44118-4320

AMC Rambler Club [21567], c/o Brian Yacino, Pres., 6 Murolo Rd., North Grosvenordale, CT 06255-1814, (860)923-0485

AMC Rambler Club [IO], North Grosvenordale, CT, United States

AMC World Clubs - Defunct.

AMCHA, the Natl. Israeli Centre for Psychosocial Support of Holocaust Survivors and the Second Generation [IO], Jerusalem, Israel

AMCinstitute [314], 100 N 20th St., 4th Fl., Philadelphia, PA 19103-1443, (215)564-3484

Amcot, Inc. [4301], PO Box 259, Bakersfield, CA 93302, (661)327-5961

Amdahl Users Group - Address unknown since 2005.

AME Assn. (Atlantic) [IO], Fredericton, NB, Canada

AME Church; Women's Missionary Soc., [20627]

Amegroid
Amegroid Soc. of Am. [9366]

Amegroid Soc. of Am. [9366], 3 Woodthorne Ct., No. 12, Owings Mills, MD 21117, (410)363-6187

Ameinu [19174], c/o Doni Remba, Exec. Dir., 114 W 26th St., Ste. 1005, New York, NY 10001-6708, (212)675-5138

Amelia Earhart Collectors Club - Address unknown since 2007.

Amelia Earhart Res. Consortium - Address unknown since 1995.

AMEND [12020], 2727 Bryant St., Ste. 350, Denver, CO 80211, (303)832-6363

AMEND Network [★12020]

Amendment; Academics for the Second [17286]

Amendment Comm. of the U.S.A; Liberty [17296]

Amendment Lawyers Assn; First [5605]

Amendment Network; Natl. Victims' Constitutional [18779]

AMER Medical Div., Amer. Near East Refugee Aid - Defunct.

Amerasian
One Child at a Time [11642]
Pearl S. Buck Intl. [11646]

Amerasians for Intl. Aid and Adoption [★11642]

Am; Assn. of Consulting Foresters of [4680]

Am; Assn. of Indian Muslims of [19109]

America Australia Interaction Assn. - Address unknown since 1995.

Am. the Beautiful Fund [4532], 725 15th St. NW, Ste. 605, Washington, DC 20005, (202)638-1649

Am. Beautiful; Keep [4584]

Am. Bikes [17022], 1612 K St. NW, Ste. 800, Washington, DC 20006, (202)833-8080

America; Black Archives of Mid- [9400]

Am; Bnei Akiva of North [★20178]

Am. Bus. Conf. [1170], 1828 L St. NW, Ste. 908, Washington, DC 20036, (202)822-9300

America; Campaign for [18285]

Am. Celiac Soc. [★15543]

Am; Copywriter's Coun. of [875]

Am. Coun. on Educ., Center for Advancement of Racial and Ethnic Equity [8889], One Dupont Cir. NW, Washington, DC 20036-1193, (202)939-9300

Am. Coun. on Educ., Off. of Minorities in Higher Educ. [★8889]

Am. Council for Trade in Services [3837]

Am. - Ecological and Toxicological Assn. of Dyes and Organic Pigments Mfrs; ETAD North [5089]

America First - Address unknown since 1995.

America-Georgia Bus. Coun. [2296], 2300 M St. NW, Ste. 800, Washington, DC 20037, (202)416-1606

Am. Homebrewers Assn. [191], 736 Pearl St., Boulder, CO 80302, (303)447-0816

Am. Individual and Gp. Home Hea. Care Assn. [★12291]

America-Israel Chamber of Commerce and Indus. [24336], 3 New York Plz., 10th Fl., New York, NY 10004, (212)232-8440

America-Israel Coun. for Israeli-Palestinian Peace [18047], 224 Lake Dr., Kensington, CA 94708-1132, (510)526-8449

America-Israel Cultural Found. [10251], 51 E 42nd St., Ste. 400, New York, NY 10017, (212)557-1600

America-Israel Cultural Found. [IO], New York, NY, United States

America-Israel Culture House - Defunct.

America-Israel Friendship League [10252], 134 E 39th St., New York, NY 10016, (212)213-8630

America-Israel Soc. [★10251]

America-Israel Soc. [★IO]

America-Italy Soc. - Address unknown since 2003.

Am. Memorial Found; Women in Military Ser. for [6360]

America-MidEast Educational and Training Services [18048], 1730 M St. NW, Ste. 1100, Washington, DC 20036, (202)776-9600

America-MidEast Educational and Training Services [IO], Washington, DC, United States

Am. on the Move Found. [14537], 44 School St., Ste. 325, Boston, MA 02108, (617)367-6894

Am. Movement; New [★18652]

America Needs Fatima Campaign [★19763]

Am. Outdoors [23681], PO Box 10847, Knoxville, TN 37939, (865)558-3595

America Remembers - Address unknown since 1999.

Am. Rsrc. Center; Central [★17989]

Am. Scores [23772], 520 8th Ave., Ste. 801, New York, NY 10018, (212)868-9510

Am; Scriabin Soc. of [10696]

Am. Sings! [10524], 904 Polaris Way, Missoula, MT 59803, (800)372-1222

America Weeks Program - Defunct.

Am. World Adoption Assn. [11233], 6723 Whittier Ave., Ste. 202, McLean, VA 22101, (703)356-8447

Americal Div. Veterans Assn. [21385], c/o Mr. Roger Gilmore, Natl. Adjutant, PO Box 830662, Richardson, TX 75080

American
Africa Action [16918]
Africa-America Inst. [16919]
Africa-American Friendship Soc. [18862]
Alliance for Retired Americans [18543]
Allied Artists of Am. [9487]
America-Israel Chamber of Commerce and Indus. [24336]
Amer. and African Bus. Women's Alliance [691]
Amer. Arab Chamber of Commerce [24225]
Amer. Assembly [18418]
Amer. Bus. Conf. [17622]
The Amer. Cause [17642]
Amer. Civil Liberties Union [17084]
Amer. Civil Liberties Union Found. [17085]
Amer. Coun. for Capital Formation [17347]
Amer. Coun. on Consumer Interests [17305]
Amer. Culture Assn. [10886]
Amer. Defense Inst. [17373]
Amer. Fed. of Jews From Central Europe [17944]
Amer. Fed. of Ramallah, Palestine [9392]
Amer. Folklore Soc. [9953]
Amer. Ireland Fund [17929]
Amer. Patriots Assn. [21239]
Amer. Soc. for Muslim Advancement [10245]
Amer. Stud. Assn. [9367]
Americana Music Assn. [10555]
Americanism Educational League [17623]
Americans for Peace Now [17935]
Americans for Religious Liberty [17090]
America's Future [17624]
Archaeological Conservancy [6439]
Armenian Amer. Chamber of Commerce [24263]
The Asia Found. [17005]
Asian/Pacific Amer. Heritage Assn. [18972]
Assn. of Chinese Amer. Physicians [15991]
Assn. of Concerned African Scholars [16926]
Australian New Zealand - Amer. Chambers of Commerce [24248]
Austrian Assn. for Amer. Stud. [IO]
Belgian-Luxembourg Amer. Stud. Assn. [IO]
Bostonian Soc. [10097]
British Assn. for Amer. Stud. [IO]
Bulgarian-American Chamber of Commerce [24243]
Bulgarian Natl. Front [17027]
Bus. Coun. for Intl. Understanding [17862]
Bus. Executives for Natl. Security [18587]
Canadian/American Border Trade Alliance [3838]
Canadian Assn. for Amer. Stud. [IO]
Carson McCullers Soc. [11164]
Catharine Maria Sedgwick Soc. [11165]
Center for Constitutional Rights [17097]
Center for the Defense of Free Enterprise [17625]
Chinese Amer. Assn. of Engg. [7008]
Chinese-American Golf Assn. [23445]
Civil War Round Table Associates [10102]
Common Dreams [16972]
Confederate Memorial Assn. [9368]
Confederate Memorial Literary Soc. [10105]
Congressional Arts Caucus [17254]
Congressional Automotive Caucus [17255]
The Conservative Caucus [17264]
Conservative Opportunity Soc. [17257]
Cormac McCarthy Soc. [11168]
Coun. on Contemporary Families [12149]
Coun. on Foreign Relations [17608]
Croatian Amer. Assn. [17868]
Croatian-American Chamber of Commerce [24314]
Cuban Amer. Alliance Educ. Fund [19023]
Custer Battlefield Historical and Museum Assn. [10106]
Early Amer. Indus. Assn. [9481]
Eisenhower Fellowships [17884]
English in Action [17885]
Estonian Amer. Chamber of Commerce and Indus. [24318]
European Assn. for Amer. Stud. [IO]
Finnish and Amer. Women's Network [17586]
Flag Mfrs. Assn. of Am. [1487]
Foreign Policy Assn. [17610]
Free Cong. Political Action Comm. [17268]
Freedom Alliance [9369]
Freedom of Expression Found. [17116]

Reference to "IO" in place of a book number signifies that the association may be found in the 45th edition of International Organizations.

Friends of the Amer. Museum in Britain/Halcyon Found. [9370]
Friends of the Amer. Museum in Britain/Halcyon Found. [IO]
Fudan Museum Found. [10504]
German Assn. for Amer. Stud. [IO]
German Historical Inst. [10110]
Hall of Fame for Great Americans [11119]
Harriet Beecher Stowe Soc. [11173]
Hellenic Amer. Natl. Coun. [9995]
Historic Deerfield [10034]
Historical Soc. of Early Amer. Decoration [9482]
The Hospitality and Info. Ser. [17896]
Independent Americans [17294]
Inst. for Amer. Indian Stud. [6447]
Inter-American Commn. on Human Rights [17765]
Inter-American Defense Bd. [17378]
Intl. Center [17613]
Intl. Center in New York [17897]
Intl. Cultic Stud. Assn. [17368]
Iranian Amer. Bar Assn. [5504]
Irish Amer. Unity Conf. [17932]
Irish Assn. for Amer. Stud. [IO]
Japanese Assn. for Amer. Stud. [IO]
Jewish Inst. for Natl. Security Affairs [17380]
John Birch Soc. [17274]
Laotian Amer. Natl. Alliance [19192]
Laotian Amer. Soc. [19193]
League of the South [17125]
Lebanese Amer. Professional Soc. [19205]
Leuva Patidar Samaj of USA [10221]
Liberty Amendment Comm. of the U.S.A. [17296]
Lincoln Inst. for Res. and Educ. [16940]
Lithuanian-American Bar Assn. [5507]
Mgt. Educ. Alliance [8029]
Middle East Policy Coun. [18063]
Move Am. Forward [18733]
Museum of the Fur Trade [10132]
Natl. Center for Constitutional Stud. [17297]
Natl. Comm. on Amer. Foreign Policy [17615]
Natl. Comm. for an Effective Cong. [17252]
Natl. Coun. of Asian Pacific Americans [17013]
Natl. Coun. on U.S.-Arab Relations [18066]
Natl. Fed. of Croatian Americans [17362]
Natl. Justice Found. of Am. [17298]
Natl. Register of Prominent Americans and Intl. Notables [11140]
Natl. Strategy Info. Center [17383]
Natl. Trust for Historic Preservation [10051]
Nepali Amer. Friendship Assn. [19288]
Netherlands Amer. Stud. Assn. [IO]
Nordic Assn. for Amer. Stud. [IO]
Omohundro Inst. of Early Amer. History and Culture [10140]
Oper. Crossroads Africa [16932]
Org. of Chinese Americans [17065]
Pakistan Chamber of Commerce USA [24364]
Pakistani Amer. Bus. Executives Assn. [758]
Palestine Liberation Org. [18069]
Panamerican/PanAfrican Assn. [17371]
Patidar Cultural Assn. of USA [10218]
Patriots of Fort McHenry-Living Classrooms [10057]
People for the Amer. Way [17143]
People's Medical Soc. [17694]
Philip Roth Soc. [11187]
Philippine Amer. Writers and Artists [11188]
Polish Amer. Golf Assn. [23462]
Polish-American-Jewish Alliance for Youth Action [13510]
Polish Assn. for Amer. Stud. [IO]
Rolling Thunder [21265]
The Russian-American Center/Track Two Inst. for Citizen Diplomacy [17912]
Russian-American Chamber of Commerce in the USA [24371]
Salvadoran Amer. Medical Soc. [15092]
Secretary's Open Forum [17617]
Senate Tourism Caucus [17259]
Serbian-American Chamber of Commerce [24373]
Serbian Amer. Medical and Dental Soc. [14185]
Soc. for Amer. Archaeology [6455]
Soc. for Commercial Archeology [9485]
Soc. for Indonesian-Americans [19116]
Soc. for the Stud. of Amer. Women Writers [11195]

Soc. for the Stud. of Midwestern Literature [10430]
Soc. of Taiwanese Americans, Chicago Chap. [19403]
Southern Christian Leadership Conf. [17154]
Susan Glaspell Soc. [11197]
Swedish-American Bar Assn. [5532]
Taiwanese Amer. Citizens League [19404]
Thornton Wilder Soc. [11200]
Trans-Atlantic Amer. Flag Liner Operators/Trans-Pacific Amer. Flag Berth Operators [3592]
Turkish-American Chamber of Commerce and Indus. [24384]
U.S.-Asia Inst. [17009]
U.S. Assn. of Former Members of Cong. [17253]
U.S. Canada Peace Anniversary Assn. [19299]
U.S.-China Peoples Friendship Assn. [17066]
U.S.-Vietnam Trade Coun. [17010]
USA Sanatan Sports and Cultural Assn. [23787]
Washington Off. on Africa [16935]
William Dean Howells Soc. [9724]
Women in Military Ser. for Am. Memorial Found. [6360]
World Policy Inst. [17620]
Young America's Found. [17280]
Amer. Aberdeen-Angus Breeder's Assn. [★4212]
Amer. Abstract Artists [9488], 194 Powers St., Brooklyn, NY 11211
Amer. Acad. of Achievement - Defunct.
Amer. Acad. of Actuaries [2127], 1100 17th St. NW, 7th Fl., Washington, DC 20036, (202)223-8196
Amer. Acad. of Acupuncture and Oriental Medicine [13611], 1925 W County Rd., B2, Roseville, MN 55113, (651)631-0204
Amer. Acad. of Addiction Psychiatry [16062], 345 Blackstone Blvd., 2nd Fl. - RCH, Providence, RI 02906, (401)524-3076
Amer. Acad. of Adoption Attorneys [5471], PO Box 33053, Washington, DC 20033, (202)832-2222
Amer. Acad. of Advt. [7919], c/o Dr. Donald W. Jugenheimer, Exec. Dir., Coll. of Mass Communications, Texas Tech Univ., Box 43082, Lubbock, TX 79409-3082, (806)742-3385
Amer. Acad. of Algology [★15832]
Amer. Acad. of Allergy [★13592]
Amer. Acad. of Allergy, Asthma and Immunology [13592], 555 E Wells St., Ste. 1100, Milwaukee, WI 53202-3823, (414)272-6071
Amer. Acad. of Alternative Medicine [13612]
Amer. Acad. of Ambulatory Care [★13662]
Amer. Acad. of Ambulatory Care Nursing [15428], E Holly Ave., PO Box 56, Pitman, NJ 08071-0056, (856)256-2350
Amer. Acad. of Ambulatory Nursing Admin. [★15428]
Amer. Acad. of Anesthesiologist Assistants [13670], PO Box 13978, Tallahassee, FL 32317, (850)656-8848
Amer. Acad. of Anti-Aging Medicine [15125], c/o Dr. Ronald Klatz, Pres., 1510 W Montana St., Chicago, IL 60614, (773)528-1000
Amer. Acad. of Appellate Lawyers [5472], 15245 Shady Grove Rd., Ste. 130, Rockville, MD 20850, (301)258-9210
Amer. Acad. of Arts and Letters [10196], 633 W 155 St., New York, NY 10032, (212)368-5900
Amer. Acad. of Arts and Sciences [9605], 136 Irving St., Cambridge, MA 02138, (617)576-5000
Amer. Acad. of Asian Studies - Defunct.
Amer. Acad. of Audiology [16439], 11730 Plaza Am. Dr., Ste. 300, Reston, VA 20190, (703)790-8466
Amer. Acad. for Cerebral Palsy [★13934]
Amer. Acad. for Cerebral Palsy and Developmental Medicine [13934], 555 E Wells St., Ste. 1100, Milwaukee, WI 53202, (414)918-3014
Amer. Acad. of Child and Adolescent Psychiatry [16063], 3615 Wisconsin Ave. NW, Washington, DC 20016-3007, (202)966-7300
Amer. Acad. of Child Psychiatry [★16063]
Amer. Acad. of Cleft Palate Prosthesis [★14055]
Amer. Acad. of Clinical Neurophysiology [15375], Dept. of Psychiatry, Univ. of Michigan Hea. Sys., 1500 E Medical Center Dr., Ann Arbor, MI 48109-0295, (734)936-8269
Amer. Acad. of Clinical Psychiatrists [16064], PO Box 458, Glastonbury, CT 06033, (860)635-5533

Amer. Acad. of Clinical Toxicology [16657], 777 E Park Dr., PO Box 8820, Harrisburg, PA 17105-8820, (717)558-7847
Amer. Acad. on Commun. in Healthcare [15984], 16020 Swingley Ridge Rd., Ste. 300, Chesterfield, MO 63017, (636)449-5080
Amer. Acad. of Cosmetic Dentistry [14093], 5401 World Dairy Dr., Madison, WI 53718, (608)222-8583
Amer. Acad. of Cosmetic Surgery [14037], 737 N Michigan Ave., Ste. 2100, Chicago, IL 60611-5405, (312)981-6760
Amer. Acad. of Counseling Psychology [16118], c/o Steve K.D. Eichel, PhD, Pres., 409 Nottingham Rd., Newark, DE 19711, (302)598-1330
Amer. Acad. of Craniofacial Pain [15751], 1901 N Roselle Rd., Ste. 920, Schaumburg, IL 60195-3187, (847)885-1272
Amer. Acad. of Craniomandibular Disorders [★14106]
Amer. Acad. of Craniomandibular Orthopedics [★14106]
Amer. Acad. of Criminalistics - Defunct.
Amer. Acad. of Crisis Interveners - Address unknown since 2003.
Amer. Acad. of Crown and Bridge Prosthodontics [★14097]
Amer. Acad. of Dental Electrosurgery - Address unknown since 2000.
Amer. Acad. of Dental Gp. Practice [14094], 2525 E Arizona Biltmore Cir., Ste. 127, Phoenix, AZ 85016, (602)381-1185
Amer. Acad. of Dental Practice Admin. [14095], c/o Kathleen S. Uebel, Exec. Dir., 1063 Whippoorwill Ln., Palatine, IL 60067-7064, (847)934-4404
Amer. Acad. of Dental Radiology [★14104]
Amer. Acad. of Dentists - Defunct.
Amer. Acad. of Dermatology [14189], PO Box 4014, Schaumburg, IL 60168-4014, (847)240-1280
Amer. Acad. of Dermatology [IO], Schaumburg, IL, United States
Amer. Acad. of Dermatology and Syphilology [★IO]
Amer. Acad. of Dermatology and Syphilology [★14189]
Amer. Acad. of Diplomacy [5744], 1800 K St. NW, Ste. 1014, Washington, DC 20006, (202)331-3721
Amer. Acad. of Disability Evaluating Physicians [14033], 150 N Wacker Dr., Ste. 1420, Chicago, IL 60606, (312)658-1171
Amer. Acad. of Emergency Medicine [14323], 555 E Wells St., Ste. 1100, Milwaukee, WI 53202-3823, (414)276-7390
Amer. Acad. of Environmental Engineers [6982], 130 Holiday Ct., Ste. 100, Annapolis, MD 21401, (410)266-3311
Amer. Acad. of Environmental Medicine [14360], 7701 E Kellogg Dr., Ste. 625, Wichita, KS 67207-1705, (316)684-5500
Amer. Acad. of Environmental Medicine [IO], Wichita, KS, United States
Amer. Acad. of Equine Art [9410], c/o Kentucky Horse Park, 4089 Iron Works Pkwy., Lexington, KY 40511, (859)281-6031
Amer. Acad. of Estate Planning Attorneys [5473], 6050 Santo Rd., Ste. 240, San Diego, CA 92124, (858)453-2128
Amer. Acad. of Esthetic Dentistry [14096], 737 N Michigan Ave., Ste. 2100, Chicago, IL 60611, (312)981-6770
Amer. Acad. of Experts in Traumatic Stress [16685], 368 Veterans Memorial Hwy., Commack, NY 11725, (631)543-2217
Amer. Acad. of Facial Plastic and Reconstructive Surgery [14038], 310 S Henry St., Alexandria, VA 22314, (703)299-9291
Amer. Acad. of Family Physicians [14383], PO Box 11210, Shawnee Mission, KS 66207-1210, (913)906-6000
Amer. Acad. of Fed. Civil Ser. Physicians [★15998]
Amer. Acad. of Fertility Care Professionals [12634], 11700 Studt Ave., Ste. C, St. Louis, MO 63131, (402)489-3733
Amer. Acad. of Fixed Prosthodontics [14097], PO Box 1409, Bodega Bay, CA 94923-1409, (707)875-3040

A star before a book entry number signifies that the name is not listed separately, but is mentioned within the entry.

American Acad. of Floriculture [★**1493**]

Amer. Acad. of Forensic Psychology [**5746**], c/o Alan M. Goldstein, PhD, 13 Arden Dr., Hartsdale, NY 10530, (914)693-7760

Amer. Acad. of Forensic Sciences [**5747**], 410 N 21st St., Colorado Springs, CO 80904-2712, (719)636-1100

Amer. Acad. of Gen. Practice [★**14383**]

Amer. Acad. of Gnathologic Orthopedics [**14098**], Box 687, Arnold, CA 95223, (800)510-AAGO

Amer. Acad. of Gold Foil Operators [**14099**], c/o Dr. David F. Bridgeman, Pres., 701 N Main St., New Martinsville, WV 26155, (740)483-9096

Amer. Acad. of Head, Neck and Facial Pain [★**15751**]

Amer. Acad. of Health Administration - Address unknown since 1991.

Amer. Acad. of Hea. Care Providers [★**15302**]

Amer. Acad. of Hea. Care Providers in the Addictive Disorders [**15302**], 314 W Superior St., Ste. 508, Duluth, MN 55802, (218)727-3940

Amer. Acad. of Hea. Physics [**16598**], 1313 Dolley Madison Blvd., Ste. 402, McLean, VA 22101, (703)790-1745

Amer. Acad. of Healthcare Attorneys [★**5782**]

Amer. Acad. of the History of Dentistry [**14100**], c/o Marc B. Ehrlich, DMD, Sec.-Treas., 1371 Beacon St., Brookline, MA 02446, (617)566-2734

Amer. Acad. of HIV Medicine [**13556**], 1705 DeSales St. NW, Ste. 700, Washington, DC 20036, (202)659-0699

Amer. Acad. of Home Care Physicians [**14835**], PO Box 1037, Edgewood, MD 21040-0337, (410)676-7966

Amer. Acad. of Homeopathic Medicine - Address unknown since 1988.

Amer. Acad. of Homiletics [★**20081**]

Amer. Acad. of Hospice and Palliative Medicine [**15985**], 4700 W Lake Ave., Glenview, IL 60025-1485, (847)375-4712

Amer. Acad. of Hosp. Attorneys [★**5782**]

Amer. Acad. of Husband-Coached Childbirth [**15579**], PO Box 5224, Sherman Oaks, CA 91413-5224, (818)788-6662

Amer. Acad. of Implant Dentistry [**14101**], 211 E Chicago Ave., Ste. 750, Chicago, IL 60611, (312)335-1550

Amer. Acad. of Implant Dentures [★**14101**]

Amer. Acad. of Implant Prosthodontics [**14102**], 709 Haddonfield-Berlin Rd., Voorhees, NJ 08043, (856)782-3990

Amer. Acad. of Insurance Medicine [**IO**], Ottawa, ON, Canada

Amer. Acad. for Jewish Res. - Defunct.

Amer. Acad. of Kinesiology and Physical Educ. [**8978**], c/o Human Kinetics, PO Box 5076, Champaign, IL 61820-2200, (217)351-5076

Amer. Acad. of Laser Dentistry [★**14088**]

Amer. Acad. for Liberal Educ. [**8775**], 1050 17th St. NW, Ste. 400, Washington, DC 20036, (202)452-8611

Amer. Acad. of Matrimonial Lawyers [**5698**], 150 N Michigan Ave., Ste. 2040, Chicago, IL 60601, (312)263-6477

Amer. Acad. of Maxillofacial Prosthetics [**14103**], c/o Dr. Steven P. Haug, Exec. Sec., 1121 W Michigan St., Indianapolis, IN 46202, (317)274-5571

Amer. Acad. of Mechanics [**7297**], c/o Rohan Abeyaratne, Pres., Massachusetts Inst. of Technology, 77 Massachusetts Ave., Cambridge, MA 02139-4307, (617)253-2201

Amer. Acad. of Medical Acupuncture [**15740**], 4929 Wilshire Blvd., Ste. 428, Los Angeles, CA 90010, (323)937-5514

Amer. Acad. of Medical Administrators [**15045**], 701 Lee St., Ste. 600, Des Plaines, IL 60016-4516, (847)759-8601

Amer. Acad. of Medical Administrators Res. and Educational Found. [**15046**], 701 Lee St., Ste. 600, Des Plaines, IL 60016, (847)759-8601

Amer. Acad. of Medical Directors [★**15056**]

Amer. Acad. of Medical Ethics - Address unknown since 2003.

Amer. Acad. of Medical Hypnoanalysts [**14914**], 1022 Depot Hill Rd., Broomfield, CO 80020, (888)454-9766

Amer. Acad. of Medical-Legal Analysis - Address unknown since 1999.

Amer. Acad. of Medical Mgt. [**15086**], Crossville Commons, 560 W Crossville Rd., Ste. 103, Roswell, GA 30075, (770)649-7150

Amer. Acad. of Medical Preventics [★**16051**]

Amer. Acad. of Medical Preventics [★**IO**]

Amer. Acad. on Mental Retardation [★**15238**]

Amer. Acad. of Microbiology [**6559**], 1752 N St. NW, Washington, DC 20036, (202)737-3600

American Academy of Microbiology [**IO**], Washington, DC, United States

Amer. Acad. of Micropigmentation [**14039**], c/o Charles S. Zwerling, MD, Chm., 2709 Medical Off. Pl., Goldsboro, NC 27534, (919)736-3937

Amer. Acad. of Ministry [**19914**], PO Box 681868, Franklin, TN 37068-1868, (615)599-9889

Amer. Acad. of Natural Family Planning [★**12634**]

Amer. Acad. of Neurological and Orthopaedic Surgeons [**15409**], 10 Cascade Creek Ln., Las Vegas, NV 89113, (702)388-7390

American Academy of Neurological Surgery - Address unknown since 2003.

Amer. Acad. of Neurology [**15376**], 1080 Montreal Ave., St. Paul, MN 55116, (651)695-2717

Amer. Acad. of Nurse Practitioners [**15429**], PO Box 12846, Austin, TX 78711, (512)442-4262

Amer. Acad. of Nursing [**15430**], 555 E Wells St., Ste. 1100, Milwaukee, WI 53202, (414)287-0289

Amer. Acad. of Obstetrics and Gynecology [★**15584**]

Amer. Acad. of Occupational Medicine [★**15624**]

Amer. Acad. of Ophthalmology [**15656**], PO Box 7424, San Francisco, CA 94120-7424, (415)561-8500

Amer. Acad. of Optometry [**15711**], 6110 Executive Blvd., Ste. 506, Rockville, MD 20852, (301)984-1441

Amer. Acad. of Optometry [**IO**], Rockville, MD, United States

Amer. Acad. of Optometry - British Chap. [**IO**], Woodbridge, United Kingdom

Amer. Acad. of Oral and Maxillofacial Pathology [**15852**], 214 N Hale St., Wheaton, IL 60187, (630)579-3252

Amer. Acad. of Oral and Maxillofacial Radiology [**14104**], PO Box 1010, Evans, GA 30809-1010, (706)721-2607

Amer. Acad. of Oral Medicine [**14105**], PO Box 2016, Edmonds, WA 98020-9516, (425)778-6162

Amer. Acad. Oral Pathology [★**15852**]

Amer. Acad. of Oral Roentgenology [★**14104**]

Amer. Acad. of Organ - Defunct.

Amer. Acad. of Orofacial Pain [**14106**], 19 Mantua Rd., Mount Royal, NJ 08061, (856)423-3629

Amer. Acad. of Orthodontics for the Gen. Practitioner [**14107**], 9701 Wesley St., Ste. 202, Greenville, TX 75402, (800)634-2027

Amer. Acad. of Orthopaedic Manual Physical Therapists [**15971**], 2104 Delta Way, Ste. 7, Tallahassee, FL 32303, (850)222-0397

Amer. Acad. of Orthopaedic Surgeons [**15752**], 6300 N River Rd., Rosemont, IL 60018-4262, (847)823-7186

American Academy of Orthopaedic Surgeons [**IO**], Rosemont, IL, United States

Amer. Acad. of Orthotists and Prosthetists [**15782**], 526 King St., Ste. 201, Alexandria, VA 22314, (703)836-0788

Amer. Acad. of Osteopathic Surgeons [★**15792**]

Amer. Acad. of Osteopathy [**15790**], 3500 DePauw Blvd., Ste. 1080, Indianapolis, IN 46268, (317)879-1881

Amer. Acad. of Otolaryngic Allergy and Found. [**13593**], 1990 M St. NW, Ste. 680, Washington, DC 20036, (202)955-5010

Amer. Acad. of Otolaryngology - Head and Neck Surgery [**15817**], 1 Prince St., Alexandria, VA 22314-3354, (703)836-4444

Amer. Acad. of Pain Mgt. [**15831**], 13947 Mono Way, Ste. A, Sonora, CA 95370, (209)533-9744

Amer. Acad. of Pain Medicine [**15832**], 4700 W Lake Ave., Glenview, IL 60025, (847)375-4731

Amer. Acad. of Pediatric Dentistry [**14108**], 211 E Chicago Ave., Ste. 700, Chicago, IL 60611-2663, (312)337-2169

Amer. Acad. of Pediatrics [**15880**], 141 NW Point Blvd., Elk Grove Village, IL 60007-1098, (847)434-4000

Amer. Acad. of Pedodontics [★**14108**]

Amer. Acad. of Periodontology [**14109**], 737 N Michigan Ave., Ste. 800, Chicago, IL 60611-6660, (312)787-5518

Amer. Acad. of Pharmaceutical Physicians Educ. Found. [★**8840**]

Amer. Acad. of Philately [★**22783**]

Amer. Acad. of Physical Educ. [★**8978**]

Amer. Acad. of Physical Medicine and Rehabilitation [**16307**], 330 N Wabash Ave., Ste. 2500, Chicago, IL 60611-7617, (312)464-9700

Amer. Acad. of Physician Assistants [**15973**], 950 N Washington St., Alexandria, VA 22314-1552, (703)836-2272

Amer. Acad. of Physician Assistants in Occupational Medicine [**15622**], 950 N Washington St., Alexandria, VA 22314-1552, (800)596-4398

Amer. Acad. on Physician and Patients [★**15984**]

Amer. Acad. of Physiologic Dentistry - Address unknown since 2003.

Amer. Acad. for Plastics Res. in Dentistry [★**14084**]

Amer. Acad. Podiatric Admin. [★**16024**]

Amer. Acad. of Podiatric Mgt. [★**16024**]

Amer. Acad. of Podiatric Practice Mgt. [**16024**], 10 Maple St., Ste. 301, Middleton, MA 01949, (978)646-9091

Amer. Acad. of Podiatric Sports Medicine [**16471**], 109 Greenwich Dr., Walkersville, MD 21793, (301)845-9887

Amer. Acad. of Political and Social Sci. [**7520**], 3814 Walnut St., Philadelphia, PA 19104-6197, (215)746-6500

Amer. Acad. of Polygraph Examiners [★**5753**]

Amer. Acad. of Practice Mgt. in Podiatry [★**16024**]

Amer. Acad. of Procedural Coders [★**14694**]

Amer. Acad. of Professional Coders [**14694**], 2480 S 3850 W, Ste. B, Salt Lake City, UT 84120, (801)236-2200

Amer. Acad. for Professional Law Enforcement - Defunct.

Amer. Acad. of Psychiatry and the Law [**5780**], One Regency Dr., PO Box 30, Bloomfield, CT 06002-0030, (860)242-5450

Amer. Acad. of Psychoanalysis [★**16101**]

Amer. Acad. of Psychoanalysis and Dynamic Psychiatry [**16101**], PO Box 30, 1 Regency Dr., Bloomfield, CT 06002, (888)691-8281

Amer. Acad. of Psychotherapists [**16198**], 605 Poole Dr., Garner, NC 27529, (919)779-5051

Amer. Acad. of Religion [**8223**], 825 Houston Mill Rd. NE, Ste. 300, Atlanta, GA 30329, (404)727-3049

Amer. Acad. of Res. Historians of Medieval Spain [**10081**], c/o Helen Nader, Sec.-Treas., Univ. of Arizona, Dept. of History, PO Box 210027, Tucson, AZ 85721

Amer. Acad. of Restorative Dentistry [**14110**], c/o CityStar Gp., Inc., PO Box 26385, Colorado Springs, CO 80936, (719)559-1945

Amer. Acad. in Rome [**IO**], Rome, Italy

Amer. Acad. of Safety Education - Address unknown since 2007.

Amer. Acad. of Sanitarians [**16383**], c/o Gary Noonan, Exec. Sec.-Treas., 1568 LeGrand Cir., Lawrenceville, GA 30043-8191, (678)407-1051

Amer. Acad. of Sanitary Engineers [★**6982**]

Amer. Acad. of Sclerotherapy [★**15814**]

Amer. Acad. of Sleep Medicine [**16418**], One Westbrook Corporate Ctr., Ste. 920, Westchester, IL 60154, (708)492-0930

Amer. Acad. of Somnology [**16419**], PO Box 27077, Las Vegas, NV 89126-1077, (702)371-0947

Amer. Acad. of Spinal Surgeons - Address unknown since 1999.

Amer. Acad. of Sports Physicians [**16472**], 17445 Oak Creek Ct., Encino, CA 91316, (818)501-8855

Amer. Acad. of State Certified Appraisers [**270**], 1438-F W Main St., Ephrata, PA 17522-1345, (717)721-3500

Amer. Acad. of Stress Disorders - Defunct.

Amer. Acad. of Teachers of Singing [**8898**], c/o Jan Eric Douglas, Chm., 777 W End Ave., New York, NY 10025-5551, (212)666-5951

Reference to "IO" in place of a book number signifies that the association may be found in the 45th edition of International Organizations.

Amer. Acad. of Thermology - Address unknown since 2002.

Amer. Acad. of Transportation - Address unknown since 1995.

Amer. Acad. of Tropical Medicine [16692]

Amer. Acad. of Tuberculosis Physicians - Defunct.

Amer. Acad. of Veterinary and Comparative Toxicology [16736], c/o Dr. Ramesh Gupta, Pres., Murray State Univ. in Kentucky, Breathitt Veterinary Center, 715 North Dr., PO Box 2000, Hopkinsville, KY 42240, (270)886-3959

Amer. Acad. of Veterinary Dermatology - Address unknown since 2002.

Amer. Acad. of Veterinary Nutrition [16737], c/o Wilbur B. Amand, VMD, Exec. Dir., 6 N Pennel Rd., Media, PA 19063-5520, (610)892-4812

Amer. Acad. of Veterinary Pharmacology and Therapeutics [16738], c/o Dr. Joe S. Gloyd, Sec.-Treas., Gloyd Gp., 3 Penny Lane Ct., Wilmington, DE 19803-4023, (302)761-9690

Amer. Acad. of Wine - Defunct.

Amer. Acad. of Wound Mgt. [16686], 1155 15th St. NW, Ste. 500, Washington, DC 20005, (202)457-8408

Amer. Accordion Musicological Soc. [10525], c/o Joanna Arnold Darrow, 322 Haddon Ave., Westmont, NJ 08108, (856)854-6628

Amer. Accordionists' Assn. [10526], 152 Home Fair Dr., Fairfield, CT 06825, (203)335-2045

Amer. Accounting Assn. [7], 5717 Bessie Dr., Sarasota, FL 34233-2330, (941)921-7747

Amer. Accreditation Healthcare Commn. [14679], 1220 L St. NW, Ste. 400, Washington, DC 20005, (202)216-9010

Amer. Action Fund for Blind Children and Adults [16821], 1800 Johnson St., Ste. 100, Baltimore, MD 21230, (410)659-9315

Amer. Acupuncture Assn. [15741], 4262 Kissena Blvd., Flushing, NY 11355, (718)886-4431

Amer. Adoption Cong. [11234], PO Box 42730, Washington, DC 20015, (202)483-3399

American Advent Mission Society [★19442]

American Advent Mission Society [★IO]

Amer. Advt. Fed. [83], 1101 Vermont Ave. NW, Ste. 500, Washington, DC 20005-6306, (202)898-0089

Amer. Advt. Fed. Educ. Services [24393], 1101 Vermont Ave. NW, Ste. 500, Washington, DC 20005, (202)898-0089

Amer. Affenpinscher Assn. - Address unknown since 1995.

Amer. Affiliation of Tall Clubs [★13300]

Amer. Affiliation of Tall Clubs [★IO]

Amer. Affiliation of Visiting Nurses Associations and Services [★15532]

Amer. Afghan Education Fund - Address unknown since 1999.

Amer.-African Affairs Assn. - Address unknown since 2001.

Amer. and African Bus. Women's Alliance [691], 1100 17th St. NW, Ste. 1100, Washington, DC 20036, (202)263-3520

Amer. and African Bus. Women's Alliance [IO], Washington, DC, United States

Amer. Agents Assn. [2128]

Amer. Aging Assn. [14507], c/o The Sally Balin Medical Center, 110 Chesley Dr., Media, PA 19063, (610)627-2626

American Aging Association [IO], Media, PA, United States

Amer. Agri-Women [16948], 11425 Pedee Creek Rd., Monmouth, OR 97361, (503)581-6610

Amer. Agri-Women Rsrc. Center [16949], c/o Eleanor Kiner, Dir., 27703 Kiner Rd. N, Almira, WA 99103

Amer. Agricultural Economics Assn. [6867], 555 E Wells, Ste. 1100, Milwaukee, WI 53202, (414)918-3190

Amer. Agricultural Economics Assn. [IO], Milwaukee, WI, United States

Amer. Agricultural Editors' Assn. [3076], PO Box 156, New Prague, MN 56071, (952)758-6502

Amer. Agricultural Law Assn. [5431], PO Box 2025, Eugene, OR 97402-0009, (541)485-1090

Amer. Agricultural Marketing Assn. - Address unknown since 2001.

Amer. Agricultural Movement [★16950]

Amer. Agriculture Movement [16950], c/o Larry Matlack, Pres., 13118 E Stroud Rd., Burrton, KS 67020, (620)463-3513

Amer. Aid Soc. of German Descendants [19071], 6540 N Milwaukee Ave., Chicago, IL 60631-1750, (773)763-9554

Amer. Aid Soc. of German Descendants [IO], Chicago, IL, United States

Amer. Aid Soc. for the West Indies - Defunct.

Amer. Aid to Ulster - Address unknown since 1994.

Amer. Air Mail Soc. [22780], c/o Stephen Reinhard, Treas., PO Box 110, Mineola, NY 11501

Amer. Airborne Assn. [20699], 10301 McKinstry Mill Rd., New Windsor, MD 21776-7903, (888)567-2927

Amer. Airgun Field Target Assn. [22976], c/o Steve Schulz, Sec.-Treas., 7223 Barnett Rd., Bethesda, MD 20817

American-Albanian Catholic Charity [★18506]

American-Albanian Catholic Charity [★IO]

Amer. Albino Assn. [★4855]

Amer. Albino Horse Club [★4855]

Amer. Alfalfa Processors Assn. [★1357]

Amer. Allergy Assn. - Defunct.

Amer. Alliance Against Violence [★17589]

American Alliance of Cancer Pain Initiatives [★15830]

Amer. Alliance of Ethical Movers [13346], 1200 DeKalb Pike, Center Square, PA 19422

Amer. Alliance for Hea., Physical Educ. and Recreation [★8979]

Amer. Alliance for Hea., Physical Educ., Recreation and Dance [★8979]

Amer. Alliance for Hea., Physical Educ., Recreation and Dance [8979], 1900 Assn. Dr., Reston, VA 20191-1598, (703)476-3400

Amer. Alliance for Medical Cannabis [15020], 44500 Tide Ave., Arch Cape, OR 97102, (503)436-1882

Amer. Alliance of Paralegals, Inc. [6149], 16815 E Shea Blvd., Ste. 110, PBM No. 101, Fountain Hills, AZ 85268

Amer. Alliance for Rights and Responsibilities [★17096]

Amer. Alliance for Theatre and Educ. [10998], 7475 Wisconsin Ave., Ste. 300A, Bethesda, MD 20814, (301)951-7977

Amer. Alligator Coun. - Defunct.

Amer. Alligator Farmers Assn. - Defunct.

Amer. Alpine Club [7074], 710 10th St., Ste. 100, Golden, CO 80401, (303)384-0110

Amer. Alternative Medical Assn. [13613], 2200 Market St., Ste. 329, Galveston, TX 77550-1530, (409)621-2600

Amer. Alternative Medicine Assn. [★13641]

Amer. Alumni Coun. [★8245]

Amer. Amaryllis Soc. Gp. [★6637]

Amer. Amaryllis Soc. Gp. [★IO]

Amer. Amateur Baseball Cong. [23100], 100 W Broadway, Farmington, NM 87401, (505)327-3120

Amer. Amateur Inventors Club - Defunct.

Amer. Amateur Karate Fed. [23559], 1930 Wilshire Blvd., Ste. 1007, Los Angeles, CA 90057, (213)483-8262

Amer. Amateur Press Assn. [22910], c/o Ivan D. Snyder, Sec.-Treas., 2951 Archer Dr., Springfield, OH 45503-1209, (937)390-3499

Amer. Amateur Racquetball Assn. [★23678]

Amer. Ambulance Assn. [14313], 8201 Greensboro Dr., Ste. 300, McLean, VA 22102, (703)610-9018

Amer. Ambulance and Rescue Assn. - Defunct.

Amer. Ambulatory Fracture Assn. [★15756]

Amer. Amputee Found. [11916], PO Box 250218, Little Rock, AR 72225, (501)666-2523

Amer. Amputee Hockey Assn. [23799], 150 York St., Stoughton, MA 02072, (781)297-1393

Amer. Amputee Soccer Assn. [23773], 1022 Creekside Dr., Wilmington, DE 19804, (302)683-0997

Amer. Amusement Machine Assn. [1296], 450 E Higgins Rd., Ste. 201, Elk Grove Village, IL 60007, (847)290-9088

American Amusement Machine Association [IO], Elk Grove Village, IL, United States

American Amusement Machine Charitable Foundation [★IO]

American Amusement Machine Charitable Foundation [★1296]

Amer. Andalusian Assn. [★4894]

Amer. Andalusian Assn. [★IO]

Amer. Angora Goat Breeder's Assn. [4122], PO Box 195, Rocksprings, TX 78880, (830)683-4483

Amer. Angus Assn. [4212], 3201 Frederick Ave., St. Joseph, MO 64506, (816)383-5100

Amer. Animal Health Pharmaceutical Assn. - Defunct.

Amer. Animal Hosp. Assn. [16739], 12575 W Bayaud Ave., Lakewood, CO 80228, (303)986-2800

Amer. Animal Welfare Assn. - Defunct.

Amer. Anorexia Bulimia Assn. [★14302]

Amer. Anorexia Bulimia Assn. [★14302]

Amer. Antarctic Assn. - Defunct.

Amer. Anthropological Assn. [6402], 2200 Wilson Blvd., Ste. 600, Arlington, VA 22201-3357, (703)528-1902

Amer. Anthropological Assn; Gen. Anthropology Division of the [6417]

Amer. Anti-Terrorism Inst. - Defunct.

Amer. Anti-Vivisection Soc. [11345], 801 Old York Rd., Ste. 204, Jenkintown, PA 19046, (215)887-0816

Amer. Antiquarian Soc. [10008], 185 Salisbury St., Worcester, MA 01609-1634, (508)755-5221

Amer. Antique Graphics Soc. - Address unknown since 2003.

Amer. Antique Playing Card Collector's Club [★21955]

Amer. Antiques and Crafts Soc. - Defunct.

Amer. Apitherapy Soc. [13614], 4835 Van Nuys Blvd. 100, Sherman Oaks, CA 91403, (818)501-0446

Amer. Appaloosa Assn. Worldwide [4809], PO Box 429, Republic, MO 65738-0429, (417)466-2046

American Appaloosa Association Worldwide [IO], Republic, MO, United States

Amer. Apparel Contractors Assn. [★IO]

Amer. Apparel Contractors Assn. [★222]

Amer. Apparel and Footwear Assn. [221], 1601 N Kent St., Ste. 1200, Arlington, VA 22209, (703)524-1864

Amer. Apparel and Footwear Manufacturers Assn. [★221]

Amer. Apparel Machinery Trade Assn. [1990]

Amer. Apparel Manufacturers Assn. [★221]

Amer. Apparel Producers Assn. [★222]

Amer. Apparel Producers Assn. [★IO]

American Apparel Producers Network [IO], Atlanta, GA, United States

Amer. Apparel Producers' Network [222], PO Box 720693, Atlanta, GA 30358, (404)843-3171

Amer. Aquarist Soc. - Address unknown since 2007.

Amer. Aquarium Societies; Fed. of [7173]

Amer. Arab Affairs Coun. [★18063]

Amer. Arab Affairs Coun. [★IO]

American-Arab Anti-Discrimination Comm. [17082], 1732 Wisconsin Ave. NW, Washington, DC 20007, (202)244-2990

American-Arab Assn. for Commerce and Indus. [★24357]

Amer. Arab Chamber of Commerce [24225], 12740 W Warren Ave., Ste. 101, Dearborn, MI 48126, (313)945-1700

Amer.-Arab Relations Comm. - Address unknown since 2002.

Amer. Arab Relief Agency - Defunct.

Amer. Arabic Assn. - Address unknown since 2001.

Amer. Arbitration Assn. [5448], 1633 Broadway, 10th Fl., New York, NY 10019, (212)716-5800

Amer. Archery Coun. - Defunct.

Amer. Architectural Found. [★6461]

Amer. Architectural Found. [6461], 1799 New York Ave. NW, Washington, DC 20006, (202)626-7318

Amer. Architectural Manufacturers Assn. [588], 1827 Walden Off. Sq., Ste. 550, Schaumburg, IL 60173-4287, (847)303-5664

Amer. Archives Assn. - Defunct.

Amer. Armsport Assn. [23059], 176 Dean Rd., Mooresburg, TN 37811, (423)272-6162

Amer. Art; Archives of [9419]

Amer. Art Deco Dealers Assn. [295], PO Box 2454, Cordova, TN 38088-2454

A star before a book entry number signifies that the name is not listed separately, but is mentioned within the entry.

Amer. Art Pottery Assn. [9411], c/o Marie Latta, 907 Maurer, Wilton, IA 52778

Amer. Art Therapy Assn. [16199], 5999 Stevenson Ave., Alexandria, VA 22304, (703)212-2238

Amer. Artists of Chinese Brush Painting [9538], PO Box 4256, Huntington Beach, CA 92605

Amer. Artists Professional League [9489], 47 5th Ave., New York, NY 10003, (212)645-1345

Amer. Arts Alliance [9539], 1112 16th St. NW, Ste. 400, Washington, DC 20036, (202)207-3850

Amer. Arts and Crafts Alliance [9824], PO Box 250826, New York, NY 10025, (212)866-2239

Amer.-ASEAN Trade Coun. - Address unknown since 1999.

Amer.-Asian Educational Exchange - Defunct.

Amer. Asiatic Assn. - Address unknown since 1995.

Amer. Assembly [18418], 475 Riverside Dr., Ste. 456, New York, NY 10115-0456, (212)870-3500

Amer. Assembly of Collegiate Schools of Bus. [★8010]

Amer. Assembly of Collegiate Schools of Bus. [★IO]

Amer. Assembly for Men in Nursing [15431], c/o Byron McCain, PO Box 130220, Birmingham, AL 35213, (205)802-7551

Amer. Assisted Living Nurses Assn. [15432], PO Box 10469, Napa, CA 94581, (760)510-6624

Amer. Assoc. Rental Operators [★3377]

Amer. Associates, Ben-Gurion Univ. of the Negev [8673], 1430 Broadway, 8th Fl., New York, NY 10018, (212)687-7721

Amer. Assn. of Aardvark Aficionados - Address unknown since 1999.

Amer. Assn. for the Abolition of Involuntary Mental Hospitalization - Defunct.

Amer. Assn. of Academic Editors - Address unknown since 1995.

Amer. Assn. for Accreditation of Ambulatory Plastic Surgery Facilities [★16557]

Amer. Assn. for Accreditation of Ambulatory Surgery Facilities [16557], 5101 Washington St., Ste. 2F, Gurnee, IL 60031, (847)775-1970

Amer. Assn. for Accreditation of Lab. Animal Care [★13695]

Amer. Assn. for Accreditation of Lab. Animal Care [★IO]

Amer. Assn. for Active Lifestyles and Fitness; School and Community Safety Soc. of Am. of the [12989]

Amer. Assn. for Acupuncture and Oriental Medicine [★15742]

Amer. Assn. for Acupuncture and Oriental Medicine [★IO]

Amer. Assn. of adaptedSPORTS Programs [23333], PO Box 451047, Atlanta, GA 31145, (404)294-0070

Amer. Assn. for Adult and Continuing Educ. [8146], 10111 Martin Luther King, Jr. Hwy., Ste. 200C, Bowie, MD 20720, (301)459-6261

Amer. Assn. for the Advancement of Atheism - Address unknown since 2003.

Amer. Assn. for the Advancement of Core Curriculum - Address unknown since 2003.

Amer. Assn. for the Advancement of the Humanities - Defunct.

Amer. Assn. for Advancement of Physical Educ. [★8979]

Amer. Assn. for the Advancement of Sci. [7596], 1200 New York Ave. NW, Washington, DC 20005, (202)326-6400

Amer. Assn. for the Advancement of Slavic Stud. [10966], 8 Story St., Cambridge, MA 02138, (617)495-0677

Amer. Assn. of Advt. Agencies [84], 405 Lexington Ave., 18th Fl., New York, NY 10174-1801, (212)682-2500

Amer. Assn. for Aerosol Res. [6662], 15000 Commerce Pkwy., Ste. C, Mount Laurel, NJ 08054, (856)439-9080

Amer. Assn. for Affirmative Action [12066], 888 16th St. NW, Ste. 800, Washington, DC 20006, (202)349-9855

Amer. Assn. Against Addiction - Defunct.

Amer. Assn. of Agricultural Coll. Editors [★4098]

Amer. Assn. of Agricultural Communicators of Tomorrow [★8714]

Amer. Assn. for Agricultural Educ. [7933], c/o Tim Murphy, Treas., Rm. 229 Scoates Hall, Campus Mail 2116, Texas A&M Univ., College Station, TX 77843-2116, (979)862-3419

Amer. Assn. for Agricultural Engg. and Vocational Agriculture [★9298]

American Assn. of AIDS Executives - Address unknown since 2000.

Amer. Assn. of Airport Executives [138], 601 Madison St., Ste. 400, Alexandria, VA 22314, (703)824-0500

Amer. Assn. of Alternative Healers - Address unknown since 2006.

Amer. Assn. of Ambulatory Surgery Centers [16558], PO Box 5271, Johnson City, TN 37602-5271, (423)915-1001

Amer. Assn. of Anatomists [13667], 9650 Rockville Pike, Bethesda, MD 20814-3998, (301)634-7910

Amer. Assn. of Anger Mgt. Providers [15185], 12301 Wilshire Blvd., Ste. 418, Brentwood, CA 94513, (310)207-3591

Amer. Assn. for Applied Linguistics [10397], 3416 Primm Ln., Birmingham, AL 35216, (205)824-7700

Amer. Assn. of Applied and Preventive Psychology [16119], PO Box 3822, Tucson, AZ 85722, (520)621-9182

American Association of Applied and Preventive Psychology [IO], Tucson, AZ, United States

Amer. Assn. of Architectural Bibliographers - Defunct.

Amer. Assn. for Artificial Intelligence [6483], 445 Burgess Dr., Ste. 100, Menlo Park, CA 94025, (650)328-3123

Amer. Assn. of Attorney-Certified Public Accountants [8], 3921 Old Lee Hwy., Ste. 71A, Fairfax, VA 22030, (703)352-8064

Amer. Assn. of Audio Analgesia - Defunct.

Amer. Assn. of Automatic Door Mfrs. [1163], 1300 Sumner Ave., Cleveland, OH 44115-2851, (216)241-7333

Amer. Assn. for Automotive Medicine [★12951]

Amer. Assn. of Avian Pathologists [16740], 953 Coll. Sta. Rd., Athens, GA 30602-4875, (706)542-5645

Amer. Assn. of Ayurvedic Medicine - Defunct.

Amer. Assn. of Backgammon Clubs - Address unknown since 1999.

Amer. Assn. of Baggage Traffic Managers - Defunct.

Amer. Assn. of Bank Directors [456], 4701 Sangamore Rd., Ste. P-15, Bethesda, MD 20816, (301)263-9841

Amer. Assn. of Behavioral and Social Sciences [6522], c/o Diane Keffer, Dept. of SSME, Univ. of Tampa, 401 W Kennedy Blvd., Tampa, FL 33606-1490

Amer. Assn. of Behavioral Therapists [13744], PO Box 1737, Ormond Beach, FL 32175-1737, (386)767-4060

Amer. Assn. of Bible Colleges [★8080]

Amer. Assn. of Bicycle Importers - Address unknown since 2003.

Amer. Assn. of Billing Professionals - Address unknown since 1999.

Amer. Assn. of Bioanalysts [14989], 906 Olive St., Ste. 1200, St. Louis, MO 63101-1434, (314)241-1445

Amer. Assn. of Bioanalysts Bd. of Registry [15126], 906 Olive St., Ste. 1200, St. Louis, MO 63101-1434, (314)241-1445

Amer. Assn. of Biofeedback Clinicians - Defunct.

Amer. Assn. of Birth Centers [15580], 3123 Gottschall Rd., Perkiomenville, PA 18074, (215)234-8068

Amer. Assn. of Black Russian Terriers [22185], c/o Karen Magill, Treas., 341 Laurel Dr., Danville, CA 94526, (925)820-1636

Amer. Assn. of Blacks in Energy [6936], 927 15th St. NW, Ste. 200, Washington, DC 20005-2321, (202)371-9530

Amer. Assn. of Blood Banks [13761], 8101 Glenbrook Rd., Bethesda, MD 20814-2749, (301)907-6977

Amer. Assn. of Book Wholesalers - Address unknown since 1995.

Amer. Assn. of Botanical Gardens and Arboreta [★4973]

Amer. Assn. of Botanical Gardens and Arboretums [★4973]

Amer. Assn. of Bovine Practitioners [16741], PO Box 3610, Auburn, AL 36831-3610, (334)821-0442

Amer. Assn. of Breeders of Holsteiner Horses [★4824]

Amer. Assn. for Budget and Prog. Anal. [6201], PO Box 1157, Falls Church, VA 22041, (703)941-4300

Amer. Assn. of Business Brokers - Defunct.

Amer. Assn. of Bus. Valuation Specialists [692], PO Box 13089, Tallahassee, FL 32317, (850)878-3134

Amer. Assn. of Cable T.V. Owners - Address unknown since 1999.

Amer. Assn. for Cancer Educ. [13789], c/o Paula Brown, Exec. Asst., San Diego Hospice and Palliative Care, 4311 3rd Ave., San Diego, CA 92103-1407, (619)278-6164

Amer. Assn. for Cancer Res. [15635], 615 Chestnut St., 17th Fl., Philadelphia, PA 19106-4406, (215)440-9300

Amer. Assn. for Cancer Res. [IO], Philadelphia, PA, United States

Amer. Assn. of Candy Technologists [7087], 175 Rock Rd., Glen Rock, NJ 07452, (201)652-2655

Amer. Assn. of Cardiovascular Nurses [★15433]

Amer. Assn. of Cardiovascular and Pulmonary Rehabilitation [13886], 401 N Michigan Ave., Ste. 2200, Chicago, IL 60611-4267, (312)321-5146

Amer. Assn. for Career Educ. [8046], 2900 Amby Pl., Hermosa Beach, CA 90254-2216, (310)376-7378

Amer. Assn. of Caregiving Youth [13466], 3998 FAU Blvd., No. 307, Boca Raton, FL 33481-1525, (561)391-7401

Amer. Assn. of Cat Enthusiasts [21899], PO Box 321, Ledyard, CT 06339, (973)658-5198

Amer. Assn. of Ceramic Dealers - Defunct.

Amer. Assn. of Ceramic Indus. [★786]

Amer. Assn. of Cereal Chemists [★6660]

Amer. Assn. of Cereal Chemists [★IO]

Amer. Assn. of Cereal Chemists; Milling and Baking Division of [★7095]

Amer. Assn. of Certified Allergists [13594]

Amer. Assn. of Certified Allied Hea. Personnel in Ophthalmology [★15674]

Amer. Assn. of Certified Orthoptists [15657], c/o Ronald Biernacki, CO, Pres., Vanderbilt Univ., 104 MAB TN Lions EYE Center, Nashville, TN 37212, (615)936-2250

Amer. Assn. of Chairmen of Medical School Departments of Pathology [★15863]

Amer. Assn. of Chairs of Departments of Psychiatry [16065], c/o Lucille F. Meinsler, Exec. Sec., 1594 Cumberland St., Lebanon, PA 17042, (717)270-1673

Amer. Assn. of Chamber Magazines - Defunct.

Amer. Assn. of Cheerleading Coaches and Advisors [23061], 6745 Lenox Center Ct., Ste. 318, Memphis, TN 38115, (800)533-6583

Amer. Assn. for Child Psychoanalysis [★16106]

Amer. Assn. of Children's Residential Centers [13467], 11700 W Lake Park Dr., Milwaukee, WI 53224, (877)332-2272

Amer. Assn. for Chinese Companies - Defunct.

Amer. Assn. for Chinese Stud. [8074], c/o Prof. Peter C.Y. Chow, Exec. Dir., The City Coll. - CUNY, NAC R4/116, Convent Ave. and 138th St., New York, NY 10031, (212)650-6206

Amer. Assn. of Christian Counselors [19862], PO Box 739, Forest, VA 24551, (434)525-9470

Amer. Assn. of Christian Counselors [IO], Forest, VA, United States

Amer. Assn. of Christian Schools [7875], Natl. Off., 602 Belvoir Ave., East Ridge, TN 37412, (423)629-4280

Amer. Assn. of Christian Schools of Higher Learning - Defunct.

Amer. Assn. for Chronic Fatigue Syndrome [★14266]

Amer. Assn. of Classified School Employees [24041], 555 New Jersey Ave. NW, Washington, DC 20001, (800)879-4597

Amer. Assn. of Cleaning Equipment Manufacturers - Address unknown since 2002.

Amer. Assn. for Cleft Palate Rehabilitation [★14055]

Amer. Assn. of Clinic Physicians and Surgeons - Defunct.

Amer. Assn. of Clinical Anatomists [13668], c/o Brian R. MacPherson, PhD, Sec., Univ. of Kentucky Coll. of Medicine, Anatomy and Neurobiology, MN225 Chandler Medical Ctr., Lexington, KY 40536-0298, (859)323-5539

Reference to "IO" in place of a book number signifies that the association may be found in the 45th edition of International Organizations.

Amer. Assn. for Clinical Chemistry [13936], 1850 K St. NW, Ste. 625, Washington, DC 20006, (202)857-0717

American Association for Clinical Chemistry [IO], Washington, DC, United States

Amer. Assn. of Clinical Chemists [★IO]

Amer. Assn. of Clinical Chemists [★13936]

Amer. Assn. of Clinical Directors [15986], 520 N Northwest Hwy., Park Ridge, IL 60068-2573, (847)825-5586

Amer. Assn. of Clinical Endocrinologists [14350], 245 Riverside Ave., Ste. 200, Jacksonville, FL 32202, (904)353-7878

Amer. Assn. for Clinical Histocompatibility Testing [★14931]

Amer. Assn. for Clinical Immunology and Allergy [★13596]

Amer. Assn. of Clinical Lab. Supervisors and Administrators [★14993]

Amer. Assn. of Clinical Urologists [16698], 1100 E Woodfield Rd., Ste. 520, Schaumburg, IL 60173, (847)517-7225

Amer. Assn. of Code Enforcement [5959], 5310 E Main St., Ste. 104, Columbus, OH 43213, (614)552-2633

Amer. Assn. of Coll. Baseball Coaches [★23101]

Amer. Assn. of Coll. Baseball Coaches [★IO]

Amer. Assn. of Coll. Bus. Officers [★7897]

Amer. Assn. of Coll. and Univ. Bus. Officers [★7897]

American Assn. of Colleges [★12721]

Amer. Assn. of Colleges of Chiropody [★16025]

Amer. Assn. of Colleges of Nursing [8842], 1 Dupont Cir. NW, Ste. 530, Washington, DC 20036, (202)463-6930

Amer. Assn. of Colleges of Osteopathic Medicine [15791], 5550 Friendship Blvd., Ste. 310, Chevy Chase, MD 20815-7231, (301)968-4100

Amer. Assn. of Colleges of Pharmacy [15909], 1426 Prince St., Alexandria, VA 22314, (703)739-2330

Amer. Assn. of Colleges of Podiatric Medicine [16025], 15850 Crabbs Br. Way, Ste. 320, Rockville, MD 20855, (301)948-9760

Amer. Assn. of Colleges of Podiatry [★16025]

Amer. Assn. of Colleges for Teacher Educ. [9208], 1307 New York Ave. NW, Ste. 300, Washington, DC 20005-4701, (202)293-2450

Amer. Assn. for Collegiate Independent Stud. [7944], c/o Lisa Bourlier, Pres., PO Box 888400, Lincoln, NE 68588-8400, (402)472-4338

Amer. Assn. of Collegiate Registrars [★7910]

Amer. Assn. of Collegiate Registrars and Admissions Officers [7910], 1 Dupont Cir. NW, Ste. 520, Washington, DC 20036, (202)293-9161

Amer. Assn. of Collegiate Schools of Bus. [★8010]

Amer. Assn. of Collegiate Schools of Bus. [★IO]

Amer. Assn. of Commerce Publications [★24257]

Amer. Assn. of Commercial Executives [★24251]

Amer. Assn. of Commodity Traders - Defunct.

Amer. Assn. of Community Colleges [8117], 1 Dupont Cir. NW, Ste. 410, Washington, DC 20036-1176, (202)728-0200

Amer. Assn. of Community Dental Programs [14111], 635 W 7th St., Ste. 309, Cincinnati, OH 45203, (513)621-0248

Amer. Assn. of Community and Junior Colleges [★8117]

Amer. Assn. of Community Psychiatrists [16066], c/o Francis M. Bell, Admin. Dir., PO Box 570218, Dallas, TX 75357-0218, (972)613-0985

Amer. Assn. of Community Theatre [10999], 8402 Briar Wood Cir., Lago Vista, TX 78645, (512)267-0711

Amer. Assn. for the Comparative Stud. of Law [★5865]

Amer. Assn. for Comprehensive Hea. Planning [★14542]

Amer. Assn. of Computer Professionals - Address unknown since 1988.

Amer. Assn. of Cmpt. Rental Professionals [895], Adams Hill Rd., Box 34, South Newfane, VT 05351, (877)846-6404

Amer. Assn. of Concerned Engineers - Defunct.

Amer. Assn. for Conservation Info. [★4358]

Amer. Assn. of Conservators and Restorers - Defunct.

Amer. Assn. for Consumer Benefits - Address unknown since 2006.

Amer. Assn. for Contamination Control [★7570]

Amer. Assn. for Contamination Control [★IO]

Amer. Assn. for Continuity of Care [14836]

Amer. Assn. of Convention Planners - Defunct.

Amer. Assn. for Corporate Contributions - Defunct.

Amer. Assn. of Correctional Facility Officers [★11870]

Amer. Assn. for Correctional and Forensic Psychology [11853], c/o Mr. David Randall, Sec.-Treas., PO Box 7642, Wilmington, NC 28406, (805)489-0665

Amer. Assn. of Correctional Officers [★11870]

Amer. Assn. of Correctional Psychologists [★11853]

Amer. Assn. Correctional Training Personnel [★11871]

Amer. Assn. Correctional Training Personnel [★IO]

Amer. Assn. of Cosmetic Surgeons [★14037]

Amer. Assn. of Cosmetology Schools/Cosmetology Educators of Am. [8160], 15825 N 71st St., Ste. 100, Scottsdale, AZ 85254, (480)281-0431

Amer. Assn. of Cost Engineers [★6842]

Amer. Assn. of Cost Engineers [★IO]

Amer. Assn. for Counseling and Development [★11815]

Amer. Assn. of Creative Artists - Address unknown since 1995.

Amer. Assn. of Credit Counselors - Defunct.

Amer. Assn. of Credit Union Leagues [1102], c/o Credit Union Natl. Assn., PO Box 4312, Madison, WI 53701-0431, (608)231-4000

Amer. Assn. of Crimean Turks - Address unknown since 2001.

Amer. Assn. of Critical-Care Nurses [15433], 101 Columbia, Aliso Viejo, CA 92656-4109, (949)362-2000

Amer. Assn. for Critical Sci. Investigation into Claimed Hauntings [7437], PO Box 22772, Denver, CO 80222-0772, (720)837-6565

Amer. Assn. of Crop Insurers [2129], 1 Massachusetts Ave. NW, Ste. 800, Washington, DC 20001, (202)789-4100

Amer. Assn. for Crystal Growth [6851], 25 4th St., Somerville, NJ 08876-3205, (908)575-0649

Amer. Assn. of Daily Money Managers [1453], 174 Crestview Dr., Bellefonte, PA 16823, (877)326-5991

Amer. Assn. of the Deaf-Blind [14737], 8630 Fenton St., Ste. 121, Silver Spring, MD 20910-4500, (301)495-4403

Amer. Assn. of Dealers in Ancient, Oriental, and Primitive Art - Address unknown since 1994.

Amer. Assn. of Dental Consultants [2130], 10032 Wind Hill Dr., Greenville, IN 47124, (812)923-2600

Amer. Assn. of Dental Editors [3077], 750 N Lincoln Memorial Dr., Ste. 422, Milwaukee, WI 53202, (414)272-2759

Amer. Assn. of Dental Examiners [14112], 211 E Chicago Ave., Ste. 760, Chicago, IL 60611, (312)440-7464

Amer. Assn. for Dental Res. [14113], 1619 Duke St., Alexandria, VA 22314-3406, (703)548-0066

Amer. Assn. Dental Schools [★8193]

Amer. Assn. Dental Schools [★IO]

Amer. Assn. of Dental Victims - Address unknown since 2002.

Amer. Assn. of Diabetes Educators [14217], 100 W Monroe St., Ste. 400, Chicago, IL 60603-1901, (800)338-3633

Amer. Assn. of Direct Human Service Personnel - Address unknown since 2002.

Amer. Assn. of Directors of Psychiatric Residency Training [16067], c/o Lucille F. Meinsler, Admin. Mgr., Executive Off., 1594 Cumberland St., Lebanon, PA 17042, (717)270-1673

Amer. Assn. of Disability Communicators - Defunct.

Amer. Assn. of Disabled Persons - Address unknown since 2002.

Amer. Assn. of Dispensing Ophthalmologists [15658], PO Box 655, Jarrettsville, MD 21084, (800)705-2236

Amer. Assn. of Doctors' Nurses - Address unknown since 1995.

Amer. Assn. of Drilling Engineers [7460], PO Box 940069, Houston, TX 77094, (281)293-9800

Amer. Assn. of Drugless Practitioners [13615], 2200 Market St., Ste. 329, Galveston, TX 77550-1530, (409)621-2600

Amer. Assn. of Early Childhood Educators - Defunct.

Amer. Assn. of Economic Developers - Defunct.

Amer. Assn. of Economic Entomologists and Entomological Society of America [★7062]

Amer. Assn. of Electromyography and Electrodiagnosis [★15303]

Amer. Assn. of Electronic Reporters and Transcribers [3180], 23812 Rock Cir., Bothell, WA 98021-8573, (800)233-5306

Amer. Assn. - Electronic Voice Phenomena [★7469]

Amer. Assn. - Electronic Voice Phenomena [7469], PO Box 13111, Reno, NV 89507

Amer. Assn. - Electronic Voice Phenomena [★IO]

American Association of Electronic Voice Phenomena [IO], Reno, NV, United States

Amer. Assn. of Elementary/Kindergarten/Nursery Educators - Defunct.

Amer. Assn. for Employment in Educ. [8994], 3040 Riverside Dr., Ste. 125, Columbus, OH 43221-2550, (614)485-1111

Amer. Assn. of Endodontists [14114], 211 E Chicago Ave., Ste. 1100, Chicago, IL 60611-2691, (312)266-7255

Amer. Assn. of Engg. Societies [6983], 1620 I St. NW, Ste. 210, Washington, DC 20006, (202)296-2237

Amer. Assn. of Engineers [★7035]

Amer. Assn. of English Jewish Newspapers [★3081]

American Assn. of Enterprise Zones - Address unknown since 2003.

Amer. Assn. of Entrepreneurial Dentists - Address unknown since 1999.

Amer. Assn. of Equine Practitioners [16742], 4075 Iron Works Pkwy., Lexington, KY 40511, (859)233-0147

Amer. Assn. of Equine Veterinary Technicians [16743], 2604 Lake Cove, Highland Village, TX 75077, (972)966-3440

Amer. Assn. of Equine Veterinary Technicians [IO], Highland Village, TX, United States

Amer. Assn. of Equip. Lessors [★IO]

Amer. Assn. of Equip. Lessors [★3381]

Amer. Assn. for Ethiopian Jews - Address unknown since 1999.

Amer. Assn. of Evangelical Students - Defunct.

Amer. Assn. of Examiners and Administrators of Educational Personnel [★7883]

Amer. Assn. of Examiners and Administrators of Educational Personnel [★IO]

Amer. Assn. of Exporters and Importers [2297], 1050 17th St. NW, Ste. 810, Washington, DC 20036, (202)857-8009

Amer. Assn. for Extension Education - Defunct.

Amer. Assn. of Eye and Ear Hospitals [14859], 1100 Wilson Blvd., Ste. 1200, Arlington, VA 22209, (703)243-8848

American Association of Eye and Ear Hospitals [IO], Arlington, VA, United States

American Assn. of Family Businesses - Address unknown since 2004.

Amer. Assn. of Family and Consumer Sciences [12285], 400 N Columbus St., Ste. 202, Alexandria, VA 22314, (703)706-4600

Amer. Assn. of Feed Exporters - Defunct.

Amer. Assn. of Feed Microscopists Div. [★4662]

Amer. Assn. of Feline Practitioners [16744], 203 Towne Centre Dr., Hillsborough, NJ 08844-4693, (908)359-9351

Amer. Assn. of Felt and Straw Goods Importers - Defunct.

Amer. Assn. of Financial Professionals - Defunct.

Amer. Assn. of First Responders [★14320]

Amer. Assn. of Food Hygiene Veterinarians [16745], c/o Linda Tollefson, Immediate Past Pres., U.S. Food and Drug Admin., 5600 Fishers Ln., Rm. 14C06 HF33, Rockville, MD 20857, (301)827-3040

Amer. Assn. of Food Stamp Directors [6261], c/o Kathy Link, Pres., Utah Dept. of Workforce Services, 140 E 300 S, 5th Fl., Salt Lake City, UT 84111-2305, (801)526-9230

Amer. Assn. of Foot Specialists - Defunct.

Amer. Assn. of Foreign Medical Graduates - Defunct.

A star before a book entry number signifies that the name is not listed separately, but is mentioned within the entry.

Amer. Assn. of Former Soviet Political Prisoners [★17766]

Amer. Assn. of Former Soviet Political Prisoners [★IO]

Amer. Assn. of Forms Executives - Defunct.

Amer. Assn. of Franchisees and Dealers [1665], 3500 5th Ave., Ste. 103, PO Box 81887, San Diego, CA 92138-1887, (619)209-3775

Amer. Assn. for Fuel Cells [6937], 50 San Miguel Ave., Daly City, CA 94015, (650)992-3963

Amer. Assn. for Functional Orthodontics [14115], 106 S Kent St., Winchester, VA 22601, (540)662-2200

Amer. Assn. of Functional Orthodontists [★14115]

Amer. Assn. of Fundraising Counsel [★1686]

Amer. Assn. of Genito-Urinary Surgeons [16699], Univ. of Michigan, Dept. of Urology, 3875 Taubman Center SPC 5330, 1500 E Medical Center Dr., Ann Arbor, MI 48109-5330, (734)232-4943

Amer. Assn. for Geodetic Surveying [7716], c/o Ronnie Taylor, Sec., Natl. Geodetic Survey/NOAA, 2905 Carnaby Ct., Tallahassee, FL 32308, (850)245-2606

Amer. Assn. for Geriatric Psychiatry [16068], 7910 Woodmont Ave., Ste. 1050, Bethesda, MD 20814-3069, (301)654-7850

Amer. Assn. for Gifted Children [8463], c/o Duke Univ., PO Box 90270, Durham, NC 27708-0270, (919)783-6152

Amer. Assn. of Grain Inspection and Weighing Agencies [1747], c/o Bob Peterson, 20610 NE 157th St., Kearney, MO 64060, (816)810-5000

Amer. Assn. of Grant Professionals [12708], c/o Gail Vertz, Exec. Dir., 1333 Meadowlark Ln., Ste. 206, Kansas City, KS 66102, (913)788-3000

Amer. Assn. of Gravity Field Energy - Defunct.

Amer. Assn. of Gp. Workers [★13206]

Amer. Assn. of Gynecologic Laparoscopists [15581], 6757 Katella Ave., Cypress, CA 90630-5105, (714)503-6200

Amer. Assn. of Gynecological Laparoscopists [★15581]

Amer. Assn. for Hand Surgery [14522], 20 N Michigan Ave., Ste. 700, Chicago, IL 60602, (312)236-3307

Amer. Assn. of Handwriting Analysts [11205], c/o Ed Jackson, Pres., 1060 Grandeview Blvd., Apt. 622, Huntsville, AL 35824, (256)772-5326

Amer. Assn. for the Hard of Hearing [★16442]

Amer. Assn. of Health Data Systems - Defunct.

Amer. Assn. on Hea. and Disability [14235], 110 N Washington St., Ste. 340, Rockville, MD 20850, (301)545-6140

Amer. Assn. for Hea. Educ. [16234], 1900 Assn. Dr., Reston, VA 20191-1599, (703)476-3437

Amer. Assn. for Hea. Freedom [16049], PO Box 458, Great Falls, VA 22066, (703)294-6244

Amer. Assn. of Health and Medical Museums - Defunct.

Amer. Assn. for Hea., Physical Educ. and Recreation [★8979]

Amer. Assn. of Healthcare Administrative Mgt. [15047], 11240 Waples Mill Rd., Ste. 200, Fairfax, VA 22030, (703)281-4043

Amer. Assn. of Healthcare Consultants [14860], 5938 N Drake Ave., Chicago, IL 60659, (888)350-2242

Amer. Assn. of Heart Failure Nurses [15434], 15000 Commerce Pkwy., Ste. C, Mount Laurel, NJ 08054, (856)642-4422

Amer. Assn. of Hebrew Teachers Colls. - Defunct.

Amer. Assn. of Hide, Skin and Leather Merchants [★2421]

Amer. Assn. for Higher Educ. [8478]

Amer. Assn. of Hip and Knee Surgeons [16559], 6300 N River Rd., Ste. 615, Rosemont, IL 60018-4237, (847)698-1200

Amer. Assn. of Hispanic CPAs [★16]

Amer. Assn. for the History of Medicine [10082], c/o Chris Crenner, MD, Sec.-Treas., Univ. of Kansas Medical Center, Dept. of History and Philosophy, 3901 Rainbow Blvd., MS 1025, Kansas City, KS 66160, (913)588-7040

Amer. Assn. for the History of Nursing [10083], PO Box 175, Lanoka Harbor, NJ 08734-0175, (609)693-7250

American Assn. for Holistic Health - Address unknown since 2001.

Amer. Assn. of Home Based Businesses [1917], c/o Beverley Williams, Founder, 285 Red Run Heights Rd., Oakland, MD 21550-7907

Amer. Assn. for Home-Based Early Interventionists [17056], Utah State Univ., 6500 Old Main Hill, Logan, UT 84322-6500, (800)396-6144

Amer. Assn. for Homecare [14670], 2011 Crystal Dr., Ste. 725, Arlington, VA 22202, (703)836-6263

Amer. Assn. of Homeopathic Pharmacists - Address unknown since 1994.

Amer. Assn. for Homes for the Aging [★11273]

Amer. Assn. for Homes for the Aging [★IO]

American Association of Homes and Services for the Aging [IO], Washington, DC, United States

Amer. Assn. of Homes and Services for the Aging [11273], 2519 Connecticut Ave. NW, Washington, DC 20008-1520, (202)783-2242

Amer. Assn. for Horsemanship Safety [12946], PO Box 39, Fentress, TX 78622, (512)488-2220

Amer. Assn. of Hosp. Accountants [★15066]

Amer. Assn. of Hosp. Consultants [★14860]

Amer. Assn. of Hosp. Dental Chiefs [★14116]

Amer. Assn. of Hosp. Dentists [★14186]

Amer. Assn. of Hosp. Dentists [14116], c/o Special Care Dentistry Assn., 401 N Michigan Ave., Ste. 2200, Chicago, IL 60611, (312)527-6764

Amer. Assn. of Hosp. Podiatrists [16026], c/o Frank Rinaldi, Exec. Dir., 8508 18th Ave., Brooklyn, NY 11214, (718)259-1822

Amer. Assn. of Housecall Veterinarians [16746]

Amer. Assn. of Housing Educators [12303], c/o Jean A. Memken, PhD, Exec. Dir., 5060 FCS Dept., Illinois State Univ., Normal, IL 61790-5060, (309)438-5802

Amer. Assn. of Human-Animal Bond Veterinarians [13702], c/o Dr. Thomas Krall, DVM, Treas., PO Box 13489, St. Petersburg, FL 33733-3489

Amer. Assn. for Human Design Practitioners [1151], PO Box 1716, Taos, NM 87571

Amer. Assn. for Humanistic Psychology [★16140]

Amer. Assn. of Immunologists [14929], 9650 Rockville Pike, Bethesda, MD 20814-3998, (301)634-7178

Amer. Assn. of Imported Car Dealers - Defunct.

Amer. Assn. of Importers and Breeders of Belgian Draft Horses [★4865]

Amer. Assn. for the Improvement of Boxing [23259], 86 Fletcher Ave., Mount Vernon, NY 10552-3319, (914)664-4571

Amer. Assn. of Independent Coll. and Univ. Presidents [★8534]

Amer. Assn. of Independent News Distributors [3078], c/o Erik Zenhausern, Exec. Dir., 93 Second St., Harrison, NY 10528, (877)GO-AAIND

Amer. Assn. on Indian Affairs [★18092]

Amer. Assn. of Individual Investors [8422], 625 N Michigan Ave., Chicago, IL 60611, (312)280-0170

Amer. Assn. of Industrial Dentists - Defunct.

Amer. Assn. of Indus. Editors [★879]

Amer. Assn. of Indus. Editors [★IO]

Amer. Assn. of Indus. Mgt. [2480], PO Box 924, Agawam, MA 01001, (413)737-8766

Amer. Assn. of Indus. Nurses [★15439]

Amer. Assn. of Industrial Veterinarians - Address unknown since 2005.

Amer. Assn. of Inhalation Therapists [★16599]

Amer. Assn. for Inhalation Therapy [★16599]

Amer. Assn. of Insurance Mgt. Consultants [953], c/o Mr. Thomas M. Braniff, Pres., 8980 Lakes at 610 Dr., Ste. 100, Houston, TX 77054, (713)664-6424

Amer. Assn. of Insurance Services [2131], 1745 S Naperville Rd., Wheaton, IL 60187-8132, (630)681-8347

Amer. Assn. of Integrated Healthcare Delivery Systems [15048], 4435 Waterfront Dr., Ste. 101, PO Box 4913, Glen Allen, VA 23060, (804)747-5823

Amer. Assn. of Integrative Medicine [15152], 2750 E Sunshine St., Springfield, MO 65804, (417)881-9995

Amer. Assn. on Intellectual and Developmental Disabilities [15239], 444 N Capitol St. NW, Ste. 846, Washington, DC 20001-1512, (202)387-1968

Amer. Assn. for Intl. Aging [11274]

Amer. Assn. for the Intl. Commn. of Jurists [17742], 280 Madison Ave., Ste. 1102, New York, NY 10016, (212)972-0883

Amer. Assn. for the Intl. Commn. of Jurists [IO], New York, NY, United States

Amer. Assn. of Inventors [IO], Saginaw, MI, United States

Amer. Assn. of Inventors [7225], 2309 State St., Saginaw, MI 48602, (989)793-5319

Amer. Assn. of IV Therapy - Defunct.

Amer. Assn. of Jesuit Scientists - Defunct.

Amer. Assn. for Jewish Educ. [★8692]

Amer. Assn. of Junior Colleges [★8117]

Amer. Assn. for Justice [6328], 1050 31st St. NW, Washington, DC 20007-4405, (202)965-3500

Amer. Assn. of Kidney Patients [15283], 3505 E Frontage Rd., Ste. 315, Tampa, FL 33607, (813)636-8100

Amer. Assn. for Klinefelter Syndrome Info. and Support [14538], c/o Roberta Rappaport, Founding Pres., 2945 W Farwell Ave., Chicago, IL 60645-2925, (888)466-5747

Amer. Assn. for Lab. Accreditation [7234], 5301 Buckeystown Pike., Ste. 350, Frederick, MD 21704, (301)644-3248

Amer. Assn. for Lab. Animal Sci. [13693], 9190 Crestwyn Hills Dr., Memphis, TN 38125-8538, (901)754-8620

Amer. Assn. of Language Specialists [3852], PO Box 39339, Washington, DC 20016-9339, (301)365-9088

Amer. Assn. of Language Specialists [IO], Washington, DC, United States

Amer. Assn. of Law Libraries [10316], 53 W Jackson Blvd., Ste. 940, Chicago, IL 60604, (312)939-4764

Amer. Assn. of Legal Nurse Consultants [14999], 401 N Michigan Ave., Chicago, IL 60611, (312)321-5177

Amer. Assn. for Leisure and Recreation and Amer. Assn. for Active Lifestyles and Fitness [★12793]

Amer. Assn. of Lib. Trustees [★10335]

Amer. Assn. of LifeStyle Counselors [14053], PO Box 610410, Dallas, TX 75261-0410, (817)545-3220

Amer. Assn. of Limited Partners - Defunct.

Amer. Assn. for Long-Term Care Insurance [2132], 3835 E Thousand Oaks Blvd., Ste. 336, Westlake Village, CA 91362, (818)597-3227

Amer. Assn. for Lost Children [12607], 539 Fred Rogers Dr., Latrobe, PA 15650, (724)537-6970

Amer. Assn. of Machinery Importers - Defunct.

Amer. Assn. of Managed Care Nurses [15435], 4435 Waterfront Dr., Ste. 101, Glen Allen, VA 23060, (804)747-9698

Amer. Assn. of Managing Gen. Agents [2133], 150 S Warner Rd., Ste. 156, King of Prussia, PA 19406, (610)225-1999

Amer. Assn. of Marriage Counselors [★16200]

Amer. Assn. of Marriage and Family Counselors [★16200]

Amer. Assn. for Marriage and Family Therapy [16200], 112 S Alfred St., Alexandria, VA 22314-3061, (703)838-9808

Amer. Assn. for Maternal and Child Health - Defunct.

Amer. Assn. of Meat Processors [2656], PO Box 269, Elizabethtown, PA 17022, (717)367-1168

Amer. Assn. of Media Specialists and Librarians - Defunct.

Amer. Assn. of Medical Assistants [15081], 20 N Wacker Dr., Ste. 1575, Chicago, IL 60606, (312)899-1500

Amer. Assn. of Medical Audit Specialists [15049], PO Box 47609, San Antonio, TX 78265-8609, (210)590-2666

Amer. Assn. of Medical Billers [15050]

Amer. Assn. for Medical Chronobiology and Chronotherapeutics [13751], c/o Erhard Haus, PhD, Pres., Univ. of Minnesota, Dept. of Pathology, 640 Jackson St., St. Paul, MN 55101, (651)254-9630

Amer. Assn. of Medical Clinics [★14717]

Amer. Assn. of Medical Dosimetrists [15116], One Physics Ellipse, College Park, MD 20740, (301)209-3320

Amer. Assn. of Medical Milk Commissions [16384], c/o Dr. Paul Fleiss, MD, Pres., 1824 N Hillhurst Ave., Los Angeles, CA 90027, (323)664-1977

Reference to "IO" in place of a book number signifies that the association may be found in the 45th edition of International Organizations.

Amer. Assn. of Medical Record Librarians [★15097]

Amer. Assn. of Medical Rev. Officers [14695], PO Box 12873, Research Triangle Park, NC 27709, (800)489-1839

Amer. Assn. of Medical Social Workers [★13206]

Amer. Assn. of Medical Soc. Executives [15153], 555 E Wells St., Ste. 1100, Milwaukee, WI 53202, (414)221-9275

Amer. Assn. for Medical Systems and Informatics [★14079]

Amer. Assn. for Medical Transcription [★15084]

Amer. Assn. of Medico-Legal Consultants - Defunct.

Amer. Assn. on Mental Deficiency [★15239]

Amer. Assn. of Mental Hea. Professionals in Corrections [15186], PO Box 160208, Sacramento, CA 95816-0208

Amer. Assn. on Mental Retardation [★15239]

Amer. Assn. of Meta-Science - Address unknown since 1999.

Amer. Assn. of Microcomputer Investors - Defunct.

Amer. Assn. for Middle East Studies - Defunct.

Amer. Assn. of Minority Businesses [2760], c/o Charles L. Kelly, Pres./CEO, PO Box 35432, Charlotte, NC 28235, (704)596-1870

Amer. Assn. of Minority Enterprise Small Bus. Investment Companies [★2764]

Amer. Assn. of Motor Vehicle Administrators [5535], 4301 Wilson Blvd., Ste. 400, Arlington, VA 22203, (703)522-4200

Amer. Assn. of Multiple Enchondroma Diseases; AAMED - The [15749]

Amer. Assn. for Museum Volunteers [10489], c/o Victoria B. Wilson, Membership Sec., PO Box 9494, Washington, DC 20016

Amer. Assn. of Museums [10490], 1575 Eye St. NW, Ste. 400, Washington, DC 20005, (202)289-1818

Amer. Assn. of Music Festivals - Defunct.

Amer. Assn. for Music Therapy [★16205]

Amer. Assn. of Naturopathic Physicians [15280], 4435 Wisconsin Ave. NW, Ste. 403, Washington, DC 20016, (202)237-8150

Amer. Assn. of Nephrology Nurses and Technicians [★15286]

Amer. Assn. of Neurological Surgeons [15410], 5550 Meadowbrook Dr., Rolling Meadows, IL 60008, (847)378-0500

American Association of Neurological Surgeons [IO], Rolling Meadows, IL, United States

Amer. Assn. of Neuromuscular and Electrodiagnostic Medicine [15303], 2621 Superiod Dr. NW, Rochester, MN 55901, (507)288-0100

Amer. Assn. of Neuropathologists [15853], c/o Dr. George Perry, Sec.-Treas., Univ. of Texas at San Antonio, Coll. of Sciences, 6900 N Loop 1604 W, San Antonio, TX 78249-0661, (216)368-3671

Amer. Assn. of Neuroscience Nurses [15436], 4700 W Lake Ave., Glenview, IL 60025, (847)375-4733

Amer. Assn. of Neuroscience Nurses [IO], Glenview, IL, United States

Amer. Assn. for Nude Recreation [10760], 1703 N Main St., Ste. E, Kissimmee, FL 34744, (407)933-2064

Amer. Assn. of Nurse Anesthetists [15437], 222 S Prospect Ave., Park Ridge, IL 60068, (847)692-7050

Amer. Assn. of Nurse Assessment Coordinators [14608], 1873 S Bellaire St., Ste. 800, Denver, CO 80222, (303)758-7647

Amer. Assn. of Nurse Attorneys [15000], PO Box 515, Columbus, OH 43216-0515, (877)538-2262

Amer. Assn. of Nurse Life Care Planners [15438], 3267 E 3300 S, No. 309, Salt Lake City, UT 84109, (801)274-1184

Amer. Assn. of Nurse-Midwives [★15447]

Amer. Assn. of Nurserymen [★5042]

Amer. Assn. of Nurserymen, Florists and Seedsmen [★5042]

Amer. Assn. of Nursing Homes [★14540]

Amer. Assn. of Nutritional Consultants [15540], 401 Kings Hwy., Winona Lake, IN 46590, (888)828-2262

Amer. Assn. of Obstetricians and Gynecologists [★15587]

Amer. Assn. of Occupational Hea. Nurses [15439], 2920 Brandywine Rd., Ste. 100, Atlanta, GA 30341, (770)455-7757

Amer. Assn. of Off. Nurses [15440]

Amer. Assn. of Oilwell Drilling Contractors [★2930]

Amer. Assn. of Oilwell-Drilling Contractors [★IO]

Amer. Assn. for Ophthalmic Standardized Echography [15659], c/o Karl C. Ossoinig, MD, Pres., 1345 Cedar St., Iowa City, IA 52245, (319)337-4066

Amer. Assn. of Ophthalmology [★15656]

Amer. Assn. of Oral and Maxillofacial Surgeons [15732], 9700 W Bryn Mawr Ave., Rosemont, IL 60018-5701, (847)678-6200

Amer. Assn. of Oral and Plastic Surgeons [★14040]

Amer. Assn. of Oriental Healing Arts [★15024]

Amer. Assn. of Oriental Medicine [15742], PO Box 162340, Sacramento, CA 95816, (916)443-4770

American Association of Oriental Medicine [IO], Sacramento, CA, United States

Amer. Assn. of Orthodontists [14117], 401 N Lindbergh Blvd., St. Louis, MO 63141-7816, (314)993-1700

Amer. Assn. of Orthomolecular Medicine - Defunct.

Amer. Assn. of Orthopedic Medicine [15753], 600 Pembrook Dr., Woodland Park, CO 80863, (800)992-2063

Amer. Assn. of Orthopic Technicians [★15657]

Amer. Assn. of Osteopathic Colleges [★15791]

Amer. Assn. of Osteopathic Examiners - Address unknown since 2001.

Amer. Assn. of Osteopathic Specialists [★15792]

Amer. Assn. of Owners and Breeders of Peruvian Paso Horses [4810]

Amer. Assn. of Paging Carriers [872], 441 N Crestwood Dr., Wilmington, NC 28405, (866)301-2272

Amer. Assn. for Paralegal Educ. [8759], 19 Mantua Rd., Mount Royal, NJ 08061, (856)423-2829

Amer. Assn. of Paranormal Investigators [2896], 13973 E Utah Cir., Aurora, CO 80012, (303)482-6897

Amer. Assn. for Parapsychology [7441], Box 225, Canoga Park, CA 91305, (818)883-0887

Amer. Assn. of Parenthood Physicians [★12177]

Amer. Assn. of Partial Hospitalization [★16080]

Amer. Assn. of Passenger Rate Men - Defunct.

Amer. Assn. of Passenger Traffic Officers - Defunct.

Amer. Assn. of Pastoral Counselors [19863], 9504A Lee Hwy., Fairfax, VA 22031-2303, (703)385-6967

Amer. Assn. of Pathologists [★15860]

Amer. Assn. of Pathologists' Assistants [15854], Rosewood Off. Plz., 1711 W County Rd. B, Ste. 300 N, Roseville, MN 55113-4036, (651)697-9264

Amer. Assn. of Pathologists and Bacteriologists [★15860]

Amer. Assn. of Pediatric Ophthalmology [★15660]

Amer. Assn. for Pediatric Ophthalmology and Strabismus [15660], PO Box 193832, San Francisco, CA 94119-3832, (415)561-8505

Amer. Assn. of People with Disabilities [11917], 1629 K St. NW, Ste. 503, Washington, DC 20006, (202)457-0046

Amer. Assn. of Personal Financial Planners - Defunct.

Amer. Assn. of Pesticide Safety Educators [4627], c/o Carol Ramsay, Washington State Univ., PO Box 646382, Pullman, WA 99164-6382, (509)335-9222

Amer. Assn. of Petroleum Geologists [7125], 1444 S Boulder Ave., Tulsa, OK 74119, (918)584-2555

Amer. Assn. of Petroleum Landmen [★2913]

Amer. Assn. of Pharmaceutical Scientists [7467], 2107 Wilson Blvd., Ste. 700, Arlington, VA 22201-3042, (703)243-2800

American Association of Pharmaceutical Scientists [IO], Arlington, VA, United States

Amer. Assn. of Pharmacy Technicians [15910], PO Box 1447, Greensboro, NC 27402, (336)333-9356

Amer. Assn. of Philosophy Teachers [8964], c/o Betsy Decyk, Exec. Dir., Off. of Univ. Ombuds, 6300 State Univ. Dr., No. 140, Long Beach, CA 90815

Amer. Assn. of Phonetic Sciences [10842], Dept. of Commun. Disorders, 3750 Lindell Blvd., St. Louis, MO 63108, (314)977-2825

Amer. Assn. for Physical Activity and Recreation [12793], 1900 Assn. Dr., Reston, VA 20191-1598, (703)476-3400

Amer. Assn. of Physical Anthropologists [6403], PO Box 7050, Lawrence, KS 66044, (800)627-0326

Amer. Assn. of Physician-Hospital Organizations [★15048]

Amer. Assn. of Physician Offices and Labs. [14990], 10401 Kingston Pike, Knoxville, TN 37922, (865)470-9605

Amer. Assn. of Physician Specialists [15792], 5550 W Executive Dr., Ste. 400, Tampa, FL 33609, (813)433-2277

Amer. Assn. of Physicians' Assistants - Defunct.

Amer. Assn. of Physicians for Human Rights [★14431]

Amer. Assn. of Physicians of Indian Origin [15987], 600 Enterprise Dr., Ste. 108, Oak Brook, IL 60523, (630)530-2277

Amer. Assn. of Physicists in Medicine [16014], One Physics Ellipse, College Park, MD 20740, (301)209-3350

American Association of Physicists in Medicine [IO], College Park, MD, United States

Amer. Assn. of Physics Teachers [8993], 1 Physics Ellipse, College Park, MD 20740-3845, (301)209-3300

Amer. Assn. of Plastic Surgeons [14040], 900 Cummings Ctr., Ste. 221-U, Beverly, MA 01915, (978)927-8330

Amer. Assn. of Podiatric Physicians and Surgeons - Address unknown since 2007.

Amer. Assn. of Poison Control Centers [16658], 3201 New Mexico Ave., Ste. 330, Washington, DC 20016, (202)362-7217

Amer. Assn. of Police Polygraphists [5748], PO Box 657, Waynesville, OH 45068-0657, (888)743-5479

Amer. Assn. of Political Consultants [18342], 600 Pennsylvania Ave. SE, Ste. 330, Washington, DC 20003, (202)544-9815

Amer. Assn. of Port Authorities [5778], 1010 Duke St., Alexandria, VA 22314-3589, (703)684-5700

Amer. Assn. of Port Authorities [IO], Alexandria, VA, United States

Amer. Assn. of Preferred Provider Organizations [14680], 222 S First St., Ste. 303, Louisville, KY 40202, (502)403-1122

Amer. Assn. of Premium Incentive, Travel Suppliers and Agents [3904], PO Box 35189, Chicago, IL 60707-0189, (708)453-0080

Amer. Assn. of Presidents of Independent Colleges and Universities [8534], Box 7070, Provo, UT 84602, (801)422-5625

Amer. Assn. of Private Railroad Car Owners [3276], 630 Constitution Ave. NE, Ste. B, Washington, DC 20002-6036, (202)547-5696

Amer. Assn. of Pro Life Obstetricians and Gynecologists [18545], 339 River Ave., Holland, MI 49423, (616)546-2639

Amer. Assn. of Pro-Life Pediatricians [18546]

Amer. Assn. of Professional Apiculturists [4162], c/o Eric Mussen, PhD, UC Davis, Dept. of Entomology, One Shields Ave., Davis, CA 95616-8584, (530)752-0472

Amer. Assn. of Professional Bridal Consultants [★533]

Amer. Assn. of Professional Bridal Consultants [★IO]

Amer. Assn. of Professional Consultants [★960]

Amer. Assn. of Professional Hypnologists - Defunct.

Amer. Assn. of Professional Hypnotherapists [14915], 4149-A El Camino Way, Palo Alto, CA 94306-4036, (650)323-3224

Amer. Assn. of Professional Landmen [2913], 4100 Fossil Creek Blvd., Fort Worth, TX 76137-2723, (817)847-7700

Amer. Assn. of Professional Ringside Physicians [15988], 40 Heights Rd., Ste. 201, Darien, CT 06820, (203)662-8900

Amer. Assn. of Professional Sales Engineers [3462]

Amer. Assn. of Professional Schools of Accountancy - Defunct.

Amer. Assn. of Professional Standards Rev. Organizations [★16262]

Amer. Assn. of the Professions - Defunct.

Amer. Assn. of Professors of Yiddish - Address unknown since 1999.

Amer. Assn. to Promote the Teaching of Speech to the Deaf [★14736]

Amer. Assn. to Promote the Teaching of Speech to the Deaf [★IO]

A star before a book entry number signifies that the name is not listed separately, but is mentioned within the entry.

Amer. Assn. for Protecting Children [★11556]

Amer. Assn. of Psychiatric Administrators [14861], c/o Frances M. Bell, Exec. Dir., PO Box 570218, Dallas, TX 75357-0218, (800)650-5888

Amer. Assn. of Psychiatric Services for Children - Address unknown since 2001.

Amer. Assn. of Psychiatric Social Workers [★13206]

Amer. Assn. of Psychiatric Technicians [16069], 1220 S St., Ste. 100, Sacramento, CA 95811-7138, (916)443-1701

Amer. Assn. of Psychiatrists from India - Address unknown since 1999.

Amer. Assn. of Psychoanalytic Physicians [★16104]

Amer. Assn. of Public Hea. Dentistry [14118], PO Box 7536, Springfield, IL 62791-7536, (217)391-0218

Amer. Assn. of Public Hea. Dentists [★14118]

Amer. Assn. of Public Hea. Physicians [16235], 3433 Kirchoff Rd., Rolling Meadows, IL 60008-1842, (847)371-1502

Amer. Assn. of Public Hea. Veterinarians [16747]

Amer. Assn. of Public Human Services - Defunct.

Amer. Assn. for Public Opinion Res. [18368], PO Box 14263, Lenexa, KS 66285-4263, (913)310-0118

Amer. Assn. of Public Welfare Info. Systems Mgt. [★13152]

Amer. Assn. of Rabbis - Address unknown since 2004.

Amer. Assn. of Radon Scientists and Technologists [7108], PO Box 2109, Fletcher, NC 28732, (866)772-2778

Amer. Assn. of Railroad Superintendents [3277], PO Box 456, Tinley Park, IL 60477-0456, (708)342-0210

Amer. Assn. of Railroad Ticket Agents - Defunct.

Amer. Assn. of Railway Surgeons - Defunct.

Amer. Assn. of the Red Cross [★12830]

Amer. Assn. of Registration Executives [★6218]

Amer. Assn. for Rehabilitation Therapy - Defunct.

Amer. Assn. of Released/Retired Military Educators - Defunct.

Amer. Assn. of Religious Crusaders - Defunct.

Amer. Assn. of Religious Therapists - Address unknown since 1995.

Amer. Assn. for Respiratory Care [16599], 9425 N MacArthur Blvd., Ste. 100, Irving, TX 75063-4706, (972)243-2272

Amer. Assn. for Respiratory Therapy [★16599]

Amer. Assn. of Retired Veterinarians [16748]

Amer. Assn. of Retirement Communities [12896], Univ. of Oklahoma, 1600 S Jenkins Ave., Norman, OK 73072, (405)325-3489

Amer. Assn. of Riding Schools [22582], 8375 Coldwater Rd., Davison, MI 48423-8966, (810)496-0360

Amer. Assn. of Safety Councils [12947], c/o Toni Burrows, Pres., 770 S Military Trail, West Palm Beach, FL 33415, (561)689-4733

Amer. Assn. of Safety Councils [IO], West Palm Beach, FL, United States

Amer. Assn. of School Administrators [7882], 801 N Quincy St., Ste. 700, Arlington, VA 22203, (703)528-0700

Amer. Assn. of School Librarians [10317], 50 E Huron St., Chicago, IL 60611-2729, (312)280-4382

Amer. Assn. of School Personnel Administrators [7883], 533-B N Mur-Len Rd., Olathe, KS 66062, (913)829-2007

Amer. Assn. of School Personnel Administrators [IO], Olathe, KS, United States

Amer. Assn. of School Photographers [★IO]

Amer. Assn. of School Photographers [★3012]

Amer. Assn. of School Physicians [★14718]

Amer. Assn. of Schools and Dept. of Journalism [★7893]

Amer. Assn. of Schools of Theological Schools [★9270]

Amer. Assn. of Schools of Theological Schools [★IO]

Amer. Assn. of Sci. Workers [★7634]

Amer. Assn. of Senior Physicians [★15155]

Amer. Assn. of Ser. Coordinators [1985], PO Box 1178, Powell, OH 43065-1178, (614)848-5958

Amer. Assn. of Sex Educators and Counselors [★16398]

Amer. Assn. of Sexuality Educators, Counselors and Therapists [16398], PO Box 1960, Ashland, VA 23005-4960, (804)752-0026

Amer. Assn. of Sheep and Goat Practitioners [★16749]

Amer. Assn. of Sheriff Posses and Riding Clubs - Defunct.

Amer. Assn. of Shotgunning - Defunct.

Amer. Assn. of Sleep Disorders [★16418]

Amer. Assn. of Sleep Disorders Centers [★16418]

Amer. Assn. for Small Dredging and Marine Constr. Companies [★2576]

Amer. Assn. of Small Property Owners [18379], 4200 Cathedral Ave. NW, Ste. 515, Washington, DC 20016, (202)625-8330

Amer. Assn. of Small Res. Companies - Defunct.

Amer. Assn. of Small Ruminant Practitioners [16749], 2413 Nashville Rd., Ste. 112 MS-C13, Bowling Green, KY 42101, (270)793-0781

Amer. Assn. of Snowboard Instructors [23765], 133 S Van Gordon St., Ste. 102, Lakewood, CO 80228, (303)987-2700

Amer. Assn. of Social Directories - Address unknown since 1995.

Amer. Assn. for Social Psychiatry - Address unknown since 1999.

Amer. Assn. for Social Security - Defunct.

Amer. Assn. of Social Workers [★13206]

Amer. Assn. of Spanish Timbrado Breeders [21834], 6831 El Banquero Pl., San Diego, CA 92119, (619)582-9698

Amer. Assn. of Special Educators - Defunct.

Amer. Assn. of Specialized Colls. and Schools - Address unknown since 1995.

Amer. Assn. of Spinal Cord Injury Nurses [15441], 75-20 Astoria Blvd., East Elmhurst, NY 11370, (718)803-3782

Amer. Assn. of Spinal Cord Injury Psychologists and Social Workers [16459], 75-20 Astoria Blvd., Jackson Heights, NY 11372, (718)803-3782

Amer. Assn. State Boards, Veterinary [★16755]

Amer. Assn. of State Climatologists [7324], c/o Paul Knight, Pres., Pennsylvania State Climatologist, Dept. of Meteorology, 503 Walker Bldg., University Park, PA 16802

Amer. Assn. of State Colleges and Universities [8096], 1307 New York Ave. NW, 5th Fl., Washington, DC 20005-4701, (202)293-7070

Amer. Assn. of State Compensation Insurance Funds [2134], 7501 E Lowry Blvd., Denver, CO 80230, (303)361-4890

Amer. Assn. of State Compensation Insurance Funds [IO], Austin, TX, United States

Amer. Assn. of State Counseling Boards [14054], 5999 Stevenson Ave., Alexandria, VA 22304, (703)212-2239

Amer. Assn. of State Highway Officials [★6312]

Amer. Assn. of State Highway and Trans. Officials [6312], 444 N Capitol St. NW, Ste. 249, Washington, DC 20001-1539, (202)624-5800

Amer. Assn. for State and Local History [10084], 1717 Church St., Nashville, TN 37203-2921, (615)320-3203

Amer. Assn. of State Psychology Boards [★16144]

Amer. Assn. of State Psychology Boards [★IO]

Amer. Assn. of State Ser. Commissions [6189], 1400 I St. NW, Ste. 560, Washington, DC 20005-6526, (202)729-8263

Amer. Assn. of State Social Work Boards [★13200]

Amer. Assn. of State Troopers [5960], 1949 Raymond Diehl Rd., Tallahassee, FL 32308, (850)385-7904

Amer. Assn. of Stomatologists - Defunct.

Amer. Assn. of Stratigraphic Palynologists [7434], c/o Dr. Thomas D. Demchuk, Sec.-Treas., PO Box 2197, Houston, TX 77252-2197

Amer. Assn. of Stratigraphic Palynologists [IO], Houston, TX, United States

Amer. Assn. of Students of German - Defunct.

Amer. Assn. for the Stud. of Allergy [★13592]

Amer. Assn. for the Stud. of the Feebleminded [★15239]

Amer. Assn. for the Stud. of Goiter [★16646]

Amer. Assn. for the Stud. of Headache [★14531]

Amer. Assn. for the Stud. of Liver Diseases [14801], 1001 N Fairfax, Ste. 400, Alexandria, VA 22314, (703)299-9766

Amer. Assn. for the Study of Neoplastic Diseases - Defunct.

Amer. Assn. for Study of the U.S. in World Affairs - Defunct.

Amer. Assn. of Subscription Agencies - Defunct.

Amer. Assn. of Suicidology [13286], 5221 Wisconsin Ave. NW, Washington, DC 20015, (202)237-2280

Amer. Assn. of Sunday and Feature Editors [3079], c/o Kalyani Chadha, Exec. Dir., Coll. of Journalism, Univ. of Maryland, 1117 Journalism Bldg., College Park, MD 20742-7111, (301)314-2631

Amer. Assn. in Support of Ecological Initiatives - Address unknown since 2001.

Amer. Assn. of Surgeon Assistants [★16560]

Amer. Assn. for the Surgery of Trauma [16687], 633 N St. Clair St., No. 2600, Chicago, IL 60611, (312)202-5468

Amer. Assn. of Surgical Physician Assistants [16560], 4267 NW Fed. Hwy., PMB 201, Jensen Beach, FL 34957, (888)882-2772

Amer. Assn. of Swine Practitioners [★16750]

Amer. Assn. of Swine Practitioners [★IO]

American Association of Swine Veterinarians [IO], Perry, IA, United States

Amer. Assn. of Swine Veterinarians [16750], 902 1st Ave., Perry, IA 50220-1703, (515)465-5255

Amer. Assn. of Swiss Alpine Club Members - Defunct.

Amer. Assn. of Teacher Educators in Agriculture [★7933]

Amer. Assn. of Teachers of Arabic [7958], Dept. of Modern Languages and Literatures, Coll. of William and Mary, PO Box 8795, Williamsburg, VA 23187-8795, (757)221-3145

Amer. Assn. of Teachers of Chinese Language and Culture [★8074]

Amer. Assn. of Teachers Colleges [★9208]

Amer. Assn. of Teachers of Esperanto [8403], c/o Sally Lawton, 12 Stage Rd., Westhampton, MA 01027-9603, (413)527-3579

Amer. Assn. of Teachers of French [8448], Southern Illinois Univ., Mail Code 4510, Carbondale, IL 62901, (618)453-5731

Amer. Assn. of Teachers of French [IO], Carbondale, IL, United States

Amer. Assn. of Teachers of German [8460], 112 Haddontowne Ct., No. 104, Cherry Hill, NJ 08034-3668, (856)795-5553

Amer. Assn. of Teachers of Italian [8680], c/o Edoardo Lebano, Exec. Dir., Indiana Univ., Dept. of French and Italian, Ballentine 642, Bloomington, IN 47405, (812)855-2508

Amer. Assn. of Teachers of Italian [IO], Bloomington, IN, United States

Amer. Assn. of Teachers of Journalism [★8706]

Amer. Assn. of Teachers of Korean - Defunct.

Amer. Assn. of Teachers of Slavic and East European Languages [9125], PO Box 569, Beloit, WI 53512-0569, (608)361-9697

Amer. Assn. of Teachers of Spanish and Portuguese [8725], 900 Ladd Rd., Walled Lake, MI 48390, (248)960-2180

Amer. Assn. of Teachers of Spanish and Portuguese [IO], Exton, PA, United States

Amer. Assn. of Teachers of Turkic Languages [9282], Princeton Univ., Near Eastern Stud., 110 Jones Hall, Princeton, NJ 08544-1008, (609)258-1435

Amer. Assn. of Teachers of Turkish [★9282]

Amer. Assn. of Teaching and Curriculum [9209], c/o Marcella L. Kysilka, Exec. Sec., 4240 Yorketowne Rd., Orlando, FL 32812-7958

Amer. Assn. of Tech. High Schools and Inst. [★9228]

Amer. Assn. of Tech. High Schools and Inst. [★IO]

Amer. Assn. for Tech. in Psychiatry [16070], PO Box 11, Bronx, NY 10464-0011, (718)502-9469

Amer. Assn. of Temporary and Contract Employees - Address unknown since 1986.

Amer. Assn. of Testifying Physicians - Address unknown since 1994.

Amer. Assn. of Textile Chemists and Colorists [7794], PO Box 12215, Research Triangle Park, NC 27709-2215, (919)549-8141

American Association of Textile Chemists and Colorists [IO], Research Triangle Park, NC, United States

Reference to "IO" in place of a book number signifies that the association may be found in the 45th edition of International Organizations.

Amer. Assn. for Textile Technology - Defunct.

Amer. Assn. of Theatre Organ Enthusiasts [★10553]

Amer. Assn. of Theological Schools [★9270]

Amer. Assn. of Theological Schools [★IO]

Amer. Assn. for Therapeutic Humor [★16605]

Amer. Assn. for Thoracic Surgery [16640], 900 Cummings Ctr., Ste. 221U, Beverly, MA 01915-6183, (978)927-8330

Amer. Assn. of Tissue Banks [16663], 1320 Old Chain Bridge Rd., Ste. 450, McLean, VA 22101, (703)827-9582

Amer. Assn. of Trauma Specialists - Defunct.

Amer. Assn. of Traveling Passenger Agents - Defunct.

Amer. Assn. for the Treatment of Opioid Dependence [16499], 217 Broadway, Ste. 304, New York, NY 10007, (212)566-5555

Amer. Assn. for Ukrainian Stud. [8650], 1583 Massachusetts Ave., Cambridge, MA 02138, (617)495-4053

Amer. Assn. for Ukrainian Stud. [IO], Cambridge, MA, United States

Amer. Assn. for the United Nations [★18770]

Amer. Assn. of Univ. Administrators [7884], PO Box 630101, Little Neck, NY 11363, (347)235-4822

Amer. Assn. of Univ. Affiliated Programs for the Developmentally Disabled [★12563]

Amer. Assn. of Univ. Affiliated Programs for Persons With Developmental Disabilities [★12563]

Amer. Assn. of Univ. Instructors in Accounting [★7]

Amer. Assn. of Univ. Professors [9022], 1012 14th St. NW, Ste. 500, Washington, DC 20005, (202)737-5900

Amer. Assn. of Univ. Professors Found. - Address unknown since 1995.

Amer. Assn. of Univ. Professors of Urban Affairs and Environmental Sciences - Address unknown since 1995.

Amer. Assn. of Univ. Students - Address unknown since 2003.

Amer. Assn. of Univ. Teachers of Insurance [★8574]

Amer. Assn. of Univ. Women [9311], 1111 16th St. NW, Washington, DC 20036, (202)785-7700

Amer. Assn. of Univ. Women Educational Found. [9312], 1111 16th St. NW, Washington, DC 20036, (202)728-7602

Amer. Assn. of Univ. Women Legal Advocacy Fund [6358], 1111 16th St. NW, Washington, DC 20036, (202)785-7750

Amer. Assn. of Utilization Mgt. Nurses - Defunct.

Amer. Assn. of Variable Star Observers [6497], 49 Bay State Rd., Cambridge, MA 02138, (617)354-0484

Amer. Assn. of Veterinary Anatomists - Defunct.

Amer. Assn. of Veterinary Bacteriologists - Defunct.

Amer. Assn. of Veterinary Clinicians [16751], 37 W Broad St., Ste. 480, Columbus, OH 43215-4132, (614)358-0417

Amer. Assn. of Veterinary Immunologists [16752], c/o Eileen L. Thacker, PhD, Sec.-Treas., 2118 Vet Med Bldg., Veterinary Microbiology and Preventive Medicine, Iowa State Univ., Ames, IA 50011, (515)294-5097

Amer. Assn. of Veterinary Lab. Diagnosticians [16753], PO Box 1770, Davis, CA 95617, (530)754-9719

Amer. Assn. of Veterinary Nutritionists [★16737]

Amer. Assn. of Veterinary Parasitologists [16754], c/o Dr. Alan A. Marchiondo, Sec.-Treas., IVX Animal Hea., Inc., 3915 S 48th St. Terr., St. Joseph, MO 64503-4711, (816)676-6171

Amer. Assn. of Veterinary State Boards [16755], 4106 Central St., Kansas City, MO 64111, (816)931-1504

Amer. Assn. of Visually Impaired Attorneys [5474], c/o Amer. Coun. of the Blind, 1155 15th St. NW, Ste. 1004, Washington, DC 20005, (202)467-5081

Amer. Assn. for Vital Records and Public Hea. Statistics [★6218]

Amer. Assn. for Vocational Instructional Materials [9298], 220 Smithonia Rd., Winterville, GA 30683, (706)742-5355

Amer. Assn. of Wardens and Superintendents [★11884]

Amer. Assn. of Wardens and Superintendents [★IO]

Amer. Assn. of Webmasters [896], 7017 Litchfield Rd., No. 331, Glendale, AZ 85307, (623)202-5613

Amer. Assn. of Wedding Planners [2654], c/o Weddings Beautiful Worldwide, 1004 N Thompson St., Ste. 205, Richmond, VA 23230, (804)342-6061

Amer. Assn. of Wildlife Veterinarians [16756], c/o Dr. Mark Cunningham, Sec., Florida Fish and Wildlife Conservation Commn., 4005 S Main St., Gainesville, FL 32601

Amer. Assn. of Women [18419], 337 Washington Blvd., Ste. 1, Marina del Rey, CA 90292, (310)822-4449

Amer. Assn. for Women in Community Colleges [9313], PO Box 336603, Greeley, CO 80633-0611, (970)352-2079

Amer. Assn. for Women in Community and Junior Colleges [★9313]

Amer. Assn. of Women Dentists [14119], 216 W Jackson Blvd., Ste. 625, Chicago, IL 60606, (800)920-2293

Amer. Assn. of Women Emergency Physicians [14324], c/o Amer. Coll. of Emergency Physicians, PO Box 619911, Dallas, TX 75261-9911, (972)550-0911

Amer. Assn. for Women Podiatrists [16027], c/o Kathleen Satterfield, DPM, Pres., 138 Dresden Wood, Boerne, TX 78006, (830)229-5444

Amer. Assn. of Women Radiologists [★16271]

Amer. Assn. for Women Radiologists [16271], 4550 Post Oak Pl., Ste. 342, Houston, TX 77027, (713)965-0566

Amer. Assn. of Women Voters [★18419]

Amer. Assn. of Woodworkers [9825], 222 Landmark Ctr., 75 W 5th St., St. Paul, MN 55102, (651)484-9094

American Association of Woodturners [IO], St. Paul, MN, United States

Amer. Assn. of Workers for the Blind [★16833]

Amer. Assn. of Working People [12067], 4435 Waterfront Dr., Ste. 101, Glen Allen, VA 23060, (804)527-1905

Amer. Assn. for World Hea. - Defunct.

Amer. Assn. of Yellow Pages Publishers [★3261]

Amer. Assn. of Youth Museums [★10495]

Amer. Assn. of Zoo Keepers [7855], 3601 SW 29th St., Ste. 133, Topeka, KS 66614-2054, (785)273-9149

Amer. Assn. of Zoo Veterinarians [16757], c/o Dr. Robert Hilsenroth, Exec. Dir., 581705 White Oak Rd., Yulee, FL 32097, (904)225-3275

Amer. Assn. for Zoological Nomenclature [7859], c/o Eric Hoberg, Treas., USDA Agricultural Res. Ser., BARC E No. 1180, 10300 Baltimore Ave., Beltsville, MD 20705

Amer. Assn. of Zoological Parks and Aquariums [★7857]

Amer. Associations of Spanish Speaking CPA's [★16]

Amer. Astrological Assn. - Defunct.

Amer. Astronautical Fed. - Defunct.

Amer. Astronautical Soc. [6368], 6352 Rolling Mill Pl., Ste. 102, Springfield, VA 22152-2354, (703)866-0020

Amer. Astronautical Soc. [IO], Springfield, VA, United States

Amer. Astronomical Soc. [6498], 2000 Florida Ave. NW, Ste. 400, Washington, DC 20009-1231, (202)328-2010

Amer. Atheist Women - Defunct.

Amer. Atheists [19463], PO Box 5733, Parsippany, NJ 07054-6733, (908)276-7300

Amer. Athletic Assn. for the Deaf [★23369]

Amer. Athletic Trainers Assn. and Certification Bd. [23953], 146 E Duarte Rd., Arcadia, CA 91006, (626)445-1978

Amer. Auction Bridge League [★21893]

Amer. Auction Bridge League [★IO]

Amer. Audiology Soc. [★14738]

Amer. Auditory Soc. [14738], 352 Sundial Ridge Cir., Dammeron Valley, UT 84783-5196, (435)574-0062

Amer. Austin/Bantam Club [21568], c/o Marilyn Sanson, Treas., 724 Maple Dr., Kirkville, NY 13082, (315)656-7568

Amer. Australian Assn. [18975], 599 Lexington Ave., 18th Fl., New York, NY 10022, (212)338-6860

Amer. Australian Bicentennial Found. - Defunct.

American-Austrian Soc. [18976], c/o Mrs. Urlike Wiesner, Sec., 5618 Dover Ct., Alexandria, VA 22312

Amer. Auto Racing Writers and Broadcasters Assn. [23069], 922 N Pass Ave., Burbank, CA 91505-2703, (818)842-7005

Amer. Autoduel Assn. [22456], c/o Steve Jackson Games, PO Box 18957, Austin, TX 78760, (512)447-7866

Amer. Autoimmune Related Diseases Assn. [14930], 22100 Gratiot Ave., Eastpointe, MI 48021-2227, (586)776-3900

Amer. Automatic Control Coun. - Address unknown since 2001.

Amer. Auto. Assn. [403], c/o AAA Mid-Atlantic, One River Pl., Wilmington, DE 19801, (302)299-4700

Amer. Automobile Mfrs. Assn. - Defunct.

Amer. Auto. Touring Alliance [3905], c/o Natl. Auto. Club, 1151 E Hillsdale Blvd., Foster City, CA 94404, (650)294-7000

Amer. Automotive Leasing Assn. [3375], 675 N Washington St., Ste. 410, Alexandria, VA 22314, (703)548-0777

Amer. Autonomic Soc. [15406], c/o Ms. Anita Zeller, Exec. Sec., 18915 Inca Ave., Lakeville, MN 55044, (952)469-5837

Amer. Avalanche Assn. [12948], c/o Mark Mueller, Exec. Dir., PO Box 2831, Pagosa Springs, CO 81147, (970)946-0822

Amer. Aviation Historical Soc. [21426], 2333 Otis St., Santa Ana, CA 92704-3846, (714)549-4818

Amer. Award Manufacturers Assn. [★441]

Amer. Azteca Horse Intl. Assn. [4811], PO Box 1577, Rapid City, SD 57709, (605)342-2322

American Azteca Horse International Association [IO], Rapid City, SD, United States

Amer. Bach Found. [★IO]

Amer. Bach Found. [★10690]

Amer. Back Soc. [15754], 2647 Intl. Blvd., Ste. 401, Oakland, CA 94601, (510)536-9929

Amer. Backflow Prevention Assn. [7818], PO Box 3051, Bryan, TX 77805-3051, (979)846-7606

American Backflow Prevention Association [IO], Bryan, TX, United States

Amer. Backgammon Players Assn. - Defunct.

Amer. Bahraini Friendship Soc. [19150], PO Box 5934, Friendship Sta. 234, Washington, DC 20016, (301)897-2162

Amer. Bail Bondsman Assn. - Address unknown since 1988.

Amer. Bail Coalition [442], 1725 Desales St. NW, Ste. 800, Washington, DC 20036, (202)659-6547

Amer. Bakers Assn. [444], 1300 I St. NW, Ste. 700 W, Washington, DC 20005, (202)789-0300

Amer. Ballet Competition [9862], c/o Dance Affiliates, 4701 Bath St., No. 46, Philadelphia, PA 19137-2229, (215)636-9000

Amer. Ballet Theatre [★9868]

American Ballet Theatre [★9868]

Amer. Bamboo Soc. [6619], 315 S Coast Hwy. 101, Ste. U, PMB 212, Encinitas, CA 92024-3555

American Bamboo Society [IO], Encinitas, CA, United States

Amer. Bandmasters Assn. [10527], c/o Dr. William J. Moody, Sec.-Treas., 4250 Shorebrook Dr., Columbia, SC 29206, (803)787-6540

Amer. Bandstand Fan Club [25024], c/o David Frees, Pres., PO Box 131, Adamstown, PA 19501, (717)738-2513

Amer. Bandstand Fan Club; 1950s [★25024]

Amer. Bandstand Memory Club [★25024]

Amer. Banjo Fraternity [10528], 636 Pelis Rd., Newark, NY 14513, (315)331-6717

Amer. Bankers Assn. [457], 1120 Connecticut Ave. NW, Washington, DC 20036, (202)663-5000

Amer. Bankruptcy Inst. [5574], 44 Canal Center Plz., Ste. 404, Alexandria, VA 22314, (703)739-0800

Amer. Bantam Assn. [5102], PO Box 127, Augusta, NJ 07822, (973)383-8633

Amer. Baptist Black Caucus - Address unknown since 1999.

American Baptist Churches in the U.S.A. [★19470]

Amer. Baptist Education Assn. - Defunct.

Amer. Baptist Foreign Mission Soc. [★19483]

A star before a book entry number signifies that the name is not listed separately, but is mentioned within the entry.

Amer. Baptist Foreign Mission Soc. [★IO]

Amer. Baptist Historical Soc. [19470], PO Box 851, Valley Forge, PA 19482-0851, (610)768-2269

Amer. Baptist Home Mission Societies [★19484]

Amer. Baptist Home Mission Soc. [★19484]

Amer. Baptist Homes and Hospitals Assn. [19471], PO Box 851, Valley Forge, PA 19482-0851, (800)ABC-3USA

Amer. Baptist Missionary Union [★19483]

Amer. Baptist Missionary Union [★IO]

Amer. Baptist Natl. Ministries [★19484]

Amer. Baptist Women [★19468]

Amer. Baptists Concerned [20048], c/o Chris Boisvert, Communications Coor., PO Box 3183, Walnut Creek, CA 94598, (925)459-9053

Amer. Bar Assn. [5475], 321 N Clark St., Chicago, IL 60610, (312)988-5000

Amer. Bar Assn. Center on Children and the Law [11555], 740 15th St. NW, Washington, DC 20005-1019, (202)662-1720

Amer. Bar Assn. Center for Professional Responsibility [5476], 321 N Clark St., 15th Fl., Chicago, IL 60610-4714, (312)988-5325

Amer. Bar Assn. Commn. on Homelessness and Poverty [12286], 740 15th St. NW, Washington, DC 20005-1022, (202)662-1694

Amer. Bar Assn. - Commn. on Mental and Physical Disability Law [5781], 740 15th St. NW, 9th Fl., Washington, DC 20005, (202)662-1571

Amer. Bar Assn. Comm. on the Resolution of Minor Disputes [★5449]

Amer. Bar Assn. Criminal Justice Sect. [5922], 740 15th St. NW, 10th Fl., Washington, DC 20005-1019, (202)662-1510

Amer. Bar Assn; Hea. Law Sect. - [5783]

Amer. Bar Assn. Representation of the Homeless Proj. [★12286]

Amer. Bar Assn. Sect. of Dispute Resolution [5449], 740 15th St. NW, Washington, DC 20005-1019, (202)662-1680

Amer. Bar Assn. Sect. of Intl. Law [5863], 740 15th St. NW, Washington, DC 20005, (202)662-1661

Amer. Bar Assn. Sect. of Intl. Law [IO], Washington, DC, United States

Amer. Bar Assn. Special Comm. on Dispute Resolution [★5449]

Amer. Bar Assn. Standing Comm. on Dispute Resolution [★5449]

Amer. Bar Assn; Traffic Court Prog. of the [6310]

Amer. Bar Assn. Young Lawyers Div. [5477], 321 N Clark, Chicago, IL 60610, (312)988-5614

Amer. Bar Found. [5923], 750 N Lake Shore Dr., Chicago, IL 60611, (312)988-6500

Amer. Bar Found; Fellows of the [5494]

Amer. Barefoot Club [23974], c/o Kerry Ross, Sec.-Treas., PO Box 1203, Frederick, CO 80530-1203, (303)833-5450

Amer. Barred Plymouth Rock Bantam Club - Defunct.

Amer. Barred Plymouth Rock Club [★5114]

Amer. Barrel Racing Assn. [23492], PO Box 203, Collinsville, TX 76233, (817)790-4446

Amer. Bartenders' Assn. [192]

Amer. Baseball Coaches Assn. [23101], 108 S Univ. Ave., Ste. 3, Mount Pleasant, MI 48858-2327, (989)775-3300

American Baseball Coaches Association [IO], Mount Pleasant, MI, United States

Amer. Baseball Cong. [★23100]

Amer. Baseball Fans Assn. - Defunct.

Amer. Baseball Found. [23102], 2660 10th Ave. S, Ste. 620, Birmingham, AL 35205, (205)558-4235

Amer. Bashkir Curly Registry [4812], PO Box 151029, Ely, NV 89315, (775)289-4999

Amer. Basketball Assn. [★23134]

Amer. Bat Conservation Soc. - Address unknown since 2003.

Amer. Battleship Assn. [21210], PO Box 711247, San Diego, CA 92171, (858)271-6106

Amer. Bay Horse Assn. - Defunct.

Amer. Bay Horse Registry - Defunct.

Amer. Beagle Club - Defunct.

Amer. Bearing Mfrs. Assn. [1991], 2025 M St. NW, Ste. 800, Washington, DC 20036-2422, (202)367-1155

Amer. Beauty Assn. [★1086]

Amer. Bed and Breakfast Assn. - Address unknown since 2003.

Amer. Bee Breeders Assn. - Defunct.

Amer. Beefalo Assn. [★4123]

Amer. Beefalo Assn. [★IO]

Amer. Beefalo World Registry [IO], Laramie, WY, United States

Amer. Beefalo World Registry [4123], 10892 Yakima Valley Hwy., Zillah, WA 98953, (866)374-2297

Amer. Beekeeping Fed. [502], PO Box 1337, Jesup, GA 31598-1038, (912)427-4233

Amer. Beethoven Soc. [9803], c/o Ira F. Brilliant Center for Beethoven Stud., San Jose State Univ., 1 Washington Sq., San Jose, CA 95192-0171, (408)808-2058

Amer. Begonia Soc. [22482], PO Box 471651, San Francisco, CA 94147-1651, (918)333-1587

Amer. Behcet's Assn. [★13746]

Amer. Behcet's Disease Assn. [13746], PO Box 19952, Amarillo, TX 79114-9952, (800)7BEHCETS

Amer. Behcet's Found. [★13746]

Amer. Belarussian Relief Org. [12828], PO Box 365, Zebulon, NC 27597, (919)269-6033

Amer. Belgian Blue Assn. [★4213]

Amer. Belgian Blue Breeders [4213], PO Box 154, Hedrick, IA 52563, (641)661-2332

Amer. Belgian Blue Breeders Assn. [★4213]

Amer. Belgian Hare Club [5131], c/o Linda Telega, 6456 Spencer Clark Rd., Fowler, OH 44418, (330)722-2817

Amer. Belgian Malinois Club [22186], 21710 Cove Point Farm Rd., Tilghman, MD 21671, (410)886-2232

American Belgian Malinois Club [IO], Tilghman, MD, United States

Amer. Belgian Tervuren Club - Defunct.

Amer. Bell Assn. Intl. [21958], 7210 Bellbrook Dr., San Antonio, TX 78227-1002

Amer. Bell Assn. Intl. [IO], San Antonio, TX, United States

Amer. Belted Galloway Cattle Breeders' Assn. [★4256]

Amer. Benedictine Acad. [19566], c/o Adel Sautner, OSB, Exec. Sec., St. Benedict's House, 415 S Crow St., Pierre, SD 57501, (605)224-0969

Amer. Benefits Coun. [6169], 1212 New York Ave. NW, Ste. 1250, Washington, DC 20005-3987, (202)289-6700

Amer. Berkshire Assn. [5230], PO Box 2436, West Lafayette, IN 47996, (765)497-3618

Amer. Berlin Opera Found. [10529], c/o Mannheim LLC, 712 5th Ave., 32nd Fl., New York, NY 10019, (212)664-8843

Amer. Beverage Alcohol Assn. - Defunct.

Amer. Beverage Assn. [503], 1101 16th St. NW, Washington, DC 20036-4803, (202)463-6732

Amer. Beverage Inst. [504], 1090 Vermont Ave. NW, Ste. 800, Washington, DC 20005, (202)463-7110

Amer. Beverage Licensees [193], 5101 River Rd., Ste. 108, Bethesda, MD 20816-1560, (301)656-1494

Amer. Beveren Rabbit Club [22917], c/o Kim Calloway, Pres., 6010 S County Rd., 100 W, Frankfort, IN 46041, (765)659-4906

Amer. Bible Soc. [19504], 1865 Broadway, New York, NY 10023-7505, (212)408-1200

Amer. Bible Soc. [IO], New York, NY, United States

Amer. Biblical Encyclopedia Soc. - Defunct.

Amer. Bicentennial Commemorative Soc. - Defunct.

Amer. Bicycle Assn. [23305], PO Box 718, Chandler, AZ 85244, (480)961-1903

Amer. Bicycle Polo Assn. [23658], c/o Bicycle Polo Assn. of Am., 305 Magnolia Lake Ct., Aiken, SC 29803, (803)648-4993

Amer. Bicycle Racing [23667], PO Box 487, Tinley Park, IL 60477-0487, (708)532-7204

Amer. Bike Month Comm. - Defunct.

Amer. Bikeways Found. - Defunct.

Amer. Bill of Rights Day Assn. - Defunct.

Amer. Billiard Assn. [★23146]

Amer. Biographical Inst. Res. Assn. [21097], c/o Amer. Biographical Inst., PO Box 31226, Raleigh, NC 27622, (919)781-8710

Amer. Biological Safety Assn. [3436], 1200 Allanson Rd., Mundelein, IL 60060-3808, (847)949-1517

Amer. Biological Soc. - Defunct.

Amer. Bird Beer Label Assn. [★21491]

Amer. Bird Beer Label Assn. [★IO]

Amer. Bird Conservancy [5290], PO Box 249, The Plains, VA 20198-0249, (540)253-5780

Amer. Bird Conservation Assn. [21835]

Birders' Exchange - Defunct.

Amer. Birding Assn. [7411], 4945 N 30th St., Ste. 200, Colorado Springs, CO 80919, (719)578-9703

American Birding Association [IO], Colorado Springs, CO, United States

Amer. Birkebeiner Ski Found. [23749], PO Box 911, Hayward, WI 54843, (715)634-5025

Amer. Birth Control League [★12187]

Amer. Bison Assn. [★4139]

Amer. Black Book Writers Assn. - Address unknown since 1999.

Amer., Black, Chicano, Puerto Rican, Asian Americans; Natl. Assn. of Interdisciplinary Stud. for Native [★9919]

Amer. Black Chiropractors Assn. - Address unknown since 1999.

Amer. Black Hereford Assn. [4214], 25333 Wolcott Rd., Leavenworth, KS 66048, (913)727-1266

Amer. Black Maine-Anjou Assn. - Defunct.

Amer. Black and Tan Coonhound Assn. - Address unknown since 2001.

Amer. Bladesmith Soc. [9826], PO Box 1481, Cypress, TX 77410-1481, (281)225-9159

Amer. Blake Found. - Defunct.

Amer. Blasting Assn. [★7020]

Amer. Blasting Assn. [★IO]

Amer. Blind Bowling Assn. [23334], c/o Linda Keeney, Pres., 320 S Gramercy Pl., Apt. 205, Los Angeles, CA 90020, (213)384-9613

Amer. Blind and Disabled Golf Assn. [★23335]

Amer. Blind Golf Assn. [23335], 7634 Benassi Dr., Gilroy, CA 95020, (408)842-3369

Amer. Blind Lawyers Assn. [★5474]

Amer. Blind Skiing Found. [23336], 2228 Grand Pointe Trail, Aurora, IL 60504, (312)409-1605

Amer. Blonde d'Aquitaine Assn. [4215], 7407 VZ County Rd. 1507, Grand Saline, TX 75140, (903)570-0568

Amer. Blood Commn. - Defunct.

Amer. Blood Resources Assn. [★13765]

Amer. Bloodhound Club [22187], c/o Jan Rothwell, 193 Captain Clark Hwy., Wilton, NH 03086-5727

Amer. Blue Cheese Assn. - Defunct.

Amer. Blue and White Rabbit Club - Address unknown since 1999.

Amer. Bd. of Abdominal Surgery [16561], 1 E Emerson St., Melrose, MA 02176, (781)665-6102

Amer. Bd. of Allergy and Immunology [13595], 111 S Independence Mall E, Ste. 701, Philadelphia, PA 19106-2512, (215)592-9466

Amer. Bd. of Alternative Medicine [13616], c/o Dr. B. Alli, PO Box 24224, Detroit, MI 48224-0224, (313)882-0641

Amer. Bd. of Alternative Medicine [IO], Detroit, MI, United States

Amer. Bd. of Anesthesiology [13671], 4101 Lake Boone Trail, Ste. 510, Raleigh, NC 27607-7506, (919)881-2570

Amer. Bd. of Bariatric Medicine [15573], 2821 S Parker Rd., Ste. 625, Aurora, CO 80014, (303)752-4000

Amer. Bd. of Bioanalysis [7235], 906 Olive St., Ste. 1200, St. Louis, MO 63101-1434, (314)241-1445

Amer. Bd. of Bioanalysts [★7235]

Amer. Bd. of Bionic Rehabilitative Psychology - Address unknown since 1999.

Amer. Bd. of Blood-Transfusionless Medicine and Surgery - Address unknown since 1999.

Amer. Bd. of Cardiovascular Perfusion [13887], 207 N 25th Ave., Hattiesburg, MS 39401, (601)582-2227

Amer. Bd. of Certification [5478], 101 2nd St. SE, Ste. 904, Cedar Rapids, IA 52401, (319)365-2222

Amer. Bd. for Certification in Orthotics, Prosthetics and Pedorthics [15783], 330 John Carlyle St., Ste. 210, Alexandria, VA 22314, (703)836-7114

Amer. Bd. of Certified and Registered Encephalographic Technicians and Technologists - Address unknown since 2002.

Reference to "IO" in place of a book number signifies that the association may be found in the 45th edition of International Organizations.

Encyclopedia of Associations, 46th Edition

2967

Amer. Board of Certified Social Services Designees - Address unknown since 2005.

Amer. Bd. of Chelation Therapy [★16659]

Amer. Bd. of Chiropractic Independent Examiners [13987], 3343 Montrose Ave., Laureldale, PA 19605, (610)929-9882

Amer. Bd. of Clinical Biofeedback - Defunct.

Amer. Bd. of Clinical Chemistry - Address unknown since 1994.

Amer. Bd. of Clinical Child and Adolescent Psychology [★16121]

Amer. Bd. of Clinical Hea. Psychology [★16121]

Amer. Bd. of Clinical Immunology and Allergy - Defunct.

American Bd. of Clinical Metal Toxicology [16659], c/o James Smith, DO, Treas., 4889 Smith Rd., West Chester, OH 45069, (513)863-6277

Amer. Bd. of Clinical Neuropsychology [★16121]

Amer. Bd. of Clinical Psychology [★16121]

Amer. Bd. of Cognitive and Behavioral Psychology [★16121]

Amer. Bd. of Colon and Rectal Surgery [16059], 20600 Eureka Rd., Ste. 600, Taylor, MI 48180, (734)282-9400

Amer. Bd. of Counseling Psychology [★16121]

Amer. Bd. on Counseling Services [★8169]

Amer. Bd. on Counseling Services [★IO]

Amer. Bd. of Criminal Lawyers - Address unknown since 1990.

Amer. Bd. of Criminalistics [5749], PO Box 1123, Wausau, WI 54402-1123, (715)845-3684

Amer. Bd. of Dental Medicine and Surgery - Address unknown since 1999.

Amer. Bd. of Dental Public Hea. [14120], c/o Robert H. Dumbaugh, DDS, Exec. Sec., 5274 Island View Cir. N, Polk City, FL 33868, (863)984-9278

Amer. Bd. of Dermatology [14190], Henry Ford Hea. Sys., 1 Ford Pl., Detroit, MI 48202-3450, (313)874-1088

Amer. Bd. of Disability Analysts [16308], 345 24th Ave. N, Ste. 200, Park Plaza Medical Bldg., Nashville, TN 37203, (615)327-2984

Amer. Bd. of Emergency Medicine [14325], 3000 Coolidge Rd., East Lansing, MI 48823-6319, (517)332-4800

Amer. Bd. of Endodontics [14121], 211 E Chicago Ave., Ste. 1100, Chicago, IL 60611-2691, (312)266-7255

Amer. Bd. of Examiners in Pastoral Counseling [19864], c/o Fred Clark, Credentials Comm. Chm., 261 Spring St., Cheshire, CT 06410, (203)271-3733

Amer. Bd. of Examiners in Professional Psychology [★16121]

Amer. Bd. of Examiners in Professional Psychology [★16121]

Amer. Bd. of Examiners of Psychodrama, Sociometry, and Gp. Psychotherapy [16201], c/o Amer. Bd. of Examiners, PO Box 15572, Washington, DC 20003-0572, (202)483-0514

Amer. Bd. of Examiners in Psychological Hypnosis [★14917]

Amer. Bd. of Facial Plastic and Reconstructive Surgery [16562], 115C S St. Asaph St., Alexandria, VA 22314, (703)549-3223

Amer. Bd. of Family Dentistry [14122], 1501 Camp Mohave Rd., No. 1, Fort Mohave, AZ 86426

Amer. Bd. of Family Medicine [14384], 2228 Young Dr., Lexington, KY 40505-4294, (859)269-5626

Amer. Bd. of Family Practice [★14384]

Amer. Bd. of Family Psychology [★16121]

Amer. Bd. of Forensic Anthropology [14400], c/o Elizabeth A. Murray, PhD, Sec., Coll. of Mount St. Joseph, Dept. of Biology, 5701 Delhi Rd., Cincinnati, OH 45233-1670, (513)244-4948

Amer. Bd. of Forensic Document Examiners [5750], 7887 San Felipe, Ste. 122, Houston, TX 77063, (713)784-9537

Amer. Bd. of Forensic Examiners [★5751]

Amer. Bd. of Forensic Examiners [★IO]

Amer. Bd. of Forensic Odontology [14401], c/o The Forensic Sciences Found., PO Box 669, Colorado Springs, CO 80901-0669, (719)636-1100

Amer. Bd. of Forensic Psychiatry - Defunct.

Amer. Bd. of Forensic Psychology [★16121]

American Bd. of Forensic Toxicology [★5767]

Amer. Bd. of Funeral Ser. Educ. [8896], c/o Dr. Michael Smith, Exec. Dir., 3432 Ashland Ave., Ste. U, St. Joseph, MO 64506, (816)233-3747

Amer. Bd. of Genetic Counseling [14492], PO Box 14216, Lenexa, KS 66285, (913)895-4617

Amer. Bd. of Gp. Psychology [★16121]

Amer. Bd. of Hair Restoration Surgery [14518], c/o The Amer. Bd. of Hair Restoration, 18525 S Torrence Ave., Lansing, IL 60438, (708)474-2600

Amer. Bd. of Hea. Physics [16015], 1313 Dolley Madison Blvd., Ste. 402, McLean, VA 22101, (703)790-1745

Amer. Bd. of Homeopathic Medicine - Address unknown since 1988.

Amer. Bd. of Hypnotherapy [14916], PO Box 531605, Henderson, NV 89053

Amer. Bd. of Independent Medical Examiners [8877], 1338 3rd Ave., Huntington, WV 25701, (304)523-1415

American Board of Independent Medical Examiners [IO], Huntington, WV, United States

Amer. Bd. of Indus. Hygiene [15623], 6015 W St. Joseph, Ste. 102, Lansing, MI 48917, (517)321-2638

Amer. Bd. of Industrial Medicine and Surgery - Address unknown since 2001.

Amer. Bd. of Internal Medicine [14965], 510 Walnut St., Ste. 1700, Philadelphia, PA 19106-3699, (215)446-3500

Amer. Bd. of Lab. Animal Medicine [★16762]

Amer. Bd. of Lower Extremities Surgery [16028], 6421 Inkster Rd., Ste. 102, Bloomfield Hills, MI 48301, (248)855-7740

Amer. Bd. of Managed Care Nursing [15442], 4435 Waterfront Dr., Ste. 101, Glen Allen, VA 23060, (804)527-1905

Amer. Bd. of Master Educators - Address unknown since 2002.

Amer. Bd. of Medical Genetics [14493], 9650 Rockville Pike, Bethesda, MD 20814-3998, (301)634-7315

American Bd. of Medical Lab. Immunology [★6559]

American Bd. of Medical Lab. Immunology [★IO]

Amer. Bd. of Medical-Legal Analysis in Medicine and Surgery - Address unknown since 1999.

American Bd. of Medical Microbiology [★6559]

American Bd. of Medical Microbiology [★IO]

Amer. Bd. of Medical Psychotherapists and Psychodiagnosticians [16202], 345 24th Ave. N, Ste. 200, Park Plaza Medical Bldg., Nashville, TN 37203-1520, (615)327-2984

Amer. Bd. of Medical Specialties [15117], 1007 Church St., Ste. 404, Evanston, IL 60201-5913, (847)491-9091

Amer. Bd. of Medical Specialties in Podiatry [★16029]

Amer. Bd. of Medical Toxicology [★16660]

Amer. Bd. of Missions to the Jews [★19998]

Amer. Bd. of Multiple Specialties in Podiatry [16029], 1350 Broadway, Ste. 1705, New York, NY 10018, (212)356-0690

Amer. Bd. of Neurological Microsurgery - Address unknown since 1999.

Amer. Bd. of Neurological/Orthopaedic Laser Surgery - Address unknown since 1999.

Amer. Bd. of Neurological and Orthopaedic Medicine and Surgery - Address unknown since 1999.

Amer. Bd. of Neurological Surgery [15411], 6550 Fannin St., Ste. 2139, Houston, TX 77030, (713)441-6015

Amer. Bd. of Neuroscience Nursing [15443], 4700 W Lake Ave., Glenview, IL 60025, (847)375-4733

Amer. Bd. of Nuclear Medicine [15419], 4555 Forest Park Blvd., Ste. 119, St. Louis, MO 63108, (314)367-2225

Amer. Bd. of Nursing Specialties [15444], 610 Thornhill Ln., Aurora, OH 44202, (330)995-9172

Amer. Bd. of Nutrition [15541], Univ. of Alabama at Birmingham, 1675 Univ. Blvd., 439 Susan Mott Webb Nutrition Sciences Bldg., Birmingham, AL 35294-3360, (205)996-2513

Amer. Bd. of Obstetrics and Gynecology [15582], 2915 Vine St., Dallas, TX 75204, (214)871-1619

Amer. Bd. for Occupational Hea. Nurses [15445], 201 E Ogden Ave., Ste. 114, Hinsdale, IL 60521-3652, (630)789-5799

Amer. Bd. of Operative Dentistry [14123], c/o Clyde Roggenkamp, DDS, Sec.-Treas., LLU School of Dentistry, Loma Linda, CA 92350, (909)558-4640

Amer. Bd. for Ophthalmic Examinations [★15661]

Amer. Bd. of Ophthalmology [15661], 111 Presidential Blvd., Ste. 241, Bala Cynwyd, PA 19004-1075, (610)664-1175

Amer. Bd. of Opticianry [15704], 6506 Loisdale Rd., Ste. 209, Springfield, VA 22150-1815, (703)719-5800

Amer. Bd. of Opticianry [★15707]

Amer. Bd. of Opticianry [IO], Springfield, VA, United States

Amer. Bd. of Oral and Maxillofacial Pathology [15855], PO Box 25915, Tampa, FL 33622-5915, (813)286-2444

Amer. Bd. of Oral and Maxillofacial Surgery [15733], 625 N Michigan Ave., Ste. 1820, Chicago, IL 60611, (312)642-0070

American Bd. of Oral Medicine [★8197]

Amer. Bd. of Oral Pathology [★15855]

Amer. Bd. of Oral Surgery [★15733]

Amer. Bd. of Organizational and Bus. Consulting [★16121]

Amer. Bd. of Orthodontia [★14124]

Amer. Bd. of Orthodontics [14124], 401 N Lindbergh Blvd., Ste. 308, St. Louis, MO 63141-7839, (314)432-6130

Amer. Bd. of Orthodontics; Coll. of Diplomates of the [14149]

Amer. Bd. of Orthopaedic Microneurosurgery - Address unknown since 1999.

Amer. Bd. of Orthopaedic Surgery [15755], 400 Silver Cedar Ct., Chapel Hill, NC 27514, (919)929-7103

Amer. Bd. of Otolaryngology [15818], 5615 Kirby Dr., Ste. 600, Houston, TX 77005, (713)850-0399

Amer. Bd. of Pain Medicine [15833], 4700 W Lake Ave., Glenview, IL 60025-1468, (847)375-4726

Amer. Bd. of Pathology [15856], PO Box 25915, Tampa, FL 33622-5915, (813)286-2444

Amer. Bd. of Pediatric Dentistry - Defunct.

Amer. Bd. of Pediatrics [15881], 111 Silver Cedar Ct., Chapel Hill, NC 27514, (919)929-0461

Amer. Bd. of Perianesthesia Nursing Certification [15446], 475 Riverside Dr., 6th Fl., New York, NY 10115-0089, (800)6ABPANC

Amer. Bd. of Periodontology [14125], 4157 Mountain Rd., PBN 249, Pasadena, MD 21122, (410)437-3749

Amer. Bd. of Physical Medicine and Rehabilitation [16309], 3015 Allegro Park Ln. SW, Rochester, MN 55902-4139, (507)282-1776

Amer. Bd. of Physician Nutrition Specialists [15542], c/o Univ. of Alabama at Birmingham, 439 Susan Mott Webb Nutrition Sciences Bldg., 1675 Univ. Blvd., Birmingham, AL 35294-3360, (205)996-2513

Amer. Bd. of Plastic Surgery [14041], 7 Penn Center, Ste. 400, 1635 Market St., Philadelphia, PA 19103-2204, (215)587-9322

Amer. Bd. of Podiatric Dermatology - Defunct.

Amer. Bd. of Podiatric Orthopedics [★16030]

Amer. Bd. of Podiatric Orthopedics and Primary Medicine [★16030]

Amer. Bd. of Podiatric Orthopedics and Primary Podiatric Medicine [16030], 3812 Sepulvada Blvd., Ste. 530, Torrance, CA 90505, (310)375-0700

Amer. Bd. of Podiatric Surgery [16031], c/o James A. Lamb, Exec. Dir., 445 Fillmore St., San Francisco, CA 94117-3404, (415)553-7800

Amer. Bd. of Preventive Medicine [16050], 330 S Wells St., Ste. 1018, Chicago, IL 60606, (312)939-2276

Amer. Bd. of Preventive Medicine and Public Hea. [★16050]

Amer. Bd. of Proctology [★16059]

Amer. Bd. of Professional Disability Consultants [6040]

Amer. Bd. of Professional Liability Attorneys [6041], 170 Wright Ave., Malverne, NY 11565, (516)599-7700

Amer. Bd. of Professional Neuropsychology [16120], c/o Michael J. Raymond, PhD, Exec. Dir., John Heinz Rehabilitation Inst., 150 Mundy St., Wilkes-Barre, PA 18702, (570)826-3771

A star before a book entry number signifies that the name is not listed separately, but is mentioned within the entry.

Amer. Bd. of Professional Psychology [16121], 300 Drayton St., 3rd Fl., Savannah, GA 31401, (912)234-5477

Amer. Bd. of Professional Psychology in Hypnosis [★14917]

Amer. Bd. on Professional Standards in Vocational Counseling [★8169]

Amer. Bd. on Professional Standards in Vocational Counseling [★IO]

Amer. Bd. of Prosthodontics [14126], PO Box 271894, West Hartford, CT 06127-1894, (860)679-2649

Amer. Bd. of Psychiatry and Neurology [16071], 500 Lake Cook Rd., Ste. 335, Deerfield, IL 60015-5635, (847)945-7900

Amer. Bd. of Psychoanalysis in Psychology [★16121]

Amer. Bd. of Psychological Hypnosis [14917], c/o Samuel M. Migdole, EdD, Pres., North Shore Counseling Ctr., 23 Broadway, Beverly, MA 01915, (978)922-2280

Amer. Bd. for Psychological Services - Defunct.

Amer. Bd. of Quality Assurance and Utilization Rev. Physicians [16260], 6640 Cong. St., New Port Richey, FL 34653, (727)569-0190

Amer. Bd. of Rabbis - Vaad Harabonim of Am. [20111], 292 5th Ave., 4th Fl., New York, NY 10001, (212)714-3598

Amer. Bd. of Radiology [16272], 5441 E Williams Blvd., Ste. 200, Tucson, AZ 85711, (520)790-2900

Amer. Bd. of Registration of EEG and EP Technologists [14305], 1904 Croydon Dr., Springfield, IL 62703, (217)553-3758

Amer. Bd. of Registration of EEG Technologists [★14305]

Amer. Bd. of Rehabilitation Psychology [★16121]

Amer. Bd. of Ringside Medicine and Surgery - Address unknown since 1999.

Amer. Bd. of School Psychology [★16121]

Amer. Bd. of Sci. in Nuclear Medicine [15420], 1850 Samuel Morse Dr., Reston, VA 20190, (703)708-9000

Amer. Bd. of Sexology [16399], PO Box 1166, Winter Park, FL 32790-1166, (407)645-1641

Amer. Bd. of Sleep Medicine [16420], One Westbrook Corporate Ctr., Ste. 920, Westchester, IL 60154, (708)492-1290

American Bd. of Somnology [★16419]

Amer. Bd. of Surgery [16563], 1617 John F. Kennedy Blvd., Ste. 860, Philadelphia, PA 19103, (215)568-4000

Amer. Bd. of Thoracic Neurological Orthopaedic Medicine and Surgery - Address unknown since 1999.

Amer. Bd. of Thoracic Surgery [16641], 633 N St. Clair St., Ste. 2320, Chicago, IL 60611, (312)202-5900

Amer. Bd. of Toxicology [7799], PO Box 30054, Raleigh, NC 27622-0054, (919)841-5022

Amer. Bd. of Toxicology [IO], Raleigh, NC, United States

Amer. Bd. of Trial Advocates [6329], 2001 Bryan St., Bryan Tower, Ste. 3000, Dallas, TX 75201-3078, (214)871-7523

Amer. Bd. of Trial Advocates; Found. of the [5495]

Amer. Bd. of Tropical Medicine - Defunct.

Amer. Bd. of Urgent Care Medicine [13662], c/o Amer. Acad. of Urgent Care Medicine, 2813 S Hiawassee Rd., Ste. 206, Orlando, FL 32835, (407)521-5789

Amer. Bd. of Urologic Allied Hea. Professionals [★16706]

Amer. Bd. of Urology [16700], 2216 Ivy Rd., Ste. 210, Charlottesville, VA 22903, (434)979-0059

Amer. Bd. of Veterinary Practitioners [16758], c/o Jeff Allen, Exec. Dir., 618 Church St., Ste. 220, Nashville, TN 37219, (615)250-7794

Amer. Bd. of Veterinary Radiology [★16770]

Amer. Bd. of Veterinary Specialties [16759], c/o Amer. Veterinary Medical Assn., 1931 N Meacham Rd., Ste. 100, Schaumburg, IL 60173, (847)925-8070

Amer. Bd. of Veterinary Toxicology [16760], c/o Dr. Randall A. Lovell, Candidate Coor., FDA/Center for Veterinary Medicine, Division of Animal Feeds, HFV-222, 7519 Standish Pl., Rm. 226, Rockville, MD 20855, (240)453-6857

Amer. Bd. of Vocational Experts [9299], 3540 Soquel Ave., Ste. A, Santa Cruz, CA 95062-1769, (831)464-4890

Amer. Boarding Kennels Assn. [2954], 1702 E Pikes Peak Ave., Colorado Springs, CO 80909-5717, (719)667-1600

Amer. Boardsailing Industries Assn. - Address unknown since 1988.

Amer. Boat Builders and Repairers Assn. [2568], 50 Water St., Warren, RI 02885, (401)247-0318

Amer. Boat and Yacht Coun. [2569], 613 Third St., Ste. 10, Annapolis, MD 21403, (410)990-4460

Amer. Boccaccio Assn. [9629], c/o Dr. Janet Smarr, Pres., Univ. of California at San Diego, Dept. of Theatre - 0344, 9500 Gilman Dr., La Jolla, CA 92093-0344, (858)454-7683

Amer. Boiler Mfrs. Assn. [1992], 8221 Old Courthouse Rd., Ste. 207, Vienna, VA 22182, (703)356-7172

Amer. Bonanza Soc. [21427], PO Box 12888, Wichita, KS 67277, (316)945-1700

American Bonanza Society [IO], Wichita, KS, United States

Amer. Bone Marrow Donor Registry [13768], PO Box 8841, Mandeville, LA 70470-8841, (985)626-1749

Amer. Bonsai Soc. [22483], PO Box 351604, Toledo, OH 43635-1604

Amer. Book Center for War Devastated Libraries [★10392]

Amer. Book Coun. - Defunct.

Amer. Book Producers Assn. [3200], 381 Park Ave., New York, NY 10016, (212)645-2368

Amer. Book Publishers Coun. [★3206]

Amer. Booksellers Assn. [3396], 200 White Plains Rd., Tarrytown, NY 10591, (800)637-0037

Amer. Booksellers Found. for Free Expression [17641], 275 7th Ave., 15th Fl., New York, NY 10001, (212)587-4025

Amer. Bop Assn. [9863], c/o Jim Laux, Pres., 125 Red River Dr., Sherwood, AR 72120, (501)834-8609

Amer. Border Fancy Canary Club - Defunct.

Amer. Border Leicester Assn. [5177], c/o Polly Hopkins, Treas., 494 Evans Rd., Chepachet, RI 02814, (401)949-4619

Amer. Botanical Coun. [6620], PO Box 144345, Austin, TX 78714-4345, (512)926-4900

Amer. Bottled Water Assn. [★509]

Amer. Bottled Water Assn. [★IO]

Amer. Bottlers of Carbonated Beverages [★503]

Amer. Bouvier des Flandres Club [22188], c/o David Raper, Treas., 1718 Trinity Rd., Raleigh, NC 27607-4920

Amer. Bowhunters Assn. - Defunct.

Amer. Bowling Cong. [★23255]

Amer. Bowling Cong. [★IO]

Amer. Box Shook Export Assn. - Defunct.

Amer. Boxer Club [22189], c/o Sandy Orr, Sec., 7106 N 57th St., Omaha, NE 68152-2301, (402)571-0389

Amer. Boxer Rescue Assn. [11346], c/o Beth Moody, Membership Chair, PO Box 134, Mount Morris, MI 48458, (334)272-2590

Amer. Boxwood Soc. [22484], PO Box 85, Boyce, VA 22620-0085

Amer. Brachytherapy Soc. [13790], 12100 Sunset Hills Rd., Ste. 130, Reston, VA 20190, (703)234-4078

Amer. Brahma Club - Address unknown since 1995.

Amer. Brahman Breeders Assn. [4216], 3003 S Loop W, Ste. 520, Houston, TX 77054, (713)349-0854

Amer. Brahmental Assn. - Defunct.

Amer. Brahmousin Coun. [4217], PO Box 88, Whitesboro, TX 76273, (903)564-3995

Amer. Brahms Soc. [9804], c/o George S. Bozarth, Exec. Dir., School of Music, Univ. of Washington, Box 353450, Seattle, WA 98195-3450, (206)543-0400

Amer. Braille Press for War and Civilian Blind [★16854]

Amer. Braille Press for War and Civilian Blind [★IO]

Amer. Brain Tumor Assn. [13791], 2720 River Rd., Des Plaines, IL 60018, (847)827-9910

Amer. Bralers Assn. - Address unknown since 2002.

Amer. Brangus Breeders Assn. [★4265]

Amer. Brazilian Assn. - Defunct.

Amer. Breed Assn. - Address unknown since 2003.

Amer. Breeders Assn. [★7111]

Amer. Breweriana Assn. [21828], PO Box 595767, Fort Gratiot, MI 48059-5767, (810)385-7101

Amer. Bridge Assn. [21891], 2828 Lakewood Ave. SW, Atlanta, GA 30315, (404)768-5517

Amer. Bridge League [★21893]

Amer. Bridge League [★IO]

Amer. Bridge Teachers' Assn. [21892], 1254 26th Ave., San Francisco, CA 94122-1505, (415)566-4592

Amer. Bridge, Tunnel, and Turnpike Assn. [★6318]

Amer. Bridge, Tunnel, and Turnpike Assn. [★IO]

Amer. British Numismatic Soc. - Defunct.

Amer. British White Park Assn. [4218], PO Box 957, Harrison, AR 72602, (877)900-BEEF

Amer. Brittany Club [22190], c/o Mary Jo Trimble, Sec., 10370 Fleming Rd., Carterville, IL 62918, (618)985-2336

Amer. Brittle Bone Soc. - Defunct.

American Broadcasting Network [★17625]

Amer. Broncho-Esophagological Assn. [13778], c/o Dr. Peter J. Koltai, Sec., Stanford Univ. School of Medicine, Division of Pediatric Otolaryngology, 801 Welch Rd., Stanford, CA 94305

Amer. Bronchoscopic Soc. [★13778]

Amer. Brotherhood for the Blind [★16821]

Amer. Brown Leghorn Club - Defunct.

Amer. Brugmansia and Datura Soc. [22455], 51431 State Hwy. 14, Chariton, IA 50049

Amer. Brush Mfrs. Assn. [1968], 2111 Plum St., Ste. 274, Aurora, IL 60506, (630)631-5217

Amer. Brussels Griffon Assn. [22191], c/o Linda Vance, Sec., PO Box 11, Shirley, IL 61772-0011, (309)828-4311

Amer. Bryological and Lichenological Soc. [6621], Dept. of Biology, Univ. of Nebraska, Omaha, NE 68182-0040, (402)554-2491

American Bryological and Lichenological Society [IO], Omaha, NE, United States

Amer. Bryological Soc. [★IO]

Amer. Bryological Soc. [★6621]

Amer. Buckskin Registry Assn. [4813], PO Box 493850, Redding, CA 96049, (530)223-1420

Amer. Buddhist Acad. [★19542]

Amer. Buddhist Assn. [19540], c/o Bright Dawn Home Spread, W7136 County Rd. U, Plymouth, WI 53073-4538, (920)528-1364

Amer. Buddhist Movement [19541], 301 W 45th St., New York, NY 10036, (212)489-1075

Amer. Buddhist Stud. Center [19542], 331 Riverside Dr., New York, NY 10025, (212)864-7424

Amer. Budgerigar Soc. [21836], c/o Dinah Moore, Sec., 521 Westview St., Lenoir, NC 28645, (828)754-2480

Amer. Buff Plymouth Rock Club - Address unknown since 1995.

Amer. Buff Wyandotte Club - Defunct.

Amer. Buffalo Assn. [★4139]

Amer. Bugatti Club [21569], 600 Lakeview Terr., Glen Ellyn, IL 60137, (630)469-4920

Amer. Building Contractors Assn. - Address unknown since 2001.

Amer. Bulgarian League - Defunct.

Amer. Bullmastiff Assn. [22192], c/o Walker Weeks, Membership Chm., 2425 Therese St., Jefferson City, MO 65101, (573)635-0088

Amer. Bunka Embroidery Assn. [22721], c/o Nancy Vicari, Treas., PO Box 233, Gloucester, MA 01931-0233

Amer. Bunka Embroidery Assn. [IO], Fort Myers, FL, United States

Amer. Bur. for Medical Advancement in China - Defunct.

Amer. Bur. of Metal Statistics [7309], PO Box 805, Chatham, NJ 07928, (973)701-2299

Amer. Bur. of Metal Statistics [★7309]

Amer. Bur. of Shipping [2600], 16855 Northchase Dr., Houston, TX 77060, (281)877-5800

Amer. Burn Assn. [13781], 625 N Michigan Ave., Ste. 2550, Chicago, IL 60611, (312)642-9260

Amer. Bus Assn. [3859], 700 13th St. NW, Ste. 575, Washington, DC 20005-5934, (202)842-1645

Reference to "IO" in place of a book number signifies that the association may be found in the 45th edition of International Organizations.

Amer. Bus. Assn. of Russian Professionals [3181], 1290 Oakmead Pkwy., Ste. 118, Sunnyvale, CA 94085

Amer. Business Card Club - Address unknown since 2002.

Amer. Bus. Clubs Spastic Paralysis Fund [★11964]

Amer. Bus. Commun. Assn. [★8014]

Amer. Bus. Conf. [17622], 1828 L St. NW, Ste. 908, Washington, DC 20036, (202)822-9300

Amer. Bus. Coun. of Dubai and the Northern Emirates [IO], Dubai, United Arab Emirates

Amer. Bus. Coun. of the Gulf Countries [IO], Riyadh, Saudi Arabia

Amer. Bus. Coun., Malaysia [★IO]

Amer. Bus. Coun. of Pakistan [IO], Karachi, Pakistan

Amer. Bus. Coun. of Singapore [★IO]

Amer. Business Found. for Cancer Res. - Defunct.

Amer. Bus. Law Assn. [★8757]

Amer. Bus. Law Assn. [★IO]

Amer. Bus. Media [3201], 675 3rd Ave., New York, NY 10017-5704, (212)661-6360

Amer. Business Media Coun. - Defunct.

Amer. Bus. Men's Res. Found. [★13217]

American Bus. Network [★24301]

Amer. Bus. Press [★3201]

Amer. Bus. Women's Assn. [693], 9100 Ward Pkwy., PO Box 8728, Kansas City, MO 64114-0728, (816)361-6621

Amer. Bus. Writing Assn. [★8014]

Amer. Businessmen of Jeddah [IO], Jeddah, Saudi Arabia

Amer. Businessmen's Club - Address unknown since 2001.

Amer. Businessmen's Club of the Netherlands - Defunct.

Amer. Businesspersons Assn. [694], Hillsboro Executive Ctr. N, 350 Fairway Dr., Ste. 200, Deerfield Beach, FL 33441-1834, (954)571-1877

Amer. Butter Inst. [1128], 2101 Wilson Blvd., Ste. 400, Arlington, VA 22201, (703)243-5630

Amer. Buyers Fed. [★1454]

Amer. Buyers of Meeting and Incentive Travel - Defunct.

Amer.-Byelorussian Cultural Relief Assn. - Address unknown since 1995.

Amer. Byron Soc. [★9641]

Amer. Cable Assn. [779], One Parkway Ctr., Ste. 212, Pittsburgh, PA 15220, (412)922-8300

Amer. Cadet Alliance [20718], PO Box 144, Sea Girt, NJ 08750-0144, (732)840-4500

Amer. Camaro Assn. [21570], 5786 Buckeye Rd., Macungie, PA 18062

Amer. Camellia Soc. [22485], Massee Lane Gardens, 100 Massee Ln., Fort Valley, GA 31030, (478)967-2358

Amer. Camp Assn. [23268], 5000 State Rd. 67 N, Martinsville, IN 46151-7902, (765)342-8456

Amer. Campaign for Prevention of Child Abuse and Family Violence [★12035]

Amer. Camping Assn. [★23268]

American-Canadian Genealogical Soc. [21098], PO Box 6478, Manchester, NH 03108-6478, (603)622-1554

American-Canadian Genealogical Soc. [IO], Manchester, NH, United States

Amer. Canal Soc. [IO], Freemansburg, PA, United States

Amer. Canal Soc. [9772], c/o Charles W. Derr, Sec.-Treas., 117 Main St., Freemansburg, PA 18017, (610)691-0956

Amer. Canary Fanciers Assn. [21837], c/o Ralph Tepedino, Pres., 4503 West Ave. 40, Los Angeles, CA 90065, (323)255-2679

Amer. Cancer Soc. [13792], PO Box 22718, Oklahoma City, OK 73123-1718, (800)ACS-2345

Amer. Canine Educ. Found. [22193], c/o Lt. Col. Wallace H. Pede, CEO, 7200 Tanager St., Springfield, VA 22150, (703)451-5656

Amer. Canine Educ. Fund [★22193]

Amer. Canine Sports Medicine Assn. [16761], PO Box 07412, Fort Myers, FL 33919

Amer. Canna Soc. - Address unknown since 2007.

Amer. Cannabis Res. Experiment - Address unknown since 1999.

Amer. Canoe Assn. [23278], 7432 Alban Sta. Blvd., Ste. B-232, Springfield, VA 22150, (703)451-0141

Amer. Canoe Mfrs. Union - Defunct.

Amer. Canvas Inst. - Defunct.

Amer. Canyoneering Assn. [21949], PO Box 1208, Cedar City, UT 84720, (435)590-8889

Amer. Capon Producers Assn. - Address unknown since 1995.

Amer. Car Rental Assn. [3376], 12324 E 86th St. N, No. 130, Owasso, OK 74055-2543, (888)200-2795

Amer. Car Rental Assn. - Defunct.

Amer. Carbon Comm. [★6663]

Amer. Carbon Soc. [6663], c/o Dr. Wesley Hoffman, Chm., Air Force Research Laboratory, AFRL/PRSM, 10 E Saturn Blvd., Edwards, CA 93524-7680, (661)275-5768

Amer. Cardiology Technologists Assn. [★13885]

Amer. Cargo War Risk Reinsurance Exchange - Defunct.

Amer. Carnation Soc. - Defunct.

Amer. Carnival Glass Assn. [22549], c/o Dolores Wagner, Sec., 5951 Fredericksburg Rd., Wooster, OH 44691-9491, (330)264-3703

Amer. Carnivals Assn. - Defunct.

Amer. Carousel Soc. - Defunct.

Amer. Carp Soc. [22448], PO Box 1502, Bartlesville, OK 74005-1502, (315)764-5654

Amer. Carpal Tunnel Syndrome Assn. [★15631]

Amer. Carpet Inst. [★2254]

Amer. Cartographic Assn. [★6654]

Amer. Case Mgt. Assn. [15051], 10310 W Markham St., Ste. 209, Little Rock, AR 72205, (501)907-2262

Amer. Cash Flow Inst. - Address unknown since 2006.

American Casket Retailers Assn. - Address unknown since 2006.

Amer. Cast Metals Assn. [★9227]

Amer. Casting Assn. [23406], c/o Dale Lanser, Exec. Sec., 1773 Lance End Ln., Fenton, MO 63026-2674, (636)225-9443

Amer. Cat Assn. [21900]

Amer. Cat Fanciers Assn. [21901], PO Box 1949, Nixa, MO 65714-1949, (417)725-1530

Amer. Cat Fanciers Assn. [IO], Nixa, MO, United States

Amer. Catholic Church Assn. - Defunct.

Amer. Catholic Comm. - Address unknown.

Amer. Catholic Conf. - Defunct.

Amer. Catholic Correctional Chaplains Assn. [19741], c/o Rev. Thomas R. Houle, Treas., 210 W 31st St., New York, NY 10001, (212)564-9070

Amer. Catholic Historical Assn. [10085], Mullen Lib., Rm. 320, Catholic Univ. of Am., Washington, DC 20064, (202)319-5079

Amer. Catholic Historical Soc. [10086], 263 S 4th St., Philadelphia, PA 19106, (856)424-4728

American Catholic Historical Society [IO], Philadelphia, PA, United States

Amer. Catholic Lawyers Assn. [5558], PO Box 10092, Fairfield, NJ 07004, (973)244-9895

Amer. Catholic Philosophical Assn. [8965], Univ. of St. Thomas, Centre for Thomistic Stud., 3800 Mohtrose Blvd., Houston, TX 77006, (713)942-3483

Amer. Catholic Prison Chaplains Assn. [★19741]

Amer. Catholic Psychological Assn. [★16132]

Amer. Catholic Sociological Soc. [★7661]

Amer. Catholic Truth Soc. - Defunct.

Amer. Catholic Union [19567], PO Box 2622, Richmond, CA 94802-1622, (415)232-3323

The Amer. Cause [17642], 501 Church St., Ste. 217, Vienna, VA 22180, (703)255-2632

Amer. Cause - Defunct.

Amer. Cavalier King Charles Spaniel Club [22194], c/o Luanne K. Dunham, Corresponding Sec., 2 Bud Davis Rd., Newnan, GA 30263

Amer. Cave Conservation Assn. [4345], PO Box 409, 119 E Main St., Horse Cave, KY 42749, (270)786-1466

Amer. Cave and Karst Center [★4345]

American Cave and Karst Center [★4345]

Amer. Cave Museum [★4345]

Amer. Cavy Breeders Assn. [4124], c/o James D. Nielsen, Sec.-Treas., 1157 E San Angelo Ave., Gilbert, AZ 85234, (480)545-1785

Amer. CB Radio Assn. [21493]

Amer. Celiac Society/Dietary Support Coalition [15543], PO Box 23455, New Orleans, LA 70183-0455, (504)737-3293

Amer. Cement Alliance [★915]

Amer. Cement Trade Alliance [★915]

Amer. Cemetery Assn. [★2781]

Amer. Cemetery Assn. [★IO]

Amer. Cemetery-Mortuary Comm. - Defunct.

Amer. Center for the Alexander Technique [13617], 39 W 14th St., Rm. 507, New York, NY 10011, (212)633-2229

Amer. Center for Chinese Medical Sciences - Address unknown since 1999.

Amer. Center for Design - Defunct.

Amer. Center for Intl. Leadership - Address unknown since 1999.

Amer. Center for Law and Justice [12901], PO Box 90555, Washington, DC 20090-0555, (757)226-2489

Amer. Center for Physics [7498], 1 Physics Ellipse, College Park, MD 20740, (301)209-3100

Amer. Center for Polish Culture [★10879]

Amer. Center for Polish Culture [★IO]

Amer. Center for the Quality of Work Life - Address unknown since 1999.

Amer. Center for Stanislavski Theatre Art - Defunct.

Amer. Center of the Union Internationale de la Marionnette; UNIMA-U.S.A., [22916]

Amer. Central European Dental Inst. [14127], 60 Fed. St., Boston, MA 02110-2510, (617)423-6165

Amer. Central European Dental Inst. [IO], Boston, MA, United States

Amer. Ceramic Soc. [IO], Westerville, OH, United States

Amer. Ceramic Soc. [6657], 735 Ceramic Pl., Ste. 100, Westerville, OH 43081-8728, (614)794-5855

Amer. Certified Morticians Assn. - Defunct.

Amer. Certified Shake and Shingle Bur. - Address unknown since 1995.

Amer. Cetacean Soc. [7258], PO Box 1391, San Pedro, CA 90733-1391, (310)548-6279

Amer. Chain Assn. [1993], 4724 Lone Oak Blvd., Naples, FL 34109, (239)514-3441

Amer. Chain of Warehouses [3976], 156 Flamingo Dr., Beecher, IL 60401-9725, (708)946-9792

Amer. Chamber of Commerce [★24305]

Amer. Chamber of Commerce [★IO]

Amer. Chamber of Commerce in Argentina [IO], Buenos Aires, Argentina

Amer. Chamber of Commerce in Australia [IO], Sydney, Australia

Amer. Chamber of Commerce in Australia - Melbourne Br. [IO], Melbourne, Australia

Amer. Chamber of Commerce in Australia - National/New South Wales Off. [IO], Sydney, Australia

Amer. Chamber of Commerce in Australia - Perth Br. [IO], Perth, Australia

Amer. Chamber of Commerce in Austria [IO], Vienna, Austria

Amer. Chamber of Commerce in Azerbaijan [IO], Baku, Azerbaijan

Amer. Chamber of Commerce in Belgium [IO], Brussels, Belgium

Amer. Chamber of Commerce of Bolivia [IO], La Paz, Bolivia

Amer. Chamber of Commerce of Bolivia - Address unknown since 1995.

Amer. Chamber of Commerce of Brazil - Rio de Janeiro [IO], Rio de Janeiro, Brazil

Amer. Chamber of Commerce of Brazil - Sao Paulo [IO], Sao Paulo, Brazil

Amer. Chamber of Commerce in Bulgaria [IO], Sofia, Bulgaria

Amer. Chamber of Commerce of Cuba in the U.S. [IO], Bethesda, MD, United States

Amer. Chamber of Commerce of Cuba in the U.S. [24258]

Amer. Chamber of Commerce in the Czech Republic [IO], Prague, Czech Republic

Amer. Chamber of Commerce of the Dominican Republic [IO], Santo Domingo, Dominican Republic

Amer. Chamber of Commerce in Egypt [IO], Cairo, Egypt

A star before a book entry number signifies that the name is not listed separately, but is mentioned within the entry.

Amer. Chamber of Commerce of El Salvador [IO], San Salvador, El Salvador

Amer. Chamber of Commerce Estonia [IO], Tallinn, Estonia

Amer. Chamber of Commerce to the European Union [IO], Brussels, Belgium

Amer. Chamber of Commerce Executives [24251], 4875 Eisenhower Ave., Ste. 250, Alexandria, VA 22304, (703)998-0072

Amer. Chamber of Commerce in France [IO], Paris, France

Amer. Chamber of Commerce in Germany [IO], Frankfurt am Main, Germany

Amer. Chamber of Commerce in Germany - Frankfurt [IO], Frankfurt, Germany

Amer. Chamber of Commerce in Guangdong [IO], Guangzhou, People's Republic of China

Amer. Chamber of Commerce of Guatemala [IO], Guatemala City, Guatemala

Amer. Chamber of Commerce in Hong Kong [IO], Hong Kong, People's Republic of China

Amer. Chamber of Commerce in Hungary [IO], Budapest, Hungary

Amer. Chamber of Commerce in Indonesia [IO], Jakarta, Indonesia

Amer. Chamber of Commerce and Indus. of Panama [IO], Panama City, Panama

Amer. Chamber of Commerce Ireland [IO], Dublin, Ireland

Amer. Chamber of Commerce in Italy [IO], Milan, Italy

Amer. Chamber of Commerce in Italy - Florence - Defunct.

Amer. Chamber of Commerce in Italy - Rome - Defunct.

Amer. Chamber of Commerce of Jamaica [IO], Kingston, Jamaica

Amer. Chamber of Commerce in Japan [IO], Tokyo, Japan

Amer. Chamber of Commerce in Korea [IO], Seoul, Republic of Korea

Amer. Chamber of Commerce in Latvia [IO], Riga, Latvia

Amer. Chamber of Commerce in Lithuania [IO], Vilnius, Lithuania

Amer. Chamber of Commerce in Luxembourg [IO], Luxembourg, Luxembourg

Amer. Chamber of Commerce of Mexico - Guadalajara [IO], Guadalajara, Mexico

Amer. Chamber of Commerce of Mexico - Mexico City [IO], Mexico City, Mexico

Amer. Chamber of Commerce in Morocco - Address unknown since 1994.

Amer. Chamber of Commerce in the Netherlands [IO], Amsterdam, Netherlands

Amer. Chamber of Commerce in New Zealand [IO], Auckland, New Zealand

Amer. Chamber of Commerce in Nicaragua [IO], Managua, Nicaragua

Amer. Chamber of Commerce in Norway [IO], Oslo, Norway

Amer. Chamber of Commerce in Okinawa [IO], Okinawa, Japan

Amer. Chamber of Commerce - People's Republic of China [IO], Beijing, People's Republic of China

Amer. Chamber of Commerce of Peru [IO], Lima, Peru

Amer. Chamber of Commerce of the Philippines [IO], Makati City, Philippines

Amer. Chamber of Commerce in Poland [IO], Warsaw, Poland

Amer. Chamber of Commerce in Portugal [IO], Lisbon, Portugal

Amer. Chamber of Commerce Researchers Assn. [★7561]

Amer. Chamber of Commerce Researchers Assn. [★24272]

Amer. Chamber of Commerce in Romania [IO], Bucharest, Romania

Amer. Chamber of Commerce in Russia [IO], Moscow, Russia

Amer. Chamber of Commerce in Shanghai [IO], Shanghai, People's Republic of China

Amer. Chamber of Commerce in Singapore [IO], Singapore, Singapore

Amer. Chamber of Commerce in the Slovak Republic [IO], Bratislava, Slovakia

Amer. Chamber of Commerce in South Africa [IO], Johannesburg, Republic of South Africa

Amer. Chamber of Commerce in South Africa [★IO], Johannesburg, Republic of South Africa

Amer. Chamber of Commerce in Spain - Barcelona [IO], Barcelona, Spain

Amer. Chamber of Commerce in Spain - Madrid [IO], Madrid, Spain

Amer. Chamber of Commerce in Sri Lanka [IO], Colombo, Sri Lanka

Amer. Chamber of Commerce in Sweden [IO], Stockholm, Sweden

Amer. Chamber of Commerce in Switzerland [★24378]

Amer. Chamber of Commerce in Taipei [IO], Taipei, Taiwan

Amer. Chamber of Commerce, Taipei, Republic of China [★IO]

Amer. Chamber of Commerce in Thailand [IO], Bangkok, Thailand

Amer. Chamber of Commerce in Thailand - Address unknown since 1994.

Amer. Chamber of Commerce - Trinidad and Tobago [IO], Port of Spain, Trinidad and Tobago

Amer. Chamber of Commerce in the Ukraine [IO], Kiev, Ukraine

Amer. Chamber of Commerce - United Kingdom [★IO]

Amer. Chamber of Commerce in Vietnam - Hanoi [IO], Hanoi, Vietnam

Amer. Chamber of Commerce in Vietnam - Ho Chi Minh City [IO], Ho Chi Minh City, Vietnam

Amer. Chambers of Commerce in Latin Am; Assn. of [24352]

Amer. Chaplain's Assn. - Address unknown since 1989.

Amer. Chap., Intl. Real Estate Fed. [★3310]

Amer. Charbray Breeders Assn. [★4228]

Amer. Charbray Breeders Assn. [★IO]

Amer. Charities for Reasonable Fundraising Regulation [12195], 9112 Tetterton Ave., Vienna, VA 22182, (703)938-1809

Amer. Charolais Breeders Assn. [★4228]

Amer. Charolais Breeders Assn. [★IO]

Amer. Chautauquas [★10901]

Amer. Checker Assn. [★22457]

Amer. Checker Assn. [★IO]

Amer. Checker Fed. [IO], Louisville, KY, United States

Amer. Checker Fed. [22457], c/o Jonathan Chappell, Treas., 3721 Falcon Crest Dr., Apt. 201, Louisville, KY 40219

Amer. Checkered Giant Club [★5132]

Amer. Checkered Giant Rabbit Club [5132], 542 Aspen St. NW, Toledo, OR 97391

Amer. Cheese Soc. [1129], 304 W Liberty St., Ste. 201, Louisville, KY 40202, (502)583-3783

Amer. Chem. Coun. [★798]

Amer. Chem. Soc. [6664], 1155 16th St. NW, Washington, DC 20036, (202)872-4600

Amer. Chem. Soc; Rubber Div., [3433]

Amer. Chemistry Coun. [798], 1300 Wilson Blvd., Arlington, VA 22209, (703)741-5000

Amer. Chen Style Tai Chi Assn. [23578], 300 NE 12 Ave., No. 601, Hallandale Beach, FL 33009

Amer. Chesapeake Club [22195], PO Box 58082, Salt Lake City, UT 84158

Amer. Chess Assn. [21942], 3612 N Silver Sand Ct., North Las Vegas, NV 89032-7688

Amer. Chess Found. [★21945]

Amer. Chesterton Soc. [9630], 4117 Pebblebrook Cir., Minneapolis, MN 55437, (952)831-3096

Amer. Chesterton Soc. [IO], Minneapolis, MN, United States

The Amer. Chestnut Found. [6622], PO Box 4044, 469 Main St., Ste. 1, Bennington, VT 05201-4044, (802)447-0110

Amer. Chevelle Enthusiasts Soc. [21571], 2576 Memorial Blvd., No. 167, Springfield, TN 37172, (615)643-2237

Amer. Cheviot Sheep Soc. [5178], c/o Jo Bernard, Sec.-Treas., PO Box 367, New Richland, MN 56072, (507)465-8474

Amer. Chianina Assn. [4219], 1708 N Prairie View Rd., PO Box 890, Platte City, MO 64079, (816)431-2808

Amer. Child Care Services - Defunct.

Amer. Child Custody Alliance - Address unknown since 1989.

Amer. Child Guidance Found. - Defunct.

Amer. Children of SCORE [10530], 8031 Great Run Ln., PO Box 3423, Warrenton, VA 20188, (540)428-2313

Amer. Chile Center - Defunct.

Amer.-Chilean Coun. - Defunct.

Amer. Chinchilla Rabbit Breeders Assn. - Address unknown since 2003.

Amer. Chinese Medical Soc. [★15163]

Amer. Chinese Pharmaceutical Assn. [15911], PO Box 2623, Cherry Hill, NJ 08034, (609)394-6121

American-Chinese Professionals; Assn. of [★19012]

Amer. Chiropractic Assn. [13988], 1701 Clarendon Blvd., Arlington, VA 22209, (703)276-8800

Amer. Chiropractic Assn. Coun. on Sports Injuries and Physical Fitness [13989], c/o ACA Sports Coun., PO Box 400, Norwalk, IA 50211, (515)981-9340

Amer. Chiropractic Coll. of Radiology [13990], PO Box 3053, La Habra, CA 90632-3053, (562)947-8755

Amer. Chiropractic Coun. on Roentgenology [★16288]

Amer. Chiropractic Registry of Radiologic Technologists [16273], 52 W Colfax St., Palatine, IL 60067, (847)705-1178

Amer. Choral Directors Assn. [10531], PO Box 2720, Oklahoma City, OK 73101-2720, (405)232-8161

Amer. Choral Found. - Defunct.

Amer. Choral Found. Lib. [★10588]

Amer. Christian Fiction Writers [11156], PO Box 101066, Palm Bay, FL 32910-1066

Amer. Christian Missionary Soc. [★19856]

Amer. Christian Palestine Comm. - Defunct.

Amer. Christians for the Abolition of Torture - Defunct.

Amer. Christmas Crib Soc. - Defunct.

Amer. Chronic Pain Assn. [15834], PO Box 850, Rocklin, CA 95677, (800)533-3231

Amer. Church Building Fund Commn. [★19952]

Amer. Cichlid Assn. [22433], c/o Claudia Dickinson, Ambassador-at-Large, PO Box 5078, Montauk, NY 11954, (631)668-5125

Amer. Cinema Editors [1376], 100 Universal City Plz., 2282 Verna Fields Bldg., Rm. 190, Universal City, CA 91608, (818)777-2900

Amer. Circus Memorial Assn. - Address unknown since 1995.

Amer. Citizens Abroad [18949], 1051 N George Mason Dr., Arlington, VA 22205, (703)276-0949

Amer. Citizens Abroad [IO], Geneva, Switzerland

American Citizens Abroad

Amer. Citizens Abroad [IO]

Amer. Club of Paris [IO]

Amer. Soc. of Sydney [IO]

Assn. of Americans and Canadians in Israel [IO]

Assn. of Americans Resident Overseas [IO]

Amer. Citizen's Comm. of Inquiry Into President Kennedy's Assassination - Defunct.

Amer. Citizens Comm. on Reducing Debt - Defunct.

Amer. Citizens Concerned for Life Education Fund/ ACCL Communications Center - Defunct.

Amer. Citizens for Honesty in Govt. - Defunct.

Amer. Citizens for Justice [17083], PO Box 2735, Southfield, MI 48037

Amer. Citizens for Justice; Asian Amer. Center for Justice of the [17094]

Amer. Citizens and Lawmen Assn. - Address unknown since 1991.

Amer. Citizens Together - Address unknown since 2001.

Amer. Citizenship Center [17067], 2501 E Memorial Rd., Box 11000, Oklahoma City, OK 73136-1100, (405)425-5032

Amer. Civic Assn. [12403], 131 Front St., Binghamton, NY 13905-3193, (607)723-9419

The Amer. Civil Defense Assn. [5559], 11576 S State St., Ste. 502, Draper, UT 84020, (800)425-5397

Amer. Civil Liberties Union [17084], 125 Broad St., 18th Fl., New York, NY 10004, (212)549-2500

Amer. Civil Liberties Union Found. [17085], 125 Broad St., 18th Fl., New York, NY 10004, (212)549-2500

Reference to "IO" in place of a book number signifies that the association may be found in the 45th edition of International Organizations.

Amer. Civil Rights Inst. [17086], PO Box 188350, Sacramento, CA 95818-8350, (916)444-2278

Amer. Civil War Assn. [10087], c/o Debi Casey, Treas., 547C Morse Ave., Sacramento, CA 95864, (301)399-3702

Amer. Civil War Round Table - United Kingdom [IO], Uxbridge, United Kingdom

Amer. Clan Gregor Soc. [20780], c/o Lois Ann Garlitz, Registrar, 238 W 1220 N, American Fork, UT 84003, (801)763-0663

Amer. Classical League [8726], Miami Univ., 422 Wells Mills Dr., Oxford, OH 45056-1694, (513)529-7741

Amer. Clean Water Assn. - Defunct.

Amer. Cleft Palate Assn. [★14055]

Amer. Cleft Palate-Craniofacial Assn. [14055], 1504 E Franklin St., Ste. 102, Chapel Hill, NC 27514-2820, (919)933-9044

Amer. Cleft Palate Educational Found. [★14058]

Amer. Clematis Soc. [4672], c/o Edith Malek, Pres., PO Box 17085, Irvine, CA 92623-7085

Amer. Clergy Leadership Conf. [19858], 3224 16th St. NW, Washington, DC 20010, (202)319-3200

Amer. CLG of Foot Orthopedists [★16032]

Amer. Clinical and Climatological Assn. [14018], c/o Herbert L. DuPont, MD, Pres., 6720 Bertner Ave., MC 1-164, Houston, TX 77030, (832)355-4122

Amer. Clinical Lab. Assn. [14991], 1250 H St. NW, Ste. 880, Washington, DC 20005, (202)637-9466

Amer. Clinical Neurophysiology Soc. [14306], PO Box 30, Bloomfield, CT 06002, (860)243-3977

Amer. Clipper Owners Club [22942], 1880 Countrywood Ct., Walnut Creek, CA 94598

Amer. Cloak and Suit Mfrs. Assn. [223]

Amer. Club of Lyon [IO], Lyon, France

Amer. Club of Paris [IO], Paris, France

Amer. Clydesdale Assn. [★4872]

Amer. Coal Ash Assn. [3986], 15200 E Girard Ave., Ste. 3050, Aurora, CO 80014, (720)870-7897

Amer. Coal Coun. [6702], 2980 E Northern Ave., Ste. B5, Phoenix, AZ 85028, (602)485-4737

Amer. Coal Found. [837], 101 Constitution Ave. NW, Ste. 525 E, Washington, DC 20001-2133, (202)463-9875

Amer. Coal Sales Assn. [★846]

Amer. Coalition of Citizens With Disabilities - Defunct.

Amer. Coalition for Life - Address unknown since 1994.

Amer. Coalition of Patriotic Societies - Defunct.

Amer. Coalition on Trade Expansion With Canada - Address unknown since 1989.

Amer. Coalition of Unregistered Churches [20520]

Amer. Coaster Enthusiasts [22970], 1100-H Brandywine Blvd., Zanesville, OH 43701-7303, (740)450-1560

Amer. Cockatiel Soc. [21838], c/o Gerald Oldberg, Pres., 511 NE Orchard Dr., Lee's Summit, MO 64063, (816)524-3785

Amer. Cocoa Res. Comm. [★6545]

Amer. Cocoa Res. Inst. [★6545]

Amer. Coke and Coal Chemicals Inst. [838], 1140 Connecticut Ave. NW, Ste. 705, Washington, DC 20036, (202)452-7198

Amer. Collection Assn. - Address unknown since 1990.

Amer. Collectors Assn. [★1144]

Amer. Collectors Assn. [★IO]

American Collectors of Infant Feeders [IO], Buffalo, MO, United States

Amer. Collectors of Infant Feeders [21959], c/o Shirley Hickman, Sec., 18 Fountain Lake Ln., Buffalo, MO 65622

Amer. Coll. of Addiction Treatment Administrators [13219], c/o Ronald J. Hunsicker, Pres./CEO, 313 W Liberty St., Ste. 129, Lancaster, PA 17603-2748, (717)392-8480

Amer. Coll. Admissions Advisory Center [★7911]

Amer. Coll. Admissions Center [★7911]

Amer. Coll. for Advancement in Medicine [16051], 24411 Ridge Rte., Ste. 115, Laguna Hills, CA 92653, (949)309-3520

Amer. Coll. for Advancement in Medicine [IO], Laguna Hills, CA, United States

Amer. Coll. of Allergists [★13596]

Amer. Coll. of Allergy, Asthma and Immunology [13596], 85 W Algonquin Rd., Ste. 550, Arlington Heights, IL 60005-4425, (847)427-1200

Amer. Coll. of Allergy and Immunology [★13596]

Amer. Coll. of Angiology [16719]

Amer. Coll. of Apothecaries [15912], PO Box 341266, Memphis, TN 38184, (901)383-8119

Amer. Coll. of Bankruptcy [5575], 11350 Random Hills Rd., Ste. 800, Fairfax, VA 22030-6044, (703)934-6154

Amer. Coll. of Cardiology [13888], 2400 N St. NW, Washington, DC 20037-1153, (202)375-6000

Amer. Coll. of Cardiovascular Administrators [15052], c/o Amer. Acad. of Medical Administrators, 701 Lee St., Ste. 600, Des Plaines, IL 60016-4516, (847)759-8601

Amer. Coll. of Cardiovascular Invasive Specialists [★13885]

Amer. Coll. and Career Counseling Center [7911], 2401 Pennsylvania Ave., Ste. 10-C-51, Philadelphia, PA 19130, (215)235-5855

Amer. Coll. of Chemosurgery [★15636]

Amer. Coll. of Chest Physicians [13889], 3300 Dundee Rd., Northbrook, IL 60062, (847)498-1400

Amer. Coll. of Chest Physicians [IO], Northbrook, IL, United States

Amer. Coll. of Chiropractic Consultants [13991], 28 E Jackson Bldg., 10th Fl., Ste. 1020, Chicago, IL 60604, (708)895-3141

Amer. Coll. of Chiropractic Obstetricians and Gynecologists - Defunct.

Amer. Coll. of Chiropractic Orthopedists [13992], c/o Dr. David Swensen, Treas., 40 W Foster St., Melrose, MA 02176, (781)665-1497

American College of Chiropractic Orthopedists [IO], El Centro, CA, United States

Amer. Coll. of Chiropractic Specialists [★IO]

Amer. Coll. of Chiropractic Specialists [★13992]

Amer. Coll. of Clinic Administrators - Defunct.

Amer. Coll. of Clinic Managers [★15054]

Amer. Coll. of Clinical Hypnosis - Defunct.

Amer. Coll. of Clinical Pharmacology [15913], 3 Ellinwood Ct., New Hartford, NY 13413-1105, (315)768-6117

Amer. Coll. of Clinical Pharmacy [15914], 13000 W 87th St. Pkwy., Lenexa, KS 66215-4530, (913)492-3311

Amer. Coll. of Computer Lawyers - Defunct.

Amer. Coll. of Constr. Lawyers [323], 1030 15th St. NW, Ste. 870, Washington, DC 20005

Amer. Coll. of Contingency Planners [14609], 701 Lee St., Ste. 600, Des Plaines, IL 60016-4516, (847)759-8601

Amer. Coll. for Continuing Education - Defunct.

Amer. Coll. Counseling Assn. [8162], PO Box 791006, Baltimore, MD 21279-1006, (703)823-9800

American College Counseling Association [IO], Baltimore, MD, United States

Amer. Coll. of Counselors [12137], 2750 E Sunshine St., Springfield, MO 65804-2047, (317)826-3168

American Coll. of Critical Care Medicine [★14071]

American Coll. of Critical Care Medicine [★IO]

Amer. Coll. Dance Festival Assn. [9864], 225 Rockville Pike, Ste. L10-B, Rockville, MD 20850, (301)251-1848

Amer. Coll. of Dentists [14128], 839J Quince Orchard Blvd., Gaithersburg, MD 20878-1614, (301)977-3223

Amer. Coll. of Domiciliary Midwives [15583], 3889 Middlefield Rd., Palo Alto, CA 94303-4718, (650)328-8491

Amer. Coll. of Ecology - Defunct.

Amer. Coll. of Emergency Physicians [14326], 1125 Executive Cir., Irving, TX 75038-2522, (972)550-0911

Amer. Coll. of Epidemiology [14373], 1500 Sunday Dr., Ste. 102, Raleigh, NC 27607, (919)861-5573

Amer. Coll. of Eye Surgeons [16564], 334 E Lake Rd., No. 135, Palm Harbor, FL 34685-2427, (727)366-1487

Amer. Coll. of Foot and Ankle Orthopedics and Medicine [16032], 5272 River Rd., Ste. 630, Bethesda, MD 20816, (301)718-6505

Amer. Coll. of Foot and Ankle Pediatrics [16033]

Amer. Coll. of Foot and Ankle Surgeons [16034], 8725 W Higgins Rd., Ste. 555, Chicago, IL 60631-2724, (773)693-9300

Amer. Coll. of Foot Surgeons [★16034]

Amer. Coll. of Forensic Examiners [★5751]

Amer. Coll. of Forensic Examiners [★IO]

Amer. Coll. of Forensic Examiners Intl. [IO], Springfield, MO, United States

Amer. Coll. of Forensic Examiners Intl. [5751], 2750 E Sunshine, Springfield, MO 65804, (417)881-3818

Amer. Coll. of Forensic Psychiatry [5752], PO Box 130458, Carlsbad, CA 92013-0458, (760)929-9777

Amer. Coll. of Forensic Psychology [14402], PO Box 130458, Carlsbad, CA 92013-0458, (760)929-9777

Amer. Coll. of Gastroenterology [14405], PO Box 342260, Bethesda, MD 20827-2260, (301)263-9000

Amer. Coll. of Gen. Practitioners in Osteopathic Medicine and Surgery [★15793]

Amer. Coll. of Hea. Assn. [14714], PO Box 28937, Baltimore, MD 21240-8937, (410)859-1500

Amer. Coll. of Hea. Care Administrators [15535], 300 N Lee St., Ste. 301, Alexandria, VA 22314, (703)739-7900

Amer. Coll. of Hea. Plan Mgt. [15053], c/o Amer. Acad. of Medical Administrator, 701 Lee St., No. 600, Des Plaines, IL 60016-4516, (847)759-8601

Amer. Coll. of Healthcare Architects [14610], PO Box 14548, Lenexa, KS 66285-4548, (913)492-4307

Amer. Coll. of Healthcare Architects [IO], Lenexa, KS, United States

Amer. Coll. of Healthcare Executives [14862], 1 N Franklin, Ste. 1700, Chicago, IL 60606, (312)424-2800

Amer. Coll. of Healthcare Info. Administrators [14611], 701 Lee St., Ste. 600, Des Plaines, IL 60016-4516, (847)759-8601

Amer. Coll. of Heraldry [21099], 1643-B Savannah Hwy., Ste. 396, Charleston, SC 29407

Amer. Coll. of Home Health Administrators - Address unknown since 2003.

Amer. Coll. of Home Obstetrics - Address unknown since 2004.

Amer. Coll. of Hosp. Administrators [★14862]

Amer. Coll. of Intl. Physicians [14973], 9323 Old Mt. Vernon Rd., Alexandria, VA 22309, (703)221-1500

Amer. Coll. of Intl. Physicians [IO], Alexandria, VA, United States

Amer. Coll. of Lab. Animal Medicine [16762], c/o Dr. Melvin W. Balk, Exec. Dir., 96 Chester St., Chester, NH 03036, (603)887-2467

Amer. Coll. of Legal Medicine [15001], 2 Woodfield Lake, 1100 E Woodfield Rd., Ste. 520, Schaumburg, IL 60173, (847)969-0283

Amer. Coll. of Managed Care Administrators [★15053]

Amer. Coll. of Managed Care Medicine [14681], PO Box 4765, Glen Allen, VA 23058-4765, (804)527-1906

Amer. Coll. of Managed Care Medicine [IO], Glen Allen, VA, United States

Amer. Coll. of Medical Genetics [14494], 9650 Rockville Pike, Bethesda, MD 20814-3999, (301)634-7127

Amer. Coll. of Medical Gp. Administrators [★15054]

Amer. Coll. of Medical Informatics [★14079]

Amer. Coll. of Medical Physics [16016], 12100 Sunset Hills Rd., Ste. 130, Reston, VA 20190-5202, (703)481-5001

Amer. Coll. of Medical Practice Executives [15054], 104 Inverness Terr. E, Englewood, CO 80112-5306, (303)799-1111

Amer. Coll. of Medical Practice Mgt. [★15086]

Amer. Coll. of Medical Quality [16261], 4334 Montgomery Ave., Ste. B, Bethesda, MD 20814, (301)913-9149

Amer. Coll. of Medical Staff Development [★15086]

Amer. Coll. of Medical Technologists - Defunct.

Amer. Coll. of Medical Toxicology [16660], 1901 N Roeselle Rd., Ste. 920, Schaumburg, IL 60195, (847)885-0674

Amer. Coll. of Medicine - Address unknown since 2004.

Amer. Coll. of Mental Hea. Admin. [15187], 7804 Lorma del Norte Rd. NE, Albuquerque, NM 87109, (505)822-5038

A star before a book entry number signifies that the name is not listed separately, but is mentioned within the entry.

Amer. Coll. of Mohs Micrographic Surgery and Cutaneous Oncology [15636], 555 E Wells St., Ste. 1100, Milwaukee, WI 53202-3823, (414)347-1103

Amer. Coll. of Musicians [8899], PO Box 1807, Austin, TX 78767, (512)478-5775

Amer. Coll. of Neuropsychiatrists [16072], 28595 Orchard Lake Rd., Ste. 200, Farmington Hills, MI 48334, (248)553-0010

Amer. Coll. of Neuropsychopharmacology [15915], 545 Mainstream Dr., Ste. 110, Nashville, TN 37228, (615)324-2360

Amer. Coll. of Nuclear Medicine [15421], c/o Robert P. Powell, Exec. Dir., 101 W Broad St., Ste. 614, Hazleton, PA 18201, (570)501-9661

Amer. Coll. of Nuclear Physicians [15422], 1850 Samuel Morse Dr., Reston, VA 20190-5316, (703)326-1190

Amer. Coll. of Nurse-Midwifery [★15447]

Amer. Coll. of Nurse-Midwives [15447], 8403 Colesville Rd., Ste. 1550, Silver Spring, MD 20910, (240)485-1800

Amer. Coll. of Nurse Practitioners [15448], 1501 Wilson Blvd., Ste. 509, Arlington, VA 22209, (703)740-2529

Amer. Coll. of Nursing Home Administrators [★15535]

Amer. Coll. of Nutrition [15544], 300 S Duncan Ave., Ste. 225, Clearwater, FL 33755, (727)446-6086

Amer. Coll. of Nutrition [IO], Clearwater, FL, United States

Amer. Coll. of Obstetricians and Gynecologists [15584], PO Box 96920, Washington, DC 20090-6920, (202)638-5577

Amer. Coll. of Occupational and Environmental Medicine [15624], 25 NW Point Blvd., Ste. 700, Elk Grove Village, IL 60007-1030, (847)818-1800

Amer. Coll. of Occupational Medicine [★15624]

Amer. Coll. of Oncology Administrators [15055], c/o Amer. Acad. of Medical Administrators, 701 Lee St., Ste. 600, Des Plaines, IL 60016-4516, (847)759-8601

Amer. Coll. of Optometric Physicians - Address unknown since 1990.

Amer. Coll. of Oral and Maxillofacial Surgeons [15734], 2025 M St. NW, Washington, DC 20036, (202)367-1182

American College of Oral and Maxillofacial Surgeons [IO], Washington, DC, United States

Amer. Coll. of Orgonomy [15738], PO Box 490, Princeton, NJ 08542, (732)821-1144

Amer. Coll. of Osteopathic Emergency Physicians [14327], 142 E Ontario St., Ste. 1250, Chicago, IL 60611, (312)587-3709

Amer. Coll. of Osteopathic Family Physicians [15793], 330 E Algonquin Rd., Ste. 1, Arlington Heights, IL 60005, (847)952-5108

Amer. Coll. of Osteopathic Hosp. Administrators [★14876]

Amer. Coll. of Osteopathic Internists [15794], 3 Bethesda Metro Ctr., Ste. 508, Bethesda, MD 20814, (301)656-8877

Amer. Coll. of Osteopathic Neurologists and Psychiatrists [15377], 28595 Orchard Lake Rd., Ste. 200, Farmington Hills, MI 48334, (248)553-0010

Amer. Coll. of Osteopathic Obstetricians and Gynecologists [15585], 8851 Camp Bowie W, Ste. 120, Fort Worth, TX 76116, (817)377-0421

Amer. Coll. of Osteopathic Pain Mgt. and Sclerotherapy [★15796]

Amer. Coll. of Osteopathic Pediatricians [15795], 2209 Dickens Rd., Richmond, VA 23230-2005, (877)231-ACOP

Amer. Coll. of Osteopathic Sclerotherapeutic Pain Mgt. [15796], 303 S Ingram Ct., Middletown, DE 19709, (302)376-8080

Amer. Coll. of Osteopathic Surgeons [15797], 123 N Henry St., Alexandria, VA 22314-2903, (703)684-0416

Amer. Coll. of Otorhinolaryngologists - Defunct.

Amer. Coll. of Pain Medicine [★15833]

Amer. Coll. Personnel Assn. [8961], 1 Dupont Cir. NW, Ste. 300, Washington, DC 20036-1188, (202)835-2272

Amer. Coll. of Pharmacists - Address unknown since 1995.

Amer. Coll. of Phlebology [16720], 100 Webster St., Ste. 101, Oakland, CA 94607-3724, (510)834-6500

Amer. Coll. of Physician Executives [15056], 4890 W Kennedy Blvd., Ste. 200, Tampa, FL 33609, (813)287-2000

Amer. Coll. of Physicians [★14966]

Amer. Coll. of Physicians-American Soc. of Internal Medicine [14966], 190 N Independence Mall W, Philadelphia, PA 19106-1572, (215)351-2600

Amer. Coll. of Physicians Assistants - Defunct.

Amer. Coll. of Podiatric Medical Rev. [16035], c/o Dr. Craig Gastwirth, DPM, Sec.-Treas., 3800 Woodward Ave., Ste. 318, Detroit, MI 48201-2066, (313)833-3091

Amer. Coll. of Podiatric Radiologists - Address unknown since 2004.

Amer. Coll. of Podopediatrics [★16033]

Amer. Coll. of Preventive Medicine [16052], 1307 New York Ave. NW, No. 200, Washington, DC 20005, (202)466-2044

Amer. Coll. of Probate Counsel [★6183]

Amer. Coll. of Prosthodontists [14129], 211 E Chicago Ave., Ste. 1000, Chicago, IL 60611, (312)573-1260

The Amer. Coll. of Psychiatrists [16073], 122 S Michigan Ave., Ste. No. 1360, Chicago, IL 60603, (312)662-1020

Amer. Coll. of Psychoanalysts - Address unknown since 2004.

Amer. Coll. Public Relations Assn. [★8245]

Amer. Coll. of Radiation Oncology [16267], 5272 River Rd., Bethesda, MD 20816, (301)718-6515

Amer. Coll. of Radio Marketing - Address unknown since 1994.

Amer. Coll. of Radiology [16274], 1891 Preston White Dr., Reston, VA 20191, (703)648-8900

Amer. Coll. of Real Estate Lawyers [5479], 1 Central Plz., 11300 Rockville Pike, Ste. 903, Rockville, MD 20852, (301)816-9811

Amer. Coll. of Rheumatology [16367], 1800 Century Pl., Ste. 250, Atlanta, GA 30345-4300, (404)633-3777

American College of Rheumatology [IO], Atlanta, GA, United States

Amer. Coll. of Spine Surgeons [★IO]

Amer. Coll. of Spine Surgeons [★15402]

Amer. Coll. of Sports Medicine [16473], 401 W Michigan St., Indianapolis, IN 46202-3233, (317)637-9200

Amer. Coll. of Surgeons [16565], 633 N St. Clair St., Chicago, IL 60611-3211, (312)202-5000

Amer. Coll. of Surgeons [IO], Chicago, IL, United States

Amer. Coll. of Tax Counsel [5924], 1156 15th St. NW, Ste. 900, Washington, DC 20005-1704, (202)637-3243

Amer. Coll. Testing [★9246]

Amer. Coll. of Theriogenologists [16763], PO Box 3065, Montgomery, AL 36109, (334)395-4666

Amer. Coll. of Toxicology [7800], 9650 Rockville Pike, Bethesda, MD 20814, (301)634-7840

Amer. Coll. of Toxicology [IO], Bethesda, MD, United States

Amer. Coll. of Trial Lawyers [6330], 19900 MacArthur Blvd., Ste. 610, Irvine, CA 92612-8405, (949)752-1801

Amer. Coll. of Trust and Estate Counsel [6183], 3415 S Sepulveda Blvd., Ste. 330, Los Angeles, CA 90034-6032, (310)398-1888

Amer. Coll. of Veterinary Anesthesiologists [16764], c/o Dr. Lydia Donaldson, Exec. Sec., PO Box 1100, Middleburg, VA 20118

Amer. Coll. of Veterinary Dermatology [16765], c/o Kim Boyanowski, DVM, 1411 El Camino Real, Redwood City, CA 94063, (650)365-6826

Amer. Coll. of Veterinary Emergency and Critical Care [16766], c/o Dr. Armelle de Laforcade, DVM, Exec. Sec., Tufts Cummings School of Veterinary Medicine, 200 Westboro Rd., North Grafton, MA 01536, (508)839-5395

Amer. Coll. of Veterinary Internal Medicine [16767], 1997 Wadsworth Blvd., Ste. A, Lakewood, CO 80214-5293, (303)231-9933

Amer. Coll. of Veterinary Microbiologists - Address unknown since 1989.

Amer. Coll. of Veterinary Ophthalmologists [16768], PO Box 1311, Meridian, ID 83680, (208)466-7624

Amer. Coll. of Veterinary Pathologists [16769], 2810 Crossroads Dr., Ste. 3800, Madison, WI 53718-7961, (608)443-2466

Amer. Coll. of Veterinary Radiology [16770], PO Box 8820, Harrisburg, PA 17105-8820, (717)558-7865

Amer. Coll. of Veterinary Surgeons [16771], 11 N Washington St., Ste. 720, Rockville, MD 20850, (301)610-2000

Amer. Coll. of Veterinary Toxicologists [★16736]

Amer. Collegians for Life [★12928]

Amer. Collegiate Horsemen's Assn. [4814], PO Box 1322, Findlay, OH 45840, (740)361-9411

Amer. Collegiate Retailing Assn. [8815], c/o Robert Robicheaux, Membership Chm., 219 Business-Engineering Complex, 1150 10th Ave. S, Birmingham, AL 35294-4460, (205)934-4648

Amer. Colon Therapy Assn. [★16061]

Amer. Colon Therapy Assn. [★IO]

Amer. Colonists; Natl. Soc., Daughters of the [20746]

Amer. Colonists; Natl. Soc., Sons of the [20748]

Amer. Colonization Soc. - Charity and Social Welfare Org. - Address unknown since 1994.

Amer. Color Print Soc. [9412], c/o Elizabeth MacDonald, Treas./Membership Chair, 205 Woodside Ave., Narberth, PA 19072

Amer. Comedy Museum Assn. - Defunct.

Amer. Commerce and Shipping Assn. - Address unknown since 2003.

Amer. Commercial Collectors Assn. [★1147]

Amer. Commercial Collectors Assn. [★IO]

Amer. Commercial Rabbit Assn. - Defunct.

Amer. Comm. for the Protection and Salvage of Artistic and Historic Monuments in War Areas - Defunct.

Amer. Comm. to Advance the Study of Petroglyphs and Pictographs [6437]

Amer. Comm. for the Advancement of Torah Educ. [★8678]

Amer. Comm. on Africa [★16918]

Amer. Comm. on Africa [★IO]

Amer. Comm. for Aid to Poland - Defunct.

Amer. Comm. for the Brotherhood of Saint Andrew in Japan [★12418]

Amer. Comm. for Crystal Growth [★6851]

Amer. Comm. for Democracy and Freedom in Greece - Defunct.

Amer. Comm. for the Evangelization of the Greeks [★20298]

Amer. Comm. for the Evangelization of the Greeks [★IO]

Amer. Comm. on the History of the Second World War [★IO]

Amer. Comm. on the History of the Second World War [★10167]

Amer. Comm. for Human Rights [★17783]

Amer. Comm. for Human Rights [★IO]

Amer. Comm. for Intl. Conservation - Defunct.

Amer. Comm. for Irish Stud. [★10239]

Amer. Comm. for Irish Stud. [★IO]

Amer. Comm. on Italian Migration [19159], 25 Carmine St., New York, NY 10014, (212)247-7373

Amer. Comm. on Japan - Defunct.

Amer. Comm. for KEEP [12418], 825 Green Bay Rd., Ste. 122, Wilmette, IL 60091-2500, (847)853-2502

Amer. Comm. for the Natl. Sick Fund of Israel - Defunct.

Amer. Comm. of OSE - Defunct.

Amer. Comm. for Peace in Chechnya [18189], 1319 18th St. NW, Washington, DC 20036, (202)296-2861

American Committee for Peace In Chechnya [IO], Washington, DC, United States

Amer. Comm. to Preserve Abu Simbel - Address unknown since 1995.

Amer. Committee to Protect the Foreign Born - Defunct.

Amer. Comm. for Rescue and Resettlement of Iraqi Jews [17943], 1125 Park Ave., New York, NY 10028, (212)427-1246

Reference to "IO" in place of a book number signifies that the association may be found in the 45th edition of International Organizations.

American Committee for Rescue and Resettlement of Iraqi Jews [IO], New York, NY, United States

American Committee for Shaare Zedek Hospital in Jerusalem [IO], New York, NY, United States

Amer. Comm. for Shaare Zedek Hosp. in Jerusalem [12455], 49 W 45th St., Ste. 1100, New York, NY 10036, (212)354-8801

Amer. Comm. for Shenkar Coll. [8674], 307 7th Ave., Ste. 1805, New York, NY 10001, (212)947-1597

Amer. Comm. of Slavists [10967], c/o Prof. Michael S. Flier, Chm., Harvard Univ., Dept. of Slavic Languages and Literatures, 12 Quincy St., Barker Ctr., Cambridge, MA 02138

Amer. Comm. of the Slovak World Cong. - Defunct.

Amer. Comm. for South Asian Art [★9413]

Amer. Comm. for Ulster Justice - Defunct.

Amer. Comm. on U.S.-Soviet Relations - Defunct.

Amer. Comm. for the Weizmann Inst. of Sci. [7597], 633 3rd Ave., New York, NY 10017, (212)895-7900

Amer. Commodity Distribution Assn. [4302], c/o W. Kenneth Shifflett, Exec. Sec., 11358 Barley Field Way, Marriottsville, MD 21104, (410)442-4612

Amer. Commun. Assn. [6710], c/o Dale Cyphert, PhD, Treas., The Univ. of Northern Iowa, Coll. of Bus. Admin., 1227 W 27th St., Cedar Falls, IA 50614-0125, (319)273-6150

Amer. Commun. Assn. [IO], Cedar Falls, IA, United States

Amer. Communications; Found. for [17177]

Amer. Communism; Historians of [8506]

Amer. Community Cultural Center Assn. [9846], 149 Cannongate III, Nashua, NH 03063-1953, (603)886-2748

Amer. Community Gardening Assn. [22486], 1777 E Broad St., Columbus, OH 43203, (877)275-2242

Amer. Community Theatre Assn. [★10999]

Amer. Commuters Assn. - Address unknown since 1995.

Amer. Comparative Literature Assn. [10409], Univ. of Texas at Austin, Prog. in Comparative Literature, 1 Univ. Sta. B5003, Austin, TX 78712-0196, (512)471-8020

Amer. Compensation Assn. [★1283]

Amer. Compensation Assn. [★IO]

Amer. Competition Opportunities for Riders with Disabilities [23330], c/o Judy Serie Nagy, 5303 Felter Rd., San Jose, CA 95132, (408)261-8292

Amer. Component Dealers Assn. - Defunct.

Amer. Composers Alliance [10532], 648 Broadway, Rm. 803, New York, NY 10012, (212)362-8900

Amer. Composers Forum [9805], 332 Minnesota St., Ste. E-145, St. Paul, MN 55101-1300, (651)228-1407

Amer. Composites Mfrs. Assn. [589], 1010 N Glebe Rd., Ste. 450, Arlington, VA 22201, (703)525-0511

Amer. Cmpt. Barrel Racing Assn. [23493], c/o Charleen Ornellas, Pres., 17117 Iona Ave., Lemoore, CA 93245, (559)469-7406

Amer. Cmpt. Sci. League [8127], PO Box 521, West Warwick, RI 02893, (401)822-4312

Amer. Cmpt. Scientists Assn. [6718], c/o Andrew Vanoceur, Chm., Gen. Delivery Box ACSA, Los Alamos, NM 87544-9999, (908)272-0016

Amer. Concert Choir - Defunct.

Amer. Concord Grape Assn. [★4724]

Amer. Concrete Agricultural Pipe Assn. - Defunct.

Amer. Concrete Contractors Assn. - Defunct.

Amer. Concrete Inst. [6832], PO Box 9094, Farmington Hills, MI 48333-9094, (248)848-3700

Amer. Concrete Pavement Assn. [913], 500 New Jersey Ave. NW, 7th Fl., Washington, DC 20001, (202)638-2272

Amer. Concrete Pipe Assn. [3023], 1303 W Walnut Hill Ln., Ste. 305, Irving, TX 75038-3008, (972)506-7216

Amer. Concrete Pressure Pipe Assn. [3024], 11800 Sunrise Valley Dr., Ste. 309, Reston, VA 20191-5302, (703)391-9135

Amer. Concrete Pumping Assn. [914], 606 Enterprise Dr., Lewis Center, OH 43035-9432, (614)431-5618

Amer. Confed. of Reciprocating, Examining and Licensing Medical Boards [★15165]

Amer. Confed. of Reciprocating, Examining and Licensing Medical Boards [★IO]

Amer. Confed. of State Medical Examining Boards [★IO]

Amer. Confed. of State Medical Examining Boards [★15165]

Amer. Conf. of Academic Deans [7885], 1818 R St. NW, Washington, DC 20009, (202)884-7419

Amer. Conf. of Cantors [20112], 213 N Morgan St., Ste. 1A, Chicago, IL 60607, (312)491-1034

Amer. Conf. of Certified Cantors [★20112]

Amer. Conf. of Governmental Indus. Hygienists [15625], 1330 Kemper Meadow Dr., Cincinnati, OH 45240, (513)742-2020

Amer. Conf. for Irish Stud. [10239], c/o Prof. Jose Lanters, Pres., Univ. of Wisconsin-Milwaukee, Dept. of English, PO Box 413, Milwaukee, WI 53201, (912)871-1755

Amer. Conf. for Irish Stud. [IO], Milwaukee, WI, United States

Amer. Conf. of Pharmaceutical Faculties [★15909]

Amer. Conf. of Real Estate Investment Trusts - Defunct.

Amer. Conf. of Therapeutic Selfhelp/Selfhealth Social Action Clubs - Defunct.

Amer. Congregation of Jews From Austria - Address unknown since 1999.

Amer. Congregational Assn. [19859], 14 Beacon St., 2nd Fl., Boston, MA 02108, (617)523-0604

Amer. Cong. of Community Supports and Employment Services [17206], 1501 M St. NW, 7th Fl., Washington, DC 20005, (202)466-3355

Amer. Cong. of Exhibitors - Defunct.

Amer. Cong. of Physical Medicine [★16310]

Amer. Cong. of Physical Medicine and Rehabilitation [★16310]

Amer. Cong. of Rehabilitation Medicine [16310], 6801 Lake Plaza Dr., Ste. B-205, Indianapolis, IN 46220, (317)915-2250

Amer. Cong. on Surveying and Mapping [7717], 6 Montgomery Village Ave., Ste. 403, Gaithersburg, MD 20879, (240)632-9716

Amer. Cong. on Surveying and Mapping; Control Surveys Division of the [★7716]

Amer. Conifer Soc. [5253], c/o John Martin, Off. Mgr., 175 Charisma Ln., Lewisville, NC 27023-9611, (336)945-0483

Amer. Connemara Pony Soc. [4815], c/o Marynell Eyles, Sec., PO Box 100, Middlebrook, VA 24459

Amer. Conservation Assn. [4346]

Amer. Conservative Trust - Address unknown since 1988.

Amer. Conservative Union [17261], 1007 Cameron St., Alexandria, VA 22314, (703)836-8602

Amer. Conservatives for Freedom - Defunct.

Amer. Conservatory Theater Found. [11000], 30 Grant Ave., 6th Fl., San Francisco, CA 94109-5800, (415)834-3200

Amer. Constitution Soc. for Law and Policy [5603], 1333 H St. NW, 11th Fl., Washington, DC 20005, (202)393-6181

Amer. Constitutional and Civil Rights Union - Defunct.

Amer. Constitutional Law Found. - Address unknown since 1999.

Amer. Constitutional Rights Assn. - Address unknown since 1989.

Amer. Constitutional Rights Protection Assn. - Defunct.

Amer. Constr. Inspectors Assn. [937], 12995 6th St., Ste. 69, Yucaipa, CA 92399-2549, (909)795-3039

Amer. Construction Owners Assn. - Defunct.

Amer. Consular Assn. [★24070]

Amer. Consultants League [954], c/o ETR, 245 NE 4th Ave., Ste. 102, Delray Beach, FL 33483, (866)344-7200

Amer. Consultants League [IO], Delray Beach, FL, United States

Amer. Consumer Alliance - Address unknown since 2006.

Amer. Consumer Service - Defunct.

Amer. Consumers Assn. [17304], 2633 Flossmoor Rd., Flossmoor, IL 60422, (708)957-2900

Amer. Consumers and Travelers; Fed. of [13342]

Amer. Contact Dermatitis Soc. [14191], 138 Palm Coast Pkwy. NE, No. 333, Palm Coast, FL 32137, (386)437-4405

Amer. Contemplative Soc. - Defunct.

Amer. Contract Bridge League [21893], 2990 Airways Blvd., Memphis, TN 38116-3847, (901)332-5586

Amer. Contract Bridge League [IO], Memphis, TN, United States

Amer. Contract Compliance Assn. [17493], PO Box 65586, St. Paul, MN 55165-0586, (866)222-2298

Amer. Cookie Jar Assn. [22577], c/o Gary Cottrell, Membership Chm., 304 Clinton St., Fayetteville, NY 13066

Amer. Coon Hunters Assn. [23541], c/o WCCHR Registration Off., PO Box 453, Grayson, KY 41143, (606)474-9740

Amer. Cooperative Coun. on Compensation Tech. [4059], 7701 France Ave., Ste. 450, Minneapolis, MN 55435, (952)897-1737

Amer. Coordinating Comm. for Equality in Sport and Soc. - Defunct.

Amer. Copper Coun. [2694], 2 S End Ave., No. 4C, New York, NY 10280, (212)945-4990

Amer. Coptic Assn. [19018], 582 Bergen Ave., Jersey City, NJ 07304, (201)451-0972

Amer. Copy Editors Soc. [3080], c/o Carol DeMasters, Admin., 7 Avenida Vista Grande, Ste. B7, No. 467, Santa Fe, NM 87508

Amer. Copyright Coun. - Defunct.

Amer. Copyright Soc. - Defunct.

Amer. Cordage and Netting Manufacturers [★1075]

Amer. Cormo Sheep Assn. [5179], HC 59, Box 25, Broadus, MT 59317, (406)427-5449

Amer. Corn Millers' Fed. [★2738]

Amer. Corn Millers' Fed. - Defunct.

Amer. Corporate Counsel Assn. [★5614]

Amer. Correctional Assn. [11854], 206 N Washington St., Ste. 200, Alexandria, VA 22314, (301)918-1800

Amer. Correctional Chaplains Assn. [19742], c/o Laurie Etter, Sec., PO Box 422, East Lyme, CT 06333, (860)691-6549

Amer. Correctional Food Ser. Assn. [★1577]

American Correctional Food Service Association [IO], Minneapolis, MN, United States

Amer. Correctional Hea. Services Assn. [14715], 250 Gatsby Pl., Alpharetta, GA 30022-6161, (877)918-1842

Amer. Corrective Therapy Assn. [★16311]

Amer. Corriedale Assn. [5180], c/o Marcia E. Craig, Exec. Sec., PO Box 391, Clay City, IL 62824, (618)676-1046

Amer. Cotswold Record Assn. [5181], PO Box 59, Plympton, MA 02367, (781)585-2026

Amer. Cotswold Sheep Assn. [★5181]

Amer. Cotton Cooperative [★4301]

Amer. Cotton Linter Assn. - Defunct.

Amer. Cotton Mfrs. Assn. [★3772]

Amer. Cotton Mfrs. Inst. [★3772]

Amer. Cotton Shippers Assn. [1089], 88 Union Ave., Ste. 1204, Memphis, TN 38103, (901)525-2272

Amer. Cotton Waste Exchange - Defunct.

Amer. Coun. for the Advancement of Human Rights - Address unknown since 1999.

Amer. Coun. on Alcohol Problems [13220], 2376 Lakeside Dr., Birmingham, AL 35244, (205)989-8177

Amer. Coun. on Alcoholism [13221], 1000 E Indian School Rd., Phoenix, AZ 85014, (800)527-5344

Amer. Coun. of Applied Clinical Nutrition [15545], PO Box 509, Florissant, MO 63032, (314)921-3997

Amer. Coun. for the Arts [★9546]

Amer. Coun. for the Arts in Education - Defunct.

Amer. Coun. for Better Broadcasts [★9766]

Amer. Coun. of the Blind [16822], 1155 15th St. NW, Ste. 1004, Washington, DC 20005, (202)467-5081

Amer. Coun. of the Blind Enterprises and Services [16823], 120 S 6th St., Ste. 1005, Minneapolis, MN 55402, (612)332-3242

Amer. Coun. of Blind Fed. Employees [★16824]

Amer. Coun. of the Blind; Friends-in-Art of [9504]

Amer. Coun. of Blind Govt. Employees [16824], c/o Billie Jean Keith, Pres., 737 N Buchanan St., Arlington, VA 22203

Amer. Coun. of the Blind Lions [16825], c/o Alan Beatty, Pres., PO Box 2312, Fort Collins, CO 80522, (970)484-2598

Amer. Coun. of the Blind Parents [★16844]

A star before a book entry number signifies that the name is not listed separately, but is mentioned within the entry.

Amer. Coun. for Capital Formation [17347], 1750 K St. NW, Ste. 400, Washington, DC 20006-2302, (202)293-5811

Amer. Coun. on Capital Gains and Estate Taxation [★17347]

Amer. Coun. for Career Women - Address unknown since 1994.

Amer. Coun. of Certified Podiatric Physicians and Surgeons [★16028]

Amer. Coun. on Chiropractic Physiotherapy [★13999]

Amer. Coun. on Chiropractic Roentgenology [★16288]

Amer. Coun. of Christian Churches [19761], PO Box 5455, Bethlehem, PA 18015-0455, (610)865-3009

American Coun. for Collaboration and Language Stud; Amer. Coun. of Teachers of Russian/ [★8226]

Amer. Coun. of Commercial Labs. [★7236]

Amer. Coun. for Competitive Telecommunications [★3955]

Amer. Coun. for Constr. Educ. [8141], 1717 N Loop 1604 E, Ste. 320, San Antonio, TX 78232-1570, (210)495-6161

Amer. Coun. on Consumer Interests [17305], 555 E Wells St., Ste. 1100, Milwaukee, WI 53202, (414)918-3189

Amer. Coun. for Coordinated Action - Defunct.

Amer. Coun. on Cosmetology Education - Defunct.

Amer. Coun. for Drug Educ. [13222], 164 W 74th St., New York, NY 10023, (646)505-2061

Amer. Coun. on Educ. [8224], 1 Dupont Cir. NW, Washington, DC 20036-1193, (202)939-9300

Amer. Coun. on Educ. for Journalism [★8703]

Amer. Coun. on Educ; Off. of Women in Higher Educ., [9324]

Amer. Coun. for Emigres in the Professions - Defunct.

Amer. Coun. for an Energy-Efficient Economy [6938], 1001 Connecticut Ave. NW, Ste. 801, Washington, DC 20036, (202)429-8873

Amer. Coun. of Engg. Companies [6984], 1015 15th St., 8th Fl. NW, Washington, DC 20005-2605, (202)347-7474

Amer. Coun. on the Environment - Address unknown since 2003.

Amer. Coun. of Executives in Religion - Defunct.

Amer. Coun. on Exercise [15958], 4851 Paramount Dr., San Diego, CA 92123, (858)279-8227

Amer. Coun. for Fitness and Nutrition [15959], PO Box 33396, Washington, DC 20033-3396, (800)953-1700

Amer. Coun. for Free Asia - Address unknown since 1994.

Amer. Coun. on Germany [19072], 14 E 60th St., Ste. 1000, New York, NY 10022, (212)826-3636

Amer. Coun. on Germany [IO], New York, NY, United States

Amer. Coun. for Headache Educ. [14530], 19 Mantua Rd., Mount Royal, NJ 08061, (856)423-0258

Amer. Coun. for Health Care Reform - Address unknown since 2004.

Amer. Coun. for Healthful Living - Address unknown since 1999.

Amer. Coun. of Highway Advertisers [85]

Amer. Coun. of Human Rights - Defunct.

Amer. Coun. of Hypnotist Examiners [14918], 700 S Central Ave., Glendale, CA 91204, (818)242-1159

Amer. Coun. of Independent Labs. [7236], 1629 K St. NW, Ste. 400, Washington, DC 20006-1633, (202)887-5872

Amer. Coun. of Independent Labs. [★7236]

Amer. Coun. of Independent Savings and Loan Assns. - Defunct.

Amer. Coun. of Indus. Arts Supervisors [★9232]

Amer. Coun. of Indus. Arts Supervisors [★IO]

Amer. Coun. on Indus. Arts Teacher Educ. [★IO]

Amer. Coun. on Indus. Arts Teacher Educ. [★8543]

Amer. Coun. of the Intl. Inst. of Welding [7846], 550 NW LeJeune Rd., Miami, FL 33126, (305)443-9353

Amer. Coun. on Intl. Intercultural Educ. [8651], Oakton Community Coll., 1600 E Golf Rd., Des Plaines, IL 60016, (847)635-2605

American Council on International Intercultural Education [IO], Des Plaines, IL, United States

Amer. Coun. on Intl. Personnel [IO], Washington, DC, United States

Amer. Coun. on Intl. Personnel [1252], 1212 New York Ave. NW, Ste. 800, Washington, DC 20005, (202)371-6789

Amer. Coun. on Intl. Sports - Address unknown since 1995.

Amer. Coun. for Intl. Stud. [8592], 343 Cong. St., Ste. 3100, Boston, MA 02210, (617)236-2051

Amer. Coun. for Intl. Stud. [IO], Boston, MA, United States

Amer. Coun. for Judaism [20113], c/o Rabbi Howard A. Berman, Exec. Dir., PO Box 300537, Jamaica Plain Sta., Boston, MA 02130, (617)983-1400

Amer. Coun. for Judaism Philanthropic Fund [★12803]

Amer. Coun. of Learned Societies [10197], 633 3rd Ave., New York, NY 10017-6795, (212)697-1505

Amer. Coun. of Life Insurers [2135], 101 Constitution Ave. NW, Washington, DC 20001-2133, (202)624-2000

Amer. Coun. on Marijuana and Other Psychoactive Drugs [★13222]

Amer. Coun. on the Middle East - Defunct.

Amer. Coun. of Nanny Schools - Defunct.

Amer. Coun. of Parent Cooperatives [★8070]

Amer. Coun. of Parent Cooperatives [★IO]

Amer. Coun. on Pharmaceutical Educ. [★15907]

Amer. Coun. of Polish Cultural Clubs [★19301]

Amer. Coun. for Polish Culture [19301], c/o Deborah M. Majka, Pres., 812 Lombard St., Apt. 12, Philadelphia, PA 19147-1308

Amer. Coun. on Public Relations [★3195]

Amer. Coun. for Quebec Stud. [★8044]

Amer. Coun. for Quebec Stud. [★IO]

Amer. Coun. of Railroad Women - Address unknown since 2002.

Amer. Coun. for Reclamation Res. [★6114]

Amer. Coun. for Relief of Refugee Rabbis in Israel - Defunct.

Amer. Coun. on Renewable Energy [6939], PO Box 33518, Washington, DC 20033-3518, (202)393-0001

Amer. Coun. for Romanians - Defunct.

Amer. Coun. on Rural Special Educ. [9137], Montana Center on Disabilities/MSU-Billings, 1500 Univ. Dr., Billings, MT 59101, (406)657-2312

Amer. Coun. on Schools and Colls. [8225]

Amer. Coun. on Sci. and Hea. [14539], 1995 Broadway, 2nd Fl., New York, NY 10023-5882, (212)362-7044

Amer. Coun. of the Slovak World Cong. - Defunct.

Amer. Coun. of Snowmobile Associations [23766], 271 Woodland Pass, Ste. 216, East Lansing, MI 48823, (517)351-4362

Amer. Coun. for Southern Asian Art [9413], c/o Joan Cummins, Sec., 133 W 17th St., No. 6D, New York, NY 10011

Amer. Coun. of Spotted Asses [4125], c/o Coreen Eaton, Sec.-Treas., 914 Riske Ln., Wentzville, MO 63385, (636)828-5955

Amer. Coun. of State Savings Supervisors [458], c/o Andrea M. Falzarano, CAE, Exec. Dir., PO Box 1904, Leesburg, VA 20177, (703)669-5440

Amer. Coun. of Taxpayers - Address unknown since 1995.

Amer. Coun. of Teachers of Russian/American Coun. for Collaboration and Language Stud. [★8226]

Amer. Coun. of Teachers of Russian/American Coun. for Collaboration and Language Stud. [★IO]

Amer. Coun. of Teachers of Uncommonly Taught Asian Languages - Defunct.

Amer. Coun. on the Teaching of Foreign Languages [8727], 700 S Washington St., Ste. 210, Alexandria, VA 22314, (703)894-2900

Amer. Coun. for Tech. [5813], 11350 Random Hills Rd., Ste. 120, Fairfax, VA 22030, (703)218-1955

Amer. Coun. on Transplantation - Defunct.

Amer. Coun. of Trustees and Alumni [7869], 1726 M St. NW, Ste. 802, Washington, DC 20036-4525, (202)467-6787

Amer. Coun. for Turfgrass - Defunct.

Amer. Coun. for Univ. Planning and Academic Excellence - Address unknown since 1994.

Amer. Coun. of Vedic Astrology [★21548]

Amer. Coun. of Venture Clubs [★13068]

Amer. Coun. for World Freedom - Defunct.

Amer. Coun. of Young Political Leaders [18000], 1717 K St. NW, Ste. 500, Washington, DC 20036, (202)857-0999

Amer. Coun. of Young Political Leaders [IO], Washington, DC, United States

Amer. Councils for Intl. Educ. [IO], Washington, DC, United States

Amer. Councils for Intl. Educ. [8226], 1776 Massachusetts Ave. NW, Ste. 700, Washington, DC 20036, (202)833-7522

Amer. Counseling Assn. [11815], 5999 Stevenson Ave., Alexandria, VA 22304, (800)347-6647

Amer. Countertrade Assn. [★2305]

Amer. Country Life Assn. - Defunct.

Amer. Court and Commercial Newspapers [3202], c/o Public Notice Rsrc. Center, PO Box 5337, Arlington, VA 22205, (703)812-0561

Amer. Cowboy Culture Assn. [9379], c/o Natl. Cowboy Symposium and Celebration, PO Box 6638, Lubbock, TX 79493, (806)787-8871

Amer. Craft Assn. - Defunct.

Amer. Craft Coun. [9827], 72 Spring St., 6th Fl., New York, NY 10012-4019, (212)274-0630

Amer. Crafts Coun. [★9827]

Amer. Craftsmen's Coun. [★9827]

Amer. Cranberry Growers Assn. [4702]

Amer. CranioSacral Therapy Assn. [14822], c/o Upledger Inst., 11211 Prosperity Farms Rd., Ste. D-325, Palm Beach Gardens, FL 33410, (561)622-4334

Amer. Crape Myrtle Soc. [★4976]

Amer. Crappie Assn. [22449], 125 Ruth Ave., Benton, KY 42025, (270)395-4204

Amer. Cream Draft Horse Assn. [4816], 193 Crossover Rd., Bennington, VT 05201, (802)447-7612

Amer. Cream Draft Horse Assn. of Am. [★4816]

Amer. Creativity Assn. [10168], Drexel Univ., Goodwin Coll., 3001 Market St., Philadelphia, PA 19104, (866)616-4492

Amer. Credit Card Collectors Soc. [17357], PO Box 2465, Midland, MI 48641

Amer. Credit Union Mortgage Assn. [1103], PO Box 400955, Las Vegas, NV 89140, (702)933-2007

Amer. Credit Union Mortgage Assn. and Amer. CU Housing Alliance [★1103]

Amer. Cricket Growers Assn. - Defunct.

Amer. Criminal Justice Assn. (Lambda Alpha Epsilon) [11855], PO Box 601047, Sacramento, CA 95860-1047, (916)484-6553

Amer. Croatian Academic Soc. - Address unknown since 1995.

Amer. Crop Protection Assn. [★807]

Amer. Cross Country Skiers [23750], PO Box 604, Bend, OR 97709, (541)317-0217

Amer. Crossbow Assn. - Address unknown since 2003.

Amer. Crossbow Fed. [23542], PO Box 251, Glenwood, MN 56334, (320)634-3660

Amer. Crossbred Pony Registry - Address unknown since 2007.

Amer. Crossbreed Dairy Cattle Club - Defunct.

Amer. Crossword Fed. [22458], PO Box 69, Massapequa Park, NY 11762, (516)795-8823

Amer. Cryonics Soc. [14073], PO Box 1509, Cupertino, CA 95015, (408)446-9001

Amer. Cryptogram Assn. [22178], 3300 Darby Rd., Apt. 7114, Haverford, PA 19041

Amer. Crystallographic Assn. [6852], PO Box 96, Buffalo, NY 14207-0090, (716)898-8690

Amer. Cuemakers Assn. [518], c/o Russ Espiritu, Chm., 6162 Hwy. 18, Brandon, MS 39042, (601)825-7077

Amer. CueSports Alliance [23144], 101 S Military Ave., Ste. P - No. 131, Green Bay, WI 54303, (920)662-1705

Amer. Culinary Fed. [790], 180 Center Place Way, St. Augustine, FL 32095, (904)824-4468

Amer. Cultural Exchange [★8176]

Amer. Cultural Resources Assn. [9540], PO Box 4020, Ithaca, NY 14852, (801)394-0013

Amer. Culture Assn. [10886], c/o John F. Bratzel, Exec. Dir., Michigan State Univ., 276 Bessey Hall, East Lansing, MI 48824, (517)355-6660

Reference to "IO" in place of a book number signifies that the association may be found in the 45th edition of International Organizations.

Amer. Cultured Dairy Products Inst. - Address unknown since 1994.

Amer. Cultures; The Assn. of [9554]

Amer. Cultures; Inst. for the Stud. of [10746]

Amer. Custard Glass Collectors - Defunct.

Amer. Custom Gunmakers Guild [1477], 22 Vista View Ln., Cody, WY 82414-9606, (307)587-4297

Amer. Cut Glass Assn. [22550], c/o Kathy Emmerson, Exec. Sec., PO Box 482, Ramona, CA 92065-0482

Amer. Cutlery Manufacturers Assn. [★3708]

Amer. Cutting Horse Assn. [23520], PO Box 2443, Brenham, TX 77834, (979)836-3370

Amer. Cycling Union - Address unknown since 2001.

Amer. Czech and Slovak Assn. - Address unknown since 2004.

Amer. Daffodil Soc. [22487], PO Box 522, Hawkinsville, GA 31036, (614)451-4747

American Daffodil Society [IO], Hawkinsville, GA, United States

Amer. Dahlia Soc. - Defunct.

Amer. Dairy Assn. - Defunct.

Amer. Dairy Cattle Club - Defunct.

Amer. Dairy Goat Assn. [4126], PO Box 865, 209 W Main St., Spindale, NC 28160, (828)286-3801

Amer. Dairy Goat Products Assn. - Defunct.

Amer. Dairy Products Inst. [1130], 116 N York St., Elmhurst, IL 60126, (630)530-8700

Amer. Dairy Sci. Assn. [4485], c/o Peter Studney, Exec. Dir., 1111 N Dunlap Ave., Savoy, IL 61874, (217)356-5146

Amer. Dance Festival [9865], Box 90772, Durham, NC 27708-0772, (919)684-6402

Amer. Dance Festival [★9865]

Amer. Dance Friendship Tour - Address unknown since 2004.

Amer. Dance Guild [9866], PO Box 2006, Lenox Hill Sta., New York, NY 10021, (212)932-2789

Amer. Dance Therapy Assn. [16203], 2000 Century Plz., Ste. 108, 10632 Little Patuxent Pkwy., Columbia, MD 21044, (410)997-4040

Amer. Dart Assn. - Defunct.

Amer. Darters Assn. [23327], 1000 Lake St. Louis Blvd., Ste. 310, Lake St. Louis, MO 63367-9932, (636)625-8621

Amer. Dartmoor Pony Assn. [4817], 203 Kendall Oaks Dr., Boerne, TX 78006

Amer. Darts Org. [23328], c/o Katie Harris, 230 N Crescent Way, Ste. K, Anaheim, CA 92801-6707, (714)254-0212

Amer. Deaf Volleyball Assn. - Address unknown since 2001.

Amer. Deafness and Rehabilitation Assn. [★14735]

Amer. Debate Assn. [9151], c/o Univ. of Mary Washington, Combs Hall, 1301 Colorado Ave., Fredericksburg, VA 22401, (540)654-1252

Amer. Decency Assn. [17281], PO Box 202, Fremont, MI 49412, (231)924-4010

Amer. Decentralized Wastewater Assn. [4006], 918 Cong. Ave., Ste. 200, Austin, TX 78701, (800)993-5002

Amer. Defenders Against Animal Mistreatment - Address unknown since 1995.

Amer. Defenders of Bataan and Corregidor [21386], c/o Everett D. Reamer, Natl. Commander, 2301 Jamaica Blvd. S, Lake Havasu City, AZ 86406

Amer. Defenders - Defunct.

Amer. Defense Inst. [17373], 1055 N Fairfax St., Ste. 200, Alexandria, VA 22314, (703)519-7000

Amer. Dehydrated Onion and Garlic Assn. - Address unknown since 2000.

Amer. Delaine and Merino Record Assn. [5182], c/o Connie M. King, Sec., 59419 Walters Rd., Jacobsburg, OH 43933-9731, (740)686-2172

Amer. Democratic Political Action Comm. - Address unknown since 2000.

Amer. Dental Assistants Assn. [14130], 35 E Wacker Dr., Ste. 1730, Chicago, IL 60601-2211, (312)541-1550

Amer. Dental Assistants Assn; Certifying Bd. of the [★14151]

Amer. Dental Assn. [14131], 211 E Chicago Ave., Chicago, IL 60611-2678, (312)440-2500

Amer. Dental Assn; Alliance of the [14092]

Amer. Dental Assn; Auxiliary to the [★14092]

Amer. Dental Assn; Women's Auxiliary to the [★14092]

Amer. Dental Educ. Assn. [8193], 1400 K St. NW, Ste. 1100, Washington, DC 20005, (202)289-7201

Amer. Dental Educ. Assn. [IO], Washington, DC, United States

Amer. Dental Hygienists' Assn. [14132], 444 N Michigan Ave., Ste. 3400, Chicago, IL 60611, (312)440-8911

Amer. Dental Inst. - Defunct.

Amer. Dental Interfraternity Coun. - Address unknown since 2005.

Amer. Dental Lab. Assn. [★14170]

Amer. Dental Soc. of Anesthesiology [14133], 211 E Chicago Ave., Ste. 780, Chicago, IL 60611, (312)664-8270

Amer. Dental Trade Assn. [★1859]

Amer. Dentists for Foreign Service - Address unknown since 1995.

Amer. Deputy Sheriffs' Assn. [5961], 3001 Armand St., Ste. B, Monroe, LA 71201, (800)937-7940

Amer. Dermatologic Soc. of Allergy and Immunology - Defunct.

Amer. Dermatological Assn. [14192], c/o Julie Odessky, Exec. Mgr., PO Box 551301, Davie, FL 33355, (954)452-1113

Amer. Desalting Assn. [★7824]

Amer. Desalting Assn. [★IO]

Amer. Deserters Comm. - Address unknown since 1995.

Amer. Deserters Comm., France - Address unknown since 1995.

Amer. Design Bicentennial - Defunct.

Amer. Design Drafting Assn. [7152], 105 E Main St., Newbern, TN 38059, (731)627-0802

Amer. Development Group - Address unknown since 2003.

Amer. Devon Cattle Assn. [4220], c/o Martha Trantham, Exec. Sec., 43 Lenoir Ln., Canton, NC 28716, (828)235-8269

Amer. Devon Cattle Club [★4220]

Amer. Dexter Cattle Assn. [4221], 4150 Merino Ave., Watertown, MN 55388, (952)215-2206

Amer. Diabetes Assn. [14218], 1701 N Beauregard St., Alexandria, VA 22311, (800)342-2383

Amer. Dialect Soc. [10398], c/o Allan A. Metcalf, Exec. Sec., MacMurray Coll., Dept. of English, Jacksonville, IL 62650-2590, (217)479-7117

Amer. Diamond Industry Assn. [2355]

Amer. Dianthus Soc. [★22507]

Amer. Die Casting Inst. [★2054]

Amer. Dietetic Assn. [15546], 120 S Riverside Plz., Ste. 2000, Chicago, IL 60606-6995, (312)899-0040

Amer. Digestive Disease Soc. - Address unknown since 1991.

Amer. Digestive Hea. Found. [★14417]

Amer. Dinner Theatre Inst. [1297], 1275 E Waterloo Rd., Akron, OH 44306, (330)724-9855

Amer. Diopter and Decibel Soc. - Address unknown since 2001.

Amer. Directors Inst. - Address unknown since 1990.

Amer. Disability Assn. [11918], 2201 Sixth Ave. S, Birmingham, AL 35233, (205)328-9090

Amer. Disabled for Accessible Public Transit [★17413]

Amer. Disabled for Attendant Prog. Today [17413], 201 S Cherokee St., Denver, CO 80223, (303)733-9324

Amer. Disaster Reserve [12000], 3355 N Acad. Blvd., No. 232, Colorado Springs, CO 80917-5103

Amer. Disc Jockey Assn. [2796], 20118 N 67th Ave., Ste. 300-605, Glendale, AZ 85308, (623)882-8048

Amer. Distance Educ. Consortium [8227], C218 Animal Sci. Bldg., Univ. of Nebraska, Lincoln, NE 68583-0952, (402)472-7000

Amer. Ditchley Found. [17857], 445 Park Ave., 9th Fl., New York, NY 10022, (212)541-3791

Amer. Diversified Dog Soc. - Defunct.

Amer. Divorce Assn. of Men Intl. - Address unknown since 2005.

Amer. Dobermann Assn. [22196], PO Box 2231, Snohomish, WA 98291-2231, (425)397-7630

Amer. Document Network - Defunct.

Amer. Documentation Inst. [★7188]

Amer. Dog Breeders Assn. [22197], PO Box 1771, Salt Lake City, UT 84110, (801)936-7513

Amer. Dog Feed Inst. - Defunct.

Amer. Dog Owner's Assn. [11347], PO Box 186, Castleton, NY 12033, (518)732-7600

Amer. Dog Show Judges [22198], c/o Carl G. Leipmann, Sec., 9144 W Mt. Morris Rd., Flushing, MI 48433, (810)639-7075

Amer. Dog Trainers Network [3851]

Amer. Donkey and Mule Soc. [4127], PO Box 1210, Lewisville, TX 75067, (972)219-0781

Amer. Dorper Sheep Breeders' Soc. [5183], PO Box 796, Columbia, MO 65201, (573)442-8257

Amer. Double Dutch League [23697], PO Box 567, Cherry Hill, NJ 08003-0567, (800)982-ADDL

Amer. Dove Assn. [21839], 7037 Haynes Rd., Georgetown, IN 47122

Amer. Down Assn. [★2258]

Amer. Down Assn. - Defunct.

Amer. Drag Racing Assn. [★23071]

Amer. Drag Racing Assn. [★IO]

Amer. Dream; Center for a New [17260]

Amer. Drive-In Operators Assn. - Defunct.

Amer. Driver Educ. Assn. [★8210]

Amer. Driver and Safety Educ. Assn. [★8210]

Amer. Driver and Traffic Safety Educ. Assn. [8210], Highway Safety Center, Indiana Univ. of Pennsylvania, R & P Bldg., Indiana, PA 15705, (724)357-4051

Amer. Driving Soc. [23491], PO Box 278, Cross Plains, WI 53528, (608)237-7382

Amer. Drug Mfrs. Assn. [★2980]

Amer. Druze Public Affairs Comm. - Address unknown since 1987.

Amer. Druze Soc. [20095], 2239 Merton Ave., Los Angeles, CA 90041-1914, (323)255-1455

Amer. Dry Milk [★1130]

Amer. Dutch Bantam Soc. [5103], c/o Kristi van Greunen, Pres., 1910 Union St., Alameda, CA 94501

Amer. Dutch Rabbit Club [5133], c/o Barb Kline, Sec.-Treas., 4664 S C Rd. 591, New Riegel, OH 44853, (419)595-2050

Amer. Dwarf Hotot Rabbit Club - Address unknown since 2002.

Amer. Dye Mfrs. Inst. - Defunct.

Amer. Ear Assn. for Res. - Address unknown since 2002.

Amer. Ecological Engg. Soc. [6864], PO Box 116350, Gainesville, FL 32611-6350

Amer. Economic Assn. [6868], 2014 Broadway, Ste. 305, Nashville, TN 37203, (615)322-2595

Amer. Economic Development Coun. [★5812]

Amer. Economic Development Coun. [★IO]

Amer. Economic Found. - Address unknown since 2001.

Amer. Edge Collectors Assn. [22612], PO Box 2565, Country Club Hills, IL 60478, (708)868-7784

Amer. Edged Products Manufacturers Assn. [3708], 21165 Whitfield Pl., No. 105, Potomac Falls, VA 20165, (703)433-9281

Amer. Education Coalition - Defunct.

Amer. Educ. Finance Assn. [8342], PO Box 117049, Gainesville, FL 32611-7049, (352)392-2391

Amer. Education Forum - Defunct.

Amer. Educational Gender Info. Ser. [★13090]

Amer. Educational Publishers Inst. [★3206]

Amer. Educational Res. Assn. [9053], 1430 K St. NW, Ste. 1200, Washington, DC 20005, (202)238-3200

Amer. Educational Res. Assn. Women's Caucus [★9328]

Amer. Educational Soc. - Address unknown since 1994.

Amer. Educational Stud. Assn. [8228], c/o Rhonda Jeffries, Sec., Dept. of Instruction and Teacher Educ., Wardlaw Coll. of Educ., Univ. of South Carolina, Columbia, SC 29208, (803)777-5270

Amer. Educational Stud. Assn. [IO], Columbia, SC, United States

Amer. Educational Trust [18049], PO Box 53062, Washington, DC 20009, (202)939-6050

Amer. Egg Bd. [5104], 1460 Renaissance Dr., Ste. 301, Park Ridge, IL 60068, (847)296-7043

Amer. Egyptian Chamber of Commerce - Address unknown since 2003.

Amer. Egyptian Cooperation Found. [17481], 235 E 40th St., Ste. 22A, New York, NY 10016, (212)867-2323

A star before a book entry number signifies that the name is not listed separately, but is mentioned within the entry.

Amer. Egyptian Cooperation Found. [IO], New York, NY, United States

Amer. Egyptian Soc. [★24357]

Amer. Elasmobranch Soc. [7278], c/o Julie A. Neer, Treas., NOAA Fisheries, 3500 Delwood Beach Rd., Panama City, FL 32408, (850)234-6541

Amer. Election Commn. - Defunct.

Amer. Electrochemical Soc. [★6680]

Amer. Electroencephalographic Soc. [★14306]

Amer. Electrology Assn. [14308], c/o Patsy Kirby, CPE, Exec. Dir., PO Box 687, Bodega Bay, CA 94923, (707)875-9135

Amer. Electrolysis Assn. [★14308]

Amer. Electrophoresis Soc. [6900], 1201 Ann St., Madison, WI 53713, (608)258-1565

Amer. Embryo Transfer Assn. [4149], 1111 N Dunlap Ave., Savoy, IL 61874, (217)398-2217

Amer. Emergency Comm. for Tibetan Refugees - Defunct.

Amer. Emigrants' League - Defunct.

Amer. Emu Assn. [4993], PO Box 2502, San Angelo, TX 76902-2502, (541)332-0675

Amer. Endodontic Soc. [14134], 265 N Main St., Glen Ellyn, IL 60137, (773)519-4879

Amer. Endurance Ride Conf. [23933], PO Box 6027, Auburn, CA 95604, (530)823-2260

Amer. Energy Month - Defunct.

Amer. Engg. Alliance [6985], Bowling Green Sta., PO Box 1446, New York, NY 10274-1446, (212)606-4053

Amer. Engg. Assn. [6986], 4116 S Carrier Pkwy., Ste. 280-809, Grand Prairie, TX 75052, (201)664-6954

Amer. Engineering Model Soc. - Defunct.

Amer. Engg. Standards Comm. [★6267]

Amer. English Spot Rabbit Club [5134], c/o Rosalie Berry, Sec.-Treas., 513 E Kent Rd., Lubbock, TX 79403, (806)762-1918

Amer. Enterprise Assn. [★18420]

Amer. Enterprise Inst. for Public Policy Res. [18420], 1150 17th St. NW, Washington, DC 20036, (202)862-5800

Amer. Entrepreneurs Assn. - Defunct.

Amer. Entrepreneurs for Economic Growth [695], 1655 N Fort Myer Dr., Ste. 850, Arlington, VA 22209, (703)524-3743

Amer. Envelope Mfrs. Assn. [★3681]

Amer. Environmental Hea. Found. [14361], 8345 Walnut Hill Ln., Ste. 225, Dallas, TX 75231, (214)361-9515

Amer. Environmental Safety Coun. [★5694]

Amer. Epilepsy Soc. [14379], 342 N Main St., West Hartford, CT 06117-2507, (860)586-7505

Amer. Equestrian Alliance [1923], PO Box 6230, Scottsdale, AZ 85261, (602)992-1570

Amer. Equestrian Trade Assn. [4818], 591 North Ave., Ste. 3-2, Wakefield, MA 01880-1617, (781)246-0486

Amer. Equilibration Soc. [14135], 207 E Ohio St., Ste. 399, Chicago, IL 60611, (847)965-2888

Amer. Equine Assn. [4819]

Amer. Escrow Assn. [1398], 211 N Union St., Ste. 100, Alexandria, VA 22314, (703)519-1240

Amer. Eskimo Dog Club of Am. [22199], c/o Lynn McClure, Pres., 3242 S 187th St., Seatac, WA 98188, (206)242-9944

Amer. Ethical Union [20083], 2 W 64th St., New York, NY 10023-7104, (212)873-6500

Amer. Ethnological Soc. [6404], c/o Member Services - Amer. Anthropological Assn., 4350 N Fairfax Dr., Ste. 640, Arlington, VA 22203-1620, (703)528-1902

Amer. Eugenics Soc. [★6862]

American-European Greyhound Alliance [17678], c/o Louise Coleman, Pres., 167 Saddle Hill Rd., Hopkinton, MA 01748, (508)435-5969

American-European Greyhound Alliance [IO], Hopkinton, MA, United States

American-European Soda Ash Shipping Assn. - Address unknown since 2003.

Amer. European Translators Assn. - Defunct.

Amer. Euthanasia Found. - Defunct.

Amer. Evaluation Assn. [7071], 16 Sconticut Neck Rd., No. 290, Fairhaven, MA 02719, (508)748-3326

Amer. Ex-Prisoners of War [21262], 3201 E Pioneer Pkwy., No. 40, Arlington, TX 76010-5396, (817)649-2979

Amer. Excess Insurance Assn. - Address unknown since 2001.

Amer. Executives for Mgt. Excellence - Defunct.

Amer. Experiment; Center of the [17262]

Amer. Exploration and Production Coun. [2914], 101 Constitution Ave. NW, Ste. 800, Washington, DC 20001-2133, (202)742-4300

Amer. Fabricating Inst. of Technology - Defunct.

Amer. Face Brick Assn. [★604]

Amer. Facsimile Assn. [3732], 2200 Benjamin Franklin Pkwy., Ste. E105A, Philadelphia, PA 19130, (215)981-0292

Amer. Faculty Coun. for the Gradualist Way to Peace - Defunct.

Amer. Fair Trade Coun. - Address unknown since 1994.

Amer. Family Assn. [17162], PO Drawer 2440, Tupelo, MS 38803, (662)844-5036

Amer. Family Communiversity [12138], PO Box 121187, Chicago, IL 60612, (312)738-2275

Amer. Family Farm Found. - Address unknown since 2003.

Amer. Family Farm and Ranch Assn. - Defunct.

Amer. Family Found. [★17368]

Amer. Family Heritage Soc. - Defunct.

Amer. Family Records Assn. [21100]

Amer. Family Rights Assn. [17508], c/o Nev Moore, Co-Founder, PO Box 1560, Cotuit, MA 02635

Amer. Family Soc. - Defunct.

Amer. Family Therapy Acad. [11816], 1608 20th St. NW, 4th Fl., Washington, DC 20009, (202)483-8001

Amer. Family Therapy Assn. [★11816]

Amer. Fan Assn. - Address unknown since 1995.

Amer. Fan Collectors Assn. [★21533]

Amer. Fancy Rat and Mouse Assn. [22704], 9230 64th St., Riverside, CA 92509-5924, (909)238-5231

Amer. Fans of Jon Pertwee - Defunct.

Amer. Far Eastern Soc. - Address unknown since 2003.

Amer. Farm Bur. Fed. [4642], 600 Maryland Ave. SW, Ste. 1000W, Washington, DC 20024, (202)406-3600

Amer. Farm Bur. Found. for Agriculture [4095], 600 Maryland Ave. SW, Ste. 100W, Washington, DC 20024, (202)406-3662

Amer. Farm Bur. Res. Found. [★4095]

Amer. Farm Economic Assn. [★6867]

Amer. Farm Economic Assn. [★IO]

Amer. Farm Found. - Defunct.

Amer. Farm Mgt. Assn. [★6867]

Amer. Farm Mgt. Assn. [★IO]

Amer. Farm Res. Assn. [★4095]

Amer. Farmland Trust [16951], 1200 18th St. NW, Ste. 800, Washington, DC 20036, (202)331-7300

Amer. Farrier's Assn. [522], 4059 Iron Works Pkwy., Ste. 1, Lexington, KY 40511, (859)233-7411

Amer. Fashion Assn. - Defunct.

Amer. Fastener and Closure Assn. - Defunct.

Amer. Fathers Coalition [12660], c/o Amer. Coalition for Fathers and Children, 1718 M St. NW, Ste. 187, Washington, DC 20036, (800)978-3237

Amer. Federalist Party - Address unknown since 2001.

Amer. Fed. for Aging Res. [14508], 55 W 39th St., 16th Fl., New York, NY 10018, (212)703-9977

Amer. Fed. of Arts [9541], 305 E 47th St., 10th Fl., New York, NY 10017, (212)988-7700

Amer. Fed. of Astrologers [6488], 6535 S Rural Rd., Tempe, AZ 85283-3746, (480)838-1751

Amer. Fed. of Aviculture [21840], PO Box 7312, North Kansas City, MO 64116, (816)421-2473

Amer. Fed. for Clinical Res. [★14019]

Amer. Fed. of Film Societies - Defunct.

Amer. Fed. for the Furtherance of Torah - Address unknown since 1995.

Amer. Fed. of Govt. Employees [24068], 80 F St. NW, Washington, DC 20001, (202)737-8700

Amer. Fed. of Grain Millers - Defunct.

Amer. Fed. of Home Health Agencies - Address unknown since 2005.

Amer. Fed. of Information Processing Societies - Defunct.

Amer. Fed. of Intl. Institutes [★12404]

Amer. Fed. of Intl. Institutes [★IO]

Amer. Fed. of Jazz Societies [10270], c/o Jim Jones, Pres., 1400 16th St., Ste. 420, Washington, DC 20036, (310)831-3372

Amer. Fed. of Jewish Fighters, Camp Inmates and Nazi Victims - Defunct.

Amer. Fed. of Jews From Central Europe [17944], 570 7th Ave., New York, NY 10018, (212)921-3871

American Federation of Jews From Central Europe [IO], New York, NY, United States

Amer. Fed. of Labor [★24096]

Amer. Fed. of Labor and Cong. of Indus. Organizations [★24096]

Amer. Fed. of Medical Accreditation - Address unknown since 1999.

Amer. Fed. for Medical Res. [14019], 900 Cummings Ctr., Ste. 221-U, Beverly, MA 01915, (978)927-8330

Amer. Fed. of Mineralogical Societies [7339], PO Box 302, Glyndon, MD 21071-0302, (410)833-7926

Amer. Fed. of Motorcyclists [22664], 6167 Jarvis Ave., No. 333, Newark, CA 94560, (510)796-7005

Amer. Fed. of Musicians of the U.S. and Canada [24149], 1501 Broadway, Ste. 600, New York, NY 10036, (212)869-1330

Amer. Fed. of Musicians of the U.S. and Canada [IO], New York, NY, United States

Amer. Fed. of New Zealand Rabbit Breeders [5135], c/o John Neff, 1351 Holder Ln., Geneva, FL 32732, (407)349-0450

Amer. Fed. of Organizations for the Hard of Hearing [★16442]

Amer. Fed. of Police [★5962]

Amer. Fed. of Police and Concerned Citizens [5962], 6350 Horizon Dr., Titusville, FL 32780, (305)573-0070

Amer. Fed. of Polish Jews [19302]

Amer. Fed. of Poultry Producers Assns. - Defunct.

Amer. Fed. of Priests - Address unknown since 1995.

Amer. Fed. of Pueri Cantores - Address unknown since 2001.

Amer. Fed. of Radio Artists [★24022]

Amer. Fed. of Railroad Police - Defunct.

Amer. Fed. of Ramallah, Palestine [9392], 27484 Ann Arbor Trail, Westland, MI 48185, (734)425-1600

Amer. Fed. of Reformed Young Men Societies [★19831]

Amer. Fed. of Reformed Young Women Societies [★19831]

Amer. Fed. of Representatives of Intl. Companies in Africa [★3903]

Amer. Fed. of Representatives of Intl. Companies in Africa [★IO]

Amer. Fed. of Retail Kosher Butchers - Address unknown since 1995.

Amer. Fed. of School Administrators [7886], 1101 17th St. NW, Ste. 408, Washington, DC 20036, (202)986-4209

Amer. Fed. of Security Officers [24184], 4311 Wilshire Blvd., Ste. 302, Los Angeles, CA 90028, (323)461-3441

Amer. Fed. of Small Business - Address unknown since 1994.

Amer. Fed. of Soroptimist Clubs [★13065]

Amer. Fed. of Soroptimist Clubs [★IO]

Amer. Fed. of State, County and Municipal Employees [24069], 1625 L St. NW, Washington, DC 20036-5687, (202)429-1000

Amer. Fed. of Survivors - Defunct.

Amer. Fed. of Teachers [24042], 555 New Jersey Ave. NW, Washington, DC 20001, (202)879-4400

Amer. Fed. of Teachers Educational Found; Center for the Child Care Workforce, A Proj. of the [12072]

Amer. Fed. of Tech. Engineers [★24052]

Amer. Fed. of TV and Radio Artists [24022], 260 Madison Ave., 9th Fl., New York, NY 10016-2401, (212)532-0800

Amer. Fed. of TV Recording Artists [★17981]

Reference to "IO" in place of a book number signifies that the association may be found in the 45th edition of International Organizations.

Encyclopedia of Associations, 46th Edition

2977

Amer. Fed. of Violin and Bow Makers [2797], 321 Columbus Ave., Boston, MA 02116

Amer. Feed Indus. Assn. [1357], 1501 Wilson Blvd., Ste. 1100, Arlington, VA 22209, (703)524-0810

Amer. Feed Indus. Assn. [★1357]

Amer. Feed Manufacturers Assn. [★1357]

Amer. Feline Soc. - Defunct.

Amer. Female Impersonators Assn. - Address unknown since 1991.

Amer. Fence Assn. [938], 800 Roosevelt Rd., Bldg. C-312, Glen Ellyn, IL 60137, (630)942-6598

Amer. Fence Assn. [IO], Glen Ellyn, IL, United States

Amer. Fern Soc. [6623], c/o Dr. George Yatskievych, Membership Sec., PO Box 299, St. Louis, MO 63166-0299, (314)577-9522

Amer. Ferret Assn. [22415], PMB 255, 626-C Admiral Dr., Annapolis, MD 21401, (888)FERRET-1

Amer. Fertility Assn. [14388], 305 Madison Ave., Ste. 449, New York, NY 10165, (888)917-3777

Amer. Fertility Soc. [★14389]

Amer. Fertility Soc. [★IO]

Amer. Festival of Microtonal Music [10533], c/o Johnny Reinhard, Dir., 318 E 70th St., Ste. 5FW, New York, NY 10021, (212)517-3550

Amer. Fiber Mfrs. Assn. [3769], 1530 Wilson Blvd., Ste. 690, Arlington, VA 22209, (703)875-0432

Amer. Fiber, Textile, Apparel Coalition - Defunct.

Amer. Fiberboard Assn. [590], 853 N Quentin Rd., Ste. 317, Palatine, IL 60067, (847)934-8394

American Fiberboard Association [IO], Palatine, IL, United States

Amer. Fibromyalgia Syndrome Assn. [14395], 7371 E Tanque Verde Rd., Tucson, AZ 85715, (520)733-1570

Amer. Field Ser. [★8589]

Amer. Field Ser. [★8175]

Amer. Field Ser. [★IO]

Amer. Field Ser. [★IO]

Amer. Fighter Aces Assn. [20647], 9404 E Marginal Way S, Seattle, WA 98108-4907, (206)768-7155

Amer. Fighter Aces Museum Found. - Address unknown since 2007.

Amer. Film Export Assn. - Address unknown since 1995.

Amer. Film Inst. [9927], 2021 N Western Ave., Los Angeles, CA 90027-1625, (323)856-7600

Amer. Film Inst. Alumni Assn. Writers Workshop [★11203]

Amer. Film Marketing Assn. [★1382]

Amer. Film Marketing Assn. [★IO]

Amer. Film and Video Assn. - Address unknown since 2003.

Amer. Filtration and Separations Soc. [7724], 7608 Emerson Ave. S, Richfield, MN 55423, (612)861-1277

Amer. Finance Assn. [1399], c/o Blackwell Publishing, Membership Services, 350 Main St., Malden, MA 02148, (781)388-8532

Amer. Financial Services Assn. [2422], 919 18th St. NW, Ste. 300, Washington, DC 20006-5517, (202)296-5544

Amer. Fine Arts Soc. [★9496]

Amer. Fine China Guild - Address unknown since 2003.

Amer. Finnsheep Breeders Assn. [5184], c/o Cynthia Smith, Sec., HC 65, Box 517, Hominy, OK 74035, (918)519-4140

Amer. Fire Prevention Soc. - Defunct.

Amer. Fire Safety Coun. [799], 1909 K St. NW, Ste. 400, Washington, DC 20006, (202)419-3269

Amer. Fire Sprinkler Assn. [3437], 12750 Merit Dr., Ste. 350, Dallas, TX 75251, (214)349-5965

Amer. Firearm Assn. - Address unknown since 1990.

Amer. Firearms Industry Assn. - Defunct.

Amer. Fired Arts Alliance [9542], PO Box 202, Iola, WI 54945-0202, (800)331-0038

Amer. First Day Cover Found. - Defunct.

Amer. First Day Cover Soc. [22781], PO Box 16277, Tucson, AZ 85732-6277, (520)321-0880

Amer. Fish Decoy Assn. [21960], 624 Merritt St., PO Box 250, Fife Lake, MI 49633, (231)879-3912

Amer. Fish Farmers Fed. - Defunct.

Amer. Fisheries Soc. [7169], 5410 Grosvenor Ln., Ste. 110, Bethesda, MD 20814-2199, (301)897-8616

Amer. Fisheries Soc. [IO], Bethesda, MD, United States

Amer. Flag Assn. - Defunct.

Amer. Flag Assn. of the U.S. - Defunct.

Amer. Flag Berth Operators; Trans-Atlantic Amer. Flag Liner Operators/Trans-Pacific [3592]

Amer. Flag Comm. - Address unknown since 1995.

Amer. Flag Inst. - Defunct.

Amer. Flag Liner Operators/Trans-Pacific Amer. Flag Berth Operators; Trans-Atlantic [3592]

Amer. Flame Res. Comm. - Address unknown since 1995.

Amer. Flight Strips Assn. - Defunct.

Amer. Flint Glass Workers of North Am. [★24067]

Amer. Flock Assn. [3770], 6 Beacon St., Ste. 1125, Boston, MA 02108, (617)303-6288

Amer. Floorcovering Alliance [2250], 210 W Cuyler St., Dalton, GA 30720, (706)278-4101

Amer. Floorcovering Assn. [★3431]

Amer. Floorcovering Assn. [★IO]

Amer. Floral Indus. Assn. [1489], PO Box 420244, Dallas, TX 75342-0244, (214)742-2747

Amer. Floral Marketing Coun. - Defunct.

Amer. Florists Assn. - Defunct.

Amer. Florists and Ornamental Horticulturists; Soc. of [★1493]

Amer. Florists; Soc. of [1493]

Amer. Flower Importers Assn. [★1489]

Amer. Flute Guild [10534], PO Box 1515, South Pasadena, CA 91031, (626)441-6314

Amer. Fly-Fishing Trade Assn. [3635], 940 Hill St., Athens, GA 30606, (706)355-3804

Amer. Flyer Assn. - Defunct.

Amer. Folklore Soc. [9953], c/o Timothy Lloyd, Exec. Dir., Ohio State Univ., Mershon Center, 1501 Neil Ave., Columbus, OH 43201-2602, (614)292-3375

Amer. Food for Peace Coun. - Defunct.

Amer. Foot Care Inst. - Defunct.

Amer. Foot Health Found. - Defunct.

Amer. Football Coaches Assn. [23427], 100 Legends Ln., Waco, TX 76706, (254)754-9900

American Football Conf. [★23432]

American Football League [★23432]

Amer. Football League Players Assn. [★23434]

Amer. Footwear Inst. - Defunct.

Amer. Forage and Grassland Coun. [5165], 350 Poplar Ave., Elmhurst, IL 60126, (630)941-3240

Amer. Forces Guild for Infant Survival [★16522]

Amer. and Foreign Christian Union [19762], PO Box 1254, Summerfield, FL 34492-1254

Amer. Foreign Law Assn. [5864], c/o Michael D. Patrick, Treas., Fragomen, Del Rey, Bernsen and Loewy, LLP, 515 Madison Ave., New York, NY 10022

Amer. Foreign Policy Inst. - Defunct.

Amer. Foreign Ser. Assn. [24070], 2101 E St. NW, Washington, DC 20037, (202)338-4045

Amer. Foreign Ser. Protective Assn. [19118], 1716 N St. NW, Washington, DC 20036-2902, (202)833-4910

Amer. Forensic Assn. [9152], Box 256, River Falls, WI 54022, (715)425-3198

Amer. Forensic Nurses [15449], 255 N El Cielo, Ste. 195, Palm Springs, CA 92262, (760)322-9925

Amer. Forest Adventures - Defunct.

Amer. Forest Coun. [★4679]

Amer. Forest History Found. [★10109]

Amer. Forest and Paper Assn. [4679], 1111 19th St. NW, Ste. 800, Washington, DC 20036, (202)463-2700

Amer. Forestry Assn. [★4347]

Amer. Forests [4347], PO Box 2000, Washington, DC 20013, (202)737-1944

Amer. Forged Fitting and Flange Assn. - Defunct.

Amer. Formalwear Assn. [★242]

Amer. Formalwear Assn. [★IO]

Amer. Forsythia Soc. - Address unknown since 2007.

Amer. Forum: Educ. in a Global Age [★8593]

Amer. Forum for Global Educ. [8593], 120 Wall St., Ste. 2600, New York, NY 10005, (212)624-1300

Amer. Forum for Jewish-Christian Cooperation [19887], c/o Dr. David Z. Ben-Ami, 1407 Montfort Dr., Harrisburg, PA 17110, (717)236-0437

Amer. Forum for Jewish-Christian Cooperation [IO], Harrisburg, PA, United States

Amer. Found. for Aging Res. [14509], North Carolina State Univ., Biochemistry Dept., Campus Box 7622, Raleigh, NC 27695-7622, (919)515-5679

Amer. Found. for AIDS Res. [13557], 120 Wall St., 13th Fl., New York, NY 10005-3908, (212)806-1600

Amer. Found. for AIDS Res. [IO], New York, NY, United States

Amer. Found. for Allergic Diseases [★13598]

Amer. Found. for Alternative Health Care, Res. and Development - Defunct.

Amer. Found. for the Blind [16826], 11 Penn Plz., Ste. 300, New York, NY 10001, (212)502-7600

Amer. Found. for Continuing Education - Defunct.

Amer. Found. for Health - Address unknown since 2008.

Amer. Found. for Health Care Reform - Address unknown since 2001.

Amer. Found. for Homeopathy - Address unknown since 1993.

Amer. Found. for Mgt. Res. [★2481]

Amer. Found. for Mgt. Res. [★IO]

Amer. Found. for Maternal and Child Health [15586]

Amer. Found. for Negro Affairs [★8045]

American Found. for Negro Affairs Natl. Educ. and Res. Fund [★8045]

Amer. Found. for Overseas Blind [★16854]

Amer. Found. for Overseas Blind [★IO]

Amer. Found. for Pharmaceutical Educ. [15916], 1 Church St., Ste. 202, Rockville, MD 20850-4184, (301)738-2160

Amer. Found. for the Prevention of Venereal Disease [16409]

Amer. Found. for Psychoanalysis and Psychoanalysis in Groups [★16101]

American Found. for Res. and Consumer Educ. in Social Work Regulation [★13200]

Amer. Found. for Resistance Intl. - Defunct.

Amer. Found. for Suicide Prevention [13287], 120 Wall St., 22nd Fl., New York, NY 10005, (212)363-3500

Amer. Found. for Surgery of the Hand [14523], 6300 N River Rd., Ste. 600, Rosemont, IL 60018-4256, (847)384-8300

Amer. Foundation of Traditional Chinese Medicine - Address unknown since 2004.

Amer. Found. for Tropical Medicine - Defunct.

Amer. Found. for Urologic Diseases [★16705]

Amer. Found. for Vision Awareness - Defunct.

Amer. Found. for World Youth Understanding - Defunct.

Amer. Foundry Soc. [9227], 1695 N Penny Ln., Schaumburg, IL 60173, (847)824-0181

Amer. Foundrymen's Assn. [★9227]

Amer. Foundrymen's Soc. [★9227]

Amer. Fox Terrier Club [22200], c/o Mrs. Anne E. Smith, 6838 Lake Shore Rd., Derby, NY 14047, (717)292-5259

Amer. Fox Trotting Horse Breed Assn. - Address unknown since 1994.

Amer. Fracture Assn. [15756]

Amer. Franchise Assn. - Address unknown since 1994.

Amer. Franchisee Assn. [1666], 53 W Jackson Blvd., Ste. 1157, Chicago, IL 60604, (312)431-0545

Amer. Fraternal Insurance Company [★19146]

Amer. Fraternal Snowshoe Union - Address unknown since 1990.

Amer. Fraternal Union [19119], PO Box 59, Ely, MN 55731-0059, (218)365-3143

Amer. Freedom Alliance [18507], 11500 W Olympic Blvd., Ste. 400, Los Angeles, CA 90064, (310)444-3085

Amer. Freedom Center [18421]

Amer. Freedom Coalition - Defunct.

Amer. Freedom from Hunger Found. [★12394]

Amer. Freedom of Residence Fund - Defunct.

American-French Genealogical Soc. [21101], 78 Earle St., PO Box 830, Woonsocket, RI 02895-0870, (401)765-6141

Amer. Friends of the Alliance Israelite Universelle [8675], 15 W 16th St., 6th Fl., New York, NY 10011-6301, (917)606-8260

Amer. Friends of ALYN Hosp. [12825], 51 E 42nd St., Ste. 308, New York, NY 10017, (212)869-8085

A star before a book entry number signifies that the name is not listed separately, but is mentioned within the entry.

American Friends of ALYN Hospital [IO], New York, NY, United States

Amer. Friends of the Anglican Centre in Rome [IO], Providence, RI, United States

Amer. Friends of the Anglican Centre in Rome [19451], c/o Rev. Norman J. Catir, Jr., Exec. Sec., 31 John St., Providence, RI 02906, (401)831-4285

Amer. Friends of the Anne Frank Center [★17713]

Amer. Friends of the Anne Frank Center [★IO]

Amer. Friends of the Anti-Bolshevik Bloc of Nations - Address unknown since 1994.

Amer. Friends of the Australian Natl. Gallery Found. [★10492]

Amer. Friends of Beth Hatefutsoth [10253], 633 3rd Ave., 21st Fl., New York, NY 10017, (212)339-6034

Amer. Friends of Boys Town Jerusalem [★13473]

Amer. Friends of Cambridge Univ. [★9284]

Amer. Friends of the Captive Nations - Defunct.

Amer. Friends of Chung-Ang Univ. - Defunct.

Amer. Friends of Covent Garden and the Royal Ballet - Address unknown since 2002.

Amer. Friends of the Fed. of Jewish Organizations and Communities of Russia - Defunct.

Amer. Friends of Greece - Defunct.

Amer. Friends of the Gutenberg Museum - Defunct.

Amer. Friends of the Haifa Maritime Museum - Address unknown since 2002.

Amer. Friends of the Hakluyt Soc. [10410], c/o Clare Flemming, Explorers Club, 46 E 70th St., New York, NY 10021

Amer. Friends of Henry Irving [24727], Penthouse North, 29 Washington Sq. W, New York, NY 10011, (212)533-5018

Amer. Friends of Israel - Address unknown since 1989.

Amer. Friends of the Israel Museum [10491], 500 5th Ave., Ste. 2540, New York, NY 10110, (212)997-5611

Amer. Friends of the Jerusalem Inst. for Talmudic Res. - Address unknown since 1991.

Amer. Friends of the Jewish Museum of Greece - Address unknown since 2002.

Amer. Friends of Julio Iglesias Fan Club [24833], PO Box 1425, La Mirada, CA 90637-1425

Amer. Friends of Lafayette [11102], 316 Markle Hall, Lafayette Coll., Easton, PA 18042

Amer. Friends of the Middle East [★18048]

Amer. Friends of the Middle East [★IO]

Amer. Friends of the Natl. Gallery of Australia [10492], c/o Amer. Australian Assn., 599 Lexington Ave., 17th Fl., New York, NY 10022, (212)338-6860

Amer. Friends of Neot Kedumim [19505], PO Box 236, Howes Cave, NY 12092, (518)296-8673

Amer. Friends of Neot Kedumim [IO], Howes Cave, NY, United States

Amer. Friends of the Paris Opera and Ballet [9543], 972 5th Ave., New York, NY 10021, (212)439-1426

Amer. Friends of Religious Freedom in Israel - Defunct.

Amer. Friends of Rhodesia, South Africa, and Southwest Africa - Defunct.

Amer. Friends of Romania [19331], PO Box 5884, Bethesda, MD 20824, (202)966-1922

Amer. Friends of the Royal Shakespeare Theatre - Address unknown since 1995.

Amer. Friends of St. David's Cathedral [10009], St. David's Episcopal Church, 5150 Macomb St. NW, Washington, DC 20016, (434)978-4552

Amer. Friends of Scottish Opera [★10570]

Amer. Friends of Scottish Opera [★IO]

Amer. Friends of Scottish War Blinded - Defunct.

Amer. Friends Ser. Comm. [13148], 1501 Cherry St., Philadelphia, PA 19102, (215)241-7000

Amer. Friends Ser. Comm. [IO], Philadelphia, PA, United States

Amer. Friends Ser. Comm; Mississippi Surveillance Proj. of the [★17093]

Amer. Friends of the Shakespeare Birthplace Trust [11157], c/o John Chwat, Pres., 625 Slaters Ln., Ste. 103, Alexandria, VA 22314-1176, (703)684-7703

Amer. Friends of the Shakespeare Birthplace Trust [IO], Alexandria, VA, United States

Amer. Friends of Switzerland [★IO]

Amer. Friends of Switzerland [★19398]

Amer. Friends of the Tel Aviv Univ. [★8679]

Amer. Friends of The Hebrew Univ. [8676], 1 Battery Park Plz., 25th Fl., New York, NY 10004, (212)607-8500

Amer. Friends of Turkey [18752], 1111 14th St. NW, Ste. 1050, Washington, DC 20005, (202)783-0483

Amer. Friends of Turkey [IO], Washington, DC, United States

Amer. Friends of the Univ. of the Negev [★8673]

Amer. Friends of the Vatican Lib. [10318], 3535 Indian Trail, Orchard Lake, MI 48324, (248)683-0311

Amer. Friends of Vietnam - Defunct.

Amer. Friends of the Wildfowl and Wetlands Trust - Defunct.

Amer. Frontier; Museum Assn. of the [★10132]

Amer. Frozen Food Export Assn. - Defunct.

Amer. Frozen Food Inst. [1496], 2000 Corporate Ridge, Ste. 1000, McLean, VA 22102, (703)821-0770

Amer. Fruit and Vegetable Shippers Assn. [★4766]

Amer. Fuchsia Soc. [22488], c/o Judy Salome, 6979 Clark Rd., Paradise, CA 95969, (530)876-8517

Amer. Fund for Alternatives to Animal Res. - Defunct.

Amer. Fund for Czechoslovak Relief [12802], Bohemian Natl. Hall, 321 E 73rd St., New York, NY 10021, (212)452-3015

American Fund for Czechoslovak Relief [IO], New York, NY, United States

Amer. Fund for Czechosloval Refugees [★IO]

Amer. Fund for Czechosloval Refugees [★12802]

Amer. Fund for Dental Educ. [★8196]

Amer. Fund for Dental Hea. [★8196]

Amer. Fund for Israel Institutions [★10251]

Amer. Fund for Israel Institutions [★IO]

Amer. Fund for Palestine Institutions [★IO]

Amer. Fund for Palestine Institutions [★10251]

Amer. Fund for Slovak Refugees - Defunct.

Amer. Funeral Directors and Embalmers Assn. - Address unknown since 1995.

Amer. Funny Car Series [23070], 4003 Freeport Rd., Sterling, IL 61081, (815)626-2537

Amer. Fur Indus. [★236]

Amer. Fur Liner Contractors Assn. - Defunct.

Amer. Fur Merchants' Assn. - Address unknown since 2003.

Amer. Fur Resources Inst. - Defunct.

Amer. Furniture Mfrs. Assn. [★1690]

Amer. Fuzzy Lop Rabbit Club [22918], c/o Muriel Keyes, Sec., 14255 SE Stephens, Portland, OR 97233

Amer. Galloway Breeders' Assn. [4222], 310 W Spruce, Missoula, MT 59802, (406)728-5719

Amer. Galvanizers Assn. [850], 6881 S Holy Cir., Ste. 108, Centennial, CO 80112, (720)554-0900

American Galvanizers Association [IO], Centennial, CO, United States

Amer. Game Collectors Assn. [★22460]

Amer. Game Fowl Soc. [4190], PO Box 800, Belton, SC 29627, (864)237-5280

Amer. Game Protective Assn. [★5308]

Amer. Gaming Assn. [1718], 1299 Pennsylvania Ave. NW, Ste. 1175, Washington, DC 20004, (202)552-2675

Amer. Gas Assn. [1676], 400 N Capitol St. NW, Ste. 400, Washington, DC 20001, (202)824-7000

Amer. Gasoline Dealers Assn. - Address unknown since 1995.

Amer. Gastroenterological Assn. [14406], 4930 Del Ray Ave., Bethesda, MD 20814, (301)654-2055

Amer. Gastroscopic Club [★14409]

Amer. Gastroscopic Soc. [★14409]

Amer. Gathering of Jewish Holocaust Survivors [17712], 122 W 30th St., Ste. 205, New York, NY 10001, (212)239-4230

Amer. Gay/Lesbian Atheists - Address unknown since 1999.

Amer. Gear Mfrs. Assn. [1994], 500 Montgomery St., Ste. 350, Alexandria, VA 22314-1581, (703)684-0211

Amer. Gear Mfrs. Assn. [IO], Alexandria, VA, United States

Amer. Gelbvieh Assn. [4223], 10900 Dover St., Westminster, CO 80021, (303)465-2333

Amer. Gem and Mineral Suppliers Assn. - Address unknown since 2004.

Amer. Gem Soc. [2356], 8881 W Sahara Ave., Las Vegas, NV 89117, (702)255-6500

Amer. Gem Trade Assn. [2357], 3030 LBJ Fwy., Ste. 840, Dallas, TX 75234, (214)742-4367

Amer. Genetic Assn. [7111], PO Box 257, Buckeystown, MD 21717-0257, (301)695-9292

Amer. Geographical Soc. [7120], 120 Wall St., Ste. 100, New York, NY 10005, (212)422-5456

Amer. Geological Inst. [7126], 4220 King St., Alexandria, VA 22302-1502, (703)379-2480

Amer. Geophysical Union [7136], 2000 Florida Ave. NW, Washington, DC 20009-1277, (202)462-6900

Amer. Gerbil Soc. [21515], 18893 Lawrence 2100, Mount Vernon, MO 65712

Amer. Geriatrics Soc. [14510], c/o The Empire State Building, 350 5th Ave., Ste. 801, New York, NY 10118, (212)308-1414

Amer. German Shepherd Rescue Assn. [11348], c/o Linda Kury, Pres., PO Box 7113, Clearlake, CA 95422, (707)994-5241

Amer. Ghost Soc. [7438], 15 Forest Knolls Estates, Decatur, IL 62521, (217)422-1002

Amer. GI Forum of U.S. [21280], 2870 N Speer Blvd., Ste. 103, Denver, CO 80211, (303)458-1700

Amer. GI Forum Women - Address unknown since 2001.

Amer. Ginseng Soc. - Address unknown since 2003.

Amer. Glassware Assn. - Defunct.

Amer. Glove Importers Assn. - Defunct.

Amer. Glovebox Soc. [7384], PO Box 9099, Santa Rosa, CA 95405, (800)530-1022

Amer. Gloxinia Soc. [★22515]

Amer. Gloxinia Soc. [★IO]

Amer. Gloxinia and Gesneriad Soc. [★IO]

Amer. Gloxinia and Gesneriad Soc. [★22515]

Amer. Go Assn. [22459], PO Box 397, New York, NY 10113-0397, (917)817-7080

Amer. Goat Soc. [4128], c/o Amy Kowalik, Off. Mgr., 735 Oakridge Ln., Pipe Creek, TX 78063, (830)535-4247

Amer. Goiter Assn. [★16646]

Amer. Gold Assn. - Defunct.

Amer. Gold Star Mothers [21188], 2128 Leroy Pl. NW, Washington, DC 20008, (202)265-0991

American Golf Players Assn. - Address unknown since 2006.

Amer. Golf Sponsors [★23461]

Amer. Good Govt. Soc. - Defunct.

Amer. Gotland Horse Assn. - Address unknown since 1985.

Amer. Gourd Soc. [22489], PO Box 2186, Kokomo, IN 46904-2186

Amer. Grain Products Processing Inst. - Defunct.

Amer. Grandprix Assn. - Defunct.

Amer. Granite Assn. [★2772]

Amer. Graniteware Assn. [★22083]

Amer. Grape Growers Alliance for Fair Trade - Defunct.

Amer. Graphological Soc. - Defunct.

Amer. Grassfed Assn. [2438], 1648 Gaylord St., Denver, CO 80206, (877)774-7277

Amer. Grassland Coun. [★5165]

Amer./Greek Exchange Soc. - Defunct.

Amer. Green Movement [★18325]

Amer. Greenhouse Vegetable Growers Assn. - Defunct.

American Greenways [★4380]

Amer. Greyhound Track Operators Assn. [23391], Palm Beach Kennel Club, 1111 N Cong. Ave., West Palm Beach, FL 33409, (561)688-5799

Amer. Groomer's Guild - Defunct.

Amer. Grooming Shop Assn. - Defunct.

Amer. Ground Flat Stock Assn. - Address unknown since 1995.

Amer. Ground Water Trust [4007], 16 Centre St., Concord, NH 03301, (603)228-5444

Amer. Gp. Gymnastics Assn. [23473], c/o USA Gymnastics, 201 S Capitol Ave., Pan Am Plz., Ste. 300, Indianapolis, IN 46225, (317)237-5050

Amer. Gp. Practice Assn. [★14717]

Amer. Gp. Psychotherapy Assn. [16204], 25 E 21st St., 6th Fl., New York, NY 10010, (212)477-2677

Reference to "IO" in place of a book number signifies that the association may be found in the 45th edition of International Organizations.

Encyclopedia of Associations, 46th Edition

2979

Amer. Guernsey Assn. **[4224]**, 7614 Slate Ridge Blvd., Reynoldsburg, OH 43068, (614)864-2409

Amer. Guernsey Cattle Club **[★4224]**

Amer. Guides Assn. - Defunct.

Amer. Guild of Animal Artists - Address unknown since 1995.

Amer. Guild of Authors and Composers **[★5859]**

Amer. Guild of Banjoists, Mandolinists and Guitarists **[★10536]**

Amer. Guild of Court Videographers **[6019]**, 1628 E Third St., Casper, WY 82601, (307)472-9600

Amer. Guild of English Handbell Ringers **[10535]**, 1055 E Centerville Sta. Rd., Dayton, OH 45459, (937)438-0085

Amer. Guild of Hypnotherapists **[14919]**, 2200 Veterans Blvd., Ste. 108, Kenner, LA 70062-4005

Amer. Guild for Infant Survival **[16522]**, 301 Eastwood Cir., Virginia Beach, VA 23454-4014, (757)463-3845

Amer. Guild of Judaic Art **[9414]**, 15 Greenspring Valley Rd., Owings Mills, MD 21117, (410)902-0411

Amer. Guild of Music **[10536]**, PO Box 599, Warren, MI 48090-0599, (248)686-1975

Amer. Guild of Musical Artists **[24150]**, 1430 Broadway, 14th Fl., New York, NY 10018, (212)265-3687

Amer. Guild of Organists **[10537]**, 475 Riverside Dr., Ste. 1260, New York, NY 10115, (212)870-2310

Amer. Guild of Patient Account Mgt. **[★15047]**

Amer. Guild of Patient Account Managers **[★15047]**

Amer. Guild of Town Criers **[10896]**, c/o John Karsten, Pres., 121 S Div. Ave., Holland, MI 49424, (616)396-1943

Amer. Guild of Variety Artists **[24151]**

Amer. Guinea Hog Assn. **[5231]**, PO Box 719, New Boston, NH 03070

Amer. Gulf War Veterans Assn. **[21281]**, PO Box 85, Versailles, MO 65084, (573)378-6049

Amer. Gun Dealers Assn. - Address unknown since 1995.

Amer. Guppy Assn. **[★22442]**

Amer. Guppy Assn. **[★IO]**

Amer. Gymnastic Union **[★23802]**

Amer. Gynecological and Obstetrical Soc. **[15587]**, c/o Cassandra Larkins, Admin. Dir., 409 12th St. SW, Washington, DC 20024-2125, (202)863-1648

Amer. Gynecological Soc. **[★15587]**

Amer. Hackney Horse Soc. **[4820]**, 4059 Iron Works Pkwy., A-3, Lexington, KY 40511-8462, (859)255-8694

Amer. Haflinger Registry **[4821]**, 1686 E Waterloo Rd., Akron, OH 44306, (330)784-0000

Amer. Hair Loss Assn. **[14519]**, 23679 Calabasas Rd., No. 254, Calabasas, CA 91302-1502

Amer. Hair Loss Coun. **[14193]**, 30 S Main St., Shenandoah, PA 17976-2331, (412)765-3666

Amer. Hair Replacement Assn. - Defunct.

Amer. Half-Paso Assn. - Defunct.

Amer. Half-Quarter Horse Registry **[4822]**, PO Box 1198, Apache Junction, AZ 85217-1198, (480)982-1551

Amer. Hampshire Sheep Assn. **[5185]**, 15603 173rd Ave., Milo, IA 50166-8940, (641)942-6402

Amer. Handel Soc. **[9806]**, Univ. of Maryland, School of Music, College Park, MD 20742, (909)607-3568

Amer. Handwriting Anal. Found. **[11206]**, PO Box 6201, San Jose, CA 95150-6201, (800)826-7774

Amer. Hanoverian Soc. **[4823]**, 4067 Iron Works Pkwy., Ste. 1, Lexington, KY 40511-8483, (859)255-4141

Amer. Hardboard Assn. **[★1643]**

Amer. Hardboard Assn. **[★IO]**

Amer. Hardboard Assn. - Defunct.

Amer. Hardware Mfrs. Assn. **[1815]**, 801 N Plaza Dr., Schaumburg, IL 60173, (847)605-1025

Amer. Hardwood Export Coun. **[1603]**, 1111 19th St. NW, Ste. 800, Washington, DC 20036, (202)463-2720

Amer. Hardwood Info. Center **[4054]**, c/o Hardwood Mfrs. Assn., 400 Penn Center Blvd., Ste. 530, Pittsburgh, PA 15235, (412)829-0770

Amer. Harlequin Rabbit Club **[5136]**, c/o Judy Bustle, Sec.-Treas., 132 Farmers Ln., State Road, NC 28676, (336)874-7438

Amer. Harp Soc. **[10538]**, c/o Kathleen Moon, Exec. Sec., PO Box 38334, Los Angeles, CA 90038-0334, (323)469-3050

Amer. Hatpin Soc. **[21961]**, c/o Cathy Miller, VP, 2505 Indian Creek Rd., Diamond Bar, CA 91765-3307

American Hatpin Society **[IO]**, Diamond Bar, CA, United States

Amer. Head and Neck Soc. **[15819]**, 11300 W Olympic Blvd., Ste. 600, Los Angeles, CA 90064, (310)437-0559

Amer. Headache Soc. **[14531]**, 19 Mantua Rd., Mount Royal, NJ 08061, (856)423-0043

Amer. Healing Assn. - Defunct.

Amer. Hea. Assistance Found. **[15100]**, 22512 Gateway Center Dr., Clarksburg, MD 20871-2005, (301)948-3244

Amer. Health Assn. - Address unknown since 1999.

Amer. Hea. and Beauty Aids Inst. **[1841]**, PO Box 19510, Chicago, IL 60619-0510, (708)333-8740

Amer. Health Care Advisory Assn. - Address unknown since 2004.

Amer. Hea. Care Assn. **[14540]**, 1201 L St. NW, Washington, DC 20005, (202)842-4444

Amer. Hea. Care Assn. **[★14652]**

Amer. Hea. Decisions **[14541]**, The Hastings Center, 21 Malcolm Gordon Rd., Garrison, NY 10524, (845)424-0005

Amer. Health Industries Inst. - Defunct.

Amer. Hea. Info. Mgt. Assn. **[15097]**, 233 N Michigan Ave., 21st Fl., Chicago, IL 60601, (312)233-1100

Amer. Hea. Lawyers Assn. **[5782]**, 1025 Connecticut Ave. NW, Ste. 600, Washington, DC 20036-5405, (202)833-1100

Amer. Hea. Planning Assn. **[14542]**, 7245 Arlington Blvd., Ste. 300, Falls Church, VA 22042, (703)573-3103

Amer. Hea. Quality Assn. **[16262]**, 1155 21st St. NW, Washington, DC 20036, (202)331-5790

Amer. Hea. and Temperance Assn. **[13303]**, c/o Dr. DeWitt S. Williams, Dir., 12501 Old Columbia Pike, Silver Spring, MD 20902, (301)680-6733

Amer. Hea. and Temperance Soc. **[★13303]**

Amer. Healthcare Inst. **[★14597]**

Amer. Healthcare Radiology Administrators **[16275]**, 490B Boston Post Rd., No. 101, Sudbury, MA 01776, (978)443-7591

Amer. Hearing Aid Associates **[14739]**, 1380 Wilmington Pike, West Chester, PA 19382, (800)984-3272

Amer. Hearing Impaired Hockey Assn. **[23337]**, 1143 W Lake St., Chicago, IL 60607, (312)226-5880

Amer. Hearing Res. Found. **[14740]**, 8 S Michigan Ave., Ste. 814, Chicago, IL 60603-4539, (312)726-9670

Amer. Hearing Soc. **[★16442]**

Amer. Heart Assn. **[13890]**, 7272 Greenville Ave., Dallas, TX 75231, (301)223-2307

Amer. Heart Assn; Coun. on Arteriosclerosis, Thrombosis and Vascular Biology of the **[13902]**

Amer. Heartworm Soc. **[16772]**, PO Box 667, Batavia, IL 60510, (630)262-1997

Amer. Hebrew Congregations; Religious Action Center of the Union of **[★17954]**

Amer. Helicopter Soc. **[139]**, 217 N Washington St., Alexandria, VA 22314-2538, (703)684-6777

Amer. Helicopter Soc. **[IO]**, Alexandria, VA, United States

Amer. Hellenic Alliance - Defunct.

American-Hellenic Chamber of Commerce **[IO]**, Athens, Greece

Amer. Hellenic Cong. - Defunct.

Amer. Hellenic Educational Progressive Assn. **[19083]**, 1909 Q St. NW, Ste. 500, Washington, DC 20009, (202)232-6300

Amer. Hellenic Inst. **[24325]**, 1220 16th St. NW, Washington, DC 20036, (202)785-8430

Amer. Helvetia Philatelic Soc. **[22782]**, c/o Richard Hall, Sec., PO Box 15053, Asheville, NC 28813-0053

Amer. Helvetia Philatelic Soc. **[IO]**, Asheville, NC, United States

Amer. Hemerocallis Soc. **[22490]**, c/o Kevin P. Walek, Pres., 9122 John Way, Fairfax Station, VA 22039-3042, (703)798-5501

Amer. Hemisphere Assn. of the Intl. Cooperative Insurance Fed. **[★2141]**

Amer. Hemochromatosis Soc. **[14543]**, c/o Sandra Thomas, Pres./Founder, 4044 W Lake Mary Blvd., Unit No. 104, PMB 416, Lake Mary, FL 32746-2012, (407)829-4488

Amer. Hepatic Found. - Defunct.

Amer. Hepatitis Assn. - Address unknown since 1995.

Amer. Hepato-Pancreato-Biliary Assn. **[14802]**, 341 N Maitland Ave., Ste. 130, Maitland, FL 32751, (407)647-8839

Amer. Hepato-Pancreato-Biliary Assn. **[IO]**, Maitland, FL, United States

Amer. Heraldry Soc. **[21102]**, 2011 I St., Sacramento, CA 95814

Amer. Herb Assn. **[6624]**, PO Box 1673, Nevada City, CA 95959, (530)265-9552

Amer. Herbal Products Assn. **[1904]**, 8484 Georgia Ave., Ste. 370, Silver Spring, MD 20910-5606, (301)588-1171

Amer. Herbalists Guild **[14817]**, 141 Nob Hill Rd., Cheshire, CT 06410, (203)272-6731

Amer. Hereford Assn. **[4225]**, PO Box 014059, Kansas City, MO 64101, (816)842-3757

Amer. Herens Assn. **[4226]**

Amer. Heritage Alliance - Defunct.

Amer. Heritage Assn. Intl. **[★8590]**

Amer. Heritage Assn. Intl. **[★IO]**

Amer. Heritage Found. - Address unknown since 1995.

Amer. Heritage Soc. - Defunct.

Amer. Hernia Soc. **[16566]**, PO Box 4834, Englewood, CO 80155, (303)567-7899

American Hernia Society **[IO]**, Englewood, CO, United States

American Hibiscus Society **[IO]**, Venice, FL, United States

Amer. Hibiscus Soc. **[22491]**, PO Box 1580, Venice, FL 34284-1580, (941)484-6459

Amer. Highland Cattle Assn. **[4227]**, 200 Livestock Exchange Bldg., 4701 Marion St., Denver, CO 80216, (303)292-9102

Amer. Highway Freight Assn. **[★3863]**

Amer. Highway Proj. **[10010]**, 15 Church St., Le Roy, NY 14482, (585)768-8354

Amer. Highway Sign Assn. **[★85]**

Amer. Highway Users Alliance **[12949]**, 1101 14th St. NW, Ste. 750, Washington, DC 20005, (202)857-1200

Amer. Hiking Soc. **[23934]**, 1422 Fenwick Ln., Silver Spring, MD 20910, (301)565-6704

Amer. Himalayan Rabbit Assn. **[5137]**, c/o Errean Kratochvil, Sec.-Treas., 7715 Callan Ct., New Port Richey, FL 34654, (727)847-1001

American Himalayan Rabbit Association **[IO]**, New Port Richey, FL, United States

Amer. Hindu Assn. **[20077]**, PO Box 55405, Madison, WI 53705, (608)848-9046

Amer. Hippotherapy Assn. **[16600]**, 136 Bush Rd., Damascus, PA 18415, (888)851-4592

American Hippotherapy Association **[IO]**, Damascus, PA, United States

Amer.-Hispanic Owned Radio Assn. - Address unknown since 1999.

Amer. Histadrut Cultural Exchange Inst. - Defunct.

Amer. Histadrut Development Found. **[★12458]**

Amer. Histadrut Development Found. **[★IO]**

Amer. Historians; Org. of **[10142]**

Amer. Historic Inns **[1909]**, PO Box 669, Dana Point, CA 92629, (949)497-2232

Amer. Historic Monument Soc. **[★2785]**

Amer. Historic Racing Motorcycle Assn. **[22665]**, 2375 Midway Rd. SE, Bolivia, NC 28422, (910)253-8012

Amer. Historical Assn. **[10088]**, 400 A St. SE, Washington, DC 20003-3889, (202)544-2422

Amer. Historical Philatelic Soc. - Defunct.

Amer. Historical Print Collectors Soc. **[21523]**, 94 Marine St., Farmingdale, NY 11735-5605

Amer. Historical Soc. of Germans From Russia **[19073]**, 631 D St., Lincoln, NE 68502-1199, (402)474-3363

Amer. Historical Soc. of Germans From Russia **[IO]**, Lincoln, NE, United States

A star before a book entry number signifies that the name is not listed separately, but is mentioned within the entry.

Amer. Historical Soc; Natl. Japanese [10267]

American Historical Soc; Swedish- [10989]

Amer. History Forum and Civil War Educ. Assn. [8500], PO Box 78, Winchester, VA 22604, (540)678-8598

Amer. Hobbit Assn. [9631], 6068 Tarn Cir., Mason, OH 45040, (513)398-8058

Amer. Hobby Fed. - Defunct.

Amer. Hockey Coaches Assn. [23481], c/o Joe Bertagna, Exec. Dir., 7 Concord St., Gloucester, MA 01930, (781)245-4177

Amer. Hockey League [23482], 1 Monarch Pl., Ste. 2400, Springfield, MA 01144-4004, (413)781-2030

Amer. Hockey League [IO], Springfield, MA, United States

Amer. Holistic Hea. Assn. [14823], PO Box 17400, Anaheim, CA 92817, (714)779-6152

Amer. Holistic Health Sciences Assn. - Defunct.

Amer. Holistic Medical Assn. [14824], PO Box 2016, Edmonds, WA 98020, (425)967-0737

Amer. Holistic Medical Found. - Defunct.

Amer. Holistic Nurses' Assn. [14825], 323 N San Francisco St., Ste. 201, Flagstaff, AZ 86001, (928)526-2196

Amer. Holistic Veterinary Medical Assn. [16773], 2218 Old Emmorton Rd., Bel Air, MD 21015, (410)569-0795

Amer. Holstein Horse Assn. [★4824]

Amer. Holsteiner Horse Assn. [4824], 222 E Main St., Ste. 1, Georgetown, KY 40324-1712, (502)863-4239

Amer. Home Bus. Assn. [1918], 965 E 4800 S, Ste. 3c, Salt Lake City, UT 84117, (866)396-7773

Amer. Home Economics Assn. [★12285]

Amer. Home Furnishings Alliance [1690], 317 W High Ave., 10th Fl., High Point, NC 27260, (336)884-5000

Amer. Home Laundry Manufacturers Assn. [★264]

Amer. Home Laundry Mfrs. Assn. and the Consumer Products Division of the Natl. Elecl. Mfrs. Assn. [★6114]

Amer. Home Life Intl. [8594], 1725A Oregon Pike, Lancaster, PA 17601-4206, (717)560-2840

Amer. Home Life Intl. [IO], Lancaster, PA, United States

Amer. Home Lighting Assn. [★2431]

Amer. Home Sewing Coun. [★3784]

Amer. Home Sewing and Craft Assn. [★3784]

Amer. Homeowners Assn. [2458], PO Box 16817, Stamford, CT 06905, (203)323-7715

Amer. Homeowners Found. [3296], 6776 Little Falls Rd., Arlington, VA 22213-1213, (800)489-7776

Amer. Homeowners Grassroots Alliance [17727], 6776 Little Falls Rd., Arlington, VA 22213-1213, (800)489-7776

Amer. Homeowners' Rsrc. Center [17743], PO Box 97, San Juan Capistrano, CA 92693, (949)366-2125

Amer. Hominological Assn. - Defunct.

Amer. Honey Producers Assn. [4163], c/o Mark Brady, Pres., 3307 Sanger Creek Way, Waxahachie, TX 75165, (972)937-2022

Amer. Horizons - Defunct.

Amer. Horse Coun. [4825], 1616 H St. NW, 7th Fl., Washington, DC 20006, (202)296-4031

Amer. Horse Defense Fund [4826], 1718 M St. NW, Unit 191, Washington, DC 20036-4505, (202)609-8198

Amer. Horse Protection Assn. [5291]

Amer. Horse Publications [3203], 49 Spinnaker Cir., South Daytona, FL 32119, (386)760-7743

Amer. Horse Shows Assn. [★23534]

Amer. Horse Trials Found. [23521], 221 Grove Cove Rd., Centreville, MD 21617, (443)262-9555

Amer. Horseman Alliance [1924], 7550 IH-10 W, 14th Fl., San Antonio, TX 78229, (210)541-7127

Amer. Horticultural Marketing Coun. - Defunct.

Amer. Horticultural Soc. [22492], 7931 E Boulevard Dr., Alexandria, VA 22308-1300, (703)768-5700

Amer. Horticultural Therapy Assn. [16601], 201 E Main St., Ste. 1405, Lexington, KY 40507-2004, (859)514-9177

Amer. Hosp. Assn. [14863], 1 N Franklin, Chicago, IL 60606-3421, (312)422-3000

Amer. Hosp. Assn; Amer. Soc. for Healthcare Environmental Services of the [14866]

Amer. Hosp. Assn; Educational Trust of the [★14884]

Amer. Hosp. Assn; Natl. Soc. of Patient Representatives of the [★15005]

Amer. Hosp. Assn; Soc. for Healthcare Consumer Advocacy of the [15005]

Amer. Hosp. Radiology Administrators [★16275]

Amer. Host Found. - Address unknown since 2002.

Amer. Hosta Soc. [22493], c/o Sandie Markland, Membership Sec., 8702 Pinnacle Rock Ct., Lorton, VA 22079-3029, (703)690-3021

Amer. Hostage Comm. - Defunct.

Amer. Hot Dip Galvanizers Assn. [★850]

Amer. Hot Dip Galvanizers Assn. [★IO]

Amer. Hot Rod Assn. [IO], Spokane, WA, United States

Amer. Hot Rod Assn. [23071], N 102 Hayford Rd., Spokane, WA 99224, (509)244-3663

Amer. Hotel Assn. [★1927]

Amer. Hotel Found. [★1928]

Amer. Hotel and Lodging Assn. [1927], 1201 New York Ave. NW, No. 600, Washington, DC 20005-3931, (202)289-3100

Amer. Hotel and Lodging Educational Found. [1928], 1201 New York Ave. NW, Ste. 600, Washington, DC 20005-3931, (202)289-3100

Amer. Hotel and Motel Assn. [★1927]

Amer. Hotel and Motel Brokers [★3311]

Amer. Hotel and Motel Brokers [★IO]

Amer. Hovercraft Assn. [★22589]

Amer. Hull Insurance Syndicate [2136], 30 Broad St., New York, NY 10004, (212)405-2803

Amer. Humane Assn. [13149], 63 Inverness Dr. E, Englewood, CO 80112-5117, (303)792-9900

Amer. Humane Assn. Children's Div. [★11556]

Amer. Humane Assn. Children's Services [11556], 63 Inverness Dr. E, Englewood, CO 80112-5117, (303)792-9900

Amer. Humane Educ. Soc. [★11429]

Amer. Humanics [8743], 1100 Walnut St., Ste. 1900, Kansas City, MO 64106, (816)561-6415

Amer. Humanics Found. [★8743]

Amer. Humanist Assn. [20084], 1777 T St. NW, Washington, DC 20009-7125, (202)238-9088

Amer. Humor Stud. Assn. [10207], c/o Janice McIntire-Strasburg, PhD, Exec. Dir., St. Louis Univ., Dept. of English, 3800 Lindell Blvd., St. Louis, MO 63108-3414

Amer. Hungarian Catholic Soc. [★19144]

Amer. Hungarian Educators' Assn. [8533], c/o Eniko Molnar Basa, Exec. Dir., 4515 Willard Ave., No. 2210, Chevy Chase, MD 20815-3685, (301)657-4757

Amer. Hungarian Educators' Assn. [IO], Chevy Chase, MD, United States

Amer. Hungarian Fed. [19104], c/o Atilla Kocsis, Dir., 809 Natl. Press Bldg., Washington, DC 20045, (202)737-0127

Amer. Hungarian Folklore Centrum [10213], 178 Oakdene Ave., Teaneck, NJ 07666, (201)836-4869

Amer. Hungarian Found. [10214], PO Box 1084, New Brunswick, NJ 08903, (732)846-5777

Amer. Hungarian Lib. and Historical Soc. [10215], 213 E 82nd St., New York, NY 10028-2701, (212)249-9360

Amer.-Hungarian Medical Assn. - Address unknown since 1995.

Amer. Hungarian Stud. Found. [★10214]

American Hungarians; Natl. Fed. of [19108]

Amer. Hydrangea Soc. [22494], PO Box 986, Grayson, GA 30017

Amer. Hydrogen Assn. [6940], 2350 W Shangri La Rd., Phoenix, AZ 85029-4724, (602)328-4238

Amer. Hyperlexia Assn. [13940], 195 W Spangler, Ste. B, Elmhurst, IL 60126, (630)415-2212

Amer. Hypnodontic Soc. - Defunct.

Amer. Hypnosis Assn. [14920], c/o Hypnosis Motivation Inst., 18607 Ventura Blvd., Ste. 310, Tarzana, CA 91356, (818)758-2747

Amer. Hypnotists' Assn. - Address unknown since 1994.

Amer. Imagery Assn. - Defunct.

Amer. Immigration and Citizenship Conf. [★17806]

Amer. Immigration and Citizenship Conf. [★IO]

Amer. Immigration Control Found. [17800], PO Box 525, 222 W Main St., Monterey, VA 24465, (540)468-2022

Amer. Immigration Law Found. [5806], 918 F St. NW, 6th Fl., Washington, DC 20004, (202)742-5600

Amer. Immigration Lawyers Assn. [5807], 918 F St. NW, Washington, DC 20004-1400, (202)216-2400

Amer. Immigration Reform; Fed. for [17805]

Amer. Impact Found. - Defunct.

Amer. Import Shippers Assn. [3557], 662 Main St., New Rochelle, NY 10801, (914)633-3770

Amer. Imported Auto. Dealers Assn. [★404]

Amer. Imported Auto. Dealers Assn. [★IO]

Amer. Importers Assn. [★2297]

Amer. Importers Assn. of the U.S. [2298], 214 7th St. N, Safety Harbor, FL 34695, (727)204-8500

Amer. Importers and Exporters Meat Products Group - Address unknown since 2001.

Amer. Impressionist Soc. [9490], 856 5th Pl., Vero Beach, FL 32962, (772)569-0597

Amer. In-Vitro Allergy/Immunology Soc. - Address unknown since 2006.

Amer. Incense Mfrs. Assn. - Defunct.

Amer. Independent Bus. Alliance [3602], 222 S Black Ave., Bozeman, MT 59715, (406)582-1255

Amer. Independent Cockpit Alliance [24008], PO Box 220670, St. Louis, MO 63122-0670, (603)528-2552

Amer. Independent Dentist's Assn. [14136], c/o K. Randall Groh, DDS, Acting Chm., 336 Alhambra Cir., Coral Gables, FL 33134, (305)442-1177

Amer. Independent Designers Assn. - Defunct.

Amer. Independent Refiners Assn. - Defunct.

American Indian

Advancing Native Missions [19833]

Affiliated Tribes of Northwest Indians [18948]

Alliance of Tribal Tourism Advocates [19267]

Amer. Indian Culture Res. Center [10731]

Amer. Indian Heritage Found. [10732]

Amer. Indian Law Alliance [16973]

Amer. Indian Liberation Crusade [12622]

Amer. Indian Lib. Assn. [10319]

Amer. Indian Youth Running Strong [12623]

Americans for Indian Opportunity [12624]

Archaeological Conservancy [6439]

Assoc. Comm. of Friends on Indian Affairs [20039]

Assn. of Amer. Indian Physicians [15989]

Assn. of Kannada Kootas of Am. [19111]

Assn. of Native Amer. Medical Students [15087]

Assn. for the Stud. of Amer. Indian Literatures [10734]

Bear Butte Intl. Alliance [19446]

Black and Indian Mission Off. [19587]

Black Indians and Intertribal Native Amer. Assn. [19269]

Bur. of Catholic Indian Missions [19591]

Cherokee Natl. Historical Soc. [10735]

Citizens Equal Rights Alliance [5800]

Consortia of Administrators for Native Amer. Rehabilitation [19270]

Continental Confed. of Adopted Indians [10737]

Coun. for Indian Educ. [8937]

Crazy Horse Memorial Found. [10739]

Creek Indian Memorial Assn. [10740]

First Nations Development Inst. [12625]

Gamma Delta Pi [24710]

Gathering of Nations [10742]

Heritage Inst. [19271]

Indian Arts and Crafts Assn. [10743]

Indian Defense League of Am. [19273]

Indian Heritage Coun. [10744]

Indian Youth of Am. [12626]

Inst. of Amer. Indian Arts [10745]

Inst. for Amer. Indian Stud. [6447]

Inst. for the Stud. of Amer. Cultures [10746]

Inst. for Tribal Environmental Professionals [19274]

Inter-Tribal Indian Ceremonial Assn. [10747]

Iroquois Stud. Assn. [10748]

Lakota Student Alliance [19275]

Maniilaq Assn. [12627]

Midwest Treaty Network [19276]

Natl. Amer. Indian Housing Coun. [5791]

Natl. Assn. of PreCollege Directors [8371]

Natl. Assn. of Tribal Historic Preservation Officers [10047]

Reference to "IO" in place of a book number signifies that the association may be found in the 45th edition of International Organizations.

Encyclopedia of Associations, 46th Edition

2981

Natl. Center for Amer. Indian and Alaska Native Mental Hea. Res. [15220]
Natl. Center for Neurogenic Commun. Disorders [16449]
Natl. Coun. of Urban Indian Hea. [15277]
Natl. Indian Bus. Assn. [751]
Natl. Indian Child Welfare Assn. [19277]
Natl. Indian Gaming Assn. [5771]
Natl. Indian Hea. Bd. [12629]
Natl. Indian Wars Assn. [9371]
Natl. Native Amer. EMS Assn. [14341]
Natl. Soc. for Amer. Indian Elderly [19279]
Natl. Tribal Child Support Assn. [11713]
Natl. Tribal Development Assn. [19280]
Nations Ministries [20370]
Native Amer. Bus. Alliance [19281]
Native Amer. Church of North Am. of the Cowlitz Indians [19447]
Native Amer. Community Bd. [12630]
Native Amer. Fatherhood and Families Assn. [12681]
Native Amer. Fish and Wildlife Soc. [4595]
Native Amer. Indian Info. and Trade Center [24358]
Native Amer. Inst. [10751]
Native Amer. Leadership Alliance [20455]
Native Amer. Public Telecommunications [9767]
Native Amer. Recreation and Sport Inst. [23631]
Native Amer. Sports Coun. [23632]
Native Amer. Water Assn. [4012]
Native Tourism Alliance [24381]
North Am. Native Amer. (Indian) Info. and Trade Center [10752]
North Amer. Alliance for the Advancement of Native Peoples [12631]
Old Sleepy Eye Collectors' Club of Am. [21934]
Order of the Indian Wars [10479]
Oyate [19284]
Pan Amer. Indian Assn. [10753]
Phi Sigma Nu Native Amer. Fraternity [24647]
Punjabi-American Cultural Assn. [10223]
Seva Found. [12443]
Sikh Amer. Legal Defense and Educ. Fund [18600]
Trail of Tears Assn. [11057]
Tree of Peace Soc. [9913]
United Indian Missions, Intl. [20405]
United South and Eastern Tribes [12632]
World Emergency Relief [12885]
Amer. Indian Affairs; Assn. on [18092]
Amer. Indian and Alaska Native Mental Hea. Res; Natl. Center for [15220]
Amer. Indian/Alaska Native Nurses Assn. - Defunct.
Amer. Indian Archaeological Inst. [★6447]
Amer. Indian Arts Center - Defunct.
Amer. Indian Arts Coun. [10730], 725 Preston Forest Shopping Ctr., Ste. B, Dallas, TX 75230, (214)891-9640
Amer. Indian Arts; Inst. of [10745]
Amer. Indian Bus. Leaders [2830], c/o Tina Begay, Exec. Dir., Gallagher Bus. Bldg., Ste. 366, Missoula, MT 59812, (406)243-4879
Amer. Indian Cattlemen's Assn; Natl. [4273]
Amer. Indian Coun. of Architects and Engineers [6462], c/o Jefferson Begay, Pres., 1707 E Highland Ave., Ste. 200, Phoenix, AZ 85016, (602)222-5300
Amer. Indian Court Judges Assn; Natl. [5905]
Amer. Indian Culture Res. Center [10731], PO Box 98, Marvin, SD 57251-0098, (605)398-9200
Amer. Indian Defense Assn. [★18092]
Amer. Indian Development Assn. - Defunct.
Amer. Indian Elderly; Natl. Soc. for [19279]
Amer. Indian Enterprise Development; Natl. Center for [12628]
Amer. Indian Environmental Coun. - Defunct.
Amer. Indian and Eskimo Cultural Found. - Defunct.
Amer. Indian Ethnohistoric Conf. [★9918]
Amer. Indian Graduate Center [8426], 4520 Montgomery Blvd. NE, Ste. 1B, Albuquerque, NM 87109, (505)881-4584
Amer. Indian Health Care Assn. - Address unknown since 1999.
Amer. Indian Heritage Found. [10732], PO Box 6301, Falls Church, VA 22040, (703)819-0979

Amer. Indian Higher Educ. Consortium [8935], 121 Oronoco St., Alexandria, VA 22314, (703)838-0400
Amer. Indian Historical Assn. - Address unknown since 1995.
Amer. Indian Historical Soc. - Defunct.
Amer. Indian Horse Registry [4827], Rancho San Francisco, 9028 State Park Rd., Lockhart, TX 78644, (512)398-6642
Amer. Indian Housing Coun; Natl. [5791]
Amer. Indian Information Center - Defunct.
Amer. Indian Inst. [10733], Univ. of Oklahoma, Coll. of Continuing Educ., 555 Constitution St., Ste. 227, Norman, OK 73072-7820, (405)325-4127
Amer. Indian Law Alliance [16973], 11 Broadway, 2nd Fl., New York, NY 10004, (212)477-9100
Amer. Indian Law Students Assn. [★8772]
Amer. Indian Liberation Crusade [12622], 4009 S Halldale Ave., Los Angeles, CA 90062-1851, (323)299-1810
Amer. Indian Lib. Assn. [10319], c/o Ms. Rhonda Harris Taylor, Newsl. Ed., Univ. of Oklahoma, School of Lib. and Info. Stud., 401 W Brooks, Norman, OK 73019, (405)325-3921
Amer. Indian Lore Assn. [★10751]
Amer. Indian Movement [18090], Grand Governing Coun., PO Box 13521, Minneapolis, MN 55414, (612)721-3914
Amer. Indian Natl. Bank Scholarship Fund - Defunct.
Amer. Indian Philosophy Assn. [19268], Univ. of New Mexico, Philosophy Dept., Albuquerque, NM 87131
Amer. Indian Physicians; Assn. of [15989]
Amer. Indian Press Assn. - Defunct.
Amer. Indian Projects Found. - Defunct.
Amer. Indian Refugees - Address unknown since 1989.
Amer. Indian Registry for the Performing Arts - Address unknown since 1994.
Amer. Indian Res. and Development [8464]
Amer. Indian Ritual Object Repatriation Found. [18091], 463 E 57th St., New York, NY 10022-3003, (212)980-9441
Amer. Indian Scholarships [★8426]
Amer. Indian Science and Education Center - Defunct.
Amer. Indian Sci. and Engg. Soc. [6987], PO Box 9828, Albuquerque, NM 87119-9828, (505)765-1052
Amer. Indian Stud; Inst. for [6447]
Amer. Indian Summer Seminar - Defunct.
Amer. Indian Trade and Info. Center; North [★10750]
Amer. Indian Travel Commn. - Defunct.
Amer. Indian Youth Running Strong [12623], 2550 Huntington Ave., Ste. 200, Alexandria, VA 22303-1499, (703)317-9881
Amer. Indians; Coun. for Native [10738]
Amer. Indians; Natl. Cong. of [18096]
Amer. Indians for Sobriety - Address unknown since 1991.
Amer. Indonesian Chamber of Commerce [24332], 317 Madison Ave., Ste. 1619, New York, NY 10017, (212)687-4505
Amer. Indoor Air Quality Coun. [5082], PO Box 11599, Glendale, AZ 85318-1599, (623)582-0832
Amer. Indoor Archery Assn. - Defunct.
Amer. Indus. Arts Assn. [★9231]
Amer. Indus. Arts Assn. [★IO]
Amer. Indus. Arts Student Assn. [★8547]
Amer. Indus. Bankers Assn. [★2422]
Amer. Indus. Development Coun. [★5812]
Amer. Indus. Development Coun. [★IO]
Amer. Indus. Extension Alliance [2546], c/o Dr. Ronald A. Cox, Pres., Center for Indus. Res. and Ser., 2272 Howe Hall, Ste. 2620, Ames, IA 50011-2272, (515)294-9592
Amer. Industrial Health Coun. [15626]
Amer. Indus. Hygiene Assn. [15627], 2700 Prosperity Ave., Ste. 250, Fairfax, VA 22031, (703)849-8888
Amer. Industrial Music Assn. - Defunct.
Amer. Indus. Radium and X-Ray Soc. [★7787]
Amer. Infertility Assn. [★14388]
Amer. Information Network - Address unknown since 1991.
Amer. Inland Waterways Assn. - Defunct.

Amer. Innerspring Manufacturers [1969], 1918 N Pkwy., Memphis, TN 38112, (901)274-9030
Amer. Inst. of Actuaries [★2239]
Amer. Inst. of Aeronautics and Astronautics [6369], 1801 Alexander Bell Dr., Ste. 500, Reston, VA 20191-4344, (703)264-7500
Amer. Inst. of Architects [6463], 1735 New York Ave. NW, Washington, DC 20006-5292, (202)626-7300
Amer. Inst. of Architects Found. [★6461]
Amer. Inst. of Architecture Students [288], 1735 New York Ave. NW, Washington, DC 20006, (202)626-7472
Amer. Inst. of Baking [445], 1213 Bakers Way, PO Box 3999, Manhattan, KS 66505-3999, (785)537-4750
Amer. Inst. of Bangladesh Stud. [7996], c/o Prof. Guy Welbon, PhD, Pres., South Asia Ctr., 820 Williams Hall, 36th & Spruce St., Univ. of Pennsylvania, Philadelphia, PA 19104-6305, (215)898-7475
American Inst. of Banking [★457]
Amer. Inst. of Biological Sciences [6560], 1444 I St. NW, Ste. 200, Washington, DC 20005, (202)628-1500
Amer. Inst. of Biomedical Climatology - Defunct.
Amer. Inst. of Bolt, Nut and Rivet Mfrs. [★1823]
Amer. Inst. of Building Design [6464], 7059 Blair Rd. NW, Ste. 201, Washington, DC 20012, (800)366-2423
Amer. Inst. for Cancer Res. [13793], 1759 R St. NW, Washington, DC 20009, (202)328-7744
Amer. Inst. of Certified Planners [5585], 1776 Massachusetts Ave. NW, Washington, DC 20036-1904, (202)872-0611
Amer. Inst. of Certified Public Accountants [9], 1211 Ave. of the Americas, New York, NY 10036-8775, (212)596-6001
Amer. Inst. of Ceylonese Studies - Defunct.
Amer. Inst. for Chartered Property Casualty Underwriters [★2137]
Amer. Inst. of Chem. Engineers [6665], 3 Park Ave., New York, NY 10016-5991, (212)591-8100
Amer. Inst. of Chemists [6666], 315 Chestnut St., Philadelphia, PA 19106-2702, (215)873-8224
Amer. Inst. of Child Care Centers - Defunct.
Amer. Inst. of Commemorative Art [2771], 11003 Fellswood Ct., Louisville, KY 40243-0602, (502)254-1375
Amer. Inst. of Computerized Accounting Professionals - Defunct.
Amer. Inst. for Conservation of Historic and Artistic Works [10011], 1717 K St. NW, Ste. 200, Washington, DC 20036, (202)452-9545
American Institute for Conservation of Historic and Artistic Works [IO], Washington, DC, United States
Amer. Inst. of Constructors [6833], PO Box 26334, Alexandria, VA 22314, (703)683-4999
Amer. Inst. of Consulting Engineers [★6984]
Amer. Inst. for Contemporary German Stud. [9976], 1755 Massachusetts Ave. NW, Ste. 700, Washington, DC 20036-2121, (202)332-9312
Amer. Inst. for Contemporary German Stud. [IO], Washington, DC, United States
Amer. Inst. of Cooperation - Defunct.
Amer. Inst. for CPCU [2137], 720 Providence Rd., Ste. 100, PO Box 3016, Malvern, PA 19355-0716, (610)644-2100
Amer. Inst. of Crop Ecology - Defunct.
Amer. Inst. for Decision Sciences [★8021]
Amer. Inst. of Decorators [★2251]
Amer. Inst. for Design and Drafting [★7152]
Amer. Inst. for Economic Development - Address unknown since 1995.
Amer. Inst. for Economic Res. [6869], PO Box 1000, Great Barrington, MA 01230, (413)528-1216
Amer. Inst. of Elecl. Engineers [★6926]
Amer. Inst. of Employment Counseling [★1272]
Amer. Inst. of Engineers [6988], 4630 Appian Way, Ste. 206, El Sobrante, CA 94803-1875, (510)758-6240
Amer. Inst. for Exploration - Defunct.
Amer. Inst. of Fellows in Free Enterprise - Defunct.
Amer. Inst. of Financial Brokers - Address unknown since 1991.
Amer. Inst. of Fishery Res. Biologists [7170], c/o Dr. Linda Jones, Pres., 14931 73rd Ave. NE, Kenmore, WA 98028

A star before a book entry number signifies that the name is not listed separately, but is mentioned within the entry.

Amer. Inst. of Floral Designers **[1490]**, 720 Light St., Baltimore, MD 21230, (410)752-3318

Amer. Inst. of Food Distribution **[1497]**, 1 Broadway, 2nd Fl., Elmwood Park, NJ 07407, (201)791-5570

Amer. Inst. of Food Distribution **[IO]**, Elmwood Park, NJ, United States

Amer. Inst. for Foreign Stud. **[8652]**, River Plz., 9 W Broad St., Stamford, CT 06902-3788, (203)399-5000

Amer. Inst. for Foreign Stud. Found. **[8595]**, 9 W Broad St., River Plz., Stamford, CT 06902, (203)399-5414

Amer. Inst. for Foreign Stud. Scholarship Found. **[★8595]**

Amer. Inst. of France - Defunct.

Amer. Inst. for Free Labor Development - Address unknown since 2001.

Amer. Inst. for Full Employment **[12068]**, 2636 Biehn St., Klamath Falls, OR 97601, (541)273-6731

Amer. Inst. for Full Employment **[IO]**, Klamath Falls, OR, United States

Amer. Inst. of Graphic Arts **[1757]**, 164 5th Ave., New York, NY 10010, (212)807-1990

Amer. Inst. of Grapho Anal. **[★11210]**

Amer. Inst. of Grapho Anal. **[★IO]**

Amer. Inst. of Group Counseling - Defunct.

Amer. Inst. of the History of Pharmacy **[15917]**, 777 Highland Ave., Madison, WI 53705-2222, (608)262-5378

Amer. Inst. of Homeopathy **[14845]**, 801 N Fairfax St., Ste. 306, Alexandria, VA 22314, (888)445-9988

Amer. Inst. for Human Engineering and Development - Address unknown since 1995.

Amer. Inst. of Hydrology **[7823]**, 300 Village Green Cir., Ste. 201, Smyrna, GA 30080, (770)384-1634

Amer. Inst., Inc. - Address unknown since 2000.

Amer. Inst. of Indian Stud. **[8541]**, 1130 E 59th St., Chicago, IL 60637, (773)702-8638

Amer. Inst. of Indus. Engineers **[★7016]**

Amer. Inst. of Inspectors **[2116]**, PO Box 248, Lower Lake, CA 95457, (800)877-4770

Amer. Inst. for Intl. Steel **[2695]**, 8201 Greensboro Dr., Ste. 300, McLean, VA 22102, (703)245-8075

Amer. Inst. for Intl. Steel **[IO]**, Washington, DC, United States

Amer. Inst. of Iranian Stud. **[IO]**, New York, NY, United States

Amer. Inst. of Iranian Stud. **[10237]**, c/o Dr. Erica Ehrenberg, Exec. Dir., 118 Riverside Dr., No. 13A, New York, NY 10024

Amer. Inst. for Islamic Affairs **[★18062]**

Amer. Inst. for Islamic Affairs **[★IO]**

Amer. Inst. of Islamic Studies - Address unknown since 2004.

Amer. Inst. of Kitchen Dealers **[★2271]**

Amer. Inst. of Landscape Architects **[★6466]**

Amer. Inst. of Laundering **[★2405]**

Amer. Inst. of Laundering **[★IO]**

Amer. Inst. of Leisuretime - Address unknown since 1995.

Amer. Inst. of Life Threatening Illness and Loss (Division of Found. of Thanatology) **[11908]**, c/o Dr. Austin H. Kutscher, Pres., Columbia-Presbyterian Medical Ctr., 630 W 168th St., New York, NY 10032, (718)601-4453

Amer. Inst. for Maghrib Stud. **[7927]**, Center for Middle Eastern Stud., Marshall Bldg., Rm. 477, 845 N Park Ave., PO Box 210158-B, Tucson, AZ 85721-0158, (520)626-6498

Amer. Inst. for Maghrib Stud. **[IO]**, Tucson, AZ, United States

Amer. Inst. of Maintenance **[★2462]**

Amer. Inst. of Mgt. - Address unknown since 1999.

Amer. Inst. for Managing Diversity **[17369]**, 1200 W Peachtree St. NW, Ste. 3, Atlanta, GA 30309, (404)575-2131

Amer. Inst. of Marine Underwriters **[2138]**, 14 Wall St., New York, NY 10005, (212)233-0550

Amer. Inst. for Marxist Studies - Defunct.

Amer. Inst. for Medical and Biological Engg. **[7112]**, 1901 Pennsylvania Ave. NW, Ste. 401, Washington, DC 20001, (202)496-9660

Amer. Inst. of Medical Ethics **[12122]**

Amer. Inst. for the Medical Res. of Trauma - Defunct.

Amer. Inst. of Merchant Shipping **[★6059]**

Amer. Inst. of Mind Development and Control **[★7447]**

Amer. Inst. of Mining and Metallurgical Engineers **[★7346]**

Amer. Inst. of Mining, Metallurgical, and Petroleum Engineers **[7346]**, PO Box 270728, Littleton, CO 80127-0013, (303)948-4255

Amer. Inst. of Mining, Metallurgical and Petroleum Engineers; Mining Br., **[★7349]**

Amer. Inst. of Mortgage Brokers **[★489]**

Amer. Inst. of Musical Stud. **[8900]**, 28 E 69th St., Kansas City, MO 64113, (816)268-3657

Amer. Inst. of Musical Stud. **[IO]**, Kansas City, MO, United States

Amer. Inst. of Nail and Tack Mfrs. - Defunct.

Amer. Inst. of Nautical Archeology **[★6448]**

Amer. Inst. of Nautical Archeology **[★IO]**

Amer. Inst. of Nutrition **[★15548]**

Amer. Inst. of Nutrition **[★15547]**

Amer. Inst. of Oral Biology **[14137]**, PO Box 7184, Loma Linda, CA 92354-7184, (909)558-4671

Amer. Inst. of Organbuilders **[2798]**, PO Box 130982, Houston, TX 77219, (713)529-2212

Amer. Inst. of Park Executives **[★6153]**

Amer. Inst. of Parliamentarians **[10770]**, 550M Richie Hwy. No. 271, Severna Park, MD 21146, (888)664-0428

Amer. Inst. of Pathologic Science - Defunct.

Amer. Inst. for Patristic and Byzantine Stud. **[9770]**, 12 Minuet Ln., Kingston, NY 12401, (845)336-8797

Amer. Inst. for Patristic and Byzantine Stud. **[IO]**, Kingston, NY, United States

Amer. Inst. of Philanthropy **[12709]**, PO Box 578460, Chicago, IL 60657, (773)529-2300

Amer. Inst. of Physics **[7499]**, 1 Physics Ellipse, College Park, MD 20740, (301)209-3000

Amer. Inst. of Planners **[★5585]**

Amer. Inst. of Planners **[★5586]**

Amer. Inst. of Plant Engineers **[★7003]**

Amer. Inst. of Polish Culture **[10876]**, 1440 79th St. Causeway, Ste. 117, Miami, FL 33141, (305)864-2349

Amer. Inst. of Polish Culture **[IO]**, Miami, FL, United States

Amer. Inst. for Preventive Medicine **[IO]**, Farmington Hills, MI, United States

Amer. Inst. for Preventive Medicine **[16053]**, 30445 Northwestern Hwy., Ste. 350, Farmington Hills, MI 48334, (248)539-1800

Amer. Inst. of Professional Geologists **[★7127]**

Amer. Inst. of Professional Geologists **[7127]**, 1400 W 122nd Ave., Ste. 250, Westminster, CO 80234, (303)412-6205

Amer. Inst. for Property and Liability Underwriters **[★2137]**

Amer. Inst. for Public Ser. **[13150]**, 100 W 10th St., Ste. 215, Wilmington, DE 19801-1665, (302)622-9101

Amer. Inst. of Real Estate Appraisers **[★275]**

Amer. Inst. of Reciprocators - Defunct.

Amer. Inst. for Res. and Education in Naturopathy - Address unknown since 1985.

Amer. Inst. for Shippers' Associations **[3558]**, PO Box 33457, Washington, DC 20033-0457, (202)628-0933

Amer. Inst. of Steel Constr. **[6834]**, 1 E Wacker Dr., Ste. 700, Chicago, IL 60601-1802, (312)670-2400

Amer. Inst. of Stress **[16487]**, 124 Park Ave., Yonkers, NY 10703, (914)963-1200

Amer. Inst. for Stuttering Treatment and Professional Training **[16440]**, 27 W 20th St., Ste. 1203, New York, NY 10011-3707, (212)633-6400

Amer. Inst. of Supply Associations **[★3061]**

Amer. Inst. of Swedish Arts, Literature, and Sci. **[★10988]**

Amer. Inst. of Swedish Arts, Literature, and Sci. **[★IO]**

Amer. Inst. of Tax Practice - Address unknown since 1995.

Amer. Inst. of Technical Illustrators Assn. - Defunct.

American Institute for Teen AIDS Prevention **[13558]**

Amer. Inst. for Teen Aids Prevention **[★13558]**

Amer. Inst. of Timber Constr. **[1633]**, 7012 S Revere Pkwy., Ste. 140, Centennial, CO 80112, (303)792-9559

Amer. Inst. of Ultrasound in Medicine **[16436]**, 14750 Sweitzer Ln., Ste. 100, Laurel, MD 20707-5906, (301)498-4100

Amer. Inst. for Verdi Stud. **[10539]**, Dept. of Music, Faculty of Arts and Sci., 24 Waverly Pl., Rm. 268, New York, NY 10003, (212)998-2587

Amer. Inst. of Weights and Measures - Defunct.

Amer. Inst. of Wine and Food **[22568]**, 213-37 39th Ave., Box 216, Bayside, NY 11361, (800)274-2493

Amer. Inst. of Wood Engg. **[★7100]**

Amer. Institutes for Res. **[7560]**, 1000 Thomas Jefferson St. NW, Washington, DC 20007, (202)403-5000

Amer. Institutes for Res. **[★6523]**

Amer. Institutes for Res. in the Behavioral Sciences **[6523]**, 1000 Thomas Jefferson St. NW, Washington, DC 20007-3835, (202)342-5000

Amer. Institutions Food Service Assn. - Defunct.

Amer. Instructors of the Deaf **[★14750]**

Amer. Insurance Assn. **[★2139]**

Amer. Insurance Assn. **[2139]**, 1130 Connecticut Ave. NW, Ste. 1000, Washington, DC 20036, (202)828-7100

American Insurance Highway Safety Association **[★12964]**

American Insurance Marketing and Sales Soc. **[2140]**, PO Box 35718, Richmond, VA 23235, (804)674-6466

Amer. Insurers Highway Safety Alliance - Address unknown since 2002.

Amer. Integrative Medical Assn. **[15034]**, PO Box 3204, Norfolk, VA 23514-3204, (757)623-1200

Amer. Intellectual Property Assn. **[★5837]**

Amer. Intellectual Property Law Assn. **[5835]**, 241 18th St. S, Ste. 700, Arlington, VA 22202, (703)415-0780

Amer. Intercultural Student Exchange **[8596]**, 707 Lakehall Rd., Lake Village, AR 71653, (870)265-5050

Amer. Intl. Acad. - Defunct.

Amer. Intl. Assn. for Economic and Social Development - Defunct.

Amer. Intl. Auto. Dealers Assn. **[404]**, 211 N Union St., Ste. 300, Alexandria, VA 22314, (703)519-7800

Amer. Intl. Auto. Dealers Assn. **[IO]**, Alexandria, VA, United States

Amer. Intl. Chamber of Commerce **[IO]**, Alhambra, CA, United States

Amer. Intl. Chamber of Commerce **[24247]**, 1000 S Fremont Ave., A1 Bldg., Ste. 1220-99, Alhambra, CA 91803, (213)255-2066

American-International Charolais Assn. **[4228]**, 11700 NW Plaza Cir., Kansas City, MO 64153, (816)464-5977

American-International Charolais Association **[IO]**, Kansas City, MO, United States

Amer. Intl. Checkers Soc. - Address unknown since 2001.

Amer. Intl. Dragon Assn. - Address unknown since 1999.

Amer. Intl. Freight Assn. - Defunct.

Amer. Intl. Hea. Alliance **[14716]**, 1250 Eye St. NW, Ste. 350, Washington, DC 20005, (202)789-1136

Amer. Intl. Hea. Alliance **[IO]**, Washington, DC, United States

Amer. Intl. Homestays - Address unknown since 1994.

Amer. Intl. Marchigiana Soc. **[★4271]**

Amer. Intl. Marchigiana Soc. **[4229]**, PO Box 198, Walton, KS 67151-0198, (620)837-3303

Amer. Intl. Music Fund - Defunct.

American/International Reiki Assn. **[★13648]**

American/International Reiki Assn. **[★IO]**

Amer. Intl. Shuffleboard **[23734]**

Amer. Intl. Tennis Teams - Address unknown since 2004.

Amer. Intl. Women's Assn. of Rabat **[IO]**, Rabat, Morocco

American/International Women's Club of Casablanca **[IO]**, Casablanca, Morocco

Amer. Intl. Women's Club of Genoa **[IO]**, Genoa, Italy

Amer. Intl. Women's Club of Torino **[IO]**, Turin, Italy

Amer. Interprofessional Inst. - Defunct.

Amer. Intersociety Acad. for Certification of Sanitarians **[★16383]**

Reference to "IO" in place of a book number signifies that the association may be found in the 45th edition of International Organizations.

Amer. Intra-Ocular Implant Soc. [★15665]

Amer. Iranian Coun. [17926], 29 A Wiggins St., Princeton, NJ 08542, (609)252-9099

Amer. Iranian Coun. [IO], Princeton, NJ, United States

Amer. Ireland Education Found.-Political Education Comm. - Address unknown since 2006.

Amer. Ireland Fund [17929], 211 Cong. St., 10th Fl., Boston, MA 02110, (617)574-0720

Amer. Ireland Fund [IO], Boston, MA, United States

American Iris Society [IO], Cedar Hill, MO, United States

Amer. Iris Soc. [22495], c/o Tom Gormley, Membership Sec., 10606 Timber Ridge St., Dubuque, IA 52001-8268, (563)513-0504

Amer. Irish Bicentennial Comm. - Defunct.

Amer. Irish Historical Soc. [10240], 991 5th Ave., New York, NY 10028, (212)288-2263

Amer. Irish Unity Comm. - Defunct.

Amer. Iron Ore Assn. [2696], 614 Superior Ave. W, Ste. 915, Cleveland, OH 44113-1383, (216)241-8261

Amer. Iron Ore Assn. [IO], Cleveland, OH, United States

Amer. Iron and Steel Assn. [★2697]

Amer. Iron and Steel Inst. [2697], 1140 Connecticut Ave. NW, Ste. 705, Washington, DC 20036, (202)452-7100

Amer. Islamic Chamber of Commerce [24259], PO Box 93033, Albuquerque, NM 87199-3033

Amer. Islamic Chamber of Commerce [IO], Albuquerque, NM, United States

American-Islamic Relations; Coun. on [19156]

Amer.-Israel Anti-Smoking Soc. - Defunct.

American-Israel Chamber of Commerce and Indus. [★24336]

Amer. Israel Chamber of Commerce - Southeast Region [24260], 1150 Lake Hearn Dr., Ste. 130, Atlanta, GA 30342, (404)843-9426

Amer. Israel Chamber of Commerce - Southeast Region [IO], Atlanta, GA, United States

American-Israel Environmental Coun. [IO], New York, NY, United States

American-Israel Environmental Coun. [10254], c/o Perry Davis Associates, Inc., 25 W 45th St., Ste. 1405, New York, NY 10036, (212)840-1166

American-Israel Numismatic Assn. [22723], PO Box 13063, Silver Spring, MD 20911-0063

Amer. Israel Opera Found. - Address unknown since 2000.

Amer. Israel Public Affairs Comm. [18050], 440 1st St. NW, Ste. 600, Washington, DC 20001, (202)639-5200

Amer. Israeli Civil Liberties Coalition - Address unknown since 1999.

Amer. Israeli Lighthouse [16827]

Amer. Israeli Lighthouse [IO], New York, NY, United States

Amer.-Israeli Ophthalmological Soc. - Address unknown since 2007.

Amer. - Israeli Orthopaedic Soc. - Address unknown since 1999.

Amer. Italian Cong. - Defunct.

Amer. Italian Historical Assn. [10256], c/o The John D. Calandra Italian Amer. Inst., Queens Coll./City Univ. of New York, 25 W 43rd St., 17th Fl., New York, NY 10036, (708)756-7168

Amer. Italian Historical Assn. [IO], Chicago Heights, IL, United States

Amer. Italian Historical Soc. [★IO]

Amer. Italian Historical Soc. [★10261]

Amer. Ivy Soc. [22496], PO Box 2123, Naples, FL 34106-2123

Amer. Ivy Soc. [IO], Naples, FL, United States

Amer. Jail Assn. [11856], 1135 Professional Ct., Hagerstown, MD 21740-5853, (301)790-3930

Amer. Japanese Trade Comm. - Defunct.

Amer. Jazz Alliance - Defunct.

Amer. Jeepster Club [21572], c/o Jim Serr, Pres., PO Box 653, Lincoln, CA 95648-8761

Amer. Jersey Cattle Assn. [4230], 6486 E Main St., Reynoldsburg, OH 43068-2362, (614)861-3636

Amer. Jersey Cattle Club [★4230]

Amer. Jesuit Missionary Assn. [★19643]

Amer. Jewelers Protective Assn. [★2374]

Amer. Jewelry Marketing Assn. - Defunct.

Amer. Jewish Alternatives to Zionism - Address unknown since 1999.

Amer. Jewish Archives [★10285]

Amer. Jewish Archives; Marcus Center of the [10285]

Amer. Jewish Commn. on the Holocaust - Defunct.

Amer. Jewish Comm. [20114], 165 E 56 St., New York, NY 10022, (212)751-4000

Amer. Jewish Conf. on Soviet Jewry [★17448]

Amer. Jewish Conf. on Soviet Jewry [★IO]

Amer. Jewish Cong. [20115], 825 Third Ave., New York, NY 10022, (212)879-4500

Amer. Jewish Correctional Chaplains Assn. - Address unknown since 2004.

Amer. Jewish Heritage Comm. - Address unknown since 1999.

Amer. Jewish Historical Soc. [10272], 15 W 16th St., New York, NY 10011, (212)294-6160

Amer. Jewish History Center of the Jewish Theological Seminary - Defunct.

Amer. Jewish Joint Distribution Comm. [12464], 711 3rd Ave., 10th Fl., New York, NY 10017-4014, (212)687-6200

Amer. Jewish Joint Distribution Comm. [IO], New York, NY, United States

Amer. Jewish Joint Distribution Comm; Migration Dept. of the [★12471]

Amer. Jewish Leadership Conf. - Address unknown since 1989.

Amer. Jewish League Against Communism - Address unknown since 1989.

Amer. Jewish League for Israel [20116], 450 7th Ave., Ste. 808, New York, NY 10123, (212)371-1583

Amer. Jewish Military History; Natl. Museum of [21312]

Amer. Jewish Philanthropic Fund [12803]

Amer. Jewish Physicians' Comm. [★8676]

Amer. Jewish Press Assn. [3081], PO Box 19121, Washington, DC 20036, (202)250-6144

Amer. Jewish Public Relations Soc. - Address unknown since 1995.

Amer. Jewish Publication Soc. [★10283]

Amer. Jewish Relief Comm. [★12464]

Amer. Jewish Relief Comm. [★IO]

Amer. Jewish Soc. for Ser. [12465], 10319 Westlake Blvd., Ste. 193, Bethesda, MD 20817, (240)205-5940

Amer. Jewish Vegetarian Soc. [★11068]

Amer. Jewish World Ser. [12829], 45 W 36th St., 10th Fl., New York, NY 10018-7904, (212)792-2900

Amer. Jewish World Ser. [IO], New York, NY, United States

Amer. Joint Comm. on Cancer [15637], 633 N St. Clair St., Chicago, IL 60611, (312)202-5313

Amer. Joint Comm. for Cancer Staging and End Results Reporting [★15637]

Amer. Journalism Historians Assn. [8501], c/o Carol Sue Humphrey, Admin. Sec., OBU Box 61201, 500 W Univ., Shawnee, OK 74804-2590, (405)878-2221

Amer. Judges Assn. [5892], 300 Newport Ave., Williamsburg, VA 23185-4147, (757)259-1841

Amer. Judicature Soc. [5893], Drake Univ., The Opperman Ctr., 2700 Univ. Ave., Des Moines, IA 50311, (515)271-2281

Amer. Judo Assn. [23552], PO Box 1568, Santa Barbara, CA 93102, (805)569-1388

Amer. Judo and Jujitsu Fed. [23553], c/o Central Off. Admin., PO Box 8392, Medford, OR 97504, (800)850-AJJF

American Junior Acad. of Sci. [★7617]

Amer. Junior Brahman Assn. [4231], c/o Amer. Brahman Breeders Assn., 3003 S Loop W, Ste. 520, Houston, TX 77054, (713)349-0854

Amer. Junior Chianina Assn. [4232], c/o Amer. Chianina Assn., 1708 N Prairie View Rd., PO Box 890, Platte City, MO 64079, (816)431-2808

Amer. Junior Golf Assn. [23444], 1980 Sports Club Dr., Braselton, GA 30517, (770)868-4200

Amer. Junior Hereford Assn. [★4276]

Amer. Junior Paint Horse Assn. [4828], PO Box 961023, Fort Worth, TX 76161-0023, (817)834-2742

Amer. Junior Quarter Horse Assn. [★4839]

Amer. Junior Rodeo Assn. [23684], 4501 Armstrong St., San Angelo, TX 76903, (325)658-8868

Amer. Junior Shorthorn Assn. [4233], c/o Amer. Shorthorn Assn., 8288 Hascall St., Omaha, NE 68124, (402)393-7200

Amer. Junior Simmental Assn. [★4248]

Amer. Justice Inst. [11835], 349 Main St., Ste. 104, Laurel, MD 20707, (301)725-5858

Amer. Juvenile Arthritis Org. [16368], 1330 W Peachtree St., Ste. 100, Atlanta, GA 30309, (404)965-7535

Amer. Karakul Fur Sheep Registry [★5186]

Amer. Karakul Sheep Registry [5186], 11500 Hwy. 5, Boonville, MO 65233, (660)838-6340

Amer. Kart Mfrs. Assn. - Defunct.

Amer. Kempo-Karate Assn. [23579], c/o Acad. of Kempo-Karate, 5760 Oak Dr., Charlotte, NC 28216, (704)393-1077

Amer. Kennel Club [22201], 260 Madison Ave., New York, NY 10016, (212)696-8200

Amer. Kenpo Karate Intl. [23560], PO Box 768, Evanston, WY 82931, (307)789-4124

Amer. Kerry Bog Pony Soc. [4829], c/o Linda C. Ashar, Pres., 13010 W Darrow Rd., Vermilion, OH 44089, (440)967-2680

American Kerry Bog Pony Society [IO], Vermilion, OH, United States

Amer. Kerry and Dexter Club [★4221]

Amer. Keuda Cat Assn. [4204], PO Box 636, Palmer, TX 75152, (866)841-2813

Amer. Kiddie Ride Assn. - Defunct.

Amer. Kidney Fund [15284], 6110 Executive Blvd., Ste. 1010, Rockville, MD 20852, (301)881-3052

Amer. Kiko Goat Assn. [4780], c/o Jean Thomure, Sec., 295 Cardinal Ln., Trenton, GA 30752, (706)657-8649

Amer. Killifish Assn. [22434], c/o Monty Lehmann, Chm., 17386 Days Point Rd., Smithfield, VA 23430

Amer. Kinesiotherapy Assn. [16311], 118 Coll. Dr., No. 5142, Hattiesburg, MS 39406, (800)296-AKTA

Amer. Kitefliers Assn. [23569], PO Box 1614, Walla Walla, WA 99362, (800)252-2550

Amer. Knowledge Rescue [★12287]

Amer.-Korean Friendship and Information Center - Defunct.

Amer. Kurdish Info. Network [17967], c/o Kani Xulam, Dir., 2722 Connecticut Ave. NW, No. 42, Washington, DC 20008-5316, (202)483-6444

Amer. Kurdish Info. Network [IO], Washington, DC, United States

Amer. Kuvasz Assn. [12015], c/o Agi Hejja, 3831 Broad St. Rd., Gum Spring, VA 23065-2135

American-Kuwaiti Alliance [2299], 2550 M St. NW, Washington, DC 20037, (202)429-4999

Amer. Labor Alliance; Asian Pacific [24003]

Amer. Labor Education Center [8720]

Amer. Labor Education Service - Defunct.

Amer. Labyrinth Assn. - Address unknown since 2001.

Amer. Ladder Inst. [1816], 401 N Michigan Ave., Chicago, IL 60611, (312)644-6610

Amer. LaMancha Club - Address unknown since 1994.

Amer. Lamb Coun. [5187], c/o Amer. Sheep Indus. Assn., 9785 Maroon Cir., Ste. 360, Englewood, CO 80112, (303)771-3500

Amer. Laminators Assn. - Defunct.

Amer. Lancia Club [21573], c/o Neil Pering, Membership Sec., 27744 Via Ventana, Los Altos Hills, CA 94022, (650)941-7497

Amer. Land Alliance - Defunct.

Amer. Land Conservancy [4348], 250 Montgomery St., Ste. 210, San Francisco, CA 94104, (415)912-3660

Amer. Land Development Assn. [★3298]

Amer. Land Resource Assn. - Defunct.

Amer. Land Rights Assn. [6187], PO Box 400, Battle Ground, WA 98604, (360)687-3087

Amer. Land Title Assn. [3297], 1828 L St. NW, Ste. 705, Washington, DC 20036-5182, (202)296-3671

Amer. Landrace Assn. [5232], c/o Natl. Swine Registry, PO Box 2417, West Lafayette, IN 47996, (765)463-3594

Amer. Lands Access Assn. [22937], c/o Norman W. Hanschu, Treas., 6607 Sturbridge Ln., Canton, MI 48187-2638

A star before a book entry number signifies that the name is not listed separately, but is mentioned within the entry.

Amer. Lands Alliance [4533], 726 7th St. SE, Washington, DC 20003, (202)547-9400

Amer. Landscape Horticulture Assn. - Address unknown since 2001.

Amer. Langshan Club [5105], c/o Forrest Beauford, Sec.-Treas., 18077 S Hwy. 88, Claremore, OK 74017, (918)341-2238

Amer. Language Acad. [★8785]

Amer. Laryngeal Papilloma Found. - Defunct.

Amer. Laryngological Assn. [15820], c/o Ms. Maxine Cunningham, Admin., Vanderbilt Univ. Medical Ctr., Dept. of Otolaryngology, 1215 21st Ave. S, 7302 MCE S, Nashville, TN 37232-8783, (615)322-6326

Amer. Laryngological, Rhinological and Otological Soc. [15821], 555 N 30th St., Omaha, NE 68131, (402)346-5500

Amer. Latex Allergy Assn. [13597], PO Box 198, Slinger, WI 53086, (262)677-9707

Amer. Latvian Assn. [19198], 400 Hurley Ave., Rockville, MD 20850-3121, (301)340-1914

American Laundry and Linen College [★2401]

Amer. Law Enforcement Officers Assn. [★5962]

Amer. Law Firms for African Relief - Defunct.

Amer. Law Inst. [5925], 4025 Chestnut St., Philadelphia, PA 19104-3099, (215)243-1600

Amer. Law Student Assn. [★8769]

Amer. Lawn Bowls Assn. [★23256]

Amer. Lawyers Auxiliary [5480], 2010 E 46th St., Tulsa, OK 74105

American Lawyers; Incorporated Soc. of Irish/ [5939]

Amer. Leadership Forum [18001], PO Box 980365, Houston, TX 77098, (713)807-1253

Amer. League to Abolish Capital Punishment - Defunct.

Amer. League Against Epilepsy [★14379]

Amer. League of Anglers and Boaters [23407], 225 Reinekers Ln., Ste. 420, Alexandria, VA 22314, (703)519-9691

Amer. League of Anglers - Defunct.

Amer. League for Deaf-Blind [★14737]

Amer. League for Exports and Security Assistance - Address unknown since 2002.

Amer. League of Families of POWs - Address unknown since 1988.

Amer. League of Financial Institutions [459]

Amer. League of Lobbyists [18343], PO Box 30005, Alexandria, VA 22310, (703)960-3011

Amer. League of Professional Baseball Clubs [★23113]

Amer. Leather Belting Assn. [★2051]

Amer. Leather Chemists Assn. [6667], 1314 50th St., Ste. 103, Lubbock, TX 79412-2940, (806)744-1798

Amer. Lebanese Engg. Soc. [6989], PO Box 585, Norwood, MA 02062, (617)642-7185

Amer. Lebanese League - Address unknown since 1989.

Amer. Lebanese Medical Assn. [15154], 6302 Princeville Cir., Huntington Beach, CA 92648, (714)960-0564

Amer. Legacy Found. [18743], 2030 M St. NW, 6th Fl., Washington, DC 20036, (202)454-5555

Amer. Legal Found. [★6229]

Amer. Legal Studies Assn. - Defunct.

Amer. Legation Museum Soc; Tangier [10068]

Amer. Legend [4129], c/o Motorcycle Trailers Inc., 903 S Prairieview Rd., Mahomet, IL 61853, (217)586-2201

Amer. Legion [20666], c/o Public Relations Div., PO Box 1055, Indianapolis, IN 46206, (317)630-1200

American Legion [20666]
  Amer. Legion [20666]
  Amer. Legion Auxiliary [21189]
  Forty and Eight [20667]
  Natl. Amer. Legion Press Assn. [20668]
  Sons of the Amer. Legion [21201]

Amer. Legion Auxiliary [21189], 777 N Meridian St., 3rd Fl., Indianapolis, IN 46204-1420, (317)955-3845

Amer. Legion Auxiliary Girls Nation [17068], Natl. 4-H Conf. Center, 7100 Connecticut Ave., Chevy Chase, MD 20815, (317)955-3845

Amer. Legion Baseball [23103], 700 N Pennsylvania St., Indianapolis, IN 46204

Amer. Legion Press Assn. [★20668]

Amer. Legion; Sons of the [21201]

Amer. Legislative Exchange Coun. [18422], 1129 20th St. NW, Ste. 500, Washington, DC 20036, (202)466-3800

Amer. Legislators Assn. [★6273]

Amer. Leprosy Found. [★15010]

Amer. Leprosy Found. [★IO]

Amer. Leprosy Missions [IO], Greenville, SC, United States

Amer. Leprosy Missions [15007], 1 ALM Way, Greenville, SC 29601, (864)271-7040

Amer. Lessing Soc. [★9680]

Amer. Lhasa Apso Club [22202], c/o Joyce Johanson, Membership Chair, 126 Kurlene Dr., Macomb, IL 61455, (309)837-1665

Amer. Liberal Assn. - Address unknown since 1995.

Amer. Lib. Assn. [10320], 50 E Huron St., Chicago, IL 60611, (312)944-6780

Amer. Lib. Assn; Black Caucus of the [10343]

Amer. Lib. Association/Gay, Lesbian, Bisexual and Transgendered Round Table [12214], c/o Norman Eriksen, Asst. Div. Mgr., Brooklyn Public Lib., Brooklyn, NY 11238, (718)230-2716

Amer. Lib. Assn. - Off. for Res. and Statistics [10934], 50 E Huron St., Chicago, IL 60611-2795, (312)280-4273

Amer. Lib. Assn. - Public Info. Off. [10897], 50 E Huron St., Chicago, IL 60611, (800)545-2433

Amer. Lib. Assn; Reference and User Services Assn. of [10383]

Amer. Library Soc. - Defunct.

Amer. Lib. Trustee Assn. [★10335]

Amer. Licensed Practical Nurses Assn. [15450]

Amer. Life Educ. and Res. Trust [★12902]

Amer. Life Found. - Address unknown since 2001.

Amer. Life League [12902], PO Box 1350, Stafford, VA 22555, (540)659-4171

Amer. Lifesaving Emergency Response Team [★12894]

Amer. Lighting Assn. [2431], PO Box 420288, Dallas, TX 75342-0288, (214)698-9898

Amer. Limited Edition Assn. - Defunct.

Amer. Liszt Soc. [9807], c/o Justin Kolb, Exec. Membership Sec., 1136 Hog Mountain Rd., Fleischmanns, NY 12430, (845)586-4457

Amer. Literacy Coun. [8785], 1441 Mariposa Ave., Boulder, CO 80302, (303)440-7385

Amer. Literary Soc. - Defunct.

Amer. Literary Translators Assn. [11058], Univ. of Texas at Dallas, PO Box 830688, Richardson, TX 75083-0688, (972)883-2093

Amer. Literature Assn. [10411], c/o Alfred Bendixen, Exec. Dir., Dept. of English, Texas A&M Univ., College Station, TX 77843-4227

Amer. Lithotripsy Soc. [15285], 305 Second Ave., Ste. 200, Waltham, MA 02451-1122, (781)895-9098

Amer. Lithuanian Found. - Defunct.

Amer. Lithuanian Musicians Alliance [10540], 7310 S California Ave., Chicago, IL 60629, (708)687-1430

Amer. Lithuanian Organist Musicians Alliance [★10540]

Amer. Lithuanian Press and Radio Assn. - Viltis [19207], PO Box 19010, Cleveland, OH 44119-0010, (216)531-8150

Amer. Lithuanian Press and Radio Assn. - Viltis [IO], Cleveland, OH, United States

Amer. Lithuanian Roman Catholic Organist Alliance [★10540]

Amer. Lithuanian Roman Catholic Women's Alliance [★19211]

Amer. Lithuanian Workers Literary Assn. - Defunct.

Amer. Littoral Soc. - Northeast Region [7269], 28 W 9th Rd., Broad Channel, NY 11693, (718)318-9344

Amer. Livebearer Assn. [22435], 5 Zerbe St., Cressona, PA 17929-1513, (570)385-0573

Amer. Livebearer Assn. [IO], Cressona, PA, United States

Amer. Liver Found. [14803], 75 Maiden Ln., Ste. 603, New York, NY 10038, (212)668-1000

Amer. Lives Endowment - Defunct.

Amer. Livestock Breeds Conservancy [4994], PO Box 477, Pittsboro, NC 27312, (919)542-5704

Amer. Lock Collectors Assn. [21962], 8576 Barbara Dr., Mentor, OH 44060, (440)257-2346

Amer. Log Homes Coun. [★2525]

Amer. Loggers Coun. [1604], PO Box 966, Hemphill, TX 75948, (409)625-0206

Amer. Logistics Assn. [6064], 1133 15th St. NW, Ste. 640, Washington, DC 20005, (202)466-2520

Amer. Longevity Assn. - Defunct.

Amer. Loudspeaker Mfrs. Assn. [★1206]

Amer. Low Power TV Assn. - Defunct.

Amer. Luggage Dealers Assn. - Defunct.

Amer. Luggage Dealers Cooperative [2439], 20 First Plaza Ctr. NW, Ste. 310, Albuquerque, NM 87102, (505)246-0087

Amer. Lumber Standard Comm. [1634], PO Box 210, Germantown, MD 20875-0210, (301)972-1700

American Lumber Standard Committee [IO], Germantown, MD, United States

Amer. Lumberjack Assn. [23800], c/o Andrea Furber, Treas., 213 Somerville Rd., Santa Rosa, CA 95409

Amer. Lunar Soc. [6499], c/o Eric Douglas, VP, 10326 Tarleton Dr., Mechanicsville, VA 23116, (804)550-1211

American Lunar Society [IO], Mechanicsville, VA, United States

Amer. Lung Assn. [16354], 61 Broadway, 6th Fl., New York, NY 10006, (212)315-8700

Amer. Lutheran Church [★20224]

Amer. Lutheran Church Men [★20224]

Amer. Lutheran Church Women - Defunct.

Amer. Lutheran Educ. Assn. [★8802]

Amer. Lutheran Publicity Bur. [20212], c/o Donna Roche, Off. Mgr., PO Box 327, Delhi, NY 13753-0327, (607)746-7511

Amer. Lyceum Assn. [★10901]

Amer. Lyme Disease Found. [14249], PO Box 466, Lyme, CT 06371, (800)876-LYME

Amer. Machine Tool Distributors' Assn. [1995], 1445 Res. Blvd., Ste. 450, Rockville, MD 20850, (301)738-1200

Amer. Machine Tool Export Associates - Address unknown since 1995.

Amer. Magnolia Soc. [★6643]

Amer. Mail-Order Merchants Assn. - Address unknown since 1995.

Amer. Mailorder Assn. [2457], 2272 Colorado Blvd., No. 1228, Los Angeles, CA 90041

Amer. Maine-Anjou Assn. [4234], 204 Marshall Rd., PO Box 1100, Platte City, MO 64079-1100, (816)431-9950

Amer. Malacological Soc. [7254], c/o Dr. Dawn E. Dittman, Treas., Tunison Lab. of Aquatic Sci., 3075 Gracie Rd., Cortland, NY 13045

Amer. Malacological Union [★7254]

American-Malaysian Chamber of Commerce [IO], Kuala Lumpur, Malaysia

Amer. Maltese Assn. [22203], c/o Richard Glenn, Pres., 10175 Reese Rd., Clarkston, MI 48348

Amer. Malting Barley Assn. [4303], 740 N Plankinton Ave., Ste. 830, Milwaukee, WI 53203-2403, (414)272-4640

Amer. Mammoth Jack Stock Registry [★4130]

Amer. Mammoth Jackstock Registry [4130], PO Box 1723, Johnson City, TX 78636, (830)868-2357

Amer. Managed Behavioral Healthcare Assn. [★24088]

Amer. Managed Care Pharmacy Assn. [★2988]

Amer. Mgt. Assn. [2481], 1601 Broadway, New York, NY 10019-7420, (212)586-8100

Amer. Mgt. Assn. [IO], New York, NY, United States

Amer. Manchester Terrier Club [22204], c/o Paula Hradkowsky, 1st VP, 2274 Broomstick Ln., Green Lane, PA 18054, (215)679-4607

Amer. Manganese Producers Assn. - Defunct.

Amer. Manual Medicine Assn. [13618], c/o Marie A. Ruberto, Managing Dir., 1845 Lakeshore Dr., Ste. 7, Muskegon, MI 49441, (888)375-7245

Amer. Mfrs. Assn. and Affiliated Indus. [★1992]

Amer. Mfrs. Assn. of Products From Corn [★1508]

Amer. Manufacturers of Toilet Articles [★1845]

Amer. Mfg. Trade Action Coalition [2547], 910 16th St. NW, Ste. 760, Washington, DC 20006, (202)452-0866

Amer. Marine Drilling and Exploration Assn. - Defunct.

Amer. Marine Hull Insurance Syndicate [★2136]

Amer. Marine Insurance CH - Defunct.

Reference to "IO" in place of a book number signifies that the association may be found in the 45th edition of International Organizations.

Amer. Marine Insurance Forum - Address unknown since 1994.

Amer. Marine Insurance Syndicate [★2136]

Amer. Marine Insurance Syndicate for Insurance of Builder's Risks - Defunct.

Amer. Marinelife Dealers Assn. [5007], c/o Liz Harris, Sec., Creatures Featured, PO Box 1052, Madison, FL 32341, (850)973-3488

Amer. Maritain Assn. [10782], c/o John Trapani, Jr., Pres., Walsh Univ., 2020 Easton St. NW, North Canton, OH 44720-3336

Amer. Maritime Assn. [6056]

Amer. Maritime Cong. [6057], 400 N Capitol St. NW, Ste. G-50, Washington, DC 20001, (202)347-8020

Amer. Maritime Museums; Coun. of [10501]

Amer. Maritime Officers Ser. [6058], 490 L'Enfant Plz. SW, Ste. 7204, Washington, DC 20024, (202)479-1133

Amer. Maritime Safety, Inc. [2570], 445 Hamilton Ave., Ste. 1204, White Plains, NY 10601-1833, (914)997-2916

Amer. Marketing Assn. [2613], 311 S Wacker Dr., Ste. 5800, Chicago, IL 60606, (312)542-9000

Amer. Marketing Soc. [★2613]

Amer. Massage and Therapy Assn. [★15022]

Amer. Massage Therapy Assn. [15022], 500 Davis St., Ste. 900, Evanston, IL 60201-4695, (847)864-0123

Amer. Masters of Foxhounds Assn. [★23546]

Amer. Match Coun. - Defunct.

Amer. Matchcover Collecting Club [21963], PO Box 18481, Asheville, NC 28814-0481, (828)254-4487

Amer. Matchcover Collecting Club [★21963]

Amer. Material Handling Soc. [★7282]

Amer. Material Handling Soc. [★IO]

Amer. Mathematical Assn. of Two-Year Colleges [8821], Southwest Tennessee Community Coll., 5983 Macon Cove, Memphis, TN 38134, (901)333-4643

Amer. Mathematical Soc. [7286], 201 Charles St., Providence, RI 02904-2213, (401)455-4000

Amer. Mathematics Project - Defunct.

Amer. Matthay Assn. [8901], c/o George Loring, Pres., 232 Pond Brook Rd., West Chesterfield, NH 03466

Amer. McAll Assn. - Address unknown since 2001.

Amer. Mead Assn. - Address unknown since 1999.

Amer. Measuring Tool Mfrs. Assn. [7694], 8652 E Ave., Mentor, OH 44060, (440)974-6829

Amer. Meat Goat Assn. [2657], PO Box 676, Sonora, TX 76950, (325)387-6100

Amer. Meat Inst. [2658], 1150 Connecticut Ave. NW, 12th Fl., Washington, DC 20036, (202)587-4200

Amer. Meat Inst. Found. - Defunct.

Amer. Meat Packers Assn. [★2658]

Amer. Meat Sci. Assn. [7088], 1111 N Dunlap Ave., Savoy, IL 61874, (217)356-5368

Amer. Medallic Sculpture Assn. - Defunct.

Amer. Medical Assn. [15155], 515 N State St., Chicago, IL 60610, (312)464-5000

Amer. Medical Assn. Alliance [15156], 515 N State St., 9th Fl., Chicago, IL 60610, (312)464-4470

Amer. Medical Assn. Auxiliary [★15156]

Amer. Medical Assn. Comm. on the Medical Aspects of Sports - Defunct.

Amer. Medical Assn. for the Conservation of Vision [★16882]

Amer. Medical Assn; Coun. on Medical Educ. of the [8836]

Amer. Medical Assn. Educ. and Res. Found. [★8843]

Amer. Medical Assn. Found. [8843], 515 N State St., Chicago, IL 60610, (312)464-4200

Amer. Medical Assn; Student [★8844]

Amer. Medical Assn; Women's Auxiliary to the [★15156]

Amer. Medical Athletic Assn. [23650], 4405 East-West Hwy., Ste. 405, Bethesda, MD 20814, (301)913-9517

Amer. Medical Authors - Defunct.

Amer. Medical Billing Assn. [15057], 4297 Forrest Dr., Sulphur, OK 73086, (580)622-2624

Amer. Medical Center for Burma - Defunct.

Amer. Medical Curling Assn. - Address unknown since 1995.

Amer. Medical Directors Assn. [15536], 11000 Broken Land Pkwy., Ste. 400, Columbia, MD 21044, (410)740-9743

Amer. Medical Educ. Found. [★8843]

Amer. Medical Electroencephalographic Assn. - Address unknown since 2004.

Amer. Medical Equestrian Assn. [★16474]

Amer. Medical Equestrian Association/Safe Riders Found. [16474], PO Box 91883, Albuquerque, NM 87199, (866)441-2632

Amer. Medical Fly Fishing Assn. [4349], c/o Dr. Veryl F. Frye, Sec.-Treas., PO Box 768, Lock Haven, PA 17745, (570)769-7375

Amer. Medical Golf Assn. - Defunct.

Amer. Medical Gp. Assn. [14717], 1422 Duke St., Alexandria, VA 22314-3403, (703)838-0033

Amer. Medical Informatics Assn. [14079], 4915 St. Elmo Ave., Ste. 401, Bethesda, MD 20814, (301)657-1291

Amer. Medical Joggers Assn. [★23650]

Amer. Medical Massage Assn. [15023], 801 W Norton Ave., Ste. 420, Muskegon, MI 49441, (231)733-0717

Amer. Medical Network - Defunct.

Amer. Medical Peer Rev. Assn. [★16262]

Amer. Medical Political Action Comm. [18279], c/o Amer. Medical Assn., 515 N State St., Chicago, IL 60610, (800)621-8335

Amer. Medical Publishers' Assn. [3204], 308 E Lancaster Ave., Ste. 110, Wynnewood, PA 19096, (610)642-2810

Amer. Medical Records Assn. [★15097]

Amer. Medical Rehabilitation Providers Assn. [16312], 1710 North St. NW, Washington, DC 20036, (202)223-1920

Amer. Medical Res. Found. [★8843]

Amer. Medical Resources Found. [14974], PO Box 3609, Brockton, MA 02304-3609, (508)580-3301

Amer. Medical Resources Found. [IO], Brockton, MA, United States

Amer. Medical Soc. on Alcoholism and Other Drug Dependencies [★16501]

Amer. Medical Soc. for Sports Medicine [16475], 11639 Earnshaw, Overland Park, KS 66210, (913)327-1415

Amer. Medical Student Assn. [8844], 1902 Assn. Dr., Reston, VA 20191, (703)620-6600

Amer. Medical Technologists [15127], 10700 W Higgins Rd., Rosemont, IL 60018, (847)823-5169

Amer. Medical Tennis Assn. [23898], 1803 Cobblestone Dr., Provo, UT 84604, (800)326-2682

Amer. Medical Women's Assn. [14696], 211 N Union St., Ste. 100, Alexandria, VA 22314, (703)838-0500

Amer. Medical Writers Assn. [3082], 40 W Gude Dr., No. 101, Rockville, MD 20850-1192, (301)294-5303

Amer. Medico Psychological Assn. [★16076]

Amer. Membrane Tech. Assn. [7824], 2409 SE Dixie Hwy., Stuart, FL 34996, (772)463-0820

American Membrane Technology Association [IO], Stuart, FL, United States

Amer. Menopause Found. [16894], 350 5th Ave., Ste. 2822, New York, NY 10118, (212)714-2398

Amer. Men's Stud. Assn. [12341], 22 East St., Northampton, MA 01060, (336)323-2672

Amer. Mensa [9981], 1229 Corporate Dr. W, Arlington, TX 76006-6103, (817)607-0060

Amer. Mental Hea. Alliance [15188], PO Box 4075, Portland, OR 97208-4075, (503)279-8160

Amer. Mental Hea. Counselors Assn. [15189], 801 N Fairfax St., Ste. 304, Alexandria, VA 22314, (703)548-6002

Amer. Mental Health Found. - Address unknown since 2001.

Amer. Merchant Marine Inst. [★6059]

Amer. Merchant Marine Lib. Assn. [10321], 635 Fourth Ave., Brooklyn, NY 11232, (718)369-3818

Amer. Merchant Marine Veterans [21387], PO Box 151205, Cape Coral, FL 33915-1205, (239)549-1010

Amer. Messianic Fellowship [★19988]

Amer. Messianic Fellowship [★IO]

Amer. Metal Detector Mfrs. Assn. [1817], 1881 W State St., Garland, TX 75042, (972)494-6151

Amer. Metal Etching Mfrs. Trade Assn. [★2720]

Amer. Metal Importers Assn. - Defunct.

Amer. Metal Repair Assn. - Defunct.

Amer. Metal Stamping Assn. [★2726]

Amer. Metaphysical Assn. - Address unknown since 1994.

Amer. Meteor Soc. [6500], c/o Karl Simmons, Treas., 44017 Woodland Ct., Callahan, FL 32011

Amer. Meteorological Soc. [7325], 45 Beacon St., Boston, MA 02108-3693, (617)227-2425

Amer. Metered Postage Soc. - Defunct.

Amer. Methanol Inst. [★7110]

Amer. MGB Assn. [21574], PO Box 11401, Chicago, IL 60611, (773)878-5055

Amer. MGC Register [21575], 2809 Copter Rd., Pensacola, FL 32514, (850)478-3171

Amer. Microchemical Soc. [6668], c/o Herk Felder, Treas., 2 June Way, Middlesex, NJ 08846

Amer. Microscopical Soc. [7332], c/o Dr. Stephen L. Gardiner, PhD, Sec., Bryn Mawr Coll., Dept. of Biology, 101 N Merion Ave., Bryn Mawr, PA 19010, (610)526-5094

Amer. Mideast Bus. Associates [24357], 4 Kansas Rd., Little Egg Harbor Township, NJ 08087-1037, (609)296-4783

Amer. Military History Found. [★10482]

Amer. Military Inst. [★10482]

Amer. Military Medical Impression [6111]

Amer. Military Precision Flying Teams Assn. - Defunct.

Amer. Military Retirees Assn. [21282], 5436 Peru St., Ste. 1, Plattsburgh, NY 12901, (518)563-9479

Amer. Military Soc. [6065], PO Box 98186, Washington, DC 20090-8186, (800)379-6128

Amer. Military Uniform Collectors; Assn. of [22628]

Amer. Milking Devon Cattle Assn. [4235], c/o Sue Randall, Registrar, 135 Old Bay Rd., New Durham, NH 03855, (603)859-6611

Amer. Milking Shorthorn Junior Soc. [4236], 800 Pleasant St., Beloit, WI 53511-5456, (608)365-3332

Amer. Milking Shorthorn Soc. [4237], c/o David J. Kendall, Exec. Sec., 800 Pleasant St., Beloit, WI 53511-5456, (608)365-3332

Amer. Millinery Mfrs. Assn. - Defunct.

Amer. Miniature Cheviot Sheep Breeders Assn. [5188], 403 Cheryl Way, Silver Springs, NV 89429, (775)629-1211

Amer. Miniature Horse Assn. [4830], 5601 S Interstate 35 W, Alvarado, TX 76009, (817)783-5600

Amer. Miniature Jersey Cattle Registry [4238]

Amer. Miniature Llama Assn. [21513], PO Box 8, Kalispell, MT 59903, (406)755-3438

Amer. Miniature Racing Car Assn. - Defunct.

Amer. Miniature Schnauzer Club [22205], 105 Fite's Creek Rd., Mount Holly, NC 28120-1149, (704)827-6544

Amer. Mining Cong. - Defunct.

Amer. Minor Breeds Conservancy [★4994]

Amer. Miscellaneous Soc. - Defunct.

Amer. Mission to the Chinese and Asian - Defunct.

Amer. Mission to Greeks [★20298]

Amer. Mission to Greeks [★IO]

Amer. Missionary Fellowship [20296], PO Box 370, Villanova, PA 19085-0370, (610)527-4439

Amer. Mizrachi Women [★20119]

Amer. Mobile Groomers Assn. [2955], c/o Barkleigh Mgt. Gp., Inc., 970 W Trindle Rd., Mechanicsburg, PA 17055, (717)691-3388

Amer. Mobile Telecommunications Assn. [★3742]

Amer. Mobile Telecommunications Assn. - Defunct.

Amer. Mobilehome Assn. - Defunct.

Amer. Mock Trial Assn. [9281], 2700 Westown Pkwy., Ste. 220, West Des Moines, IA 50266-1411, (515)283-0803

Amer. Model Soldier Soc. and Amer. Military Historical Soc. - Address unknown since 1999.

Amer. Model Yachting Assn. [22642], c/o Michelle Dannenhoffer, Membership Sec., 558 Oxford Ave., Melbourne, FL 32935-3010, (888)237-9524

Amer. Mold Builders Assn. [1996], 701 E Irving Park Rd., No. 207, Roselle, IL 60172, (630)980-7667

Amer. Monetary Found. [★17298]

Amer. Money Mgt. Assn. [★1454]

Amer. Money Mgt. Gp. [1454], 5755 N Point Pkwy., Ste. 57, Alpharetta, GA 30022-1145, (678)297-9500

A star before a book entry number signifies that the name is not listed separately, but is mentioned within the entry.

Amer. Montessori Consulting [8890], PO Box 5062, Rossmoor, CA 90720, (562)598-2321

Amer. Montessori Soc. [8891], 281 Park Ave. S, New York, NY 10010-6102, (212)358-1250

Amer. Monument Assn. [2772], c/o Pennie Sabel, Exec. Dir., 30 Eden Alley, Ste. 301, Columbus, OH 43215, (614)461-5852

Amer. Mookee Assn. [4191], Rte. 1, Box 4050, Clinton, OK 73601, (864)876-2543

Amer. Morgan Horse Assn. [4831], 122 Bostwick Rd., Shelburne, VT 05482-4417, (802)985-4944

Amer. Morphological Soc. [★7867]

Amer. Mosquito Control Assn. [5072], 15000 Commerce Pkwy., Ste. C, Mount Laurel, NJ 08054, (856)439-9222

American Mosquito Control Association [IO], Mount Laurel, NJ, United States

Amer. Motel Assn. - Address unknown since 1995.

Amer. Mothers Comm. [★12139]

Amer. Mothers, Inc. [12139], Carlyle Crescent Center, 1940 Duke St., Ste. 200, Alexandria, VA 22314, (703)486-5760

Amer. Mothers of Korean Orphans - Address unknown since 1995.

Amer. Motility Soc. [★14407]

Amer. Motivational Assn. - Defunct.

Amer. Motorcycle Assn. [★23622]

Amer. Motorcycle Heritage Found. [23621], 13515 Yarmouth Dr., Pickerington, OH 43147, (614)856-2222

Amer. Motorcyclist Assn. [23622], 13515 Yarmouth Dr., Pickerington, OH 43147-8214, (614)856-1900

Amer. Motors Drag Racing Assn. [★23080]

Amer. Motors Drivers and Racers Assn; Natl. [23080]

Amer. Motors Owners Assn. [21576], c/o Don P. Loper, 1615 Purvis Ave., Janesville, WI 53548, (608)752-8247

Amer. Motorsport Intl. - Defunct.

Amer. Mountain Guides Assn. [23284], PO Box 1739, Boulder, CO 80306-1739, (303)271-0984

Amer. Mouse Lovers - Defunct.

Amer. Movement for World Govt. - Address unknown since 1989.

Amer. Movers Conf. [★3559]

Amer. Movers Conf. [★IO]

Amer. Movers Inst. [★IO]

Amer. Movers Inst. [★3559]

Amer. Moving and Storage Assn. [3559], 1611 Duke St., Alexandria, VA 22314-3406, (703)683-7410

American Moving and Storage Association [IO], Alexandria, VA, United States

Amer. Moving and Storage Tech. Found. [★IO]

Amer. Moving and Storage Tech. Found. [★3559]

Amer. Mule Assn. [4131], PO Box 1349, Yerington, NV 89447, (775)463-1922

Amer. Mule Racing Assn. [23668], PO Box 660651, Sacramento, CA 95866-0651, (916)263-1529

Amer. Municipal Assn. [★6130]

Amer. Murray Grey Assn. [4239], PO Box 60748, Reno, NV 89506, (775)972-7526

Amer. Museum of Natural History [7357], Central Park W at 79th St., New York, NY 10024-5192, (212)769-5100

Amer. Museum of Negro History [★9360]

Amer. Mushroom Inst. [4703], Washington, D.C. Off., 1 Massachusetts Ave. NW, Ste. 800, Washington, DC 20001, (202)842-4344

Amer. Music Center [10541], 30 W 26th St., Ste. 1001, New York, NY 10010-2011, (212)366-5260

Amer. Music Conf. [10542], 5790 Armada Dr., Carlsbad, CA 92008-4391, (760)431-9124

Amer. Music Festival Assn. [10543], 10 N 2nd St., Ste. 401, Harrisburg, PA 17101, (717)255-3020

Amer. Music; Inst. for Stud. in [8911]

Amer. Music Scholarship Assn. [★10726]

Amer. Music Therapy Assn. [16205], 8455 Colesville Rd., Ste. 1000, Silver Spring, MD 20910, (301)589-3300

Amer. Music; U.S. Info. Center for [★10541]

Amer. Musical Instrument Soc. [10544], 389 Main St., Ste. 202, Malden, MA 02148, (781)397-8870

Amer. Musicians Union [24152]

Amer. Musicological Soc. [10545], 6010 College Sta., Brunswick, ME 04011, (207)798-4243

Amer. Muslim Alliance [18083], 39675 Cedar Blvd., Ste. 220 E, Newark, CA 94560, (510)252-9858

Amer. Muslim Assn; United [20441]

Amer. Muslim Coun. [19262], 1005 W Webster Ave., Ste. 3, Chicago, IL 60614, (773)248-3390

Amer. Muslim Support Group - Address unknown since 2001.

Amer. Muslims for Global Peace and Justice - Defunct.

Amer. Muslims Intent on Learning and Activism [10728], PO Box 2216, Los Gatos, CA 95031

Amer. Mustang Assn. [4832]

Amer. Mustang and Burro Assn. [4833], PO Box 1013, Grass Valley, CA 95945-1013

Amer. Mutual Life Assn. [19368], 19424 S Waterloo Rd., Cleveland, OH 44119, (216)531-1900

Amer. Mycological Soc. [★6632]

Amer. Nail Producers Coun. - Defunct.

Amer. Name Soc. [10764], c/o Dr. Michael F. McGoff, Vice Provost/Treas., Off. of the Provost, Binghamton Univ., State Univ. of New York, Binghamton, NY 13902-6000, (607)777-2143

American Name Society [IO], Binghamton, NY, United States

Amer. Naprapathic Assn. [15276], 164 Div. St., Ste. 714, Elgin, IL 60120, (847)214-8642

Amer. Narcolepsy Assn. - Address unknown since 1999.

Amer. Natl. CattleWomen [4240], PO Box 3881, Englewood, CO 80155, (303)694-0313

Amer. Natl. Commn. for the Accreditation of Colleges and Universities - Defunct.

Amer. Natl. Comm. to Aid Homeless Armenians - Address unknown since 1999.

Amer. Natl. Coun. for Health Education of the Public - Defunct.

Amer. Natl. CowBelles [★4240]

Amer. Natl. Heritage Assn. - Address unknown since 2001.

Amer. Natl. Metric Coun. [18678], 900 Mix Ave., Ste. 1, Hamden, CT 06514-5106, (203)287-9849

Amer. Natl. Postal Employees Retirees Assn. - Address unknown since 1995.

Amer. Natl. Red Cross [★12830]

Amer. Natl. Standards Comm. on Pulp, Paper and Paperboard - Defunct.

Amer. Natl. Standards Comm. - Z39 [★7206]

Amer. Natl. Standards Inst. [6267], 1819 L St. NW, 6th Fl., Washington, DC 20036, (202)293-8020

Amer. Natl. Theatre and Acad. - Defunct.

Amer. Nationalist Union [18319], PO Box 426, Allison Park, PA 15101-0426, (412)443-7300

Amer. Nationalities Coun. - Address unknown since 1989.

Amer. Native Press Res. Assn. - Defunct.

Amer. Natural Childbirth Assn. - Defunct.

Amer. Natural Hygiene Soc. [★15279]

Amer. Natural Soda Ash Corp. [1725], 15 Riverside Ave., 2nd Fl., Westport, CT 06880, (203)226-9056

Amer. Nature Assn. - Defunct.

Amer. Nature Stud. Soc. [7358], c/o Pocono Environmental Educ. Center, RR 2, Box 1010, Dingmans Ferry, PA 18328

Amer. Naturopathic Assn. - Address unknown since 2006.

Amer. Naturopathic Medical Assn. [15281], PO Box 96273, Las Vegas, NV 89193, (702)897-7053

Amer. Naturopathic Practitioners Assn. - Address unknown since 2000.

Amer. Nautical Alliance [★20718]

Amer. Nautical Cadets [★20718]

Amer. Naval and Marine Scouts [★20718]

Amer. Navion Soc. [21428], PMB 335, 16420 SE McGillivray, Ste. 103, Vancouver, WA 98683-3461, (360)833-9921

Amer. Nazi Party [★18805]

Amer. Nazi Party [★IO]

Amer. Near East Refugee Aid [IO], Washington, DC, United States

Amer. Near East Refugee Aid [12804], 1522 K St. NW, Ste. 600, Washington, DC 20005, (202)842-2766

Amer. Needlepoint Guild [22148], 2810 Crossroads Dr., Ste. 3800, Madison, WI 53718, (608)443-2476

Amer. Nephrology Nurses' Assn. [15286], E Holly Ave., Box 56, Pitman, NJ 08071, (856)256-2320

Amer. Netherland Dwarf Rabbit Club [5138], c/o Sue Travis-Shutter, Sec.-Treas., 326 Travis Ln., Rockwall, TX 75032, (925)687-7656

Amer. Netherlands Club of Rotterdam [IO], Rotterdam, Netherlands

Amer. Network of Community Options and Resources [12560], 1101 King St., Ste. 380, Alexandria, VA 22314, (703)535-7850

Amer. Neuroendocrine Soc. [15035], c/o Dr. Susan Wray, Sec., Cellular and Developmental Neurobiology Sect., NIH, NINDS, Bldg. 35, Rm. 3A-1012, Bethesda, MD 20892, (301)496-8129

Amer. Neurogastroenterology and Motility Soc. [14407], 45685 Harmony Ln., Belleville, MI 48111, (734)699-1130

Amer. Neurological Assn. [15378], 5841 Cedar Lake Rd. S, Ste. 204, Minneapolis, MN 55416, (952)545-6284

Amer. Neuromodulation Soc. [★15847]

Amer. Neuropsychiatric Assn. [16074], 700 Ackerman Rd., Ste. 625, Columbus, OH 43202, (614)447-2077

Amer. Neurotology Soc. [16441], c/o Shirley Gossard, Admin., 3096 Riverdale Rd., The Villages, FL 32162, (352)751-0932

Amer. Newcomen [★10138]

Amer. News Women's Club [3083], 1607 22nd St. NW, Washington, DC 20008, (202)332-6770

Amer. Newspaper Guild [★24140]

Amer. Newspaper Publishers Assn. [★3244]

Amer. Newspaper Women's Club [★3083]

Amer. Nickel Collectors' Assn. - Address unknown since 1999.

Amer. Nihilism Assn. [8966]

Amer. Nobel Center - Defunct.

American Nonsmokers' Rights Foundation [★16432]

Amer. Nordic Walking Assn. [15960], PO Box 24205, Los Angeles, CA 90024-0205, (310)388-0344

Amer. Normande Assn. [★4281]

Amer. North Country Cheviot Sheep Assn. [5189], c/o Sandy Thomas, Sec.-Treas., 10506 S 875 E, Walkerton, IN 46574, (574)586-3778

Amer. Norwich Soc. - Defunct.

Amer. Nouthetic Psychology Assn. - Address unknown since 2007.

Amer. Nuclear Energy Coun. [★6969]

Amer. Nuclear Energy Coun. - Defunct.

Amer. Nuclear Insurers [3948], 95 Glastonbury Blvd., Glastonbury, CT 06033-4438, (860)682-1301

Amer. Nuclear Soc. [7385], 555 N Kensington Ave., La Grange Park, IL 60526, (708)352-6611

Amer. Numismatic and Archaeological Soc. [★22725]

Amer. Numismatic Assn. [22724], 818 N Cascade Ave., Colorado Springs, CO 80903-3279, (719)632-2646

Amer. Numismatic Soc. [22725], 96 Fulton St., New York, NY 10038, (212)571-4470

Amer. Nursery and Landscape Assn. [5042], 1000 Vermont Ave. NW, Ste. 300, Washington, DC 20005-4914, (202)789-2900

Amer. Nurses Assn. [15451], 8515 Georgia Ave., Ste. 400, Silver Spring, MD 20910, (301)628-5000

Amer. Nurses in Business Assn. - Address unknown since 2002.

Amer. Nurses Credentialing Center [2838], 8515 Georgia Ave., Ste. 400, Silver Spring, MD 20910-3492, (301)628-5250

Amer. Nurses Found. [15452], 8515 Georgia Ave., Ste. 400 W, Silver Spring, MD 20910, (301)628-5227

Amer. Nursing Assistant's Assn. - Address unknown since 1999.

Amer. Nursing Assistant's Found. - Address unknown since 1999.

Amer. Nursing Home Assn. [★14540]

Amer. Nursing Informatics Assn. [15453], 1908 S El Camino Real, Ste. H, San Clemente, CA 92672

Amer. Nutraceutical Assn. [14612], 5120 Selkirk Dr., Ste. 100, Birmingham, AL 35242, (205)980-5710

Amer. Nutrition Soc. - Address unknown since 1995.

Amer. Nyckelharpa Assn. [10546], c/o John Wendell, Sec.-Treas., 1486 Ulupuni St., Kailua, HI 96734

American Nyckelharpa Association [IO], Kailua, HI, United States

Reference to "IO" in place of a book number signifies that the association may be found in the 45th edition of International Organizations.

Amer. Nystagmus Network [16828], 303-D Beltline Pl., No. 321, Decatur, AL 35603

Amer. Oat Assn. [★2738]

Amer. Oat Assn. - Defunct.

Amer. Obesity Assn. [15574], 1250 24th St. NW, Ste. 300, Washington, DC 20037, (202)776-7711

Amer. Occupational Medical Assn. [★15624]

Amer. Occupational Therapy Assn. [16602], 4720 Montgomery Ln., PO Box 31220, Bethesda, MD 20824-1220, (301)652-2682

Amer. Occupational Therapy Certification Bd. [★16625]

Amer. Occupational Therapy Found. [15628], 4720 Montgomery Ln., PO Box 31220, Bethesda, MD 20824-1220, (301)652-6611

Amer. Oceanic Org. - Address unknown since 1995.

Amer. Oceans Campaign - Defunct.

Amer. Office Supplies Exporters Assn. - Defunct.

Amer. Officers of the Great War [★21417]

Amer. Officers of the Great War [★IO]

American Oil Chemists' Society [IO], Urbana, IL, United States

Amer. Oil Chemists' Soc. [6669], PO Box 17190, Urbana, IL 61803-7190, (217)359-2344

Amer. Oil and Gas Historical Soc. [2915], 1201 15th St. NW, Ste. 300, Washington, DC 20005, (202)857-4785

Amer. Old Time Fiddlers Assn. - Defunct.

Amer. Olive Oil Assn. [★2859]

Amer. Olive Oil Assn. [★IO]

Amer. Olympic Assn. [★23637]

Amer. Ontoanalytic Assn. - Defunct.

Amer. Opera Soc. - Defunct.

Amer. Ophthalmological Soc. [15662], PO Box 193940, San Francisco, CA 94119-3940, (415)561-8578

Amer. Opportunity Found. - Address unknown since 1988.

Amer. Optical Assn. [★15712]

Amer. Optometric Assn. [15712], 243 N Lindbergh Blvd., 1st Fl., St. Louis, MO 63141-7881, (314)991-4100

Amer. Optometric Found. [15713], 6110 Executive Blvd., Ste. 506, Rockville, MD 20852, (240)880-3088

Amer. Optometric Student Assn. [15714], c/o Amer. Optometric Assn., 243 N Lindbergh, St. Louis, MO 63141, (800)365-2291

Amer. Orchid Soc. [6625], 16700 AOS Ln., Delray Beach, FL 33446-4351, (561)404-2000

American Orchid Society [IO], Delray Beach, FL, United States

Amer. Order of Corpsmen and Combat Medics - Address unknown since 2001.

Amer. Order of the French Croix de Guerre - Defunct.

Amer. Ordnance Assn. [★6089]

Amer. Orff-Schulwerk Assn. [10547], PO Box 391089, Cleveland, OH 44139-8089, (440)543-5366

Amer. Organ Transplant Assn. [16664], 21175 Tomball Pkwy., No. 194, Houston, TX 77070, (713)344-2402

Amer. Org. for Bodywork Therapies of Asia [15024], 1010 Haddonfield-Berlin Rd., Ste. 408, Voorhees, NJ 08043-3514, (856)782-1616

Amer. Org. of Nurse Executives [15454], c/o Executive Off., 325 Seventh St. NW, Liberty Pl., Washington, DC 20004, (202)626-2240

Amer. Org. of Tour Operators to Israel - Defunct.

Amer. Oriental Bodywork Therapy Assn. [★15024]

Amer. Oriental Soc. [9614], Univ. of Michigan, Hatcher Graduate Lib., Ann Arbor, MI 48109-1205, (734)647-4760

Amer. Oriental Soc. [IO], Ann Arbor, MI, United States

Amer. Ornithologists' Union [7412], 1313 Dolley Madison Blvd., Ste. 402, McLean, VA 22101, (703)790-1745

Amer. Ort Fed. [★12480]

Amer. Ort Fed. [★IO]

Amer. ORT and Women's Amer. ORT [★IO]

Amer. ORT and Women's Amer. ORT [★12480]

Amer. Orthodontic Soc. [14138], 11884 Greenville Ave., Ste. 112, Dallas, TX 75243-3537, (800)448-1601

Amer. Orthopaedic Assn. [15757], 6300 N River Rd., Ste. 505, Rosemont, IL 60018, (847)318-7330

Amer. Orthopaedic Foot and Ankle Soc. [15758], 6300 N River Rd., Ste. 510, Rosemont, IL 60018, (847)698-4654

Amer. Orthopaedic Foot Soc. [★15758]

Amer. Orthopaedic Soc. [★15750]

Amer. Orthopaedic Soc. for Sports Medicine [16476], 6300 N River Rd., Ste. 500, Rosemont, IL 60018, (847)292-4900

Amer. Orthopsychiatric Assn. [16075], Arizona State Univ., Dept. of Psychology, Box 871104, Tempe, AZ 85287-1104, (480)727-7518

Amer. Orthoptic Coun. [15663], c/o Ms. Leslie France, CO, Admin., 3914 Nakoma Rd., Madison, WI 53711, (608)233-5383

Amer. Orthotic and Prosthetic Assn. [1855], 330 John Carlyle St., Ste. 200, Alexandria, VA 22314, (571)431-0876

Amer. Osler Soc. [15157], c/o Charles S. Bryan, MD, Sec.-Treas., Univ. of South Carolina School of Medicine, Dept. of Medicine, 2 Medical Park, Ste. 502, Columbia, SC 29203, (803)540-1000

Amer. Osteopathic Acad. of Addiction Medicine [16500], 142 E Ontario St., Chicago, IL 60611, (800)621-1773

Amer. Osteopathic Acad. Addictionology [★16500]

Amer. Osteopathic Acad. of Geriatrics - Defunct.

Amer. Osteopathic Acad. of Orthopedics [15759], PO Box 291690, Davie, FL 33329-1690, (954)262-1700

Amer. Osteopathic Acad. of Physical Medicine and Rehabilitation [★15805]

Amer. Osteopathic Acad. of Public Hea. and Preventive Medicine [★15802]

Amer. Osteopathic Acad. of Sclerotherapy [★15814]

Amer. Osteopathic Acad. of Sports Medicine [16477], 2810 Crossroads Dr., Ste. 3800, Madison, WI 53718, (608)443-2477

Amer. Osteopathic Assn. [15798], 142 E Ontario St., Chicago, IL 60611, (312)202-8000

Amer. Osteopathic Assn; Auxiliary to the [★15789]

Amer. Osteopathic Assn; Bur. of Professional Educ. of the [15810]

Amer. Osteopathic Bd. of Emergency Medicine [14328], c/o Josette M. Fleming, Mgr., 142 E Ontario St., Chicago, IL 60611, (312)335-1065

Amer. Osteopathic Bd. of Family Physicians [15799], 330 E Algonquin Rd., Ste. 6, Arlington Heights, IL 60005, (847)640-8477

Amer. Osteopathic Bd. of Gen. Practice [★15799]

Amer. Osteopathic Bd. of Pediatrics [15800], 142 E Ontario St., 4th Fl., Chicago, IL 60611, (312)202-8267

Amer. Osteopathic Bd. of Preventive Medicine [15801], 142 E Ontario St., 4th Fl., Chicago, IL 60611-2864, (800)621-1773

American Osteopathic Bd. of Rehabilitation Medicine [★15805]

Amer. Osteopathic Coll. of Allergy and Immunology - Address unknown since 2000.

Amer. Osteopathic Coll. of Anesthesiologists [13672], 6500 NW Tower Dr., Ste. 103, Kansas City, MO 64151-4414, (816)584-2622

Amer. Osteopathic Coll. of Dermatology [14194], PO Box 7525, Kirksville, MO 63501, (660)665-2184

Amer. Osteopathic Coll. of Nuclear Medicine - Defunct.

Amer. Osteopathic Coll. of Occupational and Preventive Medicine [15802], c/o Mr. Jeffrey J. LeBoeuf, Pres., Associates Innovators, LCC, 5620 Cedar Park Dr., Ste. 1-B, Jackson, MS 39206, (800)558-8686

Amer. Osteopathic Coll. of Ophthalmology and the Amer. Osteopathic Coll. of Otolaryngology-Head and Neck Surgery [15803], 4764 Fishburg Rd., Ste. F, Huber Heights, OH 45424, (800)455-9404

Amer. Osteopathic Coll. of Pathologists [15804], 142 E Ontario St., Chicago, IL 60611-8224, (312)202-8197

Amer. Osteopathic Coll. of Physical Medicine and Rehabilitation [15805], PO Box 732, Dover, NH 03821-0732, (603)343-1937

Amer. Osteopathic Coll. of Physical Medicine and Rehabilitation [★15805]

Amer. Osteopathic Coll. of Preventive Medicine [★15802]

Amer. Osteopathic Coll. of Proctology - Address unknown since 2003.

Amer. Osteopathic Coll. of Radiology [16276], 119 E 2nd St., Milan, MO 63556-1331, (660)265-4011

Amer. Osteopathic Coll. of Rehabilitation Medicine [★15805]

Amer. Osteopathic Coll. of Rheumatology - Defunct.

Amer. Osteopathic Colleges of Ophthalmology and Otolaryngology-Head and Neck Surgery [15664], 4764 Fishburg Rd., Ste. F, Huber Heights, OH 45424, (937)233-5653

Amer. Osteopathic Found. [15806], 142 E Ontario St., Ste. 502, Chicago, IL 60611, (312)202-8234

Amer. Osteopathic Healthcare Assn. - Address unknown since 2006.

Amer. Osteopathic Historical Soc. - Defunct.

Amer. Osteopathic Occupational Medical Assn. [★15802]

Amer. Osteopathic Soc. of Anesthesiologists [★13672]

Amer. Osteopathic Soc. of Herniologists [★15814]

Amer. Ostrich Assn. [4132], PO Box 166, Ranger, TX 76470

Amer. Otological Soc. [15822], c/o Ms. Shirley Gossard, Admin., 3096 Riverdale Rd., The Villages, FL 32162, (352)751-0932

Amer. Otorhinologic Soc. for Plastic Surgery [★14038]

Amer. Outreach Assn. [13223], 5490 Delhart Rd., Ste. 205, Galax, VA 24333, (276)236-5934

Amer. Overseas Assn. [★12831]

Amer. Overseas Res. Centers; Coun. of [7566]

Amer. Overseas Schools Historical Soc. [10012], PO Box 1500, Wichita, KS 67201, (316)265-6837

Amer. Oxford Down Record Assn. [★5190]

Amer. Oxford Sheep Assn. [5190], 1960 E 2100 North Rd., Stonington, IL 62567, (217)325-3515

Amer. Pain Found. [15835], 201 N Charles St., Ste. 710, Baltimore, MD 21201-4111, (888)615-7246

Amer. Pain Soc. [15836], 4700 W Lake Ave., Glenview, IL 60025, (847)375-4715

Amer. Paint Horse Assn. [4834], PO Box 961023, Fort Worth, TX 76161-0023, (817)834-2742

Amer. Paint Horse Assn. [★4828]

Amer. Paint Mfrs. Assn. [★2884]

Amer. Paint Quarter Horse Assn. [★4834]

Amer. Paint Stock Horse Assn. [★4834]

Amer. Paintball Players Assn. [23645], c/o Chris Raehl, Coor., 1133 Indus. Blvd., No. 6, Chippewa Falls, WI 54729, (715)720-9131

Amer. Palestine Comm. - Defunct.

Amer. Palestine Fund [★10251]

Amer. Palestine Fund [★IO]

Amer. Pancreatic Assn. - Address unknown since 2002.

Amer. Paper Inst. [★4679]

Amer. Paper Machinery Assn. [★2003]

Amer. Paperweight Guild - Defunct.

American-Paraguayan Cultural Center [IO], Asuncion, Paraguay

Amer. Paralysis Assn. [★16463]

Amer. Paraplegia Soc. [16460], 75-20 Astoria Blvd., Jackson Heights, NY 11372, (718)803-3782

Amer. Parapsychological Res. Assn. [★7441]

Amer. Parents Comm. - Defunct.

Amer. Park and Recreation Soc. [6153], c/o Mike Moran, CPRP, Pres., 220 S Gilbert St., Iowa City, IA 52240, (319)356-5100

Amer. Parkinson Disease Assn. [15304], Natl. Off., 135 Parkinson Ave., Staten Island, NY 10305, (718)981-8001

Amer. Parliamentary Debate Assn. [9153], 401 Alfred Lerner Hall, MC 2602, 2920 Broadway, New York, NY 10027

Amer. Parole Assn. [★11843]

Amer. Parquet Assn. - Defunct.

Amer. Part-Blooded Horse Registry [4835], 12294 SE 104th Ct., Portland, OR 97086, (503)698-9615

Amer. Partners - Defunct.

Amer. Partnership for Eosinophilic Disorders [14408], 3419 Whispering Way Dr., Richmond, TX 77469, (713)498-8216

Amer. Partridge Plymouth Rock Club - Defunct.

A star before a book entry number signifies that the name is not listed separately, but is mentioned within the entry.

Amer. Paso Fino Horse Assn. **[4836]**, PO Box 2363, Pittsburgh, PA 15230, (724)437-5170

Amer. Pastured Poultry Producers Assn. **[5106]**, 36475 Norton Creek Rd., Blodgett, OR 97326, (541)453-4557

Amer. Patent Law Assn. **[★5835]**

Amer. Pathology Found. **[15857]**, 1540 S Coast Hwy., No. 203, Laguna Beach, CA 92651, (949)464-9810

Amer. Patients Assn. - Address unknown since 1995.

Amer. Patriots Assn. **[21239]**, c/o Terry Lynch, Pres./ Founder, PO Box 241035, Montgomery, AL 36124-1035

Amer. Pavement Marking Assn. - Defunct.

Amer. Pawnbrokers Assn. - Address unknown since 1990.

Amer. Pax Assn. **[★18121]**

Amer. Payroll Assn. **[1253]**, 660 N Main Ave., Ste. 100, San Antonio, TX 78205-1217, (210)226-4600

Amer. Peace Soc. **[17858]**

Amer. Peace Test - Defunct.

Amer. Peanut Coun. **[5049]**, 1500 King St., Ste. 301, Alexandria, VA 22314, (703)838-9500

Amer. Peanut Coun. - European Off. **[IO]**, London, United Kingdom

Amer. Peanut Product Mfrs. - Address unknown since 2003.

Amer. Peanut Res. and Educ. Assn. **[★5050]**

Amer. Peanut Res. and Educ. Soc. **[5050]**, c/o Dr. J. Ronald Sholar, Exec. Off., Oklahoma State Univ., 376 AG Hall, Stillwater, OK 74078, (405)372-3052

Amer. Peanut Shellers Assn. **[5051]**, 2336 Lake Park Dr., Albany, GA 31707, (229)888-2508

Amer. Pedestrian Assn. - Address unknown since 1999.

Amer. Pediatric Soc. **[15882]**, 3400 Res. Forest Dr., Ste. B-7, The Woodlands, TX 77381, (281)419-0052

Amer. Pediatric Surgical Assn. **[15883]**, 60 Revere Dr., Ste. 500, Northbrook, IL 60062, (847)480-9576

Amer. Pediatric Surgical Nurses Assn. **[15455]**, PO Box 1605, Lansdale, PA 19446, (614)722-3900

Amer. Pencil Collectors Soc. **[21964]**, c/o Andrew L. Westberg, Pres., 916 Wall St., North Mankato, MN 56003, (507)344-0643

Amer. Penstemon Soc. **[22497]**, c/o Dwayne Dickerson, Membership Sec., 600 S Cherry St., Ste. 127, Denver, CO 80246

Amer. Peony Soc. **[22498]**, c/o Claudia Schroer, Membership Sec./Ed., 713 White Oak Ln., Kansas City, MO 64116-4607

Amer. People for Amer. Prisoners - Address unknown since 1995.

Amer. Performance Horse Assn. - Address unknown since 2001.

Amer. Personal Chef Assn. **[★791]**

Amer. Personal and Private Chef Assn. **[791]**, 4572 Delaware St., San Diego, CA 92116, (800)644-8389

Amer. Personnel and Guidance Assn. **[★11815]**

Amer. Peruvian Paso Horse Registry **[★4934]**

Amer. Peruvian Paso Horse Registry **[★IO]**

Amer. Pet Boarding Assn. - Address unknown since 2002.

Amer. Pet Products Mfrs. Assn. **[2956]**, 255 Glenville Rd., Greenwich, CT 06831, (203)532-0000

Amer. Pet Soc. **[11349]**, c/o World Wide Pet Indus. Assn., 135 W Lemon Ave., Monrovia, CA 91016, (626)447-2222

Amer. Pet Stock Assn. **[★5139]**

Amer. Petanque Assn. U.S.A. **[★23649]**

Amer. Petroleum Credit Assn. **[★1427]**

Amer. Petroleum Credit Assn. **[★IO]**

Amer. Petroleum Equip. Suppliers **[★2942]**

Amer. Petroleum Inst. **[2916]**, 1220 L St. NW, Washington, DC 20005-4070, (202)682-8000

Amer. Pewter Guild - Defunct.

Amer. Pharmaceutical Assn. - Acad. of Pharmacy Practice and Mgt. **[★15918]**

Amer. Pharmaceutical Assn. Acad. of Students of Pharmacy **[★15919]**

Amer. Pharmaceutical Assn. Student Sect. **[★15919]**

Amer. Pharmaceutical Mfrs. Assn. **[★2980]**

Amer. Pharmacists Assn. - Acad. of Pharmacy Practice and Mgt. **[15918]**, c/o APhA, 1100 15th St. NW, Ste. 400, Washington, DC 20005-1707, (202)628-4410

Amer. Pharmacists Assn. Acad. of Student Pharmacists **[15919]**, c/o Amer. Pharmacists Assn., 1100 15th St. NW, Ste. 400, Washington, DC 20005-1707, (202)628-4410

Amer. Pheasant Soc. **[★5292]**

Amer. Pheasant and Waterfowl Soc. **[5292]**, c/o E.T. Trader, Treas., 6220 Bullbeggar Rd., Withams, VA 23488

Amer. Philatelic Cong. **[22783]**, c/o Mr. Ross A. Towle, Sec.-Treas., 400 Clayton St., San Francisco, CA 94117-1912

Amer. Philatelic Res. Lib. **[22784]**, 100 Match Factory Pl., Bellefonte, PA 16823, (814)933-3803

Amer. Philatelic Soc. **[22785]**, 100 Match Factory Pl., Bellefonte, PA 16823, (814)933-3803

Amer. Philatelic Soc; Junior Writers Unit, **[★22837]**

Amer. Philatelic Soc. Writers Unit **[22786]**, c/o Mr. George B. Griffenhagen, 2501 Drexel St., Vienna, VA 22180-6906

American Philatelic Society Writers Unit **[IO]**, Vienna, VA, United States

Amer.-Philippine Science Found. - Address unknown since 1995.

Amer. Philological Assn. **[10296]**, c/o Univ. of Pennsylvania, 292 Logan Hall, 249 S 36th St., Philadelphia, PA 19104-6304, (215)898-4975

Amer. Philosophical Assn. **[10783]**, Univ. of Delaware, 31 Amstel Ave., Newark, DE 19716-4797, (302)831-1112

Amer. Philosophical Soc. **[7598]**, 104 S 5th St., Philadelphia, PA 19106-3387, (215)440-3400

Amer. Philosophy; Soc. for the Advancement of **[10828]**

Amer. Phlox Soc. - Address unknown since 2006.

Amer. Photographic Artisans Guild **[★2990]**

Amer. Photographic Artists Guild **[2990]**, c/o D. John McCarthy, Pres., 568 Main St., Wilbraham, MA 01095-1604, (413)596-8752

Amer. Photographic Artists Guild **[★2990]**

Amer. Photographic Historical Soc. **[10843]**, 28 Marksman Ln., Levittown, NY 11756-5110, (516)796-7280

Amer. Photoplatemakers Assn. **[★7154]**

Amer. Photoplatemakers Assn. **[★IO]**

Amer. Physical Educ. Assn. **[★8979]**

Amer. Physical Fitness Res. Inst. - Defunct.

Amer. Physical Soc. **[7500]**, One Physics Ellipse, College Park, MD 20740-3844, (301)209-3200

Amer. Physical Soc. **[IO]**, College Park, MD, United States

Amer. Physical Therapy Assn. **[16603]**, 1111 N Fairfax St., Alexandria, VA 22314-1488, (703)684-2782

Amer. Physical Therapy Assn; Orthopaedic Sect., **[16630]**

American Physical Therapy Assn; Private Practice Section/ **[16633]**

Amer. Physician Art Assn. **[9415]**, c/o Dr. Lawrence Travis, MD, Sec.-Treas., 2410 Patterson St., Ste. 202, Nashville, TN 37203, (615)327-4944

Amer. Physicians Assn. of Computer Medicine - Defunct.

Amer. Physicians and Dentists; Union of **[24092]**

Amer. Physicians Fellowship for the Israel Medical Assn. **[★12456]**

Amer. Physicians Fellowship for the Israel Medical Assn. **[★IO]**

Amer. Physicians Fellowship for Medicine in Israel **[IO]**, Boston, MA, United States

Amer. Physicians Fellowship for Medicine in Israel **[12456]**, 2001 Beacon St., Ste. 210, Boston, MA 02135, (617)232-5382

Amer. Physicians Poetry Assn. - Address unknown since 1994.

Amer. Physicians' Soc. for Physiologic Tension Control - Defunct.

Amer. Physiological and Natural Hygiene Soc. **[★15279]**

Amer. Physiological Soc. **[7510]**, 9650 Rockville Pike, Bethesda, MD 20814-3991, (301)634-7164

Amer. Physiotherapy Assn. **[★16603]**

Amer. Phyto Aromatherapy Assn. - Address unknown since 1999.

Amer. Phytopathological Soc. **[6626]**, 3340 Pilot Knob Rd., St. Paul, MN 55121, (651)454-7250

Amer. Pianists Assn. **[22709]**, 4603 Clarendon Rd., Ste. 030, Indianapolis, IN 46208, (317)940-9945

Amer. PIE **[★17500]**

Amer. Pie Coun. **[446]**, PO Box 368, Lake Forest, IL 60045, (847)371-0170

Amer. Piedmontese Assn. **[★4287]**

Amer. Pilots' Assn. **[2571]**, 499 S Capitol St. SW, Ste. 409, Washington, DC 20003, (202)484-0700

Amer. Pinto Arabian Registry **[4837]**, 608 Pecan, Ferris, TX 75125, (972)544-2717

Amer. Pinzgauer Assn. **[4241]**, PO Box 147, Bethany, MO 64424, (660)425-8617

Amer. Pioneer Trails Assn. - Defunct.

Amer. Pioneers **[★21067]**

Amer. Pipe Fittings Assn. **[3025]**

Amer. Pistol and Revolver Assn. - Defunct.

American Pit Bull Terrier
    Amer. Dog Breeders Assn. **[22197]**
    Working Pit Bull Terrier Club of Am. **[22385]**

Amer. Pit Bull Terrier Assn; Natl. **[22311]**

Amer. Planning Assn. **[5586]**, 122 S Michigan Ave., Ste. 1600, Chicago, IL 60603-6107, (312)431-9100

Amer. Plant Life Soc. **[★6637]**

Amer. Plant Life Soc. **[★IO]**

Amer. Plant Selections - Defunct.

Amer. Plastics Coun. **[3044]**, 1300 Wilson Blvd., Arlington, VA 22209, (703)741-5000

Amer. Plate Number Single Soc. **[22787]**, c/o Rick Burdsall, Sec., PO Box 1023, Palatine, IL 60078-1023

Amer. Platform Tennis Assn. **[23899]**, 530 Woodland Ln. S, Northfield, IL 60093, (847)446-9737

Amer. Play Money Soc. - Defunct.

Amer. Playwrights Theatre - Defunct.

Amer. Plywood Assn. **[★1637]**

Amer. Podiatric Circulatory Soc. **[16036]**, c/o Dr. Stanley Goldstein, Pres., 5704 18th Ave., Brooklyn, NY 11204, (718)236-7952

Amer. Podiatric Medical Assn. **[16037]**, 9312 Old Georgetown Rd., Bethesda, MD 20814-1621, (301)571-9200

Amer. Podiatric Medical Assn. Auxilliary - Defunct.

Amer. Podiatric Medical Students' Assn. **[16038]**, 9312 Old Georgetown Rd., Bethesda, MD 20814, (301)493-9667

Amer. Podiatric Medical Writers Assn. **[16039]**, PO Box 750129, Forest Hills, NY 11375, (718)897-9700

Amer. Podiatric Multiple Specialties Bd. **[★16029]**

Amer. Podiatric Students Assn. **[★16038]**

Amer. Podiatry Assn. **[★16037]**

Amer. Poetry Assn. - Address unknown since 1994.

Amer. Poetry League - Address unknown since 1995.

Amer. Poets; Acad. of **[10859]**

Amer. Poinsettia Soc. - Defunct.

Amer. Pointer Club **[22206]**, c/o Susan Bleckley, Recording Sec., 327 Lugonia St., Newport Beach, CA 92663, (949)515-4454

Amer. Polar Soc. **[7515]**, PO Box 300, Searsport, ME 04974

Amer. Polar Soc. **[IO]**, Searsport, ME, United States

Amer. Polarity Therapy Assn. **[13619]**, 122 N Elm St., Ste. 512, Greensboro, NC 27401, (336)574-1121

Amer. Police Acad. - Defunct.

Amer. Police Hall of Fame and Museum **[★5962]**

Amer.-Polish Natl. Relief for Poland - Defunct.

Amer. Polish Rabbit Club - Defunct.

Amer. Political Items Collectors **[22903]**, PO Box 55, Avon, NY 14414, (585)226-2236

Amer. Political Sci. Assn. **[7521]**, 1527 New Hampshire Ave. NW, Washington, DC 20036-1206, (202)483-2512

Amer. Polled Hereford Assn. **[★4225]**

Amer. Polled Shorthorn Soc. - Defunct.

Amer. Polocrosse Assn. **[23338]**, PO Box 915, New Hampton, NY 10958, (843)825-2686

Amer. Polygraph Assn. **[5753]**, PO Box 8037, Chattanooga, TN 37414-0037, (423)892-3992

Amer. Polypay Sheep Assn. **[5191]**, c/o Karey Claghorn, Sec., 15603 173rd Ave., Milo, IA 50166, (641)942-6402

Amer. Pomeranian Club **[22207]**, c/o Annette Davis, Membership Sec., 391 N Mink Creek Rd., Pocatello, ID 83204, (208)234-0932

Amer. Pomological Soc. **[4704]**, c/o R.M. Crassweller, Treas., 103 Tyson Bldg., University Park, PA 16802-4200, (814)863-6163

Reference to "IO" in place of a book number signifies that the association may be found in the 45th edition of International Organizations.

Amer. Porphyria Found. [15243], PO Box 22712, Houston, TX 77227, (713)266-9617

Amer. Portland Cement Alliance [★915]

Amer. Portland Cement Assn. [915], 1330 Connecticut Ave. NW, Ste. 1250, Washington, DC 20036, (202)408-9494

Amer. Portrait Soc. - Address unknown since 1987.

Amer. Portuguese Cultural Soc. [★10889]

Amer. Portuguese Cultural Soc. [★IO]

Amer. Portuguese Engg. and Architecture Soc. [7530], 56 Cong. St., Newark, NJ 07105, (973)344-9224

Amer. Portuguese Soc. [10889]

Amer. Portuguese Soc. [IO], New York, NY, United States

Amer. Portuguese Stud. Assn. [9004], PO Box 1158, Ames, IA 50014

Amer. Postal Chess League - Defunct.

Amer. Postal Chess Tournaments [21943], PO Box 147, Western Springs, IL 60558-0147, (630)268-8287

Amer. Postal Workers Union [24166], 1300 L St. NW, Washington, DC 20005, (202)842-4200

Amer. Potash Inst. [★4107]

Amer. Poultry Assn. [5107], c/o Dave Anderson, Pres., 947 Grand Ave., Fillmore, CA 93015, (805)524-4046

Amer. Poultry Historical Soc. - Address unknown since 2002.

Amer. Poultry Intl. [5108], PO Box 16805, Jackson, MS 39236, (601)956-1715

Amer. Poultry Intl. [IO], Jackson, MS, United States

Amer. POW-MIA Coalition - Address unknown since 2003.

Amer. Powder Metallurgy Inst. [★7310]

Amer. Powder Metallurgy Inst. [★IO]

Amer. Power Boat Assn. [23152], PO Box 377, Eastpointe, MI 48021, (586)773-9700

Amer. POWER Comm. - Address unknown since 2002.

Amer. Power Net Assn. [★3780]

Amer. Pre-Veterinary Medical Assn. [16774], c/o Arvind Badrinarayanan, Sec., 303 W Green St., Champaign, IL 61820

Amer. Precision Optics Mfrs. Assn. [3480], PO Box 20001, Rochester, NY 14602, (585)292-2676

Amer. Pregnancy Assn. [15588], 1425 Greenway Dr., Ste. 440, Irving, TX 75038, (972)550-0140

Amer. Prepaid Legal Services Inst. [6020], 321 N Clark St., Chicago, IL 60610, (312)988-5751

Amer. Press Inst. [8704], 11690 Sunrise Valley Dr., Reston, VA 20191-1498, (703)620-3611

American Press Syndicate [★17625]

Amer. Preventive Medical Assn. [★16049]

Amer. Primrose Soc. [22499], c/o Julia Haldorson, Treas., PO Box 210913, Auke Bay, AK 99821

Amer. Print Alliance [9544], 302 Larkspur Turn, Peachtree City, GA 30269-2210

American Print Alliance [IO], Peachtree City, GA, United States

Amer. Printed Fabrics Coun. - Address unknown since 2000.

Amer. Printing History Assn. [9989], PO Box 4519, Grand Central Sta., New York, NY 10163-4519, (212)930-9220

Amer. Printing House for the Blind [16829], PO Box 6085, 1839 Frankfort Ave., Louisville, KY 40206-0085, (502)895-2405

Amer. Prison Assn. [★11854]

Amer. Prison Ministry - Address unknown since 1995.

Amer. Pro Life Coun. - Address unknown since 2004.

Amer. Pro Se Assn. [6021], 1441 Prospect Ave., Plainfield, NJ 07060, (908)753-4516

Amer. Probation and Parole Assn. [6164], 2760 Res. Park Dr., Lexington, KY 40511-8482, (859)244-8203

Amer. Produce - Address unknown since 1995.

Amer. Producers of Italian Type Cheese Assn. - Defunct.

Amer. Production and Inventory Control Soc. [★7181]

Amer. Production and Inventory Control Soc. [★IO]

Amer. Productivity Center [★2482]

Amer. Productivity & Quality Center [★2482]

Amer. Professional Assn. - Defunct.

Amer. Professional Faceters Assn. - Defunct.

Amer. Professional Needlework Retailers - Address unknown since 1999.

Amer. Professional Pet Distributors - Defunct.

Amer. Professional Practice Assn. [14697], Assn. Member Ser. Center, Hillsboro Executive Center N, 350 Fairway Dr., Ste. 200, Deerfield Beach, FL 33441-1834, (800)221-2168

Amer. Professional Racquetball Org. - Address unknown since 1995.

Amer. Professional Soc. on the Abuse of Children [11557], PO Box 30669, Charleston, SC 29417, (843)764-2905

Amer. Professional Soc. of the Deaf - Defunct.

Amer. Professional Wedding Photographers Assn. [2991], 1155 Sherman St., No. 203, Denver, CO 80203, (800)725-1650

Amer. Professional Wound Care Assn. [16688], 853 Second St. Pike, Ste. A1, Richboro, PA 18954, (215)364-4100

Amer. Professors for Peace in the Middle East - Defunct.

Amer. Prosecutors Res. Inst. [5481], 99 Canal Center Plz., Ste. 510, Alexandria, VA 22314, (703)549-9222

Amer. Prospect Res. Assn. [★12198]

Amer. Prostate Soc. [16701], PO Box 870, Hanover, MD 21076, (410)859-3735

Amer. Prosthodontic Soc. [14139], 426 Hudson St., Hackensack, NJ 07601, (201)440-7699

Amer. Protestant Correctional Chaplains Assn. - Address unknown since 1999.

Amer. Protestant Health Assn. - Defunct.

Amer. Protestants for Truth About Ireland - Defunct.

Amer. Pseudo-Obstruction and Hirschsprung's Disease Soc. [★14419]

Amer. Pseudo-Obstruction and Hirschsprung's Disease Soc. [★IO]

Amer. Pseudo-Obstruction and Hirschsprung's Disease Soc. - Defunct.

Amer. Psychiatric Assn. [16076], 1000 Wilson Blvd., Ste. 1825, Arlington, VA 22209-3901, (703)907-7300

Amer. Psychiatric Assn. Alliance [16077], c/o Angela Poblocki, Exec. Dir., PO Box 285, North Boston, NY 14110

Amer. Psychiatric Assn; Caucus of Gay, Lesbian, and Bisexual Members of the [★12217]

Amer. Psychiatric Assn; Gay Caucus of Members of the [★12217]

Amer. Psychiatric Assn; Gay, Lesbian, and Bisexual Caucus of the [★12217]

American Psychiatric Assn; Inst. on Psychiatric Services/ [16085]

Amer. Psychiatric Nurses Assn. [15456], 1555 Wilson Blvd., Ste. 602, Arlington, VA 22209, (703)243-2443

Amer. Psychoanalytic Assn. [16102], 309 E 49th St., New York, NY 10017-1601, (212)752-0450

Amer. Psychoanalytic Found. [16103], c/o Amer. Psychoanalytic Assn., 309 E 49th St., New York, NY 10017, (212)752-0450

American Psychological Association [★16145]

Amer. Psychological Assn. [16122], 750 First St. NE, Washington, DC 20002-4242, (202)336-5500

Amer. Psychological Assn. - Addictions Div. [16123], c/o Dr. Kim Fromme, Pres., Univ. of Texas at Austin, 1 Univ. Sta., A8000, Austin, TX 78712, (512)471-0039

American Psychological Association Division 31 - State, Provincial, and Territorial Psychological Association Affairs [16124], c/o Michael O. Ranney, MPA, Exec. Dir., 400 E Town St., Ste. 200, Columbus, OH 43215-1599, (614)224-0034

Amer. Psychological Assn. - Division of Family Psychology [16125], c/o Amer. Psychological Assn., 750 First St. NE, Washington, DC 20002-4242, (202)336-6013

Amer. Psychological Assn. Division of Independent Practice [16126], c/o Jeannie Beeaff, Div. 42, Central Off., 919 W Marshall Ave., Phoenix, AZ 85013, (602)246-6768

Amer. Psychological Assn. - Div. of Intl. Psychology [16127], c/o Uwe Gielen, PhD, Pres.-Elect, St. Francis Coll., 180 Remsen St., Brooklyn, NY 11201, (718)489-5386

Amer. Psychological Assn. - Division of Psychotherapy [16206], c/o Tracey Martin, Div. 29 Central Off., 6557 E Riverdale St., Mesa, AZ 85215-0722, (602)363-9211

Amer. Psychological Assn. - Div. of Trauma Psychology [16128], c/o Judith L. Alpert, PhD, Pres., New York Univ., 239 Greene St., 5th Fl., New York, NY 10003, (212)691-6587

Amer. Psychological Assn. of Graduate Students [16129], 750 1st St. NE, Washington, DC 20002-4242, (202)336-6014

Amer. Psychological Assn. - Hea. Psychology Div. [16130], PO Box 1838, Ashland, VA 23005-4838, (804)752-4987

Amer. Psychological Assn. - Media Psychology Div. [16131], 750 First St. NE, Washington, DC 20002-4242

Amer. Psychological Assn. - Psychology of Religion (Division 36) [16132], Div. Services Off., 750 1st St. NE, Washington, DC 20002-4242, (202)218-3599

Amer. Psychological Practitioners Assn. - Address unknown since 2002.

Amer. Psychological Soc. [★16142]

Amer. Psychology-Law Soc. [16133], c/o Ms. Lynn Peterson, Admin. Asst., PO Box 638, Niwot, CO 80544, (303)652-9154

Amer. Psychopathological Assn. [16190], c/o Linda B. Cottler, PhD, Treas., Dept. of Psychiatry, Washington Univ. School of Medicine, 40 N Kings Hwy., Ste. 4, St. Louis, MO 63108

Amer. Psychosocial Oncology Soc. [15638], 2365 Hunters Way, Charlottesville, VA 22911, (434)293-5350

Amer. Psychosomatic Soc. [16196], 6728 Old McLean Village Dr., McLean, VA 22101, (703)556-9222

Amer. Psychotherapy Assn. [16207], 2750 E Sunshine St., Springfield, MO 65804, (417)823-0173

Amer. Public Communications Coun. [3733], 625 Slaters Ln., Ste. 104, Alexandria, VA 22314, (703)739-1322

Amer. Public Gardens Assn. [4973], 100 W 10th St., Ste. 614, Wilmington, DE 19801-6604, (302)655-7100

Amer. Public Gas Assn. [3951], 201 Massachusetts Ave. NE, Ste. C-4, Washington, DC 20002, (202)464-2742

Amer. Public Hea. Assn. [16236], 800 I St. NW, Washington, DC 20001, (202)777-2742

Amer. Public Human Services Assn. [13151], 810 1st St. NE, Ste. 500, Washington, DC 20002, (202)682-0100

Amer. Public Human Services Assn. - Info. Systems Mgt. [13152], c/o Marquett Youngblood, Chm., Oklahoma Dept. of Human Services, 2400 N Lincoln Blvd., Oklahoma City, OK 73105, (405)521-6602

Amer. Public Info. on the Env. [17500], PO Box 676, Northfield, MN 55057-0676, (800)320-2743

Amer. Public Policy Assn. [★6201]

Amer. Public Power Assn. [6336], 2301 M St. NW, Washington, DC 20037-1427, (202)467-2900

Amer. Public Relations Assn. [★3195]

Amer. Public Transit Assn. [★3860]

Amer. Public Transit Assn. [★IO]

American Public Transportation Association [IO], Washington, DC, United States

Amer. Public Trans. Assn. [3860], 1666 K St. NW, Ste. 1100, Washington, DC 20006, (202)496-4800

Amer. Public Welfare Assn. [★13151]

Amer. Public Works Assn. [6233], 2345 Grand Blvd., Ste. 700, Kansas City, MO 64108-2625, (816)472-6100

Amer. Publicists Guild - Defunct.

Amer. Puerto Rican Action League - Address unknown since 1995.

Amer. Puffer Alliance - Defunct.

Amer. Pulp and Paper Mill Superintendents Assn. [★2893]

A star before a book entry number signifies that the name is not listed separately, but is mentioned within the entry.

Amer. Pulpwood Assn. [★1607]

Amer. Puppet Arts Coun. - Defunct.

Amer. Purchasing Soc. [3262], PO Box 256, Aurora, IL 60506, (630)859-0250

Amer. Pyrotechnics Assn. [3267], PO Box 30438, Bethesda, MD 20824, (301)907-8181

Amer. Qigong Assn. [13620], 117 Topaz Way, San Francisco, CA 94131, (415)285-9400

Amer. Quarter Horse Assn. [4838], PO Box 200, Amarillo, TX 79168, (806)376-4811

Amer. Quarter Horse Youth Assn. [4839], c/o Amer. Quarter Horse Assn., 1600 Quarter Horse Dr., PO Box 200, Amarillo, TX 79104, (806)376-4811

Amer. Quarter Pony Assn. [4840], PO Box 30, New Sharon, IA 50207, (641)675-3669

Amer. Quaternary Assn. [7359], c/o Cary Cock, Treas., Dept. of Geography, Univ. of South Carolina, Columbia, SC 29208, (803)777-1211

Amer. Quick Printing Assn. - Defunct.

Amer. Quicksilver Inst. - Defunct.

Amer. Quilt Study Group [9828], 1610 L St., Lincoln, NE 68508-2509, (402)477-1181

Amer. Quilter's Soc. [22149], PO Box 3290, Paducah, KY 42002-3290, (270)898-7903

Amer. Quilts; Alliance for [9823]

Amer. Rabbit Breeders Assn. [5139], PO Box 5667, Bloomington, IL 61702, (309)664-7500

Amer. Rabbit and Cavy Breeders Assn. [★5139]

Amer. Racing Driver's Club - Address unknown since 1995.

Amer. Racing Pigeon Union [22894], PO Box 18465, Oklahoma City, OK 73154-0465, (405)848-5801

Amer. Radio Assn. [24023], c/o John F. Lindner, Admin., 360 W 31st St., 3rd Fl., New York, NY 10001-2727, (212)239-8600

Amer. Radio Coun. - Defunct.

Amer. Radio Importers Assn. - Defunct.

Amer. Radio Relay League [21494], 225 Main St., Newington, CT 06111-1494, (860)594-0200

Amer. Radiological Nurses Assn. [15457], 7794 Grow Dr., Pensacola, FL 32514, (850)474-7292

Amer. Radium Soc. [15639], 11300 W Olympic Blvd., Ste. 600, Los Angeles, CA 90064, (310)437-0581

Amer. Rafting Assn. - Defunct.

Amer. Railroad Found. - Defunct.

Amer. Railway and Airline Supervisors Assn. [★24180]

Amer. Railway Bridge and Building Assn. [★3280]

Amer. Railway Bridge and Building Assn. [★IO]

Amer. Railway Car Export Assn. - Defunct.

Amer. Railway Car Inst. [3278], 29W 140 Butterfield Rd., Ste. 103-A, Warrenville, IL 60555, (630)393-0106

Amer. Railway Development Assn. [3279], PO Box 1025, Paoli, PA 19301, (484)467-1414

Amer. Railway Development Assn. [IO], Paoli, PA, United States

Amer. Railway Engg. and Maintenance Assn. [★IO]

Amer. Railway Engg. and Maintenance Assn. [★3280]

Amer. Railway Engg. and Maintenance of Way Assn. [3280], 10003 Derekwood Ln., Ste. 210, Lanham, MD 20706-4875, (301)459-3200

American Railway Engineering and Maintenance of Way Association [IO], Lanham, MD, United States

Amer. Rainwater Catchment Systems Assn. [7825], 4065 Broadway, San Antonio, TX 78209

Amer. Rambouillet Sheep Breeders' Assn. [5192], 1610 S State Rd. 3261, Levelland, TX 79336-9230, (806)894-3081

Amer. Ranch Horse Assn. [4841], PO Box 186, Nancy, KY 42544, (606)872-2742

Amer. Rare Breed Assn. [4496], 9921 Frank Tippett Rd., Cheltenham, MD 20623, (301)868-5718

Amer. Rationalist Fed. - Address unknown since 1995.

Amer. Rayon Inst. - Defunct.

Amer. Reading Coun. - Defunct.

Amer. Real Estate Soc. [9049], c/o Diane Quarles, Membership Services Mgr., Clemson Univ., Box 341323, Clemson, SC 29634, (864)656-1373

Amer. Real Estate and Urban Economics Assn. [9050], PO Box 9958, Richmond, VA 23228, (866)273-8321

Amer. Reciprocal Insurance Assn. - Defunct.

Amer. Record Merchandisers and Distributors Assn. - Defunct.

Amer. Record Soc. - Defunct.

Amer. Recorder Soc. [10548], 1129 Ruth Dr., St. Louis, MO 63122-1019, (314)966-4082

Amer. Recorder Teachers Assn. [8902], c/o Susan P. Groskreutz, Pres., 1355 Westminster Ln., Bourbonnais, IL 60914-1633, (815)937-9936

Amer. Records Mgt. Assn. [★2096]

Amer. Records Mgt. Assn. [★IO]

Amer. Recovery Assn. [1145], 5525 N MacArthur Blvd., Ste. 135, Irving, TX 75038, (972)755-4755

Amer. Recreation Coalition [12794], 1225 New York Ave. NW, Ste. 450, Washington, DC 20005-6405, (202)682-9530

Amer. Recreation Soc. [★6153]

Amer. Recreational Equip. Assn. [★1298]

Amer. Recreational Equip. Assn. [★IO]

Amer. Recreational Golf Assn. [3636], 7300 W Fullerton Ave., PO Box 35215, Chicago, IL 60707-0215, (708)453-0080

Amer. Recreational Racket Sports Assn. [3637], 7115 W North Ave., Ste. 272, Oak Park, IL 60302, (708)453-0080

American Recreational Sports Association [★3636]

American Recreational Sports Association [★3637]

Amer. Recreational Vehicle Living Assn. - Defunct.

Amer. Red Brangus Assn. [4242], 3995 E Hwy. 290, Dripping Springs, TX 78620, (512)858-7285

Amer. Red Cross Natl. HQ [12830], 2025 E St. NW, Washington, DC 20006, (202)303-4498

Amer. Red Cross Overseas Assn. [12831], 200 S Lebanon Rd., Loveland, OH 45140, (770)427-4943

Amer. Red Magen David for Israel - Amer. Friends of Magen David Adom [12832], 888 7th Ave., Ste. 403, New York, NY 10106, (212)757-1627

Amer. Red Magen David for Israel - Amer. Friends of Magen David Adom [IO], New York, NY, United States

Amer. Red Poll Assn. [4243], PO Box 147, Bethany, MO 64424, (660)425-7318

Amer. Reflexology Certification Bd. [13621], PO Box 740879, Arvada, CO 80006-0879, (303)933-6921

Amer. Refugee Comm. [12805], 430 Oak Grove St., Ste. 204, Minneapolis, MN 55403, (612)872-7060

Amer. Refugee Comm. [IO], Minneapolis, MN, United States

Amer. Registry of Clinical Radiography Technologists - Defunct.

Amer. Registry of Diagnostic Medical Sonography [16437], 51 Monroe St., Plz. East One, Rockville, MD 20850-2400, (301)738-8401

Amer. Registry of Inhalation Therapists [★16626]

Amer. Registry of Medical Assistants [15082], 69 Southwick Rd., Westfield, MA 01085-4729, (413)562-7336

Amer. Registry of Pathology [15858], c/o Armed Forces Inst. of Pathology, 14th St. and Alaska Ave. NW, Bldg. 54, Washington, DC 20306-6000, (301)578-1646

Amer. Registry of Physical Therapists - Defunct.

Amer. Registry of Professional Animal Scientists [215], 1111 N Dunlap Ave., Savoy, IL 61874, (217)356-5390

Amer. Registry of Professional Entomologists [★7062]

Amer. Registry of Radiologic Technologists [15128], 1255 Northland Dr., St. Paul, MN 55120-1155, (651)687-0048

Amer. Registry of Radiological Technicians [★15128]

Amer. Registry of X-Ray Technicians [★15128]

Amer. Rehabilitation Assn. [★16312]

Amer. Rehabilitation Comm. [★12075]

Amer. Rehabilitation Counseling Assn. [16313], c/o Irmo Marini, PhD, Pres., Univ. of Texas, Pan Amer. Dept. of Rehabilitation, Coll. of Hea. Sciences and Human Services, 1201 W Univ. Dr., Edinburg, TX 78539-2999, (956)316-7035

Amer. Rehabilitation Economics Assn. [16314], 127 N Westwind Dr., El Cajon, CA 92020-2955, (800)317-AREA

Amer. Rehabilitation Found. [★16335]

Amer. Reiki Assn. [★13648]

Amer. Reiki Assn. [★IO]

Amer. Reiki Master Assn. [13622], c/o Cheri L. Robertson, Pres., PO Box 130, Lake City, FL 32056-0130, (904)755-9638

Amer. Relief for Italy [★13474]

Amer. Relief for Korea - Defunct.

Amer. Relief for Poland - Defunct.

Amer. Reloaders Assn. - Defunct.

Amer. Remittances Everywhere; Cooperative for [★12838]

Amer. Remount Assn. Half-Thoroughbred Registry - Address unknown since 2007.

Amer. Renewal Found. [18280], PO Box 54, Corbin, VA 22446

Amer. Rental Assn. [3377], 1900 19th St., Moline, IL 61265, (800)334-2177

Amer. Repossessors Assn. [★1145]

Amer. Rescue Dog Assn. [12889], PO Box 613, Bristow, VA 20136

Amer. Rescue Dog Assn. [IO], Bristow, VA, United States

Amer. Rescue Team Intl. [12287], PO Box 237, San Francisco, CA 94127, (415)533-2231

Amer. Rescue Workers [13153], 25 Ross St., Williamsport, PA 17701, (570)323-8693

Amer. Res. Inst. for Community Development - Address unknown since 1995.

Amer. Res. Inst. in Turkey [11060], c/o Univ. of Pennsylvania Museum, 3260 South St., Philadelphia, PA 19104-6324, (215)898-3474

Amer. Res. Inst. in Turkey [IO], Philadelphia, PA, United States

Amer. Resort Development Assn. [3298], 1201 15th St. NW, No. 400, Washington, DC 20005-2842, (202)371-6700

Amer. Resort and Residential Development Assn. [★3298]

Amer. Resources Gp. [4350], 374 Maple Ave. E, Ste. 310, Vienna, VA 22180-4751, (703)255-2700

Amer. Restaurant China Coun. - Address unknown since 2006.

Amer. Restaurant Inst. [★1957]

Amer. Restitution Assn. - Defunct.

Amer. Retail Assn. Executives - Defunct.

Amer. Retail Coal Assn. - Defunct.

Amer. Retail Fed. [★3423]

Amer. Retirees Assn. [21184], PO Box 2333, Redlands, CA 92373-0781, (909)557-0107

Amer. Retreaders Assn. [★3813]

Amer. Retreaders Assn. [★IO]

Amer. Reusable Textile Assn. [3771], PO Box 1053, Mulberry, FL 33860-1053, (863)660-5350

Amer. Revenue Assn. [22788], c/o Eric Jackson, Pres., PO Box 728, Leesport, PA 19533-0728, (610)926-6200

American Revenue Association [IO], Leesport, PA, United States

American Revolution

Aaron Burr Accord [11097]

Amer. Friends of Lafayette [11102]

Amer. Revolution Round Table [9372]

Black Revolutionary War Patriots Found. [20669]

Bostonian Soc. [10097]

Centennial Legion of Historic Military Commands [21240]

Colonial Order of the Acorn [20735]

Colonial Soc. of Massachusetts [10104]

Daughters of the Cincinnati [20670]

Descendants of the Signers of the Declaration of Independence [20671]

Flagon and Trencher - Descendants of Colonial Tavern Keepers [20737]

Friends of Patrick Henry [11115]

Gen. Soc. of Colonial Wars [20738]

Gen. Soc. of Mayflower Descendants [21247]

Gen. Soc., Sons of the Revolution [20672]

Hereditary Order of Descendants of the Loyalists and Patriots of the Amer. Revolution [20673]

H.M. 10th Regiment of Foot, Amer. Contingent [9373]

Holland Soc. of New York [20740]

Jamestowne Soc. [20742]

Johannes Schwalm Historical Assn. [21128]

Junior Amer. Citizens [11335]

Natl. Center for the Amer. Revolution [10134]

Natl. Soc. of the Children of the Amer. Revolution [20674]

Reference to "IO" in place of a book number signifies that the association may be found in the 45th edition of International Organizations.

Natl. Soc. of the Colonial Dames of Am. [20743]
Natl. Soc. Colonial Dames XVII Century [20744]
Natl. Soc., Daughters of the Amer. Colonists [20746]
Natl. Soc., Daughters of the Amer. Revolution [20675]
Natl. Soc., Sons of the Amer. Revolution [20676]
Natl. Soc. Women Descendants of the Ancient and Honorable Artillery Company [20749]
Natl. Temple Hill Assn. [10050]
Northwest Territory Alliance [9374]
Order of Americans of Armorial Ancestry [20750]
Order of the Founders and Patriots of Am. [20755]
Patriotic Order Sons of Am. [21242]
Soc. of the Ark and the Dove [20758]
Soc. of the Cincinnati [20677]
Soc. of the Cincinnati [IO]
Soc. of Daughters of Holland Dames [20759]
Soc. of the Descendants of the Colonial Clergy [20760]
Soc. of the Descendants of Washington's Army at Valley Forge [20678]
Soc. of the Founders and Friends of Norwich, Connecticut [10063]
Valley Forge Historical Soc. [9375]
Veteran Corps of Artillery, State of New York, Constituting the Military Soc. of the War of 1812 [21204]
Amer. Revolution Bicentennial Administration - Defunct.
Amer. Revolution; Hereditary Order of Descendants of the Loyalists and Patriots of the [20673]
Amer. Revolution Round Table [9372], c/o Mr. David W. Jacobs, Chm., 6 Grovedale Rd., Niantic, CT 06357, (718)762-2817
Amer. Reye's Syndrome Assn. - Defunct.
Amer. Reye's Syndrome Soc. [★16366]
Amer. Rheumatism Assn. [★16367]
Amer. Rheumatism Assn. [★IO]
Amer. Rhinologic Soc. [15823], c/o Wendi Perez, Exec. Dir., 9 Sunset Terr., Warwick, NY 10990, (845)988-1631
Amer. Rhododendron Soc. [22500], PO Box 525, Niagara Falls, NY 14304, (416)424-1942
Amer. Rice Growers Cooperative Assn. - Defunct.
Amer. Riding Instructors Assn. [22583], 28801 Trenton Ct., Bonita Springs, FL 34134-3337, (239)948-3232
Amer. Right to Read - Defunct.
Amer. Right of Way Assn. [★6246]
Amer. Right of Way Assn. [★IO]
Amer. Rights Coalition - Address unknown since 2006.
Amer. Rights at Work [17968], 1100 17th St. NW, Ste. 950, Washington, DC 20036, (202)822-2127
Amer. Risk and Insurance Assn. [8574], 716 Providence Rd., Malvern, PA 19355-3402, (610)640-1997
Amer. River Touring Assn. [936], 24000 Casa Loma Rd., Groveland, CA 95321, (209)962-7873
Amer. Rivers [4351], 1101 14th St. NW, Ste. 1400, Washington, DC 20005, (202)347-7550
Amer. Rivers Conservation Coun. [★4351]
Amer. Road Builders Assn. [★6313]
Amer. Road Makers [★6313]
Amer. Road Racing Assn. - Address unknown since 1999.
Amer. Road and Trans. Builders Assn. [6313], The ARTBA Bldg., 1219 28th St. NW, Washington, DC 20007-3389, (202)289-4434
Amer. Robot Soc. - Address unknown since 1986.
Amer. Rock Art Res. Assn. [6438], Arizona State Museum, Univ. of Arizona, Box 210026, Tucson, AZ 85721-0026, (888)668-0052
Amer. Rock Garden Soc. [★22535]
Amer. Rock Garden Soc. [★IO]
Amer. Rock Mechanics Assn. [3690], c/o Peter H. Smeallie, Exec. Dir., 600 Woodland Terr., Alexandria, VA 22302, (703)683-1808
Amer. Rocket Soc. [★6369]
Amer. Roentgen Ray Soc. [16277], 44211 Slatestone Ct., Leesburg, VA 20176-5109, (703)729-3353
American Roentgen Ray Society [IO], Leesburg, VA, United States

Amer. Romagnola Assn. [4244], 3815 Touzalin, Ste. 104, Lincoln, NE 68507, (402)466-3334
Amer. Roman Catholic Women's Alliance; Lithuanian [19211]
Amer. Romanian Acad. of Arts and Sciences [9606], c/o Dr. Nicolae H. Pavel, Sec. Gen., Ohio Univ., Dept. of Mathematics, Athens, OH 45701, (740)593-1267
Amer. Romanian Acad. of Arts and Sciences [IO], Athens, OH, United States
Amer. Romanian Comm. for Assistance to Refugees - Address unknown since 2001.
Amer. Romanian Orthodox Youth [20540], c/o John E. Lazar, Pres., 18430 W Nine Mile Rd., Southfield, MI 48075, (734)646-6420
American Romanian Orthodox Youth [IO], Southfield, MI, United States
Amer. Romney Breeders' Assn. [5193], 744 Riverbanks Rd., Grants Pass, OR 97527-9607, (541)476-6428
Amer. Roque and Croquet Assn. [23090], PO Box 2304, Richmond, IN 47375-2304, (765)962-7191
Amer. Roque League [★23090]
Amer. Rose Coun. - Defunct.
Amer. Rose Found. [★22501]
Amer. Rose Soc. [22501], 8877 Jefferson Paige Rd., PO Box 30000, Shreveport, LA 71119, (318)938-5402
Amer. Rosie the Riveter Assn. [21388], c/o Dr. Frances T. Carter, Founder/Natl. Exec. Dir. Emeritus, 3470 Loch Ridge Dr., Birmingham, AL 35216-4475, (205)822-4106
American Rosie the Riveter Association [IO], Birmingham, AL, United States
Amer. Rottweiler Club [22208], c/o Diane Garnett, Pres., 18182 E Euclid Pl., Aurora, CO 80016-1100, (303)699-5029
Amer. Rowing Assn. - Address unknown since 1989.
Amer. Royal Assn. [4995], 1701 Amer. Royal Ct., Kansas City, MO 64102, (816)221-9800
Amer. RSROA Roller Hockey Assn. - Address unknown since 1995.
Amer. Rubberband Duckpin Bowling Cong. - Address unknown since 2002.
Amer. Running Assn. [23651], 4405 East-West Hwy., Ste. 405, Bethesda, MD 20814, (301)913-9517
Amer. Rural Hea. Assn. [★16248]
Amer. Russian Aid Assn. - Address unknown since 1999.
American-Russian Chamber of Commerce and Indus. [24261], Aon Center, 200 E Randolph St., Ste. 2200, Chicago, IL 60601, (312)494-6562
Amer. Russian Slavonic Democratic Club - Address unknown since 1995.
Amer. Russian Theatrical Alliance [11001], 1409 Midvale Ave., Ste. 105, Los Angeles, CA 90024, (310)312-4989
Amer. Sabbath Tract and Commun. Coun. [★20545]
Amer. Sabbath Tract Soc. [★20545]
Amer. Sable Rabbit Soc. - Defunct.
Amer. Saddle Horse Breeders Assn. [★4842]
Amer. Saddle Horse Youth Club - Defunct.
Amer. Saddlebred Horse Assn. [4842], 4083 Iron Works Pkwy., Lexington, KY 40511, (859)259-2742
Amer. Saddlebred Pleasure Horse Assn. [★4842]
Amer. Saddlebred Sporthorse Assn. [4843], 520 Byers Rd., Chester Springs, PA 19425, (610)458-8652
Amer. Safe Climbing Assn. [21950], PO Box 1814, Bishop, CA 93515, (650)843-1473
The Amer. Safe Deposit Assn. [460], PO Box 519, Franklin, IN 46131, (317)738-4432
Amer. Safety Belt Coun. [★377]
Amer. Sail Training Assn. [23153], PO Box 1459, Newport, RI 02840, (401)846-1775
Amer. Sailing Assn. [23154], 5301 Beethoven St., Ste. 265, Los Angeles, CA 90066, (310)822-7171
Amer. Sailing Assn. Found. [23155], c/o Amer. Sailing Assn., 5301 Beethoven St., Ste. 265, Los Angeles, CA 90066-7052, (310)822-7171
Amer. Sailing Educ. Assn. [★8811]
Amer. St. Boniface Soc. [19568], PO Box 1352, Bronx, NY 10466, (718)994-0989
Amer. Salers Assn. [4245], 19590 E Main St., No. 202, Parker, CO 80138, (303)770-9292

Amer. Salers Junior Assn. [4246], c/o Amer. Salers Assn., 19590 E Main St., No. 202, Parker, CO 80138, (303)770-9292
Amer. Sales Assn. - Defunct.
Amer. Saluki Assn. - Address unknown since 2005.
Amer. Salvage Pool Assn. [342], PMB 709, 2100 Roswell Rd., Ste. 200 C, Marietta, GA 30062, (678)560-6678
Amer. Salvation Army [★13153]
Amer. Sambo Assn. [23580], PO Box 5773, Long Island City, NY 11105, (718)728-8054
Amer. Samoa Natl. Olympic Comm. [IO], Pago Pago, American Samoa
Amer. Samoa Track and Field Assn. [IO], Pago Pago, American Samoa
Amer. Sanatorium Assn. [★IO]
Amer. Sanatorium Assn. [★16642]
Amer. Sanctuary Assn. [4156], 2308 Chatfield, Las Vegas, NV 89128, (702)804-8562
Amer. Santal Mission [★20234]
Amer. Santal Mission [★IO]
Amer. Satellite TV Alliance - Defunct.
Amer. Satin Rabbit Breeders' Assn. [5140], c/o Clarence Linsey, Sec.-Treas., 316 S Mahaffie, Olathe, KS 66061-4756, (913)764-1531
Amer./Saudi Business Roundtable - Defunct.
Amer. Savings Educ. Coun. [8440], 1100 13th St. NW, Ste. 878, Washington, DC 20005-4204, (202)659-0670
Amer. Savings and Loan Leagues [★459]
Amer. Scallop Assn. [3491], c/o Harvey Mickelson, Gen. Counsel, 30 Cornell St., New Bedford, MA 02740, (508)993-8800
American-Scandinavian Found. [10942], 58 Park Ave., New York, NY 10016, (212)879-9779
American-Scandinavian Found. [IO], New York, NY, United States
Amer. Scandinavian Student Exchange [★IO]
Amer. Scandinavian Student Exchange [★8600]
Amer. Scenic and Historic Preservation Soc. - Defunct.
Amer. Schizophrenia Assn. - Defunct.
American/Schleswig-Holstein Heritage Soc. [19066], PO Box 506, Walcott, IA 52773-0506, (563)284-4184
Amer. Scholastic Associates Intl. [★8230]
Amer. Scholastic Associates Intl. [★IO]
Amer. School Band Directors' Assn. [8903], PO Box 696, Guttenberg, IA 52052, (563)252-2500
Amer. School and Community Safety Assn. [★12989]
Amer. School Counselor Assn. [8163], 1101 King St., Ste. 625, Alexandria, VA 22314, (703)683-2722
American School Counselor Association [IO], Alexandria, VA, United States
Amer. School Food Ser. Assn. [★9173]
Amer. School Hea. Assn. [14718], PO Box 708, Kent, OH 44240, (330)678-1601
Amer. Schools Assn. [8164], PO Box 577820, Chicago, IL 60657-7820, (800)230-2263
Amer. Schools for the Deaf; Assn. of Superintendents and Principals of [★14749]
Amer. Schools for the Deaf; Conf. of Executives of [★14749]
Amer. Schools of Oriental Res. [9615], 656 Beacon St., 5th Fl., Boston, MA 02215-2006, (617)353-6570
Amer. Schools of Oriental Res. [IO], Boston, MA, United States
Amer. Schools in South Am; Assn. of [8642]
Amer. Schooner Assn. - Address unknown since 1995.
Amer. Science Film Assn. - Defunct.
Amer. Sci. Affiliation [20546], PO Box 668, Ipswich, MA 01938, (978)356-5656
Amer. Sci. Glassblowers Soc. [3481], PO Box 778, Madison, NC 27025, (336)427-2406
Amer. Scientists; Fed. of [18445]
Amer. Scotch Highland Breeders Assn. [★4227]
Amer. Scottish Found. [19347], 575 Madison Ave., Ste. 1006, New York, NY 10022-2511, (212)605-0338
Amer. Scouting Traders Assn. [★22057]
Amer. Scouting Traders Assn. [★IO]
Amer. Screenwriters Assn. [IO], Beverly Hills, CA, United States

---

A star before a book entry number signifies that the name is not listed separately, but is mentioned within the entry.

Amer. Screenwriters Assn. [4060], 269 S Beverly Dr., Ste. 2600, Beverly Hills, CA 90212-3807, (866)265-9091

Amer. Seafood Distributors Assn. - Defunct.

Amer. Seafood Retailers Assn. - Address unknown since 1994.

Amer. Sealyham Terrier Club [22209], c/o Sharon Yard, Pres., 14111 Rehoboth Church Rd., Lovettsville, VA 20180-3217, (540)882-3492

Amer. Seamen's Friend Soc. - Defunct.

Amer. in Search - Defunct.

Amer. Seat Belt Coun. [★377]

Amer. Seat Belt Coun. [★377]

Amer. Secretaries of State; Assn. of [★6277]

Amer. Sect., Intl. Assn. for Testing Materials [★7789]

Amer. Sect. of the Intl. Solar Energy Soc. [★7676]

Amer. Secularist Assn. - Defunct.

Amer. Security Coun. [18586], 1239 Pennsylvania Ave. SE, Washington, DC 20003, (202)546-5200

Amer. Security Coun. Educ. Found. [★16986]

Amer. Security Coun. Found. [16986], 1239 Pennsylvania Ave. SE, Washington, DC 20003, (202)546-5200

Amer. Seed Res. Found. [5173], 225 Reinekers Ln., Ste. 650, Alexandria, VA 22314-2875, (703)837-8140

Amer. Seed Trade Assn. [5174], 225 Reinekers Ln., Ste. 650, Alexandria, VA 22314-2875, (703)837-8140

Amer. Self-Help CH [★13013]

Amer. Self-Help Gp. CH [13013], 100 E Hanover Ave., Ste. 202, Cedar Knolls, NJ 07927-2020, (973)326-6789

Amer. Self-Protection Assn. [23712], c/o Dr. Evan S. Baltazzi, Founder/Chm., 825 Greengate Oval, Sagamore Hills, OH 44067-2311

Amer. Seminar Leaders Assn. [8147], 2405 E Washington Blvd., Pasadena, CA 91104, (626)791-1211

Amer. Senior Citizens Assn. - Defunct.

Amer. Senior Fitness Assn. [15961], PO Box 2575, New Smyrna Beach, FL 32170, (386)423-6634

Amer. Seniors Housing Assn. [12304], 5100 Wisconsin Ave. NW, Ste. 307, Washington, DC 20016, (202)237-0900

Amer. Sephardi Fed. [20117], 15 W 16th St., New York, NY 10011-6301, (212)294-8350

Amer. Sepsis Alliance [14946], c/o Dr. Carl Flatley, Chm., DDS, 1865 Salem Ct., Dunedin, FL 34698, (727)460-7765

Amer.-Serbian Cultural Assn. - Address unknown since 1995.

Amer. Service Veterans Assn. - Address unknown since 2004.

Amer. Servicemen's Union - Address unknown since 1995.

Amer. Sewing Guild [22150], 9660 Hillcroft, Ste. 510, Houston, TX 77096, (713)729-3000

Amer. Shagya Arabian Verband [4844], 15918 Porter Rd., Verona, KY 41092

Amer. Shark Assn. [23156], 5435 Wells Curtice Rd., Canandaigua, NY 14424

Amer. Sheep Indus. Assn. [5194], 9785 Maroon Cir., Ste. 360, Centennial, CO 80112, (303)771-3500

Amer. Sheep Producers' Coun. [★5194]

Amer. Shetland Pony Club/American Miniature Horse Registry [4845], 81-B Queenwood Rd., Morton, IL 61550, (309)263-4044

Amer. Shetland Sheepdog Assn. [22210], c/o Mrs. Susan Christie, Treas., 41044 Savage Rd., Antioch, IL 60002-7222, (847)838-3049

Amer. Shetland Sheepdog Assn. - Defunct.

Amer. Shiatsu Assn. [★15024]

Amer. Shih Tzu Club [22211], 279 Sun Valley Ct., Ripon, CA 95366

Amer. Shipbuilding Assn. [591], 600 Pennsylvania Ave. SE, Ste. 305, Washington, DC 20003-4345, (202)544-8170

Amer. Shire Horse Assn. [4846], c/o Pamela Correll, Admin. Sec., 1211 Hill Harrell Rd., Effingham, SC 29541, (843)629-0072

Amer. Shooting Sports Coun. - Defunct.

American Shore and Beach Preservation Association [4352], 5460 Beaujolais Ln., Fort Myers, FL 33919-2704, (239)489-2616

Amer. Shorin Kempo Karate Assn. [23581], c/o Terry L. Bryan, Pres., 1587 York St., Colorado Springs, CO 80918, (719)598-0398

American Shorin Kempo Karate Association [IO], Colorado Springs, CO, United States

Amer. Short Line Railroad Assn. [★3281]

Amer. Short Line and Regional Railroad Assn. [3281], 50 F St. NW, Ste. 7020, Washington, DC 20001-1507, (202)628-4500

Amer. Shorthorn Assn. [4247], 8288 Hascall St., Omaha, NE 68124-3234, (402)393-7200

Amer. Shorthorn Breeders Assn. [★4247]

Amer. Shortwave Listeners Club [21495], 16182 Ballad Ln., Huntington Beach, CA 92649-2272, (714)846-1685

Amer. Shotcrete Assn. [916], 38800 Country Club Dr., Farmington Hills, MI 48331, (248)848-3780

Amer. Shoulder and Elbow Surgeons [16567], 6300 N River Rd., Ste. 727, Rosemont, IL 60018-4226, (847)698-1629

Amer. Shrimp Processors Assn. - Address unknown since 2007.

Amer. Shrimpboat Assn. - Defunct.

Amer. Shropshire Registry Assn. [5195], c/o Mark McCabe, Youth Page Coor., 5154 Nickelson Rd., Prospect, OH 43342, (740)494-2969

Amer. Shuffleboard Company [★23734]

Amer. Siam Soc. - Defunct.

Amer. Sickle Cell Anemia Assn. [16415], 10300 Carnegie Ave., Cleveland Clinic/East Off. Bldg. (EEb18), Cleveland, OH 44106, (216)229-8600

Amer. Sickle Cell Anemia Soc. [★16415]

Amer. Sickle Cell Soc. [★16415]

Amer. SIDS Inst. [★16523]

Amer. Sighthound Field Assn. [22212], c/o Marilyn Standerford, Pres., 15054 Dayton St., Omaha, NE 68137, (402)895-4626

Amer. Sightseeing Assn. [★IO]

Amer. Sightseeing Intl. [IO], Toronto, ON, Canada

Amer. Sign Language Teachers Assn. [14741], PO Box 92445, Rochester, NY 14692

Amer. Silk Coun. - Defunct.

Amer. Silkie Bantam Club [5109], c/o Sheila Gordon, Sec.-Treas., 41429 Butler Ct., Indio, CA 92203, (760)342-1649

Amer. Simmental Assn. [4248], 1 Simmental Way, Bozeman, MT 59715, (406)587-4531

Amer. Singers Club [21841], c/o Ron Moy, Sec.-Treas., 1141 Norwood Ave., Oakland, CA 94610-1837, (510)524-4077

Amer. Single Shot Rifle Assn. [23714], c/o Keith Foster, Membership Admin., 15770 Rd. 1037, Oakwood, OH 45873, (419)393-2976

American Single Shot Rifle Association [IO], Oakwood, OH, United States

Amer. Singles Golf Assn. [13106], PO Box 848, Pineville, NC 28134, (704)889-4600

Amer. Ski-Bike Assn. [23801], PO Box 40, Lake George, CO 80827

Amer. Ski Fed. - Address unknown since 2001.

Amer. Ski Mfrs. Assn. - Defunct.

Amer. Ski Teachers Assn. of Natur Teknik - Defunct.

Amer. Skin Assn. [14195], 346 Park Ave. S, New York, NY 10010, (212)889-4858

Amer. Sleep Apnea Assn. [16421], 1424 K St. NW, Ste. 302, Washington, DC 20005, (202)293-3650

American-Slovenian Polka Found. [10549], 605 E 222nd St., Euclid, OH 44123, (216)261-3263

Amer. Slow Sand Assn. - Defunct.

Amer. Small Bus. Assn. [★3603]

Amer. Small Bus. Travel Alliance [3906], PO Box 270543, Flower Mound, TX 75027-0543, (469)648-0190

Amer. Small Businesses Assn. [3603], 206 E Coll. St., Ste. 201, Grapevine, TX 76051, (800)942-2722

Amer. Small and Rural Hosp. Assn. [★16248]

Amer. Smoking Pipe Mfrs. Assn. - Defunct.

Amer. Snowmobile Assn. - Defunct.

Amer. Snowplowing Assn. - Defunct.

Amer. Social Hea. Assn. [16410], PO Box 13827, Research Triangle Park, NC 27709, (919)361-8400

Amer. Social Hea. Assn; Herpes Rsrc. Center - [16412]

Amer. Social Hea. Assn; HPV Support Prog. - [16413]

Amer. Social Hygiene Assn. [★16410]

Amer. Soc. of Abdominal Surgeons [16568], 1 E Emerson St., Melrose, MA 02176, (781)665-6102

Amer. Soc. for Abrasive Methods [★1989]

Amer. Soc. for Abrasive Methods [★IO]

Amer. Soc. for Abrasives [★IO]

Amer. Soc. for Abrasives [★1989]

Amer. Soc. of Access Professionals [5814], 1444 I St. NW, Ste. 700, Washington, DC 20005-6542, (202)712-9054

Amer. Soc. of Addiction Medicine [16501], 4601 N. Park Ave., Upper Arcade No. 101, Chevy Chase, MD 20815, (301)656-3920

Amer. Soc. for Adolescent Psychiatry [16078], PO Box 570218, Dallas, TX 75357-0218, (972)686-6166

American Society for Adolescent Psychiatry [IO], Dallas, TX, United States

Amer. Soc. of Adults with Pseudo-Obstruction [★IO]

Amer. Soc. of Adults with Pseudo-Obstruction [★14410]

Amer. Soc. for Advancement of Anesthesia in Dentistry [★13673]

Amer. Soc. for Advancement of Anesthesia in Dentistry [★IO]

Amer. Soc. for Advancement of Anesthesia and Sedation in Dentistry [IO], Bound Brook, NJ, United States

Amer. Soc. for Advancement of Anesthesia and Sedation in Dentistry [13673], 6 E Union Ave., Bound Brook, NJ 08805, (732)469-9050

Amer. Soc. for Advancement of Gen. Anesthesia in Dentistry [★13673]

Amer. Soc. for Advancement of Gen. Anesthesia in Dentistry [★IO]

Amer. Soc. for Advancement of Haifa Inst. of Tech. [★IO]

Amer. Soc. for Advancement of Haifa Inst. of Tech. [★8677]

Amer. Soc. for the Advancement of Pharmacotherapy [16134], c/o Keith Cooke, Div. Services Off., Amer. Psychological Assn., 750 1st St. NE, Washington, DC 20002-4242, (202)216-7602

Amer. Soc. for the Advancement of Proj. Mgt. [2519], 6547 N Acad., No. 404, Colorado Springs, CO 80918, (931)647-7373

American Society for the Advancement of Project Management [IO], Colorado Springs, CO, United States

Amer. Soc. for the Advancement of Violin Making [★10720]

Amer. Soc. of Aeronautical Engineers [★6520]

Amer. Soc. of Aeronautical Engineers [★IO]

Amer. Soc. of Aerospace Pilots - Defunct.

Amer. Soc. for Aesthetic Plastic Surgery [14042], 11081 Winners Cir., Los Alamitos, CA 90720-2813, (562)799-2356

Amer. Soc. for Aesthetics [9545], Armstrong Atlantic State Univ., 11935 Abercorn St., Savannah, GA 31419, (912)921-2124

Amer. Soc. for Aesthetics [IO], Savannah, GA, United States

Amer. Soc. of African Culture - Defunct.

Amer. Soc. on Aging [11275], 833 Market St., Ste. 511, San Francisco, CA 94103-1824, (415)974-9600

Amer. Soc. of Agricultural Appraisers [271], PO Box 186, Twin Falls, ID 83303-0186, (208)733-2323

Amer. Soc. of Agricultural and Biological Engineers [6990], 2950 Niles Rd., St. Joseph, MI 49085-8607, (269)429-0300

Amer. Soc. of Agricultural and Biological Engineers [IO], St. Joseph, MI, United States

Amer. Soc. of Agricultural Consultants [IO], Denver, CO, United States

Amer. Soc. of Agricultural Consultants [4074], N78W14573 Appleton Ave., No. 287, Menomonee Falls, WI 53051, (262)253-6902

Amer. Soc. of Agricultural Engineers [★6990]

Amer. Soc. of Agricultural Engineers [★IO]

Amer. Soc. of Agronomy [4096], 677 S Segoe Rd., Madison, WI 53711, (608)273-8080

Amer. Soc. of Alderian Psychology [★16162]

Amer. Soc. for the Alexander Technique [13623], PO Box 60008, Florence, MA 01062-0008, (413)584-2359

Reference to "IO" in place of a book number signifies that the association may be found in the 45th edition of International Organizations.

Amer. Soc. of Allied Hea. Professions [★8855]

Amer. Soc. of Alternative Therapists [13624], PO Box 703, Rockport, MA 01966, (978)281-4400

Amer. Soc. for Amusement Park Safety and Security [3526], c/o George Hull, Treas., Brookfield Zoo, 3300 Golf Rd., Brookfield, IL 60513, (708)485-0023

Amer. Soc. of Ancient Instruments - Defunct.

Amer. Soc. of Andrology [16702], 1100 E Woodfield Rd., Ste. No. 520, Schaumburg, IL 60173, (847)619-4909

Amer. Soc. of Anesthesia Technologists and Technicians [15083], 7044 S 13th St., Oak Creek, WI 53154-1429, (414)908-4942

Amer. Soc. of Anesthesiologists [13674], 520 N Northwest Hwy., Park Ridge, IL 60068-2573, (847)825-5586

Amer. Soc. of Anesthetists [★13674]

Amer. Soc. of Animal Sci. [4150], 1111 N Dunlap Ave., Savoy, IL 61874, (217)356-9050

Amer. Soc. of Anthropometric Medicine and Nutrition - Defunct.

Amer. Soc. for Apheresis [13706]

Amer. Soc. of Appraisers [272], 555 Herndon Pkwy., Ste. 125, Herndon, VA 20170, (703)478-2228

Amer. Soc. of Architectural Hardware Consultants [★1821]

Amer. Soc. of Architectural Hardware Consultants [★IO]

Amer. Soc. of Architectural Illustrators [289], 3301 N Garden Ln., Avondale, AZ 85392, (623)433-8782

Amer. Soc. of Arms Collectors - Address unknown since 1997.

Amer. Soc. of Artists [9491], PO Box 1326, Palatine, IL 60078, (312)751-2500

Amer. Soc. of Assn. Executives [315], 1575 I St. NW, Washington, DC 20005, (202)371-0940

Amer. Soc. of Assn. Executives [IO], Washington, DC, United States

Amer. Soc. for Assn. Publishing - Address unknown since 2003.

Amer. Soc. of Auctioneers - Defunct.

Amer. Soc. for Automation in Pharmacy [2969], 492 Norristown Rd., Ste. 160, Blue Bell, PA 19422, (610)825-7783

Amer. Soc. of Bakery Engineers [★447]

Amer. Soc. of Baking [447], 533 1st St. E, Sonoma, CA 95476, (707)935-0103

Amer. Soc. of Bank Directors - Address unknown since 2003.

Amer. Soc. of Bariatric Physicians [15575], 2821 S Parker Rd., Ste. 625, Aurora, CO 80014, (303)770-2526

Amer. Soc. for Bariatric Surgery [16569], 100 SW 75th St., Ste. 201, Gainesville, FL 32607, (352)331-4900

Amer. Soc. of Barmasters - Defunct.

Amer. Soc. for Biochemistry and Molecular Biology [6546], 9650 Rockville Pike, Bethesda, MD 20814-3996, (301)634-7145

Amer. Soc. for Bioethics and Humanities [8845], 4700 W Lake Ave., Glenview, IL 60025-1485, (847)375-4745

Amer. Soc. of Biological Chemists [★6546]

Amer. Soc. of Biomechanics [6561], c/o Max Kurz , PhD, Membership Chm., Univ. of Houston, Dept. of Hea. and Human Performance, 104S Garrison, 3855 Holman St., Houston, TX 77004, (713)743-2274

Amer. Soc. for Blood and Marrow Transplantation [16665], 85 W Algonquin Rd., Ste. 550, Arlington Heights, IL 60005, (847)427-0224

Amer. Soc. of Body and Design Engineers - Address unknown since 2001.

Amer. Soc. for Bone and Mineral Res. [15787], 2025 M St. NW, Ste. 800, Washington, DC 20036-3309, (202)367-1161

Amer. Soc. for Bookplate Collectors and Designers [21965], PO Box 14964, Tucson, AZ 85732-4964, (781)393-9970

American Society of Bookplate Collectors and Designers [IO], Cambridge, MA, United States

Amer. Soc. of Botanical Artists [9492], 47 5th Ave., New York, NY 10003, (212)691-9080

Amer. Soc. of Breast Disease [13772], PO Box 140186, Dallas, TX 75214, (214)368-6836

Amer. Soc. of Breast Surgeons [16570], 5950 Symphony Woods Rd., Ste. 212, Columbia, MD 21044, (410)992-5470

Amer. Soc. of Brewing Chemists [6670], 3340 Pilot Knob Rd., St. Paul, MN 55121-2097, (651)454-7250

American Society of Brewing Chemists [IO], St. Paul, MN, United States

Amer. Soc. of Bus. Press Editors [★3084]

Amer. Soc. of Bus. Publication Editors [3084], 214 N Hale St., Wheaton, IL 60187, (630)510-4588

Amer. Soc. of Camera Collectors [10844], 6445 Antiqua Pl., West Hills, CA 91307, (818)888-1125

Amer. Soc. of Cardiovascular Professionals/Society for Cardiovascular Mgt. [★13885]

Amer. Soc. of Cartographers - Defunct.

Amer. Soc. of Cataract and Refractive Surgery [15665], 4000 Legato Rd., Ste. 700, Fairfax, VA 22033, (703)591-2220

Amer. Soc. for Cell Biology [6562], 8120 Woodmont Ave., Ste. 750, Bethesda, MD 20814-2762, (301)347-9300

Amer. Soc. of Certified Engg. Technicians [6991], PO Box 1536, Brandon, MS 39043, (601)824-8991

Amer. Soc. of Check Collectors [22726], 473 E Elm St., Sycamore, IL 60178

Amer. Soc. of Childbirth Educators [15589], PO Box 2282, Sedona, AZ 86339, (928)284-9897

Amer. Soc. of Chinese Medicine - Defunct.

Amer. Soc. of Christian Ethics [★12128]

Amer. Soc. of Christian Social Ethics in the U.S. and Canada [★12128]

Amer. Soc. for Church Growth [19841], c/o Dr. Alan McMahan, School of Intercultural Stud., Biola Univ., 13800 Biola Ave., La Mirada, CA 90639-0001, (562)944-0351

Amer. Soc. of Church History [20078], c/o Yale Divinity School, 409 Prospect St., Rm. S127, New Haven, CT 06511, (203)432-3158

American Society of Church History [IO], New Haven, CT, United States

Amer. Soc. of Cinematographers [1377], PO Box 2230, Hollywood, CA 90078, (323)969-4333

Amer. Soc. of Civil Engineers [6992], 1801 Alexander Bell Dr., Reston, VA 20191-4400, (703)295-6300

Amer. Soc. for Clinical Evoked Potentials - Defunct.

Amer. Soc. of Clinical Hypnosis [14921], 140 N Bloomingdale Rd., Bloomingdale, IL 60108-1017, (630)980-4740

Amer. Soc. of Clinical Hypnosis - Educ. and Res. Found. [14922], 140 N Bloomingdale Rd., Bloomingdale, IL 60108-1017, (630)980-4740

Amer. Soc. for Clinical Investigation [14020], 35 Res. Dr., Ste. 300, Ann Arbor, MI 48103, (734)222-6050

Amer. Soc. for Clinical Lab. Sci. [14992], 6701 Democracy Blvd., Ste. 300, Bethesda, MD 20817, (301)657-2768

Amer. Soc. of Clinical Lab. Technicians [★14992]

Amer. Soc. for Clinical Nutrition [15547], 9650 Rockville Pike, Bethesda, MD 20814-3998, (301)634-7110

Amer. Soc. of Clinical Oncology [15640], 1900 Duke St., Ste. 200, Alexandria, VA 22314, (703)299-0150

Amer. Soc. of Clinical Pathologists [★15859]

Amer. Soc. for Clinical Pathology [15859], 33 W Monroe, Ste. 1600, Chicago, IL 60603, (312)541-4999

Amer. Soc. of Clinical Pharmacology and Chemotherapy [★15920]

Amer. Soc. for Clinical Pharmacology and Therapeutics [15920], 528 N Washington St., Alexandria, VA 22314-2314, (703)836-6981

Amer. Soc. of Clinical Psychopharmacology [15921], PO Box 40395, Glen Oaks, NY 11004, (718)470-4007

Amer. Soc. of CLU and ChFC [★2240]

Amer. Soc. of CLU and ChFC [★IO]

Amer. Soc. of Colon and Rectal Surgeons [16060], 85 W Algonquin Rd., Ste. 550, Arlington Heights, IL 60005, (847)290-9184

Amer. Soc. for Colposcopy and Cervical Pathology [15590], 20 W Washington St., Ste. 1, Hagerstown, MD 21740, (301)733-3640

Amer. Soc. for Colposcopy and Colpomicroscopy [★15590]

Amer. Soc. of Comparative Law [5865], c/o Symeon C. Symeonides, Pres., Willamette Univ. Coll. of Law, 245 Winter St. SE, Salem, OR 97301, (503)370-6402

Amer. Soc. for Competitiveness [8007], PO Box 1658, Indiana, PA 15705, (724)357-5928

Amer. Soc. of Composers, Authors and Publishers [5836], 1 Lincoln Plz., New York, NY 10023, (212)621-6000

Amer. Soc. for Composites [6651], c/o Prof. James M. Whitney, Treas., Dept. of Civil Engg., 422 Kettering Lab., Univ. of Dayton, 300 Coll. Park, Dayton, OH 45469-0243, (937)229-2979

Amer. Soc. of Cmpt. Dealers [★897]

Amer. Soc. for Concrete Constr. [★1001]

Amer. Soc. of Concrete Contractors [1001], 2025 S Brentwood Blvd., Ste. 105, St. Louis, MO 63144, (314)962-0210

Amer. Soc. for Conservation Archaeology - Address unknown since 2003.

Amer. Soc. of Construction Inspectors - Address unknown since 1995.

Amer. Soc. of Consultant Pharmacists [15922], 1321 Duke St., Ste. 400, Alexandria, VA 22314-3563, (703)739-1300

Amer. Soc. of Consulting Arborists [5254], 15245 Shady Grove Rd., Ste. 130, Rockville, MD 20850, (301)947-0483

Amer. Soc. of Consulting Planners [5587], 1776 Massachusetts Ave. NW, Washington, DC 20036-1904, (202)872-0611

Amer. Soc. of Contemporary Artists [9493], c/o Harriet FeBland, 245 E 63rd St., No. 1803, New York, NY 10021, (212)759-2215

Amer. Soc. of Contemporary Medicine, Surgery, and Ophthalmology [15666], 7250 N Cicero Ave., Lower Level 6, Lincolnwood, IL 60712, (312)440-0699

Amer. Soc. of Contemporary Ophthalmology [★15666]

Amer. Soc. of Contrarian Speakers and Writers [5601]

Amer. Soc. for the Control Cancer [★13792]

Amer. Soc. for Corporate Historians, Archivists and Librarians - Defunct.

Amer. Soc. of Corporate Secretaries [★75]

Amer. Soc. of Cosmetic Surgeon [★14037]

Amer. Soc. of Country Music - Address unknown since 1988.

Amer. Soc. of Crime Lab. Directors [5754], 139K Tech. Dr., Garner, NC 27529, (919)773-2044

Amer. Soc. of Criminology [11899], 1314 Kinnear Rd., Ste. 212, Columbus, OH 43212-1156, (614)292-9207

Amer. Soc. for Crippled Children in Israel - Defunct.

Amer. Soc. of Critical Care Anesthesiologists [13675], 520 N Northwest Hwy., Park Ridge, IL 60068-2573, (847)825-5586

Amer. Soc. for Cybernetics [6719], 2033 K St. NW, Ste. 230, Washington, DC 20052, (202)994-1642

Amer. Soc. of Cytology [★14075]

Amer. Soc. of Cytopathology [14075], 400 W 9th St., Ste. 201, Wilmington, DE 19801, (302)429-8802

Amer. Soc. for Cytotechnology [14076], 1500 Sunday Dr., Ste. 102, Raleigh, NC 27607, (919)861-5571

Amer. Soc. of Danish Engineers [6993]

Amer. Soc. for Deaf Children [14742], 3820 Hartzdale Dr., Camp Hill, PA 17011, (717)703-0073

Amer. Soc. for the Defense of Tradition, Family and Property [★19763]

Amer. Soc. for the Defense of Tradition, Family and Property - Defunct.

Amer. Soc. for Dental Aesthetics [14140], 635 Madison Ave., New York, NY 10022, (212)751-3263

American Society for Dental Aesthetics [IO], New York, NY, United States

Amer. Soc. of Dental Ceramics [★14110]

Amer. Soc. of Dentist Anesthesiologists [14141], c/o Dr. Lee Lichtenstein, Treas., 723 N Beers St., Holmdel, NJ 07733, (732)739-3337

Amer. Soc. of Dentistry for Children - Defunct.

A star before a book entry number signifies that the name is not listed separately, but is mentioned within the entry.

Amer. Soc. for Dermatologic Surgery [14196], 5550 Meadowbrook Dr., Ste. 120, Rolling Meadows, IL 60008, (847)956-0900

Amer. Soc. of Dermatological Retailers [86], c/o Dr. Jeffrey Lauber, MD, Medical Dir., 320 Superior Ave., No. 395, Newport Beach, CA 92663-2511, (949)646-9098

Amer. Soc. of Dermatology [14197], 2721 Capital Ave., Sacramento, CA 95816-6004, (916)446-5054

Amer. Soc. of Dermatopathology [14198], 60 Revere Dr., Ste. 500, Northbrook, IL 60062, (847)400-5820

Amer. Soc. of Design Engineers - Defunct.

Amer. Soc. of Diagnostic and Interventional Nephrology [15287], c/o Dianna Garvey, 131 Continental Dr., Ste. 405, Newark, DE 19713, (302)658-7596

Amer. Soc. of Directors of Volunteer Services [13382], One N Franklin, Ste. 2800, Chicago, IL 60606, (312)422-3938

Amer. Soc. of Disk Jockeys - Defunct.

Amer. Soc. of Dowsers [7470], PO Box 24, Danville, VT 05828, (802)684-3417

Amer. Soc. for Eastern Arts - Defunct.

Amer. Soc. for Echocardiography [13891], 1500 Sunday Dr., Ste. 102, Raleigh, NC 27607, (919)861-5574

Amer. Soc. for Eighteenth-Century Stud. [10089], Wake Forest Univ., PO Box 7867, Winston-Salem, NC 27109, (336)727-4694

Amer. Soc. of Electroencephalographic Technologists [★14307]

Amer. Soc. of Electroneurodiagnostic Technologists [14307], 6501 E Commerce Ave., Ste. 120, Kansas City, MO 64120, (816)931-1120

Amer. Soc. of Embalmers [2773], PO Box 0685, Forest Park, IL 60130-0685, (800)728-9185

Amer. Soc. of Emergency Radiology [16278], 4550 Post Oak Pl., Ste. 342, Houston, TX 77027, (713)965-0566

Amer. Soc. of Employee Suggestion Professionals - Address unknown since 2003.

Amer. Soc. of Employers [1251], 23815 Northwestern Hwy., Southfield, MI 48075-7713, (248)353-4500

Amer. Soc. for Engg. Educ. [8366], 1818 N St. NW, Ste. 600, Washington, DC 20036-2479, (202)331-3500

Amer. Soc. for Engg. Educ. [IO], Washington, DC, United States

Amer. Soc. for Engg. Mgt. [6994], PO Box 820, Rolla, MO 65402-0820, (573)341-2101

Amer. Soc. of Enologists [★5407]

Amer. Soc. for Enology and Viticulture [5407], PO Box 1855, Davis, CA 95617-1855, (530)753-3142

Amer. Soc. for Environmental Education - Address unknown since 1991.

Amer. Soc. for Environmental History [8383], c/o Interdisciplinary Arts and Sciences Prog., Univ. of Washington, Box 358436, Tacoma, WA 98402-3100

American Society for Environmental History [IO], Tacoma, WA, United States

Amer. Soc. for Ethnohistory [9918], c/o Duke Univ. Press, PO Box 906660, Durham, NC 27708-0660, (919)687-3602

Amer. Soc. of Exercise Physiologists [16019], c/o The Coll. of St. Scholastica, 1200 Kenwood Ave., Duluth, MN 55811, (218)723-6297

Amer. Soc. of Exodontists [★15732]

Amer. Soc. for Experimental Neuro Therapeutics [15379], 342 N Main St., Ste. 301, West Hartford, CT 06117-2507, (860)586-7570

Amer. Soc. for Experimental Pathology [★15860]

Amer. Soc. for Extra-Corporeal Tech. [15129], 2209 Dickens Rd., Richmond, VA 23230-2005, (804)565-6363

Amer. Soc. for Extracorporeal Circulation Technicians [★15129]

Amer. Soc. of Facial Plastic Surgery [★14038]

Amer. Soc. of Farm Equip. Appraisers [273], PO Box 186, Twin Falls, ID 83303-0186, (208)733-2323

Amer. Soc. of Farm Managers [★274]

Amer. Soc. of Farm Managers and Rural Appraisers [274], 950 S Cherry St., Ste. 508, Denver, CO 80246-2664, (303)758-3513

Amer. Soc. of Forensic Geologists [7128], c/o Jeffrey C. Reid, PhD, Pres., 8401 Summerspring Ln., Raleigh, NC 27615-3015, (919)618-0810

Amer. Soc. of Forensic Odontology [14142], c/o Dr. Bruce A. Schrader, Exec. Dir., 13048 N Res. Blvd., Ste. B, Austin, TX 78750

Amer. Soc. of the French Legion of Honor [19061]

American Society of the French Order of Merit [9967]

Amer. Soc. of French-Speaking Health Professionals - Address unknown since 2003.

Amer. Soc. for Friendship with Switzerland [★19398]

Amer. Soc. for Friendship with Switzerland [★IO]

Amer. Soc. of Furniture Designers [1691], 144 Woodland Dr., New London, NC 28127, (910)576-1273

Amer. Soc. of Gas Engineers [6941], PO Box 66, Artesia, CA 90702, (949)733-4304

Amer. Soc. for Gastrointestinal Endoscopy [14409], 1520 Kensington Rd., Ste. 202, Oak Brook, IL 60523, (630)573-0600

Amer. Soc. of Gene Therapy [14495], 555 E Wells St., Ste. 1100, Milwaukee, WI 53202, (414)278-1341

American Society of Gene Therapy [IO], Milwaukee, WI, United States

American Society of Genealogists [IO], Derry, NH, United States

Amer. Soc. of Genealogists [21103], PO Box 1515, Derry, NH 03038-1515

Amer. Soc. of Gen. Surgeons [16571], PO Box 4834, Englewood, CO 80155, (303)771-5948

Amer. Soc. for Genomic Medicine [14496], The Stefan Univ., PO Box 2946, La Jolla, CA 92038

Amer. Soc. for Genomic Medicine [IO], La Jolla, CA, United States

Amer. Soc. of Geolinguistics [IO], New York, NY, United States

Amer. Soc. of Geolinguistics [10399], c/o Prof. Wayne Finke, Ed., Dept. of Modern Languages, Baruch Coll., B6-280, 17 Lexington Ave., New York, NY 10010-5585, (646)312-4420

Amer. Soc. for Geriatric Dentistry [★14186]

Amer. Soc. for German Literature of the 16th and 17th Centuries - Address unknown since 1989.

Amer. Soc. of Golf Course Architects [6465], 125 N Executive Dr., Ste. 106, Brookfield, WI 53005, (262)786-5960

Amer. Soc. for Gravitational and Space Biology Student Assn. [6563], Bone/Signal Lab., NASA Ames Res. Center, Mail Stop 236-7, Moffett Field, CA 94035, (650)604-6014

Amer. Soc. of Greek and Latin Epigraphy [11207], c/o Prof. Paul Iversen, Sec.-Treas., CWRU Dept. of Classics, 111 Mather House, 11201 Euclid Ave., Cleveland, OH 44106-7111

Amer. Soc. of the Greek Order of Saint Dennis of Zante - Address unknown since 1995.

Amer. Soc. of Gp. Psychotherapy and Psychodrama [16208], 301 N Harrison St., Ste. 508, Princeton, NJ 08540, (609)452-1339

Amer. Soc. of Hair Restoration Surgery [14520], c/o Amer. Acad. of Cosmetic Surgery, 737 N Michigan Ave., Ste. 2100, Chicago, IL 60611, (312)981-6760

Amer. Soc. of Hair Restoration Surgery [IO], Chicago, IL, United States

Amer. Soc. of Hand Therapists [14524], 401 N Michigan Ave., Chicago, IL 60611-4267, (312)321-6866

Amer. Soc. of Handicapped Physicians [11919]

Amer. Soc. for the Hard of Hearing [★16442]

Amer. Soc. of Head and Neck Radiology [16279], 2210 Midwest Rd., Ste. 207, Oak Brook, IL 60523-8205, (630)574-0220

Amer. Soc. of Head and Neck Surgeons [★15819]

Amer. Soc. for Head and Neck Surgery [★15819]

Amer. Soc. of Hea. Sys. Pharmacists [15923], 7272 Wisconsin Ave., Bethesda, MD 20814, (301)657-3000

Amer. Soc. for Healthcare Central Ser. Professionals [14864], 1 N Franklin, No. 2800, Chicago, IL 60606, (312)422-3700

Amer. Soc. for Healthcare Education and Training of the Amer. Hospital Assn. - Defunct.

Amer. Soc. for Healthcare Engg. of the Amer. Hosp. Assn. [14865], c/o Amer. Hosp. Assn., One N Franklin, 28th Fl., Chicago, IL 60606, (312)422-3800

Amer. Soc. for Healthcare Environmental Services of the Amer. Hosp. Assn. [14866], 1 N Franklin St., Ste. 2800, Chicago, IL 60606, (312)422-3860

American Society for Healthcare Environmental Services of the American Hospital Association [IO], Chicago, IL, United States

Amer. Soc. for Healthcare Food Ser. Administrators [14867], 455 S Fourth St., Ste. 650, Louisville, KY 40202, (502)583-3783

Amer. Soc. for Healthcare Human Resources Admin. [14868], c/o Amer. Hosp. Assn., 1 N Franklin, 31st Fl., Chicago, IL 60606, (312)422-3720

Amer. Soc. for Healthcare Marketing and Public Relations [★14896]

Amer. Soc. for Healthcare Materials Mgt. [★14872]

Amer. Soc. of Healthcare Publication Editors [14613], 8870 Darrow Rd., Ste. F106-155, Twinsburg, OH 44087, (330)487-0344

Amer. Soc. for Healthcare Risk Mgt. [14869], 1 N Franklin St., Chicago, IL 60606, (312)422-3980

Amer. Soc. Heating and Air-Conditioning Engineers [★6995]

Amer. Soc. Heating and Air-Conditioning Engineers [★IO]

American Society of Heating, Refrigerating and Air-Conditioning Engineers [IO], Atlanta, GA, United States

Amer. Soc. of Heating, Refrigerating and Air-Conditioning Engineers [6995], 1791 Tullie Cir. NE, Atlanta, GA 30329, (404)636-8400

Amer. Soc. of Hematology [14783], 1900 M St. NW, Ste. 200, Washington, DC 20036, (202)776-0544

Amer. Soc. for Histocompatibility and Immunogenetics [14931], 15000 Commerce Pkwy., Ste. C, Mount Laurel, NJ 08054, (856)638-0428

Amer. Soc. of Home Inspectors [592], 932 Lee St., Ste. 101, Des Plaines, IL 60016-6546, (847)759-2820

Amer. Soc. for Horticultural Sci. [6627], 113 SW St., Ste. 200, Alexandria, VA 22314-2851, (703)836-4606

Amer. Soc. of Hospice Care - Defunct.

Amer. Soc. of Hosp. Attorneys [★5782]

Amer. Soc. of Hospital-Based Emergency Air Medical Services [★14314]

Amer. Soc. of Hospital-Based Emergency Air Medical Services [★IO]

Amer. Soc. for Hosp. Central Ser. Personnel [★14864]

Amer. Soc. for Hosp. Engg. [★14865]

Amer. Soc. for Hosp. Food Ser. Administrators [★14867]

Amer. Soc. for Hosp. Marketing and Public Relations [★14896]

Amer. Soc. for Hosp. Materials Mgt. [★14872]

Amer. Soc. of Hosp. Nursing Ser. Administrators [★15454]

Amer. Soc. of Hosp. Pharmacists Res. and Educ. Found. [★15926]

Amer. Soc. of Hosp. Public Relations [★14896]

Amer. Soc. for Hosp. Purchasing Agents [★14872]

Amer. Soc. for Hosp. Purchasing and Materials Mgt. [★14872]

Amer. Soc. of Human Genetics [7113], 9650 Rockville Pike, Bethesda, MD 20814-3998, (301)634-7300

Amer. Soc. of Hypertension [14905], 148 Madison Ave., 5th Fl., New York, NY 10016-6700, (212)696-9099

Amer. Soc. of Hypertension [IO], New York, NY, United States

Amer. Soc. of Ichthyologists and Herpetologists [7158], c/o Maureen A. Donnelly, Sec., Dept. of Biological Sciences, Coll. of Arts and Sci., Florida Intl. Univ., 11200 SW 8th St., Miami, FL 33199, (305)348-1235

Amer. Soc. of Independent Business - Defunct.

Amer. Soc. of Indexers [10322], 10200 W 44th Ave., Ste. 304, Wheat Ridge, CO 80033, (303)463-2887

Amer. Soc. of Industrial Auctioneers - Address unknown since 1995.

Amer. Soc. of Industrial Medicine - Address unknown since 2002.

Amer. Soc. for Indus. Security [★2083]

Amer. Soc. for Indus. Security [★IO]

Reference to "IO" in place of a book number signifies that the association may be found in the 45th edition of International Organizations.

Amer. Soc. for Info. Sci. and Tech. [7188], 1320 Fenwick Ln., Ste. 510, Silver Spring, MD 20910, (301)495-0900

Amer. Soc. of Inspectors of Plumbing and Sanitary Engg. [★7590]

Amer. Soc. of Instrument Engineers [★7220]

Amer. Soc. of Instrument Engineers [★IO]

Amer. Soc. of Insurance Mgt. [★2235]

Amer. Soc. of Interior Designers [2251], 608 Massachusetts Ave. NE, Washington, DC 20002-6006, (202)546-3480

American Soc. of Internal Medicine; Amer. Coll. of Physicians- [14966]

Amer. Soc. of Internal Medicine - Defunct.

Amer. Soc. of Intl. Executives - Defunct.

Amer. Soc. of Intl. Law [5866], 2223 Massachusetts Ave. NW, Washington, DC 20008, (202)939-6000

Amer. Soc. of Intl. Law [IO], Washington, DC, United States

Amer. Soc. of Interpreters - Defunct.

Amer. Soc. of Interventional Pain Physicians [15837], 81 Lakeview Dr., Paducah, KY 42001, (270)554-9412

Amer. Soc. of Interventional and Therapeutic Neuroradiology [16280], 3975 Fair Ridge Dr., Ste. 400 N, Fairfax, VA 22033, (703)691-2272

Amer. Soc. of Inventors [7226], PO Box 58426, Philadelphia, PA 19102, (215)546-6601

Amer. Soc. for Investigative Pathology [15860], 9650 Rockville Pike, Bethesda, MD 20814-3993, (301)634-7130

Amer. Soc. of Irrigation Consultants [7826], 125 Paradise Ln., PO Box 426, Rochester, MA 02770, (508)763-8140

Amer. Soc. of the Italian Legions of Merit - Address unknown since 1995.

Amer. Soc. of Jewelry Historians [10271], 1333A North Ave., No. 103, New Rochelle, NY 10804, (914)235-0983

Amer. Soc. of Jewelry Historians [IO], New Rochelle, NY, United States

Amer. Soc. for Jewish Heritage in Poland [IO], New York, NY, United States

Amer. Soc. for Jewish Heritage in Poland [10273], 1202 Lexington Ave., No. 121, New York, NY 10028-1425, (212)330-6588

Amer. Soc. for Jewish Music [10550], Center for Jewish History, 15 W 16th St., New York, NY 10011, (212)294-8328

Amer. Soc. of Journalism School Administrators [★7893]

Amer. Soc. of Journalists and Authors [11158], 1501 Broadway, Ste. 302, New York, NY 10036, (212)997-0947

Amer. Soc. of Knitting Technologists [7795]

Amer. Soc. for Kurds [13154], 227 N Bronough St., Ste. 1001, Tallahassee, FL 32301

Amer. Soc. for Kurds [IO], Tallahassee, FL, United States

Amer. Soc. of Landscape Architects [6466], 636 Eye St. NW, Washington, DC 20001-3736, (202)898-2444

Amer. Soc. of Landscape Architects Found. [★6476]

Amer. Soc. for Laser Medicine and Surgery [14997], 2100 Stewart Ave., Ste. 240, Wausau, WI 54401, (715)845-9283

Amer. Soc. of Law Enforcement Trainers [★5963]

Amer. Soc. of Law Enforcement Training [5963]

Amer. Soc. of Law and Medicine [15002]

Amer. Soc. of Law, Medicine and Ethics [15002], 765 Commonwealth Ave., Ste. 1634, Boston, MA 02215, (617)262-4990

Amer. Soc. for Legal History [10090], c/o William P. LaPiana, Treas., New York Law School, 57 Worth St., New York, NY 10013, (212)431-1830

Amer. Soc. of Limnology and Oceanography [7393], 5400 Bosque Blvd., Ste. 680, Waco, TX 76710-4446, (254)399-9635

American Society of Limnology and Oceanography [IO], Waco, TX, United States

Amer. Soc. for Lipo-Suction Surgery [16572], c/o Amer. Acad. of Cosmetic Surgery, 737 N Michigan Ave., Ste. 2100, Chicago, IL 60611-5405, (312)981-6760

Amer. Soc. of Local Officials - Defunct.

Amer. Soc. of Lubrication Engineers [★7047]

Amer. Soc. of Lubrication Engineers [★IO]

Amer. Soc. of Magazine Editors [3085], 810 7th Ave., 24th Fl., New York, NY 10019, (212)872-3700

Amer. Soc. of Magazine Photographers [★2992]

Amer. Soc. of Mammalogists [7259], PO Box 1897, Lawrence, KS 66044-8897, (785)843-1235

Amer. Soc. of Marine Artists [9494], PO Box 369, Ambler, PA 19002

Amer. Soc. for Mass Spectrometry [7688], 2019 Galisteo St., Bldg. I-1, Santa Fe, NM 87505, (505)989-4517

Amer. Soc. of Master Dental Technologists [14143], 146-21 13th Ave., Whitestone, NY 11357-2420, (718)746-8355

Amer. Soc. of Matrix Biology [6564], c/o Delores M. Francis, Admin., 9650 Rockville Pike, Bethesda, MD 20814, (301)634-7120

Amer. Soc. of Mature Catholics - Defunct.

Amer. Soc. of Maxillofacial Surgeons [15735], 444 E Algonquin Rd., Arlington Heights, IL 60005, (847)228-3338

Amer. Soc. for Measurement Control [★7220]

Amer. Soc. for Measurement Control [★IO]

Amer. Soc. of Mech. Engineers [7298], 3 Park Ave., New York, NY 10016-5990, (973)882-1170

Amer. Soc. of Mech. Engineers Auxiliary [7299], 3 Park Ave., 23rd Fl., New York, NY 10016-5990, (212)591-7846

Amer. Soc. of Mech. Engineers; Woman's Auxiliary to the [★7299]

Amer. Soc. of Media Photographers [2992], 150 N 2nd St., Philadelphia, PA 19106, (215)451-2767

Amer. Soc. of Medical Missionaries - Address unknown since 2004.

Amer. Soc. of Medical Technologists [★14992]

Amer. Soc. for Medical Tech. [★14992]

Amer. Soc. for Medicine and Science - Address unknown since 2006.

Amer. Soc. of Mental Hea. Bus. Administrators [★15191]

Amer. Soc. for Metals [★7311]

Amer. Soc. for Metals [★IO]

Amer. Soc. for Microbiology [6565], 1752 N St. NW, Washington, DC 20036, (202)737-3600

Amer. Soc. of Military Comptrollers [6066], 415 N Alfred St., Alexandria, VA 22314, (703)549-0360

Amer. Soc. of Military Insignia Collectors [22627], c/o George Duell, Membership Sec., 526 Lafayette Ave., Palmerton, PA 18071-1621, (610)826-5067

Amer. Soc. of Milling and Baking Tech. [★6660]

Amer. Soc. of Milling and Baking Tech. [★IO]

Amer. Soc. of Mining and Reclamation [6114], 3134 Montavesta Rd., Lexington, KY 40502-3548, (859)351-9032

Amer. Soc. of Minority Hea. and Transplant Professionals [★16666]

Amer. Soc. of Missiology [20297], c/o Austin Presbyterian Theological Seminary, 100 E 27th St., Austin, TX 78705, (512)404-4855

Amer. Soc. for Mohs Histotechnology [15130], 555 E Wells St., Ste. 1100, Milwaukee, WI 53202, (414)347-1103

Amer. Soc. for Mohs Surgery [15641], Private Mail Box 391, 5901 Warner Ave., Huntington Beach, CA 92649-4659, (714)379-6262

Amer. Soc. for Mohs Surgery [IO], Huntington Beach, CA, United States

Amer. Soc. of Multicultural Hea. and Transplant Professionals [16666], 700 N 4th St., Richmond, VA 23219, (866)276-4871

Amer. Soc. of Municipal Engineers [★6233]

Amer. Soc. of Music Arrangers [★10551]

Amer. Soc. of Music Arrangers and Composers [10551], PO Box 17840, Encino, CA 91416, (818)994-4661

Amer. Soc. of Music Copyists - Address unknown since 2002.

Amer. Soc. for Muslim Advancement [10245], 475 Riverside Dr., Ste. 248, New York, NY 10115, (212)870-2552

Amer. Soc. of Naturalists [7360], c/o Univ. of Chicago Press, PO Box 37005, Chicago, IL 60637, (773)753-3347

Amer. Soc. of Naval Engineers [7270], 1452 Duke St., Alexandria, VA 22314-3458, (703)836-6727

Amer. Soc. for Neo-Hellenic Stud. [★9770]

Amer. Soc. for Neo-Hellenic Stud. [★IO]

Amer. Soc. of Nephrology [15288], 1725 I St. NW, Ste. 510, Washington, DC 20006, (202)659-0599

Amer. Soc. for Netherlands Philately - Defunct.

Amer. Soc. for Neural Transplantation [★15380]

Amer. Soc. for Neural Transplantation and Repair [15380], c/o Donna C. Morrison, Conf. Coor./Office Mgr., Dept. of Neurosurgery, MDC-78, Center for Aging and Brain Repair, Univ. of South Florida, 12901 Bruce B. Downs Blvd., Tampa, FL 33612-4799, (813)974-3154

Amer. Soc. for Neurochemistry [7374], 9037 Ron Den Ln., Windermere, FL 34786-8328, (407)876-0750

Amer. Soc. of Neuroimaging [16281], 5841 Cedar Lake Rd., Ste. 204, Minneapolis, MN 55416, (952)545-6291

Amer. Soc. of Neurophysiological Monitoring [15381], 20 N Michigan Ave., Ste. 700, Chicago, IL 60602, (800)479-7979

Amer. Soc. of Neuroradiology [16282], 2210 Midwest Rd., Ste. 207, Oak Brook, IL 60523, (630)574-0220

Amer. Soc. of Neurorehabilitation [15382], 5841 Cedar Lake Rd., Ste. 204, Minneapolis, MN 55416, (952)545-6324

Amer. Soc. of Newspaper Editors [3086], 11690B Sunrise Valley Dr., Reston, VA 20191-1409, (703)453-1122

Amer. Soc. for Nondestructive Testing [7787], PO Box 28518, Columbus, OH 43228-0518, (614)274-6003

Amer. Soc. of Notaries [6146], PO Box 5707, Tallahassee, FL 32314-5707, (850)671-5164

Amer. Soc. of Nuclear Cardiology [13892], 4550 Montgomery Ave., Ste. 780 N, Bethesda, MD 20814-3304, (301)215-7575

Amer. Soc. for Nursing Ser. Administrators [★15454]

Amer. Soc. for Nutrition [15548], 9650 Rockville Pike, Ste. 4500, Bethesda, MD 20814-3998, (301)634-7050

Amer. Soc. for Nutritional Sciences [★15548]

Amer. Soc. for Oceanography [★7273]

Amer. Soc. of Ocularists [15118], PO Box 608, Earlysville, VA 22936-0608, (434)973-4066

Amer. Soc. of Onomatologists - Defunct.

Amer. Soc. of Ophthalmic Administrators [15058], 4000 Legato Rd., Ste. 700, Fairfax, VA 22033, (703)591-2220

Amer. Soc. of Ophthalmic Plastic and Reconstructive Surgery [14043], 5841 Cedar Lake Rd., Ste. 204, Minneapolis, MN 55416, (952)646-2038

Amer. Soc. of Ophthalmic Registered Nurses [15458], PO Box 193030, San Francisco, CA 94119-3030, (415)561-8513

Amer. Soc. for Ophthalmic Ultrasonography [15667], c/o Suzanne W. Daly, BSN, Sec.-Treas., Weill Cornell Medical Coll., Dept. of Ophthalmology, 1300 York Ave., Box 112, New York, NY 10021, (212)746-2504

Amer. Soc. of Ophthalmologic and Otolaryngologic Allergy [★13593]

Amer. Soc. of Oral Surgeons [★15732]

Amer. Soc. of Orthodontists [★14117]

Amer. Soc. of Orthopaedic Physician's Assistants [15760], 8365 Keystone Crossing, Ste. 107, Indianapolis, IN 46240, (800)280-2390

Amer. Soc. of Orthopedic Professionals [15761], PO Box 7440, Seminole, FL 33775, (727)394-1700

Amer. Soc. of Outpatient Surgeons [★16558]

Amer. Soc. of Pain Educators [15838], PO Box 1548, Montclair, NJ 07042, (973)233-5570

Amer. Soc. for Pain Mgt. Nursing [15459], PO Box 15473, Lenexa, KS 66285-5473, (913)895-4606

Amer. Soc. of Papyrologists [10769], c/o Univ. of Cincinnati, U.S. Department of Classics ML 226, 410 Blegen Lib., Cincinnati, OH 45221-0226, (513)556-4366

Amer. Soc. for Parenteral and Enteral Nutrition [15549], 8630 Fenton St., Ste. 412, Silver Spring, MD 20910-3805, (301)587-6315

American Soc. for Payroll Management - Address unknown since 2006.

A star before a book entry number signifies that the name is not listed separately, but is mentioned within the entry.

Amer. Soc. of Pediatric Hematology/Oncology [14784], 4700 W Lake Ave., Glenview, IL 60025-1485, (847)375-4716

Amer. Soc. of Pediatric Nephrology [15289], 3400 Res. Forest Dr., Ste. B7, The Woodlands, TX 77381, (281)419-0052

Amer. Soc. of Pediatric Neuroradiology [16283], 2210 Midwest Rd., Ste. 207, Oak Brook, IL 60523-8205, (630)574-0220

Amer. Soc. for Pediatric Neurosurgery - Address unknown since 2001.

Amer. Soc. of Pension Actuaries [★1233]

Amer. Soc. of Pension Professionals and Actuaries [1233], 4245 N Fairfax Dr., Ste. 750, Arlington, VA 22203, (703)516-9300

Amer. Soc. for Performance Improvement - Address unknown since 2002.

Amer. Soc. of Perfumers [1659], PO Box 1551, West Caldwell, NJ 07007, (201)991-0040

Amer. Soc. of PeriAnesthesia Nurses [15460], 10 Melrose Ave., Ste. 110, Cherry Hill, NJ 08003-3696, (856)616-9600

American Society of PeriAnesthesia Nurses [IO], Cherry Hill, NJ, United States

Amer. Soc. of Periodontists [★14109]

Amer. Soc. for Personnel Admin. [★2908]

Amer. Soc. for Personnel Admin. Intl. [★2907]

Amer. Soc. for Personnel Admin. Intl. [★IO]

Amer. Soc. of Petroleum Operations Engineers - Address unknown since 2002.

Amer. Soc. of Pharmacognosy [15924], c/o David J. Slatkin, Treas., 3149 Dundee Rd., No. 260, Northbrook, IL 60062, (773)995-3748

American Society of Pharmacognosy [IO], Northbrook, IL, United States

Amer. Soc. for Pharmacology and Experimental Therapeutics [15925], 9650 Rockville Pike, Bethesda, MD 20814-3995, (301)634-7060

Amer. Soc. for Pharmacy Law [15003], 3085 Stevenson Dr., Ste. 200, Springfield, IL 62703, (217)529-6948

Amer. Soc. for Philatelic Pages and Panels - Address unknown since 2002.

Amer. Soc. for Philosophy Counseling and Psychotherapy [16209], c/o Dr. Samuel Zinaich, Sec.-Treas./Pres., Purdue Univ. Calumet, 2200 169th St., Hammond, IN 46323-2094

Amer. Soc. for Photobiology [6566], PO Box 1897, Lawrence, KS 66044, (800)627-0629

American Society for Photobiology [IO], Lawrence, KS, United States

Amer. Soc. of Photogrammetry [★7495]

Amer. Soc. for Photogrammetry and Remote Sensing [★7495]

Amer. Soc. of Photographers [10845], c/o Doug Box, Exec. Dir., PO Box 1120, Caldwell, TX 77836-6120, (979)272-5555

Amer. Soc. of Physical Medicine and Rehabilitation [★16307]

Amer. Soc. of Physician Analysts [★16104]

Amer. Soc. of Physicians in Chronic Disease Facilities - Defunct.

Amer. Soc. of Piano Technicians [★2822]

Amer. Soc. of Picture Professionals [2993], 117 S St. Asaph St., Alexandria, VA 22314, (703)299-0219

Amer. Soc. of Planning Officials [★5586]

Amer. Soc. of Plant Biologists [6628], 15501 Monona Dr., Rockville, MD 20855-2768, (301)251-0560

Amer. Soc. of Plant Physiologists [★6628]

Amer. Soc. of Plant Taxonomists [6629], Dept. of Botany 3165, Univ. of Wyoming, 1000 E Univ. Ave., Laramie, WY 82071, (307)766-2556

Amer. Soc. of Plastic and Reconstructive Surgeons [★14045]

Amer. Soc. of Plastic and Reconstructive Surgical Nurses [★15461]

Amer. Soc. of Plastic Surgeons [14044], 444 E Algonquin Rd., Arlington Heights, IL 60005, (847)228-9900

Amer. Soc. of Plastic Surgeons and Plastic Surgery Educ. Found. [14045], 444 E Algonquin Rd., Arlington Heights, IL 60005, (847)228-9900

Amer. Soc. of Plastic Surgical Nurses [15461], 7794 Grow Dr., Pensacola, FL 32514, (850)473-2443

Amer. Soc. for Plasticulture [4097], 526 Brittany Dr., State College, PA 16803-1420, (814)238-7045

Amer. Soc. of Plumbing Engineers [6996], 8614 Catalpa Ave., Ste. 1007, Chicago, IL 60656-1116, (773)693-2773

American Soc. of Plumbing Engineers Res. Foundation [★6996]

Amer. Soc. of Podiatric Dermatology - Address unknown since 2004.

Amer. Soc. of Podiatric Medical Assistants [16040], 2124 S Austin Blvd., Cicero, IL 60804, (708)863-6303

Amer. Soc. of Podiatric Medicine - Address unknown since 2004.

Amer. Soc. of Podiatrists and Chiropractors [16041], PO Box 35215, Chicago, IL 60707-0215, (708)453-0080

Amer. Soc. of Polar Philatelists [22789], c/o Alan Warren, Sec., PO Box 39, Exton, PA 19341-0039, (610)321-0740

Amer. Soc. of Portrait Artists [9495], PO Box 230216, Montgomery, AL 36106, (800)62-ASOPA

Amer. Soc. for Portuguese Numismatics - Address unknown since 1999.

Amer. Soc. of Post Anesthesia Nurses [★15460]

Amer. Soc. of Post Anesthesia Nurses [★IO]

Amer. Soc. of Pre-Dental Students - Defunct.

Amer. Soc. for Precision Engg. [6997], PO Box 10826, Raleigh, NC 27605-0826, (919)839-8444

Amer. Soc. for Precision Nailmakers - Defunct.

Amer. Soc. for the Preservation of Sacred, Patriotic and Operatic Music - Address unknown since 1995.

Amer. Soc. for the Prevention of Crime - Defunct.

Amer. Soc. for the Prevention of Cruelty to Animals [11350], 424 E 92nd St., New York, NY 10128-6804, (212)876-7700

Amer. Soc. for Preventive Dentistry - Defunct.

Amer. Soc. of Preventive Oncology [15642], c/o Heidi Sahel, Exec. Dir., 330 WARF Bldg., 610 Walnut St., Madison, WI 53726, (608)263-9515

Amer. Soc. of Primatologists [6405], c/o Karen L. Bales, Treas., Univ. of California, Dept. of Psychology, 1 Shields Ave., Davis, CA 95616, (530)754-5890

Amer. Soc. of Professional Appraisers - Defunct.

Amer. Soc. of Professional Biologists [★6560]

Amer. Soc. of Professional Communicators [873], 4885 McKnight Rd., Ste. 325, Pittsburgh, PA 15237, (412)625-4094

Amer. Soc. of Professional Draftsmen and Artists - Address unknown since 1995.

Amer. Soc. of Professional Ecologists - Defunct.

Amer. Soc. of Professional Estimators [8142], 2525 Perimeter Place Dr., Ste. 103, Nashville, TN 37214, (615)316-9200

Amer. Soc. of Professional and Executive Women - Defunct.

Amer. Soc. of Professional Graphologists [1812], 23 South Dr., Great Neck, NY 11021

Amer. Soc. for the Protection of Nature in Israel [4353], 28 Arrandale Ave., Great Neck, NY 11024-1804, (800)411-0966

Amer. Soc. for the Protection of Nature in Israel [IO], Great Neck, NY, United States

Amer. Soc. for Psychical Res. [7442], 5 W 73rd St., New York, NY 10023, (212)799-5050

Amer. Soc. of Psychoanalytic Physicians [16104], 13528 Wisteria Dr., Germantown, MD 20874, (301)540-3197

Amer. Soc. of Psychopathology of Expression [16191], c/o Dr. Irene Jakab, Pres., 74 Lawton St., Brookline, MA 02446, (617)738-9821

Amer. Soc. for Psychoprophylaxis in Obstetrics [★15608]

Amer. Soc. for Psychoprophylaxis in Obstetrics [★IO]

American Society for Public Administration [IO], Washington, DC, United States

Amer. Soc. for Public Admin. [6190], 1301 Pennsylvania Ave. NW, Ste. 840, Washington, DC 20004-1735, (202)393-7878

Amer. Soc. for Quality [7552], PO Box 3005, Milwaukee, WI 53201-3005, (414)272-8575

Amer. Soc. for Quality Control [★7552]

Amer. Soc. of Questioned Document Examiners [5755], PO Box 18298, Long Beach, CA 90807, (562)901-3376

Amer. Soc. of Radiographers [★15131]

Amer. Soc. of Radiologic Technologists [15131], 15000 Central Ave. SE, Albuquerque, NM 87123-3909, (505)298-4500

Amer. Soc. of Range Mgt. [★5166]

Amer. Soc. of Real Estate Counselors [★3308]

Amer. Soc. of Real Estate Counselors [★IO]

American Society for Reconstructive Microsurgery [IO], Chicago, IL, United States

Amer. Soc. for Reconstructive Microsurgery [16573], 20 N Michigan Ave., Ste. 700, Chicago, IL 60602, (312)456-9579

Amer. Soc. for Reconstructive Surgery [16574], 20 N Michigan Ave., Ste. 700, Chicago, IL 60602, (312)456-9579

Amer. Soc. for Reformation Res. [★10931]

Amer. Soc. of Refrigerating Engineers [★6995]

Amer. Soc. of Refrigerating Engineers [★IO]

Amer. Soc. of Regional Anesthesia and Pain Medicine [IO], Park Ridge, IL, United States

Amer. Soc. of Regional Anesthesia and Pain Medicine [13676], 520 N Northwest Hwy., Park Ridge, IL 60068-2573, (847)825-7246

Amer. Soc. of Regional Anesthesia and Pain Practice [★13676]

Amer. Soc. of Regional Anesthesia and Pain Practice [★IO]

American Society for Reproductive Medicine [IO], Birmingham, AL, United States

Amer. Soc. for Reproductive Medicine [14389], 1209 Montgomery Hwy., Birmingham, AL 35216-2809, (205)978-5000

Amer. Soc. for Res. in Psychosomatic Problems [★16196]

Amer. Soc. of Retired Dentists [19330]

Amer. Soc. of Rio de Janeiro - Address unknown since 1995.

Amer. Soc. of Roommate Services [12305], c/o Ms. Susan Stein, 5353 N Fed. Hwy., No. 212, Fort Lauderdale, FL 33308, (212)362-0162

Amer. Soc. for Russian Naval History - Defunct.

Amer. Soc. of Safety Engineers [7586], 1800 E Oakton St., Des Plaines, IL 60018, (847)699-2929

Amer. Soc. of Saint Caecilia [★20428]

Amer. Soc. of Sanitary Engg. [7590], 901 Canterbury, Ste. A, Westlake, OH 44145, (440)835-3040

Amer. Soc. of Senior Wire Rope Engineers - Address unknown since 2001.

Amer. Soc. of Separated and Divorced Men [12005]

Amer. Soc. of Sephardic Studies - Address unknown since 2006.

Amer. Soc. of Spine Radiology [16284], 2210 Midwest Rd., Ste. 207, Oak Brook, IL 60523-8205, (630)574-0220

Amer. Soc. for Steel Treating [★7311]

Amer. Soc. for Steel Treating [★IO]

American Society for Stereotactic and Functional Neurosurgery [IO], Newark, NJ, United States

Amer. Soc. for Stereotactic and Functional Neurosurgery [15412], c/o Dr. Michael Schulder, Pres., North Shore Univ. Hosp., Dept. of Neurosurgery, 9 Tower 300 Community Dr., Manhasset, NY 11030, (516)562-3065

Amer. Soc. for the Stud. of Arteriosclerosis [★13902]

Amer. Soc. for the Study of Ideological Belief Systems - Defunct.

Amer. Soc. for the Stud. of Orthodontics [14144], 70-15 164th St., Flushing, NY 11365, (718)591-6411

Amer. Soc. for the Study of Religion - Address unknown since 1994.

Amer. Soc. for the Stud. of Sterility [★14389]

Amer. Soc. for the Stud. of Sterility [★IO]

Amer. Soc. of Sugar Beet Technologists [7089], 800 Grant St., Ste. 300, Denver, CO 80203-2944, (303)832-4460

Amer. Soc. of Sugar Cane Technologists [3700], c/o Dr. Denver T. Loupe, Gen. Sec.-Treas., PO Box 25100, Baton Rouge, LA 70894-5100, (225)578-6930

Amer. Soc. for Surface Mining and Reclamation [★6114]

Reference to "IO" in place of a book number signifies that the association may be found in the 45th edition of International Organizations.

Amer. Soc. for Surgery of the Hand [14525], 6300 N River Rd., Ste. 600, Rosemont, IL 60018, (847)384-8300

Amer. Soc. of Swedish Engineers [6998], 780 3rd Ave., King of Prussia, PA 19406, (610)265-4352

Amer. Soc. of Sydney [IO], Sydney, Australia

Amer. Soc. of Tax Problem Solvers [6290], 2250 Wehrle Dr., Ste. 3, Williamsville, NY 14221, (716)630-1650

Amer. Soc. of Tax Professionals [10], PO Box 1213, Lynnwood, WA 98046-1213, (425)774-1996

Amer. Soc. of Teachers of Dancing - Address unknown since 1995.

Amer. Soc. of Tech. Appraisers [★272]

Amer. Soc. for Technion-Israel Inst. of Tech. [8677], 55 E 59th St., No. 124, New York, NY 10022-1112, (212)407-6300

Amer. Soc. for Technion-Israel Inst. of Tech. [IO], New York, NY, United States

Amer. Soc. of Test Engineers [7788], PO Box 389, Nutting Lake, MA 01865-0389

Amer. Soc. for Testing and Materials [7789], PO Box C700, West Conshohocken, PA 19428-2959, (610)832-9500

Amer. Soc. of Theatre Consultants [955], c/o Edgar L. Lustig, Sec./CFO, 12226 Mentz Hill Rd., St. Louis, MO 63128, (314)843-9218

American Society of Theatre Consultants [IO], St. Louis, MO, United States

Amer. Soc. for Theatre Res. [11002], PO Box 1798, Boulder, CO 80306-1798, (303)530-1838

Amer. Soc. of Therapeutic Radiologists [★16285]

Amer. Soc. for Therapeutic Radiology and Oncology [16285], 8280 Willow Oaks Corporate Dr., Ste. 500, Fairfax, VA 22031, (703)502-1550

Amer. Soc. of Tool Engineers [★7268]

Amer. Soc. of Tool and Mfg. Engineers [★7268]

Amer. Soc. of Traffic and Trans. [★3861]

Amer. Soc. for Training and Development [★8018]

Amer. Soc. for Training and Development [3182], 1640 King St., Box 1443, Alexandria, VA 22313-2043, (703)683-8100

American Society for Training and Development [IO], Alexandria, VA, United States

Amer. Soc. of Training Directors [★8018]

Amer. Soc. of Transplant Surgeons [16667], 2461 S Clark St., Ste. 640, Arlington, VA 22202, (703)414-7870

Amer. Soc. of Transplantation [16668], 15000 Commerce Pkwy., Ste. C, Mount Laurel, NJ 08054, (856)439-9986

Amer. Soc. of Trans. and Logistics [3861], 1400 Eye St. NW, Ste. 1050, Washington, DC 20005, (202)580-7270

Amer. Soc. of Travel Agents [3907], 1101 King St., Ste. 200, Alexandria, VA 22314, (703)739-2782

Amer. Soc. of Trial Consultants [6524], 1941 Greenspring Dr., Timonium, MD 21093, (410)560-7949

Amer. Soc. of Tropical Medicine [★16693]

Amer. Soc. of Tropical Medicine and Hygiene [16693], 60 Revere Dr., Ste. 500, Northbrook, IL 60062, (847)480-9592

Amer. Soc. of T.V. Cameramen and Intl. Soc. of Videographers - Address unknown since 2002.

Amer. Soc. of Ultrasound Tech. Specialists [★16438]

Amer. Soc. of Univ. Composers [★9817]

Amer. Soc. of Utility Investors - Defunct.

Amer. Soc. of Validation Engineers [1289]

Amer. Soc. for Value Inquiry [10784], c/o Joram G. Haber, Sec.-Treas., Dept. of Philosophy, Bergen Community Coll., 400 Paramus Rd., Paramus, NJ 07652-1595, (201)447-9282

Amer. Soc. of Veterinary Ethology [★16780]

Amer. Soc. of Veterinary Ophthalmology [16775], 1416 W Liberty Ave., Stillwater, OK 74075

Amer. Soc. of Veterinary Physiologists and Pharmacologists - Defunct.

Amer. Soc. of Victimology [13360], c/o Division of Continuing Educ., Washburn Univ., 1700 SW Coll. Ave., Topeka, KS 66621, (785)231-1010

Amer. Soc. for Virology [6547], c/o Dorothea L. Sawicki, PhD, Sec.-Treas., Dept. of Medical Microbiology and Immunology, Univ. of Toledo Coll. of Medicine, 3000 Arlington Ave., Mail Stop 1021, Toledo, OH 43614, (419)383-5173

Amer. Soc. of Wedding Professionals [532], 268 Griggs Ave., Teaneck, NJ 07666, (973)472-1800

Amer. Soc. of Wireless Pioneers of the Seven Seas [★3757]

Amer. Soc. of Women Accountants [11], 8405 Greensboro Dr., Ste. 800, McLean, VA 22102-5120, (703)506-3265

Amer. Soc. of Writers on Legal Subjects [★5584]

Amer. Soc. for X-Ray and Electron Diffraction [★6852]

Amer. Soc. of X-Ray Technicians [★15131]

Amer. Soc. of Zoologists [★7867]

Amer. Sociological Assn. [7658], 1307 New York Ave. NW, Ste. 700, Washington, DC 20005, (202)383-9005

Amer. Sociological Assn; Honors Prog. Student Assn. of the [24702]

Amer. Sociological Soc. [★7658]

Amer. Sociological Soc; Rural Sect. of the [★7667]

Amer. Sociometric Assn. - Defunct.

Amer. Sod Producers Assn. [★4799]

Amer. Sod Producers Assn. [★IO]

Amer. Software Users Group - Defunct.

Amer. Soil Survey Assn. [★7674]

Amer. Sokol Educational and Physical Culture Org. [19025], 122 W 22nd St., Oak Brook, IL 60523-1557, (630)368-0771

Amer. Solar Energy Assn. [★7676]

Amer. Solar Energy Soc. [7676], 2400 Central Ave., Ste. A, Boulder, CO 80301, (303)443-3130

Amer. Solidarity Movement - Defunct.

Amer. Sommelier Assn. [194], 580 Broadway, Ste. 716, New York, NY 10012, (212)226-6805

Amer. Sons of Liberty [17087], 1142 S Diamond Bar Blvd., Ste. 305, Diamond Bar, CA 91765

American South
Center for Southern Folklore [9376]
Inst. for Southern Stud. [9377]
Southern Historical Assn. [9378]
Swedish Assn. for Amer. Stud. [IO]

Amer. Southdown Breeders' Assn. [5196], 100 Cornerstone Rd., Fredonia, TX 76842, (325)429-6226

Amer.-Southern Africa Chamber of Trade and Indus. [24375]

Amer.-Southern Africa Coun. - Defunct.

Amer. Sovereignty Task Force [17859], c/o State Dept. Watch, PO Box 65398, Washington, DC 20035

Amer.-Soviet Exchanges; Org. for [★17905]

Amer.-Soviet Textbook Study Project - Defunct.

Amer. Soybean Assn. [4304], 12125 Woodcrest Executive Dr., Ste. 100, St. Louis, MO 63141-5009, (314)576-1770

Amer. Soybean Inst. - Defunct.

Amer. Spa and Hea. Resort Assn. [3352], PO Box 585, Lake Forest, IL 60045, (847)234-8851

Amer. Space Found. - Defunct.

Amer. Space Frontier Comm. - Defunct.

Amer. Spaniel Club [22213], c/o Kathleen L. Patterson, Sec., PO Box 4194, Frankfort, KY 40604-4194, (502)352-4290

Amer. Spaniel Club [IO], Frankfort, KY, United States

Amer. Spanish Comm. [17088], PO Box 42, Leonia, NJ 07605-0042, (201)567-7417

Amer. Spasmodic Torticollis Assn. [★15353]

Amer. Specialty Toy Retailing Assn. [2385], 116 W Illinois St., Ste. 5E, Chicago, IL 60610, (312)222-0984

Amer. Specification Inst. - Defunct.

Amer. Speech Language Hearing Assn. [16442], 10801 Rockville Pike, Rockville, MD 20852, (800)638-8255

Amer. Speed Assn. [23072], c/o Racing Speed Associates, LLC dba ASA Racing, 457 S Ridgewood Ave., Ste. 101, Daytona Beach, FL 32114, (386)258-2221

Amer. Spelean Historical Assn. [10091], 6304 Kaybro St., Laurel, MD 20707, (301)725-5877

Amer. Spice Trade Assn. [1498], 2025 M St. NW, Ste. 800, Washington, DC 20036, (202)367-1127

Amer. Spinal Injury Assn. [16461], 2020 Peachtree Rd. NW, Atlanta, GA 30309-1402, (404)355-9772

Amer. Spoon Collectors [21966], PO Box 243, Rhinecliff, NY 12574, (845)876-0303

Amer. Spoon Collectors [IO], Rhinecliff, NY, United States

Amer. Sport Fishing Assn. [★23408]

Amer. Sport Horse Registry - Defunct.

Amer. Sport Touring Rider's Assn. - Address unknown since 2007.

Amer. Sportfishing Assn. [23408], 225 Reinekers Ln., Ste. 420, Alexandria, VA 22314, (703)519-9691

Amer. Sportpony Registry [★4851]

Amer. Sports Assn. [3656], 2 Sarah Ln., Monroe, NJ 08831, (732)446-8794

Amer. Sports Builders Assn. [1002], 8480 Baltimore Natl. Pike, No. 307, Ellicott City, MD 21043, (410)730-9595

Amer. Sports Education Inst./Boosters Clubs of America - Defunct.

Amer. Sports Inst. [8229], PO Box 1837, Mill Valley, CA 94942, (415)383-5750

Amer. Sports Medicine Assn. Bd. of Certification - Address unknown since 2006.

Amer. Sports Medicine Inst. [16478], 2660 10th Ave. S, Ste. 505, Birmingham, AL 35205, (205)918-0000

Amer. Sports Org. [23993], 40 E Highlands Ranch Pkwy., Highlands Ranch, CO 80126, (303)471-4035

Amer. Sportscasters Assn. [544], 225 Broadway, Ste. 2030, New York, NY 10007, (212)227-8080

Amer. Sportsman's Club - Address unknown since 1995.

Amer. Spotted Poland China Record [★5239]

Amer. Sprocket Chain Mfrs. Assn. [★1993]

Amer. Squadron of Aviation Historians - Address unknown since 1995.

Amer. Squid Marketing Assn. - Defunct.

Amer. Staffing Assn. [1254], 277 S Washington St., Ste. 200, Alexandria, VA 22314-3675, (703)253-2020

Amer. Stage Network - Address unknown since 2006.

Amer. Stamp Dealers Assn. [1910], 3 School St., Ste. 205, Glen Cove, NY 11542-2548, (516)759-7000

Amer. Standard Chinchilla Assn. [★5141]

Amer. Standard Chinchilla Rabbit Assn. [★5141]

Amer. Standard Chinchilla Rabbit Breeders Assn. [5141], c/o Patricia Gest, Sec.-Treas., 1607 9th St. W, Palmetto, FL 34221, (941)729-1184

Amer. Standardbred Breeders Assn. - Defunct.

Amer. Standards Assn. [★6267]

Amer. State Geologists; Assn. of [7129]

Amer. Sta. Wagon Owners Assn. [21577], PO Box 914, Matthews, NC 28106, (704)847-7510

Amer. Statistical Assn. [7702], 732 N Washington St., Alexandria, VA 22314-1943, (703)684-1221

Amer. Steamship Historical Soc. [★22980]

Amer. Steamship and Tourist Agents Assn. [★3907]

Amer. Steamship Traffic Executives Comm. - Defunct.

Amer. Steel Treaters' Soc. [★7311]

Amer. Steel Treaters' Soc. [★IO]

Amer. Sternwheel Assn. - Defunct.

Amer. Stock Exchange [3507], 86 Trinity Pl., New York, NY 10006, (212)306-1000

Amer. Stock Yards Assn. - Address unknown since 2003.

Amer. Street Machines - Defunct.

Amer. String Teachers Assn. [8904], 4153 Chain Bridge Rd., Fairfax, VA 22030, (703)279-2113

Amer. Striped Bass Soc. - Defunct.

Amer. Stroke Assn. [16492], Natl. Center, 7272 Greenville Ave., Dallas, TX 75231, (214)706-1890

Amer. Student Assn. - Address unknown since 1988.

Amer. Student Assn. of Community Colleges [9174], 2250 N Univ. Pkwy., Ste. 4865, Provo, UT 84604-1510, (801)863-8620

American Student Coun. Association [★9014]

Amer. Student Dental Assn. [8194], 211 E Chicago Ave., Ste. 700, Chicago, IL 60611-2687, (312)440-2795

Amer. Student Govt. Assn. [9175], 412 NW 16th Ave., Gainesville, FL 32601-4203, (352)373-6907

Amer. Student Hea. Assn. [★14714]

Amer. Student Media Assn. - Defunct.

A star before a book entry number signifies that the name is not listed separately, but is mentioned within the entry.

American Studies
Amer. History Forum and Civil War Educ. Assn. **[8500]**
Amer. Overseas Schools Historical Soc. **[10012]**
Amer. Portuguese Stud. Assn. **[9004]**
Amer. Stud. Assn. **[9367]**
Friends of the Amer. Museum in Britain/Halcyon Found. **[9370]**
Soc. for the Anthropology of North Am. **[6425]**
Statue of Liberty - Ellis Island Found. **[10066]**
Amer. Stud. Assn. **[9367]**, 1120 19th St. NW, Ste. 301, Washington, DC 20036, (202)467-4783
Amer. Subacute Care Assn. - Address unknown since 2004.
Amer. Subcontractors Assn. **[1003]**, 1004 Duke St., Alexandria, VA 22314-3588, (703)684-3450
Amer. Sudden Infant Death Syndrome Inst. **[16523]**, 509 Augusta Dr., Marietta, GA 30067, (770)426-8746
Amer. Suffolk Horse Assn. **[4847]**, c/o Mary Margaret M. Read, Sec., 4240 Goehring Rd., Ledbetter, TX 78946-5004
Amer. Suffolk Sheep Soc. **[★5219]**
Amer. Sugar Alliance **[1499]**, 2111 Wilson Blvd., Ste. 600, Arlington, VA 22201, (703)351-5055
Amer. Sugar Beet Industry Policy Comm. - Defunct.
Amer. Sugar Cane League of the U.S.A. **[5225]**, PO Drawer 938, Thibodaux, LA 70301, (985)448-3707
Amer. Sugarbeet Growers Assn. **[5226]**, 1156 15th St. NW, Ste. 1101, Washington, DC 20005, (202)833-2398
Amer. Sulphur Horse Assn. **[22585]**, 2180 Mt. Olive Ch. Rd., Taylorsville, NC 28681
American Sulphur Horse Association **[IO]**, Taylorsville, NC, United States
Amer. Sunbathers Stamp Club - Defunct.
Amer. Sunbathing Assn. **[★10760]**
Amer. Sunday School Union **[★20296]**
Amer. Supercharger Club and Owner's Assn. - Address unknown since 2001.
Amer. Supplier Inst. **[7725]**, 38705 7 Mile Rd., Ste. 345, Livonia, MI 48152, (734)464-1395
Amer. Supply Assn. **[3061]**, 222 Merchandise Mart Plz., Ste. 1400, Chicago, IL 60654, (312)464-0090
Amer. Supply and Machinery Mfrs. Assn. **[★2027]**
Amer. Surgical Assn. **[16575]**, 900 Cummings Ctr., Ste. 221-U, Beverly, MA 01915, (978)927-8330
Amer. Surgical Hosp. Assn. **[15036]**, 910 E 20th St., Sioux Falls, SD 57105, (605)275-5349
Amer. Surgical Trade Assn. **[★1860]**
Amer. Survival Assn. - Defunct.
Amer. Swan Boat Assn. **[23669]**, 312 Duff Ave., Wenonah, NJ 08090, (856)468-4646
Amer. Swedish Historical Museum **[10987]**, 1900 Pattison Ave., Philadelphia, PA 19145-5901, (215)389-1776
Amer. Swedish Inst. **[10988]**, 2600 Park Ave., Minneapolis, MN 55407-1090, (612)871-4907
Amer. Swedish Inst. **[IO]**, Minneapolis, MN, United States
Amer. Swimming Coaches Assn. **[23882]**, 5101 NW 21st Ave., Ste. 200, Fort Lauderdale, FL 33309, (954)563-4930
Amer. Swimming Pool Res. Org. - Defunct.
American-Swiss Assn. **[★19398]**
American-Swiss Assn. **[★IO]**
American-Swiss Found. **[IO]**, New York, NY, United States
American-Swiss Found. **[19398]**, 232 E 66th St., New York, NY 10021, (212)754-0130
Amer. Swiss Found. for Scientific Exchange - Address unknown since 1995.
Amer. Symphony Orchestra League **[10552]**, 33 W 60th St., 5th Fl., New York, NY 10023, (212)262-5161
Amer. Syringomyelia Alliance Proj. **[15305]**, PO Box 1586, Longview, TX 75606-1586, (903)236-7079
Amer. Tai Chi Assn. **[16593]**, 2465 Centreville Rd., No. J17, Ste. 150, Herndon, VA 20171, (703)477-8878
Amer. Tan Rabbit Specialty Club - Address unknown since 1995.
Amer. Tang Soo Do Assn. - Defunct.
Amer. Tapestry Alliance **[9416]**, PO Box 28600, San Jose, CA 95159-8600

American Tapestry Alliance **[IO]**, San Jose, CA, United States
Amer. Tarantula Soc. - Defunct.
Amer. Tarentaise Assn. **[4249]**, PO Box 594, Red Oak, IA 51566, (402)639-9808
Amer. Tarot Assn. **[22983]**, 2901 Richmond Rd., Ste. 130, No. 123, Lexington, KY 40509-1763, (800)372-1524
Amer. Tarot Assn. **[IO]**, Lexington, KY, United States
Amer. Tarpan Studbook Assn. - Address unknown since 1987.
Amer. Task Force for Lebanon **[19204]**, 2213 M St. NW, 3rd Fl., Washington, DC 20037, (202)223-9333
Amer. Task Force on Palestine **[17860]**, 815 Connecticut Ave., Ste. 200, Washington, DC 20006, (202)887-0177
Amer. Tax Policy Inst. **[18701]**, 1156 15th St. NW, Ste. 900, Washington, DC 20005, (202)637-3243
Amer. Tax Reduction Movement - Address unknown since 1994.
Amer. Tax Token Soc. **[22727]**, c/o Carl L. Cochrane, Sec.-Treas., 12 Pheasant Dr., Asheville, NC 28803
Amer. Taxation Assn. **[6291]**, c/o Amer. Accounting Assn., 5717 Bessie Dr., Sarasota, FL 34233-2399, (941)921-7747
Amer. Taxicab Assn. **[★3894]**
Amer. Taxicab Assn. **[★IO]**
Amer. Taxpayers Assn. - Defunct.
Amer. Teachers Assn. **[★24045]**
Amer. Teachers Assn. of the Martial Arts **[23582]**, c/o Dr. T.R. Crimi, PhD, Pres., 11990 Sunset Hill Rd., Penn Valley, CA 95946, (530)432-5588
Amer. Tech. Educ. Assn. **[9228]**, c/o North Dakota State Coll. of Sci., 800 N 6th St., Wahpeton, ND 58076-0002, (701)671-2240
Amer. Tech. Educ. Assn. **[IO]**, Wahpeton, ND, United States
Amer. Technical Soc. - Address unknown since 1995.
Amer. Technion Soc. **[★8677]**
Amer. Technion Soc. **[★IO]**
Amer. Teilhard Assn. **[9632]**, PO Box 280, Lewisburg, PA 17837, (570)523-0929
Amer. Teilhard Assn. for the Future of Man **[★9632]**
Amer. Teilhard de Chardin Assn. **[★9632]**
Amer. TeleEdCommunications Alliance **[7766]**, c/o Clancy DeLong, 1500 W High St., Mount Pleasant, MI 48858, (888)870-8677
Amer. Telemarketing Assn. **[★2614]**
Amer. Telemedicine Assn. **[16595]**, 1100 Connecticut Ave. NW, Ste. 540, Washington, DC 20036, (202)223-3333
Amer. Teleservices Assn. **[2614]**, 3815 River Crossing Pkwy., Ste. 20, Indianapolis, IN 46240, (317)816-9336
Amer. TV Soc. **[★563]**
Amer. Telugu Assn. **[9848]**, PO Box 4496, Naperville, IL 60567, (630)783-2250
Amer. Temperance Soc. **[★13303]**
Amer. Tennessee Fainting Goat Assn. **[4781]**
Amer. Tennis Assn. **[23900]**, 1100 Mercantile Ln., Ste. 115A, Largo, MD 20774, (301)583-4631
Amer. Tennis Indus. Fed. **[★3653]**
Amer. Textbook Coun. **[9258]**, 475 Riverside Dr., Rm. 1948, New York, NY 10115, (212)870-2760
Amer. Textile Machinery Assn. **[1997]**, 201 Park Washington Ct., Falls Church, VA 22046, (703)538-1789
Amer. Textile Mfrs. Inst. **[3772]**, 1130 Connecticut Ave. NW, Washington, DC 20036-3954, (202)862-0500
Amer. TFP **[19763]**, PO Box 251, Spring Grove, PA 17362, (717)225-7147
Amer. Theatre Arts for Youth **[11003]**, 1429 Walnut St., Philadelphia, PA 19102, (215)563-3501
Amer. Theatre Assn. **[★9262]**
Amer. Theatre Critics Assn. **[11004]**, c/o Kathryn Burger, Admin., 773 Nebraska Ave. W, St. Paul, MN 55117, (651)261-7804
Amer. Theatre and Drama Soc. **[11005]**, c/o Ken Bright, Membership Sec., 325 Clearview Ave., Apt. No. 2, Crafton, PA 15205
Amer. Theatre and Drama Soc. **[IO]**, Crafton, PA, United States

Amer. Theatre Organ Enthusiasts **[★10553]**
Amer. Theatre Organ Soc. **[10553]**, c/o Jim Merry, Exec. Sec., PO Box 5327, Fullerton, CA 92838-0327, (714)773-4354
American Theatre Society **[★11049]**
Amer. Theological Lib. Assn. **[10323]**, 300 S Wacker Dr., Ste. 2100, Chicago, IL 60606-6701, (312)454-5100
Amer. Theological Soc. - Midwest Div. - Address unknown since 2001.
Amer. Therapeutic Assn. - Address unknown since 2001.
Amer. Therapeutic Recreation Assn. **[16315]**, 1414 Prince St., Ste. 204, Alexandria, VA 22314, (703)683-9420
Amer. Therapeutic Soc. **[★15920]**
Amer. Thoracic Soc. **[16642]**, 61 Broadway, New York, NY 10006, (212)315-8600
Amer. Thoracic Soc. **[IO]**, New York, NY, United States
Amer. Thoroughbred Breeders Assn. **[★23515]**
Amer. Thoroughbred Owners Assn. **[★23515]**
Amer. Thyroid Assn. **[16646]**, 6066 Leesburg Pike, Ste. 550, Falls Church, VA 22041, (703)998-8890
Amer. Tilapia Assn. **[4666]**, 111 W Washington St., Ste. 1, Charles Town, WV 25414-1529, (304)728-2167
Amer. Time Travel Soc. - Defunct.
Amer. Tin Trade Assn. **[2698]**
Amer. Tinnitus Soc. **[16443]**, PO Box 5, Portland, OR 97207-0005, (503)248-9985
Amer. Tire Mfrs. Export Assn. - Defunct.
Amer. Title Assn. **[★3297]**
Amer. Tolkien Soc. - Address unknown since 2003.
Amer. Toll Bridge Assn. **[★6318]**
Amer. Toll Bridge Assn. **[★IO]**
Amer. Topical Assn. **[IO]**, Arlington, TX, United States
Amer. Topical Assn. **[22790]**, PO Box 57, Arlington, TX 76004-0057, (817)274-1181
Amer. Topical Assn., Americana Unit **[22791]**, 17 Peckham Rd., Poughkeepsie, NY 12603, (845)452-2126
Amer. Topical Assn., Biology Unit **[22792]**, c/o Christopher Dahle, Sec., 1401 Linmar Dr. NE, Cedar Rapids, IA 52402, (319)364-4999
Amer. Topical Assn; Fine Arts Unit of **[★22819]**
Amer. Torah Shelemah Comm. - Defunct.
Amer. Torch Soc. - Address unknown since 1995.
Amer. Tort Reform Assn. **[5926]**, 1101 Connecticut Ave. NW, Ste. 400, Washington, DC 20036, (202)682-1163
Amer. Tour Managers Assn. - Defunct.
Amer. Toy Fox Terrier Club **[22214]**, c/o Dr. Richard Lichty, Pres., 7522 Barrs Lake Rd., Duluth, MN 55803-9738, (218)525-3449
Amer. Toy Manchester Terrier Club **[★22204]**
Amer. Toy Retailers Assn. - Address unknown since 1995.
Amer. Track Racing Assn. **[23306]**, c/o Kathy Volski, Pres., 18203 Groeschke Rd., Houston, TX 77084, (281)578-0693
Amer. Tract Soc. **[19987]**, 1624 N 1st St., PO Box 462008, Garland, TX 75046-2008, (972)276-9408
Amer. Tractor Pullers Assn. **[★23929]**
Amer. Trade Assn. **[★IO]**
Amer. Trade Assn. for British Woolens - Defunct.
Amer. Trade Assn. Executives **[★315]**
Amer. Trade Assn. Executives **[★IO]**
Amer. Trade Union Coun. for Histadrut - Address unknown since 1999.
Amer. Traffic Safety Control Devices Assn. **[★3438]**
Amer. Traffic Safety Services Assn. **[3438]**, 15 Riverside Pkwy., Ste. 100, Fredericksburg, VA 22406-1077, (540)368-1701
Amer. Traffic Services Assn. **[★3438]**
Amer. Trails **[23935]**, PO Box 491797, Redding, CA 96049-1797, (530)547-2060
Amer. Trails Found. - Defunct.
Amer. Trails Network **[★23935]**
Amer. Train Dispatchers Assn. **[★24175]**
Amer. Train Dispatchers Dept. of the BLE **[24175]**, 1370 Ontario St., Ste. 1040, Cleveland, OH 44113-1736, (216)241-2770
Amer. Trainers Assn. - Defunct.

Reference to "IO" in place of a book number signifies that the association may be found in the 45th edition of International Organizations.

Amer. Trakehner Assn. [4848], 1536 W Church St., Newark, OH 43055, (740)344-1111

American Trakehner Association [IO], Newark, OH, United States

Amer. Tramp Shipowners Assn. - Defunct.

Amer. Transit Assn. [★3860]

Amer. Transit Assn. [★IO]

Amer. Transit Collectors' Assn. - Defunct.

Amer. Transit Service Coun. [6314]

Amer. Translators Assn. [3853], 225 Reinekers Ln., Ste. 590, Alexandria, VA 22314-2875, (703)683-6100

Amer. Transplant Assn. [16669], 47 W Polk St., Ste. 100-133, Chicago, IL 60605, (800)494-4527

Amer. Trans. Bowling Assn. [23249]

Amer. Trauma Soc. [16689], 8903 Presidential Pkwy., Ste. 512, Upper Marlboro, MD 20772, (301)420-4189

Amer. Travel Assn. [★1929]

Amer. Travel Inns [1929]

Amer. Trial Lawyers Assn. [★6328]

Amer. Trote and Trocha Assn. [4849], 17050 SW 20th Avenue Rd., Ocala, FL 34473-8808, (352)347-7761

Amer. Trotting Assn. [★23519]

Amer. Truck Dealers [3862], c/o Natl. Auto. Dealers Assn., 8400 Westpark Dr., McLean, VA 22102, (703)821-7000

Amer. Truck Historical Soc. [23021], PO Box 901611, Kansas City, MO 64190-1611, (816)891-9900

Amer. Truck Stop Owners Assn. [3397], PO Box 4949, Winston-Salem, NC 27115-4949, (336)744-5555

Amer. Truckers Benevolent Assn. - Defunct.

Amer. Trucking Associations [3863], 950 N Glebe Rd., Ste. 210, Arlington, VA 22203-4181, (703)838-1700

American Trucking Associations Foundation [★3863]

Amer. Trucking Associations; The Maintenance Coun. of the [★3895]

Amer. Trucking Associations; Tech. and Maintenance Coun. of the [3895]

Amer. Trudeau Soc. [★16642]

Amer. Trudeau Soc. [★IO]

Amer. Tube Assn. and Tube and Pipe Fabricators Assn., Intl. [★IO]

Amer. Tube Assn. and Tube and Pipe Fabricators Assn., Intl. [★3040]

Amer. Tunaboat Assn. - Defunct.

Amer. Tung Oil Assn., AAL - Defunct.

Amer. Tunis Sheep Breeders' Assn. [★5208]

Amer. Turkey Hunters Assn. - Defunct.

American-Turkish Coun. [18753], 1111 14th St. NW, Washington, DC 20005, (202)783-0483

American-Turkish Coun. [IO], Washington, DC, United States

American-Turkish Friendship Coun. [★IO]

American-Turkish Friendship Coun. [★18753]

Amer. Turkish Soc. [19407], 3 Dag Hammarskjold Plz., New York, NY 10017, (212)583-7614

Amer. Turkish Soc. [IO], New York, NY, United States

Amer. Turnerbund [★23802]

Amer. Turners [23802], 1127 E Kentucky St., PO Box 4216, Louisville, KY 40204, (502)636-2395

Amer. Turpentine Farmers Assn. Cooperative - Address unknown since 2003.

Amer. Type Culture Coll. [6567], PO Box 1549, Manassas, VA 20108, (703)365-2700

Amer. Typecasting Fellowship [9990], PO Box 263, Terra Alta, WV 26764, (304)789-2455

American Typecasting Fellowship [IO], Terra Alta, WV, United States

Amer. Ukrainian Medical Soc. [★15182]

Amer. Ukrainians; Self Reliance Assn. of [19414]

Amer. Underground Assn. [★7715]

Amer. Underground Constr. Assn. [7715], 3001 Hennepin Ave. S, Ste. D202, Minneapolis, MN 55408, (212)465-5541

American-Underground-Space Assn. [★7715]

Amer. Union of Men [18036], PO Box 80131, Santa Barbara, CA 93117

Amer. Union of Pizza Delivery Drivers [24062], PO Box 15172, Pensacola, FL 32514, (850)665-3494

Amer. Union of Students - Defunct.

Amer. Union of Swedish Singers - Defunct.

Amer. Unity Coun; Mexican [12277]

Amer. Universities; Assn. of [8099]

Amer. Universities Field Staff -Institute of World Affairs [★8663]

Amer. Universities Field Staff -Institute of World Affairs [★IO]

Amer. Univ. in Moscow [IO], Washington, DC, United States

Amer. Univ. in Moscow [8597], 1800 Connecticut Ave. NW, Washington, DC 20009, (202)364-0200

Amer. Urogynecologic Soc. [16703], 2025 M St. NW, Ste. 800, Washington, DC 20036-2422, (202)367-1167

Amer. Urological Assn. [16704], 1000 Corporate Blvd., Linthicum, MD 21090, (410)689-3700

Amer. Urological Assn. Found. [16705], 1000 Corporate Blvd., Linthicum, MD 21090, (410)689-3700

Amer. Uveitis Soc. [15668], c/o Rudolph M. Franklin, MD, Exec. Sec., 3535 Bienville Ave., Ste. W380, New Orleans, LA 70119

American-Uzbekistan Chamber of Commerce [24262], 1717 N St. NW, Washington, DC 20036, (202)828-4111

American-Uzbekistan Chamber of Commerce [IO], Washington, DC, United States

Amer. Vacuum Soc. [★7822]

Amer. Values; Inst. for [12158]

Amer. Vaulting Assn. [23967], 8205 Santa Monica Blvd., No. 1-288, West Hollywood, CA 90046, (323)654-0800

Amer. Vecturist Assn. [23006], c/o Richard Mallicote, Sec., 655 Wintergate Ct., Alpharetta, GA 30022-5584

Amer. Vegan Soc. [11067], 56 Dinshah Ln., PO Box 369, Malaga, NJ 08328, (856)694-2887

Amer. Vegetarian - Address unknown since 1989.

Amer. Vegetarian Union - Defunct.

Amer. Veneer Package Assn. - Defunct.

Amer. Venereal Disease Assn. - Address unknown since 1999.

Amer. Venous Forum [16721], 203 Washington St., PMB 311, Salem, MA 01970, (978)744-5005

Amer. Ventilation Assn. - Defunct.

Amer. Veterans Alliance [21283], 818 Concord St. NE, Salem, OR 97301, (503)391-2981

Amer. Veterans; AMVETS - [21285]

Amer. Veterans Assn. - Natl. HQ [21284]

Amer. Veterans Auxiliary; Disabled [20764]

Amer. Veterans Comm. - Defunct.

Amer. Veterans; Disabled [20763]

Amer. Veterans for Equal Rights [12215], PO Box 1490, Washington, DC 20006, (718)849-5665

Amer. Veterans of Foreign Ser. [★21331]

Amer. Veterans of Israel [21165], 136 E 39th St., New York, NY 10016-0914, (212)685-8548

Amer. Veterans Medical Airlift Ser. [6342], 931 Flanders Rd., PO Box 1065, La Canada Flintridge, CA 91011, (818)952-6212

Amer. Veterans Soc. of Artists - Address unknown since 1995.

Amer. Veterans That Enlisted Underage - Address unknown since 2008.

Amer. Veterans, U.S.A., Ladies Auxiliary; Polish Legion of [21260]

American Veterans of World War II, Korea and Vietnam; AMVETS [★21285]

Amer. Veterinarian Ser. Assn. [16776], 7115 W North Ave., Ste. 272, Oak Park, IL 60302, (708)453-0080

Amer. Veterinary Chiropractic Assn. [16777], 442154 E 140 Rd., Bluejacket, OK 74333, (918)784-2231

Amer. Veterinary Dental Soc. [16778], PO Box 803, Fayetteville, TN 37334, (931)438-0238

Amer. Veterinary Distributors Assn. [2957], 2105 Laurel Bush Rd., Ste. 200, Bel Air, MD 21015, (443)640-1040

Amer. Veterinary Exhibitors Assn. [1334]

Amer. Veterinary Holistic Medical Assn. [★16773]

Amer. Veterinary Medical Assn. [16779], 1931 N Meacham Rd., Ste. 100, Schaumburg, IL 60173, (847)925-8070

American Veterinary Medical Assn. Found. [★16779]

Amer. Veterinary Medical Assn; Student [16809]

Amer. Veterinary Medical Law Assn. [5927], c/o Karen M. Wernette, DVM, Exec. Dir., 511 N Country Ridge Ct., Lake Zurich, IL 60047-2824, (847)719-1810

Amer. Veterinary Neurology Assn. - Defunct.

Amer. Veterinary Radiology Soc. - Defunct.

Amer. Veterinary Soc. of Animal Behavior [16780], c/o Lisa Radosta, DVM, Sec.-Treas., PO Box 210636, Royal Palm Beach, FL 33421-0636

Amer. Veterinary Soc. for Computer Medicine - Address unknown since 1995.

Amer. Veterinary Soc. for the Stud. of Breeding Soundness [★16806]

Amer. Victims of Abortion [12903], 419 7th St. NW, Ste. 500, Washington, DC 20004, (202)626-8800

Amer. Video Assn. - Defunct.

Amer. Viewcard Club - Address unknown since 1995.

Amer. Viewpoint [★17072]

Amer. Viewpoint Soc. [★17072]

Amer. Vineyard Found. [5408], PO Box 5779, Napa, CA 94581, (707)252-6911

Amer. Vinland Assn. [19460], 537 Jones St., PMB 2154, San Francisco, CA 94102-2007

Amer. Viola Soc. [10554], 14070 Proton Rd., Ste. 100, Dallas, TX 75244-3601, (972)233-9107

Amer. Vision [19764], PO Box 220, Powder Springs, GA 30127, (770)222-7266

Amer. Viticultural Area Assn. - Defunct.

Amer. Vocational Assn. [★9300]

Amer. Vocational Education Personnel Development Assn. - Defunct.

Amer. Vocational Educ. Res. Assn. [★9301]

Amer. Volkssport Assn. [23803], 1001 Pat Booker Rd., Ste. 101, Universal City, TX 78148, (210)659-2112

Amer. Volleyball Coaches Assn. [23969], 2365 Harrodsburg Rd., Ste. A325, Lexington, KY 40504, (859)226-4315

Amer. Voyager Assn. [22666], 2015 Powers Dr., Lewiston, ID 83501, (208)746-3530

Amer. Voyager Assn. [IO], Lewiston, ID, United States

American Wagyu Association [IO], Pullman, WA, United States

Amer. Wagyu Assn. [4250], c/o Ms. Jeanene de Avila, PO Box 547, Pullman, WA 99163, (509)397-1011

Amer. Waldensian Aid Soc. [★20612]

Amer. Waldensian Soc. [20612], PO Box 398, Valdese, NC 28690, (336)716-4745

Amer. Walking Horse Assn. - Address unknown since 1995.

Amer. Walking Pony Assn. [4850], PO Box 5282, Macon, GA 31208, (478)743-2321

Amer. Walnut Manufacturers Assn. [1635], PO Box 5046, Zionsville, IN 46077, (317)873-8780

Amer. War Dads - Address unknown since 2003.

Amer. War Dads Auxiliary - Address unknown since 1995.

Amer. War Mothers [21190], 5415 Connecticut Ave. NW, Ste. L30, Washington, DC 20015, (202)362-0090

Amer. Warehouse Assn. [★3979]

Amer. Warehouse Assn. [★IO]

Amer. Warehousemen's Assn. [★IO]

Amer. Warehousemen's Assn. [★3979]

Amer. Wargaming Assn. [★22475]

Amer. Warmblood Registry [4851], PO Box 197, Carter, MT 59420, (406)734-5499

Amer. Warmblood Soc. [4852], 2 Buffalo Run Rd., Center Ridge, AR 72027-8347, (501)893-2777

Amer. Warmblood and Sport Horse Guild [4853]

Amer. Watch Assemblers Assn. [★2358]

Amer. Watch Assn. [2358]

Amer. Watch Workers Union - Defunct.

Amer. Watchmaker Inst. [★2359]

Amer. Watchmakers-Clockmakers Inst. [2359], 701 Enterprise Dr., Harrison, OH 45030, (513)367-9800

Amer. Watchmakers Inst. [★2359]

Amer. Water Buffalo Assn. [4996], c/o Dr. Hugh Popenoe, Pres., PO Box 13533, Gainesville, FL 32604, (352)392-2643

American Water Buffalo Association [IO], Gainesville, FL, United States

A star before a book entry number signifies that the name is not listed separately, but is mentioned within the entry.

Amer. Water Resources Assn. **[IO]**, Middleburg, VA, United States

Amer. Water Resources Assn. **[7827]**, PO Box 1626, Middleburg, VA 20118-1626, (540)687-8390

Amer. Water Ski Assn. **[★23979]**

Amer. Water Ski Educational Found. **[23975]**, 1251 Holy Cow Rd., Polk City, FL 33868-8200, (863)324-2472

Amer. Water Spaniel Club **[22215]**, c/o Jean Wright, Pres., 37499 Farris Rd., Scio, OR 97374, (503)394-3047

Amer. Water Spaniel Club **[IO]**, Fallbrook, CA, United States

Amer. Water Works Assn. **[IO]**, Denver, CO, United States

Amer. Water Works Assn. **[4008]**, 6666 W Quincy Ave., Denver, CO 80235-3098, (303)794-7711

Amer. Watercolor Soc. **[9417]**, 47 5th Ave., New York, NY 10003, (212)206-8986

Amer. Watercraft Assn. **[23980]**, PO Box 1993, Ashburn, VA 20147-9998, (800)913-2921

Amer. Waterpark Assn. **[★1329]**

Amer. Waterpark Assn. **[★IO]**

Amer. Watershed Coun. - Defunct.

Amer. Waterslager Soc. **[21842]**, c/o Tom Trujillo, Pres., 556 S Cactus Wren St., Gilbert, AZ 85296, (480)892-5464

American Waterslager Society **[IO]**, Gilbert, AZ, United States

Amer. Waterways Operators **[2601]**, 801 N Quincy St., Ste. 200, Arlington, VA 22203, (703)841-9300

Amer. Wax Importers and Refiners Assn. - Address unknown since 1995.

Amer. Weather Observers Supplemental Observation Network - Address unknown since 2003.

Amer. Weight Lifting Assn. - Defunct.

Amer. Welara Pony Soc. **[4854]**, PO Box 401, Yucca Valley, CA 92286-0401

American Welara Pony Society **[IO]**, Yucca Valley, CA, United States

Amer. Welders Assn. - Defunct.

Amer. Welding Inst. - Address unknown since 2001.

Amer. Welding Soc. **[7847]**, 550 NW Le Jeune Rd., Miami, FL 33126, (305)443-9353

Amer. Welding Soc. **[IO]**, Miami, FL, United States

American West

   Amer. Cowboy Culture Assn. **[9379]**

   Buffalo Bill Historical Center **[11105]**

   Cowboy Mounted Shooting Assn. **[23716]**

   Natl. Assn. for Outlaw and Lawman History **[9380]**

   Natl. Cowboy and Western Heritage Museum **[9381]**

   Natl. Fed. of Professional Bullriders **[23688]**

   Oregon-California Trails Assn. **[10056]**

   PEN Center U.S.A. **[11186]**

   Pony Express Historical Assn. **[10145]**

   Ranching Heritage Assn. **[10148]**

   Rodeo Historical Soc. **[9382]**

   Soc. of Private and Pioneer Numismatists **[22758]**

   Superstition Mountain Historical Soc. **[9383]**

   Western Cover Soc. **[22890]**

   Western Gamebird Alliance **[4466]**

   Western History Assn. **[9384]**

   Western Literature Assn. **[10434]**

   Westerners Intl. **[9385]**

   Women Writing the West **[4071]**

   Zane Grey's West Soc. **[9728]**

Amer. West African Freight Conf. **[★3597]**

Amer. West Overseas Assn. - Defunct.

Amer. Wheelchair Bowling Assn. **[23339]**, c/o Dave Roberts, Exec. Sec.-Treas., PO Box 69, Clover, VA 24534-0069, (434)454-2269

Amer. Whippet Club **[22216]**, c/o Kay Nierengarten, Membership Chair, 5654 Chalston Dr., Saginaw, MN 55779

Amer. White Horse and Amer. Creme Horse Registry **[4855]**, 90000 Edwards Rd., Naper, NE 68755, (402)832-5560

Amer. White Shepherd Assn. **[22217]**, c/o Melanie Fuellgraf, Membership Chair, 316 N Trail, Butler, PA 16002

Amer. Whitewater **[23682]**, PO Box 1540, Cullowhee, NC 28723, (828)293-9791

Amer. Whitewater Affiliation **[★23682]**

Amer. Wholesale Booksellers Assn. **[3398]**, c/o Patty Walsh, Exec. Sec., 702 S Michigan, South Bend, IN 46601, (574)288-4141

Amer. Wholesale Marketers Assn. **[1500]**, 2750 Prosperity Ave., Ste. 530, Fairfax, VA 22031, (703)208-3358

Amer. Widows of World War II **[★21195]**

Amer. Wild Equine Coun. - Defunct.

Amer. Wilderness Alliance **[★4354]**

Amer. Wildlands **[4354]**, PO Box 6669, Bozeman, MT 59771, (406)586-8175

Amer. Wildlife Education Found. - Defunct.

Amer. Wildlife Found. **[★5308]**

Amer. Wildlife Inst. **[★4471]**

Amer. Wildlife Inst. **[★5308]**

Amer. Willow Growers Network **[5255]**, c/o English Basketry Willows, 412 County Rd. 31, Norwich, NY 13815-3149, (607)336-9031

Amer. Wind Energy Assn. **[7852]**, 1101 14th St. NW, 12th Fl., Washington, DC 20005, (202)383-2500

Amer. Window Covering Mfrs. Assn. **[★2279]**

Amer. Wine Alliance for Res. and Educ. **[5409]**, PO Box 765, Washington, DC 20004-0765, (800)700-4050

Amer. Wine Assn. - Defunct.

Amer. Wine Soc. **[5410]**, c/o Mary Ann Coskery, Exec. Dir., 113 S Perry St., Lawrenceville, GA 30045, (678)377-7070

Amer. Wire Cloth Inst. **[1998]**, 25 N Broadway, Tarrytown, NY 10591, (914)332-0040

Amer. Wire Producers Assn. **[1999]**, 801 N Fairfax St., Ste. 211, Alexandria, VA 22314-1757, (703)299-4434

Amer. Wire Rope Mfrs. Assn. - Defunct.

Amer. Woman's Assn. - Defunct.

Amer. Woman's Economic Development Corp. **[3604]**, 216 E 45th St., 10th Fl., New York, NY 10017, (917)368-6100

Amer. Women's Soc. of Certified Public Accountants **[12]**, 136 S Keowee St., Dayton, OH 45402, (937)222-1872

Amer. Women of Berkshire and Surrey **[IO]**, Virginia Water, United Kingdom

Amer. Women Buyers Club - Defunct.

Amer. Women Composers - Address unknown since 2003.

Amer. Women Overseas Domestic Violence Fund **[12021]**

Amer. Women Overseas Domestic Violence Fund **[IO]**, Portland, OR, United States

Amer. Women Playwrights Assn. - Address unknown since 1995.

Amer. Women and Politics; Center for **[17516]**

Amer. Women in Radio and TV **[545]**, 8405 Greensboro Dr., Ste. 800, McLean, VA 22102, (703)506-3290

Amer. Women of Surrey **[IO]**, Cobham, United Kingdom

Amer. Women of Ticino **[IO]**, Carona, Switzerland

Amer. Women's Assn. of Hong Kong **[IO]**, Hong Kong, People's Republic of China

Amer. Women's Assn. of Kenya **[IO]**, Nairobi, Kenya

Amer. Women's Assn. for Renewable Energy - Address unknown since 2001.

Amer. Women's Assn. of Rome **[IO]**, Rome, Italy

Amer. Women's Assn. of Vienna **[IO]**, Vienna, Austria

Amer. Women's Auxiliary to the Royal Children's Hosp. Melbourne **[IO]**, Toorak, Australia

Amer. Women's Clergy Assn. **[★20615]**

Amer. Women's Clergy Assn; African- **[20615]**

Amer. Women's Club of Amsterdam **[IO]**, Amsterdam, Netherlands

Amer. Women's Club of Antigua and Barbuda **[IO]**, St. Johns, Antigua-Barbuda

Amer. Women's Club Antwerp **[IO]**, Brasschaat, Belgium

Amer. Women's Club of Basel **[IO]**, Basel, Switzerland

Amer. Women's Club of Berlin **[IO]**, Berlin, Germany

Amer. Women's Club of Bogota **[IO]**, Bogota, Colombia

Amer. Women's Club of Brussels **[IO]**, Brussels, Belgium

Amer. Women's Club of Cairo **[IO]**, Cairo, Egypt

Amer. Women's Club of Central Scotland **[IO]**, Edinburgh, United Kingdom

Amer. Women's Club of Cologne **[IO]**, Cologne, Germany

Amer. Women's Club of Curacao **[IO]**, Curacao, Netherlands Antilles

Amer. Women's Club of Dublin **[IO]**, Dublin, Ireland

Amer. Women's Club of Dusseldorf **[IO]**, Dusseldorf, Germany

Amer. Women's Club in Finland **[IO]**, Helsinki, Finland

Amer. Women's Club of Gothenburg **[IO]**, Goteborg, Sweden

Amer. Women's Club of Hamburg **[IO]**, Hamburg, Germany

Amer. Women's Club of Lausanne **[IO]**, Lausanne, Switzerland

Amer. Women's Club of Liechtenstein **[IO]**, Schaan, Liechtenstein

Amer. Women's Club of London **[IO]**, London, United Kingdom

Amer. Women's Club of Luxembourg **[IO]**, Luxembourg, Luxembourg

Amer. Women's Club of Madrid **[IO]**, Madrid, Spain

Amer. Women's Club Malmo **[IO]**, Malmo, Sweden

Amer. Women's Club of Oslo **[IO]**, Oslo, Norway

Amer. Women's Club of Perth **[IO]**, Perth, Australia

Amer. Women's Club of the Philippines **[IO]**, Makati City, Philippines

Amer. Women's Club of Shanghai **[IO]**, Shanghai, People's Republic of China

Amer. Women's Club in Stockholm **[IO]**, Stockholm, Sweden

Amer. Women's Club of the Taunus **[IO]**, Oberursel, Germany

Amer. Women's Club of Thailand **[IO]**, Wattana, Thailand

Amer. Women's Club of The Hague **[IO]**, The Hague, Netherlands

Amer. Women's Club of Zurich **[IO]**, Zurich, Switzerland

Amer. Women's Gp. of Languedoc-Roussillon **[IO]**, Baillargues, France

Amer. Women's Gp. in Paris **[IO]**, Paris, France

Amer. Women's Hospitals **[★14870]**

Amer. Women's Hospitals Ser. **[★14870]**

Amer. Women's Hospitals Ser. Comm. of AMWA **[14870]**, 801 N Fairfax St., Ste. 400, Alexandria, VA 22302, (703)838-0500

Amer. Women's Lawn Bowls Assn. **[★23256]**

Amer. Women's League of Kuwait **[IO]**, Bayan, Kuwait

Amer. Women's Org. of Greece **[IO]**, Athens, Greece

Amer. Women's Org. of Moscow **[IO]**, Moscow, Russia

Amer. Women's Physical Therapeutic Assn. **[★16603]**

Amer. Women's Self-Defense Assn. **[13010]**, 556 Rte. 17 N, Ste. 7-209, Paramus, NJ 07652, (888)STOP-RAPE

Amer. Women's Self-Defense Assn. **[IO]**, Lindenhurst, NY, United States

Amer. Women's Voluntary Services - Address unknown since 1995.

Amer. Wood Chip Export Assn. - Defunct.

Amer. Wood Fabric Inst. - Defunct.

Amer. Wood-Preservers' Assn. **[1636]**, PO Box 361784, Birmingham, AL 35236-1784, (205)733-4077

Amer. Wood Preservers Bur. - Defunct.

Amer. Wood Preservers Inst. - Defunct.

Amer. Wooden Money Guild **[22728]**

Amer. Wool Coun. **[3773]**, c/o Amer. Sheep Indus. Assn., 9785 Maroon Cir., Ste. 360, Englewood, CO 80112, (303)771-3500

Amer. Workers Party **[★18802]**

Amer. Workers Party **[★IO]**

Amer. Workforce Alliance for Responsible Economics; A.W.A.R.E. - **[1258]**

Amer. Working Collie Assn. **[22218]**, c/o Judy Cummings, Sec., 26695 Snell Ln., Los Altos Hills, CA 94022, (650)941-1022

Amer. Working Dog Fed. **[21516]**, c/o Al Govednik, Pres., 4282 Illinois Hwy. 17, Alpha, IL 61413, (309)334-3403

Amer. Working Malinois Assn. **[21517]**, c/o Dana Williams, Membership Chair, 12683 8th St., Garden Grove, CA 92840, (909)556-4212

Amer. Working Terrier Assn. - Address unknown since 1991.

Reference to "IO" in place of a book number signifies that the association may be found in the 45th edition of International Organizations.

Amer. World War II Orphans Network [11235], 5745 Lee Rd., Indianapolis, IN 46216, (540)310-0750

Amer. World War II Orphans Network [IO], Indianapolis, IN, United States

Amer. Wrestling Coaches and Officials Assn. [★23987]

Amer. Writers; Friends of [11171]

Amer. Wu Shu Soc. [23583], PO Box 5898, Long Island City, NY 11105-5898

Amer. Wu Shu Soc. [IO], Long Island City, NY, United States

Amer. Y-Flyer Yacht Racing Assn. [23157], 7349 Scarborough Blvd., East Dr., Indianapolis, IN 46256-2052, (317)849-7588

Amer. Yachtmen's Assn. [★23160]

Amer. Yangjia Michuan Taijiquan Assn. [23584], PO Box 173, Grand Haven, MI 49417

Amer. Yankee Assn. [21429], PO Box 1531, Cameron Park, CA 95682-1531, (530)676-4292

Amer. Yarn Spinners Assn. [3774], 2500 Lowell Rd., Gastonia, NC 28053, (704)824-3522

Amer. Yoga Assn. [11216], PO Box 19986, Sarasota, FL 34276, (941)927-4977

Amer. Yorkshire Club [5233], c/o Natl. Swine Registry, PO Box 2417, West Lafayette, IN 47996, (765)463-3594

Amer. Young Mensa - Defunct.

Amer. Youth Circus Org. [9795], PO Box 96, Temple, NH 03084, (603)654-5523

Amer. Youth Football [23428], 1000 S Point Dr., TH-9, Miami, FL 33139, (305)535-6591

Amer. Youth Found. [20638], 8706 Manchester Rd., Ste. 102, St. Louis, MO 63144, (314)963-1321

Amer. Youth Horse Coun. [4856], 6660 No. D-451 Delmonico, Colorado Springs, CO 80919, (719)594-9778

Amer. Youth Hostels [★12797]

Amer. Youth Hostels [★IO]

Amer. Youth Policy Forum [13468], 1836 Jefferson Pl. NW, Washington, DC 20036, (202)775-9731

Amer. Youth Soccer Org. [23774], 12501 S Isis Ave., Hawthorne, CA 90250, (800)872-2976

Amer. Youth Understanding Diabetes Abroad [14219], 1700 N Moore St., Ste. 2000, Arlington, VA 22209, (703)527-3860

Amer. Youth Understanding Diabetes Abroad [IO], Arlington, VA, United States

Amer. Youth Work Center [13469], 1200 17th St. NW, 4th Fl., Washington, DC 20036, (202)785-0764

Amer. Yugoslav Claims Comm. - Defunct.

Amer. Zinc Assn. [2699], 2025 M St. NW, Ste. 800, Washington, DC 20036, (202)367-1151

Amer. Zionist Comm. for Public Affairs [★18050]

Amer. Zionist Coun. [★20118]

Amer. Zionist Emergency Coun. [★20118]

Amer. Zionist Fed. [★20118]

Amer. Zionist Movement [20118], 633 3rd Ave., New York, NY 10017, (212)318-6100

Amer. Zionist Youth Coun. - Address unknown since 2000.

Amer. Zionist Youth Found. - Address unknown since 2004.

Amer. Zombie Assn. - Defunct.

Amer. Zoo and Aquarium Assn. [★7857]

Americana Music Assn. [10555], PO Box 128077, Nashville, TN 37212, (615)386-6936

Americanism Educational League [17623], PO Box 1287, Monrovia, CA 91017, (626)357-7733

Americanism Found. - Address unknown since 2002.

Americans Against Bombing; Americans Against World Empire/ [18794]

Americans Against Union Control of Govt. [17979], c/o Public Ser. Res. Coun., 320-D Maple Ave. E, Vienna, VA 22180-4742, (703)242-3575

Amers. Against Violence; Silent March: [17599]

Americans Against World Empire/Americans Against Bombing [18794]

Americans for the Arts [9546], 1000 Vermont Ave. NW, 6th Fl., Washington, DC 20005, (202)371-2830

Americans for Balanced Energy Choices [17495], PO Box 1638, Alexandria, VA 22313, (703)684-7473

Americans to Ban Cloning [17089], 1100 H St. NW, Ste. 700, Washington, DC 20005, (202)347-6840

Americans for Better Care [★17329]

Americans for Better Care of the Dying [13313], 1700 Diagonal Rd., Ste. 635, Alexandria, VA 22314, (703)647-8505

Americans for Better Immigration [17801], c/o Roy Beck, Pres., 1601 N Kent St., Ste. 1100, Arlington, VA 22209, (703)816-8820

Amers. for Budget Equity - Defunct.

Americans Caring for Children Worldwide [★20562]

Americans Caring for Children Worldwide [IO], Redlands, CA, United States

Amers. for Children's Relief - Defunct.

Amers. by Choice - Address unknown since 1990.

Americans for Civic Participation [★18364]

Americans; Coalition for Healthy Korean [14988]

Amers. for a Common Sense Budget - Defunct.

Amers. for Common Sense - Defunct.

Amers. Concerned About Corporate Power - Defunct.

Amers. for Constitutional Action - Address unknown since 1995.

Amers. for Constitutional Democracy - Address unknown since 2006.

Americans for Constitutional Freedom [★17126]

Americans for Constitutional Freedom; Media Coalition/ [★17126]

Amers. for Constitutional Integrity - Address unknown since 2004.

Americans for Constitutional Justice - Defunct.

Amers. for Constitutional Training - Address unknown since 1988.

Americans for Customary Weight and Measure [18679], PO Box 24A, Wiscasset, ME 04578

Amers. for Death with Dignity - Address unknown since 2001.

Americans for Decency [17282], 3431 W Thunderbird Rd., No. 13-275, Phoenix, AZ 85053-5641, (602)993-4353

Amers. for Democracy in Ukraine - Address unknown since 2004.

Americans for Democratic Action [18009], 1625 K St. NW, Ste. 210, Washington, DC 20006, (202)785-5980

Amers. for a Democratic Soc. - Defunct.

Amers. for Economic Freedom - Address unknown since 1995.

Amers. for Economic Reform.- Defunct.

Americans for Effective Law Enforcement [5652], 841 W Touhy Ave., Park Ridge, IL 60068-3351, (847)685-0700

Amers. for Energy Independence - Defunct.

Americans for the Enforcement of Attorney Ethics [12123], PO Box 35189, Chicago, IL 60707-0189, (773)283-3880

Americans for the Enforcement of Intellectual Property Rights [5837], PO Box 35215, Chicago, IL 60707-0215, (773)453-0080

Americans for the Enforcement of Judicial Ethics [12124], PO Box 35215, Chicago, IL 60707-0215, (708)453-0080

Amers. for the Environment - Address unknown since 2004.

Americans for Fair Electronic Commerce Transactions [17441], 1615 New Hampshire Ave. NW, Washington, DC 20009

Americans for Free Choice in Medicine [15158], 1525 Superior Ave., Ste. 101, Newport Beach, CA 92663

Amers. for Generational Equity - Defunct.

Amers. for God - Defunct.

Americans; Hall of Fame for Great [11119]

Amers. for Historic Preservation - Address unknown since 1995.

Amers. for Historical Accuracy - Defunct.

Amers. for Human Rights and Social Justice - Defunct.

Amers. for Human Rights in Ukraine [17744]

Amers. for Human Rights in Ukraine [IO], Newark, NJ, United States

Americans for Immigration Control [17802], PO Box 738, Monterey, VA 24465, (540)468-2023

Americans for Indian Opportunity [12624], 1001 Marquette Ave. NW, Albuquerque, NM 87102, (505)842-8677

Americans for Informed Democracy [5660], 45 Court St., New Haven, CT 06511, (203)773-1202

Americans for Intl. Aid [★11642]

Amers. of Italian Descent - Address unknown since 1999.

Amers. for Justice on the Job - Defunct.

Amers. of Lebanese-Syrian Ancestry for America - Address unknown since 1995.

Americans for Legal Reform; HALT - [★17961]

Americans for Legal Reform; HALT - An Org. of [17961]

Americans for Libraries Coun. [10324], 27 Union Sq. W, Ste. 204, New York, NY 10003, (646)336-6236

Amers. for Medical Freedom - Defunct.

Americans for Medical Progress [★13694]

Americans for Medical Progress Educational Found. [13694], 908 King St., Ste. 301, Alexandria, VA 22314, (703)836-9595

Americans for Middle East Understanding [18051], 475 Riverside Dr., Rm. 245, New York, NY 10115-0245, (212)870-2053

Americans for Middle East Understanding [IO], New York, NY, United States

Amers. for More Power Sources - Defunct.

Amers. for a Music Library in Israel - Defunct.

Amers. Mutually Interested in Giving Others a Start - Defunct.

Amers. for the Natl. Interest - Defunct.

Amers. for the Natl. Voter Initiative Amendment - Defunct.

Americans; New York Assn. for New [12479]

Americans for a Non-Violent Soc. - Defunct.

Americans for Nonsmokers' Rights [16432], 2530 San Pablo Ave., Ste. J, Berkeley, CA 94702, (510)841-3032

Amers. for Nuclear Energy - Address unknown since 1999.

Americans for Our Heritage and Recreation [4355], c/o The Conservation Fund, 1800 N Kent St., Ste. 1120, Arlington, VA 22209-2156, (703)525-6300

Americans Overseas
Amer. Citizens Abroad [18949]

Amers. for Peace in the Americas - Address unknown since 1988.

Amers. for Peace - Defunct.

Amers. for Peace and Democracy in the Middle East - Address unknown since 1986.

Americans for Peace Now [17935], 1101 14th St. NW, 6th Fl., Washington, DC 20005, (202)728-1893

Americans for Peace Now [IO], Washington, DC, United States

Amers. for the Presidency - Defunct.

Amers. for President Reagan's Foreign Policy - Defunct.

Amers. for Progressive Israel - Address unknown since 2001.

Americans for Reform - Address unknown since 2008.

Americans for Religious Liberty [17090], PO Box 6656, Silver Spring, MD 20916, (301)260-2988

Amers. for Responsible Govt. - Defunct.

Amers. for Safe and Competitive Trucking - Address unknown since 2001.

Americans for a Safe Israel [18052], 1751 2nd Ave., New York, NY 10128-5363, (212)828-2424

Americans for a Safe Israel [IO], New York, NY, United States

Americans for a Sound AIDS/HIV Policy [★IO]

Americans for a Sound AIDS/HIV Policy [★16962]

Americans for a Sound AIDS Policy [★16962]

Americans for a Sound AIDS Policy [★IO]

Amers. for Substance Abuse Prevention and Treatment - Address unknown since 1995.

Americans for Tax Reform [18702], 1920 L St. NW, Ste. 200, Washington, DC 20036, (202)785-0266

Americans for Trans. Mobility [6315], U.S. Chamber of Commerce, Congressional and Public Affairs, Trans. and Infrastructure, 1615 H St. NW, Washington, DC 20062, (202)463-5600

Amers. for Undivided Israel U.S.A. - Address unknown since 1990.

Americans for UNESCO [18760], The George Washington Univ., 2131 G St. NW, Washington, DC 20052, (202)994-0506

Amers. United for God and Country [17287]

Americans United for Israel [19157]

A star before a book entry number signifies that the name is not listed separately, but is mentioned within the entry.

Americans United for Life [12904], 310 S Peoria St., Ste. 300, Chicago, IL 60607-3534, (312)492-7234

Amers. United to Outlaw Fluoridation - Defunct.

Amers. United Res. Found. - Defunct.

Americans United for Separation of Church and State [19836], 518 C St. NE, Washington, DC 20002, (202)466-3234

Americans; United Services for New [★12471]

Amers. United for a Smoke Free Soc. - Defunct.

Americans for the Universality of UNESCO [★18760]

Amers. Want to Know - Defunct.

Americans With Disabilities Act [11920], 9841 SW 100 Ave., Miami, FL 33176, (305)271-0012

AmeriCares Found. [12833], 88 Hamilton Ave., Stamford, CT 06902, (203)658-9500

Americas

Americas Soc. [16974]

Americas Soc. [IO]

Council on Hemispheric Affairs [IO]

Coun. on Hemispheric Affairs [16975]

Inst. for the Stud. of Amer. Cultures [10746]

Inter-American Commn. on Human Rights [17765]

Inter-American Defense Bd. [17378]

Interamerican Assn. for Environmental Defense [4630]

Intl. Relations Center [16976]

Intl. Relations Center [IO]

North Amer. Cong. on Latin Am. [16977]

Org. of Amer. States [16978]

Org. of Amer. States [IO]

Pan Amer. Development Found. [IO]

Pan Amer. Development Found. [16979]

Partners of the Americas [16980]

Partners of the Americas [IO]

America's Angel [12140], PO Box 3124, San Diego, CA 92103

Americas Assn. of Cooperative/Mutual Insurance Societies [2141], 8201 Greensboro Dr., Ste. 300, McLean, VA 22102, (703)245-8077

America's Athletes with Disabilities [23340], 8630 Fenton St., Ste. 920, Silver Spring, MD 20910, (301)589-9402

America's Blood Centers [13762], 725 15th St. NW, Ste. 700, Washington, DC 20005, (202)393-5725

Americas Boychoir Fed. - Address unknown since 2003.

America's Carriers Telecommunication Assn. - Address unknown since 2002.

America's Charities [12196], 14150 Newbrook Dr., Ste. 110, Chantilly, VA 20151, (800)458-9505

America's Children Hunger Network [11558], c/o Ruby J. Aime, Pres., 25263 N 67th Dr., Peoria, AZ 85383, (623)376-0727

America's Children Hunger Network [IO], Peoria, AZ, United States

America's Community Bankers [461], 900 19th St. NW, Ste. 400, Washington, DC 20006, (202)857-3100

America's Conscience Fund - Defunct.

America's Development Found. [17387], 101 N Union St., Ste. 200, Alexandria, VA 22314, (703)836-2717

America's Earners' Protective Conf. - Defunct.

America's Ekiden Fed. - Defunct.

America's Estuaries; Restore [5278]

America's Found. [20709], 100 Front St., Ste. 1440, West Conshohocken, PA 19428, (601)825-7033

America's Freedom Ride - Defunct.

America's Fund for Afghan Children [11265], c/o The White House, 1600 Pennsylvania Ave. NW, Washington, DC 20500, (202)456-1111

America's Future [17624], 7800 Bonhomme Ave., St. Louis, MO 63105, (314)725-6003

America's Future; Campaign for [18388]

America's Future; Inst. for [18353]

America's Future Trees Found. - Defunct.

America's Hea. Insurance Plans [14682], 601 Pennsylvania Ave. NW, Ste. 500, Washington, DC 20004, (202)778-3200

America's Hea. Together [14614], 3220 Ordway St. NW, Washington, DC 20008, (202)966-1138

America's Nazi Party [★18802]

America's Nazi Party [★IO]

America's Promise - The Alliance for Youth [13470], 909 N Washington Ave., Ste. 400, Alexandria, VA 22314-1556, (703)684-4500

America's Second Harvest [12388], 35 E Whacker Dr., No. 2000, Chicago, IL 60601, (312)263-2303

America's Ser. Commissions [★6189]

America's Small Business Political Action Comm. - Defunct.

Americas Soc. [16974], 680 Park Ave., New York, NY 10021, (212)249-8950

Americas Soc. [IO], New York, NY, United States

Am'.s Soc. of Divorced Men [★12005]

America's Sound Transportation Review Org. - Defunct.

America's Sports Stars for POW's-MIA's - Defunct.

America's Victory Force [21343]

AmeriCorps VISTA [13383], 1201 New York Ave. NW, Washington, DC 20005, (202)606-5000

Amerifax Cattle Assn. [4251]

Amerika Katolika Esperanto-Societo - Defunct.

Amerikaanse Kamer van Koophandel [★IO]

Amerikos Lietuviu Taryba [★19210]

Amerikos Lietuviu Tautine Sajunga [★19215]

Amerind Found. [6406], PO Box 400, 2100 N Amerind Rd., Dragoon, AZ 85609, (520)586-3666

Amerind Found. [IO], Dragoon, AZ, United States

AMERPO Unit - Defunct.

Amertool Services - Defunct.

AMF Alcort Sailfish-Sunfish Class [★23194]

AMF Alcort Sailfish-Sunfish Class [★IO]

AMF Intl. [IO], Lansing, IL, United States

AMF Intl. [19988], PO Box 5470, Lansing, IL 60438-5470, (708)418-0020

AMF Sunfish Racing Class Assn. [★23194]

AMF Sunfish Racing Class Assn. [★IO]

AMG Intl. [IO], Chattanooga, TN, United States

AMG Intl. [20298], 6815 Shallowford Rd., Chattanooga, TN 37421, (423)894-6060

AMHS [11817], c/o Integrity Intl., 15702 Tasa Pl., Laurel, MD 20707, (301)953-7353

AMHS Inst. [★14597]

AMHS Inst; Assn. [★14597]

Amici della Terra - Italia [★IO]

Amici Thomae Mori [★IO]

AMICUS: Commun. Managers Assn. [IO], London, United Kingdom

Amicus Inst. of America - Defunct.

Amigos de las Americas [13384], 5618 Star Ln., Houston, TX 77057, (713)782-5290

Amigos de las Americas [IO], Houston, TX, United States

AMIGOS Bibliographic Coun. [★10325]

AMIGOS Lib. Services [10325], 14400 Midway Rd., Dallas, TX 75244-3509, (972)851-8000

Amigos da Terra - Brasil [★IO]

Amigos de la Tierra [★IO]

Amigos de la Tierra - Argentina [★IO]

Amigos de la Tierra El Salvador [★IO]

Amigos de la Tierra - Espana [★IO]

Amigos de la Tierra - Uruguay [★IO]

Amigu di Tera [★IO]

Amis de Cliff Richard and The Shadows [IO], Vif, France

Amis d'Escoffier Soc. of New York; Les [1535]

Amis de le Louisiene [★IO]

Amis de Panhard and Deutsch Bonnet; Les [21686]

Amis de la Reliure d'Art [★IO]

Amis de la Terre [★IO]

Amis de la Terre - Togo [★IO]

Amish

Anabaptist Sociology and Anthropology Assn. [7559]

Lancaster Mennonite Historical Soc. [21130]

Natl. Comm. for Amish Religious Freedom [19448]

AMISTAD Am. [8502], 746 Chapel St., Ste. 300, New Haven, CT 06510, (203)495-1839

AMIT [20119], 817 Broadway, New York, NY 10003, (212)477-4720

AMITA - Defunct.

Amity Alliances/Amity Intl. [IO], Viskhapatnam, India

Amity Found. [★IO]

Amity Found. [★12423]

Amity Fund; Sino-American [19016]

Amizade Global Service-Learning and Volunteer Programs [13385], PO Box 110107, Pittsburgh, PA 15232, (412)441-6655

Amizade Global Service-Learning and Volunteer Programs [IO], Pittsburgh, PA, United States

Amman World Trade Center [IO], Amman, Jordan

Ammunitions Mfrs. Inst; Sporting Arms and [1482]

Amnesty Information and Action Center - Defunct.

Amnesty Intl. - Algeria [IO], Algiers, Algeria

Amnesty Intl. - Argentina [IO], Buenos Aires, Argentina

Amnesty Intl. - Aruba [IO], Oranjestad, Aruba

Amnesty Intl. Asia Pacific [IO], Hong Kong, People's Republic of China

Amnesty Intl. Australia - NSW Br. [IO], Broadway, Australia

Amnesty Intl. - Austria [IO], Vienna, Austria

Amnesty Intl. - Bahamas [IO], Nassau, Bahamas

Amnesty Intl. - Barbados [IO], Bridgetown, Barbados

Amnesty Intl. - Belgium [IO], Antwerp, Belgium

Amnesty Intl. - Benin [IO], Cotonou, Benin

Amnesty Intl. - Bermuda [IO], Hamilton, Bermuda

Amnesty Intl. - Burkina Faso [IO], Ouagadougou, Burkina Faso

Amnesty Intl. - Canadian Sect. [IO], Ottawa, ON, Canada

Amnesty Intl. - Chile [IO], Santiago, Chile

Amnesty Intl. - Cote d'Ivoire [IO], Abidjan, Cote d'Ivoire

Amnesty Intl. - Croatia [IO], Zagreb, Croatia

Amnesty Intl. - Czech Republic [IO], Prague, Czech Republic

Amnesty Intl. Danish Sect. [IO], Copenhagen, Denmark

Amnesty Intl. - England [★IO]

Amnesty Intl. European Union Assn. [IO], Brussels, Belgium

Amnesty Intl. - Faroe Islands [IO], Torshavn, Faroe Islands

Amnesty Intl., Finnish Sect. [IO], Helsinki, Finland

Amnesty Intl. France [IO], Paris, France

Amnesty Intl. - Gambia [IO], Banjul, Gambia

Amnesty Intl. - Ghana [IO], Accra, Ghana

Amnesty Intl. - Grenada [IO], St. George's, Grenada

Amnesty Intl. - Guyana [IO], Georgetown, Guyana

Amnesty Intl. Hong Kong [IO], Hong Kong, People's Republic of China

Amnesty Intl. - Hungary [IO], Budapest, Hungary

Amnesty Intl. - Icelandic Sect. [IO], Reykjavik, Iceland

Amnesty Intl. - Intl. Secretariat [IO], London, United Kingdom

Amnesty Intl. - Ireland [IO], Dublin, Ireland

Amnesty Intl. Israel Sect. [IO], Tel Aviv, Israel

Amnesty Intl. - Italy [IO], Rome, Italy

Amnesty Intl. - Jamaica [IO], Kingston, Jamaica

Amnesty Intl. Japan [IO], Tokyo, Japan

Amnesty Intl. - Korea [★IO]

Amnesty Intl. Luxembourg [IO], Luxembourg, Luxembourg

Amnesty Intl. Malaysia [IO], Selangor, Malaysia

Amnesty Intl. - Mali [IO], Bamako, Mali

Amnesty Intl. Mexican Sect. [IO], Mexico City, Mexico

Amnesty Intl. - Mongolia [IO], Ulan Bator, Mongolia

Amnesty Intl. New Zealand Sect. [IO], Auckland, New Zealand

Amnesty Intl. Norge [★IO]

Amnesty Intl. - Norway [IO], Oslo, Norway

Amnesty Intl. Osterreich [★IO]

Amnesty Intl. - Pakistan [IO], Karachi, Pakistan

Amnesty Intl. - Paraguay [IO], Asuncion, Paraguay

Amnesty Intl. - Peru [IO], Lima, Peru

Amnesty Intl. - Philippines [IO], Quezon City, Philippines

Amnesty Intl. - Poland [IO], Warsaw, Poland

Amnesty Intl. - Puerto Rico [IO], Rio Piedras, PR, United States

Amnesty Intl. - Puerto Rico [17745], Calle Robles, No. 54 - Altos, Oficina 11, Rio Piedras, PR 00925

Amnesty Intl. - Russia [IO], Moscow, Russia

Amnesty Intl. Sect. Francaise [★IO]

Amnesty Intl. - Senegal [IO], Dakar, Senegal

Amnesty Intl. - Sierra Leone [IO], Freetown, Sierra Leone

Amnesty Intl. - South Africa [IO], Pretoria, Republic of South Africa

Amnesty Intl. - South Korean Sect. [IO], Seoul, Republic of Korea

Amnesty Intl. - Spain [IO], Madrid, Spain

Reference to "IO" in place of a book number signifies that the association may be found in the 45th edition of International Organizations.

Amnesty Intl., Suomen Osasto [★IO]
Amnesty Intl. - Swiss Sect. [IO], Bern, Switzerland
Amnesty Intl. - Taiwan [IO], Taipei, Taiwan
Amnesty Intl. - Thailand [IO], Bangkok, Thailand
Amnesty Intl. - Tunisia [IO], Tunis, Tunisia
Amnesty Intl. - Turkey [IO], Istanbul, Turkey
Amnesty Intl. - Ukraine [IO], Kiev, Ukraine
Amnesty Intl. - United Kingdom [IO], London, United Kingdom
Amnesty Intl. - United Kingdom Scottish Off. [IO], Edinburgh, United Kingdom
Amnesty Intl. of the U.S.A. [IO], New York, NY, United States
Amnesty Intl. of the U.S.A. [17746], 5 Penn Plz., New York, NY 10001, (212)807-8400
Amnesty Intl. - Zambia [IO], Kitwe, Zambia
Amnesty Intl. - Zimbabwe [IO], Harare, Zimbabwe
Amnesty for Women [IO], Hamburg, Germany
Amnet - Defunct.
Amnistia Internacional [★IO]
Amnistia Internacional Argentina [★IO]
Amnistia Internacional - Chile [★IO]
Amnistia Internacional - Paraguay [★IO]
Amnistia Internacional, Seccion Mexicana [★IO]
AMOA Intl. Flipper Pinball Assn. - Defunct.
AMOA Natl. Dart Assn. [23329], c/o Leslie Murphy, CAE, Exec. Dir., 7150 Winton Dr., Ste. 300, Indianapolis, IN 46268, (317)387-1299
AMOA National Dart Association [IO], Indianapolis, IN, United States
AMORC English Grand Lodge; Rosicrucian Order, [19336]
Amorphia - Defunct.
Amorphous Silica and Silicates Industry Assn; Synthetic [826]
AMP Soc. Staff Assn. [★IO]
Amphibian Veterinarians; Assn. of Reptilian and [16783]
Amphibians and Reptiles; Soc. for the Stud. of [7160]
Amphibious Auto Club of America - Defunct.
Amphicar Owners Club - Defunct.
Amputation Found; Natl. [11965]
Amputee Athletic Assn; U.S. [★23343]
Amputee Coalition of Am. [14236], 900 E Hill Ave., Ste. 285, Knoxville, TN 37915-2568, (865)524-8772
Amputee Found; Amer. [11916]
Amputee Golf Assn; Eastern [23446]
Amputee Golf Assn; Natl. [23349]
Amputee Hockey Assn; Amer. [23799]
Amputee Network; Intl. Child [11954]
Amputee Services Assn; United [15080]
Amputee Shoe and Glove Exchange - Defunct.
Amputee Skiers Assn; Natl. [★23343]
Amputee Soccer Assn; Amer. [23773]
Amputee Sports Assn; Canadian [IQ]
Amputee Sports Assn. - Defunct.
Amputees in Motion [★11921]
Amputees in Motion, Intl. [11921], c/o Amputee Coalition of Am., 900 E Hill Ave., Ste. 205, Knoxville, TN 37915-2566, (865)524-8772
Amsbaugh Family Assn. - Address unknown since 2002.
Amsterdam Coun. for Port and Industry - Address unknown since 1995.
Amtrak Historical Soc. - Address unknown since 1994.
Amtralease [3378]
AMURT [IO], Brussels, Belgium
Amusement Bus. Assn; Outdoor [1324]
Amusement Indus. Mfrs. and Suppliers Intl. [1298], Banco Bus. Park, 1061 Main St., Bin No. 28, North Huntingdon, PA 15642, (724)864-3862
Amusement Indus. Manufacturers and Suppliers Intl. [IO], Port St. Lucie, FL, United States
Amusement Machine Assn; Amer. [1296]
Amusement Machine Charitable Foundation; American [★1296]
Amusement Machine Charitable Foundation; American [★IO]
Amusement and Music Operators Assn. [1299], 33 W Higgins Rd., Ste. 830, South Barrington, IL 60010, (847)428-7699
Amusement Park Club Intl. - Defunct.

Amusement Park Safety and Security; Amer. Soc. for [3526]
Amusement Parks
Amer. Soc. for Amusement Park Safety and Security [3526]
Amusement Indus. Mfrs. and Suppliers Intl. [1298]
Amusement and Music Operators Assn. [1299]
Australian Amusement Leisure and Recreation Assn. [IO]
City Parks Alliance [18184]
Darkride and Funhouse Enthusiasts [21511]
European Fed. of Amusement and Leisure Parks [IO]
Intl. Assn. of Amusement Parks and Attractions [1303]
Natl. Amusement Park Historical Assn. [21512]
Natl. Assn. of Amusement Ride Safety Officials [214]
Natl. Fantasy Fan Club for Disneyana Enthusiasts [24791]
Outdoor Amusement Bus. Assn. [1324]
World Waterpark Assn. [1329]
Amusement Parks; Intl. Assn. of [★1303]
Amusement Parks; Mfrs. Div., Natl. Assn. of [★1298]
Amusement Parks; Natl. Assn. of [★1303]
Amusement Parks, Pools, and Beaches; Natl. Assn. of [★1303]
Amusement and Vending Machine Distributors Assn. - Defunct.
AMVETS - Amer. Veterans [21285], 4647 Forbes Blvd., Lanham, MD 20706-4380, (301)459-9600
AMVETS (American Veterans of World War II, Korea and Vietnam) [★21285]
AMVETS Auxiliary - Address unknown since 1995.
AMWA; Amer. Women's Hospitals Ser. Comm. of [14870]
Amy Beth Fan Club [24841], c/o T. Parravano, Dir., Peridot Records, PO Box 8846, Cranston, RI 02920, (401)785-2677
Amyloidosis Support Groups [14250], c/o Muriel Finkel, Pres., 232 Orchard Dr., Wood Dale, IL 60191, (847)350-7540
Amyloidosis Support Network [14251], 1490 Herndon Ln., Marietta, GA 30062, (770)977-1500
Amyotrophic Lateral Sclerosis
ALS March of Faces [13666]
Amyotrophic Lateral Sclerosis Assn. [15306], 27001 Agoura Rd., Ste. 150, Calabasas Hills, CA 91301-5104, (818)880-9007
Amyotrophic Lateral Sclerosis; Brazilian Assn. of [IO]
Amyotrophic Lateral Sclerosis Soc. of Am. [★15306]
Amyotrophic Lateral Sclerosis Soc. of Canada [IO], Toronto, ON, Canada
Amy's Doll Lover's Club [22391], 399 Winfield Rd., Rochester, NY 14622, (585)266-4956
Anabaptist Assn. of Australia and New Zealand [IO], Sutherland, Australia
Anabaptist Sociology and Anthropology Assn. [7559], c/o James P. Hurd, Chm., Bethel Univ., Dept. of Anthropology and Sociology, 3900 Bethel Dr., St. Paul, MN 55112, (651)638-6329
Anachronism; Soc. for Creative [10463]
Anaerobe Soc. of the Americas [6568], PO Box 452058, Los Angeles, CA 90045, (310)216-9265
Anaerobe Soc. of the Americas [IO], Los Angeles, CA, United States
Anaesthesia and Intensive Care; European Soc. for Computing and Tech. in [IO]
Anaesthesia Sect. of the Canadian Medical Assn. [★IO]
Anaesthetic Res. Soc. [IO], Nottingham, United Kingdom
Analyse des Reseaux Sociaux; Reseau Intl. pour l' [★7651]
Analyses of Behavior; Soc. for Quantitative [6541]
Analyses; Inst. for Defense [6256]
Anal. Assn; U.S.A. Transactional [13743]
Anal; Center for Expressive [★16217]
Anal. and Educ. Found; The Conservative Caucus Res., [17265]
Anal; Inst. for Expressive [16217]
Anal; Natl. Assn. for Bank Cost [★464]
Analysts and Advocates; Tax [★18718]
Analysts Fed; Financial [★2331]
Analysts; Inst. of Chartered Financial [★2331]

Analysts; Natl. Fed. of Municipal [749]
Analysts; New York Soc. of Security [3519]
Analysts Soc; Fixed Income [1462]
Analysts; Tax [18718]
Analytical Chemistry; Center for Process [6675]
Analytical Chemistry and Spectroscopy Societies; Fed. of [6682]
Analytical Chemists; Assn. of Official [★6671]
Analytical Development [★13427]
Analytical Development [★IO]
Analytical Lab. Managers Assn. [7237], 2019 Galisteo St., Bldg. I-1, Santa Fe, NM 87505, (505)989-4683
Analytical Life Sci. Systems Association [★3488]
Analytical Psychology; C.G. Jung Found. for [16147]
Analytical Psychology; Intl. Assn. for [IO]
Ananda Marga [IO], New Delhi, India
Ananda Marga [20633], 97-38 42nd Ave., 1F, Corona, NY 11368, (718)898-1603
Ananda Marga Pracarka Samgha - Berlin Sector [IO], Mainz, Germany
Ananda Marga Universal Relief Team - Brazil [IO], Sao Paulo, Brazil
Ananda Marga Yoga Soc. [★20633]
Ananda Yoga Teachers Assn. [11217], c/o The Expanding Light, 14618 Tyler Foote Rd., Nevada City, CA 95959, (530)478-7518
Anaphylaxis Australia Inc. [IO], Hornsby Heights, Australia
Anaphylaxis Canada [IO], Toronto, ON, Canada
Anaphylaxis Network; Food Allergy and [13600]
Anarchism
Intl. Centre for Res. on Anarchism [IO]
Voluntary Cooperation Movement [IO]
Voluntary Cooperation Movement [16981]
Workers Solidarity Alliance [16982]
Anarchist Assn. of the Americas - Defunct.
Anarchist Black Cross - Address unknown since 1995.
Anatomical Soc. [IO], Halle, Germany
Anatomical Soc. of Great Britain and Ireland [IO], Falmer, United Kingdom
Anatomical Soc. of Paris [IO], Paris, France
Anatomische Gesellschaft [★IO]
Anatomists; Amer. Assn. of [13667]
Anatomy
Amer. Assn. of Anatomists [13667]
Amer. Assn. of Clinical Anatomists [13668]
Anatomical Soc. [IO]
Anatomical Soc. of Great Britain and Ireland [IO]
Anatomical Soc. of Paris [IO]
British Assn. of Clinical Anatomists [IO]
Byelorussian Anatomical Soc. [IO]
Cajal Club [15385]
Canadian Assn. for Anatomy, Neurobiology and Cell Biology [IO]
European Assn. of Clinical Anatomy [IO]
European Fed. for Experimental Morphology [IO]
Human Anatomy and Physiology Soc. [7951]
Hungarian Anatomical Soc. [IO]
Intl. Acad. of Gnathology-American Sect. [14158]
Intl. Soc. for Plastination [15870]
Italian Soc. of Anatomy [IO]
Pan Amer. Assn. of Anatomy [13669]
Spanish Soc. of Anatomy [IO]
Anatomy and Physiology Soc; Human [7951]
Ancestry; Order of Americans of Armorial [20750]
Ancestry Res. Club - Defunct.
Anchor Block Found. - Address unknown since 2000.
Ancient Accepted Scottish Rite of Free-Masonry (Northern Masonic Jurisdiction); Supreme Coun., [19252]
Ancient Arabic Order of the Nobles of the Mystic Shrine for North Am; Imperial Coun. of the [19238]
Ancient Astronaut Soc. - Defunct.
Ancient Coin Collectors Guild [22729], PO Box 911, Gainesville, MO 65655, (417)679-2142
Ancient Egypt and Middle East Soc. [IO], Skegness, United Kingdom
Ancient Egyptian Arabic Order Nobles of the Mystic Shrine [19227], 2239 Democrat Rd., Memphis, TN 38132-1802, (901)395-0150
Ancient Egyptian Order of Sciots [19228], PO Box 501801, San Diego, CA 92150-1801, (858)755-0931

A star before a book entry number signifies that the name is not listed separately, but is mentioned within the entry.

Ancient Forest Intl. [4356], PO Box 1850, Redway, CA 95560, (707)923-4475
Ancient Forest Intl. [IO], Redway, CA, United States
Ancient Greek Philosophy; Soc. for [10830]
Ancient Historians; Assn. of [10093]
Ancient and Honorable Artillery Company of Massachusetts [21191], Armory Faneuil Hall, 4th Fl., Boston, MA 02109, (617)227-1638
Ancient and Honorable Artillery Company; Natl. Soc. Women Descendants of the [20749]
Ancient and Honorable Artillery Company; Order of Descendants of the [20751]
Ancient and Honourable Order of Small Castle Owners of Great Britain - Defunct.
Ancient and Illustrious Order Knights of Malta [19325]
Ancient Mediterranean Res. Assn. - Address unknown since 1988.
Ancient Military Historians; Soc. of [10481]
Ancient Monuments Soc. [IO], London, United Kingdom
Ancient Mystic Order of Bagmen of Bagdad Imperial Guild - Defunct.
Ancient Mystic Order of Samaritans - Address unknown since 2001.
Ancient Mystical Order Rosae Crucis [★19336]
Ancient Order of Foresters of the Pacific Coast Jurisdiction - Defunct.
Ancient Order of Gleaners [★19124]
Ancient Order of Hibernians in Am. [19152], 31 Logan St., Auburn, NY 13021-3925, (315)252-3895
Ancient Order United Workmen - Defunct.
Ancients [★21191]
And Justice for All [18639], PO Box 53079, Washington, DC 20009, (202)547-0508
Andalusian Assn; Amer. [★4894]
Andalusian and Lusitano Horse Assn; Intl. [4894]
Andean
  Inst. of Andean Res. [9386]
  Inst. of Andean Stud. [9387]
  Inst. of Andean Stud. [IO]
Andean Commn. of Jurists [IO], Lima, Peru
Andean Community - Gen. Secretariat [IO], Lima, Peru
Andean Cooperation in Health - Address unknown since 2002.
Andean Found. - Address unknown since 1995.
Andean Info. Network [IO], Cochabamba, Bolivia
Andean Rural Health Care - Address unknown since 2005.
Andelin Found. for Education in Family Living - Address unknown since 1995.
Anderson Soc; Clan [10953]
Andhra Pradesh Oil Millers' Assn. [IO], Hyderabad, India
Andlauer Family Assn. [20781], 3929 Milton Dr., Independence, MO 64055-4043, (816)373-5309
Andolan - Organizing South Asian Workers [24138], PO Box 720364, Jackson Heights, NY 11372, (718)426-2774
Andorra Chamber of Commerce, Indus. and Services [IO], Andorra la Vella, Andorra
Andorra DanceSport Fed. [IO], Andorra la Vella, Andorra
Andorra Natl. Comm. for UNICEF [IO], Andorra la Vella, Andorra
Andorra Radioamateur Union [IO], Andorra la Vella, Andorra
Andorra Squash Rackets Assn. [IO], Andorra la Vella, Andorra
Andorran Coll. of Dentists [IO], Andorra la Vella, Andorra
Andorran Philately Study Circle - Defunct.
Andover Distributors Assn. - Defunct.
Andre Agassi Fan Club [IO], Reading, United Kingdom
Andre Agassi Official Intl. Fan Club - Defunct.
Andrea McArdle Fan Club [24728], 2352 B South St., Elgin, IL 60123, (847)695-3163
Andrew the Apostle; Order of Saint [20073]
Andrew; Brotherhood of Saint [19946]
Andrew Furuseth Found. for Maritime Res. [★3593]
Andrew Jackson Papers Proj. [★11133]
Andrew W. Mellon Found. [10777], 140 E 62nd St., New York, NY 10065-8124, (212)838-8400

Andrews Sisters Fan Club - Address unknown since 1989.
Andrew's Soc. of the State of New York; Saint [19355]
Androgen Insensitivity Syndrome Support Gp. - USA [14441], PO Box 2148, Duncan, OK 73534-2148
Andrology; Amer. Soc. of [16702]
Andrology; Intl. Soc. of [IO]
Andrology; Nordic Assn. for [IO]
Andrology Soc; British [IO]
Andy Griffith Show Appreciation Soc. - Address unknown since 1995.
The Andy Griffith Show Rerun Watchers Club [25025], 9 Music Sq. S, PMB 146, Nashville, TN 37203-3286
Anemia Action Coun; Natl. [14794]
Anemia Assn; Amer. Sickle Cell [16415]
Anemia Blood and Res. Found. for Children; Cooley's [★14788]
Anemia Found; Cooley's [14788]
Anemia and MDS Intl. Found; Aplastic [14785]
Anemia and Myelodysplasia Assn. of Canada; Aplastic [IO]
Anemia Res. Fund; Fanconi [14450]
Anemia Soc; Amer. Sickle Cell [★16415]
Anemia Support Gp; Fanconi's [★14450]
Anesthesia Awareness Campaign [13677], PO Box 8592, Reston, VA 20195-2492, (703)437-7327
Anesthesia and Critical Care Soc; Intl. Trauma [13686]
Anesthesia and Critical Care; Soc. of Neurosurgical [15417]
Anesthesia in Dentistry; Amer. Soc. for Advancement of [★13673]
Anesthesia Educational Programs; Coun. on Accreditation of Nurse [8835]
Anesthesia History Assn. [13678], 200 Medical Arts Bldg., 200 Delafield Ave., Ste. 2070, Pittsburgh, PA 15215, (412)784-5343
Anesthesia Nurses; Amer. Soc. of Peri [15460]
Anesthesia Nurses; Amer. Soc. of Post [★15460]
Anesthesia Overseas [★15778]
Anesthesia Overseas [★IO]
Anesthesia and Pain Practice; Amer. Soc. of Regional [★13676]
Anesthesia Patient Safety Found. [13679], 8007 S Meridian St., Bldg. 1, Ste. 2, Indianapolis, IN 46217-2922
Anesthesia and Perinatology; Soc. for Obstetric [15903]
Anesthesia; Soc. for Educ. in [13690]
Anesthesia Soc; Navy [13687]
Anesthesia; Soc. for Pediatric [13691]
Anesthesia Technologists and Technicians; Amer. Soc. of [15083]
Anesthesiological Training Similator Program - Defunct.
Anesthesiologists; Amer. Coll. of Veterinary [16764]
Anesthesiologists; Amer. Osteopathic Soc. of [★13672]
Anesthesiologists; Soc. of Air Force [★13683]
Anesthesiology
  Amer. Acad. of Anesthesiologist Assistants [13670]
  Amer. Assn. of Nurse Anesthetists [15437]
  Amer. Bd. of Anesthesiology [13671]
  Amer. Coll. of Veterinary Anesthesiologists [16764]
  Amer. Dental Soc. of Anesthesiology [14133]
  Amer. Osteopathic Coll. of Anesthesiologists [13672]
  Amer. Soc. for Advancement of Anesthesia and Sedation in Dentistry [13673]
  Amer. Soc. for Advancement of Anesthesia and Sedation in Dentistry [IO]
  Amer. Soc. of Anesthesiologists [13674]
  Amer. Soc. of Critical Care Anesthesiologists [13675]
  Amer. Soc. of Interventional Pain Physicians [15837]
  Amer. Soc. of Regional Anesthesia and Pain Medicine [13676]
  Amer. Soc. of Regional Anesthesia and Pain Medicine [IO]
  Anaesthetic Res. Soc. [IO]

Anesthesia Awareness Campaign [13677]
Anesthesia History Assn. [13678]
Anesthesia Patient Safety Found. [13679]
Assn. of Anaesthetists of Great Britain and Ireland [IO]
Assn. of Cardiothoracic Anaesthetists [IO]
Assn. for Low Flow Anaesthesia [IO]
Assn. of Paediatric Anaesthetists of Great Britain and Ireland [IO]
Assn. of Univ. Anesthesiologists [13680]
Assn. of Veterans Affairs Anesthesiologists [13681]
Australia and New Zealand Coll. of Anaesthetists [IO]
Australian Soc. of Anaesthetists [IO]
Belgian Assn. of Regional Anesthesia [IO]
British Assn. of Indian Anaesthetists [IO]
Canadian Anesthesiologists' Soc. [IO]
Confed. of Latin Amer. Societies of Anesthesiology [IO]
Congenital Cardiac Anesthesia Soc. [13682]
Coun. on Accreditation of Nurse Anesthesia Educational Programs [8835]
Coun. on Certification of Nurse Anesthetists [15475]
Dannemiller Memorial Educational Found. [13683]
European Soc. of Anaesthesiology [IO]
European Soc. for Computing and Tech. in Anaesthesia and Intensive Care [IO]
European Soc. of Intravenous Anaesthesia [IO]
Fed. of European Associations of Paediatric Anaesthesia [IO]
Finnish Soc. of Anaesthesiologists [IO]
French Soc. of Anesthesia and Intensive Care [IO]
German Soc. of Anaesthesiology and Intensive Care Medicine [IO]
Indian Assn. of Cardiovascular Thoracic Anaesthesiologists [IO]
Intl. Anesthesia Res. Soc. [IO]
Intl. Anesthesia Res. Soc. [13684]
Intl. Soc. for Anaesthetic Pharmacology [13685]
International Society for Anaesthetic Pharmacology [IO]
International Trauma Anesthesia and Critical Care Society [IO]
Intl. Trauma Anesthesia and Critical Care Soc. [13686]
Israel Soc. of Anesthesiologists [IO]
Japanese Soc. of Anesthesiologists [IO]
Korean Soc. of Anesthesiologists [IO]
Malaysian Soc. of Anaesthesiologists [IO]
Malignant Hyperthermia Assn. of the U.S. [14464]
Navy Anesthesia Soc. [13687]
Obstetric Anaesthetists' Assn. [IO]
Philippine Soc. of Anesthesiologists [IO]
Royal Coll. of Anaesthetists [IO]
Sociedad de Anestesiologia de Chile [IO]
Soc. for the Advancement of Anaesthesia in Dentistry [IO]
Soc. for Ambulatory Anesthesia [13688]
Soc. of Cardiovascular Anesthesiologists [13689]
Soc. of Cardiovascular Anesthesiologists [IO]
Soc. for Computing and Tech. in Anaesthesia [IO]
Soc. for Educ. in Anesthesia [13690]
Soc. for Obstetric Anesthesia and Perinatology [15903]
Soc. for Pediatric Anesthesia [13691]
Soc. for Tech. in Anesthesia [13692]
Soc. for Tech. in Anesthesia [IO]
World Fed. of Societies of Anaesthesiologists [IO]
Anesthesiology; Amer. Dental Soc. of [14133]
Anesthetists; Amer. Assn. of Nurse [15437]
Anesthetists; Amer. Soc. of [★13674]
Anesthetists; Assn. of Univ. [★13680]
Anesthetists; Coun. on Certification of Nurse [15475]
Anesthetists; Long Island Soc. of [★13674]
Anesthetists; New York Soc. of [★13674]
Aneurysm Outreach Inc. [14544], 17222 Hwy. 929, Prairieville, LA 70769, (225)622-1577
A.N.G. Fan Club - Address unknown since 2006.
Angel Collectors Club of America - Address unknown since 2004.
Angel Flight Am. [★14312]
Angel Flight/Silver Wings [★24549]

Reference to "IO" in place of a book number signifies that the association may be found in the 45th edition of International Organizations.

Angel Flight West [12512], 3161 Donald Douglas Loop S, Santa Monica, CA 90405, (310)390-2958
Angel Network; Corporate [13817]
The Angel Planes [★14319]
Angel Tree Program; Prison Fellowship [★11888]
Angela Thirkell Soc. [9633], PO Box 7109, San Diego, CA 92167, (619)222-8143
Angelcare [11672], PO Box 600370, San Diego, CA 92160-0370, (619)795-6234
Angelcare [IO], San Diego, CA, United States
Angele Fernande Daniel Family Org. - Address unknown since 2003.
Angeles que Aguardan [★IO]
Angelic Warfare Confraternity - Defunct.
Angelman Syndrome Assn. [IO], Sutherland, Australia
Angelman Syndrome Found. [16528], 3015 E New York St., Ste. A2265, Aurora, IL 60504, (630)978-4245
Angelo State Univ. Alumni Assn. [18874], ASU Station No. 11049, San Angelo, TX 76909, (325)942-2122
Angelo State Univ. Ex-Students Assn. [★18874]
The Angels [★20684]
Anger Mgt. Providers; Amer. Assn. of [15185]
Angevin History; Haskins Soc. for Viking, Anglo-Saxon, Anglo-Norman, and [★10459]
Angiography and Interventions; Soc. for Cardiac [13924]
Angioma Alliance [15307], 107 Quaker Meeting House Rd., Williamsburg, VA 23188, (757)258-3355
Angioma Alliance [IO], Williamsburg, VA, United States
Anglers' Assn; Natl. Professional [23420]
Anglers and Boaters; Amer. League of [23407]
Anglers; Natl. Fed. of [IO]
Anglers Sportsman Soc; Bass [23410]

Anglican
Anglican Assn. of Biblical Scholars [19449]
Anglican Assn. of Biblical Scholars [IO]
Anglican Fellowship of Prayer [19452]
Anglican Order of Archbishop Robert Leighton [19453]
Anglican Soc. [19942]
Anglican Use Assn. [19450]
Assn. of Anglican Musicians [20425]
Colleges and Universities of the Anglican Communion [7952]
Colleges and Universities of the Anglican Communion [IO]
Commn. of the Churches on Intl. Affairs [20094]
Fellowship of Concerned Churchmen [19454]
Found. for Christian Theology [19960]
Intl. Order of St. Vincent [19963]
Sharing of Ministries Abroad U.S.A. [20393]
Soc. for Promoting and Encouraging Arts and Knowledge of the Church [19972]
South Amer. Missionary Soc. - USA [20398]
Anglican Assn. of Biblical Scholars [19449], c/o Kevin A: Wilson, Sec.-Treas., 2 Museum Sq., Lawrence, MA 01840
Anglican Assn. of Biblical Scholars [IO], Tewksbury, MA, United States
Anglican Bookstore, Oper. Pass-Along [★19972]

Anglican Catholic
Amer. Friends of the Anglican Centre in Rome [19451]
Amer. Friends of the Anglican Centre in Rome [IO]
Anglican Church in Japan [IO]
Anglican Fellowship of Prayer [19452]
Anglican Found. of Canada [IO]
Anglican Order of Archbishop Robert Leighton [19453]
Church Army in Canada [IO]
Fellowship of Concerned Churchmen [IO]
Fellowship of Concerned Churchmen [19454]
Modern Churchpeople's Union [IO]
Sharing of Ministries Abroad U.S.A. [20393]
Soc. of King Charles the Martyr [19455]
South Amer. Missionary Soc. - USA [20398]
Anglican Church in Japan [IO], Tokyo, Japan
Anglican Fellowship of Prayer [19452], 1106 Mansfield Ave., Indiana, PA 15701, (724)463-6436

Anglican Found. of Canada [IO], Toronto, ON, Canada
Anglican Musicians; Assn. of [20425]
Anglican Order of Archbishop Robert Leighton [19453]
Anglican Pacifist Fellowship [IO], Milton Keynes, United Kingdom
Anglican Soc. [19942], c/o Rev. J. Robert Wright, Pres., The Gen. Theological Seminary, 175 9th Ave., New York, NY 10011
Anglican Soc. in North America [★19942]
Anglican Use Assn. [19450]
Anglicans for Life [12905], 405 Frederick Ave., Sewickley, PA 15143-1522, (412)749-0455
Anglicans United [19943], PO Box 763217, Dallas, TX 75376-3217, (972)293-7443
Angling Assn; U.S. Shore [23425]
Angling Found. [★IO]
Angling Trades Assn. [IO], Kenilworth, United Kingdom
Anglo-Amer. Associates - Address unknown since 1991.
Anglo-Amer.-Hellenic Bur. of Education - Defunct.
Anglo-Austrian Music Soc. [IO], London, United Kingdom
Anglo Chilean Soc. [IO], London, United Kingdom
Anglo Danish Soc. [IO], Derby, United Kingdom
Anglo-European Coll. of Chiropractic [IO], Bournemouth, United Kingdom
Anglo-German Found. for the Stud. of Indus. Soc. [IO], London, United Kingdom
Anglo-Jewish Assn. [★IO]
Anglo-Jewish Assn. [IO], London, United Kingdom
Anglo-Jewish Assn. [★17947]
Anglo-Norman, and Angevin History; Haskins Soc. for Viking, Anglo-Saxon, [★10459]
Anglo-Saxon, Anglo-Norman, and Angevin History; Haskins Soc. for Viking, [★10459]
Anglo-Saxon Christian Patriot - Address unknown since 1999.
Angolan Taekwondo Fed. [IO], Luanda, Angola
Angora Goat Breeder's Assn; Amer. [4122]
Angora Goat Breeders Assn; Colored [4782]
Angora Goat Record and Registry - Defunct.
Angora Rabbit Breeders Club; Natl. [5150]

Anguilla
Anguilla Tourist Bd. [24224]
Anguilla Amateur Athletic Fed. [IO], The Valley, Anguilla
Anguilla Financial Services Assn. [IO], The Valley, Anguilla
Anguilla Natl. Trust [IO], The Valley, Anguilla
Anguilla Tourist Bd. [24224], c/o Mrs. Marie Walker, 246 Central Ave., White Plains, NY 10606, (914)287-2400
Anguilla Tourist Info. Off. [★24224]
Anguilla Tourist Info. and Reservation Off. [★24224]
Angus Assn. of Am; Red [4291]
Angus Assn; Amer. [4212]
Angus Assn; Natl. Junior [4275]
Angus Assn; North Amer. Romagnola and Rom [4283]
Angus Breeder's Assn; Amer. Aberdeen- [★4212]
Angus Soc. of Australia [IO], Armidale, Australia
Angus Youth Australia [IO], Armidale, Australia
Anheuser-Busch Collectors Club [21967], c/o Steinland Gifts and Collectibles, 14 N 679 Rte. 25, Ste. A, East Dundee, IL 60118, (847)428-3150
Aniline Assn. - Address unknown since 2003.
Animal Agriculture Alliance [1501], PO Box 9522, Arlington, VA 22219, (703)562-5160
Animal Agriculture; Natl. Inst. for [5003]
Animal Air Trans. [★11361]
Animal Alliance of Canada [IO], Toronto, ON, Canada
Animal Alternatives - Address unknown since 1999.
Animal Artists; Soc. of [9526]
Animal Assisted Therapy Found. [16604], 15632 Hwy. 110 S, Ste. 7, Whitehouse, TX 75791
Animal Behavior; Amer. Veterinary Soc. of [16780]
Animal Behavior Mgt. Alliance [7860], 3650 S Pointe Cir., No. 205, Laughlin, NV 89029
Animal Behavior Soc. [7861], Indiana Univ., 2611 E 10th St., Bloomington, IN 47408-2603, (812)856-5541

Animal Bond; Intl. Soc. for the Stud. of the Human-Companion [★16615]
Animal Breeders Assn. of Estonia [IO], Rapla, Estonia
Animal Breeders; Natl. Assn. of [5002]

Animal Breeding
Afghan Hound Club of Am. [22179]
African Love Bird Soc. [21832]
African Parrot Soc. [21833]
Airedale Terrier Club of Am. [22180]
Akhal-Teke Assn. of Am. [4808]
Akita Club of Am. [22181]
Akita Rescue Soc. of Am. [11341]
Alaskan Malamute Assistance League [11342]
Alaskan Malamute Club of Am. [22182]
All Amer. Premier Breeds Admin. [22183]
Alley Cat Allies [11343]
Alliance for Animals [11344]
Alpaca Assn. New Zealand [IO]
Alpaca Owners and Breeders Assn. [4120]
Alpines Intl. [4121]
Alpines Intl. [IO]
Amateur Field Trial Clubs of Am. [22184]
Amer. Angora Goat Breeder's Assn. [4122]
Amer. Appaloosa Assn. Worldwide [4809]
Amer. Assn. of Black Russian Terriers [22185]
Amer. Assn. of Cat Enthusiasts [21899]
Amer. Assn. of Owners and Breeders of Peruvian Paso Horses [4810]
Amer. Assn. of Spanish Timbrado Breeders [21834]
Amer. Azteca Horse Intl. Assn. [4811]
Amer. Bashkir Curly Registry [4812]
Amer. Beefalo World Registry [4123]
Amer. Beefalo World Registry [IO]
Amer. Belgian Blue Breeders [4213]
Amer. Belgian Hare Club [5131]
Amer. Berkshire Assn. [5230]
Amer. Black Hereford Assn. [4214]
Amer. Border Leicester Assn. [5177]
Amer. Bouvier des Flandres Club [22188]
Amer. Boxer Club [22189]
Amer. Boxer Rescue Assn. [11346]
Amer. Brahman Breeders Assn. [4216]
Amer. Brahmousin Coun. [4217]
Amer. British White Park Assn. [4218]
Amer. Brittany Club [22190]
Amer. Brussels Griffon Assn. [22191]
Amer. Buckskin Registry Assn. [4813]
Amer. Budgerigar Soc. [21836]
Amer. Bullmastiff Assn. [22192]
Amer. Canary Fanciers Assn. [21837]
Amer. Canine Educ. Found. [22193]
Amer. Cat Assn. [21900]
Amer. Cat Fanciers Assn. [21901]
Amer. Cavy Breeders Assn. [4124]
Amer. Checkered Giant Rabbit Club [5132]
Amer. Chesapeake Club [22195]
Amer. Cheviot Sheep Soc. [5178]
Amer. Cockatiel Soc. [21838]
Amer. Coll. of Theriogenologists [16763]
Amer. Connemara Pony Soc. [4815]
Amer. Cormo Sheep Assn. [5179]
Amer. Cotswold Record Assn. [5181]
Amer. Coun. of Spotted Asses [4125]
Amer. Cream Draft Horse Assn. [4816]
Amer. Dairy Goat Assn. [4126]
Amer. Dartmoor Pony Assn. [4817]
Amer. Delaine and Merino Record Assn. [5182]
Amer. Devon Cattle Assn. [4220]
Amer. Dexter Cattle Assn. [4221]
Amer. Dobermann Assn. [22196]
Amer. Dog Show Judges [22198]
Amer. Donkey and Mule Soc. [4127]
Amer. Dorper Sheep Breeders' Soc. [5183]
Amer. Dove Assn. [21839]
Amer. Dutch Bantam Soc. [5103]
Amer. Dutch Rabbit Club [5133]
Amer. English Spot Rabbit Club [5134]
Amer. Eskimo Dog Club of Am. [22199]
Amer. Fancy Rat and Mouse Assn. [22704]
Amer. Fed. of Aviculture [21840]
Amer. Fed. of New Zealand Rabbit Breeders [5135]
Amer. Ferret Assn. [22415]

A star before a book entry number signifies that the name is not listed separately, but is mentioned within the entry.

Amer. Finnsheep Breeders Assn. [5184]
Amer. Fox Terrier Club [22200]
Amer. Galloway Breeders' Assn. [4222]
Amer. Game Fowl Soc. [4190]
Amer. Gelbvieh Assn. [4223]
Amer. Gerbil Soc. [21515]
Amer. German Shepherd Rescue Assn. [11348]
Amer. Goat Soc. [4128]
Amer. Guernsey Assn. [4224]
Amer. Guinea Hog Assn. [5231]
Amer. Hackney Horse Soc. [4820]
Amer. Haflinger Registry [4821]
Amer. Half-Quarter Horse Registry [4822]
Amer. Hampshire Sheep Assn. [5185]
Amer. Hanoverian Soc. [4823]
Amer. Harlequin Rabbit Club [5136]
Amer. Hereford Assn. [4225]
Amer. Highland Cattle Assn. [4227]
Amer. Himalayan Rabbit Assn. [5137]
Amer. Holsteiner Horse Assn. [4824]
Amer. Horse Coun. [4825]
Amer. Indian Horse Registry [4827]
American-International Charolais Assn. [4228]
Amer. Jersey Cattle Assn. [4230]
Amer. Junior Shorthorn Assn. [4233]
Amer. Kennel Club [22201]
Amer. Kerry Bog Pony Soc. [4829]
Amer. Keuda Cat Assn. [4204]
Amer. Killifish Assn. [22434]
Amer. Kuvasz Assn. [12015]
Amer. Landrace Assn. [5232]
Amer. Legend [4129]
Amer. Lhasa Apso Club [22202]
Amer. Maine-Anjou Assn. [4234]
Amer. Maltese Assn. [22203]
Amer. Mammoth Jackstock Registry [4130]
Amer. Manchester Terrier Club [22204]
Amer. Milking Shorthorn Junior Soc. [4236]
Amer. Milking Shorthorn Soc. [4237]
Amer. Miniature Cheviot Sheep Breeders Assn.
  [5188]
Amer. Miniature Jersey Cattle Registry [4238]
Amer. Miniature Llama Assn. [21513]
Amer. Miniature Schnauzer Club [22205]
Amer. Mookee Assn. [4191]
Amer. Morgan Horse Assn. [4831]
Amer. Mule Assn. [4131]
Amer. Murray Grey Assn. [4239]
Amer. Mustang Assn. [4832]
Amer. Natl. CattleWomen [4240]
Amer. North Country Cheviot Sheep Assn. [5189]
Amer. Ostrich Assn. [4132]
Amer. Oxford Sheep Assn. [5190]
Amer. Paint Horse Assn. [4834]
Amer. Part-Blooded Horse Registry [4835]
Amer. Pinzgauer Assn. [4241]
Amer. Pointer Club [22206]
Amer. Pomeranian Club [22207]
Amer. Quarter Pony Assn. [4840]
Amer. Racing Pigeon Union [22894]
Amer. Rambouillet Sheep Breeders' Assn. [5192]
Amer. Ranch Horse Assn. [4841]
Amer. Rare Breed Assn. [4496]
Amer. Red Brangus Assn. [4242]
Amer. Red Poll Assn. [4243]
Amer. Romagnola Assn. [4244]
Amer. Romney Breeders' Assn. [5193]
Amer. Rottweiler Club [22208]
Amer. Saddlebred Horse Assn. [4842]
Amer. Saddlebred Sporthorse Assn. [4843]
Amer. Salers Assn. [4245]
Amer. Satin Rabbit Breeders' Assn. [5140]
Amer. Sealyham Terrier Club [22209]
Amer. Shagya Arabian Verband [4844]
Amer. Sheep Indus. Assn. [5194]
Amer. Shetland Pony Club/American Miniature
  Horse Registry [4845]
Amer. Shetland Sheepdog Assn. [22210]
Amer. Shih Tzu Club [22211]
Amer. Shorthorn Assn. [4247]
Amer. Shropshire Registry Assn. [5195]
Amer. Simmental Assn. [4248]
Amer. Singers Club [21841]
Amer. Southdown Breeders' Assn. [5196]
Amer. Spaniel Club [22213]

Amer. Standard Chinchilla Rabbit Breeders Assn.
  [5141]
Amer. Sulphur Horse Assn. [22585]
Amer. Tarentaise Assn. [4249]
Amer. Tilapia Assn. [4666]
Amer. Toy Fox Terrier Club [22214]
Amer. Trakehner Assn. [4848]
Amer. Trote and Trocha Assn. [4849]
Amer. Wagyu Assn. [4250]
Amer. Walking Pony Assn. [4850]
Amer. Warmblood Registry [4851]
Amer. Warmblood Soc. [4852]
Amer. Warmblood and Sport Horse Guild [4853]
Amer. Water Spaniel Club [22215]
Amer. Waterslager Soc. [21842]
Amer. Welara Pony Soc. [4854]
Amer. Whippet Club [22216]
Amer. White Horse and Amer. Creme Horse
  Registry [4855]
Amer. White Shepherd Assn. [22217]
Amer. Working Collie Assn. [22218]
Amer. Working Dog Fed. [21516]
Amer. Working Malinois Assn. [21517]
Amer. Yorkshire Club [5233]
Amerifax Cattle Assn. [4251]
Animal Breeders Assn. of Estonia [IO]
Animal Rights Coalition [11356]
Animal Rights Intl. [11357]
Ankole Watusi Intl. Registry [4252]
Anti-Cruelty Soc. [11364]
Arabian F.O.A.L. Assn. [11365]
Arabian Horse Breeders Alliance [4859]
Arabian Horse Trust [4861]
Arabian Professional and Amateur Horseman's
  Assn. [4862]
ARCA: Amer. Romeldale/CVM Assn. [5197]
Arizona Canine Acad. [22219]
Asiatic Breeders Assn. [4192]
Assoc. Koi Clubs of Am. [22437]
Assn. for People with Dogs Named Marty [22220]
Australian Cattle Dog Club of Am. [22221]
Australian Shepherd Club of Am. [22222]
Australian Soc. of Animal Production (Sydney Br.)
  [IO]
Australian Terrier Club of Am. [22223]
Authentic Hovawarts of North Am. [22224]
Ayrshire Breeders' Assn. [4253]
Barbados Blackbelly Sheep Assn. Intl. [5198]
Barzona Breeders Assn. of Am. [4254]
Basenji Club of Am. [22225]
Basset Hound Club of Am. [22226]
Bearded Collie Club of Am. [22227]
Beefmaster Breeders United [4255]
Belgian Draft Horse Corp. of Am. [4865]
Belgian Sheepdog Club of Am. [22228]
Belted Galloway Soc. [4256]
Berger Picard Club of Am. [22229]
Bernese Mountain Dog Club of Am. [22230]
Bichon Frise Club of Am. [22231]
Bird Clubs of Am. [21843]
Black Russian Terrier Club of Am. [22232]
Black Top and Natl. Delaine Merino Sheep Assn.
  [5199]
Bluefaced Leicester Union of North Am. [5200]
Bluetick Breeders of Am. [22233]
Border Terrier Club of Am. [22234]
Borzoi Club of Am. [22235]
Boston Terrier Club of Am. [22236]
Brotogeris Soc. Intl. [4194]
Brown Swiss Cattle Breeders Assn. of the U.S.A.
  [4258]
Buelingo Beef Cattle Soc. [4259]
Bull Terrier Club of Am. [22237]
Bulldog Club of Am. Rescue Network [11372]
Cairn Terrier Club of Am. [22238]
Californian Rabbit Specialty Club [5142]
Canada Fox Breeders Assn. [IO]
Canadian Swine Breeder Assn. [IO]
Canadian Swine Exporters Assn. [IO]
Canary and Finch Soc. [4195]
Canine Defense Fund [11373]
Cardigan Welsh Corgi Club of Am. [22240]
Carver-Scott Humane Soc. [11374]
Caspian Horse Soc. of the Americas [4869]
Cat Fanciers' Assn. [21903]

Cat Fanciers' Fed. [21904]
Caucasian Ovcharka Club of Am. [22241]
Cavalier King Charles Spaniel Club of Am.
  [22242]
Central States Roller Canary Breeders Assn.
  [21844]
Champagne d'Argent Rabbit Fed. [5143]
Champagne Horse Breeders' and Owners' Assn.
  [4870]
Chester White Swine Record Assn. [5234]
Chihuahua Club of Am. [22243]
Chinchilla Breeders' Gp. [IO]
Chinese Shar-Pei Club of Am. [22244]
Chow Chow Club, Inc. [22245]
Cinnamon Rabbit Breeders Assn. [5144]
Citizens to End Animal Suffering and Exploitation
  [11375]
Cleveland Bay Horse Soc. of North Am. [4871]
Clumber Spaniel Club of Am. [22246]
Clydesdale Breeders of the U.S.A. [4872]
Cockapoo Club of Am. [22247]
Collie Club of Am. [22248]
Colorado Ranger Horse Assn. [4873]
Colored Angora Goat Breeders Assn. [4782]
Columbia Sheep Breeders Assn. of Am. [5201]
COM-U.S.A. [21845]
Compassion for Animals Campaign [11381]
Continental Dorset Club [5202]
Continental Mi-Ki Assn. [22250]
Cotswold Breeders Assn. [4133]
Curly-Coated Retriever Club of Am. [22252]
Curly Sporthorse Intl. [4874]
Dachshund Club of Am. [22253]
Dales Pony Assn. of North Am. [4875]
Dales Pony Soc. of Am. [4876]
Dalmatian Club of Am. [22254]
Dandie Dinmont Terrier Club of Am. [22255]
Dartmoor Sheep Breeders' Assn. [IO]
Desert German Shorthaired Pointer Club [22256]
The Designer Cat Assn. [21906]
Doberman Pinscher Club of Am. [22257]
Dogs for the Deaf [14754]
Dogue de Bordeaux Soc. of Am. [22258]
Dohne Merino Breed Soc. of South Africa [IO]
Doris Day Animal League [11387]
Dutch Goatbreeders' Assn. [IO]
Echo Dogs White Shepherd Rescue [11388]
Egyptian Arabian Horse Alliance [4877]
Empress Chinchilla Breeders Cooperative [4134]
English Cocker Spaniel Club of Am. [22259]
English Setter Assn. of Am. [22260]
English Shepherd Club [22261]
English Springer Spaniel Field Trial Assn. [22262]
English Toy Spaniel Club of Am. [22263]
Epagneul Breton USA [22264]
Estrela Mountain Dog Assn. of Am. [22265]
European Fur Breeders Assn. [IO]
European Soc. of Domestic Animal Reproduction
  [IO]
Exotic Bird Soc. of Am. [21846]
Farm Sanctuary [11395]
Fed. for the Amer. Staffordshire Terrier [21518]
Fell Pony Soc. and Conservancy of the Americas
  [4878]
Fell Pony Soc. of North Am. [4879]
Ferret Fanciers Club [22416]
Fidelco Guide Dog Found. [16846]
Field Spaniel Soc. of Am. [22266]
Finnish Fur Breeders' Assn. [IO]
Fitzgerald's Fancys: Rat and Mouse Info. [22705]
Flat-Coated Retriever Soc. of Am. [22268]
Florida Keys Wild Bird Rehabilitation Center
  [5317]
French Brittany Gun Dog Assn. [22270]
French Bull Dog Club of Am. [22271]
French League for Animal Rights [IO]
Galiceno Horse Breeders Assn. [4883]
Gelbray Intl. [4262]
German Shepherd Dog Club of Am. [22272]
German Shorthaired Pointer Club of Am. [22274]
German Wirehaired Pointer Club of Am. [22275]
Golden Retriever Club of Am. [22277]
Goldfish Soc. of Am. [22439]
Gordon Setter Club of Am. [22278]
Gotland-Russ Assn. of North Am. [4885]

Reference to "IO" in place of a book number signifies that the association may be found in the 45th edition of International Organizations.

Grayson-Jockey Club Res. Found. [4886]
Great Dane Club of Am. [22279]
Great Pyrenees Club of Am. [22280]
Greyhound Adoption Center [11401]
Greyhound Club of Am. [22281]
Greyhound Racing Assn. of Am. [23392]
Guide Dogs of Am. [16851]
Guinea Fowl Breeders Assn. [4196]
Guinea Fowl Intl. Assn. [4197]
Half Saddlebred Registry of Am. [4889]
Harness Horsemen Intl. [23497]
Harness Racing Museum and Hall of Fame
  [23498]
Hartz Club of Am. [22772]
Havana Rabbit Breeders Assn. [5145]
Havana Silk Dog Assn. of Am. [22282]
Holland Lop Rabbit Specialty Club [5146]
Holstein Assn. USA [4263]
Hooved Animal Humane Soc. [11407]
Hotot Rabbit Breeders Intl. [5147]
Hovawart Club of Am. [22283]
Humane Farming Assn. [11411]
Hungarian Pumi Club of Am. [22284]
Hunting Retriever Club [22285]
Icelandic Horse Trekkers [4893]
Icelandic Sheepdog Assn. of Am. [22286]
Inst. for Lab. Animal Res. [13698]
Intl. Arabian Horse Assn. [4895]
Intl. Assn. of Butterfly Exhibitions [1341]
Intl. Assn. of Canine Professionals [1161]
The Intl. Bengal Breeders' Assn. [4205]
The Intl. Bengal Cat Soc. [4206]
Intl. Betta Cong. [22441]
Intl. Borzoi Coun. [22287]
Intl. Brangus Breeders Assn. [4265]
Intl. Buckskin Horse Assn. [4896]
The Intl. Cat Assn. [21910]
Intl. Colored Appaloosa Assn. [4897]
Intl. Conure Assn. [21848]
Intl. Curly Horse Org. [4898]
Intl. Desert Lynx Cat Assn. [4207]
Intl. Embryo Transfer Soc. [16794]
Intl. Fainting Goat Assn. [4784]
Intl. Fed. of Amer. Homing Pigeon Fanciers
  [22895]
Intl. French Brittany Club of Am. [22288]
Intl. Goat Assn. [4785]
Intl. Junior Brangus Breeders Assn. [4266]
Intl. Kennel Club of Chicago [22289]
Intl. Miniature Zebu Assn. [4268]
Intl. Modena Club [22896]
Intl. Morab Breeders' Assn. [4900]
Intl. Morab Registry [4901]
Intl. Nubian Breeders Assn. [4135]
Intl. Nubian Breeders Assn. [IO]
Intl. Pedigree Assignment and Bloodline Res.
  Assn. [4902]
Intl. Quarab Horse Assn. [4903]
The Intl. Savannah Breeders' Assn. [4208]
Intl. Seppala Assn. [22291]
Intl. Texas Longhorn Assn. [4269]
Intl. Trotting and Pacing Assn. [23501]
Intl. Wild Waterfowl Assn. [5331]
Intl. Yak Assn. [5001]
Intertribal Bison Cooperative [5036]
Irish Blacks Assn. [4270]
Irish Draught Horse Soc. of North Am. [4909]
Irish Terrier Club of Am. [22293]
Irish Water Spaniel Club of Am. [22294]
Irish Wolfhound Club of Am. [22295]
Jack Russell Terrier Club of Am. [22297]
Jacob Sheep Breeders Assn. [5203]
Japanese Akita Club of Am. [22298]
Japanese Chin Club of Am. [22299]
Japanese Soc. of Breeding [IO]
Jews for Animal Rights [11422]
The Jockey Club [23502]
Johns Hopkins Center for Alternatives to Animal
  Testing [11423]
Keeshond Club of Am. [22300]
Kiger Mesteno Assn. [4910]
Kuvasz Club of Am. [22302]
Ladies Kennel Assn. of Am. [22303]
LaPerm Soc. of Am. [21912]
Lippitt Morgan Breeders Assn. [4912]

Llama Assn. of North Am. [4136]
Lop Rabbit Club of Am. [5148]
Maremma Sheepdog Club of Am. [22304]
Marky Cattle Assn. [4271]
Mastiff Club of Am. [22305]
Miniature Australian Shepherd Club of Am.
  [22306]
Miniature Bull Terrier Club of Am. [22307]
Miniature Donkey Registry [4137]
Miniature Hereford Breeders Assn. [4272]
Miniature and Novelty Sheep Breeders Assn. and
  Registry [5204]
Miniature Pinscher Club of Am. [22308]
Missouri Fox Trotting Horse Breed Assn. [4913]
Mohair Coun. of Am. [4138]
Montadale Sheep Breeders Assn. [5205]
Natl. Alliance of Burmese Breeders [4210]
Natl. Amateur Retriever Club [22309]
Natl. Amer. Eskimo Dog Assn. [22310]
Natl. Amer. Indian Cattlemen's Assn. [4273]
Natl. Amer. Pit Bull Terrier Assn. [22311]
Natl. Angora Rabbit Breeders Club [5150]
Natl. Assn. of Animal Breeders [5002]
Natl. Assn. of Dog Obedience Instructors [22312]
Natl. Assn. of Louisiana Catahoulas [22313]
Natl. Beagle Club of Am. [22314]
Natl. Birman Fanciers [21913]
Natl. Bison Assn. [4139]
Natl. Bucking Bull Assn. [23687]
Natl. Cesky Terrier Club of Am. [22316]
Natl. Chicken Coun. [5111]
Natl. Cockatiel Soc. [21852]
Natl. Color-Bred Assn. [21853]
Natl. Comm. on Pot Bellied Pigs [4140]
Natl. Cutting Horse Assn. [4918]
Natl. Entlebucher Mountain Dog Assn. [22317]
Natl. Fed. of Flemish Giant Rabbit Breeders
  [5151]
Natl. Greyhound Assn. [22318]
Natl. Horse Show Commn. [4919]
Natl. Inst. of Red Orange Canaries and All Other
  Cage Birds [21855]
Natl. Junior Angus Assn. [4275]
Natl. Lilac Rabbit Club of Am. [5153]
Natl. Lincoln Sheep Breeders' Assn. [5207]
Natl. Museum of Racing and Hall of Fame
  [23508]
Natl. Mustang Assn. [4921]
Natl. Ornamental Goldfish Growers Assn. [4181]
Natl. Pedigreed Livestock Coun. [4141]
Natl. Pet Alliance [11441]
Natl. Pigeon Assn. [21856]
Natl. Poultry Improvement Plan [5112]
Natl. Pygmy Goat Assn. [4142]
Natl. Quarter Horse Registry [4922]
Natl. Quarter Pony Assn. [4923]
Natl. Rex Rabbit Club [5155]
Natl. Saanen Breeders Assn. [4143]
Natl. Show Pig Assn. [22982]
Natl. Silver Rabbit Club [5156]
Natl. Snaffle Bit Assn. [4926]
Natl. Spotted Saddle Horse Assn. [4927]
Natl. Spotted Swine Record [5239]
Natl. Swine Registry [5241]
Natl. Toy Fox Terrier Assn. [22321]
Natl. Tunis Sheep Registry, Inc. [5208]
Natl. Walking Horse Assn. [4928]
Natural Colored Wool Growers Assn. [5209]
New Zealand Soc. of Animal Production [IO]
Nigerian Dwarf Goat Assn. [4788]
North Amer. Babydoll Southdown Sheep Assn.
  and Registry [5211]
North Amer. Border Terrier Welfare [12019]
North Amer. Clun Forest Assn. [5212]
North Amer. Cockatiel Soc. [21857]
North Amer. Corriente Assn. [4278]
North Amer. Danish Warmblood Assn. [4930]
North Amer. Dept. of the Royal Warmblood
  Studbook of the Netherlands [4931]
North Amer. Deutsch Kurzhaar Club [22323]
North Amer. Equine Ranching Info. Coun. [1926]
North Amer. Falconers Assn. [23398]
North Amer. Fish Breeders Guild [22444]
North Amer. Gamebird Assn. [4144]
North Amer. Horsemen's Assn. [4932]

North Amer. Jack Russell Terrier Assn. [22324]
North Amer. Limousin Found. [4279]
North Amer. Limousin Junior Assn. [4280]
North Amer. Lionhead Rabbit Club [5157]
North Amer. Llewellin Breeders Assn. [22326]
North Amer. Model Horse Shows Assn. [22587]
North Amer. Mustang Assn. and Registry [4933]
North Amer. Normande Assn. [4281]
North Amer. Peruvian Horse Assn. [4934]
North Amer. Piedmontese Assn. [4282]
North Amer. Potbellied Pig Assn. [4145]
North Amer. Romagnola and RomAngus Assn.
  [4283]
North Amer. Shagya-Arabian Soc. [4936]
North Amer. Sheep Dog Soc. [22328]
North Amer. Single-footing Horse Assn. [4937]
North Amer. South Devon Assn. [4284]
North Amer. Spotted Draft Horse Assn. [4938]
North Amer. Teckel Club [22329]
North Amer. Tuli Assn. [4285]
North Amer. Wensleydale Sheep Assn. [5214]
North Amer. Working Bouvier Assn. [22330]
Norwegian Elkhound Assn. of Am. [22331]
Norwegian Forest Cat Breed Coun. [21914]
Norwegian Lundehund Assn. of Am. [22332]
Norwich and Norfolk Terrier Club [22333]
Oberhasli Breeders of Am. [4146]
Old English Sheepdog Club of Am. [22334]
OPP Concerned Sheep Breeders Soc. [16803]
Oregon Horsemen's Benevolent Protective Assn.
  [23512]
Painted Desert Sheep Soc. [5215]
Palomino Horse Breeders of Am. [4942]
Palomino Rabbit Co-Breeders Assn. [5158]
Paso Fino Horse Assn. [4943]
Patterdale Terrier Club of Am. [22338]
Pekingese Club of Am. [22339]
Pembroke Welsh Corgi Club of Am. [22340]
Performing Animal Welfare Soc. [11446]
Peruvian Inca Orchid Dog Club of Am. [22341]
Pet Care Trust [11447]
Pet Savers Found. [11449]
Piedmontese Assn. of the U.S. [4287]
PIGS - A Sanctuary [4147]
Pinto Horse Assn. of Am. [4944]
Pionus Breeders Assn. [21859]
Plymouth Rock Fanciers Club [5114]
Poland China Record Assn. [5242]
Polish Tatra Sheepdog Club of Am. [22342]
Pony of the Americas Club [4945]
Poodle Club of Am. [22343]
Portuguese Podengo Club of Am. [22344]
Portuguese Water Dog Club of Am. [22345]
Poultry Breeders of Am. [5115]
Prevent a Litter Coalition [11451]
Primarily Primates, Inc. [11452]
Professional Handlers Assn. [22346]
Pug Dog Club of Am. [22347]
Pure Puerto Rican Paso Fino Fed. of Am. [4946]
Purebred Dairy Cattle Assn. [4288]
Purebred Dexter Cattle Assn. of North Am. [4289]
Pyrenean Mastiff Club of Am. [22349]
Quaker Parakeet Soc. [4200]
Racking Horse Breeders' Assn. of Am. [4948]
RagaMuffin Cat Lovers Soc. [22777]
Ranchers-Cattlemen Action Legal Fund, United
  Stockgrowers of Am. [4290]
Rat, Mouse, and Hamster Fanciers [22708]
Rat Terrier Club of Am. [22350]
Red Angus Assn. of Am. [4291]
Rex Breeders United [21915]
Rhinelander Rabbit Club of Am. [5159]
Rhodesian Ridgeback Club of the U.S. [22351]
Rocky Mountain Horse Assn. [4949]
Rocky Mountain Llama and Alpaca Assn. [4148]
Sacred Cat of Burma Fanciers [21916]
Saint Bernard Club of Am. [22352]
Samoyed Club of Am. [22354]
Santa Gertrudis Breeders Intl. [4292]
Savannah Cat Club [4211]
Scottish Blackface Sheep Breeder's Assn. [5216]
Scottish Deerhound Club of Am. [22356]
Scottish Terrier Club of Am. [22357]
Sebright Club of Am. [5117]
Selkirk Rex Breed Club [21917]

A star before a book entry number signifies that the name is not listed separately, but is mentioned within the entry.

Senepol Cattle Breeders Assn. [4293]
Senior Conformation Judges Assn. [22358]
Serama Coun. of North Am. [4201]
Siberian Husky Club of Am. [22359]
Silky Terrier Club of Am. [22360]
Silver Marten Rabbit Club [5160]
Silver Wyandotte Club of Am. [5118]
Skye Terrier Club of Am. [22361]
Soays of Am. [5218]
Soc. Against Vivisection [11458]
Soc. of Border Leicester Sheep Breeders [IO]
Soc. of Parrot Breeders and Exhibitors [21860]
Soc. for the Stud. of Reproduction [16350]
Soc. for Theriogenology [16806]
Somali Cat Club of Am. [21918]
Somali Intl. Cat Club [21919]
Spanish-Barb Breeders Assn. [4952]
Spanish Mustang Registry [4953]
Spanish Water Dog Assn. of Am. [22362]
Spotted Saddle Horse Breeders' and Exhibitors'
  Assn. [4955]
Stafford Canary Club of Am. [21861]
Staffordshire Terrier Club of Am. [22364]
Standard Schnauzer Club of Am. [22365]
Standardbred Owners Assn. [23513]
Striped Bass Growers Assn. [4670]
Support Dogs, Inc. [11990]
Swedish Warmblood Assn. of North Am. [4958]
Tennessee Walking Horse Breeders' and Exhibi-
  tors' Assn. [4959]
Texas Longhorn Breeders Assn. of Am. [4294]
Thoroughbred Club of Am. [23514]
Thoroughbred Owners and Breeders Assn.
  [23515]
Thoroughbred Racing Associations [23516]
Thoroughbred Racing Protective Bur. [23517]
Tibetan Spaniel Club of Am. [22366]
Tibetan Terrier Club of Am. [22367]
Tiger Horse Assn. [4960]
Toledo Bird Assn., Zebra Finch Club of America
  [21862]
Traditional Cat Assn. [21920]
Traditional and Classic Cat Intl. [21921]
Tree House Animal Found. [11464]
Treeing Walker Breeders and Fanciers Assn.
  [22368]
Tufts Center for Animals and Public Policy
  [11466]
United Animal Nations [11470]
United Braford Breeders [4295]
United Burmese Cat Fanciers [21922]
United Cat Fed. [21923]
United Doberman Club [22369]
United Gloster Breeders [21863]
United Kennel Club [22370]
United Silver Fanciers [21924]
U.S. Animal Hea. Assn. [16811]
U.S. Assn. of Roller Canary Culturists [21864]
U.S. Boer Goat Assn. [4789]
U.S. Border Collie Club [22372]
U.S. Boxer Assn. [22373]
U.S. Kerry Blue Terrier Club [22374]
U.S. Lakeland Terrier Club [22375]
U.S. Lipizzan Registry [4963]
U.S. Mondioring Assn. [23389]
U.S. Neapolitan Mastiff Club [22376]
U.S. Peruvian Horse Assn. [4964]
U.S. Poultry and Egg Assn. [5122]
U.S. Rottweiler Club [22377]
U.S. Trotting Assn. [23519]
United Suffolk Sheep Assn. [5219]
Virginia Poultry Breeders Assn. [5124]
Viva! USA [11484]
Vizsla Club of Am. [22378]
Warmblood Breeders of North Am. [4968]
Weimaraner Club of Am. [22379]
Welsh Springer Spaniel Club of Am. [22380]
Wensleydale Longwool Sheep Breeders' Assn.
  [IO]
West Highland White Terrier Club of Am. [22381]
Western Intl. Walking Horse Assn. [4970]
Westminster Kennel Club [22382]
White German Shepherd Dog Club of Am.
  [22383]
Wild Canid Survival and Res. Center [5393]

Wildlife Trust [5402]
Wirehaired Vizsla Club of Am. [22384]
Working Pit Bull Terrier Club of Am. [22385]
Working Riesenschnauzer Fed. [22386]
World Bulldog Alliance [22387]
World Wide Kennel Club [22388]
WTCARES [22389]
Yorkshire Terrier Club of Am. [22390]
Animal Care; Amer. Assn. for Accreditation of Lab.
  [★13695]
Animal Care Coll. [IO], Ascot, United Kingdom
Animal Care Comm. [★11460]
Animal Care Panel [★13693]
Animal Care Trust; Farm [★4997]
Animal Concerns Trust; Food [4997]
Animal Control Acad; HSUS [★11412]
Animal Damage Control Assn; Natl. [5076]
Animal Defence League of Canada [IO], Ottawa,
  ON, Canada
Animal Diseases; Conf. of Res. Workers in [16790]
Animal Educational League - Defunct.
Animal Feed Mfrs. Assn. [IO], Centurion, Republic of
  South Africa
Animal Freedom Found. [IO], Groningen,
  Netherlands
Animal Guild of America - Defunct.
Animal Hea. Assn; U.S. [16811]
Animal Hea. Distributors Assn. [IO], Woodbridge,
  United Kingdom
Animal Hea. Found. [16781], 3615 Bassett Rd.,
  Pacific, MO 63069
Animal Hea. Info. Specialists [IO], Hatfield, United
  Kingdom
Animal Hea. Inst. [2970], c/o Ron Phillips, VP,
  Legislative and Public Affairs, 1325 G St. NW, Ste.
  700, Washington, DC 20005-3127, (202)637-2440
Animal Hea. Trust [IO], Newmarket, United Kingdom
Animal Hosp. Assn; Amer. [16739]
Animal Indus. Hea. [★1501]
Animal Indus. Veterinarians; Bur. of [★16799]
Animal Indus. Veterinarians; Natl. Assn. of Bur. of
  [★16799]
Animal Legal Defense Fund [11351], 170 E Cotati
  Ave., Cotati, CA 94931, (707)795-2533
Animal Liberation [IO], Courtenay, BC, Canada
Animal Liberation Action Gp. [11352], Univ. of
  Wisconsin Oshkosh, Campus Connection, Reeve
  Memorial Union, 748 Algoma Blvd., Oshkosh, WI
  54901-3512, (920)424-0265
Animal Liberation from Laboratories Coalition -
  Defunct.
Animal Managers Assn; Lab. [★13699]
Animal Medical Center [11353], 510 E 62nd St.,
  New York, NY 10021-8314, (212)838-8100
Animal Medicine; Amer. Bd. of Lab. [★16762]
Animal Medicine; Amer. Coll. of Lab. [16762]
Animal Mission [IO], Tadworth, United Kingdom
Animal Nutrition and Animal Products Inst. [IO], Pre-
  toria, Republic of South Africa
Animal Nutrition Assn. of Canada [IO], Ottawa, ON,
  Canada
Animal Nutrition Res. Coun. - Defunct.
Animal Place [11354], PO Box 5910, Vacaville, CA
  95696-5910, (707)449-4814
Animal and Plant Hea. Assn. [IO], Blackrock, Ireland
Animal Political Action Comm. - Address unknown
  since 1995.
Animal Protection Inst. of Am. [11355], PO Box
  22505, Sacramento, CA 95822, (916)447-3085
Animal Protection Soc. of Am. [★11469]
Animal Protective Assn. [★11404]
Animal Relief Effort; Rare [★5373]

Animal Research
Alley Cat Allies [11343]
Alliance for Animals [11344]
Alliance of Marine Mammal Parks and Aquariums
  [5006]
Amer. Assn. for Lab. Animal Sci. [13693]
Amer. Assn. of Retired Veterinarians [16748]
Amer. Coll. of Veterinary Anesthesiologists
  [16764]
Americans for Medical Progress Educational
  Found. [13694]
Animal Rights Coalition [11356]
Animal Rights Intl. [11357]

Anti-Cruelty Soc. [11364]
Assn. for Assessment and Accreditation of Lab.
  Animal Care Intl. [13695]
Assn. for Assessment and Accreditation of Lab.
  Animal Care Intl. [IO]
Carver-Scott Humane Soc. [11374]
Citizens to End Animal Suffering and Exploitation
  [11375]
Coalition to Protect Animals in Entertainment
  [11378]
Comparative Cognition Soc. [6400]
Compassion for Animals Campaign [11381]
Doing Things for Animals [11386]
Doris Day Animal League [11387]
Found. for Biomedical Res. [13696]
Fur Commn. U.S.A. [11399]
German Shepherd Dog Club of Am. - Working
  Dog Assn. [22273]
Grayson-Jockey Club Res. Found. [4886]
Hawk Mountain Sanctuary [5324]
Hooved Animal Humane Soc. [11407]
Humane Farming Assn. [11411]
Incurably Ill for Animal Res. [13697]
Inst. for Lab. Animal Res. [13698]
Intl. Assn. of Animal Behavior Consultants [7864]
Intl. Assn. for Bear Res. and Mgt. [5325]
Intl. Found. for Ethical Res. [11415]
Intl. Goat Assn. [4785]
Intl. Pedigree Assignment and Bloodline Res.
  Assn. [4902]
Jews for Animal Rights [11422]
Johns Hopkins Center for Alternatives to Animal
  Testing [11423]
Lab. Animal Mgt. Assn. [13699]
Natl. Assn. for Biomedical Res. [13700]
Nature of Wellness [13701]
Nature of Wellness [IO]
Performing Animal Welfare Soc. [11446]
Pet Savers Found. [11449]
Primarily Primates, Inc. [11452]
Public Responsibility in Medicine and Res.
  [18585]
Shark Res. Inst. [5019]
Sirenian Intl. [5016]
Soc. Against Vivisection [11458]
Tree House Animal Found. [11464]
Tufts Center for Animals and Public Policy
  [11466]
United Activists for Animal Rights [11469]
United Animal Nations [11470]
U.S. Animal Hea. Assn. [16811]
Walking Horse Trainers Assn. [4967]
Animal Res. and Conservation Center [★4469]
Animal Resources; Inst. of Lab. [★13698]
Animal Rights
2nd Chance 4 Pets [11481]
Activists for Protective Animal Legislation [11338]
Actors and Others for Animals [11339]
Akita Rescue Soc. of Am. [11341]
Alaskan Malamute Assistance League [11342]
Alley Cat Allies [11343]
Alliance for Animals [11344]
Alliance For Animal Rights [IO]
Amer. Anti-Vivisection Soc. [11345]
Amer. Assn. for Lab. Animal Sci. [13693]
Amer. Dog Owner's Assn. [11347]
Amer. German Shepherd Rescue Assn. [11348]
Amer. Horse Defense Fund [4826]
Amer. Mobile Groomers Assn. [2955]
Amer. Pet Soc. [11349]
Amer. Sanctuary Assn. [4156]
Amer. Soc. for the Prevention of Cruelty to
  Animals [11350]
Americans for Medical Progress Educational
  Found. [13694]
Animal Legal Defense Fund [11351]
Animal Liberation Action Gp. [11352]
Animal Medical Center [11353]
Animal Place [11354]
Animal Protection Inst. of Am. [11355]
Animal Rights Coalition [11356]
Animal Rights Intl. [11357]
Animal Rights Network/Institute for Animals and
  Soc. [11359]
Animal Trans. Assn. [11361]

Reference to "IO" in place of a book number signifies that the association may be found in the 45th edition of International Organizations.

Animal Welfare Inst. [11362]
Animals Australia [IO]
Animals Voice [11363]
Anti-Cruelty Soc. [11364]
Appalachian Bear Rescue [5293]
Assoc. Humane Societies [11366]
Assn. for Assessment and Accreditation of Lab. Animal Care Intl. [13695]
Assn. of Professional Humane Educators [12058]
The Assn. of Sanctuaries [11367]
Australians for Animals [IO]
Avian Welfare Coalition [4193]
Back in the Saddle Horse Adoption [4864]
Bide-A-Wee Home Assn. [11371]
Bulldog Club of Am. Rescue Network [11372]
Canine Defense Fund [11373]
Carver-Scott Humane Soc. [11374]
Chimp Haven [11729]
Choose Cruelty Free [IO]
Citizens to End Animal Suffering and Exploitation [11375]
Coalition to Protect Animals in Entertainment [11378]
Coalition to Protect Animals in Parks and Refuges [11379]
Comm. to Abolish Sport Hunting [11380]
Compassion for Animals Campaign [11381]
Compassion Over Killing [11382]
Concern for Helping Animals in Israel [11383]
Culture and Animals Found. [11384]
Dogs Deserve Better [12017]
Doing Things for Animals [11386]
Doris Day Animal League [11387]
Echo Dogs White Shepherd Rescue [11388]
Eco-Animal Allies [11773]
Equus Sanctuary [16983]
FARM (Farm Animal Reform Movement) [11394]
Farm Sanctuary [11395]
Found. for Biomedical Res. [13696]
Friends of Animals [11397]
Front Range Equine Rescue [4881]
Fund for Animals [11398]
Fund for Horses [4159]
Fur Commn. U.S.A. [11399]
Fur Free Alliance [4153]
Great Ape Proj. [11400]
GREY2K USA [4800]
Greyhound Adoption Center [11401]
Harmony House for Cats [11404]
Heart Bandits Amer. Eskimo Dog Rescue [12018]
Hearts United for Animals [11405]
Helping Hands Rescue [11406]
Hooved Animal Humane Soc. [11407]
Humane Farming Assn. [11411]
Humane Soc. of the U.S. [11412]
Incurably Ill for Animal Res. [13697]
Inst. for Lab. Animal Res. [13698]
Intl. Defenders of Animals [11414]
Intl. Found. for Ethical Res. [11415]
Intl. Fund for Animal Welfare [11416]
Intl. Primate Protection League [11418]
Intl. Soc. for Animal Rights [11419]
Intl. Soc. for Cow Protection [4155]
Intl. Veterinary Assistance [11420]
Jehovah's Witnesses for Animal Rights [11421]
Jews for Animal Rights [11422]
Johns Hopkins Center for Alternatives to Animal Testing [11423]
Mercy For Animals [11336]
Morris Animal Found. [11428]
MSPCA-Angell [11429]
Natl. Animal Control Assn. [11430]
Natl. Anti-Vivisection Soc. [11432]
Natl. Assn. for Biomedical Res. [13700]
Natl. Assn. for Humane and Environmental Educ. [11433]
Natl. Cat Protection Soc. [11434]
Natl. Cong. of Animal Trainers and Breeders [11435]
Natl. Dog Registry [11436]
Natl. Endowment for the Animals [11437]
Natl. Greyhound Adoption Prog. [11438]
Natl. Horse Protection Coalition [11439]
Natl. Humane Educ. Soc. [11440]
Natl. Opossum Soc. [4160]

Natl. Pet Alliance [11441]
Natl. Stinson Club [21467]
North Amer. Border Terrier Welfare [12019]
North Amer. Kai Assn. [22325]
Oregon Horsemen's Benevolent Protective Assn. [23512]
People for the Ethical Treatment of Animals [11444]
People Protecting Animals and Their Habitats [11445]
Performing Animal Welfare Soc. [11446]
Pet Care Trust [11447]
Pet Pride [11448]
Pet Savers Found. [11449]
Polar Bears Intl. [5367]
Political Assn. for Animal Rights in Europe [IO]
Prevent a Litter Coalition [11451]
Primarily Primates, Inc. [11452]
Sanctuary Workers and Volunteers Assn. [11455]
Save the Chimps [4298]
Scientists Center for Animal Welfare [11456]
Shark Res. Inst. [5019]
Soc. Against Vivisection [11458]
Soc. for Animal Protective Legislation [11459]
Soc. and Animals Forum [11460]
Stampe Club Intl. [21479]
Stolen Horse Intl. [11461]
Student Animal Rights Alliance [11337]
Sumatran Orangutan Soc. USA [5384]
Support Our Shelters [11462]
Tattoo-a-Pet [11463]
Tree House Animal Found. [11464]
Tufts Center for Animals and Public Policy [11466]
Unexpected Wildlife Refuge [11467]
United Action for Animals [11468]
United Activists for Animal Rights [11469]
United Animal Nations [11470]
United Humanitarians [11471]
U.S. Animal Hea. Assn. [16811]
U.S. Sportsmen's Alliance [23550]
U.S.A. Defenders of Greyhounds [11473]
Vegetarian Rsrc. Gp. [11073]
Viva! USA [11484]
Women's Humane Soc. Animal Shelter [11479]
Animal Rights America - Address unknown since 2004.
Animal Rights Aruba [IO], Oranjestad, Aruba
Animal Rights; Attorneys for [★11351]
Animal Rights Coalition [11356], PO Box 8750, Minneapolis, MN 55408, (612)822-6161
Animal Rights Information and Education Service - Address unknown since 2003.
Animal Rights Info. Ser. [★11465]
Animal Rights Intl. [11357], PO Box 1292, Middlebury, CT 06762, (203)598-0554
Animal Rights Intl. [IO], Middlebury, CT, United States
Animal Rights Kollective [IO], Toronto, ON, Canada
Animal Rights Mobilization [11358], PO Box 805859, Chicago, IL 60680, (773)282-8918
Animal Rights Network/Animals' Agenda [★11359]
Animal Rights Network/Institute for Animals and Soc. [11359], 3500 Boston St., Ste. 325, Baltimore, MD 21224, (410)675-4566
Animal Rights; Soc. for [★11419]
Animal Rights Sweden [IO], Alvsjo, Sweden
Animal Samaritans [IO], Bexleyheath, United Kingdom

Animal Science

Amer. Assn. for Lab. Animal Sci. [13693]
Amer. Assn. of Retired Veterinarians [16748]
Amer. Embryo Transfer Assn. [4149]
Amer. Registry of Professional Animal Scientists [215]
Amer. Soc. of Animal Sci. [4150]
Amer. Soc. for Reproductive Medicine [14389]
Animal Behavior Mgt. Alliance [7860]
Animal Nutrition and Animal Products Inst. [IO]
Assn. for Assessment and Accreditation of Lab. Animal Care Intl. [13695]
Australasian Soc. for the Stud. of Animal Behaviour [IO]
Australian Pork [IO]
British Chelonia Gp. [IO]

British Soc. of Animal Sci. [IO]
Canadian Assn. for Lab. Animal Sci. [IO]
Canadian Soc. of Animal Sci. [IO]
Champagne Horse Breeders' and Owners' Assn. [4870]
Comparative Cognition Soc. [6400]
European Assn. for Animal Production [IO]
Fed. of Animal Sci. Societies [4151]
Fed. of European Lab. Animal Sci. Associations [IO]
Fertility Res. Found. [14391]
Found. for Biomedical Res. [13696]
Inst. for Lab. Animal Res. [13698]
Intl. Comm. for Animal Recording [IO]
International Marine Animal Trainers Association [IO]
Intl. Marine Animal Trainers Assn. [6401]
Intl. Soc. for Animal Genetics [IO]
Japanese Soc. of Animal Sci. [IO]
Lab. Animal Mgt. Assn. [13699]
Lab. Animal Sci. Assn. [IO]
Natl. Animal Interest Alliance [11431]
Natl. Animal Supplement Coun. [4152]
Natl. Assn. for Biomedical Res. [13700]
Natl. Block and Bridle Club [24401]
Netherlands Centre Alternatives to Animal Use [IO]
Nordic Coun. for Reindeer Husbandry Res. [IO]
Poultry Sci. Assn. [5116]
Res. Inst. for Animal Hea. [IO]
Resolve, The Natl. Infertility Assn. [14394]
Scandinavian Soc. for Lab. Animal Sci. [IO]
Soc. for Lab. Animal Sci. [IO]
Spanish Ethological Soc. [IO]
World Assn. for Animal Production [IO]
World Rabbit Sci. Assn. [IO]
World's Poultry Sci. Assn., U.S.A. Br. [5125]
The Animal Soc. [11360], 723 S Casino Center Blvd., 2nd Fl., Las Vegas, NV 89101, (702)477-9677
The Animal Soc. [IO], Las Vegas, NV, United States
Animal Supplement Coun; Natl. [4152]
Animal Task Force; Farm [★11394]
Animal Technician Certification Program [★13693]
Animal Traction Network for Eastern and Southern Africa [IO], Nairobi, Kenya
Animal Trans. Assn. [11361], 111 East Loop N, Houston, TX 77029, (713)532-2177
Animal Trans. Assn. - European Off. [IO], Redhill, United Kingdom
Animal Trans. Assn. Intl; Independent Pet and [2958]

Animal Welfare

2nd Chance 4 Pets [11481]
Action Volunteers for Animals [IO]
Activists for Protective Animal Legislation [11338]
Actors and Others for Animals [11339]
Adopt A Husky [11340]
Advocates for Animals [IO]
African Love Bird Soc. [21832]
African Parrot Soc. [21833]
African Wild Dog Conservancy [5288]
Akhal-Teke Assn. of Am. [4808]
Akita Rescue Soc. of Am. [11341]
Alaskan Malamute Assistance League [11342]
Alley Cat Allies [11343]
Alliance for Animals [11344]
Amer. Anti-Vivisection Soc. [11345]
Amer. Appaloosa Assn. Worldwide [4809]
Amer. Assn. of Black Russian Terriers [22185]
Amer. Assn. of Cat Enthusiasts [21899]
Amer. Assn. of Equine Veterinary Technicians [16743]
Amer. Assn. of Housecall Veterinarians [16746]
Amer. Assn. of Human-Animal Bond Veterinarians [13702]
Amer. Assn. for Lab. Animal Sci. [13693]
Amer. Assn. of Retired Veterinarians [16748]
Amer. Assn. of Spanish Timbrado Breeders [21834]
Amer. Azteca Horse Intl. Assn. [4811]
Amer. Bashkir Curly Registry [4812]
Amer. Black Hereford Assn. [4214]
Amer. Boxer Rescue Assn. [11346]
Amer. Budgerigar Soc. [21836]

A star before a book entry number signifies that the name is not listed separately, but is mentioned within the entry.

Amer. Bullmastiff Assn. [22192]
Amer. Canary Fanciers Assn. [21837]
Amer. Cat Assn. [21900]
Amer. Cat Fanciers Assn. [21901]
Amer. Cockatiel Soc. [21838]
Amer. Dog Owner's Assn. [11347]
Amer. Dove Assn. [21839]
Amer. Dutch Bantam Soc. [5103]
Amer. Equestrian Alliance [1923]
Amer. Fed. of Aviculture [21840]
Amer. Ferret Assn. [22415]
Amer. Game Fowl Soc. [4190]
Amer. Gerbil Soc. [21515]
Amer. German Shepherd Rescue Assn. [11348]
Amer. Holsteiner Horse Assn. [4824]
Amer. Horse Defense Fund [4826]
Amer. Humane Assn. [13149]
Amer. Kerry Bog Pony Soc. [4829]
Amer. Keuda Cat Assn. [4204]
Amer. Kuvasz Assn. [12015]
Amer. Miniature Jersey Cattle Registry [4238]
Amer. Mobile Groomers Assn. [2955]
Amer. Mookee Assn. [4191]
Amer. Pet Soc. [11349]
Amer. Pheasant and Waterfowl Soc. [5292]
Amer. Ranch Horse Assn. [4841]
Amer. Rare Breed Assn. [4496]
Amer. Saddlebred Sporthorse Assn. [4843]
Amer. Sanctuary Assn. [4156]
Amer. Shagya Arabian Verband [4844]
Amer. Shetland Sheepdog Assn. [22210]
Amer. Singers Club [21841]
Amer. Soc. for the Prevention of Cruelty to
  Animals [11350]
Amer. Sulphur Horse Assn. [22585]
Amer. Toy Fox Terrier Club [22214]
Amer. Trote and Trocha Assn. [4849]
Amer. Wagyu Assn. [4250]
Amer. Water Spaniel Club [22215]
Amer. Waterslager Soc. [21842]
Amer. Working Collie Assn. [22218]
Animal Alliance of Canada [IO]
Animal Behavior Mgt. Alliance [7860]
Animal Defence League of Canada [IO]
Animal Freedom Found. [IO]
Animal Hea. Found. [16781]
Animal Legal Defense Fund [11351]
Animal Liberation [IO]
Animal Liberation Action Gp. [11352]
Animal Medical Center [11353]
Animal Mission [IO]
Animal Place [11354]
Animal Protection Inst. of Am. [11355]
Animal Rights Aruba [IO]
Animal Rights Coalition [11356]
Animal Rights Intl. [11357]
Animal Rights Intl. [IO]
Animal Rights Kollective [IO]
Animal Rights Mobilization [11358]
Animal Rights Network/Institute for Animals and
  Soc. [11359]
Animal Rights Sweden [IO]
Animal Samaritans [IO]
The Animal Soc. [IO]
The Animal Soc. [11360]
Animal Trans. Assn. [11361]
Animal Trans. Assn. - European Off. [IO]
Animal Welfare Inst. [11362]
Animalia- Fed. for the Protection of Animals [IO]
Animals in Distress Sanctuary [IO]
Animals First [11482]
Animals in Mind [IO]
Animals Voice [IO]
Animals Voice [11363]
Anonymous [IO]
Anti-Cruelty Soc. [11364]
Appalachian Bear Rescue [5293]
Arabian F.O.A.L. Assn. [11365]
Arabian Professional and Amateur Horseman's
  Assn. [4862]
Arcus Found. [18266]
Arizona Canine Acad. [22219]
Asiatic Breeders Assn. [4192]
Assoc. Humane Societies [11366]
Assn. for Assessment and Accreditation of Lab.
  Animal Care Intl. [13695]

Assn. for People with Dogs Named Marty [22220]
Assn. of Professional Humane Educators [12058]
Assn. for the Protection of Fur-Bearing Animals
  [IO]
The Assn. of Sanctuaries [11367]
Assn. of Shelter Veterinarians [16784]
Assn. of Veterinarians for Animal Rights [11368]
Australian Animal Protection Soc. [IO]
Australian Assn. for Humane Res. [IO]
Australian and New Zealand Coun. for the Care of
  Animals in Res. and Teaching [IO]
Australian Shepherd Club of Am. [22222]
Avian Welfare Coalition [4193]
Back in the Saddle Horse Adoption [4864]
Bear Trust Intl. [5297]
Beardies and Others Needing Emissaries [11369]
Beaver Water World [IO]
Best Friends Animal Soc. [11370]
Bide-A-Wee Home Assn. [11371]
Bide Awhile Animal Shelter Soc. [IO]
Bird Clubs of Am. [21843]
Blackwater Wildlife Rescue [IO]
Blue Cross [IO]
Bonefish and Tarpon Unlimited [4987]
Boreal Songbird Initiative [5302]
Born Free Found. [IO]
British Columbia Soc. for the Prevention of
  Cruelty to Animals [IO]
British Union for the Abolition of Vivisection [IO]
Brotogeris Soc. Intl. [4194]
Buelingo Beef Cattle Soc. [4259]
Bulgarian Animal Defence League [IO]
Bulgarian Soc. for the Protection of Birds [IO]
Bulldog Club of Am. Rescue Network [11372]
Calico Cat Registry Intl. [21902]
Canadian Assn. for Humane Trapping [IO]
Canadian Assn. for Shar-Pei Rescue [IO]
Canadian Coun. on Animal Care [IO]
Canadian Farm Animal Care Trust [IO]
Canadian Fed. of Humane Societies [IO]
Canadian Hedgehog Assn. [IO]
Canadians for Ethical Treatment of Food Animals
  [IO]
Canary and Finch Soc. [4195]
Canine Cancer Awareness [16788]
Canine Defense Fund [11373]
Carriage Operators of North Am. [783]
Carver-Scott Humane Soc. [11374]
Caspian Horse Soc. of the Americas [4869]
Cat Fanciers' Assn. [21903]
Cat Fanciers' Fed. [21904]
Cats Protection [IO]
Central States Roller Canary Breeders Assn.
  [21844]
Chimp Haven [11729]
Chinese Shar-Pei Club of Am. [22244]
Christians Helping Animals and People [19456]
Citizens to End Animal Suffering and Exploitation
  [11375]
Civitas [11376]
Clare Animal Welfare [IO]
Coalition for Non-Violent Food [11377]
Coalition to Protect Animals in Entertainment
  [11378]
Coalition to Protect Animals in Parks and Refuges
  [11379]
COM-U.S.A. [21845]
Comm. to Abolish Sport Hunting [11380]
Compassion for Animals Campaign [11381]
Compassion In World Farming - Ireland [IO]
Compassion Over Killing [11382]
Compassion in World Farming [IO]
Concern for Helping Animals in Israel [IO]
Concern for Helping Animals in Israel [11383]
Culture and Animals Found. [11384]
Curly Sporthorse Intl. [4874]
Dachshund Rescue of North Am. [11385]
Dales Pony Assn. of North Am. [4875]
Dales Pony Soc. of Am. [4876]
Dog Scouts of Am. [12016]
Dogs Deserve Better [12017]
Dogs Trust [IO]
Dogue de Bordeaux Soc. of Am. [22258]
Doing Things for Animals [11386]
Donkey Breed Soc. [IO]

Donkey Sanctuary [IO]
Doris Day Animal League [11387]
Echo Dogs White Shepherd Rescue [11388]
Eco-Animal Allies [11773]
Egyptian Arabian Horse Alliance [4877]
Elephant Care Intl. [5313]
Elephant Managers Assn. [4158]
Elephant Sanctuary in Tennessee [11389]
English Springer Rescue Am. [11390]
Epagneul Breton USA [22264]
Equine Advocates [11391]
Equine Rescue League [11392]
Equus Sanctuary [16983]
European Coalition to End Animal Experiments
  [IO]
European Rsrc. Centre for Alternatives in Higher
  Educ. [IO]
Exotic Bird Rescue [11393]
Exotic Bird Soc. of Am. [21846]
FARM (Farm Animal Reform Movement) [11394]
Farm Sanctuary [11395]
Fell Pony Soc. and Conservancy of the Americas
  [4878]
Fell Pony Soc. of North Am. [4879]
Feminists for Animal Rights [11396]
Field Spaniel Soc. of Am. [22266]
Fight Against Animal Cruelty in Europe [IO]
Food Animal Concerns Trust [4997]
Found. for Biomedical Res. [13696]
Freshwater Mollusk Conservation Soc. [5034]
Friends of Animals [11397]
Friends of the Sea Otter [5320]
Front Range Equine Rescue [4881]
Fund for Animals [11398]
Fund for Horses [4159]
Fur Commn. U.S.A. [11399]
Fur Free Alliance [4153]
Fur Free Alliance [IO]
Grassroots Endangered Species Coalition [4154]
Great Ape Proj. [11400]
Great Ape Proj. [IO]
Greek Animal Rescue [IO]
Greenpeace U.S.A. [4571]
GREY2K USA [4800]
Greyhound Adoption Center [11401]
Greyhound Friends [11402]
Greyhound Racing Assn. of Am. [23392]
Habitat for Horses [11403]
Harmony House for Cats [11404]
Harness Horsemen Intl. [23497]
Harness Racing Museum and Hall of Fame
  [23498]
Heart Bandits Amer. Eskimo Dog Rescue [12018]
Hearts United for Animals [11405]
Helping Hands Rescue [11406]
Helping Hands Rescue [IO]
Hooved Animal Humane Soc. [11407]
Horse Lovers United [17730]
Horseaid Equine Relief Programme [11408]
House Rabbit Network [11409]
House Rabbit Soc. [11410]
Human-Animal Bond Assn. of Canada [IO]
Humane Farming Assn. [11411]
Humane Slaughter Assn. [IO]
Humane Soc. of Dominica [IO]
Humane Soc. Intl. - Australia [IO]
Humane Soc. of the U.S. [11412]
In Defense of Animals [11413]
Incurably Ill for Animal Res. [13697]
Inst. for Animal Hea. [IO]
Inst. of Animal Tech. [IO]
Inst. for Lab. Animal Res. [13698]
Intl. Alliance for Animal Therapy and Healing
  [13703]
Intl. Animal Rescue - UK [IO]
Intl. Assn. Against Painful Experiments on Animals
  [IO]
Intl. Assn. for Bear Res. and Mgt. [5325]
Intl. Assn. of Canine Professionals [1161]
Intl. Assn. of Human-Animal Interaction Organiza-
  tions [16615]
The Intl. Bengal Breeders' Assn. [4205]
The Intl. Bengal Cat Soc. [4206]
The Intl. Cat Assn. [21910]
Intl. Colored Appaloosa Assn. [4897]

Reference to "IO" in place of a book number signifies that the association may be found in the 45th edition of International Organizations.

Intl. Conure Assn. [21848]
Intl. Curly Horse Org. [4898]
Intl. Defenders of Animals [11414]
Intl. Defenders of Animals [IO]
Intl. Desert Lynx Cat Assn. [4207]
Intl. Found. for Ethical Res. [11415]
Intl. Found. for Ethical Res. [IO]
Intl. Fund for Animal Welfare [IO]
Intl. Fund for Animal Welfare [11416]
Intl. Hedgehog Assn. [11417]
Intl. Hedgehog Assn. [IO]
Intl. Livestock Identification Assn. [4998]
Intl. Miniature Zebu Assn. [4268]
Intl. Order of the Armadillo [22597]
Intl. Otter Survival Fund [IO]
Intl. Primate Protection League [IO]
Intl. Primate Protection League [11418]
Intl. Quarab Horse Assn. [4903]
The Intl. Savannah Breeders' Assn. [4208]
Intl. Seppala Assn. [22291]
Intl. Soc. for Animal Rights [11419]
Intl. Soc. for Animal Rights [IO]
Intl. Soc. for Cow Protection [IO]
Intl. Soc. for Cow Protection [4155]
Intl. Soc. for Endangered Cats [4209]
Intl. Sugar Glider Assn. [11483]
Intl. Texas Longhorn Assn. [4269]
Intl. Trotting and Pacing Assn. [23501]
Intl. Veterinary Assistance [11420]
Intl. Veterinary Assistance [IO]
InterNICHE [IO]
Intertribal Bison Cooperative [5036]
Irish Blue Cross [IO]
Irish Draught Horse Soc. of North Am. [4909]
Irish Soc. for the Prevention of Cruelty to Animals
    [IO]
Jehovah's Witnesses for Animal Rights [11421]
Jews for Animal Rights [11422]
The Jockey Club [23502]
Johns Hopkins Center for Alternatives to Animal
    Testing [11423]
Kiger Mesteno Assn. [4910]
LaPerm Soc. of Am. [21912]
Last Chance for Animals [11424]
Last Chance Corral [11425]
Latham Found. [11426]
Lippitt Morgan Breeders Assn. [4912]
Llama RescueNet [11427]
London Animal Action [IO]
Mercy For Animals [11336]
Miniature Australian Shepherd Club of Am.
    [22306]
Missing Pet Partnership [12707]
Morris Animal Found. [11428]
Morris Animal Found. [IO]
MSPCA-Angell [11429]
Natl. Alliance of Burmese Breeders [4210]
Natl. Animal Control Assn. [11430]
Natl. Animal Interest Alliance [11431]
Natl. Animal Supplement Coun. [4152]
Natl. Animal Welfare Trust [IO]
Natl. Anti-Vivisection Soc. [IO]
Natl. Anti-Vivisection Soc. [11432]
Natl. Assn. for Biomedical Res. [13700]
Natl. Assn. for Humane and Environmental Educ.
    [11433]
Natl. Cat Protection Soc. [11434]
Natl. Cesky Terrier Club of Am. [22316]
Natl. Circus Preservation Soc. [9799]
Natl. Cockatiel Soc. [21852]
Natl. Color-Bred Assn. [21853]
Natl. Comm. on Pot Bellied Pigs [4140]
Natl. Cong. of Animal Trainers and Breeders
    [11435]
Natl. Dog Registry [11436]
Natl. Dog Wardens Assn. [IO]
Natl. Endangered Species Act Reform Coalition
    [17504]
Natl. Endowment for the Animals [11437]
Natl. Entlebucher Mountain Dog Assn. [22317]
Natl. Greyhound Adoption Prog. [11438]
Natl. Horse Protection Coalition [11439]
Natl. Humane Educ. Soc. [11440]
Natl. Inst. of Red Orange Canaries and All Other
    Cage Birds [21855]

Natl. Museum of Racing and Hall of Fame
    [23508]
Natl. Mustang Assn. [4921]
Natl. Opossum Soc. [4160]
Natl. Pet Alliance [11441]
Natl. Pigeon Assn. [21856]
Natl. Veterinarian Ser. Assn. [16801]
Natl. Walking Horse Assn. [4928]
NAUCRATES [IO]
New Zealand Ferret Protection and Welfare Soc.
    [IO]
North Amer. Border Terrier Welfare [12019]
North Amer. Cockatiel Soc. [21857]
North Amer. Falconers Assn. [23398]
North Amer. Fish Breeders Guild [22444]
North Amer. Fur Trade [IO]
North Amer. Grouse Partnership [5354]
North Amer. Kai Assn. [22325]
North Amer. Piedmontese Assn. [4282]
North Amer. Potbellied Pig Assn. [4145]
North Amer. Romagnola and RomAngus Assn.
    [4283]
North Amer. Teckel Club [22329]
North Amer. Tuli Assn. [4285]
North Amer. Wildlife Enforcement Officers Assn.
    [5357]
North Amer. Wolf Assn. [5359]
Norwegian Forest Cat Breed Coun. [21914]
OPP Concerned Sheep Breeders Soc. [16803]
Options for Animals Intl. [16804]
Oregon Horsemen's Benevolent Protective Assn.
    [23512]
Patriotic Pets [11442]
Patterdale Terrier Club of Am. [22338]
PAWS For A Cause [11443]
People for the Ethical Treatment of Animals
    [11444]
People for the Ethical Treatment of Animals
    Europe [IO]
People Protecting Animals and Their Habitats [IO]
People Protecting Animals and Their Habitats
    [11445]
Peoples Dispensary for Sick Animals [IO]
Performing Animal Welfare Soc. [11446]
Pet Care Trust [11447]
Pet Pride [11448]
Pet Savers Found. [11449]
PETA India [IO]
PIGS - A Sanctuary [4147]
Pionus Breeders Assn. [21859]
Polar Bears Intl. [5367]
Pot Belly Pig Rescue [11450]
Prevent a Litter Coalition [11451]
Primarily Primates, Inc. [11452]
Primate Rescue Center [11453]
Pure Puerto Rican Paso Fino Fed. of Am. [4946]
Purebred Dexter Cattle Assn. of North Am. [4289]
Pyrenean Mastiff Club of Am. [22349]
Quaker Parakeet Soc. [4200]
Rabbits Unlimited Inc. [4161]
RagaMuffin Cat Lovers Soc. [22777]
ReRun [17731]
Return to Freedom [16984]
Rex Breeders United [21915]
Royal Humane Soc. [IO]
Royal Soc. for the Prevention of Cruelty to
    Animals [IO]
Safe Harbour Animal Refuge [11454]
Sanctuary Workers and Volunteers Assn. [11455]
Savannah Cat Club [4211]
Save the Chimps [4298]
Scientists Center for Animal Welfare [11456]
Scottish Soc. for the Prevention of Cruelty to
    Animals [IO]
Scottish SPCA [IO]
Selkirk Rex Breed Club [21917]
Senepol Cattle Breeders Assn. [4293]
Serama Coun. of North Am. [4201]
Shark Res. Inst. [5019]
Simian Soc. of Am. [11457]
Soc. Against Vivisection [11458]
Soc. for Animal Protective Legislation [11459]
Soc. and Animals Forum [11460]
Soc. for the Protection of Animals Abroad [IO]
Somali Cat Club of Am. [21918]

Somali Intl. Cat Club [21919]
Spotted Saddle Horse Breeders' and Exhibitors'
    Assn. [4955]
Stafford Canary Club of Am. [21861]
Standardbred Owners Assn. [23513]
Stolen Horse Intl. [11461]
Stolen Horse Intl. [IO]
Student Animal Rights Alliance [11337]
Sumatran Orangutan Soc. - UK [IO]
Sumatran Orangutan Soc. USA [5384]
Support Our Shelters [11462]
Swedish Soc. Against Painful Experiments on
    Animals [IO]
Swiss Lab. Animal Sci. Assn. [IO]
Tattoo-a-Pet [11463]
Thai Soc. for the Prevention of Cruelty to Animals
    [IO]
Thoroughbred Club of Am. [23514]
Thoroughbred Owners and Breeders Assn.
    [23515]
Thoroughbred Racing Associations [23516]
Thoroughbred Racing Protective Bur. [23517]
Thoroughbred Retirement Found. [16985]
Tibetan Spaniel Club of Am. [22366]
Tiger Horse Assn. [4960]
Toledo Bird Assn., Zebra Finch Club of America
    [21862]
TortoiseAid Intl. [5385]
Traditional and Classic Cat Intl. [21921]
Tree House Animal Found. [11464]
The True Nature Network [11465]
Tufts Center for Animals and Public Policy
    [11466]
Unexpected Wildlife Refuge [11467]
United Action for Animals [11468]
United Activists for Animal Rights [11469]
United Animal Nations [11470]
United Burmese Cat Fanciers [21922]
United Cat Fed. [21923]
United Gloster Breeders [21863]
United Humanitarians [11471]
United Poultry Concerns [11472]
United Producers [5030]
U.S. Animal Hea. Assn. [16811]
U.S. Assn. of Roller Canary Culturists [21864]
U.S.-Mexico Border Hea. Assn. [16256]
U.S. Neapolitan Mastiff Club [22376]
U.S. Rottweiler Club [22377]
U.S. Sportsmen's Alliance [23550]
U.S. Trotting Assn. [23519]
Universities Fed. for Animal Welfare [IO]
U.S.A. Defenders of Greyhounds [11473]
Viva! USA [11484]
Viva! USA [IO]
Vivisection Investigation League [11474]
Voice for Animals [11475]
Warmblood Breeders of North Am. [4968]
Wild Animal Orphanage [11476]
Wild Burro Rescue and Preservation Proj. [11517]
Wild Canid Survival and Res. Center [5393]
Wild Horse Organized Assistance [5394]
Wild Horse Sanctuary [11477]
Wild Horse Spirit [11478]
Wild Horses of Am. Registry [5395]
WildAid [5396]
Wildlife Aid [IO]
Wildlife Disease Assn. [5398]
Women's Humane Soc. Animal Shelter [11479]
Working Riesenschnauzer Fed. [22386]
World Assn. of Veterinary Lab. Diagnosticians
    [16819]
World Blue Chain: For the Protection of Animals
    and Nature [IO]
World Soc. for the Protection of Animals [IO]
World Soc. for the Protection of Animals [11480]
World Soc. for the Protection of Animals -
    Australia [IO]
World Soc. for the Protection of Animals - Brazil
    [IO]
World Soc. for the Protection of Animals - Canada
    [IO]
World Soc. for the Protection of Animals -
    Colombia [IO]
World Soc. for the Protection of Animals - Costa
    Rica [IO]

A star before a book entry number signifies that the name is not listed separately, but is mentioned within the entry.

World Soc. for the Protection of Animals - Denmark [IO]
World Soc. for the Protection of Animals - England [IO]
World Soc. for the Protection of Animals - Germany [IO]
World Soc. for the Protection of Animals - Netherlands [IO]
World Soc. for the Protection of Animals - New Zealand [IO]
ZooCheck New Zealand [IO]
Animal Welfare Inst. [11362], PO Box 3650, Washington, DC 20027, (703)836-4300
Animal Welfare; Natl. Catholic Soc. for [★11419]
Animalia- Fed. for the Protection of Animals [IO], Helsinki, Finland

Animals

2nd Chance 4 Pets [11481]
Activists for Protective Animal Legislation [11338]
Actors and Others for Animals [11339]
Afghan Hound Club of Am. [22179]
African Love Bird Soc. [21832]
African Parrot Soc. [21833]
African Wild Dog Conservancy [5288]
Airedale Terrier Club of Am. [22180]
Akhal-Teke Assn. of Am. [4808]
Akita Club of Am. [22181]
Akita Rescue Soc. of Am. [11341]
Alaskan Malamute Assistance League [11342]
Alaskan Malamute Club of Am. [22182]
All Amer. Premier Breeds Admin. [22183]
Alley Cat Allies [11343]
Alliance for Animals [11344]
Alliance of Marine Mammal Parks and Aquariums [5006]
Alliance of Veterinarians for the Env. [4626]
Alpaca Llama Show Assn. [21514]
Amateur Field Trial Clubs of Am. [22184]
Amer. Acad. of Veterinary and Comparative Toxicology [16736]
Amer. Acad. of Veterinary Pharmacology and Therapeutics [16738]
Amer. Angora Goat Breeder's Assn. [4122]
Amer. Angus Assn. [4212]
Amer. Animal Hosp. Assn. [16739]
Amer. Anti-Vivisection Soc. [11345]
Amer. Appaloosa Assn. Worldwide [4809]
Amer. Assn. of Avian Pathologists [16740]
Amer. Assn. of Black Russian Terriers [22185]
Amer. Assn. of Bovine Practitioners [16741]
Amer. Assn. of Cat Enthusiasts [21899]
Amer. Assn. of Equine Veterinary Technicians [16743]
Amer. Assn. of Food Hygiene Veterinarians [16745]
Amer. Assn. of Housecall Veterinarians [16746]
Amer. Assn. of Human-Animal Bond Veterinarians [13702]
Amer. Assn. for Lab. Animal Sci. [13693]
Amer. Assn. of Public Hea. Veterinarians [16747]
Amer. Assn. of Retired Veterinarians [16748]
Amer. Assn. of Small Ruminant Practitioners [16749]
Amer. Assn. of Spanish Timbrado Breeders [21834]
Amer. Assn. of Swine Veterinarians [16750]
Amer. Assn. of Veterinary Lab. Diagnosticians [16753]
Amer. Assn. of Veterinary Parasitologists [16754]
Amer. Assn. of Veterinary State Boards [16755]
Amer. Assn. of Wildlife Veterinarians [16756]
Amer. Assn. of Zoo Keepers [7855]
Amer. Assn. of Zoo Veterinarians [16757]
Amer. Assn. for Zoological Nomenclature [7859]
Amer. Azteca Horse Intl. Assn. [4811]
Amer. Bantam Assn. [5102]
Amer. Beefalo World Registry [4123]
Amer. Belgian Blue Breeders [4213]
Amer. Black Hereford Assn. [4214]
Amer. Blonde d'Aquitaine Assn. [4215]
Amer. Bd. of Veterinary Specialties [16759]
Amer. Bd. of Veterinary Toxicology [16760]
Amer. Boarding Kennels Assn. [2954]
Amer. Border Leicester Assn. [5177]
Amer. Bouvier des Flandres Club [22188]

Amer. Boxer Club [22189]
Amer. Brahman Breeders Assn. [4216]
Amer. Brittany Club [22190]
Amer. Brussels Griffon Assn. [22191]
Amer. Buckskin Registry Assn. [4813]
Amer. Budgerigar Soc. [21836]
Amer. Bullmastiff Assn. [22192]
Amer. Canary Fanciers Assn. [21837]
Amer. Canine Educ. Found. [22193]
Amer. Cat Assn. [21900]
Amer. Cat Fanciers Assn. [21901]
Amer. Chesapeake Club [22195]
Amer. Chianina Assn. [4219]
Amer. Cockatiel Soc. [21838]
Amer. Coll. of Theriogenologists [16763]
Amer. Coll. of Veterinary Anesthesiologists [16764]
Amer. Coll. of Veterinary Dermatology [16765]
Amer. Coll. of Veterinary Internal Medicine [16767]
Amer. Coll. of Veterinary Ophthalmologists [16768]
Amer. Coll. of Veterinary Pathologists [16769]
Amer. Coll. of Veterinary Radiology [16770]
Amer. Coll. of Veterinary Surgeons [16771]
Amer. Collegiate Horsemen's Assn. [4814]
Amer. Connemara Pony Soc. [4815]
Amer. Cream Draft Horse Assn. [4816]
Amer. Dairy Goat Assn. [4126]
Amer. Dartmoor Pony Assn. [4817]
Amer. Devon Cattle Assn. [4220]
Amer. Dexter Cattle Assn. [4221]
Amer. Dobermann Assn. [22196]
Amer. Dog Owner's Assn. [11347]
Amer. Dog Show Judges [22198]
Amer. Donkey and Mule Soc. [4127]
Amer. Dorper Sheep Breeders' Soc. [5183]
Amer. Dove Assn. [21839]
Amer. Dutch Bantam Soc. [5103]
Amer. Embryo Transfer Assn. [4149]
Amer. Emu Assn. [4993]
Amer. Equine Assn. [4819]
Amer. Eskimo Dog Club of Am. [22199]
Amer. Fancy Rat and Mouse Assn. [22704]
Amer. Fed. of Aviculture [21840]
Amer. Ferret Assn. [22415]
Amer. Fox Terrier Club [22200]
Amer. Galloway Breeders' Assn. [4222]
Amer. Game Fowl Soc. [4190]
Amer. Gelbvieh Assn. [4223]
Amer. Gerbil Soc. [21515]
Amer. German Shepherd Rescue Assn. [11348]
Amer. Goat Soc. [4128]
Amer. Guernsey Assn. [4224]
Amer. Guinea Hog Assn. [5231]
Amer. Hackney Horse Soc. [4820]
Amer. Haflinger Registry [4821]
Amer. Half-Quarter Horse Registry [4822]
Amer. Hanoverian Soc. [4823]
Amer. Heartworm Soc. [16772]
Amer. Hereford Assn. [4225]
Amer. Highland Cattle Assn. [4227]
Amer. Holistic Veterinary Medical Assn. [16773]
Amer. Holsteiner Horse Assn. [4824]
Amer. Horse Coun. [4825]
Amer. Horse Defense Fund [4826]
Amer. Horse Protection Assn. [5291]
Amer. Indian Horse Registry [4827]
American-International Charolais Assn. [4228]
Amer. Jersey Cattle Assn. [4230]
Amer. Kennel Club [22201]
Amer. Keuda Cat Assn. [4204]
Amer. Kiko Goat Assn. [4780]
Amer. Killifish Assn. [22434]
Amer. Kuvasz Assn. [12015]
Amer. Langshan Club [5105]
Amer. Legend [4129]
Amer. Lhasa Apso Club [22202]
Amer. Maltese Assn. [22203]
Amer. Manchester Terrier Club [22204]
Amer. Milking Shorthorn Soc. [4237]
Amer. Miniature Cheviot Sheep Breeders Assn. [5188]
Amer. Miniature Jersey Cattle Registry [4238]
Amer. Miniature Llama Assn. [21513]

Amer. Miniature Schnauzer Club [22205]
Amer. Mobile Groomers Assn. [2955]
Amer. Mookee Assn. [4191]
Amer. Morgan Horse Assn. [4831]
Amer. Mule Assn. [4131]
Amer. Mule Racing Assn. [23668]
Amer. Murray Grey Assn. [4239]
Amer. Mustang Assn. [4832]
Amer. Natl. CattleWomen [4240]
Amer. Paint Horse Assn. [4834]
Amer. Part-Blooded Horse Registry [4835]
Amer. Pastured Poultry Producers Assn. [5106]
Amer. Pet Products Mfrs. Assn. [2956]
Amer. Pet Soc. [11349]
Amer. Pinzgauer Assn. [4241]
Amer. Pointer Club [22206]
Amer. Pomeranian Club [22207]
Amer. Pre-Veterinary Medical Assn. [16774]
Amer. Racing Pigeon Union [22894]
Amer. Ranch Horse Assn. [4841]
Amer. Rare Breed Assn. [4496]
Amer. Red Brangus Assn. [4242]
Amer. Red Poll Assn. [4243]
Amer. Riding Instructors Assn. [22583]
Amer. Romagnola Assn. [4244]
Amer. Rottweiler Club [22208]
Amer. Royal Assn. [4995]
Amer. Saddlebred Horse Assn. [4842]
Amer. Saddlebred Sporthorse Assn. [4843]
Amer. Sanctuary Assn. [4156]
Amer. Sealyham Terrier Club [22209]
Amer. Shagya Arabian Verband [4844]
Amer. Shetland Pony Club/American Miniature Horse Registry [4845]
Amer. Shetland Sheepdog Assn. [22210]
Amer. Shih Tzu Club [22211]
Amer. Shire Horse Assn. [4846]
Amer. Shorthorn Assn. [4247]
Amer. Sighthound Field Assn. [22212]
Amer. Simmental Assn. [4248]
Amer. Singers Club [21841]
Amer. Soc. of Animal Sci. [4150]
Amer. Soc. for the Prevention of Cruelty to Animals [11350]
Amer. Soc. for Reproductive Medicine [14389]
Amer. Soc. of Veterinary Ophthalmology [16775]
Amer. Spaniel Club [22213]
Amer. Suffolk Horse Assn. [4847]
Amer. Sulphur Horse Assn. [22585]
Amer. Tarentaise Assn. [4249]
Amer. Toy Fox Terrier Club [22214]
Amer. Trakehner Assn. [4848]
Amer. Trote and Trocha Assn. [4849]
Amer. Veterinary Dental Soc. [16778]
Amer. Veterinary Medical Assn. [16779]
Amer. Veterinary Soc. of Animal Behavior [16780]
Amer. Wagyu Assn. [4250]
Amer. Walking Pony Assn. [4850]
Amer. Warmblood Registry [4851]
Amer. Warmblood and Sport Horse Guild [4853]
Amer. Water Spaniel Club [22215]
Amer. Waterslager Soc. [21842]
Amer. Welara Pony Soc. [4854]
Amer. Whippet Club [22216]
Amer. White Horse and Amer. Creme Horse Registry [4855]
Amer. White Shepherd Assn. [22217]
Amer. Working Collie Assn. [22218]
Amer. Working Dog Fed. [21516]
Amer. Working Malinois Assn. [21517]
Amer. Youth Horse Coun. [4856]
Americans for Medical Progress Educational Found. [13694]
Amerifax Cattle Assn. [4251]
Animal Behavior Mgt. Alliance [7860]
Animal Behavior Soc. [7861]
Animal Hea. Inst. [2970]
Animal Legal Defense Fund [11351]
Animal Medical Center [11353]
Animal Place [11354]
Animal and Plant Hea. Assn. [IO]
Animal Protection Inst. of Am. [11355]
Animal Rights Coalition [11356]
Animal Rights Intl. [11357]
Animal Rights Network/Institute for Animals and Soc. [11359]

Reference to "IO" in place of a book number signifies that the association may be found in the 45th edition of International Organizations.

Animal Trans. Assn. [11361]
Animal Welfare Inst. [11362]
Animals First [11482]
Animals as Intermediaries [4157]
Ankole Watusi Intl. Registry [4252]
Anti-Cruelty Soc. [11364]
Appalachian Bear Rescue [5293]
Appaloosa Horse Club [4857]
Aquarium and Zoo Facilities Assn. [7856]
Aquatic Animal Life Support Operators [7279]
Arabian F.O.A.L. Assn. [11365]
Arabian Horse Assn. [4858]
Arabian Horse Breeders Alliance [4859]
Arabian Horse Owners Found. [4860]
Arabian Horse Trust [4861]
Arabian Professional and Amateur Horseman's Assn. [4862]
ARCA: Amer. Romeldale/CVM Assn. [5197]
Arizona Canine Acad. [22219]
Asiatic Breeders Assn. [4192]
Assistance Dogs Intl. [11923]
Assoc. Humane Societies [11366]
Assoc. Koi Clubs of Am. [22437]
Assn. for Assessment and Accreditation of Lab. Animal Care Intl. [13695]
Assn. for Explosive Detection K-9s, Intl. [5964]
Assn. for People with Dogs Named Marty [22220]
Assn. for Pet Loss and Bereavement [12706]
Assn. of Professional Humane Educators [12058]
The Assn. of Sanctuaries [11367]
Assn. of Shelter Veterinarians [16784]
Assn. of Veterinary Hematology and Transfusion Medicine [16785]
Assn. for Women Veterinarians [16786]
Assn. of Zoological Horticulture [4974]
Assn. of Zoos and Aquariums [7857]
Australasian Pig Sci. Assn. [IO]
Australian Cattle Dog Club of Am. [22221]
Australian Shepherd Club of Am. [22222]
Australian Terrier Club of Am. [22223]
Authentic Hovawarts of North Am. [22224]
Avian Welfare Coalition [4193]
Ayrshire Breeders' Assn. [4253]
Back in the Saddle Horse Adoption [4864]
Baidarka Historical Soc. [9954]
Barbados Blackbelly Sheep Assn. Intl. [5198]
Barzona Breeders Assn. of Am. [4254]
Basenji Club of Am. [22225]
Basset Hound Club of Am. [22226]
Bat Conservation Intl. [5296]
Bear Trust Intl. [5297]
Bearded Collie Club of Am. [22227]
Beefmaster Breeders United [4255]
Belgian Draft Horse Corp. of Am. [4865]
Belgian Sheepdog Club of Am. [22228]
Belted Galloway Soc. [4256]
Berger Picard Club of Am. [22229]
Bernese Mountain Dog Club of Am. [22230]
Beyond the Pond.International Frog Collectors Club [21977]
Bichon Frise Club of Am. [22231]
Bide-A-Wee Home Assn. [11371]
Bird Clubs of Am. [21843]
Black Russian Terrier Club of Am. [22232]
Bluefaced Leicester Union of North Am. [5200]
Bluetick Breeders of Am. [22233]
Border Terrier Club of Am. [22234]
Borzoi Club of Am. [22235]
Boston Terrier Club of Am. [22236]
British Camelids Assn. [IO]
Brotogeris Soc. Intl. [4194]
Brown Swiss Cattle Breeders Assn. of the U.S.A. [4258]
Buelingo Beef Cattle Soc. [4259]
Bull Terrier Club of Am. [22237]
Bulldog Club of Am. Rescue Network [11372]
Cairn Terrier Club of Am. [22238]
Call and Whistle Collectors Assn. [21983]
Canary and Finch Soc. [4195]
Canine Assistants [11925]
Canine Cancer Awareness [16788]
Canine Defense Fund [11373]
Canines for Disabled Kids [11927]
Cardigan Welsh Corgi Club of Am. [22240]
Care Rehabilitation and Aid for Sick Hedgehogs [IO]

Carver-Scott Humane Soc. [11374]
Caspian Horse Soc. of the Americas [4869]
Cat Collectors [21990]
Cat Fanciers' Assn. [21903]
Cat Fanciers' Fed. [21904]
Caucasian Ovcharka Club of Am. [22241]
Cavalier King Charles Spaniel Club of Am. [22242]
Center for the Stud. of Natural and Historical Anomalies [7862]
Central States Roller Canary Breeders Assn. [21844]
Champagne Horse Breeders' and Owners' Assn. [4870]
Chihuahua Club of Am. [22243]
Chimp Haven [11729]
Chinese Shar-Pei Club of Am. [22244]
Chow Chow Club, Inc. [22245]
Citizens to End Animal Suffering and Exploitation [11375]
Clumber Spaniel Club of Am. [22246]
Clydesdale Breeders of the U.S.A. [4872]
Coalition to Protect Animals in Entertainment [11378]
Coalition to Protect Animals in Parks and Refuges [11379]
Cockapoo Club of Am. [22247]
Collie Club of Am. [22248]
Colorado Ranger Horse Assn. [4873]
Colored Angora Goat Breeders Assn. [4782]
COM-U.S.A. [21845]
Comm. to Abolish Sport Hunting [11380]
Comparative Cognition Soc. [6400]
Compassion for Animals Campaign [11381]
Compassion Over Killing [11382]
Concern for Helping Animals in Israel [11383]
Conf. of Res. Workers in Animal Diseases [16790]
Continental Mi-Ki Assn. [22250]
Controlled Release Soc. [6678]
Cotswold Breeders Assn. [4133]
Cow Observers Worldwide [22002]
Create A Smile Dental Found. [13318]
Culture and Animals Found. [11384]
Curly-Coated Retriever Club of Am. [22252]
Curly Sporthorse Intl. [4874]
Dachshund Club of Am. [22253]
Dales Pony Assn. of North Am. [4875]
Dales Pony Soc. of Am. [4876]
Dalmatian Club of Am. [22254]
Dandie Dinmont Terrier Club of Am. [22255]
Danish Livestock and Meat Bd. [IO]
Delta Soc. [16611]
Desert German Shorthaired Pointer Club [22256]
The Designer Cat Assn. [21906]
Doberman Pinscher Club of Am. [22257]
Dog Scouts of Am. [12016]
Dogs for the Deaf [14754]
Dogs Deserve Better [12017]
Dogs on Stamps Stud. Unit [22815]
Dogue de Bordeaux Soc. of Am. [22258]
Doing Things for Animals [11386]
Doris Day Animal League [11387]
EarthVoice [4555]
Echo Dogs White Shepherd Rescue [11388]
Eco-Animal Allies [11773]
Egyptian Arabian Horse Alliance [4877]
Elephant Care Intl. [5313]
Elephant Managers Assn. [4158]
Elephant Managers Assn. [IO]
Empress Chinchilla Breeders Cooperative [4134]
English Cocker Spaniel Club of Am. [22259]
English Setter Assn. of Am. [22260]
English Shepherd Club [22261]
English Springer Spaniel Field Trial Assn. [22262]
English Toy Spaniel Club of Am. [22263]
Epagneul Breton USA [22264]
Equine Assisted Growth and Learning Assn. [16216]
Estrela Mountain Dog Assn. of Am. [22265]
Exotic Bird Soc. of Am. [21846]
Exotic Wildlife Assn. [5316]
FARM (Farm Animal Reform Movement) [11394]
Farm Sanctuary [11395]
Fauna Found. [IO]

Fed. for the Amer. Staffordshire Terrier [21518]
Fell Pony Soc. and Conservancy of the Americas [4878]
Fell Pony Soc. of North Am. [4879]
Ferret Fanciers Club [22416]
Fertility Res. Found. [14391]
Fidelco Guide Dog Found. [16846]
Field Spaniel Soc. of Am. [22266]
Fitzgerald's Fancys: Rat and Mouse Info. [22705]
Flat-Coated Retriever Soc. of Am. [22268]
Food Animal Concerns Trust [4997]
Found. for Biomedical Res. [13696]
French Brittany Gun Dog Assn. [22270]
French Bull Dog Club of Am. [22271]
Freshwater Mollusk Conservation Soc. [5034]
Friends of Animals [11397]
Friends of the Natl. Zoo [7858]
Friends of the Sea Otter [5320]
Front Range Equine Rescue [4881]
Fuller Found. [13118]
Fund for Animals [11398]
Fund for Horses [4159]
Fund for Horses [IO]
Fur Commn. U.S.A. [11399]
Galiceno Horse Breeders Assn. [4883]
Gelbray Intl. [4262]
German Shepherd Dog Club of Am. [22272]
German Shepherd Dog Club of Am. - Working Dog Assn. [22273]
German Shorthaired Pointer Club of Am. [22274]
German Wirehaired Pointer Club of Am. [22275]
Gliding Horse and Pony Registry [4884]
Global Gecko Assn. [5169]
Golden Retriever Club of Am. [22277]
Goldfish Soc. of Am. [22439]
Gordon Setter Club of Am. [22278]
Gotland-Russ Assn. of North Am. [4885]
Grayson-Jockey Club Res. Found. [4886]
Great Ape Proj. [11400]
Great Dane Club of Am. [22279]
Great Pyrenees Club of Am. [22280]
GREY2K USA [4800]
Greyhound Adoption Center [11401]
Greyhound Club of Am. [22281]
Greyhound Racing Assn. of Am. [23392]
Guinea Fowl Breeders Assn. [4196]
Guinea Fowl Intl. Assn. [4197]
Half Saddlebred Registry of Am. [4889]
Harmony House for Cats [11404]
Harness Horsemen Intl. [23497]
Harness Racing Museum and Hall of Fame [23498]
Hartz Club of Am. [22772]
Havana Silk Dog Assn. of Am. [22282]
Hawaiian Intl. Billfish Tournament [22440]
Heart Bandits Amer. Eskimo Dog Rescue [12018]
Hearts United for Animals [11405]
Holstein Assn. USA [4263]
Hooved Animal Humane Soc. [11407]
Hovawart Club of Am. [22283]
Humane Farming Assn. [11411]
Humane Soc. of the U.S. [11412]
Hungarian Pumi Club of Am. [22284]
Hunting Retriever Club [22285]
Icelandic Horse Trekkers [4893]
Icelandic Sheepdog Assn. of Am. [22286]
Incurably Ill for Animal Res. [13697]
Independent Pet and Animal Trans. Assn. Intl. [2958]
Inst. for Lab. Animal Res. [13698]
Intl. Alliance for Animal Therapy and Healing [13703]
International Alliance for Animal Therapy and Healing [IO]
Intl. Andalusian and Lusitano Horse Assn. [4894]
Intl. Arabian Horse Assn. [4895]
Intl. Assn. of Animal Behavior Consultants [7864]
Intl. Assn. of Animal Massage and Bodywork [15028]
Intl. Assn. for Aquatic Animal Medicine [16792]
Intl. Assn. for Bear Res. and Mgt. [5325]
Intl. Assn. of Canine Professionals [1161]
Intl. Assn. of Human-Animal Interaction Organizations [16615]
Intl. Assn. for Paratuberculosis [16793]

A star before a book entry number signifies that the name is not listed separately, but is mentioned within the entry.

Intl. Assn. of Pet Cemeteries and Crematories [2959]
The Intl. Bengal Breeders' Assn. [4205]
The Intl. Bengal Cat Soc. [4206]
Intl. Betta Cong. [22441]
Intl. Borzoi Coun. [22287]
Intl. Buckskin Horse Assn. [4896]
The Intl. Cat Assn. [21910]
Intl. Colored Appaloosa Assn. [4897]
Intl. Conure Assn. [21848]
Intl. Curly Horse Org. [4898]
Intl. Defenders of Animals [11414]
Intl. Desert Lynx Cat Assn. [4207]
Intl. Embryo Transfer Soc. [16794]
Intl. Fainting Goat Assn. [4784]
Intl. Fed. of Amer. Homing Pigeon Fanciers [22895]
Intl. Found. for Ethical Res. [11415]
Intl. French Brittany Club of Am. [22288]
Intl. Fund for Animal Welfare [11416]
Intl. Goat Assn. [4785]
Intl. Kennel Club of Chicago [22289]
Intl. Lama Registry [21519]
Intl. Lama Registry [IO]
Intl. Livestock Identification Assn. [4998]
Intl. Miniature Zebu Assn. [4268]
Intl. Modena Club [22896]
Intl. Morab Breeders' Assn. [4900]
Intl. Morab Registry [4901]
Intl. Nubian Breeders Assn. [4135]
Intl. Order of the Armadillo [22597]
Intl. Pedigree Assignment and Bloodline Res. Assn. [4902]
Intl. Police Work Dog Assn. [5979]
Intl. Primate Protection League [11418]
Intl. Quarab Horse Assn. [4903]
The Intl. Savannah Breeders' Assn. [4208]
Intl. Seppala Assn. [22291]
Intl. Soc. for Adaptive Behavior [6533]
Intl. Soc. of Animal License Collectors [22058]
Intl. Soc. for Animal Rights [11419]
Intl. Soc. for Cow Protection [4155]
Intl. Soc. for Endangered Cats [4209]
Intl. Soc. of Veterinary Dermatopathology [16795]
Intl. Sugar Glider Assn. [11483]
Intl. Texas Longhorn Assn. [4269]
Intl. Trotting and Pacing Assn. [23501]
Intl. Veterinary Acupuncture Soc. [16796]
Intl. Veterinary Assistance [11420]
Intl. Veterinary Ultrasound Soc. [16797]
Intl. Weight Pull Assn. [23384]
Intl. Yak Assn. [5001]
Irish Blacks Assn. [4270]
Irish Draught Horse Soc. of North Am. [4909]
Irish Terrier Club of Am. [22293]
Irish Water Spaniel Club of Am. [22294]
Irish Wolfhound Club of Am. [22295]
Jack Russell Terrier Club of Am. [22297]
Japanese Akita Club of Am. [22298]
Japanese Chin Club of Am. [22299]
Jews for Animal Rights [11422]
The Jockey Club [23502]
Johns Hopkins Center for Alternatives to Animal Testing [11423]
Keeping Track [5335]
Keeshond Club of Am. [22300]
Kiger Mesteno Assn. [4910]
Kuvasz Club of Am. [22302]
Lab. Animal Mgt. Assn. [13699]
Ladies Kennel Assn. of Am. [22303]
LaPerm Soc. of Am. [21912]
Last Chance Corral [11425]
Lipizzan Assn. of North Am. [4911]
Lippitt Morgan Breeders Assn. [4912]
Livestock Marketing Assn. [5021]
Llama Assn. of North Am. [4136]
Maremma Sheepdog Club of Am. [22304]
Mastiff Club of Am. [22305]
Mercy For Animals [11336]
Miniature Australian Shepherd Club of Am. [22306]
Miniature Bull Terrier Club of Am. [22307]
Miniature Donkey Registry [4137]
Miniature Hereford Breeders Assn. [4272]
Miniature and Novelty Sheep Breeders Assn. and Registry [5204]

Miniature Pinscher Club of Am. [22308]
Missing Pet.Partnership [12707]
Missouri Fox Trotting Horse Breed Assn. [4913]
Morris Animal Found. [11428]
MSPCA-Angell [11429]
Musical Dog Sport Assn. [23385]
Natl. Alliance of Burmese Breeders [4210]
Natl. Amateur Retriever Club [22309]
Natl. Amer. Eskimo Dog Assn. [22310]
Natl. Amer. Pit Bull Terrier Assn. [22311]
Natl. Animal Control Assn. [11430]
Natl. Anti-Vivisection Soc. [11432]
Natl. Assn. of Animal Breeders [5002]
Natl. Assn. for Biomedical Res. [13700]
Natl. Assn. of Dog Obedience Instructors [22312]
Natl. Assn. of Fed. Veterinarians [16799]
Natl. Assn. for Humane and Environmental Educ. [11433]
Natl. Assn. of Louisiana Catahoulas [22313]
Natl. Beagle Club of Am. [22314]
Natl. Bird Dog Challenge Assn. [22315]
Natl. Birman Fanciers [21913]
Natl. Bison Assn. [4139]
Natl. Block and Bridle Club [24401]
Natl. Bucking Bull Assn. [23687]
Natl. Cat Protection Soc. [11434]
Natl. Cesky Terrier Club of Am. [22316]
Natl. Cockatiel Soc. [21852]
Natl. Color-Bred Assn. [21853]
Natl. Comm. on Pot Bellied Pigs [4140]
Natl. Cong. of Animal Trainers and Breeders [11435]
Natl. Cutting Horse Assn. [4918]
Natl. Dog Groomers Assn. of Am. [2962]
Natl. Dog Registry [11436]
Natl. Endangered Species Act Reform Coalition [17504]
Natl. Endowment for the Animals [11437]
Natl. Entlebucher Mountain Dog Assn. [22317]
Natl. Greyhound Adoption Prog. [11438]
Natl. Greyhound Assn. [22318]
Natl. Horse Protection Coalition [11439]
Natl. Horse Show Commn. [4919]
Natl. Humane Educ. Soc. [11440]
Natl. Hunter Jumper Assn. [23530]
Natl. Hunters Assn. [23547]
Natl. Inst. for Animal Agriculture [5003]
Natl. Inst. of Red Orange Canaries and All Other Cage Birds [21855]
Natl. Junior Angus Assn. [4275]
Natl. Livestock Producers Assn. [5024]
Natl. Miniature Donkey Assn. [5004]
Natl. Museum of Racing and Hall of Fame [23508]
Natl. Mustang Assn. [4921]
Natl. Narcotic Detector Dog Assn. [5997]
Natl. Opossum Soc. [4160]
Natl. Pedigreed Livestock Coun. [4141]
Natl. Pet Alliance [11441]
Natl. Pigeon Assn. [21856]
Natl. Pygmy Goat Assn. [4142]
Natl. Quarter Horse Registry [4922]
Natl. Quarter Pony Assn. [4923]
Natl. Reined Cow Horse Assn. [22586]
Natl. Reining Horse Assn. [4924]
Natl. Show Horse Registry [4925]
Natl. Show Pig Assn. [22982]
Natl. Snaffle Bit Assn. [4926]
Natl. Spotted Saddle Horse Assn. [4927]
Natl. Toy Fox Terrier Assn. [22321]
Natl. Veterinarian Ser. Assn. [16801]
Natl. Walking Horse Assn. [4928]
Nigerian Dwarf Goat Assn. [4788]
NMC [16802]
North Amer. Babydoll Southdown Sheep Assn. and Registry [5211]
North Amer. Banding Coun. [7421]
North Amer. Border Terrier Welfare [12019]
North Amer. Cockatiel Soc. [21857]
North Amer. Danish Warmblood Assn. [4930]
North Amer. Deutsch Kurzhaar Club [22323]
North Amer. Dog Agility Coun. [23387]
North Amer. Falconers Assn. [23398]
North Amer. Fish Breeders Guild [22444]
North Amer. Grouse Partnership [5354]

North Amer. Horsemen's Assn. [4932]
North Amer. Hunting Club [23548]
North Amer. Jack Russell Terrier Assn. [22324]
North Amer. Kai Assn. [22325]
North Amer. Lionhead Rabbit Club [5157]
North Amer. Llewellin Breeders Assn. [22326]
North Amer. Model Horse Shows Assn. [22587]
North Amer. Mustang Assn. and Registry [4933]
North Amer. Peruvian Horse Assn. [4934]
North Amer. Piedmontese Assn. [4282]
North Amer. Potbellied Pig Assn. [4145]
North Amer. Romagnola and RomAngus Assn. [4283]
North Amer. Saddle Mule Assn. [21520]
North Amer. Shagya-Arabian Soc. [4936]
North Amer. Sheep Dog Soc. [22328]
North Amer. Single-footing Horse Assn. [4937]
North Amer. Spotted Draft Horse Assn. [4938]
North Amer. Teckel Club [22329]
North Amer. Trap Collector Assn. [22095]
North Amer. Tuli Assn. [4285]
North Amer. Wensleydale Sheep Assn. [5214]
North Amer. Wildlife Enforcement Officers Assn. [5357]
North Amer. Wildlife Park Found. [5358]
North Amer. Wolf Assn. [5359]
North Amer. Working Bouvier Assn. [22330]
Norwegian Elkhound Assn. of Am. [22331]
Norwegian Forest Cat Breed Coun. [21914]
Norwegian Lundehund Assn. of Am. [22332]
Norwich and Norfolk Terrier Club [22333]
Old English Sheepdog Club of Am. [22334]
OPP Concerned Sheep Breeders Soc. [16803]
Options for Animals Intl. [16804]
Oregon Horsemen's Benevolent Protective Assn. [23512]
Pacific Marine Mammal Center [5361]
Painted Desert Sheep Soc. [5215]
Palomino Horse Assn. [4941]
Palomino Horse Breeders of Am. [4942]
Paso Fino Horse Assn. [4943]
Patriotic Pets [11442]
Patterdale Terrier Club of Am. [22338]
Pekingese Club of Am. [22339]
Pembroke Welsh Corgi Club of Am. [22340]
People-Animals-Love [16632]
People, Animals, Nature [13319]
People Protecting Animals and Their Habitats [11445]
Performing Animal Welfare Soc. [11446]
Peruvian Inca Orchid Dog Club of Am. [22341]
Pet Care Trust [11447]
Pet Food Inst. [2963]
Pet Indus. Distributors Assn. [2964]
Pet Indus. Joint Advisory Coun. [2965]
Pet Pride [11448]
Pet Savers Found. [11449]
Piedmontese Assn. of the U.S. [4287]
PIGS - A Sanctuary [4147]
Pinto Horse Assn. of Am. [4944]
Pionus Breeders Assn. [21859]
Polar Bears Intl. [5367]
Polish Tatra Sheepdog Club of Am. [22342]
Pony of the Americas Club [4945]
Poodle Club of Am. [22343]
Portuguese Podengo Club of Am. [22344]
Portuguese Water Dog Club of Am. [22345]
Prevent a Litter Coalition [11451]
Primarily Primates, Inc. [11452]
Princess Kitty Fan Club [24778]
Producers Livestock Marketing Assn. [5029]
Professional Handlers Assn. [22346]
Protection Sports Assn. [23848]
Pug Dog Club of Am. [22347]
Pure Puerto Rican Paso Fino Fed. of Am. [4946]
Purebred Dexter Cattle Assn. of North Am. [4289]
Pyrenean Mastiff Club of Am. [22349]
Quaker Parakeet Soc. [4200]
Rabbits Unlimited Inc. [4161]
Racking Horse Breeders' Assn. of Am. [4948]
RagaMuffin Cat Lovers Soc. [22777]
Ranchers-Cattlemen Action Legal Fund, United Stockgrowers of Am. [4290]
Rat Fan Club [22706]
Rat, Mouse, and Hamster Fanciers [22708]

Reference to "IO" in place of a book number signifies that the association may be found in the 45th edition of International Organizations.

Rat Terrier Club of Am. [22350]
Resolve, The Natl. Infertility Assn. [14394]
Rex Breeders United [21915]
Rhodesian Ridgeback Club of the U.S. [22351]
Rocky Mountain Horse Assn. [4949]
Rocky Mountain Llama and Alpaca Assn. [4148]
Sacred Cat of Burma Fanciers [21916]
Saint Bernard Club of Am. [22352]
Samoyed Club of Am. [22354]
Sanctuary Workers and Volunteers Assn. [11455]
Savannah Cat Club [4211]
Save the Chimps [4298]
Scientists Center for Animal Welfare [11456]
Scottish Deerhound Club of Am. [22356]
Scottish Terrier Club of Am. [22357]
Selkirk Rex Breed Club [21917]
Senepol Cattle Breeders Assn. [4293]
Senior Conformation Judges Assn. [22358]
Serama Coun. of North Am. [4201]
Shark Res. Inst. [5019]
Siberian Husky Club of Am. [22359]
Silky Terrier Club of Am. [22360]
Skye Terrier Club of Am. [22361]
Soays of Am. [5218]
Soc. Against Vivisection [11458]
Soc. of Animal Artists [9526]
Soc. for Animal Protective Legislation [11459]
Soc. and Animals Forum [11460]
Soc. for Integrative and Comparative Biology [7867]
Soc. of Parrot Breeders and Exhibitors [21860]
Soc. for Theriogenology [16806]
Soc. for Tropical Veterinary Medicine [16807]
Somali Cat Club of Am. [21918]
Somali Intl. Cat Club [21919]
Soul Friends [16637]
Southwestern Donkey and Mule Soc. [21521]
Spanish-Barb Breeders Assn. [4952]
Spanish Confed. of Animal Feed Manufacturers [IO]
Spanish Mustang Registry [4953]
Spanish Water Dog Assn. of Am. [22362]
Spotted Saddle Horse Breeders' and Exhibitors' Assn. [4955]
Stafford Canary Club of Am. [21861]
Staffordshire Terrier Club of Am. [22364]
Standard Schnauzer Club of Am. [22365]
Standardbred Owners Assn. [23513]
Stolen Horse Intl. [11461]
Student Animal Rights Alliance [11337]
Student Veterinary Emergency and Critical Care Soc. [16810]
Sumatran Orangutan Soc. USA [5384]
Support Dogs, Inc. [11990]
Support Our Shelters [11462]
Swedish Warmblood Assn. of North Am. [4958]
Tattoo-a-Pet [11463]
Tennessee Walking Horse Breeders' and Exhibitors' Assn. [4959]
Therapy Dogs Intl. [16638]
Thoroughbred Club of Am. [23514]
Thoroughbred Owners and Breeders Assn. [23515]
Thoroughbred Racing Associations [23516]
Thoroughbred Racing Protective Bur. [23517]
Tibetan Spaniel Club of Am. [22366]
Tibetan Terrier Club of Am. [22367]
Tiger Horse Assn. [4960]
Toledo Bird Assn., Zebra Finch Club of America [21862]
TortoiseAid Intl. [5385]
Traditional Cat Assn. [21920]
Traditional and Classic Cat Intl. [21921]
TRAFFIC North Am. [5386]
Tree House Animal Found. [11464]
Treeing Walker Breeders and Fanciers Assn. [22368]
Tufts Center for Animals and Public Policy [11466]
Turkey Vulture Soc. [5389]
Unexpected Wildlife Refuge [11467]
United Action for Animals [11468]
United Activists for Animal Rights [11469]
United Animal Nations [11470]
United Burmese Cat Fanciers [21922]

United Cat Fed. [21923]
United Doberman Club [22369]
United Gloster Breeders [21863]
United Humanitarians [11471]
United Kennel Club [22370]
United Producers [5030]
United Professional Horsemen's Assn. [4961]
United Silver Fanciers [21924]
U.S. Animal Hea. Assn. [16811]
U.S. Assn. of Roller Canary Culturists [21864]
U.S. Boer Goat Assn. [4789]
U.S. Border Collie Club [22372]
U.S. Boxer Assn. [22373]
U.S. Dog Agility Assn. [23388]
U.S. Hunter Jumper Assn. [23536]
U.S. Icelandic Horse Cong. [4962]
U.S. Kerry Blue Terrier Club [22374]
U.S. Lakeland Terrier Club [22375]
U.S.-Mexico Border Hea. Assn. [16256]
U.S. Mondioring Assn. [23389]
U.S. Neapolitan Mastiff Club [22376]
U.S. Peruvian Horse Assn. [4964]
U.S. Rottweiler Club [22377]
U.S. Sportsmen's Alliance [23550]
U.S. Team Penning Assn. [23518]
U.S. Trotting Assn. [23519]
U.S.A. Defenders of Greyhounds [11473]
Veterinary Botanical Medicine Assn. [16812]
Veterinary Orthopedic Soc. [16816]
Viva! USA [11484]
Vizsla Club of Am. [22378]
Walking Horse Owners' Assn. [4966]
Walking Horse Trainers Assn. [4967]
Warmblood Breeders of North Am. [4968]
Water Planet USA [5018]
Weimaraner Club of Am. [22379]
Welsh Pony and Cob Soc. of Am. [4969]
Welsh Springer Spaniel Club of Am. [22380]
West Highland White Terrier Club of Am. [22381]
Western Intl. Walking Horse Assn. [4970]
Western Veterinary Conf. [16817]
Westminster Kennel Club [22382]
White German Shepherd Dog Club of Am. [22383]
Wild Canid Survival and Res. Center [5393]
Wild Horse Organized Assistance [5394]
Wild Horses of Am. Registry [5395]
WildAid [5396]
Wirehaired Vizsla Club of Am. [22384]
Working Pit Bull Terrier Club of Am. [22385]
Working Riesenschnauzer Fed. [22386]
World Assn. for the Advancement of Veterinary Parasitology [16818]
World Assn. of Veterinary Lab. Diagnosticians [16819]
World Bulldog Alliance [22387]
World Canine Freestyle Org. [23390]
World Wide Kennel Club [22388]
World Wide Pet Indus. Assn. [2968]
WTCARES [22389]
Yorkshire Terrier Club of Am. [22390]
Animals Australia [IO], North Melbourne, Australia
Animals in Distress Sanctuary [IO], Irlam, United Kingdom
Animals First [11482]
Animals Found; Options for [★16804]
Animals as Intermediaries [4157], PO Box 155, Concord, MA 01742, (978)369-2585
Animals-Love; People- [16632]
Animals in Mind [IO], Worle, United Kingdom
Animals and Nature; Interfaith Coun. for the Protection of [4409]
Animals; New York Women's League for [★11353]
Animals; Options for [★16804]
Animals; Orthopedic Found. for [16805]
Animals in Politics - Defunct.
Animals for Recreational Enjoyment; I KARE - Individuals Against Killing [★5332]
Animals Voice [11363], 1354 E Ave., No. R-252, Chico, CA 95926, (530)343-2498
Animals Voice [IO], Chico, CA, United States
Animated Film Soc., ASIFA - Hollywood; Intl. [1383]

Animation

ABRADEMI - Brazilian Manga and Illustration Artists Assn. [IO]

Animators Unite [9388]
Banzai Anime Klub of Alberta [IO]
Broadcast Designer's Assn. [554]
Dedicated Otaku Anime Club [IO]
Intl. Animated Film Soc., ASIFA - Hollywood [1383]
Japanese Animation Fans Western Australia [IO]
Japanese Animation Soc. [IO]
Melbourne Anime Soc. (Australia) [IO]
Official Gumby Fan Club [24793]
Soc. for the Promotion of Japanese Animation [9473]
Walt Disney Collectors Soc. [22129]
World Chap. of Disneyana Enthusiasts [22132]
Animation Producers' Assn. - Defunct.
Animation; Soc. for the Promotion of Japanese [9473]
Animation; Women in [1372]
Animators Unite [9388], 525 85th St., Brooklyn, NY 11209
Anime UNSW [IO], Sydney, Australia
Anisa Found. [IO], Mexicali, Mexico
Anita Borg Inst. for Women and Tech. [IO], Palo Alto, CA, United States
Anita Borg Inst. for Women and Tech. [12754], 1501 Page Mill Rd., MS 1105, Palo Alto, CA 94304, (650)236-4756
Anjou Assn; Amer. Maine- [4234]
Ankina Breeders - Defunct.
Ankle Orthopedics and Medicine; Amer. Coll. of Foot and [16032]
Ankle Pediatrics; Amer. Coll. of Foot and [16033]
Ankle Soc; Amer. Orthopaedic Foot and [15758]
Ankle Surgeons; Amer. Coll. of Foot and [16034]
Ankole Watusi Intl. Registry [4252], 22484 W 239 St., Spring Hill, KS 66083-9306, (913)592-4050
Ankole Watusi Intl. Registry [IO], Spring Hill, KS, United States
Ankylosing Spondylitis Assn. [★16377]
Ankylosing Spondylitis Assn. of Ireland [IO], Dublin, Ireland
Ankylosing Spondylitis Gp. of New South Wales [IO], Royal Exchange, Australia
Ankylosing Spondylitis Soc. in Hungary [IO], Budapest, Hungary
Ankylosing Spondylitis Soc. in Italy [IO], Bologna, Italy
Ankylosing Spondylitis Soc; Natl. [IO]
Ann-Margret's Official Fan Club [24729], PO Box 2045, Toluca Lake, CA 91610
Annalee Club [22392], c/o Annalee Mobilitee Dolls, Inc., PO Box 708, Meredith, NH 03253, (603)279-3333
Annalee Doll Soc. [★22392]
Annals of Improbable Res. [7599], PO Box 380853, Cambridge, MA 02238, (617)491-4437
Annals of Improbable Res. [IO], Cambridge, MA, United States
Annapolis Naval Sailing Assn. [21867], 58 Bennion Rd., Annapolis, MD 21402-5054, (410)531-2107
Anne Christy Fan Club - Address unknown since 1989.
Anne Frank Center; Amer. Friends of the [★17713]
Anne Frank Center U.S.A. [17713], 38 Crosby St., 5th Fl., New York, NY 10013, (212)431-7993
Anne Frank Center U.S.A. [IO], New York, NY, United States
Anne Frank - Fonds [IO], Basel, Switzerland
Anne Frank House [IO], Amsterdam, Netherlands
Anne Frank Inst. of Philadelphia [★IO]
Anne Frank Inst. of Philadelphia [★17723]
Anne Frank Stichting [★IO]
Anne Murray Intl. Fan Club [IO], Toronto, ON, Canada
Anneke Jans and Everardus Bogardus Descendants Assn. [20782], c/o Mr. William Brower Bogardus, Founder, 1121 Linhof Rd., Wilmington, OH 45177-2917, (937)382-3803
Annie People - Address unknown since 2001.
Annie Sims Intl. Fan Club [24842], PO Box 816, Bastrop, TX 78602-0816
Annonsorforeningen [★IO]
Annual Charges Policy Group - Defunct.
Annual Rpt. Coun. - Defunct.
Annual Steel Guitar Convention [★10629]

A star before a book entry number signifies that the name is not listed separately, but is mentioned within the entry.

Annual Steel Guitar Convention [★IO]
Annuity Assn; Teachers Insurance and [8579]
Annuity Insurers; Comm. of [2156]
Annular Bearing Engineers Comm. [★1991]
Anodizers Coun; Aluminum [849]
Anodizers Coun; Architectural [★849]
Anodizing Assn; Intl. Hard [2710]
Anomalies; Center for the Stud. of Natural and Historical [7862]
Anomaly - Defunct.
Anonymous [IO], Tel Aviv, Israel
Anonymous Arts Recovery Soc. [10956]
Anonymous; Co-Dependents [13016]
Anonymous Families History Project - Defunct.
Anorexia Bulimia Assn; Amer. [★14302]
Anorexia Nervosa
    Alliance for Eating Disorders Awareness [14297]
    Intl. Assn. of Eating Disorders Professionals [14300]
    Natl. Eating Disorders Assn. [14302]
Anorexia Nervosa Aid Soc. [★14302]
Anorexia Nervosa and Assoc. Disorders [★14301]
Anorexia Nervosa and Assoc. Disorders; Natl. Assn. of [14301]
Anorexia Nervosa and Bulimia Assn. [IO], Kingston, ON, Canada
Anorexia Nervosa and Related Eating Disorders [14298], PO Box 5102, Eugene, OR 97405, (541)344-1144
Anorexic Aid [★IO]
Anorexic Family Aid [★IO]
Another Mother for Peace - Defunct.
Another World Fan Club - Defunct.
Ansar Burney Welfare Trust Intl. [IO], Karachi, Pakistan
Ansley Family Assn. [20783], c/o Judy Candler, Chair, 782 Wisham Rd., Thomson, GA 30824
Ansley Reunion Assn. - Address unknown since 1995.
Antarabudaya Malaysia [★IO]
Antarctic Inst. of Canada [IO], Edmonton, AB, Canada
Antarctic Prog. of the Intl. Geophysical Year [★7518]
Antarctic Prog; U.S. [7518]
Antarctic and Southern Ocean Coalition [7516], 1630 Connecticut Ave. NW, 3rd Fl., Washington, DC 20009, (202)234-2480
Antarctic and Southern Ocean Coalition [IO], Washington, DC, United States
The Antarctica Proj. [IO], Washington, DC, United States
The Antarctica Proj. [7517], c/o Antarctic and Southern Ocean Coalition, 1630 Connecticut Ave. NW, 3rd Fl., Washington, DC 20009, (202)234-2480
Antarctica Tour Operators; Intl. Assn. of [3921]
Antarctican
    Amer. Alpine Club [7074]
    Amer. Polar Soc. [7515]
    Antarctic and Southern Ocean Coalition [7516]
    Intl. Assn. of Antarctica Tour Operators [3921]
    U.S. Antarctic Prog. [7518]
Antarctican Soc. - Address unknown since 2003.
Anteater Assn. - Defunct.
Antenna Measurement Techniques Assn. [6905], c/o Jeff Guerrieri, Sec., MIST m/s 818.02, 325 Broadway, Boulder, CO 80305
Antennas and Propagation Soc; IEEE [6913]
Anthology Film Archives [9928], 32 2nd Ave., New York, NY 10003, (212)505-5181
Anthony Sharp and Rachael Ellison Family Org. - Address unknown since 2002.
Anthony Women's Spirituality Educ. Forum; Susan B. [★20628]
Anthony's Guild; St. [20388]
Anthracite Industry Assn. - Address unknown since 1994.
Anthracite Information Bur. - Defunct.
Anthracite Railroads Historical Soc. [10907], PO Box 519, Lansdale, PA 19446-0519
Anthropological Assn. of Greece [IO], Athens, Greece
Anthropological Assn. of Ireland [IO], Maynooth, Ireland
Anthropological Stud. of Play; Assn. for the [★10858]

Anthropological Vocations; Underprivileged Students of [9079]
Anthropologists; Caucus of Black [★6409]
Anthropology
    African Amer. Cultural Alliance [9351]
    Amer. Anthropological Assn. [6402]
    Amer. Assn. of Physical Anthropologists [6403]
    Amer. Bd. of Forensic Anthropology [14400]
    Amer. Ethnological Soc. [6404]
    Amer. Soc. of Primatologists [6405]
    Amer. Stud. Assn. [9367]
    Amerind Found. [6406]
    Amerind Found. [IO]
    Anabaptist Sociology and Anthropology Assn. [7559]
    Anthropological Assn. of Greece [IO]
    Anthropological Assn. of Ireland [IO]
    Anthropology Film Center [6407]
    Anthroposophical Soc. in Am. [19457]
    Archeology Div. of the American Anthropological Association [6441]
    Assn. for Africanist Anthropology [6408]
    Assn. of Black Anthropologists [6409]
    Assn. for Evolutionary Economics [6872]
    Assn. for Gravestone Stud. [10015]
    Assn. of Latina and Latino Anthropologists [6410]
    Assn. for Political and Legal Anthropology [6411]
    Assn. of Sci. Museum Directors [10498]
    Assn. of Senior Anthropologists [6412]
    Assn. of Social Anthropologists of Aoteaora/New Zealand [IO]
    Assn. of Social Anthropologists of the UK and the Commonwealth [IO]
    Assn. for Social Anthropology in Oceania [IO]
    Assn. for Social Anthropology in Oceania [6413]
    The Assn. for the Stud. of Play [10858]
    Biological Anthropology Sect. [6414]
    British Assn. for Biological Anthropology and Osteoarchaeology [IO]
    Chinese Historians in the U.S. [8503]
    Coun. on Anthropology and Educ. [6415]
    Dental Anthropology Assn. [14150]
    European Assn. of Social Anthropologists [IO]
    Evolutionary Anthropology Soc. [6416]
    Gen. Anthropology Division of the Amer. Anthropological Assn. [6417]
    Historic New England [10035]
    Human Biology Assn. [6577]
    Independent Scholars of Asia [9957]
    Inst. of Andean Res. [9386]
    Inst. for the Stud. of Amer. Cultures [10746]
    Inst. for the Stud. of Man [6418]
    Intl. Acad. for Child Brain Development [15389]
    Intl. Assn. of Coroners and Medical Examiners [15093]
    Intl. Center of Medieval Art [10461]
    Intl. Inst. of Anthropology [IO]
    Intl. Org. for the Stud. of Gp. Tensions [10189]
    Intl. Primatological Soc. [6419]
    International Primatological Society [IO]
    Intl. Soc. for Human Ethology [6534]
    Intl. Time Capsule Soc. [10041]
    Intl. Union of Anthropological and Ethnological Sciences [IO]
    Intl. Women's Anthropology Conf. [IO]
    Intl. Women's Anthropology Conf. [6420]
    Kroeber Anthropological Soc. [6421]
    Lambda Alpha [24402]
    Logical Language Gp. [10304]
    Natl. Assn. of Medical Examiners [15094]
    Natl. Assn. for the Practice of Anthropology [6422]
    Natl. Assn. of Student Anthropologists [7953]
    Natl. Bd. of Medical Examiners [15095]
    New England Antiquities Res. Assn. [6452]
    Polynesian Soc. [IO]
    Royal Anthropological Inst. of Great Britain and Ireland [IO]
    Soc. for Anthropology in Community Colleges [7954]
    Soc. for the Anthropology of Consciousness [7955]
    Soc. for the Anthropology of Europe [6423]
    Soc. for the Anthropology of Europe [IO]
    Soc. for the Anthropology of Food and Nutrition [6424]

    Soc. for the Anthropology of North Am. [6425]
    Soc. for the Anthropology of Religion [6426]
    Soc. for Applied Anthropology [6427]
    Soc. for Applied Anthropology [IO]
    Soc. for Cross-Cultural Res. [10230]
    Soc. for Cultural Anthropology [6428]
    Soc. for East Asian Anthropology [6429]
    Soc. for Economic Anthropology [6430]
    Soc. for Ethnomusicology [10701]
    Soc. for Evolutionary Anal. in Law [6539]
    Soc. for Latin Amer. Anthropology [6431]
    Soc. for Latin Amer. Anthropology [IO]
    Soc. of Lesbian and Gay Anthropologists [6432]
    Soc. for Linguistic Anthropology [6433]
    Soc. for Medical Anthropology [6434]
    Soc. for Personality Assessment [16176]
    Soc. for Psychological Anthropology [7550]
    Soc. for the Sci. Stud. of Religion [20506]
    Soc. for the Stud. of Coherence [IO]
    Soc. for Urban, Natl. and Transnational/Global Anthropology [6435]
    Soc. for Visual Anthropology [6436]
    Soc. of Woman Geographers [7124]
    Swedish Soc. for Anthropology and Geography [IO]
    Underprivileged Students of Anthropological Vocations [9079]
    World Archaeological Soc. [6460]
    World Atlatl Assn. [22611]
Anthropology; Ad Hoc Gp. on Latin Amer. [★6431]
Anthropology; Amer. Bd. of Forensic [14400]
Anthropology Assn; Canadian Sociology and [IO]
Anthropology of Consciousness; Soc. for the [7955]
Anthropology; Coun. for Museum [10502]
Anthropology in Eastern Oceania; Assn. for Social [★6413]
Anthropology Film Center [6407], HC70 Box 3209, Glorieta, NM 87535, (505)757-2219
Anthropology Film Center [★6407]
Anthropology Film Center Found. [★6407]
Anthropology Film Inst. [★6407]
Anthropology Gp; Latin Amer. [★6431]
Anthropology Resource Center - Defunct.
Anthropology of Visual Commun; Soc. for the [★6436]
Anthroposophical
    Anthroposophical Soc. in Am. [19457]
    Threefold Educational Found. and School [8529]
Anthroposophical Medicine; Physicians' Assn. for [13646]
Anthroposophical Nurses Assn. of Am. [15462], 5909 SE Div. St., Portland, OR 97206, (503)235-9067
Anthroposophical Soc. in Am. [19457], 1923 Geddes Ave., Ann Arbor, MI 48104, (734)662-9355
Anthroposophical Soc. in Canada [IO], Thornhill, ON, Canada
Anthroposophical Soc. in Great Britain [IO], London, United Kingdom
Anthroposophical Translators and Editors Assn. - Defunct.
Anthrozoology; Intl. Soc. for [IO]
Anti-Abortion League; Jewish [18555]
Anti-Aging Medicine; Amer. Acad. of [15125]
Anti-Apartheids Beweging Nederland [★IO]
Anti-Asian Violence; Comm. Against [17006]
Anti-Bureaucracy Special Interest Group - Defunct.
Anti-Catholic League - Defunct.
Anti-Censorship and Deception Union [17038], PO Box 400297, Cambridge, MA 02140, (617)491-0433
Anti-Child Pornography Org. [12766], PO Box 22338, Eagan, MN 55122-0388
Anti-Child Pornography Org. [IO], Eagan, MN, United States.
Anti-Communist Advisory Comm. - Address unknown since 1995.
Anti-Communist Confed. of Polish Freedom Fighters in U.S.A. - Address unknown since 1999.
Anti-Communist Intl. [16987]
Anti-Communist Intl. [IO], New York, NY, United States
Anti-Communist League of America - Address unknown since 1995.
Anti Copying In Design [IO], Gloucester, United Kingdom

Reference to "IO" in place of a book number signifies that the association may be found in the 45th edition of International Organizations.

Anti-Counterfeiting Gp. **[IO]**, High Wycombe, United Kingdom

Anti-Cruelty Soc. **[11364]**, 157 W Grand Ave., Chicago, IL 60610, (312)644-8338

Anti-Defamation League **[17091]**, 605 3rd Ave., New York, NY 10158, (212)885-7700

Anti Defamation League of B'nai B'rith **[★17091]**

Anti-Defamation League; Christian **[17102]**

Anti-Digit Dialing League - Address unknown since 1995.

Anti-Discrimination Comm; American-Arab **[17082]**

Anti-Drug Coalitions of Am; Community **[13233]**

Anti-Euthanasia Task Force; Intl. **[★12133]**

Anti-Fascist Network - Defunct.

Anti-Friction Bearing Distributors Assn. **[★2007]**

Anti-Friction Bearing Mfrs. Assn. **[★1991]**

Anti-Imperialist; Vietnam Veterans Against the War **[18785]**

Anti-Piracy Centre in Finland **[★IO]**

Anti-Pollution League; Seacoast **[4451]**

Anti-Racism Info. Ser. **[IO]**, Geneva, Switzerland

Anti-Racist Action-Los Angeles/People Against Racist Terror **[IO]**, Culver City, CA, United States

Anti-Racist Action-Los Angeles/People Against Racist Terror **[17092]**, PO Box 1055, Culver City, CA 90232-1055, (310)495-0299

Anti-Racist Action/People Against Racist Terror **[★17092]**

Anti-Racist Action/People Against Racist Terror **[★IO]**

Anti-Repression Rsrc. Team **[17093]**, PO Box 210, Bellefonte, PA 16823-0210

Anti-Saloon League of Am. **[★13220]**

Anti-Slavery and Aborigines' Protection Soc. **[★IO]**

Anti-Slavery Intl. **[IO]**, London, United Kingdom

Anti-Slavery Intl. **[★12371]**

Anti-Slavery Soc. for the Protection of Human Rights **[★IO]**

Anti-Vivisection Soc; Amer. **[11345]**

Anti-Vivisection Soc; Natl. **[11432]**

Anti-Vivisection Soc. of New York **[★11474]**

Antiaircraft Assn; U.S. **[★6071]**

Anti-Apartheid

Artists for a New South Africa **[11911]**

Antibiotics; Alliance for the Prudent Use of **[15908]**

Anti-Communism

Alpha-66 **[17363]**

Amer. Security Coun. Found. **[16986]**

Anti-Communist Intl. **[16987]**

Anti-Communist Intl. **[IO]**

Captive Nations Comm. **[16988]**

Cardinal Mindszenty Found. **[16989]**

CAUSA Intl. **[16990]**

CAUSA Intl. **[IO]**

Christian Anti-Communism Crusade **[16991]**

Natl. Comm. to Reopen the Rosenberg Case **[17135]**

Religious Freedom Coalition **[12880]**

Selous Found. **[16992]**

Anti-Fascism

Action Reconciliation Ser. for Peace **[IO]**

Antigua and Barbuda Assn. of Persons with Disabilities **[IO]**, St. Johns, Antigua-Barbuda

Antigua and Barbuda Red Cross Soc. **[IO]**, St. Johns, Antigua-Barbuda

Antigua and Barbuda Tennis Assn. **[IO]**, St. Johns, Antigua-Barbuda

Antigua Hotels and Tourist Assn. **[IO]**, St. Johns, Antigua-Barbuda

Antigua Planned Parenthood Assn. **[IO]**, St. Johns, Antigua-Barbuda

Antigua Squash Rackets Assn. **[IO]**, St. Johns, Antigua-Barbuda

Anti-Imperialism

Vietnam Veterans Against the War Anti-Imperialist **[18785]**

Antilles Episcopal Conf. **[IO]**, St. James, Trinidad and Tobago

Antilliaanse Gewichthef Bond **[IO]**, Curacao, Netherlands Antilles

Anti-Poverty

Community Food Security Coalition **[12192]**

Developing Technologies **[IO]**

European Anti-poverty Network **[IO]**

Inst. of Cultural Affairs - Netherlands **[IO]**

Millennium Promise **[11485]**

Mir Pace Intl. **[12872]**

NetAid **[11486]**

New Forests Proj. **[12436]**

Partnership for Sustainable Development - Nepal **[IO]**

Soc. for Welfare Awakening Training and Hea. Implementation **[IO]**

Stand Up For Africa **[IO]**

Sursawera **[IO]**

Antipsychiatry Coalition **[16079]**, c/o Carrie L. Drake, 2040 Polk St., Box 234, San Francisco, CA 94109

Antiquarian Booksellers Assn. **[IO]**, London, United Kingdom

Antiquarian Booksellers Assn. of Am. **[9740]**, 20 W 44th St., 4th Fl., New York, NY 10036-6604, (212)944-8291

Antiquarian Booksellers' Assn. of Canada **[IO]**, Ottawa, ON, Canada

Antiquarian Booksellers' Center - Address unknown since 1995.

Antiquarian Horological Soc. **[IO]**, Sussex, United Kingdom

Antiquarian Soc; Amer. **[10008]**

Antique Advt. Assn. of Am. **[21420]**, PO Box 76, Petersburg, IL 62675

Antique Airplane Assn. **[21430]**, 22001 Bluegrass Rd., Ottumwa, IA 52501-8569, (641)938-2773

Antique and Amusement Photographers Intl. **[2994]**, PO Box 150, Eureka Springs, AR 72632, (479)253-8554

Antique Appraisal Assn. of America - Defunct.

Antique and Art Dealers Assn. of Am; Natl. **[300]**

Antique and Art Glass Salt Shaker Collectors Soc. **[21968]**, c/o Leann Lindsey, Membership Chair, 25033 Ribbonwood Dr., Sun Lakes, AZ 85248

Antique Auto Racing Assn. **[21578]**, c/o Paul O'Malley, Sec.-Treas., PO Box 181, Capon Bridge, WV 26711, (304)856-2042

Antique Auto. Club of Am. **[21579]**, PO Box 417, Hershey, PA 17033, (717)534-1910

Antique Barbed Wire Soc. **[21969]**, 2720 Camino Chueco, Santa Fe, NM 87505-5250, (417)788-1111

Antique Barbed Wire Society **[IO]**, Kearney, NE, United States

Antique Bicycle Club of America - Defunct.

Antique Boat Club **[★21870]**

Antique Boat Club; Chris Craft **[21870]**

Antique Boat Soc. - Defunct.

Antique Boat and Yacht Club - Address unknown since 2001.

Antique Bottle Collectors Assns. - Defunct.

Antique Bowie Knife Assn. - Address unknown since 2005.

Antique Caterpillar Machinery Owners Club **[22619]**, PO Box 2220, East Peoria, IL 61611, (309)694-0664

Antique and Classic Boat Soc. **[21868]**, 422 James St., Clayton, NY 13624, (315)686-2628

Antique/Classic Div; EAA **[★21442]**

Antique Collectors' Club **[IO]**, Woodbridge, United Kingdom

Antique Comb Collectors Club **[★IO]**

Antique Comb Collectors Club **[★21970]**

Antique Comb Collectors Club Intl. **[21970]**

Antique Comb Collectors Club International **[IO]**, Laurel Springs, NJ, United States

Antique Dealers of Am; Branched from: Associated **[★219]**

Antique Dealers; Assn. of Art and **[IO]**

Antique Dealers Assn. of Czech Republic **[IO]**, Prague, Czech Republic

Antique Dealers Assn. of Poland **[IO]**, Krakow, Poland

Antique Dealers League of Am; Art and **[297]**

Antique and Decorative Arts League **[★297]**

Antique Doorknob Collectors of Am. **[21971]**, PO Box 31, Chatham, NJ 07928-0031, (973)635-6338

Antique Engine and Thresher Assn. - Defunct.

Antique Engine, Tractor, and Toy Assn. **[23001]**

Antique Fan Collectors Assn. **[21533]**, c/o Dick Boswell, Treas., 2245 Harrison Ave., Lincoln, NE 68502

Antique and Historic Glass Found. - Address unknown since 1994.

Antique Label Soc; Pacific **[★21995]**

Antique Modelers; Soc. of **[21477]**

Antique Motor Fire Apparatus in Am; Soc. for the Preservation and Appreciation of **[22423]**

Antique Motorcycle Club of Am. **[22667]**, c/o Dick Winger, Membership Chm., PO Box 310, Sweetser, IN 46987, (765)384-5421

Antique Motorcycle Club of America **[IO]**, Sweetser, IN, United States

Antique Oldsmobile Club; Natl. **[21726]**

Antique Outboard Motor Club **[23158]**, PO Box 2526, Walla Walla, WA 99362

Antique Phonograph Collectors Club **[22710]**, 502 E 17th St., Brooklyn, NY 11226, (718)941-6835

Antique Playing Card Collector's Club; Amer. **[★21955]**

Antique Poison Bottle Collectors Assn. **[21972]**, c/o Mary Riggin, Pres., PO Box 53, Marionville, VA 23408, (757)442-2179

Antique Powercraft Historical Soc. - Defunct.

Antique Radio Club of Am. **[★22923]**

Antique Radio Club of Am. **[★IO]**

Antique Radio Guild of America - Defunct.

Antique Reloading Tool Collector's Assn. **[22424]**, c/o Tom Quigley, PO Box 1567, Castle Rock, WA 98611

Antique Small Engine Collectors Club **[22409]**, c/o Dale Crane, Pres., 7609 State Rd. 58 E, Heltonville, IN 47436-8772

Antique Snowmobile Club of Am. **[22943]**, HCR 83, Box 1068, Pequot Lakes, MN 56472, (218)543-4146

Antique Souvenir China Collectors - Defunct.

Antique Stove Assn. **[21524]**, 2321 E Pioneer, Duluth, MN 55804

Antique Stove Info. CH **[21525]**, 421 N Main St., Monticello, IN 47960-1932, (574)583-6465

Antique Studebaker Club **[21580]**, PO Box 1743, Maple Grove, MN 55311, (763)420-7829

Antique Telephone Collectors Assn. **[22985]**, PO Box 1252, McPherson, KS 67460, (620)245-9555

Antique Telescope Soc. **[21526]**, c/o Dr. Walter H. Breyer, Sec., 1878 Robinson Rd., Dahlonega, GA 30533

Antique Tools and Indus. Assn; Potomac **[22610]**

Antique Toy Collectors of Am. **[22993]**, Crescent Springs, Covington, KY 41017

Antique Tribal Art Dealers Assn. **[296]**, 215 Sierra SE, Albuquerque, NM 87108, (415)863-3173

Antique Truck Club of Am. **[23022]**, 85 S Walnut St., Boyertown, PA 19512, (610)367-2567

Antique Valentines Assn. - Defunct.

Antique Wireless Assn. **[22923]**, PO Box 421, Bloomfield, NY 14469

Antique Wireless Association **[IO]**, Bloomfield, NY, United States

Antiques

1/87 Vehicle Club **[22641]**

1965-66 Full Size Chevrolet Club **[21557]**

Abarth Register, U.S.A. **[21562]**

Abingdon Pottery Club **[21522]**

Aeronautica and Air Label Collectors Club **[21422]**

Aeronca Lovers Club **[21423]**

Aerostar Owners Assn. **[21424]**

Airflow Club of Am. **[21563]**

Aladdin Knights of the Mystic Light **[22617]**

Alaska Collectors' Club **[22779]**

Alfa Romeo Owners Club **[21565]**

All-American Indian Motorcycle Club **[22663]**

AMC Rambler Club **[21567]**

Amer. Air Mail Soc. **[22780]**

Amer. Art Deco Dealers Assn. **[295]**

Amer. Austin/Bantam Club **[21568]**

Amer. Bell Assn. Intl. **[21958]**

Amer. Bugatti Club **[21569]**

Amer. Carnival Glass Assn. **[22549]**

Amer. Collectors of Infant Feeders **[21959]**

Amer. Cut Glass Assn. **[22550]**

Amer. Edge Collectors Assn. **[22612]**

Amer. First Day Cover Soc. **[22781]**

Amer. Helvetia Philatelic Soc. **[22782]**

Amer. Historical Print Collectors Soc. **[21523]**

American-Israel Numismatic Assn. **[22723]**

Amer. Lancia Club **[21573]**

Amer. Lock Collectors Assn. **[21962]**

A star before a book entry number signifies that the name is not listed separately, but is mentioned within the entry.

Amer. MGB Assn. [21574]
Amer. MGC Register [21575]
Amer. Motors Owners Assn. [21576]
Amer. Numismatic Assn. [22724]
Amer. Numismatic Soc. [22725]
Amer. Pencil Collectors Soc. [21964]
Amer. Philatelic Cong. [22783]
Amer. Philatelic Res. Lib. [22784]
Amer. Philatelic Soc. [22785]
Amer. Philatelic Soc. Writers Unit [22786]
Amer. Plate Number Single Soc. [22787]
Amer. Revenue Assn. [22788]
Amer. Soc. of Bookplate Collectors and Designers [21965]
Amer. Soc. of Check Collectors [22726]
Amer. Soc. of Military Insignia Collectors [22627]
Amer. Soc. of Polar Philatelists [22789]
Amer. Spoon Collectors [21966]
Amer. Sta. Wagon Owners Assn. [21577]
Amer. Tax Token Soc. [22727]
Amer. Topical Assn. [22790]
Amer. Topical Assn., Americana Unit [22791]
Amer. Topical Assn., Biology Unit [22792]
Amer. Wooden Money Guild [22728]
Amer. Yankee Assn. [21429]
Ancient Coin Collectors Guild [22729]
Antique Advt. Assn. of Am. [21420]
Antique Airplane Assn. [21430]
Antique and Art Glass Salt Shaker Collectors Soc. [21968]
Antique Auto Racing Assn. [21578]
Antique Auto. Club of Am. [21579]
Antique Barbed Wire Soc. [21969]
Antique Caterpillar Machinery Owners Club [22619]
Antique and Classic Boat Soc. [21868]
Antique Comb Collectors Club Intl. [21970]
Antique Dealers Assn. of Czech Republic [IO]
Antique Dealers Assn. of Poland [IO]
Antique Doorknob Collectors of Am. [21971]
Antique Fan Collectors Assn. [21533]
Antique Motorcycle Club of Am. [22667]
Antique Phonograph Collectors Club [22710]
Antique Reloading Tool Collector's Assn. [22424]
Antique Small Engine Collectors Club [22409]
Antique Snowmobile Club of Am. [22943]
Antique Stove Assn. [21524]
Antique Stove Info. CH [21525]
Antique Studebaker Club [21580]
Antique Telephone Collectors Assn. [22985]
Antique Telescope Soc. [21526]
Antique Toy Collectors of Am. [22993]
Antique Tribal Art Dealers Assn. [296]
Antique Truck Club of Am. [23022]
Antique Wireless Assn. [22923]
Antiques and Collectibles Associations [216]
Antiques and Collectibles Dealer Assn. [863]
Antiques and Collectibles Natl. Assn. [864]
Antiques Coun. [217]
Antiques Coun. [IO]
Arctic Cat Club of Am. [22944]
Ariel Motorcycle Club North Am. [22668]
Armed Forces Stamp Exchange Club [22793]
Armor and Arms Club [21536]
Art and Antique Dealers League of Am. [297]
Assoc. Collectors of El Salvador [22794]
Assn. of Amer. Military Uniform Collectors [22628]
Assn. of Coffee Mill Enthusiasts [21973]
Assn. of North Amer. Radio Clubs [21498]
Assn. of Ohio Longrifle Collectors [22425]
Assn. of Restorers and Coun. of Craftsmen and Artists [218]
Astronomy Stud. Unit [22795]
Austin Bantam Soc. [21583]
Austin-Healey Sports and Touring Club [21586]
Australian Antique and Art Dealers Assn. [IO]
Auto. License Plate Collectors Assn. [21587]
Bead Soc. of Los Angeles [21975]
Bellanca-Champion Club [21431]
Berkeley Exchange [21590]
Beyond the Pond. International Frog Collectors Club [21977]
Bird Airplane Club [21432]
Blue/White Pottery Club [21527]
BMW Car Club of Am. [21591]

BMW Motorcycle Owners of Am. [22670]
BMW Riders Assn. Intl. [22671]
BMW Vintage Car Club of Am. [21593]
Boss 429 Owners Dir. [21596]
Brazil Philatelic Assn. [22797]
Brewery Collectibles Club of Am. [21979]
Bricklin Intl. Owners Club [21598]
British Antique Furniture Restorers Assn. [IO]
Browning Collectors Assn. [22426]
Buick Club of Am. [21599]
Buick GS Club of Am. [21600]
Cadillac-LaSalle Club [21602]
Call and Whistle Collectors Assn. [21983]
Canadian Antique Phonograph Soc. [IO]
Canadian Corkscrew Collectors Club [21985]
Cardinal [21433]
Carriage Assn. of Am. [21987]
CartoPhilatelic Soc. [22799]
Case Collectors Club [22613]
Casey Jones Railroad Unit - ATA [22800]
Casino Chip and Gaming Token Collectors Club [21989]
Cast Iron Seat Collectors Assn. [22607]
Cat Collectors [21990]
Cessna Owner Org. [21435]
Cessna Pilots Assn. [21436]
Chemistry and Physics on Stamps Stud. Unit [22802]
Chess Collectors Intl. [21944]
Chevrolet Nomad Assn. [21607]
Chicago Map Soc. [21528]
China Stamp Soc. [22803]
Chris Craft Antique Boat Club [21870]
Christian Motorcyclists Assn. [22674]
Christmas Philatelic Club [22804]
Christmas Seal and Charity Stamp Soc. [21993]
Christopher Columbus Philatelic Soc. [22805]
Chrysler 300 Club Intl. [21611]
Chrysler Town and Country Owners Registry [21612]
Cigarette Pack Collectors Assn. [21994]
Citizens' Stamp Advisory Comm. [22806]
Citroen Quarterly Car Club [21613]
Civil Censorship Study Group [22807]
Civil War Token Soc. [22732]
Classic Chevy Intl. [21615]
Classic Jaguar Assn. [21616]
Classic Thunderbird Club Intl. [21617]
Classic Yacht Assn. [21871]
Cobra Owners Club of Am. [21619]
Coin Operated Collectors Assn. [21997]
Collectors Club [22808]
Collectors Record Club [22712]
Collectors of Religion on Stamps [22809]
Colonial Coin Collectors Club [22733]
Combined Organizations of Numismatic Error Collectors of Am. [22734]
Conestoga Soc. [21529]
Confederate Stamp Alliance [22811]
Contemporary Historical Vehicle Assn. [21620]
Cookie Cutter Collectors Club [22000]
Corben Club [21440]
Corrado Club of Am. [21621]
Corvair Soc. of Am. [21622]
Cover Collectors Circuit Club [22812]
Cow Observers Worldwide [22002]
Croatian Philatelic Soc. [22813]
Crosley Auto. Club [21624]
Crown Victoria Assn. [21625]
Cuban Numismatic Assn. [22735]
Czech Collector's Assn. [22008]
Dedicated Wooden Money Collectors [22736]
Deltiologists of Am. [22905]
DeSoto Club of Am. [21630]
Deutsches Motorrad Register [22677]
Diecast Exchange Club [22010]
Disabled Veterans Keychain Tag and Chauffeur's Badge Collectors Newsl. [22011]
Dodge Bros. Club [21632]
Dodge Pilothouse Era Truck Club of Am. [23024]
Dogs on Stamps Stud. Unit [22815]
Doll Artisan Guild [22394]
Doll Costumer's Guild [22395]
EAA Vintage Aircraft Assn. [21442]
EAA Warbirds of Am. [21443]

Early Amer. Coppers [22737]
Early Ford V-8 Club of Am. [21633]
Early Typewriter Collectors Assn. [22015]
Earth's Physical Features Stud. Unit [22816]
Edsel Club [21636]
Egg Cup Collectors' Corner [22016]
Eire Philatelic Assn. [22817]
Emergency Vehicle Owners and Operators Assn. [21639]
Ercoupe Owners Club [21444]
Errors, Freaks and Oddities Collector's Club [22818]
Erskine Registry [21640]
Fairchild Club [21446]
Fairlane Club of Am. [21641]
Fan Assn. of North Am. [22021]
Fenton Art Glass Collectors of Am. [22552]
Ferrari Owners Club [21644]
Figural Bottle Opener Collectors Club [22023]
Figural Cast Iron Collector's Club [22417]
Fine Arts Philatelists [22819]
First Flight Soc. [21447]
Flow Blue Intl. Collectors Club [22026]
Flying Apache Assn. [21448]
Ford Galaxie Club of Am. [21647]
Fostoria Glass Collectors [22553]
Fostoria Glass Soc. of Am. [22554]
Found. for the Stud. of the Arts and Crafts Movement at Roycroft [21530]
France and Colonies Philatelic Soc. [22820]
Funk Aircraft Owners Assn. [21449]
Gar Wood Soc. [21873]
Gems, Minerals and Jewelry Stud. Unit [22821]
German Colonies Collectors Gp. [22822]
Germany Philatelic Soc. [22823]
Glass Art Soc. [22555]
Golden Glow of Christmas Past [22975]
Golf Collectors Soc. [22031]
Graham Bros. Truck and Bus Club [21894]
Graham Owners Club Intl. [21650]
Graphics Philately Assn. [22824]
Gravely Tractor Club of Am. [23002]
Guild of Antique Dealers and Restorers [IO]
Gull Wing Gp. Intl. [21652]
Haiti Philatelic Soc. [22825]
Harley Hummer Club [22679]
Haynes-Apperson Owners Club [21653]
Heart of America Carnival Glass Assn. [22557]
Heisey Collectors of America/National Heisey Glass Museum [22558]
Helicopter Club of America [21450]
Hellenic Philatelic Soc. of Am. [22826]
H.H. Franklin Club [21656]
Historic Deerfield [10034]
Historic Motor Sports Assn. [21657]
Homer Laughlin China Collectors Assn. [22036]
Honda Sport Touring Assn. [22681]
Horseless Carriage Club of Am. [21658]
Howdy Doody Memorabilia Collectors Club [22038]
Hudson-Essex-Terraplane Club [21659]
Hummel Collectors Club [22040]
Hurst/Olds Club of Am. [21661]
India Stud. Circle for Philately [22828]
Indian Motor-Cycle Club of America [22682]
Inter-Governmental Philatelic Corp. [22829]
Intl. 190SL Gp. [21663]
Intl. Amphicar Owners Club [21664]
Intl. Assn. of Jazz Record Collectors [22714]
Intl. Assn. of R.S. Prussia Collectors [22043]
Intl. B and B Fly-Inn Club [21451]
Intl. Bank Note Soc. [22739]
Intl. Bond and Share Soc. [22046]
Intl. Brick Collectors' Assn. [22048]
Intl. Bus Collectors Club [21895]
Intl. Camaro Club [21665]
Intl. Carnival Glass Assn. [22559]
Intl. Cessna 120/140 Assn. [21453]
The Intl. Cessna 170 Assn. [21454]
Intl. Chinese Snuff Bottle Soc. [21890]
Intl. Collectors Guild [22051]
Intl. Correspondence of Corkscrew Addicts [22052]
Intl. Coun. of Air Shows [21455]
Intl. Doll Makers Assn. [22397]

Reference to "IO" in place of a book number signifies that the association may be found in the 45th edition of International Organizations.

Intl. Edsel Club [21666]
Intl. Fed. of Postcard Dealers [22906]
Intl. Fire Buff Associates [22421]
Intl. Handicappers' Net [21502]
Intl. King Midget Car Club [21667]
Intl. Match Safe Assn. [22053]
Intl. Mustang Bullitt Owners Club [21669]
Intl. Nippon Collectors Club [21929]
Intl. Norton Owners' Assn. [22684]
Intl. Old Lacers, Inc. [22161]
Intl. Pietenpol Assn. [21456]
Intl. Radio Club of Am. [21503]
Intl. Railroad and Transportation Postcard Collectors Club [22055]
Intl. Rose O'Neill Club Found. [22399]
Intl. Soc. of Animal License Collectors [22058]
Intl. Soc. of Antique Scale Collectors [22059]
Intl. Soc. for Japanese Philately [22830]
Intl. Soc. for Vehicle Preservation [21670]
Intl. Stamp and Coin Collectors Soc. [22832]
Intl. Stationary Steam Engine Soc. [22977]
Intl. Vintage Poster Dealers Assn. [106]
Intl. Watch Collectors Soc. [22988]
Interstate Club [21458]
Iso and Bizzarrini Owners Club [21672]
Italian Car Registry [21673]
Jack Knight Air Mail Soc. [22834]
Jaguar Clubs of North Am. [21674]
Jewett Owners Club [21676]
Jordan Register [21677]
Junior Philatelists of Am. [22837]
Kaiser-Frazer Owners Club Intl. [21680]
Karmann Ghia Club of North Am. [21681]
Kate Greenaway Soc. [22063]
Kissel Kar Klub [21682]
Knife Collectors Club [22615]
Korea Postcard Collectors Gp. [22907]
Korea Stamp Soc. [22838]
Kustom Kemps of Am. [21683]
Lamborghini Club Am. [21684]
Late Great Chevrolet Assn. [21685]
Latin Amer. Paper Money Soc. [22741]
Les Amis de Panhard and Deutsch Bonnet [21686]
Liberty Seated Collectors Club [22742]
Lighter-Than-Air Soc. [21460]
Lincoln and Continental Owners Club [21687]
Lincoln Owners' Club [21688]
Lithuanian Numismatic Assn. [22743]
Little Elegance Memories of Yesterday [22065]
Lladro Soc. [21930]
London Vintage Taxi Assn. - Amer. Sect. [21690]
Longwave Club of Am. [21505]
Lotus, Ltd. [21691]
Love Token Soc. [22744]
Luscombe Endowment [21461]
M. T. Bottle Collectors Assn. [22066]
Machine Cancel Soc. [22839]
Magic Lantern Soc. of the U.S. and Canada [21531]
Mailer's Postmark Permit Club [22840]
Man Will Never Fly Memorial Soc. Internationale [22598]
Manuscript Soc. [22068]
Marble Collectors' Soc. of Am. [22624]
Maritime Postmark Soc. [22841]
Marmon Club [21694]
Maserati Info. Exchange [21696]
Mathematical Stud. Unit [22842]
Maverick/Comet Club Intl. [21697]
Mech. Bank Collectors of Am. [21826]
Medal Collectors of Am. [22745]
Medical Subjects Unit [22843]
Mercedes-Benz Club of Am. [21699]
Meter Stamp Soc. [22844]
Metropolitan Owners Club of North Am. [21701]
Mexico Elmhurst Philatelic Soc. Intl. [22846]
Mid-Century Mercury Car Club [21704]
Midstates Jeepster Assn. [21705]
Midwest Decoy Collectors Assn. [22071]
Midwest Sunbeam Registry [21706]
Milestone Car Soc. [21707]
Military Vehicle Preservation Assn. [22630]
Mini Car Club, U.S.A. [21708]
Miniature Arms Collectors/Makers Soc. [21538]

Miniature Book Soc. [9752]
Mobile Post Off. Soc. [22848]
Model A Ford Cabriolet Club [21709]
Model A Ford Club of Am. [21710]
Model "A" Restorers Club [21712]
Model "T" Ford Club of Am. [21713]
Model "T" Ford Club Intl. [21714]
Monocoupe Club [21462]
Morgan Car Club [21717]
Morgan Plus Four Club [21718]
Morris Minor Registry [21720]
Motor Bus Soc. [21896]
Muntz Jet Registry [21721]
Napoleonic Age Philatelists [22849]
Nash Car Club of Am. [21725]
Natl. 210 Owners Assn. [21463]
Natl. Aeronca Assn. [21464]
Natl. Antique and Art Dealers Assn. of Am. [300]
Natl. Antique Doll Dealers Assn. [22402]
Natl. Antique Oldsmobile Club [21726]
Natl. Antique Tractor Pullers Assn. [23004]
Natl. Assn. of Milk Bottle Collectors [22076]
Natl. Assn. of Miniature Enthusiasts [22077]
Natl. Assn. of Paper and Advt. Collectors [22412]
Natl. Assn. of Rocketry [22650]
Natl. Assn. of Timetable Collectors [23008]
Natl. Assn. of Watch and Clock Collectors [22990]
Natl. Automatic Pistol Collectors Assn. [21539]
Natl. Button Soc. [22079]
Natl. Cambridge Collectors [22561]
Natl. Carousel Assn. [21897]
Natl. Collectors Assn. of Die Doubling [22746]
Natl. Corvette Owners Assn. [21728]
Natl. Corvette Restorers Soc. [21729]
Natl. Coun. of Corvette Clubs [21730]
Natl. Depression Glass Assn. [22562]
Natl. DeSoto Club [21731]
Natl. Duncan Glass Soc. [22563]
Natl. Firebird and T/A Club [21732]
Natl. Fishing Lure Collectors Club [22082]
Natl. Graniteware Soc. [22083]
Natl. Historical Fire Found. [22422]
Natl. Imperial Glass Collectors Soc. [22565]
Natl. Inst. of Amer. Doll Artists [22403]
Natl. Intercollegiate Flying Assn. [21466]
Natl. Knife Collectors Assn. [22616]
Natl. Mossberg Collectors Assn. [22430]
Natl. Old Timers Auto Racing Club [21737]
Natl. Pop Can Collectors [22085]
Natl. Stinson Club [21467]
Natl. St. Rod Assn. [21738]
Natl. Toothpick Holder Collectors' Soc. [22089]
Natl. Valentine Collectors' Assn. [22090]
Natl. Woodie Club [21739]
Natl. World War II Glider Pilots Assn. [21468]
Nautical Res. Guild [21880]
New England M.G. "T" Register Limited [21740]
Newspaper Collectors Soc. of Am. [22092]
Nineteen Thirty-Two Buick Registry [21741]
North Amer. Collectors [22747]
North Amer. Mini Moke Registry [21745]
North Amer. Model Boat Assn. [22654]
North Amer. Radio Archives [22926]
North Amer. Shortwave Assn. [21507]
NSU Enthusiasts U.S.A. [21746]
Numismatic Literary Guild [22749]
Numismatics Intl. [22750]
Oakland-Pontiac Enthusiast Org. [21748]
Occupied Japan Club [22098]
The Old Appliance Club [21535]
Old Sleepy Eye Collectors' Club of Am. [21934]
Oldsmobile Club of Am. [21749]
On the Lighter Side, Intl. Lighter Collectors [22100]
Opel Motorsports Club [21752]
Orders and Medals Soc. of Am. [22631]
Org. of Bricklin Owners [21753]
Original Doll Artists Coun. of Am. [22404]
Original Hobo Nickel Soc. [22752]
OX5 Aviation Pioneers [21469]
Packard Auto. Classics [21755]
Packards Intl. Motor Car Club [21758]
Pantera Intl. [21759]
Paperweight Collectors' Assn. [22102]
Peanut Pals [22104]

Perfins Club [22854]
Pewter Collectors Club of Am. [22107]
Philatelic Found. [22855]
Pierce-Arrow Soc. [21761]
Plymouth Barracuda/Cuda Owners Club [21763]
Plymouth Owners Club [21764]
Pontiac-Oakland Club Intl. [21766]
Popular Rotorcraft Assn. [21471]
Porsche Club of Am. [21767]
Porterfield Airplane Club [21472]
Postcard History Soc. [22909]
Professional Car Soc. [21768]
Professional Numismatists Guild [22754]
Quarter Century Wireless Assn. [21509]
The Questers [21532]
Radio Club of Am. [22928]
Radio Collectors of Am. [22929]
Rearwin Club [21474]
Renault Owners Club of North Am. [21769]
REO Club of Am. [21770]
Richardson Boat Owners Assn. [21884]
Rickenbacker Automobile Club of America [21771]
Rickman Owners Club Intl. [22689]
Road Race Lincoln Register [21773]
Rolls-Royce Owners' Club [21774]
Rometsch Registry [21775]
Rough and Tumble Engineers' Historical Assn. [22979]
Rudge Enthusiasts Club [22691]
Saab Club of North Am. [21778]
Sabra Automobile Connection [21779]
Saving Antiquities for Everyone [9389]
Saxon Owners Registry [21781]
Shelby Amer. Auto. Club [21782]
Ships-in-Bottles Assn. of Am. [22658]
Short Wing Piper Club [21475]
Silver Wings Fraternity [21476]
Soc. of Antique Modelers [21477]
Soc. of Automotive Historians [21785]
Soc. of Inkwell Collectors [22114]
Soc. of Lincoln Cent Collectors [22756]
Soc. of Paper Money Collectors [22757]
Soc. for the Preservation and Appreciation of Antique Motor Fire Apparatus in Am. [22423]
Soc. of Private and Pioneer Numismatists [22758]
Soc. of Ration Token Collectors [22759]
Soc. of Tobacco Jar Collectors [21936]
Soc. of U.S. Pattern Collectors [22761]
Southeastern Historical Keyboard Soc. [22720]
Spark Plug Collectors of Am. [22116]
Sports Car Club of Am. [21787]
Stampe Club Intl. [21479]
Steam Auto. Club of Am. [21789]
Stearman Restorers Assn. [21480]
Still Bank Collectors Club of Am. [21827]
Studebaker Driver's Club [21790]
Stutz Club [21791]
Subaru 360 Drivers' Club [21792]
Swift Museum Found. [21481]
Tea Leaf Club Intl. [21937]
Telephone Collectors Intl. [22986]
Texas Date Nail Collectors Assn. [22121]
Thimble Collectors Intl. [22122]
Thimble Guild [22123]
Thompson Collectors Assn. [22431]
Token and Medal Soc. [22763]
Toned Coin Collectors Soc. [22764]
Topolino Register of North Am. [21797]
Toy Stitchers Intl., Inc. [22998]
Traditional Small Craft Assn. [21885]
Travel Air Club [21482]
Triumph Register of Am. [21800]
Tucker Auto. Club of Am. [21801]
TVR Car Club North Am. [21802]
Twin Bonanza Assn. [21483]
United Fed. of Doll Clubs [22407]
United Flying Octogenarians [21485]
United Four-Wheel Drive Associations [21805]
United Sidecar Assn. [22693]
U.S. Classic Racing Assn. [22694]
U.S. Mexican Numismatic Assn. [22765]
U.S. Stamp Soc. [22888]
U.S. Ultralight Assn. [21486]
Universal Autograph Collectors Club [22126]
Unrecognised States Numismatic Soc. [22766]

A star before a book entry number signifies that the name is not listed separately, but is mentioned within the entry.

Velocette Owners Club of North Am. [22695]
Veteran Motor Car Club of Am. [21808]
Vincent Owners Club - Keystone Sect. [22697]
Vintage BMW Motorcycle Owners [22698]
Vintage Chevrolet Club of Am. [21809]
Vintage Drivers Club of Am. [21810]
Vintage Motor Bike Club [22699]
Vintage Radio and Phonograph Soc. [22931]
Vintage Sailplane Assn. [23045]
Vintage Thunderbird Club Intl. [21812]
Vintage Triumph Register [21813]
Vintage Volkswagen Club of Am. [21814]
Volkswagen Club of Am. [21815]
Volvo Club of Am. [21816]
Weatherby Collectors Assn. [22432]
Wedgwood Intl. Seminar [21939]
Western Assoc. Modelers [22661]
Whirly-Girls - Intl. Women Helicopter Pilots [21487]
Whisky Pitcher Collectors Assn. of Am. [22130]
Wills Sainte Claire Museum [21817]
Willys Overland Jeepster Club [21818]
Willys-Overland-Knight Registry [21819]
Winchester Arms Collectors Assn. [21540]
Winged Warriors/National B-Body Owners Assn. [21820]
Wooton Desk Owners Soc. [22131]
World Airline Historical Soc. [21488]
World Antique Dealers Assn. [219]
World Atlatl Assn. [22611]
World Internet Numismatic Soc. [22768]
World Proof Numismatic Assn. [22769]
World War I Aeroplanes [21490]
Worldwide Camaro Club [21821]
Worldwide Television-FM DX Assn. [21510]
Young Numismatists of Am. [22770]
Z Series Car Club of Am. [21824]
Antiques and Collectibles Associations [216], PO Box 4389, Davidson, NC 28036, (704)895-9088
Antiques and Collectibles Dealer Assn. [863], c/o Antiques and Collectibles Assn., PO Box 4389, Davidson, NC 28036, (704)895-9088
Antiques and Collectibles Natl. Assn. [864], PO Box 4389, Davidson, NC 28036, (704)895-9088
Antiques Coun. [217], PO Box 1508, Warren, MA 01083, (413)436-7064
Antiques Coun. [IO], Warren, MA, United States
Antiquities
Ancient Coin Collectors Guild [22729]
Antique Caterpillar Machinery Owners Club [22619]
Antique Small Engine Collectors Club [22409]
Armenian Numismatic Soc. [22730]
Armor and Arms Club [21536]
Colonial Coin Collectors Club [22733]
Figural Cast Iron Collector's Club [22417]
Israel Antiquities Authority [IO]
Miniature Book Soc. [9752]
Natl. Collectors Assn. of Die Doubling [22746]
Natl. Historical Fire Found. [22422]
Original Hobo Nickel Soc. [22752]
Saving Antiquities for Everyone [9389]
Soc. for the Preservation of Poultry Antiquities [5119]
Soc. of U.S. Pattern Collectors [22761]
Toned Coin Collectors Soc. [22764]
Unrecognised States Numismatic Soc. [22766]
Antiquities; Assn. for the Preservation of Virginia [★10013]
Antiquities Res. Assn; New England [6452]
Antiquities; Soc. for the Preservation of New England [★10035]
Antiquities; Soc. for the Preservation of Poultry [5119]
Anti-Racism
Anti-Racist Action-Los Angeles/People Against Racist Terror [17092]
Fed. Hispanic Law Enforcement Officers Assn. [5969]
The Generation After [17119]
Natl. Action Network [17127]
Natl. Assn. for the Advancement of Colored People [17129]
Natl. MultiCultural Inst. [11829]
Turkish Amer. Alliance for Fairness [19410]

A World of Difference Inst. [11487]
A World of Difference Inst. [IO]
Anti-Semitism
Anti-Defamation League [17091]
The Generation After [17119]
Intl. Network of Children of Jewish Holocaust Survivors [17720]
Jewish Coun. for Public Affairs [12474]
Jews Against the Occupation [17952]
Russian Amer. Jews for Israel [18576]
A World of Difference Inst. [11487]
Antitrust Coalition for Consumer Choice in Hea. Care [14615], c/o Doug Badger, Washington Coun. Ernst and Young, 1150 17th St. NW, Washington, DC 20036, (202)293-7474
Antitrust Laws; Comm. to Support the [17626]
Antitrypsin Support Gp; Alpha 1 [★16353]
Antwerp Diamond High Coun. [IO], Antwerp, Belgium
Anuvrat Global Org. [IO], Jaipur, India
Anxiety Center; Natl. [18416]
Anxiety Disorder SIG [★12744]
Anxiety Disorders
ABIL - Agoraphobics Building Independent Lives [12546]
Agoraphobics in Motion [12742]
Anxiety Disorders Assn. of Am. [12743]
Anxiety Disorders Assn. of Victoria [IO]
Anxiety Disorders Special Interest Gp. [12744]
Anxiety and Phobia Treatment Center [12745]
Anxiety Self Help Assn. [IO]
Obsessive-Compulsive Found. [15230]
Panic, Anxiety, and Depression Assistance [IO]
Panic Anxiety Disorder Assn. [IO]
Panic Anxiety Disorder Assn. (Queensland) [IO]
Selective Mutism Found. [15233]
South African Depression and Anxiety Gp. [IO]
UK Paruresis Trust [IO]
Anxiety Disorders Assn. of Am. [12743], 8730 Georgia Ave., Ste. 600, Silver Spring, MD 20910, (240)485-1001
Anxiety Disorders Assn. of Victoria [IO], Kew, Australia
Anxiety Disorders Special Interest Gp. [12744], c/o Alicia E. Meuret, PhD, Treas., Southern Methodist Univ., Hyer Hall, 6424 Hilltop Ln., Dallas, TX 75205
Anxiety and Phobia Clinic [★12745]
Anxiety and Phobia Program - Address unknown since 2008.
Anxiety and Phobia Treatment Center [12745], White Plains Hosp., Davis Ave. at E Post Rd., White Plains, NY 10601, (914)681-1038
Anxiety Self Help Assn. [IO], Nedlands, Australia
Any Boy Can Program - Defunct.
Any Soldier [11490], PO Box 29, Hoagland, IN 46745-0029
AOAC Intl. [6671], 481 N Frederick Ave., Ste. 500, Gaithersburg, MD 20877-2417, (301)924-7077
AOAC Intl. [IO], Gaithersburg, MD, United States
The AODC [★IO]
AOIP - Address unknown since 2003.
AOJS [★7601]
AOMAlliance [★13607]
Aontas Fiontair Agus Spoirt [★IO]
Aontas Innealtoireacht Bithleighis na hEireann [★IO]
Aontas Muinteoiri Eireann [★IO]
Aontas Teilgin Agus Amais na h'Eireann [★IO]
Aos-Oideachas Naisiunta Tri Aontu Soarlach [★IO]
Aosdana [IO], Dublin, Ireland
AOTCB [★16625]
Aouon Archv. [9418], c/o Michael Rossman, Dir., 1741 Virginia St., Berkeley, CA 94703, (510)849-1154
APA: The Engineered Wood Assn. [1637], 7011 S 19th, Tacoma, WA 98466, (253)565-6600
Apache Assn; Flying [21448]
Apartment Assn. of America - Defunct.
Apartment Assn; Natl. [3317]
Apartment CH; Natl. Accessible [11963]
Apartment Owners Assn; Natl. [★3317]
Apartment Owners and Managers Assn. of America - Defunct.
APB Registry [★4835]
APCA [★5081]

APCA [★IO]
APEC - Automated Procedures for Engineering Consultants [6999]
Aphasia
Acad. of Aphasia [13704]
Natl. Aphasia Assn. [13705]
Apheresis
Amer. Soc. for Apheresis [13706]
World Apheresis Assn. [IO]
Apiary Inspectors of Am. [4164], c/o Minnesota Dept. of Agriculture, 625 Robert St. N, St. Paul, MN 55155-2538, (651)201-6095
APICS Region 8 [IO], Toronto, ON, Canada
APICS - The Association for Operations Management [IO], Alexandria, VA, United States
APICS - The Assn. for Operations Mgt. [7181], 5301 Shawnee Rd., Alexandria, VA 22312-2317, (703)354-8851
APICS — The Educational Soc. for Rsrc. Mgt. [7181]
APICS — The Educational Soc. for Rsrc. Mgt. [IO]
Apicultural Soc; Eastern [★4165]
Apiculture
Amer. Assn. of Professional Apiculturists [4162]
Amer. Honey Producers Assn. [4163]
Apiary Inspectors of Am. [4164]
Asian Apicultural Assn. [IO]
Bee Improvement and Bee Breeders' Assn. [IO]
Beekeeping Extension Soc. [IO]
British Bee-Keepers' Assn. [IO]
Canadian Honey Coun. [IO]
Central Assn. of Bee-Keepers [IO]
Coun. of Natl. Beekeeping Associations in the United Kingdom [IO]
Eastern Apicultural Soc. of North Am. [4165]
European Assn. for Apitherapy [IO]
Fed. Coun. of Australian Apiarists' Assn. [IO]
Fed. of Irish Beekeepers Associations [IO]
Intl. Bee Res. Assn. [IO]
Intl. Fed. of Beekeepers' Associations [IO]
Mid-U.S. Honey Producers Marketing Assn. [4166]
Natl. Beekeepers Assn. of New Zealand [IO]
Scottish Beekeepers' Assn. [IO]
UK Apitherapy Soc. [IO]
Apio-Therapy Soc; North Amer. [★13614]
Apistogramma Study Group [22436], PO Box 504, Elkhorn, WI 53121
Apistogramma Study Group [IO], Elkhorn, WI, United States
Apitherapy; European Assn. for [IO]
Apitherapy Soc; Amer. [13614]
APIW [2142], c/o Maryanne Sherman, Pres., Sherman Think Tank, 15 Hopkins Dr., Lawrenceville, NJ 08648, (609)896-2280
APL and J Languages; Special Interest Gp. on the [7540]
Aplastic Anemia of Canada [★IO]
Aplastic Anemia Found. of Am. [★IO]
Aplastic Anemia Found. of Am. [★14785]
Aplastic Anemia and MDS Intl. Found. [14785], PO Box 310, Churchton, MD 20733, (410)867-0242
Aplastic Anemia and MDS International Foundation [IO], Churchton, MD, United States
Aplastic Anemia and Myelodysplasia Assn. of Canada [IO], Richmond Hill, ON, Canada
APMI Intl. [IO], Princeton, NJ, United States
APMI Intl. [7310], 105 Coll. Rd. E, Princeton, NJ 08540-6692, (609)452-7700
Apnea Assn; Amer. Sleep [16421]
APOG [★IO]
Apollo Class Assn. - Defunct.
Apollo Launch Tower; Save the [★9341]
Apollo Owners Register - Defunct.
Apollo Soc. [9341], PO Box 61206, Honolulu, HI 96839-1206, (808)473-3316
Apollo XI Collector Soc. - Defunct.
Apostle; Missionary Soc. of Saint Paul the [19663]
Apostleship of Prayer [19569], 3211 S Lake Dr., Ste. 216, Milwaukee, WI 53235, (414)486-1152
Apostleship of Prayer [IO], Toronto, ON, Canada
Apostleship of the Sea in the U.S.A. [19570], 3211 4th St. NE, Washington, DC 20017-1194, (202)541-3384
Apostolate; Bishops' Comm. on the Liturgical [★19585]

Reference to "IO" in place of a book number signifies that the association may be found in the 45th edition of International Organizations.

Apostolate; Center for Applied Res. in the [19608]
Apostolate for Family Consecrations [19571], 3375 Rte. 36, Bloomingdale, OH 43910, (740)765-5500
Apostolate for Inclusion Ministry; Natl. [20026]
Apostolate for the Mentally Retarded; Natl. [★20026]
Apostolate with Mentally Retarded Persons; Natl. [★20026]
Apostolate with People with Mental Retardation; Natl. [★20026]
Apostolate of the Sick and Disabled; CUSA: An [19620]
Apostolate of Suffering - Defunct.
Apostolate of the Word [★19711]
Apostolic Development; St. Vincent Pallotti Center for [20390]
Apostolic Oblates; Inst. of [19638]
Apothecaries; Amer. Coll. of [15912]
Apothecaries of London; Worshipful Soc. of [IO]
Apoyo Para el Campesino Indigena del Oriente Boliviano [★IO]
APPA: The Association of Higher Education Facilities Officers [IO], Alexandria, VA, United States
APPA: The Assn. of Higher Educ. Facilities Officers [8333], 1643 Prince St., Alexandria, VA 22314-2818, (703)684-1446
Appalachia; Catholic Comm. of [20311]
Appalachian
  Appalachian Bear Rescue [5293]
  Appalachian Consortium [9390]
  Appalachian Mountain Club [23936]
  Appalachian Stud. Assn. [9391]
  Appalachian Trail Conservancy [23937]
  Melungeon Heritage Assn. [18950]
  Southern Appalachian Dulcimer Assn. [10708]
Appalachian Bear Center [★5293]
Appalachian Bear Rescue [5293], PO Box 364, Townsend, TN 37882, (865)448-0143
Appalachian Consortium [9390], c/o Dr. Patricia D. Beaver, Dir., Center for Appalachian Stud., Appalachian State Univ., ASU Box 32018, Boone, NC 28608, (828)262-4089
Appalachian Dulcimer Assn; Southern [10708]
Appalachian Families - Defunct.
Appalachian Finance Assn. [★1414]
Appalachian Forum - Address unknown since 2001.
Appalachian Hardwood Club [★1638]
Appalachian Hardwood Manufacturers, Inc. [1638], PO Box 427, High Point, NC 27261, (336)885-8315
Appalachian Mountain Club [23936], 5 Joy St., Boston, MA 02108, (617)523-0636
Appalachian Stud. Assn. [9391], ASA Off., Marshall Univ., 111 Jenkins Hall, One John Marshall Dr., Huntington, WV 25755, (304)696-2904
Appalachian Trail Conf. [★23937]
Appalachian Trail Conservancy [23937], PO Box 807, Harpers Ferry, WV 25425-0807, (304)535-6331
Appalachian Volunteers, Inc. - Address unknown since 2002.
Appaloosa Assn; Intl. Colored [4897]
Appaloosa Assn. Worldwide; Amer. [4809]
Appaloosa Color Breeders Assn. - Address unknown since 1995.
Appaloosa Horse Assn. of New Zealand [IO], TePuke, New Zealand
Appaloosa Horse Club [IO], Moscow, ID, United States
Appaloosa Horse Club [4857], 2720 W Pullman Rd., Moscow, ID 83843, (208)882-5578
Appaloosa Horse Club of Canada [IO], Claresholm, AB, Canada
Appaloosa Pony; Natl. [★4945]
Appaloosa Sport Horse Assn. - Address unknown since 2003.
Apparatus Makers Assn. of Am. [★3488]
Apparatus Makers Assn; PMC Sect. of the Sci. [★3485]
Apparatus Ser. Assn; Elecl. [1180]
Apparel
  Accessories Coun. [220]
  Amer. Apparel and Footwear Assn. [221]
  Amer. Apparel Machinery Trade Assn. [1990]
  Amer. Apparel Producers' Network [222]
  American Apparel Producers Network [IO]

Amer. Cloak and Suit Mfrs. Assn. [223]
Amer. Fiber Mfrs. Assn. [3769]
Apparel Graphics Inst. [224]
Apparel Mfrs. Assn. [225]
Argentine Chamber of the Clothing Indus. [IO]
Asian Amer. Importers Assn. [226]
Associacao Nacional das Industrias de Vestuario e Confeccao [IO]
Associated Corset and Brassiere Mfrs. [227]
Assn. of Austrian Clothing Indus. [IO]
Assn. of Fashion Retailers in Finland [IO]
Assn. of Knitwear Designers [IO]
Assn. of Knitwear Designers [228]
Assn. des Maitres-Foureurs de Grand-Duche de Luxembourg [IO]
Assn. of Suppliers to the British Clothing Indus. [IO]
Associazione Italiana Pellicceria [IO]
Bangladesh Garment Manufacturers and Exporters Assn. [IO]
Belgian Fur Trade Fed. [IO]
Boot and Shoe Travelers Assn. of New York [1596]
British Fur Trade Assn. [IO]
British Glove Assn. [IO]
British Hat Guild [IO]
British Menswear Guild [IO]
Brotherhood of Shoe and Allied Craftsmen [24063]
Canadian Apparel Fed. [IO]
Clothing Assn. [IO]
Clothing Mfrs'. Assn. of India [IO]
Clothing Mfrs. Assn. of the U.S.A. [229]
Coun. of Fashion Designers of Am. [230]
Coun. of Textile and Fashion Indus. of Australia [IO]
Custom Tailors and Designers Assn. of Am. [231]
Cyprus Clothing Indus. Assn. [IO]
Dress for Success Worldwide [13424]
Educational Found. for the Fashion Indus. [232]
Estonian Clothing and Textile Assn. [IO]
European Apparel and Textile Org. [IO]
European Sunglass Assn. [IO]
Fashion Exports New York [IO]
Fashion Exports New York [233]
Fashion Gp. Intl. [234]
Fashion Gp. Intl. [IO]
Fashion Outreach [235]
Fed. of Clothing Designers and Executives [IO]
Fed. of Finnish Textile and Clothing Indus. [IO]
Fed. of French Ladies' Fashion [IO]
Footwear Distributors and Retailers of Am. [1597]
French Fed. of Haute Couture and Ready-to-Wear and Fashion Designers [IO]
Fur Coun. of Canada [IO]
Fur Finland [IO]
Fur Industrialists and Businessmen Assn. [IO]
Fur Info. Coun. of Am. [236]
Fur Inst. of Canada [IO]
Garment Assn. of Nepal [IO]
German Fur Assn. [IO]
German Shoe Indus. Assn. [IO]
Greater Blouse, Skirt and Undergarment Assn. [237]
Haberdashers' Company [IO]
Headwear Info. Bur. [238]
Honduran Mfrs. Assn. [IO]
Hong Kong Fashion Designers Assn. [IO]
Hong Kong Fur Fed. [IO]
Hong Kong Garment Mfrs. Assn. [IO]
Hong Kong Hide and Leather Traders' Assn. [IO]
The Hosiery Assn. [239]
Infant and Juvenile Mfrs. Assn. [240]
Intl. Apparel Fed. [IO]
Intl. Assn. of Clothing Designers and Executives [IO]
Intl. Assn. of Clothing Designers and Executives [241]
Intl. Formalwear Assn. [242]
International Formalwear Association [IO]
Intl. Fur Trade Fed. [IO]
Intl. Wooden Bow Tie Club [243]
Intimate Apparel Square Club [12201]
Japan Fur Assn. [IO]
Kopenhagen Fur [IO]

Ladies Apparel Contractors Assn. [244]
Men's Clothing Mfrs. Assn. [IO]
Merchant Taylors' Company [IO]
Mexico Apparel Chamber [IO]
Natl. Assn. of Blouse Mfrs. [245]
Natl. Assn. of Clothing Mfrs. [IO]
Natl. Assn. of Fashion and Accessory Designers [246]
Natl. Assn. of Men's Sportswear Buyers [247]
Natl. Assn. of Uniform Manufacturers and Distributors [248]
Natl. Button Soc. [22079]
Natl. Cap and Patch Assn. [22080]
Natl. Childrenswear Assn. [IO]
Natl. Costumers Assn. [249]
Natl. Fashion Accessories Assn. [250]
Natl. Knitwear and Sportswear Assn. [251]
Natl. Pitching Assn. [23121]
Natl. Shoe Retailers Assn. [1598]
Neckwear Assn. of America [252]
New York Coat and Suit Assn. [253]
New York Skirt and Sportswear Assn. [254]
Norwegian Fur Breeders' Assn. [IO]
Organizacion Empresarial Espanola de la Peleteria [IO]
Pakistan Hosiery Manufacturers Assn. [IO]
Pakistan Readymade Garments Mfrs'. and Exporters' Assn. [IO]
Pelsinform [IO]
Polish Fur Fed. [IO]
Professional Apparel Assn. [255]
Professional Assn. of Custom Clothiers [256]
Shetland Knitwear Trades Assn. [IO]
Shoe Ser. Inst. of Am. [1600]
Sojuzpushnina [IO]
Spanish Fed. of Clothing Companies [IO]
Spanish Knitting Assn. [IO]
Sunglass Assn. of Am. [257]
Swedish Fur Breeders Assn. [IO]
Taiwan Bags Assn. [IO]
Taiwan Garment Indus. Assn. [IO]
Taiwan Zippers Mfrs. Assn. [IO]
Textile Soc. of Am. [3805]
Textiles, Clothing and Leather Processing Assn. [IO]
Thai Garment Manufacturers Assn. [IO]
Turkish Clothing Manufacturers Assn. [IO]
Two/Ten Footwear Found. [1601]
UK Fashion Exports [IO]
Ukrainian Assn. of Furriers [IO]
Underfashion Club [258]
Western-English Trade Assn. [259]
World Shoe Assn. [260]
World Shoe Association [IO]
Worldwide Responsible Apparel Production [IO]
Worldwide Responsible Apparel Production [261]
Worshipful Company of Pattenmakers [IO]
Young Menswear Assn. [262]
Apparel Assn; Leather [2415]
Apparel Contractors Assn; Amer. [★222]
Apparel Contractors Assn; Southern [★222]
Apparel and Equip. Manufacturers Assn; Western [★259]
Apparel and Footwear Manufacturers Assn; Amer. [★221]
Apparel Graphics Inst. [224], 58 Boston Dr., Ste. 1000, Ocean Pines, MD 21811, (410)641-7300
Apparel Guild - Defunct.
Apparel Indus; Gen. Arbitration Coun. of the Textile and [5453]
Apparel Industries Inter-Assn. Comm. - Defunct.
Apparel Indus; Chamber of Commerce of the [24269]
Apparel Industry Comm. on Imports - Defunct.
Apparel Indus; Educational Found. for the [★232]
Apparel Indus; Young Men's Assn. of the Men's [★262]
Apparel Indus; Young Menswear Assn. of Men's [★262]
Apparel Machinery Trade Assn; Amer. [1990]
Apparel Mfrs. Assn. [225], 1601 N Kent St., Ste. 1200, Arlington, VA 22209, (703)797-9037
Apparel Manufacturers Assn; Amer. [★221]
Apparel Manufacturing Executives Assn. - Defunct.
Apparel Producers Assn; Amer. [★222]

A star before a book entry number signifies that the name is not listed separately, but is mentioned within the entry.

Apparel Res. Found. - Defunct.
Apparel Retailers of Am. [★3423]
Apparel Square Club; Intimate [12201]
Apparel; U.S. Assn. of Importers of Textiles and [3807]
APPEAL: Asian Pacific Partners for Empowerment and Leadership [11760], 300 Frank H. Ogawa Plz., Ste. 620, Oakland, CA 94612, (510)272-9536
APPEAL: Asian Pacific Partners for Empowerment and Leadership [IO], Oakland, CA, United States
Appeal; Church World Ser. Community [★12842]
Appeal of Conscience Found. [18508], 119 W 57th St., New York, NY 10019-2401, (212)535-5800
Appellate Court Clerks; Natl. Conf. of [5629]
Appellate Lawyers; Amer. Acad. of [5472]
Apperson Owners Club; Haynes- [21653]
Appita [IO], Rotorua, New Zealand
Appita - Tech. Assn. for the Australian and New Zealand Pulp and Paper Indus. [IO], Carlton, Australia
Apple
  Apple Products Res. and Educ. Coun. [4705]
  Michigan Apple Comm. [4739]
  U.S. Apple Assn. [4768]
Apple Assn; Intl. [★4768]
Apple Assn; U.S. [4768]
Apple Commn; Washington State [4773]
Apple Comm; Michigan [4739]
Apple Inst; Natl. [★4768]
Apple Octopus Now - Address unknown since 1999.
Apple and Pear Growers Assn. of South Australia [IO], Cavan, Australia
Apple Processors Assn. [1673], 1100 17th St. NW, 10th Fl., Washington, DC 20036, (202)785-6710
Apple Products Res. and Educ. Coun. [4705], 5775 Peachtree-Dunwoody Rd., Bldg. G, Ste. 500, Atlanta, GA 30342, (404)252-3663
Apples Inst; Processed [★4705]
Apples Inst; Processed [★510]
Apple's Kin - Defunct.
Appleseed: The Natl. Campaign for Public School Improvement; Proj. [8332]
AppleWorks Users Gp. [6760], PO Box 701010, Plymouth, MI 48170, (734)454-1969
Appliance and Electronic Indus. Assn. [IO], Auckland, New Zealand
Appliance Engineers Soc; Gas [★6941]
Appliance and Equip. Manufacturers; Assn. of Gas [★265]
Appliance and Limb Mfrs. Assn; Orthopedic [★1855]
Appliance Manufacturers; Inst. of [★265]
Appliance Parts Distributors Assn. [263], 4700 W Lake Ave., Glenview, IL 60025, (847)375-4713
Appliance Parts Jobbers Assn. [★263]
Appliances
  Amer. Soc. of Gas Engineers [6941]
  Antique Fan Collectors Assn. [21533]
  Antique Stove Assn. [21524]
  Appliance Parts Distributors Assn. [263]
  Assn. of Home Appliance Manufacturers [264]
  Canadian Gas Assn. [IO]
  Gas Appliance Manufacturers Assn. [265]
  Gas Appliance Mfrs. Assn. of Australia [IO]
  Hoover Historical Center [21534]
  Intl. Housewares Assn. [1972]
  Malaysian Elecl. Appliances Indus. Gp. [IO]
  Member Insurance Assn. [1827]
  Natl. Appliance Parts Suppliers Assn. [266]
  Natl. Appliance Ser. Assn. [267]
  The Old Appliance Club [21535]
  Professional Ser. Assn. [3553]
  Stove, Furnace, Energy, and Allied Appliance Workers Division of the Intl. Brotherhood of Boilermakers [24001]
  Vacuum Dealers Trade Assn. [268]
Application Programming Interface Consortium; Biometric [6572]
Application Ser. Provider Indus. Consortium [3722], c/o Computing Tech. Indus. Assn., 1815 S Meyers Rd., Ste. 300, Oakbrook Terrace, IL 60181-5228, (630)678-8300
Applications Gp; Open [890]
Applications Soc; IEEE Indus. [7183]
Applicators Assn; Interstate Professional [2909]
Applied Computational Electromagnetics Soc. [6906], c/o Dr. Richard W. Adler, Exec. Off., Naval Post Graduate School, ECE Dept., Code EC/AB, 833 Dyer Rd., Monterey, CA 93943-5121, (831)646-1111

Applied Computing; SIGAPP - Special Interest Gp. on [6821]
Applied Ekistics; Educational Center for [10228]
Applied Interactive Multimedia; Assn. for [2666]
Applied Learning Tech; Soc. for [8571]
Applied Linguistics; Amer. Assn. for [10397]
Applied Linguistics Assn. of New Zealand [IO], Auckland, New Zealand
Applied Linguistics; Center for [10401]
Applied Mathematics; Soc. for Indus. and [7294]
Applied Naturalist Guild - Defunct.
Applied Nutrition; Intl. Coll. of [★15560]
Applied Osteopathy; Acad. of [★15790]
Applied Poetry; Assn. for [16211]
Applied and Preventive Psychology; Amer. Assn. of [16119]
Applied Psychophysiology and Biofeedback; Assn. for [13749]
Applied Res. Center [18635], 900 Alice St., Ste. 400, Oakland, CA 94607, (510)653-3415
Applied Res. Centre for Archeology and Fine Arts [★IO]
Applied Res. and Development Intl. - Address unknown since 2004.
Applied Res. Ethics Natl. Assn. [15101], 126 Brookline Ave., Ste. 202, Boston, MA 02115-3920, (617)423-4112
Applied Systems Client Network [2143], 801 Douglas Ave., Ste. 205, Altamonte Springs, FL 32714, (407)869-0404
Applied Tech. Coun. [7000], 201 Redwood Shores Pkwy., Ste. 240, Redwood City, CA 94065, (650)595-1542
Applied Vision Assn. [IO], Bristol, United Kingdom
Applied Voice Input/Output Soc. [6720], PO Box 20817, San Jose, CA 95160, (408)323-1783
The Applique Soc. [22151], PO Box 89, Sequim, WA 98382-0089, (800)597-9827
The Applique Soc. [IO], Sequim, WA, United States
Appointed Democratic Officials; Natl. Assn. of Latino [★17706]
Appointed Officials; Natl. Assn. of Latino Elected and [17706]
Appointees Alumni Assn; Reagan [★18365]
Appointment Secretaries; Natl. Assn. of [★8961]
Appraisal Inst. [275], HQ Off., 550 W Van Buren St., Ste. 1000, Chicago, IL 60607, (312)335-4100
Appraisal Inst. of Canada [IO], Ottawa, ON, Canada
Appraisers
  Acad. of Experts [IO]
  Accredited Gemologists Assn. [2354]
  Accredited Rev. Appraisers Coun. [269]
  Amer. Acad. of State Certified Appraisers [270]
  Amer. Soc. of Agricultural Appraisers [271]
  Amer. Soc. of Appraisers [272]
  Amer. Soc. of Farm Equip. Appraisers [273]
  Amer. Soc. of Farm Managers and Rural Appraisers [274]
  Antique Tribal Art Dealers Assn. [296]
  Appraisal Inst. [275]
  Appraisers Assn. of Am. [276]
  Assn. of Agents, Brokers and Valuers of Wine and Foreign Spirits [IO]
  Assn. of Machinery and Equip. Appraisers [277]
  Collector Car Appraisers Assn. [278]
  Equip. Appraisers Assn. of North Am. [279]
  Equip. Appraisers Assn. of North Am. [IO]
  Found. of Real Estate Appraisers [280]
  Independent Automotive Damage Appraisers Assn. [281]
  Inst. of Bus. Appraisers [282]
  Intl. Soc. of Appraisers [283]
  Intl. Soc. of Appraisers [IO]
  Japanese Assn. of Real Estate Appraisal [IO]
  Jeweler's Advisory Gp. [2369]
  Natl. Aircraft Appraisers Assn. [188]
  Natl. Assn. of Independent Fee Appraisers [284]
  Natl. Assn. of Jewelry Appraisers [2380]
  Natl. Assn. of Master Appraisers [3321]
  Natl. Assn. of Real Estate Appraisers [285]
  Natl. Assn. of Rev. Appraisers and Mortgage Underwriters [3329]
  Natl. Soc. of Appraiser Specialists [286]
  Professional Women's Appraisal Assn. [287]
  World Assn. of Valuation Organizations [IO]

Appraisers; Amer. Inst. of Real Estate [★275]
Appraisers; Amer. Soc. of Tech. [★272]
Appraisers Assn. of Am. [276], 386 Park Ave. S, 20th Fl., Ste. 2000, New York, NY 10016, (212)889-5404
Appraisers; Assn. of Governmental [★272]
Appraisers Inst; Natl. Residential [3333]
Appraisers and Mortgage Underwriters; Natl. Assn. of Rev. [3329]
Appraisers; Natl. Assn. of Jewelry [2380]
Appraisers; Natl. Assn. of Master [3321]
Appraisers; National Soc. of Real Estate [★3323]
Appraisers; Soc. of Real Estate [★275]
Appreciation Soc; Six of One Club: The Prisoner [25043]
Apprentices of the Plumbing and Pipe Fitting Indus. of the U.S. and Canada; United Assn. of Journeymen and [★24164]
Apprentices of the Plumbing, Pipe Fitting, Sprinkler Fitting Indus. of the U.S. and Canada; United Assn. of Journeymen and [24164]
Apprenticeship
  Intl. Union of Painters and Allied Trades/Joint Apprenticeship and Training Fund [12082]
  Natl. Assn. of Field Training Officers [5987]
  Young Apprentice's Assn. [IO]
Apprenticeship and Manpower Training Fund; Intl. Joint Painting, Decorating and Drywall [★12082]
Apprenticeship Prog. for Cooks and pastry cooks; National [★790]
Apprenticeship, Referral and Outreach for Women - Defunct.
Apprenticeship and Training Comm; Natl. Joint Painting, Decorating, and Drywall [★12082]
Apprenticeship Training Prog. for Balancing Technicians [★598]
Appropriate/Alternative Tech; Trans-National Network of [★17002]
Appropriate Hea. Resources and Technologies Action Gp. [★IO]
Appropriate Rural Tech. Inst. [IO], Pune, India
Appropriate Technology
  African Centre for Tech. Stud. [IO]
  African Energy Policy Res. Network/Foundation for Woodstove Dissemination [IO]
  Amer. Rainwater Catchment Systems Assn. [7825]
  Appropriate Rural Tech. Inst. [IO]
  Appropriate Tech. ASIA [IO]
  Aprovecho Res. Center [IO]
  Aprovecho Res. Center [16993]
  APT Enterprise Development [IO]
  Asian and Pacific Centre for Transfer of Tech. [IO]
  Centre for Alternative Tech. [IO]
  Centre for Rural Tech., Nepal [IO]
  Compatible Tech. Intl. [4087]
  Domestic Technologies [16994]
  Domestic Technologies [IO]
  E. F. Schumacher Soc. [16995]
  EnterpriseWorks/VITA [16996]
  EnterpriseWorks/VITA [IO]
  Exchange Gp. for Appropriate Tech. [IO]
  German Appropriate Tech. Exchange [IO]
  Integrated Mfg. Tech. Initiative [7264]
  Intermediate Tech. Development Gp. of North Am. [16997]
  Intermediate Tech. Development Gp. - Peru [IO]
  Intl. Rainwater Catchment Systems Assn. [7832]
  Natl. Center for Appropriate Tech. [16998]
  Pakistan Coun. of Renewable Energy Tech. [IO]
  Planet Drum Found. [IO]
  Planet Drum Found. [16999]
  Practical Action [IO]
  Practical Action - Bangladesh [IO]
  Prog. for Appropriate Tech. in Hea. [IO]
  Prog. for Appropriate Tech. in Hea. [17000]
  Programme for Belize [IO]
  Res. and Technological Exchange Gp. - France [IO]
  Res. and Tech. Exchange Gp. - Vietnam [IO]
  Servants in Faith and Technology [IO]
  Servants in Faith and Tech. [17001]
  Skat Found. [IO]
  Technonet Asia [IO]
  TRANET [IO]

Reference to "IO" in place of a book number signifies that the association may be found in the 45th edition of International Organizations.

TRANET [17002]

Appropriate Tech. ASIA [IO], Chatteris, United Kingdom

Appropriate Tech. Assistance Ser; Natl. [★6951]

Appropriate Tech. Development Org. [★IO]

Appropriate Tech. Intl. [★IO]

Appropriate Tech. Intl. [★16996]

Appropriate Tech; Southern Inst. for [★17001]

Approval of Schools Comm. [★8835]

Approved Driving Instructors Natl. Joint Coun. [IO], Gloucester, United Kingdom

Approving Agencies; Natl. Assn. of State [6345]

APQC [2482], 123 N Post Oak Ln., 3rd Fl., Houston, TX 77024, (713)681-4020

Apraxia of Speech Assn; Childhood [16444]

Apricot Producers of California [4706], PO Box 974, Turlock, CA 95381, (209)632-9777

April Fan Club - Address unknown since 1994.

Aprovecho Inst. [★16993]

Aprovecho Inst. [★IO]

Aprovecho Res. Center [IO], Cottage Grove, OR, United States

Aprovecho Res. Center [16993], 80574 Hazelton Rd., Cottage Grove, OR 97424, (541)942-8198

APSE: The Network on Employment [17414], 1627 Monument Ave., Richmond, VA 23220, (804)278-9187

APT Enterprise Development [IO], Moreton-in-Marsh, United Kingdom

APVA Preservation Virginia [10013], 204 W Franklin St., Richmond, VA 23220, (804)648-1889

Aqua-Cat Catamaran Sailing Assn. - Address unknown since 1995.

Aqua Lung Dealers Assn. - Defunct.

Aquaculture

Alternative Aquaculture Assn. [4167]

Amer. Tilapia Assn. [4666]

Aquaculture Assn. of Canada [IO]

Aquaculture Assn. of Southern Africa [IO]

Aquaculture Certification Council [IO]

Aquaculture Certification Coun. [4168]

Aquaculture Intl. [4169]

Aquaculture Intl. [IO]

Aquatic Gardeners Assn. [4777]

Aquatic Res. Inst. [7171]

Asian-Pacific Regional Res. and Training Centre for Integrated Fish Farming [IO]

Australasian Soc. for Phycology and Aquatic Botany [IO]

Breeder's Registry [22438]

Canadian Aquaculture Indus. Alliance [IO]

Canadian Assn. of Aquarium Clubs [IO]

Catfish Farmers of Am. [4170]

The Catfish Inst. [4171]

European Aquaculture Soc. [IO]

Fed. of European Aquaculture Producers [IO]

Florida Tropical Fish Farms Assn. [4172]

Global Aquaculture Alliance [4173]

Global Aquaculture Alliance [IO]

Hungarian Alcological Soc. [IO]

Hydroponic Soc. of Am. [4174]

The Icelandic Aquaculture Assn. [IO]

Intl. Assn. of Meiobenthologists [IO]

Intl. Soc. for Reef Stud. [4581]

Japan Intl. Food and Aquaculture Soc. [IO]

Marine Aquarium Coun. [IO]

Marine Aquarium Coun. [4175]

Marine Aquarium Coun. - Indonesia [IO]

Marine Aquarium Societies of North Am. [4176]

Muskies Inc. [4177]

Natl. Aquaculture Assn. [4178]

Natl. Aquaculture Coun. [4179]

Natl. Assn. of State Aquaculture Coordinators [4180]

Natl. Ornamental Goldfish Growers Assn. [4181]

Pacific Shellfish Inst. [4182]

Shetland Aquaculture [IO]

Southern African Soc. of Aquatic Scientists [IO]

Striped Bass Growers Assn. [4670]

U.S. Aquaculture Soc. [4183]

U.S. Freshwater Prawn and Shrimp Growers Assn. [3505]

U.S. Trout Farmers Assn. [4184]

World Aquaculture Soc. [4185]

World Aquaculture Soc. [IO]

Aquaculture Assn. of Canada [IO], St. Andrews, NB, Canada

Aquaculture Assn; National [★4026]

Aquaculture Assn. of Southern Africa [IO], Pretoria, Republic of South Africa

Aquaculture Certification Council [IO], Kirkland, WA, United States

Aquaculture Certification Coun. [4168], 12815 72nd Ave. NE, Kirkland, WA 98034, (425)825-7935

Aquaculture Intl. [4169], c/o Charles W. Johnson, Founder/Pres., PO Box 606, Andrews, NC 28901

Aquaculture Intl. [IO], Andrews, NC, United States

Aquaculture Suppliers Assn; U.S. [4026]

Aquarian Res. Found. [18606], 5620 Morton St., Philadelphia, PA 19144, (215)848-2292

Aquarium Assn; Amer. Zoo and [★7857]

Aquarium Societies; Fed. of Amer. [7173]

Aquarium Societies of North Am; Marine [4176]

Aquarium Soc; Natl. [10442]

Aquarium and Zoo Facilities Assn. [7856], 1901 N Roselle Rd., Ste. 920, Schaumburg, IL 60195, (847)885-7400

Aquariums; Amer. Assn. of Zoological Parks and [★7857]

Aquatic Animal Life Support Operators [7279], PO Box 690067, Orlando, FL 32869-0067, (407)363-2587

Aquatic Art; Intl. Acad. of [23884]

Aquatic Babies Cong; World [★23894]

Aquatic Bodywork Assn; Worldwide [13658]

Aquatic Exercise Assn. [23652], 201 Tamiami Trail S, Ste. 3, Nokomis, FL 34275, (941)486-8600

Aquatic Gardeners Assn. [4777], c/o Cheryl Rogers, Membership Coor., PO Box 51536, Denton, TX 76206-1536

Aquatic Gardeners Assn. [IO], Denton, TX, United States

Aquatic Injury Safety Found. [★12963]

Aquatic and Marine Affairs; Women's Network in [★7277]

Aquatic Network; Women's [7277]

Aquatic Plant Mgt. Soc. [6630], PO Box 821265, Vicksburg, MS 39182-1265, (601)634-2656

Aquatic Plants

Aquatic Gardeners Assn. [4777]

Intl. Waterlily and Water Gardening Soc. [22524]

Reef Check [5012]

ReefGuardian Intl. [5014]

Aquatic Res. Inst. [7171], 2242 Davis Ct., Hayward, CA 94545, (510)782-4058

Aquatic Res. Interactive [★7171]

Aquatic Resources Educ. Assn. [7956], c/o Amanda Wuestefeld, Treas., Indiana Division of Fish and Wildlife, Natural Resources Educ. Ctr., Ft. Harrison State Park, 5785 Glenn Rd., Indianapolis, IN 46216-1066, (317)549-0206

Aquatic Sports; U.S. [23890]

Aquatics

Alliance of Marine Mammal Parks and Aquariums [5006]

Amer. Cichlid Assn. [22433]

Amer. Elasmobranch Soc. [7278]

Amer. Marinelife Dealers Assn. [5007]

Aquatic Animal Life Support Operators [7279]

Aquatic Res. Inst. [7171]

Aquatic Resources Educ. Assn. [7956]

Canadian Aquafitness Leaders Alliance [IO]

Fed. of Amer. Aquarium Societies [7173]

Intl. Assn. for Aquatic Animal Medicine [16792]

Intl. Soc. for Reef Stud. [4581]

Marine Aquarium Coun. [4175]

Marine Fish Conservation Network [4419]

Natl. Assn. of Marine Labs. [7274]

Natl. Assn. of State Aquaculture Coordinators [4180]

Pacific Coast Cichlid Assn. [22445]

Reef Check [5012]

Reef Relief [5013]

ReefGuardian Intl. [5014]

Seafood Choices Alliance [3503]

SeaWeb [5015]

U.S. Aquaculture Soc. [4183]

Worldwide Aquatic Bodywork Assn. [13658]

A.R. Stevens and the Ricochettes Fan Club - Address unknown since 1999.

ARA Intl. [IO], Niederanven, Luxembourg

ARA Res. Inst. [★IO]

ARA Res. Inst. [★9606]

Araappaloosa Found. Breeders Intl. - Address unknown since 2003.

Arab

American-Arab Anti-Discrimination Comm. [17082]

Amer. Arab Chamber of Commerce [24225]

Arab Amer. Assn. of Engineers and Architects [6467]

Arab Amer. Leadership Coun. [17003]

Arab Amer. Women's Coun. [18951]

Arab Bankers Assn. of North Am. [462]

Arab World and Islamic Resources and School Services [9393]

Arabian Jockey Club [23494]

Bilateral US-Arab Chamber of Commerce [24226]

Bilateral US-Arab Chamber of Commerce [IO]

Egyptian Student Assn. in North Am. [9179]

Free Muslims Coalition [18084]

Inst. for Palestine Stud. [9397]

Interns for Peace [17736]

Natl. Amer. Arab Nurses Assn. [15490]

Natl. Coun. on U.S.-Arab Relations [18066]

Natl. United States-Arab Chamber of Commerce [24290]

Palestine Liberation Org. [18069]

Syrian Stud. Assn. [8880]

Thought and Educ. Club [7957]

Arab Affairs Coun; Amer. [★18063]

Arab African Soc. of GE and Endoscopy [IO], Cairo, Egypt

Arab Air Carriers Org. [IO], Beirut, Lebanon

Arab Amer. Assn. of Engineers and Architects [6467], PO Box 1536, Chicago, IL 60690-1536, (312)409-8560

Arab-Amer. Democratic Fed. [★17003]

Arab-Amer. Historical Soc. - Address unknown since 2003.

Arab Amer. Inst. [18344], 1600 K St. NW, Ste. 601, Washington, DC 20006, (202)429-9210

Arab Amer. Inst. [IO], Washington, DC, United States

Arab Amer. Leadership Coun. [17003], 1600 K St. NW, Ste. 601, Washington, DC 20006, (202)429-9210

Arab-Amer. Media Soc. - Address unknown since 2003.

Arab Amer. Medical Assn. [★14707]

Arab Amer. Medical Assn; Natl. [14707]

Arab-American Press Guild [3087], 13313 Debell St., Arleta, CA 91331, (818)896-5860

Arab Amer. Republican Fed. [★17003]

Arab Amer. Republican Fed. - Defunct.

Arab-American Univ. Graduates; Assn. of [18953]

Arab Amer. Women's Coun. [18951], c/o Amer. Arab Chamber of Commerce, 12740 W Warren Ave., Ste. 101, Dearborn, MI 48126, (313)945-1700

Arab Anti-Discrimination Comm; American- [17082]

Arab Assn. for Commerce and Indus; American- [★24357]

Arab Assn. for Human Rights [★IO]

Arab Assn. for Human Rights [IO], Nazareth, Israel

Arab Atomic Energy Agency [IO], Tunis, Tunisia

Arab Bankers Assn. of North Am. [IO], New York, NY, United States

Arab Bankers Assn. of North Am. [462], c/o Brenda Murad, Exec. Dir., PO Box 2249, Grand Central Sta., New York, NY 10163, (212)599-3030

Arab Bur. of Educ. for the Gulf States [IO], Riyadh, Saudi Arabia

Arab Center for the Stud. of Arid Zones and Dry Lands [IO], Damascus, Syrian Arab Republic

Arab Chamber of Commerce; Natl. United States- [24290]

Arab Community Center for Economic and Social Services [18952], 2651 Saulino Ct., Dearborn, MI 48120, (313)842-7010

Arab Fed. for Food Indus. [IO], Damascus, Syrian Arab Republic

Arab Fed. for Food Indus. - Jordan [IO], Amman, Jordan

Arab Fertilizer Assn. [IO], Cairo, Egypt

Arab Gulf Programme for United Nations Development Organizations [IO], Riyadh, Saudi Arabia

A star before a book entry number signifies that the name is not listed separately, but is mentioned within the entry.

Arab Horse Soc. [IO], Marlborough, United Kingdom
Arab Hotel Assn. [IO], Jerusalem, Israel
Arab Inst. of Navigation [IO], Alexandria, Egypt
Arab Intl. Assn. for Tourism and Automobile Clubs [23009]
Arab Intl. Women's Forum [IO], London, United Kingdom
Arab-Israeli Relations
   Inst. for Palestine Stud. [9397]
   SHEMESH: Jewish-Arab Friendship and Coexistence in the Galilee, Israel [IO]
Arab-Jewish Women's Dialogue for Peace - Defunct.
Arab Knowledge and Mgt. Soc. [IO], Amman, Jordan
Arab Lawyers Union - Address unknown since 2002.
Arab Mahgreb Union [IO], Rabat, Morocco
Arab Network for Env. and Development [IO], Cairo, Egypt
Arab Org. for Agricultural Development [IO], Khartoum, Sudan
Arab Org. for Human Rights [IO], Cairo, Egypt
Arab Palestine Assn. [IO], Mississauga, ON, Canada
Arab Planning Inst. [IO], Safat, Kuwait
Arab Press Freedom Watch [IO], London, United Kingdom
Arab Satellite Communications Org. [IO], Riyadh, Saudi Arabia
Arab Soc. of Chemotherapy, Microbiology and Infectious Diseases [IO], Riyadh, Saudi Arabia
Arab Soc. for Intellectual Property [IO], Amman, Jordan
Arab Soc. for Plant Protection [IO], Beirut, Lebanon
Arab Thought Forum [IO], Jerusalem, Israel
Arab Towns Org. [IO], Kaifan, Kuwait
Arab Union for Cement and Building Materials [IO], Damascus, Syrian Arab Republic
Arab Union of Producers, Transporters and Distributors of Electricity [IO], Amman, Jordan
Arab Urban Development Inst. [IO], Riyadh, Saudi Arabia
Arab Women Connect - Arab States Regional Off. [IO], Amman, Jordan
Arab Women's Coun. - Address unknown since 1999.
Arab Women's Solidarity Assn. [13419], c/o Rabab Abdulhadi, Rep., New York Univ., Center for the Stud. of Gender and Sexuality, 285 Mercer St., 3rd Fl., Rm. 307, New York, NY 10003-6653, (212)992-9543
Arab Women's Solidarity Assn. [IO], New York, NY, United States
Arab World Inst. [IO], Paris, France
Arab World and Islamic Resources and School Services [IO], Abiquiu, NM, United States
Arab World and Islamic Resources and School Services [9393], PO Box 174, Abiquiu, NM 87510, (505)685-4533
Arabi Soc; Muhyiddin Ibn [20578]
Arabian F.O.A.L. Assn. [11365], PO Box 198, Parksville, NY 12768-0198, (505)531-2977
Arabian Horse Alliance; Egyptian [4877]
Arabian Horse Assn. [4858], 10805 E Bethany Dr., Aurora, CO 80014, (303)696-4500
Arabian Horse Assn; Intl. [4895]
Arabian Horse Breeders Alliance [4859], 28150 N Alma School Pkwy., Ste. 103-474, Scottsdale, AZ 85262, (480)415-8921
Arabian Horse Breeders Alliance [IO], Scottsdale, AZ, United States
Arabian Horse Club Registry of Am. [★4858]
Arabian Horse Historians Assn. [10092]
Arabian Horse Owners Found. [4860], PO Box 30924, Tucson, AZ 85751, (520)760-0682
Arabian Horse Registry of Am. and Intl. Arabian Horse Assn. [★4858]
Arabian Horse Trust [4861]
Arabian Jockey Club [23494], 10805 E Bethany Dr., Aurora, CO 80014, (303)696-4523
Arabian Professional and Amateur Horseman's Assn. [4862], 14900 N Pennsylvania Ave., No. 421, Oklahoma City, OK 73134
Arabian Registry; Amer. Pinto [4837]
Arabian Soc; North Amer. Shagya- [4936]
Arabian Verband; Amer. Shagya [4844]
Arabic
   American-Arab Anti-Discrimination Comm. [17082]

Amer. Assn. of Teachers of Arabic [7958]
Amer. Fed. of Ramallah, Palestine [9392]
Arab Community Center for Economic and Social Services [18952]
Arab Thought Forum [IO]
Arab World Inst. [IO]
Arab World and Islamic Resources and School Services [IO]
Arab World and Islamic Resources and School Services [9393]
Assn. of Arab-American Univ. Graduates [18953]
Birzeit Soc. [9394]
Canadian Arab Fed. [IO]
Canadian Arab Friendship Assn. [IO]
Canadian Palestinian Found. of Quebec [IO]
Chaldean Fed. of Am. [9395]
Coun. of Lebanese Amer. Organizations [9396]
Inst. of Islamic and Arabic Sciences in Am. [8670]
Inst. for Palestine Stud. [9397]
Inst. for Palestine Stud. [IO]
Inst. for Res. and Stud. of the Arab and Muslim World [IO]
Syrian Stud. Assn. [8880]
United North Lebanon Soc. [18954]
Arabic Order Nobles of the Mystic Shrine; Ancient Egyptian [19227]
Arabic Order of the Nobles of the Mystic Shrine for North Am; Imperial Coun. of the Ancient [19238]
Arabic Sciences in Am; Inst. of Islamic and [8670]
Arachnology
   British Arachnological Soc. [IO]
   British Tarantula Soc. [IO]
   Intl. Soc. of Arachnology [IO]
Aranzadi Zientzi Elkartea [★IO]
Ararat Found. [18963]
Arator Soc. - Defunct.
Araucanian Royalist Soc; North Amer. [10054]
Arba Sicula [19359], St. John's Univ., Languages & Literature Dept., Jamaica, NY 11439, (718)990-5203
Arba Sicula [IO], Jamaica, NY, United States
Arbeitsgemeinschaft 13 August [★IO]
Arbeitsgemeinschaft Alpenlander [★IO]
Arbeitsgemeinschaft Spina Bifida und Hydrocephalus [IO], Dortmund, Germany
Arbeitsgemeinschaft fur Sportpsychologie [★IO]
Arbeitsgemeinschaft fur Wissenschaft und Politik [★IO]
Arbeitsgemeinschaft der Wissenschaftlichen Medizinischen Fachgesellschaften [★IO]
Arbeitskreis kulinarischer Fachjournalisten [★IO]
Arbetarnas Bildningsforbund [★IO]
Arbitration Coun. of the Textile Indus; Gen. [★5453]
Arbitration Found. [★5448]
Arbitration and Mediation
   ADR Inst. of Canada [IO]
   Advocates Intl. [17998]
   Alberta Arbitration and Mediation Soc. [IO]
   Alliance for Peacebuilding [17248]
   Amer. Arbitration Assn. [5448]
   Amer. Bar Assn. Sect. of Dispute Resolution [5449]
   Asia Am. Initiative [11762]
   Assn. for Conflict Resolution [5450]
   Australian Centre for Intl. Commercial Arbitration [IO]
   Australian and New Zealand Ombudsman Assn. [IO]
   British Columbia Intl. Commercial Arbitration Centre [IO]
   British and Irish Ombudsman Assn. [IO]
   Cairo Regional Centre for Intl. Commercial Arbitration [IO]
   Center for Dispute Settlement [5451]
   Center for Medical Ethics and Mediation [5452]
   Chartered Inst. of Arbitrators [IO]
   Conflict Resolution Network Canada [IO]
   CPR Intl. Inst. for Conflict Prevention and Resolution [11488]
   Family Mediation Manitoba [IO]
   Gen. Arbitration Coun. of the Textile and Apparel Indus. [5453]
   Global Majority [17249]
   Inst. for Intl. Mediation and Conflict Resolution [5454]

Inst. for Intl. Mediation and Conflict Resolution [IO]
Inst. for Mediation and Conflict Resolution [5455]
Inter-American Commercial Arbitration Commn. [5456]
Intl. Centre for Settlement of Investment Disputes [5457]
Intl. Centre for Settlement of Investment Disputes [IO]
Intl. Ombudsman Inst. [IO]
Japan Commercial Arbitration Assn. [IO]
Lawyers Assoc. Worldwide [5505]
Mediators Without Borders [5458]
Natl. Acad. of Arbitrators [5459]
Natl. Assn. for Community Mediation [5460]
Natl. Center for Mediation Educ. [5461]
Permanent Court of Arbitration [IO]
Professional Mediation Assn. [5462]
Scottish Coun. for Intl. Arbitration [IO]
Singapore Intl. Arbitration Centre [IO]
Soc. of Maritime Arbitrators [5463]
Swiss Arbitration Assn. [IO]
Veterinary Assn. for Arbitration and Jurisprudence [IO]
Arbitration and Mediation Inst. of Canada [★IO]
Arbitration Prog; Gen. Ser. Consumer [★17330]
Arbitration Soc. of Am. [★5448]
Arbitration Soc; Swedish Peace and [IO]
Arbor Day; Comm. for Natl. [18670]
Arbor Day Found; Natl. [18673]
Arboreta; Amer. Assn. of Botanical Gardens and [★4973]
Arboretum; Friends of the Natl. [6634]
Arboretum; Friends of the U.S. Natl. [★6634]
Arboretums; Amer. Assn. of Botanical Gardens and [★4973]
Arboricultural Assn. [IO], Romsey, United Kingdom
Arborist Assn; Natl. [★5262]
Arborists; Amer. Soc. of Consulting [5254]
Arborists; Soc. of Municipal [6121]
Arborists and Urban Foresters Soc; Municipal [★6121]
Arbutus Vocational Soc. [★IO]
ARC-Institute for Tropical and Subtropical Crops [IO], Nelspruit, Republic of South Africa
Arc; Natl. Conf. of Executives of the [2506]
Arc of the U.S. [12561], 1010 Wayne Ave., Ste. 650, Silver Spring, MD 20910, (301)565-3842
ARC Videodance [★9867]
ARCA: Amer. Romeldale/CVM Assn. [5197], c/o Barbara Kloese, Registrar, 429 W US Hwy. 30, Valparaiso, IN 46385, (219)759-9665
Arcade Collectors Intl. - Address unknown since 2003.
Arcadian Fed. of Am; Pan [19090]
Arcane Order - Defunct.
Archaeological Conservancy [6439], 5301 Central Ave. NE, Ste. 902, Albuquerque, NM 87108-1517, (505)266-1540
Archaeological Inst. of Am. [6440], 656 Beacon St., 6th Fl., Boston, MA 02215-2006, (617)353-9361
Archaeological Inst. of Am. [IO], Boston, MA, United States
Archaeological Inst; Amer. Indian [★6447]
Archaeological Soc; Amer. Numismatic and [★22725]
Archaeological Soc; Near East [6451]
Archaeological Soc; Shepaug Valley [★6447]
Archaeologists; Natl. Assn. of State [6450]
Archaeologists; Register of Professional [6453]
Archaeologists; Soc. of Professional [★6453]
Archaeology
   Amer. Comm. to Advance the Study of Petroglyphs and Pictographs [6437]
   Amer. Rock Art Res. Assn. [6438]
   Amer. Schools of Oriental Res. [9615]
   Amerind Found. [6406]
   Archaeological Conservancy [6439]
   Archaeological Inst. of Am. [6440]
   Archaeological Inst. of Am. [IO]
   Archaeology Abroad [IO]
   Archeology Div. of the American Anthropological Association [6441]
   Associates for Biblical Res. [19507]
   Assn. for Environmental Archaeology [IO]

Reference to "IO" in place of a book number signifies that the association may be found in the 45th edition of International Organizations.

Assn. for Gravestone Stud. [10015]
Assn. for Roman Archaeology [IO]
Australian Archaeological Assn. [IO]
Australian Assn. of Consulting Archaeologist [IO]
Bristol Indus. Archaeological Soc. [IO]
Canadian Archaeological Assn. [IO]
Cataraqui Archaeological Res. Found. [IO]
CEDAM Intl. [4371]
Center for Amer. Archeology [6442]
Center for the Stud. of Beadwork [6443]
Center for the Study of Beadwork [IO]
Cornwall Archaeological Soc. [IO]
Coun. for British Archaeology [IO]
Coun. for Independent Archaeology [IO]
Coun. for Scottish Archaeology [IO]
Creek Indian Memorial Assn. [10740]
Dorset Natural History and Archaeological Soc.
  [IO]
Early Sites Res. Soc. [6444]
Egypt Exploration Soc. [IO]
Epigraphic Soc. [6445]
Etruscan Found. [6446]
European Architectural Endoscopy Assn. [IO]
European Assn. of Archaeologists [IO]
Fed. of Metal Detector and Archaeological Clubs
  [22578]
Fudan Museum Found. [10504]
German State Archaeologists' Assn. [IO]
Glasgow Archaeological Soc. [IO]
Greater London Indus. Archaeology Soc. [IO]
Hunter Archaeological Soc. [IO]
Indo-Pacific Prehistory Assn. [IO]
Inst. for Amer. Indian Stud. [6447]
Inst. of Andean Res. [9386]
Inst. of Field Archaeologists [IO]
Inst. of Nautical Archaeology [IO]
Inst. of Nautical Archaeology [6448]
Inst. for the Stud. of Amer. Cultures [10746]
Intl. Assn. for Classical Archaeology [IO]
Intl. Assn. of Egyptologists [IO]
Intl. Assn. for Obsidian Stud. [IO]
Intl. Assn. for Obsidian Stud. [6449]
Intl. Coun. for Archaeozoology [IO]
Intl. Time Capsule Soc. [10041]
Intl. Union for Prehistoric and Protohistoric Sci-
  ences [IO]
London and Middlesex Archaeological Soc. [IO]
Mexican Epigraphic Soc. [10130]
Museum of African Amer. History [9360]
Natl. Assn. of State Archaeologists [6450]
Nautical Archaeology Soc. [IO]
Near East Archaeological Society [IO]
Near East Archaeological Soc. [6451]
New England Antiquities Res. Assn. [6452]
New Zealand Archaeological Assn. [IO]
Register of Professional Archaeologists [6453]
Roman-Germanic Commn. of German
  Archaeological Inst. [IO]
Royal Archaeological Inst. [IO]
SEAMEO Regional Centre for Archaeology and
  Fine Arts [IO]
SEARCH Found. [6454]
Soc. for Amer. Archaeology [6455]
Soc. of Antiquaries of Scotland [IO]
Soc. of Bead Researchers [IO]
Soc. of Bead Researchers [6456]
Soc. for Church Archaeology [IO]
Soc. for Historical Archaeology [IO]
Soc. for Historical Archaeology [6457]
Soc. for Indus. Archeology [6458]
Soc. for Medieval Archaeology [IO]
Soc. of Museum Archaeologists [IO]
Soc. for Post-Medieval Archaeology [IO]
Soc. of Woman Geographers [7124]
South African Archaeological Soc. [IO]
Stonehenge Study Group [6459]
Swedish Archaeological Soc. [IO]
Trireme Trust U.S.A. [10483]
Ulster Archaeological Soc. [IO]
Valley of the Kings Found. [IO]
Women's Classical Caucus [9801]
World Archaeological Soc. [6460]
World Archaeological Soc. [IO]
World Atlatl Assn. [22611]
Archaeology Abroad [IO], London, United Kingdom

Archaeology; Assn. for Indus. [IO]
Archaeology (North Am.); Soc. for Coptic [10153]
Archaeus Proj. [13625], PO Box 7079, Kamuela, HI
  96743
Archbishop Oscar Arnulfo Romero Relief Fund
  [★18498]
Archbishop Oscar Arnulfo Romero Relief Fund [★IO]
Archconfraternity of Christian Mothers [19572], 220
  37th St., Pittsburgh, PA 15201, (412)683-2400
Archconfraternity of the Holy Ghost [19573], 6230
  Brush Run Rd., Bethel Park, PA 15102, (412)831-
  0302
Archconfraternity of Perpetual Adoration - Defunct.
Archconfraternity of Prayer for Israel - Defunct.
L'Arche Australia [IO], Hobart, Australia
Arche Noah [IO], Schiltern, Austria
Archeological Research; Scientific Exploratory
  [★6454]
Archeology; Amer. Inst. of Nautical [★6448]
Archeology Div. of the American Anthropological As-
  sociation [6441], c/o Amer. Anthropological Assn.,
  2200 Wilson Blvd., Ste. 600, Arlington, VA 22201,
  (703)528-1902
Archeology Sect. [★6441]
Archeology; Soc. for Commercial [9485]
Archer Assn. [20784], PO Box 6233, McLean, VA
  22106, (703)264-1372

Archery
  Amer. Crossbow Fed. [23542]
  Archery Australia [IO]
  Archery New Zealand [IO]
  Archery Shooters Assn. [23050]
  Archery Trade Assn. [3638]
  Assn. for Archery in Schools [IO]
  Bowhunting Preservation Alliance [22603]
  British Long-Bow Soc. [IO]
  Christian Bowhunters of Am. [23051]
  Croatian Archery Assn. [IO]
  Fed. of Canadian Archers [IO]
  Grand Natl. Archery Soc. [IO]
  Indonesia Archery Assn. [IO]
  Intl. Archery Fed. [IO]
  Intl. Bowhunting Org. [23544]
  Natl. Archery Assn. of the U.S. [23052]
  Natl. Bowhunter Educ. Found. [23053]
  The Natl. Crossbowmen of the U.S.A. [23054]
  Natl. Field Archery Assn. [23055]
  Natl. Field Archery Soc. [IO]
  North Amer. Bowhunting Coalition [22606]
  Northern Ireland Archery Soc. [IO]
  Physically Challenged Bowhunters of Am. [23549]
  Pope and Young Club [23056]
  Professional Bowhunter's Soc. [23057]
  United Sportsmans Assn. of North Am. [23058]
Archery Australia [IO], Panania, Australia
Archery Lane Operators Assn. [★3657]
Archery Manufacturers Assn. [★3638]
Archery Manufacturers Assn. [★IO]
Archery Manufacturers and Dealers Assn. [★IO]
Archery Manufacturers and Dealers Assn. [★3638]
Archery Manufacturers and Merchants Org. [★3638]
Archery Manufacturers and Merchants Org. [★IO]
Archery Manufacturers Org. [★IO]
Archery Manufacturers Org. [★3638]
Archery New Zealand [IO], Canterbury, New
  Zealand
Archery Range and Retailers Org. [3657], 156 N
  Main, Ste. D, Oregon, WI 53575, (608)835-9060
Archery Shooters Assn. [23050], PO Box 399, Ken-
  nesaw, GA 30156, (770)795-0232
Archery Trade Assn. [3638], Bus. and Trade Show
  Off., 860 E 4500 S, Ste. No. 310, Salt Lake City,
  UT 84107, (801)261-2380
Archery Trade Assn. [IO], Salt Lake City, UT, United
  States
Archie Campbell Fan Club - Defunct.
Architects; Amer. Inst. of [6463]
Architects; Amer. Soc. of Golf Course [6465]
Architects; Amer. Soc. of Landscape [6466]
Architects; Assn. of Univ. [6472]
Architects and Brokers Assn; Yacht [★2598]
Architects; Canadian Soc. of Landscape [IO]
Architects Coun. of Europe [IO], Brussels, Belgium
Architects/Designers; Intl. Fed. of Interior [IO]
Architects/Designers/Planners for Social Responsibil-
  ity [18142], PO Box 9126, Berkeley, CA 94709,
  (510)845-1000

Architect's Emergency Comm. - Address unknown
  since 1995.
Architects and Engineers; Amer. Indian Coun. of
  [6462]
Architects and Engineers; Asian Amer. [6470]
Architects, Engineers and Constr. Officers; Natl.
  Restaurant Assn. Multi-Unit [1050]
Architects, Engineers and Scientists in Am; Soc. of
  Turkish [★7048]
Architects and Engineers for Social Responsibility
  [IO], Oswaldtwistle, United Kingdom
Architects; Fed. of German Landscape [IO]
Architects Found; Amer. Inst. of [★6461]
Architects Found; Amer. Soc. of Landscape [★6476]
Architects and Marine Engineers; Soc. of Naval
  [7368]
Architects; Natl. Org. of Black [★6478]
Architects; Natl. Org. of Minority [6478]
Architects and Planners in Support of Nicaragua -
  Address unknown since 1994.
Architects Regional Coun. Asia [IO], Seoul, Republic
  of Korea
Architects Registration Bd. [IO], London, United
  Kingdom
Architects Registration Coun. of the UK [★IO]
Architects Renewal Comm. in Harlem - Defunct.
Architects for Social Responsibility [★18142]
Architects; Soc. of Amer. Registered [6480]
Architects; Soc. of Beaux-Arts [★7963]
Architects; Western Assn. of [★6463]
Architectural Acoustics Soc. - Defunct.
Architectural Aluminum Manufacturers Assn. [★588]
Architectural Anodizers Coun. [★849]
Architectural Assn. [IO], London, United Kingdom
Architectural Assn. of Ireland [IO], Dublin, Ireland
Architectural Barriers Comm. - Defunct.
Architectural Cladding Assn. [IO], Leicester, United
  Kingdom
Architectural Education
  Amer. Architectural Found. [6461]
  Amer. Soc. of Architectural Illustrators [289]
  Architectural Assn. of Ireland [IO]
  Architectural Engg. Inst. [6468]
  Carpenters' Company [10018]
  European Assn. of Architectural Educ. [IO]
  Found. for Design Integrity [1152]
  Soc. for Design Admin. [6481]
  Ulster Architectural Heritage Soc. [IO]
Architectural Educ; European Assn. of [IO]
Architectural Engineering Institute [IO], Reston, VA,
  United States
Architectural Engg. Inst. [6468], c/o Amer. Soc. of
  Civil Engineers, 1801 Alexander Bell Dr., Reston,
  VA 20191-4400, (703)295-6393
Architectural Engineers; Natl. Soc. of [★6468]
Architectural Fabric Structures Inst. - Defunct.
Architectural Glass and Metal Contractors Assn.
  [IO], Pickering, ON, Canada
Architectural Hardware Consultants; Amer. Soc. of
  [★1821]
Architectural Heritage Found. [10014], Old City Hall,
  45 School St., Boston, MA 02108-3204, (617)523-
  8678
Architectural Heritage Soc. of Scotland [IO], Edin-
  burgh, United Kingdom
Architectural Historians; Soc. of [10150]
Architectural History Found. - Defunct.
Architectural Inst. of the Republic of China [IO],
  Taipei, Taiwan
Architectural League of New York [17235], The
  Urban Center, 457 Madison Ave., New York, NY
  10022, (212)753-1722
Architectural Manufacturers Assn; Amer. [588]
Architectural Metal Mfrs; Natl. Assn. of [2719]
Architectural Photographers Assn. - Defunct.
Architectural Precast Assn. [917], 6710 Winkler Rd.,
  Ste. 8, Fort Myers, FL 33919, (239)454-6989
Architectural Products Contractors; Natl. Assn. of
  Miscellaneous, Ornamental and [1037]
Architectural Res. Centers Consortium [6469], c/o
  Prof. Stephen Weeks, Treas., Univ. of Minnesota,
  Dept. of Architecture, Rapson Hall, Rm. 145, 89
  Church St., Minneapolis, MN 55455, (612)624-
  2832
Architectural Res. Centers Consortium [IO],
  Philadelphia, PA, United States

A star before a book entry number signifies that the name is not listed separately, but is mentioned within the entry.

Architectural Soc. of China **[IO]**, Beijing, People's Republic of China

Architectural and Specialist Door Mfrs. Assn. **[IO]**, High Wycombe, United Kingdom

Architectural Spray Coaters Assn. - Address unknown since 2004.

Architectural Terra Cotta Inst. - Defunct.

Architectural Woodwork Inst. **[593]**, 46179 Westlake Dr., Ste. 120, Potomac Falls, VA 20165, (571)323-3636

Architectural Woodwork Mfrs. Assn. of Canada **[IO]**, High River, AB, Canada

Architecture

Alexander Thomson Soc. **[IO]**

Amer. Architectural Found. **[6461]**

Amer. Architectural Manufacturers Assn. **[588]**

Amer. Concrete Inst. **[6832]**

Amer. Highway Proj. **[10010]**

Amer. Indian Coun. of Architects and Engineers **[6462]**

Amer. Inst. of Architects **[6463]**

Amer. Inst. of Architecture Students **[288]**

Amer. Inst. of Building Design **[6464]**

Amer. Portuguese Engg. and Architecture Soc. **[7530]**

Amer. Soc. of Architectural Illustrators **[289]**

Amer. Soc. of Golf Course Architects **[6465]**

Amer. Soc. of Landscape Architects **[6466]**

Amer. Underground Constr. Assn. **[7715]**

Anonymous Arts Recovery Soc. **[10956]**

APEC - Automated Procedures for Engineering Consultants **[6999]**

Arab Amer. Assn. of Engineers and Architects **[6467]**

Architects Coun. of Europe **[IO]**

Architects/Designers/Planners for Social Responsibility **[18142]**

Architects Regional Coun. Asia **[IO]**

Architects Registration Bd. **[IO]**

Architectural Assn. **[IO]**

Architectural Engineering Institute **[IO]**

Architectural Engg. Inst. **[6468]**

Architectural Inst. of the Republic of China **[IO]**

Architectural League of New York **[17235]**

Architectural Res. Centers Consortium **[6469]**

Architectural Res. Centers Consortium **[IO]**

Architectural Soc. of China **[IO]**

Architectural Woodwork Inst. **[593]**

Architecture for Humanity **[11761]**

Arcosanti, A Proj. of the Cosanti Found. **[4497]**

Asian Amer. Architects and Engineers **[6470]**

Assn. for Bridge Constr. and Design **[6471]**

Assn. of Building Engineers **[IO]**

Assn. of Collegiate Schools of Architecture **[7959]**

Assn. of Consultant Architects **[IO]**

Assn. of Consulting Architects - Australia **[IO]**

Assn. of Energy Engineers **[6942]**

Assn. of Licensed Architects **[290]**

Assn. of Licensed Architects **[IO]**

Assn. of Univ. Architects **[6472]**

Assn. for Women in Architecture **[291]**

Athenaeum of Philadelphia **[10342]**

Australian Architecture Assn. **[IO]**

Buckminster Fuller Inst. **[11104]**

Building Futures Coun. **[606]**

Building Res. Coun. **[7960]**

Canadian Centre for Architecture **[IO]**

Carpenters' Company **[10018]**

Chartered Inst. of Architectural Technologists **[IO]**

Commonwealth Assn. of Architects **[IO]**

Community Associations Inst. **[17212]**

Constr. Indus. Round Table **[940]**

Constr. Specifications Inst. **[6836]**

Cool Roof Rating Coun. **[615]**

CoreNet Global **[3305]**

Coun. of Landscape Architectural Registration Boards **[6473]**

Coun. of Latin-American Students of Architecture **[292]**

Coun. on Tall Buildings and Urban Habitat **[6474]**

Council on Tall Buildings and Urban Habitat **[IO]**

Edinburgh Architectural Assn. **[IO]**

Energy Res. Gp. **[IO]**

Environmental Design Res. Assn. **[5464]**

European Coun. of Interior Architects **[IO]**

European Coun. for the Village and Small Town **[IO]**

Experimental Cities, Inc. **[17236]**

Fed. Chamber of Architects, Germany **[IO]**

Fed. of Danish Architects **[IO]**

Fed. of Swiss Architects **[IO]**

Found. for the Stud. of the Arts and Crafts Movement at Roycroft **[21530]**

Frank Lloyd Wright Assn. **[7961]**

Frank Lloyd Wright Preservation Trust **[10023]**

French Heritage Soc. **[10024]**

Friends of Cast Iron Architecture **[10025]**

Friends of Terra Cotta **[10029]**

Gen. Soc. of Mechanics and Tradesmen of the City of New York **[9229]**

Graham Found. **[293]**

Hardwood Coun. **[4056]**

Heritage Conservation Network **[10033]**

Historians of British Art **[9478]**

Historians of Eighteenth-Century Art and Architecture **[9479]**

Historians of German and Central European Art and Architecture **[9921]**

Hong Kong Inst. of Architects **[IO]**

Illuminating Engg. Soc. of North Am. **[7250]**

Indian Inst. of Architects **[IO]**

Inst. for Urban Design **[6475]**

Intelligent Building Gp. **[IO]**

Intl. Acad. of Architecture - Bulgaria **[IO]**

Intl. Architects Designers Planners for Social Responsibility **[IO]**

Intl. Assn. of Architectural Photographers **[2999]**

Intl. Assn. for Bridge Maintenance and Safety **[538]**

Intl. Coun. of the Museum of Modern Art **[9448]**

Intl. Design Conf. in Aspen **[9905]**

Intl. Fed. of High Rise Structures **[IO]**

Intl. Inst. of Site Planning **[IO]**

Intl. Inst. of Site Planning **[5465]**

Intl. Union of Architects **[IO]**

Landscape Architecture Found. **[6476]**

League of Historic Amer. Theatres **[11021]**

Malaysian Inst. of Architects **[IO]**

The Masonry Soc. **[6837]**

Metal Building Contractors and Erectors Assn. **[2528]**

Namibia Inst. of Architects **[IO]**

Natl. Architectural Accrediting Bd. **[7962]**

Natl. Assn. of Architectural Metal Mfrs. **[2719]**

Natl. Assn. of Church Design Builders **[831]**

Natl. Assn. of Miscellaneous, Ornamental and Architectural Products Contractors **[1037]**

Natl. Assn. of Norwegian Architects **[IO]**

Natl. Assn. of Swedish Architects **[IO]**

Natl. Building Museum **[6477]**

Natl. Coun. of Architectural Registration Boards **[5466]**

Natl. Coun. of Architectural Registration Boards **[IO]**

Natl. Dome Coun. **[2530]**

Natl. Inst. of Building Sciences **[6838]**

Natl. One Coat Stucco Assn. **[650]**

Natl. Org. of Minority Architects **[6478]**

Natl. Parking Assn. **[2900]**

Natl. Restaurant Assn. Multi-Unit Architects, Engineers and Constr. Officers **[1050]**

Natl. Soc. of Mural Painters **[9517]**

Natl. Tech. Assn. **[7752]**

New York New Visions **[17232]**

New Zealand Inst. of Architects **[IO]**

Phi Kappa Upsilon Fraternity **[24464]**

Preservation Action **[10058]**

Public Art Fund **[17239]**

Residential Space Planners Intl. **[2275]**

Rice Design Alliance **[6479]**

Roofing Indus. Comm. on Weather Issues **[666]**

Roofing Indus. Educational Inst. **[1064]**

Royal Architectural Inst. of Canada **[IO]**

Royal Australian Inst. of Architects **[IO]**

Royal Incorporation of Architects in Scotland **[IO]**

Royal Inst. of the Architects of Ireland **[IO]**

Royal Inst. of British Architects **[IO]**

Royal Inst. of Dutch Architects **[IO]**

Royal Oak Found. **[10060]**

Royal Soc. of Ulster Architects **[IO]**

Rural and Indus. Design and Building Assn. **[IO]**

Sculpture in the Env. **[17240]**

Singapore Inst. of Architects **[IO]**

Soc. of Amer. Registered Architects **[6480]**

Soc. of Architectural Historians **[10150]**

Soc. of Architectural Historians of Great Britain **[IO]**

Soc. of Czech Architects **[IO]**

Soc. for Design Admin. **[6481]**

Soc. for Marketing Professional Services **[2649]**

Soc. of Naval Architects and Marine Engineers **[7368]**

Soc. for the Stud. of Architecture in Canada **[IO]**

South African Inst. of Architects **[IO]**

Swiss Soc. of Engineers and Architects **[IO]**

Tau Sigma Delta **[24403]**

Theatre Historical Soc. of Am. **[11050]**

Tiles and Architectural Ceramics Soc. **[IO]**

Trinidad and Tobago Inst. of Architects **[IO]**

Twentieth Century Soc. **[IO]**

Ukrainian Engineers' Soc. of Am. **[7050]**

Union of Architects in Bulgaria **[IO]**

Union of Architects of Romania **[IO]**

Union of Architects of Russia **[IO]**

Van Alen Inst.: Projects in Public Architecture **[7963]**

Vernacular Architecture Forum **[6482]**

Victorian Soc. **[IO]**

Walter Burley Griffin Soc. of Am. **[9398]**

World Fed. of Great Towers **[IO]**

Architecture; Assn. for Cmpt. Aided Design in **[6721]**

Architecture of Cmpt. Systems; Special Interest Gp. for **[6747]**

Architecture, Educ. and Indus; School Facilities Coun. of **[★7892]**

Architecture; Friends of Cast Iron **[10025]**

Architecture for Humanity **[11761]**, 900 Bridgeway, Ste. 2, Sausalito, CA 94965-2100, (415)332-6273

Architecture for Humanity **[IO]**, Sausalito, CA, United States

Architecture School Librarians; Assn. of **[10328]**

Architecture and Surveying Inst. **[★IO]**

Archival Security Program - Defunct.

Archv; Aouon **[9418]**

Archives

Acad. of Certified Archivists **[294]**

Anthology Film Archives **[9928]**

Assn. of Canadian Archivists **[IO]**

Assn. of Catholic Diocesan Archivists **[9399]**

Assn. of Commonwealth Archivists and Records Managers **[IO]**

Assn. of German Archivists **[IO]**

Assn. for Recorded Sound Collections **[10337]**

Australian Soc. of Archivists **[IO]**

Black Archives of Mid-America **[9400]**

British Record Soc. **[IO]**

British Records Assn. **[IO]**

Bus. Archives Coun. **[IO]**

Canadian Coun. of Archives **[IO]**

Gay, Lesbian, Bisexual, Transgender Historical Soc. **[10078]**

Intl. Assn. of French Language Archives **[IO]**

Intl. Assn. of Sound and Audiovisual Archives **[IO]**

Intl. Coun. on Archives **[IO]**

Irish Soc. for Archives **[IO]**

John F. Kennedy Lib. Found. **[10365]**

Midwest Archives Conf. **[9401]**

Natl. Archives and Records Admin. Volunteer Assn. **[9402]**

Natl. Assn. of Govt. Archives and Records Administrators **[5820]**

Natl. Coalition for History **[10135]**

Pacific Regional Br. of the Intl. Coun. on Archives **[IO]**

Property Records Indus. Assn. **[3187]**

Soc. of Amer. Archivists **[9403]**

Soc. of Archivists - Ireland **[IO]**

Soc. of Archivists - United Kingdom **[IO]**

Swedish Archival Assn. **[IO]**

Archives Advisory Comm; Film and TV **[★9932]**

Archives of Amer. Art **[9419]**, PO Box 37012, Washington, DC 20013-7012, (202)633-7940

Archives; Amer. Jewish **[★10285]**

Archives Commn. of the Amer. Historical Assn; Public **[★9403]**

Reference to "IO" in place of a book number signifies that the association may be found in the 45th edition of International Organizations.

Archives and History of the United Methodist Church; Gen. Commn. on **[10467]**

Archives; Marcus Center of the Amer. Jewish **[10285]**

Archives and Museum of the Polish Catholic Union of Am. **[★10882]**

Archives; North Amer. Radio **[22926]**

Archives and Record Ser. Volunteer Assn; Natl. **[★9402]**

Archives and Records Administrators; Natl. Assn. of Govt. **[5820]**

Archives and Records Administrators; Natl. Assn. of State **[★5820]**

Archives and Res. Center; Assassination **[18787]**

Archives and Res. Libraries in Jewish Stud; Coun. of **[10351]**

Archives; Sigmund Freud **[16115]**

Archives; Southern Baptist Historical Lib. and **[19499]**

Archives for UFO Res. **[IO]**, Norrkoping, Sweden

Archivio Disarmo **[IO]**, Rome, Italy

Archivists; Assn. of Moving Image **[9932]**

Archivists and Librarians in the History of the Hea. Sciences **[10326]**, c/o Brooke Fox, Sec.-Treas., PO Box 250403, Charleston, SC 29425, (843)792-2288

Archonist Club - Defunct.

A.R.C.I Nuova Associazione **[IO]**, Rome, Italy

ARCNET Trade Assn. - Defunct.

Arcology

Arcosanti, A Proj. of the Cosanti Found. **[4497]**

Canadian Arctic Resources Comm. **[IO]**

Arcosanti **[★4497]**

Arcosanti, A Proj. of the Cosanti Found. **[4497]**, HC 74, Box 4136, Mayer, AZ 86333, (928)632-7135

Arcosanti Proj. **[★4497]**

Arctic

Amer. Alpine Club **[7074]**

Amer. Polar Soc. **[7515]**

Arctic Cat Club of Am. **[22944]**, c/o Paul Wustrack, Mgr./Webmaster, PO Box 528, Rosendale, WI 54974-0528

Arctic Club **[★7076]**

Arctic Club **[★IO]**

Arctic Inst. of North Am. **[IO]**, Calgary, AB, Canada

Arctic Missions **[★IO]**

Arctic Missions **[★20348]**

Arctic Monitoring and Assessment Programme **[IO]**, Oslo, Norway

Arctic Network - Address unknown since 2006.

Arctic Region Found. of Vocational Training **[IO]**, Overtornea, Sweden

Arctic Res. Program **[★7622]**

Arctic Slope Native Assn. - Address unknown since 1995.

Arctic Winter Games Intl. Comm. **[IO]**, Whitehorse, YT, Canada

Arcus Found. **[18266]**, 402 E Michigan Ave., Kalamazoo, MI 49007, (269)373-4373

Area Bus. Publications; Assn. of **[★3199]**

Arena Managers Assn. - Defunct.

Arena Theatres Assn; Musical **[★9594]**

ARES Case Clearinghouse **[★9049]**

ARF - Advt. Res. Found. **[87]**, 432 Park Ave. S, New York, NY 10016, (212)751-5656

ARF Tzeghagrons **[★18087]**

Argentina

Argentine-American Chamber of Commerce **[24227]**

San Martin Soc. of U.S.A., Washington DC **[11150]**

Argentina Chamber of Commerce **[IO]**, Buenos Aires, Argentina

Argentina Israel Chamber of Commerce **[IO]**, Buenos Aires, Argentina

Argentina Oils and Fats Assn. **[IO]**, Buenos Aires, Argentina

Argentine Acad. of Geophysicists and Geodesists **[IO]**, Buenos Aires, Argentina

Argentine Acad. of Letters **[IO]**, Buenos Aires, Argentina

Argentine Advt. Agencies' Assn. **[IO]**, Buenos Aires, Argentina

Argentine Agricultural Assn. **[IO]**, Buenos Aires, Argentina

Argentine-American Chamber of Commerce **[24227]**, 630 5th Ave., 25th Fl., Rockefeller Ctr., New York, NY 10111, (212)698-2238

Argentine Assn. of Biology and Nuclear Medicine **[IO]**, Buenos Aires, Argentina

Argentine Assn. of Doctors for the Env. **[IO]**, Buenos Aires, Argentina

Argentine Assn. of Ecology **[IO]**, Buenos Aires, Argentina

Argentine Assn. of Insurance Companies **[IO]**, Buenos Aires, Argentina

Argentine Assn. of Medical Informatics **[IO]**, Buenos Aires, Argentina

Argentine Assn. of Non-Destructive and Structural Evaluation **[IO]**, Buenos Aires, Argentina

Argentine Assn. for Photogrammetry and Related Sciences **[IO]**, Buenos Aires, Argentina

Argentine Assn. of Travel and Tourism Agencies **[IO]**, Buenos Aires, Argentina

Argentine Bank Marketing Assn. **[IO]**, Buenos Aires, Argentina

Argentine Bible Soc. **[IO]**, Buenos Aires, Argentina

Argentine Biochemical Assn. **[IO]**, Buenos Aires, Argentina

Argentine Cable TV Assn. **[IO]**, Buenos Aires, Argentina

Argentine Canadian Chamber of Commerce **[IO]**, Buenos Aires, Argentina

Argentine Center of Agricultural Engineers **[IO]**, Buenos Aires, Argentina

Argentine Centre of Engg. **[IO]**, Buenos Aires, Argentina

Argentine Chamber of Aerosols **[IO]**, Buenos Aires, Argentina

Argentine Chamber of the Aluminum, Metals and Related Indus. **[IO]**, Buenos Aires, Argentina

Argentine Chamber of Book Publishers **[IO]**, Buenos Aires, Argentina

Argentine Chamber of the Clothing Indus. **[IO]**, Buenos Aires, Argentina

Argentine Chamber of Constr. **[IO]**, Buenos Aires, Argentina

Argentine Chamber of Elecl. Material Distributors **[IO]**, Buenos Aires, Argentina

Argentine Chamber of Electronics Indus. **[IO]**, Buenos Aires, Argentina

Argentine Chamber of Exporters **[IO]**, Buenos Aires, Argentina

Argentine Chamber of Informatics and Communications **[IO]**, Buenos Aires, Argentina

Argentine Chamber of Limited Companies **[IO]**, Buenos Aires, Argentina

Argentine Chamber of Producers of Pharmaceutical Chemicals **[IO]**, Buenos Aires, Argentina

Argentine Chamber of Stationers, Bookshops and Related Businesses **[IO]**, Buenos Aires, Argentina

Argentine Chamber of Supermarkets **[IO]**, Buenos Aires, Argentina

Argentine Commn. for Human Rights - Address unknown since 1995.

Argentine Coun. of Shopping Centers **[IO]**, Buenos Aires, Argentina

Argentine Cricket Assn. **[IO]**, Buenos Aires, Argentina

Argentine Fiscal Associations **[IO]**, San Luis, Argentina

Argentine Franchising Assn. **[IO]**, Buenos Aires, Argentina

Argentine Game Developers Assn. **[IO]**, Buenos Aires, Argentina

Argentine Indus. Assn. **[IO]**, Buenos Aires, Argentina

Argentine Information Service Center - Defunct.

Argentine Magazine Publishers' Assn. **[IO]**, Buenos Aires, Argentina

Argentine Marketing Assn. **[IO]**, Buenos Aires, Argentina

Argentine Metallurgical Indus'. Assn. **[IO]**, Buenos Aires, Argentina

Argentine-North Amer. Assn. for the Advancement of Science, Technology and Culture - Defunct.

Argentine Oil Indus. Chamber **[IO]**, Buenos Aires, Argentina

Argentine Orthopedic and Traumatology Assn. **[IO]**, Buenos Aires, Argentina

Argentine Packaging Inst. **[IO]**, Buenos Aires, Argentina

Argentine Paleontological Assn. **[IO]**, Buenos Aires, Argentina

Argentine Republic Chamber of Importers **[IO]**, Buenos Aires, Argentina

Argentine Soc. of Bioengineering **[IO]**, Corrientes, Argentina

Argentine Soc. of Biology **[IO]**, Buenos Aires, Argentina

Argentine Soc. of Botany **[IO]**, Buenos Aires, Argentina

Argentine Soc. of Cancerology **[IO]**, Buenos Aires, Argentina

Argentine Soc. of Cardiology **[IO]**, Buenos Aires, Argentina

Argentine Soc. of Dermatology **[IO]**, Buenos Aires, Argentina

Argentine Soc. of Endocrinology and Metabolism **[IO]**, Buenos Aires, Argentina

Argentine Soc. of Gastroenterology **[IO]**, Buenos Aires, Argentina

Argentine Soc. of Geographical Stud. **[IO]**, Buenos Aires, Argentina

Argentine Soc. of Hematology **[IO]**, Buenos Aires, Argentina

Argentine Soc. of Hypertension **[IO]**, Buenos Aires, Argentina

Argentine Soc. of Infectious Diseases **[IO]**, Buenos Aires, Argentina

Argentine Soc. of Medical Genetics **[IO]**, Buenos Aires, Argentina

Argentine Soc. of Ophthalmology **[IO]**, Buenos Aires, Argentina

Argentine Soc. of Pediatrics **[IO]**, Buenos Aires, Argentina

Argentine Soc. of Psychosomatic Obstetrics and Gynaecology **[IO]**, Buenos Aires, Argentina

Argentine Soc. for Psychotrauma **[IO]**, Buenos Aires, Argentina

Argentine Sugar Center **[IO]**, Buenos Aires, Argentina

Argentine TV and Radio Assn. **[IO]**, Buenos Aires, Argentina

Argentinean League Against Epilepsy **[IO]**, Buenos Aires, Argentina

Argentinian Assn. of Dermatology **[IO]**, Buenos Aires, Argentina

Argentinian Assn. of Ethical Investigations **[IO]**, Buenos Aires, Argentina

Argentinian Soc. of EEG and Clinical Neurophysiology **[IO]**, Buenos Aires, Argentina

Arias Found. for Peace and Human Progress **[IO]**, San Jose, Costa Rica

Arica Inst. **[IO]**, Kent, CT, United States

Arica Inst. **[10169]**, PO Box 645, Kent, CT 06757-0645, (860)927-1006

Arica Inst. in Am. **[★10169]**

Arica Inst. in Am. **[★IO]**

Arid-Land Rsrc. Clearing House; Native Seeds/Southwestern Endangered **[★4429]**

Arid Lands Stud; Assn. for **[4498]**

Ariel Motorcycle Club North Am. **[22668]**, PO Box 77737, Stockton, CA 95267-1037, (714)894-5761

Ariel Owners' Motorcycle Club **[★22668]**

The Aril Soc. **[★22502]**

Aril Soc. Intl. **[22502]**, c/o Donald Eaves, Gen. Sec., 1102 County Rd. 192, Carbon, TX 76435

Arise - Address unknown since 2005.

Arise Intl. **[★20299]**

Arise Intl. **[★IO]**

ARISE Intl. Mission **[IO]**, College Park, MD, United States

ARISE Intl. Mission **[20299]**, PO Box 1014, College Park, MD 20741, (410)599-3436

Aristolochite Soc. **[★24571]**

Aristos Guild - Defunct.

Aristotelian Soc. **[IO]**, London, United Kingdom

Arizona Cactus **[★IO]**

Arizona Cactus **[★6631]**

Arizona Cactus and Native Flora Soc. **[★6633]**

Arizona Cactus and Succulent Res. **[6631]**

Arizona Cactus and Succulent Research **[IO]**, Bisbee, AZ, United States

Arizona Canine Acad. **[22219]**

Arizona Cotton Planting Seed Distributors **[★4317]**

Arizona Job Colls. - Defunct.

A star before a book entry number signifies that the name is not listed separately, but is mentioned within the entry.

Arizona Macintosh Users Gp. **[6782]**, 4331 E Baseline Rd., Ste. B-105, PMB 445, Gilbert, AZ 85234
ARJD **[★5895]**
Ark and the Dove; Soc. of the **[20758]**
Ark-La-Tex Genealogical Assn. **[21104]**, PO Box 4463, Shreveport, LA 71134-0463
Arkansas Inst. for Social Justice **[★11796]**
Arkansas Pottery Collectors; Natl. Soc. of **[22088]**
Arkivet for UFO-Forskning **[★IO]**
Arkleton Trust **[IO]**, Streatley, United Kingdom
Arktisen Laaketieteen Keskus **[★IO]**
Arktisk Institut **[★IO]**
The Arlin J. Brown Information Center - Defunct.
ARLIS/UK and Ireland: Art Libraries Soc. of the United Kingdom and Ireland **[IO]**, London, United Kingdom
Arm Trade Campaign; Disarmament and **[★18167]**
ARMA Intl. - Canadian Region **[IO]**, Calgary, AB, Canada
ARMA Intl. - The Assn. of Info. Mgt. Professionals **[IO]**, Lenexa, KS, United States
ARMA Intl. - The Assn. of Info. Mgt. Professionals **[2096]**, 13725 W 109th St., Ste. 101, Lenexa, KS 66215, (913)341-3808
Armadillo Breeders Assn. - Defunct.
Armadillo; Intl. Order of the **[22597]**
Armateurs du Saint-Laurent **[★IO]**
Armbrust Assn; U.S. **[★23058]**
Arme Schulschwestern von Unserer Lieben Frau **[★IO]**
Armed Females of Am. **[17587]**, 2702 E Univ. Dr., Ste. 103, PMB 213, Mesa, AZ 85213, (480)924-8202

Armed Forces

2nd Infantry Div. (2id), Korean War Veterans Alliance **[21167]**
29th Infantry Div. Assn. **[20679]**
33rd Infantry Div. Assn. **[20680]**
35th Div. Assn. **[20681]**
63rd Infantry Div. Assn. **[20690]**
95th Infantry Div. Assn. **[20691]**
107th Engineer Assn. **[5467]**
AdoptaPlatoon **[11489]**
AFBA, The 5Star Assn. **[18955]**
Air Force Aid Soc. **[18956]**
Air Force Public Affairs Alumni Assn. **[6200]**
All Ser. Postal Chess Club **[21941]**
Amer. Battleship Assn. **[21210]**
Amer. Cadet Alliance **[20718]**
Amer. Legion **[20666]**
Amer. Legion Auxiliary **[21189]**
Amer. Logistics Assn. **[6064]**
Amer. Registry of Pathology **[15858]**
Amer. War Mothers **[21190]**
Any Soldier **[11490]**
Armed Forces Communications and Electronics Assn. **[6067]**
Armed Forces Hostess Assn. **[6068]**
Armed Forces Inst. of Pathology **[15261]**
Armed Forces Stamp Exchange Club **[22793]**
Army and Air Force Mutual Aid Assn. **[18957]**
Army Distaff Foundation/Knollwood **[21192]**
Army Emergency Relief **[18958]**
Army Nurse Corps Assn. **[15262]**
Assn. of Amer. Military Uniform Collectors **[22628]**
Assn. for Counselors and Educators in Govt. **[11818]**
Assn. of Military Surgeons of the U.S. **[15263]**
Beirut Veterans of Am. **[21287]**
Books For Soldiers **[11491]**
Christian Military Fellowship **[19782]**
Coalition to Salute America's Heroes **[21294]**
Combat Helicopter Pilots Assn. **[20648]**
De Re Militari: The Soc. for Medieval Military History **[10474]**
Desert Storm Veterans Assn. **[21298]**
Distinguished Flying Cross Soc. **[20711]**
Empowerment Soc. of the U.S.A. **[13425]**
Freedom Is Not Free **[12596]**
Give2TheTroops **[12597]**
Hof Reunion Assn. **[20682]**
Homefront Hugs USA **[13352]**
Homes for Our Troops **[21302]**
Inter-University Seminar on Armed Forces and Soc. **[6077]**

Intl. Military Community Executives Assn. **[834]**
Iraq and Afghanistan Veterans of Am. **[21335]**
Iraq War Veterans Org. **[21304]**
Japanese Amer. Veterans Assn. **[21305]**
Jewish War Veterans of the U.S.A. - Natl. Ladies Auxiliary **[21196]**
Laptops for the Wounded **[11741]**
Marine Corps Cryptologic Assn. **[21174]**
Marine Corps Engineer Assn. **[6142]**
Marine Corps Recruiters Assn. **[5799]**
Military Benefit Assn. **[18959]**
Military Intelligence Corps Assn. **[5862]**
Military Officers Assn. of Am. **[21235]**
Military Order of the Purple Heart of the U.S.A. **[20715]**
Military Vehicle Preservation Assn. **[22630]**
Natl. Alliance of Families for the Return of America's Missing Servicemen **[21263]**
Natl. Assn. of County Veterans Ser. Officers **[21309]**
Natl. Assn. of Free Will Baptists **[19492]**
Natl. Defense Trans. Assn. **[6090]**
Natl. Museum of Amer. Jewish Military History **[21312]**
Navy-Marine Corps Relief Soc. **[18960]**
Navy Mutual Aid Assn. **[18961]**
Navy Seabee Veterans of Am. **[21217]**
Navy Wifeline Assn. **[21199]**
Oper. AC **[11492]**
Oper. Gratitude **[11493]**
Oper. Gratitude **[IO]**
Oper. Homelink **[11494]**
Oper. Sandbox **[11495]**
Oper. ShoeBox **[11496]**
Oper. Soldier Support **[11497]**
Oper.: Take a Soldier to the Movies **[11498]**
Oper. We Do Care **[11499]**
Orders and Medals Soc. of Am. **[22631]**
Professional Armed Forces Rodeo Assn. **[23693]**
Salute Our Services **[11500]**
SATS/EAF Assn. **[21179]**
Soc. of Air Force Physicians **[15264]**
Soc. of Medical Consultants to the Armed Forces **[15265]**
Soc. of Military Orthopaedic Surgeons **[15266]**
Soldiers' Angels **[19259]**
Soldiers Overseas Family Gateway **[12598]**
Soldiers for the Truth **[20683]**
A Soldier's Wish List **[11501]**
Sons and Daughters In Touch **[12599]**
Stars for Stripes **[20770]**
Support Our Soldiers Am. **[11502]**
Tee it up for the Troops **[13357]**
Tin Can Sailors - The Natl. Assn. of Destroyer Veterans **[21220]**
Tragedy Assistance Prog. for Survivors **[11503]**
United Spouses Assn. **[21202]**
U.S. Marine Corps Scout/Sniper Assn. **[21181]**
United We Serve **[21203]**
USAF Medical Ser. Corps Assn. **[13590]**
USMC Vietnam Tankers Assn. **[21337]**
USO World HQ **[18962]**
USO World HQ **[IO]**
USS Nitro (AE-2/AE-23) Assn. **[5468]**
Valley Forge Historical Soc. **[9375]**
Vietnam Era Seabees **[21339]**
Vietnam Security Police Assn. **[21340]**
Women Veterans of Am. **[21333]**
Armed Forces; Assn. of Jewish Chaplains of the **[19743]**
Armed Forces Benefit and Aid Assn. - Defunct.
Armed Forces Benefit Assn. **[★18955]**
Armed Forces Broadcasters Assn. - Address unknown since 2001.
Armed Forces Chem. Assn. **[★6089]**
Armed Forces Civilian Instructors Assn. - Defunct.
Armed Forces Communications and Electronics Assn. **[6067]**, c/o Tobey Jackson, Promotions and PR Mgr., 4400 Fair Lakes Ct., Fairfax, VA 22033-3899, (703)631-6100
Armed Forces Communications and Electronics Assn. **[IO]**, Fairfax, VA, United States
Armed Forces Communications and Electronics Assn. of Canada **[IO]**, Ottawa, ON, Canada
Armed Forces Enlisted Personnel Benefit Assn. **[★18959]**

Armed Forces Hostess Assn. **[6068]**, The Pentagon, Rm. ID110, 6604 Army Pentagon, Washington, DC 20310-6604, (703)697-3180
Armed Forces Inst. of Pathology **[15261]**, 6825 16th St. NW, Washington, DC 20306-6000, (202)782-2882
Armed Forces Judo Assn. **[★23555]**
Armed Forces Mail Call - Defunct.
Armed Forces Mgt. Assn. **[★6089]**
Armed Forces Marketing Coun. - Defunct.
Armed Forces Relief and Benefit Assn. **[★18955]**
Armed Forces Reunion Assn. - Defunct.
Armed Forces and Soc; Inter-University Seminar on **[6077]**
Armed Forces; Soc. of Medical Consultants to the **[15265]**
Armed Forces Sports **[6069]**, The Summit Center, 4700 King St., 4th Fl., Alexandria, VA 22302-4418, (703)681-7215
Armed Forces Sports Comm. **[★6069]**
Armed Forces Stamp Exchange Club **[22793]**, c/o Larry O. Sundholm, Exec. Sec., PO Box 8473, Spokane, WA 99203-0473, (509)747-0662
Armed Forces Writers League **[★5583]**
Armed Resistance Unit - Address unknown since 1997.

Armenia

Armenian Amer. Chamber of Commerce **[24263]**
Armenian Church Youth Org. of Am. **[19458]**
Armenian Missionary Assn. of Am. **[19459]**
Armenian Rugs Soc. **[9420]**
Assn. of Armenian Church Choirs of Am. **[10559]**
Armenia Skating Fed. **[IO]**, Yerevan, Armenia

Armenian

Ararat Found. **[18963]**
Armenian Amer. Chamber of Commerce **[24263]**
Armenian Assembly of Am. **[9404]**
Armenian Assembly of Am. **[IO]**
Armenian Behavioral Sci. Assn. **[6525]**
Armenian Church Youth Org. of Am. **[19458]**
Armenian Educational Found. **[8343]**
Armenian Film Found. **[9405]**
Armenian Film Found. **[IO]**
Armenian Gen. Benevolent Union **[IO]**
Armenian Gen. Benevolent Union **[18964]**
Armenian Missionary Assn. of Am. **[19459]**
Armenian Natl. Comm. of Am. **[18965]**
Armenian Natl. Comm. of Am. **[IO]**
Armenian Natl. Educ. Comm. **[IO]**
Armenian Natl. Educ. Comm. **[7964]**
Armenian Relief Soc. of Eastern USA **[18966]**
Armenian Relief Soc. of Eastern USA **[IO]**
Armenian Rugs Soc. **[9420]**
Armenian Students' Assn. of Am. **[18967]**
Armenian Women's Welfare Assn. **[18968]**
Assn. of Armenian Church Choirs of Am. **[10559]**
Assn. of Armenian Info. Professionals **[18969]**
Hairenik Assn. **[18970]**
Natl. Assn. for Armenian Stud. and Res. **[9406]**
Soc. for Armenian Stud. **[9407]**
Soc. for Armenian Stud. **[IO]**
Armenian Alumni Assn. - Address unknown since 2000.
Armenian Amer. Chamber of Commerce **[24263]**, 1141 N Brand Blvd., Ste. 309, Glendale, CA 91202, (818)247-0196
Armenian Amer. Soc. for Stud. on Stress and Genocide **[15190]**, c/o Dr. Anie Kalayjian, 185 E 85th St., Mezz No. 4, New York, NY 10028, (201)941-2266
Armenian Assembly of Am. **[9404]**, 1140 19th St. NW, Ste. 600, Washington, DC 20036, (202)393-3434
Armenian Assembly of Am. **[IO]**, Washington, DC, United States
Armenian Assembly of America, Student Affairs Div. - Defunct.
Armenian Assn. of Orthodontists **[IO]**, Yerevan, Armenia
Armenian Assn. of Women with Univ. Educ. **[IO]**, Yerevan, Armenia
Armenian Bar Assn. **[IO]**, Los Angeles, CA, United States
Armenian Bar Assn. **[5482]**, c/o Lisa Boyadjian, Admin. Asst., PO Box 29111, Los Angeles, CA 90029, (323)666-6288

Reference to "IO" in place of a book number signifies that the association may be found in the 45th edition of International Organizations.

Armenian Behavioral Sci. Assn. **[6525]**, c/o Prof. Harold Takooshian, PhD, Exec. Off., 113 W 60th St., Rm. 916, New York, NY 10023, (212)636-6393

Armenian Behavioral Sci. Assn. **[IO]**, New York, NY, United States

Armenian Cardiologists Assn. **[IO]**, Yerevan, Armenia

Armenian Church Youth Org. of Am. **[19458]**, Eastern Diocese of the Armenian Church of Am., 630 2nd Ave., New York, NY 10016, (212)686-0710

Armenian Coin Club **[★22730]**

Armenian Coin Club **[★IO]**

Armenian Dance Sport Fed. **[IO]**, Yerevan, Armenia

Armenian Draughts Fed. **[IO]**, Yerevan, Armenia

Armenian Educational Coun. - Address unknown since 2001.

Armenian Educational Found. **[8343]**, 600 W Broadway, Ste. 130, Glendale, CA 91204, (818)242-4154

Armenian Electron Microscopy Soc. **[IO]**, Yerevan, Armenia

Armenian Engineers and Scientists of Am. **[IO]**, Glendale, CA, United States

Armenian Engineers and Scientists of Am. **[7600]**, 417 W Arden Ave., Ste. 112C, Glendale, CA 91203-4046, (818)547-3372

Armenian Film Found. **[9405]**, 2219 Thousand Oaks Blvd., Ste. 292, Thousand Oaks, CA 91362, (805)495-0717

Armenian Film Found. **[IO]**, Thousand Oaks, CA, United States

Armenian Gen. Benevolent Union **[IO]**, New York, NY, United States

Armenian Gen. Benevolent Union **[18964]**, 55 E 59th St., New York, NY 10022-1112, (212)319-6383

Armenian Gen. Benevolent Union of Am. **[★18964]**

Armenian Gen. Benevolent Union of Am. **[★IO]**

Armenian Handball Fed. **[IO]**, Yerevan, Armenia

Armenian Info. Professionals; Assn. of **[18969]**

Armenian Junior Chamber **[IO]**, Yerevan, Armenia

Armenian Lib. Assn. **[IO]**, Yerevan, Armenia

Armenian Literary Soc. - Defunct.

Armenian Medical Assn. **[IO]**, Yerevan, Armenia

Armenian Missionary Assn. of Am. **[19459]**, 31 W Century Rd., Paramus, NJ 07652, (201)265-2607

Armenian Natl. Comm. of Am. **[18965]**, 1711 N St. NW, Washington, DC 20036, (202)775-1918

Armenian Natl. Comm. of Am. **[IO]**, Washington, DC, United States

Armenian Natl. Coun. of America - Address unknown since 1995.

Armenian Natl. Educ. Comm. **[7964]**, c/o The Armenian Prelacy, 138 E 39th St., New York, NY 10016, (212)689-7810

Armenian Natl. Educ. Comm. **[IO]**, New York, NY, United States

Armenian Natl. League Against Epilepsy **[IO]**, Yerevan, Armenia

Armenian Natl. Paralympic Comm. **[IO]**, Yerevan, Armenia

Armenian Numismatic Soc. **[IO]**, Pico Rivera, CA, United States

Armenian Numismatic Soc. **[22730]**, 8511 Beverly Park Pl., Pico Rivera, CA 90660-1920, (562)695-0380

Armenian Numismatics and Artifact Soc. **[★22730]**

Armenian Numismatics and Artifact Soc. **[★IO]**

Armenian Physical Soc. **[IO]**, Yerevan, Armenia

Armenian Progressive League of America - Address unknown since 1994.

Armenian Red Cross **[★18966]**

Armenian Red Cross **[★IO]**

Armenian Relief Soc. **[★IO]**

Armenian Relief Soc. **[IO]**, Yerevan, Armenia

Armenian Relief Soc. **[★18966]**

Armenian Relief Soc. of Eastern USA **[18966]**, 80 Bigelow Ave., Ste. 200, Watertown, MA 02472, (617)926-3801

Armenian Relief Soc. of Eastern USA **[IO]**, Watertown, MA, United States

Armenian Revolutionary Fed. **[IO]**, Watertown, MA, United States

Armenian Revolutionary Fed. **[18086]**, 80 Bigelow Ave., Watertown, MA 02472, (617)926-3685

Armenian Revolutionary Fed. of Am. **[★18086]**

Armenian Revolutionary Fed. of Am. **[★IO]**

Armenian Rheumatological Assn. **[IO]**, Yerevan, Armenia

Armenian Rugs Soc. **[9420]**, 939 N Amphlett Blvd., San Mateo, CA 94401, (650)343-8585

Armenian Scientific Assn. of America - Defunct.

Armenian Soc. of Cardiology **[★IO]**

Armenian Squash Fed. **[IO]**, Yerevan, Armenia

Armenian Students' Assn. of Am. **[18967]**, 333 Atlantic Ave., Warwick, RI 02888, (401)461-6114

Armenian Stud. and Res; Natl. Assn. for **[9406]**

Armenian Tech. Gp. **[4086]**, PO Box 5969, Fresno, CA 93755-5969, (559)224-1000

Armenian Tech. Gp. **[IO]**, Fresno, CA, United States

Armenian Tennis Fed. **[IO]**, Yerevan, Armenia

Armenian Women's Welfare Assn. **[18968]**, PO Box 191, Belmont, MA 02478, (617)484-2602

Armenian Youth Fed. of Am. **[★18087]**

Armenian Youth Fed. - Youth Org. of the ARF **[18087]**, 80 Bigelow Ave., Watertown, MA 02472, (617)923-1933

Armies of Tennessee, CSA and U.S.A. **[20722]**, PO Box 91, Rosedale, IN 47874, (765)548-2594

Arming Women Against Rape and Endangerment **[★13442]**

Armor and Arms Club **[21536]**, c/o Dean K. Boorman, Pres., Dean Boorman & Associates, 40 Edgemont Rd., Montclair, NJ 07042-2305, (973)744-8838

Armor Assn; U.S. **[6107]**

Armored Car Assn; Natl. **[3575]**

Armored Car Operators Assn; Independent **[3568]**

Armored Cavalry Assn; U.S. **[★6107]**

Armored Div. Assn; Fourth **[20701]**

Armored Infantry Battalion Assn; 526th **[21382]**

Armored Trans. Inst. **[3560]**, c/o James L. Dunbar, Chm., 50 Schilling Rd., Hunt Valley, MD 21031, (410)229-1929

Armorial Ancestry; Order of Americans of **[20750]**

Arms

Academics for the Second Amendment **[17286]**

Adopt-A-Minefield **[IO]**

Amer. Coll. of Heraldry **[21099]**

Amer. Heraldry Soc. **[21102]**

Antique Reloading Tool Collector's Assn. **[22424]**

Armor and Arms Club **[21536]**

Arms Control Association/Arms Control Today **[17422]**

Assn. of Maltese Arms Collectors and Shooters **[IO]**

Company of Military Historians **[22629]**

Coun. for a Livable World **[17425]**

Coun. for a Livable World Educ. Fund **[17426]**

Global Network Against Weapons and Nuclear Power in Space **[18152]**

Japanese Sword Soc. of the U.S. **[21537]**

Japanese Sword Soc. of the U.S. **[IO]**

Miniature Arms Collectors/Makers Society **[IO]**

Miniature Arms Collectors/Makers Soc. **[21538]**

Missile Defense Advocacy Alliance **[17382]**

Natl. Automatic Pistol Collectors Assn. **[21539]**

Peace Action **[18166]**

Sword Swallowers Assn. Intl. **[10776]**

Thompson Collectors Assn. **[22431]**

Weatherby Collectors Assn. **[22432]**

Winchester Arms Collectors Assn. **[21540]**

Women's Action for New Directions **[18175]**

World Armsport Fed. **[23060]**

ARMS of America - Address unknown since 1987.

Arms and Ammunitions Mfrs. Inst; Sporting **[1482]**

Arms and Armour Soc. **[IO]**, London, United Kingdom

Arms; Citizens Comm. for the Right to Keep and Bear **[17105]**

Arms Control Association/Arms Control Today **[17422]**, 1313 L St. NW, Ste. 130, Washington, DC 20005, (202)463-8270

Arms Control Computer Network - Defunct.

Arms Control Education Project - Defunct.

Arms Control and Foreign Policy Caucus - Address unknown since 2003.

Arms Control Inst; Chem. and Biological **[17023]**

ARMS/FIRMS Users Assn. - Defunct.

Arms of Friendship - Defunct.

Arms; Natl. Citizens Comm. for the Right to Keep and Bear **[★17105]**

Arms Race Education Project - Defunct.

Arms Soc; Miniature **[★21538]**

ArmSports; U.S. **[23991]**

Armstrong Clan Soc. **[10951]**, c/o Peter A. Armstrong, Membership Chm./Treas./Dir., 128 Essex Dr., Summerville, SC 29485

Armstrong Clan Soc. **[IO]**, Summerville, SC, United States

Armstrong Siddeley Owners Club **[IO]**, Sutton Coldfield, United Kingdom

Armwrestling

Amer. Armsport Assn. **[23059]**

Nova Scotia Arm Wrestling Assn. **[IO]**

World Armsport Fed. **[IO]**

World Armsport Fed. **[23060]**

Armwrestling Fed; World **[★23060]**

Army

2nd Infantry Div. (2id), Korean War Veterans Alliance **[21167]**

11th Airborne Div. Assn. **[20684]**

13th Airborne Div. Assn. **[20685]**

24th Infantry Div. Assn. **[20686]**

25th Infantry Div. Assn. **[20687]**

29th Infantry Div. Assn. **[20679]**

32nd Infantry Div. Veterans Assn. **[20688]**

43rd Infantry Div. Veterans Assn. **[20689]**

63rd Infantry Div. Assn. **[20690]**

70th Infantry Div. Assn. **[21366]**

94th Infantry Div. Assn. **[21369]**

95th Infantry Div. Assn. **[20691]**

96th Infantry Div. Assn. **[20692]**

99th Infantry Div. Assn. **[21370]**

100th Infantry Div. Assn. **[20693]**

101st Airborne Div. Assn. **[20694]**

104th Infantry Div. Natl. Timberwolf Assn. **[20695]**

107th Engineer Assn. **[5467]**

164th Infantry Assn. of the U.S. **[20696]**

187th Airborne Regimental Combat Team Assn. **[20697]**

325th Glider Infantry Assn. **[21374]**

504th Parachute Infantry Regiment Assn. **[21378]**

509th Parachute Infantry Assn. **[21380]**

517th Parachute Regimental Combat Team Assn. **[21381]**

526th Armored Infantry Battalion Assn. **[21382]**

704th Tank Destroyer Battalion Assn. **[21383]**

749th Tank Battalion Assn. Friends **[20698]**

829th Signal Ser. Assn. **[21384]**

AdoptaPlatoon **[11489]**

Amer. Airborne Assn. **[20699]**

Any Soldier **[11490]**

Armed Forces Sports **[6069]**

Army Aviation Assn. of Am. **[6070]**

Army Engineer Assn. **[5469]**

Army Historical Found. **[10471]**

Army Nurse Corps Assn. **[15262]**

Assn. of Military Surgeons of the U.S. **[15263]**

Assn. of the U.S. Army **[6071]**

Beirut Veterans of Am. **[21287]**

Books For Soldiers **[11491]**

Coalition to Salute America's Heroes **[21294]**

Desert Storm Veterans Assn. **[21298]**

DUSTOFF Assn. **[20700]**

Fourth Armored Div. Assn. **[20701]**

Freedom Is Not Free **[12596]**

George C. Marshall Found. **[11118]**

Give2TheTroops **[12597]**

Great War Assn. **[10475]**

HQ 310th Command Assn. **[20702]**

Hof Reunion Assn. **[20682]**

Homefront Hugs USA **[13352]**

Homes for Our Troops **[21302]**

Intl. Military Community Executives Assn. **[834]**

Iraq and Afghanistan Veterans of Am. **[21335]**

Iraq War Veterans Org. **[21304]**

Japanese Amer. Veterans Assn. **[21305]**

Judge Advocates Assn. **[6078]**

Merrill's Marauders Assn. **[21395]**

Military Intelligence Corps Assn. **[5862]**

Mobile Riverine Force Assn. **[21346]**

Natl. 4th Infantry (Ivy) Div. Assn. **[20703]**

Natl. Assn. of County Veterans Ser. Officers **[21309]**

A star before a book entry number signifies that the name is not listed separately, but is mentioned within the entry.

Natl. Assn. of the Sixth Infantry Div. [20704]
Natl. Counter Intelligence Corps Assn. [21164]
Natl. Guard Assn. of the U.S. [6091]
Oper. AC [11492]
Oper. Gratitude [11493]
Oper. Homelink [11494]
Oper. Sandbox [11495]
Oper. ShoeBox [11496]
Oper. Soldier Support [11497]
Oper.: Take a Soldier to the Movies [11498]
Oper. We Do Care [11499]
Patton Soc. [11141]
Polar Bear Assn. of World War II [21401]
Reserve Officers Assn. of the U.S. [6103]
Salute Our Services [11500]
Signal Corps Regimental Assn. [20705]
Soc. of the 3rd Infantry Div. [21186]
Soc. of Army Physician Assistants [15977]
Soc. of the First Infantry Div. [20706]
Soc. of Medical Consultants to the Armed Forces [15265]
Soc. of Military Otolaryngologists - Head and Neck Surgeons [15267]
Soldiers' Angels [19259]
Soldiers Overseas Family Gateway [12598]
Soldiers for the Truth [20683]
A Soldier's Wish List [11501]
Stars for Stripes [20770]
Support Our Soldiers Am. [11502]
Tee it up for the Troops [13357]
Tragedy Assistance Prog. for Survivors [11503]
U.S. Armor Assn. [6107]
U.S. Army Ranger Assn. [20707]
U.S. Army Warrant Officers Assn. [6108]
U.S. Marine Corps Scout/Sniper Assn. [21181]
United We Serve [21203]
Women Veterans of Am. [21333]
Women's Army Corps Veterans' Assn. [20708]
Army and Air Force Mutual Aid Assn. [18957], 102 Sheridan Ave., Bldg. 468, Fort Myer, VA 22211-1110, (703)522-3060
Army; Assn. of the U.S. [6071]
Army Aviation Assn. of Am. [6070], 755 Main St., Ste. 4D, Monroe, CT 06468-2830, (203)268-2450
Army Cadet League of Canada [IO], Ottawa, ON, Canada
Army; Church [19947]
Army Corps Veterans' Assn; Women's [20708]
Army Distaff Foundation/Knollwood [21192], 6200 Oregon Ave. NW, Washington, DC 20015, (202)541-0149
Army Emergency Relief [18958], 200 Stovall St., Alexandria, VA 22332-0001, (703)428-0000
Army Engineer Assn. [5469], PO Box 30260, Alexandria, VA 22310-8260, (703)428-7084
Army Families Fed. [IO], Pewsey, United Kingdom
Army Finance Assn. - Defunct.
Army Historical Found. [10471], 2425 Wilson Blvd., Arlington, VA 22201, (703)522-7901
Army Hostess Assn. [★6068]
Army Medical Museum [★15261]
Army Mutual Aid Assn. [★18957]
Army, Navy, and Air Force Veterans in Canada [IO], Ottawa, ON, Canada
Army and Navy Legion of Valor of the U.S. [★20714]
Army and Navy Union, U.S.A. [21286], c/o William Kramer, Natl. Adjutant Gen., 2178 Harmon Ave., Niles, OH 44446, (330)673-9373
Army Nurse Corps Assn. [15262], PO Box 39235, San Antonio, TX 78218-1235, (210)650-3534
Army Nurse Corps Assn; Retired [★15262]
Army Ordnance Assn. [★6089]
Army of the Philippines [★21331]
Army Physician Assistants; Soc. of [15977]
Army Records Soc. [IO], London, United Kingdom
Army Relief Soc. [★18958]
Army Soc; Church [★19947]
Army Special Forces Decade Assn; U.S. [★21270]
Army Special Forces Decade Club; U.S. [★21270]
Army of Tennessee, CSA [★20722]
Army Theatre Arts Assn. - Defunct.
Army Transport Assn. [★6090]
Army Veterans Assn. of Am; Polish [21259]
Army Warrant Officers Assn; U.S. [6108]

Army Widows' Assn. [IO], Upavon, United Kingdom
Arnold Air Soc. [24546], AFROTC Det. 770 Clemson Univ., 300 Tillman Hall, Box 341352, Clemson, SC 29634, (864)656-3254
Arnold Chiari Malformation Assn; World [16556]
Arnold and Mabel Beckman Center for History of Chemistry [★10101]
Arnolt-Bristol Registry - Address unknown since 2001.
Aromatherapists; Intl. Fed. of Professional [IO]
Aromatherapy; Natl. Assn. for Holistic [14830]
Aromatherapy Trade Coun. [IO], Ipswich, United Kingdom
Aromatic Red Cedar Closet Lining Mfrs. Assn. - Address unknown since 2002.
Aron Eisenberg Fan Club - Address unknown since 2004.
Arpad Acad. of Hungarian Scientists, Writers and Artists Abroad - Address unknown since 2002.
Arpad Fed. - Address unknown since 2002.
Arrangers; Amer. Soc. of Music [★10551]
Arrangers and Composers; Amer. Soc. of Music [10551]
ARRB Gp. [IO], Vermont South, Australia
ARRB Transport Res. [★IO]
Arrhythmia Death Syndromes Found; Sudden [14484]
Arrhythmias Res. and Educ. Found; Cardiac [13897]
ARRL Found. [21496], 225 Main St., Newington, CT 06111, (860)594-0397
ARROW - Defunct.
Arrow; Order of the [13005]
Ars Antiqua Soc. - Defunct.
Ars Baltica [IO], Vilnius, Lithuania

Arson Investigation
Intl. Assn. of Arson Investigators [5716]
Intl. Fire Photographers Assn. [3001]

Art
18th St. Arts Complex [9408]
Academie des Beaux-Arts [IO]
Affiliated Woodcarvers [9533]
African Amer. Visual Arts Assn. [9409]
Alliance for Amer. Quilts [9823]
Alliance for Cultural Democracy [9536]
Alliance of Professional Tattooists [3714]
Allied Artists of Am. [9487]
Alpha Omega Assn. [9537]
Amer. Abstract Artists [9488]
Amer. Acad. of Equine Art [9410]
Amer. Art Deco Dealers Assn. [295]
Amer. Art Pottery Assn. [9411]
Amer. Art Therapy Assn. [16199]
Amer. Artists Professional League [9489]
Amer. Arts Alliance [9539]
Amer. Bladesmith Soc. [9826]
Amer. Bonsai Soc. [22483]
Amer. Carnival Glass Assn. [22549]
Amer. Color Print Soc. [9412]
Amer. Coun. for Southern Asian Art [9413]
Amer. Cut Glass Assn. [22550]
Amer. Fired Arts Alliance [9542]
Amer. Friends of the Natl. Gallery of Australia [10492]
Amer. Gourd Soc. [22489]
Amer. Guild of Judaic Art [9414]
Amer. Historical Print Collectors Soc. [21523]
Amer. Impressionist Soc. [9490]
Amer. Inst. for Conservation of Historic and Artistic Works [10011]
Amer. Needlepoint Guild [22148]
Amer. Photographic Historical Soc. [10843]
Amer. Physician Art Assn. [9415]
Amer. Print Alliance [9544]
Amer. Quilter's Soc. [22149]
Amer. Sewing Guild [22150]
Amer. Soc. of Artists [9491]
Amer. Soc. of Greek and Latin Epigraphy [11207]
Amer. Soc. of Photographers [10845]
Amer. Tapestry Alliance [9416]
American Tapestry Alliance [IO]
Amer. Watercolor Soc. [9417]
Animators Unite [9388]
Antique and Art Glass Salt Shaker Collectors Soc. [21968]
Antique Tribal Art Dealers Assn. [296]

Aouon Archv. [9418]
Architectural League of New York [17235]
Archives of Amer. Art [9419]
ARLIS/UK and Ireland: Art Libraries Soc. of the United Kingdom and Ireland [IO]
Armenian Rugs Soc. [9420]
Art Alliance for Contemporary Glass [9421]
Art Alliance for Contemporary Glass [IO]
Art and Antique Dealers League of Am. [297]
Art Child [IO]
Art Dealers Assn. of Am. [298]
Art Dealers Assn. of Canada [IO]
Art Directors Club [IO]
Art Directors Club [9422]
Art Dreco Inst. [9423]
Art Information Center [9424]
Art Inst. of Light [9425]
Art and Sci. Collaborations [9607]
Art Services Intl. [9426]
Art Services Intl. [IO]
Art Students League of New York [9496]
Art Through Touch [IO]
Art for the World [IO]
Arthur Rackham Soc. [9427]
Artists' Assn. of Finland [IO]
Artists for a Better World Intl. [9549]
Artists Helping Artists [9498]
Artists for Israel Intl. [9428]
Artists for Israel Intl. [IO]
Artists Space [9499]
Artists in Stained Glass Canada [IO]
Arts and Bus. Coun. [9550]
Arts and Crafts Soc. [9429]
Arts Intl. [9551]
Arts in Therapy Network [13709]
The Arts We Need [13710]
Asian Amer. Arts Alliance [9552]
Asian Amer. Arts Centre [9553]
Associacao Portuguesa Antiquarios [IO]
Assn. of Art and Antique Dealers [IO]
Assn. of Art Editors [3207]
Assn. of Art Galleries in Switzerland [IO]
Assn. for Art History [9430]
Assn. of Art Museum Curators [10493]
Assn. of Art Museum Directors [10494]
Assn. des Commercants d'Art de la Suisse [IO]
Assn. of Fine Art Dealers in the Netherlands [IO]
Association of Historians of Nineteenth-Century Art [IO]
Assn. of Historians of Nineteenth-Century Art [9431]
Assn. of Intl. Photography Art Dealers [10846]
Assn. of Israel's Decorative Arts [9556]
Assn. of Medical Illustrators [13707]
Association of Medical Illustrators [IO]
Assn. of Norwegian Visual Artists [IO]
Assn. for Textual Scholarship in Art History [IO]
Assn. for Textual Scholarship in Art History [9432]
Assn. for Theatre in Higher Educ. [9262]
Assn. for Visual Arts [IO]
Associazione Antiquari d'Italia [IO]
Audubon Artists [9433]
Australian Antique and Art Dealers Assn. [IO]
Australian Rock Art Res. Assn. [IO]
Bavarian Acad. of Fine Arts [IO]
Blue Earth Alliance [10847]
Bohemia Ragtime Soc. [10568]
Bonsai Clubs Intl. [22504]
Brazilian Dimensional Embroidery Intl. Guild [22987]
British Antique Dealers' Assn. [IO]
British Art Medal Soc. [IO]
British Assn. for Modern Mosaic [IO]
British Origami Soc. [IO]
Bundesverband Deutscher Galerien E.V. [IO]
Canadian Doll Artists Assn. [IO]
Caricature Carvers of Am. [9829]
CAS Collectors [21926]
Catholic Fine Arts Soc. [9562]
Center for the Stud. of Political Graphics [9434]
Chambre Syndicale de l'Estampe, du Dessin et du Tableau [IO]
Chess Collectors Intl. [21944]
Children's Art Found. [9781]
Chinese-American Arts Coun. [9608]

Christian Comic Arts Soc. [9435]
Colonial Coverlet Guild of Am. [21998]
Colored Pencil Soc. of Am. [9436]
Colored Pencil Society of America [IO]
Commercial Photographers Intl. [2995]
Conservation Center for Art and Historic Artifacts [9437]
Contemporary Art Soc. [IO]
Coun. for Bus. and the Arts in Canada [IO]
Cow Observers Worldwide [22002]
CREATE [IO]
Crochet Assn. Intl. [22154]
Cross Cultural Collaborative [8177]
Culture and Animals Found. [11384]
Czech Collector's Assn. [22008]
Daguerreian Soc. [10848]
Dance Heritage Coalition [9877]
Dance/U.S.A. [9879]
Dansk Kunst og Antikvitetshandler Union [IO]
Dedham Pottery Collectors Soc. [22009]
Deutscher Kunsthandelsverband E.V. [IO]
Doll Artisan Guild [22394]
Doll Costumer's Guild [22395]
Doris Duke Charitable Found. [13115]
The Drawing Center [9438]
Embroiderers' Guild of Am. [22155]
Empire State Tattoo Club of Am. [10993]
Enamelist Soc. [22156]
Ethnic Cultural Preservation Coun. [9847]
Experiments in Art and Tech. [9439]
Eye Level Gallery Soc. [IO]
Fan Tek [10943]
Fed. of Modern Painters and Sculptors [9502]
Federazione Italiana Mercanti d'Arte [IO]
Fenton Art Glass Collectors of Am. [22552]
Fine Art Trade Guild [IO]
Fine Arts Philatelists [22819]
Florence Ceramics Collectors Soc. [22025]
Folk Art Soc. of Am. [9956]
Found. for Hosp. Art [13708]
Franklin Furnace Archv. [9440]
Friends of Fiber Art Intl. [9441]
Friends of French Art [10026]
Fudan Museum Found. [10504]
Gen Art [9442]
Glass Art Soc. [22555]
Global Alliance for Intelligent Arts [9443]
Global Alliance for Intelligent Arts [IO]
Graphic Artists Guild [9505]
Guild of Amer. Papercutters [22157]
Handweavers Guild of Am. [22158]
Heisey Collectors of America/National Heisey Glass Museum [22558]
Historians of British Art [9478]
Homowo African Arts and Cultures [9350]
Independent Curators Intl. [9444]
Independent Curators Intl. [IO]
Indo-American Arts Coun. [9570]
Inst. of Amer. Indian Arts [10745]
Inst. of Art Stud. [IO]
Inst. for Expressive Anal. [16217]
Inter-Tribal Indian Ceremonial Assn. [10747]
Interlochen Center for the Arts [9571]
Intermuseum Conservation Assn. [10505]
Intl. Acad. of Aquatic Art [23884]
Intl. Acad. of Ceramics [IO]
Intl. Artists Network [9506]
Intl. Assn. of Art Critics - Canada Sect. [IO]
Intl. Assn. of Art Critics - France [IO]
Intl. Assn. of Art Critics - Germany [IO]
Intl. Assn. of Duncan Certified Ceramic Teachers [21928]
Intl. Assn. of Pastel Societies [9445]
International Association of Pastel Societies [IO]
International Association for Professional Art Advisors [IO]
Intl. Assn. for Professional Art Advisors [24002]
Intl. Assn. of Sand Castle Builders [22971]
Intl. Assn. of Silver Art Collectors [22044]
Intl. Assn. for the Stud. of Ancient Mosaics [IO]
Intl. Bossons Collectors Soc. [22047]
Intl. Carnival Glass Assn. [22559]
Intl. Center of Medieval Art [10461]
Intl. Chain Saw Wood Sculptors Assn. [9446]
Intl. Comic Arts Assn. [9447]

Intl. Comic Arts Assn. [IO]
Intl. Confed. of Art Dealers [IO]
Intl. Confed. of Art Dealers - Austria [IO]
Intl. Coun. of the Museum of Modern Art [IO]
Intl. Coun. of the Museum of Modern Art [9448]
Intl. Design Conf. in Aspen [9905]
Intl. Doll Makers Assn. [22397]
Intl. Expressive Arts Therapy Assn. [13712]
Intl. Fed. of Rock Art Organizations [IO]
Intl. Fine Print Dealers Assn. [309]
Intl. Found. for Art Res. [9449]
Intl. Found. for Art Res. [IO]
Intl. Guild of Glass Artists [IO]
Intl. Guild of Glass Artists [299]
Intl. Guild of Miniature Artisans [22159]
Intl. Guild of Realism [9574]
Intl. Hajji Baba Soc. [9450]
Intl. Hajji Baba Soc. [IO]
Intl. Ivory Soc. [9832]
Intl. Kodak Historical Soc. [10850]
Intl. Machine Quilters Assn. [22160]
Intl. Network for Contemporary Iraqi Artists [IO]
Intl. Old Lacers, Inc. [22161]
Intl. Order of E.A.R.S. [10979]
Intl. Photographic Historical Org. [10851]
Intl. Quilt Assn. [22162]
Intl. Rose O'Neill Club Found. [22399]
Intl. Soc. of Fine Art Photographers [10852]
Intl. Soc. for the Stud. of Pilgrimage Art [9451]
Intl. Soc. for the Stud. of Pilgrimage Art [IO]
Intl. Tap Assn. [9888]
Inuit Art Found. [IO]
Irish Antique Dealers Assn. [IO]
Irish Arts Center - An Claidheamh Soluis [10243]
Italian Folk Art Fed. of Am. [10259]
James Renwick Alliance [9452]
Japan Art Academy [IO]
Japan Art Assn. [IO]
Japan Art History Forum [9480]
Japan Intl. League of Artists [IO]
Jargon Soc. [9958]
Junior Art Club [IO]
Kappa Pi Intl. Honorary Art Fraternity [24404]
Kinetic Art Org. [9453]
The Knitting Guild Assn. [22164]
Landscape Artists Intl. [9509]
Lesbians in the Visual Arts [9454]
Lesbians in the Visual Arts [IO]
Leslie-Lohman Gay Art Found. [9455]
Macedonian Arts Coun. [10437]
Majolica Intl. Soc. [21931]
Master Drawings Assn. [9456]
Master Painters Australia - Western Australian Assn. [IO]
McCoy Pottery Collectors' Soc. [21932]
Midmarch Associates [9510]
Mosaic Assn. of Australia [IO]
Napoleonic Age Philatelists [22849]
Natl. Antique and Art Dealers Assn. of Am. [300]
Natl. Art Museum of Sport [9457]
Natl. Artists Equity Assn. [9511]
Natl. Arts Found. [IO]
Natl. Assn. of Artists and Crafters [301]
Natl. Assn. of Artists' Organizations [9512]
Natl. Assn. of Comics Art Educators [8115]
Natl. Assn. of Independent Artists [9513]
Natl. Assn. of Miniature Enthusiasts [22077]
Natl. Assn. for the Visual Arts [IO]
Natl. Assn. of Women Artists [9514]
Natl. Cambridge Collectors [22561]
Natl. Cartoonists Soc. [9515]
Natl. Center of Afro-American Artists [9361]
Natl. Center for Film and Video Preservation [9942]
Natl. Coalition of Creative Arts Therapies Associations [16224]
Natl. Coun. for Taekwondo Masters Certification [23599]
Natl. Depression Glass Assn. [22562]
Natl. Duncan Glass Soc. [22563]
Natl. Guild of Decoupeurs [22168]
Natl. Ice Carving Assn. [9458]
Natl. Imperial Glass Collectors Soc. [22565]
Natl. Inst. of Amer. Doll Artists [24403]
Natl. Native Amer. (Indian) Cooperative [10750]

Natl. Oil and Acrylic Painters' Soc. [9459]
Natl. Park Acad. of the Arts [9460]
Natl. Polymer Clay Guild [22579]
Natl. Postal Arts Assn. [22139]
Natl. Quilting Assn. [22170]
Natl. Sculpture Soc. [10959]
Natl. Soc. of Mural Painters [9517]
Natl. Soc. of Painters in Casein and Acrylic [9518]
Natl. Watercolor Soc. [9461]
Natl. Wood Carvers Assn. [22171]
Natural Figure Art Assn. [9462]
New English Art Club [IO]
New Horizons Arts Initiative [9589]
New Zealand Antique Dealers Assn. [IO]
New Zealand Maori Arts and Crafts Inst. [IO]
Nikon Historical Soc. [10854]
Norges Kunst - og Antikvitetshandleres Forening [IO]
North Am. Native Amer. (Indian) Info. and Trade Center [10752]
North Amer. Quilling Guild [21541]
North Amer. Torquay Soc. [22094]
Northwest Regional Spinners' Assn. [22172]
Oil Painters of Am. [9520]
Omega Theatre and the Omega Arts Network [9590]
Ontario Arts Council/Ontario Arts Coun. Found. [IO]
Oriental Ceramic Soc. [IO]
Origami USA [22771]
Pacific Arts Assn. [9463]
Pacific Arts Assn. [IO]
Pastel Soc. of Am. [IO]
Pastel Soc. of Am. [9464]
Pen and Brush [9521]
Performing Arts Found. [9592]
Philip Boileau Collectors' Soc. [21542]
Phoenix Bird Collectors of Am. [21935]
The Photographic Historical Soc. [10855]
Photographic Soc. of Am. [22893]
Pictorial Photographers of Am. [10856]
Polish Arts and Culture Found. [19307]
Pomegranate Guild of Judaic Needlework [9837]
Portrait Soc. of Am. [9465]
Potters' Soc. of Australia [IO]
Prince Edward Island Coun. of the Arts [IO]
The Print Center [9522]
Print Coun. of Am. [9466]
Private Art Dealers Assn. [302]
Professional Knifemakers Assn. [9839]
Professional Picture Framers Assn. [9467]
Professional Tattoo Artists Guild [3716]
P.S.1 Contemporary Art Center [9595]
Public Art Fund [17239]
The Questers [21532]
Quilters Hall of Fame [22173]
Quimper Club Intl. [21546]
Recycled Art Assn. [9468]
The Rock Poster Soc. [9469]
Rogers Group [10960]
Rose Bowl Collectors [22112]
Royal Acad. of Dramatic Art [IO]
Royal Chamber of the Belgian Antique Dealers [IO]
Royal Soc. of Painter-Printmakers [IO]
Royal Watercolour Soc. [IO]
Roycrofters-at-Large Assn. [9840]
Salmagundi Club [9597]
Saving the Arts [9598]
Saving and Preserving Arts and Cultural Environments [9470]
Scandinavian Soc. for Prehistoric Art [IO]
Sculptors Guild [10961]
Sculpture in the Env. [17240]
Silk Painters Intl. [9524]
Silvermine Guild Arts Center [9471]
Smocking Arts Guild of Am. [22174]
Soc. of Animal Artists [9526]
Soc. for Applied Psychological Res. in the Performing Arts [16170]
Soc. for Asian Art [9472]
Soc. for Calligraphy [11213]
Soc. of Decorative Painters [22175]
Soc. for Folk Arts Preservation [9963]
Soc. of Illustrators [9527]

A star before a book entry number signifies that the name is not listed separately, but is mentioned within the entry.

Soc. of London Art Dealers **[IO]**
Soc. for the Promotion of Japanese Animation **[9473]**
Soc. of Spanish and Spanish-American Stud. **[10974]**
Soc. for the Stud. of German Art **[IO]**
Soc. of Tempera Painters **[9528]**
South African Antique Dealers Assn. **[IO]**
Space Coast Writers' Guild **[11196]**
Statue of Liberty Club **[22118]**
Stencil Artisans League, Inc. **[9474]**
Stencil Artisans League, Inc. **[IO]**
Student Photographic Soc. **[10857]**
Sumi-e Soc. of Am. **[9475]**
Sveriges Konst Och Antikhandlarforening **[IO]**
Swiss Assn. of Dealers in Antiques and Arts **[IO]**
Sword Swallowers Assn. Intl. **[10776]**
Taos Natl. Soc. of Watercolorists **[9476]**
Temple of Man **[20582]**
Thomas Nast Soc. **[9477]**
UNIMA-U.S.A., Amer. Center of the Union Internationale de la Marionnette **[22916]**
United Chainsaw Carvers Guild **[9842]**
United Fed. of Doll Clubs **[22407]**
U.S. Soc. for Educ. Through Art **[7980]**
Volunteer Committees of Art Museums of Canada and the U.S. **[10516]**
VSA arts **[11993]**
Wallace-Reader's Digest Funds **[12055]**
Ward Museum of Wildfowl Art, Salisbury Univ. **[9529]**
Water Colour Soc. of Ireland **[IO]**
Watermark Assn. of Artisans **[303]**
Westbeth Corp. **[9530]**
Western Assn. for Art Conservation **[304]**
White Ironstone China Assn. **[21940]**
Women in the Arts **[11093]**
Women's Caucus for Art **[9531]**
Women's Interart Center **[11096]**
World Acad. of Art and Sci. **[9612]**
World Org. of China Painters **[22177]**
World Sand Sculptors Assn. **[22972]**
YLEM: Artists Using Sci. and Tech. **[9532]**
Art Against Apartheid - Address unknown since 1989.
Art Alliance for Contemporary Glass **[9421]**, PO Box 7022, Evanston, IL 60201, (847)869-2018
Art Alliance for Contemporary Glass **[IO]**, Evanston, IL, United States
Art of Amer. Coun. of the Blind; Friends-in- **[9504]**
Art; Amer. Inst. of Commemorative **[2771]**
Art and Antique Dealers League of Am. **[297]**, 1040 Madison Ave., New York, NY 10021, (212)879-7558
Art Assn. of Am; Coll. **[★7969]**
Art Center; Women's Inter **[11096]**
Art Child **[IO]**, St.-Mande, France
Art Club; Auto. Objects d' **[21588]**
Art Club of the City of New York; Women's **[★9514]**
Art Collectors Club of America - Address unknown since 1995.
Art Conservators; Western Assn. of **[★304]**
Art and Craft Materials Inst. **[★1799]**
Art and Creative Materials Inst. **[1799]**, PO Box 479, Hanson, MA 02341-0479, (781)293-4100
Art, Culture and Educ; Intl. Sex Worker Found. for **[13092]**
Art, Culture and Educ; Sex Worker Found. for **[★13092]**
Art Dealers Assn. of Am. **[298]**, 575 Madison Ave., New York, NY 10022, (212)940-8590
Art Dealers Assn. of Canada **[IO]**, Toronto, ON, Canada
Art Dealers; Natl. Assn. of Fine **[★298]**
Art Deco Societies of America - Address unknown since 1990.
Art and Design Alumni Assn; Center for Creative Stud. - Coll. of **[★18888]**
Art Directors Club **[9422]**, 106 W 29th St., New York, NY 10001, (212)643-1440
Art Directors Club **[IO]**, New York, NY, United States
Art Directors Guild **[9929]**, 11969 Ventura Blvd., 2nd Fl., Studio City, CA 91604, (818)762-9995
Art Directors; Soc. of Motion Picture **[★9929]**
Art Dreco Inst. **[9423]**, PMB 131, 2570 Ocean Ave., San Francisco, CA 94132, (415)333-8372

Art Fed. of Am; Italian Folk **[10259]**
Art Found; Children's **[9781]**
Art; Friends of French **[10026]**
Art Fund; Public **[17239]**
Art Galleries
  Amer. Friends of the Natl. Gallery of Australia **[10492]**
  Amer. Guild of Judaic Art **[9414]**
  Amer. Impressionist Soc. **[9490]**
  Art Information Center **[9424]**
  Art Services Intl. **[9426]**
  Artists Space **[9499]**
  Assn. of Art Museum Curators **[10493]**
  Assn. of Coll. and Univ. Museums and Galleries **[10496]**
  Assn. of Intl. Photography Art Dealers **[10846]**
  Friends of Fiber Art Intl. **[9441]**
  Independent Curators Intl. **[9444]**
  Intl. Arts and Artists **[9572]**
  Intl. Assn. of Art Critics - U.S. Sect. **[9573]**
  Intl. Fine Print Dealers Assn. **[309]**
  Intl. Guild of Realism **[9574]**
  Oil Painters of Am. **[9520]**
  Omega Theatre and the Omega Arts Network **[9590]**
  Portrait Soc. of Am. **[9465]**
  P.S.1 Contemporary Art Center **[9595]**
  Soc. of Tempera Painters **[9528]**
  Sumi-e Soc. of Am. **[9475]**
  Taos Natl. Soc. of Watercolorists **[9476]**
Art Glass Assn. **[1726]**, PO Box 2537, Zanesville, OH 43702-2537, (740)450-6547
Art Glass Assn. **[IO]**, Zanesville, OH, United States
Art Glass Collectors of Am; Fenton **[22552]**
Art Glass Salt Shaker Collectors Soc; Antique and **[21968]**
Art Glass Suppliers Assn. **[★1726]**
Art Glass Suppliers Assn. **[★IO]**
Art Glass Suppliers Assn. Intl. **[★IO]**
Art Glass Suppliers Assn. Intl. **[★1726]**
Art Greenhaw Official Intl. Fan Club **[24843]**, c/o Marilyn McKay, Pres., 105 Broad St., Mesquite, TX 75149, (972)285-5441
Art Hazards Information Center - Defunct.
Art History
  Amer. Abstract Artists **[9488]**
  Amer. Friends of the Shakespeare Birthplace Trust **[11157]**
  Amer. Impressionist Soc. **[9490]**
  Amer. Soc. of Greek and Latin Epigraphy **[11207]**
  Art Dreco Inst. **[9423]**
  Assn. of Art Historians **[IO]**
  Assn. for Art History **[9430]**
  Assn. of Art Museum Curators **[10493]**
  Assn. of Historians of Nineteenth-Century Art **[9431]**
  The Drawing Center **[9438]**
  Eighteen Nineties Soc. **[IO]**
  Franklin Furnace Archv. **[9440]**
  Historians of British Art **[9478]**
  Historians of Eighteenth-Century Art and Architecture **[9479]**
  Historians of German and Central European Art and Architecture **[9921]**
  Intl. Found. for Art Res. **[9449]**
  Japan Art History Forum **[9480]**
  Native Amer. Art Stud. Assn. **[7965]**
  Pre-Raphaelite Soc. **[IO]**
  Print Coun. of Am. **[9466]**
  Soc. for Seventeenth-Century Music **[10705]**
  World Archaeological Soc. **[6460]**
Art Information Center **[9424]**
Art Information Center; Artists' Gallery and **[★9424]**
Art Inst. of Light **[9425]**
Art; Intl. Acad. of Aquatic **[23884]**
Art Libraries Soc. of North Am. **[IO]**, Ottawa, ON, Canada
Art Libraries Soc. of the United Kingdom and Ireland; ARLIS/UK and Ireland: **[IO]**
Art Material Mfrs. Assn. - Defunct.
Art Materials Trade Assn; Natl. **[1802]**
Art Museum Assn. of Am. **[★9541]**
Art Museum Directors; Assn. of **[10494]**
Art Museums Assn. of Australia **[★IO]**
Art Museums; Assn. of Women's Committees of **[★10516]**

Art Museums of Canada and the U.S; Volunteer Committees of **[10516]**
Art Music Composers; Christian Fellowship of **[9808]**
Art in Negro Colleges; Comm. for the Development of **[★7969]**
Art Patrons Assn. of America - Address unknown since 1995.
Art; PSI Inst. for Contemporary **[★9595]**
Art in the Public Interest **[9547]**, PO Box 68, Saxapahaw, NC 27340, (336)376-8404
Art Res. Assn; Amer. Rock **[6438]**
Art Resources in Collaboration **[9867]**, 123 W 18th St., 7th Fl., New York, NY 10011-4127, (212)206-6492
Art, Salisbury Univ; Ward Museum of Wildfowl **[9529]**
Art et de la Sci; Academie Mondiale de l' **[★9612]**
Art and Sci. Collaborations **[9607]**, 130 E End Ave. - 1A, New York, NY 10028, (941)955-5103
Art and Sci. Collaborations **[IO]**, New York, NY, United States
Art and Sci. Found; Photographic **[8975]**
Art Services Intl. **[9426]**, 1319 Powhatan St., Alexandria, VA 22314, (703)548-4554
Art Services Intl. **[IO]**, Alexandria, VA, United States
Art Soc. of Am; Folk **[9956]**
Art Soc; Glass **[22555]**
Art Space; Center for Cuban Studies/Cuban **[9845]**
Art Students League of New York **[9496]**, 215 W 57th St., New York, NY 10019, (212)247-4510
Art Teachers' Assn. **[IO]**, Halifax, NS, Canada
Art and Technology - Defunct.
Art Therapy
  Amer. Art Therapy Assn. **[16199]**
  Amer. Soc. of Psychopathology of Expression **[16191]**
  Arts in Therapy Network **[13709]**
  Arts in Therapy Network **[IO]**
  The Arts We Need **[13710]**
  British Columbia Art Therapy Assn. **[IO]**
  Inst. for Expressive Anal. **[16217]**
  Intl. Assn. for Voice Movement Therapy **[13711]**
  Intl. Assn. for Voice Movement Therapy **[IO]**
  Intl. Expressive Arts Therapy Assn. **[IO]**
  Intl. Expressive Arts Therapy Assn. **[13712]**
  Irish Assn. of Creative Arts Therapists **[IO]**
  Natl. Coalition of Creative Arts Therapies Associations **[16224]**
Art Therapy Assn; Amer. **[16199]**
Art Through Touch **[IO]**, London, United Kingdom
Art; U.S. Soc. for Educ. Through **[★7980]**
Art and Urban Resources; Inst. for **[★9595]**
Art Watch Intl. **[9548]**, c/o James Beck, Pres., Columbia Univ., 931 Schermerhorn, New York, NY 10027, (212)854-4569
Art Watch Intl. **[IO]**, New York, NY, United States
Art; Women's Caucus for **[9531]**
Art for the World **[IO]**, Milan, Italy
Art for World Friendship - Defunct.
ARTBA-PAC **[★6313]**
ARTDO Intl. **[IO]**, San Juan, Philippines
Arterial Hypertension Soc. of Mexico **[IO]**, Mexico City, Mexico
Arteriosclerosis; Amer. Soc. for the Stud. of **[★13902]**
Arteriosclerosis, Thrombosis and Vascular Biology of the Amer. Heart Assn; Coun. on **[13902]**
Artfoundation **[IO]**, London, United Kingdom
Arthacharya Found. **[IO]**, Mount Lavinia, Sri Lanka
Arthritis Care **[IO]**, London, United Kingdom
Arthritis Care - Central England **[IO]**, Nottingham, United Kingdom
Arthritis Care - North England **[IO]**, Wakefield, United Kingdom
Arthritis Care - Scotland **[IO]**, Glasgow, United Kingdom
Arthritis Care - South England **[IO]**, London, United Kingdom
Arthritis Care - Southeast England **[IO]**, London, United Kingdom
Arthritis Care - Wales **[IO]**, Newcastle Emlyn, United Kingdom
Arthritis Found. **[16369]**, PO Box 7669, Atlanta, GA 30357-0669, (404)872-7100
Arthritis Found. of Ireland **[★IO]**

Reference to "IO" in place of a book number signifies that the association may be found in the 45th edition of International Organizations.

Arthritis Hea. Professions Assn. [IO], Toronto, ON, Canada

Arthritis Hea. Professions Assn. [★16370]

Arthritis Ireland [IO], Dublin, Ireland

Arthritis and Musculoskeletal and Skin Diseases Info. CH; Natl. Inst. of [16372]

Arthritis New Zealand [IO], Hastings, New Zealand

Arthritis New Zealand - Auckland [IO], North Shore City, New Zealand

Arthritis New Zealand - Bay of Plenty [IO], Rotorua, New Zealand

Arthritis New Zealand - Gisborne [IO], Gisborne, New Zealand

Arthritis New Zealand - Hawkes Bay [IO], Hastings, New Zealand

Arthritis New Zealand - Manawatu [IO], Palmerston North, New Zealand

Arthritis New Zealand - Manukau [IO], Manukau City, New Zealand

Arthritis New Zealand - Northland [IO], Whangarei, New Zealand

Arthritis New Zealand - Taranaki [IO], New Plymouth, New Zealand

Arthritis New Zealand - Tauranga/Western Bay of Plenty [IO], Tauranga, New Zealand

Arthritis New Zealand - Waikato [IO], Hamilton, New Zealand

Arthritis New Zealand - Wairarapa [IO], Masterton, New Zealand

Arthritis New Zealand - Waitakere [IO], Auckland, New Zealand

Arthritis New Zealand - Wanganui [IO], Wanganui, New Zealand

Arthritis New Zealand - Wellington [IO], Wellington, New Zealand

Arthritis Org; Amer. Juvenile [16368]

Arthritis Res. Campaign [IO], Chesterfield, United Kingdom

Arthritis and Rheumatism Coun. for Res. [★IO]

Arthritis and Rheumatism Found. [★16369]

Arthritis and Rheumatism Natural Therapy Res. Assn. [IO], London, United Kingdom

The Arthritis Soc. [IO], Toronto, ON, Canada

The Arthritis Trust of Am. [★16375]

Arthrogryposis Assn. - Defunct.

Arthrogryposis Multiplex Congenita; Avenues, Natl. Support Gp. for [15309]

Arthroscopy 2000; European Soc. of Sports Traumatology, Knee Surgery and [IO]

Arthroscopy Assn. of North Am. [15762], 6300 N River Rd., Ste. 104, Rosemont, IL 60018, (847)292-2262

Arthur Machen Soc. - Defunct.

Arthur Miller Soc. [11159], c/o Stephen Marino, Sec.-Treas./Ed., 100-14 160th Ave., Howard Beach, NY 11414

Arthur Rackham Soc. [9427], 10 Cameron Pl., Grosse Pointe, MI 48230

The Arthur Ransome Soc. [IO], Cumbria, United Kingdom

The Arthur Ransome Soc. [★IO]

The Arthur Ransome Soc. LTD [★IO]

Arthur Rubinstein Intl. Music Soc. [IO], Tel Aviv, Israel

Arthur Szyk Soc. [9497], 1200 Edgehill Dr., Burlingame, CA 94010, (650)343-9588

Arthur Vining Davis Foundations [12048], c/o Dr. Jonathan T. Howe, Exec. Dir., 225 Water St., Ste. 1510, Jacksonville, FL 32202-5185, (904)359-0670

Article 19 - Global Campaign for Free Expression [IO], London, United Kingdom

Article Number Assn. [★IO]

Article Numbering Assn. of Bosnia and Herzegovina [IO], Sarajevo, Bosnia-Hercegovina

Article Numbering Assn. of the Czech Republic [★IO]

Article Numbering Assn. of the Dominican Republic [★IO]

Article Numbering Assn. of Iceland [★IO]

Article Numbering Assn. of Ireland [★IO]

Article Numbering Assn. of Lithuania [★IO]

Article Numbering Assn. of Macedonia [★IO]

Article Numbering Assn. of Mauritius [IO], Port Louis, Mauritius

Article Numbering Assn. of Tunisia [★IO]

Article Numbering Assn. of Ukraine [★IO]

Article Numbering Assn. of Uruguay [★IO]

Articulated Cranes Coun; Mfrs. of Telescoping and [2041]

Artifact Soc; Armenian Numismatics and [★22730]

Artifacts

Aircraft Engine Historical Soc. [9364]

Amer. Printing History Assn. [9989]

Authentic Artifact Collectors Assn. [21543]

Baidarka Historical Soc. [9954]

Barbados Museum and Historical Soc. [IO]

Black Archives of Mid-America [9400]

Chinese Historical Soc. of Am. [9789]

Church Monuments Soc. [IO]

Crazy Horse Memorial Found. [10739]

Creek Indian Memorial Assn. [10740]

Early Amer. Indus. Assn. [9481]

Eikon Gesellschaft der Freunde der Ikonenkunst e.v. [IO]

Fan Circle Intl. [IO]

Finnish Egyptological Soc. [IO]

Furniture History Soc. [IO]

Historical Soc. of Early Amer. Decoration [9482]

Holy Shroud Guild [19635]

ICOMOS Canada [IO]

Intl. Coun. on Monuments and Sites - France [IO]

Intl. Found. for Art Res. [9449]

Intl. Inst. for Conservation of Historic and Artistic Works [IO]

Intl. Photographic Historical Org. [10851]

Mai Wah Soc. [9622]

Midwest Old Settlers and Threshers Assn. [9483]

Monumental Brass Soc. [IO]

Natl. Threshers Assn. [9484]

Soc. of Antiquaries of London [IO]

Soc. for Commercial Archeology [9485]

Titanic Historical Soc. [10447]

Tool and Trades History Soc. [IO]

World Atlatl Assn. [22611]

Artificial Breeders; Natl. Assn. of [★5002]

Artificial Flower Mfrs. Bd. of Trade - Defunct.

Artificial Intelligence

Amer. Assn. for Artificial Intelligence [6483]

Assn. for Automatic Language Processing [IO]

Assn. for Lab. Automation [6515]

Canadian Info. Processing Soc. [IO]

Catalan Assn. for Artificial Intelligence [IO]

Cognitive Sci. Soc. [6484]

European Coordinating Committee for Artificial Intelligence [IO]

European Soc. for the Stud. of Cognitive Systems [IO]

Intl. Artificial Intelligence in Educ. Soc. [IO]

Intl. Assn. of Knowledge Engineers [IO]

Intl. Assn. of Knowledge Engineers [6485]

Intl. Soc. for Adaptive Behavior [6533]

Intl. Soc. of Applied Intelligence [6486]

Intl. Soc. of Applied Intelligence [IO]

Logical Language Gp. [10304]

Special Interest Gp. on Artificial Intelligence [6487]

Taiwanese Assn. for Artificial Intelligence [IO]

World Transhumanist Assn. [7163]

Artificial Life; Intl. Soc. of [6584]

Artificial Organs

European Soc. for Artificial Organs - East European Off. [IO]

Natl. Examining Bd. of Ocularists [15694]

Tissue Banks Intl. [13713]

Tissue Banks Intl. [IO]

Artificial and Synthetic Fibers Manufacturers' Assn. [IO], Sao Paulo, Brazil

Artillery Assn; 77th [21342]

Artillery Assn; U.S. Field [★6071]

Artillery Company of Massachusetts; Ancient and Honorable [21191]

Artillery Company; Natl. Soc. Women Descendants of the Ancient and Honorable [20749]

Artillery Company; Order of Descendants of the Ancient and Honorable [20751]

Artillery, State of New York, Constituting the Military Soc. of the War of 1812; Veteran Corps of [21204]

Artillery, State of New York; Veterans Corps of [★21204]

Artisan Guild; Doll [22394]

Artisans; Aid to [12415]

Artisans Guild; Amer. Photographic [★2990]

Artisans; Intl. Guild of Miniature [22159]

Artisans Order of Mutual Protection [19120], 8100 Roosevelt Blvd., Philadelphia, PA 19152, (800)551-1873

Artist-Blacksmith's Assn. of North Am. [523], c/o LeeAnn Mitchell, Central Off. Admin., PO Box 816, Farmington, GA 30638-0816, (706)310-1030

Artist-Blacksmith's Assn. of North Am. [IO], Farmington, GA, United States

Artistes Sin Fronteras [★IO]

Artistic License - Address unknown since 1999.

Artistic Works—American Gp; Intl. Inst. for Conservation of Historic and [10011]

Artistic Works; Amer. Inst. for Conservation of Historic and [10011]

Artists

Acad. of Arts and Sciences of the Americas [18830]

Actors' Equity Assn. [24148]

Adolph and Esther Gottlieb Found. [9486]

African Amer. Visual Arts Assn. [9409]

Alliance for Amer. Quilts [9823]

Alliance of Artists and Recording Companies [3346]

Alliance for the Arts [9535]

Alliance for Cultural Democracy [9536]

Alliance of Professional Tattooists [3714]

Allied Artists of Am. [9487]

Alpha Omega Assn. [9537]

Amer. Abstract Artists [9488]

Amer. Acad. of Arts and Letters [10196]

Amer. Art Deco Dealers Assn. [295]

Amer. Artists of Chinese Brush Painting [9538]

Amer. Artists Professional League [9489]

Amer. Arts Alliance [9539]

Amer. Bop Assn. [9863]

Amer. Chesterton Soc. [9630]

Amer. Color Print Soc. [9412]

Amer. Fed. of Musicians of the U.S. and Canada [24149]

Amer. Fired Arts Alliance [9542]

Amer. Flute Guild [10534]

Amer. Friends of the Paris Opera and Ballet [9543]

Amer. Guild of Judaic Art [9414]

Amer. Guild of Musical Artists [24150]

Amer. Guild of Variety Artists [24151]

Amer. Impressionist Soc. [9490]

Amer. Musicians Union [24152]

Amer. Photographic Artists Guild [2990]

Amer. Print Alliance [9544]

Amer. Russian Theatrical Alliance [11001]

Amer. Soc. of Artists [9491]

Amer. Soc. of Botanical Artists [9492]

Amer. Soc. of Contemporary Artists [9493]

Amer. Soc. of Marine Artists [9494]

Amer. Soc. of Portrait Artists [9495]

Amer. Tapestry Alliance [9416]

Amer. Theatre and Drama Soc. [11005]

Americana Music Assn. [10555]

Animators Unite [9388]

Annie Sims Intl. Fan Club [24842]

Art Dreco Inst. [9423]

Art Greenhaw Official Intl. Fan Club [24843]

Art Information Center [9424]

Art Inst. of Light [9425]

Art and Sci. Collaborations [9607]

Art Students League of New York [9496]

Arthur Szyk Soc. [9497]

Artists Against AIDS Worldwide [11325]

Artists for a Better World Intl. [9549]

Artists in Christian Testimony [19989]

Artists Helping Artists [9498]

Artists Helping Artists [IO]

Artists for Israel Intl. [9428]

Artists for a New South Africa [11911]

Artists Rights Soc. [305]

Artists Space [9499]

Artists Without Borders [IO]

A.R.T.S. Anonymous [13014]

Arts and Bus. Coun. [9550]

Arts Centre Gp. [IO]

Arts Intl. [9551]

A star before a book entry number signifies that the name is not listed separately, but is mentioned within the entry.

ArtTable [9500]
Asian Amer. Arts Centre [9553]
Assoc. Actors and Artistes of Am. [24153]
Assn. of Israel's Decorative Arts [9556]
Assn. for Korean Music Res. [10561]
Assn. of Lifecasters Intl. [10957]
Assn. of Mouth and Foot Painting Artists [IO]
Assn. of Theatrical Press Agents and Managers [24154]
Atlatl [9557]
Audubon Artists [9433]
Austin Cody's Official Intl. Fan Club [24845]
Better World Chorus [12617]
Beyond Baroque Literary/Arts Center [9559]
Black Gold Gp. [9501]
Blue Earth Alliance [10847]
Bohemia Ragtime Soc. [10568]
Branscombe Richmond Fan Club [24779]
British Doll Artists Assn. [IO]
British Soc. of Master Glass Painters [IO]
British Toymakers Guild [IO]
Broadcast Designer's Assn. [554]
Canadian Artists Representation [IO]
Canadian Soc. of Painters in Water Colour [IO]
Caricature Carvers of Am. [9829]
Center for Book Arts [9745]
Center for the Stud. of Political Graphics [9434]
Chris Young Fan Club [24862]
Christian Comic Arts Soc. [9435]
Clay Underwood Fan Club [24865]
Coalition of Asian Pacifics in Entertainment [1300]
Cooltan Arts [IO]
Creative Time [9565]
Cross Cultural Collaborative [8177]
Dance/Drill Team Directors of Am. [9876]
Dance Heritage Coalition [9877]
Dance Theater Workshop [9566]
Dance/U.S.A. [9879]
Dancers Without Borders [9880]
Delbert McClinton Intl. Fan Club [24874]
Drs. for Artists [12520]
Doll Artisan Guild [22394]
The Drawing Center [9438]
Empire State Tattoo Club of Am. [10993]
Enamelist Soc. [22156]
Ernst Bacon Soc. [10593]
European Amer. Musical Alliance [10594]
European Coun. of Artists [IO]
Experiments in Art and Tech. [9439]
Fed. Assn. of Artists of the Fine Arts [IO]
Fed. of Modern Painters and Sculptors [9502]
Filipinas Americas Sci. and Art Found. [9609]
Finnish Painters' Union [IO]
Firearms Engravers Guild of Am. [9830]
Folk Art Soc. of Am. [9956]
Fractured Atlas [9503]
Franklin Furnace Archv. [9440]
Friends of Dennis Lee Fan Club [24780]
Friends-in-Art of Amer. Coun. of the Blind [9504]
Friends of Ty Herndon Fan Club [24896]
Global Alliance of Performers [10773]
Graphic Artists Guild [9505]
Graphic Artists Guild [IO]
The Grascals Fan Club [24904]
Guild of Aviation Artists [IO]
Guild of Fine Craftsmen and Artisans [306]
Guild of Italian Amer. Actors [24155]
Guild of Natural Sci. Illustrators [7153]
Guild of Railway Artists [IO]
Hispanic Org. of Latin Actors [10001]
Indo-American Arts Coun. [9570]
Intl. Alliance of Theatrical Stage Employees, Moving Picture Technicians, Artists and Allied Crafts of the U.S., Its Territories and Canada [24156]
Intl. Artists Network [9506]
Intl. Arts and Artists [9572]
Intl. Assn. of Art Critics - U.S. Sect. [9573]
Intl. Assn. of Pastel Societies [9445]
Intl. Chain Saw Wood Sculptors Assn. [9446]
Intl. Comic Arts Assn. [9447]
Intl. Concert Alliance [10617]
Intl. Doll Makers Assn. [22397]
Intl. Guild of Artists [IO]
Intl. Guild of Glass Artists [299]
Intl. Guild of Miniature Artisans [22159]

Intl. Guild of Musicians in Dance [10774]
Intl. Guild of Realism [9574]
Intl. Guild of Symphony, Opera and Ballet Musicians [24157]
Intl. Ivory Soc. [9832]
Intl. Machine Quilters Assn. [22160]
Intl. Quilt Assn. [22162]
Intl. Rose O'Neill Club Found. [22399]
Intl. Soc. of Copier Artists [9507]
Intl. Soc. of Copier Artists [IO]
Intl. Soc. of Glass Beadmakers [311]
Intl. Soc. for the Performing Arts [9575]
Intl. Tap Assn. [9888]
Intl. Traditional Country Music Fan Club [24914]
Intl. Vintage Poster Dealers Assn. [106]
Jargon Soc. [9958]
Jeannie Seely's Circle of Friends [24917]
Jew's Harp Guild [10634]
Jim Hubbard Fan Club [24920]
Johnnie Ray Intl. Fan Club [24927]
Junior Shag Assn. [9890]
Jussi Bjorling Soc. - USA [9508]
Kelly Lang Fan Club [24932]
Kinetic Art Org. [9453]
Labor Heritage Found. [9578]
Landscape Artists Intl. [9509]
Landscape Artists Intl. [IO]
Lee's Familee [24937]
Mexican Amer. Music Assn. [10647]
Michael Crawford Intl. Fan Assn. [24760]
Michael Jackson Fan Club [24948]
Midmarch Associates [9510]
Mixed Harmony Barbershop Quartet Assn. [10648]
Movement Theatre Intl. [11025]
Musicians' Alliance for Peace [18223]
Natl. Artists Equity Assn. [9511]
Natl. Arts Found. [9582]
Natl. Assn. of Artists and Crafters [301]
Natl. Assn. of Artists' Organizations [9512]
Natl. Assn. of Independent Artists [9513]
Natl. Assn. of Latino Arts and Culture [9584]
Natl. Assn. of Women Artists [9514]
Natl. Cartoonists Soc. [9515]
Natl. Center of Afro-American Artists [9361]
Natl. Clogging Org. [9892]
Natl. Fastdance Assn. [9894]
Natl. Found. for Advancement in the Arts [9587]
Natl. Inst. of Amer. Doll Artists [22403]
Natl. League of Amer. Pen Women [9588]
Natl. New Play Network [11030]
Natl. Polymer Clay Guild [22579]
Natl. Portraiture Assn. [IO]
Natl. Soc. of Artists [9516]
Natl. Soc. of Mural Painters [9517]
Natl. Soc. of Painters in Casein and Acrylic [9518]
Natl. Watercolor Soc. [9461]
Natural Figure Art Assn. [9462]
New Horizons Arts Initiative [9589]
New York Coun. of Motion Picture and TV Unions [24056]
North Amer. British Music Stud. Assn. [10676]
North Amer. Quilling Guild [21541]
NURTUREart Non-Profit [9519]
NURTUREart Non-Profit [IO]
Official Robert Newman Fan Club [24765]
Oh Ji Ho Intl. Fan Club [24781]
Oil Painters of Am. [9520]
Omega Theatre and the Omega Arts Network [9590]
Original Doll Artists Coun. of Am. [22404]
Other Minds [10684]
Pastel Soc. [IO]
Pastel Soc. of Am. [9464]
Pen and Brush [9521]
People's News Agency [3155]
Performing Arts Found. [9592]
Performing Arts Medicine Assn. [16164]
Philip Boileau Collectors' Soc. [21542]
Philippine Amer. Writers and Artists [11188]
Pollock-Krasner Found. [17004]
Pollock-Krasner Foundation [IO]
Portrait Soc. of Am. [9465]
Positive Music Assn. [10688]
Potters Coun. [9780]

Potters for Peace [9838]
Precious Metal Clay Guild [8172]
The Print Center [9522]
The Print Center [IO]
Professional Assn. of Comics Entertainment Retailers [9523]
P.S.1 Contemporary Art Center [9595]
Public Art Fund [17239]
Recycled Art Assn. [9468]
REG - The Intl. Roger Waters Fan Club [24965]
Renaissance Artists and Writers Assn. [10202]
Richard Burgi Fan Club [24768]
The Rock Poster Soc. [9469]
Rogers Group [10960]
Romanian Stud. Assn. of Am. [10938]
Royal British Soc. of Sculptors [IO]
Royal Inst. of Oil Painters [IO]
Royal Inst. of Painters in Water Colours [IO]
Royal Soc. of British Artists [IO]
Royal Soc. of Marine Artists [IO]
Royal Soc. of Miniature Painters, Sculptors and Gravers [IO]
Royal Soc. of Portrait Painters [IO]
Rustie Blue Intl. Fan Club [24972]
Saint Andrew Abbey [11192]
Salmagundi Club [9597]
Sandicast Collectors Guild [21544]
Screen Actors Guild [24158]
Sculptors Guild [10961]
Sculpture in the Env. [17240]
Silk Painters Intl. [9524]
Silvermine Guild Arts Center [9471]
Soc. for All Artists [IO]
Soc. of Amer. Mosaic Artists [9525]
Soc. of Animal Artists [9526]
Soc. for Applied Psychological Res. in the Performing Arts [16170]
Soc. for Calligraphy [11213]
Soc. of Equestrian Artists [IO]
Society of Illustrators [IO]
Soc. of Illustrators [9527]
Soc. of Scottish Artists [IO]
Soc. of Stage Directors and Choreographers [24159]
Soc. of Tempera Painters [9528]
Soc. of Wildlife Artists [IO]
Stars for Stripes [20770]
Stencil Artisans League, Inc. [9474]
Sword Swallowers Assn. Intl. [10776]
Talent Managers Assn. [1325]
Tamizdat [9853]
Taos Natl. Soc. of Watercolorists [9476]
Tattoo Club of Great Britain [IO]
Thomas Kinkade Collectors' Soc. [21545]
Three Dog Night Fan Club [24984]
Ukraine Assn. of Cartoonists [IO]
The Unconservatory [10714]
UNIMA-U.S.A., Amer. Center of the Union Internationale de la Marionnette [22916]
Union des Artistes de la Reunion [IO]
Union of Bulgarian Artists [IO]
United Chainsaw Carvers Guild [9842]
United Fed. of Doll Clubs [22407]
United Scenic Artists [24160]
U.S. Natl. Inst. of Dance [9899]
U.S. Soc. for Educ. Through Art [7980]
Unity Corps [19017]
Victorian Artists Soc. [IO]
Visual Artists and Galleries Assn. [5861]
Visual Stud. Workshop [9950]
VSA arts [11993]
Ward Museum of Wildfowl Art, Salisbury Univ. [9529]
Westbeth Corp. [9530]
Women in the Arts [11093]
Women's Caucus for Art [9531]
Women's Interart Center [11096]
Wood Engravers Network [9843]
World Org. of China Painters [22177]
World Piano Competition [10726]
World Swing Dance Coun. [9902]
Yiddisher Kultur Farband [10291]
YLEM: Artists Using Sci. and Tech. [9532]
Young Concert Artists [10727]
Youth Educ. in the Arts [9604]

Reference to "IO" in place of a book number signifies that the association may be found in the 45th edition of International Organizations.

Artists Across Frontiers [★IO]
Artists for Africa; United Support of [★12882]
Artists Against AIDS Worldwide [11325]
Artists Against AIDS Worldwide [IO], Washington, DC, United States
Artists Against Racism [IO], Toronto, ON, Canada
Artists Aid Soc. [★19263]
Artists; Amer. Fed. of TV and Radio [24022]
Artists; Amer. Fed. of TV Recording [★17981]
Artists; Amer. Guild of Musical [24150]
Artists; Amer. Guild of Variety [24151]
Artists' Assn. of Finland [IO], Helsinki, Finland
Artists; Assn. of Restorers and Coun. of Craftsmen and [218]
Artists; Assn. of Stained Glass Lamp [2392]
Artists and Athletes Against Apartheid - Address unknown since 1999.
Artists for a Better World Intl. [9549], 4845 Fountain Ave., No. 13, Hollywood, CA 90028
Artists for a Better World Intl. [IO], Hollywood, CA, United States
Artists Betwixt and Between - Address unknown since 2007.
Artists; Brooklyn Soc. of [★9493]
Artists in Christian Testimony [19989], PO Box 1649, Brentwood, TN 37024-1649, (615)376-7861
Artists in Christian Testimony [IO], Brentwood, TN, United States
Artists Civil Rights Assistance Fund - Defunct.
Artists Confronting AIDS - Address unknown since 2000.
Artists Coun. of Am; Original Doll [22404]
Artists; Drs. for [12520]
Artists Equity Assn. [★9511]
Artists Equity Fund [★9511]
Artists' Fellowship [19263], 47 5th Ave., New York, NY 10003, (646)230-9833
Artists and Galleries Assn; Visual [5861]
Artists' Gallery and Art Information Center [★9424]
Artists Guild; Amer. Photographic [2990]
Artists Guild; Amer. Photographic [★2990]
Artists Guild of Chicago - Defunct.
Artists Guild of New York - Defunct.
Artists Guild; Original Paper Doll [22405]
Artists Guild; Professional Tattoo [3716]
Artists Helping Artists [9498], 300 Redwood Dr., Santa Cruz, CA 95060, (831)457-2476
Artists Helping Artists [IO], Santa Cruz, CA, United States
Artists; Intl. Soc. of Scientist- [★9610]
Artists for Israel Intl. [9428], PO Box 2056, New York, NY 10163-2056, (212)245-4188
Artists for Israel Intl. [IO], New York, NY, United States
Artists; Lesbian Visual [★9454]
Artists Managers Guild [★172]
Artists; Natl. Center of Afro-American [9361]
Artists; Natl. Inst. of Amer. Doll [22403]
Artists Network; Eternal [★9506]
Artists for a New South Africa [11911], 2999 Overland Ave., Ste. 102, Los Angeles, CA 90064, (310)204-1748
Artists for a New South Africa [IO], Los Angeles, CA, United States
Artists for Nuclear Disarmament - Defunct.
Artists for Peace in the Middle East; Writers and [18072]
Artists Recovering Through the Twelve Steps [★13014]
Artists' Representatives Assn. - Defunct.
Artist's Rights Assn. - Defunct.
Artists Rights Soc. [305], 536 Broadway, 5th Fl., New York, NY 10012, (212)420-9160
Artists; Silvermine Guild of [★9471]
Artists; Society of Amer. [★9496]
Artists; Soc. of Amer. Graphic [9992]
Artists Space [9499], 38 Greene St., 3rd Fl., New York, NY 10013, (212)226-3970
Artists in Stained Glass Canada [IO], Parry Sound, ON, Canada
Artists for Survival/Artists for Mideast Peace - Address unknown since 2007.
Artists Technical Res. Inst. - Defunct.
Artists United Against Apartheid - Defunct.
Artists; United Scenic [24160]

Artists Using Sci. and Tech; YLEM: [9532]
Artists Without Borders [IO], Tokyo, Japan
Artists and Writers Assn; Renaissance [10202]
Artists; Young Concert [10727]
Artmobile - Defunct.
Artnet - Defunct.
Arts
  Academia Chilena de Bellas Artes [IO]
  Acad. of Arts and Sciences of the Americas [18830]
  Actors' Equity Assn. [24148]
  Affiliated Woodcarvers [9533]
  Affiliated Woodcarvers [IO]
  African Amer. Visual Arts Assn. [9409]
  Algonquin Arts Coun. [IO]
  All-India Fine Arts and Crafts Soc. [IO]
  All Out Arts [9534]
  Alliance for Amer. Quilts [9823]
  Alliance for the Arts [9535]
  Alliance for Cultural Democracy [9536]
  Alpha Omega Assn. [9537]
  Amer. Acad. of Arts and Letters [10196]
  Amer. Acad. of Arts and Sciences [9605]
  Amer. Art Deco Dealers Assn. [295]
  Amer. Artists of Chinese Brush Painting [9538]
  Amer. Arts Alliance [9539]
  Amer. Arts and Crafts Alliance [9824]
  Amer. Assn. of Community Theatre [10999]
  Amer. Assn. of Woodturners [9825]
  Amer. Bop Assn. [9863]
  Amer. Cultural Resources Assn. [9540]
  Amer. Fed. of Arts [9541]
  Amer. Fed. of Musicians of the U.S. and Canada [24149]
  Amer. Film Inst. [9927]
  Amer. Fired Arts Alliance [9542]
  Amer. Flute Guild [10534]
  Amer. Friends of the Paris Opera and Ballet [9543]
  Amer. Friends of the Shakespeare Birthplace Trust [11157]
  Amer. Guild of Judaic Art [9414]
  Amer. Guild of Musical Artists [24150]
  Amer. Guild of Variety Artists [24151]
  Amer. Inst. of Graphic Arts [1757]
  Amer. Musicians Union [24152]
  Amer. Print Alliance [9544]
  American Print Alliance [IO]
  Amer. Russian Theatrical Alliance [11001]
  Amer. Soc. for Aesthetics [9545]
  Amer. Soc. for Aesthetics [IO]
  Amer. Soc. of Picture Professionals [2993]
  Amer. Tapestry Alliance [9416]
  Amer. Theatre and Drama Soc. [11005]
  Americans for the Arts [9546]
  Animators Unite [9388]
  Aosdana [IO]
  Architectural League of New York [17235]
  Art and Creative Materials Inst. [1799]
  Art Greenhaw Official Intl. Fan Club [24843]
  Art in the Public Interest [9547]
  Art Resources in Collaboration [9867]
  Art and Sci. Collaborations [9607]
  Art Watch Intl. [9548]
  Art Watch Intl. [IO]
  Artfoundation [IO]
  Artists for a Better World Intl. [IO]
  Artists for a Better World Intl. [9549]
  Artists Helping Artists [9498]
  Arts and Bus. [IO]
  Arts and Bus. Coun. [9550]
  Arts Coun. England [IO]
  Arts Coun. of Ireland [IO]
  Arts Coun. of Northern Ireland [IO]
  Arts Coun. of Wales [IO]
  Arts, Crafts and Theatre Safety [12950]
  Arts Educ. Partnership [7966]
  Arts Intl. [9551]
  Arts Intl. [IO]
  Arts Marketing Assn. [IO]
  Arts in Therapy Network [13709]
  The Arts We Need [13710]
  Asia/Pacific Cultural Centre for UNESCO [IO]
  Asian Amer. Arts Alliance [9552]
  Asian Amer. Arts Centre [9553]

  Asian Amer. Arts Centre [IO]
  Asian CineVision [9930]
  Assoc. Actors and Artistes of Am. [24153]
  The Assn. of Amer. Cultures [9554]
  Assn. of Arts Admin. Educators [7967]
  Assn. for the Calligraphic Arts [9555]
  Assn. of Friends of Classical Art [IO]
  Assn. of Hispanic Arts [IO]
  Assn. of Historians of Nineteenth-Century Art [9431]
  Assn. of Israel's Decorative Arts [9556]
  Assn. of Israel's Decorative Arts [IO]
  Assn. for Korean Music Res. [10561]
  Assn. of Lifecasters Intl. [10957]
  Assn. for Native Development in the Performing and Visual Arts [IO]
  Assn. of Painting Craft Teachers [IO]
  Assn. of Performing Arts Presenters [7968]
  Assn. for the Preservation and Presentation of the Arts [9355]
  Assn. of Sci. Fiction and Fantasy Artists [307]
  Assn. of Stained Glass Lamp Artists [2392]
  Assn. of Theatrical Press Agents and Managers [24154]
  Atlatl [9557]
  Audience Development Comm. [11006]
  Australia Coun. [IO]
  Australia Coun. for the Arts [IO]
  Bahrain Arts Soc. [IO]
  Ballet Theatre Found. [9868]
  Beaux Arts Alliance [9558]
  Beyond Baroque Literary/Arts Center [9559]
  Blue Earth Alliance [10847]
  Blues Heaven Found. [10567]
  BoardSource [12651]
  British and Intl. Fed. of Festivals [IO]
  British Sugarcraft Guild [IO]
  Bus. Comm. for the Arts [9560]
  Butimar Productions [9849]
  Canada Coun. for the Arts [IO]
  Canadian Arts Presenting Assn. [IO]
  Canadian Assn. of Arts Admin. Educators [IO]
  Canadian Conf. of the Arts [IO]
  Canadian Inst. of the Arts for Young Audiences [IO]
  Canadian Soc. for Educ. through Art [IO]
  Caricature Carvers of Am. [9829]
  Cartoonists Northwest [9561]
  Catholic Fine Arts Soc. [9562]
  Center for United States-China Arts Exchange [9784]
  Chinese-American Arts Coun. [9608]
  Chris Blair Fan Club [24802]
  Christians in the Visual Arts [9563]
  Coalition of Asian Pacifics in Entertainment [1300]
  Cobbett Assn. for Chamber Music Res. [10579]
  Coll. Art Assn. [7969]
  Complex Weavers [308]
  Conf. of Drama Schools [IO]
  Congressional Arts Caucus [17254]
  Coun. for Art Educ. [7970]
  Coun. of Colleges of Arts and Sciences [7971]
  Coun. for Dance Educ. and Training - UK [IO]
  Coun. of Literary Magazines and Presses [10893]
  Cowles Charitable Trust [9564]
  Craft Yarn Coun. of Am. [22153]
  Creative New Zealand [IO]
  Creative Time [9565]
  Cross Cultural Collaborative [8177]
  Culture and Animals Found. [11384]
  Dance Heritage Coalition [9877]
  Dance Theater Workshop [9566]
  Dance/U.S.A. [9879]
  Decorative Arts Trust [9567]
  Dept. for Professional Employees, AFL-CIO [24173]
  Drs. for Artists [12520]
  Doll Costumer's Guild [22395]
  Early Music Network [10591]
  Elder Craftsmen [11285]
  Enamelist Soc. [22156]
  Ernst Bacon Soc. [10593]
  Estonian Artists' Assn. [IO]
  European Amer. Musical Alliance [10594]
  European Cultural Found. [IO]

A star before a book entry number signifies that the name is not listed separately, but is mentioned within the entry.

European League of Institutes of the Arts [IO]
Fed. of British Artists [IO]
Film Arts Found. [9937]
Film/Video Arts [9938]
FilmAid Intl. [12811]
Fine Arts Assn. of Finland [IO]
Fine Arts Philatelists [22819]
Firearms Engravers Guild of Am. [9830]
Florence Ceramics Collectors Soc. [22025]
Folk Art Soc. of Am. [9956]
Fractured Atlas [9503]
Friends of Bezalel Acad. of Arts [10255]
Friends of the Kennedy Center [9568]
Getty Grant Prog. [9569]
Getty Grant Prog. [IO]
Gifts In Kind Intl. [12720]
Global Alliance of Performers [10773]
Grantmakers in the Arts [12722]
Greater Vancouver Alliance for Arts and Culture [IO]
Grolier Club [9749]
Guild of Italian Amer. Actors [24155]
Guild of Natural Sci. Illustrators [7153]
Henry Luce Found. [12050]
Hispanic Soc. of Am. [10002]
Historians of British Art [9478]
Homowo African Arts and Cultures [9350]
Hong Kong Arts Festival Soc. [IO]
Hong Kong Schools Music and Speech Assn. [IO]
Howard Gilman Foundation [IO]
Howard Gilman Found. [11504]
Independent Print Indus. Assn. [IO]
Indo-American Arts Coun. [IO]
Indo-American Arts Coun. [9570]
Inst. of Amer. Indian Arts [10745]
Inst. of Contemporary Arts [IO]
Inter-Society for the Electronic Arts [IO]
Interlochen Center for the Arts [IO]
Interlochen Center for the Arts [9571]
Intl. Acad. of Aquatic Art [23884]
Intl. Alliance of Theatrical Stage Employees, Moving Picture Technicians, Artists and Allied Crafts of the U.S., Its Territories and Canada [24156]
Intl. Artists Network [9506]
Intl. Arts and Artists [9572]
Intl. Arts and Artists [IO]
Intl. Arts Medicine Assn. [IO]
Intl. Arts Medicine Assn. [7972]
Intl. Assn. of Art Critics - Hong Kong [IO]
Intl. Assn. of Art Critics - Ireland [IO]
Intl. Assn. of Art Critics - Taiwan [IO]
Intl. Assn. of Art Critics - U.S. Sect. [9573]
Intl. Assn. of Arts and Cultural Mgt. [IO]
Intl. Assn. for Voice Movement Therapy [13711]
Intl. Assn. of Wagner Societies [IO]
Intl. Brecht Soc. [9661]
Intl. Comic Arts Assn. [9447]
Intl. Concert Alliance [10617]
Intl. Coun. of Fine Arts Deans [7973]
Intl. Coun. of Fine Arts Deans [IO]
Intl. Expressive Arts Therapy Assn. [13712]
Intl. Fed. of Arts Councils and Culture Agencies [IO]
International Fine Print Dealers Association [IO]
Intl. Fine Print Dealers Assn. [309]
Intl. Guild of Glass Artists [299]
Intl. Guild of Miniature Artisans [22159]
Intl. Guild of Musicians in Dance [10774]
Intl. Guild of Realism [9574]
Intl. Guild of Symphony, Opera and Ballet Musicians [24157]
Intl. Ivory Soc. [9832]
Intl. Machine Quilters Assn. [22160]
Intl. Network of Schools for the Advancement of Arts Educ. [7974]
Intl. Network of Schools for the Advancement of Arts Educ. [IO]
Intl. Order of E.A.R.S. [10979]
Intl. Quilt Assn. [22162]
Intl. Res. Inst. for Media, Commun. and Cultural Development [IO]
Intl. Soc. for Educ. Through Art [IO]
Intl. Soc. for Educ. Through Art - Netherlands [IO]
Intl. Soc. of Glass Beadmakers [311]
Intl. Soc. for Hildegard Von Bingen Stud. [11124]

Intl. Soc. for the Performing Arts [9575]
Intl. Soc. for the Performing Arts [IO]
Intl. Soc. for the Performing Arts Found. [IO]
Intl. Soc. for the Performing Arts Found. [9576]
Intl. Soc. of Phenomenology, Aesthetics, and the Fine Arts [9577]
Intl. Soc. of Phenomenology, Aesthetics, and the Fine Arts [IO]
Intl. Tap Assn. [9888]
Intl. Vintage Poster Dealers Assn. [106]
Jew's Harp Guild [10634]
Junior Shag Assn. [9890]
Kappa Pi Intl. Honorary Art Fraternity [24404]
Kappa Pi Intl. Honorary Art Fraternity [IO]
Kennedy Center Alliance for Arts Educ. Network [7975]
Kinetic Art Org. [9453]
The Knitting Guild Assn. [22164]
Korean Culture and Arts Found. [IO]
Labor Heritage Found. [9578]
Ladyslipper [11087]
Landscape Artists Intl. [9509]
Leonardo, The Intl. Soc. for the Arts, Sciences and Tech. [9610]
Longfellow Soc. [10863]
Macedonian Arts Coun. [10437]
Makassed Found. of Am. [12730]
McCoy Pottery Collectors' Soc. [21932]
Mid Atlantic Fiber Assn. [310]
Midori and Friends [7976]
Mixed Harmony Barbershop Quartet Assn. [10648]
Nashville Entertainment Assn. [9579]
Natl. Aboriginal Achievement Found. [IO]
Natl. Alliance for Media Arts and Culture [9580]
Natl. Art Educ. Assn. [7977]
Natl. Art Exhibitions by the Mentally Ill [9581]
Natl. Arts Coun. of Zimbabwe [IO]
Natl. Arts Coun. of Zimbabwe - Masvingo [IO]
Natl. Arts Coun. of Zimbabwe - Matabeleland North [IO]
Natl. Arts Found. [9582]
Natl. Assembly of State Arts Agencies [9583]
Natl. Assn. of Artists and Crafters [301]
Natl. Assn. of Decorative and Fine Arts Societies [IO]
Natl. Assn. of Flower Arrangement Societies [IO]
Natl. Assn. of Independent Artists [9513]
Natl. Assn. of Latino Arts and Culture [9584]
Natl. Assn. of Photographic Equip. Technicians [3004]
Natl. Assn. of Schools of Art and Design [7978]
Natl. Basketry Org. [22167]
Natl. Center of Afro-American Artists [9361]
Natl. Coalition of Creative Arts Therapies Associations [16224]
Natl. Commission for Culture and the Arts [IO]
Natl. Coun. for the Traditional Arts [9961]
Natl. Dance Assn. [9893]
Natl. Endowment for the Arts [9585]
Natl. Endowment for the Christian Arts [9586]
Natl. Fastdance Assn. [9894]
Natl. Found. for Advancement in the Arts [9587]
Natl. Guild of Community Schools of the Arts [7979]
Natl. Initiative for a Networked Cultural Heritage [9858]
Natl. League of Amer. Pen Women [9588]
Natl. New Play Network [11030]
Natl. Park Acad. of the Arts [9460]
Natl. Polymer Clay Guild [22579]
Natl. Soc. of Artists [9516]
Natl. Soc. for Educ. in Art and Design [IO]
Natl. Women's Hall of Fame [20716]
Native Hawaiian Culture and Arts Prog. [10884]
Natural Figure Art Assn. [9462]
New Horizons Arts Initiative [9589]
New York Coun. of Motion Picture and TV Unions [24056]
New Zealand Acad. of Fine Arts [IO]
North Am. Native Amer. (Indian) Info. and Trade Center [10752]
North Amer. British Music Stud. Assn. [10676]
North Amer. Fed. of German Folk Dance Groups [9965]

North Amer. Quilling Guild [21541]
North Amer. Tang Shou Tao Assn. [13645]
Oil Painters of Am. [9520]
Omega Theatre and the Omega Arts Network [9590]
Pastel Artists Canada [IO]
Pastel Soc. of Australia [IO]
Pastel Soc. of Eastern Canada [IO]
Paul VI Inst. for the Arts [9591]
Paved Arts New Media [IO]
Performing Arts Found. [9592]
Performing Arts Resources [9593]
Phi Beta [24405]
Philip Boileau Collectors' Soc. [21542]
Philippine Amer. Writers and Artists [11188]
Picture Archv. Coun. of Am. [3008]
The Players [11038]
Portobello Antique Dealers Assn. [IO]
Portrait Soc. of Am. [9465]
Positive Music Assn. [10688]
Potters Coun. [9780]
Potters for Peace [9838]
Precious Metal Clay Guild [8172]
Prince Edward Island Coun. of the Arts [IO]
Professional Arts Mgt. Inst. [9594]
Professional Knifemakers Assn. [9839]
P.S.1 Contemporary Art Center [9595]
Puppet Centre Trust [IO]
Quilters Hall of Fame [22173]
Quimper Club Intl. [21546]
Renaissance Artists and Writers Assn. [10202]
Retailers of Art Glass and Supplies [1734]
Rhizome [9596]
Rhizome [IO]
River of Words [4186]
The Rock Poster Soc. [9469]
Rotterdam Arts Coun. [IO]
Royal Acad. of Arts [IO]
Royal Acad. of Sciences, Humanities and Fine Arts of Belgium [IO]
Royal Danish Acad. of Fine Arts [IO]
Royal Over-Seas League [IO]
Royal Scottish Acad. [IO]
Roycrofters-at-Large Assn. [9840]
Salmagundi Club [9597]
Saving the Arts [9598]
Schomburg Center for Res. in Black Culture [9363]
Scottish Arts Coun. [IO]
Scottish Historic and Res. Soc. of Delaware Valley [10955]
Screen Actors Guild [24158]
Sewing Educator Alliance [9121]
Shakespeare Theatre Assn. of Am. [11042]
Silk Painters Intl. [9524]
Singapore Indian Fine Arts Soc. [IO]
Soc. of Amer. Mosaic Artists [9525]
Soc. for Applied Psychological Res. in the Performing Arts [16170]
Soc. for the Arts in Healthcare [13714]
Soc. for the Arts in Healthcare [IO]
Soc. for the Arts, Religion and Contemporary Culture [9599]
Soc. of Fine Art Auctioneers and Valuers [IO]
Soc. of Heraldic Arts [IO]
Soc. for Seventeenth-Century Music [10705]
Soc. of Stage Directors and Choreographers [24159]
Spellbinders [10984]
Stencil Artisans League, Inc. [9474]
Subud Intl. Cultural Assn. - U.S.A. [9600]
Swedish Natl. Coun. for Cultural Affairs [IO]
Sword Swallowers Assn. Intl. [10776]
Symphony for United Nations [9601]
Symphony for United Nations [IO]
Taos Natl. Soc. of Watercolorists [9476]
Textile Soc. for the Stud. of Art, Design and History [IO]
Tyrone Guthrie Centre [IO]
The Unconservatory [10714]
UNIMA-U.S.A., Amer. Center of the Union Internationale de la Marionnette [22916]
United Chainsaw Carvers Guild [9842]
United Scenic Artists [24160]
U.S. Natl. Inst. of Dance [9899]

Reference to "IO" in place of a book number signifies that the association may be found in the 45th edition of International Organizations.

U.S. Soc. for Educ. Through Art [7980]
Unity Corps [19017]
Urban Art Intl. [1811]
Verband der Internationalen Lyceum Clubs in Deutschland [IO]
Visual Arts Ontario [IO]
Volunteer Lawyers for the Arts [6036]
VSA arts [11993]
Walpole Soc. [IO]
Ward Museum of Wildfowl Art, Salisbury Univ. [9529]
Weave a Real Peace [11505]
Wolf Trap Found. for the Performing Arts [9602]
Women in the Arts [11093]
Wood Engravers Network [9843]
World Org. of China Painters [22177]
World Piano Competition [10726]
World Swing Dance Coun. [9902]
Young Audiences [9603]
Youth Educ. in the Arts [9604]
Youth Educ. in the Arts [IO]
Ziegfeld Club [11054]
Arts; Academy of Wind and Percussion [★10660]
Arts Administrators; Assn. of Coll., Univ. and Community [★7968]
Arts; All Out [9534]
Arts for Am., Natl. Assembly of Local Arts Agencies [★9546]
Arts; Amer. Inst. of Graphic [1757]
A.R.T.S. Anonymous [13014], PO Box 230175, New York, NY 10023, (212)873-7075
Arts Architects; Soc. of Beaux- [★7963]
Arts Assn; Amer. Indus. [★9231]
Arts Assn; Natl. Postal [22139]
Arts; Assn. for the Preservation and Presentation of the [9355]
Arts Assn; Zen-do Kai Martial [★23619]
Arts; Bilingual Found. of the [11007]
Arts and Bus. [IO], London, United Kingdom
Arts and Bus. Coun. [9550]
Arts; Bus. Volunteers for the [★9550]
Arts Caucus; Congressional [★17254]
Arts Center - An Claidheamh Soluis; Irish [10243]
Arts Centre Gp. [IO], London, United Kingdom
Arts; Congressional Member Org. for the [★17254]
Arts Coun; Amer. Indian [10730]
Arts Coun. England [IO], London, United Kingdom
Arts Coun. of Great Britain [★IO]
Arts Coun. of Ireland [IO], Dublin, Ireland
Arts Coun. of Northern Ireland [IO], Belfast, United Kingdom
Arts Coun; Public [★17239]
Arts Coun. of Wales [IO], Cardiff, United Kingdom

Arts and Crafts
ABC Quilts Projs. [11506]
Affiliated Woodcarvers [9533]
Aid to Artisans [12415]
Alliance for Amer. Quilts [9823]
Amer. Art Pottery Assn. [9411]
Amer. Arts and Crafts Alliance [9824]
Amer. Assn. of Woodturners [9825]
Amer. Bunka Embroidery Assn. [22721]
Amer. Craft Coun. [9827]
Amer. Fired Arts Alliance [9542]
Amer. Gourd Soc. [22489]
Amer. Needlepoint Guild [22148]
Amer. Quilt Study Group [9828]
Amer. Quilter's Soc. [22149]
Amer. Sewing Guild [22150]
Amer. Soc. of Artists [9491]
Amer. Tapestry Alliance [9416]
Artists Helping Artists [9498]
Assn. of Israel's Decorative Arts [9556]
Assn. of Stained Glass Lamp Artists [2392]
Australian Indigenous Art Trade Assn. [IO]
Brazilian Dimensional Embroidery Intl. Guild [22987]
Caricature Carvers of Am. [9829]
Colonial Coverlet Guild of Am. [21998]
Cow Observers Worldwide [22002]
Craft Org. Development Assn. [1100]
Craft Yarn Coun. of Am. [22153]
Crochet Assn. Intl. [22154]
Crochet Guild of Am. [22722]
Cross Cultural Collaborative [8177]

Doll Artisan Guild [22394]
Doll Costumer's Guild [22395]
Elder Craftsmen [11285]
Embroiderers' Guild of Am. [22155]
Enamelist Soc. [22156]
Firearms Engravers Guild of Am. [9830]
Florence Ceramics Collectors Soc. [22025]
Folk Art Soc. of Am. [9956]
Found. for the Stud. of the Arts and Crafts Movement at Roycroft [21530]
Guild of Amer. Papercutters [22157]
Handweavers Guild of Am. [22158]
Hispanic Soc. of Am. [10002]
Homeworkers Organized for More Employment [12081]
Indian Arts and Crafts Assn. [10743]
Indo-American Arts Coun. [9570]
Inst. of Amer. Indian Arts [10745]
Inter-Tribal Indian Ceremonial Assn. [10747]
Intl. Arts and Artists [9572]
Intl. Assn. of Duncan Certified Ceramic Teachers [21928]
Intl. Doll Makers Assn. [22397]
Intl. Fine Print Dealers Assn. [309]
Intl. Guild of Candle Artisans [9831]
Intl. Guild of Glass Artists [299]
Intl. Guild of Miniature Artisans [22159]
Intl. Internet Leather Crafters' Guild [2414]
Intl. Ivory Soc. [9832]
Intl. Machine Quilters Assn. [22160]
Intl. Old Lacers, Inc. [22161]
Intl. Quilt Assn. [22162]
Intl. Rose O'Neill Club Found. [22399]
Intl. Soc. of Glass Beadmakers [311]
Intl. Soc. of Glass Beadmakers [IO]
Kinetic Art Org. [9453]
Knifemakers' Guild [9834]
The Knitting Guild Assn. [22164]
Landscape Artists Intl. [9509]
Lock Museum of Am. [9835]
McCoy Pottery Collectors' Soc. [21932]
Natl. Assn. of Artists and Crafters [301]
Natl. Assn. of Independent Artists [9513]
Natl. Assn. of Miniature Enthusiasts [22077]
Natl. Basketry Org. [22167]
Natl. Coun. on Educ. for the Ceramic Arts [9836]
Natl. Guild of Decoupeurs [22168]
Natl. Inst. of Amer. Doll Artists [22403]
Natl. Pig Carvers Assn. [22169]
Natl. Polymer Clay Guild [22579]
Natl. Quilting Assn. [22170]
Natl. Wood Carvers Assn. [22171]
Native Amer. Inst. [10751]
North Am. Native Amer. (Indian) Info. and Trade Center [10752]
North Amer. Quilling Guild [21541]
Northwest Regional Spinners' Assn. [22172]
Origami USA [22771]
Pen and Brush [9521]
Philip Boileau Collectors' Soc. [21542]
Pomegranate Guild of Judaic Needlework [9837]
Potters Coun. [9780]
Potters for Peace [9838]
Precious Metal Clay Guild [8172]
Professional Knifemakers Assn. [9839]
Quilters Hall of Fame [22173]
Quimper Club Intl. [21546]
Recycled Art Assn. [9468]
Retailers of Art Glass and Supplies [1734]
Roycrofters-at-Large Assn. [9840]
Sewing Educator Alliance [9121]
Silk Painters Intl. [9524]
Smocking Arts Guild of Am. [22174]
Soc. of Amer. Mosaic Artists [9525]
Soc. of Decorative Painters [22175]
Soc. for Folk Arts Preservation [9963]
Soc. of North Amer. Goldsmiths [9841]
Soc. of Tempera Painters [9528]
Studio Art Quilt Associates [21547]
UNIMA-U.S.A., Amer. Center of the Union Internationale de la Marionnette [22916]
United Chainsaw Carvers Guild [9842]
United Fed. of Doll Clubs [22407]
Ward Museum of Wildfowl Art, Salisbury Univ. [9529]

Wood Engravers Network [9843]
Arts and Crafts Alliance; Amer. [9824]
Arts and Crafts Alumni Assn; California Coll. of [18882]
Arts and Crafts Assn; Indian [10743]
Arts and Crafts Movement at Roycroft; Found. for the Stud. of the [21530]
Arts and Crafts Soc. [9429], 828 SE 34th Ave., Ste. B, Portland, OR 97214, (503)459-4422
Arts, Crafts and Theatre Safety [12950], 181 Thompson St., Ste. 23, New York, NY 10012-2586, (212)777-0062
Arts for Crisis Training; Performing [★11830]
Arts and Culture; Alliance for Asian Amer. [★9552]
Arts and Culture Found; Polish [19307]
Arts and Cultures; Homowo African [9350]
Arts Dealers Assn; Natl. Graphic [★1804]
Arts Educ; Alliance for [★7975]
Arts Educ. Assn; Intl. Graphic [8470]
Arts Educ. Assn; Natl. Graphic [★8470]
Arts Educ. Partnership [7966], 1 Massachusetts Ave. NW, Ste. 700, Washington, DC 20001-1431
Arts Employers of Am; Graphic [24082]
Arts Exchange; Center for United States-China [9784]
Arts Fed. Intl; Ceramic [★1911]
Arts; Fellowship of United Methodists in Music and Worship [20261]
Arts; Fellowship of United Methodists in Worship, and Other [★20261]
Arts; Film/Video [9938]
Arts Found; Film [9937]
Arts; Friends of Bezalel Acad. of [10255]
Arts; GALA Performing [★10599]
Arts Guild of Am; Smocking [22174]
Arts Guild; Natl. Graphic [★8470]
Arts; Inst. of Amer. Indian [10745]
Arts Intl. [9551], 770 Broadway, 2nd Fl., New York, NY 10003-9522, (212)674-9744
Arts Intl. [IO], New York, NY, United States
Arts; Intl. Assn. for the Fantastic in the [10945]
Arts Intl. Prog. of the Inst. of Intl. Educ. [★9551]
Arts Intl. Prog. of the Inst. of Intl. Educ. [★IO]
Arts Intl. Union; Graphic [★24083]
Arts and Knowledge of the Church; Soc. for Promoting and Encouraging [19972]
Arts League; Antique and Decorative [★297]
Arts and Letters; Amer. Acad. of [10196]
Arts and Letters for Historically Black Colls. and Universities; Natl. Consortium of [8111]
Arts and Letters; Natl. Soc. of [10201]
Arts; Lutheran Soc. for Worship, Music and the [★19900]
Arts Mgt. Inst; Performing [★9594]
Arts Managers and Agent; Natl. Assn. Performing [★175]
Arts Managers and Agents; North Amer. Performing [175]
Arts Marketing Assn. [IO], Cambridge, United Kingdom
Arts, Media and Entertainment; Fellowship of Christians in the [★20024]
Arts; Natl. Assn. of Dramatic and Speech [11026]
Arts; Natl. Coun. on Educ. for the Ceramic [9836]
Arts; Natl. Coun. for the Traditional [9961]
Arts; Natl. Hispanic Found. for the [19101]
Arts Network; Omega [★9590]
Arts for a New Nicaragua - Address unknown since 1999.
Arts for the Parks [★9460]
Arts Philatelists; Fine [22819]
Arts Preservation; Soc. for Folk [9963]
Arts Prog; Native Hawaiian Culture and [10884]
Arts Programs Natl. Org. Comm; Neighborhood [★9536]
Arts Recovery Soc; Anonymous [10956]
Arts, Religion and Culture; Found. for the [★9599]
Arts Sales Found; Graphic [1768]
Arts Sans Frontieres [★IO]
Arts and Sci. of Am; Polish Inst. of [★10881]

Arts and Sciences
Amer. Acad. of Arts and Sciences [9605]
Amer. Romanian Acad. of Arts and Sciences [9606]
Amer. Romanian Acad. of Arts and Sciences [IO]

A star before a book entry number signifies that the name is not listed separately, but is mentioned within the entry.

Argentine Acad. of Letters **[IO]**
Art and Sci. Collaborations **[IO]**
Art and Sci. Collaborations **[9607]**
Assn. for Integrative Stud. **[10227]**
Canadian Commn. for UNESCO **[IO]**
Chinese-American Arts Coun. **[9608]**
Dept. for Professional Employees, AFL-CIO **[24173]**
European Acad. of Sciences and Arts **[IO]**
Filipinas Americas Sci. and Art Found. **[IO]**
Filipinas Americas Sci. and Art Found. **[9609]**
Finnish Soc. of Sciences and Letters **[IO]**
Holland Soc. of Arts and Sciences **[IO]**
Intl. Assn. of Empirical Aesthetics **[IO]**
Intl. Soc. for Hildegard Von Bingen Stud. **[11124]**
Islamic Educational, Sci., and Cultural Org. **[IO]**
Israel Natl. Commn. for UNESCO **[IO]**
Kuwait Natl. Commn. for Educ., Sci. and Culture **[IO]**
Leonardo, The International Society for the Arts, Sciences and Technology **[IO]**
Leonardo, The Intl. Soc. for the Arts, Sciences and Tech. **[9610]**
Mexican Arts and Tech. Network **[9611]**
Modernist Stud. Assn. **[8780]**
Natl. Fed. of UNESCO Associations in Japan **[IO]**
Natl. UNESCO Club for Sci. Expeditions **[IO]**
Nobel Found. **[IO]**
Norwegian Acad. of Sci. and Letters **[IO]**
Org. of Ibero-American States for Educ., Sci. and Culture - Spain **[IO]**
Phi Beta Kappa **[24406]**
Polish Inst. of Arts and Sciences of Am. **[10881]**
Royal Danish Acad. of Sciences and Letters **[IO]**
Royal Irish Acad. **[IO]**
Royal Netherlands Acad. of Arts and Sciences **[IO]**
Royal Soc. for the Encouragement of Arts, Manufactures, and Commerce **[IO]**
Slovenian Acad. of Sciences and Arts **[IO]**
Swedish Natl. Commn. for UNESCO **[IO]**
UNESCO Club - Malta **[IO]**
United Nations Educational, Sci. and Cultural Org. **[IO]**
World Acad. of Art and Sci. **[IO]**
World Acad. of Art and Sci. **[9612]**
Arts and Sciences; Acad. of Motion Picture **[1374]**
Arts and Sciences; Acad. of Psychic **[7439]**
Arts and Sciences; Acad. of TV **[542]**
Arts and Sciences in Am; Czechoslovak Soc. of **[★9860]**
Arts and Sciences in Am; Polish Amer. Historical Commn. of the Polish Inst. of **[★10880]**
Arts and Sciences of Am; Polish Inst. of **[10881]**
Arts and Sciences; Hollywood Chap. of Natl. Acad. of TV **[★542]**
Arts and Sciences; Natl. Acad. of Recording **[10929]**
Arts and Sciences; Natl. Acad. of TV **[567]**
Arts and Sciences; Natl. Accrediting Commn. of Cosmetology **[7877]**
Arts Services Div; Special **[★9491]**
Arts; Soc. for Automation in Fine **[★8132]**
Arts Soc; Percussive **[10686]**
Arts Soc; Spanish Colonial **[10005]**
Arts Student Assn; Amer. Indus. **[★8547]**
Arts Studio Collectors Assn; Ceramic **[★21926]**
Arts Suppliers Assn; Graphic **[★1804]**
Arts Suppliers Assn; North Amer. Graphic **[1804]**
Arts Tech. Found; Graphic **[1769]**
Arts Therapies Associations; Natl. Coalition of Creative **[16224]**
Arts Therapy Associations; Natl. Coalition of **[★16224]**
Arts in Therapy Network **[13709]**, c/o The Arts We Need, PO Box 2652, New York, NY 10009, (800)586-TAWN
Arts in Therapy Network **[IO]**, New York, NY, United States
Arts; Tibetan Inst. of Performing **[★11055]**
Arts Unit of Amer. Topical Assn; Fine **[★22819]**
Arts; Very Special **[★11993]**
Arts; Volunteer Lawyers for the **[6036]**
The Arts We Need **[13710]**, PO Box 2652, New York, NY 10009, (800)586-TAWN
Arts; Women in the **[11093]**

Arts for Youth; Amer. Theatre **[11003]**
ArtTable **[9500]**, 116 John St., Ste. 822, New York, NY 10038, (212)343-1735
Arturo Toscanini Soc. - Address unknown since 1995.
Aruba Amateur Athletic Assn. **[★IO]**
Aruba Amateur Radio Club **[IO]**, San Nicolas, Aruba
Aruba Athletic Fed. **[IO]**, Oranjestad, Aruba
Aruba Badminton Club **[IO]**, Noord, Aruba
Aruba Chamber of Commerce and Indus. **[IO]**, Oranjestad, Aruba
Aruba Lawn Tennis Bond **[IO]**, Oranjestad, Aruba
Aruba Secretaries Assn. **[IO]**, Oranjestad, Aruba
Aruba Squash Assn. **[IO]**, Oranjestad, Aruba
Aruba Taekwondo Assn. **[IO]**, Oranjestad, Aruba
Arubaanse Atletiek Bond **[★IO]**
Arumanian
    Soc. Farsarotul **[18971]**
Aryan Unity Party of America - Defunct.
ARZA - Canada **[IO]**, Toronto, ON, Canada
Arztinnen und Arzte fur eine Gesunde Umwelt **[★IO]**
As The World Turns Fan Club - Address unknown since 1995.
As You Sow Found. **[11812]**, 311 California St., Ste. 510, San Francisco, CA 94104, (415)391-3212
ASA Cooperative Network - Address unknown since 2003.
ASA Intl. **[8230]**, 119 Cooper St., Babylon, NY 11702, (631)893-4540
ASA Intl. **[IO]**, Babylon, NY, United States
Asa Lafitte Stark Family Assn. - Defunct.
ASA Teaching Resources Center **[★7658]**
ASAE Found. **[★315]**
ASAE Found. **[★IO]**
Asanteman Assn. - Address unknown since 1989.
ASARian **[11521]**, PO Box 605, Durham, NC 27702-0605
Asatru
    Amer. Vinland Assn. **[19460]**
    Asatru Alliance **[19461]**
Asatru Alliance **[19461]**, PO Box 961, Payson, AZ 85547
Asatru Free Assembly **[★19461]**
Asbestos
    Asbestos Cement Prdt. Producers Assn. **[312]**
    Asbestos Cement Product Producers Association **[IO]**
    Asbestos Disease Awareness Org. **[16655]**
    Asbestos Litigation Gp. **[13321]**
    Assn. of Asbestos Cement Prdt. Producers **[3026]**
    White Lung Assn. **[13332]**
Asbestos Abatement Worker and Training Prog. **[★620]**
Asbestos Cement Pipe Producers; Assn. of **[★3026]**
Asbestos Cement Prdt. Producers Assn. **[312]**, PMB 114, 1235 Jefferson Davis Hwy., Arlington, VA 22202, (514)861-1153
Asbestos Cement Prdt. Producers; Assn. of **[3026]**
Asbestos Cement Product Producers Association **[IO]**, Arlington, VA, United States
Asbestos Cement Products Assn. - Defunct.
Asbestos Coun; Natl. **[★620]**
Asbestos Disease Awareness Org. **[16655]**, 1525 Aviation Blvd., Ste. 318, Redondo Beach, CA 90278
Asbestos Disease Awareness Org. **[IO]**, Redondo Beach, CA, United States
Asbestos Info. Association/North Am. **[2740]**, PMB 114, 1235 Jefferson Davis Hwy., Arlington, VA 22202-3283, (703)560-2980
Asbestos Inst. **[★IO]**
Asbestos Litigation Gp. **[13321]**, 5113 Southwest Pkwy., No. 285, Austin, TX 78735, (512)892-6689
Asbestos Removal Contractors Assn. **[IO]**, Burton-On-Trent, United Kingdom
Asbestos Textile Inst. - Defunct.
Asbestos Tile Inst; Asphalt and Vinyl **[★665]**
Asbestos Victims of America - Address unknown since 2002.
Asbestos Workers; Intl. Assn. of Heat and Frost Insulators and **[24093]**
ASCA (acronym) **[★5254]**
Ascended Masters
    Church Universal and Triumphant **[19462]**

Ascension Poetry Reading Series - Defunct.
Ascension, and Tristan da Cunha Philatelic Soc; St. Helena, **[22866]**
Aschimici **[★IO]**
Ascociacion Peruana de Terapistas Fisicos **[IO]**, Lima, Peru
ASCP **[★13885]**
ASD-STAN **[IO]**, Brussels, Belgium
ASEAN Bankers Assn. **[IO]**, Singapore, Singapore
ASEAN Confed. of Employers **[IO]**, Makati City, Philippines
ASEAN Coun. on Petroleum - Indonesia **[IO]**, Jakarta, Indonesia
ASEAN Fed. of Elecl. Engg. Contractors **[IO]**, Quezon City, Philippines
Asean Football Fed. **[IO]**, Petaling Jaya, Malaysia
ASEAN Free Trade Area **[IO]**, Jakarta, Indonesia
ASEAN Inst. for Hea. Development **[IO]**, Bangkok, Thailand
ASEAN Inter-Parliamentary Assembly **[IO]**, Jakarta, Indonesia
ASEAN Inter-Parliamentary Org. **[★IO]**
ASEAN Network for Women in Skills Training **[IO]**, Jakarta, Indonesia
ASEAN Neurological Assn. **[IO]**, Singapore, Singapore
ASEAN Neurological Soc. **[★IO]**
ASEAN Port Authorities Assn. **[★IO]**
ASEAN Ports Assn. **[IO]**, Manila, Philippines
ASEAN Promotion Centre on Trade, Investment and Tourism **[IO]**, Tokyo, Japan
ASEAN Regional Forum **[IO]**, Jakarta, Indonesia
ASEAN Univ. Network **[IO]**, Bangkok, Thailand
ASEAN Vegetable Oils Club **[IO]**, Selangor, Malaysia
ASEIB; Roster of Certified Engineers of the **[★6982]**
Asepsis Procedures; Org. for Safety and **[14182]**
Aseptic Packaging Coun. **[2872]**, 2120 L St. NW, Ste. 400, Washington, DC 20037, (202)478-6158
Asfalttiliitto ry **[★IO]**
ASFE **[7137]**, 8811 Colesville Rd., Ste. G106, Silver Spring, MD 20910, (301)565-2733
ASFE: Professional Firms Practicing in the Geosciences **[★7137]**
ASFE/The Assn. of Engg. Firms Practicing in the Geosciences **[★7137]**
ASGCA **[★6465]**
ASGM **[19506]**, PO Box 240, Kissimmee, FL 34747, (321)284-4593
Ash Assn; Amer. Coal **[3986]**
Ash Assn; Natl. **[★3986]**
ASH Australia **[IO]**, Kings Cross, Australia
Ash Corp; Amer. Natural Soda **[1725]**
Ash Development Assn. of Australia **[IO]**, Wollongong, Australia
Ash Export Assn; U.S. Soda **[★1725]**
Ashburn Inst. for Global Stud. in Federalism and Democracy **[18308]**, PO Box 77164, Washington, DC 20013-7164, (703)728-6482
Ashburn Institute for Global Studies in Federalism and Democracy **[IO]**, Washington, DC, United States
Ashburton Jaycee **[IO]**, Ashburton, New Zealand
Ashland, The Henry Clay Estate **[★11121]**
Ashoka: Innovators for the Public **[12419]**, 1700 N More St., Ste. 2000, Arlington, VA 22209, (703)527-8300
Ashoka: Innovators for the Public **[IO]**, Arlington, VA, United States
ASHP Found. **[15926]**, 7272 Wisconsin Ave., Bethesda, MD 20814, (301)664-8612
ASHP Res. and Educ. Found. **[★15926]**
Ashram Proj; Prison- **[11886]**
Ashtray Collectors Club, Intl. - Defunct.
Asia
    Aid for Intl. Medicine **[14972]**
    Allies Building Community **[9613]**
    Amer. Buddhist Assn. **[19540]**
    Amer. Buddhist Movement **[19541]**
    Amer. Buddhist Stud. Center **[19542]**
    Amer. Comm. for KEEP **[12418]**
    Amer. Go Assn. **[22459]**
    Amer. Oriental Soc. **[9614]**
    Asia Am. Initiative **[11762]**
    The Asia Found. **[17005]**
    The Asia Found. **[IO]**

Reference to "IO" in place of a book number signifies that the association may be found in the 45th edition of International Organizations.

Asia Pacific - USA Chamber of Commerce [24264]
Asia Soc. [9616]
Asian Amer. Arts Alliance [9552]
Asian Amer. Arts Centre [9553]
Asian CineVision [9930]
Asian Indian Chamber of Commerce [24228]
Buddhist Churches of Am. Fed. of Buddhist Women's Associations [19543]
Burma-America Buddhist Assn. [19546]
Central Eurasian Stud. Soc. [10233]
Centre for Development and Population Activities [12422]
China Medical Bd. of New York [14976]
Chinese-American Arts Coun. [9608]
Comm. Against Anti-Asian Violence [17006]
Comm. on Res. Materials on Southeast Asia [10349]
Conf. on Asian History [9617]
Cultural Integration Fellowship [9618]
East-West Center [17882]
First Zen Inst. of Am. [19549]
Focus on the Global South [IO]
Free Burma Coalition [IO]
Free Burma Coalition [17007]
Gay Asian Pacific Support Network [12229]
Henry Luce Found. [12050]
Honolulu Japanese Chamber of Commerce [24348]
Independent Scholars of Asia [9957]
Indian Dental Assn., U.S.A. [14157]
Intl. Betta Cong. [22441]
Intl. Soc. for Japanese Philately [22830]
Japan Aikido Assn. U.S.A. [23595]
Japan Convention Bur. [24341]
Japan External Trade Org. [24342]
Japan Info. Access Proj. [10265]
Japan Light Machinery Info. Center of Central New York [24343]
Japan Natl. Tourist Org. [24344]
Mai Wah Soc. [9622]
Mongolia Soc. [10487]
Natl. Advisory Coun. for South Asian Affairs [17008]
Natl. Advisory Coun. for South Asian Affairs [IO]
Natl. Assn. of Asian Amer. Professionals [9623]
Occupied Japan Club [22098]
Origami USA [22771]
Pacific Asia Travel Assn. [3933]
People-to-People Hea. Found. [14984]
Soc. for Asian Art [9472]
Soc. for East Asian Anthropology [6429]
Southeast Asia Rsrc. Action Center [12820]
Sumi-e Soc. of Am. [9475]
United States-Asia Environmental Partnership [4612]
U.S.-Asia Inst. [17009]
U.S.-Asia Inst. [IO]
U.S. Natl. Comm. for Pacific Economic Cooperation [17465]
U.S.-Vietnam Trade Coun. [17010]
U.S.-Vietnam Trade Council [IO]
Vets With a Mission [IO]
Vets With a Mission [17011]
Volunteers in Asia [13407]
Western Young Buddhist League [19558]
Zen Stud. Soc. [19559]
Asia Acad. of Mgt. [IO], Hong Kong, People's Republic of China
Asia Against Child Trafficking [IO], Quezon City, Philippines
Asia Am. Initiative [IO], Washington, DC, United States
Asia Am. Initiative [11762], 1523 16th St. NW, Washington, DC 20036, (202)232-7020
Asia; Amer. Org. for Bodywork Therapies of [15024]
Asia Bottled Water Assn. [IO], Jakarta, Indonesia
Asia Center; South-East [18502]
Asia; Comm. on Amer. Lib. Resources on South [★10349]
Asia; Comm. on Amer. Lib. Resources on Southeast [★10349]
Asia Crime Prevention Found. [IO], Tokyo, Japan
The Asia Found. [IO], San Francisco, CA, United States

The Asia Found. [17005], PO Box 193223, San Francisco, CA 94119-3223, (415)982-4640
Asia Fund for Human Development [★IO]
Asia Gender and Trade Network [IO], Quezon City, Philippines
Asia Inst. - Defunct.
Asia-Japan Women's Rsrc. Center [IO], Tokyo, Japan
Asia-Josei-Siryo-Center [★IO]
Asia Keisei Zaidan [★IO]
Asia Monitor Rsrc. Center [IO], Hong Kong, People's Republic of China
Asia; NCSJ: Advocates on Behalf of Jews in Russia, Ukraine, the Baltic States and Eur [17448]
Asia-No Onnatacchi No Kai [★IO]
Asia/North Am. Communications Center [★IO]
Asia-Oceania Assn. for the Stud. of Obesity [IO], Kuala Lumpur, Malaysia
Asia and Oceania Thyroid Assn. [IO], Nagoya, Japan
Asia and Pacific Alliance of YMCAs [IO], Hong Kong, People's Republic of China
Asia/Pacific Amer. Librarians Assn. [IO], Goleta, CA, United States
Asia/Pacific Amer. Librarians Assn. [10327], c/o Michelle Baildon, VP, MIT Humanities Lib., 77 Massachusetts Ave., Rm. 14S-222, Cambridge, MA 02139, (617)253-9352
Asia-Pacific Assn. of Agricultural Res. Institutions [IO], Bangkok, Thailand
Asia Pacific Assn. of Agricultural Res. Institutions - India [IO], Bangkok, Thailand
Asia Pacific Assn. for the Control of Tobacco [IO], Taipei, Taiwan
Asia-Pacific Assn. of Forestry Res. Institutions [IO], Selangor, Malaysia
Asia-Pacific Assn. for Machine Translation [IO], Kyoto, Japan
Asia Pacific Assn. of Paediatric Urologists [IO], Hong Kong, People's Republic of China
Asia-Pacific Broadcasting Union [IO], Kuala Lumpur, Malaysia
Asia Pacific Center for Justice and Peace - Address unknown since 2006.
Asia-Pacific Centre for Educational Innovation for Development [★IO]
Asia-Pacific Coun. of Amer. Chambers of Commerce [IO], Singapore, Singapore
Asia-Pacific Coun. of Optometry [IO], Forest Grove, OR, United States
Asia-Pacific Coun. of Optometry [15715]
Asia/Pacific Cultural Centre for UNESCO [IO], Tokyo, Japan
Asia Pacific Deaf Sports Confed. [IO], Kuala Lumpur, Malaysia
Asia-Pacific Economic Cooperation [IO], Singapore, Singapore
Asia-Pacific Forestry Commn. [IO], Bangkok, Thailand
Asia Pacific Forum on Women, Law and Development [IO], Chiang Mai, Thailand
Asia Pacific Found. of Canada [IO], Vancouver, BC, Canada
Asia Pacific Higher Educ. Res. Network [IO], Sydney, Australia
Asia Pacific Higher Institutions Res. Network [★IO]
Asia Pacific Hospice Palliative Care Network [IO], Singapore, Singapore
Asia-Pacific Implant Centre [IO], Hong Kong, People's Republic of China
Asia-Pacific Inst. for Broadcasting Development [IO], Kuala Lumpur, Malaysia
Asia and Pacific Internet Assn. [IO], Petaling Jaya, Malaysia
Asia Pacific Lab. Accreditation Cooperation [IO], North Melbourne, Australia
Asia Pacific League of Associations for Rheumatology [IO], Hong Kong, People's Republic of China
Asia-Pacific Legal Metrology Forum [IO], Ibaraki, Japan
Asia Pacific Loan Market Assn. [IO], Hong Kong, People's Republic of China
Asia Pacific Lottery Assn. [IO], Wayville, Australia
Asia Pacific Marketing Fed. [IO], Hong Kong, People's Republic of China

Asia Pacific Menopause Fed. [IO], Hong Kong, People's Republic of China
Asia-Pacific Migration Res. Network [IO], Canberra, Australia
Asia Pacific Mountain Network [IO], Lalitpur, Nepal
Asia Pacific Network for Food Anal. [IO], Archerfield, Australia
Asia Pacific Network for Global Change Res. [IO], Kobe, Japan
Asia-Pacific Network for Intl. Educ. and Values Educ. [IO], Mitcham, Australia
Asia-Pacific Network of People Living with HIV/AIDS [IO], Bangkok, Thailand
Asia Pacific Occupational Safety and Hea. Org. [IO], Hong Kong, People's Republic of China
Asia, Pacific and Oceania Sports Assembly [IO], Croydon South, Australia
Asia Pacific Orthopaedic Assn. [IO], Kuala Lumpur, Malaysia
Asia Pacific Paediatric Endocrine Soc. [IO], Westmead, Australia
Asia Pacific Peace Res. Assn. [IO], Quezon City, Philippines
Asia and Pacific Plant Protection Commn. [IO], Bangkok, Thailand
Asia-Pacific Population Info. Network [IO], Bangkok, Thailand
Asia-Pacific Professional Services Marketing Assn. [IO], Chatswood, Australia
Asia-Pacific Programme of Educational Innovation for Development [IO], Bangkok, Thailand
Asia Pacific Public Health Nutrition Assn. [16237]
Asia and Pacific Regional Bur. for Educ. [IO], Bangkok, Thailand
Asia-Pacific Risk and Insurance Assn. [IO], Singapore, Singapore
Asia-Pacific Satellite Communications Coun. [IO], Seoul, Republic of Korea
Asia and Pacific Seed Assn. [IO], Bangkok, Thailand
Asia Pacific Sociological Assn. [IO], Wollongong, Australia
Asia Pacific Telecommunity [IO], Bangkok, Thailand
Asia Pacific Top Level Domains Assn. [IO], Wellington, New Zealand
Asia Pacific Tourism Assn. [IO], Busan, Republic of Korea
Asia Pacific - USA Chamber of Commerce [24264], 150 S Los Robles Ave., Ste. 490, Pasadena, CA 91101, (626)795-9486
Asia Partnership for Human Development [IO], Bangkok, Thailand
Asia Rsrc. Action Center; Southeast [12820]
Asia Soc. [9616], 725 Park Ave., 70th St., New York, NY 10021, (212)327-9217
Asia Soc. [IO], New York, NY, United States
Asia Soil Conservation Network for the Humid Tropics [IO], Jakarta, Indonesia
Asia Watch Comm. [★IO]
Asia Watch Comm. [★17762]
Asia and West Pacific Network for Urban Conservation [IO], Penang, Malaysia
Asia Women's Assn. of the U.S.A; Pan-Pacific and Southeast [17907]
ASIAN [18974], 1167 Mission St., 4th Fl., San Francisco, CA 94103, (415)928-5910
Asian
  African Asian Latina Lesbians United [17649]
  Allies Building Community [9613]
  Alpha Iota Omicron [24611]
  Amer. Buddhist Assn. [19540]
  Amer. Buddhist Movement [19541]
  Amer. Buddhist Stud. Center [19542]
  Amer. Coun. for Southern Asian Art [9413]
  Amer. Go Assn. [22459]
  Amer. Oriental Soc. [9614]
  Amer. Oriental Soc. [IO]
  Amer. Schools of Oriental Res. [IO]
  Amer. Schools of Oriental Res. [9615]
  Andolan - Organizing South Asian Workers [24138]
  APPEAL: Asian Pacific Partners for Empowerment and Leadership [11760]
  The Asia Found. [17005]
  Asia/Pacific Amer. Librarians Assn. [10327]
  Asia Pacific Found. of Canada [IO]

A star before a book entry number signifies that the name is not listed separately, but is mentioned within the entry.

Asia Soc. [IO]
Asia Soc. [9616]
Asian Amer. Arts Alliance [9552]
Asian Amer. Arts Centre [9553]
Asian Amer. Justice Center [5470]
Asian Amer. Legal Defense and Educ. Fund [17095]
Asian Bus. League of San Francisco [696]
Asian Cinema Stud. Soc. [7981]
Asian Cinema Stud. Soc. [IO]
Asian CineVision [9930]
Asian Indian Chamber of Commerce [24228]
Asian/Pacific Amer. Heritage Assn. [18972]
Asian Pacific Amer. Heritage Coun. [18973]
Asian Pacific Amer. Labor Alliance [24003]
Asian Pacific Americans for Progress [17012]
Asian and Pacific Islander Amer. Vote [18345]
Asian and Pacific Islander Inst. on Domestic Violence [12022]
Asian Speakers' Bur. [17607]
Asian Stud. Assn. of Australia [IO]
Asiatic Philharmonia Soc. [10557]
Assn. for Asian Amer. Stud. [7982]
Assn. for Asian Stud. [7983]
Assn. for Asian Stud. [IO]
Assn. of South East Asian Stud. in the UK [IO]
Beta Chi Theta Natl. Fraternity [24618]
Black and Asian Stud. Assn. [IO]
Buddhist Churches of Am. Fed. of Buddhist Women's Associations [19543]
Burma-America Buddhist Assn. [19546]
Canadian Asian Stud. Assn. [IO]
Canadian Guild of Pakistani Women [IO]
Canadian Soc. for Mesopotamian Stud. [IO]
Champa Cultural Preservation Assn. of USA [11082]
China Medical Bd. of New York [14976]
China Times Cultural Found. [7984]
China Times Cultural Found. [IO]
Chinese-American Arts Coun. [9608]
Coalition of Asian Pacifics in Entertainment [1300]
Comm. on Res. Materials on Southeast Asia [10349]
Conf. on Asian History [9617]
Cultural Integration Fellowship [9618]
Delta Phi Omega Sorority [24705]
East-West Cultural Center [9619]
European Assn. for Southeast Asian Stud. [IO]
Filipinas Americas Sci. and Art Found. [9609]
First Zen Inst. of Am. [19549]
French Assn. for Res. on South-East Asia [IO]
Gay Asian Pacific Alliance [12228]
German Assn. for Asian Stud. [IO]
Honolulu Japanese Chamber of Commerce [24348]
Independent Scholars of Asia [9957]
Indian Dental Assn., U.S.A. [14157]
Indonesian Stud. Comm. [9620]
Indus Women Leaders [18003]
Inst. of Asian Res. [IO]
Inst. for the Intl. Educ. of Students [IO]
Inst. for the Intl. Educ. of Students [7985]
Intercollegiate Taiwanese Amer. Students Assn. [19401]
Intl. Assn. of Asian Crime Investigators [5636]
Intl. Assn. of Asian Stud. [7986]
Intl. Assn. of Asian Stud. [IO]
Intl. Betta Cong. [22441]
Intl. Feng Shui Guild [9906]
Intl. Soc. for Japanese Philately [22830]
Iota Nu Delta Fraternity [24631]
Japan Aikido Assn. U.S.A. [23595]
Japan Convention Bur. [24341]
Japan External Trade Org. [24342]
Japan Info. Access Proj. [10265]
Japan Light Machinery Info. Center of Central New York [24343]
Japan Natl. Tourist Org. [24344]
Kappa Phi Gamma Sorority [24712]
Law Enforcement Assn. of Asian Pacifics [19201]
Leadership Educ. for Asian Pacifics [9621]
Mai Wah Soc. [9622]
Mai Wah Soc. [IO]
Malaysia/Singapore/Brunei Stud. Gp. of the Southeast Asia Coun. Assn. for Asian Stud. [IO]

Malaysia/Singapore/Brunei Stud. Gp. of the Southeast Asia Coun. Assn. for Asian Stud. [7987]
Malaysian Br. of the Royal Asiatic Soc. [IO]
Mexican Epigraphic Soc. [10130]
Natl. Asian Pacific Center on Aging [11300]
Natl. Assn. for Asian and Pacific Amer. Educ. [7988]
Natl. Assn. for Direct Care Workers of Color [14709]
Natl. Coun. of Asian Pacific Americans [17013]
New Zealand Asian Stud. Soc. [IO]
Nordic Assn. for South Asian Stud. [IO]
Nordic Inst. of Asian Stud. [IO]
North Amer. South Asian Bar Assn. [5527]
Occupied Japan Club [22098]
Oriental Stud. Inst. [IO]
Origami USA [22771]
Pacific Asia Travel Assn. [3933]
Permanent Intl. Altaistic Conf. [7989]
Permanent Intl. Altaistic Conf. [IO]
Pi Delta Psi Fraternity [24649]
Royal Asiatic Soc. of Great Britain and Ireland [IO]
Royal Asiatic Soc. - Hong Kong Br. [IO]
Royal Soc. for Asian Affairs [IO]
Sigma Beta Rho Fraternity [24656]
Singapore Netherlands Assn. [IO]
Soc. for Asian Art [9472]
Soc. for Asian and Comparative Philosophy [10831]
Soc. for Asian Music [10699]
Soc. for East Asian Anthropology [6429]
Soc. for South Asian Stud. [IO]
South Asian Amer. Leaders of Tomorrow [18667]
Southeast Asia Rsrc. Action Center [12820]
Sumi-e Soc. of Am. [9475]
U.S.-Vietnam Trade Coun. [17010]
Vietnamese Canadian Fed. [IO]
Volunteers in Asia [13407]
Western Young Buddhist League [19558]
Zen Stud. Soc. [19559]
Asian Acad. of Aesthetic Dentistry [IO], Jakarta, Indonesia
Asian-African Legal Consultative Comm. [★IO]
Asian-African Legal Consultative Org. [IO], New Delhi, India
Asian Aid Org. [IO], Wauchope, Australia
Asian-American
Amer. Citizens for Justice [17083]
APPEAL: Asian Pacific Partners for Empowerment and Leadership [11760]
Asia Am. Initiative [11762]
The Asia Found. [17005]
ASIAN [18974]
Asian Amer. Architects and Engineers [6470]
Asian Amer. Arts Alliance [9552]
Asian Amer. Arts Centre [9553]
Asian Amer. Center for Justice of the Amer. Citizens for Justice [17094]
Asian Amer. Govt. Executives Network [5704]
Asian Amer. Journalists Assn. [3088]
Asian Amer. Legal Defense and Educ. Fund [17095]
Asian Amer. MultiTechnology Assn. [1204]
Asian Amer. Music Soc. [10556]
Asian Amer./Pacific Islander Nurses Assn. [15463]
Asian Amer. Real Estate Assn. [3299]
Asian Americans/Pacific Islanders in Philanthropy [12710]
Asian/Pacific Amer. Heritage Assn. [18972]
Asian Pacific Amer. Labor Alliance [24003]
Asian Pacific Americans for Progress [17012]
Asiatic Philharmonia Soc. [10557]
Before Columbus Found. [10416]
Iota Nu Delta Fraternity [24631]
Media Action Network for Asian Americans [18029]
Natl. Asian Amer. Pacific Islander Mental Hea. Assn. [15215]
Natl. Asian Amer. Soc. of Accountants [42]
Natl. Asian Peace Officers' Assn. [5983]
Natl. Assn. of Asian Amer. Law Enforcement Commanders [5984]
Natl. Assn. of Asian Amer. Professionals [9623]

Natl. Assn. of Medical Minority Educators [8868]
Natl. Coalition for Asian Pacific Amer. Community Development [11785]
Natl. Cong. of Vietnamese Americans [19425]
Natl. Coun. of Asian Amer. Bus. Associations [774]
Natl. Coun. of Asian Pacific Americans [17013]
Natl. Fed. of Asian-Amer. United Methodists [20266]
North Amer. South Asian Bar Assn. [5527]
Panamerican/PanAfrican Assn. [17371]
Pi Delta Psi Fraternity [24649]
Soc. for Asian Art [9472]
South Asian Amer. Leaders of Tomorrow [18667]
South Asian Amer. Voting Youth [18366]
Union of North Amer. Vietnamese Students Assn. [19426]
U.S.-Asia Inst. [17009]
Vietnamese Amer. Coun. [19427]
Vietnamese Medical Assn. of the U.S.A. [15183]
Asian Amer. Architects and Engineers [6470], c/o Samantha S. Low, Membership Chair, The Albert Gp., 114 Sansome St., Ste. 710, San Francisco, CA 94104, (415)957-8788
Asian Amer. Arts Alliance [9552], 155 Ave. of the Americas, 6th Fl., New York, NY 10013, (212)941-9208
Asian Amer. Arts Centre [9553], 26 Bowery St., New York, NY 10013, (212)233-2154
Asian Amer. Arts Centre [IO], New York, NY, United States
Asian Amer. Arts and Culture; Alliance for [★9552]
Asian Amer. Caucus for Disarmament - Address unknown since 1995.
Asian Amer. Center for Justice of the Amer. Citizens for Justice [17094]
Asian Amer. Certified Public Accountants - Address unknown since 2001.
Asian Amer. Curriculum Proj. [8598], 529 E 3rd Ave., San Mateo, CA 94401, (650)375-8286
Asian Amer. Curriculum Proj. [IO], San Mateo, CA, United States
Asian Amer. Dance Theater [★IO]
Asian Amer. Dance Theater [★9553]
Asian Amer. Free Labor Inst. - Defunct.
Asian Amer. Govt. Executives Network [5704], 1001 Connecticut Ave. NW, Ste. 530, Washington, DC 20036, (202)423-6801
Asian Amer. Govt. Executives Network [IO], Washington, DC, United States
Asian Amer. Hotel Owners Assn. [IO], Atlanta, GA, United States
Asian Amer. Hotel Owners Assn. [1930], 66 Lenox Pointe NE, Atlanta, GA 30324-3170, (404)816-5759
Asian Amer. Importers Assn. [226], 1407 Broadway, Ste. 2106, New York, NY 10018-3617, (212)239-8120
Asian Amer. Journalists Assn. [3088], 1182 Market St., Ste. 320, San Francisco, CA 94102, (415)346-2051
Asian Amer. Justice Center [5470], 1140 Connecticut Ave. NW, Ste. 1200, Washington, DC 20036, (202)296-2300
Asian Amer. Legal Defense and Educ. Fund [17095], 99 Hudson St., 12th Fl., New York, NY 10013, (212)966-5932
Asian Amer. Librarians Assn. - Defunct.
Asian Amer. MultiTechnology Assn. [1204], PO Box 7522, Menlo Park, CA 94026-7522, (650)738-1480
Asian Amer. Music Soc. [10556], 39 Eton Overlook, Rockville, MD 20850, (301)424-3379
Asian Amer./Pacific Islander Nurses Assn. [15463], c/o SeonAe Yeo, PhD, Pres., Univ. of Michigan, School of Nursing, Div. of Hea. Promotion and Risk Reduction, 400 N Ingalls St., Ste. 3160, Ann Arbor, MI 48109-0482
Asian Amer./Pacific Islander Nurses Assn. [IO], Ann Arbor, MI, United States
Asian Amer. Psychological Assn. - Defunct.
Asian Amer. Real Estate Assn. [3299], 6600 Sands Point, Ste. 210, Houston, TX 77074, (281)275-4419
Asian Amer. Telecommunications Assn; Natl. [★17166]

Reference to "IO" in place of a book number signifies that the association may be found in the 45th edition of International Organizations.

Asian-Amer. United Methodists; Natl. Fed. of [20266]

Asian Amer. Voters Coalition - Address unknown since 1999.

Asian Amer. Women; Natl. Assn. of Professional [743]

Asian Amer. Writers' Workshop [4061], 16 W 32nd St., Ste. 10A, New York, NY 10001, (212)494-0061

Asian Americans; Natl. Assn. of Interdisciplinary Stud. for Native Amer., Black, Chicano, Puerto Rican, [★9919]

Asian Americans/Pacific Islanders in Philanthropy [12710], 200 Pine St., Ste. 700, San Francisco, CA 94104, (415)273-2760

Asian Apicultural Assn. [IO], Tokyo, Japan

Asian Art; Soc. for [9472]

Asian Assn. of Agricultural Colleges and Universities [IO], Laguna, Philippines

Asian Assn. of Agricultural Engg. [IO], Pathumthani, Thailand

Asian Assn. of Convention and Visitor Bureaus [IO], Macau, Macao

Asian Assn. for Dynamic Osteosynthesis [IO], Hong Kong, People's Republic of China

Asian Assn. of Mgt. Organisations [IO], New Delhi, India

Asian Assn. of Social Psychology [IO], Wellington, New Zealand

Asian - Australasian Soc. of Neurological Surgeons [IO], Chennai, India

Asian Badminton Confed. [IO], Kuala Lumpur, Malaysia

Asian Benevolent Corps [★9613]

Asian Bus. League of San Francisco [696], 564 Market St., Ste. 404, San Francisco, CA 94104, (415)350-9023

Asian Cassava Res. Network [IO], Bangkok, Thailand

Asian Cinema Stud. Soc. [IO], Drexel Hill, PA, United States

Asian Cinema Stud. Soc. [7981], c/o Dr. John A. Lent, Chm./Ed., 669 Ferne Blvd., Drexel Hill, PA 19026, (215)204-8348

Asian CineVision [9930], 133 W 19th St., Ste. 300, New York, NY 10011-4117, (212)989-1422

Asian Clearing Union [IO], Tehran, Iran

Asian Coalition for Housing Rights [IO], Bangkok, Thailand

Asian Coalition of Human Rights Orgs. - Address unknown since 2002.

Asian Communities; CAAAV: Organizing [★17006]

Asian Community Intl. Policy Res. [★IO]

Asian and Comparative Philosophy; Soc. for [10831]

Asian Composers' League [IO], Seoul, Republic of Korea

Asian Confed. of Credit Unions [IO], Bangkok, Thailand

Asian Conservation Laboratory - Defunct.

Asian Corporate Governance Assn. [IO], Hong Kong, People's Republic of China

Asian Coun. of Logistics Mgt. [IO], Calcutta, India

Asian Cultural Forum on Development - U.S.A. - Defunct.

Asian Dermatological Assn. [IO], Hong Kong, People's Republic of China

Asian Development Bank [IO], Manila, Philippines

Asian Development Bank Staff Assn. [IO], Mandaluyong City, Philippines

Asian Disaster Preparedness Center [IO], Pathumthani, Thailand

Asian Energy Inst. [IO], New Delhi, India

Asian Fed. of Advt. Associations [IO], Petaling Jaya, Malaysia

Asian Fed. Against Involuntary Disappearances [IO], Quezon City, Philippines

Asian Financial Soc. [1400], PO Box 568, Bowling Green Sta., New York, NY 10274-0568, (212)479-8405

Asian Fisheries Soc. [IO], Quezon City, Philippines

Asian Folklore Stud. Gp. [★IO]

Asian Folklore Stud. Gp. [★9957]

Asian Food Info. Centre [IO], Singapore, Singapore

Asian Football Confed. [IO], Kuala Lumpur, Malaysia

Asian Forum of Parliamentarians on Population and Development [IO], Bangkok, Thailand

Asian Handball Fed. [IO], Safat, Kuwait

Asian Hea. Inst. [IO], Nisshin, Japan

Asian Hockey Fed. [IO], Kuala Lumpur, Malaysia

Asian Hosp. Fed. [IO], Tokyo, Japan

Asian Human Rights Commn. [IO], Hong Kong, People's Republic of China

Asian-Indian

Asian Indian Chamber of Commerce [24228]

Asian Indian Chamber of Commerce [24228], ITM Corporate Ctr., 6 Kilmer Rd., Ste. J, Edison, NJ 08817, (732)777-4666

Asian-Indian Women in America - Address unknown since 2003.

Asian Indians in Am; Assn. of [★19110]

Asian Inst. for Development Commun. [IO], Kuala Lumpur, Malaysia

Asian Inst. of Gemological Sciences, Bangkok [IO], Bangkok, Thailand

Asian Inst. of Mgt. [IO], Makati City, Philippines

Asian Inst. of Tech. [IO], Pathumthani, Thailand

Asian Inst. of Tech. Alumni Assn. [IO], Pathumthani, Thailand

Asian Inst. of Tourism [IO], Quezon City, Philippines

Asian Law Caucus [5928], 939 Market St., Ste. 201, San Francisco, CA 94103, (415)896-1701

Asian Literature Div. of MLA - Defunct.

Asian Media Coalition - Defunct.

Asian Media Info. and Commun. Centre [IO], Singapore, Singapore

Asian Medical Student's Assn. - Philippines [IO], Manila, Philippines

Asian Network for Free Elections [IO], Bangkok, Thailand

Asian NGO Coalition for Agrarian Reform and Rural Development [IO], Quezon City, Philippines

Asian-Oceanian Computing Indus. Org. [IO], Tokyo, Japan

Asian and Oceanian Epilepsy Assn. [IO], New Delhi, India

Asian Org. of Supreme Audit Institutions [IO], New Delhi, India

Asian and Pacific Amer. Educ; Natl. Assn. for [7988]

Asian Pacific Amer. Families Against Substance Abuse; Natl. [13258]

Asian/Pacific Amer. Heritage Assn. [18972], 6220 Westpark, Ste. 245B, Houston, TX 77057, (713)784-1112

Asian Pacific Amer. Heritage Coun. [18973]

Asian Pacific Amer. Labor Alliance [24003], 815 16th St. NW, Washington, DC 20006, (202)508-3733

Asian and Pacific Amers. for Nuclear Awareness - Address unknown since 1995.

Asian Pacific Americans for Progress [17012], 215 S Santa Fe Ave., No. 3, Los Angeles, CA 90012, (213)453-1986

Asian and Pacific Assn. for Social Work Educ. [IO], Hong Kong, People's Republic of China

Asian Pacific Assn. for the Stud. of the Liver [IO], New Delhi, India

Asian and Pacific Associations of Optometrists; Intl. Fed. of [★15715]

Asian Pacific Center on Aging; Natl. [11300]

Asian and Pacific Centre for Transfer of Tech. [IO], New Delhi, India

Asian and Pacific Coconut Community [IO], Jakarta, Indonesia

Asian Pacific Community Hea. Organizations; Assn. of [14719]

Asian Pacific Confed. of Chem. Engg. [IO], Barton, Australia

Asian Pacific Endodontic Confed. [IO], Dandenong, Australia

Asian and Pacific Fed. of Clinical Biochemistry [IO], Singapore, Singapore

Asian Pacific Fed. of Societies for Surgery of the Hand [IO], Bangkok, Thailand

Asian Pacific Fed. of UNESCO Clubs and Associations [IO], Seoul, Republic of Korea

Asian and Pacific Islander Amer. Hea. Forum [14545], 450 Sutter St., Ste. 600, San Francisco, CA 94108, (415)954-9988

Asian and Pacific Islander Amer. Vote [18345], 1666 K St. NW, Ste. 440, Washington, DC 20006, (202)223-9170

Asian and Pacific Islander Inst. on Domestic Violence [12022], 450 Sutter St., Ste. 600, San Francisco, CA 94108, (415)954-9988

Asian Pacific Partners for Empowerment and Leadership; APPEAL: [11760]

Asian and Pacific Professional Language and Education Services - Defunct.

Asian-Pacific Regional Res. and Training Centre for Integrated Fish Farming [IO], Wuxi, People's Republic of China

Asian-Pacific Rsrc. and Res. Centre for Women [IO], Kuala Lumpur, Malaysia

Asian Pacific Rural and Agricultural Credit Assn. [IO], Bangkok, Thailand

Asian and Pacific Skill Development Programme [IO], Bangkok, Thailand

Asian-Pacific Soc. of Digestive Endoscopy [IO], Hong Kong, People's Republic of China

Asian Pacific Soc. for Digestive Endoscopy [IO], Hong Kong, People's Republic of China

Asian-Pacific Soc. of Nephrology [IO], Parkville, Australia

Asian-Pacific Soc. of Respirology [IO], Tokyo, Japan

Asian Pacifics; Leadership Educ. for [9621]

Asian Pan-Pacific Soc. for Paediatric Gastroenterology Hepatology and Nutrition [IO], Singapore, Singapore

Asian Pan-Pacific Soc. for Paediatric Gastroenterology and Nutrition [★IO]

Asian Pan-Pacific Soc. for Pediatric Gastroenterology, Hepatology and Nutrition [IO], Brisbane, Australia

Asian People's Friendship Soc. [IO], Tokyo, Japan

Asian Physics Educ. Network - UNESCO Representative [IO], Jakarta, Indonesia

Asian Planning Schools Assn. [IO], Hong Kong, People's Republic of China

Asian Political Scientists Group in U.S.A. - Defunct.

Asian Productivity Org. [IO], Tokyo, Japan

Asian Professional Security Assn. - Hong Kong Chap. [IO], Hong Kong, People's Republic of China

Asian Professional Security Assn. - Malaysia Chap. [IO], Petaling Jaya, Malaysia

Asian Professional Security Assn. - Singapore Chap. [IO], Singapore, Singapore

Asian Racing Fed. [IO], Sydney, Australia

Asian Regional Exchange for New Alternatives [IO], Hong Kong, People's Republic of China

Asian Regional Training and Development Org. [★IO]

Asian Reinsurance Corp. [IO], Bangkok, Thailand

Asian Relations; Commn. on U.S.- [★17010]

Asian Rsrc. Center on Aging; Natl. Pacific/ [★11300]

Asian Resources [12069], 5709 Stockton Blvd., Sacramento, CA 95824, (916)454-1892

Asian Rural Inst. [IO], Tochigi, Japan

Asian Securities Analysts Fed. [IO], Tokyo, Japan

Asian Sleep Res. Soc. [IO], Nagoya, Japan

Asian Soc. for Cardiovascular Surgery [IO], Tokyo, Japan

Asian Soc. for Environmental Geotechnology [IO], Nanjing, People's Republic of China

Asian Soc. for Environmental Protection [IO], Pathumthani, Thailand

Asian Soc. for Pigment Cell Res. [IO], Chandigarh, India

Asian Speakers' Bur. [17607], 18600 Walkers Choice Rd., Ste. 4, Montgomery Village, Gaithersburg, MD 20886, (301)990-8831

Asian Statistical Inst. [★IO]

Asian Studies

Amer. Schools of Oriental Res. [9615]

Center for Teaching About China [8552]

Chinese Historians in the U.S. [8503]

Conf. on Asian History [9617]

Coun. of Teachers of Southeast Asian Languages [7990]

Gp. of Universities for the Advancement of Vietnamese Abroad [9296]

Malaysia/Singapore/Brunei Stud. Gp. of the Southeast Asia Coun. Assn. for Asian Stud. [7987]

Natl. Coun. of Japanese Language Teachers [9226]

Soc. for East Asian Anthropology [6429]

South Asian Language Teachers Assn. [7991]

Asian Stud. Assn. of Australia [IO], Canberra, Australia

A star before a book entry number signifies that the name is not listed separately, but is mentioned within the entry.

Asian Stud; Inst. of [★7985]
Asian Stud; Inst. of European and [★7985]
Asian Surgical Assn. [IO], Hong Kong, People's Republic of China
Asian TV Australia Assn. [IO], Footscray, Australia
Asian Tennis Fed. [IO], Hong Kong, People's Republic of China
Asian Vegetable Res. and Development Center [IO], Tainan, Taiwan
Asian Wetland Bur. [★IO]
Asian Women in Action; Black, Indian, Hispanic, and [13420]
Asian Women in Bus. [697], 358 5th Ave., Ste. 504, New York, NY 10001, (212)868-1368
Asian Women in Bus. [IO], New York, NY, United States
Asian Women's Assn. [★IO]
Asian Women's Human Rights Coun. [IO], Bangalore, India
Asian Women's Rsrc. Centre for Culture and Theology [IO], Kuala Lumpur, Malaysia
Asian Worldwide Elvis Fan Club [24805], PO Box 19132, Houston, TX 77224-9132
Asian Youth Centre [IO], Chennai, India
Asian Youth Orchestra [IO], Hong Kong, People's Republic of China
Asiatic Breeders Association [IO], Tucson, AZ, United States
Asiatic Breeders Assn. [4192], c/o Joyce Baum, Pres., PO Box 8265, Tucson, AZ 85738, (928)474-3322
Asiatic Parrot Assn. Intl. - Address unknown since 2006.
Asiatic Philharmonia Soc. [10557], PO Box 2799, Sunnyvale, CA 94087, (408)331-4909
ASID Educational Found. [★2251]
ASIS Intl. [2083], 1625 Prince St., Alexandria, VA 22314-2818, (703)519-6200
ASIS Intl. [IO], Alexandria, VA, United States
Ask a Friend to Explain Reconstruction - Defunct.
Ask Us - Defunct.
Askio Disabled People Switzerland [IO], Bern, Switzerland
Asleep At The Wheel Fan Club [24844], PO Box 463, Austin, TX 78767, (512)444-9885
ASM Found. for Educ. and Research [★7311]
ASM Found. for Educ. and Research [★IO]
ASM Intl. [IO], Novelty, OH, United States
ASM Intl. [7311], 9639 Kinsman Rd., Novelty, OH 44073-0002, (440)338-5151
ASME Intl. Gas Turbine Inst. [7001], 5775-C Glenridge Dr., No. 115, Atlanta, GA 30328, (404)847-0072
ASME Intl. Gas Turbine Inst. [IO], Atlanta, GA, United States
Asmita Women's Publishing House, Media and Rsrc. Org. [IO], Kathmandu, Nepal
ASMP - The Soc. of Photographers in Communications [★2992]
Asocacion Colombiana de Terapia Ocupacional [IO], Bogota, Colombia
Asociacao Fiscal Portuguesa [★IO]
Asociacao Interamericana de Engenharia Sanitaria [★IO]
Asociacao Interamericana de Engenharia Sanitaria [★7589]
Asociace fotografu [★IO]
Asociace ceskych pojistovacich makleru [★IO]
Asociace sklarskeho a keramickeho prumyslu Ceske republiky [★IO]
Asociace Ceskych Cestovnich Kancelari a Agentur [★IO]
Asociace Ceskych Reklamnich Agentur a Marketingove Komunikace [★IO]
Asociace Cestovnich Kancelari Ceske Republiky [★IO]
Asociace Skolnich Sportovnich Klubu CR [★IO]
Asociacia Marfanovho Syndromu [★IO]
Asociacia Public Relations Slovenskej Republiky [★IO]
Asociacia Slovenskych Geomorfologov [★IO]
Asociacija Lietuvos Keliai [★IO]
Asociacio Uruguaya de la Rosa [★IO]
Asociacion internacional de relaciones del trabajo [★IO]

Asociacion de Administradores de Riesgos de la Republica Argentina [IO], Buenos Aires, Argentina
Asociacion de Afectados Sindrome de Marfan [IO], Alicante, Spain
Asociacion de Amigos de los Amigos [★20045]
Asociacion Andar Costa Rica [IO], San Jose, Costa Rica
Asociacion Argentina de Agencias de Publicidad [★IO]
Asociacion Argentina de Agencias de Viajes y Turismo [★IO]
Asociacion Argentina de Aikido [IO], Buenos Aires, Argentina
Asociacion Argentina de Baile Deportivo [IO], San Isidro, Argentina
Asociacion Argentina de Biologia y Medicina Nuclear [★IO]
Asociacion Argentina de Codificacion de Productos Comerciales [★IO]
Asociacion Argentina de Companias de Seguros [★IO]
Asociacion Argentina de Dermatologia [★IO]
Asociacion Argentina de Ecologia [★IO]
Asociacion Argentina de Economia Politica [IO], Buenos Aires, Argentina
Asociacion Argentina de Editores de Revistas [★IO]
Asociacion Argentina para el Estudio del Dolor [IO], Buenos Aires, Argentina
Asociacion Argentina de Franchising [★IO]
Asociacion Argentina de Geofisicos y Geodestas [★IO]
Asociacion Argentina de Ginecologia y Obstetricia Psicosomatica [★IO]
Asociacion Argentina de Grasas y Aceites [★IO]
Asociacion Argentina de Huntington [★IO]
Asociacion Argentina de Informatica Medica [★IO]
Asociacion Argentina de Investigaciones Eticas [★IO]
Asociacion Argentina de Marketing [★IO]
Asociacion Argentina de Medicos por el Medio Ambiente [★IO]
Asociacion Argentina de Ortopedia y Traumatologia [★IO]
Asociacion Argentina de Osteologia y Metabolismo Mineral [IO], Buenos Aires, Argentina
Asociacion Argentina de Proteccion Familiar [IO], Buenos Aires, Argentina
Asociacion Argentina de Rosicultura [★IO]
Asociacion Argentina de Sedimentologia [IO], La Plata, Argentina
Asociacion Argentina de Squash Rackets [IO], Buenos Aires, Argentina
Asociacion Argentina de TV por Cable [★IO]
Asociacion Argentina de Tenis [IO], Buenos Aires, Argentina
Asociacion Argentina de Terapistas Ocupacionales [IO], Buenos Aires, Argentina
Asociacion Bancaria Costarricense [★IO]
Asociacion Bancaria de Guatemala [★IO]
Asociacion Bancaria de Panama [★IO]
Asociacion Bancaria de Venezuela [★IO]
Asociacion de Bancos de la Argentina [★IO]
Asociacion de Bancos Privados de Bolivia [★IO]
Asociacion de Bancos Privados del Ecuador [★IO]
Asociacion de Bancos Publicos y Privados de la Republica Argentina [★IO]
Asociacion de Bibliotecarios Graduados de la Republica Argentina [★IO]
Asociacion Bioquimica Argentina [★IO]
Asociacion Boliviana de Aseguradores [★IO]
Asociacion Boliviana para Estudio and Tratamiento del Dolor [IO], La Paz, Bolivia
Asociacion Boliviana de Ingenieria Geotecnica [IO], La Paz, Bolivia
Asociacion Chilena de Albergues Turisticos Juveniles [★IO]
Asociacion Chilena de Control Automatico [IO], Santiago, Chile
Asociacion Chilena de Cricket [★IO]
Asociacion Chilena de Empresas Mayoristas y Representantes de Turismo [★IO]
Asociacion Chilena de Empresas de Tecnologias de Informacion [★IO]
Asociacion Chilena de Empresas de Turismo [★IO]
Asociacion Chilena para el Estudio del Dolor [IO], Santiago, Chile

Asociacion Chilena de Proteccion de la Familia [IO], Santiago, Chile
Asociacion Chilena de la Rosa [IO], Santiago, Chile
Asociacion Chilena de Sismologia e Ingenieria Antisismica [★IO]
Asociacion Civil de Planificacion Familiar [IO], Caracas, Venezuela
Asociacion Colombiana para el Avance de la Ciencia [★IO]
Asociacion Colombiana de Baille Deportivo [IO], Manizales, Colombia
Asociacion Colombiana De Fertilidad Y Esterilidad [IO], Barranquilla, Colombia
Asociacion Colombiana de Dermatologia [★IO]
Asociacion Colombiana para el Estudio del Dolor [IO], Bogota, Colombia
Asociacion Colombiana de Exportadores de Flores [★IO]
Asociacion Colombiana de Industrias Plasticas [★IO]
Asociacion Colombiana de Musica Electroacustica [IO], Bogota, Colombia
Asociacion Colombiana de Neurofisiologia Clinica [★IO]
Asociacion Colombiana de Osteologia y Metabolismo Mineral [IO], Bogota, Colombia
Asociacion Colombiana del Petroleo [★IO]
Asociacion Colombiana de Productores de Fonogramas [IO], Bogota, Colombia
Asociacion Colombiana de Psiquiatria [★IO]
Asociacion de Combatientes de la Brigada de Asalto 2506 [★20717]
Asociacion de Comerciantes y Distribuidores de Viveres y Similares de Panama [★IO]
Asociacion de Companias Consultoras del Ecuador [★IO]
Asociacion Cosarricense de Climaterio y Menopausia [IO], San Jose, Costa Rica
Asociacion Costarricense de Badminton [IO], San Jose, Costa Rica
Asociacion Costarricense de Floricultores [★IO]
Asociacion Costarricense de Geotecnia [IO], San Jose, Costa Rica
Asociacion Costarricense de la Industria del Plastico [★IO]
Asociacion Costarricense para Organizaciones de Desarrollo [IO], San Jose, Costa Rica
Asociacion de Cricket Argentino [★IO]
Asociacion Cristiana Femenin de la Republica Argentina [★IO]
Asociacion Cristiana Femenina [★IO]
Asociacion Cristiana Femenina [★13526]
Asociacion Cristiana Femenina de Chile [★IO]
Asociacion Cristiana Femenina de Colombia [★IO]
Asociacion Cristiana Femenina Nacional de la Republica Mexicana [★IO]
Asociacion Cristiana Femenina de Peru [★IO]
Asociacion Cristiana Femenina de Uruguay [★IO]
Asociacion Cristiana Feminina Nacional del Salvador [★IO]
Asociacion Cristiana de Jovenes del Peru [★IO]
Asociacion Cubana de Reconocimiento de Patrones [★IO]
Asociacion de Cultivadores de Cana de Azucar de Colombia [★IO]
Asociacion Demografica Costarricense [★IO]
Asociacion Demografica Salvadorena [★IO]
Asociacion Dental Mexicana [IO], Mexico City, Mexico
Asociacion por los Derechos Civiles [★IO]
Asociacion de Desarrolladores de Videojuegos Argentina [★IO]
Asociacion de Diarios y Revistas del Peru [IO], Lima, Peru
Asociacion de Distribuidores de Golosinas y Afines [★IO]
Asociacion de Distribuidores de Software [★IO]
Asociacion Distrofia Muscular [IO], Buenos Aires, Argentina
Asociacion Dominicana de Empresas de Inversion Extranjera [★IO]
Asociacion Dominicana Pro-Bienestar de la Familia [IO], Santo Domingo, Dominican Republic
Asociacion de Economia de Am. Latina y el Caribe [★IO]

Reference to "IO" in place of a book number signifies that the association may be found in the 45th edition of International Organizations.

Asociacion Ecuatoriana de Editores de Periodicos [★IO]
Asociacion Ecuatoriana de Radiodifusion [★IO]
Asociacion Editores de Diarios de la Ciudad de Buenos Aires [IO], Buenos Aires, Argentina
Asociacion de Editores de Diarios Espanoles [IO], Madrid, Spain
Asociacion de Editores de los Estados [IO], Mexico City, Mexico
Asociacion Empresarial de Fabricantes y Comerciantes Mayoristas de Articulos de Regalo [★IO]
Asociacion de Empresarios Detallistas de Frutas y Hortalizas [★IO]
Asociacion de Entidades Periodisticas Argentinas [IO], Buenos Aires, Argentina
Asociacion de Entidades Periodisticas del Paraguay [IO], Asuncion, Paraguay
Asociacion de fotografos profesionales de Espana [IO], Barcelona, Spain
Asociacion Espanola de Aerosoles [★IO]
Asociacion Espanola de Agencias de Publicidad [★IO]
Asociacion Espanola de Anunciantes [IO], Madrid, Spain
Asociacion Espanola de Baile Deportivo y de Competicion [★IO]
Asociacion Espanola de Codificacion Comercial [★IO]
Asociacion Espanola de Consultores en Ingenieria [IO], Madrid, Spain
Asociacion Espanola Contra La Osteoporosis [★IO]
Asociacion Espanola de Cricket [★IO]
Asociacion Espanola para el Deficit de Alfa-1 [★IO]
Asociacion Espanola de Economia [★IO]
Asociacion Espanola para la Economia Energetica [★IO]
Asociacion Espanola de Empresas de la Carne [★IO]
Asociacion Espanola de Esclerosis Lateral Amiotrofica [IO], Madrid, Spain
Asociacion Espanola de Esclerosis Multiple [★IO]
Asociacion Espanola de Fabricantes de Automoviles y Camiones [★IO]
Asociacion Espanola de Fabricantes de Caramelos y Chicles [★IO]
Asociacion Espanola de Fabricantes Exportadores de Bisuteria [★IO]
Asociacion Espanola de Fabricantes de Juguetes [★IO]
Asociacion Espanola de Fabricantes de Pasta, Papel y Carton [★IO]
Asociacion Espanola de Fabricantes de Pinturas y Tintas de Imprimir [★IO]
Asociacion Espanola de Fisioterapeutas [IO], Madrid, Spain
Asociacion Espanola de Gerencia de Riesgos y Seguros [IO], Madrid, Spain
Asociacion Espanola de la Industria y el Comercio Exportador del Aceite de Oliva [★IO]
Asociacion Espanola de Ingenieria de Proyectos [IO], Valencia, Spain
Asociacion Espanola de Joyeros, Plateros y Relojeros [★IO]
Asociacion Espanola de Operadores de Productos Petroliferos [★IO]
Asociacion Espanola de Productores de Huevos [★IO]
Asociacion Espanola de Reconocimiento de Formas y Analisis de Imagenes [★IO]
Asociacion Espanola de la Rosa [IO], Madrid, Spain
Asociacion Espanola de Sistemas de Informacion Geografica [IO], Madrid, Spain
Asociacion Espanola de Tecnicos de Cerveza y Malta [★IO]
Asociacion Espanola de Unihockey y Floorball [★IO]
Asociacion de Estados del Caribe [★IO]
Asociacion Europea de Coleopterologia [★IO]
Asociacion Europea de Suministradores de Servicios para Personas con Minusvalias Disabilities [★IO]
Asociacion de Exportadores e Industriales de Aceitunas de Mesa [IO],
Asociacion de Exportadores de Manufacturas de Chile [★IO]
Asociacion de Fabricantes Artesanales de Helados y Afines [★IO]

Asociacion de Fabricantes de Cemento Portland [★IO]
Asociacion de Fabricantes y Comercializadores de Aditivos y Complementos Alimentarios [★IO]
Asociacion de Fabricantes de Equipos de Climatizacion [★IO]
Asociacion de Fabricantes de Harinas y Semolas de Espana [★IO]
Asociacion de Fabricantes de Pequenos Electrodomesticos [★IO]
Asociacion de Fabricantes de Riego Espanoles [★IO]
Asociacion de Fabricas de Automotores [★IO]
Asociacion Farmaceutica Mexicana [★IO]
Asociacion Feldenkrais Argentina [IO], Buenos Aires, Argentina
Asociacion Filatelica de Filipinas - Defunct.
Asociacion Filosofica de Mexico [IO], Mexico City, Mexico
Asociacion Fisica Argentina [★IO]
Asociacion de Fisioterapeutas del Uruguay [IO], Montevideo, Uruguay
Asociacion para la Formacion y Actividades Interculturales para la Juventud [★IO]
Asociacion de Gerentes de Guatemala [★IO]
Asociacion Gremial de Empresarios Hoteleros de Chile [★IO]
Asociacion Gremial de Industriales de la Goma [★IO]
Asociacion Gremial de Industriales Quimicos de Chiles [★IO]
Asociacion Gremial de Pequenos y Medianos Industriales Metalurgicos [★IO]
Asociacion Gremial de Supermercados de Chile [★IO]
Asociacion Guatemalteca De Fertilidad Y Reproduccion Humana [IO], Guatemala City, Guatemala
Asociacion Guatemalteca de Deportes Aereos [IO], Guatemala City, Guatemala
Asociacion Guatemalteca de Dermatologia [IO], Antigua, Guatemala
Asociacion Guatemalteca de Espina Bifida [IO], Guatemala City, Guatemala
Asociacion Guatemalteca de Medicina Deportiva [IO], Guatemala City, Guatemala
Asociacion Hondurena de Instituciones Bancarias [★IO]
Asociacion Hondurena de Maquiladores [★IO]
Asociacion de Hoteles de Turismo de la Republica Argentina [★IO]
Asociacion de la Industria de la Piel para el Comercio Exterior [★IO]
Asociacion de la Industria del Salmon [★IO]
Asociacion Indus. Textil de Proceso Algodonero [★IO]
Asociacion de Industriales del Estado de Mexico [★IO]
Asociacion de Industriales Metalurgico y Mineria de Venezuela [★IO]
Asociacion de Industriales Metalurgicos de la Republica Argentina [★IO]
Asociacion de Industrias de la Carne de Espana [★IO]
Asociacion de Industrias Metalurgicas y Metalmecanicas [★IO]
Asociacion de Ingenieros Cubanos [7002], PO Box 557575, Miami, FL 33255-7575
Asociacion de Ingenieros y Tecnicos del Automotor [★IO]
Asociacion de Inquilinos del Ecuador [IO], Quito, Ecuador
Asociacion Interamericana de Contabilidad [★IO]
Asociacion Interamericana de Contabilidad [★35]
Asociacion Interamericana de Intenieria Sanitaria [★7589]
Asociacion Interamericana de Intenieria Sanitaria [★IO]
Asociacion Interamericana de la Propiedad Indus. [★IO]
Asociacion Internacional de Asmologia [★IO]
Asociacion Internacional de Ecologia [★IO]
Asociacion Internacional de Estudios en Comunicacion Social [★IO]
Asociacion Internacional de Expertos Cientificos del Turismo [★IO]

Asociacion Internacional de Ferias de Am. [★IO]
Asociacion Internacional de Hidrogeologos Grupo Espanol [★IO]
Asociacion Internacional de Hispanistas [★IO]
Asociacion Internacional de Lectura [★IO]
Asociacion Internacional de Lectura [★9043]
Asociacion Intl. de Escritores Policiacos [★IO]
Asociacion Latinoamericana de Administradores de Riesgos y Seguros [IO], Sao Paulo, Brazil
Asociacion Latinoamericana de Botanica [★IO]
Asociacion Latinoamericana de Diabetes [★IO]
Asociacion Latinoamericana de Fitopatologia [★IO]
Asociacion Latinoamericana de Instituciones Financieras Para el Desarrollo [★IO]
Asociacion Latinoamericana de Investigadores de la Comunicacion [★IO]
Asociacion Latinoamericana de Organizaciones de Promocion [★IO]
Asociacion Latinoamericana del Torax [★IO]
Asociacion de Lineas Aereas Internacionales [★IO]
Asociacion de Madereros de Honduras [★IO]
Asociacion Madres de Plaza de Mayo [★IO]
Asociacion de Marketing Bancario Argentino [★IO]
Asociacion Medica Argentina [IO], Buenos Aires, Argentina
Asociacion Medica Nacional de la Republica de Panama [IO], Panama City, Panama
Asociacion Mexicana de Agencias de Investigacion de Mercado y Opinion Publica [★IO]
Asociacion Mexicana de Agencias de Investigacion de Mercado y Opinion Publica [★IO]
Asociacion Mexicana de Agencias de Publicidad [★IO]
Asociacion Mexicana Automovilistica [★IO]
Asociacion Mexicana De la Enfermidad De Huntington I.A.P. [IO], Mexico City, Mexico
Asociacion Mexicana de Distribuidores de Automotores [★IO]
Asociacion Mexicana de Distribuidores de Maquinaria [★IO]
Asociacion Mexicana de Estandares papa el Comercio Electronico [★IO]
Asociacion Mexicana de Fabricantes de Articulos para Regalo, Decoracion y Artesanias [★IO]
Asociacion Mexicana de Facultades y Escuelas de Medicina [IO], Mexico City, Mexico
Asociacion Mexicana de Hoteles y Moteles [IO], Mexico City, Mexico
Asociacion Mexicana de la Industria Automotriz [IO], Mexico City, Mexico
Asociacion Mexicana de Mecatronica [★IO]
Asociacion Mexicana de Parques Industriales [★IO]
Asociacion Mexicana de Productores de Fonogramas AC [IO], Mexico City, Mexico
Asociacion Mexicana de Profesionales de Ferias, Exposiciones y Convenciones [★IO]
Asociacion Mexicana de Restaurantes [★IO]
Asociacion Mexicana de Tecnicos de las Industrias de Celulosa y del Papel [★IO]
Asociacion Mexicana de Voluntarios [IO], Ciudad Obregon, Mexico
Asociacion de Mujeres Universitarias de El Salvador [IO], San Salvador, El Salvador
Asociacion de Mujeres Universitarias de Vizcaya [IO], Lejona, Spain
Asociacion Mundial de las Guias Scouts [★IO]
Asociacion Mundial Veterinaria de Avicola [★IO]
Asociacion de Musica Electroacustica de Espana [IO], Barcelona, Spain
Asociacion Mutual Israelita Argentina [★IO]
Asociacion Nacional de Actores [IO], San Rafael, Mexico
Asociacion Nacional de Anunciantes Colombia [IO], Bogota, Colombia
Asociacion Nacional de Anunciantes del Peru [IO], Lima, Peru
Asociacion Nacional de Anunciantes-Venezuela [★IO]
Asociacion Nacional de Anunciantes - Venezuela [IO], Caracas, Venezuela
Asociacion Nacional de Arrendadores de Vehiculos [★IO]
Asociacion Nacional de Avisadores [IO], Santiago, Chile
Asociacion Nacional de Comerciantes en Automoviles [★IO]

A star before a book entry number signifies that the name is not listed separately, but is mentioned within the entry.

Asociacion Nacional Contra el Cancer **[IO]**, Panama City, Panama
Asociacion Nacional de Cultivadores de Palma Africana **[★IO]**
Asociacion Nacional de Distribuidores de Llantas y Plantas Renovadoras **[★IO]**
Asociacion Nacional de Economistas y Contadores de Cuba **[★IO]**
Asociacion Nacional de la Empresa Privada **[★IO]**
Asociacion Nacional Empresarial de la Industria Farmaceutica **[★IO]**
Asociacion Nacional de Empresas de Aguas de Bebida Envasada **[★IO]**
Asociacion Nacional de Empresas Comercializadoras de Productores del Campo **[★IO]**
Asociacion Nacional Espanola de Distribuidores Automaticos **[★IO]**
Asociacion Nacional de Especialidades Farmaceuticas Publicitarias **[★IO]**
Asociacion Nacional de Estabelecimientos Financieros de Creditos **[★IO]**
Asociacion Nacional de Exportadores de Cacao **[★IO]**
Asociacion Nacional de Fabricantes de Bebidas Refrescantes Analcoholicas **[★IO]**
Asociacion Nacional de Fabricantes de Chocolate, Dulces y Similares **[★IO]**
Asociacion Nacional de Fabricantes e Importadores de Electrodomesticos de Linea Blanca **[★IO]**
Asociacion Nacional de Fabricantes de Pinturas y Tintas **[★IO]**
Asociacion Nacional de Fisioterapistas de Guatemala **[IO]**, Guatemala City, Guatemala
Asociacion Nacional de Hoteles y Restaurantes **[★IO]**
Asociacion Nacional de Importadores y Exportadores **[★IO]**
Asociacion Nacional de la Industria del Cafe **[★IO]**
Asociacion Nacional de la Industria Quimica **[★IO]**
Asociacion Nacional de Industriales de Honduras **[IO]**
Asociacion Nacional de Industrias de Aceites y Mantecas Comestibles **[★IO]**
Asociacion Nacional de Industrias del Plastico **[★IO]**
Asociacion Nacional de Instituciones Financieras **[★IO]**
Asociacion Nacional pro Personas Mayores - Address unknown since 2000.
Asociacion Nacional de la Prensa - Chile **[IO]**, Santiago, Chile
Asociacion Nacional de Productores de Semillas de Chile **[★IO]**
Asociacion Nacional de Proveedores de la Industria del Calzado **[★IO]**
Asociacion Nacional de Proveedores para la Industria del Calzado **[★IO]**
Asociacion Nacional de la Publicidad **[IO]**, Mexico City, Mexico
Asociacion Nacional de la Publicidad **[★IO]**
Asociacion Nacional de Scouts de Panama **[★IO]**
Asociacion Nacional de Squash de Guatemala **[IO]**, Guatemala City, Guatemala
Asociacion Nacional de Supermercados y Autoservicios **[★IO]**
Asociacion Nacional de Tiendas de Autoservicio y Departamentales **[★IO]**
Asociacion Nacional de Vendedores Vehiculos a Motor Reparacion y Recambios **[★IO]**
Asociacion Odontologica Argentina **[★IO]**
Asociacion de Orquideologia de Quito **[IO]**, Quito, Ecuador
Asociacion de Padres de Personas con Autismo **[★IO]**
Asociacion Paleontologica Argentina **[★IO]**
Asociacion Panamena de Fisioterapia Kinesiologia **[IO]**, Panama City, Panama
Asociacion Panamena de Juego de Damas **[IO]**, Panama City, Panama
Asociacion Panamena para el Planeamiento de la Familia **[★IO]**
Asociacion Panamena de Taekwondo **[IO]**, Panama City, Panama
Asociacion Panamericana de Instituciones de Credito Educativo **[★IO]**
Asociacion Paraguaya de Aikido **[IO]**, Asuncion, Paraguay

Asociacion Paraguaya de Tenis **[IO]**, Asuncion, Paraguay
Asociacion Peruana de Agencias de Publicidad **[★IO]**
Asociacion Peruana de Arquitetura del Paisaje **[IO]**, Lima, Peru
Asociacion Peruana para la Conservacion de la Naturaleza **[★IO]**
Asociacion Peruana para el Estudio del Dolor **[IO]**, Lima, Peru
Asociacion Petroquimica y Quimica Latinoamericana **[★IO]**
Asociacion de la Prensa Profesional **[★IO]**
Asociacion Pro-Bienestar de la Familia Colombiana **[IO]**, Bogota, Colombia
Asociacion Pro-Bienestar de la Familia Ecuatoriana **[IO]**, Guayaquil, Ecuador
Asociacion Pro Bienestar de la Familia de Guatemala **[IO]**, Guatemala City, Guatemala
Asociacion Pro-Bienestar de la Familia Nicaraguense **[IO]**, Managua, Nicaragua
Asociacion de Productores de Azucar de Honduras **[★IO]**
Asociacion de Productores Fonograficos de Venezuela **[IO]**, Caracas, Venezuela
Asociacion de Productores de Salmon y Trucha de Chile **[★IO]**
Asociacion de Productores de Vinos Finos de Exportacion **[★IO]**
Asociacion Puertorriquena Pro-Bienestar de la Familia **[IO]**, San Juan, PR, United States
Asociacion Puertorriquena Pro-Bienestar de la Familia **[12176]**, PO Box 192221, San Juan, PR 00919-2221, (787)765-7373
Asociacion Regional de Empresas de Petroleo, Gas Natural en Latino Am., el Caribe **[★IO]**
Asociacion de Revistas de Informacion **[IO]**, Madrid, Spain
Asociacion Rural del Paraguay **[★IO]**
Asociacion Salvadorena de Industriales **[★IO]**
Asociacion Salvemos Los Ninos de Honduras **[★IO]**
Asociacion de Teleradiodifusoras Argentinas **[★IO]**
Asociacion de TV Educativa Iberoamericana **[★IO]**
Asociacion Universitaria Iberoamericana de Postgrado **[★IO]**
Asociacion Uruguaya de Badminton **[IO]**, Montevideo, Uruguay
Asociacion Uruguaya para el Estudio del Dolor **[IO]**, Montevideo, Uruguay
Asociacion Uruguaya de Planificacion Familiar **[★IO]**
Asociacion Uruguaya de Psicoterapia Psicoanalitica **[★IO]**
Asociacion Uruguaya de Tenis **[IO]**, Montevideo, Uruguay
Asociacion Uruguaya para la Tutela Organizada de los derechos Reprograficos **[IO]**, Montevideo, Uruguay
Asociacion de Usuarios de la Zona Libre de Colon **[★IO]**
Asociacion Venezolana para el Estudio del Dolor **[IO]**, Caracas, Venezuela
Asociacion Venezolana de Exportadores **[★IO]**
Asociacion Venezolana de Fabricantes de Alimentos Concentrados para Animales **[★IO]**
Asociacion Venezolana de Fabricantes de Pastas Alimenticias **[★IO]**
Asociacion Venezolana de Huntington **[IO]**, Caracas, Venezuela
Asociacion Venezolana de la Industria Quimica y Petroquimica **[★IO]**
Asociacion Venezolana de Industrias Plasticas **[★IO]**
Asociacion Venezolana de Pilotos Privados y Propietarios de Aeronaves **[★IO]**
Asociacion Venezolana de Productores de Pulpa, Papel y Carton **[★IO]**
Asociata Femeilor Manager din Romania **[IO]**, Bucharest, Romania
Asociata Pentru Protectia Consumatorilor Din Romania **[★IO]**
Asociatia pentru Compatibiltate Electromagnetica din Romania **[★IO]**
Asociatia Femeilor din Romania **[★IO]**
Asociatia Generala a Inginerilor din Romania **[★IO]**
Asociatia Handicapatilor Neuromotor din Romania **[★IO]**

Asociatia Medicilor Stomatologi cu Practica Privada din Romania **[★IO]**
Asociatia Nationala a Internet Ser. Providerilor din Romania **[★IO]**
Asociatia Nationala Romana de Ortodontie **[IO]**, Iasi, Romania
Asociatia Presei Independente **[★IO]**
Asociatia Producatorilor si Importatorilor De Auto. **[★IO]**
Asociatia Radioamatorilor din Moldova **[★IO]**
Asociatia Romana a Bancilor **[★IO]**
Asociatia Romana de Psihologie Transpersonala **[★IO]**
Asociatia Romana pentru Telelucru si Teleactivitati **[★IO]**
Asociatia Youth Hostel Romania **[★IO]**
Asociatiei Nationale A Femeilor Cu Diploma Universitara Din Romania **[IO]**, Bucharest, Romania
Asociation Argentina Amigos de la Astronomia **[IO]**, Buenos Aires, Argentina
Asociation Argentina de Ensayos No Destructivos y Estructurales **[★IO]**
Association Colombiana de Endoscopia Digestiva **[IO]**, Bogota, Colombia
Asociation Espanola del Gas **[★IO]**
Asociation de Exportadores del Peru **[★IO]**
Asociation Ivorienne de Medicine Sportive **[IO]**, Abidjan, Cote d'Ivoire
Asociation Quimica Argentina **[IQ]**, Buenos Aires, Argentina
Asocijacija radioamatera u Bosni i Hercegovini **[★IO]**
Asosiasi Penyelenggara Jasa Internet Indonesia **[★IO]**
ASPA Accreditation Inst. **[★2902]**
Asparagus Club - Defunct.
Asparagus Growers Assn. **[IO]**, Louth, United Kingdom
Asparagus Indus. Coun; New Jersey **[4748]**
ASPECT Found. **[8599]**, 211 Sutter St., 10th Fl., San Francisco, CA 94108, (800)879-6884
Aspen Inst. **[10194]**, One Dupont Cir. NW, Ste. 700, Washington, DC 20036-1133, (202)736-5800
Aspen Inst. Berlin **[IO]**, Berlin, Germany
Aspen Inst. for Humanistic Stud. **[★10194]**
Aspen; Intl. Design Conf. in **[9905]**
Aspen Project **[★13848]**
Aspencade Motorcyclists Convention - Address unknown since 1990.
Asperger Syndrome Assn. of Ireland **[IO]**, Dublin, Ireland
Asperger Syndrome Coalition of the U.S. **[★15337]**
Asperger Syndrome; MAAP Services for Autism and **[15337]**
Asperger's Syndrome; Families of Adults Afflicted with **[16531]**
Asphalt Assn. **[★595]**
Asphalt Assn. **[★IO]**
Asphalt Assn; German **[IO]**
Asphalt Emulsion Manufacturers Assn. **[594]**, 3 Church Cir., PMB 250, Annapolis, MD 21401, (410)267-0023
Asphalt Inst. **[595]**, 2696 Res. Park Dr., Lexington, KY 40511-8480, (859)288-4960
Asphalt Inst. **[IO]**, Lexington, KY, United States
Asphalt Pavement Alliance **[596]**, c/o Asphalt Inst., PO Box 14052, Lexington, KY 40512, (859)288-4960
Asphalt Pavement Assn; Natl. **[641]**
Asphalt Paving Technologists; Assn. of **[6835]**
Asphalt Recycling and Reclaiming Assn. **[3987]**, PMB 250, 3 Church Cir., Annapolis, MD 21401, (410)267-0023
Asphalt Roofing Indus. Bur. **[★597]**
Asphalt Roofing Manufacturers Assn. **[597]**, 1156 15th St. NW, Ste. 900, Washington, DC 20005, (202)207-0917
Asphalt Rubber Producers Gp. **[★667]**
Asphalt Rubber Producers Gp. **[★IO]**
Asphalt Tile Inst. **[★665]**
Asphalt and Vinyl Asbestos Tile Inst. **[★665]**
Aspira of Am. **[★8231]**
ASPIRA Assn. **[8231]**, 1444 Eye St. NW, Ste. 800, Washington, DC 20005-2210, (202)835-3600
Aspira Public Policy Leadership Program **[★8231]**
ASPIRE - Assn. of Special People Inspired to Riding Excellence - Defunct.

Reference to "IO" in place of a book number signifies that the association may be found in the 45th edition of International Organizations.

Aspirin Found. of Am. **[2971]**, 807 Natl. Press Bldg., Washington, DC 20045-1801, (800)432-3247

Aspiring Actors Club - Address unknown since 2003.

Aspley Orchid Soc. **[IO]**, Virginia, Australia

ASPRS - Amer. Soc. of Plastic and Reconstructive Surgery **[★14044]**

ASPRS - The Imaging and Geospatial Info. Soc. **[7495]**, 5410 Grosvenor Ln., Ste. 210, Bethesda, MD 20814-2160, (301)493-0290

ASRT Educ. and Res. Foundation **[★15131]**

Assassination Archives and Res. Center **[18787]**, 1003 K St. NW, Ste. 640, Washington, DC 20001, (202)393-1921

Assassination Info. Bur. **[★18787]**

Assassinations; Comm. to Investigate **[★18787]**

Assault

Natl. Center for Assault Prevention **[12032]**

STAMP - Survivors Take Action Against Abuse by Military Personnel **[11507]**

Assault Prevention Center; Natl. **[★12032]**

Assault Prevention; Natl. Center for **[12032]**

Assault Prevention Training Proj. **[★12032]**

Assault Res. Assn; Sexual **[★6529]**

Assaulted Women's Helpline **[IO]**, Toronto, ON, Canada

Assaulted Women's Hotline **[★IO]**

ASSE Intl. Student Exchange Programs **[IO]**, Laguna Beach, CA, United States

ASSE Intl. Student Exchange Programs **[8600]**, 603 High Dr., Laguna Beach, CA 92651, (949)497-1699

Assemble Europenne des Academiques Turcs **[★IO]**

L'Assemblee Canadienne de la Danse **[★IO]**

Assemblee Des Regions D'Europe **[★IO]**

Assemblee Francaise des Chambers de Commerce et d'industrie **[★IO]**

Assemblee Nationale des Franco-Americains/Natl. Assn. of Franco-Amers. - Address unknown since 2001.

Assemblee des Ordinaires Catholiques de Terre Sainte **[★IO]**

Assemblee Parlementaire de l'Otan **[★IO]**

Assemblee des Premieres Nations **[★IO]**

Assemblee des Regions Europeennes Viticoles **[★IO]**

Assembly of Captive European Nations - Address unknown since 1995.

Assembly of Episcopal Healthcare Chaplains **[19944]**, c/o Jean Scribner, Pres., Beatrice Community Hosp., 1326 N 10th St., Beatrice, NE 68310, (402)223-7372

Assembly of European Regions **[IO]**, Strasbourg, France

Assembly of First Nations **[IO]**, Ottawa, ON, Canada

Assembly of Free Spirit Baptist Churches - Address unknown since 1995.

Assembly of French Chambers of Commerce and Indus. **[IO]**, Paris, France

Assembly of Governmental Employees - Defunct.

Assembly of Librarians of the Americas - Defunct.

Assembly of Natl. Tourist Office Representatives in New York - Defunct.

Assembly of Regional Health Planning Orgs. - Defunct.

Assembly of Turkish Amer. Associations **[19408]**, 1526 18th St. NW, Washington, DC 20036, (202)483-9090

Assembly of Wine Producing European Regions **[IO]**, Bordeaux, France

Asses; Amer. Coun. of Spotted **[4125]**

Assessing Officers; Natl. Assn. of **[★6296]**

Assessment Assn; Environmental **[4559]**

Assessment Consultants; Training Res. **[★6528]**

Assessment of Educational Progress; Natl. **[9253]**

Asset Managers Forum **[1401]**, 360 Madison Ave., New York, NY 10017-7111, (646)637-9200

Asset Managers Forum **[IO]**, New York, NY, United States

Asset Search Industry Assn. - Address unknown since 1999.

Assigned Names and Numbers; Internet Corp. for **[6813]**

Assist Card Intl. **[3908]**, 1001 Brickell Bay Dr., Ste. 2302, Miami, FL 33131, (305)381-9959

Assist Card Intl. **[IO]**, Miami, FL, United States

Assist Intl. **[IO]**, Scotts Valley, CA, United States

Assist Intl. **[12513]**, PO Box 66396, Scotts Valley, CA 95067-6396, (831)438-4582

Assistance Assn; Cambodian Mutual **[19422]**

Assistance Assn; Ethiopian Community Mutual **[19043]**

Assistance Dog Partners; Intl. Assn. of **[14241]**

Assistance Dog Services; Natl. Educ. for **[14770]**

Assistance Dogs of Am., Inc. **[11922]**, 8806 State Rte. 64, Swanton, OH 43558, (419)825-3622

Assistance Dogs Australia **[IO]**, Engadine, Australia

Assistance Dogs Intl. **[IO]**, Santa Rosa, CA, United States

Assistance Dogs Intl. **[11923]**, 1215 Sebastopol Rd., Santa Rosa, CA 95407, (707)545-3647

Assistance for Indigenous People of Eastern Bolivia **[IO]**, Santa Cruz, Bolivia

Assistance League **[13035]**, PO Box 6637, Burbank, CA 91510-6637, (818)846-3777

Assistance League; Natl. **[★13035]**

Assistance Mgt. Assn; Natl. **[★2507]**

Assistance in Ministries - Defunct.

Assistance Prog; Funeral Ser. Consumer **[17330]**

Asst. Directors Local 161 **[★24055]**

Asst. Masters and Mistresses Assn. **[★IO]**

Asst. and Pacific Regional Org. of the Intl. Fed. of Commercial, Clerical, Professional and Tech. Employers **[★IO]**

Asst. U.S. Attorneys; Natl. Assn. of **[5508]**

Assistants; Amer. Soc. of Orthopaedic Physician's **[15760]**

Assistants Assn; Intl. Virtual **[68]**

Assistants; Hea. Care Executive **[64]**

Assisted Living; Consumer Consortium on **[11283]**

Assisted Living Facilities Assn. of Am. **[★12306]**

Assisted Living Fed. of Am. **[12306]**, 1650 King St., Ste. 602, Alexandria, VA 22314-2747, (703)894-1805

Assisted Living; Natl. Center for **[14652]**

Assisted Reproductive Tech; Soc. for **[16346]**

ASSITEJ/USA **[★11051]**

ASSOCARTA - Italian Assn. of Paper, Cardboard and Pulp Mfrs. **[IO]**, Milan, Italy

Associazione Italiana di Geologia Applicata e Ambientale **[IO]**, Rome, Italy

Associacao de Atletismo de Macau **[IO]**, Macau, Macao

Associacao de Badminton de Macau **[IO]**, Macau, Macao

Associacao Brasil Huntington **[IO]**, Atibaia, Brazil

Associacao Brasileiara Interdisciplinar de AIDS **[★IO]**

Associacao Brasileira de Aerossois e Saneantes Domissanitarios **[★IO]**

Associacao Brasileira de Agentes de Viagens **[★IO]**

Associacao Brasileira de Anunciantes **[★IO]**

Associacao Brasileira de Arquitetos Paisagistas **[IO]**, Sao Paulo, Brazil

Associacao Brasileira de Aviacao Geral **[IO]**, Sao Paulo, Brazil

Associacao Brasileira de Bancos **[★IO]**

Associacao Brasileira de Bancos **[★IO]**

Associacao Brasileira de Bebidas **[★IO]**

Associacao Brasileira de Bioinformatica e Bioligia Computacional **[★IO]**

Associacao Brasileira de Cafes Especiais **[★IO]**

Associacao Brasileira de Ceramica **[★IO]**

Associacao Brasileira de Cimento Portland **[★IO]**

Associacao Brasileira do Comercio Farmaceutico **[★IO]**

Associacao Brasileira de Consultores de Engenharia **[★IO]**

Associacao Brasileira de Cosmetologia **[★IO]**

Associacao Brasileira Da Infra-Estrutura E Industrias De Base **[★IO]**

Associacao Brasileira De Shopping Centers **[★IO]**

Associacao Brasileira de Direitos Reprograficos **[IO]**, Sao Paulo, Brazil

Associacao Brasileira de Distrofia Muscular **[★IO]**

Associacao Brasileira de Ecoturismo **[★IO]**

Associacao Brasileira de Embalagem **[★IO]**

Associacao Brasileira das Empresas de Cartoes de Credito e Servicos **[★IO]**

Associacao Brasileira das Empresas de Coleta de Dados **[★IO]**

Associacao Brasileira das Empresas de Software **[★IO]**

Associacao Brasileira de Empresas de Vendas Diretas **[★IO]**

Associacao Brasileira de Engenharia Automotiva **[★IO]**

Associacao Brasileira de Esclerose Lateral Amiotrofica **[★IO]**

Associacao Brasileira de Esclerose Multipla **[IO]**, Sao Paulo, Brazil

Associacao Brasileira dos Fabricantes de Brinquedos **[★IO]**

Associacao Brasileira de Franchising **[★IO]**

Associacao Brasileira de Gerencia de Riscos **[IO]**, Sao Paulo, Brazil

Associacao Brasileira de Gerenciamento de Projetos **[★IO]**

Associacao Brasileira de Imprensa **[★IO]**

Associacao Brasileira da Industria de Aguas Minerais **[IO]**, Sao Paulo, Brazil

Associacao Brasileira da Industria de Cafe **[★IO]**

Associacao Brasileira da Industria Eletrica e Eletronica **[★IO]**

Associacao Brasileira da Industria do Fumo **[★IO]**

Associacao Brasileira da Industria de Hoteis **[★IO]**

Associacao Brasileira da Industria de Maquinas e Equipamentos **[★IO]**

Associacao Brasileira da Industria Quimica **[★IO]**

Associacao Brasileira da Industria Textil e de Confeccao **[★IO]**

Associacao Brasileira das Industrias da Alimentacao **[★IO]**

Associacao Brasileira das Industrias do Mobiliario **[★IO]**

Associacao Brasileira das Industrias de Naotecidos e Tecidos Tecnicos **[★IO]**

Associacao Brasileira das Industrias de Oleos Vegetais **[★IO]**

Associacao Brasileira de Jet Ski **[★IO]**

Associacao Brasileira de Mecanica dos Solos e Engenharia Geotecnica **[★IO]**

Associacao Brasileira de Metalurgia e Materiais **[★IO]**

Associacao Brasileira de Mulheres Universitarias **[IO]**, Porto Alegre, Brazil

Associacao Brasileira de Ortondontia e Ortopedia Facial **[★IO]**

Associacao Brasileira do Papelao Ondulado **[★IO]**

Associacao Brasileira Para o Desenvolvimento de Liderancas **[IO]**, Sao Paulo, Brazil

Associacao Brasileira de Private Equity and Venture Capital **[IO]**, Rio de Janeiro, Brazil

Associacao Brasileira dos Produtores de Discos **[IO]**, Rio de Janeiro, Brazil

Associacao Brasileira dos Produtores e Exportadores de Frangos **[★IO]**

Associacao Brasileira dos Produtores de Fibras Artificiais e Sinteticas **[★IO]**

Associacao Brasileira de Quimica **[★IO]**

Associacao Brasileira de Representantes de Veiculos de Comunicacao **[★IO]**

Associacao Brasileira de Supermercados **[★IO]**

Associacao Brasileira de Floorball **[★IO]**

Associacao Comercial Do Porto **[★IO]**

Associacao Comercial de Macau **[★IO]**

Associacao do Comercio Automovel de Portugal **[IO]**, Lisbon, Portugal

Associacao Crista Feminina do Brasil **[★IO]**

Associacao De Universidades Amazonicas **[★IO]**

Associacao dos Dirigentes de Vendas e Marketing do Brasil **[★IO]**

Associacao das Empresas de Vinho do Porto **[★IO]**

Associacao Evangelica de Acampamentos **[★IO]**

Associacao dos Exportadores e Importadores de Macau **[★IO]**

Associacao de Fabricantes para a Industria Automovel **[★IO]**

Associacao Fonografica Portuguesa **[IO]**, Lisbon, Portugal

Associacao dos Fumicultores do Brasil **[★IO]**

Associacao de Grossistas de Produtos Quimicos e Farmaceuticos **[★IO]**

Associacao dos Hoteis de Portugal **[★IO]**

Associacao de Ilusionismo de Macau **[★IO]**

Associacao de Industriais Metalurgicos, Metalomecanicos e Afins de Portugal **[IO]**, Porto, Portugal

Associacao Indus. de Macau **[★IO]**

A star before a book entry number signifies that the name is not listed separately, but is mentioned within the entry.

Associacao dos Inquilinos Lisbonenses [IO], Lisbon, Portugal

Associacao dos Inquilinos do Norte de Portugal [IO], Porto, Portugal

Associacao Internacional de Estudantes de Agricultura [★IO]

Associacao Internacional de Estudantes de Agricultura [★IO]

Associacao Internacional de Estudantes de Agricultura [★IO]

Associacao Internacional de Estudantes de Agricultura - Algarve [★IO]

Associacao Internacional de Estudantes de Agricultura - Comite de Lisboa [★IO]

Associacao Internacional de Estudantes de Agricultura - Comite Local de Santarem [★IO]

Associacao do Jovem Aprendiz [★IO]

Associacao Latinoamericana de Estradas de Ferro [★IO]

Associacao Medica Braseleira [IO], Sao Paulo, Brazil

Associacao Medica Homeopatica Brasileira [★IO]

Associacao Medico Espirita do Brasil [★IO]

Associacao Nacional dos Comerciantes Exportadores de Vinhos e Bebidas Espirituosas [★IO]

Associacao Nacional de Comerciantes e Industriais de Produtos Alimentares [★IO]

Associacao Nacional para a Difusao de Adubos [★IO]

Associacao Nacional dos Doentes com Artrite Infantil [IO], Lisbon, Portugal

Associacao Nacional de Editores de Revistas [★IO]

Associacao Nacional des Empresas do Comercio e da Reparacao Automovel [IO], Lisbon, Portugal

Associacao Nacional dos Fabricantes de Ceramica para Revestimento [★IO]

Associacao Nacional dos Fabricantes de Veiculos Automotores [★IO]

Associacao Nacional das Farmacias [★IO]

Associacao Nacional dos Industriais de Arroz [★IO]

Associacao Nacional dos Industriais de Lanificios [★IO]

Associacao Nacional dos Industriais de Refrigerantes e Sumos de Frutos [★IO]

Associacao Nacional das Industrias de Vestuario e Confeccao [IO], Porto, Portugal

Associacao Nacional de Jornais [IO], Brasilia, Brazil

Associacao Nacional do Ramo Automovel [★IO]

Associacao Nacional das industrias de Vestuario e Confeccao [★IO]

Associacao de Pilotos e Proprietarios de Aeronaves [★IO]

Associacao Portugesa Antiquarios [IO], Lisbon, Portugal

Associacao Portuguesa das Agencias de Viagens e Turismo [★IO]

Associacao Portuguesa de Anunciantes [IO], Lisbon, Portugal

Associacao Portuguesa de Centros Comerciais [★IO]

Associacao Portuguesa de Controlo Automatico [IO], Lisbon, Portugal

Associacao Portuguesa de Deficientes [IO], Lisbon, Portugal

Associacao Portuguesa de Doentes de Huntington [IO], Alvor, Portugal

Associacao Portuguesa dos Editores e Livreiros [★IO]

Associacao Portuguesa de Educacao Ambiental [★IO]

Associacao Portuguesa de Educacao Musical [★IO]

Associacao Portuguesa de Empresas de Distribuicao [★IO]

Associacao Portuguesa de Empresas Petroliferas [★IO]

Associacao Portuguesa de Fotogrammetria e Deteccao Remote [IO], Lisbon, Portugal

Associacao Portuguesa de Geomorfologos [IO], Lisbon, Portugal

Associacao Portuguesa da Industria Farmaceutica [★IO]

Associacao Portuguesa da Industria Papeleira [★IO]

Associacao Portuguesa da Industria de Plasticos [★IO]

Associacao Portuguesa dos Industriais de Aguas Minerais e de Nascente [★IO]

Associacao Portuguesa dos Industriais de Alimentos Compostos para Animais [★IO]

Associacao Portuguesa dos Industriais de Calcado, Componentes, Artigos de Pele e seus Sucedaneos [★IO]

Associacao Portuguesa dos Industriais de Curtumes [★IO]

Associacao Portuguesa de Investigacao Operacional [★IO]

Associacao Portuguesa Para o Desenvolvimento do Teletrabalho [★IO]

Associacao Portuguesa de Radiodifusao [★IO]

Associacao Portuguesa de Reconhecimento de Padroes [IO], Porto, Portugal

Associacao Portuguesa dos Tecnicos das Industrias de Celulose e Papel [★IO]

Associacao dos Profissionais e Empresas de Mediacao Imobiliaria de Portugal [★IO]

Associacao da Restauracao e Similares de Portugal [★IO]

Associacao Spina Bifida e Hidrocefalia de Portugal [IO], Lisbon, Portugal

Associacao desportiva Taekwondo de Mocambique [IO], Maputo, Mozambique

Associacao Tecnica Brasil-Alemanha [IO], Sao Paulo, Brazil

Associacao Tecnica Brasileira das Industrias Automaticas de Vidro [★IO]

Associacao das Universidades de Lingua Portuguesa [★IO]

Associacio Catalana d'Intel-ligencia Artificial [★IO]

Associacio Veterinaria per a l'Atencio de la Fauna Exotica i Salvatge [★IO]

Associacion Colombiana de Endocrinologia [IO], Bogota, Colombia

Associacion Colombiana de Facultades de Medicina [★IO]

Associacion Colombiana de Fisioterapia [IO], Bogota, Colombia

Associacion Comunitaria de Autosuficiencia [IO], Jocotepec, Mexico

Associacion Costarricense de Arquitectos Paisajistas [IO], San Jose, Costa Rica

Associacion Costarricense de Terapeutas Fisicos de Costa Rica [IO], San Jose, Costa Rica

Associacion para el Desarrollo de Microempresas [★IO]

Associacion de Diarios Colombianos [IO], Bogota, Colombia

Associacion Espafiola para la Defensa de la Competencia [IO], Madrid, Spain

Associacion de Importadores y Exportadores de la Republica Argentina [★IO]

Associacion Mexicana de Endoscopia Gastrointestinal [IO], Mexico City, Mexico

Associacion Mexicana de Fisioterapia [IO], Puebla, Mexico

Associacion Nicaraguense de Medicina del Deporte [IO], Managua, Nicaragua

Associate Collegiate Players - Defunct.

Associate Degree Nursing; Natl. Org. for [15512]

Associate Jewelers - Defunct.

Associate Missionaries of the Assumption [20300], 11 Old English Rd., Worcester, MA 01609, (508)767-1356

Associate Missionaries of the Assumption [IO], Worcester, MA, United States

Associate Reformed Presbyterian Church, World Witness [★IO]

Associate Reformed Presbyterian Church, World Witness [★20420]

Assoc. Actors and Artistes of Am. [24153], 165 W 46th St., New York, NY 10036, (212)869-0358

Assoc. Actors and Artistes of Am. [IO], New York, NY, United States

Assoc. Advt. Clubs of the World [★83]

Associated Agents of America - Defunct.

Assoc. Air Balance Coun. [598], 1518 K St. NW, Washington, DC 20005, (202)737-0202

Associated Baby Carriage Dealers - Defunct.

Assoc. Bakers of Am. [★454]

Assoc. Bakers of Am. - Retail and Wholesale [★454]

Assoc. Blind [16830], 315 5th Ave., Ste. 807, New York, NY 10016, (212)683-4950

Assoc. Boards for Christian Colleges in China [★8649]

Assoc. Boards for Christian Colleges in China [★IO]

Assoc. Bodywork and Massage Professionals [15025], 1271 Sugarbush Dr., Evergreen, CO 80439-9766, (303)674-8478

Associated Brokers of America - Defunct.

Assoc. Builders and Contractors [1004], 4250 N Fairfax Dr., 9th Fl., Arlington, VA 22203-1607, (703)812-2000

Assoc. Bus. Publications [★3201]

Assoc. Bus. Writers of Am. [★3146]

Assoc. Camera Clubs of Am. [★22893]

Associated Catholic Laymen's First Friday Clubs - Address unknown since 1995.

Assoc. Chain Drug Stores [★2972]

Assoc. Chain Drug Stores [★IO]

Assoc. Chambers of Commerce and Indus. of India [IO], New Delhi, India

Assoc. Chinese Chambers of Commerce and Indus. of Malaysia [IO], Kuala Lumpur, Malaysia

Assoc. Church Press [3205], PO Box 621001, Oviedo, FL 32762-1001, (407)341-6615

The Associated Clubs [19372]

Assoc. Coffee Indus. of Am. [★511]

Assoc. Collectors of El Salvador [22794], c/o Pierre Cahen, PO Box 02-5364, Miami, FL 33102

Assoc. Colleges of the Midwest [8097], 205 W Wacker Dr., Ste. 220, Chicago, IL 60606, (312)263-5000

Assoc. Collegiate Press [8705], Univ. of Minnesota, 2221 Univ. Ave. SE, Ste. 121, Minneapolis, MN 55414, (612)625-8335

Assoc. Comm. of Friends on Indian Affairs [20039], PO Box 2326, Richmond, IN 47375-2326

Assoc. Constr. Distributors Intl. [599], PO Box 14552, Des Moines, IA 50306-3552, (515)964-1335

Assoc. Constr. Distributors Intl. [IO], Des Moines, IA, United States

Assoc. Cooperage Indus. of Am. [972], 2100 Gardiner Ln., Ste. 100-E, Louisville, KY 40205-2947, (502)459-6113

Assoc. Corn Products Mfrs. [★1508]

Associated Corset and Brassiere Mfrs. [227]

Assoc. Court and Commercial Newspapers [★3202]

Assoc. Credit Bureaus [★1409]

Assoc. Daughters of Early Amer. Witches [21358], c/o Mrs. Marlene L. Wilkinson, Gen. Pres., 6876 Richard Wilson Dr., Millington, TN 38053-3934

Assoc. Designers of Canada [IO], Toronto, ON, Canada

Associated Dress Carriers of Brooklyn and Queens - Defunct.

Assoc. Equip. Distributors [2000], 615 W 22nd St., Oak Brook, IL 60523, (630)574-0650

Associated Exhibitors of the Amer. Alliance for Health, Physical Education, Recreation and Dance - Address unknown since 2004.

Assoc. Fraternities of Am. [★19133]

Assoc. Funeral Directors Intl. [2774], PO Box 1089, Hammonton, NJ 08037-5089, (423)392-1985

Associated Funeral Directors International [IO], Hammonton, NJ, United States

Assoc. Funeral Directors Ser. [★IO]

Assoc. Funeral Directors Ser. [★2774]

Assoc. Funeral Directors Ser. Intl. [★2774]

Assoc. Funeral Directors Ser. Intl. [★IO]

Associated Fur Mfrs. - Address unknown since 2003.

Assoc. Gen. Contractors of Am. [1005], 2300 Wilson Blvd., Ste. 400, Arlington, VA 22201, (703)548-3118

Associated Geographers of America - Defunct.

Assoc. Glass and Pottery Mfrs. [3709], 520 Westchester Dr., Greensburg, PA 15601, (724)837-2332

Assoc. Glee Clubs of Am. [★IO]

Associated Granite Craftsmens Guild - Address unknown since 1995.

Associated Graphologists Intl. - Defunct.

Assoc. Hea. Found. [18983], 2347 Jericho Tpke., 2nd Fl., New Hyde Park, NY 11040, (516)739-9500

Assoc. Hea. Systems [★14597]

Assoc. Humane Societies [11366], 124 Evergreen Ave., Newark, NJ 07114-2133, (973)824-7080

Assoc. Humane Societies of New Jersey [★11366]

Assoc. Humans [IO], Paris, France

Reference to "IO" in place of a book number signifies that the association may be found in the 45th edition of International Organizations.

Assoc. Independent Elecl. Contractors of Am. [★1018]

Associated Industrial Photographic Dealers - Defunct.

Assoc. Institutes for Lath and Plaster [★1026]

Assoc. Institutes for Lath and Plaster [★IO]

Assoc. Japan-America Societies of the U.S. [★19171]

Assoc. Koi Clubs of Am. [22437], PO Box 3345, Orange, CA 92857-0345, (714)731-5610

Associated Koi Clubs of America [IO], Orange, CA, United States

Assoc. Landscape Contractors of Am. and Professional Lawn Care Assn. of Am. [★2398]

Associated Legislative Rabbinate of America - Address unknown since 1995.

Assoc. Locksmiths of Am. [1818], 3500 Easy St., Dallas, TX 75247, (214)819-9733

Assoc. Luxury Hotels Intl. [1931], 1000 Connecticut Ave. NW, Ste. 603, Washington, DC 20036, (202)887-7020

Assoc. Mail and Parcel Centers [2446], 950 Glenn Dr., Ste. 150, Folsom, CA 95630, (707)226-9384

Assoc. Male Choruses of Am. [IO], Dunsford, ON, Canada

Assoc. Manufacturers of Elecl. and Supplies [★IO]

Assoc. Manufacturers of Elecl. and Supplies [★1191]

Assoc. Manufacturers of Toilet Articles [★1845]

Associated Master Barbers and Beauticians of America [★1079]

Assoc. Medical Services [IO], Toronto, ON, Canada

Assoc. Minority Contractors of Am. [★1036]

The Associated Missions - Address unknown since 1999.

Associated Motion Picture Advertisers - Address unknown since 1995.

Associated Motor Carriers Tariff Bur. - Defunct.

Associated Opera Companies of America - Defunct.

Associated Orgs. for Professionals in Education - Defunct.

Assoc. Owners and Developers [939], PO Box 4163, McLean, VA 22103-4163, (703)734-2397

Assoc. Parishes for Liturgy and Mission [19945], PO Box 10416, Rochester, NY 14610

Associated Photographers Intl. - Address unknown since 1995.

Associated Piece Goods Buyers of the Cloak and Suit Industry - Defunct.

Associated Pimiento Canners - Defunct.

Assoc. Pipe Organ Builders of Am. [2799], PO Box 155, Chicago Ridge, IL 60415, (800)473-5270

Assoc. Police Communications Officers [★6248]

Assoc. Police Communications Officers [★IO]

Associated Poultry and Egg Industries - Defunct.

Assoc. Press [3089], 450 W 33rd St., New York, NY 10001, (212)621-1500

Assoc. Press Broadcasters [546], c/o AP Broadcast News Center, 1825 K St. NW, Ste. 800, Washington, DC 20006-1232, (202)736-1108

Assoc. Press Broadcasters Assn. [★546]

Assoc. Press Managing Editors [3090], 19 Commerce Ct. W, Cranbury, NJ 08512-2416, (212)621-1838

Assoc. Press Radio-Television Assn. [★546]

Associated Press Sports Editors - Defunct.

Assoc. Professional Massage Therapists and Allied Hea. Practitioners Intl. [★15025]

Assoc. Professional Massage Therapists and Body-workers [★15025]

Assoc. Professional Sleep Societies [16422], 1 Westbrook Corporate Ctr., Ste. 920, Westchester, IL 60154, (708)492-0930

Assoc. Public-Safety Communications Officers [★6248]

Assoc. Public-Safety Communications Officers [★IO]

Associated Public School Systems - Defunct.

Associated Rare Breeds of New England - Defunct.

The Associated Readers of Tarot Intl. - Address unknown since 1991.

Assoc. Regional Accounting Firms [★51]

Assoc. Regional Accounting Firms [★IO]

Assoc. Retail Bakers of Am. [★454]

Assoc. Retail Confectioners of North Am. [★1561]

Assoc. Retail Confectioners of North Am. [★IO]

Assoc. Retail Confectioners of the U.S. [★IO]

Assoc. Retail Confectioners of the U.S. [★1561]

Associated Risk Managers Intl. - Address unknown since 2003.

Associated Sandblasting Contractors - Address unknown since 1999.

Assoc. Schools of Constr. [8143], c/o Colorado State Univ., Mfg. Tech. and Constr. Mgt., 102 Guggenheim, Fort Collins, CO 80523, (970)491-7958

Associated Schools of Construction [IO], Fort Collins, CO, United States

Assoc. Services for the Blind [16831], 919 Walnut St., Philadelphia, PA 19107, (215)627-0600

Assoc. Ship Chandlers [★2584]

Assoc. Soc. of Locomotive Engineers and Firemen [IO], London, United Kingdom

Assoc. Soil and Found. Engineers [★7137]

Assoc. Specialty Contractors [1006], 3 Bethesda Metro Ctr., Ste. 1100, Bethesda, MD 20814, (703)548-3118

Assoc. Stenotypists of Am. [★5630]

Assoc. Surplus Dealers [3701], c/o ASD/AMD Trade Shows, 11835 W Olympic Blvd., Ste. 550E, Los Angeles, CA 90064-5810, (310)481-7300

Assoc. Telephone Answering Exchanges [★3735]

Assoc. Telephone Answering Exchanges [★IO]

Assoc. Telephone Exchanges [★IO]

Assoc. Telephone Exchanges [★3735]

Assoc. Third Class Mail Users [★2449]

Associated Tobacco Mfrs. - Defunct.

Assoc. Traffic Clubs [★3896]

Assoc. Traffic Clubs [★IO]

The Associated Turtles - Defunct.

Associated Two-Year Schools in Construction - Defunct.

Associated Veterinary Laboratories - Defunct.

Associated Video Dealers of America - Defunct.

Assoc. Wire Rope Fabricators [2001], PO Box 748, Walled Lake, MI 48390-0748, (248)994-7753

Assoc. Writing Programs [★11160]

Associates of the Amer. Foreign Ser. Worldwide [24071], 5555 Columbia Pike, Ste. 208, Arlington, VA 22204-3117, (703)820-5420

Associates of the Amer. Foreign Ser. Worldwide [IO], Arlington, VA, United States

Associates for Biblical Res. [IO], Akron, PA, United States

Associates for Biblical Res. [19507], PO Box 144, Akron, PA 17501, (717)859-3443

Associates for Bulimia and Related Disorders - Defunct.

Associates of Clinical Pharmacology [★15927]

Associates of Clinical Pharmacology [★IO]

Associates in Cultural Exchange [8176], 200 W Mercer St., Ste. 108, Seattle, WA 98119-3958, (206)217-9644

Associates of Elvis Presley Fan Clubs - Address unknown since 1999.

Associates of the Graymoor Ecumenical Inst. - Defunct.

Associates of Vietnam Veterans of Am. [21344], 8605 Cameron St., Ste. 400, Silver Spring, MD 20910-3718, (301)585-4000

Associates for Youth Development - Defunct.

Associatiacao Das Secretaries De Angola [IO], Luanda, Angola

L'Association canadienne des sports pout paralytiques cerebraux [★IO]

Assn. canadienne des physiciens et physiciennes [★IO]

Assn. canadienne des etudes aseatiques [★IO]

L'Association professionnelle des agents du service exterieur [★IO]

Assn. cycliste canadienne [★IO]

Assn. canadienne des reviseurs [★IO]

Assn. canadienne de science politique [★IO]

Assn. canadienne de la paie [★IO]

L'Association canadienne des estudes sur les femmes [★IO]

Assn. canadienne de justice penale [★IO]

Assn. canadienne des infirmieres et infirmiers en sante communantaire [★IO]

Assn. des manufacturlers de vetements pour hommes [★IO]

Assn. canadienne des importateurs et expotateurs [★IO]

Assn. nationale des grands usagers postaux [★IO]

Assn. canadienne des professeurs de redaction technique et scientifique [★IO]

Assn. canadienne des redacteurs scientifiques [★IO]

Assn. canadienne des infirmieres en oncologie [★IO]

Assn. canadienne des professeurs de langues secondes [★IO]

Assn. canadienne des organismes de controle des regimes retraite [★IO]

Assn. canadienne des chirurgiens generaux [★IO]

Assn. canadienne des radiologistes [★IO]

Assn. canadienne en protheses et orthese [★IO]

L'Association canadienne des organismes artistiques [★IO]

Assn. canadienne de la poesie [★IO]

Assn. catholique canadienne de la sante [★IO]

Assn. canadienne des soins de sante [★IO]

Assn. canadienne des chefs de pompiers [★IO]

Assn. canadienne de gerontologie [★IO]

Assn. canadienne des automobilistes [★IO]

Assn. europeenne de societies de neurochirugie [★IO]

Assn. nationale des revetements de sol [★IO]

Assn. europeenne de demolition [★IO]

Assn. nationale des distributeurs aux petites surfaces alimentaires [★IO]

Assn. canadienne des sports en fauteuil roulant [★IO]

Assn. quebecoise de sport en fauteuil roulant [★IO]

Assn. canadienne de protection civile [★IO]

Assn. canadienne de basketball en fauteuil roulant [★IO]

Assn. canadienne de soins palliatifs [★IO]

L'Association canadienne pour la sante mentale [★IO]

Assn. canadienne des preteurs sur salaire [★IO]

Assn. europeenne des linguistes et des professeurs de langues [★IO]

Assn. canadienne des etudiantes catholiques [★IO]

Assn. canadienne des entraineurs [★IO]

Assn. europeenne des organizations nationales des detaillants en textile [★IO]

Assn. canadienne des importateurs et exportateurs [★IO]

Assn. europeenne de boxe amateur [★IO]

L'Association canadienne des specialistes en emploi et des employeurs [★IO]

Assn. canadienne pour la sante des adolescents [★IO]

Assn. canadienne des professionnels de la securite routiere [★IO]

Assn. canadienne des conseillers en management [★IO]

Assn. canadienne pour les etudes superieures [★IO]

Assn. canadienne des revues savantes [★IO]

Assn. canadienne des assistantes dentaires [★IO]

Assn. canadienne de crosse [★IO]

Assn. canadienne des fabricants de carton ondule [★IO]

Assn. canadienne des epices [★IO]

Assn. canadienne des administrateurs de regimes de retraite [★IO]

Assn. des regions frontalieres europeenes [★IO]

Assn. of 40th Infantry Div. Korean War Veterans [21168], c/o Sid Sultzbaugh, Sec., 2029 G St., Lorain, OH 44052

Assn. of Academic Agronomists [IO], Helsinki, Finland

Assn. of Academic Chairmen of Plastic Surgery [14046], c/o Michele Campbell, Mgr., 444 E Algonquin Rd., Arlington Heights, IL 60005, (800)526-9884

Assn. of Academic Hea. Centers [14546], 1400 16th St. NW, Ste. 720, Washington, DC 20036, (202)265-9600

Assn. of Academic Health Sciences Library Directors - Address unknown since 2002.

Assn. of Academic Physiatrists [16316], 1106 N Charles St., Ste. 201, Baltimore, MD 21201, (410)637-8300

Assn. for Academic Surgery [16576], 11300 W Olympic Blvd., Ste. 600, Los Angeles, CA 90064, (310)437-1606

A star before a book entry number signifies that the name is not listed separately, but is mentioned within the entry.

Association for Academic Travel Abroad [★8588]

Assn. of Academies of Sci. [★7617]

Assn. for Accounting Admin. [13], 136 S Keowee St., Dayton, OH 45402, (937)222-0030

Assn. of Accounting Administrators [★13]

Assn. of Accounting Companies in Bulgaria [IO], Sofia, Bulgaria

Assn. for Accounting Marketing [2615], 14 W Third St., Ste. 200, Kansas City, MO 64105, (816)221-1296

Assn. of Accounting Technicians [IO], London, United Kingdom

Assn. for the Accreditation of Human Res. Protection Programs [11225], 915 15th St. NW, Ste. 400, Washington, DC 20005, (202)783-1112

Assn. of Accredited Advt. Agents of Hong Kong [IO], Hong Kong, People's Republic of China

Assn. of Accredited Advt. Agents Singapore [IO], Singapore, Singapore

Assn. of Accredited Naturopathic Medical Colleges [8943], 4435 Wisconsin Ave. NW, Ste. 403, Washington, DC 20016, (202)237-8150

Assn. of Accredited School and Departments of Journalism [★7893]

Assn. for Achievement and Improvement through Assessment [IO], Wetherby, United Kingdom

Assn. Actuarielle Internationale [★IO]

Assn. for Addiction Professionals; NAADAC The [16509]

Assn. des Adjoints Administratifs [★IO]

Assn. des Administrations Portuaires Canadiennes [★IO]

Assn. of Administrative Assistants [IO], Oakville, ON, Canada

Assn. of Administrative Assistants and Secretaries to U.S. Senators - Address unknown since 1995.

Assn. of Administrative Law Judges [5894], c/o Judge Thomas Snook, Co-Chm., 1454 Mendavia Ave., Coral Gables, FL 33146, (414)297-3141

Assn. of Administrative Law Judges, Dept. of Hea. and Human Services [★5894]

Assn. of Administrative Professionals New Zealand [IO], Wellington, New Zealand

Assn. of Administrative Professionals New Zealand - Auckland Gp. [IO], Auckland, New Zealand

Assn. of Administrative Professionals New Zealand - Dunedin Gp. [IO], Dunedin, New Zealand

Assn. of Administrative Professionals New Zealand - Manawatu Gp. [IO], Palmerston North, New Zealand

Assn. of Administrative Professionals New Zealand - Marlborough Gp. [IO], Blenheim, New Zealand

Assn. of Administrative Professionals New Zealand - Porirua City Gp. [IO], Porirua, New Zealand

Assn. of Administrative Professionals New Zealand - Taranaki Gp. [IO], New Plymouth, New Zealand

Assn. of Administrators of the Interstate Compact on Adoption and Medical Assistance [11236], 810 1st St. NE, Ste. 500, Washington, DC 20002, (202)682-0100

Assn. of Administrators of the Interstate Compact on the Placement of Children [11559], c/o Amer. Public Human Services Assn., 810 1st St. NE, Ste. 500, Washington, DC 20002, (202)682-0100

Assn. of Administrators of the Interstate Compact for the Supervision of Parolees and Probationers [★6166]

Assn. of Adult Day Support Programs [IO], Edmonton, AB, Canada

Assn. for Adult Development and Aging - Address unknown since 2002.

Assn. to Advance Collegiate Schools of Bus. [8013], 777 S Harbour Island Blvd., Ste. 750, Tampa, FL 33602-5730, (813)769-6500

Assn. to Advance Ethical Hypnosis - Address unknown since 2001.

Assn. for Advanced Health Care Managers - Defunct.

Assn. for Advanced Life Underwriting [2144], 2901 Telestar Ct., Falls Church, VA 22042, (703)641-9400

Assn. of Advanced Rabbinical and Talmudic Schools [8683]

Assn. for Advanced Training in the Behavioral Sciences [8878], 5126 Ralston St., Ventura, CA 93003, (805)676-3030

Assn. for the Advancement of Aging Res. - Defunct.

Assn. for the Advancement of Applied Sport Psychology [16479], 2810 Crossroads Dr., Ste. 3800, Madison, WI 53718, (608)443-2475

Association for the Advancement of Applied Sport Psychology [IO], Madison, WI, United States

Assn. for the Advancement of Automotive Medicine [12951], PO Box 4176, Barrington, IL 60011-4176, (847)844-3880

Assn. for the Advancement of Baltic Stud. [9730], 14743 Braemar Crescent Way, Darnestown, MD 20878-3911, (301)977-8491

Assn. for the Advancement of Baltic Stud. [IO], Darnestown, MD, United States

Assn. for Advancement of Behavior Therapy [★13733]

Assn. for Advancement of the Behavioral Therapies [★13733]

Assn. for Advancement of Blind Children [★16832]

Assn. for the Advancement of Blind and Retarded [16832], PO Box 560247, College Point, NY 11356, (718)321-3800

Assn. for the Advancement of British Biotechnology [★IO]

Assn. for the Advancement of Central Asian Res. - Address unknown since 1999.

Assn. for the Advancement of Computing in Educ. [9237], PO Box 1545, Chesapeake, VA 23327-1545, (757)366-5606

The Assn. for the Advancement of Cost Engg. [★6842]

The Assn. for the Advancement of Cost Engg. [★IO]

Assn. for the Advancement of Creative Musicians [10558], 410 S Michigan Ave., Ste. 943, Chicago, IL 60680, (312)922-1900

Assn. for the Advancement of Documentation Sciences and Techniques [IO], Montreal, QC, Canada

Association for the Advancement of Dutch-American Studies [IO], Holland, MI, United States

Assn. for the Advancement of Dutch-American Stud. [9908], The Joint Archives of Holland, Hope Coll., PO Box 9000, Holland, MI 49422-9000, (616)395-7798

Assn. for the Advancement of Family Stability [★12138]

Assn. for the Advancement of Feminism [IO], Hong Kong, People's Republic of China

Assn. for the Advancement of Gestalt Therapy [16135], c/o Sylvie Falschlunger, Admin. Asst., 60 Waller Ave., White Plains, NY 10605, (914)686-3477

Assn. for the Advancement of Health Care Managers - Defunct.

Assn. for the Advancement of Hea. Educ. [★16234]

Assn. for the Advancement of Indus. Crops [4110], c/o USDA-ARS-ALARC, 21881 Cardon Ln., Maricopa, AZ 85239, (520)316-6426

Assn. for the Advancement of Intl. Educ. [8640], PO Box 1500, Sheridan, WY 82801-1500, (307)674-6446

Assn. for the Advancement of Intl. Educ. [IO], Sheridan, WY, United States

Assn. for the Advancement of Invention and Innovation - Defunct.

Assn. for the Advancement of Medical Education - Defunct.

Assn. for the Advancement of Medical Instrumentation [6606], 1110 N Glebe Rd., Ste. 220, Arlington, VA 22201-4795, (703)525-4890

Association for the Advancement of Medical Instrumentation [IO], Arlington, VA, United States

Assn. for the Advancement of Mexican Americans [11763], 6001 Gulf Fwy., Houston, TX 77023, (713)926-4756

Assn. for the Advancement of Modelling and Simulation Techniques in Enterprises - France [IO], Tassin-la-Demi-Lune, France

Assn. for Advancement of Modelling and Simulation Techniques in Enterprises - Spain [IO], Barcelona, Spain

Assn. for the Advancement of Ophthalmology - Defunct.

Assn. for the Advancement of Philosophy and Psychiatry [7487], c/o Prof. Jerome L. Kroll, MD, Pres., Univ. of Minnesota Medical School, Community-University Hea. Care Clinic, 2201 Bloomington Ave. S, Minneapolis, MN 55404

Association for the Advancement of Philosophy and Psychiatry [IO], Minneapolis, MN, United States

Assn. for the Advancement of Policy, Res. and Development in the Third World [17828]

Assn. for the Advancement of Polish Studies - Address unknown since 1989.

Assn. for the Advancement of Psychoanalysis (of the Karen Horney Psychoanalytic Inst. and Center) [16105], 329 E 62nd St., New York, NY 10021, (212)838-4333

Assn. for the Advancement of Psychology [16136], PO Box 38129, Colorado Springs, CO 80937-8129, (800)869-6595

Assn. for the Advancement of Psychotherapy [16210], c/o T. Byram Karasu, MD, Ed.-in-Chief, Belfer Educ. Ctr., Rm. 405, 1300 Morris Park Ave., Bronx, NY 10461, (718)430-3503

Assn. for Advancement of Res. on Multiple Sclerosis [★15349]

Assn. for the Advancement of Sports Potential [★16480]

Assn. for the Advancement of Sustainability in Higher Educ. [8479], 1935 SE 24th Ave., Portland, OR 97214, (503)222-7041

Assn. for the Advancement of Sustainability in Higher Educ. [IO], Portland, OR, United States

Assn. for the Advancement of Teacher Educ. in Music [★IO]

Assn. for the Advancement of Wound Care [14547], 83 Gen. Warren Blvd., Ste. 100, Malvern, PA 19355, (610)560-0484

Assn. of Adventist Forums [20554], PO Box 619047, Roseville, CA 95661-9047, (916)774-1080

Association of Adventist Forums [IO], Roseville, CA, United States

Assn. for Adventure Sports [IO], Ramelton, Ireland

Assn. of Advertisers in Ireland [IO], Blackrock, Ireland

Assn. of Advt., Commercial and Magazine Photographers of Australia [IO], North Sydney, Australia

Assn. of Advt. and Commun. Agencies [IO], Paris, France

Assn. of Advt. and Commun. Companies [★IO]

Assn. of Advertising Lawyers - Defunct.

Assn. Advisory Coun. - Address unknown since 1999.

Assn. Aeronautique et Astronautique de France [IO], Paris, France

Assn. for Aerosol Res. [IO], Karlsruhe, Germany

Assn. for Affiliated Coll. and Univ. Offices [★8341]

Assn. Africaine du Commerce des Semences [★IO]

Assn. Africaine de Credit Rural et Agricole [★IO]

Assn. Africaine De Sci. Politique [★IO]

Assn. Africaine des Formateurs au Soutien de la Paix [★IO]

Assn. of African Amer. Financial Advisors [1455], 3 Bethesda Metro Ctr., Ste. 700, Bethesda, MD 20814, (301)961-1507

Assn. of African Amer. People's Legal Coun. - Address unknown since 1995.

Assn. of African Amer. Vintners [195], PO Box 2168, Sonoma, CA 95476, (707)933-0556

Assn. of African-Amer. Women Business Owners - Address unknown since 2005.

Assn. of African Election Authorities [IO], Accra, Ghana

Assn. of African Physicians in North America - Address unknown since 1990.

Assn. of African Stud. Programs [7928], c/o Gail Vernazza, Dartmouth Coll., Dept. of History, 6107 Carson Hall, Hanover, NH 03755-3506

Assn. of African Universities [IO], Accra, Ghana

Assn. of African Women Scholars [IO], Indianapolis, IN, United States

Assn. of African Women Scholars [9071], c/o Dr. Obioma Nnaemeka, Pres., French and Women's Stud., Cavanaugh Hall, Rm. 001C, Indiana Univ., 425 Univ. Blvd., Indianapolis, IN 46202, (317)278-2038

Assn. for Africanist Anthropology [6408], c/o Amer. Anthropological Assn., 2200 Wilson Blvd., Ste. 600, Arlington, VA 22201-3357, (703)528-1902

Assn. des Agences-Conseils en Commun. [IO], Paris, France

Reference to "IO" in place of a book number signifies that the association may be found in the 45th edition of International Organizations.

Assn. des Agences Conseils en Commun. [★IO]

Assn. of Agents, Brokers and Valuers of Wine and Foreign Spirits [IO], Amsterdam, Netherlands

Assn. for Agricultural Colleges in Denmark [IO], Arhus, Denmark

Assn. of Agricultural Res. Institutions in the Near East and North Africa [IO], Amman, Jordan

Assn. for the Aid of Crippled Children [★11541]

Assn. to Aid Refugees, Japan [★IO]

Assn. for Aid and Relief, Japan [IO], Tokyo, Japan

Assn. des Aides Familiales du Quebec [IO], Montreal, QC, Canada

Assn. of Air Force Missileers [20662], PO Box 5693, Breckenridge, CO 80424, (970)453-0500

Assn. of Air Medical Services [14314], 526 King St., Ste. 415, Alexandria, VA 22314-3143, (703)836-8732

Assn. of Air Medical Services [IO], Alexandria, VA, United States

Assn. of Air Transport Unions - Defunct.

Assn. of Airborne Ranger Companies of the Korean War - Address unknown since 1995.

Assn. Albanaise Des Femmes Diplomees Des Universites [IO], Tirana, Albania

Assn. of Albanian Girls and Women [IO], Dulles, VA, United States

Assn. of Albanian Girls and Women [18382], c/o Amy L. Sebes, Founder/Dir., 9510 Tirana Pl., Dulles, VA 20189-9510, (310)291-9205

Assn. Algerienne pour la Planification Familiale [IO], Oran, Algeria

Assn. of Allergists for Mycological Investigations - Defunct.

Assn. of Alternate Postal Systems [2447], 1725 Oaks Way, Oklahoma City, OK 73131, (405)478-0161

Assn. of Alternative Newsweeklies [3091], 1250 Eye St. NW, Ste. 804, Washington, DC 20005, (202)289-8484

Assn. of Alumni of Intl. Educational and Cultural Exchange; Fulbright [★8613]

Assn. Alzheimer Suisse [IO], Yverdon-les-Bains, Switzerland

Assn. of Amateur Magicians - Defunct.

Assn. of Amazonian Universities [IO], Sao Bras, Brazil

Assn. for Ambulatory Behavioral Healthcare [16080], 247 Douglas Ave., Portsmouth, VA 23707, (757)673-3741

Assn. for Ambulatory Pediatric Services [★15879]

Assn. of Ambulatory Vaginal and Incontinence Surgeons [★IO]

Assn. of Amer. Air Travel Clubs - Defunct.

Assn. of Amer. Battery Manufacturers [★380]

Assn. of Amer. Battery Manufacturers [★IO]

Assn. of Amer. Bd. of Examiners in Veterinary Medicine [★16755]

Assn. of Amer. Cancer Institutes [13794], 200 Lothrop St., Iroquois Bldg., Ste. 308, Pittsburgh, PA 15213, (412)647-6111

Assn. of Amer. Ceramic Component Manufacturers [785], 735 Ceramic Pl., Ste. 100, Westerville, OH 43081-8720, (614)794-5821

Assn. of Amer. Chambers of Commerce in Latin Am. [24352], 1615 H St. NW, Washington, DC 20062-2000, (202)463-5485

Assn. of American-Chinese Professionals [★19012]

Assn. of Amer. Choruses [★10588]

Assn. of Amer. CIRP Industrial Sponsors - Defunct.

Assn. of Amer. Colleges [★8098]

Assn. of Amer. Colls. Arts Program - Defunct.

Assn. of Amer. Colleges and Universities [8098], 1818 R St. NW, Washington, DC 20009, (202)387-3760

Assn. of Amer. Collegiate Literary Societies [10412]

Assn. of Amer. Consumers [★13342]

The Assn. of Amer. Cultures [9554], 656 S 2nd Ave., Yuma, AZ 85364, (928)783-1757

Assn. of Amer. Dance Companies - Defunct.

Assn. for the Amer. Dance Festival [★9865]

Assn. of Amer. Dentists - Address unknown since 1995.

Assn. of Amer. Editorial Cartoonists [3092], 3899 N Front St., Harrisburg, PA 17110, (717)703-3069

Assn. of Amer. Feed Control Officials [5432], c/o Dr. Rodney J. Noel, Sec.-Treas., Purdue Univ., Off. of Indiana State Chemist, 175 S Univ. St., West Lafayette, IN 47907-2063, (765)494-1561

Assn. of Amer. Fertilizer Control Officials [★5433]

Assn. of Amer. Foreign Ser. Women [★24071]

Assn. of Amer. Foreign Ser. Women [★IO]

Assn. of Amer. Geographers [7121], 1710 16th St. NW, Washington, DC 20009-3198, (202)234-1450

Assn. of Amer. Historic Inns [★1909]

Assn. on Amer. Indian Affairs [18092], 966 Hungerford Dr., Ste. 12-B, Rockville, MD 20850, (240)314-7155

Assn. of Amer. Indian Physicians [15989], 1225 Sovereign Row, Ste. 103, Oklahoma City, OK 73108, (405)946-7072

Assn. of Amer. Intl. Colleges and Universities [8641], 1301 S Noland Rd., Independence, MO 64055, (816)461-3633

Assn. of Amer. Intl. Colleges and Universities [IO], Independence, MO, United States

Assn. of Amer. Intl. Colleges and Universitles - France [IO], Aix-en-Provence, France

Assn. of Amer. Jurists - Address unknown since 1999.

Assn. of Amer. Law Schools [8760], 1201 Connecticut Ave. NW, Ste. 800, Washington, DC 20036-2717, (202)296-8851

Assn. of Amer. Law Schools; Sect. on Gay and Lesbian Legal Issues, [★8761]

Assn. of Amer. Law Schools Sect. on Sexual Orientation and Gender Identity Issues [8761], c/o Prof. Mark E. Wojcik, Chm.-Elect, The John Marshall Law School, 315 S Plymouth Ct., Chicago, IL 60604, (312)987-2391

Assn. of Amer. Medical Book Publishers [★3204]

Assn. of Amer. Medical Colleges [8846], 2450 N St. NW, Washington, DC 20037-1126, (202)828-0400

Assn. of Amer. Medical Colleges-Women in Medicine Prog. [8847], 2450 North St. NW, Washington, DC 20037-1126, (202)828-0521

Assn. of Amer. Military Uniform Collectors [22628], PO Box 1876, Elyria, OH 44036, (440)365-5321

Assn. of Amer. Motorcycle Road Racers - Defunct.

Assn. of Amer. Pesticide Control Officials [6170], PO Box 466, Milford, DE 19963, (302)422-8152

Assn. of Amer. Physicians - Defunct.

Assn. of Amer. Physicians and Surgeons [15990], 1601 N Tucson Blvd., Ste. 9, Tucson, AZ 85716, (800)635-1196

Assn. of Amer. Plant Food Control Officials [5433], Fertilizer/Ag Lime Control Ser., Univ. of Missouri-Columbia, Columbia, MO 65211-8080, (573)882-0007

Assn. of Amer. Playing Card Mfrs. - Defunct.

Assn. of Amer. Publishers [3206], 71 5th Ave., 2nd Fl., New York, NY 10003-3004, (212)255-0200

Assn. of Amer. Railroad Dining Car Officers - Defunct.

Assn. of Amer. Railroads [3282], 50 F St. NW, Washington, DC 20001-1564, (202)639-2100

Assn. of Amer. Rhodes Scholars [19345], 1 AAA Dr., Ste. 102, Trenton, NJ 08691-1803, (866)746-0283

Assn. of Amer. Schools in Central Am., Colombia, Caribbean and Mexico [IO], Quito, Ecuador

Assn. of Amer. Schools in South Am. [8642], 12333 NW 18th St., Ste. 5, Pembroke Pines, FL 33026, (954)436-4034

Assn. of Amer. Secretaries of State [★6277]

Assn. of Amer. Seed Control Officials [5434], c/o Anita Hall, 101 E State St., No. 214, Ithaca, NY 14850, (607)256-3313

Assn. of Amer. Seed Control Officials [IO], Harrisburg, PA, United States

Assn. of Amer. Ship Owners - Defunct.

Assn. of Amer. State Geologists [7129], c/o Chacko J. John, Pres., Louisiana State Univ., 3079 Energy, Coast and Environment Bldg., Baton Rouge, LA 70803, (225)578-5320

Assn. of Amer. Sword Collectors - Defunct.

Assn. of Amer. Trial Lawyers [★6328]

Assn. of Amer. Universities [8099], 1200 New York Ave., Ste. 550, Washington, DC 20005, (202)408-7500

Assn. of Amer. Univ. Presses [8550], 71 W 23rd St., Ste. 901, New York, NY 10010-4102, (212)989-1010

Assn. of Amer. Veterinary Medical Colleges [9293], 1101 Vermont Ave. NW, Ste. 301, Washington, DC 20005, (202)371-9195

Assn. of Amer. Vintners - Address unknown since 1994.

Assn. of Amer. Volunteer Physicians - Defunct.

Assn. of Amer. Wives of Europeans [IO], Paris, France

Assn. of Amer. Women Dentists [★14119]

Assn. of Amer. Wood Pulp Importers - Defunct.

Assn. of Amer. Youth of Ukrainian Descent - Address unknown since 2001.

Assn. of Americans and Canadians in Israel [IO], Jerusalem, Israel

Assn. of Americans for Civic Responsibility [17074], 13316 Foxhall Dr., Silver Spring, MD 20906, (301)933-1494

Assn. of Americans Resident Overseas [IO], Paris, France

Assn. of America's Public TV Stations [547], 666 Eleventh St. NW, Ste. 1100, Washington, DC 20001, (202)654-4200

Assn. of America's Young Democratic Azerbaijanian Friends [IO], Baku, Azerbaijan

Assn. AMHS Inst. [★14597]

Assn. des Amidonneries de Cereales de l'UE [★IO]

Assn. des Amis de la Republique Arabe Sahraouie Democratique [IO], Paris, France

Assn. of Anaesthetists of Great Britain and Ireland [IO], London, United Kingdom

Assn. des Anciens Fonctionnaires Internationaux [★IO]

Assn. des Anciens de l'OMS [★IO]

Assn. of Ancient Historians [10093], c/o Prof. Jennifer T. Roberts, Pres., Dept. of Foreign Languages and Literatures, City Coll. of New York, NAC 5-223, Convent Ave. and 138th St., New York, NY 10031, (212)650-6731

Assn. of Anglican Musicians [20425], PO Box 7530, Little Rock, AR 72217, (828)274-2681

Assn. for the Anthropological Stud. of Play [★10858]

Assn. of Apex Clubs of Australia [IO], Nuriootpa, Australia

Assn. of Apollo-Soyuz Test Project Philatelists - Defunct.

Assn. of Appliance and Home Entertainment Distributors - Defunct.

Assn. of Applied Biologists [IO], Warwick, United Kingdom

Assn. for Applied Community Researchers [7561], PO Box 100127, Arlington, VA 22210, (703)522-4980

Assn. of Applied Geochemists [IO], Nepean, ON, Canada

Assn. of Applied Insect Ecologists [★5073]

Assn. for Applied Interactive Multimedia [2666], PO Box 182, Charleston, SC 29402-0182

Assn. of Applied IPM Ecologists [5073], PO Box 12181, Fresno, CA 93776, (559)907-4897

Assn. for Applied Poetry [16211], 81 Shadymere Ln., Columbus, OH 43213, (614)986-1881

Assn. for Applied Psychoanalysis - Defunct.

Assn. for Applied Psychophysiology and Biofeedback [13749], 10200 W 44th Ave., Ste. 304, Wheat Ridge, CO 80033, (303)422-8436

Assn. for Applied and Therapeutic Humor [16605], 65 Enterprise, Aliso Viejo, CA 92656, (949)715-4681

Assn. of Approved Tourist Guides of Ireland [IO], Dublin, Ireland

Assn. Aquacole du Canada [★IO]

Assn. of Arab-American Univ. Graduates [18953], 211 E 4th St., New York, NY 10009

Assn. of Arab Universities [IO], Amman, Jordan

Assn. for Arab Youth - Baladna [IO], Haifa, Israel

Assn. for Archery in Schools [IO], Banbury, United Kingdom

Assn. of Architectural Librarians - Defunct.

Assn. of Architecture School Librarians [10328], c/o Jennifer Benedetto Beals, Sec.-Treas., Art and Architecture Librarian, Univ. of Tennessee, 145 Hodges Lib., Knoxville, TN 37996-1000, (865)974-0014

Assn. of Area Bus. Publications [★3199]

Assn. of Argentine Banks [IO], Buenos Aires, Argentina

Assn. for Arid Lands Stud. [4498], c/o Intl. Center for Arid and Semiarid Land Stud., PO Box 41036, Lubbock, TX 79409-1036, (806)742-2218

A star before a book entry number signifies that the name is not listed separately, but is mentioned within the entry.

Assn. of Armenian Church Choirs of Am. [10559], c/o Ms. Mary Selvinazian, Treas./Ed., 5636 196th Pl., Flushing, NY 11365-2310, (718)423-5680

Assn. of Armenian Info. Professionals [18969], 139 Cedar St., Cliffside Park, NJ 07010, (201)941-2266

Assn. des Arpenteurs des Terres du Canada [★IO]

Assn. of Art and Antique Dealers [IO], London, United Kingdom

Assn. of Art Editors [3207], c/o Phil Freshman, Pres., 3912 Natchez Ave. S, St. Louis Park, MN 55416, (952)922-1374

Assn. of Art Galleries in Switzerland [IO], Basel, Switzerland

Assn. of Art Historians [IO], London, United Kingdom

Assn. for Art History [9430], Indiana Univ., Henry Radford Hope School of Fine Arts, Fine Arts 124, Bloomington, IN 47405

Assn. of Art Museum Curators [10493], 174 E 80th St., New York, NY 10021, (212)879-7582

Assn. of Art Museum Curators [IO], New York, NY, United States

Assn. of Art Museum Directors [10494], 120 E 56th St., Ste. 520, New York, NY 10022, (212)754-8084

Assn. of Artist-Run Galleries - Address unknown since 2001.

Assn. of Arts Admin. Educators [7967], c/o Andrew Taylor, Pres./Dir., Bolz Center for Arts Admin., 975 Univ. Ave., Madison, WI 53706, (608)263-4161

Assn. for the Arts and Psychology - Defunct.

Assn. of Asbestos Cement Pipe Producers [★3026]

Assn. of Asbestos Cement Prdt. Producers [3026], 1235 Jefferson Davis Hwy., PMB 114, Arlington, VA 22202-3283, (514)861-1153

Assn. of Asia Pacific Airlines [IO], Kuala Lumpur, Malaysia

Assn. of Asia Pacific Physical Societies [IO], Kanazawa, Japan

Assn. for Asian Amer. Stud. [7982], Cornell Univ., 420 Rockefeller Hall, Ithaca, NY 14853-2502, (607)255-3320

Assn. of Asian Confed. of Credit Unions [★IO]

Assn. of Asian Election Authorities - Address unknown since 2006.

Assn. of Asian Indians in Am. [★19110]

Assn. of Asian/Pacific Amer. Artists - Address unknown since 2002.

Assn. of Asian Pacific Community Hea. Organizations [14719], 300 Frank H. Ogawa Plz., Ste. 620, Oakland, CA 94612, (510)272-9536

Assn. of Asian-Pacific Operational Res. Societies [IO], Mandaluyong City, Philippines

Assn. of Asian Performing Arts Festivals [IO], Singapore, Singapore

Assn. of Asian Social Sci. Res. Councils [IO], Quezon City, Philippines

Assn. for Asian Stud. [IO], Ann Arbor, MI, United States

Assn. for Asian Stud. [7983], 1021 E Huron St., Ann Arbor, MI 48104, (734)665-2490

Assn. Asiatique des Bureaux de Congres et de Tourisme [★IO]

Assn. of Asphalt Paving Technologists [6835], 4711 Clark Ave., Ste. G, White Bear Lake, MN 55110-3268, (651)293-9188

Assn. for Assessment and Accreditation of Lab. Animal Care Intl. [13695], 5283 Corporate Dr., Ste. 203, Frederick, MD 21703, (301)696-9626

Assn. for Assessment and Accreditation of Lab. Animal Care Intl. [IO], Frederick, MD, United States

Assn. for Assessment in Counseling [★9247]

Assn. for Assessment in Counseling and Educ. [9247], c/o Amer. Counseling Assn., 5999 Stevenson Ave., Alexandria, VA 22304-3300, (800)347-6647

Assn. of Asset Mgt. Companies [IO], Bratislava, Slovakia

Assn. of Asst. Mistresses [★IO]

Assn. of Asst. Teachers in Tech. Institutes [★IO]

Assn. of Assistive Tech. Act Programs [14237], c/o Deborah Buck, Exec. Dir., PO Box 32, Delmar, NY 12054, (518)439-1263

Assn. des Assureurs Cooperatifs et Mutualistes Europeens [★IO]

Assn. of Asthma Educators [16355], 1215 Anthony Ave., Columbia, SC 29201-1701, (888)988-7747

Assn. for Astrological Networking [6489], 8306 Wilshire Blvd., PMB 537, Beverly Hills, CA 90211, (212)726-1407

Assn. for Astrological Psychology [★6490]

Assn. for Astronomy Educ. [IO], London, United Kingdom

Assn. of Astronomy Educators - Defunct.

Assn. of Atlantic Women Bus. Owners [IO], Halifax, NS, Canada

Assn. of Attenders and Alumni of The Hague Acad. of Intl. Law [IO], The Hague, Netherlands

Assn. of Attorney-Mediators [5483], PO Box 741955, Dallas, TX 75374-1955, (972)669-8101

Assn. of Audio-Visual Technicians - Defunct.

Assn. of Audiovisual and Film Indus. of Austria [IO], Vienna, Austria

L'Association des Auditeurs at Anciens Auditeurs de L'Academie de Droit Intl. de la Haye [★IO]

Assn. of Australasian Diesel Specialists [IO], Melbourne, Australia

Assn. of Australasian Palaeontologists [IO], Sydney, Australia

Assn. of Australian Boutique Winemakers [IO], Ashfield, Australia

Assn. of Australian Ports and Marine Authorities [IO], Sydney, Australia

Assn. of the Austrian Chem. Indus. [IO], Vienna, Austria

Assn. of Austrian Clothing Indus. [IO], Vienna, Austria

Assn. of the Austrian Elecl. and Electronics Indus. [IO], Vienna, Austria

Assn. of Austrian Librarians [IO], Bregenz, Austria

Assn. of the Austrian Machinery and Metalware Indus. [IO], Vienna, Austria

Assn. of the Austrian Paper Indus. [IO], Vienna, Austria

Assn. of Austrian Textile Indus. [IO], Vienna, Austria

Assn. of Authorised Public Accountants [IO], London, United Kingdom

Assn. of Authors' Agents [IO], London, United Kingdom

Assn. of Authors' Representatives [171], 676A 9th Ave., No. 312, New York, NY 10036, (212)252-3695

Assn. of Auto and Truck Recyclers [★3988]

Assn. for Automatic Identification and Mobility North Am. [336], c/o Mary Lou Bosco, 125 Warrendale-Bayne Rd., Warrendale, PA 15086, (724)934-5688

Assn. for Automatic Language Processing [IO], Paris, France

Assn. of Auto. Importers [★IO]

Assn. of Automotive Aftermarket Distributors [★370]

Assn. of Automotive Aftermarket Distributors/Parts Plus [370], 3085 Fountainside Dr., No. 210, Germantown, TN 38138, (901)682-9090

Assn. of the Automotive Indus. [IO], Frankfurt am Main, Germany

Assn. of Automotive Tech. Societies in Finland [IO], Helsinki, Finland

Assn. of Average Adjusters [IO], London, United Kingdom

Assn. of Average Adjusters of the U.S. [2145], 126 Midwood Ave., Farmingdale, NY 11735

Assn. of Avian Veterinarians - USA [16782], PO Box 811720, Boca Raton, FL 33481, (561)393-8901

Assn. of Avian Veterinarians - USA [IO], Boca Raton, FL, United States

Assn. for Aviation Psychology [6370], c/o Lori McDonnell, Membership Service Coor., NASA Ames Res. Center, Mail Stop 262-4, Moffett Field, CA 94035

Assn. of Aviation and Space Museums - Defunct.

Assn. for Baha'i Stud. [IO], Ottawa, ON, Canada

Assn. of Bakery Ingredients Mfrs. [IO], Edinburgh, United Kingdom

Assn. for Balance of Political Power - Address unknown since 1995.

Assn. of Balloon and Airship Constructors - Address unknown since 2002.

Assn. Bancaire pour l'Evro [★IO]

Assn. of Bangkok Alumni of Dermatology - Pakistan [IO], Peshawar, Pakistan

Assn. of Bank Holding Companies [★477]

Assn. of Bank Travel Bureaus - Defunct.

Assn. of Bankrupts [★IO]

Assn. of Banks in Jordan [IO], Amman, Jordan

Assn. of Banks in Lebanon [IO], Beirut, Lebanon

Assn. of Banks in Malaysia [IO], Kuala Lumpur, Malaysia

Assn. of Banks in Singapore [IO], Singapore, Singapore

Assn. of Banks in Slovakia [IO], Bratislava, Slovakia

Assn. des Banques et Banquiers Luxembourg [★IO]

Assn. des Banquiers Canadiens [★IO]

Assn. of Baptist Chaplains - Defunct.

Assn. of Baptist Homes and Hospitals [★19471]

Assn. of Baptist Professors of Religion [★9277]

Assn. of Baptists for Evangelism in the Orient [★19472]

Assn. of Baptists for Evangelism in the Orient [★IO]

Assn. of Baptists for Scouting [12995], c/o Boy Scouts of Am., PO Box 152079, Irving, TX 75015-2079

Assn. of Baptists for World Evangelism [19472], PO Box 8585, Harrisburg, PA 17105-8585, (717)774-7000

Assn. of Baptists for World Evangelism [IO], Harrisburg, PA, United States

Assn. of Baptists for World Evangelism - Canada [IO], London, ON, Canada

L'Association du Barreau Canadien [★IO]

Assn. of Baseball Leagues; George Khoury [23109]

Assn. of Battery Recyclers - Address unknown since 2001.

Assn. of Bearing Specialists [★2007]

Assn. of Beer and Malt Mfrs. [IO], Rome, Italy

Assn. for Behavior Anal. [6526], 1219 S Park St., Kalamazoo, MI 49001-5607, (269)492-9310

Assn. for Behavioral and Cognitive Therapies [13733], 305 7th Ave., 16th Fl., New York, NY 10001-6008, (212)647-1890

Assn. for Behavioral Hea. and Wellness [24088], c/o Pamela Greenberg, MPP, Pres./CEO, 1101 Pennsylvania Ave. NW, 6th Fl., Washington, DC 20004, (202)756-7726

Assn. of Behavioral Healthcare Mgt. [15191], c/o Natl. Coun. for Community Behavioral Healthcare, 12300 Twinbrook Pkwy., Ste. 320, Rockville, MD 20852, (301)984-6200

Assn. for the Behavioral Sciences and Medical Educ. [6527], 1460 N Center Rd., Burton, MI 48509, (810)715-4365

Assn. for the Behavioral Treatment of Sexual Abusers [★6529]

Assn. for the Behavioral Treatment of Sexual Aggression [★6529]

Assn. of Belarussian Amer. Veterans in America - Address unknown since 2001.

Assn. Belge des Architectes de Jardins et des Architectes Paysagistes [IO], Brussels, Belgium

Assn. Belge des Banques [★IO]

Assn. Belge de Documentation [★IO]

Assn. Belge des Journalistes Agricoles [★IO]

Assn. Belge du Marketing Direct [★IO]

Assn. Belge des patients Osteoporotiques [★IO]

Assn. Belge du Secteur des Aliments de l'Enfance et des Aliments Dietetiques [★IO]

Assn. Belge des Syndicats Medicaux [IO], Brussels, Belgium

Assn. of Belgian Pulp, Paper and Bd. Producers [IO], Brussels, Belgium

Assn. of Belgian Relocation Agents [IO], Waterloo, Belgium

Assn. for Benchmarking in Hea. Care [1848], c/o The Benchmarking Network, 4606 FM 1960 W, Ste. 250, Houston, TX 77069-9949, (281)440-5044

Assn. of Benedictin Children [★13752]

Assn. of Better Bus. Bureaus [★17309]

Assn. of Better Bus. Bureaus [★IO]

Assn. of Better Cmpt. Dealers [★898]

Assn. for Better Living and Educ. Intl; ABLE: [11756]

Assn. of Beverage Container Recyclers - Defunct.

Assn. of Bible Institutes and Bible Colleges [★8080]

Assn. for Biblical Higher Educ. [8080], 5575 S Semoran Blvd., Ste. 26, Orlando, FL 32822-1781, (407)207-0808

Assn. for the Bibliography of History [10094], c/o Charles A. D'Aniello, Exec. Sec.-Treas., State Univ. of New York at Buffalo, Lockwood Memorial Lib., Rm. 321, Buffalo, NY 14260, (716)645-2817

Reference to "IO" in place of a book number signifies that the association may be found in the 45th edition of International Organizations.

Assn. des Bibliotheques de la Sante du Canada [★IO]

Assn. of Biological Collections Appraisers - Address unknown since 2002.

Assn. of Biomedical Communications Directors [14030], c/o Manny Bekier, Dir., SUNY Downstate Medical Ctr., 450 Clarkson Ave., Brooklyn, NY 11203, (718)270-7551

Assn. for Biomedical Res. [★13700]

Assn. of Biomolecular Rsrc. Facilities [7238], 2019 Galisteo St., Bldg. I, Santa Fe, NM 87505, (505)983-8102

Assn. of Biotechnology Companies [★520]

Assn. of Biotechnology Led Enterprises [IO], Bangalore, India

Assn. of Birth Defect Children [★13752]

Assn. for Birth Psychology [16137], 444 E 82nd St., New York, NY 10028, (212)988-6617

Assn. of Bituminous Contractors [839], 815 Connecticut Ave. NW, Ste. 620, Washington, DC 20006, (202)785-4440

Assn. of Black Admissions and Financial Aid Officers of the Ivy League and Sister Schools - Address unknown since 2004.

Assn. of Black Anthropologists [6409], c/o Dana-Ain Davis, Social Sciences Div., 735 Anderson Hill Rd., Purchase, NY 10577-1402, (914)251-6624

Assn. of Black Cardiologists [13893], 5355 Hunter Rd., Atlanta, GA 30349, (404)201-6600

Assn. of Black Catholics Against Abortion - Defunct.

Assn. of Black CPA Firms - Defunct.

Assn. of Black Found. Executives - Address unknown since 2001.

Assn. of Black Motion Picture and TV Producers - Address unknown since 1991.

Assn. of Black Nursing Faculty [8848], PO Box 589, Lisle, IL 60532, (630)969-3809

Assn. of Black Psychologists [16138], PO Box 55999, Washington, DC 20040-5999, (202)722-0808

Assn. of Black Sociologists [7659], 4200 Wisconsin Ave. NW, PMB 106-257, Washington, DC 20016-2143, (202)365-1759

Assn. of Black Sporting Goods Professionals - Address unknown since 2003.

Assn. of Black Storytellers [★10981]

Assn. of Black Women Attorneys [5484], 255 W 36th St., Ste. 800, New York, NY 10018, (212)300-2193

Assn. of Black Women in Higher Educ. [9314], PO Box 210, Princeton, NJ 08540, (609)258-5494

Assn. for the Bladder Exstrophy Community [14252], 3075 First St., La Salle, MI 48145, (734)243-9912

Assn. for the Bladder Exstrophy Community [IO], La Salle, MI, United States

Association of Blauvelt Descendants [IO], Westminster, CO, United States

Assn. of Blauvelt Descendants [20785], 3367 W 113th Ave., Westminster, CO 80031-7179, (303)438-7267

Assn. of Blind and Partially Sighted Teachers and Students [IO], London, United Kingdom

Assn. of Blind Piano Tuners [IO], Darwen, United Kingdom

Assn. for the Blind of Western Australia [IO], Perth, Australia

Assn. of Blood Donor Recruiters - Defunct.

The Assn. of Boarding Schools [9018], 2141 Wisconsin Ave. NW, Ste. H, Washington, DC 20007, (202)965-8982

Assn. of Boards of Certification [6337], 208 5th St., Ames, IA 50010-6259, (515)232-3623

Assn. of Boards of Certification for Operating Personnel [★6337]

Assn. of Boards of Certification for Operating Personnel in Water and Wastewater Utilities [★6337]

Assn. of Bone and Joint Surgeons [15763], 6300 N River Rd., Ste. 727, Rosemont, IL 60018-4226, (847)698-1636

Assn. of Book Gp. Readers and Leaders [9738], Box 885, Highland Park, IL 60035, (312)337-8810

Assn. of Book Gp. Readers and Leaders [IO], Highland Park, IL, United States

Assn. of Book Travelers - Address unknown since 2000.

Assn. of Booksellers for Children [529], c/o Kristen McLean, Exec. Dir., 6538 Collin Ave., No. 168, Miami Beach, FL 33141, (617)390-7759

Assn. of Bordeaux Wine and Alcohol Wholesalers [IO], Bordeaux, France

Assn. for Borderlands Stud. [IO], Las Cruces, NM, United States

Assn. for Borderlands Stud. [8653], c/o Dr. Manuel Chavez, Pres., Center for Latin Amer. and Caribbean Stud., Michigan State Univ., 300 Intl. Center, East Lansing, MI 48824, (517)353-1960

Assn. Botanique du Canada [★IO]

Assn. of Boys and Girls Clubs Professionals - Address unknown since 2003.

Assn. of Boys and Students Clothing Mfrs. - Defunct.

Assn. for Brain Tumor Res. [★13791]

Association of Brass and Bronze Ingot Manufacturers [★2701]

Assn. for Breastfeeding Fashions - Defunct.

Assn. of Breastfeeding Mothers [IO], Bridgwater, United Kingdom

Assn. of Breeders and European Distributors of Flower Seed Varieties [★IO]

Assn. of Breeders of Thoroughbred Holstein Cattle [★4263]

Assn. of Brethren Caregivers [11276], 1451 Dundee Ave., Elgin, IL 60120-1949, (847)742-5100

Assn. of Brewers and Brewers' Assn. of Am. [★198]

Assn. of Bridal Consultants [533], 56 Danbury Rd., Ste. 11, New Milford, CT 06776, (860)355-0464

Association of Bridal Consultants [IO], New Milford, CT, United States

Assn. for Bridge Constr. and Design [6471], PO Box 23264, Pittsburgh, PA 15222-6264, (412)257-8774

Assn. of British Advt. Agents [★IO]

Assn. of British Certification Bodies [IO], Chislehurst, United Kingdom

Assn. of British Chem. Mfrs. [★IO]

Assn. of British Choral Directors [IO], Sherborne, United Kingdom

Assn. of British Climatologists [IO], Birmingham, United Kingdom

Assn. of British Columbia Drama Educators [IO], Vancouver, BC, Canada

Assn. of British Correspondence Colleges [IO], London, United Kingdom

Assn. of British Credit Unions Limited [IO], Manchester, United Kingdom

Assn. of British Detectives [★IO]

Assn. of British Dir. Publishers [★IO]

Assn. for British Dispensing Opticians [IO], London, United Kingdom

Assn. of British Drivers [IO], Kenley, United Kingdom

Assn. of British Factors and Discounters [★IO]

Assn. of British Healthcare Indus. [IO], London, United Kingdom

Assn. of British Insurers [IO], London, United Kingdom

Assn. of British Introduction Agencies [IO], London, United Kingdom

Assn. of British Investigators [IO], London, United Kingdom

Assn. of British Jazz Musicians [IO], London, United Kingdom

Assn. of British Mining Equip. Companies [IO], Wakefield, United Kingdom

Assn. of British Neurologists [IO], London, United Kingdom

Assn. of British Offshore Indus. [IO], London, United Kingdom

Assn. of British Offshore Indus. [★IO]

Assn. of British Oil Indus. [★IO]

Assn. of British Orchestras [IO], London, United Kingdom

Assn. of the British Pharmaceutical Indus. [IO], London, United Kingdom

Assn. of British Philatelic Societies [IO], Thetford, United Kingdom

Assn. of British Picture Restorers [★IO]

Assn. of British Professional Conf. Organisers [IO], Birmingham, United Kingdom

Assn. of British Riding Schools [IO], Penzance, United Kingdom

Assn. of British Sailmakers [IO], Southampton, United Kingdom

Assn. of British Sci. Writers [IO], London, United Kingdom

Assn. of British Theatre Technicians [IO], London, United Kingdom

Assn. of British Theological and Philosophical Libraries [IO], London, United Kingdom

Assn. of British Travel Agents [IO], London, United Kingdom

Assn. of British Wild Animal Keepers [IO], Upton, United Kingdom

Assn. for Broadcast Engineering Standards - Defunct.

Assn. of Broadcasting Doctors [IO], Ely, United Kingdom

Assn. of Brokers and Yacht Agents [★IO]

Assn. of Brokers and Yacht Agents [IO], Petersfield, United Kingdom

Assn. of Building Component Mfrs. [IO], Aylesford, United Kingdom

Assn. of Building Engineers [IO], Northampton, United Kingdom

Assn. of Building Hardware Mfrs. [IO], Tamworth, United Kingdom

Assn. of Bulgarians with Bronchial Asthma [IO], Sofia, Bulgaria

Assn. Burkinabe des Femmes Diplomees des Universites [IO], Ouagadougou, Burkina Faso

Assn. Burundaise des Femmes Diplomees des Universites [IO], Bujumbura, Burundi

Assn. for Bus. Commun. [8014], c/o Dr. Betty S. Johnson, Exec. Dir., PO Box 6143, Nacogdoches, TX 75962-0001, (936)468-6280

Assn. of Bus. Executives [IO], London, United Kingdom

Assn. of Business Forms Mfrs. - Defunct.

Assn. of Business Officers of Preparatory Schools - Address unknown since 1999.

Assn. of Business Products Mfrs. - Address unknown since 2005.

Assn. of Bus. Psychologists [IO], London, United Kingdom

Assn. of Bus. Publishers [★3201]

Assn. of Bus. Recovery Professionals [IO], London, United Kingdom

Assn. of Bus. Schools [IO], London, United Kingdom

Association for Business Simulation and Experiential Learning [IO], Glenside, PA, United States

Assn. for Bus. Simulation and Experiential Learning [8015], c/o Annette Halpin, VP/Exec. Dir., Dept. of Marketing, Arcadia Univ., 450 S Easton Rd., Glenside, PA 19038, (215)572-2849

Assn. for Bus. Sponsorship of the Arts [★IO]

Assn. of Business Support Services Intl. - Defunct.

Assn. of Bus. Travellers [IO], North Sydney, Australia

Assn. of Bus. Women of Serbia [IO], Belgrade, Serbia

Assn. of Buying Offices - Defunct.

Assn. of C and C Users [IO], Bexhill-on-Sea, United Kingdom

Assn. of Cable Communicators [5556], PO Box 75007, Washington, DC 20013-0007, (202)222-2370

Assn. of Cable TV Suppliers - Defunct.

Assn. des Cadres d'Institutions Culturelles [★IO]

Assn. of Call Center Managers [2520], 2505 Living Rock Ave., Las Vegas, NV 89106, (702)367-2288

Assn. for the Calligraphic Arts [9555], 26 Main St., East Greenwich, RI 02818

Assn. of Cambodian Survivors of America [12806]

Assn. Camerounaise de Femmes Diplomees des Universites [★IO]

Assn. of Camp Nurses [IO], Bemidji, MN, United States

Assn. of Camp Nurses [15464], 8630 Thorsonveien NE, Bemidji, MN 56601, (218)586-2633

Assn. of Camphill Communities [IO], Aberdeen, United Kingdom

Assn. des Camps du Canada [★IO]

Assn. du the du Canada [★IO]

Assn. mineralogique du Canada [★IO]

Assn. geologique du Canada [★IO]

L'Association des architects paysagistes du Canada [★IO]

Assn. des universites et colleges du Canada [★IO]

A star before a book entry number signifies that the name is not listed separately, but is mentioned within the entry.

L'Association internationale de la gestion du personnel - Canada [★IO]

Assn. des critiques de theatre du Canada [★IO]

Assn. of Canada Lands Surveyors [IO], Ottawa, ON, Canada

Assn. of Canadian Academic Healthcare Organizations [IO], Ottawa, ON, Canada

Assn. of Canadian Advertisers [IO], Toronto, ON, Canada

Assn. of Canadian Archivists [IO], Ottawa, ON, Canada

Assn. of Canadian Biscuit Mfrs. [IO], Don Mills, ON, Canada

Assn. of Canadian Choral Conductors [IO], Montreal, QC, Canada

Assn. of Canadian Clubs [IO], Ottawa, ON, Canada

Assn. of Canadian Coll. and Univ. Teachers of English [IO], Halifax, NS, Canada

Assn. of Canadian Community Colleges [IO], Ottawa, ON, Canada

Assn. of Canadian Distillers [IO], Ottawa, ON, Canada

Assn. of Canadian Ergonomists [IO], Calgary, AB, Canada

Assn. of Canadian Faculties of Dentistry [IO], Ottawa, ON, Canada

Assn. of Canadian Film Craftspeople [IO], Burnaby, BC, Canada

Assn. for Canadian Jewish Stud. [IO], Montreal, QC, Canada

Assn. of Canadian Knights of the Sovereign Military Order of Malta [★IO]

Assn. of Canadian Map Libraries and Archives [IO], Ottawa, ON, Canada

Assn. of Canadian Medical Colleges [★IO]

Assn. of Canadian Mountain Guides [IO], Canmore, AB, Canada

Assn. of Canadian Orchestras [★IO]

Assn. of Canadian Pension Mgt. [IO], Toronto, ON, Canada

Assn. of Canadian Port Authorities [IO], Ottawa, ON, Canada

Assn. of Canadian Publishers [IO], Toronto, ON, Canada

Assn. of Canadian Search, Employment and Staffing Services [IO], Mississauga, ON, Canada

Assn. for Canadian Stud. [IO], Montreal, QC, Canada

Assn. for Canadian Stud. in the U.S. [IO], Washington, DC, United States

Assn. for Canadian Stud. in the U.S. [8043], 1220 19th St. NW, Ste. 801, Washington, DC 20036, (202)223-9005

Assn. of Canadian Teaching Hospitals [★IO]

Assn. for Canadian Theatre Res. [IO], Toronto, ON, Canada

Assn. of Canadian Travel Agencies [IO], Ottawa, ON, Canada

Assn. of Canadian Universities for Northern Stud. [IO], Ottawa, ON, Canada

Assn. of Canadian Univ. and Coll. Teachers of French [IO], Guelph, ON, Canada

Assn. of Canadian Univ. Presses [IO], Toronto, ON, Canada

Assn. of Canadian Venture Capital Companies [★IO]

Assn. of Canadian Women Composers [IO], Toronto, ON, Canada

Assn. des chefs de choeurs Canadien [★IO]

Assn. Canadiene Des Indus. De La Musique [★IO]

Assn. Canadiene d'experts-conseils en Patrimoine [★IO]

Assn. Canadienne du soin des plaies [★IO]

Assn. Canadienne pour la recherche sur les services et les politiques de la sante [★IO]

Assn. Canadienne des employes professionels [★IO]

Assn. Canadienne et de recherche institutionelles [★IO]

Assn. Canadienne des moniteurs de surf des neiges [★IO]

Assn. Canadienne du beton prepare [★IO]

L'Association Canadienne du medicament generique [★IO]

L'Association Canadienne des utilisateurs de satellites [★IO]

Assn. Canadienne des paiements [★IO]

Assn. Canadienne des 5 Quilles [★IO]

Assn. Canadienne des Administrateurs et des Administratrices Solaires [★IO]

Assn. Canadienne des Agences de Voyages [★IO]

Assn. Canadienne des Agents de Commun. en Educ. [★IO]

Assn. Canadienne des Aliements de Sante [★IO]

Assn. Canadienne des Artistes de la Scene [★IO]

Assn. Canadienne des Ataxies Familiales [★IO]

Assn. Canadienne des Banques Alimentaires [★IO]

Assn. Canadienne des Bibliotheques, Archives et Centres de Documentation Musicaux [★IO]

Assn. Canadienne des Bibliotheques de Droit [★IO]

Assn. Canadienne du Bison [★IO]

Assn. Canadienne de la Boulangerie [★IO]

Assn. Canadienne de Boxe Amateur [★IO]

Assn. Canadienne de Cadeaux et d'accessoires de Table [★IO]

Assn. Canadienne du Camionnage d'Entreprise [★IO]

Assn. Canadienne de Canotage [★IO]

Assn. Canadienne du Capital de Risque et d'Investissement [★IO]

Assn. Canadienne de Cartographie [★IO]

L'Association Canadienne des Centres de vie Autonome [★IO]

Assn. Canadienne des Centres Contre les Agressions a Caractere Sexuel [★IO]

Assn. Canadienne des Chaines de Pharmacies [★IO]

Assn. Canadienne des Chefs de Police [★IO]

Assn. Canadienne Chirurgie Pediatrique [★IO]

Assn. Canadienne du Ciment [★IO]

L'Association Canadienne du Commerce des Semences [★IO]

Assn. Canadienne des Commisions de Police [★IO]

L'Association Canadienne des Commissions/Conseils Scolaires [★IO]

Assn. Canadienne des Compagnies d'Assurance Mutuelles [★IO]

Assn. Canadienne des Compagnies d'Assurances de Personnes [★IO]

Assn. Canadienne du Comptables d'Assurance [★IO]

L'Association Canadienne des Conseillers et Conseillers Juridiques d'Entreprises [★IO]

Assn. Canadienne des Conseillers en Genetique [★IO]

Assn. Canadienne des Conseillers Hypothecaires Accredites [★IO]

Assn. Canadienne des Conseillers Professionnels en Immigration [★IO]

Assn. Canadienne pour la Conservation et la Restauration des Biens Culturels [★IO]

Assn. Canadienne de la Constr. [★IO]

Assn. Canadienne du Contreplaque [★IO]

Assn. Canadienne du Contreplaque et des Placages de Bois Dur [★IO]

Assn. Canadienne du Controle du Trafic Aerien - Sect. Locale 5454 des TCA [★IO]

Assn. Canadienne des Cosmetiques, Produits de Toilette et Parfums [★IO]

Assn. Canadienne de Counseling [★IO]

Assn. Canadienne de Counselling Universitaire et Collegial [★IO]

Assn. Canadienne de la Courtepointe [★IO]

Assn. Canadienne des Courtiers en Valeurs Mobilieres [★IO]

Assn. Canadienne de Cricket [★IO]

Assn. Canadienne de Curling [★IO]

Assn. Canadienne D' Hydrographie [★IO]

Assn. Canadienne d'Acoustique [★IO]

Assn. Canadienne d'Acoustique [★IO]

Assn. Canadienne D'Alarme Incendie [★IO]

Assn. Canadienne des laboratoires d'analyses environmentale [★IO]

L'Association Canadienne d'Art Photographique [★IO]

Assn. Canadienne d'Articles de Sport [★IO]

Assn. Canadienne d'Auto Distribution [★IO]

L' Assn. Canadienne De Cultures Speciales [★IO]

L'Association Canadienne De Droit Maritime [★IO]

Assn. Canadienne De L'Industrie Du Caoutchouc [★IO]

Assn. Canadienne De Sante Publique [★IO]

Assn. Canadienne d'Economique [★IO]

Assn. Canadienne d'Economique de Energie [★IO]

Assn. Canadienne d'Education [★IO]

Assn. Canadienne d'Equitation Therapeutique [★IO]

Assn. Canadienne d'Ergonomie [★IO]

Assn. Canadienne de Dermatologie [★IO]

Assn. Canadienne Des Annonceurs [★IO]

Assn. Canadienne Des Barrages [★IO]

Assn. Canadienne Des Commissaires D'Ecoles Catholiques [★IO]

Assn. Canadienne Des Experts Independants [★IO]

L'Association Canadienne Des Exportateurs De Porcs [★IO]

Assn. Canadienne Des Infirmieres Et Infermiers En Pratique Avancee [★IO]

Assn. Canadienne D'etudes Cinematographiques [★IO]

Assn. Canadienne d'Etudes du Developpement Intl. [★IO]

Assn. Canadienne d'Etudes Fiscales [★IO]

Assn. Canadienne d'Habitation et de Renovation Urbaine [★IO]

Assn. Canadienne D'Histoire Ferroviaire [★IO]

Assn. Canadienne du Diabete [★IO]

Assn. Canadienne des Directeurs Medicaux en Assurance-Vie [★IO]

Assn. Canadienne de Distributeurs d'Equipement [★IO]

Assn. Canadienne des Distributeurs de Films [★IO]

L'Association Canadienne des Distributeurs de Produits Chimiques [★IO]

Assn. Canadienne de la Distribution des Fruits et Legumes [★IO]

Assn. Canadienne de Documentation Professionnelle [★IO]

Assn. Canadienne d'Oncologie Psychosociale [★IO]

Assn. Canadienne d'Orthopedie [★IO]

Assn. Canadienne Droit er Societe [★IO]

Assn. Canadienne Du Diabete [★IO]

Assn. Canadienne Du Diabete [★IO]

Assn. Canadienne Du Diabete [★IO]

Assn. Canadienne Du Diabete [★IO]

Assn. Canadienne Du Diabete [★IO]

L'Association Canadienne Du Quarter Horse [★IO]

Assn. Canadienne d'Urologie [★IO]

Assn. Canadienne de la Dyslexie [★IO]

Assn. Canadienne des Eaux Potables et Usees [★IO]

Assn. Canadienne des Eaux Souterraines [★IO]

Assn. Canadienne des Echecs par Correspondance [★IO]

Assn. Canadienne des Ecoles de sciences infirmieres [★IO]

L'Association Canadienne des Ecoles de Ser. Social [★IO]

Assn. Canadienne des Editeurs de Musique [★IO]

Assn. Canadienne des Educateurs de Musique [★IO]

Assn. Canadienne des Educateurs en Radiodiffusion [★IO]

Assn. Canadienne Embouteilleurs d'Eau [★IO]

Assn. Canadienne des Employes de Telephone [★IO]

Assn. Canadienne des Enterprises de Messagerie [★IO]

Assn. Canadienne des Entrepreneur Electriciens [★IO]

Assn. Canadienne des Entrepreneurs en Couverture [★IO]

Assn. Canadienne des Entreprises Familiales [★IO]

Assn. Canadienne des Entreprises de Geomatique [★IO]

Assn. Canadienne des Ergotherapeutes [★IO]

Assn. Canadienne des Etudes Neoplatoniciennes [★IO]

Assn. Canadienne des Etudiants et des Internes en Pharmacie [★IO]

Assn. Canadienne des Ex-Parlementaires [★IO]

Assn. Canadienne des Exportateurs d'Equipements et Services Miniers [★IO]

Assn. Canadienne des Fabricants de Brosses [★IO]

L'Association Canadienne des Fabricants Confiseries [★IO]

Assn. Canadienne de Fabricants d'Armoires de Cuisine [★IO]

Reference to "IO" in place of a book number signifies that the association may be found in the 45th edition of International Organizations.

Assn. Canadienne des Fabricants de Grignotines [★IO]

Assn. Canadienne des Fabricants des Portes et des Cadres d'Acier [★IO]

Assn. Canadienne des Fabricants de Produits Chimiques [★IO]

Assn. Canadienne des Fabricants de Produits de Quincaillerie et d'Articles Menagers [★IO]

Assn. Canadienne des Fabricants de Tuyaux de Beton [★IO]

Assn. Canadienne des Femmes Cadres et Entrepreneurs [★IO]

L'Association Canadienne des Femmes en Communications [★IO]

Assn. Canadienne des Femmes d'Assurance [★IO]

Assn. Canadienne de Financement et de Location [★IO]

Assn. Canadienne des Finisseurs de Metaux [★IO]

Assn. Canadienne des Foires et Expositions [★IO]

L'Association Canadienne des Fonds de Revenu [★IO]

Assn. Canadienne de Forage au Diamant [★IO]

Assn. Canadienne de la Formation Professionnelle [★IO]

Assn. Canadienne des Fournisseurs de laboratoire [★IO]

Assn. Canadienne de la Franchise [★IO]

Assn. Canadienne de Gastroenterologie [★IO]

Assn. Canadienne du Gaz [★IO]

Assn. Canadienne de Gerance de Tirage [★IO]

Assn. Canadienne de Gestion D'Expositions [★IO]

Assn. Canadienne de Gestion Environnementale [★IO]

Assn. Canadienne de la Gestion Parasitaire [★IO]

Assn. Canadienne de Golf des Sourds [★IO]

Assn. Canadienne des Golfeurs Professionels [★IO]

Assn. Canadienne pour les Handicapes Neurologiques [★IO]

Assn. Canadienne des Harmonies [★IO]

Assn. Canadienne des Herissons [★IO]

Assn. Canadienne de Hockey-Balle [★IO]

Assn. Canadienne des Hygienistes Dentaires [★IO]

Assn. Canadienne des Importateurs Reglementes [★IO]

Assn. Canadienne des Indus. du Recyclage [★IO]

Assn. Canadienne des Inedecins Recidents [★IO]

Assn. Canadienne des Infirmieres et Infirmiers en Orthopedie [★IO]

Assn. Canadienne des Infirmieres et Infirmiers en Sante du Travail [★IO]

Assn. Canadienne des Infirmieres et Infirmiers en Sciences Neurologiques [★IO]

Assn. Canadienne des Infirmieres et Infirmiers en Sidologie [★IO]

Assn. Canadienne des Infirmieres et Infirmiers en Soins aux Brules [★IO]

Assn. Canadienne des Infirmiers et Infirmieres en Gerontologie [★IO]

Assn. Canadienne des Informieres en Approches Holistiques de Soins [★IO]

Assn. Canadienne des Inspecteurs de Biens Immobiliers [★IO]

Assn. Canadienne des Institutions de Sante Universtaires [★IO]

Assn. Canadienne des Intervenants en Formation Policiere [★IO]

Assn. Canadienne pour les Jeunes Enfants [★IO]

L'Association Canadienne de Jouet [★IO]

L'Association Canadienne des Journalistes [★IO]

Assn. Canadienne des Journaux [★IO]

Assn. Canadienne des Juges de Cours Provinciales [★IO]

Assn. Canadienne de l' Energie Eolienne [★IO]

Assn. Canadienne de l'Autobus [★IO]

Assn. Canadienne pour l'Avancement des Femmes du Sport et de l'Activite Physique [★IO]

Assn. Canadienne de L'emballage [★IO]

Assn. Canadienne de l'enseigne [★IO]

Assn. Canadienne de l'Enseignement Cooperatif [★IO]

Assn. Canadienne pour l'Etude du Curriculum [★IO]

Assn. Canadienne pour l'Etude du Quarternaire [★IO]

Assn. Canadienne pour l'Histoire du Nursing [★IO]

Assn. Canadienne des Libertes Civiles [★IO]

Assn. Canadienne de l'Imprimerie [★IO]

Assn. Canadienne de l'Industrie du Bois [★IO]

L'Association Canadienne de l'Industrie de la Peinture et du Revetement [★IO]

Assn. Canadienne de l'industrie des Plastiques [★IO]

Assn. Canadienne de l'informatique [★IO]

Assn. Canadienne de Linguistique [★IO]

Assn. Canadienne pour l'Integration Communautaire [★IO]

Assn. Canadienne de Literature Comparee [★IO]

Assn. Canadienne pour L'Obtention de Services aux Personnes Autistiques [★IO]

Assn. Canadienne de Lutte Amateur [★IO]

Assn. Canadienne de la Maladie Coeliaque [★IO]

Assn. Canadienne des Mfrs. de Produits Nautiques [★IO]

Assn. Canadienne des Manufacturiers de Biscuits [★IO]

Assn. Canadienne des Manufacturiers de Palettes et Contenants [★IO]

L'Association Canadienne Marchands Numismatiques [★IO]

Assn. Canadienne des Marches des Capitaux [★IO]

Assn. Canadienne du Marketing [★IO]

Assn. Canadienne des Massotherapeutes du Sport [★IO]

Assn. Canadienne des Medecins d'Urgence [★IO]

Assn. Canadienne des Medecins Veterinaires [★IO]

Assn. Canadienne des Membres des Tribunaux d'Utilite Publique [★IO]

Assn. Canadienne de Microbiologie Clinique et des Maladies [★IO]

Assn. Canadienne des Mouleurs sous Pression [★IO]

L'Association Canadienne des entrepreneurs en Mousse de Polyurethane [★IO]

Assn. Canadienne pour les Nations-Unies [★IO]

Assn. Canadienne pour les Nations Unies - Div. de la Region du Saguenay-Lac-Saint-Jean [★IO]

Assn. Canadienne pour les Nations Unies - Montreal [★IO]

Assn. Canadienne pour les Nations Unies - Region de Quebec [★IO]

Assn. Canadienne des docteurs en Naturopathie [★IO]

Assn. Canadienne de Neurologie Pediatrique [★IO]

Assn. Canadienne des Neuropathologistes [★IO]

Assn. Canadienne des Optometristes [★IO]

Assn. Canadienne des Orthodontistes [★IO]

Assn. Canadienne des Orthophonistes et Audiologistes [★IO]

Assn. Canadienne des Palynologues [★IO]

L'Association Canadienne de Parachutisme Sportiff [★IO]

Assn. Canadienne des Parajuristes [★IO]

Assn. Canadienne des Paraplegiques [★IO]

Assn. Canadienne des Parcs et Loisirs [★IO]

Assn. Canadienne des Pathologistes [★IO]

Assn. Canadienne de Philosophie [★IO]

Assn. Canadienne de Photographes et Illustrateurs de Publicite [★IO]

Assn. Canadienne de Physiotherapie [★IO]

Assn. Canadienne des Pilotes de Ligne Internationale [★IO]

Assn. Canadienne de Pipelines d'Energie [★IO]

Assn. Canadienne des Plans de la Croix Bleue [★IO]

Assn. Canadienne du Plegage Humanitaire [★IO]

Assn. Canadienne des Policiers [★IO]

Assn. Canadienne Pou La Sante Mentale - Div. du Quebec [★IO]

L'Association Canadienne Pour les Etudes de Renseignment et de Securite [★IO]

Assn. Canadienne Pour La Sante Mentale [★IO]

Assn. Canadienne Pour La Sante Mentale, Filiale de Chatham-Kent [★IO]

Assn. Canadienne pour la Pratique et l'Education Pastorales [★IO]

Assn. Canadienne pour la Prevention du Suicide [★IO]

Assn. Canadienne des Producteurs de Semences [★IO]

Assn. Canadienne de Production de Film et de TV [★IO]

Assn. Canadienne des Produits de Bur. [★IO]

Assn. Canadienne des Profesionnels en dons Planifies [★IO]

Assn. Canadienne des Professeurs de Comptabilite [★IO]

L' Assn. Canadienne des Professeurs de Danse [★IO]

Assn. Canadienne des Professeurs d'Immersion [★IO]

Assn. Canadienne des Professionnels de l'Insolvabilite et de la reorganisation [★IO]

L'association Canadienne des Professionnels de la Vente [★IO]

Assn. Canadienne de Programmes en Admin. Publique [★IO]

Assn. Canadienne des Programmes de Stages [★IO]

Assn. Canadienne de Protection Medicale [★IO]

Assn. Canadienne des Radiodiffuseurs [★IO]

Assn. Canadienne de Radioprotection [★IO]

Assn. Canadienne pour la Recherche en Economie Familials [★IO]

Assn. Canadienne de Recherches Dentaires [★IO]

Assn. Canadienne de Reflexologie [★IO]

Assn. Canadienne de Rehabilitation des Sites Degrades [★IO]

Assn. Canadienne des Relations Industrielles [★IO]

Assn. Canadienne des Representants de Ventes en Gros [★IO]

Assn. Canadienne des Resources Hydriques [★IO]

Assn. Canadienne des Responsables de l'Aide Financiere au Etudiants [★IO]

Assn. Canadienne des Restaurateurs Professionnels [★IO]

Assn. Canadienne des Sage-Femmes [★IO]

Assn. Canadienne de Sante Dentaire Publique [★IO]

Assn. Canadienne pour la Sante Mentale [★IO]

Assn. Canadienne pour la Sci. des Animaux de Labatoire [★IO]

Assn. Canadienne de Sci. Economique des Affaires [★IO]

Assn. Canadienne des Sciences Geomatiques [★IO]

Assn. Canadienne des Sciences de l'Information [★IO]

L'Association Canadienne de la Securite [★IO]

Assn. Canadienne de Securite Incendie [★IO]

Assn. Canadienne de Semiotique [★IO]

Assn. Canadienne de Sensibilisation a l'Infertilite [★IO]

Assn. Canadienne des Slavistes [★IO]

Assn. Canadienne des Snowbirds [★IO]

Assn. Canadienne de Soccer [★IO]

Assn. Canadienne des Societes Elizabeth Fry [★IO]

Assn. Canadienne de Soins et Services Communautaires [★IO]

Assn. Canadienne de Soins et Services a Domicile [★IO]

Assn. Canadienne du Sport Collegial [★IO]

Assn. Canadienne des Sports pour Amputes [★IO]

Assn. Canadienne des Sports pour Skieurs Handicapes [★IO]

Assn. Canadienne du Stationnement [★IO]

Assn. Canadienne pour les Structures et Materiaux Composites [★IO]

L'Association Canadienne de la Surdicecite et de la Rubeole [★IO]

Assn. Canadienne des Surintendants de Golf [★IO]

Assn. Canadienne de la Technologie des Cartes a Memoire [★IO]

Assn. Canadienne de la Technologie de l'information [★IO]

Assn. Canadienne des Technologues en Electroneurophysiologie [★IO]

Assn. Canadienne des Technologues en Radiation Medicale [★IO]

Assn. Canadienne du Telephone Independant [★IO]

Assn. Canadienne de Tennis du Table [★IO]

Assn. Canadienne des Therapeutes du Sport [★IO]

Assn. Canadienne de Traductologie [★IO]

Assn. Canadienne de Traitement d'Images et de Reconnaissance des Formes [★IO]

Assn. Canadienne de Transport Industriel [★IO]

Assn. Canadienne du Transport Urbain [★IO]

A star before a book entry number signifies that the name is not listed separately, but is mentioned within the entry.

Assn. Canadienne des Travailleuses et Travailleurs Sociaux [★IO]

Assn. Canadienne du Vehicule Recreatif [★IO]

Assn. Canadienne des Veterans de la Coree [★IO]

Assn. Canadienne de Vexillologie [★IO]

L'Association Canadienne de Vol a Voile [★IO]

Assn. Canadienne de Yachting [★IO]

Assn. Canado Americaine [★19060]

Assn. of Cancer Executives [13795], c/o Brian J. Mandrier, Exec. Dir., 1255 Twenty-Third St. NW, Washington, DC 20037-1174, (202)521-1886

Assn. of Cancer Inst. Directors [★13794]

Assn. of Cancer Online Resources [13796], 173 Duane St., Ste. 3A, New York, NY 10013-3334, (212)226-5525

Assn. Candienne des Pepinieristes et des Paysagistes [★IO]

Assn. Cannadienne des Radio-Oncologues [★IO]

Assn. of Capitol Reporters and Editors [6181], c/o Charles Ashby, Treas., 2141 Eliot St., Denver, CO 80211, (803)771-8658

Assn. of Car Rental Indus. Systems Standards [IO], Eastbourne, United Kingdom

Assn. for Car and Truck Rental Independents and Franchisees [★3376]

Assn. Caraibe pour l'Environnement [★IO]

Assn. of Cardiologists of Bosnia and Herzegovina [IO], Sarajevo, Bosnia-Hercegovina

Assn. of Cardiothoracic Anaesthetists [IO], Hull, United Kingdom

Assn. for the Care of Asthma - Defunct.

Assn. for the Care of Children's Health - Defunct.

Assn. of Career Mgt. Consulting Firms Intl. [1255], 204 E St. NE, Washington, DC 20002, (202)547-6344

Assn. of Career Mgt. Consulting Firms Intl. [IO], Washington, DC, United States

Assn. of Career Professionals Intl. [IO], Washington, DC, United States

Assn. of Career Professionals Intl. [782], 204 E St. NE, Washington, DC 20002, (202)547-6377

Assn. for Career and Tech. Educ. [9300], 1410 King St., Alexandria, VA 22314, (703)683-3111

Assn. for Career and Tech. Educ. Res. [9301], c/o Dick Joerger, Pres., Univ. of Minnesota, 320B Vo-Tech Educ. Bldg., 1954 Buford Ave., St. Paul, MN 55108, (612)624-4298

Assn. of Career Training Schools - Defunct.

Assn. for Careers Educ. and Guidance [IO], Banbury, United Kingdom

Assn. of Caribbean Economists [IO], Kingston, Jamaica

Assn. of Caribbean Electoral Organizations [5557], c/o IFES, 1101 15th St. NW, 3rd Fl., Washington, DC 20005, (202)350-6700

Assn. of Caribbean States [IO], Port of Spain, Trinidad and Tobago

Assn. of Caribbean Studies - Address unknown since 2006.

Assn. of Caribbean Univ., Res. and Institutional Libraries [10329], PO Box 23317, San Juan, PR 00931-3317, (787)790-8054

Assn. of Caribbean Univ., Res. and Institutional Libraries [IO], San Juan, PR, United States

Assn. Cartographique Internationale [★IO]

Assn. des Cartotheques et des Archieves Cartographiques du Canada [★IO]

Assn. of Casualty Accountants and Statisticians and Insurance Accountants Assn. [★53]

Assn. of Casualty and Surety Companies [★2139]

Assn. of Catholic Colleges and Universities [8051], 1 Dupont Cir., Ste. 650, Washington, DC 20036, (202)457-0650

Assn. of Catholic Diocesan Archivists [9399]

Assn. of Catholic Institutes of Educ. [IO], Angers, France

Assn. of Catholic Trade Unionists - Address unknown since 1995.

Assn. of Catholic T.V. and Radio Syndicators - Address unknown since 2008.

Assn. of CCTV Surveyors [★IO]

Assn. of Celebrity Personal Assistants [59], 914 Westwood Blvd., PMB 507, Los Angeles, CA 90024-2905, (310)281-7755

Assn. of Centers of Medieval and Renaissance Stud. [★10458]

Assn. Centrafricaine pour le Bien-Etre Familial [IO], Bangui, Central African Republic

Assn. for Central Asian Studies - Defunct.

Assn. of Central and Eastern European Election Officials [IO], Budapest, Hungary

Assn. of Ceramic Educators [★IO]

Assn. of Ceramic Educators [★8061]

Assn. of Ceramic Tile Mfrs. of Spain [IO], Castellon, Spain

Assn. des Cercles Canadiens [★IO]

Assn. of Cereal Starch Producers in the EU [IO], Brussels, Belgium

Association of Certified Adizes Practitioners International [IO], Carpinteria, CA, United States

Assn. of Certified Adizes Practitioners Intl. [2483], 6404 Via Real, Carpinteria, CA 93013, (805)565-2901

Assn. of Certified Anti-Money Laundering Specialists [463], Brickell Bayview Center, 80 SW 8th St., Ste. 2350, Miami, FL 33130, (305)373-0020

Association of Certified Anti-Money Laundering Specialists [IO], Miami, FL, United States

Assn. of Certified Fraud Examiners [IO], Austin, TX, United States

Assn. of Certified Fraud Examiners [2084], The Gregor Bldg., 716 West Ave., Austin, TX 78701-2727, (512)478-9000

Assn. of Certified Fraud Examiners, Belgium Chap. 127 [IO], Berlaar, Belgium

Assn. of Certified Fraud Examiners, Hong Kong Chap. [IO], Hong Kong, People's Republic of China

Assn. of Certified Fraud Examiners, South African Chap. [IO], Menlo Park, Republic of South Africa

Assn. of Certified Fraud Examiners, United Kingdom Chap. [IO], Cheam, United Kingdom

Assn. of Certified Fraud Specialists [2085], PO Box 348777, Sacramento, CA 95834-8777, (916)419-6319

Assn. of Certified Liquidators - Address unknown since 2005.

Assn. of Certified Marine Surveyors [2572], 209/241 Nooseneck Hill Rd., West Greenwich, RI 02817, (401)397-1888

Assn. of Certified Professional Secretaries [60]

Assn. of Certified Public Accountant Examiners [★5428]

Assn. of Certified Servers - Address unknown since 2001.

Assn. of Certified Treasury Managers [IO], Hyderabad, India

Assn. of Certified Turnaround Professionals [956], 150 S Wacker Dr., Ste. 900, Chicago, IL 60606, (312)578-6900

Assn. of Chairmen of Departments of Mechanics [8829], Virginia Polytechnic Inst. and State Univ., Dept. of Engg. Sci. and Mechanics, 223 Norris Hall - MC 0219, Blacksburg, VA 24061, (540)231-6651

Assn. for Challenge Course Tech. [2869], c/o Sylvia Dresser, Exec. Dir., 496 Castlewood Ln., Deerfield, IL 60015, (847)945-0829

Assn. of Champagne Producers [IO], Reims, France

Assn. fiscale internationale - Chapitre Canadien [★IO]

Assn. of Charitable Foundations [IO], London, United Kingdom

Assn. of Charity Officers [IO], Potters Bar, United Kingdom

Assn. of Chartered Accountants in the U.S. [14], 341 Lafayette St., Ste. 4246, New York, NY 10012-2417, (212)334-2078

Assn. of Chartered Certified Accountants - Australia and New Zealand [IO], Sydney, Australia

Assn. of Chartered Certified Accountants - Botswana [IO], Gaborone, Botswana

Assn. of Chartered Certified Accountants - Cambodia [IO], Phnom Penh, Cambodia

Assn. of Chartered Certified Accountants Canada [IO], Toronto, ON, Canada

Assn. of Chartered Certified Accountants Caribbean [IO], Port of Spain, Trinidad and Tobago

Assn. of Chartered Certified Accountants - Central and Eastern Europe Off. [IO], Prague, Czech Republic

Assn. of Chartered Certified Accountants - Cyprus [IO], Nicosia, Cyprus

Assn. of Chartered Certified Accountants - Ethiopia [IO], Addis Ababa, Ethiopia

Assn. of Chartered Certified Accountants - Ghana [IO], Accra, Ghana

Assn. of Chartered Certified Accountants - Gulf States [IO], Dubai, United Arab Emirates

Assn. of Chartered Certified Accountants - Hong Kong [IO], Hong Kong, People's Republic of China

Assn. of Chartered Certified Accountants - Ireland [IO], Dublin, Ireland

Assn. of Chartered Certified Accountants - Kenya [IO], Nairobi, Kenya

Assn. of Chartered Certified Accountants - Malaysia [IO], Kuala Lumpur, Malaysia

Assn. of Chartered Certified Accountants - Mauritius [IO], Port Louis, Mauritius

Assn. of Chartered Certified Accountants - Poland [IO], Warsaw, Poland

Assn. of Chartered Certified Accountants - Singapore [IO], Singapore, Singapore

Assn. of Chartered Certified Accountants - South Africa [IO], Saxonwold, Republic of South Africa

Assn. of Chartered Certified Accountants - Sri Lanka [IO], Colombo, Sri Lanka

Assn. of Chartered Certified Accountants - Uganda [IO], Kampala, Uganda

Assn. of Chartered Certified Accountants - United Kingdom [IO], Glasgow, United Kingdom

Assn. of Chartered Certified Accountants - Vietnam [IO], Ho Chi Minh City, Vietnam

Assn. of Chartered Certified Accountants - Zambia [IO], Lusaka, Zambia

Assn. of Chartered Certified Accountants - Zimbabwe [IO], Harare, Zimbabwe

Assn. of Chartered Indus. Designers of Ontario [IO], Toronto, ON, Canada

Assn. of Chartered Secretaries in the U.S. - Defunct.

Assn. of Chem. and Allied Employers [★IO]

Assn. of Chem. Indus. [IO], Ljubljana, Slovenia

Assn. of Chem. Indus. of Slovenia [IO], Ljubljana, Slovenia

Assn. of Chem. Indus. of the Czech Republic [IO], Prague, Czech Republic

Assn. of Chem. Indus. of Germany [IO], Frankfurt, Germany

Assn. des Chemins de fer du Canada [★IO]

Assn. of Chemists of the Textile Indus. [IO], Clichy, France

Association for Chemoreception Sciences [IO], Minneapolis, MN, United States

Assn. for Chemoreception Sciences [13937], 5841 Cedar Lake Rd., Minneapolis, MN 55416, (952)646-2035

Assoiation des Chercheurs Iraniens [IO], London, United Kingdom

Assn. of Chess Professionals [IO], St. Petersburg, Russia

Assn. des Chevaux Morgan Canadien [★IO]

Assn. of Chief Ambulance Officers [★IO]

Assn. of Chief Estate Surveyors and Property Managers in Local Govt. [IO], Stockport, United Kingdom

Assn. Chief Executives Coun. [698]

Assn. of Chief Executives of Voluntary Organisations [IO], London, United Kingdom

Assn. of Chief Officers of Probation [★IO]

Assn. of Chief Police Officers of England, Wales and Northern Ireland [IO], London, United Kingdom

Assn. of Chief Police Officers in Scotland [IO], Glasgow, United Kingdom

Assn. of Chief State School Audiovisual Officers [★8568]

Assn. of Chief Tech. Officers [★IO]

Assn. of Chiefs and Officials of Bureaus of Labor [★5917]

Assn. of Child Abuse Lawyers [IO], Surbiton, United Kingdom

Assn. for Child and Adolescent Mental Hea. [IO], London, United Kingdom

Assn. of Child and Adolescent Psychiatric Nurses [★IO]

Assn. of Child and Adolescent Psychiatric Nurses [★15487]

Assn. of Child Advocates [★11662]

Assn. for Child Hea. [IO], Lagos, Nigeria

Reference to "IO" in place of a book number signifies that the association may be found in the 45th edition of International Organizations.

Assn. of Child Neurology Nurses [IO], Little Rock, AR, United States

Assn. of Child Neurology Nurses [15465], c/o Rita Brockway, Arkansas Children's Hosp., Div. of Neurology, 800 Marshall St., Little Rock, AR 72202-3591

Assn. for Child Psychoanalysis [16106], 7820 Enchanted Hills Blvd., No. A-233, Rio Rancho, NM 87144, (505)771-0372

Assn. for Child Psychology and Psychiatry [★IO]

Assn. of Child Psychotherapists [IO], London, United Kingdom

Assn. for Childbirth at Home [★IO]

Assn. for Childbirth at Home [★15591]

Assn. for Childbirth at Home, Intl. [15591], c/o The Natural Birth and Women's Center, 14140 Magnolia Blvd., Sherman Oaks, CA 91423, (818)386-1082

Assn. for Childbirth at Home, Intl. [IO], Sherman Oaks, CA, United States

Assn. for Childhood Educ. Intl. [IO], Olney, MD, United States

Assn. for Childhood Educ. Intl. [8064], 17904 Georgia Ave., Ste. 215, Olney, MD 20832, (301)570-2111

Assn. for Children and Adults with Learning Disabilities [★12492]

Assn. for Children with a Disability [IO], Armidale, Australia

Assn. for Children with Down Syndrome [12562], 4 Fern Pl., Plainview, NY 11803, (516)933-4700

Assn. for Children for Enforcement of Support [11673], 3474 Raymont Blvd., 2nd Fl., University Heights, OH 44118, (800)739-2237

Assn. for Children for Enforcement of Support [★11673]

Assn. for Children with Learning Disabilities [★12492]

Assn. for Children with Retarded Mental Development [★12572]

Assn. for Children with Russell-Silver Syndrome - Address unknown since 2001.

Assn. of Children's Hospices [IO], Bristol, United Kingdom

Assn. of Children's Museums [10495], 1300 L St. NW, No. 975, Washington, DC 20005, (202)898-1080

Assn. of Children's Prosthetic-Orthotic Clinics [15784], 6300 N River Rd., Ste. 727, Rosemont, IL 60018-4226, (847)698-1637

Assn. of Childrens Welfare Agencies [IO], Haymarket, Australia

Assn. of Chilean Salmon Farmers - Address unknown since 2002.

Assn. of Chilean Tourism Agencies [IO], Santiago, Chile

Assn. des Chimistes de l'Industrie Textile [★IO]

Assn. of Chinese Amer. Physicians [15991], c/o Ms. Randi Lee, PO Box 1565, New York, NY 10159-1565, (212)684-9038

Assn. of Chinese-American Professionals [19012], 10303 Westoffice Dr., Box No. 194, Houston, TX 77042-5306

Assn. for the Chinese Blind [★16854]

Assn. for the Chinese Blind [★IO]

Assn. of Chinese Finance Professionals [1402], 240 Hazelwood Ave., San Francisco, CA 94127

Assn. of Chinese Food Scientists and Technologists in Am. [★7092]

Assn. of Chinese from Indochina [★18502]

Assn. of Chinese from Indochina [★IO]

Assn. of Chinese Scientists and Engineers - U.S.A. [IO], Schaumburg, IL, United States

Assn. of Chinese Scientists and Engineers - U.S.A. [6698], PO Box 59715, Schaumburg, IL 60159

Assn. Chinoise de Handball [IO], Beijing, People's Republic of China

Assn. of Chiropractic Coll. Presidents [★IO]

Assn. of Chiropractic Coll. Presidents [★13993]

Assn. of Chiropractic Colleges [13993], c/o David S. O'Bryon, CAE, Exec. Dir., 4424 Montgomery Ave., Ste. 102, Bethesda, MD 20814, (301)652-5066

Association of Chiropractic Colleges [IO], Bethesda, MD, United States

Assn. Chiropratique Canadienne [★IO]

Assn. of the Chocolate, Biscuit and Confectionery Indus. of the EU [IO], Brussels, Belgium

Assn. of the Chocolate and Confectionery Indus. [IO], Copenhagen, Denmark

Assn. of Choral Conductors - Defunct.

Assn. of Christian Church Educators [19842], PO Box 1986, Indianapolis, IN 46206-1986, (317)713-2631

Assn. of Christian Coin Dealers and Collectors - Defunct.

Assn. for Christian Ethics [19574], PO Box 1007, New York, NY 10150, (718)357-4830

Assn. of Christian Institutes for Social Concern in Asia [IO], Chennai, India

Assn. of Christian Investigators [5876], c/o Kelly Riddle, Pres., 2553 Jackson Keller, Ste. 200, San Antonio, TX 78230, (210)342-0509

Assn. of Christian Journalists [IO], St. Petersburg, Russia

Assn. of Christian Lay Centres in Africa [IO], Nairobi, Kenya

Association of Christian Librarians [IO], Cedarville, OH, United States

Assn. of Christian Librarians [10330], PO Box 4, Cedarville, OH 45314, (937)766-2255

Assn. of Christian Rsrc. Organizations Serving Sudan [★IO]

Assn. for Christian Schools - Defunct.

Assn. for Christian Schools Intl. [8081], PO Box 65130, Colorado Springs, CO 80962-5130, (719)528-6906

Assn. of Christian Schools Intl. [IO], Colorado Springs, CO, United States

Assn. of Christian Teachers [IO], St. Albans, United Kingdom

Assn. of Christian Therapists [19765], 6728 Old McLean Village Dr., McLean, VA 22101, (703)556-9222

Assn. for Christian Training and Service - Defunct.

Assn. of Christian Truckers [20596], PO Box 187, Brownstown, IL 62418, (618)427-3737

Assn. of Christian Universities and Colleges in Asia [IO], Nakhon Pathom, Thailand

Assn. of Christians in the Mathematical Sciences [19766], c/o Dr. Robert Brabenec, Exec. Sec., Wheaton Coll., Dept. of Mathematics, 501 Coll. Ave., Wheaton, IL 60187, (630)752-5869

Assn. of Church Missions Committees [★20293]

Assn. of the Cider and Fruit Wine Indus. of the European Union [IO], Brussels, Belgium

Assn. of Cinema Labs. [★1367]

Assn. of Cinema and Video Labs. [1367], c/o Chip Wilkinson, Pres., 630 Ninth Ave., New York, NY 10036, (212)586-4822

Assn. of Cinematograph, TV and Allied Technicians [★IO]

Assn. of Cities for Recycling [★IO]

Assn. of Cities and Regions for Recycling and Sustainable Rsrc. Mgt. [IO], Skipton, United Kingdom

Assn. for Civil Rights [IO], Buenos Aires, Argentina

Assn. for Civil Rights in Israel [IO], Jerusalem, Israel

Assn. of Civilian Technicians [24072], 12620 Lake Ridge Dr., Woodbridge, VA 22192-2335, (703)494-4845

Assn. of Clandestine Radio Enthusiasts [21497], PO Box 1, Belfast, NY 14711-0001

Assn. of Classical and Christian Schools [9089], PO Box 9741, Moscow, ID 83843, (208)882-6101

Assn. of Classical and Christian Schools [IO], Moscow, ID, United States

Assn. of Classroom Teachers - of NEA - Defunct.

Assn. for Clinic Managers [★15067]

Assn. for Clinical Biochemistry [IO], London, United Kingdom

Assn. for Clinical Data Mgt. [IO], St. Albans, United Kingdom

Assn. of Clinical Embryologists [IO], Cambridge, United Kingdom

Assn. for Clinical Pastoral Educ. [19915], 1549 Clairmont Rd., Ste. 103, Decatur, GA 30033-4635, (404)320-1472

Assn. of Clinical Pastoral Educators [★19915]

Assn. of Clinical Pathologists [IO], Hove, United Kingdom

Assn. for Clinical Psychosocial Res. [16139], c/o Lisa Dixon, MD, Membership Chair, Dept. of Psychology, Univ. of Maryland, 685 W Baltimore St., Baltimore, MD 21201-1549, (215)842-4550

Assn. of Clinical Res. Organizations [14021], c/o Douglas Peddicord, PhD, Exec. Dir., 227 Massachusetts Ave. NE, Ste. 300, Washington, DC 20002, (202)543-4018

Assn. of Clinical Res. for the Pharmaceutical Indus. [★IO]

Assn. of Clinical Res. Professionals [IO], Alexandria, VA, United States

Assn. of Clinical Res. Professionals [15927], 500 Montgomery St., Ste. 800, Alexandria, VA 22314, (703)254-8100

Assn. of Clinical Scientists [14022], PO Box 1287, Middlebury, VT 05753, (802)462-2507

Assn. for Clinical Theological Training and Care [★IO]

Assn. of Clinicians for the Underserved [14616], 1420 Spring Hill Rd., Ste. 600, McLean, VA 22102, (703)442-5318

Assn. of Club Executives [1932], 4340 Beechwood Lake Dr., Naples, FL 34112, (216)965-7527

Assn. of Cocoa and Chocolate Mfrs. of the U.S. [★1506]

Assn. of Coffee Mill Enthusiasts [21973], c/o Robert P. Palmer, Treas., PO Box 86, Olivet, MI 49076-0086

Assn. of Collecting Clubs [21974], 18222 Flower Hill Way, No. 299, Gaithersburg, MD 20879, (301)926-8663

Assn. of Coll. Admin. Professionals [7887], PO Box 1389, Staunton, VA 24402, (540)885-1873

Assn. of Coll. Admissions Counselors [★7912]

Assn. of Coll. Auxiliary Services [★3478]

Assn. of Coll. Fraternities - Defunct.

Assn. of Coll. Geology Teachers [★8459]

Assn. of Coll. Honor Societies [★24470]

Assn. of Coll. Honor Societies [24501], 4990 Northwind Dr., Ste. 140, East Lansing, MI 48823-5031, (517)351-8335

Assn. of Coll. Honor Societies [★IO]

Assn. of Coll. Police Training Officials [★11899]

Assn. of Coll. Professors of Textiles and Clothing [★3791]

Assn. of Coll. Professors of Textiles and Clothing [★IO]

Assn. of Coll. and Reference Libraries [★10331]

Assn. of Coll. and Res. Libraries [10331], 50 E Huron St., Chicago, IL 60611-2795, (312)280-2523

Assn. of Coll. Unions [★9166]

Assn. of Coll. Unions [★IO]

Assn. of Coll. Unions Intl. [IO], Bloomington, IN, United States

Assn. of Coll. Unions Intl. [9166], One City Centre, Ste. 200, 120 W 7th St., Bloomington, IN 47404-3925, (812)245-2284

Assn. of Coll. and Univ. Auditors [7888], 342 N Main St., Ste. 301, West Hartford, CT 06117-2507, (860)586-7561

Association of College and University Auditors [IO], West Hartford, CT, United States

Assn. of Coll. and Univ. Clubs [IO], Alexandria, VA, United States

Assn. of Coll. and Univ. Clubs [8100], 1733 King St., Alexandria, VA 22314-2720, (703)739-4288

Assn. of Coll., Univ. and Community Arts Administrators [★7968]

Assn. of Coll. and Univ. Concert Managers [★7968]

Assn. of Coll. and Univ. Housing Officers Intl. [9167], 941 Chatham Ln., Ste. 318, Columbus, OH 43221-2416, (614)292-0099

Assn. of Coll. and Univ. Housing Officers Intl. [IO], Columbus, OH, United States

Assn. of Coll. and Univ. Museums and Galleries [10496], c/o Philip and Muriel Berman Museum of Art, Ursinus Coll., 601 E Main St., Collegeville, PA 19426, (610)409-3500

Assn. of Coll. and Univ. Offices [★8341]

Assn. of Coll. and Univ. Printers - Address unknown since 2003.

Assn. of Coll. and Univ. Religious Affairs [9168], c/o Rev. Susan Henry-Crowe, Sec.-Treas., Emory Univ., Atlanta, GA 30322, (404)727-6226

A star before a book entry number signifies that the name is not listed separately, but is mentioned within the entry.

Assn. of Colleges **[IO]**, London, United Kingdom

Assn. des Colleges Communautaires du Canada **[★IO]**

Assn. of Colls. and Secondary Schools - Defunct.

Assn. of Colls. and Universities for Intl.-Intercultural Studies - Defunct.

Assn. of Collegiate Alumnae **[★9311]**

Assn. of Collegiate Bus. Schools and Programs **[8101]**, 7007 Coll. Blvd., Ste. 420, Overland Park, KS 66211, (913)339-9356

Assn. of Collegiate Conf. and Events Directors-International **[2673]**, Colorado State Univ., 8037 Campus Delivery, Fort Collins, CO 80523-8037, (970)491-3772

Assn. of Collegiate Conf. and Events Directors-International **[IO]**, Fort Collins, CO, United States

Assn. of Collegiate Entrepreneurs - Address unknown since 2001.

Assn. of Collegiate Licensing Administrators **[★2630]**

Assn. of Collegiate Schools of Architecture **[7959]**, 1735 New York Ave. NW, 3rd Fl., Washington, DC 20006, (202)785-2324

Assn. of Collegiate Schools of Nursing **[★15510]**

Assn. of Collegiate Schools of Planning **[9285]**, c/o Donna Dodd, Mgr., 6311 Mallard Trace Dr., Tallahassee, FL 32312, (850)385-2054

Assn. of Coloproctology of Great Britain and Ireland **[IO]**, London, United Kingdom

Assn. to Combat Huntington's Disease **[★IO]**

The Assn. of Comedy Artists - Defunct.

Assn. des Comites Nationaux Olympiques **[★IO]**

Assn. des Comites Nationaux Olympiques d'Afrique **[★IO]**

Assn. des Commercants d'Art de la Suisse **[IO]**, Zurich, Switzerland

Assn. des Commercants de Vehicules Recreatifs du Canada **[★IO]**

Assn. Commercial Banks of Latvia **[IO]**, Riga, Latvia

Assn. of Commercial Diving Educators **[23960]**, c/o Santa Barbara City Coll., 721 Cliff Dr., Santa Barbara, CA 93109-2394, (805)965-0581

Assn. of Commercial Finance Attorneys **[5485]**, c/o Richard K. Brown, Sec., Kennedy Covington Lobdell & Hickman, LLP, 214 N Tryon St., Hearst Tower, 43rd Fl., Charlotte, NC 28202, (704)331-7403

Assn. of Commercial Finance Companies of New York **[★2423]**

Assn. of Commercial Finance Companies of New York **[★IO]**

Assn. of Commercial Mail Receiving Agencies - Defunct.

Assn. of Commercial Records Centers **[★2109]**

Assn. of Commercial Records Centers **[★IO]**

Assn. of Commercial Stock Image Licensors **[1378]**, 400 W 55th St., Ste. 14G, New York, NY 10019, (212)956-3893

Assn. of Commercial TV in Europe **[IO]**, Brussels, Belgium

Assn. for Common European Nursing Diagnoses, Interventions and Outcomes **[IO]**, Dublin, Ireland

Assn. of Commonwealth Archivists and Records Managers **[IO]**, London, United Kingdom

Assn. for Commonwealth Literature and Language Stud. **[IO]**, Surrey, BC, Canada

Assn. of Commonwealth Universities **[IO]**, London, United Kingdom

Assn. for Commun. Admin. **[9154]**

Assn. for Commun. Excellence in Agriculture, Natural Resources, and Life and Human Sciences **[4098]**, PO Box 110811, Gainesville, FL 32611, (352)392-9588

Assn. of Communications Enterprises **[★3955]**

Assn. for Communications Tech. Professionals in Higher Educ; ACUTA: The **[8548]**

Assn. for Community Affiliated Plans **[14617]**, 1400 Eye St. NW, Ste. 330, Washington, DC 20005, (202)331-4601

Assn. for Community Based Education **[8123]**

Assn. for Community Based Educational Institutions **[★8123]**

Assn. of Community Cancer Centers **[13797]**, 11600 Nebel St., Ste. 201, Rockville, MD 20852-2557, (301)984-9496

Assn. of Community Coll. Trustees **[8118]**, 1233 20th St. NW, Ste. 301, Washington, DC 20036, (202)775-4667

Assn. for Community Colleges **[IO]**, Arhus, Denmark

Assn. of Community and Comprehensive Schools **[IO]**, Dublin, Ireland

Assn. for Community Design - Defunct.

Assn. for Community Hea. Improvement **[16238]**, 180 Montgomery St., Ste. 1520, San Francisco, CA 94104, (415)248-8408

Assn. for Community Hea. Improvement **[IO]**, San Francisco, CA, United States

Assn. of Community Hea. Nursing Educators **[15466]**, 10200 W 44th Ave., No. 304, Wheat Ridge, CO 80033, (303)422-0769

Assn. for Community Networking **[8124]**, c/o Michael Maranda, Pres., 1375 E 54th St., No. 2, Chicago, IL 60615

Assn. for Community Networking **[IO]**, Chicago, IL, United States

Assn. for Community Org. and Social Admin. **[13198]**, 20560 Bensley Ave., Lynwood, IL 60411, (708)757-4187

Assn. of Community Organizations for Reform Now **[11749]**, 2-4 Nevin St., 2nd Fl., Brooklyn, NY 11217, (718)246-7900

Assn. of Community Organizations for Reform Now **[IO]**, Toronto, ON, Canada

Assn. of Community Rail Partnerships **[IO]**, Huddersfield, United Kingdom

Assn. of Community Tribal Schools **[8936]**, c/o Dr. Roger Bordeaux, Exec. Dir., 5320 Paragon St., Rocklin, CA 95677, (916)315-0906

Assn. of Community Trusts and Foundations **[★IO]**

Assn. for Community-Wide Protection from Nuclear Attack **[★5559]**

Assn. for Commuter Trans. **[13334]**, 1444 I St. NW, Ste. 700, Washington, DC 20005, (202)712-9021

Association for Commuter Transportation **[IO]**, Washington, DC, United States

Assn. for Comparative Economic Stud. **[6870]**, c/o Prof. Josef Brada, Exec. Sec., Arizona State Univ., Dept. of Economics, PO Box 873806, Tempe, AZ 85287-3806, (480)965-6524

Assn. for Comparative Economics **[★6870]**

Assn. for Competitive Tech. **[3723]**, 1401 K St. NW, Ste. 502, Washington, DC 20005, (202)331-2130

Assn. for Comprehensive Energy Psychology **[16192]**, PO Box 910244, San Diego, CA 92191-0244, (619)861-2237

Association for Comprehensive Energy Psychology **[IO]**, San Diego, CA, United States

Assn. for Comprehensive NeuroTherapy **[15383]**, PO Box 2198, Broken Arrow, OK 74013, (561)798-0472

Assn. of Comptrollers and Accounting Officers **[★6204]**

Assn. of Comptrollers and Accounting Officers **[★IO]**

Assn. for Computational Linguistics **[IO]**, Stroudsburg, PA, United States

Assn. for Computational Linguistics **[10400]**, c/o Priscilla Rasmussen, Bus. Mgr., 209 N Eighth St., Stroudsburg, PA 18360-1721, (570)476-8006

Assn. for Cmpt. Aided Design in Architecture **[6721]**, PO Box 218171, Columbus, OH 43221, (419)596-6095

Assn. for Computer Art and Design Education - Defunct.

Assn. of Computer and CD-ROM Users - Defunct.

Assn. for Cmpt. Educators **[★8132]**

Assn. for Cmpt. Educators **[★IO]**

Assn. of the Cmpt. and Multimedia Indus. Malaysia **[IO]**, Petaling Jaya, Malaysia

Assn. for Cmpt. Operations Mgt. **[★6781]**

Assn. of Cmpt. Professionals **[IO]**, Arlington, United Kingdom

Assn. of Cmpt. Professionals - Defunct.

Assn. of Cmpt. Support Specialists **[6809]**, c/o Edward J. Weinberg, Pres., 333 Mamaroneck Ave., No. 129, White Plains, NY 10605, (917)438-0865

Assn. of Computer Users - Defunct.

Assn. for Computing Machinery **[6783]**, 2 Penn Plz., Ste. 701, New York, NY 10121-0701, (212)869-7440

Assn. of Concerned African Scholars **[16926]**, c/o Meredeth Turshen, Co-Chair, School of Planning and Public Policy, Rutgers Univ., New Brunswick, NJ 08903

Assn. of Concerned African Scholars **[IO]**, New Brunswick, NJ, United States

Assn. of Concerned Citizens **[★19012]**

Assn. of Concert Bands **[10560]**, c/o Nada Vencl, Sec., 6613 Cheryl Ann Dr., Independence, OH 44131-3718, (216)524-1897

Assn. of Concert Bands of Am. **[★10560]**

Assn. of Conductors in the Netherlands **[IO]**, Arnhem, Netherlands

Assn. of Confectionery Indus. **[IO]**, Buenos Aires, Argentina

Assn. of Confectionery Wholesalers and Importers **[★IO]**

Assn. of Conf. Executives **[★IO]**

Assn. for Conferences and Events **[IO]**, Huntingdon, United Kingdom

Assn. for Conflict Resolution **[5450]**, 1015 18th St. NW, Ste. 1150, Washington, DC 20036, (202)667-9700

Assn. for Conflict Resolution - Defunct.

Assn. Congolaise Accompagner **[IO]**, Brazzaville, Republic of the Congo

Assn. for the Conservation of Energy **[IO]**, London, United Kingdom

Assn. of Conservation Engineers **[4357]**, c/o Greg Mihalevich, Sec., PO Box 180, Jefferson City, MO 65102, (573)522-4115

Assn. for Conservation Info. **[4358]**, c/o Randall T. Cox, Esq., Legal Counsel, First Interstate Bldg., Ste. 701, 222 S Gillette Ave., Gillette, WY 82716, (304)269-0463

Assn. des Consommateurs du Canada **[★IO]**

Assn. for Consortium Leadership **[8480]**, c/o Virginia Tidewater Consortium for Higher Educ., 4900 Powhatan Ave., Norfolk, VA 23508-1836, (757)683-3183

Assn. for Constitutional Democracy in Liberia - Address unknown since 1995.

Assn. des Constructeurs Europeens de Motocycles **[★IO]**

Assn. of Constr. Inspectors **[2117]**, 21640 N 19th Ave., Suite C-2, Phoenix, AZ 85027, (623)580-4646

Assn. of Constr. Material Producers of Estonia **[IO]**, Tallinn, Estonia

Assn. of Constr. Proj. Managers **[IO]**, Benmore, Republic of South Africa

Assn. des Constructuers Europeens d'Automobiles **[★IO]**

Assn. for Consultancy and Engg. **[IO]**, London, United Kingdom

Assn. of Consultant Architects **[IO]**, Bromley, United Kingdom

Assn. of Consultants in Access - Australia **[IO]**, Herne Hill, Australia

Assn. des Consultants et des Laboratoires Experts **[★IO]**

Assn. of Consulting Actuaries **[IO]**, London, United Kingdom

Assn. of Consulting Architects - Australia **[IO]**, Melbourne, Australia

Assn. of Consulting Chemists and Chem. Engineers **[6672]**, PO Box 297, Sparta, NJ 07871-0297, (973)729-6671

Assn. of Consulting Engineers Australia **[IO]**, Sydney, Australia

Assn. of Consulting Engineers of Australia - Australian Capital Territory **[IO]**, Manuka, Australia

Assn. of Consulting Engineers of Australia - New South Wales **[IO]**, Sydney, Australia

Assn. of Consulting Engineers of Australia - Northern Territory **[IO]**, Darwin, Australia

Assn. of Consulting Engineers of Australia - South Australia **[IO]**, Marden, Australia

Assn. of Consulting Engineers of Australia - Tasmania **[IO]**, St. Leonards, Australia

Assn. of Consulting Engineers of Australia - Victoria **[IO]**, Hawthorn West, Australia

Assn. of Consulting Engineers Botswana **[IO]**, Gaborone, Botswana

Assn. of Consulting Engineers of Canada **[IO]**, Ottawa, ON, Canada

Assn. of Consulting Engineers (India) **[★IO]**

Assn. of Consulting Engineers of Ireland **[IO]**, Dublin, Ireland

Reference to "IO" in place of a book number signifies that the association may be found in the 45th edition of International Organizations.

Assn. of Consulting Engineers of Kenya [IO], Nairobi, Kenya

Assn. of Consulting Engineers Malaysia [IO], Kuala Lumpur, Malaysia

Assn. of Consulting Engineers of Namibia [IO], Windhoek, Namibia

Assn. of Consulting Engineers New Zealand [IO], Wellington, New Zealand

Assn. of Consulting Engineers, Nigeria [IO], Lagos, Nigeria

Assn. of Consulting Engineers, Norway [IO], Oslo, Norway

Assn. of Consulting Engineers of Pakistan [IO], Karachi, Pakistan

Assn. of Consulting Engineers in Suriname [IO], Paramaribo, Suriname

Assn. of Consulting Engineers of Zambia [IO], Lusaka, Zambia

Assn. of Consulting Foresters [★4680]

Assn. of Consulting Foresters of Am. [4680], 312 Montgomery St., Ste. 208, Alexandria, VA 22314, (703)548-0990

Assn. of Consulting Mgt. Engineers [★2485]

Assn. of Consulting Scientists [IO], Colchester, United Kingdom

Association for Consumer Research [IO], Duluth, MN, United States

Assn. for Consumer Res. [17306], c/o Rajiv Vaidyanathan, Exec. Dir., Univ. of Minnesota Duluth, Labovitz School of Bus. and Economics, 11 E Superior St., Ste. 210, Duluth, MN 55802, (218)726-7853

Assn. of Contact Lens Mfrs. [IO], Devizes, United Kingdom

Assn. of Container Reconditioners [★994]

Assn. of Contemplative Sisters [20563]

Assn. for Continence Advice [IO], Bathgate, United Kingdom

Assn. for Continuing Dental Educ. [IO], Minneapolis, MN, United States

Assn. for Continuing Dental Educ. [8195], c/o Lynda Young, Pres., Univ. of Minnesota, 6-406 Moos HS Tower, 515 Delaware St. SE, Minneapolis, MN 55455, (612)625-5499

Assn. for Continuing Education - Defunct.

Assn. for Continuing Engg. Educ. in the Commonwealth of Independent States [★IO]

Assn. for Continuing Higher Educ. [8148], PO Box 118067, Charleston, SC 29423-8067, (843)574-6658

Assn. for Continuing Legal Educ. [8762], c/o Donna J. Passons, Exec. Dir., PO Box 4646, Austin, TX 78765, (512)453-4340

Assn. of Continuing Legal Educ. Administrators [★8762]

Assn. of Continuing Legal Educ. Administrators [★8762]

Assn. for Contract Textiles [3775], PO Box 101981, Fort Worth, TX 76185, (817)924-8048

Assn. of Contract Tribal Schools [★8936]

Assn. of Convenience Stores [IO], Farnborough, United Kingdom

Assn. for Convention Marketing Executives [1933], c/o Sheila Crowley, Exec. Dir., 204 E St. NE, Washington, DC 20002, (202)547-8030

Assn. for Convention Operations Mgt. [2674], 191 Clarksville Rd., Princeton Junction, NJ 08550, (609)799-3712

Association for Convention Operations Management [IO], Princeton Junction, NJ, United States

Assn. of Conveyor and Material Preparation Equip. Mfrs. [★2013]

Assn. for Convulsive Therapy [15192], 5454 Wisconsin Ave., Ste. 1220, Chevy Chase, MD 20815, (301)951-7220

Association for Convulsive Therapy [IO], Chevy Chase, MD, United States

Assn. of Cooking Schools [★IO]

Assn. of Cooking Schools [★1582]

Assn. for Cooperation in Engineering - Defunct.

Assn. of Cooperation in Tunisia [IO], Tunis, Tunisia

Assn. de Cooperation en Tunisie [★IO]

Assn. of Cooperative Banks of the EC [★IO]

Assn. of Cooperative Educators [IO], St. Paul, MN, United States

Assn. of Cooperative Educators [8156], c/o The Cooperative Found., PO Box 64047, St. Paul, MN 55164, (703)578-1820

Assn. of Cooperative Lib. Organizations [★10340]

Assn. for the Coordination of Univ. Religious Affairs [★9168]

Assn. for Core Texts and Courses [8776], Saint Mary's Coll. of California, 1928 St. Mary's Rd., Moraga, CA 94556, (925)631-8597

Assn. for Core Texts and Courses [IO], Moraga, CA, United States

Assn. for Corporate Computing Tech. Professionals [★IO]

Assn. for Corporate Computing Tech. Professionals [★6799]

Assn. of Corporate Counsel [5614], 1025 Connecticut Ave. NW, Ste. 200, Washington, DC 20036-5425, (202)293-4103

Assn. of Corporate Environmental Officers - Address unknown since 2004.

Assn. for Corporate Growth [699], 616 N North Ct., Ste. 210, Palatine, IL 60067-8156, (847)934-5425

Assn. for Corporate Growth and Diversification [★699]

Assn. for Corporate Growth - Toronto Chap. [IO], Toronto, ON, Canada

Assn. of Corporate Travel Executives [3909], 515 King St., Ste. 440, Alexandria, VA 22314, (703)683-5322

Assn. of Corporate Treasurers [IO], London, United Kingdom

Assn. of Corporate Treasurers (Singapore) [IO], Singapore, Singapore

Assn. of Corporate Treasurers of Southern Africa [IO], Cresta, Republic of South Africa

Association of Correctional Food Service Affiliates [1578], 4248 Park Glen Rd., Minneapolis, MN 55416, (952)928-4658

Assn. of Correctional Food Ser. Affiliates [1577], 406 Surrey Woods Dr., St. Charles, IL 60174, (630)513-4736

Assn. for Correctional Res. and Information Mgt. - Address unknown since 2007.

Assn. of Cosmetics and Perfume Mfrs., Importers and Distributors [IO], Geneva, Switzerland

Assn. of Cosmetologists [★1078]

Assn. of Cosmetologists and Hairdressers [1078]

Assn. of Cost Engineers [IO], Sandbach, United Kingdom

Assn. Costarricense de Taekwondo [IO], San Jose, Costa Rica

Assn. of Cotton Textile Merchants of New York [★3772]

Assn. of Cotton Yarn Distributors [★3776]

Assn. of Coun. Secretaries [★19902]

Assn. of Coun. Secretaries and Solicitors [IO], Weymouth, United Kingdom

Assn. for Counselling at Work [IO], Lutterworth, United Kingdom

Assn. for Counselor Educ. and Supervision [8165], c/o Judith C. Durham, APRN, Pres., St. Joseph College, Dept. of Counselor Education, 1678 Asylum Ave., West Hartford, CT 06117, (860)231-6778

Assn. for Counselors and Educators in Govt. [11818], 5999 Stevenson Ave., Alexandria, VA 22304-3300, (800)347-6647

Assn. of Country Entertainers - Defunct.

Assn. of County Chief Executives [IO], Chester, United Kingdom

Assn. for Couples in Marriage Enrichment [12505], PO Box 21374, Winston-Salem, NC 27120, (336)724-1526

Assn. of Coupon Professionals [3399], 200 E Howard St., Ste. 280, Des Plaines, IL 60018, (847)297-7773

Assn. for Craft Producers [IO], Kathmandu, Nepal

Assn. of Crafts and Creative Industries - Defunct.

Assn. for Creative Change - Defunct.

Assn. of Credit Card Investigators [★5881]

Assn. of Credit Card Investigators [★IO]

Assn. of Credit Union Internal Auditors [1104], PO Box 1926, Columbus, OH 43216-1926, (866)254-8128

Assn. of Credit Union League Executives - Address unknown since 2003.

Assn. of Cricket Statisticians [★IO]

Assn. of Cricket Statisticians and Historians [IO], Cardiff, United Kingdom

Assn. of Cricket Umpires and Scorers [IO], Surrey, United Kingdom

Assn. for Crime Scene Reconstruction [5634], PO Box 51376, Phoenix, AZ 85076-1376, (602)534-9280

Assn. for Cultural Economics Intl. [6871], c/o Prof. Neil O. Alper, Exec. Sec.-Treas., Dept. of Economics, Northeastern Univ., 301 Lake Hall, Boston, MA 02115, (617)373-2839

Assn. for Cultural Economics Intl. [IO], Boston, MA, United States

Assn. for Cultural Evolution [9857], PO Box 2382, Mill Valley, CA 94942, (415)409-3220

Assn. for Cultural Exchange, ACE Stud. Tours [IO], Cambridge, United Kingdom

Assn. of Cultural Executives [IO], Waterloo, ON, Canada

Assn. for Cultural Interchange - Defunct.

Association of Cultural Mythologists - Defunct.

Assn. Culturelle Suisse d'Aikido, Aikikai Suisse [IO], Effretikon, Switzerland

Assn. of the Customs Bar [★IO]

Assn. of the Customs Bar [★5659]

Assn. of Customs Brokers of Kazakhstan [IO], Almaty, Kazakhstan

Assn. of Cycle Traders [IO], Tunbridge Wells, United Kingdom

Assn. of Cytogenetic Technologists [★6569]

Assn. of Czech Advt. Agencies and Marketing Commun. [IO], Prague, Czech Republic

Assn. of Czech Insurance Brokers [IO], Prague, Czech Republic

Assn. canadienne des producteurs d'acier [★IO]

Assn. suisse d'action pour les juifs de l'ancienne Union societique [★IO]

Assn. canadienne d'agri-marketing - Alberta [★IO]

Assn. canadienne d'agri-marketing - Manitoba [★IO]

Assn. canadienne d'agri-marketing - Saskatchewan [★IO]

Assn. canadienne d'Anatomie, de Neurobiologie et de Biologie Cellulaire [★IO]

Assn. for Dance Movement Therapy - United Kingdom [IO], Torquay, United Kingdom

Assn. of Danish Advertisers [IO], Soborg, Denmark

Assn. of Danish Bus. Economists [IO], Copenhagen, Denmark

Assn. of Danish Cosmetics, Toiletries, Soap and Detergent Indus. [IO], Copenhagen, Denmark

Assn. of Danish Designers [★IO]

Assn. of Danish Energy Companies [IO], Frederiksberg, Denmark

Assn. of Danish Fish Processing Indus. and Exporters [IO], Copenhagen, Denmark

Assn. of Danish Fruit and Vegetables Indus. [IO], Copenhagen, Denmark

Assn. of Danish Landscape Architects [IO], Copenhagen, Denmark

Assn. of Danish Lawyers and Economists [IO], Copenhagen, Denmark

Assn. of Danish Oil and Oilseed Processors [IO], Arhus, Denmark

Assn. of Danish Pharmacists [IO], Hellerup, Denmark

Assn. of Danish Res. Libraries [IO], Arhus, Denmark

Assn. of Danish Shipbuilders [★IO]

Assn. of Danish Shoe Retailers [IO], Hellerup, Denmark

Assn. of Danish Travel Agents [IO], Frederiksberg, Denmark

Assn. canadienne d'archeologie [★IO]

Assn. of Dark Leaf Tobacco Dealers and Exporters [3817], c/o Hail and Cotton, Inc., PO Box 638, Springfield, TN 37172-0638, (615)384-9576

Assn. des galleries d'art du Canada [★IO]

Assn. internationale des critiques d'art - Irlande [★IO]

Assn. d'assurances du Barreau canadien [★IO]

Assn. des courtiers d'assurances du Canada [★IO]

Assn. for Data Center, Networking and Enterprise Systems [★6781]

Assn. of Data Communications Users - Defunct.

Assn. of the Deaf in Israel [IO], Tel Aviv, Israel

A star before a book entry number signifies that the name is not listed separately, but is mentioned within the entry.

Assn. of Deans of Amer. Colleges of Veterinary Medicine [★9293]

Assn. of Deans of Pharmacy of Canada [IO], Saskatoon, SK, Canada

Assn. for Death Educ. and Counseling [11909], 60 Revere Dr., Ste. 500, Northbrook, IL 60062, (847)509-0403

Assn. D'Editeurs de la Press Libre et Independante [IO], Libreville, Gabon

Assn. in Defence of the Wrongly Convicted [IO], Toronto, ON, Canada

Assn. of Defense Communities [5811], 734 15th St. NW, Ste. 900, Washington, DC 20005, (202)822-5256

Assn. of Defense Trial Attorneys [5825], c/o Glenn S. Morgan, Membership Chm., PO Box 310, Rutland, VT 05702-0310, (802)786-1045

Assn. of Defensive Spray Mfrs. [3544], 906 Olive St., Ste. 1200, St. Louis, MO 63101-1434, (314)241-1445

Assn. of Democratic Pharmacists [IO], Hamburg, Germany

Assn. Dentair Canadienne [★IO]

Assn. Dentaire Francaise [IO], Paris, France

Assn. of Dental Dealers in Europe [IO], Gumligen-Bern, Switzerland

Assn. for Dental Educ. in Europe [IO], Dublin, Ireland

Assn. for Denture Prosthesis [★IO]

Assn. of Departments and Administrators in Speech Commun. [★9154]

Assn. of Departments of English [8374], 26 Broadway, 3rd Fl., New York, NY 10004-1789, (646)576-5130

Assn. of Departments of English in Amer. Colleges and Universities [★8374]

Assn. of Departments of Foreign Languages [8728], 26 Broadway, 3rd Fl., New York, NY 10004-1789, (646)576-5140

Assn. d'equipement du transport canadienne [★IO]

Assn. of Dermato-Venerologists of Latvia [IO], Riga, Latvia

Assn. Des Banquiers Prives Suisses [★IO]

Assn. of Descendants of Defenders of Baltimore [★21354]

Assn. des Designers Canadiens [★IO]

Assn. of Desk and Derrick Clubs [2917], 5153 E 51st St., Ste. 107, Tulsa, OK 74135-7442, (918)622-1749

Assn. of Desk and Derrick Clubs of North Am. [★2917]

Assn. of Destination Mgt. Executives [3910], PO Box 2307, Dayton, OH 45401-2307, (937)586-3727

Assn. of Destination Mgt. Executives [IO], Dayton, OH, United States

Assn. of Detergent Zeolite Producers [IO], Brussels, Belgium

Assn. d'etudes canadiennes [★IO]

Assn. d'etudes juives canadiennes [★IO]

Assn. canadienne d'etudes environnementales [★IO]

Assn. d'Etudes Baha'ies [★IO]

Assn. d'Etudes Politiques Transeuropeennes [★IO]

Assn. d'Europe des Etudes feministes internationales [★IO]

Assn. for the Development of Aerospace Medicine [IO], Montreal, QC, Canada

Assn. for the Development of Children's Residential Facilities [IO], Dartmouth, NS, Canada

Assn. for the Development of Computer-Based Instructional Systems - Address unknown since 1999.

Assn. for the Development of Educ. in Africa [IO], Paris, France

Assn. of Development Financing Institutions in Asia and the Pacific [IO], Makati City, Philippines

Assn. for the Development of Human Potential [10181], 406 S Coeur d'Alene St., No. T, Spokane, WA 99204, (509)838-3575

Assn. for Development and Innovation of the Furniture Indus. [IO], Paris, France

Assn. for the Development of Intl. Exchange of Food and Agricultural Productions and Techniques [IO], Paris, France

Assn. for the Development of Microenterprise [IO], Santo Domingo, Dominican Republic

Assn. for the Development of Religious Info. Systems [20091], PO Box 210735, Nashville, TN 37221-0735, (615)301-8507

Assn. for the Development of Social Therapy - Defunct.

Assn. pour le Developpement des Echanges Electroniques Professionnels [★IO]

Assn. pour le Developpement des Echanges Internationaux de Produits et Techniques Agro-Alimentaires [★IO]

Assn. d'Experts Europeens du Batiment et de la Constr. [★IO]

Assn. des grands parcs d'expositions europeens [★IO]

Assn. des Diabetiques en Centrafrique [★IO]

Assn. of Diaconal Organizations in Europe [★IO]

Assn. of Diesel Specialists [IO], Research Triangle Park, NC, United States

Assn. of Diesel Specialists [1290], PO Box 13966, Research Triangle Park, NC 27709-3966, (919)406-8804

Assn. d'information sur l'allergie et l'asthme [★IO]

Assn. d'Instituts Europeens de Conjoncture Economique [★IO]

Assn. of Diplomates of the Amer. Bd. of Oral Surgery [★IO]

Assn. of Diplomates of the Amer. Bd. of Oral Surgery [★15734]

Assn. des Diplomes de l'Ecole des Hautes Etudes Commerciales [★IO]

Assn. des Diplomes de Polytechnique [★IO]

Assn. for Direct Instruction [8232], PO Box 10252, Eugene, OR 97440, (541)485-1293

Assn. of Direct Marketing Agencies [★2625]

Assn. des Directeurs et Coordonnateurs des Programmes de Journalisme des Universites Canadiennes [★IO]

Assn. of Directors of Children's Services [IO], Manchester, United Kingdom

Assn. of Directors of Journalism Programs in Canadian Universities [IO], Regina, SK, Canada

Assn. for Directors of Radiation Oncology Programs [3271], c/o Steven Smith, Membership Dir., 8280 Willow Oaks Corporate Dr., Ste. 500, Fairfax, VA 22031, (703)502-1550

Assn. of Directors of Social Services [IO], London, United Kingdom

Assn. of Directors of Social Work [IO], Edinburgh, United Kingdom

Assn. of Dir. Marketing [2616], 1187 Thorn Run Rd., Ste. 630, Moon Township, PA 15108-3198, (412)269-0663

Assn. of Dir. Publishers [3208], 116 Cass St., PO Box 1929, Traverse City, MI 49685-1929, (800)267-9002

Assn. of Disabled Amer. Golfers [23341], PO Box 280649, Lakewood, CO 80228-0649, (303)922-5228

Assn. of Disabled Professionals [IO], London, United Kingdom

Assn. des Distillateurs Canadiens [★IO]

Assn. of District Secretaries [★IO]

Assn. of Dive Prog. Administrators [23377], c/o Richard S. Blankfein, Membership Dir., New York Aquarium Surf Ave., W 8th St., Brooklyn, NY 11224, (718)265-4738

Assn. of Diving Contractors [★1007]

Assn. of Diving Contractors [★IO]

Assn. of Diving Contractors Intl. [IO], Houston, TX, United States

Assn. of Diving Contractors Intl. [1007], 5206 FM 1960 W, Ste. 202, Houston, TX 77069-4406, (281)893-8388

Assn. Djiboutienne pour l'Equilibre et la Promotion de la Famille [IO], Djibouti, Djibouti

Assn. of Doctors for the Env. - ISDE Italy [IO], Arezzo, Italy

Assn. canadienne des producteurs d'Oeufs d'Incubation a chair [★IO]

Assn. of Domestic Mgt. [★IO]

Assn. of Dominion Land Surveyors [★IO]

Assn. des Doyens de Pharmacie du Canada [★IO]

Assn. of Drainage Authorities [IO], Surbiton, United Kingdom

Assn. for Dressings and Sauces [1502], 1100 Johnson Ferry Rd., Ste. 300, Atlanta, GA 30342, (404)252-3663

Assn. of Drilled Shaft Contractors [★1000]

Assn. of Drilled Shaft Contractors [★IO]

Assn. of Drinkwatchers Intl. - Defunct.

Assn. of Driver Educators for the Disabled [★8209]

Assn. of Driver Educators for the Disabled [★IO]

Assn. for Driver Rehabilitation Specialists; ADED: The [8209]

Assn. de Droit Intl. [★IO]

Assn. pour le Droit de Mourir dans la Dignite [★IO]

Assn. of Ductwork Contractors and Allied Services [IO], Reading, United Kingdom

Assn. canadienne des professeures et professeurs d'universite [★IO]

Assn. of the Dutch Adhesive Indus. [IO], Leidschendam, Netherlands

Assn. of Dutch Artists [★IO]

Assn. of Dutch Businessmen in Singapore [IO], Singapore, Singapore

Assn. of the Dutch Chem. Indus. [IO], Leidschendam, Netherlands

Assn. of Dutch Designers [IO], Amsterdam, Netherlands

Assn. of Dutch Fruit and Vegetable Exporters [IO], The Hague, Netherlands

Assn. for Dutch Music History [★IO]

Assn. of the Dutch Pharmaceutical Indus. [★IO]

Assn. of Dutch Poultry Processing Indus. [IO], Houten, Netherlands

Assn. of the Dutch Univ. Libraries and the Royal Lib. [IO], The Hague, Netherlands

Assn. of Dutch Wholesalers in Paint [IO], The Hague, Netherlands

Assn. of DX Reporters - Defunct.

Assn. of Earth Sci. Editors [3093], c/o Mary Ann Schmidt, 554 Chess St., Pittsburgh, PA 15205

Association of Earth Science Editors [IO], Pittsburgh, PA, United States

Assn. of East Asian Res. Universities [IO], Hefei, People's Republic of China

Assn. of Eastern Foresters [★4689]

Assn. Echecs et Maths [★IO]

Assn. des Ecoles de Sante Publique de la Regional Europeenne [★IO]

Assn. of Economic Poisons Control Officials [★6170]

Assn. of Economic Sci. Institutions [IO], Moscow, Russia

Assn. Ecosystem [IO], Moscow, Russia

Assn. of Ecosystem Res. Centers [4499], c/o Robin Graham, Sec., Environmental Sciences Div., Oak Ridge Natl. Lab., PO Box 2008, Oak Ridge, TN 37831-2008, (865)576-7756

L'Association des Ecrivains Italo Canadiens [★IO]

Assn. of Edison Illuminating Companies [3952], c/o Earl B. Parsons, Jr., Exec. Dir./Sec.-Treas., PO Box 2641, Birmingham, AL 35291, (205)257-2530

Assn. des Editeurs Belges [★IO]

Assn. des Editeurs de la Presse Privee du Mali [IO], Bamako, Mali

Assn. of Editorial Businesses - Defunct.

Assn. for the Educ. of Children with Medical Needs [8072], 7065 Hillgreen Dr., Dallas, TX 75214, (214)456-5930

Assn. for Educ. in Healthcare Info. Tech. [15132], 401 N Michigan Ave., Ste. 2400, Chicago, IL 60611, (312)321-6839

Assn. for Educ. in Intl. Bus. [★8011]

Assn. for Educ. in Intl. Bus. [★IO]

Assn. for Educ. in Journalism [★8706]

Assn. for Educ. in Journalism and Mass Commun. [8706], 234 Outlet Pointe Blvd., Columbia, SC 29210-5667, (803)798-0271

Assn. of Educ. Practitioners and Provider [★9215]

Assn. for Educ. and Rehabilitation of the Blind and Visually Impaired [16833], 1703 N Beauregard St., Ste. 440, Alexandria, VA 22311, (703)671-4500

Assn. for the Educ. of Teachers in Sci. [★9211]

Assn. for Educ. of the Visually Handicapped [★16833]

Assn. for Educ. in World Govt. [★17620]

Assn. for Educ. in World Govt. [★IO]

Assn. for Educational Activity [IO], Helsinki, Finland

Assn. for Educational Communications and Tech. [8551], 1800 N Stonelake Dr., Ste. 2, Bloomington, IN 47404, (812)335-7675

Reference to "IO" in place of a book number signifies that the association may be found in the 45th edition of International Organizations.

Assn. for Educational Development - Defunct.

Assn. of Educational Negotiators [★24046]

Assn. of Educational Psychologists [IO], Durham, United Kingdom

Assn. of Educational Publishers [9009], 510 Heron Dr., Ste. 201, Logan Township, NJ 08085, (856)241-7772

Assn. of Educational Publishers; EdPress - The [★9009]

Assn. Educative des Amateurs d'Astronomie du Centre [IO], Orleans, France

Assn. of Educators of Gifted Children [★8465]

Assn. of Educators for Homebound and Hospitalized Children [★11998]

Assn. of Educators for Homebound and Hospitalized Children [★9141]

Assn. of Educators for Homebound and Hospitalized Children [★IO]

Assn. of Educators in Imaging and Radiologic Sciences [9096], PO Box 90204, Albuquerque, NM 87199-0204, (505)823-4740

Assn. of Educators in Private Practice [★9215]

Assn. of Educators in Radiological Sciences [★9096]

Assn. for Efficient Environmental Energy Systems [7138]

Assn. of Electoral Administrators [IO], Liverpool, United Kingdom

Assn. of Elecl. Contractors - Ireland [IO], Blackrock, Ireland

Assn. for Elecl., Electronic and Info. Technologies [IO], Frankfurt am Main, Germany

Assn. of Elecl., Electronics and Automation Societies in Finland [IO], Helsinki, Finland

Assn. of Elecl. Engineers [IO], Helsinki, Finland

Assn. of Elecl. and Mech. Trades [IO], York, United Kingdom

Assn. of Electricity Producers [IO], London, United Kingdom

Assn. of Electronic Cottagers - Defunct.

Assn. of Electronic Distributors - Address unknown since 2003.

Assn. for Electronic Hea. Care Transactions [14618], c/o Healthcare Info. and Mgt. Systems Soc., 230 E Ohio St., Ste. 500, Chicago, IL 60611, (312)664-4467

Assn. of Electronic Manufacturers [★1212]

Assn. for Electronics Mfg. of the Soc. of Mfg. Engineers [6907], c/o Soc. of Mfg. Engineers, 1 SME Dr., PO Box 930, Dearborn, MI 48121-0930, (313)425-3000

Association for Electronics Manufacturing of the Society of Manufacturing Engineers [IO], Dearborn, MI, United States

Assn. of the Electrotechnical Indus. of the Slovak Republic [IO], Bratislava, Slovakia

Assn. des Eleveurs Ayrshire du Canada [★IO]

Assn. of Emergency Physicians [14329], 911 Whitewater Dr., Mars, PA 16046, (724)772-1818

Assn. for Emissions Control by Catalyst [IO], Brussels, Belgium

Assn. for the Encouragement of Correct Punctuation, Spelling, and Usage in Public Communications - Address unknown since 1995.

Assn. for Energy Cost Allocation [★IO]

Association of Energy Engineers [IO], Atlanta, GA, United States

Assn. of Energy Engineers [6942], 4025 Pleasantdale Rd., Ste. 420, Atlanta, GA 30340, (770)447-5083

Assn. of Energy Engineers, Bulgaria/Sofia [IO], Sofia, Bulgaria

Assn. of Energy Engineers, Poland/Czestochowa [IO], Czestochowa, Poland

Assn. of Energy Engineers, Poland/Warsaw [IO], Warsaw, Poland

Assn. of Energy Engineers, West Georgia Chap. [IO], Batumi, Georgia

Assn. of Energy Ser. Companies [2918], 10200 Richmond Ave., Ste. 275, Houston, TX 77042-4140, (713)781-0758

Assn. of Energy Services Professionals [6943], 4809 E Thistle Landing Dr., Ste. 100, Phoenix, AZ 85044, (480)704-5900

Assn. of Energy Services Professionals [★6943]

Assn. of Energy Services Professionals [★IO]

Assn. of Energy Services Professionals [IO], Phoenix, AZ, United States

Assn. for Engg. Graphics and Imaging Systems [1800], c/o Intl. Reprographic Assn., 401 N Michigan Ave., Chicago, IL 60611, (312)245-1026

Assn. of Enrolled Agents [★6299]

Assn. for Enterprise Integration [700], 2111 Wilson Blvd., Ste. 400, Arlington, VA 22201, (703)247-9474

Assn. for Enterprise Opportunity [3605], 1601 N Kent St., Ste. 1101, Arlington, VA 22209, (703)841-7760

Assn. of Enterprising Mothers - Address unknown since 2000.

Assn. of Entertainers - Address unknown since 1995.

Assn. of Entertainment Industry Computer Professionals - Address unknown since 1990.

Assn. for Env. Conscious Building [IO], Llandysul, United Kingdom

Assn. for Env. and Public Hea. [IO], Ry, Denmark

Assn. for Environmental Archaeology [IO], Portsmouth, United Kingdom

Assn. for Environmental Educ., Russia [IO], Obninsk, Russia

Assn. of Environmental and Engg. Geologists [7130], PO Box 460518, Denver, CO 80246, (303)757-2926

Assn. of Environmental Engg. Professors [★9023]

Assn. of Environmental Engg. and Sci. Professors [9023], c/o Joanne Fetzner, 2303 Naples Ct., Champaign, IL 61822, (217)398-6969

Assn. for the Environmental Hea. of Soils [5221], 150 Fearing St., Amherst, MA 01002, (413)549-5170

Assn. of Environmental and Rsrc. Economists [4359], c/o Marilyn M. Voight, Exec. Dir., 1616 P St. NW, Rm. 600, Washington, DC 20036, (202)328-5125

Assn. of Environmental Scientists and Administrators - Defunct.

Assn. of Episcopal Colleges [8397], c/o Colleges and Universities of the Anglican Communion, 815 2nd Ave., New York, NY 10017-4594, (212)716-6148

Assn. of Episcopal Colleges [IO], New York, NY, United States

Assn. for Equine Sports Medicine - Address unknown since 2007.

Assn. of Equip. Lessors [★3381]

Assn. of Equip. Lessors [★IO]

Association of Equipment Management Professionals [IO], Glenwood Springs, CO, United States

Assn. of Equip. Mgt. Professionals [2442], PO Box 1368, Glenwood Springs, CO 81602-1368, (970)384-0510

Assn. of Equip. Manufacturers [177], 6737 W Washington St., Ste. 2400, Milwaukee, WI 53214, (414)272-0943

Assn. of Equip. Manufacturers [IO], Milwaukee, WI, United States

Assn. of Equip. Mfrs. - Canada [IO], Ottawa, ON, Canada

Assn. for Eradication of Heart Attack [13894], 2472 Bolsover St., No. 439, Houston, TX 77005, (713)529-4484

Assn. of Esko-Graphics' Users [6761], c/o Michael D. Meyer, Chm., 622 High St., New London, WI 54961, (920)540-2103

Assn. Espanola de Constructores de Maquinaria Textil [★IO]

Assn. Espanola de Esclerosis Lateral Amiotrofica [★IO]

Assn. of Estonian Broadcasters [IO], Tallinn, Estonia

Assn. of the Estonian Food Indus. [IO], Tallinn, Estonia

Assn. des Etats Genereaux des Etudiants de l'Europe [IO], Brussels, Belgium

Assn. des Etudiantes Infirmiereres du Canada [★IO]

Assn. of European Accumulator Mfrs. [★IO]

Assn. of European Adhesives Mfrs. [IO], Brussels, Belgium

Assn. of European Airlines [IO], Brussels, Belgium

Assn. of European Assay Offices [IO], London, United Kingdom

Assn. of European Automotive Components and Parts [★IO]

Assn. of European Border Regions [IO], Gronau, Germany

Assn. of European Building Surveyors and Constr. Experts [IO], London, United Kingdom

Assn. of European Businesses [IO], Moscow, Russia

Assn. of European Cancer Leagues [IO], Bern, Switzerland

Assn. of European Candle Mfrs. [IO], Neuilly-sur-Seine, France

Assn. of European Cartonboard and Carton Mfrs. Assn. [★IO]

Assn. of European Chambers of Commerce and Indus. [IO], Brussels, Belgium

Assn. of European Cities Interested in Elec. Vehicles [IO], Brussels, Belgium

Assn. of European Civil Engg. Faculties [IO], Prague, Czech Republic

Assn. of European Conjuncture Institutes [IO], Louvain-la-Neuve, Belgium

Assn. of European Cooperative and Mutual Insurers [IO], Brussels, Belgium

Assn. of European Correspondence Schools [★IO]

Assn. of European Elec. Machine Tool Manufacturers [★IO]

Assn. of European Fruit and Vegetable Processing Indus. [★IO]

Assn. of European Gas Meter Mfrs. [IO], Nivelles, Belgium

Assn. of European Geological Societies [IO], Essen, Germany

Assn. of European Gypsum Indus. [IO], Brussels, Belgium

Assn. of European Journalists [IO], Kraainem, Belgium

Assn. of European Mfrs. of Internal Combustion Engines [★IO]

Assn. of European Mfrs. of Sporting Ammunition [IO], Rome, Italy

Assn. of European Manufacturers of Tech. Ceramics for Electronic, Electchanical and Other Applications [★IO]

Assn. of European Market Res. Institutes [★IO]

Assn. of European Migration Institutions [IO], Alborg, Denmark

Assn. of European Operational Res. Societies within IFORS [IO], Brussels, Belgium

Assn. of European Operational Res. Societies within IFORS - France [IO], Paris, France

Assn. of European Police Colleges [IO], Warnsveld, Netherlands

Assn. of European Producers of Steel for Packaging [IO], Brussels, Belgium

Assn. of European Psychiatrists [IO], Strasbourg, France

Assn. of European Public Postal Operators [IO], Brussels, Belgium

Assn. of European Radios [IO], Brussels, Belgium

Assn. of European Railway Equip. Mfrs. [★IO]

Assn. of European Refrigeration Compressor and Controls Mfrs. [IO], Berlin, Germany

Assn. of European Schools of Planning [IO], Reims, France

Assn. of European Sci. and Tech. Transfer Professionals [IO], The Hague, Netherlands

Assn. of the European Self-Medication Indus. [IO], Brussels, Belgium

Assn. of the European Space Indus. [IO], Paris, France

Assn. of European Storage Battery Mfrs. [IO], Brussels, Belgium

Assn. of European Tomato Processing Indus. [★IO]

Assn. of European Toxicologists and European Societies of Toxicology [IO], Milan, Italy

Assn. of European Trade Mark Owners [IO], Leicester, United Kingdom

Assn. for European Transport [IO], London, United Kingdom

Association of European Universities [★IO]

Assn. of European Water Meter Mfrs. [IO], Paris, France

Assn. of European Wheel Mfrs. [IO], Ceriano Laghetto, Italy

Assn. Europeene des Centres D'Ethique Medicale [★IO]

A star before a book entry number signifies that the name is not listed separately, but is mentioned within the entry.

Assn. Europeene des Galvanisateurs [★IO]

Assn. Europeene des Jeunes Historiens [★IO]

Assn. Europeene pour l'Enseignement de l'Architecture [★IO]

Assn. Europeene des Petites et Moyennes Entreprises du PPE [★IO]

Assn. Europeene des Pharmaciens des Hopitaux [★IO]

Assn. Europeene de Sci. Regionale [★IO]

Assn. Europeene des Sous-Officiers de Reserve [★IO]

Assn. Europeene des Universites Ecoles et Colleges d'Optometrie [★IO]

Assn. Europeenne des Academiciens Turcs Belgie [★IO]

Assn. Europeenne des Acarologistes [★IO]

Assn. Europeenne des Agents Artistiques [★IO]

Assn. Europeenne de Cautionnement Mutuel [★IO]

Assn. Europeenne des Centres Anti-Poisons et de Toxicologie Clinique [★IO]

Assn. Europeenne des Centres Nationaux de Productivite [★IO]

Assn. Europeenne du Ciment [★IO]

Assn. Europeenne des Conservatoires, Academies de Musique et Musikhochschulen [★IO]

Assn. Europeenne des Conservatoires, Academies de Musique et Musikkockschulen [★IO]

Association Europeenne des Constructeurs de Material Aerospatial [★IO]

Association Europeenne des Constructeurs de Material Aerospatial [★154]

Assn. Europeenne d'Anatomie Clinique [★IO]

Assn. Europeenne d'Apitherapie [★IO]

Assn. Europeenne d'Athletisme [★IO]

Assn. Europeenne d'Emballages Alimentaires a Usage Unique [★IO]

Assn. Europeenne pour la Direction du Personnel [★IO]

Assn. Europeenne pour le Droit de l'Alimentation [★IO]

Assn. Europeenne des Ecoles d' Hotelleerie et de Tourisme [★IO]

Assn. Europeenne des Editeurs d'Annuaires et Bases de Donrees [★IO]

Assn. Europeenne des Editeurs de Journaux [★IO]

Assn. Europeenne des Enseignants [★IO]

Assn. Europeenne des Establissements d'Enseignment Veterinaire [★IO]

Assn. Europeenne des Etudes Juives [★IO]

Assn. Europeenne des Fabricants de Composants Electroniques [★IO]

Assn. Europeenne des Femmes Pour la Recherche Theologique [★IO]

Assn. Europeenne des Festivals [★IO]

Assn. Europeenne des Gaz de Petrole Liquefies [★IO]

Assn. Europeenne des Graveurs et des Flexographes [★IO]

Assn. Europeenne des Instituts Recherche et de Formation en Matiere de Developpement [★IO]

Assn. Europeenne de Laboratoires de Teledetection [★IO]

Assn. Europeenne pour l'Administration de la Recherche Industrielle [★IO]

Assn. Europeenne de l'Asphalte [★IO]

Assn. Europeenne pour l'Etude de l'Alimentation et du Developpement de l'Enfant [★IO]

Assn. Europeenne pour l'Etude de la Population [★IO]

Assn. Europeenne de Libre-Echange [★IO]

Assn. Europeenne du Loisir [★IO]

Assn. Europeenne de Mgt. et Marketing Financiers [★IO]

Assn. Europeenne des Medicins des Hopitaux [★IO]

Assn. Europeenne des Musees d'Histoire des Sciences Medicales [★IO]

Assn. Europeenne Pour L'Information Sur Le Developpement Local [★IO]

Assn. Europeenne pour la Protection Passive contre l'Incendie [★IO]

Assn. Europeenne des Syndicats de Fabricants de Bougies et de Cierges [★IO]

Assn. Europeenne de Terminologie [★IO]

Assn. Europeenne Thyroide [★IO]

Assn. Europeenne de Tisseurs de Verre [★IO]

Assn. Europeenne des Vehicules Electriques Routiers [★IO]

Assn. Europeenne de Vente par Correspondance et a Distance [★IO]

Assn. Europeenne des Voies Vertes [★IO]

Assn. Europeennee De L Universite [★IO]

Assn. of Evangelical Friends [★IO]

Assn. of Evangelical Friends [★20040]

Assn. of Evangelical Lutheran Church [★20224]

Assn. of Evangelical Relief and Development Organizations [20486], 1224 E Washington St., Phoenix, AZ 85034, (520)459-1864

Assn. of Evangelicals in Africa [IO], Nairobi, Kenya

Assn. of Evangelicals for Italian Missions - Address unknown since 2002.

Assn. des Evangeliques d'Afrique [★IO]

Assn. of Event Organisers [IO], Berkhamsted, United Kingdom

Assn. for Evolutionary Economics [6872], c/o Off. of Sec.-Treas., Bucknell Univ., Dept. of Economics, Coleman Hall 154, Lewisburg, PA 17837, (570)577-3648

Assn. of Executive Directors of Halls of Fame [★23827]

Assn. of Executive Recruiting Consultants [★1256]

Assn. of Executive Recruiting Consultants [★IO]

Assn. of Executive Search Consultants [IO], New York, NY, United States

Assn. of Executive Search Consultants [1256], 12 E 41st St., 17th Fl., New York, NY 10017, (212)398-9556

Assn. of Executive Secretaries [★19902]

Assn. Executives; Automotive Trade [349]

Assn. Executives; Food Indus. [3405]

Assn. Executives Human Rights Caucus - Defunct.

Assn. Executives; Natl. Coun. of County [5624]

Assn. Executives; Natl. Coun. of State Pharmacy [★15943]

Assn. Executives of North Am; Nursery [★5047]

Assn. Executives of North Am; Nursery and Landscape [5047]

Assn. Executives; Nursery [★5047]

Assn. of Exhibition Organisers [★IO]

Assn. of Existential Psychology and Psychiatry - Defunct.

Assn. for Experiential Educ. [8411], 3775 Iris Ave., Ste. 4, Boulder, CO 80301-2043, (303)440-8844

Assn. des Experts-Comptables Internationaux [★IO]

Assn. of Exploration Geochemists [★IO]

Assn. for Explosive Detection K-9s, Intl. [IO], Aquilla, TX, United States

Assn. for Explosive Detection K-9s, Intl. [5964], c/o Nancy Bidwell, Pres., PO Box 176, Aquilla, TX 76622, (386)788-4083

Assn. for the Export of Canadian Books [IO], Ottawa, ON, Canada

Assn. des Fabricants de Cafe Solubles des Pays de la Communaute Economique Europeenne [★IO]

Assn. de Fabricants Europeens d'Accumulateurs [★IO]

Assn. des Fabricants Europeens d'Emulsifiants Alimentaires [★IO]

Assn. des Fabricants Europeens de Rubans Auto-Adhesifs [★IO]

Assn. des Fabricants, Importateurs et Fournisseurs de Produits de Cosmetique et de Parfumerie [★IO]

Assn. des Fabricants Internationaux d'Automobiles du Canada [★IO]

Assn. des Fabricants de Pates, Papiers et Cartons de Belgique [★IO]

Assn. for Facilities Engg. [7003], 12100 Sunset Hills Rd., Ste. 130, Reston, VA 20190, (703)234-4066

Assn. des Facultes Dentaires du Canada [★IO]

Assn. des Facultes de Medecine du Canada [★IO]

Assn. des Facultes de Pharmacie du Canada [★IO]

Assn. of Faculties of Medicine of Canada [IO], Ottawa, ON, Canada

Assn. of Faculties of Pharmacy of Canada [IO], Vancouver, BC, Canada

Assn. of Fair Housing Committees - Defunct.

Assn. des Familles Ouellet-te d'Amerique [★IO]

Assn. des Familles Gosselin [★IO]

Assn. of Family and Conciliation Courts [5699], 6525 Grand Teton Plz., Madison, WI 53719-1083, (608)664-3750

Assn. of Family Farmers - Defunct.

Assn. for Family Living - Defunct.

Assn. of Family Medicine Residency Directors [15059], 11400 Tomahawk Creek Pkwy., Ste. 670, Leawood, KS 66211-2672, (913)906-6000

Assn. of Family Practice Administrators [15060], c/o Dawn Sexton, Exec. Sec., 11400 Tomahawk Creek Pkwy., Leawood, KS 66211-2672, (800)274-2237

Assn. of Family Practice Physician Assistants [14698], 295 W Crossville Rd., Ste. 130, Roswell, GA 30075, (770)640-7605

Assn. of Family Practice Residency Directors [★15059]

Assn. of Farmworker Opportunity Programs [12585], 1726 M St. NW, Ste. 800, Washington, DC 20036, (202)826-6006

Assn. of Fashion, Advt., and Editorial Photographers [★IO]

Assn. of Fashion and Image Consultants [★IO]

Assn. of Fashion and Image Consultants [★957]

Assn. of Fashion Retailers in Finland [IO], Helsinki, Finland

Assn. of Fed. Communications Consulting Engineers [7767], c/o Tom Cox, Sec., 3221 Foothill St., Clear Channel Radio, Escondido, CA 92025, (703)780-4824

Assn. of Federal Computer Users - Defunct.

Assn. of Federal Fiscal Technicians - Defunct.

Assn. for Fed. Info. Resources Mgt. [5815], PO Box 2848, Alexandria, VA 22301, (703)549-1160

Assn. of Fed. Investigators [★5653]

Assn. of Federal Photographers - Defunct.

Assn. of Federal Safety and Health Professionals - Defunct.

Assn. of Federal Woman's Award Recipients - Defunct.

Assn. des Federations Internationales Olympiques d'Ete [★IO]

Assn. des Federations Internationales des Sports d'Hiver [★IO]

Assn. of Federchimica [IO], Milan, Italy

Assn. Feline Canadienne [★IO]

Assn. of Female Exhibit Managers and Conf. Organizers - Address unknown since 2003.

Assn. Feminine d'Education et d'Action Sociale [★IO]

Assn. of Feminist Consultants - Defunct.

Assn. des Femmes Autochtones du Canada [★IO]

Assn. des Femmes Chefs d'Entreprises du Cote d'Ivoire [IO], Abidjan, Cote d'Ivoire

Assn. des Femmes Chefs d'Entreprises Maroc [IO], Casablanca, Morocco

Assn. des Femmes Compositeurs Canadiennes [★IO]

Assn. des Femmes d'Affaires et Chefs d'Entreprises du Benin [IO], Cotonou, Benin

Assn. des Femmes d'Affaires et Chefs d'Entreprises du Gabon [IO], Libreville, Gabon

Assn. des Femmes Entrepreneurs Chefs d'Entreprises [IO], Kinshasa, Democratic Republic of the Congo

Assn. des Femmes contre l'Osteoporose [IO], Neuilly-sur-Seine, France

Assn. of Feng Shui Consultants [IO], Epping, Australia

Assn. of Fertilizer and Phosphate Chemists [6673], PO Box 1645, Bartow, FL 33831

Assn. of Festival Organisers [IO], Matlock, United Kingdom

Assn. for Field Archaeology - Defunct.

Assn. of Field Ornithologists [7413], c/o Cecilia M. Riley, Pres., 103 West Hwy., Lake Jackson, TX 77566, (979)480-0999

Assn. of Field Ser. Managers, Intl. [★3545]

Assn. of Field Ser. Managers, Intl. [★IO]

Assn. of Film Commissioners [★IO]

Assn. of Film Commissioners [★1368]

Assn. of Film Commissioners Intl. [1368], 314 N Main, Helena, MT 59601, (406)495-8040

Assn. of Film Commissioners Intl. [IO], Helena, MT, United States

Assn. of Finance and Insurance Professionals [2146], PO Box 1933, Colleyville, TX 76034, (817)428-2434

Assn. of Financial Advisers [IO], Deakin West, Australia

Reference to "IO" in place of a book number signifies that the association may be found in the 45th edition of International Organizations.

Assn. for Financial Counseling and Planning Educ. **[1456]**, 1500 W 3rd Ave., Ste. 223, Columbus, OH 43212, (614)485-9650

Assn. for Financial Guaranty Insurers **[2147]**, c/o Mackin and Company, 139 Lancaster St., Albany, NY 12210-1903, (518)449-4698

Assn. for Financial Professionals **[1403]**, 4520 E West Hwy., Ste. 750, Bethesda, MD 20814, (301)907-2862

Assn. of Financial Services Holding Companies - Address unknown since 2002.

Assn. for Financial Tech. **[61]**, c/o Kurt Guenther, Pres., 230 Sci. Dr., Ste. 800, Norcross, GA 30092-2904, (800)879-1996

Assn. of Fine Art Dealers in the Netherlands **[IO]**, Amsterdam, Netherlands

Assn. for Finishing Processes of the Soc. of Mfg. Engineers **[IO]**, Dearborn, MI, United States

Assn. for Finishing Processes of the Soc. of Mfg. Engineers **[6703]**, 1 SME Dr., PO Box 930, Dearborn, MI 48121, (313)271-1500

Assn. of Finnish Advertisers **[IO]**, Helsinki, Finland

Assn. of Finnish Furniture and Joinery Indus. **[IO]**, Helsinki, Finland

Assn. of Finnish Music Schools **[IO]**, Helsinki, Finland

Assn. of Finnish Pharmacies **[IO]**, Helsinki, Finland

Assn. of Finnish Symphony Orchestras **[IO]**, Helsinki, Finland

Assn. of Firearm and Tool Mark Examiners **[7083]**, c/o Michelle N. Kuehner, Membership Sec., Forensic Lab-Firearms Sect., 10 County Office Bldg., 542 Forbes Ave., Pittsburgh, PA 15219, (412)350-3732

Assn. of First Div. Civil Servants **[IO]**, London, United Kingdom

Assn. Fiscale Internationale **[★IO]**

Assn. of Fish and Wildlife Agencies **[IO]**, Washington, DC, United States

Assn. of Fish and Wildlife Agencies **[4360]**, 444 N Capitol St. NW, Ste. 725, Washington, DC 20001, (202)624-7890

Assn. for Fitness Professionals; IDEA: The **[★15965]**

Assn. of Flight Attendants **[★24009]**

Assn. of Flight Attendants **[★IO]**

Association of Flight Attendants - CWA **[IO]**, Washington, DC, United States

Assn. of Flight Attendants - CWA **[24009]**, 501 3rd St. NW, Washington, DC 20001, (202)434-1300

Assn. of Flock Processors - Defunct.

Assn. of Flow Survey Contractors **[★IO]**

Assn. des Fonderies Canadiennes **[★IO]**

Assn. of Food Distributors **[★1503]**

Assn. of Food and Drug Officials **[5736]**, 2550 Kingston Rd., Ste. 311, York, PA 17402, (717)757-2888

Assn. of Food and Drug Officials of the U.S. **[★5736]**

Assn. of Food Indus. **[1503]**, 3301 Rte. 66, Ste. 205, Bldg. C, Neptune, NJ 07753, (732)922-3008

Assn. of Food Indus. **[IO]**, Paris, France

Assn. of Food Indus. Sanitarians **[★2463]**

Assn. of Food Journalists **[3094]**, c/o Carol DeMasters, Exec. Dir., 7 Avienda Vista Grande, Ste. B7 467, Santa Fe, NM 87508-9199

Association of Food Journalists **[IO]**, Santa Fe, NM, United States

Assn. of Football Badge Collectors **[IO]**, Liverpool, United Kingdom

Assn. of Football Statisticians **[IO]**, London, United Kingdom

Assn. of Footwear Distributors - Defunct.

Assn. For Educ. Welfare Mgt. **[IO]**, Wakefield, United Kingdom

L'Association des Forces aeriennes du Canada **[★IO]**

Assn. of Foreign Banks **[IO]**, London, United Kingdom

Assn. of Foreign Banks in Switzerland **[IO]**, Zurich, Switzerland

Assn. of Foreign Investors in Real Estate **[IO]**, Washington, DC, United States

Assn. of Foreign Investors in Real Estate **[2328]**, Ronald Reagan Bldg., 1300 Pennsylvania Ave. NW, Washington, DC 20004, (202)312-1400

Assn. of Foreign Investors in U.S. Real Estate **[★2328]**

Assn. of Foreign Investors in U.S. Real Estate **[★IO]**

Assn. of Foreign Trade Representatives - Address unknown since 2008.

Assn. of Forensic DNA Analysts and Administrators **[5756]**, Univ. of North Texas Hea. Sci. Center, 3500 Camp Bowie Blvd., Fort Worth, TX 76107, (817)735-5107

Association of Forensic DNA Analysts and Administrators **[IO]**, Fort Worth, TX, United States

Association of Forensic Document Examiners **[IO]**, Cleveland, OH, United States

Assn. of Forensic Document Examiners **[5757]**, PO Box 31402, Cleveland, OH 44131

Assn. of Forensic Physicians **[IO]**, Glasgow, United Kingdom

Assn. of Forensic Quality Assurance Managers **[IO]**, Quantico, VA, United States

Assn. of Forensic Quality Assurance Managers **[5758]**, c/o Suzanne Smith, Sec./Membership Chair, Fed. Bur. of Investigation, 2501 Investigation Pkwy., Rm. 1115, Quantico, VA 22135, (703)632-8294

Assn. of Foresters and Wood Technologists **[IO]**, Warsaw, Poland

Assn. Forestiere Canadienne **[★IO]**

Assn. for Forests, Development and Conservation **[IO]**, Beirut, Lebanon

Assn. for Formation and Activities Intercultural for Youth **[IO]**, Madrid, Spain

Assn. pour la Formation des Enseignants en Europe **[★IO]**

Assn. of Former Agents of the U.S. Secret Ser. **[5877]**, 525 SW 5th St., Ste. A, Des Moines, IA 50309-4501, (515)282-8192

Assn. of Former Intelligence Officers **[5878]**, 6723 Whittier Ave., Ste. 303 A, McLean, VA 22101, (703)790-0320

Assn. of Former Intelligence Officers **[IO]**, McLean, VA, United States

Assn. of Former Intl. Civil Servants **[IO]**, Geneva, Switzerland

Assn. of Former Intl. Civil Servants - New York **[5566]**, One United Nations Plz., Rm. DC1-580, New York, NY 10017, (212)963-2943

Assn. of Former Senate Aides - Address unknown since 1989.

Assn. of Former Students; Wayland Baptist Univ. **[18943]**

Assn. of Former Trainees of the European Union **[IO]**, Brussels, Belgium

Assn. of Former UNESCO Staff Members **[IO]**, Paris, France

Assn. of Former WHO Staff Members **[IO]**, Geneva, Switzerland

Assn. of Formulation Chemists **[6674]**

Assn. for the Foundations of Sci., Language and Cognition **[IO]**, Brussels, Belgium

Assn. Francaise des Banques **[★IO]**

Assn. Francaise d'Assurance Qualite en Anatomie et Cytologie Pathologiques **[★IO]**

Assn. Francaise d'Astronomie **[IO]**, Paris, France

Assn. Francaise Des Documentalistes Et Des Biblio the caires Specialises **[★IO]**

Assn. Francaise d'Etude de la Concurrence **[★IO]**

Assn. Francaise des Diabetiques **[★IO]**

Assn. Francaise des Femmes Diplomees des Universites **[IO]**, Paris, France

Assn. Francaise de Floorball **[★IO]**

Assn. Francaise du Froid **[★IO]**

Assn. Francaise du Froid **[IO]**, Paris, France

Assn. Francaise pour l'Etude des Sols **[IO]**, Olivet, France

Assn. Francaise de Lutte Anti-Rhumatismale **[IO]**, Paris, France

Assn. Francaise de Micromineralogie **[★IO]**

Assn. Francaise de Normalisation **[★IO]**

Assn. Francaise des Observateurs d'Etoiles Variables **[★IO]**

Assn. Francaise de Protection des Plantes **[★IO]**

Assn. Francaise pour la Reconnaisance et l'Interpretation des Formes **[★IO]**

Assn. Francaise du Syndrome de Marfan **[IO]**, Maisons-Laffitte, France

Assn. Francaise des Ynglings **[IO]**, La Rochelle, France

Assn. des malaisiens en France **[★IO]**

Assn. France Alzheimer **[IO]**, Paris, France

Assn. France-Etats-Unis **[★IO]**

Assn. Francois-Xavier Bagnoud **[IO]**, Geneva, Switzerland

Assn. Francophone Internationale des Directeurs d'Etablissements Scolaires **[★IO]**

Assn. Francophone de Mgt. de Projet **[★IO]**

Assn. Francophone pour le Savoir **[★IO]**

Assn. of Fraternity Advisors **[24475]**, 9640 N Augusta Dr., Ste. 433, Carmel, IN 46032, (317)876-1632

Assn. of Free Community Papers **[88]**, PO Box 1989, Idaho Springs, CO 80452, (877)203-2327

Association of Free Community Papers **[IO]**, Idaho Springs, CO, United States

Assn. of Free French in the U.S. - Defunct.

Assn. of Free Methodist Educational Institutions **[8447]**, PO Box 535002, Indianapolis, IN 46253-5002, (317)244-3660

Assn. of Freestanding Radiation Oncology Centers **[16268]**, 1501 M St. NW, 7th Fl., Washington, DC 20005, (202)872-6767

Assn. of French Dairy Processors **[IO]**, Paris, France

Assn. for French Language Stud. **[IO]**, Birmingham, United Kingdom

Assn. of French Mechanical Industries - Address unknown since 2003.

Assn. of French-Speaking Physicians of Canada **[IO]**, Montreal, QC, Canada

Assn. of French-Speaking Planetariums **[IO]**, Strasbourg, France

Assn. of Friends of Classical Art **[IO]**, Fribourg, Switzerland

Assn. of Fruit and Vegetable Inspection and Standardization Agencies **[1674]**, c/o Thomas Smith, Pres., 1100 Bank St., Rm. 804, Richmond, VA 23219, (804)786-3548

Assn. of Fruit and Vegetable Retailers **[IO]**, Madrid, Spain

Assn. of Fruit and Vegetable Wholesalers **[IO]**, Milan, Italy

Assn. of Full Gospel Women Clergy **[20275]**

Assn. of Fund Raisers and Direct Sellers **[★1684]**

Assn. of Fund-Raising Distributors and Suppliers **[1684]**, 1100 Johnson Ferry Rd., Ste. 300, Atlanta, GA 30342, (404)252-3663

Assn. of Fundraising List Professionals - Defunct.

Assn. of Fundraising Professional Edmonton and Area Chap. **[IO]**, Spruce Grove, AB, Canada

Assn. of Fundraising Professionals **[12197]**, 4300 Wilson Blvd., Ste. 300, Arlington, VA 22203, (703)684-0410

Assn. of Fundraising Professionals Manitoba Chap. **[IO]**, Winnipeg, MB, Canada

Assn. of Fundraising Professionals Nova Scotia **[IO]**, Halifax, NS, Canada

Assn. of Fundraising Professionals - Ottawa Chap. **[IO]**, Orleans, ON, Canada

Assn. of Fur Farm Suppliers - Defunct.

Assn. Gabonaise de Medecine du Sport **[IO]**, Libreville, Gabon

Assn. of Game and Puzzle Collectors **[22460]**, PMB 321, 197M Boston Post Rd. W, Marlborough, MA 01752

Assn. of Gardens Trusts **[IO]**, London, United Kingdom

Assn. of Gas Appliance and Equip. Manufacturers **[★265]**

Assn. of Gastroenterologists of Bosnia and Herzegovina **[IO]**, Sarajevo, Bosnia-Hercegovina

Association of Gastrointestinal Motility Disorders **[IO]**, Bedford, MA, United States

Assn. of Gastrointestinal Motility Disorders **[14410]**, 12 Roberts Dr., Bedford, MA 01730, (781)275-1300

Assn. of Gay and Lesbian Armenians France **[IO]**, Paris, France

Assn. for Gay, Lesbian, and Bisexual Issues in Counseling **[12216]**, c/o Brian Dew, PhD, Pres., 640 Glen Iris Dr., No. 510, Georgia State Univ., Atlanta, GA 30308, (404)651-3409

Assn. for Gay and Lesbian Issues in Counseling **[★12216]**

A star before a book entry number signifies that the name is not listed separately, but is mentioned within the entry.

Assn. of Gay and Lesbian Psychiatrists [12217], 4514 Chester Ave., Philadelphia, PA 19143-3707, (215)222-2800

Assn. des Gays et Lesbiennes Armeniens de France [★IO]

Assn. for Gender Equity Leadership in Educ. [8399], 317 S Div., PMB 54, Ann Arbor, MI 48104, (734)769-2456

Assn. of Genealogists and Record Agents [★IO]

Assn. of Genealogists and Researchers in Archives [IO], Horsham, United Kingdom

Assn. for Gen. and Liberal Stud. [8777], c/o Paul Ranieri, Exec. Dir., Ball State Univ., English Dept., RB 2109, Muncie, IN 47306, (765)285-8406

Assn. of Gen. Merchandise Chains [★3427]

Assn. of Gen. Retailers and Traders [★IO]

Assn. Generale Des Federations Internationales De Sports [★IO]

Assn. Generale de l'Industrie du Medicame [★IO]

Assn. of Genetic Technologists [6569], PO Box 15945, Lenexa, KS 66285-5945, (913)541-0497

Assn. for Genito-Urinary Medicine, Medical Soc. for the Stud. of Venereal Diseases [★IO]

Assn. for Geographic Info. [IO], London, United Kingdom

Assn. for the Geological Collaboration in Japan [IO], Tokyo, Japan

Assn. of Geology Teachers [★8459]

Assn. of Geomorphologists of Ukraine [IO], Kiev, Ukraine

Assn. of Geotechnical and Geoenvironmental Specialists [IO], Beckenham, United Kingdom

Assn. of German Archivists [IO], Fulda, Germany

Assn. of German Broadcasters - Defunct.

Assn. of German Chambers of Industry and Commerce - Defunct.

Assn. of German Coal Importers [IO], Hamburg, Germany

Assn. of German Concert Choirs [IO], Weimar, Germany

Assn. of German Dental Mfrs. [IO], Cologne, Germany

Assn. of German Electrocial Engineers [IO], Frankfurt am Main, Germany

Assn. of German Engineers [IO], Dusseldorf, Germany

Assn. of the German Fruit Juice Indus. [IO], Bonn, Germany

Assn. of German Home Textiles Indus. [IO], Wuppertal, Germany

Assn. of the German Hotdip Galvanizing Indus. [IO], Dusseldorf, Germany

Assn. of the German India Rubber Indus. [★IO]

Assn. of German Language Authors in America - Defunct.

Assn. of the German Leather Indus. [IO], Frankfurt am Main, Germany

Assn. of the German Leather Indus. [★IO]

Assn. of German Librarians [IO], Berlin, Germany

Assn. of German Machine Tool Factories [★IO]

Assn. of the German Margarine Indus. [IO], Bonn, Germany

Assn. of German Mortgage Banks [★IO]

Assn. of German Music Dealers [IO], Bonn, Germany

Assn. of German Music Publishers [IO], Bonn, Germany

Assn. of the German Nobility in North Am. [21105], 1101 W 2nd St., Benicia, CA 94510, (707)745-1605

Assn. of German Paper Factories [★IO]

Assn. of the German Petroleum Indus. [IO], Hamburg, Germany

Assn. of German Pfandbrief Banks [IO], Berlin, Germany

Assn. of German Public Libraries [★IO]

Assn. of the German Rubber Mfg. Indus. [IO], Frankfurt am Main, Germany

Assn. of the German Smoking Tobacco Indus. [IO], Bonn, Germany

Assn. of German Textile Machinery Mfrs. [★IO]

Assn. of the German Tobacco Indus. [★IO]

Assn. of the German Trade Fair Indus. [IO], Berlin, Germany

Assn. of German Transport Undertakings [IO], Cologne, Germany

Assn. of German Travel Agents and Tour Operators [IO], Berlin, Germany

Assn. of German Urologists [IO], Dusseldorf, Germany

Assn. of German Wine Experts [IO], Geisenheim, Germany

Assn. of German Wood Import Houses [★IO]

Assn. of the German Zinc Galvanizing Indiana [★IO]

Assn. for Gerontology Educ. in Social Work [8461], c/o Maureen Corley, 1416 Fama Dr. NE, Atlanta, GA 30329-3308, (615)256-1885

Assn. for Gerontology in Higher Educ. [8462], 1220 L St. NW, Ste. 901, Washington, DC 20005-4018, (202)289-9806

Assn. of Gerontology India [IO], Varanasi, India

Assn. de Gestion Internationale des Oeuvres Audio-visuelles [★IO]

Assn. de Gestion de Tresorerie du Canada [★IO]

Assn. of Ghana Indus. [IO], Accra, Ghana

The Assn. for the Gifted [8465], c/o Tom Southern, Pres., Miami Univ., McGuffey Hall, Rm. 156, Oxford, OH 45056, (513)529-6634

Assn. of Gifted-Creative Children - Address unknown since 2003.

Assn. for Gifted and Talented Students - Address unknown since 2004.

Assn. of Girl Scout Executive Staff [12996], 1601 N Bond St., Ste. 303, Naperville, IL 60563, (630)369-7781

Assn. of Girl Scout Professional Workers [★12996]

Assn. of the Glass and Ceramics Indus. of the Czech Republic [IO], Prague, Czech Republic

Assn. for Global Bus. [IO], Sterling, VA, United States

Assn. for Global Bus. [8016], PO Box 651166, Sterling, VA 20165, (703)421-7768

Assn. Global View [8017], PO Box 3324, Chico, CA 95927, (530)892-9696

Assn. Global View [IO], Chico, CA, United States

Assn. for Glycogen Storage Disease [15244], PO Box 896, Durant, IA 52747, (563)785-6038

Assn. for Gnotobiotics Res. and Tech. [4534], c/o Dr. Philip B. Carter, Interim Exec. Sec.-Treas., North Carolina State Univ., Coll. of Veterinary Medicine, 4700 Hillsborough St., Raleigh, NC 27606, (919)513-6278

Assn. of Golf Club Secretaries [IO], Weston-Super-Mare, United Kingdom

Assn. of Golf Exhibitors - Address unknown since 2006.

Assn. of Golf Merchandisers [3639], PO Box 7247, Phoenix, AZ 85011-7247, (602)604-8250

Assn. of Golf Writers [IO], Chilham, United Kingdom

Assn. of Gospel Rescue Missions [IO], North Kansas City, MO, United States

Assn. of Gospel Rescue Missions [13155], 1045 Swift St., North Kansas City, MO 64116, (816)471-8020

Assn. of Governing Boards of State Universities and Allied Institutions [★7889]

Assn. of Governing Boards of Universities and Colleges [7889], 1 Dupont Cir., Ste. 400, Washington, DC 20036, (202)296-8400

Assn. of Governing Bodies of Independent Schools [IO], Salisbury, United Kingdom

Assn. of Govt. Accountants [5426], 2208 Mt. Vernon Ave., Alexandria, VA 22301-1314, (703)684-6931

Assn. for Govt. Assisted Housing - Defunct.

Assn. of Govt. Marketing Assistance Specialists [1740], PO Box 1607, Orange, TX 77630, (409)886-0125

Assn. of Govt. Nursing Staff [★IO]

Assn. of Govt. Officials in Indus. of the U.S. and Canada [★5917]

Assn. of Governmental Appraisers [★272]

Assn. of Governmental Labor Officials [★5917]

Assn. for Governmental Leasing and Finance [6202], 19 Mantua Rd., Mount Royal, NJ 08061, (856)423-3259

Assn. of Grace Brethren Ministers [19533], PO Box 694, Winona Lake, IN 46590

Assn. of Graduate Careers Advisory Services [IO], Sheffield, United Kingdom

Assn. for Graduate Educ. and Res. [★8477]

Assn. of Graduate Liberal Stud. Programs [8778], c/o Duke Univ., Box 90095, Durham, NC 27708-0095, (919)684-1987

Assn. of Graduate Librarians of Argentina [IO], Buenos Aires, Argentina

Assn. of Graduate Recruiters [IO], Warwick, United Kingdom

Assn. of Graduate Schools in Assn. of Amer. Universities [7890], 1200 New York Ave. NW, Ste. 550, Washington, DC 20005, (202)408-7500

Assn. of Graduates [8882], U.S. Air Force Acad., 3116 Acad. Dr., USAF Academy, CO 80840-4475, (719)472-0300

Assn. of Graduates of the School of Advanced Bus. Stud. [IO], Montreal, QC, Canada

Assn. of Graduates of the U.S. Air Force Acad. [18875], 3116 Acad. Dr., USAF Academy, CO 80840-4475, (719)472-0300

Assn. of Graphic Arts Consultants [★1788]

Assn. for Graphic Arts Training [1758], c/o Albert LeBlanc, McNaughton and Gunn, Inc., 960 Woodland Dr., Saline, MI 48176, (734)429-5411

Assn. of Graphic Communications [1759], 330 7th Ave., 9th Fl., New York, NY 10001-5010, (212)279-2100

Assn. of Graphic Solutions Providers; IPA The [7154]

Assn. for Gravestone Stud. [10015], 278 Main St., Ste. 207, Greenfield, MA 01301-3230, (413)772-0836

Assn. of Greek Producers of Phonograms [IO], Halandri, Greece

Assn. of Greek Tourist Enterprises [IO], Athens, Greece

Assn. of Greek Women Entrepreneurs [IO], Thessaloniki, Greece

Assn. of Greeting Card Retailers - Defunct.

Assn. des Grossistes en Medicaments du Canada [★IO]

Assn. of Ground Water Scientists and Engineers - A Division of Natl. Ground Water Assn. [7828], 601 Dempsey Rd., Westerville, OH 43081-8978, (614)898-7791

Assn. for Gp. and Individual Psychotherapy [IO], London, United Kingdom

Assn. for Group Psychoanalysis and Process - Defunct.

Assn. of Group Travel Executives - Defunct.

Assn. of Guilds of Weavers, Spinners and Dyers [IO], Taunton, United Kingdom

Assn. Guineenne d'Education et d'aide aux Diabetiques [★IO]

Assn. for the Habilitation of the Mentally Handicapped [★IO]

Assn. of Haitian Physicians Abroad [15159], 1166 Eastern Pkwy., Brooklyn, NY 11213, (718)245-1015

Assn. Haitienne de Taekwondo [IO], Delmas, Haiti

Assn. of Halfway House Alcoholism Programs of North Am. [13224], 860 N Center St., Mesa, AZ 85201, (480)610-8300

Assn. for Happiness Advancement [18046]

Assn. of Head Teachers in Scotland [★IO]

Assn. of Headmasters and Directors of Educ. [★IO]

Assn. of Heads of Outdoor Educ. Centres [IO], Cumbria, United Kingdom

Assn. of Hea. Care Journalists [IO], Columbia, MO, United States

Assn. of Hea. Care Journalists [3095], 10 Neff Hall, Columbia, MO 65211, (573)884-5606

Assn. of Hea. Fac. Licensure and Certification Directors [★6210]

Assn. of Hea. Fac. Survey Agencies [6210], 5105 Solemn Grove Rd., Garner, NC 27529, (919)661-8774

Assn. of Hea. Food Mfrs. [IO], Bad Homburg, Germany

Assn. for Hea. Info. and Libraries in Africa [IO], Lusaka, Zambia

Assn. of Hea. Insurance Advisors [14958], 2901 Telestar Ct., Falls Church, VA 22042-1205, (703)770-8200

Assn. of Health Occupations Teacher Educators - Defunct.

Assn. for Hea. Services Res. [★14535]

Assn. for Healthcare Documentation Integrity [15084], 4230 Kiernan Ave., Ste. 130, Modesto, CA 95356, (209)527-9620

Reference to "IO" in place of a book number signifies that the association may be found in the 45th edition of International Organizations.

Assn. of Healthcare Internal Auditors [15061], 10200 W 44th Ave., Ste. 304, Wheat Ridge, CO 80033, (303)327-7546

Assn. for Healthcare Philanthropy [14871], 313 Park Ave., Ste. 400, Falls Church, VA 22046, (703)532-6243

Assn. for Healthcare Philanthropy [IO], Falls Church, VA, United States

Assn. of Healthcare Philanthropy Canada [IO], Toronto, ON, Canada

Assn. of Healthcare Professionals [IO], Gateshead, United Kingdom

Assn. for Healthcare Quality - Defunct.

Assn. for Healthcare Rsrc. and Materials Mgt. [14872], 1 N Franklin, Chicago, IL 60606, (312)422-3840

Assn. of Hebrew Catholics [19575], 4120 W Pine Blvd., St. Louis, MO 63108-2802

Assn. of Heliographers - Defunct.

Assn. to Help Chernobyl [IO], Nagoya, Japan

Assn. for the Help of Retarded Children [15240], 83 Maiden Ln., New York, NY 10038, (212)780-2500

Assn. for Heritage Interpretation [IO], Perth, United Kingdom

Assn. of High Medicare Hospitals - Address unknown since 1999.

Assn. of High Pressure Water Jetting Contractors [★IO]

Assn. for High Tech Distribution [★1205]

Assn. for High Tech Distributors [★1205]

Assn. for High Tech. Distribution [1205], N19 W24400 Riverwood Dr., Waukesha, WI 53188, (262)696-3490

Assn. for Higher Educ. [★8478]

Assn. for Higher Educ. Access and Disability [IO], Dublin, Ireland

Assn. for Higher Educ. and Development [IO], Addis Ababa, Ethiopia

Assn. on Higher Educ. and Disability [IO], Huntersville, NC, United States

Assn. on Higher Educ. and Disability [8201], 107 Commerce Center Dr., Ste. 204, Huntersville, NC 28078, (704)947-7779

Assn. of Higher Educ. Facilities Officers; APPA: The [8333]

Assn. for Higher Educ. of North Texas [★8477]

Assn. of Highway Steel Transporters - Defunct.

Assn. of Hillel/Jewish Campus Professionals - Address unknown since 1995.

Assn. of Himalayan Yoga Meditation Societies [11218], 631 Univ. Ave. NE, Minneapolis, MN 55413, (612)379-2386

Assn. of Himalayan Yoga Meditation Societies [IO], Minneapolis, MN, United States

Assn. of Hispanic Advt. Agencies [89], 8201 Greensboro Dr., 3rd Fl., McLean, VA 22102, (703)610-9014

Assn. of Hispanic Arts [9999], PO Box 1169, New York, NY 10029, (212)876-1242

Assn. of Hispanic Arts [IO], New York, NY, United States

Assn. of Hispanic Fed. Executives [★5711]

Assn. for Hispanic Handicapped of New Jersey - Address unknown since 2001.

Assn. of Hispanic Healthcare Executives [14699], PO Box 230832, Ansonia Sta., New York, NY 10023, (212)877-1615

Assn. of Hispanics of Great Britain and Ireland [IO], Durham, United Kingdom

Association of Historians of Nineteenth-Century Art [IO], Chicago, IL, United States

Assn. of Historians of Nineteenth-Century Art [9431], c/o Janet Whitmore, Membership Coor., 5614 N Wayne Ave., No. 1, Chicago, IL 60660

Assn. of Historic Sites Officials [★10084]

Assn. for Historical Fencing [23399], PO Box 2013, Secaucus, NJ 07096-2013

Association for Historical Fencing [IO], Secaucus, NJ, United States

Assn. for the History of Chiropractic [13994], c/o Ms. Glenda Wiese, PhD, Exec. Dir., 1000 Brady St., Davenport, IA 52803, (563)884-5894

Assn. of History and Computing (UK Br.) [IO], Liverpool, United Kingdom

Assn. for the History of Language [IO], Canberra, Australia

Assn. for the History of the Northern Seas [IO], Liverpool, United Kingdom

Assn. of Holistic Animal Practitioners - Defunct.

Assn. of Holistic Biodynamic Massage Therapists [IO], Kettering, United Kingdom

Assn. for Holistic Health - Defunct.

Assn. of Holocaust Organizations [17714], PO Box 230317, Hollis, NY 11423, (516)582-4571

Assn. of Holocaust Organizations [IO], Hollis, NY, United States

Assn. for Holotropic Breathwork Intl. [13626], PO Box 400267, Cambridge, MA 02140

Assn. of Home Appliance Manufacturers [264], 1111 19th St. NW, Ste. 402, Washington, DC 20036, (202)872-5955

Assn. of Home Info. Pack Providers [IO], Market Harborough, United Kingdom

Association of Home Office Underwriters [IO], Atlanta, GA, United States

Assn. of Home Off. Underwriters [2148], 2300 Windy Ridge Pkwy., Ste. 600, Atlanta, GA 30339, (770)984-3715

Assn. for Honest Attorneys [5486], PO Box 558, Derby, KS 67037, (316)788-0901

Assn. of Hong Kong Nursing Staff [IO], Hong Kong, People's Republic of China

Assn. of Hosp. Directors of Medical Educ. [★14873]

Assn. of Hosp. Hea. and Fitness [★15966]

Assn. for Hosp. Medical Educ. [14873], 109 Bush Creek Rd., Irwin, PA 15642, (724)864-7321

Assn. of Hosp. Superintendents of U.S. and Canada [★14863]

Assn. of Hospital TV Networks - Address unknown since 1988.

Assn. of the Hotel, Restaurant, and Tourism Indus. in Denmark [IO], Frederiksberg, Denmark

Assn. des Hotels du Canada [★IO]

Assn. Houde Intl. [IO], Glencoe, IL, United States

Assn. Houde Intl. [21106], c/o John Houde, Box 82, Glencoe, IL 60022

Assn. of House Democratic Press Assistants - Address unknown since 2005.

Assn. for Human Emergence - Defunct.

Assn. of Human Rsrc. Systems Professionals [★67]

Assn. of Human Rsrc. Systems Professionals [★IO]

Assn. of Human Resources Mgt. and Organizational Behavior [★IO]

Assn. of Human Resources Mgt. and Organizational Behavior [★6528]

Assn. of Human Rights and Torture Defenders - Cameroon [IO], Buea, Cameroon

Assn. for Humanist Sociology [7660], c/o Kathy McMahon-Klosterman, VP of Membership, Dept. of Educational Psychology, 1256 Robert Dickey Pkwy., Kettering, OH 45409, (505)538-6824

Assn. for Humanistic Education - Defunct.

Assn. for Humanistic Educ. and Development [★8527]

Assn. for Humanistic Gerontology - Defunct.

Assn. for Humanistic Psychology [16140], 1516 Oak St., No. 320A, Alameda, CA 94501-2958, (510)769-6495

Assn. of Humanistic Psychology Practitioners [IO], London, United Kingdom

Assn. of Humanistic Rabbis [20120], 28611 W 12 Mile Rd., Farmington Hills, MI 48334, (248)478-7610

Assn. of the Hungarian Automotive Indus. [IO], Budapest, Hungary

Assn. of Hungarian Consulting Engineers and Architects [IO], Budapest, Hungary

Assn. of the Hungarian Exhibition and Fair Organisers [IO], Budapest, Hungary

Assn. of Hungarian Foundries [IO], Budapest, Hungary

Assn. of Hungarian Geophysicists [IO], Budapest, Hungary

Assn. of Hungarian Inventors [IO], Budapest, Hungary

Assn. of Hungarian Journalists [IO], Budapest, Hungary

Assn. of Hungarian Librarians [IO], Budapest, Hungary

Assn. of Hungarian Medical Societies [IO], Budapest, Hungary

Assn. of Hungarian Physiotherapists [IO], Budapest, Hungary

Assn. of Hungarian Record Companies [IO], Budapest, Hungary

Assn. of Hungarian Steel Indus. [IO], Budapest, Hungary

Assn. of Hungarian Students in North America - Defunct.

Assn. Huntington France [IO], Paris, France

Assn. of Hydraulic Equip. Mfrs. [★IO]

Assn. of Iberian and Latin Amer. Stud. of Australasia [IO], Melbourne, Australia

Assn. of the Ice Cream Indus. [★IO]

Assn. of Ice Cream and Related Products Manufacturers [IO], Buenos Aires, Argentina

Assn. of Icelandic Importers, Exporters, and Wholesale Merchants [IO], Reykjavik, Iceland

Assn. of Icelandic Physiotherapists [IO], Reykjavik, Iceland

L'association de l'industrie canadienne de L'enregistrement [★IO]

Assn. of Illustrators [IO], London, United Kingdom

Assn. for Image Anal. and Recognition [IO], Minsk, Belarus

Assn. of Image Consultants [★IO]

Assn. of Image Consultants [★957]

Assn. of Image Consultants Intl. [957], 100 E Grand Ave., Ste. 330, Des Moines, IA 50309, (515)282-5500

Association of Image Consultants International [IO], Des Moines, IA, United States

Assn. for Image Processing [IO], Warsaw, Poland

Assn. of Imaging Tech. and Sound - Address unknown since 2004.

Assn. of Immigration Attorneys - Defunct.

Assn. of Immigration and Nationality Lawyers [★5807]

Assn. of Importers and Exporters of the Republic of Argentina [IO], Buenos Aires, Argentina

Assn. of Importers-Mfrs. for Muzzleloading - Defunct.

Assn. for the Improvement of Community Coll. Teaching - Defunct.

Assn. for Improvement in the Maternity Services [IO], Surbiton, United Kingdom

Assn. for the Improvement of the Mississippi River - Defunct.

Assn. for the Improvement in Production and Utilisation of Banana [IO], New Delhi, India

Assn. of Incentive Marketing - Defunct.

Assn. of Independent Art Historians - Address unknown since 2002.

Assn. of Independent Broker Dealers - Defunct.

Assn. of Independent Colls. of Art and Design - Defunct.

Assn. of Independent Commercial Producers [90], 3 W 18th St., 5th Fl., New York, NY 10011, (212)929-3000

Assn. of Independent Composers and Performers - Address unknown since 1995.

Assn. of Independent Cmpt. Specialists [IO], Stroud, United Kingdom

Assn. of Independent Consultants [IO], Markham, ON, Canada

Assn. of Independent Corrugated Converters [IO], Alexandria, VA, United States

Assn. of Independent Corrugated Converters [973], PO Box 25708, Alexandria, VA 22313, (703)836-2422

Assn. of Independent Crop Consultants [IO], Petersfield, United Kingdom

Assn. of Independent Electricity Producers [★IO]

Assn. of Independent European Lawyers [IO], London, United Kingdom

Assn. of Independent Financial Advisers [IO], London, United Kingdom

Assn. of Independent Info. Professionals [IO], Baton Rouge, LA, United States

Assn. of Independent Info. Professionals [2097], 8550 United Plaza Blvd., Ste. 1001, Baton Rouge, LA 70809, (225)408-4400

Assn. of Independent Libraries [IO], Leeds, United Kingdom

Assn. of Independent Machine Copy Dealers and Mfrs. - Address unknown since 1995.

Assn. of Independent Mailing Equip. Dealers [★2448]

A star before a book entry number signifies that the name is not listed separately, but is mentioned within the entry.

Assn. of Independent Manufacturers'/Representatives **[2534]**, One Spectrum Pointe, Ste. 150, Lake Forest, CA 92630-2283, (949)859-2884

Assn. of Independent Medical Equip. Suppliers **[★14670]**

Assn. of Independent Microdealers **[★2827]**

Assn. of Independent Museums **[IO]**, Gosport, United Kingdom

Assn. of Independent Music **[IO]**, London, United Kingdom

Assn. for Independent Music - Defunct.

Assn. of Independent Music Publishers **[2800]**, PO Box 69473, Los Angeles, CA 90069, (818)771-7301

Assn. of Independent Optical Wholesalers **[★1864]**

Assn. of Independent Optical Wholesalers **[★IO]**

Assn. of Independent Physical Therapists **[IO]**, Bochum, Germany

Assn. of Independent Railways and Preservation Societies **[★IO]**

Assn. of Independent Record Labels **[IO]**, Fortitude Valley, Australia

Assn. of Independent Res. Institutes **[7562]**, c/o DAI Mgt., Inc., PO Box 844, Westminster, MD 21158, (410)751-8900

Assn. of Independent Res. and Tech. Organisations **[IO]**, Chipping Campden, United Kingdom

Assn. of Independent Retirees **[IO]**, Deakin West, Australia

Assn. of Independent Sci. Engg. and Testing Firms **[★7236]**

Assn. of Independent Tour Operators **[IO]**, Twickenham, United Kingdom

Assn. of Independent Trust Companies **[1457]**, 8 S Michigan Ave., Ste. 1000, Chicago, IL 60603, (312)223-1611

Assn. of Independent Video and Filmmakers **[9931]**

Assn. of Independents in Radio **[548]**, PO Box 220400, Boston, MA 02122, (877)937-2477

Assn. of Independents in Radio **[IO]**, Brooklyn, NY, United States

Assn. of Indian Entomologists in North Am. **[IO]**, Manhattan, KS, United States

Assn. of Indian Entomologists in North Am. **[7057]**, c/o Seemanti Chakrabarti, Treas., 123 W Waters Hall, Dept. of Entomology, Kansas State Univ., Manhattan, KS 66506

Assn. of Indian Muslims **[★19109]**

Assn. of Indian Muslims of Am. **[19109]**, PO Box 10654, Silver Spring, MD 20904

Assn. of Indian Pathologists in North Am. **[15861]**, c/o Rajal Shah, MD, Treas., 2G332UH, 1500 E Medical Center Dr., Dept. of Pathology, Ann Arbor, MI 48109-0054

Assn. of Indian Universities **[IO]**, New Delhi, India

Assn. of Indians in Am. **[19110]**, 5415 108 St., Corona, NY 11368, (718)271-0453

Assn. for India's Development **[12420]**, PO Box F, College Park, MD 20741-3005, (301)717-1059

Assn. for India's Development **[IO]**, College Park, MD, United States

Assn. for Individually Guided Education - Defunct.

Assn. of Indonesian Furniture and Wood Products Mfrs. **[★IO]**

Assn. of Indus. Advertisers **[★IO]**

Assn. of Indus. Advertisers **[★94]**

Assn. for Indus. Archaeology **[IO]**, Leicester, United Kingdom

Assn. of Indus. Laser Users **[IO]**, Abingdon, United Kingdom

Assn. of Indus. Metallizers, Coaters and Laminators **[851]**, 201 Springs St., Fort Mill, SC 29715, (803)802-7820

Assn. of Indus. Road Safety Officers **[IO]**, Worthing, United Kingdom

Assn. des Indus. Europeennes du Platre **[★IO]**

Assn. des Indus. de Marque **[★IO]**

Assn. of the Indus. of Juices and Nectars from Fruits and Vegetables of the European Union **[IO]**, Brussels, Belgium

Assn. of Industry Mfrs. - Defunct.

Assn. of Indus. Mfrs. Representatives **[★2534]**

Assn. for Infant Massage - Defunct.

Assn. for Infant Mental Hea., United Kingdom **[IO]**, Bristol, United Kingdom

Assn. des Infirmieres et Infirmiers du Canada **[★IO]**

Assn. for Informal Logic and Critical Thinking **[10785]**, c/o Donald Hatcher, Treas., Ctr. for Critical Thinking, Baker Univ., Baldwin City, KS 66006

Assn. of Info. and Dissemination Centers **[★7189]**

Assn. of Info. and Dissemination Centers **[7189]**, PO Box 3212, Maple Glen, PA 19002-8212, (215)654-9129

Assn. of Info. and Dissemination Centers **[IO]**, Maple Glen, PA, United States

Assn. of Info. and Dissemination Centers **[★IO]**

Assn. for Info. and Image Mgt. **[★2095]**

Assn. for Info. Mgt. **[IO]**, London, United Kingdom

Assn. of Information Managers for Financial Institutions - Defunct.

Assn. for Info. Media and Equip. **[328]**, PO Box 9844, Cedar Rapids, IA 52409-9844, (319)654-0608

Assn. of Info. Officers in the Pharmaceutical Indus. **[★IO]**

Assn. of Info. Specialists **[IO]**, Tbilisi, Georgia

Assn. for Info. Systems **[6722]**, PO Box 2712, Atlanta, GA 30301-2712, (404)651-0348

Assn. of Information Systems Professionals - Defunct.

Assn. of Info. Tech. Professionals **[8128]**, 401 N Michigan Ave., Ste. 2400, Chicago, IL 60611-4267, (312)245-1070

Assn. of Informed Senior Citizens - Defunct.

Assn. des Ingenieurs-Conseils du Canada **[★IO]**

Assn. des Ingenieurs Polonais du Canada **[★IO]**

Assn. of Ingersoll-Rand Distributors **[2002]**, 1300 Sumner Ave., Cleveland, OH 44115-2851, (216)241-7333

Assn. of Innerspring Manufacturers **[★1969]**

Assn. for Innovation in Higher Education - Defunct.

Assn. for Innovative Cooperation in Europe **[★IO]**

Assn. for Innovative Marketing - Address unknown since 2001.

Assn. of Insolvency Accountants **[★15]**

Assn. of Insolvency and Restructuring Advisors **[15]**, 221 Stewart Ave., Ste. 207, Medford, OR 97501, (541)858-1665

Assn. of Inspectors Gen. **[5777]**, Historic Carpenters' Hall, 320 Chestnut St., Philadelphia, PA 19106, (360)265-7785

Assn. Inst. - Address unknown since 1986.

Assn. of the Inst. for Certification of Cmpt. Professionals **[★8129]**

Assn. of the Inst. for Certification of Computing Professionals **[8129]**, 2350 E Devon Ave., Ste. 115, Des Plaines, IL 60018-4610, (847)299-4227

Assn. of the Inst. for Certification of Computing Professionals **[★8131]**

Assn. of Institutes for Aesthetic Educ. - Address unknown since 2002.

Assn. of Institutional Res. **[8997]**, 1435 E Piedmont Dr., Ste. 211, Tallahassee, FL 32308, (850)385-4155

Assn. of Institutions for Feminist Educ. and Res. in Europe **[IO]**, Utrecht, Netherlands

Assn. des Instituts Catholiques de l'Education **[★IO]**

Assn. of Insulin-Dependent Diabetics - Defunct.

Assn. of Insurance Advertisers - Defunct.

Assn. of Insurance Attorneys **[★5825]**

Assn. of Insurance Companies - Greece **[IO]**, Athens, Greece

Assn. of Insurance and Reinsurance Companies of Turkey **[IO]**, Istanbul, Turkey

Assn. of Insurance and Risk Managers **[IO]**, London, United Kingdom

Assn. for the Integration of Mgt. - Address unknown since 1990.

Assn. for Integrative Hea. Care Practitioners **[15037]**, PO Box 3204, Norfolk, VA 23514-3204, (757)623-1200

Assn. for Integrative Stud. **[10227]**, c/o Prof. William H. Newell, Exec. Dir., Miami Univ., School of Interdisciplinary Stud., Oxford, OH 45056, (513)529-2213

Assn. for Intelligence Officers **[★5878]**

Assn. for Intelligence Officers **[★IO]**

Assn. for Intelligent Systems Technology - Defunct.

Assn. for Intelligent Transport Systems India **[IO]**, Bhopal, India

Assn. for Interactive Marketing **[3734]**, 1430 Broadway, 8th Fl., New York, NY 10018, (888)337-0008

Assn. for Interactive Media **[★3734]**

Assn. for Intercollegiate Athletics for Women - Defunct.

Assn. for Interdisciplinary Res. in Values and Social Change **[12906]**, 512 10th St. NW, Washington, DC 20004, (202)626-8800

Assn. of Interior Specialists **[IO]**, Solihull, United Kingdom

Association of Internal Management Consultants **[IO]**, Marco Island, FL, United States

Assn. of Internal Mgt. Consultants **[2484]**, 824 Caribbean Ct., Marco Island, FL 34145, (239)642-0580

Assn. of Intl. Accountants **[IO]**, Newcastle upon Tyne, United Kingdom

Assn. for Intl. Advertising Agencies - Defunct.

Assn. for Intl. Agricultural Educ. **[★7934]**

Assn. for Intl. Agricultural Educ. **[★IO]**

Assn. for Intl. Agricultural and Extension Educ. **[IO]**, Gainesville, FL, United States

Assn. for Intl. Agricultural and Extension Educ. **[7934]**, c/o Thomas Bruening, PhD, Treas., Penn State Univ., Dept. of Agricultural and Extension Educ., 335 Agricultural Admin. Bldg., University Park, PA 16802, (814)863-7420

Assn. for Intl. Agriculture and Rural Development **[7935]**, c/o Joy C. Odom, Sec.-Treas., Dept. of Agricultural Economics, Mississippi State Univ., PO Box 5187, Mississippi State, MS 39762, (662)325-0549

Assn. for Intl. Agriculture and Rural Development **[IO]**, Mississippi State, MS, United States

Assn. of Intl. Air Courier Services **[★IO]**

Assn. of Intl. Airlines **[IO]**, San Jose, Costa Rica

Assn. Intl. des Assureurs contre la Grele **[★IO]**

Assn. of Intl. Auto. Manufacturers **[IO]**, Arlington, VA, United States

Assn. of Intl. Auto. Manufacturers **[343]**, 2111 Wilson Blvd., Ste. 1150, Arlington, VA 22201, (703)525-7788

Assn. of Intl. Auto. Mfrs. of Canada **[IO]**, Toronto, ON, Canada

Assn. of Intl. Banks and Trust Companies in the Bahamas **[IO]**, Nassau, Bahamas

Assn. of Intl. Bond Dealers **[★IO]**

Assn. of Intl. Border Agencies - Address unknown since 1990.

Assn. for Intl. Bus. **[701]**, 725 G St., Salida, CO 81201, (719)539-0500

Assn. for Intl. Bus. **[IO]**, Salida, CO, United States

Assn. for Intl. Cancer Res. **[IO]**, St. Andrews, United Kingdom

Assn. of Intl. Collective Mgt. of Audiovisual Works **[IO]**, Geneva, Switzerland

Assn. of Intl. Colleges and Universities **[★IO]**

Assn. of Intl. Colleges and Universities **[★8641]**

Assn. for Intl. Cooperation of Agriculture and Forestry **[★IO]**

Assn. of Intl. Couriers and Express Services **[IO]**, Slough, United Kingdom

Assn. of the Intl. Cultural Youth Exchange in Europe **[★IO]**

Assn. for Intl. Development - Defunct.

Assn. of Intl. Educ. Administrators **[7891]**, c/o Dr. Darla K. Deardorff, Exec. Dir., Duke Univ., Campus Box 90404, Durham, NC 27708-0404, (919)668-1928

Assn. of Intl. Educ. Administrators **[IO]**, Durham, NC, United States

Assn. Intl. des Entraineurs d'Athletisme **[★IO]**

Assn. Intl. des Entraineurs d'Athletisme **[★23919]**

Assn. of Intl. Hea. Researchers **[14548]**, 2665 Pleasant Valley Rd., Mobile, AL 36606, (251)473-3946

Assn. of Intl. Hea. Researchers **[IO]**, Mobile, AL, United States

Assn. of Intl. Healthcare Recruiters and Employers - Defunct.

Assn. of Intl. Insurance Agents **[★2191]**

Assn. for Intl. Investment **[★18473]**

Assn. for Intl. Investment **[★IO]**

Assn. Intl. pour l'Etude de l'Economie de l'Assurance **[★IO]**

Reference to "IO" in place of a book number signifies that the association may be found in the 45th edition of International Organizations.

Assn. of Intl. Marathons [★IO]
Assn. of Intl. Marathons and Road Races [IO], London, United Kingdom
Assn. for Intl. Medical Study [12834]
Assn. for Intl. Medical Study - Defunct.
Assn. of Intl. Meeting Planners [2675]
Assn. for Intl. Motion Engineers [7004], Western Michigan Univ. - Kohrman Hall, 1903 W Michigan Ave., Kalamazoo, MI 49008, (269)337-7650
Assn. of Intl. Motion Engineers [IO], Kalamazoo, MI, United States
Assn. of the Intl. Olympic Winter Sports Federations [IO], Zurich, Switzerland
Assn. of Intl. Pharmaceutical Mfrs. [IO], Moscow, Russia
Assn. of Intl. Photography Art Dealers [IO], Washington, DC, United States
Assn. of Intl. Photography Art Dealers [10846], 1767 P St. NW, Ste. 200, Washington, DC 20036-1421, (202)986-0105
Assn. for Intl. Practical Training [8601], 10400 Little Patuxent Pkwy., Ste. 250, Columbia, MD 21044-3519, (410)997-2200
Assn. for Intl. Practical Training [IO], Columbia, MD, United States
Assn. of Intl. Professional and Bus. Women [IO], Oslo, Norway
Assn. of Intl. Publishers Representatives - Defunct.
Assn. of Intl. Res. Initiatives for Environmental Stud. [IO], Tokyo, Japan
Assn. of Intl. Schools in Africa [IO], Nairobi, Kenya
Assn. Intl. des Societes d'Assurance Mutuelle [★IO]
Assn. of Intl. Trade Fairs of Am. [IO], Caracas, Venezuela
Assn. of Intl. Trading Companies in Audio-Visual Equip. and Public Info. Services [IO], Paris, France
Assn. of Intl. Vehicle Mfrs. [IO], Bad Homburg, Germany
Association for International Youth Sports - Address unknown since 2003.
Assn. for Intl. Youth-work - Christian Women's Working Group [IO], Bonn, Germany
Assn. Internationale des Anatomistes du Bois [★IO]
Assn. Internationale des Anthropobiologistes [★IO]
Assn. Internationale des Approvisionneurs de Navires [★IO]
Assn. Internationale des Arbitres de Water Polo [★IO]
Assn. Internationale des Archives Francophones [★IO]
Assn. Internationale des Avocats du Monde et des Indus. du Spectacle [★IO]
Assn. Internationale du Barreau [★IO]
Assn. Internationale des Charites [★IO]
Assn. Internationale de Chirurgie Buccale et Maxillo-Faciale [★IO]
Assn. Internationale de Chirurgie Buccale et Maxillo-Faciale [★15736]
Assn. Internationale des Circuits Permanents [★IO]
Assn. Internationale de Climatologie [★IO]
Assn. Internationale Contre les Experiences Douloureuses sur les Animaux [★IO]
Assn. Internationale des Cordeliers [★IO]
Assn. Internationale de la Couleur [★IO]
Assn. Internationale des Critiques d'Art [★IO]
Assn. Internationale des Critiques d'Art - Sect. Canadienne [★IO]
Assn. Internationale des Critiques Litteraires [★IO]
Assn. Internationale de Cybernetique [★IO]
Assn. Internationale d'Ecologie [★IO]
Assn. Internationale des Demographes de Langue Francaise [★IO]
Assn. Internationale Des Etudiants en Sciences Economiques et Commerciales [★IO]
Assn. Internationale Des Etudiants en Sciences Economiques et Commerciales [★8012]
Assn. Internationale Des Magistrats De La Jeunesse Et De La Famille [★IO]
Assn. Internationale du Design Interactif [★IO]
Assn. Internationale d'Essais de Semences [★IO]
Assn. Internationale d'Esthetique Experimentale [★IO]
Assn. Internationale d'Etudes de la Genese des Minerais [★IO]
Assn. Internationale d'Etudes de la Mission [★IO]

Assn. Internationale d'Etudes Occitanes [★IO]
Assn. Internationale d'Etudes Patristiques [★IO]
Assn. Internationale d'Histoire Economique [★IO]
Assn. Internationale d'Institutions d'Histoire Ouvriere [★IO]
Assn. Internationale Droit, Ethique and Sci. [★IO]
Assn. Internationale du Droit Nucleaire [★IO]
Assn. Internationale de Droit Penal [★IO]
Assn. Internationale de Droit Penal [★IO]
Assn. Internationale pour les Echanges en Agriculture [★IO]
Assn. Internationale des Ecoles et Instituts d'Administration [★IO]
Assn. Internationale des Ecoles des Sciences de l'Information [IO], Carouge, Switzerland
Assn. Internationale des Ecoles de Travail Social [★IO]
Assn. Internationale des Ecoles de Voile [★IO]
Assn. Internationale des Egyptologues [★IO]
Assn. Internationale des Entrepreneurs en Pipelines [★IO]
Assn. Internationale des Etudes Hongroises [★IO]
Assn. Internationale des Etudes et Recherches sur L'Information et la Commun. [★IO]
Assn. Internationale des Etudiants en Siences Economiques et Commerciales [IO], Rotterdam, Netherlands
Assn. Internationale des Etudiants Veterinaires [★IO]
Assn. Internationale des Experts en Philatelie [★IO]
Assn. Internationale des Fabricants de Caisses en Carton Ondule [★IO]
Assn. Internationale des Fabricants de Caisses en Carton Ondule [★985]
Assn. Internationale des Federations di Athletisme [★IO]
Assn. Internationale du Film d'Animation [★IO]
Assn. Internationale du Film d'Animation [★IO]
Assn. Internationale Forets Mediterraneenes [★IO]
Assn. Internationale Francophone des Aines [★IO]
Assn. Internationale Futuribles [★IO]
Assn. Internationale de Geochimie et de Cosmochimie [★IO]
Assn. Internationale de Geodesie [★IO]
Assn. Internationale de Geologie de l'Ingenieur [★IO]
Assn. Internationale de Geomagnetisme et d'Aeronomie [★IO]
Assn. Internationale des Geomorphologues [★IO]
Assn. Internationale de Grands Magasins [★IO]
Assn. Internationale des Hautes Juridictions Administratives [★IO]
Assn. Internationale des Instituts de Navigation [★IO]
Assn. Internationale des Interpretes de Conf. [★IO]
Assn. Internationale des Jeunes Avocats [★IO]
Assn. Internationale des Juristes Democrates [★IO]
Assn. Internationale des Laboratoires Textiles Lainiers [★IO]
Assn. Internationale pour l'Etude des Argiles [★IO]
Assn. Internationale pour l'Etude du Foie [★IO]
Assn. Internationale pour l'Etude de la Musique Populaire [★IO]
Assn. Internationale pour l'Evaluation du Rendement Scolaire [★IO]
Assn. Internationale pour l'Histoire des Religions [★IO]
Assn. Internationale de l'Industrie des Engrais [★IO]
Assn. Internationale pour l'Informatique Statistique [★IO]
Assn. Internationale de Linguistique Appliquee [★IO]
Assn. Internationale de l'Inspection du Travail [★IO]
Assn. Internationale de Litterature Comparee [★IO]
Assn. Internationale pour l'Oceanographie Biologique [★IO]
Assn. Internationale de l'Ozone - EA3G [★IO]
Assn. Internationale des Ludotheques [★IO]
Assn. Internationale des Maires Francophones [★IO]
Assn. Internationale de Mgt. des Arts et de la Culture [★IO]
Assn. Internationale de Mecanisation des Essais en Plein Champ [★IO]
Assn. Internationale de Medecine Agricole et de Sante Rurale [★IO]

Assn. Internationale de Medecine et de Biologie de l'Environnement [★IO]
Assn. Internationale des Musees d'Agriculture [★IO]
Assn. Internationale de la Mutualite [IO], Brussels, Belgium
Assn. Internationale de Mycologie [★IO]
Assn. Internationale de Mycologie [★7351]
Assn. Internationale de Navigation [★IO]
Assn. Internationale des Numismates Professionnels [★IO]
Assn. Internationale des Organismes de Commerce pour un Monde en Developement [★IO]
Assn. Internationale de Papyrologues [★IO]
Assn. Internationale de la Presse Filmee [★IO]
Assn. Internationale de la Presse Sportive [★IO]
Assn. Internationale des Professeurs d'Anglais des Universites [★IO]
Assn. Internationale pour la Protection de la Propriete Intellectuelle [★IO]
Assn. Internationale de Psychiatrie de l'Enfant et de l'Adolescent et des Professionas Associees [★IO]
Assn. Internationale de Psychiatrie de l'Enfant et de l'Adolescent et des Professions Associees [★IO]
Assn. Internationale de Psychologie Appliquee [★IO]
Assn. Internationale de Recherche Apicole [★IO]
Assn. Internationale du Registre des Bateaux du Rhin [★IO]
Assn. Internationale des Registres du Cancer [★IO]
Assn. Internationale Sans But Lucratif [★IO]
Assn. Internationale de la Savonnerie, de la Detergence et des Produits d'Entretien [★IO]
Assn. Internationale de Sci. et de Technologie pour le Developpement [★IO]
Assn. Internationale des Sciences Economiques [★IO]
Assn. Internationale des Sciences Hydrologiques [★IO]
Assn. Internationale des Sciences Phonetiques [★IO]
Assn. Internationale de la Securite Sociale [★IO]
Assn. Internationale de Sedimentologistes [★IO]
Assn. Internationale de Semiotique [★IO]
Assn. Internationale des Services d'Installations Electriques sur lesBateaux [★IO]
Assn. Internationale de Signalisation Maritime [★IO]
Assn. Internationale de Societes s'Occupant des Agents Mutagenes Presents dans l'Environnement [★IO]
Assn. Internationale de Societes s'Occupant des Agents Mutagenes Presents dans l'Environnement [★6578]
Assn. Internationale de Sociologie [★IO]
Assn. Internationale des Sociologues de Langue Francaise [★IO]
Assn. Internationale pour le Sport des Aveugles [★IO]
Assn. Internationale des Statisticiens d'Enquetes [★IO]
Assn. Internationale pour la Taxonomie Vegetale [★IO]
Assn. Internationale des Techniciens Biologistes [★IO]
Assn. Internationale des Technologistes de Laboratoire Medical [★IO]
Assn. Internationale du Theatre Amateur [★IO]
Assn. Internationale du Theatre pour l'Enfance et la Jeunesse [★IO]
Assn. Internationale des Traducteurs de Conf. [★IO]
Assn. Internationale des Travaux en Souterrain [★IO]
Assn. Internationale des Universites [★IO]
Assn. Internationale Villes et Ports [★IO]
Assn. Internationale pour les Voiles Minces en Beton [★IO]
Assn. Internationale de Volcanologie et de Chimie de l'Interieur de la Terre [★IO]
Assn. canadienne des fournisseurs Internet [★IO]
Assn. of Internet Professionals - Address unknown since 2006.
Assn. of Interpretive Naturalists [★7363]
Assn. of Interstate Commerce Commn. Practitioners [★6316]
Assn. of Interstate Motor Carriers - Defunct.
Assn. of Invalids and Veterans of World War II from the Former USSR and Other European Countries - Address unknown since 2008.

A star before a book entry number signifies that the name is not listed separately, but is mentioned within the entry.

Assn. Inventeurs Chercheurs Suisse Romande [★IO]

Assn. of Investment Brokers - Address unknown since 1989.

Assn. of Investment Companies [IO], London, United Kingdom

Assn. for Investment Mgt. and Res. [★IO]

Assn. for Investment Mgt. and Res. [★2331]

Assn. of Investment Mgt. Sales Executives [2329], 1320 19th St. NW, Ste. 300, Washington, DC 20036-1636, (202)296-3560

Assn. of Investment Trust Companies - England [★IO]

Assn. of Irish Composers [IO], Dublin, Ireland

Assn. of Irish Humanists [★IO]

Assn. of Irish Musical Societies [IO], Thurles, Ireland

Assn. of Iron and Steel Engineers [★7312]

Assn. for Iron and Steel Tech. [7312], 186 Thorn Hill Rd., Warrendale, PA 15086, (724)776-6040

Assn. of Iroquois and Allied Indians [IO], London, ON, Canada

Assn. of Islamic Charitable Projects [20096], 4431 Walnut St., Philadelphia, PA 19104, (215)387-8888

Assn. of Israel's Decorative Arts [9556], c/o Erika Vogel, Dir., 110 E 59th St., 26th Fl., New York, NY 10022, (212)931-0089

Assn. of Israel's Decorative Arts [IO], New York, NY, United States

Assn. of Italian Canadian Writers [IO], Bright's Grove, ON, Canada

Assn. of Italian Clinical Dermatologists [IO], Bari, Italy

Assn. of Italian Confectionery Manufacturers [IO], Rome, Italy

Assn. of Italian Flour and Pasta Indus. [IO], Rome, Italy

Assn. of Italian Hosp. Dermatologists [IO], Sorrento, Italy

Assn. Ivoirienne pour le Bien-Etre Familial [IO], Abidjan, Cote d'Ivoire

Assn. Izida [IO], Plovdiv, Bulgaria

Assn. of Japan Plastics Machinery [IO], Tokyo, Japan

Assn. of Japanese Consulting Engineers [IO], Tokyo, Japan

Assn. of Japanese Geographers [IO], Tokyo, Japan

Assn. on Japanese Textile Imports - Defunct.

Assn. of Jensen Owners - Address unknown since 1999.

Assn. of Jesuit Colleges and Universities [8052], One Dupont Cir. NW, Ste. 405, Washington, DC 20036, (202)862-9893

Assn. des Jeunes pour le Developpement Pasteef [★IO]

Assn. Jeunesse Action Developpement [★IO]

Assn. Jeunesse Fransaskoise [★IO]

Assn. of Jewish Aging Services [11277], 316 Pennsylvania Ave. SE, Ste. 402, Washington, DC 20003, (202)543-7500

Assn. of Jewish Book Publishers - Defunct.

Assn. of Jewish Center Professionals [12466], 15 E 26th St., New York, NY 10010-1579, (212)786-5154

Assn. of Jewish Center Workers [★12466]

Assn. of Jewish Chaplains of the Armed Forces [19743]

Assn. of Jewish Community Relations Workers - Address unknown since 1994.

Assn. for Jewish Demography and Statistics - Amer. Br. - Address unknown since 2004.

Assn. of Jewish Ex-Servicemen and Women [IO], London, United Kingdom

Assn. of Jewish Family and Children's Agencies [12467], 620 Cranbury Rd., Ste. 102, East Brunswick, NJ 08816, (732)432-7120

Assn. of Jewish Genealogical Societies [★21122]

Assn. of Jewish Genealogical Societies [★IO]

Assn. of Jewish Libraries [IO], New York, NY, United States

Assn. of Jewish Libraries [10332], c/o NFJC, 330 7th Ave., 21st Fl., New York, NY 10001, (212)725-5359

Assn. of Jewish People for Encouragement of Jewish Agricultural Settlements - Defunct.

Assn. of Jewish Religious Professionals from the Commonwealth of Independent States and Eastern Europe [IO], Jerusalem, Israel

Assn. for Jewish Retarded [★12570]

Assn. of Jewish Sponsored Camps [23275], 130 E 59th St., New York, NY 10022, (212)751-0477

Assn. for Jewish Stud. [8684], 15 W 16th St., New York, NY 10011-6301, (917)606-8249

Assn. for Jewish Stud. [IO], New York, NY, United States

Assn. des Joueurs d'Echecs Professionnels [★IO]

Assn. des Journalistes Auto. du Canada [★IO]

Assn. des Journalistes Sportifs [★IO]

Assn. of Junior Leagues Intl. [IO], New York, NY, United States

Assn. of Junior Leagues Intl. [13386], 80 Maiden Ln., Ste. 305, New York, NY 10038, (212)951-8300

Assn. des Juristes Franco-Britanniques [★IO]

Assn. of Juvenile Compact Administrators - Defunct.

Assn. of Kannada Kootas of Am. [19111], c/o Mr. Madhu Rangaiah, 16 Patron Dr., Bloomfield, NJ 07003, (248)377-2727

Assn. of Kenya Medical Lab. Sci. Officers [IO], Nairobi, Kenya

Assn. of Kew Gardeners in America - Defunct.

Assn. of Knitted Fabrics Mfrs. - Defunct.

Assn. of Knitwear Designers [228], c/o Diane Zangl, Pres., W3090 County Rd. Y, Lomira, WI 53048, (920)583-4298

Assn. of Knitwear Designers [IO], Lomira, WI, United States

Assn. of Korean Agricultural Medicine and Rural Hea. [IO], Daegu, Republic of Korea

Assn. of Korean-Canadian Scientists and Engineers [IO], North York, ON, Canada

Assn. of Korean Geomorphologists [IO], Chinju, Republic of Korea

Assn. for Korean Music Res. [IO], Willimantic, CT, United States

Assn. for Korean Music Res. [10561], c/o Prof. Okon Hwang, Sec.-Treas., Eastern Connecticut State Univ., Performing Arts Dept., Willimantic, CT 06226, (860)465-5109

Assn. for Korean Studies - Address unknown since 2001.

Assn. for Korean Stud. in Europe [IO], Paris, France

Assn. of Labor Assistants and Childbirth Educators [13977], PO Box 390436, Cambridge, MA 02139, (617)441-2500

Assn. of Labor-Management Administrators and Consultants on Alcoholism [★13203]

Assn. of Labor Relations Agencies [24112], c/o Les Heltzer, VP of Professional Development, Natl. Labor Relations Bd., 1099 14th St. NW, Ste. 11600, Washington, DC 20570, (202)273-1067

Assn. of Labor Relations Agencies [IO], Washington, DC, United States

Assn. for Lab. Automation [IO], Geneva, IL, United States

Assn. for Lab. Automation [6515], c/o Greg Dummer, CAE, Exec. Dir., 330 W State St., Geneva, IL 60134, (630)208-6830

Assn. of Labour Providers [IO], Frimley, United Kingdom

Assn. of Ladies of Charity of the U.S. [★13173]

Assn. Laitiere Europeene [★IO]

Assn. Laitiere Francaise [★IO]

Assn. genevoise pour l'alimentation infantile [★IO]

Assn. of Land-Grant Colleges and State Universities [★8110]

Assn. of Landscape Contractors of Ireland [IO], Bangor, United Kingdom

Assn. for Language Learning [IO], Rugby, United Kingdom

Assn. of Language Testers in Europe [IO], Cambridge, United Kingdom

Assn. of Language Travel Organisations [IO], Copenhagen, Denmark

Assn. de Langue Francaise pour l'Etude du Diabete et des Maladies Metaboliques [★IO]

Assn. de Langue Francaise pour l'Etude du Stress et du Traumatisme [IO], Paris, France

Assn. of Laparoscopic Surgeons of Great Britain and Ireland [IO], London, United Kingdom

Assn. francaise pour la recherche sur l'Asie du Sud-Est [★IO]

Assn. of Late-Deafened Adults [14743], 8038 MacIntosh Ln., Rockford, IL 61107, (815)332-1515

Assn. for Latin Amer. Studies - Defunct.

Assn. for Latin Liturgy [IO], Bristol, United Kingdom

Assn. of Latina and Latino Anthropologists [6410], c/o Amer. Anthropological Assn., 2200 Wilson Blvd., Ste. 600, Arlington, VA 22201-3357, (703)528-1902

Assn. of Latino Professionals in Finance and Accounting [16], 801 S Grand Ave., Ste. 400, Los Angeles, CA 90017, (213)243-0004

Assn. of Latvian Academic Societies - Defunct.

Assn. pour l'avancement des sciences et des techniques de la documentation [★IO]

Assn. canadienne pour l'avancement des etudes Neerlandaises [★IO]

Assn. pour l'Avancement des Sciences et des Techniques de la Documentation [IO], Montreal, QC, Canada

Assn. pour l'Avancement des Techniques de Modelisation et de Simulation dans l'Enterprise [★IO]

Assn. of Law Costs Draftsmen [IO], Diss, United Kingdom

Assn. of Law Teachers [IO], Coventry, United Kingdom

Assn. of Lawyers for Children [IO], East Molesey, United Kingdom

Assn. of Leadership Educators [8744], 233 Human Environmental Sciences Bldg., Oklahoma State Univ., Stillwater, OK 74078, (405)744-6231

Assn. of Learned and Professional Soc. Publishers [IO], Brighton, United Kingdom

Assn. of Learned Societies in the Social Sciences [★IO]

Assn. of Learning Disabled Adults - Defunct.

Assn. for Learning Languages en Famille [IO], Sheffield, United Kingdom

Assn. for Learning Tech. [IO], Oxford, United Kingdom

Assn. of Leather Exporters [IO], Barcelona, Spain

Assn. canadienne sur la qualite de l'eau [★IO]

Assn. of Lebanese Industrialists [IO], Beirut, Lebanon

Assn. canadienne de l'education a distance [★IO]

Assn. pour le developpment de l'education en Afrique [★IO]

Assn. pour l'Education Permanente dans les Universites du Canada [★IO]

Association of Legal Administrators [IO], Lincolnshire, IL, United States

Assn. of Legal Administrators [5929], 75 Tri State Intl., Ste. 222, Lincolnshire, IL 60069-4435, (847)267-1252

Assn. of Legal Court Interpreters and Translators [IO], Montreal, QC, Canada

Assn. for Legal Professionals; NALS, the [71]

Assn. for the Legal Right to Abortion [IO], Claremont, Australia

Assn. canadienne de l'electricite [★IO]

Assn. pour l'Enseignement de la Pediatrie en Europe [★IO]

Assn. canadienne de la medecine du travail et de l'environnement [★IO]

Assn. of Lesbian, Gay, and Bisexual Psychologies - Europe [IO], Trier, Germany

Assn. internationale pour l'Etude de la mosaique antique [★IO]

L'Association canadienne pour l'etude pratique de la loi dans le systeme educatif [★IO]

Assn. pour l'etude du droit de la Concurrence [IO], Brussels, Belgium

Assn. pour l'Etude des Langues et Litteratures du Commonwealth [★IO]

Assn. canadienne pour l'etude de l'education des adultes [★IO]

Assn. pour l'exportation du livre canadien [★IO]

Assn. canadienne de l'hydroelectricite [★IO]

Assn. canadienne de l'hydrogene [★IO]

Assn. Libanaise des Stomises [★IO]

Assn. for the Liberation of Ukraine - Defunct.

Assn. of Libertarian Feminists [18013], 484 Lake Park Ave., No. 24, Oakland, CA 94610-2730, (925)228-0565

Assn. de la Librairie Ancienne du Canada [★IO]

Assn. of Librarians in the History of the Hea. Sciences [★10326]

Assn. of Librarians in Public Libraries [★IO]

Reference to "IO" in place of a book number signifies that the association may be found in the 45th edition of International Organizations.

Assn. for Lib. Collections and Tech. Services **[10333]**, 50 E Huron St., Chicago, IL 60611, (312)280-5037

Assn. of Lib. and Info. Professionals of the Czech Republic **[IO]**, Prague, Czech Republic

Assn. of Lib. and Info. Professionals - Germany **[IO]**, Reutlingen, Germany

Assn. for Lib. and Info. Sci. Educ. **[8782]**, 65 E Wacker Pl., Ste. 1900, Chicago, IL 60601-7246, (312)795-0996

Assn. for Lib. Ser. to Children **[10334]**, 50 E Huron St., Chicago, IL 60611-2795, (312)280-2163

Assn. for Lib. Trustees and Advocates **[10335]**, 50 E Huron St., Chicago, IL 60611, (312)280-2160

Assn. of Licensed Aircraft Engineers **[IO]**, Bagshot, United Kingdom

Assn. of Licensed Architects **[IO]**, Barrington, IL, United States

Assn. of Licensed Architects **[290]**, PO Box 687, Barrington, IL 60011-0687, (847)382-0630

Assn. of Licensed Multiple Retailers **[IO]**, London, United Kingdom

Assn. of Life Agency Officers **[★IO]**

Assn. of Life Agency Officers **[★2195]**

Assn. of Life-Giving Churches **[19843]**, c/o Karol Hobbs, Church of the Highlands, 4700 Highlands Way, Birmingham, AL 35210, (205)980-5577

Assn. of Life Insurance Counsel **[5826]**, 135 N Pennsylvania St., Ste. 1600, Indianapolis, IN 46204, (317)684-5485

Assn. of Life Insurance Medical Directors of Am. **[★IO]**

Assn. of Lifecasters Intl. **[IO]**, Summit, NJ, United States

Assn. of Lifecasters Intl. **[10957]**, c/o Edmund Mc-Cormick, Dir., 18 Bank St., Summit, NJ 07901, (908)273-5600

Assn. of Light Aviation of Kazakhstan **[IO]**, Almaty, Kazakhstan

Assn. of Light Indus. Enterprises of Lithuania **[★IO]**

Assn. of Lighting Designers **[IO]**, Oxford, United Kingdom

Assn. of Lighting and Mercury Recyclers **[5168]**, c/o Paul Abernathy, Exec. Dir., 2436 Foothill Blvd., Ste. B, Calistoga, CA 94515, (707)942-2197

Assn. of Limb Mfrs. of Am. **[★1855]**

L'Association canadienne de l'immeuble **[★IO]**

Assn. europeenne de l'industrie solaire thermique **[★IO]**

Assn. de L'Industrie Touristique du Canada **[★IO]**

Association for Linen Management **[2401]**, 2161 Lexington Rd., Ste. 2, Richmond, KY 40475, (859)624-0177

Assn. pour la microbiologie medicale et l'infectiology Canada **[★IO]**

Assn. canadienne du droit des technologies de l'information **[★IO]**

Assn. for Linguistic Typology **[IO]**, Antwerp, Belgium

Assn. de Linguistique du Canada et des Etats Unis **[★IO]**

Assn. de Linguistique du Canada et des Etats Unis **[★10405]**

Assn. for Literary and Linguistic Computing **[IO]**, Glasgow, United Kingdom

Assn. of Literary Scholars and Critics **[10413]**, 650 Beacon Ave., Ste. 510, Boston, MA 02215, (617)358-1990

Assn. of Lithuania Shipbuilders and Shiprepairers **[IO]**, Klaipeda, Lithuania

Assn. of Lithuanian Banks **[IO]**, Vilnius, Lithuania

Assn. of Lithuanian Chambers of Commerce, Indus. and Crafts **[IO]**, Vilnius, Lithuania

Assn. of Lithuanian Foresters in Exile - Defunct.

Assn. Litteraire Artistique Canadienne **[★IO]**

Assn. de Litterature et de Linguistique Computationnelles **[★IO]**

Assn. for Living Historical Farms and Agricultural Museums **[★10497]**

Assn. for Living History, Farm and Agricultural Museums **[10497]**, 8774 Rte. 45 NW, North Bloomfield, OH 44450, (440)685-4410

Assn. of Lloyd's Members **[IO]**, London, United Kingdom

Assn. of Loading and Elevating Equip. Mfrs. **[IO]**, Caterham, United Kingdom

Assn. of Local Authorities of Northern Ireland **[★IO]**

Assn. of Local Authority Chief Executives **[IO]**, Watford, United Kingdom

Assn. of Local Govt. Auditors **[5429]**, 449 Lewis Hargett Cir., Ste. 290, Lexington, KY 40503-3669, (859)276-0686

Assn. of Local Housing Finance Agencies **[★5794]**

Assn. of Local Newspapers **[IO]**, Warsaw, Poland

Assn. of Local Official Hea. Agencies **[★IO]**

Assn. of Local Public Hea. Agencies **[IO]**, Toronto, ON, Canada

Assn. of Local TV Stations - Address unknown since 2005.

Assn. of Local Transport Airlines - Defunct.

Assn. of London Burough Engineers and Surveyors **[IO]**

Assn. of London Govt. **[IO]**, London, United Kingdom

Assn. of Long Distance Telephone Companies **[★3955]**

L'Association des counsellers en orientation de l'Ontario **[★IO]**

Assn. for Loss Prevention and Security - Defunct.

Assn. of Loudspeaker Mfrs. and Acoustics Intl. **[1206]**, PO Box 180093, Boston, MA 02118, (617)314-6977

Assn. for Low Countries Stud. in Great Britain and Ireland **[IO]**, Sheffield, United Kingdom

Assn. for Low Flow Anaesthesia **[IO]**, Leeds, United Kingdom

Association of Lunar and Planetary Observers **[IO]**, Springfield, IL, United States

Assn. of Lunar and Planetary Observers **[21550]**, c/o Matthew L. Will, Sec.-Treas., PO Box 13456, Springfield, IL 62791-3456

Assn. of Lutheran Men **[★20224]**

Assn. of Lutheran Secondary Schools **[8801]**, c/o Dr. Ross Stueber, Exec. Dir., Concordia Univ. Wisconsin, 12800 N Lake Shore Dr., Mequon, WI 53097-2404, (262)243-4519

Assn. malienne de Lutte contre le Diabete **[IO]**, Bamako, Mali

Assn. Luxembourg Alzheimer **[IO]**, Luxembourg, Luxembourg

Assn. of Luxembourg Engineers, Architects and Industrialists **[IO]**, Luxembourg, Luxembourg

Assn. Luxembourg Osteoporose **[IO]**, Mamer, Luxembourg

Assn. Luxembourgeoise Des Kinesitherapeutes **[IO]**, Luxembourg, Luxembourg

Assn. Luxembourgeoise des Ingenieurs, Architectes et Industriels **[★IO]**

Assn. Luxembourgeoise de Producteurs Professionnels d'Assurances **[IO]**, Luxembourg, Luxembourg

Assn. Luxembourgeoise de Gerontologie et Geriatrie **[IO]**, Ettelbruck, Luxembourg

Assn. of Luxury Suite Directors **[3676]**, 135 Merchant St., Ste. 145, Cincinnati, OH 45246, (513)674-0555

Assn. for Machine Translation in the Americas **[7807]**, c/o Priscilla Rasmussen, Bus. Mgr., 209 N 8th St., Stroudsburg, PA 18360, (570)476-8006

Assn. for Machine Translation in the Americas **[IO]**, Stroudsburg, PA, United States

Assn. for Machine Translation and Computational Linguistics **[★IO]**

Assn. for Machine Translation and Computational Linguistics **[★10400]**

Assn. of Machinery and Equip. Appraisers **[277]**, 315 S Patrick St., Alexandria, VA 22314, (703)836-7900

Assn. of Macintosh Trainers **[6810]**, 112 Britt Ct., Chapel Hill, NC 27514, (919)370-3071

Assn. of Macintosh Trainers **[IO]**, Chapel Hill, NC, United States

Assn. for Macular Diseases **[15669]**, 210 E 64th St., 8th Fl., New York, NY 10021, (212)605-3719

Assn. of Mailing, Shipping, and Off. Automation Specialists **[2448]**, 949 Winding Brook Ln., Walnut, CA 91789, (888)750-6245

Assn. des Maitres-Foureurs de Grand-Duche de Luxembourg **[IO]**, Luxembourg, Luxembourg

Assn. of the Maize Starch Indus. of the EEC **[★IO]**

Assn. of Major City Building Officials **[★5547]**

Assn. of Major City/County Building Officials **[5547]**, 505 Huntmar Park Dr., Ste. 210, Herndon, VA 20170, (703)481-2038

Assn. of Major Symphony Orchestra Volunteers - Address unknown since 1991.

Assn. of Makers of Printings and Writings **[IO]**, Swindon, United Kingdom

Assn. of Makers of Soft Tissue Papers **[★IO]**

Assn. of Malaysian Loss Adjusters **[IO]**, Kuala Lumpur, Malaysia

L'Association des Malentendants Canadiens **[★IO]**

L'Association des Malentendants Canadiens - Branche d'Edmonton **[★IO]**

Assn. of Maltese Arms Collectors and Shooters **[IO]**, Naxxar, Malta

Assn. of Managed Care Dentists **[14145]**, 1223 Wilshire Blvd., Ste. 483, Santa Monica, CA 90403, (310)453-3439

Assn. of Managed Care Providers **[★14145]**

Assn. of Managed Healthcare Organizations **[★14680]**

Assn. of Mgt. **[★6528]**

Assn. of Mgt. **[★IO]**

Assn. of Mgt. Analysts in State and Local Govt. - Address unknown since 2002.

Assn. Mgt. Companies; Inst. of **[★314]**

Assn. of Mgt. Consultants **[★2499]**

Assn. of Mgt. Consulting Firms **[2485]**, 380 Lexington Ave., Ste. 1700, New York, NY 10168, (212)551-7887

Assn. of Mgt., Consulting and Tech. for Constr. **[IO]**, Bucharest, Romania

Assn. of Mgt. Corporations In Singapore **[IO]**, Singapore, Singapore

Assn. for Mgt. Excellence - Defunct.

Assn. for Mgt. Info. in Financial Services **[464]**, 3895 Fairfax Ct., Atlanta, GA 30339, (770)444-3557

Assn. Mgt. Inst; Multiple **[★314]**

Assn. of Management/International Assn. of Mgt. **[6528]**, PO Box 64841, Virginia Beach, VA 23467-4841, (757)482-2273

Association of Management/International Association of Management **[IO]**, Virginia Beach, VA, United States

Assn. for the Mgt. of Org. Design **[★IO]**

Assn. for the Mgt. of Org. Design **[★2510]**

Assn. of Mgt. and Professional Staffs **[IO]**, Wakefield, United Kingdom

Assn. Managers; Automotive Trade **[★349]**

Assn. of Managing Consultants - Defunct.

Assn. of Manpower Franchise Owners **[1257]**, c/o Jane A. Svinicki, CAE, Exec. Dir., 6737 W Washington St., Ste. 1420, Milwaukee, WI 53214, (414)276-2651

Assn. of Manufactured Goods Exporters **[IO]**, Santiago, Chile

Assn. of Manufacturers of Confectionary and Chocolate **[★IO]**

Assn. of Mfrs. of Confectionary and Chocolate **[★1558]**

Assn. of Mfrs. of Domestic Appliances **[IO]**, London, United Kingdom

Assn. of Mfrs. and Formulators of Enzyme Products **[IO]**, Brussels, Belgium

Assn. of Mfrs. of Household Appliances **[IO]**, Paris, France

Assn. of Manufacturers and Importers of Elecl. Household Appliances **[IO]**, Copenhagen, Denmark

Assn. of Mfrs. of Power Generating Systems **[IO]**, Peterborough, United Kingdom

Assn. of Mfrs. of Woodworking Machinery **[★2080]**

Assn. des Manufacturiers de la Menuiserie Architecturale du Canada **[★IO]**

Assn. for Mfg. Excellence **[IO]**, Arlington Heights, IL, United States

Assn. for Mfg. Excellence **[2548]**, 3115 N Wilke Rd., Ste. G, Arlington Heights, IL 60004, (224)232-5980

Assn. for Mfg. Tech. **[7262]**, 7901 Westpark Dr., McLean, VA 22102-4206, (703)893-2900

Assn. of Map Memorabilia Collectors - Defunct.

Assn. of Marian Helpers **[19576]**, Eden Hill, Stockbridge, MA 01263, (413)298-3931

Assn. of Marina Indus. **[2602]**, 50 Water St., Warren, RI 02885, (401)737-9775

Assn. of Marina Indus. **[IO]**, Washington, DC, United States

Assn. of Marine Technicians **[2573]**, 513 River Estates Pkwy., Canton, GA 30114-9419, (770)720-4234

A star before a book entry number signifies that the name is not listed separately, but is mentioned within the entry.

Assn. of Marine Underwriters of the U.S. - Defunct.

Assn. Marocaine De Squash [IO], Casablanca, Morocco

Assn. Marocaine des Exportateurs [★IO]

Assn. Marocaine pour l'Industrie et le Commerce de l'Automobile [★IO]

Assn. Marocaine de Medecine du Sport [IO], Casablanca, Morocco

Assn. of Married Women - Address unknown since 1995.

Assn. of Marshall Scholars [9072], 3100 Massachusetts Ave. NW, Washington, DC 20008-3600, (202)588-7844

Assn. of Marshall Scholars [IO], Washington, DC, United States

Assn. of Marshall Scholars and Alumnae/i [★IO]

Assn. of Marshall Scholars and Alumnae/i [★9072]

Assn. for Mascular Degeneration [★15669]

Assn. of Masonic Boards of Relief of the U.S. and Canada [19229], 3 De Saix Blvd., New Orleans, LA 70119, (504)949-6347

Assn. of Master of Business Administration Executives [702]

Assn. of Master Hypnotists - Address unknown since 2002.

Assn. of Master Upholsterers and Soft Furnishers [IO], Cardiff, United Kingdom

Assn. of Maternal and Child Hea. Programs [13947], 1220 19th St. NW, Ste. 801, Washington, DC 20036, (202)775-0436

Assn. for Mathematics Applied to Economic and Social Sciences [IO], Milan, Italy

Assn. of Mature Canadians [IO], Toronto, ON, Canada

Assn. Mauricienne Femmes Chefs d'Entreprises [IO], Port Louis, Mauritius

Assn. Mauritaninne de Medecine du Sport [IO], Nouakchott, Mauritania

Assn. of Mauritian Mfrs. [IO], Port Louis, Mauritius

Assn. canadienne des specialistes en chirurgie buccale et maxillo-faciale [★IO]

Assn. of Maximum Ser. Telecasters [★549]

Assn. for Maximum Ser. TV [549], 4100 Wisconsin Ave. NW, PO Box 9897, Washington, DC 20016, (202)966-1956

Assn. of MBA Executives [★702]

Assn. of MBA's [IO], London, United Kingdom

Assn. for Measurement and Evaluation of Commun. [IO], London, United Kingdom

Assn. for Measurement and Evaluation in Counseling and Development [★9247]

Assn. for Measurement and Evaluation in Guidance [★9247]

Assn. des Medecins Biochimistes du Canada [★IO]

Assn. des Medecins et Medecins Dentistes du Grand-Duche de Luxembourg [IO], Luxembourg, Luxembourg

Assn. for Media-Based Continuing Educ. for Engineers [8367], 888 N Euclid Ave., No. 302, PO Box 210158, Tucson, AZ 85721, (800)338-9344

Assn. for Media Literacy [IO], Toronto, ON, Canada

Assn. of Media Producers [IO]

Assn. of Media Producers [★331]

Assn. for Media Psychology - Address unknown since 1999.

L'Association des Media et de la Technologie en Educ. du Canada [★IO]

Assn. for Media and Tech. in Educ. in Canada [IO], Etobicoke, ON, Canada

Assn. for Medical Advertising Agencies - Address unknown since 1995.

Assn. for Medical and Bio-Informatics, Singapore [IO], Singapore, Singapore

Assn. of Medical Deans in Europe [★IO]

Assn. of Medical Device Reprocessors [15038], 1400 16th St. NW, Ste. 400, Washington, DC 20036, (202)518-6796

Assn. of Medical Diagnostics Mfrs. [3482], 555 13th St. NW, Ste. 7W-404, Washington, DC 20004, (202)637-6837

Assn. of Medical Directors of Info. Systems [14957], 682 Peninsula Dr., Lake Almanor, CA 96137, (530)596-4477

Assn. of Medical Doctors of Asia [IO], Okayama, Japan

Assn. of Medical Doctors of Kazakhstan [IO], Almaty, Kazakhstan

Assn. for Medical Educ. in the Eastern Mediterranean Region [IO], Irbid, Jordan

Assn. for Medical Educ. in Europe [IO], Dundee, United Kingdom

Assn. for Medical Educ. and Res. in Substance Abuse [8849], 125 Whipple, 3rd Fl., Providence, RI 02908, (401)243-8460

Assn. for Medical Educ. in the Western Pacific Region [IO], Adelaide, Australia

Assn. of Medical Group Psychoanalysts - Defunct.

Assn. for Medical Humanities [IO], Durham, United Kingdom

Association of Medical Illustrators [IO], Lawrence, KS, United States

Assn. of Medical Illustrators [13707], 810 E 10th St., Lawrence, KS 66044, (866)393-4264

Assn. of Medical Lab. Immunologists [14932], c/o Maggie Fogel, Admin., 34 W 83rd St., Ste. R, New York, NY 10024, (212)873-2955

Assn. of Medical Microbiologists [IO], London, United Kingdom

Assn. of Medical Microbiology and Infectious Disease Canada [IO], Ottawa, ON, Canada

Assn. of Medical Officers of Amer. Institutions of Idiotic and Feebleminded Children [★15239]

Assn. of Medical Physicists of India [IO], Bombay, India

Association of Medical Professionals with Hearing Losses [IO], Miamisburg, OH, United States

Assn. of Medical Professionals with Hearing Losses [14744], 4850 Reliance Rd., Front Royal, VA 22630

Assn. of Medical Publications [3209], c/o Cheryl L. Pizor, Exec. Dir., 231 N Ave. W, No. 335, Westfield, NJ 07090, (908)233-8147

Assn. of Medical Record Consultants - Defunct.

Assn. of Medical Rehabilitation Administrators - Defunct.

Assn. of Medical Res. Charities [IO], London, United Kingdom

Assn. of Medical School Pediatric Dept. Chairs [15884], c/o Jean Bartholomew, Coor., Amer. Bd. of Pediatrics, 111 Silver Cedar Ct., Chapel Hill, NC 27514-1651, (919)942-1993

Assn. of Medical Schools in Europe [IO], Lleida, Spain

Assn. of Medical Secretaries, Practice Admin. and Receptionists [★IO]

Assn. of Medical Secretaries, Practice Managers, Administrators and Receptionists [IO], London, United Kingdom

Assn. of Medical Superintendents of Amer. Institutions for Insane [★16076]

Assn. of Medical Superintendents of Mental Hospitals [★14861]

Assn. Medicale Francaise [IO], Paris, France

Assn. Medicale Franco-Americaine - Defunct.

Assn. Medicale Haitienne [IO], Port-au-Prince, Haiti

Assn. Medicale Mondiale [★IO]

Assn. Medicale Podiatrique Canadienne [★IO]

Assn. of Medicine and Psychiatry [16081], c/o Michael R. Hanlon, Exec. Dir., 3815 Kanawha Ave. SE, Charleston, WV 25304-1543, (304)925-9366

Assn. des Medicins de Langue Francaise du Canada [★IO]

Assn. of Mediterranean Chambers of Commerce and Indus. [IO], Barcelona, Spain

Assn. of Meeting Professionals [1934], 2025 M St. NW, Ste. 800, Washington, DC 20036, (202)973-8686

Assn. of Member Episcopal Conferences in Eastern Africa [IO], Nairobi, Kenya

Assn. of Members and Friends of the Historic Southern Tenant Farmers Union - Defunct.

Assn. of Membership Executives - Address unknown since 1991.

Assn. des Membres des Conferences Episcopales de l'Afrique Orientale [★IO]

Assn. of Memoirists and Family Historians - Defunct.

Assn. for Mental Health Affiliation with Israel - Defunct.

Assn. of Mental Health Librarians - Defunct.

Assn. of Mental Health Practitioners With Disabilities - Defunct.

Assn. of Mental Hea. Specialties [★11817]

Assn. of Mental Heath Administrators [★15191]

Assn. canadienne pour la sante mentale, filiale du Bas-du-Fleuve [★IO]

Assn. of Merchants and Mfg. of Textile Stores and Machinery [★IO]

Assn. of Mercy Colleges [8053], c/o Dr. Mary Ann Dillon, RSM, Pres., Mt. Aloysius Coll., 7373 Admiral Perry Hwy., Cresson, PA 16630

Assn. of Metal Sprayers [★IO]

Assn. of Methodist Historical Societies [★10467]

Assn. Metropolitan District Engineers [★IO]

Assn. of Metropolitan Planning Organizations [17207], 1029 Vermont Ave. NW, Ste. 710, Washington, DC 20005, (202)296-7051

Assn. of Metropolitan Sewerage Agencies [★6237]

Assn. of Metropolitan Water Agencies [6135], 1620 I St. NW, Ste. 500, Washington, DC 20006, (202)331-2820

Assn. for Mexican Cave Stud. [7691], PO Box 7672, Austin, TX 78713

Assn. for Mexican Cave Stud. [IO], Austin, TX, United States

Assn. of Mezzanine Mfrs. [★2071]

Assn. of Mezzanine Mfrs. - Defunct.

Assn. of Microbiological Diagnostic Mfrs. [★3482]

Assn. for Microbiological Media Mfrs. [★3482]

Assn. for Micrography, Image and Info. Mgt. [IO], Frankfurt am Main, Germany

Assn. of Microsoft Solution Providers [★IO]

Assn. of Midwest Fish and Game Commissioners [★5339]

Assn. of Midwest Fish and Wildlife Agencies [★5339]

Assn. of Midwest Fish and Wildlife Commissioners [★5339]

Assn. of Military Banks of Am. [465], PO Box 3335, Warrenton, VA 20188, (540)347-3305

Assn. of Military Colleges and Schools of the U.S. [8883], c/o Dr. Rudolph H. Ehrenberg, Jr., Exec. Dir., 3604 Glenbrook Rd., Fairfax, VA 22031-3211, (703)272-8406

Assn. of Military Colleges and Schools of the U.S. [★8883]

Assn. of Military Osteopathic Physicians and Surgeons [15807], 1796 Seven Hills Ln., Severn, MD 21144-1061, (410)519-8217

Assn. of Military Surgeons of the U.S. [15263], 9320 Old Georgetown Rd., Bethesda, MD 20814-1653, (301)897-8800

Assn. of Mill and Elevator Mutual Insurance Companies - Address unknown since 1999.

Assn. of Millwork Distributors [600], 10047 Robert Trent Jones Pkwy., New Port Richey, FL 34655-4649, (727)372-3665

Assn. of Minicomputer Users [6784]

Assn. Miniere du Canada [★IO]

Assn. of Mining Analysts [IO], London, United Kingdom

Assn. of Minor League Umpires [23104], PO Box 1571, Andover, MA 01810

Assn. of Minority Hea. Professions Schools [8850], 100 Edgewood Ave., Ste. 1020, Atlanta, GA 30303, (678)904-4217

Assn. of the Miraculous Medal [19577], 1811 W St. Joseph St., Perryville, MO 63775-1598, (573)547-2508

Assn. of Missile and Rocket Industries - Defunct.

Assn. of Missing and Exploited Children's Organizations [12601], PO Box 19668, Alexandria, VA 22320-0668, (703)838-8379

Assn. of Missing and Exploited Children's Organizations [IO], Alexandria, VA, United States

Assn. of Mobile Home Mortgage Bankers - Defunct.

Assn. of Modified Asphalt Producers [601], PO Box 270006, St. Louis, MO 63127, (314)843-2627

Assn. for Molecular Pathology [15862], 9650 Rockville Pike, Bethesda, MD 20814-3993, (301)634-7939

Assn. Mondial de Radios Communautarias [★IO]

Assn. Mondiale des Agences de Voyages [★IO]

Assn. Mondiale des Indus. de Traitement des Algues Marines [★IO]

Assn. Mondiale des Journaux [★IO]

Assn. Mondiale pour l'Advancement de Parasitologie Veterinaire [★IO]

Reference to "IO" in place of a book number signifies that the association may be found in the 45th edition of International Organizations.

Assn. Mondiale pour l'Advancement de Parasitologie Veterinaire [★16818]

Assn. Mondiale pour l'Ecole Instrument de Paix [★IO]

Assn. Mondiale des Organisations de Recherche Industrielle et Technologique [★IO]

Assn. Mondiale des Radio-Amateurs et des Radio-clubs Chretiens [★IO]

Assn. Mondiale de la Route [★IO]

Assn. Montessori International-U.S.A. [8892], 410 Alexander St., Rochester, NY 14607-1028, (585)461-5920

Assn. Montessori Internationale [★IO]

Assn. for Moral Educ. [8233], c/o Nancy Nordmann, PhD, Sec., Natl.-Louis Univ., Psychology Dept., 122 S Michigan Ave., Chicago, IL 60603

Assn. of Mormon Counselors and Psychotherapists [16212], 2540 E 1700 S, Salt Lake City, UT 84108, (801)583-6227

Assn. of Motion Picture Sound [IO], London, United Kingdom

Assn. of Motion Picture and TV Producers [★1375]

L'Association Motocycliste Canadienne [★IO]

Assn. of Motor Vehicle Importers - Representatives [IO], Athens, Greece

Assn. of Mountaineering Instructors [IO], Conwy, United Kingdom

Assn. of Mouth and Foot Painting Artists [IO], Schaan, Liechtenstein

Association of Moving Image Archivists [IO], Hollywood, CA, United States

Assn. of Moving Image Archivists [9932], 1313 N Vine St., Hollywood, CA 90028, (323)463-1500

Assn. for Multi-Media Intl. - Address unknown since 2003.

Assn. for Multicultural Counseling and Development [11819], c/o Dr. Canary Hogan, Membership Chair, 1285 Cheyenne Blvd., Madison, TN 37115, (615)876-5117

Assn. for Multicultural Sci. Educ. [9097], c/o Meg Wilder Watson, Sec., 11 Westland St., Brockton, MA 02301

Assn. of MultiEthnic Americans [12141], PO Box 29223, Los Angeles, CA 90029-0223

Assn. for Multiple Endocrine Neoplasia Disorders [IO], Tunbridge Wells, United Kingdom

Assn. of Municipal Electricity Undertakings (Southern Africa) [IO], Ferndale, Republic of South Africa

Assn. of Municipal Engineers [IO], London, United Kingdom

Assn. of Municipal Engineers [★IO]

Assn. of Municipal Equip. Professionals [IO], Montreal, QC, Canada

Assn. of Municipal Recycling Coordinators [IO], Guelph, ON, Canada

Assn. des Musees Canadiens [★IO]

Assn. of Music Producers [2801], 3 W 18th St., 5th Fl., New York, NY 10011, (212)924-4100

Assn. of Music Video Broadcasters - Address unknown since 2002.

Assn. of Music Writers and Photographers [10562], PO Box 79, Oak Lawn, IL 60454

Assn. of Music Writers and Photographers [IO], Oak Lawn, IL, United States

Assn. de Musicotherapie du Canada [★IO]

Association of Muslim Amer. Lawyers [★20097]

Assn. of Muslim Lawyers [IO], High Wycombe, United Kingdom

Assn. of Muslim Professionals [IO], Singapore, Singapore

Assn. of Muslim Scientists and Engineers [7005], PO Box 38, Plainfield, IN 46168, (517)947-6338

Assn. of Muslim Social Scientists [7646], PO Box 5502, Herndon, VA 20172

Assn. of Mutual Fire Insurance Engineers [★2178]

Assn. of Mutual Fund Plan Sponsors [★3515]

Assn. of Mutual Funds in India [IO], Bombay, India

Assn. of Mutual Insurance Engineers [★2178]

Assn. of Natl. Advertisers [91], 708 Third Ave., New York, NY 10017-4270, (212)697-5950

Assn. of Natl., European and Mediterranean Societies of Gastroenterology [IO], Vienna, Austria

Assn. of Natl. Grasslands - Address unknown since 2001.

Assn. of Natl. Health Service Corps Scholarship Recipients - Defunct.

Assn. of Natl. Numbering Agencies [IO], Frankfurt am Main, Germany

Assn. of Natl. Olympic Committees [IO], Paris, France

Assn. of Natl. Olympic Committees of Africa [IO], Yaounde, Cameroon

Assn. of Natl. Park Authorities [IO], Cardiff, United Kingdom

Assn. of Natl. Park Rangers [6154], PO Box 108, Larned, KS 67550-0108, (316)285-2107

Assn. of Natl. Parks [★IO]

Assn. for a Natl. Recycling Policy [★4000]

Assn. of Natl. Security Alumni - Address unknown since 2006.

Assn. of Natl. Tourist Off. Representatives (UK) [IO], Hove, United Kingdom

Assn. Nationale des Dieteticiens du Luxembourg [★IO]

Assn. Nationale des Editeurs de Livres [★IO]

Assn. Nationale des Enterprises en Recrutement et Placement de Personnel [★IO]

Assn. Nationale Femme et du Droit [★IO]

Assn. Nationale des Indus. Alimentaires [★IO]

Assn. Nationale des Indus. de la Neige [★IO]

Assn. Nationale pour l'Etude de la Neige et des Avalanches [★IO]

Assn. Nationale des Retraites Federaux [★IO]

Assn. of Native Amer. Medical Students [15087], 1225 Sovereign Row, Ste. 103, Oklahoma City, OK 73108, (405)946-7072

Assn. for Native Development in the Performing and Visual Arts [IO], Toronto, ON, Canada

Assn. of Natural Biocontrol Producers [5074], c/o Maclay Burt, Exec. Dir., 2230 Martin Dr., Tustin, CA 92782, (714)544-8295

Assn. of Natural Burial Grounds [IO], London, United Kingdom

Assn. of Natural Gasoline Mfrs. [★2924]

Assn. of Natural Medicine Pharmacists [15282], PO Box 150727, San Rafael, CA 94915-0727, (415)479-1512

Assn. of Natural Resource Enforcement Trainers - Defunct.

Assn. of Natural Rubber Producing Countries [IO], Kuala Lumpur, Malaysia

Assn. of Nature Reserve Burial Grounds [★IO]

Assn. of Naval ROTC Colleges and Universities [★8884]

Assn. of Navy Safety Professionals - Defunct.

Assn. of Needle-Free Injection Mfrs. [2549], c/o Linda D'Antonio, 6308 Fly Rd., East Syracuse, NY 13057, (315)463-4999

Assn. Neerlandaise d'Assistance au Developpement - Cameroon [★IO]

Assn. of Nepal and Himalayan Stud. [IO], Portland, OR, United States

Assn. of Nepal and Himalayan Stud. [8944], c/o Himalaya, Portland State Univ., Geography Dept., Box 751, Portland, OR 97207-0751, (503)725-8044

Assn. of Nepalis in the Americas [19286], c/o Anil R. Pathak, Treas., 3609 Ox Ridge Ct., Fairfax, VA 22033

Assn. of Nepalis in the Americas [IO], Fairfax, VA, United States

Assn. pour les Neurinomes Acoustiques du Canada [★IO]

Assn. for Neuro-Linguistic Programming [IO], Barnet, United Kingdom

Assn. of Neuro-Metabolic Disorders - Address unknown since 1999.

Assn. for the Neurologically Disabled of Canada [IO], Etobicoke, ON, Canada

Assn. des Neurologues Liberaux de Langue Francaise [IO], Versailles, France

Assn. of Neuromuscular Disorders [IO], Istanbul, Turkey

Assn. of Neuroscience Departments and Programs [15384], 41218 Roundup Rd., Magnolia, TX 77354, (281)259-6737

Assn. of Neurosurgical Physician Assistants [15974], 4267 NW Fed. Hwy., PMB 202, Jensen Beach, FL 34957, (888)94A-NSPA

Assn. for New Canadians [IO], St. John's, NL, Canada

Assn. of New Zealand Advertisers [IO], Auckland, New Zealand

Assn. of Newspaper Classified Advt. Managers [★3244]

Assn. of Newspaper and Magazine Wholesalers [IO], Reading, United Kingdom

Assn. of Nigerian Physicians in the Americas [IO], Charlotte, NC, United States

Assn. of Nigerian Physicians in the Americas [15992], 7221 Pineville Matthews Rd., Ste. 200, Charlotte, NC 28226, (330)677-0400

Assn. of Noise Consultants [IO], St. Albans, United Kingdom

Assn. for Non-Traditional Students in Higher Educ. [IO], Grand Junction, CO, United States

Assn. for Non-Traditional Students in Higher Educ. [7916], c/o Gabe DeGabriele, Consultant, 315 Grand View Park Dr., Grand Junction, CO 81503, (970)210-3159

Assn. for Non-White Concerns in Personnel and Guidance [★11819]

Assn. of the Nonwoven Fabrics Indus; INDA, [3785]

Assn. of Nordic Paper Historians [IO], Bromma, Sweden

Assn. Nordique d'Etudes Canadiennes [★IO]

Assn. of North Amer. Dir. Publishers [★3208]

Assn. of North Amer. Missions [20301], PO Box 8667, Longview, TX 75607-8667, (903)234-2075

Assn. of North Amer. Radio Clubs [21498], c/o Dr. Harold Cones, Chm., 2 Whits Ct., Newport News, VA 23606

Assn. of Northwest Steelheaders [23409], PO Box 22065, Milwaukie, OR 97269, (503)653-4176

Assn. of Northwest Steelheaders [IO], Milwaukie, OR, United States

Assn. of Norwegian Economists [IO], Oslo, Norway

Assn. of Norwegian Visual Artists [IO], Oslo, Norway

Assn. Nouvelle-Angleterre/Acadie - Address unknown since 2000.

Assn. of NROTC Colleges and Universities [8884], c/o Jennifer Ashbaugh, Admin. Off., Univ. of Rochester, 33A Wallis Hall, PO Box 270041, Rochester, NY 14627-0041, (585)275-2096

Assn. Nucleaire Canadienne [★IO]

Assn. of Nurse Advocates for Childbirth Solutions [13978], 916 Daleview Dr., Silver Spring, MD 20901, (301)434-5546

Assn. of Nurses in AIDS Care [13559], 3538 Ridge-wood Rd., Akron, OH 44333, (330)670-0101

Assn. of Nurses Endorsing Transplantation [15670]

Assn. de Nutrition Animale du Canada [★IO]

Assn. of Nutrition Departments and Programs [8947], c/o Dr. Connie M. Weaver, Chair, Purdue Univ., Foods and Nutrition, 700 W State St., West Lafayette, IN 47907-2059

Assn. of Nutrition Services Agencies [14720], 1634 Eye St. NW, Ste. 605, Washington, DC 20006, (202)737-1011

Assn. of Obedience Clubs and Judges - Defunct.

Assn. of Occupational and Environmental Clinics [15629], 1010 Vermont Ave. NW, Ste. 513, Washington, DC 20005, (202)347-4976

Assn. of Occupational Hea. Professionals in Healthcare [15630], 109 VIP Dr., Ste. 220, Wexford, PA 15090, (800)362-4347

Assn. of Occupational Therapists of Ireland [IO], Dublin, Ireland

Assn. for Ocular Pharmacology and Therapeutics [IO], San Diego, CA, United States

Assn. for Ocular Pharmacology and Therapeutics [15671], c/o Dr. Achim H. Krauss, PhD, Treas., Pfizer Inc., 10724 Sci. Center Dr., San Diego, CA 92121, (858)638-3748

Assn. Of British Climbing Walls [IO], London, United Kingdom

Assn. Of Danish Physiotherapists [IO], Copenhagen, Denmark

Assn. Of Hunt Saboteurs - Ireland [IO], Dublin, Ireland

Assn. of Official Agricultural Chemists [★IO]

Assn. of Official Agricultural Chemists [★6671]

Assn. of Official Analytical Chemists [★6671]

Assn. of Official Analytical Chemists [★IO]

Assn. of Official Seed Analysts [IO], Stillwater, OK, United States

Assn. of Official Seed Analysts [5435], Mail Boxes Etc., No. 285, 601 S Washington, Stillwater, OK 74074-4539, (405)780-7372

A star before a book entry number signifies that the name is not listed separately, but is mentioned within the entry.

Assn. of Official Seed Certifying Agencies [5436], 1601 52nd Ave., Ste. 1, Moline, IL 61265, (309)736-0120

Assn. des Officiers des Postes du Canada [★IO]

Assn. of Ohio Longrifle Collectors [22425], c/o Dan Smith, Sec., 23003 State Rte. 339, Beverly, OH 45715-5029, (740)984-4896

Assn. of Oil and Gas Producing Companies [IO], Hannover, Germany

Assn. of Oil Pipe Lines [2919], 1808 Eye St. NW, Washington, DC 20006, (202)408-7970

Assn. of Oilwell Servicing Contractors [★2918]

Assn. of Old Crows [6908], 1000 N Payne St., Ste. 300, Alexandria, VA 22314-1652, (703)549-1600

Assn. of Oldetime Barbell and Strongmen - Address unknown since 2003.

Assn. Olympique Canadienne [★IO]

Assn. of Oncology Social Work [13199], 100 N 20th St., 4th Fl., Philadelphia, PA 19103, (215)599-6093

Assn. of Online Insurance Agents [2149], 1440 N Harbor Blvd., Ste. 725, Fullerton, CA 92835, (888)223-4773

Assn. of Ontario Snowboarders [IO], Toronto, ON, Canada

Assn. des Operateurs Postaux Publics Europeens [★IO]

Assn. of Operatic Dancing of Great Britain [★IO]

Assn. of Operating Dept. Practitioners [★IO]

Assn. of Operating Room Nurses [★IO]

Assn. of Operating Room Nurses [★15468]

Assn. of Operating Room Technicians [★15133]

Assn. for Operations Mgt; APICS - The [7181]

Assn. of Operative Millers [★2737]

Assn. of Operative Millers [★IO]

Assn. for Ophthalmic Cooperation to Asia [IO], Hyogo, Japan

Assn. des Opticiens du Canada [★IO]

Assn. of Optometric Educators [8851], c/o Northeastern State Univ., Coll. of Optometry, Optometry Bldg. 124, 600 N Grand Ave., Tahlequah, OK 74464, (918)456-5511

Assn. of Optometrists [IO], London, United Kingdom

Assn. of Oral and Maxillofacial Surgeons of India [IO], Salem, India

Assn. of Organ Procurement Organizations [14287], 1364 Beverly Rd., Ste. 100, McLean, VA 22101, (703)556-4242

Assn. of Organisers of Exhibition Events in the Czech Republic [★IO]

Assn. of Organisers of Exhibition Events in the Czech Republic and the Slovak Republic [★IO]

Assn. of Organizations of Disabled People of Croatia [IO], Zagreb, Croatia

Assn. Orthodontique Francaise des Specialistres en Orthopedie Dento-Faciale [IO], Saintes, France

Assn. of Orthodox Jewish Scientists [7601], c/o Yossi Bennett, Exec. Dir., 1011 Moss Pl., Lawrence, NY 11559, (718)969-3669

Assn. of Orthodox Jewish Teachers [9210], 1577 Coney Island Ave., Brooklyn, NY 11230, (718)258-3585

Assn. of Orthodox Jewish Teachers of the New York City Public Schools [★9210]

Assn. of Orthodox Jews in Communications - Address unknown since 1994.

Assn. of Orthopaedic Chairmen [★15750]

Assn. of Osteopathic Directors and Medical Educators [15808], 142 E Ontario St., Chicago, IL 60611, (312)202-8211

Assn. of Osteopathic Publications - Defunct.

Assn. of Osteopathic State Executive Directors [15809], 2007 Apalache Pkwy., Tallahassee, FL 32301-4867, (850)878-7364

Assn. of Otolaryngology Administrators [15062], 1844 Ardmore Blvd., Pittsburgh, PA 15221, (412)243-5156

Assn. of Our Lady of Salvation - Defunct.

Assn. for Outdoor Educ. [★IO]

Assn. of Outdoor Recreation and Educ. [8950], 6511 Buckshore Dr., Whitmore Lake, MI 48189, (810)299-2782

Assn. of Outplacement Consulting Firms [★1255]

Assn. of Outplacement Consulting Firms [★IO]

Assn. of Outplacement Consulting Firms Intl. [★IO]

Assn. of Outplacement Consulting Firms Intl. [★1255]

Assn. of Overseas Educators - Defunct.

Assn. of Pacific Fisheries [★3502]

Assn. of Pacific Island Legislatures [5774], 181 E Marine Corps Dr., Carl Rose Bldg., Ste. 207, Hagatna, GU 96910, (671)472-2719

Assn. of Pacific Island Legislatures [IO], Hagatna, GU, United States

Assn. des musees du Pacifique Insulaire [★IO]

Assn. of Paediatric Anaesthetists of Great Britain and Ireland [IO], London, United Kingdom

Assn. of Paid Circulation Publications [★2455]

Assn. of Painting Craft Teachers [IO], London, United Kingdom

Assn. of Pakistani Physicians [★15993]

Assn. of Pakistani Physicians of North Am. [15993], 6414 S Cass Ave., Westmont, IL 60559, (630)968-8585

Assn. of Pakistani Physicians and Surgeons of the United Kingdom [IO], Manchester, United Kingdom

Assn. for Palliative Medicine of Great Britain and Ireland [IO], Southampton, United Kingdom

Assn. Pan-Africaine des Sciences Neurologiques [★IO]

Assn. of Parents Paying Child Support - Address unknown since 1994.

Assn. Parlementaire du Commonwealth [★IO]

Assn. of Paroling Authorities Intl. [IO], Wallingford, PA, United States

Assn. of Paroling Authorities Intl. [6165], c/o Bea Leopold, Exec. Dir., 233 Canterbury Dr., Wallingford, PA 19086, (610)872-4645

Assn. of Part-Time Professionals - Defunct.

Assn. for Past Life Res. and Therapies [★16617]

Assn. for Past-Life Res. and Therapies [★16617]

Assn. for Past-Life Res. and Therapy [★16617]

Assn. of Pastry Chefs [IO], Sonning on Thames, United Kingdom

Assn. of Pathology Chairmen [★15863]

Assn. of Pathology Chairs [15863], 9650 Rockville Pike, Bethesda, MD 20814-3993, (301)634-7880

Assn. for Pathology Informatics [15864], 9650 Rockville Pike, Bethesda, MD 20814-3993, (301)634-7820

Assn. for Payment Clearing Services [IO], London, United Kingdom

Assn. of Payroll and Superannuation Administrators [★IO]

Assn. for Peace [IO], Rome, Italy

Assn. of Pedestrian and Bicycle Professionals [18747], PO Box 93, Cedarburg, WI 53012-0093, (262)375-6180

Assn. for Pediatric Educ. in Europe [IO], Bordeaux, France

Assn. of Pediatric Hematology/Oncology Nurses [15467], 4700 W Lake Ave., Glenview, IL 60025-1485, (847)375-4724

Assn. of Pediatric Oncology Nurses [★15467]

Assn. of Pediatric Oncology Social Workers [15885], c/o Dr. Barbara Jones, Pres., Univ. of Texas at Austin, 1925 San Francisco Blvd., Austin, TX 78712, (512)475-9367

Assn. of Pediatric Prog. Directors [8852], 6728 Old McLean Village Dr., McLean, VA 22101-3906, (703)556-9222

Assn. of Pediatric Therapists [16606], PO Box 194191, San Francisco, CA 94119

Assn. of Pension Lawyers [IO], London, United Kingdom

Assn. for People with Dogs Named Marty [22220], c/o Marty Sheets, Exec. Dir., 22201 King Rd., Woodhaven, MI 48183

Assn. for People With Arthritis - Defunct.

Assn. of Performing Arts Presenters [7968], 1112 16th St. NW, Ste. 400, Washington, DC 20036, (202)833-2787

Assn. de Periodistas y Escritores Agrarios Españoles [IO], Madrid, Spain

Assn. for Perioperative Practice [IO], Harrogate, United Kingdom

Association of PeriOperative Registered Nurses [IO], Denver, CO, United States

Assn. of PeriOperative Registered Nurses [15468], 2170 S Parker Rd., Ste. 300, Denver, CO 80231-5711, (303)755-6304

Assn. of Personal Cmpt. User Groups [6785], 3155 E Patrick Ln., Ste. 1, Las Vegas, NV 89120-3481, (800)558-6867

Assn. of Personal Counsellors [IO], Sydney, Australia

Assn. of Personal Historians [10095], c/o Gloria Nussbaum, Membership Chair, 870 NW 178th Ave., Beaverton, OR 97006-4044, (503)645-0616

Assn. of Personal Injury Lawyers [IO], Nottingham, United Kingdom

Assn. for Persons with Developmental Disabilities and Mental Hea. Needs; NADD - An [12552]

Assn. for Persons with Severe Handicaps [★11991]

Assn. for Persons in Supported Employment [★17414]

Assn. for Persons With Special Needs [IO], Singapore, Singapore

Assn. of Peruvian Exporters [IO], Lima, Peru

Assn. of Pet Behavior Counsellors [IO], Worcester, United Kingdom

Assn. of Pet Dog Trainers [1160], 150 Executive Center Dr., Box 35, Greenville, SC 29615, (800)PET-DOGS

Assn. of Pet Dog Trainers Australia [IO], Bankstown Square, Australia

Assn. of Pet Dog Trainers - United Kingdom [IO], Kempsford, United Kingdom

Assn. for Pet Loss and Bereavement [12706], PO Box 106, Brooklyn, NY 11230, (718)382-0690

Assn. for Petroleum and Explosives Admin. [IO], Saffron Walden, United Kingdom

Assn. of Petroleum Re-Refiners - Address unknown since 2004.

Assn. of the Pharmaceutical Companies' Representatives in Poland [★IO]

Assn. of Pharmaceutical Distributors - Italy [IO], Rome, Italy

Assn. of Pharmaceutical Manufacturers [IO], Stockholm, Sweden

Assn. des Pharmaciens du Canada [★IO]

Assn. of Pharmacy Technicians of United Kingdom [IO], London, United Kingdom

Assn. of Philanthropic Counsel [958], 1901 N Roselle Rd., Ste. 920, Schaumburg, IL 60195, (704)940-7386

Assn. of Philippine-Amer. Women - Address unknown since 1995.

Assn. of Philippine Orthodontists [IO], Makati City, Philippines

Assn. of Philippine Physicians in Am. [15994]

Assn. of Philippine Practicing Physicians in Am. [★15994]

Assn. of Philosophy Journal Editors - Address unknown since 2006.

Assn. for Philosophy of the Unconscious [10786], Dept. of Philosophy, Georgetown Univ., Washington, DC 20057, (202)687-7613

Assn. Phonetique Internationale [★IO]

Assn. of Photo Sensitizers - Defunct.

Assn. of Photographers [IO], London, United Kingdom

Assn. of Photographers [IO], Prague, Czech Republic

Assn. of Photographic Importers and Distributors - Defunct.

Assn. of Physical Fitness Centers - Address unknown since 2003.

Assn. for Physical and Mental Rehabilitation [★16311]

Assn. of Physical Oceanography [★7398]

Assn. of Physical Oceanography [★IO]

Assn. of Physical Plant Administrators [★IO]

Assn. of Physical Plant Administrators [★8333]

Assn. of Physical Plant Administrators of Universities and Colleges [★8333]

Assn. of Physical Plant Administrators of Universities and Colleges [★IO]

Assn. of Physical Scientists in Medicine [IO], Dublin, Ireland

Assn. for Physical and Systems Mathematics - Address unknown since 2004.

Assn. of Physician Asst. Programs [★15976]

Assn. of Physician Assistants in Cardiovascular Surgery [13895], PO Box 4834, Englewood, CO 80155, (303)221-5651

Assn. of Physicians for the Env. of Turkey [IO], Istanbul, Turkey

Assn. of Physicians and Medical Workers for Social Responsibility [IO], Nairobi, Kenya

Reference to "IO" in place of a book number signifies that the association may be found in the 45th edition of International Organizations.

Assn. of Physiotherapists of Swaziland [IO], Manzini, Swaziland

Assn. of Physiotherapists in Tanzania [IO], Dar es Salaam, United Republic of Tanzania

Assn. des Pilotes Maritimes du Canada [★IO]

Assn. of Pizza Delivery Drivers [1579]

Assn. des Planetariums de Langue Francaise [★IO]

Assn. of Planned Parenthood Physicians [★12177]

Assn. of Planned Parenthood Professionals [★12177]

Assn. for the Planning and Development of Services for the Aged in Israel [IO], Jerusalem, Israel

Assn. of Planning Supervisors [★IO]

Assn. of Plastic Raw Material Distributors - Defunct.

Assn. for Play Therapy [16607], 2060 N Winery Ave., No. 102, Fresno, CA 93703, (559)252-2278

Assn. of Plumbing and Heating Contractors [IO], Coventry, United Kingdom

Assn. for Poetry Therapy [★16223]

Assn. of Police Authorities [IO], London, United Kingdom

Assn. of Police Surgeons [★IO]

Assn. of Policy Market Makers [IO], London, United Kingdom

Assn. of Polish Agricultural Journalists [IO], Lodz, Poland

Assn. of Polish Engineers in Canada [IO], Toronto, ON, Canada

Assn. of Polish Filmmakers [IO], Warsaw, Poland

Assn. of Polish Geomorphologists [IO], Poznan, Poland

Assn. of Polish Operational Res. Societies [IO], Warsaw, Poland

Assn. of Polish Papermakers [IO], Lodz, Poland

Assn. of Polish Women in Am. [★19311]

Assn. for Political and Legal Anthropology [6411], c/o Bill Maurer, Pres.-Elect, Univ. of California - Irvine, Dept. of Anthropology, 3272 Social Sciences Plz. B, Irvine, CA 92697-5100, (949)824-7602

Assn. of Political Science Instructors - Defunct.

Assn. for Politics and the Life Sciences [7522], Utah State Univ., Political Sci. Dept., Logan, UT 84322-0725, (435)797-8104

Assn. of Polysomnographic Technologists [16423], 1 Westbrook Corporate Ctr., Ste. 920, Westchester, IL 60154, (708)492-0796

Assn. of Polytechnic Graduates [IO], Montreal, QC, Canada

Association of Pool and Spa Professionals [IO], Alexandria, VA, United States

Assn. of Pool and Spa Professionals [3353], 2111 Eisenhower Ave., Ste. 500, Alexandria, VA 22314, (703)838-0083

Assn. for Population/Family Planning Libraries and Info. Centers-International [10336], c/o Kiet Bang, Membership Sec., The Pennsylvania State Univ., Population Res. Inst., 706 Oswald Tower, University Park, PA 16802, (814)863-6703

Assn. for Population/Family Planning Libraries and Info. Centers-International [IO], Chapel Hill, NC, United States

Assn. of Port Hea. Authorities [IO], Ipswich, United Kingdom

Assn. of Port Wine Companies [IO], Vila Nova de Gaia, Portugal

Assn. of Portuguese-Language Universities [IO], Lisbon, Portugal

Assn. for Post Natal Illness [IO], London, United Kingdom

Assn. for Postal Commerce [2449], 1901 N Ft. Myer Dr., Ste. 401, Arlington, VA 22209-1609, (703)524-0096

Assn. of Postal Officials of Canada [IO], Ottawa, ON, Canada

Assn. of Postconsumer Plastic Recyclers [3045], 2000 L St. NW, Ste. 835, Washington, DC 20006, (202)316-3046

Assn. of Poultry Slaughterhouse Operators - Address unknown since 1995.

Assn. Pour La Lutte Contre Le Psoriasis [IO], Boisemont, France

Assn. Pour La Prevention Des Infections A l'hopital et dans La Communaute [★IO]

Assn. Pour Le Commerce Et Les Services En Ligne [IO], Paris, France

Assn. of Power Producers of Ontario [IO], Toronto, ON, Canada

Assn. for Practical and Professional Ethics [8967], Indiana Univ., 618 E 3rd St., Bloomington, IN 47405-3602, (812)855-6450

Assn. for Practical Theology - Address unknown since 2001.

Assn. of Practicing Certified Public Accountants [17]

Assn. of Practitioners Before the Interstate Commerce Commn. [★6316]

Assn. of Practitioners in Infection Control [★14947]

Assn. of Pragmatic Individuals - Defunct.

Assn. de Pre-Histoire de la Regional Indo-Pacifique [★IO]

Assn. for Pre- and Perinatal Psychology and Hea. [13979], PO Box 1398, Forestville, CA 95436, (707)887-2838

Assn. for Precision Graphics - Defunct.

Assn. of Presbyterian Colleges [★9005]

Assn. of Presbyterian Colleges and Universities [9005], 100 Witherspoon St., Louisville, KY 40202-1396, (502)569-5364

Assn. of Presbyterian Univ. Pastors and Campus Ministry Assn. [★19933]

Assn. for the Preservation of Anti-Psychiatric Artifacts - Defunct.

Assn. for the Preservation of the Auction Market - Defunct.

Assn. for the Preservation of Civil War Sites [★10019]

Assn. for the Preservation and Presentation of the Arts [9355], 2011 Benning Rd. NE, Washington, DC 20002, (202)529-3244

Assn. for Preservation Tech. [★10016]

Assn. for Preservation Tech. [★IO]

Assn. for Preservation Tech. Intl. [IO], Springfield, IL, United States

Assn. for Preservation Tech. Intl. [10016], 3085 Stevenson Dr., Ste. 200, Springfield, IL 62703, (217)529-9039

Assn. for the Preservation of Virginia Antiquities [★10013]

Assn. to Preserve Cape Cod [4361], PO Box 398, 3010 Main St., Barnstable, MA 02630-0398, (508)362-4226

Assn. de la Presse Francophone [★IO]

Assn. des Presses Universitaires Canadiennes [★IO]

Assn. for the Prevention of Atmospheric Pollution [IO], Le Kremlin-Bicetre, France

Assn. pour la Prevention de la Pollution Atmospherique [★IO]

Assn. for Prevention Teaching and Res. [16054], 1001 Connecticut Ave. NW, Ste. 610, Washington, DC 20036, (202)463-0550

Assn. pour la Prevention de la Torture [★IO]

Assn. for the Prevention of Torture [IO], Geneva, Switzerland

Assn. of Principal Fire Officers [IO], Tamworth, United Kingdom

Assn. of Printed Media of Macedonia [IO], Skopje, Macedonia

Assn. of Private Banks of Ecuador [IO], Quito, Ecuador

Assn. of Private Client Investment Managers and Stockbrokers [IO], London, United Kingdom

Association of Private Enterprise Education [IO], Chattanooga, TN, United States

Assn. of Private Enterprise Educ. [9019], c/o Dr. J.R. Clark, Sec.-Treas., The Univ. of Tennessee at Chattanooga, 313 Fletcher Hall, Dept. 6106, 615 McCallie Ave., Chattanooga, TN 37403-2598, (423)425-4118

Assn. of Private Hospitals - Address unknown since 1995.

Assn. of Private Hospitals of Malaysia [IO], Kuala Lumpur, Malaysia

Assn. of Private Libraries - Address unknown since 2007.

Assn. of Private Market Operators [IO], Rotherham, United Kingdom

Assn. of Private Pension and Welfare Plans [★6169]

Assn. of Private Postal Systems [★2447]

Assn. of Private Weather Related Companies [★7326]

Assn. of Privately Owned Seventh-Day Adventist Services and Indus. [★20553]

Assn. du Prix Albert Londres [IO], Paris, France

Assn. of Problem Gambling Ser. Administrators [12208], c/o Tim Christensen, Pres., Arizona Off. of Problem Gambling, 202 E Earll Dr., Ste. 200, Phoenix, AZ 85012, (602)266-8299

Assn. of the Processed Cheese Indus. of the EU [IO], Bonn, Germany

Assn. of Procurement Tech. Assistance Specialists [★1740]

Assn. of Producers and Exporters of Fine Wines [IO], Santiago, Chile

Assn. of Producers and Merchants of Wines and Spirits in Bulgaria [IO], Sofia, Bulgaria

Association of Productivity Specialists [IO], New York, NY, United States

Assn. of Productivity Specialists [2486], 521 5th Ave., Ste. 1700, New York, NY 10175, (212)286-0943

Assn. des Produits Forestiers du Canada [★IO]

Assn. des Professeurs d'Allemand des Universites Canadiennes [★IO]

Assn. des Professeurs de Francais des Universites et des Colleges Canadiens [★IO]

Assn. des Professeurs Franco-Americains - Defunct.

Assn. des Professeurs de l'Enseignement Secondaire et Superieur [★IO]

Assn. of Professional Ball Players of Am. [23105], 1820 W Orangewood Ave., Ste. 206, Orange, CA 92868-2052, (714)935-9993

Assn. of Professional Baseball Physicians - Defunct.

Assn. of Professional Bridge Players - Address unknown since 2002.

Assn. for Professional Broadcasting Educ. [★8001]

Assn. for Professional Broadcasting Educ. [★IO]

Assn. of Professional Chaplains [19744], 1701 E Woodfield Rd., Ste. 400, Schaumburg, IL 60173, (847)240-1014

Assn. of Professional Collectors - Defunct.

Assn. of Professional Color Imagers - Defunct.

Assn. of Professional Commun. Consultants [959], c/o Dr. Kenneth W. Davis, Pres., 8910 Purdue Rd., Ste. 480, Indianapolis, IN 46268, (317)616-1810

Assn. of Professional Commun. Consultants [IO], Indianapolis, IN, United States

Assn. of Professional Cmpt. Consultants [IO], Toronto, ON, Canada

Assn. of Professional Consultants [960], PO Box 51193, Irvine, CA 92619-1193, (949)675-9222

Assn. of Professional Design Firms [1806], 1448 E 52nd St., No. 201, Chicago, IL 60615, (773)643-7052

Assn. of Professional Directors of YMCAs in the U.S. [★13460]

Assn. of Professional Directors, Young Men's Christian Associations in the U.S. [★13460]

Assn. of Professional Draftsman [★7152]

Assn. of Professional Energy Managers [6944], 3916 W Oak St., Ste. D, Burbank, CA 91505, (818)972-2159

Assn. of Professional Engineers, Geologists and Geophysicists of Alberta [IO], Edmonton, AB, Canada

Assn. of Professional Engineers, Scientists and Managers Australia [IO], Melbourne, Australia

Assn. of Professional, Executive, Clerical, and Cmpt. Staff [★IO]

Assn. of Professional, Executive, Clerical, and Cmpt. Staff and GMB [★IO]

Assn. of Professional Flight Attendants [24010], 1004 W Euless Blvd., Euless, TX 76040, (817)540-0108

Association of Professional Foresters [★IO]

Assn. of Professional Futurists [IO], Waltham, MA, United States

Assn. of Professional Futurists [7102], 681 Main St., Ste. 324, Waltham, MA 02451

Assn. of Professional Genealogists in Ireland [IO], Dublin, Ireland

Assn. of Professional Geological Scientists [★7127]

Assn. of Professional Humane Educators [12058], c/o The Latham Found., Latham Plaza Bldg., 1826 Clement Ave., Alameda, CA 94501

Assn. of Professional Insurance Women [★2142]

A star before a book entry number signifies that the name is not listed separately, but is mentioned within the entry.

Assn. of Professional Landscape Designers [2393], 4305 N Sixth St., Ste. A, Harrisburg, PA 17110, (717)238-9780

Association of Professional Landscape Designers [IO], Harrisburg, PA, United States

Assn. of Professional Landscapers [IO], Reading, United Kingdom

Assn. of Professional Material Handling Consultants [961], 8720 Red Oak Blvd., Ste. 201, Charlotte, NC 28217, (704)676-1190

Assn. of Professional Model Makers [7006], PO Box 165, Hamilton, NY 13346, (877)663-2766

Assn. of Professional Music Therapists [IO], East Barnet, United Kingdom

Assn. for Professional Observers [4667], PO Box 30167, Seattle, WA 98103

Assn. of Professional Organizers [★7166]

Assn. of Professional Piercers [3715], PO Box 1287, Lawrence, KS 66044, (785)841-6060

Assn. of Professional Placement Agencies and Consultants [★IO]

Assn. of Professional Police Investigators - Address unknown since 2003.

Assn. of Professional Recording Services [IO], Totnes, United Kingdom

Assn. of Professional Recruiters of Canada [IO], Ottawa, ON, Canada

Assn. of Professional Researchers for Advancement [12198], 401 N Michigan Ave., Ste. 2200, Chicago, IL 60611, (312)321-5196

Assn. of Professional Responsibility Lawyers [5487], 134 N LaSalle St., Ste. 1600, Chicago, IL 60602, (312)782-4396

Assn. of Professional Schools of Intl. Affairs [8654], c/o Braden Smith, Exec. Dir., 225 Eggers Hall, Syracuse, NY 13244-1090, (315)443-2113

Assn. of Professional Schools of Intl. Affairs [IO], Syracuse, NY, United States

Assn. of Professional Schools of Music - Defunct.

Assn. of Professional Sleep Societies [★16422]

Assn. for the Professional Treatment of Offenders - Defunct.

Assn. of Professional Vocal Ensembles [★10577]

Assn. of Professional Women Who are Parents - Defunct.

Assn. of Professional Writing Consultants [★959]

Assn. of Professional Writing Consultants [★IO]

Assn. for Professionals in Infection Control and Epidemiology [14947], 1275 K St. NW, Ste. 1000, Washington, DC 20005-4006, (202)789-1890

Assn. for Professionals in Services for Adolescents [IO], Whitchurch, United Kingdom

Assn. des Professionnels a l'Outillage Municipal [★IO]

Assn. Professionnelle des Opticiens et Optometristes de Belgique [IO], Brussels, Belgium

Assn. des Professionnels de l'information et de la Documentation [IO], Paris, France

Assn. of Professors of Cardiology [13896], 2400 N St. NW, Washington, DC 20037, (202)375-6191

Assn. of Professors of Gynecology and Obstetrics [15592], 2130 Priest Bridge Dr., Ste. 7, Crofton, MD 21114, (410)451-9560

Assn. of Professors of Higher Educ. [★8482]

Assn. of Professors of Human and Medical Genetics [14497], c/o Gerald Feldman, PhD, Pres., Wayne State Univ. School of Medicine, Molecular Medicine and Genetics Dept., 540 E Canfield St., 3216 Scott Hall, Detroit, MI 48201-1928, (313)577-6298

Assn. of Professors of Medicine [8853], 2501 M St. NW, Ste. 550, Washington, DC 20037-1325, (202)861-9191

Assn. of Professors of Mission [20302], c/o Ruth Tucker, PhD, Calvin Theological Seminary, 927 Giddings SE, Grand Rapids, MI 49506, (616)957-8667

Assn. of Professors, Practitioners, and Researchers in Religious Educ; Religious Educ. Assn.: An [19939]

Assn. of Professors and Researchers in Religious Educ. [★19939]

Assn. of Professors of Secondary and Higher Educ. [IO], Strassen, Luxembourg

Assn. of Profiles Consultants - Address unknown since 1999.

Assn. of Prog. Directors in Endocrinology, Diabetes and Metabolism [14351], 8401 Connecticut Ave., Ste. 900, Chevy Chase, MD 20815, (301)941-0243

Assn. of Prog. Directors in Endocrinology and Metabolism [★14351]

Assn. of Prog. Directors in Internal Medicine [14967], c/o Alliance for Academic Internal Medicine, 2501 M St. NW, Ste. 550, Washington, DC 20037-1325, (202)861-9351

Assn. of Prog. Directors in Radiology [15088], 820 Jorie Blvd., Oak Brook, IL 60523, (630)368-3737

Assn. of Prog. Directors in Surgery [16577], PO Box 342260, Bethesda, MD 20827-2260, (301)320-1200

Assn. of Prog. Directors in Vascular Surgery [16578], c/o Soc. for Vascular Surgery, 633 N St. Clair St., Chicago, IL 60611, (312)202-5600

Assn. on Programs for Female Offenders [11857], c/o Judy C. Anderson, Treas., 3119 Heyward St., Columbia, SC 29250-2632

Assn. for Progressive Communications [17163], c/o Intl. Global Communications, PO Box 29047, San Francisco, CA 94129-0047, (415)561-6100

Assn. of Progressive Rental Organizations [3379], 1504 Robin Hood Trail, Austin, TX 78703, (800)204-2776

Assn. for Proj. Mgt. [IO], High Wycombe, United Kingdom

Assn. for Proj. Mgt. Hong Kong [IO], Hong Kong, People's Republic of China

Assn. for Proj. Safety [IO], Edinburgh, United Kingdom

Assn. Promoting Educ. and Conservation in Amazonia [IO], Woodland Hills, CA, United States

Assn. Promoting Educ. and Conservation in Amazonia [5294], 21338 Dumetz Rd., Woodland Hills, CA 91364, (818)348-6614

Assn. for the Promotion of African Community Initiatives [IO], Douala, Cameroon

Assn. for the Promotion of Christian Union [★19891]

Assn. pour la Promotion de la Diffusion Internationale de la Presse [★IO]

Assn. pour la Promotion de la Famille Haitienne [IO], Port-au-Prince, Haiti

Assn. pour la Promotion des Initiatives Communautaires Africaines [★IO]

Assn. of Promotion Marketing Agencies Worldwide [★IO]

Assn. of Promotion Marketing Agencies Worldwide [★3468]

Assn. for the Promotion of the Mathematics Educ. of Girls and Women [★8828]

Assn. for Promotion of Skiing [IO], Oslo, Norway

Assn. for the Promotion of Tourism to Africa [IO], Trabuco Canyon, CA, United States

Assn. for the Promotion of Tourism to Africa [3826], c/o Nancy Decker-Davidson, Exec. Dir., 21761 Via Del Lago, Trabuco Canyon, CA 92679, (949)400-9989

Assn. of Property Unit Trusts [★IO]

Assn. of Proposal Mgt. Professionals [2487], PO Box 668, Dana Point, CA 92629-0668, (949)493-9398

Assn. pour la Protection des Automobilistes [★IO]

Assn. for the Protection of Consumers [IO], Bucharest, Romania

Assn. for Protection of Env. and Culture [IO], Kathmandu, Nepal

Assn. for the Protection of Fur-Bearing Animals [IO], Vancouver, BC, Canada

Assn. for the Protection of Nature and the Env. - Kairouan, Tunisia [IO], Kairouan, Tunisia

Assn. for the Protection of Rural Scotland [★IO]

Assn. of Protestant Churches and Missions in Germany [IO], Hamburg, Germany

Assn. of Protestant Development Organisations in Europe [★IO]

Assn. Psychanalytique Internationale [★IO]

Assn. des Psychiatres du Canada [★IO]

Assn. of Psychiatric Outpatient Centers of America - Address unknown since 1990.

Assn. for Psychoanalytic Medicine [16107], c/o Dr. Lila J. Kalinich, MD, Pres., 333 Central Park W, New York, NY 10025, (718)548-6088

Assn. for Psychoanalytic and Psychosomatic Medicine [★16107]

Assn. for Psychoanalytic Self Psychology [16141], c/o Helena Johansson, Membership Mgr., 7916 Convoy Ct., San Diego, CA 92111-1212, (858)565-9921

Assn. for Psychohistory [★10123]

Assn. for Psychological Astrology [6490], 360 Quietwood Dr., San Rafael, CA 94903, (415)479-5812

Assn. for Psychological Counseling and Training [★IO]

Assn. for Psychological Sci. [16142], 1010 Vermont Ave. NW, 11th Fl., Washington, DC 20005-4918, (202)783-2077

Assn. for Psychological Type Intl. [16143], 9650 Rockville Pike, Bethesda, MD 20814-3998, (301)634-7450

Assn. of Psychologists of Nova Scotia [IO], Halifax, NS, Canada

Assn. of Psychology Internship Centers [★8854]

Assn. of Psychology Postdoctoral and Internship Centers [8854], 10 G St. NE, Ste. 440, Washington, DC 20002, (202)589-0600

Assn. for the Psychophysiological Stud. of Sleep [★16429]

Assn. for Psychotheatrics - Defunct.

Assn. of PTL Partners - Address unknown since 1988.

Assn. of Public Analysts [IO], London, United Kingdom

Assn. for Public Broadcasting [★547]

Assn. for Public Broadcasting [★547]

Assn. of Public Corps. - Address unknown since 2003.

Assn. of Public Data Users [7190], c/o APB Associates, 28300 Franklin Rd., Southfield, MI 48034-1562, (248)354-6520

Assn. of Public Hea. Labs. [16239], 8515 Georgia Ave., Ste. 700, Silver Spring, MD 20910, (240)485-2745

Assn. of Public Hea. Labs. [IO], Silver Spring, MD, United States

Assn. for Public Justice Educ. Fund [★18431]

Assn. of Public Pension Fund Auditors [24147], PO Box 2407, ESP Sta., Albany, NY 12220

Assn. for Public Policy Anal. and Mgt. [18423], 1029 Vermont Ave. NW, Ste. 1150, Washington, DC 20005, (202)496-0130

Association for Public Policy Analysis and Management [IO], Washington, DC, United States

Assn. of Public and Private Banks of the Argentine Republic [IO], Buenos Aires, Argentina

Assn. of Public Radio Stations [★9765]

Assn. of Public-Safety Communications Officials - Intl. [6248], 351 N Williamson Blvd., Daytona Beach, FL 32114-1112, (386)322-2500

Association of Public-Safety Communications Officials - International [IO], Daytona Beach, FL, United States

Assn. for Public Ser. Excellence [IO], Manchester, United Kingdom

Assn. of Public Treasurers of the U.S. and Canada [6203], 962 Wayne Ave., Ste. 910, Silver Spring, MD 20910, (301)495-5560

Assn. of Publication Production Managers - Address unknown since 2003.

Assn. de la Publicite par l'Objet du Canada [★IO]

Assn. of Publicly Traded Companies - Address unknown since 2004.

Assn. of Publicly Traded Investment Funds [★3515]

Assn. of Publicly Traded Investment Funds - Defunct.

Assn. of Publishers' Representatives [★113]

Assn. of Publishing Agencies [IO], London, United Kingdom

Assn. of Publishing Systems Users - Defunct.

Assn. for Puerto Rican-Hispanic Culture - Address unknown since 2007.

Assn. Pulmonaire du Canada [★IO]

Assn. of the Pulp and Paper Indus. [IO], Prague, Czech Republic

Assn. for Purchasing and Supply [IO], Dublin, Ireland

Assn. of PVO Financial Managers [IO], Westport, CT, United States

Assn. of PVO Financial Managers [1458], 19 S Compo Rd., Westport, CT 06880, (203)226-3650

Reference to "IO" in place of a book number signifies that the association may be found in the 45th edition of International Organizations.

Assn. of Qualified Curative Hypnotherapists [IO], Thatcham, United Kingdom

Assn. of Qualified Volunteers in Youth Services [IO], Montreal, QC, Canada

Assn. of Qualitative Res. [IO], St. Neots, United Kingdom

Association for Quality and Participation [★7555]

Assn. Quebecoise des Critiques de Cinema [IO], Montreal, QC, Canada

Assn. Quebecoise des troubles d'apprentissage [★IO]

Assn. Quebecoise de L'Industrie du Disque, du Spectacle et de la Video [IO], Montreal, QC, Canada

Assn. Quebecoise pour la Therapie Conjugale et Familiale [★IO]

Assn. of Racing Commissioners Intl. [IO], Lexington, KY, United States

Assn. of Racing Commissioners Intl. [6240], 2343 Alexandria Dr., Ste. 200, Lexington, KY 40504-3283, (859)224-7070

Assn. of Racquetsports Mfrs. and Suppliers - Defunct.

Assn. for Radiation Res. [IO], Leicester, United Kingdom

Assn. of Radical Midwives [IO], Oxford, United Kingdom

Assn. of Radio Amateurs of Bosnia and Herzegovina [★IO]

Assn. of Radio Amateurs of Slovenia [IO], Ljubljana, Slovenia

Assn. of Radio Indus. and Businesses [IO], Tokyo, Japan

Assn. of Radio-TV News Analysts - Defunct.

Assn. of Railroad Advertising and Marketing - Defunct.

Assn. of Railway Communicators - Defunct.

Assn. of Railway Museums [10908], 1016 Rosser St., Conyers, GA 30012, (770)278-0088

Assn. of Railway Training Providers [IO], London, United Kingdom

Assn. of Railway Trainmen and Locomotive Firemen - Address unknown since 1995.

Assn. of Rain Apparel Contractors - Defunct.

Assn. for Rational Environmental Alternatives - Defunct.

Assn. for Real Change [IO], Chesterfield, United Kingdom

Assn. of Real Estate Companies of Estonia [IO], Tallinn, Estonia

Assn. of Real Estate Funds [IO], London, United Kingdom

Assn. of Real Estate License Law Officials [IO], Littleton, CO, United States

Assn. of Real Estate License Law Officials [6243], 8361 Sangre de Cristo Rd., Ste. 250, Littleton, CO 80127, (303)979-6190

Assn. of Real Estate Women [3300], 322 Eighth Ave., Ste. 501, New York, NY 10001, (212)599-6181

Assn. for Realistic Philosophy - Defunct.

Assn. des bibliotheques de Recherche du Canada [★IO]

Assn. pour la Recherche sur la Sclerose Laterale Amyotrophique [IO], Paris, France

Assn. de la Recherche Theatrale au Canada [★IO]

Assn. of Recognised English Language Services [★IO]

Assn. of Recognized IOC Intl. Sports Federations [IO], Colorado Springs, CO, United States

Assn. of Recognized IOC Intl. Sports Federations [23804], 1631 Mesa Ave., Ste. A, Colorado Springs, CO 80906, (719)636-2695

Assn. for Recognizing the Life of Stillborns [12661], 601 W Rand Rd., No. 102, Arlington Heights, IL 60004, (847)749-4258

Assn. of Record Librarians of North Am. [★15097]

Assn. for Recorded Sound Collections [10337], c/o Peter Shambarger, Exec. Dir., PO Box 543, Annapolis, MD 21404-0543, (410)757-0488

Association for Recorded Sound Collections [IO], Annapolis, MD, United States

Assn. of the Recording Indus. of Ghana [IO], Accra, Ghana

Assn. of Records Executives and Administrators [★IO]

Assn. of Records Executives and Administrators [★2096]

Assn. of Records Managers and Administrators [IO], Calgary, AB, Canada

Assn. of Recovering Motorcyclists [13225], 1503 Market St., La Crosse, WI 54601

Assn. de Recyclage du Polystyrene du Canada [★IO]

Assn. of Reflexologists [IO], Taunton, United Kingdom

Assn. of Reform Zionists of Am. [★IO]

Assn. of Reform Zionists of Am. [★20122]

Assn. of Reformed Baptist Churches of Am. [19473], PO Box 289, Carlisle, PA 17013, (717)249-7473

Assn. of Refrigerant and Desuperheating Mfg. [1877], Addison Products Co., ECU Div., PO Box 607776, 7050 Overland Rd., Orlando, FL 32810, (407)290-1329

Assn. of Regional Religious Communicators - Defunct.

Assn. of Regional Weed Control Conferences [★4109]

Assn. of Registered Bank Holding Companies [★477]

Assn. des Registraires des Universites et Colleges du Canada [★IO]

Assn. of Registrars of the Universities and Colleges of Canada [IO], Sherbrooke, QC, Canada

Assn. of Regulatory Boards of Optometry [IO], St. Louis, MO, United States

Assn. of Regulatory Boards of Optometry [15716], 1750 S Brentwood Blvd., Ste. 503, St. Louis, MO 63144, (314)785-6000

Assn. of Regulatory and Clinical Scientists Australia [IO], Crows Nest, Australia

Assn. for Regulatory Reform [★2526]

Assn. for the Rehabilitation of the Brain Injured [IO], Calgary, AB, Canada

Assn. of Rehabilitation Centers [★16312]

Assn. for Rehabilitation of Commun. and Oral Skills [IO], Malvern, United Kingdom

Assn. of Rehabilitation Facilities [★16312]

Assn. for Rehabilitation Marketing [2617], 118 Julian Pl., PMB 105, Syracuse, NY 13210

Assn. of Rehabilitation Nurses [15469], 4700 W Lake Ave., Glenview, IL 60025-1485, (847)375-4710

Assn. of Rehabilitation Programs in Cmpt. Tech. [11924], Western Michigan Univ., Educational Stud. Off., 3421 Sangren Hall, Kalamazoo, MI 49008, (269)387-2053

Assn. of Rehabilitation Programs in Data Processing [★11924]

Assn. for Religion and Intellectual Life [19916], DBA CrossCurrents, 475 Riverside Dr., Ste. 1945, New York, NY 10115-0021, (212)870-2544

Assn. for Religious and Value Issues in Counseling [★8166]

Assn. of Relocation Agents [★IO]

Assn. of Relocation Professionals [IO], Diss, United Kingdom

Assn. for Renaissance Martial Arts [IO], Hiram, GA, United States

Assn. for Renaissance Martial Arts [8820], 5220 Jimmy Lee Smith Pkwy., Ste. 104, No. 111, Hiram, GA 30141

Assn. for Repetitive Motion Syndromes [15631], PO Box 471973, Aurora, CO 80047-1973, (303)369-0803

Assn. of Reporters of Judicial Decisions [5895], 5711 Nevada St., College Park, MD 20740, (202)479-3194

Assn. of Representatives of Professional Athletes - Address unknown since 1994.

Assn. of Reproduction Materials Manufacturers [★1800]

Assn. of Reproductive Hea. Professionals [12177], 2401 Pennsylvania Ave. NW, Ste. 350, Washington, DC 20037-1718, (202)466-3825

Assn. of Reptilian and Amphibian Veterinarians [16783], c/o Wilbur B. Amand, VMD, Exec. Dir., PO Box 605, Chester Heights, PA 19017, (610)892-4812

Association of Reptilian and Amphibian Veterinarians [IO], Chester Heights, PA, United States

Assn. for Res. of Childhood Cancer [13798], PO Box 251, Buffalo, NY 14225-0251, (716)681-4433

Assn. for Res. in Cosmecology - Defunct.

Assn. of Res. Directors [7563], c/o Stephen H. Kolison, Jr., Chm.-Elect, Tennessee State Univ., 3500 John A. Merritt Blvd., Nashville, TN 37209-1561, (615)963-2194

Assn. for Res. and Enlightenment [7443], 215 67th St., Virginia Beach, VA 23451-2061, (757)428-3588

Assn. for Res. and Enlightenment [IO], Virginia Beach, VA, United States

Assn. for Res. in Growth Relationships - Defunct.

Assn. of Res. Libraries [10338], 21 Dupont Cir. NW, Ste. 800, Washington, DC 20036, (202)296-2296

Assn. for Res. in Modern History [IO], Bonn, Germany

Assn. for Res. in Nervous and Mental Disease [16082], c/o Weill Medical Coll. of Cornell Univ., Dept. of Psychiatry, 1300 York Ave., Rm. F-1231, New York, NY 10021, (570)839-0296

Assn. for Res. on Nonprofit Organizations and Voluntary Action [13387], 340 W Michigan St., Canal Level Ste. A, Indianapolis, IN 46202-3272, (317)684-2120

Association for Research on Nonprofit Organizations and Voluntary Action [IO], Indianapolis, IN, United States

Assn. for Res. in Ophthalmology [★IO]

Assn. for Res. in Ophthalmology [★15672]

Assn. for Res. in Otolaryngology [15824], 19 Mantua Rd., Mount Royal, NJ 08061, (856)423-0041

Assn. for Res. in Personality [7543], c/o R. Chris Fraley, Sec.-Treas./Webmaster, Dept. of Psychology, Univ. of Illinois, 603 E Daniel St., Champaign, IL 61820, (217)333-3486

Assn. for Res. in Vision and Ophthalmology [15672], 12300 Twinbrook Pkwy., Ste. 250, Rockville, MD 20852-1606, (240)221-2900

Association for Research in Vision and Ophthalmology [IO], Rockville, MD, United States

Assn. for Res. in the Voluntary and Community Sector [IO], London, United Kingdom

Assn. of Researchers in Medicine and Sci. [IO], London, United Kingdom

Assn. of Reserve City Bankers [★477]

Assn. of Reserve Officers of the U.S. Public Health Service - Defunct.

Assn. for Residential Care [★IO]

Assn. of Residential Letting Agents [IO], Amersham, United Kingdom

Assn. of Residential Managing Agents [IO], London, United Kingdom

Assn. of Residents in Radiation Oncology [15643], c/o Steven Smith, Prog. Mgr., 8280 Willow Oaks Corporate Dr., Ste. 500, Fairfax, VA 22031, (703)839-7326

Assn. Resource Inst. - Address unknown since 1994.

Assn. for Responsible Medicine - Address unknown since 2004.

Assn. for the Restoration of the Church and Home [19844], 2071 County Rd. 139, Ovid, NY 14521, (607)869-3586

Assn. of Restorers [★218]

Assn. of Restorers and Coun. of Craftsmen and Artists [218], 8 Medford Pl., New Hartford, NY 13413, (315)733-1952

Assn. for Restriction of Radio and TV Commercials - Defunct.

Assn. pour le Retablissement des Institutions et Oeuvres Israelites en France [20121], 645 Madison Ave., New York, NY 10022, (212)888-8123

Assn. of Retail Advisors - Defunct.

Assn. of Retail Marketing Services [3463], 10 Drs. James Parker Blvd., Ste. 103, Red Bank, NJ 07701-1500, (732)842-5070

The Assn. of Retail Marketing Services; TSIA— [3463]

Assn. of Retail Marketing Services; TSIA—The [3463]

Assn. for Retail Tech. Standards [3400], 325 7th St. NW, Ste. 1100, Washington, DC 20004-2818, (202)626-8140

Assn. of Retail Travel Agents [3911], 4320 N Miller Rd., Scottsdale, AZ 85251, (800)969-6069

A star before a book entry number signifies that the name is not listed separately, but is mentioned within the entry.

Assn. for Retarded Citizens [★12561]

Assn. for Retarded Citizens of the U.S. [★12561]

Assn. for Retinopathy of Prematurity and Related Diseases [15673], PO Box 250425, Franklin, MI 48025, (800)788-2020

Assn. of Retired Americans [12897], 6505 E 82nd St., No. 130, Indianapolis, IN 46250, (800)806-6160

Assn. of Retired Hispanic Police [6171], PO Box 1735, Cathedral Sta., New York, NY 10025, (718)246-4836

Assn. of Retired Intelligence Officers [★5878]

Assn. of Retired Intelligence Officers [★IO]

Assn. of Retirement Housing Managers [IO], London, United Kingdom

Assn. of Rheumatologists of Russia [IO], Moscow, Russia

Assn. of Rheumatology Hea. Professionals [16370], c/o Amer. Colorado of Rheumatology, 1800 Century Pl., Ste. 250, Atlanta, GA 30345-4300, (404)633-3777

Assn. of Ridesharing Professionals [★13334]

Assn. of Ridesharing Professionals [★IO]

Assn. for the Right to Die with Dignity [IO], Paris, France

Assn. for the Rights of Catholics in the Church [19578], 3150 Newgate Dr., Florissant, MO 63033, (413)477-1080

Assn. of Risk and Insurance Managers of Australasia [★IO]

Assn. of Risk Mgt. - Japan [IO], Tokyo, Japan

Assn. of Road Racing Athletes - Address unknown since 2001.

Assn. for Road Traffic Safety and Mgt. [IO], Teddington, United Kingdom

Assn. for Road Traffic Sign Makers [★IO]

Assn. of Road Users of Pakistan [IO], Islamabad, Pakistan

Assn. of Roller and Silent Chain Mfrs. [★1993]

Assn. for Roman Archaeology [IO], Swindon, United Kingdom

Assn. of Romanian Catholics of America [19579]

Assn. of Rotational Molders [★3046]

Assn. of Rotational Molders [★IO]

Association of Rotational Molders International [IO], Oak Brook, IL, United States

Assn. of Rotational Molders Intl. [3046], 800 Roosevelt Rd., Bldg. C, Ste. 312, Glen Ellyn, IL 60137, (630)571-0611

Assn. Royale Belge des Indus. du Biscuit, du Chocolat, de la Confiserie et de la Praline [★IO]

Assn. Royale de Golf du Canada [★IO]

Assn. of Rural Advisory Centres [IO], Vantaa, Finland

Assn. of Rural Cooperation in Africa and Latin Am. - Nicaragua [IO], Managua, Nicaragua

Assn. for Rural Development and Action Res. [IO], Vizianagaram, India

Assn. of Rural Surgeons of India [IO], Bombay, India

Assn. of Russian-American Scholars in the U.S.A. [10941], PO Box 180035, Richmond Hill, NY 11418

Assn. of Russian Auto. Dealers [IO], Moscow, Russia

Assn. of Russian Banks [IO], Moscow, Russia

Assn. of Russian Imperial Medical Officers - Defunct.

Assn. of Russian Imperial Naval Officers in America - Address unknown since 1995.

Assn. of Russian War Invalids of World War II - Address unknown since 1995.

Assn. for Safe Intl. Road Travel [13335], 11769 Gainsborough Rd., Potomac, MD 20854, (301)983-5252

Assn. for Safe Intl. Road Travel [IO], Potomac, MD, United States

Assn. of Safety Coun. Executives - Address unknown since 1999.

Assn. of Salaried Medical Specialists [IO], Wellington, New Zealand

Assn. of Sales Admin. Managers [3464], c/o Bill Martin, Sec.-Treas., Box 1356, Laurence Harbor, NJ 08879, (732)264-7722

Assn. for Sales Force Management - Defunct.

Assn. of Sales and Marketing Companies [★1518]

Assn. of Sales and Marketing Companies - Defunct.

The Assn. of Sanctuaries [11367], PO Box 925, Stillwater, MN 55082, (763)772-3087

Assn. for Sandwich Educ. and Training [IO], Sheffield, United Kingdom

Assn. for Sane Psychiatric Practices - Defunct.

Assn. canadienne pour la sante, l'education physique, le loisir et la danse [★IO]

Assn. of School Bus. Officials [★IO]

Assn. of School Bus. Officials [★7892]

Assn. of School Bus. Officials Intl. [7892], 11401 N Shore Dr., Reston, VA 20190-4200, (703)478-0405

Assn. of School Bus. Officials Intl. [IO], Reston, VA, United States

Assn. of School Bus. Officials of the U.S. and Canada [★IO]

Assn. of School Bus. Officials of the U.S. and Canada [★7892]

Assn. of School and Coll. Leaders [IO], Leicester, United Kingdom

Assn. for School, Coll. and Univ. Staffing [★8994]

Assn. of Schools of Allied Hea. Professions [8855], 4400 Jenifer St. NW, Ste. 333, Washington, DC 20015, (202)237-6481

Assn. of Schools of Allied Hea. Professions [★8855]

Assn. of Schools and Colleges of Optometry [15717], 6110 Executive Blvd., Ste. 420, Rockville, MD 20852, (301)231-5944

Assn. of Schools of Journalism and Mass Commun. [7893], 234 Outlet Pointe Blvd., Columbia, SC 29210-5667, (803)798-0271

Assn. of Schools of Public Hea. [16240], 1101 15th St. NW, Ste. 910, Washington, DC 20005, (202)296-1099

Assn. of Schools of Public Hea. in the European Region [IO], St. Maurice, France

Assn. for Schools of Social Work in Africa [IO], Addis Ababa, Ethiopia

Assn. of Schoolsports Clubs Czech Republic [IO], Prague, Czech Republic

Assn. for Sci. Educ. [IO], Hatfield, United Kingdom

Assn. of Sci. Fiction and Fantasy Artists [307], PO Box 15131, Arlington, TX 76015-7311

Assn. of Sci. Museum Directors [10498], c/o Bonnie W. Styles, Sec.-Treas., Illinois State Museum, 502 S Spring St., Springfield, IL 62706-5000, (217)782-7011

Assn. for Sci. Teacher Educ. [9211], c/o Dr. Eugene Wagner, Exec. Sec., 113 Radcliff Dr., Pittsburgh, PA 15237, (412)624-2861

Assn. of Science-Technology Centers [10499], 1025 Vermont Ave. NW, Ste. 500, Washington, DC 20005-6310, (202)783-7200

Assn. for Science, Technology and Innovation - Address unknown since 2006.

Assn. for Sciences and Politics [IO], Innsbruck, Austria

Assn. of the Sci. Medical Societies of Germany [IO], Dusseldorf, Germany

Assn. for the Sci. Stud. of Anomalous Phenomena [IO], London, United Kingdom

Assn. for the Sci. Stud. of Consciousness [8140], PO Box 20393, Greenville, NC 27858

Assn. for the Sci. Stud. of Near Death Phenomena [★7476]

Assn. for the Sci. Stud. of Near Death Phenomena [★IO]

Assn. of Sci. and Tech. Translators of Slovenia [IO], Ljubljana, Slovenia

Assn. Scientifique Internationale du Cafe [★IO]

Assn. Scientifique de l'Industrie Europeenne du Talc [★IO]

Assn. Scientifique Mondiale de Cuniculture [★IO]

Assn. of Scientists and Engineers of the Naval Sea Systems Command - Address unknown since 1995.

Assn. in Scotland for Tech. and Res. into Astronautics [★IO]

Assn. in Scotland for Tech. and Res. Into Astronautics [IO], Glasgow, United Kingdom

Assn. of Scottish Games and Festivals [19348], c/o Roberta M. Goss, Treas., 3000 Walnut Ave., Altoona, PA 16601-1612, (814)942-0077

Assn. for Scottish Literary Stud. [IO], Glasgow, United Kingdom

Assn. of Scottish Visitor Attractions [IO], Stirling, United Kingdom

Assn. des Scouts du Canada [★IO]

Assn. of Sea Grant Prog. Institutions [★7276]

Assn. of Seafood Importers - Defunct.

Assn. of Sealant Applicators [IO], Canvey Island, United Kingdom

Assn. of Second Class Mail Publications [★2455]

Assn. of Second Class Mail Publishers [★2455]

Assn. of Secondary Teachers [★IO]

Assn. of Secondary Teachers Ireland [IO], Dublin, Ireland

Assn. des Secretaires Generaux des Parlements [★IO]

Assn. of Secretaries and Administrative Professionals of Trinidad and Tobago [IO], Port of Spain, Trinidad and Tobago

Assn. of Secretaries Gen. of Parliaments [IO], London, United Kingdom

Assn. Secretaries; Nursery [★5047]

Assn. of Secretaries, Young Men's Christian Associations of North Am. [★13460]

Assn. paritaire pour la sante et la securite du travial Secteur fabrication de produits en metal et de produits electriques [★IO]

Assn. Sectorielle Fabrication d'Equipement de Transport et de Machines [★IO]

Assn. of Securities and Exchange Commn. Alumni [3508], PO Box 5767, Washington, DC 20016, (202)462-1211

Assn. of Security Consultants [IO], Addlestone, United Kingdom

Assn. Senegalaise des Femmes Chefs d'Entreprise [IO], Dakar, Senegal

Assn. of Senior Anthropologists [6412], c/o Paul Doughty, Chm., 1071 NW 21st Terr., Gainesville, FL 32603-1034, (904)392-2031

Assn. of Ser. and Cmpt. Dealers Intl. [897], 131 NW 1st Ave., Delray Beach, FL 33444, (561)266-9016

Assn. des Services aux Etudiants des Universites et Colleges du Canada [★IO]

Assn. for Services Mgt. Intl. [IO], Fort Myers, FL, United States

Assn. for Services Mgt. Intl. [3545], 1342 Colonial Blvd., Ste. 25D, Fort Myers, FL 33907, (239)275-7887

Assn. for Settlements and Housing Activities [IO], New Delhi, India

Assn. of Seventh-Day Adventist Educators - Defunct.

Assn. of Seventh-Day Adventist Engineers and Architects - Defunct.

Assn. of Seventh-Day Adventist Librarians [10339], Columbia Union Coll. Lib., 7600 Flower Ave., Takoma Park, MD 20912-7796, (301)891-4222

Assn. of Seventh Day Pentecostal Assemblies - Defunct.

The Assn. for the Severely Handicapped [★11991]

Assn. for the Sexually Harassed - Address unknown since 1999.

Assn. for Shared Parenting [IO], Dudley, United Kingdom

Assn. of Shareware Professionals [6762], c/o Mr. Richard Holler, Exec. Dir., PO Box 1522, Martinsville, IN 46151, (765)349-4740

Assn. of Shelter Veterinarians [16784], c/o Julie D. Dinnage, DVM, MSPCA, 350 S Huntington Ave., Boston, MA 02130

Assn. of Shelter Veterinarians [IO], Boston, MA, United States

Assn. of Ship Brokers and Agents - U.S.A. [2603], 510 Sylvan Ave., Ste. 201, Englewood Cliffs, NJ 07632, (201)569-2882

The Assn. of Shopping Centres [IO], Singapore, Singapore

Assn. for Short Term Psychotherapy - Defunct.

Assn. of Show and Agricultural Organisations [IO], Redhill, United Kingdom

Assn. for Sickle Cell Anemia - Defunct.

Assn. of SIDS and Infant Mortality Programs [16524], 8280 Greensboro Dr., Ste. 300, McLean, VA 22102-3807, (800)930-7437

Assn. for SIDS Prog. Professionals [★16524]

Assn. of Sign Language Interpreters [IO], Milton Keynes, United Kingdom

Assn. of Significant Cemeteries in Europe [IO], Bologna, Italy

Assn. of Singapore Marine Indus. [IO], Singapore, Singapore

Reference to "IO" in place of a book number signifies that the association may be found in the 45th edition of International Organizations.

Assn. of Sites Advocating Child Protection [11560], 5042 Wilshire Blvd., No. 540, Los Angeles, CA 90036-4305, (323)908-7864

Assn. for Skeptical Enquiry [IO], Ripley, United Kingdom

Assn. for Skilled and Tech. Sciences [8542], c/o Don Eshelby, Exec. Dir., 1931 Mortimer Ct., Boise, ID 83712, (703)777-1740

Assn. of Sleep Disorders Centers [★16418]

Assn. of Slovak Geomorphologists [IO], Bratislava, Slovakia

Assn. of Slovenia Entrepreneurs [IO], Ljubljana, Slovenia

Assn. for Small Business Advancement - Defunct.

Assn. of Small Bus. Development Centers [3606], 8990 Burke Lake Rd., Burke, VA 22015, (703)764-9850

Assn. of Small Foundations [18267], 1720 N St. NW, Washington, DC 20036, (202)580-6560

Assn. of Small Loan Administrators [★5610]

Assn. of Small and Medium Enterprises [IO], Singapore, Singapore

Assn. of Smoked Fish Processors - Address unknown since 2004.

Assn. for Social Advancement [IO], Dhaka, Bangladesh

Assn. of Social Anthropologists of Aoteaora/New Zealand [IO], Auckland, New Zealand

Assn. of Social Anthropologists of the UK and the Commonwealth [IO], Manchester, United Kingdom

Assn. for Social Anthropology in Eastern Oceania [★IO]

Assn. for Social Anthropology in Eastern Oceania [★6413]

Assn. for Social Anthropology in Oceania [6413], c/o Dr. Jocelyn Armstrong, Sec., Dept. of Community Hea., Univ. of Illinois MC-588, 1206 S Fourth St., Champaign, IL 61820, (217)244-1196

Assn. for Social Anthropology in Oceania [IO], Champaign, IL, United States

Assn. of Social and Behavioral Scientists - Address unknown since 1999.

Assn. for Social Economics [6873], c/o Elba K. Brown-Collier, Sec., Educ. Mgt. Info. Systems, 7116 Wandering Oak Rd., Austin, TX 78749, (512)288-5988

Assn. of Social Sci. Researchers [IO], Wellington, New Zealand

Assn. for the Social Sci. Stud. of Jewry [IO], Glassboro, NJ, United States

Assn. for the Social Sci. Stud. of Jewry [8685], c/o Prof. Harriet Hartman, PhD, Pres., Rowan Univ., Dept. of Sociology, 201 Mullica Hill Rd., Glassboro, NJ 08028, (856)256-4500

Assn. of Social Work Boards [13200], 400 S Ridge Pkwy., Ste. B, Culpeper, VA 22701, (540)829-6880

Assn. des Societes Nationales, Europeennes et Mediterraneennes de Gastroenterologie [★IO]

Assn. of Societies for Occupational Safety and Hea. [IO], Clubview, Republic of South Africa

Assn. Sociocyberneering, Inc. [★18632]

Assn. of the Sociological Stud. of Jewry [★8685]

Assn. of the Sociological Stud. of Jewry [★IO]

Assn. for the Sociology of Religion [7661], 618 SW 2nd Ave., Galva, IL 61434-1912, (309)932-2727

Assn. of Software Brokers - Defunct.

Assn. for Software Protection - Address unknown since 1985.

Assn. for Software Testing [6763], c/o Cmpt. Sciences Dept., Florida Inst. of Tech., 150 W Univ. Blvd., Melbourne, FL 32901, (317)709-2419

Assn. for Software Testing and Evaluation - Defunct.

Assn. of Soil and Found. Engineers [★7137]

Assn. for the Soldiers of Israel [IO], Toronto, ON, Canada

Assn. of Solicitors and Investment Managers [IO], Tonbridge, United Kingdom

Assn. Solidaire Defense Droits de Locataires [IO], Cotonou, Benin

Assn. Solidarite Luxembourg-Nicaragua [★IO]

Assn. of Soluble Coffee Mfrs. of the European Union [IO], Amsterdam, Netherlands

Assn. of Solution Oriented Counsellors and Hypnotherapists of Australia [IO], Bendigo, Australia

Assn. of the Sons of Poland [19303], 333 Hackensack St., Carlstadt, NJ 07072, (201)935-2807

Assn. des Sourds du Canada [★IO]

Assn. of South African Quantity Surveyors [IO], Halfway House, Republic of South Africa

Assn. of South African Women in Sci. and Engg. [IO], Rhodes Gift, Republic of South Africa

Assn. of South East Asian Stud. in the UK [IO], London, United Kingdom

Assn. of Southeast Asian Institutions of Higher Learning [IO], Manila, Philippines

Assn. of Southern Baptist Campus Ministers [19474], c/o BCM at Louisiana State Univ., PO Box 25118, Baton Rouge, LA 70894, (225)343-0408

Assn. of Southern Baptist Colleges and Schools [★9276]

Assn. pour le Soutien et l'Appui a la Femme Entrepreneur [IO], Douala, Cameroon

Assn. of Space Explorers - U.S.A. [IO], Houston, TX, United States

Assn. of Space Explorers - U.S.A. [6371], 1150 Gemini Ave., Houston, TX 77058, (281)280-8172

Assn. of Spanish Costume Jewelry Mfrs. and Exporters [IO], Mahon, Spain

Assn. of Spanish Pulp and Paper Manufactures [IO], Madrid, Spain

Assn. of Spanish Tobacconists [IO], Madrid, Spain

Assn. of Speakers Clubs [IO], Solihull, United Kingdom

Assn. for Special Children [★12562]

Assn. for Specialist Fire Protection [IO], Aldershot, United Kingdom

Assn. of Specialists in Cleaning and Restoration [★2475]

Assn. for Specialists in Gp. Work [11820], c/o Janice Delucia-Waack, Pres., Univ. of Buffalo, SUNY, Counseling, School and Educational Psychology, 409 Baldy Hall, Buffalo, NY 14260, (716)645-2484

Assn. of Specialized and Cooperative Lib. Agencies [10340], c/o Amer. Lib. Assn., 50 E Huron St., Chicago, IL 60611, (312)280-4395

Assn. of Specialized Film Exhibitors - Defunct.

Assn. of Specialized and Professional Accreditors [1174], c/o Cynthia A. Davenport, Exec. Dir., 1020 W Byron St., Ste. 8G, Chicago, IL 60613-2987, (773)525-2160

Assn. of Specialty Cut Flower Growers [1491], PO Box 268, Oberlin, OH 44074, (440)774-2887

Assn. of Specialty Professors [8587], c/o Alliance for Academic Internal Medicine, 2501 M St. NW, Ste. 550, Washington, DC 20037-1325, (202)861-9351

Assn. of Specialty Professors [IO], Washington, DC, United States

Assn. of Speech and Drama - Address unknown since 2001.

Assn. for Spina Bifida and Hydrocephalus [IO], Peterborough, United Kingdom

Assn. for Spirit at Work [IO], East Haven, CT, United States

Assn. for Spirit at Work [★20575]

Assn. for Spiritual Awareness - Address unknown since 2007.

Assn. for Spiritual, Ethical and Religious Values in Counseling [8166], PO Box 161250, Orlando, FL 32816, (800)347-6647

Assn. Sportive de Monaco - Aikido [IO], Monaco, Monaco

Assn. of Sports Information Directors - Address unknown since 1995.

Assn. of Sports Journalists [IO], Paris, France

Assn. of Sports Medicine of the Balkans [IO], Bucharest, Romania

Assn. of Sports Medicine of Ghana [IO], Accra, Ghana

Assn. of Sports Museums and Halls of Fame [★23827]

Assn. des Sports des Sourds du Canada [★IO]

Assn. of Sprocket Chain Mfrs. - Defunct.

Assn. of Sri-Lankans in Am. [19394], 2 E Glen Rd., Denville, NJ 07834, (973)627-7855

Assn. of Staff Physician Recruiters [15995], 1711 W County Rd. B, Ste. 300N, Roseville, MN 55113, (800)830-2777

Association of Staff Physician Recruiters [IO], Roseville, MN, United States

Assn. of Stained Glass Lamp Artists [2392], 5070 Cromwell Dr. NW, Gig Harbor, WA 98335

Assn. for Stamp Exhibitions - Defunct.

Assn. of State Baptist Papers [19475], c/o Alabama Baptist Newspaper, 3310 Independence Dr., Birmingham, AL 35209, (205)870-4720

Assn. of State Colleges and Universities [★8096]

Assn. of State Correctional Administrators [11858], 213 Court St., Ste. 606, Middletown, CT 06457, (860)704-6410

Assn. of State Dam Safety Officials [6249], 450 Old Vine St., Lexington, KY 40507-1544, (859)257-5140

Assn. of State Democratic Chairmen [★17399]

Assn. of State Democratic Chairs [17399], 430 S Capitol St. SE, Washington, DC 20003, (202)479-5121

Assn. of State Drinking Water Administrators [6211], 1025 Connecticut Ave. NW, Ste. 903, Washington, DC 20036, (202)293-7655

Assn. of State Energy Res. and Tech. Transfer Institutions [6945], c/o Sherry Benzmiller, Admin., 455 Sci. Dr., Ste. 200, Madison, WI 53711, (608)238-4601

Assn. of State Floodplain Managers [4362], 2809 Fish Hatchery Rd., Ste. 204, Madison, WI 53713, (608)274-0123

Assn. of State and Interstate Water Pollution Control Administrators [5688], 1221 Connecticut Ave. NW, 2nd Fl., Washington, DC 20036, (202)756-0600

Assn. of State Labor Relations Agencies - Address unknown since 1995.

Assn. of State Lib. Agencies [★10340]

Assn. of State Planning and Development Agencies [★5592]

Assn. of State and Provincial Psychology Boards [16144], PO Box 241245, Montgomery, AL 36124-1245, (334)832-4580

Assn. of State and Provincial Psychology Boards [IO], Montgomery, AL, United States

Assn. of State and Provincial Safety Officials - Address unknown since 1995.

Assn. of State Public Hea. Veterinarians [★16747]

Assn. of State Sanitary Boards [★16811]

Assn. of State Supervisors of Mathematics [8822], c/o Diane Schaefer, Pres., Rhode Island Dept. of Educ., 225 Westminster St., Providence, RI 02903-3400, (401)222-8436

Assn. of State and Territorial Chronic Disease Program Directors - Defunct.

Assn. of State and Territorial Dental Directors [14146], 105 Westerly Rd., New Bern, NC 28560, (252)637-6333

Assn. of State and Territorial Directors of Hea. Promotion and Public Hea. Educ. [★6215]

Assn. of State and Territorial Directors of Local Health Services - Defunct.

Assn. of State and Territorial Directors of Nursing - Address unknown since 2002.

Assn. of State and Territorial Directors of Public Hea. Educ. [★6215]

Assn. of State and Territorial Hea. Officers [★6212]

Assn. of State and Territorial Hea. Officials [6212], 2231 Crystal Dr., Ste. 450, Arlington, VA 22202, (202)371-9090

Assn. of State and Territorial Local Hea. Liaison Officials [6213], Empire State Plz., Corning Tower Bldg., Rm. 821, Albany, NY 12237, (518)473-4223

Assn. of State and Territorial Maternal and Child Hea. and Crippled Children's Directors [★13947]

Assn. of State and Territorial Public Health Nutrition Directors - Defunct.

Assn. of State and Territorial Public Hea. Veterinarians [★16747]

Assn. of State and Territorial Solid Waste Mgt. Officials [6353], 444 N Capitol St. NW, Ste. 315, Washington, DC 20001, (202)624-5828

Assn. of State Wetland Managers [4363], 2 Basin Rd., Windham, ME 04062, (207)892-3399

Assn. of Statisticians of Amer. Religious Bodies - Address unknown since 2000.

Assn. of Steam Boiler, Pressure Vessel and Piping Manufacturers [IO], Dusseldorf, Germany

Assn. of Steel Distributors [2700], 401 N Michigan Ave., Chicago, IL 60611, (312)644-6610

Assn. of Steel and Metal Forming Indus. [IO], Hagen, Germany

A star before a book entry number signifies that the name is not listed separately, but is mentioned within the entry.

Assn. of Sterilizer and Disinfector Equip. Mfrs. Assn. [★IO]

Assn. for Stimulating Know How [IO], Gurgaon, India

Assn. of Stock Exchange Firms [★3523]

Assn. of Storage and Retrieval Professionals; ISDA - [2847]

Assn. Strabismologique Europeene [★IO]

Assn. for Strategic Alliance Professionals [IO], Wellesley, MA, United States

Assn. for Strategic Alliance Professionals [2521], 31 Washington St., Wellesley, MA 02481, (781)972-1346

Assn. for Strategic Planning [3042], 12021 Wilshire Blvd., Ste. 286, Los Angeles, CA 90025-1200, (877)816-2080

Assn. for Strengthening Agricultural Res. in Eastern and Central Africa [IO], Entebbe, Uganda

Assn. of Stress Consultants [IO], Holsworthy, United Kingdom

Assn. of Structural Draftsmen of America - Address unknown since 1995.

Assn. for Student Counselling [★IO]

Assn. of Student Intl. Law Societies [★IO]

Assn. of Student Intl. Law Societies [★5868]

Assn. of Student Loan Administrators; Natl. [8432]

Assn. of Student and Professional Italian-Americans [19160], 115 Charles St., No. 4, New York, NY 10014, (212)242-3215

Assn. for Student Teaching [★9212]

Assn. for Stud. in the Conservation of Historic Buildings [IO], London, United Kingdom

Assn. for the Stud. of Abortion [★11223]

Assn. for the Study and Advancement of Supportive Values - Address unknown since 2001.

Assn. for the Stud. of African-American Life and History [9356], CB Powell Bldg., Howard Univ., 525 Bryant St., Ste. C142, Washington, DC 20059, (202)865-0053

Assn. for the Stud. of Afro-American Life and History [★9356]

Assn. for the Stud. of Amer. Indian Literatures [10734], c/o Siobhan Senier, Univ. of New Hampshire, Dept. of English, Hamilton Smith Hall, 95 Main St., Durham, NH 03824

Assn. for the Stud. of Animal Behaviour [IO], Cambridge, United Kingdom

Assn. for the Stud. of Asthma and Allied Conditions [★13592]

Assn. for the Stud. of Australian Literature [IO], Sydney, Australia

Assn. for the Stud. of Classical African Civilizations [9349], 2274 W 20th St., Los Angeles, CA 90018, (323)730-1155

Assn. for the Stud. of Community Org. [★13206]

Assn. for the Stud. of the Cuban Economy [8214], PO Box 28267, Washington, DC 20038-8267

Assn. for the Study of Dada and Surrealism - Address unknown since 1999.

Assn. for the Stud. of Dreams [★16426]

Assn. for the Study of European Problems - Address unknown since 1995.

Assn. for the Stud. of Food and Soc. [7090], c/o Jonathan Deutsch, Sec., Kingsborough Community Coll., CUNY, Dept. of Tourism and Hospitality (TOU), 2002 Oriental Blvd., Brooklyn, NY 11235

Assn. for the Stud. of Free Institutions [8481], c/o Carson Holloway, Exec. Dir., Univ. of Nebraska at Omaha, Dept. of Political Sci., 275 Arts and Sciences Hall, Omaha, NE 68182, (402)554-4862

Assn. for the Stud. of German Politics [IO], Brighton, United Kingdom

Assn. for the Study of the Grants Economy - Address unknown since 1995.

Assn. for the Stud. of Higher Educ. [8482], Michigan State Univ., 424 Erickson Hall, East Lansing, MI 48824, (517)432-8805

Assn. for Stud. of Internal Secretions [★14355]

Assn. for the Stud. of Intl. Relations [★IO]

Assn. for the Study of Jewish Languages - Address unknown since 2001.

Assn. for Study of Karma - Address unknown since 2001.

Assn. for the Study of Literature and Alchemy - Address unknown since 1989.

Assn. for the Stud. of Literature and Env. [10414], c/o Amy McIntyre, Managing Dir., PO Box 502, Keene, NH 03431, (603)357-7411

Assn. for the Study of Man-Environment Relations - Defunct.

Assn. for the Stud. of Medical Educ. [IO], Edinburgh, United Kingdom

Assn. for the Stud. of Modern and Contemporary France [IO], Portsmouth, United Kingdom

Assn. for the Stud. of Negro Life and History [★9356]

Assn. for the Stud. of Obesity [IO], Woodford Green, United Kingdom

Assn. for the Stud. of Peak Oil and Gas - USA [7461], PO Box 371438, Denver, CO 80237, (303)759-1998

Assn. for the Stud. of Persianate Societies [8668], c/o Habib Borjian, Sec.-Treas., 118-18 Union Tpke., Apt. 18E, Kew Gardens, NY 11415

The Assn. for the Stud. of Play [10858], c/o Dana Gross, Sec., St. Olaf Coll., 1520 St. Olaf Ave., Northfield, MN 55057-1098, (507)646-3624

Assn. for the Stud. and Preservation of Roman Mosaics [IO], Aldershot, United Kingdom

Assn. for the Stud. of Soviet-Type Economies [★6870]

Assn. for the Stud. of Travel in Egypt and the Near East [IO], Cambridge, United Kingdom

Assn. for the Stud. of the World Refugee Problem [IO], Hochberg, Germany

Assn. for the Stud. of the Worldwide African Diaspora [7929], c/o Prof. Barbara Krauthamer, Treas., NYU Dept. of History, 53 Washington Sq. S, 7th Fl., New York, NY 10012-1018

Assn. of Subscription Agents and Intermediaries [IO], High Wycombe, United Kingdom

Assn. of Sugar Cane Growers of Colombia [IO], Bogota, Colombia

Assn. of Sugar Producers of Puerto Rico - Defunct.

Assn. Suisse des Annonceurs [★IO]

Assn. Suisse pour la Cooperation Internationale [★IO]

Assn. Suisse Des Locataires [★IO]

Assn. Suisse Des Remmes Diplomees Des Universites [IO], Bivio, Switzerland

Assn. Suisse d'Etude de la Concurrence [IO], Zurich, Switzerland

Assn. Suisse des Femmes Diplomees des Universites [★IO]

Assn. Suisse de Golf [★IO]

Assn. Suisse des Insurance et Risk Managers [★IO]

Assn. Suisse Invention Romande [★IO]

Assn. Suisse des Musiciens [★IO]

Assn. Suisse des Proprietaires Yngling [IO], Oberkulm, Switzerland

Assn. Suisse de Recherche Operationnelle [IO], Basel, Switzerland

Assn. de la Suisse Romande et Italienne Contre les Myopathies [IO], Aubonne, Switzerland

Assn. of Summer Olympic Intl. Federations [IO], Lausanne, Switzerland

Assn. of Summer Sessions Deans and Directors [★9199]

Assn. of Superannuation Funds of Australia [IO], Sydney, Australia

Assn. of Superintendents of Buildings and Grounds of Universities and Colleges [★IO]

Assn. of Superintendents of Buildings and Grounds of Universities and Colleges [★8333]

Assn. of Superintendents and Principals of Amer. Schools for the Deaf [★14749]

Assn. for Supervision and Curriculum Development [8178], 1703 N Beauregard St., Alexandria, VA 22311-1714, (703)578-9600

Assn. for Supervision and Curriculum Development [IO], Alexandria, VA, United States

Assn. of Supervisors of Midwives [IO], Great Yarmouth, United Kingdom

Assn. of Suppliers to the British Clothing Indus. [IO], Halifax, United Kingdom

Assn. of Suppliers of Electronic Instruments and Components [IO], Helsinki, Finland

Assn. of Suppliers of Household Appliances in the Netherlands [IO], Zoetermeer, Netherlands

Assn. of Suppliers to the Paper Indus. [2003], 15 Tech. Pkwy. S, Ste. 500, Norcross, GA 30092, (770)209-7521

Assn. for Suppliers of Printing and Publishing and Converting Technologies [★1782]

Assn. for Suppliers of Printing, Publishing and Converting Technologies; NPES - The [1782]

Assn. of Support Professionals [3546], 122 Barnard Ave., Watertown, MA 02472-3414, (617)924-3944

Association of Support Professionals [IO], Watertown, MA, United States

Assn. for Support of Social and Community Integration [IO], Porto, Portugal

Assn. of Surf Angling Clubs - Address unknown since 1990.

Assn. of Surfing Professionals [23877], PO Box 309, Huntington Beach, CA 92648, (714)536-3500

Assn. of Surgeons of Great Britain and Ireland [IO], London, United Kingdom

Assn. for Surgical Educ. [IO], Springfield, IL, United States

Assn. for Surgical Educ. [8856], SIU School of Medicine, Dept. of Surgery, PO Box 19655, Springfield, IL 62794-9655, (217)545-3835

Assn. of Surgical Technologists [15133], 6 W Dry Creek Cir., Ste. 200, Littleton, CO 80120, (303)694-9130

Assn. for the Sustainable Use and Recovery of Resources in Europe [IO], Brussels, Belgium

Assn. of Swedish Agricultural Producers [★IO]

Assn. of Swedish Bakeries [IO], Stockholm, Sweden

Assn. of Swedish Engg. Indus. [IO], Stockholm, Sweden

Assn. of Swedish-Language Authors in Finland [★IO]

Assn. of Swedish Lighting Designers [IO], Stockholm, Sweden

Assn. of Swedish Municipalities with Nuclear Reactors [IO], Malmo, Sweden

Assn. of Swiss Advt. and Communications Agencies [★IO]

Assn. of Swiss Advt. and Communications Agencies BSW [IO], Zurich, Switzerland

Association for Symbolic Logic [IO], Poughkeepsie, NY, United States

Assn. for Symbolic Logic [7287], Vassar Coll., 124 Raymond Ave., PO Box 742, Poughkeepsie, NY 12604, (845)437-7080

Assn. of Synthetic Yarn Mfrs. [★3774]

Assn. of Systematic Kinesiology [IO], East Sussex, United Kingdom

Assn. of Systematics Collections [★6590]

Assn. for Systems Mgt. - Address unknown since 2001.

Assn. canadienne de Taekwondo WTF [★IO]

Assn. of Talent Agents [172], 9255 Sunset Blvd., Ste. 930, Los Angeles, CA 90069, (310)274-0628

Assn. of Tank and Cistern Mfrs. [IO], Chepstow, United Kingdom

Assn. of Tankcleaning Companies in the Netherlands [IO], The Hague, Netherlands

Assn. Tchadienne de lutte contre le Diabete [★IO]

Assn. Tchadienne de Medecine du Sport [IO], N'Djamena, Chad

Assn. for Teacher Educ. in Europe [IO], Brussels, Belgium

Assn. of Teacher Educators [9212], PO Box 793, Manassas, VA 20113, (703)331-0911

Assn. of Teachers Agencies of the South [★1275]

Assn. of Teachers of Educ. Institutions [★8096]

Assn. of Teachers of English in Negro Colleges [★8729]

Assn. of Teachers of Japanese [8682], 240 Humanities Bldg., 279 UCB, Boulder, CO 80309-0279, (303)492-5487

Assn. of Teachers of Latin Amer. Stud. [10309], 58th Ave., Level 1, Ste. 252, Little Neck, NY 11362, (718)428-1237

Assn. of Teachers of Latin Amer. Stud. [IO], Little Neck, NY, United States

Assn. of Teachers and Lecturers [IO], London, United Kingdom

Assn. of Teachers of Lipreading to Adults [IO], Colchester, United Kingdom

Assn. of Teachers of Mathematics [IO], Derby, United Kingdom

Assn. of Teachers of Preventive Medicine [★16054]

Assn. of Teachers of Singing [IO], Burton-On-Trent, United Kingdom

Assn. of Teachers of Tech. Writing [9332], c/o Journals Subscription Dept., LEA, Inc., 10 Indus. Ave., Mahwah, NJ 07430

Reference to "IO" in place of a book number signifies that the association may be found in the 45th edition of International Organizations.

Assn. of Teachers Training Staff [★IO]

Assn. for Teaching Aids in Mathematics [★IO]

Assn. for Teaching Psychology [IO], Leicester, United Kingdom

Assn. for the Teaching of the Social Sciences [IO], Manchester, United Kingdom

Assn. of Tech. Employees [★24024]

Assn. of Tech. Lightning and Access Specialists [IO], Nottingham, United Kingdom

Assn. of Tech. Personnel in Ophthalmology [15674], 2025 Woodlane Dr., St. Paul, MN 55125-2998, (651)731-7239

Assn. of Technical Professionals - Defunct.

Assn. of Tech. and Supervisory Professionals [5737], c/o Pete Bridgeman, Natl. Sec., 436 Park St. NE, Vienna, VA 22180

Assn. Technique Canadienne du Bitume [★IO]

Assn. Technique Internationale des Bois Tropicaux [★IO]

Assn. Technique de l'Importation Charbonniere - Address unknown since 2005.

Assn. for Tech. in Music Instruction [8905], 312 E Pine St., Missoula, MT 59802, (406)721-1152

Assn. for Telecommunication Professionals in Higher Educ; ACUTA: The [★8548]

Assn. of Telehealth Ser. Providers [15160], 4702 SW Scholls Ferry Rd., No. 400, Portland, OR 97225-2008, (503)922-0988

Assn. of Telemedicine Ser. Providers [★15160]

Assn. of Telemessaging Services Intl. [★3735]

Assn. of Telemessaging Services Intl. [★IO]

Assn. of Telephone Answering Services - Defunct.

Assn. of Telephone Messaging Suppliers - Defunct.

Assn. of TeleServices Intl. [3735], 12 Acad. Ave., Atkinson, NH 03811, (866)896-ATSI

Assn. of TeleServices Intl. [IO], Atkinson, NH, United States

Assn. for Temperate Agroforestry [4119], 203 ABNR Bldg., Univ. of Missouri, Columbia, MO 65211, (573)884-3216

Assn. of Temporary and Interim Executive Secretaries [★IO]

Assn. of Tenants - BIHUSS-Saravejo [IO], Sarajevo, Bosnia-Hercegovina

Assn. of Tenants of the Slovak Republic [IO], Zilina, Slovakia

Assn. of Tenants of Slovenia [IO], Ljubljana, Slovenia

Assn. of Tennis Professionals - Defunct.

Assn. of Tequila Producers - Defunct.

Assn. for Terminology and Knowledge Transfer [IO], Frederiksberg, Denmark

Assn. of Terrestrial Magnetism and Electricity [★IO]

Assn. for Tertiary Educ. Mgt. [IO], O'Connor, Australia

Assn. of Test Publishers [3210], 1201 Pennsylvania Ave. NW, Ste. 900, Washington, DC 20004, (866)240-7909

Assn. of Textile and Footwear Importers and Wholesalers [IO], Helsinki, Finland

Assn. of Textile Retailers - Netherlands [IO], Doorn, Netherlands

Assn. for Textual Scholarship in Art History [IO], Boston, MA, United States

Assn. for Textual Scholarship in Art History [9432], c/o Dr. Liana De Girolami Cheney, Pres., 112 Charles St., Beacon Hill, Boston, MA 02114, (617)367-1679

Assn. of Thai Cmpt. Indus. [IO], Bangkok, Thailand

Assn. of Thai Professionals in Am. and Canada [19406], 14 Doric Ave., Parsippany, NJ 07054, (973)299-7992

Assn. of Thai Textile Bleaching, Dyeing, Printing and Finishing Indus. [IO], Bangkok, Thailand

Assn. for The Advancement of Social Potential [★16480]

Assn. of Theatre Benefit Agents - Defunct.

Assn. for Theatre in Higher Educ. [9262], PO Box 1290, Boulder, CO 80306-1290, (303)530-2167

Assn. of Theatre Movement Educators [9263], c/o Annette Thornton, Sec., Lawrence Univ., Dept. of Theatre Arts, PO Box 599, Appleton, WI 54912-0599

Association of Theatre Movement Educators [IO], Newark, DE, United States

Assn. of Theatre Screen Advertising Companies - Defunct.

Assn. of Theatrical Press Agents and Managers [24154], 1560 Broadway, Ste. 700, New York, NY 10036-2501, (212)719-3666

Assn. for Theological Educ. in South East Asia [IO], Manila, Philippines

Assn. of Theological Schools in South East Asia [★IO]

Assn. of Theological Schools in the U.S. and Canada [IO], Pittsburgh, PA, United States

Assn. of Theological Schools in the U.S. and Canada [9270], 10 Summit Park Dr., Pittsburgh, PA 15275-1103, (412)788-6505

Assn. of Therapeutic Communities [IO], Cheltenham, United Kingdom

Assn. for Therapeutic Eurythmy in North Am. [IO], Chicago, IL, United States

Assn. for Therapeutic Eurythmy in North Am. [16608], c/o Susanne Zipperlen, 2110 W Arthur Ave., Apt. 2, Chicago, IL 60645, (773)761-0833

Assn. for Therapeutic Philosophy [IO], Swindon, United Kingdom

Assn. on Third World Affairs [IO], Washington, DC, United States

Assn. on Third World Affairs [17829], c/o Dr. Lorna Hahn, Exec. Dir., 1717 K St. NW, Ste. 600, Washington, DC 20036, (202)973-0157

Assn. of Third World Stud. [17830], c/o Dr. William D. Pederson, Exec. Dir., Intl. Lincoln Center for Amer. Stud., Louisiana State Univ., Shreveport, LA 71115-2301, (318)797-5349

Assn. of Third World Stud. [IO], Shreveport, LA, United States

Assn. of Tile, Terrazzo, Marble Contractors and Affiliates [★1053]

Assn. of Tongan Univ. Women [IO], Nuku'alofa, Tonga

Assn. of Tongue Depressors - Defunct.

Assn. of Tour Operators and Travel Agents of the Czech Republic [IO], Prague, Czech Republic

Assn. of Tourist Hotels of the Republic of Argentina [IO], Buenos Aires, Argentina

Assn. of Town Centre Mgt. [IO], London, United Kingdom

Assn. of Track and Field Statisticians [IO], Warrandyte, Australia

Assn. of Track and Structures Suppliers [★IO]

Assn. of Track and Structures Suppliers [★3289]

Assn. of Trade Fair and Exhibition Organisers of the Czech Republic [IO], Prague, Czech Republic

Assn. of Trade and Forfaiting in the Americas [IO], New York, NY, United States

Assn. of Trade and Forfaiting in the Americas [1404], c/o Gregory J. Bernardi, Pres./Treas., 1180 Ave. of the Americas, Ste. 2020, New York, NY 10022, (212)377-2012

Assn. of Traders and Bottlers of Wines and Spirits from Northern Portugal [IO], Porto, Portugal

Assn. des Traducteurs et Interpretes Judiciaires [★IO]

Assn. des Traducteurs et Interpretes de l'Alberta [★IO]

Assn. des Traducteurs et Traductrices Literariness du Canada [★IO]

Assn. of Training and Employment Professionals - Defunct.

Assn. du Traite Atlantique [★IO]

Assn. pour le Traitement Automatique des Langues [★IO]

Assn. de la Transformation Laitiere Francaise [★IO]

Assn. des Transitaires Internationaux Canadiens [★IO]

Assn. of Translation Companies [IO], London, United Kingdom

Assn. of Translators and Interpreters of Alberta [IO], Edmonton, AB, Canada

Assn. for Transpersonal Psychology [10170], PO Box 50187, Palo Alto, CA 94303, (650)424-8764

Assn. du Transport Aerien Intl. [★IO]

Assn. for Trans. Law, Logistics and Policy [★6316]

Assn. of Trans. Law Professionals [6316], c/o Lauren Michalski, Exec. Dir., PO Box 5407, Annapolis, MD 21403-0702, (410)268-1311

Assn. of Trans. Practitioners [★6316]

Assn. des Transports du Canada [★IO]

Assn. of Traumatic Stress Specialists [IO], Phillips, ME, United States

Assn. of Traumatic Stress Specialists [11821], PO Box 246, Phillips, ME 04966-0246, (207)639-2433

Assn. of Travel Agencies of Czech Republic [IO], Prague, Czech Republic

Assn. of Travel Marketing Executives [3912], c/o Kristin Zern, Exec. Dir., 331 W 57th St., Ste. 482, New York, NY 10019, (212)765-0625

Assn. for the Treatment of Sexual Abusers [6529], 4900 SW Griffith Dr., Ste. 274, Beaverton, OR 97005-4732, (503)643-1023

Assn. for the Treatment of Tobacco Use and Dependence [16653], c/o Ken Wassum, Pres., Free & Clear, Inc., 999 3rd Ave., Ste. 2100, Seattle, WA 98104, (206)876-2198

Assn. of Trial Behavior Consultants [★6524]

Assn. of Trial Lawyers of Am. [★6328]

Assn. of Trinidad and Tobago Insurance Companies [IO], Port of Spain, Trinidad and Tobago

Assn. for Tropical Biology [★6570]

Assn. for Tropical Biology and Conservation [6570], c/o W. John Kress, Exec. Dir., PO Box 37012, Washington, DC 20013-7012, (202)633-0920

Assn. for Tropical Lepidoptera [7058], c/o Peter J. Eliazar, Sec.-Treas., PO Box 141210, Gainesville, FL 32614-1210, (352)846-2000

Assn. Tunisienne de Mecanique des Sols [IO], Tunis, Tunisia

Assn. of Turkish Consulting Engineers and Architects [IO], Ankara, Turkey

Assn. for Two-Child Families - Defunct.

Assn. of Uganda Women Medical Doctors [IO], Kampala, Uganda

Assn. of Ukrainian Doctors [IO], Odessa, Ukraine

Assn. of Ukrainian Sports Clubs in North America - Address unknown since 2007.

Assn. of Umbrella Mfrs. and Suppliers - Defunct.

Assn. of Unclaimed Property Administrators [★6186]

Assn. for the Understanding of Man - Defunct.

Assn. des anciens fonctionnaires UNESCO [★IO]

Assn. of Union Constructors; NEA - The [1056]

Assn. for Union Democracy [24113], 104 Montgomery St., Brooklyn, NY 11225, (718)564-1114

Assn. of Unit Trusts and Investment Funds [★IO]

Assn. to Unite the Democracies [★IO]

Assn. to Unite the Democracies [★18308]

Assn. of United Contractors of America - Defunct.

Assn. of United Kingdom Media Librarians [IO], London, United Kingdom

Assn. of the U.S. Army [6071], 2425 Wilson Blvd., Arlington, VA 22201, (703)841-4300

Assn. of U.S. Chess Journalists [★3104]

Assn. of U.S. Members of the Intl. Inst. of Space Law [6372]

Assn. of U.S. Night Vision Mfrs. - Address unknown since 1999.

Assn. of U.S. Univ. Directors of Intl. Agricultural Programs [★7935]

Assn. of U.S. Univ. Directors of Intl. Agricultural Programs [★IO]

Assn. of United Ukrainian Canadians [IO], Edmonton, AB, Canada

Assn. of Unity Churches [19845], PO Box 610, Lee's Summit, MO 64063, (816)524-7414

Assn. of Unity Churches Canada [IO], Kitchener, ON, Canada

Assn. of Universalist Women [★20604]

Assn. Universelle d'Aviculture Scientifique [★IO]

Assn. Universitaire Canadienne d'Etudes Nordiques [★IO]

Assn. Universitaire Interamericaine [★IO]

Assn. des Universites Africaines [★IO]

Assn. of Universities of Asia and the Pacific [IO], Nakhon Ratchasima, Thailand

Assn. of Universities of the British Commonwealth [★IO]

Assn. of Universities and Colleges of Canada [IO], Ottawa, ON, Canada

Assn. of Universities for Res. in Astronomy [6501], 1212 New York Ave. NW, Ste. 450, Washington, DC 20005, (202)483-2101

Assn. of Univ. Administrators [IO], Manchester, United Kingdom

A star before a book entry number signifies that the name is not listed separately, but is mentioned within the entry.

Assn. of Univ. Affiliated Facilities [★12563]

Assn. of Univ. Anesthesiologists [13680], 520 N Northwest Hwy., Park Ridge, IL 60068-2573, (847)825-5586

Assn. of Univ. Anesthetists [★13680]

Assn. of Univ. Architects [6472], 1277 Univ. of Oregon, Eugene, OR 97403-1277, (541)346-3537

Assn. for Univ. Business and Economic Res. - Defunct.

Assn. of Univ. Centers on Disabilities [12563], 1010 Wayne Ave., Ste. 920, Silver Spring, MD 20910, (301)588-8252

Assn. of Univ. and Coll. Counseling Center Directors [8167], c/o Charles O. Davidshofer, PhD, Treas., Colorado State Univ., 4112 Attleboro Ct., Fort Collins, CO 80525, (970)491-0745

Assn. for Univ. and Coll. Counseling Center Directors [IO], Fort Collins, CO, United States

Assn. for Univ. and Coll. Counselling [★IO]

Assn. of Univ. and Coll. Lecturers [★IO]

Assn. of Univ. Environmental Health/Sciences Centers - Defunct.

Assn. of Univ. Evening Colleges [★8148]

Assn. of Univ. Fisheries and Wildlife Prog. Administrators [★8391]

Assn. of Univ. Interior Designers [2252], c/o Jo Morrisson, Second VP/Membership Chair, WMU Campus Architecture and Design, 1201 Oliver St., Kalamazoo, MI 49008-5313

Assn. of Univ. Leaders for a Sustainable Future [8483], 2100 L St. NW, Washington, DC 20037, (202)778-6133

Assn. of Univ. Leaders for a Sustainable Future [IO], Washington, DC, United States

Assn. of Univ. Libraries, the Royal Lib., and the Lib. of the Royal Netherlands Acad. of Sciences [★IO]

Assn. of Univ. Professors of French and Heads of Departments of French in Universities in the UK and Ireland [IO], Durham, United Kingdom

Assn. of Univ. Professors of French and Heads of French Departments [★IO]

Assn. of Univ. Professors of Ophthalmology [15675], PO Box 420369, San Francisco, CA 94142-0369, (415)561-8548

Assn. of Univ. Programs in Hea. Admin. [8857], 2000 N 14th St., Ste. 780, Arlington, VA 22201, (703)894-0940

Assn. of Univ. Programs in Hosp. Admin. [★8857]

Assn. of Univ. Radiologic Technologists [★9096]

Assn. of Univ. Radiologists [16286], 820 Jorie Blvd., Oak Brook, IL 60523, (630)368-3730

Assn. of Univ. Related Res. Parks [★9054]

Assn. of Univ. Res. and Indus. Links [IO], Belfast, United Kingdom

Assn. of Univ. and Res. Libraries [★IO]

Assn. of Univ. Res. Parks [9054], 6262 Swan Rd., Ste. 170, Tucson, AZ 85718, (520)529-2521

Assn. of Univ. Summer Sessions [9199], c/o Dr. Leslie J. Coyne, Recorder, Maxwell Hall 222, Indiana Univ., 750 E Kirkwood Ave., Bloomington, IN 47405, (812)855-5048

Assn. of Univ. Teachers - London and Univ. and Coll. Lecturers' Union [★IO]

Assn. of Univ. Teachers - Scotland [IO], Edinburgh, United Kingdom

Assn. of Univ. Tech. Managers [5838], 60 Revere Dr., Ste. 500, Northbrook, IL 60062, (847)559-0846

Assn. for Unmanned Vehicle Systems [★7580]

Assn. for Unmanned Vehicle Systems [★IO]

Association for Unmanned Vehicle Systems International [IO], Arlington, VA, United States

Assn. for Unmanned Vehicle Systems Intl. [7580], 2700 S Quincy St., Ste. 400, Arlington, VA 22206, (703)845-9671

Assn. of Upper Gastrointestinal Surgeons [IO], London, United Kingdom

Assn. of Upper Level Colleges and Universities [★8096]

Assn. of Uptown Converters - Address unknown since 1995.

Assn. of Urban Sisters - Defunct.

Assn. of Urban Universities - Defunct.

Assn. of Users of Res. Agencies [IO], Harpenden, United Kingdom

Assn. of Vacation Home Rental Managers [★3344]

Assn. for Vaccine Damaged Children [IO], Coquitlam, BC, Canada

Assn. of Vacuum Equip. Mfrs. [★IO]

Assn. of Vacuum Equip. Mfrs. [★2006]

Assn. of Vacuum Equip. Mfrs. Intl. [★2006]

Assn. of Vacuum Equip. Mfrs. Intl. [★IO]

Assn. of Valuers of Licensed Property [IO], Sudbury, United Kingdom

Assn. for Vascular Access [16722], 134 Fairmont St., Ste. B, Clinton, MS 39056, (601)924-2233

Assn. of Vascular and Interventional Radiographers [16723], 12100 Sunset Hills Rd., Ste. 130, Reston, VA 20190, (703)234-4055

Assn. of Vegetarian Dietitians and Nutrition Educators - Defunct.

Assn. of Venture Capital Clubs - Defunct.

Assn. of Venture Founders - Defunct.

Assn. for Vertical Market Computing - Defunct.

Assn. of Veterans Affairs Anesthesiologists [13681], c/o Prof. Martin J. London, MD, Pres., 4150 Clement St., San Francisco, CA 94121

Assn. of Veterans Affairs Ophthalmologists [15676], PO Box 193940, San Francisco, CA 94119-3940, (415)561-8523

Assn. of Veterans Affairs Ophthalmologists [IO], San Francisco, CA, United States

Assn. of Veterinarians for Animal Rights [11368], PO Box 208, Davis, CA 95617-0208, (530)759-8106

Assn. of Veterinary Anaesthetists [IO], Hatfield, United Kingdom

Assn. of Veterinary Anaesthetists of Great Britain and Ireland [★IO]

Assn. of Veterinary and Crop Protection Associations of Southern Africa [IO], Halfway House, Republic of South Africa

Assn. of Veterinary Hematology and Transfusion Medicine [16785], c/o Dr. Larry DeLuca, Exec. Dir., 2509 N Campbell Ave., No. 304, Tucson, AZ 85719-3304

Assn. for Veterinary Teaching and Res. Work [IO], Taunton, United Kingdom

Assn. of Veterinary Technician Educators [9294], c/o Ronald J. Epps, Sec.-Treas., McLennan Community Coll., 1400 Coll. Dr., Waco, TX 76708

Assn. for Victim-Offender Mediation [★18780]

Assn. for Victim-Offender Mediation [★IO]

Assn. europeenne contre les Violences faites aux Femmes au Travail [★IO]

Assn. of Virtual Assistants of Ireland [IO], Jordanstown, United Kingdom

Assn. of Vision Educators [IO], Kailua, HI, United States

Assn. of Vision Educators [15677], c/o Kate Keilman, 111 Hekili St., Ste. A, No. 206, Kailua, HI 96734

Assn. of Vision Sci. Librarians [10341], c/o Fong Optometry and Hea. Sciences Lib., School of Optometry, 490 Minor Hall, Berkeley, CA 94720-2020, (510)642-1020

Assn. for Visual Arts [IO], Cape Town, Republic of South Africa

Assn. of Visual Communicators [★IO]

Assn. of Visual Communicators [★1384]

Assn. of Visual Language Interpreters of Canada [IO], Edmonton, AB, Canada

Assn. of Visual Language Interpreters of New Brunswick [IO], Edmonton, AB, Canada

Assn. of Visual Merchandise Representatives [2535], c/o Tom Raguse, Pres., 307 Cove Creek Ln., Houston, TX 77042-1023, (713)782-5533

Assn. of Visual Sci. Librarians [★10341]

Assn. for Vital Records and Hea. Statistics [★6218]

Assn. of Vitamin Chemists - Defunct.

L'Association Volcanologique Europeenne [★IO]

Assn. of Volleyball Professionals [24191], 6100 Center Dr., 9th Fl., Los Angeles, CA 90045, (310)426-8000

Assn. of Voluntary Action Scholars [★13387]

Assn. of Voluntary Action Scholars [★IO]

Assn. of Voluntary Ser. Organisations [IO], Brussels, Belgium

Assn. for Voluntary Sterilization [★IO]

Assn. for Voluntary Sterilization [★12180]

Assn. for Voluntary Surgical Contraception [★12180]

Assn. for Voluntary Surgical Contraception [★IO]

Assn. for Volunteer Admin. - Defunct.

Assn. of Volunteer Bureaus [★13401]

Assn. for Volunteer Services [IO], Beirut, Lebanon

Assn. of Wa-Tan-Ye Clubs - Address unknown since 2006.

Assn. of Waldorf Schools of North Am. [8526], 337 Oak Grove St., Minneapolis, MN 55403, (612)870-8310

Assn. of Waldorf Schools of North Am. [IO], Minneapolis, MN, United States

Assn. of the Wall and Ceiling Indus. - Intl. [IO], Falls Church, VA, United States

Assn. of the Wall and Ceiling Indus. - Intl. [602], 513 W Broad St., Ste. 210, Falls Church, VA 22046, (703)538-1600

Assn. of Water Technologies [4009], 15245 Shady Grove Rd., Ste. 130, Rockville, MD 20850, (301)740-1421

Assn. of Water Transportation Accounting Officers - Defunct.

Assn. of Web Professionals - Address unknown since 2006.

Assn. of Wedding Planners Worldwide [★537]

Assn. of Wedding Planners Worldwide [★IO]

Association for Wedding Professionals International [IO], Sacramento, CA, United States

Assn. for Wedding Professionals Intl. [1935], 6700 Freeport Blvd., Ste. 202, Sacramento, CA 95822, (916)392-5000

Assn. of Welcoming and Affirming Baptists [19476], PO Box 259257, Madison, WI 53725, (608)255-2155

Assn. of Welding Distributors [IO], Telford, United Kingdom

Assn. of Wesley Founds. - Defunct.

Assn. of Western Pulp and Paper Workers [24064], 1430 SW Clay St., Portland, OR 97208-4566, (503)228-7486

Assn. of Wheelchair Children [IO], London, United Kingdom

Assn. of Wholesale Elecl. Bulk Buyers [IO], Ilkeston, United Kingdom

Assn. of Wholesalers of Chem. and Pharmaceutical Goods [IO], Lisbon, Portugal

Assn. of Winery Suppliers [196], 575 W Coll. Ave., Ste. 103, Santa Rosa, CA 95401, (707)573-3901

Assn. of Wireless Tech. [IO], Maidenhead, United Kingdom

Assn. for Women in Architecture [291], 22815 Frampton Ave., Torrance, CA 90501-5034, (310)534-8466

Assn. of Women in Architecture - Defunct.

Assn. for Women in Aviation Maintenance [4034], c/o Marcia Buckingham, Treas., PO Box 1030, Edgewater, FL 32132-1030, (386)416-0248

Assn. of Women Bus. Owners [★744]

Assn. Women and Bus. in Russia [IO], St. Petersburg, Russia

Assn. for Women in Communications [874], 3337 Duke St., Alexandria, VA 22314, (703)370-7436

Assn. for Women in Computing [6786], 41 Sutter St., Ste. 1006, San Francisco, CA 94104, (415)905-4663

Assn. of Women in Development [★IO]

Assn. of Women Educators [IO], Sandgate, Australia

Assn. of Women in Environmental Professions [4619], PO Box 748, Seattle, WA 98111-0748

Assn. of Women Gemologists - Defunct.

Assn. of Women Geoscientists [★7139]

Assn. for Women Geoscientists [7139], PO Box 30645, Lincoln, NE 68503-0645, (402)489-8122

Association for Women Geoscientists Found. [★7139]

Assn. of Women Indus. Designers [7179], PO Box 468, Old Chelsea Sta., New York, NY 10011

Assn. of Women Indus. Designers [IO], New York, NY, United States

Assn. for Women Journalists [3096], PO Box 2199, Fort Worth, TX 76113, (817)685-3876

Assn. of Women Martial Arts Instructors [23585], PO Box 7033, Houston, TX 77248-7033, (281)630-5120

Assn. of Women Mathematicians [★7288]

Assn. for Women in Mathematics [7288], 11240 Waples Mill Rd., Ste. 200, Fairfax, VA 22030, (703)934-0163

Reference to "IO" in place of a book number signifies that the association may be found in the 45th edition of International Organizations.

Assn. of Women in the Metal Indus. **[4035]**, 19 Mantua Rd., Mount Royal, NJ 08061, (856)423-3201

Assn. of Women in Natural Foods - Address unknown since 1999.

Assn. of Women Painters and Sculptors **[★9514]**

Assn. for Women Psychologists **[★16145]**

Assn. for Women in Psychology **[16145]**, c/o Prof. Suzanna Rose, PhD, Dir. of Women's Stud., Florida Intl. Univ., Women's Stud. Center, DM 212, Univ. Park, Miami, FL 33199, (305)348-2408

Assn. for Women in Sci. **[7602]**, 1200 New York Ave. NW, Ste. 650, Washington, DC 20005, (202)326-8940

Assn. for Women in the Sciences **[IO]**, Christchurch, New Zealand

Assn. of Women Shooters of Canada **[IO]**, Mississauga, ON, Canada

Assn. of Women Soil Scientists **[7672]**, c/o Kelly Counts, Sec.-Treas., USDA-NRCS Soil Survey, 621 W Fetterman St., Buffalo, WY 82834, (951)369-4820

Assn. of Women Solicitors **[IO]**, London, United Kingdom

Assn. for Women in Sports Media **[3097]**, 3899 N Front St., Harrisburg, PA 17110, (717)703-3086

Assn. for Women Students - Defunct.

Assn. of Women Surgeons **[16579]**, 5204 Fairmont Ave., Ste. 208, Downers Grove, IL 60515, (630)655-0392

Assn. of Women Surgeons **[IO]**, Downers Grove, IL, United States

Assn. for Women Veterinarians **[16786]**, c/o Bonnie Thompson, K-State Coll. of Veterinary Medicine, 228 Coles Hall, Manhattan, KS 66506-5602, (785)532-1918

Assn. for Women's Active Return to Education - Defunct.

Assn. of Women's Committees of Art Museums **[★10516]**

Assn. of Women's Hea., Obstetric and Neonatal Nurses **[15470]**, 2000 L St. NW, Ste. 740, Washington, DC 20036, (202)261-2400

Association of Women's Health, Obstetric and Neonatal Nurses **[IO]**, Washington, DC, United States

Assn. of Women's Music and Culture - Defunct.

Assn. for Women's Residential Facilities **[★IO]**

Assn. for Women's Rights in Development **[IO]**, Toronto, ON, Canada

Assn. of Woodturners of Great Britain **[IO]**, Cambridge, United Kingdom

Assn. of Woodwind Teachers **[IO]**, Kent, United Kingdom

Assn. of Woodworking and Furnishings Suppliers **[4058]**, 500 Citadel Dr., Ste. 200, Commerce, CA 90040, (323)838-9440

The Assn. for Work Process Improvement **[6787]**, 75 Fed. St., Ste. 901, Boston, MA 02110, (617)426-1167

Assn. of Workers for Children with Emotional and Behavioural Difficulties **[★IO]**

Assn. for Workplace Democracy - Defunct.

Assn. of WORKSHOP WAY Consultants **[9213]**, PO Box 850170, New Orleans, LA 70185-0170, (504)486-4871

Assn. for Worksite Hea. Promotion **[★16473]**

Assn. for Worksite Health Promotion - Defunct.

Assn. of World Citizens **[18831]**, 55 New Montgomery St., Ste. 224, San Francisco, CA 94105, (415)541-9610

Assn. of World Citizens **[IO]**, San Francisco, CA, United States

Assn. of World Coun. of Churches Related Development Organisations in Europe **[IO]**, Brussels, Belgium

Assn. for World Evangelism - Address unknown since 1991.

Assn. of World Trade Chamber Executives - Defunct.

Assn. for World Travel Exchange **[8602]**, c/o Intl. Student Center, 38 W 88th St., New York, NY 10024, (212)787-7706

Assn. for World Travel Exchange **[IO]**, New York, NY, United States

Assn. for the World Univ. - Defunct.

Assn. of Writers and Writing Programs **[11160]**, George Mason Univ., Mail Stop 1E3, Fairfax, VA 22030-4444, (703)993-4301

Assn. of Yachting Professionals **[23159]**

Assn. of Yarn Distributors **[3776]**

Assn. of Yiddish Writers and Journalists in Israel **[IO]**, Tel Aviv, Israel

Assn. of YMCA Professionals **[13460]**, 12 Broad St., Ste. 2-1, Westerly, RI 02891, (401)604-0034

Assn. of Young Economists of Georgia **[IO]**, Tbilisi, Georgia

Association of Young Journalists **[IO]**, College Park, MD, United States

Assn. of Young Journalists **[3098]**, 1117 Journalism Bldg., Univ. of Maryland, Philip Merrill Coll. of Journalism, College Park, MD 20742-7111

Assn. for Youth Action Development **[IO]**, Nouakchott, Mauritania

Assn. Youth Found; Ohio Standard Breeding **[★23496]**

Assn. of Youth Museums **[★10495]**

Assn. of Yugoslav Jews in the U.S.A. **[19175]**

Assn. Zen Internationale **[★IO]**

Assn. of Zimbabwe Advertisers **[IO]**, Harare, Zimbabwe

Assn. of Zoo Veterinary Technicians **[16787]**, c/o Mr. Joel Pond, CVT, Exec. Dir., Lincoln Park Zoo, 2001 N Clark St., Chicago, IL 60614, (312)742-7211

Assn. of Zoological Horticulture **[4974]**, PO Box 135776, Clermont, FL 34713, (407)939-1609

Assn. of Zoos and Aquariums **[7857]**, 8403 Colesville Rd., Ste. 710, Silver Spring, MD 20910-3314, (301)562-0777

Assn. des Zoos et Aquariums du Canada **[★IO]**

Associations

Alliance for Nonprofit Mgt. **[313]**

Alumni Assn. of the Universidad del Valle **[18872]**

AMC Institute **[IO]**

AMCinstitute **[314]**

American Psychological Association Division 31 - State, Provincial, and Territorial Psychological Association Affairs **[16124]**

Amer. Soc. of Assn. Executives **[315]**

Amer. Soc. of Assn. Executives **[IO]**

Assn. of Charitable Foundations **[IO]**

Assn. of Chief Executives of Voluntary Organisations **[IO]**

Assn. of Philanthropic Counsel **[958]**

Assn. du Prix Albert Londres **[IO]**

Canadian Soc. of Assn. Executives **[IO]**

Caribbean Policy Development Centre **[IO]**

Caribbean Soc. of Hotel Assn. Executives **[24330]**

Center for Excellence in Assn. Leadership **[316]**

DMA Nonprofit Fed. **[317]**

European Soc. of Assn. Executives **[IO]**

Fed. of European and Intl. Associations Established in Belgium **[IO]**

Foundation for Educational Futures **[IO]**

Found. for Educational Futures **[318]**

Inst. of Assn. Mgt. **[IO]**

Inst. of Fundraising **[IO]**

Intl. Assn. of Golf Administrators **[IO]**

The IPA Assn. of Am. **[3022]**

Military, Veterans and Patriotic Ser. Organizations of Am. **[21245]**

Natl. Assn. for Membership Development **[319]**

Natl. Coun. of Nonprofit Associations **[320]**

Natl. Coun. of State Sociological Associations **[7665]**

Partnership for Food Safety Educ. **[14399]**

Scottish Coun. for Voluntary Organisations **[IO]**

Soc. of Natl. Assn. Publications **[321]**

Soc. for Nonprofit Organizations **[322]**

Tanzania Assn. of Non Governmental Organizations **[IO]**

VUFO-NGO Rsrc. Centre **[IO]**

Associations des proprietaires de cinemas du Canada **[★IO]**

Associations Coun. of the Natl. Assn. of Mfrs. **[★2562]**

Associations Inst; Community **[17212]**

Associazione Amici de Bambini **[IO]**, Milan, Italy

Associazione Antiquari d'Italia **[IO]**, Florence, Italy

Associazione Bancaria Italia **[★IO]**

Associazione Bertoni per la Cooperazione e lo Sviluppo nel Terzo Mondo **[IO]**, Verona, Italy

Associazione Centro Aiuti Volontari Cooperazione Sviluppo Terzo Mondo **[IO]**, Trento, Italy

Associazione Compagnia Jazz Ballet **[IO]**, Turin, Italy

Associazione di Cooperazione Cristiana Internazionale **[IO]**, Trieste, Italy

Associazione di Cultura Tradizionale Giapponese - Aikikai d'Italia **[IO]**, Rome, Italy

Associazione Culturale Antonio Pedrotti **[IO]**, Trento, Italy

Associazione Dermatologi Ospedalieri Italiani **[★IO]**

Associazione Distributori Farmaceutici **[★IO]**

Associazione dei Fonografici Italiani **[★IO]**

Associazione Geotecnica Italiana **[IO]**, Rome, Italy

Associazione Grossisti Ortofrutticoli **[★IO]**

Associazione degli Industriali della Birra e del Malto **[★IO]**

Associazione degli Industriali delle Carni **[★IO]**

Associazione Industriali Mugnani e Pastai d'Italia **[★IO]**

Associazione Industrie Dolciarie Italiane **[★IO]**

Associazione Industrie per l'Aerospazio I Sistemi e la Difesa **[★IO]**

Associazione Industrie Risiere Italiane **[★IO]**

Associazione Ingegneri per l'Ambiente ed il Territorio **[★IO]**

Associazione Internazionale di Archeologia Classica **[★IO]**

Associazione Internazionale dei Professori d'Italiano **[★IO]**

Associazione Internazionale Studenti di Agraria **[★IO]**

Associazione Internazionale di Volontariato **[★IO]**

Associazione per gli Interventi di Cooperazione allo Sviluppo **[IO]**, Milan, Italy

Associazione Italian Sclerosi Laterale Amiotrofica **[IO]**, Novara, Italy

Associazione Italiana Amici di Raoul Follereau **[★IO]**

Associazione Italiana di Architettura del Paesaggio **[IO]**, Genova, Italy

Associazione Italiana Biblioteche **[★IO]**

Associazione Italiana Biblioteche **[IO]**, Rome, Italy

Associazione Italiana Classe Yngling **[IO]**, Rapallo, Italy

Associazione Italiana dei Construttori ed Operatori del Settore Oleoidraulico e Pneumatico **[★IO]**

Associazione Italiana Costruttori Autoattrezzature **[★IO]**

Associazione Italiana Costruttori Autoattrezzature **[★IO]**

Associazione Italiana dell' Industria Olearia **[IO]**, Rome, Italy

Associazione Italiana d'Ingegneria Economica **[★IO]**

Associazione Italiana per i Diritti di Riproduzione delle Opere dell'ingegno **[IO]**, Milan, Italy

Associazione Italiana Distribuzione Automatica **[★IO]**

Associazione Italiana per la Documentazione Avanzata **[★IO]**

Associazione Italiana Economisti dell'Energia **[★IO]**

Associazione Italiana Editori **[★IO]**

Associazione Italiana di Ematologia ed Oncologia Pediatrica **[★IO]**

Associazione Italiana Fioristi **[IO]**, Rome, Italy

Associazione Italiana Fioristi **[★IO]**

Associazione Italiana di Fisica Medica **[★IO]**

Associazione Italiana Fisioterapisti **[IO]**, Rome, Italy

Associazione Italiana del Franchising **[★IO]**

Associazione Italiana Guide e Scouts d'Europa Cattolici **[IO]**, Rome, Italy

Associazione Italiana per l'Idrogeno e Celle a Combustibile **[★IO]**

Associazione Italiana di Informatica Medica **[★IO]**

Associazione Italiana di Ingegneria Agraria **[IO]**, Milan, Italy

Associazione Italiana Lattiero-Casearia **[★IO]**

Associazione Italiana Manifatturieri Pelli e Succedanei **[★IO]**

Associazione Italiana di Metallurgia **[★IO]**

Associazione Italiana di Metallurgia **[IO]**, Milan, Italy

Associazione Italiana Pellicceria **[IO]**, Milan, Italy

Associazione Italiana Periti liquidatori Assicurativi Incendio e Rischi Diversi **[★IO]**

Associazione Italiana del Private Equity e Venture Capital **[★IO]**

Associazione Italiana della Rosa **[IO]**, Monza, Italy

A star before a book entry number signifies that the name is not listed separately, but is mentioned within the entry.

Associazione Italiana Sclerosi Multipla [IO], Genoa, Italy
Associazione Italiana Sindrome di Moebius [★IO]
Associazione Italiana Spondiloartriti [★IO]
Associazione Italiana per gli Studi Giapponesi [★IO]
Associazione Italiana Tecnico Economica Cemento [★IO]
Associazione Italiana di Terapia Occupazionale [IO], Rome, Italy
Associazione Italiana per la Tutela della Concorrenza [IO], Milan, Italy
Associazione Italiana del Vuoto [★IO]
Associazione Librai Italiani [★IO]
Associazione per le Malattie Infiammatorie Croniche dell'Intestino [★IO]
Associazione per la Matematica Applicata alle Scienze Economiche e Sociali [★IO]
Associazione Medici per l'Ambiente - ISDE Italia [★IO]
Associazione Nazionale fra Aziende di Vendite per Corrispondenza [IO], Milan, Italy
Associazione Nazionale Calzaturifici Italiani [★IO]
Associazione Nazionale Commercianti in Ferro e Acciai, Metalli Non-Ferrosi, Rottami Ferrosi, Ferramenta e Affini [★IO]
Associazione Nazionale del Commercio dei Prodotti Lattiero-Caseari [★IO]
Associazione Nazionale Cooperativa tra Dettaglianti [★IO]
Associazione Nazionale dell'Industria Farmaceutica [★IO]
Associazione Nazionale Editoria Periodica Specializzata [★IO]
Associazione Nazionale Editoria Specializzata [★IO]
Associazione Nazionale Esportatori Importatori Ortofrutticoli ed Agrumari [★IO]
Associazione Nazionale Fabbricanti Articoli Ottici [★IO]
Associazione Nazionale Fabbricanti Prodotti per la Casa [★IO]
Associazione Nazionale Fibre Chimiche [★IO]
Associazione Nazionale Fotografi Professionisti [IO], Milan, Italy
Associazione Nazionale Fra i Produttori di Articoli Sportivi [★IO]
Associazione Nazionale Grossisti Distributori di Apparecchi Fotografici [★IO]
Associazione Nazionale Imprese Armamento Ferroviario [IO], Rome, Italy
Associazione Nazionale Imprese Trasporti Automobilistici [★IO]
Associazione Nazionale Industriali Conserve Alimentari Vegetali [★IO]
Associazione Nazionale degli Industriali del Vetro [★IO]
Associazione Nazionale fra gli Industriali dello Zucchero, dell'Alcool e del Lievito [★IO]
Associazione Nazionale fra Industrie Automobilistiche [★IO]
Associazione Nazionale fra le Industrie della Gomma, Cavi Elettrici ed Affini [IO], Milan, Italy
Associazione Nazionale Malati Reumatici [IO], Rome, Italy
Associazione Nazionale per la tutela del Malato di Psoriasi e Vitiligine [IO], Milan, Italy
Associazione Nazionale tra i Produttori di Alimenti Zootecnici [★IO]
Associazione Nazionale Produttori Articoli per Scrittura e Affini [★IO]
Associazione Nazionale dei Produttori di Piastrelle di Ceramica e di Materiali Refrattari [IO], Sassuolo, Italy
Associazione Nazionale di Risk Managers e Responsabili Assicurazioni Aziendali [IO], Milan, Italy
Associazione Nazionale Rivenditori Specialisti di Pneumatici [★IO]
Associazione la Nostra Famiglia [IO], Ponte Lambro, Italy
Associazione per la Pace [★IO]
Associazione Studi Am. Latina [IO], Rome, Italy
Associazione per lo Studio del Problema Mondiale dei Rifugiati [★IO]
Associazione Tecnica dell'Automobile [★IO]
Associazione Tessile Italiana [★IO]
Associes Benevoles Qualifies au Ser. des Jeunes [★IO]

Associes Canadiens de l'Universite Ben-Gurion du Neguev [★IO]
AssoComunicazione Associazione delle Imprese di Comunicazione [IO], Milan, Italy
ASSUCOPIE [IO], Ottignies-Louvain-la-Neuve, Belgium
Assumption Guild [19580], 330 Market St., Brighton, MA 02135, (617)783-0400
Assurance Soc; North Amer. Union Life [★19010]
Assurandor Societet [★IO]
Assurex Intl. - Address unknown since 1995.

Assyrian
Assyrian Aid Soc. of Am. [11508]
Assyrian Aid Soc. of Am. [IO]
Assyrian Chaldean Athletics of North Am. [23062]
Assyrian Medical Soc. [13715]
Assyrian Medical Soc. [IO]
Bet-Nahrain [9624]

Assyrian Academic Soc. [10297], 8324 N Lincoln Ave., Skokie, IL 60077, (847)982-5800
Assyrian Academic Soc. [IO], Skokie, IL, United States
Assyrian Aid Soc. of Am. [IO], Berkeley, CA, United States
Assyrian Aid Soc. of Am. [11508], 350 Berkeley Park Blvd., Berkeley, CA 94707, (510)527-9997
Assyrian Chaldean Athletics of North Am. [23062], c/o Ashur Enwiya, Chm., 8018 W Lyons St., Niles, IL 60714, (847)583-8525
Assyrian Chaldean Athletics of North Am. [IO], Niles, IL, United States
Assyrian Medical Soc. [IO], Redlands, CA, United States
Assyrian Medical Soc. [13715], c/o Samir Johna, MD, Pres., 1616 W Olive Ave., Redlands, CA 92373
ASTA Chap. of Greece [IO], Athens, Greece
Astara [20443], 10700 Jersey Blvd., Ste. 450, Rancho Cucamonga, CA 91730, (909)948-7412
Astara Found. [★20443]
ASTD [8018], Box 1443, 1640 King St., Alexandria, VA 22313-2043, (703)683-8100
Asthma and Allergy Found. of Am. [13598], 1233 20th St. NW, Ste. 402, Washington, DC 20036, (202)466-7643
Asthma and Allergy Patients; Albanian Assn. in Support of [IO]
Asthma and Allied Conditions; Assn. for the Stud. of [★13592]
Asthma Care Assn. of America - Defunct.
Asthma Center; Natl. [★16361]
Asthma Center; Natl. Jewish Hospital/National [★16361]
Asthma Found. of New South Wales [IO], St. Leonards, Australia
Asthma and Immunology; Amer. Acad. of Allergy, [13592]
Asthma and Immunology; Amer. Coll. of Allergy, [13596]
Asthma and Immunology; Joint Coun. of Allergy, [13602]
Asthma Info. Assn; Allergy/ [IO]
Asthma Network Mothers of Asthmatics; Allergy and [16352]
Asthma Network; Natl. Allergy and [★16352]
Asthma Soc. of Canada [IO], Toronto, ON, Canada
Asthma Soc. of Ireland [IO], Dublin, Ireland
Aston Martin Owners Club [IO], Wallingford, United Kingdom
Aston Martin Owners Club [21581], c/o Susan Laskey, Sec., 645 5th Ave., Ste. 900, New York, NY 10022, (212)830-6160
ASTRA - Defunct.
Astro Artz [★9408]
Astro-Psychology Inst. - Defunct.
Astrologers' Guild of America [6491]
Astrologers Intl. - Defunct.
Astrological Assn. of Great Britain [IO], London, United Kingdom

Astrology
Amer. Fed. of Astrologers [6488]
Assn. for Astrological Networking [6489]
Assn. for Psychological Astrology [6490]
Astrologers' Guild of America [6491]
Astrological Assn. of Great Britain [IO]

Astromusic [6492]
British Assn. for Vedic Astrology [IO]
Coun. of Vedic Astrology [21548]
Faculty of Astrological Stud. [IO]
Fed. of Australian Astrologers [IO]
Friends of Astrology [6493]
Intl. Soc. for Astrological Res. [6494]
Intl. Soc. for Astrological Res. [IO]
Intl. Soc. of Bus. Astrologers [IO]
Org. for Professional Astrology [6495]

Astrology; Amer. Coun. of Vedic [★21548]
Astromusic [6492], PO Box 3120, Ashland, OR 97520, (541)488-3344
AstroMusical Res. [★6492]
Astronaut Coun; Young [7925]
Astronaut Program; Young [★7925]
Astronaut Scholars Honor Soc. [24584], c/o Linn LeBlanc, Exec. Dir., Astronaut Scholarship Found., 6225 Vectorspace Blvd., Titusville, FL 32780, (321)269-6101
Astronautics; Amer. Inst. of Aeronautics and [6369]
Astronautics; Intl. Acad. of [IO]
Astronauttinen Tutkimusseura [★IO]
Astronomers Assn. of New York City; Amateur [★6496]
Astronomical Assn; Rocket City [★6511]
Astronomical and Astrophysical Soc. of Am. [★6498]
Astronomical League [6502], 9201 Ward Pkwy., Ste. 100, Kansas City, MO 64114, (816)333-7759
Astronomical Soc. of Australia [IO], Epping, Australia
Astronomical Soc. of France [IO], Paris, France
Astronomical Soc. of Japan [IO], Tokyo, Japan
Astronomical Soc. of New South Wales [IO], Sydney, Australia
Astronomical Soc. of the Pacific [6503], 390 Ashton Ave., San Francisco, CA 94112, (415)337-1100
Astronomical Soc. of South Australia [IO], Adelaide, Australia
Astronomical Soc. of Southern Africa [IO], Observatory, Republic of South Africa
Astronomical Soc. of Western Australia [IO], Subiaco, Australia
Astronomisk Selskab Danmark [★IO]

Astronomy
Amateur Astronomers Assn. [6496]
Amateur Astronomers, Inc. [21549]
Amer. Assn. of Variable Star Observers [6497]
Amer. Astronomical Soc. [6498]
Amer. Lunar Soc. [6499]
American Lunar Society [IO]
Amer. Meteor Soc. [6500]
Antique Telescope Soc. [21526]
Asociation Argentina Amigos de la Astronomia [IO]
Assn. Aeronautique et Astronautique de France [IO]
Assn. Educative des Amateurs d'Astronomie du Centre [IO]
Assn. Francaise d'Astronomie [IO]
Assn. of French-Speaking Planetariums [IO]
Association of Lunar and Planetary Observers [IO]
Assn. of Lunar and Planetary Observers [21550]
Assn. of Universities for Res. in Astronomy [6501]
Astronomical League [6502]
Astronomical Soc. of Australia [IO]
Astronomical Soc. of France [IO]
Astronomical Soc. of Japan [IO]
Astronomical Soc. of New South Wales [IO]
Astronomical Soc. of the Pacific [6503]
Astronomical Soc. of South Australia [IO]
Astronomical Soc. of Southern Africa [IO]
Astronomical Soc. of Western Australia [IO]
Astronomy Ireland [IO]
Astronomy Stud. Unit [22795]
Austrian Astronomical Soc. [IO]
British Astronomical Assn. [IO]
British Interplanetary Soc. [IO]
Canadian Astronomical Soc. [IO]
Central Bur. for Astronomical Telegrams [6504]
Danish Astronomical Assn. [IO]
Dutch Youth Assn. for Astronomy [IO]
EUROAVIA - European Assn. of Aerospace Students [IO]
European Astronomical Soc. [IO]

Reference to "IO" in place of a book number signifies that the association may be found in the 45th edition of International Organizations.

European Southern Observatory [IO]
Fed. of Astronomical and Geophysical Data Anal. Services [IO]
Fed. of Astronomical Societies [IO]
Fed. of Galaxy Explorers [9136]
French Assn. of Variable Star Observers [IO]
International Amateur-Professional Photoelectric Photometry [IO]
Intl. Amateur-Professional Photoelectric Photometry [6505]
Intl. Astronomical Union [IO]
Intl. Dark-Sky Assn. [IO]
Intl. Dark-Sky Assn. [6506]
Intl. Occultation Timing Assn. [6507]
Intl. Occultation Timing Assn. [IO]
Intl. Planetarium Soc. [IO]
Intl. Planetarium Soc. [6508]
Irish Astronomical Assn. [IO]
Jordanian Astronomical Soc. [IO]
Maria Mitchell Assn. [6509]
Nederlandse Vereniging voor Weer- en Sterrenkunde [IO]
New England Antiquities Res. Assn. [6452]
North Amer. Meteor Network [7328]
Romanian Soc. for Meteors and Astronomy [IO]
Royal Astronomical Soc. [IO]
Royal Astronomical Soc. of Canada [IO]
Royal Astronomical Soc. of New Zealand [IO]
Sci. Comm. on Frequency Allocations for Radio Astronomy and Space Sci. [IO]
SETI League [6510]
Societe Astronomique de France [IO]
Soc. for Popular Astronomy [IO]
Stonehenge Study Group [6459]
Swedish Astronomical Soc. [IO]
Swiss Astronomical Soc. [IO]
Swiss Soc. of Astrophysics and Astronomy [IO]
Ursa Astronomical Assn. [IO]
Von Braun Astronomical Soc. [6511]
Webb Soc. [6512]
Webb Soc. [IO]
Astronomy Educ; Assn. for [IO]
Astronomy and Ionosphere Center; National [★7622]
Astronomy Ireland [IO], Dublin, Ireland
Astronomy Observatory; National Optical [★7622]
Astronomy Observatory; National Radio [★7622]
Astronomy Stud. Unit [22795]
Astrophysical Soc. of Am; Astronomical and [★6498]
At-one-ment Associates - Address unknown since 1999.
At-Risk Educ. Assn; Natl. [8327]
At-sea Processors Assn. [1483], c/o Stephanie Madsen, Exec. Dir., PO Box 32817, Juneau, AK 99803, (206)285-5139
ATA - A Graphic Communications Assn. - Defunct.
ATA Carnet [★766]
ATA Carnet [★IO]
ATA; Casey Jones Railroad Unit - [22800]
ATOmp;T; Lesbian, Bisexual, Gay and Transgendered United Employees at [12242]
Atari Teachers' Network - Defunct.
Atari Users Assn. - Address unknown since 2005.
Ataxia Found; Natl. [15342]
Ataxia Telangiectasia Children's Proj. [14253], 668 S Military Trail, Deerfield Beach, FL 33442-3023, (954)481-6611
Ataxia-Telangiectasia Soc. [IO], Harpenden, United Kingdom
Ataxia - UK [IO], London, United Kingdom
Atchley/Harden Family Assn. - Address unknown since 2007.
ATEGRUS: Asociacion Tecnica para la gestion de Residues y Medio Ambiente [★IO]
Ateitis Assn. of Lithuanian Catholic Alumni - Address unknown since 2001.
Ateliers du Soleil [★IO]
Atex Commercial Users Group - Address unknown since 1990.
Athanor Fellowship [★20445]

Atheist
Amer. Atheists [19463]
Atheist Alliance, Inc. [19464]
Atheists United [19465]
Center For Inquiry [17643]

Freedom From Religion Found. [19837]
Inst. for Creation Res. [20538]
Intl. League of Non-Religious and Atheists [IO]
Secular Student Alliance [17790]
Atheist Alliance, Inc. [19464], PO Box 234, Pocopson, PA 19366, (866)HERETIC
Atheist Assn. - Address unknown since 1988.
Atheista and Co. - Address unknown since 2006.
Atheists United [19465], 4773 Hollywood Blvd., Hollywood, CA 90027-5333, (323)666-4258
Athena Alliance [17468], c/o Kenan Patrick Jarboe, Pres., 911 E Capitol St. SE, Washington, DC 20003-3903, (202)547-7064
Athena; Maids of [19089]
Athenaeum of Philadelphia [10342], 219 S 6th St., Philadelphia, PA 19106-3794, (215)925-2688
Athens Chamber of Commerce and Indus. [IO], Athens, Greece
Athens Daily Newspaper Publishers Assn. [IO], Athens, Greece

Athletes
Achilles Track Club [23331]
Adirondack Forty-Sixers [23930]
Adirondack Mountain Club [23931]
Adirondack Trail Improvement Soc. [23932]
Adventure Cycling Assn. [23304]
af2 Natl. Fan Club [24829]
Aikido Assn. of Am. [23046]
Aikido Assn. of North Am. [23047]
All-Amer. Collegiate Golf Found. [23443]
All Japan Ju-Jitsu Intl. Fed. [23577]
Amateur Athletic Union [23797]
Amateur Baseball Umpires' Assn. [23798]
Amateur Ski Instructors Assn. [23748]
Amateur Softball Assn. of Am. [23788]
Am. Outdoors [23681]
Amer. Acad. of Podiatric Sports Medicine [16471]
Amer. Acad. of Sports Physicians [16472]
Amer. Amateur Baseball Cong. [23100]
Amer. Amateur Karate Fed. [23559]
Amer. Amputee Soccer Assn. [23773]
Amer. Armsport Assn. [23059]
Amer. Assn. of adaptedSPORTS Programs [23333]
Amer. Assn. for the Improvement of Boxing [23259]
Amer. Assn. of Snowboard Instructors [23765]
Amer. Athletic Trainers Assn. and Certification Bd. [23953]
Amer. Barefoot Club [23974]
Amer. Barrel Racing Assn. [23492]
Amer. Baseball Coaches Assn. [23101]
Amer. Bicycle Assn. [23305]
Amer. Bicycle Polo Assn. [23658]
Amer. Bicycle Racing [23667]
Amer. Blind Bowling Assn. [23334]
Amer. Blind Skiing Found. [23336]
Amer. Coll. of Sports Medicine [16473]
Amer. Competition Opportunities for Riders with Disabilities [23330]
Amer. CueSports Alliance [23144]
Amer. Darters Assn. [23492]
Amer. Double Dutch League [23697]
Amer. Endurance Ride Conf. [23933]
Amer. Football Coaches Assn. [23427]
Amer. Gp. Gymnastics Assn. [23473]
Amer. Hiking Soc. [23934]
Amer. Hockey Coaches Assn. [23481]
Amer. Hockey League [23482]
Amer. Hot Rod Assn. [23071]
Amer. Judo Assn. [23552]
Amer. Junior Golf Assn. [23444]
Amer. Junior Rodeo Assn. [23684]
Amer. Kempo-Karate Assn. [23579]
Amer. Kenpo Karate Intl. [23560]
Amer. Legion Baseball [23103]
Amer. Medical Athletic Assn. [23650]
Amer. Medical Tennis Assn. [23898]
Amer. Motorcycle Heritage Found. [23621]
Amer. Orthopaedic Soc. for Sports Medicine [16476]
Amer. Osteopathic Acad. of Sports Medicine [16477]
Amer. Platform Tennis Assn. [23899]
Amer. Sambo Assn. [23580]

Amer. Self-Protection Assn. [23712]
Amer. Swan Boat Assn. [23669]
Amer. Swimming Coaches Assn. [23882]
Amer. Tennis Assn. [23900]
Amer. Track Racing Assn. [23306]
Amer. Trails [23935]
Amer. Turners [23802]
Amer. Vaulting Assn. [23967]
Amer. Volkssport Assn. [23803]
Amer. Volleyball Coaches Assn. [23969]
Amer. Water Ski Educational Found. [23975]
Amer. Wheelchair Bowling Assn. [23339]
Amer. Whitewater [23682]
Amer. Wu Shu Soc. [23583]
Amer. Youth Soccer Org. [23774]
America's Angel [12140]
America's Found. [20709]
AMOA Natl. Dart Assn. [23329]
Appalachian Mountain Club [23936]
Appalachian Trail Conservancy [23937]
Aquatic Exercise Assn. [23652]
Arabian Jockey Club [23494]
Assn. of Commercial Diving Educators [23960]
Assn. of Disabled Amer. Golfers [23341]
Assn. of Dive Prog. Administrators [23377]
Assn. for Historical Fencing [23399]
Assn. of Northwest Steelheaders [23409]
Assn. of Professional Ball Players of Am. [23105]
Assn. of Surfing Professionals [23877]
Assyrian Chaldean Athletics of North Am. [23062]
Athletes Abroad for Christ [19466]
Athletes Abroad for Christ [IO]
Athletes in Action [19990]
Athletic Equip. Managers Assn. [23805]
Atlantic Coast Conf. [23806]
Australian Football Assn. of North Am. [23429]
Babe Ruth Baseball/Softball [23106]
Babe Ruth Birthplace/Sports Legends at Camden Yards [23107]
Bicycle Parking Proj. [23307]
Bicycle Ride Directors' Assn. of Am. [23308]
Big East Conf. [23807]
Big Ten Conf. [23808]
Big West Conf. [23809]
BlueRibbon Coalition [23680]
Caribbean Amer. Netball Assn. [23633]
Catalina 22 Natl. Sailing Assn. [23162]
Central Collegiate Hockey Assn. [23483]
Central Intercollegiate Athletic Assn. [23811]
CHA - Certified Horsemanship Assn. [23523]
Championship Assn. of Mechanics [23075]
Cinderella Softball Leagues [23789]
Citizenship Through Sports Alliance [23812]
Coll. Athletic Bus. Mgt. Assn. [23813]
Coll. Gymnastics Assn. [23474]
Coll. Sports Info. Directors of Am. [23814]
Coll. Swimming Coaches Assn. of Am. [23883]
Collegiate Commissioners Assn. [23815]
Collegiate Soaring Assn. [23039]
Consolidated Athletic Commn. [23816]
Continental Basketball Assn. [23129]
Continental Divide Trail Soc. [23938]
Cook Islands Touch Assn. [IO]
Cosmopolitan Soccer League [23775]
Coun. of Ivy Gp. Presidents [23817]
Cowboy Mounted Shooting Assn. [23716]
Disabled Sports USA [23343]
Divers Alert Network [23378]
Eastern Assn. of Rowing Colleges [23699]
Eastern Coll. Athletic Conf. [23484]
Eastern Coll. Soccer Assn. [23776]
Eastern Collegiate Hockey Assn. [23485]
Eastern Intercollegiate Gymnastic League [23475]
Eastern Surfing Assn. [23878]
England Touch Assn. [IO]
Fed. of Intl. Polo [23819]
Fellowship of Christian Athletes [20008]
Fiji Touch Assn. [IO]
Florida Trail Assn. [23939]
Football Writers Assn. of Am. [23430]
Free Throwers Boomerang Soc. [23247]
Future Fisherman Found. [23415]
George Khoury Assn. of Baseball Leagues [23109]
Golf Coaches Assn. of Am. [23448]

A star before a book entry number signifies that the name is not listed separately, but is mentioned within the entry.

Golf Tournament Assn. of Am. [23449]
Golf Writers Assn. of Am. [23450]
Great Lakes Sport Fishing Coun. [23416]
Gp. Fore Golf Found. [23451]
Guam Natl. Olympic Comm. [23636]
Hampton One-Design Class Racing Assn. [23173]
Handicapped Scuba Assn. [23344]
Harness Horse Youth Found. [23496]
Heritage Trails Fund [23940]
Hockey North Am. [23486]
Hong Kong Touch and Tag Rugby Assn. [IO]
Horsemanship Safety Assn. [23525]
Inland Lake Yachting Assn. [23175]
Inst. of Diving [23961]
Intercollegiate Fencing Assn. [23401]
Intercollegiate Horse Show Assn. [23526]
Intercollegiate Outing Club Assn. [23941]
Intercollegiate Rowing Assn. [23700]
Intercollegiate Tennis Assn. [23902]
Intl. 210 Assn. [23179]
Intl. 505 Yacht Racing Assn., Amer. Sect. [23180]
Intl. Acad. of Aquatic Art [23884]
Intl. Acad. for Sports Dentistry [16481]
Intl. Aikido Assn. [23048]
Intl. Alliance for Youth Sports [23994]
Intl. Assn. of Gay and Lesbian Martial Artists [23588]
Intl. Bonefishing Soc. [22452]
Intl. Boxing Fed. [23260]
Intl. Boxing Hall of Fame Museum [23261]
Intl. Dodge Ball Fed. [23821]
Intl. Fed. of Sleddog Sports [23393]
Intl. Female Boxers Assn. [23263]
Intl. Gay Figure Skating Union [23736]
Intl. Golf Associates [23452]
Intl. Golf Fed. [23453]
Intl. Hunter Educ. Assn. [23545]
Intl. J/22 Class Assn. [23187]
Intl. Lacrosse Fed. [23570]
Intl. League of Professional Baseball Clubs [23110]
Intl. Martial Arts League [23589]
Intl. Medalist Assn. [23825]
Intl. Mental Game Coaching Assn. [23289]
Intl. Mountain Bicycling Assn. [23310]
Intl. Naples Sabot Assn. [23190]
Intl. Natural Bodybuilding and Fitness Fed. [23243]
Intl. Professional Rodeo Assn. [23686]
Intl. Racquetball Fed. [23677]
Intl. Senior Softball Assn. [23790]
Intl. Seven-Star Mantis Style Lee Kam Wing Martial Art Assn. - USA [23591]
Intl. Side Saddle Org. [23529]
Intl. Ski Dancing Assn. [23751]
Intl. Skiing History Assn. [10965]
Intl. Softball Fed. [23791]
Intl. Sports Exchange [23826]
Intl. Sports Heritage Assn. [23827]
Intl. Sports Massage Fed. [16482]
Intl. Sungja-Do Assn. [23593]
Intl. Swimming Hall of Fame [23886]
Intl. Tennis Hall of Fame [23903]
Intl. Thunderbird Class Assn. [23195]
Intl. Track and Field Coaches Assn. [23919]
Intl. Traditional Karate Fed. [23562]
Intl. Unicycling Fed. [23311]
Intl. Vaulting Club [23968]
Intl. Veteran Boxers Assn. [23264]
Intl. Wheelchair Road Racers Club [23346]
Intl. Yang Style Tai Chi Chuan Assn. [23594]
IOCALUM [23942]
Japan Aikido Assn. U.S.A. [23595]
Japan Touch Assn. [IO]
Jersey Touch Assn. [IO]
The Jockey Club [23502]
Jockeys' Guild [23503]
Joint Commn. on Sports Medicine and Sci. [16483]
Keith Bulluck Fan Club [24830]
Knights Boxing Team - Intl. [23265]
Korean Amer. Professional Tennis Assn. [23904]
Ladies Professional Golf Assn. [23454]
League of Amer. Bicyclists [23312]
Light Living Library [23272]

Lincoln Heritage Trail Found. [23943]
Little League Baseball and Softball [23111]
Little League Found. [23112]
Maccabi USA/Sports for Israel [23828]
Major League Baseball [23113]
Major Wingfield Historical Soc. [23905]
Marathon Skating Intl. [23737]
Martial Arts Intl. Fed. [23596]
Martial Arts USA [23597]
Metropolitan Intercollegiate Basketball Assn. [23131]
Middle States Regatta Assn. [23701]
Montana Outfitters and Guides Assn. [23944]
Mountaineers [23945]
Mounted Games Across Am. [23830]
Multicultural Golf Assn. of Am. [23455]
Naismith Memorial Basketball Hall of Fame [23132]
Natl. Ability Center [23347]
Natl. Acad. of Sports [23831]
Natl. Advt. Golf Assn. [23456]
Natl. Alliance for Accessible Golf [23348]
Natl. Alliance for Youth Sports [23290]
Natl. Amateur Baseball Fed. [23115]
Natl. Amateur Body Builders Assn. USA [23244]
Natl. Amputee Golf Assn. [23349]
Natl. Assn. of Athletic Development Directors [23832]
Natl. Assn. of Basketball Coaches [23133]
Natl. Assn. of Collegiate Directors of Athletics [23833]
Natl. Assn. of Collegiate Gymnastics Coaches/ Women [23476]
Natl. Assn. of Collegiate Marketing Administrators [23834]
Natl. Assn. of Intercollegiate Athletics [23835]
Natl. Assn. of Left-Handed Golfers [23458]
Natl. Assn. of Professional Baseball Leagues [23116]
Natl. Assn. of Shooting Sports Athletes [23720]
Natl. Assn. of Sports Commissions [23871]
Natl. Assn. of Sports Officials [23872]
Natl. Assn. of Sports Officials - Organizations Network [23873]
Natl. Assn. of Underwater Instructors [23963]
Natl. Assn. of Women's Gymnastic's Judges [23477]
Natl. Athletic Trainers' Assn. [23954]
Natl. Baseball Cong. [23117]
Natl. Baseball Hall of Fame and Museum [23118]
Natl. Basketball Assn. [23134]
Natl. Basketball Athletic Trainers Assn. [23135]
Natl. Bicycle League [23313]
Natl. Bicycle Tour Directors Assn. [23314]
Natl. Bucking Bull Assn. [23687]
Natl. Camp Assn. [23277]
Natl. Center for Bicycling and Walking [23315]
Natl. Christian Coll. Athletic Assn. [23837]
Natl. Collegiate Athletic Assn. [23838]
Natl. Collegiate Roller Hockey Assn. [23487]
Natl. Collegiate Table Tennis Assn. [23895]
Natl. Disability Sports Alliance [23353]
Natl. Fastpitch Coaches Assn. [23840]
Natl. Fed. of Professional Bullriders [23688]
Natl. Fed. of Professional Trainers [23956]
Natl. Fed. of State High School Associations [23841]
Natl. Field Hockey Coaches Assn. [23404]
Natl. Finals Rodeo Comm. [23689]
Natl. Football Found. and Coll. Hall of Fame [23431]
Natl. Football League [23432]
Natl. Football League Alumni [23433]
Natl. Football League Players Assn. [23434]
Natl. Gym Assn. [23654]
Natl. High School Athletic Coaches Assn. [23292]
Natl. High School Baseball Coaches Assn. [23119]
Natl. High School Rodeo Assn. [23690]
Natl. Intercollegiate Rodeo Assn. [23691]
Natl. Intercollegiate Running Club Assn. [23707]
Natl. Intercollegiate Soccer Officials Assn. [23778]
Natl. Interscholastic Swimming Coaches Assn. of Am. [23887]
Natl. Intramural-Recreational Sports Assn. [23842]

Natl. Jousting Assn. [23551]
Natl. Junior Baseball League [23120]
Natl. Junior Coll. Athletic Assn. [23843]
Natl. Little Britches Rodeo Assn. [23692]
Natl. Org. for Rivers [23683]
Natl. Org. of I Walkers [23971]
Natl. Paddleball Assn. [23092]
Natl. Pitching Assn. [23121]
Natl. Public Parks Tennis Assn. [23906]
Natl. Scholastic Surfing Assn. [23880]
Natl. Semi-Professional Baseball Assn. [23122]
Natl. Senior Games Assn. [23655]
Natl. Ski Patrol Sys. [23753]
Natl. Soccer Coaches Assn. of Am. [23779]
Natl. Softball Assn. [23792]
Natl. Sporting Clays Assn. [23726]
Natl. Starwind/Spindrift Class Assn. [23207]
Natl. Steeplechase Assn. [23509]
Natl. Strength and Conditioning Assn. [23957]
Natl. Thoroughbred Racing Assn. [23510]
Natl. Throws Coaches Assn. [23293]
Natl. Tractor Pullers Assn. [23928]
Natl. Trail Ride Assn. [23946]
Natl. Wheelchair Basketball Assn. [23354]
Natl. Wheelchair Poolplayer Assn. [23355]
Natl. Wheelchair Softball Assn. [23356]
Natl. Women's Hall of Fame [20716]
Natl. Women's Martial Arts Fed. [23600]
Natl. Wrestling Coaches Assn. [23987]
Natl. Youth Sports Safety Found. [16484]
NETA - Natl. Exercise Trainers Assn. [23037]
New England Trails Conf. [23948]
New York Triathlon Club [23922]
New Zealand Touch Assn. [IO]
NFHS Coaches Assn. [23294]
NFHS Officials Assn. [23874]
Niue Touch Assn. [IO]
North Am. Wu(Hao) Taiji Fed. [23601]
North Amer. Boxing Fed. [23266]
North Amer. Chinese Soccer League [23780]
North Amer. Fishing Club [23421]
North Amer. Football League [23435]
North Amer. Formula 18 Assn. [23208]
North Amer. Kettlebell Fed. [23984]
North Amer. Natural Bodybuilding Fed. [23245]
North Amer. Network of Women Runners [23656]
North Amer. Powerlifting Fed. [23662]
North Amer. Riding for the Handicapped Assn. [23357]
North Amer. Sports Fed. [23065]
North Amer. Strongman [23246]
North Amer. Trail Ride Conf. [23949]
North Country Trail Assn. [23950]
Olson 30 Class Assn. [23210]
One-Arm Dove Hunt Assn. [23358]
Over the Hill Gang, Intl. [23846]
Pacific 10 Conf. [23847]
Pacific Northwest Ski Assn. [23754]
Pakistan Touch Ball Fed. [IO]
Pan-American Union of Karatedo Organizations [23564]
Patience T'ai Chi Assn. [23897]
PGA TOUR Tournaments Assn. [23461]
Physically Challenged Golf Assn. [23359]
Polish Amer. Golf Assn. [23462]
Pony Baseball and Softball [23124]
Positive Coaching Alliance [23296]
Pro Athletes Outreach [20029]
Pro Players Assn. [13402]
Professional Armed Forces Rodeo Assn. [23693]
Professional Assn. of Diving Instructors [23964]
Professional Assn. of Volleyball Officials [23875]
Professional Baseball Athletic Trainers Soc. [23125]
Professional Football Researchers Assn. [23438]
Professional Golfers' Assn. of Am. [23464]
Professional Putters Assn. [23465]
Professional Rodeo Cowboys Assn. [23694]
Professional Skaters Assn. [23738]
Professional Ski Instructors of Am. [23755]
Professional Tennis Registry [23909]
Qajaq USA [23981]
Rails-to-Trails Conservancy [23952]
Randonneurs USA [23316]
Recreational Scuba Training Coun. [23965]

Reference to "IO" in place of a book number signifies that the association may be found in the 45th edition of International Organizations.

RollerSoccer Intl. Fed. [23850]
Running USA [23708]
San Juan 21 Class Assn. [23215]
Scoot-Tours Touring Scooter Riders Assn. [23627]
Scotland Touch Assn. [IO]
Sheclimbs [23285]
Shudokan Martial Arts Assn. [23603]
Ski for Light [23361]
Soccer Assn. for Youth [23781]
Soc. for Amer. Baseball Res. [23126]
Soc. of Roller Skating Teachers of Am. [23741]
Sony Ericsson WTA Tour [23910]
South African Masters Sports Assn. [IO]
Southeastern Conf. [23851]
Southern Conf. [23852]
Special Olympics [23362]
Sport and Recreation Law Assn. [23870]
Sports Charities USA [23854]
Sports Hall of Oblivion [23855]
Sports Philatelists Intl. [22877]
Sportscar Vintage Racing Assn. [23085]
Surfrider Found. [23881]
Synchro Swimming U.S.A. [23889]
Tandem Club of Am. [23317]
Touch Football Australia [IO]
Touch Rugby Assn. of Thailand [IO]
Traditional Tae Kwon Do Chung Do Assn. [23604]
Ultimate Players Assn. [23375]
Underwater Soc. of Am. [23966]
Unicycling Soc. of Am. [23319]
United Fly Tyers [23424]
U.S. Adult Soccer Assn. [23857]
U.S. Adventure Racing Assn. [23672]
U.S. Amateur Confed. of Roller Skating [23742]
U.S. Amateur Tug of War Assn. [23959]
U.S.A. Cricket Assn. [23299]
U.S.A. Deaf Basketball [23136]
U.S.A. Netball Assn. [23634]
U.S.A. Wushu-Kungfu Fed. [23605]
U.S. Apnea Assn. [23380]
U.S. Aquatic Sports [23890]
U.S. ArmSports [23991]
U.S. Assn. for Blind Athletes [23363]
U.S. Barrel Jumping Assn. [23743]
U.S. Basketball Writers Assn. [23137]
U.S. Biathlon Assn. [23756]
U.S. Bicycle Polo Assn. [23660]
U.S. Blind Golf Assn. [23364]
U.S. Bobsled and Skeleton Fed. [23767]
U.S. Bocce Fed. [23241]
U.S. Broomball Assn. [23858]
U.S. Collegiate Athletic Assn. [23859]
U.S. Collegiate Ski and Snowboard Assn. [23757]
U.S. Collegiate Sports Coun. [23860]
U.S. Competitive Aerobics Fed. [23038]
U.S. Cultural Exchange and Sports Soc. [23861]
U.S. Curling Assn. [23302]
U.S. Cycling Fed. [23320]
U.S. Dental Tennis Assn. [23911]
U.S. Disc Sports [23376]
U.S. Dressage Fed. [23533]
U.S. Equestrian Fed. [23534]
U.S. Eventing Assn. [23535]
U.S. Fastpitch Assn. [23794]
U.S. Fencing Assn. [23402]
U.S. Fencing Coaches Assn. [23403]
U.S. Field Hockey Assn. [23405]
U.S. Figure Skating Assn. [23744]
U.S. Flag Football League [23440]
U.S. Flag and Touch Football League [23441]
U.S. Floorball Assn. [23093]
U.S. Football Alliance [23442]
U.S. Futsal Fed. [23862]
U.S. Girls' Wrestling Assn. [23988]
U.S. Golf Assn. [23467]
U.S. Handball Assn. [23480]
U.S. Handcycling Fed. [23321]
U.S. Helice Assn. [23729]
U.S. High School Tennis Assn. [23912]
U.S. Hydrofoil Assn. [23978]
U.S. Indoor Soccer Assn. [23782]
U.S. Intercollegiate Lacrosse Assn. [23571]
U.S. Isshinryu Karate Assn. [23565]
U.S. Judo [23554]
U.S. Judo Assn. [23555]

U.S. Lacrosse [23572]
U.S. Lacrosse Assn., Women's Div. [23573]
U.S. Luge Assn. [23575]
U.S. Martial Arts Assn. [23607]
U.S. Masters Swimming [23891]
U.S. Mirror Class Assn. [23229]
U.S. Modern Pentathlon Assn. [23925]
U.S. Muay Thai Assn. [23608]
U.S. Natl. Tennis Acad. [23913]
U.S. Olympic Comm. [23637]
U.S. Polo Assn. [23661]
U.S. Pony Clubs [23537]
U.S. Power Soccer Assn. [23783]
U.S. Professional Diving Coaches Assn. [23381]
U.S. Professional Tennis Assn. [23914]
U.S. ProMiniGolf Assn. [23469]
U.S. Quad Rugby Assn. [23705]
U.S. Racquetball Assn. [23678]
U.S. Rowing Assn. [23704]
U.S. Rugby Football Union [23706]
U.S. Ski Coaches Assn. [23758]
U.S. Ski Mountaineering Assn. [23759]
U.S. Ski and Snowboard Assn. [23760]
U.S. Ski Team Found. [23761]
U.S. Snowshoe Assn. [23769]
U.S. Soling Assn. [23234]
U.S. Specialty Sports Assn. [23795]
U.S. Speedskating [23745]
U.S. Sport Jujitsu Assn. [23609]
U.S. Sports Acad. [23864]
U.S. Sports Chiropractic Fed. [23282]
U.S. Sports Massage Fed. [16485]
U.S. Squash Racquets Assn. [23876]
U.S. Swim School Assn. [23892]
U.S. Taekwondo Union [23610]
U.S. Tchoukball Assn. [23094]
U.S. Team Penning Assn. [23518]
U.S. Telemark Ski Assn. [23762]
U.S. Tennis Assn. [23915]
U.S. Volleyball Association/USA Volleyball [23970]
U.S. Water Fitness Assn. [23657]
U.S. Water Polo [23973]
U.S. Women's Curling Assn. [23303]
U.S. Yngling Assn. [23237]
U.S. Youth Soccer Assn. [23784]
U.S. Yudo Assn. [23611]
Universal Martial Arts Brotherhood [23612]
Universal Wheelchair Football Assn. [23368]
Univ. Athletic Assn. [23865]
US Cheng Ming Martial Arts Assn. [23613]
US Club Soccer [23785]
US Log Rolling Assn. [23982]
US Soccer [23786]
U.S.A. Baseball [23127]
U.S.A. Basketball [23138]
USA Boxing [23267]
USA Broomball [23095]
USA Canoe/Kayak [23280]
USA Climbing [23286]
USA Deaf Sports Fed. [23369]
USA Diving [23382]
USA Gymnastics [23479]
USA Hockey [23488]
U.S.A. Karate Fed. [23566]
USA Powerlifting [23664]
USA Pulling [23929]
USA Roller Sports [23746]
USA Sanatan Sports and Cultural Assn. [23787]
USA Swimming [23893]
U.S.A. Table Tennis [23896]
USA Tennis - NJTL [23916]
U.S.A. Track and Field [23926]
USA Triathlon [23927]
USA Water Ski [23979]
USA Weightlifting [23985]
U.S.A. Wrestling [23989]
USGA Green Sect. [23470]
Vintage Base Ball Assn. [23128]
Virgin Islands Olympic Comm. [23638]
Western Athletic Conf. [23866]
Western Collegiate Hockey Assn. [23489]
Western Golf Assn. [23471]
Western Women Premier Bowlers [23257]
Wheelchair Sports, USA [23371]
Women Outdoors [23644]

Women's All-Star Assn. [23258]
Women's Basketball Coaches Assn. [23139]
Women's Flat Track Derby Assn. [23747]
Women's Natl. Basketball Players Assn. [23140]
Women's Professional Rodeo Assn. [23696]
Women's Sports Found. [23867]
World Aquatic Babies and Children [23894]
World Armsport Fed. [23060]
World Assn. of Benchers and Dead Lifters [23986]
World Diving Coaches Assn. [23383]
World Fast-Draw Assn. [23733]
World Freestyle Watercraft Alliance [23983]
World Head of Family Sokeship Coun. [23614]
World Jeet Kune Do Fed. [23615]
World Martial Arts Assn. [23616]
World Masters Cross-Country Ski Assn. [23763]
World Modern Arnis Alliance [23617]
World Olympians Assn. [23639]
World Sports Medicine Assn. of Registered Therapists [16486]
World Traditional Karate Org. [23567]
World Ving Tsun Athletic Assn. [23618]
Worldloppet/American Birkebeiner [23764]
Wrestlers WithOut Borders [23990]
WTA Tour Players Assn. [23917]
Zen-do Kai Martial Arts [23619]
Athletes Abroad for Christ [19466]
Athletes Abroad for Christ [IO], New Era, MI, United States
Athletes in Action [IO], Xenia, OH, United States
Athletes in Action [19990], 651 Taylor Dr., Xenia, OH 45385-7246, (937)352-1000
Athletes Against Drugs [★13260]
Athletes Against Drugs; Natl. Assn. of [13260]
Athletes Against Drunk Driving; Recording Artists, Actors and [12986]
Athletes of Am; Intercollegiate Assn. of Amateur [23820]
Athletes CAN [IO], Ottawa, ON, Canada
Athletes with Disabilities; America's [23340]
Athletes and Entertainers for Kids [★13560]
Athletes; Fellowship of Christian [20008]
Athletes Outreach; Pro [20029]
Athletes United for Peace [18190], 712 Peralta Ave., Berkeley, CA 94707, (510)273-9235
Athletes; U.S. Assn. for Blind [23363]
Athletic Administrators Assn; Natl. Interscholastic [8989]
Athletic Administrators; Coun. of Collegiate Women's [★8982]
Athletic Assn; Amer. Medical [23650]
Athletic Assn. of Antigua and Barbuda [IO], St. Johns, Antigua-Barbuda
Athletic Assn; Central Intercollegiate [23811]
Athletic Assn; Colored Intercollegiate [★23811]
Athletic Assn. for the Deaf; Amer. [★23369]
Athletic Assn. of Ireland [IO], Dublin, Ireland
Athletic Assn; Natl. Christian Coll. [23837]
Athletic Assn; Natl. Collegiate [23838]
Athletic Assn; Natl. Junior Coll. [23843]
Athletic Assn; Natl. Little Coll. [★23859]
Athletic Assn; Natl. Small Coll. [★23859]
Athletic Assn; Natl. Wheelchair [★23371]
Athletic Assn. of Sri Lanka [IO], Colombo, Sri Lanka
Athletic Assn. of Thailand [IO], Pathumthani, Thailand
Athletic Assn; U.S. Amputee [★23343]
Athletic Assn; U.S. Cerebral Palsy [★23353]
Athletic Assn; Univ. [23865]
Athletic Assn. of Wrestling Coaches and Officials; Natl. Collegiate [★23987]
Athletic Associations; Natl. Fed. of State High School [★23841]
Athletic Bus. Mgt. Assn; Coll. [23813]
Athletic Bus. Managers Assn; Coll. [★23813]
Athletic Coaches Assn; Natl. High School [23292]
Athletic Commn; Consolidated [23816]
Athletic Conf; Eastern Coll. [23484]
Athletic Conf; Southwest [23853]
Athletic Conf; Western [23866]
Athletic Development Directors; Natl. Assn. of [23832]
Athletic Directors; Natl. Coun. of Secondary School [8988]

A star before a book entry number signifies that the name is not listed separately, but is mentioned within the entry.

Athletic and Educational Opportunities/Intl. Center - Defunct.
Athletic Equip. Managers Assn. [23805]; c/o Dorothy Cutting, Off. Mgr., 460 Hunt Hill Rd., Freeville, NY 13068, (607)539-6300
Athletic Equip; Natl. Operating Comm. on Standards for [3451]
Athletic Fed. of Bosnia and Herzegovina [IO], Sarajevo, Bosnia-Hercegovina
Athletic Fed. of Georgia [IO], Tbilisi, Georgia
Athletic Fed. of Kyrgyz Republic [IO], Bishkek, Kirgizstan
Athletic Fed. of Nigeria [IO], Lagos, Nigeria
Athletic Fed. of Republic of Armenia [IO], Yerevan, Armenia
Athletic Fed. of Republic of Kazakhstan [IO], Almaty, Kazakhstan
Athletic Fed; Swiss [IO]
Athletic Fed. of Tajikistan [IO], Dushanbe, Tajikistan
Athletic Fed. of Uzbekistan [IO], Tashkent, Uzbekistan
Athletic Footwear Assn. - Defunct.
Athletic Goods Manufacturers Assn. [★3652]
Athletic Goods Manufacturers Assn. [★IO]
Athletic Goods Team Distributors [★3648]
Athletic Inst. [3658], c/o Sporting Goods Manufacturers Assn., 1150 17th St. NW, Ste. 850, Washington, DC 20036, (202)775-1762
Athletic League; Natl. Police [★13496]
Athletic Leagues; Natl. Assn. of Police [13496]
Athletic Motivation; Inst. of [★23665]
Athletic Motivation and Inst. of Athletic Motivation; Inst. for the Stud. of [★23665]
Athletic Motivation; Inst. for the Stud. of [★23665]
Athletic Solomons [IO], Honiara, Solomon Islands
Athletic Success Inst. [23665], c/o William J. Winslow, Dir., 1933 Winward Point, Discovery Bay, CA 94514, (925)516-8686
Athletic Trainers Assn. and Certification Bd; Amer. [23953]
Athletic Trainers' Assn; Natl. [23954]
Athletic Trainers Soc; Professional Baseball [23125]
Athletic Trainers Soc; Professional Football [23437]
Athletic Training Comm; NAGWS [★8987]
Athletic Training Coun. [★8987]
Athletic Training; Natl. Coun. of [8987]
Athletic Union; Amateur [23797]
Athletic Union; Competitive Swimming Comm. of the Amateur [★23893]
Athletic Union; Powerlifting Comm. of the Amateur [★23663]
Athletic Union; Synchronized Swimming Division of the Amateur [★23889]
Athletic Union Taekwondo Comm; U.S. Natl. Amateur [★23610]
Athletic Union; Water Polo Comm. of the Amateur [★23973]
Athletics
Achilles Track Club [23331]
Adirondack Forty-Sixers [23930]
Adirondack Mountain Club [23931]
Adirondack Trail Improvement Soc. [23932]
Adventure Cycling Assn. [23304]
af2 Natl. Fan Club [24829]
Aikido Assn. of Am. [23046]
Aikido Assn. of North Am. [23047]
All-Amer. Collegiate Golf Found. [23443]
All Japan Ju-Jitsu Intl. Fed. [23577]
Amateur Athletic Union [23797]
Amateur Ski Instructors Assn. [23748]
Amateur Softball Assn. of Am. [23788]
Am. Outdoors [23681]
Amer. Acad. of Podiatric Sports Medicine [16471]
Amer. Acad. of Sports Physicians [16472]
Amer. Alliance for Hea., Physical Educ., Recreation and Dance [8979]
Amer. Amateur Baseball Cong. [23100]
Amer. Amateur Karate Fed. [23559]
Amer. Amputee Soccer Assn. [23773]
Amer. Armsport Assn. [23059]
Amer. Assn. of adaptedSPORTS Programs [23333]
Amer. Assn. of Cheerleading Coaches and Advisors [23061]
Amer. Assn. for the Improvement of Boxing [23259]

Amer. Assn. of Snowboard Instructors [23765]
Amer. Athletic Trainers Assn. and Certification Bd. [23953]
Amer. Barefoot Club [23974]
Amer. Barrel Racing Assn. [23492]
Amer. Baseball Coaches Assn. [23101]
Amer. Bicycle Assn. [23305]
Amer. Bicycle Polo Assn. [23658]
Amer. Bicycle Racing [23667]
Amer. Blind Bowling Assn. [23334]
Amer. Blind Skiing Found. [23336]
Amer. Coll. of Sports Medicine [16473]
Amer. Competition Opportunities for Riders with Disabilities [23330]
Amer. CueSports Alliance [23144]
Amer. Darters Assn. [23327]
Amer. Double Dutch League [23697]
Amer. Endurance Ride Conf. [23933]
Amer. Football Coaches Assn. [23427]
Amer. Gp. Gymnastics Assn. [23473]
Amer. Hiking Soc. [23934]
Amer. Hockey Coaches Assn. [23481]
Amer. Hockey League [23482]
Amer. Hot Rod Assn. [23071]
Amer. Judo Assn. [23552]
Amer. Junior Golf Assn. [23444]
Amer. Junior Rodeo Assn. [23684]
Amer. Kempo-Karate Assn. [23579]
Amer. Kenpo Karate Intl. [23560]
Amer. Legion Baseball [23103]
Amer. Medical Athletic Assn. [23650]
Amer. Medical Tennis Assn. [23898]
Amer. Motorcycle Heritage Found. [23621]
Amer. Orthopaedic Soc. for Sports Medicine [16476]
Amer. Osteopathic Acad. of Sports Medicine [16477]
Amer. Platform Tennis Assn. [23899]
Amer. Sambo Assn. [23580]
Amer. Self-Protection Assn. [23712]
Amer. Sports Builders Assn. [1002]
Amer. Swan Boat Assn. [23669]
Amer. Swimming Coaches Assn. [23882]
Amer. Teachers Assn. of the Martial Arts [23582]
Amer. Tennis Assn. [23900]
Amer. Track Racing Assn. [23306]
Amer. Trails [23935]
Amer. Turners [23802]
Amer. Vaulting Assn. [23967]
Amer. Volkssport Assn. [23803]
Amer. Volleyball Coaches Assn. [23969]
Amer. Water Ski Educational Found. [23975]
Amer. Wheelchair Bowling Assn. [23339]
Amer. Whitewater [23682]
Amer. Wu Shu Soc. [23583]
Amer. Youth Soccer Org. [23774]
America's Found. [20709]
AMOA Natl. Dart Assn. [23329]
Appalachian Mountain Club [23936]
Appalachian Trail Conservancy [23937]
Aquatic Exercise Assn. [23652]
Arabian Jockey Club [23494]
Assn. of Commercial Diving Educators [23960]
Assn. of Disabled Amer. Golfers [23341]
Assn. of Dive Prog. Administrators [23377]
Assn. for Historical Fencing [23399]
Assn. of Northwest Steelheaders [23409]
Assn. of Professional Ball Players of Am. [23105]
Assn. of Surfing Professionals [23877]
Assn. for Women in Sports Media [3097]
Assyrian Chaldean Athletics of North Am. [23062]
Assyrian Chaldean Athletics of North Am. [IO]
Athletes in Action [19990]
Athletes CAN [IO]
Athletic Equip. Managers Assn. [23805]
Athletic Inst. [3658]
Athletic Success Inst. [23665]
Atlantic Coast Conf. [23806]
Babe Ruth Baseball/Softball [23106]
Babe Ruth Birthplace/Sports Legends at Camden Yards [23107]
Baseball Writers Assn. of Am. [3099]
Bicycle Parking Proj. [23307]
Bicycle Ride Directors' Assn. of Am. [23308]
Big East Conf. [23807]

Big Ten Conf. [23808]
Big West Conf. [23809]
BlueRibbon Coalition [23680]
Caribbean Amer. Netball Assn. [23633]
Catalina 22 Natl. Sailing Assn. [23162]
Central Collegiate Hockey Assn. [23483]
Central Intercollegiate Athletic Assn. [23811]
CHA - Certified Horsemanship Assn. [23523]
Championship Assn. of Mechanics [23075]
Cinderella Softball Leagues [23789]
Citizenship Through Sports Alliance [23812]
Coll. Athletic Bus. Mgt. Assn. [23813]
Coll. Gymnastics Assn. [23474]
Coll. Sports Info. Directors of Am. [23814]
Coll. Swimming Coaches Assn. of Am. [23883]
Collegiate Commissioners Assn. [23815]
Collegiate Soaring Assn. [23039]
Combat Martial Art Practitioners Assn. [23587]
Consolidated Athletic Commn. [23816]
Continental Basketball Assn. [23129]
Continental Divide Trail Soc. [23938]
Cosmopolitan Soccer League [23775]
Coun. of Ivy Gp. Presidents [23817]
Cowboy Mounted Shooting Assn. [23716]
Disabled Sports USA [23343]
Divers Alert Network [23378]
Dwarf Athletic Assn. of Am. [23063]
Eastern Assn. of Rowing Colleges [23699]
Eastern Coll. Athletic Conf. [23484]
Eastern Coll. Soccer Assn. [23776]
Eastern Collegiate Hockey Assn. [23485]
Eastern Intercollegiate Gymnastic League [23475]
Eastern Surfing Assn. [23878]
Federacion Dominicana de Asociaciones de Atletismo [IO]
Fed. of Intl. Polo [23819]
Fellowship of Christian Athletes [20008]
Florida Trail Assn. [23939]
Football Writers Assn. of Am. [23430]
Found. for Safer Athletic Field Environments [23064]
Free Throwers Boomerang Soc. [23247]
Future Fisherman Found. [23415]
George Khoury Assn. of Baseball Leagues [23109]
Golf Coaches Assn. of Am. [23448]
Golf Tournament Assn. of Am. [23449]
Golf Writers Assn. of Am. [23450]
Great Lakes Sport Fishing Coun. [23416]
Gp. Fore Golf Found. [23451]
Hampton One-Design Class Racing Assn. [23173]
Handicapped Scuba Assn. [23344]
Harness Horse Youth Found. [23496]
Heritage Trails Fund [23940]
Hockey North Am. [23486]
Horsemanship Safety Assn. [23525]
Inland Lake Yachting Assn. [23175]
Inst. of Diving [23961]
Intercollegiate Fencing Assn. [23401]
Intercollegiate Horse Show Assn. [23526]
Intercollegiate Outing Club Assn. [23941]
Intercollegiate Rowing Assn. [23700]
Intercollegiate Tennis Assn. [23902]
Intl. 210 Assn. [23179]
Intl. 505 Yacht Racing Assn., Amer. Sect. [23180]
Intl. Acad. of Aquatic Art [23884]
Intl. Acad. for Sports Dentistry [16481]
Intl. Aikido Assn. [23048]
Intl. Assn. of Gay and Lesbian Martial Artists [23588]
Intl. Assn. of Physical Educ. and Sport for Girls and Women [8980]
Intl. Athletic Found. [IO]
Intl. Bonefishing Soc. [22452]
Intl. Boxing Fed. [23260]
Intl. Boxing Hall of Fame Museum [23261]
Intl. Coun. for Hea., Physical Educ., Recreation, Sport, and Dance [8981]
Intl. Dodge Ball Fed. [23821]
Intl. Fed. of Sleddog Sports [23393]
Intl. Female Boxers Assn. [23263]
Intl. Golf Associates [23452]
Intl. Golf Fed. [23453]
Intl. Hunter Educ. Assn. [23545]
Intl. J/22 Class Assn. [23187]

Reference to "IO" in place of a book number signifies that the association may be found in the 45th edition of International Organizations.

Intl. Lacrosse Fed. [23570]
Intl. League of Professional Baseball Clubs [23110]
Intl. Martial Arts League [23589]
Intl. Medalist Assn. [23825]
Intl. Mental Game Coaching Assn. [23289]
Intl. Mountain Bicycling Assn. [23310]
Intl. Naples Sabot Assn. [23190]
Intl. Natural Bodybuilding and Fitness Fed. [23243]
Intl. Professional Rodeo Assn. [23686]
Intl. Racquetball Fed. [23677]
Intl. Senior Softball Assn. [23790]
Intl. Seven-Star Mantis Style Lee Kam Wing Martial Art Assn. - USA [23591]
Intl. Side Saddle Org. [23529]
Intl. Ski Dancing Assn. [23751]
Intl. Skiing History Assn. [10965]
Intl. Softball Fed. [23791]
Intl. Sports Exchange [23826]
Intl. Sports Heritage Assn. [23827]
Intl. Sports Massage Fed. [16482]
Intl. Swimming Hall of Fame [23886]
Intl. Tennis Hall of Fame [23903]
Intl. Thunderbird Class Assn. [23195]
Intl. Track and Field Coaches Assn. [23919]
Intl. Traditional Karate Fed. [23562]
Intl. Unicycling Fed. [23311]
Intl. Vaulting Club [23968]
Intl. Veteran Boxers Assn. [23264]
Intl. Wheelchair Road Racers Club [23346]
Intl. Yang Style Tai Chi Chuan Assn. [23594]
IOCALUM [23942]
Japan Aikido Assn. U.S.A. [23595]
The Jockey Club [23502]
Jockeys' Guild [23503]
Joint Commn. on Sports Medicine and Sci. [16483]
Keith Bulluck Fan Club [24830]
Knights Boxing Team - Intl. [23265]
Korean Amer. Professional Tennis Assn. [23904]
Ladies Professional Golf Assn. [23454]
League of Amer. Bicyclists [23312]
Light Living Library [23272]
Lincoln Heritage Trail Found. [23943]
Little League Baseball and Softball [23111]
Little League Found. [23112]
Maccabi USA/Sports for Israel [23828]
Major League Baseball [23113]
Major Wingfield Historical Soc. [23905]
Marathon Skating Intl. [23737]
Martial Arts Intl. Fed. [23596]
Martial Arts USA [23597]
Metropolitan Intercollegiate Basketball Assn. [23131]
Middle States Regatta Assn. [23701]
Montana Outfitters and Guides Assn. [23944]
Mountaineers [23945]
Mounted Games Across Am. [23830]
Multicultural Golf Assn. of Am. [23455]
Naismith Memorial Basketball Hall of Fame [23132]
Natl. Ability Center [23347]
Natl. Acad. of Sports [23831]
Natl. Advt. Golf Assn. [23456]
Natl. Alliance for Accessible Golf [23348]
Natl. Alliance for Youth Sports [23290]
Natl. Amateur Baseball Fed. [23115]
Natl. Amateur Body Builders Assn. USA [23244]
Natl. Amputee Golf Assn. [23349]
Natl. Assn. of Athletic Development Directors [23832]
Natl. Assn. of Basketball Coaches [23133]
Natl. Assn. of Collegiate Directors of Athletics [23833]
Natl. Assn. of Collegiate Gymnastics Coaches/ Women [23476]
Natl. Assn. of Collegiate Marketing Administrators [23834]
Natl. Assn. for Girls and Women in Sport [8983]
Natl. Assn. of Intercollegiate Athletics [23835]
Natl. Assn. for Kinesiology and Physical Educ. in Higher Educ. [8984]
Natl. Assn. of Left-Handed Golfers [23458]
Natl. Assn. for Physical Educ. in Higher Educ. [8985]

Natl. Assn. of Professional Baseball Leagues [23116]
Natl. Assn. for Sport and Physical Educ. [8986]
Natl. Assn. of Sports Commissions [23871]
Natl. Assn. of Sports Officials [23872]
Natl. Assn. of Sports Officials - Organizations Network [23873]
Natl. Assn. of Underwater Instructors [23963]
Natl. Assn. of Women's Gymnastic's Judges [23477]
Natl. Athletic Trainers' Assn. [23954]
Natl. Baseball Cong. [23117]
Natl. Baseball Hall of Fame and Museum [23118]
Natl. Basketball Assn. [23134]
Natl. Basketball Athletic Trainers Assn. [23135]
Natl. Bicycle League [23313]
Natl. Bicycle Tour Directors Assn. [23314]
Natl. Bucking Bull Assn. [23687]
Natl. Camp Assn. [23277]
Natl. Center for Bicycling and Walking [23315]
Natl. Christian Coll. Athletic Assn. [23837]
Natl. Collegiate Athletic Assn. [23838]
Natl. Collegiate Roller Hockey Assn. [23487]
Natl. Collegiate Table Tennis Assn. [23895]
Natl. Coun. of Athletic Training [8987]
Natl. Coun. of Secondary School Athletic Directors [8988]
Natl. Coun. on Strength and Fitness [23955]
Natl. Coun. for Taekwondo Masters Certification [23599]
Natl. Coun. of Youth Sports [23839]
Natl. Disability Sports Alliance [23353]
Natl. Fed. of Professional Bullriders [23688]
Natl. Fed. of Professional Trainers [23956]
Natl. Fed. of State High School Associations [23841]
Natl. Field Hockey Coaches Assn. [23404]
Natl. Finals Rodeo Comm. [23689]
Natl. Football Found. and Coll. Hall of Fame [23431]
Natl. Football League [23432]
Natl. Football League Alumni [23433]
Natl. Football League Players Assn. [23434]
Natl. Gym Assn. [23654]
Natl. High School Athletic Coaches Assn. [23292]
Natl. High School Baseball Coaches Assn. [23119]
Natl. High School Rodeo Assn. [23690]
Natl. Intercollegiate Rodeo Assn. [23691]
Natl. Intercollegiate Running Club Assn. [23707]
Natl. Intercollegiate Soccer Officials Assn. [23778]
Natl. Interscholastic Athletic Administrators Assn. [8989]
Natl. Interscholastic Swimming Coaches Assn. of Am. [23887]
Natl. Intramural-Recreational Sports Assn. [23842]
Natl. Jousting Assn. [23551]
Natl. Junior Baseball League [23120]
Natl. Junior Coll. Athletic Assn. [23843]
Natl. Little Britches Rodeo Assn. [23692]
Natl. Operating Comm. on Standards for Athletic Equip. [3451]
Natl. Org. for Rivers [23683]
Natl. Org. of I Walkers [23971]
Natl. Paddleball Assn. [23092]
Natl. Public Parks Tennis Assn. [23906]
Natl. Scholastic Surfing Assn. [23880]
Natl. Semi-Professional Baseball Assn. [23122]
Natl. Senior Games Assn. [23655]
Natl. Ski Patrol Sys. [23753]
Natl. Soccer Coaches Assn. of Am. [23779]
Natl. Softball Assn. [23792]
Natl. Sporting Clays Assn. [23726]
Natl. Sporting Goods Assn. [3647]
Natl. Starwind/Spindrift Class Assn. [23207]
Natl. Steeplechase Assn. [23509]
Natl. Strength and Conditioning Assn. [23957]
Natl. Thoroughbred Racing Assn. [23510]
Natl. Throws Coaches Assn. [23293]
Natl. Tractor Pullers Assn. [23928]
Natl. Trail Ride Assn. [23946]
Natl. Wheelchair Basketball Assn. [23354]
Natl. Wheelchair Poolplayer Assn. [23355]
Natl. Wheelchair Softball Assn. [23356]
Natl. Women's Hall of Fame [20716]

Natl. Women's Martial Arts Fed. [23600]
Natl. Wrestling Coaches Assn. [23987]
Natl. Youth Sports Safety Found. [16484]
NETA - Natl. Exercise Trainers Assn. [23037]
New England Trails Conf. [23948]
New York Triathlon Club [23922]
NFHS Coaches Assn. [23294]
NFHS Officials Assn. [23874]
North Am. Wu(Hao) Taiji Fed. [23601]
North Amer. Boxing Fed. [23266]
North Amer. Chinese Soccer League [23780]
North Amer. Fastpitch Assn. [23793]
North Amer. Fishing Club [23421]
North Amer. Football League [23435]
North Amer. Formula 18 Assn. [23208]
North Amer. Kettlebell Fed. [23984]
North Amer. Natural Bodybuilding Fed. [23245]
North Amer. Network of Women Runners [23656]
North Amer. Riding for the Handicapped Assn. [23357]
North Amer. Sports Fed. [23065]
North Amer. Sports Fed. [IO]
North Amer. Strongman [23246]
North Amer. Trail Ride Conf. [23949]
North Country Trail Assn. [23950]
NSGA Team Dealer Div. [3648]
Olson 30 Class Assn. [23210]
One-Arm Dove Hunt Assn. [23358]
Over the Hill Gang, Intl. [23846]
Pacific 10 Conf. [23847]
Pacific Northwest Ski Assn. [23754]
Pan-American Union of Karatedo Organizations [23564]
Panthessalonikan Athletic Org. of Konstantinople [IO]
Patience T'ai Chi Assn. [23897]
PGA TOUR Tournaments Assn. [23461]
Physically Challenged Golf Assn. [23359]
Polish Amer. Golf Assn. [23462]
Pony Baseball and Softball [23124]
Positive Coaching Alliance [23296]
Pro Athletes Outreach [20029]
Pro Players Assn. [13402]
Professional Armed Forces Rodeo Assn. [23693]
Professional Assn. of Diving Instructors [23964]
Professional Assn. of Volleyball Officials [23875]
Professional Baseball Athletic Trainers Soc. [23125]
Professional Football Researchers Assn. [23438]
Professional Golfers' Assn. of Am. [23464]
Professional Putters Assn. [23465]
Professional Rodeo Cowboys Assn. [23694]
Professional Skaters Assn. [23738]
Professional Ski Instructors of Am. [23755]
Professional Tennis Registry [23909]
Qajaq USA [23981]
Rails-to-Trails Conservancy [23952]
Randonneurs USA [23316]
Recreational Scuba Training Coun. [23965]
RollerSoccer Intl. Fed. [23850]
Running USA [23708]
San Juan 21 Class Assn. [23215]
Scoot-Tours Touring Scooter Riders Assn. [23627]
Scottish Athletics [IO]
Senior Roller Skaters of Am. [23739]
Sheclimbs [23285]
Shudokan Martial Arts Assn. [23603]
Sigma Delta Psi [24407]
Ski for Light [23361]
Soccer Assn. for Youth [23781]
Soc. for Amer. Baseball Res. [23126]
Soc. of Roller Skating Teachers of Am. [23741]
Soc. of State Directors of Hea., Physical Educ. and Recreation [8992]
Sony Ericsson WTA Tour [23910]
Southeastern Conf. [23851]
Southern Conf. [23852]
Special Olympics [23362]
Sport and Recreation Law Assn. [23870]
Sporting Goods Agents Assn. [176]
Sporting Goods Manufacturers Assn. Intl. [3652]
Sports Charities USA [23854]
Sports Hall of Oblivion [23855]
Sports Philatelists Intl. [22877]
Sportscar Vintage Racing Assn. [23085]

A star before a book entry number signifies that the name is not listed separately, but is mentioned within the entry.

Surfrider Found. [23881]
Synchro Swimming U.S.A. [23889]
Tandem Club of Am. [23317]
Traditional Tae Kwon Do Chung Do Assn. [23604]
Ultimate Players Assn. [23375]
Underwater Soc. of Am. [23966]
Unicycling Soc. of Am. [23319]
United Fly Tyers [23424]
U.S. Adventure Racing Assn. [23672]
U.S. Amateur Confed. of Roller Skating [23742]
U.S. Amateur Tug of War Assn. [23959]
U.S.A. Cricket Assn. [23299]
U.S.A. Deaf Basketball [23136]
U.S.A. Netball Assn. [23634]
U.S.A. Wushu-Kungfu Fed. [23605]
U.S. Apnea Assn. [23380]
U.S. Aquatic Sports [23890]
U.S. ArmSports [23991]
U.S. Assn. for Blind Athletes [23363]
U.S. Assn. of Independent Gymnastic Clubs [3673]
U.S. Barrel Jumping Assn. [23743]
U.S. Basketball Writers Assn. [23137]
U.S. Biathlon Assn. [23756]
U.S. Bicycle Polo Assn. [23660]
U.S. Blind Golf Assn. [23364]
U.S. Bobsled and Skeleton Fed. [23767]
U.S. Bocce Fed. [23241]
U.S. Broomball Assn. [23858]
U.S. Collegiate Athletic Assn. [23859]
U.S. Collegiate Ski and Snowboard Assn. [23757]
U.S. Collegiate Sports Coun. [23860]
U.S. Competitive Aerobics Fed. [23038]
U.S. Cultural Exchange and Sports Soc. [23861]
U.S. Curling Assn. [23302]
U.S. Dental Tennis Assn. [23911]
U.S. Disc Sports [23376]
U.S. Dressage Fed. [23533]
U.S. Equestrian Fed. [23534]
U.S. Eventing Assn. [23535]
U.S. Fastpitch Assn. [23794]
U.S. Fencing Assn. [23402]
U.S. Fencing Coaches Assn. [23403]
U.S. Field Hockey Assn. [23405]
U.S. Figure Skating Assn. [23744]
U.S. Flag Football League [23440]
U.S. Flag and Touch Football League [23441]
U.S. Floorball Assn. [23093]
U.S. Football Alliance [23442]
U.S. Futsal Fed. [23862]
U.S. Girls' Wrestling Assn. [23988]
U.S. Golf Assn. [23467]
U.S. Handball Assn. [23480]
U.S. Handcycling Fed. [23321]
U.S. Helice Assn. [23729]
U.S. High School Tennis Assn. [23912]
U.S. Hydrofoil Assn. [23978]
U.S. Indoor Soccer Assn. [23782]
U.S. Intercollegiate Lacrosse Assn. [23571]
U.S. Isshinryu Karate Assn. [23565]
U.S. Judo [23554]
U.S. Judo Assn. [23555]
U.S. Lacrosse [23572]
U.S. Lacrosse Assn., Women's Div. [23573]
U.S. Luge Assn. [23575]
U.S. Martial Arts Assn. [23607]
U.S. Masters Swimming [23891]
U.S. Mirror Class Assn. [23229]
U.S. Modern Pentathlon Assn. [23925]
U.S. Muay Thai Assn. [23608]
U.S. Natl. Tennis Acad. [23913]
U.S. Olympic Comm. [23637]
U.S. Polo Assn. [23661]
U.S. Pony Clubs [23537]
U.S. Power Soccer Assn. [23783]
U.S. Professional Diving Coaches Assn. [23381]
U.S. Professional Tennis Assn. [23914]
U.S. ProMiniGolf Assn. [23469]
U.S. Quad Rugby Assn. [23705]
U.S. Racquetball Assn. [23678]
U.S. Rowing Assn. [23704]
U.S. Rugby Football Union [23706]
U.S. Running Streak Assn. [23709]
U.S. Ski Coaches Assn. [23758]
U.S. Ski Mountaineering Assn. [23759]

U.S. Ski and Snowboard Assn. [23760]
U.S. Ski Team Found. [23761]
U.S. Snowshoe Assn. [23769]
U.S. Soling Assn. [23234]
U.S. Specialty Sports Assn. [23795]
U.S. Speedskating [23745]
U.S. Sport Jujitsu Assn. [23609]
U.S. Sports Acad. [23864]
U.S. Sports Massage Fed. [16485]
U.S. Squash Racquets Assn. [23876]
U.S. Swim School Assn. [23892]
U.S. Taekwondo Union [23610]
U.S. Tchoukball Assn. [23094]
U.S. Team Penning Assn. [23518]
U.S. Telemark Ski Assn. [23762]
U.S. Tennis Assn. [23915]
U.S. Volleyball Association/USA Volleyball [23970]
U.S. Water Fitness Assn. [23657]
U.S. Water Polo [23973]
U.S. Women's Curling Assn. [23303]
U.S. Yngling Assn. [23237]
U.S. Youth Soccer Assn. [23784]
U.S. Yudo Assn. [23611]
Universal Wheelchair Football Assn. [23368]
Univ. Athletic Assn. [23865]
US Cheng Ming Martial Arts Assn. [23613]
US Club Soccer [23785]
US Log Rolling Assn. [23982]
US Soccer [23786]
U.S.A. Baseball [23127]
U.S.A. Basketball [23138]
USA Boxing [23267]
USA Broomball [23095]
USA Canoe/Kayak [23280]
USA Climbing [23286]
USA Deaf Sports Fed. [23369]
USA Diving [23382]
USA Fed. of Pankration Athlima [23066]
USA Gymnastics [23479]
USA Hockey [23488]
U.S.A. Karate Fed. [23566]
USA Powerlifting [23664]
USA Pulling [23929]
USA Roller Sports [23746]
USA Sanatan Sports and Cultural Assn. [23787]
USA Swimming [23893]
U.S.A. Table Tennis [23896]
USA Tennis - NJTL [23916]
U.S.A. Track and Field [23926]
USA Triathlon [23927]
USA Water Ski [23979]
USA Weightlifting [23985]
U.S.A. Wrestling [23989]
USGA Green Sect. [23470]
Vintage Base Ball Assn. [23128]
Western Athletic Conf. [23866]
Western Collegiate Hockey Assn. [23489]
Western Golf Assn. [23471]
Western Women Premier Bowlers [23257]
Wheelchair Sports, USA [23371]
Women Involved in Sports Evolution [23067]
Women Outdoors [23644]
Women's All-Star Assn. [23258]
Women's Basketball Coaches Assn. [23139]
Women's Natl. Basketball Players Assn. [23140]
Women's Professional Rodeo Assn. [23696]
Women's Sports Found. [23867]
World Aquatic Babies and Children [23894]
World Armsport Fed. [23060]
World Assn. of Benchers and Dead Lifters [23986]
World Diving Coaches Assn. [23383]
World Fast-Draw Assn. [23733]
World Freestyle Watercraft Alliance [23983]
World Jeet Kune Do Fed. [23615]
World Martial Arts Assn. [23616]
World Masters Cross-Country Ski Assn. [23763]
World Olympians Assn. [23639]
World Sports Medicine Assn. of Registered Therapists [16486]
World Ving Tsun Athletic Assn. [23618]
Worldloppet/American Birkebeiner [23764]
WTA Tour Players Assn. [23917]
Zen-do Kai Martial Arts [23619]
Athletics Administrators; Natl. Assn. of Collegiate Women [8982]

Athletics Assn. of Malawi [IO], Blantyre, Malawi
Athletics Assn. of Maldives [IO], Male, Maldives
Athletics Associations of Guyana [IO], Georgetown, Guyana
Athletics Australia [IO], Melbourne, Australia
Athletics for the Blind - Address unknown since 1995.
Athletics Canada [IO], Ottawa, ON, Canada
The Athletics Cong. of the U.S.A. [★23926]
Athletics Cook Islands [IO], Rarotonga, Cook Islands
Athletics and Entertainers for Kids [13560], 3337 Colorado St., Long Beach, CA 90814, (562)438-5905
Athletics Fed. of India [IO], New Delhi, India
Athletics Fed. of Pakistan [IO], Islamabad, Pakistan
Athletics Fiji [IO], Suva, Fiji
Athletics Kenya [IO], Nairobi, Kenya
Athletics Namibia [IO], Windhoek, Namibia
Athletics; Natl. Assn. of Academic Advisors for [8171]
Athletics; Natl. Assn. of Collegiate Directors of [23833]
Athletics; Natl. Assn. of Intercollegiate [23835]
Athletics New Zealand [IO], Wellington, New Zealand
Athletics Samoa [IO], Apia, Western Samoa
Athletisme Canada [★IO]
Athlima; USA Fed. of Pankration [23066]
Athra Kadisha: The Soc. for the Preservation of Jewish Holy Sites [10274], 203 Penn St., Brooklyn, NY 11211, (845)783-9626
Athy Tribe of Galway - Address unknown since 2007.
Atira Women's Rsrc. Soc. [IO], Vancouver, BC, Canada
Atkins Appreciation Soc; Chet [24858]
Atlanta Blues Fan Club - Defunct.
Atlanta Flames Fan Club [24996], c/o Betsy Watkins, VP, 3297 Wiltshire Dr., Avondale Estates, GA 30002-1640
Atlantic
  Atlantic Coast Conf. [23806]
  Atlantic Coun. of the U.S. [17014]
  Club Managers Assn. of Am. [833]
Atlantic Amer. Flag Liner Operators/Trans-Pacific Amer. Flag Berth Operators; Trans- [3592]
Atlantic Assn. of Applied Economists [IO], Halifax, NS, Canada
Atlantic Center for the Env. [★IO]
Atlantic Center for the Env. [★4601]
Atlantic Center for the Env; Quebec-Labrador Foundation/ [4601]
Atlantic Coast Boat Builders and Repairers Assn. [★2568]
Atlantic Coast Conf. [23806], PO Drawer ACC, Greensboro, NC 27417-6724, (336)854-8787
Atlantic Coast Football League - Defunct.
Atlantic Coun. of Canada [IO], Toronto, ON, Canada
Atlantic Coun. of the U.S. [17014], 1101 15th St. NW, 11th Fl., Washington, DC 20005, (202)463-7226
Atlantic Deeper Waterways Assn. - Defunct.
Atlantic Economic Soc. [★6883]
Atlantic Economic Soc. [★IO]
Atlantic Equity Consortium; Mid- [8276]
Atlantic Estuarine Res. Soc. [★7271]
Atlantic Fiber Assn; Mid [310]
Atlantic Film Festival Assn. [IO], Halifax, NS, Canada
Atlantic Fisheries Assn; Middle [3493]
Atlantic Flyway Coun. [5295], Virginia Dept. of Game & Inland Fisheries, PO Box 11104, Richmond, VA 23230, (804)367-1000
Atlantic and Gulf Amer. Flag Berth Operators - Address unknown since 1995.
Atlantic and Gulf Coasts Dry Dock Assn. [★2592]
Atlantic Independent Union [24161], 520 Cinnaminson Ave., Palmyra, NJ 08065, (856)303-0776
Atlantic Information Centre for Teachers - Defunct.
Atlantic Legal Found. [5930], 330 Madison Ave., 6th Fl., New York, NY 10017, (212)867-3322
Atlantic Ocean Alliance - Defunct.
Atlantic Offshore Fish and Lobster Assn. [★5728]
Atlantic Offshore Fishermen's Assn. [★5728]
Atlantic Offshore Lobstermen's Assn. [5728], c/o Bonnie Spinazzola, Exec. Dir./Sec., 54 Chatham Dr., Bedford, NH 03110, (603)206-5468

Reference to "IO" in place of a book number signifies that the association may be found in the 45th edition of International Organizations.

Atlantic Professional Boatmans Assn. - Defunct.
Atlantic Salmon Fed. [IO], St. Andrews, NB, Canada
Atlantic States Marine Fisheries Commn. [5729],
1444 Eye St. NW, 6th Fl., Washington, DC 20005,
(202)289-6400
Atlantic Treaty Assn. [IO], Brussels, Belgium
Atlantic Waterfowl Coun. [★5295]
Atlantis Project - Defunct.
Atlantis Res. Centre - Defunct.
Atlantis Res. Group - Address unknown since 2001.
Atlantische Commissie [★IO]
Atlantsammenslutningen [★IO]
Atlas Economic Res. Found. [6874], 2000 N 14th
St., Ste. 550, Arlington, VA 22201, (703)934-6969
Atlas Educational Center - Defunct.
Atlatl [9557]
Atletska Zveza Slovenije [IO], Ljubljana, Slovenia
Atletski savez Bosne i Hercegovine [★IO]
ATM Indus. Assn. [466], PO Box 452, Brookings, SD
57006-0452
Atmospheric Policy; Alliance for Responsible [797]
Atmospheric Research; National Center for [★7622]
Atmospheric Res; Univ. Corp. for [7329]
ATOL [IO], Leuven, Belgium
Atomedic Res. Center - Address unknown since
1995.
Atomic Bomb Casualty Commn. [★IO]
Atomic Bomb Survivors in the U.S; Comm. of
[18144]
Atomic Energy Agency; Intl. [IO]
Atomic Energy Coun. [IO], Taipei, Taiwan
Atomic Energy Liability Underwriters; Mutual [2201]
Atomic Energy Soc. of Japan [IO], Tokyo, Japan
Atomic Indus. Forum [★6969]
Atomic/Nuclear Energy Study Group - Address
unknown since 1989.
Atomic Scientists; Fed. of [★18445]
Atomic Veterans; Natl. Assn. of [13353]
Attachment Parenting Intl. [12662], PO Box 4615,
Alpharetta, GA 30023, (800)520-8320
Attachment Parenting Intl. [IO], Nashville, TN, United
States
Attend [IO], London, United Kingdom
Attendance; Natl. League to Promote School
[★8326]
Attendant Prog. Today; Amer. Disabled for [17413]
Attention-Deficit Disorder Assn. [★15343]
Attention Deficit Disorder Assn; Natl. [15343]
Attention Deficit Disorder; Children and Adults With
[★15314]
Attention-Deficit Disorders; Children with [★15314]
Attention Deficit/Hyperactivity Disorder; Children and
Adults With [15314]
Attention Deficit Info. Network [15308], 58 Prince
St., Needham, MA 02492, (781)455-9895
Attitudinal Healing; Center for [★15206]
Attiyeh Found. - Address unknown since 2003.
Attorney-Certified Public Accountants; Amer. Assn. of
[8]
Attorney Ethics; Americans for the Enforcement of
[12123]
Attorney Ethics Assn. [★12123]
Attorney Ethics Assn. [★12123]
Attorneys
Advocates' Soc. [IO]
Alliance of Merger and Acquisition Advisors [54]
Amer. Acad. of Adoption Attorneys [5471]
Amer. Acad. of Appellate Lawyers [5472]
Amer. Acad. of Estate Planning Attorneys [5473]
Amer. Acad. of Matrimonial Lawyers [5698]
Amer. Assn. for Justice [6328]
Amer. Assn. of Nurse Attorneys [15000]
Amer. Assn. of Visually Impaired Attorneys [5474]
Amer. Bankruptcy Inst. [5574]
Amer. Bar Assn. [5475]
Amer. Bar Assn. Center for Professional
Responsibility [5476]
Amer. Bar Assn. Young Lawyers Div. [5477]
Amer. Bd. of Certification [5478]
Amer. Bd. of Professional Liability Attorneys
[6041]
Amer. Bd. of Trial Advocates [6329]
Amer. Catholic Lawyers Assn. [5558]
Amer. Coll. of Constr. Lawyers [323]
Amer. Coll. of Legal Medicine [15001]

Amer. Coll. of Real Estate Lawyers [5479]
Amer. Coll. of Trial Lawyers [6330]
Amer. Court and Commercial Newspapers [3202]
Amer. Foreign Law Assn. [5864]
Amer. Hea. Lawyers Assn. [5782]
Amer. Immigration Lawyers Assn. [5807]
Amer. Law Inst. [5925]
Amer. Lawyers Auxiliary [5480]
Amer. Prepaid Legal Services Inst. [6020]
Amer. Prosecutors Res. Inst. [5481]
Amer. Soc. of Access Professionals [5814]
Amer. Soc. of Law, Medicine and Ethics [15002]
Amer. Soc. for Pharmacy Law [15003]
Amer. Veterinary Medical Law Assn. [5927]
Americans for the Enforcement of Attorney Ethics
[12123]
Armenian Bar Assn. [5482]
Armenian Bar Assn. [IO]
Asian Amer. Legal Defense and Educ. Fund
[17095]
Assn. of Attorney-Mediators [5483]
Assn. of Black Women Attorneys [5484]
Assn. of Commercial Finance Attorneys [5485]
Assn. of Defense Trial Attorneys [5825]
Assn. for Honest Attorneys [5486]
Assn. of Independent European Lawyers [IO]
Assn. of Muslim Lawyers [IO]
Assn. of Pension Lawyers [IO]
Assn. of Professional Responsibility Lawyers
[5487]
Assn. of Solicitors and Investment Managers [IO]
Assn. of Women Solicitors [IO]
The Attorney's Gp. [5488]
Avocats Sans Frontieres [IO]
Bar Assn. for Local Govt. and the Public Ser. [IO]
Canadian Bar Assn. [IO]
Canadian Corporate Counsel Assn. [IO]
Center for Amer. and Intl. Law [5931]
Chinese Law Soc. of Am. [5933]
Clarity [6011]
Clinical Legal Educ. Assn. [8763]
Commonwealth Assn. of Public Sector Lawyers
[IO]
Copyright Soc. of the U.S.A. [5843]
CoreNet Global [3305]
Coun. for Court Excellence [5897]
Coun. of Parent Attorneys and Advocates [9142]
Croatian Amer. Bar Assn. [5489]
Croatian Bar Assn. [IO]
Customs and Intl. Trade Bar Assn. [5659]
Decalogue Soc. of Lawyers [5490]
Defense Res. Inst. [6042]
Educ. Law Assn. [5676]
Equal Justice Works [5898]
European Lawyers' Union [IO]
European Young Bar Assn. [IO]
Faculty of Advocates [IO]
Fair Elections Legal Network [5491]
Fed. Bar Assn. [5492]
Fed. Circuit Bar Assn. [5493]
Fed. of Defense and Corporate Counsel [5827]
Fellows of the Amer. Bar Found. [5494]
Fellows of the American Bar Foundation [IO]
Finnish Bar Assn. [IO]
First Amendment Lawyers Assn. [5605]
Found. of the Amer. Bd. of Trial Advocates [5495]
Found. of the Fed. Bar Assn. [5937]
Franco-British Lawyers Soc. [IO]
Gen. Coun. of the Bar [IO]
Gen. Coun. of the Bar of Northern Ireland [IO]
Global Lawyers and Physicians [14558]
Global Village Inst. [6235]
Guild of Catholic Lawyers [19631]
Hispanic Natl. Bar Assn. [5496]
Human Rights Advocates [5801]
Human Rights First [17759]
Incorporated Soc. of Irish/American Lawyers
[5939]
Inner Circle of Advocates [6043]
Inst. of Certified Bus. Counselors [726]
Inst. of Judicial Admin. [5902]
Inter-American Bar Assn. [5941]
Intl. Acad. of Trial Lawyers [5497]
Intl. Acad. of Trial Lawyers [IO]
Intl. Alliance of Holistic Lawyers [5498]

Intl. Alliance of Law Firms [IO]
Intl. Assn. of Defense Counsel [IO]
Intl. Assn. of Defense Counsel [5499]
Intl. Assn. of Lawyers [IO]
Intl. Assn. of Official Human Rights Agencies
[5802]
Intl. Assn. of Prosecutors [IO]
Intl. Assn. of Young Lawyers [IO]
Intl. Intellectual Property Assn. [5848]
Intl. Legal Defense Counsel [5869]
Intl. Municipal Lawyers Assn. [5500]
Intl. Municipal Lawyers Assn. [IO]
Intl. Network of Boutique Law Firms [5501]
Intl. Senior Lawyers Proj. [5502]
Intl. Senior Lawyers Proj. [IO]
Intl. Soc. of Barristers [6331]
Intl. Soc. of Primerus Law Firms [5503]
Intl. Soc. of Primerus Law Firms [IO]
Iranian Amer. Bar Assn. [5504]
ITC Trial Lawyers Assn. [6332]
Law Soc. [IO]
Law Soc. of England [IO]
Law Soc. of Scotland [IO]
Law Students for Choice [18517]
Lawyers Alliance for World Security [18158]
Lawyers Assoc. Worldwide [5505]
Lawyers for Children Am. [6026]
Lawyers for One Am. [6028]
Lawyers Without Borders [18008]
Lex Mundi [5506]
Lex Mundi [IO]
Lithuanian-American Bar Assn. [5507]
Los Angeles Copyright Soc. [5854]
Minority Corporate Counsel Assn. [5615]
Natl. Assn. of Asst. U.S. Attorneys [5508]
Natl. Assn. of Attorneys Gen. [6276]
Natl. Assn. of Bench and Bar Spouses [5509]
Natl. Assn. of Bond Lawyers [6255]
Natl. Assn. of Coll. and Univ. Attorneys [5677]
Natl. Assn. of Consumer Bankruptcy Attorneys
[5510]
National Association of Consumer Bankruptcy At-
torneys [IO]
Natl. Assn. of County Civil Attorneys [5619]
Natl. Assn. of Dealer Counsel [361]
Natl. Assn. of Muslim Lawyers [5511]
Natl. Assn. of Railroad Trial Counsel [6321]
Natl. Assn. of Republican Attorneys [5512]
Natl. Assn. of Retail Coll. Attorneys [5513]
Natl. Assn. of Women Lawyers [5514]
Natl. Bar Assn. [5515]
Natl. Bd. of Trial Advocacy [6333]
Natl. Center on Poverty Law [6030]
Natl. Conf. of Bar Examiners [5950]
Natl. Conf. of Bar Presidents [5516]
Natl. Conf. of Black Lawyers [5517]
Natl. Conf. of Black Lawyers [IO]
Natl. Conf. of Women's Bar Associations [5518]
Natl. Counsel of Black Lawyers [5519]
Natl. District Attorneys Assn. [5668]
Natl. Employment Lawyers Assn. [5520]
Natl. Hea. Law Prog. [5784]
Natl. Immigration Proj. of the Natl. Lawyers Guild
[5810]
Natl. Lawyers Assn. [5521]
Natl. Lawyers Guild [5522]
Natl. Lesbian and Gay Law Assn. [5523]
Natl. Network of Estate Planning Attorneys [5524]
Natl. Org. of Bar Counsel [5953]
Natl. South Asian Bar Assn. [6018]
Network of Trial Law Firms [5525]
Nigerian Lawyers Assn. [5526]
North Amer. South Asian Bar Assn. [5527]
North Amer. South Asian Law Student Assn.
[8773]
North Amer. Trucking Industrial Relations Assn.
[2906]
People Before Lawyers [5528]
Renaissance Lawyer Soc. [5529]
Scandinavian Amer. Lawyers Assn. [5530]
Scottish Law Agents Soc. [IO]
Serbian Bar Assn. of Am. [5531]
Singapore Corporate Counsel Assn. [IO]
Soc. for Healthcare Consumer Advocacy of the
Amer. Hosp. Assn. [15005]

A star before a book entry number signifies that the name is not listed separately, but is mentioned within the entry.

Soc. of Medical Jurisprudence [15006]
State Capital Global Law Firm Gp. [324]
State Capital Global Law Firm Group [IO]
Swedish-American Bar Assn. [5532]
Swedish Bar Assn. [IO]
Taiwanese Amer. Lawyers Assn. [5533]
Trademark Soc. [5860]
Trans. Lawyers Assn. [6326]
Trial Lawyers Marketing [2651]
U.S. Justice Found. [6228]
U.S. Law Firm Gp. [5534]
USFN-America's Mortgage Banking Attorneys [325]
Attorneys; Amer. Acad. of Adoption [5471]
Attorneys; Amer. Acad. of Healthcare [★5782]
Attorneys; Amer. Assn. of Nurse [15000]
Attorneys; Amer. Bd. of Professional Liability [6041]
Attorneys; Amer. Soc. of Hosp. [★5782]
Attorneys for Animal Rights [★11351]
Attorneys; Assn. of Defense Trial [5825]
Attorneys Assn. Found; Natl. District [★5668]
Attorneys; Assn. of Insurance [★5825]
Attorneys Assn; Natl. District [5668]
Attorneys and Executives in Corporate Real Estate; Intl. Assn. of [3314]
Attorneys Gen; Natl. Assn. of [6276]
The Attorney's Gp. [5488], Hillsboro Executive Center North, 350 Fairway Dr., Ste. 200, Deerfield Beach, FL 33441-1834, (954)571-1877
Attorneys; Natl. Acad. of Elder Law [6029]
Attorneys; Natl. Assn. of Claimants Compensation [★6328]
Attorneys; Natl. Assn. of Coll. and Univ. [5677]
Attorneys; Natl. Assn. of County Civil [5619]
Attorneys; Natl. Assn. of County and Prosecuting [★5668]
Attorneys; Natl. Assn. of Securities and Commercial Law [★5579]
Attorneys; Natl. Assn. of Shareholder and Consumer [5579]
Attorneys; Natl. Coll. of District [5667]
Attorneys; Soc. of Hosp. [★5782]
ATV
Specialty Vehicle Inst. of Am. [398]
ATV German Assn. for Water Env. [★IO]
ATV Safety Institute/Division of Specialty Vehicle Inst. of Am. [12952], 2 Jenner St., Ste. 150, Irvine, CA 92618-3806, (949)727-3727
AU [★22894]
Au Bas de l'Echelle [★IO]
Au Pair in Am. [8603], 9 W Broad St., River Plz., Stamford, CT 06902, (203)399-5000
Auburn-Cord-Duesenberg Club [21582], c/o Barbara Pietracatella, Membership Sec., 536 McClean Ave., Staten Island, NY 10305-3644, (718)981-0549
Auburn Univ. Montgomery Alumni Assn. [18876], PO Box 244023, Montgomery, AL 36124-4023, (334)244-3000
Auckland Bowls [IO], Auckland, New Zealand
Auckland Chamber of Commerce and Indus. [IO], Auckland, New Zealand
Auckland Miniature Horse Club [IO], Albany, New Zealand
Auckland Refugee Coun. [IO], Auckland, New Zealand
Auction Bridge League; Amer. [★21893]
Auction Marketing Inst. [★326]
Auctioneers Assn. of Canada [IO], Edmonton, AB, Canada
Auctioneers, Estate Agents and Valuers Inst. of Zimbabwe [★IO]
Auctioneers and Valuers Assn. of Australia [IO], Burwood, Australia
Auctions
Auctioneers Assn. of Canada [IO]
Auctioneers and Valuers Assn. of Australia [IO]
Burley Marketing Assn. [3818]
Natl. Auctioneers Assn. [326]
Natl. Auto Auction Assn. [327]
World Antique Dealers Assn. [219]
Audie Henry Fan Club - Defunct.
Audience Development Comm. [11006], PO Box 30, New York, NY 10027, (212)368-6906
Audience Screen Extras Guild; TV [55]

Audiences; Young [9603]
Audio Engg. Soc. [6909], 60 E 42nd St., Rm. 2520, New York, NY 10165-2520, (212)661-8528
Audio Engg. Soc. - British Sect. [IO], Slough, United Kingdom
Audio Publishers Assn. [3347], 191 Clarksville Rd., Princeton Junction, NJ 08550, (609)799-6327
Audio Recording Rights Coalition - Defunct.
Audio Recording Services; Soc. of Professional [3351]
Audio Recording Studios; Soc. of Professional [★3351]
Audio Special Interest Gp; Interactive [2807]
Audio-Visual Assn; Natl. [★331]
Audiological Soc. of Australia [IO], Forest Hill, Australia
Audiologists; Acad. of Dispensing [★14733]
Audiologists; British Soc. of Hearing Aid [IO]
Audiologists; Canadian Assn. of Speech-Language Pathologists and [IO]
Audiologists; Soc. of Hearing Aid [★14763]
Audiology
Acad. of Doctors of Audiology [14733]
Acad. of Rehabilitative Audiology [14734]
ADARA: Professionals Networking for Excellence in Ser. Delivery with Individuals who are Deaf or Hard of Hearing [14735]
Alexander Graham Bell Assn. for the Deaf and Hard of Hearing [14736]
Amer. Auditory Soc. [14738]
Amer. Hearing Aid Associates [14739]
Amer. Hearing Res. Found. [14740]
Amer. Neurotology Soc. [16441]
Amer. Soc. for Deaf Children [14742]
Amer. Speech Language Hearing Assn. [16442]
Audiological Soc. of Australia [IO]
Audiology Awareness Campaign [13716]
Australian Tinnitus Assn. (NSW) [IO]
Better Hearing Inst. [14745]
Conf. of Educational Administrators of Schools and Programs for the Deaf [14749]
Coun. of Amer. Instructors of the Deaf [14750]
Coun. on Educ. of the Deaf [14751]
Deaf History Intl. [14081]
Deafness Res. Found. [14753]
Dogs for the Deaf [14754]
European Fed. of Audiology Societies [IO]
HEAR Center [14756]
Hearing Loss Assn. of Am. [14759]
Helen Keller Natl. Center for Deaf-Blind Youths and Adults [14760]
House Ear Inst. [16446]
Intl. Hearing Dog, Inc. [14762]
Intl. Hearing Soc. [14763]
Military Audiology Assn. [13717]
Model Secondary School for the Deaf [14766]
Natl. Assn. of the Deaf [14767]
Natl. Assn. of Future Doctors of Audiology [13718]
Natl. Assn. of School Nurses for the Deaf [14768]
Natl. Black Assn. for Speech-Language and Hearing [16448]
Natl. Captioning Inst. [14769]
Natl. Centre for Audiology [IO]
Natl. Hearing Conservation Assn. [14772]
Natl. Ser. Dog Center [14774]
Natl. Student Speech Language Hearing Assn. [16453]
Oral Hearing-Impaired Sect. [14775]
Parents' Sect. of the Alexander Graham Bell Assn. for the Deaf and Hard of Hearing [14776]
Registry of Interpreters for the Deaf [14778]
Telecommunications for the Deaf and Hard of Hearing, Inc. [14780]
Audiology; Acad. of Rehabilitative [14734]
Audiology; Amer. Acad. of [16439]
Audiology Awareness Campaign [13716], 1 Windsor Cove, Ste. 305, Columbia, SC 29223, (800)445-8629
Audiology; Intl. Assn. of Physicians in [IO]
Audiology Soc; Amer. [★14738]
Audiovisual
Alliance for a Media Literate Am. [8830]
Assn. for Info. Media and Equip. [328]
Communications Media Mgt. Assn. [329]
European Audiovisual Entrepreneurs [IO]

Home Recording Rights Coalition [5844]
Independent Professional Representatives Org. [330]
InfoComm Intl. [331]
InfoComm Intl. [IO]
Intl. Assn. for Media and History [IO]
Intl. Soc. of Commun. Specialists [IO]
Intl. Soc. of Commun. Specialists [332]
Natl. Alliance for Media Arts and Culture [9580]
Online Audiovisual Catalogers [10379]
Other Minds [10684]
Pacific Islanders in Communications [10455]
Video Software Dealers Assn. [333]
Audiovisual Catalogers; Online [10379]
Audiovisual Communications
Alliance for a Media Literate Am. [8830]
HAVi [6513]
Media Ecology Assn. [8831]
Pacific Islanders in Communications [10455]
Visual Resources Assn. [334]
Visual Resources Assn. [IO]
Audio-Visual Credit Interchange - Defunct.
Audiovisual Instruction; Dept. of [★8551]
Audiovisual Mgt. Assn. [★329]
Audiovisual Officers; Assn. of Chief State School [★8568]
Audit Bur. of Circulations [126], 900 N Meacham Rd., Schaumburg, IL 60173-4968, (847)605-0909
Audit Bur. of Circulations - India [IO], Bombay, India
Audit Bur. of Circulations - United Kingdom [IO], Berkhamsted, United Kingdom
Audit Bur. of Marketing Services - Defunct.
Audit Bur. for Media Measurement; Traffic [123]
Audit Bur; Traffic [★123]
Audit of Circulation; Bus. Publications [★93]
Audit of Circulations; Certified [127]
Audit, Control and Oper; NABAC, The Assn. for Bank [★467]
Audit and Control; Special Interest Gp. on Security, [6752]
Audit; Controlled Circulations [★93]
Audit Gp; Healthcare Internal [★15061]
Audit Network; Catholic Healthcare [8240]
Auditing Assn; Canadian Environmental [IO]
Auditorium Managers Assn. [★IO]
Auditorium Managers Assn. [★2671]
Auditorium Managers; Intl. Assn. of [★2671]
Auditors; Assn. of Coll. and Univ. [7888]
Auditors Assn; EDP [★65]
Auditors Assn; Electronic Data Processing [★65]
Auditors; Assn. of Healthcare Internal [15061]
Auditors; Assn. of Local Govt. [5429]
Auditors, Comptrollers, and Treasurers; Natl. Assn. of State [6206]
Auditors and Controllers; Natl. Assn. for Bank [★467]
Auditors and Engineers; Natl. Assn. of Independent Insurance [2210]
Auditors; Natl. Soc. of Insurance Premium [2226]
Auditory Res. Found; Hearing Educ. Through [★14756]
Auditory Soc; Amer. [14738]
Audubon Artists [9433], 47 5th Ave., 3rd Fl., New York, NY 10003
Audubon Naturalist Soc. of the Central Atlantic States [4364], 8940 Jones Mill Rd., Chevy Chase, MD 20815, (301)652-9188
Audubon Soc. of the District of Columbia [★4364]
Audubon Soc; Natl. [4422]
AUFBAU Trust [19176], 2121 Broadway, New York, NY 10023, (212)873-7400
AUFBAU Trust [IO], New York, NY, United States
August 13 Working Comm. [IO], Berlin, Germany
August Derleth Society [IO], Sauk City, WI, United States
August Derleth Soc. [9634], PO Box 481, Sauk City, WI 53583, (608)643-3242
Augusta Huiell Seaman Soc. - Defunct.
Augustan Reprint Soc. [10415], c/o AMS Press Inc., 63 Flushing Ave., Unit No. 221, Bldg. 292, Ste. 417, Brooklyn, NY 11205-1005, (718)875-8100
Augustan Soc. [21107], PO Box 771267, Orlando, FL 32877-1267, (407)745-0848
Augustan Soc. [IO], Daggett, CA, United States
Augustana Historical Soc. [19343], Augustana Coll., 639 38th St., Rock Island, IL 61201-2296, (309)794-7000

Reference to "IO" in place of a book number signifies that the association may be found in the 45th edition of International Organizations.

Augustana Swedish Inst. [★19343]

The Augustine Fellowship [★13074]

Augustine Herman Czech Amer. Historical Soc. - Defunct.

Augustinian Educational Assn. - Defunct.

Augustinian Secondary Educational Assn. [8054], 2520 S York Town, Tulsa, OK 74114, (918)746-2600

Augusto Cesar Sandino Found. [IO], Managua, Nicaragua

Augustus Institute [★11878]

AUI Peace Language Intl. [10298]

aUI Peace Language International [★10298]

Aulton Family Assn; Allton, Alton, [20779]

AURA - Defunct.

Aurand - Aurant - Aurandt Family Assn. [20786]

Aurandt Family Assn; Aurand - Aurant - [20786]

Aurant - Aurandt Family Assn; Aurand - [20786]

Aurobindo Assn; Sri [20636]

Aurobindo Center; Matagiri Sri [★20636]

Aurora Ministries [20276], c/o Aurora Mission, PO Box 1549, Bradenton, FL 34206, (941)748-4100

Aurora Scientific Academies - Address unknown since 1999.

AUS-MEAT [IO], Brisbane, Australia

Auslandsorganisation; NSDAP [★18329]

Aussenhandelsvereinigung des Deutschen Einzel-handels Ev [★IO]

Aussies Rescue and Placement Helpline [★22222]

Ausstellungs-und Messe-Ausschuss der Deutschen Wirtschaft [★IO]

Austin/Bantam Club; Amer. [21568]

Austin Bantam Soc. [21583], 1589 N Grand Oaks Ave., Pasadena, CA 91104, (626)791-2617

Austin Bantam Soc. [IO], Pasadena, CA, United States

Austin Cody's Official Intl. Fan Club [24845], c/o Austin Cody, LLC, PO Box 21, Pomfret, MD 20675

Austin Families Genealogical Soc. [20787], 23 Allen Farm Ln., Concord, MA 01742-2202, (978)369-8591

Austin-Healey Club of Am. [21584], c/o Mr. Mike Schneider, Membership Dir., 110 N Rastetter Ave., Louisville, KY 40206, (877)5-HEALEY

Austin-Healey Club USA [21585], 8002 Northeast Hwy. 99, Ste. B, PMB 424, Vancouver, WA 98665-8813, (408)394-3444

Austin-Healey Sports and Touring Club [21586], 309 E Broad St., Quakertown, PA 18951-1703, (215)536-6912

Austin Powers Collector's Club; The Official [24826]

Austin Ten Drivers Club [IO], Ripley, United Kingdom

Austins of Am. Genealogical Soc. [★20787]

Australasian Assn. of Clinical Biochemists [IO], Mount Lawley, Australia

Australasian Assn. of Convenience Stores [IO], Melbourne, Australia

Australasian Assn. of Distance Educ. Schools [IO], Charters Towers, Australia

Australasian Assn. for Lexicography [IO], North Ryde, Australia

Australasian Assn. of Philosophy [IO], Hobart, Australia

Australasian Bioethics Assn. [IO], Sydney, Australia

Australasian Bottled Water Inst. [IO], Rosebery, Australia

Australasian Bus. Travel Assn. [IO], Rockdale, Australia

Australasian Cartridge Remanufacturers Assn. [IO], Parramatta, Australia

Australasian Cave and Karst Mgt. Assn. [IO], Williamstown, Australia

Australasian Cemeteries and Crematoria Assn. [IO], Brunswick, Australia

Australasian Ceramic Soc. [★IO]

Australasian Chap. of Intl. Geosynthetics Soc. [IO], Clayton, Australia

Australasian Coll. of Dermatologists [IO], Boronia Park, Australia

Australasian Coll. for Emergency Medicine [IO], West Melbourne, Australia

Australasian Coll. of Physical Scientists and Engineers in Medicine [IO], Melbourne, Australia

Australasian Coll. of Sexual Hea. Physicians [IO], Sydney, Australia

Australasian Coll. of Tropical Medicine [IO], Red Hill, Australia

Australasian Corrections Educ. Assn. [IO], Darling-hurst, Australia

Australasian Corrosion Assn. [IO], Kerrimuir, Australia

Australasian Critical Incident Stress Assn. [IO], Sandy Bay, Australia

Australasian Critical Incident Stress Assn. - New South Wales [IO], Hobart, Australia

Australasian Critical Incident Stress Assn. - Queens-land [IO], Moffatt Beach, Australia

Australasian Critical Incident Stress Assn. - Tasmania [IO], Hobart, Australia

Australasian Critical Incident Stress Assn. - Victoria [IO], Melbourne, Australia

Australasian Fed. of Family History Organisations [IO], Weston Creek, Australia

Australasian Fleet Managers Assn. [IO], Melbourne, Australia

Australasian Gaming Machine Mfrs. Assn. [IO], Mos-man, Australia

Australasian Hellenic Educational Progressive Assn. [IO], Kent Town, Australia

Australasian Inst. of Mining and Metallurgy [IO], Car-lton, Australia

Australasian Inst. of Radiography [★IO]

Australasian Jet Sports Boating Assn. [IO], Ash-more, Australia

Australasian Lighting Indus. Assn. [IO], Sydney, Australia

Australasian Lymphology Assn. [IO], Toowong, Australia

Australasian Marine Sciences Assn. AMSA [★IO]

Australasian Meat Indus. Employees' Union [IO], Brisbane, Australia

Australasian Mech. Copyright Owners Soc. [IO], St. Leonards, Australia

Australasian Medical Writers Assn. [IO], Chatswood, Australia

Australasian Menopause Soc. [IO], Toowoomba, Australia

Australasian Palliative Link Intl. [IO], East Mel-bourne, Australia

Australasian Performing Rights Assn. [IO], St. Le-onards, Australia

Australasian Pharmaceutical Sci. Assn. [IO], Parkville, Australia

Australasian Pig Sci. Assn. [IO], South Perth, Australia

Australasian Plant Pathology Soc. [IO], Toowoomba, Australia

Australasian Plant Soc. [IO], Cheshire, United Kingdom

Australasian Political Stud. Assn. [IO], Sydney, Australia

Australasian Promotional Products Assn. [IO], Al-phington, Australia

Australasian Quaternary Assn. [IO], Penrith, Australia

Australasian Radiation Protection Soc. [IO], Upper Ferntree Gully, Australia

Australasian Raptor Assn. [IO], Sunbury, Australia

Australasian Regional Assn. of Zoological Parks and Aquaria [IO], Mosman, Australia

Australasian Sci. Educ. Res. Assn. [IO], Armidale, Australia

Australasian Sleep Assn. [IO], Sydney, Australia

Australasian Soc. of Aerospace Medicine [IO], Bal-wyn, Australia

Australasian Soc. for Behavioural Hea. and Medicine [IO], Herston, Australia

Australasian Soc. for Biomaterials [IO], Brisbane, Australia

Australasian Soc. of Cataract and Refractive Surgeons [IO], Mount Martha, Australia

Australasian Soc. of Clinical and Experimental Pharmacologists and Toxicologists [IO], Lilydale, Australia

Australasian Soc. of Clinical Immunology and Allergy [IO], Balgowlah, Australia

Australasian Soc. for Computers in Learning in Tertiary Educ. [IO], Wollongong, Australia

Australasian Soc. for Gen. Relativity and Gravitation [IO], Canberra, Australia

Australasian Soc. for HIV Medicine [IO], Darling-hurst, Australia

Australasian Soc. for Human Biology [IO], Crawley, Australia

Australasian Soc. of Oral Medicine and Toxicology [IO], Sydney, Australia

Australasian Soc. for Phycology and Aquatic Botany [IO], Lyons, Australia

Australasian Soc. for the Stud. of Animal Behaviour [IO], Marsfield, Australia

Australasian Soc. for the Stud. of Obesity [IO], Syd-ney, Australia

Australasian Soc. for Traumatic Stress Stud. [IO], Lidcombe, Australia

Australasian Soc. for Trenchless Tech. [IO], Greenwood, Australia

Australasian Soc. for Ultrasound in Medicine [IO], Sydney, Australia

Australasian Soc. of Zoo Keeping [IO], Healesville, Australia

Australasian Sound Recordings Assn. [IO], Hepburn Springs, Australia

Australasian and South East Asian Tissue Typing Assn. [IO], Sydney, Australia

AustralAsian Specialty Coffee Assn. [IO], St. Le-onards, Australia

Australasian Tuberous Sclerosis Soc. [IO], Blaxland, Australia

Australasian Union of Jewish Students [IO], Sydney, Australia

Australasian Universities Language and Literature Assn. [IO], Sydney, Australia

Australasian Universities Modern Language Assn. [★IO]

Australasian Victorian Stud. Assn. [IO], Crawley, Australia

Australia

Amer. Friends of the Natl. Gallery of Australia [10492]

Ankylosing Spondylitis Gp. of New South Wales [IO]

ASH Australia [IO]

Australia-New Zealand Assn. [IO]

Australian Cattle Dog Club of Am. [22221]

Australian Football Assn. of North Am. [23429]

Australian New Zealand - Amer. Chambers of Commerce [24248]

Australian and New Zealand Stud. Assn. of North Amer. [8484]

Australian Terrier Club of Am. [22223]

Australian Trade Commn. [24229]

Australian Vaccination Network [IO]

Australian Wound Mgt. Assn. [IO]

Intl. Assn. of Speakers Bureaus [10900]

Miniature Australian Shepherd Club of Am. [22306]

Natl. Found. for Australian Women [IO]

Soc. of Australasian Specialists/Oceania [22871]

Australia Amateur Ice Racing Coun. [★IO]

Australia; Amer. Friends of the Natl. Gallery of [10492]

Australia Arab Chamber of Commerce and Indus. [IO], Kingston, Australia

Australia Bhutan Friendship Assn. [IO], Thimphu, Bhutan

Australia-Brazil Chamber of Commerce [IO], Artar-mon, Australia

Australia-Britain Soc. [IO], Deakin, Australia

Australia Coun. [IO], Strawberry Hills, Australia

Australia Coun. for the Arts [IO], Surry Hills, Australia

Australia Defence Assn. [IO], Wanniassa, Australia

Australia Fan Club - Address unknown since 1995.

Australia Ice Racing Coun. [IO], Brisbane, Australia

Australia-Israel Chamber of Commerce [IO], Double Bay, Australia

Australia Kangaroo Club - Defunct.

Australia New Guinea Fishes Assn. [IO], Ringwood, Australia

Australia-New Zealand Assn. [IO], Vancouver, BC, Canada

Australia and New Zealand Coll. of Anaesthetists [IO], Melbourne, Australia

Australia and New Zealand Organ Donation Registry [IO], Woodville South, Australia

A star before a book entry number signifies that the name is not listed separately, but is mentioned within the entry.

Australia New Zealand Soc. for Ecological Economics [IO], Canberra, Australia
Australia Pacific Islands Bus. Coun. [IO], Wynnum, Australia
Australia Philippines Bus. Coun. [IO], Mordialloc, Australia
Australia-Singapore Chamber of Commerce and Indus. [IO], Sydney, Australia
Australia-Taiwan Bus. Coun. [IO], Sydney, Australia
Australia Tibet Coun. [IO], Darlinghurst, Australia
Australian
   Amer. Australian Assn. [18975]
   Amer. Friends of the Natl. Gallery of Australia [10492]
   Australian Cattle Dog Club of Am. [22221]
   Australian Football Assn. of North Am. [23429]
   Australian New Zealand - Amer. Chambers of Commerce [24248]
   Australian and New Zealand Stud. Assn. of North Amer. [8484]
   Australian Terrier Club of Am. [22223]
   Coun. of Australian Powerlifting Organizations [IO]
   Intl. Percy Grainger Soc. [9810]
   Miniature Australian Shepherd Club of Am. [22306]
   Soc. of Australasian Specialists/Oceania [22871]
Australian Acad. of the Humanities [IO], Canberra, Australia
Australian Acad. of Sci. [IO], Canberra, Australia
Australian Acad. of Technological Sciences [★IO]
Australian Acad. of Technological Sciences and Engg. [IO], Parkville, Australia
Australian Acoustical Soc. [IO], Castlemaine, Australia
Australian Acupuncture and Chinese Medicine Assn. [IO], Coorparoo, Australia
Australian Addison's Disease Assn. [IO], Dorrigo, Australia
Australian Agency for Intl. Development [IO], Canberra, Australia
Australian Agricultural and Rsrc. Economics Soc. [IO], Canberra, Australia
Australian Amer. Assn. [IO], Melbourne, Australia
Australian Amer. Chamber of Commerce of Southern California - Address unknown since 2002.
Australian-American Fulbright Commission [IO], Deakin, Australia
Australian Amusement Leisure and Recreation Assn. [IO], Gold Coast, Australia
Australian Animal Protection Soc. [IO], Keysborough, Australia
Australian Antique and Art Dealers Assn. [IO], Melbourne, Australia
Australian Antique and Art Dealers Assn. [IO], Malvern, Australia
Australian Antique Dealers Assn. [★IO]
Australian Antique Dealers Assn. [★IO]
Australian Archaeological Assn. [IO], South Fremantle, Australia
Australian Architecture Assn. [IO], Sydney, Australia
Australian Assn. of Career Counsellors [IO], Alberton, Australia
Australian Assn. for Cognitive and Behaviour Therapy [IO], Nedlands, Australia
Australian Assn. of Consultant Pharmacy [IO], Canberra, Australia
Australian Assn. of Consulting Archaeologist [IO], Sydney, Australia
Australian Assn. for Corrosion Prevention [★IO]
Australian Assn. of the Deaf [IO], Stafford, Australia
Australian Assn. for Exercise and Sport Sci. [IO], Red Hill, Australia
Australian Assn. of Gerontology [IO], Belconnen, Australia
Australian Assn. of Hong Kong [IO], Hong Kong, People's Republic of China
Australian Assn. for Humane Res. [IO], Malvern, Australia
Australian Assn. of Massage Therapists [IO], Melbourne, Australia
Australian Assn. of Mathematics Teachers [IO], Adelaide, Australia
Australian Assn. of Men Barbershop Singers [IO], West Gosford, Australia
Australian Assn. for the Mentally Retarded [★IO]

Australian Assn. of Natl. Advertisers [IO], Sydney, Australia
Australian Assn. of Practice Managers [IO], Fortitude Valley, Australia
Australian Assn. for Professional and Applied Ethics [IO], Sydney, Australia
Australian Assn. for Psychological Type [IO], Loganholme, Australia
Australian Assn. of Social Workers [IO], Kingston, Australia
Australian Assn. of Social Workers - Hunter Valley Br. [IO], Newcastle, Australia
Australian Assn. of Social Workers - New South Wales Br. [IO], Rozelle, Australia
Australian Assn. of Social Workers - North Queensland Br. [IO], Mackay, Australia
Australian Assn. of Social Workers - Northern Territory Br. [IO], Nightcliff, Australia
Australian Assn. of Social Workers - South Australian Br. [IO], Adelaide, Australia
Australian Assn. of Social Workers - Tasmanian Br. [IO], Hobart, Australia
Australian Assn. of Social Workers - Victorian Br. [IO], Carlton, Australia
Australian Assn. of Somatic Psychotherapists [IO], Sydney, Australia
Australian Assn. for the Stud. of Religions [IO], Sydney, Australia
Australian Assn. for the Teaching of English [IO], Kensington Gardens, Australia
Australian Assn. of Vaginal and Incontinence Surgeons [IO], Wahroonga, Australia
Australian Athletes with a Disability [IO], Homebush, Australia
Australian Athletic Union [★IO]
Australian Auto. Assn. [IO], Canberra, Australia
Australian Automotive Aftermarket Assn. [IO], Mulgrave, Australia
Australian Banana Growers' Coun. [IO], Brisbane, Australia
Australian Bank Employees' Union [★IO]
Australian Bankers' Assn. [IO], Sydney, Australia
Australian Barramundi Farmers Assn. [IO], Toowong, Australia
Australian Bartenders Guild [IO], Sydney, Australia
Australian Baseball Fed. [IO], Southport, Australia
Australian Beef Assn. [IO], Toowoomba, Australia
Australian Beverage Coun. Ltd. [IO], Rosebery, Australia
Australian Bird Stud. Assn. [IO], Sydney, Australia
Australian Blind Sports Federations [IO], Milton, Australia
Australian Book Publishers Assn. [★IO]
Australian Booksellers Assn. [IO], Kew East, Australia
Australian Bowhunters Assn. [IO], Morayfield, Australia
Australian Braford Soc. [IO], Rockhampton, Australia
Australian Brahman Breeders' Assn. [IO], Rockhampton, Australia
Australian Braunvieh Assn. [IO], Bradford, Australia
Australian Breastfeeding Assn. [IO], Glen Iris, Australia
Australian Bus. Coun. for Sustainable Energy [IO], Carlton, Australia
Australian Bus. in Europe [IO], Melbourne, Australia
Australian Bus. Limited Incorporating the State Chamber of Commerce (NSW) [IO], North Sydney, Australia
Australian Bus. Limited and State Chamber of Commerce (New South Wales) [★IO]
Australian Businesswomen's Network [IO], Rosebery, Australia
Australian Camp Connect Assn. [IO], Kilsyth, Australia
Australian Cancer Soc. [★IO]
Australian Cane Farmers Assn. [IO], Brisbane, Australia
Australian Canegrowers Coun. [★IO]
Australian Canoe Fed. [★IO]
Australian Canoeing [IO], Silverwater, Australia
Australian Capital Territory Aeromodellers Assn. [IO], Fyshwick, Australia
Australian Capital Territory Dental Therapists' Assn. [IO], Woden, Australia

Australian Capital Territory History Teachers Assn. [IO], Phillip, Australia
Australian Casino Assn. [IO], Manuka, Australia
Australian Catholic Bishops' Conf. [IO], Canberra, Australia
Australian Catholic Relief [★IO]
Australian Catholic Social Justice Coun. [IO], North Sydney, Australia
Australian Cattle Dog Club of Am. [22221], c/o Leigh Ann Yandle-Perry, Membership Sec., 3019 Justin Braswell Rd., Monroe, NC 28110-9317
Australian Centre for Intl. Commercial Arbitration [IO], Sydney, Australia
Australian Ceramic Soc. [IO], Perth, Australia
Australian Cerebral Palsy Assn. [★IO]
Australian Chamber of Commerce and Indus. [IO], Kingston, Australia
Australian Chamber of Fruit and Vegetable Indus. [IO], Sydney, Australia
Australian Chess Fed. [IO], Avoca Beach, Australia
Australian Chicken Meat Fed. [IO], North Sydney, Australia
Australian Cinematographers Soc. [IO], Artarmon, Australia
Australian Circus and Physical Theatre Assn. [IO], North Melbourne, Australia
Australian Citrus Growers [IO], Mildura, Australia
Australian Civil Liberties Union [IO], Carlton, Australia
Australian Clay Minerals Soc. [IO], Glen Osmond, Australia
Australian Climbing Instructors Assn. [IO], Natimuk, Australia
Australian Coal Assn. [IO], Deakin, Australia
Australian Coffee Traders Assn. [IO], Leichhardt, Australia
Australian Collaborative Land Evaluation Prog. [IO], Canberra, Australia
Australian Collectors of Mech. Musical Instruments [IO], St. Ives, Australia
Australian Coll. of Educators [IO], Deakin West, Australia
Australian Coll. of Hea. Ser. Executives [IO], North Ryde, Australia
Australian Coll. of Occupational Hea. Nurses [IO], Tullamarine, Australia
Australian Coll. of Pharmacy Practice [IO], Canberra, Australia
Australian Coll. of Rural and Remote Medicine [IO], Brisbane, Australia
Australian Comm. for UNICEF [IO], Sydney, Australia
Australian Cmpt. Soc. [IO], Sydney, Australia
Australian Conservation Found. [IO], Carlton, Australia
Australian Consumers' Assn. [IO], Marrickville, Australia
Australian Copyright Coun. [IO], Strawberry Hills, Australia
Australian Coral Reef Soc. [IO], St. Lucia, Australia
Australian Corporate Lawyers Assn. [IO], Melbourne, Australia
Australian Corriedale Assn. [IO], Melbourne, Australia
Australian Coun. of Agricultural Journalists [IO], Brisbane, Australia
Australian Coun. of Deans of Sci. [IO], Sydney, Australia
Australian Coun. for Educational Leaders [IO], Winmalee, Australia
Australian Coun. for Educational Leaders - Newcastle [IO], Newcastle, Australia
Australian Coun. for Educational Leaders - South Australia [IO], Adelaide, Australia
Australian Coun. for Educational Leaders - Wagga Wagga [IO], Wagga Wagga, Australia
Australian Coun. for Educational Res. [IO], Camberwell, Australia
Australian Coun. for Hea., Physical Educ. and Recreation [IO], Hindmarsh, Australia
Australian Coun. on Healthcare Standards [IO], Sydney, Australia
Australian Coun. for Intl. Development [IO], Deakin, Australia
Australian Coun. for the Mentally Retarded [★IO]

Reference to "IO" in place of a book number signifies that the association may be found in the 45th edition of International Organizations.

Australian Coun. of Organizations for Subnormal Children [★IO]

Australian Coun. for Overseas Aid [★IO]

Australian Coun. for Private Educ. and Training [IO], Sydney, Australia

Australian Coun. on Safety and Quality in Hea. Care [IO], Sydney, Australia

Australian Coun. of Superannuation Investors [IO], Melbourne, Australia

Australian Coun. of Trade Unions [IO], Melbourne, Australia

Australian Coun. of Women and Policing [IO], Manuka, Australia

Australian Cricketers' Assn. [IO], Melbourne, Australia

Australian Croquet Assn. [IO], Brighton, Australia

Australian Curriculum Stud. Assn. [IO], Deakin West, Australia

Australian Dairy Corp. [★IO]

Australian Deaf Sports Fed. [★IO]

Australian Democrats [IO], Black Forest, Australia

Australian Dental Assn. [IO], St. Leonards, Australia

Australian Dental and Oral Hea. Therapists' Assn. [IO], Modbury North, Australia

Australian Dental Therapists' Assn. [★IO]

Australian Dental Therapists' Assn. - Northern Territory [IO], Casuarina, Australia

Australian Dermatology Nurses Assn. [IO], Salisbury Downs, Australia

Australian Die Casting Assn. [IO], Bayswater, Australia

Australian Direct Marketing Assn. [IO], Sydney, Australia

Australian Draughts Fed. [IO], Kildare, Australia

Australian Dried Fruits Assn. [IO], Mildura, Australia

Australian Drug Found. [IO], North Melbourne, Australia

Australian Early Childhood Assn. [★IO]

Australian Earthquake Engg. Soc. [IO], McKinnon, Australia

Australian Educ. Union [IO], Southbank, Australia

Australian Elecl. and Electronic Mfrs. Assn. [IO], Canberra, Australia

Australian Entertainment Indus. Assn. [★IO]

Australian Entomological Soc. [IO], Orange, Australia

Australian Environmental Pest Managers Assn. [IO], Broadway, Australia

Australian False Memory Assn. [IO], Epping, Australia

Australian Family Assn. [IO], North Melbourne, Australia

Australian Fed. Police Assn. [IO], Canberra, Australia

Australian Fed. of Airfreight Forwarders [★IO]

Australian Fed. of Bus. and Professional Women [★IO]

Australian Fed. of Civil Celebrants [IO], Bathurst, Australia

Australian Fed. of Disability Organisations [IO], Melbourne, Australia

Australian Fed. of Friends of Museums [IO], Canberra, Australia

Australian Fed. of Homelessness Organisations [IO], Dickson, Australia

Australian Fed. of Intl. Forwarders [iO], Eastgardens, Australia

Australian Fed. of Modern Language Teachers Associations [IO], West Croydon, Australia

Australian Fed. Of AIDS Organisations [IO], Newtown, Australia

Australian Fed. of SPELD Associations [IO], Spit Junction, Australia

Australian Fed. of Travel Agents [IO], Sydney, Australia

Australian Fed. of Univ. Women [IO], Canberra, Australia

Australian Fed. of Univ. Women - Tasmania [IO], Hobart, Australia

Australian Film Inst. [IO], South Melbourne, Australia

Australian Finnsheep Breeders Assn. [IO], Inglewood, Australia

Australian Floorball Assn. [IO], North Sydney, Australia

Australian Flower Export Coun. [IO], North Melbourne, Australia

Australian Flying Disc Assn. [IO], St. Leonards, Australia

Australian Fodder Indus. Assn. [IO], Balwyn, Australia

Australian Food and Grocery Coun. [IO], Kingston, Australia

Australian Football Assn. of North Am. [IO], Columbus, OH, United States

Australian Football Assn. of North Am. [23429], PO Box 27623, Columbus, OH 43227-0623, (614)571-8986

Australian Foremen Stevedores Assn. [★IO]

Australian Funeral Directors Assn. [IO], Kew East, Australia

Australian Furniture Removers Assn. [IO], Baulkham Hills, Australia

Australian Galloway Assn. [IO], Wodonga, Australia

Australian Garden History Soc. [IO], Melbourne, Australia

Australian Gas Assn. [IO], Braeside, Australia

Australian Gelbvieh Assn. [IO], Armidale, Australia

Australian Geography Teachers Assn. [IO], Launceston, Australia

Australian Geological Survey Org. [★IO]

Australian Geomechanics Soc. [IO], St. Ives, Australia

Australian Geoscience Coun. [IO], Carlton South, Australia

Australian Geoscience Info. Assn. [IO], Kensington, Australia

Australian Ginseng Growers Assn. [IO], Melbourne, Australia

Australian Glass and Glazing Assn. [IO], Melbourne, Australia

Australian Graphic Design Assn. [IO], Sydney, Australia

Australian Gynaecological Endoscopy Soc. [IO], Castlecrag, Australia

Australian Hand Therapy Assn. [IO], Brisbane, Australia

Australian Hea. Promotion Assn. [IO], Maroochydore, Australia

Australian Hereford Soc. [IO], Spring Hill, Australia

Australian Higher Educ. Indus. Assn. [IO], Melbourne, Australia

Australian Highland Cattle Soc. [IO], Ascot Vale, Australia

Australian Homoeopathic Assn. [IO], Hastings, Australia

Australian Horse Alliance [IO], Elanora, Australia

Australian Horticultural Exporters Assn. [IO], Knoxfield, Australia

Australian Hotels Assn. (NSW) [IO], Sydney, Australia

Australian Hotels Assn. (South Australian Br.) [IO], Adelaide, Australia

Australian Hotels Assn. (Tasmania) [IO], Hobart, Australia

Australian Hotels Assn. (Victoria Br.) [IO], Melbourne, Australia

Australian Human Rsrc. Inst. [IO], Melbourne, Australia

Australian Huntington Disease Assn. - New South Wales [IO], West Ryde, Australia

Australian Huntington Disease Assn. - Victoria [IO], Melbourne, Australia

Australian Huntington Disease Assn. - Western Australia [IO], Nedlands, Australia

Australian Huntington's Disease Assn. [IO], Nedlands, Australia

Australian Indigenous Art Trade Assn. [IO], Fremantle, Australia

Australian Indigenous Doctors' Assn. [IO], Manuka, Australia

Australian Indus. Gp. [IO], North Sydney, Australia

Australian Infant, Child, Adolescent and Family Mental Hea. Assn. [IO], Stepney, Australia

Australian Infection Control Assn. [IO], Eight Mile Plains, Australia

Australian Info. Indus. Assn. [IO], Deakin, Australia

Australian Information Security Assn. [IO], Sydney, Australia

Australian Inst. of Aboriginal and Torres Strait Islander Stud. [IO], Canberra, Australia

Australian Inst. of Administrative Law [IO], Canberra, Australia

Australian Inst. of Agricultural Sci. and Tech. [IO], Hawthorn, Australia

Australian Inst. of Biology [IO], Milton, Australia

Australian Inst. of Building [IO], Canberra, Australia

Australian Inst. of Company Directors [IO], Sydney, Australia

Australian Inst. of Credit Mgt. [IO], St. Leonards, Australia

Australian Inst. of Criminology [IO], Canberra, Australia

Australian Inst. of Energy [IO], Raymond Terrace, Australia

Australian Inst. of Food Sci. and Tech. [IO], Alexandria, Australia

Australian Inst. of Genealogical Stud. [IO], Blackburn, Australia

Australian Inst. of Geoscientists [IO], Perth, Australia

Australian Inst. of Intl. Affairs [IO], Deakin, Australia

Australian Inst. of Landscape Architects [IO], Canberra, Australia

Australian Inst. of Mgt. [IO], St. Kilda, Australia

Australian Inst. of Marine Sci. [IO], Townsville, Australia

Australian Inst. of Nuclear Sci. and Engg. [IO], Menai, Australia

Australian Inst. of Packaging [IO], Chatswood, Australia

Australian Inst. of Petroleum [IO], Canberra, Australia

Australian Inst. of Physics [IO], Parkville, Australia

Australian Inst. of Professional Intelligence Officers [IO], Civic Square, Australia

Australian Inst. of Professional Photography [IO], Fitzroy, Australia

Australian Inst. of Proj. Mgt. [IO], Sydney, Australia

Australian Inst. of Quantity Surveyors [IO], Deakin West, Australia

Australian Inst. of Radiography [IO], Collingwood, Australia

Australian Inst. of Steel Constr. [★IO]

Australian Inst. of Urban Stud. [IO], Melbourne, Australia

Australian Insurance Employees' Union [★IO]

Australian Insurance Law Assn. [IO], Box Hill, Australia

Australian Interactive Media Indus. Assn. [IO], Sydney, Australia

Australian Intl. Yngling Assn. [IO], Sydney, Australia

Australian Internationals - Address unknown since 1986.

Australian Kite Assn. [IO], Torquay, Australia

Australian Kitesurfing Assn. [IO], Belmont, Australia

Australian Koala Found. [IO], Brisbane, Australia

Australian Koala Found; Friends of the [5319]

Australian Labor Party [IO], Kingston, Australia

Australian Labradoodle Assn. [IO], Prospect, Australia

Australian Lancia Register [IO], Mount Waverley, Australia

Australian Lavender Indus. [IO], Leichhardt, Australia

Australian Lawyers for Human Rights [IO], Sydney, Australia

Australian Lib. and Info. Assn. [IO], Kingston, Australia

Australian Life Cycle Assessment Soc. [IO], Balwyn, Australia

Australian Linguistic Soc. [IO], Callaghan, Australia

Australian Literacy Educators' Assn. [IO], Norwood, Australia

Australian Logistics Coun. [IO], Robina, Australia

Australian Lutheran World Ser. [IO], Albury, Australia

Australian Macadamia Soc. [IO], Lismore, Australia

Australian Malaysian Singaporean Assn. [IO], Sydney, Australia

Australian Mammal Soc. [IO], Armidale, Australia

Australian Mfg. Workers' Union [IO], Granville, Australia

Australian Marine Conservation Soc. [IO], Brisbane, Australia

Australian Marine Sciences Assn. [IO], Kilkivan, Australia

Australian Market and Social Res. Soc. [IO], Glebe, Australia

Australian Mathematical Soc. [IO], Canberra, Australia

A star before a book entry number signifies that the name is not listed separately, but is mentioned within the entry.

Australian Meat Indus. Coun. [IO], Crows Nest, Australia

Australian Medical Assn. [IO], Kingston, Australia

Australian Medical Coun. [IO], Kingston, Australia

Australian Medical Students' Assn. [IO], Parkville, Australia

Australian Mensa [IO], Toorak, Australia

Australian Microscopy and Microanalysis Soc. [IO], Sydney, Australia

Australian Military Medicine Assn. [IO], Hobart, Australia

Australian Mineral Found. [IO], Glenside, Australia

Australian Mines and Metals Assn. [IO], Melbourne, Australia

Australian Miniature Enthusiasts Assn. [IO], Cherrybrook, Australia

Australian Mining Indus. Coun. [★IO]

Australian Mining and Petroleum and Law Assn. [IO], Melbourne, Australia

Australian Mobile Telecommunications Assn. [IO], Manuka, Australia

Australian Multiple Birth Assn. [IO], Coogee, Australia

Australian Municipal, Administrative, Clerical and Services Union [IO], Carlton South, Australia

Australian Mushroom Growers Assn. [IO], Windsor, Australia

Australian Music Centre [IO], Grosvenor Place, Australia

Australian Music Retailers Assn. [IO], Malvern, Australia

Australian Music Therapy Assn. [IO], Malvern, Australia

Australian Natl. Flag Assn. [IO], Sydney, Australia

Australian Natl. Gallery Found; Amer. Friends of the [★10492]

Australian Natl. Kennel Coun. [IO], Red Hill, Australia

Australian Natl. Sportfishing Assn. [IO], Matraville, Australia

Australian Natl. Sportfishing Assn. - NT Br. [IO], Darwin, Australia

Australian Natl. Sportfishing Assn. - Victoria [IO], Williamstown, Australia

Australian Natl. Sportfishing Assn. - Western Australia [IO], Claremont, Australia

Australian Native Dog Conservation Soc. [IO], Bargo, Australia

Australian Network for Plant Conservation [IO], Canberra, Australia

Australian Neuroscience Soc. [IO], Kent Town, Australia

Australian New Zealand - Amer. Chambers of Commerce [IO], Chicago, IL, United States

Australian New Zealand - Amer. Chambers of Commerce [24248], 30 N LaSalle St., Ste. 3400, Chicago, IL 60602, (312)641-5311

Australian and New Zealand Assn. for the Advancement of Sci. [IO], Adelaide, Australia

Australian and New Zealand Assn. of Antiquarian Booksellers [IO], Pokolbin, Australia

Australian and New Zealand Assn. for Leisure Stud. [IO], Canterbury, New Zealand

Australian and New Zealand Assn. for Medieval and Early Modern Stud. [IO], Crawley, Australia

Australian and New Zealand Assn. for Medieval and Renaissance Stud. [IO], Crawley, Australia

Australian and New Zealand Assn. of Oral and Maxillofacial Surgeons [IO], Crows Nest, Australia

Australian and New Zealand Assn. of Physicians in Nuclear Medicine [IO], Balmain, Australia

Australian and New Zealand Assn. of Psychotherapy [IO], Woollahra, Australia

Australian and New Zealand Assn. for the Treatment of Sexual Abuse [IO], Haymarket, Australia

Australian and New Zealand Bone and Mineral Soc. [IO], Sydney, Australia

Australian and New Zealand Coun. for the Care of Animals in Res. and Teaching [IO], Adelaide, Australia

Australian and New Zealand Ombudsman Assn. [IO], Melbourne, Australia

Australian and New Zealand Psychodrama Assn. [IO], Adelaide, Australia

Australian and New Zealand Pulp and Paper Indus. Tech. Assn. [★IO]

Australian and New Zealand Soc. of Blood Transfusion [IO], Sydney, Australia

Australian and New Zealand Soc. of Intl. Law [IO], Sydney, Australia

Australian-New Zealand Soc. of New York - Address unknown since 2001.

Australian and New Zealand Soc. of Nuclear Medicine [IO], Upper Ferntree Gully, Australia

Australian and New Zealand Soc. of Palliative Medicine [IO], Cheltenham, Australia

Australian and New Zealand Soc. of Respiratory Sci. [IO], Perth, Australia

Australian and New Zealand Solar Energy Soc. [IO], Frenchs Forest, Australia

Australian and New Zealand Sports Law Assn. [IO], Randwick, Australia

Australian and New Zealand Stud. Assn. of North Amer. [IO], Austin, TX, United States

Australian and New Zealand Stud. Assn. of North Amer. [8484], Edward A. Clark Center for Australian and New Zealand Stud., Harry Ransom Humanities Res. Ctr., Ste. 3.362, The Univ. of Texas at Austin, Austin, TX 78713-7219

Australian Newsagents' Fed. [IO], St. Leonards, Australia

Australian Nuclear Assn. [IO], Sutherland, Australia

Australian Nuclear Sci. and Tech. Org. [IO], Menai, Australia

Australian Nudist Fed. [IO], Bulahdelah, Australia

Australian Nudist Fed. Supporter Club [IO], North Parramatta, Australia

Australian Numismatic Soc. [IO], Brookvale, Australia

Australian Nurses' Cardiovascular and Hypertension Assn. [IO], Chatswood, Australia

Australian Nursing Fed. [IO], Kingston, Australia

Australian Oilseeds Fed. [IO], Royal Exchange, Australia

Australian Olive Assn. [IO], Pendle Hill, Australia

Australian Olive Oil Assn. [IO], Carlton, Australia

Australian Optical Soc. [IO], Callaghan, Australia

Australian Orthopaedic Assn. [IO], Sydney, Australia

Australian Orthopaedic Foot and Ankle Soc. [IO], Adelaide, Australia

Australian Packaging Machinery Assn. [IO], Rose Bay North, Australia

Australian Pain Soc. [IO], North Sydney, Australia

Australian Paint Mfrs. Fed. [IO], North Sydney, Australia

Australian Paralympic Comm. [IO], Homebush Bay, Australia

Australian Parkour Assn. [IO], Brunswick, Australia

Australian Pattern Recognition Soc. [IO], St. Lucia, Australia

Australian Payments Clearing Assn. [IO], Sydney, Australia

Australian People for Hea., Educ. and Development Abroad [IO], Sydney, Australia

Australian Petroleum Exploration Assn. [★IO]

Australian Petroleum Production and Exploration Assn. [IO], Canberra, Australia

Australian Pharmaceutical Mfrs. Assn. [★IO]

Australian Physiological and Pharmacological Soc. [★IO]

Australian Physiological Soc. [IO], Adelaide, Australia

Australian Physiotherapy Assn. [IO], Melbourne, Australia

Australian Pipeline Indus. Assn. [IO], Kingston, Australia

Australian Plaiters and Whipmakers Assn. [IO], Kuranda, Australia

Australian Plants Soc. [★IO]

Australian Plants Soc. - New South Wales Region [IO], Blacktown, Australia

Australian Plants Soc., South Australia [IO], Unley, Australia

Australian Plants Soc. Tasmania [IO], Hobart, Australia

Australian Poll Dorset Assn. [IO], Melbourne, Australia

The Australian Poll Hereford Soc. [★IO]

Australian Population Assn. [IO], Acton, Australia

Australian Pork [IO], Deakin West, Australia

Australian Prawn Farmers Assn. [IO], Brisbane, Australia

Australian Press Coun. [IO], Sydney, Australia

Australian Principals Assn. Professional Development Coun. [IO], Hindmarsh, Australia

Australian Private Hospitals Assn. [IO], Canberra, Australia

Australian Professional Footballers' Assn. [IO], Melbourne, Australia

Australian Property Inst. [IO], Deakin, Australia

Australian Psychological Soc. [IO], Melbourne, Australia

Australian Public Access Network Assn. [IO], Doncaster, Australia

Australian Publishers' Assn. [IO], Ultimo, Australia

Australian Pulp and Paper Indus. Tech. Assn. [★IO]

Australian Pump Mfrs'. Assn. [★IO]

Australian Quadripilegic Assn. [★IO]

Australian Red Cross ACT [IO], Mawson, Australia

Australian Red Cross Soc. [IO], Carlton, Australia

Australian Red Poll Cattle Breeders [IO], Armidale, Australia

Australian Rehabilitation and Assistive Tech. Assn. [IO], Silvan, Australia

Australian Reproductive Hea. Alliance [IO], Deakin West, Australia

Australian Res. Coun. [IO], Canberra, Australia

Australian Resuscitation Coun. [IO], Melbourne, Australia

Australian Rheumatology Assn. [IO], Sydney, Australia

Australian Rheumatology Assn. - Australian Capital Territory [IO], Canberra, Australia

Australian Rheumatology Assn. - New South Wales [IO], Eastwood, Australia

Australian Rheumatology Assn. - Queensland [IO], Woolloongabba, Australia

Australian Rheumatology Assn. - South Australia [IO], Woodville, Australia

Australian Rheumatology Assn. - Tasmania [IO], Hobart, Australia

Australian Rheumatology Assn. - Western Australia [IO], Perth, Australia

Australian Rhododendron Soc. [IO], Olinda, Australia

Australian Road Res. Bd. [★IO]

Australian Robot Assn. [★IO]

Australian Robotics and Automation Assn. [IO], Sydney, Australia

Australian Rock Art Res. Assn. [IO], Caulfield South, Australia

Australian Rural Nurses and Midwives [IO], Deakin West, Australia

Australian Sailing and Cruising Club [IO], Potts Point, Australia

Australian Salaried Medical Officers' Fed. [IO], Glebe, Australia

Australian Sci. Teachers Assn. [IO], Deakin West, Australia

Australian Screen Directors Assn. [IO], Rozelle, Australia

Australian Screen Editors Guild [IO], Paddington, Australia

Australian Seafood Indus. Coun. [IO], Ascot, Australia

Australian Seed Fed. [IO], Manuka, Australia

Australian Self-Medication Indus. [IO], North Sydney, Australia

Australian Services Union [IO], Carlton South, Australia

Australian Severe Weather Assn. [IO], Kew, Australia

Australian Shareholders' Assn. [IO], Chatswood, Australia

Australian Sheep Breeders Assn. [IO], Bendigo, Australia

Australian Shepherd Club of Am. [22222], 6091 E State Hwy. 21, Bryan, TX 77808-9652, (979)778-1082

Australian Ship Repairers Gp. [IO], Ashmore, Australia

Australian Shipbuilders Assn. [IO], Ashmore, Australia

Australian Shipowners Assn. [IO], Port Melbourne, Australia

Australian Sign Language Interpreters Assn. [IO], Wanniassa, Australia

Australian Simmental Breeders Assn. [IO], Armidale, Australia

Reference to "IO" in place of a book number signifies that the association may be found in the 45th edition of International Organizations.

Australian Skeptics - NSW Br. **[IO]**, Roseville, Australia

Australian Small Animal Veterinary Assn. **[IO]**, St. Leonards, Australia

Australian Soccer Assn. **[★IO]**

Australian Soc. of Anaesthetists **[IO]**, Edgecliff, Australia

Australian Soc. of Animal Production (Sydney Br.) **[IO]**, Kemps Creek, Australia

Australian Soc. for Antimicrobials **[IO]**, South Perth, Australia

Australian Soc. of Archivists **[IO]**, Dickson, Australia

Australian Soc. of Assn. Executives **[IO]**, Fyshwick, Australia

Australian Soc. of Authors **[IO]**, Strawberry Hills, Australia

Australian Soc. of Baking **[IO]**, Terrigal, Australia

Australian Soc. for Biochemistry and Molecular Biology **[IO]**, Kent Town, Australia

Australian Soc. for Biomaterials **[★IO]**

Australian Soc. for Biophysics **[IO]**, Canberra, Australia

Australian Soc. of Calligraphers **[IO]**, Willoughby, Australia

Australian Soc. of Certified Practising Accountants **[★IO]**

Australian Soc. for Classical Stud. **[IO]**, Bundanoon, Australia

Australian Soc. of Clinical Hypnotherapists **[IO]**, Eastwood, Australia

Australian Soc. of Clinical Neurophysiologists **[IO]**, Sydney, Australia

Australian Soc. of Cosmetic Chemists **[IO]**, Sydney, Australia

Australian Soc. Electron Microscopy **[★IO]**

Australian Soc. of Exploration Geophysicists **[IO]**, Perth, Australia

Australian Soc. for Fish Biology **[IO]**, Canberra, Australia

Australian Soc. of Hypnosis **[IO]**, Alphington, Australia

Australian Soc. of Legal Philosophy **[IO]**, Canberra, Australia

Australian Soc. for Limnology **[IO]**, Melbourne, Australia

Australian Soc. of Magicians **[IO]**, Cheltenham, Australia

Australian Soc. for Medical Res. **[IO]**, Sydney, Australia

Australian Soc. for Microbiology **[IO]**, Melbourne, Australia

Australian Soc. for Music Educ. **[IO]**, Mawson, Australia

Australian Soc. for Operations Res. **[IO]**, Adelaide, Australia

Australian Soc. for Operations Res. - ACT Chap. **[IO]**, Melbourne, Australia

Australian Soc. for Operations Res. - Melbourne Chap. **[IO]**, Melbourne, Australia

Australian Soc. for Operations Res. - Queensland Chap. **[IO]**, Brisbane, Australia

Australian Soc. for Operations Res. - South Australia Chap. **[IO]**, Adelaide, Australia

Australian Soc. for Operations Res. - Sydney Chap. **[IO]**, Sydney, Australia

Australian Soc. for Operations Res. - Western Australia Chap. **[IO]**, Perth, Australia

Australian Soc. of Orthodontists **[IO]**, Crows Nest, Australia

Australian Soc. of Otolaryngology Head and Neck Surgery **[IO]**, Sydney, Australia

Australian Soc. for Parasitology **[IO]**, Brisbane, Australia

Australian Soc. of Plant Scientists **[IO]**, Crawley, Australia

Australian Soc. of Soil Sci. **[IO]**, Warragul, Australia

Australian Soc. of Sugar Cane Technologists **[IO]**, Mackay, Australia

Australian Soc. of Teachers of the Alexander Technique **[IO]**, Darlinghurst, Australia

Australian Soc. of Viticulture and Oenology **[IO]**, Adelaide, Australia

Australian Sociological Assn. **[IO]**, Brisbane, Australia

Australian Soft Drinks Assn. **[★IO]**

Australian Sonographers Assn. **[IO]**, Moorabbin, Australia

Australian Spatial Info. Bus. Assn. **[IO]**, Deakin West, Australia

Australian Speech Sci. and Tech. Assn. **[IO]**, Canberra, Australia

Australian Spina Bifida and Hydrocephalus Assn. **[IO]**, Nedlands, Australia

Australian Sport Aviation Confed. **[IO]**, Batehaven, Australia

Australian Sports Commn. **[IO]**, Belconnen, Australia

Australian Stabilisation Indus. Assn. **[IO]**, Chatswood, Australia

Australian Stainless Steel Development Assn. **[IO]**, Brisbane, Australia

Australian Steel Inst. **[IO]**, North Sydney, Australia

Australian Stock Horse Soc. **[IO]**, Scone, Australia

Australian Subscription TV and Radio Assn. **[IO]**, Pyrmont, Australia

Australian Suburban Newspapers Assn. **[★IO]**

Australian Sugar Producers Assn. **[★IO]**

Australian Superfine Wool Growers' Assn. **[IO]**, Brooklyn, Australia

Australian Systematic Botany Soc. **[IO]**, Canberra, Australia

Australian Teachers Fed. **[★IO]**

Australian Teachers of Media **[IO]**, St. Kilda, Australia

Australian Teachers Union **[★IO]**

Australian Terrier Club of Am. **[22223]**, c/o Carol Sazama, Corresponding Sec., 3 Pin Oak Trail, Medford, NJ 08055-8836

Australian Texel Stud Breeders Assn. **[IO]**, Melbourne, Australia

Australian Textile Workers' Union **[★IO]**

Australian Tile Coun. **[IO]**, Hope Valley, Australia

Australian Tinnitus Assn. (NSW) **[IO]**, Woollahra, Australia

Australian Touch Assn. **[★IO]**

Australian Tourism Export Coun. **[IO]**, Sydney, Australia

Australian Toy Assn. **[IO]**, North Melbourne, Australia

Australian Trade Commn. **[24229]**, 150 E 42nd St., 34th Fl., New York, NY 10017-5612, (212)351-6560

Australian Traditional-Medicine Soc. **[IO]**, Meadowbank, Australia

Australian Trail Horse Riders Assn. **[IO]**, Helensburgh, Australia

Australian Trail Horse Riders Assn. - New South Wales Br. **[IO]**, Karuah, Australia

Australian Trail Horse Riders Assn. - Queensland **[IO]**, Nerang, Australia

Australian Trail Horse Riders Assn. - South Australian Br. **[IO]**, Kersbrook, Australia

Australian Trail Horse Riders Assn. - Victoria Br. **[IO]**, Karuah, Australia

Australian Trucking Assn. **[IO]**, Forrest, Australia

Australian Trust for Conservation Volunteers **[★IO]**

Australian UNIX and Open Systems Users Gp. **[IO]**, Baulkham Hills, Australia

Australian Vaccination Network **[IO]**, Bangalow, Australia

Australian Vascular Biology Soc. **[IO]**, Melbourne, Australia

Australian Vegetables and Potato Growers' Fed. **[IO]**, Mulgrave, Australia

Australian Vegetarian Soc. **[IO]**, Surry Hills, Australia

Australian Venture Capital Assn. Limited **[IO]**, Sydney, Australia

Australian Veterinary Assn. **[IO]**, St. Leonards, Australia

Australian Vice-Chancellors' Comm. **[★IO]**

Australian Volunteer Coast Guard Assn. **[IO]**, Allambie Heights, Australia

Australian Wagyu Assn. **[IO]**, Armidale, Australia

Australian Water Assn. **[IO]**, Artarmon, Australia

Australian Water Ski Fed. **[IO]**, Dickson, Australia

Australian Water and Wastewater Assn. **[★IO]**

Australian Welding Inst. **[★IO]**

Australian Welding Res. Assn. **[★IO]**

Australian White Suffolk Assn. **[IO]**, Goodwood, Australia

Australian Wildlife Protection Coun. **[IO]**, Melbourne, Australia

Australian Wind Energy Assn. **[IO]**, Melbourne, Australia

Australian Wine and Brandy Corp. **[IO]**, Kent Town, Australia

Australian Wine Consumers' Co-operative Soc. **[IO]**, Kings Cross, Australia

Australian Wine Export Coun. **[★IO]**

Australian Women in Agriculture **[IO]**, Canberra, Australia

Australian Women Lawyers **[IO]**, Canberra, Australia

Australian Women Pilots' Assn. **[IO]**, Fyshwick, Australia

Australian Women's Amateur Athletic Union **[★IO]**

Australian Women's Hea. Network **[IO]**, Noarlunga, Australia

Australian Wool Growers Assn. **[IO]**, Coolah, Australia

Australian Workers' Union **[IO]**, West Melbourne, Australia

Australian Wound Mgt. Assn. **[IO]**, West Leederville, Australia

Australian Writers' Guild **[IO]**, Surry Hills, Australia

Australians Against Racism **[IO]**, Enfield, Australia

Australians for Animals **[IO]**, Byron Bay, Australia

Australians for Constitutional Monarchy **[IO]**, Sydney, Australia

Austria

Alpine Tourist Commn. **[24223]**

Austrian Cultural Forum **[9625]**

Austrian Press and Info. Ser. **[24230]**

Austrian Tourist Off. **[24231]**

Austrian Trade Commn. **[24232]**

Center for Austrian Stud. **[9626]**

Fed. of Alpine and Schuhplattler Clubs in North Am. **[9627]**

Soc. for Austrian and Habsburg History **[9628]**

Soc. for the Development of Austrian Economics **[6894]**

U.S. Austrian Chamber of Commerce **[24233]**

Austria Natl. Comm. for UNICEF **[IO]**, Vienna, Austria

Austria Philatelic Soc. of New York - Defunct.

Austrian

American-Austrian Soc. **[18976]**

Austrian Cultural Forum **[9625]**

Austrian Cultural Forum **[IO]**

Austrian Press and Info. Ser. **[24230]**

Austrian Tourist Off. **[24231]**

Austrian Trade Commn. **[24232]**

Center for Austrian Stud. **[9626]**

Center for Austrian Stud. **[IO]**

Federation of Alpine and Schuhplattler Clubs in North America **[IO]**

Fed. of Alpine and Schuhplattler Clubs in North Am. **[9627]**

Soc. for Austrian and Habsburg History **[9628]**

Society for Austrian and Habsburg History **[IO]**

Soc. for the Development of Austrian Economics **[6894]**

U.S. Austrian Chamber of Commerce **[24233]**

Austrian Acad. of Sciences **[IO]**, Vienna, Austria

Austrian Advt. Res. Assn. **[IO]**, Vienna, Austria

Austrian Assn. for Amer. Stud. **[IO]**, Salzburg, Austria

Austrian Assn. of Music **[IO]**, Vienna, Austria

Austrian Assn. for Pattern Recognition **[IO]**, Vienna, Austria

Austrian Assn. for Theatre Technics **[IO]**, Vienna, Austria

Austrian Astronomical Soc. **[IO]**, Vienna, Austria

Austrian Auto. Touring and Motorcycle Club **[IO]**, Vienna, Austria

Austrian Badminton Assn. **[IO]**, Graz, Austria

Austrian Bankers' Assn. **[IO]**, Vienna, Austria

Austrian Baseball-Softball Fed. **[IO]**, Vienna, Austria

Austrian Bible Soc. **[IO]**, Vienna, Austria

Austrian Booksellers' and Publishers' Assn. **[IO]**, Vienna, Austria

Austrian Brewers' Assn. **[IO]**, Vienna, Austria

Austrian Cockpit Assn. **[IO]**, Vienna, Austria

Austrian Coffee and Tea Bd. **[IO]**, Vienna, Austria

Austrian Commn. on Geomorphology **[IO]**, Vienna, Austria

Austrian Composers Assn. **[IO]**, Vienna, Austria

Austrian Cmpt. Soc. **[IO]**, Vienna, Austria

A star before a book entry number signifies that the name is not listed separately, but is mentioned within the entry.

Austrian Consultants Assn. [IO], Vienna, Austria
Austrian Coun. for Agricultural Engg. and Rural Development [IO], Vienna, Austria
Austrian Cricket Assn. [IO], Vienna, Austria
Austrian Cultural Forum [IO], New York, NY, United States
Austrian Cultural Forum [9625], Austrian Cultural Inst., 11 E 52nd St., New York, NY 10022, (212)319-5300
Austrian Cultural Inst. [★9625]
Austrian Cultural Inst. [★IO]
Austrian DanceSport Fed. [IO], Vienna, Austria
Austrian Doctors for a Healthy Env. [IO], Vienna, Austria
Austrian Economic Assn. [IO], Vienna, Austria
Austrian Economic Soc. [★IO]
Austrian Fed. Economic Chamber [IO], Vienna, Austria
Austrian Fed. of Independent Loss Adjusters [IO], Vienna, Austria
Austrian Fed. of Roller Skating and Inline Skating [IO], Vienna, Austria
Austrian Fed. of Univ. Women [IO], Vienna, Austria
Austrian Floorball Fed. [IO], Leoben, Austria
Austrian Forum - Defunct.
Austrian Found. for Development Res. [IO], Vienna, Austria
Austrian Frisbee-Sport Fed. [IO], Vienna, Austria
Austrian Golf Assn. [IO], Vienna, Austria
Austrian Hotels' Assn. [IO], Vienna, Austria
Austrian Huntington Assn. [IO], Vienna, Austria
Austrian Ice Hockey Fed. [IO], Vienna, Austria
Austrian Inst. [★IO]
Austrian Inst. [★9625]
Austrian Inst. of Economic Res. [IO], Vienna, Austria
Austrian-Japan Soc. for Sci. and Art [IO], Vienna, Austria
Austrian Jet Sport Assn. [IO], Vienna, Austria
Austrian League Against Epilepsy [IO], Vienna, Austria
Austrian Ludwig Wittgenstein Soc. [IO], Kirchberg am Wechsel, Austria
Austrian Magazines Assn. [IO], Vienna, Austria
Austrian Medical Chamber [IO], Vienna, Austria
Austrian Medical Students Assn. [IO], Vienna, Austria
Austrian Member Comm. of the World Energy Coun. [IO], Vienna, Austria
Austrian Milling Assn. [IO], Vienna, Austria
Austrian Natl. Soc. of Agricultural Engineers [IO], Wieselburg, Austria
Austrian Natl. Tourist Off. [★24231]
Austrian Natl. Union of Students [IO], Vienna, Austria
Austrian Neuroscience Assn. [IO], Vienna, Austria
Austrian Newspaper Assn. [IO], Vienna, Austria
Austrian North-South Inst. for Development Cooperation [IO], Vienna, Austria
Austrian Oil Crushers and Processors [IO], Bruck an der Leitha, Austria
Austrian Olympic Comm. [IO], Vienna, Austria
Austrian Paralympic Comm. [IO], Vienna, Austria
Austrian P.E.N. Centre [IO], Vienna, Austria
Austrian Pharmacological Soc. [IO], Graz, Austria
Austrian Physical Soc. [IO], Graz, Austria
Austrian Physiological Soc. [IO], Graz, Austria
Austrian Physiotherapy Assn. [IO], Vienna, Austria
Austrian Press and Info. Ser. [24230], 3524 Intl. Ct. NW, Washington, DC 20008-3022, (202)895-6775
Austrian Professional Travel Agents and Tour Operators Assn. [IO], Vienna, Austria
Austrian Sci. Fund [IO], Vienna, Austria
Austrian Soc. for Acupuncture [IO], Vienna, Austria
Austrian Soc. of Antimicrobial Chemotherapy [IO], Vienna, Austria
Austrian Soc. for Applied Res. in Tourism [IO], Vienna, Austria
Austrian Soc. of Automotive Engineers [IO], Vienna, Austria
Austrian Soc. for Bone and Mineral Res. [IO], Vienna, Austria
Austrian Soc. of Cardiology [IO], Vienna, Austria
Austrian Soc. of Chemotherapy [★IO]
Austrian Soc. for Clinical Neurophysiology [IO], Vienna, Austria

Austrian Soc. of Dermatology and Venereology [IO], Vienna, Austria
Austrian Soc. for Electron Microscopy [IO], Vienna, Austria
Austrian Soc. for Geriatrics and Gerontology [IO], Vienna, Austria
Austrian Soc. of Hypertension [IO], Vienna, Austria
Austrian Soc. of Operations Res. [IO], Vienna, Austria
Austrian Soc. of Sports Medicine [IO], Vienna, Austria
Austrian Soc. of Sterility, Fertility and Endocrinology [IO], Graz, Austria
Austrian Sports Fed. [IO], Vienna, Austria
Austrian Statistical Soc. [IO], Vienna, Austria
Austrian Taekwondo Fed. [IO], Innsbruck, Austria
Austrian Tea Bd. [★IO]
Austrian Theatre Technicians Assn. [★IO]
Austrian Tourist Off. [24231], PO Box 1142, New York, NY 10108-1142, (212)994-6880
Austrian Trade Commn. [24232], 120 W 45th St., 9th Fl., New York, NY 10036, (212)421-5250
Austrian Trade Commissions in the U.S. [24265], 11601 Wilshire Blvd., Ste. 2420, Los Angeles, CA 90025, (310)477-9988
Austrian Trade Commissions in the U.S. [IO], Los Angeles, CA, United States
Austrian Trade Commissions in the U.S. and Canada [★IO]
Austrian Trade Commissions in the U.S. and Canada [★24265]
Austrian Trade Union Fed. - Christian Fraction [IO], Vienna, Austria
Austrian Umbrella Org. for Geographic Info. [IO], Innsbruck, Austria
Austrian Vehicle Indus. Assn. [IO], Vienna, Austria
Austrian Water Ski Fed. [IO], Leonding, Austria
Austrian Waterski Fed. [IO], Leonding, Austria
Austrian Youth Hostel Assn. [IO], Vienna, Austria
Austropapier - Vereinigung der Osterreichischen Papierindustrie [★IO]
Authentic Artifact Collectors Assn. [21543], c/o Cliff Jackson, Pres., 323 Hamme Mill Rd., Warrenton, NC 27589
Authentic Hovawarts of North Am. [22224], PO Box 527, Redwood Valley, CA 95470, (925)458-1252

Authors

Alice in Wonderland Collectors Network [21957]
Amer. Boccaccio Assn. [9629]
Amer. Chesterton Soc. [9630]
Amer. Chesterton Soc. [IO]
Amer. Christian Fiction Writers [11156]
Amer. Hobbit Assn. [9631]
Amer. Literature Assn. [10411]
Amer. Soc. of Composers, Authors and Publishers [5836]
Amer. Teilhard Assn. [9632]
Angela Thirkell Soc. [9633]
Arthur Miller Soc. [11159]
The Arthur Ransome Soc. [IO]
August Derleth Society [IO]
August Derleth Soc. [9634]
Authors Guild [11161]
Authors League of Am. [11162]
Ayn Rand Inst. [10787]
Barbara Pym Soc. [9635]
Bernard Shaw Soc. [9636]
Bertrand Russell Soc. [9637]
Betsy-Tacy Soc. [9638]
Bram Stoker Club [IO]
Bram Stoker Memorial Association [IO]
Bram Stoker Memorial Assn. [9639]
Bram Stoker Soc. - Ireland [IO]
Bronte Soc. [IO]
Burroughs Bibliophiles [9640]
Byron Soc. of Am. [9641]
Carson McCullers Soc. [11164]
Cassie Edwards Intl. Fan Club [24782]
Catharine Maria Sedgwick Soc. [11165]
Charles S. Peirce Soc. [9642]
Charles S. Peirce Soc. [IO]
Charles W. Chesnutt Assn. [11166]
Charles Williams Soc. [IO]
Christopher Morley Knothole Assn. [9643]
Comm. on Scholarly Editions [11167]

Cormac McCarthy Soc. [11168]
Dante Soc. of Am. [9644]
D.H. Lawrence Soc. of North Am. [9645]
D.H. Lawrence Soc. of North Am. [IO]
Dickens Fellowship [IO]
Dickens Soc. [9646]
Don DeLillo Soc. [11169]
Dorothy L. Sayers Soc. [IO]
Edgar Allan Poe Soc. of Baltimore [9647]
E.F. Benson Soc. [IO]
Elvish Linguistic Fellowship [10402]
Eugene O'Neill Soc. [9648]
Eugene O'Neill Society [IO]
Evelyn Scott Soc. [11170]
F. Scott Fitzgerald Soc. [9649]
F. Scott Fitzgerald Society [IO]
Francis Bacon Found. [9650]
Friends of Thomas More [IO]
Gene Stratton Porter Memorial Soc. [9651]
George MacDonald Soc. [IO]
George Sand Assn [9652]
George Sand Soc. [9653]
Georgia Writers Assn. and Young Georgia Writers [11172]
Goethe Soc. of North Am. [9654]
Gone With the Wind Soc. [24831]
Harriet Beecher Stowe Center [9655]
Harriet Beecher Stowe Soc. [11173]
Harry Stephen Keeler Soc. [9656]
Harry Stephen Keeler Society [IO]
Hegel Soc. of Am. [9657]
Hemingway Found. and Soc. [9658]
H.G. Wells Soc. [IO]
Horatio Alger Soc. [9659]
Horror Writers Assn. [11174]
Housman Soc. [IO]
Ibsen Soc. of Am. [IO]
Ibsen Soc. of Am. [9660]
Intl. Assn. of Crime Writers, North Amer. Br. [11175]
Intl. Brecht Soc. [9661]
Intl. Brecht Soc. [IO]
Intl. Dostoevsky Soc. [IO]
Intl. Friends of the London Lib. [10363]
Intl. Lawrence Durrell Soc. [9662]
International Lawrence Durrell Society [IO]
Intl. Rebecca West Soc. [11178]
Intl. Spenser Soc. [9663]
Intl. Theodore Dreiser Soc. [9664]
Intl. Theodore Dreiser Soc. [IO]
Intl. Thomas Merton Soc. [IO]
Intl. Thomas Merton Soc. [9665]
Intl. Thriller Writers [11179]
Intl. Virginia Woolf Soc. [9666]
Intl. Virginia Woolf Soc. [IO]
Intl. Vladimir Nabokov Soc. [IO]
Intl. Vladimir Nabokov Soc. [9667]
Intl. Wizard of Oz Club [9668]
Intl. Wizard of Oz Club [IO]
Jack London Res. Center [9669]
James A. Michener Soc. [9670]
James Dickey Soc. [10875]
James Joyce Soc. [9671]
James Joyce Soc. of Southern Colorado [9672]
Jane Austen Soc. of North Am. [9673]
Jane Austen Soc. of North Am. [IO]
Jane Austen Soc. of the United Kingdom [IO]
Jesse Stuart Found. [9674]
Johnson Soc. - Lichfield [IO]
Johnson Soc. of London [IO]
Joseph Conrad Soc. of Am. [9675]
Journalists, Authors and Poets on Stamps Stud. Unit [10778]
Kafka Soc. of Am. and Jour. [9676]
Kafka Soc. of Am. and Jour. [IO]
Keats-Shelley Assn. of Am. [9677]
Kipling Soc. [IO]
Langston Hughes Soc. [9678]
Laura Ingalls Wilder Memorial Soc. [9679]
Lessing Soc. [9680]
Lewis Carroll Soc. [IO]
Lewis Carroll Soc. of North Am. [9681]
Literary Source [3232]
Longfellow Soc. [10863]
Louisa May Alcott Memorial Assn. [9682]

Reference to "IO" in place of a book number signifies that the association may be found in the 45th edition of International Organizations.

Lowell Celebrates Kerouac! **[9683]**
Mark Twain Boyhood Home Associates **[9684]**
Mark Twain Circle of New York **[9685]**
Mark Twain Home Found. **[9686]**
Mark Twain House and Museum **[9687]**
Mark Twain Res. Found. **[9688]**
Marlowe Lives! Assn. **[9689]**
Marlowe Soc. of Am. **[9690]**
Melville Soc. **[9691]**
Mencken Soc. **[9692]**
Mertonvrienden of Belgium and the Netherlands **[IO]**
Milton Soc. of Am. **[9693]**
Mythopoeic Soc. **[10427]**
Nathaniel Hawthorne Soc. **[9694]**
Natl. Assn. of Women Writers **[11183]**
Natl. Assn. of Writers in Educ. **[IO]**
Natl. Steinbeck Center **[9695]**
Natl. Writers Union **[24219]**
New York C.S. Lewis Soc. **[9696]**
Noah Webster House **[10053]**
Nockian Soc. **[9697]**
North Amer. Jules Verne Soc. **[11184]**
North Amer. Sartre Soc. **[10819]**
P. N. Elrod Fan Club **[IO]**
Paul Claudel Society **[IO]**
Paul Claudel Soc. **[9698]**
Pearl S. Buck Birthplace Found. **[9699]**
PEN Center U.S.A. **[11186]**
Philip Jose Farmer Soc. **[9700]**
Philip Roth Soc. **[11187]**
Pirandello Soc. of Am. **[9701]**
Playwrights Guild of Canada **[IO]**
P.N. Elrod Fan Club **[9702]**
Poe Found. **[9703]**
Poe Stud. Assn. **[9704]**
Poets Against the War **[11189]**
Powys Soc. **[IO]**
Powys Soc. of North Am. **[9705]**
Ralph Waldo Emerson Memorial Assn. **[9706]**
Richard Jefferies Soc. **[IO]**
Richard Wright Circle **[9707]**
Robinson Jeffers Assn. **[11190]**
Rousseau Assn. **[9708]**
Rousseau Assn. **[IO]**
Saint Andrew Abbey **[11192]**
Shakespeare Birthplace Trust **[IO]**
Shakespeare Oxford Soc. **[IO]**
Shakespeare Oxford Soc. **[9709]**
Shakespeare Soc. **[9710]**
Societe des Amis d'Alexandre Dumas **[IO]**
Societe des Auteurs, Compositeurs et Editeurs de Musique **[IO]**
Societe Belge des Auteurs Compositeurs et Editeurs **[IO]**
Soc. of Children's Book Writers and Illustrators **[11194]**
Soc. of Composers, Authors and Music Publishers of Canada **[IO]**
Soc. for the History of Authorship, Reading and Publishing **[9754]**
Soc. for Reproduction Rights of Authors, Composers and Publishers in Canada **[IO]**
Soc. for the Stud. of Amer. Women Writers **[11195]**
Soc. for Textual Scholarship **[10432]**
Susan Glaspell Soc. **[11197]**
Swedenborg Found. **[9711]**
Tennyson Soc. **[IO]**
Text and Academic Authors Assn. **[11199]**
Theodore Roethke Memorial Found. **[10872]**
The Thomas Hardy Assn. **[9712]**
Thomas Hardy Soc. **[IO]**
Thomas Wolfe Soc. **[9713]**
Thoreau Soc. **[9714]**
Thorne Smith Soc. **[9715]**
Thornton Wilder Soc. **[11200]**
Tilling Soc. **[IO]**
Tolkien Soc. **[IO]**
Trollope Soc. **[9716]**
Uncle Remus Museum **[9717]**
Vachel Lindsay Assn. **[9718]**
Vergilian Soc. **[9719]**
W. T. Bandy Center for Baudelaire and Modern French Stud. **[9720]**

Walden Pond Advisory Comm. **[4464]**
Walt Whitman Birthplace Assn. **[9721]**
Willa Cather Pioneer Memorial and Educational Found. **[9722]**
William Allen White Found. **[9723]**
William Dean Howells Soc. **[9724]**
William Morris Soc. **[IO]**
William Morris Soc. in the U.S. **[9725]**
The Wodehouse Soc. **[9726]**
Wolfe Pack **[9727]**
Women's Natl. Book Assn. **[3174]**
World Antique Dealers Assn. **[219]**
Yiddisher Kultur Farband **[10291]**
Zane Grey's West Soc. **[9728]**
Zora Neale Hurston Soc. **[9729]**
Authors; Amer. Soc. of Journalists and **[11158]**
Authors Assn; Text and Academic **[11199]**
Authors Assn; Textbook **[★11199]**
Authors and Composers; Amer. Guild of **[★5859]**
Authors and Composers; Society of European Stage **[★9817]**
Authors Guild **[11161]**, 31 E 32nd St., 7th Fl., New York, NY 10016-7923, (212)563-5904
Authors League of Am. **[11162]**, c/o The Authors Guild, 31 E 32nd St., 7th Fl., New York, NY 10016-7923, (212)563-5904
Authors' Licensing and Collecting Soc. **[IO]**, London, United Kingdom
Authors; Natl. Alliance of Short Fiction **[11182]**
Authors and Poets on Stamps Stud. Unit; Journalists, **[10778]**
Authors and Publishers; Amer. Soc. of Composers, **[5836]**
Authors and Publishers Assn. **[3211]**, 8919 Friendship Rd., Houston, TX 77080-4111
Authors' Representatives; Assn. of **[171]**
Authors' Representatives; Soc. of **[★171]**
Authors; Soc. of Midland **[4070]**
Authorship, Reading and Publishing; Soc. for the History of **[9754]**

Autism

Autism Assn. Australian Capital Territory **[IO]**
Autism Assn. - Singapore **[IO]**
Autism Assn. of Western Australia **[IO]**
Autism Coun. of Australia **[IO]**
Autism-Europe **[IO]**
Autism Independent UK **[IO]**
Autism Initiatives **[IO]**
Autism Network Intl. **[IO]**
Autism Network Intl. **[13719]**
Autism Northern Territory **[IO]**
Autism Queensland **[IO]**
The Autism Res. Found. **[13720]**
Autism Res. Inst. **[13721]**
Autism Res. Inst. **[IO]**
Autism Services Center **[13722]**
Autism Soc. of Am. **[13723]**
Autism Soc. Canada **[IO]**
Autism Soc. Philippines **[IO]**
Autism Soc. of Serbia **[IO]**
Autism South Australia **[IO]**
Autism Speaks **[13724]**
Autism Spectrum Australia **[IO]**
Autism Treatment Services of Canada **[IO]**
Autism Victoria **[IO]**
Canines for Disabled Kids **[11927]**
First Signs **[13942]**
Friends of LADDERS **[12491]**
Global Autism Proj. **[13725]**
Global Autism Proj. **[IO]**
Global and Regional Asperger Syndrome Partnership **[15325]**
Intl. Autistic Res. Org. **[IO]**
Intl. Rett Syndrome Assn. **[15333]**
Irish Soc. for Autism **[IO]**
Natl. Alliance for Autism Res. **[13726]**
Natl. Autism Assn. **[13727]**
Natl. Autism Soc. of Malaysia **[IO]**
Natl. Autism Soc. of Sweden **[IO]**
Org. for Autism Res. **[13728]**
Parents and Professionals and Autism Northern Ireland **[IO]**
Scottish Soc. for Autism **[IO]**
Soc. for Helping People with Autism **[IO]**
Soc. for Treatment of Autism **[IO]**

Spanish Assn. for Parents with Autistic Children **[IO]**
Autism; Action for **[IO]**
Autism and Asperger Syndrome; MAAP Services for **[15337]**
Autism Assn. Australian Capital Territory **[IO]**, Mawson, Australia
Autism Assn. - Singapore **[IO]**, Singapore, Singapore
Autism Assn. of Western Australia **[IO]**, Perth, Australia
Autism Coun. of Australia **[IO]**, Forestville, Australia
Autism-Europe **[IO]**, Brussels, Belgium
Autism Hotline; Natl. **[★13722]**
Autism Independent UK **[IO]**, Kettering, United Kingdom
Autism Initiatives **[IO]**, Liverpool, United Kingdom
Autism Network Intl. **[IO]**, Syracuse, NY, United States
Autism Network Intl. **[13719]**, PO Box 35448, Syracuse, NY 13235-5448
Autism Northern Territory **[IO]**, Darwin, Australia
Autism; NSAC, The Natl. Soc. for Children and Adults with **[★13723]**
Autism Queensland **[IO]**, Sunnybank, Australia
The Autism Res. Found. **[13720]**, c/o Moss-Rosene Lab, 715 Albany St., W701, Boston, MA 02118, (617)414-7012
Autism Res. Inst. **[13721]**, 4182 Adams Ave., San Diego, CA 92116, (619)281-7165
Autism Res. Inst. **[IO]**, San Diego, CA, United States
Autism Services Center **[13722]**, The Keith Albee Bldg., 929 4th Ave., PO Box 507, Huntington, WV 25710-0507, (304)525-8014
Autism Soc. of Am. **[13723]**, 7910 Woodmont Ave., Ste. 300, Bethesda, MD 20814-3067, (301)657-0881
Autism Soc. of British Columbia **[IO]**, Burnaby, BC, Canada
Autism Soc. Canada **[IO]**, Ottawa, ON, Canada
Autism Soc. in Norway **[IO]**, Oslo, Norway
Autism Soc. Philippines **[IO]**, Quezon City, Philippines
Autism Soc. of Serbia **[IO]**, Belgrade, Serbia
Autism South Australia **[IO]**, Fullarton, Australia
Autism Speaks **[13724]**, 2 Park Ave., 11th Fl., New York, NY 10016, (212)252-8584
Autism Spectrum Australia **[IO]**, Sydney, Australia
Autism Treatment Services of Canada **[IO]**, Calgary, AB, Canada
Autism Victoria **[IO]**, Melbourne, Australia
Autismeforeningen i Norge **[★IO]**
Autistic Children; Natl. Soc. for **[★13723]**
Auto Auction Assn; Natl. **[327]**
Auto Body Coun; Natl. **[363]**
Auto Body Representatives Coun. - Defunct.
Auto Collision Repair; Inter-Industry Conf. on **[415]**
Auto Conf; Congressional **[★17255]**
Auto-Cycle Union - Motorcycling Great Britain **[IO]**, Rugby, United Kingdom
Auto Enthusiasts Intl. - Defunct.
Auto and Flat Glass Dealers Assn; Natl. **[★1732]**
Auto Glass Industry Coun. - Address unknown since 1991.
Auto-Insurance Reform; Coalition for **[17316]**
Auto Intl. Assn. **[371]**, 7101 Wisconsin Ave., Ste. 1300, Bethesda, MD 20814, (301)654-6664
Auto Intl. Assn. **[IO]**, Bethesda, MD, United States
Auto- ja Kuljetusalan Tyontekijaliitto **[★IO]**
Auto League; Sacred Heart **[★19711]**
Auto Mag or Automatic Magazine **[★21539]**
Auto Parts Recyclers Assn. of Australia **[IO]**, Melbourne, Australia

Auto Racing

Amer. Auto Racing Writers and Broadcasters Assn. **[23069]**
Amer. Funny Car Series **[23070]**
Amer. Hot Rod Assn. **[23071]**
Antique Auto Racing Assn. **[21578]**
Auto. Competition Comm. for the U.S. FIA **[23073]**
Championship Assn. of Mechanics **[23075]**
Championship Auto Racing Teams **[23076]**
Derrike Cope Fan Club **[24783]**
Eastern Museum of Motor Racing **[21634]**
Goodguys Rod and Custom Assn. **[21649]**

A star before a book entry number signifies that the name is not listed separately, but is mentioned within the entry.

Grand Amer. Road Racing Assn. [23068]
Historic Motor Sports Assn. [21657]
Intl. Hot Rod Assn. [23077]
Intl. Motor Contest Assn. [23078]
Intl. Motor Sports Assn. [23079]
Johnny Benson Fan Club [24784]
Natl. Amer. Motors Drivers and Racers Assn.
[23080]
Natl. Assn. for Stock Car Auto Racing [23081]
Natl. Auto Racing Historical Soc. [23082]
Natl. Elec. Drag Racing Assn. [23396]
Natl. Hot Rod Assn. [23083]
Natl. Indy 500 Collectors Club [21734]
Natl. Old Timers Auto Racing Club [21737]
Sports Car Club of Am. [21787]
Sportscar Vintage Racing Assn. [23085]
United Black Drag Racers Assn. [23397]
U.S. Auto Club [23086]
U.S. Late Model Assn. [23087]
Vintage Drivers Club of Am. [21810]
Western Assoc. Modelers [22661]
Women's Automotive Assn. Intl. [367]
Young Racers of Am. [23674]
Auto Safety; Advocates for Highway and [12944]
Auto Safety; Center for [12956]
Auto Ser. Excellence [★424]
Auto Sound Challenge Assn; Intl. [1219]
Auto Suppliers Benchmarking Assn. [703], 4606 FM
1960 W, Ste. 250, Houston, TX 77069-9949,
(281)440-5044
Auto Suppliers Benchmarking Consortium [★703]
Auto and Truck Recyclers; Assn. of [★3988]
Auto and Truck Wreckers Assn; Natl. [★3988]
Auto Workers Action Caucus - Defunct.
Auto Workers Community Action Prog; United
[★18298]
Auto Workers; United [★24004]
Auto Wreckers Assn; Natl. [★3988]
Autoalan Keskusliitto ry [★IO]
Autobody Craftsman Assn. [372], c/o Alpine Auto
Body, PO Box 820230, Vancouver, WA 98662,
(206)575-8893
Autobody Supply and Equipment Mfrs. Coun. -
Defunct.
Autoclaved Aerated Concrete Products Assn. [918],
3701 County Rd. 544 E, Haines City, FL 33844,
(863)422-6360
Autoduel Assn; Amer. [22456]
Autograph Chap. of the Amer. First Day Cover Soc. -
Defunct.
Autograph Collectors Club; Universal [22126]
Autograph Dealers Assn; Professional [865]
Autographics Intl. - Defunct.
Autoimmune Disorders
Alliance for Lupus Res. [15013]
Churg Strauss Syndrome Assn. [13729]
Intl. Org. of Multiple Sclerosis Nurses [15486]
Intl. Scleroderma Network [16387]
Natl. Sjogren's Syndrome Assn. [16373]
PBCers Org. [14816]
Platelet Disorder Support Assn. [13730]
Vasculitis Found. [16552]
Autoliito [★IO]
Automata and Computability Theory; Special Interest
Gp. on [★7539]
Automated Builders Consortium [603], 1445 Donlon
St., Ste. 16, Ventura, CA 93003, (805)642-9735
Automated Electrified Monorail Product Section -
Material Handling Inst. - Defunct.
Automated Imaging Assn. [7581], PO Box 3724, Ann
Arbor, MI 48106, (734)994-6088
Automated Material Handling Systems Assn. [IO],
Leicester, United Kingdom
Automated Procedures for Engineering Consultants;
APEC - [6999]
Automated Procedures for Engineering Consultants,
Inc. [★6999]
Automated Storage/Retrieval Systems [2004], 8720
Red Oak Blvd., Ste. 201, Charlotte, NC 28217,
(704)676-1190
Automated Systems Assn; Cmpt. and [★6737]
Automated Vision Assn. [★7581]
Automatic Control
Asociacion Chilena de Control Automatico [IO]
Associacao Portuguesa de Controlo Automatico
[IO]

Assn. for Lab. Automation [6515]
Automatic Control Soc. of Slovenia [IO]
Brazilian Automatics Soc. [IO]
Chinese Assn. of Automation [IO]
Finnish Soc. of Automation [IO]
GAMBICA, Assn. for Instrumentation, Control,
Automation and Lab. Tech. [IO]
IEEE Control Systems Soc. [6514]
Inst. of Systems, Control and Info. Engineers [IO]
Intl. Fed. of Automatic Control - Canada [IO]
Intl. Fed. of Automatic Control - Natl. Member
Org. of Hungary [IO]
Israeli Assn. of Automatic Control [IO]
Red des Automatica de Cuba [IO]
Singapore Indus. Automation Assn. [IO]
Slovak Intl. Fed. of Automatic Control - Natl.
Member Org. [IO]
Sociedade Brasileira de Automatica [IO]
Ukrainian Assn. of Automatic Control [IO]
United Kingdom Automatic Control Coun. [IO]
Automatic Control Soc. of Slovenia [IO], Maribor,
Slovenia
Automatic Damper Mfrs. Assn. - Defunct.
Automatic Door Mfrs; Amer. Assn. of [1163]
Automatic Door Suppliers Assn. [IO], Warlingham,
United Kingdom
Automatic Fire Alarm Assn. [3439], PO Box 951807,
Lake Mary, FL 32795-1807, (407)833-9133
Automatic Guided Vehicle Systems [★2005]
Automatic Guided Vehicle Systems Sect. of the
Material Handling Inst. [2005], 8720 Red Oak
Blvd., Ste. 201, Charlotte, NC 28217, (704)676-
1190
Automatic Identification
AIM [335]
Assn. for Automatic Identification and Mobility
North Am. [336]
Automatic Identification Mfrs. - Argentina [IO]
Automatic Identification Mfrs. - Belgium [IO]
Automatic Identification Mfrs. - Brazil [IO]
Automatic Identification Mfrs. - Denmark [IO]
Automatic Identification Mfrs. - Germany [IO]
Automatic Identification Mfrs. - India [IO]
Automatic Identification Mfrs. - Italia [IO]
Automatic Identification Mfrs. - United Kingdom
[IO]
EAN Argentina [IO]
EAN Azerbaijan [IO]
EAN Bahrain [IO]
EAN Belarus [IO]
EAN Croatia [IO]
GS1 [IO]
GS1 Austria GmbH [IO]
GS1 Denmark [IO]
GS1 Ireland [IO]
GS1 Malta [IO]
GS1 Mauritius [IO]
GS1 UK [IO]
GS1 US [337]
Integrated Bus. Communications Alliance [338]
Optical Prdt. Code Coun. [339]
Automatic Identification Assn. [IO], Moscow, Russia
Automatic Identification Mfrs. [★335]
Automatic Identification Mfrs. - Argentina [IO], Bue-
nos Aires, Argentina
Automatic Identification Mfrs. Assn. [★335]
Automatic Identification Mfrs. - Belgium [IO], Brus-
sels, Belgium
Automatic Identification Mfrs. - Brazil [IO], Sao
Paulo, Brazil
Automatic Identification Mfrs. - Denmark [IO], Lyn-
gby, Denmark
Automatic Identification Mfrs. - Germany [IO],
Lampertheim, Germany
Automatic Identification Mfrs. - India [IO], New Delhi,
India
Automatic Identification Mfrs. - Italia [IO], Milan, Italy
Automatic Identification Mfrs. - United Kingdom [IO],
Halifax, United Kingdom
Automatic Laundry and Cleaning Coun; Natl.
[★2402]
Automatic Merchandising Assn; Natl. [3971]
Automatic Meter Reading Assn. [3953], 60 Revere
Dr., Ste. 500, Northbrook, IL 60062, (847)480-9628
Automatic Musical Instrument Collectors Assn. Intl. -
Address unknown since 1999.

Automatic Phonograph Mfrs. Assn. - Defunct.
Automatic Pistol Collectors Assn; Natl. [21539]
Automatic Sprinkler Assn; Natl. [★3449]
Automatic Sprinkler and Fire Control Assn; Natl.
[★3449]
Automatic Transmission Rebuilders Assn. [373],
2400 Latigo Ave., Oxnard, CA 93030, (805)604-
2000
Automatic Vending Assn. [IO], Sutton, United
Kingdom
Automatic Vending Assn. of Britain [★IO]
Automatic Welding Machinery Assn. - Defunct.
Automation
Assn. for Lab. Automation [6515]
Assn. for Lab. Automation [IO]
Control and Info. Systems Integrators Assn.
[3704]
Ebix Users Assn. [340]
HAVi [6513]
Automation Assn; Home [★1178]
Automation Assn; Measurement, Control, and [3485]
Automation in Bus. Educ; Soc. for [★8132]
Automation Consortium; Electronic Design [6911]
Automation Div; Info. Sci. and [★10368]
Automation in English and the Humanities; Soc. for
[★8132]
Automation in Fine Arts; Soc. for [★8132]
Automation in Pharmacy; Amer. Soc. for [2969]
Automation in Professional Educ; Soc. for [★8132]
Automation in the Social Sciences; Soc. for [★8132]
Automation Soc. - Address unknown since 1994.
Automation Soc; IEEE Robotics and [7582]
Automation Soc; ISA - Instrumentation, Systems,
and [7220]
Automation; Special Interest Gp. for Design [6749]
Automation Specialists; Assn. of Mailing, Shipping,
and Off. [2448]
Automation Technology Services - Address unknown
since 2005.
Automedica - Defunct.
Automobilclub von Deutschland [IO], Frankfurt,
Germany
Automobile
71 429 Mustang Registry [21551]
1929 Silver Anniversary Buick Club [IO]
1937-1938 Buick Club [21552]
1948-50 Packard Convertible Roster [21553]
1953-54 Buick Skylark Club [21554]
1956 Studebaker Golden Hawk Owners Register
[21555]
1958 Cadillac Owners Assn. [21556]
1958 Cadillac Owners Association [IO]
1965-66 Full Size Chevrolet Club [21557]
1970 Dart Swinger 340s Registry [21558]
1971 GTO and Judge Convertible Registry
[21559]
1995 Corvette Pace Car Registry [21560]
66,67,68 High Country Special Mustang Registry
[21561]
AAA Found. for Traffic Safety [12943]
Abarth Register, U.S.A. [21562]
Airflow Club of Am. [21563]
Alfa Romeo Assn. [21564]
Alfa Romeo Club of Canada [IO]
Alfa Romeo Owners Club [21565]
Alliance for a New Trans. Charter [6311]
Alvis Owner Club [IO]
AMC Pacer Club [21566]
AMC Rambler Club [21567]
AMC Rambler Club [IO]
Amer. Assn. of Motor Vehicle Administrators
[5535]
Amer. Austin/Bantam Club [21568]
Amer. Auto Racing Writers and Broadcasters
Assn. [23069]
Amer. Auto. Touring Alliance [3905]
Amer. Bugatti Club [21569]
Amer. Camaro Assn. [21570]
Amer. Chevelle Enthusiasts Soc. [21571]
Amer. Funny Car Series [23070]
Amer. Highway Users Alliance [12949]
Amer. Hot Rod Assn. [23071]
Amer. Hot Rod Assn. [IO]
Amer. Jeepster Club [21572]
Amer. Lancia Club [21573]

Reference to "IO" in place of a book number signifies that the association may be found in the 45th edition of International Organizations.

Encyclopedia of Associations, 46th Edition

3097

Amer. MGB Assn. [21574]
Amer. MGC Register [21575]
Amer. Motors Owners Assn. [21576]
Amer. Salvage Pool Assn. [342]
Amer. Speed Assn. [23072]
Amer. Sta. Wagon Owners Assn. [21577]
Americans for Trans. Mobility [6315]
Antique Auto Racing Assn. [21578]
Antique Auto. Club of Am. [21579]
Antique Studebaker Club [21580]
Antique Truck Club of Am. [23022]
Armstrong Siddeley Owners Club [IO]
Assn. for the Advancement of Automotive
   Medicine [12951]
Assn. of Automotive Aftermarket Distributors/Parts
   Plus [370]
Aston Martin Owners Club [21581]
Aston Martin Owners Club [IO]
Auburn-Cord-Duesenberg Club [21582]
Austin Bantam Soc. [21583]
Austin Bantam Soc. [IO]
Austin-Healey Club of Am. [21584]
Austin-Healey Club USA [21585]
Austin-Healey Sports and Touring Club [21586]
Austin Ten Drivers Club [IO]
Autobody Craftsman Assn. [372]
Automobile Club de l'Ouest [IO]
Auto. Competition Comm. for the U.S. FIA
   [23073]
Auto. Film Club of Am. [344]
Auto. License Plate Collectors Assn. [21587]
Auto. Objects d'Art Club [21588]
Auto. Racing Club of Am. [23074]
Automotive Consumer Action Prog. [17307]
Automotive Engine Rebuilders Assn. [375]
Automotive Hall of Fame [345]
Automotive Indus. Action Gp. [346]
Automotive Lift Inst. [376]
Automotive Maintenance and Repair Assn. [407]
Automotive Oil Change Assn. [408]
Automotive Parts Remanufacturers Assn. [409]
Automotive Presidents Coun. [348]
Automotive Recyclers Assn. [3988]
Automotive Refrigeration Products Inst. [378]
Automotive Ser. Assn. [410]
Automotive Trade Assn. Executives [349]
Automotive Trade Policy Coun. [350]
Automotive Training Managers Coun. [351]
Automotive Undercar Trade Org. [352]
Avanti Owners Assn. Intl. [21589]
Avanti Owners Assn. Intl. [IO]
Aviation Safety Inst. [12953]
Bentley Drivers Club [IO]
Berkeley Enthusiasts Club [IO]
Berkeley Exchange [21590]
BMW Car Club of Am. [21591]
BMW Club of Canada [IO]
BMW CS Registry [21592]
BMW Vintage Car Club of Am. [21593]
Borgward Owners' Club [21594]
Boss 302 Registry [21595]
Boss 429 Owners Dir. [21596]
Brabham Register [21597]
Brabham Register [IO]
Bricklin Intl. Owners Club [IO]
Bricklin Intl. Owners Club [21598]
Bristol Owners' Club [IO]
British Slot Car Racing Assn. [IO]
Buick Car Club of Australia in NSW [IO]
Buick Club of Am. [21599]
Buick GS Club of Am. [21600]
Buick St. Rod Assn. [22919]
Bullnose Morris Club [IO]
Cadillac Drivers Club [21601]
Cadillac-LaSalle Club [21602]
California Assn. of Tiger-Owners [21603]
California Association of Tiger-Owners [IO]
Canadian St. Rod Assn. [IO]
Capri Club North Am. [21604]
Car Wash Owners and Suppliers Assn. [411]
Center for Auto Safety [12956]
Challenger T/A Registry [21605]
Challenger T/A Registry [IO]
Championship Assn. of Mechanics [23075]
Championship Auto Racing Teams [23076]

Championship Auto Racing Teams [IO]
Checker Car Club of Am. [21606]
Chevrolet Nomad Assn. [21607]
Chevy and Geo Club [21608]
Chevy GMC Intl. Truck Club [21609]
Christian Motorsports Ministries [21610]
Christian Motorsports Ministries [IO]
Chrysler 300 Club Intl. [IO]
Chrysler 300 Club Intl. [21611]
Chrysler Town and Country Owners Registry
   [21612]
Chrysler Town and Country Owners Registry [IO]
Citroen Car Club [IO]
Citroen Quarterly Car Club [21613]
Classic Car Club of Am. [21614]
Classic Chevy Intl. [21615]
Classic Chevy Intl. [IO]
Classic Jaguar Assn. [21616]
Classic Thunderbird Club Intl. [21617]
Classic Thunderbird Club Intl. [IO]
Club Delahaye [IO]
Club Elite North Am. [21618]
Coalition for Auto Glass Safety and Public Aware-
   ness [1727]
Coalition for Vehicle Choice [17015]
Cobra Owners Club of Am. [21619]
Collector Car Appraisers Assn. [278]
Combat Veterans Motorcycle Assn. [22675]
Commercial Vehicle Safety Alliance [355]
Contemporary Historical Vehicle Assn. [21620]
Corrado Club of Am. [21621]
Corvair Soc. of Am. [21622]
Corvette Club of Am. [21623]
Crosley Auto. Club [21624]
Crown Victoria Assn. [21625]
Cyclone Montego Torino Registry [21626]
Daimler and Lanchester Owners' Club - England
   [IO]
Danish Auto. Sports Union [IO]
DARTS Club [21627]
Davis Registry [21628]
Davis Registry [IO]
Dealers Alliance [412]
DeLorean Owners Assn. [21629]
Derrike Cope Fan Club [24783]
DeSoto Club of Am. [21630]
DKW Club of Am. [21631]
Dodge Bros. Club [21632]
Dodge Pilothouse Era Truck Club of Am. [23024]
Early Ford V-8 Club of Am. [21633]
East Coast Timing Assn. [22920]
Eastern Museum of Motor Racing [21634]
Eastern Packard Club [21635]
Edsel Club [21636]
Edsel Owner's Club [21637]
Elec. Auto Assn. [6516]
Elgin Motorcar Owners Registry [21638]
Elgin Motorcar Owners Registry [IO]
Elton Sawyer Fan Club [25005]
Elva Owners Club [IO]
Emergency Vehicle Owners and Operators Assn.
   [21639]
Erskine Registry [21640]
European Registration Plate Assn. [IO]
Fairlane Club of Am. [21641]
Falcon Club of Am. [21642]
Fed. of British Historic Vehicle Clubs [IO]
Fed. Francaise du Sport Auto. [IO]
Ferrari Club of Am. [21643]
Ferrari Owners Club [21644]
Fiero Owners Club of Am. [21645]
FoMoCo Owners Club [21646]
Ford Galaxie Club of Am. [21647]
Ford Motor Minority Dealers Assn. [413]
Gasoline and Automotive Ser. Dealers Assn. [414]
GM Futurliner [21648]
GM Futurliner [IO]
Goodguys Rod and Custom Assn. [21649]
Graham Owners Club Intl. [21650]
Graham Owners Club Intl. [IO]
Grand Amer. Road Racing Assn. [23068]
GTO Assn. of Am. [21651]
Gull Wing Gp. Intl. [21652]
Gull Wing Gp. Intl. [IO]
Haynes-Apperson Owners Club [21653]

Heartland Vintage Thunderbird Club of Am.
   [21654]
Heavy-Duty Bus. Forum [356]
Henry Nyberg Soc. [21655]
Henry Nyberg Soc. [IO]
H.H. Franklin Club [21656]
Historic Commercial Vehicle Soc. [IO]
Historic Motor Sports Assn. [21657]
Horseless Carriage Club of Am. [21658]
Hudson-Essex-Terraplane Club [21659]
Hudson-Essex-Terraplane Club [IO]
Hudson Essex Terraplane Historical Soc. [21660]
Hurst/Olds Club of Am. [21661]
Inliners Intl. [21662]
Inliners Intl. [IO]
Insurance Inst. for Highway Safety [12964]
Insurance Premium Finance Assn. [2181]
Inter-Amer. Safety Coun. [12965]
Inter-Industry Conf. on Auto Collision Repair [415]
Intl. 190SL Gp. [21663]
Intl. Amphicar Owners Club [21664]
Intl. Assn. of Lemon Law Administrators [5536]
Intl. Automotive Remarketers Alliance [359]
Intl. Camaro Club [21665]
Intl. Camaro Club [IO]
Intl. Edsel Club [IO]
Intl. Edsel Club [21666]
Intl. Hot Rod Assn. [23077]
Intl. King Midget Car Club [21667]
Intl. Mfrs. Representatives Assn. [360]
Intl. Mercury Owners Assn. [21668]
Intl. Midas Dealers Assn. [417]
Intl. Motor Contest Assn. [23078]
Intl. Motor Sports Assn. [23079]
Intl. Mustang Bullitt Owners Club [21669]
Intl. Soc. of Air Safety Investigators [12966]
Intl. Soc. for Vehicle Preservation [21670]
Intl. Soc. for Vehicle Preservation [IO]
Intl. Thunderbird Club [IO]
Intl. Thunderbird Club [21671]
Intl. Trans. Mgt. Assn. [6319]
Intl. Union, United Auto., Aerospace and
   Agricultural Implement Workers of Am. [24004]
Iso and Bizzarrini Owners Club [21672]
Iso and Bizzarrini Owners Club [IO]
Italian Car Registry [21673]
J-Road Open Club [IO]
Jaguar Clubs of North Am. [IO]
Jaguar Clubs of North Am. [21674]
Japan Auto. Mfrs. Assn., Washington Off. [389]
Jensen Healey Preservation Soc. [21675]
Jewett Owners Club [21676]
Johnny Benson Fan Club [24784]
Jordan Register [21677]
Jowett Car Club [IO]
The Judge GTO Intl. [21678]
Kaiser-Darrin Owners Roster [21679]
Kaiser-Frazer Owners Club Intl. [21680]
Kaiser-Frazer Owners Club Intl. [IO]
Karmann Ghia Club of North Am. [IO]
Karmann Ghia Club of North Am. [21681]
Kissel Kar Klub [21682]
Kissel Kar Klub [IO]
Kustom Kemps of Am. [21683]
Kustoms of Am. [22921]
Lamborghini Club Am. [21684]
Lancia Motor Club [IO]
Late Great Chevrolet Assn. [21685]
Lea-Francis Owners' Club [IO]
Les Amis de Panhard and Deutsch Bonnet
   [21686]
Limousine Indus. Mfrs. Org. [391]
Lincoln and Continental Owners Club [21687]
Lincoln Owners' Club [21688]
Lincoln Zephyr Owner's Club [21689]
Lincoln Zephyr Owner's Club [IO]
London Vintage Taxi Assn. - Amer. Sect. [21690]
Lotus, Ltd. [21691]
LOVEfords [21692]
LOVEfords [IO]
Marlin Auto Club [21693]
Marmon Club [21694]
Marmon Club [IO]
The Maserati Club [IO]
The Maserati Club [21695]

A star before a book entry number signifies that the name is not listed separately, but is mentioned within the entry.

Maserati Info. Exchange [21696]
Maverick/Comet Club Intl. [21697]
Mazda Club [21698]
McLaughlin Buick Club of Canada [IO]
Mercedes-Benz Club of Am. [21699]
Mercedes-Benz M-100 Owner's Gp. [21700]
Metropolitan Owners' Club [IO]
Metropolitan Owners Club of North Am. [21701]
MG Car Club [IO]
MG Drivers Club of North Am. [21702]
MG Octagon Car Club [IO]
MG Vintage Racers [22922]
Microcar and Minicar Club [21703]
Mid-Century Mercury Car Club [21704]
Midstates Jeepster Assn. [21705]
Midwest Sunbeam Registry [21706]
Milestone Car Soc. [21707]
Military Vehicle Preservation Assn. [22630]
Mini Car Club, U.S.A. [21708]
Model A Ford Cabriolet Club [21709]
Model A Ford Club of Am. [21710]
Model A Ford Found. [21711]
Model "A" Restorers Club [21712]
Model "T" Ford Club of Am. [21713]
Model "T" Ford Club Intl. [21714]
Model "T" Ford Club Intl. [IO]
Mopar Scat Pack Club [21715]
Morgan 3/4 Gp. [21716]
Morgan Car Club [21717]
Morgan Plus Four Club [21718]
Morgan Sports Car Club [IO]
Morgan Three-Wheeler Club [IO]
Morgan Three-Wheeler Club - USA Gp. [21719]
Morris Minor Registry [21720]
Morris Register [IO]
Mothers Against Drunk Driving [12969]
Motor Sports Assn. [IO]
Muntz Jet Registry [21721]
Mustang Club of Am. [21722]
Mustang II Network [21723]
Mustang Owners Club Intl. [21724]
Nash Car Club of Am. [21725]
Natl. Amer. Motors Drivers and Racers Assn. [23080]
Natl. Antique Oldsmobile Club [21726]
Natl. Assn. of Athletes Against Drugs [13260]
Natl. Assn. of Auto. Museums [10511]
Natl. Assn. of Investigative Specialists [2325]
Natl. Assn. for Stock Car Auto Racing [23081]
Natl. Assn. of Women Highway Safety Leaders [12971]
Natl. Auto Racing Historical Soc. [23082]
Natl. Auto. Dealers Assn. [420]
Natl. Automotive Radiator Ser. Assn. [422]
Natl. Automotive Technicians Educ. Found. [7992]
Natl. Automotive and Truck Museum of U.S. [10512]
Natl. Championship Racing Assn. [23670]
Natl. Chevy Assn. [21727]
Natl. Commn. Against Drunk Driving [12973]
Natl. Corvette Owners Assn. [21728]
Natl. Corvette Restorers Soc. [21729]
Natl. Coun. of Corvette Clubs [21730]
Natl. DeSoto Club [21731]
Natl. Elec. Drag Racing Assn. [23396]
Natl. Firebird and T/A Club [21732]
Natl. Hot Rod Assn. [23083]
Natl. Impala Assn. [21733]
Natl. Independent Auto. Dealers Assn. [423]
Natl. Indy 500 Collectors Club [21734]
Natl. Inst. for Automotive Ser. Excellence [424]
Natl. Insurance Crime Bur. [2224]
Natl. Karting Assn. [IO]
Natl. Limousine Assn. [3880]
Natl. Monte Carlo Owners Assn. [21735]
Natl. Nostalgic Nova [21736]
Natl. Old Timers Auto Racing Club [21737]
Natl. Safety Coun. [12979]
Natl. St. Rod Assn. [21738]
Natl. Transit Benefit Assn. [6324]
Natl. Woodie Club [21739]
New England M.G. "T" Register Limited [21740]
New York State Assn. of Ser. Stations and Repair Shops [426]
New Zealand Buick Enthusiasts [IO]

Nineteen Thirty-Two Buick Registry [21741]
Nissan Infiniti Car Owners Club [21742]
North Amer. Auto Union Register [21743]
North Amer. English and European Ford Registry [21744]
North Amer. Mini Moke Registry [21745]
Northern Late Model Racing Assn. [23084]
NSU Enthusiasts U.S.A. [21746]
NSX Club of Am. [21747]
Oakland-Pontiac Enthusiast Org. [21748]
Oldsmobile Club of Am. [21749]
Online Imperial Club [21750]
Opel Assn. of North Am. [21751]
Opel Motorsports Club [21752]
Opel Motorsports Club [IO]
Oper. Lifesaver [12983]
Org. of Bricklin Owners [21753]
Overseas Automotive Coun. [364]
P6 Rover Owners Club [IO]
Pacific Northwest Region of the Lincoln and Continental Owners Club [IO]
Pacific Northwest Region of the Lincoln and Continental Owners Club [21754]
Packard Auto. Classics [21755]
Packard Club [21756]
Packard Club [IO]
Packard V-8 Roster, '55-'56 [21757]
Packards Intl. Motor Car Club [21758]
Packards Intl. Motor Car Club [IO]
Pantera Intl. [IO]
Pantera Intl. [21759]
Pantera Owners Club of Am. [21760]
PGI [396]
Pierce-Arrow Soc. [21761]
Pierce-Arrow Soc. [IO]
Pioneer Auto. Touring Club [21762]
Plymouth Barracuda/Cuda Owners Club [21763]
Plymouth Owners Club [21764]
Police Car Owners of Am. [21765]
Police Car Owners of America [IO]
Polish Auto. and Motorcycle Fed. [IO]
Pontiac-Oakland Club Intl. [IO]
Pontiac-Oakland Club Intl. [21766]
Porsche Club of Am. [21767]
Professional Car Soc. [21768]
Railton Owners Club [IO]
Renault Owners Club of North Am. [21769]
REO Club of Am. [21770]
REO Club of Am. [IO]
Rickenbacker Automobile Club of America [21771]
Riviera Owners Assn. [21772]
Road Race Lincoln Register [21773]
Road Race Lincoln Register [IO]
Rolls-Royce Enthusiasts' Club [IO]
Rolls-Royce Owners' Club [21774]
Rometsch Registry [21775]
Rometsch Registry [IO]
Rover P4 Drivers Guild [IO]
Rover Saloon Touring Club of Am. [21776]
S2000 Club of Am. [21777]
Saab Club of North Am. [21778]
Sabra Automobile Connection [21779]
SAE Intl. - Soc. of Automotive Engineers [6520]
Saleen Club of Am. [21780]
Saxon Owners Registry [21781]
School and Community Safety Soc. of Am. of the Amer. Assn. for Active Lifestyles and Fitness [12989]
Seat Belt Choice Coalition [17016]
Seatbelt Law Opposition Forum [12990]
Shelby Amer. Auto. Club [21782]
Silver Ghost Assn. [21783]
Singer Owners' Club [IO]
Sir Henry Royce Memorial Found. [IO]
Slant 6 Club of Am. [21784]
Soc. of Automotive Analysts [365]
Soc. of Automotive Engineers [7632]
Soc. of Automotive Historians [21785]
Society of Automotive Historians [IO]
Soc. of Collision Repair Specialists [428]
Solid Axle Corvette Club [21786]
Solid Axle Corvette Club [IO]
SP 250 Register [IO]
Spark Plug Collectors of Am. [22116]
Specialty Equip. Market Assn. [397]

Sports Car Club of Am. [21787]
Sportscar Vintage Racing Assn. [23085]
Spring Res. Inst. [399]
Squire SS-100 Registry [21788]
Standing Up for SUV, Pickup and Van Owners of Am. [17017]
Steam Auto. Club of Am. [21789]
Studebaker Driver's Club [21790]
Students Against Destructive Decisions, Students Against Drunk Driving [12992]
Stutz Club [21791]
Subaru 360 Drivers' Club [21792]
Sunbeam Rapier Registry [21793]
Super Coupe Club of Am. [21794]
Teton Club Intl. [22632]
Thunderbird and Cougar Club of Am. [21795]
Tigers East/Alpines East [21796]
Tigers East/Alpines East [IO]
Topolino Register of North Am. [21797]
Toyota Owner's and Restorer's Club [21798]
Toyota Territory Off-Roaders Assn. [22965]
TR8 Car Club of Am. [21799]
Traffic Records Comm. [12993]
Triumph Register of Am. [21800]
Tucker Auto. Club of Am. [21801]
Tune-Up Manufacturers Coun. [402]
TVR Car Club North Am. [21802]
United Black Drag Racers Assn. [23397]
United Coun. of Corvette Clubs [21803]
United Ford Owners [21804]
United Four-Wheel Drive Associations [21805]
United Four-Wheel Drive Associations [IO]
United Mopar Club [21806]
United Speedways of North Am. [23671]
U.S. Auto Club [23086]
U.S. Late Model Assn. [23087]
United St. Machine Assn. [21807]
Veteran Motor Car Club of Am. [21808]
Vintage Austin Register [IO]
Vintage Chevrolet Club of Am. [21809]
Vintage Drivers Club of Am. [21810]
Vintage Sports Car Club of Am. [21811]
Vintage Thunderbird Club Intl. [21812]
Vintage Thunderbird Club Intl. [IO]
Vintage Triumph Register [21813]
Vintage Volkswagen Club of Am. [21814]
Volkswagen Club of Am. [21815]
Volvo Club of Am. [21816]
Western Assoc. Modelers [22661]
White Owners Register [23026]
Wills Sainte Claire Museum [21817]
Willys Overland Jeepster Club [21818]
Willys-Overland-Knight Registry [21819]
Willys-Overland-Knight Registry [IO]
Winged Warriors/National B-Body Owners Assn. [21820]
Wolseley Register [IO]
Women's Automotive Assn. Intl. [367]
Worldwide Camaro Club [21821]
WPC Club [21822]
Young Racers of Am. [23674]
Z Car Club Assn. [21823]
Z Series Car Club of Am. [21824]
Zimmerman Registry [21825]
Zimmerman Registry [IO]
Auto., Aircraft, and Agricultural Implement Workers of Am; Intl. Union, United [★24004]
Auto. Assn; Amer. [403]
Auto. Assn. of Malaysia [IO], Kuala Lumpur, Malaysia
Automobile Club of America; Rickenbacker [21771]
Auto. Club of Ecuador [IO], Quito, Ecuador
Automobile Club de l'Ouest [IO], Le Mans, France
Auto. Club Motor Sports Assn; Royal [IO]
Auto. Club of Poland [★IO]
Auto. Competition Comm. for the U.S. FIA [23073], 7800 S Elati St., Ste. 303, Littleton, CO 80120, (303)730-8100
Auto. Dealers Assn; Amer. Imported [★404]
Auto. Dealers Assn; Natl. [420]
Auto. Dealers Assn; Natl. Independent [423]
Auto. Dealers; Natl. Assn. of Minority [2765]
Auto. Engineers; Soc. of [★6520]
Auto. Film Club of Am. [344], 10 Cross St., Staten Island, NY 10304, (718)447-2255

Reference to "IO" in place of a book number signifies that the association may be found in the 45th edition of International Organizations.

Auto. Importers of Am. [★343]
Auto. Importers of Am. [★IO]
Auto. Importers' Assn. [★IO]
Automobile Importers Compliance Assn. - Defunct.
Auto. Journalists Assn. of Canada [IO], Cobourg, ON, Canada
Automobile Legal Assn. - Defunct.
Auto. License Plate Collectors Assn. [21587], 508 Coastal Dr., Virginia Beach, VA 23451
Auto. Mfrs. Assn., Washington Off; Japan [389]
Auto. Objects d'Art Club [21588], 252 N 7th St., Allentown, PA 18102, (610)432-3355
Auto. Old Timers [★345]
Automobile Owners Action Coun. - Defunct.
Auto. Protection Assn. [IO], Montreal, QC, Canada
Auto. Racing Club of Am. [23074], PO Box 5217, Toledo, OH 43611-0217, (734)847-6726
Auto. Safety Belt Inst. [★377]
Automobile Seat Cover Assn. of America - Defunct.
Auto. Theft Bur; Natl. [★2224]
Auto. Touring Alliance; Amer. [3905]
Auto. and Touring Club of Finland [IO], Helsinki, Finland
Automobile Utility Trailer Rental Assn. - Address unknown since 1995.
Auto. Workers' Unions; Confed. of Japan [IO]
Automobiles; Natl. Registry of Willys - Knight [★21819]
Automotive
  1/87 Vehicle Club [22641]
  1937-1938 Buick Club [21552]
  1948-50 Packard Convertible Roster [21553]
  1953-54 Buick Skylark Club [21554]
  1956 Studebaker Golden Hawk Owners Register [21555]
  1958 Cadillac Owners Assn. [21556]
  1965-66 Full Size Chevrolet Club [21557]
  1971 GTO and Judge Convertible Registry [21559]
  1995 Corvette Pace Car Registry [21560]
  66,67,68 High Country Special Mustang Registry [21561]
  Abarth Register, U.S.A. [21562]
  Airflow Club of Am. [21563]
  Alfa Romeo Owners Club [21565]
  AMC Pacer Club [21566]
  AMC Rambler Club [21567]
  Amer. Austin/Bantam Club [21568]
  Amer. Bugatti Club [21569]
  Amer. Lancia Club [21573]
  Amer. MGB Assn. [21574]
  Amer. MGC Register [21575]
  Amer. Motors Owners Assn. [21576]
  Amer. Sta. Wagon Owners Assn. [21577]
  Antique Auto Racing Assn. [21578]
  Antique Auto. Club of Am. [21579]
  Antique Studebaker Club [21580]
  Assn. of Automotive Aftermarket Distributors/Parts Plus [370]
  Assn. of Automotive Tech. Societies in Finland [IO]
  Austin Bantam Soc. [21583]
  Austin-Healey Sports and Touring Club [21586]
  Australasian Fleet Managers Assn. [IO]
  Auto. Film Club of Am. [344]
  Auto. License Plate Collectors Assn. [21587]
  Automotive Consumer Action Prog. [17307]
  Automotive Engine Rebuilders Assn. [375]
  Automotive Hall of Fame [345]
  Automotive Lift Inst. [376]
  Automotive Parts Remanufacturers Assn. [409]
  Automotive Presidents Coun. [348]
  Automotive Refrigeration Products Inst. [378]
  Automotive Res. Assn. of India [IO]
  Automotive Ser. Assn. [410]
  Automotive Trade Assn. Executives [349]
  Automotive Trade Policy Coun. [350]
  Automotive Undercar Trade Org. [352]
  Battery Vehicle Soc. [IO]
  Berkeley Exchange [21590]
  BMW Car Club of Am. [21591]
  BMW Vintage Car Club of Am. [21593]
  Boss 302 Registry [21595]
  Boss 429 Owners Dir. [21596]
  Bricklin Intl. Owners Club [21598]

Buick Club of Am. [21599]
Buick GS Club of Am. [21600]
Cadillac Drivers Club [21601]
Cadillac-LaSalle Club [21602]
Canadian Auto Workers [IO]
Capri Club North Am. [21604]
Chevrolet Nomad Assn. [21607]
Chevy and Geo Club [21608]
Christian Motorsports Ministries [21610]
Chrysler 300 Club Intl. [21611]
Chrysler Town and Country Owners Registry [21612]
Citroen Quarterly Car Club [21613]
Classic Chevy Intl. [21615]
Classic Jaguar Assn. [21616]
Classic Thunderbird Club Intl. [21617]
Coalition for Auto Glass Safety and Public Awareness [1727]
Cobra Owners Club of Am. [21619]
Combat Veterans Motorcycle Assn. [22675]
Confed. of Japan Auto. Workers' Unions [IO]
Congressional Automotive Caucus [17255]
Contemporary Historical Vehicle Assn. [21620]
Corrado Club of Am. [21621]
Corvair Soc. of Am. [21622]
Corvette Club of Am. [21623]
Crosley Auto. Club [21624]
Crown Victoria Assn. [21625]
Cyclone Montego Torino Registry [21626]
Dealers Alliance [412]
DeSoto Club of Am. [21630]
DKW Club of Am. [21631]
Dodge Bros. Club [21632]
Dodge Pilothouse Era Truck Club of Am. [23024]
Early Ford V-8 Club of Am. [21633]
Edsel Club [21636]
Elec. Auto Assn. [6516]
Elec. Drive Trans. Assn. [6517]
Emergency Vehicle Owners and Operators Assn. [21639]
Erskine Registry [21640]
European Assn. for Battery, Hybrid and Fuel Cell Elec. Vehicles [IO]
Fairlane Club of Am. [21641]
Federauto [IO]
Ferrari Owners Club [21644]
Ford Galaxie Club of Am. [21647]
French Soc. of Automotive Engineers [IO]
Gasoline and Automotive Ser. Dealers Assn. [414]
Graham Bros. Truck and Bus Club [21894]
Graham Owners Club Intl. [21650]
Gull Wing Gp. Intl. [21652]
Haynes-Apperson Owners Club [21653]
H.H. Franklin Club [21656]
Historic Motor Sports Assn. [21657]
Horseless Carriage Club of Am. [21658]
Hudson-Essex-Terraplane Club [21659]
Hurst/Olds Club of Am. [21661]
Intl. 190SL Gp. [21663]
Intl. Amphicar Owners Club [21664]
Intl. Assn. for Natural Gas Vehicles [IO]
Intl. Auto Sound Challenge Assn. [1219]
Intl. Automotive Remarketers Alliance [359]
Intl. Bus Collectors Club [21895]
Intl. Camaro Club [21665]
Intl. Edsel Club [21666]
Intl. King Midget Car Club [21667]
Intl. Mfrs. Representatives Assn. [360]
Intl. Mercury Owners Assn. [21668]
Intl. Midas Dealers Assn. [417]
Intl. Motor Press Assn. [3120]
Intl. Mustang Bullitt Owners Club [21669]
Intl. Soc. for Terrain-Vehicle Systems [6518]
Intl. Soc. for Terrain-Vehicle Systems [IO]
Intl. Soc. for Vehicle Preservation [21670]
Intl. Thunderbird Club [21671]
Intl. Union, United Auto., Aerospace and Agricultural Implement Workers of Am. [24004]
Iso and Bizzarrini Owners Club [21672]
Italian Car Registry [21673]
Jaguar Clubs of North Am. [21674]
Jensen Healey Preservation Soc. [21675]
Jewett Owners Club [21676]
Johnny Benson Fan Club [24784]
Jordan Register [21677]

Kaiser-Darrin Owners Roster [21679]
Kaiser-Frazer Owners Club Intl. [21680]
Karmann Ghia Club of North Am. [21681]
Kissel Kar Klub [21682]
Kustom Kemps of Am. [21683]
Lamborghini Club Am. [21684]
Late Great Chevrolet Assn. [21685]
Les Amis de Panhard and Deutsch Bonnet [21686]
Lincoln and Continental Owners Club [21687]
Lincoln Owners' Club [21688]
London Vintage Taxi Assn. - Amer. Sect. [21690]
Lotus, Ltd. [21691]
Mfrs. of Emission Controls Assn. [3072]
Marmon Club [21694]
Maserati Info. Exchange [21696]
Maverick/Comet Club Intl. [21697]
Mazda Club [21698]
Mercedes-Benz Club of Am. [21699]
Mercedes-Benz M-100 Owner's Gp. [21700]
Metropolitan Owners Club of North Am. [21701]
Microcar and Minicar Club [21703]
Mid-Century Mercury Car Club [21704]
Midstates Jeepster Assn. [21705]
Midwest Sunbeam Registry [21706]
Milestone Car Soc. [21707]
Military Vehicle Preservation Assn. [22630]
Mini Car Club, U.S.A. [21708]
MIRA [IO]
Mobile Air Conditioning Soc. Worldwide [1893]
Model A Ford Cabriolet Club [21709]
Model A Ford Club of Am. [21710]
Model "A" Restorers Club [21712]
Model "T" Ford Club of Am. [21713]
Model "T" Ford Club Intl. [21714]
Morgan Car Club [21717]
Morgan Plus Four Club [21718]
Morris Minor Registry [21720]
Motor Bus Soc. [21896]
Muntz Jet Registry [21721]
Nash Car Club of Am. [21725]
Natl. Antique Oldsmobile Club [21726]
Natl. Assn. of Auto. Museums [10511]
Natl. Assn. of Dealer Counsel [361]
Natl. Assn. of Emergency Vehicle Technicians [418]
Natl. Auto. Dealers Assn. [420]
Natl. Automotive Radiator Ser. Assn. [422]
Natl. Automotive and Truck Museum of U.S. [10512]
Natl. Corvette Owners Assn. [21728]
Natl. Corvette Restorers Soc. [21729]
Natl. Coun. of Corvette Clubs [21730]
Natl. DeSoto Club [21731]
Natl. Ethanol Vehicle Coalition [4776]
Natl. Firebird and T/A Club [21732]
Natl. Independent Auto. Dealers Assn. [423]
Natl. Inst. for Automotive Ser. Excellence [424]
Natl. Old Timers Auto Racing Club [21737]
Natl. St. Rod Assn. [21738]
Natl. Woodie Club [21739]
Natural Gas Vehicle for Am. [6519]
New England M.G. "T" Register Limited [21740]
New York State Assn. of Ser. Stations and Repair Shops [426]
Nineteen Thirty-Two Buick Registry [21741]
North Amer. Auto Union Register [21743]
North Amer. Mini Moke Registry [21745]
North Amer. Truck Camper Owners Assn. [23025]
NSU Enthusiasts U.S.A. [21746]
NSX Club of Am. [21747]
Oakland-Pontiac Enthusiast Org. [21748]
Oldsmobile Club of Am. [21749]
Opel Assn. of North Am. [21751]
Opel Motorsports Club [21752]
Org. of Bricklin Owners [21753]
Overseas Automotive Coun. [364]
Packard Auto. Classics [21755]
Packard V-8 Roster, '55-'56 [21757]
Packards Intl. Motor Car Club [21758]
Pantera Intl. [21759]
Performance Warehouse Assn. [3981]
PGI [396]
Pierce-Arrow Soc. [21761]
Plymouth Barracuda/Cuda Owners Club [21763]

A star before a book entry number signifies that the name is not listed separately, but is mentioned within the entry.

Plymouth Owners Club [21764]
Pontiac-Oakland Club Intl. [21766]
Porsche Club of Am. [21767]
Portuguese Assn. of Automotive Suppliers [IO]
Professional Car Soc. [21768]
Renault Owners Club of North Am. [21769]
REO Club of Am. [21770]
Rickenbacker Automobile Club of America [21771]
Riviera Owners Assn. [21772]
Road Race Lincoln Register [21773]
Rolls-Royce Owners' Club [21774]
Rometsch Registry [21775]
RVing Women [22962]
S2000 Club of Am. [21777]
Saab Club of North Am. [21778]
Sabra Automobile Connection [21779]
SAE Intl. - Soc. of Automotive Engineers [6520]
SAE International - Society of Automotive
    Engineers [IO]
Saleen Club of Am. [21780]
Saxon Owners Registry [21781]
SFI Found. [6521]
Shelby Amer. Auto. Club [21782]
Soc. of Automotive Engineers of China [IO]
Soc. of Automotive Engineers - Thailand [IO]
Soc. of Automotive Historians [21785]
Soc. of Collision Repair Specialists [428]
Spark Plug Collectors of Am. [22116]
Specialty Equip. Market Assn. [397]
Sports Car Club of Am. [21787]
Squire SS-100 Registry [21788]
Standing Up for SUV, Pickup and Van Owners of
    Am. [17017]
Steam Auto. Club of Am. [21789]
Studebaker Driver's Club [21790]
Stutz Club [21791]
Subaru 360 Drivers' Club [21792]
Sunbeam Rapier Registry [21793]
Super Coupe Club of Am. [21794]
Teton Club Intl. [22632]
Thunderbird and Cougar Club of Am. [21795]
Tire Soc. [7798]
Topolino Register of North Am. [21797]
Toyota Territory Off-Roaders Assn. [22965]
Triumph Register of Am. [21800]
Truck Mfrs. Assn. [366]
Tucker Auto. Club of Am. [21801]
Tune-Up Manufacturers Coun. [402]
TVR Car Club North Am. [21802]
United Coun. of Corvette Clubs [21803]
United Ford Owners [21804]
United Four-Wheel Drive Associations [21805]
U.S. Late Model Assn. [23087]
United St. Machine Assn. [21807]
Veteran Motor Car Club of Am. [21808]
Vintage Chevrolet Club of Am. [21809]
Vintage Drivers Club of Am. [21810]
Vintage Thunderbird Club Intl. [21812]
Vintage Triumph Register [21813]
Vintage Volkswagen Club of Am. [21814]
Volkswagen Club of Am. [21815]
Volvo Club of Am. [21816]
Western Assoc. Modelers [22661]
Wills Sainte Claire Museum [21817]
Willys Overland Jeepster Club [21818]
Willys-Overland-Knight Registry [21819]
Winged Warriors/National B-Body Owners Assn.
    [21820]
Worldwide Camaro Club [21821]
Z Series Car Club of Am. [21824]
Zimmerman Registry [21825]
Automotive Advertisers Coun. [★92]
Automotive Aftermarket Distributors; Assn. of [★370]
Automotive Aftermarket Indus. Assn. [374], 7101
    Wisconsin Ave., Ste. 1300, Bethesda, MD 20814-
    3415, (301)654-6664
Automotive Aftermarket Industry Association [IO],
    Bethesda, MD, United States
Automotive Battery Charger Mfrs. Coun. - Defunct.
Automotive Body Parts Assn. [405], PO Box
    820689, Houston, TX 77282-0689, (281)531-0809
Automotive Body Parts Assn. [IO], Houston, TX,
    United States
Automotive Booster Clubs Intl. - Address unknown
    since 2004.

Automotive Caucus; Congressional [17255]
Automotive Chemical Mfrs. Coun. - Defunct.
Automotive Club; Overseas [★364]
Automotive Communications Coun. [92], 7101
    Wisconsin Ave., Ste. 1300, Bethesda, MD 20814,
    (240)333-1089
Automotive Component Mfrs. Assn. of India [IO],
    New Delhi, India
Automotive Consumer Action Prog. [17307], c/o
    Washington Area New Auto. Dealers Assn., 5301
    Wisconsin Ave. NW, Ste. 210, Washington, DC
    20015, (202)237-7200
Automotive Cooling Systems Inst. - Defunct.
Automotive Damage Appraisers Assn; Independent
    [281]
Automotive Dismantlers and Recyclers of Am.
    [★3988]
Automotive Dismantlers and Recyclers Assn.
    [★3988]
Automotive Distribution Fed. [IO], Birmingham,
    United Kingdom
Automotive Education
    Coun. of Advanced Automotive Trainers [341]
    Natl. Automotive Technicians Educ. Found. [7992]
    North Amer. Coun. of Automotive Teachers [7993]
    Women's Automotive Assn. Intl. [367]
Automotive Engine Rebuilders Assn. [375], 330
    Lexington Dr., Buffalo Grove, IL 60089-6933,
    (847)541-6550
Automotive Engine Rebuilders Assn. [IO], Buffalo
    Grove, IL, United States
Automotive Engineers and Technicians Assn. [IO],
    Buenos Aires, Argentina
Automotive Exhaust Res. Inst. - Defunct.
Automotive Exhaust Systems Mfrs. Coun. - Defunct.
Automotive Filter Manufacturers Coun. [★384]
Automotive Filter Manufacturers Coun. [★IO]
Automotive Fleet and Leasing Assn. [406], c/o Paul
    Hanscom, Exec. Dir., 1000 Westgate Dr., St. Paul,
    MN 55114, (651)203-7247
Automotive Hall of Fame [345], 21400 Oakwood
    Blvd., Dearborn, MI 48124-4078, (313)240-4000
Automotive Industries
    1/87 Vehicle Club [22641]
    1937-1938 Buick Club [21552]
    1948-50 Packard Convertible Roster [21553]
    1953-54 Buick Skylark Club [21554]
    1956 Studebaker Golden Hawk Owners Register
        [21555]
    1958 Cadillac Owners Assn. [21556]
    1965-66 Full Size Chevrolet Club [21557]
    1971 GTO and Judge Convertible Registry
        [21559]
    1995 Corvette Pace Car Registry [21560]
    66,67,68 High Country Special Mustang Registry
        [21561]
    Abarth Register, U.S.A. [21562]
    ACFO [IO]
    Airflow Club of Am. [21563]
    Alberta Motor Assn. [IO]
    Alberta Motor Transport Assn. [IO]
    Alfa Romeo Owners Club [21565]
    AMC Pacer Club [21566]
    AMC Rambler Club [21567]
    Amer. Austin/Bantam Club [21568]
    Amer. Bugatti Club [21569]
    Amer. Lancia Club [21573]
    Amer. MGB Assn. [21574]
    Amer. MGC Register [21575]
    Amer. Motors Owners Assn. [21576]
    Amer. Salvage Pool Assn. [342]
    Amer. Sta. Wagon Owners Assn. [21577]
    Antique Auto Racing Assn. [21578]
    Antique Auto. Club of Am. [21579]
    Antique Studebaker Club [21580]
    Asociacion Mexicana de la Industria Automotriz
        [IO]
    Associacao do Comercio Automovel de Portugal
        [IO]
    Associacao Nacional des Empresas do Comercio
        e da Reparacao Automovel [IO]
    Assn. of the Automotive Indus. [IO]
    Assn. of European Cities Interested in Elec.
        Vehicles [IO]
    Assn. of the Hungarian Automotive Indus. [IO]

Assn. of Intl. Auto. Manufacturers [IO]
Assn. of Intl. Auto. Manufacturers [343]
Assn. of Intl. Vehicle Mfrs. [IO]
Assn. of Motor Vehicle Importers - Representa-
    tives [IO]
Austin Bantam Soc. [21583]
Austin-Healey Sports and Touring Club [21586]
Australian Automotive Aftermarket Assn. [IO]
Austrian Vehicle Indus. Assn. [IO]
Auto Parts Recyclers Assn. of Australia [IO]
Auto Suppliers Benchmarking Assn. [703]
Auto. Film Club of Am. [344]
Automotive Hall of Fame [345]
Automotive Indus. Assn. of Canada [IO]
Automotive Indus. Action Gp. [346]
Automotive Indus. Assn. of the Slovak Republic
    [IO]
Automotive Mfrs'. Assn. - Argentina [IO]
Automotive Mfrs. and Importers Assn. [IO]
Automotive Market Res. Coun. [347]
Automotive Parts Accessories Assn. [IO]
Automotive Parts Mfrs'. Assn. [IO]
Automotive Parts Mfrs. of Mexico [IO]
Automotive Presidents Coun. [348]
Automotive Retailers' Assn. [IO]
Automotive Trade Assn. Executives [349]
Automotive Trade Policy Coun. [350]
Automotive Training Managers Coun. [351]
Automotive Undercar Trade Org. [352]
Automotive Women's Alliance [353]
Automotive Women's Alliance [IO]
Belgian Fed. of Bus and Coach Operators [IO]
Berkeley Exchange [21590]
BMW Car Club of Am. [21591]
BMW Vintage Car Club of Am. [21593]
Boss 302 Registry [21595]
Boss 429 Owners Dir. [21596]
Brazilian Assn. of Motor Vehicle Manufacturers
    [IO]
Bricklin Intl. Owners Club [21598]
British Vehicle Rental and Leasing Assn. [IO]
Buick Club of Am. [21599]
Buick GS Club of Am. [21600]
Bus and Coach Assn. of New Zealand [IO]
Cadillac Drivers Club [21601]
Cadillac-LaSalle Club [21602]
Capri Club North Am. [21604]
Car Care Coun. [354]
Car Rental Coun. of Ireland [IO]
Chamber of Venezuelan Auto. Products
    Manufacturers [IO]
Chevrolet Nomad Assn. [21607]
Chevy and Geo Club [21608]
Christian Motorsports Ministries [21610]
Chrysler 300 Club Intl. [21611]
Chrysler Town and Country Owners Registry
    [21612]
Citroen Quarterly Car Club [21613]
Classic Chevy Intl. [21615]
Classic Jaguar Assn. [21616]
Classic Thunderbird Club Intl. [21617]
Coalition for Auto Glass Safety and Public Aware-
    ness [1727]
Cobra Owners Club of Am. [21619]
Combat Veterans Motorcycle Assn. [22675]
Commercial Trailer Assn. [IO]
Commercial Vehicle Safety Alliance [IO]
Commercial Vehicle Safety Alliance [355]
Comm. of French Auto. Manufacturers [IO]
Congressional Automotive Caucus [17255]
Contemporary Historical Vehicle Assn. [21620]
Corrado Club of Am. [21621]
Corvair Soc. of Am. [21622]
Corvette Club of Am. [21623]
Crosley Auto. Club [21624]
Crown Victoria Assn. [21625]
Cyclone Montego Torino Registry [21626]
DeSoto Club of Am. [21630]
DKW Club of Am. [21631]
Dodge Bros. Club [21632]
Dodge Pilothouse Era Truck Club of Am. [23024]
Early Ford V-8 Club of Am. [21633]
Edsel Club [21636]
Emergency Vehicle Owners and Operators Assn.
    [21639]

Reference to "IO" in place of a book number signifies that the association may be found in the 45th edition of International Organizations.

Erskine Registry [21640]
Fairlane Club of Am. [21641]
Fed. of Auto. Distributors [IO]
Fed. du Materiel pour l'Automobile [IO]
Ferrari Owners Club [21644]
Finnish Central Org. for Motor Trades and Repairs [IO]
Ford Galaxie Club of Am. [21647]
French Vehicle Equip. Indus. Assn. [IO]
German Fed. for Motor Trades and Repairs [IO]
Graham Bros. Truck and Bus Club [21894]
Graham Owners Club Intl. [21650]
Gull Wing Gp. Intl. [21652]
Haynes-Apperson Owners Club [21653]
Heavy-Duty Bus. Forum [356]
Heavy Duty Distribution Assn. [357]
H.H. Franklin Club [21656]
Historic Motor Sports Assn. [21657]
Horseless Carriage Club of Am. [21658]
Hudson-Essex-Terraplane Club [21659]
Hurst/Olds Club of Am. [21661]
Inst. of Automotive Engineer Assessors [IO]
Inst. of the Motor Indus. [IO]
Inst. of Vehicle Recovery [IO]
Intl. 190SL Gp. [21663]
Intl. Assn. of Quality Technicians in the Automotive Industry [358]
Intl. Assn. of Quality Technicians in the Automotive Industry [IO]
Intl. Automotive Remarketers Alliance [359]
Intl. Bus Collectors Club [21895]
Intl. Camaro Club [21665]
Intl. Edsel Club [21666]
Intl. Fed. of Automotive Aftermarket Distributors [IO]
Intl. King Midget Car Club [21667]
Intl. Mfrs. Representatives Assn. [360]
Intl. Mercury Owners Assn. [21668]
Intl. Mustang Bullitt Owners Club [21669]
Intl. Soc. for Vehicle Preservation [21670]
Intl. Thunderbird Club [21671]
Iso and Bizzarrini Owners Club [21672]
Italian Automotive Ser. Equip. Mfrs. Assn. [IO]
Italian Car Registry [21673]
Jaguar Clubs of North Am. [21674]
Japan Auto Parts Indus. Assn. [IO]
Japan Auto. Fed. [IO]
Japan Auto. Importers' Assn. [IO]
Japan Auto. Mfrs. Assn. [IO]
Japan Automotive Products' Assn. [IO]
Japan Mini Vehicles Assn. [IO]
Jensen Healey Preservation Soc. [21675]
Jewett Owners Club [21676]
Jordan Register [21677]
Kaiser-Darrin Owners Roster [21679]
Kaiser-Frazer Owners Club Intl. [21680]
Karmann Ghia Club of North Am. [21681]
Kissel Kar Klub [21682]
Korea Auto. Manufacturers' Assn. [IO]
Kustom Kemps of Am. [21683]
Lamborghini Club Am. [21684]
Late Great Chevrolet Assn. [21685]
Latvian Authorized Auto. Dealers' Assn. [IO]
Les Amis de Panhard and Deutsch Bonnet [21686]
Lincoln and Continental Owners Club [21687]
Lincoln Owners' Club [21688]
London Vintage Taxi Assn. - Amer. Sect. [21690]
Lotus, Ltd. [21691]
Malaysian Automotive Components and Parts Mfrs. Assn. [IO]
Marmon Club [21694]
Maserati Info. Exchange [21696]
Maverick/Comet Club Intl. [21697]
Mazda Club [21698]
Mercedes-Benz Club of Am. [21699]
Mercedes-Benz M-100 Owner's Gp. [21700]
Metropolitan Owners Club of North Am. [21701]
Mexican Assn. of Car Dealers [IO]
Mexican Automotive Assn. [IO]
Microcar and Minicar Club [21703]
Mid-Century Mercury Car Club [21704]
Midstates Jeepster Assn. [21705]
Midwest Sunbeam Registry [21706]
Milestone Car Soc. [21707]

Mini Car Club, U.S.A. [21708]
Model A Ford Cabriolet Club [21709]
Model A Ford Club of Am. [21710]
Model "A" Restorers Club [21712]
Model "T" Ford Club of Am. [21713]
Model "T" Ford Club Intl. [21714]
Morgan Car Club [21717]
Morgan Plus Four Club [21718]
Moroccan Automotive Indus. Assn. [IO]
Morris Minor Registry [21720]
Motor Bus Soc. [21896]
Motor Vehicle Dismantlers' Assn. of Great Britain [IO]
Muntz Jet Registry [21721]
Nash Car Club of Am. [21725]
Natl. Antique Oldsmobile Club [21726]
Natl. Assn. of Auto. Dealers [IO]
Natl. Assn. of Auto. Museums [10511]
Natl. Assn. of Automotive Component and Allied Mfrs. [IO]
Natl. Assn. of Automotive Components Mfrs. [IO]
Natl. Assn. of Car Mfrs. [IO]
Natl. Assn. of Dealer Counsel [361]
Natl. Assn. of Emergency Vehicle Technicians [418]
Natl. Assn. of Fleet Administrators [362]
Natl. Auto Body Coun. [363]
Natl. Automotive and Truck Museum of U.S. [10512]
Natl. Corvette Owners Assn. [21728]
Natl. Corvette Restorers Soc. [21729]
Natl. Coun. of Corvette Clubs [21730]
Natl. DeSoto Club [21731]
Natl. Ethanol Vehicle Coalition [4776]
Natl. Firebird and T/A Club [21732]
Natl. Motor Vehicle Assn. [IO]
Natl. Old Timers Auto Racing Club [21737]
Natl. Org. for Motor Retail Trade and Repairs [IO]
Natl. St. Rod Assn. [21738]
Natl. Union of Automotive Distributors [IO]
Natl. Woodie Club [21739]
New England M.G. "T" Register Limited [21740]
Nineteen Thirty-Two Buick Registry [21741]
North Amer. Auto Union Register [21743]
North Amer. Mini Moke Registry [21745]
North Amer. Truck Camper Owners Assn. [23025]
NSU Enthusiasts U.S.A. [21746]
NSX Club of Am. [21747]
Oakland-Pontiac Enthusiast Org. [21748]
Oldsmobile Club of Am. [21749]
Opel Club of North Am. [21751]
Opel Motorsports Club [21752]
Org. of Bricklin Owners [21753]
Overseas Automotive Coun. [364]
Packard Auto. Classics [21755]
Packard V-8 Roster, '55-'56 [21757]
Packards Intl. Motor Car Club [21758]
Pakistan Assn. of Automotive Parts and Accessories Manufacturers [IO]
Pantera Intl. [21759]
Performance Warehouse Assn. [3981]
Pierce-Arrow Soc. [21761]
Plymouth Barracuda/Cuda Owners Club [21763]
Plymouth Owners Club [21764]
Pontiac-Oakland Club Intl. [21766]
Porsche Club of Am. [21767]
Professional Car Soc. [21768]
Renault Owners Club of North Am. [21769]
REO Club of Am. [21770]
Retail Motor Indus. Fed. [IO]
Rickenbacker Automobile Club of America [21771]
Riviera Owners Assn. [21772]
Road Race Lincoln Register [21773]
Rolls-Royce Owners' Club [21774]
Rometsch Registry [21775]
RVing Women [22962]
S2000 Club of Am. [21777]
Saab Club of North Am. [21778]
Sabra Automobile Connection [21779]
Saleen Club of Am. [21780]
Saxon Owners Registry [21781]
Scottish Motor Trade Assn. [IO]
Shelby Amer. Auto. Club [21782]
Singapore Cycle and Motor Traders' Assn. [IO]
Soc. of Automotive Analysts [365]

Soc. of Automotive Historians [21785]
Spanish Motor Vehicle Manufactures' Assn. [IO]
Sports Car Club of Am. [21787]
Squire SS-100 Registry [21788]
Steam Auto. Club of Am. [21789]
Studebaker Driver's Club [21790]
Stutz Club [21791]
Subaru 360 Drivers' Club [21792]
Sunbeam Rapier Registry [21793]
Super Coupe Club of Am. [21794]
Tech. Assn. of the Automotive Indus. [IO]
Thunderbird and Cougar Club of Am. [21795]
Topolino Register of North Am. [21797]
Towing and Recovery Assn. of Am. [429]
Toyota Territory Off-Roaders Assn. [22965]
Triumph Register of Am. [21800]
Truck-Frame and Axle Repair Assn. [430]
Truck Mfrs. Assn. [366]
Truck Manufacturers Assn. [IO]
Tucker Auto. Club of Am. [21801]
TVR Car Club North Am. [21802]
United Coun. of Corvette Clubs [21803]
United Ford Owners [21804]
United Four-Wheel Drive Associations [21805]
United St. Machine Assn. [21807]
Venezuelan Chamber of the Automotive Indus. [IO]
Veteran Motor Car Club of Am. [21808]
Vintage Chevrolet Club of Am. [21809]
Vintage Drivers Club of Am. [21810]
Vintage Thunderbird Club Intl. [21812]
Vintage Triumph Register [21813]
Vintage Volkswagen Club of Am. [21814]
Volkswagen Club of Am. [21815]
Volvo Club of Am. [21816]
Wills Sainte Claire Museum [21817]
Willys Overland Jeepster Club [21818]
Willys-Overland-Knight Registry [21819]
Winged Warriors/National B-Body Owners Assn. [21820]
Women's Automotive Assn. Intl. [367]
Women's Automotive Assn. Intl. [IO]
Worldwide Camaro Club [21821]
Yugoslav Soc. of Automotive Engineers [IO]
Z Series Car Club of Am. [21824]
Zimmerman Registry [21825]
Automotive Indus. Assn. of Canada [IO], Ottawa, ON, Canada
Automotive Indus. Action Gp. [346], 26200 Lahser Rd., Ste. 200, Southfield, MI 48033-7100, (248)358-3003
Automotive Indus. Assn. [IO], Prague, Czech Republic
Automotive Indus. Assn. of the Slovak Republic [IO], Bratislava, Slovakia
Automotive Information Coun. - Address unknown since 2001.
Automotive Legislative Coun. of America - Defunct.
Automotive Lift Inst. [376], PO Box 85, Cortland, NY 13045, (607)756-7775
Automotive Lift Inst. [IO], Cortland, NY, United States
Automotive Maintenance and Repair Assn. [IO], Bethesda, MD, United States
Automotive Maintenance and Repair Assn. [407], 7910 Woodmont Ave., Ste. 760, Bethesda, MD 20814, (301)634-4955
Automotive Manufacturers
1/87 Vehicle Club [22641]
1937-1938 Buick Club [21552]
1948-50 Packard Convertible Roster [21553]
1953-54 Buick Skylark Club [21554]
1956 Studebaker Golden Hawk Owners Register [21555]
1958 Cadillac Owners Assn. [21556]
1965-66 Full Size Chevrolet Club [21557]
1971 GTO and Judge Convertible Registry [21559]
1995 Corvette Pace Car Registry [21560]
66,67,68 High Country Special Mustang Registry [21561]
Abarth Register, U.S.A. [21562]
Airflow Club of Am. [21563]
Alfa Romeo Owners Club [21565]
Alliance of Auto. Mfrs. [368]

A star before a book entry number signifies that the name is not listed separately, but is mentioned within the entry.

Alliance of Auto. Manufacturers **[IO]**
Ambulance Mfrs. Div. **[369]**
AMC Pacer Club **[21566]**
AMC Rambler Club **[21567]**
Amer. Austin/Bantam Club **[21568]**
Amer. Bugatti Club **[21569]**
Amer. Lancia Club **[21573]**
Amer. MGB Assn. **[21574]**
Amer. MGC Register **[21575]**
Amer. Motors Owners Assn. **[21576]**
Amer. Sta. Wagon Owners Assn. **[21577]**
Antique Auto Racing Assn. **[21578]**
Antique Auto. Club of Am. **[21579]**
Antique Studebaker Club **[21580]**
Assn. of Automotive Aftermarket Distributors/Parts Plus **[370]**
Assn. for Emissions Control by Catalyst **[IO]**
Assn. of European Storage Battery Mfrs. **[IO]**
Assn. of Intl. Auto. Mfrs. of Canada **[IO]**
Austin Bantam Soc. **[21583]**
Austin-Healey Sports and Touring Club **[21586]**
Auto Intl. Assn. **[371]**
Auto Intl. Assn. **[IO]**
Autobody Craftsman Assn. **[372]**
Automatic Transmission Rebuilders Assn. **[373]**
Automotive Aftermarket Indus. Assn. **[374]**
Automotive Aftermarket Industry Association **[IO]**
Automotive Component Mfrs. Assn. of India **[IO]**
Automotive Distribution Fed. **[IO]**
Automotive Engine Rebuilders Assn. **[IO]**
Automotive Engine Rebuilders Assn. **[375]**
Automotive Lift Inst. **[376]**
Automotive Lift Inst. **[IO]**
Automotive Mfrs. Assn. - Turkey **[IO]**
Automotive Manufactures' Racing Assn. **[IO]**
Automotive Occupant Restraints Coun. **[377]**
Automotive Refrigeration Products Inst. **[378]**
Automotive Undercar Trade Org. **[352]**
Automotive Warehouse Distributors Assn. **[379]**
Battery Coun. Intl. **[380]**
Battery Coun. Intl. **[IO]**
Berkeley Exchange **[21590]**
BMW Car Club of Am. **[21591]**
BMW Vintage Car Club of Am. **[21593]**
Boss 302 Registry **[21595]**
Boss 429 Owners Dir. **[21596]**
Brake Manufacturers Coun. **[381]**
Bricklin Intl. Owners Club **[21598]**
British Battery Mfrs. Assn. **[IO]**
British Indus. Truck Assn. **[IO]**
Buick Club of Am. **[21599]**
Buick GS Club of Am. **[21600]**
Cadillac Drivers Club **[21601]**
Cadillac-LaSalle Club **[21602]**
Capri Club North Am. **[21604]**
Chevrolet Nomad Assn. **[21607]**
Chevy and Geo Club **[21608]**
Christian Motorsports Ministries **[21610]**
Chrysler 300 Club Intl. **[21611]**
Chrysler Town and Country Owners Registry **[21612]**
Citroen Quarterly Car Club **[21613]**
Classic Chevy Intl. **[21615]**
Classic Jaguar Assn. **[21616]**
Classic Thunderbird Club Intl. **[21617]**
Cobra Owners Club of Am. **[21619]**
Commercial Vehicle Solutions Network **[382]**
Contemporary Historical Vehicle Assn. **[21620]**
Corvair Soc. of Am. **[21622]**
Corvette Club of Am. **[21623]**
Crosley Auto. Club **[21624]**
Crown Victoria Assn. **[21625]**
Cyclone Montego Torino Registry **[21626]**
DeSoto Club of Am. **[21630]**
DKW Club of Am. **[21631]**
Dodge Bros. Club **[21632]**
Early Ford V-8 Club of Am. **[21633]**
Edsel Club **[21636]**
Equip. and Tool Inst. **[383]**
Erskine Registry **[21640]**
European Auto. Mfrs. Assn. **[IO]**
European Union of Coachbuilders **[IO]**
Fairlane Club of Am. **[21641]**
Ferrari Owners Club **[21644]**
Filter Manufacturers Coun. **[384]**

Filter Manufacturers Coun. **[IO]**
Fire Fighting Vehicle Mfrs. Assn. **[IO]**
Ford Galaxie Club of Am. **[21647]**
Friction Materials Standards Inst. **[385]**
Graham Bros. Truck and Bus Club **[21894]**
Graham Owners Club Intl. **[21650]**
Gull Wing Gp. Intl. **[21652]**
Haynes-Apperson Owners Club **[21653]**
Heavy Duty Representatives Assn. **[386]**
H.H. Franklin Club **[21656]**
Historic Motor Sports Assn. **[21657]**
Horseless Carriage Club of Am. **[21658]**
Hudson-Essex-Terraplane Club **[21659]**
Hurst/Olds Club of Am. **[21661]**
Indus. Truck Assn. **[387]**
Inst. of Vehicle Engineers **[IO]**
Intl. 190SL Gp. **[21663]**
Intl. Bus Collectors Club **[21895]**
Intl. Camaro Club **[21665]**
Intl. Edsel Club **[21666]**
Intl. King Midget Car Club **[21667]**
Intl. Mercury Owners Assn. **[21668]**
Intl. Mustang Bullitt Owners Club **[21669]**
Intl. Org. of Motor Vehicle Mfrs. **[IO]**
Intl. Soc. for Vehicle Preservation **[21670]**
Intl. Thunderbird Club **[21671]**
Intl. Truck Parts Assn. **[388]**
Intl. Truck Parts Assn. **[IO]**
Iso and Bizzarrini Owners Club **[21672]**
Italian Car Registry **[21673]**
Jaguar Clubs of North Am. **[21674]**
Japan Auto. Mfrs. Assn., Washington Off. **[389]**
Jensen Healey Preservation Soc. **[21675]**
Jewett Owners Club **[21676]**
Jordan Register **[21677]**
Kaiser-Darrin Owners Roster **[21679]**
Kaiser-Frazer Owners Club Intl. **[21680]**
Kissel Kar Klub **[21682]**
Korea Auto Indus. Cooperative Assn. **[IO]**
Kustom Kemps of Am. **[21683]**
Lamborghini Club Am. **[21684]**
Late Great Chevrolet Assn. **[21685]**
Les Amis de Panhard and Deutsch Bonnet **[21686]**
Light Truck Accessory Alliance **[390]**
Limousine Indus. Mfrs. Org. **[391]**
Lincoln and Continental Owners Club **[21687]**
Lincoln Owners' Club **[21688]**
London Vintage Taxi Assn. - Amer. Sect. **[21690]**
Lotus, Ltd. **[21691]**
Marmon Club **[21694]**
Maserati Info. Exchange **[21696]**
Mazda Club **[21698]**
Mercedes-Benz Club of Am. **[21699]**
Mercedes-Benz M-100 Owner's Gp. **[21700]**
Metropolitan Owners Club of North Am. **[21701]**
Microcar and Minicar Club **[21703]**
Mid-Century Mercury Car Club **[21704]**
Midstates Jeepster Assn. **[21705]**
Midwest Sunbeam Registry **[21706]**
Milestone Car Soc. **[21707]**
Mini Car Club, U.S.A. **[21708]**
Model A Ford Cabriolet Club **[21709]**
Model A Ford Club of Am. **[21710]**
Model "A" Restorers Club **[21712]**
Model "T" Ford Club of Am. **[21713]**
Model "T" Ford Club Intl. **[21714]**
Morgan Car Club **[21717]**
Morgan Plus Four Club **[21718]**
Morris Minor Registry **[21720]**
Motor Bus Soc. **[21896]**
Motor and Equip. Manufacturers Assn. **[392]**
Motor and Equip. Manufacturers Assn. **[IO]**
Motor Indus. Assn. **[IO]**
Motorcycle Indus. Assn. **[IO]**
Motorcycle Indus. Coun. **[2795]**
Motorcycle Indus. in Europe **[IO]**
Muntz Jet Registry **[21721]**
Nash Car Club of Am. **[21725]**
Natl. Antique Oldsmobile Club **[21726]**
Natl. Assn. of Auto. Mfrs. of South Africa **[IO]**
Natl. Assn. of Trailer Mfrs. **[393]**
Natl. Automotive Parts Assn. **[394]**
Natl. Corvette Owners Assn. **[21728]**
Natl. Corvette Restorers Soc. **[21729]**

Natl. Coun. of Corvette Clubs **[21730]**
Natl. DeSoto Club **[21731]**
Natl. Firebird and T/A Club **[21732]**
Natl. Old Timers Auto Racing Club **[21737]**
Natl. St. Rod Assn. **[21738]**
Natl. Truck Equip. Assn. **[395]**
Natl. Woodie Club **[21739]**
New England M.G. "T" Register Limited **[21740]**
Nineteen Thirty-Two Buick Registry **[21741]**
North Amer. Auto Union Register **[21743]**
North Amer. Mini Moke Registry **[21745]**
North Amer. Truck Camper Owners Assn. **[23025]**
NSU Enthusiasts U.S.A. **[21746]**
NSX Club of Am. **[21747]**
Oakland-Pontiac Enthusiast Org. **[21748]**
Oldsmobile Club of Am. **[21749]**
Opel Assn. of North Am. **[21751]**
Opel Motorsports Club **[21752]**
Org. of Bricklin Owners **[21753]**
Packard Auto. Classics **[21755]**
Packard V-8 Roster, '55-'56 **[21757]**
Packards Intl. Motor Car Club **[21758]**
Pantera Intl. **[21759]**
PGI **[396]**
Pierce-Arrow Soc. **[21761]**
Plymouth Barracuda/Cuda Owners Club **[21763]**
Plymouth Owners Club **[21764]**
Pontiac-Oakland Club Intl. **[21766]**
Porsche Club of Am. **[21767]**
Professional Car Soc. **[21768]**
Renault Owners Club of North Am. **[21769]**
REO Club of Am. **[21770]**
Rickenbacker Automobile Club of America **[21771]**
Riviera Owners Assn. **[21772]**
Road Race Lincoln Register **[21773]**
Rolls-Royce Owners' Club **[21774]**
Rometsch Registry **[21775]**
RVing Women **[22962]**
Saab Club of North Am. **[21778]**
Sabra Automobile Connection **[21779]**
Saleen Club of Am. **[21780]**
Saxon Owners Registry **[21781]**
Shelby Amer. Auto. Club **[21782]**
Soc. of Automotive Historians **[21785]**
Soc. of Indian Auto. Mfrs. **[IO]**
Soc. of the Irish Motor Indus. **[IO]**
Soc. of Motor Mfrs. and Traders **[IO]**
Specialty Equip. Market Assn. **[397]**
Specialty Vehicle Inst. of Am. **[398]**
Sports Car Club of Am. **[21787]**
Spring Res. Inst. **[399]**
Squire SS-100 Registry **[21788]**
Steam Auto. Club of Am. **[21789]**
Studebaker Driver's Club **[21790]**
Stutz Club **[21791]**
Subaru 360 Drivers' Club **[21792]**
Sunbeam Rapier Registry **[21793]**
Super Coupe Club of Am. **[21794]**
Thunderbird and Cougar Club of Am. **[21795]**
Topolino Register of North Am. **[21797]**
Triumph Register of Am. **[21800]**
Truck Mfrs. Assn. **[366]**
Truck Mixer Mfrs. Bur. **[400]**
Truck Trailer Mfrs. Assn. **[401]**
Truck Trailer Manufacturers Association **[IO]**
Tucker Auto. Club of Am. **[21801]**
Tune-Up Manufacturers Coun. **[402]**
TVR Car Club North Am. **[21802]**
United Coun. of Corvette Clubs **[21803]**
United Ford Owners **[21804]**
United Four-Wheel Drive Associations **[21805]**
United St. Machine Assn. **[21807]**
Vehicle Builders and Repairers Assn. **[IO]**
Veteran Motor Car Club of Am. **[21808]**
Vintage Chevrolet Club of Am. **[21809]**
Vintage Drivers Club of Am. **[21810]**
Vintage Thunderbird Club Intl. **[21812]**
Vintage Triumph Register **[21813]**
Vintage Volkswagen Club of Am. **[21814]**
Volkswagen Club of Am. **[21815]**
Volvo Club of Am. **[21816]**
Wills Sainte Claire Museum **[21817]**
Willys Overland Jeepster Club **[21818]**
Willys-Overland-Knight Registry **[21819]**
Winged Warriors/National B-Body Owners Assn. **[21820]**

Reference to "IO" in place of a book number signifies that the association may be found in the 45th edition of International Organizations.

Worldwide Camaro Club [21821]
Z Series Car Club of Am. [21824]
Zimmerman Registry [21825]
Automotive Mfrs'. Assn. - Argentina [IO], Buenos Aires, Argentina
Automotive Mfrs. Assn; Speciality [★396]
Automotive Mfrs. Assn. - Turkey [IO], Istanbul, Turkey
Automotive Manufacturers EDP Coun. [★70]
Automotive Mfrs. and Importers Assn. [IO], Bucharest, Romania
Automotive Manufactures' Racing Assn. [IO], Sheffield, United Kingdom
Automotive Market Res. Coun. [347], PO Box 13966, Research Triangle Park, NC 27709-3966, (919)549-4800
Automotive Medicine; Amer. Assn. for [★12951]
Automotive Medicine; Assn. for the Advancement of [12951]
Automotive Occupant Protection Assn. - Address unknown since 2006.
Automotive Occupant Restraints Coun. [377], 1081 Dove Run Rd., Ste. 403, Lexington, KY 40502, (859)269-4240
Automotive Oil Change Assn. [408], 12810 Hillcrest, Ste. 221, Dallas, TX 75230, (972)458-9468
Automotive Old Timers [★345]
Automotive Org. Team [★345]
Automotive Parts Accessories Assn. [IO], Auckland, New Zealand
Automotive Parts Export Coun. - Defunct.
Automotive Parts Mfrs'. Assn. [IO], Toronto, ON, Canada
Automotive Parts Mfrs. of Mexico [IO], Mexico City, Mexico
Automotive Parts Rebuilders Assn. [★IO]
Automotive Parts Rebuilders Assn. [★409]
Automotive Parts Remanufacturers Assn. [409], 4215 Lafayette Center Dr., Ste. 3, Chantilly, VA 20151-1243, (703)968-2772
Automotive Parts Remanufacturers Association [IO], Chantilly, VA, United States
Automotive Presidents Coun. [348], c/o Motor and Equip. Mfrs. Assn., PO Box 13966, Research Triangle Park, NC 27709-3966, (919)549-4800
Automotive Products Emissions Comm. - Defunct.
Automotive Products Export Coun. - Defunct.
Automotive Recyclers Assn. [3988], 3975 Fair Ridge Dr., Ste. 20 N, Fairfax, VA 22033, (703)385-1001
Automotive Refrigeration Products Inst. [378]
Automotive Refurbishing Tech. Services; Dart [★21627]
Automotive Res. Assn. of India [IO], Pune, India
Automotive Retailers' Assn. [IO], Burnaby, BC, Canada
Automotive Safety Found. [★12988]
Automotive Ser. Assn. [410], PO Box 929, Bedford, TX 76095-0929, (817)283-6205
Automotive Ser. Assn; Independent [★410]
Automotive Ser. Councils [★410]
Automotive Services
   Allgemeiner Deutscher Automobil-Club [IO]
   Amer. Auto. Assn. [403]
   Amer. Intl. Auto. Dealers Assn. [404]
   Amer. Intl. Auto. Dealers Assn. [IO]
   Assn. of Automotive Aftermarket Distributors/Parts Plus [370]
   Assn. of Car Rental Indus. Systems Standards [IO]
   Assn. of Russian Auto. Dealers [IO]
   Australian Auto. Assn. [IO]
   Austrian Auto. Touring and Motorcycle Club [IO]
   Automobilclub von Deutschland [IO]
   Auto. Assn. of Malaysia [IO]
   Auto. Club of Ecuador [IO]
   Auto. Film Club of Am. [344]
   Auto. and Touring Club of Finland [IO]
   Automotive Body Parts Assn. [IO]
   Automotive Body Parts Assn. [405]
   Automotive Engine Rebuilders Assn. [375]
   Automotive Fleet and Leasing Assn. [406]
   Automotive Hall of Fame [345]
   Automotive Lift Inst. [376]
   Automotive Maintenance and Repair Assn. [407]
   Automotive Maintenance and Repair Assn. [IO]

Automotive Oil Change Assn. [408]
Automotive Parts Remanufacturers Assn. [409]
Automotive Parts Remanufacturers Association [IO]
Automotive Presidents Coun. [348]
Automotive Refrigeration Products Inst. [378]
Automotive Ser. Assn. [410]
Automotive Trade Assn. Executives [349]
Automotive Training Managers Coun. [351]
Automotive Undercar Trade Org. [352]
Automovil Club de Costa Rica [IO]
Automovil Club de El Salvador [IO]
Canadian Auto. Assn. [IO]
Canadian Auto. Dealers Assn. [IO]
Canadian Automotive Repair and Ser. Coun. [IO]
Canadian Carwash Assn. [IO]
Canadian Vehicle Mfrs. Assn. [IO]
Car Rental Assn. of Namibia [IO]
Car Wash Owners and Suppliers Assn. [411]
Christian Motorsports Ministries [21610]
Coalition for Auto Glass Safety and Public Awareness [1727]
Commercial Vehicle Solutions Network [382]
Danish Auto. Dealers Assn. [IO]
Dealer Mgt. Assn. [717]
Dealers Alliance [412]
Disabled Motorists Fed. [IO]
European Assn. of Automotive Suppliers [IO]
European Car and Truck Rental Assn. [IO]
European Transmission Sys. Operators [IO]
Ford Motor Minority Dealers Assn. [413]
Gasoline and Automotive Ser. Dealers Assn. [414]
Hong Kong Auto. Assn. [IO]
Icelandic Auto. Assn. [IO]
Inter-American Fed. of Touring and Auto. Clubs [IO]
Inter-Industry Conf. on Auto Collision Repair [415]
Intl. Auto. Fed. [IO]
Intl. Carwash Assn. [IO]
Intl. Carwash Assn. [416]
Intl. Fed. of Auto. Experts [IO]
Intl. Mfrs. Representatives Assn. [360]
Intl. Midas Dealers Assn. [417]
Intl. Midas Dealers Assn. [IO]
Intl. Truck Parts Assn. [388]
Italian Garage Equip. Mfrs. Assn. [IO]
Maserati Info. Exchange [21696]
Motorcycle Indus. Coun. [2795]
Natl. Assn. of Automotive Dealers, Repair Outlets and Component Retailers [IO]
Natl. Assn. of Dealer Counsel [361]
Natl. Assn. of Emergency Vehicle Technicians [418]
Natl. Assn. of Fleet Resale Dealers [419]
Natl. Assn. of Vehicle Rental Dealers [IO]
Natl. Auto. Dealers Assn. [420]
Natl. Automotive Finance Assn. [421]
Natl. Automotive Radiator Ser. Assn. [422]
Natl. Independent Auto. Dealers Assn. [423]
Natl. Inst. for Automotive Ser. Excellence [424]
Natl. Truck Equip. Assn. [395]
Natl. Windshield Repair Assn. [425]
New York State Assn. of Ser. Stations and Repair Shops [426]
New Zealand Auto. Assn. [IO]
Overseas Automotive Coun. [364]
Royal Irish Auto. Club [IO]
Ser. Specialists Assn. [427]
Soc. of Collision Repair Specialists [428]
Standing Up for SUV, Pickup and Van Owners of Am. [17017]
Towing and Recovery Assn. of Am. [429]
Truck-Frame and Axle Repair Assn. [430]
Truck Mixer Mfrs. Bur. [400]
Tune-Up Manufacturers Coun. [402]
Used Truck Assn. [431]
Automotive Study Unit, ATA - Defunct.
Automotive Teachers; Natl. Assn. of Coll. [★7993]
Automotive Trade Assn. Executives [349], 8400 Westpark Dr., McLean, VA 22102, (703)821-7072
Automotive Trade Assn. Managers [★349]
Automotive Trade Policy Coun. [350], 1350 I St. NW, Ste. 1060, Washington, DC 20005, (202)789-0030
Automotive Training Managers Coun. [351], 101 Blue Seal Dr. SE, Ste. 101, Leesburg, VA 20175, (703)669-6670

Automotive and Truck Museum of U.S; Natl. [10512]
Automotive Undercar Trade Org. [352], 7101 Wisconsin Ave., Ste. 1300, Bethesda, MD 20814, (301)654-6664
Automotive Warehouse Distributors Assn. [379], 7101 Wisconsin Ave., Ste. 1300, Bethesda, MD 20814, (301)654-6664
Automotive Wholesalers Assn. Executives - Defunct.
Automotive Women's Alliance [353], PO Box 4305, Troy, MI 48099-4305, (248)643-6590
Automotive Women's Alliance [IO], Troy, MI, United States
Automovil Club de Costa Rica [IO], San Jose, Costa Rica
Automovil Club del Ecuador [★IO]
Automovil Club de El Salvador [IO], San Salvador, El Salvador
AutoPrep 5000 Users Group - Defunct.
Autos; Natl. Org. for Racing Radio Control [22652]
Autosound Challenge Assn; Natl. [★1219]
Autry Family Assn. - Address unknown since 2001.
Autumn Leaf Collectors Club; Natl. [22078]
Aux-ODACA [★22404]
Auxiliaries of Our Lady of the Cenacle [19581], 513 W Fullerton Pkwy., Chicago, IL 60614-5999, (773)528-6404
Auxiliary to the Amer. Dental Assn. [★14092]
Auxiliary to the Amer. Osteopathic Assn. [★15789]
Auxiliary to the Amer. Pharmaceutical Assn. - Address unknown since 2002.
Auxiliary to the Amer. Soc. of Mech. Engineers; Woman's [★7299]
Auxiliary Mexican Border Veterans - Address unknown since 1995.
Auxiliary to the Natl. Dental Assn. - Address unknown since 2002.
Auxiliary to the Natl. Medical Assn. [15161], 1012 10th St. NW, Washington, DC 20001, (202)371-1674
Auxiliary Services; Natl. Assn. of Coll. [3478]
Auxiliary to Sons of Union Veterans of the Civil War [20723], 2449 Center Ave., Alliance, OH 44601-4531, (330)823-6919
Auxiliary of the U.S.A; Catholic War Veterans [21194]
AV Pansophic Users Group - Defunct.
AVA [★IO]
Ava Barber Fan Club - Defunct.
Avalanche Assn; Amer. [12948]
Avaliku Sona Noukogu [★IO]
Avant Ministries [20303], 10000 N Oak Trafficway, Kansas City, MO 64155, (816)734-8500
Avanti Club of Am. [★21589]
Avanti Club of Am. [★IO]
Avanti Owners Assn. Intl. [IO], Maple Grove, MN, United States
Avanti Owners Assn. Intl. [21589], c/o Cornerstone Registration, PO Box 1743, Maple Grove, MN 55311-6743, (763)420-7829
AVCARE: Natl. Assn. for Crop Production and Animal Hea. [★IO]
AVEM Intl. [IO], Albuquerque, NM, United States
AVEM Intl. [2006], 71 Pinon Hill Pl. NE, Albuquerque, NM 87122-1914, (505)856-6924
Avenues, Natl. Support Gp. for Arthrogryposis Multiplex Congenita [15309], c/o Lynn Staheli, MD, Children's Orthopedic Hosp. and Medical Center, 4800 Sand Point Way NE, Seattle, WA 98105
Average Adjusters of the U.S; Assn. of [2145]
AVERT [IO], London, United Kingdom
Avian Pathologists; Amer. Assn. of [16740]
Avian Philately Unit - Defunct.
Avian Veterinarians; Mid-Atlantic States Assn. of [16798]
Avian Welfare Coalition [4193], PO Box 40212, St. Paul, MN 55104
Aviation
   187th Airborne Regimental Combat Team Assn. [20697]
   508th Parachute Infantry Regiment Assn. [21379]
   Acad. of Model Aeronautics [21421]
   Aeronautica and Air Label Collectors Club [21422]
   Aeronca Lovers Club [21423]
   Aerospace Indus. Assn. of Am. [130]
   Aerospace Medical Assn. [13538]

A star before a book entry number signifies that the name is not listed separately, but is mentioned within the entry.

Aerostar Owners Assn. [21424]
African Civil Aviation Commn. [IO]
Agency for the Safety of Air Navigation in Africa
    and Madagascar [IO]
Air Charity Network [14312]
Air, Inc. - Aviation Info. Resources [131]
Air League [IO]
Air Line Pilots Assn., Intl. [IO]
Air Line Pilots Assn., Intl. [24005]
Air Mail Pioneers [21425]
Air and Surface Transport Nurses Assn. [15427]
Air Traffic Control Assn. [132]
Air Weather Reconnaissance Assn. [21279]
Aircraft Engine Historical Soc. [9364]
Aircraft Mechanics Fraternal Assn. [24006]
Aircraft Owners and Pilots Assn. [135]
Airlift/Tanker Assn. [20646]
Airline Pilots Security Alliance [432]
Allied Pilots Assn. [24007]
Amer. Air Mail Soc. [22780]
Amer. Assn. of Airport Executives [138]
Amer. Aviation Historical Soc. [21426]
Amer. Bonanza Soc. [21427]
Amer. Fighter Aces Assn. [20647]
Amer. Helicopter Soc. [139]
Amer. Independent Cockpit Alliance [24008]
Amer. Navion Soc. [21428]
Amer. Yankee Assn. [21429]
Antique Airplane Assn. [21430]
Army Aviation Assn. of Am. [6070]
Assn. of Air Medical Services [14314]
Assn. of Flight Attendants - CWA [24009]
Association of Flight Attendants - CWA [IO]
Assn. of Professional Flight Attendants [24010]
Assn. of U.S. Members of the Intl. Inst. of Space
    Law [6372]
Assn. for Women in Aviation Maintenance [4034]
Australasian Soc. of Aerospace Medicine [IO]
Aviation Consumer Action Proj. [17308]
Aviation Crime Prevention Inst. [433]
Aviation Development Coun. [140]
Aviation Indus. Assn. of New Zealand [IO]
Aviation Maintenance Found. Intl. [143]
Aviation Medical Soc. - New Zealand [IO]
Aviation Safety Alliance [434]
Aviation Safety Inst. [12953]
Belgian Aviation History Assn. [IO]
Belgian Cockpit Assn. [IO]
Bellanca-Champion Club [21431]
Bird Airplane Club [21432]
Bird Strike Comm. USA [5299]
Black Pilots of Am. [435]
C.A.L./N-X-211 Collectors Soc. [11106]
Canadian Air Traffic Control Assn.- CAW Local
    5454 [IO]
Canadian Union of Public Employees - Airline Div.
    [IO]
Cardinal Club [21433]
Caterpillar Club [146]
Center for Aviation Res. and Educ. [5537]
Cessna Owner Org. [21435]
Cessna Pilots Assn. [21436]
Cherokee Pilots' Assn. [21437]
Citizens Aviation Watch Assn. [11509]
Civil Air Patrol [5538]
Combat Helicopter Pilots Assn. [20648]
Corben Club [21440]
Daedalian Found. [20649]
Danish Airtaxi Assn. [IO]
EAA Vintage Aircraft Assn. [21442]
EAA Warbirds of Am. [21443]
Ercoupe Owners Club [21444]
European Civil Aviation Conf. [IO]
European Cockpit Assn. [IO]
European Org. for Civil Aviation Equip. [IO]
Experimental Aircraft Assn. [6373]
F-4 Phantom II Soc. [21445]
Fairchild Club [21446]
Fellowship of Christian Airline Personnel [20007]
Finnish Airline Pilots Assn. [IO]
First Flight Soc. [21447]
Flight Safety Found. [148]
Flying Apache Assn. [21448]
Flying Chiropractors Assn. [14002]
Flying Dentists Assn. [14153]

Flying Physicians Assn. [13731]
Funk Aircraft Owners Assn. [21449]
Helicopter Club of America [21450]
Helicopter Found. Intl. [151]
Intl. Aerobatic Club [23040]
Intl. Airline Passengers Assn. [23015]
Intl. Assn. of Flight Paramedics [14334]
Intl. Assn. of Machinists [24011]
Intl. Assn. of Machinists [IO]
Intl. Assn. of Machinists and Aerospace Workers
    [24012]
Intl. Assn. of Military Flight Surgeon-Pilots [13541]
Intl. Assn. of Natural Rsrc. Pilots [4187]
Intl. Aviation Ground Support Assn. [436]
Intl. Aviation Ground Support Assn. [IO]
International Aviation Womens Association [IO]
Intl. Aviation Womens Assn. [437]
Intl. B and B Fly-Inn Club [21451]
Intl. Bird Dog Assn. [21452]
Intl. Cessna 120/140 Assn. [21453]
The Intl. Cessna 170 Assn. [21454]
Intl. Civil Aviation Org. [IO]
Intl. Civil Aviation Org. Asia Pacific Off. [IO]
Intl. Civil Aviation Org. Eastern and Southern
    African Off. [IO]
Intl. Comm. for the Rescue of KAL 007 Survivors
    [18541]
Intl. Coun. of Air Shows [21455]
Intl. Experimental Aerospace Soc. [6375]
Intl. Org. of Masters, Mates and Pilots, ILA, AFL-
    CIO [24128]
Intl. Pietenpol Assn. [21456]
Intl. Scale Soaring Assn. [22648]
Intl. Soc. of Air Safety Investigators [12966]
Intl. Soc. of Transport Aircraft Trading [156]
Interstate Club [21458]
Jack Knight Air Mail Soc. [22834]
Jamaican Airline Pilots' Assn. [IO]
Latin Amer. Aeronautical Assn. [IO]
Latin Amer. Aeronautical Assn. [438]
Lawyer-Pilots Bar Assn. [5539]
Lighter-Than-Air Soc. [21460]
LightHawk [4418]
Luscombe Endowment [21461]
Malaysian Airlines Pilots' Assn. [IO]
Man Will Never Fly Memorial Soc. Internationale
    [22598]
MAPS Air Museum - Military Aviation Preservation
    Soc. [9342]
Marine Corps Aviation Reconnaissance Assn.
    [6052]
Metropolitan Air Post Soc. [22845]
Microlight Assn. of South Africa [IO]
Monocoupe Club [21462]
Natl. 210 Owners Assn. [21463]
Natl. Aeronca Assn. [21464]
Natl. Agricultural Aviation Assn. [4188]
National Agricultural Aviation Association [IO]
Natl. Air Disaster Alliance [11510]
Natl. Air-Racing Gp. [23041]
Natl. Air Traffic Controllers Assn. [24013]
Natl. Aircraft Appraisers Assn. [188]
Natl. Assn. of Air Traffic Specialists [24014]
Natl. Assn. of Flight Instructors [161]
Natl. Assn. of Priest Pilots [19667]
Natl. Assn. of Rocketry [22650]
Natl. Assn. of Scale Aeromodelers [22651]
Natl. Assn. of State Aviation Officials [5540]
Natl. Assn. of Timetable Collectors [23008]
Natl. Aviation and Space Educ. Alliance [7994]
Natl. Black Coalition of Fed. Aviation Employees
    [5541]
Natl. Catholic Conf. of Airport Chaplains [19754]
Natl. Coalition for Aviation Educ. [7995]
Natl. EMS Pilots Assn. [14322]
Natl. Gay Pilot's Assn. [439]
Natl. Intercollegiate Flying Assn. [21466]
Natl. Soaring Found. [23042]
Natl. Space Club [6377]
Natl. Space Soc. [6378]
Natl. World War II Glider Pilots Assn. [21468]
Negro Airmen Intl. [6380]
New Zealand Air Line Pilots' Assn. [IO]
Order of Daedalians [20650]
Org. of Black Airline Pilots [164]

OX5 Aviation Pioneers [21469]
Pilot Class 43-D Assn. [21400]
Pilots for Christ Intl. [20028]
The Planetary Soc. [6382]
Popular Rotorcraft Assn. [21471]
Porterfield Airplane Club [21472]
Professional Airways Systems Specialists [24015]
Professional Aviation Maintenance Assn. [165]
Professional Pilots Fed. [24016]
Rearwin Club [21474]
Regional Aviation Assn. of Australia [IO]
Royal Air Force Historical Soc. [IO]
Short Wing Piper Club [21475]
Silver Wings Fraternity [21476]
Soaring Soc. of Am. [23043]
Soc. of Antique Modelers [21477]
Soc. of Experimental Test Pilots [6384]
Stearman Restorers Assn. [21480]
Swedish Aviation Historical Soc. [IO]
Swift Museum Found. [21481]
Transport Workers Union of Am. [24200]
Travel Air Club [21482]
Twin Bonanza Assn. [21483]
United Flying Octogenarians [21485]
U.S. Pilots Assn. [168]
U.S. Powered Paragliding Assn. [23643]
U.S. Ultralight Assn. [21486]
USAF Medical Ser. Corps Assn. [13590]
Vintage Sailplane Assn. [23045]
Western Assoc. Modelers [22661]
Whirly-Girls - Intl. Women Helicopter Pilots
    [21487]
Women of the Natl. Agricultural Aviation Assn.
    [4189]
World Airline Entertainment Assn. [440]
World Airline Entertainment Association [IO]
World Airline Historical Soc. [21488]
World War I Aeroplanes [21490]
Zeppelin Collectors Club [22892]
Aviation Artists; Guild of [IO]
Aviation Assn. of Am; Army [6070]
Aviation Assn; European Bus. [IO]
Aviation Assn; Marine Corps [6080]
Aviation Assn; Natl. Bus. [162]
Aviation Assn; Univ. [7924]
Aviation Cadet Alumni Assn. - Defunct.
Aviation Club; Hong Kong [IO]
Aviation and Computer Enthusiasts - Defunct.
Aviation Consumer Action Proj. [17308]
Aviation Coun; Intl. Bus. [IO]
Aviation Crime Prevention Inst. [433], PMB 306, 226
    N Nova Rd., Ormond Beach, FL 32174, (386)341-
    7270
Aviation Development Coun. [140], 141-07 20th
    Ave., Ste. 404, Whitestone, NY 11357, (718)746-
    0212
Aviation Distributors and Manufacturers Assn. [141],
    100 N 20th St., 4th Fl., Philadelphia, PA 19103-
    1443, (215)564-3484
Aviation Env. Fed. [IO], London, United Kingdom
Aviation Facilities Energy Assn. - Defunct.
Aviation Fellowship; Mission [20359]
Aviation Force Veterans Assn; First Marine [★6080]
Aviation Historical Soc; Amer. [21426]
Aviation Historical Soc; Canadian [IO]
Aviation Historical Soc. - Defunct.
Aviation Indus. Assn. of New Zealand [IO], Welling-
    ton, New Zealand
Aviation Indus. CBT Comm. [142], PO Box 472,
    Sugar City, ID 83448-0472, (208)496-1136
Aviation Indus. Computer-Based Training Comm.
    [★142]
Aviation Info. Resources; Air - [★131]
Aviation Insurance Assn. [2150], 14 W 3rd St., Ste.
    200, Kansas City, MO 64105, (816)221-8488
Aviation Insurance Rating Bur. - Defunct.
Aviation Maintenance Assn; Professional [165]
Aviation Maintenance; Assn. for Women in [4034]
Aviation Maintenance Found. Intl. [143]
Aviation Manufacturers Assn; Gen. [149]
Aviation Medical Soc. - New Zealand [IO], Auckland,
    New Zealand
Aviation Museum Found; Naval [★6379]
Aviation Officials Center for Aviation Res. and Educ;
    Natl. Assn. of State [★5537]

Aviation Pioneers; OX5 [21469]
Aviation Preservation Soc; Military [★9342]
Aviation Preservation Soc. and Museum; Military
    [★9342]
Aviation Psychology; Assn. for [6370]
Aviation Safety Alliance [434], 601 Madison St., Ste.
    300, Alexandria, VA 22314, (703)739-6700
Aviation Safety and Health Assn. - Address unknown
    since 1994.
Aviation Safety Inst. [12953], PO Box 690, Worthing-
    ton, OH 43085, (614)885-4242
Aviation Sans Frontieres [IO], Orly Aerogares,
    France
Aviation Security Assn. of America - Intl. - Defunct.
Aviation/Space Writers Assn. - Address unknown
    since 2001.
Aviation Study Unit - Defunct.
Aviation Suppliers Assn. [2550], 2233 Wisconsin
    Ave. NW, Ste. 503, Washington, DC 20007,
    (202)347-6899
Aviation Technician Educ. Coun. [7921], 2090 Wex-
    ford Ct., Harrisburg, PA 17112, (717)540-7121
Aviation Theft Bur; Intl. [★433]
Aviation Trades Assn; Natl. [★160]
Aviators; California Wheelchair [★21457]
Avicultural Advancement Coun. of Canada [IO],
    Chemainus, BC, Canada
Avicultural Soc. [IO], Totnes, United Kingdom
Avicultural Soc. of Am. [IO], Riverside, CA, United
    States
Avicultural Soc. of Am. [7414], c/o Helen Hanson,
    Membership Sec., PO Box 5516, Riverside, CA
    92517-5516, (951)780-4102
Aviculture; Amer. Fed. of [21840]
Aviculturist and Cage Bird Judges Assn; Greater
    North Amer. [★21845]
Avion Travelcade Club [22945]
Avionics Maintenance Conf. [144], c/o Aeronautical
    Radio, Inc., 2551 Riva Rd., Annapolis, MD 21401,
    (410)266-2008
Avis Licensee Assn. [3380], 300 Old Country Rd.,
    Ste. 341, Mineola, NY 11501, (516)747-4951
AVKO Dyslexia Res. Found. [9138], 3084 W Willard
    Rd., Ste. W, Clio, MI 48420-7801, (810)686-9283
AVM Support Group - Defunct.
Avocado Advisory Bd; California [★4707]
Avocado Commn; California [4707]
Avocado Growers Bargaining Coun. - Defunct.
Avocado Soc; California [4708]
Avocats Sans Frontieres [IO], Brussels, Belgium
Avon and Border Counties Welsh Pony and Cob
    Assn. [IO], Malmesbury, United Kingdom
Avon Clubs; Natl. Assn. of [★22073]
Avon Collectors; Natl. Assn. of [22073]
AVS Sci. and Tech. Soc. [7822], 120 Wall St., 32nd
    Fl., New York, NY 10005, (212)248-0200
AVSC Intl. [★12180]
AVSC Intl. [★IO]
Awaiting Angels [IO], Trujillo, Peru
Awake In Am. [18601], PO Box 51601, Philadelphia,
    PA 19115-1601, (215)764-6568
A.W.A.K.E. Network [★16421]
Awana Clubs Intl. [20639], 1 E Bode Rd., Stream-
    wood, IL 60107-6658, (630)213-2000
Awana Clubs Intl. [IO], Streamwood, IL, United
    States
Awana Youth Assn. [★IO]
Awana Youth Assn. [★20639]
Awards
    Alpha Chi [24498]
    Alpha Chi Sigma [24428]
    Alpha Delta Kappa [24449]
    Alpha Epsilon [24395]
    Alpha Epsilon Delta [24541]
    Alpha Gamma Rho [24396]
    Alpha Iota Sorority [24413]
    Alpha Kappa Delta [24701]
    Alpha Kappa Psi [24414]
    Alpha Mu Gamma Natl. [24525]
    Alpha Omega Alpha Honor Medical Soc. [24542]
    Alpha Omega Intl. Dental Fraternity [24437]
    Alpha Psi Lambda Natl. [24615]
    Alpha Sigma Nu [24500]
    Alpha Tau Delta [24559]
    Alpha Zeta [24397]

Alpha Zeta Omega [24567]
Amer. Assn. of Grant Professionals [12708]
America's Found. [20709]
Arnold Air Soc. [24546]
Assn. of Coll. Honor Societies [24501]
Assn. of Fraternity Advisors [24475]
Astronaut Scholars Honor Soc. [24584]
Awards and Recognition Assn. [441]
Beta Alpha Psi [24391]
Beta Beta Beta [24408]
Beta Gamma Sigma [24415]
Beta Gamma Sigma Alumni [24416]
Beta Phi Mu [24532]
Beta Sigma Kappa [24562]
Center for the Stud. of the Coll. Fraternity [24476]
Central Off. Executives Assn. of Natl. Pan-
    Hellenic Conf. [24477]
Chi Eta Phi Sorority [24560]
Congressional Medal of Honor Soc. [20710]
Cum Laude Soc. [24503]
Delphi Found. [24451]
Delta Epsilon Sigma [24504]
Delta Kappa Epsilon [24623]
Delta Lambda Phi Natl. Social Fraternity [24624]
Delta Mu Delta Honor Soc. [24418]
Delta Omega [24582]
Delta Omicron [24550]
Delta Phi Epsilon, Professional Foreign Ser.
    Fraternity [24472]
Delta Phi Epsilon Professional Foreign Ser. Soror-
    ity [24473]
Delta Phi Upsilon [24431]
Delta Pi Epsilon [24426]
Delta Psi Omega [24444]
Delta Sigma Delta [24438]
Delta Theta Phi [24527]
Distinguished Flying Cross Soc. [20711]
Epsilon Pi Tau [24720]
Epsilon Sigma Phi [24436]
Eta Phi Beta [24419]
Eta Sigma Phi, Natl. Classics Honorary Soc.
    [24433]
Francena Purchase Applied Honors Soc. [17018]
Francena Purchase Applied Honors Society [IO]
Fraternity Executives Assn. [24479]
Gamma Iota Sigma [24520]
Gamma Sigma Delta [24398]
Gamma Theta Upsilon [24491]
Golden Key Intl. Honour Soc. [24506]
Golden Raspberry Award Found. [22419]
Green Leaf Natl. Honor Soc. [24471]
Honors Prog. Student Assn. of the Amer.
    Sociological Assn. [24702]
Horatio Alger Assn. of Distinguished Americans
    [20712]
Intl. Gold and Silver Plate Soc. [18977]
Iota Beta Sigma [24410]
Iota Phi Lambda [24421]
Kappa Delta Epsilon [24452]
Kappa Delta Pi [24453]
Kappa Mu Epsilon [24537]
Kappa Omicron Nu [24496]
Kappa Pi Intl. Honorary Art Fraternity [24404]
Kappa Psi [24568]
Kappa Tau Alpha [24522]
Ladies Auxiliary, Military Order of the Purple
    Heart, U.S.A. [20713]
Lambda Alpha Intl. [24445]
Lambda Iota Tau [24533]
Lambda Kappa Sigma [24569]
Legion of Valor of the U.S.A. [20714]
Medal Collectors of Am. [22745]
Military Order of the Purple Heart of the U.S.A.
    [20715]
Mortar Bd. [24509]
Mu Alpha Theta [24538]
Mu Beta Psi [24552]
Mu Phi Epsilon Intl. [24553]
Natl. Adult Educ. Honor Soc. [24392]
Natl. Alpha Lambda Delta [24510]
Natl. Assn. of the Knights of Scorpius, Honorary
    Leadership Soc. [24511]
Natl. Beta Club [24592]
Natl. Block and Bridle Club [24401]
Natl. Broadcasting Soc. - Alpha Epsilon Rho
    [24411]

Natl. Honor Soc. [24512]
Natl. Junior Honor Soc. [24513]
Natl. Kappa Kappa Iota [24454]
Natl. Pan-Hellenic Editors Conf. [24448]
Natl. Panhellenic Conf. [24485]
Natl. Sorority of Phi Delta Kappa [24455]
Natl. Tech. Honor Soc. [24725]
Natl. Valedictorian Honor Soc. [24514]
Natl. Women's Hall of Fame [20716]
North Amer. Interfraternal Found. [24486]
North-American Interfraternity Conf. [24487]
Omega Delta [24563]
Omicron Delta Epsilon [24446]
Omicron Delta Kappa Soc. [24515]
Omicron Kappa Upsilon [24439]
Order of the Coif [24516]
Orders and Medals Soc. of Am. [22631]
Phi Alpha Delta [24528]
Phi Alpha Sigma [24543]
Phi Alpha Theta [24495]
Phi Beta [24405]
Phi Beta Delta [24517]
Phi Beta Kappa [24406]
Phi Chi Medical Fraternity [24544]
Phi Delta Chi [24570]
Phi Delta Epsilon Medical Fraternity [24540]
Phi Delta Gamma [24577]
Phi Delta Phi Intl. Legal Fraternity [24530]
Phi Kappa Phi [24518]
Phi Mu Alpha Sinfonia Fraternity and Found. Natl.
    HQ [24555]
Phi Sigma [24409]
Phi Sigma Iota [24526]
Phi Sigma Pi Natl. Honor Fraternity [24531]
Pi Kappa Phi [24551]
Pi Omicron Natl. Sorority [24601]
Professional Fraternity Assn. [24488]
Psi Beta [24579]
Psi Omega [24440]
Sigma Alpha Iota Intl. Music Fraternity [24557]
Sigma Delta Chi Found. [24524]
Sigma Delta Epsilon, Graduate Women in Sci.
    [24587]
Silver Wings [24549]
Soc. of Professional Journalists [3164]
Tau Epsilon Rho Law Soc. [24529]
Theta Alpha Phi [24721]
Theta Psi [24566]
Theta Tau [24469]
Token and Medal Soc. [22763]
Upsilon Pi Epsilon Assn. [24435]
Xi Psi Phi [24442]
Awards and Recognition Assn. [441], 4700 W Lake
    Ave., Glenview, IL 60025, (847)375-4800
AWARE [★13442]
A.W.A.R.E. - Amer. Workforce Alliance for
    Responsible Economics [1258]
AWARE; We Are [13442]
Awareness Center - Defunct.
Awareness Gp. on AIDS Prevention [IO], Nairobi,
    Kenya
Awareness Res. Found. - Address unknown since
    1994.
AWEA [★7852]
AWill/AWay RVers Assn. - Defunct.
AWRT Educational Foundation [★545]
Axiomatic Knowledge and Educ; Inst. for [7606]
Axiomatic Knowledge and Systematic Core Educ;
    Inst. for [★7606]
Axios USA [20049], 342 E Jericho Tpke., No. 191,
    Mineola, NY 11501-2111, (917)513-9368
Axis - Address unknown since 1995.
Axis of Justice [18640], 1275 N Wilton Pl., Ste. B,
    Los Angeles, CA 90038
Axis of Justice [IO], Los Angeles, CA, United States
Axle Repair Assn; Truck-Frame and [430]
Ayn Rand Inst. [10787], 2121 Alton Pkwy., Ste. 250,
    Irvine, CA 92606-4926, (949)222-6550
Ayn Rand Memorial Library Assn. - Defunct.
Ayn Rand Soc. [10788], c/o Prof. Allan Gotthelf,
    Chm., Univ. of Pittsburgh, Dept. of History and
    Philosophy of Sci., 1017 Cathedral of Learning,
    Pittsburgh, PA 15260
Ayrshire Breeders' Assn. [4253], 1224 Alton Creek
    Rd., Ste. B, Columbus, OH 43228, (614)335-0020

A star before a book entry number signifies that the name is not listed separately, but is mentioned within the entry.

Ayrshire Breeders' Assn. of Canada [IO], St.-Hyacinthe, QC, Canada
Ayurveda; Everyday [13606]
Ayurvedic Medical Assn; Natl. [13642]
AYUSA Intl. [8444], 600 California St., 10th Fl., San Francisco, CA 94108, (800)727-4540
AYUSA Intl. [IO], San Francisco, CA, United States
Azalea Soc. of Am. [22503], c/o John Brown, Pres., 1000 Moody Bridge Rd., Cleveland, SC 29635-9789, (864)836-6898
Azerbaijan Athletics Fed. [IO], Baku, Azerbaijan
Azerbaijan Draughts Fed. [IO], Baku, Azerbaijan
Azerbaijan Gadin Ve Inkishaf Merkezi [★IO]
Azerbaijan League Against Epilepsy [IO], Baku, Azerbaijan
Azerbaijan Lib. Development Assn. [IO], Baku, Azerbaijan
Azerbaijan Medical Assn. [IO], Baku, Azerbaijan
Azerbaijan Red Crescent Soc. [IO], Baku, Azerbaijan
Azerbaijan Republic Badminton Fed. [IO], Baku, Azerbaijan
Azerbaijan Taekwondo Fed. [IO], Baku, Azerbaijan
Azerbaijan Tennis Fed. [IO], Baku, Azerbaijan
Azerbaijan Women and Development Center [IO], Baku, Azerbaijan
Azerbaijan Women's Assn. [IO], Baku, Azerbaijan
Azerbaijan Young Lawyers' Union [IO], Baku, Azerbaijan
Azerbaycan Qizil Aypara Cemiyyeti [★IO]
Azerbaycan Taekvondo Federasiyasina [★IO]
AZRA/World Union for Progressive Judaism North America [IO], New York, NY, United States
AZRA/World Union for Progressive Judaism North Am. [20122], 633 3rd Ave., New York, NY 10017-6778, (212)452-6530
Aztec Club of 1847—The Military Soc. of the Mexican War 1846-1848 - Address unknown since 2000. AztecaAzteca Horse Intl. Assn; Amer. [4811]
Azteca Horse Registry of Am. [4863], PO Box 998, Ridgefield, WA 98642-0998, (360)887-3259
AZUR Development [IO], Brazzaville, Republic of the Congo
AZUR Developpement [★IO]

B

B-26 Marauder Historical Soc. [21389], 3900 E Timerod, Tucson, AZ 85711
B-26 Marauder Historical Society [IO], Tucson, AZ, United States
B-52's U.F.O. United Fans Org. - Defunct.
B and B Fly-Inn Club; Intl. [21451]
B-Body Owners Assn; Winged Warriors/National [21820]
B. J. Thomas Fan Club - Address unknown since 1989.
BA [IO], London, United Kingdom
BAAF [★IO]
Babbage Inst. for the History of Info. Tech; Charles [10100]
Babbage Soc. - Address unknown since 1995.
Babe Ruth Baseball/Softball [23106], Babe Ruth League, Inc., 1770 Brunswick Pike, PO Box 5000, Trenton, NJ 08638, (609)695-1434
Babe Ruth Birthplace Found. [★23107]
Babe Ruth Birthplace/Sports Legends at Camden Yards [23107], 216 Emory St., Baltimore, MD 21230, (410)727-1539
Babe Ruth Museum/Sports Legends at Camden Yards [★23107]
Babies Coalition; Natl. Healthy Mothers, Healthy [15612]
Babies Cong; World Aquatic [★23894]
Babies; Parents of Premature [12686]
Babiker Badri Sci. Assn. for Women's Stud. [IO], Omdurman, Sudan
Babraham Inst. [IO], Cambridge, United Kingdom
Baby Milk Action [IO], Cambridge, United Kingdom
Baby Products Assn. [IO], Aylesbury, United Kingdom
Baby; Save-A- [★12918]
BACCHUS and Gamma Peer Educ. Network [★13226]
BACCHUS and Gamma Peer Educ. Network [★IO]
BACCHUS Network [IO], Denver, CO, United States

BACCHUS Network [13226], PO Box 100430, Denver, CO 80250-0430, (303)871-0901
BACCHUS of the U.S. [★13226]
BACCHUS of the U.S. [★IO]
Bach Elgar Choir [IO], Hamilton, ON, Canada
Bach Found; Amer. [★10690]
Bachad Org. [★20178]
Back Bay Lisa - Defunct.
Back to the City - Defunct.
Back Country Horsemen of Am. [23522], PO Box 1367, Graham, WA 98338-1367, (360)832-2461
Back to the Future.The Fan Club - Defunct.
Back in the Saddle Horse Adoption [4864], c/o Joni Fink, Exec. Dir., 1313 Youngs Rd., Linden, PA 17744, (570)974-1087
Back Soc; Amer. [15754]
BackCare, The Charity for Healthier Backs [IO], Teddington, United Kingdom
Backflow Prevention Assn; Amer. [7818]
Backgammon Assn; Intl. [22466]
Background Screeners; Natl. Assn. of Professional [1983]
Backpackers Assn; Intl. [★23934]
Backpackers Club [IO], Chatham, United Kingdom
Backscratchers Club of America - Address unknown since 1995.
Bacon Families Assn. - Defunct.
Bacon Found; Francis [9650]
Bacteriologists; Amer. Assn. of Pathologists and [★15860]
Bacteriologists; Soc. of Amer. [★6565]
Bacteriology
    Amer. Assn. of Medical Milk Commissions [16384]
Bacus/B'Gosh Families - Defunct.
BAD 2 Assn. - Address unknown since 2004.
Badan Peguam Malaysia [★IO]
Badfinger Fan Club - Address unknown since 1995.
Badge Collectors Newsl; Disabled Veterans Keychain Tag and Chaffeur's [22011]
Badger Face Welsh Mountain Sheep Soc. [IO], Hereford, United Kingdom
Badminton
    Afghanistan Badminton Fed. [IO]
    Algerian Badminton Assn. [IO]
    Aruba Badminton Club [IO]
    Asian Badminton Confed. [IO]
    Asociacion Costarricense de Badminton [IO]
    Asociacion Uruguaya de Badminton [IO]
    Associacao de Badminton de Macau [IO]
    Austrian Badminton Assn. [IO]
    Azerbaijan Republic Badminton Fed. [IO]
    Badminton Assn. of the Cook Islands [IO]
    Badminton Assn. of the Democratic People's Republic of Korea [IO]
    Badminton Assn. of Ghana [IO]
    Badminton Assn. of Iceland [IO]
    Badminton Assn. of Malawi [IO]
    Badminton Assn. of Maldives [IO]
    Badminton Assn. of Malta [IO]
    Badminton Assn. of the People's Republic of China [IO]
    Badminton Assn. of Thailand [IO]
    Badminton Bond Curacao [IO]
    Badminton Canada [IO]
    BADMINTON England [IO]
    Badminton Europe [IO]
    Badminton Fed. of Armenia [IO]
    Badminton Fed. of Cambodia [IO]
    Badminton Fed. of Cameroon [IO]
    Badminton Fed. of the Former Yugoslav Republic of Macedonia [IO]
    Badminton Fed. of Islamic Republic of Iran [IO]
    Badminton Fed. of Nigeria [IO]
    Badminton Fed. of the Republic of Moldova [IO]
    Badminton Pan Amer. Confed. [23088]
    BADMINTON Scotland [IO]
    Badminton Union of Ireland [IO]
    Badminton Union of Namibia [IO]
    Badminton World Fed. [IO]
    Badmintonsamband Foroya [IO]
    Badmintonska Zveza Slovenije [IO]
    Bangladesh Badminton Fed. [IO]
    Barbados Badminton Assn. [IO]
    Belarussian Badminton Fed. [IO]
    Bermuda Badminton Assn. [IO]

    Bhutan Badminton Fed. [IO]
    Botswana Badminton Assn. [IO]
    Brunei Natl. Badminton Assn. [IO]
    Bulgarian Badminton Fed. [IO]
    Cayman Islands Badminton Assn. [IO]
    Central African Badminton Fed. [IO]
    Chinese Taipei Badminton Assn. [IO]
    Comision Nacional de Badminton del Peru [IO]
    Commn. Adhoc Congolaise de Badminton [IO]
    Confederacao Brasileira de Badminton [IO]
    Croatian Badminton Assn. [IO]
    Cyprus Badminton Fed. [IO]
    Czech Badminton Fed. [IO]
    Deutscher Badminton Verband [IO]
    Egyptian Badminton Fed. [IO]
    Equatorial Guinea Badminton Fed. [IO]
    Eritrean Natl. Badminton Fed. [IO]
    Estonian Badminton Fed. [IO]
    Ethiopian Badminton Fed. [IO]
    Federacao Mocambicana de Badminton [IO]
    Federacao Portuguesa de Badminton [IO]
    Federacion de Badminton de Chile [IO]
    Federacion de Badminton de la Republica Argentina [IO]
    Federacion Cubana de Badminton [IO]
    Federacion Ecuatoriana de Badminton [IO]
    Federacion Espanola de Badminton [IO]
    Federacion Nacional de Badminton de Guatemala [IO]
    Federacion Nacional de Badminton de Honduras [IO]
    Federacion Salvadorena de Badminton [IO]
    Fed. Libanaise de Badminton [IO]
    Fed. Malagasy de Badminton [IO]
    Fed. Royal Marocaine de Badminton [IO]
    Fed. Togolaise de Badminton [IO]
    Federazione Italiana Badminton [IO]
    Fiji Badminton Assn. [IO]
    Finnish Badminton Assn. [IO]
    Georgian Badminton Fed. [IO]
    Gibraltar Badminton Fed. [IO]
    Greenland Badminton Fed. [IO]
    Guyana Badminton Assn. [IO]
    Hellenic Badminton Fed. [IO]
    Hong Kong Badminton Assn. [IO]
    Hungarian Badminton Assn. [IO]
    Iraqi Badminton Fed. [IO]
    Israel Badminton Assn. [IO]
    Jamaica Badminton Assn. [IO]
    Jordan Badminton Fed. [IO]
    Kazakhstan Badminton Fed. [IO]
    Kenya Badminton Assn. [IO]
    Korea Badminton Assn. [IO]
    Kuwait Badminton Fed. [IO]
    Kyrghyz Natl. Badminton Fed. [IO]
    La Federacion Dominicana de Badminton [IO]
    Lao Badminton Fed. [IO]
    Latvian Badminton Fed. [IO]
    Lesotho Badminton Assn. [IO]
    Lithuanian Badminton Fed. [IO]
    Luxembourg Badminton Fed. [IO]
    Mauritius Badminton Assn. [IO]
    Mongolian Badminton Assn. [IO]
    Myanmar Badminton Fed. [IO]
    Nauru Badminton Fed. [IO]
    Nederlandse Badminton Bond [IO]
    Nepal Badminton Assn. [IO]
    New Zealand Badminton Fed. [IO]
    Nippon Badminton Assn. [IO]
    Palestine Badminton Fed. [IO]
    Philippine Badminton Assn. [IO]
    Polski Zwiazek Badmintona [IO]
    Romanian Badminton Fed. [IO]
    Russian Badminton Fed. [IO]
    Samoa Badminton Assn. [IO]
    Singapore Badminton Assn. [IO]
    Slovak Badminton Fed. [IO]
    Somali Badminton Fed. [IO]
    Sri Lanka Badminton Assn. [IO]
    Stanley Badminton Club [IO]
    Surinaamse Badminton Bond [IO]
    Swaziland Natl. Badminton Assn. [IO]
    Syrian Arab Badminton Fed. [IO]
    Tanzania Badminton Assn. [IO]
    Trinidad and Tobago Badminton Assn. [IO]

Reference to "IO" in place of a book number signifies that the association may be found in the 45th edition of International Organizations.

Turkish Badminton Fed. [IO]
Turkmenistan Badminton Fed. [IO]
Ukrainian Badminton Fed. [IO]
USA Badminton [23089]
Uzbekistan Badminton Fed. [IO]
Vietnam Badminton Fed. [IO]
Welsh Badminton Union [IO]
Zambia Badminton Assn. [IO]
Zimbabwe Badminton Assn. [IO]
Badminton Assn. of the Cook Islands [IO], Rarotonga, Cook Islands
Badminton Assn. of the Democratic People's Republic of Korea [IO], Pyongyang, Democratic People's Republic of Korea
Badminton Assn. of England [★IO]
Badminton Assn. of Ghana [IO], Accra, Ghana
Badminton Assn. of Iceland [IO], Reykjavik, Iceland
Badminton Assn. of Malawi [IO], Zomba, Malawi
Badminton Assn. of Maldives [IO], Male, Maldives
Badminton Assn. of Malta [IO], Valletta, Malta
Badminton Assn. of the People's Republic of China [IO], Beijing, People's Republic of China
Badminton Assn. of Thailand [IO], Bangkok, Thailand
Badminton Assn; U.S. [★23089]
Badminton Bond Curacao [IO], Curacao, Netherlands Antilles
Badminton Canada [IO], Ottawa, ON, Canada
BADMINTON England [IO], Milton Keynes, United Kingdom
Badminton Europe [IO], Brondby, Denmark
Badminton Fed. of Armenia [IO], Yerevan, Armenia
Badminton Fed. of Cambodia [IO], Phnom Penh, Cambodia
Badminton Fed. of Cameroon [IO], Yaounde, Cameroon
Badminton Fed. of the Former Yugoslav Republic of Macedonia [IO], Skopje, Macedonia
Badminton Fed. of the Independent Republic of Iran [★IO]
Badminton Fed. of Islamic Republic of Iran [IO], Tehran, Iran
Badminton Fed. of Nigeria [IO], Lagos, Nigeria
Badminton Fed. of the Republic of Moldova [IO], Chisinau, Moldova
Badminton Pan Amer. Confed. [23088], 1 World Trade Ctr., Ste. 300, Long Beach, CA 90831, (714)385-1222
BADMINTON Scotland [IO], Glasgow, United Kingdom
Badminton Union of Ireland [IO], Dublin, Ireland
Badminton Union of Namibia [IO], Oranjemund, Namibia
Badminton; USA [23089]
Badminton World Fed. [IO], Kuala Lumpur, Malaysia
Badmintonsamband Foroya [IO], Torshavn, Faroe Islands
Badmintonsamband Islands [★IO]
Badmintonska Zveza Slovenije [IO], Medvode, Slovenia
Baendasamtoek Islands [★IO]
Bag Assn; Plastic [★980]
Bag and Cover Assn; Indus. [★2875]
Bag Dealers Assn; Natl. Burlap [★999]
Bag and Packaging Assn; Textile [999]
Bag Processors Assn; Textile [★999]
The Bagehot Coun. [★7528]
Bagehot Res. Coun. on Natl. Sovereignty; Walter [7528]
Bagpipe Soc. [IO], Otley, United Kingdom
Baha'i
   Assn. for Baha'i Stud. [IO]
   Baha'i Community of Canada [IO]
   European Baha'i Bus. Forum [IO]
   Natl. Spiritual Assembly of the Baha'is of India [IO]
   Natl. Spiritual Assembly of the Baha'is of New Zealand [IO]
   Natl. Spiritual Assembly of the Baha'is of the U.S. [19467]
   Natl. Spiritual Assembly of the Baha'is of Vanuatu [IO]
   Spiritual Assembly of the Baha'is of Malaysia [IO]
Baha'i Community of Canada [IO], Thornhill, ON, Canada

Baha'is of the U.S. and Canada; Natl. Spiritual Assembly of the [★19467]
Baha'is of the U.S; Natl. Spiritual Assembly of the [19467]
Bahamas Agricultural and Indus. Corp. [IO], Nassau, Bahamas
Bahamas Amateur Athletic Assn. [★IO]
Bahamas Assn. of Athletic Associations [IO], Nassau, Bahamas
Bahamas Baseball Fed. [IO], Nassau, Bahamas
Bahamas Chamber of Commerce - Nassau [IO], Nassau, Bahamas
Bahamas Crisis Centre [IO], Nassau, Bahamas
Bahamas Elecl. Workers' Union [IO], Nassau, Bahamas
Bahamas Employers' Confed. [IO], Nassau, Bahamas
Bahamas Historical Soc. [IO], Nassau, Bahamas
Bahamas Inst. of Chartered Accountants [IO], Nassau, Bahamas
Bahamas Lawn Tennis Assn. [IO], Nassau, Bahamas
Bahamas Olympic Assn. [IO], Nassau, Bahamas
Bahamas Real Estate Assn. [IO], Nassau, Bahamas
Bahamas Red Cross Soc. [IO], Nassau, Bahamas
Bahamas Sailing Assn. [IO], Nassau, Bahamas
Bahamas Squash Raquets Assn. [IO], Nassau, Bahamas
Bahamas Taekwondo Fed. [IO], Nassau, Bahamas
Bahamas Union of Teachers [IO], Nassau, Bahamas
Bahrain Arts Soc. [IO], Manama, Bahrain
Bahrain Athletics Assn. [IO], Manama, Bahrain
Bahrain Badminton and Squash Assn. [IO], Manama, Bahrain
Bahrain Bowling Assn. [IO], Manama, Bahrain
Bahrain Diabetic Assn. [IO], Bahrain, Bahrain
Bahrain Disabled Sports Fed. [IO], Manama, Bahrain
Bahrain Family Planning Assn. [IO], Manama, Bahrain
Bahrain Handball Assn. [IO], Manama, Bahrain
Bahrain Maritime Sports Assn. [IO], Manama, Bahrain
Bahrain Tennis Fed. [IO], Manama, Bahrain
Bahrain Weightlifting and Bodybuilding Assn. [IO], Manama, Bahrain
Bahrain Youth Hostels Soc. [IO], Manama, Bahrain
Baidarka Historical Soc. [9954], PO Box 5454, Bellingham, WA 98227-5454, (360)734-9226
BAIF Development Res. Found. [IO], Pune, India
Baikal Environmental Wave [IO], Irkutsk, Russia
Bail
   Amer. Bail Coalition [442]
   Professional Bail Agents of the U.S. [5542]
Bailey Fan Club; Razzy [24964]
Baja Outreach - Address unknown since 2003.
Bajoran Alliance - Defunct.
BAK - Deutsche Rheuma Liga Bundesverband e.V. [IO], Bonn, Germany
Baker Family Intl. [IO], Staunton, IL, United States
Baker Family Intl. [20788], c/o Crystal Jensen, Genealogist, 326 Panhorst, Staunton, IL 62088-1829
Baker St. Irregulars [10964], 2 Dettling Rd., Maynard, MA 01754, (717)633-8911
Baker St. Irregulars [IO], Indianapolis, IN, United States
Baker Student Program; Ella [★17097]
Bakers of Am; Assoc. [★454]
Bakers of Am; Assoc. Retail [★454]
Bakers of Am. Cooperative; Quality [453]
Bakers of Am; Retail [★454]
Bakers of Am; Retail Merchant [★454]
Bakers of Am. - Retail and Wholesale; Assoc. [★454]
Bakers Assn. of Am; Retail [★454]
Bakers Assn; Amer. [444]
Bakers Assn; Independent [452]
Bakers Assn; Wholesale Variety [455]
Bakers Club - Defunct.
Bakers, Food and Allied Workers' Union - Ireland [IO], Dublin, Ireland
Bakers, Food and Allied Workers' Union - United Kingdom [IO], Welwyn Garden City, United Kingdom

Bakers Guild of Am; Bread [451]
Bakers Inst; Biscuit [★450]
Bakery
   Allied Trades of the Baking Indus. [443]
   Amer. Bakers Assn. [444]
   Amer. Inst. of Baking [445]
   Amer. Soc. of Baking [447]
   Bakery, Confectionery, Tobacco Workers and Grain Millers Intl. Union [24017]
   Baking Indus. Sanitation Standards Comm. [448]
   Independent Bakers Assn. [452]
   Intl. Dairy-Deli-Bakery Assn. [1522]
   Natl. Assn. of Flour Distributors [1540]
   Retailer's Bakery Assn. [454]
Bakery Assn; Intl. Dairy-Deli- [1522]
Bakery Assn; Retailer's [454]
Bakery and Confectionery Indus'. Assn. [IO], Rijswijk, Netherlands
Bakery, Confectionery, Tobacco Workers and Grain Millers Intl. Union [24017], 10401 Connecticut Ave., Kensington, MD 20895, (301)933-8600
Bakery, Confectionery and Tobacco Workers Intl. Union [★24017]
Bakery and Confectionery Workers' Intl. Union of Am. [★24017]
Bakery Engineers; Amer. Soc. of [★447]
Bakery Equip. Manufacturers Assn. [★449]
Bakery Equip. Manufacturers Assn. [★IO]
Bakery Sanitarians; Natl. Assn. of [★2463]
Baking
   Allied Trades of the Baking Indus. [443]
   Amer. Bakers Assn. [444]
   Amer. Inst. of Baking [445]
   Amer. Pie Coun. [446]
   Amer. Soc. of Baking [447]
   Assn. of Bakery Ingredients Mfrs. [IO]
   Assn. of Canadian Biscuit Mfrs. [IO]
   Assn. of the Chocolate, Biscuit and Confectionery Indus. of the EU [IO]
   Assn. of the Chocolate and Confectionery Indus. [IO]
   Assn. of Confectionery Indus. [IO]
   Assn. of Italian Confectionery Manufacturers [IO]
   Assn. of Pastry Chefs [IO]
   Assn. of Swedish Bakeries [IO]
   Australian Soc. of Baking [IO]
   Bakers, Food and Allied Workers' Union - Ireland [IO]
   Bakery and Confectionery Indus'. Assn. [IO]
   Bakery, Confectionery, Tobacco Workers and Grain Millers Intl. Union [24017]
   Baking Assn. of Canada [IO]
   Baking Indus. Sanitation Standards Comm. [448]
   BEMA, The Baking Indus. Suppliers Assn. [449]
   BEMA, The Baking Indus. Suppliers Assn. [IO]
   Biscuit, Cake, Chocolate, and Confectionery Assn. [IO]
   Biscuit and Cracker Manufacturers Assn. [450]
   Bread Bakers Guild of Am. [451]
   Bread Bakers Guild of America [IO]
   British Confectioners' Assn. [IO]
   British Soc. of Baking [IO]
   Confectionery Manufacturers of Australasia [IO]
   Dutch Bakery Center [IO]
   Dutch Biscuit, Chocolate and Confectionery Indus. Assn. [IO]
   European Employers' Comm. of Yeast Manufacturers [IO]
   Fed. Bakers' Assn. [IO]
   Fed. Confectionery Assn. [IO]
   Fed. of Bakers [IO]
   Finnish Bakery Assn. [IO]
   German Assn. of the Bread and Pastry Indus. [IO]
   Home Baking Assn. [1520]
   Independent Bakers Assn. [452]
   Japan Biscuit Assn. [IO]
   Natl. Assn. of Bakery Products [IO]
   Natl. Assn. of Flour Distributors [1540]
   Natl. Assn. of Master Bakers - England [IO]
   Natl. Chamber of Sugar Confectionery Mfrs. [IO]
   Natl. Chocolate and Confectionery Producers' Assn. [IO]
   Natl. Confed. of Bakers [IO]
   Natl. Union of the Toast Indus. [IO]
   Quality Bakers of Am. Cooperative [453]

A star before a book entry number signifies that the name is not listed separately, but is mentioned within the entry.

Retailer's Bakery Assn. [454]
Royal Belgian Assn. of Biscuit, Chocolate, Pralines and Confectionery [IO]
Scottish Assn. of Master Bakers [IO]
Spanish Confed. of Bakery Organisations [IO]
Spanish Fed. of Confectionery Mfrs. [IO]
Sweets Global Network [IO]
Swiss Confectionery and Pastry Bakers' Assn. [IO]
Union of Swiss Chocolate Manufacturers [IO]
Wholesale Variety Bakers Assn. [455]
Worshipful Company of Bakers [IO]
Baking; Amer. Soc. of [447]
Baking Assn. of Canada [IO], Mississauga, ON, Canada
Baking Assn; Home [1520]
Baking Division of AACC Intl; Milling and [7095]
Baking Division of Amer. Assn. of Cereal Chemists; Milling and [★7095]
Baking Indus. Sanitation Standards Comm. [448], PO Box 3999, Manhattan, KS 66505-3999, (785)537-4750
Baking Industry and Teamster Labor Conf. - Address unknown since 2003.
Baking Tech; Amer. Soc. of Milling and [★6660]
Balalaika and Domra Assn. of Am. [10563], 2801 Warner St., Madison, WI 53713-2160, (608)259-9440
Balance Coun; Assoc. Air [598]
Balance Disorders Assn; Dizziness and [★15829]
Balancing Bur; Natl. Environmental [1895]
Balancing Technicians; Apprenticeship Training Prog. for [★598]
Bald-Headed Men of Am. [19373], 102 Bald Dr., Morehead City, NC 28557, (252)726-1855
Baldness
Amer. Hair Loss Assn. [14519]
Natl. Alopecia Areata Found. [16386]
Baldwin Found. of ACLU; Roger [★17085]
Balearic Assn. of Stutterers [IO], Palma de Mallorca, Spain
Balgarska Akademija na Naukite [★IO]
Bali/Indonesia ACM SIGGRAPH [IO], Bali, Indonesia
Balint Soc. [IO], London, United Kingdom
Balkan Acad. of Cosmetic Surgery [IO], Sofia, Bulgaria
Balkan Geophysical Soc. [IO], Bucharest, Romania
Balkan Physical Union [IO], Thessaloniki, Greece
Balkan Turks of America Assn. - Address unknown since 1994.
Ball Collectors Club [22551], c/o Mason Bright, Pres., 497 Fox Dr., Monroe, MI 48161, (734)241-0113
Ball Games
af2 Natl. Fan Club [24829]
Amer. Roque and Croquet Assn. [23090]
Australian Floorball Assn. [IO]
Austrian Floorball Fed. [IO]
Belgian Floorball Fed. [IO]
Brazilian Floorball Assn. [IO]
Camogie Assn. [IO]
Canadian Ball Hockey Assn. [IO]
Canadian Broomball Fed. [IO]
Canadian Unihockey Floorball Fed. [IO]
Caribbean Amer. Netball Assn. [23633]
Czech Floorball Union [IO]
Danish Floorball Fed. [IO]
Estonian Floorball Union [IO]
Fed. of Floorball of Russia [IO]
Fed. of Intl. Bandy [IO]
Finnish Floorball Fed. [IO]
Floorball Fed. of India [IO]
French Floorball Assn. [IO]
Georgian Floorball Assn. [IO]
German Floorball Assn. [IO]
Great Britain Floorball Fed. [IO]
Hong Kong Netball Assn. [IO]
Hungarian Floorball Fed. [IO]
Intl. Dodge Ball Fed. [23821]
Intl. Floorball Fed. [IO]
Intl. Senior Softball Assn. [23790]
Italian Unihockey and Floorball Assn. [IO]
Japan Floorball Assn. [IO]
Keith Bulluck Fan Club [24830]
Korea Floorball Fed. [IO]

Latvian Floorball Union [IO]
Liechtenstein Floorball Assn. [IO]
Malaysian Floorball Assn. [IO]
National Amateur Dodgeball Association [IO]
Natl. Amateur Dodgeball Assn. [23091]
Natl. High School Baseball Coaches Assn. [23119]
Natl. Paddleball Assn. [23092]
Natl. Rounders Assn. [IO]
Netherlands Floorball and Unihockey Assn. [IO]
Norwegian Bandy Federation/Floorball Sect. [IO]
Pakistan Fed. of Floorball [IO]
Polish Floorball Fed. [IO]
Rounders Coun. of Ireland [IO]
Singapore Floorball Assn. [IO]
Slovak Floorball Assn. [IO]
Slovenian Floorball Assn. [IO]
Spanish Unihockey and Floorball Assn. [IO]
Swedish Floorball Fed. [IO]
Swiss Floorball Assn. [IO]
Ukraine Floorball Fed. [IO]
U.S.A. Deaf Basketball [23136]
U.S. Broomball Assn. [23858]
U.S. Fastpitch Assn. [23794]
U.S. Floorball Assn. [23093]
U.S. Football Alliance [23442]
U.S. Futsal Fed. [23862]
U.S. High School Tennis Assn. [23912]
U.S. Indoor Soccer Assn. [23782]
U.S. Power Soccer Assn. [23783]
U.S. Tchoukball Assn. [23094]
Universal Wheelchair Football Assn. [23368]
US Club Soccer [23785]
USA Broomball [23095]
U.S.A Team Handball [23096]
Valley Intl. Foosball Assn. [1717]
Vintage Base Ball Assn. [23128]
Ball Intl. Fan Club; David [24871]
Ball Players of Am; Assn. of Professional [23105]
Ball and Roller Bearing Mfrs. Assn. [IO], Birmingham, United Kingdom
Ballard Fan Club; Florence [24888]
Ballet; Amer. Friends of the Paris Opera and [9543]
Ballet Competition; Amer. [9862]
Ballet Musicians; Intl. Guild of Symphony, Opera and [24157]
Ballet Org; British [IO]
Ballet Soc. - Defunct.
Ballet Theatre; American [★9868]
Ballet Theatre Found. [9868], 890 Broadway, New York, NY 10003-1278, (212)477-3030
Ballew Family Assn. of Am. [20789], c/o Paul Ballew, Treas., 4227 Sandy Br. Dr., Buford, GA 30519, (816)454-4218
Balloon
Aeronaut Soc. [23097]
Balloon Fed. of Am. [23098]
Highamerica Balloon Club [23099]
Inflatable Advt. Dealers Assn. [101]
Lighter-Than-Air Soc. [21460]
Balloon Club of America - Address unknown since 1995.
Balloon Fed. of Am. [23098], PO Box 400, Indianola, IA 50125, (515)961-8809
Balloon Mfrs. Assn. - Defunct.
Balloon Platoon of America [★23099]
Balloon Post Collectors Club - Address unknown since 2001.
Ballooning
Aeronaut Soc. [23097]
Balloon Fed. of Am. [23098]
British Assn. of Balloon Operators [IO]
British Balloon and Airship Club [IO]
Canadian Balloon Assn. [IO]
Highamerica Balloon Club [23099]
Lighter-Than-Air Soc. [21460]
Ballot Assn; Honest [17486]
Ballroom Dancers Assn; U.S. Amateur [★9900]
Ballroom Dancers' Fed. Intl. [IO], Kenley, United Kingdom
Ballroom and Entertainment Assn; Natl. [1317]
Balm in Gilead [13561], 701 E Franklin St., Ste. 1000, Richmond, VA 23219, (804)644-2256
Balm in Gilead [IO], New York, NY, United States
Baltic
Ars Baltica [IO]

Assn. for the Advancement of Baltic Stud. [IO]
Assn. for the Advancement of Baltic Stud. [9730]
Baltic Amer. Freedom League [17019]
Baltic Amer. Freedom League [IO]
Baltic Coun. of Australia [IO]
Baltic Women's Coun. [18978]
Found. for the Advancement of Sephardic Stud. and Culture [19181]
Joint Baltic Amer. Natl. Comm. [17020]
Joint Baltic Amer. Natl. Comm. [IO]
Latvian Canadian Cultural Centre [IO]
Lithuanian World Community [IO]
Lithuanian World Community [18979]
Lituanus Found. [10436]
United Baltic Appeal [18980]
United Baltic Appeal [IO]
World Fed. of Estonian Women's Clubs [IO]
World Fed. of Estonian Women's Clubs [18981]
Baltic Air Charter Assn. [IO], London, United Kingdom
Baltic Amer. Comm; Joint [★17020]
Baltic Amer. Freedom League [17019], PO Box 65056, Los Angeles, CA 90065-0056, (949)837-7135
Baltic Amer. Freedom League [IO], Los Angeles, CA, United States
Baltic Assn. to the United Nations [★IO]
Baltic Assn. to the United Nations [★18980]
Baltic Coun. of Australia [IO], Strathfield, Australia
Baltic Exchange [IO], London, United Kingdom
Baltic and Intl. Maritime Conf. [★IO]
Baltic and Intl. Maritime Coun. [IO], Bagsvaerd, Denmark
Baltic Marine Biologists [IO], Stockholm, Sweden
Baltic Marine Env. Protection Commn. - Helsinki Commn. [★IO]
Baltic Orthodontic Assn. [IO], Kaunas, Lithuania
Baltic Ports Org. [IO], Gdynia, Poland
Baltic States and Eurasia; NCSJ: Advocates on Behalf of Jews in Russia, Ukraine, the [17448]
Baltic States Freedom Coun. - Defunct.
Baltic Student Fed. - Address unknown since 1995.
Baltic and White Sea Conf. [★IO]
Baltic Women's Coun. [18978]
Baltic World Coun. - Defunct.
Baltimore Area Coun. on Alcoholism [★13221]
Baltimore; Assn. of Descendants of Defenders of [★21354]
Baltimore and Ohio Railroad Historical Soc. [10909], PO Box 24225, Baltimore, MD 21227-0725
Baltimore Publishers Assn. - Address unknown since 2003.
Baltimore Vegetarians [★11073]
Bama Band Fan Club - Address unknown since 1989.
Bamboo Soc; Amer. [6619]
Bamboo Soc. of India [IO], Bangalore, India
Bamboo of The Americas [4365], c/o Gib Cooper, Exec. Dir., 28446 Hunter Creek Loop, Gold Beach, OR 97444, (541)247-0835
Banana Assn; Intl. [4736]
Banana Link [IO], Norwich, United Kingdom
Banco Centroamericano de Integracion Economica [★IO]
Banco Interamericano de Desarrollo [★IO]
Banco Interamericano de Desarrollo [★17460]
Banco Interamericano de Desenvolvimento [★17460]
Banco Interamericano de Desenvolvimento [★IO]
Band Acad. of Am; Big [10565]
Band Assn; Lesbian and Gay [10638]
Band Assn; Natl. [10660]
Band Assn; Natl. Catholic [10661]
Band Assn; North Amer. Brass [10675]
Band and Choral Directors Hall of Fame; Natl. [★8926]
Band and Choral Directors Hall of Fame; Natl. High School [★8926]
Band Directors' Assn; Amer. School [8903]
Band Directors Natl. Assn; Coll. [8906]
Band Directors Natl. Assn; Women [★8934]
Band Inst; Natl. High School [★8926]
Band Instrument Mfrs; Natl. Assn. of [★2810]
Band Instrument Repair Technicians; Natl. Assn. of Professional [2818]

Reference to "IO" in place of a book number signifies that the association may be found in the 45th edition of International Organizations.

Band Saw Mfrs. Assn. of Am; Hack and [★1830]
Bandalag Starfsmanna Rikis og Baeja [★IO]
Bandaleg Islenskra Leikfelaga [★IO]
Banding Assn; Eastern Bird [7417]
Banding Assn; Inland Bird [7420]
Banding Coun; North Amer. [7421]
Bandmasters Assn; Amer. [10527]
Bandmasters' Assn; Natl. Catholic [★10661]
Bands
  Amer. Bandmasters Assn. [10527]
  Assn. of Concert Bands [10560]
  Bands of Am. [10564]
  The Grascals Fan Club [24904]
  Kappa Kappa Psi [24551]
  Lesbian and Gay Band Assn. [10638]
  Natl. Band Assn. [10660]
  Natl. Catholic Band Assn. [10661]
  Natl. High School Band Directors Hall of Fame
    [8926]
  North Amer. Brass Band Assn. [10675]
  Phi Beta Mu [24554]
  REG - The Intl. Roger Waters Fan Club [24965]
  Tau Beta Sigma [24558]
  Three Dog Night Fan Club [24984]
  Women Band Directors Intl. [8934]
  Youth Educ. in the Arts [9604]
Bands of Am. [10564], 39 W Jackson Pl., Ste. 150,
  Indianapolis, IN 46225, (317)636-2263
Bands of Am; Assn. of Concert [★10560]
Bands of Am; Lesbian and Gay [★10638]
Bands of Am; Marching [★10564]
Bands; Assn. of Concert [10560]
Bandstand Fan Club; Amer. [25024]
Bandstand Memory Club; Amer. [★25024]
Bandy Center for Baudelaire and Modern French
  Stud; W. T. [9720]
Bandy Center for Baudelaire Stud; W. T. [★9720]
Bandy Fed. of Canada/Floorball Sect. [★IO]
Bangalore ACM Chap. [IO], Bangalore, India
Bangkok ACM SIGGRAPH [IO], Bangkok, Thailand
Bangkok Shipowners and Agents Assn. [IO],
  Bangkok, Thailand
Bangladesh Acad. of Sciences [IO], Dhaka, Bang-
  ladesh
Bangladesh Amateur Athletic Assn. [IO], Dhaka,
  Bangladesh
Bangladesh Amateur Radio League [IO], Dhaka,
  Bangladesh
Bangladesh Assn. of Consulting Engineers [IO],
  Dhaka, Bangladesh
Bangladesh Assn. of Software and Info. Services
  [IO], Dhaka, Bangladesh
Bangladesh Assn. of Sports Medicine [IO], Dhaka,
  Bangladesh
Bangladesh Badminton Fed. [IO], Dhaka, Bang-
  ladesh
Bangladesh Bible Soc. [IO], Dhaka, Bangladesh
Bangladesh Centre for Advanced Stud. [IO], Dhaka,
  Bangladesh
Bangladesh Chem. Soc. [IO], Dhaka, Bangladesh
Bangladesh Cultural Assn. - Address unknown since
  1995.
Bangladesh Dental Soc. [IO], Dhaka, Bangladesh
Bangladesh Economic Assn. [IO], Dhaka, Bang-
  ladesh
Bangladesh Environmental Lawyers Assn. [IO],
  Dhaka, Bangladesh
Bangladesh Fed. of Univ. Women [IO], Dhaka,
  Bangladesh
Bangladesh Fertility Soc. [IO], Dhaka, Bangladesh
Bangladesh Garment Manufacturers and Exporters
  Assn. [IO], Dhaka, Bangladesh
Bangladesh Handball Fed. [IO], Dhaka, Bangladesh
Bangladesh Inst. of Development Stud. [IO], Dhaka,
  Bangladesh
Bangladesh Jute Spinners Assn. [IO], Dhaka, Bang-
  ladesh
Bangladesh Medical Assn. of North Am. [15162],
  4250 Hempstead Tpke., Ste. 17, Bethpage, NY
  11714-5707, (516)796-4245
Bangladesh Medical Stud. and Res. Inst. [IO],
  Dhaka, Bangladesh
Bangladesh Occupational Therapy Assn. [IO],
  Dhaka, Bangladesh
Bangladesh Protibandhi Kallyan Somity [IO], Dhaka,
  Bangladesh

Bangladesh Red Crescent Soc. [IO], Dhaka, Bang-
  ladesh
Bangladesh Rural Advancement Comm. [★IO]
Bangladesh Shishu Adhikar Forum [IO], Dhaka,
  Bangladesh
Bangladesh Soc. for Stud. of Pain [IO], Dhaka,
  Bangladesh
Bangladesh Squash Rackets Fed. [IO], Dhaka,
  Bangladesh
Bangladesh Taekwondo Fed. [IO], Dhaka, Bang-
  ladesh
Bangladesh Tea Bd. [IO], Chittagong, Bangladesh
Bangladesh Tennis Fed. [IO], Dhaka, Bangladesh
Bangladesh Unnayan Gobeshona Protishthan [★IO]
Bangladesh Unnayan Parishad [IO], Dhaka, Bang-
  ladesh
Bangladesh Weightlifting Fed. [IO], Dhaka, Bang-
  ladesh
Bangladeshi
  Amer. Inst. of Bangladesh Stud. [7996]
  Bangladesh Medical Assn. of North Am. [15162]
  Bangladesh Shishu Adhikar Forum [IO]
  Cultural Assn. of Bengal [9737]
Bangles N' Mash Intl. - Defunct.
Banjo Fraternity; Amer. [10528]
Banjoists, Mandolinists and Guitarists; Amer. Guild of
  [★10536]
Bank Admin. Inst. [467], 1 N Franklin St., Ste. 1000,
  Chicago, IL 60606-3421, (312)683-2464
Bank Audit, Control and Oper; NABAC, The Assn.
  for [★467]
Bank Auditors and Controllers; Natl. Assn. for
  [★467]
Bank Capital Markets Assn. - Address unknown
  since 1995.
Bank Directors; Amer. Assn. of [456]
Bank Equip. Suppliers Assn; Natl. Independent
  [★476]
Bank Holding Companies; Assn. of [★477]
Bank Holding Companies; Assn. of Registered
  [★477]
Bank Info. Center [468], 1100 H St. NW, Ste. 650,
  Washington, DC 20005, (202)737-7752
Bank Info. Center [IO], Washington, DC, United
  States
Bank Insurance and Securities Assn. [2151], 303 W
  Lancaster Ave., Ste. 2D, Wayne, PA 19087,
  (610)989-9047
Bank Loan and Credit Officers; Robert Morris
  Associates-Association of [★498]
Bank Marketing Assn. [★2611]
Bank Public Relations and Marketing Assn. [★2611]
Bank Securities Assn. [★2151]
Bank and Security Vault Mfrs. Assn. - Defunct.
Bank Servicers; Natl. Assn. of [★61]
Bank-Share Owners Advisory League - Defunct.
Bank Stationers Assn. [★3678]
Bank Women; Natl. Assn. of [★478]
Bankcard Holders of America - Address unknown
  since 2002.
Bankcard Services Assn. [★472]
Bankcard Services Assn. [★IO]
Bankers of Am; Savings and Community [★461]
Bankers Assn. of Am; Independent [★480]
Bankers Assn. of Am; Investment [★3523]
Bankers Assn; Amer. Indus. [★2422]
Bankers' Assn. for Finance and Trade [469], 1120
  Connecticut Ave. NW, 5th Fl., Washington, DC
  20036, (202)663-7575
Bankers' Assn. for Finance and Trade [IO],
  Washington, DC, United States
Bankers' Assn. for Foreign Trade [★IO]
Bankers' Assn. for Foreign Trade [★469]
Bankers Assn; Morris Plan [★470]
Bankers Assn; Natl. Negro [★492]
Bankers Assn. of the Republic of China [IO], Taipei,
  Taiwan
Bankers; Assn. of Reserve City [★477]
Bankers Assn. of Seoul [★IO]
Bankers Conf; Investment [★3517]
Bankers; Inst. of Foreign [★481]
Bankers; Natl. Assn. of Urban [★499]
Bankers; Natl. Coun. of Community [★461]
Bankers Political Action Comm. [★18281]
Banker's Round Table [★477]

Banking
ABA Marketing Network [2611]
African Export-Import Bank [IO]
Amer. Assn. of Bank Directors [456]
Amer. Bankers Assn. [457]
Amer. Coun. of State Savings Supervisors [458]
Amer. Escrow Assn. [1398]
Amer. League of Financial Institutions [459]
Amer. Money Mgt. Gp. [1454]
Amer. Numismatic Assn. [22724]
Amer. Numismatic Soc. [22725]
The Amer. Safe Deposit Assn. [460]
Amer. Soc. of Check Collectors [22726]
America's Community Bankers [461]
Ancient Coin Collectors Guild [22729]
Arab Bankers Assn. of North Am. [462]
Arab Bankers Assn. of North Am. [IO]
ASEAN Bankers Assn. [IO]
Assn. of Banks in Jordan [IO]
Assn. of Banks in Lebanon [IO]
Assn. of Banks in Slovakia [IO]
Association of Certified Anti-Money Laundering
  Specialists [IO]
Assn. of Certified Anti-Money Laundering Special-
  ists [463]
Assn. of Chinese Finance Professionals [1402]
Assn. of Foreign Banks [IO]
Assn. of Foreign Banks in Switzerland [IO]
Assn. of German Pfandbrief Banks [IO]
Assn. of Lithuanian Banks [IO]
Assn. for Mgt. Info. in Financial Services [464]
Assn. of Military Banks of Am. [465]
Assn. for Payment Clearing Services [IO]
Assn. of Russian Banks [IO]
ATM Indus. Assn. [466]
Australian Payments Clearing Assn. [IO]
Austrian Bankers' Assn. [IO]
Bank Admin. Inst. [467]
Bank Info. Center [468]
Bank Info. Center [IO]
Bankers' Assn. for Finance and Trade [IO]
Bankers' Assn. for Finance and Trade [469]
Banking Law Inst. [5543]
BANKPAC [18281]
Brazilian Assn. of Commercial Banks [IO]
Brazilian Banks Assn. [IO]
British Bankers' Assn. [IO]
Canadian Bankers Assn. [IO]
Chartered Inst. of Bankers - Scotland [IO]
Check Payment Systems Assn. [3678]
Colonial Coin Collectors Club [22733]
Comm. of Scottish Clearing Bankers [IO]
Conf. of State Bank Supervisors [5544]
Consumer Bankers Assn. [470]
Credit Inst. of Canada [IO]
Czech Banking Assn. [IO]
Danish Bankers Assn. [IO]
Dedicated Wooden Money Collectors [22736]
Development Bank of Southern Africa [IO]
Early Amer. Coppers [22737]
Electronic Funds Transfer Assn. [471]
Electronic Transactions Assn. [472]
Electronic Transactions Assn. [IO]
Environmental Bankers Assn. [473]
Euro Banking Assn. [IO]
European Assn. for Banking and Financial History
  [IO]
European Assn. of Cooperative Banks [IO]
European Banking Fed. [IO]
European Comm. for Banking Standards [IO]
European Mortgage Fed. [IO]
European Savings Banks Gp. [IO]
Farm Credit Coun. [474]
Financial Markets Assn. [1419]
Financial Markets Assn. - U.S.A. [475]
Financial and Security Products Assn. [476]
Financial Services Round Table [477]
Financial Women Intl. [478]
Financial Women Intl. [IO]
Finnish Bankers' Assn. [IO]
French Assn. of Banks [IO]
Global Assn. of Risk Professionals [1423]
Hellenic Amer. Bankers Assn. [479]
Hong Kong Assn. of Banks [IO]
Hungarian Banking Assn. [IO]

A star before a book entry number signifies that the name is not listed separately, but is mentioned within the entry.

Independent Community Bankers of Am. [480]
Indian Banks' Assn. [IO]
Insolvency Practitioners Assn. [IO]
Inst. of Bankers Malaysia [IO]
Inst. of Bankers in South Africa [IO]
Inst. of Bankers of Zimbabwe [IO]
Inst. of Certified Bus. Counselors [726]
Inst. of Financial Services - England [IO]
Inst. of Intl. Bankers [IO]
Inst. of Intl. Bankers [481]
Inst. of Intl. Finance [482]
Inst. of Intl. Finance [IO]
Inter-Governmental Philatelic Corp. [22829]
Intl. Assn. of Financial Engineers [1424]
Intl. Bank Note Soc. [22739]
Intl. Bankers Forum [IO]
Intl. Confed. of Agricultural Credit [IO]
Intl. Financial Services Assn. [483]
Intl. Union for Housing Finance [IO]
Irish Bankers Fed. [IO]
Irish Payment Services Org. [IO]
Italian Banking Assn. [IO]
Kenya Bankers Assn. [IO]
Korea Fed. of Banks [IO]
Latin Amer. Banking Fed. [IO]
Latin Amer. Paper Money Soc. [22741]
Liberty Seated Collectors Club [22742]
Liechtenstein Bankers Assn. [IO]
Lithuanian Numismatic Assn. [22743]
Loan Syndications and Trading Assn. [484]
Loan Syndications and Trading Assn. [IO]
Love Token Soc. [22744]
Luxembourg Bankers' Assn. [IO]
Mech. Bank Collectors of Am. [21826]
Mortgage Bankers Assn. [485]
NACHA: The Electronic Payments Assn. [486]
Natl. Assn. of Affordable Housing Lenders [487]
Natl. Assn. of Equity Source Banks [488]
Natl. Assn. of Labour Banks [IO]
Natl. Assn. of Mortgage Brokers [489]
Natl. Assn. of Mortgage Planners [490]
Natl. Assn. of Payment Professionals [1438]
Natl. Assn. of Professional Mortgage Women
  [491]
Natl. Bankers Assn. [492]
Natl. Collectors Assn. of Die Doubling [22746]
Natl. Finance Adjusters [493]
Natl. Home Equity Mortgage Assn. [494]
Natl. Inst. of Bank Mgt. [IO]
Natl. Marine Bankers Assn. [495]
Natl. Reverse Mortgage Lenders Assn. [2430]
New Zealand Bankers' Assn. [IO]
North Amer. Collectors [22747]
Northern Ireland Bankers' Assn. [IO]
Numismatic Literary Guild [22749]
Numismatics Intl. [22750]
Original Hobo Nickel Soc. [22752]
Payments Assn. of South Africa [IO]
Professional Currency Dealers Assn. [22753]
Professional Numismatists Guild [22754]
Professional Women's Appraisal Assn. [287]
Retired Western Union Employees Assn. [496]
Retirement Indus. Trust Assn. [497]
Risk Mgt. Assn. [498]
SIFIDA Investment Company [IO]
Singapore Investment Banking Assn. [IO]
Single Global Currency Assn. [IO]
Single Global Currency Assn. [17021]
Soc. of Lincoln Cent Collectors [22756]
Soc. of Medical Banking Excellence [1449]
Soc. of Paper Money Collectors [22757]
Soc. of Ration Token Collectors [22759]
Soc. of U.S. Pattern Collectors [22761]
Swiss Private Bankers Assn. [IO]
Token and Medal Soc. [22763]
Toned Coin Collectors Soc. [22764]
U.S. Mexican Numismatic Assn. [22765]
Unrecognised States Numismatic Soc. [22766]
Urban Financial Services Coalition [499]
Western Independent Bankers [500]
Western Payments Alliance [1451]
Women in Banking and Finance [IO]
World Internet Numismatic Soc. [22768]
World Proof Numismatic Assn. [22769]
Young Numismatists of Am. [22770]

Banking Advisory Network; Community [20]
Banking; American Inst. of [★457]
Banking Assn. of Panama [IO], Panama City,
  Panama
Banking Assn. South Africa [IO], Marshalltown,
  Republic of South Africa
Banking Assn. of Venezuela [IO], Caracas,
  Venezuela
Banking Benchmarking Assn; Financial Services and
  [721]
Banking; Coun. on Intl. [★483]
Banking Coun. of South Africa [★IO]
Banking Law Inst. [5543], c/o Arkansas Bar Assn.,
  2224 Cottondale Ln., Little Rock, AR 72202,
  (501)375-4606
Banking; Mid-America Coun. on Intl. [★483]
Banking Profession Political Action Comm. [★18281]
Banking; School of Mortgage [★485]
Banking and Securities Industry Comm. - Defunct.
Banking; U.S. Coun. on Intl. [★483]
Banking; Western Coun. on Intl. [★483]
BANKPAC [18281], c/o Amer. Bankers Assn., 1120
  Connecticut Ave. NW, Washington, DC 20036,
  (202)663-5129
Bankruptcy; Amer. Coll. of [5575]
Bankruptcy Assn. of England and Wales [IO], Lan-
  caster, United Kingdom
Bankruptcy Attorneys; Natl. Assn. of Consumer
  [5510]
Bankruptcy Inst; Amer. [5574]
Bankruptcy Judges; Natl. Conf. of [5909]
Bankruptcy Trustees; Natl. Assn. of [5578]
Banks
  Amer. Numismatic Assn. [22724]
  Amer. Numismatic Soc. [22725]
  Amer. Soc. of Check Collectors [22726]
  Ancient Coin Collectors Guild [22729]
  Arab Bankers Assn. of North Am. [462]
  Assn. of Argentine Banks [IO]
  Assn. of Banks in Malaysia [IO]
  Assn. of Banks in Singapore [IO]
  Assn. Commercial Banks of Latvia [IO]
  Assn. of Intl. Banks and Trust Companies in the
    Bahamas [IO]
  Assn. of Private Banks of Ecuador [IO]
  Assn. of Public and Private Banks of the
    Argentine Republic [IO]
  Australian Bankers' Assn. [IO]
  Bankers Assn. of the Republic of China [IO]
  Banking Assn. of Panama [IO]
  Banking Assn. South Africa [IO]
  Banking Assn. of Venezuela [IO]
  Banks Assn. of Turkey [IO]
  Belgian Bankers' Assn. [IO]
  Bolivian Private Bankers' Assn. [IO]
  Colonial Coin Collectors Club [22733]
  Conf. of State Bank Supervisors [5544]
  Costa Rican Banking Assn. [IO]
  Dedicated Wooden Money Collectors [22736]
  DTC Assn. [IO]
  Early Amer. Coppers [22737]
  Estonian Banking Assn. [IO]
  Foreign Banks' Assn. [IO]
  Guatemalan Banks' Assn. [IO]
  Honduran Assn. of Banking Institutions [IO]
  Inst. of Bankers in Ireland [IO]
  Inter-Governmental Philatelic Corp. [22829]
  Intl. Bank Note Soc. [22739]
  Jamaica Bankers' Assn. [IO]
  Japanese Bankers Assn. [IO]
  Latin Amer. Paper Money Soc. [22741]
  Liberty Seated Collectors Club [22742]
  Lithuanian Numismatic Assn. [22743]
  Love Token Soc. [22744]
  Mech. Bank Collectors of Am. [21826]
  Medal Collectors of Am. [22745]
  Natl. Collectors Assn. of Die Doubling [22746]
  Natl. Financial Institutions' Assn. [IO]
  North Amer. Collectors [22747]
  Numismatic Literary Guild [22749]
  Numismatics Intl. [22750]
  Original Hobo Nickel Soc. [22752]
  Pakistan Banks' Assn. [IO]
  Professional Currency Dealers Assn. [22753]
  Professional Numismatists Guild [22754]

Romanian Banking Assn. [IO]
Single Global Currency Assn. [17021]
Soc. of Lincoln Cent Collectors [22756]
Soc. of Medical Banking Excellence [1449]
Soc. of Paper Money Collectors [22757]
Soc. of Ration Token Collectors [22759]
Soc. of U.S. Pattern Collectors [22761]
Still Bank Collectors Club of Am. [21827]
Swedish Bankers' Assn. [IO]
Swiss Bankers Assn. [IO]
Thai Bankers' Assn. [IO]
Token and Medal Soc. [22763]
Toned Coin Collectors Soc. [22764]
U.S. Mexican Numismatic Assn. [22765]
Unrecognised States Numismatic Soc. [22766]
World Internet Numismatic Soc. [22768]
World Proof Numismatic Assn. [22769]
Young Numismatists of Am. [22770]
Banks Assn. of Turkey [IO], Istanbul, Turkey
Banks; Natl. Assn. of Supervisors of State [★5544]
Banks Prog. of The DRF; Natl. Temporal Bone
  [★15121]
Bank's Wives Assn; Inter-American Development
  [★19436]
Bankshot Operators; Natl. Assn. of [3667]
Bankshot Sports [★3667]
Bankwatch - Defunct.
Banner Project [★18196]
Banner Project [★IO]
Banque Canadienne de Tissue du Cerveau [★IO]
Banque Europeenne de Sange Congele de Groupes
  Rares [★IO]
Banque Interamericaine de Developpement [★IO]
Banque Interamericaine de Developpement
  [★17460]
Banquet Managers Guild [★1951]
Banquet Managers Guild [★IO]
Banshees - Defunct.
Bantam Assn; Amer. [5102]
Bantam Class Assn; Rhodes [23214]
Bantam Club; Amer. Austin/ [21568]
Bantam Club; Amer. Silkie [5109]
Bantam Soc; Amer. Dutch [5103]
Bantock Soc. [IO], Bristol, United Kingdom
Banzai Anime Klub of Alberta [IO], Edmonton, AB,
  Canada
Banzai Inst. for Biomedical Engineering and
  Strategic Info - Defunct.
BAPS Care Intl. [★18268]
BAPS Care Intl. [IO], Piscataway, NJ, United States
BAPS Charities [18268], 81 Suttons Ln., Ste. 103,
  Piscataway, NJ 08854, (732)777-1818
Baptist
  ABW Ministries [19468]
  All Africa Baptist Fellowship [IO]
  All-Ukrainian Evangelical Baptist Fellowship
    [19469]
  Amer. Baptist Historical Soc. [19470]
  Amer. Baptist Homes and Hospitals Assn. [19471]
  Amer. Baptists Concerned [20048]
  Assn. of Baptists for World Evangelism [19472]
  Assn. of Baptists for World Evangelism [IO]
  Assn. of Baptists for World Evangelism - Canada
    [IO]
  Assn. of Reformed Baptist Churches of Am.
    [19473]
  Assn. of Southern Baptist Campus Ministers
    [19474]
  Assn. of State Baptist Papers [19475]
  Assn. of Welcoming and Affirming Baptists
    [19476]
  Baptist Bible Fellowship Intl. [19477]
  Baptist Bible Fellowship Intl. [IO]
  Baptist Churches of New Zealand [IO]
  Baptist Communicators Assn. [19478]
  Baptist Convention of Hong Kong [IO]
  Baptist Historical Soc. [IO]
  Baptist Joint Comm. for Religious Liberty [19479]
  Baptist Mid-Missions [19480]
  Baptist Union of Australia [IO]
  Baptist Union of Denmark [IO]
  Baptist Women in Ministry/Folio [19481]
  Baptist World Alliance [19482]
  Baptist World Alliance [IO]
  Bd. of Intl. Ministries [IO]

Reference to "IO" in place of a book number signifies that the association may be found in the 45th edition of International Organizations.

Bd. of Intl. Ministries [19483]
Bd. of Natl. Ministries [19484]
Conservative Baptist Assn. of Am. [19485]
Continental Baptist Missions [19486]
Crusaders for Christ [20462]
Ethics and Religious Liberty Commn. of the
Southern Baptist Convention [19487]
European Baptist Fed. [IO]
European Baptist Mission [IO]
European Baptist Women's Union [IO]
Fed. des Eglises Evangeliques Baptistes de
France [IO]
Fellowship of Amer. Baptist Musicians [20430]
Gen. Assn. of Gen. Baptists [19488]
Gen. Assn. of Regular Baptist Churches [19489]
The Interchurch Center [19896]
Master's Men of the Natl. Assn. of Free Will
Baptists [19490]
Mission to the Americas [IO]
Missions Door [19491]
Natl. Assn. of Baptist Professors of Religion
[9277]
Natl. Assn. of Free Will Baptists [19492]
Natl. Baptist Convention, U.S.A. [19493]
New Zealand Baptist Missionary Soc. [IO]
Seventh Day Baptist Gen. Conf. [19494]
Seventh Day Baptist Historical Soc. [19495]
Seventh Day Baptist Missionary Soc. [19496]
Seventh Day Baptist World Fed. [19497]
Seventh Day Baptist World Fed. [IO]
Southern Baptist Found. [19498]
Southern Baptist Historical Lib. and Archives
[19499]
Strict Baptist Historical Soc. [IO]
Union Evangelica Bautista Espanola [IO]
William H. Whitsitt Baptist Heritage Soc. [19500]
Woman's Missionary Union, SBC [19501]
Women Nationally Active for Christ [19502]
WorldVenture [19503]
WorldVenture [IO]
Baptist Bible Fellowship Intl. [IO], Springfield, MO,
United States
Baptist Bible Fellowship Intl. [19477], PO Box 191,
Springfield, MO 65801-0191, (417)862-5001
Baptist Church; Master's Men of the Free Will
[★19490]
Baptist Churches of New Zealand [IO], South Auck-
land, New Zealand
Baptist Churches in the U.S.A; American [★19470]
Baptist Communicators Assn. [19478], 1715K S Ru-
therford Blvd., No. 295, Murfreesboro, TN 37130,
(615)904-0152
Baptist Convention; Historical Commn., Southern
[★19499]
Baptist Convention of Hong Kong [IO], Hong Kong,
People's Republic of China
Baptist Convention; Natl. [★19493]
Baptist Denomination in the U.S. for Foreign Mis-
sions; Gen. Convention of the [★19483]
Baptist Educational Convention; Natl. [★19493]
Baptist Foreign Mission Convention [★19493]
Baptist Foreign Mission Soc; Amer. [★19483]
Baptist Foreign Mission Soc; Woman's Amer.
[★19483]
Baptist Gen. Conf. of the U.S. and Canada; Seventh
Day [20545]
Baptist Historical Soc. [IO], Didcot, United Kingdom
Baptist Home Mission Societies; Amer. [★19484]
Baptist Home Mission Soc; Amer. [★19484]
Baptist Home Mission Soc; Conservative [★19491]
Baptist Home Mission Soc; Woman's Amer.
[★19484]
Baptist Homes and Hospitals; Assn. of [★19471]
Baptist Hospital Assn. - Address unknown since
2001.
Baptist Joint Comm. on Public Affairs [★19479]
Baptist Joint Comm. for Religious Liberty [19479],
200 Maryland Ave. NE, Washington, DC 20002,
(202)544-4226
Baptist Mid-Missions [19480], PO Box 308011,
Cleveland, OH 44130-8011, (440)826-3930
Baptist Mission; Hiawatha [★19486]
Baptist Mission of North America - Defunct.
Baptist Missionary Union; Amer. [★19483]
Baptist Missions; Gen. Coun. of Cooperating
[★19480]

Baptist Musicians; Fellowship of Amer. [20430]
Baptist Natl. Ministries; Amer. [★19484]
Baptist Peace Fellowship of North Am. [18191],
4800 Wedgewood Dr., Charlotte, NC 28210,
(704)521-6051
Baptist Peace Fellowship of North Am. [IO],
Charlotte, NC, United States
Baptist Press Assn; Southern [★19475]
Baptist Professors of Religion; Assn. of [★9277]
Baptist Professors of Religion; Natl. Assn. of [9277]
Baptist Public Relations Assn. [★19478]
Baptist Reformation Rev. [★19909]
Baptist Sociology and Anthropology Assn; Ana
[7559]
Baptist Students Concerned - Defunct.
Baptist Union of Australia [IO], Eastwood, Australia
Baptist Union of Denmark [IO], Copenhagen,
Denmark
Baptist Union and Missionary Soc. of New Zealand
[★IO]
Baptist Union of New Zealand [★IO]
Baptist Univ. Alumni Assn; Oklahoma [18917]
Baptist Univ. Alumni Assn; Ouachita [18920]
Baptist Univ. Assn. of Former Students; Wayland
[18943]
Baptist Women; Amer. [★19468]
Baptist Women in Ministry [★19481]
Baptist Women in Ministry/Folio [19481], c/o McAfee
School of Theology, 3001 Mercer Univ. Dr., Atlanta,
GA 30341
Baptist Women; Natl. Coun. of Amer. [★19468]
Baptist World Aid Australia [IO], Frenchs Forest,
Australia
Baptist World Alliance [IO], Falls Church, VA, United
States
Baptist World Alliance [19482], 405 N Washington
St., Falls Church, VA 22046, (703)790-8980
Baptistkirken i Danmark [★IO]
Baptists; Bd. of Home Missions of the Natl. Assn. of
Free Will [★19492]
Baptists Concerned; Amer. [20048]
Baptists for Evangelism in the Orient; Assn. of
[★19472]
Baptists for Life [12907], PO Box 3158, Grand
Rapids, MI 49501, (616)257-6800
Baptists for Scouting; Assn. of [12995]
Baqura [★20095]
Bar Assn; Amer. [5475]
Bar Assn; Canadian [IO]
Bar Assn. Center on Children and the Law; Amer.
[11555]
Bar Assn. Center for Professional Responsibility;
Amer. [5476]
Bar Assn. Commn. on Homelessness and Poverty;
Amer. [12286]
Bar Assn. Criminal Justice Sect; Amer. [5922]
Bar; Assn. of the Customs [★5659]
Bar Assn; Energy [5683]
Bar Assn; Fed. [5492]
Bar Assn; Fed. Communications [5580]
Bar Assn; Fed. Power [★5683]
Bar Assn; Found. of the Fed. [5937]
Bar Assn; Guam [6024]
Bar Assn; Hispanic Natl. [5496]
Bar Assn; La Raza Natl. [★5496]
Bar Assn; Lawyer-Pilots [5539]
Bar Assn. for Local Govt. and the Public Ser. [IO],
Birmingham, United Kingdom
Bar Assn; NACCA [★6328]
Bar Assn; Natl. [5515]
Bar Assn; Natl. Asian Pacific Amer. [5947]
Bar Assn; Natl. Crime Victim [6349]
Bar Assn; Natl. Italian Amer. [5952]
Bar Assn. Sect. of Dispute Resolution; Amer. [5449]
Bar Assn; Traffic Court Prog. of the Amer. [6310]
Bar Assn. Young Lawyers Div; Amer. [5477]
Bar Associations; Natl. Conf. of Women's [5518]
Bar/Bat Mitzvah Pilgrimage World Zionist Org. -
Defunct.
Bar Code Alliance; Indus. [★338]
Bar Code Coun; Hea. Indus. [★14080]
Bar Coding
Natl. Assn. of Campus Card Users [3707]
Bar Coun. [★IO]
Bar Counsel; Natl. Org. of [5953]

Bar Entertainment and Dance Assn. [IO], Stockport,
United Kingdom
Bar Examiners; Natl. Conf. of [5950]
Bar Executives; Natl. Assn. of [5948]
Bar Executives; Natl. Conf. of [★5948]
Bar Found; Amer. [5923]
Bar Found; Fellows of the Amer. [5494]
Bar Mills; Steel [★2732]
Bar Presidents; Natl. Conf. of [5516]
Bar-Related Title Insurers; Natl. Assn. of [2204]
Bar-Related Title Insurers; Natl. Conf. of [★2204]
Bar Secretaries; Natl. Conf. of [★5948]
Bar Spouses; Natl. Assn. of Bench and [5509]
Bar and Tavern Owners; Natl. Assn. of [205]
BARA: The Assn. for Robotics and Automation [IO],
Coventry, United Kingdom
Baraga Assn. and Archives; Bishop [19583]
Barb Landers Fund [★8399]
Barbados
Barbados Blackbelly Sheep Assn. Intl. [5198]
Barbados Tourism Authority [24234]
Natl. Assn. of Barbados Organizations [9731]
Barbados Amateur Weightlifting Assn. [IO], Christ
Church, Barbados
Barbados Assn. of Medical Practitioners [IO], St.
Michael, Barbados
Barbados Assn. of Off. Professionals [IO], Bridge-
town, Barbados
Barbados Badminton Assn. [IO], Bridgetown,
Barbados
Barbados Blackbelly Sheep Assn. Intl. [5198], 815
Bell Hill Rd., Cobden, IL 62920, (618)893-4568
Barbados Bd. of Tourism [★24234]
Barbados Cancer Soc. [IO], St. Michael, Barbados
Barbados Chamber of Commerce and Indus. [IO],
St. Michael, Barbados
Barbados Customs Brokers and Clerks Assn. [IO],
St. Michael, Barbados
Barbados Dental Assn. [IO], St. Michael, Barbados
Barbados Employers' Confed. [IO], St. Michael,
Barbados
Barbados Family Planning Assn. [IO], St. Michael,
Barbados
Barbados Hotel and Tourism Assn. [IO], Bridgetown,
Barbados
Barbados Labour Party [IO], Bridgetown, Barbados
Barbados Lawn Tennis Assn. [★IO]
Barbados Mfrs'. Assn. [IO], St. Michael, Barbados
Barbados Museum and Historical Soc. [IO], St.
Michael, Barbados
Barbados Natl. Org. For The Disabled [IO], Bridge-
town, Barbados
Barbados Natl. Trust [IO], St. Michael, Barbados
Barbados Olympic Assn. [IO], St. Michael, Barbados
Barbados Physical Therapy Assn. [IO], St. Michael,
Barbados
Barbados Sailing Assn. [IO], Bridgetown, Barbados
Barbados Secondary Teachers' Union [IO], St.
Michael, Barbados
Barbados Sport Medicine Assn. [IO], St. Michael,
Barbados
Barbados Squash Rackets Assn. [IO], Bridgetown,
Barbados
Barbados Taekwondo Assn. [IO], Christ Church,
Barbados
Barbados Tennis Assn. [IO], Bridgetown, Barbados
Barbados Tourism Authority [24234], 800 2nd Ave.,
New York, NY 10017, (212)986-6516
Barbados Union of Teachers [IO], St. Michael,
Barbados
Barbados Workers' Union [IO], St. Michael,
Barbados
Barbara Bain Intl. [IO], River Falls, WI, United States
Barbara Bain Intl. [24730], c/o Ms. Terry S. Bowers,
Pres., 603 N Clark St., River Falls, WI 54022-1404
Barbara Bush Found. for Family Literacy [8786],
1201 15th St. NW, Ste. 420, Washington, DC
20005, (202)955-6183
Barbara Eden Intl. Fan Club [★24731]
Barbara Eden's Official Fan Club [24731], PO Box
5556, Sherman Oaks, CA 91403
Barbara Pym Soc. [9635], c/o Ellen Miller, 145
Indian Hill Rd., Carlisle, MA 01741, (978)287-4776
Barbecue Assn; Natl. [1542]
Barbecue Indus. Assn. [★1679]

A star before a book entry number signifies that the name is not listed separately, but is mentioned within the entry.

Barbed Wire
  Antique Barbed Wire Soc. [21969]
  New Mexico Barbed Wire Collectors Assn.
    [22091]
Barbed Wire Collectors Assn; New Mexico [22091]
Barbeque Assn; Hearth, Patio and [1679]
Barbeque Cookers Assn; Intl. [22570]
Barbeque Soc; Kansas City [22573]
Barber Boards of Am; Natl. Assn. of [1083]
Barber Boards; Natl. Assn. of [★1083]
Barber Coin Collector Soc. - Address unknown since
  1999.
Barber Mfrs. Assn; Natl. Beauty and [★1086]
Barber Shop Quartet Singing in Am; Soc. for the
  Preservation and Encouragement of [10704]
Barbers, Beauticians and Allied Indus. Intl. Assn.
  [★24061]
Barbers and Beauticians of America; Associated
  Master [★1079]
Barbers and Beauticians of America; Hair Intl./As-
  sociated Master [1079]
Barbers Company [IO], London, United Kingdom
Barbers Examiners of Am; Natl. Assn. of Boards of
  [★1083]
Barbershop Harmony Soc. [★10704]
Barbie Lovers Club [★22391]
BARCO Graphics User Assn. [★6761]
Bardin Inst; Brandeis - [8687]
Barefoot Club; Amer. [23974]
BAREMA [IO], Oxford, United Kingdom
Bargaining Assn; Raisin [4759]
Barh Koh Env. and Sustainable Development Aid
  [IO], Toronto, ON, Canada
Bariatric Medicine; Amer. Bd. of [15573]
Bariatric Physicians; Amer. Soc. of [15575]
Bariatric Surgery; Amer. Soc. for [16569]
Bariloche Found. [IO], Bariloche, Argentina
Barisal Young Men's Christian Association [IO], Bar-
  isal, Bangladesh
Bark Producers Assn; Natl. [★1651]
Bark and Soil Producers Assn; Natl. [★1651]
Barley Assn; Amer. Malting [4303]
Barley Foods Coun; Natl. [1751]
Barley Growers Assn; Natl. [4663]
Barley Improvement Assn; Malting [★4303]
Barley and Malt Inst. - Defunct.
Barne- og ungdomsrevmatikergruppe [★IO]
Barney Family Historical Assn. [20790], 7503 Ridge-
  brook Dr., Springfield, VA 22153
Barnham/Barnum Bunch - Address unknown since
  1995.
Barnsley Chamber of Commerce and Indus. [IO],
  Barnsley, United Kingdom
Baromedical Nurses Assn. [15471], PO Box 531190,
  San Diego, CA 92153, (303)918-9686
Baronial Order of Magna Charta and the Military
  Order of Crusades [10096], 14115 41st Ave. N,
  Plymouth, MN 55446
Baronial Order of Magna Charta and the Military
  Order of Crusades [IO], Wyncote, PA, United
  States
Baronial Order of Runnemede [★IO]
Baronial Order of Runnemede [★10096]
Barons Booster Club; Cleveland [★25001]
Baroque Found; Beyond [★9559]
Baroque Literary/Arts Center; Beyond [9559]
Barra Found. - Defunct.
Barracuda/Cuda Owners Club; Plymouth [21763]
Barre Granite Assn. [3691], PO Box 481, Barre, VT
  05641, (802)476-4131
Barrel and Drum Assn; Natl. [★994]
Barrel Futurities of Am. [23495], c/o Ross Wright,
  Sec.-Treas., 5650 N Broadway, Norman, OK
  73069, (405)364-0274
Barrel Horse Assn; Natl. [23506]
Barrel Jumping Assn; Michigan [★23743]
Barrel Jumping Assn; U.S. [23743]
Barrel Racers Assn; Natl. Christian [23507]
Barrel Racing Assn; Amer. [23492]
Barrel Racing Assn; Amer. Cmpt. [23493]
Barrel Racing Assn; Intl. [23500]
Barren Found. - Defunct.
Barrie Constr. Assn. [IO], Barrie, ON, Canada
Barrier Islands Coalition - Defunct.
Barrier Paper Mfrs. Assn. - Defunct.

Barristers' Wives; Natl. [★5509]
Barry All The Time - Address unknown since 2007.
Barry Bostwick Fan Club - Address unknown since
  2008.
Barry Morse Fan Club - Address unknown since
  1989.
Bars; Order of the Stars and [★20729]
Bartenders' Assn; Amer. [192]
Bartenders Guild; United Kingdom [IO]
Bartenders Intl. Union; Hotel and Restaurant
  Employees and [★24095]
Bartenieff Inst. of Movement Stud; Laban/ [9891]
Barter Assn; Natl. Commodity and [18411]
Barty Found; Billy [13104]
Barzona Breeders Assn. of Am. [4254], 480 Jason
  Rd., Fort Collins, CO 80524, (970)498-9306
BASE Assn; U.S. [23647]
Baseball
  Amateur Baseball Assn. of Thailand [IO]
  Amateur Baseball Umpires' Assn. [23798]
  Amer. Amateur Baseball Cong. [23100]
  Amer. Baseball Coaches Assn. [23101]
  American Baseball Coaches Association [IO]
  Amer. Baseball Found. [23102]
  Amer. Legion Baseball [23103]
  Assn. of Minor League Umpires [23104]
  Assn. of Professional Ball Players of Am. [23105]
  Atlantic Coast Conf. [23806]
  Australian Baseball Fed. [IO]
  Austrian Baseball-Softball Fed. [IO]
  Babe Ruth Baseball/Softball [23106]
  Babe Ruth Birthplace/Sports Legends at Camden
    Yards [23107]
  Bahamas Baseball Fed. [IO]
  Baseball Canada [IO]
  Baseball Fed. of Armenia [IO]
  Baseball Fed. of Georgia [IO]
  Baseball Fed. of Islamic Republic of Iran [IO]
  Baseball Fed. of Kenya [IO]
  Baseball Ireland [IO]
  Baseball Nova Scotia [IO]
  Baseball and Softball Assn. of the Republic of
    Moldova [IO]
  Baseball Softball Assn. of Slovenia [IO]
  Baseball and Softball Cook Islands Assn. [IO]
  Baseball and Softball Fed. of the Republic of Ka-
    zakhstan [IO]
  Baseball Writers Assn. of Am. [3099]
  Belarus Baseball and Softball Fed. [IO]
  Big East Conf. [23807]
  Big Ten Conf. [23808]
  British Baseball Fed. [IO]
  British Virgin Islands Baseball Fed. [IO]
  Brunei Amateur Softball and Baseball Assn. [IO]
  Bulgarian Baseball Fed. [IO]
  Cameroon Baseball and Softball Fed. [IO]
  Canadian Fed. of Amateur Baseball [IO]
  Chinese Baseball Assn. [IO]
  Confed. of European Baseball [IO]
  Cosmic Baseball Assn. [23108]
  Coun. of Ivy Gp. Presidents [23817]
  Croatian Baseball Assn. [IO]
  Cyprus Amateur Baseball Fed. [IO]
  Czech Baseball Fed. [IO]
  Danish Baseball Softball Fed. [IO]
  Eastern Collegiate Hockey Assn. [23485]
  Estonian Baseball and Softball Fed. [IO]
  Federacion Argentina de Beisbol [IO]
  Federacion Boliviana de Beisbol y Softbol [IO]
  Federacion Costarricense de Beisbol Aficionado
    [IO]
  Federacion Cubana de Beisbol [IO]
  Federacion Ecuatoriana de Beisbol [IO]
  Federacion Hondurena de Beisbol Aficionado [IO]
  Federacion Mexicana de Beisbol [IO]
  Federacion Nacional de Beisbol de Guatemala
    [IO]
  Federacion Nicaraguense de Beisbol Asociada
    [IO]
  Federacion Panamena de Beisbol Aficionado [IO]
  Federacion Salvadorena de Beisbol [IO]
  Federacion Venezolana de Beisbol [IO]
  Fed. of Baseball of Chile [IO]
  Fed. of Baseball Malaysia [IO]
  Fed. Baseball Softball Ukraine [IO]

  Fed. Malienne de Base-Ball et de Softball [IO]
  Fed. Togolaise de Base-ball et Soft-ball [IO]
  Fed. Tunisienne de Baseball et Softball [IO]
  Fiji Islands Baseball Assn. [IO]
  George Khoury Assn. of Baseball Leagues
    [23109]
  Ghana Baseball and Softball Assn. [IO]
  Hellenic Amateur Baseball Fed. [IO]
  Hungarian Natl. Baseball and Softball Fed. [IO]
  Indonesia Amateur Baseball and Softball Fed. [IO]
  Intl. Baseball Fed. [IO]
  Intl. League of Professional Baseball Clubs
    [23110]
  Israel Assn. of Baseball [IO]
  Jamaica Baseball Assn. [IO]
  Koninklijke Belgische Baseball en Softball Feder-
    atie [IO]
  Korean Baseball Assn. [IO]
  Leo Lassen Legacy Proj. [24789]
  Lesotho Baseball and Softball Assn. [IO]
  Liberia Baseball and Softball Assn. [IO]
  Lithuanian Baseball Assn. [IO]
  Little League Baseball and Softball [IO]
  Little League Baseball and Softball [23111]
  Little League Found. [23112]
  Luxembourg Baseball Fed. [IO]
  Major League Baseball [23113]
  Major League Baseball Players Alumni Assn.
    [23114]
  Major League Baseball Players Assn. [24018]
  Mongolian Natl. Fed. of Baseball [IO]
  Morocco Baseball Fed. [IO]
  Namibia Baseball Assn. [IO]
  Natl. Amateur Baseball Fed. [23115]
  Natl. Assn. of Intercollegiate Athletics [23835]
  Natl. Assn. of Professional Baseball Leagues
    [23116]
  National Association of Professional Baseball
    Leagues [IO]
  Natl. Baseball Cong. [23117]
  Natl. Baseball Hall of Fame and Museum [23118]
  Natl. Cap and Patch Assn. [22080]
  Natl. Christian Coll. Athletic Assn. [23837]
  Natl. Collegiate Athletic Assn. [23838]
  Natl. High School Baseball Coaches Assn.
    [23119]
  Natl. Junior Baseball League [23120]
  Natl. Junior Coll. Athletic Assn. [23843]
  Natl. Pitching Assn. [23121]
  Natl. Semi-Professional Baseball Assn. [23122]
  Negro Leagues Baseball Museum [23123]
  Netherlands Antillean Baseball Fed. [IO]
  New Zealand Baseball Fed. [IO]
  Nigerian Baseball and Softball Assn. [IO]
  North Amer. Sports Fed. [23065]
  Pacific 10 Conf. [23847]
  Pakistan Fed. Baseball and Softball [IO]
  Papua New Guinea Baseball Fed. [IO]
  Philippine Amateur Baseball Assn. [IO]
  Polish Baseball and Softball Fed. [IO]
  Pony Baseball and Softball [23124]
  Professional Baseball Athletic Trainers Soc.
    [23125]
  Republic of the Marshall Islands Baseball Fed.
    [IO]
  Reviving Baseball in Inner Cities [13512]
  Romanian Baseball and Softball Fed. [IO]
  Singapore Baseball and Softball Assn. [IO]
  Slovak Baseball Fed. [IO]
  Soc. for Amer. Baseball Res. [23126]
  Southeastern Conf. [23851]
  Southern Conf. [23852]
  Sri Lanka Amateur Baseball and Softball Assn.
    [IO]
  Swedish Baseball and Softball Fed. [IO]
  Uganda Baseball and Softball Assn. [IO]
  U.S. Collegiate Athletic Assn. [23859]
  U.S. Collegiate Sports Coun. [23860]
  U.S.A. Baseball [23127]
  Uzbekistan Baseball Fed. [IO]
  Vintage Base Ball Assn. [23128]
  World Umpires Assn. [24019]
  World Umpires Association [IO]
  Zambia Softball and Baseball Assn. [IO]
  Zimbabwe Baseball and Softball Assn. [IO]

Reference to "IO" in place of a book number signifies that the association may be found in the 45th edition of International Organizations.

Baseball Assn; Natl. Beep [23350]
Baseball; Boys [★23124]
Baseball Canada [IO], Ottawa, ON, Canada
Baseball Coaches; Amer. Assn. of Coll. [★23101]
Baseball Cong; Amer. [★23100]
Baseball Fed. of Armenia [IO], Yerevan, Armenia
Baseball Fed. of Georgia [IO], Tbilisi, Georgia
Baseball Fed. of Islamic Republic of Iran [IO], Te-hran, Iran
Baseball Fed. of Kenya [IO], Nairobi, Kenya
Baseball Fed; U.S. [★23127]
Baseball Hall of SHAME - Defunct.
Baseball in Inner Cities; Reviving [13512]
Baseball Ireland [IO], Cabinteely, Ireland
Baseball; Natl. Comm. for Amateur [★23127]
Baseball Nova Scotia [IO], Halifax, NS, Canada
Baseball Players Assn; Major League [24018]
Baseball; Pony and Colt Boys [★23124]
Baseball and Softball Assn. of the Republic of Moldova [IO], Chisinau, Moldova
Baseball Softball Assn. of Slovenia [IO], Ljubljana, Slovenia
Baseball and Softball Cook Islands Assn. [IO], Raro-tonga, Cook Islands
Baseball and Softball Fed. of the Republic of Kaza-khstan [IO], Almaty, Kazakhstan
Baseball Writers Assn. of Am. [3099], PO Box 610611, Bayside, NY 11361, (718)767-2582
Baseball Writers Assn; Natl. Collegiate [3135]
Basel Action Network [18797], c/o Earth Economics, 122 S Jackson, Ste. 320, Seattle, WA 98104, (206)652-5555
Basel Action Network [IO], Seattle, WA, United States
Basel Club - Address unknown since 1986.
Basenji Club of Am. [22225], c/o Anne L. Graves, Sec., 5102 Darnell, Houston, TX 77096-1404
Bases Proj; Foreign [17609]
Bashkir Curly Registry; Amer. [4812]
Basic Acrylic Monomer Mfrs. [800], 17260 Vannes Ct., Hamilton, VA 20158, (540)751-2093
Basic Acrylic Monomer Mfrs. Assn. [★800]
Basic Education
  Girlstart [8468]
  Learning First Alliance [8273]
  Natl. Assn. for the Educ. of Young Children [8069]
  Phonics Inst. [9046]
  Room to Read [12053]
Basic Human Needs Assn. [IO], Tokyo, Japan
Basic and Traditional Food Assn. - Defunct.
Basic Youth Conflicts; Inst. in [★13489]
Basingstoke Conservation Volunteers [IO], Basing-stoke, United Kingdom
Basketball
  Assyrian Chaldean Athletics of North Am. [23062]
  Atlantic Coast Conf. [23806]
  Basketball Nova Scotia [IO]
  Basketball Scotland [IO]
  Big East Conf. [23807]
  Big Ten Conf. [23808]
  British Columbia Wheelchair Basketball Soc. [IO]
  Calgary Minor Basketball Assn. [IO]
  Canada Basketball [IO]
  Canadian Wheelchair Basketball Assn. [IO]
  Continental Basketball Assn. [23129]
  Coun. of Ivy Gp. Presidents [23817]
  Danish Basketball Fed. [IO]
  Dr. James Naismith Basketball Found. [IO]
  Eastern Collegiate Hockey Assn. [23485]
  England Basketball [IO]
  FIBA Oceania [IO]
  Hong Kong Basketball Assn. [IO]
  Intl. Assn. of Approved Basketball Officials [IO]
  Intl. Assn. of Approved Basketball Officials [23130]
  Intl. Basketball Fed. [IO]
  Metropolitan Intercollegiate Basketball Assn. [23131]
  Mini-Basketball England [IO]
  Naismith Memorial Basketball Hall of Fame [23132]
  Natl. Assn. of Bankshot Operators [3667]
  Natl. Assn. of Basketball Coaches [23133]
  Natl. Assn. of Intercollegiate Athletics [23835]
  Natl. Basketball Assn. [23134]

  Natl. Basketball Athletic Trainers Assn. [23135]
  Natl. Basketball Players Assn. [24192]
  Natl. Christian Coll. Athletic Assn. [23837]
  Natl. Collegiate Athletic Assn. [23838]
  Natl. Junior Coll. Athletic Assn. [23843]
  Natl. Wheelchair Basketball Assn. [23354]
  North Amer. Sports Fed. [23065]
  Pacific 10 Conf. [23847]
  Schweiz Basketball-Verband [IO]
  Southeastern Conf. [23851]
  Southern Conf. [23852]
  U.S.A. Deaf Basketball [23136]
  U.S. Basketball Writers Assn. [23137]
  U.S. Collegiate Athletic Assn. [23859]
  U.S. Collegiate Sports Coun. [23860]
  U.S.A. Basketball [23138]
  Women's Basketball Coaches Assn. [23139]
  Women's Natl. Basketball Players Assn. [23140]
Basketball Assn. of Am. [★23134]
Basketball Assn; Amer. [★23134]
Basketball Assn; Natl. Wheelchair [23354]
Basketball Assn. of the U.S.A; Amateur [★23138]
Basketball Fed. of the U.S.A. - Defunct.
Basketball Found; Dr. James Naismith [IO]
Basketball Hall of Fame; Naismith Memorial [23132]
Basketball League; Natl. [★23134]
Basketball; Natl. Assn. of Intercollegiate [★23835]
Basketball Nova Scotia [IO], Halifax, NS, Canada
Basketball Players Assn; Natl. [24192]
Basketball Scotland [IO], Edinburgh, United Kingdom
Basketmakers' Assn. [IO], Cheltenham, United Kingdom
BASO - Assn. for Cancer Surgery [IO], London, United Kingdom
Basque
  Basque Educational Org. [9732]
  Soc. of Basque Stud. in Am. [9733]
  Soc. of Basque Stud. in Am. [IO]
Basque Cultural Center [★9732]
Basque Educational Org. [9732], PO Box 31861, San Francisco, CA 94131-0861
B.A.S.S. [★23410]
Bass Anglers Sportsman Soc. [23410], PO Box 10000, Lake Buena Vista, FL 32830, (334)409-5329
Bass; Intl. Inst. for the String [★10625]
Bass Res. Found. - Address unknown since 2000.
Basset Hound Club of Am. [22226], c/o Bobby Brandt, Corresponding Sec., 11401 Gamache Dr., Anchorage, AK 99516, (907)346-1849
Bassett Family Org; Lorin Elias [20982]
Bass'n Gal - Defunct.
Bastard Nation: The Adoptee Rights Org. [11237], PO Box 1469, Edmond, OK 73083-1469, (415)704-3166
Bat Conservation Intl. [5296], PO Box 162603, Austin, TX 78716, (512)327-9721
Bat Conservation Intl. [IO], Austin, TX, United States
Bat Conservation Trust - England [★IO]
Bat Conservation Trust - UK [IO], London, United Kingdom
Bataan and Corregidor; Amer. Defenders of [21386]
Bataan Relief Org. [★21262]
Bater Surname Org. [20791]
Bates Assn. of Great Britain [★IO]
Bates Assn. for Vision Educ. [IO], London, United Kingdom
Batey Relief Alliance [IO], Brooklyn, NY, United States
Batey Relief Alliance [12835], PO Box 300565, Brooklyn, NY 11230-5656, (917)627-5026
Bath Assn; Natl. Kitchen and [2271]
Bath Enclosure Mfrs. Assn. [3062], c/o Christopher E. Birch, Exec. Dir., PO Box 4730, Topeka, KS 66604, (785)273-0393
Bath Inst. for Rheumatic Diseases [IO], Bath, United Kingdom
Bathroom Mfrs. Assn. [IO], Stoke-On-Trent, United Kingdom
Baton Twirling
  Canadian Baton Twirling Fed. [IO]
  Global Alliance of Natl. Baton Twirling and Majorette Associations [23141]
  Natl. Baton Twirling Assn. Intl. [23142]

  U.S. Twirling Assn. [23143]
Baton Twirling Assn. Intl; Natl. [23142]
Baton Twirling and Majorette Associations; World Fed. of [★23141]
Battalion Assn; 86th Chem. Mortar [21368]
Battalion Assn; 526th Armored Infantry [21382]
Battalion Assn; 704th Tank Destroyer [21383]
Batten Disease Support and Res. Assn. [15310], 166 Humphries Dr., Reynoldsburg, OH 43068, (740)927-4298
Batten Disease Support and Res. Assn. - Australia [IO], Killarney Vale, Australia
Batterers Anonymous - Beyond Abuse [12023], c/o Sojourner Truth House, Inc., PO Box 080319, Milwaukee, WI 53208, (414)643-4799
Batteries
  Battery Assn. of Japan [IO]
  European Portable Battery Assn. [IO]
  Portable Rechargeable Battery Assn. [501]
Battery Assn. of Japan [IO], Tokyo, Japan
Battery Coun. Intl. [IO], Chicago, IL, United States
Battery Coun. Intl. [380], 401 N Michigan Ave., 24th Fl., Chicago, IL 60611-4267, (312)644-6610
Battery Vehicle Soc. [IO], Dorchester, United Kingdom
Batting Inst; Natl. Cotton [1094]
Battle of the Bulge; Veterans of the [21412]
Battle of Ormoc Bay Assn. [21390], c/o Mr. William M. Dallam, Sec.-Treas., 117 Tuscarora St., Har-risburg, PA 17104
Battlefield Campaign; Civil War [★4380]
Battlefield Coalition; Save the [10061]
Battlefield Commissions; Natl. Order of [21237]
Battleship Assn; Amer. [21210]
Battleship Assn; USS North Carolina [21411]
Baubiologie and Ecology; Intl. Inst. for [4513]
Bauddha-Grantha-Prakasana Samitiya [★IO]
Baudelaire and Modern French Stud; W. T. Bandy Center for [9720]
Baudelaire Stud; W. T. Bandy Center for [★9720]
Baudreau Graveline Genealogical Assn; Urbain [21074]
Bauersachs Genealogical Soc. - Address unknown since 1995.
Baum, L. Frank
  Intl. Wizard of Oz Club [9668]
Bautz Descendants - Defunct.
Bavarian Acad. of Fine Arts [IO], Munich, Germany
Bavarian Acad. of Sciences and Humanities [IO], Munich, Germany
Bavarian Festival Soc. - Defunct.
Bay Area Cryonics Soc. [★14073]
Bay Area Independent Publishers Assn. [3212], PO Box E, Corte Madera, CA 94976, (415)456-0247
Bay Area Photographica Assn. [★10851]
Bay Area Photographica Assn. [★IO]
Bay Area Physicians for Human Rights [12218], PO Box 14188, San Francisco, CA 94114-0188
Bay Area Printmakers [★1762]
Bay Horse Soc. of North Am; Cleveland [4871]
Bay of Pigs
  Bay of Pigs Veterans Assn. [20717]
Bay of Pigs Veterans Assn. [20717], 1821 SW 9th St., Miami, FL 33135, (305)649-4719
Bay of Plenty Miniature Horse Club [IO], Tauranga, New Zealand
Bay Tiger Class Assn. - Defunct.
Bayerische Akademie der Schonen Kunste [★IO]
Bayerische Akademie der Wissenschaften [★IO]
Bayou Fan Club - Defunct.
Bazelon Center for Mental Hea. Law; Judge David L. [17123]
BBB Wise Giving Alliance [17309], 4200 Wilson Blvd., Ste. 800, Arlington, VA 22203-1838, (703)276-0100
BBB Wise Giving Alliance [IO], Arlington, VA, United States
BBM Bur. of Measurement [★IO]
BBM Canada [IO], Toronto, ON, Canada
B.C. Assn. of Clinical Counsellors [IO], Victoria, BC, Canada
BC Assn. of Social Workers [IO], Vancouver, BC, Canada
BC Innovation Coun. [IO], Vancouver, BC, Canada
B.C. Road Builders and Heavy Constr. Assn. [IO], Burnaby, BC, Canada

A star before a book entry number signifies that the name is not listed separately, but is mentioned within the entry.

BC Salmon Farmers Assn. [IO], Vancouver, BC, Canada
BC Wheelchair Sports Assn. [IO], Vancouver, BC, Canada
The BCA [★1122]
BCA-Credit Info. [★552]
BCM Intl. [19508], PO Box 249, Akron, PA 17501-0249, (717)859-6404
BCM Intl. [IO], Akron, PA, United States
BCPC [IO], Alton, United Kingdom
BCR Natl. Laboratory - Defunct.
BDA Intl. [★554]
BDA Intl. [★IO]
BDPA Info. Tech. Thought Leaders [★62]
Be Active, Be Emancipated [IO], Zagreb, Croatia
Be and See Inspirations [IO], Lagos, Nigeria
Be Somebody, Be Yourself Inst. [12342]
Beach Boys
　Friends of Dennis Wilson [24892]
Beach Boys Britain Fan Club [IO], Lutterworth, United Kingdom
Beach Boys Fan Club [24846], 631 N Stephanie St., No. 546, Henderson, NV 89014
Beach Boys Freaks United [★24846]
Beach Educ. Advocates for Culture, Hea., Env. and Safety [10761], PO Box 530702, Miami Shores, FL 33153, (305)620-7090
Beach Movie Fan Club - Defunct.
Beach Preservation Association; American Shore and [4352]
Beach Ultimate Gp. Portugal [IO], Parede, Portugal
Beaches Documentation Center; Free [★10763]
B.E.A.C.H.E.S. Found. Inst. [★10761]
Beaches Info. Center; Free [★10763]
Beaches; Natl. Assn. of Amusement Parks, Pools, and [★1303]
BeachFront USA [10762], PO Box 328, Moreno Valley, CA 92556, (949)240-3183
Beacon Coll. - Defunct.
Beacon for Freedom of Expression [IO], Oslo, Norway
The Bead Soc. [★21975]
Bead Soc. of Los Angeles [21975], PO Box 241874, Los Angeles, CA 90024-9674
Bead and Stone Importers Assn. - Defunct.
Beadle Bumble Fund - Address unknown since 1995.
Beadwork; Center for the Stud. of [6443]
Beagle Club of Am; Natl. [22314]
Beale Cipher Assn. [6848]
Beall Family Assn. [20792], 30 SE Gilham, Portland, OR 97215-1366
Beam Bottle and Specialties Clubs; Natl. Assn. of Jim [★21889]
BEAMA Capacitor Manufacturer's Assn. [IO], London, United Kingdom
BEAMA Installation [IO], London, United Kingdom
BEAMA Metering and Communications Assn. [IO], London, United Kingdom
BEAMA Transmission and Distribution Assn. [IO], London, United Kingdom
Beamtenbund und Tarifunion [★IO]
Bean Advisory Bd; California Dry [4713]
Bean Assn. [★1503]
Bean Assn; Amer. Soy [4304]
Bean Assn; Southern [21057]
Bean Coun; Natl. Dry [★4769]
Bear Assn; Intl. [★5325]
Bear Biology Assn. [★5325]
Bear Biology Assn. [★IO]
Bear Butte Intl. Alliance [19446], PO Box 4232, Sturgis, SD 57785
Bear Center; Appalachian [★5293]
Bear Center; North Amer. [5350]
Bear Club; Coney Island Polar [★23888]
Bear Club - U.S.A; Polar [23888]
Bear Club - Winter Swimmers; Polar [★23888]
Bear Found; Great [5322]
Bear Res. and Mgt; Intl. Assn. for [5325]
Bear Res. and Mgt; Intl. Assn. for [★5325]
Bear Soc; North Amer. [5351]
Bear Survival Alliance - Defunct.
Bear Trust Intl. [5297], PO Box 4006, Missoula, MT 59806-4006, (406)523-7779
Bear Trust Intl. [IO], Missoula, MT, United States

Beard Found; James [11125]
Bearded Collie Club of Am. [22227], c/o Carol Sirrine, Corresponding Sec., 5652 Clinton Ave. S, Minneapolis, MN 55419, (612)866-9014
Beardies and Others Needing Emissaries [11369], 6357 Chestnut Pkwy., Flowery Branch, GA 30542
Bearing Distributors Assn; Anti-Friction [★2007]
Bearing Engineers Comm; Annular [★1991]
Bearing Engineers Comm; Roller [★1991]
Bearing Inst; Cast Bronze [★2008]
Bearing Mfrs. Assn; Amer. [1991]
Bearing Mfrs. Assn; Anti-Friction [★1991]
Bearing Specialists; Assn. of [★2007]
Bearing Specialists Assn. [2007], 800 Roosevelt Rd., Bldg. C, Ste. 312, Glen Ellyn, IL 60137, (630)858-3838
Bearings
　Japan Bearing Indus. Assn. [IO]
Bearings for Re-Establishments - Defunct.
Bears Intl; Polar [5367]
Bears Intl. Soc. - Defunct.
Beatles
　Beatles Connection [24785]
　Beatles Fan Club: Good Day Sunshine [24786]
　Beatles Fans Unite [24787]
　Working Class Hero Beatles Club [24788]
Beatles Connection [24785]
Beatles Fan Club: Good Day Sunshine [24786], 315 Derby Ave., Orange, CT 06477, (203)891-8131
Beatles Fans Unite [24787], c/o Maureen A. Lowry, Pres., PO Box 50123, Cicero, IL 60804-0123
Beatles Info. Center [IO], Stockholm, Sweden
Beatles Live Peace in Pepperland [★24788]
Beatles Now [★IO]
Beatles Peace Followers [★24788]
Beatles Unlimited [IO], Nieuwegein, Netherlands
Beaton Inst. of Cape Breton Stud. [IO], Sydney, NS, Canada
Beatrice M. Murphy Found. - Address unknown since 1995.
Beaudet Surname Org. - Address unknown since 2002.
Beaumont Soc. [IO], London, United Kingdom
Beauticians and Allied Indus. Intl. Assn; Barbers, [★24061]
Beauticians of America; Associated Master Barbers and [★1079]
Beauticians of America; Hair Intl./Associated Master Barbers and [1079]
Beautiful Music Friends - Address unknown since 2008.
Beauty Aids Inst; Amer. Hea. and [1841]
Beauty Assn; Amer. [★1086]
Beauty Assn; United [★1086]
Beauty and Barber Mfrs. Assn; Natl. [★1086]
Beauty and the Beast Intl. - Defunct.
Beauty; Coalition for Scenic [★4606]
Beauty Culture; Natl. Coun. of Boards of [★5616]
Beauty Culturists' League; Natl. [1084]
Beauty; Natl. Coalition to Preserve Scenic [★4606]
Beauty Salon Chain Assn; Natl. [★1081]
Beauty Without Cruelty U.S.A. - Defunct.
Beaux Arts Alliance [9558], 119 E 74th St., New York, NY 10021, (212)639-9120
Beaux-Arts Architects; Soc. of [★7963]
Beaux-Arts Inst. of Design [★7963]
Beaver Ambassador Club [22946], c/o Iris Schmidt, Membership Dir., 3590 Round Bottom Rd., Cincinnati, OH 45244-3026, (760)946-0581
Beaver Water World [IO], Westerham, United Kingdom
Because I Love You: The Parent Support Gp. [13293], PO Box 2062, Winnetka, CA 91396-2062, (818)884-8242
Becket Fund for Religious Liberty [18509], 1350 Connecticut Ave. NW, Ste. 605, Washington, DC 20036, (202)955-0095
Beckman Center for History of Chemistry; Arnold and Mabel [★10101]
Beckwith-Wiedemann Support Network [14442], c/o Bruce Beckwith, MD, 88 Brookside, Missoula, MT 59802
Bed-and-Breakfast Assn; Natl. [1954]
Bed and Breakfast League [★1936]
Bed and Breakfast League/Sweet Dreams and Toast [1936]

Bed & Breakfast Reservation Services World-Wide - Defunct.
Bed Fed; Natl. [IO]
Bedding and Furniture Law Officials; Intl. Assn. of [5823]
Bedding Mfrs; Better Sleep Coun. of the Natl. Assn. of [★16424]
Bedding Mfrs; Natl. Assn. of [★1974]
Bedding Plants Intl. - Defunct.
Bedford Systems Users Group - Defunct.
Bedfordshire and Luton Chamber of Commerce, Training and Enterprise [IO], Luton, United Kingdom
Bedlington Terrier Club of America - Defunct.
Bedside Network; Veterans [12116]
Bee Improvement and Bee Breeders' Assn. [IO], Northampton, United Kingdom
Bee Industries Assn. - Defunct.
Bee Res. Assn. [★IO]
Beecham Soc; Sir Thomas [10697]
Beecher Stowe Center; Harriet [9655]
Beef Breeders Intl; Red Poll [★4243]
Beef Cattle Soc; Buelingo [4259]
Beef Coun; Natl. [★5023]
Beef Export Fed; Canada [IO]
Beef Friesian Soc. [★4270]
Beef Improvement Fed. [7091], c/o Dr. Twig Marston, Exec. Dir., 222 Weber Hall, Manhattan, KS 66506, (785)532-5428
Beef Info. Centre [IO], Mississauga, ON, Canada
Beef Promotion and Res. Bd. [★4261]
Beefalo Assn; Amer. [★4123]
Beefalo Assn; World [★4123]
Beefalo Breeders Registry; Intl. [★4123]
Beefmaster Breeders United [4255], 6800 Park 10 Blvd., Ste. 290 W, San Antonio, TX 78213, (210)732-3132
Beefmaster Breeders Universal [★4255]
Beekeepers Assn. of New Zealand; Natl. [IO]
Beekeepers Associations; Natl. Fed. of [★502]
Beekeeping
　Amer. Apitherapy Soc. [13614]
　Amer. Beekeeping Fed. [502]
　Amer. Honey Producers Assn. [4163]
　Apiary Inspectors of Am. [4164]
　Eastern Apicultural Soc. of North Am. [4165]
Beekeeping Extension Soc. [IO], Zaria, Nigeria
Beep Baseball Assn; Natl. [23350]
Beer
　Amer. Breweriana Assn. [21828]
　Amer. Soc. of Brewing Chemists [6670]
　Beer Inst. [197]
　Brewers Assn. [198]
　Brewery Collectibles Club of Am. [21979]
　Brewmeisters Anonymous [21829]
　Eastern Coast Breweriana Assn. [21830]
　Intl. Bird Beer Label Assn. [21491]
　Master Brewers Assn. of the Americas [6544]
　Minnesota Beer Wholesalers Assn. [204]
　Natl. Assn. of Breweriana Advt. [22074]
　North Amer. Brewers' Assn. [208]
Beer Assn. of Executives of Am; State [★204]
Beer Assn. Executives of Am; Wholesale [★204]
Beer Assn. Secretaries; Natl. Assn. of State [★204]
Beer Can Collectors of Am. [★21979]
Beer Distributors Secretaries of Am. [★204]
Beer Inst. [197], 122 C St. NW, Ste. 350, Washington, DC 20001, (202)737-2337
Beer Trade Assn; Home Wine and [202]
Beer Wholesalers' Assn. of Am; Natl. [★207]
Beer Wholesalers Assn; Minnesota [204]
Beer Wholesalers Assn; Natl. [207]
Beer Wholesalers Secretaries; State [★204]
Beet Growers Assn; Amer. Sugar [5226]
Beet Growers Assn; Red River Valley Sugar [5229]
Beet Sugar Assn; U.S. [1567]
Beet Sugar Development Found. [5227], 800 Grant St., Ste. 300, Denver, CO 80203, (303)832-4460
Beet Sugar Indus; U.S. [★1567]
Beet Technologists; Amer. Soc. of Sugar [7089]
Beethoven in Am; Friends of [★9803]
Beethoven Assn. - Defunct.
Beethoven Found. [★22709]
Beethoven Soc; Amer. [9803]
Beethoven Studies; Ira F. Brilliant Center for [★9803]

Reference to "IO" in place of a book number signifies that the association may be found in the 45th edition of International Organizations.

Before Columbus Found. [10416], 655-13th St., Ste. 302, Oakland, CA 94612, (510)268-9775
Befrienders Intl. [★IO]
Befrienders Intl. Samaritans Worldwide [★IO]
Befrienders Worldwide [IO], Ewell, United Kingdom
BEGIN - Defunct.
Beginnings Institute [★19698]
Begonia Soc; Amer. [22482]
Begonia Soc; California [★22482]
Behavior; Amer. Veterinary Soc. of Animal [16780]
Behavior Anal; Midwestern Assn. for [★6526]
Behavior Consultants; Assn. of Trial [★6524]
Behavior Genetics Assn. [14498], c/o Stacey Cherny, Treas., Univ. of Colorado, Inst. for Behavioral Genetics, 447 UCB, Boulder, CO 80309-0447
Behavior Genetics Assn. [IO], Boulder, CO, United States
Behavior; Inst. for the Advancement of Human [13735]
Behavior Soc; Animal [7861]
Behavior Therapy and Res. Soc. - Address unknown since 1990.
Behavioral Disorders; Coun. for Children with [9140]
Behavioral Hea. Directors; Natl. Assn. of County [14708]
Behavioral Hea. Nurses and Associates; Consortium of [15474]
Behavioral Healthcare Assn; Amer. Managed [★24088]
Behavioral Healthcare Mgt; Assn. of [15191]
Behavioral Healthcare; Natl. Coun. for Community [15223]
Behavioral Medicine
  Acad. of Behavioral Medicine Res. [13732]
  Acad. of Psychosomatic Medicine [16195]
  Albert Ellis Inst. [16197]
  Amer. Acad. of Psychoanalysis and Dynamic Psychiatry [16101]
  Amer. Acad. of Psychotherapists [16198]
  Amer. Acad. of Sleep Medicine [16418]
  Amer. Art Therapy Assn. [16199]
  Amer. Assn. of LifeStyle Counselors [14053]
  Amer. Assn. for Marriage and Family Therapy [16200]
  Amer. Assn. for Medical Chronobiology and Chronotherapeutics [13751]
  Amer. Assn. of Mental Hea. Professionals in Corrections [15186]
  Amer. Assn. of Psychiatric Technicians [16069]
  Amer. Correctional Hea. Services Assn. [14715]
  Amer. Dance Therapy Assn. [16203]
  Amer. Gp. Psychotherapy Assn. [16204]
  Amer. Mental Hea. Alliance [15188]
  Amer. Mental Hea. Counselors Assn. [15189]
  Amer. Music Therapy Assn. [16205]
  Amer. Psychoanalytic Assn. [16102]
  Amer. Psychopathological Assn. [16190]
  Amer. Psychosomatic Soc. [16196]
  Amer. Psychotherapy Assn. [16207]
  Amer. Soc. for the Advancement of Pharmacotherapy [16134]
  Amer. Soc. of Psychoanalytic Physicians [16104]
  Amer. Veterinary Soc. of Animal Behavior [16780]
  Assoc. Professional Sleep Societies [16422]
  Assn. for Advancement of Psychoanalysis (of the Karen Horney Psychoanalytic Inst. and Center) [16105]
  Assn. for the Advancement of Psychotherapy [16210]
  Assn. for Behavioral and Cognitive Therapies [13733]
  Assn. of Behavioral Healthcare Mgt. [15191]
  Assn. for Child Psychoanalysis [16106]
  Assn. of Medicine and Psychiatry [16081]
  Assn. for Psychoanalytic Medicine [16107]
  Australasian Soc. for Behavioural Hea. and Medicine [IO]
  Autism Res. Inst. [13721]
  Behavior Genetics Assn. [14498]
  Better Sleep Coun. [16424]
  Community Guidance Ser. [16214]
  Devereux Natl. [13734]
  Dyspraxia Found. County Durham [IO]
  Equine Assisted Growth and Learning Assn. [16216]

Global Alliance of Mental Illness Advocacy Networks [15200]
Global and Regional Asperger Syndrome Partnership [15325]
Hispanic Neuropsychological Soc. [15388]
Inst. for the Advancement of Human Behavior [13735]
Inst. for the Development of Emotional and Life Skills/National Inst. of Relationship Enhancement [15201]
Inst. for Expressive Anal. [16217]
Inst. for Labor and Mental Health [15202]
Intercontinental Fed. of Behavioral Optometry [15719]
Intl. Alliance for Child and Adolescent Mental Hea. and Schools [15204]
Intl. Assn. for Cognitive Psychotherapy [16218]
Intl. Assn. for Relational Psychoanalysis and Psychotherapy [16108]
Intl. Assn. for Voice Movement Therapy [13711]
Intl. Center for Attitudinal Healing [15206]
Intl. Comm. Against Mental Illness [15207]
Intl. Fed. for Psychoanalytic Educ. [9028]
Intl. REST Investigators Soc. [16220]
Intl. Soc. for Adaptive Behavior [6533]
Intl. Soc. of Behavioral Medicine [IO]
Intl. Soc. for Comparative Psychology [16152]
Intl. Soc. for Developmental Psychobiology [16153]
Intl. Soc. of Psychiatric Genetics [14502]
Intl. Transactional Anal. Assn. [16089]
Karen Horney Clinic [16109]
Mental Hea. Am. [15211]
Mental Hea. Corporations of Am. [13736]
Mental Res. Inst. [13737]
Milton H. Erickson Found. [16221]
Natl. Acad. of Neuropsychology [16158]
Natl. Alliance of Advocates for Buprenorphine Treatment [16511]
Natl. Alliance on Mental Illness [15214]
Natl. Assn. for the Advancement of Psychoanalysis [16110]
Natl. Assn. for Drama Therapy [16222]
Natl. Assn. for Poetry Therapy [16223]
Natl. Assn. of Psychiatric Hea. Systems [16091]
Natl. Assn. for Rural Mental Hea. [15217]
Natl. Assn. of State Mental Hea. Prog. Directors [15219]
Natl. Assn. of Therapeutic Schools and Programs [13738]
Natl. Educ. Alliance for Borderline Personality Disorder [15224]
Natl. Inst. for the Clinical Application of Behavioral Medicine [13739]
Natl. Latino Behavioral Hea. Assn. [15227]
Natl. Psychological Assn. for Psychoanalysis [16111]
Org. for Autism Res. [13728]
Postgraduate Center for Mental Hea. [16227]
Psychohistory Forum [16113]
Psychotherapy Network [16228]
Rabbinic Center for Res. and Counseling [16229]
Radical Caucus in Psychiatry [16092]
Recovery, Inc. [16230]
Sigmund Freud Archives [16115]
Sleep Res. Soc. [16429]
Social Psychiatry Res. Inst. [16094]
Social/Vocational Rehabilitation Clinic [16231]
Soc. of Behavioral Medicine [13740]
Soc. for Behavioral Neuroendocrinology [13741]
Soc. of Biological Psychiatry [16095]
Soc. for Developmental and Behavioral Pediatrics [15898]
Soc. for Pediatric Psychology [16175]
Soc. of Professors of Child and Adolescent Psychiatry [16096]
Soc. for the Sci. Stud. of Religion [20506]
Soc. for the Stud. of Ingestive Behavior [13742]
Somatics Soc. [12363]
Swedish Soc. of Behavioral Medicine [IO]
Treatment and Res. Advancements Assn. for Personality Disorder [15235]
U.S.A. Transactional Anal. Assn. [13743]
U.S. Psychiatric Rehabilitation Assn. [16336]
William Glasser Inst. [16233]

World Assn. of Cultural Psychiatry [16097]
World Assn. for Infant Mental Hea. [16098]
World Assn. of Sleep Medicine [16430]
World Assn. for Social Psychiatry [16099]
World Fed. for Mental Hea. [15237]
Zero to Three: Natl. Center for Infants, Toddlers and Families [13944]
Behavioral Medicine Res; Acad. of [13732]
Behavioral Neuropsychology Special Interest Group - Defunct.
Behavioral Pediatrics; Soc. for [★15898]
Behavioral Pediatrics; Soc. for Developmental and [15898]
Behavioral Pharmacology Soc. - Address unknown since 2002.
Behavioral Res. Coun. - Defunct.
Behavioral Sci. Computing; Special Interest Gp. for Social and [★6542]
Behavioral Sci; Natl. Inst. for Applied [★8415]
Behavioral Sciences
  Acad. of Behavioral Medicine Res. [13732]
  Acad. of Psychosomatic Medicine [16195]
  Albert Ellis Inst. [16197]
  Amer. Acad. of Psychoanalysis and Dynamic Psychiatry [16101]
  Amer. Acad. of Psychotherapists [16198]
  Amer. Acad. of Sleep Medicine [16418]
  Amer. Art Therapy Assn. [16199]
  Amer. Assn. of Anger Mgt. Providers [15185]
  Amer. Assn. of Behavioral and Social Sciences [6522]
  Amer. Assn. of Behavioral Therapists [13744]
  Amer. Assn. of LifeStyle Counselors [14053]
  Amer. Assn. for Marriage and Family Therapy [16200]
  Amer. Assn. for Medical Chronobiology and Chronotherapeutics [13751]
  Amer. Assn. of Mental Hea. Professionals in Corrections [15186]
  Amer. Assn. of Psychiatric Technicians [16069]
  Amer. Correctional Hea. Services Assn. [14715]
  Amer. Dance Therapy Assn. [16203]
  Amer. Gp. Psychotherapy Assn. [16204]
  Amer. Institutes for Res. in the Behavioral Sciences [6523]
  Amer. Mental Hea. Alliance [15188]
  Amer. Mental Hea. Counselors Assn. [15189]
  Amer. Music Therapy Assn. [16205]
  Amer. Psychoanalytic Assn. [16102]
  Amer. Psychological Assn. - Hea. Psychology Div. [16130]
  Amer. Psychopathological Assn. [16190]
  Amer. Psychosomatic Soc. [16196]
  Amer. Psychotherapy Assn. [16207]
  Amer. Soc. for the Advancement of Pharmacotherapy [16134]
  Amer. Soc. of Psychoanalytic Physicians [16104]
  Amer. Soc. of Trial Consultants [6524]
  Amer. Veterinary Soc. of Animal Behavior [16780]
  Animal Behavior Mgt. Alliance [7860]
  Armenian Behavioral Sci. Assn. [6525]
  Armenian Behavioral Sci. Assn. [IO]
  Assoc. Professional Sleep Societies [16422]
  Assn. for Advanced Training in the Behavioral Sciences [8878]
  Assn. for Advancement of Psychoanalysis (of the Karen Horney Psychoanalytic Inst. and Center) [16105]
  Assn. for the Advancement of Psychotherapy [16210]
  Assn. for Africanist Anthropology [6408]
  Assn. for Behavior Anal. [6526]
  Assn. of Behavioral Healthcare Mgt. [15191]
  Assn. for the Behavioral Sciences and Medical Educ. [6527]
  Assn. for Child Psychoanalysis [16106]
  Assn. of Latina and Latino Anthropologists [6410]
  Assn. of Management/International Assn. of Mgt. [6528]
  Association of Management/International Association of Management [IO]
  Assn. of Medicine and Psychiatry [16081]
  Assn. for Psychoanalytic Medicine [16107]
  Assn. for Res. in Personality [7543]
  The Assn. for the Stud. of Play [10858]

A star before a book entry number signifies that the name is not listed separately, but is mentioned within the entry.

Assn. for the Treatment of Sexual Abusers [6529]
Awake In Am. [18601]
Because I Love You: The Parent Support Gp. [13293]
Behavior Genetics Assn. [14498]
Better Sleep Coun. [16424]
Community Guidance Ser. [16214]
Consciousness-Based Educ. Assn. [9029]
Consortium of Social Sci. Associations [7649]
European Assn. for Behavioural and Cognitive Therapies [IO]
Evolutionary Anthropology Soc. [6416]
Fed. of Behavioral, Psychological, and Cognitive Sciences [6530]
Global Alliance of Mental Illness Advocacy Networks [15200]
Hispanic Neuropsychological Soc. [15388]
Hong Kong Soc. for Quality of Life [IO]
Human Behavior and Evolution Soc. [6531]
Human Resources Res. Org. [6532]
Inst. for the Development of Emotional and Life Skills/National Inst. of Relationship Enhancement [15201]
Inst. for Expressive Anal. [16217]
Inst. for Labor and Mental Health [15202]
Intercontinental Fed. of Behavioral Optometry [15719]
Intl. Alliance for Child and Adolescent Mental Hea. and Schools [15204]
Intl. Assn. of Animal Behavior Consultants [7864]
Intl. Assn. for Cognitive Psychotherapy [16218]
Intl. Assn. for Relational Psychoanalysis and Psychotherapy [16108]
Intl. Behavioral Neuroscience Soc. [15408]
Intl. Center for Attitudinal Healing [15206]
Intl. Comm. Against Mental Illness [15207]
Intl. Fed. for Psychoanalytic Educ. [9028]
Intl. Inst. of Forecasters [7106]
Intl. Org. for the Stud. of Gp. Tensions [10189]
Intl. REST Investigators Soc. [16220]
Intl. Soc. for Adaptive Behavior [6533]
Intl. Soc. for Adaptive Behavior [IO]
Intl. Soc. for Behavioral Nutrition and Physical Activity [13745]
Intl. Soc. for Comparative Psychology [16152]
Intl. Soc. for Developmental Psychobiology [16153]
Intl. Soc. for Dialogical Sci. [7544]
Intl. Soc. for Human Ethology [6534]
Intl. Soc. for Human Ethology [IO]
Intl. Soc. of Neuro-Semantics [16396]
Intl. Soc. for Neuroimmunomodulation [15395]
Intl. Soc. of Psychiatric Genetics [14502]
Intl. Soc. for Quality-of-Life Stud. [7997]
International Society for Quality-of-Life Studies [IO]
International Society for Research on Aggression [IO]
Intl. Soc. for Res. on Aggression [6535]
Intl. Soc. for Self and Identity [7546]
Intl. Soc. for the Stud. of Behavioural Development [IO]
Intl. Transactional Anal. Assn. [16089]
Japanese Assn. for Behavior Anal. [IO]
Karen Horney Clinic [16109]
Laban/Bartenieff Inst. of Movement Stud. [9891]
Mental Hea. Am. [15211]
Mental Res. Inst. [13737]
Milton H. Erickson Found. [16221]
Natl. Acad. of Neuropsychology [16158]
Natl. Alliance on Mental Illness [15214]
Natl. Assn. for the Advancement of Psychoanalysis [16110]
Natl. Assn. for Drama Therapy [16222]
Natl. Assn. for Poetry Therapy [16223]
Natl. Assn. of Psychiatric Hea. Systems [16091]
Natl. Assn. for Rural Mental Hea. [15217]
Natl. Assn. of State Mental Hea. Prog. Directors [15219]
Natl. Character Lab. [6536]
Natl. Coun. of State Sociological Associations [7665]
Natl. Educ. Alliance for Borderline Personality Disorder [15224]
Natl. Latino Behavioral Hea. Assn. [15227]

Natl. Psychological Assn. for Psychoanalysis [16111]
Northamerican Assn. of Masters in Psychology [9030]
Ophelia Proj. [13509]
Organizational Behavior Teaching Soc. [6537]
Postgraduate Center for Mental Hea. [16227]
Psychohistory Forum [16113]
Psychometric Soc. [16166]
Psychotherapy Network [16228]
Rabbinic Center for Res. and Counseling [16229]
Radical Caucus in Psychiatry [16092]
Recovery, Inc. [16230]
Sigmund Freud Archives [16115]
Sleep Res. Soc. [16429]
Social Psychiatry Res. Inst. [16094]
Social/Vocational Rehabilitation Clinic [16231]
Soc. for the Advancement of Behavior Anal. [6538]
Soc. for the Anthropology of North Am. [6425]
Soc. for Behavioral Neuroendocrinology [13741]
Soc. of Biological Psychiatry [16095]
Soc. of Consulting Psychology [16172]
Soc. for Consumer Psychology [17344]
Soc. for Cross-Cultural Res. [10230]
Soc. for Evolutionary Anal. in Law [6539]
Soc. for Evolutionary Anal. in Law [IO]
Soc. for the History of Psychology [7548]
Soc. for Human Performance in Extreme Environments [6540]
Soc. for Pediatric Psychology [16175]
Soc. of Professors of Child and Adolescent Psychiatry [16096]
Soc. of Psychological Hypnosis [16178]
Soc. for the Psychological Stud. of Ethnic Minority Issues [16179]
Soc. for Quantitative Analyses of Behavior [6541]
Soc. for the Sci. Stud. of Religion [20506]
Soc. for Theoretical and Philosophical Psychology [16186]
Soc. for Vocational Psychology [7551]
Somatics Soc. [12363]
Special Interest Gp. on Cmpt. and Human Interaction [6542]
U.S.A. Transactional Anal. Assn. [13743]
U.S. Psychiatric Rehabilitation Assn. [16336]
William Glasser Inst. [16233]
World Assn. of Cultural Psychiatry [16097]
World Assn. for Infant Mental Hea. [16098]
World Assn. of Sleep Medicine [16430]
World Assn. for Social Psychiatry [16099]
World Fed. for Mental Hea. [15237]
Zero to Three: Natl. Center for Infants, Toddlers and Families [13944]
Behavioral Sciences; Assn. for Advanced Training in the [8878]
Behavioral Sciences; NTL Inst. for Applied [8415]
Behavioral and Social Sciences Survey Comm. - Defunct.
Behavioral Teratology Soc; Neuro [15356]
Behavioral Therapists; Natl. Assn. of Cognitive- [16193]
Behavioral Toxicology Soc. [16661], Wayne State Univ., 5057 Woodward Ave., 7th Fl., Detroit, MI 48202
Behavioral Treatment of Sexual Abusers; Assn. for the [★6529]
Behavioral Treatment of Sexual Aggression; Assn. for the [★6529]
Behaviorists for Social Action [★18607]
Behaviorists for Social Responsibility [18607], c/o Dr. Mark Mattaini, Chm., 1040 W Harrison St., Chicago, IL 60607, (312)996-4629
Behavioural and Cognitive Psychotherapies; British Assn. for [IO]
Behcet's Assn; Amer. [★13746]
Behcet's Found; Amer. [★13746]
Behcet's Syndrome
  Amer. Behcet's Disease Assn. [13746]
Beijing ACM SIGGRAPH [IO], Beijing, People's Republic of China
Beirut Veterans of Am. [21287], c/o Debra Reisert, 8219 Sara Ln., Georgetown, IN 47122
Bela Lugosi Soc. - Defunct.
Belarus
  Belarusian Inst. of Arts and Sci. [9734]

North Amer. Assn. for Belarusian Stud. [9735]
Belarus Athletic Fed. [IO], Minsk, Belarus
Belarus Baseball and Softball Fed. [IO], Minsk, Belarus
Belarus Draughts Fed. [IO], Minsk, Belarus
Belarus Sailing Union [IO], Minsk, Belarus
Belarus Tennis Assn. [IO], Minsk, Belarus
Belarusian Acad. of Sciences [★IO]
Belarusian-Amer. Assn. in the U.S.A. - Address unknown since 2002.
Belarusian Assn. of Consulting Engineers [IO], Minsk, Belarus
Belarusian Canadian Alliance [IO], Toronto, ON, Canada
Belarusian Cong. Comm. of America - Address unknown since 2003.
Belarusian Dance Sport Fed. [IO], Minsk, Belarus
Belarusian Fed. of Air Sports [IO], Minsk, Belarus
Belarusian Inst. of Arts and Sci. [IO], Jamaica, NY, United States
Belarusian Inst. of Arts and Sci. [9734], 166-34 Gothic Dr., Jamaica, NY 11432, (201)244-0776
Belarusian Lib. Assn. [IO], Minsk, Belarus
Belarusian Physical Soc. [IO], Minsk, Belarus
Belarusian Republican Taekwondo Fed. [IO], Minsk, Belarus
Belarusian Sci. Rheumatological Soc. [IO], Minsk, Belarus
Belarusian Students Assn. [IO], Minsk, Belarus
Belarussian
  Amer. Belarussian Relief Org. [12828]
  Belarusian Inst. of Arts and Sci. [9734]
  Belarusian Inst. of Arts and Sci. [IO]
  North Amer. Assn. for Belarusian Stud. [IO]
  North Amer. Assn. for Belarusian Stud. [9735]
Belarussian Badminton Fed. [IO], Minsk, Belarus
Belarussian Physiological Soc. [IO], Minsk, Belarus
Beldon Fund [4535], 99 Madison Ave., 8th Fl., New York, NY 10016, (212)616-5600
Belgian
  Amer. Bouvier des Flandres Club [22188]
  Belgian Amer. Assn. [18982]
  Belgian Amer. Chamber of Commerce in the U.S. [24235]
  Belgian Amer. Educational Found. [9736]
  Belgian Sheepdog Club of Am. [22228]
  Belgian Tourist Off. [24236]
Belgian Aerospace Indus. Assn. [IO], Brussels, Belgium
Belgian Aikikai [IO], Bevel, Belgium
Belgian Amer. Assn. [18982]
Belgian Amer. Chamber of Commerce in the U.S. [24235], c/o FORTIS Bank, 153 E 53rd St., 27th Fl., New York, NY 10022, (212)340-6271
Belgian Amer. Educational Found. [9736], 195 Church St., New Haven, CT 06510, (203)777-5765
Belgian Assn. of Baby and Dietetic Food [IO], Brussels, Belgium
Belgian Assn. for Documentation [IO], Brussels, Belgium
Belgian Assn. for Osteoporosis Patients [IO], Antwerp, Belgium
Belgian Assn. of Plastics Converters [★IO]
Belgian Assn. of Plastics and Rubber Converters [IO], Brussels, Belgium
Belgian Assn. of Regional Anesthesia [IO], Leuven, Belgium
Belgian Assn. for the Stud. of the Liver [IO], Leuven, Belgium
Belgian Assn. for the Stud. of Obesity [IO], Brussels, Belgium
Belgian Assn. of Teachers of the Alexander Technique [IO], Groot-Bijgaarden, Belgium
Belgian Aviation History Assn. [IO], Temse, Belgium
Belgian Bankers' Assn. [IO], Brussels, Belgium
Belgian Begonia Growers Assn. - Defunct.
Belgian Blue Breeders; Amer. [4213]
Belgian Blue Breeders Assn; Amer. [★4213]
Belgian Bone Club [IO], Liege, Belgium
Belgian Brewers [IO], Brussels, Belgium
Belgian Catholic Scouts [★IO]
Belgian Center for Corrosion Stud. [IO], Brussels, Belgium
Belgian Centre for Music Documentation [IO], Brussels, Belgium

Reference to "IO" in place of a book number signifies that the association may be found in the 45th edition of International Organizations.

Belgian Chamber of Inventors [IO], Brussels, Belgium

Belgian Clayshooting Fed. [IO], Schilde, Belgium

Belgian Cockpit Assn. [IO], Brussels, Belgium

Belgian Confed. of the Dairy Indus. [IO], Leuven, Belgium

Belgian Cricket Fed. [IO], Antwerp, Belgium

Belgian Dance Sport Fed. [IO], Houthalen, Belgium

Belgian Direct Marketing Assn. [IO], Brussels, Belgium

Belgian Draft Horse Corp. of Am. [4865], PO Box 335, Wabash, IN 46992, (260)563-3205

Belgian Draft Horses; Amer. Assn. of Importers and Breeders of [★4865]

Belgian Electrotechnical Comm. [IO], Brussels, Belgium

Belgian EMG and Clinical Neurophysiology Soc. [IO], Brussels, Belgium

Belgian Engineers in North America - Defunct.

Belgian Fed. of Bus and Coach Operators [IO], Brussels, Belgium

Belgian Fed. of Distributors [IO], Brussels, Belgium

Belgian Fed. of the Footwear Indus. [IO], Brussels, Belgium

Belgian Fed. of Psychologists [IO], Brussels, Belgium

Belgian Fed. of Univ. Graduate Women [IO], Alsemberg, Belgium

Belgian Finer Foods Coun. - Defunct.

Belgian Floorball Fed. [IO], Iddergem, Belgium

Belgian Flying Disc Fed. [IO], Brussels, Belgium

Belgian Franchise Fed. [IO], Brussels, Belgium

Belgian Fur Trade Fed. [IO], Brussels, Belgium

Belgian Geological Soc. [IO], Brussels, Belgium

Belgian Geosynthetics Soc. [IO], Brussels, Belgium

Belgian Hare Club; Amer. [5131]

Belgian Heart League [IO], Brussels, Belgium

Belgian Hypertension Comm. [IO], Esneux, Belgium

Belgian League Against Epilepsy [IO], Gent, Belgium

Belgian-Luxembourg Amer. Stud. Assn. [IO], Brussels, Belgium

Belgian Luxembourg Chamber of Commerce in Great Britain [IO], Hessle, United Kingdom

Belgian Malinois Club; Amer. [22186]

Belgian Mathematical Soc. [IO], Brussels, Belgium

Belgian Medical Informatics Assn. [IO], Baisy-Thy, Belgium

Belgian Natl. Comm. for UNICEF [IO], Brussels, Belgium

Belgian Natl. Taekwondo Union [IO], Brussels, Belgium

Belgian Natl. Tourist Off. [★24236]

Belgian Neurological Soc. [IO], Liege, Belgium

Belgian Operations Res. Soc. [IO], Diepenbeek, Belgium

Belgian Org. for Fish Producers [★IO]

Belgian Packaging Inst. [IO], Zellik-Asse, Belgium

Belgian Pain Soc. [IO], Leuven, Belgium

Belgian Paralympic Comm. [IO], Brussels, Belgium

Belgian Periodical Press Fed. [IO], Brussels, Belgium

Belgian Pharmaceutical Indus. Assn. [IO], Brussels, Belgium

Belgian Physical Soc. [IO], Brussels, Belgium

Belgian Pool Billiard Fed. [IO], Westende, Belgium

Belgian Publishers' Assn. [IO], Brussels, Belgium

Belgian Risk Mgt. Assn. [IO], Brussels, Belgium

Belgian Royal Soc. of Rheumatology [IO], Brussels, Belgium

Belgian Sheepdog Club of Am. [22228], c/o Shelly Brosnan, Corresponding Sec., 3499 Marthaler Rd. NE, Woodburn, OR 97071-9524

Belgian Sheepdogs
 Belgian Sheepdog Club of Am. [22228]

Belgian Soc. of Cardiology [IO], Brussels, Belgium

Belgian Soc. of Clinical Neurophysiology [IO], Liege, Belgium

Belgian Soc. of Digestive Endoscopy [IO], Brussels, Belgium

Belgian Soc. of Fundamental and Clinical Physiology and Pharmacology [IO], Liege, Belgium

Belgian Soc. of Gerontology and Geriatrics [IO], Wetteren, Belgium

Belgian Soc. of Human Genetics [IO], Brussels, Belgium

Belgian Soc. for Microscopy [IO], Antwerp, Belgium

Belgian Teleworking Assn. [IO], Brussels, Belgium

Belgian Tourist Off. [24236], 220 E 42nd St., Ste. 3402, New York, NY 10017, (212)758-8130

Belgian Transplantation Soc. [IO], Brussels, Belgium

Belgian Veterinary Cmpt. Assn. [IO], Liege, Belgium

Belgian Wallonia-Brussels Discgolf Assn. [IO], Namur, Belgium

Belgisch Verpakkingsinstituut [★IO]

Belgische Bontfederatie [★IO]

Belgische Confederatie van de Zuivelindustrie [IO], Leuven, Belgium

Belgische DansSport Federatie [★IO]

Belgische Vereniging voor Gerontologie en Geriatrie [★IO]

Belgische Vereniging voor Neurologie [★IO]

Belgische Vereniging Sport-Geneeskunde and Sportwetenschappen [★IO]

Belgische Vereniging Voor Tuinarchitecten En Landschapsarchitecten [★IO]

Belgium
 Amer. Bouvier des Flandres Club [22188]
 Belgian Amer. Chamber of Commerce in the U.S. [24235]
 Belgian Amer. Educational Found. [9736]
 Belgian Sheepdog Club of Am. [22228]
 Belgian Tourist Off. [24236]

Belgium Assn. of Agricultural Journalists [IO], Brussels, Belgium

Belgium; Commission for Relief in [★9736]

Belgium Convention and Incentive Bur. [★IO]

Belgium Fed. of Fuel Suppliers [IO], Brussels, Belgium

Belgium-Japan Assn. and Chamber of Commerce [IO], Brussels, Belgium

Belgium-Luxembourg Chamber of Commerce in Hong Kong [IO], Hong Kong, People's Republic of China

Belgium Philatelic Soc. - Defunct.

Belgium Soc. for Reproductive Medicine [IO], Ternat, Belgium

Belgium Squash Fed. [IO], Herentals, Belgium

Belgo-Canadian Assn. [IO], Scarborough, ON, Canada

Believe the Children - Address unknown since 2003.

Believe In Tomorrow Natl. Children's Found. [11674], 6601 Frederick Rd., Baltimore, MD 21228, (410)744-1032

Belize Amateur Athletic Assn. [IO], Belize City, Belize

Belize Chamber of Commerce and Indus. [IO], Belize City, Belize

Belize Citrus Growers Assn. [IO], Dangriga, Belize

Belize Family Life Assn. [IO], Belize City, Belize

Belize Natl. Teachers' Union [IO], Belize City, Belize

Belize Red Cross [IO], Belize City, Belize

Belize Taekwondo Fed. [IO], Belize City, Belize

Belize Tennis Assn. [IO], Belize City, Belize

Belize Tourism Indus. Assn. [IO], Belize City, Belize

Bell Assn. for the Deaf; Alexander Graham [★14736]

Bell Assn. for the Deaf and Hard of Hearing; Parents' Sect. of the Alexander Graham [14776]

Bell Assn. for the Deaf; Parents' Sect. of the Alexander Graham [★14776]

Bell Family Assn. of the U.S. [20793], c/o Alta Jean Ginn, Membership Sec., 12147 Holly Knoll Cir., Great Falls, VA 22066, (703)430-6745

Bellamy Brothers Fan Club - Address unknown since 1999.

Bellanca-Champion Club [21431], PO Box 100, Coxsackie, NY 12051, (518)731-6800

Bellanca-Champion Club [IO], Coxsackie, NY, United States

Bellanet [IO], Ottawa, ON, Canada

Belleek Collectors' Intl. Soc. [IO], Great Falls, VA, United States

Belleek Collectors' Intl. Soc. [21925], PO Box 1498, Great Falls, VA 22066, (703)272-6270

Belleek Collectors' Soc. [★21925]

Belleek Collectors' Soc. [★IO]

Bellona [★IO]

Bellona Europa [★IO]

Bellona Europe [IO], Brussels, Belgium

Bells
 Amer. Bell Assn. Intl. [21958]

Amer. Guild of English Handbell Ringers [10535]
 North Amer. Guild of Change Ringers [10678]

Bellwoods Centres for Community Living [IO], Toronto, ON, Canada

Belorussian Sci. Soc. of Cardiologists [IO], Minsk, Belarus

Below/Hook Lifters Sect. of the Material Handling Inst. [★2042]

Belt Assn. - Defunct.

Belt and Button Assn. [2836]

Belt Coun; Amer. Safety [★377]

Belt Coun; Amer. Seat [★377]

Belt Inst; Auto. Safety [★377]

Belted Galloway Soc. [4256], c/o Laura Glassmann, Sec., PO Box 316, Bendersville, PA 17306-0316, (717)677-9655

Belting Assn; Amer. Leather [★2051]

Belting Assn; Natl. Indus. [2051]

Belting Mfrs. Assn; Woven Fabric [★3792]

BEMA [★449]

BEMA [★IO]

BEMA, The Baking Indus. Suppliers Assn. [IO], Overland Park, KS, United States

BEMA, The Baking Indus. Suppliers Assn. [449], 7101 Coll. Blvd., Ste. 1505, Overland Park, KS 66210, (913)338-1300

BEMFAM (Sociedade Civil Bem-Estar Familiar no Brazil) [IO], Rio de Janeiro, Brazil

Ben Franklin Soc. - Defunct.

Ben-Gurion Inst. and Archives [★8673]

Ben-Gurion Univ. of the Negev; Amer. Associates, [8673]

Bench and Bar Spouses; Natl. Assn. of [5509]

Bench Rest Shooters Assn; Natl. [23721]

Benchers and Dead Lifters; World Assn. of [23986]

Benchmarking Assn; Auto Suppliers [703]

Benchmarking Assn; Elec. Utility [6901]

Benchmarking Assn; Financial Services and Banking [721]

Benchmarking Assn; Human Resources [723]

Benchmarking Assn; Procurement and Supply Chain [760]

Benchmarking Consortium; Accounting and Finance [690]

Benchmarking Consortium; Agile Mfg. [2545]

Benchmarking Consortium; Auto Suppliers [★703]

Benchmarking Consortium; Info. Systems Mgt. [725]

Benchmarking in Hea. Care; Assn. for [1848]

Benchmarking Intl. Gp; Telecommunications [3758]

Benchmarking Network [2834], 4606 FM 1960 W, Ste. 250, Houston, TX 77069, (281)440-5044

Benchmarking Network; Call Center [★731]

Benedict Coll. Natl. Alumni Soc. [18877], 1600 Harden St., Columbia, SC 29204, (803)253-5000

Benedictin Children; Assn. of [★13752]

Benedictine Acad; Amer. [19566]

Benedictine Liturgical Conf. [★19900]

Benedictine Liturgical Conf. [★IO]

Benedictines for Peace [19582], c/o Carol Ann Wassmuth, OSB, 465 Keuterville Rd., Cottonwood, ID 83522-5183, (208)962-5032

Beneficial Assn; Polish [19309]

Benefit Administrators; Soc. of Professional [1245]

Benefit and Aid Soc; Mutual [★19146]

Benefit Assn; Armed Forces [★18955]

Benefit Assn; Armed Forces Enlisted Personnel [★18959]

Benefit Assn; Armed Forces Relief and [★18955]

Benefit Assn; Loyal Christian [19129]

Benefit Assn; Military [18959]

Benefit Assn; Natl. Transit [6324]

Benefit Assn; North Amer. [★19145]

Benefit Assn; Slovenian Mutual [★19368]

Benefit Assn; U.S. Letter Carriers Mutual [19142]

Benefit Assn; Woman's [★19145]

Benefit Fund of the U.S.A; Workmen's [19146]

Benefit Res. Inst; Employee [1235]

Benefit Soc; Slovene Natl. [19369]

Benefits Coalition for Affordable Choice and Quality; Hea. [14688]

Benefits Coun; Amer. [6169]

Benefits; Coun. on Employee [1234]

Benefits Inst; Natl. Employee [1243]

Benelli Owner's Club of America - Defunct.

BeNeLux Assn. of Bariatric Surgeons [IO], Gent, Belgium

A star before a book entry number signifies that the name is not listed separately, but is mentioned within the entry.

Benelux Assn. for Energy Economics [IO], Petten, Netherlands
Benelux Economic Union [IO], Brussels, Belgium
Benelux Economische Unie [★IO]
Benesh Inst. [IO], London, United Kingdom
Benevolent and Aid Assn. of Am. and Swedish-Finnish Temperance Assn; Swedish-Finnish [★9952]
Benevolent Assn; Chinese Consolidated [19015]
Benevolent Assn. of the Christian Church; Natl. [13177]
Benevolent Corps; Asian [★9613]
Benevolent Fund of the Coll. of Optometrists [★IO]
Benevolent Fund of the Coll. of Optometrists and the Assn. of Optometrists [IO], Swanley, United Kingdom
Benevolent Institutions; Commn. on [★13165]
Benevolent and Loyal Order of Pessimists [22591], PO Box 1945, Iowa City, IA 52244, (319)351-2973
Benevolent Order of the State of Texas; Slavonic [★19139]
Benevolent Org. for Development, Hea., and Insight [IO], Campbell Town, Australia
Benevolent Protective Assn; Oregon Horsemen's [23512]
Benevolent and Protective Order of Elks [19035], 2750 N Lakeview Ave., Chicago, IL 60614-1889, (773)755-4700
Benevolent and Protective Order of Elks of Canada [IO], Regina, SK, Canada
Benevolent Soc. of California [★19131]
Benevolent Soc; Maltese-Amer. [19222]
Benevolent Soc. of New York; Swiss [19400]
Bengal
   Cultural Assn. of Bengal [9737]
Bengal Breeders' Assn; The Intl. [4205]
Bengal Cat Soc; The Intl. [4206]
Benign Essential Blepharospasm Res. Found. [15311], PO Box 12468, Beaumont, TX 77726-2468, (409)832-0788
Benjamin Franklin Educ. Found. [8234], 6275 Hazeltine Natl. Dr., Orlando, FL 32822, (407)240-8009
Benjamin Franklin Literary and Medical Soc. [14549], 1100 Waterway Blvd., Indianapolis, IN 46202, (317)634-1100
Benjamin Franklin Stamp Club - Defunct.
Benjamin Gender Dysphoria Assn; Natl. Harry [★13103]
Benjamin Harrison Found; Pres. [11142]
Bennington Bunch - Defunct.
Benny Wilson Fan Club - Address unknown since 1989.
Bentgrass Commn; Oregon Highland [4797]
Benthological Soc; Midwest [★4516]
Benthological Soc; North Amer. [4516]
Bentley Drivers Club [IO], Branbury, United Kingdom
Benton Found. [11764], 1625 K St. NW, 11th Fl., Washington, DC 20006, (202)638-5770
Benvenuto Club of Milan [IO], Milan, Italy
Berean Bible Soc. [IO], Germantown, WI, United States
Berean Bible Soc. [19509], PO Box 756, Germantown, WI 53022, (262)255-4750
Berean Mission, Inc. [★20326]
Berean Mission, Inc. [★IO]
Bereaved Parents - Defunct.
Bereaved Parents of the USA [11512], c/o John Goodrich, PO Box 95, Park Forest, IL 60466-0095, (708)748-7866
Bereavement
   AARP Grief and Loss Prog. [13414]
   Alive Alone [11511]
   Assn. for Death Educ. and Counseling [11909]
   Assn. for Pet Loss and Bereavement [12706]
   Bereaved Parents of the USA [11512]
   Center for Death Educ. and Bioethics [13314]
   Children's Grief Educ. Assn. [12265]
   Cruse Bereavement Care Scotland [IO]
   RAINBOWS [11718]
   Ray of Hope [13291]
   Violent Death Bereavement Soc. [11513]
Bereavement Services [12663], c/o Gundersen Lutheran Medical Found., 1900 S Ave., La Crosse, WI 54601, (608)775-4747
Bereavement Services; RTS [★12663]

Berger Picard Club of Am. [22229], c/o Maria Leana, Treas., 607 Barretts Run Rd., Bridgeton, NJ 08302
Beritashvili Physiological Soc. of Georgia [IO], Tbilisi, Georgia
Berkeley Enthusiasts Club [IO], Oswaldkirk, United Kingdom
Berkeley Exchange [21590]
Berkeley Macintosh Users Gp. - Defunct.
Berkeley Newsletter - Address unknown since 2002.
Berkeley Soc; Intl. [10798]
Berkshire Assn; Amer. [5230]
Berkshire Conservation Volunteers [IO], Reading, United Kingdom
Berlin Fan Club - Defunct.
Berlin Opera Found; Amer. [10529]
Berlin U.S. Military Veterans Assn. [★21288]
Berlin Veterans Assn. [21288], 244 E Hamel Rd., Huachuca City, AZ 85616-8140, (520)456-1910
Bermuda
   Bermuda Dept. of Tourism [24237]
Bermuda Anglers Club [IO], Hamilton, Bermuda
Bermuda Assn. of Landscape Architects [IO], Hamilton, Bermuda
Bermuda Badminton Assn. [IO], Devonshire, Bermuda
Bermuda Bar Assn. [IO], Hamilton, Bermuda
Bermuda Chamber of Commerce [IO], Hamilton, Bermuda
Bermuda Dental Assn. [IO], Hamilton, Bermuda
Bermuda Dept. of Tourism [24237], 675 3rd Ave., 20th Fl., New York, NY 10017, (212)818-9800
Bermuda Employers' Coun. [IO], Hamilton, Bermuda
Bermuda Hotel Assn. [IO], Hamilton, Bermuda
Bermuda Intl. Bus. Assn. [IO], Hamilton, Bermuda
Bermuda Lawn Tennis Assn. [IO], Hamilton, Bermuda
Bermuda Occupational Therapy Assn. [IO], Devonshire, Bermuda
Bermuda Olympic Assn. [IO], Hamilton, Bermuda
Bermuda Physiotherapy Assn. [IO], Hamilton, Bermuda
Bermuda Public Services Union [IO], Hamilton, Bermuda
Bermuda Sailing Assn. [IO], Hamilton, Bermuda
Bermuda Squash Racquets Assn. [IO], Hamilton, Bermuda
Bermuda Taekwondo Assn. [IO], Hamilton, Bermuda
Bermuda Trade Development Bd. [★24237]
Bermuda Union of Teachers [IO], Hamilton, Bermuda
Bernard Herrmann Soc. - Address unknown since 1994.
Bernard van Leer Found. [IO], The Hague, Netherlands
Bernard Shaw Soc. [9636], PO Box 1159, Madison Square Sta., New York, NY 10159-1159, (212)982-9885
Berne Declaration [IO], Zurich, Switzerland
Bernese Mountain Dog
   Bernese Mountain Dog Club of Am. [22230]
Bernese Mountain Dog Club of Am. [22230], c/o Stephanie Sotiros, Membership Chair, 3109 Leahey, Stevens Point, WI 54481
Bernoulli Soc. for Mathematical Statistics and Probability [IO], Voorburg, Netherlands
Beroepsorganisatie Nederlandse Ontwerpers [★IO]
Beroepsvereniging van de Experten B.O.A.R. [IO], Brussels, Belgium
Berry Surname Org. - Address unknown since 2007.
Berth Operators; Trans-Atlantic Amer. Flag Liner Operators/Trans-Pacific Amer. Flag [3592]
Bertrand Russell Soc. [9637], c/o Dennis Darland, 1406 26th St., Rock Island, IL 61201-2837
Berufsverband der Deutschen Urologen [★IO]
Berufsverband Deutscher Markt- und Sozialforscher [★IO]
Berufsverband Info. Bibliothek [★IO]
Berufsverband der Pharmaberater [IO], Worms, Germany
Berufsverband der Yogalehrenden in Deutschland e.V. [★IO]
Bessie Smith Soc. [24847]
Best Buddies Intl. [12564], 100 SE Second St., Ste. 2200, Miami, FL 33131, (305)374-2233

Best Buddies Intl. [IO], Miami, FL, United States
Best Candidate Comm. - Address unknown since 2000.
BEST Employers Assn. [3607], 2505 McCabe Way, Irvine, CA 92614, (949)253-4080
Best Friends Animal Sanctuary [★11370]
Best Friends Animal Soc. [11370], 5001 Angel Canyon Rd., Kanab, UT 84741-5000, (435)644-2001
Best Holiday Trav-L-Park Assn. [3354], 545 Lonely Cottage Dr., Upper Black Eddy, PA 18972, (866)665-5448
Bet-Nahrain [9624], PO Box 4116, Modesto, CA 95352, (209)538-4130
Beta Alpha Psi [24391], Palladian I, 220 Leigh Farm Rd., Durham, NC 27707, (919)402-4044
Beta Beta Beta [24408], c/o Kathy W. Roush, Sec.-Treas., Univ. of North Alabama, PO Box 5079, Florence, AL 35632, (256)765-6220
Beta Chi Theta Natl. Fraternity [24618], 9663 Santa Monica Blvd., Ste. 498, Beverly Hills, CA 90210
Beta Gamma Sigma [24415], 125 Weldon Pkwy., Maryland Heights, MO 63043, (314)432-5650
Beta Gamma Sigma [IO], Maryland Heights, MO, United States
Beta Gamma Sigma Alumni [24416], c/o Beta Gamma Sigma, 125 Weldon Pkwy., Maryland Heights, MO 63043, (314)432-5650
Beta Gamma Sigma Alumni in New York City [★24416]
Beta Gamma Upsilon - Address unknown since 1995.
Beta Kappa Chi [24585], c/o Ms. Deadra James Mackie, Exec. Sec., PO Box 10046, Baton Rouge, LA 70813, (225)771-4845
Beta Phi Alpha [★24686]
Beta Phi Gamma - Defunct.
Beta Phi Mu [24532], Florida State Univ., School of Info. Stud., Tallahassee, FL 32306-2100, (850)644-8123
Beta Phi Mu [IO], Tallahassee, FL, United States
Beta Pi Sigma Sorority [24417], 256 Waterville, Chicago, IL 60619
Beta Sigma Kappa [24562], c/o Todd Fleischer, Exec. Dir., PO Box 5886, Topeka, KS 66605
Beta Sigma Omicron - Defunct.
Beta Sigma Phi [24596], PO Box 8500, Kansas City, MO 64114, (816)444-6800
Beta Sigma Psi [★24619]
Beta Sigma Psi Natl. Lutheran Fraternity [24619], 2408 Lebanon Ave., Belleville, IL 62221, (618)235-0014
Beta Sigma Rho [★24652]
Beta Theta Pi [24620], PO Box 6277, 5134 Bonham Rd., Oxford, OH 45056, (513)523-7591
Beth Din of Am. [20123], 305 7th Ave., 12th Fl., New York, NY 10001-6008, (212)807-9042
Beth Fan Club; Amy [24841]
Beth Hatefutsoth; Amer. Friends of [10253]
Beth Jacob Schools; Federated Coun. of [8691]
Bethany Care Soc. [IO], Calgary, AB, Canada
Bethany Christian Services Intl. [IO], Grand Rapids, MI, United States
Bethany Christian Services Intl. [11561], 901 Eastern Ave. NE, PO Box 294, Grand Rapids, MI 49501-0294, (616)224-7610
Bethany Fellowship Missions [★20304]
Bethany Fellowship Missions [★IO]
Bethany International [★IO]
Bethany International [★20304]
Bethany Intl. Missions [20304], 6820 Auto Club Rd., Ste. M, Bloomington, MN 55438, (952)944-2121
Bethany Intl. Missions [IO], Bloomington, MN, United States
Bethel Ministries [★19874]
Bethesda Lutheran Home and Services [★12565]
Bethesda Lutheran Homes and Services [12565], 600 Hoffman Dr., Watertown, WI 53094, (920)261-3050
Bethesda Natl. Found. of Massachusetts [★15652]
Bethesda Natl. Found. of Massachusetts [★IO]
Bethlehem Assn. [18053], PO Box 1111, Media, PA 19063, (610)353-2010
Bethlehem Mission Immense [IO], Immensee, Switzerland

Reference to "IO" in place of a book number signifies that the association may be found in the 45th edition of International Organizations.

Bethlehem Mission Soc. [★IO]
Bethune-Cookman Coll. Natl. Alumni Assn. [18878], 640 Dr. Mary McLeod Bethune Blvd., Daytona Beach, FL 32114-3099, (386)481-2985
Betonelement-Foreningen [★IO]
Bets' Pets [★24732]
Betsy-Tacy Soc. [9638], PO Box 94, Mankato, MN 56002-0094, (507)345-9777
Better Am; Citizens for a [17103]
Better Boys Found. [11675], 1512 S Pulaski Rd., Chicago, IL 60623, (773)277-9582
Better Bus. Bur; Natl. [★17309]
Better Bus. Bureaus; Assn. of [★17309]
Better Bus. Bureaus Found; Coun. of [★17309]
Better Bus. Bureaus; Natl. Advt. Div. Coun. of [111]
Better Bus. Bureaus; U.S. Coun. of [765]
A Better Chance [8321], 240 W 35th St., 9th Fl., New York, NY 10001-2506, (646)346-1310
Better Education thru Simplified Spelling - Address unknown since 2001.
Better Env; Citizens for a [★5095]
Better Govt. Assn. [18282], 11 E Adams St., Ste. 608, Chicago, IL 60603, (312)427-8330
Better Hearing Australia [IO], Prahran, Australia
Better Hearing Inst. [14745], 515 King St., Ste. 420, Alexandria, VA 22314, (703)684-3391
Better Heating-Cooling Coun. [★1884]
Better Highway Info. Found. [★6313]
Better Humanity League - Address unknown since 1999.
Better Lawn and Turf Institute/American Sod Producers Assn. [★4794]
Better Lawn and Turf Institute/American Sod Producers Assn. [★IO]
Better Light Better Sight Bur. - Defunct.
Better Packaging Advisory Coun. - Address unknown since 1995.
Better Postcard Collectors' Club [★22905]
Better Sleep Coun. [16424], 501 Wythe St., Alexandria, VA 22314-1917, (202)828-8833
Better Sleep Coun. (of the Intl. Sleep Products Assn.) [★16424]
Better Sleep Coun. (of the Natl. Assn. of Bedding Mfrs.) [★16424]
Better Vision Inst. [15678], c/o Vision Coun. of Am., 1700 Diagonal Rd., Ste. 500, Alexandria, VA 22314, (703)548-4560
Better World Builders J. L. Inst. [★12142]
Better World Chorus [12617], PO Box 20934, Park West Finance Sta., New York, NY 10025
Better World Chorus [IO], New York, NY, United States
Better World J. L. Inst. [12142]
Better World J. N. L. Found. [★12142]
Better World Soc. - Defunct.
Betting; Natl. Assn. of Off-Track [23505]
Betty Boop Fan Club; Official [24792]
Betty Boop Intl. Collectible Club [21976]
Betty White Fan Club [24732], c/o Kay Daly, 3552 Fed. Ave., Los Angeles, CA 90066
Beverage Assn; Natl. Licensed [★193]
Beverage Container Manufacturers Assn; Carbonated [★974]
Beverage Control Assn; Natl. Alcohol [5446]
Beverage Importers; Natl. Assn. of [206]
Beverage Importers; Natl. Assn. of Alcoholic [★206]
Beverage Indus; Licensed [★199]
Beverage Indus; Natl. Women's Assn. of Allied [★213]
Beverage Indus; Tax Council-Alcoholic [★199]
Beverage Indus. Env. Coun. [IO], Glebe, Australia
Beverage Laws; Joint Comm. of the States to Stud. Alcohol [★5445]
Beverage Legislative Coun; Alcohol [5444]
Beverage Licensees; Amer. [193]
Beverage Mfrs. Agents Assn. - Defunct.
Beverage Network [505], c/o John Craven, Ed., 1 Miffin Pl., 3rd Fl., Cambridge, MA 02138, (617)715-9670
Beverage Packaging Assn; Brewers and [★508]
Beverage Retailers; Natl. Assn. of [★193]
Beverage Ser. Assn. [IO], Northwood, United Kingdom
Beverages
Alberta Bottle Depot Assn. [IO]

All Star Dairy Assn. [1126]
Amer. Beverage Assn. [503]
Amer. Beverage Inst. [504]
Amer. Sommelier Assn. [194]
Aseptic Packaging Coun. [2872]
Assn. of the German Fruit Juice Indus. [IO]
Australian Beverage Coun. Ltd. [IO]
Beverage Indus. Env. Coun. [IO]
Beverage Network [505]
Beverage Ser. Assn. [IO]
Brewery and Soft Drink Workers Conf. - U.S.A. and Canada [24020]
British Columbia Bottle Depot Assn. [IO]
British Soft Drinks Assn. [IO]
Caffeine Awareness Alliance [13747]
Cavanagh's Coca-Cola Collectors' Soc. [21991]
Chamber of Soft Drink and Related Mfrs. [IO]
Comm. of European Coffee Associations [IO]
Confed. of Intl. Soft Drinks Associations [IO]
Culligan Dealers Assn. of North Am. [1667]
Dr Pepper Bottlers Assn. [506]
Dutch Soft Drinks Assn. [IO]
European Coffee Fed. [IO]
European Fed. of Associations of Coffee Roasters [IO]
Fed. of French Maltsters [IO]
Free the Grapes! [16971]
German Coffee Assn. [IO]
Inter-African Coffee Org. [IO]
Intl. Assn. on Coffee Sci. [IO]
International Beverage Dispensing Equipment Association [IO]
Intl. Beverage Dispensing Equip. Assn. [507]
Intl. Beverage Packaging Assn. [508]
Intl. Bottled Water Assn. [509]
Intl. Bottled Water Assn. [IO]
Intl. Coffee Org. [IO]
Intl. Dairy Foods Assn. [1134]
Intl. Fed. of Fruit Juice Producers [IO]
Intl. Org. of Vine and Wine [IO]
Intl. Soc. of Beverage Technologists [IO]
Intl. Soc. of Beverage Technologists [6543]
Intl. Tea Comm. [IO]
Intl. Women's Coffee Alliance [11783]
Italian Fed. of the Mineral and Soft Drinks Indus. [IO]
Japan Soft Drinks Assn. [IO]
Juice Products Assn. [510]
Koninklijke Nederlandse Vereniging voor de Koffiehandel [IO]
Master Brewers Assn. of the Americas [IO]
Master Brewers Assn. of the Americas [6544]
Natl. Assn. of Bar and Tavern Owners [205]
Natl. Assn. of German Non-Alcoholic Beverage Indus. [IO]
Natl. Coffee Assn. of U.S.A. [511]
Natl. Pop Can Collectors [22085]
Natl. Soft Drink Manufacturers' Assn. [IO]
New Zealand Juice and Beverage Assn. [IO]
North Amer. Brewers' Assn. [208]
Organic Grapes Into Wine Alliance [5418]
Portuguese Mineral Water Producers' Assn. [IO]
Refreshments Canada [IO]
Responsible Hospitality Inst. [11985]
Royal Crown Bottlers Assn. [512]
Royal Fed. of Water and Soft Drinks Indus. [IO]
Santa Cruz Mountains Winegrowers Assn. [5420]
Soft Drink and Fruit Juice Producers' Assn. [IO]
Spanish Bottled Water Assn. [IO]
Specialty Coffee Assn. of Am. [513]
Specialty Wine Retailers Assn. [4031]
Swiss Mineral Water and Soft Drink Producers' Assn. [IO]
Tea Assn. of the U.S.A. [514]
Tea Bd. of India [515]
Tea Bd. of Kenya [IO]
Tea Coun. [IO]
Tea Coun. of the U.S.A. [IO]
Tea Coun. of the U.S.A. [516]
Thai Coffee Exporters Assn. [IO]
Union of European Beverages Assn. [IO]
United Kingdom Tea Assn. [IO]
World Alliance of Gourmet Robustas [1738]
World Cocoa Found. [6545]
Beverages; Amer. Bottlers of Carbonated [★503]

Beveren Rabbit Club; Amer. [22917]
Beveren Rabbit Club - Defunct.
Beverly Found. [11278], 566 El Dorado St., No. 100, Pasadena, CA 91101-2505, (626)792-2292
Bewitched Fan Club; Magic of [25034]
Beyaz Esya Yan Sanayicileri Dernegi [★IO]
Beyond Baroque Found. [★9559]
Beyond Baroque Literary/Arts Center [9559], 681 Venice Blvd., Venice, CA 90291, (310)822-3006
Beyond Beef - Address unknown since 2003.
Beyond Baroque Found. [★9559]
Beyond Pesticides - Natl. Coalition Against the Misuse of Pesticides [13322], 701 E St. SE, Ste. 200, Washington, DC 20003, (202)543-5450
Beyond the Pond.International Frog Collectors Club [21977], PO Box 201413, Bloomington, MN 55420
Beyond the Rainbow [24733], PO Box 31672, St. Louis, MO 63131-0672, (314)799-1724
Beyond War Found. [★18203]
Beyondblue [IO], Hawthorn West, Australia
Beyster Inst. [704], UC Washington Ctr., 1608 Rhode Island Ave. NW, Washington, DC 20036, (202)833-4617
Bezalel Acad. of Arts; Friends of [10255]
BFG Owners Club, U.S.A. - Defunct.
BGSA Chap. [★24416]
Bharatiya Agro Indus. Found. [★IO]
Bharatiya Janata Party [IO], New Delhi, India
BHHMA [★IO]
Bhojpuri Assn. of North Am. [IO], East Windsor, NJ, United States
Bhojpuri Assn. of North Am. [10299], 50 Tennyson Rd., East Windsor, NJ 08520, (972)948-0996
BHR Gp. [IO], Bedford, United Kingdom
Bhutan Amateur Athletic Assn. [IO], Thimphu, Bhutan
Bhutan Badminton Fed. [IO], Thimphu, Bhutan
Bhutan Chamber of Commerce and Indus. [IO], Thimphu, Bhutan
Bhutan Philatelic Soc. - Address unknown since 1985.
Bhutan Soc. of the United Kingdom [IO], London, United Kingdom
Bhutan Taekwondo Fed. [IO], Thimphu, Bhutan
Bhutan Tennis Fed. [IO], Thimphu, Bhutan
Bhutan Women and Children Org. [IO], Kathmandu, Nepal
Bi-Partisan Budget Appeal - Defunct.
Bi Without Borders [17024], PO Box 581037, Minneapolis, MN 55458
Bi Women's Cultural Alliance [12219], PO Box 2254, Washington, DC 20013-2254, (202)828-3065
BIA Educators; Natl. Coun. of [★8938]
BIA - Ottawa Valley [★IO]
Biafra Assn. in the Americas - Defunct.
Biafran Medical Assn. in the Americas - Defunct.
Biathlon Assn; U.S. [23756]
Biathlon Assn; U.S. Modern Pentathlon and [★23925]
Bibi Besch Fan Club - Address unknown since 1989.
Bible
Adult Christian Educ. Found. [19913]
Africa Inland Mission Intl. [20294]
Alliance for Life Ministries [19760]
Amer. Bible Soc. [19504]
Amer. Bible Soc. [IO]
Amer. Clergy Leadership Conf. [19858]
Amer. Congregational Assn. [19859]
Amer. Coun. of Christian Churches [19761]
Amer. Family Assn. [17162]
Amer. and Foreign Christian Union [19762]
Amer. Friends of Neot Kedumim [19505]
Amer. Friends of Neot Kedumim [IO]
Amer. Indian Liberation Crusade [12622]
Amer. Missionary Fellowship [20296]
AMF Intl. [19988]
Anglican Assn. of Biblical Scholars [19449]
Argentine Bible Soc. [IO]
Artists for Israel Intl. [9428]
ASGM [19506]
Associates for Biblical Res. [19507]
Associates for Biblical Res. [IO]
Assn. for Biblical Higher Educ. [8080]
Assn. of Classical and Christian Schools [9089]
Assn. of Life-Giving Churches [19843]
Assn. of State Baptist Papers [19475]

A star before a book entry number signifies that the name is not listed separately, but is mentioned within the entry.

Austrian Bible Soc. [IO]
Awana Clubs Intl. [20639]
Bangladesh Bible Soc. [IO]
Baptist Bible Fellowship Intl. [19477]
BCM Intl. [19508]
BCM Intl. [IO]
Berean Bible Soc. [IO]
Berean Bible Soc. [19509]
Bethany Intl. Missions [20304]
Bible Believers Fellowship [20477]
Bible League [19510]
Bible League [IO]
Bible League of Canada [IO]
Bible Sabbath Assn. [20543]
Bible Soc. in Angola [IO]
Bible Soc. of Armenia [IO]
Bible Soc. in Australia [IO]
Bible Soc. of Benin [IO]
Bible Soc. in Botswana [IO]
Bible Soc. of Brazil [IO]
Bible Soc. of Burkina Faso [IO]
Bible Soc. in Burundi [IO]
Bible Soc. in Cambodia [IO]
Bible Soc. of Cameroon [IO]
Bible Soc. in Central African Republic [IO]
Bible Soc. of Chad [IO]
Bible Soc. in Congo [IO]
Bible Soc. of Costa Rica [IO]
Bible Soc. of Cote d'Ivoire [IO]
Bible Soc. of Cyprus [IO]
Bible Soc. of Democratic Republic of Congo [IO]
Bible Soc. of Egypt [IO]
Bible Soc. of El Salvador [IO]
Bible Soc. of Eritrea [IO]
Bible Soc. of Ethiopia [IO]
Bible Soc. in Gabon [IO]
Bible Soc. of Ghana [IO]
Bible Soc. of Guinea [IO]
Bible Soc. of Honduras [IO]
Bible Soc. of India [IO]
Bible Soc. in Jordan [IO]
Bible Soc. work in Kazakhstan [IO]
Bible Soc. of Kenya [IO]
Bible Soc. in Lebanon [IO]
Bible Soc. in Lesotho [IO]
Bible Soc. in Liberia [IO]
Bible Soc. of Lithuania [IO]
Bible Soc. of Mali [IO]
Bible Soc. of Mexico [IO]
Bible Soc. in Mozambique [IO]
Bible Soc. of Myanmar [IO]
Bible Soc. in Namibia [IO]
Bible Soc. in Netherlands Antilles [IO]
Bible Soc. in New Zealand [IO]
Bible Soc. in Nicaragua [IO]
Bible Soc. of Nigeria [IO]
Bible Soc. of Panama [IO]
Bible Soc. of Papua New Guinea [IO]
Bible Soc. in Poland [IO]
Bible Soc. of Portugal [IO]
Bible Soc. of Republic of Belarus [IO]
Bible Soc. in Rwanda [IO]
Bible Soc. of Senegal [IO]
Bible Soc. in Sierra Leone [IO]
Bible Soc. of Singapore [IO]
Bible Soc. of Spain [IO]
Bible Soc. in Sudan [IO]
Bible Soc. in Swaziland [IO]
Bible Soc. in Taiwan [IO]
Bible Soc. of Tanzania [IO]
Bible Soc. of Togo [IO]
Bible Soc. of Uzbekistan [IO]
Bible Soc. of Zambia [IO]
Bible Soc. of Zimbabwe [IO]
Bibles for the Blind and Visually Handicapped [19511]
Bibles For The World [20305]
Biblical Witness Fellowship [20606]
Billy Graham Evangelistic Assn. [19992]
BLI [19512]
BLI [IO]
Bolivian Bible Soc. [IO]
Braille Bible Found. [19513]
Bulgarian Bible Soc. [IO]
Canadian Bible Soc. [IO]

Canadian Soc. of Biblical Stud. [IO]
Catholic Biblical Assn. of Am. [9272]
Chalcedon Found. [20535]
Child Evangelism Fellowship [19997]
Chilean Bible Soc. [IO]
Christ for the Nations [20314]
Christ Truth Ministries [19514]
Christian Bus. Men's Comm. [19771]
Christian Century Found. [19772]
Christian Chiropractors Assn. [19773]
Christian Communications, Inc. [19774]
Christian Educators Fellowship of the United Methodist Church [19923]
Christian Family Renewal [19776]
Christian Holiness Partnership [19779]
Christian Literature and Bible Center [20317]
Christian Media Assn. [20237]
Christian Record Services [16842]
Christian Res. Inst. [19785]
Christian Ser. Club [19515]
Christian Stewardship Assn. [20512]
Christian TV Mission [19536]
Christians in Govt. [19516]
Colombian Bible Soc. [IO]
Commun. Commn. [19537]
Concordia Gospel Outreach [20214]
Congregation Shema Yisrael [20135]
Connecting Church Assn. [19846]
Creation Health Found. [20547]
Creation Res. Soc. [20548]
Croatian Bible Soc. [IO]
Crusaders for Christ [20462]
Czech Bible Soc. [IO]
Danish Bible Soc. [IO]
Dawn Bible Students Assn. [19517]
Dominican Republic Bible Soc. [IO]
Ecuadorian Bible Soc. [IO]
Electronic Bible Soc. [19518]
Estonian Bible Soc. [IO]
Ethics and Religious Liberty Commn. of the Southern Baptist Convention [19487]
Evangelical Missiological Soc. [20334]
Evangelical Theological Soc. [19980]
Evangelical Training Assn. [19925]
Fellowship of Christian Magicians [19797]
Fellowship of Christian Peace Officers - U.S.A. [19798]
Fellowship Intl. Mission [20338]
Finnish Bible Soc. [IO]
Full Gospel Bus. Men's Fellowship Intl. [19801]
Gen. Assn. of Regular Baptist Churches [19489]
Genesis Inst. [20549]
German Bible Soc. [IO]
The Gideons Intl. [20011]
Greek Bible Soc. [IO]
Haitian Bible Soc. [IO]
High School Evangelism Fellowship [20013]
Hindustan Bible Inst. [19927]
Hong Kong Bible Soc. [IO]
Hungarian Bible Soc. [IO]
Icelandic Bible Soc. [IO]
IFCA Intl. [19849]
Inst. for Biblical Res. [19519]
Interact Ministries [20348]
Interdisciplinary Biblical Res. Inst. [19928]
Intl. Assn. of Biblical Counselors [19867]
Intl. Bible Soc. [19520]
Intl. Bible Soc. [IO]
Intl. Bible Students Assn. [IO]
Intl. Bible Students Assn. [19521]
Intl. Convention of Faith Ministries [19807]
Intl. Coun. of Christian Churches [20015]
Intl. Coun. of Community Churches [19850]
Intl. Fed. of Messianic Jews [20255]
Intl. Order of the King's Daughters and Sons [19810]
Intl. Org. for Septuagint and Cognate Stud. [19522]
Intl. Org. for Septuagint and Cognate Stud. [IO]
Intl. Soc. of Bible Collectors [IO]
Intl. Soc. of Bible Collectors [19523]
Irish Biblical Assn. [IO]
Korean Bible Soc. [IO]
Kristana Esperantista Ligo Internacia [19812]
Latvian Bible Soc. [IO]

Life Action Revival Ministries [20020]
Literacy and Evangelism Intl. [8791]
Lord's Day Alliance of the U.S. [20544]
Luis Palau Assn. [20022]
Lutheran Bible Translators [19524]
Lutheran Bible Translators of Canada [IO]
Lutheran Braille Workers [16867]
The Mailbox Club [19525]
The Mailbox Club [IO]
Malagasy Bible Soc. [IO]
Malta Bible Soc. [IO]
MOMS in Touch Intl. [20621]
Narramore Christian Found. [19815]
Natl. Assn. of Professors of Hebrew [8695]
Natl. Bible Assn. [20205]
Natl. Coun. of Churches of Christ in the U.S.A. [19905]
Natl. Coun. On Bible Curriculum In Public Schools [9052]
Natl. Religious Broadcasters [19539]
The Navigators [19817]
Near East Archaeological Soc. [6451]
Neighborhood Bible Stud. [19526]
Nepal Bible Soc. [IO]
Netherlands Bible Soc. [IO]
New Hope Intl. [20372]
New Horizon World Center [19527]
Non-Denominational Bible Prophecy Stud. Assn. [19528]
Non-Denominational Bible Prophecy Study Association [IO]
Norwegian Bible Soc. [IO]
OMS Intl. [20379]
Paraguayan Bible Soc. [IO]
Peale Center for Christian Living [19825]
Personal Freedom Outreach [19875]
Peruvian Bible Soc. [IO]
Philippine Bible Soc. [IO]
Plymouth Rock Found. [8302]
Pocket Testament League [19529]
Pocket Testament League [IO]
Presbyterian Evangelistic Fellowship [20471]
Rosicrucian Fellowship [20541]
SEARCH Found. [6454]
Searching Together Educational Ministries [19909]
Seventh Day Baptist Gen. Conf. [19494]
Seventh Day Baptist Gen. Conf. of the U.S. and Canada [20545]
Seventh Day Baptist Historical Soc. [19495]
Seventh Day Baptist Missionary Soc. [19496]
Seventh Day Baptist World Fed. [19497]
Sharing of Ministries Abroad U.S.A. [20393]
Slavic Gospel Assn. [20395]
Soc. of Biblical Literature [19530]
Soc. for New Testament Stud. [IO]
Southern Baptist Found. [19498]
Swiss Bible Soc. [IO]
Teen Challenge Intl. [20643]
Truth Missionaries Chap. of Positive Accord [20585]
Tyndale Soc. [20530]
United Bible Societies [IO]
United Bible Societies in Venezuela [IO]
The Way Intl. [20411]
Westar Inst. [20509]
Woman's Missionary Union, SBC [19501]
Women Nationally Active for Christ [19502]
World Archaeological Soc. [6460]
World Literature Ministries [19832]
World's Christian Endeavor Union [19829]
Wycliffe Bible Translators [19531]
Bible Assn; Natl. [20205]
Bible Believers [IO], Currabubula, Australia
Bible Believers Fellowship [20477], PO Box 0065, Baldwin, NY 11510-0065, (516)739-7746
Bible Broadcast; Prisoners [★19514]
Bible Centered Ministries [★19508]
Bible Centered Ministries [★IO]
Bible Christian Union [★20331]
Bible Club [★19825]
Bible Club Movement [★19508]
Bible Club Movement [★IO]
Bible Colleges; Accrediting Assn. of [★8080]
Bible Colleges; Accrediting Assn. of [★8080]
Bible Colleges; Amer. Assn. of [★8080]

Reference to "IO" in place of a book number signifies that the association may be found in the 45th edition of International Organizations.

Bible Colleges; Assn. of Bible Institutes and [★8080]
Bible Comm; Laymen's Natl. [★20205]
Bible Holiness Movement [IO], Vancouver, BC, Canada
Bible Inst; Hindustan [19927]
Bible Inst; Moody [20368]
Bible League [19510], PO Box 28000, Chicago, IL 60628, (708)367-8500
Bible League [IO], Chicago, IL, United States
Bible League of Canada [IO], Burlington, ON, Canada
Bible League; World Home [★19510]
Bible Literature Intl. [★19512]
Bible Literature Intl. [★IO]
Bible Mediation League [★IO]
Bible Mediation League [★19512]
Bible Memory Assn., Intl. - Defunct.
Bible Mission; Eastern European [★20372]
Bible Mission, Inc; Children's [★19995]
Bible Protestant Missions - Address unknown since 1995.
Bible Sabbath Assn. [20543], 802 NW 21st Ave., Battle Ground, WA 98604, (307)686-5191
Bible Schools; Vacation [★19483]
Bible-Science Assn. - Defunct.
Bible Soc. in Angola [IO], Luanda, Angola
Bible Soc. of Armenia [IO], Yerevan, Armenia
Bible Soc. in Australia [IO], Canberra, Australia
Bible Soc. of Benin [IO], Cotonou, Benin
Bible Soc. in Botswana [IO], Gaborone, Botswana
Bible Soc. of Brazil [IO], Barueri, Brazil
Bible Soc. of Burkina Faso [IO], Ouagadougou, Burkina Faso
Bible Soc. in Burundi [IO], Bujumbura, Burundi
Bible Soc. in Cambodia [IO], Phnom Penh, Cambodia
Bible Soc. of Cameroon [IO], Yaounde, Cameroon
Bible Soc. in Central African Republic [IO], Bangui, Central African Republic
Bible Soc. of Chad [IO], N'Djamena, Chad
Bible Soc. in Congo [IO], Brazzaville, Republic of the Congo
Bible Soc. of Costa Rica [IO], San Jose, Costa Rica
Bible Soc. of Cote d'Ivoire [IO], Abidjan, Cote d'Ivoire
Bible Soc. of Cyprus [IO], Nicosia, Cyprus
Bible Soc. of Democratic Republic of Congo [IO], Kinshasa, Democratic Republic of the Congo
Bible Soc. of Egypt [IO], Cairo, Egypt
Bible Soc. of El Salvador [IO], San Salvador, El Salvador
Bible Soc. of Eritrea [IO], Asmara, Eritrea
Bible Soc. of Ethiopia [IO], Addis Ababa, Ethiopia
Bible Soc. in Gabon [IO], Libreville, Gabon
Bible Soc. of Ghana [IO], Accra, Ghana
Bible Soc. of Guinea [IO], Conakry, Guinea
Bible Soc. of Honduras [IO], Tegucigalpa, Honduras
Bible Soc. of India [IO], Bangalore, India
Bible Soc. Intl; New York [★19520]
Bible Soc. in Jordan [IO], Amman, Jordan
Bible Soc. work in Kazakhstan [IO], Almaty, Kazakhstan
Bible Soc. of Kenya [IO], Nairobi, Kenya
Bible Soc. in Lebanon [IO], Beirut, Lebanon
Bible Soc. of Lesotho [IO], Maseru, Lesotho
Bible Soc. in Liberia [IO], Monrovia, Liberia
Bible Soc. of Lithuania [IO], Vilnius, Lithuania
Bible Soc. of Mali [IO], Bamako, Mali
Bible Soc. of Mexico [IO], Mexico City, Mexico
Bible Soc. in Mozambique [IO], Maputo, Mozambique
Bible Soc. of Myanmar [IO], Yangon, Myanmar
Bible Soc. in Namibia [IO], Windhoek, Namibia
Bible Soc. in Netherlands Antilles [IO], Curacao, Netherlands Antilles
Bible Soc; New York [★19520]
Bible Soc; New York City Intl. [★19520]
Bible Soc. in New Zealand [IO], Wellington, New Zealand
Bible Soc. in Nicaragua [IO], Managua, Nicaragua
Bible Soc. of Nigeria [IO], Lagos, Nigeria
Bible Soc. of Panama [IO], Panama City, Panama
Bible Soc. of Papua New Guinea [IO], Port Moresby, Papua New Guinea

Bible Soc. in Poland [IO], Warsaw, Poland
Bible Soc. of Portugal [IO], Lisbon, Portugal
Bible Soc. of Republic of Belarus [IO], Minsk, Belarus
Bible Soc. in Rwanda [IO], Kigali, Rwanda
Bible Soc; Scottish [IO]
Bible Soc. of Senegal [IO], Dakar, Senegal
Bible Soc. in Sierra Leone [IO], Freetown, Sierra Leone
Bible Soc. of Singapore [IO], Singapore, Singapore
Bible Soc. of Spain [IO], Madrid, Spain
Bible Soc. in Sudan [IO], Khartoum, Sudan
Bible Soc. in Swaziland [IO], Manzini, Swaziland
Bible Soc. in Taiwan [IO], Taipei, Taiwan
Bible Soc. of Tanzania [IO], Dodoma, United Republic of Tanzania
Bible Soc. of Togo [IO], Lome, Togo
Bible Soc. of Uzbekistan [IO], Tashkent, Uzbekistan
Bible Soc. of Zambia [IO], Lusaka, Zambia
Bible Soc. of Zimbabwe [IO], Harare, Zimbabwe
The Bible Standard [★IO]
The Bible Standard [★20018]
Bible Study League of America - Defunct.
Bible and Tract Soc. of New York; Watchtower [20109]
Bible Translators of Canada; Lutheran [IO]
Bible Translators; Messengers of Christ-Lutheran [★19524]
Bibles for the Blind and Visually Handicapped [19511], 3228 E Rosehill Ave., Terre Haute, IN 47805-1297, (812)466-4899
Bibles For The World [20305], PO Box 49759, Colorado Springs, CO 80949-9759, (888)382-4253
Bibles For The World [IO], Colorado Springs, CO, United States
Bibles Intl; Living [★19520]
Biblical Am. Resistance Front - Defunct.
Biblical Assn. of Am; Catholic [9272]
Biblical Colloquium - Defunct.
Biblical Concerns; Presbyterians for [★20476]
Biblical Evangelism - Defunct.
Biblical Fine Arts Assn. - Address unknown since 1999.
Biblical Higher Educ; Assn. for [8080]
Biblical Inst. for Social Change [20490], c/o Rev. Dr. Cain Hope Felder, Founder/Chm./CEO, Howard Univ. School of Divinity, 1400 Shepherd St. NE, Ste. 264 and 266, Washington, DC 20017, (202)269-4311
Biblical Instructors; Natl. Assn. of [★8223]
Biblical Ministries Worldwide [19991], 1595 Herrington Rd., Lawrenceville, GA 30043-5616, (770)339-3500
Biblical Ministries Worldwide [IO], Lawrenceville, GA, United States
Biblical Numismatic Soc. - Defunct.
Biblical Res. Inst; Interdisciplinary [19928]
Biblical Stud; Canadian Soc. of [IO]
Biblical Topics Study Unit - Defunct.
Biblical Witness Fellowship [20606], PO Box 102, 182 High St., Candia, NH 03034-0102, (800)494-9172
Biblical Witness; United Church People for [★20606]
Biblijos skaitymo draugija [★IO]
Biblio/Poetry Therapy; Natl. Fed. for [16225]
Bibliographic Coun; AMIGOS [★10325]
Bibliographical Soc. of Am. [9741], PO Box 1537, Lenox Hill Sta., New York, NY 10021, (212)452-2710
Bibliographical Soc. of Australia and New Zealand [IO], Wagga Wagga, Australia
Bibliographical Soc. of Canada [IO], Toronto, ON, Canada
Bibliographical Soc. - United Kingdom [IO], London, United Kingdom
Bibliographical Soc. of the Univ. of Virginia [9742], c/o Anne Ribble, Sec.-Treas., Alderman Lib., PO Box 400152, Charlottesville, VA 22904, (434)924-7013
Bibliography of History; Assn. for the [10094]
Bibliomania Soc; Numismatic [22748]
Bibliophiles of Am; Taurine [9755]
Bibliophiles; Burroughs [9640]
Biblioteca de Mujeres [IO], Madrid, Spain
Bibliotheques Europeennes de Theologie [★IO]

Bicentennial Coun. of the Thirteen Original States - Defunct.
Bichon
  Bichon Frise Club of Am. [22231]
  Bichon Frise Club of Am. [22231], c/o Cyndie Adams, Corresponding Sec., 1039 Windsor St., Reading, PA 19604-2334, (610)374-7293
BICSI [3736], World HQ, 8610 Hidden River Pkwy., Tampa, FL 33637-1000, (813)979-1991
BICSI [IO], Tampa, FL, United States
Bicycle
  Adventure Cycling Assn. [23304]
  Am. Bikes [17022]
  Amer. Bicycle Assn. [23305]
  Amer. Bicycle Polo Assn. [23658]
  Amer. Bicycle Racing [23667]
  Amer. Track Racing Assn. [23306]
  Amer. Volkssport Assn. [23803]
  Assn. of Pedestrian and Bicycle Professionals [18747]
  Bicycle Fed. of Australia [IO]
  Bicycle Helmet Safety Inst. [12954]
  Bicycle Network [13336]
  Bicycle New South Wales [IO]
  Bicycle Nova Scotia [IO]
  Bicycle Parking Proj. [23307]
  Bicycle Queensland [IO]
  Bicycle Ride Directors' Assn. of Am. [23308]
  Bicycle Stamps Club [22796]
  Bicycle Trans. Alliance [IO]
  Bike and Build [11514]
  Bikes Belong Coalition [21831]
  BlueRibbon Coalition [23680]
  Caesarean Cycling Club [IO]
  Calgary Mountain Bike Alliance [IO]
  Cycle Polo Fed. of India [IO]
  Cycling Australia [IO]
  Downed Bikers Assn. [12612]
  European Cycling Union [IO]
  Human Powered Vehicle Assn. [7811]
  Icelandic Mountainbike Club [IO]
  Intl. Fed. of Bike Messenger Associations [IO]
  Intl. Fed. of Bike Messenger Associations [517]
  Intl. Mountain Bicycling Assn. [23310]
  Intl. Unicycling Fed. [23311]
  Italian Fed. of Urban Cyclists and Bicycle Tourism [IO]
  League of Amer. Bicyclists [23312]
  Mountain Bike Orienteering Australia [IO]
  Natl. Bicycle Dealers Assn. [3645]
  Natl. Bicycle League [23313]
  Natl. Bicycle Tour Directors Assn. [23314]
  Natl. Center for Bicycling and Walking [23315]
  Newcastle Cycleways Movement [IO]
  Pedal Power ACT [IO]
  Randonneurs USA [23316]
  Russian Cycle Touring Club [IO]
  Tandem Club of Am. [23317]
  Thunderhead Alliance [18751]
  Tricycle Assn. [IO]
  Unicycling Soc. of Am. [23319]
  U.S. Bicycle Polo Assn. [23660]
  U.S. Cycling Fed. [23320]
  Veteran-Cycle Club [IO]
  The Wheelmen [23322]
Bicycle Africa [★13338]
Bicycle Africa [★IO]
Bicycle Assn; Amer. [23305]
Bicycle Assn; China [IO]
Bicycle Assn. of Great Britain [IO], Coventry, United Kingdom
Bicycle Assn; U.S. [★23305]
Bicycle Dealers Assn; Natl. [3645]
Bicycle Education and Legal Found. - Defunct.
Bicycle Fed. of Am. [★23315]
Bicycle Fed. of Australia [IO], Canberra, Australia
Bicycle Forum [★23304]
Bicycle Helmet Safety Inst. [12954], 4611 7th St. S, Arlington, VA 22204-1419, (703)486-0100
Bicycle Inst. of America - Defunct.
Bicycle League of Am; Amateur [★23320]
Bicycle League; Natl. [23313]
Bicycle Mfrs. Assn. of America - Address unknown since 2001.
Bicycle Network [13336], PO Box 8194, Philadelphia, PA 19101, (215)222-1253

A star before a book entry number signifies that the name is not listed separately, but is mentioned within the entry.

Bicycle Network [IO], Philadelphia, PA, United States
Bicycle New South Wales [IO], Sydney, Australia
Bicycle Nova Scotia [IO], Halifax, NS, Canada
Bicycle Parking Proj. [23307], PO Box 7342, Philadelphia, PA 19101, (215)222-1253
Bicycle Polo Assn; U.S. [23660]
Bicycle Prdt. Suppliers Assn. [3640], PO Box 187, Montgomeryville, PA 18936, (215)393-3144
Bicycle Queensland [IO], West End, Australia
Bicycle Ride Directors' Assn. of Am. [23308], c/o Sheila Lyons, 755 N Leafwood Ave., Brea, CA 92821, (562)690-9693
Bicycle Stamps Club [22796], c/o Bill Eubanks, 21304 2nd Ave. SE, Bothell, WA 98021-7550
Bicycle Study Unit - Address unknown since 2001.
Bicycle Tasmania [IO], Hobart, Australia
Bicycle Transportation Action - Defunct.
Bicycle Trans. Alliance [IO], West Perth, Australia
Bicycle Travel Assn; Bikecentennial: The [★23304]
Bicycle U.S.A; League of Amer. Wheelmen/ [★23312]
Bicycle Wholesale Distributors Assn. [★3640]
Bicycling Assn; Intl. Mountain [23310]
Bicycling Assn; Natl. Off-Road [★23320]
Bicycling Parking Found. [★23307]
Bicycling Parking Proj. [★23307]
Bicycling and Walking; Natl. Center for [23315]
Bicyclist Assn; Helmet Comm., Washington Area [★12954]
Bicyclist Association; Washington Area [★12954]
Bicyclists Educational and Legal Foundation - Defunct.
Bicyclists; League of Amer. [23312]
Biddy Basketball - Address unknown since 1995.
Bide-A-Wee Home Assn. [11371], 410 E 38th St., New York, NY 10016, (212)532-6395
Bide Awhile Animal Shelter Soc. [IO], Dartmouth, NS, Canada
BIE Mint Oddity Collectors Guild - Defunct.
Biehn Fan Club; Official Michael [24764]
Biennial Coun. of Community Churches [★19850]
Biennial Coun. of Community Churches [★IO]
Bienvenue a l'Association canadienne des telecommunications sans fil [★IO]
Bifida Assn. of Am; Spina [16458]
Big Apple Triathlon Club [★23922]
Big Band Acad. of Am. [10565], c/o David Bernhart, Pres., 1438 N Pepper St., Burbank, CA 91505-1835, (818)559-1313

Big Band Music
Big Band Acad. of Am. [10565]
Collectors Record Club [22712]
Glenn Miller Birthplace Soc. [24902]

Big Bend Natural History Assn. [7361], PO Box 196, Big Bend National Park, TX 79834-0196, (432)477-2236
Big Bros. of Am. [★11676]
Big Bros. Big Sisters of Am. [11676], 230 N 13th St., Philadelphia, PA 19107, (215)567-7000
Big Bros. Big Sisters of Canada [IO], Burlington, ON, Canada
Big Deal - Defunct.
Big East Conf. [23807], 222 Richmond St., Ste. 110, Providence, RI 02903, (401)272-9108
Big Eight Conf. - Defunct.
Big Eight Coun. on Black Student Govt. - Address unknown since 1999.
Big Island Rainforest Action Gp. [4366], PO Box 341, Kurtistown, HI 96760, (808)966-7622
Big Little Book Collector's Club [21978], PO Box 1242, Danville, CA 94526, (925)837-2086
Big Little Book Collector's Club of Am. [★21978]
Big M Mercury Club - Defunct.
Big Man's Fan Club - Address unknown since 1995.
Big Picture Alliance [16480], c/o Jeffrey A. Seder, Exec. Dir./Co-Founder, 501 Hicks Rd., West Grove, PA 19390, (610)383-6000
Big Picture Company [8353], 325 Public St., Providence, RI 02905, (401)752-3528
Big Salmon River Angling Assn. [IO], St. John, NB, Canada
Big Seven Restorers Club - Defunct.
Big Sisters of Am; Big Bros. [11676]
Big Sisters, Intl. [★11676]

Big Ten Communications Department [★23808]
Big Ten Conf. [23808], 1500 W Higgins Rd., Park Ridge, IL 60068-6300, (847)696-1010
Big Thicket Assn. [4367], PO Box 198, Saratoga, TX 77585, (409)382-5102
Big Thicket Conservation Assn. - Address unknown since 2000.
Big Thicket Coordinating Comm. - Defunct.
Big Thicket Natural Heritage Trust [4368], PO Box 1049, Kountze, TX 77625
Big Vote; Oper. [18362]
Big West Conf. [23809], 2 Corporate Park, Irvine, CA 92606, (949)261-2525
Bigelow Soc. [20794], PO Box 1909, Eugene, OR 97440, (541)741-6969
Bigelow Soc. [IO], Springfield, OR, United States
Bigfoot Info. Center; Michigan [★7480]
Bigfoot Res. Team; Southwestern [★7472]
Bigfoot Stud; Center for [7472]
Bigger League; Little [★23106]
Bighelp for Educ. [IO], Hyderabad, India
Bighorn Sheep; Soc. for the Conservation of [5381]
Bihar Assn. of North Am. [10220], 1823 Mustang Crossing, Missouri City, TX 77459, (281)416-2234
Bihar Assn. of North Am. [IO], Missouri City, TX, United States
Bike Assn; Amer. Ski- [23801]
Bike Assn; Intl. Police Mountain [6172]
Bike and Build [11514], 20 Jay St., Ste. M08, Brooklyn, NY 11211, (718)599-5925
Bike Club; Vintage Motor [22699]
Bike; Pro [★23315]
Bike and Tea Soc; Women's Mountain [23323]
Bikecentennial [★23304]
Bikecentennial: The Bicycle Travel Assn. [★23304]
Bikes Belong Coalition [21831], PO Box 2359, Boulder, CO 80306, (303)449-4893
Bikes Not Bombs [18103], 284 Amory St., Jamaica Plain, MA 02130, (617)522-0222
Bikes Not Bombs [IO], Jamaica Plain, MA, United States
Bikeways - Defunct.
Bilateral Safety Corridor Coalition [12368], 1132 E Plaza Blvd., No. 203, National City, CA 91950, (619)336-0770
Bilateral US-Arab Chamber of Commerce [24226], PO Box 571870, Houston, TX 77257-1870
Bilateral US-Arab Chamber of Commerce [IO], Houston, TX, United States
Bildkonst Upphovsratt i Sverige [IO], Stockholm, Sweden
Biliary Assn; Intl. [★14802]
Biliary Assn; Intl. Hepato-Pancreato- [★14802]
Biliary Atresia and Liver Transplant Network [16529], 3835 Richmond Ave., Box 190, Staten Island, NY 10312, (718)987-6200
Biliary Pancreatic Assn; Intl. Hepato- [★14802]
Bilingual Educ; Natl. CH for [★8287]
Bilingual Found. of the Arts [11007], 421 North Ave. 19, Los Angeles, CA 90031, (323)225-4044

Bilingualism
Center for Applied Linguistics [10401]
Intercultural Development Res. Assn. [7998]
Intercultural Development Res. Assn. [IO]
Natl. Assn. for Bilingual Educ. [7999]
Natl. CH for English Language Acquisition and Language Instruction Educational Programs [8287]
Puerto Rican Traveling Theatre Company [11040]

Bilkent Turkey ACM SIGART [IO], Ankara, Turkey
Bill Deal and the Rhondels Fan Club [24848], c/o Robert J. McKenzie, Pres., 114 Prince George Dr., Hampton, VA 23669-3604, (757)838-2059
Bill Farrar Fan Club - Address unknown since 1989.
Bill Glass Evangelistic Assn. [★19996]
Bill Glass Evangelistic Assn. [★IO]
Bill Glass Ministries [★IO]
Bill Glass Ministries [★19996]
Bill and Melinda Gates Found. [12273], PO Box 23350, Seattle, WA 98102, (206)709-3140
Bill Raskob Found. [17479], PO Box 507, Crownsville, MD 21032-0507, (410)923-9123
Bill of Rights Assn. - Address unknown since 2003.
Billers; Amer. Assn. of Medical [15050]
The Billfish Found. [5298], 2161 E Commercial Blvd., 2nd Fl., Fort Lauderdale, FL 33308, (954)938-0150

Billiard Assn; Amer. [★23146]
Billiard and Bowling Inst. of Am. [3641], PO Box 6573, Arlington, TX 76005, (800)343-1329
Billiard Cong. of Am. [23145], 12303 Airport Way, Ste. 290, Broomfield, CO 80021, (866)852-0999
Billiard Fed. of the U.S.A. [★23146]
Billiard Players Assn. of America - Address unknown since 1995.

Billiards
Amer. Cuemakers Assn. [518]
Amer. CueSports Alliance [23144]
Amer. Roque and Croquet Assn. [23090]
Belgian Pool Billiard Fed. [IO]
Billiard Cong. of Am. [23145]
British Professional Pool Players Assn. [IO]
Canadian Poolplayers Assn. [IO]
English Pool Assn. [IO]
European Pocket Billiard Fed. [IO]
Finnish Billiard Fed. [IO]
Hellenic Billiard Fed. [IO]
Intl. Cuemakers Assn. [IO]
Intl. Cuemakers Assn. [519]
Natl. Wheelchair Poolplayer Assn. [23355]
Norwegian Billiard Fed. [IO]
Russian Natl. Billiard Fed. [IO]
Ukrainian Natl. Sportive Billiard Fed. [IO]
U.S. Billiard Assn. [23146]
U.S. Professional Poolplayers Assn. [23147]
U.S. Snooker Assn. [23148]
Women's Professional Billiard Assn. [23149]
World Confed. of Billiard Sports [23150]
World Confed. of Billiard Sports [IO]
World Snooker [IO]

Billie Jo Spears Fan Club - Defunct.
Billing Assn; Amer. Medical [15057]
Billing and Mgt. Assn; Healthcare [15169]
Billings Ovulation Method Assn. - USA [12635], PO Box 2135, St. Cloud, MN 56302, (651)699-8139
Billionaire Boys Club - Address unknown since 1997.
Billy Barty Found. [13104], 929 W Olive Ave., Ste. C, Burbank, CA 91506, (818)953-5410
Billy Barty Found. for Little People [★13104]
Billy Blanton Fan Club Intl. - Defunct.
Billy Cate Fan Club - Address unknown since 1989.
Billy "Crash" Craddock Fan Club [24849], c/o Judy Plummer, Pres., 4101 Pickfair Rd., Springfield, IL 62703
Billy Graham Evangelistic Assn. [19992], 1 Billy Graham Pkwy., Charlotte, NC 28201, (704)401-2432
Billy Ray Cyrus Spirit [24850], PO Box 1206, Franklin, TN 37065, (931)486-3326
Billy Troy Fan Club - Defunct.
Bimetallic Question [IO], Montreal, QC, Canada
Bina; Congregation [10277]
Binders' Guild [9743], 2925 Powell St., Eugene, OR 97405, (541)485-6527
Binding Indus. of Am. [★1760]
Binding Indus. of Am. [★IO]
Binding Indus. Assn. Intl. [IO], Sewickley, PA, United States
Binding Indus. Assn. Intl. [1760], 200 Deer Run Rd., Sewickley, PA 15143, (412)259-1802
BiNet USA [12220], 4201 Wilson Blvd., No. 110, Box 311, Arlington, VA 22203-1859, (800)585-9368
Bing Crosby Historical Soc. - Defunct.
Bing's Friends and Collectors Soc. [24851], c/o Hobie Wilson, Pres./Ed., 236 Andrieux St., Sonoma, CA 95476-6909, (707)996-0257
Bingthings Soc. - Defunct.
Bio-Dynamic Agricultural Assn. [IO], Stroud, United Kingdom
Bio-Dynamics; Josephine Porter Inst. for Applied [4104]
Bio-Electro-Magnetics Inst. - Defunct.
Bio-Energy Coun. - Defunct.
Bio-Ethical Reform; Center for [18547]
Bio-Gro New Zealand [IO], Wellington, New Zealand
Bio-Integral Rsrc. Center [5075], PO Box 7414, Berkeley, CA 94707, (510)524-2567
Bio-Magnetics; Intl. Found. of [16654]
Bio-Technology Purchasing Mgt. Assn. - Defunct.
BIO Ventures for Global Hea. [14975], 1225 Eye St. NW, Ste. 1010, Washington, DC 20005, (202)312-9260

Reference to "IO" in place of a book number signifies that the association may be found in the 45th edition of International Organizations.

BIO Ventures for Global Hea. [IO], Washington, DC, United States
Bioanalysis; Amer. Bd. of [7235]
Bioanalysts; Amer. Assn. of [14989]
Bioanalysts; Amer. Bd. of [★7235]
Bioanalysts Bd. of Registry; Amer. Assn. of [15126]
BIOCAV [★10484]
Biochemical, Biophysical and Microbiological Soc. of Finland [IO], Helsinki, Finland
Biochemical Societies; Pan Amer. Assn. of [★6551]
Biochemical Soc. - England [IO], London, United Kingdom
Biochemical Soc. of Israel [★IO]
Biochemical Soc; Latvian [IO]
Biochemistry
   Amer. Oil Chemists' Soc. [6669]
   Amer. Soc. for Biochemistry and Molecular Biology [6546]
   Amer. Soc. of Plant Biologists [6628]
   Amer. Soc. for Virology [6547]
   Argentine Biochemical Assn. [IO]
   Asian and Pacific Fed. of Clinical Biochemistry [IO]
   Assn. for Clinical Biochemistry [IO]
   Australasian Assn. of Clinical Biochemists [IO]
   Australian Soc. for Biochemistry and Molecular Biology [IO]
   Biochemical Soc. - England [IO]
   Bioelectrochemical Soc. [IO]
   Biophysical Soc. [6612]
   Canadian Assn. of Medical Biochemists [IO]
   Canadian Soc. of Biochemistry, Molecular and Cellular Biology [IO]
   European Chemoreception Res. Org. [IO]
   Fed. of African Societies of Biochemistry and Molecular Biology [IO]
   Fed. of Amer. Societies for Experimental Biology [6576]
   Fed. of European Biochemical Societies [IO]
   Finnish Biochemical Soc. [IO]
   German Soc. for Biochemistry and Molecular Biology [IO]
   Indian Peptide Soc. [IO]
   Intl. Coenzyme Q10 Assn. [IO]
   Intl. Isotope Soc. [IO]
   Intl. Isotope Soc. [6548]
   Intl. Maillard Reaction Soc. [6683]
   Intl. Proteolysis Soc. [6549]
   Intl. Proteolysis Soc. [IO]
   Intl. Soc. of Chem. Ecology [IO]
   Intl. Soc. of Chem. Ecology [6550]
   Intl. Union of Biochemistry and Molecular Biology [IO]
   Israel Soc. for Biochemistry and Molecular Biology [IO]
   Japanese Peptide Soc. [IO]
   Malaysian Assn. of Clinical Biochemists [IO]
   Natl. Acad. of Clinical Biochemistry [13748]
   Norwegian Biochemical Soc. [IO]
   Pan-American Assn. for Biochemistry and Molecular Biology [IO]
   Pan-American Assn. for Biochemistry and Molecular Biology [6551]
   Phi Lambda Upsilon [24430]
   Protein Soc. [6552]
   Protein Soc. [IO]
   Protein Soc. of Thailand [IO]
   RNA Soc. [6553]
   Slovenian Biochemical Soc. [IO]
   Soc. for Molecular Biology and Evolution [6601]
   South African Soc. of Biochemistry and Molecular Biology [IO]
   Spanish Soc. of Proteomics [IO]
   Swiss Biochemical Soc. [IO]
   Swiss Soc. for Biochemistry [IO]
Bioclimatological Commn. of Acad. of Sciences [★IO]
Bioclimatological Gp. of Czechoslovak Soc. of Meteorology [★IO]
BioCommunications Assn. [IO], Hillsborough, NC, United States
BioCommunications Assn. [14031], 220 Southwind Ln., Hillsborough, NC 27278, (919)245-0906
Biocontrol Producers; Assn. of Natural [5074]
Biodiversity Action Network - Address unknown since 2004.

Biodynamic Agriculture Australia [IO], Bellingen, Australia
Biodynamic Craniosacral Therapy Assn. of North Am. [14069], 852 Don Diego Ave., Santa Fe, NM 87505, (505)820-1335
Bio-Dynamic Farming
   Josephine Porter Inst. for Applied Bio-Dynamics [4104]
Biodynamic Farming and Gardening Assn. [4643], 25844 Butler Rd., Junction City, OR 97448, (541)998-0105
Bioelectrical Repair and Growth Soc. [★6554]
Bioelectrical Repair and Growth Soc. [★IO]
Bioelectrics
   Soc. for Physical Regulation in Biology and Medicine [IO]
   Soc. for Physical Regulation in Biology and Medicine [6554]
Bioelectrochemical Soc. [IO], Paris, France
Bioelectromagnetics
   Bioelectromagnetics Soc. [6555]
   Bioelectromagnetics Special Interest Gp. [6556]
Bioelectromagnetics Soc. [6555], 2412 Cobblestone Way, Frederick, MD 21702-2626, (301)663-4252
Bioelectromagnetics Special Interest Gp. [6556], c/o Amer. Mensa, 1229 Corporate Dr. W, Arlington, TX 76006-6103, (817)607-0060
Bioenergy Assn. of New Zealand [IO], Wellington, New Zealand
Bioethics
   Center for Applied Christian Ethics [19975]
   Center for Bio-Ethical Reform [18547]
   Center for Bioethics [6557]
   Center for Bioethics [6558]
   Intl. Assn. of Bioethics [IO]
   Scottish Coun. on Human Bioethics [IO]
Bioethics; Center for Death Educ. and [13314]
Bioethics; Center for Interdisciplinary Res. in [IO]
Bioethics Consultation; Soc. for [★8845]
Bioethics and Humanities; Amer. Soc. for [8845]
Bioethics; Network on Feminist Approaches to [★12126]
Biofeedback
   Archaeus Proj. [13625]
   Assn. for Applied Psychophysiology and Biofeedback [13749]
   Assn. of Polysomnographic Technologists [16423]
   Biofeedback Certification Inst. of Am. [13750]
   Intl. REST Investigators Soc. [16220]
   Soc. for Psychophysiological Res. [16183]
Biofeedback; Assn. for Applied Psychophysiology and [13749]
Biofeedback Certification Inst. of Am. [13750], 10200 W 44th Ave., Ste. 310, Wheat Ridge, CO 80033-2840, (303)420-2902
Biofeedback Found. of Europe [IO], Amersfoort, Netherlands
Biofeedback Res. Soc. [★13749]
Biofeedback Soc. of Am. [★13749]
Biographical Inst. Res. Assn; Amer. [21097]
Biographical Soc; New York Genealogical and [21137]
Biophysics Conf; Natl. [★6612]
BioIndustry Assn. [IO], London, United Kingdom
Bioinformatics Italian Soc. [IO], Bari, Italy
Bioinstrumentation Advisory Coun. - Defunct.
Biokemisk Forening [★IO]
Biological Anthropology Sect. [6414], c/o Jim Bindon, Univ. of Alabama, Dept. of Anthropology, PO Box 870210, Tuscaloosa, AL 35487, (205)348-1958
Biological Arms Control Inst; Chem. and [17023]
Biological Chemists; Amer. Soc. of [★6546]
Biological Coun. [★IO]
Biological Editors; Conf. of [★3108]
Biological Engg; Amer. Inst. for Medical and [7112]
Biological Engg. Soc. [★IO]
Biological Farmers of Australia [IO], Chermside, Australia
Biological Field Stations; Org. of Inland [★6591]
Biological Husbandry Gp. [★IO]
Biological Info. Processing Org. [★6783]
Biological Inst. of Tropical America - Address unknown since 1994.
Biological Photographic Assn. [★14031]

Biological Photographic Assn. [★IO]
Biological Res. Inst. - Address unknown since 1995.
Biological Rhythms; Soc. for Light Treatment and [16636]
Biological Safety Assn; Amer. [3436]
Biological Stain Commn. [6571], Univ. of Rochester, Medical Center, Pathology Dept., 575 Elmwood Ave., Box 626, Rochester, NY 14642-0001, (585)275-2751
Biological Stains; Commn. on Standardization of [★6571]
Biological Therapy of Cancer; Intl. Soc. for [13835]
Biological Weapons
   BioWeapons Prevention Proj. [IO]
   Chem. and Biological Arms Control Inst. [17023]
   Nuclear Threat Initiative [18164]
   Sunshine Proj. [IO]
Biologics Evaluation and Res; Center for [14671]
Biologie and Ecology; Intl. Inst. for Bau [4513]
Biologists; Amer. Inst. of Fishery Res. [7170]
Biologists; Amer. Soc. of Plant [6628]
Biologists; Amer. Soc. of Professional [★6560]
Biologists; Soc. of Systematic [7868]
Biology
   Acad. for Ethics in Medicine [IO]
   Acarological Soc. of Am. [7056]
   Adhesion Soc. [6661]
   Amer. Acad. of Microbiology [6559]
   American Academy of Microbiology [IO]
   Amer. Assn. for Medical Chronobiology and Chronotherapeutics [13751]
   Amer. Assn. of Stratigraphic Palynologists [7434]
   Amer. Cetacean Soc. [7258]
   Amer. Coll. of Toxicology [7800]
   Amer. Elasmobranch Soc. [7278]
   Amer. Fern Soc. [6623]
   Amer. Fisheries Soc. [7169]
   Amer. Genetic Assn. [7111]
   Amer. Inst. of Biological Sciences [6560]
   Amer. Inst. of Fishery Res. Biologists [7170]
   Amer. Inst. of Oral Biology [14137]
   Amer. Littoral Soc. - Northeast Region [7269]
   Amer. Marinelife Dealers Assn. [5007]
   Amer. Microscopical Soc. [7332]
   Amer. Museum of Natural History [7357]
   Amer. Oil Chemists' Soc. [6669]
   Amer. Philosophical Soc. [7598]
   Amer. Quaternary Assn. [7359]
   Amer. Soc. for Biochemistry and Molecular Biology [6546]
   Amer. Soc. of Biomechanics [6561]
   Amer. Soc. for Cell Biology [6562]
   Amer. Soc. for Gravitational and Space Biology Student Assn. [6563]
   Amer. Soc. for Matrix Biology [6564]
   Amer. Soc. for Microbiology [6565]
   Amer. Soc. for Photobiology [6566]
   American Society for Photobiology [IO]
   Amer. Soc. of Plant Biologists [6628]
   Amer. Soc. of Primatologists [6405]
   Amer. Type Culture Coll. [6567]
   Americans to Ban Cloning [17089]
   Anaerobe Soc. of the Americas [6568]
   Anaerobe Soc. of the Americas [IO]
   Animal Behavior Mgt. Alliance [7860]
   Animal Behavior Soc. [7861]
   Aquatic Animal Life Support Operators [7279]
   Aquatic Res. Inst. [7171]
   Arab Soc. for Plant Protection [IO]
   Argentine Soc. of Biology [IO]
   Assn. of Applied Biologists [IO]
   Assn. of Earth Sci. Editors [3093]
   Assn. of Genetic Technologists [6569]
   Assn. of Indian Entomologists in North Am. [7057]
   Assn. for Mexican Cave Stud. [7691]
   Assn. of Sci. Museum Directors [10498]
   Assn. for Tropical Biology and Conservation [6570]
   Australasian Bioethics Assn. [IO]
   Australasian Soc. for Human Biology [IO]
   Australian Inst. of Biology [IO]
   Australian Soc. for Microbiology [IO]
   Babraham Inst. [IO]
   Beta Beta Beta [24408]
   Biological Anthropology Sect. [6414]

A star before a book entry number signifies that the name is not listed separately, but is mentioned within the entry.

Biological Stain Commn. [6571]
Biomedical Engg. Soc. [6607]
Biometric Application Programming Interface Consortium [6572]
Biophysical Soc. [6612]
Brazilian Soc. of Biochemistry and Molecular Biology [IO]
British Aerobiology Fed. [IO]
British Soc. for Cell Biology [IO]
Canadian Fed. of Biological Societies [IO]
Canadian Soc. of Environmental Biologists [IO]
Canadian Soc. of Microbiologists [IO]
Carnegie Institution of Washington [7564]
Cell Proliferation Soc. [6573]
Cell Stress Soc. Intl. [16488]
Center for Bioethics [6558]
Center for Bioethics [6557]
Center for Interdisciplinary Res. in Bioethics [IO]
Center for the Stud. of Natural and Historical Anomalies [7862]
Centre for Bioethics [IO]
Classification Soc. of North Am. [7456]
Colombian Assn. of Medical Schools [IO]
Comm. for Mapping the Flora of Europe [IO]
Comm. on the Status of Women in Microbiology [6574]
Coun. for Biotechnology Info. [6614]
Coun. of Entomology Dept. Administrators [7060]
Coun. of Sci. Editors [3108]
Coun. on Undergraduate Res. [9059]
The Crustacean Soc. [7863]
Cushman Found. for Foraminiferal Res. [7428]
Danish Coun. of Ethics [IO]
Danish Soc. for Biochemistry and Molecular Biology [IO]
EarthWave Soc. [4556]
Environmental Careers Org. [8388]
Environmental Mutagen Soc. [6575]
Estuarine Res. Fed. [7271]
Ethics Inst. [IO]
Eugenics Special Interest Gp. [7114]
European Cell Death Org. [IO]
European Culture Collections' Org. [IO]
European Fed. of Biotechnology [IO]
European Fed. of Biotechnology - Germany [IO]
European Fed. of Cytology Societies [IO]
European Life Scientist Org. [IO]
European Molecular Biology Lab. [IO]
European Molecular Biology Org. [IO]
European Soc. for Animal Cell Tech. [IO]
European Soc. for Evolutionary Biology [IO]
European Soc. for Photobiology [IO]
Fed. of Amer. Societies for Experimental Biology [6576]
Fed. of Asian and Oceanian Biochemists and Molecular Biologists [IO]
Fed. of European Microbiological Societies [IO]
Fiber Soc. [7078]
Freshwater Biological Assn. [IO]
Freshwater Mollusk Conservation Soc. [5034]
Friends of the Natl. Zoo [7858]
Geochemical Soc. [7141]
Global Assn. for Interpersonal Neurobiology Stud. [7375]
Hawkwatch Intl. [7419]
Hong Kong Bioethics Assn. [IO]
Human Biology Assn. [6577]
Inst. of Biology [IO]
Inst. of Human Origins [7072]
Inst. for the Stud. of Man [6418]
Intl. Assn. of Animal Behavior Consultants [7864]
Intl. Assn. of Astacology [7174]
Intl. Assn. of Biological Technicians [IO]
Intl. Assn. for Biologicals [IO]
International Association of Environmental Mutagen Societies [IO]
Intl. Assn. of Environmental Mutagen Societies [6578]
Intl. Assn. of Human Biologists [IO]
Intl. Assn. for Lichenology [IO]
Intl. Bioacoustics Coun. [IO]
Intl. Biodeterioration and Biodegradation Soc. [IO]
Intl. Biogeography Soc. [7122]
Intl. Biometric Soc. [7707]
Intl. Biometric Soc., Eastern North Amer. Region [7708]

Intl. Biometric Soc., Western North Amer. Region [7709]
Intl. Canopy Network [6579]
International Canopy Network [IO]
Intl. Cell Death Soc. [6854]
Intl. Cell Res. Org. [IO]
International Cytokine Society [IO]
Intl. Cytokine Soc. [6580]
Intl. Endotoxin and Innate Immunity Soc. [7803]
Intl. Fed. of Cell Biology [6581]
International Federation of Cell Biology [IO]
Intl. Maillard Reaction Soc. [6683]
Intl. Org. for Biotechnology and Bioengineering [IO]
Intl. Org. for Mycoplasmology [IO]
Intl. Org. for Mycoplasmology [6582]
Intl. Org. of Plant Biosystematists [6639]
Intl. Soc. for Analytical Cytology [6583]
Intl. Soc. for Analytical Cytology [IO]
International Society of Artificial Life [IO]
Intl. Soc. of Artificial Life [6584]
Intl. Soc. of Bioethics [IO]
Intl. Soc. for Biological and Environmental Repositories [IO]
Intl. Soc. for Biological and Environmental Repositories [6585]
Intl. Soc. for Bioluminescence and Chemiluminescence [7612]
Intl. Soc. for Biosafety Res. [6586]
Intl. Soc. for Biosafety Res. [IO]
Intl. Soc. of Chem. Ecology [6550]
Intl. Soc. for Chronobiology [6587]
Intl. Soc. for Chronobiology [IO]
Intl. Soc. for Computational Biology [2094]
Intl. Soc. of Cryptozoology [7865]
Intl. Soc. of Developmental Biologists [IO]
Intl. Soc. for Developmental Psychobiology [16153]
Intl. Soc. of Differentiation [6588]
Intl. Soc. of Differentiation [IO]
Intl. Soc. for the History, Philosophy, and Social Stud. of Biology [8507]
Intl. Soc. for Interferon and Cytokine Res. [16351]
Intl. Soc. for Phylogenetic Nomenclature [7116]
Intl. Soc. for Plant Molecular Biology [6589]
Intl. Soc. for Plant Molecular Biology [IO]
Intl. Soc. of Protistologists [7866]
Intl. Union of Biological Sciences [IO]
Intl. Union of Microbiological Societies [IO]
The Israel Soc. for Developmental Biology [IO]
Japanese Soc. of Developmental Biologists [IO]
Japanese Soc. for Plant Systematics [IO]
Life Extension Soc. [14074]
Membrane Soc. of Japan [IO]
Microscopy Soc. of Am. [7335]
Natl. Assn. of Biology Teachers [8000]
Natl. Coun. on Ethics in Human Res. [IO]
Natl. Inst. for Biological Standards and Control [IO]
Natl. Speleological Soc. [7693]
Natural Sci. Collections Alliance [6590]
Netherlands Biotechnological Soc. [IO]
North Amer. Forensic Entomology Assn. [7064]
North Amer. Native Fishes Assn. [7175]
North Amer. Vascular Biology Org. [16728]
Nuffield Coun. on Bioethics [IO]
Oceanic Soc. Expeditions [23016]
Org. of Biological Field Stations [6591]
Org. for Human Brain Mapping [7379]
PACON Intl. [5011]
Pan-American Aerobiology Assn. [6592]
Pan-American Aerobiology Assn. [IO]
Pan-American Assn. for Biochemistry and Molecular Biology [6551]
Phi Sigma [24409]
Proteome Soc. [7119]
Radiation Res. Soc. [7557]
Samuel Roberts Noble Found. [4082]
Scottish Microbiology Soc. [IO]
Sicilian Bioethical Inst. [IO]
Sociedad de Biologia de Chile [IO]
Sociedad Espanola de Bioquimica y Biologia Molecular [IO]
Soc. for Applied Microbiology [IO]
Soc. for Biological Engg. [6593]

Soc. for Conservation Biology [6594]
Soc. for Conservation Biology [IO]
Soc. for Cryobiology [6847]
Soc. for Developmental Biology [6595]
Society for Developmental Biology [IO]
Society of Ethnobiology [IO]
Soc. of Ethnobiology [6596]
Soc. for Experimental Biology [IO]
Soc. for Experimental Biology and Medicine [6597]
Soc. For Biomaterials [6609]
Soc. for Free Radical Biology and Medicine [6613]
Soc. for Gen. Microbiology [IO]
Soc. of Gen. Physiologists [7511]
Soc. for In Vitro Biology [6598]
Soc. for Indus. Microbiology [6599]
Soc. for Integrative and Comparative Biology [7867]
Soc. for Marine Mammalogy [5017]
Soc. for Mathematical Biology [6600]
Soc. for Molecular Biology and Evolution [6601]
Soc. for Molecular Imaging [15181]
Soc. of Nematologists [7371]
Soc. for Neuroscience [7380]
Soc. for Northwestern Vertebrate Biology [7364]
Soc. of Rheology [7579]
Soc. for the Stud. of Evolution [7073]
Soc. for the Stud. of Human Biology [IO]
Soc. for the Stud. of Social Biology [6862]
Soc. of Systematic Biologists [7868]
Soc. of Woman Geographers [7124]
South African Assn. for Marine Biological Res. [IO]
Suomen Biologian Seura Vanamo [IO]
Swiss Soc. for Biomedical Ethics [IO]
Swiss Soc. for Microbiology [IO]
Systematics Assn. of New Zealand [IO]
Teratology Soc. [6602]
Tropical Biology Assn. [IO]
United Kingdom Environmental Mutagen Soc. [IO]
U.S. Fed. for Culture Collections [6603]
U.S. Human Proteome Org. [6604]
United States Human Proteome Organization [IO]
Waksman Found. for Microbiology [6605]
Wilderness Medical Soc. [15184]
The Wildlife Soc. [5401]
World Assn. for Chinese Biomedical Engineers [6611]
World Environmental Org. [4475]
World Fed. for Culture Collections [IO]
Biology of the Amer. Heart Assn; Coun. on Arteriosclerosis, Thrombosis and Vascular [13902]
Biology; Amer. Inst. of Oral [14137]
Biology; Amer. Soc. for Biochemistry and Molecular [6546]
Biology Editors; Coun. of [★3108]
Biology; Found. for Micro [★6605]
Biology; Intl. Soc. for Cell [★6581]
Biology; Israel Soc. for Biochemistry and Molecular [IO]
Biology and Medicine; Soc. for Free Radical [6613]
Biology; Soc. for Integrative and Comparative [7867]
Biology; Soc. for Leukocyte [16365]
Biology; Soc. for Northwestern Vertebrate [7364]
Biology; Soc. for the Stud. of Social [6862]
Biology; Soc. for Vascular Medicine and [16729]
Biomagnetic Therapy Assn. [16609], PO Box 394, Lyons, CO 80540, (303)823-0307
Biomass Energy Res. Assn. [6946], 901 D St. SW, Ste. 100, Washington, DC 20024, (847)381-6320
Biomaterials; European Soc. for [IO]
Biomaterials; Soc. For [6609]
Biomechanics; Amer. Soc. of [6561]
Biomechanics; European Soc. of [IO]
Biomedical Communications Directors; Assn. of [14030]
Biomedical Computing Soc. [★6783]
Biomedical Computing; Special Interest Gp. on [★6783]

Biomedical Engineering
Ad Hoc Gp. for Medical Res. Funding [17686]
Argentine Soc. of Bioengineering [IO]
Association for the Advancement of Medical Instrumentation [IO]

Reference to "IO" in place of a book number signifies that the association may be found in the 45th edition of International Organizations.

Assn. for the Advancement of Medical Instrumentation [6606]
Australasian Soc. for Biomaterials [IO]
BioCommunications Assn. [14031]
Biomedical Engg. Assn. of Ireland [IO]
Biomedical Engineering Society [IO]
Biomedical Engg. Soc. [6607]
BIOTECanada [IO]
Brazilian Soc. of Biomedical Engg. [IO]
Bulgarian Sci. Soc. of Virology [IO]
Canadian Medical and Biological Engg. Soc. [IO]
Canadian Soc. for Biomechanics [IO]
Colombian Assn. of Bioengineering and Medical Electronics [IO]
Cyprus Assn. of Medical Physics and Biomedical Engg. [IO]
Danish Soc. for Biomedical Engg. [IO]
Diagnostic Marketing Assn. [2624]
DICOM Standards Comm. [7178]
Dutch Soc. for Biomaterials and Tissue Engg. [IO]
European Biomedical Res. Assn. [IO]
European Soc. of Biomechanics [IO]
German Assn. of Biomedical Engg. [IO]
IEEE Engg. in Medicine and Biology Soc. [IO]
IEEE Engg. in Medicine and Biology Soc. [6608]
Inst. of Biomedical Sci. [IO]
Inst. of Physics and Engg. in Medicine [IO]
Intl. Fed. for Medical and Biological Engg. [IO]
Intl. Functional Elecl. Stimulation Soc. [15390]
Intl. Soc. of Artificial Life [6584]
Intl. Soc. of Biomechanics [IO]
Intl. Soc. for Electrophysiology and Kinesiology [IO]
Intl. Soc. for Interferon and Cytokine Res. [16351]
Japanese Biochemical Soc. [IO]
Japanese Soc. for Tissue Engg. [IO]
Norwegian Soc. for Biomedical Engg. [IO]
Slovak Soc. of Biomedical Engg. and Medical Informatics [IO]
Sociedad Mexicana de Ingenieria Biomedica [IO]
Soc. for Biological Engg. [6593]
Soc. for Biomedical Engg. [IO]
Soc. for Biotechnology, Japan [IO]
Soc. For Biomaterials [6609]
Spanish Soc. of Biomedical Engg. [IO]
Tissue Engg. Soc. Intl. [IO]
Tissue Engg. Soc. Intl. [6610]
World Assn. for Chinese Biomedical Engineers [6611]
World Assn. for Chinese Biomedical Engineers [IO]
Biomedical Engg. Assn. of Ireland [IO], Blanchardstown, Ireland
Biomedical Engineering Society [IO], Landover, MD, United States
Biomedical Engg. Soc. [6607], 8401 Corporate Dr., Ste. 140, Landover, MD 20785-2224, (301)459-1999
Biomedical Ethics; Swiss Soc. for [IO]
Biomedical Info. Processing; Special Interest Gp. for [★6783]
Biomedical Marketing Assn. [★2624]
Biomedical Res; Assn. for [★13700]
Biomedical Res. Defense Fund - Defunct.
Biomedical Res. and Experimental Therapeutics Soc. of Singapore [IO], Singapore, Singapore
Biomedical Res; Found. for [13696]
Biomedical Res; Natl. Assn. for [13700]
Biometric Application Programming Interface Consortium [6572], c/o Steve Vinsik, Sec., 11491 Sunset Hills Rd., Reston, VA 20190, (703)579-3064
Biometric Indus. Assn; Intl. [7743]
The Biometric Soc. [★7707]
The Biometric Soc. [★IO]
Biometric Soc., Eastern North Amer. Region; Intl. [7708]
Biometric Soc., Western North Amer. Region [★7709]
Biometric Soc., Western North Amer. Region [★IO]
Biometrics Inst. [IO], Crows Nest, Australia
Biomimetics New Zealand [IO], Christchurch, New Zealand
Biomolecular Rsrc. Facilities; Assn. of [7238]
Biomolecular Sciences; Soc. for [6694]

Bionomics Inst. [1171], 2173 E Francisco Blvd., Ste. C, San Rafael, CA 94901, (415)454-1800
Bionomy Intl; Soc. of Ortho- [13767]
Biophysical Soc. [6612], 9650 Rockville Pike, Bethesda, MD 20814, (301)634-7114
Biophysical Soc. of Argentina [IO], Buenos Aires, Argentina
Biophysical Soc. of Canada [IO], Trois-Rivieres, QC, Canada
Biophysical Soc. of China [IO], Beijing, People's Republic of China
Biophysics
  Australian Soc. for Biophysics [IO]
  Biophysical Soc. [6612]
  Biophysical Soc. of Argentina [IO]
  Biophysical Soc. of Canada [IO]
  Biophysical Soc. of China [IO]
  British Biophysical Soc. [IO]
  European Biophysical Societies' Assn. [IO]
  Hungarian Biophysical Soc. [IO]
  Indian Biophysical Soc. [IO]
  Intl. Inst. of Biophysics [IO]
  Intl. Union for Pure and Applied Biophysics [IO]
  Italian Soc. of Biophysics [IO]
  Society for Free Radical Biology and Medicine [IO]
  Soc. for Free Radical Biology and Medicine [6613]
  Soc. for Molecular Biology and Evolution [6601]
Bioplaneta Network, Mexico [IO], Mexico City, Mexico
Biopolitics Intl. Org. [IO], Athens, Greece
BioProcess Engineering Soc. Intl. - Address unknown since 1987.
BiOptic Driving Network - USA [15705], 5520 Ridgeton Hill Ct., Fairfax, VA 22032
Bioregional Project - Address unknown since 2001.
Bioregionalism
  Planet Drum Found. [16999]
Biosciences Fed. [IO], Cambridge, United Kingdom
Biosophical Inst. - Defunct.
Biostatistics; Intl. Soc. for Clinical [IO]
BIOTECanada [IO], Ottawa, ON, Canada
Biotech Medical Mgt. Assn. [14683], 10592 Perry Hwy., No. 300, Wexford, PA 15090, (724)934-8440
Biotech Trainers; Soc. of Pharmaceutical and [3475]
Biotechnological Soc; Netherlands [IO]
Biotechnology
  All India Biotech Assn. [IO]
  Alliance for Better Foods [4674]
  Assn. of Biotechnology Led Enterprises [IO]
  Biometrics Inst. [IO]
  Biomimetics New Zealand [IO]
  Biotechnology Indus. Org. [520]
  Coun. for Biotechnology Info. [6614]
  Coun. for Biotechnology Info. [IO]
  DECHEMA [IO]
  European Assn. for Bioindustries [IO]
  European Biosafety Assn. [IO]
  Genetic Engg. Action Network [6615]
  Indigenous Peoples Coun. on Biocolonialism [12407]
  Intl. Biopharmaceutical Assn. [15936]
  Intl. Ser. for the Acquisition of Agri-biotech Applications [6398]
  Intl. Soc. for Biosafety Res. [6586]
  Intl. Soc. for Computational Biology [2094]
  Intl. Soc. of Lyophilization - Freeze Drying [6616]
  Japan Soc. for Bioscience, Biotechnology and Agrochemistry [IO]
  New Zealand's Biotech Indus. Org. [IO]
  Norwegian Bioindustry Assn. [IO]
  Org. of Regulatory and Clinical Associates [521]
  Spanish Assn. of Bioenterprises [IO]
  Surfaces in Biomaterials Found. [6617]
  Women in Bio [6618]
Biotechnology Assn; Indus. [★520]
Biotechnology and Bioengineering; Intl. Org. for [IO]
Biotechnology Companies; Assn. of [★520]
Biotechnology; European Fed. of [IO]
Biotechnology Indus. Org. [520], 1201 Maryland Ave. SW, Ste. 900, Washington, DC 20024, (202)962-9200
Bioterrorism
  Chem. and Biological Arms Control Inst. [17023]

Nuclear Threat Initiative [18164]
BioWeapons Prevention Proj. [IO], Geneva, Switzerland
Biphenyl Work Group - Defunct.
Biplane Assn; Natl. [21465]
Bipolar Support Alliance; Depression and [15196]
Birch Soc; John [17274]
Bird
  African Bird Club [IO]
  African Love Bird Soc. [21832]
  African Parrot Soc. [21833]
  Amateur Field Trial Clubs of Am. [22184]
  Amer. Assn. of Spanish Timbrado Breeders [21834]
  Amer. Bird Conservancy [5290]
  Amer. Bird Conservation Assn. [21835]
  Amer. Birding Assn. [7411]
  Amer. Budgerigar Soc. [21836]
  Amer. Canary Fanciers Assn. [21837]
  Amer. Cockatiel Soc. [21838]
  Amer. Dove Assn. [21839]
  Amer. Fed. of Aviculture [21840]
  Amer. Game Fowl Soc. [4190]
  Amer. Mookee Assn. [4191]
  Amer. Ornithologists' Union [7412]
  Amer. Ostrich Assn. [4132]
  Amer. Pastured Poultry Producers Assn. [5106]
  Amer. Poultry Intl. [5108]
  Amer. Racing Pigeon Union [22894]
  Amer. Singers Club [21841]
  Amer. Waterslager Soc. [21842]
  American Waterslager Society [IO]
  Asiatic Breeders Association [IO]
  Asiatic Breeders Assn. [4192]
  Assn. of Avian Veterinarians - USA [16782]
  Assn. of Field Ornithologists [7413]
  Audubon Naturalist Soc. of the Central Atlantic States [4364]
  Australasian Raptor Assn. [IO]
  Australian Bird Stud. Assn. [IO]
  Avian Welfare Coalition [4193]
  Avicultural Soc. of Am. [7414]
  Big Thicket Assn. [4367]
  Bird Airplane Club [21432]
  Bird Clubs of Am. [21843]
  Bird Conservation Soc. of Thailand [IO]
  Bird Observers Club of Australia [IO]
  BirdLife Belarus [IO]
  BirdLife Botswana [IO]
  BirdLife Malta [IO]
  Birdlife South Africa [IO]
  Birds Australia [IO]
  Birds of Prey Found. [5300]
  BirdWatch Ireland [IO]
  Boreal Songbird Initiative [5302]
  Brooks Bird Club [5304]
  Brotogeris Soc. Intl. [4194]
  Brotogeris Soc. Intl. [IO]
  Budgerigar and Foreign Bird Soc. [IO]
  Call and Whistle Collectors Assn. [21983]
  Canadian Dove Assn. [IO]
  Canadian Peregrine Found. [IO]
  Canadian Racing Pigeon Union [IO]
  Canary and Finch Soc. [4195]
  Canberra Ornithologists Gp. [IO]
  Central States Roller Canary Breeders Assn. [21844]
  COM-U.S.A. [21845]
  Cooper Ornithological Soc. [7415]
  Cornell Lab. of Ornithology [7416]
  Doga Dernegi [IO]
  Dove Sportsman's Soc. [IO]
  Dove Sportsman's Soc. [11515]
  Ducks Unlimited [5311]
  European Ornithologists' Union [IO]
  Exotic Bird Soc. of Am. [21846]
  Fatal Light Awareness Prog. [IO]
  Florida Keys Wild Bird Rehabilitation Center [5317]
  Ghana Wildlife Soc. [IO]
  Guinea Fowl Breeders Assn. [4196]
  Guinea Fowl Intl. Assn. [4197]
  Hartz Club of Am. [22772]
  Hawk Migration Assn. of North Am. [7418]
  Hawk Mountain Sanctuary [5324]

A star before a book entry number signifies that the name is not listed separately, but is mentioned within the entry.

Hawkwatch Intl. [7419]
Hummingbird Soc. [4198]
Hunting Retriever Club [22285]
Inland Bird Banding Assn. [7420]
Intl. Assn. of Avian Trainers and Educators [21847]
Intl. Assn. of Avian Trainers and Educators [IO]
Intl. Aviculturists Soc. [IO]
Intl. Aviculturists Soc. [4199]
Intl. Bird Beer Label Assn. [21491]
Intl. Bird Rescue Res. Center [5326]
Intl. Center for the Stud. of Bird Migration, Latrun [IO]
International Conure Association [IO]
Intl. Conure Assn. [21848]
Intl. Crane Found. [5327]
Intl. Fed. of Amer. Homing Pigeon Fanciers [22895]
Intl. Gloster Breeders Assn. [21849]
Intl. Modena Club [22896]
Intl. Parrotlet Soc. [21850]
International Parrotlet Society [IO]
Intl. Wild Waterfowl Assn. [5331]
Mid-Atlantic States Assn. of Avian Veterinarians [16798]
Natl. Amateur Retriever Club [22309]
Natl. Audubon Soc. [4422]
Natl. Beagle Club of Am. [22314]
Natl. Cage Bird Show [21851]
Natl. Chicken Coun. [5111]
Natl. Cockatiel Soc. [21852]
Natl. Color-Bred Assn. [21853]
Natl. Finch and Softbill Soc. [21854]
Natl. Inst. of Red Orange Canaries and All Other Cage Birds [21855]
Natl. Parrot Sanctuary [IO]
Natl. Pigeon Assn. [21856]
North Amer. Banding Coun. [7421]
North Amer. Bluebird Soc. [5352]
North Amer. Cockatiel Soc. [21857]
North American Cockatiel Society [IO]
North Amer. Crane Working Group [5353]
North Amer. Falconers Assn. [23398]
North Amer. Gamebird Assn. [4144]
North Amer. Grouse Partnership [5354]
North Amer. Loon Fund [5355]
North Amer. Parrot Soc. [21858]
North Amer. Rhea Assn. [5005]
Nuttall Ornithological Club [7422]
Ornithological Soc. of New Zealand [IO]
Pacific Seabird Gp. [5362]
Parrot Soc. of Australia [IO]
Parrots and People [11516]
Pelican Man's Bird Sanctuary [5364]
The Peregrine Fund [5365]
Pionus Breeders Assn. [21859]
Pionus Breeders Assn. [IO]
Poultry Sci. Assn. [5116]
Purple Martin Conservation Assn. [5369]
Quail Unlimited [5370]
Quaker Parakeet Soc. [4200]
Quaker Parakeet Society [IO]
Raptor Res. Found. [5372]
Ruffed Grouse Soc. [5376]
Russian Bird Conservation Union [IO]
Serama Coun. of North Am. [4201]
SOC [IO]
Soc. of Canadian Ornithologists [IO]
Soc. of Parrot Breeders and Exhibitors [21860]
Soc. for the Preservation of Birds of Prey [5382]
Soc. of Tympanuchus Cupido Pinnatus [5383]
Stafford Canary Club of Am. [21861]
Stafford Canary Club of America [IO]
Tanygnathus Soc. [4202]
Toledo Bird Assn., Zebra Finch Club of America [21862]
The Trumpeter Swan Soc. [5388]
Turkey Vulture Soc. [5389]
United Gloster Breeders [21863]
United Gloster Breeders [IO]
U.S. Assn. of Roller Canary Culturists [21864]
U.S. Poultry and Egg Assn. [5122]
Virginia Poultry Breeders Assn. [5124]
Ward Museum of Wildfowl Art, Salisbury Univ. [9529]

Waterfowl U.S.A. [4465]
Western Gamebird Alliance [4466]
Whooping Crane Conservation Assn. [5392]
Wild Bird Feeding Indus. [1361]
Wilson Ornithological Soc. [7424]
Wobbly Parrot Rescue [IO]
Bird Airplane Club [21432], c/o Jeannie Hill, PO Box 328, Harvard, IL 60033-0328, (815)943-7205
Bird Assn. of California - Address unknown since 1995.
Bird Assn; North Amer. Game [4144]
Bird Banding Assn; Eastern [7417]
Bird Banding Assn; Inland [7420]
Bird-Banding Assn; Northeastern [★7413]
Bird Club; Brooks [5304]
Bird Clubs of Am. [21843], c/o Georgi Higel, Dir., PO Box 1433, Waldorf, MD 20604-1433, (301)843-3683
Bird Conservancy; Amer. [5290]
Bird Conservation; Rare Center for Tropical [★5373]
Bird Conservation Soc. of Thailand [IO], Bangkok, Thailand
Bird Dog Assn; Intl. [21452]
Bird Feeding Indus; Wild [1361]
Bird Friends Soc. - Defunct.
Bird Gp; Pacific Sea [5362]
Bird Life Intl. - United Kingdom [IO], Cambridge, United Kingdom
Bird and Mammal Soc; Pacific Northwest [★7364]
Bird Observers Club of Australia [IO], Nunawading, Australia
Bird Preservation; Intl. Coun. for [★5290]
Bird Rehabilitation Center; Florida Keys Wild [5317]
Bird Sanctuary; Pelican Man's [5364]
Bird Strike Comm. Europe [★IO]
Bird Strike Comm. USA [5299], 6100 Columbus Ave., Sandusky, OH 44870, (419)625-0242
Bird Stud. Canada [IO], Port Rowan, ON, Canada
Birding Assn; Amer. [7411]
BirdLife Belarus [IO], Minsk, Belarus
BirdLife Botswana [IO], Mogoditshane, Botswana
BirdLife Cyprus [IO], Nicosia, Cyprus
BirdLife Intl. [IO], Cambridge, United Kingdom
BirdLife Malta [IO], Ta'Xbiex, Malta
Birdlife South Africa [IO], Johannesburg, Republic of South Africa
Birds in Am; More Game [★5311]
Birds Australia [IO], Carlton, Australia
Birds of Prey
  Amer. Poultry Intl. [5108]
  Birds of Prey Found. [5300]
  Hawk Mountain Sanctuary [5324]
  Intl. Bird Rescue Res. Center [5326]
  The Intl. Osprey Found. [5328]
  Last Chance Forever [5336]
  Natl. Audubon Soc. [4422]
  North Amer. Falconers Assn. [23398]
  The Peregrine Fund [5365]
  Poultry Sci. Assn. [5116]
  Raptor Educ. Found. [5371]
  Raptor Res. Found. [5372]
  Soc. for the Preservation of Birds of Prey [5382]
  Turkey Vulture Soc. [5389]
  U.S. Poultry and Egg Assn. [5122]
  Virginia Poultry Breeders Assn. [5124]
Birds of Prey Found. [5300], 2290 S 104th St., Broomfield, CO 80020, (303)460-0674
The Birds of Prey Soc. [★5382]
Birds of Prey; Soc. for the Preservation of [5382]
Birds of Prey Working Group [IO], Johannesburg, Republic of South Africa
BirdWatch Ireland [IO], Newtownmountkennedy, Ireland
Birkebeiner Ski Found; Amer. [23749]
Birman Fanciers; Natl. [21913]
Birmingham Chamber of Commerce and Indus. [IO], Birmingham, United Kingdom
Birmingham Natural History Soc. [IO], Birmingham, United Kingdom
Birney Intl. Fan Club; David [24737]
Birth; Amer. Acad. of Husband-Coached Child [15579]
Birth; Center for Loss in Multiple [12665]
Birth Center Network; Cooperative [★15580]
Birth; Center for the Stud. of Multiple [15272]

Birth Control League; Amer. [★12187]
Birth Defect and Clinical Genetic Soc. - Defunct.
Birth Defect Res. for Children [13752], 800 Celebration Ave., Ste. 225, Celebration, FL 34747, (407)566-8304
Birth Defects
  AboutFace Intl. [IO]
  Angelman Syndrome Found. [16528]
  Assn. for the Bladder Exstrophy Community [14252]
  Birth Defect Res. for Children [13752]
  CHERUBS - Assn. of Congenital Diaphragmatic Hernia Res., Advocacy and Support [13753]
  CHERUBS - Association of Congenital Diaphragmatic Hernia Research, Advocacy and Support [IO]
  Children's Craniofacial Assn. [14057]
  Cornelia de Lange Syndrome Found. [13754]
  Erb's Palsy Assn. of Ireland [IO]
  FACES: The Natl. Craniofacial Assn. [14061]
  Fatty Oxidation Disorders (FOD) Family Support Gp. [16532]
  FG Syndrome Family Alliance [16533]
  Five P Minus Soc. [16534]
  FRAXA Res. Found. [16535]
  Intl. Fed. of Teratology Societies [IO]
  Klippel-Trenaunay Support Gp. [13755]
  March of Dimes Birth Defects Found. [13756]
  MUMS Natl. Parent-to-Parent Network [16541]
  Myotubular Myopathy Rsrc. Gp. [16542]
  Natl. Birth Defects Prevention Network [13757]
  Nevus Network [16545]
  Org. of Teratology Info. Services [13758]
  Pierre Robin Network [14473]
  Prader-Willi Syndrome Assn. (U.S.A.) [14475]
  Reach Ireland [IO]
  Rubinstein-Taybi Parent Gp. U.S.A. [13759]
  Spina Bifida Assn. of Am. [16458]
  Support Org. for Trisomy 18, 13, and Related Disorders [14485]
  Uplift Internationale [15737]
  Wide Smiles [16554]
Birth Defects Found; March of Dimes [13756]
Birth Educators; Amer. Soc. of Child [15589]
Birth Educators; Assn. of Labor Assistants and Child [13977]
Birth Experiences; Center for Humane Options in Child [15594]
Birth; Informed Home [★15602]
Birth Intl; Water [13984]
Birth and Parenting; Informed Homebirth/Informed [15602]
Birth and Postpartum Professional Assn; Child [13980]
Birth Psychology; Assn. for [16137]
Birth Support Providers, Intl. - Address unknown since 2001.
Birth Without Pain Educ. Assn; Child [★15607]
Birthparent Support Network; Adoptee- [11228]
Birthparents; Concerned United [11241]
Birthright Intl. [IO], Toronto, ON, Canada
Birthright U.S.A. [12908], PO Box 98363, Atlanta, GA 30359-2063, (800)550-4900
Birzeit Soc. [9394], PO Box 1822, Norwalk, CA 90651, (714)996-3389
Biscuit Bakers Inst. [★450]
Biscuit, Cake, Chocolate, and Confectionery Assn. [IO], London, United Kingdom
Biscuit and Cracker Distributors Assn. - Defunct.
Biscuit and Cracker Manufacturers Assn. [450], 6325 Woodside Ct., Ste. 125, Columbia, MD 21046, (443)545-1645
Bisexual
  Affirmation: United Methodists for Lesbian, Gay and Bisexual Concerns [20047]
  Alliance for Full Acceptance [12213]
  Alpha Lambda Tau Intl. Social Fraternity [24613]
  Assn. for Gay, Lesbian, and Bisexual Issues in Counseling [12216]
  Assn. of Welcoming and Affirming Baptists [19476]
  Bi Without Borders [17024]
  BiNet USA [12220]
  Blind Friends of Lesbian, Gay, Transgender and Bisexual People [12221]

Reference to "IO" in place of a book number signifies that the association may be found in the 45th edition of International Organizations.

Brethren/Mennonite Coun. for Lesbian, Gay, Bisexual and Transgender Interest [20050]
FireFlag/EMS [5773]
Friends for Lesbian, Gay, Bisexual, Transgender, and Queer Concerns [20056]
Gay Asian Pacific Alliance [12228]
Gay, Lesbian and Affirming Disciples Alliance [20057]
Gay, Lesbian, Bisexual, Transgender Historical Soc. [10078]
Gay, Lesbian, Bisexual, and Transgendered Disabled Veterans of Am. [20765]
HeartStrong [12232]
Interfaith Working Group [12887]
Intl. Fed. of Black Prides [12238]
Intl. Gay Figure Skating Union [23736]
Interweave Continental (Unitarian Universalists for Lesbian, Gay, Bisexual and Transgender Concerns) [20059]
Lesbian, Bisexual, Gay and Transgendered United Employees at AT&T [12242]
Lesbian, Gay, Bisexual, and Transgender People in Medicine [12243]
Lesbian, Gay, Bisexual and Transgender US Peace Corps Alumni [18260]
Marriage Equality USA [12506]
More Light Presbyterians for Lesbian, Gay, Bisexual and Transgender Concerns [20063]
Natl. Assn. of Lesbian, Gay, Bisexual and Trans-gender Community Centers [11804]
Natl. Assn. of Social Workers Natl. Comm. on Lesbian, Gay and Bisexual Issues [12245]
Natl. Coalition for LGBT Hea. [12247]
Natl. Gay and Lesbian Chamber of Commerce [24321]
Racial Justice 911 [18493]
Sigma Phi Beta Fraternity [24659]
Soc. for the Psychological Stud. of Lesbian, Gay and Bisexual Issues [16180]
Soulforce [17657]
United Church of Christ Coalition for Lesbian, Gay, Bisexual and Transgender Concerns [20067]
Bisexual Caucus of the Amer. Psychiatric Assn; Gay, Lesbian, and [★12217]
Bisexual Center - Defunct.
Bisexual Concerns; Affirmation: United Methodists for Lesbian, Gay and [20047]
Bisexual, Gay and Transgendered United Employees at ATOmp;T; Lesbian, [12242]
Bisexual Issues in Counseling; Assn. for Gay, Lesbian, and [12216]
Bisexual Issues; Natl. Assn. of Social Workers Natl. Comm. on Lesbian, Gay and [12245]
Bisexual Issues; Soc. for the Psychological Stud. of Lesbian, Gay and [16180]
Bisexual Members of the Amer. Psychiatric Assn; Caucus of Gay, Lesbian, and [★12217]
Bisexual People in Medicine; Lesbian, Gay and [★12243]
Bisexual Returned Peace Corps Volunteers; Lesbian, Gay and [★18260]
Bisexual and Transgender Concerns; Interweave Continental Unitarian Universalists for Lesbian, Gay, [20059]
Bisexual and Transgender Concerns; More Light Presbyterians for Lesbian, Gay, [20063]
Bisexual and Transgender Concerns; United Church of Christ Coalition for Lesbian, Gay, [20067]
Bisexual and Transgender Interest; Brethren/Men-nonite Coun. for Lesbian, Gay, [20050]
Bisexual, and Transgender Org; Natl. Latina/o Lesbian, Gay, [9972]
Bisexual, and Transgender People in Medicine; Lesbian, Gay, [12243]
Bisexual and Transgender US Peace Corps Alumni; Lesbian, Gay, [18260]
Bisexual, and Transgendered Disabled Veterans of Am; Gay, Lesbian, [20765]
Bisexual Veterans of Am; Gay, Lesbian, and [★12215]
Bishop Baraga Assn. [★19583]
Bishop Baraga Assn. and Archives [19583], 347 Rock St., Marquette, MI 49855, (906)225-1141
Bishop Fan Club; Bonnie Lou [★24853]

Bishop Hill Heritage Assn. [21108], PO Box 92, Bishop Hill, IL 61419-0092, (309)927-3899
Bishop Intl. Fan Club; Bonnie Lou [24853]
Bishop Pike Found. [★12364]
Bishops' Comm. for Ecumenical Affairs [★19584]
Bishops' Comm. for Ecumenical and Interreligious Affairs [19584], 3211 4th St. NE, Washington, DC 20017-1194, (202)541-3000
Bishops' Comm. on the Liturgical Apostolate [★19585]
Bishops' Comm. on the Liturgy [19585], 3211 4th St. NE, Washington, DC 20017-1194, (202)541-3000
Bishops' Comm. for Migrant Workers [★12282]
Bishops' Comm. on Priestly Formation [19917], c/o U.S. Conf. of Catholic Bishops, 3211 4th St. NE, Washington, DC 20017-1194, (202)541-3033
Bishops' Comm. on Scouting [★13001]
Bishops' Comm. for the Spanish Speaking [★12282]
Bishops' Comm. on Vocations [19586], c/o U.S. Conferences of Catholic Bishops, 3211 4th St. NE, Washington, DC 20017, (202)541-3033
Bishops' Conf. of Scotland [IO], Airdrie, United Kingdom
Bishops; Natl. Conf. of Catholic [★19735]
Bishops; Secretariat for Hispanic Affairs, U.S. Conf. of Catholic [12282]
Bishops; U.S. Conf. of Catholic [19735]
Bison Assn; Natl. [4139]
Bison Cooperative; Intertribal [5036]
Bison Hybrid Intl. Assn. [★4123]
Bison Hybrid Intl. Assn. [★IO]
Bit Assn; Natl. Snaffle [4926]
Bitterroot Outfitters [★23944]
Bitumen Waterproofing Assn. [IO], Nottingham, United Kingdom
Bituminous Coal Assn; Keystone [★847]
Bituminous Coal Inst. [★846]
Bituminous Coal Operators' Assn. [840], 1500 K St. NW, Washington, DC 20005-1209, (202)783-3195
Bituminous Concrete Assn; Natl. [★641]
Bituminous Contractors; Assn. of [839]
Bituminous Pipe Inst. - Defunct.
Bivex and Nationaal Verbond van Slachthuizen en Vleesuitsnijderijen-Boviqual [★IO]
Biye Beekeepers Soc. [★IO]
Bizzarrini Owners Club; Iso and [21672]
BKR Intl. [18], 19 Fulton St., Ste. 306, New York, NY 10038, (212)964-2115
BKR Intl. [IO], New York, NY, United States
B.K.S. Iyengar Yoga Natl. Assn. of the U.S. [23992], c/o Adriana De Franco, Membership Chair, 3940 Laurel Canyon Blvd., No. 947, Studio City, CA 91604, (800)889-9642
BKSTS - The Moving Image Soc. [IO], Iver Heath, United Kingdom
Black Acad. of Arts and Letters - Defunct.
Black Accountants; Natl. Assn. of [44]
Black Affairs Center for Training and Organizational Development - Address unknown since 2002.
Black Aged; Natl. Caucus on the [★11306]
Black Aged; Natl. Caucus and Center on [11306]
Black Aged; Natl. Center on [★11306]
The Black Agenda [16937], PO Box 9726, Columbus, OH 43209, (614)338-8383
Black Airline Pilots; Org. of [164]
Black Alcoholism and Addiction Coun; Natl. [13265]
Black Alliance for Educational Options [8322], 1710 Rhode Island Ave. NW, 12th Fl., Washington, DC 20036, (202)429-2236
Black Amer. Cinema Soc. [★9926]
Black Amer. Law Students Assn. [★8771]
Black Amer. Response to the African Community - Address unknown since 2003.
Black Amer. Travel Assn. - Defunct.
Black Amers. for Bush - Defunct.
Black Americans for Life [12909], 512 10th St. NW, Washington, DC 20004, (202)378-8858
Black Americans; Prog. for Res. on [6396]
Black Anthropologists; Caucus of [★6409]
Black Architects; Natl. Org. of [★6478]
Black Archives of Mid-America [9400], 2033 Vine St., Kansas City, MO 64108, (816)483-1300
Black and Asian Stud. Assn. [IO], London, United Kingdom
Black Assn. for Speech-Language and Hearing; Natl. [16448]

Black Awareness in TV [17164], 30 Josephine St., 3rd Fl., Detroit, MI 48202-1810, (313)871-3333
Black Bass Found. - Defunct.
Black Belt Fed. of the U.S.A; Judo [★23556]
Black on Black Love Campaign; Natl. [11842]
Black Broadcasters Alliance [550]
Black Bus. and Professional Assn. [IO], Toronto, ON, Canada
Black Cardiologists; Assn. of [13893]
Black Career Women [19323], PO Box 19332, Cincinnati, OH 45219-0332, (513)531-1932
Black Catholic Clergy Caucus; Natl. [19669]
Black Catholic Cong; Natl. [19670]
Black Catholics; Natl. Off. for [19691]
Black Caucus of the Amer. Lib. Assn. [10343], c/o Karolyn S. Thompson, VP, 118 Coll. Dr., No. 5053, Hattiesburg, MS 39406-0001, (601)266-5111
Black Caucus; Congressional [17256]
Black Caucus of Local Elected Officials; Natl. [6127]
Black Caucus of State Legislators; Natl. [6281]
Black Chamber of Commerce; Natl. [24250]
Black Chemists and Chem. Engineers; Natl. Org. of [★6689]
Black Chemists and Chem. Engineers; Natl. Org. for the Professional Advancement of [6689]
Black, Chicano, Puerto Rican, Asian Americans; Natl. Assn. of Interdisciplinary Stud. for Native Amer., [★9919]
Black Child Development Inst; Natl. [11542]
Black Church Appeal; United [16947]
Black Churches; Cong. of Natl. [19890]
Black Citizens Action; Natl. Assn. of [16942]
Black Citizens for a Fair Media - Address unknown since 1999.
Black Civic Participation; Natl. Coalition on [18358]
Black Coaches Assn. [23287], Pan Amer. Plz., 201 S Capitol Ave., Ste. 495, Indianapolis, IN 46225, (317)829-5600
Black Coalition for 1984 - Address unknown since 1995.
Black Coalition for AIDS Prevention [IO], Toronto, ON, Canada
Black Coalition of Fed. Aviation Employees; Natl. [5541]
Black Coll. Alumni Hall of Fame Found; Natl. [18911]
Black Coll. Radio Org. [551], PO Box 3191, Atlanta, GA 30302, (404)523-6136
Black Colleges of the Natl. Assn. of State Universi-ties and Land-Grant Colleges; Off. for the Advancement of Public [8112]
Black Colls. and Universities; Natl. Consortium of Arts and Letters for Historically [8111]
Black Community Crusade for Children [11562], 25 E St. NW, Washington, DC 20001, (202)628-8787
Black Concern - Defunct.
Black Cops Against Police Brutality [5965], PO Box 4256, East Orange, NJ 07019, (973)926-5717
Black Country Chamber of Commerce [IO], Brierley Hill, United Kingdom
Black County Officials; Natl. Assn. of [5617]
Black County Officials; Natl. Org. of [★5617]
Black Culinarian Alliance [1122], 55 W 116th St., Ste. 234, New York, NY 10026, (646)548-2949
Black Data Processing Associates [62], 6301 Ivy Ln., Ste. 700, Greenbelt, MD 20770, (301)220-2180
Black Deaf Advocates; Natl. [17418]
Black Designers; Org. of [9907]
Black Devils [★IO]
Black Economic Res. Center - Defunct.
Black Educators Assn. of Nova Scotia [IO], Halifax, NS, Canada
Black Efforts for Soul in TV - Address unknown since 1995.
Black Engineers; Natl. Soc. of [7034]
Black Engineers and Scientists; Natl. Coun. of [7618]
Black Entertainment Lawyers Assn. [★5687]
Black Entertainment and Sports Lawyers Assn. [5687], PO Box 441485, Fort Washington, MD 20749-1485, (301)248-1818
Black Family Life and Culture; Inst. for the Advanced Stud. of [9359]
Black Family Res. Org. - Address unknown since 1991.

A star before a book entry number signifies that the name is not listed separately, but is mentioned within the entry.

Black Farmers and Agriculturists Assn. [4111], PO Box 61, Tillery, NC 27887, (252)826-2800

Black Filmmaker Found. [9933], 11 W 42nd St., 9th Fl., New York, NY 10036, (212)253-1690

Black Flight Attendants of Am. [18866], 1060 Crenshaw Blvd., Ste. 202, Los Angeles, CA 90019, (888)682-2322

Black Flight Attendants of America [IO], Los Angeles, CA, United States

Black Fund of Am; United [★12204]

Black Fund; United [12204]

Black Gay Archives - Defunct.

Black Gold Gp. [9501], c/o Windsor Artworks, 123 Cedar Landing Rd., Windsor, NC 27983, (252)794-9764

Black Graduate Student Assn; Natl. [18869]

Black Health Res. Found. - Address unknown since 1994.

Black Hereford Assn; Amer. [4214]

Black History Month Assn. [IO], Halifax, NS, Canada

Black Holocaust Soc. [16938], 6622 N Bourbon St., Rm. 16, Milwaukee, WI 53224, (414)446-4377

Black Human Resources Network [2901]

Black, Indian, Hispanic, and Asian Women in Action [13420], 1830 James Ave. N, Minneapolis, MN 55417, (612)521-2986

Black and Indian Mission Off. [19587]

Black Indians and Intertribal Native Amer. Assn. [19269], PO Box 143, Upperstrasburg, PA 17265, (717)491-1065

Black Info. Tech. Forum [IO], Gauteng, Republic of South Africa

Black Informed Professionals - Defunct.

Black Interpreters; Natl. Alliance of [3854]

Black Journalists; Natl. Assn. of [3129]

Black Justice Coalition; Natl. [18643]

Black Law Enforcement Executives; Natl. Org. of [5999]

Black Law Students Assn; Natl. [8771]

Black Lawyers; National Conference of [★5519]

Black Lawyers; Natl. Counsel of [5519]

Black Leadership Forum [18867], 910 17th St. NW, Ste. 317, Washington, DC 20006, (202)789-1965

Black Leadership Initiative on Cancer; Natl. [13847]

Black Liberation Army - Address unknown since 1997.

Black Lung Assn. [13323], c/o Bill Bailey, PO Box 872, Crab Orchard, WV 25827, (304)252-9654

Black Mayors; Natl. Conf. of [6129]

Black Mayors; Southern Conf. of [★6129]

Black MBA Assn; Natl. [8035]

Black McDonald's Operators Assn; Natl. [1955]

Black Meeting Planners Coalition; Natl. [★2687]

Black Meeting Planners; Natl. Coalition of [2687]

Black Memorabilia Collectors - Defunct.

Black Mental Hea. Alliance [15193], 733 W 40th St., Ste. 10, Baltimore, MD 21211, (410)338-2642

Black Mesa Defense Fund - Defunct.

Black Methodists for Church Renewal [20260], 201 8th Ave. S, PO Box 801, Nashville, TN 37202-0801, (615)749-6351

Black Military History Inst. of Am. [10472], c/o Col. William A. De Shields, Exec. Off., PO Box 1134, Fort Meade, MD 20755, (410)757-4250

Black Ministries; Episcopal Commn. for [★19968]

Black Music Assn. - Defunct.

Black Music Caucus of the Music Educators Natl. Conf; Natl. [★8922]

Black and Non-White YMCA Volunteers and Staff - Defunct.

Black Nurses Assn; Natl. [15505]

Black Nursing Faculty; Assn. of [8848]

Black Owned Broadcasters Assn; Natl. [★568]

Black Owned Broadcasters; Natl. Assn. of [568]

Black PAC - Defunct.

Black Panther Party - Defunct.

Black Participation Project - Defunct.

Black Patriots Found. [★20669]

Black Perspective - Address unknown since 1995.

Black Physicists; Natl. Soc. of [7504]

Black Pilots of Am. [435], PO Box 7463, Pine Bluff, AR 71611, (504)214-7346

Black Police Assn; Natl. [5990]

Black-Polish Conf. of Greater Detroit - Defunct.

Black Press of Am. [★3241]

Black Professional Development; Natl. Consortium for [8049]

Black Programming Consortium; Natl. [9764]

Black Psychiatrists of America - Address unknown since 2000.

Black Psychologists; Assn. of [16138]

Black Public Administrators; Natl. Forum for [6196]

Black Public Relations Soc; Natl. [3194]

Black Radical Cong. [18868], PO Box 24795, St. Louis, MO 63115, (314)307-3441

Black Resources Information Coordinating Services - Address unknown since 2003.

Black Retail Action Gp. [3401], c/o Rockefeller Center Sta., PO Box 1192, New York, NY 10185, (212)319-7751

Black Revolutionary War Patriots Found. [20669]

Black Rhino Vegetarian Soc. - Defunct.

Black Rock Coalition [17499], PO Box 1054, Cooper Sta., New York, NY 10276, (212)713-5097

Black Russian Terrier Club of Am. [22232], c/o Dana F. Kellerman, Sec., 5621 N Kenmore Ave., Chicago, IL 60660, (773)271-5407

Black Russian Terriers; Amer. Assn. of [22185]

Black Salesmen and Black Saleswomen; Natl. Alliance of [3469]

Black Saleswomen; Natl. Alliance of Black Salesmen and [3469]

Black Sash [★IO]

Black Sash Trust [IO], Cape Town, Republic of South Africa

Black School Educators; Natl. Alliance of [9217]

Black School Superintendents; Natl. Alliance of [★9217]

Black Scientists Assn; NIH [6395]

Black Sea Economic Cooperation [★IO]

Black Secretaries of America - Address unknown since 1995.

Black Security Executives; Intl. Org. of [3533]

Black Silent Majority Comm. of the U.S.A. - Address unknown since 1999.

Black Sisters' Conf; Natl. [19671]

Black Social Workers; Natl. Assn. of [13204]

Black Sociologists; Assn. of [7659]

Black Sociologists; Caucus of [★7659]

Black Solidarity Political Party - Address unknown since 1995.

Black State Troopers Coalition; Natl. [5430]

Black Storytellers; Assn. of [★10981]

Black Storytellers; Natl. Assn. of [10981]

Black Students Psychological Assn. - Defunct.

Black Stuntmen's Assn. [1379]

Black Survival Fund; Emergency [★12780]

Black Survival Fund; Natl. [12780]

Black Tennis and Sports Found. - Address unknown since 1995.

Black Theater Alliance - Defunct.

Black Theatre Network [11008], c/o Dr. La Tanya Reese, Bus. Mgr., 2609 Douglas Rd. SE, Ste. 102, Washington, DC 20020-6540, (202)274-5667

Black-Top Delaine Merino Sheep Breeders' Assn. - Defunct.

Black Top and Natl. Delaine Merino Sheep Assn. [5199]

Black Trade Unionists; Coalition of [24202]

Black United Fed. of Charities; Natl. [16943]

Black United Fund; Natl. [12656]

Black Veterans [★21289]

Black Veterans; Natl. Assn. for [21308]

Black Veterans for Social Justice [21289], 665 Willoughby Ave., Brooklyn, NY 11206, (718)852-6004

Black Voter Participation; Natl. Coalition on [★18358]

Black Wings in Aviation [★6380]

Black Women Attorneys; Assn. of [5484]

Black Women in Church and Soc. [20617], 700 Martin Luther King Jr. Dr. SW, Atlanta, GA 30314, (404)527-5713

Black Women Empowerment Program - Defunct.

Black Women of Essence [11269], PO Box 471001, Lake Monroe, FL 32747-1001, (321)279-8784

Black Women in Higher Educ; Assn. of [9314]

Black Women; Natl. Coalition of 100 [17552]

Black Women; Natl. Hook-Up of [17559]

Black Women Organized for Educational Development [13421], c/o Black Women Organized for Political Action, 449 15th St., 3rd Fl., Oakland, CA 94612, (510)763-9523

Black Women Publishing - Address unknown since 2003.

Black Women in Sisterhood for Action [13422], PO Box 1592, Washington, DC 20013, (202)543-6013

Black Women United for Action [13423], 6551 Loisdale Ct., Ste. 400, Springfield, VA 22150, (703)922-5757

Black Women United for Action [IO], Springfield, VA, United States

Black Women for Wages for Housework; Intl. [18811]

Black Women's Agenda [13456], 1090 Vermont Ave. NW, Ste. 800, Washington, DC 20005, (202)216-5797

Black Women's Assn. - Address unknown since 1985.

Black Women's Community Development Assn. - Address unknown since 1995.

Black Women's Cong; Intl. [17542]

Black Women's Consciousness Raising Assn; Natl. [17551]

Black Women's Educational Alliance - Address unknown since 1999.

Black Women's Hea. Imperative [16895], 1420 K St. NW, 10th Fl., Ste. 1000, Washington, DC 20005, (202)548-4000

Black Women's Hea. Proj. [★16895]

Black Women's Hea. Proj; Natl. [★16895]

Black Women's House of Culture [IO], Santos, Brazil

Black Women's Inst. - Defunct.

Black Women's Network - Address unknown since 1995.

Black Women's Rsrc. Center [★13421]

Black Women's Roundtable on Voter Participation [18346], c/o Natl. Coalition on Black Civic Participation, 1900 L St. NW, Ste. 700, Washington, DC 20036, (202)659-4929

Black Women's Wellness; Center for [★16895]

Black World [IO], Madrid, Spain

Black World Found. [9357], PO Box 22869, Oakland, CA 94609, (734)213-2400

Black Writers Alliance - Defunct.

Black Writers Conf; Intl. [★11177]

Blackburn Family Assn. [20795], 608 S 16th St., Philadelphia, PA 19146, (215)893-9343

Blackface Sheep Breeder's Assn; Scottish [5216]

Blackfriars' Guild - Defunct.

Blackhawk Standbys, Inc. [24997], c/o Nika Alex, Financial Sec., 11555 Settlers Pond Way, Unit 2B, Orland Park, IL 60467, (708)479-7967

Blacks Against Nukes - Address unknown since 1999.

Blacks in Criminal Justice; Natl. Assn. of [11877]

Blacks in Energy; Amer. Assn. of [6936]

Blacks in Govt; Natl. Org. of [5571]

Blacks in Law Enforcement [5966], 591 Vanderbilt Ave., Ste. 133, Brooklyn, NY 11238, (718)455-9059

Blacks in Law Enforcement [★5966]

Blacks for Reparations in Am; Natl. Coalition of [16944]

Blacksmiths

Amer. Bladesmith Soc. [9826]

Amer. Farrier's Assn. [522]

Artist-Blacksmith's Assn. of North Am. [523]

Artist-Blacksmith's Assn. of North Am. [IO]

Guild of Professional Farriers [1354]

Intl. Brotherhood of Boilermakers, Iron Ship Builders, Blacksmiths, Forgers and Helpers [24021]

Natl. Blacksmiths and Weldors Assn. [524]

Sisterhood of Shoers [1355]

Blackwater Wildlife Rescue [IO], Blackwater, United Kingdom

Bladder Cancer Advocacy Network [13799], 4813 St. Elmo Ave., Bethesda, MD 20814, (301)215-9099

Blade; Natl. Soc. of Scabbard and [24548]

Bladesmith Soc; Amer. [9826]

Blair Chiropractic Soc. [13995], c/o Dr. John Hilpisch, Pres., 8603 34th St. N, Lake Elmo, MN 55042, (651)748-5731

Blair House Library Found. - Defunct.

Blair Soc. for Genealogical Res. [20796], c/o Bryce D. Blair, Pres., 726 Falling Oaks Dr., Medina, OH 44256-2778

Blair Society for Genealogical Research [IO], Medina, OH, United States

---

Reference to "IO" in place of a book number signifies that the association may be found in the 45th edition of International Organizations.

Blankets for Canada Soc. **[IO]**, Lethbridge, AB, Canada

Blast Furnace Res. - Defunct.

Blasting Assn; Amer. **[★7020]**

Blaustein Inst. for the Advancement of Human Rights; Jacob **[17771]**

Blaustein Inst. for Desert Research; Jacob **[★8673]**

Blauvelt Descendants; Assn. of **[20785]**

Blazer Horse Assn. **[4866]**, 820 N Can-Ada Rd., Star, ID 83669, (208)286-7267

BLC Leather Tech. Centre **[IO]**, Northampton, United Kingdom

Blencowe Families Assn. **[20797]**, c/o Helen B. Simpson, Sec., 550 N Darlington St., Rosemead, CA 91770-4312, (626)280-2506

Blepharospasm Res. Found; Benign Essential **[15311]**

Blessed Kateri Tekakwitha League **[19588]**, Martyrs Shrine, Off. of the Vice-Postulur, 136 Shrine Rd., Auriesville, NY 12016, (518)853-3153

Blessed Martin Guild **[★20389]**

Blessed Sacrament; Confraternity of the **[19951]**

Blessed Sacrament; Congregation of the **[19617]**

Blessed Trinity Soc. - Defunct.

Blessings Intl. **[12514]**, PO Box 35292, Tulsa, OK 74153-0292, (918)250-8101

Blessings Intl. **[IO]**, Tulsa, OK, United States

BLI **[IO]**, Colorado Springs, CO, United States

BLI **[19512]**

Blind

ADARA: Professionals Networking for Excellence in Ser. Delivery with Individuals who are Deaf or Hard of Hearing **[14735]**

Amer. Assn. of the Deaf-Blind **[14737]**

Amer. Assn. of Visually Impaired Attorneys **[5474]**

Amer. Blind Bowling Assn. **[23334]**

Amer. Blind Golf Assn. **[23335]**

Amer. Blind Skiing Found. **[23336]**

Amer. Coun. of the Blind **[16822]**

Amer. Coun. of the Blind Enterprises and Services **[16823]**

Amer. Coun. of Blind Govt. Employees **[16824]**

Amer. Found. for the Blind **[16826]**

Amer. Israeli Lighthouse **[16827]**

Amer. Printing House for the Blind **[16829]**

Assoc. Blind **[16830]**

Assoc. Services for the Blind **[16831]**

Assn. for the Advancement of Blind and Retarded **[16832]**

Assn. for the Blind of Western Australia **[IO]**

Assn. for Educ. and Rehabilitation of the Blind and Visually Impaired **[16833]**

Assn. for Retinopathy of Prematurity and Related Diseases **[15673]**

Bibles for the Blind and Visually Handicapped **[19511]**

Blind Children's Fund **[16834]**

Blind Friends of Lesbian, Gay, Transgender and Bisexual People **[12221]**

Blind Info. Tech. Specialists **[16835]**

Blind Sailing Intl. **[23151]**

Blind Sailing Intl. **[IO]**

Blind Ser. Assn. **[16836]**

Blinded Veterans Assn. **[16837]**

Braille Authority of North Am. **[16838]**

Braille Bible Found. **[19513]**

Braille Revival League **[16839]**

Braille Without Borders **[IO]**

Care Ministries **[19532]**

Carroll Center for the Blind **[16840]**

Challenge Aspen at Snowmass **[23342]**

Christian Record Services **[16842]**

Christian Services for the Blind **[16843]**

Coun. of Families with Visual Impairment **[16844]**

Disabled Sports USA **[23343]**

Elwyn **[12383]**

Fidelco Guide Dog Found. **[16846]**

Found. Fighting Blindness **[16847]**

Friends of Libraries for Blind and Physically Handicapped Individuals in North America **[10357]**

Guide Dog Found. for the Blind **[16849]**

Guide Dog Users, Inc. **[16850]**

Guide Dogs of Am. **[16851]**

Guide Dogs for the Blind **[16852]**

Guiding Eyes for the Blind **[16853]**

Helen Keller Intl. **[16854]**

Helping Hands for the Blind **[13379]**

Independent Visually Impaired Enterprisers **[16855]**

Intl. Fed. of Ophthalmological Societies **[15686]**

Intl. Perimetric Soc. **[15688]**

Intl. Trachoma Initiative **[16858]**

InTouch Networks **[16860]**

JBI Intl. - Jewish Braille Inst. of Am. **[16861]**

Jewish Guild for the Blind **[16862]**

Leader Dogs for the Blind **[16864]**

Lib. Users of Am. **[10370]**

Lutheran Braille Evangelism Assn. **[16866]**

Lutheran Braille Workers **[16867]**

MAB Community Services **[16868]**

Malaysian Assn. for the Blind **[IO]**

Natl. Accreditation Coun. for Agencies Serving the Blind and Visually Impaired **[16870]**

Natl. Alliance of Blind Students **[16871]**

Natl. Assn. of Blind Merchants **[525]**

Natl. Assn. for Parents of Children With Visual Impairments **[16873]**

Natl. Braille Assn. **[16875]**

Natl. Braille Press **[16876]**

Natl. Fed. of the Blind **[16877]**

Natl. Indus. for the Blind **[16878]**

Natl. Org. of Parents of Blind Children **[16879]**

ORBIS Intl. **[15697]**

Pan-American Assn. of Ophthalmology **[15699]**

Pilot Dogs **[16881]**

Prevent Blindness Am. **[16882]**

Protestant Guild for Human Services **[16884]**

Randolph-Sheppard Vendors of Am. **[3973]**

Recording for the Blind and Dyslexic **[16885]**

Res. to Prevent Blindness **[16886]**

Sea to See Proj. **[13760]**

Seedlings Braille Books for Children **[9297]**

Seva Found. **[12443]**

Skating Assn. for the Blind and Handicapped **[23740]**

Ski for Light **[23361]**

Theosophical Book Assn. for the Blind **[20592]**

Unite for Sight **[13381]**

U.S. Assn. for Blind Athletes **[23363]**

U.S. Blind Golf Assn. **[23364]**

U.S. Braille Chess Assn. **[21947]**

Vision Australia **[IO]**

Visually Impaired Veterans of Am. **[16891]**

Wheelchair Sports, USA **[23371]**

Xavier Soc. for the Blind **[16892]**

Blind; All Russia Assn. of the **[IO]**

Blind; Amer. Assn. of the Deaf- **[14737]**

Blind; Amer. Assn. of Workers for the **[★16833]**

Blind; Amer. Braille Press for War and Civilian **[★16854]**

Blind; Amer. Coun. of the **[16822]**

Blind; Amer. Found. for the **[16826]**

Blind; Amer. Found. for Overseas **[★16854]**

Blind; Amer. League for Deaf- **[★14737]**

Blind; Amer. Printing House for the **[16829]**

Blind; Assoc. **[16830]**

Blind; Assoc. Services for the **[16831]**

Blind; Assn. for the Chinese **[★16854]**

Blind Assn; U.S. Venetian **[★2279]**

Blind Athletes; U.S. Assn. for **[23363]**

Blind Bowling Assn; Amer. **[23334]**

Blind in Canada; John Milton Soc. for the **[IO]**

Blind; Canadian Natl. Inst. for the **[IO]**

Blind; Carroll Center for the **[16840]**

Blind; Catholic Guild for All the **[★16840]**

Blind Children and Adults; Amer. Action Fund for **[16821]**

Blind Children; Assn. for Advancement of **[★16832]**

Blind Children; Keren-Or Center for Multi-Handicapped **[★16863]**

Blind Children; Keren-Or Center for Multi-Handicapped **[★IO]**

Blind Children's Fund **[16834]**, 201 S Univ. St., Mount Pleasant, MI 48858, (989)779-9966

Blind; Christian Fellowship for the **[★16843]**

Blind; Christian Services for the **[16843]**

Blind Citizens Australia **[IO]**, Kensington, Australia

Blind; Computerized Books for the **[★16885]**

Blind and Dyslexic; Recording for the **[16885]**

Blind Enterprises and Services; Amer. Coun. of the **[16823]**

Blind; Ephphatha Services for the Deaf and **[★20216]**

Blind; Friends-in-Art of Amer. Coun. of the **[9504]**

Blind Friends of Lesbian, Gay, Transgender and Bisexual People **[12221]**, 4802 Holder Ave., Baltimore, MD 21214-3009, (410)254-1972

Blind Golf Assn; U.S. **[23364]**

Blind; Gospel Assn. for the **[16848]**

Blind Govt. Employees; Amer. Coun. of **[16824]**

Blind; Guide Dog Found. for the **[16849]**

Blind; Guiding Eyes for the **[16853]**

Blind and Handicapped; Carleton E. Morse Radio Programs for the **[★22929]**

Blind and Handicapped; Skating Assn. for the **[23740]**

Blind Info. Tech. Specialists **[16835]**, c/o Robert R. Rogers, Treas., 1121 Morado Dr., Cincinnati, OH 45238-4436, (513)921-3186

Blind Info. Tech. Specialists **[IO]**, Cincinnati, OH, United States

Blind of Ireland; Natl. Coun. for the **[IO]**

Blind; Jerusalem Institutions for the **[★16863]**

Blind; Jewish Guild for the **[16862]**

Blind Lawyers Assn; Amer. **[★5474]**

Blind; Leader Dog League for the **[★16864]**

Blind; Leader Dogs for the **[16864]**

Blind Lions; Amer. Coun. of the **[16825]**

Blind; Natl. Church Conf. of the **[13380]**

Blind; Natl. Comm. for Recording for the **[★16885]**

Blind; Natl. Fed. of the **[16877]**

Blind; Natl. Indus. for the **[16878]**

Blind; New York Guild for the Jewish **[★16862]**

Blind Outdoor Leisure Development **[★23342]**

Blind Parents; Amer. Coun. of the **[★16844]**

Blind People; Action for **[IO]**

Blind and Physically Handicapped Individuals in North America; Friends of Libraries for **[10357]**

Blind Piano Tuners; Assn. of **[IO]**

Blind; Protestant Guild for the **[★16884]**

Blind; Radio Info. Center for the **[★16831]**

Blind; Recording for the **[★16885]**

Blind Relief War Fund; Permanent **[★16854]**

Blind and Retarded; Assn. for the Advancement of **[16832]**

Blind Sailing Intl. **[23151]**, c/o Carroll Center for the Blind, 770 Centre St., Newton, MA 02458

Blind Sailing Intl. **[IO]**, Newton, MA, United States

Blind Ser. Assn. **[16836]**, 17 N State St., Ste. 1050, Chicago, IL 60602-3510, (312)236-0808

Blind Skiing Found; Amer. **[23336]**

Blind Sport New Zealand **[IO]**, Auckland, New Zealand

Blind Students; Natl. Alliance of **[16871]**

Blind Teachers; Natl. Assn. of **[9220]**

Blind; Theosophical Book Assn. for the **[20592]**

Blind Union - Uruguay; Latin Amer. **[IO]**

Blind; Vision Community Services - A Division of the Massachusetts Assn. for the **[★16868]**

Blind and Vision Found; Massachusetts Assn. for the **[★16868]**

Blind and Visually Handicapped; Bibles for the **[19511]**

Blind and Visually Handicapped; Natl. Accreditation Coun. for Agencies Serving the **[★16870]**

Blind and Visually Impaired; Assn. for Educ. and Rehabilitation of the **[16833]**

Blind and Visually Impaired; Natl. Accreditation Coun. for Agencies Serving the **[16870]**

Blind; Volunteer Services for the **[★16831]**

Blind; Xavier Soc. for the **[16892]**

Blind Youth; Vision Found. for the **[★15724]**

Blind Youths and Adults; Helen Keller Natl. Center for Deaf- **[14760]**

Blinded Amer. Veterans Found. **[20762]**, PO Box 65900, Washington, DC 20035-5900, (202)462-4430

Blinded Veterans Assn. **[16837]**, 477 H St. NW, Washington, DC 20001-2694, (202)371-8880

Blindness Am; Prevent **[16882]**

Blindness; Found. Fighting **[16847]**

Blindness; Natl. Comm. for the Prevention of **[★16882]**

Blindness; Natl. Soc. to Prevent **[★16882]**

A star before a book entry number signifies that the name is not listed separately, but is mentioned within the entry.

Blindness; Natl. Soc. for the Prevention of [★16882]
Blindness; New York State Comm. for the Prevention of [★16882]
Blindness; Res. to Prevent [16886]
Bliss Classification Assn. [IO], Cambridge, United Kingdom
Blissymbolics Commun. Intl. [IO], Toronto, ON, Canada
Blizzard Men and Ladies of 1888 - Address unknown since 1995.
Bloch Cancer Found; R.A. [13867]
Block Booking Conf. [★9169]
Block and Bridle Club; Natl. [24401]
Block Grants; Ad Hoc Coalition on [★13161]
Block Grants and Human Needs; Coalition on [★13161]
Block Parent Prog. of Canada [IO], Barrie, ON, Canada
Blonde d'Aquitaine Assn; Amer. [4215]
Blonde D'Aquitaine Found; Natl. [★4215]
Blondie
  Debbie Harry Collector's Soc. [24872]
Blondin [★20799]
Blood
  Amer. Assn. of Blood Banks [13761]
  American Bd. of Clinical Metal Toxicology [16659]
  Amer. Soc. for Apheresis [13706]
  Amer. Soc. of Hematology [14783]
  America's Blood Centers [13762]
  Assoc. Hea. Found. [18983]
  Australian and New Zealand Soc. of Blood Transfusion [IO]
  British Blood Transfusion Soc. [IO]
  Children's Blood Found. [14786]
  Coalition for Hemophilia B [14787]
  European Bank of Frozen Blood of Rare Groups [IO]
  Friends of the Jose Carreras Intl. Leukemia Found. [13825]
  Hemophilia Fed. of Am. [14789]
  HHT Found. Intl. [14454]
  Intl. Fed. of Blood Donor Organizations [IO]
  Intl. Plasma Fractionation Assn. [IO]
  Intl. Soc. of Blood Transfusion [IO]
  Intl. Soc. of Radiolabeled Blood Elements [IO]
  Intl. Soc. of Radiolabeled Blood Elements [13763]
  Intl. Soc. on Thrombosis and Haemostasis [14793]
  Japan Soc. of Blood Transfusion [IO]
  Miracle Flights for Kids [14319]
  Natl. Alliance for Thrombosis and Thrombophilia [13931]
  Natl. Blood Found. [13764]
  Natl. Hemophilia Found. [14795]
  Neutropenia Support Assn. [IO]
  North Amer. Specialized Coagulation Lab. Assn. [14996]
  Plasma Protein Therapeutics Assn. [13765]
  Platelet Disorder Support Assn. [13730]
  Sickle Cell Disease Assn. of Am. [14797]
  Soc. for the Advancement of Blood Mgt. [14798]
  USBloodDonors.org [13766]
Blood Centers; America's [13762]
Blood Donor Program; Ferret [★22416]
Blood Found; Children's [14786]
Blood and Marrow Transplantation; Amer. Soc. for [16665]
Blood and Res. Found. for Children; Cooley's Anemia [★14788]
Blood Res. Found. - Defunct.
Blood Resources Assn; Amer. [★13765]
Bloodhound Assn; Eastern Police [★6000]
Bloodhound Assn; Natl. Police [6000]
Bloodhound Club; Amer. [22187]
Bloodstain Pattern Analysts; Intl. Assn. of [5637]
Bloom County Fan Club of America - Defunct.
Bloomsday Club - Address unknown since 2001.
Bloss-Pyles-Ross-Sellards Family [20798], 4031 Grand Ave., DeLand, FL 32720, (386)985-0909
Blossom [IO], Virudhunagar, India
Blount Found. for the Eradication of Rheumatoid Disease; Roger Wyburn-Mason and Jack M. [16375]
Blouse Mfrs; Natl. Assn. of [245]
Blouse and Skirt Contractors Assn; Greater [★237]

Blouse, Skirt and Undergarment Assn; Greater [237]
Blue Anchor, Inc. - Defunct.
Blue Army of Our Lady of Fatima, U.S.A. [19589], 674 Mountain View Rd. E, PO Box 976, Washington, NJ 07882, (908)689-1700
Blue Blue Violet [★24454]
Blue Book; Proj. [7483]
The Blue Card [12468], 171 Madison Ave., Ste. 1405, New York, NY 10016-5115, (212)239-2251
Blue Collar Caucus - Defunct.
Blue Crab Industry Assn; Natl. [3495]
Blue Cross [IO], Burford, United Kingdom
Blue Cross Assn. [★14959]
Blue Cross and Blue Shield Assn. [14959], 225 N Michigan Ave., Chicago, IL 60601, (312)297-6000
Blue Diamond Growers [5052], PO Box 1768, Sacramento, CA 95814, (916)442-0771
Blue Dolphin Alliance [5008], PO Box 2481, Harmony, CA 93435, (877)257-6265
Blue Earth Alliance [10847], PO Box 94388, Seattle, WA 98124-6688
Blue Heron Support Services Assn. [IO], Barrhead, AB, Canada
Blue Intl. Collectors Club; Flow [22026]
Blue Key Honor Soc. [24502], c/o Dr. Christopher M. Sieverdes, Exec. Dir., 7501 Whitehill Ln., Whitehill Farm, Millersburg, OH 44654-9270, (330)674-2570
Blue Knights [★22669]
Blue Knights [★IO]
Blue Knights Intl. Law Enforcement Motorcycle Club [IO], Bangor, ME, United States
Blue Knights Intl. Law Enforcement Motorcycle Club [22669], 38 Alden St., Bangor, ME 04401, (207)947-4600
Blue Print and Allied Indus; Intl. Assn. of [★1801]
Blue-ray Disc Assn. [1207], c/o Makoto Morise, Sec., 10 Universal City Plz., T-100, Universal City, CA 91608, (818)301-1891
Blue-ray Disc Association [IO], Universal City, CA, United States
Blue Ribbon Coalition [★23680]
Blue Shield Assn. [★14959]
Blue Shield Assn; Blue Cross and [14959]
Blue Star Mothers of Am. [21193], c/o Karen Stevens, Pres., PO Box 471, Hazel Green, AL 35750
Blue Terrier Club; U.S. Kerry [22374]
Blue Ventures Conservation - Madagascar [IO], London, United Kingdom
Blue/White Pottery Club [21527], PO Box 460517, Aurora, CO 80015, (303)690-8649
Blue Willow Collectors Soc. - Defunct.
Bluebell Railway Preservation Soc. [IO], Lewes, United Kingdom
Blueberry Assn. of North Am; Wild [4775]
Blueberry Coun; North Amer. [4749]
Bluebird Soc; North Amer. [5352]
Bluefaced Leicester Sheep Breeders Assn. [IO], Castle Douglas, United Kingdom
Bluefaced Leicester Union of North Am. [5200], c/o Kelly Ward, Sec.-Treas., 760 W VW Ave., Schoolcraft, MI 49087, (269)679-5497
Bluegrass
  Americana Music Assn. [10555]
  Country Legends Assn. [10583]
  The Grascals Fan Club [24904]
  Intl. Bluegrass Music Assn. [10615]
  Natl. Traditional Country Music Assn. [10670]
  Southwest Bluegrass Assn. [10709]
Bluegrass Assn; Southwest [10709]
Bluegrass Music Assn; Intl. [10615]
Bluegrass Music Trust Fund [★10615]
Bluegrass Music Trust Fund [★IO]
Blueliners [24998], PO Box 805, St. Louis, MO 63188
Blueliners; Saint Louis [★24998]
Bluenose Soaring Club [IO], Halifax, NS, Canada
Blueprint Assn; Intl. Reprographic [★1801]
Blueprint and Diazotype Coaters; Natl. Assn. of [★1800]
BlueRibbon Coalition [23680], 4555 Burley Dr., Ste. A, Pocatello, ID 83202-1945, (208)237-1008
Blues
  Americana Music Assn. [10555]
  Bessie Smith Soc. [24847]

The Blues Found. [10566]
Blues Heaven Found. [10567]
Delbert McClinton Intl. Fan Club [24874]
Intl. Blues Soc. [21865]
Natl. Assn. of Rhythm and Blues Dee Jay's [10659]
Rhythm and Blues Rock and Roll Soc., Inc. [10692]
The Blues Found. [10566], 49 Union Ave., Memphis, TN 38103, (901)527-2583
Blues Heaven Found. [10567], 2120 Michigan Ave., Chicago, IL 60616, (312)808-1286
Blues Music Assn. [2802]
Blues Rock and Roll Soc., Inc; Rhythm and [10692]
Bluetick Breeders of Am. [22233], c/o Marty Waddell, Membership Chm., 1089 Jackson Ave., Tipton, IA 52772, (563)886-6855
Bluewater Bus. Card Club [IO], Sarnia, ON, Canada
Bluewater Cruising Assn. [IO], Vancouver, BC, Canada
Bluewater Sportfishing Club [IO], Hyde Park, Australia
Blunden Family History Assn. [20799], 12041 Royce Waterford Cir., Tampa, FL 33626, (813)792-2562
Blur Fan Club [IO], Stoke-On-Trent, United Kingdom
B'Man Family Assn. [20800], c/o Chris Beeman, Founder, 3416 Mayhurst Dr., Indian Trail, NC 28079, (704)882-5676
BMMF International/USA [★20351]
BMMF International/USA [★IO]
BMUG - Berkeley Macintosh Users Gp. [★6819]
BMW-507 Owner Register - Defunct.
BMW 507 Register [★21593]
BMW 700 Register - Address unknown since 1995.
BMW Car Club of Am. [21591], 640 S Main St., Ste. 201, Greenville, SC 29601, (864)250-0022
BMW Club of Canada [IO], Port Coquitlam, BC, Canada
BMW Club; The Vintage [★22698]
BMW CS Registry [21592], c/o Art Wegweiser, 5341 Gibson Hill Rd., Edinboro, PA 16412, (814)734-5107
BMW Motorcycle Owners of Am. [22670], PO Box 3982, Ballwin, MO 63022, (636)394-7277
BMW Motorcycle Owners; Vintage [22698]
BMW Riders Assn. Intl. [22671], PO Box 599, Troy, OH 45373-0599, (937)339-7100
BMW Riders Assn. Intl. [IO], West Melbourne, FL, United States
BMW RT Owners' Club - Defunct.
BMW; Vintage [★22698]
BMW Vintage Car Club of Am. [21593], PO Box S, San Rafael, CA 94913, (415)897-0220
B'Nai Birth Intl; Community Volunteer Services Commn. of [★11766]
B'nai B'rith [★20125]
B'nai B'rith [20124], 2020 K St. NW, 7th Fl., Washington, DC 20006, (202)857-6600
B'nai B'rith [IO], Washington, DC, United States
B'nai B'rith [★IO]
B'nai B'rith; Anti Defamation League of [★17091]
B'nai Brith Canada [IO], Toronto, ON, Canada
B'nai B'rith; Independent Order of [★20125]
B'nai B'rith Intl. [20125], 2020 K St. NW, 7th Fl., Washington, DC 20006, (202)857-6600
B'nai B'rith Intl. [IO], Washington, DC, United States
B'nai B'rith Intl. Commn. on Adult Jewish Educ. [★IO]
B'nai B'rith Intl. Commn. on Adult Jewish Educ. [★8686]
B'nai B'rith Intl. Senior Citizens Housing Comm. [★12469]
B'nai B'rith International's Center for Jewish Identity [8686], c/o B'nai B'rith Intl., 2020 K St. NW, 7th Fl., Washington, DC 20006, (202)857-6600
B'nai B'rith International's Center for Jewish Identity [IO], Washington, DC, United States
B'nai B'rith Senior Citizens Housing Comm. [12469]
B'nai B'rith Women [★20153]
B'nai B'rith Women [★IO]
B'nai Brith Women of Canada [★IO]
B'nai B'rith Youth Org. [20126], 2020 K St. NW, 7th Fl., Washington, DC 20006, (202)857-6633
B'nai Yiddish Soc. - Defunct.
Bnai Zion Found. [19177], 136 E 39th St., New York, NY 10016, (212)725-1211

Reference to "IO" in place of a book number signifies that the association may be found in the 45th edition of International Organizations.

Bnei Akiva; Hashomer Hadati, [★20178]
Bnei Akiva of North Am. [★20178]
Bnei Akiva of the U.S. and Canada; Religious Zionist Youth Movement - [20178]
Bnei Akiva; World Org. of [★20178]
B'nei Torah Movement; Iranian [20145]
B'nei Torah Sedaka Fund [★20145]
Bnos Agudath Israel [20127], 42 Broadway, New York, NY 10004, (212)797-9000
Boar; Fellowship of the White [★11145]
Bd. of Acquisitions of Lib. Materials - of ALA [★10333]
Bd. of Airline Representatives in the United Kingdom [IO], London, United Kingdom
Bd. of Brethren Homes and Older Adult Ministries [★11276]
Bd. of Canadian Registered Safety Professionals [IO], Mississauga, ON, Canada
Bd. for Certification of Genealogists [21109], PO Box 14291, Washington, DC 20044
Bd. for Certification in Pedorthics and Amer. Bd. for Certification in Orthotics, Prosthetics and Pedorthics [★15783]
Bd. of Certified Hazard Control Mgt. [3440], PO Box 1662, Pelham, AL 35124, (202)987-9836
Bd. of Certified Prdt. Safety Mgt. [3441], PO Box 1662, Pelham, AL 35124, (205)987-9836
Bd. of Certified Safety Professionals [7587], 208 Burwash Ave., Savoy, IL 61874, (217)359-9263
Bd. of Church and Soc. of the United Methodist Church; Gen. [20263]
Bd. of Criminalistics; Amer. [5749]
Board of Deputies of British Jews [★20124]
Board of Deputies of British Jews [★IO]
Board of Examiners in Psychotherapy [★16207]
Bd. of External Trade [IO], Dar es Salaam, United Republic of Tanzania
Bd. of Global Ministries of the United Methodist Church; Women's Division of the Gen. [20269]
Bd. of Governors of the European Schools [IO], Brussels, Belgium
Bd. of Higher Educ. [★19854]
Bd. of Home Missions of the Natl. Assn. of Free Will Baptists [★19492]
Bd. of Hospitals and Homes of The Methodist Church [★14602]
Bd. of Intl. Ministries [19483], c/o Amer. Baptist Churches in the U.S.A., PO Box 851, Valley Forge, PA 19482-0851, (800)222-3872
Bd. of Intl. Ministries [IO], Valley Forge, PA, United States
Bd. of Investment of Sri Lanka [IO], Colombo, Sri Lanka
Bd. of Marine Underwriters of San Francisco [★3576]
Bd. on Medicine of the Natl. Acad. of Sciences [★7607]
Bd. of Natl. Ministries [19484], c/o Amer. Baptist Churches in the U.S.A., PO Box 851, Valley Forge, PA 19482-0851, (610)768-2000
Bd. of Nephrology Examiners - Nursing and Tech. [★15290]
Bd. of Nephrology Examiners Nursing and Tech. [15290], 1901 Pennsylvania Ave. NW, Ste. 607, Washington, DC 20006, (202)462-1252
Bd. for Orthotist/Prosthetist Certification [15785], 7150 Columbia Gateway Dr., Ste. G, Columbia, MD 21046-1151, (443)539-3810
Bd. of Registered Polysomnographic Technologists [15134], 8201 Greensboro Dr., Ste. 300, McLean, VA 22102, (703)610-9020
Bd. Retailers Assn. [3402], PO Box 1170, Wrightsville Beach, NC 28480, (910)509-0109
Bd. of Schools of the ASCP [★15141]
Bd. of Schools of Inhalation Therapy [★16610]
Bd. of Schools of Medical Tech. [★15141]
Bd. on Science and Technology for Intl. Development - Defunct.
Bd. of Thoracic Surgery [★16641]
Bd. of Trade of Kansas City, Missouri [★4327]
Bd. of Trade; New Orleans [4331]
Bd. of Trade; Salina [4334]
Bd. of Trade of the Wholesale Seafood Merchants [4323]
Bd. of Trustees and Directors of Missions [★19496]

Bd. of Underwriters of New York - Defunct.
Bd. of Urologic Allied Hea. Professionals; Amer. [★16706]
Boardgame Players Assn. [22461], 1541 Redfield Rd., Bel Air, MD 21015
Boarding for Breast Cancer Found. [13800], 6230 Wilshire Blvd., No. 179, Los Angeles, CA 90048, (323)571-2197
Boarding Kennels Assn; Amer. [2954]
Boarding Schools; The Assn. of [9018]
Boarding Schools Assn. [IO], London, United Kingdom
Boarding Schools; Comm. on [★9018]
Boards of Certification; Assn. of [6337]
Boards of Certification for Operating Personnel; Assn. of [★6337]
Boards of Certification for Operating Personnel in Water and Wastewater Utilities; Assn. of [★6337]
Boards, Commissions, and Councils of Catholic Educ; Natl. Assn. of [8056]

Boards of Education
Natl. Assn. of Charter School Authorizers [8281]
Boards of Educ; Natl. Assn. of State [9082]
Boards of Hea; Natl. Assn. of Local [16244]
BoardSource [12651], 1828 L St. NW, Ste. 900, Washington, DC 20036-5114, (202)452-6262
Boat Assn. of Am; Elec. [★21872]
Boat Builders and Repairers Assn; Amer. [2568]
Boat Builders and Repairers Assn; Atlantic Coast [★2568]
Boat Mfrs. Assn. [★2587]
Boat Mfrs; Natl. Assn. of Engine and [★2587]
Boat Mission; Oriental [★20315]
Boat Owners Alliance; Natl. Party [3359]
Boat Owners Assn. of the U.S. [23160], 880 S Pickett St., Alexandria, VA 22304, (703)823-9550
Boat Owners Coun. of America - Defunct.
Boat People SOS Comm. - Defunct.
Boat Rental Assn; Delta House [3367]
Boat and Travel Club; Vagabundos Del Mar RV, [22966]
Boat and Yacht Coun; Amer. [2569]
Boaters Against Drunk Driving [12955], 344 Clayton Ave., Battle Creek, MI 49017-5218, (269)963-7068
Boaters; Amer. League of Anglers and [23407]
Boaters Assn; Christian [20000]

Boating
Alberg 37 Intl. Owners Assn. [21866]
Amateur Yacht Res. Soc. [IO]
Amer. Boat Builders and Repairers Assn. [2568]
Amer. Boat and Yacht Coun. [2569]
Amer. League of Anglers and Boaters [23407]
Amer. Model Yachting Assn. [22642]
Amer. Pilots' Assn. [2571]
Amer. Power Boat Assn. [23152]
Amer. Sail Training Assn. [23153]
Amer. Sailing Assn. [23154]
Amer. Sailing Assn. Found. [23155]
Amer. Shark Assn. [23156]
Amer. Swan Boat Assn. [23669]
Amer. Y-Flyer Yacht Racing Assn. [23157]
Annapolis Naval Sailing Assn. [21867]
Antique and Classic Boat Soc. [21868]
Antique Outboard Motor Club [23158]
Assn. Francaise des Ynglings [IO]
Assn. of Marina Indus. [2602]
Assn. Suisse des Proprietaires Yngling [IO]
Assn. of Yachting Professionals [23159]
Associazione Italiana Classe Yngling [IO]
Australasian Jet Sports Boating Assn. [IO]
Australian Intl. Yngling Assn. [IO]
Australian Sailing and Cruising Club [IO]
Austrian Jet Sport Assn. [IO]
Bahamas Sailing Assn. [IO]
Bahrain Maritime Sports Assn. [IO]
Baidarka Historical Soc. [9954]
Barbados Sailing Assn. [IO]
Belarus Sailing Union [IO]
Bermuda Sailing Assn. [IO]
Blind Sailing Intl. [23151]
Bluewater Cruising Assn. [IO]
Boat Owners Assn. of the U.S. [23160]
Boaters Against Drunk Driving [12955]
Boating Writers Intl. [3100]
Brazilian Jet Sports Assn. [IO]

British Finn Assn. [IO]
Bulgarian Sailing Fed. [IO]
Bullseye Assn. [23161]
Canadian Boating Fed. [IO]
Canadian Power and Sail Squadrons [IO]
Canadian Yachting Assn. [IO]
Catalina 22 Natl. Sailing Assn. [23162]
Catboat Assn. [23163]
Cayman Islands Sailing Club [IO]
Center for Wooden Boats [21869]
Chinese Taipei Yachting Assn. [IO]
Chinese Yachting Assn. [IO]
Chris Craft Antique Boat Club [21870]
Christian Boaters Assn. [20000]
Classic Yacht Assn. [21871]
Club Managers Assn. of Am. [833]
Coronado 15 Natl. Assn. [23164]
Coun. of Amer. Master Mariners [2575]
Coun. of Sailing Associations [23165]
Croatian Sailing Fed. [IO]
Cruising Assn. [IO]
Cruising Club of Am. [23166]
Cyprus Yachting Assn. [IO]
Czech Sailing Assn. [IO]
Danish Sailing Assn. [IO]
Dansk Yngling Klub [IO]
Day Sailer Assn. [23167]
Delta Houseboat Rental Assn. [3367]
Deutsche Yngling Klassenvereinigung e.V [IO]
Deutscher Segler-Verband [IO]
Egyptian Yachting and Water Ski Fed. [IO]
El Toro Intl. Yacht Racing Assn. [23168]
Elec. Boat Assn. of the Americas [21872]
Estonian Windsurfing Assn. [IO]
European Boating Assn. [IO]
European Dragon Boat Fed. [IO]
Federacao Angolana de Vela [IO]
Federacao Brasileira de Vela e Motor [IO]
Federacio Andorrana de Vela [IO]
Federacion Argentina de Yachting [IO]
Federacion Colombiana de Vela [IO]
Federacion Dominicana de Vela [IO]
Federacion Ecuatoriana de Yachting [IO]
Federacion Mexicana de Vela [IO]
Federacion Nautica de Cuba [IO]
Federacion Venezolana de Vela [IO]
Fed. Algerienne de Voile [IO]
Fed. Francaise de Voile [IO]
Fed. Libanaise de Yachting [IO]
Fed. Royale Belge du Yachting [IO]
Fed. Royale Marocaine de Yachting a Voile [IO]
Fedevela El Portal de la vela Chilena [IO]
Fiji Yachting Assn. [IO]
Finnish Yachting Assn. [IO]
FJ U.S. [23169]
The Floating Hosp. [14882]
Flying Fifteen Intl. [IO]
Flying Scot Sailing Assn. [23170]
Force 5 Class Assn. [23171]
French Sailing Fed. [IO]
Gar Wood Soc. [IO]
Gar Wood Soc. [21873]
Geary 18 Intl. Yacht Racing Assn. [23172]
Gulf Yachting Assn. [21874]
Hampton One-Design Class Racing Assn. [23173]
Hebe Haven Yacht Club [IO]
Highlander Class Intl. Assn. [23174]
Hong Kong Dragon Boat Assn. [IO]
Hong Kong Sailing Fed. [IO]
Hungarian Yachting Assn. [IO]
Icelandic Sailing Fed. [IO]
Inland Lake Yachting Assn. [23175]
Inter-Collegiate Sailing Assn. of North Am. [23176]
Inter-Lake Yachting Assn. [23177]
Interlake Sailing Class Assn. [23178]
Intl. 5.5 Class Assn. [IO]
Intl. 210 Assn. [23179]
Intl. 505 Yacht Racing Assn., Amer. Sect. [23180]
Intl. Blue Jay Class Assn. [23181]
Intl. Blue Jay Class Assn. [IO]
Intl. Catalina 27/270 Assn. [23182]
Intl. Catalina 400 Assn. [21875]
Intl. D.N. Ice Yacht Racing Assn. [23183]

A star before a book entry number signifies that the name is not listed separately, but is mentioned within the entry.

Intl. D.N. Ice Yacht Racing Assn. [IO]
Intl. Etchells Class Assn. [IO]
Intl. Etchells Class Assn. [23184]
Intl. Finn Assn. [IO]
Intl. Finn Assn. - Antigua [IO]
Intl. Finn Assn. - Argentina [IO]
Intl. Finn Assn. - Australia [IO]
Intl. Finn Assn. - Austria [IO]
Intl. Finn Assn. - Belarus [IO]
Intl. Finn Assn. - Belgium [IO]
Intl. Finn Assn. - Bermuda [IO]
Intl. Finn Assn. - Brazil [IO]
Intl. Finn Assn. - Canada [IO]
Intl. Finn Assn. - Costa Rica [IO]
Intl. Finn Assn. - Croatia [IO]
Intl. Finn Assn. - Czech Republic [IO]
Intl. Finn Assn. - Denmark [IO]
Intl. Finn Assn. - Estonia [IO]
Intl. Finn Assn. - Finland [IO]
Intl. Finn Assn. - France [IO]
Intl. Finn Assn. - Germany [IO]
Intl. Finn Assn. - Greece [IO]
Intl. Finn Assn. - Hong Kong [IO]
Intl. Finn Assn. - Hungary [IO]
Intl. Finn Assn. - Iceland [IO]
Intl. Finn Assn. - India [IO]
Intl. Finn Assn. - Japan [IO]
Intl. Finn Assn. - Lithuania [IO]
Intl. Finn Assn. - Mexico [IO]
Intl. Finn Assn. - Monaco [IO]
Intl. Finn Assn. - Netherlands [IO]
Intl. Finn Assn. - New Zealand [IO]
Intl. Finn Assn. - Philippines [IO]
Intl. Finn Assn. - Poland [IO]
Intl. Finn Assn. - Portugal [IO]
Intl. Finn Assn. - Romania [IO]
Intl. Finn Assn. - Russia [IO]
Intl. Finn Assn. - Slovakia [IO]
Intl. Finn Assn. - Slovenia [IO]
Intl. Finn Assn. - South Africa [IO]
Intl. Finn Assn. - Spain [IO]
Intl. Finn Assn. - Switzerland [IO]
Intl. Finn Assn. - Thailand [IO]
Intl. Finn Assn. - Turkey [IO]
Intl. Finn Assn. - Ukraine [IO]
Intl. Finn Assn. - Zimbabwe [IO]
Intl. Flying Dutchman Class Assn. of the U.S. [IO]
Intl. Flying Dutchman Class Assn. of the U.S. [23185]
Intl. Hobie Class Assn. [23186]
Intl. Hobie Class Assn. [IO]
Intl. Hydrofoil Soc. [IO]
Intl. Hydrofoil Soc. [21876]
Intl. J/22 Class Assn. [23187]
Intl. J/22 Class Assn. [IO]
Intl. Jet Sports Boating Assn. and Amer. Watercraft Assn. [23976]
Intl. Lightning Class Assn. [23188]
Intl. Lightning Class Assn. [IO]
International Mobjack Association [IO]
Intl. Mobjack Assn. [23189]
Intl. Model Power Boat Assn. [22645]
Intl. Naples Sabot Assn. [23190]
Intl. Penguin Class Dinghy Assn. [23191]
Intl. Penguin Class Dinghy Assn. [IO]
Intl. Prindle Class Racing Assn. [23192]
Intl. Sailing Fed. [IO]
Intl. Sailing Schools Assn. [IO]
Intl. Ship Masters' Assn. [2579]
Intl. Star Class Yacht Racing Assn. [23193]
International Star Class Yacht Racing Association [IO]
Intl. Sunfish Class Assn. [IO]
Intl. Sunfish Class Assn. [23194]
Intl. Thunderbird Class Assn. [23195]
Irish Jet Sport Assn. [IO]
Irish Sailing Assn. [IO]
Israel Yachting Assn. [IO]
Italian Sailing Fed. [IO]
Jamaica Yachting Assn. [IO]
Japan Sailing Fed. [IO]
Jet 14 Class Assn. [23196]
Jet Sports Boating Assn. of Serbia and Montenegro [IO]
Joshua Slocum Soc. Intl. [23197]

Kazakhstan Sailing Fed. [IO]
Kenya Yachting Assn. [IO]
Korean Sailing Fed. [IO]
Kuwait Jet Ski Fed. [IO]
Libyan Sailing Fed. [IO]
Lido 14 Intl. Class Assn. [23198]
Lithuanian Yachting Union [IO]
Lyman Boat Owners Assn. [21877]
Marine Retailers Assn. of Am. [2580]
Marine Soc. of the City of New York [2581]
Mauritius Yachting Assn. [IO]
MC Sailing Assn. [23199]
Metal Boat Soc. [526]
Metal Boat Soc. [IO]
Middle Atlantic Fisheries Assn. [3493]
Midget Ocean Racing Club [23200]
Myanmar Yachting Fed. [IO]
Namibia Sailing Assn. [IO]
Natl. Assn. of Charterboat Operators [2582]
Natl. Assn. of Marine Services [2584]
Natl. Assn. of State Boating Law Administrators [5545]
Natl. Boating Fed. [23201]
Natl. Boating Safety Advisory Coun. [5546]
Natl. Butterfly Assn. [23202]
Natl. C Scow Sailing Assn. [23203]
National C Scow Sailing Association [IO]
Natl. Class E Scow Assn. [23204]
Natl. Fisheries Inst. [3496]
Natl. Marine Bankers Assn. [495]
Natl. Marine Distributors Assn. [2585]
Natl. Marine Electronics Assn. [2586]
Natl. Marine Mfrs. Assn. [2587]
Natl. Marine Representatives Assn. [2588]
Natl. Offshore Dept. [23205]
Natl. One Design Racing Assn. [23206]
Natl. Party Boat Owners Alliance [3359]
Natl. Pearson Yacht Owners Assn. [21878]
Natl. Piers Soc. [IO]
Natl. Safe Boating Coun. [12977]
Natl. School Sailing Assn. [IO]
Natl. Starwind/Spindrift Class Assn. [23207]
Natl. Teen Anglers [22454]
Natl. Water Safety Cong. [12981]
Natl. Women's Sailing Assn. [21879]
Nautical Res. Guild [21880]
Nautical Research Guild [IO]
Norsk Yngling Klubb [IO]
North Amer. Formula 18 Assn. [23208]
North Amer. Model Boat Assn. [22654]
North Amer. Steam Boat Assn. [21881]
North Amer. Steam Boat Assn. [IO]
North Amer. Tasar Assn. [IO]
North Amer. Tornado Assn. [23209]
Northwest Marine Trade Assn. [2589]
Northwest Schooner Soc. [21882]
Olson 30 Class Assn. [23210]
One-Design Class Coun. [23211]
Pacific Dragon Boat Assn. [21883]
Paddle Steamer Preservation Soc. [IO]
Pakistan Sailing Fed. [IO]
Papua New Guinea Yachting Assn. [IO]
Passenger Vessel Assn. [2591]
Personal Watercraft Assn. of Bermuda [IO]
Philippine Sailing Assn. [IO]
Prindle Class Assn. [23212]
Qatar Sailing and Rowing Fed. [IO]
Residential Boat Owners Assn. [IO]
Rhodes 19 Class Assn. [23213]
Rhodes Bantam Class Assn. [23214]
Richardson Boat Owners Assn. [21884]
Royal British Virgin Islands Yacht Club [IO]
Royal Yachting Assn. [IO]
Sail Am. [527]
Sailing Assn. of the Principality of Liechtenstein [IO]
Sailing Assn. of Zimbabwe [IO]
Sailing Fed. of Azerbaijan [IO]
Sailing Fed. of Peru [IO]
Saint Lucia Sailing Assn. [IO]
Salvador Sailing Fed. [IO]
Samoa Sailing Assn. [IO]
San Juan 21 Class Assn. [23215]
Santana 20 Class Assn. [23216]
Scale Ship Modelers Assn. of North Am. [22656]

Scottish Canoe Assn. [IO]
Seven Seas Cruising Assn. [23217]
Seychelles Yachting Assn. [IO]
Shields Natl. Class Assn. [23218]
Shipbuilders Coun. of Am. [2592]
Shipowners Claims Bur. [2238]
Ships-in-Bottles Assn. of Am. [22658]
Ships on Stamps Unit [22870]
Shorthanded Sailing Assn. of Australia [IO]
Singapore Sailing Fed. [IO]
Snipe Class Intl. Racing Assn. [IO]
Snipe Class Intl. Racing Assn. [23219]
Soc. of Boat and Yacht Designers [1154]
Soc. of Small Craft Designers [2593]
Solomon Islands Yachting Assn. [IO]
Sonar Class Assn. [23220]
States Org. for Boating Access [528]
Steamboat Assn. of Sweden [IO]
Svenska Yngling Forbundet [IO]
Swan Owners Assn. of Am. [23221]
Swedish Finn Assn. [IO]
T-Ten Class Assn. [23222]
Tanzer 16 Class Assn. [23223]
Tanzer 22 Class Assn. [IO]
Thai Jet Sports Boating Assn. [IO]
Thistle Class Assn. [23224]
Traditional Boat Squadron of Australia - Australian Capital Territory [IO]
Traditional Small Craft Assn. [21885]
Tugboat Enthusiasts Soc. of the Americas [21886]
U.K. Sailing Acad. [IO]
Union Internationale Motonautique [IO]
United Kingdom Wayfarer Assn. [IO]
U.S. A-Class Catamaran Assn. [23225]
U.S. Albacore Assn. [23226]
U.S. J/24 Class Assn. [23227]
United States J/24 Class Association [IO]
U.S. Life-Saving Ser. Heritage Assn. [10072]
U.S. Mariner Class Assn. [23228]
U.S. Mirror Class Assn. [23229]
U.S. Optimist Dinghy Assn. [23230]
U.S. Power Squadrons [23231]
U.S. Sailing Assn. [23232]
U.S. Sailing Found. [23233]
U.S. Soling Assn. [23234]
U.S. Tuna Found. [3506]
U.S. Wayfarer Assn. [23235]
U.S. Windsurfing Assn. [23236]
U.S. Yngling Assn. [23237]
U.S.A. Finn Assn. [23238]
USS Wainwright Veterans Assn. [21329]
Vintage Wooden Boat Assn. [IO]
West African Discussion Agreement [3597]
West Gulf Maritime Assn. [2595]
Western Assoc. Modelers [22661]
Windmill Class Assn. [23239]
Wooden Boat Assn. of New South Wales [IO]
Wooden Boat Assn. - Queensland [IO]
Wooden Boat Assn. - Victoria [IO]
Wooden Boat Guild of Tasmania [IO]
Wooden Canoe Heritage Assn. [21887]
World Ship Soc. [IO]
Yacht Brokers Assn. of Am. [2598]
Yacht Club Uruguayo [IO]
Yacht Racing Assn. of Thailand Under Royal Patronage [IO]
Yachting Assn. of India [IO]
Yachting Assn. of Sri Lanka [IO]
Yachting Club of Am. [23240]
Yachting New Zealand [IO]
Yachting Union of Latvia [IO]
Yngling Assn. of Canada [IO]
Yngling Club Holland [IO]
Yngling Club Osterreich [IO]
Boating Anti-Pollution Coun. - Address unknown since 1995.
Boating Assn; Intl. Jet Ski [★23976]
Boating Comm; Natl. Safe [★12977]
Boating Coun; Natl. Safe [12977]
Boating Indus. Associations [★2587]
Boating Week Comm; Natl. Safe [★12977]
Boating; Western Coun. of Model [★22654]
Boating Writers Intl. [3100], 108 9th St., Wilmette, IL 60091, (847)736-4142
Boating Writers Intl. [IO], Wilmette, IL, United States

Reference to "IO" in place of a book number signifies that the association may be found in the 45th edition of International Organizations.

Boatowners Unlimited - Defunct.
Boats All Hands; PT [★21402]
Boats, Bases and Tenders; PT [★21402]
Boats, Tenders and Bases; WWII PT [★21402]
Bob Crane Memorial Fan Club - Address unknown
    since 2006.
Bob Dylan Newsletter - Address unknown since
    2001.
Bob Hastings Fan Club - Address unknown since
    2001.
Bob Homan Fan Club [24852], PO Box 653,
    Yakima, WA 98907-0653, (509)453-1228
Bob und Schlittenverband fur Deutschland e.V. [IO],
    Berchtesgaden, Germany
Bobath Alumni Assn.; Intl. [★15399]
Bobby Bare Fan Club - Defunct.
Bobby Blue Fan Club - Address unknown since
    2003.
Bobby "C" Fan Club - Defunct.
Bobby Darin Fan Club - Address unknown since
    1988.
Bobby Driscoll Fan Club - Address unknown since
    2004.
Bobby Fuller Four-Ever Intl. Fan Club - Defunct.
Bobby Goldsboro Fan Club - Address unknown
    since 1989.
Bobby Labonte Fan Club [24999], PO Box 358, Trin-
    ity, NC 27370
Bobby Vinton Booster Club - Address unknown since
    2004.
Bobby Vinton Intl. Fan Club - Address unknown
    since 2001.
Bobby Wright Intl. Fan Club; Kitty Wells-Johnny
    Wright- [24936]
Bobs Intl. - Address unknown since 2007.
Bobsled Fed; Natl. [★23767]
Bobsled and Skeleton Fed; U.S. [23767]
Bobsleigh
    Bob und Schlittenverband fur Deutschland e.V.
        [IO]
    British Bobsleigh Assn. [IO]
    Fed. Internationale de Bobsleigh et de Toboggan-
        ing [IO]
    U.S. Bobsled and Skeleton Fed. [23767]
Bobsleigh Canada Skeleton [IO], Calgary, AB,
    Canada
Boccaccio Assn; Amer. [9629]
Bocce
    Bocce Fed. of Australia [IO]
    Intl. Fed. of Petanque and Provencal Games [IO]
    U.S. Bocce Fed. [23241]
    World Bocce League [23242]
    World Bocce League [IO]
Bocce Fed. of Australia [IO], Kew East, Australia
Bocce; U.S.A. Fed. of [★23241]
Bockus Intl. Soc. of Gastroenterology [14411], c/o
    David E. Bernstein, MD, Treas., North Shore Univ.
    Hosp., 300 Community Dr., Manhasset, NY 11030,
    (516)562-4281
Bockus Intl. Soc. of Gastroenterology [IO], Manhas-
    set, NY, United States
BOCS Found. [IO], Szekesfehervar, Hungary
Body Chemistry; HELP - Inst. for [14928]
Body Positive - Defunct.
Body Positive Tayside [IO], Dundee, United Kingdom
Body Psychotherapy; U.S. Assn. for [16188]
Body Stress Release Assn. - UK [IO], Lightwater,
    United Kingdom
Body Therapy
    Amer. Center for the Alexander Technique [13617]
    Amer. Soc. for the Alexander Technique [13623]
    Assoc. Bodywork and Massage Professionals
        [15025]
    Intl. Assn. of Animal Massage and Bodywork
        [15028]
    Intl. Assn. of Structural Integrators [13638]
    Radix Inst. [13649]
    Rolf Inst. of Structural Integration [13652]
    Soc. of Ortho-Bionomy Intl. [13767]
    Society of Ortho-Bionomy International [IO]
    Worldwide Aquatic Bodywork Assn. [13658]
Body Tomography and Magnetic Resonance; Soc. of
    Computed [16297]
Bodybuilding
    Intl. Natural Bodybuilding and Fitness Fed.
        [23243]

Intl. Natural Bodybuilding and Fitness Fed. [IO]
Natl. Amateur Body Builders Assn. USA [23244]
Natl. Gym Assn. [23654]
North Amer. Natural Bodybuilding Fed. [23245]
North Amer. Powerlifting Fed. [23662]
North Amer. Sports Fed. [23065]
North Amer. Strongman [23246]
USA Powerlifting [23664]
Bodyguard Assn; Professional [IO]
Bodymind Acupressure; Jin Shin Do Found. for
    [15746]
BODYWHYS: Help, Support, Understanding for An-
    orexia and Bulimia Nervosa [★IO]
BODYWHYS: The Eating Disorders Assn. of Ireland
    [IO], Dublin, Ireland
Bodywork
    Intl. Assn. of Animal Massage and Bodywork
        [15028]
    Intl. Center for Reiki Training [22969]
    North Amer. Strongman [23246]
    Soc. of Ortho-Bionomy Intl. [13767]
Bodywork Assn; Worldwide Aquatic [13658]
Bodywork and Massage Professionals; Assoc.
    [15025]
Bodywork Therapies of Asia; Amer. Org. for [15024]
Bodywork Therapy Assn; Amer. Oriental [★15024]
Bodyworkers; Assoc. Professional Massage
    Therapists and [★15025]
Boer Goat Breeders Assn. of Australia [IO], Armi-
    dale, Australia
Boerenbond [IO], Leuven, Belgium
Boersenverein des Deutschen Buchhandels e.V.
    [★IO]
Boethius Soc; Intl. [10799]
Bogardus Descendants Assn; Anneke Jans and
    Everardus [20782]
Boggess Family Assn. [20801], 2811 Hwy. 59 S, No.
    400, Livingston, TX 77351, (281)799-1444
Bogguss Fan Club; Suzy [24978]
Bogra Young Men's Christian Association [IO],
    Bogra, Bangladesh
Bohemia Ragtime Soc. [10568], 4501 Palm Ave.,
    Des Moines, IA 50310-3790
Bohemian Catholic Union; Western [★18998]
Bohemian Free Thinking School Soc. - Address
    unknown since 1995.
Boiler Mfrs. Assn; Amer. [1992]
Boiler Owners; Coun. of Indus. [2015]
Boiler and Pressure Vessel Inspectors; Natl. Bd. of
    [5824]
Boiler and Radiator Manufacturers Assn. [IO], Glas-
    gow, United Kingdom
Boiler and Radiator Mfrs; Inst. of [★1884]
Boilermakers' Assn; Master [★3283]
Boilermakers; Intl. Brotherhood of [★24001]
Boilermakers, Iron Ship Builders, Blacksmiths, Forg-
    ers and Helpers; Intl. Brotherhood of [24021]
Boilermakers; Stove, Furnace, Energy, and Allied
    Appliance Workers Division of the Intl. Brotherhood
    of [24001]
Boise Peace Quilt Proj. [18192], PO Box 6469,
    Boise, ID 83707, (208)378-0293
Boissons rafraichissantes [★IO]
Bol Chumann na h Eireann [IO], Carrigtwohill,
    Ireland
BOLD/Challenge Aspen [★23342]
Bolivarian Soc. of the U.S. [11103]
Bolivian Assn. of Insurance Companies [IO], La Paz,
    Bolivia
Bolivian Bible Soc. [IO], Cochabamba, Bolivia
Bolivian Forestry Assn. [IO], Santa Cruz, Bolivia
Bolivian Inst. of Foreign Trade [IO], Santa Cruz,
    Bolivia
Bolivian Private Bankers' Assn. [IO], La Paz, Bolivia
Bolivian Soc. of Clinical Neurophysiology [IO], La
    Paz, Bolivia
Bolling Family Assn. [20802], PO Box 591, Vienna,
    VA 22183-0591, (703)281-7489
Bolt, Nut and Rivet Mfrs; Amer. Inst. of [★1823]
Bolted Structural Joints; Res. Coun. on Riveted and
    [★7712]
Bolton Platinum Club; Michael [24947]
Bomb Gp. Assn; 6th [21362]
Bomb Gp. Assn; 22nd [21364]
Bomb Gp. Assn; 43rd [20653]

Bomb Gp. Assn; 397th [21375]
Bomb Gp. Memorial Assn; 381st [20655]
Bomb Gp. Reunion Assn; 17th [20652]
Bomb Survivors in the U.S; Comm. of Atomic
    [18144]
Bomb Wing/Group Assn; 452nd [21376]
Bombadiers Alumni Assn. - Defunct.
Bombardiers Inc. - Defunct.
Bombardment Assn; Second [20664]
Bombardment Gp. Assn; 461st [20657]
Bombardment Gp. (H) Assn. 7th Air Force; 494th
    [20658]
Bombardment Gp. (H) Assn; 483rd [21377]
Bombardment Gp. (Heavy) Assn; 401st [20656]
Bombay Natural History Soc. [IO], Bombay, India
Bombing; Americans Against World Empire/
    Americans Against [18794]
Bonaire Govt. Tourist Off. [24361], c/o Adams
    Unlimited Public Relations and Marketing, 80
    Broad St., 32nd Fl., Ste. 3202, New York, NY
    10004, (212)956-5912
Bonaire Tourist Boards; Curacao and [★24362]
Bonaire Tourist Info. Off. [★24361]
Bonanza Assn; Twin [21483]
Bonanza Soc; Amer. [21427]
Bond Club of New York - Defunct.
Bond; Intl. Soc. for the Stud. of the Human-
    Companion Animal [★16615]
Bond Issuers; Coun. of Indus. Development
    [★17458]
Bond Lawyers; Natl. Assn. of [6255]
Bond van Orkestdirigenten en Instructeurs [★IO]
Bond Producers; Natl. Assn. of Surety [2219]
Bond and Share Soc. [★22046]
Bond and Share Soc. [★IO]
Bondurant Family Assn. [20803], c/o Jack Bondu-
    rant, Treas., 5112 Mt. Vernon Memorial Hwy.,
    Alexandria, VA 22309
Bone
    Amer. Bone Marrow Donor Registry [13768]
    Amer. Soc. for Bone and Mineral Res. [15787]
    Aplastic Anemia and MDS Intl. Found. [14785]
    Bone Marrow Found. [13769]
    Bones Soc. [15764]
    Brittle Bone Soc. [IO]
    Caitlin Raymond Intl. Registry [13770]
    Center for Intl. Blood and Marrow Transplant Res.
        [13771]
    Center for Intl. Blood and Marrow Transplant Res.
        [IO]
    Hip Soc. [15769]
    Intl. Pelvic Pain Soc. [15843]
    Intl. Soc. for Clinical Densitometry [15788]
    MHE Coalition [14465]
    Natl. Osteoporosis Found. [15775]
    Osteoporosis Australia [IO]
    Osteoporosis Australian Capital Territory [IO]
    Osteoporosis New South Wales [IO]
    Osteoporosis Northern Territory [IO]
    Osteoporosis South Australia [IO]
    Osteoporosis Tasmania [IO]
    Osteoporosis Victoria [IO]
    Osteoporosis Western Australia [IO]
    Paget Found. for Paget's Disease of Bone and
        Related Disorders [15256]
    Progressive Osseous Heteroplasia Assn. [14477]
    Prune Belly Syndrome Network [14478]
    Stickler Involved People [14483]
Bone Banks Prog. of The DRF; Natl. Temporal
    [★15121]
Bone, Hearing and Balance Pathology Rsrc.
    Registry; Natl. Temporal [★15121]
Bone, Hearing and Balance Pathology Rsrc.
    Registry; NIDCD - Natl. Temporal [15121]
Bone and Joint Surgeons; Assn. of [15763]
Bone Marrow Donor Registry-American [★13768]
Bone Marrow Donor Registry; Natl. [★14292]
Bone Marrow Donors Worldwide [IO], Leiden,
    Netherlands
Bone Marrow Found. [13769], 337 E 88th St., Ste.
    1B, New York, NY 10128, (212)838-3029
Bone Marrow Transplant Link; Natl. [16676]
Bone and Mineral Res; Amer. Soc. for [15787]
Bone and Related Disorders; Paget Found. for Pag-
    et's Disease of [15256]

A star before a book entry number signifies that the name is not listed separately, but is mentioned within the entry.

Bone Res. Soc. [IO], Bristol, United Kingdom
Bonefish and Tarpon Unlimited [4987], c/o Aaron
    Adams, PhD, Dir. of Operations and Res., PO Box
    2197, Pineland, FL 33945, (239)283-1622
Bonefishing Soc; Intl. [22452]
Bones Soc. [15764], 6300 N River Rd., Ste. 727,
    Rosemont, IL 60018-4226, (800)247-9699
Boniface Soc; Amer. St. [19568]
Bonnechere Soaring [IO], Petawawa, ON, Canada
Bonnet; Les Amis de Panhard and Deutsch [21686]
Bonnie Hartle Fan Club - Address unknown since
    1989.
Bonnie Lou Bishop Fan Club [★24853]
Bonnie Lou Bishop Intl. Fan Club [24853]
Bonsai Clubs Assn. [★22504]
Bonsai Clubs Assn. [★IO]
Bonsai Clubs Intl. [IO], Metairie, LA, United States
Bonsai Clubs Intl. [22504], PO Box 8445, Metairie,
    LA 70011-8445, (504)832-8071
Bonsai and Orchid Assn. [4975], 26 Pine St., Dover,
    DE 19901, (302)736-6781
Bonsai and Orchid Assn. [IO], Dover, DE, United
    States
Bonsai Soc; Amer. [22483]
Bonus Families [12143], PO Box 1926, Discovery
    Bay, CA 94514, (925)516-2681
Bonus Presskopia [IO], Stockholm, Sweden
Boogie People - Address unknown since 1999.
Book Aid Intl. [IO], London, United Kingdom
Book Assn. of Am; Periodical and [3247]
Book Assn. for the Blind; Theosophical [20592]
Book Assn; Women's Natl. [3174]
Book; Center for the [10417]
Book Center; Natl. Yiddish [10288]
Book Center for War Devastated Libraries; Amer.
    [★10392]
Book Club; Episcopal [★19972]
Book Club; Tzivos Hashem [★10290]
Book Clubs
    Assn. of Book Gp. Readers and Leaders [9738]
    Assn. of Book Gp. Readers and Leaders [IO]
    Single Booklovers [22142]
    Soc. of Phantom Friends [9739]
    Society of Phantom Friends [IO]
    Welsh Books Coun. [IO]
Book Collective; Boston Women's Hea. [★16909]
Book Collector's Club of Am; Big Little [★21978]
Book Collector's Club; Big Little [21978]
Book Components Manufacturers Assn. - Defunct.
Book Coun; Amer. Text [9258]
Book Distribution Program - Defunct.
Book Exchange; Natl. Yiddish [★10288]
Book Exchange; U.S. [10392]
Book Exchange; U.S. [★10392]
Book Exchange; Universal Serials and [★10392]
Book Indus. Study Group [3213], 370 Lexington
    Ave., Ste. 900, New York, NY 10017, (646)336-
    7141
Book Indus. Study Group [IO], New York, NY, United
    States
Book Manufacturers' Inst. [1761], Two Armand
    Beach Dr., Ste. 1B, Palm Coast, FL 32137-2612,
    (386)986-4552
Book and Periodical Coun. [IO], Toronto, ON,
    Canada
Book and Periodical Development Coun. [★IO]
Book Producers Assn; Amer. [3200]
Book Publishers Assn. of Alberta [IO], Edmonton,
    AB, Canada
Book Publishers; Assn. of Amer. Medical [★3204]
Book Publishers Assn; Catholic [3214]
Book Publishers Assn. of Israel [IO], Tel Aviv, Israel
Book Publishers Assn. of New Zealand [IO], Auck-
    land, New Zealand
Book Publishers' Fed. of Luxembourg [IO],
    Luxembourg, Luxembourg
Book Publishers' Professional Assn. [IO], Toronto,
    ON, Canada
Book Publishers' Representatives Assn. [★IO]
Book Writers and Illustrators; Soc. of Children's
    [11194]
Book Writers; Soc. of Children's [★11194]
Bookbinders of Amer; Employing [★1761]
Booker T. Washington Found. - Address unknown
    since 1999.

Booklet Pane Soc. - Defunct.
Booklovers; Single [22142]
Bookplate Collectors and Designers; Amer. Soc. of
    [21965]
Bookplate Soc. [IO], Reading, United Kingdom
Bookplates
    Amer. Soc. of Bookplate Collectors and Designers
    [21965]
Books
    About Books, Inc. [3198]
    African Books Collective [IO]
    Afro-Asian Book Coun. [IO]
    Alcuin Soc. [IO]
    Alice in Wonderland Collectors Network [21957]
    Amer. Soc. of Bookplate Collectors and Designers
    [21965]
    Amer. Textbook Coun. [9258]
    Antiquarian Booksellers Assn. of Am. [9740]
    ARA Intl. [IO]
    Argentine Chamber of Book Publishers [IO]
    Assn. of Amer. Publishers [3206]
    Assn. of Booksellers for Children [529]
    Australian and New Zealand Assn. of Antiquarian
    Booksellers [IO]
    Belgian Publishers' Assn. [IO]
    Bibliographical Soc. of Am. [9741]
    Bibliographical Soc. of Canada [IO]
    Bibliographical Soc. - United Kingdom [IO]
    Bibliographical Soc. of the Univ. of Virginia [9742]
    Big Little Book Collector's Club [21978]
    Binders' Guild [9743]
    Book Indus. Study Group [3213]
    Book Manufacturers' Inst. [1761]
    Book Publishers' Fed. of Luxembourg [IO]
    Books for the Barrios [12049]
    Books For Africa [9744]
    Books For Africa [IO]
    Books For Soldiers [11491]
    Canadian Bookbinders and Book Artists Guild [IO]
    Canadian Children's Book Centre [IO]
    Catholic Book Publishers Assn. [3214]
    Catholic Press Assn. [3215]
    CBA [3403]
    Center for the Book [10417]
    Center for Book Arts [9745]
    Children's Book Coun. [9746]
    Children's Book Coun. of Australia [IO]
    Children's Book Coun. of Iran [IO]
    Children's Books History Soc. [IO]
    Children's Books Ireland [IO]
    Christian Bookselling Assn. of Australia [IO]
    The Christian Sci. Publishing Soc. [3216]
    Christian Small Publishers Assn. [3217]
    Colombian Book Chamber [IO]
    Danish Publishers' Assn. [IO]
    Dictionary Soc. of North Am. [9747]
    Dutch Alliance of Booksellers [IO]
    Dutch Publishers' Assn. [IO]
    Educational Paperback Assn. [3221]
    English Language Editors' Assn. [IO]
    Fans of Oz [25048]
    Fed. of Children's Book Groups [IO]
    Fed. of Spanish Publishers' Associations [IO]
    Finnish Booksellers' Assn. [IO]
    First Book [8789]
    Gen. Egyptian Book Org. [IO]
    Georgia Writers Assn. and Young Georgia Writers
    [11172]
    Great Books Found. [9748]
    Grolier Club [9749]
    Guild of Book Workers [9750]
    Guild of Book Workers [IO]
    Hungarian Publishers and Booksellers Assn. [IO]
    Independent Online Booksellers Assn. [530]
    Indian Heritage Coun. [10744]
    Indonesian Book Publishers' Assn. [IO]
    Intl. Artists Network [9506]
    Intl. Assn. of Cross-Reference Dir. Publishers
    [3228]
    Intl. Bd. on Books for Young People [IO]
    Intl. Board on Books for Young People - Dutch
    Section [IO]
    Intl. Book Proj. [8620]
    Intl. Friends of the London Lib. [10363]
    Intl. Inst. for Frame Stud. [9991]

    Intl. Thriller Writers [11179]
    Italian Booksellers' Assn. [IO]
    Japan Audio Visual Educ. Assn. [IO]
    Jewish Book Coun. [9751]
    Latvian Publishers' Assn. [IO]
    Lib. Binding Inst. [1778]
    Literary Source [3232]
    Miniature Book Soc. [9752]
    Miniature Book Soc. [IO]
    Natl. Assn. of Independent Publishers [3238]
    Natl. Book Critics Circle [9753]
    Natl. Book Development Coun. of Singapore [IO]
    Natl. Book Trust India [IO]
    Natl. Braille Press [16876]
    Natl. Chamber of the Mexican Publishing Indus.
    [IO]
    Natl. Union of Publishing [IO]
    New Zealand Book Coun. [IO]
    Nordic Assn. of Lexicography [IO]
    Norwegian Publishers' Assn. [IO]
    Overseas Press Club of Am. [3154]
    Periodical and Book Assn. of Am. [3247]
    Philomathean Soc. of the Univ. of Pennsylvania
    [10429]
    PMA - Independent Book Publishers Assn. [3248]
    Polish Chamber of Books [IO]
    Portuguese Assn. of Booksellers and Publishers
    [IO]
    Publishers' and Booksellers' Assn. of Macedonia
    [IO]
    Reading Is Fundamental [9047]
    Renaissance English Text Soc. [10932]
    Seedlings Braille Books for Children [9297]
    Single Booklovers [22142]
    Soc. of Children's Book Writers and Illustrators
    [11194]
    Soc. for the History of Authorship, Reading and
    Publishing [9754]
    Society for the History of Authorship, Reading and
    Publishing [IO]
    Soc. of Scribes [11214]
    Soc. for Textual Scholarship [10432]
    Stelios M. Stelson Found. [8631]
    Support Our Soldiers Am. [11502]
    Taurine Bibliophiles of Am. [9755]
    U.S. Bd. on Books for Young People [9756]
    U.S. Book Exchange [10392]
    Universal Autograph Collectors Club [22126]
    Women Writing the West [4071]
    Women's Natl. Book Assn. [3174]
    Young Australians Best Book Award Coun. [IO]
Books Across Ghana - Address unknown since
    2007.
Books for Babies [★10358]
Books for the Barrios [12049], 2350 Whitman Rd.,
    Ste. D, Concord, CA 94518-2541, (925)687-7701
Books for the Barrios [IO], Concord, CA, United
    States
Books for a Better World [IO], Mesa, AZ, United
    States
Books for a Better World [8235], PO Box 30848,
    Mesa, AZ 85275, (480)628-2300
Books for the Blind; Computerized [★16885]
Books for Equal Education - Defunct.
Books For Africa [9744], 253 E 4th St., Ste. 200, St.
    Paul, MN 55101, (651)602-9844
Books For Africa [IO], St. Paul, MN, United States
Books For Soldiers [11491], 353 Jonestown Rd., No.
    123, Winston-Salem, NC 27104
Books, Inc; About [3198]
Books for Keeps [IO], London, United Kingdom
Books for the People Fund - Defunct.
Booksellers Assn; Amer. [3396]
Booksellers Assn; Amer. Wholesale [3398]
Booksellers Assn; Christian [★3403]
Booksellers Assn; Great Lakes [3225]
Booksellers Assn; Mountains and Plains [741]
Booksellers Assn. of the United Kingdom and Ireland
    [IO], London, United Kingdom
Booksellers Found. for Free Expression; Amer.
    [17641]
Booksellers New Zealand [IO], Wellington, New
    Zealand
Bookstore Assn; Coll. [★3415]
Bookstore, Oper. Pass-Along; Anglican [★19972]

Reference to "IO" in place of a book number signifies that the association may be found in the 45th edition of International Organizations.

Boomerang Assn. of Australia [IO], Huntingdale, Australia

Boomerangs
Boomerang Assn. of Australia [IO]
Free Throwers Boomerang Soc. [23247]
U.S. Boomerang Assn. [23248]

Boone and Crockett Club [5301], 250 Sta. Dr., Missoula, MT 59801, (406)542-1888

Boone Fan Club; Natl. Pat [24949]

Boone Fan Clubs; Natl. Assn. of Pat [★24949]

Boone and Frontier Families Res. Assn; Daniel [10107]

Boone Soc. [20804], 40 Church Ct., Sumter, SC 29150-4257

Boone Soc. [IO], Sumter, SC, United States

Boop Intl. Collectible Club; Betty [21976]

Booster Club; Buffalo Sabres [25000]

Booster Club; Cleveland Hockey [25001]

Booster Club; Hartford Whalers [25006]

Booster Club; Los Angeles Kings [25007]

Booster Club; New York Islanders [25009]

Booster Club; Pittsburgh Hornets [★25012]

Booster Club; Pittsburgh Penguins [25012]

Booster Clubs Assn; Natl. Hockey League [25008]

Boot and Shoe Mfrs'. Assn. [IO], London, United Kingdom

Boot and Shoe Travelers Assn. of New York [1596], 50 W 34th St., Ste. 8A6, New York, NY 10001, (212)564-1069

Bord na gCon [★IO]

Border Caucus; Congressional [5598]

Border Collie Club; U.S. [22372]

Border Collie Rescue [IO], Richmond, United Kingdom

Border Control; U.S. [17810]

Border Leicester Assn; Amer. [5177]

Border Patrol Coun; Natl. [24123]

Border Terrier Club of Am. [22234], PO Box 641044, Beverly Hills, FL 34464, (802)253-9450

Border Terrier Welfare; North Amer. [12019]

Borderland Sciences Res. Found. [7471], PO Box 6250, Eureka, CA 95502, (707)445-2247

Boreal Songbird Initiative [5302], 1904 Third Ave., Ste. 305, Seattle, WA 98101, (206)956-9040

Boreal Songbird Initiative [IO], Seattle, WA, United States

Boredom Anonymous - Defunct.

Borgward Owners' Club [21594], 77 New Hampshire Ave., Bay Shore, NY 11706, (516)273-0458

Boring Inst. - Defunct.

Boris Becker Fan Club - Defunct.

Born Again Pagans - Address unknown since 1995.

Born Free Found. [IO], Horsham, United Kingdom

Born Young [★20865]

Born Young Newsletter [★21091]

Borreliosis Found; Lyme [★14272]

Borzoi Club of Am. [22235], c/o Shen Smith, Treas., PO Box 175, Elk Rapids, MI 49629, (231)264-6665

Bosher Family Org; John [20960]

Bosnia and Herzegovina Soc. of Gastroenterologist [★IO]

Bosnia and Herzegovina Sports Medicine Assn. [IO], Sarajevo, Bosnia-Hercegovina

Bosnian-Canadian Relief Assn. [IO], Toronto, ON, Canada

BOSPO [IO], Tuzla, Bosnia-Hercegovina

Boss 302 Registry [21595], c/o Randy Ream, 1817 Janet Ave., Lebanon, PA 17046-1845, (717)274-5280

Boss 429 Owners Dir. [21596], PO Box 8035, Spokane, WA 99203, (509)448-0252

Bosses Intl; Sons of [★748]

Bossons Collectors Soc; Intl. [22047]

Boston Bruins Hockey Fan Club - Defunct.

Boston Computer Soc. - Defunct.

Boston Grain and Flour Exchange - Address unknown since 1995.

Boston Intl. Found. for Medical Education/Exchange [15089], c/o Joseph J. Vitale, MD, Chm., 160 Heritage Ln., Weymouth, MA 02189-1061, (617)414-4829

Boston Intl. Found. for Medical Education/Exchange [IO], Weymouth, MA, United States

Boston Intl. Found. for Medical Exchange [★IO]

Boston Intl. Found. for Medical Exchange [★15089]

Boston Shipping Assn. [3561]

Boston Star Trek Assn. - Address unknown since 2003.

Boston Terrier Club of Am. [22236], c/o Joyce Fletcher, Corresponding Sec., 3878 Banks Rd., Cincinnati, OH 45245-2602, (513)943-9432

Boston Theological Inst. [9271], 210 Herrick Rd., Newton Centre, MA 02459, (617)527-4880

Boston Theological Inst. Black Seminarians - Defunct.

Boston Univ. Washington Journalism Prog. [★8719]

Boston Women's Hea. Book Collective [★16909]

Boston Wool Trade Assn. [3777]

Bostonian Soc. [10097], Old State House, 206 Washington St., Boston, MA 02109-1713, (617)720-1713

Botanical Artists; Amer. Soc. of [9492]

Botanical Exchange Club [★IO]

Botanical Gardens
Amer. Ivy Soc. [22496]
Amer. Penstemon Soc. [22497]
Amer. Public Gardens Assn. [4973]
Amer. Topical Assn., Biology Unit [22792]
Australian Garden History Soc. [IO]
Bromeliad Soc. Intl. [22505]
Center for Plant Conservation [4372]
Natl. Garden Clubs [22528]

Botanical Gardens and Arboreta; Amer. Assn. of [★4973]

Botanical Gardens Conservation Intl. [IO], Richmond, United Kingdom

Botanical and Horticultural Libraries; Coun. on [10352]

Botanical Soc. [★6632]

Botanical Soc. of Am. [6632], PO Box 299, St. Louis, MO 63166, (314)577-9566

Botanical Soc. of Am; Mycological Sect., [★7352]

Botanical Soc. of the British Isles [IO], London, United Kingdom

Botanical Soc. of Edinburgh [★IO]

Botanical Soc. of Japan [IO], Tokyo, Japan

Botanical Soc. of London [★IO]

Botanical Soc. of Lund [IO], Lund, Sweden

Botanical Soc. of Scotland [IO], Edinburgh, United Kingdom

Botanical Soc. of South Africa [IO], Claremont, Republic of South Africa

Botaniese Vereniging van Suid-Afrika [★IO]

Botany
African Violet Soc. of Am. [22480]
Akerne Orchids [IO]
All-America Gladiolus Selections [22481]
Amer. Bamboo Soc. [6619]
American Bamboo Society [IO]
Amer. Begonia Soc. [22482]
Amer. Bonsai Soc. [22483]
Amer. Botanical Coun. [6620]
Amer. Boxwood Soc. [22484]
Amer. Brugmansia and Datura Soc. [22455]
Amer. Bryological and Lichenological Soc. [6621]
American Bryological and Lichenological Society [IO]
The Amer. Chestnut Found. [6622]
Amer. Community Gardening Assn. [22486]
Amer. Daffodil Soc. [22487]
Amer. Fern Soc. [6623]
Amer. Fuchsia Soc. [22488]
Amer. Genetic Assn. [7111]
Amer. Gourd Soc. [22489]
Amer. Hemerocallis Soc. [22490]
Amer. Herb Assn. [6624]
Amer. Hibiscus Soc. [22491]
Amer. Horticultural Soc. [22492]
Amer. Hosta Soc. [22493]
Amer. Iris Soc. [22495]
Amer. Ivy Soc. [22496]
Amer. Orchid Soc. [6625]
American Orchid Society [IO]
Amer. Penstemon Soc. [22497]
Amer. Peony Soc. [22498]
Amer. Phytopathological Soc. [6626]
Amer. Primrose Soc. [22499]
Amer. Public Gardens Assn. [4973]
Amer. Rhododendron Soc. [22500]
Amer. Rose Soc. [22501]

Amer. Soc. for Horticultural Sci. [6627]
Amer. Soc. of Plant Biologists [6628]
Amer. Soc. of Plant Taxonomists [6629]
Aquatic Plant Mgt. Soc. [6630]
Argentine Soc. of Botany [IO]
Aril Soc. Intl. [22502]
Arizona Cactus and Succulent Res. [6631]
Arizona Cactus and Succulent Research [IO]
Asociacion de Orquideologia de Quito [IO]
Aspley Orchid Soc. [IO]
Australasian Plant Pathology Soc. [IO]
Australian Systematic Botany Soc. [IO]
Bamboo Soc. of India [IO]
Bamboo of The Americas [4365]
Bonsai Clubs Intl. [22504]
Botanical Soc. of Am. [6632]
Botanical Soc. of the British Isles [IO]
Botanical Soc. of Japan [IO]
Botanical Soc. of Lund [IO]
Botanical Soc. of Scotland [IO]
Botanical Soc. of South Africa [IO]
Brisbane Orchid Soc. [IO]
British Bryological Soc. [IO]
British Lichen Soc. [IO]
British Phycological Soc. [IO]
British Pteridological Soc. [IO]
British Soc. for Plant Pathology [IO]
Bromeliad Soc. Intl. [22505]
Cactus and Succulent Soc. of Am. [22506]
Canadian Botanical Assn. [IO]
Canadian Phytopathological Soc. [IO]
Chinese Bamboo Soc. [IO]
Chinese Soc. for Plant Pathology [IO]
CJM Orquideas [IO]
Colomborquideas [IO]
Coun. on Botanical and Horticultural Libraries [10352]
Cymbidium Soc. of Am. [22508]
Desert Botanical Garden [6633]
Epiphyllum Soc. of Am. [22510]
EUCARPIA [IO]
European Botanical and Horticultural Libraries Gp. [IO]
European and Mediterranean Cereal Rusts Found. [IO]
Forest Gold Products [IO]
Friends of the Natl. Arboretum [6634]
Garden Club of Am. [22511]
Garden Conservancy [4402]
Garden Writers Assn. [22512]
The Gardeners of Am. [22513]
Gesneriad Hybridizers Assn. [22514]
Gesneriad Soc. [22515]
Herb Res. Found. [6635]
Herb Soc. of Am. [6636]
Heritage Roses Gp. [22517]
Indoor Gardening Soc. of Am. [22519]
InterAmerican Soc. for Tropical Horticulture [4979]
Intl. Aroid Soc. [22520]
Intl. Assn. of Botanical and Mycological Societies [IO]
Intl. Assn. for Plant Taxonomy [IO]
Intl. Assn. for Vegetation Sci. [IO]
Intl. Bulb Soc. [IO]
Intl. Bulb Soc. [6637]
Intl. Carnivorous Plant Soc. [22521]
Intl. Herb Assn. [1907]
Intl. Lilac Soc. [22522]
Intl. Oleander Soc. [22523]
Intl. Org. for the Ornamental Plants Indus. [IO]
Intl. Org. of Citrus Virologists [IO]
Intl. Org. of Citrus Virologists [6638]
Intl. Org. of Plant Biosystematists [6639]
Intl. Org. of Plant Biosystematists [IO]
Intl. Org. for Succulent Plant Stud. [IO]
Intl. Palm Soc. [IO]
Intl. Palm Soc. [6640]
Intl. Plant Genetic Resources Inst. [IO]
Intl. Soc. of Environmental Botanists [IO]
Intl. Soc. for Horticultural Sci. [IO]
International Society for Molecular Plant Microbe Interactions [IO]
Intl. Soc. for Molecular Plant Microbe Interactions [6641]
Intl. Soc. of Photosynthesis Res. [IO]

A star before a book entry number signifies that the name is not listed separately, but is mentioned within the entry.

Intl. Soc. for Plant Molecular Biology [6589]
Intl. Soc. of Plant Morphologists [IO]
Intl. Union for the Protection of New Varieties of
    Plants [IO]
Invasive Species Specialist Gp. [IO]
Israeli Soc. of Plant Sciences [IO]
Japan Bamboo Soc. [IO]
Japanese Soc. of Plant Physiologists [IO]
Kultana Orchids [IO]
Lady Bird Johnson Wildflower Center [6642]
Latin Amer. Botanical Assn. [IO]
Latin Amer. Phytopathology Assn. [IO]
Le Paradis Des Orchidees [IO]
Magnolia Soc. Intl. [6643]
Median Iris Soc. [22525]
Milo's Bali Orchids [IO]
Musser Intl. Turfgrass Found. [IO]
Musser Intl. Turfgrass Found. [6644]
Mycological Soc. of Japan [IO]
Natl. Chrysanthemum Soc. [22526]
Natl. Fuchsia Soc. [22527]
Natl. Garden Clubs [22528]
Natl. Gardening Assn. [22529]
Natl. Inst. of Agricultural Botany [IO]
New Zealand Soc. of Plant Biologists [IO]
Norsk Botanisk Forening [IO]
North Amer. Fruit Explorers [22531]
North Amer. Gladiolus Coun. [22532]
North Amer. Heather Soc. [22533]
North Amer. Lily Soc. [22534]
North Amer. Mycological Assn. [7353]
North Amer. Plant Preservation Coun. [5356]
North Amer. Rock Garden Soc. [22535]
Orchids Dominican, S.A. [IO]
Org. for Flora Neotropica [IO]
Org. for Flora Neotropica [6645]
Org. for the Phyto-Taxonomic Investigation of the
    Mediterranean Area [IO]
Org. for Tropical Stud. - Costa Rica [IO]
Orquidario Quinta do Lago [IO]
Orquideas Del Valle [IO]
Pacific Orchid Soc. of Hawaii [22536]
Paramount Orchids [IO]
Passiflora Soc. Intl. [4673]
Phycological Soc. of Am. [6646]
Phycological Soc. of Am. [IO]
Phytochemical Soc. of Europe [IO]
Phytopathological Soc. of Japan [IO]
Plant Growth Regulation Soc. of Am. [6647]
Plantio La Orquidea [IO]
Plumeria Soc. of Am. [22537]
Reblooming Iris Soc. [22538]
Rhododendron Species Found. [6648]
Ricsel Orchids [IO]
Rose Hybridizers Assn. [22539]
Scandinavian Plant Physiology Soc. [IO]
Seed Savers Exchange [22540]
Soc. of Applied Botany [IO]
Soc. for Economic Botany [6649]
Soc. for Japanese Irises [22541]
Soc. for Louisiana Irises [22542]
Soc. for Pacific Coast Native Iris [22543]
Soc. for Siberian Irises [22544]
South African Assn. of Botanists [IO]
South African Natl. Biodiversity Inst. [IO]
South African Protea Producers and Exporters
    Assn. [IO]
Southern African Soc. for Plant Pathology [IO]
Species Iris Gp. of North Am. [22545]
Swiss Botanical Soc. [IO]
Tahi Flores Exoticas [IO]
Tall Bearded Iris Soc. [22547]
Terrarium Assn. [22548]
Tucker's Orchid Nursery [IO]
World Bamboo Org. [5041]
Both ENDS [IO], Amsterdam, Netherlands
Botswana Athletics Assn. [IO], Gaborone, Botswana
Botswana Badminton Assn. [IO], Gaborone,
    Botswana
Botswana Physiotherapy Assn. [IO], Gaborone,
    Botswana
Botswana Soc. [IO], Gaborone, Botswana
Botswana Squash Rackets Assn. [IO], Gaborone,
    Botswana
Botswana-Sweden Friendship Assn. [IO], Stockholm,
    Sweden

Botswana Tennis Assn. [IO], Gaborone, Botswana
Bottle Caps
    Crowncap Collectors Soc. Intl. [22005]
    Figural Bottle Opener Collectors Club [22023]
    Natl. Pop Can Collectors [22085]
Bottle Collectors Assn; Intl. Perfume and Scent
    [★22054]
Bottle Collectors Assn; M. T. [22066]
Bottle Collectors; Fed. of Historical [21888]
Bottle Collectors; Natl. Assn. of Milk [22076]
Bottle Collectors; Perfume and Scent [★22054]
Bottle Opener Collectors Club; Figural [22023]
Bottle Soc; Chinese Snuff [★21890]
Bottle and Specialties Clubs; Natl. Assn. of Jim
    Beam [★21889]
Bottled Water Assn; Amer. [★509]
Bottlers Assn; Dr Pepper [506]
Bottlers Assn; Natl. [★503]
Bottlers Assn; Royal Crown [512]
Bottlers of Carbonated Beverages; Amer. [★503]
Bottlers Protective Assn; Natl. [★503]
Bottles
    Antique Poison Bottle Collectors Assn. [21972]
    Fed. of Historical Bottle Collectors [21888]
    Figural Bottle Opener Collectors Club [22023]
    Intl. Assn. of Jim Beam Bottle and Specialties
        Clubs [21889]
    Intl. Assn. of Jim Beam Bottle and Specialties
        Clubs [IO]
    Intl. Chinese Snuff Bottle Soc. [IO]
    Intl. Chinese Snuff Bottle Soc. [21890]
    Intl. Correspondence of Corkscrew Addicts
        [22052]
    M. T. Bottle Collectors Assn. [22066]
    Natl. Assn. of Avon Collectors [22073]
    Natl. Pop Can Collectors [22085]
    Ships-in-Bottles Assn. of Am. [22658]
    Western Assoc. Modelers [22661]
Bottles Assn. of Am; Ships-in- [22658]
Boule Foundation [★24663]
Bounders United [23010], 42700 Via del Campo,
    Temecula, CA 92592-2157, (480)782-6088
Bounty Info. Ser. [★5303]
Bounty Wildlife Info. Ser. [5303]
Bourbon Inst. [★199]
Bourgogne Wine Producers' Assn. [IO], Beaune,
    France
Bourse de Commerce Europeenne [★IO]
Bouvier des Flandres Club; Amer. [22188]
Bovine Practitioners; Amer. Assn. of [16741]
Bow Makers; Amer. Fed. of Violin and [2797]
Bow Tie Mfrs. Assn. - Address unknown since 2003.
Bowery Corp; Manhattan [★13277]
Bowfishing Assn. of Am. [23411], c/o Mark Lee,
    Pres., 5 Eldon Starr Ln., Conway, AR 72032,
    (501)730-3169
Bowhunter Educ. Found; Natl. [23053]
Bowhunter Educ. Program; International [★23053]
Bowhunters of Am; Christian [23051]
Bowhunters of America - Defunct.
Bowhunters of Am; Physically Challenged [23549]
Bowhunter's Soc; Professional [23057]
Bowhunting Org; Intl. [23544]
Bowhunting Preservation Alliance [22603], PO Box
    258, Comfrey, MN 56019, (507)877-5300
Bowlers to Veterans Link [23250], 11350 Random
    Hills Rd., Ste. 800, Fairfax, VA 22030, (703)934-
    6039
Bowlers' Victory League [★23250]
Bowlers; Western Women [★23257]
Bowlers; Worldwide Women Professional [★23257]
Bowling
    Aberfeldie Bowls Club [IO]
    Amer. Blind Bowling Assn. [23334]
    Amer. Trans. Bowling Assn. [23249]
    Amer. Wheelchair Bowling Assn. [23339]
    Auckland Bowls [IO]
    Bahrain Bowling Assn. [IO]
    Bol Chumann na h Eireann [IO]
    Bowlers to Veterans Link [23250]
    Bowling Inc. [23810]
    Bowling Proprietors' Assn. of Am. [3659]
    Bowling Writers Assn. of Am. [3101]
    Bowls Australia [IO]
    Bowls British Columbia [IO]

Bowls Canada Boulingrin [IO]
Bowls Manitoba [IO]
Bowls SA [IO]
Bowls Saskatchewan [IO]
Bowls South Africa [IO]
British Tenpin Bowling Assn. [IO]
Canadian 5 Pin Bowlers' Assn. [IO]
Canadian Tenpin Fed. [IO]
English Bowling Assn. [IO]
English Indoor Bowling Assn. [IO]
English Women's Bowling Assn. [IO]
European Bowling Proprietors Assn. [IO]
Guernsey Indoor Bowling Assn. [IO]
Hong Kong Lawn Bowls Assn. [IO]
Hong Kong Tenpin Bowling Cong. [IO]
Intl. Bowling Fed. [IO]
Intl. Bowling Pro Shop and Instructors Assn. [531]
Intl. Gay Bowling Org. [23251]
Lawn Bowls Assn. of Alberta [IO]
Natl. Assn. of Independent Resurfacers [642]
The Natl. Bowling Assn. [23252]
Natl. Duckpin Bowling Cong. [23253]
New South Wales Women's Bowling Assn. [IO]
Ontario Lawn Bowls Assn. [IO]
Professional Bowlers Assn. of Am. [23254]
Professional Bowls Assn. [IO]
Royal New South Wales Bowling Assn. [IO]
Royal Victorian Bowls Assn. [IO]
Scottish Bowling Assn. [IO]
Scottish Women's Indoor Bowling Assn. [IO]
U.S. Bowling Cong. [IO]
U.S. Bowling Cong. [23255]
U.S. Lawn Bowls Assn. [23256]
Victorian Ladies' Bowling Assn. [IO]
Western Women Premier Bowlers [23257]
Women's All-Star Assn. [23258]
World Bowling Writers [3175]
World Ninepin Bowling Assn. [IO]
Bowling Apparel Mfrs. of America - Defunct.
Bowling Assn; Amer. Blind [23334]
Bowling Assn; Amer. Wheelchair [23339]
Bowling Assn; Natl. Deaf Women's [23352]
Bowling Assn; Negro Natl. [★23252]
Bowling Assn; U.S. Seniors [★23255]
Bowling Inc. [23810], 5301 S 76th St., Greendale,
    WI 53129, (800)514-2695
Bowling Inst. of Am; Billiard and [3641]
Bowling Pro Shop and Instructors Assn; Natl. [★531]
Bowling Proprietors' Assn. of Am. [3659], 615 Six
    Flags Dr., Arlington, TX 76011, (800)343-1329
Bowling Proprietors Assn. of America - Duckpin
    Activities - Defunct.
Bowling Proprietors' Assn. of Canada [IO],
    Markham, ON, Canada
Bowling Writers Assn. of Am. [3101], 8501 N Manor
    Ln., Fox Point, WI 53217-2348, (414)351-6085
Bowling Writers Assn. of Am. and Natl. Women
    Bowling Writers Assn. [★3101]
Bowling Writers Assn; Bowling Writers Assn. of Am.
    and Natl. Women [★3101]
Bowls Assn; Amer. Lawn [★23256]
Bowls Assn; Amer. Women's Lawn [★23256]
Bowls Assn; U.S. Lawn [23256]
Bowls Australia [IO], Hawthorn, Australia
Bowls British Columbia [IO], Vancouver, BC, Canada
Bowls Canada Boulingrin [IO], Ottawa, ON, Canada
Bowls Manitoba [IO], Winnipeg, MB, Canada
Bowls SA [IO], Brooklyn Park, Australia
Bowls Saskatchewan [IO], Regina, SK, Canada
Bowls South Africa [IO], Parklands, Republic of
    South Africa
Box Assn. of America - Address unknown since
    1995.
Box Assn. of Am; Folding Paper [★2877]
Box Assn; Fibre [2887]
Box Assn; Natl. Paper [987]
Box Assn; Natl. Wooden [★989]
Box Cookers Intl; Solar [★5100]
Box Culvert Assn. [IO], Leicester, United Kingdom
Box Mfrs. Assn. of Greater New York - Defunct.
Box Mfrs'. Assn; Pacific Coast Paper [990]
Box Off. Mgt. Intl. [★1312]
Box Off. Mgt. Intl. [★IO]
Box Proj. [IO], Ormond Beach, FL, United States
Box Proj. [12836], 100 Bus. Center Dr., Ste. 26, Or-
    mond Beach, FL 32174, (386)677-8094

Reference to "IO" in place of a book number signifies that the association may be found in the 45th edition of International Organizations.

Boxboard Res. and Development Assn. [★993]
Boxer Club; Amer. [22189]
Boxer Club - Denmark [IO], Vaerlose, Denmark
Boxer Klubben [★IO]
Boxer Rescue Assn; Amer. [11346]
Boxing
   Alberta Amateur Boxing Assn. [IO]
   Amateur Boxing Assn. of England [IO]
   Amer. Assn. for the Improvement of Boxing [23259]
   Boxing BC [IO]
   Boxing Newfoundland [IO]
   Boxing Nova Scotia [IO]
   Boxing Ontario [IO]
   Boxing Saskatchewan [IO]
   Canadian Amateur Boxing Assn. [IO]
   European Amateur Boxing Assn. [IO]
   Intl. Boxing Fed. [IO]
   Intl. Boxing Fed. [23260]
   Intl. Boxing Hall of Fame Museum [23261]
   Intl. Chinese Boxing Assn. [23262]
   Intl. Chinese Boxing Assn. [IO]
   Intl. Female Boxers Assn. [IO]
   Intl. Female Boxers Assn. [23263]
   Intl. Veteran Boxers Assn. [23264]
   Knights Boxing Team - Intl. [23265]
   Manitoba Amateur Boxing Assn. [IO]
   North Amer. Boxing Fed. [IO]
   North Amer. Boxing Fed. [23266]
   USA Boxing [23267]
   World Boxing Coun. [IO]
   World Robotic Boxing Assn. [1328]
Boxing BC [IO], Burnaby, BC, Canada
Boxing Comm. of the Amateur Athletic Union; Senior Men's [★23267]
Boxing Fed; U.S.A. Amateur [★23267]
Boxing Fed; U.S. of Amer. Amateur [★23267]
Boxing Newfoundland [IO], St. John's, NL, Canada
Boxing Nova Scotia [IO], Bedford, NS, Canada
Boxing Ontario [IO], Toronto, ON, Canada
Boxing Saskatchewan [IO], Regina, SK, Canada
Boxing Writers Assn. - Address unknown since 1995.
Boxleitner's Official Fan Club; Bruce [24734]
Boxwood Soc; Amer. [22484]
Boy Love Assn; North Amer. Man/ [13099]
Boy Savior Youth Movement - Defunct.
Boy Scouts of Am. [12997], PO Box 152079, Irving, TX 75015-2079, (972)580-2000
Boy Scouts of America Alumni Family - Defunct.
Boy Scouts Assn. of Zimbabwe [IO], Harare, Zimbabwe
Boycott SDI; Campaign to [18143]
Boyet/t/e Assn; Boyt/e - [20805]
Boys Baseball [★23124]
Boys Baseball; Pony and Colt [★23124]
Boys' Brigade [IO], Hemel Hempstead, United Kingdom
Boys' Club Fed. of Am. [★13471]
Boys Clubs of Am. [★13471]
Boys Found; Better [11675]
Boys' and Girls' Brigades of America - Address unknown since 2002.
Boys and Girls; Camp Fire [★13475]
Boys and Girls Clubs of Am. [13471], 1275 Peachtree St. NE, Atlanta, GA 30309-3506, (404)487-5700
Boys and Girls Clubs of Canada [IO], Markham, ON, Canada
Boys' and Girls' Clubs of Northern Ireland [IO], Belfast, United Kingdom
Boys and Girls Intl. Floor Hockey - Address unknown since 2001.
Boys Hope [★13472]
Boys Hope Girls Hope [13472], 12120 Bridgeton Square Dr., Bridgeton, MO 63044-2607, (314)298-1250
Boys Hope Girls Hope - Ireland [IO], Galway, Ireland
Boys; Natl. Assn. of Homes for [★13501]
Boys Town; Girls and [12934]
Boys Town Jerusalem; Amer. Friends of [★13473]
Boys Town Jerusalem Found. of Am. [13473], 1 Penn Plz., Ste. 6250, New York, NY 10119, (212)244-2766
Boys' Town of Rome [★13474]
Boys' Towns of Italy [13474], 250 E 63rd St., Ste. 204, New York, NY 10021, (212)980-8770

Boys of Woodcraft Auxiliary of the Woodmen of the World [★19440]
Boys of Woodcraft Sportsmen's Clubs/Girl of Woodcraft Sportsmen's Clubs [★19440]
Boys' and Young Men's Apparel Buyers' Assn. - Defunct.
Boys and Young Men's Apparel Mfrs. Assn. - Defunct.
Boyt/e - Boyet/t/e Assn. [20805], c/o Wendy Bebout Elliott, Pres., 1060 Magnolia Ave., Placentia, CA 92870-4423, (714)993-1168
Boyz II Men VIP Club - Address unknown since 2002.
BP Amoco Marketers Assn. [2920], 15 Lake St., Ste. 280, Savannah, GA 31411-2971, (912)598-7939
BP and Amoco Oil Marketers Assn. [★2920]
BPA Intl. [★93]
BPA Intl. [★IO]
BPA Worldwide [IO], Shelton, CT, United States
BPA Worldwide [93], Two Corporate Dr., 9th Fl., Shelton, CT 06484, (203)447-2800
BPIF Cartons [IO], Coventry, United Kingdom
BPW Canada [★IO]
Brabham Owners Register [★IO]
Brabham Owners Register [★21597]
Brabham Register [21597], c/o John Hafkenshiel, Founder, 1611 Alvina Ave., Sacramento, CA 95822, (916)454-1115
Brabham Register [IO], Sacramento, CA, United States
BRAC [IO], Dhaka, Bangladesh
Brachial Plexus-Erb's Palsy Assn; Natl. [14277]
Brachytherapy Soc; Amer. [13790]
Bradford Chamber of Commerce [IO], Bradford, United Kingdom
Bradford Compact; Governor William [21248]
Bradford Family Compact [★21248]
Bradley Commn. on History in Schools [★8508]
Bradley Family Org; Robert Bruce [21036]
Bradley Method
   Amer. Acad. of Husband-Coached Childbirth [15579]
Brady Campaign to Prevent Gun Violence [17588], 1225 Eye St. NW, Ste. 1100, Washington, DC 20005, (202)898-0792
Brady Center to Prevent Gun Violence [17589], 1225 Eye St. NW, Ste. 1100, Washington, DC 20005, (202)289-7319
Braford Assn; Intl. [★4295]
Braford Breeders; United [4295]
Brahman Assn; Amer. Junior [4231]
Brahman Breeders Assn; Amer. [4216]
Brahman Samaj of North Am. [9998], PO Box 716, Belle Mead, NJ 08502, (908)431-9845
Brahman Samaj of North Am. [IO], Belle Mead, NJ, United States
Brahmousin Coun; Amer. [4217]
Brahms Soc; Amer. [9804]
Braided Rug Mfrs. Assn. - Defunct.
Braided Trimming Mfrs. Assn. [★3780]
Braille Assn; Natl. [16875]
Braille Authority of North Am. [16838], c/o Judith Dixon, Chair, 1805 N Oakland St., Arlington, VA 22207, (617)972-7249
Braille Authority of North Am. [IO], Watertown, MA, United States
Braille Bible Found. [19513], PO Box 948307, Maitland, FL 32794-8307, (407)834-3628
Braille Books for Children; Seedlings [9297]
Braille Chess Assn. [IO], Lincoln, United Kingdom
Braille Chess Assn; U.S. [21947]
Braille Evangelism Assn; Lutheran [16866]
Braille Found; Christian Record [★16842]
Braille Found. of Uruguay [IO], Montevideo, Uruguay
Braille Inst. of Am; Jewish [★16861]
Braille Poets' Guild - Defunct.
Braille Press; Natl. [16876]
Braille Press for War and Civilian Blind; Amer. [★16854]
Braille Revival League [16839], 57 Grandview Ave., Watertown, MA 02472, (617)926-9198
Braille Technical Press - Defunct.
Braille Without Borders [IO], Swisttal, Germany
Brain and Behaviour Soc; European [IO]
Brain Coalition; Decade of the [★15397]

Brain Information Service - Address unknown since 2001.
Brain Injured; Assn. for the Rehabilitation of the [IO]
Brain Injury Assn. [★14528]
Brain Injury Assn. of Alberta [IO], Red Deer, AB, Canada
Brain Injury Assn. of Am. [14528], 1608 Spring Hill Rd., Ste. 110, Vienna, VA 22182, (703)761-0750
Brain Injury Assn. of Chatham-Kent [IO], Chatham, ON, Canada
Brain Injury Assn; Danish [IO]
Brain Injury Assn. of London and Region [IO], London, ON, Canada
Brain Injury Assn. of New South Wales [IO], Epping, Australia
Brain Injury Assn. of New Zealand [IO], Auckland, New Zealand
Brain Injury Assn. of New Zealand - Auckland [IO], Auckland, New Zealand
Brain Injury Assn. of New Zealand - Bay of Plenty [IO], Mount Maunganui, New Zealand
Brain Injury Assn. of New Zealand - Canterbury [IO], Christchurch, New Zealand
Brain Injury Assn. of New Zealand - Central Districts [IO], Palmerston North, New Zealand
Brain Injury Assn. of New Zealand - Eastern Bay of Plenty [IO], Whakatane, New Zealand
Brain Injury Assn. of New Zealand - Gisborne [IO], Gisborne, New Zealand
Brain Injury Assn. of New Zealand - Hawkes Bay [IO], Hastings, New Zealand
Brain Injury Assn. of New Zealand - Nelson [IO], Nelson, New Zealand
Brain Injury Assn. of New Zealand - Northland [IO], Whangarei, New Zealand
Brain Injury Assn. of New Zealand - Rotorua [IO], Rotorua, New Zealand
Brain Injury Assn. of New Zealand - Taranaki [IO], New Plymouth, New Zealand
Brain Injury Assn. of New Zealand - Waikato [IO], Hamilton, New Zealand
Brain Injury Assn. of New Zealand - Wellington [IO], Wellington, New Zealand
Brain Injury Assn. of New Zealand - Whanganui [IO], Wanganui, New Zealand
Brain Injury Assn. of Niagara [IO], St. Catharines, ON, Canada
Brain Injury Assn. of North Bay [IO], North Bay, ON, Canada
Brain Injury Assn. of Nova Scotia [IO], Halifax, NS, Canada
Brain Injury Assn. of Peel and Halton [IO], Mississauga, ON, Canada
Brain Injury Assn. of Queensland [IO], Brisbane, Australia
Brain Injury Assn. of Sarnia and Lambton [IO], Sarnia, ON, Canada
Brain Injury Assn. of Sault Ste. Marie and District [IO], Sault Ste. Marie, ON, Canada
Brain Injury Assn. of Southeastern Ontario [IO], Kingston, ON, Canada
Brain Injury Assn. of Sudbury and District [IO], Sudbury, ON, Canada
Brain Injury Assn. of Tasmania [IO], Moonah, Australia
Brain Injury Assn. of Waterloo-Wellington [IO], Kitchener, ON, Canada
Brain Injury Assn. of Windsor-Essex County [IO], Windsor, ON, Canada
Brain Injury Australia [IO], Northcote, Australia
Brain Injury Network of South Australia [IO], Adelaide, Australia
Brain Injury Rsrc. Center [16317], PO Box 84151, Seattle, WA 98124-5451, (206)621-8558
Brain Injury Soc. of Toronto [IO], Toronto, ON, Canada
Brain Mapping; Org. for Human [7379]
Brain and Pituitary Found. of America - Defunct.
Brain Res; Natl. Found. for [15397]
Brain Res. Soc. of Finland [IO], Helsinki, Finland
Brain Tissue Bank; Canadian [IO]
Brain Tumor Assn; Amer. [13791]
Brain Tumor Coalition; North Amer. [13860]
Brain Tumor Found. of Am. [★15344]
Brain Tumor Found. of Canada [IO], London, ON, Canada

A star before a book entry number signifies that the name is not listed separately, but is mentioned within the entry.

Brain Tumor Found; Childhood [14257]

Brain Tumor Found. for Children [13948], 6065 Roswell Rd. NE, Ste. 505, Atlanta, GA 30328, (404)252-4107

Brain Tumor Found; Children's [13952]

Brain Tumor Found. of the U.S; Pediatric [13863]

Brain Tumor Res; Assn. for [★13791]

Brain Tumor Soc. [14254], 124 Watertown St., Ste. 3H, Watertown, MA 02472, (617)924-9997

Brain Tumour Australia [IO], Kotara, Australia

Brainard-Brainerd-Braynard Family Assn. [20806]

Brainerd-Braynard Family Assn; Brainard- [20806]

BrainTrust Canada Assn. [IO], Kelowna, BC, Canada

Brainwave The Irish Epilepsy Assn. [IO], Dublin, Ireland

Brake Assn; Air [3274]

Brake Lining Manufacturers Assn. [★385]

Brake Lining Standards Inst; Clutch Facing and [★385]

Brake Manufacturers Coun. [381], PO Box 13966, Research Triangle Park, NC 27709-3966, (919)549-4800

Brake Sys. Parts Manufacturers Coun. [★381]

Brakemen; Order of Railway Conductors and [★24181]

Bram Stoker Club [IO], Dublin, Ireland

Bram Stoker Memorial Association [IO], New York, NY, United States

Bram Stoker Memorial Assn. [9639], 29 Washington Sq. W, Penthouse N, New York, NY 10011

Bram Stoker Soc. - Ireland [IO], Dublin, Ireland

Bramble Growers Res. Found; North Amer. [1675]

Br. Brook Park; Friends of [★4407]

Br. Warehouse Assn. - Defunct.

Branchaud Family Assn; Brancheau- [20807]

Brancheau-Branchaud Family Assn. [20807], c/o Douglas J. Miller, Pres., 22023 W Sunrise View Pl., Santa Clarita, CA 91390, (661)296-8740

Branched from: Associated Antique Dealers of Am. [★219]

Brancheforening for Frugd og Grongindustrien [★IO]

Brancheforeningen for Saebe-, Parfumeri-, Toilet- og Kemisk-teknisk Artikler [★IO]

Brand-Beskermingsvereniging van Suider-Afraid [★IO]

Brand Conf; Intl. Livestock [★4998]

Brand Conf; Natl. Livestock [★4998]

Brand Names Educ. Found. [5839], 1133 Ave. of the Americas, New York, NY 10036-6710, (212)768-9885

Brand Names Found. - Defunct.

Brand and Theft Conf; Intl. Livestock [★4998]

Branded Goods Assn. Hungary [IO], Budapest, Hungary

Brandeis - Bardin Inst. [8687], 1101 Peppertree Ln., Brandeis, CA 93064, (805)582-4450

Brandeis Camp Inst. of the West [★8687]

Brandeis Inst. [★8687]

Brandeis Univ. Alumni Assn. [18879], PO Box 549110, Waltham, MA 02454-9110, (781)736-4100

Branding Assn. of Malaysia [IO], Petaling Jaya, Malaysia

Brandon Call Fan Club - Address unknown since 1990.

Brangus Assn; Amer. Red [4242]

Brangus Breeders Assn; Intl. [4265]

Brangus Breeders Assn; Intl. Junior [4266]

Brangus Soc. of South Africa [IO], Bloemfontein, Republic of South Africa

Branham Fan Club; Shon [24803]

Brann-Brawn Family History Assn. - Address unknown since 2007.

Branschforeningen Ljud, Ljus och Bild for professionellt bruk [★IO]

Branscombe Richmond Fan Club [24779], c/o Valerie La Rue, Pres., 1706 Palo Verde Dr., Alamogordo, NM 88310-5254

Brantley Assn. of Am. [20808], 4750 Oakleigh Manor Dr., Powder Springs, GA 30127, (770)428-4402

Brasilian League Against Epilepsy [IO], Sao Paulo, Brazil

Brass Band Assn; North Amer. [10675]

Brass and Bronze Ingot Industry [2701]

Brass and Bronze Ingot Institute [★2701]

Brass and Bronze Ingot Manufacturers [★2701]

Brass and Bronze Ingot Manufacturers; Association of [★2701]

Brass Fabricators Coun; Copper and [2704]

Brass Fabricators Foreign Trade Assn; Copper and [★2704]

Brass Gas Stop Inst. [★3066]

Brass Gas Stop Inst. [★IO]

Brass Inst; Plumbing [★3066]

Brass Inst; Sanitary [★3066]

Brass Inst; Tubular [★3066]

Brass Res. Assn; Copper and [★2750]

Brass Ring Soc. [11677], 500 Macaw Ln., No. 5, Fern Park, FL 32730, (407)339-6188

Brass Servicenter Assn; Copper and [2705]

Brass Soc; Historic [10608]

Brasseurs du Canada [★IO]

Brassiere Assn. of Am; Corset and [★221]

Brassiere Mfrs; Associated Corset and [227]

Brassiere Women's Club; Corset and [★258]

Braun Center for Holocaust Stud. [★17715]

Braun Holocaust Inst. [17715], c/o Anti-Defamation League, PO Box 96226, Washington, DC 20090-6226

Braunvieh Assn. of Am. [4257], 3815 Touzalin Ave., Ste. 103, Lincoln, NE 68507-1600, (402)466-3292

Brave Kids [13949], 1223 Wilshire Blvd., No. 1411, Santa Monica, CA 90403, (800)568-1008

Bray Sea Anglers [IO], Bray, Ireland

Braynard Family Assn; Brainard-Brainerd- [20806]

Brazer Guild; Esther Stevens [★9482]

Brazil

    Brazil Philatelic Assn. [22797]

    Brazil Tourism Off. [24238]

    Brazil-U.S. Bus. Coun. [24266]

    Brazilian-American Chamber of Commerce [24239]

    Brazilian-American Cultural Inst. [9757]

    Brazilian Dimensional Embroidery Intl. Guild [22987]

    Brazilian Govt. Trade Bur. of the Consulate Gen. of Brazil in New York [24240]

    Brazilian Stud. Assn. [8604]

    Oper. Crossroads Africa [16932]

    Villa-Lobos Music Soc. [10717]

Brazil-Canada Chamber of Commerce [IO], Toronto, ON, Canada

Brazil Labor Information and Resource Center - Defunct.

Brazil Network - Address unknown since 2003.

Brazil Nut Advertising Fund - Defunct.

Brazil Philatelic Assn. [22797], c/o Mr. Kurt Ottenheimer, 462 W Walnut St., Long Beach, NY 11561-3133

Brazil Philatelic Assn. [IO], Long Beach, NY, United States

Brazil Specialty Coffee Assn. [IO], Areado, Brazil

Brazil Tourism Off. [24238], c/o Brazil Info. Center, 2141 Wisconsin Ave. NW, Ste. M, Washington, DC 20007, (800)727-2945

Brazil-U.S. Bus. Coun. [24266], 1615 H St. NW, Washington, DC 20062, (202)463-5485

Brazilian

    Brazil Philatelic Assn. [22797]

    Brazil-U.S. Bus. Coun. [24266]

    Brazilian-American Chamber of Commerce [24239]

    Brazilian-American Cultural Inst. [9757]

    Brazilian-American Cultural Inst. [IO]

    Brazilian Dimensional Embroidery Intl. Guild [22987]

    Brazilian Govt. Trade Bur. of the Consulate Gen. of Brazil in New York [24240]

    Villa-Lobos Music Soc. [10717]

Brazilian Acad. of Letters [IO], Rio de Janeiro, Brazil

Brazilian Acad. of Sciences [IO], Rio de Janeiro, Brazil

Brazilian Agricultural Assn. [IO], Sao Paulo, Brazil

Brazilian Agricultural Res. Corp. [IO], Brasilia, Brazil

Brazilian Agroforestry Network [IO], Rio de Janeiro, Brazil

Brazilian-American Chamber of Commerce [24239], 509 Madison Ave., Ste. 304, New York, NY 10022, (212)751-4691

Brazilian-American Cultural Inst. [9757], 4719 Wisconsin Ave. NW, Washington, DC 20016, (202)362-8334

Brazilian-American Cultural Inst. [IO], Washington, DC, United States

Brazilian-Amer. Soc. - Defunct.

Brazilian Assn. of Advertisers [IO], Sao Paulo, Brazil

Brazilian Assn. of the Aerosol Indus. [IO], Sao Paulo, Brazil

Brazilian Assn. of Amyotrophic Lateral Sclerosis [IO], Sao Paulo, Brazil

Brazilian Assn. of the Automated Glass Indus. [IO], Sao Paulo, Brazil

Brazilian Assn. of Automotive Engg. [IO], Sao Paulo, Brazil

Brazilian Assn. for Bioinformatics and Computational Biology [IO], Sao Paulo, Brazil

Brazilian Assn. of Ceramic Tile Mfrs. [IO], Sao Paulo, Brazil

Brazilian Assn. for Citrus Exporters [IO], Sao Paulo, Brazil

Brazilian Assn. of the Coffee Roasting and Grinding Indus. [IO], Rio de Janeiro, Brazil

Brazilian Assn. of Commercial Banks [IO], Sao Paulo, Brazil

Brazilian Assn. of Commercial Banks and Multiple Banks [★IO]

Brazilian Assn. of Credit Card Companies and Services [IO], Sao Paulo, Brazil

Brazilian Assn. of Drinks Producers [IO], Sao Paulo, Brazil

Brazilian Assn. of Engg. Consultants [IO], Rio de Janeiro, Brazil

Brazilian Assn. of Furniture Indus. [IO], Sao Paulo, Brazil

Brazilian Assn. of Homeopathic Medicine [IO], Belo Horizonte, Brazil

Brazilian Assn. of Infrastructure and Basic Indus. [IO], Sao Paulo, Brazil

Brazilian Assn. of Media Companies Representatives [IO], Sao Paulo, Brazil

Brazilian Assn. of Motor Vehicle Manufacturers [IO], Sao Paulo, Brazil

Brazilian Assn. of the Nonwoven and Tech. Textiles Indus. [IO], Sao Paulo, Brazil

Brazilian Assn. of Orthodontics and Facial Orthopedics [IO], Goiania, Brazil

Brazilian Assn. for Proj. Mgt. [IO], Curitiba, Brazil

Brazilian Assn. of Sales and Marketing Directors [IO], Sao Paulo, Brazil

Brazilian Assn. of Shopping Centers [IO], Sao Paulo, Brazil

Brazilian Assn. of Software Companies [IO], Sao Paulo, Brazil

Brazilian Assn. of the Textile Indus. [★IO]

Brazilian Assn. of Vegetable Oil Indus. [IO], Sao Paulo, Brazil

Brazilian Automatics Soc. [IO], Sao Jose dos Campos, Brazil

Brazilian Banks Assn. [IO], Sao Paulo, Brazil

Brazilian Book Chamber [IO], Sao Paulo, Brazil

Brazilian Cement Manufacturers' Assn. [IO], Sao Paulo, Brazil

Brazilian Center of New York - Defunct.

Brazilian Center for Planning and Anal. [IO], Sao Paulo, Brazil

Brazilian Ceramics' Assn. [IO], Sao Paulo, Brazil

Brazilian Chamber of Commerce in Great Britain [IO], London, United Kingdom

Brazilian Chamber of Publishers [★IO]

Brazilian Chem. Assn. [IO], Rio de Janeiro, Brazil

Brazilian Chem. Indus. Assn. [IO], Sao Paulo, Brazil

Brazilian Chicken Producers and Exporters Assn. [IO], Sao Paulo, Brazil

Brazilian Coffee Inst. - Defunct.

Brazilian Corrugated Bd. Assn. [IO], Sao Paulo, Brazil

Brazilian Cosmetics Assn. [★IO]

Brazilian Cosmetology Assn. [IO], Sao Paulo, Brazil

Brazilian Dimensional Embroidery Intl. Guild [IO], Lynnwood, WA, United States

Brazilian Dimensional Embroidery Intl. Guild [22987], c/o Debbie Goff, Membership Chair, 13013 89th Ave. N, Seminole, FL 33776, (727)391-9207

Brazilian Direct Selling Assn. [IO], Sao Paulo, Brazil

Reference to "IO" in place of a book number signifies that the association may be found in the 45th edition of International Organizations.

Brazilian Elecl. and Electronics Indus. Assn. **[IO]**, Sao Paulo, Brazil

Brazilian Floorball Assn. **[IO]**, Sao Paulo, Brazil

Brazilian Food Indus. Assn. **[IO]**, Sao Paulo, Brazil

Brazilian Found. for Nature Conservation **[IO]**, Rio de Janeiro, Brazil

Brazilian Franchising Assn. **[IO]**, Sao Paulo, Brazil

Brazilian Genetics Soc. **[IO]**, Ribeirao Preto, Brazil

Brazilian Geomorphological Union **[IO]**, Uberlandia, Brazil

Brazilian Geophysical Soc. **[IO]**, Rio de Janeiro, Brazil

Brazilian Govt. Trade Bur. of the Consulate Gen. of Brazil in New York **[24240]**, 1185 Ave. of the Americas, 21st Fl., New York, NY 10036, (917)777-7777

Brazilian Hotels' Assn. **[IO]**, Rio de Janeiro, Brazil

Brazilian Ice Sports Fed. **[IO]**, Rio de Janeiro, Brazil

Brazilian Inst. of Economics **[IO]**, Rio de Janeiro, Brazil

Brazilian Inst. of History and Geography **[IO]**, Rio de Janeiro, Brazil

Brazilian Inst. for Info. in Sci. and Tech. **[IO]**, Brasilia, Brazil

Brazilian Interdisciplinary AIDS Assn. **[IO]**, Rio de Janeiro, Brazil

Brazilian Jet Sports Assn. **[IO]**, Sao Paulo, Brazil

Brazilian Machinery Builders' Assn. **[IO]**, Sao Paulo, Brazil

Brazilian Medical Spiritist Assn. **[IO]**, Sao Paulo, Brazil

Brazilian Metallurgy and Materials Assn. **[IO]**, Sao Paulo, Brazil

Brazilian Muscular Dystrophy Assn. **[IO]**, Sao Paulo, Brazil

Brazilian Olympic Comm. **[IO]**, Rio de Janeiro, Brazil

Brazilian Org. for Agricultural Res. **[★IO]**

Brazilian Packaging Assn. **[IO]**, Sao Paulo, Brazil

Brazilian Pharmaceutical Assn. **[IO]**, Sao Paulo, Brazil

Brazilian Press Assn. **[IO]**, Rio de Janeiro, Brazil

Brazilian Soc. for the Advancement of Sci. **[IO]**, Sao Paulo, Brazil

Brazilian Soc. of Aesthetic Dentistry **[IO]**, Rio de Janeiro, Brazil

Brazilian Soc. of Aesthetic Medicine **[IO]**, Rio de Janeiro, Brazil

Brazilian Soc. for Automation **[★IO]**

Brazilian Soc. of Biochemistry and Molecular Biology **[IO]**, Sao Paulo, Brazil

Brazilian Soc. of Biomedical Engg. **[IO]**, Rio de Janeiro, Brazil

Brazilian Soc. of Cardiology **[IO]**, Sao Paulo, Brazil

Brazilian Soc. of Clinical Neurophysiology **[IO]**, Sao Paulo, Brazil

Brazilian Soc. of Dermatology **[IO]**, Rio de Janeiro, Brazil

Brazilian Soc. of Entomology **[IO]**, Curitiba, Brazil

Brazilian Soc. of Hea. Informatics **[IO]**, Sao Paulo, Brazil

Brazilian Soc. of Hypertension **[IO]**, Sao Paulo, Brazil

Brazilian Soc. for Metrology **[IO]**, Rio de Janeiro, Brazil

Brazilian Soc. for Microscopy and Microanalysis **[IO]**, Rio de Janeiro, Brazil

Brazilian Soc. of Operational Res. **[IO]**, Rio de Janeiro, Brazil

Brazilian Soc. of Osteoporosis **[IO]**, Campinas, Brazil

Brazilian Soc. of Pharmacology and Experimental Therapeutics **[IO]**, Sao Paulo, Brazil

Brazilian Soc. of Physiology **[IO]**, Sao Paulo, Brazil

Brazilian Soc. for Soil Mechanics and Geotechnical Engg. **[IO]**, Sao Paulo, Brazil

Brazilian Stud. Assn. **[IO]**, Nashville, TN, United States

Brazilian Stud. Assn. **[8604]**, Vanderbilt Univ., 2301 Vanderbilt Pl., VU Sta., B 350031, Nashville, TN 37235-0031, (615)322-2527

Brazilian Supermarkets' Assn. **[IO]**, Sao Paulo, Brazil

Brazilian Textile and Apparel Indus. Assn. **[IO]**, Sao Paulo, Brazil

Brazilian Tobacco Indus. Assn. **[IO]**, Brasilia, Brazil

Brazilian Tourism Authority **[★24238]**

Brazilian Tourism Found. **[★24238]**

Brazilian Travel Agencies' Assn. **[IO]**, Sao Paulo, Brazil

Brazilian Water Ski Confed. **[IO]**, Sao Paulo, Brazil

The BRC **[★17499]**

Bread Bakers Guild of Am. **[451]**, 3203 Maryland Ave., North Versailles, PA 15137, (412)823-2080

Bread Bakers Guild of America **[IO]**, North Versailles, PA, United States

Bread for the Journey Intl. **[IO]**, Mill Valley, CA, United States

Bread for the Journey Intl. **[12711]**, 267 Miller Ave., Mill Valley, CA 94941, (415)383-4600

Bread Loaf Writers Conf. **[11163]**, Middlebury Coll., Middlebury, VT 05753, (802)443-5286

Bread Machine Industry Assn. - Defunct.

Bread and Roses **[12113]**, 233 Tamalpais Dr., Ste. 100, Corte Madera, CA 94925-1415, (415)945-7120

Bread on the Waters **[19993]**, 615 N Pleasant Ave., Lodi, CA 95240, (209)369-3202

Bread for the World **[17792]**, 50 F St. NW, Ste. 500, Washington, DC 20001, (202)639-9400

Bread for the World **[IO]**, Washington, DC, United States

Break Away **[★12795]**

Break Away: The Alternative Break Connection **[12795]**, 2451 Cumberland Pkwy., Ste. 3124, Atlanta, GA 30339, (800)903-0646

Break the Cycle **[12024]**, 5200 W Century Blvd., Ste. 300, Los Angeles, CA 90045, (310)286-3383

Breakdown and Legal Assistance for Motorcyclists - Address unknown since 2007.

Breakfast Assn; Natl. Bed-and- **[1954]**

Breakfast Cereal Manufacturers of Canada **[IO]**, Don Mills, ON, Canada

Breakfast Clubs of North Am; Credit Women's **[★1411]**

Breakfast League; Bed and **[★1936]**

Breakfast League/Sweet Dreams and Toast; Bed and **[1936]**

Breakthrough Collaborative **[8236]**, 545 Sansome St., Ste. 700, San Francisco, CA 94111, (415)442-0600

Breakthrough For Youth - Address unknown since 2003.

Breakthroughs Abroad **[9176]**

Breakthroughs Abroad **[IO]**, Estes Park, CO, United States

Breast Cancer Action **[13801]**, 55 New Montgomery St., Ste. 323, San Francisco, CA 94105, (415)243-9301

Breast Cancer Advisory Center **[★13870]**

Breast Cancer Advisory Center; Rose Kushner **[13870]**

Breast Cancer Advisory Center; Women's **[★13870]**

Breast Cancer Alliance; African Amer. **[13786]**

Breast Cancer Care **[IO]**, London, United Kingdom

Breast Cancer Coalition; Natl. **[13848]**

Breast Cancer Found; Susan G. Komen **[13878]**

Breast Cancer Info. and Support; Y-Me Natl. Org. for **[★13882]**

Breast Cancer; Men Against **[13843]**

Breast Cancer; Mothers Supporting Daughters with **[13844]**

Breast Cancer Network Australia **[IO]**, Camberwell, Australia

Breast Cancer Org; Y-ME Natl. **[13882]**

Breast Cancer Orgs; Natl. Alliance of **[13846]**

Breast Cancer Soc. of Canada **[IO]**, Sarnia, ON, Canada

Breast Cancer Support Ser. - Northern Ireland **[IO]**, Belfast, United Kingdom

Breast Cancer Support; Y-Me **[★13882]**

Breast Care and Masectomy Assn. **[★IO]**

Breast Care and Mastectomy Support Ser. **[★IO]**

Breast Disease; Amer. Soc. of **[13772]**

Breast Disease; Soc. for the Stud. of **[★13772]**

Breast Diseases

African Amer. Breast Cancer Alliance **[13786]**

Amer. Soc. of Breast Disease **[13772]**

Amer. Soc. of Breast Surgeons **[16570]**

European Soc. of Breast Imaging **[IO]**

European Soc. of Mastology **[IO]**

Facing Our Risk of Cancer Empowered **[13823]**

Natl. Alliance of Breast Cancer Orgs. **[13846]**

Natl. Breast Cancer Centre **[IO]**

Natl. Consortium of Breast Centers **[13773]**

Radiology Mammography Intl. **[13774]**

Rose Kushner Breast Cancer Advisory Center **[13870]**

Sharsheret **[13872]**

Soc. of Breast Imaging **[16295]**

Young Survival Coalition **[13883]**

Breast Imaging; Soc. of **[16295]** .

Breast Implants

Amer. Soc. of Breast Surgeons **[16570]**

Command Trust Network **[16896]**

Breastfeeding

Breastfeeding Promotion Network of India **[IO]**

Human Lactation Center **[12409]**

Intl. Bd. of Lactation Consultant Examiners **[13775]**

Intl. Bd. of Lactation Consultant Examiners **[IO]**

Intl. Lactation Consultant Assn. **[12410]**

Intl. Soc. for Res. in Human Milk and Lactation **[13776]**

International Society for Research in Human Milk and Lactation **[IO]**

La Leche League Intl. **[12411]**

Natl. Alliance for Breastfeeding Advocacy **[13777]**

Nursing Mothers Counsel **[12414]**

World Alliance for Breastfeeding Action **[IO]**

Breastfeeding Assn; Australian **[IO]**

Breastfeeding Promotion Network of India **[IO]**, New Delhi, India

Breathe-Free Plan to Stop Smoking - Address unknown since 1991.

Breathwork Intl; Assn. for Holotropic **[13626]**

Brecht Forum **[13111]**, 451 West St., New York, NY 10014, (212)242-4201

Brecht Forum **[IO]**, New York, NY, United States

Brecht Soc. of America - Defunct.

Breck Fan Club; Peter **[24766]**

Brecknock Fed. of Young Farmers Clubs **[IO]**, Brecon, United Kingdom

Brecon and Borders Welsh Pony and Cob Breeders Assn. **[IO]**, Brecon, United Kingdom

Breed Assn; Missouri Fox Trotting Horse **[4913]**

Breed Coun; Norwegian Forest Cat **[21914]**

Breeders of Am; Bluetick **[22233]**

Breeders of Am; Oberhasli **[4146]**

Breeders of Am; Palomino Horse **[4942]**

Breeders of Am; Poultry **[5115]**

Breeders; Amer. Assn. of Spanish Timbrado **[21834]**

Breeders; Amer. Fed. of New Zealand Rabbit **[5135]**

Breeders Assn. of Am; Barzona **[4254]**

Breeders Assn. of Am; Columbia Sheep **[5201]**

Breeders' Assn. of Am; Racking Horse **[4948]**

Breeders' Assn. of Am; Tennessee Walking Horse **[★4959]**

Breeders Assn. of Am; Texas Longhorn **[4294]**

Breeders Assn; Amer. **[★7111]**

Breeder's Assn; Amer. Aberdeen-Angus **[★4212]**

Breeder's Assn; Amer. Angora Goat **[4122]**

Breeders' Assn; Amer. Belted Galloway Cattle **[★4256]**

Breeders Assn; Amer. Brahman **[4216]**

Breeders Assn; Amer. Cavy **[4124]**

Breeders Assn; Amer. Charbray **[★4228]**

Breeders Assn; Amer. Charolais **[★4228]**

Breeders Assn; Amer. Dog **[22197]**

Breeders Assn; Amer. Finnsheep **[5184]**

Breeders' Assn; Amer. Galloway **[4222]**

Breeders Assn; Amer. Rabbit **[5139]**

Breeders Assn; Amer. Rabbit and Cavy **[★5139]**

Breeders' Assn; Amer. Rambouillet Sheep **[5192]**

Breeders' Assn; Amer. Romney **[5193]**

Breeders' Assn; Amer. Saddle Horse **[★4842]**

Breeders' Assn; Amer. Satin Rabbit **[5140]**

Breeders Assn; Amer. Scotch Highland **[★4227]**

Breeders Assn; Amer. Shorthorn **[★4247]**

Breeders' Assn; Amer. Southdown **[5196]**

Breeders' Assn; Amer. Thoroughbred **[★23515]**

Breeders Assn; Asiatic **[4192]**

Breeders' Assn; Ayrshire **[4253]**

Breeders Assn; Central States Roller Canary **[21844]**

Breeders Assn; Cinnamon Rabbit **[5144]**

A star before a book entry number signifies that the name is not listed separately, but is mentioned within the entry.

Breeders Assn; Colored Angora Goat [4782]
Breeders Assn; Emba Mink [★4129]
Breeders Assn; Galiceno Horse [4883]
Breeders Assn; Guinea Fowl [4196]
Breeders Assn; Havana Rabbit [5145]
Breeders Assn; Intl. Brangus [4265]
Breeders Assn; Intl. Butterfly [4203]
Breeders Assn; Intl. Gloster [21849]
Breeders Assn; Intl. Junior Brangus [4266]
Breeders Assn; Jacob Sheep [5203]
Breeders Assn; Kinder Goat [4786]
Breeders Assn; Montadale Sheep [5205]
Breeders' Assn; Natl. Lincoln Sheep [5207]
Breeders Assn; Natl. Saanen [4143]
Breeders Assn; North Amer. Elk [4028]
Breeders Assn; Palomino Rabbit Co- [5158]
Breeders Assn; Parthenais Cattle [4286]
Breeders Assn; Paso Fino Owners and [★4943]
Breeder's Assn; Scottish Blackface Sheep [5216]
Breeders Assn; Spanish-Barb [4952]
Breeders Assn; Sport Horse Owners and [23539]
Breeders Assn; Thoroughbred Owners and [23515]
Breeders Assn. of the U.S; Clydesdale [★4872]
Breeders Assn. of the U.S.A; Brown Swiss Cattle [4258]
Breeders Assn; Virginia Poultry [5124]
Breeders of Belgian Draft Horses; Amer. Assn. of Importers and [★4865]
Breeders' Chester White Record Assn. - Defunct.
Breeders Club; Natl. Angora Rabbit [5150]
Breeders Club; Virginia Poultry [★5124]
Breeders Consortium; Morab [4914]
Breeders Cooperative; Empress Chinchilla [4134]
Breeders' and Exhibitors' Assn; Spotted Saddle Horse [4955]
Breeders' and Exhibitors' Assn; Tennessee Walking Horse [4959]
Breeders and Exhibitors; Soc. of Parrot [21860]
Breeders and Fanciers Assn; Natl. [★5139]
Breeders and Fanciers Assn; Traditional Siamese [★21920]
Breeders and Fanciers Assn; Treeing Walker [22368]
Breeder's Found; Fidelco [★16846]
Breeders Guild; North Amer. Fish [22444]
Breeders of Holsteiner Horses; Amer. Assn. of [★4824]
Breeders Intl; Hotot Rabbit [5147]
Breeders Intl; Red Poll Beef [★4243]
Breeders; Natl. Assn. of Animal [5002]
Breeders; Natl. Assn. of Artificial [★5002]
Breeders; Natl. Cong. of Animal Trainers and [11435]
Breeders; Natl. Coun. of Commercial Plant [5175]
Breeders; Natl. Fed. of Flemish Giant [★5151]
Breeders; Natl. Fed. of Flemish Giant Rabbit [5151]
Breeders of North Am; Warmblood [4968]
Breeders Org; Haflinger [4888]
Breeders of Peruvian Paso Horses; Amer. Assn. of Owners and [4810]
Breeder's Registry [22438], 5541 Columbia Dr. N, Fresno, CA 93727
Breeders Registry; Intl. Beefalo [★4123]
Breeders and Shooting Preserve Assn; North Amer. Game [★4144]
Breeders Soc. and Registry; Intl. Miniature Cattle [4267]
Breeders' Soc; Swedish Gotland [4957]
Breeders United; Beefmaster [4255]
Breeders; United Braford [4295]
Breeders Universal; Beefmaster [★4255]
Breeders of the U.S.A; Clydesdale [4872]
Breeding Assn. Youth Found; Ohio Standard [★23496]
Breeding Soundness; Amer. Veterinary Soc. for the Stud. of [★16806]
Breeds Conservancy; Amer. Livestock [4994]
Breeds Conservancy; Amer. Minor [★4994]
Bremer Inst; Ron [★21146]
Bremer Seminars; Ron [21146]
Brenda Lee Fan Club - Address unknown since 2001.
Brennan Center for Justice at NYU School of Law [6176], c/o NYU School of Law, 161 Ave. of the Americas, 12th Fl., New York, NY 10013, (212)998-6730

Bret Hart Fan Club - Address unknown since 1999.
Brethern Church Missionary Bd. [★20307]
Brethern Church Missionary Bd. [★IO]
Brethren
Anabaptist Sociology and Anthropology Assn. [7559]
Assn. of Grace Brethren Ministers [19533]
Brethren/Mennonite Coun. for Lesbian, Gay, Bisexual and Transgender Interest [20050]
Brethren Peace Fellowship [19534]
Center for the Evangelical United Brethren Heritage [19976]
Church of the Brethren Gen. Bd. Global Mission Partnership [19535]
Progressive, Radically Inclusive Student Ministry [19938]
Brethren Caregivers; Assn. of [11276]
Brethren in Christ Missions [★20306]
Brethren in Christ Missions [★IO]
Brethren in Christ World Missions [IO], Grantham, PA, United States
Brethren in Christ World Missions [20306], PO Box 390, Grantham, PA 17027, (717)697-2634
Brethren Church; Historical Soc. of the Evangelical United [★10467]
Brethren Church Missionary Ministries [20307], 524 Coll. Ave., Ashland, OH 44805, (419)289-1708
Brethren Church Missionary Ministries [IO], Ashland, OH, United States
Brethren Gen. Bd. Global Mission Partnership; Church of the [19535]
Brethren Gen. Bd. World Ministries Commn; Church of the [★19535]
Brethren Homes and Hospitals Assn; Church of the [★11276]
Brethren Homes and Older Adult Ministries [★11276]
Brethren Homes and Older Adult Ministries; Bd. of [★11276]
Brethren/Mennonite Coun. for Gay Concerns [★20050]
Brethren/Mennonite Coun. for Lesbian, Gay, Bisexual and Transgender Interest [20050], PO Box 6300, Minneapolis, MN 55406, (612)343-2060
Brethren/Mennonite Coun. for Lesbian and Gay Concerns [★20050]
Brethren Missions [★20307]
Brethren Missions [★IO]
Brethren Peace Fellowship [19534], Box 455, New Windsor, MD 21776, (410)848-5631
Brethren Ser. Commn. [★19535]
Brethren Volunteer Ser. [13388], 1451 Dundee Ave., Elgin, IL 60120, (847)742-5100
Brethren Volunteer Ser. [IO], Elgin, IL, United States
Breton
U.S. Br. of the Intl. Comm. for the Defense of the Breton Language [IO]
U.S. Br. of the Intl. Comm. for the Defense of the Breton Language [9758]
Breton Democratic Union [IO], Lorient, France
Bretton Woods Comm. [17453], 1726 M St. NW, Ste. 200, Washington, DC 20036, (202)331-1616
Bretton Woods Fund - Defunct.
Bretton Woods Proj. [IO], London, United Kingdom
Breweriana Advt; Natl. Assn. of [22074]
Breweriana Assn; Amer. [21828]
Breweriana Assn; Eastern Coast [21830]
Breweriana Openers Collectors Club - Defunct.
Breweries Central Off. [IO], Amsterdam, Netherlands
Brewers Assn. [198], PO Box 1679, Boulder, CO 80306, (303)447-0816
Brewers Assn; Am. Home [191]
Brewers Assn. of Canada [IO], Ottawa, ON, Canada
Brewers Assn. of Japan [IO], Tokyo, Japan
Brewers Assn; Small [★198]
Brewers' Assn; Swedish [IO]
Brewers and Beverage Packaging Assn. [★508]
Brewers Comm; Small [★198]
Brewers of Europe [IO], Brussels, Belgium
Brewers Grain Inst. - Defunct.
Brewers Grains and Yeast Coun. - Defunct.
Brewers and Licensed Retailers Assn. [★IO]
Brewers of Spain [IO], Madrid, Spain
Brewers Yeast and Grains Coun. - Defunct.
Brewery Collectibles Club of Am. [21979], 747 Merus Ct., Fenton, MO 63026-2092, (636)343-6486

Brewery and Distillery Workers; Canadian [★24061]
Brewery, Flour, Cereal, Soft Drink and Distillery Workers of Am. (AFL-CIO); Intl. Union of United [★24020]
Brewery and Soft Drink Workers Conf. - U.S.A. and Canada [24020], 25 Louisiana Ave. NW, Washington, DC 20001, (202)624-6921
Brewing Chemists; Amer. Soc. of [6670]
Brewing, Food and Beverage Indus. Suppliers Assn. [IO], Wolverhampton, United Kingdom
Brewing Industries Res. Inst. - Defunct.
Brewing and Malting Barley Res. Inst. [IO], Winnipeg, MB, Canada
Brewmeisters Anonymous [21829], 20634 W Narramore Rd., Buckeye, AZ 85326, (623)561-1931
Brewster Kaleidoscope Soc. [21980], PO Box 95, Damascus, MD 20872, (706)348-6950
Brewster Soc; Elder [20893]
Brian McKnight's Official Fan Club - Address unknown since 2006.
Brian Nolan Spradlin Intl. Fan Club Org. - Defunct.
Brice Henderson Fan Club - Address unknown since 1991.
Brick Assn; Amer. Face [★604]
Brick Assn; Natl. Paving [★604]
Brick Collectors' Assn; Intl. [22048]
Brick Development Assn. [IO], Windsor, United Kingdom
Brick Distributors; Natl. Assn. of [★604]
Brick Indus. Assn. [604], 1850 Centennial Park Dr., Ste. 301, Reston, VA 20191, (703)620-0010
Brick Inst. of Am. [★604]
Brick Manufacturers Assn. [★604]
Brickish Assn. [IO], Northwich, United Kingdom
Bricklayers and Allied Craftsmen; Intl. Union of [★24027]
Bricklayers and Allied Craftsworkers; Intl. Coun. of Employers of [★1029]
Bricklayers and Allied Craftsworkers; Intl. Union of [1029]
Bricklayers and Allied Craftworkers; Intl. Union of [24027]
Bricklayers, Masons and Plasterers Intl. of Amer. [★24027]
Bricklin Club; NEA [★21598]
Bricklin Intl. [21598]
Bricklin Intl. [★IO]
Bricklin Intl. Owners Club [IO], Streetsboro, OH, United States
Bricklin Intl. Owners Club [21598], 664 Hickory Hill Ct., Streetsboro, OH 44241, (330)474-1153
Bricklin Owners; Org. of [21753]
Bridal Assn. of Am. [534], 531 H St., Bakersfield, CA 93304, (661)633-1949
Bridal and Bridesmaids Apparel Assn. - Address unknown since 1991.
Bridal Consultants; Amer. Assn. of Professional [★533]
Bridal Coun. - Defunct.
Bridal Industry Assn. - Address unknown since 1988.
Bridal Services
Amer. Professional Wedding Photographers Assn. [2991]
Amer. Soc. of Wedding Professionals [532]
Assn. of Bridal Consultants [533]
Association of Bridal Consultants [IO]
Bridal Assn. of Am. [534]
Natl. Black Bridal Assn. [535]
Natl. Bridal Ser. [536]
Weddings Beautiful Worldwide [537]
Weddings Beautiful Worldwide [IO]
Bridge
Amer. Bridge Assn. [21891]
Amer. Bridge Teachers' Assn. [21892]
Amer. Contract Bridge League [21893]
Amer. Contract Bridge League [IO]
Amer. Inst. of Steel Constr. [6834]
Amer. Railway Engg. and Maintenance of Way Assn. [3280]
Assn. for Bridge Constr. and Design [6471]
Bridge Grid Flooring Mfrs. Assn. [605]
Canadian Bridge Fed. [IO]
English Bridge Union [IO]
European Bridge League [IO]
Intl. Assn. for Bridge Maintenance and Safety [IO]

Reference to "IO" in place of a book number signifies that the association may be found in the 45th edition of International Organizations.

Intl. Assn. for Bridge Maintenance and Safety [538]

Intl. Assn. of Bridge, Structural, Ornamental and Reinforcing Iron Workers [24134]

Intl. Bridge Press Assn. [IO]

Natl. Soc. for the Preservation of Covered Bridges [10049]

Natl. Steel Bridge Alliance [539]

Bridge - A Center for the Advancement of Intercultural Studies - Address unknown since 1995.

Bridge Across the Pond/Tom Jones Fan Club - Defunct.

The Bridge - Address unknown since 2003.

Bridge Assn; U.S. [★21893]

Bridge and Building Assn; Amer. Railway [★3280]

Bridge and Building Supply Assn. - Defunct.

Bridge Constr. and Design; Assn. for [6471]

Bridge the Gap; Campus Comm. to [★18145]

Bridge the Gap; Comm. to [18145]

Bridge Grid Flooring Mfrs. Assn. [605], 300 E Cherry St., North Baltimore, OH 45872, (419)257-3561

Bridge Joint Assn. [IO], Camberley, United Kingdom

Bridge League; Amer. [★21893]

Bridge League; Amer. Auction [★21893]

Bridge Line Historical Soc. [22932], PO Box 13324, Albany, NY 12212

Bridge Pastoral Found. [IO], Birkenhead, United Kingdom

Bridge Program; Project [★11715]

Bridge Prosthodontics; Amer. Acad. of Crown and [★14097]

Bridge, Structural, Ornamental and Reinforcing Iron Workers; Intl. Assn. of [24134]

Bridges to Community [13389], 95 Croton Ave., Ossining, NY 10562, (914)923-2200

Bridges of Hope [★11672]

Bridges of Hope [★IO]

Bridges; Natl. Soc. for the Preservation of Covered [10049]

Bridging Nations [17861], 1800 K St. NW, Ste. 622, Washington, DC 20006, (202)741-3870

Bridging Nations [IO], Washington, DC, United States

Bridle Club; Natl. Block and [24401]

Brigade Assn; Hood's Texas [20726]

Bright Belt Warehouse Assn. - Defunct.

Bright Futures Farm [4867], 44793 Harrison Rd., Spartansburg, PA 16434-1809, (814)827-8270

Bright Hope Intl. [20466], 2060 Stonington Ave., Hoffman Estates, IL 60169, (224)520-6100

Bright Hope Intl. [IO], Hoffman Estates, IL, United States

Bright Wire Goods Mfrs. Service Bur. - Defunct.

Brighten the Night Program - Defunct.

Brighton Body Positive [IO], Brighton, United Kingdom

Brilliant Center for Beethoven Studies; Ira F. [★9803]

Brine Cavity Res. Gp. [★2755]

Bring Back Mark Lindsay Campaign - Address unknown since 1989.

Brinton Assn. of Am. [21110], 21 Oakland Rd., West Chester, PA 19382, (610)399-0913

Brisbane Orchid Soc. [IO], Brisbane, Australia

Brisbane Water Ski Club [IO], Brisbane, Australia

Bristol Chamber of Commerce and Initiative [IO], Bristol, United Kingdom

Bristol Indus. Archaeological Soc. [IO], Bath, United Kingdom

Bristol Owners' Club [IO], Petersfield, United Kingdom

Bristol Owners Club, U.S. Br. - Address unknown since 2001.

Britain Assn. for Ethiopian Jewry [★IO]

Britain Correspondence Club; Great [★22032]

Britain and Ireland Assn. of Aquatic Sciences Libraries and Info. Centres [IO], Suffolk, United Kingdom

Britain-Nepal Chamber of Commerce [IO], Burnham-on-Crouch, United Kingdom

Britain - Nepal Medical Trust [IO], Tonbridge, United Kingdom

Britain's Toy Soldier Club - Defunct.

Britenburg Surname Org. [20809]

Brith Abraham [★19177]

B'Rith Christian Union [★19800]

Brith Sholom [19178], 3939 Conshohocken Ave., Philadelphia, PA 19131, (215)878-5696

Brith Sholom; Independent Order of [★19178]

British

Berkeley Exchange [21590]

British Biker Cooperative [22672]

British Intl. Motorcycle Assn. [22673]

British Schools and Universities Club of New York [18984]

British Schools and Universities Found. [8102]

British Trade Off. at Consulate-General [24241]

British Universities North Am. Club [8606]

Churchill Centre [11109]

Cornish Amer. Heritage Soc. [9759]

Historians of British Art [9478]

H.M. 10th Regiment of Foot, Amer. Contingent [9373]

Intl. Educator's Inst. [8645]

Intl. Friends of the London Lib. [10363]

Intl. Rebecca West Soc. [11178]

Intl. Soc. of Anglo-Saxonists [8379]

Intl. Soc. for British Genealogy and Family History [21123]

London Vintage Taxi Assn. - Amer. Sect. [21690]

Michael Crawford Intl. Fan Assn. [24760]

Natl. Soc., Daughters of the British Empire in the U.S.A. [18985]

North Amer. Brass Band Assn. [10675]

North Amer. British Music Stud. Assn. [10676]

North Amer. Conf. on British Stud. [9760]

North Amer. Mini Moke Registry [21745]

North Amer. Torquay Soc. [22094]

Peter Sellers Appreciation Soc. [24767]

Polanyi Soc. [10826]

REG - The Intl. Roger Waters Fan Club [24965]

Richard III Soc., Amer. Br. [11145]

Sabra Automobile Connection [21779]

St. Helena, Ascension, and Tristan da Cunha Philatelic Soc. [22866]

Surtees Soc. [IO]

The Thomas Hardy Assn. [9712]

Velocette Owners Club of North Am. [22695]

VisitBritain [24242]

VisitBritain [IO]

Wedgwood Intl. Seminar [21939]

Winant and Clayton Volunteers [13409]

British Abrasives Fed. [IO], Hurst, United Kingdom

British Acad. [IO], London, United Kingdom

British Acad. of Composers and Songwriters [IO], London, United Kingdom

British Acad. of Dramatic Combat [IO], Hemsley, United Kingdom

The British Acad. of Experts [★IO]

British Acad. of Film and TV Arts [IO], London, United Kingdom

British Acad. of Film and TV Arts - Scotland [IO], Glasgow, United Kingdom

British Acad. of Forensic Sciences [IO], London, United Kingdom

British Acad. of Songwriters, Composers and Authors [★IO]

British ACM Chap. [IO], London, United Kingdom

British Activity Holiday Assn. [IO], Chester, United Kingdom

British Actors' Equity Assn. [★IO]

British Actors' Equity Assn. [IO], London, United Kingdom

British Acupuncture Coun. [IO], London, United Kingdom

British Adhesives and Sealants Assn. [IO], Worksop, United Kingdom

British Aerobiology Fed. [IO], Derby, United Kingdom

British Aerosol Mfrs'. Assn. [IO], London, United Kingdom

British Agricultural and Garden Machinery Assn. [IO], Uxbridge, United Kingdom

British Agricultural History Soc. [IO], Exeter, United Kingdom

British Agrochemicals Assn. [★IO]

British Aikido Assn. [IO], Ilkley, United Kingdom

British Air Line Pilots Assn. [IO], West Drayton, United Kingdom

British Airports Gp. [IO], London, United Kingdom

British Amateur Gymnastics Assn. [★IO]

British Amateur Rugby League Assn. [IO], Huddersfield, United Kingdom

British-American Bus. Coun. [IO], New York, NY, United States

British-American Bus. Coun. [705], 52 Vanderbilt Ave., 20th Fl., New York, NY 10017, (212)661-5660

British-American Chamber of Commerce [★24267]

British Amer. Educational Found. [8605], 520 Summit Ave., Oradell, NJ 07649, (201)261-4438

British-Amer. Rhykenological Soc. - Defunct.

British Amer. Security Info. Coun. [17374], 110 Maryland Ave. NE, Ste. 205, Washington, DC 20002, (202)546-8055

British Amer. Security Info. Coun. [IO], Washington, DC, United States

British Amer. Security Info. Coun. - United Kingdom [IO], London, United Kingdom

British Amusement Catering Trade Assn. [IO], London, United Kingdom

British Anaesthetic and Respiratory Equip. Mfrs. Assn. [★IO]

British Andrology Soc. [IO], Sheffield, United Kingdom

British Angora Goat Soc. [IO], Warwick, United Kingdom

British Antique Dealers' Assn. [IO], London, United Kingdom

British Antique Furniture Restorers Assn. [IO], Dorchester, United Kingdom

British Appaloosa Soc. [IO], Carlisle, United Kingdom

British Approvals Bd. for Telecommunications [IO], Walton-On-Thames, United Kingdom

British Approvals for Fire Equip. [IO], Kingston Upon Thames, United Kingdom

British Arachnological Soc. [IO], St. Neots, United Kingdom

British Art Medal Soc. [IO], London, United Kingdom

British Artist Blacksmiths Assn. [IO], Glasgow, United Kingdom

British Arts Festivals Assn. [IO], London, United Kingdom

British Assn. of Academic Phoneticians [IO], Glasgow, United Kingdom

British Assn. for Accident and Emergency Medicine [★IO]

British Assn. for Adoption and Fostering [IO], London, United Kingdom

British Assn. for the Advancement of Sci. [★IO]

British Assn. of Aesthetic Plastic Surgeons [IO], London, United Kingdom

British Assn. for Amer. Stud. [IO], Preston, United Kingdom

British Assn. for Applied Linguistics [IO], London, United Kingdom

British Assn. of Art Therapists [IO], London, United Kingdom

British Assn. of Audiological Physicians [IO], London, United Kingdom

British Assn. of Aviation Consultants [IO], London, United Kingdom

British Assn. of Balloon Operators [IO], Pewsey, United Kingdom

British Assn. of Barbershop Singers [IO], Bristol, United Kingdom

British Assn. of Beauty Therapy and Cosmetology [IO], Gloucester, United Kingdom

British Assn. of Behavioral Optometrists [IO], Cheltenham, United Kingdom

British Assn. for Behavioural and Cognitive Psychotherapies [IO], Bury, United Kingdom

British Assn. for Biological Anthropology and Osteoarchaeology [IO], Durham, United Kingdom

British Assn. of Brain Injury Case Managers [IO], Cranbrook, United Kingdom

British Assn. for Canadian Stud. [IO], London, United Kingdom

British Assn. for Cancer Res. [IO], Sutton, United Kingdom

British Assn. for Cemeteries in South Asia [IO], London, United Kingdom

British Assn. for Chem. Specialties [IO], Harrogate, United Kingdom

British Assn. for Chinese Stud. [IO], Colchester, United Kingdom

A star before a book entry number signifies that the name is not listed separately, but is mentioned within the entry.

British Assn. of Clinical Anatomists [IO], Norwich, United Kingdom

British Assn. and Coll. of Occupational Therapists [IO], London, United Kingdom

British Assn. of Colliery Mgt. [★IO]

British Assn. of Colliery Mgt. - Tech., Energy and Administrative Mgt. [IO], Doncaster, United Kingdom

British Assn. of Communicators in Bus. [IO], Milton Keynes, United Kingdom

British Assn. of Concert Agents [★IO]

British Assn. of Conf. Destinations [IO], Birmingham, United Kingdom

British Assn. of Cosmetic Doctors [IO], London, United Kingdom

British Assn. for Counselling [★IO]

British Assn. for Counselling and Psychotherapy [IO], Lutterworth, United Kingdom

British Assn. of Crystal Growth [IO], Nottingham, United Kingdom

British Assn. of Day Surgery [IO], London, United Kingdom

British Assn. of Dental Nurses [IO], Thornton-Cleveleys, United Kingdom

British Assn. of Dermatologists [IO], London, United Kingdom

British Assn. of Dramatherapists [IO], Cheltenham, United Kingdom

British Assn. for Early Childhood Educ. [IO], London, United Kingdom

British Assn. for Emergency Medicine [IO], London, United Kingdom

British Assn. for Fair Trade Shops [IO], Oxford, United Kingdom

British Assn. in Forensic Medicine [IO], Cardiff, United Kingdom

British Assn. of Former United Nations Civil Servants [IO], London, United Kingdom

British Assn. of Friends of Museums [IO], Whitchurch, United Kingdom

British Assn. of Golf Course Constructors [IO], Bexhill-on-Sea, United Kingdom

British Assn. of Green Crop Driers [IO], Hythe, United Kingdom

British Assn. of the Hard of Hearing [★IO]

British Assn. of Head and Neck Oncologists [IO], Sunderland, United Kingdom

British Assn. of Homoeopathic Veterinary Surgeons [IO], Bedworth, United Kingdom

British Assn. of Hospitality Accountants [IO], Wimborne, United Kingdom

British Assn. of Hotel Accountants [★IO]

British Assn. for Immediate Care [IO], Ipswich, United Kingdom

British Assn. of Indian Anaesthetists [IO], Wakefield, United Kingdom

British Assn. of Indus. Editors [★IO]

British Assn. for Info. and Lib. Educ. [★IO]

British Assn. for Info. and Lib. Educ. Res. [IO], Liverpool, United Kingdom

British Assn. for Japanese Stud. [IO], Colchester, United Kingdom

British Assn. of Journalists [IO], London, United Kingdom

British Assn. of Landscape Indus. [IO], Coventry, United Kingdom

British Assn. of Leisure Parks, Piers and Attractions [IO], London, United Kingdom

British Assn. for Local History [IO], Ashbourne, United Kingdom

British Assn. for Lung Res. [IO], London, United Kingdom

British Assn. of Medical Managers [IO], Stockport, United Kingdom

British Assn. for Modern Mosaic [IO], Exeter, United Kingdom

British Assn. Mountain Guides [IO], Conwy, United Kingdom

British Assn. of Neuroscience Nurses [IO], Sheffield, United Kingdom

British Assn. of Numismatic Societies [IO], London, United Kingdom

British Assn. for Nutritional Therapy [IO], London, United Kingdom

British Assn. of Occupational Therapists [IO], London, United Kingdom

British Assn. for Open Learning [★IO]

British Assn. of Oral and Maxillofacial Surgeons [IO], London, United Kingdom

British Assn. of Otorhinolaryngologists - Head and Neck Surgeons [IO], London, United Kingdom

British Assn. for Paediatric Nephrology [IO], Glasgow, United Kingdom

British Assn. of Paediatric Surgeons of England [IO], London, United Kingdom

British Assn. of Paintings Conservator-Restorers [IO], Norwich, United Kingdom

British Assn. of Paper Historians [IO], Alnwick, United Kingdom

British Assn. for Performing Arts Medicine [IO]

British Assn. for Performing Arts Medicine [IO], London, United Kingdom

British Assn. of Perinatal Medicine [IO], London, United Kingdom

British Assn. of Pharmaceutical Physicians [IO], Reading, United Kingdom

British Assn. of Pharmaceutical Wholesalers [IO], London, United Kingdom

British Assn. of Picture Libraries and Agencies [IO], London, United Kingdom

British Assn. of Plastic, Reconstructive and Aesthetic Surgeons [IO], London, United Kingdom

British Assn. of Play Therapists [IO], Weybridge, United Kingdom

British Assn. of Prosthetists and Orthotists [IO], Paisley, United Kingdom

British Assn. for Psychopharmacology [IO], Cambridge, United Kingdom

British Assn. of Psychotherapists [IO], London, United Kingdom

British Assn. of Radiologists [★IO]

British Assn. of Record Dealers [IO], Bournemouth, United Kingdom

British Assn. of Removers [★IO]

British Assn. of Removers [IO], Watford, United Kingdom

British Assn. of Res. Quality Assurance [IO], Ipswich, United Kingdom

British Assn. of Retinal Screeners [IO], Dundee, United Kingdom

British Assn. for Robotics and Automation [★IO]

British Assn. of Settlements and Social Action Centres [IO], London, United Kingdom

British Assn. for Sexual Hea. and HIV [IO], London, United Kingdom

British Assn. for Sexual and Marital Therapy [★IO]

British Assn. for Sexual and Relationship Therapy [IO], London, United Kingdom

British Assn. for Shooting and Conservation [IO], Wrexham, United Kingdom

British Assn. of Ski Instructors [★IO]

British Assn. of Ski Patrollers [IO], Argyllshire, United Kingdom

British Assn. of Skin Camouflage [IO], Macclesfield, United Kingdom

British Assn. for Slavonic and East European Stud. [IO], Aberystwyth, United Kingdom

British Assn. of Snowsport Instructors [IO], Aviemore, United Kingdom

British Assn. of Social Workers [IO], Birmingham, United Kingdom

British Assn. for South Asian Stud. [IO], Lancaster, United Kingdom

British Assn. of Sport and Exercise Sciences [IO], Leeds, United Kingdom

British Assn. of Sport Rehabilitators and Trainers [IO], Salford, United Kingdom

British Assn. of Stroke Physicians [IO], Ashford, United Kingdom

British Assn. for the Stud. of Headache [IO], London, United Kingdom

British Assn. for the Stud. of Religions [IO], Milton Keynes, United Kingdom

British Assn. of Surgical Oncology [★IO]

British Assn. of Symphonic Bands and Wind Ensembles [IO], Colchester, United Kingdom

British Assn. of Teachers of Dancing [IO], Glasgow, United Kingdom

British Assn. of Teachers of the Deaf [IO], High Wycombe, United Kingdom

British Assn. of Urological Surgeons [IO], London, United Kingdom

British Assn. for Vedic Astrology [IO], Romsey, United Kingdom

British Assn. of Veterinary Ophthalmologists [IO], Solihull, United Kingdom

British Assn. of Women Entrepreneurs [IO], Stirling, United Kingdom

British Astronomical Assn. [IO], London, United Kingdom

British Atherosclerosis Soc. [IO], Bristol, United Kingdom

British Athletic Fed. [★IO]

British Audio Dealers Assn. [★IO]

British Audio-Visual Dealers Assn. [IO], London, United Kingdom

British Automatic Fire Sprinkler Assn. [IO], Ely, United Kingdom

British Automatic Sprinkler Assn. [★IO]

British Ballet Org. [IO], London, United Kingdom

British Balloon and Airship Club [IO], Bristol, United Kingdom

British Bankers' Assn. [IO], London, United Kingdom

British Baseball Fed. [IO], London, United Kingdom

British Battery Mfrs. Assn. [IO], London, United Kingdom

British Beatles Fan Club [IO], Croydon, United Kingdom

British Bedding and Pot Plant Assn. [IO], Huntingdon, United Kingdom

British Bee-Keepers' Assn. [IO], Kenilworth, United Kingdom

British Beer and Pub Assn. [IO], London, United Kingdom

British Beermat Collectors Soc. [IO], Worcester, United Kingdom

British Belgian Blue Cattle Soc. [IO], Penrith, United Kingdom

British Biker Cooperative [IO], Milwaukee, WI, United States

British Biker Cooperative [22672], PO Box 371021, Milwaukee, WI 53237-2121

British Biophysical Soc. [IO], Harlow, United Kingdom

British Blind and Shutter Assn. [IO], Tamworth, United Kingdom

British Blind Sport [IO], Leamington Spa, United Kingdom

British Blood Transfusion Soc. [IO], Manchester, United Kingdom

British Bluegrass Music Assn. [IO], Liverpool, United Kingdom

British Bd. of Film Classification [IO], London, United Kingdom

British Bobsleigh Assn. [IO], Horsham, United Kingdom

British Boot, Shoe and Allied Trades Res. Assn. [★IO]

British Box and Packaging Assn. [★IO]

British Brands Gp. [IO], London, United Kingdom

British Bryological Soc. [IO], Torquay, United Kingdom

British Bus. and Gen. Aviation Assn. [IO], Aylesbury, United Kingdom

British Cable Makers Confed. [★IO]

British Cables Assn. [IO], East Molesey, United Kingdom

British Cactus and Succulent Soc. [IO], Hornchurch, United Kingdom

British Camelids Assn. [IO], Shipston-on-Stour, United Kingdom

British Camelids Owners and Breeders Assn. [★IO]

British Canadian Chamber of Trade and Commerce [IO], Beaconsfield, QC, Canada

British Canoe Union [IO], Nottingham, United Kingdom

British Cardiac Soc. [★IO]

British Cardiovascular Soc. [IO], London, United Kingdom

British Cartographic Soc. [IO], Wellington, United Kingdom

British Carton Assn. [★IO]

British Casino Assn. [IO], London, United Kingdom

British Cast Concrete Fed. [★IO]

British Cattle Veterinary Assn. [IO], Gloucester, United Kingdom

British Cave Res. Assn. [IO], Buxton, United Kingdom

Reference to "IO" in place of a book number signifies that the association may be found in the 45th edition of International Organizations.

British Caving Assn. [IO], Buxton, United Kingdom
British Caving Assn. [IO], Swansea, United Kingdom
British Cement Assn. [IO], Surrey, United Kingdom
British Centre of the Intl. Theatre Inst. [IO], London, United Kingdom
British Ceramic Confed. [IO], Stoke-On-Trent, United Kingdom
British Ceramic Plant and Machinery Manufacturers' Assn. [IO], Stoke-On-Trent, United Kingdom
British Ceramics Res. [★IO]
British Chamber of Commerce in Belgium [IO], Brussels, Belgium
British Chamber of Commerce in China [IO], Beijing, People's Republic of China
British Chamber of Commerce in Germany [IO], Berlin, Germany
British Chamber of Commerce in Hong Kong [IO], Hong Kong, People's Republic of China
British Chamber of Commerce in Hungary [IO], Budapest, Hungary
British Chamber of Commerce for Italy [IO], Milan, Italy
British Chamber of Commerce in Latvia [IO], Riga, Latvia
British Chamber of Commerce for Luxembourg [IO], Luxembourg, Luxembourg
British Chamber of Commerce in Spain [IO], Barcelona, Spain
British Chambers of Commerce [IO], London, United Kingdom
British Cheerleading Assn. [IO], Windsor, United Kingdom
British Chelonia Gp. [IO], Chippenham, United Kingdom
British Chem. Engg. Contractors Assn. [IO], London, United Kingdom
British Cheque Cashers Assn. [IO], Chester, United Kingdom
British Chess Fed. [★IO]
British-Chilean Chamber of Commerce [IO], London, United Kingdom
British Chiropractic Assn. [IO], Reading, United Kingdom
British Christmas Tree Growers Assn. [IO], Edinburgh, United Kingdom
British Cleaning Coun. [IO], Kidderminster, United Kingdom
British Clematis Assn. [★IO]
British Clematis Soc. [IO], Burford, United Kingdom
British Coatings Fed. [IO], Leatherhead, United Kingdom
British Coll. of Optometrists [★IO]
British Colour Makers Assn. [IO], Derbyshire, United Kingdom
British Columbia Art Teachers' Assn. [IO], Vancouver, BC, Canada
British Columbia Art Therapy Assn. [IO], Vancouver, BC, Canada
British Columbia Assn. for Marriage and Family Therapy [IO], Vancouver, BC, Canada
British Columbia Assn. for Play Therapy [IO], Vancouver, BC, Canada
British Columbia Assn. of Teachers of Modern Languages [IO], Vancouver, BC, Canada
British Columbia Bottle Depot Assn. [IO], Burnaby, BC, Canada
British Columbia Chefs' Assn. [IO], Vancouver, BC, Canada
British Columbia Constr. Assn. [IO], Victoria, BC, Canada
British Columbia Folklore Soc. [IO], Saanich, BC, Canada
British Columbia Herb Growers Assn. [IO], Kelowna, BC, Canada
British Columbia Historical Fed. [IO], Victoria, BC, Canada
British Columbia Hospice Palliative Care Assn. [IO], Vancouver, BC, Canada
British Columbia Intl. Commercial Arbitration Centre [IO], Vancouver, BC, Canada
British Columbia Primary Teachers' Assn. [IO], Fort Nelson, BC, Canada
British Columbia Psychological Assn. [IO], Vancouver, BC, Canada
British Columbia Schizophrenia Soc. [IO], Richmond, BC, Canada

British Columbia School Counsellors' Assn. [IO], Vancouver, BC, Canada
British Columbia Snowboard Assn. [IO], Kelowna, BC, Canada
British Columbia Soc. for the Prevention of Cruelty to Animals [IO], Vancouver, BC, Canada
British Columbia Teachers' Fed. [IO], Vancouver, BC, Canada
British Columbia Tech. Indus. Assn. [IO], Vancouver, BC, Canada
British Columbia Water and Wastewater Assn. [IO], Burnaby, BC, Canada
British Columbia Wheelchair Basketball Soc. [IO], Vancouver, BC, Canada
British Combustion Equip. Mfrs. Assn. [★IO]
British Commonwealth Numismatic Soc. - Defunct.
British Comparative Literature Assn. [IO], Manchester, United Kingdom
British Compressed Air Soc. [IO], London, United Kingdom
British Compressed Gases Assn. [IO], Derby, United Kingdom
British Cmpt. Assn. of the Blind [IO], Birmingham, United Kingdom
British Cmpt. Soc. [IO], Swindon, United Kingdom
British Confectioners' Assn. [IO], Tadworth, United Kingdom
British Constructional Steelwork Assn. [IO], London, United Kingdom
British Consultants and Constr. Bur. [★IO]
British Contact Lens Assn. [IO], London, United Kingdom
British Contract Furnishing Assn. [IO], High Wycombe, United Kingdom
British Contract Mfrs. and Packers Assn. [IO], Amersham, United Kingdom
British Copyright Coun. [IO], London, United Kingdom
British Coun. [IO], London, United Kingdom
British Coun. of Ballroom Dancing [★IO]
British Coun. Canada [IO], Ottawa, ON, Canada
British Coun. of Churches [★IO]
British Coun. of Disabled People [★IO]
British Coun. for Offices [IO], London, United Kingdom
British Coun. of Organisations of Disabled People [★IO]
British Coun. for Rehabilitation of the Disabled [★IO]
British Coun. of Shopping Centres [IO], London, United Kingdom
British Crop Protection Coun. [★IO]
British Cryoengineering Soc. [★IO]
British Cryogenics Coun. [IO], Leatherhead, United Kingdom
British Crystallographic Assn. [IO], Glasgow, United Kingdom
British Cycle Speedway Commn. [IO], Norwich, United Kingdom
British Cycling [IO], Manchester, United Kingdom
British Dam Soc. [IO], London, United Kingdom
British Dance Coun. [IO], London, United Kingdom
British Deaf Assn. [IO], London, United Kingdom
British Deaf Sports Coun. [IO], Ipswich, United Kingdom
British Decorators Assn. [★IO]
British Deer Soc. [IO], Fordingbridge, United Kingdom
British Dental Assn. [IO], London, United Kingdom
British Dental Practice Managers' Assn. [IO], Gloucester, United Kingdom
British Dental Trade Assn. [IO], Chesham, United Kingdom
British Design and Art Direction [IO], London, United Kingdom
British Detectives Assn. [★IO]
British Dietetic Assn. [IO], Birmingham, United Kingdom
British Disabled Angling Assn. [IO], Walsall, United Kingdom
British Disabled Water Ski Assn. [IO], Wraysbury, United Kingdom
British Disc Golf Assn. [IO], Warwickshire, United Kingdom
British Disinfectant Mfrs. Assn. [★IO]
British Display Soc. [IO], Essex, United Kingdom

British Disposable Products Assn. [★IO]
British Doll Artists Assn. [IO], Rudgwick, United Kingdom
British Dragonfly Soc. [IO], Peterborough, United Kingdom
British Dried Flowers Assn. [IO], Canterbury, United Kingdom
British Drilling Assn. [IO], Daventry, United Kingdom
British Driving Soc. [IO], Stowmarket, United Kingdom
British Dyslexia Assn. [IO], Reading, United Kingdom
British Ecological Soc. [IO], London, United Kingdom
British Educational Communications and Tech. Agency [IO], Coventry, United Kingdom
British Educational Leadership, Mgt. and Admin. Soc. [IO], Sheffield, United Kingdom
British Educational Res. Assn. [IO], Macclesfield, United Kingdom
British Educational Suppliers Assn. [IO], London, United Kingdom
British Effluent Water Assn. and British Water Indus. Gp. [★IO]
British Egg Indus. Coun. [IO], London, United Kingdom
British Electrostatic Control Assn. [IO], Birmingham, United Kingdom
British Electrostatic Mfrs. Assn. [IO], Birmingham, United Kingdom
British Electrotechnical and Allied Mfrs'. Assn. [IO], London, United Kingdom
British Electrotechnical Approvals Bd. [IO], Guildford, United Kingdom
British Empire Games [★IO]
British Endodontic Soc. [IO], Gerrards Cross, United Kingdom
British Engraved Stationery Assn. [IO], London, United Kingdom
British Entomological and Natural History Soc. [IO], Reading, United Kingdom
British Epilepsy Assn. [IO], Leeds, United Kingdom
British Equestrian Fed. [IO], Kenilworth, United Kingdom
British Equestrian Trade Assn. [IO], Wetherby, United Kingdom
British Equine Veterinary Assn. [IO], Fordham, United Kingdom
British and European Geranium Soc. [IO], Wellingborough, United Kingdom
British Exhibition Contractors Assn. [IO], London, United Kingdom
British Expertise [IO], London, United Kingdom
British Exporters Assn. [IO], London, United Kingdom
British Exports Marketing Advisory Comm. - Defunct.
British False Memory Soc. [IO], Bradford-on-Avon, United Kingdom
British Fantasy Soc. [IO], Cheadle, United Kingdom
British Fed. of Audio [IO], Farnham, United Kingdom
British Fed. of Brass Bands [IO], Barnsley, United Kingdom
British Fed. of Film Societies [IO], Sheffield, United Kingdom
British Fed. of Printing Machinery and Supplies [★IO]
British Fed. of Univ. Women [★IO]
British Fed. of Women Graduates [IO], London, United Kingdom
British Fed. of Young Choirs [★IO]
British Fencing Assn. [IO], London, United Kingdom
British Fertility Soc. [IO], Bristol, United Kingdom
British Fibreboard Packaging Assn. [★IO]
British Film Inst. [IO], London, United Kingdom
British Finn Assn. [IO], Worthing, United Kingdom
British Fire Protection Systems Assn. [IO], Kingston Upon Thames, United Kingdom
British Flue and Chimney Mfrs'. Assn. [IO], Reading, United Kingdom
British Fluid Power Assn. [IO], Chipping Norton, United Kingdom
British Fluid Power Distributors Assn. [IO], Chipping Norton, United Kingdom
British Fluoridation Soc. [IO], Manchester, United Kingdom
British Flute Soc. [IO], Twickenham, United Kingdom

A star before a book entry number signifies that the name is not listed separately, but is mentioned within the entry.

British Footwear Assn. [IO], Wellingborough, United Kingdom
British and Foreign Anti-Slavery Soc. [★IO]
British Forging Indus. Assn. [★IO]
British Foundry Assn. [★IO]
British Fragrance Assn. [IO], Surrey, United Kingdom
British Franchise Assn. [IO], Henley-On-Thames, United Kingdom
British Frozen Food Fed. [IO], Grantham, United Kingdom
British Fur Trade Assn. [IO], London, United Kingdom
British Furniture Mfrs. [IO], High Wycombe, United Kingdom
British Gear Assn. [IO], Burton-On-Trent, United Kingdom
British Gear Assn. [★IO]
British Geological Survey [IO], Nottingham, United Kingdom
British Geomorphological Res. Gp. [★IO]
British Geophysical Assn. [IO], Edinburgh, United Kingdom
British Geotechnical Assn. [IO], London, United Kingdom
British Geotechnical Soc. [★IO]
British Geriatrics Soc. [IO], London, United Kingdom
British - German Jurists Assn. [IO], London, United Kingdom
British Glaciological Soc. [★IO]
British Glass [IO], Sheffield, United Kingdom
British Glass Indus. Res. Assn. [★IO]
British Glass Mfrs'. Confed. [★IO]
British Gliding Assn. [IO], Leicester, United Kingdom
British Glove Assn. [IO], Bromley, United Kingdom
British Goat Soc. [IO], Newton Abbot, United Kingdom
British Grassland Soc. [IO], Cirencester, United Kingdom
British Guild of Travel Writers [IO], London, United Kingdom
British Gymnastics [IO], Newport, United Kingdom
British Hallmarking Coun. [IO], Birmingham, United Kingdom
British Hand Knitting Confed. [IO], Bingley, United Kingdom
British Hang Gliding and Paragliding Assn. [IO], Leicester, United Kingdom
British Hardmetal Assn. [IO], Sheffield, United Kingdom
The British Hardmetal Assn. and British Engineers' Cutting Tool Assn. [★IO]
British Hardmetal and Engineers' Cutting Tool Assn. [IO], Sheffield, United Kingdom
British Hardware Fed. [IO], Birmingham, United Kingdom
British Hardware and Housewares Mfrs'. Assn. [IO], Northampton, United Kingdom
British Harness Racing Club [IO], Goole, United Kingdom
British Hat Guild [IO], London, United Kingdom
British Hea. Care Assn. [IO], Kettering, United Kingdom
British Healthcare Bus. Intelligence Assn. [IO], St. Albans, United Kingdom
British Heart Found. [IO], London, United Kingdom
British Hedgehog Preservation Soc. [IO], Ludlow, United Kingdom
British Helicopter Advisory Bd. [IO], Woking, United Kingdom
British Hellenic Chamber of Commerce [IO], Athens, Greece
British Herb Trade Assn. [IO], Louth, United Kingdom
British Herbal Medicine Assn. [IO], Bournemouth, United Kingdom
British Herpetological Soc. [IO], Montrose, United Kingdom
British HIV Assn. [IO], London, United Kingdom
British Holiday and Home Parks Assn. [IO], Gloucester, United Kingdom
British Holistic Medical Assn. [IO], Bridgwater, United Kingdom
British Homeopathic Assn. [IO], London, United Kingdom
British Horn Soc. [IO], West Malling, United Kingdom

British Horological Fed. [IO], Newark, United Kingdom
British Horological Inst. [IO], Newark, United Kingdom
British Horse Soc. [IO], Kenilworth, United Kingdom
British Horse Soc. - Pony Club [★23537]
British Hospitality Assn. [IO], London, United Kingdom
British Hospitals Contributory Schemes Assn. [★IO]
British Hosta and Hemerocallis Soc. [IO], Westbury-on-Severn, United Kingdom
British Housewives' League [IO], London, United Kingdom
British Humanist Assn. [IO], London, United Kingdom
British Hydrological Soc. [IO], London, United Kingdom
British Hydromechanics Res. Assn. [★IO]
British Hydropower Assn. [IO], Wimborne, United Kingdom
British Hypertension Soc. [IO], Leicester, United Kingdom
British Iceberg Growers' Assn. [★IO]
British In-Vitro Diagnostics Assn. [IO], London, United Kingdom
British Incoming Tour Operators Assn. [★IO]
British Independent Steel Producers Assn. [★IO]
British Indian Psychiatric Assn. [IO], Kent, United Kingdom
British Indoor Cricket Assn. [IO], Sutton Coldfield, United Kingdom
British Indus. Furnace Constructors Assn. [IO], West Bromwich, United Kingdom
British Indus. Truck Assn. [IO], Ascot, United Kingdom
British Infection Soc. [IO], Naphill, United Kingdom
British Infertility Counselling Assn. [IO], Sheffield, United Kingdom
British Inline Puck Hockey Assn. [IO], Rotherham, United Kingdom
British Inline Skater Hockey Assn. [IO], Brixham, United Kingdom
British Inst. of Agricultural Consultants [IO], Sittingbourne, United Kingdom
British Inst. of Architectural Technicians [★IO]
British Inst. of Architectural Technologists [★IO]
British Inst. of Cleaning Sci. [IO], Northampton, United Kingdom
British Inst. of Dental and Surgical Technologists [IO], Shipley, United Kingdom
British Inst. of Energy Economics [IO], Aylesbury, United Kingdom
British Inst. of Facilities Mgt. [IO], Saffron Walden, United Kingdom
British Inst. of Graphologists [IO], Gerrards Cross, United Kingdom
British Inst. of Human Rights [IO], London, United Kingdom
British Inst. of Innkeeping [IO], Camberley, United Kingdom
British Inst. of Intl. and Comparative Law [IO], London, United Kingdom
British Inst. of Learning Disabilities [IO], Kidderminster, United Kingdom
British Inst. of Musculoskeletal Medicine [IO], Bushey, United Kingdom
British Inst. of Non-Destructive Testing [IO], Northampton, United Kingdom
British Inst. of Organ Stud. [IO], Cambridge, United Kingdom
British Inst. of Persian Stud. [IO], Tehran, Iran
British Inst. of Persian Stud. - United Kingdom [IO], London, United Kingdom
British Inst. of Professional Photography [IO], Ware, United Kingdom
British Inst. of Radiology [IO], London, United Kingdom
British Inst. of Surgical Technologists [★IO]
British Insurance Broker's Assn. [IO], London, United Kingdom
British Insurance and Investment Brokers' Assn. [★IO]
British Insurance Law Assn. [IO], Stowmarket, United Kingdom
British Interactive Media Assn. [IO], Billericay, United Kingdom

British Interior Design Assn. [IO], London, United Kingdom
British Interior Textiles Assn. [IO], London, United Kingdom
British Interlining Mfrs. Assn. [★IO]
British and Intl. Fed. of Festivals [IO], Macclesfield, United Kingdom
British Intl. Freight Assn. [IO], Feltham, United Kingdom
British and Intl. Golf Greenkeepers Assn. [IO], York, United Kingdom
British Intl. Motorcycle Assn. [IO], Plympton, MA, United States
British Intl. Motorcycle Assn. [★IO]
British Intl. Motorcycle Assn. [22673], PO Box 158, Plympton, MA 02367-0158, (508)946-1144
British Intl. Motorcycle Assn. [★22673]
British and Intl. Sailors Soc. [IO], Southampton, United Kingdom
British Intl. Spa Assn. [IO], Goudhurst, United Kingdom
British Intl. Stud. Assn. [IO], Stafford, United Kingdom
British Interplanetary Soc. [IO], London, United Kingdom
British Investment Casting Trade Assn. [★IO]
British Iris Soc. [IO], Surrey, United Kingdom
British and Irish Assn. of Law Librarians [IO], Warwick, United Kingdom
British and Irish Law, Educ. and Tech. Assn. [IO], Coventry, United Kingdom
British and Irish Ombudsman Assn. [IO], Twickenham, United Kingdom
British and Irish Orthoptic Soc. [IO], London, United Kingdom
British Iron and Steel Producers Assn. [★IO]
British Isles Bee Breeders' Assn. [★IO]
British-Israel Chamber of Commerce [IO], London, United Kingdom
British-Israel-World Fed. (Canada) [IO], Toronto, ON, Canada
British Jewellers' Assn. [IO], Birmingham, United Kingdom
British Jewellery and Giftware Fed. [★IO]
British Jewellery, Giftware and Finishing Fed. [IO], Birmingham, United Kingdom
British Jews; Board of Deputies of [★IO]
British Jews; Board of Deputies of [★20124]
British Judo Assn. [IO], Loughborough, United Kingdom
British Kendo Assn. [IO], Sutton, United Kingdom
British Killifish Assn. [IO], Lymington, United Kingdom
British Kinematograph Sound and TV Soc. [★IO]
British Kite Surfing Assn. [IO], Hayling Island, United Kingdom
British Korfball Assn. [IO], Chatham, United Kingdom
British Ladder Mfrs. Assn. [IO], Leeds, United Kingdom
British Laminate Fabricators Assn. [IO], Nottingham, United Kingdom
British Laminated Plastic Fabricators Assn. [★IO]
British Leafy Salads Assn. [IO], Louth, United Kingdom
British Learning Assn. [IO], Letchworth Garden City, United Kingdom
British Leprosy Relief Assn. [IO], Colchester, United Kingdom
British Leyland
  TR8 Car Club of Am. [21799]
British Lichen Soc. [IO], London, United Kingdom
British Lift Assn. [★IO]
British Lime Assn. [IO], London, United Kingdom
British Llama and Alpaca Assn. [IO], Tredington, United Kingdom
British Long-Bow Soc. [IO], Manchester, United Kingdom
British Long Distance Swimming Assn. [IO], Northwich, United Kingdom
British Luggage and Leathergoods Assn. [★IO]
British Lung Found. [IO], London, United Kingdom
British Machine Vision Assn. and Soc. for Pattern Recognition [IO], Bristol, United Kingdom
British Magical Soc. [IO], Birmingham, United Kingdom

Reference to "IO" in place of a book number signifies that the association may be found in the 45th edition of International Organizations.

British Marine Equip. Coun. [★IO]

British Marine Fed. [IO], Egham, United Kingdom

British Marine Fed. - Scotland [IO], Dunoon, United Kingdom

British Marine Life Stud. Soc. [IO], Shoreham-by-Sea, United Kingdom

British Maritime Law Assn. [IO], London, United Kingdom

British Masonry Soc. [IO], Whyteleafe, United Kingdom

British Materials Handling Fed. [IO], West Bromwich, United Kingdom

British Measurement and Testing Assn. [IO], East Malling, United Kingdom

British Mech. Power Transmission Assn. [★IO]

British Medical Acupuncture Soc. [IO], Northwich, United Kingdom

British Medical Assn. [IO], London, United Kingdom

British Medical Laser Assn. [IO], Cleveland, United Kingdom

British Medical Ultrasound Gp. [★IO]

British Medical Ultrasound Soc. [IO], London, United Kingdom

British Menopause Soc. [IO], Marlow, United Kingdom

British Menswear Guild [IO], London, United Kingdom

British Merchants Banking and Securities Houses Assn. [★IO]

British Metals Recycling Assn. [IO], Huntingdon, United Kingdom

British Mexican Soc. [IO], London, United Kingdom

British Microcirculation Soc. [IO], Bristol, United Kingdom

British Microlight Aircraft Assn. [IO], Banbury, United Kingdom

British Migraine Assn. [★IO]

British Military Historical Soc. of the U.S. - Address unknown since 1995.

British Model Flying Assn. [IO], Leicester, United Kingdom

British Model Soldier Soc. [IO], Denham, United Kingdom

British Motorcyclists Fed. [IO], Leicester, United Kingdom

British Mountaineering Coun. [IO], Manchester, United Kingdom

British Mule Soc. [IO], Swindon, United Kingdom

British Music Hall Soc. [IO], Whitstable, United Kingdom

British Music Info. Centre [IO], London, United Kingdom

British Music Rights [IO], London, United Kingdom

British Music Soc. [IO], Upminster, United Kingdom

British Mycological Soc. [IO], Guildford, United Kingdom

British Natl. Comm. on Large Dams [★IO]

British Natural Hygiene Soc. [IO], Newark-on-Trent, United Kingdom

British Naturalists' Assn. [IO], Corby, United Kingdom

British Naturism [IO], Northampton, United Kingdom

British Nautical Instrument Trade Assn. [★IO]

British Naval Equip. Assn. [IO], London, United Kingdom

British Neuropathological Soc. [IO], Plymouth, United Kingdom

British Neuropsychiatry Assn. [IO], London, United Kingdom

British Neuroscience Assn. [IO], Liverpool, United Kingdom

British North Am. Philatelic Soc. [IO], Surrey, BC, Canada

British Nuclear Energy Soc. [IO], London, United Kingdom

British Nuclear Medicine Soc. [IO], London, United Kingdom

British Numismatic Soc. [IO], London, United Kingdom

British Numismatic Trade Assn. [IO], Rye, United Kingdom

British Nutrition Found. [IO], London, United Kingdom

British Obesity Surgery Patient Assn. [IO], Taunton, United Kingdom

British Occupational Hygiene Soc. [IO], Derby, United Kingdom

British Octopush Assn. [IO], Reading, United Kingdom

British Off. Supplies and Services Fed. [IO], High Wycombe, United Kingdom

British Off. Systems and Stationery Fed. [★IO]

British Oil Spill Control Assn. [IO], London, United Kingdom

British Olympic Assn. [IO], London, United Kingdom

British Oncology Data Managers' Assn. [IO], Banbridge, United Kingdom

British Orchid Growers Assn. [IO], Sandhurst, United Kingdom

British Organ Grinders Assn. [IO], Wincanton, United Kingdom

British Orienteering Fed. [IO], Matlock, United Kingdom

British Origami Soc. [IO], Leicester, United Kingdom

British Ornithologists' Union [IO], Oxford, United Kingdom

British Orthodontic Soc. [IO], London, United Kingdom

British Orthopaedic Assn. [IO], London, United Kingdom

British Orthopaedic Foot and Ankle Soc. [IO], London, United Kingdom

British Orthopaedic Foot Surgery Soc. [★IO]

British Orthoptic Soc. [★IO]

British Osteopathic Assn. [IO], Luton, United Kingdom

British Overseas NGOs for Development [IO], London, United Kingdom

British Packaging Assn. [IO], Glasgow, United Kingdom

British Paediatric Assn. [★IO]

British Pain Soc. [IO], London, United Kingdom

British Palomino Soc. [IO], Llandysul, United Kingdom

British Paper Machinery Mfrs. Assn. [★IO]

British Parachute Assn. [IO], Leicester, United Kingdom

British Paralympic Assn. [IO], London, United Kingdom

British Parking Assn. [IO], Haywards Heath, United Kingdom

British Peanut Coun. [IO], London, United Kingdom

British Pelargonium and Geranium Soc. [IO], Guildford, United Kingdom

British Pensioners Assn. [★IO]

British Performing Arts Medicine Trust [★IO]

British Pest Control Assn. [IO], Derby, United Kingdom

British Pharmacological Soc. [IO], London, United Kingdom

British Philosophical Assn. [IO], London, United Kingdom

British Phonographic Indus. [IO], London, United Kingdom

British Photodermatology Gp. [IO], Gloucester, United Kingdom

British Phycological Soc. [IO], Lancaster, United Kingdom

British Pig Assn. [IO], Cambridge, United Kingdom

British Plastics Fed. [IO], London, United Kingdom

British Polish Chamber of Commerce [IO], Warsaw, Poland

British Polish Makers Assn. [★IO]

British Porphyria Assn. [IO], Durham, United Kingdom

British Ports Assn. [IO], London, United Kingdom

British Poultry Coun. [IO], London, United Kingdom

British Poultry Meat Fed. [★IO]

British Precast Concrete Fed. [IO], Leicester, United Kingdom

British Press Photographers Assn. [IO], London, United Kingdom

British Printing Indus. Fed. [IO], London, United Kingdom

British Production and Inventory Control Soc. [★IO]

British Professional Pool Players Assn. [IO], Manchester, United Kingdom

British Professional Toastmasters' Authority [IO], London, United Kingdom

British Promotional Merchandise Assn. [IO], London, United Kingdom

British Property Fed. [IO], London, United Kingdom

British Psychoanalytical Soc. [IO], London, United Kingdom

British Psychodrama Assn. [IO], Glasgow, United Kingdom

British Psychological Soc. [IO], Leicester, United Kingdom

British Psychosocial Oncology Soc. [IO], Nottingham, United Kingdom

British Pteridological Soc. [IO], Isle of Skye, United Kingdom

British Pump Mfrs'. Assn. [IO], West Bromwich, United Kingdom

British Puppet and Model Theatre Guild [IO], London, United Kingdom

British Pyrotechnists Assn. [IO], Cambridge, United Kingdom

British Rabbit Coun. [IO], Newark, United Kingdom

British Radio and Electronic Equip. Mfrs'. Association [★IO]

British Ready Mixed Concrete Assn. [★IO]

British Record Soc. [IO], London, United Kingdom

British Records Assn. [IO], London, United Kingdom

British Recovered Paper Assn. [IO], Swindon, United Kingdom

British Red Cross [IO], London, United Kingdom

The British Red Cross Soc. of New Hebrides [★IO]

British Reflexology Assn. [IO], Worcester, United Kingdom

British Refrigeration Assn. [IO], Reading, United Kingdom

British Resorts Assn. [★IO]

British Resorts and Destinations Assn. [IO], Southport, United Kingdom

British Retail Consortium [IO], London, United Kingdom

British Retailers Assn. [★IO]

British Retinitis Pigmentosa Soc. [IO], Buckingham, United Kingdom

British Rheumatism and Arthritis Assn. [★IO]

British Rig Owners' Assn. [IO], London, United Kingdom

British Robot Assn. [★IO]

British Rubber Manufacturers' Assn. [IO], London, United Kingdom

British Safety Coun. [IO], London, United Kingdom

British Sandwich Assn. [IO], Chepstow, United Kingdom

British Schools and Universities Club of New York [18984], c/o The Williams Club, 24 E 39th St., New York, NY 10016, (212)713-5713

British Schools and Universities Found. [8102], 575 Madison Ave., Ste. 1006, New York, NY 10022-2511, (212)662-5576

British Schools and Universities Found. [IO], New York, NY, United States

British Sci. Fiction Assn. [IO], New Barnet, United Kingdom

British Sect. of Soc. of Protozoologists [IO], Swansea, United Kingdom

British Security Indus. Assn. [IO], Worcester, United Kingdom

British Sheep Dairying Assn. [IO], Sittingbourne, United Kingdom

British Shingon Buddhist Assn. [IO], Dereham, United Kingdom

British Shoe Repair Assn. [★IO]

British Shooting Sports Coun. [IO], London, United Kingdom

British Shops and Stores Assn. [IO], Banbury, United Kingdom

British Show Jumping Assn. [IO], Kenilworth, United Kingdom

British Show Pony Soc. [IO], Huntingdon, United Kingdom

British Sign Assn. [★IO]

British Sign and Graphics Assn. [IO], Peterborough, United Kingdom

British Ski Fed. [★IO]

British Ski and Snowboard Fed. [★IO]

British Sleep Soc. [IO], Huntingdon, United Kingdom

British Slot Car Racing Assn. [IO], Burton-On-Trent, United Kingdom

British Small Animal Veterinary Assn. [IO], Gloucester, United Kingdom

A star before a book entry number signifies that the name is not listed separately, but is mentioned within the entry.

British Snowboard Assn. **[IO]**, Midlothian, United Kingdom

British Soc. for Allergy and Clinical Immunology **[IO]**, London, United Kingdom

British Soc. for Allergy, Environmental and Nutritional Medicine **[IO]**, Knighton, United Kingdom

British Soc. of Animal Sci. **[IO]**, Penicuik, United Kingdom

British Soc. for Antimicrobial Chemotherapy **[IO]**, Birmingham, United Kingdom

British Soc. of Audiology **[IO]**, Reading, United Kingdom

British Soc. of Baking **[IO]**, Bicester, United Kingdom

British Soc. for Cell Biology **[IO]**, Cambridge, United Kingdom

British Soc. of Cinematographers **[IO]**, Gerrards Cross, United Kingdom

British Soc. for Clinical Cytology **[IO]**, London, United Kingdom

British Soc. for Clinical Neurophysiology **[IO]**, Oxford, United Kingdom

British Soc. for Clinical Psychophysiology **[IO]**, Birkenhead, United Kingdom

British Soc. of Criminology **[IO]**, London, United Kingdom

British Soc. of Dental Hygiene and Therapy **[IO]**, Gloucester, United Kingdom

British Soc. of Dental Hypnosis **[★IO]**

British Soc. for Dental and Maxillofacial Radiology **[IO]**, Manchester, United Kingdom

British Soc. for Dental Res. **[IO]**, Newcastle upon Tyne, United Kingdom

British Soc. for Disability and Oral Hea. **[IO]**, Oxford, United Kingdom

British Soc. of Dowsers **[IO]**, Malvern, United Kingdom

British Soc. of Echocardiography **[IO]**, London, United Kingdom

British Soc. for Eighteenth Century Stud. **[IO]**, Leicester, United Kingdom

British Soc. of Enamellers **[IO]**, London, United Kingdom

British Soc. of Experimental and Clinical Hypnosis **[IO]**, Grimsby, United Kingdom

British Soc. of Flavourists **[IO]**, Brentwood, United Kingdom

British Soc. of Gastroenterology **[IO]**, London, United Kingdom

British Soc. for Geomorphology **[IO]**, London, United Kingdom

British Soc. of Gerontology **[IO]**, Guildford, United Kingdom

British Soc. of Gerontology **[★IO]**

British Soc. for Haematology **[IO]**, London, United Kingdom

British Soc. of Hearing Aid Audiologists **[IO]**, Essex, United Kingdom

British Soc. for Histocompatibility and Immunogenetics **[IO]**, Aberdeen, United Kingdom

British Soc. for the History of Mathematics **[IO]**, Exeter, United Kingdom

British Soc. for the History of Medicine **[IO]**, Abingdon, United Kingdom

British Soc. for the History of Pharmacy **[IO]**, Leicester, United Kingdom

British Soc. for the History of Sci. **[IO]**, Fleet, United Kingdom

British Soc. for Human Genetics **[IO]**, Birmingham, United Kingdom

British Soc. of Hypnotherapists **[IO]**, London, United Kingdom

British Soc. for Immunology **[IO]**, London, United Kingdom

British Soc. of Magazine Editors **[IO]**, Middlesex, United Kingdom

British Soc. of Magazine Editors **[IO]**, Edgware, United Kingdom

British Soc. of Master Glass Painters **[IO]**, Minehead, United Kingdom

British Soc. of Medical and Dental Hypnosis **[IO]**, Leeds, United Kingdom

British Soc. for Medical Mycology **[IO]**, Leeds, United Kingdom

British Soc. for Middle Eastern Stud. **[IO]**, Durham, United Kingdom

British Soc. for Music Therapy **[IO]**, East Barnet, United Kingdom

British Soc. for Neuroendocrinology **[IO]**, Nottingham, United Kingdom

British Soc. for Oral Medicine **[IO]**, Liverpool, United Kingdom

British Soc. for Parasitology **[IO]**, Sandy, United Kingdom

British Soc. of Periodontology **[IO]**, Hook, United Kingdom

British Soc. of Plant Breeders **[IO]**, Ely, United Kingdom

British Soc. for Plant Pathology **[IO]**, Reading, United Kingdom

British Soc. of Psychosomatic Obstetrics, Gynaecology and Andrology **[IO]**, Sheffield, United Kingdom

British Soc. of Rehabilitation Medicine **[IO]**, London, United Kingdom

British Soc. for Res. on Ageing **[IO]**, London, United Kingdom

British Soc. for Restorative Dentistry **[IO]**, Manchester, United Kingdom

British Soc. of Rheology **[IO]**, Aberystwyth, United Kingdom

British Soc. for Rheumatology **[IO]**, London, United Kingdom

British Soc. of Sci. Glassblowers **[IO]**, Thurso, United Kingdom

British Soc. of Soil Sci. **[IO]**, Aberdeen, United Kingdom

British Soc. of Sports History **[IO]**, Ambleside, United Kingdom

British Soc. for Strain Measurement **[IO]**, Flitwick, United Kingdom

British Soc. for the Stud. of Infection **[★IO]**

British Soc. for the Stud. of Prosthetic Dentistry **[IO]**, Newcastle upon Tyne, United Kingdom

British Soc. for Surgery of the Hand **[IO]**, London, United Kingdom

British Soc. of Toxicological Pathologists **[IO]**, Harrogate, United Kingdom

British Sociological Assn. **[IO]**, Durham, United Kingdom

British Soft Drinks Assn. **[IO]**, London, United Kingdom

British Sound Recording Assn. **[IO]**, Milton Keynes, United Kingdom

British Sports Assn. for the Disabled **[★IO]**

British Sports Trust **[★IO]**

British Stainless Steel Assn. **[IO]**, Sheffield, United Kingdom

British Stammering Assn. **[IO]**, London, United Kingdom

British Stammering Assn. - Scotland **[IO]**, Edinburgh, United Kingdom

British Standards Institution **[IO]**, London, United Kingdom

British Stationary Engine Res. Gp. **[★IO]**

British Stationary Engine Res. Gp. **[★22977]**

British Stickmakers Guild **[IO]**, Chesterfield, United Kingdom

British Stud; Conf. on **[★9760]**

British Studies Intelligencer - Defunct.

British Stud; North Amer. Conf. on **[9760]**

British Sub-Aqua Club **[IO]**, Ellesmere Port, United Kingdom

British Sugarcraft Guild **[IO]**, London, United Kingdom

British Sundial Soc. **[IO]**, Crowthorne, United Kingdom

British Surface Treatment Suppliers Assn. **[★IO]**

British Surfing Assn. **[IO]**, Cornwall, United Kingdom

British Suzuki Inst. **[IO]**, London, United Kingdom

British-Swedish Chamber of Commerce in Sweden **[IO]**, Stockholm, Sweden

British-Swiss Chamber of Commerce **[IO]**, Zurich, Switzerland

British Taekwondo Control Bd. **[IO]**, Mansfield, United Kingdom

British Tarantula Soc. **[IO]**, East Sussex, United Kingdom

British Tattoo Artists Fed. **[★IO]**

British TV Shopping Assn. **[IO]**, Woking, United Kingdom

British Tenpin Bowling Assn. **[IO]**, Ilford, United Kingdom

British Textile Machinery Assn. **[IO]**, Warrington, United Kingdom

British Thematic Assn. **[IO]**, Bishops Stortford, United Kingdom

British Tinnitus Assn. **[IO]**, Sheffield, United Kingdom

British Toilet Assn. **[IO]**, Winchester, United Kingdom

British Tourist Authority **[★IO]**

British Tourist Authority **[★24242]**

British Toxicology Soc. **[IO]**, Macclesfield, United Kingdom

British Toy and Hobby Assn. **[IO]**, London, United Kingdom

British Toy Importers Assn. **[★IO]**

British Toy Importers and Distributors Assn. **[★IO]**

British Toymakers Guild **[IO]**, Uckfield, United Kingdom

British Trade Development Off. **[★24241]**

British Trade and Investment Off. **[★24241]**

British Trade Off. at Consulate-General **[24241]**, c/o British Consulate-General, New York, 845 3rd Ave., 9th Fl., New York, NY 10022, (212)745-0200

British Transplantation Soc. **[IO]**, Macclesfield, United Kingdom

British Travel Assn. **[★IO]**

British Travel Assn. **[★24242]**

British Travel and Holiday Assn. **[★24242]**

British Travel and Holiday Assn. **[★IO]**

British Travelgoods and Accessories Assn. **[IO]**, Birmingham, United Kingdom

British Triathlon Assn. **[IO]**, Loughborough, United Kingdom

British Trombone Soc. **[IO]**, Coventry, United Kingdom

British Trout Assn. **[IO]**, Midlothian, United Kingdom

British Trust for Conservation Volunteers **[★IO]**

British Trust for Conservation Volunteers **[IO]**, Doncaster, United Kingdom

British Trust for Ornithology **[IO]**, Thetford, United Kingdom

British Tunnelling Soc. **[IO]**, London, United Kingdom

British Turf and Landscape Irrigation Assn. **[IO]**, Preston, United Kingdom

British Turned-Parts Mfrs. Assn. **[IO]**, Warwick, United Kingdom

British UFO Res. Assn. **[IO]**, London, United Kingdom

British Union for the Abolition of Vivisection **[IO]**, London, United Kingdom

British Universities Film Coun. **[★IO]**

British Universities Film and Video Coun. **[IO]**, London, United Kingdom

British Universities Film and Video Coun. and Soc. for Screen-Based Learning **[IO]**, London, United Kingdom

British Universities Film and Video Coun. and Soc. for Screen-Based Learning **[★IO]**

British Universities Indus. Relations Assn. **[IO]**, Bristol, United Kingdom

British Universities North Am. Club **[8606]**, PO Box 430, Southbury, CT 06488, (203)264-0901

British Urban Regeneration Assn. **[IO]**, London, United Kingdom

British Vacuum Coun. **[IO]**, London, United Kingdom

British Valve and Actuator Assn. **[IO]**, Banbury, United Kingdom

British Valve and Actuator Assn. **[★IO]**

British Vehicle Rental and Leasing Assn. **[IO]**, Amersham, United Kingdom

British Venture Capital Assn. **[IO]**, London, United Kingdom

British Veterinary Assn. **[IO]**, London, United Kingdom

British Veterinary Dental Assn. **[IO]**, Chorley, United Kingdom

British Veterinary Nursing Assn. **[IO]**, Harlow, United Kingdom

British Video Assn. **[IO]**, London, United Kingdom

British Vintage Wireless Soc. **[IO]**, Swindon, United Kingdom

British Violin Making Assn. **[IO]**, Redhill, United Kingdom

British Virgin Islands Amateur Athletic Fed. **[IO]**, Tortola, British Virgin Islands

British Virgin Islands Baseball Fed. **[IO]**, Tortola, British Virgin Islands

---

Reference to "IO" in place of a book number signifies that the association may be found in the 45th edition of International Organizations.

British Virgin Islands Lawn Tennis Assn. [IO], Tortola, British Virgin Islands
British War Veterans of America - Address unknown since 2001.
British Waste Paper Assn. [★IO]
British Water [IO], London, United Kingdom
British Water Indus. Gp. [★IO]
British Water Ski [IO], Chertsey, United Kingdom
British Web Design and Marketing Assn. [IO], London, United Kingdom
British Weight Lifters' Assn. [IO], Newport, United Kingdom
British Wheelchair Sports Found. [★IO]
British Wind Energy Assn. [IO], London, United Kingdom
British Women Pilots' Assn. [IO], Weybridge, United Kingdom
British Wood Preserving and Damp-Proofing Assn. [IO], Derby, United Kingdom
British Wood Pulp Assn. [IO], Oxted, United Kingdom
British Woodworking Fed. [IO], London, United Kingdom
British Wool Marketing Bd. [IO], Bradford, United Kingdom
British Wrestling Assn. [IO], Chesterfield, United Kingdom
British-Yemeni Soc. [IO], London, United Kingdom
BritishAmerican Bus. Inc. [IO], London, United Kingdom
BritishAmerican Bus. Inc. of New York and London [24267], 52 Vanderbilt Ave., 20th Fl., New York, NY 10017, (212)661-4060
Britsh Chem. Distributors and Traders Assn. [★IO]
Brittany
   Amer. Brittany Club [22190]
   Honolulu Japanese Chamber of Commerce [24348]
   U.S. Br. of the Intl. Comm. for the Defense of the Breton Language [9758]
Brittany Club; Amer. [22190]
Brittany Spaniel
   French Brittany Gun Dog Assn. [22270]
   Intl. French Brittany Club of Am. [22288]
Brittany Spaniel Club of Am. [★22190]
Brittle Bone Soc. [IO], Dundee, United Kingdom
Broad Universe [23034], 1121 E Vienna Ave., Milwaukee, WI 53212
Broadband Content Delivery Forum [★3737]
Broadband Services Forum [3737], 48377 Fremont Blvd., Ste. 117, Fremont, CA 94538, (510)492-4025
Broadband Wireless Assn. [IO], Atherstone, United Kingdom
Broadcast Advt. Bur. [★117]
Broadcast Cable Credit Assn. [552], 550 W Frontage Rd., Ste. 3600, Northfield, IL 60093, (847)881-8757
Broadcast Cable Financial Mgt. Assn. [553], 550 W Frontage Rd., Ste. 3600, Northfield, IL 60093, (847)716-7000
Broadcast Credit Assn. [★552]
Broadcast Designer's Assn. [554], 9000 W Sunset Blvd., Ste. 900, Los Angeles, CA 90069, (310)788-7600
Broadcast Designer's Assn. [IO], Los Angeles, CA, United States
Broadcast Designers Assn. Intl. [★IO]
Broadcast Designers Assn. Intl. [★554]
Broadcast Editorial Assn; Natl. [★3136]
Broadcast Educ. Assn. [8001], 1771 N St. NW, Washington, DC 20036-2891, (202)429-3935
Broadcast Education Association [IO], Washington, DC, United States
Broadcast Educators Assn. of Canada [IO], Toronto, ON, Canada
Broadcast Financial Mgt. Assn. [★553]
Broadcast FOCUS [★8002]
Broadcast Found. of College/University Students [8002], 89 Longview Rd., Port Washington, NY 11050, (516)883-0159
Broadcast Music, Inc. [10569], 320 W 57th St., New York, NY 10019-3790, (212)586-2000
Broadcast Pioneers [★555]
Broadcast Promotion and Marketing Executives [★577]

Broadcast Promotion and Marketing Executives [★IO]
Broadcast Rating Coun. [★566]
Broadcast Satellite Assn; Direct [★3754]
Broadcast Tech. Soc; IEEE [7768]
Broadcasters
   Air Force Public Affairs Alumni Assn. [6200]
   Amer. Auto Racing Writers and Broadcasters Assn. [23069]
   Amer. CB Radio Assn. [21493]
   Amer. Fed. of TV and Radio Artists [24022]
   Amer. Radio Assn. [24023]
   Amer. Radio Relay League [21494]
   Amer. Shortwave Listeners Club [21495]
   America's Angel [12140]
   Antique Wireless Assn. [22923]
   ARRL Found. [21496]
   Assn. of North Amer. Radio Clubs [21498]
   Christian TV Mission [19536]
   Collegiate Broadcasters, Inc. [540]
   Commun. Commn. [19537]
   Earth Communications Off. [4547]
   Friends of Old-Time Radio [22924]
   Garden Writers Assn. [22512]
   Intl. Amateur Radio Union [21501]
   Intl. Handicappers' Net [21502]
   Intl. Radio Club of Am. [21503]
   Intl. Webcasting Assn. [2667]
   Iota Beta Sigma [24410]
   Leo Lassen Legacy Proj. [24789]
   Longwave Club of Am. [21505]
   Natl. Assn. Broadcast Employees and Technicians - Communications Workers of Am. [24024]
   Natl. Assn. of Shortwave Broadcasters [541]
   Natl. Broadcasting Soc. - Alpha Epsilon Rho [24411]
   Natl. Lum and Abner Soc. [22925]
   Natl. Religious Broadcasters [19539]
   North Amer. Radio Archives [22926]
   North Amer. Shortwave Assn. [21507]
   Old Old Timers Club [21508]
   Quarter Century Wireless Assn. [21509]
   Radio Club of Am. [22928]
   Radio Collectors of Am. [22929]
   Traffic Directors Guild of Am. [584]
   Vintage Radio and Phonograph Soc. [22931]
   Worldwide Television-FM DX Assn. [21510]
Broadcasters Assn; Amer. Auto Racing Writers and [23069]
Broadcasters Assn; Assoc. Press [★546]
Broadcasters Assn; Catholic [★9761]
Broadcasters Assn; Daytime [★569]
Broadcasters Assn; Economics News [★3164]
Broadcasters Assn; Natl. Black Owned [★568]
Broadcasters Assn; Natl. Radio [★569]
Broadcasters Assn; TV [★569]
Broadcasters' Found. [★555]
Broadcasters' Found. of Am. [555], 7 Lincoln Ave., Greenwich, CT 06830, (203)862-8577
Broadcasters; Natl. Assn. of Radio and TV [★569]
Broadcasters; Org. of Country Radio [★557]
Broadcasters' Promotion Assn. [★577]
Broadcasters' Promotion Assn. [★IO]
Broadcasting
   Acad. of TV Arts and Sciences [542]
   Advanced TV Systems Comm. [543]
   African Coun. for Commun. Educ. [IO]
   Air Force Public Affairs Alumni Assn. [6200]
   Alliance for Children and TV [IO]
   Amer. Auto Racing Writers and Broadcasters Assn. [23069]
   Amer. Cable Assn. [779]
   Amer. CB Radio Assn. [21493]
   Amer. Fed. of TV and Radio Artists [24022]
   Amer. Radio Assn. [24023]
   Amer. Radio Relay League [21494]
   Amer. Shortwave Listeners Club [21495]
   Amer. Sportscasters Assn. [544]
   Amer. Women in Radio and TV [545]
   Antique Wireless Assn. [22923]
   Argentine Cable TV Assn. [IO]
   ARRL Found. [21496]
   Asia-Pacific Broadcasting Union [IO]
   Asia-Pacific Inst. for Broadcasting Development [IO]

Assoc. Press Broadcasters [546]
Assn. of America's Public TV Stations [547]
Assn. of Broadcasting Doctors [IO]
Assn. of Commercial TV in Europe [IO]
Assn. of Estonian Broadcasters [IO]
Assn. of European Radios [IO]
Assn. of Independents in Radio [IO]
Assn. of Independents in Radio [548]
Assn. for Maximum Ser. TV [549]
Assn. of North Amer. Radio Clubs [21498]
Assn. of Radio Indus. and Businesses [IO]
Australian Subscription TV and Radio Assn. [IO]
BKSTS - The Moving Image Soc. [IO]
Black Broadcasters Alliance [550]
Black Coll. Radio Org. [551]
Broadcast Cable Credit Assn. [552]
Broadcast Cable Financial Mgt. Assn. [553]
Broadcast Designer's Assn. [554]
Broadcast Designer's Assn. [IO]
Broadcast Education Association [IO]
Broadcast Educ. Assn. [8001]
Broadcast Educators Assn. of Canada [IO]
Broadcast Found. of College/University Students [8002]
Broadcasters' Found. of Am. [555]
Broadcasting Entertainment Cinematograph and Theatre Union [IO]
Cable and Satellite Broadcasting Assn. of Asia - Hong Kong Off. [IO]
Canadian Assn. of Broadcasters [IO]
Canadian Assn. of Ethnic Radio Broadcasters [IO]
Canadian Assn. of Labour Media [IO]
Canadian Broadcast Standards Coun. [IO]
Canadian Disc Jockey Assn. [IO]
Canadian Media Guild [IO]
Canadian Retransmission Collective [IO]
Caribbean Broadcasting Union [IO]
Catholic Acad. for Commun. Arts Professionals [9761]
Center for Commun. [8003]
Center for Media and Public Affairs [17169]
Christian European Visual Media Assn. [IO]
Christian Media Assn. [20237]
Christian TV Mission [19536]
Citizens Communications Center Proj. of the Inst. for Public Representation [17171]
Citizens for Independent Public Broadcasting [17025]
Coalition Opposing Signal Theft [556]
Collegiate Broadcasters, Inc. [540]
Commercial Radio Australia [IO]
Commonwealth Broadcasting Assn. [IO]
Commun. Commn. [19537]
Community Broadcasting Assn. of Australia [IO]
Community Broadcasting Found. [IO]
Corp. for Public Broadcasting [9762]
Country Radio Broadcasters [557]
CTAM - Cable and Telecommunications Assn. for Marketing [558]
Digital Video Broadcasting [IO]
Earth Communications Off. [4547]
Ecuadorian Broadcasting Assn. [IO]
Educational Broadcasting Corp. [9763]
European Broadcasting Union [IO]
Foreign Press Assn. [3113]
Frequency Coordination Sys. Assn. [IO]
Friends of Canadian Broadcasting [IO]
Friends of Old-Time Radio [22924]
Garden Writers Assn. [22512]
Guild of TV Cameramen [IO]
Guild of Vision Mixers [IO]
Hollywood Radio and TV Soc. [559]
Iberoamerican Assn. of Educational TV [IO]
Intercollegiate Broadcasting Sys. [8004]
Intl. Acad. of Broadcasting [IO]
Intl. Acad. of TV Arts and Sciences [IO]
Intl. Acad. of TV Arts and Sciences [560]
Intl. Amateur Radio Union [21501]
Intl. Assn. of Broadcast Monitors [561]
Intl. Assn. of Broadcast Monitors [IO]
Intl. Assn. of Broadcasting Mfrs. [IO]
Intl. Assn. of Women in Radio and TV [IO]
Intl. Christian Media Commn. [IO]
Intl. Christian Media Commn. [19538]
Intl. DJ Guild [2812]

A star before a book entry number signifies that the name is not listed separately, but is mentioned within the entry.

Intl. Handicappers' Net [21502]
Intl. Nanocasting Assn. [562]
Intl. Press Inst., Amer. Comm. [3123]
Intl. Radio Club of Am. [21503]
Intl. Radio and TV Soc. Found. [563]
Intl. Webcasting Assn. [2667]
Iota Beta Sigma [24410]
Junior Hollywood Radio and TV Soc. [564]
Just Think [18852]
Longwave Club of Am. [21505]
Low Power Radio Assn. [IO]
Manufacturers Radio Frequency Advisory Comm. [565]
Media Inst. of Southern Africa - Namibia [IO]
Media Inst. of Southern Africa - South Africa [IO]
Media Inst. of Southern Africa - Swaziland [IO]
Media Inst. of Southern Africa - Tanzania [IO]
Media Inst. of Southern Africa - Zambia [IO]
Media Rating Coun. [566]
Mediawatch - UK [IO]
Natl. Acad. of TV Arts and Sciences [567]
Natl. Assn. of Black Owned Broadcasters [568]
Natl. Assn. Broadcast Employees and Technicians - Communications Workers of Am. [24024]
Natl. Assn. of Broadcasters [569]
Natl. Assn. of Broadcasters of South Africa [IO]
Natl. Assn. of Farm Broadcasting [570]
Natl. Assn. of Public Affairs Networks [17026]
Natl. Assn. of Shortwave Broadcasters [541]
Natl. Assn. of TV Prog. Executives [571]
National Association of Television Program Executives [IO]
Natl. Black Programming Consortium [9764]
Natl. Broadcast Assn. for Community Affairs [572]
Natl. Broadcasting Soc. - Alpha Epsilon Rho [24411]
Natl. Cable and Telecommunications Assn. [573]
Natl. Cable TV Assn. [IO]
Natl. Cable TV Inst. [574]
Natl. Chamber of Radio and TV Indus. [IO]
Natl. Club Indus. Assn. of Am. [1320]
Natl. Community Radio Forum [IO]
Natl. Fed. of Community Broadcasters [575]
Natl. Lum and Abner Soc. [22925]
Natl. Public Radio [9765]
Natl. Religious Broadcasters [19539]
Natl. Religious Broadcasters [IO]
Natl. Telemedia Coun. [9766]
Natl. Translator Assn. [576]
Native Amer. Public Telecommunications [9767]
NEXUS - Intl. Broadcasting Assn. [IO]
North Amer. Broadcasters Assn. [IO]
North Amer. Radio Archives [22926]
North Amer. Shortwave Assn. [21507]
Norwegian Cable-TV Assn. [IO]
Old Old Timers Club [21508]
Org. of News Ombudsmen [3152]
Pacific Broadcasting Assn. [IO]
Producers Alliance for Cinema and TV [IO]
PROMAX [IO]
PROMAX [577]
Public Broadcasting Mgt. Assn. [578]
Public Broadcasting Ser. [9768]
Public Radio News Directors Incorporated [579]
Quarter Century Wireless Assn. [21509]
Radio Club of Am. [22928]
Radio Collectors of Am. [22929]
Radio-Television Correspondents Assn. [580]
Radio-Television News Directors Assn. [581]
Radio-Television News Directors' Assn. [IO]
Royal TV Soc. [IO]
Sigma Delta Chi Found. [24524]
Soc. of Broadcast Engineers [582]
Society of Broadcast Engineers [IO]
Soc. of TV Lighting Directors [IO]
South African Broadcasting Corp. [IO]
Southern African Digital Broadcasting Assn. [IO]
Spanish World Ministries [20399]
Syndicated Network TV Assn. [120]
Talk Show Hosts.com [IO]
TV Operators Caucus [583]
Traffic Directors Guild of Am. [584]
U.S. Online Disc Jockey Assn. [2825]
Vintage Radio and Phonograph Soc. [22931]
Voice of the Listener and Viewer [IO]

Women in Cable Telecommunications [585]
World Assn. of Community Radio Broadcasters [IO]
World Commun. Assn. [IO]
World Commun. Assn. [8005]
Worldwide Television-FM DX Assn. [21510]
Broadcasting; Assn. for Public [★547]
Broadcasting Consortium; Native Amer. Public [★9767]
Broadcasting Educ; Assn. for Professional [★8001]
Broadcasting Entertainment Cinematograph and Theatre Union [IO], London, United Kingdom
Broadcasting and Entertainment Trades Alliance [★IO]
Broadcasting and Film Commn. [★19537]
Broadcasting Financial Mgt; Inst. of [★553]
Broadcasting Found. of America - Defunct.
Broadcasting Freedom; Campaign for Press and [IO]
Broadcasting Hall of Fame [★569]
Broadcasts; Amer. Coun. for Better [★9766]
Broadway Cares/Equity Fights AIDS [11326], 165 W 46th St., Ste. 1300, New York, NY 10036, (212)840-0770
Broadway Dozen [★11029]
Brody and Eleni Global Fan Club; Official Lane [24953]
Broeders van de Onbevlekte Ontvangenis der Heilige Maagd Maria [★IO]
Broiler Assn; Natl. [★5111]
Broiler Coun; Natl. [★5111]
Broker Mgt. Coun. [1937], c/o Jake Buckner, CPFB, Pres., 5809 Reeds Rd., Shawnee Mission, KS 66202, (913)432-9500
Broker; NAGMR Consumer Products [★2541]
Brokerage Agencies; Natl. Assn. of Independent Life [2211]
Brokerage Assn; Printing [★1786]
Brokerage/Buyers Assn. Intl; Printing [★1786]
Brokerage/Buyers Assn; Printing [1786]
Brokerage Coun; Real Estate [★3306]
Brokerage Institute; Real Estate [★3323]
Brokerage Managers Coun; Real Estate [★3306]
Brokers and Agents - U.S.A; Assn. of Ship [2603]
Brokers and Agents of the West; Insurance [2173]
Brokers of Am; Hotel Motel [★3311]
Brokers of Am; Independent Insurance Agents and [2169]
Brokers; Amer. Hotel and Motel [★3311]
Brokers; Amer. Inst. of Mortgage [★489]
Brokers Assn. of Am; Motel [★3311]
Brokers Assn; Food [★1503]
Brokers Assn; New York Customs [★2309]
Brokers Assn; New York Foreign Freight Forwarders and [★3582]
Brokers Assn; New York/New Jersey Foreign Freight Forwarders and [3582]
Brokers and Forwarders Assn. of Am; Customs [★2309]
Brokers and Forwarders Assn. of Am; Natl. Customs [2309]
Brokers Institute; Real Estate Mgt. [★3323]
Brokers; Intl. Assn. of Independent Info. [★2097]
Brokers; Natl. Assn. of Bus. [★3322]
Brokers; Natl. Assn. of Equip. Leasing [3382]
Brokers; Natl. Assn. of Media [3322]
Brokers; Natl. Assn. of Real Estate [3323]
Brokers; Natl. Assn. of Real Estate Buyer [3324]
Brokers; Natl. Inst. of Farm and Land [★3342]
Bromeliad Identification Center [★22505]
Bromeliad Identification Center [★IO]
Bromeliad Soc. [★IO]
Bromeliad Soc. [★22505]
Bromeliad Soc. Intl. [22505], c/o Joyce Brehm, Pres., 5088 Dawne St., San Diego, CA 92117-1352
Bromeliad Soc. Intl. [IO], San Diego, CA, United States

Bronchoesophagology
Amer. Broncho-Esophagological Assn. [13778]
Canadian Network for Asthma Care [IO]
Esophageal Cancer Awareness Assn. [13822]
Intl. Bronchoesophagological Soc. [13779]
Intl. Bronchoesophagological Soc. [IO]
World Org. for Specialized Stud. on Diseases of the Esophagus [IO]

Bronchoscopic Soc; Amer. [★13778]
Bronte Soc. [IO], Keighley, United Kingdom
Bronze Bearing Inst; Cast [★2008]
Bronze Ingot Industry; Brass and [2701]
Bronze Ingot Institute; Brass and [★2701]
Bronze Ingot Manufacturers; Association of Brass and [★2701]
Bronze Ingot Manufacturers; Brass and [★2701]
Bronze Inst; Cast [2008]
Brookdale Found. [12260], 950 3rd Ave., 19th Fl., New York, NY 10022, (212)308-7355
Brooke Shields Fan Club - Defunct.
Brookings Graduate School of Economics and Govt; Robert [★18424]
Brookings Institution [18424], 1775 Massachusetts Ave. NW, Washington, DC 20036-2188, (202)797-6000
Brookings Tax Policy Center; Urban- [18722]
Brooklyn Clubs Intl. - Defunct.
Brooklyn Coll. of the City Univ. of New York Alumni Assn. [18880], 2900 Bedford Ave., 1239 Ingersoll Hall, Brooklyn, NY 11210, (718)951-5065
Brooklyn Etchers; Soc. of [★9992]
Brooklyn Soc. of Artists [★9493]
Brooks Bird Club [5304], PO Box 4077, Wheeling, WV 26003
Brooks and Dunn Fan Club [24854], PO Box 120669, Nashville, TN 37212-0669, (615)248-6772
Brooks Memorial Fund; Walter R. [★24821]
Brooks, Walter R.
Friends of Freddy [24821]
Brotherhood in Am; Danish [19031]
Brotherhood of Am; Sephardic Jewish [20179]
Brotherhood of the Amer. Lutheran Church [★20224]
Brotherhood of the Chain of Roasters [★22569]
Brotherhood Commn. - Defunct.
Brotherhood of the Footboard [★24176]
Brotherhood of the Footboard [★IO]
Brotherhood Found; Lutheran [★19218]
Brotherhood of the Jungle Cock [23412]
Brotherhood of the Knights of the Vine [5411], 3343 Indus. Dr., Ste. 2, Santa Rosa, CA 95403, (707)579-3781
Brotherhood of Locomotive Engineers, Intl. [★24176]
Brotherhood of Locomotive Engineers, Intl. [★IO]
Brotherhood of Locomotive Engineers and Trainmen, A Division of the Rail Conf. of the Intl. Brotherhood of Teamsters [IO], Cleveland, OH, United States
Brotherhood of Locomotive Engineers and Trainmen, A Division of the Rail Conf. of the Intl. Brotherhood of Teamsters [24176], 1370 Ontario St., Mezzanine, Cleveland, OH 44113-1701, (216)241-2630
Brotherhood of Locomotive Firemen and Enginemen [★24181]
Brotherhood of Magicians; Intl. [22620]
Brotherhood of Maintenance of Way Employees [24177], 20300 Civic Center Dr., Ste. 320, Southfield, MI 48076-4169, (248)948-1010
Brotherhood of Merchant Seamen and Privateers [★21408]
Brotherhood of Motorcycle Campers [★23624]
Brotherhood of Motorcycle Campers [★IO]
Brotherhood Org. of a New Destiny [IO], Los Angeles, CA, United States
Brotherhood Org. of a New Destiny [18608], PO Box 35090, Los Angeles, CA 90035-0090, (323)782-1980
Brotherhood of Painters, Decorators and Paperhangers of Am. [★12082]
Brotherhood of Painters, Decorators and Paperhangers of Am. [★IO]
Brotherhood of Pottery and Allied Workers; Intl. [★24066]
Brotherhood of Railroad Signalmen [24178], 917 Shenandoah Shores Rd., Front Royal, VA 22630-6418, (540)622-6522
Brotherhood of Railroad Trainmen [★24181]
Brotherhood of Railway, Airline and Steamship Clerks, Freight Handlers, Express and Sta. Employees [★24180]
Brotherhood of Railway, Airline and Steamship Clerks, Freight Handlers, Express and Sta. Employees; Carmen Division of the [★24179]
Brotherhood Railway Carmen [★24180]

Brotherhood Railway Carmen of Am. [★24179]
Brotherhood Railway Carmen Division/Transportation Communications Union [24179], c/o Trans. Communications Union, 3 Res. Pl., Rockville, MD 20850, (301)948-4910
Brotherhood Railway Carmen of the U.S. and Canada [★24179]
Brotherhood of Railway and Steamship Clerks, Freight Handlers, Express and Sta. Employees [★24180]
Brotherhood of Saint Andrew [19946], PO Box 632, Ambridge, PA 15003, (724)266-5810
Brotherhood of Saint Andrew in Japan; Amer. Comm. for the [★12418]
Brotherhood of Shoe and Allied Craftsmen [24063]
Brotherhood of Sleeping Car Porters [★24180]
Brotherhood of Traveling Jewelers - Address unknown since 2003.
Brotherhood of Utility Workers of New England [24215]
Brotherhood; Viking [★19461]
Brotherhood of Working Farriers Assn. [1353], c/o Ralph Casey, Pres./Exec. Dir., 14013 E Hwy. 136, Lafayette, GA 30728, (706)397-8047
Brotherhoods; Natl. Fed. of Temple [★20160]
Brotherhoods; North Amer. Fed. of Temple [★20160]
Bros. Big Sisters of Am; Big [11676]
Brother's Brother Found. [12837], 1200 Galveston Ave., Pittsburgh, PA 15233-1604, (412)321-3160
Brother's Brother Found. [IO], Pittsburgh, PA, United States
Bros. of Charity [IO], Rome, Italy
Bros. of Christian Instruction of Saint Gabriel [IO], Rome, Italy
Bros. of the Christian Schools [IO], Rome, Italy
Bros. Conf; Christian [19921]
Bros. Conf; Religious [19707]
Bros. Educ. Assn; Christian [★8060]
Bros. of the Immaculate Conception of the Blessed Virgin Mary [IO], Maastricht, Netherlands
Brother's Keeper; Oper. [★12837]
Bros; Natl. Assn. of Religious [★19707]
Bros; Natl. Educ. Coun. of the Christian [★8060]
Bros. of Our Lady, Mother of Mercy [IO], Tilburg, Netherlands
Bros., and Priest and Brother Associates; Maryknoll Priests, [★19658]
Bros; Regional Educ. Coun. of the Christian [★8060]
Bros. and Sisters in Christ [19767], PO Box 431, Kiln, MS 39556, (228)255-9251
Bros. and Sisters in Christ [IO], Kiln, MS, United States
Bros. and Sisters of Penance [★19616]
Bros. and Sisters of Penance [★19590]
Bros. and Sisters of Penance of St. Francis [19590], 20939 Quadrant Ave. N, Scandia, MN 55073, (651)433-2753
Brothers United for Future Foreskins - Address unknown since 1990.
Brotogeris Soc. Intl. [4194], PO Box 14891, Shawnee Mission, KS 66285-4891
Brotogeris Soc. Intl. [IO], Shawnee Mission, KS, United States
Brough/Nielsen/Wilson/Willson Family Org. [★20810]
Brough/Wilson/Willson Family Org. [20810]
Brougham Owners Assn. [★21602]
Brown Assn. - Address unknown since 1999.
Brown Bag Inst. - Defunct.
Brown Fan Club; Sawyer [★24974]
Brown Intl. Fan Club; Sawyer [24974]
Brown Lung Assn. - Defunct.
Brown Swiss Cattle Breeders Assn. of the U.S.A. [4258], 800 Pleasant St., Beloit, WI 53511-5456, (608)365-4474
Brown Trout Club - Defunct.
Browning Collectors Assn. [22426], 711 Scott St., Covington, KY 41011
Browning Collectors Association [IO], Covington, KY, United States
Browning Fund; Peggy [6362]
Browning Inst. - Defunct.
Brownstone Revival Coalition - Address unknown since 2006.
Brownsville Maritime Assn. [★2595]

Brownsville and Texas Southmost Coll. Alumni Assn; Univ. of Texas at [18938]
Bruce Boxleitner Fan Club - Address unknown since 2001.
Bruce Boxleitner's Official Fan Club [24734], PO Box 5513, Sherman Oaks, CA 91403
Bruce Intl., USA Br. [10952], c/o Polly Tilford, Sec., 5561 Earl Young Rd., Bloomington, IN 47408
Bruce Trail Assn. [IO], Hamilton, ON, Canada
Bruckner Soc. of America - Defunct.
Bruderhof Communities [20481], Woodcrest Bruderhof, 2032 Rte. 213, Rifton, NY 12471, (845)658-8351
Brunei Amateur Athletic Assn. [IO], Bandar Seri Begawan, Brunei Darussalam
Brunei Amateur Softball and Baseball Assn. [IO], Tutong, Brunei Darussalam
Brunei Darussalam Tennis Assn. [IO], Bandar Seri Begawan, Brunei Darussalam
Brunei Natl. Badminton Assn. [IO], Bandar Seri Begawan, Brunei Darussalam
Brunei Squash Rackets Assn. [IO], Berakas, Brunei Darussalam
Brush Mfrs. Assn; Amer. [1968]
Brush Owner's Assn. - Defunct.
Brush Painting; Amer. Artists of Chinese [9538]
Brush; Pen and [9521]
Brussels Griffon
   Amer. Brussels Griffon Assn. [22191]
Brussels Griffon Assn; Amer. [22191]
Brussels Sprouts Program Comm. - Defunct.
Brutus Defense Comm; Dennis [★17740]
Bryan Adams BadNews [IO], Vancouver, BC, Canada
Bryan Adams Fan Club [★IO]
Bryggeriforeningen [★IO]
Bryological and Lichenological Soc; Amer. [6621]
BSHAA [★IO]
BTCV [IO], Doncaster, United Kingdom
BTCV Scotland [IO], Edinburgh, United Kingdom
Buccale et Maxillo-Faciale; Assn. Internationale de Chirurgie [★15736]
Buccaneer Natl. Class Assn. - Address unknown since 1999.
Buchanan Found; James [★11126]
Buchanan Found. for the Preservation of Wheatland; James [11126]
Bucher Workmen of North Am; Amalgamated Meat Cutters and [★24061]
Buchereiverband Osterreichs [★IO]
Buck Birthplace Found; Pearl S. [9699]
Buck Found; Pearl S. [★11646]
Buck Jones Western Corral No. 1 - Address unknown since 2007.
Buck Owens Fan Club - Defunct.
Bucket Mfrs. Bur. - Defunct.
Buckeye DeSoto Club [★21731]
Buckle Assn. of New York; Covered Button and [★2836]
Buckminster Fuller Found; Friends of [★11104]
Buckminster Fuller Inst. [11104], 181 N 11th St., Ste. 402, Brooklyn, NY 11211, (718)290-9280
Buckskin Horse Assn; Intl. [4896]
Buckskin Horse Registry; Intl. [★4896]
Buckskin Registry Assn. [★4813]
Buckskin Registry Assn; Amer. [4813]
Buddhist
   Amer. Buddhist Assn. [19540]
   Amer. Buddhist Movement [19541]
   Amer. Buddhist Stud. Center [19542]
   British Shingon Buddhist Assn. [IO]
   Buddhist Churches of Am. Fed. of Buddhist Women's Associations [19543]
   Buddhist Churches of Canada [IO]
   Buddhist Mission [IO]
   Buddhist Publication Soc. [IO]
   Buddhist Soc. for Compassionate Wisdom [IO]
   Buddhist Soc. UK [IO]
   Buddhist Text Translation Soc. [19544]
   Buddhist Vihara [19545]
   Burma-America Buddhist Assn. [19546]
   Cambodian Buddhist Soc. [9769]
   Cambodian Buddhist Soc. [IO]
   Cambridge Buddhist Assn. [19547]
   Church Universal and Triumphant [19462]

   Dharma Realm Buddhist Assn. [19548]
   European Buddhist Union [IO]
   First Zen Inst. of Am. [19549]
   Found. for the Preservation of the Mahayana Tradition [19550]
   Friends of the Western Buddhist Order [19551]
   Friends of the Western Buddhist Order [IO]
   Hong Kong Buddhist Assn. [IO]
   Intl. Assn. of Buddhist Stud. [IO]
   Intl. Zen Assn. [IO]
   Jewel Heart [19552]
   Kunzang Palyul Choling [19553]
   Lotus Lantern Intl. Buddhist Center [IO]
   Mid-America Buddhist Assn. [19554]
   Nichiren Buddhist Assn. of Am. [19555]
   Pali Text Soc. [IO]
   Soka Gakkai International-United States of Am. [IO]
   Soka Gakkai International-United States of Am. [19556]
   Supreme Master Ching Hai Meditation Assn. [19557]
   Supreme Master Ching Hai Meditation Association [IO]
   Western Young Buddhist League [19558]
   World Fellowship of Buddhists [IO]
   Zen Stud. Soc. [19559]
Buddhist Acad; Amer. [★19542]
Buddhist Assn; Sino-American [★19548]
Buddhist Center of the U.S.A. - Defunct.
Buddhist Churches of Am. Fed. of Buddhist Women's Associations [19543], c/o Buddhist Churches of Am., 1710 Octavia St., San Francisco, CA 94109, (415)776-5600
Buddhist Churches of Canada [IO], Richmond, BC, Canada
Buddhist Coun. for Refugee Rescue and Resettlement - Defunct.
Buddhist Mission [IO], Budapest, Hungary
Buddhist Peace Fellowship [IO], Berkeley, CA, United States
Buddhist Peace Fellowship [18193], PO Box 3470, Berkeley, CA 94703, (510)655-6169
Buddhist Publication Soc. [IO], Kandy, Sri Lanka
Buddhist Soc. of Am. [★19549]
Buddhist Soc. for Compassionate Wisdom [IO], Toronto, ON, Canada
Buddhist Soc. UK [IO], London, United Kingdom
Buddhist Text Translation Soc. [19544], c/o Intl. Translation Inst., 1777 Murchison Dr., Burlingame, CA 94010-4504, (415)332-6221
Buddhist Vihara [19545], 5017 16th St. NW, Washington, DC 20011, (202)723-0773
Buddhist Women's Associations; Natl. Fed. of [★19543]
Buddhists Concerned for Animals - Defunct.
Buddies of the Hour Glass Assn; Friends and [21299]
Buddy Clark Fan Club - Defunct.
Buddy DeFranco Appreciation Soc. - Address unknown since 1989.
Buddy Holly Memorial Soc. - Address unknown since 2008.
Buddy Max Fan Club - Address unknown since 1994.
Budgerigar and Foreign Bird Soc. [IO], Markham, ON, Canada
Budgerigar Soc; Amer. [21836]
Budget; Comm. for a Responsible Fed. [18405]
Budget Furniture Forum [★1704]
Budget Officers; Natl. Assn. of State [6207]
Budget and Policy Priorities; Center on [18403]
Budget and Prog. Anal; Amer. Assn. for [6201]
Budget Proj; Defense [★18075]
Budi aktivna. Budi emancipirana [★IO]
Buelingo Beef Cattle Soc. [4259], 15904 W Warren Rd., Warren, IL 61087-9601, (815)745-2311
Buff and Polishing Wheel Mfrs. Assn. - Defunct.
Buffalo Assn; Amer. [★4139]
Buffalo Assn; Amer. Water [4996]
Buffalo Bill Historical Center [11105], 720 Sheridan Ave., Cody, WY 82414-3428, (307)587-4771
Buffalo Sabres Booster Club [25000], PO Box 1065, Cheektowaga, NY 14225
Buffers, Platers and Allied Workers Intl. Union; Metal Polishers, [★24021]

A star before a book entry number signifies that the name is not listed separately, but is mentioned within the entry.

Buffoons of America - Address unknown since 1985.

Buford's Boosters Fan Club - Address unknown since 1995.

Bugatti Club; Amer. **[21569]**

Bugatti Owners Club - Address unknown since 1995.

Bugday Assn. for Supporting Ecological Living **[IO]**, Istanbul, Turkey

Buick Car Club of Australia in NSW **[IO]**, Merrylands, Australia

Buick Club; 1937-1938 **[21552]**

Buick Club of Am. **[21599]**, PO Box 360775, Columbus, OH 43236-0775, (614)472-3939

Buick Collector's Club of America - Defunct.

Buick Compact Club - Defunct.

Buick GS Club of Am. **[21600]**, 625 Pine Point Cir., Valdosta, GA 31602, (229)244-0577

Buick Registry; Nineteen Thirty-Two **[21741]**

Buick Skylark Club; 1953-54 **[21554]**

Buick St. Rod Assn. **[22919]**, c/o Carter G. Hampton, Sr., Pres., 824 Kay Cir., Chattanooga, TN 37421-4218

Builders of Am; Golf Course **[★3662]**

Builders Assn. of Am; Golf Course **[3662]**

Builders Assn; Amer. Mold **[1996]**

Builders Assn; Amer. Road **[★6313]**

Builders Assn; Amer. Road and Trans. **[6313]**

Builders Assn; Golf Course **[★3662]**

Builders Assn; Natl. Frame **[1047]**

Builders Assn. of North Am; Log Home **[1031]**

Builder's Assn. of North Am; Log House **[★1031]**

Builders Assn; North Amer. Sys. **[★3706]**

Builders Assn; Systems **[★2528]**

Builders Assn; Wire Machinery **[★2079]**

Builders and Contractors; Assoc. **[1004]**

Builders Council; National Commercial **[★1035]**

Builders Exchange Executives; Intl. **[1024]**

The Builders Exchange Network **[★1024]**

The Builders Exchange Network **[★IO]**

Builders' Hardware Assn; Natl. **[★1821]**

Builders Hardware Mfrs. Assn. **[1819]**, 355 Lexington Ave., 15th Fl., New York, NY 10017, (212)297-2122

Builders and Integrators; NASBA - The Assn. of Sys. **[3706]**

Builders Merchants Fed. **[IO]**, London, United Kingdom

Builders; Natl. Assn. of Home **[1035]**

Builders of North Am; Monument **[2785]**

Builders and Repairers Assn; Amer. Boat **[2568]**

Builders of the U.S; Natl. Assn. of Home **[★1035]**

Builders Without Borders **[12307]**, 119 Main St., Kingston, NM 88042, (505)895-5400

Builders Without Borders **[IO]**, Kingston, NM, United States

Building and Allied Trades' Union **[IO]**, Dublin, Ireland

Building Assn; Energy Efficient **[★619]**

Building Codes

Assn. of Major City/County Building Officials **[5547]**

Building Officials and Code Administrators Intl. **[5548]**

Building Officials and Code Administrators Intl. **[IO]**

Constr. Specifications Canada **[IO]**

Coun. on Tall Buildings and Urban Habitat **[6474]**

EIFS Indus. Members Assn. **[618]**

European Union of Agreement **[IO]**

Expanded Shale Clay and Slate Inst. **[621]**

Intl. Assn. of Plumbing and Mech. Officials **[5549]**

Intl. Assn. of Plumbing and Mech. Officials **[IO]**

Intl. Code Coun. **[IO]**

Intl. Code Coun. **[5550]**

Intl. Conf. of Building Officials **[5551]**

Intl. Conf. of Building Officials **[IO]**

Natl. Conf. of States on Building Codes and Standards **[5552]**

Natl. Standard Plumbing Code Comm. **[5553]**

New Buildings Inst. **[5554]**

Southern Building Code Cong. Intl. **[5555]**

Southern Building Code Cong. Intl. **[IO]**

Building Collectors Soc; Souvenir **[22115]**

Building and Constr. Trades Dept. - AFL-CIO **[24025]**, 815 16th St., Ste. 600, Washington, DC 20006, (202)347-1461

Building and Constr. Trades Dept. - Canadian Off. **[IO]**, Ottawa, ON, Canada

Building Contractors and Erectors Assn; Metal **[2528]**

Building Contractors Fed. **[★IO]**

Building Cost Info. Ser. of the Royal Institution of Chartered Surveyors **[IO]**, London, United Kingdom

Building Dealers Assn; Metal **[★2528]**

Building Design; Amer. Inst. of **[6464]**

Building Designers Assn. of Australia **[IO]**, Strathpine, Australia

Building Division of the Soc. of the Plastics Indus; Thermoplastic Exterior **[★685]**

Building Fund Commn; Amer. Church **[★19952]**

Building Fund; Episcopal Church **[19952]**

Building Futures Coun. **[606]**, 2300 Wilson Blvd., Ste. 400, Arlington, VA 22201, (703)837-5365

Building Granite Quarries Assn; Natl. **[3697]**

Building Industries

ADSC: The Intl. Assn. of Found. Drilling **[1000]**

Affordable Housing Tax Credit Coalition **[586]**

Air Barrier Assn. of Am. **[587]**

Alliance of Deep Found. Testing Professionals **[6650]**

Amer. Architectural Manufacturers Assn. **[588]**

Amer. Composites Mfrs. Assn. **[589]**

Amer. Concrete Pumping Assn. **[914]**

Amer. Engg. Alliance **[6985]**

Amer. Fence Assn. **[938]**

Amer. Fiberboard Assn. **[590]**

American Fiberboard Association **[IO]**

Amer. Inst. of Building Design **[6464]**

Amer. Rock Mechanics Assn. **[3690]**

Amer. Shipbuilding Assn. **[591]**

Amer. Soc. for Composites **[6651]**

Amer. Soc. of Home Inspectors **[592]**

Architectural Cladding Assn. **[IO]**

Architectural Glass and Metal Contractors Assn. **[IO]**

Architectural Precast Assn. **[917]**

Architectural and Specialist Door Mfrs. Assn. **[IO]**

Architectural Woodwork Inst. **[593]**

Asphalt Emulsion Manufacturers Assn. **[594]**

Asphalt Inst. **[595]**

Asphalt Inst. **[IO]**

Asphalt Pavement Alliance **[596]**

Asphalt Recycling and Reclaiming Assn. **[3987]**

Asphalt Roofing Manufacturers Assn. **[597]**

Assoc. Air Balance Coun. **[598]**

Assoc. Constr. Distributors Intl. **[599]**

Assoc. Constr. Distributors Intl. **[IO]**

Assoc. Gen. Contractors of Am. **[1005]**

Assoc. Specialty Contractors **[1006]**

Assn. of Building Component Mfrs. **[IO]**

Assn. of Ceramic Tile Mfrs. of Spain **[IO]**

Assn. for Env. Conscious Building **[IO]**

Assn. of European Building Surveyors and Constr. Experts **[IO]**

Assn. of Licensed Architects **[290]**

Assn. of Millwork Distributors **[600]**

Assn. of Modified Asphalt Producers **[601]**

Assn. for Proj. Safety **[IO]**

Assn. of Sealant Applicators **[IO]**

Assn. of Tank and Cistern Mfrs. **[IO]**

Assn. of the Wall and Ceiling Indus. - Intl. **[IO]**

Assn. of the Wall and Ceiling Indus. - Intl. **[602]**

Assn. of Welding Distributors **[IO]**

Australian Inst. of Building **[IO]**

Automated Builders Consortium **[603]**

Automatic Door Suppliers Assn. **[IO]**

B.C. Road Builders and Heavy Constr. Assn. **[IO]**

Bitumen Waterproofing Assn. **[IO]**

Brick Development Assn. **[IO]**

Brick Indus. Assn. **[604]**

Bridge Grid Flooring Mfrs. Assn. **[605]**

Bridge Joint Assn. **[IO]**

British Blind and Shutter Assn. **[IO]**

British Constructional Steelwork Assn. **[IO]**

British Flue and Chimney Mfrs'. Assn. **[IO]**

Builders Merchants Fed. **[IO]**

Building Cost Info. Ser. of the Royal Institution of Chartered Surveyors **[IO]**

Building Designers Assn. of Australia **[IO]**

Building Futures Coun. **[606]**

Building Material Dealers Assn. **[607]**

Building Materials Reuse Assn. **[608]**

Building Owners and Managers Assn. Intl. **[3301]**

Building Res. Est. **[IO]**

Building Societies Assn. - England **[IO]**

Building Soc. **[IO]**

Building Systems Councils of NAHB **[2524]**

Building Trades Employers' Assn. **[609]**

Canadian Assn. for Composite Structures and Materials **[IO]**

Canadian Condominium Inst. **[IO]**

Canadian Constr. Assn. **[IO]**

Canadian Farm Builders Assn. **[IO]**

Canadian Home Builders' Assn. **[IO]**

Canadian Inst. of Steel Constr. **[IO]**

Canadian Roofing Contractors Assn. **[IO]**

Canadian Sheet Steel Building Inst. **[IO]**

Canadian Steel Door Mfrs. Assn. **[IO]**

Canadian Window and Door Mfrs. Assn. **[IO]**

Carpenters' Company **[IO]**

Ceilings and Interior Systems Constr. Assn. **[1008]**

Cellulose Insulation Manufacturers Assn. **[610]**

Cement Employers Assn. **[920]**

Cementitious Slag Makers Assn. **[IO]**

Ceramic Tile Distributors Assn. **[611]**

Chain Link Fence Manufacturers Inst. **[1362]**

Chartered Inst. of Building **[IO]**

Clay Roof Tile Coun. **[IO]**

Common Ground Alliance **[12958]**

Composite Lumber Mfrs. Assn. **[1642]**

Concrete Block Assn. **[IO]**

Concrete Reinforcing Steel Inst. **[612]**

Concrete Repair Assn. **[IO]**

Concrete Sawing and Drilling Assn. **[923]**

Concrete Tile Manufacturers Assn. **[924]**

Confed. of Intl. Contractors' Associations **[IO]**

Consortium of European Building Control **[IO]**

Constr. Assn. of Korea **[IO]**

Constr. Confed. **[IO]**

Constr. Employers Assn. **[613]**

Constr. Employers' Fed. **[IO]**

Constr. Financial Mgt. Assn. **[1012]**

Constr. Fixings Assn. **[IO]**

Constr. Owners Assn. of Am. **[614]**

Constr. Products Assn. **[IO]**

Continental Automated Buildings Assn. **[IO]**

Cool Roof Rating Coun. **[615]**

Cooling Tech. Inst. **[616]**

Coun. on Tall Buildings and Urban Habitat **[6474]**

Danish Assn. for Prdt. Modelling **[IO]**

Danish Constr. Assn. **[IO]**

Deep Foundations Inst. **[1013]**

Design-Build Inst. of Am. **[617]**

Door and Hardware Fed. **[IO]**

Draught Proofing Advisory Assn. **[IO]**

Drilling and Sawing Assn. **[IO]**

Dry Stone Walling Assn. of Great Britain **[IO]**

EFNARC **[IO]**

EIDD - Design for All Europe **[IO]**

EIFS Indus. Members Assn. **[618]**

Energy and Environmental Building Assn. **[619]**

Engg. Constr. Indus. Assn. **[IO]**

Environmental Info. Assn. **[620]**

European Assn. for Prdt. and Process Modelling in the Building Indus. **[IO]**

European Ceramic Tile Mfrs. Assn. **[IO]**

European Constr. Indus. Fed. **[IO]**

European Fed. of Associations of Insulation Contractors **[IO]**

European Fed. of Building Societies **[IO]**

European Fed. of Found. Contractors **[IO]**

European Garage Equip. Assn. **[IO]**

European Mortar Indus. Org. **[IO]**

European Network of Building Res. Institutes **[IO]**

European Phenolic Foam Assn. **[IO]**

European Tech. Contractors Comm. for the Constr. Indus. **[IO]**

European Tile and Brick Producers Fed. **[IO]**

European Union of Developers and House Builders **[IO]**

Expanded Shale Clay and Slate Inst. **[621]**

Fed. Natl. Assn. of the German Brick and Tile Indus. **[IO]**

Fed. of European Window and Curtain Wall Mfrs. Associations **[IO]**

Reference to "IO" in place of a book number signifies that the association may be found in the 45th edition of International Organizations.

Fed. of Master Builders [IO]
Fed. of Piling Specialists [IO]
Fed. of Plastering and Drywall Contractors [IO]
Fencing Contractors Assn. [IO]
FeRFA Resin Flooring Assn. [IO]
Finishing Contractors Assn. [622]
Finnish Asphalt Assn. [IO]
First Nations Natl. Building Officers Assn. [IO]
Flat Roofing Alliance [IO]
Floor Installation Association of North America [IO]
Floor Installation Assn. of North Am. [623]
Found. of the Wall and Ceiling Indus. [624]
Garage Equip. Assn. [IO]
Gen. Building Contractors Assn. [625]
German Prefab. Constr. Assn. [IO]
Glazing Indus. Code Comm. [626]
Hardwood Coun. [4056]
HAVi [6513]
Healthy Building Network [4629]
Home Builders Inst. [627]
Homeowners Against Deficient Dwellings [12314]
House Builders Fed. [IO]
Hungarian Sci. Soc. for Building [IO]
Indian Plumbing Assn. [IO]
Indus. Union of Marine and Ship Building Workers of Am. [24125]
Inst. of Carpenters [IO]
Inst. of Plumbing - Australia [IO]
Inst. of Plumbing and Heating Engg. [IO]
Inst. of Roofing [IO]
Inst. of Vitreous Enamellers [IO]
Insulated Render and Cladding Assn. [IO]
Insulated Steel Door Inst. [628]
Insulating Concrete Form Assn. [925]
Intl. Alliance for Interoperability [7018]
Intl. Assn. for Bridge Maintenance and Safety [538]
Intl. Assn. of Building Services Contractors [IO]
Intl. Assn. for the Retractable Awning Industry [IO]
Intl. Assn. for the Retractable Awning Industry [629]
Intl. Brick Collectors' Assn. [22048]
Intl. Builders Exchange Executives [1024]
Intl. Building Performance Simulation Assn. [6652]
International Building Performance Simulation Association [IO]
Intl. Cast Polymer Assn. [IO]
Intl. Cast Polymer Assn. [630]
Intl. Certified Floorcovering Installers Assn. [1025]
Intl. Door Assn. [631]
Intl. Door Assn. [IO]
Intl. Fed. of Asian and Western Pacific Contractors' Associations [IO]
Intl. Fed. for the Roofing Trade [IO]
Intl. Grooving and Grinding Assn. [928]
Intl. Playground Contractors Assn. [1028]
Intl. Slurry Surfacing Assn. [632]
Intl. Slurry Surfacing Assn. [IO]
Intl. Soc. of Coating Sci. and Tech. [6705]
Intl. Union of Building Centres [IO]
International Window Film Association [IO]
Intl. Window Film Assn. [633]
Intervention and Coiled Tubing Assn. [7512]
Irish Home Builders Assn. [IO]
Italian Trade Commn. [634]
Lead Contractors Assn. [IO]
Log Home Builders Assn. of North Am. [1031]
Log Homes Coun. [2525]
Lumber and Building Materials Assn. of Ontario [IO]
Manufactured Housing Inst. [2527]
Maple Flooring Manufacturers Assn. [635]
Maple Flooring Manufacturers Association [IO]
Master Builders Assn. - Australian Capital Territory [IO]
Master Builders Assn. - Malaysia [IO]
Master Builders Assn. - New South Wales [IO]
Master Builders Assn. - South Australia [IO]
Master Builders Assn. - Tasmania [IO]
Master Builders Assn. - Victoria [IO]
Master Builders Assn. - Western Australia [IO]
Master Builders Australia [IO]
Master Plumbers and Mech. Services Assn. of Australia [IO]

Materials and Methods Standards Assn. [636]
Mech. Contractors Assn. of Canada [IO]
Metal Building Contractors and Erectors Assn. [2528]
Metal Building Manufacturers Assn. [637]
Metal Buildings Inst. [8006]
Metal Constr. Assn. [638]
Metal Framing Manufacturers Assn. [639]
Modular Building Systems Coun. [2529]
Modular and Portable Building Assn. [IO]
Mortar Indus. Assn. [IO]
Natl. Acad. of Building Inspection Engineers [640]
Natl. Alliance for Fair Contracting [24030]
Natl. Apartment Assn. [3317]
Natl. Asphalt Pavement Assn. [641]
Natl. Assn. of Building Cooperatives Soc. [IO]
Natl. Assn. of Certified Home Inspectors [2121]
Natl. Assn. of Church Design Builders [831]
Natl. Assn. of Independent Resurfacers [642]
Natl. Assn. of Miscellaneous, Ornamental and Architectural Products Contractors [1037]
Natl. Assn. of the Remodeling Indus. [643]
Natl. Assn. of State Contractors Licensing Agencies [1040]
Natl. Assn. of Store Fixture Manufacturers [644]
Natl. Assn. of the Swedish Joinery Factories [IO]
Natl. Assn. of Tower Erectors [6653]
Natl. Assn. of Waterproofing and Structural Repair Contractors [645]
Natl. Concrete Masonry Assn. [929]
Natl. Coun. of Acoustical Consultants [646]
Natl. Coun. of Erectors, Fabricators and Riggers [1042]
Natl. Coun. of the Housing Indus. [647]
Natl. Dome Coun. [2530]
Natl. Fed. of Builders [IO]
Natl. Fed. of Demolition Contractors [IO]
Natl. Fed. of Roofing Contractors [IO]
Natl. Fenestration Rating Coun. [648]
Natl. Home Improvement Coun. [IO]
Natl. House-Building Coun. [IO]
Natl. Housing Endowment [649]
Natl. Inst. of Building Sciences [6838]
Natl. Insulation Assn. [1048]
Natl. Multi Housing Coun. [3332]
Natl. One Coat Stucco Assn. [650]
Natl. Pavement Contractors Assn. [651]
Natl. Precast Concrete Assn. [930]
Natl. Ready Mixed Concrete Assn. [931]
Natl. Register of Warranted Builders [IO]
Natl. Restaurant Assn. Multi-Unit Architects, Engineers and Constr. Officers [1050]
Natl. Slag Assn. [652]
Natl. Soc. of Master Thatchers [IO]
Natl. Specialist Contractors Coun. [IO]
Natl. Steel Bridge Alliance [539]
Natl. Sunroom Assn. [653]
Natl. Town Builders' Assn. [654]
Natl. Utility Locating Contractors Assn. [1055]
Natl. Wood Flooring Assn. [655]
National Wood Flooring Association [IO]
New Zealand Green Building Coun. [IO]
New Zealand Masonry Trades Registration Bd. [IO]
Newcastle Master Builders Assn. [IO]
NOFMA: The Wood Flooring Manufacturers Assn. [656]
North Amer. Assn. of Floor Covering Distributors [657]
North Amer. Building Material Distribution Assn. [658]
North Amer. Insulation Manufacturers Assn. [659]
North Amer. Laminate Flooring Assn. [660]
North Amer. Laminate Flooring Assn. [IO]
Panelized Building Systems Coun. [2531]
Pipe Jacking Assn. [IO]
Plastics Window Fed. [IO]
Plumbers' Company [IO]
Polyisocyanurate Insulation Mfrs. Assn. [661]
Porcelain Enamel Inst. [662]
Post-Tensioning Inst. [663]
Power Fastenings Assn. [IO]
Precast/Prestressed Concrete Inst. [934]
Professional Union of the Building Sector [IO]
Professional Women in Constr. [1062]

Proj. Exports Promotion Coun. of India [IO]
Queensland Master Builders Assn. [IO]
Registered Master Builders Fed. [IO]
Residential Constr. Workers' Assn. [948]
Residential Energy Services Network [664]
Resilient Floor Covering Inst. [665]
Road Surface Dressing Assn. [IO]
Roof Consultants Inst. [1063]
Roofing Indus. Comm. on Weather Issues [666]
Roofing Indus. Educational Inst. [1064]
Rubber Pavements Assn. [667]
Rubber Pavements Assn. [IO]
Safety Glazing Certification Coun. [668]
Scaffold Indus. Assn. [669]
Scaffolding, Shoring and Forming Inst. [670]
Scottish Building [IO]
Scottish Building Contractors Assn. [IO]
Scottish Building Employers' Fed. [IO]
Scottish Master Wrights and Builders Assn. [IO]
Scottish and Northern Ireland Plumbing Employers' Fed. [IO]
Sheet Metal Industry Promotion Plan [1065]
Singapore Contractors Assn. Ltd. [IO]
Single Ply Roofing Assn. [IO]
Slag Cement Assn. [935]
Soc. of Building Sci. Educators [8363]
South Africa Stainless Steel Development Assn. [IO]
Souvenir Building Collectors Soc. [22115]
Steel Constr. Inst. [IO]
Steel Deck Inst. [671]
Steel Door Inst. [672]
Steel Erectors Assn. of Am. [6839]
Steel Framing Alliance [2731]
Steel Joist Inst. [673]
Steel Truss and Component Assn. [2733]
Steel Window Assn. [IO]
Steel Window Inst. [674]
Structural Bd. Assn. [IO]
Structural Insulated Panel Assn. [675]
Stucco Manufacturers Assn. [676]
Submersible Wastewater Pump Assn. [677]
Sump and Sewage Pump Mfrs. Assn. [678]
Sump and Sewage Pump Manufacturers Association [IO]
Sustainable Buildings Indus. Coun. [7682]
Swedish Assn. of Door and Shutter Suppliers [IO]
Swedish Chimney Sweep Masters Assn. [IO]
Swedish Flooring Trade Assn. [IO]
Tech. Center for Clay, Tiles, and Bricks [IO]
Tesla Engine Builders Assn. [679]
Thermal Insulation Mfrs. and Suppliers Assn. [IO]
The Tile Assn. [IO]
Tile Coun. of North Am. [680]
Tile Roofing Inst. [681]
Timber Frame Bus. Coun. [682]
Truss Plate Inst. [683]
Turkish Contractors Assn. [IO]
UK Timber Frame Assn. [IO]
US Green Building Coun. [684]
Value Engg. Soc. Intl. [7052]
Vinyl Siding Inst. [685]
Welders Without Borders [7850]
Window and Door Manufacturers Assn. [686]
Wire Reinforcement Inst. [687]
Women Constr. Owners and Executives, U.S.A. [1068]
Women and Manual Trades [IO]
Wood Moulding and Millwork Producers Association [IO]
Wood Moulding and Millwork Producers Assn. [688]
Wood Truss Coun. of Am. [689]
World Fed. of Building Ser. Contractors [2479]
Building Indus. Fed. South Africa [★IO]
Building Maintenance Contractors Assn. of Canada [IO], Montreal, QC, Canada
Building Mfrs; Natl. Assn. of [★2524]
Building Material Assn; Western [1629]
Building Material Dealers Assn. [607], 12540 SW Main St., Ste. 200, Tigard, OR 97223-6198, (503)624-0561
Building Material Dealers Assn; Natl. Lumber and [1653]
Building Material Exhibitors Assn. - Defunct.

A star before a book entry number signifies that the name is not listed separately, but is mentioned within the entry.

Building Materials Fed. [IO], Dublin, Ireland
Building Materials Reuse Assn. [608], 545 Ridge Ave., State College, PA 16803, (800)990-2672
Building Museum; Natl. [6477]
Building Network; Natl. Community [11786]
Building Officials; Assn. of Major City [★5547]
Building Officials and Code Administrators Intl. [5548], c/o Intl. Code Coun., Chicago District Off., 4051 W Flossmoor Rd., Country Club Hills, IL 60478, (888)422-7233
Building Officials and Code Administrators Intl. [IO], Country Club Hills, IL, United States
Building Officials Conf. of Am. [★IO]
Building Officials Conf. of Am. [★5548]
Building Officials Conf; Pacific Coast [★5551]
Building Officials; Natl. Assn. of School [★7892]
Building Operators; Natl. Uniform Certification of [2472]
Building Owners Fed. of Mutual Insurance - Defunct.
Building Owners and Managers Assn. Intl. [3301], 1201 New York Ave. NW, Ste. 300, Washington, DC 20005-3966, (202)408-2662
Building Owners and Managers Assn. Intl. [IO], Washington, DC, United States
Building Owners and Managers Inst. Intl. [9027], 1521 Ritchie Hwy., Arnold, MD 21012, (800)235-2664
Building Owners and Managers; Natl. Assn. of [★3301]
Building Professionals' Consortium [IO], Winnipeg, MB, Canada
Building Prog; Adopt a [★11842]
Building Res. Bd. - Defunct.
Building Res. Coun. [7960], c/o School of Architecture, Univ. of Illinois at Urbana-Champaign, Coll. of Fine and Applied Arts, 117 Temple Hoyne Buell Hall, 611 Lorado Taft Dr., MC-621, Champaign, IL 61820, (217)333-1330
Building Res. Est. [IO], Watford, United Kingdom
Building Sciences; Natl. Inst. of [6838]
Building Ser. Contractors Assn. Intl. [2459], 401 N Michigan Ave., Ste. 2200, Chicago, IL 60611-4267, (312)321-5167
Building Ser. Contractors Assn. Intl. [IO], Chicago, IL, United States
Building Ser. Contractors; Natl. Assn. of [★2459]
Building Ser. Employees' Intl. Union [★24189]
Building Ser. Employees' Intl. Union [★IO]
Building Services Res. and Info. Assn. [IO], Bracknell, United Kingdom
Building Societies Assn. - England [IO], London, United Kingdom
Building Soc. [IO], Copenhagen, Denmark
Building Stone Inst. [3692], 551 Tollgate Rd., Ste. C, Elgin, IL 60123, (847)695-0170
Building Systems Coun; Modular [2529]
Building Systems Coun; Panelized [2531]
Building Systems Councils of NAHB [2524], c/o Natl. Assn. of Home Builders, 1201 15th St. NW, Washington, DC 20005, (202)266-8200
Building Systems Industry Forum - Defunct.
Building Trades
  ACV - Bouw en Industrie [IO]
  ADSC: The Intl. Assn. of Found. Drilling [1000]
  Air Barrier Assn. of Am. [587]
  Alliance of Deep Found. Testing Professionals [6650]
  Asphalt Pavement Alliance [596]
  Assoc. Gen. Contractors of Am. [1005]
  Assoc. Specialty Contractors [1006]
  Assn. of Modified Asphalt Producers [601]
  Automated Builders Consortium [603]
  Building and Constr. Trades Dept. - AFL-CIO [24025]
  Building and Constr. Trades Dept. - Canadian Off. [IO]
  Building Futures Coun. [606]
  Building Materials Reuse Assn. [608]
  Building Systems Councils of NAHB [2524]
  Building Trades Employers' Assn. [609]
  Ceilings and Interior Systems Constr. Assn. [1008]
  Constr. Financial Mgt. Assn. [1012]
  Constr., Forestry, Mining and Energy Union [IO]
  Constr. Indus. Trade Alliance [IO]

Constr. Specifications Inst. [6836]
Cool Roof Rating Coun. [615]
Deep Foundations Inst. [1013]
Employer Assn. Gp. [2555]
Expanded Shale Clay and Slate Inst. [621]
Fed. of Danish Painting Contractors [IO]
Indus. Union of Marine and Ship Building Workers of Am. [24125]
Intl. Assn. for Bridge Maintenance and Safety [538]
Intl. Assn. of Machinists and Aerospace Workers, Woodworkers District Lodge W1 [24026]
Intl. Brick Collectors' Assn. [22048]
Intl. Brotherhood of Boilermakers, Iron Ship Builders, Blacksmiths, Forgers and Helpers [24021]
Intl. Builders Exchange Executives [1024]
Intl. Fed. of Building and Wood Workers [IO]
Intl. Slurry Surfacing Assn. [632]
Intl. Union of Bricklayers and Allied Craftworkers [24027]
Intl. Union of Operating Engineers [24028]
Intervention and Coiled Tubing Assn. [7512]
Laborers' Intl. Union of North Am. [24029]
Laborers' Intl. Union of North Am. [IO]
Log Home Builders Assn. of North Am. [1031]
Log Homes Coun. [2525]
Mfrs'. Agents Natl. Assn. [2537]
Mfrs. Representatives Educational Res. Found. [2539]
Maple Flooring Manufacturers Assn. [635]
Master Builders South Africa [IO]
Materials and Methods Standards Assn. [636]
Metal Building Contractors and Erectors Assn. [2528]
Metal Building Manufacturers Assn. [637]
Metal Framing Manufacturers Assn. [639]
Natl. Alliance for Fair Contracting [24030]
Natl. Assn. of Mfrs. [2561]
Natl. Assn. of Miscellaneous, Ornamental and Architectural Products Contractors [1037]
Natl. Assn. of the Remodeling Indus. [643]
Natl. Assn. of Tower Erectors [6653]
Natl. Coun. of Erectors, Fabricators and Riggers [1042]
Natl. Insulation Assn. [1048]
Natl. One Coat Stucco Assn. [650]
Natl. Steel Bridge Alliance [539]
Natl. Town Builders' Assn. [654]
Natl. Utility Locating Contractors Assn. [1055]
New Zealand Building Trades Union [IO]
North Amer. Building Material Distribution Assn. [658]
North Amer. Laminate Flooring Assn. [660]
Operative Plasterers and Cement Masons Intl. Assn. of U.S. and Canada [24031]
Operative Plasterers and Cement Masons Intl. Assn. of U.S. and Canada [IO]
Plastic Lumber Trade Assn. [3055]
Residential Constr. Workers' Assn. [948]
Residential Energy Services Network [664]
Resilient Floor Covering Inst. [665]
Roofing Indus. Comm. on Weather Issues [666]
Roofing Indus. Educational Inst. [1064]
Scaffold Indus. Assn. [669]
Sheet Metal Industry Promotion Plan [1065]
Slag Cement Assn. [935]
Steel Deck Inst. [671]
Steel Framing Alliance [2731]
Sustainable Buildings Indus. Coun. [7682]
Traditional Small Craft Assn. [21885]
United Assn. Mfrs. Representatives [2544]
United Brotherhood of Carpenters and Joiners of Am. [24032]
United Union of Roofers, Waterproofers and Allied Workers [24033]
Building Trades Employers' Assn. [609], 1430 Broadway, 8th Fl., New York, NY 10018, (212)704-9745
Building Waterproofers Assn. - Defunct.
Buildings Indus. Coun; Sustainable [7682]
Buildings; Joint Comm. on Tall [★6474]
Buildings; Natl. Coun. for Historic Sites and [★10051]
Buildings and Urban Habitat; Coun. on Tall [6474]
Built-In Cleaning Systems Inst. - Defunct.

Bukovina Soc. of the Americas [4260], PO Box 81, Ellis, KS 67637
Bulb Soc. - Defunct.
Bulb Wholesalers Assn; North Amer. Flower [4983]
Bulgaria
  Bulgarian-American Chamber of Commerce [24243]
  Bulgarian Natl. Front [17027]
  Bulgarian Natl. Front [IO]
  North American-Bulgarian Chamber of Commerce [24291]
  U.S. Coun. for Human Rights in the Balkans [17787]
Bulgaria Squash Fed. [IO], Sofia, Bulgaria
Bulgarian
  Bulgarian-American Chamber of Commerce [24243]
  Bulgarian Natl. Front [17027]
  Bulgarian-U.S. Bus. Coun. [24244]
  Inst. of Balkan Stud. [IO]
  Latin Chamber of Commerce of U.S.A. [24354]
  North American-Bulgarian Chamber of Commerce [24291]
Bulgarian Acad. of Sciences [IO], Sofia, Bulgaria
Bulgarian ACM Chap. [IO], Varna, Bulgaria
Bulgarian Aikido Fed. [IO], Sofia, Bulgaria
Bulgarian-American Chamber of Commerce [24243], 1427 N Wilcox Ave., Hollywood, CA 90028-8123, (323)962-2414
Bulgarian Animal Defence League [IO], Sofia, Bulgaria
Bulgarian Assn. Against Epilepsy [IO], Sofia, Bulgaria
Bulgarian Assn. on Aging [IO], Sofia, Bulgaria
Bulgarian Assn. for Alternative Tourism [IO], Sofia, Bulgaria
Bulgarian Assn. of Consulting Engineers and Architects [IO], Sofia, Bulgaria
Bulgarian Assn. of Info. Technologies [IO], Sofia, Bulgaria
Bulgarian Assn. of Kinesitherapists and Rehabilitators [IO], Sofia, Bulgaria
Bulgarian Assn. of Music Producers [IO], Sofia, Bulgaria
Bulgarian Assn. of Pattern Recognition [IO], Sofia, Bulgaria
Bulgarian Assn. of Sterility and Reproductive Hea. [IO], Sofia, Bulgaria
Bulgarian Assn. of Travel Agents [IO], Sofia, Bulgaria
Bulgarian Assn. of Univ. Women [IO], Sofia, Bulgaria
Bulgarian Athletics Fed. [IO], Sofia, Bulgaria
Bulgarian Badminton Fed. [IO], Sofia, Bulgaria
Bulgarian Baseball Fed. [IO], Sofia, Bulgaria
Bulgarian Baseball and Softball Fed. [★IO]
Bulgarian Bible Soc. [IO], Sofia, Bulgaria
Bulgarian Book Assn. [IO], Sofia, Bulgaria
Bulgarian Bookpublishers Assn. [★IO]
Bulgarian Chamber of Commerce and Indus. [IO], Sofia, Bulgaria
Bulgarian Constr. Chamber [IO], Sofia, Bulgaria
Bulgarian Dance Sport Fed. [IO], Sofia, Bulgaria
Bulgarian Fed. of Baseball and Softball [★IO]
Bulgarian Fed. of Speleology [IO], Sofia, Bulgaria
Bulgarian Geological Soc. [IO], Sofia, Bulgaria
Bulgarian Geophysical Soc. [IO], Sofia, Bulgaria
Bulgarian Handball Fed. [IO], Sofia, Bulgaria
Bulgarian Hypertension League [IO], Sofia, Bulgaria
Bulgarian Ice Hockey Fed. [IO], Zurich, Switzerland
Bulgarian Indus. Assn. [IO], Sofia, Bulgaria
Bulgarian League for the Prevention of Osteoporosis [IO], Sofia, Bulgaria
Bulgarian Medical Assn. [IO], Sofia, Bulgaria
Bulgarian Mineralogical Soc. [IO], Sofia, Bulgaria
Bulgarian Natl. Comm. - Address unknown since 1994.
Bulgarian Natl. Fed. of Karate-Do [IO], Sofia, Bulgaria
Bulgarian Natl. Front [IO], Chicago, IL, United States
Bulgarian Natl. Front [17027], PO Box 46250, Chicago, IL 60646, (847)692-5460
Bulgarian Olympian Comm. [IO], Sofia, Bulgaria
Bulgarian Operational Res. Soc. [IO], Sofia, Bulgaria
Bulgarian Orienteering Fed. [IO], Sofia, Bulgaria
Bulgarian Orthodontic Soc. [IO], Sofia, Bulgaria

Reference to "IO" in place of a book number signifies that the association may be found in the 45th edition of International Organizations.

Bulgarian Paralympic Comm. [IO], Sofia, Bulgaria
Bulgarian Red Cross [IO], Sofia, Bulgaria
Bulgarian Red Cross Youth [IO], Sofia, Bulgaria
Bulgarian Sailing Fed. [IO], Sofia, Bulgaria
Bulgarian Sci. Dental Assn. [IO], Sofia, Bulgaria
Bulgarian Sci. Soc. of Virology [IO], Sofia, Bulgaria
Bulgarian Skating Fed. [IO], Sofia, Bulgaria
Bulgarian Socialist Labor Fed. - Defunct.
Bulgarian Soc. of Cardiology [IO], Sofia, Bulgaria
Bulgarian Soc. of Chemotherapy [IO], Sofia,
   Bulgaria
Bulgarian Soc. for Clinical Densitometry [IO], Sofia,
   Bulgaria
Bulgarian Soc. for Electron Microscopy [IO], Sofia,
   Bulgaria
Bulgarian Soc. of Endocrinology [IO], Sofia, Bulgaria
Bulgarian Soc. of Gastroenterology [IO], Sofia,
   Bulgaria
Bulgarian Soc. of Ophthalmology [IO], Sofia,
   Bulgaria
Bulgarian Soc. for the Protection of Birds [IO], Sofia,
   Bulgaria
Bulgarian Soc. for Rheumatology [IO], Sofia,
   Bulgaria
Bulgarian Sociological Assn. [IO], Sofia, Bulgaria
Bulgarian Taekwondo Fed. [IO], Sofia, Bulgaria
Bulgarian Telework Assn. [IO], Sofia, Bulgaria
Bulgarian Tennis Fed. [IO], Sofia, Bulgaria
Bulgarian-U.S. Bus. Coun. [IO], Washington, DC,
   United States
Bulgarian-U.S. Bus. Coun. [24244], c/o Chamber of
   Commerce of the U.S., 1615 H St. NW,
   Washington, DC 20062-2000, (202)463-5460
Bulgarian Volleyball Fed. [IO], Sofia, Bulgaria
Bulgarian Water Polo Fed. [IO], Sofia, Bulgaria
Bulgarian Web Assn. [IO], Sofia, Bulgaria
Bulgarska Federacia Volleyball [★IO]
Bulimia
   Alliance for Eating Disorders Awareness [14297]
   Anorexia Nervosa and Related Eating Disorders
      [14298]
   Intl. Assn. of Eating Disorders Professionals
      [14300]
   Natl. Assn. of Anorexia Nervosa and Assoc.
      Disorders [14301]
   Natl. Eating Disorders Assn. [14302]
Bulimia Assn; Amer. Anorexia [★14302]
Bulk Drug Manufacturers' Assn. [IO], Hyderabad,
   India
Bulk Packaging and Containerization Inst. [★978]
Bulk Vendors Assn; Natl. [3972]
Bull Dog Club of Am; French [22271]
Bull Elephants - Address unknown since 1999.
Bull Terrier Club of Am. [22237], c/o Naomi Waynee,
   Exec. Sec., 1122 E Carol Ave., Phoenix, AZ
   85020-2611, (602)943-6027
Bull Terrier Club of Am; Miniature [22307]
Bull Users Soc. - Defunct.
Bulldog
   Bulldog Club of Am. Rescue Network [11372]
   French Bull Dog Club of Am. [22271]
   Recreation Vehicle Indus. Assn. [3371]
   World Bulldog Alliance [22387]
Bulldog Club of America - Address unknown since
   1995.
Bulldog Club of Am. Rescue Network [11372], c/o
   Robert A. Cocks, Treas., PO Box 403, Hazelwood,
   MO 63042, (410)549-2554
Bullet Assn; Cast [23715]
Bulletin of the Atomic Scientists [7603], 6042 S Kim-
   bark Ave., Chicago, IL 60637, (773)702-2555
Bullfighting
   Fund for Animals [11398]
   Taurine Bibliophiles of Am. [9755]
Bullmastiff Assn; Amer. [22192]
Bullnose Morris Club [IO], Chelmsford, United
   Kingdom
Bullseye Assn. [23161], 203 Washington St., Marble-
   head, MA 01945, (508)252-3442
Bullseye Cancel Collectors' Club [22798], c/o Stan
   Vernon, Sec.-Treas., 2749 Pine Knoll Dr., No. 4,
   Walnut Creek, CA 94595-2044
Bullseye Class Assn. [★23161]
Bum Wrap Intl. - Address unknown since 2000.
Bunbury Chamber of Commerce and Indus. [IO],
   Bunbury, Australia

Bund der Deutschen Katholischen Jugend [★IO]
Bund der Deutschen Landjugend [★IO]
Bund Deutscher Innenarchitekten [★IO]
Bund Deutscher Landschaftsarchitekten [★IO]
Bund Deutscher Oenologen [★IO]
Bund Freiberuflicher Hebammen Deutschlands eV
   [★IO]
Bund Freischaffender Foto-Designer [IO], Stuttgart,
   Germany
BUND - Friends of the Earth Germany [IO], Berlin,
   Germany
Bund fur Lebensmittelrecht und Lebensmittelkunde
   e.V. [★IO]
Bund Osterreichischer Innenarchitekten [IO], Vienna,
   Austria
Bund der Steuerzahler Europa [★IO]
Bund fur Umwelt und Naturschutz Deutschland
   [★IO]
Bundersarztekammer [★IO]
Bundesarchitektenkammer [★IO]
Bundesfachverband Fleisch eV [★IO]
Bundesforschungsanstalt fur Ernahrung und Lebens-
   mittel [IO], Detmold, Germany
Bundesfraktion Christlicher Gewerkschaftsbund
   [★IO]
Bundesgremium des Einrichtungsfachhandels [★IO]
Bundesgremium des Lebensmittelhandels [★IO]
Bundesgremium des Lederwaren-, Spielwaren- und
   Sportartikelhandels [★IO]
Bundesgremium des Radio- und Elektrohandels
   [★IO]
Bundesgremium des Textilhandels [★IO]
Bundesinnung der Baecker Osterreichs [★IO]
Bundesinnung der Chemischen Gewerbe [★IO]
Bundesinnung der Fleischer [★IO]
Bundesinnung der Konditoren (Zuckerbaecker)
   [★IO]
Bundesrechtsanwaltskammer [★IO]
Bundesverband der Agraringenieure [★IO]
Bundesverband Bildender Kuenstlerinnen und Kuen-
   stler [★IO]
Bundesverband des Deutschen Exporthandels [★IO]
Bundesverband der Deutschen Fleischwarenindus-
   trie [★IO]
Bundesverband der Deutschen Industrie [★IO]
Bundesverband der Deutschen Kies- und Sandin-
   dustrie [★IO]
Bundesverband der Deutschen Luft-und Raumfahr-
   tindustrie [★IO]
Bundesverband der Deutschen Spirituosen-Industrie
   und -Importeure e. V. [★IO]
Bundesverband der Deutschen Zahnarzte [★IO]
Bundesverband der Deutschen Zementindustrie
   [★IO]
Bundesverband der Deutschen Ziegelindustrie [★IO]
Bundesverband Deutscher Fertigbau [★IO]
Bundesverband Deutscher Galerien E.V. [IO],
   Cologne, Germany
Bundesverband Deutscher Kapitalbeteiligungsgesell-
   schaften e.V. [★IO]
Bundesverband Deutscher Tabakwaren-
   Grosshandler und Automatenaufsteller e.V. [★IO]
Bundesverband Deutscher Unternehmensberater
   [★IO]
Bundesverband Deutscher Versicherungskaufleute
   e.V. [IO], Bonn, Germany
Bundesverband Deutscher Zeitungsverleger [★IO]
Bundesverband Druck und Medien [★IO]
Bundesverband der Edelstein- und Diamantindustrie
   [★IO]
Bundesverband Finanzdienstleistungen [★IO]
Bundesverband Glasindustrie [★IO]
Bundesverband des Gross- und Aussenhandels mit
   Molkereiprodukten [★IO]
Bundesverband der Hersteller- und Errichterfirmen
   von Sicherheitssystemen [★IO]
Bundesverband Kamera [★IO]
Bundesverband Medizintechnologie e.V. [★IO]
Bundesverband Molkereiprodukte eV [IO], Bonn,
   Germany
Bundesverband der Phonographischen Wirtschaft
   [★IO]
Bundesverband Praktizierender Tierarzte [★IO]
Bundesverband Regie [★IO]
Bundesverband Selbstandiger Physiotherapeuten
   [★IO]

Bundesverband der Steuerberater e.V. [★IO]
Bundesverband Wind Energie e.V. [★IO]
Bundesverband der Zigarrenindustrie [★IO]
Bundesverbandes des Deutschen Briefmarkenhan-
   dels [★IO]
Bundesvereinigung der Deutschen Arbeitgeberver-
   bande [★IO]
Bundesvereinigung der Deutschen Ernahrungsindus-
   trie [★IO]
Bundesvereinigung Lebenshilfe fur Menschen mit
   geistiger Behinderung [★IO]
BundeszahnArztekammer-BZAK [★IO]
BUNDjugend [IO], Berlin, Germany
Bunker Family Assn. of Am. [IO], Milton, WA, United
   States
Bunker Family Assn. of Am. [20811], c/o LiAnn Pen-
   nington, Treas., PO Box 337961, Greeley, CO
   80633
Bunnie Mills Fan Club - Address unknown since
   1991.
Bunyad Literacy Community Coun. [IO], Lahore,
   Pakistan
Burak Havacilik [★IO]
Bur. des radiocommunications [★IO]
Bur. des Activities Socio-Caritatives - Caritas Camer-
   oun [IO], Yaounde, Cameroon
Bur. of the Advancement of Independent Retailing -
   Defunct.
Bur. of Animal Indus. Veterinarians [★16799]
Bur. of the Budget in Exile Unrequited Marching and
   Chowder Soc. - Defunct.
Bur. Canadien de l'Education Internationale [★IO]
Bur. for Careers in Jewish Service - Defunct.
Bur. of Catholic Indian Missions [19591]
Bur. of Contract Information - Defunct.
Bur. de la Coordination des Affaires Humanitaires
   [★IO]
Bur. D'Assurance du Canada [★IO]
Bur. of Envelope Mfrs. of Am. [★3681]
Bur. of European Designers Associations [IO], Bar-
   celona, Spain
Bur. Europeen pour les Langues Moins Repandues
   [★IO]
Bur. Europeen de l'Environnement [★IO]
Bur. Europeen de l'Objection de Conscience [★IO]
Bur. Europeene des Unions de Consommateurs
   [★IO]
Bur. du Fonds des Nations Unies pour la Population
   en Algerie [★IO]
Bur. of Freelance Photographers [IO], London,
   United Kingdom
Bur. of French-Speaking Higher Educ. and Res. -
   Arab Off. [IO], Beirut, Lebanon
Bur. of French-Speaking Higher Educ. and Res. -
   Central and East European Off. [IO], Bucharest,
   Romania
Bur. of French-Speaking Higher Educ. and Res. -
   Delegation to the European Union [IO], Brussels,
   Belgium
Bur. of French-Speaking Universities Agency - South
   Asian and Pacific Off. [IO], Hanoi, Vietnam
Bur. Gravimetrique Intl. [★IO]
Bur. of Inspection of Bd. of Underwriters of New York
   [★3576]
Bur. Intl. du Beton Manufacture [★IO]
Bur. Intl. Catholique de l'Enfance [★IO]
Bur. Intl. Catholique de l'Enfance [★IO]
Bur. Intl. d'Education [★IO]
Bur. Intl. des Expositions [★IO]
Bur. Intl. de la Paix [★IO]
Bur. Intl. des Poids et Mesures [★IO]
Bur. Intl. des Producteurs d'Assurances et de Reas-
   surances [★IO]
Bur. Intl. de la Recuperation [★IO]
Bur. of Intl. Recycling [IO], Brussels, Belgium
Bur. Intl. pour la Standardisation des Fibres Artifi-
   cielles [★IO]
Bur. Intl. des Tarifs Douaniers [★IO]
Bur. Intl. du Tourisme Social [★IO]
Bur. Interprofessionnel des Vins de Bourgogne
   [★IO]
Bur. Issues Assn. [★22888]
Bureau of Land Mgt. [★5128]
Bureau of Land Mgt. [★4468]
Bureau of Land Mgt. [★IO]

A star before a book entry number signifies that the name is not listed separately, but is mentioned within the entry.

Bur. of Land Mgt. Natl. Wild Horse and Burro Prog.
[4868], c/o US Bur. of Land Mgt., Off. of Public
Affairs, 1849 C St., Rm. 406-LS, Washington, DC
20240, (202)452-5125
Bur. of Laundry and Dry Cleaning Standards -
Defunct.
Bur. Mondial du Scoutisme [★IO]
Bur. Moyen-Orient de l'Agence universitaire de la
Francophonie [★IO]
Bur. of Municipal Res. [★IO]
Bur. of Municipal Res. [★6192]
Bur. Natl. Interprofessionnel du Cognac [★IO]
Bur. of Professional Educ. of the Amer. Osteopathic
Assn. [15810], Amer. Osteopathic Assn., 142 E
Ontario St., Chicago, IL 60611, (312)202-8000
Bur. Quaker aupres des Nations Unies [★IO]
Bur. of Raw Materials for Amer. Vegetable Oils and
Fats Industries - Defunct.
Bur. Regional de l'UICN pour l'Afrique Centrale [IO],
Yaounde, Cameroon
Bur. Regional de l'UICN pour l'Afrique de l'Ouest
[IO], Ouagadougou, Burkina Faso
Bur. Technique des Femmes du Pacifique [★IO]
Bur. de la normalisation des Telecommunications
[★IO]
Bur. Togolais du Droit d'Auteur [IO], Lome, Togo
Bur. of Urethane [★3057]
Bur. of Wholesale Sales Representatives - Address
unknown since 2006.
Bureaucrats; Intl. Assn. of Professional [22595]
Bureaucrats; Natl. Assn. of Professional [★22595]
Bureaus; Assoc. Credit [★1409]
Bureaus; Intl. Gp. of Agencies and [★10900]
Bureaus of Labor; Assn. of Chiefs and Officials of
[★5917]
Burgee Data Archives [IO], Toronto, ON, Canada
Burgess Soc; Thornton W. [4608]
Burglar and Fire Alarm Assn; Natl. [3538]
Burial Assn; Hebrew Free [20141]
Burial Vault Assn; Natl. Concrete [2787]
Burkina Faso League Against Epilepsy [IO], Ouaga-
dougou, Burkina Faso
Burkina Insurance Union [IO], Ouagadougou,
Burkina Faso
Burlap Bag Dealers Assn; Natl. [★999]
Burlap and Jute Assn. [3778], c/o Susan Spiegel,
PO Box 8, Dayton, OH 45401, (937)258-8000
Burlap and Jute Assn; Jute Carpet Backing Coun.
and [2266]
Burleson Family Assn. [20812], 5810 Make Peace
Ln., Corpus Christi, TX 78414, (903)677-1565
Burlesque Historical Soc. [11009], c/o Burlesque
Hall of Fame, PO Box 1437, Las Vegas, NV 89125
Burley Auction Warehouse Assn. [★3818]
Burley and Dark Leaf Tobacco Assn. - Address
unknown since 2003.
Burley Leaf Tobacco Dealers Assn. - Address
unknown since 1994.
Burley Marketing Assn. [3818], 620 S Broadway St.,
Lexington, KY 40508-3126, (859)255-4504
Burley Stabilization Corp. [5245], PO Box 6447,
Knoxville, TN 37914, (865)525-9381
Burley Tobacco Growers Cooperative Assn. [5246],
620 S Broadway, Lexington, KY 40508, (859)252-
3561
Burlington Liars Club [22592], PO Box 156, Burling-
ton, WI 53105-0156, (262)763-4640
Burma
Burma-America Buddhist Assn. [19546]
Burma Action Ireland [IO], Dublin, Ireland
Burma-America Buddhist Assn. [19546], 1708
Powder Mill Rd., Silver Spring, MD 20903,
(301)439-4035
Burma Fanciers; Sacred Cat of [21916]
Burma-India Hump Pilot Assn; China- [21391]
Burmese Breeders; Natl. Alliance of [4210]
Burn Assn; Amer. [13781]
Burn Found; Alisa Ann Ruch [13780]
Burnett Family Genealogy Assn. - Defunct.
Burnett Fund for Responsible Journalism; Carol
[8707]
Burnett Valley Olive Growers Assn. [IO], Kingaroy,
Australia
Burns
Alisa Ann Ruch Burn Found. [13780]

Amer. Burn Assn. [13781]
Burns United Support Groups [13782]
Chinese Burn Assn. of the Integration of
Traditional and Western Medicine [IO]
European Burns Assn. [IO]
European Fed. of Associations of Burned Persons
[IO]
Intl. Soc. for Burn Injuries [IO]
Intl. Soc. for Burn Injuries [13783]
Natl. Burn Victim Found. [13784]
Phoenix Soc. for Burn Survivors [13785]
Shriners Hospitals for Children [13973]
Burns Inst. for Children; Shriner's [★24605]
Burns Soc. of the City of New York - Address
unknown since 1994.
Burns United Support Groups [13782], PO Box
36416, Detroit, MI 48236, (313)881-5577
Burr Accord; Aaron [11097]
Burr Assn; Aaron [11098]
Burro
Amer. Mustang and Burro Assn. [4833]
Bur. of Land Mgt. Natl. Wild Horse and Burro
Prog. [4868]
Wild Burro Rescue and Preservation Proj. [11517]
Wild Horse Organized Assistance [5394]
Wild Horse Sanctuary [11477]
Wild Horses of Am. Registry [5395]
Burro Assn; Amer. Mustang and [4833]
Burro Prog; Bur. of Land Mgt. Natl. Wild Horse and
[4868]
Burroughs Assn; John [7362]
Burroughs Bibliophiles [9640], c/o George T.
McWhorter, Treas., Univ. of Louisville, Rare Book
Rm., Ekstrom Lib., Louisville, KY 40292, (502)852-
8729
Burroughs Memorial Assn; John [★7362]
Burrup Family Org; William [21084]
Burton Family Org. (Burten/Burtin/Berton) - Address
unknown since 2001.
Burundi Youth For Christ [IO], Bujumbura, Burundi
Bus
Amer. Bus Assn. [3859]
Automotive Recyclers Assn. [3988]
Buses Intl. Assn. [3864]
Graham Bros. Truck and Bus Club [21894]
Intl. Bus Collectors Club [21895]
Motor Bus Soc. [21896]
Motor Bus Soc. [IO]
Natl. Assn. of Timetable Collectors [23008]
Natl. Bus Traffic Assn. [3878]
Natl. School Trans. Assn. [3882]
Soc. of Professional Drivers [3893]
Traffic Audit Bur. for Media Measurement [123]
Trans. Clubs Intl. [3896]
United Motorcoach Assn. [3900]
Bus Assn; Amer. [3859]
Bus Assn; Natl. Motor [★21896]
Bus and Coach Assn. of New Zealand [IO], Welling-
ton, New Zealand
Bus History Assn. [IO], Windsor, ON, Canada
Bus Traffic Assn; Natl. [3878]
Bus Users UK [IO], Portsmouth, United Kingdom
Buses Intl. Assn. [IO], Spokane, WA, United States
Buses Intl. Assn. [3864], PO Box 9337, Spokane,
WA 99209, (509)328-2494
Bush Found. for Family Literacy; Barbara [8786]
Bush Official Fan Club - Address unknown since
2002.
Bushmiller Soc. [24790], PO Box 2250, Amherst,
MA 01004-2250, (413)259-1627
Business
1394 High Performance Serial Bus Trade Assn.
[3720]
AACSB Intl. - Assn. to Advance Collegiate
Schools of Bus. [8010]
Acad. of Accounting Historians [10079]
Acad. of Intl. Bus. [8011]
Acad. of Legal Stud. in Bus. [8757]
Accounting and Finance Benchmarking
Consortium [690]
ACT and Region Chamber of Commerce and
Indus. [IO]
Advancing Canadian Entrepreneurship [IO]
Adventist-Laymen's Services and Indus. [20553]
Advt. Club of New York [77]

Afghan-American Chamber of Commerce [24222]
African Amer. Alliance for Homeownership [1975]
African-American Female Entrepreneurs Alliance
[4033]
African Bus. Roundtable [IO]
Agile Mfg. Benchmarking Consortium [2545]
AIESEC - U.S. [8012]
Aircraft Carrier Indus. Base Coalition [1148]
Alliance of Area Bus. Publications [3199]
Alliance of Merger and Acquisition Advisors [54]
Alliance of Minority Women for Bus. and Political
Development [2759]
Alliance for Responsible Trade [3836]
Alliance in Support of Independent Res. [3390]
Allied Bd. of Trade [2249]
Alpha Beta Gamma Intl. [24425]
Alpha Iota Delta [24412]
Alpha Iota Sorority [24413]
Alpha Iota Sorority [IO]
Alpha Kappa Psi [24414]
America-Georgia Bus. Coun. [2296]
America-Israel Chamber of Commerce and Indus.
[24336]
Amer. and African Bus. Women's Alliance [691]
Amer. and African Bus. Women's Alliance [IO]
Amer. Alliance of Ethical Movers [13346]
Amer. Art Deco Dealers Assn. [295]
Amer. Assn. of Bus. Valuation Specialists [692]
Amer. Assn. of Franchisees and Dealers [1665]
Amer. Assn. of Home Based Businesses [1917]
Amer. Assn. for Long-Term Care Insurance [2132]
Amer. Assn. of Minority Businesses [2760]
Amer. Bus. Assn. of Russian Professionals [3181]
Amer. Bus. Conf. [17622]
Amer. Bus. Media [3201]
Amer. Bus. Women's Assn. [693]
Amer. Businesspersons Assn. [694]
Amer. Contract Compliance Assn. [17493]
Amer. Coun. for Capital Formation [17347]
Amer. Entrepreneurs for Economic Growth [695]
Amer. Equestrian Trade Assn. [4818]
Amer. Exploration and Production Coun. [2914]
Amer. Hellenic Inst. [24325]
Amer. Home Bus. Assn. [1918]
Amer. Indian Bus. Leaders [2830]
Amer. Indonesian Chamber of Commerce [24332]
Amer. Indus. Extension Alliance [2546]
Amer. Intl. Chamber of Commerce [24247]
American-Kuwaiti Alliance [2299]
Amer. Mfg. Trade Action Coalition [2547]
Amer. Mideast Bus. Associates [24357]
American-Russian Chamber of Commerce and
Indus. [24261]
Amer. Small Bus. Travel Alliance [3906]
Amer. Small Businesses Assn. [3603]
Amer. Soc. for the Advancement of Proj. Mgt.
[2519]
Amer. Soc. of Bus. Publication Editors [3084]
Amer. Soc. for Competitiveness [8007]
Amer. Soc. for Training and Development [3182]
Amer.-Southern Africa Chamber of Trade and
Indus. [24375]
Amer. Woman's Economic Development Corp.
[3604]
Americanism Educational League [17623]
Americans for Fair Electronic Commerce Transac-
tions [17441]
Antiques and Collectibles Dealer Assn. [863]
Antiques and Collectibles Natl. Assn. [864]
Antiques Coun. [217]
Arab Intl. Women's Forum [IO]
Argentina Israel Chamber of Commerce [IO]
Argentine-American Chamber of Commerce
[24227]
Argentine Canadian Chamber of Commerce [IO]
Argentine Chamber of Limited Companies [IO]
Argentine Fiscal Associations [IO]
Argentine Indus. Assn. [IO]
Armenian Amer. Chamber of Commerce [24263]
Arts and Bus. Coun. [9550]
Asia Pacific - USA Chamber of Commerce
[24264]
Asian Amer. Real Estate Assn. [3299]
Asian Bus. League of San Francisco [696]
Asian Indian Chamber of Commerce [24228]

Reference to "IO" in place of a book number signifies that the association may be found in the 45th edition of International Organizations.

Asian Women in Bus. [697]
Asian Women in Bus. [IO]
Asociata Femeilor Manager din Romania [IO]
Assn. of African Amer. Financial Advisors [1455]
Assn. of Amer. Chambers of Commerce in Latin Am. [24352]
Assn. for Automatic Identification and Mobility North Am. [336]
Assn. for Bus. Simulation and Experiential Learning [8015]
Assn. of Bus. Women of Serbia [IO]
Assn. of Call Center Managers [2520]
Assn. of Certified Turnaround Professionals [956]
Assn. Chief Executives Coun. [698]
Assn. of Chinese Finance Professionals [1402]
Assn. of Club Executives [1932]
Assn. for Consumer Res. [17306]
Assn. for Corporate Growth [699]
Assn. for Enterprise Integration [700]
Assn. of European Businesses [IO]
Assn. des Femmes Chefs d'Entreprises du Cote d'Ivoire [IO]
Assn. des Femmes Chefs d'Entreprises Maroc [IO]
Assn. des Femmes d'Affaires et Chefs d'Entreprises du Benin [IO]
Assn. des Femmes d'Affaires et Chefs d'Entreprises du Gabon [IO]
Assn. des Femmes Entrepreneurs Chefs d'Entreprises [IO]
Assn. of Ghana Indus. [IO]
Assn. for Global Bus. [8016]
Assn. Global View [8017]
Assn. of Greek Women Entrepreneurs [IO]
Assn. for Intl. Bus. [IO]
Assn. for Intl. Bus. [701]
Assn. of Luxury Suite Directors [3676]
Assn. of Master of Business Administration Executives [702]
Assn. Mauricienne Femmes Chefs d'Entreprises [IO]
Assn. of Modified Asphalt Producers [601]
Assn. of Needle-Free Injection Mfrs. [2549]
Assn. of Real Estate Funds [IO]
Assn. of School Bus. Officials Intl. [7892]
Assn. Senegalaise des Femmes Chefs d'Entreprise [IO]
Assn. of Slovenia Entrepreneurs [IO]
Assn. of Small Bus. Development Centers [3606]
Assn. of Small and Medium Enterprises [IO]
Assn. for Strategic Planning [3042]
Assn. of Trade and Forfaiting in the Americas [1404]
Assn. Women and Bus. in Russia [IO]
Australian-American Fulbright Commission [IO]
Australian Bus. in Europe [IO]
Australian Indus. Gp. [IO]
Australian New Zealand - Amer. Chambers of Commerce [24248]
Australian Trade Commn. [24229]
Austrian Press and Info. Ser. [24230]
Austrian Trade Commn. [24232]
Auto Suppliers Benchmarking Assn. [703]
Automotive Trade Policy Coun. [350]
Bahamas Agricultural and Indus. Corp. [IO]
BBB Wise Giving Alliance [17309]
BC Innovation Coun. [IO]
Bermuda Intl. Bus. Assn. [IO]
BEST Employers Assn. [3607]
Beta Gamma Sigma [24415]
Beta Gamma Sigma [IO]
Beta Gamma Sigma Alumni [24416]
Beta Pi Sigma Sorority [24417]
Beyster Inst. [704]
Bilateral US-Arab Chamber of Commerce [24226]
Bd. Retailers Assn. [3402]
Brazil-U.S. Bus. Coun. [24266]
Brazilian-American Chamber of Commerce [24239]
Brazilian Govt. Trade Bur. of the Consulate Gen. of Brazil in New York [24240]
British-American Bus. Coun. [705]
British-American Bus. Coun. [IO]
British Assn. of Women Entrepreneurs [IO]
British Trade Off. at Consulate-General [24241]

BritishAmerican Bus. Inc. of New York and London [24267]
Bulgarian-American Chamber of Commerce [24243]
Bulgarian-U.S. Bus. Coun. [24244]
Bulgarian-U.S. Bus. Coun. [IO]
Bunbury Chamber of Commerce and Indus. [IO]
Bus. Alliance for Local Living Economies [887]
Bus. Assn. Italy Am. [2300]
Bus. Comm. for the Arts [9560]
Bus. and Community Found. [IO]
Bus. Coun. [18401]
Bus. Coun. of Australia [IO]
Bus. Coun. for Intl. Understanding [17862]
Bus. Espionage Controls and Countermeasures Assn. [2086]
Bus. Executives for Natl. Security [18587]
Business-Higher Educ. Forum [8008]
Bus. History Conf. [10098]
Bus. Leaders for Sensible Priorities [18387]
Bus. Modeling and Integration Domain Task Force [706]
Bus. and Professional Women Australia [IO]
Bus. and Professional Women Intl. [IO]
Bus. and Professional Women the Netherlands [IO]
Bus. and Professional Women - UK [IO]
Bus. and Professional Women's Found. [11084]
Bus. Roundtable [18402]
Bus. for Social Responsibility [707]
Bus. Travel Coalition [24382]
Bus. Volunteers Unlimited [13390]
Bus. Women's Network [4036]
Businesswomen's Assn. [IO]
Buying Influence [17310]
Byron Bay Chamber of Commerce and Indus. [IO]
Cairns Chamber of Commerce [IO]
Call Center Assn. [IO]
Camara de Comercio Argentino-Brasilena [IO]
Camara de Comercio Argentino-Britanica en la Republica Argentina [IO]
Camara de Comercio Argentino-Venezolana [IO]
Camara de Comercio Exterior de Rosario [IO]
Camara de Comercio Exterior de Salta [IO]
Camara de Comercio e Industria de Angola [IO]
Camara de Comercio e Industria de Trenque Lauquen [IO]
Camara de Comercio, Industria Y Servicios de Carlos Casares [IO]
Camara de Comercio Italiana de Rosario [IO]
Camara de Comercio Sueco Argentina [IO]
Camara Empresaria Parque Indus. de Pilar [IO]
Camara Espanola de Comercio de la Republica Argentina [IO]
Camara de Exportadores del El Rosario [IO]
Camara de Industria y Comercio Argentino-Alemana [IO]
Camara de Industria y Comercio de Matanza [IO]
Camara de La Industria El Trebol [IO]
Camara de la Produccion, la Industria y el Comercio Argentino-China [IO]
Camara de Produccion Y Servicios de La Provincia de Buenos Aires [IO]
Cameroon-USA Chamber of Commerce [24249]
Canada-Arab Bus. Coun. [IO]
Canada-China Bus. Coun. [IO]
Canada-India Bus. Coun. [IO]
Canada - Japan Soc. of British Columbia [IO]
Canada-United States Bus. Assn. [2301]
Canadian/American Border Trade Alliance [3838]
Canadian-American Bus. Coun. [708]
Canadian-American Bus. Coun. [IO]
Canadian Assn. of Women Executives and Entrepreneurs [IO]
Canadian Coun. for Aboriginal Bus. [IO]
Canadian Coun. of Chief Executives [IO]
Canadian Fed. of Bus. and Professional Women's Clubs [IO]
Canadian Fed. of Independent Bus. [IO]
Canadian Inst. of Chartered Bus. Valuators [IO]
Canadian Netherlands Bus. and Professional Assn. [IO]
Career Women's Forum [IO]
Caribbean-Central Amer. Action [12421]
Catalyst [11085]

CDS Intl. [8019]
Center for the Defense of Free Enterprise [17625]
Center for Family Business [709]
Center for Intl. Private Enterprise [710]
Center for Intl. Private Enterprise [IO]
Center for Intl. Private Enterprise - Egypt Off. [IO]
Center for Intl. Private Enterprise - Romania Off. [IO]
Center for Intl. Private Enterprise - Russia Off. [IO]
Center for Regional Development/Transparency Intl. - Armenia [IO]
Center for Women's Bus. Res. [4037]
Central Am. - U.S. Chamber of Commerce [24245]
Central Am. - U.S. Chamber of Commerce [IO]
Central Assn. of Women Entrepreneurs [IO]
Centre for Interfirm Comparison [IO]
Centre for Women in Bus. [IO]
Chamber of Commerce and Indus. of Korca [IO]
Chamber of Commerce and Indus. of Tirana [IO]
Chambre Nationale des Femmes Chefs d'Entreprise [IO]
Chartered Alternative Investment Analyst Assn. [2332]
Chief Executive Officers Club [711]
Chief Executives Org. [712]
Chile-U.S. Chamber of Commerce [24270]
China-Britain Bus. Coun. [IO]
China Productivity Center [IO]
Chinese Amer. Assn. of Commerce [24308]
Chinese Amer. Assn. of Engg. [7008]
Chinese Amer. Semiconductor Professional Assn. [1208]
Chinese Chamber of Commerce of Hawaii [24309]
Chinese Entrepreneurs Soc. of Canada [IO]
Chinese Women's Bus. Assn., ROC [IO]
Christian Bus. Men's Comm. [19771]
Christian Chamber of Commerce [24311]
City Women's Network [IO]
Coalition Against Insurance Fraud [2155]
Coalition for Govt. Procurement [1741]
Coffs Harbour Chamber of Commerce and Indus. [IO]
Coleman Found. [13162]
Colombian Amer. Assn. [24312]
Colombian Govt. Trade Bur. [24271]
CommerceNet [7727]
Commercial Off. of Spain [24376]
Commercial Photographers Intl. [2995]
Comm. of 200 [713]
Comm. for the Economic Growth of Israel [24337]
Confed. of Bolivian Private Entrepreneurs [IO]
Confed. of British Indus. [IO]
Confed. of Indian Indus. - United Kingdom [IO]
Confed. of Norwegian Bus. and Indus. [IO]
Confed. of Swedish Enterprise [IO]
Confed. of Tanzania Indus. [IO]
Confed. of Zimbabwe Indus. [IO]
Conf. Bd. Europe [IO]
Consumer Energy Coun. of Am. Res. Found. [17496]
Consumer Trends Forum Intl. [970]
Consuming Indus. Trade Action Coalition [771]
Cooperative Bus. Intl. [1071]
Cooperative Grocers' Info. Network [1072]
Coordinating Comm. of Agriculture, Commercial, Indus. and Financial Associations [IO]
Corporate Coun. on Africa [169]
Corrugated Packaging Coun. [2874]
Costa Rican Union of Chambers of Private Sector Enterprises [IO]
Coun. for the Advancement of Consumer Policy [17326]
Coun. of the Americas [24353]
Coun. for Ethical Leadership [714]
Coun. on Foreign Relations [17608]
Coun. of Growing Companies [715]
Coun. of Intl. Restaurant Real Estate Brokers [3392]
Croatian-American Chamber of Commerce [24314]
CrossRef [3220]
Culligan Dealers Assn. of North Am. [1667]

A star before a book entry number signifies that the name is not listed separately, but is mentioned within the entry.

Customer Satisfaction Measurement Assn. [716]
Czech-North Amer. Chamber of Commerce [24274]
Danish Amer. Chamber of Commerce [24316]
Dealer Mgt. Assn. [717]
Delta Mu Delta Honor Soc. [24418]
Delta Pi Epsilon [24426]
Diversity Info. Resources [2761]
Dominicans on Wall St. [1413]
Dublin City Bus. Assn. [IO]
Dvorak Intl. [2846]
Ebix Users Assn. [340]
Editorial Photographers [2996]
eMarketing Assn. [1166]
Emerging Markets Private Equity Assn. [1415]
Employers of Am. [3608]
Energy Future Coalition [6952]
EnterpriseWorks - Benin [IO]
EnterpriseWorks - Burkina Faso [IO]
EnterpriseWorks - Ghana [IO]
EnterpriseWorks - Guinea [IO]
EnterpriseWorks - Guinea-Bissau [IO]
EnterpriseWorks - Mali [IO]
EnterpriseWorks - Philippines [IO]
EnterpriseWorks - Senegal [IO]
EnterpriseWorks - Tanzania [IO]
Entrepreneurs Assn. of Slovakia [IO]
Entrepreneurs' Org. [718]
The Entrepreneurship Inst. [719]
Environmental Bus. Coun. of New England [4560]
Environmental Entrepreneurs [4392]
Environmental Indus. Commn. [IO]
Estonian Amer. Chamber of Commerce and Indus. [24318]
Estonian Bus. Assn. [IO]
Eta Phi Beta [24419]
Ethics and Compliance Officer Assn. [720]
Ethics Rsrc. Center [17072]
Euro-American Women's Coun. [17530]
European Aluminum Foil Assn. [IO]
European Assn. of Craft, Small and Medium-Sized Enterprises [IO]
European Bus. Angel Network [IO]
European Bus. Ethics Network [IO]
European Bus. History Assn. [IO]
European Bus. and Innovation Centre Network [IO]
European Confed. of Junior Enterprises [IO]
European Intl. Bus. Acad. [IO]
European Professional Women's Network [IO]
European Round Table of Industrialists [IO]
Executive Leadership Coun. [2762]
Executive Women Intl. [63]
Executives Assn. of Great Britain [IO]
Fabless Semiconductor Assn. [1215]
Fan Makers' Company [IO]
Fed. of European Private Port Operators [IO]
Fed. of Indus. Products Systems and Services for Constr. [IO]
Fed. of Philippine Amer. Chambers of Commerce [24277]
Fed. of Thai Indus. [IO]
Fellowship of Companies for Christ Intl. [19799]
Female Europeans of Medium and Small Enterprises [IO]
Financial Services and Banking Benchmarking Assn. [721]
Financial Women's Assn. of New York [1421]
Finnish Amer. Chamber of Commerce [24319]
Fisher Inst. for Medical Res. [17628]
Fitness Indus. Suppliers Assn. - North Am. [3020]
Flag Mfrs. Assn. of Am. [1487]
Foodservice Sales and Marketing Assn. [1581]
Found. ICPR Junior Coll. [8022]
Franco-Argentina Chamber of Commerce and Indus. [IO]
Free the Grapes! [16971]
French-American Chamber of Commerce [24320]
Future Bus. Leaders of Am. - Phi Beta Lambda [24420]
Geelong Chamber of Commerce [IO]
Georgia-USA Chamber of Commerce [24278]
German Amer. Chamber of Commerce [24323]
German-Chinese Bus. Assn. [IO]
German Indus. UK [IO]

German Soc. for Documentation [IO]
German Venture Capital Assn. [IO]
Ghana-USA Chamber of Commerce [24279]
Gifts In Kind Intl. [12720]
Global Bus. Coalition on HIV/AIDS [11329]
Global Bus. and Tech. Assn. [778]
Global Environmental Mgt. Initiative [4628]
Global Equity Org. [1239]
Graduate Mgt. Admission Coun. [8807]
Greek Amer. Chamber of Commerce [24280]
Green Meeting Indus. Coun. [2681]
Gp. Underwriters Assn. of Am. [2167]
Groupement des Femmes d'Affaires du Cameroun [IO]
Groupement des Femmes d'Affaires de la Guinee [IO]
Guam Chamber of Commerce [IO]
Guam Chamber of Commerce [24246]
Handcrafted Soap Makers Guild [1155]
Hellenic-American Chamber of Commerce [24326]
High Coun. for Private Enterprise [IO]
Hispanic Marketing and Commun. Assn. [2628]
Home-Based Working Moms [722]
Home Office Assn. of Am. [1919]
Honduran Private Enterprise Coun. [IO]
Hong Kong Trade Development Coun. [24329]
Hong Kong Women Professionals and Entrepreneurs Assn. [IO]
Hospitality Asset Managers Assn. [1942]
Human Resources Benchmarking Assn. [723]
Hungarian-U.S. Bus. Coun. [724]
Hungarian-U.S. Bus. Coun. [IO]
Iceland Assn. of Women Entrepreneurs FKA [IO]
Independent Online Booksellers Assn. [530]
Independent Textile Rental Assn. [3786]
Indus. Minerals Assn. - North Am. [2742]
Indus. Soc. [IO]
Industrialists' Assn. of Panama [IO]
Info. Systems Mgt. Benchmarking Consortium [725]
Info. Tech. Solution Provider Alliance [2102]
Innovation Norway - U.S. [24283]
Inst. of Certified Bus. Counselors [726]
Inst. of Certified Professional Managers [2497]
Inst. for Intl. Entrepreneurship [727]
Inst. for Operations Res. and the Mgt. Sciences [2500]
Insurance Marketplace Standards Assn. [2180]
Interactive Travel Services Assn. [3946]
Intl. Alliance of Avaya Users [3745]
The Intl. Alliance for Women [728]
The Intl. Alliance for Women [IO]
Intl. Anticounterfeiting Coalition [17333]
Intl. Assn. of Administrative Professionals [66]
Intl. Assn. of Bus. Communicators [879]
Intl. Assn. of Bus. Communicators [IO]
Intl. Assn. of Bus. Communicators - Hong Kong [IO]
Intl. Assn. for Bus. Organizations [3610]
Intl. Assn. for Contract and Commercial Mgt. [772]
Intl. Assn. of Dinnerware Matchers [1971]
Intl. Assn. for Documentation Technologies [729]
Intl. Assn. of Hispanic Meeting Professionals [2684]
Intl. Assn. for Info. and Data Quality [7197]
Intl. Assn. of Jesuit Bus. Schools [8026]
Intl. Assn. of Merger and Acquisition Professionals [730]
Intl. Assn. of Merger and Acquisition Professionals [IO]
Intl. Assn. of Outsourcing Professionals [2871]
Intl. Assn. of Privacy Professionals [2104]
Intl. Assn. for Prdt. Development [3177]
Intl. Assn. of Protocol Consultants [965]
Intl. Assn. of Ser. Evaluators [3269]
Intl. Assn. of Space Entrepreneurs [3634]
Intl. Bus. Brokers Assn. [3315]
Intl. Call Center Benchmarking Consortium [731]
Intl. Call Center Benchmarking Consortium [IO]
Intl. Coun. for Small Bus. [3611]
Intl. Design Guild [2263]
Intl. Downtown Assn. [732]
Intl. Downtown Assn. [IO]
Intl. Executive Ser. Corps [IO]

Intl. Executive Ser. Corps [733]
Intl. Experiential Marketing Assn. [2631]
Intl. Fed. of Bike Messenger Associations [517]
Intl. Food and Agribusiness Mgt. Assn. [1524]
Intl. Function Point Users Gp. [734]
Intl. Mgt. Development Assn. [735]
Intl. Mgt. Development Assn. [IO]
Intl. Medical Spa Assn. [1870]
Intl. Mystery Shopping Alliance [3412]
Intl. Ombudsman Assn. [736]
Intl. Peace Operations Assn. [18213]
Intl. Photonics Commercialization Alliance [2862]
Intl. Play Equip. Manufacturers Assn. [3060]
Intl. Security Mgt. Assn. [3534]
Intl. Soc. of Agile Mfg. [2558]
Intl. Soc. for New Institutional Economics [6885]
Intl. Soc. of Six Sigma Professionals [7534]
Intl. Vintage Poster Dealers Assn. [106]
Internet Alliance [737]
Internet Alliance [IO]
Invest to Compete Alliance [738]
Iota Phi Lambda [24421]
IPREX [3193]
Iraqi Amer. Chamber of Commerce and Indus. [24285]
Irish Bus. and Employers' Confed. [IO]
Italian-American Chamber of Commerce [24338]
Italian Chamber of Commerce and Indus. in Australia - SA [IO]
Italian Chamber of Commerce and Indus. in Queensland [IO]
Italian Confed. of Retailers, Commerce, Tourism and Ser. [IO]
Italy-America Chamber of Commerce [24339]
Jamaica Mfrs'. Assn. [IO]
Jamaica USA Chamber of Commerce [24287]
Japan Assn. of Corporate Executives [IO]
Japan Assn. of New Bus. Incubation Org. [IO]
Japan External Trade Org. [24342]
Japan Info. Access Proj. [10265]
Japan Soc. of Bus. Admin. [IO]
Japanese Chamber of Commerce and Industry of Hawaii [24345]
Jefferson Educational Found. [17273]
Jeweler's Advisory Gp. [2369]
Jordan Info. Bur. [24349]
Kauffman Center for Entrepreneurial Leadership [739]
Kazakhstan Assn. of Bus. Incubators and Innovation Centers [IO]
The Korea Soc. [24350]
Korea Trade Promotion Center [24351]
Korean Amer. Soc. of Entrepreneurs [773]
Korean Standards Assn. [IO]
Korean Women Entrepreneurs Assn. [IO]
Latin Amer. Venture Capital Assn. [1431]
Latin Bus. Assn. [740]
Latin Chamber of Commerce of U.S.A. [24354]
Leading Edge Alliance [39]
Life Insurance Settlement Assn. [2193]
Loan Syndications and Trading Assn. [484]
Logistics Mgt. Inst. [5607]
Malta Assn. of Women in Bus. [IO]
Mgt. Educ. Alliance [8029]
Medical Gp. Mgt. Assn. [15067]
Medical Spa Soc. [1871]
Mexican Industrialists' Assn. [IO]
Mid-Atlantic Equity Consortium [8276]
Minority Corporate Counsel Assn. [5615]
Moscow Intl. Bus. Assn. [IO]
Mountains and Plains Booksellers Assn. [741]
Movement of French Businesses [IO]
My Own Bus., Inc. [8030]
NanoBusiness Alliance [7750]
NASD [3517]
Natl. Advt. Div. Coun. of Better Bus. Bureaus [111]
Natl. African-American Insurance Assn. [2202]
Natl. Alliance of Clean Energy Bus. Incubators [1287]
Natl. Alliance for Fair Competition [3613]
Natl. Asian Amer. Soc. of Accountants [42]
Natl. Assn. of Blind Merchants [525]
Natl. Assn. for Bus. Economics [6886]
Natl. Assn. for Bus. Organizations [3615]

Reference to "IO" in place of a book number signifies that the association may be found in the 45th edition of International Organizations.

Natl. Assn. for Bus. Teacher Educ. [8032]
Natl. Assn. of Chamber Ambassadors [789]
Natl. Assn. of Coll. and Univ. Bus. Officers [7897]
Natl. Assn. for Community Coll. Entrepreneurship [8033]
Natl. Assn. of Condo Hotel Owners [1952]
Natl. Assn. of Entrepreneurial Parents [12675]
Natl. Assn. of Equity Source Banks [488]
Natl. Assn. of Executive Secretaries and Administrative Assistants [72]
Natl. Assn. for Female Executives [742]
Natl. Assn. of Firearms Retailers [1479]
Natl. Assn. of Home Based Businesses [1921]
Natl. Assn. for Industry-Education Cooperation [8048]
Natl. Assn. of Latina Leaders [2411]
Natl. Assn. of Minority Women in Business [2766]
Natl. Assn. of Payment Professionals [1438]
Natl. Assn. of Private Enterprise [3616]
Natl. Assn. of Private Enterprise [IO]
Natl. Assn. of Professional Asian Amer. Women [743]
Natl. Assn. of Purchasing Card Professionals [3264]
Natl. Assn. of Railway Bus. Women [3285]
Natl. Assn. of Real Estate Investment Trusts [3327]
Natl. Assn. of Responsible Loan Officers [1978]
Natl. Assn. for the Self-Employed [3617]
Natl. Assn. of Small Bus. Investment Companies [3618]
Natl. Assn. of Student Loan Administrators [8432]
Natl. Assn. of Supervisors of Bus. Educ. [8034]
Natl. Assn. of Women Bus. Owners [744]
Natl. Assn. of Women MBAs [745]
Natl. Assn. of Workforce Boards [12087]
Natl. Black MBA Assn. [8035]
Natl. Bus. Educ. Assn. [8036]
Natl. Bus. Incubation Assn. [746]
Natl. Bus. Initiative [IO]
Natl. Business League [2767]
Natl. Bus. Officers Assn. [8009]
Natl. Bus. Owners Assn. [3620]
Natl. Bus. Travel Assn. [3929]
Natl. Center for Fair Competition [3621]
Natl. Chamber of Commerce for Women [24388]
Natl. Collegiate Inventors and Innovators Alliance [7218]
Natl. Consumers League [17338]
Natl. Cooperative Bus. Assn. [1073]
Natl. Cooperative Grocers Assn. [1074]
Natl. Coun. of Asian Amer. Bus. Associations [774]
Natl. Coun. of Private Enterprises - Dominican Republic [IO]
Natl. Coun. of Private Enterprises - Panama [IO]
Natl. Development Coun. [17463]
Natl. Economic Assn. [6888]
Natl. Energy Marketers Assn. [1288]
Natl. Executive Ser. Corps [747]
Natl. Family Bus. Coun. [748]
Natl. Fed. of Independent Bus. [3622]
Natl. Fed. of Municipal Analysts [749]
Natl. Healthcare Collectors Assn. [1869]
Natl. Hispanic Bus. Assn. [8039]
Natl. Hispanic Corporate Coun. [750]
Natl. Independent Concessionaires Assn. [1591]
Natl. Indian Bus. Assn. [751]
Natl. Introducing Brokers Assn. [1714]
Natl. Justice Found. of Am. [17298]
Natl. Mgt. Assn. [2509]
Natl. Marine Charter Assn. [2610]
Natl. Nurses in Bus. Assn. [752]
Natl. Retail Hobby Stores Assn. [753]
Natl. Retail Hobby Stores Assn. [IO]
Natl. Retail Tenants Assn. [3383]
Natl. Small Bus. Assn. [3623]
Natl. Soc. of Certified Healthcare Bus. Consultants [14711]
Natl. Soc. of Hispanic MBAs [754]
Natl. Soc. for Hispanic Professionals [1908]
Natl. United States-Arab Chamber of Commerce [24290]
Natl. Women's Hall of Fame [20716]
Natl. Work at Home Mom Assn. [1922]

Natl. Writers Assn. [3146]
Native Amer. Bus. Alliance [19281]
Native Amer. Indian Info. and Trade Center [24358]
Native Financial Educ. Coalition [8442]
Netherlands Chamber of Commerce in the U.S. [24360]
Netherlands Soc. for Indus. and Trade [IO]
Network [IO]
Network Branded Prepaid Card Assn. [1443]
New Am. Alliance [1169]
New Socialist Network [IO]
North Am. Chinese Semiconductor Assn. [1226]
North America-Mongolia Bus. Coun. [2310]
North Amer. Assn. of Inventory Services [755]
North Amer. Assn. of Subway Franchisees [1670]
North American-Bulgarian Chamber of Commerce [24291]
North Amer. Celtic Buyers Assn. [784]
North American-Chilean Chamber of Commerce [24307]
North Amer. Importers Assn. [2311]
Norwegian Amer. Chamber of Commerce - New York City [24292]
NuBian Exchange News [2770]
Optical Storage Tech. Assn. [2860]
Organic Exchange [2864]
Org. of Pakistani Entrepreneurs of North Am. [756]
Original Equip. Suppliers Assn. [777]
Outsourcing Inst. [757]
Pakistan Assn. for Small and Medium Enterprises [IO]
Pakistan Chamber of Commerce USA [24364]
Pakistani Amer. Bus. Executives Assn. [758]
Pakistani Amer. Bus. Executives Assn. [IO]
Paraguayan Indus. Union [IO]
Partnership for Food Safety Educ. [14399]
PET Resin Assn. [3054]
Phi Chi Theta [24422]
Phi Delta Kappa [24578]
Phi Gamma Nu [24423]
Phi Theta Pi [24424]
Philippine-Amer. Chamber of Commerce [24365]
Plastic Optical Fiber Trade Org. [2863]
Polish Amer. Chamber of Commerce [24293]
Polish-U.S. Bus. Coun. [24366]
Portuguese Chamber [IO]
Portuguese Confed. of Bus. and Services [IO]
POWERLUNCH! [759]
Presbyterian Church Bus. Administrators' Assn. [20470]
Private Enterprise Res. Center [17635]
Private Equity CFO Assn. [1445]
Procurement and Supply Chain Benchmarking Assn. [760]
Professional Accounting Soc. of Am. [1]
Professional Scripophily Trade Assn. [761]
Professional Services Mgt. Assn. [2513]
Professional and Tech. Consultants Assn. [969]
Professional Women in Healthcare [4045]
Public Art Fund [17239]
Public Relations Soc. of Am. [3195]
PUSH Commercial Div. [12098]
Queensland Chamber of Commerce and Indus. [IO]
Real Estate Services Providers Coun. [3341]
Representative of German Indus. and Trade [762]
Representative of German Indus. and Trade [IO]
Res. Inst. for Small and Emerging Bus. [3624]
Rocky Mountain Inst. [18101]
Romanian-U.S. Bus. Coun. [24370]
Russian Acad. of Entrepreneurship [IO]
Russian-American Chamber of Commerce [24294]
Russian-American Chamber of Commerce in the USA [24371]
Sales Exchange for Refugee Rehabilitation and Vocation [3846]
Sales Professionals USA [3474]
Salvadoran Assn. of Industrials [IO]
SCORE [3625]
Search Engine Marketing Professional Org. [2648]
Self Storage Assn. of the United Kingdom [IO]

Serbian-American Chamber of Commerce [24373]
Shareholders Res. Alliance [3391]
Singapore Amer. Bus. Assn. [763]
Singapore Amer. Bus. Assn. [IO]
Singapore Productivity Assn. [IO]
Small Bus. Legislative Coun. [3627]
Small Bus. Ser. Bur. [3628]
Small Bus. in Telecommunications [3629]
Small Firms Assn. [IO]
Social Enterprise Alliance [3633]
Social Venture Network [764]
Soc. for Advancement of Mgt. [2515]
Soc. of Amer. Bus. Editors and Writers [3161]
Soc. for Bus. Ethics [12127]
Soc. of Consumer Affairs Professionals in Bus. [3196]
Soc. for Consumer Psychology [17344]
Soc. of Corporate Secretaries and Governance Professionals [75]
Soc. for Info. Mgt. [2516]
Soc. of Registered Professional Adjusters [2242]
Soc. of Trust and Estate Practitioners USA [1332]
South African USA Chamber of Commerce [24295]
South Australia Arts and Industry Development [IO]
South Australian Employers Chamber of Commerce [IO]
Southern Africa Bus. Forum [IO]
Spain-United States Chamber of Commerce [24296]
Spanish Confed. of Bus. Organisations [IO]
Specialty Wine Retailers Assn. [4031]
Sport Marketing Assn. [3672]
Sporting Goods Shippers Assn. [3590]
Springboard Enterprises [4046]
Standards, Productivity and Innovation Bd. of Singapore [IO]
State Chamber of Commerce (New South Wales) [IO]
Structured Employment Economic Development Corp. [12045]
Students in Free Enterprise [17637]
Submarine Indus. Base Coun. [1149]
Support Services Alliance [3631]
Swedish-American Chambers of Commerce, USA [24297]
Swedish Bus. Assn. of Singapore [IO]
Swedish Trade Coun. [3847]
Swiss-American Bus. Coun. [2314]
Swiss-Argentine Chamber of Commerce [IO]
Swiss-Australian Chamber of Commerce and Indus. [IO]
Swiss Bus. Assn. Singapore [IO]
Swiss Bus. Fed. [IO]
Swiss Malaysian Bus. Assn. [IO]
Taipei Bus. Assn. in Singapore [IO]
Taiwan Venture Capital Assn. [IO]
Tasmanian Chamber of Commerce and Indus. [IO]
Transparency, Consciousness and Citizenship [IO]
Transparency Intl. - Argentina [IO]
Transparency Intl. - Australia [IO]
Transparency Intl. - Azerbaijan [IO]
Transparency Intl. - Bangladesh [IO]
Transparency Intl. - Benin [IO]
Transparency Intl. - Bosnia and Herzegovina [IO]
Transparency Intl. - Botswana [IO]
Transparency Intl. - Brazil [IO]
Transparency Intl. - Brussels [IO]
Transparency Intl. - Bulgaria [IO]
Transparency Intl. - Canada [IO]
Transparency Intl. - Chile [IO]
Transparency Intl. - Colombia [IO]
Transparency Intl. - Costa Rica [IO]
Transparency Intl. - Croatia [IO]
Transparency Intl. - Czech Republic [IO]
Transparency Intl. - Denmark [IO]
Transparency Intl. - Fiji [IO]
Transparency Intl. - France [IO]
Transparency Intl. - Gambia [IO]
Transparency Intl. - Georgia [IO]
Transparency Intl. - Germany [IO]
Transparency Intl. - Greece [IO]

A star before a book entry number signifies that the name is not listed separately, but is mentioned within the entry.

Transparency Intl. - Hungary [IO]
Transparency Intl. - India [IO]
Transparency Intl. - Indonesia [IO]
Transparency Intl. - Initiative Madagascar [IO]
Transparency Intl. - Israel [IO]
Transparency Intl. - Italy [IO]
Transparency Intl. - Kazakhstan [IO]
Transparency Intl. - Kenya [IO]
Transparency Intl. - Korea [IO]
Transparency Intl. - Lithuania [IO]
Transparency Intl. - Malaysia [IO]
Transparency Intl. - Mauritius [IO]
Transparency Intl. - Moldova [IO]
Transparency Intl. - Mongolia [IO]
Transparency Intl. - Nepal [IO]
Transparency Intl. - New Zealand [IO]
Transparency Intl. - Nigeria [IO]
Transparency Intl. - Philippine Chap. [IO]
Transparency Intl. - Poland [IO]
Transparency Intl. - Romania [IO]
Transparency Intl. - Russia [IO]
Transparency Intl. - Slovakia [IO]
Transparency Intl. - South Africa [IO]
Transparency Intl. - Sri Lanka [IO]
Transparency Intl. - Sweden [IO]
Transparency Intl. - Switzerland [IO]
Transparency Intl. - Taiwan [IO]
Transparency Intl. - Tanzania [IO]
Transparency Intl. - Thailand [IO]
Transparency Intl. - Turkey [IO]
Transparency Intl. - UK [IO]
Transparency Intl. - Ukraine [IO]
Transparency Intl. - Vanuatu [IO]
Transparency Intl. - Yemen [IO]
Transparency Intl. - Zambia [IO]
Transparency Intl. - Zimbabwe [IO]
Triangle Coalition for Sci. and Tech. Educ. [9116]
Trickle Up Prog. [12446]
Trinidad and Tobago/USA Chamber of Commerce [24298]
Trust Companies' Assn. of Japan [IO]
Turkish-American Chamber of Commerce and Indus. [24384]
UCA Intl. Users Gp. [7820]
Union Mauritanienne des Femmes d'Entreprise et de Commerce [IO]
United Kingdom Forum for Organisational Hea. [IO]
United Kingdom Sci. Park Assn. [IO]
U.S. of America-China Chamber of Commerce [24310]
U.S. Assn. for Small Bus. and Entrepreneurship [3632]
U.S.-Bahrain Bus. Coun. [2315]
U.S. Bus. and Indus. Coun. [17639]
U.S. Chamber of Commerce [24301]
U.S. Coun. of Better Bus. Bureaus [765]
U.S. Coun. for Intl. Bus. [766]
U.S. Coun. for Intl. Bus. [IO]
U.S.-Cuba Trade Assn. [2316]
U.S. Freshwater Prawn and Shrimp Growers Assn. [3505]
U.S. Hispanic Chamber of Commerce [24327]
U.S. Indian Amer. Chamber of Commerce [24331]
United States-Indonesia Soc. [775]
U.S. Indus. Coalition [7637]
U.S.-Kazakhstan Bus. Assn. [2317]
United States-Mexico Chamber of Commerce [24302]
U.S. Women's Chamber of Commerce [24389]
Univ. Economic Development Assn. [9309]
US-Ireland Alliance [776]
US-Vietnam Chamber of Commerce [24387]
U.S.A. - Bus. and Indus. Advisory Comm. to the OECD [17466]
UWC - Strategic Services on Unemployment and Workers' Compensation [13348]
Venezuelan Amer. Assn. of the U.S. [24386]
Venezuelan Confed. of Indus. [IO]
Victorian Employers' Chamber of Commerce and Indus. [IO]
Volunteers in Tech. Assistance [12448]
Wales North Am. Bus. Chamber [24306]
WECAI Network [1167]
Women in Bio [6618]

Women Chiefs of Enterprises Intl. [IO]
Women Entrepreneurs of Canada [IO]
Women Entrepreneurs in Sci. and Tech. [4050]
Women Executives in Public Relations [3197]
Women in Govt. Relations [17676]
Women in Govt. Relations LEADER Found. [17677]
Women in Mgt. [2518]
Women's Creative Network [IO]
Women's Economic Round Table [18484]
Word of Mouth Marketing Assn. [2653]
Workflow and Reengineering Intl. Assn. [767]
Workflow and Reengineering Intl. Assn. [IO]
World Alliance of Gourmet Robustas [1738]
World Assn. for Small and Medium Enterprises [IO]
World Presidents' Org. [IO]
World Presidents' Org. [768]
Worldwide Responsible Apparel Production [261]
Young Entrepreneurs Assn. of Canada [IO]
Young Presidents' Org. [769]
Young Women Social Entrepreneurs [770]
Youth Venture [4072]
Zurich Chamber of Commerce [IO]
Bus; Acad. of Legal Stud. in [8757]
Bus. and Accounting Software Developers Assn. [★IO]
Bus. Admin; Natl. Assn. of Church [20513]
Bus. Administrators; Amer. Soc. of Mental Hea. [★15191]
Bus. Administrators; Natl. Assn. of Church [★20513]
Bus. Admission Coun; Graduate [★8807]
Bus. Advisory Coun. [★18401]
Bus. Aircraft Assn; Natl. [★162]
Bus. Alliance; Amer. Independent [3602]
Bus. Alliance for Commerce in Hemp [18283], PO Box 1716, El Cerrito, CA 94530, (510)215-8326
Business Alliance on Govt. Competition - Defunct.
Bus. Alliance; Independent [★3602]
Bus. Alliance for Intl. Economic Development - Address unknown since 2007.
Bus. Alliance; Internet [3730]
Bus. Alliance for Local Living Economies [887], 165 11th St., San Francisco, CA 94103, (415)255-1108
Bus. Alliance for Local Living Economies [IO], San Francisco, CA, United States
Bus; Amer. Assembly of Collegiate Schools of [★8010]
Bus; Amer. Assn. of Collegiate Schools of [★8010]
Bus. Application Software Developers Assn. [IO], Great Missenden, United Kingdom
Bus. Appraisers; Inst. of [282]
Bus. Archives Coun. [IO], Glasgow, United Kingdom
Bus. Assistance Center; Small [★3628]
Bus. Associates; Amer. Mideast [24357]
Bus. Associates; Medical Dental Hosp. [40]
Business Assn; e [98]
Bus. Assn; Amer. Home [1918]
Bus. Assn; Canada-United States [2301]
Bus; Assn. for Educ. in Intl. [★8011]
Bus. Assn. Italy Am. [2300], 199 Fremont St., 21st Fl., San Francisco, CA 94105, (415)992-7454
Business Assn. of Latin Amer. Studies - Defunct.
Bus. Assn; Mennonite Indus. and [★20249]
Bus. Assn; Natl. [3619]
Bus. Assn; Natl. Cooperative [1073]
Bus. Assn; Natl. Small [3623]
Bus. Assn; Outdoor Amusement [1324]
Bus. Aviation Assn; Natl. [162]
Business for Beauty - Defunct.
Bus. Brokers; Natl. Assn. of [★3222]
Bus. Bur; Natl. Better [★17309]
Bus. Bureaus; Assn. of Better [★17309]
Bus. Bureaus Found; Coun. of Better [★17309]
Bus. Bureaus; Natl. Advt. Div. Coun. of Better [111]
Business Card Collectors Intl. - Address unknown since 1995.
Business Card Museum - Defunct.
Bus. Circulation Assn; Natl. [★3242]
Bus. Coalition for Fair Competition [★3621]
Business Coalition on Freedom of Information - Defunct.
Business and Commerce
   Afghan-American Chamber of Commerce [24222]
   African-American Female Entrepreneurs Alliance [4033]

Alliance of Minority Women for Bus. and Political Development [2759]
Alliance for Responsible Trade [3836]
America-Georgia Bus. Coun. [2296]
America-Israel Chamber of Commerce and Indus. [24336]
Amer. Assn. for Long-Term Care Insurance [2132]
Amer. Bus. Assn. of Russian Professionals [3181]
Amer. Bus. Women's Assn. [693]
Amer. Equestrian Trade Assn. [4818]
Amer. Hellenic Inst. [24325]
Amer. Indonesian Chamber of Commerce [24332]
Amer. Indus. Extension Alliance [2546]
Amer. Intl. Chamber of Commerce [24247]
Amer. Intl. Chamber of Commerce [IO]
American-Kuwaiti Alliance [2299]
Amer. Mideast Bus. Associates [24357]
American-Russian Chamber of Commerce and Indus. [24261]
Amer.-Southern Africa Chamber of Trade and Indus. [24375]
Amer. Woman's Economic Development Corp. [3604]
Argentine-American Chamber of Commerce [24227]
Armenian Amer. Chamber of Commerce [24263]
Asia Pacific - USA Chamber of Commerce [24264]
Asian Bus. League of San Francisco [696]
Asian Indian Chamber of Commerce [24228]
Assn. of Amer. Chambers of Commerce in Latin Am. [24352]
Assn. for Corporate Growth [699]
Assn. for Enterprise Integration [700]
Assn. for Strategic Alliance Professionals [2521]
Assn. of Trade and Forfaiting in the Americas [1404]
Australian New Zealand - Amer. Chambers of Commerce [24248]
Australian New Zealand - Amer. Chambers of Commerce [IO]
Australian Trade Commn. [24229]
Austrian Press and Info. Ser. [24230]
Austrian Trade Commn. [24232]
Belgian Amer. Chamber of Commerce in the U.S. [24235]
Bilateral US-Arab Chamber of Commerce [24226]
Brazil-U.S. Bus. Coun. [24266]
Brazilian-American Chamber of Commerce [24239]
Brazilian Govt. Trade Bur. of the Consulate Gen. of Brazil in New York [24240]
British Trade Off. at Consulate-General [24241]
BritishAmerican Bus. Inc. of New York and London [24267]
Bulgarian-American Chamber of Commerce [24243]
Bus. Alliance for Local Living Economies [887]
Bus. Assn. Italy Am. [2300]
Bus. Leaders for Sensible Priorities [18387]
Bus. NZ [IO]
Buying Influence [17310]
Cameroon-USA Chamber of Commerce [24249]
Cameroon-USA Chamber of Commerce [IO]
Canadian/American Border Trade Alliance [3838]
Chile-U.S. Chamber of Commerce [24270]
Chinese Amer. Assn. of Commerce [24308]
Chinese Chamber of Commerce of Hawaii [24309]
Coalition for Govt. Procurement [1741]
Colombian Amer. Assn. [24312]
Colombian Govt. Trade Bur. [24271]
CommerceNet [7727]
Commercial Off. of Spain [24376]
Commercial Photographers Intl. [2995]
Comm. for the Economic Growth of Israel [24337]
Confed. of Nordic Bank, Finance and Insurance Employees' Unions [IO]
Consuming Indus. Trade Action Coalition [771]
Corporate Coun. on Africa [169]
Coun. of the Americas [24353]
Croatian-American Chamber of Commerce [24314]
Czech-North Amer. Chamber of Commerce [24274]

Reference to "IO" in place of a book number signifies that the association may be found in the 45th edition of International Organizations.

Danish Amer. Chamber of Commerce [24316]
eMarketing Assn. [1166]
Emerging Markets Private Equity Assn. [1415]
Estonian Amer. Chamber of Commerce and
Indus. [24318]
Fed. of Philippine Amer. Chambers of Commerce
[24277]
Finance Sector Union of Australia [IO]
Finnish Amer. Chamber of Commerce [24319]
FinSec, Finance and Info. Union [IO]
Flag Mfrs. Assn. of Am. [1487]
French-American Chamber of Commerce [24320]
Georgia-USA Chamber of Commerce [24278]
German Amer. Chamber of Commerce [24323]
German Professional Women's Assn. [4039]
Ghana-USA Chamber of Commerce [24279]
Global Environmental Mgt. Initiative [4628]
Greek Amer. Chamber of Commerce [24280]
Hellenic-American Chamber of Commerce
[24326]
Hong Kong Trade Development Coun. [24329]
Honolulu Japanese Chamber of Commerce
[24348]
Innovation Norway - U.S. [24283]
Inst. of Certified Bus. Counselors [726]
Intl. Assn. for Contract and Commercial Mgt. [772]
International Association for Contract and Com-
mercial Management [IO]
Intl. Assn. for Info. and Data Quality [7197]
Intl. Assn. of Ser. Evaluators [3269]
Intl. Assn. of Space Entrepreneurs [3634]
Intl. Christian Union of Bus. Executives [IO]
Intl. Coun. for Small Bus. [3611]
Intl. Downtown Assn. [732]
Intl. Experiential Marketing Assn. [2631]
Intl. Mystery Shopping Alliance [3412]
Intl. Photonics Commercialization Alliance [2862]
Intl. Soc. for New Institutional Economics [6885]
Iran Small Indus. and Indus. Parks Org. [IO]
Iraqi Amer. Chamber of Commerce and Indus.
[24285]
Ireland China Assn. [IO]
Ireland Japan Assn. [IO]
Italian-American Chamber of Commerce [24338]
Italy-America Chamber of Commerce [24339]
Jamaica USA Chamber of Commerce [24287]
Japan External Trade Org. [24342]
Japanese Chamber of Commerce and Industry of
Hawaii [24345]
Jordan Info. Bur. [24349]
The Korea Soc. [24350]
Korea Trade Promotion Center [24351]
Korean Amer. Soc. of Entrepreneurs [773]
Latin Amer. Venture Capital Assn. [1431]
Leading Edge Alliance [39]
Loan Syndications and Trading Assn. [484]
Malaysia South-South Assn. [IO]
Mobile Marketing Assn. [110]
My Own Bus., Inc. [8030]
Natl. Alliance for Fair Competition [3613]
Natl. Alliance for Food Safety and Security [1537]
Natl. Assn. of Chamber Ambassadors [789]
Natl. Assn. of Condo Hotel Owners [1952]
Natl. Assn. of Latina Leaders [2411]
Natl. Assn. of Payment Professionals [1438]
Natl. Assn. of Purchasing Card Professionals
[3264]
Natl. Assn. of Responsible Loan Officers [1978]
Natl. Black Chamber of Commerce [24250]
Natl. Business League [2767]
Natl. Coun. of Asian Amer. Bus. Associations
[774]
Natl. Energy Marketers Assn. [1288]
Natl. Gay and Lesbian Chamber of Commerce
[24321]
Natl. Introducing Brokers Assn. [1714]
Natl. Org. for Diversity in Sales and Marketing
[2644]
Natl. United States-Arab Chamber of Commerce
[24290]
Natl. Women's Bus. Coun. [4044]
Native Amer. Indian Info. and Trade Center
[24358]
Netherlands Chamber of Commerce in the U.S.
[24360]

Network Branded Prepaid Card Assn. [1443]
North America-Mongolia Bus. Coun. [2310]
North American-Bulgarian Chamber of Commerce
[24291]
North American-Chilean Chamber of Commerce
[24307]
North Amer. Importers Assn. [2311]
Norwegian Amer. Chamber of Commerce - New
York City [24292]
OASIS PKI Member Sect. [7780]
Pakistan Chamber of Commerce USA [24364]
Pakistani Amer. Bus. Executives Assn. [758]
PET Resin Assn. [3054]
Philippine-Amer. Chamber of Commerce [24365]
Polish Amer. Chamber of Commerce [24293]
Polish-U.S. Bus. Coun. [24366]
Res. Inst. for Small and Emerging Bus. [3624]
Romanian-U.S. Bus. Coun. [24370]
Russian-American Chamber of Commerce
[24294]
Russian-American Chamber of Commerce in the
USA [24371]
Search Engine Marketing Professional Org.
[2648]
Serbian-American Chamber of Commerce [24373]
Shareholders Res. Alliance [3391]
Shop, Distributive, and Allied Employees' Assn.
[IO]
Social Venture Network [764]
South African USA Chamber of Commerce
[24295]
Spain-United States Chamber of Commerce
[24296]
Springboard Enterprises [4046]
Support Services Alliance [3631]
Swedish-American Chambers of Commerce, USA
[24297]
Swedish Trade Coun. [3847]
Swiss-American Bus. Coun. [2314]
Trinidad and Tobago/USA Chamber of Commerce
[24298]
Turkish-American Chamber of Commerce and
Indus. [24384]
UCA Intl. Users Gp. [7820]
Union of Shop, Distributive and Allied Workers
[IO]
U.S. of America-China Chamber of Commerce
[24310]
U.S. Assn. for Small Bus. and Entrepreneurship
[3632]
U.S.-Bahrain Bus. Coun. [2315]
U.S. Chamber of Commerce [24301]
U.S. Coun. of Better Bus. Bureaus [765]
U.S.-Cuba Trade Assn. [2316]
U.S. Hispanic Chamber of Commerce [24327]
U.S. Indian Amer. Chamber of Commerce [24331]
United States-Indonesia Soc. [775]
U.S.-Kazakhstan Bus. Assn. [2317]
United States-Mexico Chamber of Commerce
[24302]
U.S. Women's Chamber of Commerce [24389]
US-Ireland Alliance [776]
US-Vietnam Chamber of Commerce [24387]
Venezuelan Amer. Assn. of the U.S. [24386]
Wales North Am. Bus. Chamber [24306]
WECAI Network [1167]
WineAmerica Natl. Assn. of Amer. Wineries [4032]
Women in Bio [6618]
Women Entrepreneurs in Sci. and Tech. [4050]
Worldwide Responsible Apparel Production [261]
Zambia Union of Financial Institutions and Allied
Workers [IO]
Bus. Comm. for the Arts [9560], 29-27 Queens Plz.
N, 4th Fl., Long Island City, NY 11101, (718)482-
9900
Bus. Commun. Assn; Amer. [★8014]
Bus. Communications Alliance; Integrated [338]
Bus. Communications Coun; Hea. Indus. [14080]
Bus. and Community Found. [IO], New Delhi, India
Bus. Conf; Am. [1170]
Bus. Conf; Amer. [17622]
Bus. Coun. [18401], PO Box 20147, Washington,
DC 20041, (202)298-7650
Business Coun; Agri [4073]
Bus. Coun. of Am; Small [17350]

Bus. Coun. of Australia [IO], Melbourne, Australia
Bus. Coun; Brazil-U.S. [24266]
Bus. Coun; Czech and Slovak-U.S. [2302]
Business Coun. for Effective Literacy - Defunct.
Business Coun. for Improved Transport Policies -
Defunct.
Bus. Coun; Intl. [★2284]
Bus. Coun. for Intl. Understanding [17862], 1212
Ave. of the Americas, 10th Fl., New York, NY
10036, (212)490-0460
Bus. Coun. for Intl. Understanding [IO], New York,
NY, United States
Bus. Coun. Midamerica; Intl. [★2284]
Bus. Coun. on Natl. Issues [★IO]
Bus. Coun; Natl. Minority [2768]
Bus. Coun; Natl. Women's [4044]
Bus. Coun. of New England; Environmental [4560]
Bus. Coun; Polish-U.S. [24366]
Bus; Coun. for Professional Educ. for [★8010]
Bus. Coun; Romanian-U.S. [24370]
Bus. Coun. for Sustainable Energy [1285], 1620 Eye
St. NW, Ste. 501, Washington, DC 20006,
(202)785-0507
Bus. Coun; U.S.-Japan [24347]
Bus. Coun; US-China [2319]
Bus. Coun; World [★768]
Business Data Processing and Mgt; Special Interest
Group for [76]
Bus. Designers, Coun. for Fed. Interior Designers;
Inst. of [★2265]
Business Development Center [★21280]
Bus. Development Centers; Assn. of Small [3606]
Bus. and Disability Coun; Natl. [12089]
Bus. and Economic Writers; Soc. of Amer. [★3161]
Bus. Economics; Natl. Assn. for [6886]
Bus. Economists; Conf. of [6878]
Bus. Economists; Natl. Assn. of [★6886]
Bus. Editors and Writers; Soc. of Amer. [3161]
Business Education
AACSB Intl. - Assn. to Advance Collegiate
Schools of Bus. [8010]
AACSB Intl. - Assn. to Advance Collegiate
Schools of Bus. [IO]
Acad. of Intl. Bus. [IO]
Acad. of Intl. Bus. [8011]
AIESEC - U.S. [8012]
AIESEC - U.S. [IO]
Alpha Beta Gamma Intl. [IO]
Alpha Beta Gamma Intl. [24425]
Amer. Soc. for Training and Development [3182]
Assn. to Advance Collegiate Schools of Bus.
[8013]
Assn. for Bus. Commun. [8014]
Assn. for Bus. Simulation and Experiential Learn-
ing [8015]
Association for Business Simulation and
Experiential Learning [IO]
Assn. of Danish Bus. Economists [IO]
Assn. for Global Bus. [IO]
Assn. for Global Bus. [8016]
Assn. Global View [8017]
Assn. Global View [IO]
ASTD [8018]
Bus. Alliance for Local Living Economies [887]
Bus. Educators Australasia [IO]
CDS Intl. [IO]
CDS Intl. [8019]
Community Coll. Bus. Officers [8020]
Decision Sciences Inst. [8021]
Delta Pi Epsilon [24426]
Economics and Bus. Educ. Assn. [IO]
Edexcel Intl. [IO]
European Consortium for the Learning Org. [IO]
European Marketing Acad. [IO]
Found. ICPR Junior Coll. [IO]
Found. ICPR Junior Coll. [8022]
Found. for Student Commun. [8023]
Intl. Assembly for Collegiate Bus. Educ. [8024]
International Assembly for Collegiate Business
Education [IO]
Intl. Assn. for Bus. and Soc. [IO]
Intl. Assn. for Bus. and Soc. [8025]
Intl. Assn. of Jesuit Bus. Schools [8026]
Intl. Assn. of Jesuit Bus. Schools [IO]
Intl. Assn. of Privacy Professionals [2104]

A star before a book entry number signifies that the name is not listed separately, but is mentioned within the entry.

Intl. Mgt. Development Assn. [735]
Intl. Soc. for Bus. Educ. [8027]
Intl. Soc. for Bus. Educ. [IO]
Irish Inst. of Training and Development [IO]
Junior Achievement [IO]
Junior Achievement [8028]
Junior Achievement China [IO]
Junior Achievement Ireland [IO]
Junior Achievement Russia [IO]
Mgt. Educ. Alliance [8029]
My Own Bus., Inc. [8030]
NASBITE Intl. [8031]
NASBITE Intl. [IO]
Natl. Assn. for Bus. Teacher Educ. [8032]
Natl. Assn. for Community Coll. Entrepreneurship [8033]
Natl. Assn. of Supervisors of Bus. Educ. [8034]
Natl. Black MBA Assn. [8035]
Natl. Bus. Educ. Assn. [8036]
Natl. Certification Commn. [8037]
Natl. Found. for Teaching Entrepreneurship [8038]
Natl. Hispanic Bus. Assn. [8039]
Native Financial Educ. Coalition [8442]
Pi Omega Pi [24427]
Russian Assn. of Bus. Educ. [IO]
Seton Hill University's E-magnify [8040]
Soc. for Judgement and Decision Making [8041]
Society for Judgement and Decision Making [IO]
Southwest Case Res. Assn. [8042]
Triangle Coalition for Sci. and Tech. Educ. [9116]
Trickle Up Prog. [12446]
Work Found. [IO]
Bus. Educ. Assn; United [★8036]
Bus. Educ; Natl. Coun. for [★8036]
Bus. Educ. of the Natl. Educ. Assn; Dept. of [★8036]
Business Educ. Res. Foundation [★8032]
Bus. Educ; Soc. for Automation in [★8132]
Bus. and Educational Radio and Assn. of Communications Technicians; Natl. Assn. of [★3752]
Bus. Educators Australasia [IO], Abbotsford, Australia
Bus. Enterprise Legal Defense and Educ. Fund; Minority [2763]
Business Enterprise Trust - Address unknown since 2004.
Bus. Equip. Mfrs. Assn. [★904]
Bus. Equip. Mfrs. Assn; Cmpt. and [★904]
Bus. Espionage Controls and Countermeasures Assn. [2086], PO Box 55582, Shoreline, WA 98155-0582
Business Espionage Controls and Countermeasures Association [IO], Shoreline, WA, United States
Bus. Ethics; Soc. for [12127]
Bus. Executives for Natl. Security [18587], 1717 Pennsylvania Ave. NW, Ste. 350, Washington, DC 20006-4620, (202)296-2125
Business Executives for Natl. Security Education Fund - Defunct.
Bus. Exporters Assn; Small [★2313]
Bus. Exporters Assn. of the U.S; Small [2313]
Bus. Forms Assn; Natl. [★3679]
Business Forms Industries; Intl. [★729]
Business Forms Inst. - Defunct.
Bus. Forms Mgt. Assn. [3677], 319 SW Washington, No. 710, Portland, OR 97204-2618, (503)227-3393
Bus. Forum; Heavy-Duty [356]
Bus. Found. of Am; Small [★3624]
Business-Higher Educ. Forum [8008], 2025 M St. NW, Ste. 800, Washington, DC 20036-1193, (202)367-1189
Bus. History Conf. [10098], c/o Roger Horowitz, Sec.-Treas., Hagley Museum and Lib., PO Box 3630, Wilmington, DE 19807-0630, (302)658-2400
Business History Found. - Defunct.
Bus. and Home Safety; Inst. for [2171]
Bus. and Indus. Coun; U.S. [★17639]
Bus. and Indus. Advisory Comm. to the OECD [IO], Paris, France
Bus. and Indus. Advisory Comm. to the OECD; U.S.A. - [17466]
Bus. and Indus. Coun; U.S. [17639]
Business-Industry Political Action Comm. [18284], 888 16th St. NW, Ste. 305, Washington, DC 20006, (202)833-1880

Business-Industry Sect. of Natl. Sci. Teachers Assn. [★8048]
Bus. and Institutional Furniture Manufacturer's Assn. [1692], 2680 Horizon Dr. SE, Ste. A-1, Grand Rapids, MI 49546-7500, (616)285-3963
Bus. Investment Companies; Amer. Assn. of Minority Enterprise Small [★2764]
Bus. Investment Companies; Natl. Assn. of Small [3618]

Business Law
Assn. of Corporate Counsel [5614]
Assn. for Enterprise Integration [700]
Minority Corporate Counsel Assn. [5615]
Natl. Assn. of Blind Merchants [525]
Natl. Fraud Info. Center/Internet Fraud Watch [17339]
Bus. Law Assn; Amer. [★8757]
Business Leader Group - Defunct.
Business Leaders; Natl. Assn. of [3614]
Bus. Leaders for Sensible Priorities [18387], c/o Duane Peterson, Exec. Dir., 191 Bank St., 3rd Fl., Burlington, VT 05401
Business Leadership Forum - Defunct.
Bus. Leadership South Africa [IO], Johannesburg, Republic of South Africa
Business League; Natl. [2767]
Business League; Natl. Negro [★2767]
Bus. Legislative Coun; Small [3627]
Bus. Magazine Editors; Soc. of [★3084]
Bus. Mail Found. [★2625]
Bus. Mgt. Assn; Coll. Athletic [23813]
Bus. Mgt. Assn; Distribution [4019]
Bus. Mgt. Assn; Professional Services [★2513]
Bus. Mgt. Assn; Radiology [15074]
Bus. Mgt. Development; Natl. Comm. for Small [★3611]
Bus. Mgt. Educ. Assn; Natl. Farm and Ranch [4639]
Bus. Managers Assn; Coll. Athletic [23813]
Bus. Managers Assn; Radiologists [★15074]
Business Market Assn. - Address unknown since 2003.
Bus. Marketing Assn. [94], 401 N Michigan Ave., Ste. 1200, Chicago, IL 60611, (312)822-0005
Business Marketing Association [IO], Chicago, IL, United States
Bus. Media; Amer. [3201]
Bus. Men's Comm; Christian [19771]
Bus. Men's Comm. Intl; Christian [★19771]
Business Men's League of the U.S. - Address unknown since 1995.
Bus. Men's Res. Found; Amer. [★13217]

Business, Minority
Amer. and African Bus. Women's Alliance [691]
Amer. Indian Bus. Leaders [2830]
Bus. Women's Network [4036]
German Professional Women's Assn. [4039]
Natl. Assn. of Black Hotel Owners, Operators and Developers [1950]
Natl. Assn. of Investment Companies [2764]
Natl. Assn. of Minority Auto. Dealers [2765]
Natl. Black Chamber of Commerce [24250]
Natl. Gay and Lesbian Chamber of Commerce [24321]
Natl. Hispanic Bus. Assn. [8039]
Natl. Indian Bus. Assn. [751]
Natl. Minority Bus. Coun. [2768]
Natl. Minority Supplier Development Coun. [2769]
Natl. Org. for Diversity in Sales and Marketing [2644]
Native Amer. Bus. Alliance [19281]
PUSH Commercial Div. [12098]
U.S. Hispanic Chamber of Commerce [24327]
Women in Progress [13446]
Bus. Modeling and Integration Domain Task Force [706], Bldg. A, Ste. 300, 140 Kendrick St., Needham, MA 02494, (781)444-0404
Business; Natl. Assn. of Minority Women in [2766]
Bus; Natl. Fed. of Independent [3622]
Bus. for Negros; Consortium for Graduate Stud. in [★8806]
Business Network - Address unknown since 2006.
Bus. Network; American [★24301]
Bus. Network; Mothers' Home [1920]
Bus. NZ [IO], Wellington, New Zealand
Bus. and Off. Educ; Natl. Assn. of Supervisors of [★8034]

Bus. Officers; Amer. Assn. of Coll. [★7897]
Bus. Officers; Amer. Assn. of Coll. and Univ. [★7897]
Bus. Officers Associations; Natl. Fed. of Coll. and Univ. [★7897]
Bus. Officers; Natl. Assn. of Coll. and Univ. [7897]
Bus. Officials; Assn. of School [★7892]
Bus. Officials; Natl. Assn. of School [★7892]
Bus. Officials of Public Schools; Natl. Assn. of School Accounting and [★7892]
Bus. Officials of the U.S. and Canada; Assn. of School [★7892]
Bus. Organizations; Natl. Assn. for [3615]
Bus. Owners Assn; Natl. [3620]
Bus. Owners; Natl. Found. for Women [★4037]
Business Partnership for Peace - Defunct.
Bus. Political Action Committees; Natl. Assn. of [18300]
Bus. and Political Development; Alliance of Minority Women for [2759]
Bus. Press; Amer. [★3201]
Bus. Press Editors; Amer. Soc. of [★3084]
Bus. Process Mgt. Initiative and Object Mgt. Gp. [★706]

Business Products
Air Barrier Assn. of Am. [587]
Craft Org. Development Assn. [1100]
Handcrafted Soap Makers Guild [1155]
Intl. Assn. for Prdt. Development [3177]
Original Equip. Suppliers Assn. [777]
RSPA [910]
Bus. Products Credit Assn. [1405], 607 Westridge Dr., O'Fallon, MO 63366, (636)272-3005
Bus. Products Indus. Assn. [★1698]
Bus. Products Indus. Assn. Dealers Alliance; Off. Products of the [★3685]
Business/Professional Advt. Assn. [★94]
Business/Professional Advt. Assn. [★IO]
Bus. and Professional Women Australia [IO], Surrey Hills, Australia
Bus. and Professional Women Intl. [IO], Horsham, United Kingdom
Bus. and Professional Women the Netherlands [IO], Amsterdam, Netherlands
Bus. and Professional Women - UK [IO], Chesterfield, United Kingdom
Bus. and Professional Women of the United Kingdom [★IO]
Bus. and Professional Women/USA [17515], 1900 M St. NW, Ste. 310, Washington, DC 20036, (202)293-1100
Bus. and Professional Women's Clubs; Natl. Assn. of Negro [13053]
Bus. and Professional Women's Clubs; Natl. Fed. of [★17515]
Bus. and Professional Women's Found. [11084], 1900 M St. NW, Ste. 310, Washington, DC 20036, (202)293-1100
Bus. Professionals of Am. [9302], 5454 Cleveland Ave., Columbus, OH 43231-4021, (614)895-7277
Bus. Professionals; Consumer Sci. [★970]
Bus. Publication Editors; Amer. Soc. of [3084]
Bus. Publications; Assoc. [★3201]
Bus. Publications; Assn. of Area [★3199]
Bus. Publications Audit of Circulation [★93]
Bus. Publications Audit of Circulation [★IO]
Bus. Publications; Natl. [★3201]
Bus. Publishers; Assn. of [★3201]
Bus. Res; Center for Women's [4037]
Bus; Res. Inst. for Small and Emerging [3624]
Bus. Roundtable [18402], 1717 Rhode Island Ave. NW, Ste. 800, Washington, DC 20036, (202)872-1260
Bus. Schools and Programs; Assn. of Collegiate [8101]
Bus. Ser. Bur; Small [3628]
Bus. for Social Responsibility [707], 111 Sutter St., 12th Fl., San Francisco, CA 94104, (415)984-3200
Bus; Soc. of Consumer Affairs Professionals in [3196]
Bus. Software Alliance [5840], c/o BSA U.S., 1150 18th St. NW, Ste. 700, Washington, DC 20036, (202)872-5500
Bus. Software Alliance Australia [IO], North Ryde, Australia

Reference to "IO" in place of a book number signifies that the association may be found in the 45th edition of International Organizations.

Bus. Software Assn. [★5840]
Bus. Software Assn. of Australia [★IO]
Business Studies
    Amer. Indian Bus. Leaders [2830]
    Assn. for Global Bus. [8016]
    Bus. Leaders for Sensible Priorities [18387]
    Financial Mgt. Assn. Intl. [8441]
    Global Bus. and Tech. Assn. [778]
    Global Bus. and Tech. Assn. [IO]
    Mgt. Educ. Alliance [8029]
    My Own Bus., Inc. [8030]
Business Systems Assn. - Defunct.
Business and Tax Planning Bd. - Defunct.
Business and Taxpayers Coalition for Affordable
    Housing - Address unknown since 2003.
Bus. Teacher Educ; Natl. Assn. for [8032]
Bus. Teachers Assn; Natl. [★8036]
Bus. Tech. Assn. [2844], 12411 Wornall Rd., Ste.
    200, Kansas City, MO 64145-1212, (816)941-3100
Bus. and Tech. Educ. Coun. [★IO]
Bus. and Tech; U.S. - ASEAN Coun. for [★3848]
Business Tourism
    Amer. Chamber of Commerce Executives [24251]
    Assoc. Luxury Hotels Intl. [1931]
    Caribbean-Central Amer. Action [12421]
    Sustainable Travel Intl. [5252]
Bus. Travel Assn; Natl. [3929]
Bus. Travel Coalition [24382], 214 Grouse Ln., Rad-
    nor, PA 19087-2730, (610)341-1850
Bus. United; Natl. Small [★3623]
Bus. United; Small [★3623]
Bus. Volunteers for the Arts [★9550]
Bus. Volunteers Unlimited [13390], 200 Public Sq.,
    Ste. 2650, Cleveland, OH 44114-2383, (216)736-
    7711
Business; Women in Agri [4085]
Bus. Women; Natl. Assn. of Railway [3285]
Bus. Women's Assn; Railway [★3285]
Bus. Women's Network [4036], 1990 M St. NW, Ste.
    700, Washington, DC 20036, (202)466-8209
Bus. Writers; Soc. of Amer. [★3161]
Bus. Writing Assn; Amer. [★8014]
Businesses; Amer. Assn. of Home Based [1917]
Businesses; Amer. Assn. of Minority [2760]
Businesses Assn; Amer. Small [3603]
Businesses; Natl. Assn. of Cmpt. Consultant [968]
Businesses; Natl. Assn. of Home Based [1921]
BusinessEurope [IO], Brussels, Belgium
Businesspersons Assn; Disabled [12076]
Businesswomen's Assn. [IO], Killarney, Republic of
    South Africa
Buster Keaton Soc; Damfinos: The Intl. [24797]
Butchers' Company [IO], London, United Kingdom
Butimar Productions [9849], PO Box 609, Menlo
    Park, CA 94026-0609, (650)327-7908
Butler, Jr. Found. for Educ. in World Law; Pierce
    [★18834]
Butsuri Tansa Gakkai [★IO]
Butter, Cheese, and Egg Exchange of the City of
    New York [★4333]
Butter and Egg Bd; Chicago [★4324]
Butter Inst; Amer. [1128]
Butter Pat Patter Assn. [21981], c/o Mary Dessoie,
    Founder, 265 Eagle Bend Dr., Bigfork, MT 59911-
    6235
Butterfield Trail Antique Auto Club - Defunct.
Butterfly
    Butterfly Lovers Intl. [7248]
    Butterfly Soc. of Japan [IO]
    Heterocera Sumatrana Soc. [IO]
    Intl. Assn. of Butterfly Exhibitions [1341]
    Intl. Butterfly Breeders Assn. [4203]
    International Butterfly Breeders Association [IO]
    Japan Heterocerists' Soc. [IO]
    Lepidopterological Soc. of Finland [IO]
    Natl. Butterfly Assn. [23202]
    North Amer. Butterfly Assn. [7249]
    Xerces Soc. [5405]
Butterfly Assn; Natl. [23202]
Butterfly Assn; North Amer. [7249]
Butterfly Conservation [IO], Wareham, United
    Kingdom
Butterfly Lovers Intl. [7248]
Butterfly and Moth Stamp Soc. - Address unknown
    since 2001.

Butterfly Soc. of Japan [IO], Tokyo, Japan
Button Assn; Belt and [2836]
Button Assn. of New York; Covered [★2836]
Button and Buckle Assn. of New York; Covered
    [★2836]
Button Soc; Natl. [22079]
Buttonhook Soc. [IO], Maidstone, United Kingdom
Buxom Belles, Intl. - Address unknown since 1995.
Buy-Black Campaign; Natl. [★2761]
Buyer Agents; Natl. Assn. of Exclusive [18495]
Buyer Brokers; Natl. Assn. of Real Estate [3324]
Buyer's Agent Coun; Real Estate [3337]
Buyers' Assn; Debt [1146]
Buyers Assn; Educational [★7899]
Buyers Assn; Intl. Entertainment [1306]
Buyers Assn. Intl; Printing Brokerage/ [★1786]
Buyers Assn; Mountain State Organic Growers and
    [5068]
Buyers Assn; Organic Growers and [5070]
Buyers Assn; Printing Brokerage/ [1786]
Buyers' Boycott - Address unknown since 1985.
Buyers Fed; Amer. [★1454]
Buyers; Natl. Assn. of Educational [★7899]
Buyers; Natl. Assn. of Men's Sportswear [247]
Buyers and Suppliers; Cosmetic Indus. [1843]
Buying Influence [17310], 801 W 47th St., Ste. 110,
    Country Club Plz., Kansas City, MO 64112,
    (816)931-7896
Buzzcocks Fan Club/Harmony in My Head - Address
    unknown since 1999.
BVWS [★IO]
BWHBC [★16909]
By Hand and Foot: Tools Dependent on Human
    Energy - Defunct.
By-Products Assn; Textile Fibers and [3803]
By Word of Mouth Storytelling Guild [10978], c/o
    Truman Coggswell, Sr., PO Box 56, Frankford, MO
    63441, (573)784-2589
Byam Caravan Club Intl; Wally [22967]
Byelorussian-Amer. Veteran Assn. - Defunct.
Byelorussian-Amer. Women Assn. - Defunct.
Byelorussian-Amer. Youth Org. - Address unknown
    since 2004.
Byelorussian Anatomical Soc. [IO], Minsk, Belarus
Byelorussian Assn. of the Physicians [IO], Minsk,
    Belarus
Byelorussian Liberation Front - Defunct.
Byelorussian Operational Res. Soc. [IO], Minsk, Be-
    larus
Byggesocietetet [★IO]
Byrd Online Fan Club; Tracy [24987]
Byron Bay Chamber of Commerce and Indus. [IO],
    Byron Bay, Australia
Byron Soc. of Am. [9641], c/o Charles E. Robinson,
    Exec. Dir., Univ. of Delaware, Dept. of English,
    Newark, DE 19716-2537, (302)831-3654
Bytown Railway Soc. [IO], Ottawa, ON, Canada
Byzantine
    Amer. Inst. for Patristic and Byzantine Stud. [IO]
    Amer. Inst. for Patristic and Byzantine Stud.
    [9770]
    North Amer. Patristics Soc. [20460]
    Soc. for the Promotion of Byzantine Stud. [IO]
    Stud. for the Promotion of Byzantine Stud. [IO]
    U.S. Natl. Comm. for Byzantine Stud. [9771]

C

C. D. Howe Memorial Found. [★IO]
C-PRO Users' Group - Defunct.
C. S. Owner's Assn. - Address unknown since 1991.
C Scow Sailing Assn; Natl. [23203]
C/SEC [15593], 13 Alfred Rd., Framingham, MA
    01701, (508)877-8266
C/SEC (Cesarean Sections: Educ. and Concern)
    [★15593]
C3: Colorectal Cancer Coalition [13802], 4301 Con-
    necticut Ave. NW, Ste. 404, Washington, DC
    20008, (202)244-2906
CAA/AAA Found. for Traffic Safety [★12943]
CAAAV: Organizing Asian Communities [★17006]
Cab Res. Bur. [★3894]
Cab Res. Bur. [★IO]

Cabbage/Cabage Surname Org. - Address unknown
    since 2007.
Cabbage Patch Kids Collectors Club [21982], c/o
    BabyLand Gen. Hosp., PO Box 714, Cleveland,
    GA 30528, (706)865-2171
Cabell Soc. - Defunct.
CABI Bioscience [IO], Wallingford, United Kingdom
CABI Bioscience Pakistan Centre [IO], Rawalpindi,
    Pakistan
CABI Bioscience Switzerland Centre [IO], Delemont,
    Switzerland
Cabin Fed; Log [★18523]
Cabin Republicans; Log [18523]
Cabinet Assn; Natl. Kitchen [★2267]
Cabinet Mfrs. Assn; Kitchen [2267]
Cabinets; Natl. Inst. of Wood Kitchen [★2267]
Cable Credit Assn; Broadcast [552]
Cable Engineers Assn; Insulated [7017]
Cable Engineers Assn; Insulated Power [★7017]
Cable Europe [IO], Brussels, Belgium
Cable Financial Mgt. Assn; Broadcast [553]
Cable Indus. Suppliers Assn; Wire and [1231]
Cable Positive [11327], 1775 Broadway, Ste. 433,
    New York, NY 10019, (212)459-1605
Cable Programmers; Natl. Fed. of Local [★17161]
Cable and Satellite Broadcasting Assn. of Asia -
    Hong Kong Off. [IO], Hong Kong, People's
    Republic of China
Cable and Telecommunications: A Marketing Soc.
    [★558]
Cable Telecommunications Assn. - Defunct.
Cable and Telecommunications Assn. for Marketing;
    CTAM - [558]
Cable and Telecommunications Assn; Natl. [573]
Cable Telecommunications Engineers; Soc. of
    [7040]
Cable and Telecommunications Human Resources
    Assn. [1980], 1755 Park St., Ste. 260, Naperville,
    IL 60563, (630)416-1166
Cable Television
    Alliance for Community Media [17161]
    Amer. Cable Assn. [779]
    Assn. of Cable Communicators [5556]
    Broadcast Cable Financial Mgt. Assn. [553]
    Cable Positive [11327]
    Cable and Telecommunications Human
        Resources Assn. [1980]
    Cable TV Labs. [780]
    Cabletelevision Advt. Bur. [95]
    CTAM - Cable and Telecommunications Assn. for
        Marketing [558]
    Free Speech TV [18726]
    Media Rating Coun. [566]
    Natl. Assn. of TV Prog. Executives [571]
    Natl. Cable and Telecommunications Assn. [573]
    Natl. Cable TV Cooperative [781]
    Natl. Cable TV Inst. [574]
    PROMAX [577]
    Syndicated Network TV Assn. [120]
    Telecommunications Res. and Action Center
        [17195]
    TV Operators Caucus [583]
    Wireless Communications Assn. Intl. [3764]
    Women in Cable Telecommunications [585]
Cable TV Admin. and Marketing Soc. [★558]
Cable TV Assn; Natl. [★573]
Cable TV Engineers; Soc. of [★7040]
Cable TV Information Center - Defunct.
Cable TV Inst; Natl. [574]
Cable TV Labs. [780], c/o Michael M. Schwartz, Sr.
    VP for Communications, 858 Coal Creek Cir.,
    Louisville, CO 80027-9750, (303)661-9100
Cable TV Public Affairs Assn. [★5556]
Cabletelevision Advt. Bur. [95], 830 Third Ave., 2nd
    Fl., New York, NY 10022, (212)508-1200
Cabrini Mission Corps [20308], 610 King of Prussia
    Rd., Radnor, PA 19087-3623, (610)971-0821
Cabriolet Club; Model A 68-B [★21709]
Cabriolet Club; Model A Ford [21709]
Cactus and Native Flora Soc; Arizona [★6633]
Cactus and Succulent Res; Arizona [6631]
Cactus and Succulent Soc. of Am. [22506], c/o Clif-
    ford Meng, Treas., PO Box 2615, Pahrump, NV
    89041-2615, (775)751-1320
CAD Soc. [6764], 8220 Stone Trail Dr., Bethesda,
    MD 20817-4556, (301)365-4585

A star before a book entry number signifies that the name is not listed separately, but is mentioned within the entry.

Cadenhead Family Assn. - Address unknown since 2006.

Cadet Exchange; International Air [★5538]

Cadets
Amer. Cadet Alliance [20718]

Cadillac Convertible Owners of America - Address unknown since 2003.

Cadillac Drivers Club [21601], c/o Wray Tibbs, Pres., 5825 Vista Ave., Sacramento, CA 95824-1428, (916)421-3193

Cadillac-LaSalle Club [21602], PO Box 360835, Columbus, OH 43236-0835, (614)478-4622

Cadillac Owners Assn; 1958 [21556]

Cadmium Coun., Inc. [★IO]

Cadwalader Park; Friends of [★4407]

CAE [IO], Melbourne, Australia

CAEF - The European Foundry Assn. [IO], Dusseldorf, Germany

Caesarean Cycling Club [IO], Jersey, United Kingdom

Caffeine Awareness Alliance [13747], 32 Saddleview Dr., Royersford, PA 19468

CAFPRS [★IO]

Cage Bird Judges Assn; Greater North Amer. Aviculturist and [★21845]

Cage Bird Show; Natl. [21851]

Cage Birds; Natl. Inst. of Red Orange Canaries and All Other [21855]

Cagney Fan Club; Sharon Gless as [★24771]

Cagney and Lacey
Sharon Gless Fan Club (U.S.) [24771]

Cagney and Lacey Fan Club - Defunct.

Cahill Cooperative [★20813]

Cahill Cooperative Ancestors [20813], 2050 Cedar Johnson Rd., West Branch, IA 52358, (319)643-2829

Cahill Immigrant Info. Exchange [★20813]

Cairn Terrier Club of Am. [22238], 37667 Timber Dr., Elizabeth, CO 80107, (303)646-9657

Cairns Chamber of Commerce [IO], Cairns, Australia

Cairo Regional Centre for Intl. Commercial Arbitration [IO], Cairo, Egypt

Caisses en Carton Ondule; Assn. Internationale des Fabricants de [★985]

Caithness Paperweight Collectors Soc. [IO], Perth, United Kingdom

Caitlin Raymond Intl. Registry [13770], UMass Memorial Medical Center, 55 Lake Ave. N, Worcester, MA 01655, (508)334-8969

Cajal Club [15385], c/o Dr. Charles E. Ribak, Sec.-Treas., Univ. of California at Irvine, School of Medicine, Dept. of Anatomy and Neurobiology, Irvine, CA 92697-1275

C.A.L./N-X-211 Collectors Soc. [11106]

Cal Owner's Assn. - Defunct.

Cal State San Marcos Alumni Assn. [18881], Off. of Alumni Relations, CSU San Marcos, San Marcos, CA 92096-0001, (760)750-4405

Calavo Growers of California - Address unknown since 2001.

Calcium Chloride Inst. - Defunct.

Caleb Campaign - Address unknown since 2003.

Caleb Smith Family Assn. - Defunct.

Caledonian Found. USA [10570], PO Box 1242, Edgartown, MA 02539-1242

Caledonian Found. USA [IO], Edgartown, MA, United States

Calendar
Calendar Marketing Assn. [2618]
Comm. for Crescent Observation Intl. [10246]
Promotional Products Assn. Intl. [116]

Calendar Marketing Assn. [2618], 214 N Hale St., Wheaton, IL 60187, (630)510-4564

Calendar Reform Found. - Defunct.

Calendar Reform Political Action Group - Defunct.

Calf Ropers Assn; U.S. [23695]

Calgary Acad. of Chefs and Cooks [IO], Calgary, AB, Canada

Calgary Amateur Radio Assn. [IO], Calgary, AB, Canada

Calgary Apartment Assn. [IO], Calgary, AB, Canada

Calgary Beach Volleyball Assn. [IO], Calgary, AB, Canada

Calgary BMX Assn. [IO], Calgary, AB, Canada

Calgary Cerebral Palsy Assn. [IO], Calgary, AB, Canada

Calgary Chinese Elderly Citizens' Assn. [IO], Calgary, AB, Canada

Calgary Constr. Assn. [IO], Calgary, AB, Canada

Calgary Coun. for Advanced Tech. [IO], Calgary, AB, Canada

Calgary Down Syndrome Assn. [IO], Calgary, AB, Canada

Calgary Folkdance Fridays Club [★IO]

Calgary Immigrant Women's Assn. [IO], Calgary, AB, Canada

Calgary Minor Basketball Assn. [IO], Calgary, AB, Canada

Calgary Mountain Bike Alliance [IO], Calgary, AB, Canada

Calgary Musicians' Assn. [IO], Calgary, AB, Canada

Calgary Recreational Intl. Folkdance Club [IO], Calgary, AB, Canada

Calgary Seniors Rsrc. Soc. [IO], Calgary, AB, Canada

Calgary Ultimate Assn. [IO], Calgary, AB, Canada

Calgary United Soccer Assn. [IO], Calgary, AB, Canada

Calgary Women's Soccer Assn. [IO], Calgary, AB, Canada

Calibre Audio Lib. [IO], Aylesbury, United Kingdom

CALIBRE - Cassette Lib. for the Blind and Print Handicapped [★IO]

Calico Cat Registry Intl. [IO], Morongo Valley, CA, United States

Calico Cat Registry Intl. [21902], PO Box 944, Morongo Valley, CA 92256, (760)363-6511

California Advt. Agencies Assn; Southern [★107]

California Almond Growers Exchange [★5052]

California Alumni Assn; St. Mary's Coll. of [18922]

California Apricot Advisory Bd. - Defunct.

California; Apricot Producers of [4706]

California Artichoke Advisory Bd. - Defunct.

California Asparagus Advisory Bd. - Defunct.

California Assn. of Parking Controllers - Address unknown since 1991.

California Assn. of Pet Professionals [★2968]

California Assn. of Pet Professionals [★IO]

California Assn. of Sanitarians [★14367]

California Assn. of Tiger-Owners [21603], 18771 Paseo Picasso, Irvine, CA 92603, (949)854-2561

California Association of Tiger-Owners [IO], Irvine, CA, United States

California Assn. of Winegrape Growers [5412], 601 Univ. Ave., Ste. 135, Sacramento, CA 95825, (916)924-5370

California Avocado Advisory Bd. [★4707]

California Avocado Assn. [★4708]

California Avocado Commn. [4707], 38 Discovery, Ste. 150, Irvine, CA 92618, (949)341-1955

California Avocado Export Assn. - Defunct.

California Avocado Soc. [4708], PO Box 1317, Carpinteria, CA 93014, (805)684-2804

California Begonia Soc. [★22482]

California Brandy Advisory Bd. - Defunct.

California Bush Berry Advisory Bd. - Defunct.

California Cactus Growers Assn. - Defunct.

California Canning Peach Assn. [4709], 2300 River Plaza Dr., Ste. 110, Sacramento, CA 95833, (916)925-9131

California Cling Peach Advisory Bd. [★4710]

California Cling Peach Bd. [4710], c/o Jim Melban, 531-D N Alta Ave., Dinuba, CA 93618-3203, (559)595-1425

California Coastal Commn. [★4669]

California Coll. of Arts and Crafts Alumni Assn. [18882], c/o Jessica Russell, Alumni Relations Mgr., 5212 Broadway, Oakland, CA 94618, (510)594-3788

California Conservation Proj. [★4460]

California Coun. Against Hea. Fraud [★17692]

California Date Administrative Comm. [4711], PO Box 1736, Indio, CA 92202-1736, (760)347-4510

California Date Administrative Comm. [★4711]

California Date Commn. [★4711]

California Date Growers Assn. - Defunct.

California Depopulation Commn. - Defunct.

California; DFA of [4726]

California Dried Fig Advisory Bd. [★4714]

California; Dried Fruit Assn. of [★4726]

California Dried Fruit Export Assn. [★4761]

California Dried Plum Bd. [4712], 3840 Rosin Ct., Ste. 170, Sacramento, CA 95834, (916)565-6232

California Dry Bean Advisory Bd. [4713], 531-D N Alta Ave., Dinuba, CA 93618-3203, (559)591-4866

California Educational Computing Consortium - Address unknown since 2004.

California Engg. Found. [7007], 2700 Zinfandel Dr., Rancho Cordova, CA 95670-4827, (916)853-1914

California Fashion Creators - Defunct.

California Fed. of Legal Secretaries [★71]

California Fed. of Legal Secretaries [★IO]

California Fig Advisory Bd. [4714], 7395 N Palm Bluffs Ave., Ste. 106, Fresno, CA 93711-5767, (559)440-5400

California Fig Inst. [4715], 7395 N Palm Bluffs Ave., Ste. 106, Fresno, CA 93711-5767, (559)440-5400

California Forest Protective Assn. [★1605]

California Forestry Assn. [1605], 1215 K St., Ste. 1830, Sacramento, CA 95814-3947, (916)444-6592

California Freezers Assn. [★1496]

California Frozen Vegetable Coun. - Defunct.

California Fruit Growers Exchange [★4763]

California Grape and Tree Fruit Assn. [★4716]

California Grape and Tree Fruit League [4716], 978 W Alluvial, Ste. 107, Fresno, CA 93711-5700, (559)226-6300

California Gp. Against Smoking Pollution [★16432]

California Growers and Shippers Protective League [★4716]

California Hang Glider Assn; Southern [★23044]

California Helicopter Assn. [★150]

California Helicopter Assn. [★IO]

California Hungarian Amer. Cultural Found. - Defunct.

California Iceberg Lettuce Commn. - Address unknown since 1994.

California Independent Almond Growers - Defunct.

California Investment Real Estate Forum - Defunct.

California Kiwifruit Commn. [4717], 770 E Shaw, Ste. 220, Fresno, CA 93710

California Macadamia Soc. [5053], PO Box 1298, Fallbrook, CA 92088-1298, (760)728-8081

California Melon Res. Bd. [4718], 531-D N Alta Ave., Dinuba, CA 93618, (559)591-0435

California Motorama Corp. [★23623]

California Natl. Watercolor Soc. [★9461]

California Olallie Berry Advisory Bd. - Defunct.

California Olive Assn. [1504], 980 9th St., Ste. 230, Sacramento, CA 95814, (916)444-9260

California Persimmon Growers Assn. - Address unknown since 1995.

California Pioneers; Soc. of [21255]

California Pistachio Commn. [5054], 1318 E Shaw Ave., Ste. 420, Fresno, CA 93710, (559)221-8294

California Prune Advisory Bd. [★4712]

California Prune Bd. [★4712]

California Public Employee Relations Prog. [17969], c/o Inst. for Res. on Labor and Employment, 2521 Channing Way, No. 5555, Berkeley, CA 94720-5555, (510)643-7096

California Raisin Advisory Bd. - Defunct.

California Rare Fruit Growers [4719], The Fullerton Arboretum-CSUF, PO Box 6850, Fullerton, CA 92834-6850, (415)839-0102

California Redwood Assn. [1639], 405 Enfrente Dr., Ste. 200, Novato, CA 94949, (415)382-0662

California Soc. of Etchers [★1762]

California Soc. of Printmakers [1762], PO Box 475422, San Francisco, CA 94147, (415)905-4296

California State Univ. - Northridge Alumni Assn. [18883], 18111 Nordhoff St., Northridge, CA 91330-8385, (818)677-2137

California State Univ. of San Marcos Alumni Assn. [★18881]

California State Univ. - Stanislaus Alumni Assn. [18884], One Univ. Cir., Turlock, CA 95382, (209)667-3131

California Strawberry Advisory Bd. [★4720]

California Strawberry Commn. [4720], PO Box 269, Watsonville, CA 95077, (831)724-1301

California; Sun-Maid Growers of [4762]

California Table Grape Commn. [4721], 392 W Fallbrook, Ste. 101, Fresno, CA 93711-6150, (559)447-8350

California; Timber Assn. of [★1605]

Reference to "IO" in place of a book number signifies that the association may be found in the 45th edition of International Organizations.

California Tobacco Educ. Clearinghouse [★8556]
California Tomorrow - Defunct.
California Traffic Safety Found. - Defunct.
California Trails Assn; Oregon- [10056]
California Vehicle Leasing Assn. [★3385]
California Vintage Race Gp. [★22665]
California Walnut Growers Assn. [★5055]
California Water Color Soc. [★9461]
California Wheelchair Aviators [★21457]
California Wheelchair Aviators [★IO]
California Wilderness Survival League [9202], 395
    Rio St., Redding, CA 96001-3611, (530)247-0632
Californian
    Los Californianos [20719]
    Native Daughters of the Golden West [18986]
    Native Sons of the Golden West [18987]
Californian Rabbit Specialty Club [5142], c/o Donald
    Mersiovsky, Sec.-Treas., 1156 Elm Grove Spur,
    Belton, TX 76513, (254)939-0345
Californians for Nonsmokers' Rights [★16432]
Californians for Responsible Res. [★11413]
Calix Soc. [13227], 2555 Hazelwood Ave., St. Paul,
    MN 55109-2030, (651)773-3117
Calix Soc. [IO], St. Paul, MN, United States
Calkins Clancaller - Address unknown since 1994.
Call Assn. - Address unknown since 1995.
Call Center Assn. [IO], Glasgow, United Kingdom
Call Center Benchmarking Network [★IO]
Call Center Benchmarking Network [★731]
Call Centre Assn. [★IO]
Call Centre Assn. of India [IO], Gurgaon, India
Call Centre Mgt. Assn. [IO], Sandbach, United
    Kingdom
Call Centre Mgt. Assn., Ireland [IO], Kilkenny,
    Ireland
Call For Action [IO], Bethesda, MD, United States
Call For Action [11802], 5272 River Rd., Ste. 300,
    Bethesda, MD 20816, (301)657-8260
Call Girls United Against Repression; Johns and
    [13094]
Call to Renewal [18376], 3333 14th St. NW, Ste.
    200, Washington, DC 20010, (202)328-8745
Call and Response [20309], c/o Mary Lou Doran,
    Dir., 10636 N 37th Ave., Phoenix, AZ 85029
A Call to Serve Intl. [11765], 601 Bus. Loop 70 W,
    Ste. 153-A, Columbia, MO 65203, (573)874-0268
Call and Whistle Collectors Assn. [21983], c/o
    James C. Fitch, 2839 E 26th Pl., Tulsa, OK 74114,
    (918)747-3202
Callerlab - Intl. Assn. of Square Dance Callers
    [9869], 467 Forrest Ave., Ste. 118, Cocoa, FL
    32922, (321)639-0039
Callerlab - Intl. Assn. of Square Dance Callers [IO],
    Cocoa, FL, United States
Calligraphers; Australian Soc. of [IO]
Calligraphers Guild; Washington [11215]
Calligraphic Arts; Assn. for the [9555]
Calligraphy and Lettering Arts Soc. [IO], London,
    United Kingdom
Calligraphy; Soc. for [11213]
Callmakers and Collectors Assn. of Am. [21984], c/o
    Herb Ohley, Membership Chm., 2925 Ethel Ave.,
    Alton, IL 62002, (618)465-5235
Calmeadow Charitable Found. [IO], Toronto, ON,
    Canada
Calorie Control Coun. [1505], 5775 Peachtree-
    Dunwoody Rd., Ste. 500-G, Atlanta, GA 30342,
    (404)252-3663
Calorimetry Conf. [7796], c/o Michael Frenkel, Chm.,
    Natl. Inst. of Standards and Tech., Thermodynam-
    ics Res. Center, Physical and Chem. Properties
    Div. 838, 325 Broadway, Rm. 2-1010, Boulder, CO
    80308-3328, (303)497-3952
Calorimetry Conf; Low Temperature [★7796]
Calvin Coolidge Memorial Found. [11107], PO Box
    97, Plymouth, VT 05056, (802)672-3389
Calvinist Fed; Young [★19831]
CAM Intl. [20310], 8625 La Prada Dr., Dallas, TX
    75228, (214)327-8206
CAM Intl. [IO], Dallas, TX, United States
Camanachd Assn. [IO], Inverness, United Kingdom
Camanachd Assn. - Address unknown since 1995.
Camara Americana de Comercio de Bolivia [★IO]
Camara Americana de Comercio de El Salvador
    [★IO]

Camara Americana de Comercio de la Republica
    Dominicana [★IO]
Camara de Anunciantes del Paraguay [IO], Asun-
    cion, Paraguay
Camara Anunciantes del Uruguay [IO], Montevideo,
    Uruguay
Camara Argentina del Aerosol [★IO]
Camara Argentina de Anunciantes [IO], Buenos
    Aires, Argentina
Camara Argentina de Comercio [★IO]
Camara Argentina de la Construccion [★IO]
Camara Argentina de Distribuidores de Materiales
    Electricos [★IO]
Camara Argentina de la Industria del Aluminio y Met-
    ales Afines [★IO]
Camara Argentina de la Industria Plastica [★IO]
Camara Argentina de Industrias Electronicas [★IO]
Camara Argentina del Libro [★IO]
Camara Argentina de Papelerias, Librerias y Afines
    [★IO]
Camara Argentina de Productores Avicolas [★IO]
Camara Argentina de Productores de Drogas Far-
    maceuticas [★IO]
Camara Argentina de Shopping Centers [★IO]
Camara Argentina de Supermercados [★IO]
Camara de Aseguradores de Venezuela [★IO]
Camara Automotriz de Venezuela [★IO]
Camara de Azucareros [★IO]
Camara Brasileira do Livro [★IO]
Camara Chilena de la Construccion [★IO]
Camara Chilena del Libro A.G. [★IO]
Camara Chileno Norteamericana de Comercio [★IO]
Camara Colombiana de Informatica y Telecomunica-
    ciones [★IO]
Camara Colombiana del Libro [★IO]
Camara de Comercio Americana del Peru [★IO]
Camara de Comercio Argentino-Brasilena [IO], Bue-
    nos Aires, Argentina
Camara de Comercio Argentino-Britanica en la Re-
    publica Argentina [IO], Buenos Aires, Argentina
Camara de Comercio Argentino-Canadiense [★IO]
Camara de Comercio Argentino-Israeli [★IO]
Camara de Comercio Argentino-Venezolana [IO],
    Buenos Aires, Argentina
Camara de Comercio de Costa Rica [★IO]
Camara de Comercio Ecuatoriano- Americana [★IO]
Camara de Comercio de los Estados Unidos en la
    Republica Argentina [★IO]
Camara de Comercio Exterior de Rosario [IO], Ro-
    sario, Argentina
Camara de Comercio Exterior de Salta [IO], Salta,
    Argentina
Camara de Comercio Guatemalteco-Americana
    [★IO]
Camara de Comercio Hondureno-Americana [★IO]
Camara de Comercio e Industria de Angola [IO],
    Luanda, Angola
Camara de Comercio e Industria de El Salvador
    [★IO]
Camara de Comercio e Industria Franco-Argentina
    [★IO]
Camara de Comercio e Industria Peruano-Alemana
    [★IO]
Camara de Comercio e Industria Peruano-Francesa
    [★IO]
Camara do Comercio e Industria de Ponta Delgada
    [★IO]
Camara de Comercio e Industria de Trenque Lau-
    quen [IO], Buenos Aires, Argentina
Camara de Comercio, Industria Y Servicios de Car-
    los Casares [IO], Carlos Casares, Argentina
Camara de Comercio Italiana de Rosario [IO], Rosa-
    rio, Argentina
Camara de Comercio Latina de los EEUU [★24354]
Camara de Comercio de Lima [★IO]
Camara de Comercio de Mocambique [★IO]
Camara de Comercio Paraguaya Americana [★IO]
Camara de Comercio y Produccion de Santiago
    [★IO]
Camara de Comercio y Produccion de Santo Dom-
    ingo [★IO]
Camara de Comercio de Santiago [★IO]
Camara de Comercio Sueco Argentina [IO], Buenos
    Aires, Argentina
Camara de Comercio Suizo Argentina [★IO]

Camara de Comercio Uruguay - Estados Unidos
    [★IO]
Camara de la Construccion de Quito [★IO]
Camara Costarricense de la Construccion [★IO]
Camara De Comercio Colombo Americana - Bogota
    [★IO]
Camara Empresaria Parque Indus. de Pilar [IO],
    Buenos Aires, Argentina
Camara de Empresarios Madereros y Afines [★IO]
Camara de Empresas de Servicios de Telecomuni-
    caciones [★IO]
Camara de Empresas de Software y Servicios Infor-
    maticos [★IO]
Camara Espanola de Comercio de la Republica
    Argentina [IO], Buenos Aires, Argentina
Camara de Exportadores del El Rosario [IO], Rosa-
    rio, Argentina
Camara de Exportadores de la Republica Argentina
    [★IO]
Camara de Fabricantes de Refrescos y Afines [★IO]
Camara de Fabricantes Venezolanos de Productos
    Automotores [★IO]
Camara Forestal de Bolivia [★IO]
Camara de Importadores de la Republica Argentina
    [★IO]
Camara de la Industria Aceitera de la Republica
    Argentina [★IO]
Camara de la Industria del Calzado del Estado de
    Guanajuato [★IO]
Camara de Industria y Comercio Argentino-Alemana
    [IO], Buenos Aires, Argentina
Camara de Industria y Comercio de Matanza [IO],
    Buenos Aires, Argentina
Camara Indus. Argentina de Indumentaria [★IO]
Camara de Informatica y Comunicaciones de la Re-
    publica Argentina [★IO]
Camara Junior de Argentina [IO], Rosario, Argentina
Camara Junior Internacional Colombia [★IO]
Camara Junior Internacional de Ecuador [★IO]
Camara Junior Internacional de Republica Domini-
    cana [★IO]
Camara Junior Internacional de Venezuela [★IO]
Camara Junior del Paraguay [IO], Asuncion,
    Paraguay
Camara Junor de Guatemala [IO], Guatemala City,
    Guatemala
Camara de La Industria El Trebol [IO], Santa Fe,
    Argentina
Camara Madrid [★IO]
Camara Mercantil de Productos del Pais [★IO]
Camara Mexicana de la Industria de la Construccion
    [★IO]
Camara Nacional de Agricultura y Agroindustria
    [★IO]
Camara Nacional de Comercio - Bolivia [★IO]
Camara Nacional de Comercio y Servicios del
    Uruguay [★IO]
Camara Nacional de Empresas Comercializadoras
    de Seguros [★IO]
Camara Nacional de Empresas de Consultoria
    [★IO]
Camara Nacional de la Industria Editorial Mexicana
    [★IO]
Camara Nacional de la Industria de Farmaceutica
    [★IO]
Camara Nacional de la Industria Panificadora y
    Similares de Mexico [★IO]
Camara Nacional de la Industria de Perfumeria,
    Cosmetica y Articulos de Tocador e Higiene [★IO]
Camara Nacional de la Industria Pesquera [★IO]
Camara Nacional de la Industria de Radio y TV
    [★IO]
Camara Nacional de la Industria de Restaurantes y
    Alimentos Condimentados [★IO]
Camara Nacional de la Industria de Telecomunica-
    ciones por Cable [★IO]
Camara Nacional de la Industria de la Transforma-
    cion [★IO]
Camara Nacional de la Industria del Vestido [★IO]
Camara Nacional de las Industrias Azucarera y Alco-
    holera [★IO]
Camara Nacional de Manufacturas Electricas [★IO]
Camara Nacional de Pesqueria [★IO]
Camara Nacional de Productores de Leche [★IO]
Camara Oficial de Comercio de Espana en Gran
    Bretana [★IO]

A star before a book entry number signifies that the name is not listed separately, but is mentioned within the entry.

Camara Paraguaya de Exportadores de Cereales y Oleaginosas [★IO]

Camara Peruana de la Construccion [★IO]

Camara Petrolera de Venezuela [★IO]

Camara de la Produccion, la Industria y el Comercio Argentino-China [IO], Buenos Aires, Argentina

Camara de Produccion Y Servicios de La Provincia de Buenos Aires [IO], La Plata, Argentina

Camara Salvadorena de la Industria de la Construccion [★IO]

Camara Salvadorena de Turismo [★IO]

Camara de Sociedades Anonimas [★IO]

Camara Textil Costarricense [★IO]

Camara Uruguaya del Libro [IO], Montevideo, Uruguay

Camara Venezolana de Empresas de Tecnologias de la Informacion [★IO]

Camara Venezolana de la Industria de Alimentos [★IO]

Camara Venezolano Americana de Comercio e Industria [★IO]

Camara Venezolano Americana de Comercio e Industria [★24305]

Camaro Assn; Amer. [21570]

Camaro Assn; Worldwide [★21821]

Camaro Club; U.S. [★21821]

Camaro Club; Worldwide [21821]

Camaro Owners of America - Defunct.

Cambodia; 11th Armored Cavalry's Veterans of Vietnam and [21341]

Cambodia Crisis Center - Defunct.

Cambodia Medical Assn. [IO], Phnom Penh, Cambodia

Cambodia Tennis Fed. [IO], Phnom Penh, Cambodia

Cambodian
Light of Cambodian Children [11617]

Cambodian Appeal - Defunct.

Cambodian Buddhist Soc. [9769], 13800 New Hampshire Ave., Silver Spring, MD 20904, (301)622-6544

Cambodian Buddhist Soc. [IO], Silver Spring, MD, United States

Cambodian Children; Light of [11617]

Cambodian Crisis Comm. - Address unknown since 1999.

Cambodian Disabled People's Org. [IO], Phnom Penh, Cambodia

Cambodian, Laotian, and Vietnamese Americans; Natl. Assn. for the Educ. and Advancement of [19424]

Cambodian Mutual Assistance Assn. [19422], 787 E Broad St., Columbus, OH 43205, (614)224-8888

Cambodian People's Party [IO], Phnom Penh, Cambodia

Cambodian Religio-Cultural Assn. of America - Defunct.

Cambodian Survivors of America; Assn. of [12806]

Cambra De Comerc Industria Serveis D' Andorra [★IO]

Cambridge in Am. [9284], 100 Ave. of the Americas, 4th Fl., New York, NY 10013, (212)984-0960

Cambridge Buddhist Assn. [19547], 75 Sparks St., Cambridge, MA 02138-2215, (617)491-8857

Cambridge Collectors; Natl. [22561]

Cambridge Mission to Delhi [★IO]

Cambridge Philosophical Soc. [IO], Cambridge, United Kingdom

Cambridge Refrigeration Tech. [IO], Cambridge, United Kingdom

Cambridge Univ; Amer. Friends of [★9284]

Cambridgeshire Area Campaign for Nuclear Disarmament [IO], St. Neots, United Kingdom

Cambridgeshire Chamber of Commerce and Indus. [IO], Cambridge, United Kingdom

Camel Hair Mfrs. Inst; Cashmere and [3779]

Camellia Soc; Amer. [22485]

Camelopard Soc. - Defunct.

Camelot Res. Comm. - Defunct.

CAMERA [★18055]

CAMERA [★IO]

Camera Clubs of Am; Assoc. [★22893]

Camera Collectors; Amer. Soc. of [10844]

Camera de Comercio Espana - Estados Unidos [★24296]

Camera de Comercio Espana - Estados Unidos [★IO]

Camera de Comert si Industrie a Romaniei si a Municipiului Bucuresti [★IO]

Camera Industries of West Germany - Defunct.

Camera and Movie Collectors; Valley [★10844]

Cameroon Assn. for the Protection and Educ. of the Child [IO], Yaounde, Cameroon

Cameroon Assn. of Univ. Women [IO], Bamenda, Cameroon

Cameroon Baseball and Softball Fed. [IO], Yaounde, Cameroon

Cameroon Diabetes Assn. [IO], Yaounde, Cameroon

Cameroon Soc. of Physiological Sciences [IO], Yaounde, Cameroon

Cameroon Soc. of Physiotherapy [IO], Yaounde, Cameroon

Cameroon-USA Chamber of Commerce [IO], Jacksonville, FL, United States

Cameroon-USA Chamber of Commerce [24249], PO Box 8842, Jacksonville, FL 32239-0842, (904)553-4095

Cameroonian Paralympic Comm. [IO], Yaounde, Cameroon

Camex Users Group - Defunct.

Camille and Henry Dreyfus Found. [8237], 555 Madison Ave., 20th Fl., New York, NY 10022-3301, (212)753-1760

Camogie Assn. [IO], Dublin, Ireland

Camp and Cabin Assn. of New Zealand [★IO]

Camp Directors Assn. of Am. [★23268]

Camp Fire Boys and Girls [★13475]

Camp Fire Club of Am. [4369], 230 Camp Fire Rd., Chappaqua, NY 10514, (914)769-5508

Camp Fire Conservation Fund [4370]

Camp Fire Girls [★13475]

Camp Fire USA [13475], 1100 Walnut St., Ste. 1900, Kansas City, MO 64106-2197, (816)285-2010

Camp Horsemanship Assn. [★23523]

Camp Info. Services; Jewish [★23275]

Campaign 1980 - Defunct.

Campaign for the Accountability of Amer. Bases [IO], Otley, United Kingdom

Campaign Against Arms Trade [IO], London, United Kingdom

Campaign Against Investment in South Africa - Defunct.

Campaign Against Nuclear War - Defunct.

Campaign Against U.S. Military Bases in the Philippines - Defunct.

Campaign for America [18285]

Campaign for America's Future [18388], 1825 K St. NW, Ste. 400, Washington, DC 20006, (202)955-5665

Campaign for Amnesty and Human Rights for Political Prisoners - Defunct.

Campaign to Boycott SDI [18143], c/o John B. Kogut, Co-Founder, 1110 W Green St., Univ. of Illinois, Urbana, IL 61801, (217)333-1060

Campaign to Check the Population Explosion - Defunct.

Campaign for Child Survival - Defunct.

Campaign Comm; Democratic Senatorial [17405]

Campaign of Concern [★14179]

Campaign for the Creation of the Natl. Youth Advisor - Defunct.

Campaign for a Democratic Foreign Policy - Defunct.

Campaign to End the Death Penalty [17028], PO Box 25730, Chicago, IL 60625, (773)955-4841

Campaign For Our Children [13476], c/o Hal Donofrio, Pres./CEO, One N Charles St., 11th Fl., Baltimore, MD 21201, (410)576-9015

Campaign Fund for Republican Women - Defunct.

Campaign Fund; Women's [17576]

Campaign for a Fur Free Am. [★11358]

Campaign for Human Development [★12713]

Campaign for Indus. [★IO]

Campaign to Label Genetically Engineered Foods [17604], PO Box 55699, Seattle, WA 98155, (425)771-4049

Campaign Life Coalition Canada [IO], Toronto, ON, Canada

Campaign for Nuclear Disarmament [IO], London, United Kingdom

Campaign for a Nuclear Free Future - Defunct.

Campaign for Nuclear Phaseout [IO], Ottawa, ON, Canada

Campaign to Oppose Bank Loans to South Africa - Defunct.

Campaign for Peace and Democracy - Defunct.

Campaign for the Peace and Reunification of Korea [★17966]

Campaign for the Peace and Reunification of Korea [★IO]

Campaign for Political Rights - Defunct.

Campaign for Press and Broadcasting Freedom [IO], London, United Kingdom

Campaign for Prosperity - Address unknown since 1990.

Campaign to Protect Rural England [IO], London, United Kingdom

Campaign for the Protection of Rural Wales [IO], Welshpool, United Kingdom

Campaign to Save the People of Palestine - Defunct.

Campaign for Space Political Action Comm. - Defunct.

Campaign for Surplus Rosaries - Defunct.

Campaign for Tobacco-Free Kids [★16433]

Campaign for a U.N. Global Communications System [★18763]

Campaign for a U.N. Global Communications System [★IO]

Campaign for U.N. Reform [★18762]

Campaign for Working Families [18286], PO Box 97163, Washington, DC 20090-7163, (703)671-8800

Campaign for a World Constituent Assembly - Defunct.

Campaign for World Govt. - Defunct.

Campaigners, U.S.A; Open Air [20027]

Campana de Solidaridad con Nicaragua [★IO]

Campbell Contacts in America - Address unknown since 2003.

Campbell Found; Joseph [9206]

Campbell River Head Injury Support Soc. [IO], Campbell River, BC, Canada

Campbell Soc; Clan [★20819]

Campbell Soc., North Am; Clan [20819]

Campden and Chorleywood Food Res. Assn. [IO], Gloucester, United Kingdom

Campers and Hikers Assn; Natl. [★23271]

Campground Owners Assn; Natl. [★3357]

Campgrounds
Best Holiday Trav-L-Park Assn. [3354]

Campgrounds; Natl. Assn. of RV Parks and [3357]

Camping
Alpine Coach Assn. [22941]
Amer. Camp Assn. [23268]
Amer. Clipper Owners Club [22942]
Assn. of Camp Nurses [15464]
Assn. for Challenge Course Tech. [2869]
Assn. of Girl Scout Executive Staff [12996]
Assn. of Jewish Sponsored Camps [23275]
California Wilderness Survival League [9202]
Camp Fire USA [13475]
Camping Women [23269]
Canadian Camping Assn. [IO]
Canadian Family Camping Fed. [IO]
Christian Camping Intl. Australia [IO]
Christian Camping Intl. - Brazil [IO]
Christian Camping Intl. - India [IO]
Christian Camping Intl. - Jamaica [IO]
Christian Camping Intl. - Japan [IO]
Christian Camping Intl. Korea [IO]
Christian Camping Intl. Polska [IO]
Christian Camping Intl. Romania [IO]
Christian Camping Intl. - Russia [IO]
Christian Camping Intl. - United Kingdom [IO]
Christian Camping International/U.S.A. [23270]
Christian Camping New Zealand [IO]
Discovery Owners Assn., Inc. [22947]
Escapees [22948]
Family Campers and RVers [23271]
Family Motor Coach Assn. [22949]
Girl Scouts of the U.S.A. [12998]
Good Sam Recreational Vehicle Club [22951]
Intl. Brotherhood of Motorcycle Campers [23624]
Intl. Fed. of Camping and Caravanning [IO]
Jayco Travel Club [22955]
Light Living Library [23272]
Loners of Am. [22956]

Reference to "IO" in place of a book number signifies that the association may be found in the 45th edition of International Organizations.

Loners on Wheels **[22957]**
Natl. African-American RV'ers Assn. **[22958]**
Natl. Assn. of RV Parks and Campgrounds **[3357]**
Natl. Assn. of Therapeutic Wilderness Camps **[23276]**
Natl. Assn. of Trailer Owners **[22959]**
Natl. Camp Assn. **[23277]**
Natl. Lutheran Outdoors Ministry Assn. **[20231]**
North Amer. Family Campers Assn. **[23273]**
North Amer. Truck Camper Owners Assn. **[23025]**
Order of the Arrow **[13005]**
Prairie Club **[12799]**
Recreation Vehicle Dealers Assn. of Am. **[3370]**
Retreat Assn. **[IO]**
RV Mfrs'. Clubs Assn. **[22961]**
SunnyTravelers **[22963]**
Wally Byam Caravan Club Intl. **[22967]**
Wilderness Classroom Org. **[8951]**
Wilderness Educ. Assn. **[8952]**
Wilderness Inquiry **[23274]**
Wilderness Volunteers **[22774]**
Winnebago-Itasca Travelers **[22968]**
Camping Assn; Natl. **[★23277]**
Camping Intl; Christian **[★23270]**
Camping and Outdoor Leisure Assn. **[★IO]**
Camping Women **[23269]**, PO Box 13261, Sacramento, CA 95813
Campingul Crestin Interconfesional **[★IO]**
Camps
Amer. Camp Assn. **[23268]**
Amer. Jewish Soc. for Ser. **[12465]**
Amer. Missionary Fellowship **[20296]**
Assn. of Camp Nurses **[15464]**
Assn. of Girl Scout Executive Staff **[12996]**
Assn. of Jewish Center Professionals **[12466]**
Assn. of Jewish Sponsored Camps **[23275]**
Boy Scouts of Am. **[12997]**
Camp Fire USA **[13475]**
Camping Women **[23269]**
Christian Camping International/U.S.A. **[23270]**
Family Campers and RVers **[23271]**
Girl Scouts of the U.S.A. **[12998]**
Hungarian Scouts Assn. **[12999]**
Interlochen Center for the Arts **[9571]**
Intl. Brotherhood of Motorcycle Campers **[23624]**
Natl. African-American RV'ers Assn. **[22958]**
Natl. Assn. of RV Parks and Campgrounds **[3357]**
Natl. Assn. of Therapeutic Wilderness Camps **[23276]**
Natl. Baton Twirling Assn. Intl. **[23142]**
Natl. Camp Assn. **[23277]**
Natl. Eagle Scout Assn. **[13002]**
Natl. Forest Recreation Assn. **[3358]**
Natl. Jewish Comm. on Scouting **[13003]**
Natl. Lutheran Outdoors Ministry Assn. **[20231]**
North Amer. Family Campers Assn. **[23273]**
Order of the Arrow **[13005]**
Prairie Club **[12799]**
Subud Youth Assn. **[13516]**
Wilderness Classroom Org. **[8951]**
Wilderness Volunteers **[22774]**
Campus Action Network - Defunct.
Campus Activities Assn; Natl. Entertainment and **[★9169]**
Campus Activities; Natl. Assn. for **[9169]**
Campus Americans for Democratic Action - Defunct.
Campus Card Users; Natl. Assn. of **[3707]**
Campus Child Care; Natl. Coalition for **[★11535]**
Campus Children's Centers; Natl. Coalition for **[11535]**
Campus Coalition - Address unknown since 1995.
Campus Coalition for Democracy **[★8490]**
Campus Comm. to Bridge the Gap **[★18145]**
Campus Compact **[8238]**, Brown Univ., PO Box 1975, Providence, RI 02912, (401)867-3950
Campus Crusade for Christ Intl. **[19994]**, 100 Lake Hart Dr., Orlando, FL 32832, (407)826-2000
Campus Crusade for Christ Intl. **[IO]**, Orlando, FL, United States
Campus Freethought Alliance **[★17643]**
Campus Greens **[18320]**, c/o Green Party of the U.S., PO Box 57065, Washington, DC 20037
Campus Ministers; Assn. of Southern Baptist **[19474]**
Campus Ministries of America - Address unknown since 2000.

Campus Ministries; Natl. Inst. for **[★19916]**
Campus Ministry Assn; Catholic **[19595]**
Campus Ministry Assn; Natl. **[19933]**
Campus Ministry Women **[19918]**, c/o Rev. Ann Marie Coleman, Sr. Minister, Univ. Church, 5655 S Univ. Ave., Chicago, IL 60637, (773)363-8142
Campus Organizing; Center for **[18195]**
Campus Outreach Opportunity League **[★17640]**
Campus Outreach Opportunity League **[★IO]**
Campus Partnerships For Hea; Community- **[11744]**
Campus Safety, Hea. and Environmental Mgt. Assn. **[4300]**, c/o Rebecca Page, 12100 Sunset Hills Rd., Ste. 130, Reston, VA 20190-3221, (703)234-4141
Campus; Security on **[11846]**
Campus Teens **[★13489]**
CAMUS Intl. **[2551]**, 505 Beach St., Ste. 130, San Francisco, CA 94133, (415)647-4503
CAMUS Intl. **[IO]**, San Francisco, CA, United States
Camus Stud. Assn. **[7488]**, c/o Prof. Raymond Gay-Crosier, Univ. of Florida, Dept. of Romance Languages and Literatures, Gainesville, FL 32611
Can Collectors; Natl. Pop **[22085]**
Can Makers **[IO]**, London, United Kingdom
Can Manufacturers Inst. **[974]**, 1730 Rhode Island Ave. NW, Ste. 1000, Washington, DC 20036, (202)232-4677
Can Recycling Inst; Steel **[★4004]**
Can and Tube Assn; Natl. Fibre **[★976]**
Can and Tube Inst; Composite **[976]**
Canaan Dog Club of Am. **[22239]**, c/o Judy Rosenthal, Corresponding Sec., PO Box 177, Stowe, VT 05672
Canada
Amer. Assn. of Port Authorities **[5778]**
American-Canadian Genealogical Soc. **[21098]**
American-French Genealogical Soc. **[21101]**
Assn. of Amer. Seed Control Officials **[5434]**
Assn. of Racing Commissioners Intl. **[6240]**
Assn. of Thai Professionals in Am. and Canada **[19406]**
Canada West Found. **[IO]**
French/Canadian/Metis Genealogical Soc. **[IO]**
French/Canadian/Metis Genealogical Soc. **[20720]**
Inst. of World Affairs **[8663]**
Intl. Assn. of Speakers Bureaus **[10900]**
Intl. Joint Commn. **[5040]**
Mine Inspectors' Inst. of Am. **[6117]**
Natl. Assn. of Coll. and Univ. Attorneys **[5677]**
U.S.-Vietnam Trade Coun. **[17010]**
Canada; Aerospace Indus. Assn. of **[★154]**
Canada; Aerospace Indus. Assn. of **[★IO]**
Canada-Arab Bus. Coun. **[IO]**, Toronto, ON, Canada
Canada Asia Accord Assn. **[IO]**, Edmonton, AB, Canada
Canada-Asia Working Group **[IO]**, Toronto, ON, Canada
Canada Assn. on Water Pollution Res. and Control **[★IO]**
Canada Atlantic Region of Narcotics Anonymous **[IO]**, St. John, NB, Canada
Canada Basketball **[IO]**, Toronto, ON, Canada
Canada Beef Export Fed. **[IO]**, Calgary, AB, Canada
Canada; Central Rabbinical Cong. of the U.S.A. and **[20130]**
Canada-China Bus. Coun. **[IO]**, Toronto, ON, Canada
Canada; Corporate Communicators **[★879]**
Canada Coun. for the Arts **[IO]**, Ottawa, ON, Canada
Canada-Czech Republic Chamber of Commerce **[IO]**, Toronto, ON, Canada
Canada Earth Energy Assn. **[★IO]**
Canada Earthsave Soc. **[★IO]**
Canada Employment and Immigration Union **[IO]**, Ottawa, ON, Canada
Canada-Finland Chamber of Commerce **[IO]**, Toronto, ON, Canada
Canada Fox Breeders Assn. **[IO]**, Dunsford, ON, Canada
Canada Games Coun. **[IO]**, Ottawa, ON, Canada
Canada Grains Coun. **[IO]**, Winnipeg, MB, Canada
Canada Hippique **[★IO]**
Canada-India Bus. Coun. **[IO]**, Toronto, ON, Canada
Canada India Village Aid Assn. **[IO]**, Vancouver, BC, Canada

Canada Indus. Innovation Centre **[★IO]**
Canada Inst. for Radiation Safety **[★IO]**
Canada-Israel Comm. **[IO]**, Ottawa, ON, Canada
Canada; Israeli Students' Org. in the U.S.A. and **[19158]**
Canada - Japan Soc. of British Columbia **[IO]**, Vancouver, BC, Canada
Canada Language Coun. **[IO]**, Gatineau, QC, Canada
Canada; Masonic Relief Assn. of U.S.A. and **[★19229]**
Canada Natl. Comm. of the Intl. Assn. on Water Pollution Res. and Control **[★IO]**
Canada-Pakistan Bus. Coun. **[IO]**, Thornhill, ON, Canada
Canada Peace Anniversary Assn; U.S. **[19299]**
Canada Porc Intl. **[★IO]**
Canada Pork Intl. **[IO]**, Ottawa, ON, Canada
Canada Safety Coun. **[IO]**, Ottawa, ON, Canada
Canada; Screen Printing Assn. of **[★1792]**
Canada-Singapore Bus. Assn. **[IO]**, Vancouver, BC, Canada
Canada Taiwan Trade Assn. **[IO]**, Vancouver, BC, Canada
Canada Tibet Comm. **[IO]**, Montreal, QC, Canada
Canada-UK Chamber of Commerce **[IO]**, London, United Kingdom
Canada-United States Bus. Assn. **[2301]**, 600 Renaissance Ctr., Ste. 1100, Detroit, MI 48243, (313)446-7013
Canada-U.S. Environmental Coun. - Defunct.
Canada West Equip. Dealers Assn. **[IO]**, Calgary, AB, Canada
Canada West Found. **[IO]**, Calgary, AB, Canada
Canada World Youth **[IO]**, Montreal, QC, Canada
Canada's Assn. for the Fifty-Plus **[IO]**, Toronto, ON, Canada
Canada's Aviation Hall of Fame **[IO]**, Wetaskiwin, AB, Canada
Canada's Natl. History Soc. **[IO]**, Winnipeg, MB, Canada
Canada's Research-Based Pharmaceutical Companies **[IO]**, Ottawa, ON, Canada
Canada's Venture Capital and Private Equity Assn. **[IO]**, Toronto, ON, Canada
Canadian
American-Canadian Genealogical Soc. **[21098]**
American-French Genealogical Soc. **[21101]**
Assn. for Canadian Stud. **[IO]**
Assn. for Canadian Stud. in the U.S. **[IO]**
Assn. for Canadian Stud. in the U.S. **[8043]**
Canadian/American Border Trade Alliance **[3838]**
Canadian Children's Opera Chorus **[IO]**
Canadian Club of New York **[18988]**
Canadian Corkscrew Collectors Club **[21985]**
Canadian Inst. **[IO]**
Canadian - Palestinian Educational Exchange **[IO]**
Canadian Serbian Natl. Comm. **[IO]**
Center for the Stud. of Canada **[IO]**
Center for the Stud. of Canada **[8044]**
Champlain Soc. **[IO]**
Echo Res. Inst. **[IO]**
Nordic Assn. for Canadian Stud. **[IO]**
Quebec dans le Monde **[IO]**
Rousseau Proj. **[IO]**
U.S. Canada Peace Anniversary Assn. **[19299]**
Canadian 4-H Coun. **[IO]**, Ottawa, ON, Canada
Canadian 5 Pin Bowlers' Assn. **[IO]**, Ottawa, ON, Canada
Canadian Aberdeen Angus Assn. **[IO]**, Calgary, AB, Canada
Canadian Academic Accounting Assn. **[IO]**, Toronto, ON, Canada
Canadian Acad. of Endodontics **[IO]**, Winnipeg, MB, Canada
Canadian Acad. of Engg. **[IO]**, Ottawa, ON, Canada
Canadian Acad. of Facial, Plastic and Reconstructive Surgery **[IO]**, Toronto, ON, Canada
Canadian Acad. of Periodontology **[IO]**, Ottawa, ON, Canada
Canadian Acad. of Recording Arts and Sciences **[IO]**, Toronto, ON, Canada
Canadian Acad. of Sport Medicine **[IO]**, Ottawa, ON, Canada
Canadian Acoustical Assn. **[IO]**, Ottawa, ON, Canada

A star before a book entry number signifies that the name is not listed separately, but is mentioned within the entry.

Canadian Acoustical Assn. - Toronto [IO], Ottawa, ON, Canada

Canadian Actors' Equity Assn. [IO], Toronto, ON, Canada

Canadian Addison Soc. [IO], Goderich, ON, Canada

Canadian Administrative Housekeepers' Assn. [★IO]

Canadian Adult Congenital Heart Network [IO], Mississauga, ON, Canada

Canadian Adult Recreational Hockey Assn. [IO], Ottawa, ON, Canada

Canadian Advanced Tech. Alliance [IO], Ottawa, ON, Canada

Canadian Advanced Tech. Assn. [★IO]

Canadian Advt. Res. Found. [IO], Toronto, ON, Canada

Canadian Aerial Applicators Assn. [IO], Edmonton, AB, Canada

Canadian Aeronautics and Space Inst. [IO], Ottawa, ON, Canada

Canadian Aerophilatelic Soc. [IO], Nepean, ON, Canada

Canadian Agri-Marketing Assn. - Alberta [IO], Calgary, AB, Canada

Canadian Agri-Marketing Assn. - Manitoba [IO], Winnipeg, MB, Canada

Canadian Agri-Marketing Assn. - Ontario [IO], Wasaga Beach, ON, Canada

Canadian Agri-Marketing Assn. - Saskatchewan [IO], Regina, SK, Canada

Canadian Agricultural Economics Soc. [IO], Victoria, BC, Canada

Canadian AIDS Soc. [IO], Ottawa, ON, Canada

Canadian AIDS Treatment Info. Exchange [IO], Toronto, ON, Canada

Canadian Air Cushion Tech. Soc. [IO], Ottawa, ON, Canada

Canadian Air Line Pilots Assn. [★IO]

Canadian Air Line Pilots Assn. [★24005]

Canadian Air Mail Collectors Club [IO], Nepean, ON, Canada

Canadian Air Traffic Control Assn.- CAW Local 5454 [IO], Ottawa, ON, Canada

Canadian Airports Coun. [IO], Ottawa, ON, Canada

Canadian All-Terrain Vehicle Distribution Coun. [★IO]

Canadian All-Terrain Vehicle Distributors Coun. [★IO]

Canadian Alliance Against Software Theft [IO], Toronto, ON, Canada

Canadian Alliance of British Pensioners [IO], Toronto, ON, Canada

Canadian Alliance of Franchise Operators [IO], Midhurst, ON, Canada

Canadian Alliance of French-Language Teachers and Administrators [IO], Ottawa, ON, Canada

Canadian Alliance of Home Schoolers [IO], Toronto, ON, Canada

Canadian Alliance of Physiotherapy Regulators [IO], Etobicoke, ON, Canada

Canadian Alliance of Student Associations [IO], Ottawa, ON, Canada

Canadian Amateur Boxing Assn. [IO], Ottawa, ON, Canada

Canadian Amateur Dancesport Assn. [IO], Pickering, ON, Canada

Canadian Amateur Diving Assn. [IO], Ottawa, ON, Canada

Canadian Amateur Musicians [IO], Harrington, QC, Canada

Canadian Amateur Rowing Assn. [★IO]

Canadian Amateur Synchronized Swimming Assn. [★IO]

Canadian Amateur Wrestling Assn. [IO], Gloucester, ON, Canada

Canadian/American Border Trade Alliance [IO], Lewiston, NY, United States

Canadian/American Border Trade Alliance [3838], PO Box 929, Lewiston, NY 14092, (716)754-8824

Canadian-American Bus. Coun. [708], 1900 K St. NW, Washington, DC 20006, (202)496-7430

Canadian-American Bus. Coun. [IO], Washington, DC, United States

Canadian-Amer. Motor Carriers Assn. - Defunct.

Canadian-Amer. Women's Assn., Amer. Sect. - Defunct.

Canadian Amputee Sports Assn. [IO], Toronto, ON, Canada

Canadian Anaesthetists' Soc. [★IO]

Canadian Anesthesiologists' Soc. [IO], Toronto, ON, Canada

Canadian Angus Assn. [IO], Calgary, AB, Canada

Canadian Angus Assn. [★IO]

Canadian Animal Hea. Inst. [IO], Guelph, ON, Canada

Canadian Antique Phonograph Soc. [IO], Toronto, ON, Canada

Canadian Apparel Fed. [IO], Ottawa, ON, Canada

Canadian Apparel Mfrs. Inst. [★IO]

Canadian Aquaculture Indus. Alliance [IO], Ottawa, ON, Canada

Canadian Aquafitness Leaders Alliance [IO], Toronto, ON, Canada

Canadian Arab Fed. [IO], Toronto, ON, Canada

Canadian Arab Friendship Assn. [IO], Edmonton, AB, Canada

Canadian Arabian Horse Registry [IO], Sherwood Park, AB, Canada

Canadian Archaeological Assn. [IO], Regina, SK, Canada

Canadian Arctic Resources Comm. [IO], Ottawa, ON, Canada

Canadian Art Museum Directors' Org. [IO], Ottawa, ON, Canada

Canadian Artists Representation [IO], Ottawa, ON, Canada

Canadian Arts Presenting Assn. [IO], Ottawa, ON, Canada

Canadian Asbestos Info. Centre [★IO]

Canadian Asian Stud. Assn. [IO], Montreal, QC, Canada

Canadian Associates of the Ben-Gurion Univ. of the Negev [IO], Toronto, ON, Canada

Canadian Assn. of Accredited Mortgage Professionals [IO], Toronto, ON, Canada

Canadian Assn. for Adolescent Hea. [IO], Montreal, QC, Canada

Canadian Assn. of Advanced Practice Nurses [IO], Mississauga, ON, Canada

Canadian Assn. for the Advancement of Netherlandic Stud. [IO], Wellington, ON, Canada

Canadian Assn. for the Advancement of Women and Sport and Physical Activity [IO], Ottawa, ON, Canada

Canadian Assn. for Amer. Stud. [IO], Kingston, ON, Canada

Canadian Assn. for Anatomy, Neurobiology and Cell Biology [IO], Kingston, ON, Canada

Canadian Assn. of Aquarium Clubs [IO], Hamilton, ON, Canada

Canadian Assn. of Arts Admin. Educators [IO], Waterloo, ON, Canada

Canadian Assn. of Blue Cross Plans [IO], Etobicoke, ON, Canada

Canadian Assn. of Broadcasters [IO], Ottawa, ON, Canada

Canadian Assn. of Burn Nurses [IO], Calgary, AB, Canada

Canadian Assn. for Bus. Economics [IO], Ottawa, ON, Canada

Canadian Assn. of Cardiac Rehabilitation [IO], Winnipeg, MB, Canada

Canadian Assn. of Cardio-Pulmonary Technologists [IO], Toronto, ON, Canada

Canadian Assn. of Career Educators and Employers [IO], Toronto, ON, Canada

Canadian Assn. of Chain Drug Stores [IO], Toronto, ON, Canada

Canadian Assn. of Chem. Distributors [IO], Oakville, ON, Canada

Canadian Assn. of Chiefs of Police [IO], Ottawa, ON, Canada

Canadian Assn. for Child Neurology [IO], Calgary, AB, Canada

Canadian Assn. for Child and Play Therapy [IO], Ottawa, ON, Canada

Canadian Assn. for Children and Adults with Learning Disabilities [★IO]

Canadian Assn. of Children's Librarians [IO], Dartmouth, NS, Canada

Canadian Assn. for Clinical Microbiology and Infectious Diseases [IO], Hamilton, ON, Canada

Canadian Assn. for Co-operative Educ. [IO], Toronto, ON, Canada

Canadian Assn. of Coll. and Univ. Libraries [IO], Toronto, ON, Canada

Canadian Assn. of Coll. and Univ. Student Services [IO], Kingston, ON, Canada

Canadian Assn. for Commonwealth Literature and Language [★IO]

Canadian Assn. for Commonwealth Literature and Language Stud. [IO], Ottawa, ON, Canada

Canadian Assn. of Communicators in Educ. [IO], Ottawa, ON, Canada

Canadian Assn. for Community Care [IO], Ottawa, ON, Canada

Canadian Assn. for Community Living [IO], Toronto, ON, Canada

Canadian Assn. for Composite Structures and Materials [IO], Montreal, QC, Canada

Canadian Assn. for Conservation of Cultural Property [IO], Ottawa, ON, Canada

Canadian Assn. of Critical Care Nurses [IO], London, ON, Canada

Canadian Assn. for Curriculum Stud. [IO], Calgary, AB, Canada

Canadian Assn. of the Deaf [IO], Ottawa, ON, Canada

Canadian Assn. of Defence and Security Indus. [IO], Ottawa, ON, Canada

Canadian Assn. for Dental Res. [IO], London, ON, Canada

Canadian Assn. for Disabled Skiing [IO], Ottawa, ON, Canada

Canadian Assn. for Distance Educ. [IO], Ottawa, ON, Canada

Canadian Assn. of Drilling Engineers [IO], Calgary, AB, Canada

Canadian Assn. of Electroneurophysiology Technologists [IO], Moncton, NB, Canada

Canadian Assn. of Elizabeth Fry Societies [IO], Ottawa, ON, Canada

Canadian Assn. of Emergency Physicians [IO], Ottawa, ON, Canada

Canadian Assn. of Energy Ser. Companies [IO], Toronto, ON, Canada

Canadian Assn. for Enterostomal Therapy [IO], Mississauga, ON, Canada

Canadian Assn. for Environmental Analytical Labs. [IO], Ottawa, ON, Canada

Canadian Assn. Environmental Mgt. [IO], New Glasgow, NS, Canada

Canadian Assn. of Equip. Distributors [IO], Ottawa, ON, Canada

Canadian Assn. of Ethnic Radio Broadcasters [IO], Toronto, ON, Canada

Canadian Assn. of Exposition Mgt. [IO], Toronto, ON, Canada

Canadian Assn. of Fairs and Exhibitions [IO], Ottawa, ON, Canada

Canadian Assn. for Familial Ataxia [IO], Montreal, QC, Canada

Canadian Assn. of Family Enterprise [IO], Oakville, ON, Canada

Canadian Assn. of Family Rsrc. Programs [IO], Ottawa, ON, Canada

Canadian Assn. of Family Rsrc. Programs [★IO]

Canadian Assn. of Farm Advisors [IO], Winnipeg, MB, Canada

Canadian Assn. of Fire Chiefs [IO], Ottawa, ON, Canada

Canadian Assn. of Food Banks [IO], Toronto, ON, Canada

Canadian Assn. of Footwear Importers [IO], Toronto, ON, Canada

Canadian Assn. of Former Parliamentarians [IO], Ottawa, ON, Canada

Canadian Assn. for Free Expression [IO], Etobicoke, ON, Canada

Canadian Assn. of Friedreich's Ataxia [★IO]

Canadian Assn. of Gastroenterology [IO], Oakville, ON, Canada

Canadian Assn. of Gen. Surgeons [IO], Ottawa, ON, Canada

Canadian Assn. of Genetic Counsellors [IO], Oakville, ON, Canada

Canadian Assn. of Geographers [IO], Montreal, QC, Canada

Reference to "IO" in place of a book number signifies that the association may be found in the 45th edition of International Organizations.

Canadian Assn. of Geophysical Contractors **[IO]**, Calgary, AB, Canada

Canadian Assn. of Gerontology **[IO]**, Ottawa, ON, Canada

Canadian Assn. of Gift Planners **[IO]**, Ottawa, ON, Canada

Canadian Assn. for Graduate Stud. **[IO]**, Ottawa, ON, Canada

Canadian Assn. for Hea., Physical Educ., Recreation and Dance **[IO]**, Ottawa, ON, Canada

Canadian Assn. for Hea. Services and Policy Res. **[IO]**, Ottawa, ON, Canada

Canadian Assn. for the History of Nursing **[IO]**, Lethbridge, AB, Canada

Canadian Assn. of Home Inspectors **[★IO]**

Canadian Assn. of Home and Property Inspectors **[IO]**, Ottawa, ON, Canada

Canadian Assn. for Humane Trapping **[IO]**, Burlington, ON, Canada

Canadian Assn. of Immersion Teachers **[IO]**, Nepean, ON, Canada

Canadian Assn. of Importers and Exporters **[IO]**, Toronto, ON, Canada

Canadian Assn. of Income Funds **[IO]**, Toronto, ON, Canada

Canadian Assn. of Independent Living Centres **[IO]**, Ottawa, ON, Canada

Canadian Assn. of Independent Schools **[IO]**, Toronto, ON, Canada

Canadian Assn. for Info. Sci. **[IO]**, London, ON, Canada

Canadian Assn. of Insolvency and Restructuring Professionals **[IO]**, Toronto, ON, Canada

Canadian Assn. of Insurance and Financial Advisors **[★IO]**

Canadian Assn. of Insurance Women **[IO]**, Halifax, NS, Canada

Canadian Assn. of Intl. Development Consultants **[IO]**, Ottawa, ON, Canada

Canadian Assn. of Internet Providers **[IO]**, Ottawa, ON, Canada

Canadian Assn. of Interns and Residents **[IO]**, Ottawa, ON, Canada

Canadian Assn. for Internship Programs **[IO]**, Toronto, ON, Canada

Canadian Assn. for Irish Stud. **[IO]**, St. John's, NL, Canada

Canadian Assn. of Journalists **[IO]**, Ottawa, ON, Canada

Canadian Assn. for Lab. Animal Sci. **[IO]**, Toronto, ON, Canada

Canadian Assn. of Labour Media **[IO]**, Toronto, ON, Canada

Canadian Assn. of Landscape Architecture **[★IO]**

Canadian Assn. of Law Libraries **[IO]**, Kingston, ON, Canada

Canadian Assn. of Learned Journals **[IO]**, Vancouver, BC, Canada

Canadian Assn. of Logistics Mgt. **[★IO]**

Canadian Assn. of Mgt. Consultants **[IO]**, Toronto, ON, Canada

Canadian Assn. for Masorti Judaism **[★IO]**

Canadian Assn. of Media Educ. Organizations **[IO]**, Toronto, ON, Canada

Canadian Assn. of Medical Biochemists **[IO]**, Kingston, ON, Canada

Canadian Assn. of Medical Microbiologists and Canadian Infectious Disease Soc. **[★IO]**

Canadian Assn. of Medical Radiation Technologists **[IO]**, Ottawa, ON, Canada

Canadian Assn. of Members of Public Utility Tribunals **[IO]**, Calgary, AB, Canada

Canadian Assn. for the Mentally Retarded **[★IO]**

Canadian Assn. of Message Exchanges **[★IO]**

Canadian Assn. of Metal Finishers **[IO]**, St. Catharines, ON, Canada

Canadian Assn. of Midwives **[IO]**, Montreal, QC, Canada

Canadian Assn. for Mine and Explosive Ordnance Security **[IO]**, Cornwall, ON, Canada

Canadian Assn. of Mining Equip. and Services for Export **[IO]**, Markham, ON, Canada

Canadian Assn. of Moldmakers **[IO]**, Windsor, ON, Canada

Canadian Assn. of Music Libraries, Archives, and Documentation Centres **[IO]**, Ottawa, ON, Canada

Canadian Assn. for Music Therapy **[IO]**, Waterloo, ON, Canada

Canadian Assn. of Mutual Insurance Companies **[IO]**, Ottawa, ON, Canada

Canadian Assn. of Naturopathic Doctors **[IO]**, Toronto, ON, Canada

Canadian Assn. of Nephrology Nurses and Technologists **[IO]**, Barrie, ON, Canada

Canadian Assn. of Neuropathologists **[IO]**, Halifax, NS, Canada

Canadian Assn. of Neuroscience Nurses **[IO]**, North Delta, BC, Canada

Canadian Assn. of Numismatic Dealers **[IO]**, Stoney Creek, ON, Canada

Canadian Assn. of Nurses in AIDS Care **[IO]**, Pontypool, ON, Canada

Canadian Assn. of Nurses in Oncology **[IO]**, Vancouver, BC, Canada

Canadian Assn. of Occupational Therapists **[IO]**, Ottawa, ON, Canada

Canadian Assn. of Oilwell Drilling Contractors **[IO]**, Calgary, AB, Canada

Canadian Assn. of Optometrists **[IO]**, Ottawa, ON, Canada

Canadian Assn. of Oral and Maxillofacial Surgeons **[IO]**, Ottawa, ON, Canada

Canadian Assn. of Orthodontists **[IO]**, Toronto, ON, Canada

Canadian Assn. of Paediatric Surgeons **[IO]**, Ottawa, ON, Canada

Canadian Assn. of Palynologists **[IO]**, Toronto, ON, Canada

Canadian Assn. of Paralegals **[IO]**, Montreal, QC, Canada

Canadian Assn. for Pastoral Practice and Educ. **[IO]**, Halifax, NS, Canada

Canadian Assn. of Pathologists **[IO]**, Ottawa, ON, Canada

Canadian Assn. of Pension Supervisory Authorities **[IO]**, North York, ON, Canada

Canadian Assn. for People Who Stutter **[★IO]**

Canadian Assn. of Petroleum Landmen **[IO]**, Calgary, AB, Canada

Canadian Assn. of Petroleum Producers **[IO]**, Calgary, AB, Canada

Canadian Assn. of Petroleum Production Accounting **[IO]**, Calgary, AB, Canada

Canadian Assn. for Pharmacy Distribution Mgt. **[IO]**, Woodbridge, ON, Canada

Canadian Assn. of Pharmacy in Oncology **[IO]**, Hamilton, ON, Canada

Canadian Assn. of Pharmacy Students and Interns **[IO]**, Toronto, ON, Canada

Canadian Assn. of Pharmacy Technicians **[IO]**, Toronto, ON, Canada

Canadian Assn. of Photographers and Illustrators in Communications **[IO]**, Toronto, ON, Canada

Canadian Assn. for Photographic Art **[IO]**, Logan Lake, BC, Canada

Canadian Assn. of Physical Medicine and Rehabilitation **[IO]**, Ottawa, ON, Canada

Canadian Assn. of Physicians for the Env. **[IO]**, Toronto, ON, Canada

Canadian Assn. of Physicists **[IO]**, Ottawa, ON, Canada

Canadian Assn. of Police Boards **[IO]**, Ottawa, ON, Canada

Canadian Assn. of Police Educators **[IO]**, Charlottetown, PE, Canada

Canadian Assn. for the Practical Stud. of Law in Educ. **[IO]**, Georgetown, ON, Canada

Canadian Assn. of Pre-Retirement Planners **[IO]**, Stratford, ON, Canada

Canadian Assn. of Principals **[IO]**, Kanata, ON, Canada

Canadian Assn. of Professional Conservators **[IO]**, Ottawa, ON, Canada

Canadian Assn. of Professional Dance Organizations **[★IO]**

Canadian Assn. of Professional Employees **[IO]**, Ottawa, ON, Canada

Canadian Assn. of Professional Heritage Consultants **[IO]**, Toronto, ON, Canada

Canadian Assn. of Professional Immigration Consultants **[IO]**, Toronto, ON, Canada

Canadian Assn. of Professional Pet Dog Trainers **[IO]**, Shelburne, ON, Canada

Canadian Assn. of Professional Speakers **[IO]**, Toronto, ON, Canada

Canadian Assn. of Programs in Public Admin. **[IO]**, Toronto, ON, Canada

Canadian Assn. for Prosthetics and Orthotics **[IO]**, Winnipeg, MB, Canada

Canadian Assn. of Provincial Court Judges **[IO]**, St. John's, NL, Canada

Canadian Assn. of Psychoanalytic Child Therapists **[IO]**, Brampton, ON, Canada

Canadian Assn. of Psychosocial Oncology **[IO]**, Toronto, ON, Canada

Canadian Assn. of Public Hea. Dentistry **[IO]**, Nepean, ON, Canada

Canadian Assn. of Public Libraries **[IO]**, Dartmouth, NS, Canada

Canadian Assn. of Radiation Oncologists **[IO]**, Vancouver, BC, Canada

Canadian Assn. of Radiologists **[IO]**, St. Laurent, QC, Canada

Canadian Assn. of Recycling Indus. **[IO]**, Ajax, ON, Canada

Canadian Assn. of Regulated Importers **[IO]**, Ottawa, ON, Canada

Canadian Assn. of Rehabilitation Personnel **[★IO]**

Canadian Assn. of Rehabilitation Professionals **[IO]**, Toronto, ON, Canada

Canadian Assn. for Renewable Energies **[IO]**, Ottawa, ON, Canada

Canadian Assn. for Res. in Home Economics **[IO]**, Halifax, NS, Canada

Canadian Assn. of Res. Libraries **[IO]**, Ottawa, ON, Canada

Canadian Assn. for Retarded Children **[★IO]**

Canadian Assn. of Retired Persons **[★IO]**

Canadian Assn. of Road Safety Professionals **[IO]**, Saskatoon, SK, Canada

Canadian Assn. of Rocketry **[IO]**, Edmonton, AB, Canada

Canadian Assn. of School Administrators **[IO]**, Oakville, ON, Canada

Canadian Assn. for School Hea. **[IO]**, Surrey, BC, Canada

Canadian Assn. for School Libraries **[IO]**, Langley, BC, Canada

Canadian Assn. of Schools of Nursing **[IO]**, Ottawa, ON, Canada

Canadian Assn. of Schools of Social Work **[IO]**, Ottawa, ON, Canada

Canadian Assn. of Second Language Teachers **[IO]**, Nepean, ON, Canada

Canadian Assn. for Security and Intelligence Stud. **[IO]**, Ottawa, ON, Canada

Canadian Assn. of Sexual Assault Centres **[IO]**, Vancouver, BC, Canada

Canadian Assn. for Shar-Pei Rescue **[IO]**, Mansfield, ON, Canada

Canadian Assn. of Slavists **[IO]**, Toronto, ON, Canada

Canadian Assn. of Snowboard Instructors **[IO]**, Montreal, QC, Canada

Canadian Assn. of Social Workers **[IO]**, Ottawa, ON, Canada

Canadian Assn. of the Sovereign Military Order of Malta **[IO]**, Ottawa, ON, Canada

Canadian Assn. of Special Libraries and Info. Services **[IO]**, Toronto, ON, Canada

Canadian Assn. of Specialized Kinesiology **[IO]**, Coquitlam, BC, Canada

Canadian Assn. of Speech-Language Pathologists and Audiologists **[IO]**, Ottawa, ON, Canada

Canadian Assn. of Student Activity Advisors **[IO]**, Guelph, ON, Canada

Canadian Assn. of Student Financial Aid Administrators **[IO]**, Fredericton, NB, Canada

Canadian Assn. for Stud. on the Baha'i Faith **[★IO]**

Canadian Assn. for the Stud. of Adult Educ. **[IO]**, Ottawa, ON, Canada

Canadian Assn. for the Stud. of Intl. Development **[IO]**, Ottawa, ON, Canada

Canadian Assn. for Suicide Prevention **[IO]**, Edmonton, AB, Canada

Canadian Assn. of Teachers of Tech. Writing **[IO]**, Toronto, ON, Canada

A star before a book entry number signifies that the name is not listed separately, but is mentioned within the entry.

Canadian Assn. of Token Collectors **[IO]**, Acton, ON, Canada

Canadian Assn. of Toy Libraries and Parent Rsrc. Centers **[★IO]**

Canadian Assn. for Translation Stud. **[IO]**, Ottawa, ON, Canada

Canadian Assn. of Univ. Bus. Officers **[IO]**, Ottawa, ON, Canada

Canadian Assn. for Univ. Continuing Educ. **[IO]**, Saskatoon, SK, Canada

Canadian Assn. of Univ. Teachers **[IO]**, Ottawa, ON, Canada

Canadian Assn. of Univ. Teachers of German **[IO]**, Guelph, ON, Canada

Canadian Assn. on Water Quality **[IO]**, Burlington, ON, Canada

Canadian Assn. of Wholesale Sales Representatives **[IO]**, Toronto, ON, Canada

Canadian Assn. of Women Executives and Entrepreneurs **[IO]**, Toronto, ON, Canada

Canadian Assn. of Wooden Money Collectors **[IO]**, Newmarket, ON, Canada

Canadian Assn. of Wound Care **[IO]**, Toronto, ON, Canada

Canadian Assn. for Young Children **[IO]**, Corner Brook, NL, Canada

Canadian Assn. of Zoological Parks **[★IO]**

Canadian Assn. of Zoos and Aquariums **[IO]**, Ottawa, ON, Canada

Canadian Astronomical Soc. **[IO]**, Kingston, ON, Canada

Canadian Athletic Therapists Assn. **[IO]**, Calgary, AB, Canada

Canadian Authors Assn. **[IO]**, Campbellford, ON, Canada

Canadian Auto Workers **[IO]**, Toronto, ON, Canada

Canadian Automatic Merchandising Assn. **[IO]**, Mississauga, ON, Canada

Canadian Automatic Sprinkler Assn. **[IO]**, Markham, ON, Canada

Canadian Auto. Assn. **[IO]**, Ottawa, ON, Canada

Canadian Auto. Dealers Assn. **[IO]**, Markham, ON, Canada

Canadian Automotive Repair and Ser. Coun. **[IO]**, Ottawa, ON, Canada

Canadian Avalanche Assn. **[IO]**, Revelstoke, BC, Canada

Canadian Aviation Historical Soc. **[IO]**, Toronto, ON, Canada

Canadian Aviation Maintenance Coun. **[IO]**, Ottawa, ON, Canada

Canadian Badminton Assn. **[★IO]**

Canadian Ball Hockey Assn. **[IO]**, Concord, ON, Canada

Canadian Balloon Assn. **[IO]**, Vankleek Hill, ON, Canada

Canadian Band Assn. **[IO]**, Winnipeg, MB, Canada

Canadian Bankers Assn. **[IO]**, Toronto, ON, Canada

Canadian Baptist Intl. Ministries **[★IO]**

Canadian Baptist Ministries **[IO]**, Mississauga, ON, Canada

Canadian Baptist Overseas Mission Bd. **[★IO]**

Canadian Bar Assn. **[IO]**, Ottawa, ON, Canada

Canadian Bar Insurance Assn. **[IO]**, Toronto, ON, Canada

Canadian Baton Twirling Fed. **[IO]**, Winnipeg, MB, Canada

Canadian Battle of Normandy Found. **[★IO]**

Canadian Battlefields Found. **[IO]**, Ottawa, ON, Canada

Canadian Beef Breeds Coun. **[IO]**, Calgary, AB, Canada

Canadian Belgian Horse Assn. **[IO]**, Schomberg, ON, Canada

Canadian Bible Soc. **[IO]**, Toronto, ON, Canada

Canadian Bison Assn. **[IO]**, Regina, SK, Canada

Canadian Blonde d'Aquitaine Assn. **[IO]**, Ottawa, ON, Canada

Canadian Bd. of Marine Underwriters **[IO]**, Mississauga, ON, Canada

Canadian Boating Fed. **[IO]**, Salaberry-de-Valleyfield, QC, Canada

Canadian Boiler Soc. **[IO]**, Toronto, ON, Canada

Canadian Bookbinders and Book Artists Guild **[IO]**, Toronto, ON, Canada

Canadian Booksellers Assn. **[IO]**, Toronto, ON, Canada

Canadian Botanical Assn. **[IO]**, Halifax, NS, Canada

Canadian Bottled Water Assn. **[IO]**, Richmond Hill, ON, Canada

Canadian Brain Tissue Bank **[IO]**, Toronto, ON, Canada

Canadian Breast Cancer Found. **[IO]**, Toronto, ON, Canada

Canadian Brewery and Distillery Workers **[★24061]**

Canadian Bridge Fed. **[IO]**, Regina, SK, Canada

Canadian Broadcast Standards Coun. **[IO]**, Ottawa, ON, Canada

Canadian Broiler Hatching Eggs Producers' Assn. **[IO]**, Ottawa, ON, Canada

Canadian Broomball Fed. **[IO]**, Winnipeg, MB, Canada

Canadian Brown Swiss and Braunvieh Assn. **[IO]**, Guelph, ON, Canada

Canadian Brush, Broom and Mop Mfrs. Assn. **[★IO]**

Canadian Brush Mfrs. Assn. **[IO]**, Toronto, ON, Canada

Canadian Bur. for Intl. Educ. **[IO]**, Ottawa, ON, Canada

Canadian Bus Assn. **[IO]**, Ottawa, ON, Canada

Canadian Bus. Aircraft Operators **[★IO]**

Canadian Bus. Aviation Assn. **[IO]**, Ottawa, ON, Canada

Canadian Bus. Press **[IO]**, Toronto, ON, Canada

Canadian Call Mgt. Assn. **[IO]**, Grimsby, ON, Canada

Canadian Camping Assn. **[IO]**, St.-Donat, QC, Canada

Canadian Cancer Soc. **[IO]**, Toronto, ON, Canada

Canadian Canoe Assn. **[IO]**, Ottawa, ON, Canada

Canadian Canoe Assn., Atlantic Div. **[IO]**, Halifax, NS, Canada

Canadian Canon Law Soc. **[IO]**, Ottawa, ON, Canada

Canadian Capital Markets Assn. **[IO]**, Toronto, ON, Canada

Canadian Cardiovascular Soc. **[IO]**, Ottawa, ON, Canada

Canadian Career Development Found. **[IO]**, Ottawa, ON, Canada

Canadian Career Info. Assn. **[IO]**, Toronto, ON, Canada

Canadian Carpet Inst. **[IO]**, Ottawa, ON, Canada

Canadian Cartographic Assn. **[IO]**, Victoria, BC, Canada

Canadian Carwash Assn. **[IO]**, Mississauga, ON, Canada

Canadian Casting Fed. **[IO]**, Willowdale, ON, Canada

Canadian Cat Assn. **[IO]**, Brampton, ON, Canada

Canadian Catholic Historical Assn. **[IO]**, Toronto, ON, Canada

Canadian Catholic Org. for Development and Peace **[IO]**, Toronto, ON, Canada

Canadian Catholic Org. for Development and Peace - Alberta **[IO]**, Edmonton, AB, Canada

Canadian Catholic Org. for Development and Peace - British Columbia **[IO]**, Abbotsford, BC, Canada

Canadian Catholic Org. for Development and Peace - Manitoba **[IO]**, Winnipeg, MB, Canada

Canadian Catholic Org. for Development and Peace - Montreal **[IO]**, Montreal, QC, Canada

Canadian Catholic Org. for Development and Peace - Newfoundland and Labrador **[IO]**, Halifax, NS, Canada

Canadian Catholic Org. for Development and Peace - Nova Scotia **[IO]**, Halifax, NS, Canada

Canadian Catholic Org. for Development and Peace - Ontario **[IO]**, Toronto, ON, Canada

Canadian Catholic Org. for Development and Peace - Quebec **[IO]**, Sillery, QC, Canada

Canadian Catholic Org. for Development and Peace - Saskatchewan **[IO]**, Saskatoon, SK, Canada

Canadian Catholic School Trustees Assn. **[IO]**, Nepean, ON, Canada

Canadian Catholic Students' Assn. **[IO]**, Toronto, ON, Canada

Canadian Cattlemen's Assn. **[IO]**, Calgary, AB, Canada

Canadian Celiac Assn. **[IO]**, Mississauga, ON, Canada

Canadian Celtic Arts Assn. **[IO]**, Toronto, ON, Canada

Canadian Centre for Architecture **[IO]**, Montreal, QC, Canada

Canadian Centre for Bus. in the Community **[★IO]**

Canadian Centre for Ecumenism **[IO]**, Montreal, QC, Canada

Canadian Centre for Ethics and Corporate Policy **[★IO]**

Canadian Centre for Ethics in Sport **[IO]**, Ottawa, ON, Canada

Canadian Centre of Intl. PEN **[★IO]**

Canadian Centre for Intl. Stud. and Cooperation - Asia **[IO]**, Montreal, QC, Canada

Canadian Centre for Intl. Stud. and Cooperation - Bolivia **[IO]**, La Paz, Bolivia

Canadian Centre for Intl. Stud. and Cooperation - Burkina Faso **[IO]**, Ouagadougou, Burkina Faso

Canadian Centre for Intl. Stud. and Cooperation - Cambodia **[IO]**, Phnom Penh, Cambodia

Canadian Centre for Intl. Stud. and Cooperation - Ecuador **[IO]**, Quito, Ecuador

Canadian Centre for Intl. Stud. and Cooperation - India **[IO]**, New Delhi, India

Canadian Centre for Intl. Stud. and Cooperation - Kosovo **[IO]**, Kosovo, Serbia

Canadian Centre for Intl. Stud. and Cooperation - Nepal **[IO]**, Kathmandu, Nepal

Canadian Centre for Intl. Stud. and Cooperation - Republic of Guinea **[IO]**, Conakry, Guinea

Canadian Centre for Intl. Stud. and Cooperation - Senegal **[IO]**, Dakar, Senegal

Canadian Centre for Marine Communications **[IO]**, St. John's, NL, Canada

Canadian Centre for Occupational Hea. and Safety **[IO]**, Hamilton, ON, Canada

Canadian Centre for Philanthropy **[★IO]**

Canadian Centre for Policy Alternatives **[IO]**, Ottawa, ON, Canada

Canadian Centre for Pollution Prevention **[IO]**, Sarnia, ON, Canada

Canadian Centre for Stress and Well-Being/Stress Mgt. Center **[IO]**, Toronto, ON, Canada

Canadian Centre on Substance Abuse **[IO]**, Ottawa, ON, Canada

Canadian Centre for Victims of Torture **[IO]**, Toronto, ON, Canada

Canadian Cerebral Palsy Sports Assn. **[IO]**, Ottawa, ON, Canada

Canadian Chamber of Commerce **[IO]**, Ottawa, ON, Canada

Canadian Charolais Assn. **[IO]**, Calgary, AB, Canada

Canadian Chem. Producers' Assn. **[IO]**, Ottawa, ON, Canada

Canadian Child Care Fed. **[IO]**, Ottawa, ON, Canada

Canadian Children's Book Centre **[IO]**, Toronto, ON, Canada

Canadian Children's Opera Chorus **[IO]**, Toronto, ON, Canada

Canadian Chinese Kuo Shu Fed. **[IO]**, Agincourt, ON, Canada

Canadian Chiropractic Assn. **[IO]**, Toronto, ON, Canada

Canadian Chiropractic Examining Bd. **[IO]**, Calgary, AB, Canada

Canadian Christian and Jews **[★IO]**

Canadian Churches' Forum for Global Ministries **[IO]**, Toronto, ON, Canada

Canadian Circulation Mgt. Assn. **[IO]**, Moncton, NB, Canada

Canadian Citizenship Fed. **[IO]**, St. John, NB, Canada

Canadian Civil Liberties Assn. **[IO]**, Toronto, ON, Canada

Canadian Clinical Nurse Specialist Gp. **[★IO]**

Canadian Club of New York **[18988]**

Canadian Co-operative Assn. **[IO]**, Ottawa, ON, Canada

Canadian Co-Operative Assn. **[★IO]**

Canadian Co-Operative Wool Growers **[IO]**, Carleton Place, ON, Canada

Canadian Coalition Against the Death Penalty **[IO]**, Toronto, ON, Canada

Canadian Coalition Against Insurance Fraud **[IO]**, Toronto, ON, Canada

Reference to "IO" in place of a book number signifies that the association may be found in the 45th edition of International Organizations.

Canadian Coalition for High Blood Pressure Prevention and Control **[IO]**, London, ON, Canada

Canadian Coalition for Nuclear Responsibility **[IO]**, Montreal, QC, Canada

Canadian Coll. of Hea. Ser. Executives **[IO]**, Ottawa, ON, Canada

Canadian Coll. of Medical Geneticists **[IO]**, Ottawa, ON, Canada

Canadian Coll. of Naturopathic Medicine **[IO]**, Toronto, ON, Canada

Canadian Coll. of Physicists in Medicine **[IO]**, Kanata, ON, Canada

Canadian Coll. of Teachers **[IO]**, Ottawa, ON, Canada

Canadian Colleges Athletic Assn. **[IO]**, Cornwall, ON, Canada

Canadian Commn. for UNESCO **[IO]**, Ottawa, ON, Canada

Canadian Comm. on Cataloguing **[IO]**, Ottawa, ON, Canada

Canadian Comm. on Irrigation and Drainage **[★IO]**

Canadian Comm. on Labour History **[IO]**, St. John's, NL, Canada

Canadian Comm. on MARC **[IO]**, Ottawa, ON, Canada

Canadian Comm. for Pacific Economic Cooperation **[IO]**, Vancouver, BC, Canada

Canadian Community Newspapers Assn. **[IO]**, Toronto, ON, Canada

Canadian Comparative Literature Assn. **[IO]**, Prince George, BC, Canada

Canadian Concrete Pipe Assn. **[IO]**, Halton Hills, ON, Canada

Canadian Condominium Inst. **[IO]**, Toronto, ON, Canada

Canadian Conf. of the Arts **[IO]**, Ottawa, ON, Canada

Canadian Conf. of Catholic Bishops **[IO]**, Ottawa, ON, Canada

Canadian Conf. of Mennonite Brethren Churches **[IO]**, Winnipeg, MB, Canada

Canadian Cong. of Neurological Sciences **[★IO]**

Canadian Conservation Inst. **[IO]**, Ottawa, ON, Canada

Canadian Constr. Assn. **[IO]**, Ottawa, ON, Canada

Canadian Consulting Agrologists Assn. **[IO]**, Saskatoon, SK, Canada

Canadian Consumer Specialty Products Assn. **[IO]**, Ottawa, ON, Canada

Canadian Continence Found. **[IO]**, Peterborough, ON, Canada

Canadian Copper and Brass Development Assn. **[IO]**, Don Mills, ON, Canada

Canadian Copyright Inst. **[IO]**, Toronto, ON, Canada

Canadian Corkscrew Collectors Club **[IO]**, East Rutherford, NJ, United States

Canadian Corkscrew Collectors Club **[21985]**, c/o Milt Becker, Membership Coor., One Madison St., 5B, East Rutherford, NJ 07073, (973)773-9224

Canadian Corporate Counsel Assn. **[IO]**, Toronto, ON, Canada

Canadian Corps of Commissionaires **[IO]**, Ottawa, ON, Canada

Canadian Correspondence Chess Assn. **[IO]**, Ottawa, ON, Canada

Canadian Corrugated Case Assn. **[IO]**, North York, ON, Canada

Canadian Cosmetic, Toiletry and Fragrance Assn. **[IO]**, Mississauga, ON, Canada

Canadian Coun. for Aboriginal Bus. **[IO]**, Toronto, ON, Canada

Canadian Coun. for Accreditation of Pharmacy Programs **[IO]**, Vancouver, BC, Canada

Canadian Coun. for the Advancement of Educ. **[IO]**, Ottawa, ON, Canada

Canadian Coun. on Animal Care **[IO]**, Ottawa, ON, Canada

Canadian Coun. of Archives **[IO]**, Ottawa, ON, Canada

Canadian Coun. of Better Bus. Bureaus **[IO]**, Toronto, ON, Canada

Canadian Coun. of the Blind **[IO]**, Ottawa, ON, Canada

Canadian Coun. of Cardiovascular Nurses **[IO]**, Ottawa, ON, Canada

Canadian Coun. of Chief Executives **[IO]**, Ottawa, ON, Canada

Canadian Coun. on Child Welfare **[★IO]**

Canadian Coun. of Christian Charities **[IO]**, Elmira, ON, Canada

Canadian Coun. of Christians and Jews **[IO]**, Toronto, ON, Canada

Canadian Coun. of Churches **[IO]**, Toronto, ON, Canada

Canadian Coun. on Continuing Educ. in Pharmacy **[IO]**, Regina, SK, Canada

Canadian Coun. on Ecological Areas **[IO]**, Ottawa, ON, Canada

Canadian Coun. for Exceptional Children **[IO]**, Milton, ON, Canada

Canadian Coun. of Financial Analysts - Address unknown since 2005.

Canadian Coun. of Grocery Distributors **[IO]**, Montreal, QC, Canada

Canadian Coun. on Hea. Facilities Accreditation **[★IO]**

Canadian Coun. on Hea. Services Accreditation **[IO]**, Ottawa, ON, Canada

Canadian Coun. for Human Resources in the Env. Indus. **[★IO]**

Canadian Coun. of Independent Labs. **[IO]**, Ottawa, ON, Canada

Canadian Coun. for Intl. Co-operation **[IO]**, Ottawa, ON, Canada

Canadian Coun. on Intl. Law **[IO]**, Ottawa, ON, Canada

Canadian Coun. of Land Surveyors **[IO]**, Ottawa, ON, Canada

Canadian Coun. of Ministers of the Env. **[IO]**, Winnipeg, MB, Canada

Canadian Coun. of Montessori Administrators **[IO]**, Toronto, ON, Canada

Canadian Coun. of Motor Transport Administrators **[IO]**, Ottawa, ON, Canada

Canadian Coun. of Muslim Women **[IO]**, Gananoque, ON, Canada

Canadian Coun. of Professional Certification **[IO]**, Toronto, ON, Canada

Canadian Coun. of Professional Engineers **[★IO]**

Canadian Coun. of Professional Fish Harvesters **[IO]**, Ottawa, ON, Canada

Canadian Coun. for Public-Private Partnerships **[IO]**, Toronto, ON, Canada

Canadian Coun. for Reform Judaism **[IO]**, Toronto, ON, Canada

Canadian Coun. for Refugees **[IO]**, Montreal, QC, Canada

Canadian Coun. on Rehabilitation and Work **[IO]**, Toronto, ON, Canada

Canadian Coun. on Smoking and Hea. **[★IO]**

Canadian Coun. of Snowmobile Organizations **[IO]**, Thunder Bay, ON, Canada

Canadian Coun. on Social Development **[IO]**, Ottawa, ON, Canada

Canadian Coun. of Teachers of English Language Arts **[IO]**, Winnipeg, MB, Canada

Canadian Coun. of Technicians and Technologists **[IO]**, Ottawa, ON, Canada

Canadian Coun. for Tobacco Control **[IO]**, Ottawa, ON, Canada

Canadian Counselling Assn. **[IO]**, Ottawa, ON, Canada

Canadian Country Music Assn. **[IO]**, Toronto, ON, Canada

Canadian Courier and Logistics Assn. **[IO]**, Toronto, ON, Canada

Canadian Courier and Messenger Assn. **[★IO]**

Canadian Craft and Hobby Assn. **[IO]**, Calgary, AB, Canada

Canadian Crafts Coun. **[★IO]**

Canadian Crafts Fed. **[IO]**, Toronto, ON, Canada

Canadian Credit Inst. Educational Found. **[IO]**, Toronto, ON, Canada

Canadian Cricket Assn. **[IO]**, Toronto, ON, Canada

Canadian Criminal Justice Assn. **[IO]**, Ottawa, ON, Canada

Canadian Critical Care Soc. **[IO]**, Toronto, ON, Canada

Canadian Crossroads Intl. **[IO]**, Toronto, ON, Canada

Canadian Culinary Fed. **[IO]**, Timberlea, NS, Canada

Canadian Culinary Fed. North Vancouver Island **[IO]**, Vancouver, BC, Canada

Canadian Culinary Fed. Saskatoon Br. **[IO]**, Saskatoon, SK, Canada

Canadian Cultural Soc. of The Deaf **[IO]**, Toronto, ON, Canada

Canadian Curling Assn. **[IO]**, Cumberland, ON, Canada

Canadian Cutting Horse Assn. **[IO]**, Innisfail, AB, Canada

Canadian Cycling Assn. **[IO]**, Ottawa, ON, Canada

Canadian Cystic Fibrosis Found. **[IO]**, Toronto, ON, Canada

Canadian Dairy Commn. **[IO]**, Ottawa, ON, Canada

Canadian Dairy and Food Supply Assn. **[★IO]**

Canadian Dam Assn. **[IO]**, Edmonton, AB, Canada

Canadian Dance Assembly **[IO]**, Toronto, ON, Canada

Canadian Dance Teachers' Assn. **[IO]**, Pitt Meadows, BC, Canada

Canadian Deaf Curling Assn. **[IO]**, Vancouver, BC, Canada

Canadian Deaf Golf Assn. **[IO]**, Edmonton, AB, Canada

Canadian Deaf Sports Assn. **[IO]**, Montreal, QC, Canada

Canadian Deafblind and Rubella Assn. **[IO]**, Port Morien, NS, Canada

Canadian Decorating Products Assn. **[★IO]**

Canadian Decorating Products Assn. **[★2274]**

Canadian Defence Indus. Assn. **[★IO]**

Canadian Defence Preparedness Assn. **[★IO]**

Canadian Dental Assistants' Assn. **[IO]**, Ottawa, ON, Canada

Canadian Dental Assn. **[IO]**, Ottawa, ON, Canada

Canadian Dental Hygienists' Assn. **[IO]**, Ottawa, ON, Canada

Canadian Dental Protective Assn. **[IO]**, Richmond Hill, ON, Canada

Canadian Dental Therapists Assn. **[IO]**, Winnipeg, MB, Canada

Canadian Dermatology Assn. **[IO]**, Ottawa, ON, Canada

Canadian Dexter Cattle Assn. **[IO]**, Ottawa, ON, Canada

Canadian Diabetes Assn. **[IO]**, Toronto, ON, Canada

Canadian Diabetes Assn. - Barrie and District Br. **[IO]**, Barrie, ON, Canada

Canadian Diabetes Assn. - Belleville/Quinte Br. **[IO]**, Belleville, ON, Canada

Canadian Diabetes Assn. - Brantford Br. **[IO]**, Brantford, ON, Canada

Canadian Diabetes Assn. - Brockville/Tri-County Br. **[IO]**, Brockville, ON, Canada

Canadian Diabetes Assn. - Calgary and District Br. **[IO]**, Calgary, AB, Canada

Canadian Diabetes Assn. - Cambridge and District Br. **[IO]**, Kitchener, ON, Canada

Canadian Diabetes Assn. - Cape Breton Br. **[IO]**, Sydney, NS, Canada

Canadian Diabetes Assn. - Chatham and District Br. **[IO]**, Chatham, ON, Canada

Canadian Diabetes Assn. - Cornwall and District Br. **[IO]**, Cornwall, ON, Canada

Canadian Diabetes Assn. - Diabetes Educator Sect. **[IO]**, Toronto, ON, Canada

Canadian Diabetes Assn. - Durham Region Br. **[IO]**, Toronto, ON, Canada

Canadian Diabetes Assn. - Eastman District Region **[IO]**, Winnipeg, MB, Canada

Canadian Diabetes Assn. - Edmonton and District Br. **[IO]**, Edmonton, AB, Canada

Canadian Diabetes Assn. - Elliot Lake/Blind River **[IO]**, Sudbury, ON, Canada

Canadian Diabetes Assn. - Elmira and District Br. **[IO]**, Kitchener, ON, Canada

Canadian Diabetes Assn. - Fredericton and District Br. **[IO]**, Fredericton, NB, Canada

Canadian Diabetes Assn. - Grand Falls and District Br. **[IO]**, Grand Falls, NB, Canada

Canadian Diabetes Assn. - Greater Vancouver and District Br. **[IO]**, Vancouver, BC, Canada

Canadian Diabetes Assn. - Guelph and South Wellington Br. **[IO]**, Kitchener, ON, Canada

A star before a book entry number signifies that the name is not listed separately, but is mentioned within the entry.

Canadian Diabetes Assn. - Haldimand/Norfolk Community Gp. **[IO]**, Dunnville, ON, Canada

Canadian Diabetes Assn. - Hamilton and District Br. **[IO]**, Hamilton, ON, Canada

Canadian Diabetes Assn. - Kawarthas Br. **[IO]**, Peterborough, ON, Canada

Canadian Diabetes Assn. - Kelowna and District Br. **[IO]**, Kelowna, BC, Canada

Canadian Diabetes Assn. - Kingston and District Br. **[IO]**, Kingston, ON, Canada

Canadian Diabetes Assn. - Kitchener-Waterloo Br. **[IO]**, Kitchener, ON, Canada

Canadian Diabetes Assn. - Lakeshore Br. **[IO]**, Peterborough, ON, Canada

Canadian Diabetes Assn. - Lethbridge and District Br. **[IO]**, Lethbridge, AB, Canada

Canadian Diabetes Assn. - Lindsay Br. **[IO]**, Lindsay, ON, Canada

Canadian Diabetes Assn. - London Br. **[IO]**, London, ON, Canada

Canadian Diabetes Assn. - Medicine Hat and District Br. **[IO]**, Medicine Hat, AB, Canada

Canadian Diabetes Assn. - Midland/Penetanguishene Br. **[IO]**, Penetanguishene, ON, Canada

Canadian Diabetes Assn. - Miramichi and District Br. **[IO]**, Miramichi, NB, Canada

Canadian Diabetes Assn. - Moncton and District Br. **[IO]**, Moncton, NB, Canada

Canadian Diabetes Assn. - Nanaimo and District Br. **[IO]**, Nanaimo, BC, Canada

Canadian Diabetes Assn. - New Brunswick **[IO]**, Fredericton, NB, Canada

Canadian Diabetes Assn. - Newfoundland and Labrador Region **[IO]**, St. John's, NL, Canada

Canadian Diabetes Assn. - Niagara Br. **[IO]**, St. Catharines, ON, Canada

Canadian Diabetes Assn. - North Bay and District Br. **[IO]**, Sudbury, ON, Canada

Canadian Diabetes Assn. - North Perth/North Wellington Br. **[IO]**, Harriston, ON, Canada

Canadian Diabetes Assn. - Nova Scotia **[IO]**, Halifax, NS, Canada

Canadian Diabetes Assn. - Oakville Br. **[IO]**, Oakville, ON, Canada

Canadian Diabetes Assn. - Orangeville and District Br. **[IO]**, Kitchener, ON, Canada

Canadian Diabetes Assn. - Ottawa and District Br. **[IO]**, Ottawa, ON, Canada

Canadian Diabetes Assn. - Peel Region Br. **[IO]**, Toronto, ON, Canada

Canadian Diabetes Assn. - Pembroke and District Br. **[IO]**, Pembroke, ON, Canada

Canadian Diabetes Assn. - Prince Edward Island **[IO]**, Charlottetown, PE, Canada

Canadian Diabetes Assn. - Prince George and District Br. **[IO]**, Prince George, BC, Canada

Canadian Diabetes Assn. - Red Deer and District Br. **[IO]**, Red Deer, AB, Canada

Canadian Diabetes Assn. - Regina Br. **[IO]**, Regina, SK, Canada

Canadian Diabetes Assn. - Sackville and District Br. **[IO]**, Sackville, NB, Canada

Canadian Diabetes Assn. - Sarnia and District Br. **[IO]**, Sarnia, ON, Canada

Canadian Diabetes Assn. - Saskatoon Br. **[IO]**, Saskatoon, SK, Canada

Canadian Diabetes Assn. - Sault Ste. Marie and District Br. **[IO]**, Sault Ste. Marie, ON, Canada

Canadian Diabetes Assn. - Sect. de Bathurst **[IO]**, Fredericton, NB, Canada

Canadian Diabetes Assn. - Sect. du Madawaska **[IO]**, Edmundston, NB, Canada

Canadian Diabetes Assn. - South Parklands Br. **[IO]**, Dauphin, MB, Canada

Canadian Diabetes Assn. - Sudbury and District Br. **[IO]**, Sudbury, ON, Canada

Canadian Diabetes Assn. - Sussex and District Br. **[IO]**, Sussex, NB, Canada

Canadian Diabetes Assn. - Thunder Bay and District Br. **[IO]**, Thunder Bay, ON, Canada

Canadian Diabetes Assn. - Timmins and District Br. **[IO]**, Timmins, ON, Canada

Canadian Diabetes Assn. - Toronto Br. **[IO]**, Toronto, ON, Canada

Canadian Diabetes Assn. - Victoria and District Br. **[IO]**, Victoria, BC, Canada

Canadian Diabetes Assn. - Westman Br. **[IO]**, Brandon, MB, Canada

Canadian Diabetes Assn. - Williams Lake and District Br. **[IO]**, Williams Lake, BC, Canada

Canadian Diabetes Assn. - Windsor and District Br. **[IO]**, Windsor, ON, Canada

Canadian Diabetes Assn. - Woodstock and District Br. **[IO]**, Woodstock, NB, Canada

Canadian Diabetes Assn. - York Region Br. **[IO]**, Toronto, ON, Canada

Canadian Diamond Drilling Assn. **[IO]**, North Bay, ON, Canada

Canadian Die Casters Assn. **[IO]**, Ottawa, ON, Canada

Canadian Direct Marketing Assn. **[★IO]**

Canadian Disarmament Info. Ser. **[IO]**, Toronto, ON, Canada

Canadian Disc Jockey Assn. **[IO]**, Arva, ON, Canada

Canadian Doll Artists Assn. **[IO]**, Ottawa, ON, Canada

Canadian Dove Assn. **[IO]**, Plattsville, ON, Canada

Canadian Down Syndrome Soc. **[IO]**, Calgary, AB, Canada

Canadian Dressage Owners and Riders Assn. **[IO]**, Hamilton, ON, Canada

Canadian Drilling Assn. **[★IO]**

Canadian Driving Soc. **[★IO]**

Canadian Dyslexia Assn. **[IO]**, Ottawa, ON, Canada

Canadian Economics Assn. **[IO]**, Ottawa, ON, Canada

Canadian Educ. Assn. **[IO]**, Toronto, ON, Canada

Canadian Educ. Centre Network **[IO]**, Vancouver, BC, Canada

Canadian Educational Ensembles **[IO]**, Winnipeg, MB, Canada

Canadian Educational Standards Inst. **[IO]**, Toronto, ON, Canada

Canadian Egg Marketing Agency **[IO]**, Ottawa, ON, Canada

Canadian Ehlers Danlos Assn. **[IO]**, Bolton, ON, Canada

Canadian Elec. Railway Assn. **[★IO]**

Canadian Elecl. Contractors Assn. **[IO]**, Toronto, ON, Canada

Canadian Elecl. Mfrs. Representatives Assn. **[★IO]**

Canadian Electricity Assn. **[IO]**, Ottawa, ON, Canada

Canadian Electronic and Appliance Ser. Assn. **[IO]**, Mississauga, ON, Canada

Canadian Emergency Preparedness Assn. **[IO]**, Chilliwack, BC, Canada

Canadian Energy Pipeline Assn. **[IO]**, Calgary, AB, Canada

Canadian Energy Res. Inst. **[IO]**, Calgary, AB, Canada

Canadian Energy Workers Assn. **[IO]**, Edmonton, AB, Canada

Canadian Environmental Auditing Assn. **[IO]**, Oakville, ON, Canada

Canadian Environmental Defence Fund **[★IO]**

Canadian Environmental Law Assn. **[IO]**, Toronto, ON, Canada

Canadian Environmental Law Res. Found. **[★IO]**

Canadian Environmental Network **[IO]**, Ottawa, ON, Canada

Canadian Equestrian Fed. **[★IO]**

Canadian Esperanto Assn. **[IO]**, Sidney, BC, Canada

Canadian Ethnic Stud. Assn. **[IO]**, Winnipeg, MB, Canada

Canadian Ethnocultural Coun. **[IO]**, Ottawa, ON, Canada

Canadian Evaluation Soc. **[IO]**, Ottawa, ON, Canada

Canadian Executive Ser. Org. **[IO]**, Toronto, ON, Canada

Canadian Family Camping Fed. **[IO]**, Rexdale, ON, Canada

Canadian Farm Animal Care Trust **[IO]**, Barrie, ON, Canada

Canadian Farm Builders Assn. **[IO]**, Stratford, ON, Canada

Canadian Farm and Indus. Equip. Inst. **[★IO]**

Canadian Farm Writers' Fed. **[IO]**, Surrey, BC, Canada

Canadian Fed. of Amateur Baseball **[★IO]**

Canadian Fed. of Amateur Baseball **[IO]**, Ottawa, ON, Canada

Canadian Fed. of Aromatherapists **[IO]**, Waterloo, ON, Canada

Canadian Fed. of Biological Societies **[IO]**, Ottawa, ON, Canada

Canadian Fed. of Bus. and Professional Women's Clubs **[IO]**, Ottawa, ON, Canada

Canadian Fed. of Bus. School Deans **[IO]**, Montreal, QC, Canada

Canadian Fed. of Chefs **[★IO]**

Canadian Fed. of Earth Sciences **[IO]**, Calgary, AB, Canada

Canadian Fed. of Engg. Students **[IO]**, Ottawa, ON, Canada

Canadian Fed. of Friends of Museums **[IO]**, Toronto, ON, Canada

Canadian Fed. of Humane Societies **[IO]**, Ottawa, ON, Canada

Canadian Fed. for the Humanities and Social Sciences **[IO]**, Ottawa, ON, Canada

Canadian Fed. of Independent Bus. **[IO]**, Willowdale, ON, Canada

Canadian Fed. of Independent Grocers **[IO]**, Willowdale, ON, Canada

Canadian Fed. of Junior Leagues **[IO]**, Calgary, AB, Canada

Canadian Fed. of Medical Students **[IO]**, Ottawa, ON, Canada

Canadian Fed. of Mental Hea. Nurses **[IO]**, Toronto, ON, Canada

Canadian Fed. of Music Teachers' Associations **[IO]**, London, ON, Canada

Canadian Fed. of Nurses Unions **[IO]**, Ottawa, ON, Canada

Canadian Fed. of Poets **[IO]**, Burlington, ON, Canada

Canadian Fed. for Sexual Hea. **[IO]**, Ottawa, ON, Canada

Canadian Fed. of Students **[IO]**, Ottawa, ON, Canada

Canadian Fed. of Trading House Associations **[IO]**, Montreal, QC, Canada

Canadian Fed. of Univ. Women **[IO]**, Ottawa, ON, Canada

Canadian Feed Indus. Assn. **[★IO]**

Canadian Feed The Children **[IO]**, Toronto, ON, Canada

Canadian Fencing Fed. **[IO]**, Laval, QC, Canada

Canadian Fertility and Andrology Soc. **[IO]**, Montreal, QC, Canada

Canadian Fertilizer Inst. **[IO]**, Ottawa, ON, Canada

Canadian Figure Skating Assn. **[★IO]**

Canadian Film Centre **[IO]**, Toronto, ON, Canada

Canadian Film Inst. **[IO]**, Ottawa, ON, Canada

Canadian Film and TV Production Assn. **[IO]**, Ottawa, ON, Canada

Canadian Filmmakers Distribution Centre **[IO]**, Toronto, ON, Canada

Canadian Finance and Leasing Assn. **[IO]**, Toronto, ON, Canada

Canadian Fire Alarm Assn. **[IO]**, Markham, ON, Canada

Canadian Fire Safety Assn. **[IO]**, North York, ON, Canada

Canadian Firefighters Curling Assn. **[IO]**, Winnipeg, MB, Canada

Canadian Fitness and Lifestyle Res. Inst. **[IO]**, Ottawa, ON, Canada

Canadian Fjord Horse Assn. **[IO]**, Killarney, MB, Canada

Canadian Flag Assn. **[IO]**, Scarborough, ON, Canada

Canadian Folk Arts Coun. **[★IO]**

Canadian Folk Music Soc. **[★IO]**

Canadian Food Exporters Assn. **[IO]**, Don Mills, ON, Canada

Canadian Food for the Hungry Intl. **[IO]**, Abbotsford, BC, Canada

Canadian Football Hall of Fame and Museum **[IO]**, Hamilton, ON, Canada

Canadian Football League **[IO]**, Toronto, ON, Canada

Canadian Football League Players Assn. **[IO]**, Oakville, ON, Canada

Canadian Foresters Life Insurance Soc. - Address unknown since 1994.

Reference to "IO" in place of a book number signifies that the association may be found in the 45th edition of International Organizations.

Canadian Forestry Assn. [IO], Pembroke, ON, Canada

Canadian Found. for AIDS Res. [IO], Toronto, ON, Canada

Canadian Found. for the Americas [IO], Ottawa, ON, Canada

Canadian Found. for the Awareness of Miracles [IO], Lefaivre, ON, Canada

Canadian Found. for Dietetic Res. [IO], Toronto, ON, Canada

Canadian Found. for Drug Policy [IO], Ottawa, ON, Canada

Canadian Found. for Economic Educ. [IO], Toronto, ON, Canada

Canadian Found. for the Love of Children [★IO]

Canadian Found. for Masorti Judaism [IO], Toronto, ON, Canada

Canadian Found. for Physically Disabled Persons [IO], Toronto, ON, Canada

Canadian Found. for the Stud. of Infant Deaths [IO], Toronto, ON, Canada

Canadian Found. for Ukrainian Stud. [IO], Toronto, ON, Canada

Canadian Foundry Assn. [IO], Ottawa, ON, Canada

Canadian Franchise Assn. [IO], Toronto, ON, Canada

Canadian and French Heritage Center; Northwest Territory, [★20720]

Canadian Friends of the Alliance Israelite Universelle [★17947]

Canadian Friends of the Alliance Israelite Universelle [★IO]

Canadian Friends of Bar-Ilan Univ. [IO], Concord, ON, Canada

Canadian Friends of Boys' Town Jerusalem [IO], Toronto, ON, Canada

Canadian Friends of Burma [IO], Ottawa, ON, Canada

Canadian Friends of Givat Haviva [IO], Toronto, ON, Canada

Canadian Friends of the Hebrew Univ. of Jerusalem [IO], Toronto, ON, Canada

Canadian Friends Historical Assn. [IO], Newmarket, ON, Canada

Canadian Friends of Mine - Address unknown since 2002.

Canadian Friends of Peace Now [IO], Thornhill, ON, Canada

Canadian Friends Ser. Comm. [IO], Toronto, ON, Canada

Canadian Friends of Soviet People [IO], Toronto, ON, Canada

Canadian Fur Trade Development Inst. [★IO]

Canadian Galloway Assn. [IO], Ottawa, ON, Canada

Canadian Gas Assn. [IO], Ottawa, ON, Canada

Canadian Gelbvieh Assn. [IO], Calgary, AB, Canada

Canadian Gemmological Assn. [IO], Toronto, ON, Canada

Canadian Gen. Standards Bd. [IO], Gatineau, QC, Canada

Canadian Generic Pharmaceutical Assn. [IO], Toronto, ON, Canada

Canadian Genetic Diseases Network [IO], Vancouver, BC, Canada

Canadian Geomorphological Res. Gp. [IO], Kanata, ON, Canada

Canadian Geophysical Union [IO], Calgary, AB, Canada

Canadian Geoscience Coun. [★IO]

Canadian Geotechnical Soc. [IO], Alliston, ON, Canada

Canadian Geriatrics Soc. [IO], Kanata, ON, Canada

Canadian German Chamber of Indus. and Commerce [IO], Toronto, ON, Canada

Canadian Gerontological Nursing Assn. [IO], Vancouver, BC, Canada

Canadian Gift and Tableware Assn. [IO], Toronto, ON, Canada

Canadian Ging Wu Kung Fu Martial Art Assn. [IO], Edmonton, AB, Canada

Canadian Girls Rodeo Assn. [IO], Calgary, AB, Canada

Canadian Goat Soc. [IO], Ottawa, ON, Canada

Canadian Golf Superintendents Assn. [IO], Mississauga, ON, Canada

Canadian Good Roads Assn. [★IO]

Canadian Gospel Music Assn. [★IO]

Canadian Grand Masters Fiddling Championship [IO], Nepean, ON, Canada

Canadian Ground Water Assn. [IO], Bedford, NS, Canada

Canadian Guernsey Assn. [IO], Guelph, ON, Canada

Canadian Guidance and Counseling Assn. [★IO]

Canadian Guidance and Counselling Found. [★IO]

Canadian Guide Dogs for the Blind [IO], Manotick, ON, Canada

Canadian Guild of Pakistani Women [IO], Willowdale, ON, Canada

Canadian Hackney Soc. [IO], Brampton, ON, Canada

Canadian Haflinger Assn. [IO], Ariss, ON, Canada

Canadian Hard of Hearing Assn. [IO], Ottawa, ON, Canada

Canadian Hard of Hearing Assn. - Alberni Valley Br. [IO], Port Alberni, BC, Canada

Canadian Hard of Hearing Assn. - BC Parents' Br. [IO], Chilliwack, BC, Canada

Canadian Hard of Hearing Assn. - British Columbia Chap. [IO], Chilliwack, BC, Canada

Canadian Hard of Hearing Assn. - Calgary Br. [IO], Calgary, AB, Canada

Canadian Hard of Hearing Assn. - Edmonton Br. [IO], Edmonton, AB, Canada

Canadian Hard of Hearing Assn. - Fredericton Br. [IO], Fredericton, NB, Canada

Canadian Hard of Hearing Assn. - Kamloops Br. [IO], Kamloops, BC, Canada

Canadian Hard of Hearing Assn. - Kelowna Br. [IO], Kelowna, BC, Canada

Canadian Hard of Hearing Assn. - Lethbridge Br. [IO], Lethbridge, AB, Canada

Canadian Hard of Hearing Assn. - Manitoba Chap. [IO], Winnipeg, MB, Canada

Canadian Hard of Hearing Assn. - Moncton Br. [IO], Dieppe, NB, Canada

Canadian Hard of Hearing Assn. - Nanaimo Br. [IO], Nanaimo, BC, Canada

Canadian Hard of Hearing Assn. - New Brunswick Chap. [IO], St. John, NB, Canada

Canadian Hard of Hearing Assn. - Newfoundland and Labrador Chap. [IO], St. John's, NL, Canada

Canadian Hard of Hearing Assn. - North Shore Br. [IO], North Vancouver, BC, Canada

Canadian Hard of Hearing Assn. - Ontario Chap. [IO], Sudbury, ON, Canada

Canadian Hard of Hearing Assn. - Orillia and District Br. [IO], Orillia, ON, Canada

Canadian Hard of Hearing Assn. - Outaouais Br. [IO], Gatineau, QC, Canada

Canadian Hard of Hearing Assn. - Prince George Br. [IO], Prince George, BC, Canada

Canadian Hard of Hearing Assn. - Quebec Chap. [IO], Gatineau, QC, Canada

Canadian Hard of Hearing Assn. - Regina and District Br. [IO], Regina, SK, Canada

Canadian Hard of Hearing Assn. - Saskatoon Br. [IO], Saskatoon, SK, Canada

Canadian Hard of Hearing Assn. - Sudbury Br. [IO], Sudbury, ON, Canada

Canadian Hard of Hearing Assn. - Vancouver Br. [IO], Vancouver, BC, Canada

Canadian Hard of Hearing Assn. - Victoria Br. [IO], Victoria, BC, Canada

Canadian Hard of Hearing Assn. - Yellowknife Br. [IO], Yellowknife, NT, Canada

Canadian Hardware and Housewares Mfrs. Assn. [IO], Scarborough, ON, Canada

Canadian Hardwood Plywood and Veneer Assn. [IO], Chambly, QC, Canada

Canadian Harvard Aircraft Assn. [IO], Tillsonburg, ON, Canada

Canadian Hays Converter Assn. [IO], Calgary, AB, Canada

Canadian Hea. Coalition [IO], Ottawa, ON, Canada

Canadian Hea. Food Assn. [IO], Toronto, ON, Canada

Canadian Hea. Info. Mgt. Assn. [IO], London, ON, Canada

Canadian Hea. Libraries Assn. [IO], Toronto, ON, Canada

Canadian Hea. Record Assn. [★IO]

Canadian Healthcare Assn. [IO], Ottawa, ON, Canada

Canadian Healthcare Engg. Soc. [IO], Kingston, ON, Canada

Canadian Healthcare Info. Tech. Trade Assn. [IO], Edmonton, AB, Canada

Canadian Hearing Soc. [IO], Toronto, ON, Canada

Canadian Hearing Soc. Found. [★IO]

Canadian Heat Exchanger and Vessel Mfrs. Assn. [IO], Mississauga, ON, Canada

Canadian Hedgehog Assn. [IO], Miramichi, NB, Canada

Canadian Hematology Soc. [IO], Ottawa, ON, Canada

Canadian Hemochromatosis Soc. [IO], Richmond, BC, Canada

Canadian Hemophilia Soc. [IO], Montreal, QC, Canada

Canadian Hereford Assn. [IO], Calgary, AB, Canada

Canadian Heritage Info. Network [IO], Gatineau, QC, Canada

Canadian Highland Cattle Soc. [IO], Smithers, BC, Canada

Canadian Historical Assn. [IO], Ottawa, ON, Canada

Canadian Historical Soc. [★IO]

Canadian HIV/AIDS Legal Network [IO], Toronto, ON, Canada

Canadian Hockey Assn. [★IO]

Canadian Hockey League [IO], Scarborough, ON, Canada

Canadian Holistic Nurses Assn. [IO], Calgary, AB, Canada

Canadian Home Builders' Assn. [IO], Ottawa, ON, Canada

Canadian Home Care Assn. [IO], Ottawa, ON, Canada

Canadian Home and School Fed. [IO], Ottawa, ON, Canada

Canadian Honey Coun. [IO], Calgary, AB, Canada

Canadian Horticultural Coun. [IO], Ottawa, ON, Canada

Canadian Hospice Palliative Care Assn. [IO], Ottawa, ON, Canada

Canadian Hosp. Engg. Soc. [★IO]

Canadian Host Family Assn. [IO], Chestermere, AB, Canada

Canadian Housing and Renewal Assn. [IO], Ottawa, ON, Canada

Canadian Human-Computer Communications Soc. [IO], Mississauga, ON, Canada

Canadian Human Rights Found. [★IO]

Canadian Hunger Found. [★IO]

Canadian Hydrogen Assn. [IO], Ottawa, ON, Canada

Canadian Hydrographic Assn. [IO], Burlington, ON, Canada

Canadian Hydrographic Assn. - Ottawa Br. [IO], Ottawa, ON, Canada

Canadian Hydrographic Assn. - Prairie Schooner Br. [IO], Calgary, AB, Canada

Canadian Hydropower Assn. [IO], Ottawa, ON, Canada

Canadian Hypertension Soc. [IO], Kingston, ON, Canada

Canadian Icelandic Horse Fed. [IO], Vanscoy, SK, Canada

Canadian Image Processing and Pattern Recognition Soc. [IO], London, ON, Canada

Canadian Imaging Trade Assn. [IO], Newmarket, ON, Canada

Canadian Immigration Historical Soc. [IO], Ottawa, ON, Canada

Canadian Importers Assn. [★IO]

Canadian Independent Adjusters' Assn. [IO], Etobicoke, ON, Canada

Canadian Independent Film Caucus [★IO]

Canadian Independent Record Production Assn. [IO], Toronto, ON, Canada

Canadian Independent Telephone Assn. [IO], Alton, ON, Canada

Canadian Indus. Relations Assn. [IO], Ste.-Foy, QC, Canada

Canadian Indus. Trans. Assn. [IO], Ottawa, ON, Canada

A star before a book entry number signifies that the name is not listed separately, but is mentioned within the entry.

Canadian Info. Processing Soc. [IO], Mississauga, ON, Canada

Canadian Injured Workers Alliance [IO], Thunder Bay, ON, Canada

Canadian Injury Prevention Found. [★IO]

Canadian Innovation Centre [IO], Waterloo, ON, Canada

Canadian Inst. [IO], Toronto, ON, Canada

Canadian Inst. of Actuaries [IO], Ottawa, ON, Canada

Canadian Inst. for the Admin. of Justice [IO], Montreal, QC, Canada

Canadian Inst. for Advanced Res. [IO], Toronto, ON, Canada

Canadian Inst. of the Arts for Young Audiences [IO], Vancouver, BC, Canada

Canadian Inst. of Certified Administrative Managers [IO], Toronto, ON, Canada

Canadian Inst. of Chartered Accountants [IO], Toronto, ON, Canada

Canadian Inst. of Chartered Bus. Valuators [IO], Toronto, ON, Canada

Canadian Inst. of Chartered Life Underwriters and Chartered Financial Consultants [★IO]

Canadian Inst. of Child Hea. [IO], Ottawa, ON, Canada

Canadian Inst. for Climate Stud. [IO], Victoria, BC, Canada

Canadian Inst. for Conflict Resolution [IO], Ottawa, ON, Canada

Canadian Inst. of Cultural Affairs [IO], Toronto, ON, Canada

Canadian Inst. of Energy [IO], North Vancouver, BC, Canada

Canadian Inst. for Energy Training [IO], Orangeville, ON, Canada

Canadian Inst. for Environmental Law and Policy [IO], Toronto, ON, Canada

Canadian Inst. of Financial Planning [IO], Mississauga, ON, Canada

Canadian Inst. of Food Sci. and Tech. [IO], Toronto, ON, Canada

Canadian Inst. of Forestry [IO], Ottawa, ON, Canada

Canadian Inst. of Gemmology [IO], Vancouver, BC, Canada

Canadian Inst. of Geomatics [IO], Ottawa, ON, Canada

Canadian Inst. of Hea. Care and Bus. [IO], Toronto, ON, Canada

Canadian Inst. for Hea. Info. [IO], Ottawa, ON, Canada

Canadian Inst. for Historical Microreproductions [★IO]

Canadian Inst. of Intl. Affairs [IO], Toronto, ON, Canada

Canadian Inst. for Jewish Res. [IO], Montreal, QC, Canada

Canadian Inst. of Mgt. [IO], Barrie, ON, Canada

Canadian Inst. of Marketing [IO], Halton Hills, ON, Canada

Canadian Inst. of Mining, Metallurgy, and Petroleum [IO], Montreal, QC, Canada

Canadian Inst. of Mortgage Brokers and Lenders [★IO]

Canadian Inst. for NDE [IO], Hamilton, ON, Canada

Canadian Inst. of Planners [IO], Ottawa, ON, Canada

Canadian Inst. of Plumbing and Heating [IO], Toronto, ON, Canada

Canadian Inst. of Professional Home Inspectors [IO], Vancouver, BC, Canada

Canadian Inst. of Public Hea. Inspectors [IO], White Rock, BC, Canada

Canadian Inst. of Public and Private Real Estate Companies [★IO]

Canadian Inst. of Quantity Surveyors [IO], Markham, ON, Canada

Canadian Inst. of Resources Law [IO], Calgary, AB, Canada

Canadian Inst. of Steel Constr. [IO], Willowdale, ON, Canada

Canadian Inst. of Strategic Stud. [IO], Toronto, ON, Canada

Canadian Inst. of Stress [IO], Toronto, ON, Canada

Canadian Inst. of Surveying [★IO]

Canadian Inst. of Surveying and Mapping [★IO]

Canadian Inst. for Theatre Tech. [IO], Ottawa, ON, Canada

Canadian Inst. of Traffic and Trans. [IO], Toronto, ON, Canada

Canadian Inst. of Travel Counsellors [IO], Toronto, ON, Canada

Canadian Inst. of Treated Wood [IO], Ottawa, ON, Canada

Canadian Inst. of Ukrainian Stud. [IO], Edmonton, AB, Canada

Canadian Institutional Res. and Planning Assn. [IO], Edmonton, AB, Canada

Canadian Insurance Accountants Assn. [IO], Toronto, ON, Canada

Canadian Insurance Claims Managers' Assn. [IO], Toronto, ON, Canada

Canadian Intl. Dragon Boat Festival Soc. [IO], Vancouver, BC, Canada

Canadian Intl. DX Club [IO], St. Lambert, QC, Canada

Canadian Intl. Freight Forwarders Assn. [IO], Toronto, ON, Canada

Canadian Intl. Grains Inst. [IO], Winnipeg, MB, Canada

Canadian Intl. Inst. of Applied Negotiation [IO], Ottawa, ON, Canada

Canadian Interuniversity Athletic Union [★IO]

Canadian Interuniversity Sport [IO], Ottawa, ON, Canada

Canadian Intravenous Nurses Assn. [IO], Toronto, ON, Canada

Canadian Investor Relations Inst. [IO], Mississauga, ON, Canada

Canadian Iris Soc. [IO], Brantford, ON, Canada

Canadian IT Law Assn. [IO], Toronto, ON, Canada

Canadian Jackie Chan Fan Club [IO], Scarborough, ON, Canada

Canadian Jesuits Intl. [IO], Toronto, ON, Canada

Canadian Jewellers Assn. [IO], Toronto, ON, Canada

Canadian Jewish Cong. [IO], Ottawa, ON, Canada

Canadian Jewish Historical Soc. [★IO]

Canadian Journalists for Free Expression [IO], Toronto, ON, Canada

Canadian Junior Football League [IO], Calgary, AB, Canada

Canadian Kendo Fed. [IO], Stouffville, ON, Canada

Canadian Kennel Club [IO], Etobicoke, ON, Canada

Canadian Kitchen Cabinet Assn. [IO], Ottawa, ON, Canada

Canadian Lab. Suppliers Assn. [IO], Kitchener, ON, Canada

Canadian Labour and Bus. Centre [IO], Ottawa, ON, Canada

Canadian Labour Cong. [IO], Ottawa, ON, Canada

Canadian Labour Market and Productivity [★IO]

Canadian Lacrosse Assn. [IO], Ottawa, ON, Canada

Canadian Land Reclamation Assn. [IO], Calgary, AB, Canada

Canadian Landmine Found. [IO], Toronto, ON, Canada

Canadian Law and Economics Assn. [IO], Toronto, ON, Canada

Canadian Law and Soc. Assn. [IO], Toronto, ON, Canada

Canadian Lawyers' Assn. for Intl. Human Rights [★IO]

Canadian Lawyers for Intl. Human Rights [IO], Ottawa, ON, Canada

Canadian League Against Epilepsy [IO], London, ON, Canada

Canadian League of Composers [IO], Toronto, ON, Canada

Canadian Lebanon Soc. of Halifax [IO], Halifax, NS, Canada

Canadian Lib. Assn. [IO], Ottawa, ON, Canada

Canadian Lib. Trustees Assn. [IO], Saskatoon, SK, Canada

Canadian Life and Hea. Insurance Assn. [IO], Toronto, ON, Canada

Canadian Life Insurance Medical Officers Assn. [IO], Ottawa, ON, Canada

Canadian Lifeboat Inst. [IO], Vancouver, BC, Canada

Canadian Limousin Assn. [IO], Calgary, AB, Canada

Canadian Linguistic Assn. [IO], St. John's, NL, Canada

Canadian Liver Found. [IO], Toronto, ON, Canada

Canadian Livestock Records Corp. [IO], Ottawa, ON, Canada

Canadian Llama and Alpaca Assn. [IO], Calgary, AB, Canada

Canadian Long Distance Riding Assn. [IO], Wellesley, ON, Canada

Canadian Long Term Care Assn. [★IO]

Canadian Lumbermen's Assn. [IO], Ottawa, ON, Canada

Canadian Lung Assn. [IO], Ottawa, ON, Canada

Canadian Lutheran World Relief [IO], Winnipeg, MB, Canada

Canadian Magazine Publishers Assn. [★IO]

Canadian Maine-Anjou Assn. [IO], Calgary, AB, Canada

Canadian Mgt. Centre [IO], Toronto, ON, Canada

Canadian Manufactured Housing Inst. [IO], Ottawa, ON, Canada

Canadian Mfrs. of Chem. Specialties Assn. [★IO]

Canadian Mfrs. and Exporters [IO], Ottawa, ON, Canada

Canadian Marfan Assn. [IO], Mississauga, ON, Canada

Canadian Marine Mfrs. Assn. [IO], Oakville, ON, Canada

Canadian Marine Officers' Union [IO], Thorold, ON, Canada

Canadian Marine Pilots' Assn. [IO], Ottawa, ON, Canada

Canadian Maritime Law Assn. [IO], Montreal, QC, Canada

Canadian Marketing Assn. [IO], Don Mills, ON, Canada

Canadian Massage Therapist Alliance [IO], Oakville, ON, Canada

Canadian Masters' Cross Country Ski Assn. [IO], St.-Romuald, QC, Canada

Canadian Mathematical Soc. [IO], Ottawa, ON, Canada

Canadian Meat Coun. [IO], Ottawa, ON, Canada

Canadian Media Guild [IO], Toronto, ON, Canada

Canadian Medical Assn. [IO], Ottawa, ON, Canada

Canadian Medical and Biological Engg. Soc. [IO], Orleans, ON, Canada

Canadian Medical Protective Assn. [IO], Ottawa, ON, Canada

Canadian MedicAlert Found. [IO], Toronto, ON, Canada

Canadian Mental Hea. Assn. [IO], Toronto, ON, Canada

Canadian Mental Hea. Assn. - Alberta Div. [IO], Edmonton, AB, Canada

Canadian Mental Hea. Assn., Barrie - Simcoe Br. [IO], Barrie, ON, Canada

Canadian Mental Hea. Assn., Bas-du-Fleuve Br. [IO], Rimouski, QC, Canada

Canadian Mental Hea. Assn. - Battlefords Br. [IO], North Battleford, SK, Canada

Canadian Mental Hea. Assn. - BC Div. [IO], Vancouver, BC, Canada

Canadian Mental Hea. Assn. - Brant County Br. [IO], Brantford, ON, Canada

Canadian Mental Hea. Assn. - Calgary Region [IO], Calgary, AB, Canada

Canadian Mental Hea. Assn. - Central Region [IO], Red Deer, AB, Canada

Canadian Mental Hea. Assn., Chatham - Kent Br. [IO], Chatham, ON, Canada

Canadian Mental Hea. Assn., Chaudiere - Appalaches Br. [IO], Levis, QC, Canada

Canadian Mental Hea. Assn. - Cochrane Timiskaming Br. [IO], Timmins, ON, Canada

Canadian Mental Hea. Assn. - Courtenay Br. [IO], Courtenay, BC, Canada

Canadian Mental Hea. Assn. - Cowichan Valley Br. [IO], Duncan, BC, Canada

Canadian Mental Hea. Assn. - Dartmouth Br. [IO], Dartmouth, NS, Canada

Canadian Mental Hea. Assn. - Durham Br. [IO], Oshawa, ON, Canada

Canadian Mental Hea. Assn. - East Central Region [IO], Camrose, AB, Canada

Reference to "IO" in place of a book number signifies that the association may be found in the 45th edition of International Organizations.

Canadian Mental Hea. Assn. - Edmonton Region **[IO]**, Edmonton, AB, Canada

Canadian Mental Hea. Assn. - Elgin County Br. **[IO]**, St. Thomas, ON, Canada

Canadian Mental Hea. Assn. - Estevan Br. **[IO]**, Estevan, SK, Canada

Canadian Mental Hea. Assn. - Fredericton/Oromocto Region **[IO]**, Fredericton, NB, Canada

Canadian Mental Hea. Assn., Grey - Bruce Br. **[IO]**, Owen Sound, ON, Canada

Canadian Mental Hea. Assn. - Hamilton Br. **[IO]**, Hamilton, ON, Canada

Canadian Mental Hea. Assn. - Hastings and Prince Edward Br. **[IO]**, Belleville, ON, Canada

Canadian Mental Hea. Assn., Haut-Richelieu Br. **[IO]**, St. Jean-sur-Richelieu, QC, Canada

Canadian Mental Hea. Assn., Huron - Perth Br. **[IO]**, Stratford, ON, Canada

Canadian Mental Hea. Assn. - Interlake Region **[IO]**, Selkirk, MB, Canada

Canadian Mental Hea. Assn. - Kamloops Br. **[IO]**, Kamloops, BC, Canada

Canadian Mental Hea. Assn. - Kelowna Br. **[IO]**, Kelowna, BC, Canada

Canadian Mental Hea. Assn. - Kingston Br. **[IO]**, Kingston, ON, Canada

Canadian Mental Hea. Assn. for the Kootenays **[IO]**, Cranbrook, BC, Canada

Canadian Mental Hea. Assn. - Lac St. Jean Br. **[IO]**, Roberval, QC, Canada

Canadian Mental Hea. Assn. - Lambton County Br. **[IO]**, Sarnia, ON, Canada

Canadian Mental Hea. Assn., Leeds - Grenville Br. **[IO]**, Brockville, ON, Canada

Canadian Mental Hea. Assn., London - Middlesex Br. **[IO]**, London, ON, Canada

Canadian Mental Hea. Assn. - Manitoba Div. **[IO]**, Winnipeg, MB, Canada

Canadian Mental Hea. Assn. - Melfort Br. **[IO]**, Melfort, SK, Canada

Canadian Mental Hea. Assn., Mid-Island Br. **[IO]**, Nanaimo, BC, Canada

Canadian Mental Hea. Assn. - Moncton Region **[IO]**, Moncton, NB, Canada

Canadian Mental Hea. Assn. - Montreal Br. **[IO]**, Montreal, QC, Canada

Canadian Mental Hea. Assn. - Moose Jaw Br. **[IO]**, Moose Jaw, SK, Canada

Canadian Mental Hea. Assn. - New Brunswick Div. **[IO]**, Fredericton, NB, Canada

Canadian Mental Hea. Assn. - Newfoundland and Labrador Div. **[IO]**, St. John's, NL, Canada

Canadian Mental Hea. Assn. - Niagara Br. **[IO]**, St. Catharines, ON, Canada

Canadian Mental Hea. Assn. - Nipissing Regional Br. **[IO]**, North Bay, ON, Canada

Canadian Mental Hea. Assn. - North and South Okanagan Br. **[IO]**, Kelowna, BC, Canada

Canadian Mental Hea. Assn. - North West Region **[IO]**, Grande Prairie, AB, Canada

Canadian Mental Hea. Assn. - North and West Vancouver Br. **[IO]**, North Vancouver, BC, Canada

Canadian Mental Hea. Assn. - Northwest Territories Div. **[IO]**, Yellowknife, NT, Canada

Canadian Mental Hea. Assn. - Nova Scotia Div. **[IO]**, Dartmouth, NS, Canada

Canadian Mental Hea. Assn. - Ontario Div. **[IO]**, Toronto, ON, Canada

Canadian Mental Hea. Assn. - Ottawa Br. **[IO]**, Ottawa, ON, Canada

Canadian Mental Hea. Assn. - Oxford County Br. **[IO]**, Woodstock, ON, Canada

Canadian Mental Hea. Assn. - Peel Br. **[IO]**, Brampton, ON, Canada

Canadian Mental Hea. Assn. - Peterborough Br. **[IO]**, Peterborough, ON, Canada

Canadian Mental Hea. Assn. - Pincher Creek Br. **[IO]**, Pincher Creek, AB, Canada

Canadian Mental Hea. Assn. - Port Alberni Br. **[IO]**, Port Alberni, BC, Canada

Canadian Mental Hea. Assn. - Prince Albert Br. **[IO]**, Prince Albert, SK, Canada

Canadian Mental Hea. Assn. - Prince County Br. **[IO]**, Summerside, PE, Canada

Canadian Mental Hea. Assn. - Prince Edward Island Div. **[IO]**, Charlottetown, PE, Canada

Canadian Mental Hea. Assn. - Prince George Br. **[IO]**, Prince George, BC, Canada

Canadian Mental Hea. Assn. - Quebec Div. **[IO]**, Montreal, QC, Canada

Canadian Mental Hea. Assn. - Regina Br. **[IO]**, Regina, SK, Canada

Canadian Mental Hea. Assn. - Region I Moncton **[IO]**, Moncton, NB, Canada

Canadian Mental Hea. Assn. - Region III Br. **[IO]**, Fredericton, NB, Canada

Canadian Mental Hea. Assn. - Region IV Edmundston **[IO]**, Edmundston, NB, Canada

Canadian Mental Hea. Assn. - Region V Campbellton **[IO]**, Campbellton, NB, Canada

Canadian Mental Hea. Assn. - Region VII Miramichi **[IO]**, Miramichi, NB, Canada

Canadian Mental Hea. Assn. - Richmond Br. **[IO]**, Richmond, BC, Canada

Canadian Mental Hea. Assn., Rive-Sud de Montreal Br. **[IO]**, Longueuil, QC, Canada

Canadian Mental Hea. Assn., S. D. and G. Prescott - Russel Br. **[IO]**, Cornwall, ON, Canada

Canadian Mental Hea. Assn. - Saint John Br. **[IO]**, St. John, NB, Canada

Canadian Mental Hea. Assn. - Saskatchewan Div. **[IO]**, Regina, SK, Canada

Canadian Mental Hea. Assn. - Saskatoon Br. **[IO]**, Saskatoon, SK, Canada

Canadian Mental Hea. Assn. - Sault Ste. Marie Br. **[IO]**, Sault Ste. Marie, ON, Canada

Canadian Mental Hea. Assn. - Simon Fraser Br. **[IO]**, New Westminster, BC, Canada

Canadian Mental Hea. Assn. - South East Region **[IO]**, Medicine Hat, AB, Canada

Canadian Mental Hea. Assn. - South Okanagan Similkameen Br. **[IO]**, Penticton, BC, Canada

Canadian Mental Hea. Assn. - South Region **[IO]**, Lethbridge, AB, Canada

Canadian Mental Hea. Assn. - Swift Current Br. **[IO]**, Swift Current, SK, Canada

Canadian Mental Hea. Assn. - Thompson Region **[IO]**, Thompson, MB, Canada

Canadian Mental Hea. Assn. - Thunder Bay Br. **[IO]**, Thunder Bay, ON, Canada

Canadian Mental Hea. Assn. - Toronto Br. **[IO]**, Toronto, ON, Canada

Canadian Mental Hea. Assn. - Vancouver/Burnaby Br. **[IO]**, Vancouver, BC, Canada

Canadian Mental Hea. Assn. - Vernon District Br. **[IO]**, Vernon, BC, Canada

Canadian Mental Hea. Assn. - Waterloo Regional Br. **[IO]**, Guelph, ON, Canada

Canadian Mental Hea. Assn., Wellington - Dufferin Br. **[IO]**, Guelph, ON, Canada

Canadian Mental Hea. Assn. - Westman Region **[IO]**, Brandon, MB, Canada

Canadian Mental Hea. Assn. - Weyburn Br. **[IO]**, Weyburn, SK, Canada

Canadian Mental Hea. Assn., Windsor - Essex County Br. **[IO]**, Windsor, ON, Canada

Canadian Mental Hea. Assn. - Winnipeg Region **[IO]**, Winnipeg, MB, Canada

Canadian Mental Hea. Assn. - Yorkton Br. **[IO]**, Yorkton, SK, Canada

Canadian Mental Hea. Assn. - Yukon Div. **[IO]**, Whitehorse, YT, Canada

Canadian Merchant Ser. Guild **[IO]**, Ottawa, ON, Canada

Canadian Meteorological and Oceanographic Soc. **[IO]**, Ottawa, ON, Canada

Canadian Micro Mineral Assn. **[IO]**, Toronto, ON, Canada

Canadian Milking Shorthorn Soc. **[IO]**, Guelph, ON, Canada

Canadian Mineral Analysts **[IO]**, Winnipeg, MB, Canada

Canadian Modern Pentathlon Assn. **[IO]**, Quebec, QC, Canada

Canadian Morgan Horse Assn. **[IO]**, Port Perry, ON, Canada

Canadian Motion Picture Distribution Assn. **[IO]**, Toronto, ON, Canada

Canadian Motorcycle Assn. **[IO]**, Hamilton, ON, Canada

Canadian MTDM Fed. **[★IO]**

Canadian Murray Grey Assn. **[IO]**, Stettler, AB, Canada

Canadian Museum of Nature **[IO]**, Ottawa, ON, Canada

Canadian Museums Assn. **[IO]**, Ottawa, ON, Canada

Canadian Mushroom Growers' Assn. **[IO]**, Guelph, ON, Canada

Canadian Music Centre **[IO]**, Toronto, ON, Canada

Canadian Music Educators Assn. **[IO]**, Waterloo, ON, Canada

Canadian Music Publishers Assn. **[IO]**, Toronto, ON, Canada

Canadian Musical Reproduction Rights Agency **[IO]**, Toronto, ON, Canada

Canadian Natl. Exhibition **[IO]**, Toronto, ON, Canada

Canadian Natl. Fed. of Independent Unions **[IO]**, Stoney Creek, ON, Canada

Canadian Natl. Inst. for the Blind **[IO]**, Toronto, ON, Canada

Canadian Natl. Soc. of the Deaf-Blind **[IO]**, North York, ON, Canada

Canadian Native Arts Found. **[★IO]**

Canadian Native Friendship Centre **[IO]**, Edmonton, AB, Canada

Canadian Nature Fed. **[★IO]**

Canadian Naturopathic Assn. **[★IO]**

Canadian Nautical Res. Soc. **[IO]**, Kingston, ON, Canada

Canadian Navigation Soc. **[IO]**, Ottawa, ON, Canada

Canadian Netherlands Bus. and Professional Assn. **[IO]**, Toronto, ON, Canada

Canadian Network for Asthma Care **[IO]**, Bolton, ON, Canada

Canadian Network of Toxicology Centres **[IO]**, Guelph, ON, Canada

Canadian Neurological Sciences Fed. **[IO]**, Calgary, AB, Canada

Canadian Neuropathy Assn. **[IO]**, Pefferlaw, ON, Canada

Canadian Neurosurgical Soc. **[IO]**, Calgary, AB, Canada

Canadian Newspaper Assn. **[IO]**, Toronto, ON, Canada

Canadian Northern Soc. **[IO]**, Camrose, AB, Canada

Canadian Norwegian Bus. Assn. **[IO]**, Sandvika, Norway

Canadian Nuclear Assn. **[IO]**, Ottawa, ON, Canada

Canadian Nuclear Soc. **[IO]**, Toronto, ON, Canada

Canadian Numismatic Assn. **[IO]**, Markham, ON, Canada

Canadian Numismatic Res. Soc. **[IO]**, Victoria, BC, Canada

Canadian Nursery Landscape Assn. **[IO]**, Milton, ON, Canada

Canadian Nursery Trades Assn. **[★IO]**

Canadian Nurses Assn. **[IO]**, Ottawa, ON, Canada

Canadian Nurses Found. **[IO]**, Ottawa, ON, Canada

Canadian Nurses Protective Soc. **[IO]**, Ottawa, ON, Canada

Canadian Nurses Respiratory Soc. **[IO]**, Ottawa, ON, Canada

Canadian Nursing Students' Assn. **[IO]**, Ottawa, ON, Canada

Canadian Occupational Hea. Nurses Assn. **[IO]**, Calgary, AB, Canada

Canadian Occupational Therapy Found. **[IO]**, Ottawa, ON, Canada

Canadian Off-Highway Vehicle Distributors Coun. **[IO]**, North York, ON, Canada

Canadian Off. Products Assn. **[IO]**, Toronto, ON, Canada

Canadian Oil Heat Assn. **[IO]**, Markham, ON, Canada

Canadian Oilseed Processors Assn. **[IO]**, Winnipeg, MB, Canada

Canadian Olympic Comm. **[IO]**, Toronto, ON, Canada

Canadian Opera Volunteer Comm. **[IO]**, Toronto, ON, Canada

Canadian Operational Res. Soc. **[IO]**, Ottawa, ON, Canada

Canadian Ophthalmological Soc. **[IO]**, Ottawa, ON, Canada

Canadian Oral History Assn. **[IO]**, Winnipeg, MB, Canada

A star before a book entry number signifies that the name is not listed separately, but is mentioned within the entry.

Canadian Organic Growers [IO], Ottawa, ON, Canada

Canadian Org. for Advancement of Computers in Hea. [★IO]

Canadian Org. for Development Through Educ. [IO], Ottawa, ON, Canada

Canadian Org. for Rare Disorders [IO], Toronto, ON, Canada

Canadian Org. of Zoologists [★IO]

Canadian Orienteering Fed. [IO], Calgary, AB, Canada

Canadian Ornamental Plant Found. [IO], North Bay, ON, Canada

Canadian Orthopaedic Assn. [IO], Westmount, QC, Canada

Canadian Orthopaedic Found. [IO], Innisfil, ON, Canada

Canadian Orthopaedic Nurses Assn. [IO], London, ON, Canada

Canadian Orthopractic Manual Therapy Assn. [IO], Edmonton, AB, Canada

Canadian Orthoptic Coun. [IO], Calgary, AB, Canada

Canadian Osteopathic Aid Soc. [IO], London, ON, Canada

Canadian Osteopathic Assn. [IO], London, ON, Canada

Canadian Overseas Telecommunications Union [IO], Montreal, QC, Canada

Canadian Owners and Pilots Assn. [IO], Ottawa, ON, Canada

Canadian Paediatric Soc. [IO], Ottawa, ON, Canada

Canadian Pain Soc. [IO], Whitby, ON, Canada

Canadian Paint and Coatings Assn. [IO], St. Laurent, QC, Canada

Canadian - Palestinian Educational Exchange [IO], Ottawa, ON, Canada

Canadian Palestinian Found. of Quebec [IO], Montreal, QC, Canada

Canadian Pallet Coun. [IO], Cobourg, ON, Canada

Canadian Palomino Horse Assn. [IO], Hannon, ON, Canada

Canadian Paper Box Mfrs. Assn. [IO], Toronto, ON, Canada

Canadian Paper Money Soc. [IO], Pickering, ON, Canada

Canadian Paperworks Union [★IO]

Canadian Paralympic Comm. [IO], Ottawa, ON, Canada

Canadian Paraplegic Assn. [IO], Ottawa, ON, Canada

Canadian Parents for French [IO], Ottawa, ON, Canada

Canadian Parking Assn. [IO], Ottawa, ON, Canada

Canadian Parks and Recreation Assn. [IO], Ottawa, ON, Canada

Canadian Parks and Wilderness Soc. [IO], Ottawa, ON, Canada

Canadian Payday Loan Assn. [IO], Hamilton, ON, Canada

Canadian Payments Assn. [IO], Ottawa, ON, Canada

Canadian Payroll Assn. [IO], Toronto, ON, Canada

Canadian Peace Alliance [IO], Toronto, ON, Canada

Canadian Peace Res. and Educational Assn. [IO], Regina, SK, Canada

Canadian Peacebuilding Coordinating Comm. [IO], Ottawa, ON, Canada

Canadian Peacekeeping Veterans Assn. [IO], Kingston, ON, Canada

Canadian Pension and Benefits Inst. [IO], Montreal, QC, Canada

Canadian Pensioners Concerned [IO], Toronto, ON, Canada

Canadian Peregrine Found. [IO], Toronto, ON, Canada

Canadian Pest Control Assn. [★IO]

Canadian Pest Mgt. Assn. [IO], Anjou, QC, Canada

Canadian Pharmaceutical Assn. [★IO]

Canadian Pharmacists Assn. [IO], Ottawa, ON, Canada

Canadian Philosophical Assn. [IO], Ottawa, ON, Canada

Canadian Philosophical Association [★10785]

Canadian Physicians for Aid and Relief [IO], Toronto, ON, Canada

Canadian Physicians for Aid and Relief - Malawi [IO], Lilongwe, Malawi

Canadian Physicians for Aid and Relief - Uganda [IO], Kampala, Uganda

Canadian Physiological Soc. [IO], Halifax, NS, Canada

Canadian Physiotherapy Assn. [IO], Toronto, ON, Canada

Canadian Phytopathological Soc. [IO], Morden, MB, Canada

Canadian Picture Pioneers [IO], Toronto, ON, Canada

Canadian Pinto Horse Assn. [IO], Spruce Grove, AB, Canada

Canadian Pinzgauer Assn. [IO], Olds, AB, Canada

Canadian Plastics Indus. Assn. [IO], Mississauga, ON, Canada

Canadian Plowing Org. [IO], Salisbury, NB, Canada

Canadian Plywood Assn. [IO], North Vancouver, BC, Canada

Canadian Podiatric Medical Assn. [IO], Sherwood Park, AB, Canada

Canadian Poetry Assn. [IO], Moncton, NB, Canada

Canadian Police Assn. [IO], Ottawa, ON, Canada

Canadian Polish Cong. [IO], Toronto, ON, Canada

Canadian Political Sci. Assn. [IO], Ottawa, ON, Canada

Canadian Polo Assn. [IO], Calgary, AB, Canada

Canadian Polystyrene Recycling Assn. [IO], Mississauga, ON, Canada

Canadian Pony Club [IO], Baldur, MB, Canada

Canadian Poolplayers Assn. [IO], Walkerton, ON, Canada

Canadian Population Soc. [IO], London, ON, Canada

Canadian Pork Coun. [IO], Ottawa, ON, Canada

Canadian Porphyria Found. [IO], Neepawa, MB, Canada

Canadian Port and Harbour Assn. [★IO]

Canadian Portland Cement Assn. [★IO]

Canadian Post-MD Educ. Registry [IO], Ottawa, ON, Canada

Canadian Postmasters and Assistants Assn. [IO], Ottawa, ON, Canada

Canadian Poultry and Egg Processors Coun. [IO], Ottawa, ON, Canada

Canadian Power and Sail Squadrons [IO], Scarborough, ON, Canada

Canadian Powerlifting Union [IO], Moose Jaw, SK, Canada

Canadian Precast/Prestressed Concrete Inst. [IO], Ottawa, ON, Canada

Canadian Prestressed Concrete Inst. [★IO]

Canadian Printing Indus. Assn. [IO], Ottawa, ON, Canada

Canadian Printing Ink Mfrs'. Assn. [IO], Oakville, ON, Canada

Canadian Process Control Assn. [IO], Oakville, ON, Canada

Canadian Produce Marketing Assn. [IO], Ottawa, ON, Canada

Canadian Professional Golfers' Assn. [IO], Acton, ON, Canada

Canadian Professional Logistics Inst. [IO], Toronto, ON, Canada

Canadian Professional Police Assn. [★IO]

Canadian Professional Rodeo Assn. [IO], Calgary, AB, Canada

Canadian Professional Sales Assn. [IO], Toronto, ON, Canada

Canadian Progress Charitable Found. [★IO]

Canadian Progress Club [IO], Toronto, ON, Canada

Canadian Property Tax Assn. [IO], Toronto, ON, Canada

Canadian Prostate Cancer Network [IO], Lakefield, ON, Canada

Canadian Psychiatric Assn. [IO], Ottawa, ON, Canada

Canadian Psychoanalytic Soc. [IO], Montreal, QC, Canada

Canadian Psychological Assn. [IO], Ottawa, ON, Canada

Canadian Public Hea. Assn. [IO], Ottawa, ON, Canada

Canadian Public Personnel Mgt. Assn. [★IO]

Canadian Public Relations Soc. [IO], Toronto, ON, Canada

Canadian Publishers' Coun. [IO], Toronto, ON, Canada

Canadian Pulp and Paper Assn. [★IO]

Canadian Quarter Horse Assn. [IO], Carberry, MB, Canada

Canadian Quaternary Assn. [IO], St. John's, NL, Canada

Canadian Quilters' Assn. [IO], Pasadena, NL, Canada

Canadian Racing Pigeon Union [IO], Tillsonburg, ON, Canada

Canadian Racquetball Assn. [★IO]

Canadian Radiation Protection Assn. [IO], Toronto, ON, Canada

Canadian Railroad Historical Assn. [IO], St. Constant, QC, Canada

Canadian Ready-Mixed Concrete Assn. [IO], Mississauga, ON, Canada

Canadian Real Estate Assn. [IO], Ottawa, ON, Canada

Canadian Recording Indus. Assn. [IO], Toronto, ON, Canada

Canadian Recreational Canoeing Assn. [★IO]

Canadian Recreational Vehicle Assn. [IO], Toronto, ON, Canada

Canadian Red Angus Promotion Soc. [IO], Taber, AB, Canada

Canadian Red Cross [IO], Ottawa, ON, Canada

Canadian Red Poll Cattle Assn. [IO], Ottawa, ON, Canada

Canadian Register of Hea. Ser. Providers in Psychology [IO], Ottawa, ON, Canada

Canadian Rehabilitation Coun. for the Disabled [IO], Fredericton, NB, Canada

Canadian Reiki Assn. [IO], Burnaby, BC, Canada

Canadian Religious Conf. [IO], Montreal, QC, Canada

Canadian Remote Sensing Soc. [IO], Ottawa, ON, Canada

Canadian Renewable Fuels Assn. [IO], Toronto, ON, Canada

Canadian Res. Inst. for the Advancement of Women [IO], Ottawa, ON, Canada

Canadian Res. Mgt. Assn. [★IO]

Canadian Resort Development Assn. [IO], Toronto, ON, Canada

Canadian Restaurant and Foodservices Assn. [IO], Toronto, ON, Canada

Canadian Retransmission Collective [IO], Toronto, ON, Canada

Canadian Rheumatology Assn. [IO], Newmarket, ON, Canada

Canadian Roofing Contractors Assn. [IO], Ottawa, ON, Canada

Canadian Rose Soc. [IO], Kingston, ON, Canada

Canadian Sanitation Supply Assn. [IO], Toronto, ON, Canada

Canadian Satellite Users Assn. [IO], Mississauga, ON, Canada

Canadian-Scandinavian Found. [IO], Montreal, QC, Canada

Canadian Schizophrenia Found. [★IO]

Canadian School Boards Assn. [IO], Ottawa, ON, Canada

Canadian School Lib. Assn. and Assn. for Teacher-Librarianship in Canada [★IO]

Canadian School Sport Fed. [IO], Gloucester, ON, Canada

Canadian School Trustees' Assn. [★IO]

Canadian Sci. Writers' Assn. [IO], Toronto, ON, Canada

Canadian Sci. Pollution and Env. Control Soc. [★IO]

Canadian Securities Inst. [IO], Toronto, ON, Canada

Canadian Security Assn. [IO], Markham, ON, Canada

Canadian Seed Growers' Assn. [IO], Ottawa, ON, Canada

Canadian Seed Trade Assn. [IO], Ottawa, ON, Canada

Canadian Semiotic Assn. [IO], Edmonton, AB, Canada

Canadian Serbian Natl. Comm. [IO], Toronto, ON, Canada

Reference to "IO" in place of a book number signifies that the association may be found in the 45th edition of International Organizations.

Canadian ShareOwners Assn. **[IO]**, Toronto, ON, Canada

Canadian Sheep Breeders' Assn. **[IO]**, Deerville, NB, Canada

Canadian Sheep Fed. **[IO]**, Guelph, ON, Canada

Canadian Sheet Steel Building Inst. **[IO]**, Cambridge, ON, Canada

Canadian Shipowners Assn. **[IO]**, Ottawa, ON, Canada

Canadian Shire Horse Assn. **[IO]**, Edmonton, AB, Canada

Canadian Shooting Sports Assn. **[IO]**, Vaughan, ON, Canada

Canadian Shorthorn Assn. **[IO]**, Regina, SK, Canada

Canadian Simmental Assn. **[IO]**, Calgary, AB, Canada

Canadian Ski Coaches Fed. **[★IO]**

Canadian Ski Coun. **[IO]**, Mississauga, ON, Canada

Canadian Ski Council **[★3660]**

Canadian Ski Instructors' Alliance **[IO]**, Montreal, QC, Canada

Canadian Ski Patrol Sys. **[IO]**, Ottawa, ON, Canada

Canadian Ski and Snowboard Professionals **[IO]**, Montreal, QC, Canada

Canadian Sleep Soc. **[IO]**, Montreal, QC, Canada

Canadian Snack Food Assn. **[IO]**, Don Mills, ON, Canada

Canadian Snowbird Assn. **[IO]**, Toronto, ON, Canada

Canadian Snowboard Fed. **[IO]**, Vancouver, BC, Canada

Canadian Soccer Assn. **[IO]**, Ottawa, ON, Canada

Canadian Soc. for 18th Century Stud. **[IO]**, Burnaby, BC, Canada

Canadian Soc. for Aesthetic (Cosmetic) Plastic Surgery **[IO]**, Pickering, ON, Canada

Canadian Soc. for Aesthetics **[IO]**, Westmount, QC, Canada

Canadian Soc. of Agricultural Engg. **[★IO]**

Canadian Soc. of Agronomy **[IO]**, Pinawa, MB, Canada

Canadian Soc. of Air Safety Investigators **[IO]**, Vancouver, BC, Canada

Canadian Soc. of Allergy and Clinical Immunology **[IO]**, Ottawa, ON, Canada

Canadian Soc. of Anaesthetists **[★IO]**

Canadian Soc. for Analytical Sciences and Spectroscopy **[IO]**, Winnipeg, MB, Canada

Canadian Soc. of Animal Sci. **[IO]**, Lacombe, AB, Canada

Canadian Soc. of Assn. Executives **[IO]**, Toronto, ON, Canada

Canadian Soc. of Atherosclerosis, Thrombosis and Vascular Biology **[IO]**, Ste.-Foy, QC, Canada

Canadian Soc. of Biblical Stud. **[IO]**, Vancouver, BC, Canada

Canadian Soc. of Biochemistry, Molecular and Cellular Biology **[IO]**, Kingston, ON, Canada

Canadian Soc. for Bioengineering **[IO]**, Winnipeg, MB, Canada

Canadian Soc. for Biomechanics **[IO]**, Windsor, ON, Canada

Canadian Soc. for Brain, Behaviour and Cognitive Sci. **[IO]**, Hamilton, ON, Canada

Canadian Soc. of Cardiology Technologists **[IO]**, Winnipeg, MB, Canada

Canadian Soc. for Chem. Engg. **[IO]**, Ottawa, ON, Canada

Canadian Soc. for Chem. Tech. **[IO]**, Ottawa, ON, Canada

Canadian Soc. for Chemistry **[IO]**, Ottawa, ON, Canada

Canadian Soc. of Children's Authors, Illustrators and Performers **[IO]**, Toronto, ON, Canada

Canadian Soc. for Chinese Stud. **[IO]**, Thornhill, ON, Canada

Canadian Soc. of Church History **[IO]**, Langley, BC, Canada

Canadian Soc. of Cinematographers **[IO]**, Toronto, ON, Canada

Canadian Soc. for Civil Engg. **[IO]**, Montreal, QC, Canada

Canadian Soc. of Clinical Chemists **[IO]**, Kingston, ON, Canada

Canadian Soc. for Clinical Investigation **[IO]**, Ottawa, ON, Canada

Canadian Soc. of Clinical Neurophysiologists **[IO]**, Calgary, AB, Canada

Canadian Soc. for Clinical Pharmacology **[IO]**, Hamilton, ON, Canada

Canadian Soc. of Club Managers **[IO]**, Toronto, ON, Canada

Canadian Soc. of Customs Brokers **[IO]**, Ottawa, ON, Canada

Canadian Soc. of Diagnostic Medical Sonographers **[IO]**, Kemptville, ON, Canada

Canadian Soc. of Dowsers **[IO]**, Brantford, ON, Canada

Canadian Soc. for Educ. through Art **[IO]**, Thunder Bay, ON, Canada

Canadian Soc. of Endocrinology and Metabolism **[IO]**, Toronto, ON, Canada

Canadian Soc. of Environmental Biologists **[IO]**, Toronto, ON, Canada

Canadian Soc. of Exploration Geophysicists **[IO]**, Calgary, AB, Canada

Canadian Soc. of Forensic Sci. **[IO]**, Ottawa, ON, Canada

Canadian Soc. of Gastroenterology Nurses and Associates **[IO]**, Hamilton, ON, Canada

Canadian Soc. of Geriatric Medicine **[★IO]**

Canadian Soc. of the History of the Catholic Church - French Sect. **[IO]**, Trois-Rivieres, QC, Canada

Canadian Soc. for the History and Philosophy of Sci. **[IO]**, Edmonton, AB, Canada

Canadian Soc. of Hosp. Pharmacists **[IO]**, Ottawa, ON, Canada

Canadian Soc. for Immunology **[IO]**, Saskatoon, SK, Canada

Canadian Soc. for Independent Radio Production **[IO]**, Ottawa, ON, Canada

Canadian Soc. for Indus. Security **[IO]**, Hamilton, ON, Canada

Canadian Soc. of Internal Medicine **[IO]**, Ottawa, ON, Canada

Canadian Soc. for Intl. Hea. **[IO]**, Ottawa, ON, Canada

Canadian Soc. for the Investigation of Child Abuse **[IO]**, Calgary, AB, Canada

Canadian Soc. for Italian Stud. **[IO]**, Toronto, ON, Canada

Canadian Soc. of Landscape Architects **[IO]**, Ottawa, ON, Canada

Canadian Soc. of Mayflower Descendants **[IO]**, Milton, ON, Canada

Canadian Soc. for Mech. Engg. **[IO]**, Kingston, ON, Canada

Canadian Soc. for Medical Lab. Sci. **[IO]**, Hamilton, ON, Canada

Canadian Soc. for Mesopotamian Stud. **[IO]**, Toronto, ON, Canada

Canadian Soc. of Microbiologists **[IO]**, Vancouver, BC, Canada

Canadian Soc. for Mucopolysaccharide and Related Diseases **[IO]**, North Vancouver, BC, Canada

Canadian Soc. for Musical Traditions **[★IO]**

Canadian Soc. for Neoplatonic Stud. **[IO]**, Quebec, QC, Canada

Canadian Soc. of New York - Address unknown since 1995.

Canadian Soc. of Nuclear Medicine **[IO]**, Ottawa, ON, Canada

Canadian Soc. for Nutritional Sciences **[IO]**, Toronto, ON, Canada

Canadian Soc. of Occupational Scientists **[IO]**, London, ON, Canada

Canadian Soc. of Orthopaedic Technologists **[IO]**, North York, ON, Canada

Canadian Soc. of Otolaryngology - Head and Neck Surgery **[IO]**, Elora, ON, Canada

Canadian Soc. of Painters in Water Colour **[IO]**, Toronto, ON, Canada

Canadian Soc. of Petroleum Geologists **[IO]**, Calgary, AB, Canada

Canadian Soc. of Plant Physiologists **[IO]**, Regina, SK, Canada

Canadian Soc. of Plastic Surgeons **[IO]**, Montreal, QC, Canada

Canadian Soc. for the Prevention of Cruelty to Children **[IO]**, Midland, ON, Canada

Canadian Soc. of Professional Engineers **[IO]**, Toronto, ON, Canada

Canadian Soc. for Psychomotor Learning and Sport Psychology **[IO]**, Windsor, ON, Canada

Canadian Soc. of Questers **[IO]**, Vancouver, BC, Canada

Canadian Soc. of Respiratory Therapists **[IO]**, Ottawa, ON, Canada

Canadian Soc. of Safety Engg. **[IO]**, Toronto, ON, Canada

Canadian Soc. of Soil Sci. **[IO]**, Pinawa, MB, Canada

Canadian Soc. for the Stud. of Diseases of Children **[★IO]**

Canadian Soc. for the Stud. of Educ. **[IO]**, Ottawa, ON, Canada

Canadian Soc. for the Stud. of Higher Educ. **[IO]**, Winnipeg, MB, Canada

Canadian Soc. for the Stud. of Religion **[IO]**, Halifax, NS, Canada

Canadian Soc. of Teachers of the Alexander Technique **[IO]**, Montreal, QC, Canada

Canadian Soc. for Traditional Music **[IO]**, Calgary, AB, Canada

Canadian Soc. for Training and Development **[IO]**, Toronto, ON, Canada

Canadian Soc. for Women in Philosophy **[IO]**, London, ON, Canada

Canadian Soc. of Zoologists **[IO]**, Edmonton, AB, Canada

Canadian Sociology and Anthropology Assn. **[IO]**, Montreal, QC, Canada

Canadian Soft Drink Assn. **[★IO]**

Canadian Spa Assn. **[★IO]**

Canadian Space Soc. **[IO]**, Toronto, ON, Canada

Canadian Special Crops Assn. **[IO]**, Winnipeg, MB, Canada

Canadian Sphagnum Peat Moss Assn. **[IO]**, St. Albert, AB, Canada

Canadian Spice Assn. **[IO]**, Don Mills, ON, Canada

Canadian Sport Aeroplane Assn. **[★IO]**

Canadian Sport Horse Assn. **[IO]**, Richmond, ON, Canada

Canadian Sport Massage Therapists Assn. **[IO]**, Toronto, ON, Canada

Canadian Sport Parachuting Assn. **[IO]**, Russell, ON, Canada

Canadian Sporting Goods Assn. **[IO]**, Montreal, QC, Canada

Canadian Standards Assn. **[★IO]**

Canadian Steel Door Mfrs. Assn. **[IO]**, Toronto, ON, Canada

Canadian Steel Producers Assn. **[IO]**, Ottawa, ON, Canada

Canadian St. Railway Assn. **[★IO]**

Canadian St. Rod Assn. **[IO]**, Toronto, ON, Canada

Canadian Stud. and Intl. Programs; Center for **[★8044]**

Canadian Stud. of Parliament Gp. **[IO]**, Ottawa, ON, Canada

Canadian Stuttering Assn. **[IO]**, Sherwood Park, AB, Canada

Canadian Sugar Inst. **[IO]**, Toronto, ON, Canada

Canadian Swine Breeder Assn. **[IO]**, Ottawa, ON, Canada

Canadian Swine Exporters Assn. **[IO]**, Woodstock, ON, Canada

Canadian Table Tennis Assn. **[IO]**, Ottawa, ON, Canada

Canadian Tanzer 16 Assn. **[★23223]**

Canadian Tarentaise Assn. **[IO]**, Shellbrook, SK, Canada

Canadian Tax Found. **[IO]**, Toronto, ON, Canada

Canadian Taxicab Assn. **[IO]**, Toronto, ON, Canada

Canadian Taxpayers' Fed. **[IO]**, Ottawa, ON, Canada

Canadian Teachers' Fed. **[IO]**, Ottawa, ON, Canada

Canadian Team Handball Fed. **[IO]**, Sherbrooke, QC, Canada

Canadian Tech. Asphalt Assn. **[IO]**, Victoria, BC, Canada

Canadian Telecommunications Consultants Assn. **[IO]**, Brampton, ON, Canada

Canadian Telecommunications Employees' Assn. **[IO]**, Toronto, ON, Canada

Canadian Telephone Employees' Assn. **[★IO]**

Canadian Tennis Assn. **[★IO]**

Canadian Tenpin Fed. **[IO]**, Lethbridge, AB, Canada

A star before a book entry number signifies that the name is not listed separately, but is mentioned within the entry.

Canadian Testing Assn. [IO], Montreal, QC, Canada
Canadian Texel Assn. [IO], Middlesex Centre, ON, Canada
Canadian Textiles Inst. [IO], Ottawa, ON, Canada
Canadian Theatre Critics Assn. [IO], Toronto, ON, Canada
Canadian Therapeutic Riding Assn. [IO], Guelph, ON, Canada
Canadian Thoracic Soc. [IO], Ottawa, ON, Canada
Canadian Thoroughbred Horse Soc. [IO], Toronto, ON, Canada
Canadian Tooling and Machining Assn. [IO], Cambridge, ON, Canada
Canadian Tourism Res. Inst. [IO], Ottawa, ON, Canada
Canadian Toy Assn. [IO], Concord, ON, Canada
Canadian Toy Collectors' Soc. [IO], Scarborough, ON, Canada
Canadian Toy Testing Coun. [IO], Ottawa, ON, Canada
Canadian Tract Soc. [IO], Brampton, ON, Canada
Canadian Trakehner Horse Soc. [IO], New Hamburg, ON, Canada
Canadian Transit Assn. [★IO]
Canadian Translators, Terminologists and Interpreters Coun. [IO], Ottawa, ON, Canada
Canadian Transplant Assn. [IO], Edmonton, AB, Canada
Canadian Trans. Equip. Assn. [IO], St. Thomas, ON, Canada
Canadian Traumatic Stress Network [IO], Ottawa, ON, Canada
Canadian Trucking Alliance [IO], Ottawa, ON, Canada
Canadian Trucking Human Resources Coun. [IO], Ottawa, ON, Canada
Canadian Turkey Marketing Agency [IO], Mississauga, ON, Canada
Canadian Ukrainian Immigrant Aid Soc. [IO], Toronto, ON, Canada
Canadian Ultimate Players Assn. [IO], Toronto, ON, Canada
Canadian Unihockey Floorball Fed. [IO], Edmonton, AB, Canada
Canadian Union of Operating Engineers and Gen. Workers [IO], Mississauga, ON, Canada
Canadian Union of Postal Workers [IO], Ottawa, ON, Canada
Canadian Union of Professional and Tech. Employees [★IO]
Canadian Union of Public Employees [IO], Ottawa, ON, Canada
Canadian Union of Public Employees - Airline Div. [IO], Etobicoke, ON, Canada
Canadian Unitarian Coun. [IO], Toronto, ON, Canada
Canadian Univ. and Coll. Counselling Assn. [IO], Kingston, ON, Canada
Canadian Univ. Football Coaches Assn. [IO], Waterloo, ON, Canada
Canadian Univ. Music Soc. [IO], Toronto, ON, Canada
Canadian Univ. Press [IO], Toronto, ON, Canada
Canadian Urban Transit Assn. [IO], Toronto, ON, Canada
Canadian Urethane Foam Contractors Assn. [IO], Winnipeg, MB, Canada
Canadian Urethane Mfrs. Assn. [IO], Waterloo, ON, Canada
Canadian Urologic Oncology Gp. [IO], Vancouver, BC, Canada
Canadian Urological Assn. [IO], Montreal, QC, Canada
Canadian Vehicle Mfrs. Assn. [IO], Toronto, ON, Canada
Canadian Veterinary Medical Assn. [IO], Ottawa, ON, Canada
Canadian Vintage Wireless Assn. - Defunct.
Canadian Viola Soc. [IO], Brossard, QC, Canada
Canadian Vocational Assn. [IO], Longueuil, QC, Canada
Canadian Voice of Women for Peace [IO], Toronto, ON, Canada
Canadian Water Quality Assn. [IO], Toronto, ON, Canada

Canadian Water Resources Assn. [IO], Ottawa, ON, Canada
Canadian Water and Wastewater Assn. [IO], Ottawa, ON, Canada
Canadian Welding Bur. [IO], Mississauga, ON, Canada
Canadian Welfare Coun. [★IO]
Canadian Well Logging Soc. [IO], Calgary, AB, Canada
Canadian Welsh Black Cattle Soc. [IO], Ottawa, ON, Canada
Canadian Western Agribition [IO], Regina, SK, Canada
Canadian Western Horse Assn. [IO], Dugald, MB, Canada
Canadian Wheat Bd. [IO], Winnipeg, MB, Canada
Canadian Wheelchair Basketball Assn. [IO], Ottawa, ON, Canada
Canadian Wheelchair Sports Assn. [IO], Ottawa, ON, Canada
Canadian Wheelchair Sports Assn. [★IO]
Canadian Wheelchair Swimming Assn. [★IO]
Canadian Wheelmen's Assn. [★IO]
Canadian Wholesale Drug Assn. [★IO]
Canadian Wildlife Fed. [IO], Kanata, ON, Canada
Canadian Wind Energy Assn. [IO], Ottawa, ON, Canada
Canadian Window and Door Mfrs. Assn. [IO], Ottawa, ON, Canada
Canadian Wireless Telecommunications Assn. [IO], Ottawa, ON, Canada
Canadian Women in Communications [IO], Toronto, ON, Canada
Canadian Women's Found. [IO], Toronto, ON, Canada
Canadian Women's Hea. Network [IO], Winnipeg, MB, Canada
Canadian Women's Stud. Assn. [IO], Toronto, ON, Canada
Canadian Wood Coun. [IO], Ottawa, ON, Canada
Canadian Wood Preservers Bur. [IO], Ottawa, ON, Canada
Canadian Wooden Pallet and Container Assn. [IO], Fenelon Falls, ON, Canada
Canadian Writers Found. [IO], Ottawa, ON, Canada
Canadian Yachting Assn. [IO], Kingston, ON, Canada
Canadian Zionist Fed. [IO], Montreal, QC, Canada
Canadiana.org [IO], Ottawa, ON, Canada
Canadians Concerned About Violence in Entertainment [IO], Toronto, ON, Canada
Canadians for Ethical Treatment of Food Animals [IO], Vancouver, BC, Canada
Canadians for Hea. Res. [IO], Westmount, QC, Canada
Canadienne Croix-Rouge [★IO]
Canadiens pour la Recherche Medicale [★IO]
Canal Soc. of New York State [9773], c/o Michele D. Beilman, Exec. Dir., 2527 Cherry Valley Tpke., Marcellus, NY 13108, (315)730-4495
Canal Zone Study Group - Address unknown since 1995.
Canals
   Amer. Canal Soc. [9772]
   Amer. Canal Soc. [IO]
   Canal Soc. of New York State [9773]
CANARIE [IO], Ottawa, ON, Canada
Canaries and All Other Cage Birds; Natl. Inst. of Red Orange [21855]
Canary Breeders Assn; Central States Roller [21844]
Canary Club of Am; Stafford [21861]
Canary Culturists; U.S. Assn. of Roller [21864]
Canary Fanciers Assn; Amer. [21837]
Canary and Finch Soc. [4195], c/o Ray Terrazas, Treas., PO Box 79311, Houston, TX 77279, (409)744-3141
Canberra Ornithologists Gp. [IO], Civic Square, Australia
Cancel Collectors' Club; Bullseye [22798]
Cancel Soc; Machine [22839]
Cancellation Club; U.S. [22886]
Cancellation Soc., Savannah Chap; Universal Ship [★22841]
Cancellation Soc; Universal Ship [22889]

Cancer
AACR-Women in Cancer Res. [16893]
Action Cancer [IO]
African Amer. Breast Cancer Alliance [13786]
Alliance for Childhood Cancer [13787]
Alliance for Lung Cancer Advocacy, Support and Educ. [13788]
Alliance of State Pain Initiatives [15830]
Amer. Assn. for Cancer Educ. [13789]
Amer. Assn. for Cancer Res. [15635]
Amer. Brachytherapy Soc. [13790]
Amer. Brain Tumor Assn. [13791]
Amer. Cancer Soc. [13792]
Amer. Coll. of Mohs Micrographic Surgery and Cutaneous Oncology [15636]
Amer. Head and Neck Soc. [15819]
Amer. Headache Soc. [14531]
Amer. Inst. for Cancer Res. [13793]
Amer. Joint Comm. on Cancer [15637]
Amer. Psychosocial Oncology Soc. [15638]
Amer. Radium Soc. [15639]
Amer. Soc. of Breast Disease [13772]
Amer. Soc. of Clinical Oncology [15640]
Amer. Soc. of Cytopathology [14075]
Amer. Soc. for Cytotechnology [14076]
Amer. Soc. for Mohs Histotechnology [15130]
Amer. Soc. for Mohs Surgery [15641]
Amer. Soc. of Pediatric Hematology/Oncology [14784]
Amer. Soc. of Preventive Oncology [15642]
Amer. Soc. for Therapeutic Radiology and Oncology [16285]
Amer. Urological Assn. Found. [16705]
Argentine Soc. of Cancerology [IO]
Asociacion Nacional Contra el Cancer [IO]
Assn. of Amer. Cancer Institutes [13794]
Assn. of Cancer Executives [13795]
Assn. of Cancer Online Resources [13796]
Assn. of Community Cancer Centers [13797]
Assn. of European Cancer Leagues [IO]
Assn. of Freestanding Radiation Oncology Centers [16268]
Assn. for Intl. Cancer Res. [IO]
Assn. of Oncology Social Work [13199]
Assn. of Pediatric Hematology/Oncology Nurses [15467]
Assn. of Pediatric Oncology Social Workers [15885]
Assn. for Res. of Childhood Cancer [13798]
Assn. of Univ. Radiologists [16286]
Barbados Cancer Soc. [IO]
BASO - Assn. for Cancer Surgery [IO]
Bladder Cancer Advocacy Network [13799]
Boarding for Breast Cancer Found. [13800]
Brain Tumor Found. of Canada [IO]
Brain Tumour Australia [IO]
Breast Cancer Action [13801]
Breast Cancer Care [IO]
Breast Cancer Network Australia [IO]
Breast Cancer Soc. of Canada [IO]
Breast Cancer Support Ser. - Northern Ireland [IO]
British Assn. for Cancer Res. [IO]
British Assn. of Head and Neck Oncologists [IO]
British Assn. for Lung Res. [IO]
C3: Colorectal Cancer Coalition [13802]
Canadian Breast Cancer Found. [IO]
Canadian Cancer Soc. [IO]
Canadian Prostate Cancer Network [IO]
Cancer Assn. of South Africa [IO]
Cancer Care [13803]
Cancer Care Ontario [IO]
Cancer Control Soc. [13804]
Cancer Coun. Australia [IO]
Cancer Coun. Australian Capital Territory [IO]
Cancer Coun. Tasmania [IO]
Cancer Coun. Western Australia [IO]
Cancer Fed. [13805]
Cancer Hope Network [13806]
Cancer Info. Ser. [13807]
Cancer Prevention Coalition [13808]
Cancer Prevention Coalition [IO]
Cancer Quality Alliance [13809]
Cancer Registry of Norway [IO]
Cancer Res. Soc. [IO]

Reference to "IO" in place of a book number signifies that the association may be found in the 45th edition of International Organizations.

Cancer Soc. of Finland [IO]
Cancer Soc. of New Zealand [IO]
Candlelighters Childhood Cancer Found. [13810]
Canine Cancer Awareness [16788]
Carcinoid Cancer Found. [13811]
Chemotherapy Found. [15644]
Childhood Cancer Found. - Candlelighters
   Canada [IO]
Childhood Eye Cancer Trust [IO]
Children's Blood Found. [14786]
Children's Cause for Cancer Advocacy [13812]
Children's Leukemia Res. Assn. [13813]
Chinese Anti-Cancer Assn. [IO]
City of Hope Natl. Medical Center [15102]
CLIC Sargent [IO]
Coalition of Cancer Cooperative Groups [13814]
Coleman Found. [13162]
Colorectal Cancer Network [13815]
Computerized Medical Imaging Soc. [16287]
Concern Found. [13816]
Connective Tissue Oncology Soc. [15645]
Corporate Angel Network [13817]
Coun. on Diagnostic Imaging [16288]
Cure Res. Found. [13818]
Damon Runyon Cancer Res. Found. [13819]
Dana-Farber Cancer Inst. [13820]
Dana-Farber Cancer Inst. [IO]
Danish Cancer Soc. [IO]
DES Action, U.S.A. [13821]
Dutch Cancer Soc. [IO]
Esophageal Cancer Awareness Assn. [13822]
European Assn. for Cancer Res. [IO]
European Assn. of Dermato-Oncology [IO]
European Network of Cancer Registries [IO]
European Org. for Res. and Treatment of Cancer
   [IO]
Facing Our Risk of Cancer Empowered [13823]
Fertile Hope [14390]
Found. for Advancement in Cancer Therapy
   [13824]
Friends of the Jose Carreras Intl. Leukemia
   Found. [13825]
Friends of the Jose Carreras International
   Leukemia Foundation [IO]
Gerson Inst. [13632]
Gilda Radner Familial Ovarian Cancer Registry
   [13826]
Gilda Radner Familial Ovarian Cancer Registry
   [IO]
Gilda's Club [13827]
Gynaecological Cancer Soc. [IO]
Haitian Amer. Assn. Against Cancer [13828]
Hereditary Colon Cancer Assn. [13829]
Hong Kong Anti-Cancer Soc. [IO]
Indian Cancer Soc. [IO]
Intercultural Cancer Coun. [IO]
Intercultural Cancer Coun. [13830]
Intl. Agency for Res. on Cancer [IO]
Intl. Assn. of Cancer Registries [IO]
Intl. Assn. of Cancer Victors and Friends [IO]
Intl. Assn. of Cancer Victors and Friends [13831]
Intl. Assn. for Comparative Res. on Leukemia and
   Related Diseases [15647]
Intl. Assn. for the Stud. of Lung Cancer [13832]
Intl. Brain Tumour Alliance [IO]
Intl. Myeloma Found. [IO]
Intl. Myeloma Found. [13833]
Intl. Network for Cancer Treatment and Res. [IO]
Intl. Psycho-Oncology Soc. [IO]
Intl. Psycho-Oncology Soc. [13834]
Intl. Skeletal Soc. [16289]
Intl. Soc. for Biological Therapy of Cancer [13835]
International Society for Biological Therapy of
   Cancer [IO]
Intl. Soc. of Oncology Pharmacy Practitioners
   [15937]
Intl. Union Against Cancer [IO]
Irish Cancer Soc. [IO]
Israel Cancer Assn. [IO]
Jamaica Cancer Soc. [IO]
Kidney Cancer Assn. [13836]
Kidney Cancer UK [IO]
Kids Konnected [11706]
KIDSCOPE [11518]
Leukemia and Lymphoma Soc. [13837]

Life Raft Gp. [13838]
Lung Cancer Alliance [13839]
Lymphoma Res. Found. [13840]
Make Today Count [13841]
Marie Curie Cancer Care [IO]
Mautner Proj. for Lesbian Hea. [14433]
Melanoma Res. Found. [13842]
Men Against Breast Cancer [13843]
Mothers Supporting Daughters with Breast Cancer
   [13844]
Multiple Myeloma Res. Found. [13845]
Natl. Alliance of Breast Cancer Orgs. [13846]
Natl. Assn. for Proton Therapy [15649]
Natl. Black Leadership Initiative on Cancer
   [13847]
Natl. Breast Cancer Coalition [13848]
Natl. Cancer Center [15650]
Natl. Cancer Coun. [IO]
Natl. Cancer Inst. of Canada [IO]
Natl. Cancer Registrars Assn. [15651]
Natl. Cervical Cancer Coalition [13849]
Natl. Childhood Cancer Found. [13850]
Natl. Children's Cancer Soc. [13851]
Natl. Coalition for Cancer Res. [17691]
Natl. Coalition for Cancer Survivorship [13852]
Natl. Comprehensive Cancer Network [13853]
Natl. Found. for Cancer Res. [15652]
Natl. Headache Found. [14533]
Natl. Immunotherapy Cancer Res. Found. [14940]
Natl. Lung Cancer Partnership [13854]
Natl. Ovarian Cancer Assn. [IO]
Natl. Ovarian Cancer Coalition [13855]
Natl. Prostate Cancer Coalition [13856]
Native Amer. Cancer Res. [13857]
NCI Alliance for Nanotechnology in Cancer
   [15110]
Neuroblastoma Children's Cancer Soc. [13858]
Neurofibromatosis [14471]
Nevus Outreach [14284]
North Amer. Assn. of Central Cancer Registries
   [13859]
North Amer. Assn. of Central Cancer Registries
   [IO]
North Amer. Brain Tumor Coalition [13860]
Oncology Nursing Soc. [15521]
Org. of European Cancer Institutes [IO]
Ovarian Cancer Natl. Alliance [13861]
Pancreatic Cancer Action Network [15851]
Patient Advocates for Advanced Cancer Treat-
   ments [13862]
Pediatric Brain Tumor Found. of the U.S. [13863]
People Against Cancer [13864]
Portuguese Cancer Soc. [IO]
Pregnant With Cancer Network [13865]
Prevent Cancer Found. [13866]
Prostate Cancer Alliance of Canada [IO]
Prostate Cancer Res. Found. of Canada [IO]
Prostate Cancer Support Assn. [IO]
R.A. Bloch Cancer Found. [13867]
Radiation and Public Hea. Proj. [16270]
Radiation Therapy Oncology Gp. [15653]
Radiological Soc. of North Am. [16293]
Radiology Mammography Intl. [13774]
Reach to Recovery [13868]
Reel Recovery [11519]
Retinoblastoma Intl. [13869]
Retinoblastoma Intl. [IO]
Rose Kushner Breast Cancer Advisory Center
   [13870]
Sarcoma Alliance [13871]
Sharsheret [13872]
Sisters Network [13873]
Skin Cancer Found. [13874]
Soc. of Gynecologic Oncologists [15654]
Soc. of Interventional Radiology [16300]
Soc. for Leukocyte Biology [16365]
Soc. for Melanoma Res. [13875]
Soc. for Radiation Oncology Administrators
   [16302]
Soc. of Surgical Oncology [15655]
Sun Safety Alliance [13876]
Sunshine Found. [11726]
Support for People with Oral and Head and Neck
   Cancer [13877]
Susan G. Komen Breast Cancer Found. [13878]

Swiss Inst. for Experimental Cancer Res. [IO]
Terry Fox Found. [IO]
Thyroid Cancer Survivors' Assn. [16648]
Ulster Cancer Found. [IO]
Us TOO Intl. [IO]
Us TOO Intl. [13879]
Veterinary Cancer Soc. [16813]
William H. Donner Found. [13880]
Women's Cancer Network [13881]
World Cancer Res. Fund [IO]
World Fed. of Surgical Oncology Societies [IO]
Y-ME Natl. Breast Cancer Org. [13882]
Young Survival Coalition [13883]
Young Survival Coalition [IO]
Cancer Advisory Center; Women's Breast [★13870]
Cancer; Amer. Joint Comm. on [15637]
Cancer Assn. of South Africa [IO], Bedfordview,
   Republic of South Africa
Cancer Biotherapy Research Group - Address
   unknown since 2006.
Cancer Book House [★13804]
Cancer Care [13803], 275 7th Ave., New York, NY
   10001-6708, (212)712-8400
Cancer Care Found; Natl. [★13803]
Cancer Care Ontario [IO], Toronto, ON, Canada
Cancer Center; Natl. [15650]
Cancer Connection [★13867]
Cancer Control Soc. [13804], 2043 N Berendo St.,
   Los Angeles, CA 90027, (323)663-7801
Cancer Coordinators [★13789]
Cancer Coun. Australia [IO], Sydney, Australia
Cancer Coun. Australian Capital Territory [IO], Fair-
   bairn, Australia
Cancer Coun. Tasmania [IO], Hobart, Australia
Cancer Coun. Western Australia [IO], Perth,
   Australia
Cancer Cytology Center; Natl. [★15650]
Cancer Cytology Found. of Am. [★15650]
Cancer Fed. [13805], PO Box 1298, Banning, CA
   92220-0009, (951)849-4325
Cancer Found; Eugene L. Garey [★15650]
Cancer Found; Natl. [★13803]
Cancer Found; Natl. Childhood [★13850]
Cancer Fund; Damon Runyon - Walter Winchell
   [★13819]
Cancer Home; Holy Family [★19027]
Cancer Hope Network [13806], 2 North Rd., Ste. A,
   Chester, NJ 07930, (908)879-4039
Cancer Hopefuls United for Mutual Support -
   Defunct.
Cancer Hot Line [★13867]
Cancer Info. Ser. [13807], c/o Natl. Cancer Inst.,
   6116 Executive Blvd., Ste. 3036 A, MSC 8322, Be-
   thesda, MD 20892-8322, (800)4-CANCER
Cancer Info. and Support; Y-Me Natl. Org. for Breast
   [★13882]
Cancer; Mautner Proj. for Lesbians with [★14433]
Cancer Prevention Coalition [13808], c/o Dr. Samuel
   S. Epstein, MD, Chm./Founder, Univ. of Illinois at
   Chicago, Scholarship of Public Hea., MC 922,
   2121 W Taylor St., Chicago, IL 60612, (312)996-
   2297
Cancer Prevention Coalition [IO], Chicago, IL,
   United States
Cancer Quality Alliance [13809], 1900 Duke St., Ste.
   200, Alexandria, VA 22314, (703)299-1050
Cancer Registrars Assn; Natl. [15651]
Cancer Registry of Norway [IO], Oslo, Norway
Cancer Res; Damon Runyon Found. for [★13819]
Cancer Res; Damon Runyon Memorial Fund for
   [★13819]
Cancer Res. Found; Natl. Immunotherapy [14940]
Cancer Res. Fund; Damon Runyon - Walter Winch-
   ell [★13819]
Cancer Res; Natl. Coalition for [17691]
Cancer Res. and Prevention Found. [★13866]
Cancer Res. Soc. [IO], Montreal, QC, Canada
Cancer Societies; Fed. of European [IO]
Cancer Soc. of Finland [IO], Helsinki, Finland
Cancer Soc. of New Zealand [IO], Wellington, New
   Zealand
Cancer Soc; Veterinary [16813]
Cancer Staging and End Results Reporting; Amer.
   Joint Comm. for [★15637]
Cancer Support; Y-Me Breast [★13882]

A star before a book entry number signifies that the name is not listed separately, but is mentioned within the entry.

Cancer Therapies; Found. for Alternative [★13824]
Cancer Therapy; Comm. for Freedom of Choice in [★13628]
Cancer Victims and Friends; Intl. Assn. of [★13831]
Candle Assn; Natl. [2268]
Candle Mfrs. Assn. [★2268]
Candlelighters Childhood Cancer Found. [13810], PO Box 498, Kensington, MD 20895-0498, (301)962-3520
Candlelighters Found. [★13810]
CANDLES - Address unknown since 1995.
CANDU Owners Gp. [IO], Toronto, ON, Canada
Candy, Chocolate and Confectionery Inst. - Defunct.
Candy Container Collectors of Am. [21986], c/o Jim Olean, Membership Chm./Treas., 115 MacBeth Dr., Lower Burrell, PA 15068-2628
Candy Technologists; Amer. Assn. of [7087]
Candy Wholesalers Assn; Natl. [★1500]
Cane Growers Assn. and; Louisiana Sugar Planters Assn., Amer. [★5225]
Canegrowers [IO], Brisbane, Australia
Canfield Family Assn. - Defunct.
Canhelp, Tajikistan [IO], Khujand, Tajikistan
Canid Survival and Res. Center; Wild [5393]
Canine Acad; Arizona [22219]
Canine Assistants [11925], 3160 Francis Rd., Alpharetta, GA 30004, (770)664-7178
Canine Assn; U.S. Police [6008]
Canine Assn. of Western Australia [IO], Canning Vale, Australia
Canine Behavior Inst. - Address unknown since 1995.
Canine Cancer Awareness [16788], 340 Oak Hill Rd., Litchfield, ME 04350
Canine Companions for Independence [11926], PO Box 446, Santa Rosa, CA 95402-0446, (707)577-1700
Canine Defense Fund [11373], c/o Amer. Dog Owners Assn., PO Box 186, Castleton, NY 12033, (518)732-7600
Canine Educ. Found; Amer. [22193]
Canine Educ. Fund; Amer. [★22193]
Canine Eye Registration Found. - Defunct.
Canine Sports Medicine Assn; Amer. [16761]
Canines for Disabled Kids [11927], 299 Redemption Rock Trail S, Princeton, MA 01541, (978)422-5299
Cannabis Action Network - Address unknown since 1994.
Cannabis Consumers; Friends and Families of [18023]
Cannabis; Pay for Schools by Regulating [18302]
Canned Chop Suey Foods Industry - Defunct.
Canned Food Information Coun. - Address unknown since 1999.
Canned Fruit Promotion Service - Defunct.
Canned Vegetable Coun. [3969]
Canners Assn; Natl. Meat [★2664]
Canning Peach Assn; California [4709]
Cannon Hunters Assn. of Seattle - Defunct.
Canoe Assn; Scottish [IO]
Canoe Assn; U.S. [23279]
Canoe Heritage Assn; Wooden [21887]
Canoe Kayak Nova Scotia [IO], Halifax, NS, Canada
Canoe Liveries and Outfitters; Natl. Associations of [★3650]

Canoeing
 Alberta Recreational Canoe Assn. [IO]
 Amer. Canoe Assn. [23278]
 Australian Canoeing [IO]
 British Canoe Union [IO]
 Camping Women [23269]
 Canadian Canoe Assn. [IO]
 Canadian Canoe Assn., Atlantic Div. [IO]
 Canoe Kayak Nova Scotia [IO]
 Croatian Canoe Fed. [IO]
 European Canoe Assn. [IO]
 Irish Canoe Union [IO]
 New Zealand Recreational Canoeing Assn. [IO]
 Norwegian Canoe Assn. [IO]
 Ontario Recreational Canoeing Assn. [IO]
 Paddle Canada [IO]
 Paddle Manitoba [IO]
 Polish Canoe Fed. [IO]
 Professional Paddlesports Assn. [3650]
 Qajaq USA [23981]
 Recreational Canoeing Assn. of British Columbia [IO]
 Swedish Canoe Fed. [IO]
 Swiss Canoe Fed. [IO]
 Trade Assn. of Paddlesports [3654]
 Tumblehome Recreational Canoe Club [IO]
 U.S. Canoe Assn. [23279]
 USA Canoe/Kayak [23280]
 Wooden Canoe Heritage Assn. [21887]
Canola Assn. of Australia [IO], Royal Exchange, Australia
Canola Assn; U.S. [1568]
Canola Coun. of Canada [IO], Winnipeg, MB, Canada
Canolfan Gymreig Materion Rhyngwladol [★IO]
Canon Collins Educational Trust for Southern Africa [IO], London, United Kingdom
Canon Law Soc. of Am. [19592], The Hecker Center, Ste. 111, 3025 Fourth St., NE, Washington, DC 20017-1102, (202)832-2350
Canon Law Soc. of the Orthodox Catholic Church [19593], PO Box 16201, Duluth, MN 55816, (218)624-0207
Canon Law Society of the Orthodox Catholic Church [IO], Duluth, MN, United States
Canopy Network; Intl. [6579]
Canseil Canadien des distributeurs en Alimentation [★IO]
Canterbury Historical Assn. [IO], Christchurch, New Zealand
Cantonese Language Assn. [7242], c/o Prof. Dana Bourgerie, Gen. Sec., Brigham Young Univ., 4064 JKHB, Provo, UT 84602, (801)378-4952
Cantors; Amer. Conf. of [20112]
Cantors; Amer. Conf. of Certified [★20112]
Cantors Assembly [20128], 3080 Broadway, Ste. 606, New York, NY 10027, (212)678-8834
Cantors Assembly [IO], New York, NY, United States
Canvas Goods Mfrs. Assn; Natl. [★3787]
Canvas Products Intl. [★3787]
Canvas Products Intl. [★IO]
Canvasback Soc. - Address unknown since 2006.
Canyoneering Assn; Amer. [21949]
Canyonlands Field Inst. [4500], PO Box 68, Moab, UT 84532, (435)259-7750
Cap and Patch Assn; Natl. [22080]
Cap Screw and Special Threaded Products Bur. - Defunct.
CAP Unit Veterans Assn. - Address unknown since 1999.
CAPCOM - Address unknown since 2006.
Cape Cod; Assn. to Preserve [4361]
Cape Lancia Club [IO], Cape Town, Republic of South Africa
Cape Town Regional Chamber of Commerce and Indus. [IO], Cape Town, Republic of South Africa
Cape Verdian League Assn. - Address unknown since 1995.
Capital Alliance; Community Development Venture [11771]
Capital Assn; Natl. Community [★17233]
Capital Assn; Natl. Venture [2348]
Capital Formation; Amer. Coun. for [17347]
Capital Gains and Estate Taxation; Amer. Coun. on [★17347]
Capital PC User Gp. [6788], 19209 Mt. Airey Rd., Brookeville, MD 20833, (301)762-9372
Capital PC User Gp. [IO], Brookeville, MD, United States
Capital Press Club [3102], PO Box 19403, Washington, DC 20036-9403, (202)628-1122

Capital Punishment
 Agape: Gospel of Life Disciples [19562]
 Campaign to End the Death Penalty [17028]
 Capital Punishment Proj. [17029]
 Death Penalty Info. Center [17030]
 Human Writes [IO]
 Lamp of Hope Proj. [17031]
 Murder Victims' Families for Reconciliation [17032]
 Natl. Coalition to Abolish the Death Penalty [17033]
 People of Faith Against the Death Penalty [17034]
 Proj. Hope to Abolish the Death Penalty [17035]
 Southern Center for Human Rights [17036]
Capital Punishment Proj. [17029], c/o John Holdridge, Dir., 201 W Main St., Ste. 402, Durham, NC 27701, (919)682-5659
Capital Quarter Horse Registry [★4922]
Capital Speakers Assn; Natl. [10902]
Capital Speakers Club - Address unknown since 1999.
Capitals Fan Club; Washington [25014]
Capitol Hill Burro Club - Address unknown since 1991.
Capitol Hill Club [★18526]
Capitol Hill Restoration Soc. [10017], 420 10th St. SE, PO Box 15264, Washington, DC 20003-0264, (202)543-0425
Capitol Hill Women's Political Caucus - Address unknown since 2003.
Capitol Historical Soc; U.S. [10164]
A Cappella Soc. of Am; Contemporary [10582]
Capri Class Assn. - Address unknown since 2001.
Capri Club North Am. [21604], PO Box 701, Johnstown, OH 43031
Capsule Soc; Intl. Time [10041]
Captain Cook Soc. [IO], Thornhill, United Kingdom
Captain Eddie Premier Gala [11108]
Captain James Smith Memorial Found. - Address unknown since 1994.
Caption Center [★12487]
Captioning Inst; Natl. [14769]
Captive Daughters [18383], 3500 Overland Ave., No. 110-108, Los Angeles, CA 90034, (310)669-4400
Captive Insurance Companies Assn. [2152], 4248 Park Glen Rd., Minneapolis, MN 55416, (952)928-4655
Captive Nations Comm. [16988], PO Box 540, Gracie Sta., New York, NY 10028-0005
Captive Nations Comm. New York [★16988]
Capuchin-Franciscans (Province of Saint Joseph) [19594], 1820 Mt. Elliott St., Detroit, MI 48207, (313)579-2100
CAPUTO [★1534]
Car Appraisers Assn; Collector [278]
Car Assn; Natl. Armored [3575]
Car Care Coun. [354], 7101 Wisconsin Ave., Ste. 1300, Bethesda, MD 20814, (240)333-1088
Car Club of Am; BMW [21591]
Car Club of Am; Checker [21606]
Car Club of Am; Classic [21614]
Car Club of Am; Nash [21725]
Car Club of America; Rickenbacker [★21771]
Car Club of Am; Sports [21787]
Car Club of Am; TR8 [21799]
Car Club of Am; Veteran Motor [21808]
Car Club of Am; Vintage Sports [21811]
Car Club; Citroen Quarterly [21613]
Car Club of England, U.S. Area; TVR [★21802]
Car Club; Mid-Century Mercury [21704]
Car Club; Morgan [21717]
Car Club North Am; TVR [21802]
Car Club; TVR [★21802]
Car Club, U.S.A; Mini [21708]
Car Collectors Assn; Toy [22997]
Car Dealers Assn; Natl. Used [★423]
Car Dept. Officers Assn. - Address unknown since 2002.
Car Gp; Imported [★343]
Car Inst; Amer. Railway [3278]
Car Mfrs. Assn; Railway [★3278]
Car Operators Assn; Independent Armored [3568]
Car Owners of Am; Police [21765]
Car Owners; Amer. Assn. of Private Railroad [3276]
Car Owners Club; Nissan Infiniti [21742]
Car Registry; Italian [21673]
Car Rent Assn. - Defunct.
Car Rental Assn. of Namibia [IO], Windhoek, Namibia
Car Rental Coun. of Ireland [IO], Dublin, Ireland
Car Soc; Milestone [21707]
Car Soc; Professional [21768]
Car and Truck Rental Independents and Franchisees; Assn. for [★3376]
Car and Truck Renting and Leasing Assn. - Address unknown since 1997.
Car Wash Mfrs. and Suppliers Assn. [★411]
Car Wash Owners and Suppliers Assn. [411], 1822 South St., Racine, WI 53404, (262)639-4393

Reference to "IO" in place of a book number signifies that the association may be found in the 45th edition of International Organizations.

Cara Irish Housing Assn. [IO], London, United Kingdom
Carabao; Military Order of the [21246]
Caracas ACM SIGGRAPH [IO], Caracas, Venezuela
Caravan America-China - Defunct.
Caravan Club Intl; Wally Byam [22967]
Caravan Farm Theatre [IO], Armstrong, BC, Canada
Carbide Engineers; Soc. of [★7322]
Carbide Producers Assn; Cemented [2702]
Carbide and Tool Engineers; Soc. of [7322]
Carbon Black Export - Defunct.
Carbon Comm; Amer. [★6663]
Carbon Paper and Inked Ribbon Assn. - Defunct.
Carbon Soc; Amer. [6663]
Carbonated Beverage Container Manufacturers Assn. [★974]
Carbonated Beverages; Amer. Bottlers of [★503]
Carcinogen Information Program - Defunct.
Carcinoid Cancer Found. [13811], 333 Mamaroneck Ave., No. 492, White Plains, NY 10605; (914)683-1001
Card Assn; Greeting [3682]
Card Clothing Mfrs. Assn. - Defunct.
Card Collectors Assn; Trade [22124]
Card Collectors; Chicago Playing [21992]
Card Collectors Club; Chrome [★22905]
Card Collectors Club; Post [22908]
Card Professionals; Natl. Assn. of Purchasing [3264]
Card Publishers; Natl. Assn. of Greeting [★3682]
Carded Yarn Assn. [★3774]
Cardiac Angiography and Interventions; Soc. for [13924]
Cardiac Arrhythmias Res. and Educ. Found. [13897], PO Box 369, Duvall, WA 98019, (425)788-1987
Cardiac Catheterization
    Soc. for Cardiac Angiography and Interventions [13924]
Cardiac Imaging; North Amer. Soc. for [13920]
Cardiac Soc. of Australia and New Zealand [IO], Sydney, Australia
Cardiac Soc. - Defunct.
Cardiac Soc. of Myanmar Medical Assn. [IO], Yangon, Myanmar
Cardiac Soc. of Nepal [IO], Kathmandu, Nepal
Cardiac Surgery; Intl. Soc. for Minimally Invasive [★13914]
Cardiff Chamber of Commerce [IO], Cardiff, United Kingdom
Cardiff Conservation Volunteers [IO], Cardiff, United Kingdom
Cardigan Welsh Corgi Club of Am. [22240], c/o Tricia Olson, Pres., 7446 Park Pl., Boulder, CO 80301-3959, (303)530-7107
Cardinal Club [21433], PO Box 6806, Santa Maria, CA 93456, (805)922-1146
Cardinal Key Natl. Honor Soc. - Address unknown since 2002.
Cardinal Mindszenty Found. [16989], PO Box 11321, St. Louis, MO 63105, (314)727-6279
Cardio-Pulmonary Technologists; Canadian Assn. of [IO]
Cardiology
    Adult Congenital Heart Assn. [13884]
    Albanian Soc. of Cardiology [IO]
    Algerian Soc. of Cardiology [IO]
    Alliance of Cardiovascular Professionals [13885]
    Amer. Assn. of Cardiovascular and Pulmonary Rehabilitation [13886]
    Amer. Assn. of Heart Failure Nurses [15434]
    Amer. Bd. of Cardiovascular Perfusion [13887]
    Amer. Coll. of Cardiology [13888]
    Amer. Coll. of Cardiovascular Administrators [15052]
    Amer. Coll. of Chest Physicians [13889]
    Amer. Coll. of Chest Physicians [IO]
    Amer. Coll. of Veterinary Internal Medicine [16767]
    Amer. Heart Assn. [13890]
    Amer. Soc. of Echocardiography [13891]
    Amer. Soc. of Nuclear Cardiology [13892]
    Argentine Soc. of Cardiology [IO]
    Armenian Cardiologists Assn. [IO]
    Assn. of Black Cardiologists [13893]
    Assn. of Cardiologists of Bosnia and Herzegovina [IO]

Assn. for Eradication of Heart Attack [13894]
Assn. of Physician Assistants in Cardiovascular Surgery [13895]
Assn. of Professors of Cardiology [13896]
Assn. of Prog. Directors in Vascular Surgery [16578]
Austrian Soc. of Cardiology [IO]
Belgian Heart League [IO]
Belgian Soc. of Cardiology [IO]
Belorussian Sci. Soc. of Cardiologists [IO]
Brazilian Soc. of Cardiology [IO]
British Cardiovascular Soc. [IO]
British Heart Found. [IO]
Bulgarian Soc. of Cardiology [IO]
Canadian Adult Congenital Heart Network [IO]
Canadian Assn. of Cardiac Rehabilitation [IO]
Canadian Cardiovascular Soc. [IO]
Canadian Soc. of Cardiology Technologists [IO]
Cardiac Arrhythmias Res. and Educ. Found. [13897]
Cardiac Soc. of Australia and New Zealand [IO]
Cardiac Soc. of Myanmar Medical Assn. [IO]
Cardiac Soc. of Nepal [IO]
Cardiovascular Credentialing Intl. [IO]
Cardiovascular Credentialing Intl. [13898]
Cardiovascular and Interventional Radiological Soc. of Europe [IO]
Children's HeartLink [13899]
Chilean Soc. of Cardiology and Cardiovascular Surgery [IO]
Colombian Soc. of Cardiology [IO]
Congenital Cardiac Anesthesia Soc. [13682]
Congenital Heart Defects Awareness [13900]
Congenital Heart Info. Network [13901]
Congenital Heart Info. Network [IO]
Coronary Artery Disease Res. Assn. [IO]
Coun. on Arteriosclerosis, Thrombosis and Vascular Biology of the Amer. Heart Assn. [13902]
Croatian Cardiac Soc. [IO]
CTSNet: Cardiothoracic Surgery Network [16643]
Cyprus Soc. of Cardiology [IO]
Czech Soc. of Cardiology [IO]
Danish Soc. of Cardiology [IO]
Dominican Soc. of Cardiology [IO]
Donald W. Reynolds Found. [13903]
Egyptian Soc. of Cardiology [IO]
Emirates Cardiac Soc. [IO]
Estonian Heart Assn. [IO]
Estonian Soc. of Cardiology [IO]
European Bd. of Cardiovascular Perfusion [IO]
European Coun. for Cardiovascular Res. [IO]
European Heart Network [IO]
European Soc. of Cardiology [IO]
European Soc. for Cardiovascular Surgery [IO]
European Soc. for Noninvasive Cardiovascular Dynamics [IO]
Finnish Cardiac Soc. [IO]
Finnish Heart Assn. [IO]
French Soc. of Cardiology [IO]
Georgian Assn. of Cardiology [IO]
German Cardiac Soc. [IO]
Ghana Soc. of Hypertension and Cardiology [IO]
Heart Assn. of Thailand [IO]
Heart Care Intl. [IO]
Heart Care Intl. [13904]
Heart Disease Res. Found. [13905]
Heart Failure Soc. of Am. [13906]
Heart Found. of Australia [IO]
Heart Rhythm Soc. [IO]
Heart Rhythm Soc. [13907]
Heart and Stroke Found. of Canada [IO]
Hellenic Cardiological Soc. [IO]
Hypertrophic Cardiomyopathy Assn. [14782]
Icelandic Cardiac Soc. [IO]
Icelandic Heart Assn. [IO]
Indo-Amer. Soc. of Interventional Cardiology [IO]
Indo-Amer. Soc. of Interventional Cardiology [13908]
Indonesian Heart Assn. [IO]
Inst. of HeartMath [10174]
Inter-American Soc. of Cardiology [IO]
InterAmerican Heart Found. [13909]
Intl. Atherosclerosis Soc. [13910]
Intl. Atherosclerosis Soc. [IO]

Intl. Bundle Br. Block Assn. [IO]
Intl. Bundle Br. Block Assn. [13911]
Intl. Heart Hea. Soc. [IO]
Intl. Soc. for Adult Congenital Cardiac Disease [IO]
Intl. Soc. for Adult Congenital Cardiac Disease [13912]
Intl. Soc. for Computerized Electrocardiology [13913]
International Society for Computerized Electrocardiology [IO]
Intl. Soc. of Electrocardiology [IO]
Intl. Soc. for Heart Res. [IO]
International Society for Minimally Invasive Cardiothoracic Surgery [IO]
Intl. Soc. for Minimally Invasive Cardiothoracic Surgery [13914]
Intl. Union of Angiology [IO]
Iranian Heart Assn. [IO]
Irish Cardiac Soc. [IO]
Israel Heart Soc. [IO]
Japanese Circulation Soc. [IO]
Japanese Soc. of Hypertension [IO]
Kids With Heart Natl. Assn. for Children's Heart Disorders [13915]
Korean Soc. of Circulation [IO]
Latin Amer. Soc. for Interventional Cardiology [IO]
Latvian Soc. of Cardiology [IO]
Lithuanian Heart Assn. [IO]
Lithuanian Soc. of Cardiology [IO]
Mended Hearts, Inc. [13916]
Michael E. DeBakey Intl. Surgical Soc. [13917]
Michael E. DeBakey International Surgical Society [IO]
Moldavian Soc. of Cardiology [IO]
Natl. Emergency Medicine Assn. [14340]
Natl. Heart Assn. of Malaysia [IO]
Natl. Heart Coun. [13918]
Natl. Heart Forum [IO]
Natl. Heart Savers Assn. [13919]
Natl. Soc. of Cardiology of the Former Yugoslav Republic of Macedonia [IO]
Netherlands Soc. of Cardiology [IO]
North American Society for Cardiac Imaging [IO]
North Amer. Soc. for Cardiac Imaging [13920]
Norwegian Coun. On Cardiovascular Diseases [IO]
Norwegian Soc. of Cardiology [IO]
Pakistan Cardiac Soc. [IO]
Pediatric Cardiac Intensive Care Soc. [15892]
Perfusion Prog. Directors' Coun. [13921]
Peripheral Arterial Disease Coalition [13922]
Peruvian Heart Assn. [13923]
Peruvian Heart Assn. [IO]
Peruvian Soc. of Cardiology [IO]
Polish Cardiac Soc. [IO]
Portuguese Soc. of Cardiology [IO]
Romanian Soc. of Cardiology [IO]
Slovak Soc. of Cardiology [IO]
Slovenian Soc. of Cardiology [IO]
Soc. for Cardiac Angiography and Interventions [13924]
Soc. of Cardiovascular Anesthesiologists [13689]
Soc. for Cardiovascular Pathology [13925]
Society for Cardiovascular Pathology [IO]
Soc. for Clinical Vascular Surgery [13926]
Soc. of Geriatric Cardiology [13927]
Soc. of Invasive Cardiovascular Professionals [13928]
Spanish Soc. of Cardiology [IO]
Sri Lanka Heart Assn. [IO]
Sudden Cardiac Arrest Assn. [13933]
Swedish Soc. of Cardiology [IO]
Swiss Soc. of Cardiology [IO]
Syrian Cardiovascular Assn. [IO]
Taiwan Soc. of Cardiology [IO]
Tunisian Soc. of Cardiology and Cardiovascular Surgery [IO]
Turkish Soc. of Cardiology [IO]
Ukrainian Soc. of Cardiology [IO]
Uruguayan Soc. of Cardiology [IO]
Vietnam Natl. Heart Assn. [IO]
WomenHeart: Natl. Coalition for Women with Heart Disease [13929]
World Coun. for Cardiovascular and Pulmonary Rehabilitation [13930]

A star before a book entry number signifies that the name is not listed separately, but is mentioned within the entry.

World Coun. for Cardiovascular and Pulmonary Rehabilitation [IO]
World Heart Fed. [IO]
Cardiology Found; Interamerican Heart [★13909]
Cardiology Found; Intl. [★13909]
Cardiology; Soc. of Geriatric [13927]
Cardiology Technologists Assn; Amer. [★13885]
Cardiomyopathy Assn. of Australia [IO], Melbourne, Australia
Cardiomyopathy Assn; Hypertrophic [14782]
Cardio-Pulmonary
  Alliance of Cardiovascular Professionals [13885]
  British Lung Found. [IO]
  Cardiomyopathy Assn. of Australia [IO]
  Natl. Alliance for Thrombosis and Thrombophilia [13931]
  Natl. Emphysema Found. [13932]
  Soc. of Chest Pain Centers and Providers [15849]
  Soc. of Invasive Cardiovascular Professionals [13928]
Cardiopulmonary Credentialing; Natl. Bd. for [★13898]
Cardiopulmonary Technologists; Natl. Soc. of [★13885]
Cardiopulmonary Tech; Natl. Soc. for [★13885]
Cardiothoracic Res. and Education Found. - Address unknown since 2002.
Cardiothoracic Surgery; Intl. Soc. for Minimally Invasive [13914]
CardioThoracic Surgery; Scandinavian Soc. for Res. in [IO]
Cardiovascular Administrators; Amer. Coll. of [15052]
Cardiovascular Credentialing Intl. [13898], 1500 Sunday Dr., Ste. 102, Raleigh, NC 27607, (919)861-4539
Cardiovascular Credentialing Intl. [★13898]
Cardiovascular Credentialing Intl. [IO], Raleigh, NC, United States
Cardiovascular Credentialing Intl. [★IO]
Cardiovascular Credentialing International/Board of Cardiovascular Tech. [★IO]
Cardiovascular Credentialing International/Board of Cardiovascular Tech. [★13898]
Cardiovascular Disease
  Adult Congenital Heart Assn. [13884]
  Alliance of Cardiovascular Professionals [13885]
  Amer. Assn. of Cardiovascular and Pulmonary Rehabilitation [13886]
  Amer. Assn. of Heart Failure Nurses [15434]
  Amer. Assn. for Thoracic Surgery [16640]
  Amer. Bd. of Cardiovascular Perfusion [13887]
  Amer. Bd. of Thoracic Surgery [16641]
  Amer. Coll. of Cardiology [13888]
  Amer. Coll. of Cardiovascular Administrators [15052]
  Amer. Coll. of Chest Physicians [13889]
  Amer. Soc. of Echocardiography [13891]
  Amer. Thoracic Soc. [16642]
  Assn. for Eradication of Heart Attack [13894]
  Assn. of Physician Assistants in Cardiovascular Surgery [13895]
  Cardiovascular Credentialing Intl. [13898]
  Congenital Cardiac Anesthesia Soc. [13682]
  Congenital Heart Defects Awareness [13900]
  Congenital Heart Info. Network [13901]
  Coun. on Arteriosclerosis, Thrombosis and Vascular Biology of the Amer. Heart Assn. [13902]
  CTSNet: Cardiothoracic Surgery Network [16643]
  Heart Care Intl. [13904]
  Heart Disease Res. Found. [13905]
  Heart Failure Soc. of Am. [13906]
  Heart Rhythm Soc. [13907]
  Hypertrophic Cardiomyopathy Assn. [14782]
  Indo-Amer. Soc. of Interventional Cardiology [13908]
  InterAmerican Heart Found. [13909]
  Intl. Bundle Br. Block Assn. [13911]
  Intl. EECP Therapists Assn. [16619]
  Intl. Pediatric Hypertension Assn. [14907]
  Mended Hearts, Inc. [13916]
  Michael E. DeBakey Intl. Surgical Soc. [13917]
  Pediatric Cardiac Intensive Care Soc. [15892]
  Perfusion Prog. Directors' Coun. [13921]
  Peripheral Arterial Disease Coalition [13922]

Soc. of Cardiovascular Anesthesiologists [13689]
  Soc. for Cardiovascular Pathology [13925]
  Soc. of Interventional Radiology [16300]
  Soc. of Invasive Cardiovascular Professionals [13928]
  Soc. of Thoracic Surgeons [16644]
  Stroke Awareness for Everyone [16495]
  Sudden Cardiac Arrest Assn. [13933]
  Thoracic Surgery Residents Assn. [16645]
  WomenHeart: Natl. Coalition for Women with Heart Disease [13929]
  World Coun. for Cardiovascular and Pulmonary Rehabilitation [13930]
Cardiovascular and Interventional Radiological Soc. of Europe [IO], Vienna, Austria
Cardiovascular and Interventional Radiology; Soc. of [★16300]
Cardiovascular Invasive Specialists; Amer. Coll. of [★13885]
Cardiovascular Mgt; Amer. Soc. of Cardiovascular Professionals/Society for [★13885]
Cardiovascular Nurses; Amer. Assn. of [★15433]
Cardiovascular Nurses Assn; Preventive [15523]
Cardiovascular Nurses; Canadian Coun. of [IO]
Cardiovascular Professionals/Society for Cardiovascular Mgt; Amer. Soc. of [★13885]
Cardiovascular and Pulmonary Credentialing; Natl. Bd. for [★13898]
Cardiovascular Soc; Michael E. DeBakey Intl. [★13917]
Cardiovascular Surgery; Asian Soc. for [IO]
Cardiovascular Technologists; Natl. Alliance of [★13885]
Cardiovascular Tech; Cardiovascular Credentialing International/Board of [★13898]
Cardiovascular Tech; Natl. Soc. for [★13885]
Care Alliance; Natl. School-Age [★11528]
Care Assn; Natl. Subacute [★14728]
CARE Austria [IO], Vienna, Austria
CARE Britain [★IO]
CARE Canada [IO], Ottawa, ON, Canada
CARE Canada - Defunct.
Care for Children Intl. [11563], c/o Neuropsychological and Family Therapy Associates, 400 S Washington St., Alexandria, VA 22314, (703)548-0721
Care for Children Intl. [IO], Alexandria, VA, United States
CARE Danmark [IO], Copenhagen, Denmark
Care Dentistry; Special [14186]
CARE Deutschland (Germany) [IO], Bonn, Germany
CARE Egypt [IO], Cairo, Egypt
Care Found. [★13897]
Care Found; Child [★11701]
CARE France [IO], Paris, France
CARE Guatemala [IO], Guatemala City, Guatemala
CARE Honduras [IO], Tegucigalpa, Honduras
CARE India [IO], New Delhi, India
CARE Intl. - Belgium [IO], Brussels, Belgium
CARE Intl. UK [IO], London, United Kingdom
CARE Intl. USA [IO], Atlanta, GA, United States
CARE Intl. USA [12838], 151 Ellis St. NE, Atlanta, GA 30303, (404)681-2552
CARE Japan [IO], Tokyo, Japan
Care for Life [★IO]
Care for Life [★11981]
Care Ministries [19532], PO Box 1830, Starkville, MS 39760-1830, (662)323-4999
Care; Natl. Assn. of Subacute and Post-Acute [14728]
Care; Natl. Inst. on Community-Based Long-Term [11312]
CARE Nederland [★IO]
CARE Nepal [IO], Kathmandu, Nepal
Care Net [17283], 44180 Riverside Pkwy., Ste. 200, Lansdowne, VA 20176, (703)478-5661
CARE Netherlands [IO], The Hague, Netherlands
CARE Norge (Norway) [IO], Oslo, Norway
Care Organizations in Dentistry; Fed. of Special [★14186]
CARE Osterreich [★IO]
Care Panel; Animal [★13693]
CARE Peru [IO], Lima, Peru
CARE Philippines [IO], Quezon City, Philippines
Care Rehabilitation and Aid for Sick Hedgehogs [IO], Poole, United Kingdom

Care Soc; Intl. Trauma Anesthesia and Critical [13686]
Care USA [17311], 151 Ellis St. NE, Atlanta, GA 30303-2420, (404)681-2552
Care for the Wild Germany [IO], Stuttgart, Germany
Care for the Wild India [IO], Bhopal, India
Care for the Wild Intl. [IO], Horsham, United Kingdom
Care for the Wild Kenya [IO], Nairobi, Kenya
Care4Dystonia [15312], c/o Beka Serdans, RN, Founder/Acting Exec. Dir., 440 E 78th St., New York, NY 10021, (800)984-0433
Career Advancement Network - Defunct.
Career Apparel Inst. - Defunct.
Career Assessment Professionals; Vocational Evaluation and [16337]
Career Coaches; Professional Assn. of Resume Writers and [12097]
Career Coll. Assn. [9303], 1101 Connecticut Ave. NW, Ste. 900, Washington, DC 20036, (202)336-6700
Career and Community Leaders of Am; Family, [8417]
Career Counseling
  Abilities! [11913]
  Assn. of Career Professionals Intl. [782]
  Assn. of Career Professionals Intl. [IO]
  Australian Assn. of Career Counsellors [IO]
  Career Development Assn. of Alberta [IO]
  Career Planning and Adult Development Network [12070]
  Compete Am. [8365]
  Corporate and Found. Relations [12075]
  Div. on Career Development and Transition [9143]
  Feminist Center for Human Growth and Development [13426]
  Girls Inc. [13486]
  Intl. Mentoring Network Org. [11520]
  Intl. Mentoring Network Org. [IO]
  Job Accommodation Network [11955]
  Just One Break [11957]
  Natl. Assn. of Blacks in Criminal Justice [11877]
  Natl. Bd. for Certified Counselors and Affiliates [11828]
  Natl. Career Development Assn. [12090]
  Natl. Employment Counseling Assn. [12091]
  Nurses for a Healthier Tomorrow [15517]
  Professional Assn. of Resume Writers and Career Coaches [12097]
  PUSH Commercial Div. [12098]
  SER - Jobs for Progress Natl. [12100]
  Soc. for Vocational Psychology [7551]
  Vocational Found., Inc. [12103]
  WAVE [12105]
  Wider Opportunities for Women [12106]
  Wildcat Ser. Corp. [12107]
Career Counseling Center; Amer. Coll. and [7911]
Career Development Assn. of Alberta [IO], Edmonton, AB, Canada
Career Development Assn; Natl. [12090]
Career Development of The Coun. for Exceptional Children; Div. on [★9143]
Career Development and Transition of the Coun. for Exceptional Children; Div. on [★9143]
Career Development and Transition; Div. on [9143]
Career Education
  AFNA Natl. Educ. and Res. Fund [8045]
  Amer. Assn. for Career Educ. [8046]
  Black Women in Sisterhood for Action [13422]
  Canadian Assn. of Career Educators and Employers [IO]
  Career Planning and Adult Development Network [12070]
  Compete Am. [8365]
  Corporate and Found. Relations [12075]
  Coun. on Career for Minorities [8047]
  Div. on Career Development and Transition [9143]
  Inst. for Women in Trades, Tech. and Sci. [4042]
  Intl. Mentoring Network Org. [11520]
  My Own Bus., Inc. [8030]
  Natl. Assn. of Blacks in Criminal Justice [11877]
  Natl. Assn. of Career Colleges [IO]
  Natl. Assn. for Industry-Education Cooperation [8048]
  Natl. Bd. for Certified Counselors and Affiliates [11828]

Reference to "IO" in place of a book number signifies that the association may be found in the 45th edition of International Organizations.

Natl. Career Development Assn. [12090]
Natl. Consortium for Black Professional Development [8049]
Natl. Hispanic Employee Assn. [12279]
Nurses for a Healthier Tomorrow [15517]
Wildcat Ser. Corp. [12107]
Career Gear [12705], Natl. HQ, 120 Broadway, 36th Fl., New York, NY 10271, (212)577-6190
Career Mgt. Professionals; Intl. Assn. of [★782]
Career Planning and Adult Development Network [12070], c/o Administrative Off., PO Box 1484, Pacifica, CA 94044, (650)359-6911
Career Schools and Colleges of Tech; Accrediting Commn. of [7873]
Career and Tech. Educ; Assn. for [9300]
Career Training Found. - Address unknown since 1991.
Career Transition For Dancers [12071], c/o The Caroline and Theodore Newhouse Centre for Dancers, The Actors' Equity Bldg., 165 W 46th St., Ste. 701, New York, NY 10036-2501, (212)764-0172
Career Women; Black [19323]
Career Women; Cosmetic [★1842]
Career Women's Forum [IO], Geneva, Switzerland
Careers Org; Environmental [8388]
Careers Program; National Health [★8231]
Careers Res. and Advisory Centre [IO], Cambridge, United Kingdom
Caregivers; Assn. of Brethren [11276]
Caregivers Assn; Natl. Family [14841]
Caregivers; Natl. Org. For Empowering [13295]
Caregiving; Natl. Alliance for [12163]
Carers Assn. [IO], Kilkenny, Ireland
Carers Assn. of South Australia [IO], Goodwood, Australia
Carers Australia [IO], Deakin West, Australia
Carers Australian Capital Territory [IO], Canberra, Australia
Carers Natl. Assn. [★IO]
Carers New South Wales [IO], Sydney, Australia
Carers Northern Ireland [IO], Belfast, United Kingdom
Carers Queensland [IO], Holland Park, Australia
Carers Queensland - Brisbane North and Sunshine Coast [IO], Maroochydore, Australia
Carers Queensland - Brisbane South and Gold Coast [IO], Holland Park, Australia
Carers Queensland - Brisbane West [IO], Holland Park, Australia
Carers Queensland - Central Queensland [IO], Rockhampton, Australia
Carers Queensland - Darling Downs/South West Queensland [IO], Dalby, Australia
Carers Queensland - Far North Queensland [IO], Cairns, Australia
Carers Queensland - Mackay [IO], Mackay, Australia
Carers Queensland - North Queensland [IO], Thuringowa, Australia
Carers Queensland - Toowoomba/Ipswich [IO], Toowoomba, Australia
Carers Queensland - Wide Bay [IO], Hervey Bay, Australia
Carers Tasmania [IO], Hobart, Australia
Carers UK [IO], London, United Kingdom
Carers Victoria [IO], Melbourne, Australia
Carers Western Australia [IO], Perth, Australia
Caret Family History Assn. - Address unknown since 2007.
Caretakers of the Env. Intl. [IO], Bergen, Netherlands
Caretakers of the Env. Intl. - Cameroon [IO], Yaounde, Cameroon
Caretakers of the Env. Intl. - Canada (Nova Scotia) [IO], Halifax, NS, Canada
Caretakers of the Env. Intl. - Portugal [IO], Lisbon, Portugal
Caretakers of the Env. Intl. - Scotland [IO], Aberdeen, United Kingdom
CARF, Commn. on Accreditation of Rehabilitation Facilities [★16318]
Cargo Airline Assn. [145], 1220 19th St. NW, Ste. 400, Washington, DC 20036, (202)293-1030
Cargo Assn; The Intl. Air [3873]
Cargo Bur; Natl. [3576]

Cargo Reinsurance Assn. - Defunct.
Cargo Security Coun; Intl. [3530]
Caribbean
   Amer. Assn. of Port Authorities [5778]
   Anguilla Tourist Bd. [24224]
   Assn. of Caribbean Electoral Organizations [5557]
   Caribbean Amer. Intercultural Org. [9774]
   Caribbean Amer. Intercultural Org. [IO]
   Caribbean-Central Amer. Action [12421]
   Caribbean Cultural Comm. [IO]
   Caribbean Culture Center [9775]
   Caribbean Soc. of Hotel Assn. Executives [24330]
   Caribbean Stud. Assn. [8050]
   Caribbean Stud. Assn. [IO]
   Caribbean Tourism Org., Amer. Br. [24252]
   Center for Intl. Policy [17748]
   DOCARE Intl., N.F.P. [12518]
   Food for the Poor [12772]
   Grenada Bd. of Tourism [24253]
   Hermandad [17046]
   Inter-American Commn. on Human Rights [17765]
   Inter-American Parliamentary Gp. on Population and Development [12432]
   Latin Amer. Venture Capital Assn. [1431]
   Natl. Assn. of Barbados Organizations [9731]
   RARE [5373]
   Saint Kitts Tourism Authority [24254]
   Saint Lucia Tourist Bd. [24255]
   Seminar on the Acquisition of Latin Amer. Lib. Materials [10386]
   TransAfrica Forum [16934]
   United Confed. of Taino People [18989]
Caribbean Action Lobby - Address unknown since 1999.
Caribbean and African Chamber of Commerce of Ontario [IO], Toronto, ON, Canada
Caribbean Agricultural Res. and Development Inst. [★IO]
Caribbean Amer. Chamber of Commerce and Indus. [IO], Brooklyn, NY, United States
Caribbean Amer. Chamber of Commerce and Indus. [24268], 63 Flushing Ave., Brooklyn Navy Yard, Bldg. No. 5, Unit 239, Brooklyn, NY 11205, (718)834-4544
Caribbean Amer. Intercultural Org. [9774], PO Box 55395, Washington, DC 20040, (202)720-3900
Caribbean Amer. Intercultural Org. [IO], Washington, DC, United States
Caribbean Amer. Netball Assn. [23633], PO Box 250-057, Lefferts Sta., Brooklyn, NY 11225, (347)221-0050
Caribbean Assn. for Feminist Res. and Action [IO], Tunapuna, Trinidad and Tobago
Caribbean Assn. of Home Economists [IO], St. Michael, Barbados
Caribbean Assn. of Indus. and Commerce [IO], Maraval, Trinidad and Tobago
Caribbean Assn. of Natl. Telecommunication Organizations [IO], Port of Spain, Trinidad and Tobago
Caribbean Assn. of Sports Medicine [IO], St. Thomas, Barbados
Caribbean Assn. for Tech. and Vocational Educ. and Training [★IO]
Caribbean Assn. of Theological Schools [IO], St. John, Barbados
Caribbean Banana Exporters Assn. [IO], London, United Kingdom
Caribbean Broadcasting Union [IO], Bridgetown, Barbados
Caribbean-Central Amer. Action [IO], Washington, DC, United States
Caribbean/Central Amer. Action [★IO]
Caribbean-Central Amer. Action [12421], 1818 N St. NW, Ste. 310, Washington, DC 20036, (202)466-7464
Caribbean/Central Amer. Action [★12421]
Caribbean; Comm. for the [★12421]
Caribbean Community [IO], Georgetown, Guyana
Caribbean Conf. of Churches [IO], Port of Spain, Trinidad and Tobago
Caribbean Conservation Assn. [IO], St. Michael, Barbados
Caribbean Conservation Corporation and Sea Turtle Survival League [IO], Gainesville, FL, United States

Caribbean Conservation Corp. and Sea Turtle Survival League [5305], 4424 NW 13th St., Ste. B-11, Gainesville, FL 32609, (352)373-6441
Caribbean Cultural Comm. [IO], Toronto, ON, Canada
Caribbean Culture Center [9775], 408 W 58th St., New York, NY 10019, (212)307-7420
Caribbean Development Bank [IO], St. Michael, Barbados
Caribbean Educational Service - Address unknown since 1995.
Caribbean Employers' Confed. [IO], Port of Spain, Trinidad and Tobago
Caribbean Engg. and Tech. Professionals [IO], Carapichaima, Trinidad and Tobago
Caribbean Environmental Hea. Inst. [IO], Castries, St. Lucia
Caribbean Examinations Coun. [IO], St. Michael, Barbados
Caribbean Export Development Agency [IO], Christ Church, Barbados
Caribbean Family Planning Affiliation [IO], St. Johns, Antigua-Barbuda
Caribbean Fisheries Inst; Gulf and [4668]
Caribbean Fruit Network [IO], St. Augustine, Trinidad and Tobago
Caribbean Gamefishing Assn. - Address unknown since 1995.
Caribbean Gender and Trade Network [IO], Tunapuna, Trinidad and Tobago
Caribbean Group for Cooperation in Economic Development - Address unknown since 1999.
Caribbean Hospitality Training Institute [★3913]
Caribbean Hospitality Training Institute [★IO]
Caribbean Hotel Assn. [IO], San Juan, PR, United States
Caribbean Hotel Assn. [3913], 1000 Ponce de Leon Ave., 5th Fl., San Juan, PR 00907-3668, (787)725-9139
Caribbean Hotel Coun. of the Caribbean Travel Assn. [★3913]
Caribbean Hotel Coun. of the Caribbean Travel Assn. [★IO]
Caribbean Hotel Foundation [★IO]
Caribbean Hotel Foundation [★3913]
Caribbean Inst. for Meteorology and Hydrology [IO], Bridgetown, Barbados
Caribbean/Latin Amer. Action [★IO]
Caribbean/Latin Amer. Action [★12421]
Caribbean Meteorological Inst. [★IO]
Caribbean Meteorological Inst. [★IO]
Caribbean Meteorological Org. [IO], Port of Spain, Trinidad and Tobago
Caribbean Natural Resources Inst. [IO], Laventille, Trinidad and Tobago
Caribbean Network for Integrated Rural Development - Trinidad and Tobago [IO], St. Augustine, Trinidad and Tobago
Caribbean Policy Development Centre [IO], St. Michael, Barbados
Caribbean Regional Coun. for Adult Educ. [IO], Port of Spain, Trinidad and Tobago
Caribbean Soc. of Hotel Assn. Executives [IO], San Juan, PR, United States
Caribbean Soc. of Hotel Assn. Executives [24330], c/o Caribbean Hotel Assn., 1000 Ponce De Leon Ave., 5th Fl., San Juan, PR 00907, (787)725-9139
Caribbean Solidarity Assn. [★18104]
Caribbean Solidarity Assn. [★IO]
Caribbean Solidarity Assn; Latin Amer. and [★18104]
Caribbean Stud. Assn. [8050], c/o Dr. Percy C. Hintzen, Pres., Univ. of California, 660 Barrows Hall, No. 2572, Berkeley, CA 94720, (510)642-0303
Caribbean Stud. Assn. [IO], Berkeley, CA, United States
Caribbean Stud; Inst. of [12430]
Caribbean Tourism Assn. [★24252]
Caribbean Tourism Assn. [★IO]
Caribbean Tourism Org. [IO], St. Michael, Barbados
Caribbean Tourism Organization [★24252]
Caribbean Tourism Org., Amer. Br. [24252], 80 Broad St., 32nd Fl., New York, NY 10004, (212)635-9530

A star before a book entry number signifies that the name is not listed separately, but is mentioned within the entry.

Caribbean Tourism Res. and Development Center [★24252]
Caribbean Tourism Res. and Development Centre [★IO]
Caribbean Tourist Assn. [★24252]
Caribbeana Coun. - Defunct.
Caribou Carnival Assn. [IO], Yellowknife, NT, Canada
Caricature Carvers of Am. [9829], PO Box 565, Derby, KS 67037
Caricaturist Network; Natl. [1318]
Caricaturists Soc. of America - Address unknown since 1994.
Carillonneurs in North Am; Guild of [10604]
Caring - Defunct.
Caring Together; Protecting and [★11565]
Caring Voice Coalition [12712], 8249 Meadowbridge Rd., Mechanicsville, VA 23116, (804)427-6468
Caritas Andorrana [IO], Andorra la Vella, Andorra
Caritas de Angola [IO], Luanda, Angola
Caritas Aotearoa New Zealand [IO], Wellington, New Zealand
Caritas Argentina [IO], Buenos Aires, Argentina
Caritas Australia [IO], North Sydney, Australia
Caritas Azerbaijan [IO], Baku, Azerbaijan
Caritas Bangladesh [IO], Dhaka, Bangladesh
Caritas Belarus [IO], Minsk, Belarus
Caritas Benin [IO], Cotonou, Benin
Caritas Bolivia [IO], La Paz, Bolivia
Caritas Bulgaria [IO], Sofia, Bulgaria
Caritas Caboverdeana [IO], Santiago, Cape Verde
Caritas Cambodia [IO], Phnom Penh, Cambodia
Caritas Catholica Belgica [IO], Brussels, Belgium
Caritas Centrafrique [IO], Bangui, Central African Republic
Caritas Colombia [IO], Santa Fe de Bogota, Colombia
Caritas Comores [IO], Moroni, Comoros
Caritas Coreana [IO], Seoul, Republic of Korea
Caritas Cote d'Ivoire [IO], Abidjan, Cote d'Ivoire
Caritas Cuba [IO], Havana, Cuba
Caritas Denmark [IO], Copenhagen, Denmark
Caritas Djibouti [IO], Djibouti, Djibouti
Caritas Dominicana [IO], Santo Domingo, Dominican Republic
Caritas Ecuador [IO], Quito, Ecuador
Caritas Egypte [IO], Cairo, Egypt
Caritas El Salvador [IO], San Salvador, El Salvador
Caritas Eritrea [IO], Asmara, Eritrea
Caritas Ethiopia [IO], Addis Ababa, Ethiopia
Caritas Gabon [IO], Libreville, Gabon
Caritas Gambia [IO], Serrekunda, Gambia
Caritas Georgia [IO], Tbilisi, Georgia
Caritas Guinea Ecuatorial [IO], Malabo, Equatorial Guinea
Caritas Hellas [IO], Athens, Greece
Caritas de Honduras [IO], Tegucigalpa, Honduras
Caritas Hong Kong [IO], Hong Kong, People's Republic of China
Caritas Hungarica [IO], Budapest, Hungary
Caritas Iceland [IO], Reykjavik, Iceland
Caritas Ile Maurice [IO], Port Louis, Mauritius
Caritas India [IO], New Delhi, India
Caritas Indonesia [IO], Jakarta, Indonesia
Caritas Internationalis - Vatican City [IO], Vatican City, Vatican City
Caritas Iran [IO], Tehran, Iran
Caritas Iraq [IO], Baghdad, Iraq
Caritas Italiana [IO], Rome, Italy
Caritas Jordan [IO], Amman, Jordan
Caritas Karuna Myanmar [IO], Yangon, Myanmar
Caritas Kazakhstan [IO], Karaganda, Kazakhstan
Caritas Kenya [IO], Nairobi, Kenya
Caritas Latvia [IO], Riga, Latvia
Caritas Lesotho [IO], Maseru, Lesotho
Caritas Liberia [IO], Monrovia, Liberia
Caritas Libie [IO], Tripoli, Libyan Arab Jamahiriya
Caritas Macedonia [IO], Skopje, Macedonia
Caritas Maroc [IO], Rabat, Morocco
Caritas Mauritanie [IO], Nouakchott, Mauritania
Caritas Mocambicana [IO], Maputo, Mozambique
Caritas Moldova [IO], Chisinau, Moldova
Caritas Monaco [IO], Monaco, Monaco
Caritas Mongolia [IO], Ulan Bator, Mongolia
Caritas Nepal [IO], Kathmandu, Nepal

Caritas Nicaragua [IO], Managua, Nicaragua
Caritas Niger [IO], Niamey, Niger
Caritas Nigeria [IO], Lagos, Nigeria
Caritas Pakistan [IO], Lahore, Pakistan
Caritas Paraguay [IO], Asuncion, Paraguay
Caritas Puerto Rico [12839], PO Box 8812, San Juan, PR 00910-0812, (787)727-7373
Caritas Republique du Congo [IO], Brazzaville, Republic of the Congo
Caritas Rwanda [IO], Kigali, Rwanda
Caritas Sao Tome and Principe [IO], Sao Tome, Sao Tome and Principe
Caritas Senegal [IO], Dakar, Senegal
Caritas Seychelles [IO], Victoria, Seychelles
Caritas South Africa [IO], Pretoria, Republic of South Africa
Caritas Swaziland [IO], Manzini, Swaziland
Caritas Switzerland [IO], Lucerne, Switzerland
Caritas Tanzania [IO], Dar es Salaam, United Republic of Tanzania
Caritas Tunisie [IO], Tunis, Tunisia
Caritas Uganda [IO], Kampala, Uganda
Caritas Ukraine [IO], Kiev, Ukraine
Carl Duisberg Soc. [★IO]
Carl Duisberg Soc. [★8019]
Carl Neilsen Soc. of America - Address unknown since 1995.
Carl Neuberg Soc. for Intl. Relations - Defunct.
Carl Orff Canada - Music for Children [IO], Delta, BC, Canada
Carl Orff Canada Musique pour Enfants [★IO]
Carl Perkins Fan Club - Defunct.
Carla Riggs-Hall Intl. Fan Club [24855], 202 Master St., Elizabethtown, KY 42701
Carleton E. Morse Radio Programs for the Blind and Handicapped [★22929]
Carlton/Reed/Ashley/Williams/ Bradford/McGoffier/ Mattews/Reade Family Org. - Defunct.
Carly Simon Intl. Fan Club - Defunct.
Carmarthenshire Welsh Pony and Cob Assn. [IO], Ammanford, United Kingdom
Carmelite Order of the Blessed Virgin Mary of Mount Carmel; Lay [19647]
Carmelites; Lay [★19647]
Carmen of Am; Brotherhood Railway [★24179]
Carmen Division of the Brotherhood of Railway, Airline and Steamship Clerks, Freight Handlers, Express and Sta. Employees [★24179]
Carmen Division/Transportation Communications Union; Brotherhood Railway [24179]
Carmen of the U.S. and Canada; Brotherhood Railway [★24179]
Carmichael U.S.A; Clan [20820]
Carn Surname Org. - Address unknown since 2004.
Carnegie Clan Soc. - Address unknown since 2000.
Carnegie Commn. on Educational TV - Defunct.
Carnegie Commn. on Higher Education - Defunct.
Carnegie Commn. on Science, Technology, and Govt. - Defunct.
Carnegie Corp. of New York [8239], 437 Madison Ave., New York, NY 10022, (212)371-3200
Carnegie Coun. on Adolescent Development [13477], PO Box 753, Waldorf, MD 20604, (212)207-6275
Carnegie Coun. for Ethics in Intl. Affairs [20093], Merrill House, 170 E 64th St., New York, NY 10021-7478, (212)838-4120
Carnegie Coun. for Ethics in Intl. Affairs [IO], New York, NY, United States
Carnegie Coun. of Policy Studies - Defunct.
Carnegie Endowment for Intl. Peace [17863], 1779 Massachusetts Ave. NW, Washington, DC 20036-2103, (202)483-7600
Carnegie Endowment for Intl. Peace [IO], Washington, DC, United States
Carnegie Forum on Educ. and the Economy [★8283]
Carnegie Found. for the Advancement of Teaching [9214], 51 Vista Ln., Stanford, CA 94305-8703, (650)566-5100
Carnegie Hall - Jeunesses Musicales - Defunct.
Carnegie Hero Fund Commn. [13036], 425 6th Ave., Ste. 1640, Pittsburgh, PA 15219-1823, (412)281-1302
Carnegie Institution of Washington [7564], 1530 P St. NW, Washington, DC 20005, (202)387-6400

Carnival Glass Assn; Amer. [22549]
Carnival Glass Assn; Heart of America [22557]
Carnivorous Plant Soc; Intl. [22521]
Carol Burnett Fund for Responsible Journalism [8707], c/o Prof. Tom Brislin, Admin., Univ. of Hawaii, Scholarship of Communications, 2550 Campus Rd., Honolulu, HI 96822-2217, (808)956-8881
Carol Lawrence Natl. Fan Club - Defunct.
Carolina Alumni Assn; Coastal [★18887]
Carolina Peanut Assn; Virginia- [5063]
Carolina Peanut Promotions; Virginia- [5064]
Carolina Univ. Alumni Assn; Coastal [18887]
Caroline Munro Fan Club - Defunct.
Carousel Organ Assn. of Am. [22711], c/o Marge Waters, Treas., 7552 Beach Rd., Wadsworth, OH 44281
Carousel Roundtable; Natl. [★21897]
Carousel Theatre Soc. [IO], Vancouver, BC, Canada
Carousels
    Darkride and Funhouse Enthusiasts [21511]
    Natl. Carousel Assn. [21897]
Carp Anglers Gp. [22450], c/o Neil Stern, 3804 Yacht Club Dr., Arlington, TX 76016-2560, (888)227-7118
Carpal Tunnel Syndrome Assn; Amer. [★15631]
Carpatho-Russian Benevolent Assn. Liberty - Address unknown since 1999.
Carpenters for Christmas - Defunct.
Carpenters' Company [10018], c/o Carpenters' Hall, 320 Chestnut St., Philadelphia, PA 19106, (215)925-0167
Carpenters' Company [IO], London, United Kingdom
Carpenters' Company of the City and County of Philadelphia [★10018]
Carpenters Fan Club - Defunct.
Carpenters and Joiners of Am; United Brotherhood of [24032]
Carper Family Assn. - Defunct.
Carpet Backing Coun. and Burlap and Jute Assn; Jute [2266]
Carpet Cleaners Inst. of the Northwest [832], PMB 40, 2421 S Union Ave., Ste. L-1, Tacoma, WA 98405, (253)759-5762
Carpet Cushion Coun. [2253], 23 Courtney Cir., Bryn Mawr, PA 19010, (610)527-3880
Carpet Export Promotion Coun. [IO], New Delhi, India
Carpet Inst. of Australia [IO], Melbourne, Australia
Carpet and Rug Industry Consumer Action Panel - Defunct.
Carpet and Rug Inst. [2254], PO Box 2048, Dalton, GA 30722-2048, (706)278-3176
Carpet Wool Coun. - Defunct.
Carpet Yarn Assn. [★3774]
Carr-Loker Descendants Assn. - Defunct.
CARR Support Gp. [IO], Toronto, ON, Canada
Carrefour Canadien Intl. [★IO]
Carreras Intl. Leukemia Found; Friends of the Jose [13825]
Carriage Assn. of Am. [21987], 3915 Jay Trump Rd., Lexington, KY 40511-8936, (859)231-0971
Carriage Club of Am; Horseless [21658]
Carriage Operators of North Am. [783], PO Box 554, Norfolk, CT 06058, (860)542-5222
Carriage Operators of North Am. [IO], Norfolk, CT, United States
Carriage Travel Club [23011], PO Box 246, Millersburg, IN 46543-0246, (574)642-3622
Carriages
    Amer. Driving Soc. [23491]
    Carriage Assn. of Am. [21987]
    Carriage Operators of North Am. [783]
    Carriage Operators of North Am. [IO]
Carrie Estelle Doheny Found. [13156], 707 Wilshire Blvd., Ste. 4960, Los Angeles, CA 90017, (213)488-1122
Carrier Assn; Natl. Air [159]
Carrier Conf; Contract [★3899]
Carrier Conf. -Irregular Route; Common [★3899]
Carrier Liaison Comm. [★3731]
Carrier Soc; Navy [22653]
Carriers' Assn; Lake [2606]
Carriers Conf; Heavy Specialized [★3589]
Carriers Conf; Interstate [★3899]

Reference to "IO" in place of a book number signifies that the association may be found in the 45th edition of International Organizations.

Carriers Container Coun. - Address unknown since 2006.

Carriers and Locals Soc. [22904], c/o Martin D. Richardson, Sec.-Treas., PO Box 74, Grosse Ile, MI 48138

Carriers; Natl. Assn. of Letter [★24168]

Carriers; Natl. Tank Truck [3580]

Carriers Sect. - Local Cartage Natl. Conf; Heavy Specialized [★3589]

Carroll Center for the Blind [16840], 770 Centre St., Newton, MA 02458, (617)969-6200

Carroll Club - Address unknown since 1995.

Carroll Rehabilitation Center for the Visually Impaired [★16840]

Carroll Soc. of North Am; Lewis [9681]

Carrom Assn; U.S. [22476]

Carruthers Clan Soc. - Defunct.

Carrying Capacity [★6859]

Carrying Capacity Network [6859], 2000 P St. NW, Ste. 310, Washington, DC 20036-5915, (202)296-4548

The Cars Fan Club - Address unknown since 1989.

Cars of the Past - Defunct.

Carson Coun; Rachel [13330]

Carson Homestead Assn; Rachel [11143]

Carson Intl. Fan Club; Jeff [24918]

Carson McCullers Soc. [11164], c/o James Mayo, Dept. of English and Foreign Languages, Jackson State Community Coll., 2046 N Pkwy., Jackson, TN 38301, (800)355-5722

Carson Trust for the Living Env; Rachel [★13330]

Carter Center [18389], One Copenhill, 453 Freedom Pkwy., Atlanta, GA 30307, (404)420-5100

Carter Family Fan Club - Address unknown since 2007.

Cartercar Registry - Defunct.

Carto-Philatelists [★22799]

Cartographic Assn; Amer. [★6654]

Cartographic Assn. of Tanzania [IO], Dar es Salaam, United Republic of Tanzania

Cartographic Soc. of the Slovak Republic [IO], Bratislava, Slovakia

Cartography
African Assn. of Remote Sensing of the Env. [IO]
Amer. Cong. on Surveying and Mapping [7717]
British Cartographic Soc. [IO]
Canadian Cartographic Assn. [IO]
Canadian Inst. of Geomatics [IO]
Cartographic Assn. of Tanzania [IO]
Cartographic Soc. of the Slovak Republic [IO]
Cartography and Geographic Info. Soc. [6654]
CartoPhilatelic Soc. [22799]
Chicago Map Soc. [21528]
Commn. for the Geological Map of the World [IO]
Consultant Quantity Surveyors Assn. [IO]
French Inst. of Pondicherry [IO]
Geomatics Indus. Assn. of Canada [IO]
Indian Soc. of Geomatics [IO]
Intl. Cartographic Assn. [IO]
Intl. Coronelli Soc. for the Stud. of Globes [IO]
Intl. Map Trade Assn. [IO]
Intl. Map Trade Assn. [6655]
Japan Cartographers Assn. [IO]
Mapping Sciences Inst., Australia [IO]
New Zealand Cartographic Soc. [IO]
North Amer. Cartographic Info. Soc. [6656]
Regional Centre for Mapping of Resources for Development [IO]
Soc. of Cartographers [IO]
Soc. for Conservation GIS [6831]
Swedish Cartographic Soc. [IO]
Swiss Soc. of Cartography [IO]
Western Assn. of Map Libraries [10394]

Cartography Division of the Amer. Cong. on Surveying and Mapping [★6654]

Cartography and Geographic Info. Soc. [6654], c/o Aileen R. Buckley, Pres., ESRI, Inc., 380 New York St., Redlands, CA 92373, (909)793-2853

Carton Ondule; Assn. Internationale des Fabricants de Caisses en [★985]

Cartoon/Fantasy Org. - Defunct.

Cartooning
Assn. of Amer. Editorial Cartoonists [3092]
Christian Comic Arts Soc. [9435]
Natl. Cartoonists Soc. [9515]

Thomas Nast Soc. [9477]

Cartoonist Guild of New York [★9505]

Cartoonist Guild of New York [★IO]

Cartoonists; Assn. of Amer. Editorial [3092]

Cartoonists' Club of Great Britain [IO], Sandy, United Kingdom

Cartoonists Northwest [9561], PO Box 31122, Seattle, WA 98103, (425)226-7623

Cartoonists Soc; Natl. [9515]

Cartoons
Animators Unite [9388]
Assn. of Amer. Editorial Cartoonists [3092]
Betty Boop Intl. Collectible Club [21976]
Bushmiller Soc. [24790]
Cartoonists' Club of Great Britain [IO]
Christian Comic Arts Soc. [9435]
Gridiron Club of Washington, DC [3114]
Intl. Comic Arts Assn. [9447]
Natl. Cartoonists Soc. [9515]
Natl. Fantasy Fan Club for Disneyana Enthusiasts [24791]
Official Betty Boop Fan Club [24792]
Official Betty Boop Fan Club [IO]
Official Gumby Fan Club [24793]
Pogo Fan Club and Walt Kelly Soc. [24794]
Popular Culture Assn. [10888]
Promotional Glass Collectors Assn. [22109]
Walt Disney Collectors Soc. [22129]
World Chap. of Disneyana Enthusiasts [22132]

CartoPhilatelic Soc. [22799], c/o Mr. Alf Jordan, Sec.-Treas., 156 W Elm St., Yarmouth, ME 04096

Carver Family Org; John [20961]

Carver-Scott Humane Soc. [11374], PO Box 215, Chaska, MN 55318, (952)368-3553

Carvers; Affiliated Wood [9533]

Carvers Assn; Natl. Pig [22169]

Carvers Assn; Natl. Wood [22171]

Carwash Assn; Intl. [★416]

Carwash Coun; Natl. [★416]

Carwash Operators Assn. - Defunct.

CAS Collectors [21926], 2000 Wisconsin Ave. N, Golden Valley, MN 55427

CAS Forum [★10571]

CAS Forum of the Violin Soc. of Am. [10571], c/o Violin Soc. of Am., 48 Acad. St., Poughkeepsie, NY 12601, (845)452-7557

Casa Ananda, A.C. of Mexico [IO], Mexico City, Mexico

CASA Assn; Natl. [★11636]

Casa de Cultura da Mulher Negra [★IO]

Casa El Salvador - Defunct.

Casa Vacanza [★22580]

Cascade Holistic Economic Consultants [★4696]

Cascade Living Lightly Assn. - Defunct.

Case Clearinghouse; ARES [★9049]

Case Collectors Club [22613], PO Box 4000, Bradford, PA 16701, (800)523-6350

Case Mgt. Soc. of Am. [15063], 6301 Ranch Dr., Little Rock, AR 72223, (501)225-2229

Case Management Society of America [IO], Little Rock, AR, United States

Case Mgt. Soc. of Australia [IO], Melbourne, Australia

Case Manager Certification; Commn. for [14703]

CASE Matching Gifts CH [12199], 1307 New York Ave. NW, Ste. 1000, Washington, DC 20005-4701, (202)478-5656

Case Res. Assn. [★4065]

Case Res. Assn; North Amer. [4065]

Case Res. Assn; Southwest [8042]

Casein and Acrylic; Natl. Soc. of Painters in [9518]

Casein Importers Assn. - Address unknown since 1995.

Casey Jones Railroad Unit [★22800]

Casey Jones Railroad Unit - ATA [22800], PO Box 18615, Rochester, NY 14618-8615

Cash-for-Cash-Off Prog. [★17327]

Cash Free America - Defunct.

Cash Mgt. Assn; Natl. Corporate [★1403]

Cash Mgt. Practitioners Assn. [★1403]

Cash Registers Collectors Club of Am. [21988], PO Box 20534, Dayton, OH 45420-0534

Cashew Export Promotion Coun. of India [IO], Cochin, India

Cashmere and Camel Hair Mfrs. Inst. [3779], 6 Beacon St., Ste. 1125, Boston, MA 02108, (617)542-7481

Casing Inst; Natural [★2659]

Casino Assn. of South Africa [IO], Vlaeberg, Republic of South Africa

Casino Chip and Gaming Token Collectors Club [21989], c/o Sunday Silverman, Membership Off., 100 S Sunrise Way, Ste. A, No. 199, Palm Springs, CA 92262-6737, (877)4CC-GTCC

Casino Operators Assn. of the UK [IO], Chard, United Kingdom

Casino Party Operators; Natl. Assn. of [1313]

Casino and Theme Party Operators; Natl. Assn. of [★1313]

Casket and Funeral Supply Assn. of Am. [2775], 49 Sherwood Terr., Ste. Y, Lake Bluff, IL 60044-2231, (847)295-6630

Casket Hardware Mfrs. Assn. - Defunct.

Casket Manufacturers Assn. of Am. [★2775]

Casket Retailers Assn; Natl. [2786]

Caspian Breed Soc. (UK) [IO], Chippenham, United Kingdom

Caspian Horse Soc. of the Americas [4869], PO Box 1589, Brenham, TX 77834-1589, (979)251-7305

Cassandra: Radical Feminist Nurses Network - Address unknown since 1995.

Cassidy Clan Fan Club - Defunct.

Cassidy Class - Address unknown since 1999.

Cassidy Fan Club; Friends of Hopalong [24742]

Cassidy Fan Club; Friends of Shaun [★24891]

Cassidys; Friends of the [24891]

Cassie Edwards Intl. Fan Club [24782], c/o Tammy Russotto, Pres., 208 NW 80th Terr., Margate, FL 33063

Cast Bronze Bearing Inst. [★2008]

Cast Bronze Bearings Inst. [★2053]

Cast Bronze Inst. [2008]

Cast Bullet Assn. [23715], c/o Ronald Klerk de Reus, Membership Dir., 12857 S Rd., Hoyt, KS 66440-9116, (785)986-6675

Cast Iron Architecture; Friends of [10025]

Cast Iron Cookware Assn; Griswold and [22588]

Cast Iron Pipe Inst. [★3029]

Cast Iron Pipe Publicity Bur. [★3029]

Cast Iron Pipe Res. Assn. [★3029]

Cast Iron Seat Collectors Assn. [22607], 604 Washington St., Woodstock, IL 60098-2251, (815)338-6464

Cast Iron Soil Pipe Found. - Defunct.

Cast Iron Soil Pipe Inst. [3027], 5959 Shallowford Rd., Ste. 419, Chattanooga, TN 37421, (423)892-0137

Cast Metals
Figural Cast Iron Collector's Club [22417]
Cast Metals Assn; Amer. [★9227]
Cast Metals Fed. [IO], West Bromwich, United Kingdom
Cast Metals Inst. [★9227]
Cast Stone and Concrete Fed. [★IO]
Cast Stone Inst. [919], PO Box 68, Lebanon, PA 17042, (717)272-3744
Castalia Found. - Defunct.
Caster Assn. of Am. - Address unknown since 2001.
Caster and Floor Truck Manufacturers Assn. [★2028]
Caster Manufacturers; Inst. of [2028]
Casting Assn; Amer. [23406]
Casting Engineers; Soc. of Die [★2054]
Casting Indus. Suppliers Assn. [2009], 14175 W Indian School Rd., Ste. B4-504, Goodyear, AZ 85395, (623)547-0920
Casting Inst; Alloy [★2070]
Casting Inst; Amer. Die [★2054]
Casting Proj; Non-Traditional [★10996]
Castings Development Centre [★IO]
Castings Tech. Intl. [IO], Sheffield, United Kingdom
Castings Tech. Intl. [★IO]

Castles
Intl. Assn. of Sand Castle Builders [22971]
Castor Seed Assn. of New York; Linseed [★2852]
Casual Furniture Mfrs. Assn; Summer and [1706]
Casual Furniture Retailers [1693], 214 N Hale St., Wheaton, IL 60187, (630)510-4562
Casual Furniture Retailers; Natl. Assn. of [★1693]
Casualty Accountants and Statisticians and Insurance Accountants Assn; Assn. of [★53]
Casualty Actuarial Soc. [2153], 4350 N Fairfax Dr., Ste. 250, Arlington, VA 22203, (703)276-3100

A star before a book entry number signifies that the name is not listed separately, but is mentioned within the entry.

Casualty Reinsurers; Natl. Assn. of Property and [★2234]
Casualty and Surety Agents; Natl. Assn. of [★2159]
Casualty and Surety Companies; Assn. of [★2139]
Casualty and Surety Conf; Southern [★2194]
Casualty Underwriters; Amer. Inst. for Chartered Property [★2137]
Casualty Underwriters; Soc. of Chartered Property and [★2160]
Cat
   Abyssinian Cat Club of Am. [21898]
   All Breeds Cat Club [IO]
   Alley Cat Allies [11343]
   Amer. Assn. of Cat Enthusiasts [21899]
   Amer. Assn. of Feline Practitioners [16744]
   Amer. Cat Assn. [21900]
   Amer. Cat Fanciers Assn. [21901]
   Amer. Cat Fanciers Assn. [IO]
   Amer. Keuda Cat Assn. [4204]
   Calico Cat Registry Intl. [21902]
   Calico Cat Registry Intl. [IO]
   Canadian Cat Assn. [IO]
   Cat Collectors [21990]
   Cat Fanciers' Assn. [21903]
   Cat Fanciers' Fed. [21904]
   Cats Protection [IO]
   Cornell Feline Hea. Center [16791]
   Cornish Rex Soc. [21905]
   The Designer Cat Assn. [21906]
   Feline Control Coun. of Victoria [IO]
   Feline Control Coun. of Western Australia [IO]
   Feral Cat Friends [21907]
   Friends of Feral Felines [21908]
   Happy Household Pet Cat Club [21909]
   Harmony House for Cats [11404]
   Hearts United for Animals [11405]
   Home for Unwanted and Lost Animals [IO]
   The International Bengal Breeders' Association [IO]
   The Intl. Bengal Breeders' Assn. [4205]
   The Intl. Bengal Cat Soc. [4206]
   The International Bengal Cat Society [IO]
   The Intl. Cat Assn. [IO]
   The Intl. Cat Assn. [21910]
   Intl. Desert Lynx Cat Assn. [4207]
   International Desert Lynx Cat Association [IO]
   The International Savannah Breeders' Association [IO]
   The Intl. Savannah Breeders' Assn. [4208]
   Intl. Soc. for Endangered Cats [4209]
   International Society for Endangered Cats [IO]
   Intl. Sphynx Soc. [IO]
   Intl. Sphynx Soc. [21911]
   LaPerm Soc. of Am. [21912]
   Lib. Cat Soc. [10367]
   Malta Feline Guardians Club [IO]
   Natl. Alliance of Burmese Breeders [4210]
   Natl. Birman Fanciers [21913]
   Natl. Cat Protection Soc. [11434]
   Natl. Pet Alliance [11441]
   Norwegian Forest Cat Breed Coun. [21914]
   Pet Food Inst. [2963]
   Pet Savers Found. [11449]
   Princess Kitty Fan Club [24778]
   RagaMuffin Cat Lovers Soc. [22777]
   Rex Breeders United [21915]
   Sacred Cat of Burma Fanciers [21916]
   Savannah Cat Club [4211]
   Selkirk Rex Breed Club [21917]
   Somali Cat Club of Am. [21918]
   Somali Intl. Cat Club [21919]
   Southern Africa Cat Coun. [IO]
   Traditional Cat Assn. [21920]
   Traditional and Classic Cat Intl. [21921]
   Traditional and Classic Cat Intl. [IO]
   United Action for Animals [11468]
   United Burmese Cat Fanciers [21922]
   United Cat Fed. [21923]
   United Silver Fanciers [21924]
Cat Allies; Alley [11343]
Cat Club; Somali Intl. [21919]
Cat Collectors [21990], PO Box 2738, Parker, CO 80134, (303)805-5884
Cat Fanciers' Assn. [21903], PO Box 1005, Manasquan, NJ 08736-0805, (732)528-9797

Cat Fanciers' Fed. [21904], PO Box 661, Gratis, OH 45330, (937)787-9009
Cat Fund [★11448]
Cat Protection Soc; Natl. [11434]
Cat Soc; Lib. [10367]
Catacomb Soc; Intl. [10039]
Catacombs in Italy; Intl. Comm. to Preserve [★10039]
Catahoulas; Natl. Assn. of Louisiana [22313]
Catalan Assn. for Artificial Intelligence [IO], Bellaterra, Spain
Catalina 22 Natl. Sailing Assn. [23162], c/o Dora McGee, Sec.-Treas., 3790 Post Gate Dr., Cumming, GA 30040, (770)887-9728
Catalina 25 Natl. Assn. - Address unknown since 1995.
Catalina 27/270 Assn; Intl. [23182]
Catalina 27 Assn; Intl. [★23182]
Catalina 27 Natl. Assn. [★23182]
Catalog Managers Assn; Natl. [3134]
Catalog and Multichannel Marketing Coun. [1763], 1120 Ave. of the Americas, New York, NY 10036-6700, (212)768-7277
Catalog Services Assn. - Defunct.
Catalogers; Online Audiovisual [10379]
Cataloging and Classification - of ALA; Division of [★10333]
Catalysis Soc. [★7624]
Catalysis Soc. (North Am.) - Defunct.
Catalysis Soc; North Amer. [7624]
Catalysis Soc; Organic Reactions [6692]
Catalyst [11085], 120 Wall St., 5th Fl., New York, NY 10005-3904, (212)514-7600
Cataract and Refractive Surgeons; European Soc. for [IO]
Cataract and Refractive Surgery; Amer. Soc. of [15665]
Cataraqui Archaeological Res. Found. [IO], Kingston, ON, Canada
Catastrophe Adjusters; Natl. Assn. of [2205]
Catboat Assn. [23163], c/o John L. Greene, Membership Sec., PO Box 246, Cataumet, MA 02534-0246, (508)947-5093
Catch Soc. of America - Defunct.
Catching the Dream [8427], 8200 Mountain Rd. NE, Ste. 203, Albuquerque, NM 87110, (505)262-2351
Catchment Systems Assn; Amer. Rainwater [7825]
Catchment Systems Assn; Intl. Rainwater [7832]
Catechetical Directors; Natl. Assn. of Parish [19932]
Catechetical Leaders; Natl. Conf. for [★19934]
Catechetical Leadership; Natl. Conf. for [19934]
Catecholamine Club - Address unknown since 2004.
Catechumenate; North Amer. Forum on the [19698]
Caterers Assn; Executive Stewards and [★1584]
Caterers Assn; Intl. Stewards and [★1584]
Caterers' Assn; Mobile Indus. [★1938]
Catering Equip. Distributors Assn. of Great Britain [IO], Bingley, United Kingdom
Catering Equip. Importers Assn. [★IO]
Catering Equip. Suppliers Assn. [IO], London, United Kingdom
Catering Executives; Natl. Assn. of [1951]
Catering Intl. Mgt. Assn; Hotel and [IO]
Catering Trade Assn; British Amusement [IO]
Caterpillar Club [146], c/o Milkweed Cafe, 901 Wilson St., Pinckneyville, IL 62274-1552
Catfish Assn. of North Am. - Address unknown since 2003.
Catfish Farmers of Am. [4170], 1100 Hwy. 82 E, Ste. 202, Indianola, MS 38751, (662)887-2699
The Catfish Inst. [4171], 5420 I-55 N, Ste. F, Jackson, MS 39211, (601)977-9559
Catharine Maria Sedgwick Soc. [11165], c/o Deborah Gussman, VP - Membership and Finance, 619 Wayne Ave., Haddonfield, NJ 08033
Catharsis Found. [IO], Calgary, AB, Canada
Cathedral; Amer. Friends of St. David's [10009]
Cathedral Assn; Natl. [19903]
Cathedral Found. [★19903]
Cather Found; Willa [★9722]
Cather Pioneer Memorial and Educational Found; Willa [9722]
Cather Soc; Willa [★9722]
Cathodic Protection Industry Assn. - Defunct.
Catholic
   Acad. of Amer. Franciscan History [19560]

ADOREMUS - Soc. for the Renewal of the Sacred Liturgy [19561]
ADOREMUS - Society for the Renewal of the Sacred Liturgy [IO]
Agape: Gospel of Life Disciples [19562]
Agustinians of the Assumption [IO]
Aid to the Church in Need [IO]
Aid to the Church in Need [19563]
All Roads Ministry [19564]
Alliance of the Orders of St. John of Jerusalem [IO]
Ambassadors of Mary [19565]
Amer. Benedictine Acad. [19566]
Amer. Catholic Historical Assn. [10085]
Amer. Catholic Historical Soc. [10086]
Amer. Catholic Lawyers Assn. [5558]
Amer. Catholic Philosophical Assn. [8965]
Amer. Catholic Union [19567]
Amer. Maritain Assn. [10782]
Amer. St. Boniface Soc. [19568]
Anglican Use Assn. [19450]
Antilles Episcopal Conf. [IO]
Apostleship of Prayer [19569]
Apostleship of the Sea in the U.S.A. [19570]
Apostolate for Family Consecrations [19571]
Archconfraternity of Christian Mothers [19572]
Archconfraternity of the Holy Ghost [19573]
Assn. of Catholic Colleges and Universities [8051]
Assn. of Catholic Diocesan Archivists [9399]
Assn. for Christian Ethics [19574]
Assn. of Hebrew Catholics [19575]
Assn. of Jesuit Colleges and Universities [8052]
Assn. for Latin Liturgy [IO]
Assn. of Marian Helpers [19576]
Assn. of Mercy Colleges [8053]
Assn. of the Miraculous Medal [19577]
Assn. for the Rights of Catholics in the Church [19578]
Assn. of Romanian Catholics of America [19579]
Assn. of Theological Schools in the U.S. and Canada [9270]
Assumption Guild [19580]
Augustinian Secondary Educational Assn. [8054]
Australian Catholic Bishops' Conf. [IO]
Australian Catholic Social Justice Coun. [IO]
Auxiliaries of Our Lady of the Cenacle [19581]
Benedictines for Peace [19582]
Bishop Baraga Assn. and Archives [19583]
Bishops' Comm. for Ecumenical and Interreligious Affairs [19584]
Bishops' Comm. on the Liturgy [19585]
Bishops' Comm. on Priestly Formation [19917]
Bishops' Comm. on Vocations [19586]
Bishops' Conf. of Scotland [IO]
Black and Indian Mission Off. [19587]
Blessed Kateri Tekakwitha League [19588]
Blue Army of Our Lady of Fatima, U.S.A. [19589]
Bros. of Charity [IO]
Bros. of Christian Instruction of Saint Gabriel [IO]
Bros. of the Christian Schools [IO]
Bros. of the Immaculate Conception of the Blessed Virgin Mary [IO]
Bros. of Our Lady, Mother of Mercy [IO]
Bros. and Sisters of Penance of St. Francis [19590]
Bur. of Catholic Indian Missions [19591]
Cabrini Mission Corps [20308]
Calix Soc. [13227]
Campus Ministry Women [19918]
Canadian Assn. of the Sovereign Military Order of Malta [IO]
Canadian Catholic Historical Assn. [IO]
Canadian Catholic Org. for Development and Peace [IO]
Canadian Catholic Org. for Development and Peace - Alberta [IO]
Canadian Catholic Org. for Development and Peace - British Columbia [IO]
Canadian Catholic Org. for Development and Peace - Manitoba [IO]
Canadian Catholic Org. for Development and Peace - Montreal [IO]
Canadian Catholic Org. for Development and Peace - Newfoundland and Labrador [IO]
Canadian Catholic Org. for Development and Peace - Nova Scotia [IO]

Reference to "IO" in place of a book number signifies that the association may be found in the 45th edition of International Organizations.

Canadian Catholic Org. for Development and Peace - Ontario [IO]
Canadian Catholic Org. for Development and Peace - Quebec [IO]
Canadian Catholic Org. for Development and Peace - Saskatchewan [IO]
Canadian Catholic School Trustees Assn. [IO]
Canadian Catholic Students' Assn. [IO]
Canadian Conf. of Catholic Bishops [IO]
Canon Law Soc. of Am. [19592]
Canon Law Soc. of the Orthodox Catholic Church [19593]
Canon Law Society of the Orthodox Catholic Church [IO]
Capuchin-Franciscans (Province of Saint Joseph) [19594]
Catholic Acad. for Commun. Arts Professionals [9761]
Catholic Acad. of Sciences in the U.S.A. [19919]
Catholic Action for St. Children [IO]
Catholic Agency for Overseas Development [IO]
Catholic Aid Assn. [18990]
Catholic Assn. of Foresters [18991]
Catholic Biblical Assn. of Am. [9272]
Catholic Biblical Fed. [IO]
Catholic Bishops' Conf. of England and Wales [IO]
Catholic Bishops' Conf. of India [IO]
Catholic Bishops' Conf. of Malaysia, Singapore, and Brunei [IO]
Catholic Bishops' Conf. of Nigeria [IO]
Catholic Bishops' Conf. of the Philippines [IO]
Catholic Book Publishers Assn. [3214]
Catholic Campaign for Human Development [12713]
Catholic Campus Ministry Assn. [19595]
Catholic Cemetery Conf. [2776]
Catholic Central Union of Am. [13157]
Catholic Charities USA [13158]
Catholic Church Extension Soc. of the U.S.A. [19596]
Catholic Daughters of the Americas [18992]
Catholic Educational Assn. of the Philippines [IO]
Catholic Family Life Insurance [18993]
Catholic Golden Age [19597]
Catholic Guardian Soc. [11564]
Catholic Hea. Assn. of the U.S. [14874]
Catholic Inst. of the Food Indus. [19598]
Catholic Intl. Educ. Off. [IO]
Catholic Knights [18994]
Catholic Knights of America [18995]
Catholic Kolping Soc. of Am. [19599]
Catholic League for Religious and Civil Rights [19600]
Catholic Legal Immigration Network [20089]
Catholic Lib. Assn. [10344]
Catholic Life Insurance Union [18996]
Catholic Medical Assn. [15996]
Catholic Missions In Canada [IO]
Catholic Negro-Amer. Mission Bd. [19601]
Catholic Network of Volunteer Ser. [19602]
Catholic News Ser. [3103]
Catholic Order of Foresters [18997]
Catholic Pamphlet Soc. of the U.S. [19603]
Catholic Parents Network [12664]
Catholic Press Assn. [3215]
Catholic Record Soc. [IO]
Catholic Relief Services (U.S. Catholic Conf.) [12807]
Catholic Theological Soc. of Am. [9776]
Catholic Traditionalist Movement [19604]
Catholic Truth Soc. [IO]
Catholic War Veterans Auxiliary of the U.S.A. [21194]
Catholic War Veterans of the U.S.A. [21290]
Catholic Women's League Australia [IO]
Catholic Women's League of Canada [IO]
Catholic Women's League of New Zealand [IO]
Catholic Worker Movement [18109]
Catholic Workman [18998]
Catholics Speak Out [19605]
Catholics Speak Out [IO]
Catholics United for the Faith [IO]
Catholics United for the Faith [19606]
Catholics United for Life [12910]

CCVI Incarnate Word Missionaries - Congregation of the Sisters of Charity of the Incarnate Word [19607]
CCVI Incarnate Word Missionaries - Congregation of the Sisters of Charity of the Incarnate Word [IO]
Center for Applied Res. in the Apostolate [19608]
Central Assn. of the Miraculous Medal [19609]
Central Bur., Catholic Central Union of Am. [19610]
Centre Natl. de Pastorale Liturgique [IO]
Children's Friendship Proj. for Northern Ireland [13478]
Christian Life Community [IO]
The Christophers [19611]
Church Music Assn. of Am. [20428]
Claretian Volunteers and Lay Missionaries [19612]
Club of Catholic Intelligentsia [IO]
Coll. of St. Scholastica Alumni Assn. [18889]
Columbian Squires [18999]
Columbian Squires [IO]
Comm. on Social Development and World Peace of the U.S. Catholic Conf. [IO]
Comm. on Social Development and World Peace of the U.S. Catholic Conf. [19613]
Company of Saint Paul [19614]
Conf. for Catholic Lesbians [20051]
Conf. of Major Superiors of Men [19615]
Confraternity of Penitents [19616]
Congregation of the Blessed Sacrament [19617]
Congregation of the Holy Spirit [IO]
Congregation of La Retraite [IO]
Congregation of Saint Basil [IO]
Congregation of Sisters of Saint Agnes [19618]
CORPUS - Natl. Assn. for an Inclusive Priesthood [19619]
Corrosion Prevention Assn. [IO]
Coun. of European Bishops' Conferences [IO]
Courage [20052]
Crosier Missions [20325]
CUSA: An Apostolate of the Sick and Disabled [19620]
Daughters of Isabella, Intl. Circle [19000]
Daughters of Isabella, Intl. Circle [IO]
Daughters of Saint Paul - European Off. [IO]
Dignity/USA [20053]
Discalced Bros. of the Most Blessed Virgin Mary of Mount Carmel [IO]
Disciples Ecumenical Consultative Coun. [19848]
Dominican Mission Found. [20328]
Edith Stein Guild [19621]
European Comm. for Catholic Educ. [IO]
Family Rosary [19622]
Fed. of Diocesan Liturgical Commissions [19623]
Fellowship of Catholic Scholars [9777]
Fellowship of Concerned Churchmen [19454]
Fellowship of Saint James [19800]
Focolare Movement [19624]
Focolare Movement [IO]
Focolare Movement - Italy [IO]
Foundations and Donors Interested in Catholic Activities [19625]
Friends of Old St. Ferdinand [19626]
FutureChurch [19627]
Glenmary Res. Center [19628]
Good Tidings [19629]
Grailville [19630]
Guild of Catholic Lawyers [19631]
Help the Helpless [12405]
Holy Childhood Assn. [19632]
Holy Cross Foreign Mission Soc. [19633]
Holy Face Assn. [19634]
Holy Face Assn. [IO]
Holy Shroud Guild [19635]
Holy Spirit Stud. Centre [IO]
Humility of Mary Ser. [IO]
Humility of Mary Ser. [19636]
Hungarian Catholic Priests' Assn. in Am. [19637]
IHM Volunteer Prog. of the Sisters, Servants of the Immaculate Heart of Mary [20346]
Independent Catholic Churches Intl. [20497]
Inst. of Apostolic Oblates [19638]
Inst. on Religious Life [19639]
Instituto Nacional Hispano de Liturgia [19640]

Inter-American Confed. for Catholic Educ. [IO]
Intl. Assn. of Jesuit Bus. Schools [8026]
Intl. Assn. for Patristic Stud. [IO]
Intl. Catholic Child Bur. - Switzerland [IO]
Intl. Catholic Deaf Assn. - U.S. Sect. [19641]
Intl. Catholic Esperanto Assn. [9915]
Intl. Catholic Stewardship Coun. [IO]
Intl. Catholic Stewardship Coun. [19642]
Intl. Fed. of Catholic Parochial Youth Communities [IO]
Intl. Fed. of Catholic Universities [IO]
Intl. Fed. of Rural Adult Catholic Movements [IO]
Intl. Kolping Soc. [IO]
Intl. Movement of Catholic Agricultural and Rural Youth [IO]
Intl. Movement of Catholic Students - African Secretariat [IO]
Intl. Movement of Catholic Students - Pax Romana [IO]
International Order of Alhambra [IO]
Intl. Order of Alhambra [19001]
Intl. Young Catholic Students [IO]
Istituto Internazionale Suore di Santa Marcellina [IO]
Jesuit Conf. [19643]
Jesuit Philosophical Assn. [9778]
Jesuit Secondary Educ. Assn. [8055]
Jesuit Volunteer Corps: Northwest [19644]
John La Farge Inst. [19645]
Joint Action in Community Ser. [11803]
Junior Daughters of Peter Claver [19002]
Junior Knights of Peter Claver [19003]
Kappa Gamma Pi [24508]
Katholiek Vormingswerk van Landelijke Vrouwen [IO]
Knights of Columbus [IO]
Knights of Columbus [19004]
Knights of Peter Claver [19005]
Knights of Saint John Intl. [19006]
Knights of Saint John Intl. [IO]
Kreis Katholischer Frauen im Heliand-Bund [IO]
Ladies of Charity of the U.S.A. [13173]
Lasallian Volunteers [20352]
Latin Liturgy Assn. [19646]
Latin Mass Soc. [IO]
Lay Carmelite Order of the Blessed Virgin Mary of Mount Carmel [19647]
Lay Mission-Helpers Assn. [19648]
Lay Mission-Helpers Assn. [IO]
Leadership Conf. of Women Religious [19649]
League of St. Dymphna [19650]
League of Tarcisians [19651]
Legatus [19652]
Lithuanian Catholic Religious Aid [19653]
Little Apostoles of Charity [IO]
Little Company of Mary Generalate [IO]
Little Flower Mission League [19654]
Little Sisters of the Assumption - France [IO]
Little Sisters of Jesus [IO]
Lollard Soc. [20524]
Louis Finkelstein Inst. for Religious and Social Stud. at the Louis Stein Center [19931]
Madonna House Apostolate [IO]
Mariannhill Mission Soc. [19655]
Mariological Soc. of Am. [19656]
Marist Bros. of the Schools [IO]
Marriage Care [IO]
Maryheart Crusaders [19657]
Maryknoll Fathers and Bros. [19658]
Maryknoll Fathers and Bros. [IO]
Maryknoll Mission Assn. of the Faithful [20354]
Maryknoll Mission Center of New England [8660]
Maryknoll Sisters of Saint Dominic [20355]
Men of the Sacred Heart [19659]
Militia of the Immaculata Movement [19660]
Mission Doctors Assn. [12532]
Missionary Sisters of the Catholic Apostolate [IO]
Missionary Sisters of the Immaculate Heart of Mary [IO]
Missionary Sisters of Our Lady of the Holy Rosary [IO]
Missionary Sisters of Our Lady of the Holy Rosary [19661]
Missionary Sisters of the Precious Blood [IO]
Missionary Sisters of Saint Peter Claver [IO]

A star before a book entry number signifies that the name is not listed separately, but is mentioned within the entry.

Missionary Sisters of the Soc. of Mary - Marist Missionary Sisters [20365]
Missionary Soc. of Saint Columban [19662]
Missionary Soc. of Saint Columban [IO]
Missionary Soc. of Saint Paul the Apostle [19663]
Missionary Vehicle Assn. [20367]
Natl. Assn. of Boards, Commissions, and Councils of Catholic Educ. [8056]
Natl. Assn. of Catholic Family Life Ministers [20288]
Natl. Assn. of Catholic Homes and Educators [8057]
Natl. Assn. of Catholic Nurses - USA [15491]
Natl. Assn. of Catholic School Teachers [8058]
Natl. Assn. of Diaconate Directors [19664]
Natl. Assn. of Diocesan Ecumenical Officers [19901]
Natl. Assn. of Hispanic Priests of the USA [19665]
Natl. Assn. of the Holy Name Soc. [19666]
Natl. Assn. of Parish Catechetical Directors [19932]
Natl. Assn. of Pastoral Musicians [8920]
Natl. Assn. of Priest Pilots [19667]
Natl. Assn. of State Catholic Conf. Directors [19668]
Natl. Black Catholic Clergy Caucus [19669]
Natl. Black Catholic Cong. [19670]
Natl. Black Sisters' Conf. [19671]
Natl. Catholic Band Assn. [10661]
Natl. Catholic Coll. Admission Assn. [19672]
Natl. Catholic Conf. of Airport Chaplains [19754]
Natl. Catholic Conf. for Interracial Justice [17133]
Natl. Catholic Conf. for Total Stewardship [19673]
Natl. Catholic Coun. on Alcoholism and Related Drug Problems [13266]
Natl. Catholic Development Conf. [19674]
Natl. Catholic Educational Assn. [8059]
Natl. Catholic Educational Exhibitors [1347]
Natl. Catholic Forensic League [9156]
Natl. Catholic Off. for the Deaf [19675]
Natl. Catholic Partnership on Disability [19676]
Natl. Catholic Pharmacists Guild of the U.S. [15945]
Natl. Catholic Rural Life Conf. [19677]
National Catholic Rural Life Conference [IO]
Natl. Catholic Soc. of Foresters [19007]
Natl. Catholic Women's Union [19678]
Natl. Christ Child Soc. [19679]
Natl. Christian Life Community of the U.S.A. [19680]
Natl. Comm. of Catholic Laymen [19681]
Natl. Conf. for Catechetical Leadership [19934]
Natl. Conf. of Diocesan Vocation Directors [19682]
Natl. Coun. of Bishops, USA [19683]
Natl. Coun. of Catholic Women [19684]
Natl. Cursillo Movement [19685]
Natl. Enthronement Center [19686]
Natl. Evangelization Teams [19687]
Natl. Fed. for Catholic Youth Ministry [19688]
Natl. Fed. of Priests' Councils [19689]
Natl. Inst. for the Word of God [19690]
Natl. Off. for Black Catholics [19691]
Natl. Org. for Continuing Educ. of Roman Catholic Clergy [19936]
Natl. Religious Vocation Conf. [19692]
Natl. Right to Life Comm. [12923]
Natl. Ser. Committee/Chariscenter USA [19693]
Natl. Shrine of St. Elizabeth Ann Seton [19694]
NETWORK, A Natl. Catholic Social Justice Lobby [18624]
New Ways Ministry [20064]
Night Adoration in the Home [19695]
Nocturnal Adoration Soc. [19696]
North Amer. Assn. for the Catechumenate [19697]
North Amer. Assn. for the Catechumenate [IO]
North Amer. Conf. of Separated and Divorced Catholics [12013]
North Amer. Forum on the Catechumenate [19698]
Ontario Conf. of Catholic Bishops [IO]
ORACLE Religious Assn. [20070]
Order of the Canons Regular of Premontre [IO]
Order of Friars Minor [IO]
Order of Saint Augustine [IO]

Order of St. Lazarus [IO]
Ordinary Assembly of Catholics of the Holy Land [IO]
Passionists Intl. [IO]
Paul VI Inst. for the Arts [9591]
Paulist Memorial Soc. [19699]
Paulist Natl. Catholic Evangelization Assn. [19700]
Pax Romana, Intl. Catholic Movement for Intellectual and Cultural Affairs [IO]
Pious Union of Prayer [19701]
Pius X Secular Inst. [19702]
Pius X Secular Inst. [IO]
Pontifical Coun. for Culture [IO]
Pontifical Mission Societies - Canada [IO]
Pontifical Mission Societies in the U.S. [19703]
Pontifical Mission Soc. [IO]
Poor Cleric Regulars of the Mother of God of the Pious Schools [IO]
Presentation Bros. of Mary [IO]
Pro Maria Comm. [19704]
Pro Sanctity Movement [19705]
Proj. Children [11717]
Quixote Center [18628]
Raskob Found. for Catholic Activities [19706]
Raskob Found. for Catholic Activities [IO]
Regional Educ. Bd. of the Christian Bros. [8060]
Religious Bros. Conf. [19707]
Religious Formation Conf. [19708]
Religious and Military Order of Knights of the Holy Sepulchre of Jerusalem [19008]
Religious and Military Order of Knights of the Holy Sepulchre of Jerusalem [IO]
Reparation Soc. of the Immaculate Heart of Mary [19709]
Response-Ability [20386]
Retreats Intl. [19710]
Retreats Intl. [IO]
Sacred Heart League [19711]
St. Ansgar's Scandinavian Catholic League [19712]
St. Ansgar's Scandinavian Catholic League [IO]
St. Anthony's Guild [20388]
St. Joan's Intl. Alliance U.S. Sect. [17570]
Saint Joseph Congregation [IO]
St. Jude League [19713]
St. Martin De Porres Guild [20389]
Saint Patrick's Missionary Soc. [IO]
St. Thomas Aquinas Found. [19714]
St. Vincent Pallotti Center for Apostolic Development [20390]
Saints' Stories [19715]
Scandinavian Bishops Conf. [IO]
School Sisters of Notre Dame [IO]
Secretariat for Catholic-Jewish Relations [19910]
Secretariat for Family, Laity, Women, and Youth [12167]
Secular Inst. of Saint Francis de Sales [19716]
Secular Institute of Saint Francis de Sales [IO]
Secular Order of Discalced Carmelites [IO]
Serra Intl. [IO]
Serra Intl. [19717]
Sisters of Charity - Halifax [IO]
Sisters of Charity of Saint Jeanne Antide Thouret [IO]
Sisters of the Cross of Chavanod [IO]
Sisters of Divine Providence [IO]
Sisters of Our Lady of Charity of the Good Shepherd [IO]
Sisters of Saint Joseph of the Sacred Heart [IO]
Sisters of Saint Louis [IO]
Slovene Franciscan Fathers [19718]
SMA Lay Missionaries [20396]
Soc. of African Missions [19719]
Soc. of African Missions [IO]
Soc. of the Little Flower [19720]
Soc. of Missionaries of Africa [19721]
Soc. of Our Lady of the Most Holy Trinity [19722]
Soc. for the Propagation of the Faith [19723]
Soc. of Saint Mary Magdalene [19724]
Soc. of Saint Peter Apostle [19725]
Soc. of Saint Pius X [IO]
Soc. of St. Vincent de Paul Coun. of the U.S. [13190]
Soc. of Traditional Roman Catholics [19726]

Sons of Charity [IO]
Southern African Catholic Bishops' Conf. [IO]
Sozialdienst Katholischer Frauen [IO]
Support Our Aging Religious [11321]
Supreme Ladies Auxiliary Knights of Saint John [19009]
Survivors Network of Those Abused by Priests [13372]
Tekakwitha Conf. Natl. Center [19727]
Tertiary Capuchins of Our Lady of Sorrows [IO]
Third Order of Carmel [IO]
Third Order of Mary/Marists [19728]
Thomas More Assn. [19729]
Trinity Hea. Intl. [14731]
Ukrainian Patriarchal World Fed. [19730]
Union of German Catholic Women [IO]
United Catholic Music and Video Assn. [19731]
United Hasroun Men's and St. Laba Ladies Charity Societies [19732]
U.S. Assn. of Consecrated Virgins [19733]
U.S. Catholic Conference/Migration and Refugee Services [12823]
U.S. Catholic Mission Assn. [19734]
U.S. Conf. of Catholic Bishops [19735]
Unmarried-Catholics Correspondence Club [22145]
Volunteer Missionary Movement - U.S. Off. [19736]
Wanderer Forum Found. [19737]
We Believe! [19738]
Western Catholic Union [19010]
Women Affirming Life [12931]
Women for Faith and Family [19739]
Women's Ordination Conf. [19740]
World Union of Catholic Women's Organisations [IO]
Worldwide Marriage Encounter [12510]
Xavier Soc. for the Blind [16892]
Catholic Acad. for Commun. Arts Professionals [9761], 1645 Brook Lynn Dr., Ste. 2, Dayton, OH 45432-1933, (937)458-0265
Catholic Acad. of Sciences in the U.S.A. [19919], PO Box 9611, Washington, DC 20016
Catholic Access Network - Deus Lumen Est! - Address unknown since 2001.
Catholic Accountants Guild - Defunct.
Catholic Action for St. Children [IO], Accra, Ghana
Catholic Actors Guild of America - Address unknown since 2002.
Catholic Agency for Overseas Development [IO], London, United Kingdom
Catholic Aid Assn. [18990], 3499 Lexington Ave. N, St. Paul, MN 55126, (651)490-0170
Catholic AIDS Network; Natl. [13579]
Catholic Alliance of Am; Lithuanian [★19212]
Catholic Alliance for Communications - Defunct.
Catholic Alliance; Lithuanian [19212]
Catholic Alumni Clubs, Intl. [18885], c/o Mr. Michael Coogan, Pres., 13517 Teakwood Ln., Germantown, MD 20874-1034, (301)916-6336
Catholic Alumni Clubs, Intl. [IO], Germantown, MD, United States
Catholic Anthropological Assn. - Defunct.
Catholic Apostolate of Radio, TV and Advertising - Defunct.
Catholic Art Assn. - Defunct.
Catholic Artists of America - Defunct.
Catholic Assn. for Communicators; UNDA U.S.A. Natl. [★9761]
Catholic Assn. of Foreign Language Teachers - Defunct.
Catholic Assn. of Foresters [18991], 182 Forbes Rd., Ste. 119, Braintree, MA 02184-2693, (781)848-8221
Catholic Assn. for Intl. Peace - Defunct.
Catholic Assn. of Persons With Visual Impairment - Defunct.
Catholic Audio Visual Educators Assn. - Address unknown since 2001.
Catholic Aviation League of Our Lady of Loreto - Defunct.
Catholic Band Assn; Natl. [10661]
Catholic Bandmasters' Assn; Natl. [★10661]
Catholic Benevolent Assn; Ladies [★19129]
Catholic Benevolent Legion; Supreme Coun. [★19004]

Reference to "IO" in place of a book number signifies that the association may be found in the 45th edition of International Organizations.

Catholic Bible Soc. of America - Defunct.

Catholic Biblical Assn. of Am. [9272], c/o Catholic Univ. of Am., 433 Caldwell Hall, Washington, DC 20064, (202)319-5519

Catholic Biblical Fed. [IO], Stuttgart, Germany

Catholic Bishops' Conf. of England and Wales [IO], London, United Kingdom

Catholic Bishops' Conf. of India [IO], New Delhi, India

Catholic Bishops' Conf. of Malaysia, Singapore, and Brunei [IO], Kuala Lumpur, Malaysia

Catholic Bishops' Conf. of Nigeria [IO], Lagos, Nigeria

Catholic Bishops' Conf. of the Philippines [IO], Manila, Philippines

Catholic Bishops; Natl. Conf. of [★19735]

Catholic Bishops; Secretariat for Hispanic Affairs/ National Conf. of [★12282]

Catholic Bishops; Secretariat for Hispanic Affairs, U.S. Conf. of [12282]

Catholic Bd. for Mission Work Among the Colored People [★19601]

Catholic Book Publishers Assn. [3214], 8404 Jamesport Dr., Rockford, IL 61108-7030, (815)332-3245

Catholic Broadcasters Assn. [★9761]

Catholic Campaign for Human Development [12713], 3211 4th St. NE, Washington, DC 20017-1194, (202)541-3210

Catholic Campus Ministry Assn. [19595], 1118 Pendleton St., Ste. 300, Cincinnati, OH 45202-8805, (513)842-0167

Catholic Cemetery Conf. [2776], 1400 S Wolf Rd., Bldg. No. 3, Hillside, IL 60162-2197, (708)202-1242

Catholic Cemetery Conf; National [★2776]

Catholic Central Union [★18997]

Catholic Central Union of Am. [13157], 3835 Westminster Pl., St. Louis, MO 63108, (314)371-1653

Catholic Central Verein of Am. [★13157]

Catholic Central Youth Union of America - Defunct.

Catholic Chaplains; Natl. Assn. of [19753]

Catholic Charities; Natl. Conf. of [★13158]

Catholic Charities USA [13158], 1731 King St., Alexandria, VA 22314, (703)549-1390

Catholic Charity; American-Albanian [★18506]

Catholic Church Extension Soc. of Canada [★IO]

Catholic Church Extension Soc. of the U.S.A. [19596], 150 S Wacker Dr., 20th Fl., Chicago, IL 60606, (888)473-2484

Catholic Civics Clubs of America - Defunct.

Catholic Clergy; Natl. Org. for Continuing Educ. of Roman [19936]

Catholic Coll. Teachers of Sacred Doctrine; Soc. of [★9273]

Catholic Commn. for Development - Zambia [IO], Lusaka, Zambia

Catholic Commn. on Intellectual and Cultural Affairs - Defunct.

Catholic Commn. for Justice, Peace and Development [★IO]

Catholic Comm. of Appalachia [20311], 213 Orchard Run Rd., Spencer, WV 25276, (304)927-5798

Catholic Comm. on Scouting [★13001]

Catholic Comm. on Scouting; Natl. [13001]

Catholic Comm. on Urban Ministry - Defunct.

Catholic Communications Foundation [★18994]

Catholic Conf. of Airport Chaplains; Natl. [19754]

Catholic Conf; Family Life Div., U.S. [★12167]

Catholic Conf; Family Life Ministry, U.S. [★12167]

Catholic Conf. on Family Life; Natl. [★12167]

Catholic Conf. for Interracial Justice; Natl. [17133]

Catholic Conference/Migration and Refugee Services; U.S. [12823]

Catholic Conference/Migration and Refugee Services; U.S. [★12823]

Catholic Conf. Migration and Refugee Services; U.S. [★12823]

Catholic Conf; U.S. [★19735]

Catholic Conf; Youth Ministry, U.S. [★12167]

Catholic Coordinating Center for Lay Missioners; Intl. Liaison U.S. [★19602]

Catholic Coordinating Center for Lay Volunteer Ministries; Intl. Liaison, U.S. [★19602]

Catholic Correctional Chaplains Assn; Amer. [19741]

Catholic Coun. on Alcoholism and Related Drug Problems; Natl. [13266]

Catholic Coun. on Civil Liberties - Defunct.

Catholic Coun. on Working Life - Address unknown since 2008.

Catholic Counselors in APGA [★8166]

Catholic Daughters of Am. [★18992]

Catholic Daughters of the Americas [18992], 10 W 71st St., New York, NY 10023, (212)877-3041

Catholic Dept. of Defense [★19564]

Catholic Development Commn. - Caritas Zimbabwe [IO], Harare, Zimbabwe

Catholic Development Commn. in Malawi - Caritas Malawi [IO], Lilongwe, Malawi

Catholic Diocesan Archivists; Assn. of [9399]

Catholic Diocesan Family Life Ministers; Natl. Assn. of [★20288]

Catholic Economic Assn. [★6873]

Catholic Educ. Assn. [★8059]

Catholic Educ. Assn; Coll. and Univ. Dept. of the Natl. [★8051]

Catholic Educational Assn. of the Philippines [IO], Quezon City, Philippines

Catholic Educational Exhibitors; Natl. [1347]

Catholic Esperanto Union; Intl. [★9915]

Catholic Evidence Guild - Defunct.

Catholic Evidence Guild, Natl. Center - Defunct.

Catholic Evidence Guild of New York - Defunct.

Catholic Extension [★19596]

Catholic Family History Soc. [IO], Enfield, United Kingdom

Catholic Family Life Insurance [18993], PO Box 11563, Milwaukee, WI 53211-0563, (414)961-0500

Catholic Family Life Ministers; Natl. Assn. of [20288]

Catholic Family Protective Life Assurance Soc. [★18993]

Catholic Family Services of Regina [IO], Regina, SK, Canada

Catholic Family Services Windsor-Essex County [IO], Windsor, ON, Canada

Catholic Fed. of America; Lithuanian Roman [19214]

Catholic Fed. of Am; Slovak [★19364]

Catholic Fed. Central Coun; Italian [19163]

Catholic Fed; Slovak [19364]

Catholic Fine Arts Soc. [9562]

Catholic Forensic League; Natl. [9156]

Catholic Golden Age [19597], PO Box 249, Olyphant, PA 18447, (800)836-5699

Catholic Golden Age Found. [★19597]

Catholic Guardian Soc. [11564], 1011 1st Ave., New York, NY 10022, (212)371-1000

Catholic Guidance Conf; Natl. [★8166]

Catholic Guidance Councils; Natl. Conf. of [★8166]

Catholic Guild for All the Blind [★16840]

Catholic Hea. Assn. of Canada [IO], Ottawa, ON, Canada

Catholic Hea. Assn. of the U.S. [14874], 4455 Woodson Rd., St. Louis, MO 63134-3797, (314)427-2500

Catholic Healthcare Audit Network [8240], 231 S Bemiston Ave., Ste. 300, Clayton, MO 63105, (314)802-2000

Catholic Historical Assn; Amer. [10085]

Catholic Historical Soc; Amer. [10086]

Catholic Homesteading Movement [11742]

Catholic Hosp. Assn. [★14874]

Catholic Hosp. Assn. of U.S. and Canada [★14874]

Catholic Info. Center; Albanian [★18506]

Catholic Information Soc. - Defunct.

Catholic Inst. of the Food Indus. [19598]

Catholic Inst. for Intl. Relations [★IO]

Catholic Intelligentsia Clubs [★IO]

Catholic Inter-Amer. Cooperation Program - Defunct.

Catholic Intl. Educ. Off. [IO], Brussels, Belgium

Catholic Interracial Coun. of Chicago - Address unknown since 1995.

Catholic Interracial Coun. of New York - Defunct.

Catholic-Jewish Relations; Secretariat for [19910]

Catholic-Jewish Relations; Subcommn. for [★19910]

Catholic Knights [18994], 1100 W Wells St., Milwaukee, WI 53233, (414)273-6266

Catholic Knights of America [18995]

Catholic Knights Insurance Soc. [★18994]

Catholic Knights of Saint George [★19144]

Catholic Kolping Soc. of Am. [19599], c/o Patricia Farkas, Natl. Admin., 9 E 8th St., Clifton, NJ 07011, (201)712-9550

Catholic League for Religious Assistance to Poland - Address unknown since 1999.

Catholic League for Religious and Civil Rights [19600], 450 Seventh Ave., New York, NY 10123, (212)371-3191

Catholic Legal Immigration Network [20089], 415 Michigan Ave. NE, Ste. 150, Washington, DC 20017, (202)635-2556

Catholic Lesbians; Conf. for [20051]

Catholic Lib. Assn. [10344], 100 North St., Ste. 224, Pittsfield, MA 01201-5109, (413)443-2252

Catholic Life Insurance Union [18996], PO Box 659527, San Antonio, TX 78265-9527, (210)828-9921

Catholic Major Markets Newspaper Assn. - Defunct.

Catholic Marriage Advisory Coun. [★IO]

Catholic Media Coun. [IO], Aachen, Germany

Catholic Medical Assn. [15996], 333 E Lancaster Ave., No. 348, Wynnewood, PA 19096-1929, (215)877-9099

Catholic Medical Mission Bd. [12515], 10 W 17th St., New York, NY 10011-5765, (212)242-7757

Catholic Medical Mission Bd. [IO], New York, NY, United States

Catholic Microfilm Center - Defunct.

Catholic Mission Coun; U.S. [★19734]

Catholic Missions In Canada [IO], Toronto, ON, Canada

Catholic Music Educators Assn; Natl. [★8920]

Catholic Mutual Aid Soc. of U.S.A; Russian Orthodox [19341]

Catholic Near East Welfare Assn. [18054], 1011 1st Ave., New York, NY 10022-4195, (212)826-1480

Catholic Near East Welfare Assn. [IO], New York, NY, United States

Catholic Negro-Amer. Mission Bd. [19601]

Catholic Network of Lay Mission Programs; Intl. Liaison of Lay Volunteers in Mission U.S. [★19602]

Catholic Network of Volunteer Ser. [19602], 6930 Carroll Ave., Ste. 506, Takoma Park, MD 20912-4423, (301)270-0900

Catholic News Ser. [3103], 3211 4th St. NE, Washington, DC 20017, (202)541-3250

Catholic Order of Foresters [18997], PO Box 3012, Naperville, IL 60566-7012, (630)983-4900

Catholic Order of Foresters; Massachusetts [★18991]

Catholic Order of Foresters; Women's [★19007]

Catholic Organist Alliance; Amer. Lithuanian Roman [★10540]

Catholic Org. for Joint Financing of Development Programmmes [★IO]

Catholic Pamphlet Soc. of the U.S. [19603]

Catholic Parents Network [12664], 4012 29th St., Mount Rainier, MD 20712, (301)277-5674

Catholic Peace Fellowship [18194], PO Box 4232, South Bend, IN 46634, (574)232-2811

Catholic Pharmacists Guild of the U.S; Natl. [15945]

Catholic Philosophical Assn; Amer. [8965]

Catholic Physicians Guilds; Natl. Fed. of [★15996]

Catholic Poetry Soc. of America - Defunct.

Catholic Press Assn. [3215], 3555 Veterans Memorial Hwy., Unit O, Ronkonkoma, NY 11779, (631)471-4730

Catholic Press Soc; Lithuanian [19213]

Catholic Prison Chaplains Assn; Amer. [★19741]

Catholic Psychological Assn; Amer. [★16132]

Catholic Record Soc. [IO], Durham, United Kingdom

Catholic Relief Services - El Salvador [IO], San Salvador, El Salvador

Catholic Relief Services - Natl. Catholic Welfare Conf. [★IO]

Catholic Relief Services - Natl. Catholic Welfare Conf. [★12807]

Catholic Relief Services (U.S. Catholic Conf.) [12807], 228 W Lexington St., Baltimore, MD 21201-3413, (410)625-2220

Catholic Relief Services (U.S. Catholic Conf.) [IO], Baltimore, MD, United States

Catholic Renascence Soc. - Defunct.

Catholic Scholarships for Negroes - Defunct.

Catholic School Press Assn. - Defunct.

Catholic Slovak Ladies Assn; First [19361]

Catholic Slovak Union of the U.S.A. and Canada; First [19362]

A star before a book entry number signifies that the name is not listed separately, but is mentioned within the entry.

Catholic Social Justice Lobby; NETWORK, A Natl. **[18624]**

Catholic Soc; Amer. Hungarian **[★19144]**

Catholic Soc. for Animal Welfare; Natl. **[★11419]**

Catholic Sociological Soc; Amer. **[★7661]**

Catholic Sokol; Junior Slovak **[★19365]**

Catholic Sokol; Slovak **[19365]**

Catholic Stewardship Coun; Natl. **[★19642]**

Catholic Students Mission Crusade - Defunct.

Catholic Tape Recorders, Intl. - Defunct.

Catholic Theological Soc. of Am. **[9776]**, c/o Dr. Dolores Christie, Exec. Dir., John Carroll Univ., 20700 N Park Blvd., University Heights, OH 44118, (216)397-1631

Catholic Thought Soc. - Defunct.

Catholic Total Abstinence Union of America - Address unknown since 1995.

Catholic Traditionalist Movement **[19604]**, 210 Maple Ave., Westbury, NY 11590-3117, (516)333-6470

Catholic Truth Soc. **[IO]**, London, United Kingdom

Catholic Union of Am; Archives and Museum of the Polish **[★10882]**

Catholic Union of Am; Polish Roman **[19314]**

Catholic Union; Czech **[19027]**

Catholic Union of the Sick in Am. **[★19620]**

Catholic Union; South Slavonic **[★19119]**

Catholic Union; Supreme Coun. of the Western **[★19010]**

Catholic Union of U.S.A. and Canada; Croatian **[19021]**

Catholic Union of the U.S.A; Croatian **[★19021]**

Catholic Union of the U.S.A; Greek **[19088]**

Catholic Union; Western Bohemian **[★18998]**

Catholic Unity; Comm. for **[★19726]**

Catholic Unity League - Defunct.

Catholic War Veterans Auxiliary of the U.S.A. **[21194]**, 441 N Lee St., Alexandria, VA 22314-2301, (703)549-3622

Catholic War Veterans of the U.S.A. **[21290]**, 441 N Lee St., Alexandria, VA 22314, (703)549-3622

Catholic War Veterans of the U.S.A. Auxiliary **[★21194]**

Catholic Welfare Conf; Catholic Relief Services - Natl. **[★12807]**

Catholic Welfare Conf; War Relief Services - Natl. **[★12807]**

Catholic Women for the ERA - Address unknown since 2003.

Catholic Women's Alliance; Lithuanian Amer. Roman **[19211]**

Catholic Women's Benevolent Legion - Address unknown since 1995.

Catholic Women's League Australia **[IO]**, Braddon, Australia

Catholic Women's League of Canada **[IO]**, Winnipeg, MB, Canada

Catholic Women's League of New Zealand **[IO]**, Hamilton, New Zealand

Catholic Women's Seminary Fund - Defunct.

Catholic Worker Movement **[18109]**, 36 E 1st St., New York, NY 10003, (212)777-9617

Catholic Workman **[18998]**, 1201 1st St. NE, New Prague, MN 56071, (952)758-2229

Catholic Writers' Guild of America - Defunct.

Catholic Youth Adoration Soc. - Defunct.

Catholic Youth Councils; Natl. Fed. of Diocesan **[★19688]**

Catholic Youth League; Ukrainian **[★19411]**

Catholics of Am; League of Ukrainian **[19411]**

Catholics in Am; Providence Assn. of Ukrainian **[19413]**

Catholics for Chile - Defunct.

Catholics for Christian Political Action - Defunct.

Catholics Correspondence Club; Unmarried- **[22145]**

Catholics for a Free Choice **[18515]**, 1436 U St. NW, Ste. 301, Washington, DC 20009-3997, (202)986-6093

Catholics; Natl. Alliance of Czech **[19029]**

Catholics; North Amer. Conf. of Separated and Divorced **[12013]**

Catholics Speak Out **[19605]**, PO Box 5206, Hyattsville, MD 20782, (301)699-0042

Catholics Speak Out **[IO]**, Hyattsville, MD, United States

Catholics United for the Faith **[IO]**, Steubenville, OH, United States

Catholics United for the Faith **[19606]**, 827 N 4th St., Steubenville, OH 43952, (740)283-2484

Catholics United for Life **[12910]**, 3050 Gap Knob Rd., New Hope, KY 40052-6927, (502)325-3061

Catholics United for Spiritual Action **[★19620]**

Cathy Buchanan Fan Club - Address unknown since 1989.

Cathy Collectors Club; Chatty **[22393]**

Cationic Flocculant Producers Assn. - Defunct.

Catlow/Whitney Family Org. - Defunct.

CatNet Echo Mail Network - Address unknown since 1999.

Cato Inst. **[18425]**, 1000 Massachusetts Ave. NW, Washington, DC 20001-5401, (202)842-0200

Caton Family Assn. **[20814]**

Cats and Cat Owners Aid - Defunct.

Cats; Harmony House for **[11404]**

Cats Protection **[IO]**, Sussex, United Kingdom

Cats Protection **[IO]**, Haywards Heath, United Kingdom

Cats on Stamps Stud. Unit **[22801]**, c/o Mary Ann Brown, Sec.-Treas., 3006 Wade Rd., Durham, NC 27705

Cattle

Aberdeen-Angus Cattle Soc. **[IO]**

Alberta Angus Assn. **[IO]**

Amer. Angus Assn. **[4212]**

Amer. Beefalo World Registry **[4123]**

Amer. Belgian Blue Breeders **[4213]**

Amer. Black Hereford Assn. **[4214]**

Amer. Blonde d'Aquitaine Assn. **[4215]**

Amer. Brahman Breeders Assn. **[4216]**

Amer. Brahmousin Coun. **[4217]**

Amer. British White Park Assn. **[4218]**

Amer. Chianina Assn. **[4219]**

Amer. Devon Cattle Assn. **[4220]**

Amer. Dexter Cattle Assn. **[4221]**

Amer. Galloway Breeders' Assn. **[4222]**

Amer. Gelbvieh Assn. **[4223]**

Amer. Guernsey Assn. **[4224]**

Amer. Hereford Assn. **[4225]**

Amer. Herens Assn. **[4226]**

Amer. Highland Cattle Assn. **[4227]**

American-International Charolais Assn. **[4228]**

American-International Charolais Association **[IO]**

Amer. Intl. Marchigiana Soc. **[4229]**

Amer. Jersey Cattle Assn. **[4230]**

Amer. Junior Brahman Assn. **[4231]**

Amer. Junior Chianina Assn. **[4232]**

Amer. Junior Shorthorn Assn. **[4233]**

Amer. Maine-Anjou Assn. **[4234]**

Amer. Milking Devon Cattle Assn. **[4235]**

Amer. Milking Shorthorn Junior Soc. **[4236]**

Amer. Milking Shorthorn Soc. **[4237]**

Amer. Miniature Jersey Cattle Registry **[4238]**

Amer. Murray Grey Assn. **[4239]**

Amer. Natl. CattleWomen **[4240]**

Amer. Pinzgauer Assn. **[4241]**

Amer. Red Brangus Assn. **[4242]**

Amer. Red Poll Assn. **[4243]**

Amer. Romagnola Assn. **[4244]**

Amer. Salers Assn. **[4245]**

Amer. Salers Junior Assn. **[4246]**

Amer. Shorthorn Assn. **[4247]**

Amer. Simmental Assn. **[4248]**

Amer. Tarentaise Assn. **[4249]**

Amer. Wagyu Assn. **[4250]**

American Wagyu Association **[IO]**

Amerifax Cattle Assn. **[4251]**

Angus Soc. of Australia **[IO]**

Angus Youth Australia **[IO]**

Ankole Watusi Intl. Registry **[IO]**

Ankole Watusi Intl. Registry **[4252]**

Australian Beef Assn. **[IO]**

Australian Braford Soc. **[IO]**

Australian Brahman Breeders' Assn. **[IO]**

Australian Braunvieh Assn. **[IO]**

Australian Cattle Dog Club of Am. **[22221]**

Australian Galloway Assn. **[IO]**

Australian Gelbvieh Assn. **[IO]**

Australian Hereford Soc. **[IO]**

Australian Highland Cattle Soc. **[IO]**

Australian Red Poll Cattle Breeders **[IO]**

Australian Simmental Breeders Assn. **[IO]**

Australian Wagyu Assn. **[IO]**

Ayrshire Breeders' Assn. **[4253]**

Ayrshire Breeders' Assn. of Canada **[IO]**

Barzona Breeders Assn. of Am. **[4254]**

Beefmaster Breeders United **[4255]**

Belted Galloway Soc. **[4256]**

Brangus Soc. of South Africa **[IO]**

Braunvieh Assn. of Am. **[4257]**

British Belgian Blue Cattle Soc. **[IO]**

Brown Swiss Cattle Breeders Assn. of the U.S.A. **[4258]**

Buelingo Beef Cattle Soc. **[4259]**

Bukovina Soc. of the Americas **[4260]**

Canadian Aberdeen Angus Assn. **[IO]**

Canadian Angus Assn. **[IO]**

Canadian Beef Breeds Coun. **[IO]**

Canadian Blonde d'Aquitaine Assn. **[IO]**

Canadian Brown Swiss and Braunvieh Assn. **[IO]**

Canadian Cattlemen's Assn. **[IO]**

Canadian Charolais Assn. **[IO]**

Canadian Dexter Cattle Assn. **[IO]**

Canadian Galloway Assn. **[IO]**

Canadian Gelbvieh Assn. **[IO]**

Canadian Guernsey Assn. **[IO]**

Canadian Hays Converter Assn. **[IO]**

Canadian Hereford Assn. **[IO]**

Canadian Highland Cattle Soc. **[IO]**

Canadian Limousin Assn. **[IO]**

Canadian Maine-Anjou Assn. **[IO]**

Canadian Milking Shorthorn Soc. **[IO]**

Canadian Murray Grey Assn. **[IO]**

Canadian Pinzgauer Assn. **[IO]**

Canadian Red Angus Promotion Soc. **[IO]**

Canadian Red Poll Cattle Assn. **[IO]**

Canadian Shorthorn Assn. **[IO]**

Canadian Simmental Assn. **[IO]**

Canadian Tarentaise Assn. **[IO]**

Canadian Welsh Black Cattle Soc. **[IO]**

Cattle Breeders' Assn. of Turkey **[IO]**

Cattlemen's Beef Promotion and Res. Bd. **[4261]**

Charolais Soc. of Australia **[IO]**

CME Group **[4324]**

Cowboys for Christ **[19792]**

Danish Galloway Soc. **[IO]**

Dexter Cattle Soc. New Zealand **[IO]**

Food Safety Consortium **[5031]**

Galloway Cattle and Beef Marketing Assn. **[IO]**

Galloway Cattle Soc. of Great Britain and Ireland **[IO]**

Gelbray Intl. **[IO]**

Gelbray Intl. **[4262]**

German Holstein Assn. **[IO]**

Herefords Australia Ltd. **[IO]**

Highland Cattle Soc. **[IO]**

Holstein Assn. USA **[4263]**

Holstein Cattle Breeders' Assn. of the Czech Republic **[IO]**

Holstein Junior Prog. **[4264]**

Intl. Brangus Breeders Assn. **[4265]**

Intl. Junior Brangus Breeders Assn. **[4266]**

International Junior Brangus Breeders Association **[IO]**

Intl. Miniature Cattle Breeders Soc. and Registry **[4267]**

Intl. Miniature Zebu Assn. **[4268]**

Intl. Soc. for Cow Protection **[4155]**

Intl. Texas Longhorn Assn. **[4269]**

International Texas Longhorn Association **[IO]**

Intl. Yak Assn. **[5001]**

Irish Angus Cattle Soc. **[IO]**

Irish Blacks Assn. **[4270]**

Irish Holstein Friesian Assn. **[IO]**

Irish Moiled Cattle Soc. **[IO]**

Lithuanian Assn. of Beef Cattle Breeders and Improvers **[IO]**

Longhorn Cattle Soc. **[IO]**

Marky Cattle Assn. **[4271]**

Miniature Hereford Breeders Assn. **[4272]**

Natl. Amer. Indian Cattlemen's Assn. **[4273]**

Natl. Beef Assn. **[IO]**

Natl. Bison Assn. **[4139]**

Natl. Coun. of Brown Swiss Cattle Breeders of Australia **[IO]**

Natl. Dairy Herd Improvement Assn. **[4274]**

Natl. Junior Angus Assn. **[4275]**

Natl. Junior Hereford Assn. **[4276]**

Reference to "IO" in place of a book number signifies that the association may be found in the 45th edition of International Organizations.

Natl. Junior Santa Gertrudis Assn. **[4277]**
Natl. Reined Cow Horse Assn. **[22586]**
New Zealand Holstein Friesian Assn. **[IO]**
North Amer. Corriente Assn. **[4278]**
North Amer. Limousin Found. **[4279]**
North Amer. Limousin Junior Assn. **[4280]**
North Amer. Normande Assn. **[4281]**
North Amer. Piedmontese Assn. **[4282]**
North American Piedmontese Association **[IO]**
North Amer. Romagnola and RomAngus Assn. **[4283]**
North Amer. South Devon Assn. **[4284]**
North Amer. Tuli Assn. **[4285]**
Parthenais Cattle Breeders Assn. **[4286]**
Piedmontese Assn. of the U.S. **[4287]**
Public Lands Coun. **[5127]**
Purebred Dairy Cattle Assn. **[4288]**
Purebred Dexter Cattle Assn. of North Am. **[4289]**
Ranchers-Cattlemen Action Legal Fund, United Stockgrowers of Am. **[4290]**
Red Angus Assn. of Am. **[4291]**
Red Poll Cattle Soc. **[IO]**
Salers Assn. of Canada **[IO]**
Salers Cattle Soc. of the UK and Ireland **[IO]**
Santa Gertrudis Breeders Intl. **[IO]**
Santa Gertrudis Breeders Intl. **[4292]**
Saskatchewan Angus Assn. **[IO]**
Senepol Cattle Breeders Assn. **[4293]**
South African Holstein Breeders' Assn. **[IO]**
Texas Longhorn Breeders Assn. of Am. **[4294]**
United Braford Breeders **[4295]**
U.S. Calf Ropers Assn. **[23695]**
Welsh Black Cattle Soc. **[IO]**
Whitebred Shorthorn Assn. **[IO]**
Women in Livestock Development **[IO]**
Women in Livestock Development **[4296]**
World Holstein-Friesian Fed. **[IO]**
World Jersey Cattle Bur. **[IO]**
World Watusi Assn. **[IO]**
World Watusi Assn. **[4297]**
Cattle Assn. of Am; White Park **[★4218]**
Cattle Breeders' Assn; Amer. Belted Galloway **[★4256]**
Cattle Breeders' Assn. of Turkey **[IO]**, Ankara, Turkey
Cattle Club of Am; Red Poll **[★4243]**
Cattle Club; Amer. Devon **[★4220]**
Cattle Club; Amer. Guernsey **[★4224]**
Cattle Club; Amer. Jersey **[★4230]**
Cattle Dog Club of Am; Australian **[22221]**
Cattle Veterinary Assn; British **[IO]**
Cattlemen's Beef Assn; Natl. **[5023]**
Cattlemen's Beef Promotion and Res. Bd. **[4261]**, 9000 E Nichols Ave., Ste. 303, Centennial, CO 80112-3450, (303)220-9890
Cattlett Fan Club; Mary Jo **[24759]**
CattleWomen; Amer. Natl. **[4240]**
Catweazle Fan Club **[IO]**, Blackburn, United Kingdom
Caucasian Ovcharka Club of Am. **[22241]**, PO Box 227, Chardon, OH 44024, (440)286-2374
Caucasus Environmental NGO Network **[IO]**, Tbilisi, Georgia
Caucus-Association of High Tech Procurement Professionals **[7373]**, Drawer 2970, Winter Park, FL 32790-2970, (407)740-5600
Caucus of Black Anthropologists **[★6409]**
Caucus of Black Economists **[★6888]**
Caucus of Black Sociologists **[★7659]**
Caucus on Children's Rights **[★11583]**
Caucus on Children's Rights **[★IO]**
Caucus of Gay Counselors **[★12216]**
Caucus of Gay, Lesbian, and Bisexual Members of the Amer. Psychiatric Assn. **[★12217]**
Caucus for a New Political Sci. **[7523]**, c/o Meredith Reid Sarkees, 4802 Wyoming Way, Crystal Lake, IL 60012-2037, (815)444-0692
Caucus of Radical Engineers - Defunct.
Caucus for TV Producers, Writers, and Directors **[17165]**, PO Box 11236, Burbank, CA 91510-1236, (818)843-7572
Caucus for Women in Statistics **[7703]**, c/o Anna Nevius, Treas., 7732 Rydal Terr., Rockville, MD 20855-2057, (301)827-0170
Caucus for Women in Statistics **[IO]**, Rockville, MD, United States

CAUSA Inst. - Address unknown since 1999.
CAUSA Intl. **[16990]**, 401 5th Ave., New York, NY 10016
CAUSA Intl. **[IO]**, New York, NY, United States
CAUSA USA - Defunct.
Cause for Concern - Defunct.
Cavalier King Charles Spaniel Club of Am. **[22242]**, PO Box 330, Conway, NH 03818, (603)447-5218
Cavalier King Charles Spaniel Club; Amer. **[22194]**
Cavalry Assn. and Memorial Res. Lib; U.S. **[10484]**
Cavalry Assn; U.S. **[★6107]**
Cavalry Assn; U.S. Armored **[★6107]**
Cavalry Assn; U.S. Horse **[★10484]**
Cavanagh's Coca-Cola Collectors' Soc. **[21991]**, 11455 Lakefield Dr., Ste. 400, Duluth, GA 30097, (678)366-2800
CAVDA-Citizens AIDS Proj. **[13562]**, 800 W Central Rd., Ste. 128, Mount Prospect, IL 60056, (847)398-3378
Cave Conservation Assn; Amer. **[4345]**
Cave Diving; Natl. Assn. for **[23962]**
Cave Res. Associates - Defunct.
Cave Res. Assn; British **[IO]**
Cave Res. Found. **[7692]**, c/o Bob Hoke, Treas., 6304 Kaybro St., Laurel, MD 20707-2621
Cave Survey; Guadalupe **[★7692]**
CAVEAT BC (Canadians Against Violence) **[IO]**, Langley, BC, Canada
Caveat (Canadians Against Violence Everywhere Advocating its Termination) **[★IO]**
Caves Assn; Natl. **[1319]**
Cavity Res. Gp; Brine **[★2755]**
Cavy Breeders Assn; Amer. **[4124]**
Cavy Breeders Assn; Amer. Rabbit and **[★5139]**
Cayman Golf Assn. - Address unknown since 2000.
Cayman Insurance Managers Assn. **[★IO]**

Cayman Islands
Cayman Islands Dept. of Tourism **[24256]**
Cayman Islands Amateur Athletic Assn. **[IO]**, Grand Cayman, Cayman Islands
Cayman Islands Badminton Assn. **[IO]**, Grand Cayman, Cayman Islands
Cayman Islands Chamber of Commerce **[IO]**, Grand Cayman, Cayman Islands
Cayman Islands Dept. of Tourism **[24256]**, 3 Park Ave., 39th Fl., New York, NY 10016, (212)889-9009
Cayman Islands Real Estate Brokers Assn. **[IO]**, Grand Cayman, Cayman Islands
Cayman Islands Sailing Club **[IO]**, Grand Cayman, Cayman Islands
CB Radio Assn; Amer. **[21493]**
CB Radio Patrol of Amer. Fed. of Police **[★5962]**
CBA **[3403]**, PO Box 62000, Colorado Springs, CO 80962-2000, (719)265-9895
CBA **[IO]**, Colorado Springs, CO, United States
CBA/ALERT - Defunct.
CBAmerica **[★19485]**
CBHL **[★10352]**
CBHL **[★IO]**
CBI Center for Environmental Stud. in Tel Aviv **[★IO]**
CBI Center for Environmental Stud. in Tel Aviv **[★10254]**
CBInternational **[★19503]**
CBInternational **[★IO]**
CBM Ministries **[19995]**, PO Box 278, Townsend, TN 37882, (865)448-1200
CBM Ministries **[★19486]**
CCCO/An Agency for Military and Draft Counseling **[★17439]**
CCDR **[★9874]**
CCDR **[★IO]**
CCF Brandon Br. **[IO]**, Brandon, MB, Canada
CCF Edmonton Br. **[IO]**, Edmonton, AB, Canada
CCF Fredericton Br. **[IO]**, Fredericton, NB, Canada
CCF Halifax Br. **[IO]**, Mineville, NS, Canada
CCF Kamloops Br. **[IO]**, Kamloops, BC, Canada
CCF Kingston Br. **[IO]**, Kingston, ON, Canada
CCF Lethbridge Assn. **[IO]**, Lethbridge, AB, Canada
CCF London Br. **[IO]**, London, ON, Canada
CCF Moncton Br. **[IO]**, Moncton, NB, Canada
CCF Okanagan Br. **[IO]**, Kelowna, BC, Canada
CCF Ottawa Br. **[IO]**, Ottawa, ON, Canada
CCF Regina Br. **[IO]**, Regina, SK, Canada
CCF St. John's Br. **[IO]**, St. John's, NL, Canada

CCF Sarnia Br. **[IO]**, Sarnia, ON, Canada
CCF Waterloo Br. **[IO]**, Waterloo, ON, Canada
CCF Winnipeg Br. **[IO]**, Winnipeg, MB, Canada
CCHS Family Network **[14255]**, c/o Al Pope, Treas., 11201 Fairfield, Livonia, MI 48150
CCIM Inst. **[3302]**, 430 N Michigan Ave., Ste. 800, Chicago, IL 60611-4092, (312)321-4460
CCIM Inst. **[IO]**, Chicago, IL, United States
CCNG Intl. **[2619]**, PO Box 92790, Southlake, TX 76092, (800)840-2264
CCVI Incarnate Word Missionaries - Congregation of the Sisters of Charity of the Incarnate Word **[19607]**
CCVI Incarnate Word Missionaries - Congregation of the Sisters of Charity of the Incarnate Word **[IO]**, San Antonio, TX, United States
CCVI Volunteers in Mission - Congregation of the Sisters of Charity of the Incarnate Word **[★IO]**
CCVI Volunteers in Mission - Congregation of the Sisters of Charity of the Incarnate Word **[★19607]**
C.D. Howe Inst. **[IO]**, Toronto, ON, Canada
CDA Natl. Credentialing Prog. **[★11526]**
CDB Volunteers - Address unknown since 1995.
CDC Natl. Prevention Info. Network **[13563]**, PO Box 6003, Rockville, MD 20849-6003, (800)458-5231
CDG Family Network Found. **[16530]**, c/o Cynthia Wren-Gray, Pres., PO Box 860847, Plano, TX 75074, (800)250-5273
CDMA Development Gp. **[7726]**, 575 Anton Blvd., Ste. 560, Costa Mesa, CA 92626, (714)545-5211
CDPD Forum - Address unknown since 2003.
CDS Intl. **[8019]**, 871 United Nations Plz., 1st Ave., 49th St., New York, NY 10017-1814, (212)497-3500
CDS Intl. **[IO]**, New York, NY, United States
Ceardchumann Teicniuil, Innealtoireachta and Leictreachais **[★IO]**
CEC ArtsLink **[IO]**, New York, NY, United States
CEC ArtsLink **[17370]**, 435 Hudson St., 8th Fl., New York, NY 10014, (212)643-1985
CEC Intl. Partners **[★17370]**
CEC Intl. Partners **[★IO]**
Cecchetti Coun. of Am. **[8183]**, 23393 Meadows Ave., Flat Rock, MI 48134, (734)379-6710
Cecilia Lee Fan Club **[★24856]**
Cecilia Lee Intl. Fan Club **[24856]**
CED - Caritas Burundi **[IO]**, Bujumbura, Burundi
CEDAM Intl. **[IO]**, Croton-on-Hudson, NY, United States
CEDAM Intl. **[4371]**, 1 Fox Rd., Croton-on-Hudson, NY 10520, (914)271-5365
Cedar Shake Assn; Handsplit Red **[★1640]**
Cedar Shake and Shingle Bur. **[1640]**, PO Box 1178, Sumas, WA 98295-1178, (604)820-7700
Cedar Shake and Shingle Bur. **[IO]**, Sumas, WA, United States
Cedar Shingle Bur; Red **[★1640]**
Cedar Shingle and Handsplit Shake Bur; Red **[★1640]**
Cedars of Lebanon of North Am; Tall **[19255]**
Cedars of Lebanon of the U.S.A; Tall **[★19255]**
Cedefop - European Centre for the Development of Vocational Training **[IO]**, Thessaloniki, Greece
CEGA Services - Address unknown since 2002.
Ceiling Indus; Found. of the Wall and **[624]**
Ceilings and Interior Systems Constr. Assn. **[1008]**, 1500 Lincoln Hwy., Ste. 202, St. Charles, IL 60174, (630)584-1919
Ceilings and Interior Systems Contractors Assn. **[★1008]**
CEIP Fund **[★8388]**
Celebrate Adoption **[★11247]**
Celebration; Community of **[19790]**
Celebrity Access - Defunct.
Celebrity Personal Assistants; Assn. of **[59]**
Celiac Assn; Canadian **[IO]**
Celiac Disease Found. **[14412]**, 13251 Ventura Blvd., No. 1, Studio City, CA 91604, (818)990-2354
Celiac Soc; Am. **[★15543]**
Celiac Society/Dietary Support Coalition; Amer. **[15543]**
Celiac Sprue Assn; Midwestern **[★14413]**
Celiac Sprue Association/United States of Am. **[14413]**, PO Box 31700, Omaha, NE 68131-0700, (402)558-0600

A star before a book entry number signifies that the name is not listed separately, but is mentioned within the entry.

Ce.L.I.M. Milano Volunteers for Intl. Ser. **[IO]**, Milan, Italy
Cell Biology; Amer. Soc. for **[6562]**
Cell Biology; Intl. Fed. of **[6581]**
Cell Biology; Intl. Soc. for **[★6581]**
Cell Disease Assn. of Am; Sickle **[14797]**
Cell Disease; Natl. Assn. for Sickle **[★14797]**
Cell Family Assn. - Address unknown since 1995.
Cell Kinetics Soc. **[★6573]**
Cell Proliferation Soc. **[6573]**, c/o Yuriy Gusev, Johns Hopkins Univ. School of Medicine, 720 Rutland Ave., Ross Bldg., Rm. 764, Baltimore, MD 21205, (410)502-6987
Cell Res; Comm. for the Advancement of Stem **[18542]**
Cell Res; Intl. Soc. for Stem **[14503]**
Cell Res; PanAmerican Soc. for Pigment **[15111]**
Cell Res; Student Soc. for Stem **[15114]**
Cell Stress Soc. Intl. **[16488]**, c/o MCB Dept., The Univ. of Connecticut, 91 N Eagleville Rd., Storrs Mansfield, CT 06269-3125
Cell Stress Soc. Intl. **[IO]**, Storrs Mansfield, CT, United States
Cell(e)/Sell(s) Family Assn. - Address unknown since 2003.
Cellular Agents; Natl. Assn. of **[★3765]**
Cellular Communications Indus. Assn. **[★3741]**
Cellular Concrete Assn. - Defunct.
Cellular Operators Assn. of India **[IO]**, New Delhi, India
Cellular Radio Communications Assn. **[★3741]**
Cellular Telecommunications Indus. Assn. **[★3741]**
Cellulose Indus. Standards Enforcement Prog. **[★610]**
Cellulose Insulation Manufacturers Assn. **[610]**, 136 S Keowee St., Dayton, OH 45402, (937)222-2462
Cellulose Mfrs. Assn. - Defunct.
Cellulose Sponge Inst. - Defunct.
Celtic
   Canadian Celtic Arts Assn. **[IO]**
   Celtic Coun. of Australia **[IO]**
   Celtic League **[IO]**
   Celtic League, Amer. Br. **[19011]**
   Dalriada Celtic Heritage Trust **[IO]**
   North Amer. Celtic Buyers Assn. **[IO]**
   North Amer. Celtic Buyers Assn. **[784]**
   Royal Celtic Soc. **[IO]**
   Southwest Celtic Music Assn. **[9779]**
Celtic Coun. of Australia **[IO]**, Mosman, Australia
Celtic Film and TV Assn. **[★IO]**
Celtic Film and TV Festival **[IO]**, Glasgow, United Kingdom
Celtic Intl. Res. Coun. - Address unknown since 2003.
Celtic Language Teachers; North Amer. Assn. for **[8741]**
Celtic League **[IO]**, Caerphilly, United Kingdom
Celtic League, Amer. Br. **[19011]**, PO Box 20153, Dag Hammarskjold Ctr., New York, NY 10017, (800)626-CELT
Celtic Soc; Royal **[IO]**
CEMAFON: European Comm. Material Products for Foundries **[IO]**, Frankfurt, Germany
Cement Admixtures Assn. **[IO]**, Solihull, United Kingdom
Cement Alliance; Amer. **[★915]**
Cement Alliance; Amer. Portland **[★915]**
Cement Assn; Amer. Portland **[915]**
Cement Assn. of Canada **[IO]**, Ottawa, ON, Canada
Cement Assn; Portland **[933]**
Cement and Concrete Assn. **[★IO]**
Cement and Concrete Assn. of Malaysia **[IO]**, Petaling Jaya, Malaysia
Cement and Concrete Assn. of New Zealand **[IO]**, Wellington, New Zealand
Cement and Concrete Inst. **[IO]**, Gauteng, Republic of South Africa
Cement Employers Assn. **[920]**, 122 E Broad St., 2nd Fl., Bethlehem, PA 18018, (610)868-8060
Cement Indus; Natl. Assn. of the German **[IO]**
Cement Indus; Res. Inst. of the Assn. of the Austrian **[IO]**
Cement Kiln Recycling Coalition **[4337]**, 1001 Connecticut Ave. NW, Ste. 615, Washington, DC 20036, (202)466-6802

Cement, Lime, Gypsum, and Allied Workers Div. **[24038]**, c/o James Hickenbotham, Intl. VP, 3112 Peters Creek Rd. N, Roanoke Plz., Roanoke, VA 24019, (540)362-7110
Cement Makers' Fed. **[★IO]**
Cement Mfrs'. Assn. **[IO]**, Noida, India
Cement Pipe Producers; Assn. of Asbestos **[★3026]**
Cement Producers; Colombian Inst. of **[IO]**
Cement Prdt. Producers Assn; Asbestos **[312]**
Cement Prdt. Producers; Assn. of Asbestos **[3026]**
Cement Trade Alliance; Amer. **[★915]**
Cement Users; Natl. Assn. of **[★6832]**
Cement Works Assn; German **[IO]**
Cemented Carbide Producers Assn. **[2702]**, 30200 Detroit Rd., Cleveland, OH 44145-1967, (440)899-0010
Cementitious Slag Makers Assn. **[IO]**, Oxted, United Kingdom
Cemeteries; Natl. Assn. of **[★2781]**
Cemeteries; Natl. Assn. of Pet **[★2959]**
Cemetery Assn; Amer. **[★2781]**
Cemetery Conf; Catholic **[2776]**
Cemetery Conf; National Catholic **[★2776]**
Cemetery Consumer Ser. Coun. **[17312]**, 107 Carpenter Dr., Ste. 100, Sterling, VA 20164, (703)391-8400
Cemetery Soc; Accredited Pet **[2953]**
Cemetery Supply Assn. **[★2782]**
Cemetery Supply Assn. **[★IO]**
Cemetery Supply Assn; Intl. **[★2782]**
Cemetery Support Comm; Abraham Lincoln Natl. **[21160]**
Cenacle; Aggregation of Congregation of Our Lady of **[★19581]**
Cenacle; Auxiliaries of Our Lady of the **[19581]**
Censeil des Editeurs Europeens **[★IO]**
Censorship
   Adult Video Assn. **[17037]**
   Anti-Censorship and Deception Union **[17038]**
   Enough Is Enough **[17923]**
   Families Against Internet Censorship **[17039]**
   Feminists for Free Expression **[17534]**
   Freedom to Read Found. **[17040]**
   Intl. Freedom to Publish Comm. **[17041]**
   Intl. Freedom to Publish Comm. **[IO]**
   Natl. Coalition Against Censorship **[17042]**
   Proj. Censored **[17043]**
   Radio Free Europe/Radio Liberty **[17191]**
   Rock Out Censorship **[17044]**
   Rock the Vote **[17045]**
   SavetheInternet.com Coalition **[17924]**
Censorship and Deception Union; Anti- **[17038]**
Censorship Study Group; Civil **[22807]**
Cent 1851-57 Unit; The Three **[★22887]**
Cent Collectors; Soc. of Lincoln **[22756]**
Centar Za Prava Deteta **[★IO]**
Centar Za Zene Rosa **[★IO]**
Centenary Coll. of Louisiana Alumni Assn. **[18886]**, c/o Saige Wilhite, Asst. Dir. of Alumni Relations, 2911 Centenary Blvd., Shreveport, LA 71104, (318)869-5028
Centenary Unit; Stamps on Stamps - **[★22878]**
Centenary Unit; Stamps on Stamps - **[★6937]**
Centennial Comm; Swedish Pioneer **[★10989]**
Centennial Legion of Historic Military Commands **[21240]**, c/o Capt. Richard Lynch, 46 Highland Ave., Jaffrey, NH 03452, (603)532-6415
Centennial Youth Proj; Roosevelt **[★13070]**
Center for Academic Ethics - Defunct.
Center for Acid Rain and Clean Air Policy Analyses **[★5083]**
Center for Action on Endangered Species - Defunct.
Center for Adaptive Learning **[★7104]**
Center for Adaptive Learning **[★IO]**
Center for Adult Learning and Educational Credentials **[★8406]**
Center to Advance Palliative Care **[14875]**, 1255 5th Ave., Ste. C-2, New York, NY 10029-3852, (212)201-2670
Center for Advanced Res. in Phenomenology - Defunct.
Center for the Advancement of the Covenant - Defunct.
Center for the Advancement of Human Service Practice - Defunct.

Center for Advancement of Public Policy **[18426]**, 323 Morning Sun Trail, Corrales, NM 87048
Center for Advancement of Racial and Ethnic Equity **[8887]**, One Dupont Cir. NW, Washington, DC 20036-1193, (202)939-9395
Center for Advancement of Racial and Ethnic Equity; Am. Coun. on Educ., **[8889]**
Center for Advocacy for the Rights and Interests of the Elderly **[11279]**, 100 N 17th St., Ste. 600, Philadelphia, PA 19103, (215)545-5728
Center for Alternative Mining Development Policy **[4536]**, 210 Avon St., Ste. 4, La Crosse, WI 54603, (608)784-4399
Center for Alternatives to Animal Testing; Johns Hopkins **[11423]**
Center for Amer. Archeology **[6442]**, PO Box 366, Kampsville, IL 62053, (618)653-4316
Center of the Amer. Experiment **[17262]**, 12 S 6th St., Minneapolis, MN 55402, (612)338-3605
Center for the Amer. Founding - Address unknown since 2008.
Center for Amer. and Intl. Law **[5931]**, 5201 Democracy Dr., Plano, TX 75024-3561, (972)244-3400
Center for Amer. and Intl. Law **[IO]**, Plano, TX, United States
Center for Amer. Women and Politics **[17516]**, Eagleton Inst. of Politics, Rutgers Univ., 191 Ryders Ln., New Brunswick, NJ 08901-8557, (732)932-9384
Center for Animals and Public Policy; Tufts **[11466]**
Center for Applications of Psychological Type **[16146]**, 2815 NW 13th St., Ste. 401, Gainesville, FL 32609-2865, (352)375-0160
Center for Applied Christian Ethics **[19975]**, Wheaton Coll., 501 Coll. Ave., Wheaton, IL 60187-5593, (630)752-5886
The Center for Applied Judaism **[★20202]**
Center for Applied Linguistics **[10401]**, 4646 40th St. NW, Washington, DC 20016-1859, (202)362-0700
Center for Applied Res. in the Apostolate **[19608]**, 2300 Wisconsin Ave. NW, Ste. 400, Washington, DC 20007, (202)687-8080
Center for the Applied Stud. of Ethnoviolence; Prejudice Institute/ **[17146]**
Center for the Applied Stud. of Prejudice and Ethnoviolence **[★17146]**
Center for Arab-Islamic Studies - Address unknown since 1999.
Center for Architectural and Design Res. - Defunct.
Center for Arts Information - Defunct.
Center for Asian Amer. Media **[17166]**, 145 9th St., Ste. 350, San Francisco, CA 94103, (415)863-0814
Center for Assessment and Policy Development **[18636]**, 268 Barren Hill Rd., Conshohocken, PA 19428, (610)828-1063
Center for Athletes Rights and Education - Defunct.
Center for Atomic Radiation Studies - Address unknown since 1999.
Center for Attitudinal Healing **[★15206]**
Center for Attitudinal Healing **[IO]**, Sausalito, CA, United States
Center for Austrian Stud. **[IO]**, Minneapolis, MN, United States
Center for Austrian Stud. **[9626]**, Univ. of Minnesota, 314 Social Sci. Bldg., 267 19th Ave. S, Minneapolis, MN 55455, (612)624-9811
Center for Auto Safety **[12956]**, 1825 Connecticut Ave. NW, Ste. 330, Washington, DC 20009-5708, (202)328-7700
Center for Aviation Res. and Educ. **[5537]**, 1010 Wayne Ave., Ste. 930, Silver Spring, MD 20910, (301)495-2848
Center for Bead Res. - Defunct.
Center for Beethoven Studies; Ira F. Brilliant **[★9803]**
Center for Bigfoot Stud. **[7472]**, 10926 Milano Ave., Norwalk, CA 90650-1638, (909)509-2951
Center for Bio-Ethical Reform **[18547]**, PO Box 219, Lake Forest, CA 92609, (949)206-0600
Center for Bioethics **[6557]**, Univ. of Minnesota, N504 Boynton Hea. Center, 410 Church St. SE, Minneapolis, MN 55455-0346, (612)624-9440
Center for Bioethics **[6558]**, Univ. of Pennsylvania, 3401 Market St., Ste. 320, Philadelphia, PA 19104-3308, (215)898-7136

Reference to "IO" in place of a book number signifies that the association may be found in the 45th edition of International Organizations.

Center for Biologics Evaluation and Res. [14671], Food and Drug Admin., 1401 Rockville Pike, Ste. 200N, Rockville, MD 20852-1428, (301)827-1800

Center for Black Education - Defunct.

Center for Black Women's Wellness [★16895]

Center for the Book [10417], c/o Lib. of Cong., 101 Independence Ave. SE, Washington, DC 20540-4920, (202)707-5221

Center for Book Arts [9745], 28 W 27th St., 3rd Fl., New York, NY 10001-6906, (212)481-0295

Center on Budget and Policy Priorities [18403], 820 1st St. NE, Ste. 510, Washington, DC 20002, (202)408-1080

Center for Campus Organizing [18195], Box 748, Cambridge, MA 02142, (617)354-9363

Center for Canadian Stud. and Intl. Programs [★8044]

Center for Canadian Stud. and Intl. Programs [★IO]

Center for Career Management Professionals - Address unknown since 2006.

Center for Chem. Plant Safety [★801]

Center for Chem. Process Safety [801], 3 Park Ave., 19th Fl., New York, NY 10016-5991, (212)591-7237

Center for the Child [★20166]

Center for the Child Care Workforce [★12072]

Center for the Child Care Workforce, A Proj. of the Amer. Fed. of Teachers Educational Found. [12072], 555 New Jersey Ave. NW, Washington, DC 20001, (202)662-8005

Center for Children with Chronic Illness and Disability - Defunct.

Center for Children's Media - Address unknown since 1990.

Center for Chinese Res. Materials [9783], PO Box 3090, Oakton, VA 22124, (703)715-2688

Center for Chinese Res. Materials [IO], Oakton, VA, United States

Center for Chinese Studies [IO], Taipei, Taiwan

Center for Christian Conservative Studies - Defunct.

Center for Christian/Jewish Understanding [★19888]

Center for Christian/Jewish Understanding of Sacred Heart Univ. [19888], c/o Sacred Heart Univ., 5151 Park Ave., Fairfield, CT 06825-1000, (203)365-7592

Center for Christian Stud. [19768], c/o Fifth Ave. Presbyterian Church, 7 W 55th St., New York, NY 10019, (212)247-0490

Center for Citizen Initiatives [17879], c/o The Presidio of San Francisco, PO Box 29912, San Francisco, CA 94129, (415)561-7777

Center for Citizen Initiatives [IO], San Francisco, CA, United States

Center for Citizenship Educ. of Mongolia [IO], Ulan Bator, Mongolia

Center for Civic Network - Defunct.

Center for Civic Networking - Defunct.

Center for Civil and Human Rights [12369], Notre Dame Law School, 301 Law School, Notre Dame, IN 46556, (574)631-8555

Center for Civil Soc. Intl. [★17445]

Center for Civil Soc. Intl. [★IO]

Center for Clean Air Policy [5083], 750 First St. NE, Ste. 940, Washington, DC 20002, (202)408-9260

Center for Clinical Integration [★14713]

Center for Commercial Floriculture; SAF - The [★1493]

Center for Commercial-Free Public Educ. [8241], 1714 Franklin St., Ste. 100-306, Oakland, CA 94612, (510)268-1100

Center for Commun. [8003], 110 E 23rd St., Ste. 900, New York, NY 10010, (212)686-5005

Center for Commun. Programs [12755], Johns Hopkins Bloomberg School of Public Hea., 111 Market Pl., Ste. 310, Baltimore, MD 21202, (410)659-6300

Center for Commun. Programs [IO], Baltimore, MD, United States

Center for Communications Ministry - Defunct.

Center for Community Action of B'Nai B'rith Intl. [11766], 2020 K St. NW, 7th Fl., Washington, DC 20006, (202)857-6600

Center for Community Action of B'Nai B'rith Intl. [IO], Washington, DC, United States

Center for Community Change [12769], 1536 U St. NW, Washington, DC 20009, (202)339-9300

Center for Community Change; Planning and Mgt. Assistance Proj. of the [★12655]

Center for Community Economic Development - Defunct.

Center for Community Education Facility Planning - Defunct.

Center for the Community Interest [17096], Lincoln Bldg., 60 E 42nd St., Ste. 2112, New York, NY 10165, (212)909-2620

Center for Community Justice [★5451]

Center for Community and Org. Development [11750], DePaul Univ., 2219 N Kenmore Ave., Chicago, IL 60614-3504, (773)325-4250

Center for Community Solutions [17517], 4508 Mission Bay Dr., San Diego, CA 92109, (858)272-5777

Center for Compliance Information - Address unknown since 1995.

Center for Computer-Assisted Legal Instruction [6789], 565 W Adams St., Chicago, IL 60661-3691, (312)906-5307

Center for Computer Law - Address unknown since 2003.

Center of Concern [17747], 1225 Otis St. NE, Washington, DC 20017-2516, (202)635-2757

Center of Concern [IO], Washington, DC, United States

Center for Concerned Engineering - Defunct.

Center for Conflict Mgt. - Address unknown since 2002.

Center for Confucian Sci. [19879], c/o Dr. Thomas Hosuck Kang, Pres., 1318 Randolph St. NE, Washington, DC 20017, (202)526-6818

Center on Conscience and War [17438], 1830 Connecticut Ave. NW, Washington, DC 20009-5732, (202)483-2220

Center on Conscience and War [IO], Washington, DC, United States

Center for Conscious Evolution - Address unknown since 1995.

Center for Constitutional Rights [17097], 666 Broadway, 7th Fl., New York, NY 10012, (212)614-6464

Center for Constructive Change [★8453]

Center for Consumer Affairs, Univ. of Wisconsin-Milwaukee [17313], c/o UWM School of Continuing Educ., 161 W Wisconsin Ave., Ste. 6000, Milwaukee, WI 53203-2602, (414)227-3200

Center for Contemporary Celebration - Defunct.

Center for Contemporary Opera [10572], PO Box 258, New York, NY 10044-0205, (212)785-2757

Center for the Coordination of Foreign Manuscript Copying - Defunct.

Center for Corporate Economics and Strategy - Defunct.

Center for Corporate Public Involvement - Defunct.

Center for Correctional Justice [★5451]

Center for Craniofacial Development and Disorders [14056], 733 N Broadway, Ste. 411, Rm. 419, Baltimore, MD 21205, (410)955-4160

Center for Creative Leadership [2488], PO Box 26300, Greensboro, NC 27438-6300, (336)545-2810

Center for Creative Leadership [IO], Greensboro, NC, United States

Center for Creative Stud. - Coll. of Art and Design Alumni Assn. [★18888]

Center for Critical Thinking [8179], PO Box 220, Dillon Beach, CA 94929, (707)878-9100

Center for Critical Thinking and Moral Critique [★8179]

Center for Cuban Stud. [★9845]

Center for Cuban Studies/Cuban Art Space [9845], 124 W 23rd St., New York, NY 10011, (212)242-0559

Center for Cultural and Tech. Interchange Between East and West [★17882]

Center for Cultural and Tech. Interchange Between East and West [★IO]

Center for Curriculum Design - Defunct.

Center for Dao-Confucianism [★19879]

Center for Death Educ. and Bioethics [13314], c/o Gerry Cox, PhD, Dir., Univ. of Wisconsin - La Crosse, SOC/ARC Dept. - 435 NH, 1725 State St., La Crosse, WI 54601-3742, (608)785-6784

Center for Death Educ. and Res. [★13314]

Center for the Defense of Free Enterprise [17625], Liberty Park, 12500 NE 10th Pl., Bellevue, WA 98005, (425)455-5038

Center for Defense Info. [17375], 1779 Massachusetts Ave. NW, Washington, DC 20036-2109, (202)332-0600

Center for Democracy [5932]

Center for Democracy and Free Enterprise [IO], Prague, Czech Republic

Center for Democracy and Tech. [17167], 1634 Eye St. NW, Ste. 1100, Washington, DC 20006, (202)637-9800

Center for Democratic Alternatives - Defunct.

Center for Democratic Renewal [17098], PO Box 50469, Atlanta, GA 30303, (404)221-0025

Center for Design and Mgt. Resources [★1807]

Center for Design Planning [5588], 4224 Spanish Trail Pl., Pensacola, FL 32504, (850)484-4100

Center on Destructive Cultism - Defunct.

Center for Development Policy [★17613]

Center for Development Policy [★IO]

Center for Dispute Settlement [5451], 1666 Connecticut Ave. NW, Washington, DC 20009-1039, (202)265-9572

Center for Documentation and Res. of Peace and Conflicts [IO], Lyon, France

Center for Dream Drama [★16425]

Center for Early Adolescence - Address unknown since 2000.

Center for Ecoliteracy [4501], 2528 San Pablo Ave., Berkeley, CA 94702, (510)845-4595

Center for Economic Conversion [17423], 222 View St., Mountain View, CA 94041-1344, (650)968-8798

Center for Economic Options [12073], 910 Quarrier St., Ste. 206, Charleston, WV 25301, (304)345-1298

Center for Economic and Policy Res. [17469], 1611 Connecticut Ave. NW, Ste. 400, Washington, DC 20009, (202)293-5380

Center for Economic and Social Justice [12046], PO Box 40711, Washington, DC 20016, (703)243-5155

Center for Editions of Amer. Authors [★11167]

Center for Educating African-Amer. Males - Address unknown since 2003.

Center for Educ. and Res. in Free Enterprise [★17635]

Center for Educ. Studies [★9258]

Center on Educ. and Training for Employment [9304], Ohio State Univ., 1900 Kenny Rd., Columbus, OH 43210-1016, (614)292-6991

Center for the Educ. of Women [9315], 330 E Liberty St., Ann Arbor, MI 48104, (734)998-7080

Center for Educational Reform - Defunct.

Center for Electronic Packaging Res. [7425], c/o Dept. of Elecl. and Cmpt. Engg., Univ. of Arizona, PO Box 210104, 1230 E Speedway Blvd., Tucson, AZ 85721-0104, (520)621-2434

Center for Energy Efficiency and Renewable Technologies [4526], 1100 11th St., Ste. 311, Sacramento, CA 95814, (916)442-7785

Center for Energy Information - Defunct.

Center for Energy Policy and Res. [6947], c/o New York Inst. of Tech., Dept. of Energy Mgt., Harry Schure Hall, Rm. 116, Old Westbury, NY 11568-8000, (516)686-7578

Center for Entrepreneurial Mgt. [★711]

Center for Environmental Educ. [★4435]

Center for Environmental Educ. [★IO]

Center for Environmental Info. [4537], 55 St. Paul St., Rochester, NY 14604, (585)262-2870

Center for Environmental Intern Programs [★8388]

Center for Environmental Investigation and Planning [IO], Santiago, Chile

Center for Environmental Stud. [4538]

Center for Equal Opportunity [10216], 7700 Leesburg Pike, Ste. 2341, Falls Church, VA 22043, (703)442-0066

Center for Ergonomic Res. [7565], Benton Hall, Miami Univ., Oxford, OH 45056

Center for the Evangelical United Brethren Heritage [19976], 4501 Denlinger Rd., Trotwood, OH 45426, (937)529-2201

Center for Excellence in Assn. Leadership [316], 236 W Portal Ave., No. 782, San Francisco, CA 94127, (650)355-4094

A star before a book entry number signifies that the name is not listed separately, but is mentioned within the entry.

Center for Excellence in Govt. [★5705]

Center for Excellence in Hea. Care Journalism [★3095]

Center for Excellence in Hea. Care Journalism [★IO]

Center for Exhibition Indus. Res. [1335], 8111 LBJ Fwy., Ste. 750, Dallas, TX 75251, (972)687-9242

Center for Experiential Educ. [★8388]

Center for Expressive Anal. [★16217]

Center for Expressive Psychotherapy [★16217]

Center for Faith Development [★20534]

Center for Family Business [709]

Center for Family Planning Prog. Development [★12175]

Center for Family Support [12566], 333 7th Ave., 9th Fl., New York, NY 10001-5004, (212)629-7939

Center for Farm Hea. and Safety [12188], Eastern Washington Univ., 526 5th St., Cheney, WA 99004, (509)359-6200

Center for Federal Policy Review - Address unknown since 1995.

Center for Field Res. at Earthwatch Inst. [★7574]

Center for Field Res. at Earthwatch Inst. [★IO]

Center for Financial Freedom and Accuracy in Financial Reporting [18404], PO Box 37812, Cincinnati, OH 45222, (513)475-0100

Center for Food Safety [4675], Natl. HQ, 660 Pennsylvania Ave. SE, Ste. 302, Washington, DC 20003, (202)547-9359

Center For Education Alternatives - Address unknown since 2004.

Center For Hea., Env. and Justice [5266], PO Box 6806, Falls Church, VA 22040-6806, (703)237-2249

Center For Inquiry [17643], PO Box 741, Amherst, NY 14228, (716)636-7571

Center for Renewable Energy and Sustainable Tech; Renewable Energy Policy Proj. - [6970]

Center For Sex and Culture [9122], c/o Dr. Carol Queen, Founder, 2215-R Market St., PMB 455, San Francisco, CA 94114, (415)255-1155

Center for Foreign Journalists [★3117]

Center for Foreign Journalists [★IO]

Center for Foreign Policy Development - Defunct.

Center for Free Market Environmentalism; Political Economy Res. Center - The [4600]

Center for Global Educ. [8662], Augsburg Coll., 2211 Riverside Ave., Minneapolis, MN 55454, (612)330-1159

Center for Global Educ. [IO], Minneapolis, MN, United States

Center on Govt. Repression - Defunct.

Center for Governmental Res. [18427], 1 S Washington St., Ste. 400, Rochester, NY 14614-1125, (585)325-6360

Center for Growth Alternatives - Defunct.

Center for Hazardous Materials Res. - Defunct.

Center for Health Action - Address unknown since 2001.

Center for Hea. Affairs [★14984]

Center for Hea. Affairs [★IO]

Center for Hea. Design [14619], 1850 Gateway Blvd., Ste. 1083, Concord, CA 94520, (925)521-9404

Center for Hea. and the Global Env. [14362], Harvard Medical School, 401 Park Dr., 2nd Fl. E, Boston, MA 02115, (617)384-8530

Center for Health and the Global Environment [IO], Boston, MA, United States

Center for the History of Amer. Needlework - Defunct.

Center for History of Chemistry [★10101]

Center for Holistic Mgt. [★4408]

Center for Holistic Mgt; Allan Savory [★4408]

Center for Hosp. Mgt. Engg. [★14885]

Center for Hospitality Res. and Service - Defunct.

Center on Human Policy [11928], Syracuse Univ., 805 S Crouse Ave., Syracuse, NY 13244-2280, (315)443-3851

Center for Human Services [13112], 7200 Wisconsin Ave., Ste. 600, Bethesda, MD 20814, (301)654-8338

Center for Human Services [IO], Bethesda, MD, United States

Center for Humane Options in Childbirth Experiences [15594], 3474 N High St., Columbus, OH 43214, (614)263-2229

Center for Immigrants Rights - Address unknown since 2000.

Center for Immigration Stud. [17803], 1522 K St. NW, Ste. 820, Washington, DC 20005-1202, (202)466-8185

Center to Improve Care of the Dying [★14082]

Center for Improved Learning Environments [★9085]

Center for Independent Action - Defunct.

Center for Independent Documentary [9934], 680 S Main St., Sharon, MA 02067, (781)784-3627

Center for Individual and Community Development [★12365]

Center for Information on America - Defunct.

Center for Innovative Diplomacy - Defunct.

Center for Institutional and Intl. Initiatives [★8745]

Center for Integral Medicine - Defunct.

Center for Integrative Education - Defunct.

Center for Intelligence Studies - Address unknown since 1994.

Center for Interdisciplinary Res. in Bioethics [IO], Brussels, Belgium

Center for Intl. Affairs [★IO]

Center for Intl. Affairs [★17878]

Center for Intl. Blood and Marrow Transplant Res. [13771], Hea. Policy Inst., Medical Coll. of Wisconsin, PO Box 26509, Milwaukee, WI 53226, (414)456-8325

Center for Intl. Blood and Marrow Transplant Res. [IO], Milwaukee, WI, United States

Center for Intl. Development and Environment [★IO]

Center for Intl. Development and Environment [★4477]

Center for Intl. Disaster Info. [12001], 4100 N Fairfax Dr., Ste. 302, Arlington, VA 22203-1629, (703)276-1914

Center for Intl. Disaster Info. [IO], Arlington, VA, United States

Center for Intl. Economic Growth - Defunct.

Center for Intl. Env. Info. [★4474]

Center for Intl. Env. Info. [★IO]

Center for Intl. Environmental Law [IO], Washington, DC, United States

Center for Intl. Environmental Law [5689], 1350 Connecticut Ave. NW, Ste. 1100, Washington, DC 20036, (202)785-8700

Center for Intl. Initiatives [8745], c/o Amer. Coun. on Educ., 1 Dupont Cir. NW, Washington, DC 20036, (202)939-9313

Center for Intl. Policy [17748], 1717 Massachusetts Ave. NW, Ste. 801, Washington, DC 20036, (202)232-3317

Center for Intl. Policy [IO], Washington, DC, United States

Center for Intl. Private Enterprise [IO], Washington, DC, United States

Center for Intl. Private Enterprise [710], 1155 15th St. NW, Ste. 700, Washington, DC 20005, (202)721-9200

Center for Intl. Private Enterprise - Egypt Off. [IO], Cairo, Egypt

Center for Intl. Private Enterprise - Romania Off. [IO], Bucharest, Romania

Center for Intl. Private Enterprise - Russia Off. [IO], Moscow, Russia

Center for Intl. Security - Defunct.

Center for Intl. and Security Stud. at Maryland [★18598]

Center for Intl. and Security Stud. at Maryland [★IO]

Center for Investigation and Development of Educ. [IO], Santiago, Chile

Center for Investigative Reporting [17168], 2927 Newbury St., Ste. A, Berkeley, CA 94703-2565, (510)809-3160

Center for Jewish Community Stud. [17945], Baltimore Hebrew Univ., 5800 Park Heights Ave., Baltimore, MD 21215, (410)664-5222

Center for Jewish History [19179], 15 W 16th St., New York, NY 10011, (212)294-8301

Center for Judicial Accountability [17956], PO Box 8220, White Plains, NY 10602, (914)421-1200

Center for Judicial Conduct Organizations [★5893]

Center for Judicial Studies - Defunct.

Center on Juvenile and Criminal Justice [5640], 54 Dore St., San Francisco, CA 94103, (415)621-5661

Center for Labor and Community Res. [17970], 3411 W Diversey Ave., Ste. 10, Chicago, IL 60647-6207, (773)278-5418

Center for Labor Res. and Educ. [8721], c/o Inst. of Indus. Relations, 2521 Channing Way, No. 5555, Berkeley, CA 94720-5555, (510)642-0323

Center for Law and Educ. [5675], 1875 Connecticut Ave. NW, Ste. 510, Washington, DC 20009, (202)986-3000

Center for Law and Justice Intl. [6017], 6375 New Hope Rd., New Hope, KY 40052, (502)549-5454

Center on Law and Pacifism - Defunct.

Center for Law in the Public Interest - Defunct.

Center for Law and Religious Freedom [18510], c/o Christian Legal Soc., 8001 Braddock Rd., Springfield, VA 22151, (703)642-1070

Center for Law and Social Policy [6220], 1015 15th St. NW, Ste. 400, Washington, DC 20005-2605, (202)906-8000

Center for Leadership Development and Academic Admin. [★8745]

Center for Learning and Telecommunications - Defunct.

Center for Lesbian and Gay Stud. [12222], City Univ. of New York, Graduate Center, Rm. 7115, 365 Fifth Ave., New York, NY 10016, (212)817-1955

Center for Liberal Strategies [IO], Sofia, Bulgaria

Center for Libertarian Stud. [18014], PO Box 4231, Burlingame, CA 94011, (800)325-7257

Center for Lifelong Learning [8406], c/o Amer. Coun. on Educ., One Dupont Cir. NW, Washington, DC 20036-1193, (202)939-9486

Center for Light Res. - Defunct.

Center for Living Democracy - Address unknown since 2004.

Center for Local Tax Res. [★18704]

Center for Loss in Multiple Birth [12665], PO Box 91377, Anchorage, AK 99509, (907)222-5321

Center for Machine Learning and Inference - Address unknown since 2003.

Center for Maghrib Stud. in Tunis [★7927]

Center for Maghrib Stud. in Tunis [★IO]

Center for Mgt. Effectiveness [2489], 15332 Antioch St., Ste. 46, Pacific Palisades, CA 90272, (310)459-6052

Center for Mgt. Tech. [2490], 16 E 96th St., Apt. 4A, New York, NY 10128-0784, (212)730-5430

Center for Marine Conservation [★4435]

Center for Marine Conservation [★IO]

Center for Marketing Commun. [★87]

Center for Marxist Res. - Defunct.

Center for Media Educ. - Address unknown since 2007.

Center for Media and Public Affairs [17169], 2100 L St. NW, Ste. 300, Washington, DC 20037, (202)223-2942

Center for Medical Consumers [14550], 239 Thompson St., New York, NY 10012, (212)674-7105

Center for Medical Consumers and Hea. Care Info. [★14550]

Center for Medical Ethics and Mediation [5452], PO Box 86110, San Diego, CA 92138-6110, (619)296-7268

Center for Medicare Advocacy [14684], PO Box 350, Willimantic, CT 06226, (860)456-7790

Center for Medieval and Early Renaissance Stud. [★10456]

Center for Medieval and Renaissance Stud. [10457], Ohio State Univ., 308 Dulles Hall, 230 W 17th Ave., Columbus, OH 43210-1361, (614)292-7495

Center for Medieval and Renaissance Stud. [10456], PO Box 6000, Binghamton, NY 13902-6000, (607)777-2730

Center for Middle East Policy - Defunct.

Center for Migration Stud. of New York [10468], 27 Carmine St., New York, NY 10014, (718)351-8800

Center for Migration Stud. of New York [IO], New York, NY, United States

Center for Military History [★10471]

Center for the Ministry of Teaching [19920], 3737 Seminary Rd., Alexandria, VA 22304, (703)461-1885

Center for Moral Democracy [★17090]

Center for Multicultural Leadership - Defunct.

Center for Multinational Studies - Defunct.

Center on Natl. Labor Policy [17980]

Reference to "IO" in place of a book number signifies that the association may be found in the 45th edition of International Organizations.

Center for Natl. Policy [18428], 1 Massachusetts Ave. NW, Ste. 333, Washington, DC 20001, (202)682-1800

Center for Natl. Policy Review - Defunct.

Center for Natl. Security Stud. [18588], 1120 19th St. NW, 8th Fl., Washington, DC 20036, (202)721-5650

Center for Nationalist Studies - Address unknown since 2003.

Center for Native Lands [★5692]

Center for Native Lands [★IO]

Center for Natural Areas - Defunct.

Center for Neighborhood Enterprise [17208], 1625 K St. NW, Ste. 1200, Washington, DC 20006, (202)518-6500

Center for Neighborhood Tech. [17209], 2125 W North Ave., Chicago, IL 60647, (773)278-4800

Center for Neo-Hellenic Studies - Address unknown since 2000.

Center for a New Amer. Dream [17260], 6930 Carroll Ave., Ste. 900, Takoma Park, MD 20912-4466, (301)891-3683

Center for New Community [17210], PO Box 479327, Chicago, IL 60647, (312)266-0319

Center for New Corporate Priorities - Defunct.

Center for New Creation - Defunct.

Center for a New Democracy - Address unknown since 1999.

Center for the New Leadership - Address unknown since 2001.

Center for New Natl. Security [17864], 664 Cherry Run Rd., Harpers Ferry, WV 25425, (304)876-9400

Center for New Schools - Defunct.

Center for Non-Broadcast TV - Defunct.

Center for Nonprofit Orgs. - Defunct.

Center for Nonviolent Alternatives - Defunct.

Center for Nonviolent Commun. [18110], PO Box 6384, Albuquerque, NM 87197, (505)244-4041

Center for Nonviolent Persuasion [★18110]

Center for Nonviolent Social Change; Martin Luther King, Jr. [18116]

Center for Nonviolent Studies - Address unknown since 1994.

Center for Occupational Res. and Development [8354], PO Box 21689, Waco, TX 76702-1689, (254)772-8756

Center for Oceans Law and Policy [7394], Univ. of Virginia, School of Law, 580 Massie Rd., Charlottesville, VA 22903, (434)924-7441

Center for Office Technology - Address unknown since 2004.

Center for Optimum Environments - Address unknown since 1995.

Center for Organ Recovery and Educ. [16670], 204 Sigma Dr., RIDC Park, Pittsburgh, PA 15238, (800)366-6777

Center for Organizational and Ministry Development [19769], PO Box 49488, Colorado Springs, CO 80949, (719)590-8808

Center for Pacific Northwest Stud. [7647], Goltz-Murray Archives Bldg., Western Washington Univ., Bellingham, WA 98225-9123, (360)650-7747

Center for Packaging Education - Address unknown since 2003.

Center for Parapsychological Res. - Defunct.

Center for Patient Advocacy [14620]

Center for Peace Educ. - Address unknown since 2003.

Center Perzent - Karakalpak Center for Reproductive Hea. and Env. [IO], Karakalpakstan, Uzbekistan

Center for Philosophy, Law, Citizenship [18271]

Center for Philosophy and Public Policy [★18454]

Center for Plant Conservation [4372], PO Box 299, St. Louis, MO 63166-0299, (314)577-9450

Center for Policy Alternatives [18429], 1875 Connecticut Ave. NW, Ste. 710, Washington, DC 20009, (202)387-6030

Center for Policy Anal. on Palestine [★8627]

Center for Policy Process - Defunct.

Center for Political and Strategic Stud. - Address unknown since 2004.

Center for Political Stud. [★7650]

Center for the Polyurethanes Indus. [3047], 1300 Wilson Blvd., Arlington, VA 22209, (703)741-5656

Center for Popular Economics [6875], Box 785, Amherst, MA 01004, (413)545-0743

Center for Population Options [★12173]

Center for Population Options [★IO]

Center for Population Options' Media Proj. [★12174]

Center to Prevent Handgun Violence [★17589]

Center for Process Analytical Chemistry [6675], Univ. of Washington, 160 Chemistry Lib. Bldg., Box 351700, Seattle, WA 98195-1700, (206)685-2326

Center for Process Stud. [10789], 1325 N Coll. Ave., Claremont, CA 91711, (909)621-5330

Center for Professional Well-Being [14700], 21 W Colony Pl., Ste. 150, Durham, NC 27705, (919)489-9167

Center to Protect Workers' Rights [24039], 8484 Georgia Ave., Ste. 1000, Silver Spring, MD 20910, (301)578-8500

Center to Protect Workers Rights [★24025]

Center for the Protection of Children's Rights Found. [IO], Bangkok, Thailand

Center for Psychological and Spiritual Hea. [15194], 1453 Mission St., San Francisco, CA 94109, (415)575-6299

Center for Public Dialogue [18430], 3152 Gracefield Rd., No. 519, Silver Spring, MD 20904, (301)890-8578

Center for Public Integrity [17667], 910 17th St. NW, Ste. 700, Washington, DC 20006, (202)466-1300

Center for Public Interest Research [★9192]

Center for Public Justice [18431], PO Box 48368, Washington, DC 20002-0368, (410)571-6300

Center for Public Photography - Defunct.

Center for Public Policy, Union Inst. - Address unknown since 1999.

Center for Public Resources [★11488]

Center for Rate Controlled Recordings - Defunct.

Center for Reclaiming Am. - Defunct.

Center for Reduction of Religious-Based Conflict [18504], 649 5th Ave. S, Ste. 201, Naples, FL 34102-6601, (239)821-4850

Center for Reduction of Religious-Based Conflict [IO], Naples, FL, United States

Center for Reflection on the Second Law - Address unknown since 1999.

Center for Reflective Community Practice [17211], Massachusetts Inst. of Tech., Dept. of Urban Stud. and Planning, Rm. 7-307, 77 Massachusetts Ave., Cambridge, MA 02139, (617)253-3216

Center for Reformation Res. [10930], 801 Seminary Pl., St. Louis, MO 63105-3168

Center of Regional Cooperation for Adult Educ. in Latin Am. and the Caribbean [IO], Patzcuaro, Mexico

Center for Regional Development/Transparency Intl. - Armenia [IO], Yerevan, Armenia

Center for Rehabilitation Hospitals and Services [★14894]

Center for Religion, Ethics and Social Policy [18609], 117 Anabel Taylor Hall, Cornell Univ., Ithaca, NY 14853, (607)255-5027

Center on Religion and Soc. [20491], c/o Reformed Theological Seminary, 2101 Carmel Rd., Charlotte, NC 28226-6399, (704)366-5066

Center for Religious Freedom, Freedom House [17749], c/o Hudson Institute, Inc., 1015 15th St. NW, 6th Fl., Washington, DC 20005, (202)974-2400

Center for Religious Freedom, Freedom House [IO], Washington, DC, United States

Center for Renewable Resources [★IO]

Center for Renewable Resources [★7677]

Center for Reproductive and Family Hea. [IO], Hanoi, Vietnam

Center for Reproductive Hea. and Family Hea. [★IO]

Center for Reproductive Law and Policy [★IO]

Center for Reproductive Law and Policy [★18516]

Center for Reproductive Rights [18516], 120 Wall St., New York, NY 10005, (917)637-3600

Center for Reproductive Rights [IO], New York, NY, United States

Center for Reproductive and Sexual Health - Defunct.

Center for Res. in Ambulatory Hea. Care Admin. [15064], 104 Inverness Terr. E, Englewood, CO 80112-5306, (303)799-1111

Center for Res. in Coll. Instruction of Science and Math - Defunct.

Center for Res. and Documentation on Intl. Language Problems [IO], Berlin, Germany

Center for Res. on Educ., Diversity and Excellence [★10401]

Center for Res. in Faith and Moral Development [20534], Candler Scholarship of Theology, Bishops Hall, Ste. 10, Atlanta, GA 30322, (404)727-2277

Center for Res. Libraries [10345], 6050 S Kenwood Ave., Chicago, IL 60637-2804, (773)955-4545

Center for Rsrc. Mgt. [4373], 200 Intl. Dr., Ste. 201, Portsmouth, NH 03801, (603)427-0206

Center for Resourceful Building Tech. - Defunct.

Center for Respect of Life and Env. [4620], 2100 L St. NW, Washington, DC 20037, (202)778-6133

Center for Responsive Design - Defunct.

Center for Responsive Governance - Defunct.

Center for Responsive Politics [18347], 1101 14th St. NW, Ste. 1030, Washington, DC 20005-5635, (202)857-0044

Center for Responsive Psychology - Defunct.

Center for the Rights of Campus Journalists - Defunct.

Center for the Rights of the Terminally Ill - Defunct.

Center for Rural Affairs [16952], PO Box 136, Lyons, NE 68038-0136, (402)687-2100

Center for Russian and East European Jewry [17946]

Center for Russian and East European Jewry [IO], New York, NY, United States

Center for Safety in the Arts - Address unknown since 2006.

Center for Scholarly Editions [★11167]

Center for School Change [8242], Univ. of Minnesota, Twin Cities (West Bank), Hubert H. Humphrey Inst. of Public Affairs, 301 19th Ave. S, Rm. 234, Minneapolis, MN 55455, (612)626-1834

Center for Science Information - Address unknown since 1994.

Center for Sci. in the Public Interest [17314], 1875 Connecticut Ave. NW, Ste. 300, Washington, DC 20009, (202)332-9110

Center for Sci. in the Public Interest - Alcohol Policies Proj. [18703], 1875 Connecticut Ave. NW, Ste. 300, Washington, DC 20009-5728, (202)332-9110

Center for Scientific Information on Vivisection - Address unknown since 1999.

Center for Seafarers' Rights [6053], c/o Seamen's Church Inst. of New York/New Jersey, 241 Water St., New York, NY 10038, (212)349-9090

Center for Security Policy [18589], 1901 Pennsylvania Ave. NW, Ste. 201, Washington, DC 20006, (202)835-9077

Center for Self-Governance [★18453]

Center for Self-Sufficiency [11743], PO Box 416, Denver, CO 80201-0416, (303)575-5676

Center for Short Lived Phenomena - Defunct.

The Center for Social Gerontology [11280], 2307 Shelby Ave., Ann Arbor, MI 48103, (734)665-1126

Center for Social and Legal Res. [5841], 2 Univ. Plz., Ste. 414, Hackensack, NJ 07601, (201)996-1154

Center for Social and Legal Res. [IO], Hackensack, NJ, United States

Center for Social Res. and Education - Address unknown since 2003.

Center for Social Stud. Educ. [9127], 901 Old Hickory Rd., Pittsburgh, PA 15243, (412)341-1967

Center on Social Welfare Policy and Law [★6232]

Center for Socialist History [10099], PO Box 626, Alameda, CA 94501-8626, (510)601-6460

Center for Southern Folklore [9376], PO Box 226, Memphis, TN 38101, (901)525-3655

Center for Soviet-Amer. Dialogue - Address unknown since 1994.

Center for Special Education Technology - Defunct.

Center for Speech Pathology [★16450]

Center for Sports and Osteopathic Medicine [16055], c/o Dr. Richard M. Bachrach, DO, Pres., 317 Madison Ave., New York, NY 10017, (212)685-8113

Center for Sports Sponsorship - Address unknown since 1999.

Center for Statistics [★8284]

A star before a book entry number signifies that the name is not listed separately, but is mentioned within the entry.

Center for Strategic and Budgetary Assessments [18075], 1667 K St. NW, Ste. 900, Washington, DC 20006, (202)331-7990

Center for Strategic and Intl. Stud. [18390], 1800 K St. NW, Ste. 400, Washington, DC 20006, (202)887-0200

Center for Strategic and Intl. Stud. [IO], Washington, DC, United States

Center for Stud. in Criminal Justice [11859], c/o The Univ. of Chicago Law School, 1111 E 60th St., Chicago, IL 60637, (773)702-9494

Center of Stud. of Disaster and Prevention [IO], Lima, Peru

Center for Stud. on the Holocaust [★17715]

Center for the Studies of Human Communities in Space [★6387]

Center for Stud. and Publications [IO], San Jose, Costa Rica

Center for the Stud. of Aging of Albany [11281], 706 Madison Ave., Albany, NY 12208, (518)465-4927

Center for the Study of the Amer. Family Farm - Address unknown since 2001.

Center for the Study of Automation and Soc. - Defunct.

Center for the Stud. of Beadwork [6443], PO Box 13719, Portland, OR 97213, (503)655-3078

Center for the Study of Beadwork [IO], Portland, OR, United States

Center for the Stud. of Canada [IO], Plattsburgh, NY, United States

Center for the Stud. of Canada [8044], c/o Christopher Kirkey, PhD, Dir., Plattsburgh State Univ. of New York, 133 Court St., Plattsburgh, NY 12901, (518)564-2086

Center for the Stud. of the Coll. Fraternity [24476], Indiana Univ., 900 E 7th St., Ste. 371, Bloomington, IN 47405, (812)855-1228

Center for the Study of Commercialism - Defunct.

Center for the Stud. of Democracy [IO], Sofia, Bulgaria

Center for the Study of Democratic Institutions - Address unknown since 2008.

Center for the Stud. of Democratic Societies [17388], Box 475, Manhattan Beach, CA 90267-0475, (310)798-2737

Center for the Study of Democratic Societies [IO], Manhattan Beach, CA, United States

Center for the Stud. of Economics [18704], 1518 Walnut St., Ste. 604, Philadelphia, PA 19102, (215)545-6004

Center for the Study of Education and Politics - Defunct.

Center for the Study of Foreign Affairs - Address unknown since 1999.

Center for the Study of the Future - Address unknown since 1999.

Center for the Stud. of Gp. Processes [7648], Univ. of Iowa, Dept. of Sociology, Iowa City, IA 52242-1401, (319)335-2503

Center for the Stud. of Human Rights [17750], Columbia Univ., Mail Code: 3365, 420 W 118th St., Rm. 1108 IAB, New York, NY 10027, (212)854-2479

Center for the Stud. of Law and Politics [★5693]

Center for the Study of Legal Authority and Mental Patient Status - Defunct.

Center for the Study of Liberal Education for Adults - Defunct.

Center for the Study of Market Alternatives - Address unknown since 2004.

Center for the Stud. of Multiple Birth [15272], 333 E Superior St., Ste. 464, Chicago, IL 60611, (312)695-1677

Center for Stud. of Multiple Gestation [★15272]

Center for the Stud. of Natural and Historical Anomalies [7862]

Center for the Study of Parent Involvement - Defunct.

Center for the Stud. of Political Graphics [9434], 8124 W 3rd St., Ste. 211, Los Angeles, CA 90048-4340, (323)653-4662

Center for the Stud. of the Presidency [17069], 1020 19th St. NW, Ste. 250, Washington, DC 20036, (202)872-9800

Center for the Stud. of Psychiatry [★16086]

Center for the Stud. bf Psychiatry [★IO]

Center for the Stud. of Psychiatry and Psychology [★IO]

Center for the Stud. of Psychiatry and Psychology [★16086]

Center for Stud. of Responsive Law [17315], PO Box 19367, Washington, DC 20036, (202)387-8030

Center for the Stud. of Sci. and Historical Anomalies [★7862]

Center for the Stud. of Social Policy [18432], 1575 Eye St. NW, Ste. 500, Washington, DC 20005, (202)371-1565

Center for the Stud. of States [★6275]

Center for the Stud. of Welfare Policy [★18432]

Center for the Study of World Survival and Prosperity - Address unknown since 2001.

Center for Studying Hea. Sys. Change [14621], 600 Maryland Ave. SW, Ste. 550, Washington, DC 20024, (202)484-5261

Center for Substance Abuse Prevention [16502], c/o SAMHSA, 1 Choke Cherry Rd., Rockville, MD 20857, (240)276-2420

Center for Surrogate Parenting [13297], West Coast Off., 15821 Ventura Blvd., Ste. 675, Encino, CA 91436, (818)788-8288

Center for the Survival of Western Democracies - Address unknown since 2002.

Center for Sustainable Agriculture - Defunct.

Center for Sustainable Transportation - Defunct.

Center for Sutton Movement Writing [11208], PO Box 517, La Jolla, CA 92038-0517, (858)456-0098

Center for Taiwan Intl. Relations [18691], 110 Maryland Ave. NE, Ste. 206, Washington, DC 20002-5626, (202)543-6287

Center for Taiwan Intl. Relations [IO], Washington, DC, United States

Center for Teaching About China [8552], c/o Kathleen Trescott, 1214 W Schwartz St., Carbondale, IL 62901, (618)549-1555

Center for Third World Organizing [17099], 1218 E 21st St., Oakland, CA 94606, (510)533-7583

Center for Third World Organizing [IO], Oakland, CA, United States

Center for the Transitional Person - Defunct.

Center for UFO Stud. [★7479]

Center for UFO Stud; J. Allen Hynek [7479]

Center for U.N. Reform Educ. [18761], 211 E 43rd St., Ste. 1801, New York, NY 10017, (212)682-6958

Center for Understanding Aging [★11297]

Center for Understanding Aging [★11297]

Center for Understanding Media - Defunct.

Center for Unified Sci. [★9102]

Center for U.S. Capital Markets - Address unknown since 2001.

Center for United States-China Arts Exchange [9784], 423 W 118th St., No. 1E, New York, NY 10027, (212)280-4648

Center for U.S.-Mexican Stud. [17700], c/o Univ. of California, San Diego, 9500 Gilman Dr., Dept. 0510, La Jolla, CA 92093-0510, (858)534-4503

Center for U.S.-Mexican Stud. [IO], La Jolla, CA, United States

Center for U.S. -USSR Initiatives [★IO]

Center for U.S. -USSR Initiatives [★17879]

Center for Urban Black Studies - Address unknown since 2002.

Center for Urban Education - Defunct.

Center for Urban Hospitals [★14895]

Center on Urban Poverty and Community Development [18377], Mandel School of Applied Social Sciences, Case Western Reserve Univ., 10900 Euclid Ave., Cleveland, OH 44106-7164, (216)368-6946

Center on Urban Poverty and Social Change [★18377]

Center for Urban and Regional Stud. [11066], 108 Battle Ln., Campus Box 3410, UNC, Chapel Hill, NC 27599-3410, (919)962-3074

Center for Urban and Regional Studies [IO], Chapel Hill, NC, United States

Center for Urban Res. [IO], Quito, Ecuador

Center for Venture Res. [2330], Univ. of New Hampshire, Whittemore School of Bus. and Economics, 15 Coll. Rd., Durham, NH 03824-3593, (603)862-3885

Center for Veterans Issues [21291], 3312 W Wells St., PO Box 080168, Milwaukee, WI 53208, (414)345-3917

Center for Veterinary Medicine [16789], c/o Food and Drug Admin., Communications Staff, 7519 Standish Pl., HFV-12, Rockville, MD 20855, (240)276-9300

Center for Victims of Torture [13361], 717 E River Pkwy., Minneapolis, MN 55455, (612)436-4800

Center for Visionary Leadership [18002], PO Box 2241, Arlington, VA 22202, (202)237-2800

Center for Vocational Educ. [★9304]

Center for a Voluntary Soc. - Defunct.

Center for Voting and Democracy [18348], 6930 Carroll Ave., Ste. 610, Takoma Park, MD 20912, (301)270-4616

Center on War and the Child - Address unknown since 2002.

Center for War, Peace, and the News Media [17170], 418 Lafayette St., Ste. 518, New York, NY 10003, (212)998-7960

Center for War, Peace, and the News Media [IO], New York, NY, United States

Center for War/Peace Stud. [17865], 330 E 38th St., Ste. 19Q, New York, NY 10016, (212)490-6494

Center for Waste Reduction Technologies [3989], c/o Amer. Inst. of Chem. Engineers, 3 Park Ave., New York, NY 10016-5991, (800)242-4363

Center for the Well-Being of Hea. Professionals [★14700]

Center for the Well Being of Hea. Professionals [14701], 21 W Colony Pl., Ste. 150, Durham, NC 27705-5589, (919)489-9167

Center for Whale Res. [7260], PO Box 1577, Friday Harbor, WA 98250-1577, (360)378-5835

Center for a Woman's Own Name - Defunct.

Center for Women Policy Stud. [17518], 1776 Massachusetts Ave. NW, Ste. 450, Washington, DC 20036, (202)872-1770

Center for Women and Sport - Defunct.

Center for Women Veterans [21292], c/o Dept. of Veteran Affairs-Central Off., 810 Vermont Ave. NW, Washington, DC 20420, (202)273-6193

Center for Women War Victims [IO], Zagreb, Croatia

Center for Women's Bus. Res. [4037], 1411 K St. NW, Ste. 1350, Washington, DC 20005, (202)638-3060

Center for Women's Stud. [★17517]

Center for Women's Stud. and Services [★17517]

Center for Wooden Boats [21869], 1010 Valley St., Seattle, WA 98109-4468, (206)382-2628

Center for Work and the Family [12144], c/o Leah Fisher, Co-Dir., 910 Tulare Ave., Berkeley, CA 94707, (925)258-5400

Center for Workers with Disabilities [11929], 810 1st St. NE, Ste. 500, Washington, DC 20002, (202)682-0100

Center for World Christian Interaction - Address unknown since 2003.

Center for World Indigenous Stud. [17812], PMB 214, 1001 Cooper Point Rd. SW, Ste. 140, Olympia, WA 98502-1107, (360)586-0656

Center for World Indigenous Stud. [IO], Olympia, WA, United States

Center for World Thanksgiving [★IO]

Center for World Thanksgiving [★20584]

Center for Youth Development and Policy Res. [18845], Acad. for Educational Development, 1875 Connecticut Ave. NW, Washington, DC 20009-5721, (202)884-8267

Center for Youth as Resources - Defunct.

Center for Zoroastrian Res. - Address unknown since 2001.

Centered Riding [22584], PO Box 157, Perkiomenville, PA 18074, (610)754-0633

Centers for Hea. Res; CIIT [7801]

Centers and Regional Associations [10458], c/o The Medieval Acad. of Am., 104 Mt. Auburn St., 5th Fl., Cambridge, MA 02138-5019, (617)491-1622

Centra Cam Vocational Training Assn. [IO], Camrose, AB, Canada

Centraal Brouwerij Kantoor [★IO]

Centraal Bur. Levensmiddelenhandel [★IO]

Central Africa Diabetes Assn. [IO], Bangui, Central African Republic

Reference to "IO" in place of a book number signifies that the association may be found in the 45th edition of International Organizations.

Central African Badminton Fed. [IO], Bangui, Central African Republic

Central Agency for Jewish Educ. [19180], 12 Millstone Campus Dr., St. Louis, MO 63146-5576, (314)432-0020

Central Alberta Brain Injury Soc. [IO], Red Deer, AB, Canada

Central Alliance of Furniture Mfrs. [IO], Haarlem, Netherlands

Central America
Center for Intl. Policy [17748]
El Rescate [12809]
Empowerment Proj. [17174]
Hermandad [17046]
Hermandad [IO]
Humanitarian Law Proj. - Intl. Educ. Development [18498]
Inst. for Regional and Intl. Stud. [17047]
Inst. for Regional and Intl. Stud. [IO]
Inter-American Commn. on Human Rights [17765]
Katalysis Partnership [17048]
Katalysis Partnership [IO]
May I Speak Freely Media [18028]
Natl. Labor Comm. for Worker and Human Rights [17049]
National Labor Committee for Worker and Human Rights [IO]
Neighbor to Neighbor [IO]
Neighbor to Neighbor [17050]
Off. of the Americas [17051]
Off. of the Americas [IO]
Religious Task Force on Central Am. and Mexico [IO]
Religious Task Force on Central Am. and Mexico [17052]
Sustainable Harvest Intl. [4115]

Central Am. Educ. Fund [★18104]
Central Am. Educ. Fund [★IO]
Central America Information Center - Address unknown since 1999.
Central America Information Office - Defunct.
Central America Peace Campaign - Defunct.
Central Am; Religious Task Force on [★17052]
Central America Res. Inst. - Address unknown since 1991.
Central Am. Rsrc. Center [★17989]
Central Am. Rsrc. Center [★IO]
Central Am. - U.S. Chamber of Commerce [IO], Coral Gables, FL, United States
Central Am. - U.S. Chamber of Commerce [24245], 3400 Coral Way, Ste. No. 602, Coral Gables, FL 33145, (305)569-9113

Central American
DOCARE Intl., N.F.P. [12518]
Inter-American Tropical Tuna Commn. [5730]
Central Amer. Action; Caribbean/ [★12421]
Central Amer. Bank for Economic Integration [IO], Tegucigalpa, Honduras
Central Amer. Club of New York - Address unknown since 1995.
Central Amer. Hea. Inst. [IO], Managua, Nicaragua
Central Amer. Mission [★IO]
Central Amer. Mission [★20310]
Central Amer. Refugee Center [★18496]
Central Amer. Refugee Center [★IO]
Central American Resource Center [IO], Washington, DC, United States
Central Amer. Rsrc. Center [18496], 1459 Columbia Rd. NW, Washington, DC 20009, (202)328-9799
Central Asian Found. for Mgt. Development [IO], Almaty, Kazakhstan
Central Assn. of Agricultural Valuers [IO], Coleford, United Kingdom
Central Assn. of Bee-Keepers [IO], Upminster, United Kingdom
Central Assn. of Commercial Secretaries [★24251]
Central Assn. of Earth Moving Contractors in Finland [IO], Helsinki, Finland
Central Assn. of the German Auto. Indus. [★IO]
Central Assn. of the German Fruit Importer and Wholesaler [★IO]
Central Assn. of German Pork Producers [IO], Bonn, Germany
Central Assn. of the Miraculous Medal [19609], 475 E Chelten Ave., Philadelphia, PA 19144-5758, (800)523-3674

Central Assn. of Sci. and Mathematics Teachers [★9115]
Central Assn. of Sci. and Mathematics Teachers [★IO]
Central Assn. of Women Entrepreneurs [IO], Helsinki, Finland
Central British Fund for World Jewish Relief [★IO]
Central Bur. for Astronomical Telegrams [6504], Mail Stop 18, Smithsonian Astrophysical Observatory, 60 Garden St., Cambridge, MA 02138, (617)495-7281
Central Bur., Catholic Central Union of Am. [19610], 3835 Westminster Pl., St. Louis, MO 63108-3409, (314)371-1653
Central Canadian Fed. of Mineralogical Societies [IO], North York, ON, Canada
Central Carpet Indus. Assn. [IO], Kathmandu, Nepal
Central Chamber of Commerce of Finland [IO], Helsinki, Finland
Central Citroen Club - Defunct.
Central Collegiate Hockey Assn. [23483], 23995 Freeway Park Dr., Ste. 201, Farmington Hills, MI 48335, (248)888-0600
Central Commn. for the Navigation on the Rhine [IO], Strasbourg, France
Central Comm. of British Commonwealth War Veterans Assn. - Defunct.
Central Comm. for Conscientious Objectors [17439], 1515 Cherry St., Philadelphia, PA 19102, (215)563-8787
Central Comm. of Forest Ownership in the EEC [★IO]
Central Comm. of Lithuanian Jurists - Address unknown since 1995.
Central Comm. on Lumber Standards [★1634]
Central Comm. on Lumber Standards [★IO]
Central Confed. of the Textile Indus. in Germany [IO], Eschborn, Germany
Central Conference of American Rabbis [IO], New York, NY, United States
Central Conf. of Amer. Rabbis [20129], 355 Lexington Ave., New York, NY 10017, (212)972-3636
Central Coun. for the Disabled [★IO]
Central Coun. of Physical Recreation [IO], London, United Kingdom
Central Dredging Assn. [IO], Delft, Netherlands
Central and East European Mgt. Development Assn. [IO], Bled, Slovenia
Central and Eastern European Networking Assn. [IO], Warsaw, Poland
Central and Eastern European Schools Assn. [IO], Rotterdam, Netherlands
Central Elec. Railfans' Assn. [22933], PO Box 503, Chicago, IL 60690, (312)346-3723
Central Entertainment Agents Coun. [★IO]
Central Eurasian Stud. Soc. [IO], Cambridge, MA, United States
Central Eurasian Stud. Soc. [10233], c/o Harvard Prog. on Central Asia and the Caucasus, 1730 Cambridge St. - CGIS S, Rm. S-326, Cambridge, MA 02138, (617)496-2643
Central Europe; Amer. Fed. of Jews From [17944]
Central European Fed. of Christian Trade Unions - Defunct.
Central Finland Chamber of Commerce [IO], Jyvaskyla, Finland
Central Forms Comm. - Defunct.
Central House for Deaconesses [★19967]
Central Inst. of Medical Medicinal and Aromatic Plants [IO], Lucknow, India
Central Intelligence Retirees Assn. - Address unknown since 1999.
Central Inter-Scholastic Press Assn. [★8713]
Central Intercollegiate Athletic Assn. [23811], 303 Butler Farm Rd., Ste. 102, PO Box 7349, Hampton, VA 23666, (757)865-0071
Central Israel ACM SIGGRAPH [IO], Herzlia, Israel
Central Marine Chamber of Commerce - Defunct.
Central Neuropsychiatric Assn. - Address unknown since 1995.
Central Off. for Bus. and Trade in Food [IO], Leidschendam, Netherlands
Central Off. Executives Assn. of Natl. Pan-Hellenic Conf. [24477], 3905 Vincennes Rd., Ste. 105, Indianapolis, IN 46268-3000, (317)872-3185

Central Okanagan Brain Injury Soc. [★IO]
Central Opera Ser. [★10681]
Central Org. for the Meat Indus. [IO], Zoetermeer, Netherlands
Central Org. for Jewish Educ. [8688], 770 Eastern Pkwy., Brooklyn, NY 11213, (718)953-2353
Central Org. of Trade Unions (Kenya) [IO], Nairobi, Kenya
Central Park; Friends of [★4407]
Central Premonitions Registry - Address unknown since 1988.
Central Psi Res. Inst. - Address unknown since 1990.
Central Rabbinical Cong. of the U.S.A. and Canada [20130], 85 Division Ave., Brooklyn, NY 11211, (212)384-6765
Central Registry of Magazine Subscription Solicitors - Defunct.
Central Registry of the Missing; Search Reports, Inc./ [12611]
Central Registry of World Dancers - Defunct.
Central Relief Comm. [★12464]
Central Relief Comm. [★IO]
Central Russia ACM SIGCHI [IO], Moscow, Russia
Central Sephardic Jewish Community of America - Address unknown since 1995.
Central Ser. Professionals; Amer. Soc. for Health-care [14864]
Central Shippers - Defunct.
Central Soc. for Clinical Res. [14023], 555 E Wells St., Ste. 1100, Milwaukee, WI 53202-3823, (414)273-2209
Central States Anthropological Soc. - Address unknown since 2002.
Central States Assn. [21434], 9283 Lindbergh Blvd., Olmsted Falls, OH 44138-2407, (440)826-3055
Central States Coll. Assn. - Defunct.
Central States; Independent Schools Assn. of the [8538]
Central States Osteopathic Herniologists [★15814]
Central States Retreaders' Assn. [★3813]
Central States Retreaders' Assn. [★IO]
Central States Roller Canary Breeders Assn. [21844], c/o Robert W. Wild, Sec.-Treas., 305 Grosvenor St., Bolingbrook, IL 60440-1043
Central Sta. Alarm Assn. [3442], 440 Maple Ave., Ste. 201, Vienna, VA 22180-4723, (703)242-4670
Central Sta. Elecl. Protection Assn. [★3442]
Central Supply Assn. [★3061]
Central Union of Agricultural Producers and Forest Owners [IO], Helsinki, Finland
Central Union for Child Welfare [IO], Helsinki, Finland
Central Union of Swedish-Speaking Agricultural Producers in Finland [IO], Helsinki, Finland
Central Union of Tenants [IO], Helsinki, Finland
Central Victorian Olive Growers Assn. [IO], Strathdale, Australia
Central and West Lancashire Chamber of Commerce and Indus. [IO], Preston, United Kingdom
Central West Olive Growers Assn. [IO], Orange, Australia
Central Wholesalers Assn. [★3064]
Central Yiddish Culture Org. [10275], Publishing House and Book Distribution Ctr., 25 E 21st St., New York, NY 10010, (212)505-8305
Centrale des Auberges de Jeunesse Luxembourgeoises [★IO]
Centrale Bond van Meubelfabrikanten [★IO]
Centrale Organisatie voor de Vleessector [★IO]
Centrale des Syndicats du Quebec [★IO]
Centre for Adult Educ. [★IO]
Centre for the Advancement and Stud. of the European Currency [★IO]
Centre Africain des Applications de la Meteorologie pour le Developpement [★IO]
Centre Africain de Formation et de Recherche Administratives pour le Developpement [★IO]
Centre for African Family Stud. [IO], Nairobi, Kenya
Centre for Agricultural Strategy [IO], Reading, United Kingdom
Centre for Alternative Tech. [IO], Machynlleth, United Kingdom
Centre for Animation, Development, and Res. in Educ. [IO], Montreal, QC, Canada

A star before a book entry number signifies that the name is not listed separately, but is mentioned within the entry.

Centre for Application of Sci. and Tech. for Rural Development [★IO]
Centre for Applied Stud. in Intl. Negotiations [IO], Geneva, Switzerland
Centre for Arctic Medicine [IO], Oulu, Finland
Centre des Auteurs Dramatiques [★IO]
Centre Belge d'Etude de la Corrosion [★IO]
Centre for Bio-ethics and Hea. Law [★IO]
Centre for Bioethics [IO], Montreal, QC, Canada
Centre for Bus. Transformation [IO], Chelmsford, United Kingdom
Centre syndicat et patronal du Canada [★IO]
Centre Canadien d'Architecture [★IO]
Centre Canadien d'Etude et de Cooperation Internationale - Burkina Faso [★IO]
Centre Canadien D'Etude Et De Cooperation Internationale [★IO]
Centre Canadien D'Etude Et De Cooperation Internationale [★IO]
Centre Canadien d'Hygiene et de Securite au Travail [★IO]
Centre Canadien d'Oecumenisme [★IO]
Centre Canadien du Film [★IO]
Centre Canadien pour l'Ethique dans le Sport [★IO]
Centre Canadien de Politiques Alternatives [★IO]
Centre Canadien de Prevention de la Pollution [★IO]
Centre for Commun. and Development [IO], Calcutta, India
Centre de Cooperation Internationale en Recherche Agronomique pour le Developpement [★IO]
Centre de Cooperation pour les Recherches Scientifiques Relatives au Tabac [★IO]
Centre d'Activites Francaises [★IO]
Centre d'Animation, de Developpement et de Recherche en Educ. [★IO]
Centre De Bioethique [★IO]
Centre for Deaf Stud. [IO], Bristol, United Kingdom
Centre d'Etudes de la Famille Africaine [★IO]
Centre d'Etudes Oecumeniques [★IO]
Centre d'Etudes Pratiques de la Negociation Internationale [★IO]
Centre d'Etudis Historics Internacionals [★IO]
Centre for Development Alternatives [IO], Chennai, India
Centre for Development and Population Activities [12422], 1133 21st St. NW, Ste. 800, Washington, DC 20036, (202)667-1142
Centre for Development and Population Activities - Egypt [IO], Cairo, Egypt
Centre for Development and Population Activities - Nigeria [IO], Abuja, Nigeria
Centre for Development Res. [★IO]
Centre d'Information sur le Boeuf [★IO]
Centre de documentation, de recherches et d'experimentations sur les pollutions accidentelles des eaux [★IO]
Centre de Documentation et de Recherche sur la Paix et les Conflits [★IO]
Centre for Documentation, Res. and Experimentation on Accidental Water Pollution [IO], Brest, France
Centre for Early Childhood Development [IO], Clareinch, Republic of South Africa
Centre Ecologique Albert Schweitzer [★IO]
Centre for Ecology and Hydrology [IO], Huntingdon, United Kingdom
Centre for Economic Policy Res. [IO], London, United Kingdom
Centre for Educ. and Documentation [IO], Bombay, India
Centre for Educational Res. and Innovation [IO], Paris, France
Centre for Env. and Development [★IO]
Centre Europeen des Entreprises a Participation Publique et des Enterprises d Interet Economique Gen. [★IO]
Centre Europeen de Formation et de Recherche en Action Social [★IO]
Centre Europeen pour l'Enseignement Superieur [★IO]
Centre Europeen de Recherche et de Documentation Parlementaires [★IO]
Centre Europeen de Recherche en Politique Sociale [★IO]
Centre Europeen des Silicones [IO], Brussels, Belgium

Centre of Films for Children and Young People in Germany [IO], Remscheid, Germany
Centre de Formation et de Recherche Cooperatives [★IO]
Centre for Hea. Educ., Training and Nutrition Awareness [IO], Ahmedabad, India
Centre for Human Rights Res. and Development [IO], Ibadan, Nigeria
Centre for Importers of Paraguay [IO], Asuncion, Paraguay
Centre for Indian Medical Heritage [IO], Coimbatore, India
Centre for Indian Scholars [IO], Terrace, BC, Canada
Centre of Indian Trade Unions [IO], New Delhi, India
Centre for Indigenous Theatre [IO], Toronto, ON, Canada
Centre for Info. on Language Teaching and Res. [★IO]
Centre for Info. Media and Tech. [★IO]
Centre for Interfirm Comparison [IO], Winchester, United Kingdom
Centre Internacional Escarre per a les Minories Etniques i les Nacions [★IO]
Centre Intl. pour le credit Communal [★IO]
Centre Intl. de Criminologie Comparee [★IO]
Centre Intl. d'Etude de Tantale et de Niobium [★IO]
Centre Intl. de recherches et d'Etudes touristiques [★IO]
Centre Intl. d'Etudes Agricoles [★IO]
Centre Intl. d'Etudes pour la Conservation et la Restauration des Biens Culturels [★IO]
Centre Intl. d'Etudes Monetaires et Bancaires [★IO]
Centre for Intl. Educ. [★IO]
Centre Intl. du Film pour l'Enfance et la Jeunesse [★IO]
Centre Intl. pour la Formation et les Echanges Geosciences [★IO]
Centre Intl. de Hautes Etudes Agronomiques Mediterraneennes [★IO]
Centre for Intl. Historical Stud. [IO], Barcelona, Spain
Centre Intl. de l'Eau et l'Assainissement [★IO]
Centre Intl. de Liaison des Ecoles de Cinema et de TV [★IO]
Centre Intl. des Marees Terrestres [★IO]
Centre Intl. de Mathematiques Pures et Appliquees [★IO]
Centre for Intl. Peacebuilding - Address unknown since 1987.
Centre Intl. de Recherche sur le Cancer [★IO]
Centre Intl. de Recherches et d'Information sur l'Economie Publique, Sociale et Cooperative [★IO]
Centre Intl. des Sciences Mecaniques [★IO]
Centre for Investigative Journalism [★IO]
Centre Islamique pour le Developpement du Commerce [★IO]
Centre du riz pour l'Afrique de l'Ouest [★IO]
Centre canadien de lutte contre l'alcoolisme et les toxicomanies [★IO]
Centre international de recherches sur l'anarchisme [★IO]
Centre for Latin Amer. Monetary Stud. [IO], Mexico City, Mexico
Centre for Latin Amer. Res. and Documentation [IO], Amsterdam, Netherlands
Centre of Mgt. in Agriculture [★IO]
Centre for Medical, Legal and Cultural Assistance for Foreigners in Austria [IO], Graz, Austria
Centre de Musique Canadienne [★IO]
Centre Natl. des Crimes Economiques du Canada [★IO]
Centre Natl. Interprofessionnel de l'Economie Laitiere [IO], Paris, France
Centre Natl. de Pastorale Liturgique [IO], Paris, France
Centre for Organisational Res. [★IO]
Centre du Patrimoine Mondial [★IO]
Centre for Photographic Conservation [IO], London, United Kingdom
Centre for Policy on Ageing [IO], London, United Kingdom
Centre for the Promotion of Imports from Developing Countries Netherlands [IO], Rotterdam, Netherlands

Centre pour la Recherche et l'Innovation dans l'Enseignement [★IO]
Centre de Recherches Interdisciplinaires en Bioethique [★IO]
Centre de Recherches pour l'Expansion de l'Economie et le Developpment des Enterprises [★IO]
Centre de Recherches sur l'histoire, l'art et la Culture Islamiques [★IO]
Centre de Recherches sur les Meningites et les Schistosomiases [★IO]
Centre de Recuperation Nutritionnelle [IO], Bangui, Central African Republic
Centre for Res. Ethics [IO], Uppsala, Sweden
Centre de Ressources sur la non-violence [★IO]
Centre for Rural Tech. [★IO]
Centre for Rural Tech., Nepal [IO], Kathmandu, Nepal
Centre for Sci. and Indus. Policy Res. [IO], Dehradun, India
Centre Scientifique de Monaco [★IO]
Centre Seismologique Intl. [★IO]
Centre Sismologique Euro-Mediterraneen [★IO]
Centre for Stud. and Res. in Intl. Law and Intl. Relations [IO], The Hague, Netherlands
Centre for the Stud. of Developing Societies [IO], New Delhi, India
Centre for Tech. Geosciences [IO], Delft, Netherlands
Centre Technique du Papier [★IO]
Centre Technique des Tuiles et Briques [★IO]
Centre Tribune Internationale de la Femme [★IO]
Centre Tribune Internationale de la Femme [★17544]
Centre for Women in Bus. [IO], Halifax, NS, Canada
Centre for Women's Development Stud. [IO], New Delhi, India
Centre for Women's Hea. [IO], Glasgow, United Kingdom
Centro Administracion de Derechos Reprograficos Asociacion Civil [IO], Buenos Aires, Argentina
Centro Agronomico Tropical de Investigacion y Ensenanza [★IO]
Centro Andino de Accion Popular [IO], Quito, Ecuador
Centro de Apoyo al Nino de la Calle de Oaxaca [IO], Oaxaca, Mexico
Centro Argentino de Arquitectos Paisajistas [IO], Buenos Aires, Argentina
Centro Argentino de Ingenieros [★IO]
Centro Azucarero Argentino [★IO]
Centro Brasileiro de Analise e Planejamento [★IO]
Centro Canadiense de Estudios y Cooperacion Internacional - Bolivia [★IO]
Centro Canadiense de Estudios y Cooperacion Internacional - Ecuador [★IO]
Centro Cientifico Tropical [★IO]
Centro de Cooperacion del Mediterraneo de la UICN [★IO]
Centro de Cooperacion Regional para la Educacion de Adultos en Am. Latina y el Caribe [★IO]
Centro Cultural Paraguayo Americano [★IO]
Centro De Investigacion y Accion Social [IO], Buenos Aires, Argentina
Centro de Derecho Ambiental y de los Recursos Naturales [★IO]
Centro de Desarrollo y Asesoria Psicosocial [★IO]
Centro de Documentacao e Pesquisa para a Africa Austral [★IO]
Centro de Documentacion de Honduras [★IO]
Centro Documentacion Sobre la Mujer [★IO]
Centro Ecologico Akumal [IO], Akumal, Mexico
Centro Espanol de Derechos Reprograficos [★IO]
Centro de Esploro kaj Dokumentado pri la Monda Lingvo-Problemo [★IO]
Centro de Estudios para el Desarrollo de la Mujer [IO], Santiago, Chile
Centro de Estudios y Documentacion Latinoamericanos [★IO]
Centro de Estudios Latinoamericanos - Justo Arosemena [IO], Panama City, Panama
Centro de Estudios Monetarios Latinoamericanos [★IO]
Centro de Estudios de Poblacion y Desarrollo Social [★IO]

Reference to "IO" in place of a book number signifies that the association may be found in the 45th edition of International Organizations.

Centro de Estudios y Prevencion de Desastres [★IO]
Centro de Estudios y Promocion del Desarrollo [★IO]
Centro de Estudios y Publicaciones [★IO]
Centro de Estudios, Recursos y Servicios a la Mujer/ Centro de Investigaciones Sociales - Address unknown since 2004.
Centro Experimental de la Vivienda Economica [IO], Cordoba, Argentina
Centro Gerontologico Latino [★IO]
Centro Gerontologico Latino [★11292]
Centro Hispano Catolico - Defunct.
Centro Humboldt [★IO]
Centro de Importadores del Paraguay [★IO]
Centro de la Industria Lechera [★IO]
Centro de Informacao Lisboa [IO], Lisbon, Portugal
Centro de Informacion y Documentacion Africana [★IO]
Centro Informazione ed Educazione allo Sviluppo [IO], Rome, Italy
Centro Inox [★IO]
Centro Interamericano de Investigacion y Documentacion Sobre Formacion Profesional [★IO]
Centro Interamericano de Libros Academicos - Address unknown since 1995.
Centro Internacional de Agricultura Tropical [★IO]
Centro Internacional de Informacion Sobre Cultivos de Cobertura [★IO]
Centro Internacional de Mejoramiento de Maiz y Trigo [★IO]
Centro Internacional de la Papa [★IO]
Centro Internazionale di Ipnosi Medica e Psicologica [★IO]
Centro de Investigacion y Desarrollo de la Educacion [★IO]
Centro de Investigacion y Documentacion para el Desarrollo del Beni [IO], Trinidad, Bolivia
Centro de Investigacion, Educacion y Servicios [IO], La Paz, Bolivia
Centro de Investigacion para la Paz [★IO]
Centro de Investigacion y Planificacion del Medio Ambiente [★IO]
Centro de Investigaciones Ciudad [★IO]
Centro Italiano di Solidarieta [★IO]
Centro Laici Italiani per le Missioni [★IO]
Centro Latino Americano de Ecologia Social [★IO]
Centro Latinoamericano de Administracion para el Desarrollo [★IO]
Centro Latinoamericano y Caribeno de Demografia [★IO]
Centro Latinoamericano de Fisica [★IO]
Centro Nacional para el Desarrollio del Acero inoxidable [IO], San Luis Potosi, Mexico
Centro Nacional para la Prevencion y Control del VIH/SIDA [★IO]
Centro Panamericano de Fiebre Aftosa [★IO]
Centro Panamericano de Ingenieria Sanitaria y Ciencias del Ambiente [★IO]
Centro Paraguayo de Estudios de Poblacion [IO], Asuncion, Paraguay
Centro de Pesquisas e Conservacao Iracambi [★IO]
Centro Regional de Sismologia para Am. del Sur [★IO]
Centro Studi Americanistici [★IO]
Centro Tribuna Internacional de la Mujer [★IO]
Centro Tribuna Internacional de la Mujer [★17544]
Centro Uruguayo de Tecnologias Apropiadas [IO], Montevideo, Uruguay
CENTROMARCA - Associacao Portuguesa de Empresas de Produtos de Marca [★IO]
Centrum pro demokracii a svobodne podnikani [★IO]
Centurion-6 Security Ser. Intl. Assn. [IO], Moscow, Russia
Centurions of the Deafness Res. Foundation [★14753]
Century Coun. [13591], 1310 G St. NW, Ste. 600, Washington, DC 20005, (202)637-0077
The Century Found. [18433], 41 E 70th St., New York, NY 10021, (212)535-4441
Century III Found. - Address unknown since 2001.
CEPS - The European Spirits Org. [IO], Brussels, Belgium
CERAM [IO], Stoke-On-Trent, United Kingdom

CERAM Res. [★IO]
Ceramic and Allied Trades Union [IO], Stoke-On-Trent, United Kingdom
Ceramic Arts Fed. Intl. [★1911]
Ceramic Arts; Natl. Coun. on Educ. for the [9836]
Ceramic Arts Studio Collectors Assn. [★21926]
Ceramic Assn; Natl. [★787]
Ceramic Dealers Assn; Natl. [★1911]
Ceramic Decorators; Soc. of Glass and [1735]
Ceramic Distributors of Am. [★1911]
Ceramic Educational Coun. [8061], c/o R. Allen Kimel, Sec.-Treas., Pennsylvania State Univ., 212A Steidle Bldg., University Park, PA 16802, (814)865-5397
Ceramic Educational Council [IO], Pell City, AL, United States
Ceramic Educators; Assn. of [★8061]
Ceramic Indus; Amer. Assn. of [★786]
Ceramic Mfrs. Assn. [786], c/o Myra Warne, Exec. Dir., 47 N Fourth St., Zanesville, OH 43701, (740)588-0828
Ceramic Mfrs. Assn; Natl. [★1911]
Ceramic Sanitary Wares Mfrs'. Assn. [IO], Istanbul, Turkey
Ceramic Soc. of Japan [IO], Tokyo, Japan
Ceramic Soc; Oriental [IO]
Ceramic Teachers Assn; Natl. [★1911]
Ceramic Tile Distributors of Am. [★611]
Ceramic Tile Distributors Assn. [611], 800 Roosevelt Rd., Bldg. C, Ste. 312, Glen Ellyn, IL 60137, (800)938-CTDA
Ceramic Tile Inst. of Am. [1009], 12061 Jefferson Blvd., Culver City, CA 90230-6219, (310)574-7800
Ceramic Tile Marketing Fed. - Defunct.
Ceramic Tiles Mfrs'. Assn. [IO], Istanbul, Turkey
Ceramics
   Abingdon Pottery Club [21522]
   Advt. Cup and Mug Collectors of Am. [21956]
   Amer. Art Pottery Assn. [9411]
   Amer. Ceramic Soc. [6657]
   Amer. Ceramic Soc. [IO]
   Amer. Collectors of Infant Feeders [21959]
   Assn. of Amer. Ceramic Component Manufacturers [785]
   Associazione Nazionale dei Produttori di Piastrelle di Ceramica e di Materiali Refrattari [IO]
   Australian Ceramic Soc. [IO]
   Australian Tile Coun. [IO]
   Belleek Collectors' Intl. Soc. [IO]
   Belleek Collectors' Intl. Soc. [21925]
   Blue/White Pottery Club [21527]
   Brazilian Assn. of Ceramic Tile Mfrs. [IO]
   Brazilian Ceramics' Assn. [IO]
   British Ceramic Confed. [IO]
   British Ceramic Plant and Machinery Manufacturers' Assn. [IO]
   CAS Collectors [21926]
   CERAM [IO]
   Ceramic and Allied Trades Union [IO]
   Ceramic Educational Council [IO]
   Ceramic Educational Coun. [8061]
   Ceramic Mfrs. Assn. [786]
   Ceramic Sanitary Wares Mfrs'. Assn. [IO]
   Ceramic Soc. of Japan [IO]
   Ceramic Tile Distributors Assn. [611]
   Ceramic Tile Inst. of Am. [1009]
   Ceramic Tiles Mfrs'. Assn. [IO]
   Chinese Ceramic Soc. [IO]
   Dedham Pottery Collectors Soc. [22009]
   Egg Cup Collectors' Corner [22016]
   European Ceramic Soc. [IO]
   EuTeCer - European Tech. Ceramics Fed. [IO]
   Florence Ceramics Collectors Soc. [22025]
   French Ceramic Soc. [IO]
   German Ceramic Soc. [IO]
   Glass Molders, Pottery, Plastics, and Allied Workers Intl. Union [24066]
   Haviland Collectors Intl. Found. [21927]
   Hummel Collectors Club [22040]
   Indian Ceramic Soc. [IO]
   International Association of Duncan Certified Ceramic Teachers [IO]
   Intl. Assn. of Duncan Certified Ceramic Teachers [21928]
   Intl. Assn. of R.S. Prussia Collectors [22043]

   Intl. Ceramic Assn. [787]
   Intl. Ceramic Assn. [IO]
   Intl. Collectors Guild [22051]
   Intl. Nippon Collectors Club [21929]
   Intl. Nippon Collectors Club [IO]
   Liaison Off. of the European Ceramic Indus. [IO]
   Lladro Soc. [21930]
   Majolica Intl. Soc. [21931]
   Majolica Intl. Soc. [IO]
   McCoy Pottery Collectors' Soc. [21932]
   M.I. Hummel Club [21933]
   Natl. Coun. on Educ. for the Ceramic Arts [9836]
   Natl. Inst. of Ceramic Engineers [6658]
   Natl. Shaving Mug Collectors Assn. [22086]
   North Amer. Torquay Soc. [22094]
   Old Sleepy Eye Collectors' Club of Am. [21934]
   Phoenix Bird Collectors of Am. [21935]
   Potters Coun. [9780]
   Potters Coun. [IO]
   Potters for Peace [9838]
   Quimper Club Intl. [21546]
   The Refractories Inst. [6659]
   Refractory Ceramic Fibers Coalition [788]
   Rose Bowl Collectors [22112]
   Soc. of Tobacco Jar Collectors [21936]
   Spanish Soc. of Ceramic and Glass [IO]
   Tea Leaf Club Intl. [21937]
   Torquay Pottery Collectors' Soc. [IO]
   Transferware Collectors Club [21938]
   Wedgwood Intl. Seminar [21939]
   Wedgwood Intl. Seminar [IO]
   Wedgwood Soc. of Great Britain [IO]
   White Ironstone China Assn. [21940]
   World Org. of China Painters [22177]
Ceramics Advanced Manufacturing Development Engineering Center - Defunct.
Ceramics; Amer. Soc. of Dental [★14110]
Ceramics Assn; Ohio [★786]
Ceramics Engineering
   Ceramic Tile Distributors Assn. [611]
   Keramos [24461]
Ceramics Intl. Assn. - Defunct.
Cercle des Benevoles du Musee des Beaux-Arts du Canada [★IO]
Cercle Intl. pour la Promotion de la Creation [★IO]
Cercles des Jeunes Naturalistes [★IO]
Cereal Chemists; Amer. Assn. of [★6660]
Cereal Chemists; Milling and Baking Division of Amer. Assn. of [★7095]
Cereal Inst. - Defunct.
Cereal, Soft Drink and Distillery Workers of Am. (AFL-CIO); Intl. Union of United Brewery, Flour, [★24020]
Cereals, Pulses, Oily Seeds and Products Exporter Union [IO], Istanbul, Turkey
Cerebral Giantism
   Sotos Syndrome Support Assn. [14482]
Cerebral Palsy
   Amer. Acad. for Cerebral Palsy and Developmental Medicine [13934]
   Calgary Cerebral Palsy Assn. [IO]
   Cerebral Palsy Soc. of New Zealand [IO]
   Children's Hemiplegia and Stroke Assn. [16493]
   CP Australia [IO]
   Inter-American Conductive Educ. Assn. [9146]
   Korean Soc. for the Cerebral Palsied [IO]
   Natl. Disability Sports Alliance [23353]
   Scope [IO]
   United Cerebral Palsy Associations [13935]
Cerebral Palsy; Amer. Acad. for [★13934]
Cerebral Palsy Athletic Assn; U.S. [★23353]
Cerebral Palsy Intl. Sports and Recreation Assn. [IO], Bad Neuenahr-Ahrweiler, Germany
Cerebral Palsy; Natl. Assn. of Sports for [★23353]
Cerebral Palsy Res. and Educational Found; United [★13935]
Cerebral Palsy Soc. of New Zealand [IO], Auckland, New Zealand
Cerebral Palsy Sports Assn; Canadian [IO]
Cerebral Palsy Sports; U.S. Assn. of [★23353]
Cerebrals Soc. [IO], Brussels, Belgium
Ceredigion Welsh Pony and Cob Assn. [IO], Lampeter, United Kingdom
CERF/IIEC [★6699]
Certificated Bailiffs' Assn. [★IO]

A star before a book entry number signifies that the name is not listed separately, but is mentioned within the entry.

Certification of Acupuncturists; Natl. Commn. for the [★15747]

Certification Agency for Medical Lab Personnel; Natl. [★15145]

Certification; Amer. Bd. of [5478]

Certification Assn. of Am; Crane [942]

Certification; Assn. of Boards of [6337]

Certification Bd; Amer. Athletic Trainers Assn. and [23953]

Certification Bd. for Diabetes Educators; Natl. [14229]

Certification Bd; Electronic Components [1210]

Certification Bd. of Infection Control and Epidemiology [14702], PO Box 19554, Lenexa, KS 66285-9554, (913)895-4607

Certification Bd. for Music Therapists [16213], 506 E Lancaster Ave., Ste. 102, Downingtown, PA 19335, (610)269-8900

Certification Bd. Perioperative Nursing [★14878]

Certification Bd. for Sterile Processing and Distribution [15119], 2 Indus. Park Rd., Ste. 3, Alpha, NJ 08865, (908)454-9555

Certification Bd. for Urologic Nurses and Associates [16706], Box 56, East Holly Ave., Pitman, NJ 08071-0056, (856)256-2351

Certification of Building Operators; Natl. Uniform [2472]

Certification Commn; Natl. [8037]

Certification; Commn. on Rehabilitation Counselor [11822]

Certification of Computing Professionals; Assn. of the Inst. for [8129]

Certification of Computing Professionals; Inst. for [8131]

Certification Consortium; Intl. Info. Systems Security [6758]

Certification Corp; Solar Rating and [7681]

Certification Coun; Aquaculture [4168]

Certification Coun; Insulating Glass [1731]

Certification Coun; Safety Glazing [668]

Certification in Dental Lab. Tech; Natl. Bd. for [14172]

Certification in Dental Tech; Natl. Bd. for [14173]

Certification Directors; Assn. of Hea. Fac. Licensure and [★6210]

Certification of Disability Mgt. Specialists Commn. [13531], 300 N Martingale Rd., Ste. 460, Schaumburg, IL 60173, (847)944-1335

Certification of Engg. Technicians; Inst. for the [★7033]

Certification in Engg. Technologies; Natl. Inst. for [7033]

Certification of Family Law, Criminal and Civil Trial Advocates Program; National [★6333]

Certification of Genealogists; Bd. for [21109]

Certification of Hea., Environmental and Safety Technologists; Coun. on [14552]

Certification Inst. of Am; Biofeedback [13750]

Certification Inst; Engg. Technologist [★7033]

Certification Inst; Human Rsrc. [2902]

Certification; Natl. Assn. of State Directors of Teacher Educ. and [9224]

Certification; Natl. Coun. for Therapeutic Recreation [16627]

Certification for Operating Personnel; Assn. of Boards of [★6337]

Certification for Operating Personnel in Water and Wastewater Utilities; Assn. of Boards of [★6337]

Certification of Orthopaedic Technologists; Natl. Bd. for [15774]

Certification of Physician Assistants; Natl. Commn. on [15975]

Certification of Physician's Assistants; Natl. Commn. on [★15975]

Certification Service; Kosher [★20170]

Certified Allergists; Amer. Assn. of [13594]

Certified Appraisers; Amer. Acad. of State [270]

Certified Archivists; Acad. of [294]

Certified Audit of Circulations [127], 155 Willowbrook Blvd., 4th Fl., Wayne, NJ 07470, (973)785-3000

Certified Automotive Repairmen's Soc. - Defunct.

Certified Ballast Mfrs. Assn. - Address unknown since 2003.

Certified Builders Assn. of New Zealand [IO], Tauranga, New Zealand

Certified Bus. Counselors; Inst. of [726]

Certified Ceramic Teachers; Intl. Assn. of Duncan [21928]

Certified Claims Professional Accreditation Coun. [3865], PO Box 550922, Jacksonville, FL 32255-0922, (904)390-1506

Certified Cold Fur Storage Assn. - Address unknown since 1995.

Certified Color Mfrs. Assn. [★869]

Certified Color Manufacturers Assn. [★IO]

Certified Consultants Intl. - Defunct.

Certified Contractor's Network [1010], 134 Sibley Ave., Ardmore, PA 19003, (866)868-7895

Certified Counselors and Affiliates; Natl. Bd. for [11828]

Certified Counselors; Natl. Bd. for [★11828]

Certified Credit Executives; Soc. of [1447]

Certified Engg. Technicians; Amer. Soc. of [6991]

Certified Exchangors [3303], c/o Doris Grutzmacher, Exec. Officer, PO Box 12490, Scottsdale, AZ 85267-2490, (480)860-8838

Certified Financial Planner Bd. of Standards [1459], 1670 Broadway, Ste. 600, Denver, CO 80202-4809, (303)830-7500

Certified Financial Planners; Intl. Bd. of Standards and Practices for [★1459]

Certified Floorcovering Installers Assn; Intl. [1025]

Certified Hazard Control Mgt; Bd. of [3440]

Certified Home Inspectors; Natl. Assn. of [2121]

Certified Horsemanship Assn; CHA - [23523]

Certified Insurance Counselors; Soc. of [8577]

Certified Interior Decorators Intl. [2255], 649 SE Central Pkwy., Stuart, FL 34994, (772)287-1855

Certified Interior Decorators Intl. [IO], Stuart, FL, United States

Certified Investment Mgt. Consultants; Inst. for [★2336]

Certified Kitchen Designers; Soc. of [2277]

Certified Marine Surveyors; Assn. of [2572]

Certified Metrication Specialist Bd. [★7701]

Certified Milk Producers Assn. of America - Defunct.

Certified Orthoptists; Amer. Assn. of [15657]

Certified Perinatal Educators Assn. - Address unknown since 2001.

Certified Pipe Welding Bur; Natl. [3033]

Certified Planners; Amer. Inst. of [5585]

Certified Practising Accountants Papua New Guinea [IO], Port Moresby, Papua New Guinea

Certified Prdt. Safety Mgt; Bd. of [3441]

Certified Professional Insurance Agents Soc. [★2140]

Certified Public Accountant Examiners; Assn. of [★5428]

Certified Public Accountants; Alliance of Practicing [6]

Certified Public Accountants; Amer. Assn. of Attorney- [8]

Certified Public Accountants; Amer. Inst. of [9]

Certified Public Accountants; Amer. Woman's Soc. of [12]

Certified Public Accountants; Assn. of Practicing [17]

Certified Public Accountants Inst. in Germany [★IO]

Certified Records Managers; Inst. of [2103]

Certified Travel Agents; Inst. of [3918]

Certified Turnaround Professionals; Assn. of [956]

Certifying Agencies; Assn. of Official Seed [5436]

Certifying Agencies; Natl. Comm. for [16916]

Certifying Bd. of the Amer. Dental Assistants Assn. [★14151]

Certifying Bd. of Gastroenterology Nurses and Associates [15472], 401 N Michigan Ave., Chicago, IL 60611-4267, (800)245-SGNA

Cerveceros de Espana [★IO]

Cerveceros Latinoamericanos [★IO]

Cervical Cancer Coalition; Natl. [13849]

Cervical Chiropractic Assn; Natl. Upper [14012]

Cervical Chiropractic Organizations; Acad. of Upper [13986]

Cervical Pathology; Amer. Soc. for Colposcopy and [15590]

Cervical Pathology and Colposcopy; Intl. Fed. for [IO]

Cervical Spine Res. Soc. [IO], Rosemont, IL, United States

Cervical Spine Res. Soc. [16462], 6300 N River Rd., Ste. 727, Rosemont, IL 60018-4226, (847)698-1628

Cervid Livestock [★4654]

Cesarean Connection - Defunct.

Cesarean Prevention Movement [★15604]

Cesarean Prevention Movement [★IO]

Cesarean Sections: Educ. and Concern; C/SEC [★15593]

Cesareans/Support, Educ. and Concern [★15593]

Ceska asociace konzultacnich inzenyru [★IO]

Ceska gerontologicka a geriatricka spolecnost [★IO]

Ceska asociace franchisingu [★IO]

Ceska asociace pojistoven [★IO]

Ceska spolecnost pro mechaniku [★IO]

Ceska fyziologicka spolecnost [★IO]

Ceska meteorologicka spolecnost [★IO]

Ceska Advokatni Komora [★IO]

Ceska Asociace pro Geoinformace [★IO]

Ceska Asociace Geomorfologu [★IO]

Ceska Asociace Squashe [★IO]

Ceska Bankovni Asociace [★IO]

Ceska Biblicka Spolecnost [★IO]

Ceska Bioklimatologicka Spolecnost [★IO]

Ceska Florbalova Unie [★IO]

Ceska Gynekologicka a Porodnicka Spolecnost [★IO]

Ceska Hostelova Asociace [★IO]

Ceska Lekarska Spolecnost J.E. Purkyne [★IO]

Ceska Liga proti Epilepsii [★IO]

Ceska Radiologicka Spolecnost [★IO]

Ceska Spolecnost Chemicka [★IO]

Ceska Spolecnost pro Experimentalni a Klinickou Farmakologii a Toxicologii [★IO]

Ceska Spolecnost pro Kybernetiku a Informatiku [★IO]

Ceska Spolecnost Telovychovneho Lekarstvi [★IO]

Ceska Stomatologicka Komora [★IO]

Ceske hnuti specialnich olympiad [★IO]

Ceske sdruzeni pro znackove vyrobky [★IO]

Ceske A Slovenske Sdruzeni V Kanade [★IO]

Ceskeho Olmpijskeho Vyboru [★IO]

Ceskeho Paralympijskeho Vyboru [★IO]

Cesko Moravska Slechtitelska a Semenarska Asociace [★IO]

Ceskomoravska psychologicka spolecnost [★IO]

Ceskomoravska Elektrotechnicka Asociace [★IO]

Ceskomoravska Slechtitelska A Semenarska Asociace [★IO]

Ceskoslovenska mikroskopicka spolecnost [★IO]

Cesky radioklub [★IO]

Cesky svaz vynalezcu a zlepsovatelu [★IO]

Cesky krasobruslarsky svaz [★IO]

Cesky Badmintonovy Svaz [★IO]

Cesky Plynarensky Svaz [★IO]

Cesky Svaz Biatlonu [★IO]

Cesky Svaz Tanecniho Sportu [★IO]

Cesky svaz Taekwondo WTF [★IO]

Cessna 120/140 Assn. [★IO]

Cessna 120/140 Assn. [★21453]

Cessna 182 Assn. of Australia [IO], Helensburgh, Australia

Cessna 190-195 Owners Assn. - Defunct.

Cessna Centurion Soc. [★21435]

Cessna Owner Org. [21435], PO Box 5000, Iola, WI 54945, (888)692-3776

Cessna Pilots Assn. [21436], 3940 Mitchell Rd., Santa Maria, CA 93455, (805)934-0493

Cessna Skyhawk Assn. [★21435]

Cessna Skylane Soc. [★21435]

Ceta-Research [IO], Trinity, NL, Canada

Cetacean Soc; Amer. [7258]

Cetacean Soc; Connecticut [★5306]

Cetacean Soc. Intl. [5306], PO Box 953, Georgetown, CT 06829, (203)770-8615

Cetacean Soc. Intl. [IO], Georgetown, CT, United States

Cetaceans

Amer. Cetacean Soc. [7258]

Dolphin Res. Center [7261]

European Cetacean Soc. [IO]

Cevre Icin Hekimler Dernegi [★IO]

Ceylon Chamber of Commerce [IO], Colombo, Sri Lanka

Ceylon (Sri Lanka) Tourist Dept. [24377], Embassy of Sri Lanka, 2148 Wyoming Ave. NW, Washington, DC 20008, (202)483-4025

Cezky svaz vodniho lyzovani [★IO]

Reference to "IO" in place of a book number signifies that the association may be found in the 45th edition of International Organizations.

CFA Inst. [IO], Charlottesville, VA, United States

CFA Inst. [2331], 560 Ray C. Hunt Dr., Charlottesville, VA 22903-2981, (434)951-5499

CFA Singapore [IO], Singapore, Singapore

CFA Soc. of the Netherlands [IO], Amsterdam, Netherlands

CFC Financial Communications - Address unknown since 1995.

CFC Intl. [14435], 183 Brown Rd., Vestal, NY 13850, (607)772-9666

CFC Policy; Alliance for Responsible [★797]

C.F.E.-C.G.C. Fed. de la Metallurgie [★IO]

C.FF.I. Ceredigion Y.F.C. [IO], Aberaeron, United Kingdom

CFIDS Assn. [★14256]

CFIDS Assn. of Am. [14256], PO Box 220398, Charlotte, NC 28222-0398, (704)365-2343

CFIDS Found; Natl. [15345]

CFU Junior Cultural Fed. [9844], c/o Croatian Fraternal Union, 100 Delaney Dr., Pittsburgh, PA 15235, (412)843-0380

CFU Scholarship Foundation [★19022]

C.G. Jung Found. for Analytical Psychology [16147], 28 E 39th St., New York, NY 10016-2587, (212)697-6430

CHA-Association for Horsemanship Safety and Educ. [★23523]

CHA - Certified Horsemanship Assn. [23523], c/o Polly Barger, Prog. Dir., 4037 Iron Works Pkwy., Ste. 180, Lexington, KY 40511, (859)259-3399

Chabad Lubavitch [20131], 770 Eastern Pkwy., Brooklyn, NY 11213, (718)774-4000

Chabad Movement [★20131]

Chabad Res. Center [★8688]

Chad Assn. for the Fight against Diabetes [IO], N'Djamena, Chad

Chaffeur's Badge Collectors Newsl; Disabled Veterans Keychain Tag and [22011]

Chain Assn; Amer. [1993]

Chain Drug Marketing Associates [★2972]

Chain Drug Marketing Associates [★IO]

Chain Drug Marketing Assn. [IO], Novi, MI, United States

Chain Drug Marketing Assn. [2972], 43157 W Nine Mile Rd., PO Box 995, Novi, MI 48376-0995, (248)449-9300

Chain Drug Stores; Assoc. [★2972]

Chain Drug Stores; Natl. Assn. of [2985]

Chain Link Fence Manufacturers Inst. [1362], 10015 Old Columbia Rd., Ste. B-215, Columbia, MD 21046, (301)596-2583

Chain Mfrs. Assn; Amer. Sprocket [★1993]

Chain Mfrs; Assn. of Roller and Silent [★1993]

Chain Mfrs. Inst; Malleable [★1993]

Chain of Roasters; Brotherhood of the [★22569]

Chain Stores; Intl. Assn. of [★3404]

Chain Stores; Natl. Assn. of Shoe [★1597]

Chaine Bleue Mondiale pour la Protection des Animaux et de la Nature [★IO]

Chaine d'approvisionement et logistique Canada [★IO]

Chaine Educ. Fund [★22569]

Chaine des Rotisseurs, Bailliage des U.S.A; Confrerie de la [22569]

Chains; Assn. of Gen. Merchandise [★3427]

Chains; Natl. Assn. of Food [★3406]

Chaipattana Found. [IO], Bangkok, Thailand

Chairman's Assn; Aerospace Dept. [7920]

Chairmen; Assn. of State Democratic [★17399]

Chairmen of Departments of Mechanics; Assn. of [8829]

Chairmen; Natl. Assn. of Credit Union [1112]

Chairs; Assn. of Medical School Pediatric Dept. [15884]

Chairs; Assn. of Pathology [15863]

Chairs of Departments of Psychiatry; Amer. Assn. of [16065]

Chalcedon Found. [20535], PO Box 158, Vallecito, CA 95251, (209)736-4365

Chaldean Fed. of Am. [9395], 30777 Northwestern Hwy., Ste. 300, Farmington Hills, MI 48334, (248)851-3023

Chalice Center for the Arts - Address unknown since 2001.

Challenge Aspen at Snowmass [23342], PO Box M, Aspen, CO 81612, (970)923-0578

Challenge Assn; Intl. Auto Sound [1219]

Challenge Coin Assn. [22731], 1375 Mistletoe Ridge Pl. NW, Concord, NC 28027, (704)723-1170

Challenge Comm. on Disability; Natl. [★17415]

Challenge Comm. of the Disabled; Natl. [★17415]

Challenge; Drug Free Kids: America's [18687]

Challenge Intl. [17415], 1204 Ina Ln., McLean, VA 22102-1704, (703)821-3385

Challenge Intl. [IO], McLean, VA, United States

Challenged Am. [14238], c/o Disabled Businesspersons Assn., 3590 Camino del Rio N, San Diego, CA 92108, (619)594-8805

Challenged Conquistadors [11930], c/o Shaun Best, Pres./Founder, 1110 Pine Cir., Smackover, AR 71762, (870)725-3612

Challenged Homeschoolers Assoc. Network; Natl. [8520]

Challenger Soc. [★IO]

Challenger Soc. for Marine Sci. [IO], Southampton, United Kingdom

Challenger T/A Car Club [★IO]

Challenger T/A Car Club [★21605]

Challenger T/A Registry [21605], PO Box 9632, Ketchikan, AK 99901-4632, (907)225-2709

Challenger T/A Registry [IO], Ketchikan, AK, United States

Challenges Worldwide [IO], Edinburgh, United Kingdom

CHALLENGES - Youth Action for Sustainable Development [IO], Lome, Togo

Chama Cha Wakutubi Tanzania [★IO]

Chama Cha Wanariadha [★IO]

Chamber of Argentine Plastics Indus. [IO], Buenos Aires, Argentina

Chamber of Commerce, Agriculture, Indus., and Handicrafts of Niger [IO], Niamey, Niger

Chamber of Commerce; Amer. [★24305]

Chamber of Commerce; Amer. Indonesian [24332]

Chamber of Commerce of the Americas - Defunct.

Chamber of Commerce Amsterdam [IO], Amsterdam, Netherlands

Chamber of Commerce of the Apparel Indus. [24269]

Chamber of Commerce; Argentine-American [24227]

Chamber of Commerce; Asian Indian [24228]

Chamber of Commerce; Brazilian-American [24239]

Chamber of Commerce; British-American [★24267]

Chamber of Commerce; Christian [24311]

Chamber of Commerce; Colombian-American [★24312]

Chamber of Commerce of Costa Rica [IO], San Jose, Costa Rica

Chamber of Commerce; Danish Amer. [24316]

Chamber of Commerce and Economy of Serbia [IO], Belgrade, Serbia

Chamber of Commerce Executives; Amer. [24251]

Chamber of Commerce; Finnish Amer. [24319]

Chamber of Commerce; French-American [24320]

Chamber of Commerce; German Amer. [24323]

Chamber of Commerce of Greater Miami; Colombian-American [24313]

Chamber of Commerce of Greater Miami; Ecuadorian-American [24317]

Chamber of Commerce; Hellenic-American [24326]

Chamber of Commerce, Herefordshire and Worcestershire [IO], Worcester, United Kingdom

Chamber of Commerce; Honolulu Japanese [24348]

Chamber of Commerce, Indus. and Agriculture of Beirut and Mount Lebanon [IO], Beirut, Lebanon

Chamber of Commerce and Indus; America-Israel [24336]

Chamber of Commerce and Indus; American-Israel [★24336]

Chamber of Commerce and Indus. of the Azores [IO], Ponta Delgada, Portugal

Chamber of Commerce and Indus. of El Salvador [IO], San Salvador, El Salvador

Chamber of Commerce and Industry of Hawaii; Japanese [24345]

Chamber of Commerce and Indus. of Korca [IO], Korca, Albania

Chamber of Commerce and Indus. of Mali [IO], Bamako, Mali

Chamber of Commerce and Indus. of New York; Japanese [24346]

Chamber of Commerce and Indus. of Romania and Bucharest [IO], Bucharest, Romania

Chamber of Commerce and Indus. of Slovenia [IO], Ljubljana, Slovenia

Chamber of Commerce and Indus. - Suriname [IO], Paramaribo, Suriname

Chamber of Commerce and Indus. of Tirana [IO], Tirana, Albania

Chamber of Commerce, Indus., and Trades of Burkina Faso [IO], Ouagadougou, Burkina Faso

Chamber of Commerce and Indus. of Western Australia [IO], East Perth, Australia

Chamber of Commerce; Italian-American [24338]

Chamber of Commerce; Italy-America [24339]

Chamber of Commerce of Latin America - Address unknown since 1988.

Chamber of Commerce of New York; Japanese [★24346]

Chamber of Commerce of North Am; North Amer. Indian [★24358]

Chamber of Commerce; North American-Chilean [24307]

Chamber of Commerce; Philippine-Amer. [24365]

Chamber of Commerce and Production of Santiago [IO], Santiago, Dominican Republic

Chamber of Commerce Researchers Assn; Amer. [★24272]

Chamber of Commerce; Romanian-American [24369]

Chamber of Commerce; Swedish-American [★24297]

Chamber of Commerce; Swiss-American [24378]

Chamber of Commerce in Switzerland; Amer. [★24378]

Chamber of Commerce - The Hague [IO], The Hague, Netherlands

Chamber of Commerce of the U.S.A. in the Republic of Chile [★IO]

Chamber of Commerce; U.S. Associates of the Intl. [★766]

Chamber of Commerce; U.S. Austrian [24233]

Chamber of Commerce in the U.S; Belgian Amer. [24235]

Chamber of Commerce; U.S. Coun. of the Intl. [★766]

Chamber of Commerce in the U.S; French-American [★24320]

Chamber of Commerce; U.S. Hispanic [24327]

Chamber of Commerce; U.S. Junior [★24390]

Chamber of Commerce; U.S. Junior [24390]

Chamber of Commerce in the U.S; Netherlands [24360]

Chamber of Commerce of the U.S. in Okinawa [★IO]

Chamber of Commerce of the U.S. - U.S. Chamber [★24301]

Chamber of Commerce of the U.S; Venezuelan [★24386]

Chamber of Commerce Uruguay - USA [IO], Montevideo, Uruguay

Chamber of Commerce of U.S.A; Latin [24354]

Chamber of Commerce of the U.S.A. in Uruguay [★IO]

Chamber of Commerce; Venezuelan-American [24305]

Chamber of Commerce in Washington, DC; European-American [★24275]

Chamber of Commerce for Women; Natl. [24388]

Chamber of Crafts of Luxembourg [IO], Luxembourg, Luxembourg

Chamber of Exporters of the Argentine Republic [★IO]

Chamber of Food Indus. [IO], Cairo, Egypt

Chamber of the Footwear Indus. in the State of Guanajuato [IO], Leon, Mexico

Chamber Found; Natl. [18464]

Chamber of Furniture Indus. of the Philippines [IO], Pasig City, Philippines

Chamber of Furniture Mfrs. [IO], Buenos Aires, Argentina

Chamber of Geological Engineers of Turkey [★IO]

Chamber of Geological Engineers of Turkey [IO], Ankara, Turkey

Chamber of Geophysical Engineers [IO], Ankara, Turkey

A star before a book entry number signifies that the name is not listed separately, but is mentioned within the entry.

Chamber of Mech. Engineers [IO], Ankara, Turkey
Chamber of Mines of Namibia [IO], Windhoek, Namibia
Chamber of Mines of South Africa [IO], Marshalltown, Republic of South Africa
Chamber Music Am. [10573], 305 7th Ave., New York, NY 10001-6008, (212)242-2022
Chamber Music Assn; Fischoff Natl. [10596]
Chamber of Petfood Mfrs. [IO], Paris, France
Chamber of Shipping [IO], London, United Kingdom
Chamber of Shipping of Am. [6059], 1730 M St. NW, Ste. 407, Washington, DC 20036-4517, (202)775-4399
Chamber of Soft Drink and Related Mfrs. [IO], Buenos Aires, Argentina
Chamber of Software Businesses and Info. Services [IO], Buenos Aires, Argentina
Chamber of Sugar Producers [IO], San Jose, Costa Rica
Chamber of Tax Advisors of the Czech Republic [IO], Brno, Czech Republic
Chamber of Telecommunications Businesses [IO], Caracas, Venezuela
Chamber of Venezuelan Auto. Products Manufacturers [IO], Caracas, Venezuela
Chamberlain Genealogical Soc; World [21157]

Chambers of Commerce
Aberdeen and Grampian Chamber of Commerce [IO]
ACCE Communications Coun. [24257]
Addis Ababa Chamber of Commerce [IO]
Afghan-American Chamber of Commerce [24222]
All China Fed. of Indus. and Commerce [IO]
Amer. Bus. Coun. of Dubai and the Northern Emirates [IO]
Amer. Bus. Coun. of the Gulf Countries [IO]
Amer. Bus. Coun. of Pakistan [IO]
Amer. Businessmen of Jeddah [IO]
Amer. Chamber of Commerce in Argentina [IO]
Amer. Chamber of Commerce in Australia [IO]
Amer. Chamber of Commerce in Australia - Melbourne Br. [IO]
Amer. Chamber of Commerce in Australia - National/New South Wales Off. [IO]
Amer. Chamber of Commerce in Australia - Perth Br. [IO]
Amer. Chamber of Commerce in Austria [IO]
Amer. Chamber of Commerce in Azerbaijan [IO]
Amer. Chamber of Commerce in Belgium [IO]
Amer. Chamber of Commerce of Bolivia [IO]
Amer. Chamber of Commerce of Brazil - Rio de Janeiro [IO]
Amer. Chamber of Commerce of Brazil - Sao Paulo [IO]
Amer. Chamber of Commerce in Bulgaria [IO]
Amer. Chamber of Commerce of Cuba in the U.S. [IO]
Amer. Chamber of Commerce of Cuba in the U.S. [24258]
Amer. Chamber of Commerce in the Czech Republic [IO]
Amer. Chamber of Commerce of the Dominican Republic [IO]
Amer. Chamber of Commerce in Egypt [IO]
Amer. Chamber of Commerce of El Salvador [IO]
Amer. Chamber of Commerce Estonia [IO]
Amer. Chamber of Commerce to the European Union [IO]
Amer. Chamber of Commerce in France [IO]
Amer. Chamber of Commerce in Germany [IO]
Amer. Chamber of Commerce in Germany - Frankfurt [IO]
Amer. Chamber of Commerce in Guangdong [IO]
Amer. Chamber of Commerce of Guatemala [IO]
Amer. Chamber of Commerce in Hong Kong [IO]
Amer. Chamber of Commerce in Hungary [IO]
Amer. Chamber of Commerce in Indonesia [IO]
Amer. Chamber of Commerce and Indus. of Panama [IO]
Amer. Chamber of Commerce Ireland [IO]
Amer. Chamber of Commerce in Italy [IO]
Amer. Chamber of Commerce of Jamaica [IO]
Amer. Chamber of Commerce in Japan [IO]
Amer. Chamber of Commerce in Korea [IO]
Amer. Chamber of Commerce in Latvia [IO]

Amer. Chamber of Commerce in Lithuania [IO]
Amer. Chamber of Commerce in Luxembourg [IO]
Amer. Chamber of Commerce of Mexico - Guadalajara [IO]
Amer. Chamber of Commerce of Mexico - Mexico City [IO]
Amer. Chamber of Commerce in the Netherlands [IO]
Amer. Chamber of Commerce in New Zealand [IO]
Amer. Chamber of Commerce in Nicaragua [IO]
Amer. Chamber of Commerce in Norway [IO]
Amer. Chamber of Commerce in Okinawa [IO]
Amer. Chamber of Commerce - People's Republic of China [IO]
Amer. Chamber of Commerce of Peru [IO]
Amer. Chamber of Commerce of the Philippines [IO]
Amer. Chamber of Commerce in Poland [IO]
Amer. Chamber of Commerce in Portugal [IO]
Amer. Chamber of Commerce in Romania [IO]
Amer. Chamber of Commerce in Russia [IO]
Amer. Chamber of Commerce in Shanghai [IO]
Amer. Chamber of Commerce in Singapore [IO]
Amer. Chamber of Commerce in the Slovak Republic [IO]
Amer. Chamber of Commerce in South Africa [IO]
Amer. Chamber of Commerce in Spain - Barcelona [IO]
Amer. Chamber of Commerce in Spain - Madrid [IO]
Amer. Chamber of Commerce in Sri Lanka [IO]
Amer. Chamber of Commerce in Sweden [IO]
Amer. Chamber of Commerce in Taipei [IO]
Amer. Chamber of Commerce in Thailand [IO]
Amer. Chamber of Commerce - Trinidad and Tobago [IO]
Amer. Chamber of Commerce in the Ukraine [IO]
Amer. Chamber of Commerce in Vietnam - Hanoi [IO]
Amer. Chamber of Commerce in Vietnam - Ho Chi Minh City [IO]
American-Hellenic Chamber of Commerce [IO]
Amer. Intl. Chamber of Commerce [24247]
Amer. Islamic Chamber of Commerce [24259]
Amer. Islamic Chamber of Commerce [IO]
Amer. Israel Chamber of Commerce - Southeast Region [IO]
Amer. Israel Chamber of Commerce - Southeast Region [24260]
American-Malaysian Chamber of Commerce [IO]
American-Russian Chamber of Commerce and Indus. [24261]
Amer.-Southern Africa Chamber of Trade and Indus. [24375]
American-Uzbekistan Chamber of Commerce [24262]
American-Uzbekistan Chamber of Commerce [IO]
Andorra Chamber of Commerce, Indus. and Services [IO]
Argentina Chamber of Commerce [IO]
Argentine Republic Chamber of Importers [IO]
Armenian Amer. Chamber of Commerce [24263]
Aruba Chamber of Commerce and Indus. [IO]
Asia-Pacific Coun. of Amer. Chambers of Commerce [IO]
Asia Pacific - USA Chamber of Commerce [24264]
Asian Assn. of Convention and Visitor Bureaus [IO]
Assembly of French Chambers of Commerce and Indus. [IO]
Assoc. Chambers of Commerce and Indus. of India [IO]
Assoc. Chinese Chambers of Commerce and Indus. of Malaysia [IO]
Assn. of Amer. Chambers of Commerce in Latin Am. [24352]
Assn. of European Chambers of Commerce and Indus. [IO]
Assn. of Lithuanian Chambers of Commerce, Indus. and Crafts [IO]
Assn. of Mediterranean Chambers of Commerce and Indus. [IO]
Athens Chamber of Commerce and Indus. [IO]

Auckland Chamber of Commerce and Indus. [IO]
Australia Arab Chamber of Commerce and Indus. [IO]
Australia-Brazil Chamber of Commerce [IO]
Australia-Israel Chamber of Commerce [IO]
Australia Philippines Bus. Coun. [IO]
Australia-Singapore Chamber of Commerce and Indus. [IO]
Australia-Taiwan Bus. Coun. [IO]
Australian Bus. Limited Incorporating the State Chamber of Commerce (NSW) [IO]
Australian Chamber of Commerce and Indus. [IO]
Australian New Zealand - Amer. Chambers of Commerce [24248]
Austrian Fed. Economic Chamber [IO]
Austrian Tourist Off. [24231]
Austrian Trade Commn. [24232]
Austrian Trade Commissions in the U.S. [24265]
Austrian Trade Commissions in the U.S. [IO]
Bahamas Chamber of Commerce - Nassau [IO]
Barbados Chamber of Commerce and Indus. [IO]
Barnsley Chamber of Commerce and Indus. [IO]
Bedfordshire and Luton Chamber of Commerce, Training and Enterprise [IO]
Belgian Luxembourg Chamber of Commerce in Great Britain [IO]
Belgium-Japan Assn. and Chamber of Commerce [IO]
Belgium-Luxembourg Chamber of Commerce in Hong Kong [IO]
Belize Chamber of Commerce and Indus. [IO]
Bermuda Chamber of Commerce [IO]
Bhutan Chamber of Commerce and Indus. [IO]
Bilateral US-Arab Chamber of Commerce [24226]
Birmingham Chamber of Commerce and Indus. [IO]
Black Country Chamber of Commerce [IO]
Bradford Chamber of Commerce [IO]
Brazil-Canada Chamber of Commerce [IO]
Brazil-U.S. Bus. Coun. [24266]
Brazilian Chamber of Commerce in Great Britain [IO]
Brazilian Govt. Trade Bur. of the Consulate Gen. of Brazil in New York [24240]
Bristol Chamber of Commerce and Initiative [IO]
Britain-Nepal Chamber of Commerce [IO]
British Canadian Chamber of Trade and Commerce [IO]
British Chamber of Commerce in Belgium [IO]
British Chamber of Commerce in China [IO]
British Chamber of Commerce in Germany [IO]
British Chamber of Commerce in Hong Kong [IO]
British Chamber of Commerce in Hungary [IO]
British Chamber of Commerce for Italy [IO]
British Chamber of Commerce in Latvia [IO]
British Chamber of Commerce for Luxembourg [IO]
British Chamber of Commerce in Spain [IO]
British Chambers of Commerce [IO]
British-Chilean Chamber of Commerce [IO]
British Hellenic Chamber of Commerce [IO]
British-Israel Chamber of Commerce [IO]
British Polish Chamber of Commerce [IO]
British-Swedish Chamber of Commerce in Sweden [IO]
British-Swiss Chamber of Commerce [IO]
BritishAmerican Bus. Inc. [IO]
BritishAmerican Bus. Inc. of New York and London [24267]
Bulgarian-American Chamber of Commerce [24243]
Bulgarian Chamber of Commerce and Indus. [IO]
Cambridgeshire Chamber of Commerce and Indus. [IO]
Cameroon-USA Chamber of Commerce [24249]
Canada-Czech Republic Chamber of Commerce [IO]
Canada-Finland Chamber of Commerce [IO]
Canada-Pakistan Bus. Coun. [IO]
Canada-UK Chamber of Commerce [IO]
Canadian Chamber of Commerce [IO]
Canadian German Chamber of Indus. and Commerce [IO]
Cape Town Regional Chamber of Commerce and Indus. [IO]

Reference to "IO" in place of a book number signifies that the association may be found in the 45th edition of International Organizations.

Cardiff Chamber of Commerce **[IO]**
Caribbean and African Chamber of Commerce of Ontario **[IO]**
Caribbean Amer. Chamber of Commerce and Indus. **[IO]**
Caribbean Amer. Chamber of Commerce and Indus. **[24268]**
Cayman Islands Chamber of Commerce **[IO]**
Central Chamber of Commerce of Finland **[IO]**
Central Finland Chamber of Commerce **[IO]**
Central and West Lancashire Chamber of Commerce and Indus. **[IO]**
Ceylon Chamber of Commerce **[IO]**
Chamber of Commerce, Agriculture, Indus., and Handicrafts of Niger **[IO]**
Chamber of Commerce Amsterdam **[IO]**
Chamber of Commerce of the Apparel Indus. **[24269]**
Chamber of Commerce of Costa Rica **[IO]**
Chamber of Commerce and Economy of Serbia **[IO]**
Chamber of Commerce, Herefordshire and Worcestershire **[IO]**
Chamber of Commerce, Indus. and Agriculture of Beirut and Mount Lebanon **[IO]**
Chamber of Commerce and Indus. of the Azores **[IO]**
Chamber of Commerce and Indus. of El Salvador **[IO]**
Chamber of Commerce and Indus. of Mali **[IO]**
Chamber of Commerce and Indus. of Romania and Bucharest **[IO]**
Chamber of Commerce and Indus. of Slovenia **[IO]**
Chamber of Commerce and Indus. - Suriname **[IO]**
Chamber of Commerce, Indus., and Trades of Burkina Faso **[IO]**
Chamber of Commerce and Indus. of Western Australia **[IO]**
Chamber of Commerce and Production of Santiago **[IO]**
Chamber of Commerce - The Hague **[IO]**
Chamber of Commerce Uruguay - USA **[IO]**
Chambers of Commerce of Ireland **[IO]**
Chambre de Commerce et d'Industrie de Nouvelle-Caledonie **[IO]**
Channel Chamber of Commerce **[IO]**
Chile-U.S. Chamber of Commerce **[24270]**
Chilean Amer. Chamber of Commerce **[IO]**
Chinese Amer. Assn. of Commerce **[24308]**
Chinese Gen. Chamber of Commerce **[IO]**
Chinese Natl. Assn. of Indus. and Commerce **[IO]**
Clonmel Chamber of Commerce **[IO]**
Colombian-American Chamber of Commerce **[IO]**
Colombian-American Chamber of Commerce - Bogota **[IO]**
Colombian-American Chamber of Commerce - Cali **[IO]**
Colombian-American Chamber of Commerce - Cartagena **[IO]**
Colombian Govt. Trade Bur. **[IO]**
Colombian Govt. Trade Bur. **[24271]**
Comite Espanol de la Camara de Comercio Internacional **[IO]**
Commerce Queensland **[IO]**
Commercial Assn. of Portugal **[IO]**
Commercial Off. of Spain **[24376]**
Confed. of Asian-Pacific Chambers of Commerce and Indus. **[IO]**
Confed. of Indus. Chambers **[IO]**
Congleton Chamber of Commerce and Enterprise **[IO]**
Costa Rican-American Chamber of Commerce **[IO]**
Coun. for Community and Economic Res. **[24272]**
Coun. of EU Chambers of Commerce in India **[IO]**
Coventry and Warwickshire Chamber of Commerce **[IO]**
Croatian-American Chamber of Commerce **[24314]**
Croydon Chamber of Commerce and Indus. **[IO]**
Curacao Chamber of Commerce and Indus. **[IO]**
Cyprus Chamber of Commerce and Indus. **[IO]**
Cyprus Embassy Trade Center **[IO]**

Cyprus Embassy Trade Center **[24273]**
Czech Confed. of Commerce and Tourism **[IO]**
Czech-North Amer. Chamber of Commerce **[24274]**
Danish Chamber of Commerce **[IO]**
Danish-UK Chamber of Commerce **[IO]**
Derbyshire Chamber and Bus. Link **[IO]**
Doncaster Chamber **[IO]**
Dorset Bus., The Chamber of Commerce and Indus. **[IO]**
Dublin Chamber of Commerce **[IO]**
Dundee and Tayside Chamber of Commerce and Indus. **[IO]**
East Lancashire Chamber of Commerce **[IO]**
Economic Chamber of the Czech Republic **[IO]**
Ecuadorian-American Chamber of Commerce - Quito **[IO]**
Edinburgh Chamber of Commerce **[IO]**
Edmonton Chamber of Commerce/World Trade Center Edmonton **[IO]**
Essex Chamber of Commerce **[IO]**
Estonian Amer. Chamber of Commerce and Indus. **[24318]**
Estonian Chamber of Commerce and Indus. **[IO]**
European - Amer. Bus. Coun. **[IO]**
European - Amer. Bus. Coun. **[24275]**
European Amer. Chamber of Commerce (France) **[IO]**
European-American Chamber of Commerce in the U.S. **[IO]**
European-American Chamber of Commerce in the U.S. **[24276]**
European Coun. of Amer. Chambers of Commerce **[IO]**
Famagusta Chamber of Commerce and Indus. **[IO]**
Fed. of Bangladesh Chambers of Commerce and Indus. **[IO]**
Fed. of Chambers of Commerce and Indus. of Belgium **[IO]**
Fed. of Chambers of Commerce and Indus. of Sri Lanka **[IO]**
Fed. of Egyptian Chambers of Commerce **[IO]**
Fed. of Indian Chambers of Commerce and Indus. **[IO]**
Fed. of Israeli Chambers of Commerce **[IO]**
Fed. of Nepalese Chambers of Commerce and Indus. **[IO]**
Fed. of Pakistan Chambers of Commerce and Indus. **[IO]**
Fed. of Philippine Amer. Chambers of Commerce **[24277]**
Fed. of Syrian Chambers of Commerce **[IO]**
Fed. of United Arab Emirates Chambers of Commerce and Indus. **[IO]**
Fife Chamber of Commerce and Enterprise **[IO]**
Foreign Investors' Chamber of Commerce and Indus. **[IO]**
Franco-British Chamber of Commerce and Indus. **[IO]**
Franco-Peruvian Chamber of Commerce and Indus. **[IO]**
French Chamber of Commerce in Great Britain **[IO]**
Galway Chamber of Commerce and Indus. **[IO]**
Gambia Chamber of Commerce and Indus. **[IO]**
Georgia-USA Chamber of Commerce **[24278]**
German-Australian Chamber of Indus. and Commerce **[IO]**
German-British Chamber of Indus. and Commerce **[IO]**
German-Peruvian Chamber of Commerce and Indus. **[IO]**
Ghana Natl. Chamber of Commerce and Indus. **[IO]**
Ghana-USA Chamber of Commerce **[24279]**
Glasgow Chamber of Commerce **[IO]**
Grand Bahama Chamber of Commerce **[IO]**
Grand Duchy of Luxembourg Chamber of Commerce **[IO]**
Greek Amer. Chamber of Commerce **[24280]**
Grenada Chamber of Indus. and Commerce **[IO]**
Guernsey Chamber of Commerce **[IO]**
Haitian-American Chamber of Commerce and Indus. **[IO]**

Hemispheric Cong. of Latin Chambers of Commerce **[IO]**
Hemispheric Cong. of Latin Chambers of Commerce **[24281]**
Hertfordshire Chamber of Commerce and Indus. **[IO]**
Honduran Amer. Chamber of Commerce - Tegucigalpa **[IO]**
Hong Kong Gen. Chamber of Commerce **[IO]**
Hong Kong Trade Development Coun. **[24329]**
Hull and Humber Chamber of Commerce, Indus. and Shipping **[IO]**
Iceland Chamber of Commerce **[IO]**
Icelandic Amer. Chamber of Commerce **[IO]**
Icelandic Amer. Chamber of Commerce **[24282]**
Indian Chamber of Commerce - Calcutta **[IO]**
Indian Chamber of Commerce Hong Kong **[IO]**
Indian Merchants' Chamber **[IO]**
Indo-American Chamber of Commerce **[IO]**
Indo-French Chamber of Commerce and Indus. **[IO]**
Indo-German Chamber of Commerce **[IO]**
Indonesian Chamber of Commerce and Indus. **[IO]**
Innovation Norway - U.S. **[IO]**
Innovation Norway - U.S. **[24283]**
Intl. Chamber of Commerce - Austria **[IO]**
Intl. Chamber of Commerce - Belgium **[IO]**
Intl. Chamber of Commerce - Czech Republic **[IO]**
Intl. Chamber of Commerce - Deutschland **[IO]**
Intl. Chamber of Commerce - Finland **[IO]**
Intl. Chamber of Commerce - France **[IO]**
Intl. Chamber of Commerce - Georgia **[IO]**
Intl. Chamber of Commerce - Hellas **[IO]**
Intl. Chamber of Commerce - Hrvatska **[IO]**
Intl. Chamber of Commerce - Hungary **[IO]**
Intl. Chamber of Commerce - Italia **[IO]**
Intl. Chamber of Commerce - Lithuania **[IO]**
Intl. Chamber of Commerce - Luxembourg **[IO]**
Intl. Chamber of Commerce - Netherlands **[IO]**
Intl. Chamber of Commerce - UK **[IO]**
Intl. Chamber of Commerce - USA **[IO]**
Intl. Chamber of Commerce - USA **[24284]**
Iraqi Amer. Chamber of Commerce and Indus. **[24285]**
Ireland Chamber of Commerce U.S.A. **[24286]**
Ireland Chamber of Commerce U.S.A. **[IO]**
Irish Australian Chamber of Commerce **[IO]**
Islamic Chamber of Commerce and Indus. **[IO]**
Isle of Man Chamber of Commerce **[IO]**
Isle of Wight Chamber of Commerce **[IO]**
Israel-American Chamber of Commerce and Indus. **[IO]**
Istanbul Chamber of Commerce **[IO]**
Italian Chamber of Commerce and Indus. for the UK **[IO]**
Jamaica USA Chamber of Commerce **[24287]**
Japan Convention Bur. **[24341]**
Jersey Chamber of Commerce and Indus. **[IO]**
Johannesburg Metropolitan Chamber of Commerce and Indus. **[IO]**
Jordan Info. Bur. **[24349]**
Killarney Chamber of Commerce **[IO]**
Korea Chamber of Commerce and Indus. **[IO]**
The Korea Soc. **[24350]**
Korea Trade Promotion Center **[24351]**
Korean Chamber of Commerce in Hong Kong **[IO]**
Kowloon Chamber of Commerce **[IO]**
Kuwait Chamber of Commerce and Indus. **[IO]**
Lancaster District Chamber of Commerce, Trade and Indus. **[IO]**
Lao Natl. Chamber of Commerce and Indus. **[IO]**
Latino Amer. Mgt. Assn. **[24288]**
Latvian Chamber of Commerce and Indus. **[IO]**
Leeds Chamber of Commerce **[IO]**
Leicestershire Chamber of Commerce and Indus. **[IO]**
Liberia Chamber of Commerce **[IO]**
Lima Chamber of Commerce **[IO]**
Limerick Chamber of Commerce **[IO]**
Lincolnshire Chamber of Commerce and Indus. **[IO]**
Lithuanian-U.S. Bus. Coun. **[IO]**
Lithuanian-U.S. Bus. Coun. **[24289]**
Liverpool Chamber of Commerce and Indus. **[IO]**

A star before a book entry number signifies that the name is not listed separately, but is mentioned within the entry.

London Chamber of Commerce and Indus. [IO]
Londonderry Chamber of Commerce [IO]
Macao Chamber of Commerce [IO]
Macclesfield Chamber of Commerce and Enterprise [IO]
Madrid Chamber of Commerce and Indus. [IO]
Malay Chamber of Commerce Malaysia [IO]
Malaysian Assoc. Indian Chambers of Commerce and Indus. [IO]
Malaysian Intl. Chamber of Commerce and Indus. [IO]
Malta Chamber of Commerce and Enterprise [IO]
Manchester Chamber of Commerce and Indus. [IO]
Mauritius Chamber of Commerce and Indus. [IO]
Milano Chamber of Commerce [IO]
Milton Keynes and North Buckinghamshire Chamber of Commerce [IO]
Mongolian Natl. Chamber of Commerce and Indus. [IO]
Mozambique Chamber of Commerce [IO]
MYCCI [IO]
Natl. Assn. of Chamber Ambassadors [789]
Natl. Chamber of Commerce - Algeria [IO]
Natl. Chamber of Commerce - Bolivia [IO]
Natl. Chamber of Commerce and Indus. of Malaysia [IO]
Natl. Chamber of Commerce and Ser. of Uruguay [IO]
Natl. Chamber of Commerce of Sri Lanka [IO]
Natl. Confed. of Commerce [IO]
Natl. Gay and Lesbian Chamber of Commerce [24321]
Natl. United States-Arab Chamber of Commerce [24290]
Nepal Chamber of Commerce [IO]
Netherlands British Chamber of Commerce [IO]
Netherlands Chamber of Commerce Australia [IO]
New Zealand Chambers of Commerce and Indus. [IO]
Nigerian Assn. of Chambers of Commerce, Indus., Mines, and Agriculture [IO]
Norfolk Chamber of Commerce and Indus. [IO]
North American-Bulgarian Chamber of Commerce [24291]
North East Chamber of Commerce [IO]
North Hampshire Chamber of Commerce and Indus. [IO]
North Staffordshire Chamber of Commerce and Indus. [IO]
Northamptonshire Chamber of Commerce [IO]
Northern Ireland Chamber of Commerce and Indus. [IO]
Norwegian Amer. Chamber of Commerce - New York City [IO]
Norwegian Amer. Chamber of Commerce - New York City [24292]
Nottinghamshire Chamber of Commerce and Indus. [IO]
Oman Chamber of Commerce and Indus. [IO]
Osaka Chamber of Commerce and Indus. [IO]
Oslo Chamber of Commerce [IO]
Overseas Investors Chamber of Commerce and Indus. [IO]
Pakistan Chamber of Commerce USA [24364]
Papua New Guinea Chamber of Commerce and Indus. [IO]
Paraguayan-American Chamber of Commerce [IO]
Paris Chamber of Commerce and Indus. [IO]
Philippine Chamber of Commerce and Indus. [IO]
Polish Amer. Chamber of Commerce [24293]
Polish Chamber of Commerce [IO]
Polish Chamber of Commerce of Importers, Exporters and Cooperation [IO]
Portsmouth and South East Hampshire Chamber of Commerce and Indus. [IO]
Portuguese Chamber of Commerce in Britain [IO]
Qatar Chamber of Commerce and Indus. [IO]
Rauma Chamber of Commerce [IO]
Romanian-U.S. Bus. Coun. [24370]
Rotherham Chamber of Commerce [IO]
Russian-American Chamber of Commerce [24294]
Russian-American Chamber of Commerce in the USA [24371]

Russo-British Chamber of Commerce [IO]
St. Helens Chamber of Commerce [IO]
St. Kitt-Nevis Chamber of Indus. and Commerce [IO]
St. Lucia Chamber of Commerce, Indus. and Agriculture [IO]
Santiago Chamber of Commerce [IO]
Santo Domingo Chamber of Commerce and Production [IO]
Serbian-American Chamber of Commerce [24373]
Sheffield Chamber of Commerce and Indus. [IO]
Shropshire Chamber of Commerce and Enterprise [IO]
Sialkot Chamber of Commerce and Indus. [IO]
Singapore Chamber of Commerce - Hong Kong [IO]
Singapore Chinese Chamber of Commerce and Indus. [IO]
Singapore Indian Chamber of Commerce and Indus. [IO]
Singapore Intl. Chamber of Commerce [IO]
Sligo Chamber of Commerce and Indus. [IO]
Slovak Chamber of Commerce and Indus. [IO]
Somerset Chamber of Commerce and Indus. [IO]
South African Chamber of Bus. [IO]
South African USA Chamber of Commerce [24295]
South Chesire Chamber [IO]
South Dublin Chamber of Commerce [IO]
Southampton and Fareham Chamber of Commerce and Indus. [IO]
Spain-United States Chamber of Commerce [IO]
Spain-United States Chamber of Commerce [24296]
Spanish Chamber of Commerce in Great Britain [IO]
Stockholm Chamber of Commerce [IO]
Suffolk Chamber of Commerce [IO]
Surrey Chambers of Commerce [IO]
Sussex Chamber of Commerce and Enterprise [IO]
Swedish-American Chambers of Commerce, USA [IO]
Swedish-American Chambers of Commerce, USA [24297]
Swedish-Canadian Chamber of Commerce [IO]
Swedish Trade Coun. [3847]
Swiss - Amer. Chamber of Commerce [IO]
Taiwan External Trade Development Coun. [IO]
Taiwan Handicraft Promotion Center [IO]
Thai Chamber of Commerce [IO]
Thames Valley Chamber of Commerce [IO]
Thanet and East Kent Chamber [IO]
Tonga Chamber of Commerce and Indus. [IO]
Trinidad and Tobago Chamber of Indus. and Commerce [IO]
Trinidad and Tobago/USA Chamber of Commerce [24298]
Turkish-American Chamber of Commerce and Indus. [24384]
Turkish British Chamber of Commerce and Indus. [IO]
Union of European Chambers of Commerce and Indus. of the Rhine, Rhone, Danube and the Alps [IO]
U.S. of America-China Chamber of Commerce [24310]
U.S. - Angola Chamber of Commerce [24299]
U.S. - Angola Chamber of Commerce [IO]
U.S. - Azerbaijan Chamber of Commerce [IO]
U.S. - Azerbaijan Chamber of Commerce [24300]
U.S. Chamber of Commerce [24301]
U.S. Coun. for Intl. Bus. [766]
U.S. Indian Chamber of Commerce [24331]
United States-Mexico Chamber of Commerce [24302]
United States-Mexico Chamber of Commerce [IO]
U.S. Pan Asian Amer. Chamber of Commerce [IO]
U.S. Pan Asian Amer. Chamber of Commerce [24303]
United States-Qatar Bus. Coun. [24304]
United States-Qatar Bus. Coun. [IO]
U.S. Women's Chamber of Commerce [24389]
US-Vietnam Chamber of Commerce [24387]
Venezuelan Amer. Assn. of the U.S. [24386]

Venezuelan-American Chamber of Commerce [24305]
Venezuelan-American Chamber of Commerce and Indus. [IO]
Vilnius Chamber of Commerce, Indus., and Crafts [IO]
Wales North Am. Bus. Chamber [24306]
Warrington Chamber of Commerce and Indus. [IO]
Waterford Chamber [IO]
West Kent Chamber of Commerce and Indus. [IO]
West Wales Chamber of Commerce [IO]
Wexford Chamber of Indus. and Commerce [IO]
Wirral Chamber of Commerce and Indus. [IO]
Zambia Assn. of Chambers of Commerce and Indus. [IO]
Chambers of Commerce of Ireland [IO], Dublin, Ireland
Chambers Ireland [★IO]
Chambley Air Base Reunion Assn. - Address unknown since 2007.
Chambre Algerienne de Commerce et d'Industrie [★IO]
Chambre Belge des Inventeurs [★IO]
Chambre de Commerce du Canada [★IO]
Chambre de Commerce, d'Agriculture, d'Industrie et d'Artisanat du Niger [★IO]
Chambre de Commerce, d'Industrie et d'Artisanat du Burkina Faso [★IO]
Chambre de Commerce et d'Industrie de l'Ile Maurice [★IO]
Chambre de Commerce et d'Industrie du Mali [★IO]
Chambre de Commerce et d'Industrie de Nouvelle-Caledonie [IO], Noumea, New Caledonia
Chambre de Commerce et d'Industrie de Paris [★IO]
Chambre de Commerce Francaise de Grande Bretagne [★IO]
Chambre de Commerce du Grand-Duche de Luxembourg [★IO]
Chambre de Commerce Intl. [★IO]
Chambre des Ingenieurs-Conseils de France [IO], Paris, France
Chambre Internationale de la Marine Marchande [★IO]
Chambre Islamique de Commerce et d'Industrie [★IO]
Chambre des Metiers du Grand-Duche de Luxembourg [★IO]
Chambre Nationale des Femmes Chefs d'Entreprise [IO], Tunis, Tunisia
Chambre des Notaires du Grand-Duche de Luxembourg [★IO]
Chambre Royale des Antiquaires de Belgique [★IO]
Chambre Syndicale des Emballages en Matiere Plastique [★IO]
Chambre Syndicale des Fabricants d'Aliments pour Chiens, Chats, Oiseaux et autres Animaux Familiers [★IO]
Chambre Syndicale de l'Estampe, du Dessin et du Tableau [IO], Paris, France
Chambre Syndicale Nationale des Fabricants de Confiserie [★IO]
Chambre Syndicale de la Repartition Pharmaceutique [★IO]
Chamois Inst; Sponge and [2420]
Champa Cultural Preservation Assn. of USA [11082], PO Box 62061, Sunnyvale, CA 94088-2061, (408)258-4202
Champagne d'Argent Fed. [★5143]
Champagne d'Argent Rabbit Fed. [5143]
Champagne Horse Breeders' and Owners' Assn. [4870], 2033 Meander Run Rd., Locust Dale, VA 22948, (910)892-2332
Champagne Wines Information Bur. - Defunct.
Champe Surname Org. [20815]
Champion Economics and Business Assn. - Address unknown since 2004.
Champions for Life Intl. [19996], PO Box 761101, Dallas, TX 75376-1101, (972)298-1101
Champions for Life International [IO], Dallas, TX, United States
Championship Assn. of Mechanics [23075]
Championship Auto Racing Teams [23076], 5350 Lakeview Pkwy., South Dr., Indianapolis, IN 46268-5129, (317)715-4100

Reference to "IO" in place of a book number signifies that the association may be found in the 45th edition of International Organizations.

Championship Auto Racing Teams [IO], Indianapolis, IN, United States
Champlain Soc. [IO], Toronto, ON, Canada
Chandler Travelling Notebook - Defunct.
Chandlers; Assoc. Ship [★2584]
Change; Center for Constructive [★8453]
Change for Children - Defunct.
Change Design [IO], Newtown, Australia
Change for Good [12840], c/o UNICEF House, 3 United Nations Plz., New York, NY 10017, (212)326-7000
Change Ringers; North Amer. Guild of [10678]
Change; Training for [13134]
Change to Win [24201], 1900 L St. NW, Ste. 900, Washington, DC 20036, (202)721-0660
Change to Win [IO], Washington, DC, United States
Channel Chamber of Commerce [IO], Folkestone, United Kingdom
Channel Crossing Assn. [IO], Ashford, United Kingdom
Channel Swimming Assn. [IO], Loughborough, United Kingdom
Chaordic Commons [7409], 875 Island Dr., No. 243, Alameda, CA 94502-6781, (415)457-3670
CHAOS in Depth - Defunct.
Chaos Theory in Psychology and Life Sciences; Soc. for [7547]
Chaplaincy; Commn. on Jewish [★19751]
Chaplaincy; HealthCare [16340]
Chaplains
  African-Amer. Women's Clergy Assn. [20615]
  Amer. Bd. of Examiners in Pastoral Counseling [19864]
  Amer. Catholic Correctional Chaplains Assn. [19741]
  Amer. Correctional Chaplains Assn. [19742]
  Apostleship of the Sea in the U.S.A. [19570]
  Assembly of Episcopal Healthcare Chaplains [19944]
  Assn. for Clinical Pastoral Educ. [19915]
  Assn. of Jewish Chaplains of the Armed Forces [19743]
  Assn. of Professional Chaplains [19744]
  Christian Chaplain Sers. [19745]
  Christian Mgt. Assn. [20511]
  CREDO [19746]
  Fed. of Fire Chaplains [19747]
  Good News Jail and Prison Ministry [11869]
  Intl. Assn. of Christian Chaplains [19748]
  Intl. Assn. of Civil Aviation Chaplains [IO]
  Intl. Assn. of Women Ministers [20619]
  Intl. Commn. of Catholic Prison Pastoral Care [IO]
  International Conference of Police Chaplains [IO]
  Intl. Conf. of Police Chaplains [19749]
  Intl. Police and Fire Chaplain's Assn. [19750]
  JWB Jewish Chaplains Coun. [19751]
  Military Chaplains Assn. of the U.S.A. [19752]
  Natl. Assn. of Catholic Chaplains [19753]
  Natl. Assn. of Church Bus. Admin. [20513]
  Natl. Assn. of Church Facilities Managers [20514]
  Natl. Assn. of Church Personnel Administrators [20515]
  Natl. Assn. of Free Will Baptists [19492]
  Natl. Campus Ministry Assn. [19933]
  Natl. Catholic Conf. of Airport Chaplains [19754]
  Natl. Comm. for Amish Religious Freedom [19448]
  Pediatric Chaplains Network [19755]
  Presbyterian Church Bus. Administrators' Assn. [20470]
  Race Track Chaplaincy of Am. [19756]
  Seafarers and Intl. House [20232]
  Trinity Medical Center [14900]
Chaplains' Aid Assn./Seminary Education Fund - Defunct.
Chaplains of the Armed Forces; Assn. of Jewish [19743]
Chaplains; Assembly of Episcopal Healthcare [19944]
Chaplains Assn; Amer. Catholic Prison [★19741]
Chaplains Assn. of the Amer. Protestant Hosp. Assn. [★19744]
Chaplains Assn; Natl. [19855]
Chaplains' Assn. of U.S. [★19752]
Chaplains; Coll. of [★19744]

Chaplain's Corps; Junior [★19855]
Chaplains and Directors of Religious Life; National Assn. of Coll. and Univ. [★9168]
Chaplains Emergency Fund [★21193]
Chaplains; Fellowship of Fire [★19747]
Chaplains; Intl. Conf. of Police [19749]
Chaplains Religious Enrichment Development Operation [★19746]
Chapman Family Assn. [20816], c/o Robert L. Sonfield, Jr., Exec. Dir., 770 S Post Oak Ln., Ste. 435, Houston, TX 77056-1913, (713)877-8333
Chap. 13 Trustees; Natl. Assn. of [★5578]
Chap. of Agassiz Assn. [★7424]
Char-Swiss Breeders Assn. - Defunct.
Character Education Inst. - Defunct.
Character Educ. Partnership [17476], 1025 Connecticut Ave. NW, Ste. 1011, Washington, DC 20036, (202)296-7743
Character Lab; Natl. [6536]
Charbonneau Connection - Defunct.
Charbray Breeders Assn; Amer. [★4228]
Charcoal Grill Mfrs. Assn. - Defunct.
Charcot Found; European [IO]
Charcot-Marie-Tooth Assn. [15313], 2700 Chestnut St., Chester, PA 19013-4867, (610)499-9264
Charcot-Marie-Tooth Disease
  Charcot-Marie-Tooth Assn. [15313]
Chariot Racing
  World Championship Cutter and Chariot Racing Assn. [23281]
Chariscenter USA; Natl. Ser. Committee/ [19693]
Charismatic Renewal Services [★19693]
Charitable Foundation; American Amusement Machine [★1296]
Charitable Foundation; American Amusement Machine [★IO]
Charitable Projects; Assn. of Islamic [20096]
Charitable Statistics; Natl. Center for [12731]
Charitable Trust for Vietnam War Art - Address unknown since 1994.
Charitable Trusts; Pew [13129]
Charities Aid Found. [★13139]
Charities Aid Found. Am. [13139], King St. Sta., 1800 Diagonal Rd., Ste. 150, Alexandria, VA 22314-2840, (703)549-8931
Charities of Am; Independent [1688]
Charities of Am; Italian [19164]
Charities of Am; Local Independent [12729]
Charities of Am; Women, Children and Family Ser. [12207]
Charities in Brooklyn; Fed. of Jewish [★12482]
Charities; Conservative Mennonite Bd. of Missions and [★20253]
Charities Info. Bur; Natl. [★17309]
Charities; Natl. Conf. of Catholic [★13158]
Charities for Reasonable Fundraising Regulation; Amer. [12195]
Charities USA; Catholic [13158]
Charities USA; Sports [23854]
Charity Institutions of Jerusalem; United [12462]
Charity Law Assn. [IO], Portsmouth, United Kingdom
Charity Officials; Natl. Assn. of State [5769]
Charity Societies; United Hasroun Men's and St. Laba Ladies [19732]
Charity; United Sisters of [20406]
Charity of the U.S.A; Ladies of [13173]
Charity of the U.S; Assn. of Ladies of [★13173]
Charity and Welfare Center; Italian [★19164]
Charlebois/Shalibo Family Assn. - Address unknown since 2004.
Charlene Tilton Fan Club - Defunct.
Charles A. and Anne Morrow Lindbergh Found. [4539], 2150 3rd Ave. N, Ste. 310, Anoka, MN 55303-2200, (763)576-1596
Charles A. Lindbergh Assn. - Defunct.
Charles A. Lindbergh Collectors Club - Address unknown since 2007.
Charles A. Lindbergh Fund [★4539]
Charles Babbage Inst. for the History of Info. Tech. [10100], Univ. of Minnesota, 211 Andersen Lib., 222 21st Ave. S, Minneapolis, MN 55455, (612)624-5050
Charles Darwin Found. [★4401]
Charles Darwin Found. for the Galapagos Islands [IO], Quito, Ecuador

Charles Darwin Found. for the Galapagos Isles [★4401]
Charles Edison Memorial Youth Fund [★8747]
Charles Edison Memorial Youth Fund [★IO]
Charles Edison Youth Fund [★IO]
Charles Edison Youth Fund [★8747]
Charles F. Kettering Found. [★8263]
Charles H. Wright Museum of African Amer. History [9358], 315 E Warren Ave., Detroit, MI 48201-1443, (313)494-5800
Charles H. Wright Museum of African Amer. History [IO], Detroit, MI, United States
Charles Homer Haskins Society [IO], Muncie, IN, United States
Charles Homer Haskins Soc. [10459], c/o Frederick Suppe, Treas., Ball State Univ., Dept. of History, Muncie, IN 47306, (765)285-8783
Charles Ives Soc. [10574], c/o Indiana Univ., School of Music, Bloomington, IN 47405, (812)855-7097
Charles Lamb Soc. [IO], Waltham Cross, United Kingdom
Charles the Martyr; Soc. of King [19455]
Charles Ray III Diabetes Assn. [14220], PO Box 792, Apex, NC 27502, (919)303-6949
Charles Ray III Diabetes Assn. [IO], Apex, NC, United States
Charles Rennie Mackintosh Soc. [IO], Glasgow, United Kingdom
Charles S. Peirce Soc. [IO], Carrollton, GA, United States
Charles S. Peirce Soc. [9642], c/o Robert Lane, Sec.-Treas., Philosophy Prog., Univ. of West Georgia, 1601 Maple St., Carrollton, GA 30118, (678)839-4745
Charles Schwab Found; Schwab Learning - A Prog. of the [12496]
Charles Stewart Mott Found. [13113], Mott Found. Bldg., 503 S Saginaw St., Ste. 1200, Flint, MI 48502-1851, (810)238-5651
Charles W. Chesnutt Assn. [11166], c/o Susan Prothro Wright, Clark Atlanta Univ., Dept. of English, Atlanta, GA 30314
Charles Williams Soc. [IO], Milton Keynes, United Kingdom
Charleson Fan Club; Leslie [24752]
Charleston Cotton Exchange - Address unknown since 1995.
Charley Pride Fan Club [24857], PO Box 670507, Dallas, TX 75367, (214)350-8477
Charlie Hodge Fan Club Internationale - Address unknown since 1994.
Charlie Rich Fan Club - Address unknown since 1987.
Charlie Sheen Fan Club - Address unknown since 2003.
Charlmers; Intersure - Singer Nelson [2191]
Charlotte W. Newcombe Found. [12749], c/o Woodrow Wilson Natl. Fellowship Found., PO Box 5281, Princeton, NJ 08543, (609)452-7007
Charolais Assn; American-International [4228]
Charolais Breeders Assn; Amer. [★4228]
Charolais Soc. of Australia [IO], Armidale, Australia
Charollaise Assn; Intl. [★4228]
Chart and Nautical Instrument Trade Assn. [IO], London, United Kingdom
Charted Designers of Am. [★2833]
Charted Designers Assn. [2833], c/o Designs with TLC, 7310 W Roosevelt St., Ste. 6, Phoenix, AZ 85043, (623)936-9900
Charter Group for a Pledge of Conscience - Address unknown since 1995.
Charterboat Operators; Natl. Assn. of [2582]
Chartered Alternative Investment Analyst Assn. [2332], 29 S Pleasant St., Amherst, MA 01002, (413)253-7373
Chartered Assn. of Lib. and Info. Professionals [★IO]
Chartered Inst. of Arbitrators [IO], London, United Kingdom
Chartered Inst. of Architectural Technologists [IO], London, United Kingdom
Chartered Inst. of Bankers - England [★IO]
Chartered Inst. of Bankers - Scotland [IO], Edinburgh, United Kingdom
Chartered Inst. of Building [IO], Ascot, United Kingdom

A star before a book entry number signifies that the name is not listed separately, but is mentioned within the entry.

Chartered Inst. of Environmental Hea. [IO], London, United Kingdom
Chartered Inst. of Housing [IO], Coventry, United Kingdom
Chartered Inst. of Journalists [IO], London, United Kingdom
Chartered Inst. of Lib. and Info. Professionals [IO], London, United Kingdom
Chartered Inst. of Lib. and Info. Professionals in Scotland [IO], Hamilton, United Kingdom
Chartered Inst. of Linguists [IO], London, United Kingdom
Chartered Inst. of Logistics and Transport [IO], Corby, United Kingdom
Chartered Inst. of Logistics Transport [IO], London, United Kingdom
Chartered Inst. of Logistics and Transport in Australia [IO], Sydney, Australia
Chartered Inst. of Logistics and Transport in Hong Kong [IO], Hong Kong, People's Republic of China
Chartered Inst. of Logistics and Transport in Ireland [IO], Dublin, Ireland
Chartered Inst. of Logistics and Transport in North America [IO], Ottawa, ON, Canada
Chartered Inst. of Logistics and Transport - Zimbabwe [IO], Harare, Zimbabwe
Chartered Inst. of Loss Adjusters [IO], London, United Kingdom
Chartered Inst. of Mgt. Accountants [IO], London, United Kingdom
Chartered Inst. of Mgt. Accountants - Australia [IO], Sydney, Australia
Chartered Inst. of Mgt. Accountants - Hong Kong Div. [IO], Hong Kong, People's Republic of China
Chartered Inst. of Mgt. Accountants - Ireland [IO], Ballsbridge, Ireland
Chartered Inst. of Marketing [IO], Maidenhead, United Kingdom
Chartered Inst. of Patent Agents [IO], London, United Kingdom
Chartered Inst. of Personnel and Development [IO], London, United Kingdom
Chartered Inst. of Public Finance and Accountancy [IO], London, United Kingdom
Chartered Inst. of Public Relations [IO], London, United Kingdom
Chartered Inst. of Purchasing and Supply [IO], Stamford, United Kingdom
Chartered Inst. of Taxation [IO], London, United Kingdom
Chartered Inst. of Transport - New Zealand [★IO]
Chartered Inst. of Transport in North America [★IO]
Chartered Inst. of Transport - Zimbabwe [★IO]
Chartered Institution of Building Services [★IO]
Chartered Institution of Building Services Engineers - England [IO], London, United Kingdom
Chartered Institution of Wastes Mgt. [IO], Northampton, United Kingdom
Chartered Institution of Water and Environmental Mgt. [IO], London, United Kingdom
Chartered Insurance Inst. [IO], London, United Kingdom
Chartered Property Casualty Underwriter Soc. [★2160]
Chartered Property Casualty Underwriters; Amer. Inst. for [★2137]
Chartered Quality Inst. [IO], London, United Kingdom
Chartered Secretaries Australia [IO], Sydney, Australia
Chartered Secretaries Australia - Queensland Br. [IO], Brisbane, Australia
Chartered Secretaries Australia - South Australia Br. [IO], Kent Town, Australia
Chartered Secretaries Australia - Tasmania Br. [IO], Melbourne, Australia
Chartered Secretaries Australia - Victoria Br. [IO], Melbourne, Australia
Chartered Secretaries Australia - Western Australia Br. [IO], Perth, Australia
Chartered Secretaries New Zealand [IO], Auckland, New Zealand
Chartered Soc. of Designers [IO], London, United Kingdom
Chartered Soc. of Physiotherapy [IO], London, United Kingdom

Chartier Family Assn. [IO], Beaverton, OR, United States
Chartier Family Assn. [20817], 13095 SW Glenn Ct., Beaverton, OR 97008-5664, (503)646-8186
Chase Purinton Family Assn. - Defunct.
Chastain Family Assn; Pierre [21023]
Chatham House [IO], London, United Kingdom
Chatham House Found. - Defunct.
Chatlos Found. [20591], PO Box 915048, Longwood, FL 32791-5048, (407)862-5077
Chatlos Found. [IO], Longwood, FL, United States
Chatty Cathy Collectors Club [22393], PO Box 4426, Seminole, FL 33775-1426
Chauffeurs, Stablemen and Helpers of Am; Intl. Brotherhood of Teamsters, [★24198]
Chautauqua Literary and Scientific Circle - Address unknown since 2002.
Chautauqua Soc; Jewish [20147]
Chautauquas; Amer. [★10901]
CHEA of CA [★8516]
CHEA of California [★8516]
Cheap Trick Intl. - Address unknown since 2001.
CHEC/America's Found. - Address unknown since 2003.
Chechnya; Amer. Comm. for Peace in [18189]
Check Collectors; Amer. Soc. of [22726]
Check Collectors Roundtable [★22726]
Check Payment Systems Assn. [3678], 2025 M St. NW, Ste. 800, Washington, DC 20036, (202)367-1144
Checker Assn; Amer. [★22457]
Checker Assn; Natl. [★22457]
Checker Car Club of Am. [21606], 2616 Kopson Ct., Bloomfield Hills, MI 48304
Checkered Giant Club; Amer. [★5132]
Checkered Giant Rabbit Club; Amer. [5132]
Checks Anonymous - Defunct.

Cheerleading
Amer. Assn. of Cheerleading Coaches and Advisors [23061]
British Cheerleading Assn. [IO]
Marching New Zealand [IO]
NFHS Spirit Assn. [23295]
Pop Warner Football [23436]
Cheese of Choice Coalition [4492], c/o Oldways Preservation and Exchange Trust, 266 Beacon St., Boston, MA 02116, (617)421-5500
Cheese and Deli Assn; Intl. [★1522]
Cheese and Deli Seminar; Intl. [★1522]
Cheese, and Egg Exchange of the City of New York; Butter, [★4333]
Cheese Importers Assn. of Am. [1131], 204 E St. NE, Washington, DC 20002, (202)547-0899
Cheese Inst; Natl. [1136]
Cheese Makers' Assn; Wisconsin [1141]
Cheese Seminar; Natl. [★1522]
Cheese Seminar; Wisconsin [★1522]
Cheese Soc; Amer. [1129]
Cheetah Cat Catamaran Assn. - Defunct.

Chefs
Amer. Culinary Fed. [790]
Amer. Personal and Private Chef Assn. [791]
British Columbia Chefs' Assn. [IO]
Calgary Acad. of Chefs and Cooks [IO]
Canadian Culinary Fed. [IO]
Canadian Culinary Fed. North Vancouver Island [IO]
Canadian Culinary Fed. Saskatoon Br. [IO]
CCF Brandon Br. [IO]
CCF Edmonton Br. [IO]
CCF Fredericton Br. [IO]
CCF Halifax Br. [IO]
CCF Kamloops Br. [IO]
CCF Kingston Br. [IO]
CCF Lethbridge Assn. [IO]
CCF London Br. [IO]
CCF Moncton Br. [IO]
CCF Okanagan Br. [IO]
CCF Ottawa Br. [IO]
CCF Regina Br. [IO]
CCF St. John's Br. [IO]
CCF Sarnia Br. [IO]
CCF Waterloo Br. [IO]
CCF Winnipeg Br. [IO]
Chefs de Cuisine Assn. of Am. [792]

Culinary Guild of Windsor [IO]
Escoffier Soc. of Toronto [IO]
FCC Chapitre Montreal [IO]
Hamilton District Soc. of Chefs and Cooks [IO]
Hong Kong Chefs Assn. [IO]
Muskoka and District Chefs Assn. [IO]
New Zealand Chefs Assn. [IO]
Northern Ireland Assn. of Chefs and Cooks [IO]
Prince Edward Island Assn. of Chefs and Cooks [IO]
Res. Chefs Assn. [1124]
Singapore Chefs Assn. [IO]
Singapore Junior Chefs Club [IO]
South African Chefs Assn. [IO]
U.S. Personal Chef Assn. [793]
Women Chefs and Restaurateurs [794]
Chefs Assn; Res. [1124]
Chefs de Cuisine Assn. of Am. [792]
Chefs de Cuisine Assn. of Am; Executive [★792]
Chefs and Restaurateurs; Intl. Assn. of Women [★794]
Chefspeare Soc. - Defunct.
Chelation Therapy; Amer. Bd. of [★16659]
Chemical Advertisers Group of New York - Address unknown since 1987.
Chem. and Allied Indus. Assn. [IO], Johannesburg, Republic of South Africa
Chem. and Allied Trades Assn; Drug, [★2974]
Chem. and Assoc. Technologies Assn; Drug, [2974]
Chem. Assn; Armed Forces [★6089]
Chem. Atrocities; Comm. to Stop [★18463]
Chem. and Biological Arms Control Inst. [17023]
Chem. Bus. Assn. [IO], Crewe, United Kingdom
Chem. Coater Assn. [★802]
Chem. Coaters Assn. Intl. [802], PO Box 54316, Cincinnati, OH 45254, (513)624-6767
Chemical Communications Assn. - Address unknown since 2004.
Chem. Contamination; Citizens for Alternatives to [5084]
Chem. Coun; Amer. [★798]
Chem. Credit Assn; Natl. [1440]
Chem. Dependency Nurses; Natl. Consortium of [★15474]
Chem. Development Assn; Commercial [★6677]
Chem. Educ; Inst. for [8062]
Chem. and Energy Workers Intl. Union; Paper, Allied-Indus., [24211]

Chemical Engineering
Bangladesh Chem. Soc. [IO]
Chem. Heritage Found. [10101]
Chem. Indus. and Engg. Soc. of China [IO]
Chem. Soc. of Pakistan [IO]
Chem. Soc. of Vietnam [IO]
Company Chemists Assn. [IO]
Fed. of Asian Chem. Societies [IO]
Institution of Chem. Engineers [IO]
Iranian Chemists' Assn. of the Amer. Chem. Soc. [6687]
Jordanian Chem. Soc. [IO]
Natl. Registry of Environmental Professionals [4593]
North Amer. Membrane Soc. [7307]
Omega Chi Epsilon [24462]
Phi Lambda Upsilon [24430]
Chem. Engg; Canadian Soc. for [IO]
Chem. Engineers; Amer. Inst. of [6665]
Chem. Engineers; Assn. of Consulting Chemists and [6672]
Chem. Engineers Club; India Chemists and [★6685]
Chem. Engineers; Natl. Org. for the Professional Advancement of Black Chemists and [6689]
Chem. Fabrics and Film Assn. [3048], 1300 Sumner Ave., Cleveland, OH 44115-2851, (216)241-7333
Chemical Fabrics and Film Association [IO], Cleveland, OH, United States
Chem. Fiber Indus. Assn. [IO], Frankfurt am Main, Germany
Chem. Hazards Commun. Soc. [IO], Lymington, United Kingdom
Chem. Heritage Found. [10101], 315 Chestnut St., Philadelphia, PA 19106-2702, (215)925-2222
Chem. and Indus. Consultants Assn. [IO], Oswestry, United Kingdom
Chem. Indus. Assn. [IO], London, United Kingdom

Reference to "IO" in place of a book number signifies that the association may be found in the 45th edition of International Organizations.

Chem. Indus. Coun. of Malaysia [IO], Kuala Lumpur, Malaysia
Chem. Indus. Assn. [IO], Santiago, Chile
Chem. Indus. and Engg. Soc. of China [IO], Beijing, People's Republic of China
Chem. Indus. Fed. of Finland [IO], Helsinki, Finland
Chem. Indus. Inst. of Toxicology [★7801]
Chemical Industry for Minorities in Engineering - Address unknown since 2006.
Chem. Indus; Salesmen's Assn. of the Amer. [★819]
Chem. Injury Info. Network [16656], PO Box 301, White Sulphur Springs, MT 59645, (406)547-2255
Chem. Injury Info. Network [IO], White Sulphur Springs, MT, United States
Chem. Inst. of Canada [★IO]
Chem. Inst. of Canada [IO], Ottawa, ON, Canada
Chemical Machining Inst; Photo- [2725]
Chem. Mgt. and Resources Assn. [★6677]
Chem. Manufacturers Assn. [★798]
Chem. Mortar Battalion Assn; 86th [21368]
Chem. Org. of Mexico [IO], Mexico City, Mexico
Chem., Paper, and Ceramic Workers' Indus. Union [★IO]
Chem. Pharmaceutical Generic Assn. [IO], Milan, Italy
Chem. Plant Safety; Center for [★801]
Chem. Producers and Distributors Assn. [803], 1430 Duke St., Alexandria, VA 22314, (703)548-7700
Chemical Res. Applied to World Needs Committee [★6697]
Chemical Res. Applied to World Needs Committee [★IO]
Chem. Res; Coun. for [6679]
Chemical Societies; Pan Amer. Assn. of Bio [★6551]
Chem. Soc. [★IO]
Chem. Soc; Amer. [6664]
Chemical Soc; Amer. Micro [6668]
Chemical Soc; Electro [6680]
Chem. Soc. of Ethiopia [IO], Addis Ababa, Ethiopia
Chemical Soc; Geo [7141]
Chemical Soc; Histo [13938]
Chem. Soc. of Japan [IO], Tokyo, Japan
Chem. Soc. of Pakistan [IO], Islamabad, Pakistan
Chem. Soc; Rubber Div., Amer. [3433]
Chem. Soc. of Vietnam [IO], Hanoi, Vietnam
Chem. Sources Assn. [1660], c/o Diane Davis, 3301 Rte. 66, Ste. 205, Bldg. C, Neptune, NJ 07753, (732)922-3008
Chem. Specialties Manufacturers Assn. [★806]
Chem. Stud; Natl. Inst. for [13326]
Chemical Toilet Assn. - Address unknown since 1995.
Chem. Waste Trans. Inst. [★3579]
Chemical Weapons
  Amer. Collectors of Infant Feeders [21959]
  Chem. and Biological Arms Control Inst. [17023]
  Nuclear Threat Initiative [18164]
Chem. Workers Union; Intl. [★24061]
Chemicals
  Acrylonitrile Gp. [795]
  Aerosol Assn. of Australia [IO]
  Agricultural Lime Assn. [IO]
  Alkylphenols and Ethoxylates Res. Coun. [796]
  Alliance for Responsible Atmospheric Policy [797]
  Amer. Chemistry Coun. [798]
  Amer. Coke and Coal Chemicals Inst. [838]
  Amer. Fire Safety Coun. [799]
  Argentine Chamber of Aerosols [IO]
  Asociation Quimica Argentina [IO]
  Assn. of the Austrian Chem. Indus. [IO]
  Assn. of Chem. Indus. [IO]
  Assn. of Chem. Indus. of Slovenia [IO]
  Assn. of Chem. Indus. of the Czech Republic [IO]
  Assn. of Chem. Indus. of Germany [IO]
  Assn. of the Dutch Chem. Indus. [IO]
  Assn. of Fertilizer and Phosphate Chemists [6673]
  Assn. of Veterinary and Crop Protection Associations of Southern Africa [IO]
  Assn. of Wholesalers of Chem. and Pharmaceutical Goods [IO]
  Atlantic Independent Union [24161]
  Basic Acrylic Monomer Mfrs. [800]
  Brazilian Assn. of the Aerosol Indus. [IO]
  Brazilian Chem. Assn. [IO]

Brazilian Chem. Indus. Assn. [IO]
British Aerosol Mfrs'. Assn. [IO]
British Assn. for Chem. Specialties [IO]
Canadian Assn. of Chem. Distributors [IO]
Canadian Chem. Producers' Assn. [IO]
Canadian Consumer Specialty Products Assn. [IO]
Center for Chem. Process Safety [801]
Centre Europeen des Silicones [IO]
Chem. and Allied Indus. Assn. [IO]
Chem. Bus. Assn. [IO]
Chem. Coaters Assn. Intl. [802]
Chem. Fiber Indus. Assn. [IO]
Chem. Hazards Commun. Soc. [IO]
Chem. Indus. Assn. [IO]
Chem. Indus. Coun. of Malaysia [IO]
Chem. Indus. Assn. [IO]
Chem. Indus. Fed. of Finland [IO]
Chem. Injury Info. Network [16656]
Chem. Inst. of Canada [IO]
Chem. Org. of Mexico [IO]
Chem. Producers and Distributors Assn. [803]
Chem. Soc. of Ethiopia [IO]
Chemicals and Allied Products Export Promotion Coun. [IO]
Chinese Chem. Soc., Taipei [IO]
Chlorinated Paraffins Indus. Assn. [804]
Chlorine Chemistry Coun. [6676]
Chlorine Inst. [805]
Citizens Against Chemtrails U.S. [17053]
Consumer Specialty Products Assn. [806]
Crop Protection Assn. [IO]
CropLife Am. [807]
Ethylene Oxide Sterilization Assn. [808]
Euro Chlor [IO]
European Aerosol Fed. [IO]
European Assn. of Chem. Distributors [IO]
European Calcium Soc. [IO]
European Catalysts Mfrs. Assn. [IO]
European Centre of Stud. on Linear Alkylbenzene [IO]
European Chem. Indus. Coun. [IO]
European Chem. Marketing and Strategy Assn. [IO]
European Chlorinated Solvent Assn. [IO]
European Citric Acid Mfrs. Assn. [IO]
European Food Phosphates Producers' Assn. [IO]
European Fuel Oxygenates Assn. [IO]
European Isocyanate and Polyol Producers Assn. [IO]
European Mine, Chem., and Energy Workers' Fed. [IO]
European Oleochemicals and Allied Products Gp. [IO]
European Pure Phosphoric Acid Producers' Assn. [IO]
European Sulphuric Acid Assn. [IO]
European Wax Fed. [IO]
Fed. Assn. of the Chem. Trade [IO]
Fed. of the Belgian Chem. Indus. [IO]
Fed. of the Estonian Chem. Indus. [IO]
German Chem. Soc. [IO]
Halogenated Solvents Indus. Alliance [809]
Handcrafted Soap Makers Guild [1155]
Hellenic Aerosol Assn. [IO]
Hungarian Chem. Indus. Assn. [IO]
Indian Chem. Coun. [IO]
Indian Chem. Soc. [IO]
Industrial Chemical Res. Assn. [810]
Inst. for Polyacrylate Absorbents [811]
Institute for Polyacrylate Absorbents [IO]
Intl. Assn. of Used Equip. Dealers [3052]
Intl. Brotherhood of DuPont Workers [24034]
Intl. Fed. of Chem., Energy, Mine and Gen. Workers' Unions [IO]
Israeli Assn. for Aerosol Res. [IO]
Italian Chem. Soc. [IO]
Italian Fed. of the Chem. Indus. [IO]
Japan Chem. Indus. Assn. [IO]
Japan Lime Assn. [IO]
Latvian Biochemical Soc. [IO]
Materials Tech. Inst. [812]
Methacrylate Producers Assn. [813]
Methyl Chloride Indus. Assn. [814]
Mining, Chem., and Energy Indus. Union [IO]

Natl. Assn. of Chem. Distributors [815]
Natl. Assn. of Sci. Materials Managers [3487]
Natl. Chem. Indus. Assn. [IO]
Natl. Lime Assn. [816]
Natl. Registry of Certified Chemists [13939]
New Zealand Chem. Indus. Coun. [IO]
North Amer. Alliance of Chem. Engineers [6690]
Norwegian Chem. Soc. [IO]
Paper, Allied-Indus., Chem. and Energy Workers Intl. Union [24211]
The Pesticide Stewardship Alliance [7068]
PET Resin Assn. [3054]
Phosphate Chemicals Export Assn. [817]
Phosphoric Acid and Phosphates Producers Assn. [IO]
Phytochemical Soc. of Europe - United Kingdom [IO]
Pine Chemicals Assn. [818]
Polish Chamber of the Chem. Indus. [IO]
Responsible Indus. for a Sound Env. [2912]
Sales Assn. of the Chem. Indus. [819]
SB Latex Coun. [820]
SGCI Chemie Pharma Schweiz [IO]
Silicones Environmental, Hea. and Safety Coun. [821]
Soap and Detergent Assn. [822]
Soc. of Flavor Chemists [6696]
Soc. of Leather Technologists and Chemists (South African Sect.) [IO]
Solvent Extractors' Assn. of India [IO]
Solvents Indus. Assn. [IO]
Spanish Aerosols Assn. [IO]
Styrene Info. and Res. Center [823]
The Sulphur Inst. [824]
The Sulphur Inst. [IO]
Swimming Pool Water Treatment Professionals [825]
Synthetic Amorphous Silica and Silicates Industry Assn. [826]
Synthetic Organic Chem. Manufacturers Assn. [827]
Titanium Dioxide Mfrs. Sector Gp. [IO]
Tributyl Phosphate Task Force [828]
Turkish Chem. Mfrs'. Assn. [IO]
US Fuel Cell Coun. [6976]
Venezuelan Assn. of the Chem. and Petrochemical Indus. [IO]
Wire Assn. Intl. [7323]
Chemicals and Allied Products Export Promotion Coun. [IO], Calcutta, India
Chemicals Assn; Natl. Agricultural [★807]
Chemicals Assn; Pulp [★818]
Chemicals Inst; Amer. Coke and Coal [838]
Chemistry
  AACC Intl. [6660]
  AACC Intl. [IO]
  Adhesion Soc. [6661]
  Alpha Chi Sigma [24428]
  Amer. Assn. for Aerosol Res. [6662]
  Amer. Assn. for Clinical Chemistry [13936]
  American Association for Clinical Chemistry [IO]
  Amer. Assn. for Crystal Growth [6851]
  Amer. Assn. of Textile Chemists and Colorists [7794]
  Amer. Bd. of Toxicology [7799]
  Amer. Carbon Soc. [6663]
  Amer. Chem. Soc. [6664]
  Amer. Coll. of Toxicology [7800]
  Amer. Crystallographic Assn. [6852]
  Amer. Inst. of Chem. Engineers [6665]
  Amer. Inst. of Chemists [6666]
  Amer. Leather Chemists Assn. [6667]
  Amer. Microchemical Soc. [6668]
  Amer. Nuclear Soc. [7385]
  Amer. Oil Chemists' Soc. [6669]
  American Oil Chemists' Society [IO]
  Amer. Soc. for Biochemistry and Molecular Biology [6546]
  Amer. Soc. of Brewing Chemists [6670]
  American Society of Brewing Chemists [IO]
  Amer. Soc. for Mass Spectrometry [7688]
  Amer. Soc. for Neurochemistry [7374]
  AOAC Intl. [6671]
  AOAC Intl. [IO]
  Asian Pacific Confed. of Chem. Engg. [IO]

A star before a book entry number signifies that the name is not listed separately, but is mentioned within the entry.

Assn. for Aerosol Res. [IO]
Association for Chemoreception Sciences [IO]
Assn. for Chemoreception Sciences [13937]
Assn. of Consulting Chemists and Chem. Engineers [6672]
Assn. of Fertilizer and Phosphate Chemists [6673]
Assn. of Formulation Chemists [6674]
Australian Soc. of Cosmetic Chemists [IO]
Biomedical Engg. Soc. [6607]
Canadian Soc. for Chem. Tech. [IO]
Canadian Soc. for Chemistry [IO]
Canadian Soc. of Clinical Chemists [IO]
Center for Process Analytical Chemistry [6675]
Chem. Heritage Found. [10101]
Chem. Soc. of Japan [IO]
Chemistry and Physics on Stamps Stud. Unit [22802]
Chinese Chem. Soc. [IO]
Chlorine Chemistry Coun. [6676]
Chromatographic Soc. [IO]
CIIT Centers for Hea. Res. [7801]
Collaborative Intl. Pesticides Analytical Coun. [IO]
Combustion Inst. [6709]
Commercial Development and Marketing Assn. [6677]
Controlled Release Soc. [6678]
Coun. for Chem. Res. [6679]
Coun. on Undergraduate Res. [9059]
Czech Chem. Soc. [IO]
Danish Chem. Soc. [IO]
Electrochemical Soc. [6680]
Emulsion Polymers Inst. [6681]
European Assn. for Chem. and Molecular Sciences [IO]
European Centre for Ecotoxicology and Toxicology of Chemicals [IO]
European Chem. Soc. [IO]
European Fed. of Chem. Engg. [IO]
European Photochemistry Assn. [IO]
European Rare-Earth Actinide Soc. [IO]
Federacion Empresarial de la Industria Quimica Espanola [IO]
Fed. of Analytical Chemistry and Spectroscopy Societies [6682]
Fed. of Societies for Coatings Tech. [6704]
French Chem. Soc. [IO]
Geochemical Soc. [7141]
German Bunsen Soc. for Physical Chemistry [IO]
Histochemical Soc. [13938]
Hong Kong Soc. of Clinical Chemistry [IO]
Hungarian Chem. Soc. [IO]
Institut de Biologie Physico-Chimique [IO]
Inst. for Chem. Educ. [8062]
Inst. of Chemistry of Ireland [IO]
Intl. Assn. of Environmental Analytical Chemistry [IO]
Intl. Assn. of Environmental Mutagen Societies [6578]
Intl. Fed. of Clinical Chemistry and Lab. Medicine [IO]
Intl. Liquid Crystal Soc. [6853]
Intl. Maillard Reaction Soc. [6683]
Intl. Org. for Chem. Sciences in Development [6684]
Intl. Org. for Chem. Sciences in Development [IO]
Intl. Proteolysis Soc. [6549]
Intl. Soc. for Aerosols in Medicine [IO]
Intl. Soc. for Bioluminescence and Chemiluminescence [7612]
Intl. Soc. of Chem. Ecology [6550]
Intl. Soc. of Electrochemistry [IO]
Intl. Soc. for Fat Res. [7405]
Intl. Soc. for Fluoride Res. [IO]
Intl. Soc. of Heterocyclic Chemistry [IO]
Intl. Soc. of India Chemists and Chem. Engineers [IO]
Intl. Soc. of India Chemists and Chem. Engineers [6685]
Intl. Soc. for the Philosophy of Chemistry [IO]
Intl. Union of Pure and Applied Chemistry [IO]
Intl. Union of Pure and Applied Chemistry [6686]
Iota Sigma Pi [24429]
Iranian Chemists' Assn. of the Amer. Chem. Soc. [6687]

Israel Chem. Soc. [IO]
Japan Assn. for Intl. Chem. Info. [IO]
Japan Oil Chemists' Soc. [IO]
Japan Soc. for Analytical Chemistry [IO]
Japan Soc. of Nuclear and Radiochemical Sciences [IO]
Korean Chem. Soc. [IO]
Milling and Baking Division of AACC Intl. [7095]
Natl. Inst. of Packaging, Handling and Logistics Engineers [7427]
Natl. Mole Day Found. [6688]
Natl. Org. for the Professional Advancement of Black Chemists and Chem. Engineers [6689]
Natl. Registry of Certified Chemists [13939]
New Zealand Inst. of Chemistry [IO]
Nordic Soc. of Clinical Chemistry [IO]
North Amer. Alliance of Chem. Engineers [6690]
North Amer. Chinese Clinical Chemists Assn. [6691]
North American Chinese Clinical Chemists Association [IO]
Organic Reactions Catalysis Soc. [6692]
Pan-American Assn. for Biochemistry and Molecular Biology [6551]
PET Resin Assn. [3054]
Phi Lambda Upsilon [24430]
Polanyi Soc. [10826]
Polish Chem. Soc. [IO]
Radiation Res. Soc. [7557]
Royal Australian Chem. Inst. [IO]
Royal Australian Chem. Inst. - ACT Br. [IO]
Royal Australian Chem. Inst. - NSW Br. [IO]
Royal Australian Chem. Inst. - NT Br. [IO]
Royal Australian Chem. Inst. - SA Br. [IO]
Royal Australian Chem. Inst. - Tasmanian Br. [IO]
Royal Australian Chem. Inst. - Victorian Br. [IO]
Royal Australian Chem. Inst. - WA Br. [IO]
Royal Netherlands Chem. Soc. [IO]
Royal Soc. of Chemistry [IO]
Rubber Div., Amer. Chem. Soc. [3433]
Salters' Inst. [IO]
Societe de Chimie Industrielle, Amer. Sect. [IO]
Societe de Chimie Industrielle, Amer. Sect. [6693]
Societe de Chimie Industrielle - French Sect. [IO]
Societe Royale de Chimie [IO]
Soc. of Biological Chemists, India [IO]
Society for Biomolecular Sciences [IO]
Soc. for Biomolecular Sciences [6694]
Soc. for Chem. Engg. and Biotechnology [IO]
Soc. of Chem. Indus. [IO]
Soc. of Cosmetic Chemists [6695]
Soc. of Flavor Chemists [6696]
Soc. for Free Radical Biology and Medicine [6613]
Soc. for the History of Alchemy and Chemistry [IO]
Soc. for Indus. Microbiology [6599]
Soc. of Mineral Analysts [7345]
Soc. of Rheology [7579]
Soc. of Toxicology [7804]
Soil Sci. Soc. of Am. [7674]
South African Chem. Inst. [IO]
Spanish Soc. of Real Chemistry [IO]
Swiss Chem. Soc. [IO]
Thermoset Resin Formulators Assn. [857]
Toxicological History Soc. [7805]
Union of Chemists in Bulgaria [IO]
U.S. Natl. Comm. for the Intl. Union of Pure and Applied Chemistry [IO]
U.S. Natl. Comm. for the Intl. Union of Pure and Applied Chemistry [6697]
Women Members Network of the Royal Soc. of Chemistry [IO]
World Assn. of Theoretically Oriented Chemists [IO]
Chemistry; Arnold and Mabel Beckman Center for History of [★10101]
Chemistry; Center for History of [★10101]
Chemistry Consortium - Defunct.
Chemistry Coun; Amer. [798]
Chemistry; HELP - Inst. for Body [14928]
Chemistry and Molecular Biology; Amer. Soc. for Bio [6546]
Chemistry; Natl. Found. for History of [★10101]
Chemistry; Natl. Registry in Clinical [★13939]

Chemistry and Physics on Stamps Stud. Unit [22802], c/o Prof. Foil A. Miller, Ed.-Emeritus, 960 Lakemont Dr., Pittsburgh, PA 15243
Chemistry and Physics Stud. Unit [★22802]
Chemistry; Soc. of Environmental Toxicology and [14370]
Chemistry Stud. Unit [★22802]
Chemists; Amer. Assn. of Clinical [★13936]
Chemists; Amer. Soc. of Biological [★6546]
Chemists; Assn. of Official Agricultural [★6671]
Chemists; Assn. of Official Analytical [★6671]
Chemists and Chem. Engineers Club; India [★6685]
Chemists and Chem. Engineers; Natl. Org. of Black [★6689]
Chemists' Club [19374], 40 W 45th St., New York, NY 10036, (212)626-9300
Chemists and Colorists; Amer. Assn. of Textile [7794]
Chemists; Milling and Baking Division of Amer. Assn. of Cereal [★7095]
CHEMOcare [★13806]
Chemoreception Sciences; Assn. for [13937]
Chemosurgery; Amer. Coll. of [★15636]
Chemotherapists Assn. of Ukraine [IO], Kiev, Ukraine

Chemotherapy
African Soc. of Chemotherapy [IO]
Amer. Coll. of Mohs Micrographic Surgery and Cutaneous Oncology [15636]
Amer. Radium Soc. [15639]
Amer. Soc. of Clinical Oncology [15640]
Amer. Soc. of Cytopathology [14075]
Amer. Soc. for Cytotechnology [14076]
Amer. Soc. for Mohs Histotechnology [15130]
Amer. Soc. for Mohs Surgery [15641]
Arab Soc. of Chemotherapy, Microbiology and Infectious Diseases [IO]
Austrian Soc. of Antimicrobial Chemotherapy [IO]
British Soc. for Antimicrobial Chemotherapy [IO]
Bulgarian Soc. of Chemotherapy [IO]
Chemotherapists Assn. of Ukraine [IO]
Croatian Soc. of Chemotherapy [IO]
Cyprus Soc. of Chemotherapy and Infectious Diseases [IO]
Czech Soc. of Chemotherapy [IO]
Found. for Advancement in Cancer Therapy [13824]
Georgian Soc. of Paediatric Chemotherapy [IO]
Hellenic Soc. for Chemotherapy [IO]
Hong Kong Cancer Chemotherapy Soc. [IO]
Hong Kong Soc. for Microbiology and Infection [IO]
Hungarian Soc. for Chemotherapy [IO]
Indian Soc. for Antimicrobial Chemotherapy [IO]
Indonesian Soc. for Chemotherapy [IO]
Intl. Soc. of Chemotherapy [IO]
Interregional Assn. for Clinical Microbiology and Antimicrobial Chemotherapy [IO]
Italian Soc. of Chemotherapy [IO]
Japanese Soc. for Chemotherapy [IO]
KIDSCOPE [11518]
Korean Soc. of Chemotherapy [IO]
Malaysian Soc. of Infectious Diseases and Chemotherapy [IO]
Mediterranean Soc. of Chemotherapy [IO]
Moroccan Soc. of Chemotherapy [IO]
Natl. Soc. of Chemotherapy of the Russian Fed. [IO]
Paul-Ehrlich-Gesellschaft fur Chemotherapie [IO]
Polish Medical Assn., Sect. of Chemotherapy [IO]
Scandinavian Soc. of Antimicrobial Chemotherapy [IO]
Slovak Soc. of Chemotherapy [IO]
Slovenian Soc. of Chemotherapy [IO]
Soc. of Chemotherapeutists in Bulgaria [IO]
Turkish Soc. of Antimicrobial Chemotherapy [IO]
Turkish Soc. of Chemotherapy [IO]
Chemotherapy; Amer. Soc. of Clinical Pharmacology and [★15920]
Chemotherapy Found. [15644], 183 Madison Ave., Rm. 403, New York, NY 10016, (212)213-9292
Chemtrails U.S; Citizens Against [17053]
Chemtrec Center Non-Emergency Services - Defunct.
Chen Style Tai Chi Assn; Amer. [23578]

Reference to "IO" in place of a book number signifies that the association may be found in the 45th edition of International Organizations.

Chen Wen-Chen Memorial Found; Professor [18694]
Cher: The Fan Club - Address unknown since 2000.
Cher'd Interest - Defunct.
Cherish [★IO]
Chernobyl; Assn. to Help [IO]
Chernobyl Children Fund [★IO]
Chernobyl Children's Fund - Japan [IO], Tokyo, Japan
Cherokee Heritage Center [★10735]
Cherokee Natl. Historical Soc. [10735], PO Box 515, Tahlequah, OK 74465-0515, (918)456-6007
Cherokee Pilots' Assn. [21437], PO Box 1996, Lutz, FL 33549, (813)242-7814
Cherry Central Cooperative [4722], PO Box 988, Traverse City, MI 49685-0988, (231)946-1860
Cherry Growers and Indus. Found. [★4741]
Cherry Growers and Indus. Found; Natl. [4741]
Cherry Growers; Northwest [4751]
Cherry Inst; Natl. Red [★4723]
Cherry Marketing Inst. [4723], PO Box 30285, Lansing, MI 48909-7785, (517)669-4264
Cherry Producers; Michigan Assn. of [4740]
CHERUBS - Assn. of Congenital Diaphragmatic Hernia Res., Advocacy and Support [13753], 270 Coley Rd., Henderson, NC 27537, (252)492-9066
CHERUBS - Association of Congenital Diaphragmatic Hernia Research, Advocacy and Support [IO], Henderson, NC, United States
Cheryl Hale Fan Club - Defunct.
Cheryl K. Warner Fan Club - Defunct.
Cheryl Roth Intl. Fan Club - Defunct.
Chesapeake Bay Seafood Industries Assn. - Address unknown since 1995.
Chesapeake Bay Yacht Racing Association [★23173]
Chesapeake Club; Amer. [22195]
Chesapeake and Ohio Historical Soc. [10910], PO Box 79, Clifton Forge, VA 24422, (540)862-2210
Cheshire Found. in Ireland [★IO]
Cheshire Ireland [IO], Sandyford, Ireland
Chesney Fan Club; Kenny [24933]
Chesnutt Assn; Charles W. [11166]

Chess

All India Chess Fed. for the Blind [IO]
All Ser. Postal Chess Club [21941]
Amer. Chess Assn. [21942]
Amer. Postal Chess Tournaments [21943]
Assn. of Chess Professionals [IO]
Australian Chess Fed. [IO]
Braille Chess Assn. [IO]
Canadian Correspondence Chess Assn. [IO]
Chess Collectors Intl. [IO]
Chess Collectors Intl. [21944]
Chess in the Schools [21945]
Chess Scotland [IO]
Chess'n Math Assn. [IO]
Correspondence Chess League of Am. [21946]
Croatian Chess Fed. [IO]
English Chess Fed. [IO]
Intl. Cmpt. Games Assn. [IO]
Scottish Correspondence Chess Assn. [IO]
U.S. Braille Chess Assn. [21947]
U.S. Chess Fed. [21948]
World Chess Fed. [IO]

Chess Assn; U.S. Braille [21947]
Chess Collectors Assn. - Defunct.
Chess Collectors Intl. [21944], c/o Floyd Sarisohn, Membership Chm., PO Box 166, Commack, NY 11725, (631)543-7667
Chess Collectors Intl. [IO], Commack, NY, United States
Chess Journalists of Am. [3104], c/o Jerry Hanken, Pres., 2012 Yosemite Dr., No. 1, Los Angeles, CA 90041, (323)257-9839
Chess Journalists; Assn. of U.S. [★3104]
Chess in the Schools [21945], 520 8th Ave., 2nd Fl., New York, NY 10018, (212)643-0225
Chess Scotland [IO], Glasgow, United Kingdom
Chess on Stamps Unit - Defunct.
Chess'n Math Assn. [IO], Toronto, ON, Canada
Chest Pain Centers and Providers; Soc. of [15849]
Chester White Swine Record Assn. [5234], PO Box 9758, Peoria, IL 61612-9758, (309)691-0151
Chesterfield Kings - Address unknown since 2001.

Chesterton, Gilbert Keith

Amer. Chesterton Soc. [9630]

Chestnut Found; The Amer. [6622]
Cheswick Historical Soc. - Address unknown since 2005.
Chet Atkins Appreciation Soc. [24858], c/o Mark Pritcher, Pres., 3716 Timberlake Rd., Knoxville, TN 37920
Chevelle Enthusiasts Soc; Amer. [21571]
Cheviot Sheep Assn; Amer. North Country [5189]
Cheviot Sheep Soc; Amer. [5178]
Chevra Agudath Achim Chesed Shel Emeth [★20141]

Chevrolet

1965-66 Full Size Chevrolet Club [21557]
Chevrolet Nomad Assn. [21607]
Chevy GMC Intl. Truck Club [21609]
Classic Chevy Intl. [21615]
Corvette Club of Am. [21623]
Intl. Camaro Club [21665]
Late Great Chevrolet Assn. [21685]
Natl. Impala Assn. [21733]
Natl. Monte Carlo Owners Assn. [21735]
Natl. Nostalgic Nova [21736]
Vintage Chevrolet Club of Am. [21809]

Chevrolet Assn; Late Great [21685]
Chevrolet Club; 1965-66 Full Size [21557]
Chevrolet Club of Am; Vintage [21809]
Chevrolet Dealers Alliance [★412]
Chevrolet Nomad Assn. [21607], PO Box 265, Davenport, NE 68335, (740)967-1955
Chevy Assn; Natl. [21727]
Chevy Club; Geo and [★21608]
Chevy Club Intl; Classic [★21615]
Chevy and Geo Club [21608], PO Box 11238, Chicago, IL 60611, (773)769-6262
Chevy GMC Intl. Truck Club [21609], PO Box 7411, Midland, TX 79708-7411
Chewing Gum Mfrs; Natl. Assn. of [1538]
Chewings Fescue and Creeping Red Fescue Commn. [4792], c/o Oregon Seed Coun., 1193 Royvonne Ave. S, Ste. 11, Salem, OR 97302, (503)585-1157
CHExchange Network - Defunct.
CHF Intl. [★12309]
CHF - Partners in Rural Development [IO], Ottawa, ON, Canada
ChFC; Amer. Soc. of CLU and [★2240]
Chi Beta Phi - Address unknown since 2001.
Chi Delta Phi - Defunct.
Chi Eta Phi Sorority [24560], 3029 13th St. NW, Washington, DC 20009, (202)232-3858
Chi Kung Assn; Natl. Qigong [13644]
Chi Omega [24681], 3395 Players Club Pkwy., Memphis, TN 38125, (901)748-8600
Chi Phi [24621], 850 Indian Trail Rd. NW, Lilburn, GA 30047, (404)231-1824
Chi Psi [24622], Jeffrey Hall, 45 Rutledge St., Nashville, TN 37210, (615)736-2520
Chi Psi Educational Trust [★24622]
Chi Sigma Iota [1099], PO Box 35448, Greensboro, NC 27425-5448, (336)841-8180
Chian Fed. of Am. [19084], 44-01 Broadway, Astoria, NY 11103, (718)204-2550
Chianina Assn; Amer. [4219]
Chianina Assn; Amer. Junior [4232]
Chicago Action for Jews in the Former Soviet Union [17444], 555 Vine St., Ste. 111, Highland Park, IL 60035, (847)433-0144
Chicago Action for Jews in the Former Soviet Union [IO], Highland Park, IL, United States
Chicago Alliance for VD Awareness [★16411]
Chicago Area Agricultural Advt. Assn. [★2640]
Chicago Blackhawk Standbys [★24997]
Chicago Bd. Options Exchange [3509], 400 S La-Salle St., Chicago, IL 60605, (312)786-5600
Chicago Butter and Egg Bd. [★4324]
Chicago Fan Club [24859], PO Box 195, Landing, NJ 07850
Chicago Hebrew Mission [★19988]
Chicago Hebrew Mission [★IO]
Chicago; Intl. Kennel Club of [22289]
Chicago Map Soc. [21528], c/o Newberry Lib., 60 W Walton St., Chicago, IL 60610, (312)255-3689
Chicago Mercantile Exchange and Chicago Board of Trade [★4324]
Chicago and Midwest Envelope Mfrs. Assn. - Defunct.

Chicago Playing Card Collectors [21992], 1319 E Sanborn, Palatine, IL 60067, (770)992-7478
Chicago Religious Task Force on Central America - Address unknown since 2001.
Chicago Saab Club [★21778]
Chicago Standbys Fan Club [★24997]
Chicago Stock Exchange [3510], One Financial Pl., 440 S LaSalle St., Chicago, IL 60605, (312)663-2222
Chicago; Textile Merchants and Assoc. Indus. of [★221]
Chicago Training Center [★17701]
Chicago Training Center [★IO]
Chicago True Advocates [24860], PO Box 195, Landing, NJ 07850, (516)933-7153
Chicago VD Alliance Comm. [★16411]
Chicana and Chicano Stud; Natl. Assn. for [8498]
Chicana Res. and Learning Center - Address unknown since 2001.
Chicana Rights Project - Defunct.
Chicano Education Project - Defunct.
Chicano Family Center [17701]
Chicano Family Center [IO], Houston, TX, United States
Chicano Legal Defense Fund - Defunct.
Chicano Org. for Political Awareness - Defunct.
Chicano Press Assn. - Address unknown since 1995.
Chicano, Puerto Rican, Asian Americans; Natl. Assn. of Interdisciplinary Stud. for Native Amer., Black, [★9919]
Chicano Stud; Natl. Assn. for [★8498]
Chicano Stud; Natl. Assn. for Chicana and [8498]
Chicano Teachers of English - Defunct.
Chicanos and Native Americans in Sci; Soc. for Advancement of [7630]
Chickasaw Horse Assn. - Defunct.
Chicken Coun; Natl. [5111]
Chicos Perdidos in Argentina [★IO]
Chicos Perdidos in Argentina and Latin Am. and Europe [IO], Mendoza, Argentina
Chief Cultural and Leisure Officers Assn. [IO], Hexham, United Kingdom
Chief Executive Officers Club [711], 4 W 22nd St., 10th Fl., New York, NY 10010, (212)925-7911
Chief Executives Forum [★712]
Chief Executives Org. [712], 7920 Norfolk Ave., Ste. 400, Bethesda, MD 20814-2507, (301)656-9220
Chief Jules Strongbow Fan Club - Defunct.
Chief Justices; Conf. of [5896]
Chief Officers of State Lib. Agencies [10346], 201 E Main St., Ste. 1405, Lexington, KY 40507, (859)514-9151
Chief Petty Officers' Assn; Natl. [21214]
Chief Petty Officers Assn; U.S. Coast Guard [20734]
Chief State School Audiovisual Officers; Assn. of [★8568]
Chief State School Officers; Coun. of [8246]
Chief Warrant and Warrant Officers Assn., U.S. Coast Guard [6072], 200 V St. SW, Washington, DC 20024, (202)554-7753
Chiefs and Officials of Bureaus of Labor; Assn. of [★5917]
Chiefs of Police; Natl. Assn. of [6173]
Chiefs of Police; Natl. Assn. of [★5972]
Chiefs of Police Union; Natl. [★5972]
Chiefs of Police of the U.S. and Canada [★5972]
Chiefs of Police of the U.S. and Canada [★IO]
Chiens Guides Canadiens pour Aveugles [★IO]
Chigaku Dantai Kenkyu-Kai [★IO]
Chihuahua Club of Am. [22243], c/o Bruce Shirky, Pres., 11489 S Foster Rd., San Antonio, TX 78218
Chihuahuan Desert Res. Inst. [4374], PO Box 905, Fort Davis, TX 79734, (432)364-2499

Child Abuse

Amer. Humane Assn. Children's Services [11556]
Amer. Professional Soc. on the Abuse of Children [11557]
Anti-Child Pornography Org. [12766]
ASARian [11521]
Assn. of Administrators of the Interstate Compact on the Placement of Children [11559]
Assn. of Sites Advocating Child Protection [11560]
Bilateral Safety Corridor Coalition [12368]
Catharsis Found. [IO]

A star before a book entry number signifies that the name is not listed separately, but is mentioned within the entry.

Catholic Guardian Soc. [11564]
Child Welfare Info. Gateway [11570]
Child Welfare Inst. [11571]
Child Welfare League of Am. [11572]
Childhelp USA [11680]
Children of the Americas [11574]
Children Now [11575]
Children's Defense Fund [11685]
Darkness to Light [11590]
Family Violence Prevention Fund [12028]
Fight Against Child Exploitation [IO]
Foster Grandparent Prog. [11693]
Good Bears of the World [13041]
Innocence in Danger - USA [11601]
Intl. Child Rsrc. Inst. [11604]
Karen Horney Clinic [16109]
Leadership Coun. on Child Abuse and
  Interpersonal Violence [12031]
LifeWorks Inst. [12551]
The Linkup - Survivors of Clergy Abuse [11522]
Love Our Children USA [11619]
Love146 [11620]
Male Survivor: The Natl. Org. Against Male
  Sexual Victimization [13077]
Molesters Anonymous [13024]
Mothers Against Sexual Abuse [13078]
Mothers Against Sexual Predators At Large
  [13079]
Natl. Abandoned Infants Assistance Rsrc. Center
  [12412]
Natl. Assn. to Protect Children [11628]
Natl. Assn. of Public Child Welfare Administrators
  [11629]
Natl. Assn. of State VOCAL Orgs. [13365]
Natl. Center for Missing and Exploited Children
  [11630]
Natl. Center for Prosecution of Child Abuse
  [11631]
Natl. Center for Youth Law [5700]
Natl. Child Abuse Defense and Rsrc. Center
  [13367]
Natl. Children's Alliance [11633]
Natl. Coalition for Child Protection Reform [11634]
Natl. Court Appointed Special Advocate Assn.
  [11636]
Natl. Exchange Club Found. [11637]
Natl. Indian Child Welfare Assn. [19277]
Natl. Org. to Halt the Abuse and Routine Mutila-
  tion of Males [11733]
Orphan Found. of Am. [11715]
Pact Training [11830]
Parents and Teachers Against Violence in Educ.
  [8208]
Parents United [13081]
Paul and Lisa Prog. [13082]
People for Children [11716]
Polly Klaas Found. [12604]
Prevent Child Abuse [11647]
Ray Helfer Soc. [13976]
RUGMARK Found. [11523]
RUGMARK Found. [IO]
STAMP - Survivors Take Action Against Abuse by
  Military Personnel [11507]
Stop it Now! [11653]
Survivors And Victims Empowered [11656]
Survivors Network of Those Abused by Priests
  [13372]
Take Root [12605]
Village of Childhelp West [11661]
VOICES in Action [13086]
Voices for America's Children [11662]
WINGS Found. [13087]
Youth Law Center [13522]
Child Abuse Defense and Rsrc. Center; Natl.
  [13367]
Child Abuse and Family Violence; Natl. Coun. on
  [12035]
Child Abuse Inst. of Res. - Defunct.
Child Abuse Laws; Victims of [★13365]
Child Abuse Listening and Mediation [11565], 1236
  Chapala St., PO Box 90754, Santa Barbara, CA
  93101, (805)965-2376
Child Abuse; Natl. Exchange Club Found. for the
  Prevention of [★11637]
Child Abuse and Neglect Info; CH on [★11570]

Child Abuse and Neglect; Kempe Natl. Center for
  the Prevention and Treatment of [★11609]
Child Abuse; Prevent [★11647]
Child Abuse Prevention Research; National Center
  on [★11647]
Child Abuse Prevention Research; National Center
  on [★IO]
Child Action Nepal [IO], London, United Kingdom
Child and Adolescent Psychiatric Nurses; Assn. of
  [★15487]
Child and Adolescent Psychiatry; Amer. Acad. of
  [16063]
Child and Adolescent Psychiatry; Soc. of Professors
  of [16096]
Child Advocacy Organizations; Natl. Assn. of State-
  Based [★11662]
Child Advocacy and Protection; Natl. Legal Rsrc.
  Center for [★11555]
Child Advocates; Assn. of [★11662]
Child Aid [14746], 917 SW Oak St., Ste. 320,
  Portland, OR 97205, (503)223-3008
Child Aid [IO], Portland, OR, United States
Child Assault Prevention [★12032]
Child Behavior Therapy Special Interest Group -
  Defunct.

Child Care
Action for Child Protection [11553]
Action for Healthy Kids [13945]
Adolescent Scoliosis Soc. of North Am. [16392]
Adopt Am. Network [11227]
Adoption Info. Services [11230]
Adoptions Together [11231]
Afterschool Alliance [11524]
Aid to Incarcerated Mothers [11851]
Alliance for Transforming the Lives of Children
  [11554]
ALSAC/Saint Jude Children's Res. Hosp. [13946]
Am. World Adoption Assn. [11233]
Amer. Assn. of Children's Residential Centers
  [13467]
Amer. Assn. for Lost Children [12607]
Amer. Bar Assn. Center on Children and the Law
  [11555]
Amer. Friends of ALYN Hosp. [12825]
Amer. Professional Soc. on the Abuse of Children
  [11557]
Angelcare [11672]
Anti-Child Pornography Org. [12766]
Assn. of Administrators of the Interstate Compact
  on the Placement of Children [11559]
Assn. for the Educ. of Children with Medical
  Needs [8072]
Assn. of Maternal and Child Hea. Programs
  [13947]
Assn. for Women in Psychology [16145]
Attachment Parenting Intl. [12662]
Au Pair in Am. [8603]
Believe In Tomorrow Natl. Children's Found.
  [11674]
Better Boys Found. [11675]
Better World J. L. Inst. [12142]
Blind Children's Fund [16834]
Boys Hope Girls Hope [13472]
Boys' Towns of Italy [13474]
Brass Ring Soc. [11677]
Brave Kids [13949]
Canadian Child Care Fed. [IO]
Catholic Guardian Soc. [11564]
Center for the Child Care Workforce, A Proj. of
  the Amer. Fed. of Teachers Educational Found.
  [12072]
CFC Intl. [14435]
Child Care Law Center [11525]
The Child Connection [12602]
Child Family Hea. Intl. [11551]
Child-Friendly Initiative [11678]
Child Relief and You Am. [11569]
Child Support Resistance [12006]
Child Welfare League of Am. [11572]
Childhelp USA [11680]
Childminding Ireland [IO]
Children of the Americas [11574]
Children, Inc. [11683]
Children Now [11575]
Children's Creative Response to Conflict Prog.
  [11684]

Children's Defense Fund [11685]
Children's Hemiplegia and Stroke Assn. [16493]
Children's HopeChest [11578]
Children's Relief Network [11581]
Children's Wish Found. Intl. [11687]
CHOICE [12178]
Christian Children's Fund [11688]
Coalition to End Childhood Lead Poisoning [4543]
Comprehensive Day Care Programs [11539]
Coun. for Professional Recognition [11526]
Dads Rights [12008]
Darkness to Light [11590]
Daycare Trust [IO]
Disabled and Alone/Life Services for the
  Handicapped [11941]
Dream Factory [11691]
Every Person Influences Children [11540]
Families for Private Adoption [11244]
Family and Home Network [12669]
Family Support Am. [12154]
Fatherhood Proj. [12670]
Floating Harbor Syndrome Support Gp. of North
  Am. [14451]
Food for the Hungry [12391]
Foster Care Alumni of Am. [11592]
Foster Grandparent Prog. [11693]
Friends in Adoption [11245]
Friends of Karen [11694]
Futures for Children [11695]
Global Autism Proj. [13725]
Global Neuro Rescue [15324]
God's Child Proj. [11597]
Guardian Assn. of Pinellas County [12266]
Healing the Children [11697]
Holistic Moms Network [12673]
Holt Intl. Children's Services [11698]
Humanity United in Giving Internationally [11699]
Indian Youth of Am. [12626]
Innocence in Danger - USA [11601]
Intl. Aid Serving Kids [11603]
Intl. Child Rsrc. Inst. [11604]
Intl. Coalition for Genital Integrity [11731]
Intl. Comm. for the Children of Chechnya [11605]
Intl. Nanny Assn. [11527]
Intl. Nanny Assn. [IO]
Intl. Org. for Adolescents [11606]
Intl. Rett Syndrome Assn. [15333]
Irish Foster Care Assn. [IO]
Jack and Jill of Am. [11702]
Jack and Jill of Am. Found. [11703]
JARC [12570]
Kempe Children's Center [11609]
Kids Fund [11704]
Kids In Danger [11612]
Kids Without Borders [11614]
Kidsave Intl. [11251]
Kindness in Suffering [11616]
A Leg To Stand On [12659]
Love Humanity - USA [11618]
Love146 [11620]
Mail for Me Club [11621]
Make-A-Wish Found. of Am. [11707]
Make a Child Smile [11708]
Meds and Food for Kids [11622]
Miracles of Hope Network [11623]
Mothers Against Sexual Abuse [13078]
Mothers Against Sexual Predators At Large
  [13079]
Mothers Without Borders [11624]
Multicultural Educ., Training, and Advocacy
  [11625]
Natl. Abandoned Infants Assistance Rsrc. Center
  [12412]
Natl. AfterSchool Assn. [11528]
Natl. Assn. of At-Home Mothers [12674]
Natl. Assn. of Child Care Professionals [11529]
Natl. Assn. of Child Care Rsrc. and Referral Agen-
  cies [11530]
Natl. Assn. of Counsel for Children [11711]
Natl. Assn. for Family and Child Care [12171]
Natl. Assn. of Former Foster Care Children of Am.
  [11626]
Natl. Assn. of Nannies [829]
Natl. Assn. for Nanny Care [11531]
Natl. Assn. of Non-Custodial Moms [11538]

Reference to "IO" in place of a book number signifies that the association may be found in the 45th edition of International Organizations.

Encyclopedia of Associations, 46th Edition

3209

Natl. Assn. to Protect Children [11628]
Natl. Assn. of Public Child Welfare Administrators [11629]
Natl. Assn. for Sick Child Daycare [11532]
Natl. Black Child Development Inst. [11542]
Natl. Center for Educ. in Maternal and Child Hea. [13969]
Natl. Center for Missing and Exploited Children [11630]
Natl. Center for Prosecution of Child Abuse [11631]
Natl. Child Care Assn. [11533]
Natl. Child Care and Family Development [11534]
Natl. Childminding Assn. [IO]
Natl. Children's Alliance [11633]
Natl. Children's Nurseries Assn. [IO]
Natl. Coalition for Campus Children's Centers [11535]
Natl. Coun. of Voluntary Child Care Organisations [IO]
Natl. Court Appointed Special Advocate Assn. [11636]
Natl. Drowning Prevention Alliance [12974]
Natl. Exchange Club Found. [11637]
Natl. Fellowship of Child Care Executives [13501]
Natl. Foster Parent Assn. [12677]
Natl. Healthy Start Assn. [15613]
Natl. Initiative for Children's Healthcare Quality [13970]
Natl. Org. of Circumcision Info. Rsrc. Centers [11732]
Natl. Org. of Mothers of Twins Clubs [12613]
Natl. Parents Assn. [12680]
Natl. Rsrc. Center for Hea. and Safety in Child Care and Early Educ. [11536]
Natl. Tribal Child Support Assn. [11713]
Natl. Work at Home Mom Assn. [1922]
Native Amer. Community Bd. [12630]
Neuroblastoma Children's Cancer Soc. [13858]
New Zealand Childcare Assn. [IO]
NIPPA - Early Years Org. [IO]
Nonverbal Learning Disorders Assn. [14998]
North Amer. Reggio Emilia Alliance [11641]
The Nurturing Network [13434]
Only a Child [11643]
Org. for the Lifelong Establishment of Paternity [11714]
Orphan Found. of Am. [11715]
Orphan Resources Intl. [11644]
Our Little Bros. and Sisters [20380]
Parents' Action For Children [12682]
Parents of Infants and Children with Kernicterus [15358]
Parents of Kids with Infectious Diseases [14954]
Partners in Foster Care [12193]
Pediatric Cardiac Intensive Care Soc. [15892]
Pediatric Infectious Diseases Soc. [14955]
Pilot Parents of Southern Arizona [12581]
Prevent Child Abuse [11647]
Proj. Children [11717]
Ray Helfer Soc. [13976]
Safe Kids Worldwide [11651]
Safe Sitter [11537]
Save the Children [11720]
Scottish Childminding Assn. [IO]
Scottish Out of School Care Network [IO]
Single and Custodial Fathers Network [12691]
Single Parent Rsrc. Center [12693]
Smile Alliance Intl. [11721]
Soc. of Clinical Child and Adolescent Psychology [16171]
Southern Early Childhood Assn. [11722]
Special Needs Advocate for Parents [11652]
Starlight Starbright Children's Found. [11724]
Sunshine Found. [11726]
Support A Child Intl. [11655]
Survivors And Victims Empowered [11656]
The Triplet Connection [12614]
Twins Found. [12616]
United Fathers of Am. [12014]
United Jewish Appeal - Fed. of Jewish Philanthropies of New York [12482]
U.S.A. Toy Lib. Assn. [11548]
Village of Childhelp West [11661]
Voices for America's Children [11662]

War Child USA [11663]
Watchlist on Children and Armed Conflict [11664]
A Wish With Wings [11728]
WishKids Intl. [11665]
Working Families [IO]
World Orphans [11667]
Youth Advocate Prog. Intl. [11668]
Child Care Action Campaign - Defunct.
Child Care; East Bay Workers in [★12072]
Child Care Employee Proj. [★12072]
Child Care Executives; Natl. Fellowship of [13501]
Child Care Found. [★11701]
Child Care Found. [★IO]
Child Care Law Center [11525], 221 Pine St., 3rd Fl., San Francisco, CA 94104, (415)394-7144
Child Care; Natl. Assn. for Family and [12171]
Child; Center for the [★20166]
Child to Child Gp. [IO], Belgrade, Serbia
The Child Connection [IO], Louisville, KY, United States
The Child Connection [12602], 2210 Meadow Dr., Ste. 28, Louisville, KY 40218, (502)459-6888

Child Custody

Action for Child Protection [11553]
Adoptee-Birthparent Support Network [11228]
Adoption Info. Services [11230]
ALMA Soc. - Adoptees' Liberty Movement Assn. [11232]
Amer. Adoption Cong. [11234]
Amer. Humane Assn. Children's Services [11556]
Amer. Soc. of Separated and Divorced Men [12005]
Assn. of Administrators of the Interstate Compact on the Placement of Children [11559]
Catholic Guardian Soc. [11564]
Child Support Resistance [12006]
Child Welfare Inst. [11571]
Childhelp USA [11680]
Children of the Americas [11574]
Children's Defense Fund [11685]
Comm. for Mother and Child Rights [11689]
Concerned Persons for Adoption [11240]
Concerned United Birthparents [11241]
Dads Rights [12008]
Families Adopting Children Everywhere [11242]
Friends in Adoption [11245]
Guardian Assn. of Pinellas County [12266]
Intl. Aid Serving Kids [11603]
Intl. Soundex Reunion Registry [11248]
Kidsave Intl. [11251]
Latin Am. Parents Assn. [11252]
Liberal Educ. for Adoptive Families [11253]
Natl. Action for Former Military Wives [12012]
Natl. Adoption Center [11254]
Natl. Assn. of Non-Custodial Moms [11538]
Natl. Center for Lesbian Rights [12246]
Natl. Center for Missing and Exploited Children [11630]
Natl. Coun. for Adoption [11255]
Natl. Council for Single Adoptive Parents [11256]
Natl. Court Appointed Special Advocate Assn. [11636]
Natl. Exchange Club Found. [11637]
North Amer. Coun. on Adoptable Children [11257]
Org. for the Lifelong Establishment of Paternity [11714]
Organized Adoption Search Info. Services [11259]
ORIGINS [11260]
Orphan Found. of Am. [11715]
Orphan Voyage [11261]
Parents Without Partners [12688]
Prevent Child Abuse [11647]
Search Reports, Inc./Central Registry of the Missing [12611]
Single and Custodial Fathers Network [12691]
Single Mothers By Choice [12692]
Societe de Chimie Therapeutique [IO]
United Fathers of Am. [12014]
Village of Childhelp West [11661]
Voices for America's Children [11662]

Child Development

Ackerman Inst. for the Family [12134]
Adopt Am. Network [11227]
Afterschool Alliance [11524]
Alliance for Transforming the Lives of Children [11554]

Amer. Acad. of Pediatrics [15880]
Amer. Bd. of Pediatrics [15881]
Amer. Found. for Maternal and Child Health [15586]
Amer. Humane Assn. Children's Services [11556]
Amer. Hyperlexia Assn. [13940]
Amer. Pediatric Soc. [15882]
Amer. Professional Soc. on the Abuse of Children [11557]
Amer. Youth Policy Forum [13468]
America's Angel [12140]
Angelcare [11672]
Assn. of Administrators of the Interstate Compact on the Placement of Children [11559]
Assn. for Birth Psychology [16137]
Assn. of Medical School Pediatric Dept. Chairs [15884]
Assn. of Pediatric Oncology Social Workers [15885]
Attachment Parenting Intl. [12662]
Autism Network Intl. [13719]
Autism Services Center [13722]
Autism Soc. of Am. [13723]
Bernard van Leer Found. [IO]
Better Boys Found. [11675]
Better World J. L. Inst. [12142]
Big Bros. Big Sisters of Am. [11676]
Birth Defect Res. for Children [13752]
Blind Children's Fund [16834]
Books for the Barrios [12049]
Canadian Assn. of Family Rsrc. Programs [IO]
Carnegie Coun. on Adolescent Development [13477]
Centre for Early Childhood Development [IO]
Child-Friendly Initiative [11678]
Child Neurology Soc. [15386]
Child Welfare League of Am. [11572]
Childhelp USA [11680]
Children and Adults With Attention Deficit/ Hyperactivity Disorder [15314]
Children, Inc. [11683]
Children of Persia [11576]
Children's Creative Response to Conflict Prog. [11684]
Children's Defense Fund [11685]
Children's Grief Educ. Assn. [12265]
Children's HopeChest [11578]
Children's Intl. Summer Villages - Canada [IO]
Children's Intl. Summer Villages - England [IO]
Children's Intl. Summer Villages - Japan [IO]
Children's Intl. Summer Villages - Netherlands [IO]
Children's Intl. Summer Villages - Norway [IO]
Children's Intl. Summer Villages - Sweden [IO]
Children's Relief Network [11581]
Community of Caring [11588]
Compassionate Kids [8384]
Comprehensive Day Care Programs [11539]
Cornelia de Lange Syndrome Found. [13754]
Coun. of Families with Visual Impairment [16844]
Coun. for Professional Recognition [11526]
Developmental Delay Resources [13941]
Divya Disha [IO]
Early Childhood Australia [IO]
Early Childhood Music and Movement Assn. [12618]
Every Person Influences Children [11540]
Family and Home Network [12669]
Family Support Am. [12154]
Fatherhood Proj. [12670]
Fight Crime: Invest in Kids [17057]
First Book [8789]
First Signs [13942]
Foster Care Alumni of Am. [11592]
Foster Grandparent Prog. [11693]
Found. for Child Development [11541]
Friends of the Children [11594]
Friends of LADDERS [12491]
Fundacion Paniamor [IO]
Gateway Intl. Center [IO]
Global Autism Proj. [13725]
Great Dads [12672]
Guitars Not Guns [18114]
Hispanic Coun. for Reform and Educational Options [8260]

A star before a book entry number signifies that the name is not listed separately, but is mentioned within the entry.

Human Growth Found. [16020]
Humanity United in Giving Internationally [11699]
Innocence in Danger - USA [11601]
Institutes for the Achievement of Human Potential [11700]
Intl. Acad. for Child Brain Development [15389]
Intl. Aid Serving Kids [11603]
Intl. Alliance for Youth Sports [23994]
Intl. Child Rsrc. Inst. [11604]
Intl. Org. for Adolescents [11606]
Jack and Jill of Am. [11702]
Jack and Jill of Am. Found. [11703]
Jaffa Inst. [IO]
Kidpower Teenpower Fullpower Intl. [12967]
Kids 4 Afghan Kids [11610]
Kids Fund [11704]
Kids Konnected [11706]
Kids Without Borders [11614]
Kindness in Suffering [11616]
Love Humanity - USA [11618]
Love146 [11620]
March of Dimes Birth Defects Found. [13756]
Miracles of Hope Network [11623]
Natl. Abandoned Infants Assistance Rsrc. Center [12412]
Natl. Assn. of At-Home Mothers [12674]
Natl. Assn. of Child Care Rsrc. and Referral Agencies [11530]
Natl. Assn. for Child Development [13943]
Natl. Assn. of Former Foster Care Children of Am. [11626]
Natl. Assn. of Mothers' Centers [12676]
Natl. Assn. of Nannies [829]
Natl. Assn. for Nanny Care [11531]
Natl. Assn. for Parents of Children With Visual Impairments [16873]
Natl. Assn. of Therapeutic Schools and Programs [13738]
Natl. Attention Deficit Disorder Assn. [15343]
Natl. Autism Assn. [13727]
Natl. Black Child Development Inst. [11542]
Natl. Center for Missing and Exploited Children [11630]
Natl. Center for Stuttering [16450]
Natl. Child Care and Family Development [11534]
Natl. Child Labor Comm. [13500]
Natl. Coalition for Campus Children's Centers [11535]
Natl. Exchange Club Found. [11637]
Natl. Fellowship of Child Care Executives [13501]
Natl. Foster Parent Assn. [12677]
Natl. Healthy Start Assn. [15613]
Natl. Inst. on Out-of-School Time [11543]
Natl. Kindergarten Alliance [9007]
Natl. Network for Youth [12935]
Natl. Org. of Mothers of Twins Clubs [12613]
Natl. Organizations for Youth Safety [13502]
Natl. Work at Home Mom Assn. [1922]
Natl. Youth Employment Coalition [13506]
Native Amer. Community Bd. [12630]
New Zealand Playcentre Fed. [IO]
North Amer. Reggio Emilia Alliance [11641]
Ophelia Proj. [13509]
Org. of Parents Through Surrogacy [13299]
Parents' Action For Children [12682]
Partners in Foster Care [12193]
Paul and Lisa Prog. [13082]
Pilot Parents of Southern Arizona [12581]
Playing for Keeps [11544]
Prevent Child Abuse [11647]
Prospect Hill Found. [11545]
Psychosocial Development and Advisory Center [IO]
Pull-thru Network [14427]
Reach the Children [11649]
Reading Recovery Coun. of North Am. [9048]
Rolling Readers [12502]
Safe Sitter [11537]
Save the Child [IO]
Save the Children [11720]
Seedlings Braille Books for Children [9297]
Soccer in the Streets [11789]
Soc. for Pediatric Radiology [16301]
Soc. for Pediatric Res. [15899]
Soc. for Res. on Adolescence [13515]

Soc. for Res. in Child Development [11546]
Society for Research in Child Development [IO]
Solidarity for Children in Africa and the World [IO]
Southern Early Childhood Assn. [11722]
Spellbinders [10984]
Students Helping St. Kids Intl. [11725]
Support A Child Intl. [11655]
Supporting Our Sons [11547]
Teachers Resisting Unhealthy Children's Entertainment [11657]
The Triplet Connection [12614]
Tuesday's Children [12003]
U.S.A. Toy Lib. Assn. [11548]
Village of Childhelp West [11661]
VOICES in Action [13086]
VOICES Assn. [13211]
William T. Grant Found. [11549]
William T. Grant Foundation [IO]
A Wish With Wings [11728]
Work for Human Development [IO]
World Org. for Human Potential [IO]
World Org. for Human Potential [11550]
World Orphans [11667]
Youth Advocate Prog. Intl. [11668]
Youth Impact Intl. [13521]
Zero to Three: Natl. Center for Infants, Toddlers and Families [13944]
Child Development Associate Consortium [★11526]
Child Development Associate Natl. Credentialing Program [★11526]
Child Development Associate Natl. Credentialing Prog. [★11526]
Child Evangelism Fellowship [19997], PO Box 348, Warrenton, MO 63383-0348, (636)456-4321
Child Evangelism Fellowship [IO], Warrenton, MO, United States
Child Evangelism Fellowship of Canada [IO], Winnipeg, MB, Canada
Child Evangelism Fellowship Intl. [★IO]
Child Evangelism Fellowship Intl. [★19997]
Child Family Hea. Intl. [11551], 995 Market St., Ste. 1104, San Francisco, CA 94103, (415)957-9000
Child Family Hea. Intl. [IO], San Francisco, CA, United States
Child and Family Policy Center [12145], 218 6th Ave., Ste. 1021, Des Moines, IA 50309-4013, (515)280-9027
Child Find [★11566]
Child Find of Am. [11566], PO Box 277, New Paltz, NY 12561-0277, (845)691-4666
Child Find Canada [IO], Winnipeg, MB, Canada
Child Focus [IO], Brussels, Belgium
Child-Friendly Initiative [11678], 210 W Hamilton Ave., Ste. 183, State College, PA 16801, (877)448-0500

Child Health
Action for Child Protection [11553]
Action for Healthy Kids [13945]
Adolescent Scoliosis Soc. of North Am. [16392]
Aicardi Syndrome Newsl. [14437]
AIDS Alliance for Children, Youth and Families [13548]
Alliance for Childhood Cancer [13787]
Alliance for Healthy Homes [13320]
ALSAC/Saint Jude Children's Res. Hosp. [13946]
Ambulatory Pediatric Assn. [15879]
Amer. Acad. of Child and Adolescent Psychiatry [16063]
Amer. Acad. of Pediatrics [15880]
Amer. Assn. of Children's Residential Centers [13467]
Amer. Assn. for Lost Children [12607]
Amer. Assn. for Pediatric Ophthalmology and Strabismus [15660]
Amer. Bd. of Pediatrics [15881]
Amer. Bd. of Psychiatry and Neurology [16071]
Amer. Center for Law and Justice [12901]
Amer. Coll. of Foot and Ankle Pediatrics [16033]
Amer. Coll. of Osteopathic Pediatricians [15795]
Amer. Found. for Maternal and Child Health [15886]
Amer. Humane Assn. Children's Services [11556]
Amer. Juvenile Arthritis Org. [16368]
Amer. Osteopathic Bd. of Pediatrics [15800]
Amer. Pediatric Soc. [15882]

Amer. Professional Soc. on the Abuse of Children [11557]
Amer. Soc. for Adolescent Psychiatry [16078]
Amer. Soc. for Deaf Children [14742]
Amer. Sudden Infant Death Syndrome Inst. [16523]
America's Fund for Afghan Children [11265]
Angelcare [11672]
Angelman Syndrome Found. [16528]
Assn. of Administrators of the Interstate Compact on the Placement of Children [11559]
Assn. for Birth Psychology [16137]
Assn. of Child Neurology Nurses [15465]
Assn. for Child Psychoanalysis [16106]
Assn. of Children's Prosthetic-Orthotic Clinics [15784]
Assn. for the Educ. of Children with Medical Needs [8072]
Assn. of Maternal and Child Hea. Programs [13947]
Assn. of Medical School Pediatric Dept. Chairs [15884]
Assn. of Pediatric Hematology/Oncology Nurses [15467]
Assn. of Pediatric Oncology Social Workers [15885]
Assn. of Pediatric Therapists [16606]
Assn. for Res. of Childhood Cancer [13798]
Assn. for Retinopathy of Prematurity and Related Diseases [15673]
Assn. of SIDS and Infant Mortality Programs [16524]
Athletics and Entertainers for Kids [13560]
Autism Network Intl. [13719]
Autism Services Center [13722]
Autism Soc. of Am. [13723]
Autism Speaks [13724]
Believe In Tomorrow Natl. Children's Found. [11674]
Better Boys Found. [11675]
Birth Defect Res. for Children [13752]
Blind Children's Fund [16834]
Boys Hope Girls Hope [13472]
Brain Tumor Found. for Children [13948]
Brass Ring Soc. [11677]
Brave Kids [13949]
Canadian Assn. for Adolescent Hea. [IO]
Canadian Inst. of Child Hea. [IO]
Cancer Care [13803]
Candlelighters Childhood Cancer Found. [13810]
Carnegie Coun. on Adolescent Development [13477]
Catholic Guardian Soc. [11564]
CCHS Family Network [14255]
Center for the Stud. of Multiple Birth [15272]
CFC Intl. [14435]
Child Family Hea. Intl. [11551]
Child Family Hea. Intl. [IO]
Child Hea. Found. [IO]
Child Hea. Found. [13950]
Child Life Coun. [13951]
Child Life Coun. [IO]
Child Neurology Soc. [15386]
Child Trends [11679]
Child Welfare Info. Gateway [11570]
Child Welfare Inst. [11571]
Child Welfare League of Am. [11572]
Childhelp USA [11680]
Childhood Arthritis and Rheumatology Res. Alliance [16371]
Childhood Brain Tumor Found. [14257]
Children and Adults With Attention Deficit/Hyperactivity Disorder [15314]
Children of the Americas [11574]
Children, Inc. [11683]
Children Now [11575]
Children of Persia [11576]
Children's Brain Tumor Found. [13952]
Children's Cause for Cancer Advocacy [13812]
Children's Craniofacial Assn. [14057]
Children's Creative Response to Conflict Prog. [11684]
Children's Cross Connection Intl. [11552]
Children's Cross Connection Intl. [IO]
Children's Defense Fund [11685]

Reference to "IO" in place of a book number signifies that the association may be found in the 45th edition of International Organizations.

Children's Eye Found. [15679]
Children's Hea. Environmental Coalition [13953]
Children's Hea. Fund [13954]
Children's HeartLink [13899]
Children's Hemiplegia and Stroke Assn. [16493]
Children's Hospice Intl. [14853]
Children's Leukemia Res. Assn. [13813]
Children's Liver Assn. for Support Services [14804]
Children's Medical Ministries [13955]
Children's Organ Transplant Assn. [13956]
Children's Relief Network [11581]
Children's Wish Found. Intl. [11687]
Christian Children's Fund [11688]
Christina Noble Children's Found. - Vietnam [IO]
Chromosome 9P Network [14443]
CityMatch [13957]
Comprehensive Day Care Programs [11539]
Congenital Heart Defects Awareness [13900]
Cornelia de Lange Syndrome Found. [13754]
Coun. of Families with Visual Impairment [16844]
Coun. of Pediatric Subspecialties [15886]
Coun. for Professional Recognition [11526]
Crigler-Najjar Assn. [14805]
Cyclic Vomiting Syndrome Assn. [14415]
Cystinosis Found. [15246]
Cystinosis Res. Network [15247]
Disabled and Alone/Life Services for the Handicapped [11941]
Docs for Tots [13958]
Dream Factory [11691]
Dysautonomia Youth Network of Am. [15318]
Emergency Relief Response Fund [20562]
Epilepsy Therapy Development Proj. [14381]
Evans Syndrome Res. and Support Gp. [14934]
Every Child By Two [13959]
Fairview Pregnancy and Newborn Loss Information [12668]
Families for Private Adoption [11244]
Family and Home Network [12669]
Family Violence Prevention Fund [12028]
Family Voices [13960]
Famous Fone Friends [11692]
Fanconi Anemia Res. Fund [14450]
Fatherhood Proj. [12670]
Fatty Oxidation Disorders (FOD) Family Support Gp. [16532]
Fed. for Children with Special Needs [12569]
Fed. of Pediatric Organizations [15887]
Feed the Children [12854]
FG Syndrome Family Alliance [16533]
First Candle/SIDS Alliance [16525]
First Signs [13942]
Five P Minus Soc. [16534]
Floating Harbor Syndrome Support Gp. of North Am. [14451]
The Floating Hosp. [14882]
Foster Grandparent Prog. [11693]
FRAXA Res. Found. [16535]
Friends of Karen [11694]
Futures for Children [11695]
Generation Green [17054]
Gift from the Heart Found. [13961]
Gift from the Heart Found. [IO]
Giving Children Hope [11596]
Global Neuro Rescue [15324]
God's Child Proj. [11597]
Gp. B Strep Assn. [13962]
Harvard Injury Control Res. Center [16690]
Healing the Children [11697]
Heart Care Intl. [13904]
Heather's Teddy Bear Org. [22035]
Holt Intl. Children's Services [11698]
Human Growth Found. [16020]
Indian Youth of Am. [12626]
Innocence in Danger - USA [11601]
Institutes for the Achievement of Human Potential [11700]
Intl. Acad. for Child Brain Development [15389]
Intl. Alliance for Child and Adolescent Mental Hea. and Schools [15204]
Intl. Assn. for Adolescent Hea. [IO]
Intl. Assn. of Pediatric Lab. Medicine [15888]
Intl. Child Amputee Network [11954]
Intl. Child Rsrc. Inst. [11604]

Intl. Children's Anophthalmia Network [16857]
Intl. Coalition for Genital Integrity [11731]
Intl. Org. for Adolescents [11606]
Intl. Pediatric Hypertension Assn. [14907]
Intl. Pediatric Nephrology Assn. [15292]
Intl. Pediatric Transplant Assn. [16673]
Intl. Relief Friendship Found. [13171]
Intl. Rett Syndrome Assn. [15333]
Intl. Soc. for Adolescent Psychiatry and Psychology [16087]
Intl. Soc. on Infant Stud. [13963]
Intl. Soc. on Infant Stud. [IO]
Jack and Jill of Am. [11702]
Jack and Jill of Am. Found. [11703]
JARC [12570]
Jewish Women Intl. [20153]
Karen Horney Clinic [16109]
KDWB Variety Family Center [13964]
Kempe Children's Center [11609]
Kids 4 Afghan Kids [11610]
Kids Fund [11704]
Kids In Danger [11612]
Kids With A Cause [11613]
Kids With Food Allergies [13603]
Kids With Heart Natl. Assn. for Children's Heart Disorders [13915]
Kids Without Borders [11614]
Kindness in Suffering [11616]
Klingenstein Third Generation Found. [13965]
Leadership to Keep Children Alcohol Free [11334]
Liberty Godparent Home [12918]
Little Hearts [13966]
Locks of Love [17055]
Love Humanity - USA [11618]
Love146 [11620]
MAGIC Found. [13967]
Mail for Me Club [11621]
Make-A-Wish Found. of Am. [11707]
Make a Child Smile [11708]
Make Today Count [13841]
March of Dimes Birth Defects Found. [13756]
Meds and Food for Kids [11622]
Molesters Anonymous [13024]
MOMS in Touch Intl. [20621]
Mothers Against Munchausen Syndrome by Proxy Allegations [13968]
Multicultural Educ., Training, and Advocacy [11625]
MUMS Natl. Parent-to-Parent Network [16541]
Myotubular Myopathy Rsrc. Gp. [16542]
Natl. Abandoned Infants Assistance Rsrc. Center [12412]
Natl. AfterSchool Assn. [11528]
Natl. Assn. of At-Home Mothers [12674]
Natl. Assn. of Child Care Professionals [11529]
Natl. Assn. of Child Care Rsrc. and Referral Agencies [11530]
Natl. Assn. for Children's Behavioral Hea. [16090]
Natl. Assn. of Counsel for Children [11711]
Natl. Assn. for Family and Child Care [12171]
Natl. Assn. of Mothers' Centers [12676]
Natl. Assn. for Parents of Children With Visual Impairments [16873]
Natl. Assn. of Public Child Welfare Administrators [11629]
Natl. Assn. for Sick Child Daycare [11532]
Natl. Assn. of State VOCAL Orgs. [13365]
Natl. Assn. of Youth Clubs [13498]
Natl. Attention Deficit Disorder Assn. [15343]
Natl. Autism Assn. [13727]
Natl. Black Child Development Inst. [11542]
Natl. Center for Educ. in Maternal and Child Hea. [13969]
Natl. Center for Missing and Exploited Children [11630]
Natl. Center for Prosecution of Child Abuse [11631]
Natl. Center for Stuttering [16450]
Natl. Child Care Assn. [11533]
Natl. Child Care and Family Development [11534]
Natl. Child Labor Comm. [13500]
Natl. Childhood Cancer Found. [13850]
Natl. Christ Child Soc. [19679]
Natl. Coalition for Campus Children's Centers [11535]

Natl. Court Appointed Special Advocate Assn. [11636]
Natl. Exchange Club Found. [11637]
Natl. Foster Parent Assn. [12677]
Natl. Healthy Start Assn. [15613]
Natl. Infant Torticollis Assn. [14945]
Natl. Initiative for Children's Healthcare Quality [13970]
Natl. Inst. of Child Hea. and Human Development [13971]
Natl. Network for Youth [12935]
Natl. Org. Caring for Kids [11638]
Natl. Org. of Circumcision Info. Rsrc. Centers [11732]
Natl. Org. to Halt the Abuse and Routine Mutilation of Males [11733]
Natl. Org. of Mothers of Twins Clubs [12613]
Natl. Parents Assn. [12680]
Natl. Prog. for Playground Safety [18578]
Natl. Rsrc. Center for Hea. and Safety in Child Care and Early Educ. [11536]
Natl. Reye's Syndrome Found. [16366]
Natl. SIDS/Infant Death Rsrc. Center [16526]
Natl. Vaccine Info. Center [13972]
Neuroblastoma Children's Cancer Soc. [13858]
New South Wales Assn. for Adolescent Hea. [IO]
New Zealand Assn. for Adolescent Hea. and Development Otago/Southland [IO]
New Zealand Assn. for Adolescent Hea. and Development - Wellington [IO]
Nonverbal Learning Disorders Assn. [14998]
North Amer. Soc. for Pediatric Gastroenterology, Hepatology and Nutrition [14424]
North Amer. Soc. for Pediatric Medicine [15891]
The Nurturing Network [13434]
Oper. Smile [12534]
Organic Acidemia Assn. [14472]
Org. for the Lifelong Establishment of Paternity [11714]
Org. of Parents Through Surrogacy [13299]
Orphan Found. of Am. [11715]
Our Little Bros. and Sisters [20380]
Parents Against Childhood Epilepsy [14382]
Parents of Infants and Children with Kernicterus [15358]
Parents of Kids with Infectious Diseases [14954]
Parents Network for the Post Institutionalized Child [16546]
Pediatric/Adolescent Gastroesophageal Reflux Assn. [14426]
Pediatric Cardiac Intensive Care Soc. [15892]
Pediatric Infectious Diseases Soc. [14955]
Pediatric Keratoplasty Assn. [15700]
Pediatric Neurotransmitter Disease Assn. [15361]
Pediatric Nursing Certification Bd. [15522]
Pediatric Orthopedic Soc. of North Am. [15780]
Pediatric Pharmacy Advocacy Gp. [15896]
Pilot Parents of Southern Arizona [12581]
Postgraduate Center for Mental Hea. [16227]
Prevent Child Abuse [11647]
Proj. Children [11717]
Pull-thru Network [14427]
Ray Helfer Soc. [13976]
Reach the Children [11649]
Restoration Proj. Intl. [12441]
Retinoblastoma Intl. [13869]
Safe Kids Worldwide [11651]
Save the Children [11720]
School Nurse Achievement Prog. [15525]
Sea to See Proj. [13760]
Selective Mutism Found. [15233]
Shriners Hospitals for Children [13973]
Smile Alliance Intl. [11721]
Social Relief Intl. [12445]
Soc. for Adolescent Medicine [13974]
Soc. of Clinical Child and Adolescent Psychology [16171]
Soc. of Pediatric Nurses [15527]
Soc. for Pediatric Psychology [16175]
Soc. for Pediatric Radiology [16301]
Soc. for Pediatric Res. [15899]
Soc. for Pediatric Urology [16715]
Soc. of Professors of Child and Adolescent Psychiatry [16096]
Soc. for Res. in Child Development [11546]

A star before a book entry number signifies that the name is not listed separately, but is mentioned within the entry.

Southern Early Childhood Assn. [11722]
Special Needs Advocate for Parents [11652]
A Special Wish Found. [11723]
Starlight Starbright Children's Found. [11724]
Sunshine Found. [11726]
Support A Child Intl. [11655]
Support Org. for Trisomy 18, 13, and Related Disorders [14485]
Survivors of Incest Anonymous [13085]
Task Force for Child Survival and Development [12542]
The Triplet Connection [12614]
U.S.A. Toy Lib. Assn. [11548]
Variety Intl. - The Children's Charity [11660]
Village of Childhelp West [11661]
Vitamin Angel Alliance [15571]
Voices for America's Children [11662]
VOICES Assn. [13211]
A Wish With Wings [11728]
WishKids Intl. [11665]
World Assn. for Infant Mental Hea. [16098]
World Org. for Human Potential [11550]
Zero to Three: Natl. Center for Infants, Toddlers and Families [13944]
Child Health; Amer. Found. for Maternal and [15586]
Child Hea. and Crippled Children's Directors; Assn. of State and Territorial Maternal and [★13947]
Child Hea. Found. [13950], 10630 Little Patuxent Pkwy., Ste. 126, Columbia, MD 21044, (410)992-5512
Child Hea. Found. [IO], Columbia, MD, United States
Child Hea. Found; Intl. [★13950]
CHILD, Inc. [★15004]
Child Keyppers' Intl. - Address unknown since 2003.
Child Labor Coalition [★17338]
Child Labor Coalition [11567], c/o Natl. Consumers League, 1701 K St. NW, Ste. 1200, Washington, DC 20006, (202)835-3323
Child Labor Comm; Natl. [13500]
Child Labor Comm; Natl. Comm. on the Educ. of Migrant Children of the Natl. [12593]
Child Life Activity Stud. Sect. [★13951]
Child Life Activity Stud. Sect. [★IO]
Child Life Coun. [IO], Rockville, MD, United States
Child Life Coun. [13951], 11820 Parklawn Dr., Ste. 240, Rockville, MD 20852-2529, (301)881-7090
Child Life Specialist Comm. [★13951]
Child Life Specialist Comm. [★IO]
Child Life Task Force [★IO]
Child Life Task Force [★13951]
Child Mirror Liberia [IO], Monrovia, Liberia
Child; National Humanitarian Proj. for the Physically Challenged [★19231]
Child Neurology Soc. [15386], 1000 W County Rd. E, Ste. 290, St. Paul, MN 55126, (651)486-9447
Child Nutrition Forum - Address unknown since 2001.
Child Proj; God's [11597]
Child Protection Alliance [IO], Bakau, Gambia
Child Psychiatric Nursing; Advocates for [★15487]
Child Psychiatry; Amer. Acad. of [★16063]
Child Psychiatry; Soc. of Professors of [★16096]
Child Psychoanalysis; Amer. Assn. for [★16106]
Child Psychoanalysis; Assn. for [16106]
Child Quest Intl. [11568], 1060 N 4th St., Ste. 200, San Jose, CA 95112, (408)287-4673
Child Quest Intl. [IO], San Jose, CA, United States
Child Reach [★IO]
Child Reach [★11681]
Child Relief and You Am. [11569], PO Box 850948, Braintree, MA 02185-0948, (339)235-0792
Child Relief and You Am. [IO], Braintree, MA, United States
Child Relief and You - Mumbai [IO], Bombay, India
Child Rights Centre [IO], Belgrade, Serbia
Child Rights; Comm. for Mother and [11689]
Child Rights Info. Network [IO], London, United Kingdom
Child Safety Coun. [★12972]
Child Safety Coun; Natl. [12972]
Child Sexual Abuse Treatment Program [★13081]
Child Study Assn. of America/Wel-Met - Defunct.
Child Support Enforcement Assn; Natl. [5701]
Child Support Network - Defunct.

Child Support Resistance [12006], 1464 Ticond-eroga Dr., Southaven, MS 38671
Child Survival and Development; Task Force for [12542]
Child Trends [11679], 4301 Connecticut Ave. NW, Ste. 350, Washington, DC 20008, (202)572-6000
Child Welfare
    Action for Child Protection [11553]
    Action Children Aid [IO]
    Action for Sick Children [IO]
    Adopt Am. Network [11227]
    Adoptee-Birthparent Support Network [11228]
    Adoption Info. Services [11230]
    Adoptions Together [11231]
    Advocates for Survivors of Child Abuse [IO]
    African Child Assn. [IO]
    African Network for Prevention and Protection Against Child Abuse and Neglect [IO]
    Afterschool Alliance [11524]
    Against Child Abuse [IO]
    Alliance for Transforming the Lives of Children [11554]
    ALMA Soc. - Adoptees' Liberty Movement Assn. [11232]
    ALSAC/Saint Jude Children's Res. Hosp. [13946]
    Am. World Adoption Assn. [11233]
    Amer. Adoption Cong. [11234]
    Amer. Assn. of Children's Residential Centers [13467]
    Amer. Assn. for Home-Based Early Intervention-ists [17056]
    Amer. Assn. for Lost Children [12607]
    Amer. Bar Assn. Center on Children and the Law [11555]
    Amer. Center for Law and Justice [12901]
    Amer. Friends of ALYN Hosp. [12825]
    Amer. Humane Assn. [13149]
    Amer. Humane Assn. Children's Services [11556]
    Amer. Jewish World Ser. [12829]
    Amer. Professional Soc. on the Abuse of Children [11557]
    Amer. Soc. for Adolescent Psychiatry [16078]
    Amer. Youth Work Center [13469]
    America's Angel [12140]
    America's Children Hunger Network [11558]
    America's Children Hunger Network [IO]
    America's Fund for Afghan Children [11265]
    America's Promise - The Alliance for Youth [13470]
    Angelcare [11672]
    Anti-Child Pornography Org. [12766]
    Asia Against Child Trafficking [IO]
    Assn. of Administrators of the Interstate Compact on the Placement of Children [11559]
    Assn. of Childrens Welfare Agencies [IO]
    Assn. for the Development of Children's Residential Facilities [IO]
    Assn. of Independent Commercial Producers [90]
    Assn. of Jewish Family and Children's Agencies [12467]
    Assn. of Maternal and Child Hea. Programs [13947]
    Assn. of Missing and Exploited Children's Organizations [12601]
    Assn. of Sites Advocating Child Protection [11560]
    Assn. for Vaccine Damaged Children [IO]
    Associazione Amici de Bambini [IO]
    Australian Comm. for UNICEF [IO]
    Autism Soc. of Am. [13723]
    Autism Speaks [13724]
    Because I Love You: The Parent Support Gp. [13293]
    Believe In Tomorrow Natl. Children's Found. [11674]
    Bethany Christian Services Intl. [11561]
    Bethany Christian Services Intl. [IO]
    Big Bros. Big Sisters of Am. [11676]
    Black Community Crusade for Children [11562]
    Blind Children's Fund [16834]
    Block Parent Prog. of Canada [IO]
    Books for the Barrios [12049]
    Boys Hope Girls Hope [13472]
    Boys' Towns of Italy [13474]
    Brass Ring Soc. [11677]
    British Assn. for Adoption and Fostering [IO]

Camp Fire USA [13475]
Canadian Friends of Boys' Town Jerusalem [IO]
Canadian Soc. for the Investigation of Child Abuse [IO]
Canadian Soc. for the Prevention of Cruelty to Children [IO]
Canines for Disabled Kids [11927]
Care for Children Intl. [11563]
Care for Children Intl. [IO]
Carnegie Coun. on Adolescent Development [13477]
Catholic Guardian Soc. [11564]
Center for the Protection of Children's Rights Found. [IO]
Central Union for Child Welfare [IO]
Centre de Recuperation Nutritionnelle [IO]
Child Abuse Listening and Mediation [11565]
The Child Connection [12602]
Child Family Hea. Intl. [11551]
Child and Family Policy Center [12145]
Child Find of Am. [11566]
Child Focus [IO]
Child-Friendly Initiative [11678]
Child Labor Coalition [11567]
Child Life Coun. [13951]
Child Mirror Liberia [IO]
Child Quest Intl. [IO]
Child Quest Intl. [11568]
Child Relief and You Am. [11569]
Child Relief and You Am. [IO]
Child Relief and You - Mumbai [IO]
Child Rights Info. Network [IO]
Child Support Resistance [12006]
Child Trends [11679]
Child Welfare Info. Gateway [11570]
Child Welfare Inst. [11571]
Child Welfare League of Am. [11572]
Child Welfare League of Canada [IO]
Child Workers in Nepal Concerned Centre [IO]
Childcare Worldwide [IO]
Childcare Worldwide [11573]
ChildFund Ireland [IO]
ChildFund New Zealand [IO]
Childhelp USA [11680]
Childhope - Zambia [IO]
Children of the Americas [IO]
Children of the Americas [11574]
Children, Inc. [11683]
Children of the Night [12933]
Children in Northern Ireland [IO]
Children Now [11575]
Children of Persia [11576]
Children at Risk in Ireland [IO]
Children of Russia [IO]
Children of Russia [11577]
Children's Creative Response to Conflict Prog. [11684]
Children's Cross Connection Intl. [11552]
Children's Defense Fund [11685]
Children's Fund of the Slovak Republic [IO]
Children's Hea. Environmental Coalition [13953]
Children's Hea. Fund [13954]
Children's Healthcare Is a Legal Duty [15004]
Children's HopeChest [11578]
Children's Legal Centre [IO]
Children's Network Intl. [IO]
Children's Network Intl. [11579]
The Children's Partnership [11580]
Children's Relief Network [11581]
Children's Relief Network [IO]
Children's Rights of America [11582]
Children's Rights Div. - Human Rights Watch [11583]
Children's Rights Div. - Human Rights Watch [IO]
Children's Safety Network [11584]
Children's Watch Intl. [11585]
Children's Watch Intl. [IO]
Children's Wish Found. Intl. [11687]
Childwatch Intl. Res. Network [IO]
Christian Children's Fund [11688]
Christian Children's Fund of Canada [IO]
Churches' Coun. for Child and Youth Care [IO]
CoMamas Assn. [12148]
Commn. on Missing and Exploited Children [11586]

Reference to "IO" in place of a book number signifies that the association may be found in the 45th edition of International Organizations.

Comm. for Children [11587]
Comm. for Missing Children [12603]
Community of Caring [11588]
Comprehensive Day Care Programs [11539]
Computers for Children [8137]
Concern for Children Trust [IO]
Concerned Persons for Adoption [11240]
Concerned United Birthparents [11241]
Conrad N. Hilton Found. [13163]
Coptic Orphans Support Assn. [11589]
Coptic Orphans Support Assn. [IO]
Coun. of Families with Visual Impairment [16844]
Coun. for Professional Recognition [11526]
CURE Intl. [13975]
CURE Intl. [IO]
CyberAngels [12452]
Darkness to Light [11590]
Defence for Children Intl. - Bolivia [IO]
Defence for Children Intl. - Canada [IO]
Defence for Children Intl. - Chile [IO]
Defence for Children Intl. - Colombia [IO]
Defence for Children Intl. - Costa Rica [IO]
Defence for Children Intl. - Czech Republic [IO]
Defence for Children Intl. - Lebanon [IO]
Defence for Children Intl. - Netherlands [IO]
Defence for Children Intl. - Palestine Sect. [IO]
Defence for Children Intl. - Switzerland [IO]
Deliver the Dream [13019]
Disabled and Alone/Life Services for the
    Handicapped [11941]
Dream Factory [11691]
Elwyn [12383]
Emergency Relief Response Fund [20562]
Empower Prog. [8945]
Empowerment Soc. Intl. [11775]
End Child Prostitution, Child Pornography and
    Trafficking of Children for Sexual Purposes -
    New Zealand [IO]
End Child Prostitution, Pornography and Traffick-
    ing [IO]
Enfants and Developpement [IO]
Enfants du Monde [IO]
Entertainment Indus. Found. [12114]
European Children's Network [IO]
European Found. for St. Children Worldwide [IO]
Every Person Influences Children [11540]
Fairview Pregnancy and Newborn Loss Informa-
    tion [12668]
FaithTrust Inst. [12027]
Families Adopting Children Everywhere [11242]
Families for Private Adoption [11244]
Family and Home Network [12669]
Family Violence Prevention Fund [12028]
Famous Fone Friends [11692]
Farm Safety 4 Just Kids [12961]
Fatherhood Proj. [12670]
Feed the Children [12854]
Feeding Hungry Children Intl. [12390]
Fellowship of St. Nicholas [IO]
Fight Crime: Invest in Kids [17057]
Find the Children [11591]
Finnish Comm. for UNICEF [IO]
First Signs [13942]
Food for the Hungry [12391]
Foster Care Alumni of Am. [11592]
Foster Family-Based Treatment Assn. [11593]
Foster Grandparent Prog. [11693]
Foster Parents Plan of Belgium [IO]
Foster Parents Plan of Germany [IO]
Free The Children [IO]
Friends in Adoption [11245]
Friends of the Children [11594]
Friends of Gracious [IO]
Friends of Karen [11694]
Friends of Rwanda Assn. [11595]
Friends of Rwanda Assn. [IO]
Futures for Children [11695]
Generation Green [17054]
Genesis Expeditions [IO]
Giving Children Hope [IO]
Giving Children Hope [11596]
Global March Against Child Labor [IO]
God's Child Proj. [11597]
Good Bears of the World [13041]
Grandparents United for Children's Rights [17058]

Guitars Not Guns [18114]
Hamro Jivan Child Care House [IO]
Healing the Children [11697]
Healthy Schools Network [4635]
Heart of Romania's Children Found. [11598]
Help Liberia Found. [IO]
Herbalife Family Found. [IO]
Herbalife Family Found. [11599]
Holistic Moms Network [12673]
Holt Intl. Children's Services [11698]
Homeless Children Intl. [20080]
Hong Kong Comm. for UNICEF [IO]
Hong Kong Soc. for the Protection of Children
    [IO]
HOPE [IO]
House of Ruth [12029]
Hug-A-Tree and Survive [11600]
Humanity United in Giving Internationally [11699]
Icelandic Comm. for UNICEF [IO]
IFS Nepal Children Welfare Prog. [IO]
Indian Children's Fund Australia [IO]
Indian Youth of Am. [12626]
Innocence in Danger - USA [11601]
Innocence in Danger - USA [IO]
Inst. for Amer. Values [12158]
Inst. for Children and Poverty [11602]
Institutes for the Achievement of Human Potential
    [11700]
Inter-American Parliamentary Gp. on Population
    and Development [12432]
Intl. Aid Serving Kids [11603]
Intl. Aid Serving Kids [IO]
Intl. Catholic Child Bur. [IO]
Intl. Child Amputee Network [11954]
Intl. Child Rsrc. Inst. [11604]
Intl. Child Rsrc. Inst. [IO]
Intl. Coalition for Genital Integrity [11731]
Intl. Comm. for the Children of Chechnya [11605]
Intl. Comm. for the Children of Chechnya [IO]
International Organization for Adolescents [IO]
Intl. Org. for Adolescents [11606]
Intl. Soc. for Prevention of Child Abuse and
    Neglect [11607]
Intl. Soc. for Prevention of Child Abuse and
    Neglect [IO]
Intl. Soundex Reunion Registry [11248]
Intimate Apparel Square Club [12201]
Jack and Jill of Am. [11702]
Jack and Jill of Am. Found. [11703]
Jackie Chan Charitable Found. [IO]
Jacob Wetterling Found. [11608]
Jewish Women Intl. [20153]
Justice for Children Intl. [IO]
Kempe Children's Center [11609]
Kidpower Teenpower Fullpower Intl. [12967]
Kids 4 Afghan Kids [11610]
Kids 4 Afghan Kids [IO]
KIDS COUNT [11611]
Kids Fund [11704]
Kids In Danger [11612]
Kids Konnected [11706]
Kids Need Both Parents [17509]
Kids With A Cause [11613]
Kids Without Borders [11614]
Kids Without Borders [IO]
Kidsave Intl. [11251]
KidsPeace [11615]
Kindernothilfe e.V. [IO]
Kindness in Suffering [IO]
Kindness in Suffering [11616]
KNH Austria [IO]
Korea Welfare Found. [IO]
Krousar Thmey [IO]
Latin Am. Parents Assn. [11252]
Lawyers for Children Am. [6026]
A Leg To Stand On [12659]
Legal Services for Children [12498]
Liberal Educ. for Adoptive Families [11253]
Liberty Godparent Home [12918]
LifeWorks Inst. [12551]
Light of Cambodian Children [11617]
Lotus Outreach [13143]
Love Humanity [IO]
Love Humanity Intl. [IO]
Love Humanity - USA [IO]

Love Humanity - USA [11618]
Love Our Children USA [11619]
Love146 [11620]
Magic Bus, India [IO]
Magicians Without Borders [12503]
Mail for Me Club [11621]
Make-A-Wish Found. of Am. [11707]
Make a Child Smile [11708]
Male Survivor: The Natl. Org. Against Male
    Sexual Victimization [13077]
Mannerheim League for Child Welfare [IO]
Marine Toys for Tots Found. [11709]
Meds and Food for Kids [11622]
Meds and Food for Kids [IO]
Mir Pace Intl. [12872]
Miracles of Hope Network [11623]
Miracles of Hope Network [IO]
Molesters Anonymous [13024]
MOMS in Touch Intl. [20621]
Mothers Against Sexual Abuse [13078]
Mothers Against Sexual Predators At Large
    [13079]
Mothers and Fathers Aligned Saving Kids [17059]
Mothers Without Borders [11624]
Mothers Without Borders [IO]
Multicultural Educ., Training, and Advocacy
    [11625]
Myanmar Maternal and Child Welfare Assn. [IO]
Natl. Abandoned Infants Assistance Rsrc. Center
    [12412]
Natl. Adoption Center [11254]
Natl. AfterSchool Assn. [11528]
Natl. Alliance to Nurture the Aged and the Youth
    [12358]
Natl. Amer. Indian Court Judges Assn. [5905]
Natl. Assn. of At-Home Mothers [12674]
Natl. Assn. of Child Care Professionals [11529]
Natl. Assn. of Child Care Rsrc. and Referral Agen-
    cies [11530]
Natl. Assn. of Counsel for Children [11711]
Natl. Assn. for Family and Child Care [12171]
Natl. Assn. of Former Foster Care Children of Am.
    [11626]
Natl. Assn. of Mothers' Centers [12676]
Natl. Assn. of Nannies [829]
Natl. Assn. for Nanny Care [11531]
Natl. Assn. for Native Amer. Children of Alcoholics
    [11627]
Natl. Assn. for Parents of Children With Visual
    Impairments [16873]
Natl. Assn. to Protect Children [11628]
Natl. Assn. of Public Child Welfare Administrators
    [11629]
Natl. Assn. for Sick Child Daycare [11532]
Natl. Assn. of State VOCAL Orgs. [13365]
Natl. Autism Assn. [13727]
Natl. Black Child Development Inst. [11542]
Natl. Center for Educ. in Maternal and Child Hea.
    [13969]
Natl. Center for Homeless Educ. [12295]
Natl. Center for Missing and Exploited Children
    [11630]
Natl. Center for Prosecution of Child Abuse
    [11631]
Natl. Child Abuse Defense and Rsrc. Center
    [13367]
Natl. Child Care Assn. [11533]
Natl. Child Care Development Assn. [11632]
Natl. Child Care and Family Development [11534]
Natl. Child Labor Comm. [13500]
Natl. Child Support Enforcement Assn. [5701]
Natl. Children's Alliance [11633]
Natl. Children's Bur. [IO]
Natl. Christ Child Soc. [19679]
Natl. Coalition Against Domestic Violence [12034]
Natl. Coalition for Campus Children's Centers
    [11535]
Natl. Coalition for Child Protection Reform [11634]
Natl. Collaboration for Youth [11635]
Natl. Conf. of the Bishop of Brazil-Pastoral of the
    Child [IO]
Natl. Coun. for Adoption [11255]
Natl. Coun. on Child Abuse and Family Violence
    [12035]
Natl. Coun. for Families and TV [17186]

A star before a book entry number signifies that the name is not listed separately, but is mentioned within the entry.

Natl. Council for Single Adoptive Parents [11256]
Natl. Court Appointed Special Advocate Assn. [11636]
Natl. Drowning Prevention Alliance [12974]
Natl. Exchange Club Found. [11637]
Natl. Fellowship of Child Care Executives [13501]
Natl. Foster Parent Assn. [12677]
Natl. Indian Child Welfare Assn. [19277]
Natl. Initiative for Children's Healthcare Quality [13970]
Natl. Inst. on Out-of-School Time [11543]
Natl. Juvenile Court Services Assn. [5702]
Natl. Network for Youth [12935]
Natl. Org. Caring for Kids [11638]
Natl. Org. of Circumcision Info. Rsrc. Centers [11732]
Natl. Org. to Halt the Abuse and Routine Mutilation of Males [11733]
Natl. Org. of Mothers of Twins Clubs [12613]
Natl. Organizations for Youth Safety [13502]
Natl. Parents Assn. [12680]
Natl. Prog. for Playground Safety [18578]
Natl. Rsrc. Center for Hea. and Safety in Child Care and Early Educ. [11536]
Natl. Rsrc. Center for Youth Services [11639]
Natl. Runaway Switchboard [12936]
Natl. Soc. for the Prevention of Cruelty to Children [IO]
Natl. Tribal Child Support Assn. [11713]
Natl. Work at Home Mom Assn. [1922]
Natl. Youth Employment Coalition [13506]
Nationwide Patrol [11640]
North Amer. Coun. on Adoptable Children [11257]
North Amer. Reggio Emilia Alliance [11641]
Nuestros Pequenos Hermanos [IO]
Nurses for the Rights of the Child [11737]
One Child at a Time [11642]
Only a Child [11643]
Only a Child [IO]
Oper. Kid-To-Kid [19757]
Org. for the Lifelong Establishment of Paternity [11714]
Org. for the Protection of Children's Rights [IO]
Org. for the Relief of Underprivileged Women and Children in Africa [12876]
Organized Adoption Search Info. Services [11259]
ORIGINS [11260]
Orphan Found. of Am. [11715]
Orphan Resources Intl. [11644]
Orphan Resources Intl. [IO]
Orphan Voyage [11261]
Orr Shalom Children's Homes [IO]
PACT [12439]
Parbatya Bouddha Mission [IO]
Parentless Children's Comm. [IO]
Parents' Action For Children [12682]
Parents Anonymous [11645]
Parents Helping Parents [12684]
Parents of Murdered Children [12685]
Parents Network for the Post Institutionalized Child [16546]
Parents Without Partners [12688]
Partners in Foster Care [12193]
Paul and Lisa Prog. [13082]
Pearl S. Buck Intl. [11646]
Pearl S. Buck Intl. [IO]
People for Children [11716]
Pilot Parents of Southern Arizona [12581]
Plan Japan [IO]
Playing for Keeps [11544]
PLAYLINK [IO]
Polaris Proj. Combating Trafficking of Women and Children [17784]
Polly Klaas Found. [12604]
Prepare Tomorrow's Parents [13511]
Prevent Child Abuse [11647]
Prevent Child Abuse [IO]
Proj. Children [11717]
Proj. Cuddle [11648]
Ray Helfer Soc. [13976]
Reach the Children [11649]
Reach the Children [IO]
Relief Found. [IO]
Restoration Proj. Intl. [12441]
Right for Children, Youth and Social Development [IO]

Robert F. Kennedy Memorial [13513]
Rosenberg Fund for Children [11719]
Russian Children's Welfare Soc. [11650]
Russian Children's Welfare Soc. [IO]
Safe Kids Canada [IO]
Safe Kids Worldwide [11651]
Safe Sitter [11537]
Sambhav [IO]
Save the Children [11720]
Save the Children Australia [IO]
Save the Children Australia - New South Wales [IO]
Save the Children Australia - South Australia [IO]
Save the Children Australia - Tasmania Div. [IO]
Save the Children Australia - Victoria Div. [IO]
Save the Children Australia - Western Australia Div. [IO]
Save the Children Canada [IO]
Save the Children Denmark [IO]
Save the Children Dominican Republic [IO]
Save the Children Egypt [IO]
Save the Children Finland [IO]
Save the Children Fund - Swaziland [IO]
Save the Children Honduras [IO]
Save the Children Hong Kong [IO]
Save the Children Italia [IO]
Save the Children - Korea [IO]
Save the Children Macedonia [IO]
Save the Children Netherlands [IO]
Save the Children New Zealand [IO]
Save the Children - Norway [IO]
Save the Children Spain [IO]
Save the Children - Sweden [IO]
Save the Children - UK [IO]
Save The Children India [IO]
Seedlings Braille Books for Children [9297]
Shared Hope Intl. [13457]
Single Mothers By Choice [12692]
Situational Mgt. and Inter-Learning Est. Soc. [IO]
Smile Alliance Intl. [11721]
Social Relief Intl. [12445]
Soc. of Professors of Child and Adolescent Psychiatry [16096]
SOS Children's Villages of India [IO]
SOS Children's Villages - Jamaica [IO]
SOS Children's Villages - Kenya [IO]
South African Soc. for the Prevention of Child Abuse and Neglect [IO]
Southern Early Childhood Assn. [11722]
Special Needs Advocate for Parents [11652]
A Special Wish Found. [11723]
Starlight Starbright Children's Found. [11724]
Stop it Now! [11653]
St. Child Rescue Ghana [IO]
Students Helping St. Kids Intl. [11725]
Sunshine Found. [11726]
Supervised Visitation Network [11654]
Supervised Visitation Network [IO]
Support A Child Intl. [IO]
Support A Child Intl. [11655]
Supporting Our Sons [11547]
Survivors And Victims Empowered [11656]
Survivors of Incest Anonymous [13085]
Task Force for Child Survival and Development [12542]
Teachers Resisting Unhealthy Children's Entertainment [11657]
Touching Hearts [11267]
The Triplet Connection [12614]
Tunas Harapan Found. [IO]
Uganda Women's Effort to Save Orphans [IO]
UNICEF Austria [IO]
UNICEF Belgium [IO]
UNICEF Bolivia [IO]
UNICEF Denmark [IO]
UNICEF Hungary [IO]
UNICEF Ireland [IO]
UNICEF Israel [IO]
UNICEF Japan [IO]
UNICEF Jordan [IO]
UNICEF Latvia [IO]
UNICEF Lithuania [IO]
UNICEF Luxembourg [IO]
UNICEF Mauritius [IO]
UNICEF New Zealand [IO]

UNICEF Norway [IO]
UNICEF Republic of Korea [IO]
UNICEF San Marino [IO]
UNICEF Slovakia [IO]
UNICEF Somalia [IO]
UNICEF Turkey Natl. Comm. [IO]
UNICEF United Kingdom [IO]
United Fathers of Am. [12014]
United Nations Children's Fund - Armenia [IO]
United Nations Children's Fund - Botswana [IO]
U.S. Fund for UNICEF [IO]
U.S. Fund for UNICEF [11658]
Uplift Internationale [15737]
U.S.A. Toy Lib. Assn. [11548]
Vanished Children's Alliance [11659]
Variety Intl. - The Children's Charity [11660]
Variety International - The Children's Charity [IO]
Village of Childhelp West [11661]
Vitamin Angel Alliance [15571]
VOICE [IO]
VOICES in Action [13086]
Voices for America's Children [11662]
VOICES Assn. [13211]
War Child USA [11663]
War Child USA [IO]
Warm Blankets Orphan Care Intl. [11727]
Watchlist on Children and Armed Conflict [11664]
Watchlist on Children and Armed Conflict [IO]
Welfare Res., Inc. [13193]
A Wish With Wings [11728]
WishKids Intl. [11665]
World Assn. for Children and Parents [11666]
World Assn. for Children and Parents [IO]
World Assn. for Infant Mental Hea. [16098]
World of Dreams Found. Canada [IO]
World Orphans [IO]
World Orphans [11667]
World Vision - Canada [IO]
World Vision Found. of Thailand [IO]
World Vision Intl. - Azerbaijan [IO]
World Vision Intl. - Brazil [IO]
World Vision Intl. - Romania [IO]
World Vision - New Zealand [IO]
World Vision - United Kingdom [IO]
Yeladim Coun. for the Child in Placement [IO]
Youth Advocate Prog. Intl. [IO]
Youth Advocate Prog. Intl. [11668]
Youth for Human Rights Intl. [12382]
Youth Law Center [13522]
Child Welfare Assn; Natl. Indian [19277]
Child Welfare Info. Gateway [11570], c/o Children's Bureau/ACYF, 1250 Maryland Ave. SW, 8th Fl., Washington, DC 20024, (703)385-7565
Child Welfare Inst. [11571], 111 E Wacker Dr., Ste. 325, Chicago, IL 60601, (312)949-5640
Child Welfare League of Am. [11572], 2345 Crystal Dr., Ste. 250, Arlington, VA 22202, (703)412-2400
Child Welfare League of America/Canada [★IO]
Child Welfare League of Canada [IO], Ottawa, ON, Canada
Child Workers in Asia [IO], Bangkok, Thailand
Child Workers in Nepal Concerned Centre [IO], Kathmandu, Nepal
Childbearing Centers; Natl. Assn. of [★15580]

Childbirth
Aiding Mothers and Fathers Experiencing Neonatal Death [11907]
Amer. Assn. of Birth Centers [15580]
Amer. Assn. of Gynecologic Laparoscopists [15581]
Amer. Bd. of Obstetrics and Gynecology [15582]
Amer. Coll. of Nurse-Midwives [15447]
Amer. Coll. of Obstetricians and Gynecologists [15584]
Amer. Coll. of Osteopathic Obstetricians and Gynecologists [15585]
Amer. Found. for Maternal and Child Health [15586]
Amer. Gynecological and Obstetrical Soc. [15587]
Amer. Pregnancy Assn. [15588]
Amer. Soc. of Childbirth Educators [15589]
Amer. Soc. for Colposcopy and Cervical Pathology [15590]
Amer. Soc. for Reproductive Medicine [14389]
Assn. for Childbirth at Home, Intl. [15591]

Reference to "IO" in place of a book number signifies that the association may be found in the 45th edition of International Organizations.

Assn. of Labor Assistants and Childbirth Educators [13977]
Assn. of Nurse Advocates for Childbirth Solutions [13978]
Assn. for Post Natal Illness [IO]
Assn. for Pre- and Perinatal Psychology and Hea. [13979]
Assn. of Professors of Gynecology and Obstetrics [15592]
Assn. of Women's Hea., Obstetric and Neonatal Nurses [15470]
C/SEC [15593]
Center for Humane Options in Childbirth Experiences [15594]
Childbirth Connection [15595]
Childbirth and Postpartum Professional Assn. [13980]
Childbirth and Postpartum Professional Association [IO]
Citizens for Midwifery [13981]
Coalition for Improving Maternity Services [15596]
Coun. on Resident Educ. in Obstetrics and Gynecology [15597]
Coun. of Women's and Infants' Specialty Hospitals [14880]
Endometriosis Assn. [15599]
Fertility Res. Found. [14391]
HELLP Syndrome Soc. [14906]
Home Birth Assn. of Ireland [IO]
Informed Homebirth/Informed Birth and Parenting [15602]
Intl. Cesarean Awareness Network [15604]
Intl. Childbirth Educ. Assn. [15605]
Intl. Coun. on Infertility Info. Dissemination [14392]
Intl. Stillbirth Alliance [13982]
Lamaze Birth Without Pain Educ. Assn. [15607]
Maternal Life Intl. [16341]
Midwest Parentcraft Center [15609]
Midwifery Educ. Accreditation Coun. [8063]
Midwives Alliance of North Am. [15610]
Natl. Campaign to Prevent Teen Pregnancy [13499]
Natl. Healthy Start Assn. [15613]
Natl. Perinatal Assn. [15900]
North Amer. Registry of Midwives [13983]
North Amer. Soc. of Obstetric Medicine [15615]
North Amer. Soc. for the Stud. of Hypertension in Pregnancy [16342]
Ovulation Method Res. and Reference Centre of Australia [IO]
Peaceful Beginnings [11669]
Post Natal Depression Support Assn. [IO]
Radiation and Public Hea. Proj. [16270]
Resolve, The Natl. Infertility Assn. [14394]
Soc. for Gynecologic Investigation [15618]
Soc. for Menstrual Cycle Res. [15619]
Soc. for Natal Effects on Hea. in Adult Life [IO]
Soc. for Obstetric Anesthesia and Perinatology [15903]
Waterbirth Intl. [13984]
Waterbirth International [IO]
Childbirth; Amer. Acad. of Husband-Coached [15579]
Childbirth by Choice Trust [IO], Toronto, ON, Canada
Childbirth Connection [15595], 281 Park Ave. S, 5th Fl., New York, NY 10010, (212)777-5000
Childbirth Education Found. - Address unknown since 1999.
Childbirth Educator Training Program [★15602]
Childbirth Educators; Amer. Soc. of [15589]
Childbirth Experiences; Center for Humane Options in [15594]
Childbirth at Home; Assn. for [★15591]
Childbirth; Natl. Assn. of Parents and Professionals for Safe Alternatives in [★15603]
Childbirth and Postpartum Professional Assn. [13980], PO Box 491448, Lawrenceville, GA 30049, (888)MY-CAPPA
Childbirth and Postpartum Professional Association [IO], Lawrenceville, GA, United States
Childbirth Trust; Natl. [IO]
Childbirth Without Pain Educ. Assn. [★15607]
Childcare Intl. [★11573]

Childcare Intl. [★IO]
Childcare Worldwide [IO], Bellingham, WA, United States
Childcare Worldwide [11573], 1971 Midway Ln., Ste. N, Bellingham, WA 98226, (360)647-2283
ChildFree Network - Address unknown since 2003.
ChildFund Australia [IO], Surry Hills, Australia
ChildFund Ireland [IO], Dublin, Ireland
ChildFund New Zealand [IO], Auckland, New Zealand
Childhelp USA [11680], 15757 N 78th St., Scottsdale, AZ 85260, (480)922-8212
Childhelp West; Village of [11661]
Childhood Apraxia of Speech Assn. [16444], 1151 Freeport Rd., No. 243, Pittsburgh, PA 15238, (412)767-6589
Childhood Arthritis and Rheumatology Res. Alliance [16371], Dept. of Pediatrics, Div. of Rheumatology, Boswell Bldg. A081, 300 Pasteur Dr., Stanford, CA 94305-5208, (650)736-4364
Childhood Assn; Holy [19632]
Childhood Assn; Southern Early [11722]
Childhood Brain Tumor Found. [14257], 20312 Watkins Meadow Dr., Germantown, MD 20876, (301)515-2900
Childhood Cancer; Assn. for Res. of [13798]
Childhood Cancer Found; Candlelighters [13810]
Childhood Cancer Found. - Candlelighters Canada [IO], Toronto, ON, Canada
Childhood Cancer Found; Natl. [★13850]
Childhood Cancer Found; Natl. [13850]
Childhood of the Coun. for Exceptional Children; Div. for Early [9144]

Childhood Education

4Children [IO]
African Child Found. [IO]
Assn. for Achievement and Improvement through Assessment [IO]
Assn. for Childhood Educ. Intl. [IO]
Assn. for Childhood Educ. Intl. [8064]
Assn. for the Educ. of Children with Medical Needs [8072]
Assn. of WORKSHOP WAY Consultants [9213]
Big Picture Company [8353]
Blind Children's Fund [16834]
British Assn. for Early Childhood Educ. [IO]
Children, Inc. [11683]
Children's Creative Response to Conflict Prog. [11684]
Christian Children's Fund [11688]
Compassionate Kids [8384]
Delta Phi Upsilon [24431]
First Book [8789]
For Inspiration and Recognition of Sci. and Tech. [8319]
Futures for Children [11695]
GalaxyGoo [8065]
God's Child Proj. [11597]
GreatSchools [8066]
Hands On Sci. Outreach [8067]
Hands On Sci. Outreach [IO]
Holt Intl. Children's Services [11698]
Indian Youth of Am. [12626]
Inst. for Childhood Resources [8068]
Intl. Centre for Child Stud. [IO]
Intl. Child Rsrc. Inst. [11604]
Intl. Relief Friendship Found. [13171]
Intl. Step by Step Assn. [IO]
Jack and Jill of Am. [11702]
Jack and Jill of Am. Found. [11703]
Kids Fund [11704]
Kids Universe, Inc. [8320]
Learning First Alliance [8273]
Military Child Educ. Coalition [8886]
Natl. Assn. for the Educ. of Young Children [8069]
Natl. Campaign for Real Nursery Educ. [IO]
Natl. Inst. on Out-of-School Time [11543]
Natl. Jewish Coalition for Literacy [8795]
Natl. Kindergarten Alliance [9007]
Natl. Urban Alliance for Effective Educ. [9291]
North Amer. Reggio Emilia Alliance [11641]
Only a Child [11643]
Parent Cooperative Preschools Intl. [8070]
Parent Cooperative Preschools Intl. [IO]
Pre-school Learning Alliance [IO]

Reading Recovery Coun. of North Am. [9048]
Room to Read [12053]
Scottish Pre-School Play Assn. [IO]
South African Cong. for Early Childhood Development [IO]
Southern Early Childhood Assn. [11722]
Stop the Violence, Face The Music [13376]
Sudan-American Found. for Educ. [8073]
Van Andel Educ. Inst. [8312]
Volunteers and Interns for Balinese Educ. Found. [IO]
World Org. for Early Childhood Educ. [IO]
World Org. for Early Childhood Educ. U.S. Natl. Comm. [8071]
World Org. for Human Potential [11550]
Childhood Eye Cancer Trust [IO], London, United Kingdom
Childhood Onset Schizophrenia; North Amer. Soc. for [15229]
Childhood Sensuality Circle - Defunct.
Childhood Teacher Educators; Natl. Assn. of Early [9222]
Childhope - Zambia [IO], Lusaka, Zambia
Childless By Choice - Defunct.
Childminding Ireland [IO], Kilcoole, Ireland
Childreach, U.S. Member of Plan Intl. [IO], Warwick, RI, United States
Childreach, U.S. Member of Plan Intl. [11681], 155 Plan Way, Warwick, RI 02886, (401)738-5600
Children
ABLE: Assn. for Better Living and Educ. Intl. [11756]
Abwenzi African Stud. [18863]
Acoustic Neuroma Assn. [15816]
Action for Child Protection [11553]
Action for Children in Conflict [IO]
Action for Healthy Kids [13945]
Adolescent Scoliosis Soc. of North Am. [16392]
Adopt Am. Network [11227]
Adoptee-Birthparent Support Network [11228]
Adoption Identity Movement [11229]
Adoption Info. Services [11230]
Adoptions Together [11231]
Adult Children of Alcoholics World Ser. Org. [13012]
Advocates for Youth [12173]
Advocates for Youth's Media Proj. [12174]
African Cradle [11670]
Afterschool Alliance [11524]
Aicardi Syndrome Newsl. [14437]
Aid to Incarcerated Mothers [11851]
Airline Ambassadors Intl. [13147]
A.L. Mailman Family Found. [11671]
Alan Guttmacher Inst. [12175]
Alliance for Childhood Cancer [13787]
Alliance for Children and Families [12136]
Alliance for Eating Disorders Awareness [14297]
Alliance for Healthy Homes [13320]
Alliance for Transforming the Lives of Children [11554]
ALMA Soc. ∗ Adoptees' Liberty Movement Assn. [11232]
ALSAC/Saint Jude Children's Res. Hosp. [13946]
Ambulatory Pediatric Assn. [15879]
Am. World Adoption Assn. [11233]
Amer. Acad. of Child and Adolescent Psychiatry [16063]
Amer. Acad. of Pediatric Dentistry [14108]
Amer. Acad. of Pediatrics [15880]
Amer. Adoption Cong. [11234]
Amer. Assn. of Caregiving Youth [13466]
Amer. Assn. of Children's Residential Centers [13467]
Amer. Assn. for Lost Children [12607]
Amer. Assn. for Pediatric Ophthalmology and Strabismus [15660]
Amer. Bar Assn. Center on Children and the Law [11555]
Amer. Belarussian Relief Org. [12828]
Amer. Bd. of Pediatrics [15881]
Amer. Bd. of Psychiatry and Neurology [16071]
Amer. Camp Assn. [23268]
Amer. Center for Law and Justice [12901]
Amer. Children of SCORE [10530]
Amer. Civil Liberties Union [17084]

A star before a book entry number signifies that the name is not listed separately, but is mentioned within the entry.

Amer. Civil Liberties Union Found. [17085]
Amer. Coll. of Foot and Ankle Pediatrics [16033]
Amer. Coll. of Osteopathic Pediatricians [15795]
Amer. Found. for Maternal and Child Health [15586]
Amer. Friends of ALYN Hosp. [12825]
Amer. Hackney Horse Soc. [4820]
Amer. Humane Assn. Children's Services [11556]
Amer. Jewish World Ser. [12829]
Amer. Junior Brahman Assn. [4231]
Amer. Juvenile Arthritis Org. [16368]
Amer. Orthodontic Soc. [14138]
Amer. Osteopathic Bd. of Pediatrics [15800]
Amer. Otological Soc. [15822]
Amer. Pediatric Soc. [15882]
Amer. Professional Soc. on the Abuse of Children [11557]
Amer. Soc. for Adolescent Psychiatry [16078]
Amer. Soc. for Deaf Children [14742]
Amer. Sudden Infant Death Syndrome Inst. [16523]
Amer. Youth Work Center [13469]
America's Angel [12140]
America's Children Hunger Network [11558]
America's Fund for Afghan Children [11265]
Andorra Natl. Comm. for UNICEF [IO]
Angelcare [IO]
Angelcare [11672]
Anti-Child Pornography Org. [12766]
Assn. of Administrators of the Interstate Compact on the Placement of Children [11559]
Assn. for Birth Psychology [16137]
Assn. of Child Neurology Nurses [15465]
Assn. for Child Psychoanalysis [16106]
Assn. for Children with Down Syndrome [12562]
Assn. for Children for Enforcement of Support [11673]
Assn. of Children's Museums [10495]
Assn. of Children's Prosthetic-Orthotic Clinics [15784]
Assn. of Directors of Children's Services [IO]
Assn. for the Educ. of Children with Medical Needs [8072]
Assn. of Jewish Family and Children's Agencies [12467]
Assn. for Lib. Ser. to Children [10334]
Assn. of Maternal and Child Hea. Programs [13947]
Assn. of Medical School Pediatric Dept. Chairs [15884]
Assn. of Missing and Exploited Children's Organizations [12601]
Assn. Montessori International-U.S.A. [8892]
Assn. of Pediatric Hematology/Oncology Nurses [15467]
Assn. of Pediatric Oncology Social Workers [15885]
Assn. of Pediatric Therapists [16606]
Assn. for Res. of Childhood Cancer [13798]
Assn. of SIDS and Infant Mortality Programs [16524]
Assn. of Sites Advocating Child Protection [11560]
Attachment Parenting Intl. [12662]
Austria Natl. Comm. for UNICEF [IO]
Autism Network Intl. [13719]
Autism Services Center [13722]
Autism Soc. of Am. [13723]
Autism Speaks [13724]
Belgian Natl. Comm. for UNICEF [IO]
Believe In Tomorrow Natl. Children's Found. [11674]
Bereaved Parents of the USA [11512]
Better Boys Found. [11675]
Bhutan Women and Children Org. [IO]
Big Bros. Big Sisters of Am. [11676]
Birth Defect Res. for Children [13752]
Black Alliance for Educational Options [8322]
Blind Children's Fund [16834]
Bonus Families [12143]
Books for the Barrios [12049]
Boys Hope Girls Hope [13472]
Boys' Towns of Italy [13474]
Brass Ring Soc. [11677]
Brave Kids [13949]
Bread and Roses [12113]

Cameroon Assn. for the Protection and Educ. of the Child [IO]
Camp Fire USA [13475]
Campaign For Our Children [13476]
Canadian Assn. for Young Children [IO]
Cancer Care [13803]
Candlelighters Childhood Cancer Found. [13810]
Canines for Disabled Kids [11927]
Captive Daughters [18383]
Carnegie Coun. on Adolescent Development [13477]
Catholic Guardian Soc. [11564]
Catholic Parents Network [12664]
CCHS Family Network [14255]
Center for Assessment and Policy Development [18636]
Center for the Child Care Workforce, A Proj. of the Amer. Fed. of Teachers Educational Found. [12072]
Center for the Stud. of Multiple Birth [15272]
Center for Surrogate Parenting [13297]
CFC Intl. [14435]
Child Action Nepal [IO]
Child to Child Gp. [IO]
The Child Connection [12602]
Child Family Hea. Intl. [11551]
Child-Friendly Initiative [11678]
Child Life Coun. [13951]
Child Neurology Soc. [15386]
Child Protection Alliance [IO]
Child Rights Centre [IO]
Child Support Resistance [12006]
Child Trends [11679]
Child Welfare Info. Gateway [11570]
Child Welfare Inst. [11571]
Child Welfare League of Am. [11572]
Child Workers in Asia [IO]
ChildFund Australia [IO]
Childhelp USA [11680]
Childhood Arthritis and Rheumatology Res. Alliance [16371]
Childreach, U.S. Member of Plan Intl. [11681]
Childreach, U.S. Member of Plan Intl. [IO]
Children and Adults With Attention Deficit/Hyperactivity Disorder [15314]
Children of the Americas [11574]
Children of the Andes [IO]
Children Before Dogs [11682]
Children of Deaf Adults [14747]
Children of the Earth [12696]
Children of the Earth United [4621]
Children, Inc. [11683]
Children of the Night [12933]
Children Now [11575]
Children of Persia [11576]
Children in Wales [IO]
Children's Advt. Rev. Unit [96]
Children's Art Found. [9781]
Children's Book Coun. [9746]
Children's Cause for Cancer Advocacy [13812]
Children's Craniofacial Assn. [14057]
Children's Creative Response to Conflict Prog. [11684]
Children's Cross Connection Intl. [11552]
Children's Defense Fund [11685]
Children's Eye Found. [15679]
Children's Hea. Environmental Coalition [13953]
Children's Hea. Fund [13954]
Children's Hemiplegia and Stroke Assn. [16493]
Children's HopeChest [11578]
Children's Hospice Intl. [14853]
Children's Leukemia Res. Assn. [13813]
Children's Literature Assn. [10418]
Children's Liver Assn. for Support Services [14804]
Children's Network Intl. [11579]
Children's Relief Network [11581]
Children's Rights [17100]
Children's Rights Alliance [IO]
Children's Rights Alliance for England [IO]
Children's Rights Div. - Human Rights Watch [11583]
Children's Television Rsrc. and Educ. Center [11686]

Children's Wish Found. of Canada [IO]
Children's Wish Found. Intl. [IO]
Children's Wish Found. Intl. [11687]
CHOICE [12178]
Choristers Guild [20426]
Christian Children's Fund [11688]
Christian Children's Fund [IO]
Christian Found. for Children and Aging [13159]
Christian Ser. Club [19515]
Christian Sports Intl. [23298]
Chromosome 9P Network [14443]
CityKids Found. [13479]
CityMatch [13957]
Clowns Without Borders - USA [11768]
Coalition to Stop the Use of Child Soldiers [IO]
Coffee Kids [11769]
COLAGE [12223]
Comm. for Missing Children [12603]
Comm. for Mother and Child Rights [11689]
The Compassionate Friends [12666]
Compassionate Kids [8384]
Comprehensive Day Care Programs [11539]
Computers for Children [8137]
Concerned Persons for Adoption [11240]
Concerned United Birthparents [11241]
Cornelia de Lange Syndrome Found. [13754]
Coun. on Accreditation [13164]
Coun. of Administrators of Special Educ. [9139]
Coun. for Children with Behavioral Disorders [9140]
Coun. of Families with Visual Impairment [16844]
Coun. of Parent Attorneys and Advocates [9142]
Coun. for Professional Recognition [11526]
Coun. of Women's and Infants' Specialty Hospitals [14880]
Couple to Couple League [12636]
Covering Kids and Families [12271]
Crigler-Najjar Assn. [14805]
Cyclic Vomiting Syndrome Assn. [14415]
Cystinosis Found. [15246]
Cystinosis Res. Network [15247]
Dads Rights [12008]
Danny Found. [12959]
Darkness to Light [11590]
The Dawkins Project [11690]
DB-Link: The Natl. Info. CH On Children Who Are Deaf-Blind [16845]
Delta Phi Upsilon [24431]
Disabled and Alone/Life Services for the Handicapped [11941]
Div. for Early Childhood of the Coun. for Exceptional Children [9144]
Docs for Tots [13958]
Donors' Offspring [13298]
Dream Factory [11691]
Dysautonomia Youth Network of Am. [15318]
Ear Found. [15825]
Education-A-Must [12056]
Educ. and Enrichment Sect. of the Natl. Coun. on Family Relations [12151]
Emergency Relief Response Fund [20562]
Empower Prog. [8945]
Empowerment Soc. Intl. [11775]
Enough Is Enough [17923]
Entertainment Indus. Found. [12114]
Ethiopian North Amer. Hea. Professionals Assn. [14629]
Every Person Influences Children [11540]
Fair Play for Children Assn. [IO]
Fairview Pregnancy and Newborn Loss Information [12668]
Families Adopting Children Everywhere [11242]
Families for Private Adoption [11244]
Family of the Americas Found. [12637]
Family and Home Network [12669]
Family Rsrc. Center on Disabilities [8202]
Family Supports [12155]
Family Violence Prevention Fund [12028]
Famous Fone Friends [11692]
Fanconi Anemia Res. Fund [14450]
Father Matters [18180]
Fatherhood Proj. [12670]
Fed. for Children with Special Needs [12569]
Fed. of Families for Children's Mental Hea. [12550]

Reference to "IO" in place of a book number signifies that the association may be found in the 45th edition of International Organizations.

Fed. of Galaxy Explorers [9136]
Fed. of Pediatric Organizations [15887]
Feed the Children [12854]
Feeding Hungry Children Intl. [12390]
First Book [8789]
First Candle/SIDS Alliance [16525]
First Signs [13942]
Floating Harbor Syndrome Support Gp. of North Am. [14451]
The Floating Hosp. [14882]
Focus on the Family [12157]
For Inspiration and Recognition of Sci. and Tech. [8319]
Foster Care Alumni of Am. [11592]
Foster Grandparent Prog. [11693]
Friends in Adoption [11245]
Friends of Karen [11694]
Friends of LADDERS [12491]
Futures for Children [11695]
Generation Green [17054]
Gift of Life Intl. [12524]
Girls Inc. [13486]
Girlstart [8468]
Give Kids the World Village [11696]
Give Kids the World Village [IO]
Giving Children Hope [11596]
Global Autism Proj. [13725]
Global Movement for Children [IO]
Global Neuro Rescue [15324]
Global Nomads Gp. [9336]
God's Child Proj. [11597]
Grandparents Rights Org. [12264]
Grandparents United for Children's Rights [17058]
Grantmakers for Children, Youth, and Families [12723]
Great Books Found. [9748]
Great Dads [12672]
GreatSchools [8066]
Guardian Assn. of Pinellas County [12266]
Guitars Not Guns [18114]
Hands On Sci. Outreach [8067]
Harvard Injury Control Res. Center [16690]
Healing the Children [11697]
Healthy Schools Network [4635]
Heather's Teddy Bear Org. [22035]
Hispanic Coun. for Reform and Educational Options [8260]
Holistic Moms Network [12673]
Hollingworth Center for Highly Gifted Children [9982]
Holt Intl. Children's Services [11698]
Holt Intl. Children's Services [IO]
HOPE for Children [IO]
House of Ruth [12029]
Human Growth Found. [16020]
Humanity United in Giving Internationally [11699]
Humanity United in Giving Internationally [IO]
Indian Youth of Am. [12626]
Infant and Juvenile Mfrs. Assn. [240]
Innocence in Danger - USA [11601]
Inst. for the Advancement of Philosophy for Children [10796]
Inst. for Amer. Values [12158]
Inst. in Basic Life Principles [13489]
Institutes for the Achievement of Human Potential [11700]
Inter-American Parliamentary Gp. on Population and Development [12432]
Intl. Acad. for Child Brain Development [15389]
Intl. Aid Serving Kids [11603]
Intl. Alliance for Child and Adolescent Mental Hea. and Schools [15204]
Intl. Alliance for Youth Sports [23994]
Intl. Assn. of Orofacial Myology [15869]
Intl. Assn. of Pediatric Lab. Medicine [15888]
Intl. Assn. for Truancy and Dropout Prevention [8326]
Intl. Child Amputee Network [11954]
Intl. Child Care U.S.A. [11701]
Intl. Child Care U.S.A. [IO]
Intl. Child Rsrc. Inst. [11604]
Intl. Children's Anophthalmia Network [16857]
Intl. Coalition for Children and the Env. [4636]
Intl. Comm. for the Children of Chechnya [11605]
Intl. DOVE Assn. [IO]

Intl. Fed. Terre des Hommes [IO]
Intl. Found. for Terror Act Victims [12942]
Intl. Inst. for Children's Literature and Reading Res. [IO]
Intl. Network of Children's Ministry [IO]
Intl. Network of Children's Ministry [19758]
Intl. Org. for Adolescents [11606]
Intl. Pediatric Hypertension Assn. [14907]
Intl. Pediatric Nephrology Assn. [15292]
Intl. Pediatric Transplant Assn. [16673]
Intl. Res. Soc. for Children's Literature [IO]
Intl. Rett Syndrome Assn. [15333]
Intl. Soc. for Adolescent Psychiatry and Psychology [16087]
Intl. Soundex Reunion Registry [11248]
Intl. Youth Lib. [IO]
Interracial Family Circle [12161]
Intimate Apparel Square Club [12201]
Islamic Amer. Relief Agency [12864]
Jack and Jill of Am. [11702]
Jack and Jill of Am. Found. [11703]
Jackie Robinson Found. [13491]
JARC [12570]
Jewish Women Intl. [20153]
Jobs for America's Graduates [12084]
Joint Custody Assn. [12011]
Juvenile Diabetes Res. Found. Intl. [14228]
Juvenile Products Mfrs. Assn. [2388]
Karen Horney Clinic [16109]
Kempe Children's Center [11609]
Kidpower Teenpower Fullpower Intl. [12967]
Kids 4 Afghan Kids [11610]
Kids for a Clean Env. [4585]
Kids Fund [11704]
Kids at Hope [11705]
Kids In Danger [11612]
Kids Konnected [11706]
Kids Kottage Found. [IO]
Kids Need Both Parents [17509]
Kids Universe, Inc. [8320]
Kids With A Cause [11613]
Kids With Food Allergies [13603]
Kids With Heart Natl. Assn. for Children's Heart Disorders [13915]
Kids Without Borders [11614]
Kidsave Intl. [11251]
KIDSCOPE [11518]
KidsPeace [11615]
Kindness in Suffering [11616]
Latin Am. Parents Assn. [11252]
Lawyers for Children Am. [6026]
League of Tarcisians [19651]
Learning Disabilities Assn. of Am. [12492]
A Leg To Stand On [12659]
Liberal Educ. for Adoptive Families [11253]
Liberty Godparent Home [12918]
Light of Cambodian Children [11617]
Love Humanity - USA [11618]
Love146 [11620]
Magicians Without Borders [12503]
Mail for Me Club [11621]
Make-A-Wish Found. of Am. [11707]
Make a Child Smile [11708]
Make Today Count [13841]
March of Dimes Birth Defects Found. [13756]
Marine Toys for Tots Found. [11709]
Meds and Food for Kids [11622]
Middle East Children's Alliance [17774]
Midori and Friends [7976]
Military Child Educ. Coalition [8886]
Mir Pace Intl. [12872]
Miracles of Hope Network [11623]
Molesters Anonymous [13024]
MOMS in Touch Intl. [20621]
Mothers Against Sexual Abuse [13078]
Mothers Against Sexual Predators At Large [13079]
Mothers Against Violence in Am. [13375]
Mothers of Murdered Youth [11710]
MOVE Intl.: Mobility Opportunities Via Educ. - USA [11962]
Ms. Found. for Women [17549]
Multicultural Educ., Training, and Advocacy [11625]
MUMS Natl. Parent-to-Parent Network [16541]

Natl. Abandoned Infants Assistance Rsrc. Center [12412]
Natl. Adoption Center [11254]
Natl. AfterSchool Assn. [11528]
Natl. Assn. of At-Home Mothers [12674]
Natl. Assn. of Child Care Professionals [11529]
Natl. Assn. of Child Care Rsrc. and Referral Agencies [11530]
Natl. Assn. for Children's Behavioral Hea. [16090]
Natl. Assn. of Counsel for Children [11711]
Natl. Assn. for the Educ. of African Amer. Children with Learning Disabilities [12493]
Natl. Assn. for Family and Child Care [12171]
Natl. Assn. of Former Foster Care Children of Am. [11626]
Natl. Assn. of Mothers' Centers [12676]
Natl. Assn. of Nannies [829]
Natl. Assn. for Nanny Care [11531]
Natl. Assn. of Non-Custodial Moms [11538]
Natl. Assn. for Parents of Children With Visual Impairments [16873]
Natl. Assn. of Private Special Educ. Centers [9147]
Natl. Assn. of Public Child Welfare Administrators [11629]
Natl. Assn. for Sick Child Daycare [11532]
Natl. Assn. of State VOCAL Orgs. [13365]
Natl. Attention Deficit Disorder Assn. [15343]
Natl. Autism Assn. [13727]
Natl. Black Child Development Inst. [11542]
Natl. Bd. for Certified Counselors and Affiliates [11828]
Natl. Center for Children in Poverty [11712]
Natl. Center for Educ. in Maternal and Child Hea. [13969]
Natl. Center for Lesbian Rights [12246]
Natl. Center for Missing and Exploited Children [11630]
Natl. Center for Prosecution of Child Abuse [11631]
Natl. Center for Stuttering [16450]
Natl. Child Abuse Defense and Rsrc. Center [13367]
Natl. Child Care Assn. [11533]
Natl. Child Care and Family Development [11534]
Natl. Child Labor Comm. [13500]
Natl. Child Safety Coun. [12972]
Natl. Children's Alliance [11633]
Natl. Christ Child Soc. [19679]
Natl. Coalition Against Domestic Violence [12034]
Natl. Coalition for Campus Children's Centers [11535]
Natl. Comm. on the Educ. of Migrant Children (of the Natl. Child Labor Comm.) [12593]
Natl. Coun. for Adoption [11255]
Natl. Council for Single Adoptive Parents [11256]
Natl. Court Appointed Special Advocate Assn. [11636]
Natl. Dissemination Center for Children with Disabilities [11971]
Natl. Drowning Prevention Alliance [12974]
Natl. Exchange Club Found. [11637]
Natl. Fellowship of Child Care Executives [13501]
Natl. Foster Parent Assn. [12677]
Natl. Head Start Assn. [9006]
Natl. Healthy Start Assn. [15613]
Natl. Infant Torticollis Assn. [14945]
Natl. Infertility Network Exchange [12678]
Natl. Initiative for Children's Healthcare Quality [13970]
Natl. Kindergarten Alliance [9007]
Natl. Network for Youth [12935]
Natl. Org. Caring for Kids [11638]
Natl. Org. of Circumcision Info. Rsrc. Centers [11732]
Natl. Org. of Mothers of Twins Clubs [12613]
Natl. Org. of Parents of Blind Children [16879]
Natl. Organizations for Youth Safety [13502]
Natl. Parent Network on Disabilities [14245]
Natl. Parents Assn. [12680]
Natl. PTA - Natl. Cong. of Parents and Teachers [8954]
Natl. Rsrc. Center for Hea. and Safety in Child Care and Early Educ. [11536]
Natl. Reye's Syndrome Found. [16366]

A star before a book entry number signifies that the name is not listed separately, but is mentioned within the entry.

Natl. Runaway Switchboard [12936]
Natl. Rural Educ. Advocacy Coalition [9068]
Natl. SIDS/Infant Death Rsrc. Center [16526]
Natl. Tribal Child Support Assn. [11713]
Natl. Vaccine Info. Center [13972]
Natl. Work at Home Mom Assn. [1922]
Natl. Youth Employment Coalition [13506]
Natl. Youth Sports Safety Found. [16484]
Native Amer. Fatherhood and Families Assn.
    [12681]
Neuroblastoma Children's Cancer Soc. [13858]
New Parents Network [8956]
Nile Children and Family Support Org. [IO]
Nongovernmental Organizations Comm. on Youth
    [13508]
Nonverbal Learning Disorders Assn. [14998]
North Amer. Coun. on Adoptable Children [11257]
North Amer. Man/Boy Love Assn. [13099]
North Amer. Reggio Emilia Alliance [11641]
North Amer. Soc. for Childhood Onset
    Schizophrenia [15229]
North Amer. Soc. for Pediatric Gastroenterology,
    Hepatology and Nutrition [14424]
North Amer. Soc. for Pediatric Medicine [15891]
The Nurturing Network [13434]
Only a Child [11643]
Oper. Smile [12534]
Organic Acidemia Assn. [14472]
Org. for the Lifelong Establishment of Paternity
    [11714]
Org. of Parents Through Surrogacy [13299]
Org. for the Relief of Underprivileged Women and
    Children in Africa [12876]
Organized Adoption Search Info. Services [11259]
ORIGINS [11260]
Orphan Found. of Am. [11715]
Orphan Resources Intl. [11644]
Orphan Voyage [11261]
Our Little Bros. and Sisters [20380]
OutProud [12252]
PACER Center - Parent Advocacy Coalition for
    Educational Rights [14246]
Parent Cooperative Preschools Intl. [8070]
Parents' Action For Children [12682]
Parents Against Childhood Epilepsy [14382]
Parents' Choice Found. [12683]
Parents of Infants and Children with Kernicterus
    [15358]
Parents of Kids with Infectious Diseases [14954]
Parents of Murdered Children [12685]
Parents for Public Schools [12052]
Parents Rights Coalition [12687]
Parents Without Partners [12688]
Partners in Foster Care [12193]
Paul and Lisa Prog. [13082]
PE4life [8991]
Pediatric AIDS Found. [13582]
Pediatric Cardiac Intensive Care Soc. [15892]
Pediatric Chaplains Network [19755]
Pediatric Infectious Diseases Soc. [14955]
Pediatric Keratoplasty Assn. [15700]
Pediatric Neurotransmitter Disease Assn. [15361]
Pediatric Nursing Certification Bd. [15522]
Pediatric Orthopedic Soc. of North Am. [15780]
People Against Rape [13083]
People for Children [11716]
People for Children [IO]
Pilot Parents of Southern Arizona [12581]
Plan Intl. [IO]
Play for Peace [12699]
Playing for Keeps [11544]
Postgraduate Center for Mental Hea. [16227]
Prepare Tomorrow's Parents [13511]
Prevent Child Abuse [11647]
PRISMS: Parents and Researchers Interested In
    Smith-Magenis Syndrome [14476]
Prog. for Appropriate Tech. in Hea. [17000]
Proj. Children [11717]
Proj. Children [IO]
Pull-thru Network [14427]
Railway Children [IO]
RAINBOWS [IO]
RAINBOWS [11718]
Ray Helfer Soc. [13976]
Reach the Children [11649]

Reading Recovery Coun. of North Am. [9048]
Restoration Proj. Intl. [12441]
Retinoblastoma Intl. [13869]
River of Words [4186]
Robert F. Kennedy Memorial [13513]
Rosenberg Fund for Children [11719]
Safe Kids Worldwide [11651]
Safe Sitter [11537]
Save the Children [11720]
School Nurse Achievement Prog. [15525]
Sea to See Proj. [13760]
Search Reports, Inc./Central Registry of the Miss-
    ing [12611]
Seedlings Braille Books for Children [9297]
Selective Mutism Found. [15233]
Sesame Workshop [9782]
Shriners Hospitals for Children [13973]
Single and Custodial Fathers Network [12691]
Single Mothers By Choice [12692]
Single Parent Rsrc. Center [12693]
Smile Alliance Intl. [11721]
Soccer in the Streets [11789]
Social Policy Action Network [13138]
Social Relief Intl. [12445]
Soc. of Children's Book Writers and Illustrators
    [11194]
Soc. of Clinical Child and Adolescent Psychology
    [16171]
Soc. for Ear, Nose, and Throat Advances in
    Children [15827]
Soc. of Environmental Understanding and Sus-
    tainability [5274]
Soc. of Military Otolaryngologists - Head and
    Neck Surgeons [15267]
Soc. for Pediatric Dermatology [14215]
Soc. of Pediatric Nurses [15527]
Soc. for Pediatric Psychology [16175]
Soc. for Pediatric Radiology [16301]
Soc. for Pediatric Res. [15899]
Soc. for Pediatric Urology [16715]
Soc. of Phantom Friends [9739]
Soc. of Professors of Child and Adolescent
    Psychiatry [16096]
Soc. for Protecting the Rights of the Child [IO]
Soc. for Res. in Child Development [11546]
Soc. of Univ. Otolaryngologists - Head and Neck
    Surgeons [15828]
Southern Early Childhood Assn. [11722]
Special Needs Advocate for Parents [11652]
A Special Wish Found. [11723]
Spellbinders [10984]
Starlight Starbright Children's Found. [11724]
Stepfamily Found. [12168]
Stop the Violence, Face The Music [13376]
Students Helping St. Kids Intl. [11725]
Students Helping Street Kids International [IO]
Subud Youth Assn. [13516]
Sudan-American Found. for Educ. [8073]
Sunshine Found. [11726]
Support A Child Intl. [11655]
Support Org. for Trisomy 18, 13, and Related
    Disorders [14485]
Supporting Our Sons [11547]
Survivors And Victims Empowered [11656]
Take Root [12605]
Task Force for Child Survival and Development
    [12542]
Teachers Resisting Unhealthy Children's
    Entertainment [11657]
Terre des Hommes Germany [IO]
Terre des Hommes Germany - Cambodia [IO]
Terre des Hommes Germany - India [IO]
Terre des Hommes Germany - Indonesia [IO]
Terre des Hommes Germany - Philippines [IO]
Terre des Hommes Germany - Southeast Asia
    [IO]
Terre des Hommes Germany - Vietnam [IO]
Terre des Hommes Germany - Zimbabwe and
    Zambia [IO]
Toughlove Intl. [12694]
Toy Indus. Assn. [3832]
Tree Musketeers [4459]
The Triplet Connection [12614]
Twins Found. [12616]
UK Comm. for UNICEF [IO]

UNICEF - Afghanistan [IO]
UNICEF - Albania [IO]
UNICEF - Algeria [IO]
UNICEF - Angola [IO]
UNICEF - Antigua and Barbuda [IO]
UNICEF - Argentina [IO]
UNICEF - Azerbaijan [IO]
UNICEF - Bahrain [IO]
UNICEF - Bangladesh [IO]
UNICEF - Barbados [IO]
UNICEF - Belarus [IO]
UNICEF - Belize [IO]
UNICEF - Benin [IO]
UNICEF - Bhutan [IO]
UNICEF - Bolivia [IO]
UNICEF - Bosnia and Herzegovina [IO]
UNICEF, Brazil-Brasilia [IO]
UNICEF, Brazil-Fortaleza [IO]
UNICEF, Brazil-Recife [IO]
UNICEF, Brazil-Rio de Janeiro [IO]
UNICEF, Brazil-Salvador [IO]
UNICEF, Brazil-Sao Luis [IO]
UNICEF - Bulgaria [IO]
UNICEF - Burkina Faso [IO]
UNICEF - Burundi [IO]
UNICEF - Cambodia [IO]
UNICEF - Cameroon [IO]
UNICEF - Cape Verde [IO]
UNICEF - Central African Republic [IO]
UNICEF - Chad [IO]
UNICEF - Chile [IO]
UNICEF - China [IO]
UNICEF - Colombia [IO]
UNICEF - Comoros [IO]
UNICEF - Costa Rica [IO]
UNICEF - Cote d'Ivoire [IO]
UNICEF - Croatia [IO]
UNICEF - Cuba [IO]
UNICEF - Czech Republic [IO]
UNICEF - Djibouti [IO]
UNICEF - Dominican Republic [IO]
UNICEF - Ecuador [IO]
UNICEF - Egypt [IO]
UNICEF - El Salvador [IO]
UNICEF - Equatorial Guinea [IO]
UNICEF - Estonia [IO]
UNICEF - Ethiopia [IO]
UNICEF - Fiji [IO]
UNICEF - Finland [IO]
UNICEF - France [IO]
UNICEF - Gabon [IO]
UNICEF - Gambia [IO]
UNICEF - Georgia [IO]
UNICEF - Germany [IO]
UNICEF - Ghana [IO]
UNICEF - Greece [IO]
UNICEF - Grenada [IO]
UNICEF - Guatemala [IO]
UNICEF - Guinea [IO]
UNICEF - Guinea-Bissau [IO]
UNICEF - Guyana [IO]
UNICEF - Iceland [IO]
UNICEF - Madagascar [IO]
UNICEF - Malawi [IO]
UNICEF - Malaysia [IO]
UNICEF - Mali [IO]
UNICEF - Mauritania [IO]
UNICEF - Mexico [IO]
UNICEF - Mongolian [IO]
UNICEF - Mozambique [IO]
UNICEF - Myanmar [IO]
UNICEF - Nepal [IO]
UNICEF - Netherlands [IO]
UNICEF - Nicaragua [IO]
UNICEF - Niger [IO]
UNICEF - Nigeria [IO]
UNICEF - Oman [IO]
UNICEF - Pakistan [IO]
UNICEF - Panama [IO]
UNICEF - Papua New Guinea [IO]
UNICEF - Paraguay [IO]
UNICEF - Peru [IO]
UNICEF - Philippines [IO]
UNICEF - Poland [IO]
UNICEF - Portugal [IO]

Reference to "IO" in place of a book number signifies that the association may be found in the 45th edition of International Organizations.

UNICEF - Republic of the Congo [IO]
UNICEF - Republic of Moldova [IO]
UNICEF - Romania [IO]
UNICEF - Russia [IO]
UNICEF - Rwanda [IO]
UNICEF - Saudi Arabia [IO]
UNICEF - Senegal [IO]
UNICEF - South Africa [IO]
UNICEF - Spain [IO]
UNICEF - Sri Lanka [IO]
UNICEF - Sudan [IO]
UNICEF - Swaziland [IO]
UNICEF - Sweden [IO]
UNICEF - Switzerland [IO]
UNICEF - Syria [IO]
UNICEF - Tajikistan [IO]
UNICEF - Thailand [IO]
UNICEF - Togo [IO]
UNICEF - Tunisia [IO]
UNICEF - Turkey [IO]
UNICEF - Uganda [IO]
UNICEF - Ukraine [IO]
UNICEF - United Republic of Tanzania [IO]
UNICEF - Uruguay [IO]
UNICEF - Uzbekistan [IO]
UNICEF - Venezuela [IO]
UNICEF - Vietnam [IO]
UNICEF - Yemen [IO]
UNICEF - Zambia [IO]
UNICEF - Zimbabwe [IO]
United Fathers of Am. [12014]
United League Toy Representatives Associations [3833]
United Nations Children's Fund - Namibia [IO]
United Nations Women's Guild [13066]
U.S. Bd. on Books for Young People [9756]
Uplift Internationale [15737]
U.S.A. Toy Lib. Assn. [11548]
Village of Childhelp West [11661]
Vitamin Angel Alliance [15571]
VOICES in Action [13086]
Voices for America's Children [11662]
VOICES Assn. [13211]
War Child USA [11663]
Warm Blankets Orphan Care Intl. [11727]
Watchlist on Children and Armed Conflict [11664]
What Kids Can Do [18859]
A Wish With Wings [11728]
WishKids Intl. [11665]
Women in Toys [3834]
World Assn. for Infant Mental Hea. [16098]
World Craniofacial Found. [14068]
World Org. for Human Potential [11550]
World Orphans [11667]
Young Racers of Am. [23674]
Youth Advocate Prog. Intl. [11668]
Youth for Human Rights Intl. [12382]
Youth Organizations U.S.A. [13523]
Zero to Three: Natl. Center for Infants, Toddlers and Families [13944]
Children and Adults with Autism; NSAC, The Natl. Soc. for [★13723]
Children and Adults with Learning Disabilities; Assn. for [★12492]
Children and Adults With Attention Deficit Disorder [★15314]
Children and Adults With Attention Deficit/Hyperactivity Disorder [15314], 8181 Professional Pl., Ste. 150, Landover, MD 20785, (301)306-7070
Children of Aging Parents [11282], PO Box 167, Richboro, PA 18954, (800)227-7294
Children; Aiding Leukemia Stricken Amer. [★13946]
Children with AIDS Proj. of Am. [11238], PO Box 23778, Tempe, AZ 85285-3778, (480)774-9718
Children; AIDS Rsrc. Found. for [13553]
Children of Alcoholic Parents - Defunct.
Children of Alcoholics, Central Ser. Bd; Adult [★13012]
Children of Alcoholics Found. [13228], 164 W 74th St., New York, NY 10023-2301, (646)505-2060
Children of Alcoholics; Natl. Assn. for [13261]
Children of Alcoholics; Natl. Assn. for Native Amer. [11627]
Children of Alcoholics World Ser. Org; Adult [13012]

Children; Amer. Assn. for Gifted [8463]
Children; Amer. Assn. for Lost [12607]
Children; Amer. Assn. for Protecting [★11556]
Children; Amer. Professional Soc. on the Abuse of [11557]
Children of the Amer. Revolution; Natl. Soc. of the [20674]
Children; Amer. Soc. for Deaf [14742]
Children of the Americas [11574], c/o W.O. Mills, III, Pres., PO Box 140165, Dallas, TX 75214-0165, (214)823-7000
Children of the Americas [IO], Dallas, TX, United States
Children; America's Fund for Afghan [11265]
Children of the Andes [IO], London, United Kingdom
Children; Assn. of Administrators of the Interstate Compact on the Placement of [11559]
Children; Assn. for Advancement of Blind [★16832]
Children; Assn. of Benedictin [★13752]
Children; Assn. of Booksellers for [529]
Children; Assn. of Educators of Gifted [★8465]
Children; Assn. of Educators for Homebound and Hospitalized [★11998]
Children; Assn. of Educators for Homebound and Hospitalized [★9141]
Children; Assn. for the Help of Retarded [15240]
Children; Assn. for Lib. Ser. to [10334]
Children; Assn. of Medical Officers of Amer. Institutions of Idiotic and Feebleminded [★15239]
Children; Assn. for Special [★12562]
Children with Attention-Deficit Disorders [★15314]
Children Awaiting Parents [11239], 595 Blossom Rd., Ste. 306, Rochester, NY 14610, (585)232-5110
Children Before Dogs [11682]
Children with Behavioral Disorders; Coun. for [9140]
Children; Black Community Crusade for [11562]
Children of Chernobyl [IO], Minsk, Belarus
Children; Christian Found. for [★13159]
Children; Commn. on Missing and Exploited [11586]
Children; Comm. for [11587]
Children; Comm. on Christian Literature for Women and [★12376]
Children of the Confederacy [20724], c/o Harold J. Trammel, UDC Bus. Off., 328 N Blvd., Richmond, VA 23220-4009, (804)355-1636
Children; Cooley's Anemia Blood and Res. Found. for [★14788]
Children; Coun. on Accreditation of Services for Families and [★13164]
Children; Coun. for Exceptional [9141]
Children of the Dawn [IO], Illovo, Republic of South Africa
Children of Deaf Adults [14747], PO Box 30715, Santa Barbara, CA 93130-0715, (805)682-0997
Children with Disabilities; Natl. Dissemination Center for [11971]
Children; Div. on Career Development of The Coun. for Exceptional [★9143]
Children; Div. on Career Development and Transition of the Coun. for Exceptional [★9143]
Children with Down Syndrome; Assn. for [12562]
Children with Down Syndrome; Parents of [★12579]
Children of the Earth [12696], 26 Baycrest Dr., South Burlington, VT 05403, (802)862-1936
Children of the Earth [IO], South Burlington, VT, United States
Children of the Earth - Italian Michael Jackson Fan Club [IO], Bari, Italy
Children of the Earth United [IO], Columbia, MD, United States
Children of the Earth United [4621], PO Box 816, Columbia, MD 21044, (443)321-4617
Children Endowment Fund; Shriners Hospitals for [★13973]
Children Everywhere; Families Adopting [11242]
Children and Families; Alliance for [12136]
Children and Families; Natl. Coalition for the Protection of [18374]
Children and Families; Natl. Law Center for [5703]
Children and Family Ser. Charities of Am; Women, [12207]
Children; Fed. of Institutes Caring for Protestant [★20482]
Children; Find the [11591]

Children; Found. for Exceptional [★11998]
Children; French-American Aid for [19064]
Children Fund; China's [★11688]
Children of Gay Parentage - Address unknown since 1986.
Children of the Green Earth - Address unknown since 1994.
Children; Gp. Proj. for Holocaust Survivors and Their [17716]
Children; Heal the [★11697]
Children; Hollingworth Center for Highly Gifted [9982]
Children of the Holocaust Assn. in Poland [IO], Warsaw, Poland
Children in Hospitals - Address unknown since 2001.
Children, Inc. [11683], 4205 Dover Rd., Richmond, VA 23221-3267, (804)359-4562
Children; Inst. for the Advancement of Philosophy for [10796]
Children Intl. [20312], PO Box 219055, Kansas City, MO 64121, (816)942-2000
Children Intl. [IO], Kansas City, MO, United States
Children; Intl. Soc. for Crippled [★16333]
Children; Keren-Or Center for Multi-Handicapped Blind [★16863]
Children; Keren-Or Center for Multi-Handicapped Blind [★IO]
Children and the Law; Amer. Bar Assn. Center on [11555]
Children with Learning Disabilities; Assn. for [★12492]
Children with Learning Disabilities; Div. for [★12490]
Children with Learning Disabilities; Found. for [★12494]
Children; Legal Services for [12498]
Children of Lesbians and Gays Everywhere [★12223]
Children Living with Inherited Metabolic Diseases [IO], Crewe, United Kingdom
Children; Natl. Assn. for the Educ. of Young [8069]
Children; Natl. Assn. for Gifted [8466]
Children; Natl. Assn. of Homes for [★12136]
Children; Natl. Assn. of Homes and Services for [★12136]
Children; Natl. Assn. of Parents and Friends of Mentally Retarded [★12561]
Children; Natl. Assn. of Private Schools for Exceptional [★9147]
Children; Natl. Assn. of Psychiatric Treatment Centers for [★16090]
Children; Natl. Assn. for Retarded [★12561]
Children; Natl. Center for Missing and Exploited [11630]
Children; Natl. Cong. for Fathers and [12172]
Children; Natl. Org. for Mentally Ill [★15211]
Children Natl; Teachers Saving [18569]
Children of the Night [12933], 14530 Sylvan St., Van Nuys, CA 91411, (818)908-4474
Children; North Amer. Coun. on Adoptable [11257]
Children in Northern Ireland [IO], Belfast, United Kingdom
Children Now [11575], 1212 Broadway, 5th Fl., Oakland, CA 94612, (510)763-2444
Children (of the Natl. Child Labor Comm.); Natl. Comm. on the Educ. of Migrant [12593]
Children Out of Detention [IO], Neutral Bay, Australia
Children; Parents of Down Syndrome [★12579]
Children; Parents of Galactosemic [15257]
Children; Parents of Murdered [12685]
Children as the Peacemakers [18196], 1243 Lago Vista Dr., Beverly Hills, CA 90210, (310)859-1325
Children as the Peacemakers [IO], Beverly Hills, CA, United States
Children as the Peacemakers Found. [★IO]
Children as the Peacemakers Found. [★18196]
Children of Persia [11576], PO Box 2602, Montgomery Village, MD 20886, (301)315-0750
Children and Poverty; Inst. for [11602]
Children: Priority One; Young [★13047]
Children: Priority One; Young [★IO]
Children; Rainbows for All God's [★11718]
Children with Retarded Mental Development; Assn. for [★12572]
Children at Risk in Ireland [IO], Dublin, Ireland
Children of the Rosary [18548], PO Box 1028, Scottsdale, AZ 85252-1028, (602)548-3131

A star before a book entry number signifies that the name is not listed separately, but is mentioned within the entry.

Children of Russia [11577], 4117 Kahala Ave., Honolulu, HI 96816, (808)737-5248
Children of Russia [IO], Honolulu, HI, United States
Children of SCORE; Amer. [10530]
Children in Scotland [IO], Edinburgh, United Kingdom
Children; Shriner's Burns Inst. for [★24605]
Children; Shriners Hospitals for [13973]
Children; Soc. for Ear, Nose, and Throat Advances in [15827]
Children, Sons and Daughters of the U.S.A. [★11335]
Children with Special Needs; Fed. for [12569]
Children as Teachers of Peace [★18196]
Children as Teachers of Peace [★IO]
Children and TV; Natl. Coun. for [★17186]
Children Under Six; Southern Assn. on [★11722]
Children of the Universe - Defunct.
Children in Wales [IO], Cardiff, United Kingdom
The Children of War [IO], Reston, VA, United States
The Children of War [18197], 1608 Washington Plz. N, 3rd Fl., Reston, VA 20190, (703)923-0455
Children and Young People of the Amer. Lib. Assn; Sect. of the Division of Libraries for [★10317]
Children and Youth with Disabilities; Natl. Info. Center for [★11971]
Children, Youth, and Families; Grantmakers for [12723]
Children and Youth; Grantmakers for [★12723]
Children and Youth with Handicaps; Natl. Info. Center for [★11971]
Children and Youth; Natl. Info. Center for Handicapped [★11971]
Children and Youth; Parents Campaign for Handicapped [★11971]
Children's Action Network - Defunct.
Children's Advt. Rev. Unit [96], 70 W 36th St., New York, NY 10018, (866)334-6272
Children's Advocacy Center - Defunct.
Children's Agencies; Assn. of Jewish Family and [12467]
Children's Aid Intl. [★11672]
Children's Aid Intl. [★IO]
Children's Aid Soc; New York [★21140]
Children's AIDS Fund [16962], PO Box 16433, Washington, DC 20041, (703)433-1560
Children's AIDS Fund [IO], Washington, DC, United States
Children's Alliance for Protection of the Environment - Defunct.
Children's Alliance; Vanished [11659]
Children's Angelcare Aid Intl. [★11672]
Children's Angelcare Aid Intl. [★IO]
Children's Art Found. [9781], PO Box 83, Santa Cruz, CA 95063, (831)426-5557
Children's Better Hea. Institute [★14549]
Children's Bible Mission, Inc. [★19995]
Children's Blood Found. [14786], 111 W 57th St., Ste. 420, New York, NY 10019, (212)297-4336
Children's Book Coun. [9746], 12 W 37th St., 2nd Fl., New York, NY 10018-7480, (212)966-1990
Children's Book Coun. of Australia [IO], Norwood, Australia
Children's Book Coun. of Iran [IO], Tehran, Iran
Children's Book Writers and Illustrators; Soc. of [11194]
Children's Book Writers; Soc. of [★11194]
Children's Books History Soc. [IO], Devon, United Kingdom
Children's Books Ireland [IO], Dublin, Ireland
Children's Brain Tumor Found. [13952], 274 Madison Ave., Ste. 1004, New York, NY 10016, (866)228-4673
Children's Campaign for Nuclear Disarmament - Defunct.
Children's Campaign for a Positive Future - Address unknown since 2006.
Children's Cancer Fund of America - Defunct.
Children's Caucus; Senate [17258]
Children's Cause for Cancer Advocacy [13812], 1010 Wayne Ave., Ste. 770, Silver Spring, MD 20910, (301)562-2765
Children's Centers; Natl. Coalition for [★11535]
Children's Centers; Natl. Coalition for Campus [11535]

Children's Charity; Variety Intl. - The [11660]
Children's Comm. 10 - Defunct.
Children's Corrective Surgery Soc. [16580], 338 W 3rd Ave., Escondido, CA 92025, (760)735-9065
Children's Counseling Center; James Weldon Johnson Family and [★12785]
Children's Craniofacial Assn. [14057], 13140 Coit Rd., Ste. 307, Dallas, TX 75240, (214)570-9099
Children's Creative Response to Conflict Prog. [11684], 521 N Broadway, Box 271, Nyack, NY 10960, (845)353-1796
Children's Cross Connection Intl. [11552], 101 Yorktown Dr., Ste. 201, Fayetteville, GA 30214, (770)716-1926
Children's Cross Connection Intl. [IO], Fayetteville, GA, United States
Children's Defense Fund [11685], 25 E St. NW, Washington, DC 20001, (202)628-8787
Children's Defense Fund of the Washington Res. Proj. [★11685]
Children's Emergency Fund; United Nations Intl. [★11658]
Children's Environmental Hea. Network [14363], 110 Maryland Ave. NE, Ste. 505, Washington, DC 20002, (202)543-4033
Children's Equality; Parents and [★18040]
Children's Exocrine Found. [16358]
Children's Express Found. - Defunct.
Children's Eye Care Found. [★15679]
Children's Eye Found. [15679], 1527 W State Hwy. 114, Ste. 500, No. 216, Grapevine, TX 76051, (817)891-1144
Children's Film Soc., India [IO], Bombay, India
Children's Film and TV Center - Defunct.
Children's Found. - Defunct.
Children's Friendship Proj. for Northern Ireland [13478], c/o Glenn A. Martinsen, Treas., 7 Old Manchester Rd., Derry, NH 03038-7312, (603)432-4301
Children's Fund; Blind [16834]
Children's Fund; Migrant [★12593]
Children's Fund of the Slovak Republic [IO], Bratislava, Slovakia
Children's Grief Educ. Assn. [12265], PO Box 21876, Denver, CO 80221, (303)722-2319
Children's Growth; MAGIC Found. for [★13967]
Children's Hea. Environmental Coalition [13953], 12300 Wilshire Blvd., Ste. 410, Los Angeles, CA 90025, (310)820-2030
Children's Health and Fitness Fund - Address unknown since 1999.
Children's Hea. Fund [13954], 215 W 125th St., Ste. 301, New York, NY 10027, (212)535-9400
Children's Healthcare Is a Legal Duty [15004], PO Box 2604, Sioux City, IA 51106, (712)948-3500
Children's Heart Fund [★13899]
Children's HeartLink [13899], 5075 Arcadia Ave., Minneapolis, MN 55436, (952)928-4860
Children's Hemiplegia and Stroke Assn. [16493], 4101 W Green Oaks Blvd., Ste. 305, No. 149, Arlington, TX 76016, (817)492-4325
Children's HIV Assn. of UK and Ireland [IO], London, United Kingdom
Children's Holistic Inst. for Life Development - Defunct.
Children's HopeChest [11578], PO Box 8627, Pueblo, CO 81008, (719)487-7800
Children's Hospice Intl. [14853], 1101 King St., Ste. 360, Alexandria, VA 22314, (703)684-0330
Children's Hospice Intl. [IO], Alexandria, VA, United States
Children's Hospitals and Related Institutions; Natl. Assn. of [14889]
Children's Intl. Summer Villages - Canada [IO], Toronto, ON, Canada
Children's Intl. Summer Villages - England [IO], Newcastle upon Tyne, United Kingdom
Children's Intl. Summer Villages - Japan [IO], Tokyo, Japan
Children's Intl. Summer Villages - Netherlands [IO], The Hague, Netherlands
Children's Intl. Summer Villages - Norway [IO], Oslo, Norway
Children's Intl. Summer Villages - Sweden [IO], Spanga, Sweden

Children's Legal Centre [IO], Colchester, United Kingdom
Children's Legal Found. - Address unknown since 1999.
Children's Legal Rights Information and Training Program - Defunct.
Children's Leukemia Res. Assn. [13813], 585 Stewart Ave., Ste. 18, Garden City, NY 11530, (516)222-1944
Children's Lib. Assn. [★10334]
Children's Literacy Initiative [8787], 2314 Market St., Philadelphia, PA 19103, (215)561-4676
Children's Literacy Proj; Natl. Cued Speech Association/Deaf [16452]
Children's Literature Assn. [10418], PO Box 138, Battle Creek, MI 49016-0138, (269)965-8180
Children's Liver Assn. for Support Services [14804], 27023 McBean Pkwy., No. 126, Valencia, CA 91355, (661)263-9099
Children's Liver Found. - Address unknown since 1994.
Children's Medical Ministries [13955], PO Box 3382, Crofton, MD 21114, (301)261-3211
Children's Medical Relief Intl. - Defunct.
Children's Mental Hea; Fed. of Families for [12550]
Children's Museums; Assn. of [10495]
Children's Network Intl. [11579], PO Box 911607, Los Angeles, CA 90091, (323)980-9870
Children's Network Intl. [IO], Los Angeles, CA, United States
Children's Oncology Gp; Found. for the [★13850]
Children's Organ Transplant Assn. [13956], 2501 COTA Dr., Bloomington, IN 47403, (800)366-2682
Children's Org. for Peace and Brotherhood - Defunct.
The Children's Partnership [11580], 2000 P St. NW, Ste. 330, Washington, DC 20036, (202)429-0033
Children's Peace Union - Defunct.
Children's PKU Network [15245], 3790 Via De La Valle, Ste. 120, Del Mar, CA 92014, (858)509-0767
Children's Proj; Ataxia Telangiectasia [14253]
Children's Project; Paul Andrew Dawkins [★11690]
Children's Prosthetic-Orthotic Clinics; Assn. of [15784]
Children's Protective Soc. [★11565]
Children's Relief Network [11581], PO Box 668, Deerfield Beach, FL 33443, (561)620-2970
Children's Relief Network [IO], Deerfield Beach, FL, United States
Children's Res. Hosp; ALSAC/Saint Jude [13946]
Children's Residential Centers; Amer. Assn. of [13467]
Children's Rights [17100], 330 7th Ave., 4th Fl., New York, NY 10001, (212)683-2210
Children's Rights Alliance [IO], Dublin, Ireland
Children's Rights Alliance for England [IO], London, United Kingdom
Children's Rights of America [11582]
Children's Rights; Caucus on [★11583]
Children's Rights Coalition - Address unknown since 2002.
Children's Rights Coun. [12007], 6200 Editors Park Dr., Ste. 103, Hyattsville, MD 20782, (301)559-3120
Children's Rights Div. - Human Rights Watch [11583], c/o Human Rights Watch, 350 5th Ave., 34th Fl., New York, NY 10118, (212)290-4700
Children's Rights Div. - Human Rights Watch [IO], New York, NY, United States
Children's Rights of Florida [★11582]
Children's Rights; Grandparents United for [17058]
Children's Rights Group - Defunct.
Children's Rights, Inc. [★11587]
Children's Rights; Natl. Coun. for [★12007]
Children's Rights Org. - Defunct.
Children's Rights Proj. - ACLU [★17100]
Children's Safety Network [11584], c/o Educ. Development Center, Inc., 55 Chapel St., Newton, MA 02458-1060, (617)618-2230
Children's Services Div. [★10334]
Children's Television Rsrc. and Educ. Center [11686]
Children's TV Workshop [★9782]
Children's Transplant Assn. - Address unknown since 1994.
Children's Tumor Found. [15315], 95 Pine St., 16th Fl., New York, NY 10005, (212)344-6633

Reference to "IO" in place of a book number signifies that the association may be found in the 45th edition of International Organizations.

Children's Village U.S.A. [★11680]
Children's Village U.S.A. [★11661]
Children's Watch Intl. [11585], 2918 Yarling Ct., Falls Church, VA 22042
Children's Watch Intl. [IO], Falls Church, VA, United States
Children's Wish Found. [★IO]
Children's Wish Found. [★11687]
Children's Wish Found. of Canada [IO], Ajax, ON, Canada
Children's Wish Found. Intl. [IO], Atlanta, GA, United States
Children's Wish Found. Intl. [11687], 8615 Roswell Rd., Atlanta, GA 30350-7526, (770)393-9474
Childrenswear Marketing Div. of the Amer. Apparel Mfrs. Assn. - Address unknown since 2004.
A Child's Wish Come True - Address unknown since 1990.
Childsave Project - Defunct.
Childsearch - Defunct.
Childsight Program [★16854]
Childsight Program [★IO]
Childwatch Intl. Res. Network [IO], Oslo, Norway

Chile
    Chile-U.S. Chamber of Commerce [24270]
    North American-Chilean Chamber of Commerce [24307]
    Physicians for Human Rights [17783]
Chile Alert - Defunct.
Chile-Amer. Assn. - Address unknown since 1995.
Chile Democratico - Address unknown since 1995.
Chile; Intl. Connoisseurs of Green and Red [22572]
Chile Legislative Center - Defunct.
Chile Resource Center and Clearinghouse - Address unknown since 1989.
Chile-U.S. Chamber of Commerce [24270], 1814 NE Miami Gardens Dr., No. 1207, North Miami Beach, FL 33179, (786)419-2092

Chilean
    Chile-U.S. Chamber of Commerce [24270]
Chilean Acad. of History [IO], Santiago, Chile
Chilean Amer. Chamber of Commerce [IO], Santiago, Chile
Chilean Article Numbering Assn. [★IO]
Chilean Assn. of Publishers, Distributors and Booksellers [IO], Santiago, Chile
Chilean Assn. of Seismology and Earthquake Engg. [IO], Santiago, Chile
Chilean Assn. of Tourism Wholesalers and Representatives [IO], Santiago, Chile
Chilean Bible Soc. [IO], Santiago, Chile
Chilean Cmpt. Sci. Soc. [IO], Santiago, Chile
Chilean Constr. Chamber [IO], Santiago, Chile
Chilean Cricket Assn. [IO], Santiago, Chile
Chilean Hotels' Assn. [IO], Santiago, Chile
Chilean Iodine Educational Bur. - Defunct.
Chilean Salmon Indus. Assn. [IO], Santiago, Chile
Chilean Salmon and Trout Farmers' Assn. [IO], Santiago, Chile
Chilean Seed Producers' Assn. [IO], Santiago, Chile
Chilean Soc. of Cardiology and Cardiovascular Surgery [IO], Santiago, Chile
Chilean Soc. of Clinical Neurophysiology [IO], Santiago, Chile
Chilean Soc. of Dermatology and Venereology [IO], Santiago, Chile
Chilean Soc. of Hypertension [IO], Santiago, Chile
Chilean Soc. of Infectious Diseases [IO], Santiago, Chile
Chilean Soc. of Info. Tech. Companies [IO], Santiago, Chile
Chilean Soc. of Obstetrics and Gynecology [IO], Santiago, Chile
Chilean Soc. of Osteology and Mineral Metabolism [IO], Santiago, Chile
Chilean Soc. of Pharmacology [IO], Concepcion, Chile
Chilean Soc. of Physiological Sciences [IO], Santiago, Chile
Chilean Supermarkets' Assn. [IO], Santiago, Chile
Chilean Textile Inst. [IO], Santiago, Chile
Chilean Wood Corp. [IO], Santiago, Chile
Chili Appreciation Soc. Intl. [★IO]
Chili Appreciation Soc. Intl. [★22574]
CHILI-U.S.A. - Address unknown since 1991.

Chilled Food Assn. [IO], Kettering, United Kingdom
Chilled Foods Assn. - Defunct.
Chilterns Amer. Women's Club [IO], Gerrards Cross, United Kingdom
Chilton Assn; USS [21224]
Chimera Educational Found. [★13436]
Chimes Hour Youth Caravan [★20411]
Chimes Hour Youth Caravan [★IO]
Chimney Rock Found. [★20469]
Chimney Safety Inst. of Am. [2460], 2155 Commercial Dr., Plainfield, IN 46168, (317)837-5362
Chimney Sweep Guild [★2471]
Chimney Sweep Guild; Natl. [2471]
Chimp Haven [11729], 13600 Chimpanzee Pl., Keithville, LA 71047, (318)925-9575

Chimpanzee
    Chimp Haven [11729]
    Jane Goodall Inst. for Wildlife Res., Educ., and Conservation [5334]
    Save the Chimps [4298]
Chin Club of Am; Japanese [22299]
Chin Human Rights Org. [IO], Nepean, ON, Canada

China
    Amer. Go Assn. [22459]
    Asia Pacific - USA Chamber of Commerce [24264]
    Blue/White Pottery Club [21527]
    Center for Chinese Res. Materials [9783]
    Center for United States-China Arts Exchange [9784]
    China Inst. in Am. [9785]
    China Medical Bd. of New York [14976]
    China Stamp Soc. [22803]
    Chinese for Affirmative Action [17101]
    Chinese Amer. Assn. of Commerce [24308]
    Chinese Amer. Assn. of Engg. [7008]
    Chinese Amer. Forum [9786]
    Chinese-American Golf Assn. [23445]
    Chinese Amer. Medical Soc. [15163]
    Chinese Chamber of Commerce of Hawaii [24309]
    Chinese Christian Mission [20313]
    Chinese Culture Assn. [9787]
    Chinese Culture Found. of San Francisco [9788]
    Chinese Historical Soc. of Am. [9789]
    Chinese Law Soc. of Am. [5933]
    Chinese Professionals Assn. of Canada [IO]
    Conf. for Chinese Oral and Performing Literature [9790]
    Falun Data Info. Center [17757]
    Families with Children from China [11243]
    Flow Blue Intl. Collectors Club [22026]
    Free the Fathers [17060]
    Friends of Falun Gong [17061]
    Fudan Museum Found. [10504]
    Human Rights in China [12373]
    Independent Fed. of Chinese Students and Scholars [17062]
    Independent Fed. of Chinese Students and Scholars [IO]
    Intl. Chinese Snuff Bottle Soc. [21890]
    Intl. Fed. of Martial Arts and Oriental Medicine [15021]
    Intl. Nippon Collectors Club [21929]
    Intl. Yan Xin Qigong Assn. [13640]
    June 4th Found. [17063]
    Mai Wah Soc. [9622]
    Natl. Comm. on United States-China Relations [17064]
    National Committee on United States-China Relations [IO]
    North Amer. Chinese Soccer League [23780]
    North Amer. Tang Shou Tao Assn. [13645]
    Org. of Chinese Americans [17065]
    Org. of Chinese Americans [IO]
    Origami USA [22771]
    Phoenix Bird Collectors of Am. [21935]
    Press Div., Taipei Economic and Cultural Off. in New York [9792]
    Sino-Amer. Cultural Soc. [9793]
    Tea Leaf Club Intl. [21937]
    United Bd. for Christian Higher Educ. in Asia [8649]
    U.S. of America-China Chamber of Commerce [24310]

    U.S. of America-China Chamber of Commerce [IO]
    U.S.-China Peoples Friendship Association [IO]
    U.S.-China Peoples Friendship Assn. [17066]
    US Cheng Ming Martial Arts Assn. [23613]
    Volunteers in Asia [13407]
    Wedgwood Intl. Seminar [21939]
    White Ironstone China Assn. [21940]
    Wildflowers Inst. [9794]
    World Assn. for Chinese Biomedical Engineers [6611]
    World Org. of China Painters [22177]
    World Ving Tsun Athletic Assn. [23618]
China Acad. of Sciences [★IO]
China Acad. of Traditional Chinese Medicine [IO], Beijing, People's Republic of China
China ACM SIGCHI [IO], Beijing, People's Republic of China
China AIDS Network [IO], Beijing, People's Republic of China
China Arts Exchange; Center for United States- [9784]
China; Assoc. Boards for Christian Colleges in [★8649]
China Assn. of Amusement Parks and Attractions [IO], Beijing, People's Republic of China
China Assn. of Inventions [IO], Beijing, People's Republic of China
China Assn. of the Lighting Indus. [IO], Beijing, People's Republic of China
China Assn. for Medical Devices Indus. [IO], Beijing, People's Republic of China
China Assn. for Medical Equip. Indus. [★IO]
China Assn. for NGO Cooperation [IO], Beijing, People's Republic of China
China Assn. for Sci. and Tech. [IO], Beijing, People's Republic of China
China Assn; White Ironstone [21940]
China Assn; Yale- [8637]
China Audio Indus. Assn. [IO], Shanghai, People's Republic of China
China Bearing Indus. Assn. [IO], Beijing, People's Republic of China
China Bicycle Assn. [IO], Beijing, People's Republic of China
China-Britain Bus. Coun. [IO], London, United Kingdom
China-Burma-India Hump Pilot Assn. [21391], 3509 Huntington Dr., Amarillo, TX 79109-4043, (806)352-4449
China-Burma-India Veterans Assn. - Defunct.
China Bus. Coun. for Sustainable Development [IO], Beijing, People's Republic of China
China Bus. Coun; US- [2319]
China Center; Indo [10122]
China; Center for Teaching About [8552]
China Centre for Intl. Stud. [IO], Beijing, People's Republic of China
China Chain Store and Franchise Assn. [IO], Beijing, People's Republic of China
China Chamber of Commerce for Import and Export of Machinery and Electronic Products [IO], Beijing, People's Republic of China
China Chamber of Commerce of Machinery and Electronic Products Importers and Exporters [★IO]
China Civil Engg. Soc. [IO], Beijing, People's Republic of China
China Clay Producers Assn. [2748], 113 Arkwright Landing, Macon, GA 31210, (478)757-1211
China Clay Producers Trade Assn. [★2748]
China Coach Assn. [IO], Hong Kong, People's Republic of China
China Collectors Assn; Homer Laughlin [22036]
China Connection [12423], c/o Kathy Call, Founder/ Exec. Dir., 458 S Pasadena Ave., Pasadena, CA 91105-1838, (626)793-3737
China Connection [IO], Pasadena, CA, United States
China Coun. [★IO]
China Coun. [★9616]
China Coun. for the Promotion of Intl. Trade [IO], Beijing, People's Republic of China
China Customs Brokers Assn. [IO], Beijing, People's Republic of China
China Disabled Persons' Fed. [IO], Beijing, People's Republic of China

---

A star before a book entry number signifies that the name is not listed separately, but is mentioned within the entry.

China Educ. Assn. for Intl. Exchange **[IO]**, Beijing, People's Republic of China
China Engg. Cost Assn. **[IO]**, Beijing, People's Republic of China
China Enterprise Confed. **[IO]**, Beijing, People's Republic of China
China External Trade Development Coun. **[★IO]**
China Family Planning Assn. **[IO]**, Beijing, People's Republic of China
China Feather and Down Indus. Assn. **[IO]**, Beijing, People's Republic of China
China Fed. of Indus. Economics **[IO]**, Beijing, People's Republic of China
China Food and Packaging Machinery Indus. Assn. **[IO]**, Beijing, People's Republic of China
China Foundry Assn. **[IO]**, Beijing, People's Republic of China
China, Glass and Giftware Assn. - Defunct.
China; Human Rights in **[12373]**
China Information Center - Defunct.
China Inland Mission **[★20378]**
China Inland Mission **[★IO]**
China Inland Mission **[★IO]**
China Inland Mission **[★IO]**
China Inland Mission Overseas Missionary Fellowship **[★IO]**
China Inland Mission Overseas Missionary Fellowship **[★20378]**
China Inst. **[★9785]**
China Inst. **[★IO]**
China Inst. in Am. **[IO]**, New York, NY, United States
China Inst. in Am. **[9785]**, 125 E 65th St., New York, NY 10021, (212)744-8181
China Inst; Indo **[★10122]**
China Intl. Found. **[★12434]**
China Intl. Found. **[★IO]**
China Law Soc. **[IO]**, Beijing, People's Republic of China
China Medical Bd. of New York **[14976]**, c/o Inst. for Intl. Medical Educ., 750 Third Ave., 23rd Fl., New York, NY 10017, (212)661-7375
China Medical Informatics Assn. **[IO]**, Beijing, People's Republic of China
China Natl. Assn. of Engg. Consultants **[IO]**, Beijing, People's Republic of China
China Natl. Light Indus. Coun. **[IO]**, Beijing, People's Republic of China
China Nonferrous Metals Soc. **[★IO]**
China Optical Goods' Indus. Assn. **[IO]**, Beijing, People's Republic of China
China Optometric and Optical Assn. **[IO]**, Beijing, People's Republic of China
China Packaging Fed. **[IO]**, Beijing, People's Republic of China
China Packaging Tech. Assn. **[★IO]**
China Peniel Missionary Soc. **[★IO]**
China Peniel Missionary Soc. **[★20409]**
China Philatelic Study Group - Defunct.
China Printed Circuit Assn. **[IO]**, Shanghai, People's Republic of China
China Productivity Center **[IO]**, Taipei, Taiwan
China Record; Amer. Spotted Poland **[★5239]**
China Record Assn; Poland **[5242]**
China Record; Natl. Spotted Poland **[★5239]**
China Recorder Indus. Assn. **[★IO]**
China Rose Soc. **[IO]**, Beijing, People's Republic of China
China School Sport Fed. **[IO]**, Beijing, People's Republic of China
China Sewing Machinery Assn. **[IO]**, Beijing, People's Republic of China
China Soc. of America - Defunct.
China Soc. of Plant Protection **[IO]**, Beijing, People's Republic of China
China; Soc. for the Stud. of Pre-Han **[★8077]**
China Soc. for Trenchless Tech. **[IO]**, Beijing, People's Republic of China
China Software Indus. Assn. **[IO]**, Beijing, People's Republic of China
China Solidarity Comm. - Defunct.
China Stamp Soc. **[22803]**, c/o Paul H. Gault, Sec., PO Box 20711, Columbus, OH 43220, (614)451-8034
China Stamp Soc. **[IO]**, Columbus, OH, United States

China Times Cultural Found. **[IO]**, Flushing, NY, United States
China Times Cultural Found. **[7984]**, PO Box 1234, Flushing, NY 11352, (718)460-4900
China Toothpaste Indus. Assn. **[IO]**, Beijing, People's Republic of China
China Toy Assn. **[IO]**, Beijing, People's Republic of China
China Trade; Natl. Coun. for US- **[★2319]**
China Triathlon Sports Assn. **[IO]**, Beijing, People's Republic of China
China; United Bd. for Christian Colleges in **[★8649]**
China Users Assn. for Satellite Communications, Broadcasting and TV **[IO]**, Beijing, People's Republic of China
China Venture Capital Assn. **[IO]**, Beijing, People's Republic of China
China Welding Assn. **[IO]**, Harbin, People's Republic of China
China Zoological Soc. **[IO]**, Beijing, People's Republic of China
China's Children Fund **[★IO]**
China's Children Fund **[★11688]**
Chinchilla Assn; Amer. Standard **[★5141]**
Chinchilla Breeders Cooperative; Empress **[4134]**
Chinchilla Breeders' Gp. **[IO]**, Cape Town, Republic of South Africa
Chinchilla Rabbit Assn; Amer. Standard **[★5141]**
Chincoteague Pony Assn; Natl. **[4917]**
Chinese
  Amer. Assn. for Chinese Stud. **[8074]**
  Amer. Chen Style Tai Chi Assn. **[23578]**
  Amer. Go Assn. **[22459]**
  Amer. Tai Chi Assn. **[16593]**
  Amer. Wu Shu Soc. **[23583]**
  Amer. Yangjia Michuan Taijiquan Assn. **[23584]**
  Asian Amer. Arts Centre **[9553]**
  Asian Amer. Curriculum Proj. **[8598]**
  Assn. of Chinese Amer. Physicians **[15991]**
  Assn. of Chinese-American Professionals **[19012]**
  Assn. of Chinese Finance Professionals **[1402]**
  Assn. of Chinese Scientists and Engineers - U.S.A. **[6698]**
  Assn. of Chinese Scientists and Engineers - U.S.A. **[IO]**
  British Assn. for Chinese Stud. **[IO]**
  Canadian Intl. Dragon Boat Festival Soc. **[IO]**
  Canadian Soc. for Chinese Stud. **[IO]**
  Center for Chinese Res. Materials **[IO]**
  Center for Chinese Res. Materials **[9783]**
  Center for Chinese Studies **[IO]**
  Center for United States-China Arts Exchange **[9784]**
  China Inst. in Am. **[9785]**
  China Inst. in Am. **[IO]**
  China Medical Bd. of New York **[14976]**
  Chinese for Affirmative Action **[17101]**
  Chinese Amer. Assn. of Commerce **[24308]**
  Chinese Amer. Assn. of Engg. **[7008]**
  Chinese Amer. Citizens Alliance **[19013]**
  Chinese Amer. Civic Coun. **[19014]**
  Chinese Amer. Cmpt. Assn. **[6811]**
  Chinese-Amer. Educational Found. **[8428]**
  Chinese Amer. Food Soc. **[7092]**
  Chinese Amer. Forum **[9786]**
  Chinese-American Golf Assn. **[23445]**
  Chinese Amer. Librarians Assn. **[10347]**
  Chinese Amer. Medical Soc. **[15163]**
  Chinese Amer. Semiconductor Professional Assn. **[1208]**
  Chinese Canadian Natl. Coun. **[IO]**
  Chinese Chamber of Commerce of Hawaii **[24309]**
  Chinese Christian Mission **[20313]**
  Chinese Consolidated Benevolent Assn. **[19015]**
  Chinese Culture Assn. **[9787]**
  Chinese Culture Association **[IO]**
  Chinese Culture Found. of San Francisco **[9788]**
  Chinese Economists Soc. **[6876]**
  Chinese Finance Assn. **[1406]**
  Chinese Historians in the U.S. **[8503]**
  Chinese Historical Soc. of Am. **[9789]**
  Chinese Historical Soc. of Am. **[IO]**
  Chinese Language Assn. of Secondary-Elementary Schools **[8075]**

  Chinese Language Teachers Assn. **[8076]**
  Chinese Law Soc. of Am. **[5933]**
  Chinese Music Soc. of North Am. **[10575]**
  Chinese School Assn. in the U.S. **[9090]**
  Chinese Stud. Assn. of Australia **[IO]**
  Choy Lee Fut Martial Arts Fed. of Am. **[23586]**
  Conf. for Chinese Oral and Performing Literature **[9790]**
  Conference for Chinese Oral and Performing Literature **[IO]**
  European Assn. of Chinese Stud. **[IO]**
  European Found. for Chinese Music Res. **[IO]**
  Falun Data Info. Center **[17757]**
  Fed. of Chinese Amer. and Chinese Canadian Medical Societies **[13985]**
  Fed. of Chinese Amer. and Chinese Canadian Medical Societies **[IO]**
  Focus on the Chinese Family **[20496]**
  Inst. of Chinese Culture **[9791]**
  Intl. Chinese Boxing Assn. **[23262]**
  Intl. Chinese Snuff Bottle Soc. **[21890]**
  Intl. Fed. of Martial Arts and Oriental Medicine **[15021]**
  Intl. Yan Xin Qigong Assn. **[13640]**
  Jin Shin Do Found. for Bodymind Acupressure **[15746]**
  Mai Wah Soc. **[9622]**
  Natl. Chinese Honor Soc. **[24432]**
  Natl. Comm. on United States-China Relations **[17064]**
  Nordic Assn. for China Stud. **[IO]**
  North Am. Chinese Semiconductor Assn. **[1226]**
  North Am. Wu(Hao) Taiji Fed. **[23601]**
  North Amer. Chinese Soccer League **[23780]**
  North Amer. Tang Shou Tao Assn. **[13645]**
  Org. of Chinese Americans **[17065]**
  Origami USA **[22771]**
  Overseas Chinese Physics Assn. **[7507]**
  Press Div., Taipei Economic and Cultural Off. in New York **[9792]**
  QiGong Res. Soc. **[13647]**
  Sino-American Amity Fund **[19016]**
  Sino-Amer. Cultural Soc. **[9793]**
  Sino-Amer. Cultural Soc. **[IO]**
  Sino-American Pharmaceutical Professionals Assn. **[15951]**
  Soc. of Intl. Chinese in Educational Tech. **[9236]**
  Soc. for the Stud. of Early China **[8077]**
  Soc. for the Stud. of Early China **[IO]**
  Travel China Roads **[8078]**
  U.S. of America-China Chamber of Commerce **[24310]**
  U.S.-China Educ. Found. **[8632]**
  U.S.-China Peoples Friendship Assn. **[17066]**
  US Cheng Ming Martial Arts Assn. **[23613]**
  Vancouver Chinese Choir Assn. **[IO]**
  Wildflowers Inst. **[IO]**
  Wildflowers Inst. **[9794]**
  World Assn. for Chinese Biomedical Engineers **[6611]**
  World Ving Tsun Athletic Assn. **[23618]**
  Yale-China Assn. **[8637]**
Chinese Acad. of Agricultural Sciences **[IO]**, Beijing, People's Republic of China
Chinese Acad. of Forestry **[IO]**, Beijing, People's Republic of China
Chinese Acad. of Meteorological Sciences **[IO]**, Beijing, People's Republic of China
Chinese Acad. of Sciences **[IO]**, Beijing, People's Republic of China
Chinese Acad. of Social Sciences **[IO]**, Beijing, People's Republic of China
Chinese Acad. of Space Tech. **[IO]**, Beijing, People's Republic of China
Chinese for Affirmative Action **[17101]**, 17 Walter U. Lum Pl., San Francisco, CA 94108, (415)274-6750
Chinese Alliance for Democracy - Address unknown since 1994.
Chinese-American Arts Coun. **[9608]**, 456 Broadway, 3rd Fl., New York, NY 10013-5800, (212)431-9740
Chinese Amer. Assn. of Commerce **[24308]**
Chinese Amer. Assn. of Engg. **[7008]**, PO Box 869, New York, NY 10268, (718)591-6012
Chinese Amer. Citizens Alliance **[19013]**, 1044 Stockton St., San Francisco, CA 94108, (415)434-2222

Reference to "IO" in place of a book number signifies that the association may be found in the 45th edition of International Organizations.

Chinese Amer. Civic Coun. [19014]

Chinese Amer. Cmpt. Assn. [6811], 5027 Merrill St., Torrance, CA 90503

Chinese-Amer. Educational Found. [8428]

Chinese Amer. Food Soc. [7092], c/o Dr. Vivian Wu, Treas., Univ. of Maine, 5735 Hitchner Hall 101A, Orono, ME 04469-5735

Chinese Amer. Forum [9786]

Chinese-American Golf Assn. [23445], 2 Doloree Dr., East Brunswick, NJ 08816, (732)422-6738

Chinese Amer. Librarians Assn. [10347], c/o Jian Anna Xiong, Membership Chair, Southern Illinois Univ. - Carbondale, Morris Lib., 605 Agriculture Dr., Mailcode 6632, Carbondale, IL 62901

Chinese Amer. Librarians Assn; Mid-West [★10347]

Chinese Amer. Medical Soc. [15163], c/o Dr. Hsueh-hwa Wang, MD, Exec. Dir., 281 Edgewood Ave., Teaneck, NJ 07666, (201)833-1506

Chinese Amer. Professors and Scientists; Soc. of [9024]

Chinese Amer. Restaurant Assn. - Address unknown since 1994.

Chinese Amer. Semiconductor Professional Assn. [1208], 3555 Ryder St., Santa Clara, CA 95051, (408)245-5638

Chinese American Semiconductor Professional Association [IO], Santa Clara, CA, United States

Chinese Amer. Women; Org. of [17567]

Chinese Anti-Cancer Assn. [IO], Beijing, People's Republic of China

Chinese Assn. of Automation [IO], Beijing, People's Republic of China

Chinese Assn. of Integrated Traditional and Western Medicine [IO], Beijing, People's Republic of China

Chinese Assn. for Physiological Sciences [IO], Beijing, People's Republic of China

Chinese Assn. for the Stud. of Pain, People's Republic of China [IO], Beijing, People's Republic of China

Chinese Assn. for the Stud. of Pain, Taiwan [IO], Tainan, Taiwan

Chinese Athletic Assn. [IO], Beijing, People's Republic of China

Chinese Bamboo Soc. [IO], Fuyang, People's Republic of China

Chinese Banknote Collectors Soc. - Defunct.

Chinese Baseball Assn. [IO], Beijing, People's Republic of China

Chinese Blind; Assn. for the [★16854]

Chinese Brush Painting; Amer. Artists of [9538]

Chinese Burn Assn. of the Integration of Traditional and Western Medicine [IO], Beijing, People's Republic of China

Chinese Canadian Natl. Coun. [IO], Toronto, ON, Canada

Chinese Ceramic Soc. [IO], Beijing, People's Republic of China

Chinese Chamber of Commerce of Hawaii [24309], 76 N King St., Ste. 202, Honolulu, HI 96817, (808)533-3181

Chinese Chem. Soc. [IO], Taipei, Taiwan

Chinese Chem. Soc., Taipei [IO], Taipei, Taiwan

Chinese Christian Mission [20313], PO Box 750759, Petaluma, CA 94975-0759, (707)762-1314

Chinese Clinical Chemists Assn; North Amer. [6691]

Chinese Consolidated Benevolent Assn. [19015], 62 Mott St., New York, NY 10013, (212)226-6280

Chinese Coordination Centre of World Evangelism [IO], Hong Kong, People's Republic of China

Chinese Coordination Centre of World Evangelism - Address unknown since 1999.

Chinese Cultural Center [★9792]

Chinese Culture Assn. [9787]

Chinese Culture Association [IO], Los Altos, CA, United States

Chinese Culture Center of San Francisco [★9788]

Chinese Culture Found. of San Francisco [9788], 750 Kearny St., 3rd Fl., San Francisco, CA 94108-1809, (415)986-1822

Chinese DanceSport Fed. [IO], Beijing, People's Republic of China

Chinese Dermatological Soc., Taipei [IO], Taipei, Taiwan

Chinese Economists Soc. [IO], Washington, DC, United States

Chinese Economists Soc. [6876], 733 15th St. NW, Ste. 910, Washington, DC 20005, (202)347-8588

Chinese Educ. Assn. for Intl. Exchange [★IO]

Chinese-English Translation Assistance Group - Defunct.

Chinese Entrepreneurs Soc. of Canada [IO], Vancouver, BC, Canada

Chinese Family; Focus on the [20496]

Chinese Figure Skating Assn. [IO], Beijing, People's Republic of China

Chinese Finance Assn. [1406], c/o Guang Guo, Membership Off., Moody's KMV, 100 Broadway, 12th Fl., New York, NY 10005

Chinese Food Scientists and Technologists in Am; Assn. of [★7092]

Chinese Foreign Missionary Union - Address unknown since 1995.

Chinese Forum [★9791]

Chinese Gen. Chamber of Commerce [IO], Hong Kong, People's Republic of China

Chinese Geophysical Soc. [IO], Beijing, People's Republic of China

Chinese Historians in the U.S. [IO], Selinsgrove, PA, United States

Chinese Historians in the U.S. [8503], c/o George Wei, Pres., Susquehanna Univ., Dept. of History, Selinsgrove, PA 17870, (570)372-4194

Chinese Historical Soc. of Am. [9789], 965 Clay St., San Francisco, CA 94108, (415)391-1188

Chinese Historical Soc. of Am. [IO], San Francisco, CA, United States

Chinese Hydraulic Engg. Soc. [IO], Beijing, People's Republic of China

Chinese Hypertension League [IO], Beijing, People's Republic of China

Chinese from Indochina; Assn. of [★18502]

Chinese Info. Ser. [★9792]

Chinese Inst. of Certified Public Accountants [IO], Beijing, People's Republic of China

Chinese Inst. of Electronics [IO], Beijing, People's Republic of China

Chinese Inst. of Engineers [IO], Taipei, Taiwan

Chinese Inst. of Engineers - U.S.A. - Address unknown since 1995.

Chinese Inst. of Food Sci. and Tech. [IO], Beijing, People's Republic of China

Chinese Internet Tech. Assn. - Address unknown since 2008.

Chinese Language Assn. of Secondary-Elementary Schools [8075], c/o Chih-Wen Su, Membership Coor., 14 Pebble Ridge Rd., Amherst, MA 01002

Chinese Language and Culture; Amer. Assn. of Teachers of [★8074]

Chinese Language Teachers Assn. [8076], c/o Center for Chinese Stud., Univ. of Hawaii, Moore Hall No. 416, 1890 East-West Rd., Honolulu, HI 96822, (808)956-2692

Chinese Laundry Assn. - Address unknown since 1995.

Chinese Law Soc. of Am. [5933], c/o Dr. C. Stephen Hsu, Chm., 1285 Ave. of the Americas, New York, NY 10019-6064, (212)373-3128

Chinese Librarians Assn. [★10347]

Chinese Mfrs. Assn. of Hong Kong [IO], Hong Kong, People's Republic of China

Chinese Material Res. Soc. [IO], Beijing, People's Republic of China

Chinese Mathematical Soc. [IO], Beijing, People's Republic of China

Chinese Mech. Engg. Soc. [IO], Beijing, People's Republic of China

Chinese Medical Assn. [IO], Beijing, People's Republic of China

Chinese Medical Soc; Amer. [★15163]

Chinese Medicine and Acupuncture Assn. of Canada [IO], London, ON, Canada

Chinese Music Soc. of North Am. [10575], PO Box 5275, Woodridge, IL 60517, (630)910-1551

Chinese Musical and Theatrical Assn. - Address unknown since 2003.

Chinese Natl. Assn. of Indus. and Commerce [IO], Taipei, Taiwan

Chinese Natl. Export Enterprises Assn. [IO], Taipei, Taiwan

Chinese News Ser. [★9792]

Chinese Nuclear Soc. [IO], Beijing, People's Republic of China

Chinese Olympic Comm. [IO], Beijing, People's Republic of China

Chinese Orienteering Comm. [IO], Beijing, People's Republic of China

Chinese Orthodontic Soc. [IO], Beijing, People's Republic of China

Chinese Pharmaceutical Assn; Amer. [15911]

Chinese Pharmacological Soc. [IO], Beijing, People's Republic of China

Chinese Professionals; Assn. of American- [★19012]

Chinese Professionals Assn. of Canada [IO], Scarborough, ON, Canada

Chinese Psychological Soc. [IO], Beijing, People's Republic of China

Chinese Radio Sports Assn. [IO], Beijing, People's Republic of China

Chinese Refugee Relief - Defunct.

Chinese Rural Hea. Assn. China [IO], Beijing, People's Republic of China

Chinese School Assn. in the U.S. [9090], 385 Fox Run, Powell, OH 43065

Chinese Shar-Pei Club of Am. [22244], c/o Jo Ann T. Redditt, Sec., 3510 Washington Ct., Alexandria, VA 22302, (217)498-6850

Chinese Snuff Bottle Soc. [★21890]

Chinese Snuff Bottle Soc. [★IO]

Chinese Soc. of Aeronautics and Astronautics [IO], Beijing, People's Republic of China

Chinese Soc. of Digestive Endoscopy [IO], Beijing, People's Republic of China

Chinese Soc. of Elecl. Engg. [IO], Beijing, People's Republic of China

Chinese Soc. of EMG and Clinical Neurophysiology [IO], Beijing, People's Republic of China

Chinese Soc. for EU Stud. [IO], Shanghai, People's Republic of China

Chinese Soc. of Forestry [IO], Beijing, People's Republic of China

Chinese Soc. for Metals [IO], Beijing, People's Republic of China

Chinese Soc. of Mineralogy, Petrology, and Geochemistry [IO], Beijing, People's Republic of China

Chinese Soc. of Plant Nematologists [IO], Guangzhou, People's Republic of China

Chinese Soc. for Plant Pathology [IO], Beijing, People's Republic of China

Chinese Soc. of Theoretical and Applied Mechanics [IO], Beijing, People's Republic of China

Chinese Soc. of Toxicology [IO], Beijing, People's Republic of China

Chinese Squash Assn. [IO], Beijing, People's Republic of China

Chinese Stud. Assn. of Australia [IO], Parkville, Australia

Chinese Taekwondo Assn. [IO], Beijing, People's Republic of China

Chinese Taipei Aeromodelling Assn. [IO], Kaohsiung, Taiwan

Chinese Taipei Badminton Assn. [IO], Taipei, Taiwan

Chinese Taipei DanceSport Fed. [IO], Taipei, Taiwan

Chinese Taipei Flying Disc Assn. [IO], Taipei, Taiwan

Chinese Taipei Microlight Assn. [IO], Kaohsiung, Taiwan

Chinese Taipei Olympic Comm. [IO], Taipei, Taiwan

Chinese Taipei Paralympic Comm. [IO], Taipei, Taiwan

Chinese Taipei Pediatric Assn. [★IO]

Chinese Taipei Soc. of Photogrammetry and Remote Sensing [IO], Taipei, Taiwan

Chinese Taipei Sports Fed. for the Disabled [IO], Taipei, Taiwan

Chinese Taipei Tennis Assn. [IO], Taipei, Taiwan

Chinese Taipei Track and Field Assn. [IO], Taipei, Taiwan

Chinese Taipei Water Ski Assn. [IO], Taipei, Taiwan

Chinese Taipei Weightlifting Assn. [IO], Taipei, Taiwan

Chinese Taipei Yachting Assn. [IO], Taipei, Taiwan

Chinese Taipei Youth Hostel Assn. [IO], Taipei, Taiwan

Chinese Taiwan Landscape Architects Soc. [IO], Taipei, Taiwan

A star before a book entry number signifies that the name is not listed separately, but is mentioned within the entry.

Chinese Taiwan Osteoporosis Assn. [IO], Tainan, Taiwan
Chinese Taiwan Soc. of Digestive Endoscopy [IO], Taipei, Taiwan
Chinese Women's Assn. - Address unknown since 1995.
Chinese Women's Benevolent Assn. - Address unknown since 2003.
Chinese Women's Bus. Assn., ROC [IO], Taipei, Taiwan
Chinese Yachting Assn. [IO], Beijing, People's Republic of China
Chinese Young Economists Soc. [★IO]
Chinese Young Economists Soc. [★6876]
Ching Hai Meditation Assn; Supreme Master [19557]
Chinook Area of Narcotics Anonymous [IO], Calgary, AB, Canada
Chios Societies of America & Canada - Address unknown since 2001.
ChiroFeed Intl. [13996]
Chiropodists; Natl. Assn. of [★16037]
Chiropractic
Acad. of Forensic and Indus. Chiropractic Consultants [830]
Acad. of Upper Cervical Chiropractic Organizations [13986]
Alliance for Alternatives in Healthcare [13609]
Amer. Bd. of Chiropractic Independent Examiners [13987]
Amer. Chiropractic Assn. [13988]
Amer. Chiropractic Assn. Coun. on Sports Injuries and Physical Fitness [13989]
Amer. Chiropractic Coll. of Radiology [13990]
Amer. Chiropractic Registry of Radiologic Technologists [16273]
Amer. Coll. of Chiropractic Consultants [13991]
Amer. Coll. of Chiropractic Orthopedists [13992]
American College of Chiropractic Orthopedists [IO]
Amer. Soc. of Podiatrists and Chiropractors [16041]
Anglo-European Coll. of Chiropractic [IO]
Association of Chiropractic Colleges [IO]
Assn. of Chiropractic Colleges [13993]
Assn. for the History of Chiropractic [13994]
Blair Chiropractic Soc. [13995]
British Chiropractic Assn. [IO]
Canadian Chiropractic Assn. [IO]
ChiroFeed Intl. [13996]
Chiropractic Assn. of South Africa [IO]
Chiropractic Doctors' Assn. of Hong Kong [IO]
Chiropractors' Assn. of Australia [IO]
Christian Chiropractors Assn. [19773]
Cong. of Chiropractic State Associations [13997]
Conservative Orthopedics Intl. Assn. [15767]
Coun. on Chiropractic Educ. [13998]
Coun. on Chiropractic Educ. Australasia [IO]
Coun. on Chiropractic Orthopedics [15768]
Coun. of Chiropractic Physiological Therapeutics and Rehabilitation [13999]
Coun. on Diagnostic Imaging [16288]
Craniosacral Therapy Assn. of the UK [IO]
European Coun. on Chiropractic Educ. [IO]
Federation of Chiropractic Licensing Boards [IO]
Fed. of Chiropractic Licensing Boards [14000]
Fed. of Straight Chiropractors and Organizations [14001]
Flying Chiropractors Assn. [14002]
Found. for the Advancement of Chiropractic Educ. [8079]
Found. for the Advancement of Chiropractic Tenets and Sci. [14003]
Found. for Chiropractic Educ. and Res. [14004]
Gen. Chiropractic Coun. [IO]
Gonstead Clinical Stud. Soc. [14005]
Inst. of Chiropodists and Podiatrists [IO]
Intl. Acad. of Olympic Chiropractic Officers [IO]
Intl. Acad. of Olympic Chiropractic Officers [14006]
Intl. Chiropractic Pediatric Assn. [14007]
Intl. Chiropractic Pediatric Assn. [IO]
Intl. Chiropractors Assn. [IO]
Intl. Chiropractors Assn. [14008]
Japanese Assn. of Chiropractors [IO]
Natl. Assn. for Chiropractic Medicine [14009]

Natl. Bd. of Chiropractic Examiners [14010]
Natl. Board of Forensic Chiropractors [14011]
Natl. Upper Cervical Chiropractic Assn. [14012]
Options for Animals Intl. [16804]
ProChiropractic Europe [IO]
Sacro Occipital Res. Soc. Intl. [IO]
Sacro Occipital Res. Soc. Intl. [14013]
Soc. of Chiropractic Orthospinology [14014]
U.S. Sports Chiropractic Fed. [23282]
Victims of Chiropractic [14015]
Women's Auxiliary of the ICA [14016]
World Chiropractic Alliance [14017]
World Chiropractic Alliance [IO]
World Fed. of Chiropractic [IO]
Chiropractic Assn; Amer. Veterinary [16777]
Chiropractic Assn; Coun. on Roentgenology to the Amer. [★16288]
Chiropractic Assn; Natl. [★13988]
Chiropractic Assn. of South Africa [IO], Bethlehem, Republic of South Africa
Chiropractic Coll. Presidents; Assn. of [★13993]
Chiropractic Coun. on Roentgenology; Amer. [★16288]
Chiropractic Doctors' Assn. of Hong Kong [IO], Hong Kong, People's Republic of China
Chiropractic Educ; Found. for Accredited [★14004]
Chiropractic Hea. Bur. [★14008]
Chiropractic Hea. Bur. [★IO]
Chiropractic Hosp. and Sanitaria; Natl. Coun. of [★13988]
Chiropractic Organizations; Fed. of Straight [★14001]
Chiropractic Orthopedics; Coun. on [15768]
Chiropractic Physiotherapy; Amer. Coun. on [★13999]
Chiropractic Registry of Radiologic Technologists; Amer. [16273]
Chiropractic Res. Found. [★14004]
Chiropractic Roentgenologists; Natl. Coun. of [★16288]
Chiropractic Roentgenology; Amer. Coun. on [★16288]
Chiropractors; Amer. Soc. of Podiatrists and [16041]
Chiropractors' Assn. of Australia [IO], Penrith, Australia
Chiropractors Assn; Christian [19773]
Chiropractors Res. Found; Intl. [★14003]
Chiropraktiese Vereniging van Suid-Afrika [★IO]
Chirurgie Buccale et Maxillo-Faciale; Assn. Internationale de [★15736]
Chirurgiens; Order of Descendants of Colonial Physicians and [20752]
Chisholm Soc. - U.S. Br; Clan [20821]
Chittagong Young Men's Christian Association [IO], Chittagong, Bangladesh
Chittenden Family Assn. - Address unknown since 2007.
Chlorinated Paraffins Indus. Assn. [804], 1250 Connecticut Ave. NW, Ste. 700, Washington, DC 20036, (202)419-1500
Chlorinators; Natl. Assn. of Gas [★825]
Chlorine Chemistry Coun. [6676], 1300 Wilson Blvd., Arlington, VA 22209, (703)741-5000
Chlorine Inst. [805], 1300 Wilson Blvd., Arlington, VA 22209, (703)741-5760
Chlorobenzene Producers Assn. - Defunct.
Chlorofluorocarbons
Alliance for Responsible Atmospheric Policy [797]
Chocolate; Assn. of Mfrs. of Confectionary and [★1558]
Chocolate Mfrs. Assn. of the U.S.A. [1506], 8320 Old Courthouse Rd., Ste. 300, Vienna, VA 22182, (703)790-5750
Chocolate Mfrs. of the U.S; Assn. of Cocoa and [★1506]
Chocolate Milk Found. - Defunct.
Chocosuisse [★IO]
CHOICE [★IO]
CHOICE [12178], 1233 Locust St., Ste. 301, Philadelphia, PA 19107, (215)985-3355
Choice Am; NARAL Pro- [18518]
Choice; Catholics for a Free [18515]
Choice in Dying - Defunct.
Choice Emergency Task Force; Republicans for [★18520]

Choice/Friends of Family Planning; Voters for [18521]
Choice-in-Currency Res. Inst. - Address unknown since 1991.
Choice in Personal Safety [IO], Middlesborough, United Kingdom
Choice Public Educ. Proj; Pro- [11224]
Choice; Religious Coalition for Reproductive [18519]
Choice; Republican Coalition for [★18533]
Choice; Republicans for [18520]
Choir Assn. of the U.S; Latvian [10637]
Choir; Natl. Christian [20433]
Choir Schools Assn. [IO], Winchester, United Kingdom
Choirs
Am. Sings! [10524]
Amer. Children of SCORE [10530]
Amer. Choral Directors Assn. [10531]
Amer. Guild of Organists [10537]
Assn. of Anglican Musicians [20425]
Assn. of Armenian Church Choirs of Am. [10559]
Better World Chorus [12617]
Choristers Guild [20426]
Chorus Am. [10577]
Church Music Assn. of Am. [20428]
Church Music Publishers Assn. [20429]
Drinker Lib. of Choral Music [10588]
Fellowship of Amer. Baptist Musicians [20430]
Gay and Lesbian Assn. of Choruses [10599]
Hymn Soc. in the U.S. and Canada [20432]
Intercollegiate Men's Choruses, An Intl. Assn. of Male Choruses [10611]
Latvian Choir Assn. of the U.S. [10637]
Mixed Harmony Barbershop Quartet Assn. [10648]
Natl. Forum of Greek Orthodox Church Musicians [20434]
Polish Singers Alliance of Am. [10687]
Presbyterian Assn. of Musicians [20435]
Soc. for the Preservation and Encouragement of Barber Shop Quartet Singing in Am. [10704]
Sweet Adelines Intl. [10711]
Unitarian Universalist Musicians' Network [20436]
Chokolade- og Konfekture-Industriens Brancheforening [★IO]
Chol Chol Found. for Human Development [IO], Temuco, Chile
Cholesterol
HELP - Inst. for Body Chemistry [14928]
Natl. Heart Savers Assn. [13919]
Choose - Address unknown since 1995.
Choose Cruelty Free [IO], Melbourne, Australia
Chopin Found. of the U.S. [10576], 1440 79th St. Causeway, Ste. 117, Miami, FL 33141, (305)868-0624
Chopin Soc. [IO], Marianske Lazni, Czech Republic
Choral Conductors Guild - Defunct.
Choral Directors Assn; Amer. [10531]
Choral Directors Hall of Fame; Natl. Band and [★8926]
Choral Directors Hall of Fame; Natl. High School Band and [★8926]
Choral Found. Lib; Amer. [★10588]
Choral Music; Drinker Lib. of [10588]
Choreographers and Composers in Residence Program; Young [★9865]
Choreographers Found; Stage Directors and [11044]
Choreographers Guild - Address unknown since 2004.
Choreographers; Soc. of Stage Directors and [24159]
Choreographers Theatre - Address unknown since 2002.
Choreography Project; National [★9865]
Choristers Guild [20426], 2834 W Kingsley Rd., Garland, TX 75041-2498, (972)271-1521
Chorus, A Natl. Assn. of Male Choruses; Intercollegiate Men's [★10611]
Chorus Am. [10577], 1156 15th St. NW, Ste. 310, Washington, DC 20005, (202)331-7577
Chorus Am.: Assn. of Professional Vocal Ensembles [★10577]
Choruses; Assn. of Amer. [★10588]
Choruses; GALA [★10599]
Choruses; Gay and Lesbian Assn. of [10599]

Reference to "IO" in place of a book number signifies that the association may be found in the 45th edition of International Organizations.

Choruses; Intercollegiate Musical Coun., A Natl.
Assn. of Male [★10611]
CHOSEN [12516], 3638 W 26th St., Erie, PA 16506-2037, (814)833-3023
CHOSEN Mission Proj. [★12516]
Chosen People Ministries [19998], 241 E 51st St.,
New York, NY 10022, (212)223-2252
Chosin Few [21169], 238 Cornwall Cir., Chalfont, PA
18914-2318, (215)822-9093
Chosin Few [IO], Chalfont, PA, United States
Chow Chow Club, Inc. [22245], c/o Dr. Joyce A.
Dandridge, Corresponding Sec., 8132 Eastern Ave.
NW, Washington, DC 20012-1312, (202)726-9155
Choy Lee Fut Martial Arts Fed. of Am. [23586], 500
1/2E Live Oak Ave., Arcadia, CA 91006, (626)574-1523
Chris Blair Fan Club [24802], c/o Bobby Evans,
Pres., PO Box 22485, Nashville, TN 37202
Chris Craft Antique Boat Club [21870], 112 14th St.
SE, Cedar Rapids, IA 52403, (319)247-7207
Chris LeDoux Intl. Fan Club [24861], PO Box 41052,
San Jose, CA 95160, (408)997-8340
Chris Young Fan Club [24862], PO Box 14338,
Huntsville, AL 35815
Christ in Action Ministries [19999], PO Box 4200,
Manassas, VA 20108, (703)368-6286
Christ in Action Ministries [IO], Manassas, VA,
United States
Christ Alongside - Address unknown since 1999.
Christ Child Soc; Natl. [19679]
Christ for the City Intl. [20277], PO Box 241827,
Omaha, NE 68124-5827, (402)592-8332
Christ for the City Intl. [IO], Omaha, NE, United
States
Christ; Coun. for Hea. and Human Services
Ministries, United Church of [13165]
Christ; Coun. for Hea. and Welfare Services, United
Church of [★13165]
Christ; Crusaders for [20462]
Christ in India; Friends of [20090]
Christ the King Found. - Defunct.
Christ of Latter-day Saints; Genealogical Soc. of the
Church of Jesus [★21115]
Christ-Lutheran Bible Translators; Messengers of
[★19524]
Christ Ministers for Racial and Social Justice; United
Church of [★20608]
Christ for the Nations [20314], PO Box 769000, Dallas, TX 75376-9000, (214)376-1711
Christ for the Nations [IO], Dallas, TX, United States
Christ; New Transport for [★20404]
Christ; Transport for [★20404]
Christ Truth Ministries [19514], c/o Virginia O'Kane,
Pres./Exec. Dir., 1233 W 9th Ave., Upland, CA
91786, (909)981-2838
Christ Truth Radio Crusade [★19514]
Christ/U.S.A; Youth for [20645]
Christ; Women Nationally Active for [19502]
CHRISTAR [20315], Box 14866, Reading, PA
19612-4866, (610)375-0300
CHRISTAR [IO], Reading, PA, United States
Christar-North America [★IO]
Christar-North America [★20315]
Christchurch Folk Music Club [IO], Christchurch,
New Zealand
Christelijk Onderwijzersverbond van Belgie [★IO]
Christelijke Onderwijscentrale [IO], Brussels,
Belgium
Christian
ABW Ministries [19468]
Acad. of Amer. Franciscan History [19560]
Acad. of Homiletics [20081]
Acad. of Parish Clergy [20274]
Adopt-A-Church Intl. [19839]
Adult Christian Educ. Found. [19913]
Advancing Churches in Missions Commitment
[20293]
Advancing Native Missions [19833]
Advent Christian Gen. Conf. of Am. [19442]
Advocates Intl. [17998]
Affirmation: United Methodists for Lesbian, Gay
and Bisexual Concerns [20047]
Africa Inland Mission Intl. [20294]
Africa Youth Ministries [IO]
African Amer. Lutheran Assn. [20211]

African-Amer. Women's Clergy Assn. [20615]
African Peoples' Christian Org. [19759]
Aglow Intl. [20616]
Aglow New Zealand [IO]
Aid to the Church in Need [19563]
Alcuin Club [IO]
All Roads Ministry [19564]
All-Ukrainian Evangelical Baptist Fellowship
[19469]
Alliance for Life Ministries [19760]
Alpha Omega Assn. [9537]
Ambassadors of Mary [19565]
Am. World Adoption Assn. [11233]
Amer. Assn. of Christian Counselors [19862]
Amer. Assn. of Christian Schools [7875]
Amer. Baptist Historical Soc. [19470]
Amer. Baptists Concerned [20048]
Amer. Benedictine Acad. [19566]
Amer. Bible Soc. [19504]
Amer. Catholic Lawyers Assn. [5558]
Amer. Christian Fiction Writers [11156]
Amer. Coalition of Unregistered Churches [20520]
Amer. Congregational Assn. [19859]
Amer. Coun. of Christian Churches [19761]
Amer. and Foreign Christian Union [19762]
Amer. Forum for Jewish-Christian Cooperation
[19887]
Amer. Inst. for Patristic and Byzantine Stud.
[9770]
Amer. Lutheran Publicity Bur. [20212]
Amer. Missionary Fellowship [20296]
Amer. Sci. Affiliation [20546]
Amer. Soc. of Church History [20078]
Amer. Soc. of Missiology [20297]
Amer. TFP [19763]
Amer. Tract Soc. [19987]
Amer. Vision [19764]
AMG Intl. [20298]
Anabaptist Sociology and Anthropology Assn.
[7559]
Anglican Order of Archbishop Robert Leighton
[19453]
Anglican Soc. [19942]
Anglicans United [19943]
Apostleship of Prayer [19569]
Apostleship of the Sea in the U.S.A. [19570]
Apostolate for Family Consecrations [19571]
Archconfraternity of Christian Mothers [19572]
Archconfraternity of the Holy Ghost [19573]
ASGM [19506]
Assembly of Episcopal Healthcare Chaplains
[19944]
Assoc. Comm. of Friends on Indian Affairs
[20039]
Assoc. Parishes for Liturgy and Mission [19945]
Associates for Biblical Res. [19507]
Assn. of Anglican Musicians [20425]
Assn. of Armenian Church Choirs of Am. [10559]
Assn. of Baptists for World Evangelism [19472]
Assn. for Biblical Higher Educ. [8080]
Assn. of Christian Church Educators [19842]
Assn. for Christian Ethics [19574]
Assn. of Christian Investigators [5876]
Assn. of Christian Lay Centres in Africa [IO]
Assn. of Christian Librarians [10330]
Assn. of Christian Schools Intl. [8081]
Assn. of Christian Schools Intl. [IO]
Assn. of Christian Therapists [19765]
Assn. of Christians in the Mathematical Sciences
[19766]
Assn. of Classical and Christian Schools [9089]
Assn. for Clinical Pastoral Educ. [19915]
Assn. for the Development of Religious Info.
Systems [20091]
Assn. of Episcopal Colleges [8397]
Assn. of Grace Brethren Ministers [19533]
Assn. of Life-Giving Churches [19843]
Assn. of Lutheran Secondary Schools [8801]
Assn. of Marian Helpers [19576]
Assn. of North Amer. Missions [20301]
Assn. of Professional Chaplains [19744]
Assn. of Professors of Mission [20302]
Assn. of Reformed Baptist Churches of Am.
[19473]
Assn. for Religion and Intellectual Life [19916]

Assn. for the Restoration of the Church and Home
[19844]
Assn. of Romanian Catholics of America [19579]
Assn. of Southern Baptist Campus Ministers
[19474]
Assn. of State Baptist Papers [19475]
Assn. of Unity Churches [19845]
Assn. of Unity Churches Canada [IO]
Assn. of Welcoming and Affirming Baptists
[19476]
Assumption Guild [19580]
Athletes in Action [19990]
Augustinian Secondary Educational Assn. [8054]
Auxiliaries of Our Lady of the Cenacle [19581]
Awana Clubs Intl. [20639]
Baptist Bible Fellowship Intl. [19477]
Baptist Joint Comm. for Religious Liberty [19479]
Baptist Mid-Missions [19480]
Baptist Women in Ministry/Folio [19481]
Baptist World Alliance [19482]
BCM Intl. [19508]
Berean Bible Soc. [19509]
Bethany Intl. Missions [20304]
Bible Believers [IO]
Bible League [19510]
Bible Sabbath Assn. [20543]
Bibles For The World [20305]
Biblical Ministries Worldwide [19991]
Biblical Witness Fellowship [20606]
Billy Graham Evangelistic Assn. [19992]
Bishop Baraga Assn. and Archives [19583]
Bishops' Comm. for Ecumenical and Interreligious
Affairs [19584]
Bishops' Comm. on the Liturgy [19585]
Bishops' Comm. on Priestly Formation [19917]
Bishops' Comm. on Vocations [19586]
Black and Indian Mission Off. [19587]
Black Methodists for Church Renewal [20260]
Blessed Kateri Tekakwitha League [19588]
BLI [19512]
Blue Army of Our Lady of Fatima, U.S.A. [19589]
Bd. of Intl. Ministries [19483]
Bread on the Waters [19993]
Bread for the World [17792]
Brethren in Christ World Missions [20306]
Brethren/Mennonite Coun. for Lesbian, Gay,
Bisexual and Transgender Interest [20050]
Brotherhood of Saint Andrew [19946]
Bros. and Sisters in Christ [19767]
Bros. and Sisters in Christ [IO]
Bruderhof Communities [20481]
Bur. of Catholic Indian Missions [19591]
Campus Crusade for Christ Intl. [19994]
Campus Ministry Women [19918]
Canadian Tract Soc. [IO]
Canon Law Soc. of Am. [19592]
Capuchin-Franciscans (Province of Saint Joseph)
[19594]
Caribbean Conf. of Churches [IO]
Catholic Acad. of Sciences in the U.S.A. [19919]
Catholic Campus Ministry Assn. [19595]
Catholic Church Extension Soc. of the U.S.A.
[19596]
Catholic Homesteading Movement [11742]
Catholic Inst. of the Food Indus. [19598]
Catholic Kolping Soc. of Am. [19599]
Catholic League for Religious and Civil Rights
[19600]
Catholic Negro-Amer. Mission Bd. [19601]
Catholic Network of Volunteer Ser. [19602]
Catholic Pamphlet Soc. of the U.S. [19603]
Catholic Traditionalist Movement [19604]
Catholic War Veterans Auxiliary of the U.S.A.
[21194]
Catholic War Veterans of the U.S.A. [21290]
Catholics Speak Out [19605]
Catholics United for the Faith [19606]
CBM Ministries [19995]
Center for Applied Res. in the Apostolate [19608]
Center for Christian/Jewish Understanding of
Sacred Heart Univ. [19888]
Center for Christian Stud. [19768]
Center for the Evangelical United Brethren
Heritage [19976]
Center for the Ministry of Teaching [19920]

A star before a book entry number signifies that the name is not listed separately, but is mentioned within the entry.

Center for Organizational and Ministry Development [19769]
Center for Public Justice [18431]
Central Assn. of the Miraculous Medal [19609]
Central Bur., Catholic Central Union of Am. [19610]
Champions for Life Intl. [19996]
Child Evangelism Fellowship [19997]
Children's Cross Connection Intl. [11552]
Chinese Christian Mission [20313]
Choristers Guild [20426]
Christ in Action Ministries [19999]
Christ for the Nations [20314]
Christ Truth Ministries [19514]
Christian Acad. for European Dialogue [IO]
Christian Action Network [19770]
Christian Addiction Rehabilitation Assn. [13229]
Christian Aid Mission [20316]
Christian Anti-Communism Crusade [16991]
Christian Anti-Defamation League [17102]
Christian Assn. for Psychological Stud. [16148]
Christian Boaters Assn. [20000]
Christian Bus. Men's Comm. [19771]
Christian Camping International/U.S.A. [23270]
Christian Century Found. [19772]
Christian Chamber of Commerce [24311]
Christian Chaplain Sers. [19745]
Christian Chiropractors Assn. [19773]
Christian Coll. Consortium [8082]
Christian Comic Arts Soc. [9435]
Christian Communications, Inc. [19774]
Christian Conf. of Asia [IO]
Christian Connections for Intl. Hea. [14551]
Christian Coun. of Sweden [IO]
Christian Defense League [19775]
Christian Dental Soc. [14147]
Christian Educators Assn. Intl. [19922]
Christian Educators Fellowship of the United Methodist Church [19923]
Christian Family Life [12146]
Christian Family Movement [12147]
Christian Family Renewal [19776]
Christian Fencers Assn. [23400]
Christian Forum Res. Found. [20560]
Christian Freedom Intl. [20521]
Christian Friends of Israel - USA [19777]
Christian Golfers' Assn. [23283]
Christian Herald Assn. [19778]
Christian Holiness Partnership [19779]
Christian Ireland Ministries [17930]
Christian Labor Assn. of the U.S.A. [24035]
Christian Law Assn. [19780]
Christian Legal Soc. [19781]
Christian Literature and Bible Center [20317]
Christian Mgt. Assn. [20511]
Christian Media Assn. [20237]
Christian Medical and Dental Associations [20238]
Christian Military Fellowship [19782]
A Christian Ministry in the Natl. Parks [19783]
Christian Missionary Fellowship [20319]
Christian Motorcyclists Assn. [22674]
Christian Overcomers [11932]
Christian-Patriots Defense League/Citizen's Emergency Defense Sys. [17263]
Christian Record Services [16842]
Christian Res. [19784]
Christian Res. Inst. [19785]
Christian Res. Inst. [IO]
Christian Restoration Assn. [19786]
Christian Schools Australia [IO]
Christian Schools Intl. [IO]
Christian Schools Intl. [8083]
The Christian Sci. Publishing Soc. [3216]
Christian Seniors Assn. [19787]
Christian Ser. Club [19515]
Christian Services for the Blind [16843]
Christian Small Publishers Assn. [3217]
Christian Sociological Soc. [7662]
Christian Sports Intl. [23298]
Christian Stewardship Assn. [20512]
Christian TV Mission [19536]
Christians in Crisis [20555]
Christians in Govt. [19516]
Christians for Peace in El Salvador [20322]
Christians in the Visual Arts [9563]

The Christophers [19611]
Church Army [19947]
Church of the Brethren Gen. Bd. Global Mission Partnership [19535]
Church Growth Inc. [20536]
Church Music Assn. of Am. [20428]
Church Music Publishers Assn. [20429]
Church Periodical Club [19949]
Church of Scotland Guild [IO]
Church Women United [20618]
Churches Uniting in Christ [19889]
Citizens for Community Values [19788]
Claretian Volunteers and Lay Missionaries [19612]
CLOUT - Christian Lesbians Out [19789]
CLOUT - Christian Lesbians Out [IO]
Commn. of the Churches on Intl. Affairs [20094]
Comm. on Missionary Evangelism [20001]
Comm. on Social Development and World Peace of the U.S. Catholic Conf. [19613]
Commun. Commn. [19537]
Community of Celebration [19790]
Company of Saint Paul [19614]
Concerned Women for Am. [19791]
Concordia Deaconess Conf. [20213]
Concordia Gospel Outreach [20214]
Concordia Historical Inst. [20215]
Conf. on Christianity and Literature [8799]
Conf. of European Churches [IO]
Conf. on Faith and History [20079]
Confessing Synod Ministries [20561]
Confraternity of the Blessed Sacrament [19951]
Congregation of the Blessed Sacrament [19617]
Congregation of Sisters of Saint Agnes [19618]
Connecting Church Assn. [19846]
Conservative Baptist Assn. of Am. [19485]
Continental Baptist Missions [19486]
CORPUS - Natl. Assn. for an Inclusive Priesthood [19619]
Coun. for Christian Colleges and Universities [8084]
Coun. of Christian Scholarly Societies [8085]
Cowboys for Christ [19792]
Cowboys for Christ [IO]
Creation Res. Soc. [20548]
CRISTA Ministries [13166]
Crossworld [20326]
Crusaders for Christ [20462]
CSB Ministries [20640]
CUSA: An Apostolate of the Sick and Disabled [19620]
Dawn Bible Students Assn. [19517]
Dignity/USA [20053]
Disciples of Christ Historical Soc. [19853]
Disciples Ecumenical Consultative Coun. [19848]
Disciples Justice Action Network [19793]
Divine Sci. Fed. Intl. [19880]
Division of Higher Educ., Christian Church-Disciples of Christ [19854]
Dominican Mission Found. [20328]
Dynamic Youth Ministries [19831]
EAPE/Campolo Ministries - Evangelical Assn. for the Promotion of Educ. [20330]
Ecumenical Theological Seminary [19924]
Edith Stein Guild [19621]
Emergency Relief Response Fund [20562]
Engg. Ministries Intl. [19794]
Engg. Ministries Intl. [IO]
Episcopal Church Building Fund [19952]
Equestrian Ministries Intl. [20082]
European Conf. on Christian Educ. [IO]
European Fed. for Diaconia [IO]
Evangelical Christian Publishers Assn. [3223]
Evangelical Church Alliance [19977]
Evangelical Coun. for Financial Accountability [20002]
Evangelical and Ecumenical Women's Caucus [19978]
Evangelical Free Church of Am. - Intl. Mission [20333]
Evangelical Friends Intl. - North Amer. Region [20040]
Evangelical Lutheran Educ. Assn. [8802]
Evangelical Missiological Soc. [20334]
Evangelical Press Assn. [20004]

Evangelical and Reformed Historical Soc. [20607]
Evangelical Social Action Commn. [20005]
Evangelical Theological Soc. [19980]
Evangelical Training Assn. [19925]
Evangelicals Concerned [20054]
Evangelischer Frauenbund der Schweiz [IO]
Evangelism and Home Missions Assn. [20006]
Evangelistic Faith Missions [20336]
Ex-Masons for Jesus [19795]
Exodus Intl. [20055]
Faith Alive [19957]
Faith at Work [19893]
FaithWorks Intl. [11777]
Family Res. Inst. [17688]
Family Rosary [19622]
FARMS Intl. [12427]
Fed. of Protestant Welfare Agencies [20482]
Fellowship of Amer. Baptist Musicians [20430]
Fellowship of Christian Airline Personnel [20007]
Fellowship of Christian Athletes [20008]
Fellowship of Christian Cowboys [19796]
Fellowship of Christian Magicians [19797]
Fellowship of Christian Peace Officers - U.S.A. [19798]
Fellowship of Christian Released Time Ministries [19926]
Fellowship of Companies for Christ Intl. [19799]
Fellowship of Companies for Christ Intl. [IO]
Fellowship of Concerned Churchmen [19454]
Fellowship of Saint James [19800]
Fellowship of United Methodists in Music and Worship Arts [20261]
Focolare Movement [19624]
Focus on the Family [12157]
Forum for Scriptural Christianity [20262]
Forward in Faith North Am. [19959]
Found. for Amer. Christian Educ. [20086]
Found. for Christian Theology [19960]
Found. for Moral Restoration [18372]
Foundations and Donors Interested in Catholic Activities [19625]
Friends of Israel Gospel Ministry [20010]
Friends of Old St. Ferdinand [19626]
Friends of Sabeel - North Am. [18205]
Full Gospel Bus. Men's Fellowship Intl. [19801]
Full Gospel Bus. Men's Fellowship Intl. [IO]
Gen. Assn. of Regular Baptist Churches [19489]
Gen. Bd. of Church and Soc. of the United Methodist Church [20263]
The Gideons Intl. [20011]
Glenmary Res. Center [19628]
Global MissionAir [20487]
Global Univ. [19802]
Global Univ. [IO]
Good Tidings [19629]
Grailville [19630]
Graymoor Ecumenical and Interreligious Inst. [19895]
Greek Orthodox Ladies Philoptochos Soc. [20071]
Guild of Catholic Lawyers [19631]
Hagiography Soc. [20526]
Healers League of the Natl. Spiritualist Assn. of Churches [20449]
Healing Waters Intl. [13410]
Hea. Ministries [20241]
High School Evangelism Fellowship [20013]
Hindustan Bible Inst. [19927]
Historical Soc. of the Episcopal Church [19962]
Holy Childhood Assn. [19632]
Holy Cross Foreign Mission Soc. [19633]
Holy Shroud Guild [19635]
Hymn Soc. in the U.S. and Canada [20432]
IFCA Intl. [19849]
Independent Bd. for Presbyterian Foreign Missions [20467]
Inspiration Ministries [11952]
Inst. of Apostolic Oblates [19638]
Inst. for Biblical Res. [19519]
Inst. on Religious Life [19639]
Integrity [20058]
Interact Ministries [20348]
Intercessors for Am. [19803]
The Interchurch Center [19896]
Interchurch Medical Assistance [20242]
Intercristo [19804]

Reference to "IO" in place of a book number signifies that the association may be found in the 45th edition of International Organizations.

Encyclopedia of Associations, 46th Edition

3227

Interdisciplinary Biblical Res. Inst. [19928]
Intl. Assn. of Biblical Counselors [19867]
Intl. Assn. of Christian Chaplains [19748]
Intl. Assn. of Women Ministers [20619]
Intl. Bible Soc. [19520]
Intl. Bible Students Assn. [19521]
Intl. Catacomb Soc. [10039]
Intl. Catholic Deaf Assn. - U.S. Sect. [19641]
Intl. Christian Concern [19805]
Intl. Christian Concern [IO]
Intl. Christian Cycling Club USA [23309]
Intl. Christian Media Commn. [19538]
Intl. Christian Stud. Assn. [19806]
Intl. Christian Stud. Assn. [IO]
Intl. Communications Agency Network [105]
Intl. Conf. of Police Chaplains [19749]
Intl. Convention of Faith Ministries [19807]
Intl. Convention of Faith Ministries [IO]
Intl. Cops for Christ [19808]
Intl. Coun. of Christian Churches [20015]
Intl. Coun. of Community Churches [19850]
Intl. Coun. of Iranian Christians [19809]
Intl. Coun. of Iranian Christians [IO]
Intl. Disciples Women's Ministries [20620]
Intl. Lutheran Deaf Assn. [20217]
Intl. Lutheran Laymen's League [20218]
Intl. Network of Children's Ministry [19758]
Intl. Order of the King's Daughters and Sons [19810]
Intl. Order of the King's Daughters and Sons [IO]
Intl. Order of St. Vincent [19963]
Intl. Orthodox Christian Charities [19811]
Intl. Orthodox Christian Charities [IO]
Intl. Police and Fire Chaplain's Assn. [19750]
Intl. Prison Ministry [11873]
Intl. Soc. of Bible Collectors [19523]
Intl. Students, Inc. [20017]
InterServe U.S.A. [20351]
Interweave Continental (Unitarian Universalists for Lesbian, Gay, Bisexual and Transgender Concerns) [20059]
Japan Intl. Christian Univ. Found. [19929]
Jesuit Conf. [19643]
Jesuit Volunteer Corps: Northwest [19644]
John La Farge Inst. [19645]
Joni and Friends [11956]
Justice Fellowship [11875]
Kids 4 Afghan Kids [11610]
Koinonia Found. [19899]
Kristana Esperantista Ligo Internacia [19812]
Kristana Esperantista Ligo Internacia [IO]
Kyosiga Community Christians Assn. for Development [IO]
Latin Am. Mission [20353]
Latin Liturgy Assn. [19646]
Lay Carmelite Order of the Blessed Virgin Mary of Mount Carmel [19647]
Lay Mission-Helpers Assn. [19648]
Laymen's Home Missionary Movement [20018]
Leadership Conf. of Women Religious [19649]
League of St. Dymphna [19650]
League of Tarcisians [19651]
Legatus [19652]
Lesbian and Gay Christian Movement [IO]
Liberal Religious Educators Assn. [20599]
Liberty Godparent Home [12918]
Life Action Revival Ministries [20020]
Life Outreach Intl. [20021]
Lithuanian Catholic Religious Aid [19653]
Little Flower Mission League [19654]
Liturgical Conf. [19900]
Living Church Found. [19964]
Lollard Soc. [20524]
Lord's Day Alliance of the U.S. [20544]
Louis Finkelstein Inst. for Religious and Social Stud. at the Louis Stein Center [19931]
Lutheran Bible Translators [19524]
Lutheran Deaconess Assn. [20219]
Lutheran Deaconess Conf. [20220]
Lutheran Educational Conf. of North Am. [8804]
Lutheran Historical Conf. [20222]
Lutheran Human Relations Assn. [20223]
Lutheran Mission Societies [20225]
Lutheran Student Movement - U.S.A. [20227]
Lutheran Volunteer Corps [20228]

Lutheran Women's Missionary League [20229]
Lutherans Concerned/North Am. [20061]
Macedonian Orthodox Youth Assn. of North Am. [19883]
The Mailbox Club [19525]
MAP Intl. [20243]
Mariological Soc. of Am. [19656]
Maryheart Crusaders [19657]
Maryknoll Fathers and Bros. [19658]
Master's Men of the Natl. Assn. of Free Will Baptists [19490]
Media Associates Intl. [19981]
Medical Missions Response [20246]
Medical Teams Intl. [12869]
Men of the Sacred Heart [19659]
Methodist Fed. for Social Action [20264]
Metropolitan Community Churches [20062]
Military Chaplains Assn. of the U.S.A. [19752]
Mission Am. Coalition [19813]
Mission Builders Intl. [19814]
Mission to the World [20468]
Missionary Gospel Fellowship [20363]
Missionary Sisters of St. Peter Claver [20364]
Missionary Soc. of Saint Paul the Apostle [19663]
Missionary TECH Team [20366]
Missions Door [19491]
Missions Intl. [20037]
MOMS in Touch Intl. [20621]
More Light Presbyterians for Lesbian, Gay, Bisexual and Transgender Concerns [20063]
Morris Cerullo World Evangelism [20025]
Narramore Christian Found. [19815]
Natl. Alliance of Covenanting Congregations [IO]
Natl. Apostolate for Inclusion Ministry [20026]
Natl. Assn. of Catholic Family Life Ministers [20288]
Natl. Assn. of Catholic Homes and Educators [8057]
Natl. Assn. of Christian Financial Consultants [1465]
Natl. Assn. of Church Bus. Admin. [20513]
Natl. Assn. of Church Facilities Managers [20514]
Natl. Assn. of Church Personnel Administrators [20515]
Natl. Assn. of Ecumenical and Interreligious Staff [19902]
Natl. Assn. of Episcopal Schools [8398]
Natl. Assn. of Evangelicals [19982]
Natl. Assn. of Hispanic Priests of the USA [19665]
Natl. Assn. of Parish Catechetical Directors [19932]
Natl. Assn. of Priest Pilots [19667]
Natl. Assn. of State Catholic Conf. Directors [19668]
Natl. Assn. for Treasurers of Religious Institutes [20516]
Natl. Baptist Convention, U.S.A. [19493]
Natl. Bible Assn. [20205]
Natl. Black Catholic Clergy Caucus [19669]
Natl. Black Sisters' Conf. [19671]
Natl. Campus Ministry Assn. [19933]
Natl. Cathedral Assn. [19903]
Natl. Catholic Conf. for Total Stewardship [19673]
Natl. Catholic Off. for the Deaf [19675]
Natl. Catholic Rural Life Conf. [19677]
Natl. Catholic Women's Union [19678]
Natl. Christ Child Soc. [19679]
Natl. Christian Barrel Racers Assn. [23507]
Natl. Christian Choir [20433]
Natl. Christian Coll. Athletic Assn. [23837]
Natl. Christian Coun. in Japan [IO]
Natl. Christian Forensics and Communications Assn. [8521]
Natl. Christian Life Community of the U.S.A. [19680]
Natl. Coalition of Men's Ministries [19816]
Natl. Collegiate Assn. for Res. of Principles [8087]
Natl. Comm. of Catholic Laymen [19681]
Natl. Conf. for Community and Justice [19904]
Natl. Conf. of Diocesan Vocation Directors [19682]
Natl. Coun. of Bishops, USA [19683]
Natl. Coun. of Catholic Women [19684]
Natl. Coun. of Churches of Christ in the U.S.A. [19905]

Natl. Coun. of Churches, Educ. and Leadership Ministries Commn. [19935]
Natl. Coun. On Bible Curriculum In Public Schools [9052]
Natl. Cursillo Movement [19685]
Natl. Enthronement Center [19686]
Natl. Evangelization Teams [19687]
Natl. Fed. of Asian-Amer. United Methodists [20266]
Natl. Fed. of Priests' Councils [19689]
Natl. Forum of Greek Orthodox Church Musicians [20434]
Natl. Ghost Ranch Found. [20469]
Natl. Guild of Churchmen [19965]
Natl. Lutheran Outdoors Ministry Assn. [20231]
Natl. Off. for Black Catholics [19691]
Natl. Org. for Continuing Educ. of Roman Catholic Clergy [19936]
Natl. Religious Affairs Assn. [19872]
Natl. Religious Broadcasters [19539]
Natl. Religious Partnership for the Env. [19941]
Natl. Religious Vocation Conf. [19692]
Natl. Ser. Committee/Chariscenter USA [19693]
Natl. Shrine of St. Elizabeth Ann Seton [19694]
Natl. United Church Ushers Assn. of Am. [20609]
Natl. Woman's Christian Temperance Union [13306]
The Navigators [19817]
Nazarene Compassionate Ministries Intl. [19818]
Nazarene Compassionate Ministries International [IO]
Neighborhood Bible Stud. [19526]
New Zealand Coun. of Christian Social Services [IO]
Night Adoration in the Home [19695]
Nocturnal Adoration Soc. [19696]
Non-Denominational Bible Prophecy Stud. Assn. [19528]
North Amer. Acad. of Ecumenists [19906]
North Amer. Assn. for the Catechumenate [19697]
North Amer. Assn. for the Diaconate [19967]
North Amer. Coalition for Christianity and Ecology [4517]
North Amer. Forum on the Catechumenate [19698]
North Amer. Professors of Christian Educ. [8088]
Nurses Christian Fellowship [19819]
Officers' Christian Fellowship of the U.S.A. [19820]
Oper. Blessing Intl. [19821]
Oper. Blessing Intl. [IO]
ORACLE Religious Assn. [20070]
Oral Roberts Univ. Educational Fellowship [8089]
Order of Saint Andrew the Apostle [20073]
Orthodox Theological Soc. in Am. [19885]
Pan Amer. Coun. for the Preservation of the Hellenic Orthodox Church and the Hellenic Language [20074]
Paraclete [20381]
Partners Worldwide [19822]
Paulist Memorial Soc. [19699]
Paulist Natl. Catholic Evangelization Assn. [19700]
Peace Mission Movement [19823]
Peace Officers for Christ Intl. [19824]
Peace Officers for Christ Intl. [IO]
Peale Center for Christian Living [19825]
Personal Freedom Outreach [19875]
Peyote Way Church of God [20447]
Phi Beta Chi [24691]
Pilots for Christ Intl. [20028]
Pioneer Clubs [20642]
Pious Union of Prayer [19701]
Pocket Testament League [19529]
Polish-American-Jewish Alliance for Youth Action [13510]
Pontifical Mission Societies in the U.S. [19703]
Prayers for Life [19907]
Praying Hands Ranches [23360]
Presbyterian Assn. of Musicians [20435]
Presbyterian Church Bus. Administrators' Assn. [20470]
Presbyterian Evangelistic Fellowship [20471]
Presbyterian Lay Comm. [20472]
Presbyterian Men [20473]

A star before a book entry number signifies that the name is not listed separately, but is mentioned within the entry.

Presbyterian-Reformed Ministries Intl. [20474]
Presbyterian Women [20475]
Prison Fellowship Intl. [11887]
Prison Fellowship Ministries [11888]
Pro Athletes Outreach [20029]
Pro Maria Comm. [19704]
Pro Sanctity Movement [19705]
Probe Ministries Intl. [8090]
Probe Ministries Intl. [IO]
Professional Assn. of Christian Educators [19937]
Progressive, Radically Inclusive Student Ministry [19938]
Promise Keepers [19834]
Reasons to Believe [20551]
Red Sea Team Intl. [20385]
Regional Educ. Bd. of the Christian Bros. [8060]
Religious Bros. Conf. [19707]
Reparation Soc. of the Immaculate Heart of Mary [19709]
Response-Ability [20386]
Revival Fires (Christian Evangelizers Assn.) [20031]
Rosedale Mennonite Missions [20253]
Rosicrucian Fellowship [20541]
Sacred Heart League [19711]
St. Ansgar's Scandinavian Catholic League [19712]
St. Anthony's Guild [20388]
St. Jude League [19713]
St. Martin De Porres Guild [20389]
Saint Photios Found. [20075]
St. Thomas Aquinas Found. [19714]
Saints Alive in Jesus [20032]
Samaritans Intl. [20392]
Seafarers and Intl. House [20232]
Seamen's Church Inst. of New York and New Jersey [19970]
Searching Together Educational Ministries [19909]
Secretariat for Catholic-Jewish Relations [19910]
Secular Inst. of Saint Francis de Sales [19716]
Serra Intl. [19717]
Seventh Day Baptist Gen. Conf. [19494]
Seventh Day Baptist Gen. Conf. of the U.S. and Canada [20545]
Seventh Day Baptist Historical Soc. [19495]
Seventh Day Baptist Missionary Soc. [19496]
Seventh Day Baptist World Fed. [19497]
Sharing of Ministries Abroad U.S.A. [20393]
Side by Side Lay Volunteer Prog. [20394]
Significant Living [11320]
Skinner Leadership Inst. [20033]
Slavic Gospel Assn. [20395]
Smile Alliance Intl. [11721]
Soc. of African Missions [19719]
Soc. of Biblical Literature [19530]
Soc. of Christian Philosophers [10832]
Soc. of the Companions of the Holy Cross [19971]
Soc. of the Descendants of the Colonial Clergy [20760]
Soc. for Hindu-Christian Stud. [20528]
Soc. of Missionaries of Africa [19721]
Soc. of Our Lady of the Most Holy Trinity [19722]
Soc. for Promoting and Encouraging Arts and Knowledge of the Church [19972]
Soc. of Saint Stephen [20523]
Soc. for the Stud. of Christian Spirituality [19826]
Soc. of Traditional Roman Catholics [19726]
Sojourners [19827]
South Amer. Missionary Soc. - USA [20398]
Southern Baptist Found. [19498]
Southern Baptist Historical Lib. and Archives [19499]
Southern Christian Leadership Conf. [17154]
Standing Commn. on Ecumenical Relations of the Episcopal Church [19974]
Standing Conf. of the Canonical Orthodox Bishops in the Americas [19886]
STEER [20401]
Students for America [17277]
Tear Australia [IO]
Teen Challenge Intl. [20643]
Teen Missions Intl. [20402]
Theosophical Book Assn. for the Blind [20592]
Third Order of Mary/Marists [19728]

Toward Tradition [20508]
Truckers for Christ [19828]
Truth Missionaries Chap. of Positive Accord [20585]
Tyndale Soc. [20530]
Unitarian Universalist Christian Fellowship [20600]
Unitarian Universalist Historical Soc. [20601]
Unitarian Universalist Ministers Assn. [20602]
Unitarian Universalist Musicians' Network [20436]
Unitarian Universalist Ser. Comm. [20603]
Unitarian Universalist Women's Fed. [20604]
United Bd. for Christian Higher Educ. in Asia [8649]
United Christian Missionary Soc. [19856]
United Church of Christ Coalition for Lesbian, Gay, Bisexual and Transgender Concerns [20067]
United Church of Christ Justice and Witness Ministries [20608]
United Church Women [IO]
United Methodist Comm. on Relief [20267]
United Methodist Youth Org. [20268]
United Sisters of Charity [20406]
U.S. Assn. of Consecrated Virgins [19733]
U.S. Conf. of Catholic Bishops [19735]
Unity Coalition for Israel [8672]
Unity Fellowship Church Movement [20068]
Urantia Found. [20587]
Ursuline Companions in Mission [20408]
Volunteer Missionary Movement - U.S. Off. [19736]
Water Missions Intl. [13411]
The Way Intl. [20411]
We Believe! [19738]
We Care Prog. [11897]
WEC Intl. [20034]
William H. Whitsitt Baptist Heritage Soc. [19500]
Woman's Home and Foreign Mission Soc. [19443]
Woman's Missionary Union, SBC [19501]
Women for Faith and Family [19739]
Women and Men Against Sexual Harassment and Other Abuses [13088]
Women Nationally Active for Christ [19502]
Women's Ordination Conf. [19740]
World Evangelical Alliance [19983]
World Fellowship of Slavic Evangelical Christians [19984]
World Impact [20414]
World Literature Ministries [19832]
World Medical Mission [20245]
World Methodist Coun. [20272]
World Methodist Historical Soc. [20273]
World Mission Prayer League [20234]
World Team [20417]
World's Christian Endeavor Union [19829]
World's Christian Endeavor Union [IO]
WorldVenture [19503]
Writing Acad. [11204]
Wycliffe Bible Translators [19531]
Xaverian Missionaries of the U.S. [20421]
Young Life [20644]
Young Women's Christian Association - Puerto Rico [13526]
Youth for Christ/U.S.A. [20645]
Youth Evangelism Assn. [20036]
Youth Ministry [20235]
Y's Men Intl., U.S. Area [13464]
Christian Acad. for European Dialogue [IO], Leuven, Belgium
Christian Accrediting Association; International [★8089]
Christian Action for the Abolition of Torture - France [IO], Paris, France
Christian Action Coun. [★17283]
Christian Action Network [19770], PO Box 606, Forest, VA 24551-0606, (434)237-8201
Christian Addiction Rehabilitation Assn. [13229], c/o Heather Rice, Whosoever Gospel Mission, 101 E Chelten Ave., Philadelphia, PA 19144, (215)438-3094
Christian Admissions Professionals; North Amer. Coalition for [7914]
Christian Advance; Unitarian [★20600]
Christian Aid [IO], London, United Kingdom

Christian Aid Ministries [IO], Berlin, OH, United States
Christian Aid Ministries [18570], PO Box 360, Berlin, OH 44610, (330)893-2428
Christian Aid Mission [20316], PO Box 9037, Charlottesville, VA 22906, (434)977-5650
Christian Aid Mission [IO], Charlottesville, VA, United States
Christian Aid Mission - Canada [IO], Fort Erie, ON, Canada
Christian Aid for Romania [★IO]
Christian Aid for Romania [★18570]
Christian AIDS Services Alliance - Address unknown since 2001.
Christian Airline Personnel; Fellowship of [20007]
Christian Airmen's Fellowship Intl. - Defunct.
Christian Alcoholic Rehabilitation Assn. [★13229]
Christian Alliance of Am; Hebrew [★20257]
Christian Alliance; Intl. Hebrew [★20016]
Christian Amateur Radio Fellowship - Defunct.
Christian Amers. for Life - Defunct.
Christian Anti-Communism Crusade [16991], PO Box 129, Manitou Springs, CO 80829, (719)685-9043
Christian Anti-Defamation League [17102], PO Box 4, Palm Harbor, FL 34683-2141, (727)771-0635
Christian Assn. of Medicine, Psychology and Religion; Orthodox [16163]
Christian Assn. of Primetimers [★11320]
Christian Assn. for Psychological Stud. [16148], c/o Paul Regan, EdD, Exec. Dir., PO Box 365, Batavia, IL 60510-0365, (630)639-9478
Christian Assn. of Senior Adult Ministries [★11320]
Christian Assn. of the U.S.A; Young Women's [13527]
Christian Associations of North Am; Assn. of Secretaries, Young Men's [★13460]
Christian Associations in the U.S; Assn. of Professional Directors, Young Men's [★13460]
Christian Athletes; Fellowship of [20008]
Christian Benefit Assn; Loyal [19129]
Christian Blind Mission [IO], Bensheim, Germany
Christian Blind Mission Intl. [IO], Greenville, SC, United States
Christian Blind Mission Intl. [★IO]
Christian Blind Mission Intl. [16841], 450 E Park Ave., Greenville, SC 29601, (864)239-0065
Christian Blind Mission Intl. - Australia [IO], Box Hill, Australia
Christian Blind Mission Intl. - Canada [IO], Stouffville, ON, Canada
Christian Blind Mission Intl. - New Zealand [IO], Auckland, New Zealand
Christian Blind Mission Intl. - UK [IO], Cambridge, United Kingdom
Christian Boaters Assn. [20000], 112 Marshview Rd., Savannah, GA 31410, (912)897-7194
Christian Bodybuilding Assn. - Defunct.
Christian Booksellers Assn. [★3403]
Christian Booksellers Assn. [★IO]
Christian Booksellers Assn. of New Zealand [IO], Paraparaumu, New Zealand
Christian Bookselling Assn. of Australia [IO], Bargo, Australia
Christian Bowhunters of Am. [23051], 2205 State Rte. 571 W, Greenville, OH 45331-9425, (937)548-0623
Christian Broadcasting Assn. - Address unknown since 2005.
Christian Brothers Boys Assn. - Address unknown since 1995.
Christian Bros. Conf. [19921], 4351 Garden City Dr., Ste. 200, Landover, MD 20785, (301)459-9410
Christian Bros. Educ. Assn. [★8060]
Christian Bros; Natl. Educ. Coun. of the [★8060]
Christian Bros; Regional Educ. Bd. of the [8060]
Christian Bros; Regional Educ. Comm. of the [★8060]
Christian Bros; Regional Educ. Coun. of the [★8060]
Christian Bros. Volunteer [★20352]
Christian Bus. Men's Comm. [19771], PO Box 8009, Chattanooga, TN 37414-0009, (423)698-4444
Christian Bus. Men's Comm. Intl. [★19771]
Christian Camp and Conf. Assn. [★23270]
Christian Camping Intl. [★23270]

Reference to "IO" in place of a book number signifies that the association may be found in the 45th edition of International Organizations.

Christian Camping Intl. Australia [IO], South Windsor, Australia

Christian Camping Intl. - Brazil [IO], Anapolis, Brazil

Christian Camping Intl. - India [IO], Bangalore, India

Christian Camping Intl. - Jamaica [IO], Kingston, Jamaica

Christian Camping Intl. - Japan [IO], Yokohama, Japan

Christian Camping Intl. Korea [IO], Seoul, Republic of Korea

Christian Camping Intl. Polska [IO], Inowlodz, Poland

Christian Camping Intl. Romania [IO], Bucharest, Romania

Christian Camping Intl. - Russia [IO], St. Petersburg, Russia

Christian Camping Intl. - United Kingdom [IO], Milton Keynes, United Kingdom

Christian Camping International/U.S.A. [23270], PO Box 62189, Colorado Springs, CO 80962-2189, (719)260-9400

Christian Camping New Zealand [IO], Auckland, New Zealand

Christian Century Found. [19772], 104 S Michigan Ave., Ste. 700, Chicago, IL 60603-5943, (312)263-7510

The Christian Challenge [★19960]

The Christian Challenge [★IO]

Christian Chamber of Commerce [24311], PO Box 48207, Minneapolis, MN 55432, (763)792-3512

Christian Chaplain Sers. [19745]

Christian Children's Fund [11688], 2821 Emerywood Pkwy., Box 26484, Richmond, VA 23294, (804)756-2700

Christian Children's Fund [IO], Richmond, VA, United States

Christian Children's Fund of Australia [★IO]

Christian Children's Fund of Canada [IO], Markham, ON, Canada

Christian Children's Fund of Ireland [★IO]

Christian Children's Fund - New Zealand [★IO]

Christian Chiropractors Assn. [19773], 2550 Stover, No. B-102, Fort Collins, CO 80525, (970)482-1404

Christian Choir; Natl. [20433]

Christian Church-Disciples of Christ; Division of Higher Educ., [19854]

Christian Church (Disciples of Christ); Social and Hea. Services of the [★13177]

Christian Church Educators; Assn. of [19842]

Christian Church; Natl. Benevolent Assn. of the [13177]

Christian Churches; Natl. Assn. of Congregational [19861]

Christian Coalition [★17284]

Christian Coalition of Am. [17284], PO Box 37030, Washington, DC 20013-7030, (202)479-6900

Christian Coll. Alumni Assn; Nebraska [18912]

Christian Coll. Athletic Assn; Natl. [23837]

Christian Coll. Coalition [★8084]

Christian Coll. Consortium [8082], 50 Stark Hwy. S, Dunbarton, NH 03046-4406, (603)774-6623

Christian Colleges in China; Assoc. Boards for [★8649]

Christian Colleges in China; United Bd. for [★8649]

Christian Comic Arts Soc. [9435], PO Box 254, Temple City, CA 91780

Christian Comm; Unitarian [★20600]

Christian Committees of Correspondence [★8302]

Christian Commun. Centre [IO], Lira, Uganda

Christian Communications, Inc. [19774], 9600 Bellaire Blvd., No. 111, Houston, TX 77036, (713)778-1155

Christian Community Development Assn. [20278], 3555 W Ogden Ave., Chicago, IL 60623, (773)762-0994

Christian Computer Users Assn., Inc. - Address unknown since 1999.

Christian Computer Users - Defunct.

Christian Conf. of Asia [IO], Hong Kong, People's Republic of China

Christian Connections for Intl. Hea. [IO], McLean, VA, United States

Christian Connections for Intl. Hea. [14551], c/o Ray Martin, Exec. Dir., 1817 Rupert St., McLean, VA 22101, (703)556-0123

Christian Coun. on Persons with Disabilities [11931], 301 E Pine St., Ste. 150, Orlando, FL 32801, (407)210-3917

Christian Coun. on Persons with Disabilities [IO], Orlando, FL, United States

Christian Coun. of Sweden [IO], Sundbyberg, Sweden

Christian Counsellors Assn. of Australia - New South Wales [IO], Jannali, Australia

Christian Counsellors Assn. of Australia - Queensland [IO], Carindale, Australia

Christian Counsellors Assn. of Australia - South Australia [IO], Unley, Australia

Christian Counsellors Assn. of Australia - Victoria [IO], Ormond, Australia

Christian Counsellors Assn. of Australia - Western Australia [IO], Ascot, Australia

Christian Crusade - Address unknown since 2008.

Christian Dance Fellowship of Australia [IO], Drummoyne, Australia

Christian Defense League [19775], PO Box 9166, Mandeville, LA 70470-9166, (601)749-8565

Christian Democrat Intl. [IO], Brussels, Belgium

Christian Democrat Org. of Am. [IO], Santiago, Chile

Christian Democratic Intl. [★IO]

Christian Democratic Union [IO], Berlin, Germany

Christian Democratic Union of Germany [★IO]

Christian Democratic World Union [★IO]

Christian Dental Soc. [14147], PO Box 296, Sumner, IA 50674, (563)578-8887

Christian Development; Continuing [★19934]

Christian Doctors Sodality - Address unknown since 1999.

Christian Doctrine; Confraternity of [★19934]

Christian Educ. [IO], Birmingham, United Kingdom

Christian Educ. Found; Adult [19913]

Christian Educ. Movement [IO]

Christian Education; Natl. Assn. of Directors of [★19937]

Christian Educ; Natl. Assn. of Professors of [★8088]

Christian Educ; Natl. Coun. of Churches, Ministries in [★19935]

Christian Educ. of the Natl. Coun. of Churches; Professors and Res. Sect. of the Division of [★19939]

Christian Educ; North Amer. Assn. of Professors of [★8088]

Christian Educators Assn. [★19922]

Christian Educators Assn. [★IO]

Christian Educators Assn. Intl. [IO], Westlake, OH, United States

Christian Educators Assn. Intl. [19922], PO Box 45610, Westlake, OH 44145, (440)250-9566

Christian Educators Fellowship of the United Methodist Church [19923], PO Box 24930, Nashville, TN 37202, (818)248-8858

Christian Educators; Professional Assn. of [19937]

Christian Engineers in Development [IO], Aylesbury, United Kingdom

Christian Esperanto Assn; Intl. [★19812]

Christian Ethics; Amer. Soc. of [★12128]

Christian Ethics; Assn. for [19574]

Christian Ethics; Center for Applied [19975]

Christian Ethics; Soc. of [12128]

Christian European Visual Media Assn. [IO], Wetzlar, Germany

Christian Evangelizers Assn; Revival Fires [20031]

Christian Faith; Defenders of the [★19774]

Christian Family Life [12146], c/o Two Becoming One, 1021 B Maxwell Mill Rd., Fort Mill, SC 29708, (800)264-3876

Christian Family Movement [12147], PO Box 925, Evansville, IN 47706-0925, (812)962-5508

Christian Family Renewal [19776]

Christian Fellowship of Art Music Composers [9808], Greatbatch Scholarship of Music, Houghton Coll., Houghton, NY 14744, (585)567-9424

Christian Fellowship for the Blind [★16843]

Christian Fellowship; Hebrew [20012]

Christian Fellowship; Inter Varsity [20347]

Christian Fellowship; Unitarian [★20600]

Christian Fellowship; Unitarian Universalist [20600]

Christian Feminists - Defunct.

Christian Fencers Assn. [23400], c/o Rev. Robert Bruce Sikes, 912 S Rock Hill Rd., St. Louis, MO 63119

Christian Financial Executives Assn. [★20511]

Christian FOCUS on Govt. - Address unknown since 1995.

Christian Forum Res. Found. [20560]

Christian Found. for Children [★13159]

Christian Found. for Children [★IO]

Christian Found. for Children and Aging [IO], Kansas City, KS, United States

Christian Found. for Children and Aging [13159], 1 Elmwood Ave., Kansas City, KS 66103, (913)384-6500

Christian Freedom Found. - Address unknown since 1995.

Christian Freedom Institutes [★8302]

Christian Freedom Intl. [20521], PO Box 535, Front Royal, VA 22630, (540)636-8907

Christian Freedom Intl. [IO], Front Royal, VA, United States

Christian Freedom Intl; Now [★20521]

Christian Friends of Israel - USA [19777], PO Box 470258, Charlotte, NC 28247-0258, (704)552-1283

Christian Golfers' Assn. [23283], 1285 Clara Louise Kellogg Dr., Sumter, SC 29153, (800)784-2171

Christian Govt. Movement - Defunct.

Christian Hea. Assn. of Kenya [IO], Nairobi, Kenya

Christian Herald Assn. [19778], c/o The Bowery Mission, 132 Madison Ave., New York, NY 10016-7004, (212)684-2800

Christian Heritage Center [17285], 10 Croyden Ln., Staunton, VA 24401, (540)885-7333

Christian Heritage Party of Canada [IO], Ottawa, ON, Canada

Christian Historical Soc; Congregational [19860]

Christian Holiness Assn. [★19779]

Christian Holiness Partnership [19779], 263 Buffalo Rd., Clinton, TN 37716, (423)457-5978

Christian Home Educators Assn. [★8516]

Christian Home Educators Assn. of California [8516], PO Box 2009, Norwalk, CA 90651-2009, (562)864-2432

Christian Honor Student Association [★8089]

Christian Hospitals Overseas Secure Equip. Needs [★12516]

Christian Instrumental Directors Assn. [★20427]

Christian Instrumentalists and Directors Assn. [20427], c/o Andrew Kamper, Treas., 1401 Ferndale SW, Grand Rapids, MI 49504

Christian Ireland Ministries [17930], PO Box 11057, Albany, NY 12211, (518)634-7021

Christian Ireland Ministries [IO], Albany, NY, United States

Christian Jail Workers [★19745]

Christian/Jewish Understanding; Center for [★19888]

Christian/Jewish Understanding of Sacred Heart Univ; Center for [19888]

Christian Labor Assn. of the U.S.A. [24035], PO Box 65, Zeeland, MI 49464, (616)772-9164

Christian Law Assn. [19780], PO Box 4010, Seminole, FL 33775, (727)399-8300

Christian Law Inst. - Address unknown since 1994.

Christian Leadership Conf; Southern [17154]

Christian League for the Handicapped [★11952]

Christian Legal Soc. [19781], 8001 Braddock Rd., Ste. 300, Springfield, VA 22151-2110, (703)642-1070

Christian Liberty Assn. - Address unknown since 1995.

Christian Librarians; Assn. of [10330]

Christian Librarians' Fellowship [★10330]

Christian Librarians' Fellowship [★IO]

Christian Librarians Network - Australia and New Zealand [IO], Wheelers Hill, Australia

Christian Life Commn. of the Southern Baptist Convention [★19487]

Christian Life Communities; U.S. Natl. Fed. of [★19680]

Christian Life Community [IO], Rome, Italy

Christian Life Community of the U.S.A; Natl. [19680]

Christian Life and Mission; Educ. for [★19935]

Christian Literacy Associates [8788], 541 Perry Hwy., Pittsburgh, PA 15229-1851, (412)364-3777

Christian Literacy Associates [IO], Pittsburgh, PA, United States

Christian Literature and Bible Center [IO], North Augusta, SC, United States

A star before a book entry number signifies that the name is not listed separately, but is mentioned within the entry.

Christian Literature and Bible Center [20317], PO Box 7130, North Augusta, SC 29861, (803)279-1981

Christian Literature for Women and Children; Comm. on [★12376]

Christian Living; Found. for [★19825]

Christian Macintosh User Gp. [6790], 2190 Bristolwood Ln., San Jose, CA 95132

Christian Mgt. Assn. [20511], PO Box 4090, San Clemente, CA 92674, (949)487-0900

Christian Mgt. Institute [★20511]

Christian Maternity Home Assn. - Defunct.

Christian Media Assn. [20237], 176 Wayland Rd., Culpeper, VA 22701, (540)829-8101

Christian Medical Coun. - Defunct.

Christian Medical and Dental Associations [20238], PO Box 7500, Bristol, TN 37621, (423)844-1000

Christian Medical and Dental Associations [IO], Bristol, TN, United States

Christian Medical and Dental Soc. [★IO]

Christian Medical and Dental Soc. [IO], Steinbach, MB, Canada

Christian Medical and Dental Soc. [★20238]

Christian Medical Found. Intl. [20239], PO Box 152136, Tampa, FL 33684-2136, (813)932-3688

Christian Medical Found. Intl. [IO], Tampa, FL, United States

Christian Medical Soc. [★IO]

Christian Medical Soc. [★20238]

Christian Medical Work; Coun. for [★20241]

Christian Methodist Episcopal Church; Women's Missionary Coun. of the [20270]

Christian Military Fellowship [19782], PO Box 1207, Englewood, CO 80150-1207, (303)761-1959

Christian Ministries Mgt. Assn. [★20511]

A Christian Ministry in the Natl. Parks [19783], 10 Justin's Way, Freeport, ME 04032, (207)865-6436

Christian Mission Aid [IO], Nairobi, Kenya

Christian Mission; Chinese [20313]

Christian Mission for the Deaf [20318], PO Box 28005, Detroit, MI 48228-0005

Christian Mission for Deaf Africans [★20318]

Christian Mission - Defunct.

Christian Mission; Holy Land [★20312]

Christian Mission Intl; Holy Land [★20312]

Christian Missionary Fellowship [20319], PO Box 501020, Indianapolis, IN 46250-6020, (317)578-2700

Christian Missionary Fellowship [IO], Indianapolis, IN, United States

Christian Missionary Soc; Amer. [★19856]

Christian Missionary Soc; The Foreign [★19856]

Christian Missionary Soc; United [19856]

Christian Missions to the Communist World [★20410]

Christian Missions in Many Lands [20320], PO Box 13, Spring Lake, NJ 07762-0013, (732)449-8880

Christian Mothers; Archconfraternity of [19572]

Christian Motorcyclists Assn. [22674], PO Box 9, Hatfield, AR 71945, (870)389-6196

Christian Motorsports Ministries [21610], PO Box 929, Bristow, OK 74010, (607)742-3407

Christian Motorsports Ministries [IO], Mansfield, PA, United States

Christian Movement for Peace [★IO]

Christian Musicians; Fellowship of [★20427]

Christian-Muslim Dialogue Comm. - Address unknown since 2001.

Christian/Muslim Relations; Duncan Black Macdonald Center for the Stud. of Islam and [★20100]

Christian Org; Intl. [★19804]

Christian Orthopaedic Partners [15765], PO Box 4712, Crofton, MD 21114, (301)261-3211

Christian Orthopaedic Partners [IO], Crofton, MD, United States

Christian Outdoorsman Assn. - Address unknown since 1994.

Christian Outreach to the Handicapped [IO], Singapore, Singapore

Christian Overcomers [11932], PO Box 2007, Garfield, NJ 07026, (973)253-2343

Christian Patriot Assn. - Defunct.

Christian-Patriots Defense League/Citizen's Emergency Defense Sys. [17263]

Christian Peace Conf. [IO], Prague, Czech Republic

Christian Peace Officers; Fellowship of [★19798]

Christian Peace Officers - U.S.A; Fellowship of [19798]

Christian Pharmacists Fellowship Intl. [15928], PO Box 24708, West Palm Beach, FL 33416-4708, (561)803-2737

Christian Pharmacists Fellowship Intl. [IO], West Palm Beach, FL, United States

Christian Philosophers; Soc. of [10832]

Christian Pilots Assn. [20321], 4100 Newport Pl., Ste. 620, Newport Beach, CA 92660, (949)271-1587

Christian Policemen; Fellowship of [★19798]

Christian Preaching Conf. - Defunct.

Christian Publishers Assn; Evangelical [3223]

Christian Record Benevolent Assn. [★16842]

Christian Record Braille Found. [★16842]

Christian Record Services [16842], PO Box 6097, Lincoln, NE 68506-0097, (402)488-0981

Christian Record Services [IO], Oshawa, ON, Canada

Christian Reformed

Anabaptist Assn. of Australia and New Zealand [IO]

Assn. of Reformed Baptist Churches of Am. [19473]

Christian Reformed Church - Spanish and World Literature Comm. [19830]

Christian Reformed Church - Spanish and World Literature Comm. [IO]

Dynamic Youth Ministries [19831]

World Literature Ministries [19832]

World Literature Ministries [IO]

Christian Reformed Church - Spanish and World Literature Comm. [IO], Grand Rapids, MI, United States

Christian Reformed Church - Spanish and World Literature Comm. [19830], 2850 Kalamazoo Ave. SE, Grand Rapids, MI 49560, (616)241-1691

Christian Reformed Church World Literature Ministries [★19832]

Christian Reformed Church World Literature Ministries [★IO]

Christian Reformed World Relief Comm. [IO], Grand Rapids, MI, United States

Christian Reformed World Relief Comm. [12424], 2850 Kalamazoo Ave. SE, Grand Rapids, MI 49560, (616)241-1691

Christian Relief and Development Assn. [IO], Addis Ababa, Ethiopia

Christian Relief Services [IO], Alexandria, VA, United States

Christian Relief Services [12841], 2550 Huntington Ave., Ste. 200, Alexandria, VA 22303-1499, (703)317-9086

Christian Renewal Ministry - Defunct.

Christian Res. [19784], PO Box 385, Eureka Springs, AR 72632-0385, (479)253-7185

Christian Res. Assn. [IO], London, United Kingdom

Christian Res. Inst. [IO], Charlotte, NC, United States

Christian Res. Inst. [19785], PO Box 8500, Charlotte, NC 28271-8500, (704)887-8200

Christian Res. Inst. Intl. [★19785]

Christian Res. Inst. Intl. [★IO]

Christian Response Intl. [★IO]

Christian Response Intl. [★20521]

Christian Restoration Assn. [19786], 7133 Central Parke Blvd., Mason, OH 45040, (513)229-8000

Christian Road Safety Assn. [IO], Wembley, United Kingdom

Christian Rural Fellowship - Defunct.

Christian Rural Overseas Prog. [★12842]

Christian Rural Overseas Prog. [★IO]

Christian School Educ. Assn; Natl. [★8081]

Christian Schools; Amer. Assn. of [7875]

Christian Schools Australia [IO], North Ryde, Australia

Christian Schools Intl. [IO], Grand Rapids, MI, United States

Christian Schools Intl. [8083], 3350 E Paris Ave. SE, Grand Rapids, MI 49512-2907, (616)957-1070

Christian Schools; Natl. Union of [★8083]

Christian Schools; Ohio Assn. of [★8081]

Christian Schools; Western Assn. of [★8081]

The Christian Sci. Publishing Soc. [3216], Jour., Sentinel, and Herald Editorial Dept. C04-10, 1 Norway St., Boston, MA 02115, (617)450-2000

Christian Seniors Assn. [19787], 139 C St. SE, Washington, DC 20003, (202)547-4400

Christian Ser. Brigade [★20640]

Christian Ser. Club [19515]

Christian Service Corps - Defunct.

Christian Ser; United Fellowship for [★20351]

Christian Servicemen Fellowship [★19782]

Christian Services for the Blind [16843], 1124 Fair Oaks Ave., PO Box 26, South Pasadena, CA 91031-0026, (626)799-3935

Christian Slater Fan Club - Address unknown since 2000.

Christian Small Publishers Assn. [3217], PO Box 481022, Charlotte, NC 28269, (704)277-7194

Christian Social Concern; Division of [★19484]

Christian Social Ethics in the U.S. and Canada; Amer. Soc. of [★12128]

Christian Social Party [IO], Luxembourg, Luxembourg

Christian Soc. for Drama - Defunct.

Christian Sociological Soc. [7662], c/o Paul J. Serwinek, 2385 Learmonth, Milford, MI 48381, (248)363-5746

Christian Solidarity Intl. [20522], 870 Hampshire Rd., Ste. T, Westlake Village, CA 91361, (805)777-7107

Christian Solidarity Intl. [IO], Westlake Village, CA, United States

Christian Solidarity Intl. - Switzerland [IO], Binz, Switzerland

Christian Solidarity Intl., U.S.A. [★IO]

Christian Solidarity Intl., U.S.A. [★20521]

Christian Solidarity, U.S.A. [★20521]

Christian Solidarity, U.S.A. [★IO]

Christian Sports Intl. [IO], Zelienople, PA, United States

Christian Sports Intl. [23298], PO Box 254, Zelienople, PA 16063, (724)453-1400

Christian Stewardship Assn. [20512], 4700 W Lake Ave., Glenview, IL 60025, (847)375-4741

Christian Stewardship Coun. [★20512]

Christian Tapes for the Disabled - Defunct.

Christian Tattoo Assn. [20590], 115 W Mulberry St., Kokomo, IN 46901, (765)461-3081

Christian Teachers Fed. of Belgium [IO], Brussels, Belgium

Christian TV Mission [19536], PO Box 10242, Springfield, MO 65808-0242, (417)581-5777

Christian Temperance Union; Natl. Woman's [13306]

Christian Testimony; Artists in [19989]

Christian Theology; Found. for [19960]

Christian Union; Assn. for the Promotion of [★19891]

Christian Union; Bible [★20331]

Christian Union; B'Rith [★19800]

Christian Union; Coun. on [★19891]

Christian Unity; Coun. on [19891]

Christian Univ. Alumni Assn; Colorado [18890]

Christian University; International [★19929]

Christian University; International [★IO]

Christian Urgent Action Network for Emergency Support Philippines - Defunct.

Christian Vegetarian Assn. [20611], PO Box 201791, Cleveland, OH 44120, (216)283-6702

Christian Vegetarian Assn. [IO], Cleveland, OH, United States

Christian Veterinary Missions of Canada [IO], Ancaster, ON, Canada

Christian Voice - Address unknown since 1989.

Christian Woman's Bd. of Missions [★19856]

Christian Women's Club of Guam - Address unknown since 2007.

Christian Women's Natl. Concerns - Defunct.

Christian World; Laymen's Movement for a [★20588]

Christian Writers Guild [★20630]

Christian Writers Guild; Jerry B. Jenkins [20630]

Christian Yellow Pages - Address unknown since 2006.

Christianiki Enosi Neanidon [★IO]

Christianity

ABW Ministries [19468]

Acad. of Amer. Franciscan History [19560]

Reference to "IO" in place of a book number signifies that the association may be found in the 45th edition of International Organizations.

Acad. of Homiletics [20081]
Acad. of Parish Clergy [20274]
Adopt-A-Church Intl. [19839]
Adult Christian Educ. Found. [19913]
Advancing Churches in Missions Commitment
   [20293]
Advancing Native Missions [19833]
Advancing Native Missions [IO]
Advent Christian Gen. Conf. of Am. [19442]
Advocates Intl. [17998]
Affirmation: United Methodists for Lesbian, Gay
   and Bisexual Concerns [20047]
Africa Inland Mission Intl. [20294]
African Amer. Lutheran Assn. [20211]
African-Amer. Women's Clergy Assn. [20615]
Aglow Intl. [20616]
Aid to the Church in Need [19563]
All Roads Ministry [19564]
All-Ukrainian Evangelical Baptist Fellowship
   [19469]
Alpha Omega Assn. [9537]
Ambassadors of Mary [19565]
Am. World Adoption Assn. [11233]
Amer. Assn. of Christian Counselors [19862]
Amer. Baptist Historical Soc. [19470]
Amer. Baptists Concerned [20048]
Amer. Benedictine Acad. [19566]
Amer. Bible Soc. [19504]
Amer. Catholic Lawyers Assn. [5558]
Amer. Christian Fiction Writers [11156]
Amer. Coalition of Unregistered Churches [20520]
Amer. Congregational Assn. [19859]
Amer. Coun. of Christian Churches [19761]
Amer. Decency Assn. [17281]
Amer. and Foreign Christian Union [19762]
Amer. Forum for Jewish-Christian Cooperation
   [19887]
Amer. Lutheran Publicity Bur. [20212]
Amer. Missionary Fellowship [20296]
Amer. Renewal Found. [18280]
Amer. Sci. Affiliation [20546]
Amer. Soc. of Church History [20078]
Amer. Soc. of Missiology [20297]
Amer. Tract Soc. [19987]
AMG Intl. [20298]
Anabaptist Sociology and Anthropology Assn.
   [7559]
Anglican Order of Archbishop Robert Leighton
   [19453]
Anglican Soc. [19942]
Anglicans United [19943]
Apostleship of Prayer [19569]
Apostleship of the Sea in the U.S.A. [19570]
Apostolate for Family Consecrations [19571]
Archconfraternity of Christian Mothers [19572]
Archconfraternity of the Holy Ghost [19573]
ASGM [19506]
Assembly of Episcopal Healthcare Chaplains
   [19944]
Assoc. Comm. of Friends on Indian Affairs
   [20039]
Assoc. Parishes for Liturgy and Mission [19945]
Associates for Biblical Res. [19507]
Assn. of Anglican Musicians [20425]
Assn. of Armenian Church Choirs of Am. [10559]
Assn. of Baptists for World Evangelism [19472]
Assn. for Christian Ethics [19574]
Assn. of Christian Investigators [5876]
Assn. of Christian Truckers [20596]
Assn. of Classical and Christian Schools [9089]
Assn. for Clinical Pastoral Educ. [19915]
Assn. for the Development of Religious Info.
   Systems [20091]
Assn. of Grace Brethren Ministers [19533]
Assn. of Life-Giving Churches [19843]
Assn. of Marian Helpers [19576]
Assn. of North Amer. Missions [20301]
Assn. of Professional Chaplains [19744]
Assn. of Professors of Mission [20302]
Assn. of Reformed Baptist Churches of Am.
   [19473]
Assn. for Religion and Intellectual Life [19916]
Assn. for the Restoration of the Church and Home
   [19844]
Assn. of Romanian Catholics of America [19579]

Assn. of Southern Baptist Campus Ministers
   [19474]
Assn. of State Baptist Papers [19475]
Assn. of Welcoming and Affirming Baptists
   [19476]
Assumption Guild [19580]
Athletes Abroad for Christ [19466]
Athletes in Action [19990]
Australian Fed. of Civil Celebrants [IO]
Auxiliaries of Our Lady of the Cenacle [19581]
Awana Clubs Intl. [20639]
Baptist Bible Fellowship Intl. [19477]
Baptist Joint Comm. for Religious Liberty [19479]
Baptist Mid-Missions [19480]
Baptist Women in Ministry/Folio [19481]
Baptist World Alliance [19482]
BCM Intl. [19508]
Berean Bible Soc. [19509]
Bethany Intl. Missions [20304]
Bible League [19510]
Bible Sabbath Assn. [20543]
Bibles For The World [20305]
Biblical Ministries Worldwide [19991]
Biblical Witness Fellowship [20606]
Billy Graham Evangelistic Assn. [19992]
Bishop Baraga Assn. and Archives [19583]
Bishops' Comm. for Ecumenical and Interreligious
   Affairs [19584]
Bishops' Comm. on the Liturgy [19585]
Bishops' Comm. on Priestly Formation [19917]
Bishops' Comm. on Vocations [19586]
Black and Indian Mission Off. [19587]
Black Methodists for Church Renewal [20260]
Blessed Kateri Tekakwitha League [19588]
BLI [19512]
Blue Army of Our Lady of Fatima, U.S.A. [19589]
Bd. of Intl. Ministries [19483]
Bread on the Waters [19993]
Brethren in Christ World Missions [20306]
Brethren/Mennonite Coun. for Lesbian, Gay,
   Bisexual and Transgender Interest [20050]
Brotherhood of Saint Andrew [19946]
Bros. and Sisters in Christ [19767]
Bruderhof Communities [20481]
Bur. of Catholic Indian Missions [19591]
Campus Crusade for Christ Intl. [19994]
Campus Ministry Women [19918]
Canon Law Soc. of Am. [19592]
Capuchin-Franciscans (Province of Saint Joseph)
   [19594]
Care Ministries [19532]
Catholic Acad. of Sciences in the U.S.A. [19919]
Catholic Campus Ministry Assn. [19595]
Catholic Church Extension Soc. of the U.S.A.
   [19596]
Catholic Homesteading Movement [11742]
Catholic Inst. of the Food Indus. [19598]
Catholic Kolping Soc. of Am. [19599]
Catholic League for Religious and Civil Rights
   [19600]
Catholic Negro-Amer. Mission Bd. [19601]
Catholic Network of Volunteer Ser. [19602]
Catholic Pamphlet Soc. of the U.S. [19603]
Catholic Traditionalist Movement [19604]
Catholic War Veterans Auxiliary of the U.S.A.
   [21194]
Catholic War Veterans of the U.S.A. [21290]
Catholics Speak Out [19605]
Catholics United for the Faith [19606]
CBM Ministries [19995]
Center for Applied Res. in the Apostolate [19608]
Center for Christian/Jewish Understanding of
   Sacred Heart Univ. [19888]
Center for the Evangelical United Brethren
   Heritage [19976]
Center for the Ministry of Teaching [19920]
Central Assn. of the Miraculous Medal [19609]
Central Bur., Catholic Central Union of Am.
   [19610]
Champions for Life Intl. [19996]
Child Evangelism Fellowship [19997]
Children's Cross Connection Intl. [11552]
Children's HopeChest [11578]
Chinese Christian Mission [20313]
Choristers Guild [20426]

Christ in Action Ministries [19999]
Christ for the Nations [20314]
Christ Truth Ministries [19514]
Christian Aid Mission [20316]
Christian Anti-Communism Crusade [16991]
Christian Anti-Defamation League [17102]
Christian Boaters Assn. [20000]
Christian Bowhunters of Am. [23051]
Christian Bus. Men's Comm. [19771]
Christian Century Found. [19772]
Christian Chaplain Sers. [19745]
Christian Chiropractors Assn. [19773]
Christian Comic Arts Soc. [9435]
Christian Communications, Inc. [19774]
Christian Community Development Assn. [20278]
Christian Connections for Intl. Hea. [14551]
Christian Defense League [19775]
Christian Educators Assn. Intl. [19922]
Christian Educators Fellowship of the United
   Methodist Church [19923]
Christian Family Renewal [19776]
Christian Fencers Assn. [23400]
Christian Forum Res. Found. [20560]
Christian Freedom Intl. [20521]
Christian Friends of Israel - USA [19777]
Christian Golfers' Assn. [23283]
Christian Holiness Partnership [19779]
Christian Labor Assn. of the U.S.A. [24035]
Christian Literacy Associates [8788]
Christian Literature and Bible Center [20317]
Christian Mgt. Assn. [20511]
Christian Media Assn. [20237]
Christian Medical and Dental Associations [20238]
Christian Military Fellowship [19782]
Christian Missionary Fellowship [20319]
Christian Motorcyclists Assn. [22674]
Christian Orthopaedic Partners [15765]
Christian Res. [19784]
Christian Res. Inst. [19785]
Christian Ser. Club [19515]
Christian Small Publishers Assn. [3217]
Christian Stewardship Assn. [20512]
Christian Tattoo Assn. [20590]
Christian TV Mission [19536]
Christian Vegetarian Assn. [20611]
Christians in Crisis [20555]
Christians in Govt. [19516]
Christians Helping Animals and People [19456]
Christians for Peace in El Salvador [20322]
The Christophers [19611]
Church Army [19947]
Church of the Brethren Gen. Bd. Global Mission
   Partnership [19535]
Church Growth Inc. [20536]
Church Music Assn. of Am. [20428]
Church Music Publishers Assn. [20429]
Church Periodical Club [19949]
Church Women United [20618]
Churches Uniting in Christ [19889]
Claretian Volunteers and Lay Missionaries
   [19612]
Collegians Activated to Liberate Life [12911]
Commn. of the Churches on Intl. Affairs [20094]
Comm. on Missionary Evangelism [20001]
Comm. on Social Development and World Peace
   of the U.S. Catholic Conf. [19613]
Commun. Commn. [19537]
Community of Celebration [19790]
Company of Saint Paul [19614]
Concordia Deaconess Conf. [20213]
Concordia Gospel Outreach [20214]
Concordia Historical Inst. [20215]
Conf. on Faith and History [20079]
Confessing Synod Ministries [20561]
Confraternity of the Blessed Sacrament [19951]
Congregation of the Blessed Sacrament [19617]
Congregation of Sisters of Saint Agnes [19618]
Connecting Church Assn. [19846]
Conservative Baptist Assn. of Am. [19485]
Continental Baptist Missions [19486]
CORPUS - Natl. Assn. for an Inclusive Priesthood
   [19619]
Coun. of Christian Scholarly Societies [8085]
Covenant World Relief [12848]
Cowboys for Christ [19792]

A star before a book entry number signifies that the name is not listed separately, but is mentioned within the entry.

Creation Res. Soc. [20548]
Crossworld [20326]
Crusaders for Christ [20462]
CSB Ministries [20640]
CUSA: An Apostolate of the Sick and Disabled [19620]
Dawn Bible Students Assn. [19517]
Dignity/USA [20053]
Disciples Ecumenical Consultative Coun. [19848]
Disciples Justice Action Network [19793]
Divine Sci. Fed. Intl. [19880]
Division of Higher Educ., Christian Church-Disciples of Christ [19854]
Dominican Mission Found. [20328]
Dynamic Youth Ministries [19831]
EAPE/Campolo Ministries - Evangelical Assn. for the Promotion of Educ. [20330]
Ecumenical Theological Seminary [19924]
Edith Stein Guild [19621]
Emergency Relief Response Fund [20562]
Episcopal Church Building Fund [19952]
Equestrian Ministries Intl. [20082]
Evangelical Church Alliance [19977]
Evangelical Coun. for Financial Accountability [20002]
Evangelical and Ecumenical Women's Caucus [19978]
Evangelical Free Church of Am. - Intl. Mission [20333]
Evangelical Friends Intl. - North Amer. Region [20040]
Evangelical Missiological Soc. [20334]
Evangelical Press Assn. [20004]
Evangelical and Reformed Historical Soc. [20607]
Evangelical Social Action Commn. [20005]
Evangelical Theological Soc. [19980]
Evangelical Training Assn. [19925]
Evangelicals Concerned [20054]
Evangelism and Home Missions Assn. [20006]
Evangelistic Faith Missions [20336]
Faith Alive [19957]
Faith at Work [19893]
FaithWorks Intl. [11777]
Family Rosary [19622]
Fed. of Protestant Welfare Agencies [20482]
Fellowship of Amer. Baptist Musicians [20430]
Fellowship of Christian Airline Personnel [20007]
Fellowship of Christian Athletes [20008]
Fellowship of Christian Magicians [19797]
Fellowship of Christian Peace Officers - U.S.A. [19798]
Fellowship of Christian Released Time Ministries [19926]
Fellowship of Concerned Churchmen [19454]
Fellowship of Saint James [19800]
Fellowship of United Methodists in Music and Worship Arts [20261]
Focolare Movement [19624]
Focus on the Chinese Family [20496]
Forum for Scriptural Christianity [20262]
Forward in Faith North Am. [19959]
Found. for Christian Theology [19960]
Found. for Traditional Values [18505]
Foundations and Donors Interested in Catholic Activities [19625]
Friends of Israel Gospel Ministry [20010]
Friends of Old St. Ferdinand [19626]
Friends of Sabeel - North Am. [18205]
Full Gospel Bus. Men's Fellowship Intl. [19801]
Gen. Assn. of Regular Baptist Churches [19489]
Gen. Bd. of Church and Soc. of the United Methodist Church [20263]
The Gideons Intl. [20011]
Glenmary Res. Center [19628]
Global MissionAir [20487]
Good Tidings [19629]
Grailville [19630]
Graymoor Ecumenical and Interreligious Inst. [19895]
Greek Orthodox Ladies Philoptochos Soc. [20071]
Guild of Catholic Lawyers [19631]
Hagiography Soc. [20526]
Healers League of the Natl. Spiritualist Assn. of Churches [20449]
Hea. Ministries [20241]

High School Evangelism Fellowship [20013]
Hindustan Bible Inst. [19927]
Historical Soc. of the Episcopal Church [19962]
HMI Ministries [20597]
Holy Childhood Assn. [19632]
Holy Cross Foreign Mission Soc. [19633]
Holy Shroud Guild [19635]
Home School Sports Network [23490]
Human Development Rsrc. Coun. [12913]
Hymn Soc. in the U.S. and Canada [20432]
IFCA Intl. [19849]
Independent Bd. for Presbyterian Foreign Missions [20467]
Inst. of Apostolic Oblates [19638]
Inst. for Biblical Res. [19519]
Inst. on Religious Life [19639]
Integrity [20058]
Interact Ministries [20348]
The Interchurch Center [19896]
Interchurch Medical Assistance [20242]
Intercristo [19804]
Interdisciplinary Biblical Res. Inst. [19928]
Intl. Assn. of Biblical Counselors [19867]
Intl. Assn. of Christian Chaplains [19748]
Intl. Assn. of Women Ministers [20619]
Intl. Bible Soc. [19520]
Intl. Bible Students Assn. [19521]
Intl. Catholic Deaf Assn. - U.S. Sect. [19641]
Intl. Christian Media Commn. [19538]
Intl. Christian Stud. Assn. [19806]
Intl. Conf. of Police Chaplains [19749]
Intl. Convention of Faith Ministries [19807]
Intl. Cops for Christ [19808]
Intl. Coun. of Christian Churches [20015]
Intl. Coun. of Community Churches [19850]
Intl. Coun. of Iranian Christians [19809]
Intl. Disciples Women's Ministries [20620]
Intl. Lutheran Deaf Assn. [20217]
Intl. Lutheran Laymen's League [20218]
Intl. Network of Children's Ministry [19758]
Intl. Order of the King's Daughters and Sons [19810]
Intl. Order of St. Vincent [19963]
Intl. Police and Fire Chaplain's Assn. [19750]
Intl. Soc. of Bible Collectors [19523]
Intl. Students, Inc. [20017]
InterServe U.S.A. [20351]
Interweave Continental (Unitarian Universalists for Lesbian, Gay, Bisexual and Transgender Concerns) [20059]
Japan Intl. Christian Univ. Found. [19929]
Jerry B. Jenkins Christian Writers Guild [20630]
Jesuit Conf. [19643]
Jesuit Volunteer Corps: Northwest [19644]
John La Farge Inst. [19645]
Koinonia Found. [19899]
Kristana Esperantista Ligo Internacia [19812]
Latin Am. Mission [20353]
Latin Liturgy Assn. [19646]
Lay Carmelite Order of the Blessed Virgin Mary of Mount Carmel [19647]
Lay Mission-Helpers Assn. [19648]
Laymen's Home Missionary Movement [20018]
Leadership Conf. of Women Religious [19649]
League of St. Dymphna [19650]
League of Tarcisians [19651]
Legatus [19652]
Liberal Religious Educators Assn. [20599]
Life Action Revival Ministries [20020]
Life Outreach Intl. [20021]
Lithuanian Catholic Religious Aid [19653]
Little Flower Mission League [19654]
Liturgical Conf. [19900]
Living Church Found. [19964]
Lollard Soc. [20524]
Lord's Day Alliance of the U.S. [20544]
Louis Finkelstein Inst. for Religious and Social Stud. at the Louis Stein Center [19931]
Luis Palau Assn. [20022]
Lutheran Bible Translators [19524]
Lutheran Deaconess Assn. [20219]
Lutheran Deaconess Conf. [20220]
Lutheran Historical Conf. [20222]
Lutheran Human Relations Assn. [20223]
Lutheran Mission Societies [20225]

Lutheran Student Movement - U.S.A. [20227]
Lutheran Volunteer Corps [20228]
Lutheran Women's Missionary League [20229]
Lutherans Concerned/North Am. [20061]
Macedonian Orthodox Youth Assn. of North Am. [19883]
The Mailbox Club [19525]
MAP Intl. [20243]
Mariological Soc. of Am. [19656]
Maryheart Crusaders [19657]
Maryknoll Fathers and Bros. [19658]
Master's Men of the Natl. Assn. of Free Will Baptists [19490]
Media Associates Intl. [19981]
Medical Missions Response [20246]
Men of the Sacred Heart [19659]
Methodist Fed. for Social Action [20264]
Metropolitan Community Churches [20062]
Military Chaplains Assn. of the U.S.A. [19752]
Mission Builders Intl. [19814]
Mission to the World [20468]
Missionary Gospel Fellowship [20363]
Missionary Sisters of St. Peter Claver [20364]
Missionary Soc. of Saint Paul the Apostle [19663]
Missionary TECH Team [20366]
Missions Door [19491]
Missions Intl. [20037]
MOMS in Touch Intl. [20621]
More Light Presbyterians for Lesbian, Gay, Bisexual and Transgender Concerns [20063]
Morris Cerullo World Evangelism [20025]
Narramore Christian Found. [19815]
Natl. Apostolate for Inclusion Ministry [20026]
Natl. Assn. of Catholic Family Life Ministers [20288]
Natl. Assn. of Catholic Homes and Educators [8057]
Natl. Assn. of Christian Financial Consultants [1465]
Natl. Assn. of Church Bus. Admin. [20513]
Natl. Assn. of Church Facilities Managers [20514]
Natl. Assn. of Church Personnel Administrators [20515]
Natl. Assn. of Ecumenical and Interreligious Staff [19902]
Natl. Assn. of Evangelicals [19982]
Natl. Assn. of Hispanic Priests of the USA [19665]
Natl. Assn. of Parish Catechetical Directors [19932]
Natl. Assn. of Priest Pilots [19667]
Natl. Assn. of State Catholic Conf. Directors [19668]
Natl. Assn. for Treasurers of Religious Institutes [20516]
Natl. Baptist Convention, U.S.A. [19493]
Natl. Bible Assn. [20205]
Natl. Black Catholic Clergy Caucus [19669]
Natl. Black Sisters' Conf. [19671]
Natl. Campus Ministry Assn. [19933]
Natl. Cathedral Assn. [19903]
Natl. Catholic Conf. for Total Stewardship [19673]
Natl. Catholic Off. for the Deaf [19675]
Natl. Catholic Rural Life Conf. [19677]
Natl. Catholic Women's Union [19678]
Natl. Christ Child Soc. [19679]
Natl. Christian Barrel Racers Assn. [23507]
Natl. Christian Forensics and Communications Assn. [8521]
Natl. Christian Life Community of the U.S.A. [19680]
Natl. Church Conf. of the Blind [13380]
Natl. Coalition of Men's Ministries [19816]
Natl. Comm. of Catholic Laymen [19681]
Natl. Conf. for Community and Justice [19904]
Natl. Conf. of Diocesan Vocation Directors [19682]
Natl. Coun. of Bishops, USA [19683]
Natl. Coun. of Catholic Women [19684]
Natl. Coun. of Churches of Christ in the U.S.A. [19905]
Natl. Coun. of Churches, Educ. and Leadership Ministries Commn. [19935]
Natl. Coun. On Bible Curriculum In Public Schools [9052]
Natl. Cursillo Movement [19685]

Reference to "IO" in place of a book number signifies that the association may be found in the 45th edition of International Organizations.

Natl. Enthronement Center [19686]
Natl. Evangelization Teams [19687]
Natl. Fed. of Asian-Amer. United Methodists [20266]
Natl. Fed. of Priests' Councils [19689]
Natl. Forum of Greek Orthodox Church Musicians [20434]
Natl. Ghost Ranch Found. [20469]
Natl. Guild of Churchmen [19965]
Natl. Lutheran Outdoors Ministry Assn. [20231]
Natl. Off. for Black Catholics [19691]
Natl. Org. for Continuing Educ. of Roman Catholic Clergy [19936]
Natl. Religious Affairs Assn. [19872]
Natl. Religious Broadcasters [19539]
Natl. Religious Partnership for the Env. [19941]
Natl. Religious Vocation Conf. [19692]
Natl. Ser. Committee/Chariscenter USA [19693]
Natl. Shrine of St. Elizabeth Ann Seton [19694]
Natl. United Church Ushers Assn. of Am. [20609]
The Navigators [19817]
Neighborhood Bible Stud. [19526]
Night Adoration in the Home [19695]
Nocturnal Adoration Soc. [19696]
Non-Denominational Bible Prophecy Stud. Assn. [19528]
North Amer. Acad. of Ecumenists [19906]
North Amer. Assn. for the Catechumenate [19697]
North Amer. Assn. for the Diaconate [19967]
North Amer. Coalition for Christianity and Ecology [4517]
North Amer. Forum on the Catechumenate [19698]
ORACLE Religious Assn. [20070]
Order of Saint Andrew the Apostle [20073]
Orthodox Christians for Life [20478]
Orthodox Theological Soc. in Am. [19885]
Pan Amer. Coun. for the Preservation of the Hellenic Orthodox Church and the Hellenic Language [20074]
Paraclete [20381]
Paulist Memorial Soc. [19699]
Paulist Natl. Catholic Evangelization Assn. [19700]
Peale Center for Christian Living [19825]
Personal Freedom Outreach [19875]
Peyote Way Church of God [20447]
Pilots for Christ Intl. [20028]
Pioneer Clubs [20642]
Pious Union of Prayer [19701]
Pocket Testament League [19529]
Pontifical Mission Societies in the U.S. [19703]
Prayers for Life [19907]
Praying Hands Ranches [23360]
Presbyterian Assn. of Musicians [20435]
Presbyterian Church Bus. Administrators' Assn. [20470]
Presbyterian Evangelistic Fellowship [20471]
Presbyterian Lay Comm. [20472]
Presbyterian Men [20473]
Presbyterian-Reformed Ministries Intl. [20474]
Presbyterian Women [20475]
Presidential Prayer Team [20210]
Pro Athletes Outreach [20029]
Pro Maria Comm. [19704]
Pro Sanctity Movement [19705]
Progressive, Radically Inclusive Student Ministry [19938]
Promise Keepers [19834]
Religious Bros. Conf. [19707]
Reparation Soc. of the Immaculate Heart of Mary [19709]
Response-Ability [20386]
Revival Fires (Christian Evangelizers Assn.) [20031]
Rosedale Mennonite Missions [20253]
Rosicrucian Fellowship [20541]
Sacred Heart League [19711]
St. Ansgar's Scandinavian Catholic League [19712]
St. Anthony's Guild [20388]
St. Jude League [19713]
St. Martin De Porres Guild [20389]
Saint Photios Found. [20075]
St. Thomas Aquinas Found. [19714]

Saints Alive in Jesus [20032]
Samaritans Intl. [20392]
Seafarers and Intl. House [20232]
Seamen's Church Inst. of New York and New Jersey [19970]
SEARCH Found. [6454]
Searching Together Educational Ministries [19909]
Secretariat for Catholic-Jewish Relations [19910]
Secular Inst. of Saint Francis de Sales [19716]
Serra Intl. [19717]
Seventh Day Baptist Gen. Conf. [19494]
Seventh Day Baptist Gen. Conf. of the U.S. and Canada [20545]
Seventh Day Baptist Historical Soc. [19495]
Seventh Day Baptist Missionary Soc. [19496]
Seventh Day Baptist World Fed. [19497]
Sharing of Ministries Abroad U.S.A. [20393]
Skinner Leadership Inst. [20033]
Slavic Gospel Assn. [20395]
Soc. of African Missions [19719]
Soc. of Biblical Literature [19530]
Soc. of the Companions of the Holy Cross [19971]
Soc. of the Descendants of the Colonial Clergy [20760]
Soc. for Hindu-Christian Stud. [20528]
Soc. of Missionaries of Africa [19721]
Soc. of Our Lady of the Most Holy Trinity [19722]
Soc. for Promoting and Encouraging Arts and Knowledge of the Church [19972]
Soc. of Saint Stephen [20523]
Soc. for the Stud. of Christian Spirituality [19826]
Soc. of Traditional Roman Catholics [19726]
South Amer. Missionary Soc. - USA [20398]
Southern Baptist Found. [19498]
Southern Baptist Historical Lib. and Archives [19499]
Standing Commn. on Ecumenical Relations of the Episcopal Church [19974]
Standing Conf. of the Canonical Orthodox Bishops in the Americas [19886]
STEER [20401]
Teen Challenge Intl. [20643]
Teen Missions Intl. [20402]
Theosophical Book Assn. for the Blind [20592]
Third Order of Mary/Marists [19728]
Toward Tradition [20508]
Truckers for Christ [19828]
Truth Missionaries Chap. of Positive Accord [20585]
Tyndale Soc. [20530]
Unitarian Universalist Christian Fellowship [20600]
Unitarian Universalist Historical Soc. [20601]
Unitarian Universalist Ministers Assn. [20602]
Unitarian Universalist Musicians' Network [20436]
Unitarian Universalist Ser. Comm. [20603]
Unitarian Universalist Women's Fed. [20604]
United Christian Missionary Soc. [19856]
United Church of Christ Coalition for Lesbian, Gay, Bisexual and Transgender Concerns [20067]
United Church of Christ Justice and Witness Ministries [20608]
United Methodist Comm. on Relief [20267]
United Methodist Youth Org. [20268]
United Sisters of Charity [20406]
U.S. Assn. of Consecrated Virgins [19733]
U.S. Conf. of Catholic Bishops [19735]
Urantia Found. [20587]
Ursuline Companions in Mission [20408]
Volunteer Missionary Movement - U.S. Off. [19736]
The Way Intl. [20411]
We Believe! [19738]
We Care Am. [13210]
WEC Intl. [20034]
Wheels for the World [11994]
William H. Whitsitt Baptist Heritage Soc. [19500]
Woman's Home and Foreign Mission Soc. [19443]
Woman's Missionary Union, SBC [19501]
Women for Faith and Family [19739]
Women and Men Against Sexual Harassment and Other Abuses [13088]
Women Nationally Active for Christ [19502]

Women's Ordination Conf. [19740]
World Evangelical Alliance [19983]
World Fellowship of Slavic Evangelical Christians [19984]
World Impact [20414]
World Literature Ministries [19832]
World Medical Mission [20245]
World Methodist Coun. [20272]
World Methodist Historical Soc. [20273]
World Mission Prayer League [20234]
World Team [20417]
World Vision [20488]
World's Christian Endeavor Union [19829]
WorldVenture [19503]
Wycliffe Bible Translators [19531]
Xaverian Missionaries of the U.S. [20421]
Young Life [20644]
Youth for Christ/U.S.A. [20645]
Youth Evangelism Assn. [20036]
Youth Ministry [20235]
Christianity and Ecology; North Amer. Coalition for [4517]
Christianity; Forum for Scriptural [20262]
Christianity and Literature; Conf. on [8799]
Christians Abroad [IO], London, United Kingdom
Christians Afloat [★20000]
Christians Afloat [★20000]
Christians Afloat - Address unknown since 2003.
Christians in Am; Fellowship of Orthodox [20542]
Christians in the Arts, Media and Entertainment; Fellowship of [★20024]
Christians in the Arts Networking - Address unknown since 2002.
Christians Assoc. for Relationships with Eastern Europe [IO], Ancaster, ON, Canada
Christians Concerned for Israel [★IO]
Christians Concerned for Israel [★17939]
Christians in Crisis [20555], PO Box 293627, Sacramento, CA 95829, (916)682-0376
Christians in Futures - Defunct.
Christians in Govt. [19516]
Christians Helping Animals and People [19456], c/o Rev. Frances Arnetta, PO Box 272, Selden, NY 11784, (631)732-3138
Christians' Israel Public Action Campaign [17936], PO Box 18173, Washington, DC 20036-8173, (202)234-3600
Christians' Israel Public Action Campaign [IO], Washington, DC, United States
Christians and Jews; Natl. Conf. of [★19904]
Christians for Latin Amer. Study and Solidarity - Defunct.
Christians for Life; Orthodox [20478]
Christians for Peace - Defunct.
Christians for Peace in El Salvador [20322], 2 Lexington St., East Boston, MA 02128, (617)567-2900
Christians in Social Work; Natl. Assn. of [★13208]
Christians in Social Work; North Amer. Assn. of [13208]
Christians for Socialism in the U.S. - Address unknown since 1988.
Christians United for Responsible Entertainment - Address unknown since 1995.
Christians in the Visual Arts [9563], 255 Grapevine Rd., Wenham, MA 01984-1813, (978)867-4124
Christians in Visual Arts [★9563]
Christic Inst. - Defunct.
Christie Intl. Fan Club; Lou [24941]
Christina Noble Children's Found. - Vietnam [IO], Ho Chi Minh City, Vietnam
Christine Jones and Friends - Defunct.
Christlich Demokratische Union [★IO]
Christlich-Demokratische Volkspartei der Schweiz [★IO]
Christliche Europaische Arbeitsgemeinschaft fur Visuelle Medien [★IO]
Christlicher Friedensdienst e.V. [★IO]
Christmas in April - U.S.A. [★12337]
Christmas in April - U.S.A; Rebuilding Together with [★12337]
Christmas Past; Golden Glow of [22975]
Christmas Philatelic Club [22804], 312 Northwood Dr., Lexington, KY 40505-2104
Christmas Seal and Charity Stamp Soc. [21993], c/o Florence H. Wright, Sec.-Treas., PO Box 18615, Rochester, NY 14618-0615

A star before a book entry number signifies that the name is not listed separately, but is mentioned within the entry.

Christmas Seal and Charity Stamp Soc. [IO], Rochester, NY, United States
Christmas Study Unit - Defunct.
Christmas Tree Assn; Natl. [5261]
Christmas Tree Assn; Pacific Northwest [3947]
Christoffel-Blindenmission [★IO]
Christoffel Blindenmission [★IO]
Christopher Columbus Philatelic Soc. [22805], c/o Leslie Seff, 3750 Hudson Manor, Terr. E, Falls Church, VA 22042-3912
Christopher and Dana Reeve Found. [16463], 636 Morris Tpke., Ste. 3A, Short Hills, NJ 07078, (973)379-2690
Christopher Morley Knothole Assn. [9643], c/o Bryant Lib., 2 Paper Mill Rd., Roslyn, NY 11576
Christopher Reeve Found. [★16463]
Christopher Reeve Paralysis Found. [★16463]
Christopher St. Liberation Day Comm. [★12233]
The Christophers [19611], 5 Hanover Sq., 11th Fl., New York, NY 10004, (212)759-4050
Christos Stelios Ioannou Found. [IO], Nicosia, Cyprus
Christ's Ser; Roving Volunteers in [23017]
Chromatographic Soc. [IO], Glasgow, United Kingdom
Chromatosis Soc; Amer. Hemo [14543]
Chrome Card Collectors Club [★22905]
Chromopathy
 Chromosome 18 Registry and Res. Soc. [14444]
 Dinshah Hea. Soc. [13631]
Chromosome 9P Network [14443], PO Box 54, Stanley, ID 83278-0054, (435)574-1121
Chromosome 9P Network [IO], Stanley, ID, United States
Chromosome 16 Found; Disorders of [14449]
Chromosome 18 Registry and Res. Soc. [14444], 7155 Oakridge Dr., San Antonio, TX 78229, (210)657-4968
Chromosome 18 Registry and Res. Soc. [IO], San Antonio, TX, United States
Chromosome Deletion Outreach [IO], Boca Raton, FL, United States
Chromosome Deletion Outreach [14445], PO Box 724, Boca Raton, FL 33429-0724, (561)395-4252
Chronic Disorganization; Natl. Study Group on [1979]
Chronic Epstein-Barr Virus Assn; Natl. [★14278]
Chronic Fatigue Immune Dysfunction
 CFIDS Assn. of Am. [14256]
 Chronic Syndrome Support Assn. [14259]
 Fibromyalgia Network [14396]
 Natl. Fibromyalgia Partnership [14398]
Chronic Fatigue Immune Dysfunction Syndrome (CFIDS) Activation Network - Address unknown since 2004.
Chronic Fatigue Syndrome; Amer. Assn. for [★14266]
Chronic Fatigue Syndrome Assn; Natl. [★14278]
Chronic Fatigue Syndrome and Fibromyalgia Assn; Natl. [14278]
Chronic Fatigue Syndrome, Fibromyalgia, and Orthostatic Intolerance; Pediatric Network for [15895]
Chronic Fatigue Syndrome; Intl. Assn. for [14266]
Chronic Fatigue Syndrome Soc., Intl. - Address unknown since 1994.
Chronic Granulomatous Disease Assn. [14258], c/o Mary Hurley, Pres., 2616 Monterey Rd., San Marino, CA 91108-1646, (626)441-4118
Chronic Granulomatous Disease Association [IO], San Marino, CA, United States
Chronic Lymphocytic Leukaemia Support Assn. [IO], Romsey, United Kingdom
Chronic Pain Assn; Amer. [15834]
Chronic Pain Assn. of Canada [IO], Edmonton, AB, Canada
Chronic Pain Outreach Assn; Natl. [15844]
Chronic Pain Support Gp. [15839], c/o Andrea R. Kramer, Facilitator, Shady Grove Hosp., Maple Rm., 9901 Medical Center Dr., Rockville, MD 20850, (301)670-0134
Chronic Syndrome Support Assn. [14259], 801 Riverside Dr., Lumberton, NC 28358-4625
Chronically Ill Kids; Natl. Org. for [★11638]
Chrysalis - Defunct.
Chrysanthemum Soc; Natl. [22526]

Chrysler
 Airflow Club of Am. [21563]
 Christian Motorsports Ministries [21610]
 Chrysler 300 Club Intl. [21611]
 Chrysler Town and Country Owners Registry [21612]
 Mopar Scat Pack Club [21715]
 Plymouth Barracuda/Cuda Owners Club [21763]
 Plymouth Owners Club [21764]
 Slant 6 Club of Am. [21784]
 United Mopar Club [21806]
 WPC Club [21822]
Chrysler 300 Club [★21611]
Chrysler 300 Club [★IO]
Chrysler 300 Club Intl. [IO], Jonesville, MI, United States
Chrysler 300 Club Intl. [21611], 4900 Jonesville Rd., Jonesville, MI 49250, (517)849-2783
Chrysler Car Club Coun. - Address unknown since 1989.
Chrysler Power [★21610]
Chrysler Power [★IO]
Chrysler Products Owners Club - Address unknown since 2001.
Chrysler Town and Country Owners Registry [21612], c/o John Slusar, Ed., 6 S 40 St., Milwaukee, WI 53215, (414)384-1843
Chrysler Town and Country Owners Registry [IO], West Allis, WI, United States
Chrysotile Inst. [IO], Montreal, QC, Canada
C.H.U.C.K. - Defunct.
Chuck Jennings Fan Club - Defunct.
Chuck Negron Fan Club [24863], PO Box 1562, Concord, NH 03302-1562
Chuck Norris Intl. Fan Club - Address unknown since 1999.
Chud Rodo Saigai Boshi Kyokai [★IO]
CHUMS, Inc. - Address unknown since 1999.
Chung Nip Hwe Gwan [★IO]
Church Alliance; Evangelical [19977]
Church Appeal; United Black [16947]
Church Army [19947], 210 W North Ave., Pittsburgh, PA 15212-4625, (412)231-5442
Church Army in Canada [IO], St. John, NB, Canada
Church Army Soc. [★19947]
Church Assn; Missionary [★20362]
Church; Assn. for the Rights of Catholics in the [19578]
Church Assn. for Seamen's Work [★19970]
Church Benefits Assn. [20461], 15000 Commerce Pkwy., Ste. C, Mount Laurel, NJ 08054, (856)439-0500
Church of the Brethren Gen. Bd. Global Mission Partnership [19535], 1451 Dundee Ave., Elgin, IL 60120, (847)742-5100
Church of the Brethren Gen. Bd. World Ministries Commn. [★19535]
Church of the Brethren Homes and Hospitals Assn. [★11276]
Church; Brotherhood of the Amer. Lutheran [★20224]
Church Building Fund Commn; Amer. [★19952]
Church Building Fund; Episcopal [19952]
Church Bus. Admin; Natl. Assn. of [20513]
Church Bus. Administrators; Natl. Assn. of [★20513]
Church Center; The Inter [19896]
Church of Christ Coalition for Lesbian, Gay, Bisexual and Transgender Concerns; United [20067]
Church of Christ; Coun. for Hea. and Human Services Ministries, United [13165]
Church of Christ; Coun. for Hea. and Welfare Services, United [★13165]
Church of Christ; Evangelical and Reformed Historical Soc., United [★20607]
Church of Christ Gay Caucus; United [★20067]
Church of Christ Ministers for Racial and Social Justice; United [★20608]
Church Coalition; Women in the [★20624]
Church Comm. for Human Rights in Asia - Defunct.
Church; Concerned Clergy and Laity of the Episcopal [19950]
Church Conf. of the Blind; Natl. [13380]
Church Convergence; Women [20624]
Church Coun; Men of the [★20473]
Church (Disciples of Christ); Social and Hea. Services of the Christian [★13177]

Church of England Record Soc. [IO], London, United Kingdom
Church Executive Development Bd. - Address unknown since 1995.
Church Extension Soc. of the U.S.A; Catholic [19596]
Church Food Ser; Natl. Assn. of [1587]
Church Found; Living [19964]
Church Furniture Mfrs. Assn. - Defunct.
Church of God
 Assn. of Life-Giving Churches [19843]
 Women of the Church of God [19835]
Church of God, Men Intl. - Address unknown since 1995.
Church of God; Natl. Woman's Missionary Soc. of the [★19835]
Church of God Peace Fellowship - Defunct.
Church of God; Peyote Way [20447]
Church of God World Missions [20323], 2490 Keith St., PO Box 8016, Cleveland, TN 37320-8016, (423)478-7190
Church of God World Missions [IO], Cleveland, TN, United States
Church Goods Assn; Natl. [3374]
Church Growth Center [20279]
Church Growth Inc. [20536], PO Box 541, Monrovia, CA 91017-0541, (800)844-9286
Church Growth; Inst. for Amer. [★20536]
Church and the Hellenic Language; Pan Amer. Coun. for the Preservation of the Hellenic Orthodox [20074]
Church; Historical Comm. of the Mennonite [★20248]
Church Historical Soc. [★19962]
Church; Historical Soc. of the Evangelical and Reformed [★20607]
Church; Historical Soc. of the United Methodist [10113]
Church History; Amer. Soc. of [20078]
Church Inst. of New York and New Jersey; Seamen's [19970]
Church Inst. of New York; Seaman's [★19970]
Church and Institutional Financing Organizations; Natl. Assn. of [2426]
Church of Jesus Christ of Latter-day Saints; Genealogical Soc. of the [★21115]
Church of Jesus Christ of Latter-Day Saints; Young Women of the [20209]
Church League of America - Defunct.
Church Lib. Assn; Evangelical [10355]
Church Lib. Assn; Lutheran [★10375]
Church Literature Found. [★19964]
Church; Master's Men of the Free Will Baptist [★19490]
Church Men; Amer. Lutheran [★20224]
Church Mission; Evangelical Free [★20333]
Church Mission Soc. [IO], London, United Kingdom
Church Missionary Community; Episcopal [★20375]
Church Missionary Soc. [★IO]
Church Missions Committees; Assn. of [★20293]
Church of Monday Night Football - Address unknown since 2001.
Church Monuments Soc. [IO], London, United Kingdom
Church Movement; Unity Fellowship [20068]
Church Music Assn. of Am. [20428], c/o Dr. Kurt Poterack, Ed., Christendom Coll., 134 Christendom Dr., Front Royal, VA 22630, (540)636-2900
Church Music; Joint Commn. on [★19973]
Church Music Publishers Assn. [20429], PO Box 158992, Nashville, TN 37215, (615)791-0273
Church Music; Standing Commn. on [19973]
Church Musicians; Natl. Forum of Greek Orthodox [20434]
Church; Natl. Assn. of Schools, Colleges and Universities of the United Methodist [8879]
Church; Natl. Benevolent Assn. of the Christian [13177]
Church in Need; Aid to the [19563]
Church-Owned Publishers Assn; Protestant [3249]
Church and Peace [IO], Schoeffengrund, Germany
Church Peace Union [★IO]
Church Peace Union [★20093]
Church Pension Fund [19948], 445 Fifth Ave., New York, NY 10016, (212)592-1800

Reference to "IO" in place of a book number signifies that the association may be found in the 45th edition of International Organizations.

Church Pensions Conf. [★20461]
Church Periodical Club [19949], 815 2nd Ave., New York, NY 10017-4594, (212)716-6130
Church Personnel Administrators; Natl. Assn. of [20515]
Church Planting Intl. [20324], PO Box 836, Gainesville, GA 30503-0836, (770)535-7008
Church Planting Intl. [IO], Gainesville, GA, United States
Church Press; Assoc. [3205]
Church Proj. on U.S. Investments in Southern Africa [★17353]
Church Renewal; Black Methodists for [20260]
Church and School of Wicca [20613], PO Box 297, Hinton, WV 25951-0297, (304)466-2613
Church and School of Wicca [IO], Hinton, WV, United States
Church of Scientology of California - Defunct.
Church of Scotland Guild [IO], Edinburgh, United Kingdom
Church of Scotland Woman's Guild [★IO]
Church and Soc; Black Women in [20617]
Church Soc. for Coll. Work - Defunct.
Church and Soc. of the United Methodist Church; Gen. Bd. of [20263]
Church of Spiritual Discovery [20569]
Church and State
    Amer. Atheists [19463]
    Americans United for Separation of Church and State [19836]
    Atheists United [19465]
    Catholic Acad. of Sciences in the U.S.A. [19919]
    Comm. on Social Development and World Peace of the U.S. Catholic Conf. [19613]
    Fellowship of Christian Released Time Ministries [19926]
    Freedom From Religion Found. [19837]
    Interfaith Working Group [12887]
    Natl. League for the Separation of Church and State [19838]
Church and State; Natl. League for the Separation of [19838]
Church and State; Protestants and Other Americans United for Separation of [★19836]
Church and Sunday School Music Publishers Assn. [★20429]
Church of Sweden Mission [IO], Uppsala, Sweden
Church and Synagogue Librarians' Fellowship - Defunct.
Church and Synagogue Lib. Assn. [10348], 2920 SW Dolph Ct., Ste. 3A, Portland, OR 97219, (503)244-6919
Church, The Original Kleptonian; Neo-American [20456]
Church Union; Consultation on [★19889]
Church; United Missionary [★20362]
Church in the U.S; Historical Soc. of the Reformed [★20607]
Church Universal and Triumphant [19462], PO Box 5000, Gardiner, MT 59030-5000, (406)848-9500
Church (U.S.A.); Dept. of History and Records Mgt. Services of the Presbyterian [★10891]
Church Ushers Assn. of Am; Natl. United [20609]
Church Ushers Assn; Natl. United [★20609]
Church; Women of the [★20475]
Church Women of the Natl. Coun. of Churches; Dept. of United [★20618]
Church Women United [20618], 475 Riverside Dr., Ste. 1626a, New York, NY 10115, (212)870-2347
Church Women; United Coun. of [★20618]
Church Women United in the U.S.A. [★20618]
Church; Women's Missionary Coun. of the Christian Methodist Episcopal [20270]
Church Workers Among the Deaf; Conf. of [★19954]
Church World Literature Ministries; Christian Reformed [★19832]
Church World Ser. [12842], PO Box 968, Elkhart, IN 46515, (574)264-3102
Church World Ser. [IO], Elkhart, IN, United States
Church World Service Aids for the Horn of Africa - Defunct.
Church World Ser. Community Appeal [★12842]
Church World Ser. Community Appeal [★IO]
Church World Ser., Immigration and Refugee Prog. [IO], Elkhart, IN, United States

Church World Ser., Immigration and Refugee Prog. [18497], PO Box 968, Elkhart, IN 46515, (574)264-3102
Church World Ser. - Vietnam [IO], Hanoi, Vietnam
Church, World Witness; Associate Reformed Presbyterian [★20420]
Church Youth Org. of Am; Armenian [19458]
Churches
    ABW Ministries [19468]
    Acad. of Homiletics [20081]
    Acad. of Parish Clergy [20274]
    Adopt-A-Church Intl. [19839]
    Adopt-A-Church Intl. [IO]
    Adult Christian Educ. Found. [19913]
    Advancing Churches in Missions Commitment [20293]
    Adventist Community Services [20552]
    Affirmation/Gay and Lesbian Mormons [20046]
    Affirmation: United Methodists for Lesbian, Gay and Bisexual Concerns [20047]
    Africa Action [16918]
    Africa Faith and Justice Network [16920]
    Africa Inland Mission Intl. [20294]
    African Amer. Lutheran Assn. [20211]
    Aglow Intl. [20616]
    Aid to the Church in Need [19563]
    Alban Inst. [19840]
    All Roads Ministry [19564]
    All-Ukrainian Evangelical Baptist Fellowship [19469]
    Amer. Baptist Historical Soc. [19470]
    Amer. Baptist Homes and Hospitals Assn. [19471]
    Amer. Baptists Concerned [20048]
    Amer. Bd. of Examiners in Pastoral Counseling [19864]
    Amer. Clergy Leadership Conf. [19858]
    Amer. Coalition of Unregistered Churches [20520]
    Amer. Congregational Assn. [19859]
    Amer. Coun. of Christian Churches [19761]
    Amer. Ethical Union [20083]
    Amer. and Foreign Christian Union [19762]
    Amer. Forum for Jewish-Christian Cooperation [19887]
    Amer. Lutheran Publicity Bur. [20212]
    Amer. Missionary Fellowship [20296]
    Amer. Romanian Orthodox Youth [20540]
    Amer. Sci. Affiliation [20546]
    Amer. Soc. for Church Growth [19841]
    Amer. Soc. of Church History [20078]
    Amer. Soc. of Missiology [20297]
    Amer. Tract Soc. [19987]
    Americans United for Separation of Church and State [19836]
    AMG Intl. [20298]
    Anglican Assn. of Biblical Scholars [19449]
    Anglican Fellowship of Prayer [19452]
    Anglican Soc. [19942]
    Anglicans United [19943]
    Armenian Church Youth Org. of Am. [19458]
    Armenian Missionary Assn. of Am. [19459]
    Assembly of Episcopal Healthcare Chaplains [19944]
    Assoc. Comm. of Friends on Indian Affairs [20039]
    Assoc. Parishes for Liturgy and Mission [19945]
    Assn. of Anglican Musicians [20425]
    Assn. of Armenian Church Choirs of Am. [10559]
    Assn. of Brethren Caregivers [11276]
    Assn. of Christian Church Educators [19842]
    Assn. for Christian Ethics [19574]
    Assn. for Clinical Pastoral Educ. [19915]
    Assn. of Contemplative Sisters [20563]
    Assn. for the Development of Religious Info. Systems [20091]
    Assn. of Life-Giving Churches [19843]
    Assn. of North Amer. Missions [20301]
    Assn. of Professors of Mission [20302]
    Assn. of Reformed Baptist Churches of Am. [19473]
    Assn. for Religion and Intellectual Life [19916]
    Assn. for the Restoration of the Church and Home [19844]
    Assn. of State Baptist Papers [19475]
    Assn. of Unity Churches [19845]
    Awana Clubs Intl. [20639]

Baptist Joint Comm. for Religious Liberty [19479]
Baptist Mid-Missions [19480]
Baptist World Alliance [19482]
BCM Intl. [19508]
Bethany Intl. Missions [20304]
Bible Sabbath Assn. [20543]
Bibles For The World [20305]
Biblical Ministries Worldwide [19991]
Biblical Witness Fellowship [20606]
Billy Graham Evangelistic Assn. [19992]
Bishops' Comm. on the Liturgy [19585]
Bishops' Comm. on Priestly Formation [19917]
Bishops' Comm. on Vocations [19586]
Black and Indian Mission Off. [19587]
Black Women in Church and Soc. [20617]
Bread on the Waters [19993]
Brethren in Christ World Missions [20306]
Brethren/Mennonite Coun. for Lesbian, Gay, Bisexual and Transgender Interest [20050]
Brethren Peace Fellowship [19534]
Brotherhood of Saint Andrew [19946]
Bruderhof Communities [20481]
Campus Crusade for Christ Intl. [19994]
Campus Ministry Women [19918]
Catholic League for Religious and Civil Rights [19600]
Catholic Traditionalist Movement [19604]
Catholics Speak Out [19605]
Catholics United for the Faith [19606]
CBM Ministries [19995]
Center for Global Educ. [8662]
Center for New Community [17210]
Champions for Life Intl. [19996]
Child Evangelism Fellowship [19997]
Chinese Christian Mission [20313]
Choristers Guild [20426]
Christ in Action Ministries [19999]
Christ for the Nations [20314]
Christian Aid Mission [20316]
Christian Boaters Assn. [20000]
Christian Bus. Men's Comm. [19771]
Christian Century Found. [19772]
Christian Chaplain Sers. [19745]
Christian Chiropractors Assn. [19773]
Christian Communications, Inc. [19774]
Christian Defense League [19775]
Christian Educators Assn. Intl. [19922]
Christian Family Renewal [19776]
Christian Holiness Partnership [19779]
Christian Instrumentalists and Directors Assn. [20427]
Christian Literature and Bible Center [20317]
Christian Media Assn. [20237]
Christian Medical and Dental Associations [20238]
Christian Military Fellowship [19782]
Christian Missionary Fellowship [20319]
Christian Res. [19784]
Christian Res. Inst. [19785]
Christians in Crisis [20555]
Christians in Govt. [19516]
Church Army [19947]
Church Benefits Assn. [20461]
Church of England Record Soc. [IO]
Church Growth Center [20279]
Church Growth Inc. [20536]
Church Music Assn. of Am. [20428]
Church Music Publishers Assn. [20429]
Church Periodical Club [19949]
Church and Synagogue Lib. Assn. [10348]
Church Women United [20618]
Commn. of the Churches on Intl. Affairs [20094]
Comm. on Missionary Evangelism [20001]
Community of Celebration [19790]
Community for Religious Res. and Education [20537]
Concordia Gospel Outreach [20214]
Concordia Historical Inst. [20215]
Conf. for Catholic Lesbians [20051]
Conf. of Churches in Aotearoa New Zealand [IO]
Conf. on Faith and History [20079]
Confessing Synod Ministries [20561]
Confraternity of the Blessed Sacrament [19951]
Congregation of Sisters of Saint Agnes [19618]
Cong. of Natl. Black Churches [19890]
Connecting Church Assn. [19846]

A star before a book entry number signifies that the name is not listed separately, but is mentioned within the entry.

Conservative Baptist Assn. of Am. [19485]
CONTACT USA [19865]
Coun. of Churches of Malaysia [IO]
Coun. on Spiritual Practices [20564]
Covenant World Relief [12848]
Cowboys for Christ [19792]
Creation Health Found. [20547]
Crossworld [20326]
Crusaders for Christ [20462]
CSB Ministries [20640]
Dignity/USA [20053]
Disciple Nations Alliance [19847]
Disciples of Christ Historical Soc. [19853]
Disciples Ecumenical Consultative Coun. [19848]
Disciples Justice Action Network [19793]
Divine Sci. Fed. Intl. [19880]
Divine Sci. Ministers Assn. [19881]
Division of Higher Educ., Christian Church-
    Disciples of Christ [19854]
Dominican Mission Found. [20328]
Ecumenical Theological Seminary [19924]
Emergency Relief Response Fund [20562]
Episcopal Church Building Fund [19952]
Ethics and Religious Liberty Commn. of the
    Southern Baptist Convention [19487]
Evangelical Church Alliance [19977]
Evangelical Church Lib. Assn. [10355]
Evangelical Coun. for Financial Accountability
    [20002]
Evangelical and Ecumenical Women's Caucus
    [19978]
Evangelical Friends Intl. - North Amer. Region
    [20040]
Evangelical Missiological Soc. [20334]
Evangelical Press Assn. [20004]
Evangelical and Reformed Historical Soc. [20607]
Evangelical Social Action Commn. [20005]
Evangelical Theological Soc. [19980]
Evangelical Training Assn. [19925]
Evangelicals Concerned [20054]
Evangelism and Home Missions Assn. [20006]
Evangelistic Faith Missions [20336]
Faith Alive [19957]
Faith at Work [19893]
Family and Church History Dept. of the Church of
    Jesus Christ of Latter-Day Saints [21115]
Fed. of Protestant Welfare Agencies [20482]
Fellowship of Amer. Baptist Musicians [20430]
Fellowship of Christian Airline Personnel [20007]
Fellowship of Christian Magicians [19797]
Fellowship of Christian Peace Officers - U.S.A.
    [19798]
Fellowship of Christian Released Time Ministries
    [19926]
Fellowship of Concerned Churchmen [19454]
Fellowship Intl. Mission [20338]
Fellowship of Orthodox Christians in Am. [20542]
Fellowship in Prayer [19894]
Fellowship of Saint James [19800]
Fellowship of Saint Paul [19958]
Fellowship of United Methodists in Music and
    Worship Arts [20261]
Focolare Movement [19624]
Forum for Scriptural Christianity [20262]
Forward in Faith North Am. [19959]
Found. for Christian Theology [19960]
Found. for a Course in Miracles [20571]
Foundations and Donors Interested in Catholic
    Activities [19625]
Freedom From Religion Found. [19837]
Friends Comm. on Natl. Legislation [20041]
Friends Gen. Conf. [20042]
Friends Historical Assn. [20043]
Friends of Israel Gospel Ministry [20010]
Friends for Lesbian, Gay, Bisexual, Transgender,
    and Queer Concerns [20056]
Friends of Old St. Ferdinand [19626]
Full Gospel Bus. Men's Fellowship Intl. [19801]
Gen. Assn. of Regular Baptist Churches [19489]
The Gideons Intl. [20011]
Good Tidings [19629]
Graymoor Ecumenical and Interreligious Inst.
    [19895]
Greek Orthodox Ladies Philoptochos Soc. [20071]
Harvest [20280]

Healers League of the Natl. Spiritualist Assn. of
    Churches [20449]
Healing Waters Intl. [13410]
High School Evangelism Fellowship [20013]
Hindustan Bible Inst. [19927]
Historical Soc. of the Episcopal Church [19962]
Historical Soc. of the United Methodist Church
    [10113]
Hymn Soc. in the U.S. and Canada [20432]
IFCA Intl. [19849]
IFCA Intl. [IO]
Independent Bd. for Presbyterian Foreign Mis-
    sions [20467]
Independent Catholic Churches Intl. [20497]
Inst. on Religion in an Age of Sci. [20550]
Inst. on Religion and Democracy [17393]
Inst. of Singles Dynamics [20281]
Integrity [20058]
Interact Ministries [20348]
The Interchurch Center [19896]
Intercristo [19804]
Interdisciplinary Biblical Res. Inst. [19928]
Interfaith Church of Metaphysics [20573]
Intl. Assn. of Women Ministers [20619]
Intl. Bd. of Jewish Missions [20014]
Intl. Christian Media Commn. [19538]
Intl. Christian Stud. Assn. [19806]
Intl. Convention of Faith Ministries [19807]
Intl. Coun. of Christian Churches [20015]
Intl. Coun. of Community Churches [19850]
Intl. Coun. of Community Churches [IO]
Intl. Disciples Women's Ministries [20620]
Intl. Fed. of Messianic Jews [20255]
Intl. Lutheran Deaf Assn. [20217]
Intl. Lutheran Laymen's League [20218]
Intl. Order of the King's Daughters and Sons
    [19810]
Intl. Order of St. Vincent [19963]
Intl. Students, Inc. [20017]
InterServe U.S.A. [20351]
Interweave Continental (Unitarian Universalists for
    Lesbian, Gay, Bisexual and Transgender
    Concerns) [20059]
Japan Intl. Christian Univ. Found. [19929]
Koinonia Found. [19899]
Kristana Esperantista Ligo Internacia [19812]
Latin Am. Mission [20353]
Latin Liturgy Assn. [19646]
Lay Carmelite Order of the Blessed Virgin Mary of
    Mount Carmel [19647]
Laymen's Home Missionary Movement [20018]
Liberal Religious Educators Assn. [20599]
Licentiate Ministers and Certified Mediums Soc.
    [20450]
Life Action Revival Ministries [20020]
Life Outreach Intl. [20021]
Liturgical Conf. [19900]
Living Church Found. [19964]
Lollard Soc. [20524]
Lord's Day Alliance of the U.S. [20544]
Louis Finkelstein Inst. for Religious and Social
    Stud. at the Louis Stein Center [19931]
Luis Palau Assn. [20022]
Lutheran Bible Translators [19524]
Lutheran Deaconess Assn. [20219]
Lutheran Deaconess Conf. [20220]
Lutheran Historical Conf. [20222]
Lutheran Human Relations Assn. [20223]
Lutheran Mission Societies [20225]
Lutheran Student Movement - U.S.A. [20227]
Lutheran Women's Missionary League [20229]
Lutherans Concerned/North Am. [20061]
Macedonian Orthodox Youth Assn. of North Am.
    [19883]
Maclellan Found. [20502]
Manna House [12293]
Master's Men of the Natl. Assn. of Free Will
    Baptists [19490]
Media Associates Intl. [19981]
Mennonite Church USA Historical Comm. [20248]
Mennonite Educ. Agency [20250]
A Messianic Jewish Perspective [20259]
Methodist Fed. for Social Action [20264]
Metropolitan Community Churches [20062]
Mission to the World [20468]

Missionary Church Historical Soc. [19851]
Missionary Sisters of St. Peter Claver [20364]
Missionary Soc. of Saint Paul the Apostle [19663]
Missionary TECH Team [20366]
Moravian Historical Soc. [20423]
More Light Presbyterians for Lesbian, Gay,
    Bisexual and Transgender Concerns [20063]
Morris Cerullo World Evangelism [20025]
Morris Pratt Inst. Assn. [20451]
Narramore Christian Found. [19815]
Natl. Apostolate for Inclusion Ministry [20026]
Natl. Assn. of Catholic Family Life Ministers
    [20288]
Natl. Assn. of Church Bus. Admin. [20513]
Natl. Assn. of Church Design Builders [831]
Natl. Assn. of Church Facilities Managers [20514]
Natl. Assn. of Church Personnel Administrators
    [20515]
Natl. Assn. of Ecumenical and Interreligious Staff
    [19902]
Natl. Assn. of Evangelicals [19982]
Natl. Assn. of Free Will Baptists [19492]
Natl. Assn. of Parish Catechetical Directors
    [19932]
Natl. Assn. of Pastoral Musicians [8920]
Natl. Assn. for Treasurers of Religious Institutes
    [20516]
Natl. Bible Assn. [20205]
Natl. Campus Ministry Assn. [19933]
Natl. Cathedral Assn. [19903]
Natl. Catholic Conf. of Airport Chaplains [19754]
Natl. Catholic Conf. for Total Stewardship [19673]
Natl. Center for the Laity [20206]
Natl. Comm. of Catholic Laymen [19681]
Natl. Conf. for Community and Justice [19904]
Natl. Coun. of Churches [19852]
Natl. Coun. of Churches of Christ in the U.S.A.
    [19905]
Natl. Coun. of Churches, Educ. and Leadership
    Ministries Commn. [19935]
Natl. Fed. of Asian-Amer. United Methodists
    [20266]
Natl. Fed. of Priests' Councils [19689]
Natl. Forum of Greek Orthodox Church Musicians
    [20434]
Natl. Ghost Ranch Found. [20469]
Natl. Guild of Churchmen [19965]
Natl. Interfaith Coalition on Aging [11314]
Natl. League for the Separation of Church and
    State [19838]
Natl. Lutheran Outdoors Ministry Assn. [20231]
Natl. Off. for Black Catholics [19691]
Natl. Shrine of St. Elizabeth Ann Seton [19694]
Natl. Spiritualist Assn. of Churches [20453]
Natl. Spiritualist Teachers Club [20454]
Natl. United Church Ushers Assn. of Am. [20609]
The Navigators [19817]
Nazarene Missions Intl. [20371]
Neighborhood Bible Stud. [19526]
Neo-American Church, The Original Kleptonian
    [20456]
New Wineskins Missionary Network [20375]
North Amer. Acad. of Ecumenists [19906]
North Amer. Assn. for the Catechumenate [19697]
North Amer. Assn. for the Diaconate [19967]
North Amer. Patristics Soc. [20460]
Northern Far East Returned Missionaries Assn.
    [20504]
Order of Saint Andrew the Apostle [20073]
Orthodox Theological Soc. in Am. [19885]
Pan Amer. Coun. for the Preservation of the Hel-
    lenic Orthodox Church and the Hellenic
    Language [20074]
Peale Center for Christian Living [19825]
Personal Freedom Outreach [19875]
Pilots for Christ Intl. [20028]
Pioneer Clubs [20642]
Pocket Testament League [19529]
Prayers for Life [19907]
Presbyterian Assn. of Musicians [20435]
Presbyterian Church Bus. Administrators' Assn.
    [20470]
Presbyterian Evangelistic Fellowship [20471]
Presbyterian Lay Comm. [20472]
Presbyterian Men [20473]

Reference to "IO" in place of a book number signifies that the association may be found in the 45th edition of International Organizations.

Presbyterian-Reformed Ministries Intl. [20474]
Presbyterian Women [20475]
Progressive, Radically Inclusive Student Ministry
  [19938]
Ramakrishna - Vivekananda Center [20610]
Religion Communicators Coun: [20483]
Religious Bros. Conf. [19707]
Religious Res. Assn. [20539]
Religious Sci. Intl. [20525]
Revival Fires (Christian Evangelizers Assn.)
  [20031]
Rosedale Mennonite Missions [20253]
Saint Photios Found. [20075]
Saints Alive in Jesus [20032]
Salesian Missioners [20391]
Samaritans Intl. [20392]
Seafarers and Intl. House [20232]
Seamen's Church Inst. of New York and New
  Jersey [19970]
Searching Together Educational Ministries [19909]
Secretariat for Catholic-Jewish Relations [19910]
Seventh Day Baptist Gen. Conf. [19494]
Seventh Day Baptist Gen. Conf. of the U.S. and
  Canada [20545]
Seventh Day Baptist Historical Soc. [19495]
Seventh Day Baptist Missionary Soc. [19496]
Seventh Day Baptist World Fed. [19497]
Sharing of Ministries Abroad U.S.A. [20393]
Sikh Coun. on Religion and Educ. [20558]
Sikh Stud. Circle [20559]
Skinner Leadership Inst. [20033]
Slavic Gospel Assn. [20395]
Soc. of the Descendants of the Colonial Clergy
  [20760]
Soc. for Hindu-Christian Stud. [20528]
Soc. for Promoting and Encouraging Arts and
  Knowledge of the Church [19972]
Soc. for the Sci. Stud. of Religion [20506]
Soc. of Traditional Roman Catholics [19726]
South African Coun. of Churches [IO]
South Amer. Missionary Soc. - USA [20398]
Southern Baptist Found. [19498]
Southern Baptist Historical Lib. and Archives
  [19499]
Spiritual Life Inst. [20566]
Standing Commn. on Ecumenical Relations of the
  Episcopal Church [19974]
Standing Conf. of the Canonical Orthodox
  Bishops in the Americas [19886]
STEER [20401]
Teen Challenge Intl. [20643]
Theosophical Book Assn. for the Blind [20592]
Theosophical Soc. in Am. [20593]
Tithing Found. [20595]
Union for Traditional Judaism [20186]
Unitarian Universalist Christian Fellowship [20600]
Unitarian Universalist Historical Soc. [20601]
Unitarian Universalist Ministers Assn. [20602]
Unitarian Universalist Musicians' Network [20436]
Unitarian Universalist Ser. Comm. [20603]
Unitarian Universalist Women's Fed. [20604]
United Church of Christ Coalition for Lesbian,
  Gay, Bisexual and Transgender Concerns
  [20067]
United Church of Christ Justice and Witness
  Ministries [20608]
United Indian Missions, Intl. [20405]
United Lodge of Theosophists [20594]
United Methodist Assn. of Hea. and Welfare
  Ministries [14602]
United Methodist Comm. on Relief [20267]
United Methodist Youth Org. [20268]
Unity Coalition for Israel [8672]
Watchtower Bible and Tract Soc. of New York
  [20109]
WEC Intl. [20034]
Wider Quaker Fellowship [20045]
Woman's Home and Foreign Mission Soc.
  [19443]
Woman's Missionary Union, SBC [19501]
Women and Men Against Sexual Harassment and
  Other Abuses [13088]
Women Nationally Active for Christ [19502]
Women's Division of the Gen. Bd. of Global
  Ministries of the United Methodist Church
  [20269]

World Cong. of Gay, Lesbian, Bisexual, and
  Transgender Jews [20069]
World Evangelical Alliance [19983]
World Fellowship of Slavic Evangelical Christians
  [19984]
World Impact [20414]
World Literature Ministries [19832]
World Methodist Coun. [20272]
World Methodist Historical Soc. [20273]
World Mission Prayer League [20234]
World Team [20417]
World's Christian Endeavor Union [19829]
Xaverian Missionaries of the U.S. [20421]
Young Life [20644]
Youth for Christ/U.S.A. [20645]
Youth Evangelism Assn. [20036]
Youth Ministry [20235]
Churches of Am. Fed. of Buddhist Women's As-
  sociations; Buddhist [19543]
Churches; Amer. Coalition of Unregistered [20520]
Churches; Amer. Coun. of Christian [19761]
Churches; Biennial Coun. of Community [★19850]
Churches' Center for Theology and Public Policy
  [18434], c/o Wesley Theological Seminary, 4500
  Massachusetts Ave. NW, Washington, DC 20016,
  (202)885-8648

Churches of Christ—Christian Churches
Amer. Congregational Assn. [19859]
Amer. Coun. of Christian Churches [19761]
Amer. and Foreign Christian Union [19762]
Center for Organizational and Ministry Develop-
  ment [19769]
Christian Bus. Men's Comm. [19771]
Christian Century Found. [19772]
Christian Communications, Inc. [19774]
Christian Family Renewal [19776]
Christian Holiness Partnership [19779]
Christian Res. Inst. [19785]
Crusaders for Christ [20462]
Disciples of Christ Historical Soc. [19853]
Division of Higher Educ., Christian Church-
  Disciples of Christ [19854]
Fellowship of Christian Magicians [19797]
Fellowship of Christian Peace Officers - U.S.A.
  [19798]
Forward in Faith North Am. [19959]
Full Gospel Bus. Men's Fellowship Intl. [19801]
The Interchurch Center [19896]
Intl. Convention of Faith Ministries [19807]
Intl. Coun. of Community Churches [19850]
Intl. Order of the King's Daughters and Sons
  [19810]
Kristana Esperantista Ligo Internacia [19812]
Narramore Christian Found. [19815]
Natl. Chaplains Assn. [19855]
Natl. Coun. of Churches of Christ in the U.S.A.
  [19905]
The Navigators [19817]
Peale Center for Christian Living [19825]
Progressive, Radically Inclusive Student Ministry
  [19938]
United Christian Missionary Soc. [19856]
United Church of Christ Coalition for Lesbian,
  Gay, Bisexual and Transgender Concerns
  [20067]
World Convention of Churches of Christ [19857]
World Convention of Churches of Christ [IO]
World's Christian Endeavor Union [19829]
Churches of Christ in the U.S.A; Natl. Coun. of
  [19905]
Churches' Commn. for Migrants in Europe [IO],
  Brussels, Belgium
Churches Commn. on Overseas Students [★IO]
Churches Commn. on Women in Ministry; Natl.
  Coun. of [★20622]
Churches' Comm. for Migrants in European [★IO]
Churches' Comm. for Voter Registration-Education -
  Defunct.
Churches Community Assn; Midtown [★12293]
Churches; Cong. of Natl. Black [19890]
The Churches Conservation Trust [IO], London,
  United Kingdom
Churches' Coun. for Child and Youth Care [IO], Ban-
  galore, India
Churches; Coun. of Community [★19850]

Churches, Educ. and Leadership Ministries Commn;
  Natl. Coun. of [19935]
Churches; Gen. Assn. of Regular Baptist [19489]
Churches; Healers League of the Natl. Spiritualist
  Assn. of [20449]
Churches on Intl. Affairs; Commn. of the [20094]
Churches; Intl. Assn. of Religious Sci. [★20525]
Churches; Intl. Coun. of Community [★19850]
Churches and Ministers; Intl. Convention of Faith,
  [★19807]
Churches, Ministries in Christian Educ; Natl. Coun.
  of [★19935]
Churches in Missions Commitment; Advancing
  [20293]
Churches; Natl. Coun. of [★19905]
Churches; Natl. Coun. of Community [★19850]
Churches; Natl. Spiritualist Assn. of [20453]
Churches; Professors and Res. Sect. of the Division
  of Christian Educ. of the Natl. Coun. of [★19939]
Churches Together in Britain and Ireland [IO],
  London, United Kingdom
Churches; U.S. Conf. for the World Coun. of [19912]
Churches Uniting in Christ [19889], 475 E Lock-
  wood, Webster Groves, MO 63119-3124,
  (314)252-3160
Churches; Universal Fellowship of Metropolitan
  Community [★20062]
Churches - Women in Ministry Gp; Natl. Coun. of
  [20622]
Churchill Centre [11109], 1150 17th St. NW, Ste.
  307, Washington, DC 20036, (202)223-5511
Churchill Found; U.S. [★8438]
Churchill Found; Winston [8438]
Churchill Soc. London [IO], Ipswich, United Kingdom
Churchill Soc. - U.S; Intl. [★11109]
Churchman Associates - Address unknown since
  2005.
Churchmen; Natl. Guild of [19965]
Churchmen's Commn. for Decent Publications -
  Defunct.
Churg Strauss Syndrome Assn. [13729], PO Box
  671, Southampton, MA 01073-0671, (413)862-
  3636
Churro; Navajosa [★5210]
Churro Sheep Assn; Navajo- [5210]
CHVAid [★21620]
Cichlasoma Study Group - Address unknown since
  2007.
Cichlid Assn; Amer. [22433]
Cichlid Assn; Pacific Coast [22445]
Cichlid Assn; Rocky Mountain [22447]
CID Agents Assn. [21207], 1896 Carlisle Rd.,
  Traverse City, MI 49686-9156, (231)932-2388
Cider Assn. of North America - Address unknown
  since 1994.
CIDESCO U.S.A. [★1085]
CIES, Food Bus. Forum [3404], 8455 Colesville Rd.,
  Ste. 705, Silver Spring, MD 20910, (301)563-3383
CIES, Food Bus. Forum [IO], Silver Spring, MD,
  United States
Cigar Assn. of America [3819]
Cigar Box Mfrs. - Defunct.
Cigar Makers' Intl. Union of Am. [★24182]
Cigar Smokers of America - Defunct.
Cigarette Advertising Code - Defunct.
Cigarette Indus. Assn. [IO], Berlin, Germany
Cigarette Lighter Mfrs. Assn. - Defunct.
Cigarette Pack Collectors Assn. [21994], c/o Richard
  Elliot, 86 Plymouth Grove Dr., Kennebunk, ME
  04043
CIIT Centers for Hea. Res. [7801], PO Box 12137,
  Research Triangle Park, NC 27709-2137,
  (919)558-1200
CILT - The Natl. Centre for Languages [IO], London,
  United Kingdom
CIMA Marketing Communications Coun. [★82]
CIMTA [858], 4244 Spring Creek Ln., Bellingham,
  WA 98226, (360)733-5721
CIMTECH [IO], Hatfield, United Kingdom
Cincinnati Bd. of Trade - Defunct.
Cincinnati; Daughters of the [20670]
Cincinnati Music Scholarship Assn. [★10726]
Cincinnatus Soc. - Defunct.
Cinderella Softball Leagues [23789], PO Box 1411,
  Corning, NY 14830, (607)937-5469

A star before a book entry number signifies that the name is not listed separately, but is mentioned within the entry.

Cinderella Stamp Club [IO], Coventry, United Kingdom
Cinecon; Soc. for Cinephiles/ [9947]
Cinema Assn; Large Format [1387]
Cinema Editors; Amer. [1376]
Cinema Labs; Assn. of [★1367]
Cinema and Media Stud; Soc. for [9946]
Cinema Soc; African Amer. [9926]
Cinema Soc; Black Amer. [★9926]
Cinema Stud; Soc. for [★9946]
Cinema Theatre Assn. [IO], London, United Kingdom
Cinema and Video Labs; Assn. of [1367]
Cinematheque; Film-Makers' [★9928]
Cinematographers; Amer. Soc. of [1377]
Cinematographers; British Soc. of [IO]
Cinematographers; Japanese Soc. of [IO]
Cinematologists; Soc. of [★9946]
Cinemists 63 - Address unknown since 2001.
Cinephiles/Cinecon; Soc. for [9947]
CineVision; Asian [9930]
Cinnamon Rabbit Breeders Assn. [5144], c/o Nancy Searle, 550 Amherst Rd., Belchertown, MA 01007, (413)253-7721
CIO Community Services Comm. [★11801]
CIO Editors and Public Relations Conf. [★3229]
CIPA [★IO]
Cipher Assn; Beale [6848]
Cipher Soc; New York [6850]
CIPRA: Intl. Commn. for the Protection of Alpine Regions [IO], Schaan, Liechtenstein
Circle Club - The Official Fan Club of the Grand Ole Opry [24864], 2802 Opryland Dr., Nashville, TN 37214, (615)871-OPRY
Circle of Companions - Defunct.
Circle of Earth [20458], S Cannon Blvd., Kannapolis, NC 28083, (704)784-7317
Circle of Friends for Amer. Veterans [21293], 210 E Broad St., Ste. 202, Falls Church, VA 22046, (703)237-8980
Circle of Hea. Intl. [12268], c/o Leilani Johnson, Admin., 90 Coventry Wood Rd., Bolton, MA 01740-1123, (512)517-3220
Circle of Hea. Intl. [IO], Austin, TX, United States
Circle K Intl. [IO], Indianapolis, IN, United States
Circle K Intl. [13037], 3636 Woodview Trace, Indianapolis, IN 46268-3196, (317)875-8755
Circle Sanctuary [20570], PO Box 9, Barneveld, WI 53507, (608)924-2216
Circle Sanctuary [IO], Barneveld, WI, United States
Circle Sanctuary Network [★IO]
Circle Sanctuary Network [★20570]
Circle of State Librarians [★IO]
Circle of Wine Writers [IO], London, United Kingdom
Circles of Exchange [★20577]
Circolo Amatori Lancia Sicilia [IO], Palermo, Italy
Circolo Amerindiano [IO], Perugia, Italy
Circuit Club; Cover Collectors [22812]
Circuits; Inst. of Printed [★1221]
Circuits Intl. [IO], Nurburg, Germany
Circuits Soc; IEEE Solid-State [6904]
Circuits and Systems Soc; IEEE [6914]
Circulation Assn; Natl. Bus. [★3242]
Circulation; Bus. Publications Audit of [★93]
Circulation Comm; Paid [★2455]
Circulation Coun. of DMA [2620], 1120 Ave. of the Americas, New York, NY 10036-6700, (212)768-7277
Circulation Coun; Paid [★2455]
Circulation Managers Assn; Intl. [★3244]
Circulation Publications; Assn. of Paid [★2455]
Circulation Technicians; Amer. Soc. of Extracorporeal [★15129]
Circulations; Audit Bur. of [126]
Circulations Audit; Controlled [★93]
Circulations; Certified Audit of [127]
Circulatory Soc; Amer. Podiatric [16036]
Circulo de Cultura Panamericano [★10312]
Circulo de Cultura Panamericano [★IO]
Circulo Dermatologico del Peru [IO], Lima, Peru
Circulo de Escritores y Poetas Iberoamericanos - Address unknown since 1995.
Circulo Uruguayo de la Publicidad [★IO]
Circum-Pacific Council for Energy and Mineral Resources [IO], Reston, VA, United States
Circum-Pacific Coun. for Energy and Mineral Resources [7340], c/o Ms. Nancy Zeigler, Sec., 12201 Sunrise Valley Dr., MS-917, Reston, VA 20192, (703)648-6645

Circumcision
Doctors Opposing Circumcision [11730]
Intl. Coalition for Genital Integrity [11731]
International Coalition for Genital Integrity [IO]
Natl. Org. of Circumcision Info. Rsrc. Centers [IO]
Natl. Org. of Circumcision Info. Rsrc. Centers [11732]
Natl. Org. to Halt the Abuse and Routine Mutilation of Males [11733]
Natl. Org. of Restoring Men [11734]
Natl. Org. of Restoring Men - UK [IO]
Newborn Rights Soc. [12413]
Non-Circumcision Educational Found. [11735]
Non-Circumcision Info. Center [11736]
Nurses for the Rights of the Child [11737]
Women's Gp. for the Abolition of Sexual Mutilation [IO]
Circumcision Educational Found; Non- [11735]
Circumcision Info. Center; Non- [11736]
Circumnavigators Club [7075], 24 E 39th St., New York, NY 10016-2555, (201)612-9100

Circus
Amer. Youth Circus Org. [9795]
Australian Circus and Physical Theatre Assn. [IO]
Circus Educ. Specialists [9796]
Circus Ethiopia [IO]
Circus Fans Assn. of Am. [9797]
Circus Historical Soc. [9798]
Intl. Jugglers' Assn. [23557]
Natl. Circus Preservation Soc. [9799]
Natl. Circus Proj. [8286]
U.S. Sports Acrobatics [23035]
World Juggling Fed. [23558]
Circus Acad; National [★9796]
Circus Educ. Specialists [9796], 56 Lion Ln., Westbury, NY 11590, (516)334-2123
Circus Ethiopia [IO], Addis Ababa, Ethiopia
Circus Exchange; International [★9796]
Circus Fans Assn. of Am. [9797], 2704 Marshall Ave., Lorain, OH 44052-4315, (440)960-2811
Circus Fund; Natl. [★9799]
Circus Historical Soc. [9798], c/o Alan Campbell, Sec.-Treas., 600 Kings Peak Dr., Alpharetta, GA 30022-7844
Circus Model Builders, Intl. [22643], c/o Ron Hurst, Sec., 4724 W Pendleton Pl., Peoria, IL 61615-2841
Circus Model Builders, Intl. [IO], Peoria, IL, United States
Circus Proj; Natl. [8286]
CIRIA [IO], London, United Kingdom
CIRIA: Constr. Indus. Res. and Info. Assn. [★IO]
CISV Intl. [IO], Newcastle upon Tyne, United Kingdom
CISV Norge, Internasjonale Barneleire [★IO]
Cities Community Development Directors Assn; Natl. Model [★17228]
Cities Directors Assn; Natl. Model [★17228]
Cities Found; Intl. Healthy [13349]
Cities, Inc; Experimental [17236]
Cities Institute; National League of [★6130]
Cities; Natl. League of [6130]
Cities Prog. for School Improvement; Res. Coun. of the Great [★9289]
Cities in Schools [★8323]
CitiHope Intl. [12843], PO Box 38, 143 Main St., Andes, NY 13731, (845)676-4400
CitiHope Intl. [IO], Andes, NY, United States
Citizen Action Fund - Address unknown since 1999.
Citizen Action Group - Defunct.
Citizen Advocacy Center [17695], 1400 16th St. NW, Ste. 101, Washington, DC 20036, (202)462-1174
Citizen Ambassador Prog; People to People [★17908]
Citizen Diplomacy - Address unknown since 1995.
Citizen Education Assn. - Defunct.
Citizen Educ. in the Law; Natl. Inst. for [★6035]
Citizen Exchange Corps [★17370]
Citizen Exchange Corps [★IO]
Citizen Exchange Coun. [★IO]
Citizen Exchange Coun. [★17370]
Citizen, Inc; Private [17147]
Citizen Involvement Training Prog. [★11750]
Citizen/Labor Energy Coalition - Defunct.
Citizen Litigation Gp; Public [17342]

Citizen Mobilization Campaign - Defunct.
Citizen; New Age [17139]
Citizen; Public [17341]
Citizen Soldier [6073], 267 5th Ave., Ste. 901, New York, NY 10016, (212)679-2250
Citizen Utility Bd. Campaign - Defunct.
Citizens Abroad; Amer. [18949]
Citizens Action; Natl. Assn. of Black [16942]
Citizens Advice [★IO]
Citizens Advocate Center - Defunct.
Citizens Against Chemtrails U.S. [17053], c/o Clifford E. Carnicom, PO Box 4653, Santa Fe, NM 87502
Citizens Against Drug Impaired Drivers [13230], PO Box 249, Thiensville, WI 53092, (414)352-2043
Citizens Against Foreign Control of America - Address unknown since 2004.
Citizens Against Govt. Waste [17668], 1301 Connecticut Ave. NW, Ste. 400, Washington, DC 20036, (202)467-5300
Citizens Against Human Rights Abuse [★17775]
Citizens Against Human Rights Abuse [★IO]
Citizens Against Lawyer Abuse - Address unknown since 1991.
Citizens Against Legalized Murder - Defunct.
Citizens Against Military Injustice - Defunct.
Citizens Against Noise - Defunct.
Citizens Against PACs - Defunct.
Citizens Against Pornography [★18372]
Citizens Against UFO Secrecy [7473], PO Box 2443, Sedona, AZ 86339, (520)203-0567
Citizens AIDS Proj; CAVDA- [13562]
Citizens Alliance; Chinese Amer. [19013]
Citizens Alliance for VD Awareness [16411], 800 W Central Rd., Ste. 128, Mount Prospect, IL 60056, (847)398-3378
Citizens for an Alternative Tax Sys. [18705], 7825 Sudley Rd., No. 206, Manassas, VA 20109, (800)767-7577
Citizens for Alternatives to Chem. Contamination [5084], 8735 Maple Grove Rd., Lake, MI 48632-9511, (989)544-3318
Citizens for Alternatives to Trident and ELF - Defunct.
Citizens for America Educational Found. - Address unknown since 1999.
Citizens for Animals - Defunct.
Citizens for Animals, Resources and Environment - Address unknown since 2003.
Citizens Assn. for the Care of Animals - Address unknown since 1995.
Citizens Aviation Watch Assn. [11509], 97-37 63rd Rd. 15 E, Rego Park, NY 11374, (718)275-3932
Citizens for a Balanced Budget - Defunct.
Citizens for a Better Am. [17103], PO Box 7647, Van Nuys, CA 91409-7647, (818)757-1776
Citizens for a Better Env. [★5095]
Citizens for Bush - Defunct.
Citizen's Call - Address unknown since 2001.
Citizen's Choice - Defunct.
Citizens for Clean Air - Defunct.
Citizens for Clean Waters - Address unknown since 1995.
Citizens CH for Hazardous Waste [★5266]
Citizens Coal Coun. [4299], PO Box 964, Washington, PA 15301, (724)222-5602
Citizens Coalition for Nursing Home Reform; Natl. [17335]
Citizens Coalition for Rational Traffic Laws [★13340]
Citizens' Commn. on Civil Rights [17104], 2000 M St. NW, Ste. 400, Washington, DC 20036, (202)659-5565
Citizen's Commn. on Pension Policy - Defunct.
Citizens' Commn. on Science, Law and the Food Supply - Defunct.
Citizen's Comm. to Amend Title 18 - Address unknown since 2003.
Citizens Comm. on Amer. Policy in the Near East - Address unknown since 1995.
Citizens Comm. for Constitutional Liberties - Defunct.
Citizens Comm. on the Fair Labor Standards Act - Defunct.
Citizens Comm. for Food and Shelter; Natl. [★12294]
Citizens Comm. on Future Directions for the Peace Corps - Address unknown since 2003.

Reference to "IO" in place of a book number signifies that the association may be found in the 45th edition of International Organizations.

Citizens' Comm. for Immigration Reform - Defunct.
Citizens Comm. for Legislation Preventing the Unsolicited Bulk Mailing of Drugs and Other Medicines - Defunct.
Citizens Comm. on Natural Resources - Defunct.
Citizens Comm. for a Nuclear Test Ban - Defunct.
Citizens Comm. for Peace With Freedom in Vietnam - Defunct.
Citizens Comm. on Population and the Amer. Future - Defunct.
Citizens Comm. for the Right to Keep and Bear Arms [17105], Liberty Park, 12500 NE 10th Pl., Bellevue, WA 98005, (425)454-4911
Citizens Comm. for UNICEF [★11658]
Citizens Comm. for UNICEF [★IO]
Citizens Comm. on U.S. War Crimes in Indochina - Defunct.
Citizens Comm. for Victim Assistance - Defunct.
Citizens for Common Sense - Defunct.
Citizens for Common Sense in Natl. Defense - Defunct.
Citizens Commun. Center of the Inst. for Public Representation [★17171]
Citizens Communications Center Proj. of the Inst. for Public Representation [17171], c/o Georgetown Univ. Law Center, 600 New Jersey Ave. NW, Washington, DC 20001, (202)662-9535
Citizens for Community Values [19788], 11175 Reading Rd., Ste. 103, Cincinnati, OH 45241-1997, (513)733-5775
Citizens for a Competitive America - Defunct.
Citizen's Cong. For Private Enterprise - Defunct.
Citizens for Conservation [★19082]
Citizens for the Constitution of the Republic - Defunct.
Citizens for Constitutional Concerns [★17143]
Citizens for Consumer Justice [18641]
Citizens Coun. of America for Segregation - Defunct.
Citizens' Coun. Forum - Defunct.
Citizens' Coun. on Hea. Care [17696], 1954 Univ. Ave. W, Ste. 8, St. Paul, MN 55104-3460, (651)646-8935
Citizens' Councils of Am. [★18684]
Citizens Crime Commissions; Natl. Assn. of [★11840]
Citizens Crusade Against Poverty [★12769]
Citizens for a Debt Free America - Defunct.
Citizens in Defense of Civil Liberties - Defunct.
Citizens Development Corps [17831], 1726 M St. NW, Ste. 1100, Washington, DC 20036, (202)872-0933
Citizens Development Corps [IO], Washington, DC, United States
Citizen's Drinking Water Coalition - Defunct.
Citizens for a Drug Free America - Address unknown since 2001.
Citizens for Educational Freedom [8338], 9333 Clayton Rd., St. Louis, MO 63124, (314)997-6361
Citizen's Emergency Defense Sys; Christian-Patriots Defense League/ [17263]
Citizens to End Animal Suffering and Exploitation [11375], PO Box 440456, Somerville, MA 02144, (617)628-9030
Citizen's Energy Coun. - Address unknown since 2002.
Citizens' Energy Project - Defunct.
Citizens Equal Rights Alliance [5800], PO Box 93, Ronan, MT 59864, (605)374-5836
Citizens for Eye Res. to Prevent Blindness - Defunct.
Citizens for Farm Labor - Defunct.
Citizens Flag Alliance [17300], PO Box 7197, Indianapolis, IN 46207-7197, (317)630-1384
Citizens Foreign Aid Comm. - Defunct.
Citizen's Forester Training Prog. [★4460]
Citizens Forum on Self-Government/National Municipal League [★6128]
Citizens for Free Kuwait - Defunct.
Citizens Freedom Found. [★19873]
Citizens Freedom Found. [★IO]
Citizens for Global Solutions [18762], 418 7th St. SE, Washington, DC 20003-2769, (202)546-3950
Citizens for Governmental Restraint [17288], 3541 Robinwood Terr., Minnetonka, MN 55305-4327, (952)938-6472

Citizens for Hea. [13627], 2104 Stevens Ave. S, Minneapolis, MN 55404, (612)879-7585
Citizens for Hea. [IO], Minneapolis, MN, United States
Citizens for Highway Safety - Defunct.
Citizens Honest Elections Found. - Address unknown since 1995.
Citizens for Impartial Justice [17957], c/o Marianne Cammarota, CSR, Chair, 147 Columbia Tpke., Florham Park, NJ 07932, (973)660-0600
Citizens for Independent Public Broadcasting [17025], 901 Old Hickory Rd., Pittsburgh, PA 15243, (412)341-1967
Citizens for Informed Choices on Marijuana - Defunct.
Citizens for Informed Consent - Defunct.
Citizens for Justice; Asian Amer. Center for Justice of the Amer. [17094]
Citizens Law Enforcement and Res. Comm. - Defunct.
Citizens for Law and Order [17958], PO Box 412, Carlsbad, CA 92018, (760)631-2028
Citizens Law and Res. Assn. - Defunct.
Citizens Leadership Found. - Defunct.
Citizens League Against the Sonic Boom - Defunct.
Citizens League; Japanese Amer. [19170]
Citizens; League of United Latin Amer. [19099]
Citizens for a Lebanon-Grenada Natl. Memorial - Defunct.
Citizens Legal Protective League - Defunct.
Citizens for Legitimate Govt. [17663], PO Box 1142, Bristol, CT 06011-1142
Citizens for Media Responsibility Without Law - Address unknown since 2002.
Citizens for Midwifery [13981], PO Box 82227, Athens, GA 30608-2227, (888)CFM-4880
Citizens Network for Foreign Affairs [17866], 1828 L St. NW, Ste. 710, Washington, DC 20036, (202)296-3920
Citizens Network for Sustainable Development [11767], c/o ISF, 11426 Rockville Pike, Ste. 306, Rockville, MD 20852, (301)770-6375
Citizens for a Nuclear Freeze - Defunct.
Citizens for Nuclear Safety; Concerned [18147]
Citizens Org; Effective [★17354]
Citizens Participation Project/The Missing Half - Defunct.
Citizen's Party - Defunct.
Citizens in Politics - Defunct.
Citizens for Private Property Rights Corp. - Address unknown since 2006.
Citizens for Proportional Representation [★18348]
Citizens for Public Action on High Blood Pressure and Cholesterol - Address unknown since 2005.
Citizens for a Quieter City - Defunct.
Citizens for Rational Traffic Laws [★13340]
Citizens for Reliable and Safe Highways [18577], c/o Truck Safety Coalition, 2020 14th St. N, Ste. 720, Arlington, VA 22201, (703)294-6404
Citizens for Renewable Energy [IO], Lion's Head, ON, Canada
Citizens for the Republic - Address unknown since 1995.
Citizens' Res. Found. [18349], 104 Moses Hall, Inst. of Governmental Stud., Univ. of California, Berkeley, CA 94720-2370, (510)642-5158
Citizens Res. Found. for the Study of Degenerative Diseases; Independent [14263]
Citizen's Rights; Conservative Majority for [17266]
Citizens for Roadside Safety [12957], 3300 Robinson Pike Rd., Grandview, MO 64030
Citizens for Safe Drivers Against Drunk Drivers/Chronic Offenders - Defunct.
Citizens for Safe Government - Address unknown since 2008.
Citizens' Scholarship Found. of Am. [★9081]
Citizens for Sensible Control of Acid Rain - Defunct.
Citizens for Sensible Safeguards [17106], c/o OMB Watch, 1742 Connecticut Ave. NW, Washington, DC 20009, (202)234-8494
Citizens' Stamp Advisory Comm. [22806], c/o U.S. Postal Ser., 1735 N Lynn St., Rm. 5013, Arlington, VA 22209-6432
Citizens for Sweepstakes - Defunct.
Citizens for Tax Justice [18706], 1616 P St. NW, Ste. 200, Washington, DC 20036, (202)299-1066

Citizens for Tax Reform in 1978 - Defunct.
Citizens for a Tobacco-Free Soc. - Address unknown since 2001.
Citizens United [17664], 1006 Pennsylvania Ave. SE, Washington, DC 20003, (202)547-5420
Citizens United for Alternatives to the Death Penalty [5641], PMB 335, 2603 Dr. Martin Luther King Jr. Hwy., Gainesville, FL 32609, (800)973-6548
Citizens United to Reduce Emissions (of Formaldehyde Poisoning Assn.) [★13324]
Citizens United for Rehabilitation of Errants [11860], c/o Natl. Cure, PO Box 2310, Natl. Capitol Sta., Washington, DC 20013-2310, (202)789-2126
Citizens United Resisting Euthanasia [12129], 303 Truman St., Berkeley Springs, WV 25411, (304)258-5433
Citizens With Low Vision; Coun. of [★11934]
Citizens With Low Vision Intl; Coun. of [11934]
Citizenship
  Amer. Citizenship Center [17067]
  Amer. Civic Assn. [12403]
  Amer. Legion Auxiliary Girls Nation [17068]
  Architects/Designers/Planners for Social Responsibility [18142]
  Assn. for Political and Legal Anthropology [6411]
  Canadian Citizenship Fed. [IO]
  Center for Philosophy, Law, Citizenship [18271]
  Center for the Stud. of the Presidency [17069]
  Center for Stud. of Responsive Law [17315]
  Chicano Family Center [17701]
  Citizens Against Govt. Waste [17668]
  Citizens' Commn. on Civil Rights [17104]
  Citizens for Governmental Restraint [17288]
  Citizens United [17664]
  Citizenship Through Sports Alliance [23812]
  Claremont Inst. [17070]
  Close Up Found. [17071]
  Community Development Soc. [17213]
  Conservative Majority for Citizen's Rights [17266]
  Defense Orientation Conf. Assn. [18591]
  Ethics Rsrc. Center [17072]
  Foreign Policy Assn. [17610]
  Free the Eagle [17629]
  Freedoms Found. at Valley Forge [17644]
  Honest Ballot Assn. [17486]
  Immigration and Refugee Services of Am. [12404]
  Natl. Alliance Against Racist and Political Repression [17128]
  Natl. Alliance for Civic Educ. [8091]
  Natl. Comm. on Amer. Foreign Policy [17615]
  Natl. Comm. for an Effective Cong. [17252]
  Natl. Conf. on Citizenship [17073]
  People's Medical Soc. [17694]
  Public Citizen [17341]
  Public Citizen Litigation Gp. [17342]
  Public Citizen's Cong. Watch [17343]
  Southern Christian Leadership Conf. [17154]
  Trilateral Commn. [17875]
  U.S. Assn. of Former Members of Cong. [17253]
  U.S. Border Control [17810]
Citizenship; Center for Philosophy, Law, [18271]
Citizenship Conf; Amer. Immigration and [★17806]
Citizenship Educational Ser. [★17072]
Citizenship Forum; Natl. Immigration Refugee [★17806]
Citizenship Through Sports Alliance [23812], c/o Ted Breidenthal, 2537 Madison Ave., Kansas City, MO 64108, (816)474-7264
CitizensLobby.com [18435], PO Box 23037, 2020 Pennsylvania Ave. NW, No. 649, Washington, DC 20026
Citriculture; Intl. Soc. of [4737]
Citroen Car Club [IO], Steyning, United Kingdom
Citroen Quarterly Car Club [21613], PO Box 30, Boston, MA 02113-0001, (617)742-6604
Citrus Associates of the New York Cotton Exchange [★4332]
Citrus Commn; Florida [★4729]
Citrus Commission; Florida [★4729]
Citrus; Florida Dept. of [4729]
Citrus Juice Processors; Natl. Assn. of [★510]
Citrus Label Collectors; Tri-County [★21995]
Citrus Label Soc. [21995], c/o Noel Gilbert, Sec.-Treas., 131 Miramonte Dr., Fullerton, CA 92835
Citrus Marketing Bd. of Israel [IO], Beit Dagan, Israel

A star before a book entry number signifies that the name is not listed separately, but is mentioned within the entry.

Citrus Mutual; Florida [4727]
Citrus Nurserymen's Assn; Florida [4728]
City Bankers; Assn. of Reserve [★477]
City Building Officials; Assn. of Major [★5547]
City Coun; Natl. Farm- [4649]
City/County Building Officials; Assn. of Major [5547]
City and County of Philadelphia; Carpenters'
    Company of the [★10018]
City Farmer Soc. [IO], Vancouver, BC, Canada
City Hea. Officials; Natl. Assn. of County and [6217]
City of Hope Natl. Medical Center [15102], 1500 E
    Duarte Rd., Duarte, CA 91010, (626)359-8111
City Hostess Intl. - Address unknown since 1994.
City Human Services Officials; U.S. Conf. of [6263]
City Kids Coalition [★13479]
City Mgt. Assn; Intl. [★6123]
City Managers' Assn; Intl. [★6123]
City Parks Alliance [18184], 1111 16th St. NW, Ste.
    310, Washington, DC 20036, (202)223-9111
City Planning Inst. of Japan [IO], Tokyo, Japan
City Planning; Natl. Conf. on [★5586]
City and Regional Magazine Assn. [3218], 4929
    Wilshire Blvd., Ste. 428, Los Angeles, CA 90010,
    (323)937-5514
City Schools; Coun. of the Great [9289]
City Univ. of New York Alumni Assn; Brooklyn Coll.
    of the [18880]
City Univ. of New York; The Feminist Press at the
    [9317]
City Walls [★17239]
City Women's Network [IO], Uxbridge, United
    Kingdom
CityKids Found. [13479], 57 Leonard St., New York,
    NY 10013, (212)925-3320
CityMatch [13957], c/o Magda G. Peck, ScD,
    Founder/Sr. Advisor, Dept. of Pediatrics, 982170
    Nebraska Medical Ctr., Omaha, NE 68198-2170,
    (402)561-7500
CityTeam Ministries [12844], 2304 Zanker Rd., San
    Jose, CA 95131, (408)232-5600
Civic Action Inst. - Defunct.
Civic Assn; Amer. [12403]
Civic Club; Natl. Pinochle Bugs Social and [13055]
Civic Coun; Chinese Amer. [19014]
Civic League; Natl. [6128]
Civic League; Natl. Italian [★19169]
Civic Participation; Americans for [★18364]
Civic Trust [IO], London, United Kingdom
Civico-Militar Cubana; Junta [17366]
Civics
    Albanian Amer. Civic League [16970]
    Amer. Civic Assn. [12403]
    Arcus Found. [18266]
    Assn. of Americans for Civic Responsibility
        [17074]
    Center for Citizenship Educ. of Mongolia [IO]
    Center for the Stud. of the Presidency [17069]
    Citizens United [17664]
    Coun. for Educ. in World Citizenship [IO]
    Coun. on Islamic Educ. [8669]
    Experimental Cities, Inc. [17236]
    Found. for Amer. Christian Educ. [8086]
    GenerationEngage [18848]
    Immigration and Refugee Services of Am. [12404]
    Innovations in Civic Participation [17075]
    Innovations in Civic Participation [IO]
    Natl. Alliance for Civic Educ. [8091]
    Natl. Voice [17076]
    Patriotic Educ. Inc. [8092]
    Presidential Classroom [8756]
    Sam Adams Alliance [17673]
    Washington Workshops Found. [8093]
CIVICUS: World Alliance for Citizen Participation
    [18340], c/o Patricia Benton, Financial Consultant,
    1420 K St. NW, Ste. 900, Washington, DC 20005,
    (202)331-8518
CIVICUS: World Alliance for Citizen Participation
    [IO], Washington, DC, United States
Civil Affairs Assn. [IO], Columbia, MD, United States
Civil Affairs Assn. [6074], 10130 Hyla Brook Rd.,
    Columbia, MD 21044-1705, (410)992-7724
Civil Air Operations Officers Assn. of Australia [IO],
    Port Melbourne, Australia
Civil Air Patrol [5538], 105 S Hansell St., Bldg. 714,
    Maxwell AFB, AL 36112-6332, (334)953-5463

Civil Attorneys; Natl. Assn. of County [5619]
Civil Aviation Chaplains Intl. [★IO]
Civil Aviation Medical Assn. [IO], Oklahoma City,
    OK, United States
Civil Aviation Medical Assn. [13540], PO Box 23864,
    Oklahoma City, OK 73123-2864, (405)840-0199
Civil Censorship Study Group [22807], c/o Charles
    J. LaBlonde, 15091 Ridgefield Ln., Colorado
    Springs, CO 80921
Civil Censorship Study Group [IO], Colorado
    Springs, CO, United States
Civil Constr. Indus. Union of the State of Rio de Jan-
    eiro [IO], Rio de Janeiro, Brazil
Civil Defense
    All India Disaster Mitigation Inst. [IO]
    The Amer. Civil Defense Assn. [5559]
    Asian Disaster Preparedness Center [IO]
    Assn. of Drainage Authorities [IO]
    Civil Affairs Assn. [6074]
    Disaster Emergency Response Assn. [5560]
    Disaster Preparedness and Emergency Response
        Assn. [5561]
    DRI Intl. [5562]
    Emergency Planning Soc. [IO]
    GeoHazards Intl. [12633]
    Intl. Assn. Emergency Managers [5563]
    Intl. Assn. Emergency Managers [IO]
    Intl. Civil Defence Org. [IO]
    Intl. Resources Gp. [IO]
    Intl. Resources Gp. [5564]
    Local Authorities Confronting Disasters and
        Emergencies [IO]
    Minuteman Civil Defense Corps [17077]
    Natl. Emergency Mgt. Assn. [5565]
    U.S. Homeland Emergency Response Org.
        [12893]
    U.S. Naval Cryptologic Veterans Assn. [21327]
Civil Defense Awareness [★18469]
Civil Defense Coun; U.S. [★5563]
Civil Defense Directors; Natl. Assn. of State [★5565]
Civil Employees; Natl. Assn. of Retired [★5710]
Civil Engineering
    Assn. of Consulting Engineers in Suriname [IO]
    Assn. of European Civil Engg. Faculties [IO]
    Associazione Geotecnica Italiana [IO]
    Australasian Chap. of Intl. Geosynthetics Soc.
        [IO]
    Belgian Geosynthetics Soc. [IO]
    China Civil Engg. Soc. [IO]
    Civil Engg. Contractors Assn. [IO]
    Civil Engg. Forum of Innovation [6699]
    Finnish Assn. of Civil Engineers [IO]
    Intl. Assn. of Civil Engg. Students [IO]
    International Geosynthetics Society [IO]
    Intl. Geosynthetics Soc. [6700]
    Intl. Geosynthetics Soc. - Brazilian Chap. [IO]
    Intl. Geosynthetics Soc. - Chinese Chap. [IO]
    Intl. Geosynthetics Soc. - Indian Chap. [IO]
    Intl. Geosynthetics Soc. - Turkish Chap. [IO]
    Japan Chap. of Intl. Geosynthetics Soc. [IO]
    Japan Soc. of Civil Engineers [IO]
    New Zealand Soc. for Earthquake Engg. [IO]
    North American Geosynthetics Society [IO]
    North Amer. Geosynthetics Soc. [6701]
Civil Engg. Contractors Assn. [IO], London, United
    Kingdom
Civil Engg. Forum of Innovation [6699], c/o Amer.
    Soc. of Civil Engineers, 1801 Alexander Bell Dr.,
    Ste. 630, Reston, VA 20191, (703)295-6314
Civil Engg. Res. Found. [★6699]
Civil Engineers; Amer. Soc. of [6992]
Civil Intl. - U.S.A; Ser. [★13404]
Civil Justice; Lawyers for [17962]
Civil Law
    Independence Inst. [17120]
    Natural Law Soc. [10813]
    Pound Civil Justice Inst. [6335]
Civil Liberties Comm; Natl. Emergency [★17097]
Civil Liberties Educational Found. - Defunct.
Civil Liberties Inst; Meiklejohn [5804]
Civil Liberties Legal Defense Fund - Defunct.
Civil Pilots for Regulatory Reform - Address
    unknown since 1989.
Civil and Public Services Assn. [★IO]
Civil Rights; Catholic League for Religious and
    [19600]

Civil Rights Documentation Project - Defunct.
Civil Rights Legal Defense Fund [★17097]
Civil Rights and Liberties
    A. Philip Randolph Educal. Fund [17078]
    Acton Inst. for the Stud. of Religion and Liberty
        [20489]
    Advocates Intl. [17998]
    Advocating Change Together [11914]
    Afghans for Civil Soc. [17079]
    Afghans for Civil Soc. [IO]
    Albanian Amer. Civic League [16970]
    All One Heart [17080]
    All of Us or None [17081]
    Alliance for Am. [11807]
    Alliance for Full Acceptance [12213]
    Alliance for Human Res. Protection [17741]
    Alliance for Women's Equality [13455]
    American-Arab Anti-Discrimination Comm. [17082]
    Amer. Citizens for Justice [17083]
    Amer. Civil Liberties Union [17084]
    Amer. Civil Liberties Union Found. [17085]
    Amer. Civil Rights Inst. [17086]
    Amer. Constitution Soc. for Law and Policy [5603]
    Amer. Family Rights Assn. [17508]
    Amer. Freedom Center [18421]
    Amer. Indian Law Alliance [16973]
    Amer. Patriots Assn. [21239]
    Amer. Sons of Liberty [17087]
    Amer. Spanish Comm. [17088]
    Americans to Ban Cloning [17089]
    Americans for Religious Liberty [17090]
    Americans United for Separation of Church and
        State [19836]
    Americans With Disabilities Act [11920]
    Anti-Defamation League [17091]
    Anti-Racism Info. Ser. [IO]
    Anti-Racist Action-Los Angeles/People Against
        Racist Terror [IO]
    Anti-Racist Action-Los Angeles/People Against
        Racist Terror [17092]
    Anti-Repression Rsrc. Team [17093]
    Anti-Slavery Intl. [IO]
    Arcus Found. [18266]
    Armed Females of Am. [17587]
    Article 19 - Global Campaign for Free Expression
        [IO]
    Artists Against Racism [IO]
    Asian Amer. Center for Justice of the Amer.
        Citizens for Justice [17094]
    Asian Amer. Legal Defense and Educ. Fund
        [17095]
    Asian and Pacific Islander Amer. Vote [18345]
    Assn. for Civil Rights [IO]
    Assn. for Civil Rights in Israel [IO]
    Australian Civil Liberties Union [IO]
    Australians Against Racism [IO]
    Axis of Justice [18640]
    Bastard Nation: The Adoptee Rights Org. [11237]
    Black Bus. and Professional Assn. [IO]
    Black Coaches Assn. [23287]
    Black Cops Against Police Brutality [5965]
    Campaign to End the Death Penalty [17028]
    Canadian Assn. for Free Expression [IO]
    Canadian Civil Liberties Assn. [IO]
    Catholic League for Religious and Civil Rights
        [19600]
    Center for Civil and Human Rights [12369]
    Center for the Community Interest [17096]
    Center for Constitutional Rights [17097]
    Center for Democratic Renewal [17098]
    Center for Third World Organizing [17099]
    Center for Third World Organizing [IO]
    Children's Rights [17100]
    Chinese for Affirmative Action [17101]
    Christian Anti-Defamation League [17102]
    Citizens for a Better Am. [17103]
    Citizens' Commn. on Civil Rights [17104]
    Citizens Comm. for the Right to Keep and Bear
        Arms [17105]
    Citizens for Consumer Justice [18641]
    Citizens Equal Rights Alliance [5800]
    Citizens for Legitimate Govt. [17663]
    Citizens for Sensible Safeguards [17106]
    Citizens United [17664]
    Coalition to Abolish Slavery and Trafficking
        [12370]

Reference to "IO" in place of a book number signifies that the association may be found in the 45th edition of International Organizations.

Coalition for Democracy in Iran [17389]
Coalition for Genetic Fairness [17107]
Coalition of Immokalee Workers [13458]
COLAGE [12223]
Commn. for Racial Equality [IO]
Commn. for Social Justice [17108]
Comm. on the Elimination of Racial Discrimination [IO]
Comm. for Humanitarian Assistance to Iranian Refugees [12808]
Comm. for Truth in Psychiatry [15195]
Community United Against Violence [12225]
Conquistadores 1492 [18669]
Death with Dignity Natl. Center [17109]
Democracy for Am. [18291]
Dept. of Civil, Human and Women's Rights, AFL-CIO [17110]
Disability Rights Center [11939]
Discussion Club [17111]
Drug Policy Alliance [17112]
Educating for Justice [9126]
Equal Justice Soc. [6258]
European/American Issues Forum [17113]
European-American Unity and Rights Org. [17114]
Falun Data Info. Center [17757]
Filipinos for Affirmative Action [18270]
First Amendment Found. [17115]
Found. Against Trafficking in Women [IO]
Free the Fathers [17060]
Free the Slaves [12371]
Freedom of Expression Found. [17116]
Freedom Forum [17117]
Freedom Forum [IO]
Freedom From Religion Found. [19837]
Freedom Org. for the Right to Enjoy Smoking Tobacco [IO]
Friedrich Naumann Found. - Africa Regional Off. [IO]
Gay and Lesbian Advocates and Defenders [17118]
Gender Action [18825]
The Generation After [17119]
GenerationEngage [18848]
Global Alliance Against Traffic in Women [IO]
Global Workers Justice Alliance [18074]
Global Youth Connect [18851]
Good Shepherd Volunteers [13394]
Hate Free Zone [17392]
Heritage Preservation Assn. [20721]
Heritage of Pride [12233]
Hispanas Organized for Political Equality [17703]
Human and Civil Rights Organizations of Am. [11738]
Independence Inst. [17120]
Inst. of Race Relations [IO]
Intellectual Disability Rights Ser. [IO]
Intelligence Proj. [17121]
Intl. Fed. of Black Prides [12238]
Intl. Inst. for Ethnic Gp. Rights and Regionalism [IO]
Intl. Movement Against All Forms of Discrimination and Racism [IO]
Intl. Org. for the Elimination of All Forms of Racial Discrimination [IO]
Intl. People's Democratic Uhuru Movement [17395]
Intl. Possibilities Unlimited [18642]
InterPride [12240]
IP Justice [5852]
Iranian Refugees' Alliance [12813]
Iraq Occupation Focus [IO]
Irish Coun. for Civil Liberties [IO]
Jews Against the Occupation [17952]
Jews for the Preservation of Firearms Ownership [17122]
John M. Olin Found. [12047]
Judge David L. Bazelon Center for Mental Hea. Law [17123]
Justice Without Borders [6025]
L. Mike Assn. [13124]
Law Students for Choice [18517]
Leadership Conf. on Civil Rights [17124]
Leadership Conf. Educ. Fund [8094]
League of the South [17125]

League of Young Voters [18356]
Lelio Basso Intl. Found. for the Rights and Liberation of Peoples [IO]
Liberty [IO]
Life After Exoneration Prog. [17360]
Marriage Equality USA [12506]
A Matter of Justice Coalition [6012]
Media Access Proj. [17182]
Media Coalition [17126]
Meiklejohn Civil Liberties Inst. [5804]
Mental Disability Rights Intl. [12574]
Mexican Amer. Legal Defense and Educational Fund [17705]
Minority Rights Gp. Intl. [IO]
Minuteman Civil Defense Corps [17077]
Mission for Est. of Human Rights in Iran [17777]
Movement Against Racism and for Friendship Between Peoples [IO]
Natl. Action Network [17127]
Natl. Alliance Against Racist and Political Repression [17128]
Natl. Alliance of Sentencing Advocates and Mitigation Specialists [5645]
Natl. Assn. of ADA Coordinators [11966]
Natl. Assn. for the Advancement of Colored People [17129]
Natl. Assn. for the Advancement of Colored People Legal Defense and Educational Fund [17130]
Natl. Assn. of Black Citizens Action [16942]
Natl. Assn. of Korean Americans [17131]
Natl. Assn. for Rights Protection and Advocacy [17132]
Natl. Assn. of Social Workers Natl. Comm. on Lesbian, Gay and Bisexual Issues [12245]
Natl. Assn. of State Sentencing Commissions [5650]
Natl. Assn. to Stop Guardian Abuse [12059]
Natl. Black Justice Coalition [18643]
Natl. Catholic Conf. for Interracial Justice [17133]
Natl. Coalition of Concerned Legal Professionals [12501]
Natl. Comm. Against Repressive Legislation [17134]
Natl. Comm. on Pay Equity [17553]
Natl. Comm. to Reopen the Rosenberg Case [17135]
Natl. Cong. of Vietnamese Americans [19425]
Natl. Drug Strategy Network [17136]
Natl. Economic and Social Rights Initiative [17778]
Natl. Fair Housing Alliance [17733]
Natl. Image [19102]
Natl. Juneteenth Observance Found. [16945]
Natl. Latina/Latino Law Student Assn. [17996]
Natl. League for the Separation of Church and State [19838]
Natl. Legal Sanctuary for Community Advancement [6015]
Natl. Mobilization Against Sweatshops [17975]
Natl. Org. for Mexican Amer. Rights [17709]
Natl. Org. for the Reform of Marijuana Laws [17137]
Natl. Rsrc. and Info. Center [18814]
Natl. Urban League [17138]
Natl. Voice [17076]
Natl. Youth Rights Assn. [18855]
New Age Citizen [17139]
No Peace Without Justice [18227]
November Coalition [18690]
Nurses for the Rights of the Child [11737]
Omega First Amendment Legal Fund [17140]
Online Privacy Alliance [17141]
OutProud [12252]
Parents Rights Coalition [12687]
Partners for Peace [18230]
Partnership for Civil Justice Legal Defense and Educ. Fund [17142]
People for the Amer. Way [17143]
People's Decade of Human Rights Educ. [17782]
People's Rights Fund [17144]
Peoples Rights Org. [17145]
Prejudice Institute/Center for the Applied Stud. of Ethnoviolence [17146]
Privacy Intl. [IO]

Private Citizen, Inc. [17147]
Proj. Equality [17148]
Protection Proj. [12377]
Puerto Rican Legal Defense and Educ. Fund [17149]
Racial Justice 911 [18493]
Rebuilding Alliance [12336]
Refugee Coun. USA [18500]
Resisting Defamation [17150]
Results Australia [IO]
Results - Canada [IO]
Results - United Kingdom [IO]
Rigoberta Menchu Tum Found. [IO]
Rigoberta Menchu Tum Found. [17151]
Rutherford Inst. [18513]
Sam Adams Alliance [17673]
Scouting For All [13006]
Seat Belt Choice Coalition [17016]
Second Amendment Found. [17152]
Sect. of Individual Rights and Responsibilities [17153]
Sikh Amer. Legal Defense and Educ. Fund [18600]
Sociologists Without Borders [18664]
Soulforce [17657]
South Asian Amer. Leaders of Tomorrow [18667]
South Asian Amer. Voting Youth [18366]
Southern Center for Human Rights [17036]
Southern Christian Leadership Conf. [17154]
Southern Poverty Law Center [17155]
Southern Poverty Law Center [IO]
Southern Regional Coun. [17156]
Sovereignty Intl. [17873]
Special Comm. on the Situation with Regard to the Implementation of the Declaration on the Granting of Independence to Colonial Countries and Peoples [17157]
Special Comm. on the Situation with Regard to the Implementation of the Declaration on the Granting of Independence to Colonial Countries and Peoples [IO]
Sportsmen's Assn. for Firearms Educ. [17600]
Student Assn. for Voter Empowerment [17490]
Students for the Second Amendment [17602]
Torture Abolition and Survivors Support Coalition Intl. [17786]
Trade Union Leadership Coun. [17158]
TransAfrica Forum [16934]
Turkish Amer. Alliance for Fairness [19410]
U.S. Farmers Assn. [16958]
Urban Alliance on Race Relations [IO]
Watchlist on Children and Armed Conflict [11664]
Women's Intl. Coalition for Economic Justice [17475]
Workers' Defense League [17159]
World Org. for Human Rights USA [12381]
Young Koreans United [12485]
Youth for Human Rights Intl. [12382]
Civil Rights Mobilization [★17124]
Civil Rights Trail [★17071]
Civil Rights Under Law; Lawyers' Comm. for [6027]
Civil Service
African Civil Ser. Observatory [IO]
Amer. Assn. of State Ser. Commissions [6189]
Assn. of Former Intl. Civil Servants - New York [5566]
Coun. of Jewish Orgs. in Civil Service [5567]
Fed. of Associations of Former Intl. Civil Servants [IO]
Natl. Assn. of Civil Service Employees [5568]
Natl. Assn. of State Retirement Administrators [5569]
Natl. Conf. on Public Employee Retirement Systems [5570]
Natl. Org. of Blacks in Govt. [5571]
Public Employees Roundtable [5572]
Civil Ser. Alliance [★IO]
Civil Ser. Employees Assn. [24073], PO Box 7125, Capitol Sta., Albany, NY 12224-0125, (518)257-1000
Civil Ser. Gp. [★IO]
Civil Soc. - Address unknown since 1986.
Civil Soc. Intl. [17445], 38 Miller Ave., No. 155, Mill Valley, CA 94941, (206)523-4755
Civil Soc. Intl. [IO], Mill Valley, CA, United States

A star before a book entry number signifies that the name is not listed separately, but is mentioned within the entry.

Civil Soc. of Multimedia Authors [IO], Paris, France
Civil Trial Advocates Program; National Certification of Family Law, Criminal and [★6333]
Civil War
   Abraham Lincoln Assn. [11100]
   Amer. Civil War Assn. [10087]
   Amer. History Forum and Civil War Educ. Assn. [8500]
   Armies of Tennessee, CSA and U.S.A. [20722]
   Auxiliary to Sons of Union Veterans of the Civil War [20723]
   Children of the Confederacy [20724]
   Civil War Round Table Associates [10102]
   Civil War Soc. [10103]
   Civil War Token Soc. [22732]
   Confederate Memorial Assn. [9368]
   Confederate Memorial Literary Soc. [10105]
   Custer Battlefield Historical and Museum Assn. [10106]
   Daughters of Union Veterans of the Civil War, 1861-1865 [20725]
   Friends of the Abraham Lincoln Museum [11113]
   Hood's Texas Brigade Assn. [20726]
   Jefferson Davis Assn. [11129]
   John Pelham Historical Assn. [11131]
   Ladies of the Grand Army of the Republic [20727]
   Love Token Soc. [22744]
   Military Order of the Loyal Legion of the U.S. [20728]
   Military Order of the Stars and Bars [20729]
   North-South Skirmish Assn. [23727]
   Robert E. Lee Memorial Assn. [11146]
   Sam Davis Memorial Assn. [11149]
   Save the Battlefield Coalition [10061]
   Soc. of Civil War Historians [10151]
   Sons of Confederate Veterans [20730]
   Sons of Union Veterans of the Civil War [20731]
   Ulysses S. Grant Assn. [11154]
   United Daughters of the Confederacy [20732]
Civil War Assn; Amer. [10087]
Civil War Battlefield Campaign [★4380]
Civil War Centennial Commn. [★11129]
Civil War Coun; Natl. Lincoln [★11113]
Civil War Historians; Soc. of [10151]
Civil War Preservation Trust [10019], 1331 H St. NW, Ste. 1001, Washington, DC 20005, (202)367-1861
Civil War Press Corps - Address unknown since 2003.
Civil War Round Table Associates [10102], PO Box 7281, Little Rock, AR 72217
Civil War Sites; Assn. for the Preservation of [★10019]
Civil War Soc. [10103], 33756 Black Mountain Rd., Tollhouse, CA 93667, (559)855-8637
Civil War Soc; Virginia Country [★10103]
Civil War; Sons of Union Veterans of the [20731]
Civil War Token Soc. [22732], c/o Dale Cade, Sec., 26548 Mazur Dr., Rancho Palos Verdes, CA 90275, (310)378-4182
Civil War Trust [★10019]
Civilian Administrators Assn; Naval [★6094]
Civilian-Based Defense Assn. - Defunct.
Civilian Blind; Amer. Braille Press for War and [★16854]
Civilian Casualty Fund - Defunct.
Civilian Cong. [17251]
Civilian Conservation Corps Alumni; Natl. Assn. of [19082]
Civilian Employees Assn; Natl. Guard [★24072]
Civilian Managers Assn; Naval [6094]
Civilian Material Assistance - Address unknown since 2001.
Civilian Technicians; Assn. of [24072]
Civilization; The Comm. for Western [8243]
Civilokonomerne [★IO]
Civitan Intl. [IO], Birmingham, AL, United States
Civitan Intl. [13038], PO Box 130744, Birmingham, AL 35213-0744, (205)591-8910
Civitas [11376], 2210 W North Ave., Chicago, IL 60647, (312)226-6700
CIVITAS: Citizens for Planetary Hea. [★11379]
Civitas Found. for the Civil Soc. [IO], Cluj-Napoca, Romania
CJM Orquideas [IO], Lima, Peru

Cladan Cultural Exchange Inst. of Australia [IO], Double Bay, Australia
An Claidheamh Soluis; Irish Arts Center - [10243]
Claim Coun., Inc; Shippers Natl. Freight [★3595]
Claimants Compensation Attorneys; Natl. Assn. of [★6328]
Claimants' Representatives; Natl. Org. of Social Security [18650]
Claims Assistance Professionals; Alliance of [2126]
Claims Conf; Eastern [2163]
Claims Coun; Natl. Truck and Heavy Equip. [2228]
Claims of the Paranormal; Comm. for the Sci. Investigation of [7444]
Claims and Prevention Coun; Trans. [★3595]
Claims Professional Accreditation Coun; Certified [3865]
Claims Support Professional Assn. [2154], 6451 N Fed. Hwy., Ste. 121, Fort Lauderdale, FL 33308, (800)523-3680
CLAL: Natl. Jewish Center for Learning and Leadership [20132], 440 Park Ave. S, 4th Fl., New York, NY 10016-8012, (212)779-3300
Clan in Am; MacLellan [20988]
Clan Anderson Soc. [10953], c/o H. Wesley Weaver, Pres., 19411 Center St., Cornelius, NC 28031, (704)892-5608
Clan Archibald Family Assn. - Defunct.
Clan Arthur Assn., USA [19349], 6430 Princeton Dr., Alexandria, VA 22307, (703)765-6593
Clan Associations; Coun. of Scottish [★19352]
Clan Bell Descendants - Address unknown since 2001.
Clan Boyd [★20945]
Clan Boyd [★IO]
Clan Brown Soc. [20818], c/o Jaythomas J. Brown, 38 High Rock St., Lynn, MA 01902-3815
Clan Buchanan Soc. in America - Address unknown since 2006.
Clan Campbell Soc. [★20819]
Clan Campbell Soc., North Am. [20819], 3704 Kantrel Pl., Valrico, FL 33594-6920, (813)685-4638
Clan Carmichael U.S.A. [20820], c/o Kathy Gambill, Membership Chair, 3298 S Beddow St., Terre Haute, IN 47802, (812)894-2336
Clan Chisholm in Am. [★20821]
Clan Chisholm Soc. [IO], Sidney, BC, Canada
Clan Chisholm Soc., Australia [IO], Panorama, Australia
Clan Chisholm Soc., Canada [IO], Okotoks, AB, Canada
Clan Chisholm Soc., New Zealand [IO], Palmerston North, New Zealand
Clan Chisholm Soc., Nova Scotia [IO], Antigonish, NS, Canada
Clan Chisholm Soc., United Kingdom [IO], Inverness, United Kingdom
Clan Chisholm Soc. - U.S. Br. [20821], PO Box 940147, Houston, TX 77094-7147
Clan Colquhoun Soc. of North Am. [20822], 2984 Mike Dr., Marietta, GA 30064
Clan Craig Assn. of Am. [19350], c/o Gloria Craig, Treas., 10002 Aurora Ave. N, Ste. 4423, Seattle, WA 98133
Clan Cunning Assn. - Defunct.
Clan Cunningham Soc. of Am. [20823], 4575 W 111th Ave., Westminster, CO 80031-2025
Clan Currie Soc. [20824], PO Box 541, Summit, NJ 07902-0541, (908)273-3509
Clan Currie Soc. [IO], Summit, NJ, United States
Clan Davidson Soc. [20825], c/o Elaine Davidson, Sec.-Treas., 235 Fairmont Dr., North Wilkesboro, NC 28659
Clan Donald Canada [IO], Trenton, NS, Canada
Clan Douglas Soc. of North Am. [20826], c/o John Douglas, Sec., 116 Wake Forest Dr., Warner Robins, GA 31093, (770)949-4797
Clan Drummond Soc. of North Am. [20827], c/o Charles McRobbie, 6 Bernard Ln., Methuen, MA 01844, (978)682-0130
Clan Ewing in Am. [19351], 513 Cherokee Dr., Erie, PA 16505
Clan Farquharson Assn. of Canada [IO], Dartmouth, NS, Canada
Clan Fergusson Soc. of North Am. [IO], Sisters, OR, United States

Clan Fergusson Soc. of North Am. [21111], 15079 Wagonwheel, Sisters, OR 97759
Clan Forrester Soc. [20828], c/o Ben Forrester, Pres., 1034 Blue Heron Dr., Commerce, GA 30529, (706)335-7688
Clan Forsyth Soc. of Canada [IO], Toronto, ON, Canada
Clan Fraser Soc. of Canada [IO], Toronto, ON, Canada
Clan Fraser Soc. of North Am. - Canadian Region [★IO]
Clan Graham Soc. [20829], c/o Norris Graham, Membership VP, PO Box 70, Yucca, AZ 86438
Clan Gregor Soc; Amer. [20780]
Clan Guthrie USA [20830], c/o Carrie Guthrie-Whitlow, Treas., PO Box 121, Port Orchard, WA 98366
Clan Hamilton Soc. [20831], c/o Philip G. Dixon, Sec., PO Box 1245, Summerville, SC 29484-1245, (803)873-2430
Clan Hunter Assn. [IO], West Kilbride, United Kingdom
Clan Hunter Assn. USA [20832], 3583 Dumbarton Rd., Atlanta, GA 30327-2613
Clan Irwin Assn. [20833], c/o Guy C. Irvin, Chm., 226 1750th Ave., Mount Pulaski, IL 62548-6635, (217)792-5226
Clan Johnston(e) in Am. [20834], c/o Dr. Stephen A. Johnston, Pres., 215 SE Maynard Rd., Cary, NC 27511, (919)380-7707
Clan Johnston(e) in America [IO], Cary, NC, United States
Clan Keith Soc. [20835], c/o Sandra K. Glasscock, Natl. Sec., 1809 N Sandal, Mesa, AZ 85205-3559, (757)479-5141
Clan Leslie Soc. [★20836]
Clan Leslie Soc. Intl. [20836], PO Box 845, Jackson, NJ 08527
Clan MacAlpine Soc. [19049], 32682 Rosemont Dr., Trabuco Canyon, CA 92679-3386
Clan MacDuff Soc. of Am. [20837], c/o Kim Duprest, Membership Chm., 526 E Charleston Ave., Phoenix, AZ 85022, (602)866-2570
Clan MacGillivray Soc. - Australia [IO], Seaford, Australia
Clan MacInnes Soc. [★20951]
Clan MacIntyre Assn. [20838], c/o Carole M. McIntyre, VP of Membership, 617 E 400 N, Centerville, UT 84014-1956
Clan MacIntyre Soc. [20839], c/o Barbara Carmel, Pres., PO Box 1199, Long Beach, CA 90801-1199, (206)362-1822
Clan Mackay Assn. of Canada [IO], Etobicoke, ON, Canada
Clan MacKay Soc. [20840], c/o David R. McKay, Pres., 5461 Poplar Dr., Monroe, MI 48161, (734)457-1772
Clan MacKenzie Soc. in the Americas [20841], PO Box 300337, Waterford, MI 48330
Clan Mackenzie Soc. in the Americas - Canada [IO], Oakville, ON, Canada
Clan MacKinnon Soc. [19050], PO Box 832, Wilton, CA 95693
Clan Mackintosh of North Am. [20842], c/o Carl R. McIntosh, Pres., 133 Steeplechase N, Columbia, SC 29209, (803)647-7573
Clan MacLennan Assn., U.S.A. [20843], c/o Winton D. MacLennan, Pres., 1032 Lockridge Ln., Ashland City, TN 37015
Clan MacLennan, Central Ontario Br. [IO], Burlington, ON, Canada
Clan Macneil Assn. of Am. [20844], c/o Ms. Rhonwn Darby McNeill, Membership VP, PO Box 230693, Montgomery, AL 36123-0693, (334)834-0612
Clan MacNeil in Canada [IO], Aurora, ON, Canada
Clan Macpherson Association [IO], Seattle, WA, United States
Clan Macpherson Assn. [20845], c/o William MacPherson, Chm., 2728 Fairview Ave. E, No. 303, Seattle, WA 98102
Clan MacRae Soc. of North Am. [20846], c/o Capt. John M. MacRae-Hall, Pres., PO Box 404, Westminster, SC 29693-0404
Clan MacThomas Soc. [★20989]
Clan Maitland Soc. of North Am. [20847], c/o Rosemary Maitland Thom, Sec., 7016 Carrondale Way, Las Vegas, NV 89128-3339

Reference to "IO" in place of a book number signifies that the association may be found in the 45th edition of International Organizations.

Clan Matheson Soc. [20848], c/o Malcolm Matheson, III, Chief Lieutenant, PO Box 307, The Plains, VA 20198

Clan Maxwell Soc. of the USA [20849], c/o Nancy Dirkes, Sec., 803 Armstrong Dr., Georgetown, TX 78628

Clan McAlister of Am. [19051], c/o S.M. McAllister, Treas., 2360 Len Cir. NW, Hartselle, AL 35640-7769, (256)773-7823

Clan McLaren Assn. of North America [20850]

Clan Menzies Soc., North Amer. Br. [20851], c/o Dr. David A. Mathewes, Commissioner, 323 Rough Water Point, Canton, NC 28716-8196, (828)648-4255

Clan Moffat Soc. [20852], c/o Roger Moffat, 3020 76th SE, Caledonia, MI 49316-8398

Clan Moncreiffe Soc. of North Am. [20853], c/o Mike W. Moncrief, Membership Chm., 1405 Plaza St. SE, Decatur, AL 35603

Clan Moncreiffe Soc. of North Am. [IO], Decatur, AL, United States

Clan Montgomery Intl. [★IO]

Clan Montgomery Intl. [★20854]

Clan Montgomery Soc. Intl. [20854], c/o Alice Montgomery, Treas., 2071 State Hwy. 29, Johnstown, NY 12095

Clan Montgomery Society International [IO], Newark, DE, United States

Clan Munro Assn. [20855], c/o Doris Munro Small, Membership Sec., 176 Neptune Rd., Orange Park, FL 32073-3231, (904)272-2931

Clan Munro Assn. of Canada [IO], Toronto, ON, Canada

Clan Napier in North America [20856], c/o Brig. Gen. John H. Napier, III, Lieutenant to the Chief, Kilmahew, Rte. 2, Box 614, Ramer, AL 36069-9254

Clan of North America; Dobie [20884]

Clan Phail Soc. in North America [19052], c/o Bill McPhail, 403 1/2 Garfield St. S, Apt. 16, Tacoma, WA 98444

Clan Pollock [20857], 300 Hillwood Blvd., Nashville, TN 37205-1308, (615)456-1699

Clan Ramsey Assn. of North Am. [20858], c/o David F. Ramsey, Membership Chm./Treas., 434 Skinner Blvd., Ste. 105, Dunedin, FL 34698, (727)734-7020

Clan Rose Soc. of Am. [20859], c/o Dorothy Blount, Sec.-Treas., 5530 Truman Mountain Rd., Gainesville, GA 30506-3842

Clan Ross Assn. of Canada [IO], Winnipeg, MB, Canada

Clan Ross Assn. of the U.S. [20860], c/o W. Hugh Ross, Pres., 1004 N Bowen Rd., Arlington, TX 76012, (303)237-0650

Clan Scott Soc. [20861], c/o Mr. David M. Scott, Membership Sec., PO Box 13021, Austin, TX 78711-3021

Clan Scott Soc. of the Americas [★20861]

Clan Scott, U.S.A. [★20861]

Clan Shaw Soc. [20862], c/o Mr. Meredith L. Shaw, Pres., 3031 Appomattox Ave., No. 102, Olney, MD 20832-1498

Clan Sinclair Assn. of Canada [IO], Toronto, ON, Canada

Clan Sinclair Assn. U.S.A. [20863], c/o Mel Sinclair, Pres., 224 Bransfield Rd., Greenville, SC 29615, (864)268-3550

Clan Soc; Innes [20950]

Clan Soc; MacCartney [20986]

Clan Soc. North Am; Murray [21005]

Clan Sutherland Soc. of North Am. [20864], c/o George W. Sutherland, VP, 9301 Harris Glen Dr., Charlotte, NC 28269

Clan Young [20865], c/o Mr. Charles A. Pickering, Treas., 84 Columbus Ave., West Bridgewater, MA 02379

Clan Young Soc. [★20865]

Clandestine Radio Enthusiasts; Assn. of [21497]

Clanranald Trust for Scotland [IO], Kincardine, United Kingdom

Clans and Associations; Coun. of Scottish [19352]

Clanwilliam Inst. [IO], Dublin, Ireland

Clara Bow Fan Club - Defunct.

Clare Animal Welfare [IO], Ennis, Ireland

Claremont Inst. [17070], 937 W Foothill Blvd., Ste. E, Claremont, CA 91711, (909)621-6825

Claretian Volunteers [★19612]

Claretian Volunteers and Lay Missionaries [19612], 205 W Monroe St., Chicago, IL 60606, (312)236-7782

Clarinet Intl. [★10616]

Clarinet Intl. [★IO]

Clarinet and Saxophone Soc. of Great Britain [IO], Hampton, United Kingdom

Clarinet Society/Clarinetwork Intl; Intl. [★10616]

Clarinetwork Intl; Intl. Clarinet Society/ [★10616]

Clarion Music Soc. - Address unknown since 2003.

Clarity [6011], c/o Prof. Joseph Kimble, Membership Sec., Box 13038, Lansing, MI 48901-3038, (517)371-5140

Clark Fan Club; Terri [24981]

Clark Found; Robert Sterling [11902]

Clark; Friends of Guy [24893]

Clark Trail Heritage Found; Lewis and [10128]

Clarsach Soc. [IO], Edinburgh, United Kingdom

Class of '74 [★18288]

Class E Scow Assn; Natl. [23204]

Classic AMX Club Intl. - Defunct.

Classic and Antique Motorcycles of America - Defunct.

Classic Bicycle and Whizzer Club of America - Defunct.

Classic Boat Soc; Antique and [21868]

Classic Car Club of Am. [21614], 1645 Des Plaines River Rd., Ste. 7A, Des Plaines, IL 60018-2206, (847)390-0443

Classic Chevy Club Intl. [★21615]

Classic Chevy Club Intl. [★IO]

Classic Chevy Intl. [IO], Titusville, FL, United States

Classic Chevy Intl. [21615], 5140 S Washington Ave., Titusville, FL 32780, (321)269-9680

Classic Comet Club of America - Defunct.

Classic Corvette Club 53-55 - Defunct.

Classic Jaguar Assn. [21616], c/o Dick Strever, 4515 N Bank Rd., Crescent City, CA 95531

Classic Racing Motorcycle Club - Defunct.

Classic Thunderbird Club Intl. [21617], 1308 E 29th St., Signal Hill, CA 90755-1842, (562)426-2709

Classic Thunderbird Club Intl. [IO], Signal Hill, CA, United States

Classic Yacht Assn. [21871], 5267 Shilshole Ave. NW, Ste. 107, Seattle, WA 98107, (206)937-6211

Classical America - Address unknown since 2001.

Classical Assn. of Ireland [IO], Dublin, Ireland

Classical Assn. of South Africa [IO], Durban, Republic of South Africa

Classical League; Amer. [8726]

Classical League; Junior [★8095]

Classical Music Broadcasters Assn. - Defunct.

Classical Music Lovers' Exchange [10578], PO Box 275, Santa Barbara, CA 93102-0275

Classical Studies

Amer. Philological Assn. [10296]

Assn. of Classical and Christian Schools [9089]

Australian Soc. for Classical Stud. [IO]

Classical Assn. of Ireland [IO]

Classical Assn. of South Africa [IO]

Early Music Network [10591]

Eta Sigma Phi, Natl. Classics Honorary Soc. [24433]

European Amer. Musical Alliance [10594]

Hellenic Philatelic Soc. of Am. [22826]

Intl. Assn. for Neo-Latin Stud. [IO]

Intl. Fed. of the Societies of Classical Stud. [IO]

Intl. Inst. for Ligurian Stud. [IO]

Mediterranean Stud. Assn. [10466]

Modern Greek Stud. Assn. [9996]

Mozart Soc. of Am. [9814]

Mycenaean Commn. [IO]

Natl. Comm. for Latin and Greek [9800]

Natl. Junior Classical League [8095]

Schubert Soc. of the USA [9816]

Soc. for Ancient Greek Philosophy [10830]

Soc. for Ancient Hellenic Stud. [IO]

Soc. for the Preservation of the Greek Heritage [9997]

Soc. for the Promotion of Hellenic Stud. [IO]

Soc. for the Promotion of Roman Stud. [IO]

Women's Classical Caucus [9801]

Classics 1946 Car Club - Defunct.

Classics Action Network [★9800]

Classics Honorary Soc; Eta Sigma Phi, Natl. [24433]

Classics Soc; U.S. Philatelic [22887]

Classification - of ALA; Division of Cataloging and [★10333]

Classification and Compensation Soc. - Defunct.

Classification Mgt. Soc; Natl. [★2092]

Classification Soc. of North Am. [7456], c/o Stanley L. Sclove, Sec.-Treas., IDS Dept., (MC 294), Univ. of Illinois - Chicago, 601 S Morgan St., Chicago, IL 60607-7100, (312)996-2676

Classified Advt. Managers; Assn. of Newspaper [★3244]

Classified Advt. Managers Assn; Southern [119]

Classified Dir. Subscribers Assn. - Defunct.

Classified School Employees; Amer. Assn. of [24041]

Classroom; Presidential [8756]

Classroom Publishers Assn. and Assn. of Educational Publishers [★9009]

Classrooms Abroad - Defunct.

Classy Bum Soc. - Address unknown since 2001.

Claudel Soc; Paul [9698]

Claver; Junior Daughters of Peter [19002]

Claver; Junior Knights of Peter [19003]

Claver; Knights of Peter [19005]

Claver; Missionary Sisters of St. Peter [20364]

Clay Flue Lining Inst. - Defunct.

Clay Guild; Natl. Polymer [22579]

Clay Memorial Found; Henry [11121]

Clay Minerals of the Natl. Acad. of Sciences—National Res. Coun; Comm. on [7341]

Clay Minerals Soc. [7341], 3635 Concorde Pkwy., Ste. 500, Chantilly, VA 20151-1125, (703)652-9960

Clay Pigeon Shooting Assn. [IO], Woking, United Kingdom

Clay Pipe Development Assn. [IO], Chesham, United Kingdom

Clay Pipe Inst; Natl. [3034]

Clay Pipe Mfrs; Natl. [★3034]

Clay Pot Mfrs; Natl. [183]

Clay Producers Assn; China [2748]

Clay Producers Trade Assn; China [★2748]

Clay Products Inst; Structural [★604]

Clay Products Res. Found; Structural [★604]

Clay Roof Tile Coun. [IO], Stoke-On-Trent, United Kingdom

Clay and Slate Inst; Expanded Shale [621]

Clay Target Shooting Assn. South Africa [IO], Great Brak River, Republic of South Africa

Clay Tile Assn; Structural [★604]

Clay Underwood Fan Club [24865], PO Box 46716, Mount Clemens, MI 48046, (586)463-5566

Clayton Fund [12179], 3505-M Cadillac Ave., Costa Mesa, CA 92626, (714)751-7433

Clean Air Policy Analyses; Center for Acid Rain and [★5083]

Clean Air Policy; Center for [5083]

Clean Air Soc. of Australia and New Zealand [IO], Toowong, Australia

Clean Air Soc. in the Netherlands [★IO]

Clean Air Trust [5085], 1625 K St. NW, Ste. 790, Washington, DC 20006, (301)941-1987

Clean Air Working Group - Defunct.

Clean Beaches Coun. [4540], 1225 New York Ave. NW, Ste. 450, Washington, DC 20005, (202)682-9507

Clean Calgary Assn. [IO], Calgary, AB, Canada

Clean Coal Coalition - Defunct.

Clean Energy Gp. [6948], 50 State St., Ste. 1, Montpelier, VT 05602, (802)223-2554

Clean Energy States Alliance [6949], c/o Clean Energy Gp., 50 State St., Ste. 1, Montpelier, VT 05602, (802)223-2554

Clean Fuels Development Coalition [5086], c/o Douglas A. Durante, Exec. Dir., 4641 Montgomery Ave., Ste. 350, Bethesda, MD 20814, (301)718-0077

Clean Harbors Cooperative [3070], 4601 Tremley Point Rd., Linden, NJ 07036, (908)862-7500

Clean Islands Intl. [4541], 8219 Elvaton Dr., Pasadena, MD 21122-3903, (410)647-2500

Clean Islands Intl. [IO], Pasadena, MD, United States

Clean Production Action [IO], Spring Brook, NY, United States

---

A star before a book entry number signifies that the name is not listed separately, but is mentioned within the entry.

Clean Production Action [4631], PO Box 153, Spring Brook, NY 14140, (716)805-1056
Clean Sites, Inc. - Defunct.
Clean Up Australia [IO], Glebe, Australia
Clean Up T.V. Campaign - Defunct.
Clean Up the World [IO], Sydney, Australia
Clean Water Action [5087], 4455 Connecticut Ave. NW, Ste. A300, Washington, DC 20008-2328, (202)895-0420
Clean Water Action Proj. [★5087]
Clean Water Coun. [5281], c/o Natl. Utility Contractors Assn., 4301 N Fairfax Dr., Ste. 360, Arlington, VA 22203-1627, (703)358-9300
Clean Water Fund [5088], 4455 Connecticut Ave. NW, Ste. A300-16, Washington, DC 20008-2328, (202)895-0432
Cleaner Manufacturers Assn; Vacuum [★264]
Cleaners Allied Trades Assn; Laundry and [★2407]
Cleaners Assn; Natl. Air Duct [2470]
Cleaners Machinery Mfrs. Assn; Laundry and Dry [★2407]
Cleaning Coun; Natl. Automatic Laundry and [★2402]
Cleaning Equip. Trade Assn. [2461], 968 Lake St. S, Ste. 202, Forest Lake, MN 55025, (651)982-0010
Cleaning Equipment Trade Association [IO], Forest Lake, MN, United States
Cleaning and Hygiene Suppliers' Assn. [IO], Marlow, United Kingdom
Cleaning Industry
   Carpet Cleaners Inst. of the Northwest [832]
   Cleaning Equip. Trade Assn. [2461]
   Cleaning Mgt. Inst. [2462]
   Intl. Executive Housekeepers Assn. [2464]
   Intl. Sanitary Supply Assn. [2466]
   Master Window Cleaners of Am. [2469]
   North Amer. Power Sweeping Assn. [2473]
   Restoration Indus. Assn. [2475]
   Sanitary Supply Wholesaling Assn. [2476]
Cleaning Inst; Indus. Gas [★3071]
Cleaning Mgt. Inst. [2462], 13 Century Hill Dr., Latham, NY 12110, (518)783-1281
Cleaning and Support Services Assn. [IO], London, United Kingdom
Cleaning Technicians; Intl. Soc. of [★2477]
Cleaning Technicians; Soc. of [★2477]
Clear Channel Broadcasting Service - Address unknown since 2003.
Clear Path Intl. [17424], 321 High School Rd. NE, No. 574, Bainbridge Island, WA 98110, (206)780-5964
Clear Path Intl. [IO], Bainbridge Island, WA, United States
Clearance Center; Copyright [5842]
Clearer Vision Ministries [13378], PO Box 2085, Sanford, FL 32772-2085, (352)475-2742
Clearer Vision Ministries [IO], Sanford, FL, United States
Clearing House for Foreign Group Visits - Defunct.
CH; Amer. Self-Help [★13013]
CH; Amer. Self-Help Gp. [13013]
CH for Bilingual Educ; Natl. [★8287]
Clearinghouse on Business Coalitions for Health Action - Defunct.
CH on Child Abuse and Neglect Info. [★11570]
Clearinghouse for Community Based Free Standing Educational Institutions [★8123]
Clearinghouse on Development Communication - Address unknown since 1999.
CH on Disability Info. [11933], Off. of Special Educ. and Rehabilitative Services, Commun. and Media Support Services, U.S. U.S. Department of Educ., 500 12th St. SW, Rm. 5133, Washington, DC 20202-2550, (202)245-7307
CH for English Language Acquisition and Language Instruction Educational Programs; Natl. [8287]
Clearinghouse on Family Violence Information - Defunct.
CH on the Handicapped [★11933]
Clearinghouse and Laboratory for Census Data - Defunct.
CH on Languages and Linguistics; ERIC [8730]
CH; Off. of Population Affairs [12757]
CH for Volunteer Accounting Services [19], 920 Hampshire Rd., Ste. A-29, Westlake Village, CA 91361, (805)495-6755

CH on Women's Issues [17519], PO Box 70603, Friendship Heights, Bethesda, MD 20813, (202)362-5717
Clearpoint Financial Solutions [1407], 8000 Franklin Farms Dr., Richmond, VA 23229, (877)877-1995
Clefs d'Or U.S.A; Les [1949]
Cleft Lip and Palate Assn. [IO], London, United Kingdom
Cleft Lip and Palate Assn. of Ireland [IO], Dublin, Ireland
Cleft Palate Assn; Amer. [★14055]
Cleft Palate-Craniofacial Assn; Amer. [14055]
Cleft Palate Found. [14058], 1504 E Franklin St., Ste. 102, Chapel Hill, NC 27514-2820, (919)933-9044
Cleft Palate Prosthesis; Amer. Acad. of [★14055]
Cleft Palate Rehabilitation; Amer. Assn. for [★14055]
Clematis Soc; Amer. [4672]
Clemens, Samuel
   Mark Twain Boyhood Home Associates [9684]
   Mark Twain Circle of New York [9685]
   Mark Twain House and Museum [9687]
   Mark Twain Res. Found. [9688]
Clergy
   Acad. of Parish Clergy [20274]
   African-Amer. Women's Clergy Assn. [20615]
   Amer. Clergy Leadership Conf. [19858]
   Amer. Forum for Jewish-Christian Cooperation [19887]
   Assn. for Clinical Pastoral Educ. [19915]
   Assn. of Professional Chaplains [19744]
   Assn. of Southern Baptist Campus Ministers [19474]
   Christian Mgt. Assn. [20511]
   Intl. Assn. of Christian Chaplains [19748]
   Intl. Assn. of Women Ministers [20619]
   Intl. Conf. of Police Chaplains [19749]
   Intl. Police and Fire Chaplain's Assn. [19750]
   The Linkup - Survivors of Clergy Abuse [11522]
   Lithuanian Catholic Religious Aid [19653]
   Liturgical Conf. [19900]
   Louis Finkelstein Inst. for Religious and Social Stud. at the Louis Stein Center [19931]
   Military Chaplains Assn. of the U.S.A. [19752]
   Natl. Assn. of Church Bus. Admin. [20513]
   Natl. Assn. of Church Facilities Managers [20514]
   Natl. Assn. of Church Personnel Administrators [20515]
   Natl. Campus Ministry Assn. [19933]
   Natl. Comm. for Amish Religious Freedom [19448]
   Natl. Org. for Continuing Educ. of Roman Catholic Clergy [19936]
   Presbyterian Church Bus. Administrators' Assn. [20470]
   Priests for Life [18564]
   Soc. of the Descendants of the Colonial Clergy [20760]
Clergy Abuse; The Linkup - Survivors of [11522]
Clergy; Acad. of Parish [20274]
Clergy Assn; African-Amer. Women's [20615]
Clergy Assn; Recovered Alcoholic [13278]
Clergy Associations; Natl. Network of Episcopal [19966]
Clergy Caucus; Natl. Black Catholic [19669]
Clergy Conf. on Alcoholism; Natl. [★13266]
Clergy Consultation Service on Abortion - Defunct.
Clergy Coun. on Alcoholism and Related Drug Problems; Natl. [★13266]
Clergy Counseling Service for Problem Pregnancies - Defunct.
Clergy Couples of the Presbyterian Family - Defunct.
Clergy and Laity Concerned - Address unknown since 2000.
Clergy and Laity of the Episcopal Church; Concerned [19950]
Clergy; Natl. Org. for Continuing Educ. of Roman Catholic [19936]
Clergy; Soc. of the Descendants of the Colonial [20760]
Clergy; Soc. of St. Peter the Apostle for Native [★19725]
Clergy in U.S.A; Missionary Union of the [★19703]
Clerks Assn; Fed. Court [5626]
Clerks Assn. of the Port of New York; Customs [★2309]

Clerks, Freight Handlers, Express and Sta. Employees; Brotherhood of Railway, Airline and Steamship [★24180]
Clerks, Freight Handlers, Express and Sta. Employees; Brotherhood of Railway and Steamship [★24180]
Clerks, Freight Handlers, Express and Sta. Employees; Carmen Division of the Brotherhood of Railway, Airline and Steamship [★24179]
Clerks; Natl. Assn. of County Recorders and [★5621]
Clerks; Natl. Assn. of County Recorders, Election Officials, and [5621]
Clerks; Natl. Conf. of Appellate Court [5629]
Clerks; United Fed. of Postal [★24166]
Clerkship Directors in Internal Medicine [14968], 2501 M St. NW, Ste. 550, Washington, DC 20037-1325, (202)861-9351
Clerkship Directors in Internal Medicine [IO], Washington, DC, United States
Cleveland Barons Booster Club [★25001]
Cleveland Bay Horse Soc. of Australasia [IO], Herne Hill, Australia
Cleveland Bay Horse Soc. of North Am. [4871], PO Box 483, Goshen, NH 03752, (352)489-2768
Cleveland Hockey Booster Club [25001], c/o Dorothy Michalko, First VP, 13118 Tyler Ave., Cleveland, OH 44111
Cleveland Vessel Owners Assn. [★2606]
CLFMA of India [IO], Bombay, India
CLG of Foot Orthopedists; Amer. [★16032]
CLIC Sargent [IO], Glasgow, United Kingdom
clickITnigeria [IO], Ile-Ife, Nigeria
Client Protection Org; Natl. [5949]
Client Specific Planning Prog. [★11878]
Cliff Richard Fan Club of Am. [24866], 3 Kelley Rd., Acton, MA 01720-3614
Cliff Richard Movement of New Zealand [IO], Auckland, New Zealand
Cliff Richard Movement - USA [★24866]
Climate Action Network Australia [IO], Ultimo, Australia
Climate Action Network Europe [IO], Brussels, Belgium
Climate Inst. [4542], 1785 Massachusetts Ave. NW, Washington, DC 20036, (202)547-0104
Climatic Data Center; National [★4590]
Climatological Assn; Amer. Clinical and [14018]
Climatologists; Amer. Assn. of State [7324]
Climb Nova Scotia [IO], Halifax, NS, Canada
Climbing
   Access Fund [23796]
   Adirondack Forty-Sixers [23930]
   Adirondack Mountain Club [23931]
   Adirondack Trail Improvement Soc. [23932]
   Amer. Canyoneering Assn. [21949]
   Amer. Endurance Ride Conf. [23933]
   Amer. Hiking Soc. [23934]
   Amer. Mountain Guides Assn. [23284]
   Amer. Safe Climbing Assn. [21950]
   Amer. Trails [23935]
   Appalachian Mountain Club [23936]
   Appalachian Trail Conservancy [23937]
   Assn. Of British Climbing Walls [IO]
   Australian Climbing Instructors Assn. [IO]
   Climb Nova Scotia [IO]
   Continental Divide Trail Soc. [23938]
   Florida Trail Assn. [23939]
   Highpointers Club [23014]
   Intercollegiate Outing Club Assn. [23941]
   IOCALUM [23942]
   Lincoln Heritage Trail Found. [23943]
   Montana Outfitters and Guides Assn. [23944]
   Mountaineers [23945]
   New England Trails Conf. [23948]
   North Amer. Trail Ride Conf. [23949]
   North Country Trail Assn. [23950]
   Outfitters Assn. of Am. [23642]
   Rails-to-Trails Conservancy [23952]
   Sheclimbs [23285]
   Sport Climbing Australia [IO]
   U.S. Adventure Racing Assn. [23672]
   U.S. Ski Mountaineering Assn. [23759]
   USA Climbing [23286]
Cline World Wide Fan Org; Always Patsy [24840]

Reference to "IO" in place of a book number signifies that the association may be found in the 45th edition of International Organizations.

Cling Peach Advisory Bd. [★4710]
Cling Peach Advisory Bd; California [★4710]
Cling Peach Bd; California [4710]
Clinic Found. of Am; Natl. Free [14585]
Clinic; Karen Horney [16109]
Clinic; Karen Horney Psychoanalytic [★16109]
Clinic Managers; Amer. Coll. of [★15054]
Clinic Managers; Assn. of [★15067]
Clinical Anatomists; Amer. Assn. of [13668]
Clinical Associates; Org. of Regulatory and [521]
Clinical Biochemistry; Natl. Acad. of [13748]
Clinical Chemistry; Amer. Assn. for [13936]
Clinical Chemistry; Natl. Registry in [★13939]
Clinical Chemists; Amer. Assn. of [★13936]
Clinical Cytometry Soc. [15865], 5 Revere Dr., Ste.
   200, Northbrook, IL 60062, (312)283-0900
Clinical Data Mgt; Soc. For [2982]
Clinical Dental Technicians Assn. [IO], Longfield,
   United Kingdom
Clinical Directors; Amer. Assn. of [15986]
Clinical Directors Network [14721], 5 W 37th St.,
   10th Fl., New York, NY 10018, (212)382-0699
Clinical Ecology; Soc. for [★14360]
Clinical Endocrinologists; Amer. Assn. of [14350]
Clinical Epidemiology Network; Intl. [14375]
Clinical and Experimental Hypnosis; Soc. for [14927]
Clinical Genetics Soc. [IO], Birmingham, United
   Kingdom
Clinical Hypnosis; Amer. Soc. of [14921]
Clinical Hypnosis - Educ. and Res. Found; Amer.
   Soc. of [14922]
Clinical Hypnotherapists; Natl. Bd. for Certified
   [14925]
Clinical Immunology and Allergy; Amer. Assn. for
   [★13596]
Clinical Immunology; Intl. Assn. of Allergology and
   [★13605]
Clinical Immunology Societies; Fed. of [14935]
Clinical Immunology Soc. [14933], 555 E Wells St.,
   Ste. 1100, Milwaukee, WI 53202-3823, (414)224-
   8095
Clinical Infant Programs; Natl. Center for [★13944]
Clinical Investigation; Amer. Soc. for [14020]
Clinical Lab. Assn; Amer. [14991]
Clinical Lab. Mgt. Assn. [14993], 989 Old Eagle
   School Rd., Ste. 815, Wayne, PA 19087, (610)995-
   9580
Clinical Lab. Sci; Amer. Soc. for [14992]
Clinical Lab. Sciences; Natl. Accrediting Agency for
   [15141]
Clinical and Lab. Standards Inst. [14994], 940 W
   Valley Rd., Ste. 1400, Wayne, PA 19087-1898,
   (610)688-0100
Clinical and Lab. Standards Inst. [IO], Wayne, PA,
   United States
Clinical Lab. Standards; Natl. Comm. for [★14994]
Clinical Lab. Standards; Natl. Comm. for [★14994]
Clinical Lab. Supervisors and Administrators; Amer.
   Assn. of [★14993]
Clinical Lab. Technicians; Amer. Soc. of [★14992]
Clinical Legal Educ. Assn. [8763], c/o Paula Galow-
   itz, Sec., New York Univ. School of Law, 245 Sulli-
   van St., 5th Fl., New York, NY 10012, (212)998-
   6441
Clinical Ligand Assay Soc. [14995], 3139 S Wayne
   Rd., Wayne, MI 48184, (734)722-6290
Clinical Magnetic Resonance Soc. [14024], 5620 W
   Sligh Ave., Tampa, FL 33634-4490, (813)806-1080
Clinical Managers; Natl. Assn. of [★15067]
Clinical and Medical Electrologists; Soc. of [★14310]
Clinical and Medical Hair Removal; Soc. for [14310]
Clinical Mental Hea. Counselors; Acad. of [★11828]
Clinical Neurophysiology; Amer. Acad. of [15375]
Clinical Neurophysiology Soc; Amer. [14306]
Clinical Nurse Specialists; Natl. Assn. of [15492]
Clinical Nutrition; Amer. Coun. of Applied [15545]
Clinical Nutrition; Amer. Soc. for [15547]
Clinical Oncology; Amer. Soc. of [15640]
Clinical Orthopaedic Soc. [15766], 2209 Dickens
   Rd., Richmond, VA 23230-2005, (804)565-6366
Clinical Pastoral Educ; Assn. for [19915]
Clinical Pastoral Educators; Assn. of [★19915]
Clinical Pathologists; Amer. Soc. of [★15859]
Clinical Pathology Accreditation [IO], Sheffield,
   United Kingdom

Clinical Pathology; Amer. Soc. for [15859]
Clinical Pharmacology; Amer. Coll. of [15913]
Clinical Pharmacology and Chemotherapy; Amer.
   Soc. of [★15920]
Clinical Pharmacology and Therapeutics; Amer. Soc.
   for [15920]
Clinical Pharmacy; Amer. Coll. of [15914]
Clinical Psychiatrists; Amer. Acad. of [16064]
Clinical Psychology; Soc. for a Sci. of [16184]
Clinical Psychopharmacology; Amer. Soc. of [15921]
Clinical Psychosocial Res; Assn. for [16139]
Clinical Radioassay Soc. [★14995]
Clinical Res; Amer. Fed. for [★14019]
Clinical Res. Associates [14148], 3707 N Canyon
   Rd., Ste. 6, Provo, UT 84604, (801)226-2121
Clinical Res. Assn; Osteopathic Manipulative
   Therapeutic and [★15790]
Clinical Sci. Club [★14022]
Clinical Scientists; Assn. of [14022]
Clinical Simulation and Learning; Intl. Nursing Assn.
   for [15485]
Clinical Social Work Fed. [13201], PO Box 3740,
   Arlington, VA 22203, (703)522-3866
Clinical Social Work; Natl. Fed. of Societies for
   [★13201]
Clinical Social Workers; Natl. Fed. of [★13201]
Clinical Soc; U.S. Public Hea. Ser. [★6214]
Clinical Sociology Assn. [★7670]
Clinical Studies
   Accreditation Rev. Comm. on Educ. in Surgical
      Tech. [15123]
   Amer. Assn. of Bioanalysts [14989]
   Amer. Assn. of Bioanalysts Bd. of Registry
      [15126]
   Amer. Assn. for Clinical Chemistry [13936]
   Amer. Clinical and Climatological Assn. [14018]
   Amer. Clinical Lab. Assn. [14991]
   Amer. Coll. of Angiology [16719]
   Amer. Fed. for Medical Res. [14019]
   Amer. Soc. for Clinical Investigation [14020]
   Amer. Soc. for Clinical Lab. Sci. [14992]
   Assn. of Clinical Res. Organizations [14021]
   Assn. of Clinical Scientists [14022]
   Assn. of Medical Lab. Immunologists [14932]
   Assn. of Polysomnographic Technologists [16423]
   Central Soc. for Clinical Res. [14023]
   Clinical Lab. Mgt. Assn. [14993]
   Clinical and Lab. Standards Inst. [14994]
   Clinical Legal Educ. Assn. [8763]
   Clinical Ligand Assay Soc. [14995]
   Clinical Magnetic Resonance Soc. [14024]
   Clinical Res. Associates [14148]
   Coalition of Cancer Cooperative Groups [13814]
   Forbes Norris MDA/ALS Res. Center [15323]
   Found. for Advances in Medicine and Sci. [14025]
   Gait and Clinical Movement Anal. Soc. [14557]
   Global Perioperative Res. Org. [14026]
   Intl. Assn. for Human Caring [14640]
   Intl. Biopharmaceutical Assn. [15936]
   Intl. Clinical Epidemiology Network [14375]
   Intl. Complement Soc. [14938]
   Intl. Nursing Assn. for Clinical Simulation and
      Learning [15485]
   Intl. Soc. for Biological Therapy of Cancer [13835]
   Natl. Acad. of Clinical Biochemistry [13748]
   Natl. Accrediting Agency for Clinical Lab. Sciences
      [15141]
   Natl. Credentialing Agency for Lab. Personnel
      [15145]
   Natl. Guideline CH [14654]
   Natl. Inst. of Electromedical Info. [14311]
   Natl. Soc. for Histotechnology [15146]
   Res. Soc. on Alcoholism [16517]
   Soc. for Applied Immunohistochemistry [15873]
   Soc. of Clinical Res. Associates [14027]
   Soc. of Clinical Res. Associates [IO]
   Soc. for Clinical Trials [14028]
Clinical Stud. Soc; Gonstead [14005]
Clinical Surgeons; Soc. of Air Force [16587]
Clinical Toxicology; Amer. Acad. of [16657]
Clinical Training; Coun. for [★19915]
Clinical Trials Gp; AIDS [13549]
Clinical Trials Project [★13848]
Clinical Urologists; Amer. Assn. of [16698]
Clinical Vascular Surgery; Soc. for [13926]

Clinicians; Amer. Assn. of Veterinary [16751]
Clinicians for Choice [13528], c/o Natl. Abortion
   Fed., 1755 Massachusetts Ave. NW, Ste. 600,
   Washington, DC 20036, (202)667-5881
Clinicians Program; International [★14163]
Clinicians Program; International [★IO]
Clinicians for the Underserved; Assn. of [14616]
Clinics; Amer. Assn. of Medical [★14717]
Clinics; Assn. of Occupational and Environmental
   [15629]
Clint Ritchie Official Fan Club - Defunct.
Clinton Investigative Commission [★18309]
Clinton for President - Defunct.
Cliometric Soc. [17454], Dept. of Economics,
   Campus Box 8110, North Carolina State Univ.,
   Raleigh, NC 27695-8110, (919)513-2870
Clipper Owners Club; Amer. [22942]
Cloak and Suit Mfrs. Assn; Amer. [223]
Cloak, Suit and Skirt Mfrs; Industrial Coun. of
   [★253]
Cloak and Suit Trucking Assn. - Address unknown
   since 2002.
Clock Assemblers and Importers Assn. - Address
   unknown since 1995.
Clock Assn; Self Winding [22991]
Clock Collectors; Natl. Assn. of Watch and [22990]
Clock Mfrs. and Marketing Assn. - Defunct.
Clock and Watch Mfrs. Assn. of America - Defunct.
Clockmakers Inst; Amer. Watchmakers- [2359]
Clogging Org; Natl. [9892]
Cloisonne Collectors Club [21996]
Cloning
   Americans to Ban Cloning [17089]
   Genetics Policy Inst. [14499]
Clonmel Chamber of Commerce [IO], Clonmel,
   Ireland
Close Up Found. [17071], 44 Canal Center Plz.,
   Alexandria, VA 22314-1592, (703)706-3300
Closed Circuit TV Mfrs. Assn. - Defunct.
Closure Comm. of the Glass Packaging Inst. [★975]
Closure Liner Mfrs. Assn. - Defunct.
Closure Manufacturers Assn. [975], PO Box 1358,
   Kilmarnock, VA 22482, (804)435-9580
Cloth Glove Mfrs; Natl. Assn. of Cotton [★2030]
Cloth Inst; Amer. Wire [1998]
Cloth Inst; Indus. Wire [★1998]
Cloth Mfrs; Intl. Assn. of Wiping [★2066]
Clothespin and Veneer Products Assn. - Defunct.
Clothiers; Professional Assn. of Custom [256]
Clothing
   Amer. Cloak and Suit Mfrs. Assn. [223]
   Amer. Sewing Guild [22150]
   Associated Corset and Brassiere Mfrs. [227]
   Career Gear [12705]
   Chamber of Commerce of the Apparel Indus.
      [24269]
   Clothing Mfrs. Assn. of the U.S.A. [229]
   Clothworkers' Company [IO]
   Coun. of Fashion Designers of Am. [230]
   Dress for Success Worldwide [13424]
   Educational Found. for the Fashion Indus. [232]
   French Fed. of Lingerie and Swimwear [IO]
   Fur Info. Coun. of Am. [236]
   Greater Blouse, Skirt and Undergarment Assn.
      [237]
   The Hosiery Assn. [239]
   Infant and Juvenile Mfrs. Assn. [240]
   Intl. Wooden Bow Tie Club [243]
   Ladies Apparel Contractors Assn. [244]
   Natl. Assn. of Blouse Mfrs. [245]
   Natl. Assn. of Fashion and Accessory Designers
      [246]
   Natl. Button Soc. [22079]
   Natl. Cap and Patch Assn. [22080]
   Natl. Knitwear and Sportswear Assn. [251]
   Neckwear Assn. of America [252]
   New York Coat and Suit Assn. [253]
   New York Skirt and Sportswear Assn. [254]
   Sew Much Comfort [11739]
   Textile Soc. of Am. [3805]
   Worldwide Responsible Apparel Production [261]
   Young Menswear Assn. [262]
Clothing Assn. [IO], Zellik, Belgium
Clothing; Assn. of Coll. Professors of Textiles and
   [★3791]

A star before a book entry number signifies that the name is not listed separately, but is mentioned within the entry.

Clothing Coun; Paper Machine [2056]
Clothing Designers; Natl. Assn. of [★241]
Clothing Mfrs'. Assn. of India [IO], Bombay, India
Clothing Mfrs. Assn. of the U.S.A. [229]
Clothworkers' Company [IO], London, United Kingdom
Cloud Family Assn. [20866], c/o Linda Boose, Sec.-Treas., 508 Crestwood Dr., Eastland, TX 76448
Clough Genealogical Soc; John [20962]
CLOUT - Christian Lesbians Out [19789], PO Box 2494, Decatur, GA 30030, (740)592-6424
CLOUT - Christian Lesbians Out [IO], Athens, OH, United States
Clown Assn; World [21953]
Clown Club of Am. [★21951]
Clown Club of Am. [★IO]
Clowner Utan Granser [★IO]
Clowns
    Clowns of Am., Intl. [IO]
    Clowns of Am., Intl. [21951]
    Clowns Without Borders - Canada [IO]
    Clowns Without Borders - Sweden [IO]
    Intl. Shrine Clown Assn. [IO]
    Intl. Shrine Clown Assn. [21952]
    World Clown Assn. [21953]
    World Clown Association [IO]
Clowns of Am. [★IO]
Clowns of Am. [★21951]
Clowns of Am., Intl. [21951], PO Box C, Richeyville, PA 15358-0532, (724)938-8765
Clowns of Am., Intl. [IO], Richeyville, PA, United States
Clowns Sans Frontieres [★IO]
Clowns Without Borders [IO], Barcelona, Spain
Clowns Without Borders - Canada [IO], Montreal, QC, Canada
Clowns Without Borders - Sweden [IO], Norsborg, Sweden
Clowns Without Borders - USA [IO], San Francisco, CA, United States
Clowns Without Borders - USA [11768], 540 Alabama, No. 215, San Francisco, CA 94110, (415)626-7737
CLU and ChFC; Amer. Soc. of [★2240]
Club Alpin Francais [★IO]
Club de las Americas - Defunct.
Club Anri - Address unknown since 1999.
Club Aquarius - Address unknown since 2002.
Club Artritas [IO], Kaunas, Lithuania
Club de Aviacion de Cuba [IO], Havana, Cuba
Club du Basset Hound [IO], St. Maur des Fosses, France
Club du Braque Francais [IO], Grasse, France
Club of Budapest [IO], Neuss, Germany
Club Canin Canadien [★IO]
Club of Catholic Intelligentsia [IO], Warsaw, Poland
Club of Channel Islands Collectors - Defunct.
Club des Chiens Tibetains de France [IO], Nyons, France
Club Delahaye [IO], Dunkirk, France
Club D.J. - Address unknown since 1989.
Club Du Vieux Manoir [IO], Pontpoint, France
Club E: The Dale Earnhardt Fan Club [25002]
Club Elite - Address unknown since 1995.
Club Elite North Am. [21618], c/o Michael Ostrov, Sec., 6238 Ralston Ave., Richmond, CA 94805-1519, (510)232-7764
Club des Epagneuls Nains Anglais [IO], Cuers, France
Club Executives; Assn. of [1932]
Club Francais du Braqwue Hongrois [★IO]
Club Francais du Bullmastiff et du Mastiff [★IO]
Club Francais d'Amerique [8449], 944 Market St., Ste. 210, San Francisco, CA 94102, (415)981-9088
Club Francais de l'Airedale Terrier et de Divers Terriers [★IO]
Club of the Friends of Ancient Smoothing Irons - Defunct.
Club Garcons and Filles du Canada [★IO]
Club de Inventores Espanoles [IO]
Club Managers Assn. of Am. [833], 1733 King St., Alexandria, VA 22314, (703)739-9500
Club Managers Assn. Australia [IO], Auburn, Australia

Club of Neuropathologists [★15853]
Club; Ogden House Seniors 50 [IO]
Club for Philately in Gerontology - Defunct.
Club Pool Assn. - Address unknown since 2006.
Club di Roma [★IO]
Club of Rome [IO], Hamburg, Germany
Club Shoe - Address unknown since 2002.
Club; Radio Executives [★563]
Clubmakers' Soc; Professional [3649]
Clubs
    Achilles Track Club [23331]
    Adirondack Forty-Sixers [23930]
    Adirondack Mountain Club [23931]
    Adirondack Trail Improvement Soc. [23932]
    Alfa Romeo Assn. [21564]
    Am. Outdoors [23681]
    Amer. Armsport Assn. [23059]
    Amer. Athletic Trainers Assn. and Certification Bd. [23953]
    Amer. Barefoot Club [23974]
    Amer. Bicycle Assn. [23305]
    Amer. Camaro Assn. [21570]
    Amer. Chevelle Enthusiasts Soc. [21571]
    Amer. Endurance Ride Conf. [23933]
    Amer. Hiking Soc. [23934]
    Amer. Hot Rod Assn. [23071]
    Amer. Junior Rodeo Assn. [23684]
    Amer. Kenpo Karate Intl. [23560]
    Amer. Medical Tennis Assn. [23898]
    Amer. Motorcycle Heritage Found. [23621]
    Amer. Platform Tennis Assn. [23899]
    Amer. Swimming Coaches Assn. [23882]
    Amer. Tennis Assn. [23900]
    Amer. Trails [23935]
    Amer. Turners [23802]
    Amer. Vaulting Assn. [23967]
    Amer. Volleyball Coaches Assn. [23969]
    Amer. Water Ski Educational Found. [23975]
    Amer. Whitewater [23682]
    AMOA Natl. Dart Assn. [23329]
    Anime UNSW [IO]
    Appalachian Mountain Club [23936]
    Appalachian Trail Conservancy [23937]
    Aquatic Exercise Assn. [23652]
    Arabian Jockey Club [23494]
    Assn. of Commercial Diving Educators [23960]
    Assn. of Northwest Steelheaders [23409]
    Assn. of Surfing Professionals [23877]
    Assn. of YMCA Professionals [13460]
    Aston Martin Owners Club [21581]
    Austin-Healey Club USA [21585]
    Babe Ruth Birthplace/Sports Legends at Camden Yards [23107]
    Benevolent and Loyal Order of Pessimists [22591]
    Bicycle Parking Proj. [23307]
    Bicycle Ride Directors' Assn. of Am. [23308]
    Big West Conf. [23809]
    BlueRibbon Coalition [23680]
    Boy Scouts of Am. [12997]
    Boys and Girls Clubs of Am. [13471]
    Camp Fire USA [13475]
    Canadian Soc. of Club Managers [IO]
    Catalina 22 Natl. Sailing Assn. [23162]
    Central Collegiate Hockey Assn. [23483]
    Championship Assn. of Mechanics [23075]
    Cinderella Softball Leagues [23789]
    CityKids Found. [13479]
    Club Managers Assn. of Am. [833]
    Club Managers Assn. Australia [IO]
    Coll. Gymnastics Assn. [23474]
    Coll. Swimming Coaches Assn. of Am. [23883]
    Collegiate Soaring Assn. [23039]
    Continental Divide Trail Soc. [23938]
    DeLorean Owners Assn. [21629]
    Direction Sports [13482]
    Divers Alert Network [23378]
    Eastern Surfing Assn. [23878]
    Extra Miler Club [23013]
    Federated Mountain Clubs of New Zealand [IO]
    Fed. of Metal Detector and Archaeological Clubs [22578]
    Florida Trail Assn. [23939]
    Free Throwers Boomerang Soc. [23247]
    Future Fisherman Found. [23415]

    Great Lakes Sport Fishing Coun. [23416]
    Hampton One-Design Class Racing Assn. [23173]
    Harness Horse Youth Found. [23496]
    Heritage Trails Fund [23940]
    Highpointers Club [23014]
    Hungarian Scouts Assn. [12999]
    Indoor Sports Club [11951]
    Inland Lake Yachting Assn. [23175]
    Inst. of Diving [23961]
    Inst. of Totally Useless Skills [22593]
    Intercollegiate Outing Club Assn. [23941]
    Intercollegiate Tennis Assn. [23902]
    Intl. 210 Assn. [23179]
    Intl. 505 Yacht Racing Assn., Amer. Sect. [23180]
    Intl. Acad. of Aquatic Art [23884]
    Intl. Assn. of Gay and Lesbian Martial Artists [23588]
    Intl. Assn. of People Who Dine Over the Kitchen Sink [22594]
    Intl. Boxing Fed. [23260]
    Intl. Boxing Hall of Fame Museum [23261]
    Intl. Fed. of Sleddog Sports [23393]
    Intl. Game Fish Assn. [23417]
    Intl. Hunter Educ. Assn. [23545]
    Intl. J/22 Class Assn. [23187]
    Intl. Lacrosse Fed. [23570]
    Intl. Military Community Executives Assn. [834]
    Intl. Military Community Executives Assn. [IO]
    Intl. Model Power Boat Assn. [22645]
    Intl. Mountain Bicycling Assn. [23310]
    Intl. Naples Sabot Assn. [23190]
    Intl. Plastic Modelers Society/United States Br. [22646]
    Intl. Racquetball Fed. [23677]
    Intl. Sports Exchange [23826]
    Intl. Sports Heritage Assn. [23827]
    Intl. Swimming Hall of Fame [23886]
    Intl. Tennis Hall of Fame [23903]
    Intl. Thunderbird Class Assn. [23195]
    Intl. Track and Field Coaches Assn. [23919]
    IOCALUM [23942]
    Japan Aikido Assn. U.S.A. [23595]
    Kiwanis Club of Te Awamutu [IO]
    Light Living Library [23272]
    Lincoln Heritage Trail Found. [23943]
    Maccabi USA/Sports for Israel [23828]
    Major Wingfield Historical Soc. [23905]
    McDonald's Collectors Club [22070]
    Montana Outfitters and Guides Assn. [23944]
    Mountaineers [23945]
    Multicultural Golf Assn. of Am. [23455]
    Natl. Ability Center [23347]
    Natl. Acad. of Sports [23831]
    Natl. Assn. of Athletic Development Directors [23832]
    Natl. Assn. of Collegiate Marketing Administrators [23834]
    Natl. Assn. of Sports Commissions [23871]
    Natl. Assn. of Sports Officials [23872]
    Natl. Assn. of Sports Officials - Organizations Network [23873]
    Natl. Assn. of Underwater Instructors [23963]
    Natl. Assn. of Youth Clubs [13498]
    Natl. Athletic Trainers' Assn. [23954]
    Natl. Baseball Hall of Fame and Museum [23118]
    Natl. Basketball Athletic Trainers Assn. [23135]
    Natl. Camp Assn. [23277]
    Natl. Club Assn. [835]
    Natl. Disability Sports Alliance [23353]
    Natl. Eagle Scout Assn. [13002]
    Natl. Fed. of Professional Trainers [23956]
    Natl. Football League Players Assn. [23434]
    Natl. History Club [8509]
    Natl. Interscholastic Swimming Coaches Assn. of Am. [23887]
    Natl. Jewish Comm. on Scouting [13003]
    Natl. Jewish Girl Scout Comm. [13004]
    Natl. Junior Baseball League [23120]
    Natl. Org. for Rivers [23683]
    Natl. Org. of I Walkers [23971]
    Natl. Public Parks Tennis Assn. [23906]
    Natl. Scholastic Surfing Assn. [23880]
    Natl. Senior Games Assn. [23655]
    Natl. Softball Assn. [23792]
    Natl. Sporting Clays Assn. [23726]

Reference to "IO" in place of a book number signifies that the association may be found in the 45th edition of International Organizations.

Natl. Starwind/Spindrift Class Assn. [23207]
Natl. Strength and Conditioning Assn. [23957]
Natl. Thoroughbred Racing Assn. [23510]
Natl. Tractor Pullers Assn. [23928]
Natl. Women's Martial Arts Fed. [23600]
Natl. Wrestling Coaches Assn. [23987]
NETA - Natl. Exercise Trainers Assn. [23037]
New England Trails Conf. [23948]
New York Triathlon Club [23922]
NFHS Officials Assn. [23874]
North Amer. Fishing Club [23421]
North Amer. Network of Women Runners [23656]
North Amer. Trail Ride Conf. [23949]
North Country Trail Assn. [23950]
Norwegian Forest Cat Breed Coun. [21914]
The Old Appliance Club [21535]
Olson 30 Class Assn. [23210]
Order of the Arrow [13005]
Over the Hill Gang, Intl. [23846]
Pan-American Union of Karatedo Organizations [23564]
Pantera Owners Club of Am. [21760]
Patience T'ai Chi Assn. [23897]
Professional Assn. of Diving Instructors [23964]
Professional Assn. of Volleyball Officials [23875]
Professional Baseball Athletic Trainers Soc. [23125]
Professional Tennis Registry [23909]
Rails-to-Trails Conservancy [23952]
Rat Fan Club [22706]
Recreational Scuba Training Coun. [23965]
San Juan 21 Class Assn. [23215]
Scoot-Tours Touring Scooter Riders Assn. [23627]
Single Booklovers [22142]
Somali Cat Club of Am. [21918]
Sony Ericsson WTA Tour [23910]
Sports Hall of Oblivion [23855]
Sportscar Vintage Racing Assn. [23085]
Surfrider Found. [23881]
Synchro Swimming U.S.A. [23889]
Tall Clubs Intl. [13300]
Tandem Club of Am. [23317]
Ultimate Players Assn. [23375]
Underwater Soc. of Am. [23966]
United Fly Tyers [23424]
U.S. Amateur Tug of War Assn. [23959]
U.S. Aquatic Sports [23890]
U.S. ArmSports [23991]
U.S. Blind Golf Assn. [23364]
U.S. Bobsled and Skeleton Fed. [23767]
U.S. Bocce Fed. [23241]
U.S. Competitive Aerobics Fed. [23038]
U.S. Cultural Exchange and Sports Soc. [23861]
U.S. Dental Tennis Assn. [23911]
U.S. Disc Sports [23376]
U.S. Flag and Touch Football League [23441]
U.S. Judo [23554]
U.S. Judo Assn. [23555]
U.S. Masters Swimming [23891]
U.S. Mirror Class Assn. [23229]
U.S. Natl. Tennis Acad. [23913]
U.S. Professional Diving Coaches Assn. [23381]
U.S. Professional Tennis Assn. [23914]
U.S. Ski and Snowboard Assn. [23760]
U.S. Soling Assn. [23234]
U.S. Sports Acad. [23864]
U.S. Squash Racquets Assn. [23876]
U.S. Swim School Assn. [23892]
U.S. Tennis Assn. [23915]
U.S. Volleyball Association/USA Volleyball [23970]
U.S. Water Fitness Assn. [23657]
U.S. Yngling Assn. [23237]
Univ. Athletic Assn. [23865]
USA Canoe/Kayak [23280]
USA Diving [23382]
U.S.A. Karate Fed. [23566]
USA Swimming [23893]
U.S.A. Table Tennis [23896]
USA Tennis - NJTL [23916]
U.S.A. Track and Field [23926]
USA Triathlon [23927]
USA Water Ski [23979]
USA Weightlifting [23985]
U.S.A. Wrestling [23989]
USGA Green Sect. [23470]

Western Athletic Conf. [23866]
Western Collegiate Hockey Assn. [23489]
Western Women Premier Bowlers [23257]
Women Outdoors [23644]
Women's All-Star Assn. [23258]
Women's Sports Found. [23867]
World Aquatic Babies and Children [23894]
World Armsport Fed. [23060]
World Diving Coaches Assn. [23383]
World Fast-Draw Assn. [23733]
World Masters Cross-Country Ski Assn. [23763]
WTA Tour Players Assn. [23917]
Y's Men Intl., U.S. Area [13464]
Clubs; IRSA, The Assn. of Quality [★3021]
Clubs for Young People [IO], London, United Kingdom
Clubul Roman de Presa [★IO]
Cluid Housing Assn. - North East [IO], Dublin, Ireland
Clumber Spaniel Club of Am. [22246], c/o Vonda Poole, Membership Sec., 874 Orchard Terrace Dr., New Wilmington, PA 16142-4222
Clun Forest Assn; North Amer. [5212]
Clutch Facing and Brake Lining Standards Inst. [★385]
Clutterers Anonymous [13015], PO Box 91413, Los Angeles, CA 90009-1413, (310)281-6064
Clwyd Welsh Pony and Cob Assn. [IO], Ruthin, United Kingdom
Clyde Bowling Fan Club - Defunct.
Clydesdale Assn; Amer. [★4872]
Clydesdale Breeders of the U.S. [★4872]
Clydesdale Breeders of the U.S.A. [4872], 17346 Kelley Rd., Pecatonica, IL 61063, (815)247-8780
Clydesdale Runners Assn. - Defunct.
CME Group [4324], 20 S Wacker Dr., Chicago, IL 60606, (312)930-1000
CN Lines Special Interest Gp. [IO], Winnipeg, MB, Canada
CNR Books [★IO]
CNR Books [★18126]
CNR Ministries - Defunct.
Co-Anon Family Groups [13231], PO Box 12722, Tucson, AZ 85732-2722, (520)513-5028
Co-Dependents Anonymous [13016], PO Box 33577, Phoenix, AZ 85067-3577, (602)277-7991
Co-Dependents of Sex Addicts [★13072]
Co-Dependents of Sex Addicts [★IO]
Co-Ette Club - Address unknown since 2004.
Co-op Am. [1069], 1612 K St. NW, Ste. 600, Washington, DC 20006, (202)872-5307
Co-Op Network; Newspaper Advt. [★3244]
Co-Op Users Group - Address unknown since 1995.
Co-operative Citrus Growers' Assn. of Trinidad and Tobago [IO], Port of Spain, Trinidad and Tobago
Co-operative Union of Tanzania [★IO]
Co-operative Women's Guild [IO], Manchester, United Kingdom
Co-Operettes [★IO]
Co-Operettes [★13048]
Coach Assn; Family Motor [22949]
Coach Assn; Recreational Vehicle Division of the Trailer [★3371]
Coach Assn; Trailer [★2527]
COACH: Canada's Hea. Informatics Assn. [IO], Toronto, ON, Canada
Coach Lace Inst. - Defunct.
Coach Mfrs. Assn; Trailer [★2527]
Coach Operators Fed. [IO], Sidmouth, United Kingdom
Coaches; Amer. Assn. of Coll. Baseball [★23101]
Coaches Assn. of Am; Coll. Swimming [23883]
Coaches Assn. of Am; Golf [23448]
Coaches Assn. of Am; Natl. Fencing [★23403]
Coaches Assn. of Am; Natl. Interscholastic Swimming [23887]
Coaches Assn. of Am; Natl. Soccer [23779]
Coaches Assn; Amer. Baseball [23101]
Coaches Assn; Amer. Football [23427]
Coaches Assn; Amer. Hockey [23481]
Coaches Assn; Amer. Swimming [23882]
Coaches Assn; Amer. Volleyball [23969]
Coaches Assn; Black [23287]
Coaches Assn; Natl. Collegiate Cross Country [★23924]

Coaches Assn; Natl. Collegiate Tennis [★23902]
Coaches Assn; Natl. Fed. [★23294]
Coaches Assn; Natl. Strength [★23957]
Coaches Assn; Natl. Wrestling [23987]
Coaches Assn; Natl. Youth Sports [★23290]
Coaches Assn; NCAA Golf [★23448]
Coaches Assn; U.S. Cross Country [23924]
Coaches Assn; U.S. Fencing [23403]
Coaches Assn; U.S. Professional Diving [23381]
Coaches Assn; U.S. Ski [23758]
Coaches Assn; Women's Basketball [23139]
Coaches; Natl. Assn. of Basketball [23133]
Coaches and Officials Assn; Amer. Wrestling [★23987]
Coaches and Officials; Natl. Collegiate Athletic Assn. of Wrestling [★23987]
Coaches and Teachers; Org. of Professional Acting [9267]
Coaches/Women; Natl. Assn. of Collegiate Gymnastics [23476]
Coaching
    Amateur Ski Instructors Assn. [23748]
    Amer. Assn. of Cheerleading Coaches and Advisors [23061]
    Amer. Assn. of Snowboard Instructors [23765]
    Amer. Baseball Coaches Assn. [23101]
    Amer. Football Coaches Assn. [23427]
    Amer. Gp. Gymnastics Assn. [23473]
    Amer. Hockey Coaches Assn. [23481]
    Amer. Riding Instructors Assn. [22583]
    Assn. of Professional Ball Players of Am. [23105]
    Black Coaches Assn. [23287]
    Canadian Univ. Football Coaches Assn. [IO]
    China Coach Assn. [IO]
    Citizenship Through Sports Alliance [23812]
    Coaching Assn. of Canada [IO]
    Empowerment Soc. of the U.S.A. [13425]
    European Athletics Coaches Assn. [IO]
    Golf Coaches Assn. of Am. [23448]
    Indoor Soccer Coaches Assn. [23288]
    Intl. Assn. of Integrative Coaches [11740]
    Intl. Assn. of Integrative Coaches [IO]
    Intl. Coach Fed. [IO]
    Intl. Coach Fed. [836]
    Intl. Coach Fed. - Australasian Region [IO]
    Intl. Mental Game Coaching Assn. [23289]
    Naismith Memorial Basketball Hall of Fame [23132]
    Natl. Alliance for Youth Sports [23290]
    Natl. Assn. of Basketball Coaches [23133]
    Natl. Assn. of Collegiate Gymnastics Coaches/Women [23476]
    Natl. Assn. for Girls and Women in Sport [8983]
    Natl. Assn. of Golf Coaches and Educators [23291]
    Natl. Fastpitch Coaches Assn. [23840]
    Natl. Field Hockey Coaches Assn. [23404]
    Natl. Football Found. and Coll. Hall of Fame [23431]
    Natl. High School Athletic Coaches Assn. [23292]
    Natl. High School Baseball Coaches Assn. [23119]
    Natl. Pitching Assn. [23121]
    Natl. Soccer Coaches Assn. of Am. [23779]
    Natl. Throws Coaches Assn. [23293]
    NFHS Coaches Assn. [23294]
    NFHS Spirit Assn. [23295]
    Positive Coaching Alliance [23296]
    Professional Golf Teachers Assn. of Am. [23463]
    Sports Coach UK [IO]
    U.S. Barrel Jumping Assn. [23743]
    U.S. Elite Coaches' Assn. for Women's Gymnastics [23297]
    U.S. Fencing Coaches Assn. [23403]
    U.S. High School Tennis Assn. [23912]
    U.S. Ski Coaches Assn. [23758]
    U.S. Twirling Assn. [23143]
    U.S. Water Polo [23973]
    USA Boxing [23267]
    USA Gymnastics [23479]
    Women's Basketball Coaches Assn. [23139]
Coaching Assn. of Canada [IO], Ottawa, ON, Canada
Coachmakers' and Coach Harness Makers' Company [IO], Chalfont St. Giles, United Kingdom

A star before a book entry number signifies that the name is not listed separately, but is mentioned within the entry.

Coady Intl. Inst. **[IO]**, Antigonish, NS, Canada
Coal
  Amer. Coal Ash Assn. **[3986]**
  Amer. Coal Coun. **[6702]**
  Amer. Coal Found. **[837]**
  Amer. Coke and Coal Chemicals Inst. **[838]**
  Americans for Balanced Energy Choices **[17495]**
  Assn. of Bituminous Contractors **[839]**
  Assn. of German Coal Importers **[IO]**
  Australian Coal Assn. **[IO]**
  Bituminous Coal Operators' Assn. **[840]**
  Black Lung Assn. **[13323]**
  Citizens Coal Coun. **[4299]**
  Coal Assn. of Canada **[IO]**
  Coal Exporters Assn. of the U.S. **[841]**
  Coal Merchants' Fed. - England **[IO]**
  Coal Tech. Assn. **[842]**
  Coal Trading Assn. **[843]**
  European Assn. for Coal and Lignite **[IO]**
  Intl. Humic Substances Soc. **[7610]**
  Japan Coal Energy Center **[IO]**
  Natl. Coal Trans. Assn. **[844]**
  Natl. Coun. of Coal Lessors **[845]**
  Natl. Mining Assn. **[846]**
  Pennsylvania Coal Assn. **[847]**
  Rocky Mountain Coal Mining Inst. **[848]**
  South African Coal Processing Soc. **[IO]**
  World Coal Inst. **[IO]**
Coal Ash Assn; Amer. **[3986]**
Coal Assn. of Canada **[IO]**, Calgary, AB, Canada
Coal Assn; Keystone Bituminous **[★847]**
Coal Assn; Natl. **[★846]**
Coal Coun. Mission; Western **[★6702]**
Coal Employment Project - Address unknown since
  1994.
Coal Exporters Assn. of the U.S. **[841]**, c/o Natl.
  Mining Assn., 101 Constitution Ave. NW, Ste. 500
  E, Washington, DC 20001-2133, (202)463-2600
Coal Exporters of the U.S. **[★841]**
Coal Fuel Mixtures Assn. - Defunct.
Coal Inst; Bituminous **[★846]**
Coal Merchants' Fed. - England **[IO]**, Alfreton,
  United Kingdom
Coal Mining Assn; Pennsylvania **[★847]**
Coal Sales Assn; Amer. **[★846]**
Coal Tar Pitch Emulsion Coun. - Defunct.
Coal Tech. Assn. **[842]**, 601 Suffield Dr., Gaithers-
  burg, MD 20878, (301)294-6080
Coal Trading Assn. **[843]**, 2001 Jefferson Davis
  Hwy., Ste. 1004, Arlington, VA 22202-3617,
  (703)418-0392
Coalition of 9/11 Families **[13307]**, 2640 Hwy. 70,
  Bldg. 1A, Manasquan, NJ 08736, (732)292-2910
Coalition to Abolish the LD50 - Address unknown
  since 2003.
Coalition to Abolish Slavery and Trafficking **[12370]**,
  5042 Wilshire Blvd., No. 586, Los Angeles, CA
  90036, (213)365-1906
Coalition for the Abolition of Marijuana Prohibition -
  Defunct.
Coalition for the Advancement of Jewish Educ.
  [8689], 520 Eighth Ave., North Tower, 2nd Fl., New
  York, NY 10018, (212)268-4210
Coalition for the Advancement of Medical Res.
  [15103], 2021 K St. NW, Ste. 305, Washington,
  DC 20006, (202)293-2856
Coalition Against Bigger Trucks **[13337]**, 901 N Pitt
  St., Ste. 310, Alexandria, VA 22314, (703)535-3131
Coalition Against Childhood Lead Poisoning and
  Parents Against Lead **[★4543]**
Coalition Against Double Taxation - Defunct.
Coalition Against Insurance Fraud **[2155]**, 1012 14th
  St. NW, Ste. 200, Washington, DC 20005,
  (202)393-7330
Coalition Against Noneffective Lightning Protection
  Technologies - Address unknown since 1994.
Coalition Against Pipeline Pollution - Defunct.
Coalition Against Regressive Taxation - Address
  unknown since 2002.
Coalition Against Sexual Harassment - Defunct.
Coalition Against the SST - Defunct.
Coalition Against Trafficking in Women **[17751]**, c/o
  Norma Ramos, Esq., Co-Exec. Dir., PO Box 7427,
  New York, NY 10116
Coalition Against Trafficking in Women **[IO]**, North
  Amherst, MA, United States

Coalition Against Unsolicited Commercial Email
  [6933], PO Box 727, Trumansburg, NY 14886,
  (303)800-6345
Coalition for Alternatives in Jewish Educ. **[★8689]**
Coalition of Am; Amputee **[14236]**
Coalition for Amer. Leadership Abroad **[17867]**, 2101
  E St. NW, Washington, DC 20037, (202)944-5519
Coalition for Amer. Leadership Abroad **[IO]**,
  Washington, DC, United States
Coalition of Amer. Pro-Life Univ. Students **[★12928]**
Coalition of Amer. Public Employees - Defunct.
Coalition of Amers. to Save the Economy - Address
  unknown since 1999.
Coalition for America's Children - Defunct.
Coalition of Asian Pacifics in Entertainment **[1300]**,
  PO Box 251855, Los Angeles, CA 90025,
  (310)278-2313
Coalition for Asian Peace and Security - Defunct.
Coalition for Auto Glass Safety and Public Aware-
  ness **[1727]**, c/o Natl. Glass Assn., 8200
  Greensboro Dr., Ste. 302, McLean, VA 22102-
  3881, (717)558-0939
Coalition for Auto-Insurance Reform **[17316]**, 7310
  Stafford Rd., Alexandria, VA 22307, (703)660-0799
Coalition for Auto Repair Choice - Defunct.
Coalition of Automotive Assns. - Defunct.
Coalition for Better TV - Defunct.
Coalition of Black Trade Unionists **[24202]**, PO Box
  66268, Washington, DC 20036-6268, (202)429-
  1203
Coalition on Block Grants and Human Needs
  [★13161]
Coalition Building Inst; Natl. **[17227]**
Coalition Canadienne Contre La Fraude A
  L'Assurance **[★IO]**
Coalition Canadienne pour la Prevention et le Con-
  trole de l'Hypertension Arterielle **[★IO]**
Coalition Canadienne de la Sante **[★IO]**
Coalition of Cancer Cooperative Groups **[13814]**,
  1818 Market St., No. 1100, Philadelphia, PA
  19103, (215)789-3600
Coalition for Children and Youth - Defunct.
Coalition for Christian Colleges and Universities
  [★8084]
Coalition for Common Courtesy - Defunct.
Coalition for Common Sense in Govt. Procurement
  [★17741]
Coalition for a Competitive Food and Agricultural
  Sys. **[4075]**
Coalition for Consumer Health and Safety - Defunct.
Coalition for Consumer Justice - Defunct.
Coalition for Corporate Responsibility - Defunct.
Coalition for a Decent U.S.A. - Defunct.
Coalition for Democracy in Iran **[17389]**
Coalition for a Democratic Majority - Defunct.
Coalition of Digestive Disease Organizations
  [★14416]
Coalition for Drug-Free Horse Racing - Defunct.
Coalition for a Drug-Free Workplace - Defunct.
Coalition of Eastern Native Americans - Defunct.
Coalition for Economic Survival **[13160]**, 514 Shatto
  Pl., Ste. 270, Los Angeles, CA 90020, (213)252-
  4411
Coalition for Educ. in the Life Sciences **[9098]**, c/o
  Dr. Louise W. Liao, Prog. Dir., Univ. of Wisconsin -
  Madison, Center for Biology Educ., 425 Henry
  Mall, 1271 Genetics/Biotechnology Bldg., Madison,
  WI 53706, (608)262-5266
Coalition for Education and Self-help Training
  Advocates - Address unknown since 2004.
Coalition to End Childhood Lead Poisoning **[4543]**,
  2714 Hudson St., Baltimore, MD 21224, (410)534-
  6447
Coalition for Environmentally Responsible
  Economies **[4544]**, 99 Chauncy St., 6th Fl.,
  Boston, MA 02111, (617)247-0700
Coalition for Environmentally Safe Communities
  [12118], 6642 Fisher Ave., Falls Church, VA
  22046, (703)534-8334
Coalition for the Equitable Treatment of Publicly
  Traded Limited Partnerships **[★2343]**
Coalition for Equitable Truck Taxes - Defunct.
Coalition of Essential Schools **[8180]**, 1814 Franklin
  St., Ste. 700, Oakland, CA 94612, (510)433-1451
Coalition of Exclusive Agent Associations **[173]**, c/o
  Donald P. Cassell, Pres., 791 Aquahart Rd., Ste.
  101, Glen Burnie, MD 21061, (410)768-5040

Coalition for Fair Copyright Protection - Defunct.
Coalition for Fair Lumber Imports **[1641]**, 975 F St.
  NW, Washington, DC 20004, (202)862-3686
Coalition for Fire-Safe Cigarettes **[12191]**, c/o Natl.
  Fire Protection Assn., 1 Batterymarch Park,
  Quincy, MA 02169, (617)984-7275
Coalition for Food Irradiation - Defunct.
Coalition For Heritable Disorders Of Connective Tis-
  sue **[14446]**, 4301 Connecticut Ave. NW, Ste. 404,
  Washington, DC 20008, (202)362-9599
Coalition for Free and Open Elections - Address
  unknown since 2003.
Coalition to Free Petkus and Gajauskas - Defunct.
Coalition for Freedom - Address unknown since
  1999.
Coalition for Genetic Fairness **[17107]**, 4301 Con-
  necticut Ave. NW, No. 404, Washington, DC
  20008-2369, (202)966-5557
Coalition on Govt. Information - Defunct.
Coalition for Govt. Procurement **[1741]**, 1990 M St.
  NW, Ste. 450, Washington, DC 20036, (202)331-
  0975
Coalition to Halt Auto Theft - Defunct.
Coalition for Harmony of Races in the U.S. **[18198]**,
  2 Gienhurst Ct., Darnestown, MD 20878, (301)948-
  7272
Coalition for Health and the Environment - Defunct.
Coalition for Health Funding - Address unknown
  since 1994.
Coalition for Healthcare Commun. **[14622]**, c/o John
  Kamp, Exec. Dir., 405 Lexington Ave., New York,
  NY 10174-1801, (212)850-0708
Coalition for Healthcare eStandards **[14623]**, 3300
  Washtenaw Ave., Ste. 222, Ann Arbor, MI 48104-
  4250, (734)677-3300
Coalition for Healthy Korean Americans **[14988]**, c/o
  Koh Memorial Hea. Center, 41 Montvale Ave., Ste.
  450, Stoneham, MA 02180, (781)438-6060
Coalition for Hemophilia B **[14787]**, 825 Third Ave.,
  Ste. 226, New York, NY 10022, (212)520-8272
Coalition of Higher Educ. Assistance Organizations
  [8344], 1101 Vermont Ave. NW, Ste. 400,
  Washington, DC 20005-3586, (202)289-3910
Coalition of Holistic Health Organizations - Defunct.
Coalition on Human Needs **[13161]**, 1120 Con-
  necticut Ave. NW, Ste. 910, Washington, DC
  20036, (202)223-2532
Coalition of Immokalee Workers **[13458]**, PO Box
  603, Immokalee, FL 34143, (239)657-8311
Coalition for Improving Maternity Services **[15596]**,
  PO Box 2346, Ponte Vedra Beach, FL 32004,
  (904)285-1613
Coalition Interagence Sida Et Developpement **[★IO]**
Coalition for Intl. Cooperation and Peace - Defunct.
Coalition for an Intl. Criminal Court **[17361]**, c/o
  World Federalist Movement, 708 3rd Ave., 24th Fl.,
  New York, NY 10017, (212)687-2863
Coalition for an Intl. Criminal Court **[IO]**, New York,
  NY, United States
Coalition for Intl. Justice **[IO]**, Washington, DC,
  United States
Coalition for Intl. Justice **[5934]**
Coalition for Jobs, Peace, and Freedom in the
  Americas **[★18463]**
Coalition for Justice in the Maquiladoras **[18610]**,
  912 Donaldson, Apt. D, San Antonio, TX 78228,
  (210)732-8957
Coalition for Justice in the Maquiladoras **[IO]**, San
  Antonio, TX, United States
Coalition for Juvenile Justice **[5915]**, 1710 Rhode
  Island Ave. NW, 10th Fl., Washington, DC 20036,
  (202)467-0864
Coalition to Keep Alaska Oil - Defunct.
Coalition to Keep Am. Connected **[18724]**, 4121
  Wilson Blvd., 10th Fl., Arlington, VA 22203-1801,
  (703)351-2148
Coalition of Labor Union Women **[24203]**, 815 16th
  St. NW, 2nd Fl. S, Washington, DC 20006,
  (202)508-6969
Coalition of Labor Union Women Center for Educ.
  and Res. **[24204]**, 815 16th St. NW, 2nd Fl. S,
  Washington, DC 20006, (202)508-6969
Coalition for Literacy **[★8794]**
Coalition of Minority Policy Professionals - Address
  unknown since 1999.

Reference to "IO" in place of a book number signifies that the association may be found in the 45th edition of International Organizations.

Coalition of Minority Women in Business - Address unknown since 1991.
Coalition Mondiale Pour L'Afrique [★16930]
Coalition Mondiale Pour L'Afrique [★IO]
Coalition of Municipalities to Ban Animal Trafficking - Address unknown since 2003.
Coalition of Natl. Hea. Educ. Organizations [8858], c/o Kathleen M. Conley, PhD, Coor., Eastern Michigan Univ., School of Hea. Promotion and Human Performance, 318 Porter Bldg., Ypsilanti, MI 48197, (734)487-7120
Coalition for a Natl. Health System - Address unknown since 1999.
Coalition of Natl. Voluntary Organizations [★12725]
Coalition for Networked Info. [7191], 21 Dupont Cir., Ste. 800, Washington, DC 20036, (202)296-5098
Coalition for a New Foreign Policy - Defunct.
Coalition of Non-Postal Media - Defunct.
Coalition for Non-Violent Food [11377], c/o Animal Rights Intl., PO Box 1292, Middlebury, CT 06762, (203)598-0554
Coalition for Nonprofit Health Care - Defunct.
Coalition for a Nuclear Free Harbor - Address unknown since 1994.
Coalition to Oppose the Arms Trade [IO], Ottawa, ON, Canada
Coalition Opposing Signal Theft [556], 1724 Massachusetts Ave. NW, Washington, DC 20036, (202)775-3684
Coalition for Peace Through Strength [★18586]
Coalition for the Peaceful Uses of Space - Address unknown since 1999.
Coalition on Political Assassinations - Address unknown since 2002.
Coalition for Positive Sexuality [13480], PO Box 77212, Washington, DC 20013-8212, (773)604-1654
Coalition to Preserve the Amer. Copyright - Defunct.
Coalition for Prompt Pay [1742], c/o ICIA, 11242 Waples Mill Rd., Ste. 200, Fairfax, VA 22030, (703)273-7200
Coalition to Protect Animals in Entertainment [11378]
Coalition to Protect Animals in Parks and Refuges [11379], PO Box 26, Swain, NY 14884-0026
Coalition for the Protection of Human Life [★IO]
Coalition of Public Employee Organizations - Address unknown since 1985.
Coalition of Publicly Traded Limited Partnerships [★2343]
Coalition of Publicly Traded Partnerships [★2343]
Coalition for Pulmonary Fibrosis [16356], 1659 Branham Ln., Ste. F, No. 227, San Jose, CA 95118, (888)222-8541
Coalition for Quality in Care [IO], London, United Kingdom
Coalition of Ratepayers for Affordable Green Electricity [★18134]
Coalition to Reduce Nuclear Dangers - Defunct.
Coalition for Religious Freedom [★18511]
Coalition for Religious Freedom [★IO]
Coalition for the Reproductive Rights of Workers - Defunct.
Coalition for Responsible Genetics [★18584]
Coalition for Responsible Mining Law - Defunct.
Coalition for Responsible Waste Incineration [3990], 1615 L St. NW, Ste. 1350, Washington, DC 20036, (202)452-1241
Coalition for Retirement Income Security - Address unknown since 1999.
Coalition for Safe Drinking Water - Defunct.
Coalition for Safe Food - Defunct.
Coalition for Safety of Abortion Clinics - Defunct.
Coalition to Salute America's Heroes [21294], 100 Broadway, Ossining, NY 10562, (914)432-5400
Coalition to Save America's Music - Defunct.
Coalition to Save Our Documentary Heritage - Defunct.
Coalition for Scenic Beauty [★4606]
Coalition of Ser. Indus. [3547], 1090 Vermont Ave. NW, Ste. 420, Washington, DC 20005, (202)289-7460
Coalition on Sexuality and Disability - Address unknown since 1999.
Coalition of Small and Independent Business Assns. - Defunct.

Coalition on Smoking or Health - Defunct.
Coalition for Sound Money - Address unknown since 1999.
Coalition on Southern Africa - Address unknown since 1995.
Coalition of Spanish Speaking Mental Hea. Organizations [★13176]
Coalition for State Prompt Pay - Defunct.
Coalition to Stop Gun Violence [17590], 1023 15th St. NW, Ste. 301, Washington, DC 20005, (202)408-0061
Coalition to Stop Trident - Defunct.
Coalition to Stop the Use of Child Soldiers [IO], London, United Kingdom
Coalition for the Strategic Defense Initiative - Defunct.
Coalition for Strategic Stability in the Middle East - Defunct.
Coalition for Student and Academic Rights [7870], PO Box 491, Solebury, PA 18963, (215)862-9096
Coalition for Student Loan Reform - Address unknown since 2004.
Coalition to Support Cuban Detainees - Defunct.
Coalition for Unborn Children [★12902]
Coalition for Uniform Product Liability Law - Address unknown since 2002.
Coalition on Urban Renewal and Educ. [18774], 1300 Pennsylvania Ave. NW, Ste. 700, Washington, DC 20004, (202)204-2575
Coalition for Vehicle Choice [17015], c/o E. Bruce Harrison & Co., 1440 New York Ave. NW, Washington, DC 20005, (800)288-6411
Coalition of Visionary Resources [2835], 194 Main St., Butler, NJ 07405, (973)838-2280
Coalition of Visionary Retailers [★2835]
Coalition for Vocational Home Economics Education - Address unknown since 2007.
Coalition for the War on Poverty - Defunct.
Coalition on Women and the Budget - Defunct.
Coalition for Women in the Humanities and Social Sciences - Defunct.
Coalition for Women in Intl. Development - Defunct.
Coalition of Women in Natl. and Intl. Business - Address unknown since 1991.
Coalition on Women and Religion - Defunct.
Coalition for Women's Appointments [17520], PO Box 50476, Washington, DC 20091, (202)785-1100
Coalition of Women's Art Orgs. - Defunct.
Coalition for Workplace Technology - Defunct.
Coalitions for America - Address unknown since 2008.
Coalitions for Health Care - Defunct.
COAR Peace Mission [17482], 4395 Rocky River Dr., Cleveland, OH 44135, (216)252-5572
Coast Alliance [4375], 3331/2 Pennsylvania Ave. SE, Washington, DC 20003, (202)546-9554
Coast Boat Builders and Repairers Assn; Atlantic [★2568]
Coast Defense Study Group [10473], 634 Silver Dawn Ct., Zionsville, IN 46077-9088
Coast Garment Manufacturers Assn; Pacific [★221]
Coast Guard
  AdoptaPlatoon [11489]
  Amer. Maritime Safety, Inc. [2570]
  Amer. Merchant Marine Lib. Assn. [10321]
  Any Soldier [11490]
  Australian Volunteer Coast Guard Assn. [IO]
  Beirut Veterans of Am. [21287]
  Books For Soldiers [11491]
  Chief Warrant and Warrant Officers Assn., U.S. Coast Guard [6072]
  Coast Defense Study Group [10473]
  Coast Guard Auxiliary Assn. [20733]
  Coast Guard Combat Veterans Assn. [21295]
  Intl. Military Community Executives Assn. [834]
  Military Officers Assn. of Am. [21235]
  Natal Sharks Bd. [IO]
  Natl. Boating Safety Advisory Coun. [5546]
  Natl. Chief Petty Officers' Assn. [21214]
  Natl. Naval Officers Assn. [6093]
  Navy Seabee Veterans of Am. [21217]
  Navy Wifeline Assn. [21199]
  Oper. AC [11492]
  Oper. Homelink [11494]
  Oper. Sandbox [11495]

  Oper. ShoeBox [11496]
  Oper. Soldier Support [11497]
  Oper.: Take a Soldier to the Movies [11498]
  Oper. We Do Care [11499]
  Salute Our Services [11500]
  Support Our Soldiers Am. [11502]
  Tin Can Sailors - The Natl. Assn. of Destroyer Veterans [21220]
  Tragedy Assistance Prog. for Survivors [11503]
  U.S. Coast Guard Chief Petty Officers Assn. [20734]
  U.S. Life-Saving Ser. Heritage Assn. [10072]
Coast Guard Auxiliary Assn. [20733], 9449 Watson Indus. Park, St. Louis, MO 63126, (314)962-8828
Coast Guard; Chief Warrant and Warrant Officers Assn., U.S. [6072]
Coast Guard Combat Veterans Assn. [21295], PO Box 544, Westfield Center, OH 44251, (330)887-5539
Coast Guard League - Address unknown since 1995.
Coast Seamen's Union [★24131]
Coast-to-Coast Bikers - Defunct.
Coastal Carolina Alumni Assn. [★18887]
Coastal Carolina Univ. Alumni Assn. [18887], Coastal Carolina Univ., PO Box 261954, Conway, SC 29528-6054, (843)347-3161
Coastal Commn; California [★4669]
Coastal Conservation Assn. [4376], 6919 Portwest Dr., Ste. 100, Houston, TX 77024, (713)626-4234
Coastal Engineering Res. Coun. - Address unknown since 2004.
The Coastal Soc. [7395], c/o Judy Tucker, CAE, Exec. Dir., PO Box 3590, Williamsburg, VA 23187-3590, (757)565-0999
Coastal States Org. [7396], Hall of States, 444 N Capitol St. NW, Ste. 322, Washington, DC 20001, (202)508-3860
Coaster Enthusiasts; Amer. [22970]
Coastwise-Great Lakes and Inland Hull Assn. - Defunct.
Coat and Suit Assn; New York [253]
Coated Abrasives Fabricators Assn. - Defunct.
Coated Abrasives Mfrs. Inst. [★2567]
Coated and Processed Paper Assn. - Defunct.
Coater Assn; Chem. [★802]
Coaters Assn. Intl; Chem. [802]
Coaters and Laminators; Assn. of Indus. Metallizers, [851]
Coaters; Natl. Assn. of Blueprint and Diazotype [★1800]
Coatings
  Aluminum Anodizers Coun. [849]
  Amer. Galvanizers Assn. [850]
  American Galvanizers Association [IO]
  Assn. for Finishing Processes of the Soc. of Mfg. Engineers [IO]
  Assn. for Finishing Processes of the Soc. of Mfg. Engineers [6703]
  Assn. of Indus. Metallizers, Coaters and Laminators [851]
  Canadian Paint and Coatings Assn. [IO]
  European Coil Coating Assn. [IO]
  European Gen. Galvanizers Assn. [IO]
  European Surface Treatment on Aluminium [IO]
  Fed. of Societies for Coatings Tech. [IO]
  Fed. of Societies for Coatings Tech. [6704]
  Hot Dip Galvanizers Assn. of Southern Africa [IO]
  Intl. Enamellers Inst. [IO]
  Intl. Soc. of Coating Sci. and Tech. [IO]
  Intl. Soc. of Coating Sci. and Tech. [6705]
  Natl. Assn. of Pipe Coating Applicators [852]
  National Association of Pipe Coating Applicators [IO]
  Natl. Coil Coating Assn. [853]
  Natl. One Coat Stucco Assn. [650]
  Powder Coating Inst. [854]
  Roof Coatings Manufacturers Assn. [855]
  Soc. of Vacuum Coaters [856]
  Surface Coatings Assn. Australia [IO]
  Surface Coatings Assn. New Zealand [IO]
  Surface Engg. Coating Assn. [6706]
  Thermal Spraying and Surface Engg. Assn. [IO]
  Thermoset Resin Formulators Assn. [857]
Coatings Assn; Natl. Paint and [2884]

A star before a book entry number signifies that the name is not listed separately, but is mentioned within the entry.

Coatney/Courtney Family Assn. **[20867]**, c/o Carol Kosanke Peterson, AG, 499 N Trellis Ct., Newport News, VA 23608, (757)369-0511

Cob Soc. of Am; Welsh Pony and **[★4969]**

Cob Soc. of Am; Welsh Pony and **[4969]**

Cobalt Development Inst. **[IO]**, Guildford, United Kingdom

Cobbett Assn. for Chamber Music Res. **[10579]**, 601 Timber Trail, Riverwoods, IL 60015-3846, (847)374-1800

Cobequid Salmon Assn. **[IO]**, Truro, NS, Canada

Coblentz Soc. **[7689]**, c/o Mary W. Carrabba, PhD, Pres., 508 Gold Terr., Rogue River, OR 97537, (541)582-2399

Cobra Club **[★21782]**

Cobra Owners Club of Am. **[21619]**, 672 N Ranchroad Dr., Orange, CA 92869, (714)546-5670

Coca-Cola Collectors Club Intl. - Address unknown since 1995.

Coca-Cola Collectors' Soc; Cavanagh's **[21991]**

Cocaine Anonymous World Services **[13232]**, PO Box 492000, Los Angeles, CA 90049-8000, (310)559-5833

Cocaine Anonymous World Services **[IO]**, Los Angeles, CA, United States

Cochlear Implant Assn., Inc. **[IO]**, Washington, DC, United States

Cochlear Implant Assn., Inc. **[14748]**, 5335 Wisconsin Ave. NW, Ste. 440, Washington, DC 20015-2052, (202)895-2781

Cochrane Collaboration **[IO]**, Oxford, United Kingdom

Cockapoo Club of Am. **[22247]**, 31766 Oak Ranch Ct., Westlake Village, CA 91361

Cockatiel Soc; Amer. **[21838]**

Cockatiel Soc; Natl. **[21852]**

Cockatiel Soc; North Amer. **[21857]**

Cockayne Syndrome Network; Share and Care **[14480]**

Cocker Spaniel

    Amer. Spaniel Club **[22213]**

    Cavalier King Charles Spaniel Club of Am. **[22242]**

    English Cocker Spaniel Club of Am. **[22259]**

Cocker Spaniel Club of Am; English **[22259]**

Cocoa and Chocolate Mfrs. of the U.S; Assn. of **[★1506]**

Cocoa Found; World **[6545]**

Cocoa Merchants' Assn. of Am. **[1507]**, World Financial Ctr., One N End Ave., 13th Fl., New York, NY 10282-1101, (212)201-8819

Cocoa Producers' Alliance **[IO]**, Lagos, Nigeria

Cocoa Res. Comm; Amer. **[★6545]**

Cocoa Res. Inst; Amer. **[★6545]**

Cocoa Res. Inst. of Ghana **[IO]**, New Tafo, Ghana

Code Comm; Glazing Indus. **[626]**

Code Coun; Uniform **[★337]**

Code Enforcement; Amer. Assn. of **[5959]**

Code Pink Women's Pre-Emptive Strike for Peace **[18199]**, 2010 Linden Ave., Venice, CA 90291, (310)827-4320

Code Pink Women's Pre-Emptive Strike for Peace **[IO]**, Venice, CA, United States

Code Talkers Assn; Navajo **[21396]**

Coders; Amer. Acad. of Procedural **[★14694]**

Coders; Amer. Acad. of Professional **[14694]**

Codes and Standards; Natl. Conf. of States on Building **[5552]**

Coe Fan Club; David Allan **[24870]**

Coeliac Soc. of Ireland **[IO]**, Dublin, Ireland

Coeliac Soc. of the United Kingdom **[★IO]**

Coeliac UK **[IO]**, High Wycombe, United Kingdom

Coercive Psychiatry; Network Against **[12554]**

The Coexistence Initiative **[★12697]**

The Coexistence Initiative **[★IO]**

Coexistence Intl. **[IO]**, Waltham, MA, United States

Coexistence Intl. **[12697]**, Mailstop 086, Waltham, MA 02454, (781)736-5017

Coffee

    Assn. of Coffee Mill Enthusiasts **[21973]**

    Assn. of Soluble Coffee Mfrs. of the European Union **[IO]**

    AustralAsian Specialty Coffee Assn. **[IO]**

    Australian Coffee Traders Assn. **[IO]**

    Brazil Specialty Coffee Assn. **[IO]**

    Brazilian Assn. of the Coffee Roasting and Grinding Indus. **[IO]**

    Caffeine Awareness Alliance **[13747]**

    Coffee Assn. of Canada **[IO]**

    Coffee Kids **[11769]**

    Coffee Trade Fed. **[IO]**

    Ethiopian Coffee Exporters' Assn. **[IO]**

    Fed. of Coffee Organisations **[IO]**

    Intl. Women's Coffee Alliance **[11783]**

    Natl. Assn. of the Coffee Indus. - Mexico **[IO]**

    Natl. Fed. of Coffee Growers of Colombia **[IO]**

    Specialty Coffee Assn. of Am. **[513]**

    Specialty Coffee Assn. of Europe **[IO]**

    World Alliance of Gourmet Robustas **[1738]**

Coffee Assn. of Am; Specialty **[513]**

Coffee Assn. of Canada **[IO]**, Toronto, ON, Canada

Coffee Assn. of U.S.A; Natl. **[511]**

Coffee Development Group - Address unknown since 1994.

Coffee Growers' Assn. of El Salvador - Defunct.

Coffee Indus. of Am; Assoc. **[★511]**

Coffee Kids **[11769]**, 1305 Luisa St., Ste. C, Santa Fe, NM 87505, (505)820-1443

Coffee Kids **[IO]**, Santa Fe, NM, United States

Coffee Mill Enthusiasts; Assn. of **[21973]**

Coffee Ser. Assn; Natl. **[★3971]**

Coffee Trade Fed. **[IO]**, London, United Kingdom

Coffin-Lowry Syndrome Found. **[14447]**, 3045 255th Ave. SE, Sammamish, WA 98075, (425)427-0939

Coffs Harbour Chamber of Commerce and Indus. **[IO]**, Coffs Harbour, Australia

COFORD: Natl. Coun. for Forest Res. and Development **[IO]**, Dublin, Ireland

Cogeneration and Competitive Power Institute **[★IO]**

Cogeneration and Competitive Power Institute **[★6942]**

Cognac Information Bur. - Defunct.

Cognitive-Behavioral Therapists; Natl. Assn. of **[16193]**

Cognitive Neuroscience Soc. **[15407]**, c/o Center for Mind and Brain, Univ. of California, Davis, One Shields Ave., Davis, CA 95616, (805)705-9014

Cognitive Neuroscience Soc. **[IO]**, Davis, CA, United States

Cognitive Sci. Soc. **[6484]**, c/o Deborah Gruber, Bus. Mgr., Univ. of Texas, Dept. of Psychology, 1 Univ. Sta. A8000, Austin, TX 78712-0187, (512)471-2030

Cognitive Sciences; Fed. of Behavioral, Psychological, and **[6530]**

Cogswell Family Assn. **[20868]**, c/o Mrs. Claire G. Cogswell-Daigle, Sec., 21 Old Belchertown Rd., Ware, MA 01082, (863)471-2735

Coif; Order of the **[24516]**

Coiffure Am; Inter **[1080]**

Coiffures de Dames; Internationale des **[★1080]**

Coil Coating Assn; Natl. **[853]**

Coil Winding Assn; Electl. Mfg. and **[1183]**

Coil Winding Assn; Intl. **[★1183]**

Coin Club; Armenian **[★22730]**

The Coin Coalition - Defunct.

Coin Laundry Assn. **[2402]**, 1315 Butterfield Rd., Ste. 212, Downers Grove, IL 60515, (630)963-5547

Coin Laundry Equip. Operators; Natl. Assn. of **[★2406]**

Coin-Op Car Wash Assn. - Address unknown since 1995.

Coin Operated Collectors Assn. **[21997]**, c/o Dan Davids, 15200 Mansel Ave., Lawndale, CA 90260

Coin Operated Collectors Assn. **[IO]**, Lawndale, CA, United States

Coins

    American-Israel Numismatic Assn. **[22723]**

    Amer. Numismatic Assn. **[22724]**

    Amer. Numismatic Soc. **[22725]**

    Amer. Tax Token Soc. **[22727]**

    Amer. Wooden Money Guild **[22728]**

    Ancient Coin Collectors Guild **[22729]**

    Challenge Coin Assn. **[22731]**

    Civil War Token Soc. **[22732]**

    Coin Operated Collectors Assn. **[21997]**

    Colonial Coin Collectors Club **[22733]**

    Combined Organizations of Numismatic Error Collectors of Am. **[22734]**

    Croatian Philatelic Soc. **[22813]**

    Cuban Numismatic Assn. **[22735]**

    Dedicated Wooden Money Collectors **[22736]**

    Early Amer. Coppers **[22737]**

    The Elongated Collectors **[22738]**

    Inter-Governmental Philatelic Corp. **[22829]**

    Intl. Bank Note Soc. **[22739]**

    Latin Amer. Paper Money Soc. **[22741]**

    Liberty Seated Collectors Club **[22742]**

    Lithuanian Numismatic Assn. **[22743]**

    Love Token Soc. **[22744]**

    Medal Collectors of Am. **[22745]**

    Natl. Collectors Assn. of Die Doubling **[22746]**

    Natl. Token Collectors Assn. **[21954]**

    North Amer. Collectors **[22747]**

    Numismatic Literary Guild **[22749]**

    Numismatics Intl. **[22750]**

    Original Hobo Nickel Soc. **[22752]**

    Professional Numismatists Guild **[22754]**

    Soc. of Lincoln Cent Collectors **[22756]**

    Soc. of Paper Money Collectors **[22757]**

    Soc. of Private and Pioneer Numismatists **[22758]**

    Soc. of Ration Token Collectors **[22759]**

    Soc. for U.S. Commemorative Coins **[22760]**

    Soc. of U.S. Pattern Collectors **[22761]**

    Token and Medal Soc. **[22763]**

    Toned Coin Collectors Soc. **[22764]**

    U.S. Mexican Numismatic Assn. **[22765]**

    Unrecognised States Numismatic Soc. **[22766]**

    Women in Numismatics **[22767]**

    World Internet Numismatic Soc. **[22768]**

    World Proof Numismatic Assn. **[22769]**

    Young Numismatists of Am. **[22770]**

Coins; Soc. for U.S. Commemorative **[22760]**

Coins on Stamps Unit - Defunct.

COINTELPRO Survivors - Defunct.

Coir Bd. of India **[IO]**, Kochi, India

Cojolya Assn. of Maya Women Weavers **[IO]**, Solola, Guatemala

Coke and Coal Chemicals Inst; Amer. **[838]**

COLA **[15039]**, 9881 Broken Land Pkwy., Ste. 200, Columbia, MD 21046, (800)981-9883

Cola Collectors Club; Pepsi- **[22106]**

COLAGE **[12223]**, 1550 Bryant St., Ste. 830, San Francisco, CA 94103, (415)861-5437

Cold Finished Steel Bar Inst. **[2703]**, c/o Kevin Van de Ven, Chm., LMP Steel Wire and Co., 20000 E First St., Maryville, MO 64468, (660)582-3127

Cold Formed Parts and Machine Inst. **[1820]**, 25 N Broadway, Tarrytown, NY 10591, (914)332-0040

Cold Spring Harbor Whaling Museum **[★10451]**

Cold Storage Contractors; Intl. Assn. of **[★1886]**

Cold Storage and Distribution Fed. **[IO]**, Reading, United Kingdom

Cold Storage Insulation Contractors; Natl. Assn. of **[★1886]**

Cold War Veterans Assn. **[21296]**, PO Box 13042, Overland Park, KS 66282-3042

Cole Country Band Fan Club - Address unknown since 1989.

Cole Soc; Descendants of Daniel **[20881]**

Colegio De Doctores En Ciencias Economicas Y Contadores Del Uruguay **[IO]**, Montevideo, Uruguay

Colegio De Economistas Del Paraguay **[IO]**, Asuncion, Paraguay

Colegio Ibero-LatinoAmericano de Dermatologia **[★IO]**

Colegio de Ingenieros de Chile A.G **[★IO]**

Colegio Internacional de Medicos Nucleares **[★IO]**

Colegio Mexicano de Interpretes de Conferencias **[★IO]**

Coleman Collectors Club; Intl. **[22049]**

Coleman Found. **[13162]**, 651 W Washington, Ste. 306, Chicago, IL 60661, (312)902-7120

Coleopterists Soc. **[7059]**, c/o Norman E. Woodley, Treas., 15703 Quince Orchard Rd., North Potomac, MD 20878-4742, (202)382-1802

Colitis and Crohn's Disease; Natl. Assn. of **[IO]**

Colitis Found. of Am; Crohn's and **[14414]**

Colitis; Found. for Ileitis and **[★14414]**

Colitis; Natl. Found. for Ileitis and **[★14414]**

Colitis; Reach Out for Youth with Ileitis and **[16548]**

Collaborative Intl. Pesticides Analytical Coun. **[IO]**, Budapest, Hungary

Reference to "IO" in place of a book number signifies that the association may be found in the 45th edition of International Organizations.

Collaborative; Organizers' [17244]
Collapsible Metal Tube Assn. [★2881]
Collapsible Tube Mfrs. Assn. - Defunct.
Collectible Club; Betty Boop Intl. [21976]
Collectibles
  1/87 Vehicle Club [22641]
  1937-1938 Buick Club [21552]
  1948-50 Packard Convertible Roster [21553]
  1953-54 Buick Skylark Club [21554]
  1956 Studebaker Golden Hawk Owners Register
    [21555]
  1958 Cadillac Owners Assn. [21556]
  1965-66 Full Size Chevrolet Club [21557]
  1971 GTO and Judge Convertible Registry
    [21559]
  1995 Corvette Pace Car Registry [21560]
  66,67,68 High Country Special Mustang Registry
    [21561]
Abarth Register, U.S.A. [21562]
Abingdon Pottery Club [21522]
A.C. Gilbert Heritage Soc. [22992]
Advt. Cup and Mug Collectors of Am. [21956]
Aeronautica and Air Label Collectors Club [21422]
Airflow Club of Am. [21563]
Aladdin Knights of the Mystic Light [22617]
Alaska Collectors' Club [22779]
Alfa Romeo Owners Club [21565]
Alice in Wonderland Collectors Network [21957]
All-American Indian Motorcycle Club [22663]
AMC Pacer Club [21566]
AMC Rambler Club [21567]
Amer. Air Mail Soc. [22780]
Amer. Art Deco Dealers Assn. [295]
Amer. Austin/Bantam Club [21568]
Amer. Bell Assn. Intl. [21958]
Amer. Bugatti Club [21569]
Amer. Carnival Glass Assn. [22549]
Amer. Coaster Enthusiasts [22970]
Amer. Collectors of Infant Feeders [21959]
Amer. Cookie Jar Assn. [22577]
Amer. Cut Glass Assn. [22550]
Amer. Edge Collectors Assn. [22612]
Amer. First Day Cover Soc. [22781]
Amer. Helvetia Philatelic Soc. [22782]
Amer. Historical Print Collectors Soc. [21523]
American-Israel Numismatic Assn. [22723]
Amer. Lancia Club [21573]
Amer. Lock Collectors Assn. [21962]
Amer. Matchcover Collecting Club [21963]
Amer. MGB Assn. [21574]
Amer. MGC Register [21575]
Amer. Motors Owners Assn. [21576]
Amer. Numismatic Assn. [22724]
Amer. Numismatic Soc. [22725]
Amer. Pencil Collectors Soc. [21964]
Amer. Philatelic Cong. [22783]
Amer. Philatelic Res. Lib. [22784]
Amer. Philatelic Soc. [22785]
Amer. Philatelic Soc. Writers Unit [22786]
Amer. Plate Number Single Soc. [22787]
Amer. Political Items Collectors [22903]
Amer. Racing Pigeon Union [22894]
Amer. Revenue Assn. [22788]
Amer. Soc. of Bookplate Collectors and Designers
    [21965]
Amer. Soc. of Check Collectors [22726]
Amer. Soc. of Military Insignia Collectors [22627]
Amer. Soc. of Polar Philatelists [22789]
Amer. Spoon Collectors [21966]
Amer. Sta. Wagon Owners Assn. [21577]
Amer. Tax Token Soc. [22727]
Amer. Topical Assn. [22790]
Amer. Topical Assn., Americana Unit [22791]
Amer. Topical Assn., Biology Unit [22792]
Amer. Wooden Money Guild [22728]
Amy's Doll Lover's Club [22391]
Ancient Coin Collectors Guild [22729]
Anheuser-Busch Collectors Club [21967]
Annalee Club [22392]
Antique Advt. Assn. of Am. [21420]
Antique and Art Glass Salt Shaker Collectors Soc.
    [21968]
Antique Auto Racing Assn. [21578]
Antique Auto. Club of Am. [21579]
Antique Barbed Wire Soc. [21969]

Antique Caterpillar Machinery Owners Club
    [22619]
Antique and Classic Boat Soc. [21868]
Antique Comb Collectors Club Intl. [21970]
Antique Doorknob Collectors of Am. [21971]
Antique Fan Collectors Assn. [21533]
Antique Motorcycle Club of Am. [22667]
Antique Phonograph Collectors Club [22710]
Antique Poison Bottle Collectors Assn. [21972]
Antique Reloading Tool Collector's Assn. [22424]
Antique Small Engine Collectors Club [22409]
Antique Stove Assn. [21524]
Antique Studebaker Club [21580]
Antique Telephone Collectors Assn. [22985]
Antique Telescope Soc. [21526]
Antique Toy Collectors of Am. [22993]
Antique Truck Club of Am. [23022]
Antique Wireless Assn. [22923]
Antiques and Collectibles Associations [216]
Antiques and Collectibles Dealer Assn. [863]
Antiques and Collectibles Natl. Assn. [864]
Antiques Coun. [217]
Arctic Cat Club of Am. [22944]
Ariel Motorcycle Club North Am. [22668]
Armed Forces Stamp Exchange Club [22793]
Armor and Arms Club [21536]
Assoc. Collectors of El Salvador [22794]
Assn. of Amer. Military Uniform Collectors [22628]
Assn. of Coffee Mill Enthusiasts [21973]
Assn. of Collecting Clubs [21974]
Assn. of Game and Puzzle Collectors [22460]
Assn. of North Amer. Radio Clubs [21498]
Assn. of Ohio Longrifle Collectors [22425]
Astronomy Stud. Unit [22795]
Austin Bantam Soc. [21583]
Austin-Healey Sports and Touring Club [21586]
Authentic Artifact Collectors Assn. [21543]
Auto. License Plate Collectors Assn. [21587]
Ball Collectors Club [22551]
Bead Soc. of Los Angeles [21975]
Berkeley Exchange [21590]
Beyond the Pond.International Frog Collectors
    Club [21977]
Bicycle Stamps Club [22796]
Big Little Book Collector's Club [21978]
Blue/White Pottery Club [21527]
BMW Car Club of Am. [21591]
BMW Motorcycle Owners of Am. [22670]
BMW Riders Assn. Intl. [22671]
BMW Vintage Car Club of Am. [21593]
Boss 302 Registry [21595]
Boss 429 Owners Dir. [21596]
Brazil Philatelic Assn. [22797]
Brewery Collectibles Club of Am. [21979]
Bricklin Intl. Owners Club [21598]
Browning Collectors Assn. [22426]
Buick Club of Am. [21599]
Buick GS Club of Am. [21600]
Bullseye Cancel Collectors' Club [22798]
Cadillac Drivers Club [21601]
Cadillac-LaSalle Club [21602]
Call and Whistle Collectors Assn. [21983]
Canadian Corkscrew Collectors Club [21985]
Capri Club North Am. [21604]
Carriage Assn. of Am. [21987]
CartoPhilatelic Soc. [22799]
CAS Collectors [21926]
Case Collectors Club [22613]
Casey Jones Railroad Unit - ATA [22800]
Casino Chip and Gaming Token Collectors Club
    [21989]
Cast Iron Seat Collectors Assn. [22607]
Cat Collectors [21990]
Cats on Stamps Stud. Unit [22801]
Cavanagh's Coca-Cola Collectors' Soc. [21991]
Center for Wooden Boats [21869]
Challenge Coin Assn. [22731]
Chatty Cathy Collectors Club [22393]
Chemistry and Physics on Stamps Stud. Unit
    [22802]
Chess Collectors Intl. [21944]
Chevrolet Nomad Assn. [21607]
Chevy and Geo Club [21608]
Chicago Map Soc. [21528]
Chicago Playing Card Collectors [21992]

China Stamp Soc. [22803]
Chris Craft Antique Boat Club [21870]
Christian Motorcyclists Assn. [22674]
Christmas Philatelic Club [22804]
Christmas Seal and Charity Stamp Soc. [21993]
Christopher Columbus Philatelic Soc. [22805]
Chrysler 300 Club Intl. [21611]
Chrysler Town and Country Owners Registry
    [21612]
Cigarette Pack Collectors Assn. [21994]
CIMTA [858]
Citizens' Stamp Advisory Comm. [22806]
Citroen Quarterly Car Club [21613]
Civil Censorship Study Group [22807]
Civil War Token Soc. [22732]
Classic Chevy Intl. [21615]
Classic Jaguar Assn. [21616]
Classic Thunderbird Club Intl. [21617]
Classic Yacht Assn. [21871]
Cobra Owners Club of Am. [21619]
Coin Operated Collectors Assn. [21997]
Collectors Club [22808]
Collectors Record Club [22712]
Collectors of Religion on Stamps [22809]
Collins Collectors Assn. [21499]
Colonial Coin Collectors Club [22733]
Colonial Coverlet Guild of Am. [21998]
Combined Organizations of Numismatic Error Col-
    lectors of Am. [22734]
Company of Military Historians [22629]
Confederate Stamp Alliance [22811]
Contemporary Historical Vehicle Assn. [21620]
Continental Luscombe Assn. [21439]
Cookie Cutter Collectors Club [22000]
Corrado Club of Am. [21621]
Corvair Soc. of Am. [21622]
Corvette Club of Am. [21623]
Cover Collectors Circuit Club [22812]
Cow Observers Worldwide [22002]
Cracker Jack Collectors Assn. [22003]
Cribbage Bd. Collectors Soc. [22004]
Croatian Philatelic Soc. [22813]
Crosley Auto. Club [21624]
Crown Victoria Assn. [21625]
Cuban Numismatic Assn. [22735]
Currier and Ives Dinnerware Collectors [22007]
Cushman Club of Am. [22676]
Cyclone Montego Torino Registry [21626]
Czech Collector's Assn. [22008]
Dedham Pottery Collectors Soc. [22009]
Dedicated Wooden Money Collectors [22736]
Deltiologists of Am. [22905]
Denver Strikers Matchcover Club [22625]
DeSoto Club of Am. [21630]
Deutsches Motorrad Register [22677]
Diecast Exchange Club [22010]
Disabled Collectors' Correspondence Club
    [22814]
Disabled Veterans Keychain Tag and Chauffeur's
    Badge Collectors Newsl. [22011]
DKW Club of Am. [21631]
Dodge Bros. Club [21632]
Dodge Pilothouse Era Truck Club of Am. [23024]
Dogs on Stamps Stud. Unit [22815]
Doll Artisan Guild [22394]
Doll Costumer's Guild [22395]
Dreamsicles Club [22013]
Early Amer. Coppers [22737]
Early Ford V-8 Club of Am. [21633]
Early Typewriter Collectors Assn. [22015]
Earth's Physical Features Stud. Unit [22816]
Edsel Club [21636]
Egg Cup Collectors' Corner [22016]
Eire Philatelic Assn. [22817]
Elgin Motorcar Owners Registry [21638]
The Elongated Collectors [22738]
Emergency Vehicle Owners and Operators Assn.
    [21639]
Errors, Freaks and Oddities Collector's Club
    [22818]
Erskine Registry [21640]
Etch-A-Sketch Club [22994]
Fairlane Club of Am. [21641]
Fairy Lamp Club [22019]
Fenton Art Glass Collectors of Am. [22552]

A star before a book entry number signifies that the name is not listed separately, but is mentioned within the entry.

Ferrari Owners Club [21644]
Figural Bottle Opener Collectors Club [22023]
Figural Cast Iron Collector's Club [22417]
Fine Arts Philatelists [22819]
Florence Ceramics Collectors Soc. [22025]
Flow Blue Intl. Collectors Club [22026]
Ford Galaxie Club of Am. [21647]
Fostoria Glass Collectors [22553]
Fostoria Glass Soc. of Am. [22554]
France and Colonies Philatelic Soc. [22820]
Friends of Old-Time Radio [22924]
Gar Wood Soc. [21873]
Gems, Minerals and Jewelry Stud. Unit [22821]
German Colonies Collectors Gp. [22822]
German Gun Collectors' Assn. [22029]
Germany Philatelic Soc. [22823]
GI Joe Collectors' Club [22996]
Gift Assn. of Am. [859]
Gift and Collectibles Guild [860]
Ginny Doll Club [22396]
Glass Art Soc. [22555]
Global Lottery Collectors Soc. [22030]
Glock Collectors Assn. [22427]
Golden Glow of Christmas Past [22975]
Golf Collectors Soc. [22031]
Goodguys Rod and Custom Assn. [21649]
Graham Bros. Truck and Bus Club [21894]
Graham Owners Club Intl. [21650]
Graphics Philately Assn. [22824]
Gravely Tractor Club of Am. [23002]
Gull Wing Gp. Intl. [21652]
Haiti Philatelic Soc. [22825]
Hammered Aluminum Collectors Assn. [22033]
Harley Hummer Club [22679]
Haynes-Apperson Owners Club [21653]
Heart of America Carnival Glass Assn. [22557]
Heather's Teddy Bear Org. [22035]
Heisey Collectors of America/National Heisey
  Glass Museum [22558]
Hellenic Philatelic Soc. of Am. [22826]
Heritage Rose Found. [22516]
H.H. Franklin Club [21656]
Historic Motor Sports Assn. [21657]
Homer Laughlin China Collectors Assn. [22036]
Honda Sport Touring Assn. [22681]
Horn and Whistle Enthusiasts Gp. [22037]
Horseless Carriage Club of Am. [21658]
Howdy Doody Memorabilia Collectors Club
  [22038]
Hudson-Essex-Terraplane Club [21659]
Hudson Essex Terraplane Historical Soc. [21660]
Hull Pottery Assn. [22039]
Hummel Collectors Club [22040]
Humor Stamp Club [22827]
Hurst/Olds Club of Am. [21661]
India Stud. Circle for Philately [22828]
Indian Motor-Cycle Club of America [22682]
Inter-Governmental Philatelic Corp. [22829]
Intl. 190SL Gp. [21663]
Intl. Amphicar Owners Club [21664]
Intl. Assn. of Jazz Record Collectors [22714]
Intl. Assn. of R.S. Prussia Collectors [22043]
Intl. Assn. of Silver Art Collectors [22044]
Intl. Autograph Collectors Club and Dealers Alli-
  ance [22045]
Intl. Bank Note Soc. [22739]
Intl. Betta Cong. [22441]
Intl. Bond and Share Soc. [22046]
Intl. Brick Collectors' Assn. [22048]
Intl. Bus Collectors Club [21895]
Intl. Camaro Club [21665]
Intl. Carnival Glass Assn. [22559]
Intl. Chinese Snuff Bottle Soc. [21890]
Intl. Coleman Collectors Club [22049]
Intl. Collectors Guild [22051]
Intl. Correspondence of Corkscrew Addicts
  [22052]
Intl. Cuemakers Assn. [519]
Intl. Doll Makers Assn. [22397]
Intl. Edsel Club [21666]
Intl. Fed. of Amer. Homing Pigeon Fanciers
  [22895]
Intl. Fed. of Postcard Dealers [22906]
Intl. Fire Buff Associates [22421]
Intl. Guild of Lamp Researchers [22618]

Intl. Handicappers' Net [21502]
Intl. Inflatable Products and Games Assn. [861]
Intl. King Midget Car Club [21667]
Intl. Match Safe Assn. [22053]
Intl. Mercury Owners Assn. [21668]
Intl. Meteorite Collectors Assn. [22981]
Intl. Mustang Bullitt Owners Club [21669]
Intl. Nippon Collectors Club [21929]
Intl. Norton Owners' Assn. [22684]
Intl. Old Lacers, Inc. [22161]
Intl. Paperweight Soc. [22776]
Intl. Radio Club of Am. [21503]
Intl. Railroad and Transportation Postcard Collec-
  tors Club [22055]
Intl. Rose O'Neill Club Found. [22399]
Intl. Sand Collectors Soc. [22056]
Intl. Soc. of Animal License Collectors [22058]
Intl. Soc. of Antique Scale Collectors [22059]
Intl. Soc. for Japanese Philately [22830]
Intl. Soc. for Vehicle Preservation [21670]
Intl. Soc. of Worldwide Stamp Collectors [22831]
Intl. Stamp and Coin Collectors Soc. [22832]
Intl. Thunderbird Club [21671]
Intl. Vintage Poster Dealers Assn. [106]
Intl. Watch Collectors Soc. [22988]
Iso and Bizzarrini Owners Club [21672]
Italian Car Registry [21673]
Jack Knight Air Mail Soc. [22834]
Jaguar Clubs of North Am. [21674]
Jensen Healey Preservation Soc. [21675]
Jewett Owners Club [21676]
John F. Kennedy First Day Cover Stud. Unit
  [22835]
Jordan Register [21677]
Junior Philatelists of Am. [22837]
Kaiser-Darrin Owners Roster [21679]
Kaiser-Frazer Owners Club Intl. [21680]
Karmann Ghia Club of North Am. [21681]
Kate Greenaway Soc. [22063]
Kissel Kar Klub [21682]
Kit Collectors Intl. [22649]
Knife Collectors Club [22615]
Korea Postcard Collectors Gp. [22907]
Korea Stamp Soc. [22838]
Kustom Kemps of Am. [21683]
Lamborghini Club Am. [21684]
Late Great Chevrolet Assn. [21685]
Latin Amer. Paper Money Soc. [22741]
Lawton Collector's Guild [22400]
L.C. Smith Collectors Assn. [22429]
Les Amis de Panhard and Deutsch Bonnet
  [21686]
Liberty Seated Collectors Club [22742]
Lincoln and Continental Owners Club [21687]
Lincoln Owners' Club [21688]
Lionel Railroader Club [22634]
Lithuanian Numismatic Assn. [22743]
Little Elegance Memories of Yesterday [22065]
Lizzie High Soc. [22401]
Lladro Soc. [21930]
London Vintage Taxi Assn. - Amer. Sect. [21690]
Lone Ranger Fan Club [25032]
Longwave Club of Am. [21505]
Lotus, Ltd. [21691]
Love Token Soc. [22744]
M. T. Bottle Collectors Assn. [22066]
Machine Cancel Soc. [22839]
Magic Collectors' Assn. [22621]
Magic Lantern Soc. of the U.S. and Canada
  [21531]
Mailer's Postmark Permit Club [22840]
Majolica Intl. Soc. [21931]
M&M's Collectors Club [22067]
Manuscript Soc. [22068]
Marble Collectors' Soc. of Am. [22624]
Maritime Postmark Soc. [22841]
Marklin Digital Special Interest Gp. [22635]
Marlin Auto Club [21693]
Marmon Club [21694]
Maserati Info. Exchange [21696]
Mathematical Stud. Unit [22842]
Maverick/Comet Club Intl. [21697]
Mazda Club [21698]
McCoy Pottery Collectors' Soc. [21932]
McDonald's Collectors Club [22070]

Mech. Bank Collectors of Am. [21826]
Medal Collectors of Am. [22745]
Medical Subjects Unit [22843]
Mercedes-Benz Club of Am. [21699]
Mercedes-Benz M-100 Owner's Gp. [21700]
Meter Stamp Soc. [22844]
Metropolitan Air Post Soc. [22845]
Metropolitan Owners Club of North Am. [21701]
Mexico Elmhurst Philatelic Soc. Intl. [22846]
Microcar and Minicar Club [21703]
Mid-Century Mercury Car Club [21704]
Midstates Jeepster Assn. [21705]
Midwest Decoy Collectors Assn. [22071]
Midwest Sunbeam Registry [21706]
Milestone Car Soc. [21707]
Military Postal History Soc. [22847]
Military Vehicle Preservation Assn. [22630]
Mini Car Club, U.S.A. [21708]
Miniature Arms Collectors/Makers Soc. [21538]
Miniature Book Soc. [9752]
Mobile Post Off. Soc. [22848]
Model A Ford Cabriolet Club [21709]
Model A Ford Club of Am. [21710]
Model "A" Restorers Club [21712]
Model "T" Ford Club of Am. [21713]
Model "T" Ford Club Intl. [21714]
Morgan Car Club [21717]
Morgan Plus Four Club [21718]
Morris Minor Registry [21720]
Motor Bus Soc. [21896]
Muntz Jet Registry [21721]
Napoleonic Age Philatelists [22849]
Nash Car Club of Am. [21725]
Natl. Antique Doll Dealers Assn. [22402]
Natl. Antique Oldsmobile Club [21726]
Natl. Assn. of Avon Collectors [22073]
Natl. Assn. of Breweriana Advt. [22074]
Natl. Assn. of Collectors [22075]
Natl. Assn. of Limited Edition Dealers [862]
Natl. Assn. of Milk Bottle Collectors [22076]
Natl. Assn. of Miniature Enthusiasts [22077]
Natl. Assn. of Paper and Advt. Collectors [22412]
Natl. Assn. of Rocketry [22650]
Natl. Assn. of Timetable Collectors [23008]
Natl. Assn. of Watch and Clock Collectors [22990]
Natl. Automatic Pistol Collectors Assn. [21539]
Natl. Autumn Leaf Collectors Club [22078]
Natl. Basketry Org. [22167]
Natl. Button Soc. [22079]
Natl. Cambridge Collectors [22561]
Natl. Cap and Patch Assn. [22080]
Natl. Carousel Assn. [21897]
Natl. Collectors Assn. of Die Doubling [22746]
Natl. Corvette Owners Assn. [21728]
Natl. Corvette Restorers Soc. [21729]
Natl. Coun. of Corvette Clubs [21730]
Natl. Depression Glass Assn. [22562]
Natl. DeSoto Club [21731]
Natl. Duck Stamp Collectors Soc. [22850]
Natl. Duncan Glass Soc. [22563]
Natl. Firebird and T/A Club [21732]
Natl. Fishing Lure Collectors Club [22082]
Natl. Graniteware Soc. [22083]
Natl. Imperial Glass Collectors Soc. [22565]
Natl. Inst. of Amer. Doll Artists [22403]
Natl. Knife Collectors Assn. [22616]
Natl. Model Railroad Assn. [22636]
Natl. Mossberg Collectors Assn. [22430]
Natl. Old Timers Auto Racing Club [21737]
Natl. Pop Can Collectors [22085]
Natl. Shaving Mug Collectors Assn. [22086]
Natl. Soc. of Arkansas Pottery Collectors [22088]
Natl. Stamp Dealers Assn. [22851]
Natl. St. Rod Assn. [21738]
Natl. Token Collectors Assn. [21954]
Natl. Toothpick Holder Collectors' Soc. [22089]
Natl. Valentine Collectors' Assn. [22090]
Natl. Woodie Club [21739]
Nautical Res. Guild [21880]
Nepal and Tibet Philatelic Stud. Circle [22852]
New England M.G. "T" Register Limited [21740]
New Mexico Barbed Wire Collectors Assn.
  [22091]
Newspaper Collectors Soc. of Am. [22092]
Nineteen Thirty-Two Buick Registry [21741]

Reference to "IO" in place of a book number signifies that the association may be found in the 45th edition of International Organizations.

North Amer. Auto Union Register [21743]
North Amer. Collectors [22747]
North Amer. Mini Moke Registry [21745]
North Amer. Model Boat Assn. [22654]
North Amer. Radio Archives [22926]
North Amer. Shortwave Assn. [21507]
North Amer. Soc. of Pipe Collectors [22093]
North Amer. Torquay Soc. [22094]
North Amer. Trap Collector Assn. [22095]
Northeastern Spoon Collectors Guild [22096]
Novelty Salt and Pepper Shakers Club [22097]
NSU Enthusiasts U.S.A. [21746]
NSX Club of Am. [21747]
Numismatic Literary Guild [22749]
Numismatics Intl. [22750]
Oakland-Pontiac Enthusiast Org. [21748]
Occupied Japan Club [22098]
The Old Appliance Club [21535]
Old Reel Collectors Assn. [22099]
Old Sleepy Eye Collectors' Club of Am. [21934]
Oldsmobile Club of Am. [21749]
On the Lighter Side, Intl. Lighter Collectors
   [22100]
Opel Assn. of North Am. [21751]
Opel Motorsports Club [21752]
Optometric Historical Soc. [15728]
Orders and Medals Soc. of Am. [22631]
Org. of Bricklin Owners [21753]
Original Doll Artists Coun. of Am. [22404]
Original Hobo Nickel Soc. [22752]
Oughtred Soc. [22101]
Packard Auto. Classics [21755]
Packard V-8 Roster, '55-'56 [21757]
Packards Intl. Motor Car Club [21758]
Pantera Intl. [21759]
Paperweight Collectors' Assn. [22102]
Peanut Pals [22104]
Pen Collectors of Am. [22105]
Perfins Club [22854]
Pewter Collectors Club of Am. [22107]
Philatelic Found. [22855]
Philatelic Friends Exchange Circuit [22856]
Philip Boileau Collectors' Soc. [21542]
Phoenix Bird Collectors of Am. [21935]
Pierce-Arrow Soc. [21761]
Plymouth Barracuda/Cuda Owners Club [21763]
Plymouth Owners Club [21764]
Polonus Philatelic Soc. [22857]
Pontiac-Oakland Club Intl. [21766]
Porsche Club of Am. [21767]
Post Mark Collectors Club [22858]
Postal Commemorative Soc. [22859]
Postal History Soc. [22860]
Postcard History Soc. [22909]
Precancel Stamp Soc. [22861]
Professional Autograph Dealers Assn. [865]
Professional Car Soc. [21768]
Professional Currency Dealers Assn. [22753]
Professional Numismatists Guild [22754]
Promotional Glass Collectors Assn. [22109]
Quarter Century Wireless Assn. [21509]
The Questers [21532]
Quimper Club Intl. [21546]
Radio Club of Am. [22928]
Radio Collectors of Am. [22929]
Renault Owners Club of North Am. [21769]
REO Club of Am. [21770]
Richardson Boat Owners Assn. [21884]
Rickenbacker Automobile Club of America [21771]
Rickman Owners Club Intl. [22689]
Riviera Owners Assn. [21772]
Road Race Lincoln Register [21773]
Rolls-Royce Owners' Club [21774]
Rometsch Registry [21775]
Rose Bowl Collectors [22112]
Rossica Soc. of Russian Philately [22862]
Rotary on Stamps Fellowship [22863]
Rudge Enthusiasts Club [22691]
Russian Zone Handoverprint Stud. and Res. Gp.
   [22864]
RVing Women [22962]
Ryukyu Philatelic Specialist Soc. [22865]
Saab Club of North Am. [21778]
Sabra Automobile Connection [21779]
Safety Razor Collectors Guild [22113]

St. Helena, Ascension, and Tristan da Cunha
   Philatelic Soc. [22866]
Saleen Club of Am. [21780]
Samuel Gompers Stamp Club [22867]
Sandicast Collectors Guild [21544]
Saxon Owners Registry [21781]
Scandinavian Collectors Club [22868]
Scouts on Stamps Soc. Intl. [22869]
Shelby Amer. Auto. Club [21782]
Ships-in-Bottles Assn. of Am. [22658]
Ships on Stamps Unit [22870]
Soc. of Amer. Magicians [22623]
Soc. of Australasian Specialists/Oceania [22871]
Soc. of Automotive Historians [21785]
Soc. for Hungarian Philately [22873]
Soc. of Inkwell Collectors [22114]
Soc. of Israel Philatelists [22874]
Soc. of Lincoln Cent Collectors [22756]
Soc. of Paper Money Collectors [22757]
Soc. for the Preservation and Appreciation of
   Antique Motor Fire Apparatus in Am. [22423]
Soc. of Private and Pioneer Numismatists [22758]
Soc. of Ration Token Collectors [22759]
Soc. for Thai Philately [22875]
Soc. of Tobacco Jar Collectors [21936]
Soc. for U.S. Commemorative Coins [22760]
Soc. of U.S. Pattern Collectors [22761]
Southeastern Historical Keyboard Soc. [22720]
Souvenir Building Collectors Soc. [22115]
Space Topic Stud. Unit [22876]
Spark Plug Collectors of Am. [22116]
Sports Car Club of Am. [21787]
Sports Philatelists Intl. [22877]
Squire SS-100 Registry [21788]
Stamps on Stamps Collectors Club [22878]
Stamps for the Wounded [22879]
State Revenue Soc. [22880]
Statue of Liberty Club [22118]
Steam Auto. Club of Am. [21789]
Steamship Historical Soc. of Am. [22980]
Still Bank Collectors Club of Am. [21827]
Strawberry Shortcake Chat Gp. [22406]
Studebaker Driver's Club [21790]
Stutz Club [21791]
Subaru 360 Drivers' Club [21792]
Sunbeam Rapier Registry [21793]
Super Coupe Club of Am. [21794]
Tea Leaf Club Intl. [21937]
Teen Assn. of Model Railroaders [22637]
Telephone Collectors Intl. [22986]
Texas Date Nail Collectors Assn. [22121]
Thimble Collectors Intl. [22122]
Thimble Guild [22123]
Thomas Kinkade Collectors' Soc. [21545]
Thompson Collectors Assn. [22431]
Thunderbird and Cougar Club of Am. [21795]
Tiffin Glass Collectors Club [22567]
Token and Medal Soc. [22763]
Toned Coin Collectors Soc. [22764]
Topolino Register of North Am. [21797]
Toy Car Collectors Assn. [22997]
Toy Stitchers Intl., Inc. [22998]
Toy Train Collectors Soc. [22638]
Toy Train Operating Soc. [22639]
Traditional Small Craft Assn. [21885]
Train Collectors Assn. [22640]
Treasures for Little Children [23000]
Triumph Register of Am. [21800]
Tucker Auto. Club of Am. [21801]
TVR Car Club North Am. [21802]
Ukrainian Philatelic and Numismatic Soc. [22883]
United Coun. of Corvette Clubs [21803]
United Fed. of Doll Clubs [22407]
United Ford Owners [21804]
United Four-Wheel Drive Associations [21805]
United Nations Philatelists, Inc. [22884]
United Postal Stationery Soc. [22885]
United Sidecar Assn. [22693]
U.S. Cancellation Club [22886]
U.S. Classic Racing Assn. [22694]
U.S. Mexican Numismatic Assn. [22765]
U.S. Stamp Soc. [22888]
United St. Machine Assn. [21807]
Universal Autograph Collectors Club [22126]
Universal Ship Cancellation Soc. [22889]

Unrecognised States Numismatic Soc. [22766]
Vaseline Glass Collectors, Inc. [22127]
Velocette Owners Club of North Am. [22695]
Veteran Motor Car Club of Am. [21808]
Vincent Owners Club - Keystone Sect. [22697]
Vintage BMW Motorcycle Owners [22698]
Vintage Chevrolet Club of Am. [21809]
Vintage Motor Bike Club [22699]
Vintage Radio and Phonograph Soc. [22931]
Vintage Thunderbird Club Intl. [21812]
Vintage Triumph Register [21813]
Vintage Volkswagen Club of Am. [21814]
Volkswagen Club of Am. [21815]
Volvo Club of Am. [21816]
Weatherby Collectors Assn. [22432]
Wedgwood Intl. Seminar [21939]
Western Assoc. Modelers [22661]
Western Cover Soc. [22890]
Whisky Pitcher Collectors Assn. of Am. [22130]
White Ironstone China Assn. [21940]
Wills Sainte Claire Museum [21817]
Willys Overland Jeepster Club [21818]
Willys-Overland-Knight Registry [21819]
Winchester Arms Collectors Assn. [21540]
Winged Warriors/National B-Body Owners Assn.
   [21820]
Women in Numismatics [22767]
Wooton Desk Owners Soc. [22131]
World Airline Historical Soc. [21488]
World Atlatl Assn. [22611]
World Chap. of Disneyana Enthusiasts [22132]
World Internet Numismatic Soc. [22768]
World Proof Numismatic Assn. [22769]
Worldwide Camaro Club [21821]
Worldwide Television-FM DX Assn. [21510]
Young Numismatists of Am. [22770]
Young Stamp Collectors of Am. [22891]
Z Series Car Club of Am. [21824]
Zeppelin Collectors Club [22892]
Zimmerman Registry [21825]
Collectibles Associations; Antiques and [216]
Collectibles and Giftmakers Guild [★860]
Collectibles Guild; Gift and [860]
Collectibles and Platemakers Guild [★860]
Collectif d'echanges pour la Technologie Appropriee
   [★IO]
Collecting Club; Amer. Matchcover [★21963]
Coll. Attorneys; Natl. Assn. of Retail [5513]
Collections Alliance; Natural Sci. [6590]
Collective Bargaining
   Amer. Union of Pizza Delivery Drivers [24062]
   Assn. of Minor League Umpires [23104]
   Intl. Assn. of EMTs and Paramedics [24051]
   Intl. Union of Indus. and Independent Workers
      [24208]
   Natl. Basketball Players Assn. [24192]
   Natl. Center for the Stud. of Collective Bargaining
      in Higher Educ. and the Professions [24036]
   Natl. Union of Law Enforcement Associations
      [24124]
   Women's Natl. Basketball Players Assn. [23140]
Collective Black Artists - Defunct.
Collector Car Appraisers Assn. [278]
Collector Circle - Defunct.
Collector Platemakers Guild [★860]
Collectors
   1/87 Vehicle Club [22641]
   52 Plus Joker [21955]
   1937-1938 Buick Club [21552]
   1948-50 Packard Convertible Roster [21553]
   1953-54 Buick Skylark Club [21554]
   1956 Studebaker Golden Hawk Owners Register
      [21555]
   1958 Cadillac Owners Assn. [21556]
   1965-66 Full Size Chevrolet Club [21557]
   1971 GTO and Judge Convertible Registry
      [21559]
   1995 Corvette Pace Car Registry [21560]
   66,67,68 High Country Special Mustang Registry
      [21561]
   Abarth Register, U.S.A. [21562]
   Abingdon Pottery Club [21522]
   A.C. Gilbert Heritage Soc. [22992]
   Advt. Cup and Mug Collectors of Am. [21956]
   Aeronautica and Air Label Collectors Club [21422]

A star before a book entry number signifies that the name is not listed separately, but is mentioned within the entry.

Aeronca Lovers Club [21423]
Aerostar Owners Assn. [21424]
Airflow Club of Am. [21563]
Aladdin Knights of the Mystic Light [22617]
Alaska Collectors' Club [22779]
Alfa Romeo Owners Club [21565]
Alice in Wonderland Collectors Network [21957]
All-American Indian Motorcycle Club [22663]
AMC Pacer Club [21566]
AMC Rambler Club [21567]
Amer. Air Mail Soc. [22780]
Amer. Art Deco Dealers Assn. [295]
Amer. Austin/Bantam Club [21568]
Amer. Bell Assn. Intl. [21958]
Amer. Bell Assn. Intl. [IO]
Amer. Breweriana Assn. [21828]
Amer. Bugatti Club [21569]
Amer. Carnival Glass Assn. [22549]
Amer. Coaster Enthusiasts [22970]
Amer. Collectors of Infant Feeders [21959]
American Collectors of Infant Feeders [IO]
Amer. Cookie Jar Assn. [22577]
Amer. Cut Glass Assn. [22550]
Amer. Edge Collectors Assn. [22612]
Amer. First Day Cover Soc. [22781]
Amer. Fish Decoy Assn. [21960]
Amer. Hatpin Soc. [21961]
American Hatpin Society [IO]
Amer. Helvetia Philatelic Soc. [22782]
Amer. Historic Racing Motorcycle Assn. [22665]
Amer. Historical Print Collectors Soc. [21523]
American-Israel Numismatic Assn. [22723]
Amer. Lancia Club [21573]
Amer. Lands Access Assn. [22937]
Amer. Lock Collectors Assn. [21962]
Amer. Matchcover Collecting Club [21963]
Amer. MGB Assn. [21574]
Amer. MGC Register [21575]
Amer. Model Yachting Assn. [22642]
Amer. Motors Owners Assn. [21576]
Amer. Numismatic Assn. [22724]
Amer. Numismatic Soc. [22725]
Amer. Pencil Collectors Soc. [21964]
Amer. Philatelic Cong. [22783]
Amer. Philatelic Res. Lib. [22784]
Amer. Philatelic Soc. [22785]
Amer. Philatelic Soc. Writers Unit [22786]
Amer. Plate Number Single Soc. [22787]
Amer. Political Items Collectors [22903]
Amer. Quilter's Soc. [22149]
Amer. Racing Pigeon Union [22894]
Amer. Revenue Assn. [22788]
Amer. Soc. of Bookplate Collectors and Designers [21965]
American Society of Bookplate Collectors and Designers [IO]
Amer. Soc. of Check Collectors [22726]
Amer. Soc. of Military Insignia Collectors [22627]
Amer. Soc. of Polar Philatelists [22789]
Amer. Spoon Collectors [21966]
Amer. Spoon Collectors [IO]
Amer. Sta. Wagon Owners Assn. [21577]
Amer. Tax Token Soc. [22727]
Amer. Topical Assn. [22790]
Amer. Topical Assn., Americana Unit [22791]
Amer. Topical Assn., Biology Unit [22792]
Amer. Vecturist Assn. [23006]
Amer. Wooden Money Guild [22728]
Amer. Yankee Assn. [21429]
Amy's Doll Lover's Club [22391]
Ancient Coin Collectors Guild [22729]
Anheuser-Busch Collectors Club [21967]
Antique Advt. Assn. of Am. [21420]
Antique and Art Glass Salt Shaker Collectors Soc. [21968]
Antique Auto Racing Assn. [21578]
Antique Auto. Club of Am. [21579]
Antique Barbed Wire Soc. [21969]
Antique Barbed Wire Society [IO]
Antique Caterpillar Machinery Owners Club [22619]
Antique and Classic Boat Soc. [21868]
Antique Collectors' Club [IO]
Antique Comb Collectors Club International [IO]
Antique Comb Collectors Club Intl. [21970]

Antique Doorknob Collectors of Am. [21971]
Antique Fan Collectors Assn. [21533]
Antique Motorcycle Club of Am. [22667]
Antique Phonograph Collectors Club [22710]
Antique Poison Bottle Collectors Assn. [21972]
Antique Reloading Tool Collector's Assn. [22424]
Antique Small Engine Collectors Club [22409]
Antique Snowmobile Club of Am. [22943]
Antique Stove Assn. [21524]
Antique Stove Info. CH [21525]
Antique Studebaker Club [21580]
Antique Telephone Collectors Assn. [22985]
Antique Telescope Soc. [21526]
Antique Toy Collectors of Am. [22993]
Antique Truck Club of Am. [23022]
Antique Wireless Assn. [22923]
Antiques and Collectibles Dealer Assn. [863]
Antiques and Collectibles Natl. Assn. [864]
Antiques Coun. [217]
Arctic Cat Club of Am. [22944]
Ariel Motorcycle Club North Am. [22668]
Armed Forces Stamp Exchange Club [22793]
Armor and Arms Club [21536]
Arms and Armour Soc. [IO]
Arthur Rackham Soc. [9427]
Assoc. Collectors of El Salvador [22794]
Assn. of Amer. Military Uniform Collectors [22628]
Assn. of Coffee Mill Enthusiasts [21973]
Assn. of Collecting Clubs [21974]
Assn. of Football Badge Collectors [IO]
Assn. of Game and Puzzle Collectors [22460]
Assn. of Israel's Decorative Arts [9556]
Assn. of North Amer. Radio Clubs [21498]
Assn. of Ohio Longrifle Collectors [22425]
Astronomy Stud. Unit [22795]
Austin Bantam Soc. [21583]
Austin-Healey Sports and Touring Club [21586]
Australian Collectors of Mech. Musical Instruments [IO]
Authentic Artifact Collectors Assn. [21543]
Auto. License Plate Collectors Assn. [21587]
Auto. Objects d'Art Club [21588]
Ball Collectors Club [22551]
Bead Soc. of Los Angeles [21975]
Bellanca-Champion Club [21431]
Berkeley Exchange [21590]
Betty Boop Intl. Collectible Club [21976]
Beyond the Pond.International Frog Collectors Club [21977]
Bicycle Stamps Club [22796]
Big Little Book Collector's Club [21978]
Bird Airplane Club [21432]
Blue/White Pottery Club [21527]
Bluewater Bus. Card Club [IO]
BMW Car Club of Am. [21591]
BMW Motorcycle Owners of Am. [22670]
BMW Riders Assn. Intl. [22671]
BMW Vintage Car Club of Am. [21593]
Bookplate Soc. [IO]
Boss 302 Registry [21595]
Boss 429 Owners Dir. [21596]
Brabham Register [21597]
Brazil Philatelic Assn. [22797]
Brewery Collectibles Club of Am. [21979]
Brewster Kaleidoscope Soc. [21980]
Bricklin Intl. Owners Club [21598]
British Beermat Collectors Soc. [IO]
Browning Collectors Assn. [22426]
Buick Club of Am. [21599]
Buick GS Club of Am. [21600]
Bullseye Cancel Collectors' Club [22798]
Butter Pat Patter Assn. [21981]
Buttonhook Soc. [IO]
Cabbage Patch Kids Collectors Club [21982]
Cadillac Drivers Club [21601]
Cadillac-LaSalle Club [21602]
Caithness Paperweight Collectors Soc. [IO]
Call and Whistle Collectors Assn. [21983]
Callmakers and Collectors Assn. of Am. [21984]
Canadian Corkscrew Collectors Club [21985]
Canadian Corkscrew Collectors Club [IO]
Candy Container Collectors of Am. [21986]
Capri Club North Am. [21604]
Cardinal Club [21433]
Carriage Assn. of Am. [21987]

CartoPhilatelic Soc. [22799]
CAS Collectors [21926]
Case Collectors Club [22613]
Casey Jones Railroad Unit - ATA [22800]
Cash Registers Collectors Club of Am. [21988]
Casino Chip and Gaming Token Collectors Club [21989]
Cast Iron Seat Collectors Assn. [22607]
Cat Collectors [21990]
Cats on Stamps Stud. Unit [22801]
Cavanagh's Coca-Cola Collectors' Soc. [21991]
Center for Wooden Boats [21869]
Cessna Owner Org. [21435]
Cessna Pilots Assn. [21436]
Challenge Coin Assn. [22731]
Chatty Cathy Collectors Club [22393]
Chemistry and Physics on Stamps Stud. Unit [22802]
Chess Collectors Intl. [21944]
Chevrolet Nomad Assn. [21607]
Chevy and Geo Club [21608]
Chicago Map Soc. [21528]
Chicago Playing Card Collectors [21992]
China Stamp Soc. [22803]
Chris Craft Antique Boat Club [21870]
Christian Motorcyclists Assn. [22674]
Christmas Philatelic Club [22804]
Christmas Seal and Charity Stamp Soc. [21993]
Christmas Seal and Charity Stamp Soc. [IO]
Christopher Columbus Philatelic Soc. [22805]
Chrysler 300 Club Intl. [21611]
Chrysler Town and Country Owners Registry [21612]
Cigarette Pack Collectors Assn. [21994]
Citizens' Stamp Advisory Comm. [22806]
Citroen Quarterly Car Club [21613]
Citrus Label Soc. [21995]
Civil Censorship Study Group [22807]
Civil War Token Soc. [22732]
Classic Chevy Intl. [21615]
Classic Jaguar Assn. [21616]
Classic Thunderbird Club Intl. [21617]
Classic Yacht Assn. [21871]
Cloisonne Collectors Club [21996]
Cobra Owners Club of Am. [21619]
Coin Operated Collectors Assn. [21997]
Coin Operated Collectors Assn. [IO]
Collectors Club [22808]
Collectors Record Club [22712]
Collectors of Religion on Stamps [22809]
Collins Collectors Assn. [21499]
Colonial Coin Collectors Club [22733]
Colonial Coverlet Guild of Am. [21998]
Combined Organizations of Numismatic Error Collectors of Am. [22734]
Commemorative Collectors Soc. [IO]
Company of Military Historians [22629]
Conchologists of Am. [21999]
Concorde Collectors Club [22810]
Confederate Stamp Alliance [22811]
Contemporary Historical Vehicle Assn. [21620]
Continental Luscombe Assn. [21439]
Cookie Cutter Collectors Club [22000]
Corben Club [21440]
Corn Items Collectors Assn. [22001]
Corrado Club of Am. [21621]
Corvair Soc. of Am. [21622]
Corvette Club of Am. [21623]
Cover Collectors Circuit Club [22812]
Cow Observers Worldwide [22002]
Cow Observers Worldwide [IO]
Cracker Jack Collectors Assn. [22003]
Cribbage Bd. Collectors Soc. [22004]
Croatian Philatelic Soc. [22813]
Crosley Auto. Club [21624]
Crown Victoria Assn. [21625]
Crowncap Collectors Soc. Intl. [22005]
Cuban Numismatic Assn. [22735]
Cupid Collectors Club [22006]
Currier and Ives Dinnerware Collectors [22007]
Cushman Club of Am. [22676]
Cyclone Montego Torino Registry [21626]
Czech Collector's Assn. [22008]
Czech Collector's Assn. [IO]
Dedham Pottery Collectors Soc. [22009]

Reference to "IO" in place of a book number signifies that the association may be found in the 45th edition of International Organizations.

Dedicated Wooden Money Collectors [22736]
Deltiologists of Am. [22905]
Denver Strikers Matchcover Club [22625]
DeSoto Club of Am. [21630]
Deutsches Motorrad Register [22677]
Diecast Exchange Club [22010]
Disabled Collectors' Correspondence Club
    [22814]
Disabled Veterans Keychain Tag and Chauffeur's
    Badge Collectors Newsl. [22011]
Divco Club of Am. [22012]
DKW Club of Am. [21631]
Dodge Bros. Club [21632]
Dodge Pilothouse Era Truck Club of Am. [23024]
Dogs on Stamps Stud. Unit [22815]
Doll Artisan Guild [22394]
Doll Costumer's Guild [22395]
Dreamsicles Club [22013]
Early Amer. Coppers [22737]
Early Amer. Pattern Glass Soc. [22014]
Early Ford V-8 Club of Am. [21633]
Early Typewriter Collectors Assn. [22015]
Earth's Physical Features Stud. Unit [22816]
Eastern Packard Club [21635]
Edsel Club [21636]
Egg Cup Collectors' Corner [22016]
Eire Philatelic Assn. [22817]
EKJ (Emmett Kelly Jr.) Collectors' Soc. [22017]
Elgin Motorcar Owners Registry [21638]
The Elongated Collectors [22738]
Emergency Vehicle Owners and Operators Assn.
    [21639]
Emmett's Elite [22018]
Ephemera Soc. [IO]
Ephemera Soc. of Am. [22411]
Ercoupe Owners Club [21444]
Errors, Freaks and Oddities Collector's Club
    [22818]
Erskine Registry [21640]
Etch-A-Sketch Club [22994]
Fairchild Club [21446]
Fairlane Club of Am. [21641]
Fairy Lamp Club [22019]
Family Circle of PenDelfin [22020]
Fan Assn. of North Am. [22021]
Fan Assn. of North Am. [IO]
Fed. of Historical Bottle Collectors [21888]
Fenton Art Glass Collectors of Am. [22552]
Ferrari Owners Club [21644]
Fiesta Collectors Club [22022]
Figural Bottle Opener Collectors Club [22023]
Figural Cast Iron Collector's Club [22417]
Figures Collectors Club [22024]
Fine Arts Philatelists [22819]
Florence Ceramics Collectors Soc. [22025]
Flow Blue Intl. Collectors Club [22026]
Flow Blue International Collectors Club [IO]
Flying Apache Assn. [21448]
Ford Galaxie Club of Am. [21647]
Fostoria Glass Collectors [22553]
Fostoria Glass Soc. of Am. [22554]
Found. for the Stud. of the Arts and Crafts Move-
    ment at Roycroft [21530]
France and Colonies Philatelic Soc. [22820]
Frankoma Family Collectors Assn. [22027]
Friends of Old-Time Radio [22924]
Funk Aircraft Owners Assn. [21449]
Gar Wood Soc. [21873]
Gartlan USA's Collectors' League [22028]
Gems, Minerals and Jewelry Stud. Unit [22821]
German Colonies Collectors Gp. [22822]
German Gun Collectors' Assn. [22029]
German Gun Collectors' Association [IO]
Germany Philatelic Soc. [22823]
GI Joe Collectors' Club [22996]
Glass Art Soc. [22555]
Global Lottery Collectors Soc. [22030]
Glock Collectors Assn. [22427]
Golden Glow of Christmas Past [22975]
Golf Collectors Soc. [22031]
Golf Collectors Soc. [IO]
Graham Bros. Truck and Bus Club [21894]
Graham Owners Club Intl. [21650]
Graphics Philately Assn. [22824]
Gravely Tractor Club of Am. [23002]

Great Britain Collectors Club [22032]
Great Britain Collectors Club [IO]
Gull Wing Gp. Intl. [21652]
Haiti Philatelic Soc. [22825]
Hammered Aluminum Collectors Assn. [22033]
Harbour Lights Collectors Soc. [22034]
Harley Hummer Club [22679]
Harley Owners Gp. [22680]
Haynes-Apperson Owners Club [21653]
Heart of America Carnival Glass Assn. [22557]
Heartland Vintage Thunderbird Club of Am.
    [21654]
Heather's Teddy Bear Org. [22035]
Heisey Collectors of America/National Heisey
    Glass Museum [22558]
Hellenic Philatelic Soc. of Am. [22826]
Heritage Rose Found. [22516]
H.H. Franklin Club [21656]
High Standard Collectors' Assn. [22428]
Historic Motor Sports Assn. [21657]
Homer Laughlin China Collectors Assn. [22036]
Homer Laughlin China Collectors Association [IO]
Honda Sport Touring Assn. [22681]
Horn and Whistle Enthusiasts Gp. [22037]
Horseless Carriage Club of Am. [21658]
Howdy Doody Memorabilia Collectors Club
    [22038]
Hudson-Essex-Terraplane Club [21659]
Hudson Essex Terraplane Historical Soc. [21660]
Hull Pottery Assn. [22039]
Hummel Collectors Club [22040]
Humor Stamp Club [22827]
Hurst/Olds Club of Am. [21661]
Ice Screamers [22041]
India Stud. Circle for Philately [22828]
Indian Motor-Cycle Club of America [22682]
Inter-Governmental Philatelic Corp. [22829]
InterCol London [IO]
Interlac [22042]
Intl. 190SL Gp. [21663]
Intl. Amphicar Owners Club [21664]
Intl. Assn. of Jazz Record Collectors [22714]
Intl. Assn. of Jim Beam Bottle and Specialties
    Clubs [21889]
Intl. Assn. of R.S. Prussia Collectors [22043]
International Association of R.S. Prussia Collec-
    tors [IO]
Intl. Assn. of Silver Art Collectors [IO]
Intl. Assn. of Silver Art Collectors [22044]
Intl. Autograph Collectors Club and Dealers Alli-
    ance [22045]
Intl. B and B Fly-Inn Club [21451]
Intl. Bank Note Soc. [22739]
Intl. Betta Cong. [22441]
Intl. Bird Dog Assn. [21452]
Intl. Bond and Share Soc. [22046]
Intl. Bond and Share Soc. [IO]
Intl. Bossons Collectors Soc. [22047]
Intl. Brick Collectors' Assn. [22048]
Intl. Bus Collectors Club [21895]
Intl. Camaro Club [21665]
Intl. Carnival Glass Assn. [22559]
Intl. Chinese Snuff Bottle Soc. [21890]
Intl. Coleman Collectors Club [22049]
Intl. Collector's Club of Hatpins and Hatpin Hold-
    ers [22050]
Intl. Collectors Guild [22051]
Intl. Collectors Guild [IO]
Intl. Correspondence of Corkscrew Addicts [IO]
Intl. Correspondence of Corkscrew Addicts
    [22052]
Intl. Doll Makers Assn. [22397]
Intl. Edsel Club [21666]
Intl. Fed. of Amer. Homing Pigeon Fanciers
    [22895]
Intl. Fed. of Postcard Dealers [22906]
Intl. Fight'n Rooster Cutlery Club [22614]
Intl. Fire Buff Associates [22421]
Intl. Guild of Lamp Researchers [22618]
Intl. Handicappers' Net [21502]
Intl. King Midget Car Club [21667]
Intl. Map Collectors' Soc. [IO]
Intl. Match Safe Assn. [IO]
Intl. Match Safe Assn. [22053]
Intl. Mercury Owners Assn. [21668]

Intl. Meteorite Collectors Assn. [22981]
Intl. Mustang Bullitt Owners Club [21669]
Intl. Nippon Collectors Club [21929]
Intl. Norton Owners' Assn. [22684]
Intl. Old Lacers, Inc. [22161]
Intl. Paperweight Soc. [22776]
Intl. Perfume Bottle Assn. [22054]
Intl. Perfume Bottle Assn. [IO]
Intl. Radio Club of Am. [21503]
Intl. Railroad and Transportation Postcard Collec-
    tors Club [22055]
Intl. Rose O'Neill Club Found. [22399]
Intl. Sand Collectors Soc. [22056]
Intl. Sand Collectors Soc. [IO]
Intl. Scouting Collectors Assn. [IO]
Intl. Scouting Collectors Assn. [22057]
Intl. Soc. of Animal License Collectors [22058]
Intl. Soc. of Animal License Collectors [IO]
Intl. Soc. of Antique Scale Collectors [IO]
Intl. Soc. of Antique Scale Collectors [22059]
Intl. Soc. of Bible Collectors [19523]
Intl. Soc. for Japanese Philately [22830]
Intl. Soc. for Vehicle Preservation [21670]
Intl. Soc. of Worldwide Stamp Collectors [22831]
Intl. Stamp and Coin Collectors Soc. [22832]
Intl. Swizzle Stick Collectors Assn. [22060]
Intl. Swizzle Stick Collectors Assn. [IO]
Intl. Thunderbird Club [21671]
Intl. Vintage Poster Dealers Assn. [106]
Intl. Watch Collectors Soc. [22988]
Intl. Watch Fob Assn. [22989]
Intl. Willow Collectors [22061]
Intl. Willow Collectors [IO]
Interstate Club [21458]
Iso and Bizzarrini Owners Club [21672]
Italian Car Registry [21673]
Jack Knight Air Mail Soc. [22834]
Jaguar Clubs of North Am. [21674]
Japanese Sword Soc. of the U.S. [21537]
Jensen Healey Preservation Soc. [21675]
Jewett Owners Club [21676]
John F. Kennedy First Day Cover Stud. Unit
    [22835]
Jordan Register [21677]
Junior Philatelists of Am. [22837]
Just for Openers [22062]
Kaiser-Darrin Owners Roster [21679]
Kaiser-Frazer Owners Club Intl. [21680]
Karmann Ghia Club of North Am. [21681]
Kate Greenaway Soc. [22063]
Kissel Kar Klub [21682]
Kit Collectors Intl. [22649]
Knife Collectors Club [22615]
Korea Postcard Collectors Gp. [22907]
Korea Stamp Soc. [22838]
Krystonia Collector's Club [22064]
Kustom Kemps of Am. [21683]
Lamborghini Club Am. [21684]
Late Great Chevrolet Assn. [21685]
Latin Amer. Paper Money Soc. [22741]
Lawton Collector's Guild [22400]
L.C. Smith Collectors Assn. [22429]
Les Amis de Panhard and Deutsch Bonnet
    [21686]
Liberty Seated Collectors Club [22742]
Lincoln and Continental Owners Club [21687]
Lincoln Owners' Club [21688]
Lionel Railroader Club [22634]
Lithuanian Numismatic Assn. [22743]
Little Elegance Memories of Yesterday [22065]
Lladro Soc. [21930]
London Vintage Taxi Assn. - Amer. Sect. [21690]
Lone Ranger Fan Club [25032]
Longwave Club of Am. [21505]
Lotus, Ltd. [21691]
Love Token Soc. [22744]
Luscombe Endowment [21461]
M. T. Bottle Collectors Assn. [22066]
Machine Cancel Soc. [22839]
Magic Collectors' Assn. [22621]
Magic Lantern Soc. of the U.S. and Canada
    [21531]
Mai Wah Soc. [9622]
Mailer's Postmark Permit Club [22840]
Majolica Intl. Soc. [21931]

A star before a book entry number signifies that the name is not listed separately, but is mentioned within the entry.

M&M's Collectors Club **[22067]**
Manuscript Soc. **[22068]**
Marble Collectors' Soc. of Am. **[22624]**
Maritime Postmark Soc. **[22841]**
Marklin Digital Special Interest Gp. **[22635]**
Marlin Auto Club **[21693]**
Marmon Club **[21694]**
Maserati Info. Exchange **[21696]**
Matchbox U.S.A. **[22069]**
Mathematical Stud. Unit **[22842]**
Maverick/Comet Club Intl. **[21697]**
Mazda Club **[21698]**
McCoy Pottery Collectors' Soc. **[21932]**
McDonald's Collectors Club **[22070]**
Mech. Bank Collectors of Am. **[21826]**
Medal Collectors of Am. **[22745]**
Medical Subjects Unit **[22843]**
Mercedes-Benz Club of Am. **[21699]**
Mercedes-Benz M-100 Owner's Gp. **[21700]**
Meter Stamp Soc. **[22844]**
Metropolitan Air Post Soc. **[22845]**
Metropolitan Owners Club of North Am. **[21701]**
Mexico Elmhurst Philatelic Soc. Intl. **[22846]**
Microcar and Minicar Club **[21703]**
Mid-Century Mercury Car Club **[21704]**
Midstates Jeepster Assn. **[21705]**
Midwest Decoy Collectors Assn. **[22071]**
Midwest Sunbeam Registry **[21706]**
Milestone Car Soc. **[21707]**
Military Postal History Soc. **[22847]**
Military Vehicle Preservation Assn. **[22630]**
Mini Car Club, U.S.A. **[21708]**
Miniature Arms Collectors/Makers Soc. **[21538]**
Miniature Book Soc. **[9752]**
Miniature Piano Enthusiast Club **[22072]**
Miniature Piano Enthusiast Club **[IO]**
Mobile Post Off. Soc. **[22848]**
Model A Ford Cabriolet Club **[21709]**
Model A Ford Club of Am. **[21710]**
Model A Ford Found. **[21711]**
Model "A" Restorers Club **[21712]**
Model "T" Ford Club of Am. **[21713]**
Model "T" Ford Club Intl. **[21714]**
Monocoupe Club **[21462]**
Morgan Car Club **[21717]**
Morgan Plus Four Club **[21718]**
Morgan Three-Wheeler Club - USA Gp. **[21719]**
Morris Minor Registry **[21720]**
Motor Bus Soc. **[21896]**
Muntz Jet Registry **[21721]**
Musical Box Soc. Intl. **[22717]**
Napoleonic Age Philatelists **[22849]**
Nash Car Club of Am. **[21725]**
Natl. 210 Owners Assn. **[21463]**
Natl. Aeronca Assn. **[21464]**
Natl. Antique Doll Dealers Assn. **[22402]**
Natl. Antique Oldsmobile Club **[21726]**
Natl. Assn. of Avon Collectors **[22073]**
Natl. Assn. of Breweriana Advt. **[22074]**
Natl. Assn. of Collectors **[22075]**
Natl. Assn. of Milk Bottle Collectors **[22076]**
Natl. Assn. of Miniature Enthusiasts **[22077]**
Natl. Assn. of Paper and Advt. Collectors **[22412]**
Natl. Assn. of Rocketry **[22650]**
Natl. Assn. of Timetable Collectors **[23008]**
Natl. Assn. of Watch and Clock Collectors **[22990]**
Natl. Automatic Pistol Collectors Assn. **[21539]**
Natl. Autumn Leaf Collectors Club **[22078]**
Natl. Basketry Org. **[22167]**
Natl. Button Soc. **[22079]**
Natl. Cambridge Collectors **[22561]**
Natl. Cap and Patch Assn. **[22080]**
Natl. Carousel Assn. **[21897]**
Natl. Collectors Assn. of Die Doubling **[22746]**
Natl. Corvette Owners Assn. **[21728]**
Natl. Corvette Restorers Soc. **[21729]**
Natl. Coun. of Corvette Clubs **[21730]**
Natl. Depression Glass Assn. **[22562]**
Natl. DeSoto Club **[21731]**
Natl. Duck Stamp Collectors Soc. **[22850]**
Natl. Duncan Glass Soc. **[22563]**
Natl. Elephant Collectors Soc. **[22081]**
Natl. Fenton Glass Soc. **[22564]**
Natl. Firearms Act Trade and Collectors Assn.
  [1480]

Natl. Firebird and T/A Club **[21732]**
Natl. Fishing Lure Collectors Club **[22082]**
Natl. Graniteware Soc. **[22083]**
Natl. Healthcare Collectors Assn. **[1869]**
Natl. Imperial Glass Collectors Soc. **[22565]**
Natl. Inst. of Amer. Doll Artists **[22403]**
Natl. Knife Collectors Assn. **[22616]**
Natl. Marble Club of America **[22084]**
Natl. Milk Glass Collectors Soc. **[22566]**
Natl. Model Railroad Assn. **[22636]**
Natl. Mossberg Collectors Assn. **[22430]**
Natl. Old Timers Auto Racing Club **[21737]**
Natl. Pop Can Collectors **[22085]**
Natl. Reamer Collectors Assn. **[22609]**
Natl. Shaving Mug Collectors Assn. **[22086]**
Natl. Shelley China Club **[22087]**
Natl. Soc. of Arkansas Pottery Collectors **[22088]**
Natl. Stinson Club **[21467]**
Natl. St. Rod Assn. **[21738]**
Natl. Token Collectors Assn. **[21954]**
Natl. Toothpick Holder Collectors' Soc. **[22089]**
Natl. Valentine Collectors' Assn. **[22090]**
Natl. Woodie Club **[21739]**
Nautical Res. Guild **[21880]**
Naval Historical Collectors and Res. Assn. **[IO]**
Nepal and Tibet Philatelic Stud. Circle **[22852]**
New England M.G. "T" Register Limited **[21740]**
New Mexico Barbed Wire Collectors Assn.
  [22091]
Newspaper Collectors Soc. of Am. **[22092]**
Nineteen Thirty-Two Buick Registry **[21741]**
Nissan Infiniti Car Owners Club **[21742]**
North Amer. Auto Union Register **[21743]**
North Amer. Collectors **[22747]**
North Amer. Mini Moke Registry **[21745]**
North Amer. Model Boat Assn. **[22654]**
North Amer. Radio Archives **[22926]**
North Amer. Shortwave Assn. **[21507]**
North Amer. Soc. of Pipe Collectors **[22093]**
North Amer. Soc. of Pipe Collectors **[IO]**
North Amer. Torquay Soc. **[IO]**
North Amer. Torquay Soc. **[22094]**
North Amer. Trap Collector Assn. **[22095]**
Northeastern Spoon Collectors Guild **[22096]**
Novelty Salt and Pepper Shakers Club **[22097]**
NSU Enthusiasts U.S.A. **[21746]**
NSX Club of Am. **[21747]**
Numismatic Literary Guild **[22749]**
Numismatics Intl. **[22750]**
Oakland-Pontiac Enthusiast Org. **[21748]**
Occupied Japan Club **[22098]**
The Old Appliance Club **[21535]**
Old Reel Collectors Assn. **[22099]**
Old Reel Collectors Association **[IO]**
Old Sleepy Eye Collectors' Club of Am. **[21934]**
Old-time Radio-Show Collectors Assn. **[IO]**
Oldsmobile Club of Am. **[21749]**
On the Lighter Side, Intl. Lighter Collectors
  [22100]
On the Lighter Side, International Lighter Collec-
  tors **[IO]**
Opel Assn. of North Am. **[21751]**
Opel Motorsports Club **[21752]**
Optometric Historical Soc. **[15728]**
Orders and Medals Soc. of Am. **[22631]**
Org. of Bricklin Owners **[21753]**
Original Doll Artists Coun. of Am. **[22404]**
Original Hobo Nickel Soc. **[22752]**
Oughtred Soc. **[22101]**
Packard Auto. Classics **[21755]**
Packard V-8 Roster, '55-'56 **[21757]**
Packards Intl. Motor Car Club **[21758]**
Pantera Intl. **[21759]**
Paperweight Collectors' Assn. **[22102]**
Partisan Prohibition Historical Soc. **[22103]**
Peanut Pals **[22104]**
Pen Collectors of Am. **[22105]**
Pepsi-Cola Collectors Club **[22106]**
Perfins Club **[22854]**
Pewter Collectors Club of Am. **[22107]**
Pewter Soc. **[IO]**
Philatelic Found. **[22855]**
Philatelic Friends Exchange Circuit **[22856]**
Phoenix Bird Collectors of Am. **[21935]**
Pickard Collectors Club **[22108]**

Pierce-Arrow Soc. **[21761]**
Plymouth Barracuda/Cuda Owners Club **[21763]**
Plymouth Owners Club **[21764]**
Polonus Philatelic Soc. **[22857]**
Pontiac-Oakland Club Intl. **[21766]**
Porsche Club of Am. **[21767]**
Porterfield Airplane Club **[21472]**
Post Card Collectors Club **[22908]**
Post Mark Collectors Club **[22858]**
Postal Commemorative Soc. **[22859]**
Postal History Soc. **[22860]**
Postcard History Soc. **[22909]**
Potomac Antique Tools and Indus. Assn. **[22610]**
Precancel Stamp Soc. **[22861]**
Professional Autograph Dealers Assn. **[865]**
Professional Autograph Dealers Association **[IO]**
Professional Car Soc. **[21768]**
Professional Currency Dealers Assn. **[22753]**
Professional Numismatists Guild **[22754]**
Professional Scripophily Trade Assn. **[761]**
Promotional Glass Collectors Assn. **[22109]**
Quarter Century Wireless Assn. **[21509]**
The Questers **[21532]**
Quimper Club Intl. **[21546]**
Radio Club of Am. **[22928]**
Radio Collectors of Am. **[22929]**
Rat Fan Club **[22706]**
Rearwin Club **[21474]**
Red Wing Collectors Soc. **[22110]**
Renault Owners Club of North Am. **[21769]**
REO Club of Am. **[21770]**
Richardson Boat Owners Assn. **[21884]**
Rickenbacker Automobile Club of America **[21771]**
Rickman Owners Club Intl. **[22689]**
Riviera Owners Assn. **[21772]**
Road Map Collectors Assn. **[22111]**
Road Map Collectors Association **[IO]**
Road Race Lincoln Register **[21773]**
Rolls-Royce Owners' Club **[21774]**
Rometsch Registry **[21775]**
Rose Bowl Collectors **[22112]**
Rossica Soc. of Russian Philately **[22862]**
Rotary on Stamps Fellowship **[22863]**
Rudge Enthusiasts Club **[22691]**
Russian Zone Handoverprint Stud. and Res. Gp.
  [22864]
RVing Women **[22962]**
Ryukyu Philatelic Specialist Soc. **[22865]**
Saab Club of North Am. **[21778]**
Sabra Automobile Connection **[21779]**
Safety Razor Collectors Guild **[22113]**
St. Helena, Ascension, and Tristan da Cunha
  Philatelic Soc. **[22866]**
Saleen Club of Am. **[21780]**
Samuel Gompers Stamp Club **[22867]**
Sandicast Collectors Guild **[21544]**
Saxon Owners Registry **[21781]**
Scandinavian Collectors Club **[22868]**
Sci. Instrument Soc. **[IO]**
Scouts on Stamps Soc. Intl. **[22869]**
Self Winding Clock Assn. **[22991]**
Shelby Amer. Auto. Club **[21782]**
Ships-in-Bottles Assn. of Am. **[22658]**
Ships on Stamps Unit **[22870]**
Short Wing Piper Club **[21475]**
Soc. of Amer. Magicians **[22623]**
Soc. of Australasian Specialists/Oceania **[22871]**
Soc. of Automotive Historians **[21785]**
Soc. for Hungarian Philately **[22873]**
Soc. of Inkwell Collectors **[22114]**
Society of Inkwell Collectors **[IO]**
Soc. of Israel Philatelists **[22874]**
Soc. of Lincoln Cent Collectors **[22756]**
Soc. of Paper Money Collectors **[22757]**
Soc. for the Preservation and Appreciation of
  Antique Motor Fire Apparatus in Am. **[22423]**
Soc. of Private and Pioneer Numismatists **[22758]**
Soc. of Ration Token Collectors **[22759]**
Soc. for Thai Philately **[22875]**
Soc. of Tobacco Jar Collectors **[21936]**
Soc. for U.S. Commemorative Coins **[22760]**
Soc. of U.S. Pattern Collectors **[22761]**
Southeastern Historical Keyboard Soc. **[22720]**
Souvenir Building Collectors Soc. **[22115]**
Space Topic Stud. Unit **[22876]**

Reference to "IO" in place of a book number signifies that the association may be found in the 45th edition of International Organizations.

Spark Plug Collectors of Am. [22116]
Sports Car Club of Am. [21787]
Sports Philatelists Intl. [22877]
Squire SS-100 Registry [21788]
Stampe Club Intl. [21479]
Stamps on Stamps Collectors Club [22878]
Stamps for the Wounded [22879]
Stangl Fulper Collectors Club [22117]
State Revenue Soc. [22880]
Statue of Liberty Club [22118]
Steam Auto. Club of Am. [21789]
Steamship Historical Soc. of Am. [22980]
Stearman Restorers Assn. [21480]
Steiff Club [22119]
Stein Collectors Intl. [22120]
Stein Collectors Intl. [IO]
Still Bank Collectors Club of Am. [21827]
Strawberry Shortcake Chat Gp. [22406]
Studebaker Driver's Club [21790]
Stutz Club [21791]
Subaru 360 Drivers' Club [21792]
Sunbeam Rapier Registry [21793]
Super Coupe Club of Am. [21794]
Tea Leaf Club Intl. [21937]
Teen Assn. of Model Railroaders [22637]
Telephone Collectors Intl. [22986]
Texas Date Nail Collectors Assn. [22121]
Thimble Collectors Intl. [22122]
Thimble Collectors Intl. [IO]
Thimble Guild [22123]
Thomas Kinkade Collectors' Soc. [21545]
Thompson Collectors Assn. [22431]
Thunderbird and Cougar Club of Am. [21795]
Tiffin Glass Collectors Club [22567]
Token and Medal Soc. [22763]
Toned Coin Collectors Soc. [22764]
Topolino Register of North Am. [21797]
Toy Car Collectors Assn. [22997]
Toy Stitchers Intl., Inc. [22998]
Toy Stores Steiff Collectors Club [22999]
Toy Train Collectors Soc. [22638]
Toy Train Operating Soc. [22639]
Toyota Owner's and Restorer's Club [21798]
Trade Card Collectors Assn. [22124]
Traditional Small Craft Assn. [21885]
Train Collectors Assn. [22640]
Transport Ticket Soc. [IO]
Travel Air Club [21482]
Treasures for Little Children [23000]
Triumph Register of Am. [21800]
Tucker Auto. Club of Am. [21801]
TVR Car Club North Am. [21802]
Twin Bonanza Assn. [21483]
Two-Cylinder Club [23005]
UHL Collectors Soc. [22125]
Ukrainian Philatelic and Numismatic Soc. [22883]
United Coun. of Corvette Clubs [21803]
United Fed. of Doll Clubs [22407]
United Flying Octogenarians [21485]
United Ford Owners [21804]
United Four-Wheel Drive Associations [21805]
United Nations Philatelists, Inc. [22884]
United Postal Stationery Soc. [22885]
United Sidecar Assn. [22693]
U.S. Cancellation Club [22886]
U.S. Classic Racing Assn. [22694]
U.S. Mexican Numismatic Assn. [22765]
U.S. Stamp Soc. [22888]
U.S. Ultralight Assn. [21486]
United St. Machine Assn. [21807]
Universal Autograph Collectors Club [22126]
Universal Ship Cancellation Soc. [22889]
Unrecognised States Numismatic Soc. [22766]
Vaseline Glass Collectors, Inc. [22127]
Velocette Owners Club of North Am. [22695]
Veteran Motor Car Club of Am. [21808]
Vincent Owners Club - Keystone Sect. [22697]
Vintage Arms Assn. [IO]
Vintage BMW Motorcycle Owners [22698]
Vintage Chevrolet Club of Am. [21809]
Vintage Fashion and Costume Jewelry Club [22128]
Vintage Fashion/Costume Jewelry Club [IO]
Vintage Motor Bike Club [22699]
Vintage Radio and Phonograph Soc. [22931]

Vintage Thunderbird Club Intl. [21812]
Vintage Triumph Register [21813]
Vintage Volkswagen Club of Am. [21814]
Volkswagen Club of Am. [21815]
Volvo Club of Am. [21816]
Walt Disney Collectors Soc. [22129]
Weatherby Collectors Assn. [22432]
Wedgwood Intl. Seminar [21939]
Western Cover Soc. [22890]
Whisky Pitcher Collectors Assn. of Am. [22130]
Whisky Pitcher Collectors Association of America [IO]
White Ironstone China Assn. [21940]
Wills Sainte Claire Museum [21817]
Willys Overland Jeepster Club [21818]
Willys-Overland-Knight Registry [21819]
Winchester Arms Collectors Assn. [21540]
Winged Warriors/National B-Body Owners Assn. [21820]
Women in Numismatics [22767]
Wooton Desk Owners Soc. [22131]
World Airline Historical Soc. [21488]
World Atlatl Assn. [22611]
World Chap. of Disneyana Enthusiasts [22132]
World Chap. of Disneyana Enthusiasts [IO]
World Internet Numismatic Soc. [22768]
World Proof Numismatic Assn. [22769]
World's Fair Collectors Soc. [IO]
Worldwide Camaro Club [21821]
Worldwide Television-FM DX Assn. [21510]
Writing Equip. Soc. [IO]
Young Numismatists of Am. [22770]
Young Stamp Collectors of Am. [22891]
Z Series Car Club of Am. [21824]
Zeiss Historical Soc. of Am. [22133]
Zeiss Historical Society of America [IO]
Zeppelin Collectors Club [22892]
Zimmerman Registry [21825]
Collectors of Am; Antique Toy [22993]
Collectors of Am; Combined Organizations of Numismatic Error [22734]
Collectors of Am; Fenton Art Glass [22552]
Collectors of Am; Mech. Bank [21826]
Collectors of America/National Heisey Glass Museum; Heisey [22558]
Collectors of Am; Radio [22929]
Collectors of Am; Souvenir Spoon [★21966]
Collectors of Amer. Art - Address unknown since 1995.
Collectors; Amer. Political Items [22903]
Collectors; Amer. Soc. of Camera [10844]
Collectors; Amer. Soc. of Check [22726]
Collectors; Amer. Soc. of Military Insignia [22627]
Collectors Assn; Amer. [★1144]
Collectors Assn; Amer. Commercial [★1147]
Collectors Assn; Amer. Edge [22612]
Collectors Assn; Amer. Fan [★21533]
Collectors Assn; Amer. Game [★22460]
Collectors; Assn. of Amer. Military Uniform [22628]
Collectors Assn; Antique Fan [21533]
Collectors Assn; Antique Telephone [22985]
Collectors Assn; Auto. License Plate [21587]
Collectors Assn; Browning [22426]
Collectors Assn; Cast Iron Seat [22607]
Collectors; Assn. of Game and Puzzle [22460]
Collectors Assn; Glock [22427]
Collectors Assn. Incorporated; Railroadiana [22936]
Collectors Assn; Intl. Perfume and Scent Bottle [★22054]
Collectors' Assn; Magic [22621]
Collectors Assn; Natl. Automatic Pistol [21539]
Collectors Assn; Natl. Knife [22616]
Collectors Assn; Natl. Mossberg [22430]
Collectors Assn; Natl. Reamer [22609]
Collectors; Assn. of Ohio Longrifle [22425]
Collectors Assn; Repossessions Division of Amer. [★1145]
Collectors Assn; Roy Rogers - Dale Evans [24971]
Collectors Assn; Winchester Arms [21540]
Collectors Circuit Club; Cover [22812]
Collectors Club [22808], 22 E 35th St., New York, NY 10016-3806, (212)683-0559
Collectors' Club; Aeronautica and Air Label [21422]
Collectors' Club; Alaska [22779]
Collector's Club of Am; Big Little Book [★21978]

Collectors Club of Am; Lionel [22633]
Collectors' Club of Am; Old Sleepy Eye [21934]
Collectors Club of Am; Still Bank [21827]
Collectors Club; Antique Phonograph [22710]
Collectors' Club; Better Postcard [★22905]
Collectors Club; Case [22613]
Collectors Club; Chrome Card [★22905]
Collectors Club; Concorde [22810]
Collector's Club; Errors, Freaks and Oddities [22818]
Collectors Club; First Day Cover [★22780]
Collectors Club; Frog Pond - Frog [★21977]
Collectors' Club; GI Joe [22996]
Collectors' Club; Goebel [★21933]
Collectors Club; Intl. Goebel [★22040]
Collectors Club; Key Chain [★22011]
Collectors Club; Key Chain Tag and Mini License Plate [★22011]
Collectors Club; Knife [22615]
Collectors Club; Liberty Seated [22742]
Collectors Club; License Plate Key Chain and Mini License Plate [★22011]
Collectors Club; Natl. Indy 500 [21734]
Collectors Club; Post Card [22908]
Collectors Club; Post Mark [22858]
Collectors Club; Salt Shaker [★21968]
Collectors Club; Transferware [21938]
Collectors Club; Zeppelin [22892]
Collectors' Correspondence Club; Disabled [22814]
Collectors; Dedicated Wooden Money [22736]
Collectors of El Salvador; Assoc. [22794]
Collectors; The Elongated [22738]
Collectors and Enthusiasts Club; Stereo Photographers, [★10853]
Collectors; Fostoria Glass [22553]
Collectors and Historians; Company of Military [★22629]
Collectors of Internal Revenue; Natl. Assn. of Employees of [★24080]
Collectors/Makers Soc; Miniature Arms [21538]
Collectors; Natl. Assn. of Paper and Advt. [22412]
Collectors; Natl. Assn. of Timetable [23008]
Collectors; Natl. Assn. of Watch and Clock [22990]
Collectors; Natl. Cambridge [22561]
Collectors; Natl. Doll and Toy [★22407]
Collectors; North Amer. [22747]
Collectors of Numismatic Errors [★22734]
Collectors Record Club [22712], 61 French Market Pl., New Orleans, LA 70116, (504)525-5000
Collectors of Religion on Stamps [22809], c/o Verna Shackleton, Sec., 425 N Linwood Ave., No. 110, Appleton, WI 54914-3476, (920)734-2417
Collectors Service Bur. - Address unknown since 2001.
Collectors' Soc. of Am; Marble [22624]
Collectors Soc; Amer. Historical Print [21523]
Collectors' Soc; Belleek [★21925]
Collectors Soc; Bing's Friends and [24851]
Collectors Soc; C.A.L./N-X-211 [11106]
Collectors; Soc. for Costa Rica [22872]
Collectors Soc; John Reich [22740]
Collectors; Soc. of Lincoln Cent [22756]
Collectors Soc; Lottery [★22030]
Collectors Soc; Natl. Imperial Glass [22565]
Collectors; Soc. of Paper Money [22757]
Collectors; Soc. of Ration Token [22759]
Collectors; Soc. of Tobacco Jar [21936]
Collectors' Soc; Toothpick Holder [★22089]
Collectors Soc; Toy Train [22638]
Collectors; Valley Camera and Movie [★10844]
Colleen Casey Fan Club - Defunct.
Coll. canadien des directeurs de services de sante [★IO]
Coll. Admin. Professionals; Assn. of [7887]
Coll. Admission Assn; Natl. Catholic [19672]
Coll. Admission Counseling; Natl. Assn. for [7912]
Coll. Admission Counselors; Natl. Assn. of [★7912]
Coll. Admissions Assistance Center - Defunct.
Coll. Age Org. of ATID - Defunct.
Coll. of Allergists; Amer. [★13596]
Coll. Alumni Hall of Fame Found; Natl. Black [18911]
Coll. of Amer. Pathologists [15866], 325 Waukegan Rd., Northfield, IL 60093-2750, (847)832-7000
College of the Ancients - Address unknown since 2000.

A star before a book entry number signifies that the name is not listed separately, but is mentioned within the entry.

Coll. Art Assn. [7969], 275 7th Ave., 18th Fl., New York, NY 10001, (212)691-1051

Coll. Art Assn. of Am. [★7969]

Coll. and Assn. of Registered Nurses of Alberta [IO], Edmonton, AB, Canada

Coll. Athletic Assn; Natl. Christian [23837]

Coll. Athletic Assn; Natl. Junior [23843]

Coll. Athletic Assn; Natl. Little [★23859]

Coll. Athletic Assn; Natl. Small [★23859]

Coll. Athletic Bus. Mgt. Assn. [23813], c/o Pat Manak, Asst. Sec., 24651 Detroit Rd., Westlake, OH 44145, (440)892-4000

Coll. Athletic Bus. Managers Assn. [★23813]

Coll. Athletic Conf; Eastern [23484]

Coll. Automotive Teachers; Natl. Assn. of [★7993]

Coll. Auxiliary Services; Assn. of [★3478]

Coll. Auxiliary Services; Natl. Assn. of [3478]

Coll. Band Directors Natl. Assn. [8906], c/o Thomas Verrier, Sec., Vanderbilt Univ., Blair School of Music, 2400 Blakemore Ave., Nashville, TN 37212, (615)322-7651

Coll. Baseball Coaches; Amer. Assn. of [★23101]

The Coll. Bd. [9248], 45 Columbus Ave., New York, NY 10023-6992, (212)713-8000

Coll. Boards; Coun. of Community [★8118]

Coll. Bookstore Assn. [★3415]

Coll. Bus. Officers; Amer. Assn. of [★7897]

Coll. Bus. Officers; Community [8020]

Coll. Canadien de Geneticiens Medicaux [★IO]

Coll. of Chaplains [★19744]

Coll. of Chaplains [★19744]

Coll. of Church Musicians - Defunct.

Coll. of Clinic Managers; Amer. [★15054]

Coll. Coalition; Christian [★8084]

Coll. Coalition; Women's [9330]

Coll. Composition and Commun; Conf. on [8376]

Coll. Consortium; Christian [8082]

Coll. Consortium for Intl. Stud. [8103], 2000 P St. NW, Ste. 503, Washington, DC 20036, (202)223-0330

Coll. Consortium for Intl. Stud. [IO], Washington, DC, United States

College Coun; Tri- [★15120]

Coll. Counseling Assn; Amer. [8162]

Coll. for Creative Stud. Alumni Assn. [18888], 201 E Kirby St., Detroit, MI 48202-4034, (313)664-7400

Coll. Dance Festival Assn; Amer. [9864]

Coll. Democrats [★17400]

Coll. Democrats of Am. [17400], 430 S Capitol St. SE, Washington, DC 20003-4024, (202)863-8018

Coll. Designers Assn; Univ. and [8572]

Coll. of Diplomates of the Amer. Bd. of Orthodontics [14149], 3260 Upper Bottom Rd., St. Charles, MO 63303, (636)922-5551

College Directors; Natl. Assn. of Pre [8371]

Coll. Editors; Amer. Assn. of Agricultural [★4098]

Coll. Educ; Police Assn. for [6004]

Coll. English Assn. [8375], c/o Joe Pestino, Treas., Nazareth Coll. of Rochester, 4245 East Ave., Rochester, NY 14618-3790, (585)389-2645

Coll. Entrance Examination Bd. [★9248]

Coll. of Family Physicians of Canada - Ontario Chap. [IO], Mississauga, ON, Canada

Coll. Football Assn. - Defunct.

Coll. Fraternity; Center for the Stud. of the [24476]

Coll. Fraternity Editors Assn. [24447], c/o Thomas C. Oliver, Pres., 5134 Bonham Rd., Oxford, OH 45056, (513)523-7591

Coll. Fraternity Secretaries Assn. [★24479]

Coll. Fund; Natl. Alumni Coun. of the United Negro [18910]

Coll. Fund; United Negro [8437]

Coll. Funds of Am; Independent [★8537]

Coll. Geology Teachers; Assn. of [★8459]

Coll. Gymnastics Assn. [23474], c/o Dr. Richard Aronson, Exec. Dir., 52 Evelyn Rd., Needham, MA 02494, (617)444-3893

Coll. Hall of Fame; Natl. Football Found. and [23431]

Coll. Hea. Assn; Amer. [14714]

Coll. of Healthcare Info. Mgt. Executives [2098], 3300 Washtenaw Ave., Ste. 225, Ann Arbor, MI 48104-5184, (734)665-0000

Coll. Honor Societies; Assn. of [24501]

Coll. Honor Societies; Assn. of [★24470]

Coll. Humanities Assn; Community [8530]

Coll. Intl. pour la Recherche en Productique [★IO]

Coll. Journalism Assn; Community [8710]

Coll. Journalism Assn; Junior [★8710]

Coll. Language Assn. [8729], c/o Booker T. Anthony, Pres., Fayetteville State Univ., Dept. of English and Foreign Languages, 1200 Murchison Rd., Fayetteville, NC 28301, (910)672-1347

Coll; League for Innovation in the Community [8120]

Coll. Magazines Associated; Engineering [3222]

Coll. des Medecins de Famille du Canada [★IO]

Coll. Media Advisers [8708], Univ. of Memphis, Dept. of Journalism, 3711 Veterans Ave., Rm. 300, Memphis, TN 38152-6661, (901)678-2403

Coll. of Medical Gp. Administrators; Amer. [★15054]

Coll. of Medical Toxicology; Amer. [16660]

Coll. Music Soc. [8907], 312 E Pine St., Missoula, MT 59802-4624, (406)721-9616

Coll. of Musicians; Amer. [8899]

Coll. of Occupational Medicine; Amer. [★15624]

Coll. of Operating Dept. Practitioners [IO], London, United Kingdom

Coll. of Optometrists [IO], London, United Kingdom

Coll. of Optometrists in Vision Development [15718], 215 W Garfield Rd., Ste. 210, Aurora, OH 44202, (330)995-0718

Coll. of Osteopathic Healthcare Executives [14876], c/o Wilson Chen, Treas., 3500 Camp Bowie, Box 300, Fort Worth, TX 76107

Coll. of Osteopathic Hosp. Administrators; Amer. [★14876]

Coll. Ouest Africain des Chirurgiens [★IO]

Coll. Parents of Am. [8485], 2000 N 14th St., Ste. 800, Arlington, VA 22201-2540, (888)761-6702

Coll. of Performance Mgt. [2491], 101 S Whiting St., Ste. 320, Alexandria, VA 22304, (703)370-7885

Coll. of Performance Mgt. [IO], Alexandria, VA, United States

Coll. Personnel Assn; Amer. [8961]

Coll. Physical Educ. Assn. for Men; Natl. [★8985]

College of Piping [IO], Glasgow, United Kingdom

Coll. Placement Coun. [★8995]

Coll. Placement Services [★8047]

College of Preachers [★19903]

College Pro-Life Network - Address unknown since 2002.

Coll. Professors of Textiles and Clothing; Assn. of [★3791]

Coll. Public Relations Assn; Amer. [★8245]

Coll. Public Relations Assn; Sports Sect., Amer. [★23814]

Coll. Publications Advisers; Natl. Coun. of [★8708]

Coll. Publishers Group - Defunct.

Coll. Radio Org; Black [551]

Coll. of Radiology; Amer. [16274]

Coll. Reading and Learning Assn. [9042], PO Box 382, El-Dorado, KS 67042, (307)382-1725

Coll. and Reference Libraries; Assn. of [★10331]

Coll. Republican Natl. Comm. [18522], 600 Pennsylvania Ave. SE, Ste. 215, Washington, DC 20003, (888)765-3564

Coll. and Res. Libraries; Assn. of [10331]

Coll. Retirement Equities Fund [★9066]

Coll. Royal des Chirurgiens Dentistes du Canada [★IO]

Coll. of St. Scholastica Alumni Assn. [18889], c/o Alumni Relations, The Coll. of St. Scholastica, Tower Hall 1410, 1200 Kenwood Ave., Duluth, MN 55811-4199, (218)723-6071

Coll. Savings Plans Network [8429], PO Box 11910, Lexington, KY 40578-1910, (859)244-8175

Coll. Science Improvement Program - Defunct.

Coll. Service Bur. - Address unknown since 1985.

Coll. Ser. Comm. of the Young Republican Natl. Fed. [★18522]

Coll. Soccer Assn; Eastern [23776]

Coll. Soccer Officials Bur; Eastern [★23776]

Coll. of Speech and Language Therapists [★IO]

Coll. of Speech Therapists [★IO]

Coll. Sports Info. Directors of Am. [23814], c/o Jeff Hodges, Sec./Digest Ed., Univ. of North Alabama, PO Box 5038, Florence, AL 35632, (256)765-4595

Coll. Stores; Natl. Assn. of [3415]

College Stores Res. and Educational Found. [★3415]

Coll. Student; Natl. Assn. on Work and the [★8996]

Coll. Student Personnel Inst. - Defunct.

Coll. Summit [8486], 1763 Columbia Rd. NW, 2nd Fl., Washington, DC 20009, (202)319-1763

Coll. Swimming Coaches Assn. of Am. [23883], c/o Phil Whitten, Exec. Dir., 10320 E Verbena Ln., Scottsdale, AZ 85255, (480)628-5488

Coll. Teacher Programs - Defunct.

Coll. of Teachers [IO], London, United Kingdom

Coll. Teachers of Sacred Doctrine; Soc. of Catholic [★9273]

Coll. Testing; Amer. [★9246]

Coll. Theology Soc. [9273], c/o Prof. Elena Procario-Foley, Sec., Iona Coll., 715 North Ave., New Rochelle, NY 10801, (914)637-2744

Coll. Trustees; Assn. of Community [8118]

Coll. and Univ. Administrators; Inst. for [★8745]

Coll. and Univ. Attorneys; Natl. Assn. of [5677]

Coll. and Univ. Auditors; Assn. of [7888]

Coll. and Univ. Bus. Officers Associations; Natl. Fed. of [★7897]

Coll. and Univ. Bus. Officers; Natl. Assn. of [7897]

Coll. and Univ. Chaplains and Directors of Religious Life; National Assn. of [★9168]

Coll., Univ. and Community Arts Administrators; Assn. of [★7968]

Coll. and Univ. Cmpt. Users Assn. [7894], c/o EDUCAUSE, 4772 Walnut St., Ste. 206, Boulder, CO 80301-2538, (303)449-4430

Coll. and Univ. Cmpt. Users Conf. [★7894]

Coll. and Univ. Concert Managers; Assn. of [★7968]

Coll. and Univ. Dept. of the Natl. Catholic Educ. Assn. [★8051]

Coll. and Univ. Educators; Nature and Environmental Writers - [8362]

Coll. and Univ. Food Services; Natl. Assn. of [1588]

Coll. and Univ. Machine Records Conf. [★7894]

Coll. and Univ. Media Centers; Consortium of [8554]

Coll. and Univ. Museums and Galleries; Assn. of [10496]

Coll. and Univ. Offices; Assn. of [★8341]

Coll. and Univ. Offices; Assn. for Affiliated [★8341]

Coll. and Univ. Personnel Assn. [★8962]

Coll. and Univ. Planning; Soc. for [9000]

Coll. and Univ. Professional Assn. for Human Resources [8962], 2607 Kingston Pike, Ste. 250, Knoxville, TN 37919, (865)637-7673

Coll. and Univ. Religious Affairs; Assn. of [9168]

College-University Rsrc. Inst. [9055]

College/University Students; Broadcast Found. of [8002]

Coll. and Univ. Summer Sessions; Natl. Assn. of [★9200]

Coll. and Univ. Systems Exchange [★8558]

Coll. Wind and Percussion Instructors; Natl. Assn. of [8919]

Coll. Women; Natl. Assn. of [★9320]

Coll. Women; Natl. Assn. for Physical Educ. of [★8985]

Coll. Women in Sport - Defunct.

Coll. Young Christian Students - Defunct.

Coll. Young Democrats of Am. [★17400]

Colleges; Accrediting Assn. of Bible [★8080]

Colleges; Accrediting Assn. of Bible [★8080]

Colleges of Acupuncture and Oriental Medicine; Coun. of [15743]

Colleges; American Assn. of [★12721]

Colleges; Amer. Assn. of Bible [★8080]

Colleges; Amer. Assn. of Community [8117]

Colleges; Amer. Assn. of Community and Junior [★8117]

Colleges; Amer. Assn. of Junior [★8117]

Colleges; Amer. Assn. of Osteopathic [★15791]

Colleges; Amer. Assn. of Teachers [★9208]

Colleges; Amer. Assn. for Women in Community [9313]

Colls; Amer. Coun. on Schools and [8225]

Colleges; Amer. Mathematical Assn. of Two-Year [8821]

Colleges of Arts and Sciences; Coun. of [7971]

Colleges; Assn. of Amer. [★8098]

Colleges; Assn. of Amer. Medical [8846]

Colleges; Assn. of Amer. Veterinary Medical [9293]

Colleges; Assn. of Bible Institutes and Bible [★8080]

Colleges; Assn. of Chiropractic [13993]

Reference to "IO" in place of a book number signifies that the association may be found in the 45th edition of International Organizations.

Colleges; Assn. of Governing Boards of Universities and **[7889]**

Colleges Assn; Great Lakes **[8106]**

Colleges; Assn. of Mercy **[8053]**

Colleges; Assn. of Physical Plant Administrators of Universities and **[★8333]**

Colleges; Assn. of Univ. Evening **[★8148]**

Colleges in China; Assoc. Boards for Christian **[★8649]**

Colleges in China; United Bd. for Christian **[★8649]**

Colleges of Chiropody; Amer. Assn. of **[★16025]**

Colleges; Comm. for the Development of Art in Negro **[★7969]**

Colleges Consortium; World Univ. **[★8114]**

Colleges Consortium; Worldwide Univ. **[★8114]**

Colleges; Coun. for the Advancement of Small **[★8535]**

Colleges; Coun. of Independent **[8535]**

Colleges and Departments of Educ; Natl. Assn. of **[★9208]**

Colleges; Eastern Assn. of Rowing **[23699]**

Colleges and Employers; Natl. Assn. of **[8995]**

Colleges; Found. for Episcopal **[★8397]**

Colleges; Fund for Episcopal **[★8397]**

Colleges; Journalism Assn. of Community **[8712]**

Colleges of Medicine of South Africa **[IO]**, Rondebosch, Republic of South Africa

Colls. of Mid-America - Address unknown since 2001.

Colleges of the Midwest; Assoc. **[8097]**

Colleges; Natl. Assn. of Physical Administrators of Universities and **[★8333]**

Colleges; Natl. Assn. of Private, Nontraditional Schools and **[7947]**

Colleges; Natl. Assn. of Schools and **[★7947]**

Colleges; Natl. Assn. of State Universities and Land-Grant **[8110]**

Colleges of the Natl. Assn. of State Universities and Land-Grant Colleges; Off. for the Advancement of Public Black **[8112]**

Colleges - of the Natl. Assn. of State Universities and Land-Grant Colleges; Off. for Advancement of Public Negro **[★8112]**

Colleges; Natl. Coun. of Acupuncture Schools and **[★15743]**

Colleges; Natl. Coun. of State Directors of Community **[8122]**

Colleges; New England Assn. of Schools and **[8296]**

Colleges of Nursing; Amer. Assn. of **[8842]**

Colleges of Optometry; Assn. of Schools and **[15717]**

Colleges of Osteopathic Medicine; Amer. Assn. of **[15791]**

Colleges of Pharmacy; Amer. Assn. of **[15909]**

Colleges of Podiatric Medicine; Amer. Assn. of **[16025]**

Colleges of Podiatry; Amer. Assn. of **[★16025]**

Colleges and Schools; Accrediting Coun. for Independent **[7874]**

Colleges and Schools Commn. on Accreditation and School Improvement; North Central Assn. of **[8297]**

Colleges and Schools; Middle States Assn. of **[8277]**

Colleges and Schools; Natl. Assn. of Trade and Tech. Schools and the Assn. of Independent **[★9303]**

Colleges and Schools; North Central Assn. of **[★8297]**

Colleges and Schools; Southern Assn. of **[8308]**

Colleges and Schools of the U.S; Assn. of Military **[8883]**

Colleges and Schools of the U.S; Assn. of Military **[★8883]**

Colleges and Secondary Schools; Middle States Assn. of **[★8277]**

Colleges; Soc. for Anthropology in Community **[7954]**

Colleges and State Universities; Assn. of Land-Grant **[★8110]**

Colleges for Teacher Educ; Amer. Assn. of **[9208]**

Colleges and Teachers of Agriculture; Natl. Assn. of **[★7942]**

Colleges and Teachers of Agriculture; North Amer. **[7942]**

Colleges of Tech; Accrediting Commn. of Career Schools and **[7873]**

Colleges and Universities

AACSB Intl. - Assn. to Advance Collegiate Schools of Bus. **[8010]**

AAUW Legal Advocacy Fund **[5573]**

Acad. of Intl. Bus. **[8011]**

Acad. of Mgt. **[8805]**

Acad. of Security Educators and Trainers **[9119]**

ACT **[9246]**

ACUO **[8341]**

ACUTA: The Assn. for Communications Tech. Professionals in Higher Educ. **[8548]**

Adult Residential Colleges Assn. **[IO]**

Agence Universitaire de la Francophone, Bur. Afrique de l'Quest **[IO]**

All-Amer. Collegiate Golf Found. **[23443]**

Alliance of Universities for Democracy **[IO]**

Alpha Lambda Tau Intl. Social Fraternity **[24613]**

Amer. Acad. of Advt. **[7919]**

Amer. Assembly **[18418]**

Amer. Associates, Ben-Gurion Univ. of the Negev **[8673]**

Amer. Assn. of Behavioral and Social Sciences **[6522]**

Amer. Assn. for Chinese Stud. **[8074]**

Amer. Assn. of Colleges of Nursing **[8842]**

Amer. Assn. of Colleges for Teacher Educ. **[9208]**

Amer. Assn. for Collegiate Independent Stud. **[7944]**

Amer. Assn. of Collegiate Registrars and Admissions Officers **[7910]**

Amer. Assn. of Community Colleges **[8117]**

Amer. Assn. for Employment in Educ. **[8994]**

Amer. Assn. for Higher Educ. **[8478]**

Amer. Assn. of Physics Teachers **[8993]**

Amer. Assn. of Presidents of Independent Colleges and Universities **[8534]**

Amer. Assn. of School Administrators **[7882]**

Amer. Assn. of State Colleges and Universities **[8096]**

Amer. Assn. of Teachers of Arabic **[7958]**

Amer. Assn. of Teachers of Slavic and East European Languages **[9125]**

Amer. Assn. of Teachers of Turkic Languages **[9282]**

Amer. Assn. of Univ. Professors **[9022]**

Amer. Assn. of Univ. Women **[9311]**

Amer. Assn. of Univ. Women Educational Found. **[9312]**

Amer. Assn. for Vocational Instructional Materials **[9298]**

Amer. Assn. for Women in Community Colleges **[9313]**

Amer. Baseball Coaches Assn. **[23101]**

Amer. Catholic Philosophical Assn. **[8965]**

Amer. Classical League **[8726]**

Amer. Collegiate Horsemen's Assn. **[4814]**

Amer. Collegiate Retailing Assn. **[8815]**

Amer. Conf. of Academic Deans **[7885]**

Amer. Coun. on Educ. **[8224]**

Amer. Coun. on Intl. Intercultural Educ. **[8651]**

Amer. Debate Assn. **[9151]**

Amer. Driver and Traffic Safety Educ. Assn. **[8210]**

Amer. Educ. Finance Assn. **[8342]**

Amer. Football Coaches Assn. **[23427]**

Amer. Forensic Assn. **[9152]**

Amer. Friends of the Alliance Israelite Universelle **[8675]**

Amer. Friends of The Hebrew Univ. **[8676]**

Amer. Inst. of Indian Stud. **[8541]**

Amer. Mathematical Assn. of Two-Year Colleges **[8821]**

Amer. Mock Trial Assn. **[9281]**

Amer. Parliamentary Debate Assn. **[9153]**

Amer. Political Sci. Assn. **[7521]**

Amer. Real Estate Soc. **[9049]**

Amer. Real Estate and Urban Economics Assn. **[9050]**

Amer. Soc. for Engg. Educ. **[8366]**

Amer. Student Govt. Assn. **[9175]**

Amer. Univ. in Moscow **[8597]**

APPA: The Assn. of Higher Educ. Facilities Officers **[8333]**

ASEAN Univ. Network **[IO]**

Asian Assn. of Agricultural Colleges and Universities **[IO]**

Assoc. Colleges of the Midwest **[8097]**

Assoc. Collegiate Press **[8705]**

Assoc. Schools of Constr. **[8143]**

Assn. of Accredited Naturopathic Medical Colleges **[8943]**

Assn. to Advance Collegiate Schools of Bus. **[8013]**

Assn. for the Advancement of Sustainability in Higher Educ. **[8479]**

Assn. of African Stud. Programs **[7928]**

Assn. of African Universities **[IO]**

Assn. of Amazonian Universities **[IO]**

Assn. of Amer. Colleges and Universities **[8098]**

Assn. of Amer. Intl. Colleges and Universities **[8641]**

Assn. of Amer. Intl. Colleges and Universities - France **[IO]**

Assn. of Amer. Universities **[8099]**

Assn. of Amer. Univ. Presses **[8550]**

Assn. of Amer. Veterinary Medical Colleges **[9293]**

Assn. of Arab Universities **[IO]**

Assn. for Assessment in Counseling and Educ. **[9247]**

Assn. for Biblical Higher Educ. **[8080]**

Assn. of Canadian Community Colleges **[IO]**

Assn. of Catholic Colleges and Universities **[8051]**

Assn. of Christian Universities and Colleges in Asia **[IO]**

Assn. of Coll. Unions Intl. **[9166]**

Assn. of Coll. and Univ. Auditors **[7888]**

Assn. of Coll. and Univ. Clubs **[8100]**

Assn. of Coll. and Univ. Clubs **[IO]**

Assn. of Coll. and Univ. Religious Affairs **[9168]**

Assn. of Colleges **[IO]**

Assn. of Collegiate Bus. Schools and Programs **[8101]**

Assn. of Collegiate Schools of Architecture **[7959]**

Assn. of Collegiate Schools of Planning **[9285]**

Assn. of Commonwealth Universities **[IO]**

Assn. for Community Based Education **[8123]**

Assn. of Community Coll. Trustees **[8118]**

Assn. of Departments of English **[8374]**

Assn. of Departments of Foreign Languages **[8728]**

Assn. for the Development of Religious Info. Systems **[20091]**

Assn. for Direct Instruction **[8232]**

Assn. of East Asian Res. Universities **[IO]**

Assn. of Episcopal Colleges **[8397]**

Assn. of Governing Boards of Universities and Colleges **[7889]**

Assn. on Higher Educ. and Disability **[8201]**

Assn. of Indian Universities **[IO]**

Assn. of Jesuit Colleges and Universities **[8052]**

Assn. for Jewish Stud. **[8684]**

Assn. for Learning Tech. **[IO]**

Assn. for Media-Based Continuing Educ. for Engineers **[8367]**

Assn. of Mercy Colleges **[8053]**

Assn. of NROTC Colleges and Universities **[8884]**

Assn. of Nutrition Departments and Programs **[8947]**

Assn. of Optometric Educators **[8851]**

Assn. of Portuguese-Language Universities **[IO]**

Assn. of Presbyterian Colleges and Universities **[9005]**

Assn. of Schools and Colleges of Optometry **[15717]**

Assn. for Social Anthropology in Oceania **[6413]**

Assn. for the Social Sci. Stud. of Jewry **[8685]**

Assn. for Tech. in Music Instruction **[8905]**

Assn. for Theatre in Higher Educ. **[9262]**

Assn. of Universities of Asia and the Pacific **[IO]**

Assn. of Universities and Colleges of Canada **[IO]**

Assn. of Universities for Res. in Astronomy **[6501]**

Assn. of Univ. Architects **[6472]**

Assn. for Univ. and Coll. Counseling Center Directors **[8167]**

Assn. of Univ. Interior Designers **[2252]**

Assn. of Univ. Leaders for a Sustainable Future **[8483]**

Assn. of Univ. Programs in Hea. Admin. **[8857]**

Assn. of Univ. Res. Parks **[9054]**

Assn. of Univ. Summer Sessions **[9199]**

Atlantic Coast Conf. **[23806]**

A star before a book entry number signifies that the name is not listed separately, but is mentioned within the entry.

Beta Chi Theta Natl. Fraternity [24618]
Big East Conf. [23807]
Big Ten Conf. [23808]
Black Coll. Radio Org. [551]
B'nai B'rith Intl. [20125]
Brandeis - Bardin Inst. [8687]
British Schools and Universities Found. [8102]
British Schools and Universities Found. [IO]
British Universities Indus. Relations Assn. [IO]
British Universities North Am. Club [8606]
Broadcast Educ. Assn. [8001]
Broadcast Found. of College/University Students [8002]
Bur. of French-Speaking Higher Educ. and Res. - Arab Off. [IO]
Bur. of French-Speaking Higher Educ. and Res. - Central and East European Off. [IO]
Bur. of French-Speaking Higher Educ. and Res. - Delegation to the European Union [IO]
Bur. of French-Speaking Universities Agency - South Asian and Pacific Off. [IO]
Business-Higher Educ. Forum [8008]
Cambridge in Am. [9284]
Campus Safety, Hea. and Environmental Mgt. Assn. [4300]
Canadian Associates of the Ben-Gurion Univ. of the Negev [IO]
Canadian Friends of Bar-Ilan Univ. [IO]
Canadian Friends of the Hebrew Univ. of Jerusalem [IO]
Career Coll. Assn. [9303]
Carnegie Corp. of New York [8239]
Catching the Dream [8427]
Center for Commun. [8003]
Center for Lifelong Learning [8406]
Center for the Stud. of the Presidency [17069]
Central Intercollegiate Athletic Assn. [23811]
Centre for Bus. Transformation [IO]
Christian Coll. Consortium [8082]
Coll. Athletic Bus. Mgt. Assn. [23813]
Coll. Band Directors Natl. Assn. [8906]
The Coll. Bd. [9248]
Coll. Consortium for Intl. Stud. [8103]
Coll. Consortium for Intl. Stud. [IO]
Coll. English Assn. [8375]
Coll. Gymnastics Assn. [23474]
Coll. Language Assn. [8729]
Coll. Media Advisers [8708]
Coll. Parents of Am. [8485]
Coll. Reading and Learning Assn. [9042]
Coll. Sports Info. Directors of Am. [23814]
Coll. Summit [8486]
Coll. Theology Soc. [9273]
Coll. and Univ. Professional Assn. for Human Resources [8962]
College-University Rsrc. Inst. [9055]
Collegiate Assn. of Table Top Gamers [22462]
Collegiate Broadcasters, Inc. [540]
Collegiate Commissioners Assn. [23815]
Collegiate Soaring Assn. [23039]
Comm. on Institutional Cooperation [8104]
Community Coll. Baccalaureate Assn. [8119]
Community Coll. Journalism Assn. [8710]
Community Colleges for Intl. Development [8607]
Compete Am. [8365]
The Conf. Bd. [6877]
Conf. on Christianity and Literature [8799]
Conf. on Coll. Composition and Commun. [8376]
Consolidated Athletic Commn. [23816]
Consortium for the Advancement of Private Higher Educ. [8105]
Consortium of Coll. and Univ. Media Centers [8554]
Consortium on Financing Higher Educ. [9057]
Coun. for Adult and Experiential Learning [8412]
Coun. for Aid to Educ. [8346]
Coun. on Career for Minorities [8047]
Coun. for Chem. Res. [6679]
Coun. for Christian Colleges and Universities [8084]
Coun. of Colleges of Arts and Sciences [7971]
Coun. for European Stud. [8404]
Coun. of Independent Colleges [8535]
Coun. of Ivy Gp. Presidents [23817]
Coun. for Jewish Educ. [8690]

Coun. for Rsrc. Development [8347]
Coun. on Undergraduate Res. [9059]
Coun. of Writing Prog. Administrators [9333]
Dow Jones Newspaper Fund [8711]
Eastern Assn. of Rowing Colleges [23699]
Eastern Coll. Athletic Conf. [23484]
Eastern Coll. Soccer Assn. [23776]
Eastern Collegiate Hockey Assn. [23485]
Editorial Projects in Educ. [8251]
Educating for Justice [9126]
Educational Res. Ser. [7895]
EDUCAUSE [8558]
Eta Sigma Alpha Natl. Home School Honor Soc. [8316]
European Univ. Assn. [IO]
Fed. for Unified Sci. Educ. [9102]
Found. ICPR Junior Coll. [8022]
Found. for Independent Higher Educ. [8537]
French-Speaking Universities Agency - Caribbean Off. [IO]
French-Speaking Univ. Agency [IO]
Future Bus. Leaders of Am. - Phi Beta Lambda [24420]
Golf Coaches Assn. of Am. [23448]
Graduate Record Examinations Bd. [9251]
Great Lakes Colleges Assn. [8106]
Higher Educ. Consortium for Urban Affairs [9286]
Hillel: The Found. for Jewish Campus Life [20142]
Hispanic Assn. of Colleges and Universities [8107]
Ibero-American Univ. Assn. for Postgraduate Universities [IO]
IES, Inst. for the Intl. Educ. of Students [8405]
INROADS [8749]
Inst. for Amer. Universities [8643]
Instructional Tech. Coun. [8565]
Inter-Collegiate Sailing Assn. of North Am. [23176]
Inter-University Consortium for Political and Social Res. [7525]
Inter-University Coun. for East Africa [IO]
Intercollegiate Broadcasting Sys. [8004]
Intercollegiate Fencing Assn. [23401]
Intercollegiate Horse Show Assn. [23526]
Intercollegiate Outing Club Assn. [23941]
Intercollegiate Rowing Assn. [23700]
Intercollegiate Stud. Inst. [17271]
Intercollegiate Tennis Assn. [23902]
Intl. Assn. of Campus Law Enforcement Administrators [9084]
Intl. Assn. for Jazz Educ. [8912]
Intl. Assn. of Professional Bureaucrats [22595]
Intl. Assn. of Universities [IO]
Intl. Coun. of Academies of Engg. and Technological Sciences [9104]
Intl. Coun. on Educ. for Teaching [9216]
Intl. Coun. of Fine Arts Deans [7973]
Intl. Coun. for Hea., Physical Educ., Recreation, Sport, and Dance [8981]
Intl. Engg. Consortium [6928]
Intl. Soc. for Educational Planning [8999]
Intl. Sports Exchange [23826]
Intl. Univ. Consortium [8566]
Intl. Univ. Found. [8648]
IOCALUM [23942]
Jesuit Assn. of Student Personnel Administrators [7896]
Joint Univ. Coun. [IO]
Journalism Assn. of Community Colleges [8712]
LASPAU: Academic and Professional Programs for the Americas [8108]
LASPAU: Academic and Professional Programs for the Americas [IO]
Leadership Enterprise for a Diverse Am. [9183]
League for Innovation in the Community Coll. [8120]
Learning Resources Network [8151]
Lisle Intercultural [8623]
Lutheran Educational Conf. of North Am. [8804]
Lutheran Student Movement - U.S.A. [20227]
Maryknoll Mission Center of New England [8660]
Mennonite Educ. Agency [20250]
Metro Intl. Prog. Services of New York [8624]
Metropolitan Intercollegiate Basketball Assn. [23131]

Mid-American Greek Coun. Assn. [24483]
Middle States Assn. of Colleges and Schools [8277]
Modern Language Assn. of Am. [8735]
Music Teachers Natl. Assn. [8918]
Natl. Acad. of Educ. [8280]
Natl. Architectural Accrediting Bd. [7962]
Natl. Assn. of Advisors for the Hea. Professions [8866]
Natl. Assn. of Baptist Professors of Religion [9277]
Natl. Assn. of Basketball Coaches [23133]
Natl. Assn. for Campus Activities [9169]
Natl. Assn. of Campus Card Users [3707]
Natl. Assn. of Coll. Auxiliary Services [3478]
Natl. Assn. of Coll. Stores [3415]
Natl. Assn. of Coll. and Univ. Bus. Officers [7897]
Natl. Assn. of Coll. and Univ. Food Services [1588]
Natl. Assn. of Coll. Wind and Percussion Instructors [8919]
Natl. Assn. of Colleges and Employers [8995]
Natl. Assn. of Collegiate Directors of Athletics [23833]
Natl. Assn. of Collegiate Marketing Administrators [23834]
Natl. Assn. for Community Coll. Entrepreneurship [8033]
Natl. Assn. of Community Coll. Teacher Educ. Programs [9221]
Natl. Assn. of Educational Off. Professionals [7898]
Natl. Assn. of Educational Procurement [7899]
Natl. Assn. for Equal Opportunity in Higher Educ. [8109]
Natl. Assn. of Geoscience Teachers [8459]
Natl. Assn. of Hea. Sci. Educ. Partnership [9107]
Natl. Assn. of Independent Colleges and Universities [8539]
Natl. Assn. of Intercollegiate Athletics [23835]
Natl. Assn. of Multicultural Engg. Prog. Advocates [8370]
Natl. Assn. for Physical Educ. in Higher Educ. [8985]
Natl. Assn. of Scholars [8490]
Natl. Assn. of Schools, Colleges and Universities of the United Methodist Church [8879]
Natl. Assn. of Self-Instructional Language Programs [8736]
Natl. Assn. of State Universities and Land-Grant Colleges [8110]
Natl. Assn. of Student Personnel Administrators [7904]
Natl. Assn. of Substance Abuse Trainers and Educators [9198]
Natl. Assn. of Univ. Women [9320]
Natl. Assn. of Veterans Prog. Administrators [9292]
Natl. Black Graduate Student Assn. [18869]
Natl. Campus Ministry Assn. [19933]
Natl. Catholic Coll. Admission Assn. [19672]
Natl. Center for Higher Educ. Mgt. Systems [7905]
Natl. Center for the Stud. of Collective Bargaining in Higher Educ. and the Professions [24036]
Natl. Christian Coll. Athletic Assn. [23837]
Natl. Coalition of Advanced Tech. Centers [9240]
Natl. Collegiate Athletic Assn. [23838]
Natl. Collegiate Paintball Assn. [23646]
Natl. Collegiate Roller Hockey Assn. [23487]
Natl. Collegiate Table Tennis Assn. [23895]
Natl. Commun. Assn. [9157]
Natl. Conf. on Student Leadership [9188]
Natl. Consortium of Arts and Letters for Historically Black Colls. and Universities [8111]
Natl. Coun. for Res. and Planning [8121]
Natl. Coun. of State Directors of Community Colleges [8122]
Natl. Coun. on Student Development [9170]
Natl. Coun. of Univ. Res. Administrators [9063]
Natl. Forensic Assn. [9158]
Natl. Intercollegiate Flying Assn. [21466]
Natl. Intercollegiate Running Club Assn. [23707]
Natl. Intercollegiate Soccer Officials Assn. [23778]
Natl. Intramural-Recreational Sports Assn. [23842]

Reference to "IO" in place of a book number signifies that the association may be found in the 45th edition of International Organizations.

Natl. Journalism Center [17634]
Natl. Junior Coll. Athletic Assn. [23843]
Natl. Orientation Directors Assn. [7907]
Natl. Parliamentary Debate Assn. [9160]
Natl. Reading Conf. [9044]
Natl. Registration Center for Stud. Abroad [8626]
Natl. Rsrc. Center for Paraprofessionals in Educ. and Related Services [9150]
Natl. Scholarship Providers Assn. [9074]
Natl. Soc. of Leadership and Success [9189]
Natl. Student Exchange [9172]
Natl. Tutoring Assn. [9283]
Natl. Writing Proj. [9334]
New England Assn. of Schools and Colleges [8296]
NFHS Music Assn. [8928]
NFHS Officials Assn. [23874]
Nordic Assn. of Univ. Administrators [IO]
North Amer. Assn. of Commencement Officers [8492]
North Amer. Assn. of Summer Sessions [9200]
North Amer. Coalition for Christian Admissions Professionals [7914]
North Central Assn. of Colleges and Schools Commn. on Accreditation and School Improvement [8297]
North Central Conf. on Summer Schools [9201]
Northwest Assn. of Accredited Schools [8298]
Oak Ridge Assoc. Universities [7625]
Off. for the Advancement of Public Black Colleges of the Natl. Assn. of State Universities and Land-Grant Colleges [8112]
Off. of Women in Higher Educ., Amer. Coun. on Educ. [9324]
O'Neill Natl. Theater Inst. [9266]
Oper. Enterprise [8808]
Org. for Tropical Stud. [7816]
Organizational Systems Res. Assn. [9234]
Pacific 10 Conf. [23847]
Pathways to Coll. Network [8493]
Peer Hea. Exchange [9338]
PEO Intl. [9325]
People to People Intl. [17909]
Phi Sigma Nu Native Amer. Fraternity [24647]
Progressive, Radically Inclusive Student Ministry [19938]
Public Leadership Educ. Network [9326]
Public Relations Student Soc. of Am. [9034]
Regional Educ. Bd. of the Christian Bros. [8060]
Religious Commun. Assn. [8116]
Royal Soc. of Edinburgh [IO]
Sallie Mae Fund [8434]
Scholars for Peace in the Middle East [18070]
School Nutrition Assn. [9173]
School Sci. and Mathematics Assn. [9115]
Scripps Assn. of Families [8113]
Security on Campus [11846]
Sigma Beta Rho Fraternity [24656]
Silver Wings [24549]
Soc. for the Advancement of Educ. [8305]
Soc. of Building Sci. Educators [8363]
Soc. for Coll. and Univ. Planning [9000]
Soc. for History Educ. [8511]
Soc. for Music Teacher Educ. [8931]
Soc. for Philosophy of Religion [8970]
Soc. for Photographic Educ. [8976]
Soc. of Professors of Educ. [8307]
Southeastern Conf. [23851]
Southeastern Regional Off. Natl. Scholarship Ser. and Fund for Negro Students [8435]
Southern Assn. of Colleges and Schools [8308]
Southern Conf. [23852]
Student African Amer. Brotherhood [19444]
Student Press Law Center [17194]
Students for America [17277]
Students for the Exploration and Development of Space [7923]
Students in Free Enterprise [17637]
Tamarind Inst. [8471]
Teachers Insurance and Annuity Assn. [8579]
Tech. Mgt. Educ. Assn. [9245]
Tel Aviv Univ.; Amer. Coun. of [8679]
Tripoli Rocketry Assn. [9117]
Union of Latin Amer. Universities [IO]
Union of North Amer. Vietnamese Students Assn. [19426]

United Bd. for Christian Higher Educ. in Asia [8649]
United Negro Coll. Fund [8437]
U.S. Basketball Writers Assn. [23137]
U.S. Collegiate Athletic Assn. [23859]
U.S. Collegiate Ski and Snowboard Assn. [23757]
U.S. Collegiate Sports Coun. [23860]
U.S. Handball Assn. [23480]
U.S. Intercollegiate Lacrosse Assn. [23571]
U.S. Lacrosse [23572]
U.S. Professional Tennis Assn. [23914]
U.S. Rowing Assn. [23704]
U.S. Ski and Snowboard Assn. [23760]
U.S. Student Assn. [9195]
Universities Coun. on Water Resources [7844]
Universities Space Res. Assn. [6392]
Univ. Athletic Assn. [23865]
Univ. and Coll. Designers Assn. [8572]
Univ. Coun. for Educational Admin. [7909]
Univ. Film and Video Assn. [8420]
Univ. Film and Video Found. [8421]
Univ. Photographers Assn. of Am. [8977]
Univ. Professors for Academic Order [9026]
University/Resident Theatre Assn. [9269]
Univ. Risk Mgt. and Insurance Assn. [8580]
Urban Affairs Assn. [9287]
U.S.A. Baseball [23127]
U.S.A. Track and Field [23926]
Western Assn. of Schools and Colleges [8314]
Western Social Sci. Assn. [7657]
Winston Churchill Found. [8438]
Women Educators [9328]
Women's Coll. Coalition [9330]
Woodrow Wilson Natl. Fellowship Found. [8439]
World Cong. of Teachers of Dancing [8192]
Worldwide Univ. Consortium [8114]
Worldwide Univ. Consortium [IO]
Yale-China Assn. [8637]
Colleges and Universities; Amer. Assn. of Presidents of Independent [8534]
Colleges and Universities; Amer. Assn. of State [8096]
Colleges and Universities of the Anglican Communion [7952], 815 2nd Ave., No. 315, New York, NY 10017-4594, (212)716-6148
Colleges and Universities of the Anglican Communion [IO], New York, NY, United States
Colleges and Universities; Assn. of Amer. [8098]
Colleges and Universities; Assn. of Catholic [8051]
Colleges and Universities; Assn. of Departments of English in Amer. [★8374]
Colleges and Universities; Assn. of Intl. [★8641]
Colleges and Universities; Assn. of Jesuit [8052]
Colleges and Universities; Assn. of Presbyterian [9005]
Colleges and Universities; Assn. of State [★8096]
Colleges and Universities; Assn. of Upper Level [★8096]
Colleges and Universities; Coun. for Christian [8084]
Colleges and Universities; Fed. of State Associations of Independent [★8539]
Colls. and Universities; Natl. Assn. of [★8225]
Colleges and Universities; Natl. Assn. of Independent [8539]
Colls. and Universities; Natl. Consortium of Arts and Letters for Historically Black [8111]
Colleges and Universities; Natl. Coun. of Independent [★8539]
Colleges and Universities; Natl. Inst. of Independent [★8539]
Colleges and Universities of the United Methodist Church; Natl. Assn. of Schools, [8879]
Colleges of Veterinary Medicine; Assn. of Deans of Amer. [★9293]
Colleges; Western Assn. of Schools and [8314]
Colleges-Women in Medicine Prog; Assn. of Amer. Medical [8847]
Collegi d-Odontolegs I Estomatolegs [★IO]
Collegians Activated to Liberate Life [12911], PO Box 259806, Madison, WI 53725, (608)256-2255
Collegians for Life; Amer. [★12928]
Collegiate Alumnae; Assn. of [★9311]
Collegiate Assn. for Res. of Principles; Natl. [8087]
Collegiate Assn. of Table Top Gamers [22462], c/o Mike Roselli, North Carolina State Univ., Campus Box 7306, Raleigh, NC 27695

Collegiate Athletic Assn.; Natl. [23838]
Collegiate Athletic Assn. of Wrestling Coaches and Officials; Natl. [★23987]
Collegiate Baseball Writers Assn; Natl. [3135]
Collegiate Basketball Assn; Metropolitan Inter [23131]
Collegiate Broadcasters, Inc. [540], UPS - Hershey Square Ctr., 1152 Mae St., Hummelstown, PA 17036, (877)ASK-CBI1
Collegiate Bus. Educ; Intl. Assembly for [8024]
Collegiate Bus. Schools and Programs; Assn. of [8101]
Collegiate Commissioners Assn. [23815], 2201 Arrington Blvd. N, Birmingham, AL 35203, (205)458-3013
Collegiate Commissioners; Natl. Assn. of [★23815]
Collegiate Cross Country Coaches Assn; Natl. [★23924]
Collegiate Directors of Athletics; Natl. Assn. of [23833]
Collegiate Equestrian Polo Assn. [23659], c/o Andres Huertas, Treas./Exec. Dir., 20317 Coulson St., Woodland Hills, CA 91367, (818)346-7648
Collegiate Flying Assn; Natl. Inter [21466]
Collegiate Golf Found; All-Amer. [23443]
Collegiate Gymnastics Assn. [★23474]
Collegiate Hockey Assn; Central [23483]
Collegiate Hockey Assn; Eastern [23485]
Collegiate Hockey Assn; Western [23489]
Collegiate Honors Coun; Natl. [8290]
Collegiate Horse Show Assn; Inter [23526]
Collegiate Literary Societies; Assn. of Amer. [10412]
Collegiate Marketing Administrators; Natl. Assn. of [23834]
Collegiate Network [8709], PO Box 4431, Wilmington, DE 19807, (302)652-4600
Collegiate Outing Club Assn; Inter [23941]
Collegiate Press; Assoc. [8705]
Collegiate Registrars and Admissions Officers; Amer. Assn. of [7910]
Collegiate Retailing Assn; Amer. [8815]
Collegiate Rodeo Assn; Natl. Inter [23691]
Collegiate Sailing Assn. of North Am; Inter- [23176]
Collegiate Scholars; Natl. Soc. of [9075]
Collegiate Schools of Architecture; Assn. of [7959]
Collegiate Schools of Bus; Amer. Assembly of [★8010]
Collegiate Schools of Bus; Amer. Assn. of [★8010]
Collegiate Schools of Planning; Assn. of [9285]
Collegiate Secretaries; Natl. Assn. of [★66]
Collegiate Ski Assn; Midwest [★23760]
Collegiate Ski Assn; Natl. [★23760]
Collegiate Ski Coaches Assn. of America - Defunct.
Collegiate Soaring Assn. [23039], 4671 Kipling St., No. 68, Wheat Ridge, CO 80033, (303)432-2137
Collegiate Sports Coun; U.S. [23860]
Collegiate Tennis Assn; Inter [23902]
Collegiate Tennis Coaches Assn; Natl. [★23902]
Collegiate Volleyball Coaches Assn. [★23969]
Collegiate Water Polo Assn. [23972], 320 W 5th St., Bridgeport, PA 19405, (610)277-6787
Collegiate Water Ski Assn; Natl. [23977]
Collegiate Women Athletics Administrators; Natl. Assn. of [8982]
Collegiate Yacht Racing Assn; Inter- [★23176]
Collegiate Yacht Racing Assn. of North Am; Inter- [★23176]
Collegium Internationale Neuro-Psychopharmacologicum [15929], c/o Oakley Ray, PhD, Exec.Sec., 1608 17th Ave. S, Nashville, TN 37203, (615)297-3144
Collegium Internationale Neuro-Psychopharmacologicum [IO], Nashville, TN, United States
Collie
Bearded Collie Club of Am. [22227]
Collie Club of Am. [22248]
North Amer. Sheep Dog Soc. [22328]
U.S. Border Collie Club [22372]
Collie Club of Am. [22248], c/o Sally Futh, Dir.-at-Large, 47 Kielwasser Rd., Washington Depot, CT 06794-1119, (860)868-2863
Collie Club of Am; Bearded [22227]
Collie Club; U.S. Border [22372]
Collingwood Rocks With Elvis Fan Club [IO], Collingwood, ON, Canada

A star before a book entry number signifies that the name is not listed separately, but is mentioned within the entry.

Collins Collectors Assn. [21499], PO Box 354, Phoenix, MD 21131
Collins Found; Treacher [14067]
Collins, Phil
 Genesis Info. [24900]
Collision Repair; Inter-Industry Conf. on Auto [415]
Collision Repair Specialists; Soc. of [428]
Colm Wilkinson Appreciation Soc. [IO], Whitby, ON, Canada
Colombia
 Colombian Amer. Assn. [24312]
 Colombian-American Chamber of Commerce of Greater Miami [24313]
 Inst. for the Stud. of Amer. Cultures [10746]
 Natl. Stamp Dealers Assn. [22851]
Colombia Human Rights Information Comm. - Address unknown since 1999.
Colombian Acad. of Exact, Physical, and Natural Sciences [IO], Bogota, Colombia
Colombian Amer. Assn. [24312], 30 Vesey St., Ste. 506, New York, NY 10007, (212)233-7776
Colombian-American Chamber of Commerce [★24312]
Colombian-American Chamber of Commerce [IO], Bogota, Colombia
Colombian-American Chamber of Commerce - Bogota [IO], Bogota, Colombia
Colombian-American Chamber of Commerce - Cali [IO], Cali, Colombia
Colombian-American Chamber of Commerce - Cartagena [IO], Cartagena, Colombia
Colombian-American Chamber of Commerce of Greater Miami [24313], 250 Catalonia Ave., Ste. 407, Coral Gables, FL 33134, (305)446-2542
Colombian Assn. for the Advancement of Sci. [IO], Bogota, Colombia
Colombian Assn. of Bioengineering and Medical Electronics [IO], Bucaramanga, Colombia
Colombian Assn. of Clinical Neurophysiology [IO], Cali, Colombia
Colombian Assn. of Dermatology [IO], Bogota, Colombia
Colombian Assn. of Flower Exporters [IO], Bogota, Colombia
Colombian Assn. of Landscape Architects [IO], Bogota, Colombia
Colombian Assn. of Medical Schools [IO], Bogota, Colombia
Colombian Assn. of Psychiatry [IO], Bogota, Colombia
Colombian Bible Soc. [IO], Bogota, Colombia
Colombian Book Chamber [IO], Bogota, Colombia
Colombian Chamber of Info. Tech. and Telecommunications [IO], Bogota, Colombia
Colombian Federations of YMCAs [IO], Bogota, Colombia
Colombian Govt. Tourist Office - Address unknown since 1994.
Colombian Govt. Trade Bur. [24271], 1901 L St. NW, Ste. 700, Washington, DC 20036, (202)887-9000
Colombian Govt. Trade Bur. [IO], Washington, DC, United States
Colombian Inst. of Cement Producers [IO], Bogota, Colombia
Colombian League Against Epilepsy [IO], Cartagena, Colombia
Colombian Olympic Comm. [IO], Bogota, Colombia
Colombian Petroleum Assn. [IO], Bogota, Colombia
Colombian Plastics Indus. Assn. [IO], Bogota, Colombia
Colombian Soc. of Cardiology [IO], Bogota, Colombia
Colombian Soc. of Engineers [IO], Bogota, Colombia
Colombian Soc. of Physics [IO], Cali, Colombia
Colombo Rubber Traders' Assn. [IO], Colombo, Sri Lanka
Colomborquideas [IO], Medellin, Colombia
Colon Cancer Assn; Hereditary [13829]
Colon Free Zone Users Assn. [IO], Colon, Panama
Colon Hydrotherapy; Intl. Assn. for [14567]
Colon and Rectal Surgeons; Amer. Soc. of [16060]
Colon and Rectal Surgery; Amer. Bd. of [16059]
Colon Therapy Assn; Amer. [★16061]
Colonel Cody's Boy Scouts [★20718]
Colonel Coon Collectors Club - Defunct.

Colong Found. for Wilderness [IO], Sydney, Australia
Colonial
 Centennial Legion of Historic Military Commands [21240]
 Colonial Coin Collectors Club [22733]
 Colonial Coverlet Guild of Am. [21998]
 Colonial Order of the Acorn [20735]
 Company of Fifers and Drummers [10580]
 Descendants of Founders of New Jersey [20736]
 Flagon and Trencher - Descendants of Colonial Tavern Keepers [20737]
 Gen. Soc. of Colonial Wars [20738]
 Gen. Soc. of Mayflower Descendants [21247]
 Hereditary Order of the First Families of Massachusetts [20739]
 Holland Soc. of New York [20740]
 Huguenot Soc. of the Founders of Manakin in the Colony of Virginia [21162]
 Intl. Soc. Daughters of Utah Pioneers [21252]
 Jacques Timothe Boucher Sieur de Montbrun Heritage Soc. [20741]
 Jamestowne Soc. [20742]
 Lock Museum of Am. [9835]
 Natl. Soc. of the Colonial Dames of Am. [20743]
 Natl. Soc. Colonial Dames XVII Century [20744]
 Natl. Soc. Colonial Daughters of the 17th Century [20745]
 Natl. Soc., Daughters of the Amer. Colonists [20746]
 Natl. Soc. of Descendants of Lords of the Maryland Manors [20747]
 Natl. Soc., Sons of the Amer. Colonists [20748]
 Natl. Soc. of the Sons of Utah Pioneers [21254]
 Natl. Soc. Women Descendants of the Ancient and Honorable Artillery Company [20749]
 Newport Restoration Found. [10052]
 Order of Americans of Armorial Ancestry [20750]
 Order of Descendants of the Ancient and Honorable Artillery Company [20751]
 Order of Descendants of Colonial Physicians and Chirurgiens [20752]
 Order of First Families of Connecticut 1631-1662 [20753]
 Order of First Families of Rhode Island and Providence Plantations [20754]
 Order of the Founders and Patriots of Am. [20755]
 Patriotic Order Sons of Am. [21242]
 Pilgrim Edward Doty Soc. [20756]
 Pilgrim Soc. [21249]
 Pilgrims of the U.S. [21250]
 Plymouth Historical Soc. [20757]
 Reynolds Family Assn. [21032]
 Soc. of the Ark and the Dove [20758]
 Soc. of California Pioneers [21255]
 Soc. of Daughters of Holland Dames [20759]
 Soc. of the Descendants of the Colonial Clergy [20760]
 Soc. of the Founders and Friends of Norwich, Connecticut [10063]
 Soc. of Indiana Pioneers [21256]
 Sons of Colonial New England Natl. Soc. [20761]
 Sons and Daughters of Oregon Pioneers [21257]
 Sons and Daughters of Pioneer Rivermen [21258]
Colonial Arts Soc; Spanish [10005]
Colonial Coin Collectors Club [22733], c/o Roger Moore, Treas., 435 Camden Ave., Moorestown, NJ 08057
Colonial Coverlet Guild of Am. [21998], c/o Laurie Coolidge, 536 Arizona Ave., Glenwood, IL 60425
Colonial New England Natl. Soc; Sons of [20761]
Colonial Order of the Acorn [20735], 20 MacKenzie Glen, Greenwich, CT 06830, (203)661-3993
Colonial Rottweiler Club [22249], c/o Anthony DiCicco, Pres., 10 Oceanview Rd., Lynbrook, NY 11563, (516)593-6392
Colonial Soc. of Massachusetts [10104], 87 Mt. Vernon St., Boston, MA 02108, (617)227-2782
Colonial Soc. of Pennsylvania - Defunct.
Colonial Soc; Swedish [10991]
Colonial Tavern Keepers; Flagon and Trencher - Descendants of [20737]
Colonial Treasure Hunters Assn. - Address unknown since 2006.
Colonialism and Indigenous Minorities Research/Action [★IO]

Colony of Virginia; Huguenot Soc. of the Founders of Manakin in the [21162]
Color
 British Colour Makers Assn. [IO]
 Color Assn. of the U.S. [866]
 Color Marketing Gp. [867]
 Color Marketing Gp. [IO]
 Color Pigments Manufacturers Assn. [868]
 Eiseman Center for Color Info. and Training [6707]
 Inter-Society Color Coun. [6708]
 Inter-Society Color Coun. [IO]
 International Association of Color Manufacturers [IO]
 Intl. Assn. of Color Mfrs. [869]
 Intl. Color Consortium [870]
 Intl. Colour Assn. [IO]
 Intl. Tech. Caramel Assn. [1532]
 Japan Fashion Color Assn. [IO]
 Soc. of Dyers and Colourists - England [IO]
 Taos Natl. Soc. of Watercolorists [9476]
Color Assn. of the U.S. [866], 315 W 39th St., Studio 507, New York, NY 10018, (212)947-7774
Color-Bred Assn; Natl. [21853]
Color-Bred Judge Assn; Greater North Amer. [★21845]
Color and Craft Inst; Crayon, Water [★1799]
Color Guild Associates [2883]
Color Inst. of America - Defunct.
Color Inst; Pantone [★6707]
Color Mfrs. Assn; Certified [★869]
Color Manufacturers Assn; Dry [★868]
Color Marketing Gp. [867], 5845 Richmond Hwy., No. 410, Alexandria, VA 22303, (703)329-8500
Color Marketing Gp. [IO], Alexandria, VA, United States
Color; Natl. Inst. for Women of [★17541]
Color Pigments Manufacturers Assn. [868], PO Box 20839, Alexandria, VA 22320-1839, (703)684-4044
Color Print Soc; Amer. [9412]
Colorado Christian Univ. Alumni Assn. [18890], c/o Alumni Relations, 8787 W Alameda Ave., Lakewood, CO 80226, (303)963-3330
Colorado Medical Alumni Assn; Univ. of [18931]
Colorado Mining Assn. [2749], 216 16th St., Ste. 1250, Denver, CO 80202, (303)575-9199
Colorado Mining Assn. Educational Found. [★2749]
Colorado Ranger Horse Assn. [4873], c/o Laurel Kosior, Newsl. Ed./Exec. Sec., 1510 Greenhouse Rd., Wampum, PA 16157, (724)535-4841
Colorado River Assn. - Address unknown since 2005.
Colorectal Cancer Network [13815], PO Box 182, Kensington, MD 20895-0182, (301)879-1500
Colored Angora Goat Breeders Assn. [4782], c/o Laurie Lee, Treas., 5390 Piney Woods Rd., Riner, VA 24149, (540)797-8601
Colored Intercollegiate Athletic Assn. [★23811]
Colored Parents and Teachers; Natl. Cong. of [★8954]
Colored Pencil Soc. of Am. [9436], c/o Cynthia L. Haase, Membership Dir., 8156-E S Wadsworth Blvd., No. 184, Littleton, CO 80128, (303)972-9210
Colored Pencil Society of America [IO], Littleton, CO, United States
Colored People; Catholic Bd. for Mission Work Among the [★19601]
Colored People Legal Defense and Educational Fund; Natl. Assn. for the Advancement of [17130]
Colored People; Natl. Assn. for the Advancement of [17129]
Colored Women's Clubs; Natl. Assn. of [13051]
Colored Women's League; Natl. [★13051]
Colored Wool Growers Assn; Natural [5209]
Colorists of Am; Natl. Professional [★2990]
Colorists; Amer. Assn. of Textile Chemists and [7794]
Colorstone Assn; Indian Diamond and [2367]
Colosseum of Motion Picture Salesmen - Address unknown since 1995.
Colpomicroscopy; Amer. Soc. for Colposcopy and [★15590]
Colposcopy and Cervical Pathology; Amer. Soc. for [15590]
Colposcopy and Colpomicroscopy; Amer. Soc. for [★15590]

Reference to "IO" in place of a book number signifies that the association may be found in the 45th edition of International Organizations.

Encyclopedia of Associations, 46th Edition

3263

Colquhoun Soc. of North Am; Clan [20822]
Colson Family History Assn; Corson/ [20870]
Colt Boys Baseball; Pony and [★23124]
Colt Commemorative Collectors' Assn. - Defunct.
Columba House Fund [★17930]
Columba House Fund [★IO]
Columban Fathers [★19662]
Columban; Missionary Soc. of Saint [19662]
Columbia Basin Trust [IO], Castlegar, BC, Canada
Columbia Coll. of Nursing Alumni Assn. [18891],
   2121 E Newport Ave., Milwaukee, WI 53211-2952,
   (414)961-3530
Columbia Gay and Lesbian Alliance [★12224]
Columbia; Gay People at [★12224]
Columbia Historical Soc. [★10114]
Columbia Natl. Fisheries Res. Lab. [★7172]
Columbia Queer Alliance [12224], c/o NYU Off. of
   LGBT Student Services, Kimmel Ctr., 60
   Washington Sq. S, Ste. 602, New York, NY 10012
Columbia River Conservation League - Defunct.
Columbia River Salmon and Tuna Packers Assn. -
   Address unknown since 1995.
Columbia Scholastic Press Advisers Assn. [9010],
   Columbia Univ., Mail Code 5711, New York, NY
   10027-6902, (212)854-9400
Columbia Scholastic Press Assn. [9011], Columbia
   Univ., Mail Code 5711, New York, NY 10027-6902,
   (212)854-9400
Columbia School Press Advisers [★9010]
Columbia School Press Specialists [★9010]
Columbia Sheep Breeders Assn. of Am. [5201],
   15603 173rd Ave., Milo, IA 50166, (641)942-6402
Columbia Soc. of Electron Microscopy [IO], Bogota,
   Colombia
Columbian Squires [IO], New Haven, CT, United
   States
Columbian Squires [18999], 1 Columbus Plz., New
   Haven, CT 06510, (203)752-4400
Columbo Newsletter - Defunct.
Columbus: Countdown 1992 - Defunct.
Columbus; Daughters of [★18998]
Columbus Found; Before [10416]
Columbus; Knights of [19004]
Columbus Philatelic Soc; Christopher [22805]
Column Res. Coun. [★7714]
COM-U.S.A. [21845], c/o Bob Garguillo, Pres., Bob's
   Auto Radiator Ser., 400 Bloomfield Ave., Bloom-
   field, NJ 07003, (973)429-9353
Coma
   Coma Recovery Assn. [14029]
Coma Recovery Assn. [14029], 8300 Republic
   Airport, Ste. 106, Farmingdale, NY 11735,
   (631)756-1826
CoMamas Assn. [12148], PO Box 231804, Encini-
   tas, CA 92023-1804, (760)942-4572
Comanche Language and Cultural Preservation
   Comm. [10736], 1375 NE Cline Rd., Elgin, OK
   73538-3086, (580)492-5126
Comb Collectors Club Intl; Antique [21970]
Combat Correspondents Assn; U.S. Marine Corps
   [3171]
Combat Helicopter Pilots Assn. [20648], PO Box
   15852, Washington, DC 20003, (630)941-9215
Combat Martial Art Practitioners Assn. [23587], c/o
   John Frank Brado, Dir./Chief Instructor, 2277 E
   Elm St., Lima, OH 45804, (419)224-1409
Combat Merchant Mariners World War II - Defunct.
Combat Team Assn; 187th Airborne Regimental
   [20697]
Combat Team Assn; 517th Parachute Regimental
   [21381]
Combat Veterans Assn; Coast Guard [21295]
Combat Veterans Motorcycle Assn. [22675], 1019
   Highland, Liberty, MO 64068
Combat Veterans; Vietnam [21350]
Combed Yarn Spinners Assn. [★3774]
Combined Black Publishers - Defunct.
Combined Campaign for Amer. Reform Judaism
   [★20176]
Combined Edible Nut Trade Assn. [IO], London,
   United Kingdom
Combined Fed. Campaign; Natl. Hea. Agencies
   Comm. for the [★12200]
Combined Health Appeal of America - Address
   unknown since 2000.

Combined Heat and Power Assn. [IO], London,
   United Kingdom
Combined North Amer. Cottage Garden Soc. and
   North Amer. Dianthus Soc. [22507]
Combined Organizations of Numismatic Error Collec-
   tors of Am. [22734], c/o Mike Diamond, Pres., PO
   Box 6351, Rock Island, IL 61201, (479)253-5055
Combined Setter Clubs of America - Defunct.
Combined Training Assn; U.S. [★23535]
Combustion
   Combustion Inst. [6709]
   Natl. Threshers Assn. [9484]
Combustion Inst. [6709], 5001 Baum Blvd., Ste.
   635, Pittsburgh, PA 15213-1851, (412)687-1366
COMCARE Alliance [14346], 1701 K St. NW, 4th Fl.,
   Washington, DC 20006, (202)429-0574
Comedian Soc. for Amateurs and Professionals -
   Defunct.
Comedy
   Abbott and Costello Intl. Fan Club [24795]
   Abbott and Costello Official Fan Club [24796]
   The Andy Griffith Show Rerun Watchers Club
      [25025]
   Damfinos: The Intl. Buster Keaton Soc. [24797]
   Intl. Jack Benny Fan Club [24798]
   Intl. Jack Benny Fan Club [24798]
   Mark Slade Fan Club [24758]
   Marx Brotherhood [24832]
   Mary Jo Cattlett Fan Club [24759]
   Natl. Phyllis Diller Fan Club [24799]
   Peter Sellers Appreciation Soc. [24767]
   Skidrow Joe Fan Club [24773]
   Three Stooges Fan Club [24800]
   W.C. Fields Fan Club [24801]
   We Love Lucy/International Lucille Ball Fan Club
      [24776]
Comedy; Soc. to Preserve and Encourage Radio
   Drama, Variety and [22930]
Comedy Writers and Performers Assn. [★10211]
Comedy Writers and Performers Assn. [★10211]
Comenius World Coun. - Address unknown since
   1995.
Comercio e Industria; Camara Venezolano
   Americana de [★24305]
Comercio Latina de los EEUU; Camara de [★24354]
Comet Media Found. of Mumbai, India [IO], Bom-
   bay, India
ComexPeru Peruvian Foreign Trading Soc. [IO],
   Lima, Peru
ComexPeru Sociedad de Comercio Exterior del Peru
   [★IO]
Comhairle Chaomhnaithe Phortaigh na hEireann
   [★IO]
Comhairle Cluiche Corr na hEireann [★IO]
Comhairle Oilimpeach na hEireann [★IO]
Comhairle Sabhailteacht Naisiunta [★IO]
Comhairle Spoirt na hEireann [★IO]
Comhairle Treidlianna na Heireann [★IO]
Comhaltas Ceoltoiri Eireann [★IO]
Comhaontas na Siochana is Neodrachta [★IO]
Comhlamh [IO], Dublin, Ireland
Comic Arts Soc; Christian [9435]
Comic Book Retailers Intl. - Address unknown since
   2003.
Comic Relief [IO], London, United Kingdom
Comics
   Alpha Omega Assn. [9537]
   Christian Comic Arts Soc. [9435]
   Comics Magazine Assn. of America [3219]
   Friends of Lulu [22134]
   Horror Writers Assn. [11174]
   Interlac [22042]
   Intl. Comic Arts Assn. [9447]
   Natl. Assn. of Comics Art Educators [8115]
Comics Code Authority [★3219]
Comics Creators Guild [IO], London, United
   Kingdom
Comics Entertainment Retailers; Professional Assn.
   of [9523]
Comics Magazine Assn. of America [3219]
Coming Out Day; Natl. [12248]
Comision Andina de Juristas [★IO]
Comision Catolica Internacional de Migracion [★IO]
Comision para la Conservacion de los Recursos Vi-
   vos Marinos Antarticos [★IO]

Comision Economica para Am. Latina y el Caribe
   [★IO]
Comision de Integracion Energetica Regional [★IO]
Comision Mexicana de Defensa y Promocion de los
   Derechos Humanos [★IO]
Comision Nacional de Badminton del Peru [IO],
   Lima, Peru
Comision Nacional de Seguridad Nuclear y Salva-
   guardias [★IO]
Comision Panamericana de Normas Tecnicas [★IO]
Comision Permanente del Pacifico Sur [★IO]
Comissione Internationale per la Protezione delle
   Alpi [★IO]
Comitato Collaborazione Medica [★IO]
Comitato di Coordinamento dell Organizzazioni per il
   Servizio Volontario [IO], Milan, Italy
Comitato Italiano Atlantico [★IO]
Comitato Italiano Paralimpico [★IO]
Comitato Olimpico Nazionale Sammarinese [IO],
   Serravalle, San Marino
Comite europeen de normalisation electrotechnique
   [★IO]
Comite europeen des constructeurs de machines
   pour plastiques et caoutchouc [★IO]
Comite canadien de catalogage [★IO]
Comite intergouvernemental de recherches urbaines
   et regionales [★IO]
Comite europeen de normalization bancaire [★IO]
Comite de Am. Latina y el Caribe para la Defensa
   de los Derechos de la Mujer [★IO]
Comite Argentino del Consejo Mundial de la Energia
   [★IO]
Comite Belge de la Distribution [★IO]
Comite Belge pour l'Investigation Scientifique des
   Phenomenes Reputes Pananormaux [IO], Brus-
   sels, Belgium
Comite Canada-Israel [★IO]
Comite Canadien d'Action sur le Statut de la Femme
   [★IO]
Comite Central des Armateurs de France [★IO]
Comite du Commerce des cereals, aliments du be-
   tail, oleagineux, huile d'olive, huiles et graisses et
   agrofourniture [★IO]
Comite des Constructeurs Francais d'Automobiles
   [★IO]
Comite Consultatif Economique et Industriel aupres
   de l'O.C.D.E. [★IO]
Comite Coordinador de Asociaciones Agricolas,
   Comerciales, Industriales y Financieras [★IO]
Comite de Coordination des Actions des ONG au
   Mali [★IO]
Comite de Coordination des Actions des Organisa-
   tions Non Gouvernementales [IO], Bamako, Mali
Comite Coordonnateur Canadien pour la Consolida-
   tion de la Paix [★IO]
Comite d'Andorra per l'UNICEF [★IO]
Comite Electrotechnique Belge [★IO]
Comite Espanol de la Camara de Comercio Interna-
   cional [IO], Barcelona, Spain
Comite Europeen des Associations de Constructeurs
   d'Engrenages et d'Elements de Transmission
   [★IO]
Comite Europeen des Associations d'interet Gen.
   [★IO]
Comite Europeen des Assurances [★IO]
Comite Europeen des Assurances [★IO]
Comite Europeen des Constructeurs de Fours et
   Equipements Thermiques Industriels [★IO]
Comite Europeen de Droit Rural [★IO]
Comite Europeen de Droit Rural [★IO]
Comite Europeen des Economistes de la Constr.
   [★IO]
Comite Europeen des Equipements Techniques du
   Batiment [★IO]
Comite Europeen des Fabricants de Sucre [★IO]
Comite Europeen des Groupements de Construc-
   teurs du Machinisme Agricole [★IO]
Comite Europeen pour l'Enseignement Catholique
   [★IO]
Comite Europeen de Liaison des Importateurs de
   Machines-Outils [★IO]
Comite Europeen de Liaison Pour la Cellulose et le
   Papier [★IO]
Comite Europeen de l'Industrie de la Robinetterie
   [★IO]

A star before a book entry number signifies that the name is not listed separately, but is mentioned within the entry.

Comite Europeen de Normalisation [★IO]

Comite des Fabricants de Levure de Panification de l'Union Europeenne [★IO]

Comite Francais de Lutte contre l'HyperTension Arterielle [★IO]

Comite Francais pour les Travaux sans Tranchee [★IO]

Comite des Indus. Lainieres de l'Union Europeenne [★IO]

Comite Intl. pour le Controle des Performances en Elevage [★IO]

Comite Intl. de Cooperation dans les Recherches Nationales en Demographie [★IO]

Comite Intl. de la Croix-Rouge [★IO]

Comite Intl. d'Histoire de la Deuxieme Guerre Mondiale [★IO]

Comite Intl. de l'Inspection Technique Auto. [★IO]

Comite Intl. de Medecine Militaire [★IO]

Comite Intl. pour la Metrologie Historique [★IO]

Comite Intl. Olympique [★IO]

Comite Intl. des Plastiques en Agriculture [★IO]

Comite Intl. pour la Protection des Cables Sousmarins [★IO]

Comite Intl. Radio-Maritime [★IO]

Comite Intl. de la Rayonne et des Fibres Synthetiques [★IO]

Comite Intl. des Sciences Historiques [★IO]

Comite Intl. du The [★IO]

Comite Intl. des Transports Ferroviaires [★IO]

Comite des eches pour l'Atlantique Centre-Est [★IO]

Comite pour l'elimination de la discrimination raciale [★IO]

Comite pour l'Europe occidentale contre la corrosion des conduites souterraines [★IO]

Comite canadien sur l'histoire du travail [★IO]

Comite Marche Commun de l'Industrie des Englais Azate [★IO]

Comite Maritime Intl. [★IO]

Comite de Mexico y Aztlan - Defunct.

Comite Mundial de Consulta de los Amigos [★IO]

Comite Nacional Pro Defensa de la Flora y Fauna [IO], Santiago, Chile

Comite Natl. pour la Cooperation Economique avec la Region du Pacifique [★IO]

Comite Nationale de Lutte contre le SIDA [★IO]

Comite Olimpico Brasileiro [★IO]

Comite Olimpico Colombiano [★IO]

Comite Olimpico Ecuatoriano [★IO]

Comite Olimpico Guatemalteco [★IO]

Comite Olimpico Mexicano [★IO]

Comite Olimpico de Portugal [★IO]

Comite Olympique Bulgare [★IO]

Comite Olympique Egyptien [★IO]

Comite Olympique Hongrois [★IO]

Comite des Organisations Professionnelles Agricoles de l'EU [★IO]

Comite Para [★IO]

Comite Paralimpico Angolano [IO], Luanda, Angola

Comite Paralimpico Espanol [★IO]

Comite Paralympique Canadien [★IO]

Comite Permanent des Indus. du Verre Europeennes [★IO]

Comite Permanent de Liaison des Orthophonistes-Logopedes de l'UE [★IO]

Comite para la Promocion y el Progreso de las Cooperativas [★IO]

Comite pour la Recherche Spatiale [★IO]

Comite Royal Belge de la Distribution [IO], Brussels, Belgium

Comite Salvadoreno Oscar Romero - Defunct.

Comite Scientifique pour l'Allocation des Frequences a la Radio Astronomie et la Recherche Spatiale [★IO]

Comite Scientifique sur les Problemes de l'Environnement [★IO]

Comite UNICEF Canada [★IO]

Comitetul Natl. Roman al Consiliului Mondial al Energiei [IO], Bucharest, Romania

Command Trust Network [16896], 11301 W Olympic Blvd., Ste. 332, Los Angeles, CA 90064

Commanderie des Cordons Bleus de France - Address unknown since 2000.

Commando Assn; Air [21277]

Commemorative Air Force [21438], PO Box 62000, Midland, TX 79711-2000, (432)563-1000

Commemorative Art; Amer. Inst. of [2771]

Commemorative Coins; Soc. for U.S. [22760]

Commemorative Collectors Soc. [IO], Newark, United Kingdom

Commemorative Soc; Postal [22859]

Commentators International; Professional Floral [★1493]

Commerce; Aftermarket Coun. on Electronic [3835]

Commerce; Alliance Against Fraud in Telemarketing and Electronic [17302]

Commerce Alumni Assn; Texas A&M Univ. - [18926]

Commerce Assn; Internet Local Advt. and [★737]

Commerce; Chinese Amer. Assn. of [24308]

Commerce Commn; Assn. of Practitioners Before the Interstate [★6316]

Commerce Commn. Practitioners; Assn. of Interstate [★6316]

Commerce in Hemp; Bus. Alliance for [18283]

Commerce and Indus; American-Arab Assn. for [★24357]

Commerce and Indus. Assn; Korea-America [★24350]

Commerce Publications; Amer. Assn. of [★24257]

Commerce Queensland [IO], Brisbane, Australia

Commerce Transactions; Americans for Fair Electronic [17441]

Commerce; U.S. Chamber of [24301]

CommerceNet [7727], 169 Univ. Ave., Palo Alto, CA 94301, (650)289-4040

Commercial Alert [18391], PO Box 19002, Washington, DC 20036, (202)387-8030

Commercial Archeology; Soc. for [9485]

Commercial Assn. Macao [★IO]

Commercial Assn. of Portugal [IO], Porto, Portugal

Commercial Boat Operators Assn. [IO], London, United Kingdom

Commercial Builders Council; National [★1035]

Commercial Chem. Development Assn. [★6677]

Commercial Collectors Assn; Amer. [★1147]

Commercial Development Assn. [★6677]

Commercial Development and Marketing Assn. [6677], 3 Park Ave., 19th Fl., New York, NY 10016-5991, (203)702-7667

Commercial Diving Educators; Assn. of [23960]

Commercial Exchange of Philadelphia - Defunct.

Commercial Executives; Amer. Assn. of [★24251]

Commercial Farmers' Bur. [★IO]

Commercial Finance Association [IO], New York, NY, United States

Commercial Finance Assn. [2423], 225 W 34th St., Ste. 1815, New York, NY 10122, (212)594-3490

Commercial Finance Assn; Natl. [★2423]

Commercial Finance Attorneys; Assn. of [5485]

Commercial Finance Companies of New York; Assn. of [★2423]

Commercial Finance Conf; Natl. [★2423]

Commercial Floriculture; SAF - The Center for [★1493]

Commercial Food Equip. Ser. Agencies of Am. [★1571]

Commercial Food Equip. Ser. Assn. [1571], 2216 W Meadowview Rd., Ste. 100, Greensboro, NC 27407, (336)346-4700

Commercial Horticultural Assn. [IO], Kenilworth, United Kingdom

Commercial and Indus. Assn. of Northern Rhodesia [★IO]

Commercial Internet Exchange Assn. [★911]

Commercial Labs; Amer. Coun. of [★7236]

Commercial Law

Amer. Bankruptcy Inst. [5574]

Amer. Coll. of Bankruptcy [5575]

Assn. of Bus. Recovery Professionals [IO]

Bankruptcy Assn. of England and Wales [IO]

Commercial Law Assn. of Australia [IO]

Commercial Law League of Am. [5576]

Forfeiture Endangers Amer. Rights [5577]

Natl. Assn. of Bankruptcy Trustees [5578]

Natl. Assn. of Shareholder and Consumer Attorneys [5579]

Commercial Law Assn. of Australia [IO], Sydney, Australia

Commercial Law League of Am. [5576], 70 E Lake St., Ste. 630, Chicago, IL 60601, (312)781-2000

Commercial Mgt; Intl. Assn. for Contract and [772]

Commercial Mortgage Securities Assn. [3304], 30 Broad St., 28th Fl., New York, NY 10004, (212)509-1844

Commercial Newspapers; Amer. Court and [3202]

Commercial Off. of Spain [24376], 405 Lexington Ave., 44th Fl., New York, NY 10174-0331, (212)661-4959

Commercial Org. Secretaries; Natl. Assn. of [★24251]

Commercial Photographers Intl. [2995], 229 Peachtree St. NE, Ste. 2200, Atlanta, GA 30303-1608, (866)886-4989

Commercial Plant Breeders; Natl. Coun. of [5175]

Commercial Producers; Assn. of Independent [90]

Commercial Product Acquisition Team - Defunct.

Commercial Radio Australia [IO], Surry Hills, Australia

Commercial Real Estate; NAIOP - The Assn. for [★3320]

Commercial Real Estate Secondary Market and Securitization Assn. - Address unknown since 2004.

Commercial Receivable Companies; Natl. Conf. of [★2423]

Commercial Records Centers; Assn. of [★2109]

Commercial Recreation Assn; Resort and [3361]

Commercial Refrigerator Mfrs. Div. [1878], 4100 N Fairfax Dr., Ste. 200, Arlington, VA 22203, (703)524-8800

Commercial Refrigerator Manufacturers Div. [★1873]

Commercial Secretaries; Central Assn. of [★24251]

Commercial Seed Technologists; Soc. of [5176]

Commercial TV Australia [★IO]

Commercial Trailer Assn. [IO], London, United Kingdom

Commercial Travelers of Am; Order of United [19135]

Commercial Travelers Assn. - Address unknown since 2002.

Commercial Travelers Insurance Fed. - Defunct.

Commercial Vehicle Safety Alliance [355], c/o Mr. Stephen F. Campbell, Exec. Dir., 1101 17th St. NW, Ste. 803, Washington, DC 20036, (202)775-1623

Commercial Vehicle Safety Alliance [IO], Washington, DC, United States

Commercial Vehicle Solutions Network [382], 5121 Bowden Rd., Ste. 303, Jacksonville, FL 32216-5950, (904)737-2900

Commercial Weather Services Assn. [7326], c/o Steven Root, CCM, Chm., WeatherBank, Inc., 1015 Waterwood Pkwy., Edmond, OK 73034

Commercial Workers Intl. Union; United Food and [24061]

Commerciales; Assn. Internationale Des Etudiants en Sciences Economiques et [★8012]

Commissie Justitia et Pax Nederland [★IO]

Commn. canadienne du lait [★IO]

Commn. for Accountability to the Public - Address unknown since 2001.

Commission on Accreditation of Allied Hea. Educ. Programs [★15123]

Commn. on Accreditation of Allied Hea. Educ. Programs [8832], 1361 Park St., Clearwater, FL 33756, (727)210-2350

Commn. on Accreditation of Ambulance Services [13532], 1926 Waukegan Rd., Ste. 1, Glenview, IL 60025-1770, (847)657-6828

Commn. on Accreditation for Law Enforcement Agencies [5967], 10302 Eaton Pl., Ste. 100, Fairfax, VA 22030-2215, (703)352-4225

Commn. on Accreditation for Marriage and Family Therapy Educ. [8819], c/o Amer. Assn. for Marriage and Family Therapy, 112 S Alfred St., Alexandria, VA 22314, (703)838-9808

Commn. on Accreditation of Rehabilitation Facilities Canada [IO], Edmonton, AB, Canada

Commn. on Accreditation of Rehabilitation Facilities; CARF, [★16318]

Commn. on Accreditation of Ser. Experiences [★8406]

Commn. of Accredited Truck Driving Schools - Defunct.

Commn. Adhoc Congolaise de Badminton [IO], Brazzaville, Republic of the Congo

Commn. on Administrative Affairs - Defunct.

Reference to "IO" in place of a book number signifies that the association may be found in the 45th edition of International Organizations.

Encyclopedia of Associations, 46th Edition

3265

Commn. for the Advancement of Public Interest Orgs. [17317]

Commn. Africaine Des Droits De L'Homme et Des Peuples [★IO]

Commn. Africaine de l'Aviation Civile [★IO]

Commn. on Air Pollution Prevention of VDI and DIN - Standards Comm. [IO], Dusseldorf, Germany

Commission on Amer. and Intl. Schools Abroad [★8296]

Commn. on Archives and History of the United Methodist Church [★10467]

Commn. on Benevolent Institutions [★13165]

Commn. of the Bishops' Conferences of the European Community [IO], Brussels, Belgium

Commn. Canadienne du Ble [★IO]

Commn. for Case Manager Certification [14703], 300 N Martingale Rd., Ste. 460, Schaumburg, IL 60173, (847)944-1330

Commn. for Certification in Geriatric Pharmacy [15930], 1321 Duke St., Alexandria, VA 22314, (703)535-3036

Commn. on Certification of Work Adjustment and Vocational Evaluation Specialists [8407], 300 N Martingale Rd., Ste. 460, Schaumburg, IL 60173, (847)944-1340

Commn. on Church Architecture - Defunct.

Commn. of the Churches on the Intl. Affairs [20094], c/o Rev. Deborah DeWinter, Programme Exec. for the U.S., 475 Riverside Dr., Rm. 1371, New York, NY 10115, (212)870-3260

Commission of the Churches on International Affairs [IO], New York, NY, United States

Commn. du Codex Alimentarius [★IO]

Commn. on Collegiate Nursing Educ. [8859], 1 Dupont Cir. NW, Ste. 530, Washington, DC 20036, (202)887-6791

Commn. for the Conservation of Antarctic Marine Living Resources [IO], North Hobart, Australia

Commn. on Correctional Facilities and Services of the Amer. Bar Assn. - Defunct.

Commn. on Crime Prevention and Criminal Justice [IO], Vienna, Austria

Commn. De la Carte Geologique du Monde [★IO]

Commission on Dental Accreditation [★14121]

Commn. on Dietetic Registration [15550], 120 S Riverside Plz., Ste. 2000, Chicago, IL 60606-6995, (312)899-0040

Commn. on Dietetic Registration [IO], Chicago, IL, United States

Commission on Disability Examiner Certification [★14575]

Commn. Du Pacific Sud [★IO]

Commn. on Education in Agriculture and Natural Resources - Defunct.

Commn. Electrotechnique Internationale [★IO]

Commission on Elementary Schools [★8277]

Commn. on Emergency Medical Services - Defunct.

Commn. des Episcopats de la Communaute Europeenne [★IO]

Commn. Europeenne Consultative pour les Peches dans les Eaux Interieures [★IO]

Commn. Europeenne du Tourisme [★IO]

Commn. on Folk Law and Legal Pluralism [★IO]

Commn. de la Fonction Publique Internationle [★IO]

Commn. de la Fonction Publique Internationle [★24143]

Commn. for Foreign Veterinary Graduates; Educational [★16779]

Commn. Francaise Justice et Paix [★IO]

Commn. on Gay/Lesbian Issues in Social work Educ. [★9132]

Commn. Generale des Peches pour la Mediterranee [★IO]

Commn. for the Geological Map of the World [IO], Paris, France

Commn. on Graduates of Foreign Nursing Schools [15473], 3600 Market St., Ste. 400, Philadelphia, PA 19104, (215)222-8454

Commn. on Hea. and Healing [★20241]

Commission on Higher Education [★8277]

Commn. on the Humanities - Defunct.

Commission on Independent Schools [★8296]

Commission on Institutions of Higher Education [★8296]

Commn. on Instructional Technology - Defunct.

Commn. on Intl. Affairs [★17832]

Commn. on Intl. Affairs [★IO]

Commn. for Intl. Development - Address unknown since 1995.

Commn. for Intl. Due Process of Law - Address unknown since 1994.

Commn. on Intl. Programs [17832], c/o Natl. Assn. of State Universities and Land-Grant Colleges, 1307 New York Ave. NW, Ste. 400, Washington, DC 20005-4722, (202)478-6040

Commn. on Intl. Programs [IO], Washington, DC, United States

Commn. on Intl. Relations [IO], Geneva, Switzerland

Commn. on Intl. Trade and Investment Policy - Defunct.

Commn. Internationale des Aumoniers Genereaux des Prisons [★IO]

Commn. Internationale pour la Conservation des Thonides de l'Atlantique [★IO]

Commn. Internationale de Demographie Historique [★IO]

Commn. Internationale d'Optique [★IO]

Commn. Internationale du Genie Rural [★IO]

Commn. Internationale des Grands Barrages [★IO]

Commn. Internationale des Indus. Agricoles et Alimentaires [★IO]

Commn. Internationale des Irrigations et du Drainage [★IO]

Commn. Internationale de Juristes [★IO]

Commn. Internationale de Juristes - Sect. Canadienne [★IO]

Commn. Internationale de l'Eclairage [★IO]

Commn. Internationale de l'Enseignement Mathematique [★IO]

Commn. Internationale de l'Etat Civil [★IO]

Commn. Internationale pour l'Histoire des Assemblees d'Etats [★IO]

Commn. Internationale pour l'Histoire des Villes [★IO]

Commn. Internationale pour l'Unification des Methodes d'Analyse du Sucre [★IO]

Commn. Internationale de Microflore du Paleozoique [IO], Nottingham, United Kingdom

Commn. Internationale de Nomenclature Zoologique [★IO]

Commn. Internationale de Numismatique [★IO]

Commn. Internationale des Oeufs [★IO]

Commn. Internationale des Peches de la Baltique [★IO]

Commn. Internationale Permanente pour l'Epreuve des Armes a Feu Portatives [★IO]

Commn. Internationale pour la Protection des Alpes [★IO]

Commn. Internationale du Riz [★IO]

Commn. Internationale de la Sante au Travail [★IO]

Commn. Internationale Technique de Sucrerie [★IO]

Commn. on Interracial Cooperation [★17156]

Commn. Intersyndicale des Deshydrateurs Europeens [★IO]

Commn. on Jewish Chaplaincy [★19751]

Commn. Justice and Peace, Netherlands [IO], The Hague, Netherlands

Commn. on Law and Aging [5935], c/o Amer. Bar Assn., 740 15th St. NW, Washington, DC 20005-1022, (202)662-8690

Commn. on Legal Pluralism [IO], Fredericton, NB, Canada

Commn. on Legal Problems of the Elderly [★5935]

Commn. for Local Admin. in England [IO], London, United Kingdom

Commn. for Local Admin. in Wales [IO], Pencoed, United Kingdom

Commn. de l'Ocean Indien [★IO]

Commn. canadienne pour l'unesco [★IO]

Commn. Luxembourgeoise - Justice et Paix [IO], Luxembourg, Luxembourg

Commn. on Marriage and Family Life - Defunct.

Commn. on Mathematics of Coll. Entrance Examination Bd. - Defunct.

Commn. on the Mentally Disabled [★5781]

Commn. des migrations, des refugies, et de la Population [★IO]

Commn. on Missing and Exploited Children [11586], 616 Adams Ave., Memphis, TN 38105, (901)405-8441

Commn. on Money and Credit - Defunct.

Commn. for Music Res. of the Austrian Acad. of Sciences [IO], Vienna, Austria

Commn. for Mycenaean Res. [★IO]

Commn. on Natl. Parks and Protected Areas [★IO]

Commn. Nationale d'Israel pour l'UNESCO [★IO]

Commn. on Nuclear Physics [IO], Adelaide, Australia

Commn. Oceanographique Intergouvernementale [★IO]

Commn. on Opticianry Accreditation [15706], c/o Ellen Stoner, Dir. of Accreditation, PO Box 4342, Chapel Hill, NC 27515, (703)468-0566

Commn. on Outreach and Synagogue Community [20133], The Union for Reform Judaism, Dept. of Outreach and Synagogue Community, 633 3rd Ave., New York, NY 10017-6778, (212)650-4230

Commn. des Pares Nationaux et [★IO]

Commn. de Pastorale Sociale - Caritas Mali [IO], Bamako, Mali

Commn. on Peace and Human Rights [★18242]

Commn. on Presidential Debates [18350], 1200 New Hampshire Ave. NW, PO Box 445, Washington, DC 20036, (202)872-1020

Commn. on Private Philanthropy and Public Needs - Defunct.

Commn. on Professional and Hospital Activities - Address unknown since 2002.

Commn. on Professional Rights and Responsibilities - Defunct.

Commn. on Professionals in Sci. and Tech. [7604], 1200 New York Ave. NW, Ste. 113, Washington, DC 20005, (202)326-7080

Commission on Public Elementary and Middle Schools [★8296]

Commission on Public Secondary Schools [★8296]

Commn. for Racial Equality [IO], London, United Kingdom

Commn. for Racial Justice [★20608]

Commn. on Rehabilitation Counselor Certification [11822], 300 N Martingale Rd., Ste. 460, Schaumburg, IL 60173, (847)944-1325

Commission for Relief in Belgium [★9736]

Commn. on Religious Counseling and Healing [19445], c/o Fr. Timothy Kjera, Moderator, PO Box 16201, Duluth, MN 55816-0201, (202)448-2948

Commission on Religious Counseling and Healing [IO], Duluth, MN, United States

Commn. on Res. in Pastoral Care and Counseling of the Congress on Ministry in specialized settings - Defunct.

Commn. on Rural Water - Defunct.

Commission on Secondary Schools [★8277]

Commn. Seismologique Europeenne [★IO]

Commn. on Sexual Orientation and Gender Expression [★9132]

Commn. on Social Action of Reform Judaism [★20177]

Commn. for Social Justice [17108], 219 E St. NE, Washington, DC 20002, (202)547-2900

Commn. on Software Issues in the 80s - Defunct.

Commn. on Standardization of Biological Stains [★6571]

Commn. on the Status of Jewish War Orphans in Europe, Amer. Sect. - Defunct.

Commn. on the Status of Women [17521], c/o Dept. of Economic and Social Affairs, Div. for the Advancement of Women, 2 UN Plz., DC2-12th Fl., New York, NY 10017, (212)963-3463

Commn. on the Status of Women [IO], New York, NY, United States

Commn. to Study the Org. of Peace - Defunct.

Commn. on the Stud. of Peace [★18242]

Commn. Syndicale Consultative aupres de l'OCDE [★IO]

Commission on Tech. and Career Institutions [★8296]

Commn. on Undergraduate Educ. in the Biological Sciences [★9098]

Commn. on U.S.-African Relations - Defunct.

Commn. on U.S.-Asian Relations [★17010]

Commn. on U.S.-Asian Relations [★IO]

Commn. on U.S.-Latin Amer. Relations - Defunct.

Commn. on U.S.-Russian Relations - Defunct.

Commn. on Voluntary Ser. and Action [★13391]

Commn. on Women in the Profession [5936], c/o Amer. Bar Assn., 321 N Clark St., 18th Fl., Chicago, IL 60610, (312)988-5715

A star before a book entry number signifies that the name is not listed separately, but is mentioned within the entry.

Comm. for Women's Equality **[17522]**, c/o Amer. Jewish Cong., 825 3rd Ave., Ste. 1800, New York, NY 10022, (212)879-4500

Comm. on the Year 2000 of the Amer. Acad. of the Arts and Sciences - Defunct.

Comm. on Youth Ser. Projects **[★13391]**

Commissionaires Canada **[★IO]**

Commissioned Officers Assn. of the U.S. Public Hea. Ser. **[6214]**, 8201 Corporate Dr., Ste. 200, Landover, MD 20785, (301)731-9080

Commissioners Assn; Collegiate **[23815]**

Commissioners; Assn. of Film **[★1368]**

Commissioners; Natl. Assn. of Securities **[★3521]**

Commissioners; Natl. Assn. of State Racing **[★6240]**

Commissioners, Secretaries and Directors of Agriculture; Natl. Assn. of **[★5439]**

Commissioners; Southeastern Assn. of Game and Fish **[★5734]**

Commissioners on Uniform State Laws; Natl. Conf. of **[6282]**

Commissions, and Councils of Catholic Educ; Natl. Assn. of Boards, **[8056]**

A Commitment to Training and Employment for Women **[IO]**, Toronto, ON, Canada

Comm. for 10 **[★18288]**

Comm. for 12 **[★18288]**

Comm. for 15 **[★18288]**

Comm. of 21 - Address unknown since 2003.

Comm. 51st State for Puerto Rico **[18490]**

Committee of 100 **[★17130]**

Committee of 100 - Address unknown since 2002.

Comm. of 100 in Finland **[IO]**, Helsinki, Finland

Comm. of 200 **[713]**, 980 N Michigan Ave., Ste. 1575, Chicago, IL 60611-7540, (312)255-0296

Comm. to Abolish the Fed - Address unknown since 1991.

Comm. to Abolish HUAC/HISC **[★17134]**

Comm. to Abolish Sport Hunting **[11380]**, PO Box 562, New Paltz, NY 12561, (845)256-1400

Committee on Accreditation of Canadian Medical Schools **[★8839]**

Comm. on Accreditation for Educational Programs for the EMS Professions **[8833]**, 1248 Hardwood Rd., Bedford, TX 76021, (817)283-9403

Comm. on Accreditation of Medical Transport Systems **[14347]**, PO Box 130, Sandy Springs, SC 29677, (864)287-4177

Committee on Accreditation of Medical Transport Systems **[IO]**, Sandy Springs, SC, United States

Comm. on Accreditation for Opthalmic Medical Personnel **[8834]**, 2025 Woodlane Dr., St. Paul, MN 55125-2998, (800)284-3937

Comm. on Accreditation for Respiratory Care **[16610]**, 1248 Harwood Rd., Bedford, TX 76021-4244, (817)283-2835

Comm. for Accuracy in Middle East Reporting in Am. **[18055]**, PO Box 35040, Boston, MA 02135-0001, (617)789-3672

Comm. for Accuracy in Middle East Reporting in Am. **[IO]**, Boston, MA, United States

Comm. for Action for Rural Indians - Defunct.

Committee for the Advancement of Cotton **[★1095]**

Comm. for the Advancement of Role-Playing Games **[22463]**, 1127 Cedar, Bonham, TX 75418, (903)583-9296

Comm. for the Advancement of Stem Cell Res. **[18542]**

Comm. of Advt. Practice **[IO]**, London, United Kingdom

Comm. Against Anti-Asian Violence **[17006]**, 2473 Valentine Ave., Bronx, NY 10458, (718)220-7391

Comm. Against Govt. Secrecy - Address unknown since 1995.

Comm. Against Govt. Waste - Defunct.

Comm. Against the Political Misuse of Psychiatry - Defunct.

Comm. Against Registration and the Draft - Defunct.

Comm. to Aid Democratic Dissidents in Yugoslavia - Defunct.

Comm. on Allied Hea. Educ. and Accreditation **[★8832]**

Comm. on Amer. East Asian Relations - Defunct.

Comm. on Amer. Lib. Resources on South Asia **[★10349]**

Comm. on Amer. Lib. Resources on South Asia **[★IO]**

Comm. on Amer. Lib. Resources on Southeast Asia **[★IO]**

Comm. on Amer. Lib. Resources on Southeast Asia **[★10349]**

Comm. for Amer. Principles - Defunct.

Comm. of Amer. Steamship Lines **[★6059]**

Comm. of Amer. Tanker Owners - Defunct.

Comm. of Amer. Youth Involvement - Defunct.

Comm. of Americans for Peace in the Middle East - Defunct.

Comm. for the Americas - Defunct.

Comm. of Annuity Insurers **[2156]**, c/o Davis and Harman LLP, 1455 Pennsylvania Ave. NW, Ste. 1200, Washington, DC 20004, (202)347-2230

Comm. for Application of Behavioral Sciences to Strategies of Peace - Defunct.

Comm. on Art Gallery of the East - Address unknown since 1995.

Comm. for Artistic and Intellectual Freedom in Iran - Address unknown since 1995.

Comm. for Asian Women **[IO]**, Bangkok, Thailand

Comm. on Assessing the Progress of Educ. **[★9253]**

Comm. to Assure the Availability of Casein - Defunct.

Comm. of Atomic Bomb Survivors in the U.S. **[18144]**, 1759 Sutter St., San Francisco, CA 94115, (562)698-0855

Comm. on Autonomous Groups - Address unknown since 1995.

Comm. to Award Miss Piggy the Oscar - Defunct.

Comm. for Awareness About Furs - Defunct.

Comm. for Better Cable TV - Defunct.

Comm. for Better Transit - Defunct.

Comm. of Black Americans for Truth About the Middle East - Defunct.

Comm. of Black Gay Men - Address unknown since 1995.

Comm. on Boarding Schools **[★9018]**

Comm. to Bridge the Gap **[18145]**, 1637 Butler Ave., Ste. 203, Los Angeles, CA 90025, (310)478-0829

Comm. to Bring Nazi War Criminals to Justice in the U.S.A. - Defunct.

Comm. on Canada-U.S. Relations - Defunct.

Comm. on Canadian Labour History **[★IO]**

Comm. to Cap the Natl. Debt - Address unknown since 1999.

Comm. on Capacity Building Sci. **[9099]**, FERMI-LAB, PO Box 500, Batavia, IL 60510-0500, (630)840-3000

Comm. on Capacity Building Sci. **[IO]**, Batavia, IL, United States

Comm. on the Care of Children - Defunct.

Comm. for the Caribbean **[★12421]**

Comm. for the Caribbean **[★IO]**

Comm. for Catholic Unity **[★19726]**

Comm. for Children **[11587]**, 568 1st Ave. S, Ste. 600, Seattle, WA 98104-2804, (206)343-1223

Comm. of Chinese Correspondence - Address unknown since 1999.

Comm. of the Christian Bros; Regional Educ. **[★8060]**

Comm. on Christian Literature for Women and Children **[★12376]**

Comm. on Christian Literature for Women and Children **[★IO]**

Comm. on Clay Minerals of the Natl. Acad. of Sciences—National Res. Coun. **[7341]**

Comm. on Codes and Standards - Defunct.

Comm. for Collective Security - Defunct.

Comm. on Common Problems of Genetics, Paleontology and Systematics of Natl. Res. Coun. **[★7073]**

Comm. on Common Security - Address unknown since 1994.

Comm. for Common Sense Divorce - Defunct.

Comm. for Common Sense Speed Laws - Defunct.

Comm. on Comparative Urban Economics - Defunct.

Comm. of Concerned Africans - Defunct.

Comm. of Concerned Artists and Professionals - Address unknown since 1995.

Comm. of Concerned Asian Scholars - Defunct.

Comm. of Concerned Catholics - Defunct.

Comm. of Concerned Journalists **[3105]**, Natl. Press Bldg., 529 14th St. NW, Ste. 450, Washington, DC 20045, (202)662-7155

Comm. of Concerned Parents **[★5869]**

Comm. of Concerned Parents **[★IO]**

Comm. of Concerned Scientists **[17752]**, 145 W 79th St., Ste. 4D, New York, NY 10024, (212)362-4441

Comm. for Conservation and Care of Chimpanzees - Defunct.

Comm. for Constitutional Govt. - Address unknown since 1995.

Comm. for Constitutional Integrity - Defunct.

Comm. on the Constitutional Sys. **[17289]**, 1400 20th St. NW, No. 912, Washington, DC 20036, (202)387-8787

Comm. for a Constructive Tomorrow **[17318]**, PO Box 65722, Washington, DC 20035, (202)429-2737

Comm. for Consumers No-Fault - Defunct.

Comm. on Continuing Education for School Personnel - Defunct.

Comm. on Contracting Out - Defunct.

Comm. for Coordination of Investigations of the Lower Mekong **[★IO]**

Comm. for the Coordination of Natl. Bibliographic Control - Defunct.

Comm. for Corporate Support of Private Universities - Defunct.

Comm. for Correspondence - Defunct.

Comm. on Cosmic Humanism - Defunct.

Comm. for Crescent Observation Intl. **[10246]**, 1069 Ellis Hollow Rd., Ithaca, NY 14850, (607)277-6706

Comm. for Crescent Observation Intl. **[IO]**, Ithaca, NY, United States

Comm. of Cuban Youth Orgs. in Exile - Address unknown since 1995.

Comm. on Data for Sci. and Tech. **[IO]**, Paris, France

Comm. to Defend the First Amendment - Defunct.

Comm. to Defend the U.S. Constitution - Defunct.

Comm. for the Defense of Human Rights in India - Address unknown since 1994.

Comm. for Defense of Human Rights in Morocco - Address unknown since 1995.

Comm. in Defense of the Palestinian and Lebanese Peoples - Defunct.

Comm. for the Defense of Persecuted Orthodox Christians - Defunct.

Comm. for the Defense of Political Prisoners in Vietnam - Address unknown since 2001.

Comm. for Defense of Soviet Political Prisoners - Defunct.

Comm. for a Democratic Majority **[17401]**, 301 4th St. NE, Ste. 202, Washington, DC 20002

Comm. for a Democratic Policy Toward Italy - Defunct.

Comm. for the Development of Art in Negro Colleges **[★7969]**

Comm. for the Development and Mgt. of Fisheries in the South China Sea **[★IO]**

Comm. on Diagnostic Reading Tests - Defunct.

Comm. for Do-It-Yourself Household Moving - Address unknown since 2003.

Comm. on Earth Observation Satellites **[IO]**, Tokyo, Japan

Comm. for Economic Development **[17455]**, 2000 L St. NW, Ste. 700, Washington, DC 20036, (202)296-5860

Comm. for Economic Development of Australia **[IO]**, Melbourne, Australia

Comm. for the Economic Growth of Israel **[24337]**, PO Box 2053, Milwaukee, WI 53217, (414)906-6250

Comm. on Education in the Basic Sciences - Defunct.

Comm. for Educ. Funding **[8345]**, 122 C St. NW, Ste. 280, Washington, DC 20001, (202)383-0083

Comm. for Effective Capital Recovery - Defunct.

Comm. for Effective Use of the Intl. Court by Repealing the Self-Judging Reservation - Defunct.

Comm. to Eliminate Legal-Size Files - Defunct.

Comm. to Eliminate Premature Christmas Advertising and Display - Defunct.

Comm. on the Elimination of Discrimination Against Women **[17523]**, c/o United Nations Div. for the Advancement of Women, 2 United Nations Plz., DC 2-12th Fl., New York, NY 10017

Reference to "IO" in place of a book number signifies that the association may be found in the 45th edition of International Organizations.

Comm. on the Elimination of Discrimination Against Women [IO], New York, NY, United States

Comm. on the Elimination of Racial Discrimination [IO], Geneva, Switzerland

Comm. on Emergency Medical Identification - Defunct.

Comm. to Encourage Corporate Philanthropy [12714], 110 Wall St., Ste. 2-1, New York, NY 10005, (212)825-1000

Comm. to End the Marion Lockdown [11861], PO Box 578172, Chicago, IL 60657-8172, (312)235-0070

Comm. to End Radiological Hazards - Defunct.

Comm. for Environmental Information - Defunct.

Comm. for Environmentally Effective Packaging - Defunct.

Comm. for Equality of Citizens Before the Courts - Address unknown since 1989.

Comm. for Equitable Access to Crude Oil - Defunct.

Comm. for Equitable Compensation - Defunct.

Comm. to Eradicate Syphilis - Defunct.

Comm. to Establish the Gold Standard - Defunct.

Comm. of European Coffee Associations [IO], Amsterdam, Netherlands

Comm. for European Constr. Equip. [IO], Brussels, Belgium

Comm. for European Foundry Assn. [★IO]

Comm. on the Exercise of the Inalienable Rights of the Palestinian People - Address unknown since 2002.

Comm. of Experts on Cosmetic Products [IO], Strasbourg, France

Comm. of Experts on Flavouring Substances [IO], Strasbourg, France

Comm. of Experts on the Hea. Control of Foodstuffs [★IO]

Comm. of Experts on the Legal Classification of Medicines as Regards Their Supply [IO], Strasbourg, France

Comm. of Experts on Materials Coming into Contact with Food [IO], Strasbourg, France

Comm. of Experts on Medicines Subject to Prescription [★IO]

Comm. of Experts on Nutrition, Food Safety and Consumer Hea. [IO], Strasbourg, France

Comm. of Experts on Pharmaceutical Questions [IO], Strasbourg, France

Comm. to Expose, Oppose, and Depose Patriarchy - Defunct.

Comm. for an Extended Lifespan - Defunct.

Comm. for Fair Insurance Rates - Defunct.

Comm. on Fair Trade with China - Address unknown since 1994.

Comm. on Federal Contracting Practices - Defunct.

Comm. on Federalism and Natl. Purpose - Defunct.

Comm. for Food and Shelter [★12294]

Comm. for Forward-Looking Republicans - Defunct.

Comm. for a Free Afghanistan - Address unknown since 1994.

Comm. for a Free China - Defunct.

Comm. for a Free Estonia - Defunct.

Comm. for a Free Gold Market - Address unknown since 1995.

Comm. for a Free Latvia - Defunct.

Comm. for a Free Lithuania - Defunct.

Comm. for a Free Mozambique - Defunct.

Comm. for a Free Namibia - Defunct.

Comm. on Free Press and Fair Trial - Defunct.

Comm. for the Free World - Defunct.

Comm. for Freedom of Choice in Cancer Therapy [★13628]

Comm. for Freedom of Choice in Medicine [13628]

Comm. of French Auto. Manufacturers [IO], Paris, France

Comm. of French Speaking Societies [19062], c/o Rubin, Bailin, Ortoli LLP, 405 Park Ave., 15th Fl., New York, NY 10022

Comm. for the Full Development of All-Channel Broadcasting - Defunct.

Comm. for Full Funding of Educ. Programs [★8345]

Comm. for the Furtherance of Torah Observance [★20169]

Comm. for the Future of America - Defunct.

Comm. for the Future - Defunct.

Comm. for the Game [22464]

Comm. for Handicapable Dancers [9870], 9354 Johnson Rd., Mobile, AL 36695, (251)633-8212

Comm. on Health and Human Rights - Defunct.

Comm. for Hispanic Arts and Res. - Address unknown since 2002.

Comm. on the History of Social Welfare [★10149]

Comm. for Honesty in Politics - Defunct.

Comm. on Human Rights [17753], c/o The Natl. Academies, 500 5th St. NW, Washington, DC 20001, (202)334-3043

Comm. for Human Rights; Amer. [★17783]

Comm. for Human Rights and Democracy in Turkey - Address unknown since 1896.

Comm. on Human Rights in Malaysia and Singapore - Defunct.

Comm. on Human Rights for the People of Nicaragua - Address unknown since 2001.

Comm. for Human Rights in Romania [★18571]

Comm. for Human Rights in Romania [★IO]

Comm. for Human Rights in Syria - Address unknown since 1995.

Comm. on Human Rights of the U.S. Natl. Acad. of Sciences [★17753]

Comm. on Human Rights of the U.S. Natl. Acad. of Sciences, Natl. Acad. of Engg., and Inst. of Medicine [★17753]

Comm. for Humane Legislation - Defunct.

Comm. for Humanitarian Assistance to Iranian Refugees [12808], PO Box 7051, New York, NY 10116, (212)747-1046

Comm. of Ice Skate Outfit Mfrs. - Defunct.

Comm. for Immediate Nuclear War - Address unknown since 2000.

Comm. for the Implementation of the Standardized Yiddish Orthography [10276], c/o League for Yiddish, Inc., 45 E 33 St., No. 203, New York, NY 10016, (212)889-0380

Comm. on Info. Systems [★5821]

Comm. on Institutional Cooperation [8104], 1819 S Neil St., Ste. D, Champaign, IL 61820-7271, (217)333-8475

Comm. for Intl. Cooperation in Natl. Res. in Demography [IO], Paris, France

Comm. on Intl. Exchange of Persons Conf. Bd. of Assoc. Res. Councils [★IO]

Comm. on Intl. Exchange of Persons Conf. Bd. of Assoc. Res. Councils [★8609]

Comm. for the Intl. Family - Defunct.

Comm. on Intl. Freedom to Publish [★17041]

Comm. on Intl. Freedom to Publish [★IO]

Comm. for Intl. Human Rights Inquiry - Defunct.

Comm. on Intl. Non-Theatrical Events [★9935]

Comm. on Intl. Non-Theatrical Events [★IO]

Comm. on Intl. Relations - Defunct.

Comm. Internationale pour la Definition des Caracteristiques Microbiologiques des Aliments [★IO]

Comm. of Interns and Residents [24089], 520 8th Ave., Ste. 1200, New York, NY 10018-4183, (212)356-8100

Comm. of Interns and Residents in New York City [★24089]

Comm. to Investigate Assassinations [★18787]

Comm. on Israeli Censorship - Address unknown since 1994.

Comm. for Italic Handwriting - Defunct.

Comm. for Jewish Claims on Austria - Address unknown since 1995.

Comm. for the Jewish Idea - Address unknown since 2001.

Comm. on Jobs, Environment and Technology - Defunct.

Comm. for Jobs Through Economic Development - Defunct.

Comm. on Justice and the Constitution - Address unknown since 2002.

Comm. for Justice for Domingo and Viernes - Defunct.

Comm. to Keep the Truth Before the Amer. People - Address unknown since 1995.

Comm. for Latvian Song Festival in U.S.A. - Address unknown since 1995.

Comm. for Legal Aid to Poor [IO], Cuttack, India

Comm. on Lesbian, Gay and Bisexual Issues; Natl. Assn. of Social Workers Natl. [12245]

Comm. of Liaison With Families of Servicemen Detained in North Vietnam - Defunct.

Comm. for the Maintenance of Jewish Standards - Defunct.

Comm. for Mapping the Flora of Europe [IO], Helsinki, Finland

Comm. on Marine Fisheries [IO], Bangkok, Thailand

Comm. on Marine Res. - Defunct.

Comm. for Medical Aid to Central America - Address unknown since 1991.

Comm. on Migration, Refugees and Demography [★IO]

Comm. on Migration, Refugees, and Population [IO], Strasbourg, France

Comm. on Militarism in Education - Defunct.

Comm. of Ministers [IO], Strasbourg, France

Comm. for Missing Children [IO], Lawrenceville, GA, United States

Comm. for Missing Children [12603], 242 Stone Mountain St., Lawrenceville, GA 30045, (678)376-6265

Comm. on Missionary Evangelism [20001], PO Box 88085, Grand Rapids, MI 49518, (616)243-0119

Comm. for Modern Courts Fund [★5901]

Comm. for the Monument of Garibaldi - Defunct.

Comm. for Mother and Child Rights [11689]

Comm. for Natl. Arbor Day [18670], 187 Ridgedale Ave., East Hanover, NJ 07936, (973)887-4510

Comm. for Natl. Health Insurance - Address unknown since 2000.

Comm. for a Natl. Land Development Policy - Defunct.

Comm. for Natl. Security - Address unknown since 2006.

Comm. of Natl. Security Companies [★3537]

Comm. for Natl. Theatre Week - Address unknown since 1988.

Comm. for a Natl. Trade Policy - Defunct.

Comm. for Netherlands Music - Defunct.

Comm. for a New Ireland - Defunct.

Comm. for a New Korea Policy - Defunct.

Comm. on Non-Market Decision Making [★7527]

Comm. for Nonviolent Action [★18123]

Comm. for Nordic Music Cooperation [★IO]

Comm. for Nuclear and Alternative Energy Systems - Defunct.

Comm. for Nuclear Responsibility [18126], PO Box 421993, San Francisco, CA 94142, (415)776-8299

Comm. for Nuclear Responsibility [IO], San Francisco, CA, United States

Comm. for Oil Pipe Lines [★2919]

Comm. for Oil Shale Development - Defunct.

Comm. On State Taxation [★18709]

Comm. for an Open Archives - Address unknown since 2004.

Comm. for Open Debate on the Holocaust - Defunct.

Comm. Opposed to Militarism and the Draft [5669], PO Box 15195, San Diego, CA 92175, (619)265-1369

Comm. on Pan-Amer. Policy - Address unknown since 1995.

Comm. on Parenthood Education - Defunct.

Comm. for Pedestrian Tolls - Defunct.

Comm. for Pets in Housing - Defunct.

Comm. for Pipe Line Companies [★2919]

Comm. on Political Educ., AFL-CIO [★18303]

Comm. for Positive Education - Defunct.

Committee on Postgraduate Educational Programs [★6559]

Committee on Postgraduate Educational Programs [★IO]

Comm. on the Present Danger - Defunct.

Comm. on Preservation of Natural Conditions Ecological Soc. of Am. [★4433]

Comm. for the Preservation of the Tule Elk - Address unknown since 2002.

Comm. to Preserve Amer. Color TV - Address unknown since 1994.

Comm. of Presidents of Statistical Societies [7704], c/o Dr. Joseph Ibrahim, Dept. of Biostatistics, Harvard School of Public Hea. and Dana Farber, CancerInstitute, 44 Binney St., Boston, MA 02115, (617)632-2472

Comm. for Prisoner Humanity and Justice - Address unknown since 1995.

Comm. for Private Offshore Rescue and Towing [2574], PO Box 4070, Annapolis, MD 21403, (866)847-3609

A star before a book entry number signifies that the name is not listed separately, but is mentioned within the entry.

Comm. of Producers of High Quality Ferrochromium - Defunct.

Comm. for Production Sharing - Defunct.

Comm. of Professional Agricultural Organisations in the EU [IO], Brussels, Belgium

Comm. for a Progressive Cong. - Address unknown since 1989.

Comm. for the Promotion and Advancement of Cooperatives [IO], Geneva, Switzerland

Comm. for the Promotion of Medical Res. [15104], c/o NYU Medical Center, School of Medicine, 530 First Ave., New York, NY 10016, (212)263-7300

Comm. to Protect Journalists [17172], 330 7th Ave., 11th Fl., New York, NY 10001, (212)465-1004

Comm. to Protect Journalists [IO], New York, NY, United States

Comm. to Protect Our Children's Teeth - Defunct.

Comm. to Protest Absurd Censorship - Address unknown since 1995.

Comm. on Public Doublespeak [17173], c/o Natl. Coun. of Teachers of English, 1111 W Kenyon Rd., Urbana, IL 61801-1096, (217)328-3870

Comm. of Publicly Owned Companies - Address unknown since 2003.

Committee for Purchase From People Who Are Blind or Severely Disabled [★16878]

Comm. to Re-Involve Ex-Offenders - Defunct.

Comm. for Real Ale - Address unknown since 1995.

Comm. for Reasonable Inventory Accounting Rules - Defunct.

Committee for Rebuilding the Home of General T. Kosciuszko - Address unknown since 2003.

Comm. to Reduce Infection Deaths [14877], 1110 Park Ave., New York, NY 10128

Comm. for the Reexamination of the History of the Second World War - Defunct.

Comm. of the Regions [IO], Brussels, Belgium

Comm. to Register and Vote the Other Half - Defunct.

Comm. on the Rehabilitation and Integration of People with Disabilities [IO], Strasbourg, France

Comm. to Release Stockpile [★2694]

Comm. for Religious Freedom [★18511]

Comm. for Religious Freedom [★IO]

Comm. on Res. in Dance [★IO]

Comm. on Res. in Dance [★9871]

Comm. on Res. Materials on Southeast Asia [10349], Harvard Coll. Lib., Harvard Univ., Cambridge, MA 02138, (617)495-0585

Comm. on Res. Materials on Southeast Asia [IO], Cambridge, MA, United States

Comm. to Resist Abortion - Address unknown since 1999.

Comm. of Responsibility - Address unknown since 1995.

Comm. for Responsible Education - Defunct.

Comm. for a Responsible Fed. Budget [18405], 1630 Connecticut Ave. NW, 7th Fl., Washington, DC 20009, (202)986-6599

Comm. for Responsible Genetics [★18584]

Comm. for Responsible Res. - Address unknown since 1994.

Comm. for Responsive Philanthropy [★12732]

Comm. for Restoration of Democracy in Burma - Address unknown since 2001.

Comm. for the Restoration of the Republic - Defunct.

Comm. to Restore the Constitution [17290]

Comm. for Return of Confiscated German and Japanese Property - Defunct.

Comm. of Returned Volunteers - Defunct.

Comm. to Reunite the Partridge Family - Defunct.

Comm. for Review of Our China Policy - Defunct.

Comm. on the Role and Status of Women in Educational Res. and Development - Address unknown since 2005.

Comm. for Safe Bicycling - Defunct.

Comm. for a SANE Nuclear Policy [★18166]

Comm. on Scholarly Editions [11167], c/o Modern Language Assn. of Am., 26 Broadway, 3rd Fl., New York, NY 10004, (646)576-5000

Committee for the Sci. Examination of Religion [★20085]

Committee for the Sci. Examination of Religion [★IO]

Comm. for the Sci. Investigation of Claims of the Paranormal [7444], PO Box 703, Amherst, NY 14226, (716)636-1425

Comm. of Sci. Soc. Presidents [★7605]

Comm. of Scottish Clearing Bankers [IO], Edinburgh, United Kingdom

Comm. on Selected Biological Problems in the Humid Tropics - Defunct.

Comm. for Self-Determination - Address unknown since 1995.

Comm. for Single Adoptive Parents [★11256]

Comm. for Single Six-Year Presidential Term - Defunct.

Comm. of Single Taxpayers - Defunct.

Comm. for Small Business Exports - Address unknown since 2003.

Comm. on Social Development and World Peace of the U.S. Catholic Conf. [19613], 3211 4th St. NE, Washington, DC 20017-1194, (202)541-3000

Comm. on Social Development and World Peace of the U.S. Catholic Conf. [IO], Washington, DC, United States

Comm. for Social Responsibility in Engineering - Defunct.

Comm. on Soc., Development and Peace - Defunct.

Comm. for Solidarity With the Bolivian People - Defunct.

Comm. in Solidarity With Latin Amer. Nonviolent Movements - Address unknown since 1994.

Comm. in Solidarity With the People of El Salvador [17483], PO Box 8560, New York, NY 10116, (212)465-8115

Comm. in Solidarity With the People of El Salvador [IO], New York, NY, United States

Comm. in Solidarity With the People of El Salvador; U.S. [★17483]

Comm. in Solidarity With the People of Guatemala - Address unknown since 1999.

Comm. in Solidarity With the People of Iran - Defunct.

Comm. on South Asian Women [17524], c/o Dr. Jyotsna Vaid, Ed., Texas A&M Univ., Dept. of Psychology, College Station, TX 77843-4235, (979)845-2576

Comm. on South Asian Women [IO], College Station, TX, United States

Committee on Soviet and East European Law [★5475]

Comm. on Space Res. [IO], Paris, France

Comm. on SST-Sonic Boom - Defunct.

Comm. on the Standardization of Hospital Graphics - Defunct.

Comm. on State Sovereignty - Defunct.

Comm. on the Status of Women in the Economics Profession [5673], c/o Lisa M. Lynch, Chair, Economic Affairs, Fletcher School of Law and Diplomacy, Tufts Univ., 160 Packard Ave., Medford, MA 02155

Comm. on the Status of Women in Microbiology [6574], c/o Dr. Lorraine Findlay, PhD, Chair, Nassau County Coll. and Medical Center, Dept. of Allied Hea. Sciences, One Educ. Dr., Garden City, NY 11530-6793, (516)572-7915

Comm. on the Status of Women in Philosophy - Defunct.

Comm. on the Status of Women in Sociology [9923], c/o Amer. Sociological Assn., 1307 New York Ave. NW, Ste. 700, Washington, DC 20005, (202)383-9005

Comm. to Stop Chem. Atrocities [★18463]

Comm. to Stop Children's Murder - Defunct.

Comm. for a Strong Peaceful America - Defunct.

Comm. for the Study of the Amer. Electorate - Address unknown since 2005.

Comm. for the Study of the Benefits and Costs of the 55 Miles Per Hour Maximum Speed Limit - Defunct.

Comm. on the Study of History - Defunct.

Comm. on Sugar Cane Diseases - Defunct.

Comm. for the Suit Against Govt. Misconduct - Defunct.

Comm. to Support the Antitrust Laws [17626], c/o Cuneo Gilbert and LaDuca, LLP, 507 C St. NE, Washington, DC 20002, (202)789-3960

Comm. in Support of Existing U.S. Tariff Policy With Respect to Honey - Defunct.

Comm. to Support Irish Political Prisoners - Defunct.

Comm. to Support Nicaragua - Defunct.

Comm. to Support the Revolution in Peru [18341], PO Box 1246, Berkeley, CA 94701, (415)252-5786

Comm. in Support of Solidarity [★17446]

Comm. in Support of Solidarity [★IO]

Comm. for the Survival of a Free Cong. [★17268]

Comm. for Sustainable Agriculture [★4100]

Comm. on the Teaching of Science of the Intl. Coun. of Scientific Unions - Defunct.

Comm. of Ten Million - Address unknown since 1987.

Comm. for a Ten Percent Flat Tax - Defunct.

Comm. for Time Uniformity - Defunct.

Comm. of Tin Mill Prdt. Producers [★977]

Comm. of Transylvania - Address unknown since 2002.

Comm. for Truth in Psychiatry [15195], PO Box 1214, New York, NY 10003, (212)473-4786

Comm. on the Undergraduate Program in Mathematics - Address unknown since 1995.

Comm. for a Unified Independent Party [18321], 225 Broadway, Ste. 2010, New York, NY 10007, (212)609-2800

Comm. on Uniform Traffic Accident Statistics [★12993]

Comm. on the Unisex Military - Defunct.

Comm. to Unite America - Defunct.

Comm. for U.S. Veterans of Hiroshima and Nagasaki [★13353]

Comm. on US/Latin Amer. Relations [19194], Cornell Univ., 316 Anabel Taylor Hall, Ithaca, NY 14853, (607)255-7293

Comm. on User Instruction for Information Literacy - Defunct.

Comm. on Vacuum Tech. [★7822]

Comm. for Vice-Chancellors and Principals [★IO]

Comm. for the Visual Arts [★9499]

Comm. for the Visual Arts/Artists Space [★9499]

Comm. for a Voluntary Census - Address unknown since 1999.

The Comm. for Western Civilization [8243], 2615 O St. NW, Washington, DC 20007, (202)338-3239

The Comm. - Witness to Reconciliation - Defunct.

Comm. on Women in Asian Studies - Address unknown since 2003.

Comm. for Women in Geophysics - Defunct.

Comm. on Women in Public Relations [★3197]

Comm. on Women's Employment and Related Social Issues - Address unknown since 1995.

Comm. of the Wool Textile Indus. in the European Economic Community [IO], Brussels, Belgium

Comm. for World Development and World Disarmament - Defunct.

Comm. on the World Food Crisis - Defunct.

Comm. on World Food Security [IO], Rome, Italy

Comm. for Zero Automobile Growth - Defunct.

Committees of Correspondence for Democracy and Socialism [5666], 545 8th Ave., 14th Fl. NE, New York, NY 10018, (212)868-3733

Comms. of Solidarity with Central America - Defunct.

Commodities

Africa Rice Center [IO]

Amcot, Inc. [4301]

Amer. Commodity Distribution Assn. [4302]

Amer. Malting Barley Assn. [4303]

Amer. Soybean Assn. [4304]

Assn. of Independent Crop Consultants [IO]

European Commodities Exchange [IO]

Federacion Nacional de Cultivadores de Cereales y Leguminosas [IO]

Fed. of Cocoa Commerce [IO]

Hong Kong Exchanges and Clearing [IO]

Hop Growers of Am. [4305]

Intl. Cotton Advisory Comm. [4306]

Intl. Cotton Advisory Comm. [IO]

Intl. Rice Commn. [IO]

Intl. Rice Res. Inst. [IO]

Intl. Wild Rice Exchange [IO]

Intl. Wild Rice Exchange [4307]

Kamut Assn. of North Am. [4308]

Natl. Assn. of Wheat Growers [4309]

Natl. Barley Growers Assn. [4663]

Natl. Corn Growers Assn. [4310]

Natl. Farmers Org. [4650]

Natl. Sorghum Producers [4311]

Natl. Sunflower Assn. [4312]

Reference to "IO" in place of a book number signifies that the association may be found in the 45th edition of International Organizations.

Natl. Sweet Sorghum Producers and Processors Assn. [871]
Northern Ireland Grain Trade Assn. [IO]
Org. for the Advancement of Knowledge [4313]
Pacific Northwest Grain and Feed Assn. [4314]
Plains Cotton Growers [4315]
Soyfoods Assn. of North Am. [4316]
Supima [4317]
Tropical Growers' Assn. [IO]
U.S. Durum Growers Assn. [4318]
U.S. Grains Coun. [4664]
U.S. Wheat Associates [4319]
U.S. Wheat Associates [IO]
United Weighers Assn. [4320]
U.S.A. Rice Coun. [4321]
Wheat Quality Coun. [4322]
Commodity and Barter Assn; Natl. [18411]
Commodity Exchange - Address unknown since 1999.

Commodity Exchanges
Bd. of Trade of the Wholesale Seafood Merchants [4323]
CME Group [4324]
Fort Worth Grain Exchange [4325]
Greenwood Cotton Exchange [4326]
Kansas City Bd. of Trade [4327]
Memphis Cotton Exchange [4328]
Minneapolis Grain Exchange [4329]
Natl. Introducing Brokers Assn. [1714]
New England Fish Exchange [4330]
New Orleans Bd. of Trade [4331]
New York Cotton Exchange [4332]
New York Mercantile Exchange [4333]
Salina Bd. of Trade [4334]
Commodity Markets Coun. [1748], 1300 L St. NW, Ste. 1020, Washington, DC 20005, (202)842-0400
Commodore Thomas Catesby Jones Soc. - Defunct.
Common [★6791]
Common-A Users Gp. [6791], 5515 N Cumberland Ave., Ste. 810, Chicago, IL 60656, (312)279-0192
Common Boundary - Defunct.
Common Carrier Conf. -Irregular Route [★3899]
Common Cause [18287], 1133 19th St. NW, 9th Fl., Washington, DC 20036, (202)833-1200
Common Cold Found. - Defunct.
Common Comm. for Amer. Unity [★12404]
Common Comm. for Amer. Unity [★IO]
Common Destiny Alliance [8244], Univ. of Maryland, 2110 Benjamin Bldg., College Park, MD 20742, (301)405-0639
Common Dreams [16972], PO Box 443, Portland, ME 04112-0443, (207)775-0488
Common Ground [★18707]
Common Ground Alliance [12958], 1421 Prince St., Ste. 410, Alexandria, VA 22314, (703)836-1709
Common Ground Prog. [IO], Kitale, Kenya
Common Ground - U.S.A. [18707], PO Box 57, Evanston, IL 60204, (847)475-0391
Common Market Comm. of the Nitrogenous and Phospatic Fertilizers Indus. [★IO]
Common Market for Eastern and Southern Africa [IO], Lusaka, Zambia
Common Market Newspaper Publishers' Org. [★IO]
Common Sense for Drug Policy [18436], 1377-C Spencer Ave., Lancaster, PA 17603, (717)299-0600
Common Sense in Govt. Procurement; Coalition for [★1741]
Common Sense about Kids and Guns [8443], 1225 I St. NW, Ste. 1100, Washington, DC 20005-3914, (202)546-0200
Common Sense Media - Defunct.
Commons, Open Spaces and Footpaths Preservation Soc. [IO], Henley-On-Thames, United Kingdom
Commonwealth
Commonwealth Inst. [IO]
Commonwealth War Graves Commn. [IO]
Royal Commonwealth Ex-Services League [IO]
Commonwealth Archivists Assn. [★IO]
Commonwealth Assn. of Architects [IO], London, United Kingdom
Commonwealth Assn. for Corporate Governance [IO], Marlborough, New Zealand
Commonwealth Assn. of Museums [IO], DeWinton, AB, Canada

Commonwealth Assn. of Non-Governmental Organisations [IO], Kaduna, Nigeria
Commonwealth Assn. of Planners [IO], Edinburgh, United Kingdom
Commonwealth Assn. for Public Admin. and Mgt. [IO], Toronto, ON, Canada
Commonwealth Assn. of Public Sector Lawyers [IO], Mosman, Australia
Commonwealth Assn. of Sci., Tech. and Mathematics Educators [IO], London, United Kingdom
Commonwealth Assn. of Surveying and Land Economy [IO], Bristol, United Kingdom
Commonwealth Assn. of Tax Administrators [IO], London, United Kingdom
Commonwealth Banana Exporters Assn. [★IO]
Commonwealth Bd. of Architectural Educ. [★IO]
Commonwealth Bd. of Surveying Educ. [★IO]
Commonwealth Broadcasting Assn. [IO], London, United Kingdom
Commonwealth Consultative Gp. on Tech. Mgt. [★IO]
Commonwealth Coun. for Educational Admin. and Mgt. [IO], Lefkosia, Cyprus
Commonwealth Countries League [IO], London, United Kingdom
Commonwealth Dental Assn. [IO], London, United Kingdom
Commonwealth Forestry Assn. [IO], Craven Arms, United Kingdom
Commonwealth Found. [IO], London, United Kingdom
Commonwealth Fund [16241], 1 E 75th St., New York, NY 10021, (212)606-3800
Commonwealth Fund for Tech. Co-Operation [IO], London, United Kingdom
Commonwealth Games Assn. of Malaysia [★IO]
Commonwealth Games Fed. [IO], London, United Kingdom
Commonwealth Hansard Editors Assn. [IO], London, United Kingdom
Commonwealth Human Ecology Coun. [IO], London, United Kingdom
Commonwealth Human Rights Initiative [IO], New Delhi, India
Commonwealth Inst. [IO], London, United Kingdom
Commonwealth Intl. Philatelic Soc. - Defunct.
Commonwealth Journalists Assn. [IO], Toronto, ON, Canada
Commonwealth Lawyers' Assn. [IO], London, United Kingdom
Commonwealth of Learning [IO], Vancouver, BC, Canada
Commonwealth Magistrates and Judges' Assn. [IO], London, United Kingdom
Commonwealth Network of Info. Tech. for Development [IO], Blata I-Bajda, Malta
Commonwealth Nurses Fed. [IO], London, United Kingdom
Commonwealth Parliamentary Assn. [IO], London, United Kingdom
Commonwealth Partnership for Tech. Mgt. [IO], London, United Kingdom
Commonwealth Pharmaceutical Assn. [IO], London, United Kingdom
Commonwealth Press Union - New Zealand Sect. [IO], Wellington, New Zealand
Commonwealth Press Union - United Kingdom [IO], London, United Kingdom
Commonwealth Sci. and Indus. Res. Org. [IO], Clayton South, Australia
Commonwealth Secretariat [IO], London, United Kingdom
Commonwealth Soc. for Deaf Charity [IO], London, United Kingdom
Commonwealth Speakers and Presiding Officers Conf. [IO], Ottawa, ON, Canada
Commonwealth Telecommunications Bd. [★IO]
Commonwealth Telecommunications Org. [IO], London, United Kingdom
Commonwealth Veterinary Assn. [IO], Bangalore, India
Commonwealth War Graves Commn. [IO], Maidenhead, United Kingdom
Commonwealth Youth Exchange Coun. [IO], London, United Kingdom

Communal Living
Communal Stud. Assn. [10020]
Lama Found. [10176]
Communal Ser. Assn. of North Am; Jewish [12472]
Communal Societies Assn; Natl. Historic [★10020]
Communal Stud. Assn. [10020], PO Box 122, Amana, IA 52203, (319)622-6446
Communaute Economique des Etats de l'Afrique de l'Ouest [★IO]
Communaute Europeenne du Rail [★IO]
Communaute Europeenne des Cooperatives de Consommateurs [★IO]
Communaute Francaise de Belgique [IO], Brussels, Belgium
Communaute du Pacifique [★IO]
Communautee Europeenne des Jeunes de l'Horticulture [★IO]
Communicating for Agriculture [★4076]
Communicating for Agriculture and the Self Employed [★4076]
Communicating for Am. [4076], PO Box 677, Fergus Falls, MN 56538-0677, (218)739-3241
Commun. and Action; Ecumenical Prog. for Inter Amer. [★17987]
Commun. Admin; Assn. for [9154]
Commun., Advt., and Marketing Educ. Found. [IO], Maidenhead, United Kingdom
Commun. Agencies Assn. of New Zealand [IO], Auckland, New Zealand
Commun. Arts Professionals; Catholic Acad. for [9761]
Commun. Assn; Amer. Bus. [★8014]
Commun. Assn. for Bus. [8014]
Commun. Assn. of Departments and Administrators in Speech [★9154]
Commun. Assn. for Educ. in Journalism and Mass [8706]
Commun. Assn; Natl. [9157]
Commun. Assn; Religious Speech Division of Speech [★8116]
Commun. Assn. of Schools of Journalism and Mass [7893]
Commun. Assn; Southern States [9162]
Commun. Assn; Speech [★9157]
Commun; Center for [8003]
Commun; Center for Marketing [★87]
Commun. Center; Mission Advanced Res. and [20358]
Commun; Center for Nonviolent [18110]
Commun. Commn. [19537], c/o Natl. Coun. of Churches U.S.A., 475 Riverside Dr., Ste. 880, New York, NY 10015, (212)870-2048
Commun. Commn; Inter-American Elecl. [★3744]
Commun. Commn; World Evangelical Fellowship [★19538]
Commun; Conf. on Coll. Composition and [8376]
Commun. Contractors Assn; Power and [1060]
Commun. Coun; Amer. Sabbath Tract and [★20545]
Commun. Coun. for Human Services; Natl. [★3195]
Commun. Coun; Indus. [★876]
Commun. Disorders Info. CH; Natl. Inst. on Deafness and Other [14773]
Commun. Disorders; Natl. Center for Neurogenic [16449]
Communication Employees Union; Transportation- [★24180]
Commun. Excellence in Agriculture, Natural Resources, and Life and Human Sciences; Assn. for [4098]
Commun; Found. for Student [8023]
Commun. Independence for the Neurologically Impaired [15316], c/o Kornreich Tech. Center, 201 I.U. Willets Rd., Albertson, NY 11507, (516)465-1629
Commun. Inst. for Online Scholarship [6899], PO Box 57, Rotterdam Junction, NY 12150, (518)887-2443
Commun; Interspecies [★7223]
Commun. and Media Law Assn. [IO], Glebe, Australia
Commun; Natl. Soc. for the Stud. of [★3748]
Commun. Soc; IEEE Professional [6923]
Commun; Special Interest Gp. on Data [★6750]
Commun. Workers' Union [IO], London, United Kingdom

A star before a book entry number signifies that the name is not listed separately, but is mentioned within the entry.

Commun. Workers' Union of Australia [IO], Carlton, Australia
Commun. Workers Union - England [IO], London, United Kingdom
Communications
  Accuracy in Media [17160]
  Alliance for Community Media [17161]
  Alliance for a Media Literate Am. [8830]
  Alliance of Rhetoric Societies [10935]
  Amer. Assn. of Paging Carriers [872]
  Amer. Commun. Assn. [6710]
  Amer. Commun. Assn. [IO]
  Amer. Family Assn. [17162]
  Amer. Lib. Assn. - Public Info. Off. [10897]
  Amer. Psychological Assn. - Media Psychology Div. [16131]
  Amer. Radio Relay League [21494]
  Amer. Soc. of Media Photographers [2992]
  Amer. Soc. of Professional Communicators [873]
  Amer. TeleEdCommunications Alliance [7766]
  Anthropology Film Center [6407]
  Antique Telephone Collectors Assn. [22985]
  Antique Wireless Assn. [22923]
  Arab Press Freedom Watch [IO]
  ARRL Found. [21496]
  Asia-Pacific Satellite Communications Coun. [IO]
  Asian Media Info. and Commun. Centre [IO]
  Assn. of Biomedical Communications Directors [14030]
  Assn. for Commun. Admin. [9154]
  Assn. of Fed. Communications Consulting Engineers [7767]
  Assn. for Media and Tech. in Educ. in Canada [IO]
  Assn. of North Amer. Radio Clubs [21498]
  Assn. of Professional Commun. Consultants [959]
  Assn. for Progressive Communications [17163]
  Assn. for Women in Communications [874]
  Benjamin Franklin Educ. Found. [8234]
  Benton Found. [11764]
  BioCommunications Assn. [14031]
  BioCommunications Assn. [IO]
  Black Awareness in TV [17164]
  British Assn. of Communicators in Bus. [IO]
  Cable Europe [IO]
  Cable and Telecommunications Human Resources Assn. [1980]
  Call Centre Mgt. Assn. [IO]
  Campaign for Press and Broadcasting Freedom [IO]
  Canadian Assn. of Communicators in Educ. [IO]
  Canadian Assn. of Photographers and Illustrators in Communications [IO]
  Canadian Women in Communications [IO]
  CANARIE [IO]
  Catholic Media Coun. [IO]
  Caucus for TV Producers, Writers, and Directors [17165]
  Center for Asian Amer. Media [17166]
  Center for Commun. [8003]
  Center for Democracy and Tech. [17167]
  Center for Investigative Reporting [17168]
  Center for Media and Public Affairs [17169]
  Center for Nonviolent Commun. [18110]
  Center for War, Peace, and the News Media [17170]
  Center for War, Peace, and the News Media [IO]
  China Users Assn. for Satellite Communications, Broadcasting and TV [IO]
  Citizens Communications Center Proj. of the Inst. for Public Representation [17171]
  Coalition for Healthcare Commun. [14622]
  Coalition to Keep Am. Connected [18724]
  Collins Collectors Assn. [21499]
  Comm. to Protect Journalists [17172]
  Comm. to Protect Journalists [IO]
  Comm. on Public Doublespeak [17173]
  Commun., Advt., and Marketing Educ. Found. [IO]
  Commun. and Media Law Assn. [IO]
  Commun. Workers' Union [IO]
  Commun. Workers' Union of Australia [IO]
  Commun. Workers Union - England [IO]
  Communications Alliance [IO]
  Communications, Elecl., Electronic, Energy, Info., Postal, Plumbing and Allied Services Union of Australia [IO]

Communications, Energy and Paperworkers Union of Canada [IO]
Communications and Info. Network Assn. of Japan [IO]
Communications Workers of Am. [24037]
CompactFlash Assn. [6723]
Cooperative Info. Superhighway [IO]
Copywriter's Coun. of Am. [875]
Coun. of Commun. Mgt. [876]
Customer Contact Assn. [IO]
Earth Communications Off. [4547]
Educational Communications [8386]
Electronics Representatives Assn. [1213]
Empowerment Proj. [17174]
Enterprise Communications Assn. [877]
Enterprise Cmpt. Telephony Forum [878]
Environmental Communicators' Org. [IO]
Essential Info. [17175]
European Consortium for Communications Res. [IO]
European Inst. for the Media [IO]
European Network for Commun. Development [IO]
Fairness and Accuracy in Reporting [17176]
Fed. Communications Bar Assn. [5580]
Federal Publishers Comm. [5581]
Fed. of Commun. Services [IO]
Film Stud. Assn. of Canada [IO]
Found. for Amer. Communications [17177]
Found. for Student Commun. [8023]
Fund for Investigative Journalism [17178]
Fund for Objective News Reporting [17179]
Genealogical Speakers Guild [10899]
Guild of Intl. Professional Toastmasters [IO]
Hea. Sci. Communications Assn. [14032]
Hispanic Marketing and Commun. Assn. [2628]
Hispanic Public Relations Assn. [17180]
HomePlug Powerline Alliance [1216]
IEEE Communications Soc. [7769]
Info. and Communications Tech. Ireland [IO]
Inst. for Public Accuracy [18456]
Inter Amer. Press Assn. [17181]
Inter Amer. Press Assn. [IO]
Intl. Alliance of Avaya Users [3745]
Intl. Amateur Radio Union [21501]
Intl. Assn. of Bus. Communicators [879]
Intl. Assn. of Bus. Communicators [IO]
Intl. Assn. of Bus. Communicators - BC Chap. [IO]
Intl. Assn. of Bus. Communicators Calgary [IO]
Intl. Assn. of Bus. Communicators Malaysia Chap. [IO]
Intl. Assn. of Bus. Communicators Manitoba [IO]
Intl. Assn. of Bus. Communicators Newfoundland and Labrador [IO]
Intl. Assn. of Bus. Communicators Ottawa [IO]
Intl. Assn. of Bus. Communicators Philippines [IO]
Intl. Assn. of Bus. Communicators Polar Chap. [IO]
Intl. Assn. of Bus. Communicators Regina [IO]
Intl. Assn. of Bus. Communicators Saskatoon [IO]
Intl. Assn. of Community TeleService Centres [IO]
Intl. Assn. for Contract and Commercial Mgt. [772]
Intl. Assn. of Film and TV Schools [IO]
Intl. Assn. of Laryngectomees [11953]
Intl. Assn. for Media and Commun. Res. [IO]
Intl. Assn. for Media and Communications Res. [IO]
Intl. Assn. of Messaging Professionals [IO]
Intl. Assn. of Messaging Professionals [6711]
Intl. Assn. of Satellite Users and Suppliers [3746]
Intl. BBSing and Electronic Communications Corp. [3747]
Intl. Commun. Assn. [3748]
Intl. Found. for Telemetering [7786]
Intl. Handicappers' Net [21502]
Intl. Inst. of Communications [IO]
Intl. Nanocasting Assn. [562]
Intl. Public Debate Assn. [9041]
Intl. Radio Club of Am. [21503]
Intl. Radio and TV Soc. Found. [563]
Intl. Soc. for Alternative and Augmentative Commun. - Finland [IO]
Intl. Soc. of Certified Electronics Technicians [1220]

Intl. Soc. of Commun. Specialists [332]
Intl. Soc. for Gesture Stud. [6712]
Intl. Soc. for Gesture Stud. [IO]
Intl. Tech. Law Assn. [5582]
Intl. Telecommunications Satellite Org. [7777]
Intl. Webcasting Assn. [2667]
Interspecies [7223]
IPREX [3193]
Joint Users of Siemens Technologies U.S. [880]
Just Think [18852]
Kappa Tau Alpha [24522]
Korean Postal Workers Union [IO]
Laptops for the Wounded [11741]
Latin Amer. Assn. of Communications Researchers [IO]
Linguistic Data Consortium [2437]
Longwave Club of Am. [21505]
Mainstream Media Proj. [18494]
Marine Corps Cryptologic Assn. [21174]
Markle Found. [6713]
Matrix Found. [18813]
Media Access Proj. [17182]
Media Alliance [17183]
Media Ecology Assn. [8831]
The Media Inst. [17184]
Media Watch [17185]
Media Watch [IO]
Mobile Satellite Users Assn. [7591]
MPLS and Frame Relay Alliance [6714]
MPLS and Frame Relay Alliance [IO]
MultiService Forum [881]
Natl. Alliance to Save Native Languages [10305]
Natl. Anxiety Center [18416]
Natl. Assn. of Baby Boomer Women [13431]
Natl. Assn. of Commun. Systems Engineers [6715]
Natl. Assn. of Govt. Communicators [5583]
Natl. Assn. of Minority Media Executives [882]
Natl. Assn. for Multi-Ethnicity in Communications [2757]
Natl. Assn. of Public Affairs Networks [17026]
Natl. Capital FreeNet [IO]
Natl. Capital Speakers Assn. [10902]
Natl. Christian Forensics and Communications Assn. [8521]
Natl. Coun. for Families and TV [17186]
Natl. Elecl. and Communications Assn. [IO]
Natl. Fed. of Abstracting and Info. Services [7205]
Natl. Hispanic Media Coalition [17187]
Natl. Info. and Communications Tech. Indus. Alliance [IO]
Natl. Marriage Encounter [12507]
Natl. Speakers Assn. [10903]
Natl. Systems Contractors Assn. [1225]
New York Women in Communications, Inc. Found. [883]
No-Code Intl. [21506]
North Amer. Assn. of Medical Educ. and Commun. Companies [8874]
North Amer. Radio Archives [22926]
North Amer. Shortwave Assn. [21507]
Old Old Timers Club [21508]
Oper. Homelink [11494]
Pacific Islanders in Communications [10455]
Pacific Telecommunications Coun. [7782]
Panos Inst. [12440]
Partnership for Food Safety Educ. [14399]
PCIA - The Wireless Infrastructure Assn. [3752]
Phone-TTY [14777]
Picture Archv. Coun. of Am. [3008]
Professional Insurance Communicators of Am. [884]
Progress and Freedom Found. [17188]
Public Conversations Proj. [17189]
Public Media Center [17190]
Public Relations Soc. of Am. [3195]
Quarter Century Wireless Assn. [21509]
Radio Amateur Satellite Corp. [7783]
Radio Club of Am. [22928]
Radio Collectors of Am. [22929]
Radio Free Europe/Radio Liberty [17191]
Religious Commun. Assn. [8116]
Reporters Comm. for Freedom of the Press [17192]
Rhetoric Soc. of Am. [10937]

Reference to "IO" in place of a book number signifies that the association may be found in the 45th edition of International Organizations.

RTCA [6308]
Satellite Indus. Assn. [885]
Scribes - The Amer. Soc. of Legal Writers [5584]
SD Card Assn. [6743]
Small Bus. in Telecommunications [3629]
Soc. of Consumer Affairs Professionals in Bus. [3196]
Soc. for the Eradication of TV [17193]
Soc. for Tech. Commun. [886]
Soc. for Tech. Commun. [IO]
Society for Technical Communication [IO]
Southern States Commun. Assn. [9162]
Special Interest Gp. on Data Communications of the Assn. for Computing Machinery [6804]
Special Interest Gp. on Design of Commun. [6823]
Student Press Law Center [17194]
Swiss Assn. for Internal Commun. [IO]
Swiss Forum for Communications Law [IO]
Tech. Communicators Assn. of New Zealand [IO]
Telecommunications Res. and Action Center [17195]
Toastmasters Intl. [10904]
Union for Democratic Communications [17196]
Union for Democratic Communications [IO]
Unison Inst. [17197]
U.S. Connected Communities Assn. [6716]
U.S. Marine Corps Combat Correspondents Assn. [3171]
U.S. Natl. Comm. of the Intl. Union of Radio Sci. [7785]
U.S. Naval Cryptologic Veterans Assn. [21327]
U.S. Soc. for Augmentative and Alternative Commun. [17198]
Vintage Radio and Phonograph Soc. [22931]
VON Coalition [2321]
Wi-Fi Alliance [6829]
Willow Mixed Media [17199]
Women Executives in Public Relations [3197]
Women's Inst. for Freedom of the Press [17200]
World Assn. for Christian Commun. [IO]
World Commun. Assn. [8005]
World Press Freedom Comm. [17201]
World Press Freedom Comm. [IO]
World Press Inst. [IO]
World Press Inst. [17202]
Worldwide Television-FM DX Assn. [21510]
Zeta Phi Eta [24434]
Communications; Accrediting Coun. on Educ. in Journalism and Mass [8703]
Communications Alliance [IO], Milsons Point, Australia
Communications Alliance; Integrated Bus. [338]
Communications on Alternatives in Education - Defunct.
Communications Arts Guild - Defunct.
Communications; ASMP - The Soc. of Photographers in [★2992]
Communications Assn., AFL-CIO/CLC; Intl. Labor [3229]
Communications Assn; Amer. Mobile Tele [★3742]
Communications Assn; Cellular Radio [★3741]
Communications Assn; Competitive Tele [★3955]
Communications Assn; Forestry Conservation [4395]
Communications; Assn. of Graphic [1759]
Communications Assn; Graphic [★1773]
Communications Assn. of Hong Kong [IO], Hong Kong, People's Republic of China
Communications Assn; Indus. [★3748]
Communications Assn; Insurance Marketing [2179]
Communications Assn; Intl. Prepaid [3767]
Communications Assn. for Marketing; CTAM - Cable and Tele [558]
Communications Assn; Microwave [★3764]
Communications Assn; Natl. Cable and Tele [573]
Communications Assn; Natl. Sound and [★1225]
Communications Assn; Portable Cmpt. and [908]
Communications Assn; Private [★9157]
Communications Consultants; Soc. of Tele [3756]
Communications Consulting Engineers; Assn. of Fed. [7767]
Communications Coordination Comm. for the United Nations [18763], 301 E 45th St., New York, NY 10017
Communications Coordination Comm. for the United Nations [IO], New York, NY, United States

Communications Corp; Intl. BBSing and Electronic [3747]
Communications Coun; ACCE [24257]
Communications Coun; AEM Marketing [★82]
Communications Coun; Amer. Public [3733]
Communications Coun; Automotive [92]
Communications Coun; CIMA Marketing [★82]
Communications Coun. - Defunct.
Communications Coun; Hea. Indus. Bus. [14080]
Communications Coun; Healthcare Marketing and [100]
Communications Coun; Land Mobile [3751]
Communications Directors; Natl. Assn. of State Tele [6306]
Communications and Elecl. Assn; Energy Tele [1185]
Communications, Elecl., Electronic, Energy, Info., Postal, Plumbing and Allied Services Union of Australia [IO], Sydney, Australia
Communications and Elecl. Workers of Canada [★IO]
Communications, Energy and Paperworkers Union of Canada [IO], Ottawa, ON, Canada
Communications Engineers; Natl. Assn. of Radio and Tele [★7773]
Communications Enterprises; Assn. of [★3955]
Communications Equipment Distributors Assn. - Defunct.
Communications Era Task Force - Defunct.
Communications; Forest Indus. Tele [1606]
Communications Fraud Control Assn. [2087], 4 Becker Farm Rd., 4th Fl., PO Box 954, Roseland, NJ 07068, (973)871-4032
Communications Fraud Control Association [IO], Roseland, NJ, United States
Communications Gp; Theatre [11047]
Communications, Inc; Christian [19774]
Communications Indus. Assn; Cellular [★3741]
Communications Indus. Assn; Cellular Tele [★3741]
Communications Indus. Assn; Cmpt. and [3739]
Communications Indus. Assn; Personal [★3752]
Communications Indus. Assn; Tele [3759]
Communications Indus. Forum; Tele [3760]
Communications Indus; Telocator, The Personal [★3752]
Communications and Info. Network Assn. of Japan [IO], Tokyo, Japan
Communications and Info. Tech. Assn. [IO], Milton Keynes, United Kingdom
Communications; Intl. Inst. of [IO]
Communications Intl. Union; Graphic [★24083]
Communications Intl. Union; Trans. [24180]
Communications Mgt. Assn. [IO], Leatherhead, United Kingdom
Communications Managers Assn. - Defunct.
Communications Market Assn. [★3738]
Communications Marketing Assn. [3738], PO Box 36275, Denver, CO 80236, (303)988-3515
Communications Media Mgt. Assn. [329], 20423 State Rd. 7, Ste. F6-491, Boca Raton, FL 33498, (561)988-2681
The Communications Network [IO], Sunbury-On-Thames, United Kingdom
Communications Network for the Elimination of Violence Against Women; Natl. [★12034]
Communications Off; Earth [4547]
Communications Officers and Advisors; Natl. Assn. of Tele [6307]
Communications Officers; Assoc. Police [★6248]
Communications Officers; Assoc. Public-Safety [★6248]
Communications Officials - Intl; Assn. of Public-Safety [6248]
Communications Project - Address unknown since 1985.
Communications Res; Coun. on [★8706]
Communications Resource Center - Defunct.
Communications Security Assn. - Address unknown since 1994.
Communications Soc; IEEE [7769]
Communications Supervisors; Natl. Comm. of [★3748]
Communications Suppliers Assn; Railway [★3291]
Communications Suppliers Assn; Railway Signal and [★3291]

Communications Supply Ser. Assn. [3954], 5700 Murray St., Little Rock, AR 72209, (501)562-7666
Communications System; Campaign for a U.N. Global [★18763]
Communications System; Campaign for a U.N. Global [★IO]
Communications Teams; Radio Emergency Assoc. [★IO]
Communications Teams; Radio Emergency Assoc. [★6254]
Communications Technicians; Natl. Assn. of Bus. and Educational Radio and Assn. of [★3752]
Communications and Tech; Assn. for Educational [8551]
Communications Tech. Professionals in Higher Educ; ACUTA: The Assn. for [8548]
Communications Trade Div. - Defunct.
Communications Union; Brotherhood Railway Carmen Division/Transportation [24179]
Communications Union; Intl. Printing and Graphics [★24083]
Communications Users Assn. of South Africa [IO], Randburg, Republic of South Africa
Communications Workers of Am. [24037], 501 3rd St. NW, Washington, DC 20001-2797, (202)434-1100
Communicative Disorders; Natl. Coalition for Res. in Neurological and [★15346]
Communicative Disorders; Natl. Comm. for Res. in Neruological and [★15346]
The Communicators - Address unknown since 1989.
Communicators of Am; Professional Insurance [884]
Communicators Assn; Baptist [19478]
Communicators Assn; Turf and Ornamental [2400]
Communicators Canada; Corporate [★879]
Communicators Coun; Religion [20483]
Communicators in Educ; Agricultural [★4098]
Communicators in Educ; Canadian Assn. of [IO]
Communicators; Episcopal [19953]
Communicators; Natl. Assn. of Govt. [5583]
Communicators of Tomorrow; Natl. Agricultural [8714]
Communicators; UNDA U.S.A. Natl. Catholic Assn. for [★9761]
Communidad de Vida Cristiana [★IO]
Communism
  Alpha-66 [17363]
  Amer. Fund for Czechoslovak Relief [12802]
  Bay of Pigs Veterans Assn. [20717]
  Captive Nations Comm. [16988]
  Christian Anti-Communism Crusade [16991]
  Natl. Comm. to Reopen the Rosenberg Case [17135]
  Progressive Labor Party [18331]
Communism, Anti-
  Amer. Security Coun. Found. [16986]
  Bay of Pigs Veterans Assn. [20717]
  Captive Nations Comm. [16988]
  Cardinal Mindszenty Found. [16989]
  CAUSA Intl. [16990]
  Christian Anti-Communism Crusade [16991]
  Natl. Comm. to Reopen the Rosenberg Case [17135]
  Selous Found. [16992]
Communism Crusade; Christian Anti- [16991]
Communism; Historians of Amer. [8506]
Communist Labor Party - Defunct.
Communist League of the U.S.A; Young [18661]
Communist Party of Australia [IO], Surry Hills, Australia
Communist Party of Bangladesh [IO], Dhaka, Bangladesh
Communist Party of Canada (Marxist-Leninist) [IO], Montreal, QC, Canada
Communist Party of India [IO], New Delhi, India
Communist Party of Nepal (Unified Marxist-Leninist) [IO], Kathmandu, Nepal
Communist Party of the U.S.A. [18322], 235 W 23rd St., New York, NY 10011, (212)989-4994
Communist Party of the U.S.A./Marxist Leninist - Defunct.
Communist World; Christian Missions to the [★20410]
Communist World; Jesus to the [★20410]
Communitarian Network [18437], 2130 H St. NW, Ste. 703, Washington, DC 20052, (202)994-6118

A star before a book entry number signifies that the name is not listed separately, but is mentioned within the entry.

Communities in Action; Alliance for [12416]
Communities Against Violence Network [13374], c/o Marc Dubin, Founder/Exec. Dir., 2711 Ordway St. NW, No. 111, Washington, DC 20008
Communities in Schools [8323], 277 S Washington St., Ste. 210, Alexandria, VA 22314, (703)519-8999
Community [IO], London, United Kingdom

Community
A. Philip Randolph Educal. Fund [17078]
ABLE: Assn. for Better Living and Educ. Intl. [11756]
AFL-CIO Community Action Field Mobilization Dept. [11801]
Amer. Civic Assn. [12403]
Asian Americans/Pacific Islanders in Philanthropy [12710]
Assn. of Americans for Civic Responsibility [17074]
Assn. for Community Affiliated Plans [14617]
Assn. for Community Hea. Improvement [16238]
Assn. of Community Organizations for Reform Now [11749]
Assn. of Jewish Center Professionals [12466]
Black Women of Essence [11269]
Bridges to Community [13389]
Catholic Homesteading Movement [11742]
Center for Community and Org. Development [11750]
Center for Neighborhood Enterprise [17208]
Center for Reflective Community Practice [17211]
Center for Self-Sufficiency [11743]
Christian Sports Intl. [23298]
Citizens for Community Values [19788]
Coalition for Environmentally Safe Communities [12118]
Communal Stud. Assn. [10020]
Community Associations Inst. [17212]
Community Built Assn. [11770]
Community-Campus Partnerships For Hea. [11744]
Community Development Soc. [17213]
Community Info. and Epidemiological Technologies [12121]
Community Leadership Assn. [11795]
Community Ser. [17214]
Community Voices [11745]
Educators Serving the Community [8318]
Experience Works [12080]
Experimental Cities, Inc. [17236]
FaithWorks Intl. [11777]
Family Justice [11865]
Family Support Am. [12154]
Fed. of Egalitarian Communities [11746]
Funders' Collaborative on Youth Organizing [12718]
Generations United [13170]
GesherCity [19183]
Globe Aware [13393]
Immigration and Refugee Services of Am. [12404]
Independence Plan for Neighborhood Councils [17219]
Indus. Areas Found. [17220]
Inst. for the Advanced Stud. of Black Family Life and Culture [9359]
Inst. for Community Economics [17221]
Inst. for Local Self-Reliance [11747]
Intermediate Tech. Development Gp. of North Am. [16997]
Intl. Alliance in Ser. and Educ. [11748]
Intl. Assn. of Character Cities [11781]
Intl. Communal Stud. Assn. [IO]
Interreligious Found. for Community Org. [11797]
Local Initiatives Support Corp. [17224]
McAuley Institute [12317]
Midwest Acad. [11751]
Natl. Alliance for Civic Educ. [8091]
Natl. Alliance to Nurture the Aged and the Youth [12358]
Natl. Assn. of Barbados Organizations [9731]
Natl. Assn. of Community Development Extension Professionals [11784]
Natl. Assn. for Community Mediation [5460]
Natl. Assn. for County Community and Economic Development [17225]
Natl. Assn. of Neighborhoods [11752]

Natl. Assn. of Planning Councils [18275]
Natl. Assn. of Students Against Violence Everywhere [18117]
Natl. Black on Black Love Campaign [11842]
Natl. Center for Urban Ethnic Affairs [11753]
Natl. Coalition for Asian Pacific Amer. Community Development [11785]
Natl. Community Action Found. [11754]
Natl. Community Building Network [11786]
Natl. Community Development Assn. [17228]
Natl. Community for Latino Leadership [19203]
Natl. Economic Development and Law Center [17464]
Natl. Latina/Latino Law Student Assn. [17996]
Natl. Latino Alliance for the Elimination of Domestic Violence [12037]
Natl. Neighborhood Coalition [17230]
Natl. Partnership for Community Leadership [11805]
Natl. People's Action [11755]
Natl. Training and Info. Center [11799]
NeighborWorks Am. [12335]
North Amer. Sankethi Assn. [9802]
Organize Training Center [11800]
People's Involvement Corp. [13183]
Pro Players Assn. [13402]
Public Dreams Soc. [IO]
Renew Am. [4336]
Sacred Dance Soc. [19878]
Seeking Common Ground [13514]
Soccer in the Streets [11789]
Somali Family Care Network [19392]
South Asian Amer. Leaders of Tomorrow [18667]
Southern Mutual Help Assn. [11790]
SustainUS [13517]
TV-Turnoff Network [12170]
U.S. Connected Communities Assn. [6716]
The Waterfront Center [11794]
Winant and Clayton Volunteers [13409]
Youth Impact Intl. [13521]
Youth Ser. Am. [13070]

Community Action
9/11 Families for a Secure Am. [18728]
A. Philip Randolph Educal. Fund [17078]
ActionAid Intl. USA [11758]
AFL-CIO Community Action Field Mobilization Dept. [11801]
Albanian Amer. Civic League [16970]
Am. Bikes [17022]
Assn. of Community Organizations for Reform Now [11749]
Bamboo of The Americas [4365]
Bike and Build [11514]
Black Women United for Action [13423]
Builders Without Borders [12307]
A Call to Serve Intl. [11765]
Center for Community Action of B'Nai B'rith Intl. [11766]
Center for Community and Org. Development [11750]
The Child Connection [12602]
City Parks Alliance [18184]
Coalition for Environmentally Safe Communities [12118]
Community Built Assn. [11770]
Community Info. and Epidemiological Technologies [12121]
Doe Network [12608]
Family Justice [11865]
Filipino Amer. Coalition for Environmental Solidarity [4634]
Free the Grapes! [16971]
Generations United [13170]
Genocide Watch [17660]
Globe Aware [13393]
Hate Free Zone [17392]
Homeowners Against Deficient Dwellings [12314]
INCITE! Women of Color Against Violence [18788]
Indicorps [12406]
Indify [13488]
Intl. Assn. of Character Cities [11781]
Intl. Fed. of Family Associations of Missing Persons from Armed Conflicts [12609]
Intl. Healthy Cities Found. [13349]

Jewish Coun. for Public Affairs [12474]
Join Hands Day [17203]
Midwest Acad. [11751]
Minuteman Civil Defense Corps [17077]
Musicians' Alliance for Peace [18223]
Natl. Assn. of African Americans for Positive Imagery [16941]
Natl. Assn. of Neighborhoods [11752]
Natl. Black on Black Love Campaign [11842]
Natl. Center for Urban Ethnic Affairs [11753]
Natl. Civic League [6128]
Natl. Coalition for Asian Pacific Amer. Community Development [11785]
Natl. Community Action Found. [11754]
Natl. Community Building Network [11786]
Natl. Community Development Org. [11798]
Natl. Haitian Soc. [17817]
Natl. Latina/Latino Law Student Assn. [17996]
Natl. Network to End Violence Against Immigrant Women [13433]
Natl. Organizers Alliance [13136]
Natl. People's Action [11755]
NeighborWorks Am. [12335]
NetAid [11486]
New York New Visions [17232]
Praxis Proj. [17204]
Refugee Coun. USA [18500]
Rising Leaders [18005]
Russian Amer. Jews for Israel [18576]
South Asian Amer. Leaders of Tomorrow [18667]
Thunderhead Alliance [18751]
Unity Corps [19017]
Voices in the Wilderness [18253]
The Waterfront Center [11794]
Community Action Agencies; Natl. Assn. of [★12770]
Community Action Agency Directors Assn; Natl. [★12770]
Community Action Agency Executive Directors Assn; Natl. [★12770]
Community Action on Latin Am. [17986], PO Box 1565, Madison, WI 53701, (608)251-3241
Community Action on Latin Am. [IO], Madison, WI, United States
Community Action Network - Address unknown since 2003.
Community Action Partnership [12770], 1140 Connecticut Ave. NW, Ste. 1210, Washington, DC 20036, (202)265-7546
Community Advice Bur. [IO], Hong Kong, People's Republic of China
Community Affairs Agencies; Coun. of State [★6272]
Community Affairs; Natl. Broadcast Assn. for [572]
Community Aid Abroad [★IO]
Community Anti-Drug Coalitions of Am. [13233], 625 Slaters Ln., Ste. 300, Alexandria, VA 22314-1176, (703)706-0560
Community Appeal; Church World Ser. [★12842]
Community Arts Administrators; Assn. of Coll., Univ. and [★7968]
Community Assistance Partnership; Rural [7841]
Community Assistance Prog; Rural [★7841]
Community Associations Inst. [17212], 225 Reinekers Ln., Ste. 300, Alexandria, VA 22314, (703)548-8600
Community Bankers of Am; Independent [480]
Community Banking Advisory Network [20], 10831 Old Mill Rd., Ste. 400, Omaha, NE 68154, (402)778-7922
Community-Based Long-Term Care; Natl. Inst. on [11312]
Community Behavioral Healthcare; Natl. Coun. for [15223]
Community Blood Bank Coun. [★13762]
Community Bd; Native Amer. [12630]
Community Broadcasters of America - Defunct.
Community Broadcasters Assn. - Defunct.
Community Broadcasters; Natl. Fed. of [575]
Community Broadcasting Assn. of Australia [IO], Alexandria, Australia
Community Broadcasting Found. [IO], Collingwood, Australia
Community Built Assn. [11770], 3375 Fairfield Pike, Bell Buckle, TN 37020, (931)389-9649
Community-Campus Partnerships For Hea. [11744], PO Box 354809, Seattle, WA 98195-4809, (206)543-8178

Reference to "IO" in place of a book number signifies that the association may be found in the 45th edition of International Organizations.

Community Cancer Centers; Assn. of [13797]
Community of Caring [11588], c/o Univ. of Utah, 1901 E South Campus Dr., No. 1120, Salt Lake City, UT 84112, (801)587-8990
Community of Celebration [19790], PO Box 309, Aliquippa, PA 15001, (724)375-1510
Community Change; Center for [12769]
Community Change; Planning and Mgt. Assistance Proj. of the Center for [★12655]
Community Chests and Councils of Am. [★12205]
Community Churches; Biennial Coun. of [★19850]
Community Churches; Coun. of [★19850]
Community Churches; Intl. Coun. of [★19850]
Community Churches; Natl. Coun. of [★19850]
Community Churches; Universal Fellowship of Metropolitan [★20062]
Community Coll. Assn. for Instruction and Technology - Defunct.
Community Coll. Baccalaureate Assn. [8119], PO Box 60210, Fort Myers, FL 33906, (239)947-8085
Community Coll. Boards; Coun. of [★8118]
Community Coll. Bus. Officers [8020], PO Box 5565, Charlottesville, VA 22905-5565, (434)293-2825
Community Coll. Humanities Assn. [8530], c/o Prof. David Berry, Exec. Dir., 303 Essex County Coll., 303 Univ. Ave., Newark, NJ 07102, (973)877-3577
Community Coll. Journalism Assn. [8710], c/o Tina Davis, Ed., 163 E Loop Dr., Camarillo, CA 93010, (805)389-3744

Community Colleges
Amer. Assn. of Community Colleges [8117]
Amer. Coun. on Intl. Intercultural Educ. [8651]
Assn. of Community Coll. Trustees [8118]
Assn. for Community Colleges [IO]
Community Coll. Baccalaureate Assn. [8119]
League for Innovation in the Community Coll. [8120]
Natl. Coun. for Marketing and Public Relations [9032]
Natl. Coun. for Res. and Planning [8121]
Natl. Coun. of State Directors of Community Colleges [8122]
Natl. Coun. for Workforce Educ. [8361]
Community Colleges; Amer. Assn. for Women in [9313]
Community Colleges; Amer. Student Assn. of [9174]
Community Colleges for Intl. Development [8607], PO Box 2068, Cedar Rapids, IA 52406-2068, (319)398-1257
Community Colleges for Intl. Development [IO], Cedar Rapids, IA, United States
Community Colleges; Journalism Assn. of [8712]
Community Colleges; Soc. for Anthropology in [7954]
Community Concern for Senior Citizens - Defunct.
Community for Creative Non-Violence [12288], 425 2nd St. NW, Washington, DC 20001, (202)393-1909
Community Creativity, Inc. - Defunct.
Community Cultural Center Assn; Amer. [9846]
Community Dental Programs; Amer. Assn. for [14111]

Community Development
ABLE: Assn. for Better Living and Educ. Intl. [11756]
ABLE: Association for Better Living and Education International [IO]
ACCION Intl. [IO]
ACCION Intl. [17205]
Acindar Found. [IO]
Action Aid - Nepal [IO]
Action for Enterprise [IO]
Action for Enterprise [11757]
Action for Market Towns [IO]
ActionAid Intl. USA [IO]
ActionAid Intl. USA [11758]
Active 20-30 Assn. of U.S./Canada [13032]
Active Learning Network for Accountability and Performance in Humanitarian Action [IO]
Adventist Development and Relief Agency - Togo [IO]
AEC - TEA Volunteer Centre [IO]
AFL-CIO Community Action Field Mobilization Dept. [11801]
Africa-America Inst. - New York [11759]

Africa-America Inst. - New York [IO]
African Amer. Criminal Justice Soc. [17359]
Africare - Angola [IO]
Africare - Benin [IO]
Africare - Nigeria [IO]
Africare - Sierra Leone [IO]
Africare - Tanzania [IO]
Afrikanerbond [IO]
Alliance for Communities in Action [12416]
Alliance of Natl. Heritage Areas [9856]
Altrusa Intl. [13033]
AMBUCS [13034]
Am. Bikes [17022]
Amer. Bar Assn. Commn. on Homelessness and Poverty [12286]
Amer. Civic Assn. [12403]
Amer. Cong. of Community Supports and Employment Services [17206]
Amer. Friends Ser. Comm. [13148]
Amer. Indian Youth Running Strong [12623]
Amer. Inst. of Certified Planners [5585]
Amer. Jewish Joint Distribution Comm. [12464]
Amer. Planning Assn. [5586]
Amer. Red Cross Overseas Assn. [12831]
Amer. Rescue Workers [13153]
Amer. Soc. of Consulting Planners [5587]
Amer. Youth Understanding Diabetes Abroad [14219]
Americans for Indian Opportunity [12624]
America's Second Harvest [12388]
AmeriCorps VISTA [13383]
APPEAL: Asian Pacific Partners for Empowerment and Leadership [11760]
APPEAL: Asian Pacific Partners for Empowerment and Leadership [IO]
Arab Urban Development Inst. [IO]
Architecture for Humanity [IO]
Architecture for Humanity [11761]
Arcus Found. [18266]
Arthacharya Found. [IO]
Artists for a Better World Intl. [9549]
Artists Helping Artists [9498]
Asia Am. Initiative [11762]
Asia Am. Initiative [IO]
ASIAN [18974]
Asian Americans/Pacific Islanders in Philanthropy [12710]
Assistance for Indigenous People of Eastern Bolivia [IO]
Assistance League [13035]
Assisted Living Fed. of Am. [12306]
Assn. for the Advancement of Mexican Americans [11763]
Assn. of Americans for Civic Responsibility [17074]
Assn. for Community Networking [8124]
Assn. of Community Organizations for Reform Now [IO]
Assn. of Gospel Rescue Missions [13155]
Assn. of Metropolitan Planning Organizations [17207]
Assn. of Pedestrian and Bicycle Professionals [18747]
Assn. Promoting Educ. and Conservation in Amazonia [5294]
Assn. for the Promotion of African Community Initiatives [IO]
Assn. for Res. on Nonprofit Organizations and Voluntary Action [13387]
Assn. of Schools of Public Hea. [16240]
Assn. for Stimulating Know How [IO]
Assn. of World Coun. of Churches Related Development Organisations in Europe [IO]
Augusto Cesar Sandino Found. [IO]
Australian Natl. Flag Assn. [IO]
Benton Found. [11764]
Bike and Build [11514]
Black Women of Essence [11269]
Blossom [IO]
Bread for the Journey Intl. [12711]
Brethren Volunteer Ser. [13388]
Bridges to Community [13389]
Builders Without Borders [12307]
Bus. Alliance for Local Living Economies [887]
Bus. Alliance for Local Living Economies [IO]

Call to Renewal [18376]
A Call to Serve Intl. [11765]
Canada India Village Aid Assn. [IO]
Canadian Inst. of Cultural Affairs [IO]
Canadian Inst. of Planners [IO]
Canadian Physicians for Aid and Relief - Malawi [IO]
Canadian Physicians for Aid and Relief - Uganda [IO]
Catholic Commn. for Development - Zambia [IO]
Center for Community Action of B'Nai B'rith Intl. [IO]
Center for Community Action of B'Nai B'rith Intl. [11766]
Center for Community and Org. Development [11750]
Center for Design Planning [5588]
Center for Neighborhood Enterprise [17208]
Center for Neighborhood Tech. [17209]
Center for New Community [17210]
Center for Reflective Community Practice [17211]
Center for Urban Res. [IO]
Center for Work and the Family [12144]
Centre for Commun. and Development [IO]
Centre for Development and Population Activities [12422]
Centre for Educ. and Documentation [IO]
Centro de Estudios Latinoamericanos - Justo Arosemena [IO]
Centro de Investigacion y Documentacion para el Desarrollo del Beni [IO]
Chaipattana Found. [IO]
Chaordic Commons [7409]
Christian Aid [IO]
Christian Community Development Assn. [20278]
Christian Engineers in Development [IO]
Christian Relief and Development Assn. [IO]
Christian Sports Intl. [23298]
Circle K Intl. [13037]
Citizens Network for Sustainable Development [11767]
CityTeam Ministries [12844]
Civic Trust [IO]
Civitan Intl. [13038]
Clowns Without Borders - USA [11768]
Clowns Without Borders - USA [IO]
Coffee Kids [IO]
Coffee Kids [11769]
Common Ground Prog. [IO]
Commonwealth Assn. of Planners [IO]
Community Advice Bur. [IO]
Community Associations Inst. [17212]
Community Built Assn. [11770]
Community Development Rsrc. Network [IO]
Community Development Soc. [IO]
Community Development Soc. [17213]
Community Development Venture Capital Alliance [11771]
Community Economics, Inc. [12308]
Community Food Security Coalition [12192]
Community Found. Network [IO]
Community Info. and Epidemiological Technologies [12121]
Community Involvement Proj. [IO]
Community Matters: The Natl. Fed. of Community Organisations [IO]
Community Ser. [17214]
Community Trans. Assn. of Am. [11772]
Conf. Bd. of Canada [IO]
Conf. on Jewish Material Claims Against Germany [12470]
Consultative Gp. on Intl. Agricultural Res. [12425]
Cooperative Housing Found. [12309]
Cosmopolitan Intl. [13039]
Coun. for Affordable and Rural Housing [12310]
Coun. on Educ. for Public Hea. [16242]
Coun. of Religious Volunteer Agencies [13391]
Coun. of State Community Development Agencies [6272]
Counterpart Intl. [12426]
Development Planning Unit [IO]
Development Stud. and Promotion Center [IO]
Development Trusts Assn. [IO]
Direct Aid Intl. [12849]
Diyalo Pariwar [IO]

A star before a book entry number signifies that the name is not listed separately, but is mentioned within the entry.

Do Something [17215]
Eco-Animal Allies [11773]
Eco-friendly Nepal [IO]
Educators Serving the Community [8318]
Egyptians Relief Assn. [11774]
El Taller [IO]
Empowerment Soc. Intl. [11775]
Emprender Found. [IO]
Engineers for a Sustainable World [IO]
Engineers for a Sustainable World [11776]
Engineers Without Borders - USA [12111]
Enterprise Community Partners [12311]
Esquel Gp. Found. - Brazil [IO]
Evangelical Lutheran Good Samaritan Soc.
  [13168]
Faith and Joy - Venezuela [IO]
FaithWorks Intl. [IO]
FaithWorks Intl. [11777]
Family Justice [11865]
FARMS Intl. [12427]
Fed. of Southern Cooperatives Land Assistance
  Fund [12937]
Fellowship for Intentional Community [17216]
Filipino Amer. Coalition for Environmental Solidar-
  ity [4634]
FilmAid Intl. [12811]
Finance Proj. [17583]
Food for Life Global [12855]
Found. for Development of Needy Communities -
  Uganda [IO]
Found. for Intl. Community Assistance [IO]
Found. for Intl. Community Assistance [17217]
Found. for People and Community Development
  [IO]
Francena Purchase Applied Honors Soc. [17018]
Fraunhofer-Information Centre for Regional Plan-
  ning and Building Constr. [IO]
Freedom from Hunger [12394]
Frontiers Found. [IO]
Frontiers Intl. [IO]
Frontiers Intl. [11778]
Funders' Collaborative on Youth Organizing
  [12718]
Fundesarrollo [IO]
Future Harvest [4089]
Futures for Children [11695]
Gems of Hope [IO]
Generations United [13170]
Genetic Engg. Action Network [6615]
German Agro Action - Germany [IO]
GesherCity [19183]
Global Harmony Found. [IO]
Global Ser. Corps [13392]
Globe Aware [13393]
Gonja Assn. of North Am. [11779]
Gonja Assn. of North Am. [IO]
Good Bears of the World [13041]
Good Fellows (Old Newsboys) [13042]
Green Empowerment [4335]
Green Empowerment [IO]
Gyro Intl. [13043]
Habitat for Humanity Intl. [12313]
Harvest Help [IO]
Hea. Educ. Coun. [14562]
Hea. Educ. Found. [16243]
Heifer Proj. Intl. [12429]
HelpArgentina [IO]
Helping Our Teen Girls in Real Life Situations
  [12261]
HELVETAS - Bhutan [IO]
HELVETAS - Mali [IO]
HELVETAS - Philippines [IO]
Hispanas Organized for Political Equality [17703]
Hmong Natl. Development [17815]
Holiday Proj. [13395]
HOPE Worldwide - Afghanistan [IO]
HOPE Worldwide - Africa [IO]
HOPE Worldwide - Australia [IO]
HOPE Worldwide - Brazil [IO]
HOPE Worldwide - Canada [IO]
HOPE Worldwide - Caribbean [IO]
HOPE Worldwide - Germany [IO]
HOPE Worldwide - Indonesia [IO]
HOPE Worldwide - Papua New Guinea [IO]
Horizons of Friendship [IO]

HOUR Money Network [17218]
Housing Assistance Coun. [12315]
Human Concern Intl. [IO]
Human Sciences Res. Coun. [IO]
ICA - Australia [IO]
Ijaw Natl. Alliance of the Americas [12639]
Immigration and Refugee Services of Am. [12404]
Independence Inst. [17120]
Independence Plan for Neighborhood Councils
  [17219]
Indicorps [12406]
Indify [13488]
Indigenous Peoples Coun. on Biocolonialism
  [12407]
Indus. Areas Found. [17220]
Innovations in Civic Participation [17075]
Inst. for Community Economics [17221]
Inst. of Cultural Affairs [12350]
Inst. of Cultural Affairs - Australia [IO]
Inst. of Cultural Affairs Intl. - Belgium [IO]
Inst. of Cultural Affairs - Japan [IO]
Inst. of Cultural Affairs - Middle East and North
  Africa [IO]
Inst. of Cultural Affairs - Mumbai [IO]
Inst. of Cultural Affairs - Pune [IO]
Inst. of Cultural Affairs - Zimbabwe [IO]
Inst. of Development Stud. [IO]
Inst. for Sustainable Communities [IO]
Inst. for Sustainable Communities [11780]
Intermediate Tech. Development Gp. of North Am.
  [16997]
Intl. Assn. of Character Cities [11781]
Intl. Assn. of Character Cities [IO]
Intl. Coalition for Children and the Env. [4636]
Intl. Coalition for Sustainable Production and
  Consumption [17222]
Intl. Coalition for Sustainable Production and
  Consumption [IO]
Intl. Fed. of Settlements and Neighbourhood Cen-
  tres [IO]
Intl. Inst. for Mgt. Development [IO]
Intl. Inst. of Rural Reconstruction, U.S. Chap.
  [12938]
Intl. Network for Urban Development [IO]
Intl. NGO Forum on Indonesian Development -
  European Liaison Off. [IO]
Intl. NGO Forum on Indonesian Development -
  Indonesia [IO]
Intl. Relief And Development [IO]
Intl. Relief And Development [11782]
Intl. Relief Friendship Found. [13171]
Intl. Relief Teams [12863]
Intl. Senior Lawyers Proj. [5502]
Intl. Soc. of City and Regional Planners [IO]
Intl. Volunteer Org. for Women, Educ. and
  Development [IO]
Intl. Women's Coffee Alliance [11783]
Interreligious Found. for Community Org. [11797]
Islamic Relief USA [12865]
Italian Center of Solidarity [IO]
Jewish Community Centers Assn. of North Am.
  [12473]
Join Hands Day [17203]
Junior Chamber Intl. [13044]
Junior Optimist Octagon Intl. [13045]
Key Club Intl. [13046]
King Baudouin Found. [IO]
Kiwanis Intl. [13047]
La Otra Bolsa de Valores [IO]
La Sertoma Intl. [13048]
Lalmba Assn. [12866]
LEAD Intl.: Leadership for Env. and Development
  [IO]
Leadership Development Network [17223]
Leap South Africa [IO]
Learning and Development Kenya [IO]
Lewa Wildlife Conservancy (USA) [5337]
Life for Relief and Development [12867]
Links [13049]
Lions Clubs Intl. [13050]
Little Bros. - Friends of the Elderly [11295]
Local Initiatives Support Corp. [17224]
Lotus Outreach [13143]
Lutheran Volunteer Corps [20228]
Ma'an Development Center [IO]

Makassed Found. of Am. [12730]
Manushi for Sustainable Development [IO]
Marga Inst., Sri Lanka Centre for Development
  Stud. [IO]
Mexican-American Opportunity Found. [12276]
Midwest Acad. [11751]
Milton S. Eisenhower Found. [11839]
Mirrer Yeshiva Central Inst. [12477]
MS - Danish Assn. for Intl. Co-operation [IO]
Musicians' Alliance for Peace [18223]
Natl. Alliance for Civic Educ. [8091]
Natl. Alliance to Nurture the Aged and the Youth
  [12358]
Natl. Alliance of Vietnamese Amer. Ser. Agencies
  [19423]
Natl. Assn. for the Advancement of Haitian
  Descendents [19097]
Natl. Assn. of Colored Women's Clubs [13051]
Natl. Assn. of Community Development Extension
  Professionals [11784]
Natl. Assn. for County Community and Economic
  Development [17225]
Natl. Assn. of County Planners [5589]
Natl. Assn. of Development Organizations [5590]
Natl. Assn. of Development Organizations Res.
  Found. [17226]
Natl. Assn. of Housing and Redevelopment Of-
  ficials [5793]
Natl. Assn. of Junior Auxiliaries [13052]
Natl. Assn. of Negro Bus. and Professional
  Women's Clubs [13053]
Natl. Assn. of Neighborhoods [11752]
Natl. Assn. for Olmsted Parks [5591]
Natl. Assn. of Planning Councils [18275]
Natl. Assn. of Rsrc. Conservation and Develop-
  ment Councils [4421]
Natl. Assn. of State Development Agencies [5592]
Natl. Assn. of Urban Hospitals [14893]
Natl. Australia Day Coun. [IO]
Natl. Benevolent Assn. of the Christian Church
  [13177]
Natl. Black on Black Love Campaign [11842]
Natl. Black Farmers Assn. [12189]
Natl. Brownfield Assn. [3191]
Natl. Center for Urban Ethnic Affairs [11753]
Natl. Coalition for Asian Pacific Amer. Community
  Development [11785]
Natl. Coalition Building Inst. [17227]
Natl. Community Action Found. [11754]
Natl. Community Building Network [11786]
Natl. Community Development Assn. [17228]
Natl. Community for Latino Leadership [19203]
Natl. Community Reinvestment Coalition [17229]
Natl. Conf. of Local Environmental Hea.
  Administrators [16246]
Natl. Coun. on Agricultural Life and Labor Res.
  Fund [12322]
Natl. Development Coun. [17463]
Natl. Exchange Club [13054]
Natl. Found. of Manufactured Home Owners
  [12323]
Natl. Haitian Soc. [17817]
Natl. Hispanic Coun. on Aging [11310]
Natl. Housing Conf. [12325]
Natl. Housing Inst. [12326]
Natl. Housing Law Proj. [5796]
Natl. Housing and Rehabilitation Assn. [12327]
Natl. Human Services Assembly [13400]
Natl. Initiative for a Networked Cultural Heritage
  [9858]
Natl. Leased Housing Assn. [12329]
Natl. Legal Sanctuary for Community Advance-
  ment [6015]
Natl. Low Income Housing Coalition [12330]
Natl. Neighborhood Coalition [17230]
Natl. Org. of African Americans in Housing
  [12331]
Natl. Organizers Alliance [13136]
Natl. Partnership for Community Leadership
  [11805]
Natl. People's Action [11755]
Natl. Policy Assn. [5593]
Natl. Puerto Rican Forum [12280]
Natl. Rural Economic Developers Assn. [18574]
Natl. Rural Hea. Assn. [16248]

Reference to "IO" in place of a book number signifies that the association may be found in the 45th edition of International Organizations.

Natl. Rural Housing Coalition [12332]
Natl. Student Campaign Against Hunger and Homelessness [12396]
Natl. Training and Info. Center [11799]
Natl. Trust Main St. Center [17231]
Natl. Youth Employment Coalition [13506]
Native Amer. Community Bd. [12630]
Neighborhood Housing Services of Am. [12334]
NeighborWorks Am. [12335]
NetAid [11486]
Netherlands Development Org. - Burkina Faso [IO]
Netherlands Development Org. - Cameroon [IO]
Netherlands Development Org. - Mali [IO]
Network Women in Development Europe [IO]
New Water Supply Coalition [7839]
New York New Visions [17232]
NGA [13056]
NSF Intl. [16249]
Omslag Workshop for Sustainable Development [IO]
OneWorld Intl. Found. [17780]
Oper. HOPE, Inc. [11787]
Ophelia Proj. [13509]
Opportunity Finance Network [17233]
Opportunity Plus [11978]
Optimist Intl. [13057]
Org. for the Relief of Underprivileged Women and Children in Africa [12876]
Organize Training Center [11800]
OXFAM Am. [12438]
Oxfam Australia [IO]
Oxfam - Quebec [IO]
PACT [12439]
Pakistan Welfare Org. [13182]
Pan African Inst. for Development - Burkina Faso [IO]
Panos Inst. - Western Africa [IO]
Partners for Livable Communities [5594]
Pasteef Youth Assn. for Development [IO]
People's Involvement Corp. [13183]
Pilot Intl. and Pilot Intl. Found. [13058]
Planet Aid [13144]
Plenty Canada [IO]
PolicyLink [18276]
Praxis Proj. [17204]
Presbyterian Hea., Educ. and Welfare Assn. [13184]
Presbyterian Hunger Prog. [12397]
Progressive Tech. Proj. [7758]
Promotora de las Comunidades Municipales [IO]
Public Citizen Hea. Res. Gp. [16250]
Public Works and Economic Development Assn. [5595]
Quota Intl. [13059]
RAFAD Found. [IO]
Rainbow/PUSH Coalition [13185]
REAP Intl. [12940]
Regional Sci. Assn. Intl. [5596]
Regional Sci. Assn. Intl. [IO]
Regional Stud. Assn. [IO]
Renew Am. [4336]
Retired and Senior Volunteer Prog. [13403]
Rigoberta Menchu Tum Found. [17151]
Rotary Intl. [13060]
Round-Table U.S.A. [13061]
Royal Dublin Soc. [IO]
Royal Town Planning Inst. [IO]
Rural Planning Organizations of Am. [6247]
Ruritan Natl. [13062]
SADC Plant Genetic Resources Centre [IO]
Salvadoran Amer. Leadership and Educational Fund [17484]
Salvation Army [13187]
Save the Children [11720]
Saving the Arts [9598]
SCI - Intl. Voluntary Ser. [13404]
Seeking Common Ground [13514]
Senior Companion Prog. [13405]
Senior Gleaners [12398]
Sertoma Intl. [13063]
Seva Found. [12443]
Singles in Ser. [13064]
Sister Island Proj. [11788]
Soccer in the Streets [11789]

Social Enterprise Alliance [3633]
Social Relief Intl. [12445]
Social Venture Network [764]
Soc. for Env. and Human Development [IO]
Soc. of Polish Town Planners [IO]
Soc. for Public Hea. Educ. [16254]
Somali Family Care Network [19392]
SOPAR [IO]
Soroptimist Intl. of the Americas [13065]
South Africa Partners [18666]
South Asian Amer. Leaders of Tomorrow [18667]
Southeast Asia Rsrc. Action Center [12820]
Southern Africa Development Community - Botswana [IO]
Southern Mutual Help Assn. [11790]
Spirit of Am. [18488]
Structured Employment Economic Development Corp. [12045]
Surface Trans. Policy Proj. [18750]
SurfAid Intl. [11791]
SurfAid Intl. [IO]
Sustainable Harvest Intl. [4115]
SustainUS [13517]
Swadhina [IO]
Swiss Assn. for Intl. Cooperation - Helvetas Vietnam [IO]
Tech. Advisors Gp. [IO]
TechnoServe - Tanzania [IO]
Teen Missions Intl. [20402]
Thunderhead Alliance [18751]
Tile Partners for Humanity [12338]
Touching Hearts [11267]
United Neighborhood Centers of Am. [11792]
U.S. Connected Communities Assn. [6716]
U.S. Junior Chamber of Commerce [24390]
U.S.-Mexico Border Hea. Assn. [16256]
Unity Corps [19017]
Urban Homesteading Assistance Bd. [12339]
Urban Land Inst. [5597]
Vietnamese Amer. Coun. [19427]
Village Earth: CSVBD [11793]
Village Earth: CSVBD [IO]
Voices in the Wilderness [18253]
Volunteer Soc. Nepal [IO]
Volunteers of Am. [13192]
Volunteers in Overseas Cooperative Assistance - USA [13408]
Volunteers in Tech. Assistance [12448]
The Waterfront Center [11794]
We Care Am. [13210]
Wimbum Cultural and Development Assn. in the U.S.A. [9344]
Winant and Clayton Volunteers [13409]
Windustry [7853]
Women for Change [IO]
Women in Show Business for Children [13069]
World Development Fed. [12449]
World Fed. of Public Hea. Associations [16258]
World Through My Eyes [IO]
World Vision Intl. - Vietnam [IO]
Youth Impact Intl. [13521]
ZHABA Facilitators Collective [IO]
Zonta Intl. [13071]
Community Development Agencies; Coun. of State [6272]
Community Development Assn; Christian [20278]
Community Development; Center for Individual and [★12365]
Community Development Coun; Ethiopian [12810]
Community Development Credit Unions; Natl. Fed. of [1118]
Community Development Directors Assn; Natl. Model Cities [★17228]
Community Development Directors; Natl. Assn. of County [★17225]
Community Development Finance Assn. [IO], London, United Kingdom
Community Development Found. [★11720]
Community Development Institute; Research and [★18840]
Community Development Org; Virginia [★11798]
Community Development Rsrc. Network [IO], Kampala, Uganda
Community Development Soc. [IO], Columbus, OH, United States

Community Development Soc. [17213], 17 S High St., Ste. 200, Columbus, OH 43215, (614)221-1900
Community Development Venture Capital Alliance [11771], 424 W 33rd St., Ste. 320, New York, NY 10001, (212)594-6747
Community Dispute Services - Defunct.
Community and District Nursing Assn. [IO], London, United Kingdom
Community Dreamsharing Network [16425]
Community Economics, Inc. [12308], 538 9th St., Ste. 200, Oakland, CA 94607, (510)832-8300
Community Education
    Amer. Cong. of Community Supports and Employment Services [17206]
    Amer. Coun. on Intl. Intercultural Educ. [8651]
    Assn. for Community Based Education [8123]
    Assn. for Community Networking [8124]
    Assn. for Community Networking [IO]
    Assn. of Schools of Public Hea. [16240]
    Center for Respect of Life and Env. [4620]
    Community-Campus Partnerships For Hea. [11744]
    Coun. on Educ. for Public Hea. [16242]
    Families for Natural Living [8416]
    First Book [8789]
    Generations United [13170]
    Hea. Educ. Found. [16243]
    Indigenous Peoples Coun. on Biocolonialism [12407]
    Intl. Alliance in Ser. and Educ. [11748]
    Intl. Assn. of Character Cities [11781]
    Literacy USA [8792]
    Milton S. Eisenhower Found. [11839]
    Natl. Center for Community Educ. [8125]
    Natl. Center for Hea. Educ. [14582]
    Natl. Center for Urban Ethnic Affairs [11753]
    Natl. Community Educ. Assn. [8126]
    Natl. Conf. of Local Environmental Hea. Administrators [16246]
    Natl. Rural Hea. Assn. [16248]
    Natl. Service-Learning Partnership [9120]
    New Road Map Found. [12360]
    NSF Intl. [16249]
    Peer Hea. Exchange [9338]
    ProEnglish [9912]
    Proj. Food, Land and People [4525]
    Public Citizen Hea. Res. Gp. [16250]
    Soc. for Public Hea. Educ. [16254]
    Supporting Our Sons [11547]
    Touching Hearts [11267]
    U.S.-Mexico Border Hea. Assn. [16256]
    World Fed. of Public Hea. Associations [16258]
Community Educ; Natl. Assn. for Family and [8513]
Community Educ. Rsrc. Center [★11750]
Community Emergency Care Assn. - Defunct.
Community Environmental Coun. [5267], 26 W Anapamu St., 2nd Fl., Santa Barbara, CA 93101, (805)884-0459
Community of E.U. Shipbuilding Assn. [★IO]
Community of European Railways [IO], Brussels, Belgium
Community of European Shipyards' Associations [IO], Brussels, Belgium
Community Fellows Prog. [★17211]
Community Financial Services Assn. [1408], 515 King St., Ste. 300, Alexandria, VA 22314, (703)684-1029
Community Food Security Coalition [12192], PO Box 209, Venice, CA 90294, (310)822-5410
Community Food Security Coalition [IO], Venice, CA, United States
Community; Found. for Global [18203]
Community Found. for Independence [★17219]
Community Found. Network [IO], London, United Kingdom
Community Foundations; Natl. Coun. on [★12652]
Community Guidance Centers; Gp. for [★16214]
Community Guidance Ser. [16214], 155 W 68th St., Ste. 1618, New York, NY 10023, (212)724-1091
Community Hea. Centers; Natl. Assn. of [14574]
Community Hea. Charities [12200], 200 N Glebe Rd., Ste. 801, Arlington, VA 22203, (703)528-1007
Community Hea; Fenway [14430]
Community Hea. Nurses Assn. of Canada [IO], Toronto, ON, Canada

---

A star before a book entry number signifies that the name is not listed separately, but is mentioned within the entry.

Community Hea. Plans; Alliance of [14678]
Community Hea. Services; Coun. of Home Hea. Agencies/ [★14840]
Community and Hosp. Infection Control Assn. - Canada [IO], Winnipeg, MB, Canada
Community Hospitals Assn. [IO], Ilminster, United Kingdom
Community Housing Fed. of Australia [IO], Woden, Australia
Community Housing for the Hearing Impaired Prog. [★14752]
Community Improvement
  Active 20-30 Assn. of U.S./Canada [13032]
  AFL-CIO Community Action Field Mobilization Dept. [11801]
  Alliance for Communities in Action [12416]
  Alliance for a Paving Moratorium [17234]
  Altrusa Intl. [13033]
  AMBUCS [13034]
  Amer. Bar Assn. Commn. on Homelessness and Poverty [12286]
  Amer. Civic Assn. [12403]
  Americans for Balanced Energy Choices [17495]
  AmeriCorps VISTA [13383]
  Architectural League of New York [17235]
  Arcus Found. [18266]
  Artists for a Better World Intl. [9549]
  Asia Am. Initiative [11762]
  Asian Americans/Pacific Islanders in Philanthropy [12710]
  Assistance League [13035]
  Assn. of Americans for Civic Responsibility [17074]
  Assn. for Community Hea. Improvement [16238]
  Assn. for Community Networking [8124]
  Assn. of Community Organizations for Reform Now [11749]
  Assn. of Gospel Rescue Missions [13155]
  Bread for the Journey Intl. [12711]
  Brethren Volunteer Ser. [13388]
  Bridges to Community [13389]
  A Call to Serve Intl. [11765]
  Center for Community and Org. Development [11750]
  Center for Work and the Family [12144]
  Christian Sports Intl. [23298]
  Christian Sports Intl. [IO]
  Circle K Intl. [13037]
  Citizens Network for Sustainable Development [11767]
  Civitan Intl. [13038]
  Coalition for Environmentally Safe Communities [12118]
  Community Built Assn. [11770]
  Community Leadership Assn. [11795]
  Cosmopolitan Intl. [13039]
  Coun. of Religious Volunteer Agencies [13391]
  Direct Aid Intl. [12849]
  Do Something [17215]
  Eco-Animal Allies [11773]
  Egyptians Relief Assn. [11774]
  Empowerment Soc. Intl. [11775]
  Engineers Without Borders - USA [12111]
  Evangelical Lutheran Good Samaritan Soc. [13168]
  Experience Works [12080]
  Experimental Cities, Inc. [17236]
  FaithWorks Intl. [11777]
  Fed. of Southern Cooperatives Land Assistance Fund [12937]
  Filipino Amer. Coalition for Environmental Solidarity [4634]
  FilmAid Intl. [12811]
  The Gardeners of America/Men's Garden Clubs of Am. [4778]
  Generations United [13170]
  Global Ser. Corps [13392]
  Global Youth Connect [18851]
  Globe Aware [13393]
  Gonja Assn. of North Am. [11779]
  Good Bears of the World [13041]
  Good Fellows (Old Newsboys) [13042]
  Gyro Intl. [13043]
  Hea. Educ. Coun. [14562]
  Holiday Proj. [13395]

Ijaw Natl. Alliance of the Americas [12639]
Immigration and Refugee Services of Am. [12404]
Intermediate Tech. Development Gp. of North Am. [16997]
Intl. Coalition for Sustainable Production and Consumption [17222]
Intl. Healthy Cities Found. [13349]
Intl. Inst. of Rural Reconstruction, U.S. Chap. [12938]
Intl. Relief Friendship Found. [13171]
Interreligious Found. for Community Org. [11797]
Join Hands Day [17203]
Junior Chamber Intl. [13044]
Junior Optimist Octagon Intl. [13045]
Key Club Intl. [13046]
Kiwanis Intl. [13047]
La Sertoma Intl. [13048]
Links [13049]
Lions Clubs Intl. [13050]
Little Bros. - Friends of the Elderly [11295]
Mental Disability Rights Intl. [12574]
Mexican-American Opportunity Found. [12276]
Midwest Acad. [11751]
Milton S. Eisenhower Found. [11839]
Natl. Alliance for Civic Educ. [8091]
Natl. Alliance for Family Court Justice [5904]
Natl. Assn. of African Americans for Positive Imagery [16941]
Natl. Assn. of Colored Women's Clubs [13051]
Natl. Assn. of Community Development Extension Professionals [11784]
Natl. Assn. of Junior Auxiliaries [13052]
Natl. Assn. of Negro Bus. and Professional Women's Clubs [13053]
Natl. Assn. of Neighborhoods [11752]
Natl. Assn. of Planning Councils [18275]
Natl. Benevolent Assn. of the Christian Church [13177]
Natl. Black on Black Love Campaign [11842]
Natl. Center for Urban Ethnic Affairs [11753]
Natl. Coalition for Asian Pacific Amer. Community Development [11785]
Natl. Coalition for the Homeless [12296]
Natl. Community Action Found. [11754]
Natl. Community Building Network [11786]
Natl. Community Development Org. [11798]
Natl. Exchange Club [13054]
Natl. Haitian Soc. [17817]
Natl. Housing Inst. [12326]
Natl. Human Services Assembly [13400]
Natl. Main St. Center [17237]
Natl. Partnership for Community Leadership [11805]
Natl. People's Action [11755]
Natl. Rural Economic Developers Assn. [18574]
Natl. Student Safety Prog. [18579]
Natl. Training and Info. Center [11799]
NeighborWorks Am. [12335]
NetAid [11486]
New Env. Assn. [4597]
New Road Map Found. [12360]
NGA [13056]
North Amer. Power Sweeping Assn. [2473]
Oper. HOPE, Inc. [11787]
Opportunity Plus [11978]
Optimist Intl. [13057]
Organize Training Center [11800]
People's Involvement Corp. [13183]
Pilot Intl. and Pilot Intl. Found. [13058]
Praxis Proj. [17204]
Presbyterian Hea., Educ. and Welfare Assn. [13184]
Progressive Tech. Proj. [7758]
Proj. for Public Spaces [17238]
Public Art Fund [17239]
Quota Intl. [13059]
Rainbow/PUSH Coalition [13185]
REAP Intl. [12940]
Renew Am. [4336]
Retired and Senior Volunteer Prog. [13403]
Rotary Intl. [13060]
Round-Table U.S.A. [13061]
Ruritan Natl. [13062]
Salvation Army [13187]
Saving the Arts [9598]

SCI - Intl. Voluntary Ser. [13404]
Sculpture in the Env. [17240]
Seeking Common Ground [13514]
Senior Companion Prog. [13405]
Sertoma Intl. [13063]
Singles in Ser. [13064]
Social Relief Intl. [12445]
Social Venture Network [764]
Soroptimist Intl. of the Americas [13065]
South Africa Partners [18666]
Southern Mutual Help Assn. [11790]
Structured Employment Economic Development Corp. [12045]
Sustainable Harvest Intl. [4115]
SustainUS [13517]
U.S. Connected Communities Assn. [6716]
U.S. Junior Chamber of Commerce [24390]
Volunteers of Am. [13192]
The Waterfront Center [11794]
We Care Am. [13210]
Wimbum Cultural and Development Assn. in the U.S.A. [9344]
Winant and Clayton Volunteers [13409]
Windustry [7853]
Women in Show Business for Children [13069]
Youth Impact Intl. [13521]
Zonta Intl. [13071]
Community Indus. Noise Control Assn. [★7383]
Community Info. and Epidemiological Technologies [12121], 511 Ave. of the Americas, No. 132, New York, NY 10011, (212)242-3428
Community Info. and Epidemiological Technologies [IO], New York, NY, United States
Community Info. Ser; European [★17507]
Community Interest; Center for the [17096]
Community Involvement Proj. [IO], Nanaimo, BC, Canada
Community and Junior Colleges; Amer. Assn. of [★8117]
Community Justice; Center for [★5451]
Community and Justice; Natl. Conf. for [19904]
Community Land Trust Center; Natl. [★17221]
Community Leadership Assn. [11795], Fanning Inst., 1240 S Lumpkin St., Univ. of Georgia, Athens, GA 30602, (706)542-0301
Community Leadership Assn. [IO], Athens, GA, United States
Community Leadership; Natl. Assn. for [★11795]
Community Leadership Organizations; Natl. Assn. of [★11795]
Community Learning and Info. Network [8334], 1750 K St. NW, Ste. 1200, Washington, DC 20006, (202)857-2330
Community Learning and Info. Network [IO], Washington, DC, United States
Community Matters: The Natl. Fed. of Community Organisations [IO], London, United Kingdom
Community Media; Alliance for [17161]
Community Media Assn. [IO], Sheffield, United Kingdom
Community Mediation; Natl. Assn. for [5460]
Community Mental Health
  Amer. Assn. of Community Psychiatrists [16066]
  Amer. Cong. of Community Supports and Employment Services [17206]
  Assn. of Schools of Public Hea. [16240]
  Community-Campus Partnerships For Hea. [11744]
  Coun. on Educ. for Public Hea. [16242]
  Hea. Educ. Found. [16243]
  Natl. Center for Victims of Crime [13366]
  Natl. Conf. of Local Environmental Hea. Administrators [16246]
  Natl. Rural Hea. Assn. [16248]
  NSF Intl. [16249]
  Public Citizen Hea. Res. Gp. [16250]
  Soc. for Public Hea. Educ. [16254]
  U.S.-Mexico Border Hea. Assn. [16256]
  World Fed. of Public Hea. Associations [16258]
Community Newspapers of Australia [IO], Sydney, Australia
Community Nutrition Inst. [15551]
Community Off. of Press and Public Affairs; European [★17507]
Community Options and Resources; Amer. Network of [12560]

Reference to "IO" in place of a book number signifies that the association may be found in the 45th edition of International Organizations.

Encyclopedia of Associations, 46th Edition

3277

Community Organization

Assn. for Community Org. and Social Admin. [13198]
Assn. of Community Organizations for Reform Now [11749]
Assn. of Jewish Center Professionals [12466]
Center for Community and Org. Development [11750]
Community Leadership Assn. [11795]
Community Leadership Assn. [IO]
Engineers for a Sustainable World [11776]
Experience Works [12080]
Homeworkers Organized for More Employment [12081]
Inst. for Social Justice [11796]
Interreligious Found. for Community Org. [11797]
Jewish Community Centers Assn. of North Am. [12473]
Midwest Acad. [11751]
Natl. Alliance for Hispanic Hea. [13176]
Natl. Assn. of Neighborhoods [11752]
Natl. Assn. of Peer Programs [11827]
Natl. Community Development Org. [11798]
Natl. Hispanic Coun. on Aging [11310]
Natl. Training and Info. Center [11799]
Natl. Youth Employment Coalition [13506]
New York New Visions [17232]
Organize Training Center [11800]
People's Involvement Corp. [13183]
South Asian Amer. Leaders of Tomorrow [18667]
Youth Ser. Am. [13070]
Community Org; Assn. for the Stud. of [★13206]
Community Org. Res. Action Project - Defunct.
Community Org. and Social Admin; Assn. for [13198]
Community Ownership Organizing Proj. [★12308]
Community Papers; Assn. of Free [88]
Community Policing Consortium [3068], 1726 M St. NW, Ste. 801, Washington, DC 20036, (800)833-3085
Community Pride Assn. - Defunct.
Community Projects; World [★12884]
Community Psychiatrists; Amer. Assn. of [16066]
Community Radio Assn. [★IO]
Community Regeneration - Defunct.
Community Relations Comm; AFL [★11801]
Community for Religious Res. and Education [20537]
Community Res. Associates - Address unknown since 1995.
Community Researchers; Assn. for Applied [7561]
Community Resources; Logan [11960]
Community Resources Workshop Assn. [★8048]
Community Safety Assn; Amer. School and [★12989]
Community School Educ. Assn; Natl. [★8126]
Community Schools of the Arts; Natl. Guild of [7979]
Community Schools; Natl. Coalition of Alternative [7948]
Community Ser. [17214], PO Box 243, Yellow Springs, OH 45387, (937)767-2161

Community Service

Action in Disabilities - India [IO]
Active 20-30 Assn. of U.S./Canada [13032]
Acupuncturists Without Borders [13536]
AFL-CIO Community Action Field Mobilization Dept. [11801]
Alliance Credit Counseling [11833]
Allies Building Community [9613]
Altrusa Intl. [13033]
AMBUCS [13034]
Amer. Bar Assn. Commn. on Homelessness and Poverty [12286]
Amer. Humane Assn. Children's Services [11556]
Amer. Inst. for Public Ser. [13150]
Amer. Red Cross Overseas Assn. [12831]
Amer. Soc. of Victimology [13360]
Amer. Youth Work Center [13469]
AmeriCorps VISTA [13383]
Architecture for Humanity [11761]
Artists for a Better World Intl. [9549]
Asia Am. Initiative [11762]
Assistance League [13035]
Assn. for the Advancement of Mexican Americans [11763]

Assn. for Community Affiliated Plans [14617]
Assn. of Girl Scout Executive Staff [12996]
Assn. of Gospel Rescue Missions [13155]
Black Women United for Action [13423]
Bread for the Journey Intl. [12711]
Break Away: The Alternative Break Connection [12795]
Brethren Volunteer Ser. [13388]
Call For Action [11802]
Call For Action [IO]
Catholic Campaign for Human Development [12713]
Center for Community Action of B'Nai B'rith Intl. [11766]
Child Relief and You Am. [11569]
Circle K Intl. [13037]
City Parks Alliance [18184]
Civitan Intl. [13038]
Coffee Kids [11769]
Community Built Assn. [11770]
Community Food Security Coalition [12192]
Convoy of Hope [12847]
Corporate and Found. Relations [12075]
Cosmopolitan Intl. [13039]
Coun. of Religious Volunteer Agencies [13391]
CRISTA Ministries [13166]
Do Something [17215]
Educators Serving the Community [8318]
Engineers for a Sustainable World [11776]
Engineers Without Borders - USA [12111]
Evangelical Lutheran Good Samaritan Soc. [13168]
Food for Life Global [12855]
Food Res. and Action Center [12393]
Funders' Collaborative on Youth Organizing [12718]
Future Harvest [4089]
Generations United [13170]
Girl Scouts of the U.S.A. [12998]
Global Envision [12194]
Global Ser. Corps [13392]
Globe Aware [13393]
Good Bears of the World [13041]
Good Fellows (Old Newsboys) [13042]
Gyro Intl. [13043]
Hea. Educ. Coun. [14562]
Help Darfur Now [12259]
Holiday Proj. [13395]
Innovations in Civic Participation [17075]
Intl. Alliance in Ser. and Educ. [11748]
Intl. Medical Volunteers Assn. [15075]
Intl. Relief And Development [11782]
Intl. Relief Friendship Found. [13171]
Intl. Relief Teams [12863]
Intl. Women's Coffee Alliance [11783]
Interreligious Found. for Community Org. [11797]
Islamic Relief USA [12865]
Jewish Communal Ser. Assn. of North Am. [12472]
Jewish Philanthropic Fund of 1933 [12475]
Joint Action in Community Ser. [11803]
Junior Chamber Intl. [13044]
Junior Optimist Octagon Intl. [13045]
Key Club Intl. [13046]
Kiwanis Intl. [13047]
La Sertoma Intl. [13048]
Links [13049]
Lions Clubs Intl. [13050]
Little Bros. - Friends of the Elderly [11295]
Lotus Outreach [13143]
Lutheran Volunteer Corps [20228]
MAD DADS (Men Against Destruction - Defending Against Drugs and Social Disorder) [12043]
Malawi Assn. of Christian Support [IO]
Mexican-American Opportunity Found. [12276]
Millennium Promise [11485]
Milton S. Eisenhower Found. [11839]
Minority Peace Corps Assn. [18261]
Natl. AIDS Housing Coalition [12319]
Natl. AMBUCS [11964]
Natl. Assn. of Colored Women's Clubs [13051]
Natl. Assn. of Junior Auxiliaries [13052]
Natl. Assn. of Lesbian, Gay, Bisexual and Trans-gender Community Centers [11804]
Natl. Assn. of Negro Bus. and Professional Women's Clubs [13053]

Natl. Assn. to Protect Children [11628]
Natl. Assn. of Senior Companion Proj. Directors [11304]
Natl. Assn. for State Community Services Programs [6279]
Natl. Benevolent Assn. of the Christian Church [13177]
Natl. Center for Victims of Crime [13366]
Natl. Coalition for the Homeless [12296]
Natl. Community Action Found. [11754]
Natl. Community Development Org. [11798]
Natl. Coun. of Jewish Women [20166]
Natl. Exchange Club [13054]
Natl. Human Services Assembly [13400]
Natl. Jewish Girl Scout Comm. [13004]
Natl. Partnership for Community Leadership [11805]
Natl. People's Action [11755]
Natl. Relief Network [12873]
Natl. Training and Info. Center [11799]
Natl. Urban League [17138]
Native Amer. Community Bd. [12630]
NGA [13056]
Opportunity Plus [11978]
Optimist Intl. [13057]
Org. for the Relief of Underprivileged Women and Children in Africa [12876]
Organize Training Center [11800]
Partners in Hea. [12270]
People's Involvement Corp. [13183]
Pilot Intl. and Pilot Intl. Found. [13058]
Points of Light Found. [13401]
Presbyterian Hea., Educ. and Welfare Assn. [13184]
Pro Players Assn. [13402]
Quota Intl. [13059]
Rebuilding Alliance [12336]
Retired and Senior Volunteer Prog. [13403]
Rotary Intl. [13060]
Round-Table U.S.A. [13061]
Ruritan Natl. [13062]
Salvation Army [13187]
SCI - Intl. Voluntary Ser. [13404]
Scottish Community Care Forum [IO]
Seeking Common Ground [13514]
Senior Companion Prog. [13405]
Sertoma Intl. [13063]
Singles in Ser. [13064]
Sister Island Proj. [11788]
Soroptimist Intl. of the Americas [13065]
Southern Mutual Help Assn. [11790]
Students Helping St. Kids Intl. [11725]
SurfAid Intl. [11791]
Survivors of Incest Anonymous [13085]
Swiss-American Coun. of Women [18815]
Tech. Without Borders [7763]
Together, Inc. [12365]
U.S. Junior Chamber of Commerce [24390]
U.S. Women of Today [13067]
U.S.A. Harvest [12402]
Vietnamese Amer. Coun. [19427]
VolunteerMatch [18793]
Volunteers of Am. [13192]
Winant and Clayton Volunteers [13409]
Women in Show Business for Children [13069]
Youth Ser. Am. [13070]
Zonta Intl. [13071]
Community Service Credit Union Coun. - Defunct.
Community Ser. Employment Prog; Senior [12099]
Community Ser; Women in [12786]
Community Services [★20552]
Community Services Activities; AFL-CIO [★11801]
Community Services; Adventist [20552]
Community Services; AFL-CIO Dept. of [★11801]
Community Services Comm; CIO [★11801]
Community Services and Continuing Educ; Natl. Coun. on [★8152]
Community Services to Intl. Visitors; Natl. Coun. for [★17903]
Community Services Programs; Natl. Assn. for State [6279]
Community for Social Justice in the Middle East and North Africa - Defunct.
Community Solutions; Center for [17517]
Community Stud; Center for Jewish [17945]

A star before a book entry number signifies that the name is not listed separately, but is mentioned within the entry.

Community Systems Found. [15552], 219 S Main St., Ste. 206, Ann Arbor, MI 48104, (734)761-1357
Community: The Union for Life [IO], London, United Kingdom
Community Theatre Assn; Amer. [★10999]
Community Training and Development - Defunct.
Community Transport Assn. [IO], Hyde, United Kingdom
Community Trans. Assn. of Am. [11772], 1341 G St. NW, 10th Fl., Washington, DC 20005, (202)628-1480
Community Tribal Schools; Assn. of [8936]
Community United Against Violence [12225], 170 A Capp St., San Francisco, CA 94110, (415)777-5500
Community and Veteran Ser. [★11766]
Community and Veteran Ser. [★IO]
Community Voices [11745], c/o Sherry Adeyemi, 210 Guilford Ave., 3rd Fl., Baltimore, MD 21202, (410)396-4502
Community Volunteer Services Commn. of B'Nai Birth Intl. [★11766]
Community Volunteer Services Commn. of B'Nai Birth Intl. [★IO]
Community Welfare; Natl. Comm. on Foundations and Trusts for [★12652]
Community of the Whole Person - Defunct.
Community World Affairs Organizations; Natl. Coun. of [★18843]
Community Youth HIV/AIDS Intervention Network [IO], Kathmandu, Nepal
Community on Youth Smoking Prevention [IO], Hong Kong, People's Republic of China
Commuter Airline Assn. [★166]
Commuter Airline Assn. of Am. [★166]
Commuter Programs; Natl. CH for [9187]
Commuter Trans; Assn. for [13334]
Como Circle; Perry [24960]
Comox Valley Head Injury Soc. [IO], Courtenay, BC, Canada
Compact Commn; Interstate Oil and Gas [5684]
Compact Data Disk Assn. - Defunct.
Compact Disc Group - Defunct.
CompactFlash Assn. [6723], PO Box 51537, Palo Alto, CA 94303, (650)843-1220
Compagnie des Experts Agrees [IO], Paris, France
Companies; Coun. of Growing [715]
Companies; Natl. Assn. of Elec. [★3956]
Companies; Natl. Assn. of Export [2307]
Companies; Natl. Conf. of Commercial Receivable [★2423]
Companion Prog; Senior [13405]
Companions of Dr. Who Fan Club - Defunct.
Companions of the Forest of America - Address unknown since 2003.
Companions of the Holy Cross; Soc. of the [19971]
Companions in Mission [★20408]
Company Chemists Assn. [IO], Milton Keynes, United Kingdom
Company of Fifers and Drummers [10580], PO Box 277, Ivoryton, CT 06442-0277, (860)767-2237
Company of Military Collectors and Historians [★22629]
Company of Military Historians [22629], PO Box 910, Rutland, MA 01543-0910, (508)845-9229
Company of Saint Paul [19614], 52 Davis Ave., White Plains, NY 10605, (914)946-1019
Company of Surgeons of London [★IO]
The Company of Veteran Motorists [★IO]
Comparative Biology; Soc. for Integrative and [7867]
Comparative Cognition Soc. [6400], c/o Jeff Katz, Sec./Conference Organizer, Dept. of Psychology, 226 Thach Hall, Auburn University, AL 36849-5214
Comparative Economic Stud; Assn. for [6870]
Comparative Economics; Assn. for [★6870]

Comparative Education
World Coun. of Comparative Educ. Societies [IO]
Comparative Educ. Soc. [★IO]
Comparative Educ. Soc. [★8655]
Comparative Educ. Soc. in Europe [IO], Freiburg, Germany
Comparative and Intl. Educ. Soc. [IO], Miami, FL, United States
Comparative and Intl. Educ. Soc. [8655], c/o Dr. Hilary Landorf, Treas., Florida International University, Coll. of Educ., Dept. of Curriculum and Instruction, 347A ZEB Bldg., Miami, FL 33199, (305)348-3488

Comparative Law
Intl. Acad. of Linguistic Law [IO]
Intl. Inst. for the Unification of Private Law [IO]
New Zealand Assn. for Comparative Law [IO]
Soc. of Comparative Legislation [IO]
Comparative Law; Amer. Soc. of [5865]
Comparative Literature Assn; Amer. [10409]
Comparative Nutrition Soc. [15553], c/o Wendy R. Hood, Sec./Webmaster, PO Box 261954, Conway, SC 29528
Comparative Philosophy; Soc. for Asian and [10831]
Comparative Stud. of Law; Amer. Assn. for the [★5865]
Comparative Stud. of Soc. and History; Soc. for the [10152]
Compassion for Animals Campaign [11381], PO Box 322, Feasterville, PA 19053, (215)721-6661
Compassion in Dying [★12130]
Compassion in Dying Fed. [12130], c/o Barbara Coombs Lee, Pres./CEO, 6312 SW Capitol Hwy., No. 415, Portland, OR 97239, (503)221-9556
Compassion In World Farming - Ireland [IO], Cork, Ireland
Compassion Intl. - Defunct.
Compassion Over Killing [11382], PO Box 9773, Washington, DC 20016, (301)891-2458
Compassion in World Farming [IO], Petersfield, United Kingdom
Compassionate Cooks [13350], PO Box 18512, Oakland, CA 94619, (510)531-2665
The Compassionate Friends [12666], PO Box 3696, Oak Brook, IL 60522-3696, (630)990-0010
Compassionate Friends; Soc. of the [★12666]
Compassionate Kids [8384], PO Box 329, Sunny Side, GA 30284-0329, (678)447-4269
Compassionate Kids [IO], Sunny Side, GA, United States
Compatible Tech. [★IO]
Compatible Tech. [★4087]
Compatible Tech. Intl. [4087], 800 Transfer Rd., Ste. 6, St. Paul, MN 55114, (651)632-3912
Compatible Tech. Intl. [IO], St. Paul, MN, United States
Compensation Administrators; Natl. Assn. of Govt. Deferred [★2340]
Compensation Assn; Amer. [★1283]
Compensation Assn; Midwest [★1283]
Compensation Attorneys; Natl. Assn. of Claimants [★6328]
Compensation Boards; Natl. Assn. of Crime Victim [13364]
Compensation; Employers Coun. on Flexible [1237]
Compensation Insurance; Natl. Coun. on [2221]
Compensation Insurance; Natl. Coun. on Workmen's [★2221]

Compensation Medicine
Amer. Acad. of Disability Evaluating Physicians [14033]
Hospitality Info. Tech. Assn. [6717]
Natl. Assn. of Disability Evaluating Professionals [14575]
Natl. Assn. of Disability Examiners [14034]
Compensation; Natl. Coun. for Uniform Interest [★486]
Compete Am. [8365], 1341 G St. NW, Ste. 1100, Washington, DC 20005
Competency Assurance; Natl. Org. for [14591]
Competency and Credentialing Inst. [14878], 2170 S Parker Rd., Ste. 295, Denver, CO 80231, (303)369-9566
Competition; Alliance for Fair [★3613]
Competition; Alliance for Rail [3275]
Competition Law Assn. [IO], London, United Kingdom
Competition Law Assn., Poland [IO], Warsaw, Poland
Competition; Natl. Alliance for Fair [3613]
Competition; Natl. Center for Fair [3621]
Competition Opportunities for Riders with Disabilities; Amer. [23330]
Competitive Intelligence Professionals; Soc. of [7211]
Competitive Livestock Marketing Assn. [★5021]
Competitive Livestock Markets Coun. - Defunct.
Competitive Markets; Org. for [4081]

Competitive Mounted Orienteering; Natl. Assn. of [23640]
Competitive Swimming Comm. of the Amateur Athletic Union [★23893]
Competitive Tech; Assn. for [3723]
Competitive Telecommunications Assn. [★3955]
Competitiveness; Amer. Soc. for [8007]
Competitiveness; Coun. on [3839]
Competitor Intelligence Professionals; Soc. of [★7211]
Complementary Alternative Medical Assn. [13629], PO Box 373478, Decatur, GA 30037
Complementary and Alternative Medicine; Natl. Center for [13643]
Complementary Medicine Assn. [13630], c/o Mary Wolken-Rodriguez, Exec. Dir., 4649 E Malvern St., Tucson, AZ 85711-4249, (520)323-6291
Completion Engg. Assn. [7182], c/o Darrell Hebert, Sec.-Treas., PO Box 1330, Houston, TX 77251-1330, (832)636-4804
Complex Weavers [308], 1615 4th Ave. N, Seattle, WA 98109
Compliance Assn; Hea. Care [14632]
Compliance; Intl. Assn. for Medicinal [15041]
Compliance Professionals; Natl. Soc. of [1745]
Component Amer. Dental Executive Secretaries - Defunct.
Component Manufacturers; Assn. of Amer. Ceramic [785]
Component Manufacturers Coun. of the Truss Plate Inst. [★683]
Components Certification Bd; Electronic [1210]
Components Mfrs. Prdt. Sect. of the Material Handling Inst; Overhead [★2042]
Components, Packaging, and Mfg. Tech. Soc; IEEE [6915]
Composer; Meet the [10643]

Composers
African Amer. Art Song Alliance [10520]
Alkan Soc. [IO]
Amer. Bandmasters Assn. [10527]
Amer. Beethoven Soc. [9803]
Amer. Brahms Soc. [9804]
Amer. Composers Alliance [10532]
Amer. Composers Forum [9805]
Amer. Festival of Microtonal Music [10533]
Amer. Handel Soc. [9806]
Amer. Inst. for Verdi Stud. [10539]
Amer. Liszt Soc. [9807]
Amer. Soc. of Composers, Authors and Publishers [5836]
Amer. Soc. of Music Arrangers and Composers [10551]
Asian Composers' League [IO]
Assn. of Canadian Women Composers [IO]
Assn. of Irish Composers [IO]
Assn. of Music Producers [2801]
Assn. of Music Writers and Photographers [10562]
Austrian Composers Assn. [IO]
Balalaika and Domra Assn. of Am. [10563]
Bantock Soc. [IO]
Bohemia Ragtime Soc. [10568]
British Music Soc. [IO]
Canadian League of Composers [IO]
Charles Ives Soc. [10574]
Christian Fellowship of Art Music Composers [9808]
Composers and Authors Soc. of Hong Kong [IO]
Composers and Authors Soc. of Singapore [IO]
Croatian Composers Soc. [IO]
Danish Soc. for Jazz, Rock, and Folk Composers [IO]
Danish Songwriters Guild [IO]
Delbert McClinton Intl. Fan Club [24874]
Delius Soc. [IO]
Donizetti Soc. [IO]
The Duke Ellington Soc. [10590]
Ernst Bacon Soc. [10593]
Frederick Chopin Soc. [IO]
Gilbert and Sullivan Soc. [9809]
Havergal Brian Soc. [IO]
Intl. Gustav Mahler Soc. [IO]
Intl. Heinrich Schutz Soc. [IO]
Intl. Kodaly Soc. [IO]

Reference to "IO" in place of a book number signifies that the association may be found in the 45th edition of International Organizations.

Intl. Percy Grainger Soc. [IO]
Intl. Percy Grainger Soc. [9810]
Intl. Salzedo Soc. [IO]
Jack Point Preservation Soc. [9811]
Johann Strauss Soc. of Great Britain [IO]
Johnnie Ray Intl. Fan Club [24927]
Korean Soc. of Woman Composers [IO]
Kurt Weill Found. for Music [10635]
Latin Amer. Art Song Alliance [10636]
Leopold Stokowski Club [9812]
Leopold Stokowski Soc. [IO]
Leschetizky Assn. [10639]
Lithuanian Composers' Union [IO]
Meet the Composer [10643]
Melodious Accord [10644]
Midwestern Gilbert and Sullivan Soc. [9813]
Mozart Soc. of Am. [9814]
MSV - Ennio Morricone Soc. [IO]
Natl. Assn. of Composers, U.S.A. [10657]
NOPA Norwegian Soc. of Composers and
    Lyricists [IO]
North Amer. British Music Stud. Assn. [10676]
Norwegian Soc. of Composers [IO]
Other Minds [10684]
Peter Warlock Soc. [IO]
Polish Composers' Union [IO]
Positive Music Assn. [10688]
Raissa Tselentis Memorial Johann Sebastian
    Bach Intl. Competitions [10690]
REG - The Intl. Roger Waters Fan Club [24965]
Roger Sessions Soc. [9815]
Schubert Soc. of the USA [9816]
Sci. Songwriters' Assn. [10693]
Scott Joplin Intl. Ragtime Found. [10694]
Soc. of Composers, Inc. [9817]
Soc. for Electro-Acoustic Music in the U.S.
    [10700]
Songwriters Assn. of Canada [IO]
Songwriters of Wisconsin Intl. [9818]
Southeastern Composers' League [10707]
Southern Songwriters Guild [2824]
Swedish Soc. of Popular Music Composers [IO]
Union of Bulgarian Composers [IO]
Villa-Lobos Music Soc. [10717]
Wilhelm Furtwangler Soc. of Am. [9819]
Yrjo Kilpinen Soc. of North Am. [9820]
Yrjo Kilpinen Soc. of North Am. [IO]
Composers Alliance; Amer. [10532]
Composers; Amer. Guild of Authors and [★5859]
Composers; Amer. Soc. of Music Arrangers and
    [10551]
Composers; Amer. Soc. of Univ. [★9817]
Composers-Authors Guild - Address unknown since
    1995.
Composers, Authors and Publishers; Amer. Soc. of
    [5836]
Composers and Authors Soc. of Hong Kong [IO],
    Hong Kong, People's Republic of China
Composers and Authors Soc. of Singapore [IO], Sin-
    gapore, Singapore
Composers' Autograph Publications - Defunct.
Composers and Conductors; Natl. Assn. for
    [★10657]
Composers' Forum for Catholic Worship - Defunct.
Composers - Intl. Soc. for Contemporary Music, U.S.
    Sect; League of [★10626]
Composers' League; Southeastern [10707]
Composers and Lyricists Guild of America - Address
    unknown since 1995.
Composers in Residence Program; Young
    Choreographers and [★9865]
Composers; Society of European Stage Authors and
    [★9817]
Composers; Soc. of Finnish [IO]
Composers Theatre - Address unknown since 2002.
Composers, U.S.A; Natl. Assn. of [10657]
Composite Can and Tube Inst. [976], 50 S Pickett
    St., Ste. 110, Alexandria, VA 22304-7206,
    (703)823-7234
Composite Can and Tube Institute [IO], Alexandria,
    VA, United States
Composite Lumber Mfrs. Assn. [1642], 1156 15th St.
    NW, Ste. 900, Washington, DC 20005, (202)207-
    0906
Composite Materials Assn; Suppliers of Advanced
    [★589]

Composite Panel Assn. [1643], 18922 Premiere Ct.,
    Gaithersburg, MD 20879-1574, (301)670-0604
Composite Panel Assn. [IO], Gaithersburg, MD,
    United States
Composite Wood Coun. [4055], 18922 Premiere Ct.,
    Gaithersburg, MD 20879-1574, (301)670-0604
Composites Assn. of New Zealand [IO], Manukau
    City, New Zealand
Composites Fabricators Assn. [★589]
Composites Mfrs. Assn; Amer. [589]
Composites Mfg. Assn. of the Soc. of Mfg.
    Engineers [2552], PO Box 930, Dearborn, MI
    48121-0930, (313)425-3000
Composites Mfg. Assn. of the Soc. of Mfg.
    Engineers [IO], Dearborn, MI, United States
Composition and Commun; Conf. on Coll. [8376]
Composition Roofers, Damp and Waterproof Work-
    ers Assn; United Slate, Tile and [★24033]
Compost Tea Coun; Intl. [5244]
Compost Tea Indus. Assn. [186], PO Box 71894,
    Eugene, OR 97401, (541)345-2855
Composting Coun. [★6356]
Composting Coun. of Canada [IO], Toronto, ON,
    Canada
Composting Coun; Solid Waste [★6356]
Compound Livestock Feed Mfrs'. Assn. of India
    [★IO]
Compounding Pharmacists; Intl. Acad. of [15935]
Comprehensive Day Care Programs [11539]
Comprehensive Hea. Educ. Found. [8860], 22419
    Pacific Hwy. S, Seattle, WA 98198-5106, (206)824-
    2907
Comprehensive Industrywide Program of Com-
    munication - Defunct.
Comprehensive Medical Soc. - Defunct.
Compress and Cotton Warehouse Assn; NA Cotton
    [★1093]
Compressed Air and Gas Inst. [2010], 1300 Sumner
    Ave., Cleveland, OH 44115-2851, (216)241-7333
Compressed Gas Assn. [1721], 4221 Walney Rd.,
    5th Fl., Chantilly, VA 20151-2923, (703)788-2700
Compressed Gas Mfrs. Assn. [★1721]
Compressor Rebuilders Assn; Refrigeration [★1887]
CompTel/ALTS [3955], 900 17th St. NW, Ste. 400,
    Washington, DC 20006, (202)296-6650
CompTel/ASCENT Alliance and Assn. for Local
    Telecommunications Services [★3955]
Compton Fan Club; Pat [24957]
Compton Found. [13114], 255 Shoreline Dr., Ste.
    540, Redwood City, CA 94065, (650)508-1181
Compton Found. [IO], Redwood City, CA, United
    States
Comptrollers and Accounting Officers; Assn. of
    [★6204]
Comptrollers; Amer. Soc. of Military [6066]
Comptrollers, and Treasurers; Natl. Assn. of State
    Auditors, [6206]
Compu-Forum - Defunct.
Compu/Graphics Users Assn. - Defunct.
Compucats' Computer Club - Defunct.
Compulsive Anonymous; Obsessive- [12555]
Compulsive Disorder Found; Obsessive [★15230]
Compulsive Found; Obsessive- [15230]
Compulsive Gambling of New Jersey; Coun. on
    [12209]
Compulsive Stutterers Anonymous - Address
    unknown since 2003.
CompuMentor [7728], 435 Brannan St., Ste. 100,
    San Francisco, CA 94107, (415)633-9300
Computability Theory; Special Interest Gp. on
    Algorithms [7539]
Computability Theory; Special Interest Gp. on
    Automata and [★7539]
Computation Theory; Special Interest Gp. on
    Algorithms and [7539]
Computational Biology; Intl. Soc. for [2094]
Computational Electromagnetics Soc; Applied [6906]
Computational Intelligence Soc. [7009], c/o James
    Keller, VP for Publications, Univ. of MO-Columbia,
    Elecl. and Cmpt. Engg. Dept., 217 Engg. Bldg. W,
    Columbia, MO 65211, (573)882-7339
Computational Linguistics; Assn. for Machine
    Translation and [★10400]
Computational Mechanics; International Assn. of
    [★7300]

Computational Mechanics; U.S. Assn. for [7300]
Computed Body Tomography and Magnetic
    Resonance; Soc. of [16297]
Computed Body Tomography; Soc. of [★16297]
Cmpt. Aid Intl. [IO], London, United Kingdom
Computer Aided Design
    Amer. Assn. of Webmasters [896]
    Interaction Design Assn. [6863]
    Intl. Assn. of Webmasters and Designers [888]
    International Association of Webmasters and
        Designers [IO]
    Intl. Building Performance Simulation Assn. [6652]
Computer-Aided Learning in Veterinary Educ. [IO],
    Edinburgh, United Kingdom
Computer Aided Manufacturing Intl. - Address
    unknown since 2007.
Cmpt. Applications in Medical Care; Symposium on
    [★14079]
Computer Applications for Ministry Network - Ad-
    dress unknown since 1995.
Cmpt. Applications in Radiology; Soc. for [★16299]
Cmpt. Assisted Language Instruction Consortium
    [8553], Texas State Univ., 214 Centennial Hall,
    601 Univ. Dr., San Marcos, TX 78666, (512)245-
    1417.
Computer Assisted Language Instruction Consortium
    [IO], San Marcos, TX, United States
Cmpt. Assisted Language, Learning and Instruction
    Consortium [★IO]
Cmpt. Assisted Language, Learning and Instruction
    Consortium [★8553]
Computer-Assisted Reporting; National Inst. for
    [★3126]
Computer-Assisted Reporting; National Inst. for
    [★IO]
Cmpt. Assn. of Nepal [IO], Kathmandu, Nepal
Cmpt. and Automated Systems Assn. [★IO]
Cmpt. and Automated Systems Assn. [★6737]
Cmpt. and Automated Systems Assn. of Soc. of Mfg.
    Engineers [★6737]
Cmpt. and Automated Systems Assn. of Soc. of Mfg.
    Engineers [★IO]
Computer-Based Music Instruction; Natl. Consortium
    for [★8905]
Computer-Based Training Comm; Aviation Indus.
    [★142]
Cmpt. and Bus. Equip. Mfrs. Assn. [★904]
Cmpt. Capacity Mgt; Inst. for [7196]
Cmpt. and Communications Indus. Assn. [3739], 900
    17th St. NW, Ste. 1100, Washington, DC 20006,
    (202)783-0070
Cmpt. Conservation Soc. [IO], Surbiton, United
    Kingdom
Cmpt. Consultant Businesses; Natl. Assn. of [968]
Computer Crime Data Center; National [★2091]
Computer Crime Data; Natl. Center for [2091]
Cmpt. Dealers; Amer. Soc. of [★897]
Cmpt. Dealers; Assn. of Better [★898]
Cmpt. Distributors' and Dealers' Assn. [IO], Makati
    City, Philippines
Cmpt. Educ. Application Network; Micro [★8557]
Cmpt. Educ; Hong Kong Assn. for [IO]
Cmpt. Educ. Mgt. Assn. - Europe [IO], High Wy-
    combe, United Kingdom
Cmpt. Educators; Assn. for [★8132]
Cmpt. Engg. Dept. Heads Assn; Elecl. and [7011]
Cmpt. Ethics Inst. [9056], c/o The Brookings Institu-
    tion, 1775 Massachusetts Ave. NW, Washington,
    DC 20036, (202)797-6183
Cmpt. Event Marketing Assn. [★2621]
Cmpt. Graphics Assn; Natl. [★894]
Cmpt. and Human Interaction; Special Interest Gp.
    on [6542]
Cmpt. Indus. Assn. [★3739]
Computer Indus. Assn; ABCD: The Micro [★898]
Cmpt. Indus. Coun. [★898]
Computer Information Exchange - Defunct.
Cmpt. Integrated Textile Design Assn. - Defunct.
Computer Investors Assn; Micro [2339]
Cmpt. Law Assn. [★5582]
Computer Literacy Coun. - Defunct.
Cmpt. Measurement Gp. [6724], PO Box 1124, 151
    Fries Mill Rd., Ste. 104, Turnersville, NJ 08012,
    (856)401-1700
Computer Micrographics Technology - Defunct.

A star before a book entry number signifies that the name is not listed separately, but is mentioned within the entry.

Cmpt. Musician Coalition [★2827]
Cmpt. Musicians Cooperative [★2827]
Computer Network Associates - Defunct.
Computer Oriented Geological Soc. [7131]
Computer Performance Evaluation Users Group - Defunct.
Cmpt. Personnel Res; Special Interest Gp. for [★6824]
Computer Press Assn. - Address unknown since 2002.
Computer Products Remanufacturing Assn; Intl. [★3996]
Cmpt. Professionals for Social Responsibility [18146], 1370 Mission St., 4th Fl., San Francisco, CA 94103, (415)839-9355

Computer Science
Afghan Cmpt. Sci. Assn. [IO]
African-American Women in Tech. [6394]
Amer. Cmpt. Sci. League [8127]
Amer. Cmpt. Scientists Assn. [6718]
Amer. Soc. for Cybernetics [6719]
Applied Voice Input/Output Soc. [6720]
Argentine Game Developers Assn. [IO]
Asia and Pacific Internet Assn. [IO]
Assn. for the Advancement of Modelling and Simulation Techniques in Enterprises - France [IO]
Assn. for Advancement of Modelling and Simulation Techniques in Enterprises - Spain [IO]
Assn. for Computational Linguistics [10400]
Assn. for Cmpt. Aided Design in Architecture [6721]
Assn. of the Cmpt. and Multimedia Indus. Malaysia [IO]
Assn. of Cmpt. Support Specialists [6809]
Assn. for Computing Machinery [6783]
Assn. for Info. Systems [6722]
Assn. of Info. Tech. Professionals [8128]
Assn. of the Inst. for Certification of Computing Professionals [8129]
Assn. for Literary and Linguistic Computing [IO]
Assn. for Software Testing [6763]
Australian Interactive Media Indus. Assn. [IO]
British Interactive Media Assn. [IO]
Bus. Application Software Developers Assn. [IO]
Bus. Software Alliance Australia [IO]
Canadian Human-Computer Communications Soc. [IO]
Chilean Cmpt. Sci. Soc. [IO]
Coll. and Univ. Cmpt. Users Assn. [7894]
CompactFlash Assn. [6723]
Cmpt. Assn. of Nepal [IO]
Cmpt. Conservation Soc. [IO]
Cmpt. Measurement Gp. [6724]
Cmpt. Sci. Teachers Assn. [8130]
Computing Res. Assn. [6725]
Coun. of European Professional Informatics Societies [IO]
Coun. of Regional Info. Tech. Associations [7192]
Cyprus Cmpt. Soc. [IO]
Czech Soc. for Cybernetics and Informatics [IO]
Digital Govt. Soc. of North Am. [7151]
Educ. Turnkey Inst. [8557]
Embedded Linux Consortium [6726]
Estonian Info. Tech. Soc. [IO]
Ethiopian Info. Tech. Professionals Assn. [IO]
EUROMICRO [IO]
European Assn. for Cmpt. Graphics [IO]
European Assn. for Cmpt. Sci. Logic [IO]
European Assn. for Theoretical Cmpt. Sci. [IO]
Finnish Info. Processing Assn. [IO]
Game Developers' Assn. of Australia [IO]
German Data Protection Org. [IO]
German Informatics Soc. [IO]
Hong Kong Assn. for Cmpt. Educ. [IO]
Icelandic Soc. for Info. Processing [IO]
IEEE Cmpt. Soc. [6727]
IEEE Systems, Man, and Cybernetics Soc. [6728]
IMAGE Soc. [6729]
Indian Soc. for Mathematical Modelling and Cmpt. Simulation [IO]
Info. Processing Soc. of Japan [IO]
Info. Resources Mgt. Assn. [2101]
Info. Tech. Solution Provider Alliance [2102]
Inst. for Certification of Computing Professionals [8131]

Inst. for Cmpt. Capacity Mgt. [7196]
Inst. for Numerical Computation and Anal. [IO]
Institution of Analysts and Programmers [IO]
Interaction Design Assn. [6863]
Intl. Assn. for Artificial Intelligence and Law [6730]
Intl. Assn. for Cmpt. Info. Systems [8132]
Intl. Assn. for Cmpt. Info. Systems [IO]
Intl. Assn. of Cmpt. Investigative Specialists [IO]
Intl. Assn. of Cmpt. Investigative Specialists [8133]
Intl. Assn. for Cybernetics [IO]
Intl. Assn. of Interaction Design [IO]
Intl. Assn. for Mathematics and Computers in Simulation [IO]
Intl. Assn. for Mathematics and Computers in Simulation [6731]
Intl. Assn. of Software Architects [6770]
Intl. Building Performance Simulation Assn. [6652]
Intl. Disk Drive Equip. and Materials Assn. [6732]
Intl. Disk Drive Equip. and Materials Assn. [IO]
Intl. Fed. for Info. Processing [IO]
Intl. Game Developers Assn. [IO]
Intl. Game Developers Assn. [6733]
Intl. Soc. of Applied Intelligence [6486]
Intl. Soc. for Ethics and Info. Tech. [7198]
Intl. Soc. of Parametric Analysts [6734]
Intl. Soc. of Parametric Analysts [IO]
Intl. Soc. for Tech. in Educ. [IO]
Intl. Soc. for Tech. in Educ. [8134]
Intl. Training and Simulation Alliance [6735]
International Training and Simulation Alliance [IO]
Intl. Visual Commun. Assn. [IO]
Internet Professional Publishers Assn. [1777]
Israel Assn. for Info. Systems [IO]
Israeli Assn. of Grid Technologies [IO]
Italian Assn. for Info. Systems [IO]
Ithaka [7200]
Korea Info. Sci. Soc. [IO]
Korea Info. Tech. Network [IO]
Korea Info. Tech. Network [6736]
Logical Language Gp. [10304]
Malaysian Natl. Cmpt. Confed. [IO]
Mfg. Integration Tech Gp. of the Soc. of Mfg. Engineers [IO]
Mfg. Integration Tech Gp. of the Soc. of Mfg. Engineers [6737]
Metro Ethernet Forum [7748]
MPLS and Frame Relay Alliance [6714]
Natl. Assn. of Commun. Systems Engineers [6715]
Natl. Assn. of Internet Ser. Providers of Romania [IO]
Natl. Info. Center for Educational Media [8569]
Natl. InStar Users Gp. [7221]
Natl. Inst. for Res. in Cmpt. Sci. and Control [IO]
Natl. Training and Simulation Assn. [6738]
Network Professional Assn. [6739]
North Amer. Chap. of the Assn. for Computational Linguistics [10408]
North Amer. Computational Social and Org. Sciences [6740]
North Amer. Fuzzy Info. Processing Soc. [6741]
Open Data Acquisition Assn. [891]
Open DeviceNet Vendor Assn. [892]
The Open Gp. [2108]
Personal Cmpt. Memory Card Intl. Assn. [6742]
Personal Cmpt. Memory Card Intl. Assn. [IO]
Programmers Guild [7757]
RapidIO Trade Assn. [889]
Rexx Language Assn. [7537]
Russian Software Developers Assn. [IO]
ScotlandIS [IO]
SD Card Assn. [6743]
Simulation Indus. Assn. of Australia [IO]
Sociedad Argentina De Informatica E Investigacion Operativa [IO]
Soc. for Computers and Law [IO]
Soc. for Computers in Psychology [6744]
Soc. for Info. Display [6745]
Society for Information Display [IO]
Soc. for Modeling and Simulation Intl. [IO]
Soc. for Modeling and Simulation Intl. [6746]
Software Contractors' Guild [1143]
Software in the Public Interest [6777]
Special Interest Gp. on Ada [7538]

Special Interest Gp. on Algorithms and Computation Theory [7539]
Special Interest Gp. for Architecture of Cmpt. Systems [6747]
Special Interest Gp. on Artificial Intelligence [6487]
Special Interest Gp. on Cmpt. Sci. Educ. [8135]
Special Interest Gp. for Computers and Soc. [6748]
Special Interest Gp. on Data Communications of the Assn. for Computing Machinery [6804]
Special Interest Gp. for Design Automation [6749]
Special Interest Gp. on Design of Commun. [6823]
Special Interest Gp. on Info. Retrieval [7212]
Special Interest Gp. on Mgt. of Data [6750]
Special Interest Gp. on Measurement and Evaluation [6751]
Special Interest Gp. on Mobility of Systems Users, Data, and Computing [6825]
Special Interest Gp. on Multimedia [6826]
Special Interest Gp. on Programming Languages [7541]
Special Interest Gp. on Security, Audit and Control [6752]
Special Interest Gp. on Simulation [6753]
SPEEDUP Soc.: Swiss Forum for GRID and High Performance Computing [IO]
Storage Networking Indus. Assn. [6754]
Transaction Processing Performance Coun. [6755]
UK Soc. for Modelling and Simulation [IO]
United Kingdom Educ. and Res. Networking Assn. [IO]
Upsilon Pi Epsilon Assn. [IO]
Upsilon Pi Epsilon Assn. [24435]
VXIbus Consortium [7793]
Web Analytics Assn. [7222]
Web3D Consortium [6828]
World Org. of Systems and Cybernetics [IO]
World Sci. and Engg. Acad. and Soc. [7054]
World Wide Web Consortium [6756]
World Wide Web Consortium [IO]
Worshipful Company of Info. Technologists [IO]
XML.org [6757]
X.Org Found. [6830]
Cmpt. Sci. Bd. [★6725]
Computer Science and Engineering Bd. of NAS - Defunct.
Cmpt. Sci. Teachers Assn. [8130], PO Box 11414, New York, NY 10286-1414, (212)626-0530

Computer Security
CyberAngels [12452]
Intl. Info. Systems Security Certification Consortium [6758]
International Information Systems Security Certification Consortium [IO]
Intl. Systems Security Engg. Assn. [7023]
People for Internet Responsibility [12453]
Special Interest Gp. on Security, Audit and Control [6752]
Cmpt. Security Inst. [2088], 600 Harrison St., San Francisco, CA 94107, (415)947-6320
Cmpt. Simulation; Soc. for [★6746]
Cmpt. Soc. of India [IO], Bombay, India
Cmpt. Soc. of South Africa [★IO]
Cmpt. Soc. of Zimbabwe [IO], Harare, Zimbabwe

Computer Software
Acacia North Amer. User Group [6759]
Advanced Media Workflow Assn. [3721]
Amer. Cooperative Coun. on Compensation Tech. [4059]
AppleWorks Users Gp. [6760]
Assn. of Cmpt. Support Specialists [6809]
Assn. of Esko-Graphics' Users [6761]
Assn. for Machine Translation in the Americas [7807]
Assn. of Public Data Users [7190]
Assn. for Retail Tech. Standards [3400]
Assn. of Shareware Professionals [6762]
Assn. for Software Testing [6763]
Biometric Application Programming Interface Consortium [6572]
CAD Soc. [6764]
China Software Indus. Assn. [IO]

Coun. of Regional Info. Tech. Associations [7192]
Danish Open Source Bus. Assn. [IO]
Distributed Computing Indus. Assn. [899]
Ebix Users Assn. [340]
Educ. Systems Exchange [8136]
Educ. Turnkey Inst. [8557]
Educational Software Cooperative [6765]
Educational Software Cooperative [IO]
Entertainment Software Assn. [6766]
European Software Assn. [IO]
Free Software Foundation [IO]
Free Software Found. [6767]
GalaxyGoo [8065]
Info. Tech. Assn. of Am. [6768]
Info. Tech. Solution Provider Alliance [2102]
Inst. for Cmpt. Capacity Mgt. [7196]
Intl. Alliance for Interoperability [7018]
Intl. Assn. for Info. and Data Quality [7197]
Intl. Assn. of Microsoft Certified Partners [6769]
Intl. Assn. of Microsoft Certified Partners [IO]
Intl. Assn. of Software Architects [IO]
Intl. Assn. of Software Architects [6770]
Intl. Building Performance Simulation Assn. [6652]
Intl. DB2 Users Gp. [6856]
Intl. .NET Assn. [6771]
Internet Professional Publishers Assn. [1777]
Internet Systems Consortium [6772]
Korea Info. Tech. Network [6736]
Legal Software Suppliers Assn. [IO]
Natl. Assn. for Justice Info. Systems [5648]
Natl. Assn. of Photoshop Professionals [1808]
Natl. Assn. for Public Hea. Info. Tech. [7203]
Natl. Assn. of Recording Merchandisers [3349]
Natl. InStar Users Gp. [7221]
Natl. MIS User Gp. [7207]
New Parents Network [8956]
NiUG Intl. [7208]
North Amer. Confed. of the Red Dragon [22479]
ODF Alliance [7209]
Open Applications Gp. [890]
Open Data Acquisition Assn. [891]
Open Data Acquisition Assn. [IO]
Open DeviceNet Vendor Association [IO]
Open DeviceNet Vendor Assn. [892]
Open Voting Consortium [17489]
Oracle Applications Users Gp. [6773]
Oracle Development Tools User Gp. [6774]
Philippine Software Indus. Assn. [IO]
Quest Intl. Users Gp. [6857]
SAS Global Forum [6802]
Soc. for Conservation GIS [6831]
Soc. for Software Quality [6775]
Software Contractors' Guild [1143]
Software Defined Radio Forum [6776]
Software in the Public Interest [6777]
Software Testing Inst. [6778]
Special Interest Gp. on Software Engg. [6779]
Systems and Software Consortium, Inc. [6780]
Text and Academic Authors Assn. [11199]
Ukrainian Assn. of Software Developers [IO]
Unicode Consortium [18683]
Unicorn Users Gp. Intl. [7214]
Vietnam Software Assn. [IO]
Virtual Private Network Consortium [2320]
World Wide Web Consortium [6756]
Zangle Natl. Users' Gp. [7216]
Cmpt. Suppliers Assn. of Zimbabwe [IO], Harare,
Zimbabwe
Cmpt. Tech. Alumni Assn; Univ. of Advancing
[18929]
Cmpt. Tech; Assn. of Rehabilitation Programs in
[11924]
Computer Users
ACM Hong Kong Chap. [IO]
ACM Japan Chap. [IO]
ACM SIGGRAPH Kuala Lumpur Professional
Chap. [IO]
AFCOM [6781]
Amer. Assn. of Cmpt. Rental Professionals [895]
Amer. Assn. of Electronic Reporters and
Transcribers [3180]
Arizona Macintosh Users Gp. [6782]
Assn. of C and C Users [IO]
Assn. of Cmpt. Professionals [IO]
Assn. for Computing Machinery [6783]

Assn. of Macintosh Trainers [6810]
Assn. of Minicomputer Users [6784]
Assn. of Personal Cmpt. User Groups [6785]
Assn. for Progressive Communications [17163]
Assn. for Software Testing [6763]
Assn. for Women in Computing [6786]
The Assn. for Work Process Improvement [6787]
Australian Cmpt. Soc. [IO]
Australian UNIX and Open Systems Users Gp.
[IO]
Austrian Cmpt. Soc. [IO]
Bali/Indonesia ACM SIGGRAPH [IO]
Bangalore ACM Chap. [IO]
Bangkok ACM SIGGRAPH [IO]
Beijing ACM SIGGRAPH [IO]
Belgian Teleworking Assn. [IO]
Bilkent Turkey ACM SIGART [IO]
Blissymbolics Commun. Intl. [IO]
British ACM Chap. [IO]
British Cmpt. Soc. [IO]
Bulgarian ACM Chap. [IO]
Bulgarian Telework Assn. [IO]
CAMUS Intl. [2551]
Capital PC User Gp. [6788]
Capital PC User Gp. [IO]
Caracas ACM SIGGRAPH [IO]
Center for Computer-Assisted Legal Instruction
[6789]
Central Israel ACM SIGGRAPH [IO]
Central Russia ACM SIGCHI [IO]
China ACM SIGCHI [IO]
Chinese Amer. Cmpt. Assn. [6811]
Christian Macintosh User Gp. [6790]
Common-A Users Gp. [6791]
Cmpt. Soc. of India [IO]
Computers for Children [8137]
Confed. of European Cmpt. User Associations
[IO]
Czech ACM SIGCHI [IO]
Ebix Users Assn. [340]
Egyptian Cmpt. Soc. [IO]
Electronic Frontiers Australia [IO]
Electronics Indus. Fed. [IO]
ENCOMPASS [6792]
Epicor Users Gp. [6793]
European Cmpt. Driving License Found. [IO]
European Inst. for Cmpt. Anti-Virus Res. [IO]
European Software Inst. [IO]
Finland ACM SIGCHI [IO]
FORTH Interest Gp. [7535]
German Chap. of the ACM [IO]
Hong Kong ACM SIGGRAPH [IO]
HUG Intl. - HTE Users' Gp. [6794]
Hungarian ACM Chap. [IO]
Info. Tech. Solution Provider Alliance [2102]
INTEREX [6795]
Intl. .NET Assn. [6771]
Intl. Oracle Users Gp. [6796]
Intl. Oracle Users Gp. [IO]
Intl. SGML/XML Users' Gp. [IO]
Intl. Tandem Users' Gp. [IO]
Intl. Tandem Users' Gp. [6797]
Internet Indus. Assn. [IO]
Internet Soc. of Australia [IO]
Irish Cmpt. Soc. [IO]
Italian ACM SIGCHI [IO]
Japan Telework Assn. [IO]
Japan UNIX Soc. [IO]
John Von Neumann Cmpt. Soc. - Hungary [IO]
Karachi ACM Chap. [IO]
Korea ACM SIGCHI [IO]
Korea Info. Tech. Network [6736]
League of Professional Sys. Administrators [6815]
Lithuanian Cmpt. Soc. [IO]
Melbourne ACM SIGGRAPH [IO]
Metro Ethernet Forum [7748]
Mexico ACM SIGCHI [IO]
Mexico City ACM SIGGRAPH [IO]
Milano ACM SIGGRAPH Professional Chap. [IO]
Moscow ACM SIGDA [IO]
Moscow ACM SIGMOD [IO]
NAQP Cmpt. Users Gp. [6798]
Natl. InStar Users Gp. [7221]
Natl. MIS User Gp. [7207]
NetAction [17242]

Netherlands ACM SIGCHI [IO]
Network and Systems Professionals Assn. [IO]
Network and Systems Professionals Assn. [6799]
New Zealand ACM SIGCHI [IO]
NiUG Intl. [7208]
North Amer. Confed. of the Red Dragon [22479]
Norwegian ACM Chap. [IO]
OASIS PKI Member Sect. [7780]
One Economy [7755]
Online Policy Gp. [17243]
People for Internet Responsibility [12453]
Personalization Consortium [6800]
Perth Australia ACM SIGGRAPH [IO]
PlanetMUG [6819]
Poland ACM Chap. [IO]
Portuguese Assn. for Telework [IO]
Professional Computing Assn. [IO]
PXI Systems Alliance [6820]
Quest Intl. Users Gp. [6857]
Regis Sys. Users' Gp. [6801]
Reporters Network [3160]
Rexx Language Assn. [7537]
Romania ACM SIGCHI [IO]
Romanian Assn. for Telework and Teleactivities
[IO]
SAS Global Forum [IO]
SAS Global Forum [6802]
SavetheInternet.com Coalition [17924]
SeniorNet [13302]
SIGAPP - Special Interest Gp. on Applied
Computing [6821]
SIMPUTER (USA) [13301]
Singapore ACM SIGGRAPH [IO]
Singapore Cmpt. Soc. [IO]
Slovenian ACM Chap. [IO]
Soc. for Modeling and Simulation Intl. [6746]
Software in the Public Interest [6777]
South Africa ACM SIGCHI [IO]
South East Queensland ACM SIGGRAPH [IO]
South India ACM SIGCHI [IO]
Special Interest Gp. on Accessible Computing
[6803]
Special Interest Gp. for Architecture of Cmpt.
Systems [6747]
Special Interest Gp. for Computers and Soc.
[6748]
Special Interest Gp. on Data Communications of
the Assn. for Computing Machinery [6804]
Special Interest Gp. on Info. Retrieval [7212]
Special Interest Gp. on Mgt. Info. Systems [6824]
Special Interest Gp. on Mobility of Systems Users,
Data, and Computing [6825]
Special Interest Gp. on Multimedia [6826]
Special Interest Gp. on Programming Languages
[7541]
Stop Net Abusers [17241]
Swiss ACM SIGCHI [IO]
Sydney ACM SIGGRAPH Chap. [IO]
Sydney SIGMOBILE ACM Chap. [IO]
Taipei/Taiwan ACM Chap. [IO]
Tehran/Iran ACM Chap. [IO]
Telework Assn. [IO]
Telework New Zealand [IO]
Thailand ACM Chap. [IO]
Tokyo ACM SIGGRAPH [IO]
Unicorn Users Gp. Intl. [7214]
UniForum Assn. [6805]
UniForum Assn. [IO]
UniForum New Zealand [IO]
United Kingdom eInformation Gp. [IO]
U.S. Internet Indus. Assn. [893]
USENIX Assn. [6806]
Vancouver ACM SIGGRAPH [IO]
Verein zur Forderung des Offentlichen Bewegten
und Unbewegten Datenverkehrs [IO]
Vivit [6807]
Web Analytics Assn. [7222]
XyUser Gp. [6808]
Zangle Natl. Users' Gp. [7216]
Cmpt. Users Assn; Coll. and Univ. [7894]
Cmpt. Users Conf; Coll. and Univ. [★7894]
Cmpt. Users Gp; NAQP [★6798]
Computer Users for Social Responsibility - Defunct.
Computer Users in Speech and Hearing - Address
unknown since 1999.

A star before a book entry number signifies that the name is not listed separately, but is mentioned within the entry.

Computer Virus Industry Assn. - Address unknown since 1994.
Cmpt. Vision and Pattern Recognition Gp. of Korea Info. Sci. Soc. [IO], Seoul, Republic of Korea
Computerized Books for the Blind [★16885]
Computerized Electrocardiology; Intl. Soc. for [13913]
Computerized Medical Imaging Soc. [16287]
Computerized Radiology Soc. [★16287]
Computerized Tax Processors; Natl. Assn. of [6298]
Computerized Tomography and Neuroimaging; Soc. for [★16281]
Computerized Tomography Soc. [★16287]
Computers
  1394 High Performance Serial Bus Trade Assn. [3720]
  ACM SIGGRAPH [894]
  ACM SIGGRAPH [IO]
  African-American Women in Tech. [6394]
  Amer. Assn. for Artificial Intelligence [6483]
  Amer. Assn. of Cmpt. Rental Professionals [895]
  Amer. Assn. of Electronic Reporters and Transcribers [3180]
  Amer. Assn. of Webmasters [896]
  Amer. Cmpt. Barrel Racing Assn. [23493]
  Amer. Literacy Coun. [8785]
  Amer. Medical Informatics Assn. [14079]
  Amer. Soc. for Automation in Pharmacy [2969]
  Americans for Fair Electronic Commerce Transactions [17441]
  Asia Pacific Top Level Domains Assn. [IO]
  Asian Amer. MultiTechnology Assn. [1204]
  Asian-Oceanian Computing Indus. Org. [IO]
  Assn. for Competitive Tech. [3723]
  Assn. for Cmpt. Aided Design in Architecture [6721]
  Assn. of Cmpt. Support Specialists [6809]
  Assn. for Computing Machinery [6783]
  Assn. of Independent Cmpt. Specialists [IO]
  Assn. for Lab. Automation [6515]
  Assn. of Macintosh Trainers [6810]
  Assn. of Macintosh Trainers [IO]
  Assn. of Minicomputer Users [6784]
  Assn. of Ser. and Cmpt. Dealers Intl. [897]
  Assn. of Shareware Professionals [6762]
  Assn. for Software Testing [6763]
  Assn. of Thai Cmpt. Indus. [IO]
  Assn. for Women in Computing [6786]
  The Assn. for Work Process Improvement [6787]
  Australian Info. Indus. Assn. [IO]
  Blue-ray Disc Assn. [1207]
  Broadband Services Forum [3737]
  Bulgarian Web Assn. [IO]
  Center for Computer-Assisted Legal Instruction [6789]
  Chilean Soc. of Info. Tech. Companies [IO]
  Chinese Amer. Cmpt. Assn. [6811]
  Coll. and Univ. Cmpt. Users Assn. [7894]
  Common Dreams [16972]
  CompactFlash Assn. [6723]
  CompuMentor [7728]
  Cmpt. Aid Intl. [IO]
  Cmpt. Assisted Language Instruction Consortium [8553]
  Cmpt. Distributors' and Dealers' Assn. [IO]
  Cmpt. Educ. Mgt. Assn. - Europe [IO]
  Cmpt. Measurement Gp. [6724]
  Cmpt. Sci. Teachers Assn. [8130]
  Cmpt. Security Inst. [2088]
  Cmpt. Soc. of Zimbabwe [IO]
  Cmpt. Suppliers Assn. of Zimbabwe [IO]
  Computers for Children [IO]
  Computers for Children [8137]
  Computing Tech. Indus. Assn. [898]
  Constr. Indus. Computing Assn. [IO]
  Corporate Event Marketing Assn. [2621]
  Coun. of European Natl. Top-Level Domain Registries [IO]
  Coun. of Regional Info. Tech. Associations [7192]
  CyberAngels [12452]
  Cyprus Info. Tech. Enterprises Assn. [IO]
  Distributed Computing Indus. Assn. [899]
  East West Educ. Development Found. [12716]
  Ebix Users Assn. [340]
  ECMA Intl. [IO]

Educ. Turnkey Inst. [8557]
Educational Software Cooperative [6765]
Electronics Representatives Assn. [1213]
Embedded Linux Consortium [6726]
ENCOMPASS [6792]
Enough Is Enough [17923]
Enterprise Cmpt. Telephony Forum [878]
Entertainment and Leisure Software Publishers Assn. [IO]
Epicor Users Gp. [6793]
Fan Tek [10943]
FORTH Interest Gp. [7535]
Geeks Without Borders [11806]
Geeks Without Borders [IO]
Geospatial Info. and Tech. Assn. [900]
German Soc. for Online Res. [IO]
Global Org. for Multi-Vendor Integration Protocol [18681]
HAVi [6513]
Hi-Ethics - Hea. Internet Ethics [14676]
HomePlug Powerline Alliance [1216]
Hong Kong Cmpt. Soc. [IO]
HTML Writers Guild [901]
IEEE Cmpt. Soc. [6727]
Independent Cmpt. Consultants Assn. [902]
Info. Indus. South Africa [IO]
Info. Storage Indus. Consortium [903]
Info. Tech. Indus. Coun. [904]
Info. Tech. Solution Provider Alliance [2102]
Inst. for Cmpt. Capacity Mgt. [7196]
Inst. for Global Communications [7772]
Interaction Design Assn. [6863]
Interactive Entertainment Assn. of Australia [IO]
Interactive Travel Services Assn. [3946]
INTEREX [6795]
Intl. Assn. for Cmpt. Info. Systems [8132]
Intl. Assn. of Cmpt. Investigative Specialists [8133]
Intl. Assn. for Cmpt. Systems Security [905]
Intl. Assn. for Cmpt. Systems Security [IO]
Intl. Assn. of Employment Web Sites [1266]
Intl. Assn. of Knowledge Engineers [6485]
Intl. Assn. for Obsidian Stud. [6449]
Intl. Assn. of Software Architects [6770]
Intl. Cartridge Recycling Assn. [3996]
Intl. Computing Centre [IO]
Intl. Disk Drive Equip. and Materials Assn. [6732]
Intl. Game Developers Assn. [6733]
Intl. Indus. Assn. for Standardizing Info. and Commun. Systems [IO]
Intl. Nanocasting Assn. [562]
Intl. .NET Assn. [6771]
Intl. Soc. of Certified Electronics Technicians [1220]
Intl. Soc. for Cmpt. Assisted Orthopaedic Surgery [15772]
Intl. Soc. for Ethics and Info. Tech. [7198]
Intl. Soc. of Parametric Analysts [6734]
Intl. Soc. for Tech. in Educ. [8134]
Intl. Tandem Users' Gp. [6797]
Intl. Training and Simulation Alliance [6735]
Intl. Webmasters Assn. [6812]
Intl. Webmasters Assn. [IO]
Intl. World Wide Web Conf. Comm. [IO]
Internet Corp. for Assigned Names and Numbers [6813]
Internet Professional Assn. [IO]
Internet Ser. Providers Assn. [IO]
Internet Soc. [IO]
Internet Soc. [906]
Internet Soc. - Republic of South Africa [IO]
IT Indus. Assn. [IO]
Ithaka [7200]
IVI Found. [6814]
Japan Video Software Assn. [IO]
Korea Info. Tech. Network [6736]
League of Professional Sys. Administrators [6815]
League of Professional Sys. Administrators [IO]
League for Programming Freedom [7536]
Legal Tech. Insider [IO]
Logical Language Gp. [10304]
Mfg. Integration Tech Gp. of the Soc. of Mfg. Engineers [6737]
Metro Ethernet Forum [7748]
MicroComputer Investors Assn. [2339]

Mobile Payment Forum [6816]
Mobile Payment Forum [IO]
NAQP Cmpt. Users Gp. [6798]
Natl. Alliance of Primary Care Informatics [14956]
Natl. Assn. of Commun. Systems Engineers [6715]
Natl. Assn. of Cmpt. Consultant Businesses [968]
Natl. Assn. of Computerized Tax Processors [6298]
Natl. Center for Computer Crime Data [2091]
Natl. Electronic Distributors Assn. [1223]
Natl. Info. Center for Educational Media [8569]
Natl. InStar Users Gp. [7221]
Natl. MIS User Gp. [7207]
NetAction [17242]
Network for Online Commerce [IO]
New Zealand Cmpt. Soc. [IO]
NiUG Intl. [7208]
North Amer. Chap. of the Assn. for Computational Linguistics [10408]
North Amer. Computational Social and Org. Sciences [6740]
North Amer. Computer Service Assn. [907]
North Amer. Confed. of the Red Dragon [22479]
North Amer. Coun. for Online Learning [7949]
OASIS PKI Member Sect. [7780]
ODF Alliance [7209]
One Economy [7755]
Online Audiovisual Catalogers [10379]
Online Policy Gp. [17243]
Open DeviceNet Vendor Assn. [892]
Open Geospatial Consortium [6817]
Oper. Homelink [11494]
Org. for the Advancement of Structured Info. Standards [7756]
Organizers' Collaborative [17244]
Pakistan Software Export Bd. [IO]
Palestinian Info. Tech. Assn. of Companies [IO]
PCI Indus. Cmpt. Mfrs. Gp. [6818]
People for Internet Responsibility [12453]
Personal Cmpt. Memory Card Intl. Assn. [6742]
PlanetMUG [6819]
Playing 2 Win [8570]
Portable Cmpt. and Communications Assn. [908]
Professional Assn. for SQL Server [909]
Progress and Freedom Found. [17188]
Progressive Tech. Proj. [7758]
PXI Systems Alliance [6820]
Quest Intl. Users Gp. [6857]
Reciclanet Hezgarri Elkartea [IO]
Rexx Language Assn. [7537]
RSPA [910]
SAS Global Forum [6802]
SavetheInternet.com Coalition [17924]
SCSI Trade Assn. [2110]
SD Card Assn. [6743]
Sea to Sky Freenet Assn. [IO]
Search Engine Marketing Professional Org. [2648]
SeniorNet [13302]
SIGAPP - Special Interest Gp. on Applied Computing [6821]
SIMPUTER (USA) [13301]
Singapore Infocomm Tech. Fed. [IO]
Singapore Microcomputer Soc. [IO]
Soc. for Info. Display [6745]
Soc. for Modeling and Simulation Intl. [6746]
Software Contractors' Guild [1143]
Software New Zealand [IO]
Software in the Public Interest [6777]
SpamCon Found. [6822]
SpamCon Found. [IO]
Special Interest Gp. on Ada [7538]
Special Interest Gp. on Algorithms and Computation Theory [7539]
Special Interest Gp. for Architecture of Cmpt. Systems [6747]
Special Interest Gp. on Artificial Intelligence [6487]
Special Interest Group for Business Data Processing and Mgt. [76]
Special Interest Gp. for Computers and Soc. [6748]
Special Interest Gp. on Data Communications of the Assn. for Computing Machinery [6804]

Reference to "IO" in place of a book number signifies that the association may be found in the 45th edition of International Organizations.

Special Interest Gp. on Design of Commun. **[6823]**
Special Interest Gp. on Info. Retrieval **[7212]**
Special Interest Gp. on Mgt. Info. Systems **[6824]**
Special Interest Gp. on Measurement and Evaluation **[6751]**
Special Interest Gp. on Mobility of Systems Users, Data, and Computing **[6825]**
Special Interest Gp. on Multimedia **[6826]**
Special Interest Gp. on Programming Languages **[7541]**
Stop Net Abusers **[17241]**
Transaction Processing Performance Coun. **[6755]**
UK Web Design Assn. **[IO]**
Unicorn Users Gp. Intl. **[7214]**
U.S. Internet Coun. **[6827]**
U.S. Internet Ser. Provider Assn. **[911]**
U.S. Prdt. Data Assn. **[2112]**
Upsilon Pi Epsilon Assn. **[24435]**
Venezuelan Chamber of Info. Tech. Businesses **[IO]**
VITA **[912]**
Volunteers in Tech. Assistance **[12448]**
VON Coalition **[2321]**
VXIbus Consortium **[7793]**
Web Analytics Assn. **[7222]**
Web3D Consortium **[6828]**
WECAI Network **[1167]**
Wi-Fi Alliance **[6829]**
XML.org **[6757]**
X.Org Found. **[6830]**
X.Org Found. **[IO]**
YLEM: Artists Using Sci. and Tech. **[9532]**
Zangle Natl. Users' Gp. **[7216]**
Computers for Children **[8137]**, 1799 Clinton St., Buffalo, NY 14206, (716)823-7248
Computers for Children **[IO]**, Buffalo, NY, United States
Computers in Educ; Intl. Coun. for **[★8134]**
Computers in Jewish Life; Inst. for **[8562]**
Computers and the Physically Handicapped; Special Interest Comm. for **[★6803]**
ComputerTown, U.S.A.! - Defunct.
Computing; Assn. for Women in **[6786]**
Computing in Educ; Assn. for the Advancement of **[9237]**
Computing in Educ; Intl. Assn. for **[★8134]**
Computing Machinery; Assn. for **[6783]**
Computing Professionals; The Intl. Assn. of Hewlett-Packard **[★6795]**
Computing Res. Assn. **[6725]**, 1100 Seventeenth St. NW, Ste. 507, Washington, DC 20036-4632, (202)234-2111
Computing Res. Bd. **[★6725]**
Computing Soc; Biomedical **[★6783]**
Computing; Special Interest Gp. for Social and Behavioral Sci. **[★6542]**
Computing Tech. Indus. Assn. **[898]**, 1815 S Meyers Rd., Ste. 300, Oakbrook Terrace, IL 60181-5228, (630)678-8300
ComSource Independent Foodservice Companies **[★1566]**
Comunicacion Intercambio y Desarrollo Humano en Am. Latina, A.C. **[IO]**, Cuernavaca, Mexico
Comunidad Andina - Secretaria Gen. **[★IO]**
Comunidad Electroacustica de Chile **[IO]**, Santiago, Chile
Comunidad Oscar A. Romero Peace Mission **[★17482]**
Comunn na Clarsaich **[★IO]**
An Comunn Gaidhealach Am. **[IO]**, Denver, CO, United States
An Comunn Gaidhealach Am. **[10954]**, PO Box 103069, Denver, CO 80250
Conaidhm Eireannach na Muinteoiri Ollscoile **[★IO]**
Concentrated Phosphate Export Assn. - Address unknown since 1995.
Concern **[4545]**, 1794 Columbia Rd. NW, Washington, DC 20009, (202)328-8160
Concern Am. **[12845]**, PO Box 1790, 2015 N Broadway Ave., Santa Ana, CA 92702, (714)953-8575
Concern Am. **[IO]**, Santa Ana, CA, United States
Concern for Children Trust **[IO]**, Karachi, Pakistan

Concern Found. **[13816]**, 8383 Wilshire Blvd., Ste. 337, Beverly Hills, CA 90211, (323)852-9844
Concern for Hea. Options - Info., Care and Educ. **[★12178]**
Concern for Helping Animals in Israel **[11383]**, PO Box 3341, Alexandria, VA 22302, (703)370-0333
Concern for Helping Animals in Israel **[IO]**, Alexandria, VA, United States
Concern; Unitarian Universalist Assn. - Washington Off. for Social **[★13135]**
Concern Worldwide **[12846]**, 104 E 40th St., Ste. 903, New York, NY 10016, (212)557-8000
Concern Worldwide **[IO]**, New York, NY, United States
Concerned Alliance of Responsible Employers - Defunct.
Concerned Amer. Indian Parents - Address unknown since 2003.
Concerned Amers. for Individual Rights - Address unknown since 1988.
Concerned Amers. for Military Improvements - Address unknown since 1999.
Concerned Broadcasters Using Inter-City Video Transmission Facilities - Defunct.
Concerned Care Intl. - Address unknown since 2001.
Concerned Children's Advertisers **[IO]**, Toronto, ON, Canada
Concerned Citizens of America - Defunct.
Concerned Citizens for Migrants - Address unknown since 1995.
Concerned Citizens for the Nuclear Breeder - Address unknown since 1995.
Concerned Citizens for Nuclear Safety **[18147]**, 107 Cienega St., Santa Fe, NM 87501, (505)986-1973
Concerned Citizens for Racially Free Am. **[17754]**, PO Box 320497, Birmingham, AL 35232-0497, (205)856-0481
Concerned Citizens for Universal Service - Defunct.
Concerned Clergy and Laity of the Episcopal Church **[19950]**, 2520 E Piedmont Rd., Ste. F-6, Marietta, GA 30062
Concerned Educators Against Forced Unionism - A Special Proj. of the Natl. Right to Work Legal Defense Found. **[17971]**, 8001 Braddock Rd., Springfield, VA 22160, (703)321-8510
Concerned Educators Allied for a Safe Env. **[18148]**, 55 Frost St., Cambridge, MA 02140, (617)661-8347
Concerned Guatemala Scholars - Defunct.
Concerned Insurance Professionals for Human Rights - Defunct.
Concerned Neighbors in Action - Address unknown since 1994.
Concerned Persons for Adoption **[11240]**, c/o Jean Giouvanos, Membership Dir., 11 Crestwood Rd., Rockaway, NJ 07866
Concerned Pet Owners' Assn. - Defunct.
Concerned Philosophers for Peace **[7489]**, c/o David Boersema, Treas., Dept. of Philosophy, Pacific Univ., 2043 Coll. Way, Forest Grove, OR 97116
Concerned Relatives of Nursing Home Patients - Address unknown since 1999.
Concerned Scientists; Comm. of **[17752]**
Concerned Scientists; Union of **[18137]**
Concerned Senators for the Arts - Address unknown since 1999.
Concerned United Birthparents **[11241]**, PO Box 503475, San Diego, CA 92150-3475, (800)822-2777
Concerned White Citizens of Alabama - Defunct.
Concerned Women for Am. **[19791]**, 1015 15th St. NW, Ste. 1100, Washington, DC 20005-2619, (202)488-7000
Concerns of Motherhood - Address unknown since 1985.
Concerns of Police Survivors **[12752]**, PO Box 3199, Camdenton, MO 65020, (573)346-4911
Concerns of Police Survivors **[★5995]**
Concert Artists; Young **[10727]**
Concert Bands of Am; Assn. of **[★10560]**
Concert Bands; Assn. of **[10560]**
Concert Managers; Assn. of Coll. and Univ. **[★7968]**
Concessionaires; Conf. of Natl. Park **[★1321]**
Concessionaires; Natl. Assn. of **[1589]**
Concessions Assn; Popcorn and **[★1589]**

Conchological Soc. of Great Britain and Ireland **[IO]**, Reading, United Kingdom
Conchologists of Am. **[21999]**, c/o Doris Underwood, Membership Dir., 698 Sheridan Woods Dr., West Melbourne, FL 32904-3302
Concierge Assn; Natl. **[1956]**
Conciliation Courts; Assn. of Family and **[5699]**
Concord **[IO]**, Brussels, Belgium
Concord Coalition **[17456]**, 1011 Arlington Blvd., Ste. 300, Arlington, VA 22209, (703)894-6222
Concord Coun. - Defunct.
Concord Grape Assn. **[4724]**, 1100 Johnson Ferry Rd., Ste. 300, Atlanta, GA 30342, (404)252-3663
Concord Grape Assn; Amer. **[★4724]**
Concord Grape Coun. **[★4724]**
Concord Video and Film Coun. **[IO]**, Ipswich, United Kingdom
Concorde Collectors Club **[22810]**
Concorde Collectors Club **[★22780]**
Concordia Deaconess Conf. **[20213]**, c/o The Lutheran Church-Missouri Synod, LMCS World Relief and Human Care, 1333 S Kirkwood Rd., St. Louis, MO 63122-7295, (314)996-1382
Concordia Gospel Outreach **[20214]**, Box 201, 3558 S Jefferson Ave., St. Louis, MO 63166, (314)268-1363
Concordia Gospel Outreach **[IO]**, St. Louis, MO, United States
Concordia Historical Inst. **[20215]**, 804 Seminary Pl., St. Louis, MO 63105-3014, (314)505-7900
Concordia Historical Soc. **[★20215]**
Concordia Mutual Life Assn. - Address unknown since 2007.
Concordia Tract Mission **[★20214]**
Concordia Tract Mission **[★IO]**
Concordia - Youth Ser. Volunteers **[IO]**, Brighton, United Kingdom

Concrete

Amer. Concrete Pavement Assn. **[913]**
Amer. Concrete Pipe Assn. **[3023]**
Amer. Concrete Pressure Pipe Assn. **[3024]**
Amer. Concrete Pumping Assn. **[914]**
Amer. Portland Cement Assn. **[915]**
Amer. Shotcrete Assn. **[916]**
Arab Union for Cement and Building Materials **[IO]**
Architectural Precast Assn. **[917]**
Asbestos Cement Prdt. Producers Assn. **[312]**
Asphalt Pavement Alliance **[596]**
Assn. of Asbestos Cement Prdt. Producers **[3026]**
Assn. of Modified Asphalt Producers **[601]**
Autoclaved Aerated Concrete Products Assn. **[918]**
Box Culvert Assn. **[IO]**
Brazilian Cement Manufacturers' Assn. **[IO]**
British Cement Assn. **[IO]**
British Precast Concrete Fed. **[IO]**
Canadian Precast/Prestressed Concrete Inst. **[IO]**
Canadian Ready-Mixed Concrete Assn. **[IO]**
Canadian Tech. Asphalt Assn. **[IO]**
Cast Stone Inst. **[919]**
Cement Admixtures Assn. **[IO]**
Cement Assn. of Canada **[IO]**
Cement and Concrete Assn. of Malaysia **[IO]**
Cement and Concrete Assn. of New Zealand **[IO]**
Cement and Concrete Inst. **[IO]**
Cement Employers Assn. **[920]**
Cement Kiln Recycling Coalition **[4337]**
Cement, Lime, Gypsum, and Allied Workers Div. **[24038]**
Cement Mfrs'. Assn. **[IO]**
Colombian Inst. of Cement Producers **[IO]**
Concrete Anchor Mfrs. Assn. **[921]**
Concrete Corrosion Inhibitors Assn. **[922]**
Concrete Inst. of Australia **[IO]**
Concrete Pipe Associations **[3028]**
Concrete Sawing and Drilling Assn. **[923]**
Concrete Sawing and Drilling Association **[IO]**
Concrete Soc. **[IO]**
Concrete Soc. of Southern Africa **[IO]**
Concrete Tile Manufacturers Assn. **[924]**
Constr. Plant-hire Assn. **[IO]**
Danish Precast Concrete Fed. **[IO]**
Danish Ready-Mixed Concrete Assn. **[IO]**
European Asphalt Pavement Assn. **[IO]**

A star before a book entry number signifies that the name is not listed separately, but is mentioned within the entry.

European Cement Assn. [IO]
European Mastic Asphalt Assn. [IO]
Fed. de l'Industrie du Beton [IO]
German Asphalt Assn. [IO]
German Cement Works Assn. [IO]
German Soc. for Concrete and Constr. Tech. [IO]
Inst. of Concrete Tech. [IO]
Insulating Concrete Form Assn. [925]
Interlocking Concrete Pavement Inst. [926]
Interlocking Concrete Pavement Institute [IO]
Intl. Bur. for Precast Concrete [IO]
Intl. Concrete Repair Inst. [IO]
Intl. Concrete Repair Inst. [927]
Intl. Grooving and Grinding Assn. [928]
Intl. Grooving and Grinding Assn. [IO]
INTERPAVE [IO]
Italian Cement Assn. [IO]
Mastic Asphalt Coun. [IO]
Natl. Assn. of the German Cement Indus. [IO]
Natl. Concrete Masonry Assn. [929]
Natl. Pavement Contractors Assn. [651]
Natl. Precast Concrete Assn. [930]
Natl. Precast Concrete Assn. Australia [IO]
Natl. Ready Mixed Concrete Assn. [931]
Ornamental Concrete Producers Assn. [932]
Portland Cement Assn. [933]
Precast Flooring Fed. [IO]
Precast/Prestressed Concrete Inst. [934]
Prestressed Concrete Assn. [IO]
Quality Scheme for Ready Mixed Concrete [IO]
Quarry Products Assn. [IO]
Res. Inst. of the Assn. of the Austrian Cement Indus. [IO]
Slag Cement Assn. [935]
Sprayed Concrete Assn. [IO]
Structural Stability Res. Coun. [7714]
Swedish Concrete Assn. [IO]
Swedish Precast Concrete Fed. [IO]
Tilt-Up Concrete Assn. [1067]
Concrete Anchor Mfrs. Assn. [921], 136 S Main St., No. 2E, St. Charles, MO 63301, (314)889-7116
Concrete Assn; Natl. Bituminous [★641]
Concrete Assn; Tilt-Up [1067]
Concrete Block Assn. [IO], Leicester, United Kingdom
Concrete Burial Vault Assn; Natl. [2787]
Concrete Constr; Amer. Soc. for [★1001]
Concrete Contractors; Amer. Soc. of [1001]
Concrete Contractors Assn; Natl. [★1001]
Concrete Contractors Assn; Poured [★1011]
Concrete Corrosion Inhibitors Assn. [922], 11836 Goya Dr., Potomac, MD 20854, (301)340-7368
Concrete Foundations Assn. [1011], PO Box 204, 113 W 1st St., Mount Vernon, IA 52314, (319)895-6940
Concrete Industries Coun. - Defunct.
Concrete Inst. [★IO]
Concrete Inst; Amer. [6832]
Concrete Inst. of Australia [IO], Rhodes, Australia
Concrete Joint Inst. - Defunct.
Concrete Paver Inst. [★929]
Concrete Pipe Assn. [IO]
Concrete Pipe Assn; Amer. [3023]
Concrete Pipe Assn. of Australasia [IO], St. Leonards, Australia
Concrete Pipe Associations [3028], 1303 W Walnut Hill Ln., Ste. 305, Irving, TX 75038-3008, (972)506-7216
Concrete Pipeline Systems Assn. [IO], Leicester, United Kingdom
Concrete Plant Manufacturers Bur. [★931]
Concrete Pressure Pipe Assn; Amer. [3024]
Concrete Pumpers Assn. of Southern California [★914]
Concrete Reinforcing Steel Inst. [612], 933 N Plum Grove Rd., Schaumburg, IL 60173-4758, (847)517-1200
Concrete Repair Assn. [IO], Aldershot, United Kingdom
Concrete Repair Specialists; Intl. Assn. of [★927]
Concrete Sawing and Drilling Assn. [923], 11001 Danka Way N, Ste. 1, St. Petersburg, FL 33716, (727)577-5004
Concrete Sawing and Drilling Association [IO], St. Petersburg, FL, United States

Concrete Soc. [IO], Camberley, United Kingdom
Concrete Soc. of Southern Africa [IO], Gauteng, Republic of South Africa
Concrete Tile Manufacturers Assn. [924], PO Box 6225, Buena Park, CA 90622, (714)535-0791
Conditioning Assn; Natl. Strength and [23957]
Conditions Ecological Soc. of Am; Comm. on Preservation of Natural [★4433]
Conductors
Assn. of Canadian Choral Conductors [IO]
Leopold Stokowski Club [9812]
Conductors and Brakemen; Order of Railway [★24181]
Conductors Guild [10581], 5300 Glenside Dr., Ste. 2207, Richmond, VA 23228, (804)553-1378
Conductors; Natl. Assn. for Composers and [★10657]
CONDUIT - Defunct.
Conestoga Soc. [21529], 16725 Collinson, Eastpointe, MI 48021
Coney Island Polar Bear Club [★23888]
Confectionary and Chocolate; Assn. of Mfrs. of [★1558]
Confectioners Assn. of the U.S; Natl. [1544]
Confectioners of North Am; Assoc. Retail [★1561]
Confectioners of the U.S; Assoc. Retail [★1561]
Confectionery Mfrs. Assn. of Canada [IO], Don Mills, ON, Canada
Confectionery Manufacturers of Australasia [IO], Camberwell, Australia
Confectionery Sales Assn. of Am; Natl. [★3419]
Confectionery Sales Assn; Natl. [3419]
Confectionery, Tobacco Workers and Grain Millers Intl. Union; Bakery, [24017]
Confectionery and Tobacco Workers Intl. Union; Bakery, [★24017]
Confectionery Workers' Intl. Union of Am; Bakery and [★24017]
Confederacao dos Agricultores de Portugal [★IO]
Confederacao das Associacoes Comerciais do Brasil [★IO]
Confederacao Brasileira de Badminton [IO], Campinas, Brazil
Confederacao Brasileira do Desporto Escolar [IO], Brasilia, Brazil
Confederacao Brasileira de Desportos no Gelo [★IO]
Confederacao Brasileira de Esqui-Aquatico [★IO]
Confederacao Brasileira de Taekwondo [IO], Rio de Janeiro, Brazil
Confederacao Brasileira de Tenis [IO], Sao Paulo, Brazil
Confederacao Brasileira de Squash [IO], Florianopolis, Brazil
Confederacao de Comercio e Servicos de Portugal [★IO]
Confederacao Nacional do Comercio [★IO]
Confederacao Nacional dos Trabalhadores em Educacao [★IO]
Confederacion Argentina de Entidades Aerodeportivas [IO], Buenos Aires, Argentina
Confederacion Atletica del Uruguay [IO], Montevideo, Uruguay
Confederacion de Camaras Industriales [★IO]
Confederacion de Empresarios Privados de Bolivia [★IO]
Confederacion Espanola de Asociaciones Profesionales de Informadores Tecnicos Sanitarios [★IO]
Confederacion Espanola de Empresarios de Plasticos [★IO]
Confederacion Espanola de Familiares de Enfermos de Alzheimer y Otras Demencias [★IO]
Confederacion Espanola de Hoteles y Alojamientos Turisticos [★IO]
Confederacion Espanola de Organizaciones Empresariales [★IO]
Confederacion Espanola de Organizaciones de Panaderia [★IO]
Confederacion Espanola de Organizaciones en favor de las Personas con Discapacidad Intelectual [IO], Madrid, Spain
Confederacion Espanola de la Pequena y Mediana Empresa [★IO]
Confederacion Indus. Argentina; Confederacion Gen. de la Industria [★IO]

Confederacion Interamericana de Educacion Catolica [★IO]
Confederacion de Kinesiologos y Fisioterapeutas de la Republica Argentina [IO], Parana, Argentina
Confederacion Latinoamericana de Sociedades de Anestesiologia [★IO]
Confederacion Medica Republica Argentina [IO], Buenos Aires, Argentina
Confederacion Mundial de Centros Comunitarios Judios [★IO]
Confederacion Nacional de Squash de Panama [IO], Panama City, Panama
Confederacion de Organizaciones Turisticas de la Am. Latina [★IO]
Confederacion Paraguaya de Taekwondo [IO], Asuncion, Paraguay
Confederacion Sudamericana de Atletismo [★IO]
Confederacion Sudamericana de Tenis [IO], Santiago, Chile
Confederacion Venezolana de Industriales [★IO]
Confederacy; Children of the [20724]
Confederacy; United Daughters of the [20732]
Confederate Air Force [★21438]
Confederate High Command, Intl. [★20722]
Confederate Memorial Assn. [9368], PO Box 6010, Washington, DC 20005, (202)483-5700
Confederate Memorial Literary Soc. [10105], The Museum of the Confederacy, 1201 E Clay St., Richmond, VA 23219, (804)649-1861
Confederate Natl. Cong. - Address unknown since 2006.
Confederate Stamp Alliance [22811], c/o Col. Richard Murphy, Sec., 501 Rosebud Ln., Greer, SC 29650
Confederate States Volunteers [★20722]
Confederate Veterans; Sons of [20730]
Confederate Veterans; United [★20730]
Confederated Spanish Societies - Defunct.
Confederated Unions of Am. [★24210]
Confed. europeenne des Administrateurs de Biens aisbl [★IO]
Confed. of Aerial Indus. [IO], Middlesex, United Kingdom
Confed. Africaine de Football [★IO]
Confed. Africaine de Tennis [★IO]
Confed. of African Medical Associations and Societies [IO], Lagos, Nigeria
Confed. of African Tennis [IO], Tunis, Tunisia
Confed. of All Type Canaries - Defunct.
Confed. of Amer. Indians - Address unknown since 1990.
Confed. of Asian Chambers of Commerce and Indus. [★IO]
Confed. of Asian and Pacific Accountants [IO], Kuala Lumpur, Malaysia
Confed. of Asian-Pacific Chambers of Commerce and Indus. [IO], Taipei, Taiwan
Confed. des Associations d'Entreprises de Commerce Intl. [★IO]
Confed. des Associations Internationales d'Entrepreneurs [★IO]
Confed. des Associations Nationales de l'Hotellerie, de la Restauration et des Cafes de l'Union Europeenne [★IO]
Confed. des Associations et Societes Medicales D'Afrique [★IO]
Confed. Belge du Commerce et de la Reparation Automobiles et des Secteurs Connexes a.s.b.l. [★IO]
Confed. Belge de l'industrie laitiere [★IO]
Confed. Belge de l'Industrie Laitiere [★IO]
Confed. of Bolivian Private Entrepreneurs [IO], La Paz, Bolivia
Confed. of Brewers of the Common Market [★IO]
Confed. of British Forgers [★IO]
Confed. of British Indus. [IO], London, United Kingdom
Confed. of British Metalforming [IO], West Bromwich, United Kingdom
Confed. of British Wool Textiles [IO], Bradford, United Kingdom
Confed. of Commercial Associations of Brazil [IO], Brasilia, Brazil
Confed. of Danish Employers [IO], Copenhagen, Denmark

Reference to "IO" in place of a book number signifies that the association may be found in the 45th edition of International Organizations.

Confed. of Danish Indus. **[IO]**, Copenhagen, Denmark

Confed. of Dental Employers **[IO]**, Holsworthy, United Kingdom

Confed. of European Baseball **[IO]**, Prague, Czech Republic

Confed. of European Cmpt. User Associations **[IO]**, Reykjavik, Iceland

Confed. of European Forest Owners **[IO]**, Brussels, Belgium

Confed. of European Paper Indus. **[IO]**, Brussels, Belgium

Confed. of European Pest Control Associations **[IO]**, Brussels, Belgium

Confed. of European Union Rectors' Conferences **[IO]**, Brussels, Belgium

Confed. Europeene de Baseball Amateur **[★IO]**

Confed. Europeene des Independents **[★IO]**

Confed. Europeene des Relations Publiques **[★IO]**

Confed. Europeenne des Associations des Technologies de l'Information **[★IO]**

Confed. Europeenne de Baseball **[★IO]**

Confed. Europeenne des Cadres **[★IO]**

Confed. Europeenne des Cooperatives de Travail Associe, des Cooperatives Sociales et des Entreprises Sociales et Participatives **[★IO]**

Confed. Europeenne des Distributeurs d'Energie Publics Communaux **[★IO]**

Confed. Europeenne des Indus. du Bois **[★IO]**

Confed. Europeenne de l'Immobilier **[★IO]**

Confed. Europeenne des Produceurs de Spiritueux **[★IO]**

Confed. Europeenne des Proprietaires Forestiers **[★IO]**

Confed. Europeenne des Syndicats Independants **[★IO]**

Confed. Europeenne des Universities du Rhin Superieur **[★IO]**

Confed. of Family Organisations in the European Union **[IO]**, Brussels, Belgium

Confed. Fiscale Europeenne **[IO]**, Berlin, Germany

Confed. of the Food and Drink Indus. of the EU **[IO]**, Brussels, Belgium

Confed. Francaise Democratique du Travail **[★IO]**

Confed. Francaise d'Ingenierie Rurale et Agricole **[IO]**, Paris, France

Confed. Francaise de L'industrie des Papiers, Cartons and Celluloses **[★IO]**

Confed. of German Employers' Associations **[IO]**, Berlin, Germany

Confed. of the German Trade Fair and Exhibition Indus. **[★IO]**

Confed. of Icelandic Employers **[IO]**, Reykjavik, Iceland

Confed. of Independent Aryan Orgs. - Defunct.

Confed. of Independent Psychoanalytic Societies of the U.S. - Address unknown since 2002.

Confed. of Independent Trade Unions in Bulgaria **[IO]**, Sofia, Bulgaria

Confed. of Indian Indus. **[IO]**, New Delhi, India

Confed. of Indian Indus. - United Kingdom **[IO]**, London, United Kingdom

Confed. of Indian Textile Indus. **[IO]**, New Delhi, India

Confed. of Indus. Chambers **[IO]**, Mexico City, Mexico

Confed. of Indus. of the Czech Republic **[IO]**, Prague, Czech Republic

Confed. of Inspection and Certification Organisations **[IO]**, Brussels, Belgium

Confed. of Intl. Contractors' Associations **[IO]**, Paris, France

Confed. of Intl. Soft Drinks Associations **[IO]**, Brussels, Belgium

Confed. Internationale des Accordeonistes **[★IO]**

Confed. Internationale des Banques Populaires **[★IO]**

Confed. Internationale des Betteraviers Europeens **[★IO]**

Confed. Internationale de la Boucherie et de la Charcuterie **[★IO]**

Confed. Internationale du Commerce et des Indus. des Legumes Secs **[★IO]**

Confed. Internationale du Credit Agricole **[★IO]**

Confed. Internationale des Fabricants de Tissus d'Ameublement **[★IO]**

Confed. Internationale des Musees d'Architecture **[★IO]**

Confed. Internationale de Musique Electroacoustique **[★IO]**

Confed. Internationale des Negociants en Oeuvres d'Art **[★IO]**

Confed. Internationale des Sages-Femmes **[★IO]**

Confed. Internationale des Societes d'Auteurs et Compositeurs **[★IO]**

Confed. Internationale des Syndicats Libres **[★IO]**

Confed. of Irish Indus. **[★IO]**

Confed. of Italian Indus. **[IO]**, Rome, Italy

Confed. of Japan Auto. Workers' Unions **[IO]**, Tokyo, Japan

Confed. of Labour "Podkrepa" Sofia, BulgariaIO

Confed. of Latin Amer. Societies of Anesthesiology **[IO]**, Buenos Aires, Argentina

Confed. of Latin Amer. Tourism Organizations **[IO]**, Buenos Aires, Argentina

Confed. des organisations familiales de l'Union europeenne **[★IO]**

Confed. Mondiale des Activites Subaquatiques **[★IO]**

Confed. Mondiale pour la Therapie Physique **[★IO]**

Confed. Mondiale du Travail **[★IO]**

Confed. of Natl. Associations of Hotels, Restaurants, Cafes and Similar Establishments **[IO]**, Brussels, Belgium

Confed. of Natl. Associations of Tanners and Dressers of the European Community **[IO]**, Brussels, Belgium

Confed. of Natl. Trade Unions **[IO]**, Montreal, QC, Canada

Confed. Nationale de la Boulangerie-Patisserie Francaise **[★IO]**

Confed. Nationale des Glaciers de France **[★IO]**

Confed. Nationale du Logement **[IO]**, Montreuil, France

Confed. of Nordic Bank Employees' Unions **[★IO]**

Confed. of Nordic Bank, Finance and Insurance Employees' Unions **[IO]**, Stockholm, Sweden

Confed. of Norwegian Bus. and Indus. **[IO]**, Oslo, Norway

Confed. of Paper Indus. **[IO]**, Wiltshire, United Kingdom

Confed. of Passenger Transport - UK **[IO]**, London, United Kingdom

Confed. of Portuguese Farmers **[IO]**, Lisbon, Portugal

Confed. of Roofing Contractors **[IO]**, Colchester, United Kingdom

Confed. of Socialist Parties of the European Community **[★IO]**

Confed. of Swedish Enterprise **[IO]**, Stockholm, Sweden

Confed. of Swiss Employers **[IO]**, Zurich, Switzerland

Confed. des Syndicats Chretiens de Belgique **[★IO]**

Confed. des Syndicats Nationaux **[★IO]**

Confed. of Taino People; United **[18989]**

Confed. of Tanners' Associations in the European Community **[★IO]**

Confed. of Tanzania Indus. **[IO]**, Dar es Salaam, United Republic of Tanzania

Confed. of Tech. Employees Organizations in Finland **[★IO]**

Confed. of Trade Unions of Monaco **[IO]**, Monaco, Monaco

Confed. of Turkish Trade Unions **[IO]**, Ankara, Turkey

Confed. of Turkish Tradesmen and Craftsmen **[IO]**, Ankara, Turkey

Confed. of Unions for Academic Professionals in Finland **[IO]**, Helsinki, Finland

Confed. of Zimbabwe Indus. **[IO]**, Bulawayo, Zimbabwe

Confed. of Zonta Clubs **[★IO]**

Confed. of Zonta Clubs **[★13071]**

Confederazione Cooperative Italiane **[★IO]**

Confederazione Generale dell'Industria Italiana **[★IO]**

Conf. of Actuaries in Public Practice **[★2157]**

Conf. of Administrators of Coll. and Univ. Counseling Services - Address unknown since 1995.

Conf. on Alternative State and Local Policies **[★18429]**

Conf. on Alternative State and Local Public Policies **[★18429]**

Conf. of Amer. Renting and Leasing Assns. - Defunct.

Conf. of Americans of Central and Eastern European Descent - Defunct.

Conf. on Asian History **[9617]**, c/o Prof. George M. Wilson, Chm., Indiana Univ., East Asian Stud. Center, Memorial Hall West 207, 1021 E Third St., Bloomington, IN 47405, (812)855-3765

Conf. on the Atlantic Community - Address unknown since 1999.

Conf. of Biological Editors **[★3108]**

The Conf. Bd. **[6877]**, 845 3rd Ave., New York, NY 10022, (212)759-0900

The Conf. Bd. **[IO]**, New York, NY, United States

Conf. Bd. of Assoc. Res. Councils **[★IO]**

Conf. Bd. of Assoc. Res. Councils **[★8609]**

Conf. Bd. of Canada **[IO]**, Ottawa, ON, Canada

Conf. Bd. Europe **[IO]**, Brussels, Belgium

Conf. Bd. of Major Printers - Defunct.

Conf. Bd. of the Mathematical Sciences **[7289]**, 1529 18th St. NW, Washington, DC 20036, (202)293-1170

Conf. on British Stud. **[★9760]**

Conf. of Bus. Economists **[6878]**, 28790 Chagrin Blvd., Ste. 350, Cleveland, OH 44122, (216)464-2137

Conf. des eveques catholiques du Canada **[★IO]**

Conf. Canadienne des arts **[★IO]**

Conf. for Catholic Lesbians **[20051]**, PO Box 853, Greenport, NY 11944, (718)680-6107

Conf. of Chief Justices **[5896]**, c/o Assn. Mgt., 300 Newport Ave., Williamsburg, VA 23185-4147, (757)259-1841

Conf. for Chinese Oral and Performing Literature **[9790]**, c/o Shu-Chu Wei, Pres., Whitman Coll., Dept. of Foreign Languages and Literature, Walla Walla, WA 99362, (509)527-5891

Conference for Chinese Oral and Performing Literature **[IO]**, Walla Walla, WA, United States

Conf. Chretienne pour la Paix **[★IO]**

Conf. on Christianity and Literature **[8799]**, c/o Prof. Paul Contino, Co-Ed., Pepperdine Univ., 24255 Pacific Coast Hwy., Malibu, CA 90263-3999, (310)506-4095

Conf. of Church Workers Among the Deaf **[★19954]**

Conf. of Churches in Aotearoa New Zealand **[IO]**, Christchurch, New Zealand

Conf. on Coll. Composition and Commun. **[8376]**, 1111 W Kenyon Rd., Urbana, IL 61801-1096, (217)328-3870

Conf. Comm. for Refugee Rabbis - Address unknown since 1995.

Conf. of Consulting Actuaries **[2157]**, 3880 Salem Lake Dr., Ste. H, Long Grove, IL 60047-6400, (847)719-6500

Conf. on Consumer Finance Law **[5608]**, c/o Prof. Alvin C. Harrell, Exec. Dir., Oklahoma City Univ. School of Law, 2501 N Blackwelder, Oklahoma City, OK 73106, (405)521-5363

Conf. of Consumer Orgs. - Address unknown since 2004.

Conf. on Critical Legal Studies - Address unknown since 1999.

Conf. on Data Systems Languages - Defunct.

Conf. des Directerus des Gymnases Suisses **[★IO]**

Conf. of Drama Schools **[IO]**, London, United Kingdom

Conf. on Dual Distribution - Address unknown since 1995.

Conf. on Economic Progress - Defunct.

Conf. of Educational Administrators of Schools and Programs for the Deaf **[14749]**, c/o Joseph P. Finnegan, Jr., Exec. Dir., PO Box 1778, St. Augustine, FL 32085-1778, (904)810-5200

Conf. of Educational Administrators Serving the Deaf **[★14749]**

Conf. on English Educ. **[8377]**, c/o Natl. Coun. of Teachers of English, 1111 W Kenyon Rd., Urbana, IL 61801-1096, (217)328-3870

Conf. on English Leadership **[1175]**, c/o Natl. Coun. of Teachers of English, 1111 W Kenyon Rd., Urbana, IL 61801-1096, (217)328-3870

Conf. of European Churches **[IO]**, Geneva, Switzerland

A star before a book entry number signifies that the name is not listed separately, but is mentioned within the entry.

Conf. of European Natl. Librarians [IO], Frankfurt am Main, Germany

Conf. of European Rabbis [IO], London, United Kingdom

Conf. of European Schools for Advanced Engg. Educ. and Res. [IO], Leuven, Belgium

Conf. Europeenne des Administrations des Postes et des Telecommunications [★IO]

Conf. Europeenne de l'Aviation Civile [★IO]

Conf. Europeenne des Ministres des Transports [★IO]

Conf. of Executives of Amer. Schools for the Deaf [★14749]

Conf. of Executives of State Associations of Counties [★5624]

Conference on Fair Foreign Investment - Defunct.

Conf. on Faith and History [20079], c/o Paul E. Michelson, Sec., Dept. of History, Huntington Univ., Huntington, IN 46750, (260)359-4242

Conf. of Funeral Ser. Examining Boards of the U.S. [★6120]

Conf. Group for Central European History - Address unknown since 1995.

Conf. Gp. on French Politics and Soc. [17621], Center for European Stud., 27 Kirkland St., Cambridge, MA 02138, (617)495-4303

Conference Group on French Politics and Society [IO], Cambridge, MA, United States

Conf. Group on Italian Politics and Soc. - Defunct.

Conf. Gp. of U.S. Natl. Organizations on the United Nations [★18770]

Conf. de la Haye de Droit Intl. Prive [★IO]

Conf. of Insurance Legislators; Natl. [5832]

Conf. of Intl. Non-Governmental Organizations [IO], Paris, France

Conf. Internationale pour les Bateaux de Sauvetage [★IO]

Conf. of Interstate Agencies - Defunct.

Conf. of Irish Indus. [★IO]

Conf; Jesuit [19643]

Conf. on Jesuit Student Personnel Administrators [★7896]

Conf. of Jewish Communal Ser. [★12472]

Conf. of Jewish Communal Ser. [★IO]

Conf. on Jewish Material Claims Against Germany [12470], 15 E 26th St., Rm. 906, New York, NY 10010, (646)536-9100

Conf. on Jewish Social Studies - Address unknown since 2007.

Conf. on Latin Amer. History [10310], c/o U.S. Department of History and Prog. in Latin Amer. Stud., Univ. of North Carolina at Charlotte, 9201 Univ. City Blvd., Charlotte, NC 28223, (704)687-2027

Conf. of Local Airlines - Defunct.

Conf. of Local Environmental Hea. Administrators [★16246]

Conf. of Major Religious Superiors of Men's Institutes of the U.S. [★19615]

Conf. of Major Religious Superiors of Women's Institutes of the United States of Am. [★19649]

Conf. of Major Superiors of Men [19615], 8808 Cameron St., Silver Spring, MD 20910, (301)588-4030

Conf. Mgt; Intl. Inst. of [★2676]

Conf. of Members of Parliament from the NATO Countries [★IO]

Conf. of Minority Public Administrators [6191], c/o Amer. Soc. for Public Admin., 1301 Pennsylvania Ave. NW, Ste. 840, Washington, DC 20004, (202)393-7878

Conf. of Minority Trans. Officials [3866], 818 18th St. NW, Ste. 850, Washington, DC 20006, (202)530-0551

Conf. of Missionary Societies in Great Britain [★IO]

Conf. of Motion Picture and TV Conf. Unions [★24056]

Conf. of Municipal Public Hea. Engineers [★16246]

Conf. of Natl. Park Concessionaires [★1321]

Conf. des Nations Unies sur le Commerce et le Developpement [★IO]

Conf. des Organisations Internationales Non-Gouvernementales [★IO]

Conference of Patriotic and Historic Societies - Defunct.

Conf. of Peripheral Maritime Regions of Europe [IO], Rennes, France

Conf. Permanente Europeenne des Associations de Professeurs d'Histoire [★IO]

Conf. Permanente Europeenne de la Probation [★IO]

Conf. on Personal Finance Law [★5608]

Conf. of Personal Managers, East [★174]

Conf. of Personal Managers, West [★174]

Conf. of Philosophical Societies [10790], c/o G. John M. Abbarno, Pres., Div. of Liberal Arts, D'Youville Coll., Buffalo, NY 14201-2486

Conf. of Podiatry Executives - Address unknown since 2002.

Conf. of Presidents of Major Amer. Jewish Organizations [20134], 633 3rd Ave., 21st Fl., New York, NY 10017, (212)318-6111

Conf. of Prince Hall Grand Masters [19230]

Conf. of Private Orgs. - Defunct.

Conf. of Professors of Preventive Medicine [★16054]

Conf. of Public Health Laboratorians - Defunct.

Conf. of Public Health Veterinarians - Address unknown since 1999.

Conf. on the Public Service - Defunct.

Conf. of Radiation Control Prog. Directors [6241], 205 Capital Ave., Frankfort, KY 40601-2832, (502)227-4543

Conf. for Reconciliation, Restitution Fund - Address unknown since 1995.

Conf. des Regions Peripheriques Maritimes d'Europe [★IO]

Conference of Research Workers in Animal Diseases [IO], Fort Collins, CO, United States

Conf. of Res. Workers in Animal Diseases [16790], c/o Dr. Robert P. Ellis, Exec. Dir., Colorado State Univ., Dept. of Microbiology, Immunology and Pathology, Microbiology Bldg., Rm. A 102, Fort Collins, CO 80523-1682, (970)491-5740

Conf. on Safe Trans. of Hazardous Articles [3562], 7803 Hill House Ct., Fairfax Station, VA 22039-2043, (703)451-4031

Conf. on Science, Philosophy and Religion - Defunct.

Conf. on Sci. and Religion [★17916]

Conf. on Sci. and Religion [★IO]

Conf. for Secondary School English Dept. Chairpersons - Address unknown since 2001.

Conf. of Small Private Colleges - Defunct.

Conf. of State Bank Supervisors [5544], 1155 Connecticut Ave. NW, 5th Fl., Washington, DC 20036-4306, (202)296-2840

Conf. of State Cemetery Assn. Secretaries - Defunct.

Conf. of State Court Administrators [5625], c/o Natl. Center for State Courts, 300 Newport Ave., Williamsburg, VA 23185, (757)259-1841

Conf. of State Health and Environmental Managers - Defunct.

Conf. of State and Provincial Health Authorities of North America - Defunct.

Conf. of State Social Security Administrators [★6259]

Conf. of State Societies [★19382]

Conf. of State and Territorial Directors of Public Hea. Educ. [★6215]

Conf. of State and Territorial Epidemiologists [★14374]

Conf. of State Utility Commn. Engineers [★6341]

Conf. for the Stud. of Political Thought [7524], c/o Prof. Sharon Snowiss, Sec.-Treas., Pitzer Coll., Dept. of Political Sci., 1050 N Mills Ave., Claremont, CA 91711, (212)854-3955

Conf. of Theological Seminaries of the U.S. and Canada [★9270]

Conf. of Theological Seminaries of the U.S. and Canada [★IO]

Conf. on Transportation Unity - Defunct.

Conf. of U.N. Representatives [★18771]

Conf. of U.N. Representatives, (CUNR), UNA-USA [★18771]

Conf. of Univ. Teachers of German in Great Britain and Ireland [IO], Exeter, United Kingdom

Conf. of Utility Commn. Engineers [★6341]

Conf. on Utopian Stud. [★10839]

Conf. on Utopian Stud. [★IO]

Conf. on Visual Literacy [★IO]

Conf. on Visual Literacy [★8271]

Conf. on World Affairs [★18832]

Conf. on World Affairs [★IO]

Conferences on Sci. and World Affairs; International Pugwash [★18842]

Conferencia de Iglesias del Caribe [★IO]

Conferencia Interamericana de Seguridad Social [★IO]

Confesercenti [★IO]

Confessing Synod Ministries [20561], East Liberty Lutheran Church, 5707 Penn Ave., Pittsburgh, PA 15206-3603, (412)362-1712

Conflict

Alliance for Peacebuilding [17248]

Asia Am. Initiative [11762]

Conflict Res. Soc. [IO]

CRU Inst. [8138]

Global Majority [17249]

HALO USA [17245]

HALO USA [IO]

Help Darfur Now [12259]

Intl. Campaign to Ban Landmines [17431]

Intl. Crisis Gp., Washington Off. [17246]

Intl. Crisis Gp., Washington Off. [IO]

Intl. Org. for the Stud. of Gp. Tensions [10189]

Intl. Peace Operations Assn. [18213]

Korean War Proj. [6344]

Mediators Without Borders [5458]

Natl. Coalition Building Inst. [17227]

Pugwash Conferences on Sci. and World Affairs [17247]

Pugwash Conferences on Sci. and World Affairs [IO]

Soc. for the Stud. of Peace, Conflict, and Violence: Peace Psychology Div. of the Amer. Psychological Assn. [16185]

Conflict Mediators Program [★8658]

Conflict Prog; Children's Creative Response to [11684]

Conflict Res. Soc. [IO], Sheffield, United Kingdom

Conflict Resolution

Advocates Intl. [17998]

Alliance for Peacebuilding [17248]

Alliance for Peacebuilding [IO]

Amer. Comm. for Peace in Chechnya [18189]

Americans United for Israel [19157]

Asia Am. Initiative [11762]

Black Holocaust Soc. [16938]

Friends of Sabeel - North Am. [18205]

Global Majority [17249]

Global Majority [IO]

Grace Contrino Abrams Peace Educ. Found. [8139]

Intl. Peace Operations Assn. [18213]

Joan B. Kroc Inst. for Intl. Peace Stud. [18216]

Justice Stud. Assn. [13109]

"Love Yourself" Stop the Violence [17250]

Mediators Without Borders [5458]

Play for Peace [12699]

Professional Mediation Assn. [5462]

Seeds of Peace [18245]

Worldwide Forgiveness Alliance [8959]

Conflict Resolution/Alternatives to Violence Training Center - Defunct.

Conflict Resolution; Assn. for [5450]

Conflict Resolution; Canadian Inst. for [IO]

Conflict Resolution Center Intl. - Defunct.

Conflict Resolution Educ. Network [★5450]

Conflict Resolution; Inst. for Mediation and [5455]

Conflict Resolution, Mediation, and Peacemaking; Training Inst. for [★8139]

Conflict Resolution; Natl. Conf. on Peacemaking and [18118]

Conflict Resolution Network Canada [IO], Waterloo, ON, Canada

Conflict Resolution Prog. [18111], c/o Laurence Berg, Prog. Dir., 15 Rutherford Pl., New York, NY 10003, (212)598-0950

Conflicts; Prog. on the Anal. and Resolution of [18242]

Confluent Education Development and Res. Center - Defunct.

Reference to "IO" in place of a book number signifies that the association may be found in the 45th edition of International Organizations.

Conformation Judges Assn. Educ. Fund; Senior [★22193]

Conformation Judges Assn; Senior [22358]

Confraternity of the Blessed Sacrament [19951], c/o Rev. William Willoughby, III, Gen. Sec., 224 E 34th St., Savannah, GA 31401

Confraternity of Christian Doctrine [★19934]

Confraternity of the Most Holy Name of Jesus [★19666]

Confraternity of Penitents [19616], 520 Oliphant Ln., Middletown, RI 02842-4600, (401)849-5421

Confraternity of Pilgrims - Address unknown since 1995.

Confrerie de la Chaine des Rotisseurs, Bailliage des U.S.A. [22569], 285 Madison Ave., Madison, NJ 07940-1099, (973)360-9200

Confrerie des Chevaliers du Tastevin [IO], Nuits-Saint-Georges, France

Confucian Sci; Center for [19879]

Congenita; Avenues, Natl. Support Gp. for Arthrogryposis Multiplex [15309]

Congenital Cardiac Anesthesia Soc. [13682], PO Box 11086, Richmond, VA 23230, (804)282-9780

Congenital Diaphragmatic Hernia Res., Advocacy and Support; CHERUBS - Assn. of [13753]

Congenital Heart Assn; Adult [13884]

Congenital Heart Defects Awareness [13900], 1996 Hartford Tpke., North Haven, CT 06473, (203)234-1371

Congenital Heart Info. Network [13901], First Fl., 600 N 3rd St., Philadelphia, PA 19123-2902, (215)627-4034

Congenital Heart Info. Network [IO], Philadelphia, PA, United States

Congleton Chamber of Commerce and Enterprise [IO], Congleton, United Kingdom

Congo Protestant Relief Agency - Defunct.

Congolese Students Union of the U.S.A. and Canada - Address unknown since 1995.

Congregation Bina [10277], 600 W End Ave., Ste. 1C, New York, NY 10024-1643, (212)873-4261

Congregation of the Blessed Sacrament [19617], 5384 Wilson Mills Rd., Cleveland, OH 44143-3023, (440)442-6311

Congregation of the Holy Spirit [IO], Rome, Italy

Congregation of La Retraite [IO], St.-Germain-en-Laye, France

Congregation of Mariannhill Missionaries; U.S. Region of [★19655]

Congregation of Our Lady of Cenacle; Aggregation of [★19581]

Congregation of the Passion of Jesus Christ [★IO]

Congregation Prog; Reconciling [★20065]

Congregation of Saint Agnes; Sisters of the [★19618]

Congregation of Saint Basil [IO], Toronto, ON, Canada

Congregation Shema Yisrael [20135], PO Box 804, Southfield, MI 48037, (248)593-5150

Congregation of the Sisters of Charity of the Incarnate Word; CCVI Incarnate Word Missionaries - [19607]

Congregation of the Sisters of Charity of the Incarnate Word; CCVI Volunteers in Mission - [★19607]

Congregation of Sisters of Saint Agnes [19618], 320 County Rd. K, Fond du Lac, WI 54935-8958, (920)907-2300

Congregational Christian

Amer. Congregational Assn. [19859]

Congregational Christian Historical Soc. [19860]

Natl. Assn. of Congregational Christian Churches [19861]

Congregational Christian Churches; Natl. Assn. of [19861]

Congregational Christian Historical Soc. [19860], 14 Beacon St., Boston, MA 02108, (617)523-0470

Congregations; Unitarian Universalist Assn. of [13135]

Congregations - Washington Off. for Faith in Action; Unitarian Universalist Assn. of [★13135]

Congres du travail du Canada [★IO]

Congres Canadien Polonais [★IO]

Congres Juif Canadien [★IO]

Congres Mondiaux du Petrole [★IO]

Congres des Peuples Autochtones [★IO]

Congress

Advisory Coun. on Historic Preservation [10007]

Amer. Conservative Union [17261]

Amer. Coun. for Capital Formation [17347]

Amer. Defense Inst. [17373]

Citizens Against Govt. Waste [17668]

Civilian Cong. [17251]

Comm. on the Constitutional Sys. [17289]

Comm. for a Responsible Fed. Budget [18405]

Congressional Arts Caucus [17254]

Congressional Border Caucus [5598]

Congressional Hispanic Caucus [17702]

Congressional Human Rights Caucus [17755]

Congressional Mgt. Found. [5599]

The Conservative Caucus [17264]

The Conservative Caucus Res., Anal. and Educ. Found. [17265]

Conservative Opportunity Soc. [17257]

Coun. for a Livable World [17425]

Coun. for a Livable World Educ. Fund [17426]

Croatian Amer. Assn. [17868]

Found. for Rational Economics and Educ. [17293]

Free Cong. Political Action Comm. [17268]

League of Conservation Voters [18312]

Liberty Amendment Comm. of the U.S.A. [17296]

Natl. Comm. for an Effective Cong. [17252]

Natl. Traditionalist Caucus [17276]

Public Citizen's Cong. Watch [17343]

U.S. Assn. of Former Members of Cong. [17253]

U.S. Capitol Historical Soc. [10164]

U.S. Holocaust Memorial Coun. [17725]

VoterWatch [5600]

Cong. of Aboriginal Peoples [IO], Ottawa, ON, Canada

Cong. of Astrological Orgs. - Defunct.

Cong. of Chiropractic State Associations [13997], PO Box 2054, Lexington, SC 29071, (803)356-6809

Cong; Comm. for the Survival of a Free [★17268]

Cong. of County Medical Societies - Defunct.

Cong; Former Members of [★17253]

Cong. Found; Free [11810]

Cong. of Independent Unions [24205]

Cong. of Indus. Organizations [★24096]

Cong. for Jewish Culture [10278], 25 E 21st St., New York, NY 10010, (212)505-8040

Cong. of Lung Assn. Staff [16357], 1150 18th St. NW, Washington, DC 20036-3816, (202)785-3355

Cong. of Natl. Black Churches [19890]

Cong. of Neurological Surgeons [15413], 10 N Martingale Rd., Ste. 190, Schaumburg, IL 60173, (847)240-2500

Cong. of Neurological Surgeons [IO], Schaumburg, IL, United States

Cong. of Orgs. of the Physically Handicapped - Defunct.

Cong. of Orgs. and Puerto Rican Hometowns - Address unknown since 1995.

Cong. Political Action Comm; Free [17268]

Cong. of Racial Equality [16939], 817 Broadway, 3rd Fl., New York, NY 10003, (212)598-4000

Congress of Religious Credit Unions - Address unknown since 2001.

Cong. on Res. in Dance [9871], State Univ. of New York, Dept. of Dance, 350 New Campus Dr., Brockport, NY 14420, (585)395-2590

Cong. on Res. in Dance [IO], Brockport, NY, United States

Cong. Res. and Educ. Found; Free [18295]

Cong. of Russian Americans [19337], 2460 Sutter St., San Francisco, CA 94115, (415)928-5841

Cong. of Scientists on Survival - Defunct.

Cong. of Secular Jewish Organizations [10279], 320 Claymore Blvd., Cleveland, OH 44143-1730, (216)481-0850

Cong. of South African Trade Unions [IO], Johannesburg, Republic of South Africa

Cong. of Southeast Asian Librarians [IO], Singapore, Singapore

Cong. Task Force - Address unknown since 1989.

Cong. to Unite Women - Defunct.

Cong. of the U.S.A; The Athletics [★23926]

Cong; Vietnam Era Veterans in [18783]

Cong. Watch [★17343]

Cong. Watch; Public Citizen's [17343]

Cong. of World Unity - Address unknown since 1995.

Congressional

Comm. on the Constitutional Sys. [17289]

Congressional Arts Caucus [17254]

Congressional Automotive Caucus [17255]

Congressional Black Caucus [17256]

Congressional Hispanic Caucus [17702]

Congressional Human Rights Caucus [17755]

Congressional Mgt. Found. [5599]

Conservative Opportunity Soc. [17257]

Free the Eagle [17629]

League of Private Property Voters [17985]

Natl. Comm. for an Effective Cong. [17252]

Public Housing Authorities Directors Assn. [5798]

Senate Children's Caucus [17258]

Senate Tourism Caucus [17259]

U.S. Assn. of Former Members of Cong. [17253]

Congressional Action Fund - Address unknown since 1995.

Congressional Advisory Bd; U.S. [18597]

Congressional Agenda: 80's [★18288]

Congressional Agenda: 90's [★18288]

Congressional Agenda: Millennium [18288], 3220 N St. NW, Ste. 178, Washington, DC 20007, (202)342-9192

Congressional Arts Caucus [★17254]

Congressional Arts Caucus [17254]

Congressional Arts Caucus Education Program - Defunct.

Congressional Auto Conf. [★17255]

Congressional Automotive Caucus [17255], c/o Dale Kildee, Co-Chm., 2107 Rayburn House Off. Bldg., Washington, DC 20515, (202)225-3611

Congressional Black Associates - Address unknown since 2001.

Congressional Black Caucus [17256], 2236 Rayburn Bldg., Washington, DC 20515-3312, (202)226-9776

Congressional Border Caucus [5598], 1527 Lonworth Bldg., Washington, DC 20515, (202)225-4831

Congressional Campaign Comm; Democratic [17402]

Congressional Caucus for Women's Issues [17525], c/o Carolyn B. Maloney, Co-Chair, 2331 Rayburn HOB, Washington, DC 20515-3214, (202)225-7944

Congressional Clearinghouse on the Future - Defunct.

Congressional Club [19434], 2001 New Hampshire Ave. NW, Washington, DC 20009, (202)332-1155

Congressional Coal Group - Address unknown since 2001.

Congressional Coalition for Soviet Jews - Defunct.

Congressional Comm; Natl. Republican [18527]

Congressional Competitiveness Caucus - Defunct.

Congressional Crime Caucus - Defunct.

Congressional Economic Leadership Inst. [18438], 201 Massachusetts Ave. NE C-6, Washington, DC 20002, (202)546-5007

Congressional Fellowship Program [★7521]

Congressional Friends of Human Rights Monitors - Address unknown since 2007.

Congressional Hispanic Caucus [17702], 1527 Longworth HOB, Washington, DC 20515, (202)225-2410

Congressional Human Rights Caucus [17755], c/o Hans Hogrefe, Dir., Off. of Congressman Tom Lantos, 2413 Rayburn HOB, Washington, DC 20515, (202)225-3531

Congressional Inst. for the Future - Address unknown since 2006.

Congressional Mgt. Found. [5599], 513 Capitol Ct. NE, Ste. 300, Washington, DC 20002, (202)546-0100

Congressional Medal of Honor Soc. [20710], 40 Patriots Point Rd., Mount Pleasant, SC 29464, (843)884-8862

Congressional Member Org. for the Arts [★17254]

Congressional Rural Caucus - Defunct.

Congressional Shipyard Coalition - Defunct.

Congressional Space Caucus - Defunct.

Congressional Staff Club - Address unknown since 2003.

A star before a book entry number signifies that the name is not listed separately, but is mentioned within the entry.

Congressional Steel Caucus - Address unknown
since 1999.
Congressional Textile Caucus - Address unknown
since 2001.
Congressional Travel and Tourism Caucus - Defunct.
Congressional Trust; Cooperative Action for [★1073]
Congressional Underwater Explorers Club - Address
unknown since 1995.
Congressional Union - Defunct.
Congressional Wives for Soviet Jewry - Defunct.
Congressional Wives Task Force - Defunct.
Congressman Club; Natl. Write Your [★18361]
Congressman; Natl. Write Your [18361]
Congresswomen's Caucus [★17525]
Congresswomen's Caucus Corp. [★17580]
The Conifer Soc. [★5253]
Conifer Soc; Amer. [5253]
Conjoined Twins Intl. [16695], PO Box 10895, Pres-
cott, AZ 86304-0895, (928)445-2777
Conjoined Twins Intl. [IO], Prescott, AZ, United
States
CONNECT: The Union for Professionals in Com-
munications [IO], London, United Kingdom
Connected Intl. Meeting Professionals Assn. [IO],
Fairfax, VA, United States
Connected Intl. Meeting Professionals Assn. [2676],
9200 Bayard Pl., Fairfax, VA 22032, (512)684-0889
Connecticut 1631-1662; Order of First Families of
[20753]
Connecticut Cetacean Soc. [★5306]
Connecticut Cetacean Soc. [★IO]
Connecticut River Watershed Coun. [4377], 15 Bank
Row, Greenfield, MA 01301, (413)772-2020
Connecticut State Univ. Alumni Assn; Southern
[18923]
Connecting Church Assn. [19846], 8001 Anderson
Blvd., Fort Worth, TX 76120, (817)274-1315
Connective Tissue; Coalition For Heritable Disorders
Of [14446]
Connective Tissue Oncology Soc. [15645], c/o
Barbara Rapp, Exec. Dir., PO Box 19611,
Alexandria, VA 22320-0611, (301)502-7371
Connective Tissue Oncology Soc. [IO], Alexandria,
VA, United States
Connector Mfrs. Assn. - Defunct.
Connector Study Group; Electronic [★6929]
Connemara Pony Breeders Soc. [IO], Clifden,
Ireland
Connemara Pony Soc; Amer. [4815]
Connexions Info. Sharing Services [IO], Toronto,
ON, Canada

Connick, Harry
Harry Connick, Jr. Fan Club [24907]
Connick, Jr. Fan Club; Harry [24907]
Connie Causey Fan Club - Address unknown since
1989.
Connie Francis Fan Club - Defunct.
Connie Francis Intl. Fan Club [24867], c/o Pat
Niglio, 100 Caton Ave., Ste. 5J, Brooklyn, NY
11218
Connie Stevens Fan Club [24868], c/o Betty A. Mo-
ran, Pres., 2500 Gaither St. SE, Hillcrest Heights,
Temple Hills, MD 20748-3030, (301)894-9342
Connoisseurs of Green and Red Chile; Intl. [22572]
Connolly Dance Company [★9872]
Connolly Dance Found. [9872], PO Box 573,
Madison, WI 53701-0573, (608)244-4328
Conquistadores 1492 [18669], PO Box 42, Leonia,
NJ 07605-0042, (201)567-7471
Conquistadors; Challenged [11930]
Conrad N. Hilton Found. [13163], 100 W Liberty St.,
Ste. 840, Reno, NV 89501, (775)323-4221
Conrad Soc. of Am; Joseph [9675]
Conrad Veidt Soc. [24735], c/o Barbara Peterson,
407 Kingston Ct., Yorktown, VA 23693
Consairway - Address unknown since 2004.
Conscience Canada [IO], Toronto, ON, Canada
Conscience Found; Appeal of [18508]
Conscience and Military Tax Campaign- U.S.
[★18716]
Conscientious Objectors
BOCS Found. [IO]
Center on Conscience and War [17438]
Central Comm. for Conscientious Objectors
[17439]

Conscientious Objectors; Natl. Interreligious Ser. Bd.
for [★17438]
Conscious Creative Action; Women In [20625]
Consciousness-Based Educ. Assn. [9029], 1100
Univ. Manor Dr., B-24, Fairfield, IA 52556,
(888)472-1677
Consciousness Res. and Training Project [12343]
Consciousness Studies
Assn. for the Sci. Stud. of Consciousness [8140]
Feathered Pipe Found. [12345]
Intl. Soc. for the Stud. of Subtle Energies and
Energy Medicine [14035]
Intl. Soc. for the Stud. of Subtle Energies and
Energy Medicine [IO]
Spiritual Frontiers Fellowship Intl. [20579]
Supreme Master Ching Hai Meditation Assn.
[19557]
Consecrations; Apostolate for Family [19571]
Conseil de la recherch en sante pur le development
[★IO]
Conseil canadien de la securite [★IO]
Conseil canadien de protection des animaux [★IO]
Conseil canadien du ski [★IO]
Conseil canadien de fromages internationaux [★IO]
Conseil canadien des professionnels en securite
agrees [★IO]
Conseil canadien pour le controle du tabac [★IO]
Conseil des 4-H du Canada [★IO]
Conseil des Aeroports du Canada [★IO]
Conseil Africain de l'Arachide [★IO]
Conseil des Barreaux Europeens [★IO]
Conseil de recherches en sciences humaines de
Canada [★IO]
Conseil national de recherches Canada [★IO]
Conseil oecumenique des chretiennes du Canada
[★IO]
Conseil Canadien des Archives [★IO]
Conseil Canadien des Aveugles [★IO]
Conseil Canadien des Bureaux d'ethique Commer-
ciale [★IO]
Conseil Canadien des Chefs d'Enterprise [★IO]
Conseil Canadien des Chretiens et des Juifs [★IO]
Conseil Canadien pour la Cooperation Internationale
[★IO]
Conseil Canadien De L'Enfrance Exceptionnelle
[★IO]
Conseil Canadien de Developpement Social [★IO]
Conseil Canadien des Eglises [★IO]
Conseil Canadien des Femmes Musulmanes [★IO]
Conseil Canadien de la Fourrure [★IO]
Conseil Canadien des Infirmieres en Nursing Cardio-
vasculaire [★IO]
Conseil Canadien des Laboratoires Independants
[★IO]
Conseil Canadien de l'Horticulture [★IO]
Conseil Canadien du Miel [★IO]
Conseil Canadien des Normes [★IO]
Conseil Canadien des Normes de la Radiotelevision
[★IO]
Conseil Canadien des Organismes de la Motoneige
[★IO]
Conseil Canadien des Pecheurs Professionnels
[★IO]
Conseil Canadien du Porc [★IO]
Conseil Canadien pour les Refugies [★IO]
Conseil Canadien des Resources Humaines en Ca-
mionnage [★IO]
Conseil Canadien des Societes Publiques-Privees
[★IO]
Conseil Canadien des Techniciens et Technologues
[★IO]
Conseil Canadien des Transformateurs d'Oeufs et
de Volailles [★IO]
Conseil des Canadiens [★IO]
Conseil de Canola du Canada [★IO]
Conseil de Commerce Canada-Inde [★IO]
Conseil de Commerce Canado-Arabe [★IO]
Conseil Commercial Canada-Chine [★IO]
Conseil du Commonwealth pour l'Ecologie Humaine
[★IO]
Conseil des Communes et Regions d'Europe [★IO]
Conseil canadien du Compostage [★IO]
Conseil Consultatif Canadiene de la Radio [★IO]
Conseil Consultatif sur la Condition de la Femme
Nouveau-Brunswick [★IO]

Conseil d'adoption du Canada [★IO]
Conseil canadien d'agrement des services de sante
[★IO]
Conseil national d'Ethique en recherche chez
l'Humain [★IO]
Conseil pour le Developpement de la Recherche en
Sciences Sociales en Afrique [★IO]
Conseil Ethnoculturel du Canada [★IO]
Conseil Europeen des Artistes [★IO]
Conseil Europeen des Associations Nationales
d'Ecoles Independantes [★IO]
Conseil Europeen De L'Information Sur
L'Alimentation [★IO]
Conseil Europeen pour les Langues [★IO]
Conseil Europeen des Producteurs de Materiaux de
Constr. [★IO]
Conseil Europeen des Urbanistes [★IO]
Conseil des Examens Chiropratique Canadien [★IO]
Conseil des Grains du Canada [★IO]
Conseil Intl. des Agence Benevoles [★IO]
Conseil Intl. des Archives [★IO]
Conseil Intl. des Associations Graphiques [★IO]
Conseil Intl. des Associations des Indus. Nautiques
[★IO]
Conseil Intl. du Batiment pour la Recherche, l'Etude
et la Documentation [★IO]
Conseil Intl. des Cereales [★IO]
Conseil Intl. de Cricket Feminin [★IO]
Conseil Intl. de la Danse [★IO]
Conseil Intl. d'Education des Adultes [★IO]
Conseil Intl. d'Etudes sur l'Europe centrale et Orien-
tale [★IO]
Conseil Intl. du Droit de l'Environnement [★IO]
Conseil Intl. d Etudes Canadiennes [★IO]
Conseil Intl. des Femmes [★IO]
Conseil Intl. des Grands Reseaux Electriques [★IO]
Conseil Intl. des Infirmieres [★IO]
Conseil Intl. de l'Action Sociale [★IO]
Conseil Intl. de la Langue Francaise [★IO]
Conseil Intl. pour l'Education Physique et la Sci. du
Sport [★IO]
Conseil Intl. de l'Enseignement a Distance [★IO]
Conseil Intl. pour l'Exploration de la Mer [★IO]
Conseil Intl. des Monuments et des Sites [★IO]
Conseil Intl. des Monuments et des Sites [★IO]
Conseil Intl. des Musees [★IO]
Conseil Intl. de la Musique [★IO]
Conseil Intl. des Normes Comptables [★IO]
Conseil Intl. de Organisations de Festivals de
Folklore et d'Arts Traditionnels [★IO]
Conseil Intl. de la Philosophie et des Sciences Hu-
maines [★IO]
Conseil Intl. sur les Problemes de l'Alcoolisme et
des Toxicomanies [★IO]
Conseil Intl. des Sciences de L'Ingenieur et de la
Technologie [★IO]
Conseil Intl. des Sciences Sociales [★IO]
Conseil Intl. du Sport Militaire [★IO]
Conseil Intl. des Tanneurs [★IO]
Conseil Interparlementaire Consultatif de Benelux
[★IO]
Conseil des Jeux du Canada [★IO]
Conseil canadien de l'education permanente en
pharmacie [★IO]
Conseil des ministres de l'Education, Canada [★IO]
Conseil canadien de l'energie [★IO]
Conseil canadien de l'entretien des aeronefs [★IO]
Conseil de l'Europe [★IO]
Conseil pour l'Homologation des Etablissements
Theologiques en Afrique [★IO]
Conseil Mondial des Associations D'education Com-
paree [★IO]
Conseil Mondial de l'Energie [★IO]
Conseil Natl. du Cuir [★IO]
Conseil Natl. des Eglises du Burundi [★IO]
Conseil Natl. des Ingenieurs et des Scientifiques de
France [IO], Paris, France
Conseil Natl. de la Recherche Scientifique [★IO]
Conseil Natl. de Recherches Canada Institut de
Recherche en Constr. [★IO]
Conseil Oecumenique des Eglises [★IO]
Conseil Oecumenique de la Jeunesse en Europe
[★IO]
Conseil Oleicole Intl. [★IO]
Conseil des Organisations Internationales des Sci-
ences Medicales [★IO]

Reference to "IO" in place of a book number signifies that the association may be found in the 45th edition of International Organizations.

Conseil des Palettes du Canada [★IO]
Conseil du Peuplier [★IO]
Conseil Superieur des Ecoles Europeennes [★IO]
Conseil des traducteurs, terminologues et interpretes du Canada [★IO]
Conseil Unitarien du Canada [★IO]
Conseil des Viandes du Canada [★IO]
Conseil de la Vie Francaise en Amerique [★IO]
Consejo Cultural Mundial [★IO]
Consejo Dominicano Contra la Osteoporosis [IO], Santo Domingo, Dominican Republic
Consejo Gen. de Colegios Oficiales de Odontologos y Estomatologos de Espana [IO], Madrid, Spain
Consejo Hondurenos de la Empresa Privada [★IO]
Consejo Interamericano de Seguridad [★12965]
Consejo Internacional de los Frutos Secos [★IO]
Consejo Latinoamericano de Iglesias [★IO]
Consejo Mundial de Boxeo [★IO]
Consejo Nacional de la Empresa Privada [★IO]
Consejo Nacional de la Empresa Privada [★IO]
Consejo Profesional de Ingeniera Agronomica [★IO]
Consejo Superior de la Empresa Privada [★IO]
Conselho Nacional de Desenvolvimento Cientifico e Tecnologico [★IO]
Conservacao Internacional - Brasil [★IO]
Conservacion Internacional Bolivia [IO], La Paz, Bolivia
ConservAmerica [4378], 3200 Carlisle Blvd. NE, Ste. 113, Albuquerque, NM 87110-1600, (505)889-4576
Conservancy; Amer. Bird [5290]
Conservancy; Amer. Livestock Breeds [4994]
Conservancy; Archaeological [6439]
Conservancy Assn. [IO], Hong Kong, People's Republic of China
Conservancy; Cultural [10741]
Conservancy Garden and Seed Bank; Southwest Traditional Crop [★4429]
Conservation
  50 Years is Enough: U.S. Network for Global Economic Justice [18829]
  Abundant Life Seed Found. [4338]
  Acres Land Trust [4339]
  Action for Solidarity, Equality, Env. and Development [IO]
  The Adirondack Coun. [4340]
  Africa Rainforest and River Conservation [4341]
  Africa Rainforest and River Conservation [IO]
  African Blackwood Conservation Proj. [IO]
  African Blackwood Conservation Proj. [4342]
  African Wild Dog Conservancy [5288]
  Alaska Coalition [4343]
  Alliance for Community Trees [4678]
  Alliance for Intl. Reforestation [4344]
  Alliance of Marine Mammal Parks and Aquariums [5006]
  Alliance of Religions and Conservation [IO]
  Alliance of Veterinarians for the Env. [4626]
  Amazon Alliance [4531]
  Am. the Beautiful Fund [4532]
  Amer. Cave Conservation Assn. [4345]
  Amer. Conservation Assn. [4346]
  Amer. Farmland Trust [16951]
  Amer. Forests [4347]
  Amer. Horse Defense Fund [4826]
  Amer. Land Conservancy [4348]
  Amer. Lands Alliance [4533]
  Amer. Marinelife Dealers Assn. [5007]
  Amer. Medical Fly Fishing Assn. [4349]
  Amer. Resources Gp. [4350]
  Amer. River Touring Assn. [936]
  Amer. Rivers [4351]
  Amer. Sanctuary Assn. [4156]
  American Shore and Beach Preservation Association [4352]
  Amer. Soc. for the Protection of Nature in Israel [4353]
  Amer. Soc. for the Protection of Nature in Israel [IO]
  Amer. Wildlands [4354]
  Americans for Our Heritage and Recreation [4355]
  Ancient Forest Intl. [4356]
  Ancient Forest Intl. [IO]
  Aquarium and Zoo Facilities Assn. [7856]
  Aquatic Resources Educ. Assn. [7956]

Arab Center for the Stud. of Arid Zones and Dry Lands [IO]
Arab Network for Env. and Development [IO]
Asian Soc. for Environmental Protection [IO]
Assn. of Conservation Engineers [4357]
Assn. for Conservation Info. [4358]
Assn. of Environmental and Rsrc. Economists [4359]
Assn. of Fish and Wildlife Agencies [4360]
Assn. of Fish and Wildlife Agencies [IO]
Assn. of Gardens Trusts [IO]
Assn. to Preserve Cape Cod [4361]
Assn. for Professional Observers [4667]
Assn. Promoting Educ. and Conservation in Amazonia [5294]
Assn. for Protection of Env. and Culture [IO]
Assn. for the Protection of Nature and the Env. - Kairouan, Tunisia [IO]
Assn. of State Floodplain Managers [4362]
Assn. of State Wetland Managers [4363]
Assn. for Strengthening Agricultural Res. in Eastern and Central Africa [IO]
Assn. for the Stud. of Peak Oil and Gas - USA [7461]
Assn. of Zoological Horticulture [4974]
Atlantic States Marine Fisheries Commn. [5729]
Audubon Naturalist Soc. of the Central Atlantic States [4364]
Australasian Cave and Karst Mgt. Assn. [IO]
Australian Conservation Found. [IO]
Australian Marine Conservation Soc. [IO]
Australian Network for Plant Conservation [IO]
Australian Plants Soc., South Australia [IO]
Australian Plants Soc. Tasmania [IO]
Baikal Environmental Wave [IO]
Bamboo of The Americas [4365]
Basingstoke Conservation Volunteers [IO]
Bat Conservation Intl. [5296]
Bear Trust Intl. [5297]
Berkshire Conservation Volunteers [IO]
Big Island Rainforest Action Gp. [4366]
Big Thicket Assn. [4367]
Big Thicket Natural Heritage Trust [4368]
Blue Dolphin Alliance [5008]
Blue Earth Alliance [10847]
Blue Ventures Conservation - Madagascar [IO]
BoardSource [12651]
Boreal Songbird Initiative [5302]
Botanical Gardens Conservation Intl. [IO]
Brazilian Found. for Nature Conservation [IO]
British Cactus and Succulent Soc. [IO]
British Naturalists' Assn. [IO]
British Trust for Conservation Volunteers [IO]
BTCV [IO]
BTCV Scotland [IO]
BUND - Friends of the Earth Germany [IO]
BUNDjugend [IO]
Bur. Regional de l'UICN pour l'Afrique Centrale [IO]
Bur. Regional de l'UICN pour l'Afrique de l'Ouest [IO]
Camp Fire Club of Am. [4369]
Camp Fire Conservation Fund [4370]
Campaign to Protect Rural England [IO]
Campaign for the Protection of Rural Wales [IO]
Canadian Assn. for Conservation of Cultural Property [IO]
Canadian Coun. of Ministers of the Env. [IO]
Canadian Environmental Network [IO]
Cardiff Conservation Volunteers [IO]
Caribbean Conservation Assn. [IO]
Caribbean Conservation Corp. and Sea Turtle Survival League [5305]
Caribbean Natural Resources Inst. [IO]
CEDAM Intl. [IO]
CEDAM Intl. [4371]
Center for Environmental Info. [4537]
Center for a New Amer. Dream [17260]
Center for Plant Conservation [4372]
Center for Rsrc. Mgt. [4373]
Charles Darwin Found. for the Galapagos Islands [IO]
Chihuahuan Desert Res. Inst. [4374]
Children of Chernobyl [IO]
Children of the Earth United [4621]

Chimp Haven [11729]
China Soc. of Plant Protection [IO]
Christian Mission Aid [IO]
CIPRA: Intl. Commn. for the Protection of Alpine Regions [IO]
Clean Air Soc. of Australia and New Zealand [IO]
Clean Beaches Coun. [4540]
Clean Water Fund [5088]
Climate Action Network Australia [IO]
Climate Action Network Europe [IO]
Coast Alliance [4375]
Coastal Conservation Assn. [4376]
Comite Nacional Pro Defensa de la Flora y Fauna [IO]
Commn. for the Conservation of Antarctic Marine Living Resources [IO]
Connecticut River Watershed Coun. [4377]
Conservacion Internacional Bolivia [IO]
ConservAmerica [4378]
Conservancy Assn. [IO]
Conservation Breeding Specialist Gp. [IO]
Conservation Breeding Specialist Gp. [4379]
Conservation Coun. of Ontario [IO]
Conservation Found. [IO]
The Conservation Fund [4380]
Conservation Intl. - Brazil [IO]
Conservation Intl. - USA [IO]
Conservation Intl. - USA [4381]
Conservation and Preservation Charities of Am. [4382]
Conservation and Res. Found. [4383]
Conservation and Res. Found. [IO]
Conservation Tech. Info. Center [4384]
Conservation Treaty Support Fund [4385]
Conservation Volunteers Alliance [IO]
Conservation Volunteers Australia [IO]
Conservation Volunteers Australia - Canberra [IO]
Conservation Volunteers Ireland [IO]
Conservation Volunteers Northern Ireland [IO]
Conservatree [4386]
Consortium for Conservation Medicine [15164]
Convention on Intl. Trade in Endangered Species of Wild Fauna and Flora [IO]
Cooperative Off. for Voluntary Organizations [18792]
Countryside Coun. for Wales [IO]
Croatian Soc. for Bird and Nature Protection [IO]
Cultural Conservancy [10741]
The Cycad Soc. [4387]
The Cycad Soc. [IO]
Danish Soc. for Nature Conservation [IO]
Defenders of Wildlife [5307]
Derbyshire Conservation Volunteers [IO]
Desert Fishes Coun. [IO]
Desert Fishes Coun. [4388]
Desert Protective Coun. [4389]
Desert Tortoise Coun. [5309]
Desert Tortoise Preserve Comm. [4390]
Double Harvest [4088]
Dove Sportsman's Soc. [11515]
Ducks Unlimited [5311]
Earth Day Canada [IO]
Earth Regeneration Soc. [4552]
Earth, Sea and Sky [IO]
EarthEcho Intl. [IO]
EarthEcho Intl. [4391]
EarthLink [IO]
EarthVoice [4555]
EarthWave Soc. [4556]
Eco-Spirit [4622]
Ecobrasil [IO]
Ecological Soc. of Am. [4506]
Ecology Action Centre [IO]
Elephant Care Intl. [5313]
Elephant Managers Assn. [4158]
Emirates Green Building Coun. [IO]
ENCAMS [IO]
English Nature [IO]
The Env. Coun. [IO]
Env. and I [IO]
Env. Liaison Centre Intl. [IO]
Environmental Alert [IO]
Environmental Alliance for Senior Involvement [11809]
Environmental Defence [IO]

A star before a book entry number signifies that the name is not listed separately, but is mentioned within the entry.

Environmental Entrepreneurs [4392]
Environmental Monitoring Gp. [IO]
Environmental Protection Res. Found. [IO]
Environmental Rights Action [IO]
Environmental Transport Assn. [IO]
Environnement Jeunesse [IO]
Epping Forest Conservation Volunteers [IO]
Equestrian Land Conservation Rsrc. [5130]
Estonian Fund for Nature [IO]
EUCC - The Coastal Union [IO]
European Centre for Nature Conservation [IO]
European Environmental Bur. [IO]
European Youth Forest Action [IO]
Fauna and Flora Intl. [IO]
Fell Pony Soc. and Conservancy of the Americas [4878]
FishAmerica Found. [4393]
Forest Action Network [IO]
Forest Guild [4394]
Forest Peoples Programme [IO]
Forest Ser. Employees for Environmental Ethics [5126]
Forest Stewardship Coun. - U.S. [4684]
ForestEthics [4685]
Forestry Conservation Communications Assn. [4395]
Found. for Res. on Economics and the Env. [4396]
Found. for Res. and Sustainable Development [IO]
Freshwater Mollusk Conservation Soc. [5034]
Friends of the Earth [4397]
Friends of the Earth - Argentina [IO]
Friends of the Earth - Australia [IO]
Friends of the Earth Austria [IO]
Friends of the Earth - Brazil [IO]
Friends of the Earth Cameroon [IO]
Friends of the Earth Costa Rica [IO]
Friends of the Earth Croatia [IO]
Friends of the Earth Curacao [IO]
Friends of the Earth - Cyprus [IO]
Friends of the Earth - Czech Republic [IO]
Friends of the Earth El Salvador [IO]
Friends of the Earth - England, Wales, and Northern Ireland [IO]
Friends of the Earth Estonia [IO]
Friends of the Earth - Europe [IO]
Friends of the Earth Finland [IO]
Friends of the Earth Flanders and Brussels [IO]
Friends of the Earth - France [IO]
Friends of the Earth Georgia [IO]
Friends of the Earth - Ghana [IO]
Friends of the Earth - Grenada [IO]
Friends of the Earth Haiti [IO]
Friends of the Earth - Hong Kong [IO]
Friends of the Earth Hungary [IO]
Friends of the Earth Indonesia [IO]
Friends of the Earth Intl. [IO]
Friends of the Earth - Ireland [IO]
Friends of the Earth - Italy [IO]
Friends of the Earth - Japan [IO]
Friends of the Earth Latvia [IO]
Friends of the Earth Luxembourg [IO]
Friends of the Earth - Macedonia [IO]
Friends of the Earth - Malaysia [IO]
Friends of the Earth Malta [IO]
Friends of the Earth Mauritius/Maudesco [IO]
Friends of the Earth Middle East - Amman [IO]
Friends of the Earth - Netherlands [IO]
Friends of the Earth - New Zealand [IO]
Friends of the Earth Nicaragua [IO]
Friends of the Earth - Papua New Guinea [IO]
Friends of the Earth Peru [IO]
Friends of the Earth Philippines [IO]
Friends of the Earth - Scotland [IO]
Friends of the Earth - Sierra Leone [IO]
Friends of the Earth Slovakia [IO]
Friends of the Earth - Spain [IO]
Friends of the Earth Sweden [IO]
Friends of the Earth - Switzerland [IO]
Friends of the Earth - Togo [IO]
Friends of the Earth - Uruguay [IO]
Friends of Env. and Development Assn. [IO]
Friends of the Everglades [4398]
Friends of the Nemaiah Valley [IO]

Friends of the River [4399]
Friends of the Trees Soc. [4400]
Front Range Equine Rescue [4881]
Fund for Horses [4159]
Fundacao Pro-TAMAR [IO]
Fundacion Natura Colombia [IO]
Galapagos Conservancy [4401]
Garden Conservancy [4402]
Global Coral Reef Alliance [4403]
Global Vision Intl. [IO]
Golondrinas Found. [IO]
Gould League [IO]
Grassland Heritage Found. [4404]
Grassroots Endangered Species Coalition [4154]
Great Lakes Commn. [6137]
Great Lakes United [4405]
Greater Yellowstone Coalition [4406]
Green Balkans Fed. [IO]
Green Dossier [IO]
Green Meeting Indus. Coun. [2681]
Green Space [IO]
Green Warriors of Norway [IO]
Green World [IO]
Green World Center [IO]
GreenNet [IO]
Greenpeace U.S.A. [4571]
Greensward Pound. [4407]
Gp. for Environmental Monitoring [IO]
Hampshire Conservation Volunteers [IO]
Haribon Found. [IO]
Harlow Conservation Volunteers [IO]
Hawk Mountain Sanctuary [5324]
Healthy Building Network [4629]
Heartland Conservation Soc. [IO]
Heritage Conservation Network [10033]
Holistic Mgt. Intl. [4408]
Inst. for Conservation Leadership [4573]
Inst. of Ecology and Environmental Mgt. [IO]
Inst. for Env. and Development Stud. [IO]
Inst. for Local Self-Reliance [11747]
Inst. for Sustainable Desert Occupancy [4510]
Inter-American Tropical Tuna Commn. [5730]
Interamerican Assn. for Environmental Defense [4630]
Interfaith Coun. for the Protection of Animals and Nature [4409]
Intergovernmental Panel on Climate Change [IO]
Intl. Assn. of Natural Rsrc. Pilots [4187]
Intl. Assn. for the Stud. of Common Property [4410]
Intl. Assn. for the Stud. of Common Property [IO]
Intl. Aviculturists Soc. [4199]
Intl. Coral Reef Action Network [IO]
The Intl. Ecotourism Soc. [3829]
Intl. Erosion Control Assn. [4411]
Intl. Erosion Control Assn. [IO]
Intl. Erosion Control Assn. - Iberoamerican [IO]
Intl. Erosion Control Assn. - Malaysia [IO]
Intl. Erosion Control Assn. - South Africa [IO]
Intl. Found. for the Conservation of Wildlife [IO]
Intl. League of Conservation Photographers [5080]
Intl. Marinelife Alliance - Philippines [IO]
Intl. Pacific Halibut Commn. [5731]
Intl. SeaKeepers Soc. [5010]
Intl. Show Caves Assn. [IO]
Intl. Soc. for Indus. Ecology [4580]
Intl. Sonoran Desert Alliance [4582]
Intl. Union for Conservation of Nature and Natural Resources - Botswana [IO]
Intl. Union for the Conservation of Nature and Natural Resources U.S. [IO]
Intl. Union for the Conservation of Nature and Natural Resources U.S. [4412]
Intl. Union for the Conservation of Nature and Natural Resources - Vietnam [IO]
Intl. Union for Conservation of Nature and Natural Resources - Zambia [IO]
Internationale AlpenschutzKomission [IO]
Iracambi Rainforest Conservation and Res. Center [IO]
Irish Peatland Conservation Coun. [IO]
IUCN: Centre for Mediterranean Cooperation of the World Conservation Union [IO]
IUCN - Environmental Law Programme Germany [IO]

IUCN - Russia [IO]
IUCN - The World Conservation Union [IO]
IUCN: The World Conservation Union Regional Off. for Southern Africa [IO]
IUCN World Conservation Union - Bangladesh [IO]
IUCN: World Conservation Union - Botswana [IO]
IUCN: World Conservation Union - Cambodia [IO]
IUCN: World Conservation Union - China [IO]
IUCN: World Conservation Union - Congo [IO]
IUCN: World Conservation Union - Ethiopia [IO]
IUCN: World Conservation Union - Guinea - Bissau [IO]
IUCN: World Conservation Union - Kenya [IO]
IUCN: World Conservation Union - Lao People's Democratic Republic [IO]
IUCN: World Conservation Union - Mali [IO]
IUCN: World Conservation Union - Mauritania [IO]
IUCN: World Conservation Union - Mozambique [IO]
IUCN: World Conservation Union - Nepal [IO]
IUCN: World Conservation Union - Niger [IO]
IUCN: World Conservation Union - Oficina Regional para Am. del Sur [IO]
IUCN: World Conservation Union - Pakistan [IO]
IUCN: World Conservation Union Programme Off. for Central Europe [IO]
IUCN: World Conservation Union - Protected Area Mgt. and Wildlife Conservation Proj. Wildlife Dept. [IO]
IUCN - World Conservation Union Regional Off. for Europe [IO]
IUCN: World Conservation Union - Senegal [IO]
IUCN: World Conservation Union - Sri Lanka [IO]
IUCN: World Conservation Union - Tanzania [IO]
IUCN: World Conservation Union - Thailand [IO]
IUCN: World Conservation Union - Uganda [IO]
IUCN: World Conservation Union - Vietnam [IO]
Izaak Walton League of Am. [4413]
Izaak Walton League of Am. Endowment [4414]
Joint Nature Conservation Comm. [IO]
Kathmandu Environmental Educ. Proj. - Nepal [IO]
Keepers of the Waters [5273]
Keeping Track [5335]
Keidanren Nature Conservation Fund [IO]
Land Improvement Contractors of Am. [4415]
Land Trust Alliance [4416]
Latvian Fund for Nature [IO]
League of Conservation Voters [18312]
League to Save Lake Tahoe [4417]
Legal Rights and Natural Resources Center - Kasama sa Kalikasan [IO]
Lewa Wildlife Conservancy (USA) [5337]
LightHawk [4418]
Lithuanian Green Movement [IO]
Live Oak Soc. [4688]
Malaysian Nature Soc. [IO]
Malta Ecological Found. [IO]
Man and the Biosphere Programme [IO]
Marine Aquarium Coun. [4175]
Marine Conservation Soc. [IO]
Marine Fish Conservation Network [4419]
Marine Stewardship Coun. [5171]
Men of the Trees (WA) [IO]
Mountain Lion Found. [5341]
Natl. Assn. of Black Scuba Divers [23711]
Natl. Assn. of Conservation Districts [4420]
Natl. Assn. of Marine Labs. [7274]
Natl. Assn. of Rsrc. Conservation and Development Councils [4421]
Natl. Audubon Soc. [4422]
Natl. Biosolids Partnership [5096]
Natl. Center for Preservation Tech. and Training [7161]
Natl. Coalition for Marine Conservation [4423]
Natl. Conservation District Employees Assn. [24209]
Natl. Coun. for the Conservation of Plants and Gardens [IO]
Natl. Coun. for Sci. and the Env. [7067]
Natl. Environmental Coalition of Native Americans [5037]
Natl. Environmental Societies Trust [IO]
Natl. Fed. of Cemetery Friends [IO]

Reference to "IO" in place of a book number signifies that the association may be found in the 45th edition of International Organizations.

Natl. Forest Found. [4424]
Natl. Forest Protection Alliance [4592]
Natl. Mitigation Banking Assn. [4425]
Natl. Movement Ekoglasnost [IO]
Natl. Parks Conservation Assn. [6160]
Natl. Soc. for Clean Air and Environmental Protection [IO]
Natl. Soc. of Conservationists [IO]
Natl. Soc. of Consulting Soil Scientists [5222]
Natl. Teen Anglers [22454]
Natl. Trust for Ireland [IO]
Natl. Wilderness Inst. [5344]
Natl. Wildlife Fed. [4426]
Natl. Wildlife Rehabilitators Assn. [5346]
Native Amer. Fish and Wildlife Soc. [4595]
Native Forest Coun. [4427]
Native Forest Network [4428]
Native Forest Network Australia [IO]
Native Seeds/SEARCH [4429]
Natural Areas Assn. [4430]
Natural Resources Coun. of Am. [4431]
Natural Resources Defense Coun. [4432]
Nature Canada [IO]
Nature Conservancy [4433]
Nature Conservation Soc. of Japan [IO]
Nature and Youth [IO]
New England Wild Flower Soc. [4434]
Next Stop - New Life [IO]
Non Guvernamental Org. BIOS [IO]
North Amer. Bluebird Soc. [5352]
North Amer. Bd. of Certified Energy Practitioners [6967]
North Amer. Grouse Partnership [5354]
North Amer. Wildlife Enforcement Officers Assn. [5357]
North Amer. Wildlife Park Found. [5358]
Northeast Sustainable Energy Assn. [6968]
Norwegian Soc. for the Conservation of Nature/Friends of the Earth Norway [IO]
Ocean Conservancy [IO]
Ocean Conservancy [4435]
Ocean Res. and Conservation Assn. [4436]
Oceana [4437]
Oceana [IO]
Ontario Nature [IO]
Open Space Inst. [4599]
Open Spaces Soc. [IO]
Organizacion PROFAUNA [IO]
Org. of Wildlife Planners [5360]
Ornamental Plant Conservation Assn. [IO]
Our Global Heritage [IO]
Ozark Soc. [4438]
Pachamama Alliance [5163]
Pacific Fishery Mgt. Coun. [5732]
Pacific Northwest Trail Assn. [23951]
Pacific Regional Env. Programme [IO]
Pacific Seabird Gp. [5362]
Pacific States Marine Fisheries Commn. [5733]
Pacific Whale Found. [5363]
PACON Intl. [5011]
Participatory Ecological Land Use Mgt. Assn. [IO]
Partners in Parks [4439]
Pele Defense Fund [4440]
Pembina Inst. for Appropriate Development [IO]
People Protecting Animals and Their Habitats [11445]
Polar Bears Intl. [5367]
Political Economy Res. Center - The Center for Free Market Environmentalism [4600]
Purple Martin Conservation Assn. [5369]
Quebec-Labrador Foundation/Atlantic Center for the Env. [4601]
Rabbits Unlimited Inc. [4161]
Rainforest Action Network [4441]
Rainforest Action Network [IO]
Rainforest Alliance [IO]
Rainforest Alliance [4442]
Rainforest Info. Centre [IO]
Rainforest Relief [5164]
RARE [5373]
Reef Check [5012]
Reef Relief [5013]
ReefGuardian Intl. [5014]
Regional Environmental Center for Central and Eastern Europe - Albania [IO]

Regional Environmental Center for Central and Eastern Europe - Country Off. Latvia [IO]
Regional Environmental Center for Central and Eastern Europe - Hungary [IO]
Renew Am. [4336]
Renewable Natural Resources Found. [4443]
Republicans for Environmental Protection [4444]
River Mgt. Soc. [4445]
River Network [4446]
A Rocha Canada [IO]
A Rocha France [IO]
A Rocha Ghana [IO]
A Rocha India [IO]
A Rocha Intl. [IO]
A Rocha Kenya [IO]
A Rocha Lebanon [IO]
Royal Soc. for Protection of Nature [IO]
Sailors for the Sea [4447]
Sarawak Campaign Comm. [IO]
Saskatchewan Environmental Soc. [IO]
Save America's Forests [4448]
Save Our Seas [4449]
Save Our Seas [IO]
Save the Redwoods League [4450]
School of Living [10178]
Scottish Natural Heritage [IO]
Scottish Wild Land Gp. [IO]
Seacoast Anti-Pollution League [4451]
Seafood Choices Alliance [3503]
SeaWeb [5015]
Shark Res. Inst. [5019]
Sheffield Conservation Volunteers [IO]
Sierra Club [4520]
Sierra Club of Canada [IO]
Sirenian Intl. [5016]
SkyTruth [4637]
Soc. for Conservation GIS [6831]
Soc. for Marine Mammalogy [5017]
Soc. for the Nature Protection of Croatia [IO]
Soc. for the Protection of Nature in Israel [IO]
Soc. for Protection of Nature in Lebanon [IO]
Soc. of Wetland Scientists [4452]
Soil and Water Conservation Soc. [4453]
The Steamboaters [4454]
Stockholm Env. Inst. - Sweden [IO]
Stockholm Environmental Inst. - Tallinn [IO]
Student Conservation Assn. [4455]
Sumatran Orangutan Soc. USA [5384]
Sustainable Buildings Indus. Coun. [7682]
Sustainable Obtainable Solutions [5129]
Sustainable Travel Intl. [5252]
Swedish Soc. for Nature Conservation [IO]
Taiga Rescue Network [IO]
Tall Timbers Land Conservancy [4456]
Tall Timbers Res. Sta. [4457]
Tanygnathus Soc. [4202]
Tanzania eco Volunteerism [IO]
Tembeza Kenya [IO]
Theodore Roosevelt Conservation Partnership [4458]
Threshold [4609]
TortoiseAid Intl. [5385]
Trail Riders of Today [23532]
Transboundary Environmental Info. Agency [IO]
Trax Programme Support of West Africa [IO]
Tread Lightly! [5167]
Tree Coun. [IO]
Tree Musketeers [4459]
Tree of Peace Soc. [9913]
TreePeople [4460]
Trees for Tomorrow [4697]
Trees, Water and People [4610]
Tropenbos Intl. [IO]
Tropical Flowering Tree Soc. [4986]
Tropical Forest Found. [4698]
Tropical Forest Rsrc. Gp. [IO]
Trust for Public Land [4461]
Union Mundial para la Naturaleza Oficina Regional para Mesoamerica [IO]
United Nations Framework Convention on Climate Change [IO]
U.S. Consortium of Soil Sci. Associations [5223]
U.S. Tourist Coun. [4462]
Upper Mississippi River Conservation Comm. [4463]

Walden Pond Advisory Comm. [4464]
WALHI [IO]
Wallace Genetic Found. [4117]
Waste Care [IO]
Waterfowl U.S.A. [4465]
Western Canada Wilderness Comm. [IO]
Western Forestry and Conservation Assn. [4700]
Western Gamebird Alliance [4466]
Wetlands Intl. Asia Pacific-Indonesia Programme [IO]
Wild Earth [IO]
Wild Earth [4467]
WildAid [5396]
The Wilderness Soc. [4468]
The Wilderness Soc. [IO]
Wildfowl and Wetlands Trust [IO]
Wildlife Conservation Soc. [4469]
Wildlife and Env. Soc. of Malawi [IO]
Wildlife Forever [5399]
Wildlife Habitat Canada [IO]
Wildlife Habitat Coun. [4470]
Wildlife Mgt. Inst. [4471]
The Wildlife Soc. [5401]
Wildlife Trusts [IO]
Wolf Haven Intl. [IO]
Wolf Haven Intl. [4472]
Women's Environmental Network [IO]
World Assn. of Soil and Water Conservation [IO]
World Assn. of Soil and Water Conservation [4473]
World Bamboo Org. [5041]
World Conservation Union [IO]
World Env. Center [IO]
World Env. Center [4474]
World Environmental Org. [4475]
World Parks [4617]
World Preserve [4476]
World Preserve [IO]
World Resources Inst. [IO]
World Resources Inst. [4477]
World Whale Police [5285]
World Wide Fund for Nature - India [IO]
World Wide Fund for Nature - Malaysia [IO]
World Wide Fund for Nature - Sweden [IO]
World Wide Fund for Nature - WWF Intl. [IO]
World Wildlife Fund [IO]
World Wildlife Fund [4478]
Worldwatch Inst. [18844]
WWF - Australia [IO]
WWF - Brasil [IO]
WWF - Piemonte e Valle d'Aosta [IO]
WWF-UK [IO]
Yukon Conservation Soc. [IO]
Conservation Assn; Amer. Bird [21835]
Conservation Assn; Gulf Coast [★4376]
Conservation Assn; Intermuseum [10505]
Conservation Assn; Natl. Parks [6160]
Conservation Assn; Natl. Parks and [★6160]
Conservation Assn; Purple Martin [5369]
Conservation Assn; Tahoe Improvement and [★4417]
Conservation Assn; Whooping Crane [5392]
Conservation of Bighorn Sheep; Soc. for the [5381]
Conservation Breeding Specialist Gp. [4379], 12101 Johnny Cake Ridge Rd., Apple Valley, MN 55124-8151, (952)997-9800
Conservation Breeding Specialist Gp. [IO], Apple Valley, MN, United States
Conservation Center; Animal Res. and [★4469]
Conservation Center for Art and Historic Artifacts [9437], 264 S 23rd St., Philadelphia, PA 19103, (215)545-0613
Conservation; Center for Marine [★4435]
Conservation Commissioners; Intl. Assn. of Game, Fish, and [★4360]
Conservation Corps Alumni; Natl. Assn. of Civilian [19082]
Conservation Corps; Natl. Assn. of Ser. and [13497]
Conservation Coun; Amer. Rivers [★4351]
Conservation Coun. of Ontario [IO], Toronto, ON, Canada
Conservation Districts; Natl. Assn. of Soil [★4420]
Conservation Districts; Natl. Assn. of Soil and Water [★4420]
Conservation Education Assn. - Defunct.

A star before a book entry number signifies that the name is not listed separately, but is mentioned within the entry.

Conservation, Educ., Diving, Awareness, Marine Res. [★4371]
Conservation, Educ., Diving, Awareness, Marine Res. [★IO]
Conservation Farmers Inc. [IO], Toowoomba, Australia
Conservation Found. [IO], London, United Kingdom
Conservation Found. [★IO]
Conservation Found. [★4478]
The Conservation Fund [4380], 1655 N Ft. Myer Dr., Ste. 1300, Arlington, VA 22209-3199, (703)525-6300
Conservation Fund; Marine Mammal [★4435]
Conservation Fund; River [★4351]
Conservation Gp; Whooping Crane [★5392]
Conservation of Historic and Artistic Works—American Gp; Intl. Inst. for [10011]
Conservation of Historic and Artistic Works; Amer. Inst. for [10011]
Conservation Info; Amer. Assn. for [★4358]
Conservation Inst; Livestock [★5003]
Conservation Intl. - Brazil [IO], Belo Horizonte, Brazil
Conservation; Intl. Inst. for Energy [6958]
Conservation Intl. - USA [4381], 2011 Crystal Dr., Ste. 500, Arlington, VA 22202, (703)341-2400
Conservation Intl. - USA [IO], Arlington, VA, United States
Conservation Intl; Wildlife [★4469]
Conservation; Jane Goodall Inst. for Wildlife Res., Educ., and [5334]
Conservation Leadership [★4380]
Conservation Leadership; Inst. for [4573]
Conservation League - Address unknown since 1995.
Conservation; Natl. Assn. of Professionals in Energy [★6942]
Conservation Northwest [4546], 1208 Bay St., No. 201, Bellingham, WA 98225-4301, (360)671-9950
Conservation Org; Environmental [4561]
Conservation and Preservation Charities of Am. [4382], 1100 Larkspur Landing Cir., Ste. 340, Larkspur, CA 94939, (800)626-6685
Conservation Program; Golden Lion Tamarin [★5321]
Conservation Proj; California [★4460]
Conservation; RARE Center for Tropical [★5373]
Conservation and Recovery Act Project; Natl. Environmental Development Assn./Resource [7835]
Conservation and Renewable Energy Inquiry and Referral Ser. [★6951]
Conservation and Res. Found. [4383], Dept. of Special Collections, Charles E. Shain Lib., Connecticut Coll., New London, CT 06320-4196
Conservation and Res. Found. [IO], New London, CT, United States
Conservation Soc; NYZS/The Wildlife [★4469]
Conservation Tech. Info. Center [4384], 1220 Potter Dr. W, Ste. 170, West Lafayette, IN 47906, (765)494-9555
Conservation Tillage Info. Center [★4384]
Conservation Treaty Support Fund [4385], 3705 Cardiff Rd., Chevy Chase, MD 20815, (301)654-3150
Conservation Trust [★IO]
Conservation of Vision; Amer. Medical Assn. for the [★16882]
Conservation Volunteers Alliance [IO], Ballarat, Australia
Conservation Volunteers Australia [IO], Ballarat, Australia
Conservation Volunteers Australia - Canberra [IO], Civic Square, Australia
Conservation Volunteers Ireland [IO], Dublin, Ireland
Conservation Volunteers Northern Ireland [IO], Belfast, United Kingdom
Conservation Voters; League of [18312]
Conservation; Western Assn. for Art [304]
Conservation; Western Found. for Raptor [★7419]
Conservationists
African Blackwood Conservation Proj. [4342]
African Wild Dog Conservancy [5288]
Alliance for Am. [11807]
Alliance for Intl. Reforestation [4344]
Am. the Beautiful Fund [4532]

Amer. Bird Conservation Assn. [21835]
Amer. Cave Conservation Assn. [4345]
Amer. Land Conservancy [4348]
Amer. Medical Fly Fishing Assn. [4349]
Amer. Resources Gp. [4350]
Amer. Soc. for the Protection of Nature in Israel [4353]
Aquarium and Zoo Facilities Assn. [7856]
Assn. of Conservation Engineers [4357]
Assn. of Fish and Wildlife Agencies [4360]
Assn. for Professional Observers [4667]
Assn. Promoting Educ. and Conservation in Amazonia [5294]
Assn. of State Wetland Managers [4363]
Atlantic States Marine Fisheries Commn. [5729]
Audubon Naturalist Soc. of the Central Atlantic States [4364]
Bamboo of The Americas [4365]
Bat Conservation Intl. [5296]
Big Thicket Assn. [4367]
Boreal Songbird Initiative [5302]
Camp Fire Conservation Fund [4370]
Children of the Earth United [4621]
Coastal Conservation Assn. [4376]
ConservAmerica [4378]
Conservation Intl. - USA [4381]
The Cycad Soc. [4387]
David and Lucile Packard Found. [11808]
David and Lucile Packard Found. [IO]
Defenders of Wildlife [5307]
Desert Tortoise Coun. [5309]
Ducks Unlimited [5311]
EarthEcho Intl. [4391]
Eco-Spirit [4622]
Ecological Soc. of Am. [4506]
Environmental Alliance for Senior Involvement [11809]
Environmental Entrepreneurs [4392]
Fed. of Amer. Consumers and Travelers [13342]
FishAmerica Found. [4393]
ForestEthics [4685]
Freshwater Mollusk Conservation Soc. [5034]
Greater Yellowstone Coalition [4406]
Greenpeace U.S.A. [4571]
Hawk Mountain Sanctuary [5324]
Intl. League of Conservation Photographers [5080]
Intl. Sonoran Desert Alliance [4582]
Izaak Walton League of Am. [4413]
Izaak Walton League of Am. Endowment [4414]
Keepers of the Waters [5273]
Land Improvement Contractors of Am. [4415]
Land Trust Alliance [4416]
League to Save Lake Tahoe [4417]
Lewa Wildlife Conservancy (USA) [5337]
Natl. Audubon Soc. [4422]
Natl. Mitigation Banking Assn. [4425]
Natl. Wildlife Fed. [4426]
Natural Areas Assn. [4430]
Natural Resources Coun. of Am. [4431]
Nature Conservancy [4433]
North Amer. Bluebird Soc. [5352]
North Amer. Wildlife Park Found. [5358]
Ocean Conservancy [4435]
Ocean Res. and Conservation Assn. [4436]
Org. of Wildlife Planners [5360]
Ozark Soc. [4438]
Pachamama Alliance [5163]
Pacific Seabird Gp. [5362]
Pacific States Marine Fisheries Commn. [5733]
Pacific Whale Found. [5363]
Republicans for Environmental Protection [4444]
Roo Rat Soc. [5375]
Save Our Seas [4449]
Save the Redwoods League [4450]
Sierra Club [4520]
Soc. for Conservation GIS [6831]
Soil and Water Conservation Soc. [4453]
Student Conservation Assn. [4455]
Sumatran Orangutan Soc. USA [5384]
Theodore Roosevelt Conservation Partnership [4458]
TortoiseAid Intl. [5385]
Trees for Tomorrow [4697]
U.S. Tourist Coun. [4462]

Walden Pond Advisory Comm. [4464]
Waterfowl U.S.A. [4465]
Western Forestry and Conservation Assn. [4700]
Wildlife Mgt. Inst. [4471]
The Wildlife Soc. [5401]
World Environmental Org. [4475]
World Parks [4617]
World Preserve [4476]
World Wildlife Fund [4478]
Conservative
The Amer. Cause [17642]
Amer. Conservative Union [17261]
Amer. Soc. of Contrarian Speakers and Writers [5601]
Amer. Sons of Liberty [17087]
Center of the Amer. Experiment [17262]
Christian-Patriots Defense League/Citizen's Emergency Defense Sys. [17263]
Christian Seniors Assn. [19787]
The Comm. for Western Civilization [8243]
The Conservative Caucus [17264]
The Conservative Caucus Res., Anal. and Educ. Found. [17265]
Conservative Majority for Citizen's Rights [17266]
Conservative Opportunity Soc. [17257]
Coun. of Volunteer Americans [18309]
Eagle Forum [17267]
Federalist Soc. for Law and Public Policy Stud. [5900]
Free Cong. Found. [11810]
Free Cong. Political Action Comm. [17268]
Freedom House [17269]
Freedom House [IO]
Frontiers of Freedom [5602]
Future of Freedom Found. [17270]
Intercollegiate Stud. Inst. [17271]
Intl. Freedom Found. [17272]
Jefferson Educational Found. [17273]
John Birch Soc. [17274]
LibertyTree [17275]
Natl. Traditionalist Caucus [17276]
North Amer. Assn. of Synagogue Executives [20517]
Public Advocate of the U.S. [18685]
Roo Rat Soc. [5375]
Students for America [17277]
Third Generation [17278]
U.S. Tourist Coun. [4462]
Upper Mississippi River Conservation Comm. [4463]
Wildlife Mgt. Inst. [4471]
The Wildlife Soc. [5401]
World Wildlife Fund [4478]
Young Americans for Freedom [17279]
Young America's Found. [17280]
Conservative Action Found. - Address unknown since 1999.
Conservative Alliance - Address unknown since 2001.
Conservative Baptist Assn. of Am. [19485], 3686 Stagecoach Rd., Ste. F, Longmont, CO 80504-5660, (720)283-3030
Conservative Baptist Foreign Mission Soc. [★19503]
Conservative Baptist Foreign Mission Soc. [★IO]
Conservative Baptist Home Mission Soc. [★IO]
Conservative Baptist Home Mission Soc. [★19491]
The Conservative Caucus [17264], 450 Maple Ave. E, Vienna, VA 22180, (703)938-9626
Conservative Caucus Found. [★17265]
The Conservative Caucus Res., Anal. and Educ. Found. [17265], 450 Maple Ave. E, Vienna, VA 22180, (703)281-6782
Conservative Citizens; Coun. of [18684]
Conservative Clubs of America - Address unknown since 1995.
Conservative Democratic Forum - Defunct.
Conservative Democratic Political Action Comm. - Address unknown since 1999.
Conservative Future [IO], London, United Kingdom
Conservative Judaism; Women's League for [20193]
Conservative Leadership Political Action Comm. - Address unknown since 2003.
Conservative Leadership Youth Found. [★8753]
Conservative Library Assn. - Defunct.
Conservative Majority for Citizen's Rights [17266], c/o Amer. Gospel Ministries, 302 Briarwood Cir. NW, Fort Walton Beach, FL 32548-3904, (850)862-6211

Reference to "IO" in place of a book number signifies that the association may be found in the 45th edition of International Organizations.

Conservative Mennonite Bd. of Missions and Charities [★20253]

Conservative Mennonite Bd. of Missions and Charities [★IO]

Conservative Network - Address unknown since 1994.

Conservative Opportunity Soc. [17257], 2418 Rayburn House Off. Bldg., Washington, DC 20515, (202)225-3501

Conservative Orthopedics Intl. Assn. [15767]

Conservative Party [18323], 486 78th St., Brooklyn, NY 11209, (718)921-2158

Conservative Party [★IO]

Conservative Party Central Off. [IO], London, United Kingdom

Conservative Party of Norway [IO], Oslo, Norway

Conservative People's Party [IO], Copenhagen, Denmark

Conservative Traditionalists
 The Amer. Cause [17642]
 Amer. Decency Assn. [17281]
 Americans for Decency [17282]
 Care Net [17283]
 Christian Coalition of Am. [17284]
 Christian Heritage Center [17285]

Conservative and Unionist Party [★IO]

Conservative Victory Comm. - Address unknown since 2007.

Conservative Youth Fed. - Defunct.

Conservatives for a Constitutional Convention - Defunct.

Conservators; Western Assn. of Art [★304]

Conservatory Theater Found; Amer. [11000]

Conservatree [4386], 100 Second Ave., San Francisco, CA 94118, (415)561-6530

Consideration; A Minor [11826]

Consiglio Mondiale dell' Energia Comitato Nazionale Italiano [★IO]

Consiglio Nazionale delle Ricerche [★IO]

Consiglio Nazionale delle Ricerche [★IO]

Consilium Conferentiarum Episcoporum Europae [★IO]

Consistent Life [18200], PO Box 9295, Silver Spring, MD 20916-9295, (641)715-3800

Consoil Associates - Defunct.

Consolidated Assn. of Nurses in Substance Abuse Intl. [★15484]

Consolidated Assn. of Nurses in Substance Abuse Intl. [★IO]

Consolidated Athletic Commn. [23816]

Consolidated Tape Assn. [3511], c/o Brian McNelis, Vendor Rep., Reuters Am., Inc., The Reuters Bldg., 3 Times Sq., 22nd Fl., New York, NY 10036, (646)223-4439

Consolidated Tenants League - Address unknown since 1986.

Consorcio Nacional de Industriales del Caucho [★IO]

Consortia of Administrators for Native Amer. Rehabilitation [19270], 105 Jefferson St., Natchitoches, LA 71457, (318)354-7400

The Consortium [8806], 5585 Pershing Ave., Ste. 240, St. Louis, MO 63112-4621, (314)877-5500

Consortium on Advanced Biosensors - Defunct.

Consortium for Advanced Mfg. Intl. [2553], 6832 Bee Cave, Ste. 256, Austin, TX 78746, (512)617-6428

Consortium for Advanced Mfg. Intl. [IO], Burleson, TX, United States

Consortium for the Advancement of Private Higher Educ. [★8535]

Consortium for the Advancement of Private Higher Educ. [8105], c/o The Coun. of Independent Colleges, 1 Dupont Cir. NW, Ste. 320, Washington, DC 20036-1142, (202)466-7230

Consortium on AIDS and Intl. Development [IO], London, United Kingdom

Consortium on Assisted Living; Consumer [11283]

Consortium of Behavioral Hea. Nurses and Associates [15474], PMB 1214, 1733 H St., Ste. 330, Blaine, WA 98230, (360)332-9105

Consortium for Citizens with Disabilities [17416], 1660 L St. NW, Ste. 700, Washington, DC 20036, (202)783-2229

Consortium of Coll. and Univ. Media Centers [8554], Iowa State Univ., 1200 Communications Bldg., Ames, IA 50011-3243, (515)294-1811

Consortium for Conservation Medicine [15164], 460 W 34th St., Fl. 17, New York, NY 10001, (212)380-4473

Consortium for Conservation Medicine [IO], New York, NY, United States

Consortium of Doctors [12074], c/o Dr. Jacqualine Desmona Myers, Dir., 501 Deerfield Dr., Montgomery, AL 36109, (334)272-1271

Consortium for Emergency Contraception; Intl. [12183]

Consortium for Energy Efficiency [1286], 98 N Washington St., Ste. 101, Boston, MA 02114-1918, (617)589-3949

Consortium of European Building Control [IO], Ipswich, United Kingdom

Consortium of European Res. Libraries [IO], London, United Kingdom

Consortium on Financing Higher Educ. [9057], 238 Main St., Ste. 402, Cambridge, MA 02142, (617)253-5030

Consortium of Graduate Liberal Studies Programs - Defunct.

Consortium for Graduate Stud. in Bus. for Negros [★8806]

Consortium for Graduate Stud. in Mgt. [★8806]

Consortium of Humanities Centers and Institutes [12386], c/o John Hope Franklin Humanities Inst., Duke Univ., Box 90403, 2204 Erwin Rd., Durham, NC 27708-0403, (919)668-0107

Consortium of Humanities Centers and Institutes [IO], Cambridge, MA, United States

Consortium of Institutes of Higher Educ. in Hea. and Rehabilitation in Europe [IO], Gent, Belgium

Consortium of Institutions for Development and Res. in Educ. in Europe [IO], Sint-Katelijne-Waver, Belgium

Consortium for Intl. Cooperation in Higher Education - Defunct.

Consortium for Intl. Crop Protection [4112], c/o Paul Jepson, Dir., Oregon State Univ., 2040 Cordley Hall, Corvallis, OR 97331-2915, (541)737-3541

Consortium for Intl. Crop Protection [IO], Corvallis, OR, United States

Consortium for Intl. Studies Education - Defunct.

Consortium Leadership; Assn. for [8480]

Consortium of Natl. Hispanic Orgs. - Defunct.

Consortium for North Amer. Higher Educ. Collaboration [8487], c/o Francisco J. Marmolejo, Exec. Dir., Univ. of Arizona, PO Box 210300, Tucson, AZ 85721-0300, (520)621-7761

Consortium for North Amer. Higher Educ. Collaboration [IO], Tucson, AZ, United States

Consortium on Peace Res., Educ. and Development [★18233]

Consortium Perfectae Caritatis - Defunct.

Consortium pour la Recherche Economique en Afrique [★IO]

Consortium of Regional Environmental Councils - Address unknown since 1995.

Consortium of Registered Nurses for Eye Acquisition [★15670]

Consortium for School Networking [8555], 1025 Vermont Ave. NW, Ste. 1010, Washington, DC 20005, (202)861-2676

Consortium of Social Sci. Associations [7649], 1522 K St. NW, Ste. 836, Washington, DC 20005, (202)842-3525

Consortium for the Stud. of Intelligence [17821], 1730 Rhode Island Ave. NW, Ste. 500, Washington, DC 20036-3117

Consortium for Sustainable Village-Based Development [★11793]

Consortium for Sustainable Village-Based Development [★IO]

Consortium of Univ. Film Centers [★8554]

Constables Assn; Natl. [5992]

Constables Assn; Natl. Police [★5992]

Constant Creative Action; Women In [★20625]

The Constant Soc. - Address unknown since 1995.

Constantian Soc. - Defunct.

Constantine - United Grand Imperial Coun; Red Cross of [19248]

Constellation Found. [★10449]

Constellation Historical Preservation Corp. [★10449]

Constituency for Africa [16927], 316 F St. NE, Ste. 100, Washington, DC 20002, (202)371-0588

Constitution
 Academics for the Second Amendment [17286]
 Amer. Constitution Soc. for Law and Policy [5603]
 Amers. United for God and Country [17287]
 Armed Females of Am. [17587]
 Citizens for Governmental Restraint [17288]
 Civilian Cong. [17251]
 Comm. on the Constitutional Sys. [17289]
 Comm. to Restore the Constitution [17290]
 Constitution Soc. [5604]
 Constitutional Rights Found. [17291]
 Constitutionists Networking Center [17292]
 Found. for Rational Economics and Educ. [17293]
 Friends of Patrick Henry [11115]
 Handgun Safety and Educ. Coun. [17684]
 Independent Americans [17294]
 Jefferson Found. [17295]
 Liberty Amendment Comm. of the U.S.A. [17296]
 Natl. Center for Constitutional Stud. [17297]
 Natl. Justice Found. of Am. [17298]
 Natl. Legal Found. [6225]
 Peoples Rights Org. [17145]
 Sportsmen's Assn. for Firearms Educ. [17600]
 Students for the Second Amendment [17602]
 Third Continental Cong. [17299]

Constitution Parties of the U.S. [★17299]

Constitution Soc. [5604], 7793 Burnet Rd., No. 37, Austin, TX 78757, (512)374-9585

Constitutional Alliance - Defunct.

Constitutional Amendment Network; Natl. Victims' [18779]

Constitutional Commn. - Address unknown since 1991.

Constitutional Concerns; Citizens for [★17143]

Constitutional Convention; World Comm. for a World [★18317]

Constitutional Freedom; Americans for [★17126]

Constitutional Freedom; Media Coalition/Americans for [★17126]

Constitutional Govt; Fund for [17669]

Constitutional Law
 Amer. Constitution Soc. for Law and Policy [5603]
 Citizens Equal Rights Alliance [5800]
 Citizens Flag Alliance [17300]
 Constitution Soc. [5604]
 Federalist Soc. for Law and Public Policy Stud. [5900]
 First Amendment Lawyers Assn. [5605]
 Peoples Rights Org. [17145]

Constitutional Lawyer's Comm. on Undeclared War - Defunct.

Constitutional Revival - Defunct.

Constitutional Rights; Center for [17097]

Constitutional Rights Found. [17291], 601 S Kingsley Dr., Los Angeles, CA 90005, (213)487-5590

Constitutional Rights; Law Center for [★17097]

Constitutional Rights Proj. [IO], Abuja, Nigeria

Constitutional Welfare Rights, U.S.A; Emergency Comm. to Defend [18443]

Constitutionists Networking Center [17292], 442 E 1250 Rd., Baldwin City, KS 66006, (785)594-3367

Constructeurs de Material Aerospatial; Association Europeenne des [★154]

Constructeurs de Material Aerospatial; Association Europeenne des [★IO]

Construction
 ADSC: The Intl. Assn. of Found. Drilling [1000]
 Aggregate and Sand Producers Assn. of South Africa [IO]
 Air Barrier Assn. of Am. [587]
 Alberta Constr. Assn. [IO]
 Alberta Constr. Safety Assn. [IO]
 Amer. Architectural Manufacturers Assn. [588]
 Amer. Concrete Inst. [6832]
 Amer. Constr. Inspectors Assn. [937]
 Amer. Coun. for Constr. Educ. [8141]
 Amer. Engg. Alliance [6985]
 Amer. Fence Assn. [938]
 Amer. Fence Assn. [IO]
 Amer. Inst. of Constructors [6833]
 Amer. Inst. of Steel Constr. [6834]
 Amer. Natl. Standards Inst. [6267]
 Amer. Railway Engg. and Maintenance of Way Assn. [3280]
 Amer. Soc. for Composites [6651]

A star before a book entry number signifies that the name is not listed separately, but is mentioned within the entry.

Amer. Soc. of Professional Estimators [8142]
Amer. Sports Builders Assn. [1002]
Amer. Underground Constr. Assn. [7715]
Argentine Chamber of Constr. [IO]
Asphalt Emulsion Manufacturers Assn. [594]
Asphalt Pavement Alliance [596]
Asphalt Recycling and Reclaiming Assn. [3987]
Assoc. Equip. Distributors [2000]
Assoc. Gen. Contractors of Am. [1005]
Assoc. Owners and Developers [939]
Assoc. Schools of Constr. [8143]
Associated Schools of Construction [IO]
Assoc. Specialty Contractors [1006]
Assn. of Asphalt Paving Technologists [6835]
Assn. of Constr. Inspectors [2117]
Assn. of Constr. Material Producers of Estonia [IO]
Assn. of Constr. Proj. Managers [IO]
Assn. of Independent Manufacturers'/Representatives [2534]
Assn. of Modified Asphalt Producers [601]
Australian Pipeline Indus. Assn. [IO]
Automated Builders Consortium [603]
Barrie Constr. Assn. [IO]
British Columbia Constr. Assn. [IO]
Builders Without Borders [12307]
Building and Allied Trades' Union [IO]
Building and Constr. Trades Dept. - AFL-CIO [24025]
Building Futures Coun. [606]
Building Materials Fed. [IO]
Building Owners and Managers Assn..Intl. [3301]
Building Services Res. and Info. Assn. [IO]
Bulgarian Constr. Chamber [IO]
Calgary Constr. Assn. [IO]
Ceilings and Interior Systems Constr. Assn. [1008]
Center to Protect Workers' Rights [24039]
Central Assn. of Earth Moving Contractors in Finland [IO]
Chilean Constr. Chamber [IO]
CIRIA [IO]
Civil Constr. Indus. Union of the State of Rio de Janeiro [IO]
College of Piping [IO]
Common Ground Alliance [12958]
Composite Lumber Mfrs. Assn. [1642]
Concrete Reinforcing Steel Inst. [612]
Concrete Tile Manufacturers Assn. [924]
Construction and Agricultural Film Mfrs. Assn. [1369]
Constr. Assn. of Bermuda [IO]
Constr. Assn. of New Brunswick [IO]
Constr. Assn. of Prince Edward Island [IO]
Constr. Chamber of Quito [IO]
Constr. Economics European Comm. [IO]
Constr. Employers Assn. [613]
Constr. Financial Mgt. Assn. [1012]
Constr. History Soc. [IO]
Constr. Indus. Coun. [IO]
Constr. Indus. Fed. [IO]
Constr. Indus. Round Table [940]
Constr. Innovation Forum [941]
Constr. Innovation Forum [IO]
Constr. Mgt. Assn. of Am. [2492]
Constr. Specifications Inst. [6836]
Constr. Writers Assn. [3106]
Cool Roof Rating Coun. [615]
Costa Rican Chamber of Constr. [IO]
Coun. of European Producers of Materials for Constr. [IO]
Coun. of Japan Constr. Indus. Employee's Unions [IO]
Coun. of Ontario Constr. Associations [IO]
Crane Certification Assn. of Am. [942]
Deep Foundations Inst. [1013]
Employers' Assn. of the Swedish Plate Works [IO]
Equip. Appraisers Assn. of North Am. [279]
Equip. Managers Coun. of Am. [943]
European Constr. Inst. [IO]
European Coun. for Constr. Res., Development and Innovation [IO]
European Org. for Tech. Approvals [IO]
Fed. Facilities Coun. [5707]
Finnish Constr. Trade Union [IO]

Firestop Contractors Intl. Assn. [IO]
Firestop Contractors Intl. Assn. [944]
Forum for the Built Env. [IO]
Found. for Pavement Preservation [945]
Fredericton Northwest Constr. Assn. [IO]
Grande Prairie Constr. Assn. [IO]
Homeowners Against Deficient Dwellings [12314]
Homes for Scotland [IO]
Hong Kong Constr. Assn. [IO]
Insulating Concrete Form Assn. [925]
Intl. Alliance for Interoperability [7018]
Intl. Assn. for Bridge Maintenance and Safety [538]
Intl. Assn. for Shell and Spatial Structures [IO]
Intl. Assn. of Used Equip. Dealers [3052]
Intl. Builders Exchange Executives [1024]
Intl. Building Performance Simulation Assn. [6652]
Intl. Coun. for Res. and Innovation in Building and Constr. [IO]
Intl. Playground Contractors Assn. [1028]
Intl. Soc. of Coating Sci. and Tech. [6705]
Intl. Soc. of Weighing and Measurement [4016]
Intl. Union of Labs. and Experts in Constr. Materials, Systems and Structures [IO]
Intl. Union of Painters and Allied Trades/Joint Apprenticeship and Training Fund [12082]
Japan Constr. Mechanization Assn. [IO]
Joiners' and Ceilers' Company [IO]
Log Home Builders Assn. of North Am. [1031]
Major Contractors' Gp. [IO]
Manufactured Housing Inst. [2527]
The Masonry Soc. [6837]
The Masonry Soc. [IO]
Masons' Company [IO]
Merit Contractors Assn. [IO]
Metal Boat Soc. [526]
Mexican Chamber of the Constr. Indus. [IO]
Modular Building Systems Coun. [2529]
Natl. Affordable Housing Network [12318]
Natl. Alliance for Fair Contracting [24030]
Natl. Assn. of Church Design Builders [831]
Natl. Assn. of Miscellaneous, Ornamental and Architectural Products Contractors [1037]
Natl. Assn. of Reinforcing Steel Contractors [1039]
Natl. Assn. of the Remodeling Indus. [643]
Natl. Assn. of State Contractors Licensing Agencies [1040]
Natl. Assn. of Tower Erectors [6653]
Natl. Building Museum [6477]
Natl. Center for Constr. Educ. and Res. [17632]
Natl. Constr. Investigators Inst. [5606]
Natl. Coun. for Cement and Building Materials [IO]
Natl. Coun. of Erectors, Fabricators and Riggers [1042]
Natl. Energy Mgt. Inst. [6961]
Natl. Inst. of Building Sciences [6838]
Natl. One Coat Stucco Assn. [650]
Natl. Pavement Contractors Assn. [651]
Natl. Res. Council's Inst. for Res. in Constr. [IO]
Natl. Restaurant Assn. Multi-Unit Architects, Engineers and Constr. Officers [1050]
Natl. Roofing Found. [8144]
Natl. Steel Bridge Alliance [539]
Natl. Stone, Sand and Gravel Assn. [3699]
Natl. Town Builders' Assn. [654]
Natl. Utility Locating Contractors Assn. [1055]
North Amer. Equip. Dealers Assn. [185]
Overseas Constr. Assn. of Japan, Inc. [IO]
Panelized Building Systems Coun. [2531]
Paviors' Company [IO]
Peruvian Constr. Indus. Chamber [IO]
Portable Sanitation Assn. Intl. [4003]
Portland Cement Mfrs'. Assn. [IO]
Professional Women in Constr. [1062]
Quartzite Rock Assn. [946]
Refined Bitumen Assn. [IO]
Residential Constr. Employers Coun. [947]
Residential Constr. Workers' Assn. [948]
Resin Flooring Assn. [IO]
Roof Consultants Inst. [1063]
Roofing Indus. Comm. on Weather Issues [666]
Roofing Indus. Educational Inst. [1064]
Salvadoran Chamber of the Constr. Indus. [IO]

Sheet Metal Industry Promotion Plan [1065]
Slag Cement Assn. [935]
Soc. of Boat and Yacht Designers [1154]
Soc. for Marketing Professional Services [2649]
South African Fed. of Civil Engg. Contractors [IO]
Specialized Carriers and Rigging Assn. [3589]
SPRI [949]
Steel Erectors Assn. of Am. [6839]
Steel Framing Alliance [2731]
Steel Truss and Component Assn. [2733]
Terrazzo Tile and Marble Assn. of Canada [IO]
Trussed Rafter Assn. [IO]
Tylers' and Bricklayers' Company [IO]
Union of Constr., Allied Trades and Technicians - United Kingdom [IO]
U.S. Soc. on Dams [7843]
United Union of Roofers, Waterproofers and Allied Workers [24033]
Western Coun. of Constr. Consumers [950]
Construction and Agricultural Film Mfrs. Assn. [1369]
Constr; Amer. Inst. of Timber [1633]
Constr; Amer. Soc. for Concrete [★1001]
Constr. Assn. of Bermuda [IO], Hamilton, Bermuda
Constr. Assn; Ceilings and Interior Systems [1008]
Constr. Assn. of Korea [IO], Seoul, Republic of Korea
Constr. Assn; Metal [638]
Constr. Assn. of New Brunswick [IO], Fredericton, NB, Canada
Constr. Assn. of Prince Edward Island [IO], Charlottetown, PE, Canada
Constr. Chamber of Quito [IO], Quito, Ecuador
Constr. Companies; Amer. Assn. for Small Dredging and Marine [★2576]
Constr. Confed. [IO], London, United Kingdom
Constr. Coun; Fed. [★5707]
Constr. and Design; Assn. for Bridge [6471]
Constr. Economics European Comm. [IO], London, United Kingdom

Construction Education

Cool Roof Rating Coun. [615]
Roofing Indus. Educational Inst. [1064]
Constr. Educ. and Res; Natl. Center for [17632]
Constr. Employers Assn. [613], 1646 N California Blvd., Ste. 500, Walnut Creek, CA 94596-4148, (925)930-8184
Constr. Employers' Fed. [IO], Belfast, United Kingdom
Constr. Equip. Advertisers [★82]
Constr. Equip. Advertisers and Public Relations Coun. [★82]
Constr. Equip. Assn. [IO], Caterham, United Kingdom
Constr. Equip; Natl. Distributors Assn. of [★2000]
Constr. Estimators Assn. of Am; Professional [1061]
Constr. Financial Mgt. Assn. [1012], 29 Emmons Dr., Ste. F-50, Princeton, NJ 08540, (609)452-8000
Constr. Fixings Assn. [IO], Oakham, United Kingdom
Constr., Forestry, Mining and Energy Union [IO], Sydney, Australia
Constr. History Soc. [IO], Ascot, United Kingdom
Constr. Indus. Computing Assn. [IO], Manchester, United Kingdom
Constr. Indus. Coun. [IO], London, United Kingdom
Constr. Indus. CPAs/Consultants Assn. [21], 15011 E Twilight View Dr., Fountain Hills, AZ 85268, (480)836-0300
Construction Industry Employers Assn. - Address unknown since 2008.
Constr. Indus; European Tech. Contractors Comm. for the [IO]
Constr. Indus. Fed. [IO], Dublin, Ireland
Construction Industry Found. - Defunct.
Construction Industry Joint Conf. - Defunct.
Construction Industry Mgt. Bd. - Defunct.
Constr. Indus. Manufacturers Assn. [★177]
Constr. Indus. Manufacturers Assn. [★IO]
Construction Industry Mfrs. Assn. - Defunct.
Construction Industry Political Action Comm. - Defunct.
Constr. Indus. Round Table [940], 1101 17th St. NW, Ste. 608, Washington, DC 20036-4734, (202)466-6777
Construction Industry Sales - Address unknown since 2003.

Reference to "IO" in place of a book number signifies that the association may be found in the 45th edition of International Organizations.

Constr. Indus. Trade Alliance **[IO]**, Carmarthen, United Kingdom
Constr. Innovation Forum **[IO]**, Canton, MI, United States
Constr. Innovation Forum **[941]**, 6494 Latcha Rd., Walbridge, OH 43465, (419)725-3108
Constr. Inspectors; Assn. of **[2117]**
Constr. Labour Relations Assn. of Manitoba **[IO]**, Winnipeg, MB, Canada
Constr. Lawyers; Amer. Coll. of **[323]**
Constr. and Maintenance Assn; Natl. Railroad **[3287]**
Constr. and Maintenance Assn; Railroad **[★3287]**
Constr. Mgt. Assn. of Am. **[2492]**, 7926 Jones Branch Dr., Ste. 800, McLean, VA 22102, (703)356-2622
Construction Marketing Research Coun. - Address unknown since 2001.
Constr; Natl. Coun. on Schoolhouse **[★8335]**
Constr. Officers; Natl. Restaurant Assn. Multi-Unit Architects, Engineers and **[1050]**
Constr. Owners Assn. of Am. **[614]**, 2859 Paces Ferry Rd., Overlook III, Ste. 420, Atlanta, GA 30339, (770)433-0820
Constr. Owners and Executives, U.S.A; Women **[1068]**
Constr. Plant-hire Assn. **[IO]**, London, United Kingdom
Constr. Products Assn. **[IO]**, London, United Kingdom
Construction Products Mfrs. Coun. - Defunct.
Constr; Professional Women in **[1062]**
Constr. Specifications Canada **[IO]**, Toronto, ON, Canada
Constr. Specifications Inst. **[6836]**, 99 Canal Center Plz., Ste. 300, Alexandria, VA 22314, (703)684-0300
Construction Tech. Laboratories **[★933]**
Constr. Trades Dept. - AFL-CIO; Building and **[24025]**
Constr. Writers Assn. **[3106]**, c/o Sheila Wertz, Exec. Dir., PO Box 5586, Buffalo Grove, IL 60089-5586, (847)398-7756
Construction Writers Association **[IO]**, Buffalo Grove, IL, United States
Constructive Action, Inc. - Defunct.
Constructive Tomorrow; Comm. for a **[17318]**
Constructors; Amer. Inst. of **[6833]**
Constructors; NEA - The Assn. of Union **[1056]**
Consular Assn; Amer. **[★24070]**
Consular Law Soc. - Address unknown since 1999.
Consular Officers, Retired; Diplomatic and **[5745]**
Consultant Dieticians Special Interest Gp. **[★15554]**
Consultant Dietitians in Hea. Care Facilities **[15554]**, 2219 Cardinal Dr., Waterloo, IA 50701, (319)235-0991
Consultant Pharmacists; Amer. Soc. of **[15922]**
Consultant Quantity Surveyors Assn. **[IO]**, Cookham, United Kingdom
Consultants
    Alliance of Professional Consultants **[952]**
    Amer. Assn. of Healthcare Consultants **[14860]**
    Amer. Assn. of Medical Billers **[15050]**
    Amer. Assn. of Wedding Planners **[2654]**
    Amer. Soc. for the Advancement of Proj. Mgt. **[2519]**
    Asian Coun. of Logistics Mgt. **[IO]**
    Assn. of Certified Turnaround Professionals **[956]**
    Assn. of Professional Futurists **[7102]**
    Assn. of WORKSHOP WAY Consultants **[9213]**
    DFK International/USA **[28]**
    Export Inst. of the U.S. **[3840]**
    Gp. of Thirty **[1172]**
    Innovation Network **[2115]**
    Inst. of Mgt. Consultants USA **[2499]**
    Intl. Assn. of Animal Behavior Consultants **[7864]**
    Intl. Assn. of Facilitators **[3183]**
    Intl. Assn. of Political Consultants **[IO]**
    Intl. Coach Fed. **[836]**
    Intl. Guild of Professional Consultants **[966]**
    Intl. Soc. of Hospitality Consultants **[967]**
    Justice Res. Assn. **[5655]**
    Leading Edge Alliance **[39]**
    Natl. Assn. of Alternative Benefits Consultants **[1867]**
    Natl. Assn. of Christian Financial Consultants **[1465]**

Natl. Assn. of Church Design Builders **[831]**
Natl. Black Bridal Assn. **[535]**
Natl. Resume Writers' Assn. **[4063]**
Natl. Soc. of Certified Healthcare Bus. Consultants **[14711]**
Natl. Soc. of Environmental Consultants **[3334]**
NHS Consultants Assn. **[IO]**
Paraclete **[20381]**
Public Safety Writers Assn. **[4068]**
Recruiters Online Network **[1281]**
Soc. of Consulting Psychology **[16172]**
Soc. of Risk Mgt. Consultants **[2244]**
Weddings Beautiful Worldwide **[537]**
Consultants; Acad. of Forensic and Indus. Chiropractic **[830]**
Consultants and Administrators; Natl. Assn. of Pension **[★17350]**
Consultants; Amer. Assn. of Healthcare **[14860]**
Consultants; Amer. Assn. of Hosp. **[★14860]**
Consultants; Amer. Assn. of Legal Nurse **[14999]**
Consultants; Amer. Assn. of Nutritional **[15540]**
Consultants; Amer. Assn. of Political **[18342]**
Consultants; Amer. Assn. of Professional Bridal **[★533]**
Consultants; Amer. Coll. of Chiropractic **[13991]**
Consultants; Amer. Soc. of Architectural Hardware **[★1821]**
Consultants; Amer. Soc. of Irrigation **[7826]**
Consultants; APEC - Automated Procedures for Engineering **[6999]**
Consultants to the Armed Forces; Soc. of Medical **[15265]**
Consultants; Assn. of Bridal **[533]**
Consultants Assn; Constr. Indus. CPAs/ **[21]**
Consultants Assn; CPA Auto Dealer **[25]**
Consultants Assn; Independent Cmpt. **[902]**
Consultants; Assn. of Internal Mgt. **[2484]**
Consultants Assn; Investment Mgt. **[2336]**
Consultants Assn; Qualitative Res. **[7573]**
Consultants; Assn. of Trial Behavior **[★6524]**
Consultants Consortium **[962]**, c/o Mr. Henry D. Lewis, CFRE, Pres., 1730 M St. NW, Ste. 801, Washington, DC 20036, (202)463-8929
Consultants, Inc; Automated Procedures for Engineering **[★6999]**
Consultants Institute **[★954]**
Consultants Institute **[★IO]**
Consultants; Inst. for Certified Investment Mgt. **[★2336]**
Consultants Inst; Roof **[1063]**
Consultants; Inst. of Tax **[6295]**
Consultants; Intl. Acad. of Nutritional **[★15540]**
Consultants; Intl. Assn. Merger and Acquisition **[★730]**
Consultants; Natl. Alliance of Independent Crop **[4078]**
Consultants; Natl. Assn. of Legal Search **[2326]**
Consultants; Natl. Assn. of State School Nurse **[15502]**
Consultants; Natl. Assn. of Vision Prog. **[★15693]**
Consultants; Natl. Bur. of Professional Mgt. **[★2505]**
Consultants; Natl. Coun. of Acoustical **[646]**
Consultants; Natl. Soc. of Environmental **[3334]**
Consultants' Network - Defunct.
Consultants Soc; Insurance **[★2244]**
Consultants; Soc. of Mortgage **[★489]**
Consultants; Soc. of Risk Mgt. **[2244]**
Consultants USA; Inst. of Mgt. **[2499]**
Consultants in World War II; Soc. of U.S. Medical **[★15265]**
Consultation Center; Alfred Adler **[★16117]**
Consultation on Church Union **[★19889]**
Consultation; Soc. for Bioethics **[★8845]**
Consultative Comm. of the Bars and Law Societies of the European Community **[★IO]**
Consultative Coun. of Jewish Organizations **[IO]**, New York, NY, United States
Consultative Coun. of Jewish Organizations **[17947]**, c/o Friends of the Alliance Israelite Universelle, 15 W 16th St., 6th Fl., New York, NY 10011, (917)606-8260
Consultative Gp. to Assist the Poor **[17833]**, 900 19th St. NW, Ste. 300, Washington, DC 20006, (202)473-9594
Consultative Group to Assist the Poor **[IO]**, Washington, DC, United States

Consultative Gp. on Intl. Agricultural Res. **[IO]**, Washington, DC, United States
Consultative Gp. on Intl. Agricultural Res. **[12425]**, World Bank, MSN G6-601, 1818 H St. NW, Washington, DC 20433, (202)473-8951
Consulting
    Airport Consultants Coun. **[951]**
    Alliance of Professional Consultants **[952]**
    Amer. Assn. of Insurance Mgt. Consultants **[953]**
    Amer. Consultants League **[954]**
    Amer. Consultants League **[IO]**
    Amer. Coun. of Engg. Companies **[6984]**
    Amer. Soc. for the Advancement of Proj. Mgt. **[2519]**
    Amer. Soc. of Agricultural Consultants **[4074]**
    Amer. Soc. of Consulting Arborists **[5254]**
    Amer. Soc. of Theatre Consultants **[955]**
    American Society of Theatre Consultants **[IO]**
    Amer. Soc. of Wedding Professionals **[532]**
    Assn. des Agences-Conseils en Commun. **[IO]**
    Assn. of Certified Turnaround Professionals **[956]**
    Assn. of Consultants in Access - Australia **[IO]**
    Association of Image Consultants International **[IO]**
    Assn. of Image Consultants Intl. **[957]**
    Assn. of Independent Consultants **[IO]**
    Assn. of Mgt. Consulting Firms **[2485]**
    Assn. of Philanthropic Counsel **[958]**
    Assn. of Professional Commun. Consultants **[959]**
    Assn. of Professional Commun. Consultants **[IO]**
    Assn. of Professional Cmpt. Consultants **[IO]**
    Assn. of Professional Consultants **[960]**
    Assn. of Professional Material Handling Consultants **[961]**
    British Expertise **[IO]**
    British Inst. of Agricultural Consultants **[IO]**
    Canadian Assn. of Intl. Development Consultants **[IO]**
    Canadian Assn. of Mgt. Consultants **[IO]**
    Canadian Telecommunications Consultants Assn. **[IO]**
    Chem. and Indus. Consultants Assn. **[IO]**
    Consultants Consortium **[962]**
    Coun. of Intl. Restaurant Real Estate Brokers **[3392]**
    Ecuadorian Consulting Companies' Assn. **[IO]**
    European Consultants Unit **[IO]**
    The Fed. of Image Consultants **[IO]**
    Finnish Assn. of Consulting Firms **[IO]**
    Foodservice Consultants Soc. Intl. **[IO]**
    Foodservice Consultants Soc. Intl. **[963]**
    Image Indus. Coun. International/Institute for Image Mgt. **[964]**
    Image Industry Council International/Institute for Image Management **[IO]**
    Inst. of Bus. Advisers **[IO]**
    Inst. of Mgt. Consultants in Ireland **[IO]**
    Inst. of Mgt. Consultants USA **[2499]**
    Inst. of Tax Consultants **[6295]**
    Intl. Assn. of Animal Behavior Consultants **[7864]**
    Intl. Assn. of Facilitators **[3183]**
    Intl. Assn. of Protocol Consultants **[965]**
    International Association of Protocol Consultants **[IO]**
    Intl. Coach Fed. **[836]**
    Intl. Guild of Professional Consultants **[966]**
    Intl. Guild of Professional Consultants **[IO]**
    Intl. Soc. of Hospitality Consultants **[IO]**
    Intl. Soc. of Hospitality Consultants **[967]**
    Leading Edge Alliance **[39]**
    Logistics Mgt. Inst. **[5607]**
    Malian Found. **[IO]**
    Municipal Consulting - Inst. for Org. and Economic Consulting **[IO]**
    Natl. Assn. of Bus. Consultants **[IO]**
    Natl. Assn. of Church Design Builders **[831]**
    Natl. Assn. of Cmpt. Consultant Businesses **[968]**
    Natl. Assn. of Cmpt. Consulting Businesses Canada **[IO]**
    Natl. Assn. of German Bus. Consultants **[IO]**
    Natl. Black Bridal Assn. **[535]**
    Natl. Chamber of Consultancy Businesses **[IO]**
    Natl. Resume Writers' Assn. **[4063]**
    Natl. Soc. of Certified Healthcare Bus. Consultants **[14711]**

A star before a book entry number signifies that the name is not listed separately, but is mentioned within the entry.

Pan-American Fed. of Consultants [IO]
Professional and Tech. Consultants Assn. [969]
Public Safety Writers Assn. [4068]
Recruitment and Consulting Services Assn. [IO]
Soc. of Consulting Psychology [16172]
Soc. of Tech. Analysts [IO]
Soc. of Turnaround Professionals [IO]
Tech. Analysts Soc. (Singapore) [IO]
Consulting Actuaries; Conf. of [2157]
Consulting Arborists; Amer. Soc. of [5254]
Consulting Assn; Action [★11757]
Consulting Chemists and Chem. Engineers; Assn. of [6672]
Consulting Comm. of the Professional Electroengineers' Organizations in Finland [★IO]
Consulting Engineers; Amer. Inst. of [★6984]
Consulting Engineers; Assn. of Fed. Communications [7767]
Consulting Engineers Assn. of India [IO], New Delhi, India
Consulting Engineers Assn. of Thailand [IO], Bangkok, Thailand
Consulting Engineers Coun. [★6984]
Consulting Firms; Assn. of Mgt. [2485]
Consulting Firms; Assn. of Outplacement [★1255]
Consulting Firms Intl; Assn. of Outplacement [★1255]
Consulting Foresters of Am; Assn. of [4680]
Consulting Planners; Amer. Soc. of [5587]
Consumer Action [17319], 221 Main St., Ste. 480, San Francisco, CA 94105, (415)777-9635
Consumer Action Now - Defunct.
Consumer Advisory Coun. - Defunct.
Consumer Advocacy of the Amer. Hosp. Assn; Soc. for Healthcare [15005]
Consumer Advocates; Natl. Assn. of State Utility [6340]
Consumer Affairs Exchange; Insurance [2174]
Consumer Affairs Internship Program; Natl. [17337]
Consumer Affairs Professionals in Bus; Soc. of [3196]
Consumer Alert [17320], 3050 K St. NW, Ste. 400, Washington, DC 20007, (202)467-5809
Consumer Alliance - Defunct.
Consumer Arbitration Prog; Gen. Ser. [★17330]
Consumer Bankers Assn. [470], 1000 Wilson Blvd., Ste. 2500, Arlington, VA 22209-3912, (703)276-1750
Consumer Behavior - Defunct.
Consumer Coalition for Health - Defunct.
Consumer Coalition for Quality Hea. Care [14624], 1101 Vermont Ave. NW, Ste. 1001, Washington, DC 20005, (202)789-3606
Consumer Commn. on the Accreditation of Health Services - Defunct.
Consumer Consortium on Assisted Living [11283], 2342 Oak St., Falls Church, VA 22046, (703)533-8121
Consumer Coun. of Denmark [IO], Copenhagen, Denmark
Consumer Coun. of Hong Kong [IO], Hong Kong, People's Republic of China
Consumer Credit Counseling Services [17358], 9009 W Loop S, Ste. 700, Houston, TX 77096, (713)923-2227
Consumer Credit Educ. Found. [★17301]
Consumer Credit Industry Association [2158], c/o William F. Burfeind, Exec. VP, 542 S Dearborn St., Ste. 400, Chicago, IL 60605
Consumer Credit Project - Defunct.
Consumer Credit Trade Assn. [IO], Shipley, United Kingdom
Consumer Data Indus. Assn. [1409], 1090 Vermont Ave. NW, Ste. 200, Washington, DC 20005-4905, (202)371-0910
Consumer Education Res. Center - Address unknown since 2003.
Consumer Educ. in Social Work Regulation; American Found. for Res. and [★13200]
Consumer Electronics Assn. [1209], 1919 S Eads St., Arlington, VA 22202, (703)907-7600
Consumer Electronics Assn. TechHome Div. [1178], 1919 S Eads St., Arlington, VA 22202, (703)907-7600
Consumer Electronics Soc; IEEE [6916]

Consumer Energy Coun. of Am. Res. Found. [17496], 2000 L St. NW, Ste. 802, Washington, DC 20036, (202)659-0404
Consumer Fed. of Am. [17321], 1620 I St. NW, Ste. 200, Washington, DC 20006, (202)387-6121
Consumer Fed. of Am. Found. [11811], 1620 I St. NW, Ste. 200, Washington, DC 20006, (202)387-6121
Consumer Finance Assn; Natl. [★2422]
Consumer Goods Coun. of South Africa [IO], Gauteng, Republic of South Africa
Consumer Hea. Educ. Coun. [14685], c/o Employee Benefit Res. Inst., 1100 13th St. NW, Ste. 878, Washington, DC 20005, (202)659-0670
Consumer Healthcare Prdt. Assn. [2973], 900 19th St. NW, Ste. 700, Washington, DC 20006, (202)429-9260
Consumer Info. Center Prog; Fed. [5817]
Consumer Info; Coun. on [★17305]
Consumer Mortgage Coalition [2424], 101 Constitution Ave. NW, 9th Fl. W, Washington, DC 20001, (202)742-4366
Consumer Orgs; Natl. Assn. of Transit [13339]
Consumer Pesticide Project - Defunct.
Consumer Products Broker; NAGMR [★2541]
Consumer Products Codification Assn. [IO], Buenos Aires, Argentina
Consumer Products Division of the Natl. Elecl. Manufacturers Assn. [★264]
Consumer Products Sales Agencies; NAGMR [★2541]
Consumer Proj. on Tech. [7542], 1621 Connecticut Ave. NW, No. 500, Washington, DC 20009, (202)332-2670
Consumer Protection Coun; Trans. [★3595]
Consumer Res. Inst. - Defunct.
Consumer Savings Alliance - Address unknown since 1999.
Consumer Sci. Bus. Professionals [★970]
Consumer Sciences; Amer. Assn. of Family and [12285]
Consumer Shows; Natl. Assn. of [1346]
Consumer Specialty Products Assn. [806], 900 17th St. NW, Ste. 300, Washington, DC 20006, (202)872-8110
Consumer Trends Forum Intl. [970], 7076 Drinkard Way, Mechanicsville, VA 23111, (804)559-6519
Consumer Web Watch [17322], c/o Consumers Union, 101 Truman Ave., Yonkers, NY 10703-1057, (914)378-2600

Consumers

AFSA Educ. Found. [17301]
Alliance Against Fraud in Telemarketing and Electronic Commerce [17302]
Alliance for Consumer Rights [17303]
Alliance Credit Counseling [11833]
Amer. Alliance of Ethical Movers [13346]
Amer. Assn. for Long-Term Care Insurance [2132]
Amer. Consumers Assn. [17304]
Amer. Coun. on Consumer Interests [17305]
Amer. Grassfed Assn. [2438]
Americans for Fair Electronic Commerce Transactions [17441]
Antitrust Coalition for Consumer Choice in Hea. Care [14615]
Assn. for Consumer Res. [17306]
Association for Consumer Research [IO]
Assn. for the Protection of Consumers [IO]
Australian Consumers' Assn. [IO]
Auto. Protection Assn. [IO]
Automotive Consumer Action Prog. [17307]
Aviation Consumer Action Proj. [17308]
BBB Wise Giving Alliance [17309]
BBB Wise Giving Alliance [IO]
Buying Influence [17310]
Canadian Coun. of Better Bus. Bureaus [IO]
Care USA [17311]
Cemetery Consumer Ser. Coun. [17312]
Center for Consumer Affairs, Univ. of Wisconsin-Milwaukee [17313]
Center for a New Amer. Dream [17260]
Center for Sci. in the Public Interest [17314]
Center for Stud. of Responsive Law [17315]
Children Before Dogs [11682]
Children's Hea. Environmental Coalition [13953]

Citizens for Consumer Justice [18641]
Coalition Against Insurance Fraud [2155]
Coalition for Auto-Insurance Reform [17316]
Coalition for Healthcare Commun. [14622]
Coalition to Keep Am. Connected [18724]
Commn. for the Advancement of Public Interest Orgs. [17317]
Comm. for a Constructive Tomorrow [17318]
Conf. on Consumer Finance Law [5608]
Consortium for Energy Efficiency [1286]
Consumer Action [17319]
Consumer Alert [17320]
Consumer Coalition for Quality Hea. Care [14624]
Consumer Consortium on Assisted Living [11283]
Consumer Coun. of Denmark [IO]
Consumer Coun. of Hong Kong [IO]
Consumer Credit Industry Association [2158]
Consumer Energy Coun. of Am. Res. Found. [17496]
Consumer Fed. of Am. [17321]
Consumer Fed. of Am. Found. [11811]
Consumer Trends Forum Intl. [970]
Consumer Web Watch [17322]
Consumers' Assn. of Canada [IO]
Consumers Assn. of Ireland [IO]
Consumers Assn. of Singapore [IO]
Consumers for Dental Choice [11912]
Consumers Educ. and Protective Assn. [17323]
Consumers Educ. and Protective Assn. [IO]
Consumers' Inst. [IO]
Consumers Intl. - Africa Off. [IO]
Consumers Intl. - Asia Pacific Off. [IO]
Consumers Intl. - England [IO]
Consumers Intl. - Regional Off. for Latin Am. and the Caribbean [IO]
Consumers' Union of Korea [IO]
Consumers Union of U.S. [17324]
Consumers for World Trade [17325]
Consumers for World Trade [IO]
Consuming Indus. Trade Action Coalition [771]
Coun. for the Advancement of Consumer Policy [17326]
Coupon Exchange Club [17327]
Customer Satisfaction Measurement Assn. [716]
Direct Selling Educ. Found. [3466]
Electricity Consumers Rsrc. Coun. [1184]
Electricity Storage Assn. [3957]
EnergyWatch [IO]
European Beer Consumers' Union [IO]
European Consumers Org. [IO]
Fed. of Malaysian Consumers Associations [IO]
Food Alliance [4676]
Food and Water [17328]
Found. Aiding the Elderly [17329]
Free the Grapes! [16971]
Funeral Ser. Consumer Assistance Prog. [17330]
Green Seal [17331]
Hea. Action Intl. [IO]
Heirs, Inc. [17332]
Homeowners Against Deficient Dwellings [12314]
Identity Theft Rsrc. Center [18007]
Indonesian Consumers Org. [IO]
Inst. of Consumer Affairs [IO]
Insurance Consumer Affairs Exchange [2174]
Insurance Marketplace Standards Assn. [2180]
Interactive Travel Services Assn. [3946]
Intl. Alliance of Avaya Users [3745]
Intl. Anticounterfeiting Coalition [17333]
International Anticounterfeiting Coalition [IO]
Intl. Assn. for Consumer Law [IO]
Intl. Assn. of Lemon Law Administrators [5536]
Intl. Coalition for Sustainable Production and Consumption [17222]
Intl. Consumer Prdt. Hea. and Safety Org. [3178]
Intl. Experiential Marketing Assn. [2631]
IP Justice [5852]
Islamic Food and Nutrition Coun. of Am. [2353]
Kids In Danger [11612]
Media Access Proj. [17182]
Metal Building Contractors and Erectors Assn. [2528]
Natl. Assn. of Consumer Advocates [17334]
Natl. Assn. of Consumer Agency Administrators [5609]
Natl. Assn. of Consumer Agency Administrators [IO]

Reference to "IO" in place of a book number signifies that the association may be found in the 45th edition of International Organizations.

Natl. Assn. of Consumer Bankruptcy Attorneys [5510]
Natl. Assn. of Consumer Credit Administrators [5610]
Natl. Assn. of Farmers' Market Nutrition Programs [4648]
Natl. Assn. of Visual Merchandisers [1153]
Natl. Black Consumers Union [IO]
Natl. Citizens Coalition for Nursing Home Reform [17335]
Natl. Coalition for Consumer Educ. [17336]
Natl. Consumer Affairs Internship Program [17337]
Natl. Consumer Forum [IO]
Natl. Consumer Law Center [5611]
Natl. Consumer's Assn. of Swaziland [IO]
Natl. Consumers League [17338]
Natl. Coun. Against Hea. Fraud [17692]
Natl. Found. for Credit Counseling [2428]
Natl. Fraud Info. Center/Internet Fraud Watch [17339]
Privacy Rights CH [3176]
Process Gas Consumers Gp. [17340]
Public Citizen [17341]
Public Citizen Litigation Gp. [17342]
Public Citizen's Cong. Watch [17343]
Residential Energy Services Network [664]
Scottish Consumer Coun. [IO]
Social Accountability Intl. [18828]
Soc. of Consumer Affairs Professionals in Bus. [3196]
Soc. for Consumer Psychology [17344]
South African Natl. Consumer Union [IO]
Southwest Res. and Info. Center [17345]
Specialty Wine Retailers Assn. [4031]
Steel Door Inst. [672]
Tanzania Consumers Protection Assn. [IO]
TeleTruth: The Alliance for Customers' Telecommunications Rights [17346]
Timeshare Consumers Assn. [IO]
Trans. and Logistics Coun. [3595]
Which [IO]
Word of Mouth Marketing Assn. [2653]
World Energy Efficiency Assn. [6978]
Consumers for Accountability Thru Nationally Driven Objectives - Address unknown since 2001.
Consumers; Assn. of Amer. [★13342]
Consumers' Assn. of Canada [IO], Ottawa, ON, Canada
Consumers' Assn. - England [★IO]
Consumers Assn. of Ireland [IO], Dublin, Ireland
Consumers Assn; Organic [5069]
Consumers Assn. of Singapore [IO], Singapore, Singapore
Consumers; Center for Medical [14550]
Consumers Cooperative Assn. [★4482]
Consumers Coun; Natl. [★13342]
Consumers for Dental Choice [11912], 316 F St. NE, Ste. 210, Washington, DC 20002, (202)544-6333
Consumers Educ. and Protective Assn. [17323], 6048 Ogontz Ave., Philadelphia, PA 19141-1347, (215)424-1441
Consumers Educ. and Protective Assn. [IO], Philadelphia, PA, United States
Consumers for the Free Market - Address unknown since 1999.
Consumers' Hea. Forum of Australia [IO], Manuka, Australia
Consumers Info. Comm; Elec. [★17321]
Consumers' Inst. [IO], Wellington, New Zealand
Consumers Intl. - Africa Off. [IO], Accra, Ghana
Consumers Intl. - Asia Pacific Off. [IO], Kuala Lumpur, Malaysia
Consumers Intl. - England [IO], London, United Kingdom
Consumers Intl. - Oficina para Am. Latina y el Caribe [★IO]
Consumers Intl. - Regional Off. for Latin Am. and the Caribbean [IO], Santiago, Chile
Consumers Opposed to Inflation in the Necessities - Defunct.
Consumers Org. for the Hearing Impaired - Defunct.
Consumers Rsrc. Coun; Electricity [1184]
Consumers' Self-Help CH; Natl. Mental Hea. [12553]
Consumers and Travelers; Fed. of Amer. [13342]

Consumers and Travelers; Natl. Assn. of [★3931]
Consumers' Union of Korea [IO], Seoul, Republic of Korea
Consumers Union of U.S. [17324], 101 Truman Ave., Yonkers, NY 10703-1057, (914)378-2000
Consumers United for Rail Equity [18289], 1050 Thomas Jefferson St. NW, 6th Fl., Washington, DC 20007, (202)298-1844
Consumers for World Trade [17325], 1707 L St. NW, Ste. 570, Washington, DC 20036, (202)293-2944
Consumers for World Trade [IO], Washington, DC, United States
Consuming Indus. Trade Action Coalition [771], 2000 L St. NW, Ste. 835, Washington, DC 20036, (202)316-3046
Contabilidad; Asociacion Interamericana de [★35]
Contact Center Associates [★2619]
Contact Centre Assn. of Singapore [IO], Singapore, Singapore
Contact Dermatitis Soc; Amer. [14191]
Contact Lens Assn. of Ophthalmologists [15680], 2025 Woodland Dr., St. Paul, MN 55125, (651)731-2944
Contact Lens Coun. [14036], 8201 Corporate Dr., Ste. 850, Landover, MD 20785, (301)459-2618
Contact Lens Examiners; Natl. [15723]
Contact Lens Mfrs. Assn. [1856], PO Box 29398, Lincoln, NE 68529, (402)465-4122
Contact Lens Mfrs. Assn. [IO], Lincoln, NE, United States
Contact Lens Soc. of Am. [1857], 441 Carlisle Dr., Herndon, VA 20170, (703)437-5100
Contact Lenses
  Assn. of Contact Lens Mfrs. [IO]
  British Contact Lens Assn. [IO]
  Contact Lens Coun. [14036]
  European Fed. of the Contact Lens Indus. [IO]
  Intl. Assn. of Contact Lens Educators [IO]
CONTACT Teleministries U.S.A. [★19865]
CONTACT Teleministry, Inc. [★19865]
CONTACT USA [19865], 11733 W 105th St., St. John, IN 46373, (219)365-9760
Container Inst; Paper Cup and [★1157]
Container Manufacturers Assn; Carbonated Beverage [★974]
Container Manufacturers Inst; Glass [★982]
Container Market Comm. [977], c/o Amer. Iron and Steel Inst., 1140 Connecticut Ave. NW, Ste. 705, Washington, DC 20036, (202)452-7100
Container Reconditioners; Assn. of [★994]
Container Recycling Alliance [4479], 700 E Butterfield Rd., Ste. 480, Lombard, IL 60148, (630)572-2480
Container Recycling Inst. [4480], 1776 Massachusetts Ave. NW, Ste. 800, Washington, DC 20036-1904, (202)263-0999
Container Resources; Natl. Assn. for PET [3997]
Containerboard and Kraft Paper Group - Defunct.
Containerization Inst. [★978]
Containerization and Intermodal Inst. [978], 960 Holmdel Rd., Bldg. 2, Ste. 201, Holmdel, NJ 07733, (732)817-9131
Containers
  Alliance for Beverage Cartons and the Env. - Belgium [IO]
  Alliance for Beverage Cartons and the Env. - United Kingdom [IO]
  Aluminum Foil Container Manufacturers Assn. [971]
  Amer. Cookie Jar Assn. [22577]
  Assoc. Cooperage Indus. of Am. [972]
  Assn. of European Producers of Steel for Packaging [IO]
  Assn. of Independent Corrugated Converters [IO]
  Assn. of Independent Corrugated Converters [973]
  Assn. of Tankcleaning Companies in the Netherlands [IO]
  Can Manufacturers Inst. [974]
  Canadian Pallet Coun. [IO]
  Canadian Wooden Pallet and Container Assn. [IO]
  Closure Manufacturers Assn. [975]
  Composite Can and Tube Inst. [976]
  Composite Can and Tube Institute [IO]

Container Market Comm. [977]
Container Recycling Alliance [4479]
Container Recycling Inst. [4480]
Containerization and Intermodal Inst. [978]
European Fed. of Corrugated Bd. Mfrs. [IO]
European Fed. of Multiwall Paper Sack Mfrs. [IO]
European Fed. of Wooden Pallet and Packaging Mfrs. [IO]
European Flexible Intermediate Bulk Container Assn. [IO]
European Secretariat of Mfrs. of Light Metal Packaging [IO]
Fiberglass Tank and Pipe Inst. [979]
Film and Bag Fed. [980]
Flexible Intermediate Bulk Container Assn. [981]
Flexible Intermediate Bulk Container Assn. [IO]
Glass Packaging Inst. [982]
Indus. Metal Containers and Wire Decking, a Prdt. Sect. of the Material Handling Indus. [983]
Inst. of Intl. Container Lessors [984]
Inst. of Intl. Container Lessors [IO]
Intl. Corrugated Case Assn. [IO]
Intl. Corrugated Case Assn. [985]
Intl. Org. of Aluminum Aerosol Can Mfrs. [IO]
Intl. Tank Container Org. [IO]
Natl. Assn. of Container Distributors [986]
Natl. Paperbox Assn. [987]
Natl. Wood Tank Inst. [988]
Natl. Wooden Pallet and Container Assn. [989]
Pacific Coast Paper Box Mfrs'. Assn. [990]
Paper Shipping Sack Manufacturers' Assn. [991]
Plastic Shipping Container Inst. [992]
Recycled Paperboard Tech. Assn. [993]
Reusable Indus. Packaging Assn. [994]
Steel Shipping Container Inst. [995]
Steel Tank Inst. and Steel Plate Fabricators Assn. [996]
Steel Tube Inst. of North Am. [997]
Steel Tube Inst. of North Am. [IO]
Tank Conf. of the Truck Trailer Mfrs. Assn. [998]
Textile Bag and Packaging Assn. [999]
Whisky Pitcher Collectors Assn. of Am. [22130]
Containers and Wire Decking, a Prdt. Sect. of the Material Handling Indus; Indus. Metal [983]
Contaminant Res. Center; Natl. Fisheries [★7172]
Contaminated Land: Applications in Real Environments [IO], London, United Kingdom
Contamination; Citizens for Alternatives to Chem. [5084]
Contamination Control; Amer. Assn. for [★7570]
Contamination Control; Scottish Soc. for [IO]
Contamination Res. Center; Environmental and [7172]
Contemplative Sisters; Assn. of [20563]
The Contemporary A Cappella Soc. [★10582]
Contemporary A Cappella Soc. of Am. [10582], 681 10th Ave., San Francisco, CA 94118, (415)358-8067
Contemporary Amer. Patriot Club [★21241]
Contemporary Art
  Amer. Print Alliance [9544]
Contemporary Art Center; P.S.1 [9595]
Contemporary Art Soc. [IO], London, United Kingdom
Contemporary Artists; Amer. Soc. of [9493]
Contemporary Arts - Defunct.
Contemporary Culture; Soc. for the Arts, Religion and [9599]
Contemporary Design Gp. [1694], c/o Lawrance Furnishings, 633 Univ. Ave., San Diego, CA 92103, (619)291-1911
Contemporary Glass; Art Alliance for [9421]
Contemporary Glass Soc. [IO], West Midlands, United Kingdom
Contemporary Historical Vehicle Assn. [21620], PO Box 493398, Redding, CA 96049-3398
Contemporary Issues Clearinghouse - Defunct.
Contemporary Music Project - Defunct.
Contemporary Music Soc. - Address unknown since 1995.
Contemporary Music, U.S. Sect; League of Composers - Intl. Soc. for [★10626]
Contemporary Problems; Acad. for [★18417]
Contemporary Quilt Art Assn. [22152], PO Box 95685, Seattle, WA 98145-2685

A star before a book entry number signifies that the name is not listed separately, but is mentioned within the entry.

Contemporary Stud; Inst. for [18453]
Content Mgt. Assn; AIIM - The Enterprise [2095]
Contests
  Amer. Canine Educ. Found. [22193]
  Amer. Fancy Rat and Mouse Assn. [22704]
  Ferret Fanciers Club [22416]
  Intl. Barbeque Cookers Assn. [22570]
  Intl. Martial Arts League [23589]
  Miss Am. Org. [22135]
  Natl. Amer. Eskimo Dog Assn. [22310]
  Natl. Birman Fanciers [21913]
  Peruvian Inca Orchid Dog Club of Am. [22341]
  Senior Conformation Judges Assn. [22358]
  Soc. of Parrot Breeders and Exhibitors [21860]
Context Inst. [18611], PO Box 946, Langley, WA
  98260, (360)221-6044
Continence; Natl. Assn. for [16709]
Continence Nurses Soc., An Assn. of E.T. Nurses;
  Wound, Ostomy and [★15533]
Continence Restored, Inc. [16707], 407 Strawberry
  Hill Ave., Stamford, CT 06902, (203)348-0601
Continence; Simon Found. for [16711]
Continental Advt. Agency Network [★79]
Continental Advt. Agency Network [★IO]
Continental Assn. of CPA Firms [★5]
Continental Assn. of Funeral and Memorial Societies
  [★2780]
Continental Assn. of Resolute Employers - Address
  unknown since 1994.
Continental Automated Buildings Assn. [IO], Ottawa,
  ON, Canada
Continental Baptist Missions [19486], 11650 North-
  land Dr., Rockford, MI 49341-8706, (616)863-2226
Continental Basketball Assn. [23129], 195
  Washington Ave., Albany, NY 12210, (518)694-
  0100
Continental Confed. of Adopted Indians [10737], 960
  Walhonding Ave., Logan, OH 43138, (740)385-
  7136
Continental Cong; Third [17299]
Continental Divide Trail Soc. [23938], 3704 N
  Charles St., No. 601, Baltimore, MD 21218,
  (410)235-9610
Continental Dorset Club [5202], PO Box 506, North
  Scituate, RI 02857-0506, (401)647-4676
Continental do Estado da California; Uniao Portu-
  guesa [★19131]
Continental European Family History Assn. [21112],
  c/o John Movius, Pres./Webmaster, PO Box 2660,
  Salt Lake City, UT 84110-2660, (801)288-1501
Continental European Family History Assn. [IO], Salt
  Lake City, UT, United States
Continental Greyhound Racing Confed. [IO], Lich,
  Germany
Continental Luscombe Assn. [21439], c/o Donna
  Boyer, 4278 Moreland Dr., Castro Valley, CA
  94546, (510)582-3683
Continental Mark II Owner's Assn. - Address
  unknown since 2003.
Continental Mi-Ki Assn. [22250], c/o Carol Wright,
  Sec., 4522 Cyclamen Way, Sacramento, CA
  95841, (916)334-1842
Continental Motosport Club [23623], PO Box 3178,
  Mission Viejo, CA 92690-3178, (949)367-1141
Continental Owners Club; Lincoln and [21687]
Continental Owners Club; Lincoln [★21687]
Continental Quilting Cong. [★22173]
Continental Service Corps - Address unknown since
  1995.
Continental Spaniel
  Papillon Club of Am. [22336]
Continental Transportation Assn. - Defunct.
Contingency Planners; Amer. Coll. of [14609]
Continued Action on Transportation - Defunct.
Continuing Care Accreditation Commn. [16318],
  4891 E Grant Rd., Tucson, AZ 85712, (520)325-
  1044
Continuing Christian Development [★19934]
Continuing Comm. on Muslim-Christian Cooperation
  - Defunct.
Continuing Comm. of the Natl. Women's Conf.
  [★17563]
Continuing Education
  Accrediting Coun. for Continuing Educ. and Train-
  ing [8145]

Amer. Assn. for Adult and Continuing Educ.
  [8146]
Amer. Seminar Leaders Assn. [8147]
Assn. for Continuing Higher Educ. [8148]
Canadian Assn. for Univ. Continuing Educ. [IO]
Elderhostel, Inc. [IO]
Elderhostel, Inc. [8149]
Global Alliance for Medical Educ. [8862]
Inst. for Retired Professionals [12898]
Intl. Assn. for Continuing Educ. and Training
  [8150]
Intl. Assn. for Continuing Educ. and Training [IO]
Learning Resources Network [8151]
Natl. Adult Educ. Honor Soc. [24392]
Natl. Assn. for Professional Development Schools
  [9091]
Natl. Coun. for Continuing Educ. and Training
  [8152]
North Amer. Assn. of Medical Educ. and Commun.
  Companies [8874]
Senior Scholars [8153]
Sloan Consortium [8304]
Soc. for Academic Continuing Medical Educ.
  [8875]
Univ. Continuing Educ. Assn. [8154]
University Continuing Education Association [IO]
Values and Visions [8155]
World Educ. [7918]
Continuing Educ. Coun. [★8145]
Continuing Educ. for Engineers; Assn. for Media-
  Based [8367]
Continuing Educ. of Roman Catholic Clergy; Natl.
  Org. for [19936]
Continuing Educ. Unit; Coun. on the [★8150]
Continuing Legal Educ. Administrators; Assn. of
  [★8762]
Continuing Legal Educ; Assn. for [8762]
Continuing Lib. Educ. Network and Exchange
  [★10350]
Continuing Lib. Educ. Network and Exchange Round
  Table [10350], c/o Jasmine Posey, Programming
  Chair, Greenwich Lib., 101 W Putnam Ave.,
  Greenwich, CT 06830-4328, (203)622-7941
Continuing Medical Educ; Alliance for [8841]
Continuing Medical Educ; Liaison Comm. on
  [★15151]
Continuing Medical Educ; Network for [15177]
Continuing the Peace Dialogue U.S.A./USSR -
  Defunct.
Continuing Professional Educ; ALI-ABA Comm. on
  [8758]
Continuity of Care; Amer. Assn. for [14836]
Contraception; Intl. Consortium for Emergency
  [12183]
Contraceptive Tech; Hea. Division of Prog. for the
  Introduction and Adaptation of [★17000]
Contraceptive Tech; Prog. for the Introduction and
  Adaptation of [★17000]
Contract Carrier Conf. [★3899]
Contract and Commercial Mgt; Intl. Assn. for [772]
Contract Flooring Assn. [IO], Nottingham, United
  Kingdom
Contract Furnishings Coun. - Defunct.
Contract Furnishings Forum [★1698]
Contract Indus. Coun; Ser. [3554]
Contract Mgt. Assn. of Am; Govt. [★1744]
Contract Mgt; Assn; Natl. [1744]
Contract Mfrs. Assn. - Address unknown since 2000.
Contract Mfg. and Packaging Assn. [★2873]
Contract Packagers Assn. [★2873]
Contract Packaging Assn. [2873], 1601 N Bond St.,
  Ste. 101, Naperville, IL 60563, (630)544-5053
Contract Packaging Assn. [★2873]
Contract Services Assn. of Am. [1743], 1000 Wilson
  Blvd., Ste. 1800, Arlington, VA 22209, (703)243-
  2020
Contract Stationers Forum [★3685]
Contract Textiles; Assn. for [3775]
Contracting; Academy of Elecl. [★1045]
Contracting and Engg. Assn; Instrument [1020]
Contracting Found; Elecl. [★1179]
Contracting Indus; Coun. of Mech. Specialty
  [★1006]
Contractor Assn; Exhibitor Appointed [1338]
Contractors
  ADSC: The Intl. Assn. of Found. Drilling [1000]

ADSC: The International Association of Founda-
  tion Drilling [IO]
Air Barrier Assn. of Am. [587]
Alliance of Deep Found. Testing Professionals
  [6650]
Amer. Cloak and Suit Mfrs. Assn. [223]
Amer. Concrete Inst. [6832]
Amer. Contract Compliance Assn. [17493]
Amer. Road and Trans. Builders Assn. [6313]
Amer. Soc. of Concrete Contractors [1001]
Amer. Sports Builders Assn. [1002]
Amer. Subcontractors Assn. [1003]
Assoc. Builders and Contractors [1004]
Assoc. Gen. Contractors of Am. [1005]
Assoc. Specialty Contractors [1006]
Assn. of Diving Contractors Intl. [1007]
Assn. of Diving Contractors Intl. [IO]
Assn. of Ductwork Contractors and Allied Services
  [IO]
Assn. of Energy Ser. Companies [2918]
Assn. of Landscape Contractors of Ireland [IO]
Building Futures Coun. [606]
Building Ser. Contractors Assn. Intl. [2459]
Canadian Assn. of Geophysical Contractors [IO]
Ceilings and Interior Systems Constr. Assn.
  [1008]
Ceramic Tile Inst. of Am. [1009]
Certified Builders Assn. of New Zealand [IO]
Certified Contractor's Network [1010]
Concrete Foundations Assn. [1011]
Confed. of Roofing Contractors [IO]
Constr. Financial Mgt. Assn. [1012]
Constr. Specifications Inst. [6836]
Cool Roof Rating Coun. [615]
Deep Foundations Inst. [1013]
Deep Foundations Institute [IO]
Directional Crossing Contractors Assn. [1014]
Dredging Contractors of Am. [2576]
Drilling Engg. Assn. [2922]
Dutch Assn. of Subcontracting Indus. [IO]
Elecl. and Communications Assn. of Western
  Australia [IO]
Elecl. Contractors Assn. of Hamilton [IO]
Elecl. Contractors Assn. of London [IO]
Elecl. Contractors Assn. of New Zealand [IO]
Elecl. Contractors Assn. of Northern Ontario [IO]
Elecl. Contractors Assn. of Ottawa [IO]
Elecl. Contractors Assn. of Quinte-St. Lawrence
  [IO]
Elecl. Contractors Assn. of Sarnia [IO]
Elecl. Contractors Assn. of Saskatchewan [IO]
Engg. Contractors Assn. [1015]
Exhibitor Appointed Contractor Assn. [1338]
Floor Covering Installation Contractors Assn.
  [1016]
Floor Installation Assn. of North Am. [623]
Gen. Contractors Assn. of Ottawa [IO]
Georgian Bay Elecl. Contractors Assn. [IO]
Glass Assn. of North Am. [1728]
Gunite/Shotcrete Contractors Assn. [1017]
Independent Contractors of Australia [IO]
Independent Elecl. Contractors [1018]
Independent Professional Painting Contractors
  Assn. of Am. [1019]
Independent Professional Painting Contractors
  Assn. of Am. [IO]
Instrument Contracting and Engg. Assn. [1020]
Instrument Technicians Labor-Mgt. Cooperation
  Fund [1021]
Insulating Concrete Form Assn. [925]
Insulation Contractors Assn. of Am. [1022]
Intl. Assn. of Geosynthetic Installers [1023]
Intl. Assn. of Geosynthetic Installers [IO]
International Builders Exchange Executives [IO]
Intl. Builders Exchange Executives [1024]
Intl. Certified Floorcovering Installers Assn. [1025]
International Certified Floorcovering Installers As-
  sociation [IO]
Intl. Consultants and Contractors Assn. of Iran
  [IO]
Intl. Ground Source Heat Pump Assn. [1889]
Intl. Inst. for Lath and Plaster [1026]
International Institute for Lath and Plaster [IO]
Intl. Masonry Inst. [IO]
Intl. Masonry Inst. [1027]

Reference to "IO" in place of a book number signifies that the association may be found in the 45th edition of International Organizations.

Intl. Playground Contractors Assn. [1028]
Intl. Playground Contractors Assn. [IO]
International Union of Bricklayers and Allied
Craftsworkers [IO]
Intl. Union of Bricklayers and Allied Craftsworkers
[1029]
Joint Indus. Bd. of the Elecl. Indus. [1030]
Ladies Apparel Contractors Assn. [244]
Log Home Builders Assn. of North Am. [1031]
Mason Contractors Assn. of Am. [1032]
Mech. Contractors Assn. of Am. [1033]
Natl. Alliance for Fair Contracting [24030]
Natl. Assn. of Elevator Contractors [1034]
Natl. Assn. of Home Builders [1035]
Natl. Assn. of Minority Contractors [1036]
Natl. Assn. of Miscellaneous, Ornamental and
Architectural Products Contractors [1037]
Natl. Assn. of Ordnance and Explosive Waste
Contractors [1038]
Natl. Assn. of Reinforcing Steel Contractors
[1039]
Natl. Assn. of State Contractors Licensing Agen-
cies [1040]
Natl. Assn. of Tower Erectors [6653]
Natl. Assn. of Women in Constr. [1041]
Natl. Assn. of Women in Constr. [IO]
Natl. Assn. of Women in Constr. - Australia [IO]
Natl. Constr. Investigators Assn. [5606]
Natl. Coun. of Erectors, Fabricators and Riggers
[1042]
Natl. Demolition Assn. [1043]
Natl. Drilling Assn. [1044]
National Drilling Association [IO]
Natl. Elecl. Contractors Assn. [1045]
Natl. Elecl. Contractors Coun. [1046]
Natl. Fireproofing Contractors Assn. [1476]
Natl. Frame Builders Assn. [1047]
Natl. Inst. of Building Sciences [6838]
Natl. Insulation Assn. [1048]
Natl. Mech. Contractors Coun. [1049]
Natl. One Coat Stucco Assn. [650]
Natl. Pavement Contractors Assn. [651]
Natl. Restaurant Assn. Multi-Unit Architects,
Engineers and Constr. Officers [1050]
Natl. Roofing Contractors Assn. [1051]
Natl. Standard Plumbing Code Comm. [5553]
Natl. Terrazzo and Mosaic Assn. [1052]
Natl. Tile Contractors Assn. [1053]
Natl. Town Builders' Assn. [654]
Natl. Utility Contractors Assn. [1054]
Natl. Utility Locating Contractors Assn. [1055]
NEA - The Assn. of Union Constructors [1056]
Netherlands Assn. of Intl. Dutch Contractors [IO]
North Amer. Alliance for Fair Employment [1277]
North Amer. Power Sweeping Assn. [2473]
Painting and Decorating Contractors of Am.
[1057]
Pile Driving Contractors Assn. [1058]
Plumbing-Heating-Cooling Contractors Assn.
[1059]
Power and Commun. Contractors Assn. [1060]
Professional Constr. Estimators Assn. of Am.
[1061]
Professional Contractors Gp. [IO]
Professional Women in Constr. [1062]
Roof Consultants Inst. [1063]
Roofing Indus. Comm. on Weather Issues [666]
Roofing Indus. Educational Inst. [1064]
Rural and Assoc. Contractors Fed. of New
Zealand [IO]
Sheet Metal Contractors Assn. of Alberta [IO]
Sheet Metal Industry Promotion Plan [1065]
Slag Cement Assn. [935]
Tile Contractors Assn. of Am. [1066]
Tilt-Up Concrete Assn. [1067]
Tilt-Up Concrete Association [IO]
Women Constr. Owners and Executives, U.S.A.
[1068]
Contractors of Am; Air Conditioning [1872]
Contractors of Am; Air Conditioning and Refrigera-
tion [★1872]
Contractors of Am; Assoc. Independent Elecl.
[★1018]
Contractors of Am; Assoc. Minority [★1036]
Contractors of Am; Dredging [2576]

Contractors of Am; Land Improvement [4415]
Contractors of Am. and Professional Lawn Care
Assn. of Am; Assoc. Landscape [★2398]
Contractors; Amer. Assn. of Oilwell Drilling [★2930]
Contractors Assn. of Am; Tile and Mantel [★1066]
Contractors Assn; Amer. Apparel [★222]
Contractors; Assn. of Bituminous [839]
Contractors Assn; British Chem. Engg. [IO]
Contractors Assn; Distribution [24162]
Contractors; Assn. of Diving [★1007]
Contractors Assn; Assn. of Drilled Shaft [★1000]
Contractors Assn; Engg. and Grading [★1015]
Contractors Assn; Exhibition Services and [★2679]
Contractors Assn; Exposition Ser. [2679]
Contractors Assn; Finishing [622]
Contractors Assn; Gen. Building [625]
Contractors Assn; Gunite [★1017]
Contractors Assn; Ladies Apparel [244]
Contractors Assn; Natl. Concrete [★1001]
Contractors Assn; Natl. Drilling [★1044]
Contractors Assn; Natl. Environmental Systems
[★1872]
Contractors Assn; Natl. Insulation [★1048]
Contractors Assn; Natl. Star Route Mail [2453]
Contractors Assn; Natl. Systems [1225]
Contractors Assn; Pipe Line [2945]
Contractors Assn; Popular Price Dress [★244]
Contractors Assn; Poured Concrete [★1011]
Contractors Assn; Southern Apparel [★222]
Contractors' Assn; Underground Engg. [★1015]
Contractors Assn; Women [4048]
Contractors Co-Op Coun. [2256]
Contractors and Erectors Assn; Metal Building
[2528]
Contractors Mutual Assn. - Defunct.
Contractors; Natl. Assn. of Building Ser. [★2459]
Contractors; Natl. Assn. of Cold Storage Insulation
[★1886]
Contractors; Natl. Assn. of Dredging [★2576]
Contractors Natl. Assn; Insulation Distributor
[★1048]
Contractors; Natl. Assn. of OEW [★1038]
Contractors; Natl. Assn. of Plumbing-Heating-Cooling
[★1059]
Contractors Natl. Assn; Sheet Metal [★1900]
Contractors' Natl. Assn; Sheet Metal and Air
Conditioning [1900]
Contractors; Natl. Assn. of Waterproofing and
Structural Repair [645]
Contractors Pump Bur. [2011], 6737 W Washington
St., Ste. 2400, Milwaukee, WI 53214-5647,
(414)272-0943
Contracts Administrators; Natl. Assn. of Professional
[★1744]
Contrarian Speakers and Writers; Amer. Soc. of
[5601]
A Contre-Courant [IO], Montreal, QC, Canada
Contribution Administrators; Natl. Assn. of Govt.
Defined [2340]
Control; Amer. Soc. for Measurement [★7220]
Control; Amer. Soc. for Quality [★7552]
Control Assn; Air Pollution [★5081]
Control Assn; Mind Development and [★7447]
Control, and Automation Assn; Measurement, [3485]
Control Coun; Calorie [1505]
Control Handguns; Natl. Coun. to [★17588]
Control and Info. Systems Integrators Assn. [3704],
640 Rice Blvd., Exton, PA 19341, (800)661-4914
Control League; Amer. Birth [★12187]
Control Prog. Directors; Conf. of Radiation [6241]
Control Surveys Division of the Amer. Cong. on
Surveying and Mapping [★7716]
Control Systems Soc; IEEE [6514]
Control Therapy, Reality Therapy, and Quality Mgt;
Inst. for [★16233]
Control of Violence and Extremism; Inst. for Preven-
tion and [★17146]
Controlled Circulations Audit [★93]
Controlled Circulations Audit [★IO]
Controlled Env. Testing Assn. [7790], 1500 Sunday
Dr., Ste. 102, Raleigh, NC 27607, (919)861-5576
Controlled Mech. Storage Systems [★2004]
Controlled Release Soc. [6678], 3340 Pilot Knob
Rd., St. Paul, MN 55121, (651)454-7250
Controlled Substances Authorities; Natl. Assn. of
State [5672]

Controllers Coun. [22], c/o Inst. of Mgt. of Ac-
countants, 10 Paragon Ave., Montvale, NJ 07645-
1718, (201)573-9000
Controllers and Financial Officers of Savings Institu-
tions; Natl. Soc. of [★1418]
Controllers Inst. of Am. [★1416]
Controllers Inst. of Am. [★IO]
Controllers Inst. Res. Found. [★1417]
Controllers; Natl. Assn. for Bank Auditors and
[★467]
Controllers; Professional Women [1446]
Controllers; Soc. of Savings and Loan [★1418]
Controllership Found. [★1417]
ControlNet Intl. [7729], 2370 E Stadium Blvd., No.
1005, Ann Arbor, MI 48104-4811, (734)922-0025
Controls Inst; Fluid [2018]
Conure Assn; Intl. [21848]
Convenience Caterers and Food Mfrs. Assn. [1938],
304 W Liberty St., Ste. 201, Louisville, KY 40202,
(502)583-3783
Convenience Store Advisory Gp; Natl. [3420]
Convenience Stores; Natl. Assn. of [3416]
Convenience Stores/Petroleum Companies; Natl.
Advisory Gp., [★3420]
Convenience Stores/Petroleum Marketers Assn;
Natl. Advisory Gp., [★3420]
Convenient Automotive Services Inst. - Defunct.
Convent General of the Knights York Cross of Ho-
nour - Address unknown since 1999.
Convention of Amer. Instructors of the Deaf
[★14750]
Convention Assn; Natl. [2688]
Convention Bur; German [24324]
Convention Bur; Japan [24341]
Convention Bur; Netherlands [★24359]
Convention Bureau/Tourist Bd; Curacao [24362]
Convention sur le Commerce Intl. des Especes de le
Faune et de Flore Sauvages Menacees
d'Extinction [★IO]
Convention Europeenne de la Constr. Metallique
[★IO]
Convention Indus. Coun. [3827], 1620 Eye St. NW,
Ste. 615, Washington, DC 20006, (202)429-8634
Convention on Intl. Trade in Endangered Species of
Wild Fauna and Flora [IO], Geneva, Switzerland
Convention on Intl. Trade in Endangered Species of
Wild Fauna and Flora [★IO]
Convention Liaison Coun. - Address unknown since
2003.
Convention Mgt. Assn; Professional [2689]
Convention Mgt; Intl. Inst. of [★2676]
Convention Managers Assn; Religious [★2690]
Convention of Natl. Societies of Elecl. Engineers of
Europe [★IO]
Convention of Natl. Societies of Elecl. Engineers of
Europe [IO], Brussels, Belgium
Convention Operations Mgt; Assn. for [2674]
Convention on the Rights of the Child [★11658]
Convention on the Rights of the Child [★IO]
Convention of Scottish Local Authorities [IO], Edin-
burgh, United Kingdom
Convention and Visitors Bur; Netherlands [★24359]
Convergencia Democratica en Uruguay - Defunct.
Conversations for the 21st Century - Sydney NSW
[IO], Drummoyne, Australia
Conversion Products Coun. Intl; Power [★1836]
Conversion Proj; Mid-Peninsula [★17423]
Convertible Registry; 1971 GTO and Judge [21559]
Convertible Roster; 1948-50 Packard [21553]
Converting Equip. Mfrs. Assn. [2012], 201 Springs
St., Fort Mill, SC 29715, (803)802-7820
Converting Technologies; NPES - The Assn. for Sup-
pliers of Printing, Publishing and [1782]
Conveyor Assn. [★2013]
Conveyor Equip. Mfrs. Assn. [2013], 6724 Lone Oak
Blvd., Naples, FL 34109, (239)514-3441
Conveyor and Material Preparation Equip. Mfrs;
Assn. of [★2013]
Conveyor Sect. of the Material Handling Inst. [2014],
8720 Red Oak Blvd., Ste. 201, Charlotte, NC
28217-3992, (704)676-1190
Convicts Assn. for a Good Environment - Defunct.
Convoy For Kids [IO], Park Orchards, Australia
Convoy of Hope [12847], 330 S Patterson Ave.,
Springfield, MO 65802, (417)823-8998

A star before a book entry number signifies that the name is not listed separately, but is mentioned within the entry.

Convulsive Therapy; Assn. for [15192]
Conway Twitty Fan Club - Defunct.
Cooder Brown Band Fan Club - Address unknown since 1989.
Cook Book Collectors Club of America - Defunct.
Cook Inlet Native Assn. - Defunct.
Cook Island Sports and Natl. Olympic Comm. [IO], Rarotonga, Cook Islands
Cook Islands Family Welfare Assn. [IO], Rarotonga, Cook Islands
Cook Islands Squash Racquets Assn. [IO], Rarotonga, Cook Islands
Cook Islands Touch Assn. [IO], Rarotonga, Cook Islands
Cook Soc; Frederick A. [11112]
Cookers Intl; Solar Box [★5100]
Cookery and Food Assn. [★IO]
Cookie Cutter Club [★22000]
Cookie Cutter Collectors Club [22000], PO Box 245, Cannon Falls, MN 55009
Cookie Jar Assn; Amer. [22577]
Cookie Manufacturers Assn; Peanut Butter Sandwich and [★1556]
Cookie and Snack Bakers Assn. - Address unknown since 2002.
Cooking
    Amer. Culinary Fed. [790]
    Amer. Inst. of Wine and Food [22568]
    Amer. Personal and Private Chef Assn. [791]
    Black Culinarian Alliance [1122]
    Chefs de Cuisine Assn. of Am. [792]
    Compassionate Cooks [13350]
    Confrerie de la Chaine des Rotisseurs, Bailliage des U.S.A. [22569]
    Cookie Cutter Collectors Club [22000]
    Cookware Mfrs. Assn. [1970]
    Griswold and Cast Iron Cookware Assn. [22588]
    Intl. Chili Soc. [22571]
    Intl. Connoisseurs of Green and Red Chile [22572]
    Kitchen Gardeners Intl. [9966]
    Soc. of German Cooks [IO]
    Solar Cookers Intl. [5100]
    Terlingua Intl. Chili Championship [22574]
    Vinegar Connoisseurs Intl. [22575]
Cooking Advancement Res. and Educ. Found. [★8174]
Cooking Advancement Res. and Educ. Found. [★IO]
Cooks and pastry cooks; National Apprenticeship Prog. for [★790]
Cooks and Stewards Union; Marine [★24132]
Cooksey Fan Club; Danny [24736]
Cookware Assn; Griswold and Cast Iron [22588]
Cookware Mfrs. Assn. [1970], PO Box 531335, Birmingham, AL 35253-1335, (205)823-3448
Cookware Mfrs. Assn; Metal [★1970]
Cool Roof Rating Coun. [615], 1738 Excelsior Ave., Oakland, CA 94602, (510)485-7175
Cooley Family Assn. of America - Address unknown since 2003.
Cooley's Anemia Blood and Res. Found. for Children [★14788]
Cooley's Anemia Found. [14788], 330 7th Ave., No. 900, New York, NY 10001, (800)522-7222
Coolidge Center for Environmental Leadership - Defunct.
Coolidge Memorial Found; Calvin [11107]
Cooling Assn; Intl. District Heating and [★1888]
Cooling Contractors Assn; Plumbing-Heating- [1059]
Cooling Contractors Assn; Natl. Assn. of Plumbing-Heating- [★1059]
Cooling Inst; Evaporative [1879]
Cooling; Natl. Solar Heating and [★6951]
Cooling Tech. Inst. [616], 2611 FM 1960 W, Ste. A-101, Houston, TX 77068-3730, (281)583-4087
Cooling Tower Inst. [★616]
Coolmine Rugby Football Club [IO], Ashbrook, Ireland
Cooltan Arts [IO], London, United Kingdom
Coon Hunters Assn; Amer. [23541]
Cooper Inst. [15962], 12330 Preston Rd., Dallas, TX 75230, (972)341-3200
Cooper Inst. [IO], Dallas, TX, United States
Cooper Inst. for Aerobics Res. [★IO]
Cooper Inst. for Aerobics Res. [★15962]

Cooper Ornithological Club [★7415]
Cooper Ornithological Club [★IO]
Cooper Ornithological Soc. [IO], Riverside, CA, United States
Cooper Ornithological Soc. [7415], c/o Eileen M. Kirsch, Sec., Upper Midwest Environmental Sciences Center, 2630 Fanta Reed Rd., La Crosse, WI 54603, (608)781-6226
Cooperage Indus. of Am; Assoc. [972]
Cooperation Centre for Sci. Res. Relative to Tobacco [IO], Paris, France
Cooperation Comm. for Folk Dance [IO], Stockholm, Sweden
Cooperation; Comm. on Institutional [8104]
Cooperation Coun; Intl. [★17916]
Cooperation for the Development of Emerging Countries [IO], Florence, Italy
Cooperation Fund; Instrument Technicians Labor-Mgt. [1021]
Cooperation Internationale pour le Developpement et la Solidarite [★IO]
Cooperation Internationale pour le Developpement et la Solidarite [★IO]
Cooperation Movement; Voluntary [16981]
Cooperation; North Amer. Students of [9190]
Cooperation Project - Address unknown since 1999.
Cooperativa Sociale Grado 16 [★IO]
Cooperativas Agrarias Federadas de Uruguay [IO], Montevideo, Uruguay
Cooperative Action for Congressional Trust [★1073]
Cooperative Alumni Assn. - Address unknown since 1999.
Cooperative for Amer. Remittances Everywhere [★12838]
Cooperative for Amer. Remittances Everywhere [★IO]
Cooperative Assistance Fund - Defunct.
Cooperative for Assistance and Relief Everywhere [★12838]
Cooperative for Assistance and Relief Everywhere [★IO]
Cooperative Assn; Dairymen's League [★4486]
Cooperative Assn; Indus. [★1249]
Cooperative Assn. of Professional Salespeople - Defunct.
Cooperative Assn. of Tractor Dealers [1070], Crescent Ctr., 6075 Poplar Ave., Ste. 125, Memphis, TN 38119, (901)333-8600
Cooperative Birth Center Network [★15580]
Cooperative Bur. for Teachers [★1263]
Cooperative Bus. Intl. [1071], 5898 Cleveland Ave., Columbus, OH 43231-6884, (614)839-2700
Cooperative Bus. Intl. [IO], Columbus, OH, United States
Cooperative; Cherry Central [4722]
Cooperative Club Intl. [★13063]
Cooperative Club Intl. [★IO]
Cooperative Coll. Registry - Defunct.
Cooperative Coll.-School Science Program - Defunct.
Cooperative Communicators Assn. - Address unknown since 1994.
Cooperative; Dairylea [4486]
Cooperative Development Intl; Agricultural [★4481]
Cooperative Dir. Assn. - Defunct.
Cooperative Education
    Assn. of Cooperative Educators [8156]
    Assn. of Cooperative Educators [IO]
    Canadian Assn. for Co-operative Educ. [IO]
    Cooperative Educ. and Internship Assn. [8157]
    Future Problem Solving Prog. Intl. [8158]
    Future Problem Solving Prog. Intl. [IO]
    Natl. Commn. for Cooperative Educ. [8159]
Cooperative Educ. Assn. [★8157]
Cooperative Educ. and Internship Assn. [8157], 16 Santa Ana Pl., Walnut Creek, CA 94598, (925)947-5581
Cooperative Extension
    Assn. for Intl. Agricultural and Extension Educ. [7934]
    Epsilon Sigma Phi [24436]
    Natl. Extension Assn. of Family and Consumer Sciences [5612]
Cooperative Extension System [★13483]
Cooperative Finance Assn. of America - Defunct.

Cooperative Finance Corp; Natl. Rural Utilities [1441]
Cooperative Food Distributors of Am. [★3421]
Cooperative Grocers' Info. Network [1072], PO Box 399, Arcata, CA 95518, (707)445-4849
Cooperative Hall of Fame [★1073]
Cooperative Housing; Found. for [★12309]
Cooperative Housing Found. [12309], 8601 Georgia Ave., Ste. 800, Silver Spring, MD 20910, (301)587-4700
Cooperative Info. Superhighway [IO], Geneva, Switzerland
Cooperative Intl. Pupil-to-Pupil Program - Address unknown since 2000.
Cooperative Learning
    Assn. of Cooperative Educators [8156]
Cooperative Lib. Agencies; Assn. of Specialized and [10340]
Cooperative Lib. Organizations; Assn. of [★10340]
Cooperative Living; New England Found. for [★18011]
Cooperative Milk Producers Fed; Natl. [★4489]
Cooperative/Mutual Insurance Societies; Americas Assn. of [2141]
Cooperative; Natl. Cable TV [781]
Cooperative; Natl. Native Amer. (Indian) [10750]
Cooperative Off. for Voluntary Organizations [18792], 199 W Town St., Norwich, CT 06360, (860)886-1986
Cooperative Org; North Amer. Student [★9190]
Cooperative Org; Sino-American [21405]
Cooperative Preservation of Architectural Records - Defunct.
Cooperative Program for Educational Opportunity - Address unknown since 1995.
Cooperative Publication Assn. - Address unknown since 1995.
Cooperative Res. Inst. - Defunct.
Cooperative Stud. of Intl. Sea-food Markets; Inst. for the [★1484]
Cooperative Stud. of Secondary School Standards [★8410]
Cooperative; Tomato Genetics [4765]
Cooperative Training and Res. Centre [IO], Kigali, Rwanda
Cooperative Union of Am; Farmers' Educational and [★4651]
Cooperative Union of Canada [★IO]
Cooperative Whole Grain Education Assn. - Address unknown since 1999.
Cooperative Work Experience Education Assn. - Address unknown since 2007.
Cooperatives
    ACDI/VOCA [4481]
    ACDI/VOCA [IO]
    Assn. of Cooperative Educators [8156]
    Bioplaneta Network, Mexico [IO]
    Canadian Co-operative Assn. [IO]
    Co-op Am. [1069]
    Cooperativas Agrarias Federadas de Uruguay [IO]
    Cooperative Assn. of Tractor Dealers [1070]
    Cooperative Bus. Intl. [1071]
    Cooperative Bus. Intl. [IO]
    Cooperative Grocers' Info. Network [1072]
    Cooperative Training and Res. Centre [IO]
    European Community of Consumer Cooperatives [IO]
    Farmland Indus. [4482]
    ICA Gender Equality Comm. [IO]
    Intl. Co-operative Alliance - Switzerland [IO]
    Intl. Raiffeisen Union [IO]
    Italian Cooperatives Assn. [IO]
    Japanese Consumers' Co-operative Union [IO]
    N.A.F. Intl. A.M.B.A. [IO]
    Natl. Cooperative Bus. Assn. [1073]
    Natl. Cooperative Grocers Assn. [1074]
    Natl. Coun. of Farmer Cooperatives [4483]
    Natl. Fed. of Agricultural Cooperative Associations [IO]
    Natl. Fed. of Agricultural Cooperators and Producers [IO]
    Natl. Fed. of Dairy Cooperatives [IO]
    Oxfam World Shops [IO]
    Savings and Credit Co-operative League of South Africa [IO]

Reference to "IO" in place of a book number signifies that the association may be found in the 45th edition of International Organizations.

Scottish Agricultural Org. Soc. [IO]
Tanzania Fed. of Cooperatives [IO]
Universal Cooperatives [4484]
Cooperatives; Fed. of Southern [★12937]
Cooperatives Land Assistance Fund; Fed. of
  Southern [12937]
Cooperatives; Natl. [★4484]
Cooperatives; Natl. Fed. of Grain [★4483]
Cooperatives; Natl. Soc. of Accountants for [49]
Cooperatives; United [★4484]
Cooperazione Internazionale - Italia [IO], Milan, Italy
Cooperazione Padania-Mondo [IO], Rome, Italy
Cooperazione per lo Sviluppo dei Paesi Emergenti
  [★IO]
Coopers Appreciation - Address unknown since
  1989.
Coopers' Company [IO], London, United Kingdom
Coopers' Intl. Union of North America - Defunct.
Coordenadora Agricola Europeia [★IO]
Coordinadora Nacional de Organizaciones Cafetal-
  eras [★IO]
Coordinadora de ONGD Para el Desarollo Espana
  [★IO]
Coordinated Hungarian Relief - Defunct.
Coordinating Bd. of Jewish Organizations [★20124]
Coordinating Bd. of Jewish Organizations [★IO]
Coordinating Comm. of Agriculture, Commercial,
  Indus. and Financial Associations [IO], Guatemala
  City, Guatemala
Coordinating Comm. for Ellis Island - Defunct.
Coordinating Comm. of Guide Dog Users [★16850]
Coordinating Comm. of Hungarian Orgs. in North
  America - Defunct.
Coordinating Comm. on Women in the Historical
  Profession/Conference Gp. on Women's History
  [★17526]
Coordinating Coun. for Handicapped Children
  [★8202]
Coordinating Coun. on Manufactured Housing
  Finance - Defunct.
Coordinating Coun. of Natl. Archaeological Societies
  - Defunct.
Coordinating Coun. of Natl. Court Organizations -
  Defunct.
Coordinating Coun. for Women in History [17526],
  c/o Jennifer R. Scanlon, Exec. Dir., Bowdoin Col-
  lege, Women's Studies Program, 7100 College
  Sta., Brunswick, ME 04011-8471, (207)725-3882
Coordinating Org. of Book Assns. - Defunct.
Coordinating Res. Coun. [2921], 3650 Mansell Rd.,
  Ste. 140, Alpharetta, GA 30022, (678)795-0506
Coordination Commn. for the Textile Indus. [★IO]
Coordination in Development - Defunct.
Coordination of Univ. Religious Affairs; Assn. for the
  [★9168]
Cootie; Supreme Pup Tent, Military Order of the
  [21323]
Copeland/Sewell Family Org. - Defunct.
Copier Dealers Assn. [2845], c/o Jeff Elkin, Dir., PO
  Box 627, Cockeysville, MD 21030-0627, (954)917-
  5510
Copper Assn; U.S. [★7309]
Copper and Brass Fabricators Coun. [2704], 1050
  17th St. NW, Ste. 440, Washington, DC 20036,
  (202)833-8575
Copper and Brass Fabricators Foreign Trade Assn.
  [★2704]
Copper and Brass Res. Assn. [★2750]
Copper and Brass Servicenter Assn. [2705], 994 Old
  Eagle School Rd., Ste. 1019, Wayne, PA 19087-
  1802, (610)971-4850
Copper Coun; Amer. [2694]
Copper Coun; Intl. Wrought [IO]
Copper Development Assn. [IO], Hemel Hempstead,
  United Kingdom
Copper Development Assn. [2750], 260 Madison
  Ave., New York, NY 10016, (212)251-7200
Copper Development Assn. - United Kingdom [IO],
  Hemel Hempstead, United Kingdom
Copper Inst. [★7309]
Copper Inst; European [IO]
Copper Plate Engravers; Natl. Assn. of Steel and
  [★3680]
Copper Poisoning
  Natl. Center for the Study of Wilson's Disease
  [15251]

Wilson's Disease Assn. Intl. [15260]
Copper Products Development Assn. [★7315]
Copper Products Development Assn. [★IO]
Copper Res. Assn; Intl. [★7315]
Copper Trade Assn. - Defunct.
Coppers; Early Amer. [22737]
Copred Consortium: Peace Res. and Educational
  Development [★18233]
Cops for Christ; Intl. [19808]
Cops for Life; Natl. [18558]
Coptic
  Amer. Coptic Assn. [19018]
Coptic Archaeology (North Am.); Soc. for [10153]
Coptic Assn; Amer. [19018]
Coptic Orphans [★11589]
Coptic Orphans [★IO]
Coptic Orphans Support Assn. [IO], Merrifield, VA,
  United States
Coptic Orphans Support Assn. [11589], PO Box
  2881, Merrifield, VA 22116, (703)641-8910
Copts Assn; U.S. [10192]
Copy-Dan [IO], Copenhagen, Denmark
Copy Editors Soc; Amer. [3080]
Copy Res. Coun. - Address unknown since 1995.
COPYGHANA [IO], Accra, Ghana
Copyright
  Advt. Club of New York [77]
  Creative Commons [5613]
  Fed. Against Copyright Theft [IO]
  Future of Music Coalition [10598]
  Intl. Fed. of Reproduction Rights Org. [IO]
  Natl. Assn. of Artists and Crafters [301]
  Natl. Assn. of Patent Practitioners [6167]
  Nordisk Copyright Bur. [IO]
Copyright Agency Limited [IO], Sydney, Australia
Copyright Bureau; Trademark and [★3802]
Copyright Clearance Center [5842], 222 Rosewood
  Dr., Danvers, MA 01923, (978)750-8400
Copyright Coun; Australian [IO]
Copyright Coun; British [IO]
Copyright Info. and Anti-piracy Centre [IO], Helsinki,
  Finland
Copyright Licensing and Admin. Soc. of Singapore
  [IO], Singapore, Singapore
Copyright Licensing Agency [IO], London, United
  Kingdom
Copyright Licensing Limited [IO], Auckland, New
  Zealand
Copyright Protection Soc; Mechanical- [IO]
Copyright Soc; Los Angeles [5854]
Copyright Soc. of the U.S.A. [5843], 352 7th Ave.,
  Ste. 739, New York, NY 10001, (212)354-6401
Copywriter's Coun. of Am. [875], CCA Bldg., PO Box
  102, Middle Island, NY 11953-0102, (631)924-8555
CORAL [IO], Oaxaca, Mexico
Coral Reef Alliance; Global [4403]
Corben Club [21440], PO Box 127, Blakesburg, IA
  52536, (641)938-2773
Corbin Res. [20869]
Cord-Duesenberg Club; Auburn- [21582]
Cordage
  Cordage Inst. [1075]
  European Assn. for the Trade in Jute and Related
    Products [IO]
  Fed. of European Rope, Twine and Netting Indus.
    [IO]
  Gold and Silver Wyre Drawers' Company [IO]
  Taiwan Elec. Wire and Cable Indus'. Assn. [IO]
Cordage Inst. [1075], 994 Old Eagle School Rd.,
  Ste. 1019, Wayne, PA 19087, (610)971-4854
Cordage and Netting Manufacturers; Amer. [★1075]
Cordaid [IO], The Hague, Netherlands
Cordell Hull Found. for Intl. Educ. [IO], New York,
  NY, United States
Cordell Hull Found. for Intl. Educ. [8656], 501 5th
  Ave., 3rd Fl., New York, NY 10017, (212)300-2138
Corduroy Coun. of America - Defunct.
Cordwainers' Company [IO], London, United
  Kingdom
CORE [IO], London, United Kingdom
Core Mfg. Credit Assn; Natl. Radiator [★1422]
COREL WTA Tour [★23910]
COREL WTA Tour [★IO]
CoreNet Global [IO], Atlanta, GA, United States
CoreNet Global [3305], 260 Peachtree St., Ste.
  1500, Atlanta, GA 30303-1237, (404)589-3200

Corgi Club of Am; Cardigan Welsh [22240]
Corgi Club of Am; Pembroke Welsh [22340]
CorgiAid [22251], c/o Joyce Trittipo, Treas., 4038
  Cherokee Dr., Madison, WI 53711
Cork Indus. Fed. [IO], Sidcup, United Kingdom
Cork Inst. of Am. [1644], c/o Dodge Regupol, Inc.,
  715 Fountain Ave., Lancaster, PA 17601, (717)295-
  3400
Cork Operative Butchers Soc. [★IO]
Cork Quality Coun. [1645], 1160 Terrace Dr.,
  Forestville, CA 95436, (707)824-5831
Corkscrew Collectors Club; Canadian [21985]
Cormac McCarthy Soc. [11168], 13850 SW 100th
  Ave., Miami, FL 33176
Cormo Sheep Assn; Amer. [5179]
Corn; Amer. Mfrs. Assn. of Products From [★1508]
Corn Growers Assn; Natl. [4310]
Corn Indus. Res. Found. [★1508]
Corn Island Storytelling Festival [★10979]
Corn Island Storytelling Festival [★IO]
Corn Items Collectors Assn. [22001]
Corn Meal Prog; Self-Rising Flour and [★1520]
Corn Products Mfrs; Assoc. [★1508]
Corn Refiners Assn. [1508], 1701 Pennsylvania
  Ave., Ste. 950, Washington, DC 20006, (202)331-
  1634
Cornea and Contact Lens Soc. of New Zealand [IO],
  Hamilton, New Zealand
Cornea Res. Found. of Am. [15105], 9002 N Merid-
  ian St., Ste. 212, Indianapolis, IN 46260, (317)814-
  2993
Cornelia de Lange Parents Gp. [★13754]
Cornelia de Lange Syndrome Found. [13754], 302
  W Main St., No. 100, Avon, CT 06001, (860)676-
  8166
Cornell Feline Hea. Center [16791], Coll. of
  Veterinary Medicine, Cornell Univ., Box 13, Ithaca,
  NY 14853-6401, (607)253-3414
Cornell Lab. of Ornithology [7416], 159 Sapsucker
  Woods Rd., Ithaca, NY 14850, (607)254-2473
Cornell Univ. Lab. of Ornithology [★7416]
Cornerstone Found. [IO], San Ignacio, Belize
Cornhusker Country Music Club [★10670]
Cornish Amer. Heritage Soc. [9759], c/o Jim
  Thomas, Treas., 8494 Wesley Dr., Flushing, MI
  48433-1165
Cornish Rex Soc. [21905], c/o Phyllis Jacobowitz,
  Ed., 57 Pires Dr., Oakdale, CT 06370
Cornwall Archaeological Soc. [IO], Helston, United
  Kingdom
Coro [18439], c/o Manatt Phelps, 700 12th St. NW,
  Ste. 1100, Washington, DC 20005-4075
Coro Found. [★18439]
Corona Worldwide [IO], London, United Kingdom
Coronado 15 Assn. [★23164]
Coronado 15 Class Racing Assn. [★23164]
Coronado 15 Natl. Assn. [23164], c/o Sue Fishman,
  Sec.-Treas., 547 Garden St., Sacramento, CA
  95815, (916)359-1442
Coronary Artery Disease Res. Assn. [IO], London,
  United Kingdom
Coronary Club - Address unknown since 2003.
Coronelli-Weltbund der Globusfreunde [★IO]
Corporacion Chilena de la Madera [★IO]
Corporacion Chilena de Prevencion del SIDA [IO],
  Santiago, Chile
Corporacion Chilena contra el SIDA [★IO]
Corporacion de Exportadores de El Salvador [★IO]
Corporal Punishment and Alternatives; Natl. Center
  for the Stud. of [8206]
Corporal Punishment in Schools; Natl. Coalition to
  Abolish [8207]
Corporate Accountability Intl. [18149], 46 Plympton
  St., Boston, MA 02118, (617)695-2525
Corporate Accountability Intl. [IO], Boston, MA,
  United States
Corporate Action Project - Defunct.
Corporate Alliance to End Partner Violence [12025],
  2416 E Washington St., Ste. E, Bloomington, IL
  61704, (309)664-0667
Corporate Angel Network [13817], Westchester
  County Airport, One Loop Rd., White Plains, NY
  10604-1215, (914)328-1313
Corporate Cash Mgt. Assn; Natl. [★1403]
Corporate Comm. of Telecommunications Users -
  Address unknown since 1999.

A star before a book entry number signifies that the name is not listed separately, but is mentioned within the entry.

Corporate Communicators Canada [★879]
Corporate Communicators Canada [★IO]
Corporate Computing Tech. Professionals; Assn. for [★6799]
Corporate Coun. on Africa [169], 1100 17th St. NW, Ste. 1100, Washington, DC 20036, (202)835-1115
Corporate Coun. on Africa [IO], Washington, DC, United States
Corporate Coun. for the Liberal Arts - Defunct.
Corporate Counsel; Fed. of Defense and [5827]
Corporate Counsel; Fed. of Insurance and [★5827]
Corporate Counsel Foundation; Federation of Defense and [★5827]
Corporate Data Exchange - Defunct.
Corporate Directors; Natl. Assn. of [2504]
Corporate Economics
    Amer. Coun. for Capital Formation [17347]
    Conf. of Bus. Economists [6878]
    Private Sector Coun. [17348]
    Rebuild Am. [17349]
    Small Bus. Coun. of Am. [17350]
Corporate Event Marketing Assn. [2621], 1512 Weiskopf Loop, Round Rock, TX 78664, (512)310-8330
Corporate and Found. Relations [12075], Univ. of Colorado Found., 4740 Walnut St., PO Box 1140, Boulder, CO 80301, (303)735-9818
Corporate Growth; Assn. for [699]
Corporate Growth and Diversification; Assn. for [★699]
Corporate Info. Center [★17353]
Corporate Law
    Assn. of Corporate Counsel [5614]
    Minority Corporate Counsel Assn. [5615]
Corporate Leadership Program; National [★12205]
Corporate Matching Gift Info; Natl. CH for [★12199]
Corporate Ombudsman Assn. [★736]
Corporate Orientation Program [★8047]
Corporate Philanthropy; Comm. to Encourage [12714]
Corporate Philanthropy; Women and Foundations/ [★17575]
Corporate and Professional Recruiters; Natl. Assn. of [★1265]
Corporate and Professional Recruitment; Intl. Assn. of [1265]
Corporate and Professional Resources; Intl. Assn. of [★1265]
Corporate Real Estate Advisors - Defunct.
Corporate Real Estate; Intl. Assn. of Attorneys and Executives in [3314]
Corporate Responsibility
    Alliance for Sustainable Jobs and the Env. [24053]
    As You Sow Found. [11812]
    Asian Corporate Governance Assn. [IO]
    Assn. of Americans for Civic Responsibility [17074]
    Australian Coun. of Superannuation Investors [IO]
    Comm. to Encourage Corporate Philanthropy [12714]
    Commonwealth Assn. for Corporate Governance [IO]
    Fund for Stockowners Rights [17351]
    Hispanic Assn. on Corporate Responsibility [17352]
    Interfaith Center on Corporate Responsibility [17353]
    Public Affairs Coun. [17354]
    Soc. for Corporate Environmental and Social Responsibility [IO]
Corporate Secretaries; Amer. Soc. of [★75]
Corporate Secretaries and Governance Professionals; Soc. of [75]
Corporate Theatre Fund [★11027]
Corporate Theatre Fund; Natl. [11027]
Corporate Transfer Agents Assn. - Address unknown since 2002.
Corporate Travel Executives; Assn. of [3909]
Corporate Treasurers; Natl. Assn. of [1435]
Corp. Aircraft Owners Assn. [★162]
Corp. for the Celebration of Jack Kerouac in Lowell [★9683]
Corp. des associations de detaillants d'automobiles [★IO]

Corp. for Enterprise Development [17457], 777 N Capitol St. NE, Ste. 800, Washington, DC 20002, (202)408-9788
Corp. for Maintaining Editorial Diversity in America - Address unknown since 1999.
Corporation for Menke's Disease - Address unknown since 2006.
Corporation for Natl. Service [★11693]
Corp. for Open Systems - Address unknown since 1994.
Corp. for Open Systems Intl. - Address unknown since 2003.
Corp. for Public Broadcasting [9762], 401 9th St. NW, Washington, DC 20004-2129, (202)879-9600
Corp. Schools; Natl. Assn. of [★2481]
Corporeal Tech; Amer. Soc. of Extra- [15129]
Corps Brandenburgia - Address unknown since 2003.
Corps Canadien des Commissionaires [★IO]
Corps of Drums Soc. [IO], Maidstone, United Kingdom
CORPUS [★19619]
Corpus Callosum; Natl. Org. for Disorders of the [15350]
Corpus Instrumentorium - Defunct.
CORPUS - Natl. Assn. for an Inclusive Priesthood [19619], 114 Sunset Dr., Raynham, MA 02767-1383, (508)822-6710
CORPUS - Natl. Assn. for a Married Priesthood [★19619]
CorpWatch [17756], 1611 Telegraph Ave., No. 702, Oakland, CA 94612, (510)271-8080
CorpWatch [IO], Oakland, CA, United States
Corrado Club of Am. [21621], PO Box 29, Bala Cynwyd, PA 19004-0029
Correctional
    All of Us or None [17081]
    Amer. Assn. for Correctional and Forensic Psychology [11853]
    Amer. Assn. of Mental Hea. Professionals in Corrections [15186]
    Amer. Correctional Assn. [11854]
    Amer. Correctional Hea. Services Assn. [14715]
    Amer. Criminal Justice Assn. (Lambda Alpha Epsilon) [11855]
    Amer. Jail Assn. [11856]
    Assn. of Correctional Food Ser. Affiliates [1577]
    Assn. on Programs for Female Offenders [11857]
    Assn. of State Correctional Administrators [11858]
    Australasian Corrections Educ. Assn. [IO]
    Center for Stud. in Criminal Justice [11859]
    Christian Chaplain Sers. [19745]
    Correctional Educ. Assn. [11862]
    Corrections Tech. Assn. [1076]
    European Prison Educ. Assn. [IO]
    Fortune Soc. [11867]
    Friends Outside [11868]
    Intl. Assn. of Correctional Officers [11870]
    Intl. Assn. of Correctional Training Personnel [11871]
    Intl. Assn. of Reentry [17355]
    Intl. Community Corrections Assn. [11872]
    Intl. Corrections and Prisons Assn. [IO]
    John Howard Assn. [11874]
    Justice Res. and Statistics Assn. [11876]
    Natl. Alliance of Police, Security and Corrections Organizations [24165]
    Natl. Alliance of Sentencing Advocates and Mitigation Specialists [5645]
    Natl. Assn. of Field Training Officers [5987]
    Natl. Assn. of State Sentencing Commissions [5650]
    Natl. Center on Institutions and Alternatives [11878]
    Natl. Center for Juvenile Justice [11879]
    Natl. Commn. on Correctional Hea. Care [14729]
    Natl. Correctional Indus. Assn. [11880]
    Natl. Coun. on Crime and Delinquency [11843]
    Natl. Criminal Justice Assn. [11881]
    Natl. Juvenile Detention Assn. [11882]
    Natl. Prison Proj. of the ACLU [11883]
    North Amer. Assn. of Wardens and Superintendents [11884]
    November Coalition [18690]
    Osborne Assn. [11885]

    Prison Fellowship Intl. [11887]
    Prison Fellowship Ministries [11888]
    Prison Ministry of Yokefellow's Intl. [11889]
    Prisoners' Rights Union [11890]
    Safer Soc. Found. [11891]
    Soc. of Correctional Physicians [16011]
    Vocational Found., Inc. [12103]
    Volunteers in Prevention, Probation, Prisons [11896]
    We Care Prog. [11897]
    Women's Prison Assn. [11898]
Correctional Administrators Assn. of Am. [★11858]
Correctional Administrators; Assn. of State [11858]
Correctional Assn; Amer. [11854]
Correctional Assn; Women's [★11857]
Correctional Chaplains Assn; Amer. [19742]
Correctional Chaplains Assn; Amer. Catholic [19741]
Correctional Educ. Assn. [11862], 8182 Lake Brown Rd., Ste. 202, Elkridge, MD 21075, (443)459-3080
Correctional Facilities Assn. - Defunct.
Correctional Facility Officers; Amer. Assn. of [★11870]
Correctional and Forensic Psychology; Amer. Assn. for [11853]
Correctional Hea. Care; Natl. Commn. on [14729]
Correctional Hea. Services Assn; Amer. [14715]
Correctional Indus. Assn; Natl. [11880]
Correctional Justice; Center for [★5451]
Correctional Officers; Amer. Assn. of [★11870]
Correctional Psychologists; Amer. Assn. of [★11853]
Correctional Reunion Assn; Islamic [20105]
Correctional Training Personnel; Intl. Assn. of [11871]
Corrections; Amer. Assn. of Mental Hea. Professionals in [15186]
Corrections Tech. Assn. [1076], c/o Paul Lewin, Pres., Colorado Dept. of Corrections, 2862 S Circle Dr., Ste. 407, Colorado Springs, CO 80906, (719)226-4811
Corrective Surgery Soc; Children's [16580]
Corrective Therapy Assn; Amer. [★16311]
Corregidor; Amer. Defenders of Bataan and [21386]
Correspondence
    All Ser. Postal Chess Club [21941]
    Amity Alliances/Amity Intl. [IO]
    Assn. of British Introduction Agencies [IO]
    Correspondence Chess League of Am. [21946]
    Cover Collectors Circuit Club [22812]
    CUSA: An Apostolate of the Sick and Disabled [19620]
    Disabled Collectors' Correspondence Club [22814]
    FIOCES [IO]
    Friends' Hea. Connection [22136]
    Golden Threads [22137]
    Golden Threads [IO]
    Intl. Correspondence of Corkscrew Addicts [22052]
    Intl. Pen Friend Ser. [IO]
    Intl. Pen Friends [IO]
    Intl. Pen Friends [22138]
    Intl. Pen Friends - Australia [IO]
    Intl. Penpal Club [IO]
    Mail for Me Club [11621]
    The Mailbox Club [19525]
    Natl. Postal Arts Assn. [22139]
    New Dawn [22140]
    Prison Pen Pals [22141]
    Single Booklovers [22142]
    Singles in Agriculture [22143]
    Student Letter Exchange [22144]
    Unmarried-Catholics Correspondence Club [22145]
    Wishing Well [22146]
    Wishing Well [IO]
    Worldwide Friendship Intl. [IO]
    Worldwide Friendship Intl. [22147]
Correspondence Chess League of Am. [21946], 15 Crossbrook Pl., Livingston, NJ 07039-3710
Correspondence Club; Disabled Collectors' [22814]
Correspondence Club; Great Britain [★22032]
Correspondence Inst; Intl. [★19802]
Correspondent Comm. - Defunct.
Correspondents Assn; Radio [★580]
Correspondents Assn; Radio-Television [580]

Reference to "IO" in place of a book number signifies that the association may be found in the 45th edition of International Organizations.

Correspondents Assn; U.S. Marine Corps Combat [3171]
Correspondents' Assn; White House [3173]
Corresponding Surveyors to the Yacht Safety Bur. [★7275]
Corriedale Assn; Amer. [5180]
Corriente Assn; North Amer. [4278]

Corrosion
Australasian Corrosion Assn. [IO]
Belgian Center for Corrosion Stud. [IO]
European Comm. for the Stud. of Corrosion and Protection of Pipes [IO]
European Fed. of Corrosion [IO]
Intl. Corrosion Coun. [IO]
NACE Intl.: The Corrosion Soc. [7027]
Natl. Assn. of Corrosion Engineers [6840]
Corrosion Engineers; Natl. Assn. of [★7027]
Corrosion Inhibitors Assn; Concrete [922]
Corrosion Prevention Assn. [IO], Aldershot, United Kingdom
Corrosion Soc; NACE Intl.: The [7027]
Corrugated Bd. Manufacturers Assn. [IO], Istanbul, Turkey
Corrugated Container Inst. - Defunct.
Corrugated Metal Pipe Assn. [★3035]
Corrugated Packaging Assn. [★IO]
Corrugated Packaging Coun. [2874], 25 Northwest Point Blvd., Ste. 510, Elk Grove Village, IL 60007, (847)364-9600
Corrugated Polyethylene Pipe Assn. [3049], c/o Plastics Pipe Inst., 1825 Connecticut Ave. NW, Ste. 680, Washington, DC 20009, (202)462-9607
Corrugated Polyethylene Pipe Association [IO], Washington, DC, United States
Corrugated Sector of the Confed. of Paper Indus. [IO], Swindon, United Kingdom
Corrugated Steel Pipe Assn; Natl. [3035]
Corset and Brassiere Assn. of Am. [★221]
Corset and Brassiere Coun. - Defunct.
Corset and Brassiere Mfrs; Associated [227]
Corset and Brassiere Women's Club [★258]
CORSO [IO], Dunedin, New Zealand
Corson/Colson Family History Assn. [20870], c/o Mrs. Iverne Corson Rinehart, VP/Ed., 2300 Cedarfield Pkwy., No. 476, Richmond, VA 23233, (804)747-8180
Corvair Model Group - Defunct.
Corvair Soc. of Am. [21622], PO Box 607, Lemont, IL 60439-0607, (630)257-6530
Corvette Club of Am. [21623], PO Box 9879, Bowling Green, KY 42102-9879, (866)482-1191
Corvette Club; Solid Axle [21786]
Corvette Clubs; Natl. Coun. of [21730]
Corvette Clubs; United Coun. of [21803]
Corvette Owners Assn; Natl. [21728]
Corvette Pace Car Registry; 1995 [21560]
Corvette Restorers Soc; Natl. [21729]
CORVUS Natl. Educational End-Users Group - Defunct.
COSA [★13072]
COSA [★IO]
COSA; Intl. Ser. Org. - [13072]
Cosanti Found; Arcosanti, A Proj. of the [4497]
COSMEP, the Intl. Assn. of Independent Publishers - Defunct.
Cosmetic Career Women [★1842]
Cosmetic Chemists; Soc. of [6695]
Cosmetic Dentistry; Amer. Acad. of [14093]
Cosmetic and Detergent Indus. Assn. - Germany [★IO]
Cosmetic Executive Women [1842], 286 Madison Ave., 19th Fl., New York, NY 10017, (212)685-5955
Cosmetic Indus. Associates; Foragers [1846]
Cosmetic Indus. Buyers and Suppliers [1843], c/o Elizabeth Mount, Treas., 17 Ridgedale Rd., Scarsdale, NY 10583, (212)319-6130
Cosmetic Ingredient Rev. [1844], 1101 17th St. NW, Ste. 412, Washington, DC 20036-4702, (202)331-0651
Cosmetic Mfrs. Assn. [IO], Bangkok, Thailand
Cosmetic Manufacturers and Distributors; Independent [1847]
Cosmetic and Perfumery Assn. of Hong Kong [IO], Hong Kong, People's Republic of China

Cosmetic Professionals; Soc. of Permanent [1087]
Cosmetic Surgeon; Amer. Soc. of [★14037]
Cosmetic Surgeons; Amer. Assn. of [★14037]

Cosmetic Surgery
Amer. Acad. of Cosmetic Surgery [14037]
Amer. Acad. of Facial Plastic and Reconstructive Surgery [14038]
Amer. Acad. of Micropigmentation [14039]
Amer. Assn. of Plastic Surgeons [14040]
Amer. Bd. of Facial Plastic and Reconstructive Surgery [16562]
Amer. Bd. of Plastic Surgery [14041]
Amer. Soc. for Aesthetic Plastic Surgery [14042]
Amer. Soc. of Hair Restoration Surgery [14520]
Amer. Soc. of Lipo-Suction Surgery [16572]
Amer. Soc. of Ophthalmic Plastic and Reconstructive Surgery [14043]
Amer. Soc. of Plastic Surgeons [14044]
Amer. Soc. of Plastic Surgeons and Plastic Surgery Educ. Found. [14045]
Amer. Soc. of Plastic Surgical Nurses [15461]
Assn. of Academic Chairmen of Plastic Surgery [14046]
Balkan Acad. of Cosmetic Surgery [IO]
British Assn. of Aesthetic Plastic Surgeons [IO]
British Assn. of Plastic, Reconstructive and Aesthetic Surgeons [IO]
Canadian Acad. of Facial, Plastic and Reconstructive Surgery [IO]
Canadian Soc. for Aesthetic (Cosmetic) Plastic Surgery [IO]
Children's Craniofacial Assn. [14057]
European Acad. of Facial Plastic Surgery [IO]
European Assn. of Plastic Surgeons [IO]
European Soc. of Ophthalmic Plastic and Reconstructive Surgery [IO]
Intl. Acad. of Cosmetic Surgery [IO]
Intl. Confed. for Plastic, Reconstructive and Aesthetic Surgery [IO]
Intl. Confed. for Plastic, Reconstructive and Aesthetic Surgery [14047]
Intl. Confed. for Plastic Reconstructive and Aesthetic Surgery Asia-Pacific Sect. [IO]
Intl. Soc. of Cosmetic and Laser Surgeons [IO]
Intl. Soc. of Cosmetic and Laser Surgeons [14048]
Interplast [14049]
Interplast [IO]
New Zealand Assn. of Plastic Surgeons [IO]
Plastic Surgery Administrative Assn. [14050]
Plastic Surgery Educational Found. [14051]
Plastic Surgery Res. Coun. [14052]
Plastic Surgery Research Council [IO]
Cosmetic, Toiletry and Fragrance Assn. [1845], 1101 17th St. NW, Ste. 300, Washington, DC 20036-4702, (202)331-1770
Cosmetic, Toiletry and Fragrance Assn. - New Zealand [IO], Auckland, New Zealand
Cosmetic, Toiletry, and Perfumery Assn. - England [IO], London, United Kingdom

Cosmetics
Amer. Acad. of Micropigmentation [14039]
Amer. Hea. and Beauty Aids Inst. [1841]
Assn. of Cosmetics and Perfume Mfrs., Importers and Distributors [IO]
Assn. of Danish Cosmetics, Toiletries, Soap and Detergent Indus. [IO]
China Toothpaste Indus. Assn. [IO]
Cosmetic Executive Women [1842]
Cosmetic Indus. Buyers and Suppliers [1843]
Cosmetic Mfrs. Assn. [IO]
Cosmetic and Perfumery Assn. of Hong Kong [IO]
Cosmetic, Toiletry and Fragrance Assn. [1845]
Cosmetic, Toiletry and Fragrance Assn. - New Zealand [IO]
Dutch Gen. Alliance of Beauty Parlours [IO]
Foragers Cosmetic Indus. Associates [1846]
Independent Cosmetic Manufacturers and Distributors [1847]
NAGMR [2541]
Natl. Beauty Culturists' League [1084]
Natl. Chamber of the Perfume and Cosmetics, Toiletries and Hygiene Prdt. [IO]
Natl. Fed. of Italian Perfume Retailers [IO]
Professional Beauty Assn. [1086]

Soc. of Cosmetic Chemists [6695]
Spanish Soc. of Cosmetic Chemists [IO]
Swedish Cosmetic, Toiletry and Household Products Suppliers' Assn. [IO]
Swiss Cosmetic and Detergent Assn. [IO]
World Intl. Nail and Beauty Assn. [1088]
Cosmetologists Assn; Natl. Hairdressers and [★1085]

Cosmetology
Aesthetics Intl. Assn. [1077]
Aesthetics Intl. Assn. [IO]
Amer. Acad. of Micropigmentation [14039]
Amer. Assn. of Cosmetology Schools/Cosmetology Educators of Am. [8160]
Assn. of Cosmetologists and Hairdressers [1078]
Barbers Company [IO]
Brazilian Cosmetology Assn. [IO]
British Assn. of Beauty Therapy and Cosmetology [IO]
British Assn. of Cosmetic Doctors [IO]
Dutch Cosmetics Assn. [IO]
Fairs and Salons of France [IO]
Hair Intl./Associated Master Barbers and Beauticians of America [1079]
Hairdressing Coun. [IO]
Intercoiffure Am. [1080]
Intl. Chain Salon Assn. [1081]
Intl. Chain Salon Assn. [IO]
Intl. Fed. of Aestheticians [IO]
Intl. Fed. of Societies of Cosmetic Chemists [IO]
Malaysian Cosmetics and Toiletries Indus. Gp. [IO]
Nail Mfrs. Coun. [1082]
Natl. Accrediting Commn. of Cosmetology Arts and Sciences [7877]
Natl. Assn. of Barber Boards of Am. [1083]
Natl. Beauty Culturists' League [1084]
Natl. Cosmetology Assn. [1085]
Natl. Fed. of French Hairdressers [IO]
Natl. Hairdressers' Fed. [IO]
Natl. - Interstate Coun. of State Boards of Cosmetology [5616]
Professional Beauty Assn. [1086]
Soc. of Cosmetic Chemists of South Africa [IO]
Soc. of Cosmetic Scientists [IO]
Soc. of Cosmetic Scientists (Singapore) [IO]
Soc. of Permanent Cosmetic Professionals [1087]
World Intl. Nail and Beauty Assn. [1088]
World Intl. Nail and Beauty Assn. [IO]
Cosmetology Accrediting Commn. [★7877]
Cosmetology Arts and Sciences; Natl. Accrediting Commn. of [7877]
Cosmetology Assn; Natl. [1085]
Cosmetology Educ; Accrediting Commn. for [★7877]
Cosmetology Educators of Am; Amer. Assn. of Cosmetology Schools/ [8160]
Cosmetology; Interstate Coun. of State Boards of [★5616]
Cosmetology; National Inst. of [★1084]
Cosmetology Schools; Natl. Accrediting Commn. for [★7877]
Cosmetology Schools; Teachers' Division of Natl. Assn. of [★8160]
Cosmetology Schools; Teachers' Educational Coun. - Natl. Assn. of [★8160]
Cosmetology Schools; Teachers' Educational Coun. - Natl. Assn. of Accredited [★8160]
Cosmic Baseball Assn. [23108], c/o Jour. of the Cosmic Baseball Assn., 907 6th St. SW, Ste. 214, Washington, DC 20024
Cosmic Corps of Engineers - Address unknown since 2001.
Cosmic Res; Natl. Coun. for Geo [6841]

Cosmology
Alexandria Soc. and Educal. Found. [8161]
Natl. Coun. for GeoCosmic Res. [6841]
Urantia Found. [20587]
Cosmopolitan Associates - Address unknown since 2004.
Cosmopolitan Clubs; Intl. Fed. of [★13039]
Cosmopolitan Intl. [13039], 7341 W 80th St., PO Box 4588, Overland Park, KS 66204, (913)648-4330
Cosmopolitan Intl. [IO], Overland Park, KS, United States

A star before a book entry number signifies that the name is not listed separately, but is mentioned within the entry.

Cosmopolitan Soccer League **[23775]**, 115 River Rd., Ste. 1029, Edgewater, NJ 07020, (201)943-3390

Cossack
  New Kuban Educ. and Welfare Assn. **[19019]**
Cossack-Amer. Citizens' Comm. - Address unknown since 1990.
Cossack Assn. New Kuban; All **[★19019]**
Cossack Natl. Press Assn. - Defunct.
Cost Accountants; Natl. Assn. of **[★34]**
Cost Anal; Inst. of **[★1448]**
Cost Engineers; Amer. Assn. of **[★6842]**
Cost Estimating and Anal; Soc. of **[1448]**
Cost Estimation
  AACE Intl. **[6842]**
  AACE Intl. **[IO]**
  Intl. Soc. of Parametric Analysts **[6734]**
  Natl. Assn. of Purchasing Card Professionals **[3264]**
  Soc. of Cost Estimating and Anal. **[1448]**
Cost Mgt. Gp. **[2493]**, c/o Inst. of Mgt. Accountants, 10 Paragon Dr., Montvale, NJ 07645-1773, (201)573-9000
Costa Rica Chap. of the ILAE **[IO]**, San Jose, Costa Rica
Costa Rica Collectors; Soc. for **[22872]**
Costa Rican-American Chamber of Commerce **[IO]**, San Jose, Costa Rica
Costa Rican Assn. of Flower Growers **[IO]**, San Jose, Costa Rica
Costa Rican Assn. of the Plastic Indus. **[IO]**, San Jose, Costa Rica
Costa Rican Banking Assn. **[IO]**, San Jose, Costa Rica
Costa Rican Chamber of the Clothing Indus. **[★IO]**
Costa Rican Chamber of Constr. **[IO]**, San Jose, Costa Rica
Costa Rican Demographic Assn. **[IO]**, San Jose, Costa Rica
Costa Rican Hypertension League **[IO]**, San Jose, Costa Rica
Costa Rican Textile Chamber **[IO]**, San Jose, Costa Rica
Costa Rican Union of Chambers of Private Sector Enterprises **[IO]**, San Jose, Costa Rica
Costello Fan Club; Abbott and **[★24795]**
Costello Fanzine **[★IO]**
Costello Intl. Fan Club; Abbott and **[24795]**
Costello Official Fan Club; Abbott and **[24796]**
Costume Coll. **[9821]**, 601 W 26th St., 3rd Fl., Ste. 325, New York, NY 10001, (212)989-5855
Costume Jewelry Bd. of Trade of New York - Defunct.
Costume Jewelry Club; Vintage Fashion and **[22128]**
Costume Jewelry Salesmen's Assn. - Defunct.
Costume Jewelry Trade Assn. - Defunct.
Costume Soc. of Am. **[9822]**, 203 Towne Centre Dr., Hillsborough, NJ 08844, (908)359-1471
Costume Study Unit - Defunct.
Costumers Assn; Natl. **[249]**
Costumes
  Costume Coll. **[9821]**
  Costume Soc. of Am. **[9822]**
  Italian Folk Art Fed. of Am. **[10259]**
Cosworth Vega Owner's Assn. - Defunct.
Cote d'Ivoire Soc. of Dermatology and Venereology **[IO]**, Abidjan, Cote d'Ivoire
COTECC **[IO]**, San Salvador, El Salvador
COTPRO **[IO]**, Harare, Zimbabwe
COTREL **[IO]**, London, United Kingdom
Cotswold Breeders Assn. **[4133]**, PO Box 441, Manchester, MD 21102
Cotswold Record Assn; Amer. **[5181]**
Cotswold Sheep Assn; Amer. **[★5181]**
Cottage Garden Soc. **[IO]**, Cheshire, United Kingdom
Cottage Garden Soc. and North Amer. Dianthus Soc; Combined North Amer. **[22507]**
Cottage Indus. Miniaturists Trade Assn. **[1162]**, 4244 Spring Creek Ln., Bellingham, WA 98226, (716)355-3651
Cottage Indus. Miniaturists Trade Assn., Inc. **[★858]**
The Cottage Prog. Intl., Inc. **[★13241]**
The Cottage Prog. Intl., Inc. **[★IO]**
Cottingham Clearinghouse - Defunct.

Cotton
  Amcot, Inc. **[4301]**
  Amer. Cotton Shippers Assn. **[1089]**
  Confed. of Indian Textile Indus. **[IO]**
  COTPRO **[IO]**
  Cotton Coun. Intl. **[IO]**
  Cotton Coun. Intl. **[1090]**
  Cotton Found. **[1091]**
  Cotton Incorporated **[1092]**
  Cotton Warehouse Assn. of Am. **[1093]**
  French Fed. of Cotton and Wool Indus. **[IO]**
  Greenwood Cotton Exchange **[4326]**
  Intl. Cotton Advisory Comm. **[4306]**
  Italian Textile Assn. **[IO]**
  Japan Cotton Traders Assn. **[IO]**
  Memphis Cotton Exchange **[4328]**
  Natl. Cotton Batting Inst. **[1094]**
  Natl. Cotton Coun. of Am. **[1095]**
  Natl. Cotton Ginners' Assn. **[1096]**
  Natl. Textile Assn. **[3795]**
  New York Cotton Exchange **[4332]**
  Organic Exchange **[2864]**
  Pakistan Cotton Ginners' Assn. **[IO]**
  Plains Cotton Growers **[4315]**
  Southern Cotton Assn. **[1097]**
  Southern Cotton Ginners' Assn. **[1098]**
  Supima **[4317]**
  Taiwan Cotton Spinners' Assn. **[IO]**
  Textile Fed. **[IO]**
Cotton Cloth Glove Mfrs; Natl. Assn. of **[★2030]**
Cotton; Committee for the Advancement of **[★1095]**
Cotton Compress and Cotton Warehouse Assn; NA **[★1093]**
Cotton Cooperative; Amer. **[★4301]**
Cotton Coun. Intl. **[1090]**, 1521 New Hampshire Ave. NW, Washington, DC 20036, (202)745-7805
Cotton Coun. Intl. **[IO]**, Washington, DC, United States
Cotton Exchange; Citrus Associates of the New York **[★4332]**
Cotton Exchange; Fort Worth Grain and **[★4325]**
Cotton Exchange; Greenwood **[4326]**
Cotton Exchange; Memphis **[4328]**
Cotton Exchange; New York **[4332]**
Cotton Found. **[1091]**, c/o Bill Norman, PO Box 820284, Memphis, TN 38112, (901)274-9030
Cotton Growers; Plains **[4315]**
Cotton Importers Assn. - Defunct.
Cotton Incorporated **[1092]**, 6399 Weston Pkwy., Cary, NC 27513, (919)678-2220
Cotton Insurance Assn. - Defunct.
Cotton Mfrs. Assn; Amer. **[★3772]**
Cotton Mfrs. Inst; Amer. **[★3772]**
Cotton Mfrs; Natl. Assn. of **[★3795]**
Cotton Planting Seed Distributors; Arizona **[★4317]**
Cotton Producers' Inst. **[★1092]**
Cotton Products Analysts; Soc. of **[★6669]**
Cotton Res. and Educ; Found. for **[★1091]**
Cotton Seed Crushers' Assn; Interstate **[★2854]**
Cotton Textile Inst. **[★3772]**
Cotton Textile Merchants of New York; Assn. of **[★3772]**
Cotton Textiles Export Promotion Coun. **[IO]**, Bombay, India
Cotton Warehouse Assn. of Am. **[1093]**, 1156 15th St. NW, Ste. 315, Washington, DC 20005, (202)331-2121
Cotton Warehouse Inspection Service - Defunct.
Cotton Yarn Distributors; Assn. of **[★3776]**
Cottonseed Products Assn; Natl. **[2854]**
Couch Potatoes - Defunct.
Cougar
  Mountain Lion Found. **[5341]**
Couleur; Assn. Internationale de la **[★IO]**
Coun. of 1890 Coll. Presidents - Address unknown since 2003.
Coun. on Abandoned Military Posts - USA **[★10021]**
Coun. of Academic and Professional Publishers **[IO]**, London, United Kingdom
Coun. of Academies of Engg. and Technological Sciences **[★IO]**
Coun. of Academies of Engg. and Technological Sciences **[★9104]**
Coun. on Accreditation **[13164]**, 120 Wall St., 11th Fl., New York, NY 10005-3902, (212)797-3000

Coun. for the Accreditation of Correspondence Colleges **[★IO]**
Coun. for Accreditation of Counseling and Related Educational Programs **[8168]**, 5999 Stevenson Ave., Alexandria, VA 22304, (703)823-9800
Coun. on Accreditation of Nurse Anesthesia Educational Programs **[8835]**, c/o Amer. Assn. of Nurse Anesthetists, 222 S Prospect Ave., Park Ridge, IL 60068, (847)692-7050
Coun. on Accreditation of Nurse Anesthesia Educational Programs/Schools **[★8835]**
Coun. for Accreditation in Occupational Hearing Conservation **[15632]**, 555 E Wells St., Ste. 1100, Milwaukee, WI 53202-3823, (414)266-5338
Coun. on Accreditation of Services for Families and Children **[★13164]**
Coun. of Active Independent Oil and Gas Producers - Defunct.
Coun. of Administrators of Special Educ. **[9139]**, c/o Dr. Luann L. Purcell, Exec. Dir., Fort Valley State Univ., 1005 State Univ. Dr., Fort Valley, GA 31030, (478)825-7667
Coun. of Adult Educ. **[★IO]**
Coun. for Adult and Experiential Learning **[8412]**, 55 E Monroe St., Ste. 1930, Chicago, IL 60603-5720, (312)499-2600
Coun. of Advanced Automotive Trainers **[341]**, 632 Gamble Dr., Lisle, IL 60532, (630)963-4051
Coun. for the Advancement of Arab-British Understanding **[IO]**, London, United Kingdom
Coun. for the Advancement of Citizenship - Defunct.
Coun. for the Advancement of Commun. with Deaf People **[IO]**, Durham, United Kingdom
Coun. for the Advancement of Consumer Policy **[17326]**
Coun. for the Advancement of Experiential Learning **[★8412]**
Coun. for the Advancement of Hospital Recreation - Defunct.
Coun. for the Advancement of Psychological Professions and Sciences **[★16136]**
Coun. for the Advancement of Sci. Writing **[3107]**, PO Box 910, Hedgesville, WV 25427, (304)754-5077
Coun. for the Advancement of Secondary Education - Defunct.
Coun. for the Advancement of Small Colleges **[★8535]**
Coun. for the Advancement of Standards in Higher Educ. **[9177]**, One Dupont Cir. NW, No. 300, Washington, DC 20036-1188, (202)862-1400
Coun. for the Advancement of Standards for Student Services/Development Programs **[★9177]**
Coun. for Advancement and Support of Educ. **[8245]**, 1307 New York Ave. NW, Ste. 1000, Washington, DC 20005-4701, (202)328-2273
Coun. of Affiliated Assns. of Jewelers of America - Defunct.
Coun. of Affiliated Marriage Enrichment Orgs. - Defunct.
Coun. for Affordable Hea. Insurance **[14686]**, 127 S Peyton St., Ste. 210, Alexandria, VA 22314, (703)836-6200
Coun. for Affordable Quality Healthcare **[14625]**, South Bldg., Ste. 500, 601 Pennsylvania Ave. NW, Washington, DC 20004, (202)861-1492
Coun. for Affordable and Rural Housing **[12310]**, 1112 King St., Alexandria, VA 22314-3022, (703)837-9001
Coun. of AFL-CIO Unions for Professional Employees **[★24173]**
Coun. for African Amer. Progress - Address unknown since 2002.
Coun. for Agricultural and Chemurgic Res. - Address unknown since 1995.
Coun. for Agricultural Sci. and Tech. **[7936]**, 4420 W Lincoln Way, Ames, IA 50014-3447, (515)292-2125
Coun. for Aid to Educ. **[8346]**, 215 Lexington Ave., 21st Fl., New York, NY 10016-6023, (212)661-5800
Coun. of Air-Conditioning and Refrigeration Industry - Address unknown since 1988.
Coun. of the Alleghenies **[9365]**, c/o Dr. Anthony Crosby, Journal Ed., PO Box 514, Frostburg, MD 21532, (301)689-8178

Reference to "IO" in place of a book number signifies that the association may be found in the 45th edition of International Organizations.

Coun. for Alternatives to Stereotyping in Entertainment - Defunct.

Coun. for Aluminium in Building [IO], Stonehouse, United Kingdom

Coun. on Amer. Affairs [★18440]

Coun. of Amer. Embroiderers - Defunct.

Coun. of Amer. Indian Artists - Address unknown since 1989.

Coun. of Amer. Instructors of the Deaf [14750], c/o Helen Lovato, Off. Mgr., PO Box 377, Bedford, TX 76095-0377, (817)354-8414

Coun. on American-Islamic Relations [19156], 453 New Jersey Ave. SE, Washington, DC 20003-4034, (202)488-8787

Coun. of Amer. Jewish Museums [10500], c/o Center for Judaic Stud., 2000 E Asbury Ave. Ste. 157, Denver, CO 80208, (303)871-3015

Coun. of Amer. Maritime Museums [10501], c/o The Whaling Museum at Cold Spring Harbor, PO Box 25, Cold Spring Harbor, NY 11724

Coun. of Amer. Master Mariners [2575], c/o Capt. Donald Moore, Sec.-Treas., PO Box 5034, Lynnwood, WA 98046-5034, (425)775-2331

Coun. of Amer. Official Poultry Tests - Defunct.

Coun. of Amer. Overseas Res. Centers [7566], PO Box 37012, Washington, DC 20013-7012, (202)633-1599

Coun. for Amer. Private Educ. [9020], 13017 Wisteria Dr., No. 457, Germantown, MD 20874-2607, (301)916-8460

Coun. of Amer. Survey Res. Organizations [18369], 170 N Country Rd., Ste. 4, Port Jefferson, NY 11777, (631)928-6954

Coun. of the Americas [24353], 680 Park Ave., New York, NY 10021, (212)249-8950

Coun. on America's Military Past [10021], PO Box 1151, Fort Myer, VA 22211

Coun. on Anthropology and Educ. [6415], c/o Amer. Anthropological Assn., 2200 Wilson Blvd., Ste. 600, Arlington, VA 22201-3357, (703)528-1902

Coun. on Anxiety Disorders - Defunct.

Coun. of Architectural Metal Trade Assns. - Defunct.

Coun. of Archives and Res. Libraries in Jewish Stud. [10351], c/o Natl. Found. for Jewish Culture, 330 7th Ave., 21st Fl., New York, NY 10001, (212)629-0500

Coun. of Armenian Amer. Nurses - Address unknown since 2002.

Coun. for Art Educ. [7970], PO Box 479, Hanson, MA 02341-0479, (781)293-4100

Coun. on Arteriosclerosis of the Amer. Heart Assn. [★13902]

Coun. on Arteriosclerosis, Thrombosis and Vascular Biology of the Amer. Heart Assn. [13902], c/o Amer. Heart Assn. Natl. Center, 7272 Greenville Ave., Dallas, TX 75231, (214)706-1293

Coun. for Asia-Europe Cooperation [IO], Tokyo, Japan

Coun. of Assn. Attorneys - Defunct.

Coun. on Atmospheric Sciences - Defunct.

Coun. of Australian Museum Associations [★IO]

Coun. of Australian Postgraduate Associations [IO], Melbourne, Australia

Coun. of Australian Powerlifting Organizations [IO], North Ipswich, Australia

Coun. of Authors and Journalists [★11172]

Coun. of the Bars and Law Societies of Europe [IO], Brussels, Belgium

Coun. of the Bars and Law Societies of the European Community [★IO]

Coun. of the Bars and Law Societies of the European Union [★IO]

Coun. for Basic Education - Defunct.

Coun. for a Beautiful Israel [★10254]

Coun. for a Beautiful Israel [★IO]

Coun. of Better Bus. Bureaus Found. [★IO]

Coun. of Better Bus. Bureaus Found. [★17309]

Coun. for Better Hearing and Speech Month - Defunct.

Coun. of Bible Believing Churches in U.S.A. - Address unknown since 2002.

Coun. of Biology Editors [★3108]

Coun. for Biomedical Communications Assns. - Address unknown since 1999.

Coun. for Biotechnology Info. [6614], 1225 Eye St. NW, Ste. 400, Washington, DC 20005, (202)962-9200

Coun. for Biotechnology Info. [IO], Washington, DC, United States

Coun. of Black Architectural Schools - Defunct.

Coun. for a Black Economic Agenda - Defunct.

Coun. of Blind Lions [★16825]

Coun. on Botanical and Horticultural Libraries [10352], c/o Ms. Gayle Bradbeer, Sec., Auraria Lib., 1100 Lawrence St., Denver, CO 80204-2095, (303)556-2791

Council on Botanical and Horticultural Libraries [IO], Denver, CO, United States

Coun. for British Archaeology [IO], York, United Kingdom

Coun. for Bus. and the Arts in Canada [IO], Toronto, ON, Canada

Coun. for Cable Information - Defunct.

Coun. of Canadians [IO], Ottawa, ON, Canada

Coun. of Car Care Centers - Address unknown since 1994.

Coun. on Career Development for Minorities [★8047]

Coun. on Career for Minorities [8047]

Coun. for Career Planning - Defunct.

Coun. on Certification of Hea., Environmental and Safety Technologists [14552], 208 Burwash Ave., Savoy, IL 61874, (217)359-2686

Coun. on Certification of Nurse Anesthetists [15475], 222 S Prospect Ave., Park Ridge, IL 60068, (847)692-7050

Coun. of Chemical Assn. Executives - Defunct.

Coun. for Chem. Res. [6679], 1730 Rhode Island Ave. NW, Ste. 302, Washington, DC 20036, (202)429-3971

Coun. of Chief State School Officers [8246], 1 Massachusetts Ave. NW, Ste. 700, Washington, DC 20001-1431, (202)336-7000

Coun. for Children with Behavioral Disorders [9140], 1110 N Glebe Rd., Ste. 300, Arlington, VA 22201-5704, (703)620-3660

Coun. on Children, Media and Merchandising - Defunct.

Coun. on Chiropractic Educ. [13998], 8049 N 85th Way, Scottsdale, AZ 85258-4321, (480)443-8877

Coun. on Chiropractic Educ. Australasia [IO], Rosewood, Australia

Coun. on Chiropractic Orthopedics [15768], c/o Gary L. Carver, Treas., 4409 Sterling Ave., Kansas City, MO 64133-1854, (816)358-5100

Coun. of Chiropractic Physiological Therapeutics and Rehabilitation [13999], c/o Dr. Donald J. Fedoryk, DC, Pres., 312 Courtyard Dr., Hillsborough, NJ 08844, (908)722-9075

Coun. for Christian Colleges and Universities [8084], 321 8th St. NE, Washington, DC 20002, (202)546-8713

Coun. for Christian Medical Work [★20241]

Coun. of Christian Scholarly Societies [8085], c/o Amy Black, Chair, Dept. of Politics and Intl. Relations, Wheaton Coll., 501 Coll. Ave., Wheaton, IL 60187, (717)291-4055

Coun. for Christian Service - Defunct.

Coun. on Christian Union [★19891]

Coun. on Christian Unity [19891], PO Box 1986, Indianapolis, IN 46206-1986, (317)713-2586

Coun. of Churches for Britain and Ireland [★IO]

Coun. of Churches of Malaysia [IO], Petaling Jaya, Malaysia

Coun. of Citizens With Low Vision [★11934]

Coun. of Citizens With Low Vision Intl. [11934], c/o Amer. Coun. of the Blind, 1155 15th St. NW, Ste. 1004, Washington, DC 20005, (703)642-1909

Coun. on Civic Education - Address unknown since 1995.

Coun. on Clinical Optometric Care - Defunct.

Coun. for Clinical Training [★19915]

Coun. of Colleges of Acupuncture and Oriental Medicine [15743], 3909 Natl. Dr., Ste. 125, Burtonsville, MD 20866, (301)476-7790

Coun. of Colleges of Arts and Sciences [7971], PO Box 8795, Williamsburg, VA 23187-8795, (757)221-1784

Coun. of Collegiate Women's Athletic Administrators [★8982]

Coun. of Commun. Mgt. [876], 65 Enterprise, Aliso Viejo, CA 92656, (973)453-8854

Coun. of Communication Societies - Defunct.

Coun. on Communications Res. [★8706]

Coun. of Community Blood Centers [★13762]

Coun. of Community Churches [★19850]

Coun. of Community Churches [★IO]

Coun. of Community Coll. Boards [★8118]

Coun. for a Community of Democracies [5661], 1801 F St. NW, Ste. 308, Washington, DC 20006, (202)789-9771

Coun. for a Community of Democracies [IO], Washington, DC, United States

Coun. for Community and Economic Res. [24272], PO Box 100127, Arlington, VA 22210, (703)522-4980

Coun. on Competitiveness [3839], 1500 K St. NW, Ste. 850, Washington, DC 20005, (202)682-4292

Coun. on Compulsive Gambling of New Jersey [12209], 3635 Quakerbridge Rd., Ste. 7, Hamilton, NJ 08619, (609)588-5515

Coun. for Computerized Library Networks - Defunct.

Coun. of Conservationists - Address unknown since 1995.

Coun. of Conservative Citizens [18684], PO Box 221683, St. Louis, MO 63122-8683, (636)940-8474

Coun. of Construction Employers - Defunct.

Coun. of Consulting Orgs. - Address unknown since 2002.

Coun. on Consumer Info. [★17305]

Coun. on Contemporary Families [12149], Univ. of Illinois at Chicago, MC 312, 1007 W Harrison St., Chicago, IL 60607, (312)996-3074

Coun. on the Continuing Educ. Unit [★8150]

Coun. on the Continuing Educ. Unit [★IO]

Coun. for Continuous Improvement - Defunct.

Coun. on Cooperation in Teacher Education - Defunct.

Coun. for Court Excellence [5897], 1111 14th St. NW, Ste. 500, Washington, DC 20005, (202)785-5917

Coun. for Culture [IO], The Hague, Netherlands

Coun. for Dance Educ. and Training - UK [IO], London, United Kingdom

Coun. of Danish Youth Organizations [★IO]

Coun. for the Defense of Freedom - Address unknown since 2002.

Coun. of Defense and Space Indus. Associations [147], 1000 Wilson Blvd., Ste. 1800, Arlington, VA 22209, (703)243-2020

Coun. for Democracy in the Americas - Defunct.

Coun. for Democracy in Korea - Defunct.

Coun. for Democratic and Secular Humanism [★20085]

Coun. for Democratic and Secular Humanism [★IO]

Council on Dental Education [★14126]

Coun. for a Dept. of Peace - Defunct.

Coun. of Development Finance Agencies [17458], 815 Superior Ave., Ste. 1301, Cleveland, OH 44114, (216)920-3073

Coun. for the Development of Social Sci. Res. in Africa [IO], Dakar, Senegal

Coun. on Diagnostic Imaging [16288], PO Box 190, Cheney, KS 67025, (316)542-3400

Coun. for Disability Rights [11935], 30 E Adams, Ste. 1130, Chicago, IL 60603, (312)444-9484

Coun. of Disabled People of Thailand [IO], Bangkok, Thailand

Council of Disabled Sailors [★23155]

Coun. for Distributive Teacher Educ. [★8818]

Coun. on Documentation Res. - Defunct.

Coun. for Early Childhood Professional Recognition [★11526]

Coun. for Eastern Orthodox Youth Leaders of the Americas - Defunct.

Coun. for Economic Growth and Security - Defunct.

Coun. on Economics and Natl. Security - Defunct.

Coun. for Educ. in the Commonwealth [IO], London, United Kingdom

Coun. on Educ. of the Deaf [14751], c/o Dr. Karen Dilka, Exec. Dir., Eastern Kentucky Univ., Wallace 245, Richmond, KY 40475, (859)622-1043

Coun. for the Educ. of the Partially Seeing [★9145]

Coun. on Educ. for Public Hea. [16242], 800 Eye St. NW, Ste. 202, Washington, DC 20001-3710, (202)789-1050

Coun. for Educ. in World Citizenship [IO], Kingston, United Kingdom

---

A star before a book entry number signifies that the name is not listed separately, but is mentioned within the entry.

Coun. for Educational Development and Res. [★9061]

Coun. of Educational Fac. Planners, Intl. [8335], 9180 E Desert Cove Dr., Ste. 104, Scottsdale, AZ 85260-6231, (480)391-0840

Coun. of Educational Fac. Planners, Intl. [IO], Scottsdale, AZ, United States

Coun. for Educational Freedom in America - Address unknown since 2004.

Coun. of Educators in Landscape Architecture [8724], PO Box 7506, Edmond, OK 73083, (405)330-4150

Coun. on Electrolysis Education - Address unknown since 1999.

Coun. for Electronic Revenue Commun. Advancement [3740], 600 Cameron St., Ste. 309, Alexandria, VA 22314, (703)340-1655

Coun. for Elementary Sci. Intl. [9100], c/o Judy Lederman, Pres., Illinois Inst. of Tech., 3424 S State St., 4th Fl., Rm. 4009, Chicago, IL 60616, (312)567-3662

Coun. for Elementary Sci. Intl. [IO], Chicago, IL, United States

Coun. for Emerging Natl. Security Affairs [18590], 1212 New York Ave. NW, Ste. 850, Washington, DC 20005, (212)678-8608

Coun. on Employee Benefit Plans [★1234]

Coun. on Employee Benefits [1234], 4910 Moorland Ln., Bethesda, MD 20814, (301)664-5940

Coun. for Energy and Mineral Resources; Circum-Pacific [7340]

Coun. of Energy Rsrc. Tribes [18093], 695 S Colorado Blvd., Ste. 10, Denver, CO 80246, (303)282-7576

Coun. on Engineering Laws - Defunct.

Coun. of Engg. and Sci. Soc. Executives [7010], c/o Corie Dacus, PO Box 130656, St. Paul, MN 55113, (952)838-3268

Coun. of Engineers and Scientists Organizations [7817], c/o Charles Bofferding, Exec. Dir., SPEEA, IFPTE Local 2001, 15205 52nd Ave. S, Seattle, WA 98188, (206)433-0991

Coun. of Entomology Dept. Administrators [7060], c/o James Harper, North Carolina State Univ., Dept. of Entomology, Box 7613, Raleigh, NC 27695-7613, (919)515-2746

Coun. for Environmental Conservation [★IO]

Coun. for Environmental Educ. [IO], Reading, United Kingdom

Coun. for Ethical Leadership [714], 92 Jefferson Ave., Ste. 108, Columbus, OH 43215, (614)221-8661

Coun. of Ethical Organizations [1333], 214 S Payne St., Alexandria, VA 22314, (703)683-7916

Coun. for Ethics in Economics [★714]

Coun. of EU Chambers of Commerce in India [IO], Bombay, India

Coun. of Europe [IO], Strasbourg, France

Coun. of European Bishops' Conferences [IO], St. Gallen, Switzerland

Coun. of European Employers of the Metal, Engg. and Technology-Based Indus. [IO], Brussels, Belgium

Coun. of European Energy Regulators [IO], Brussels, Belgium

Coun. of European Municipalities and Regions [IO], Brussels, Belgium

Coun. of European Natl. Top-Level Domain Registries [IO], Brussels, Belgium

Coun. of European Producers of Materials for Constr. [IO], Brussels, Belgium

Coun. of European Professional Informatics Societies [IO], Brussels, Belgium

Coun. for European Stud. [IO], New York, NY, United States

Coun. for European Stud. [8404], Columbia Univ., 420 W 118th St., MC 3310, New York, NY 10027, (212)854-4172

Coun. Europeen des Jeunes Agriculteurs [★IO]

Coun. for Excellence in Govt. [5705], 1301 K St. NW, Ste. 450 W, Washington, DC 20005, (202)728-0418

Coun. for Exceptional Children [9141], 1110 N Glebe Rd., Ste. 300, Arlington, VA 22201-5704, (703)620-3660

Coun. for Exceptional Children; Div. for Early Childhood of the [9144]

Coun. for Export Trading Companies - Address unknown since 1994.

Coun. of Families with Visual Impairment [16844], c/o Cindy Van Winkle, Pres., 6686 Capricorn Ln. NE, Bremerton, WA 98311

Coun. for Family Financial Education - Address unknown since 1995.

Coun. on Family Health - Defunct.

Coun. of Fashion Designers of Am. [230], 1412 Broadway, Ste. 2006, New York, NY 10018, (212)302-1821

Coun. of Federated Jewish Orgs. - Defunct.

Coun. of Federated Orgs. - Defunct.

Coun. on Fertilizer Application - Defunct.

Coun. of Film Orgs. - Address unknown since 2003.

Coun. on Fine Art Photography - Address unknown since 2001.

Council of Fleet Specialists and National Wheel and Rim Assn. [★382]

Coun. for Food, Agricultural and Rsrc. Economics [4524], c/o Tamara Wagester, Exec. Dir., 900 Second St. NE, Ste. 205, Washington, DC 20002, (202)408-8522

Coun. on Foreign Relations [17608], The Harold Pratt House, 58 E 68th St., New York, NY 10021, (212)434-9400

Coun. on Forest Engg. [4681], 620 SW 4th St., Corvallis, OR 97333, (541)754-7558

Coun. of Forest Indus. Canada [IO], Tokyo, Japan

Coun. of Forest Indus. - Canada [IO], Vancouver, BC, Canada

Coun. of Forest Indus. - UK [IO], Farnborough, United Kingdom

Coun. on Foundations [12652], 1828 L St. NW, Ste. 300, Washington, DC 20036, (202)466-6512

Coun. of French Life in Am. [IO], Quebec, QC, Canada

Coun. of Gaelic Societies - Address unknown since 1995.

Coun. of Gen. Motors Credit Unions [1105], c/o Terry Frazer, Dir., 1814 Crawford's Ferry Rd., Hartwell, GA 30643

Coun. of Georgist Organizations [18708], PO Box 57, Evanston, IL 60204, (888)262-9015

Coun. on Geriatric Cardiology [★13927]

Coun. for Govt. Reform [17665], c/o Center for Govt. Reform, 2915 Hunter Mill Rd., Ste. 23, Oakton, VA 22124-1716, (703)319-0009

Coun. on Governmental Ethics Laws [6270], PO Box 393, 196 Alps Rd., Ste. 2, Athens, GA 30606, (706)548-7758

Coun. on Governmental Relations [9058], 1200 New York Ave. NW, Ste. 750, Washington, DC 20005, (202)289-6655

Coun. of Governors' Policy Advisors - Defunct.

Coun. on Graduate Educ. for Public Admin. [★6194]

Coun. of Graduate Schools [8488], 1 Dupont Cir. NW, Ste. 430, Washington, DC 20036-1146, (202)223-3791

Coun. of Graduate Schools in the U.S. [★8488]

Coun. of Graphological Societies [11209], c/o Louie Seibert, Treas., PO Box 615, Hardy, AR 72542

Coun. of the Great City Schools [9289], 1301 Pennsylvania Ave. NW, Ste. 702, Washington, DC 20004, (202)393-2427

Coun. of Growing Companies [715]

Coun. for Hea. and Human Services [★13165]

Coun. for Hea. and Human Services Ministries, United Church of Christ [13165], 700 Prospect Ave., Cleveland, OH 44115, (866)822-8224

Coun. on Hea. Info. and Educ. [14553], 2272 Colorado Blvd., No. 1228, Los Angeles, CA 90041

Coun. on Hea. Res. for Development [IO], Geneva, Switzerland

Coun. for Hea. Ser. Accreditation of South Africa [IO], Howard Place, Republic of South Africa

Coun. for Hea. and Welfare Services, United Church of Christ [★13165]

Coun. on Hemispheric Affairs [16975], 1250 Connecticut Ave. NW, Ste. 1C, Washington, DC 20036, (202)223-4975

Council on Hemispheric Affairs [IO], Washington, DC, United States

Coun. for Higher Educ. Accreditation [8247], 1 Dupont Cir. NW, Ste. 510, Washington, DC 20036-1135, (202)955-6126

Coun. of Historical Societies [★10084]

Coun. for Holocaust Survivors With Disabilities - Defunct.

Coun. of Home Hea. Agencies/Community Hea. Services [★14840]

Coun. to Homeless Persons [IO], Fitzroy, Australia

Coun. for Hospitality Mgt. Educ. [IO], Cheltenham, United Kingdom

Coun. of Hotel and Restaurant Trainers [1939], PO Box 2835, Westfield, NJ 07091, (908)389-0757

Coun. of Housing Producers - Defunct.

Coun. for Independent Archaeology [IO], Ampthill, United Kingdom

Coun. of Independent Black Institutions - Address unknown since 2001.

Coun. of Independent Colleges [8535], 1 Dupont Cir., Ste. 320, Washington, DC 20036-1142, (202)466-7230

Coun. of Independent Petroleum Marketers [★2943]

Coun. of Independent Restaurants of Am. [1580], c/o Don Luria, Pres., 3500 E Sunrise Dr., Tucson, AZ 85718, (520)577-8181

Coun. for Indian Educ. [8937], 1240 Burlington Ave., Billings, MT 59102-4224, (406)248-3465

Coun. of Indian Employers [IO], New Delhi, India

Coun. of Indus. Arts Supervisors; Amer. [★9232]

Coun. of Indus. Boiler Owners [2015], 6035 Burke Centre Pkwy., Ste. 360, Burke, VA 22015, (703)250-9042

Coun. of Indus. Development Bond Issuers [★17458]

Coun. of Infrastructure Financing Authorities [6234], 1801 K St. NW, Ste. 500, Washington, DC 20006, (202)973-3100

Coun. of Infrastructure Financing Authorities [IO], Washington, DC, United States

Coun. of Institutional Investors [3512], 888 17th St. NW, Ste. 500, Washington, DC 20006, (202)822-0800

Coun. of Insurance Agents and Brokers [2159], 701 Pennsylvania Ave. NW, Ste. 750, Washington, DC 20004-2608, (202)783-4400

Coun. of Insurance Agents and Brokers [IO], Washington, DC, United States

Coun. for Inter-American Cooperation [★IO]

Coun. for Inter-American Cooperation [★2289]

Coun. for Inter-Amer. Security Found. - Address unknown since 1999.

Coun. on Inter-cultural Relations [★10234]

Coun. for Intercultural Studies and Programs - Defunct.

Coun. for Interdisciplinary Communication in Medicine - Address unknown since 1995.

Coun. of Intergovernmental Relations Officials [★5622]

Coun. for Interinstitutional Leadership - Address unknown since 1999.

Coun. for Interior Design Accreditation [8584], 146 Monroe Ctr. NW, Ste. 1318, Grand Rapids, MI 49503-2822, (616)458-0400

Coun. on Intl. Banking [★483]

Coun. for Intl. Business Risk Mgt. - Defunct.

Coun; Intl. Cargo Security [3530]

Coun. on Intl. Communications - Address unknown since 1995.

Coun. for Intl. Congresses of Dipterology [IO], Canberra, Australia

Coun. for Intl. Development [IO], Wellington, New Zealand

Coun. on Intl. Educational Exchange - USA [IO], Portland, ME, United States

Coun. on Intl. Educational Exchange - USA [8608], 7 Custom House St., 3rd Fl., Portland, ME 04101, (207)553-7600

Coun. for Intl. Exchange of Scholars [★8609]

Coun. for Intl. Exchange of Scholars [★IO]

Coun. for Intl. Exchange of Scholars Conf. Bd. of Assoc. Res. Councils [★IO]

Coun. for Intl. Exchange of Scholars Conf. Bd. of Assoc. Res. Councils [★8609]

Coun. for Intl. Exchange of Scholars/Institute of Intl. Educ. [8609], 3007 Tilden St. NW, Ste. 5L, Washington, DC 20008-3009, (202)686-4000

Reference to "IO" in place of a book number signifies that the association may be found in the 45th edition of International Organizations.

Coun. for Intl. Exchange of Scholars/Institute of Intl. Educ. [IO], Washington, DC, United States

Coun. of Intl. Fellowship - U.S.A. - Address unknown since 2002.

Coun. of Intl. Investigators [2322], 2150 N 107th St., Ste. 205, Seattle, WA 98133-9009, (206)361-8889

Coun. of Intl. Investigators [IO], Seattle, WA, United States

Coun. on Intl. Law Assns. - Defunct.

Coun. on Intl. Nontheatrical Events [9935], 1112 16th St. NW, Ste. 510, Washington, DC 20036, (202)785-1136

Coun. on Intl. Nontheatrical Events [IO], Washington, DC, United States

Coun. for Intl. Organizations of Medical Sciences [IO], Geneva, Switzerland

Coun. of Intl. Programs [★IO]

Coun. of Intl. Programs [★13202]

Coun. of Intl. Programs USA [13202], 1700 E 13th St., Ste. 4ME, Cleveland, OH 44114-3241, (216)566-1088

Coun. of Intl. Programs USA [IO], Cleveland, OH, United States

Coun. for Intl. Progress in Mgt. - Defunct.

Coun. on Intl. and Public Affairs [18832], 777 UN Plz., Ste. 3C, New York, NY 10017, (212)972-9877

Coun. on Intl. and Public Affairs [IO], New York, NY, United States

Coun. of Intl. Restaurant Real Estate Brokers [IO], Greensboro, NC, United States

Coun. of Intl. Restaurant Real Estate Brokers [3392], c/o William M. Kotis III, Pres., PO Box 9296, Greensboro, NC 27429, (866)247-2123

Coun. for Intl. Tax Educ. [2281], PO Box 1012, White Plains, NY 10602, (914)328-5656

Coun. for Intl. Tax Educ. [IO], White Plains, NY, United States

Coun. on Interracial Books for Children - Address unknown since 1993.

Coun. on Ionizing Radiation Measurements and Standards [7556], PO Box 1238, Duluth, GA 30096, (770)622-0026

Coun. of Islamic Affairs - Address unknown since 1995.

Coun. on Islamic Educ. [8669], PO Box 20186, Fountain Valley, CA 92728-0186, (714)839-2929

Coun. of Ivy Gp. Presidents [23817], 228 Alexander St., Princeton, NJ 08544, (609)258-6426

Coun. of Japan Auto. Workers' Unions [★IO]

Coun. of Japan Constr. Indus. Employee's Unions [IO], Tokyo, Japan

Coun. for Jewish Educ. [IO], Monsey, NY, United States

Coun. for Jewish Educ. [8690], 11 Olympia Ln., Monsey, NY 10952, (845)368-8657

Coun. of Jewish Orgs. in Civil Service [5567]

Coun. of Jewish Theaters - Address unknown since 2001.

Coun. of Jewish Women of New Zealand [IO], Lower Hutt, New Zealand

Coun. of Justice to Animals and Humane Slaughter Assn. [★IO]

Council of Khalistan/International Sikh Organization [IO], Washington, DC, United States

Coun. of Khalistan/International Sikh Org. [20557], 730 24th St. NW, No. 310, Washington, DC 20037, (202)337-1904

Coun. of Landscape Architectural Registration Boards [6473], 3949 Pender Dr., Ste. 120, Fairfax, VA 22030, (571)432-0332

Coun. for Languages and Other Intl. Stud. [★10306]

Coun. for Languages and Other Intl. Stud. [★IO]

Coun. of Large Public Housing Authorities [5788], 1250 Eye St. NW, Ste. 901, Washington, DC 20005, (202)638-1300

Coun. for Latin Am. [★24353]

Coun. of Latin-American Students of Architecture [292], 7500 Glenoaks Blvd., Burbank, CA 91510, (818)513-5372

Coun. on Law in Higher Educ. [8317], 9386 Via Classico W, Wellington, FL 33411, (561)792-4440

Coun. for Learning Disabilities [12490], 11184 Antioch Rd., Overland Park, KS 66210, (913)491-1011

Coun. of Lebanese Amer. Organizations [9396], PO Box 661823, Los Angeles, CA 90066, (919)427-8869

Coun. on Legal Educ. Opportunity [8764], 740 15th St. NW, 9th Fl., Washington, DC 20005, (202)828-6100

Coun. on Legal Education for Professional Responsibility - Defunct.

Coun. for Liberal Learning - Defunct.

Coun. on Lib. and Info. Resources [10353], 1755 Massachusetts Ave. NW, Ste. 500, Washington, DC 20036, (202)939-4750

Coun. on Library-Media Technicians [8783], c/o Margaret Barron, Exec. Dir., 28262 Chardon Rd., PMB 168, Wickliffe, OH 44092-2793, (630)257-6541

Coun. on Lib. Resources and Commn. on Preservation and Access [★10353]

Coun. on Lib. Technical-Assistants [★8783]

Coun. on Lib. Tech. [★8783]

Coun. on Licensure, Enforcement and Regulation [6271], 403 Marquis Ave., Ste. 200, Lexington, KY 40502, (859)269-1289

Coun. of Life Insurance Consultants - Address unknown since 1994.

Coun. of Literary Magazines and Presses [10893], 154 Christopher St., Ste. 3-C, New York, NY 10014-9110, (212)741-9110

Coun. for a Livable World [17425], 322 4th St. NE, Washington, DC 20002, (202)543-4100

Coun. for a Livable World [IO], Washington, DC, United States

Coun. for a Livable World Educ. Fund [IO], Washington, DC, United States

Coun. for a Livable World Educ. Fund [17426], c/o Coun. for a Livable World, 322 4th St. NE, Washington, DC 20002, (202)543-4100

Coun. for Livestock Protection - Defunct.

Coun. of the Living Theatre - Defunct.

Coun. of Logistics Mgt. [★4018]

Coun. on Lutheran Church Men - Defunct.

Coun. of Managerial and Professional Staffs [★IO]

Coun. of Mfg. Associations; Natl. Assn. of Mfrs. [2562]

Coun. for Mapping, Photogrammetry and Surveying Societies - Defunct.

Coun. for Marketing and Opinion Res. [2622], 110 Natl. Dr., 2nd Fl., Glastonbury, CT 06033, (860)657-1881

Coun. of Masajid of U.S. [20097], 45 Lilac St., Edison, NJ 08817-4254, (732)985-3304

Coun. of Mech. Specialty Contracting Indus. [★1006]

Coun. for Medical Affairs - Defunct.

Coun. on Medical Educ. of the Amer. Medical Assn. [8836], 515 N State St., Chicago, IL 60610, (312)464-4690

Coun. of Medical Specialty Societies [15120], 51 Sherwood Terr., Ste. M, Lake Bluff, IL 60044-2232, (847)295-3456

Coun. on Medical Student Educ. in Pediatrics [8861], c/o Robin Deterding, MD, Pres., Off. of Medical Affairs, Dept. of Pediatrics, 1056 E 19th Ave., B395, Denver, CO 80218-1007, (303)861-6867

Coun. on Medical TV [★14032]

Coun. of Mennonite Colls. - Address unknown since 2002.

Coun. for Middle Eastern Affairs - Defunct.

Coun. of Ministers of Educ., Canada [IO], Toronto, ON, Canada

Coun. of Mortgage Lenders [IO], London, United Kingdom

Coun. of Motion Picture Orgs. - Defunct.

Coun. on Multiemployer Pension Security - Defunct.

Coun. on Municipal Performance - Defunct.

Coun. of Musculoskeletal Specialty Societies [15273], 6300 N River Rd., Ste. 727, Rosemont, IL 60018-4226, (847)384-4330

Coun. for Museum Anthropology [10502], c/o Catherine S. Fowler, PhD, Pres., Univ. of Nevada, Dept. of Anthropology, Reno, NV 89557, (775)682-7687

Coun. for Music in Hospitals [IO], Walton-On-Thames, United Kingdom

Coun. on Music Teacher Educ. [★8931]

Coun. of Mutual Savings Institutions - Address unknown since 1995.

Coun. for Name Stud. in Great Britain and Ireland [★IO]

Coun. of Natl. Beekeeping Associations in the United Kingdom [IO], Huntly, United Kingdom

Coun. for Natl. Cooperation in Aquatics - Address unknown since 2001.

Coun. for the Natl. Interest [18056], 1250 4th St. SW, Ste. WG-1, Washington, DC 20024, (202)863-2951

Coun. of Natl. Library and Information Assns. - Address unknown since 2003.

Coun. on Natl. Literatures [10419], 6802 Metropolitan Ave., Middle Village, NY 11379, (718)821-3916

Coun. of Natl. Orgs. for Adult Education - Defunct.

Coun. for Natl. Parks [IO], London, United Kingdom

Coun. on Natl. Priorities and Resources - Defunct.

Coun. for the Natl. Register of Hea. Ser. Providers in Psychology [16149], c/o Natl. Register, 1120 G St. NW, Ste. 330, Washington, DC 20005, (202)786-7663

Coun. for Native Amer. Indians [10738]

Coun. of Natural Waters [★509]

Coun. of Natural Waters [★IO]

Coun. on Naturopathic Medical Educ. - Defunct.

Coun. for Near-Infrared Spectroscopy - Address unknown since 1994.

Coun. for Noncollegiate Continuing Educ. [★8145]

Coun. for Nongovernmental Organisations in Malawi [IO], Blantyre, Malawi

Coun. of Nordic Teachers' Unions [IO], Copenhagen, Denmark

Coun. of Nordic Trade Unions [IO], Stockholm, Sweden

Coun. on Nutritional Anthropology [★6424]

Coun. on Occupational Educ. [8248], 41 Perimeter Center East NE, Ste. 640, Atlanta, GA 30346, (770)396-3898

Coun. of Occupational Therapists for the European Countries [IO], London, United Kingdom

Coun. on Ocean Law - Address unknown since 2006.

Coun. for Old World Archaeology - Defunct.

Coun. On State Taxation [18709], 122 C St. NW, Ste. 330, Washington, DC 20001-2109, (202)484-5222

Coun. of Ontario Constr. Associations [IO], Toronto, ON, Canada

Coun. for Opportunity in Educ. [8324], 1025 Vermont Ave. NW, Ste. 900, Washington, DC 20005, (202)347-7430

Coun. for Opportunity in Graduate Mgt. Education - Defunct.

Coun. on Optometric Educ. [★15710]

Coun. on Optometric Educ; Accreditation [15710]

Coun. of Organizations [★18771]

Coun. of Orgs. Serving the Deaf - Defunct.

Coun. of Pacific Northwest Log Exporting Industries - Address unknown since 1995.

Coun. on Packaging in the Environment - Defunct.

Coun. of Parent Attorneys and Advocates [9142], PO Box 6767, Towson, MD 21285, (443)451-5270

Coun. for a Parliament of the World's Religions [20532], 70 E Lake St., Ste. 205, Chicago, IL 60601, (312)629-2990

Coun. for a Parliament of the World's Religions [IO], Chicago, IL, United States

Coun. on Peace Res. in History [★10143]

Coun. of Pediatric Subspecialties [15886], 6728 Old McLean Village Dr., McLean, VA 22101, (703)556-9222

Coun. for Periodical Distributors Assns. - Defunct.

Coun. of Petroleum Accountants Societies [23], 3900 E Mexico Ave., Ste. 602, Denver, CO 80210, (303)300-1131

Coun. of Philatelic Orgs. - Defunct.

Coun. of Philatelic Presidents - Defunct.

Coun. for Philosophical Studies - Defunct.

Coun. of Planning Librarians - Defunct.

Coun. on Podiatric Medical Educ. [16042], 9312 Old Georgetown Rd., Bethesda, MD 20814-1621, (301)581-9200

Coun. on Podiatry Educ. [★16042]

Coun. on Pollution Control Financing Agencies - Defunct.

Coun. on Postsecondary Accreditation - Defunct.

Coun. for Preservation of Rural England [★IO]

A star before a book entry number signifies that the name is not listed separately, but is mentioned within the entry.

Coun. of Presidents [★17558]
Coun. of Presidents of Women's Natl. Organizations [★17558]
Coun. for Private Enterprise [★17636]
Coun. for Private Intl. Development - Defunct.
Coun. of Professional Associations on Fed. Statistics [5816], 2121 Eisenhower Ave., Ste. 200, Alexandria, VA 22314, (703)836-0404
Coun. on Professional Certification - Address unknown since 1989.
Coun. for Professional Educ. for Bus. [★8010]
Coun. for Professional Educ. for Bus. [★IO]
Coun. for Professional Recognition [11526], 2460 16th St. NW, Washington, DC 20009, (202)265-9090
Coun. on Professional Standards in Speech-Language Pathology and Audiology - Defunct.
Coun. of Professional Surveyors [3703], 1015 15th St. NW, 8th Fl., Washington, DC 20005-2605, (202)347-7474
Coun. of Profit Sharing Indus. [★1279]
Coun. for the Protection of Human Rights of Political Refugees from Yugoslavia - Defunct.
Coun. for the Protection of Rural Wales [★IO]
Coun. of Protestant Colls. and Universities - Defunct.
Coun. of Protocol Executives [2677], 101 W 12th St., Ste. PH-H, New York, NY 10011, (212)633-6934
Coun. of Psychoanalytic Psychotherapists - Address unknown since 1995.
Coun. for Public Interest Law [★6219]
Coun. of Public Relations Firms [18487], 317 Madison Ave., Ste. 2320, New York, NY 10017, (212)922-1350
Coun. of Puerto Rican and Spanish-Amer. Orgs. of Greater New York - Defunct.
Coun. for Qualification of Residential Interior Designers [2257], PO Box 16028, High Point, NC 27261, (336)886-6100
Coun. on Quality and Leadership [12567], 100 West Rd., Ste. 406, Towson, MD 21204, (410)583-0060
Coun. on Quality and Leadership [IO], Towson, MD, United States
Coun. on Quality and Leadership in Supports for People with Disabilities [★IO]
Coun. on Quality and Leadership in Supports for People with Disabilities [★12567]
Coun. of Real Estate Brokerage Managers [3306], 430 N Michigan Ave., Chicago, IL 60611-4011, (800)621-8738
Coun. of Real Estate Brokerage Managers [IO], Chicago, IL, United States
Coun. of Regional Info. Tech. Associations [IO], Cleveland, OH, United States
Coun. of Regional Info. Tech. Associations [7192], 50 Public Sq., Ste. 200, Cleveland, OH 44113, (216)592-2295
Coun. of Regional School Accrediting Commns. - Defunct.
Coun. of Registered Engineers of Nigeria [★IO]
Coun. for Registered Gas Installers [IO], Basingstoke, United Kingdom
Coun. for the Registration of Schools Teaching Dyslexic Pupils [IO], Cheltenham, United Kingdom
Coun. for the Regulation of Engg. in Nigeria [IO], Abuja, Nigeria
Coun. on Regulatory and Information Mgt. - Address unknown since 2003.
Coun. of Rehabilitation Counselor Educators [★16329]
Coun. on Rehabilitation Educ. [16319], 300 N Martingale Rd., Ste. 460, Schaumburg, IL 60173, (847)944-1345
Coun. of Rehabilitation Specialists - Defunct.
Coun. of Relief Agencies Licensed for Operation in Germany - Defunct.
The Coun. for Religion [★8536]
Coun. on Religion and the Homosexual - Defunct.
Coun. for Religion in Independent Schools [★8536]
Coun. on Religion and Intl. Affairs [★20093]
Coun. on Religion and Intl. Affairs [★IO]
Coun. on Religion and Law - Defunct.
Coun. of Religious Jewish Workers of America - Defunct.
Coun. of Religious Volunteer Agencies [13391], c/o Dan McFadden, Dir., Brethren Volunteer Ser., 1451 Dundee Ave., Elgin, IL 60120, (847)742-5100

Coun. of Religious Volunteer Agencies [★13391]
Coun. of Reprographics Executives - Defunct.
Coun. of Republican Orgs. - Defunct.
Coun. for Res. in Glaucoma and Allied Diseases - Defunct.
Coun. for Res. in Music Educ. [8908], School of Music, 1114 W Nevada St., Urbana, IL 61801, (217)333-1027
Coun. for Res. in Music Educ. [IO], Urbana, IL, United States
Coun. on Res. and Technology - Defunct.
Coun. for Res. on Turkish History - Defunct.
Coun. for Res. in Values and Philosophy [10791], PO Box 261, Cardinal Sta., Washington, DC 20064, (202)319-6089
Coun. for Res. in Values and Philosophy [IO], Washington, DC, United States
Coun. on Resident Educ. in Obstetrics and Gynecology [15597], c/o Amer. Coll. of Obstetricians and Gynecologists, PO Box 96920, Washington, DC 20090-6920, (202)638-5577
Coun. of Resident Summer Theatres - Defunct.
Coun. of Residential Specialists [3307], 430 N Michigan Ave., 3rd Fl., Chicago, IL 60611, (312)321-4400
Coun. for Rsrc. Development [8347], 1 Dupont Cir. NW, Ste. 365, Washington, DC 20036-1176, (202)822-0750
Coun. for Responsible Genetics [18584], 5 Upland Rd., Ste. 3, Cambridge, MA 02140-2717, (617)868-0870
Coun. for Responsible Nutrition [2841], 1828 L St. NW, Ste. 900, Washington, DC 20036-5114, (202)776-7929
Coun. for Responsible Telemedicine [16596]
Coun. on Roentgenology to the Amer. Chiropractic Assn. [★16288]
Coun. for Roshei Yeshivos [★8683]
Coun. for Rural Housing and Development [★12310]
Coun. on the Safe Trans. of Hazardous Articles [★3562]
Coun. of Sailing Associations [23165], c/o U.S. Sailing Assn., PO Box 1260, 15 Maritime Dr., Portsmouth, RI 02871-0907, (401)683-0800
Coun. of Sales Promotion Agencies [★3468]
Coun. of Sales Promotion Agencies [★IO]
Coun. to Save the Postcard - Defunct.
Coun. of Savings and Loan Stock Companies - Defunct.
Coun. of Sci. Editors [3108], c/o Drohan Mgt. Gp., 12100 Sunset Hills Rd., Ste. 130, Reston, VA 20190, (703)437-4377
Coun. on Science and Technology for Development - Defunct.
Coun. of Sci. and Tech. Institutes [★IO]
Coun. for Sci. and Indus. Res. [IO], Pretoria, Republic of South Africa
Coun. of Sci. Soc. Presidents [7605], 1155 16th St. NW, Washington, DC 20036, (202)872-6230
Coun. for Scottish Archaeology [IO], Edinburgh, United Kingdom
Coun. of Scottish Clan Associations [★19352]
Coun. of Scottish Clans and Associations [19352], c/o Christie Harrison, Pres., PO Box 3774, Telluride, CO 81435, (229)985-6540
Coun. of Second Language Programs in Canada [★IO]
Council for Secular Humanism [IO], Amherst, NY, United States
Coun. for Secular Humanism [20085], PO Box 664, Amherst, NY 14226-0664, (716)636-7571
Coun. for a Secure America - Defunct.
Coun. for Sex Info. and Educ. [16400], 2272 Colorado Blvd., No. 1228, Los Angeles, CA 90041
Coun. on Sexual Orientation and Gender Expression [9132], c/o Coun. on Social Work Educ., 1725 Duke St., Ste. 500, Alexandria, VA 22314-3457, (703)683-8080
Coun. on Size and Weight Discrimination [12644], PO Box 305, Mount Marion, NY 12456-0305, (845)679-1209
Coun. of Small and Independent Business Assns. - Defunct.
Coun. for Social and Economic Stud. [18440], PO Box 34070, Washington, DC 20043, (202)371-2700

Coun. of Social Science Data Archives - Defunct.
Coun. for Social Welfare Services in Malawi [★IO]
Coun. on Social Work Educ. [9133], 1725 Duke St., Ste. 500, Alexandria, VA 22314-3457, (703)683-8080
Coun. of Societies in Dental Hypnosis - Defunct.
Coun. of Societies for the Stud. of Religion [9274], PO Box 1872, MS-156, Houston, TX 77251-1892, (713)348-5721
Coun. on Soil Testing and Plant Anal. [★7673]
Coun. on Southern Africa - Address unknown since 2001.
Coun. of the Southern Mountains - Defunct.
Coun. of Specialized Accrediting Agencies - Defunct.
Coun. for Spiritual and Ethical Educ. [8536], PO Box 19807, Portland, OR 97280, (706)354-4043
Coun. on Spiritual Practices [20564], PO Box 10086, Berkeley, CA 94709
Coun. on Sports Injuries and Physical Fitness; Amer. Chiropractic Assn. [13989]
Coun. for Standards in Human Ser. Educ. [9130], PMB 703, 1050 Larrabee Ave., Ste. 104, Bellingham, WA 98225-7367, (360)650-3531
Coun. on Standards for Intl. Educational Travel [8610], 212 S Henry St., Alexandria, VA 22314, (703)739-9050
Coun. on Standards for Intl. Educational Travel [IO], Alexandria, VA, United States
Coun. of State Administrators of Vocational Rehabilitation [16320], 4733 Bethesda Ave., Ste. 330, Bethesda, MD 20814, (301)654-8414
Coun. of State Chambers of Commerce - Address unknown since 2001.
Coun. of State Community Affairs Agencies [★6272]
Coun. of State Community Development Agencies [6272], 1825 K St., Ste. 515, Washington, DC 20006-1226, (202)293-5820
Coun. of State Education Communicators - Defunct.
Coun. of State Governments [6273], 2760 Res. Park Dr., PO Box 11910, Lexington, KY 40511-8482, (859)244-8000
Coun. of State Housing Agencies [★5795]
Coun. of State Sci. Supervisors [9101], c/o C.J. Evans, Treas., 8816 Manchester Rd., No. 261, Brentwood, MO 63144, (314)614-7707
Coun. of State and Territorial Epidemiologists [14374], 2872 Woodcock Blvd., Ste. 303, Atlanta, GA 30341, (770)458-3811
Coun. of Stock Theatres - Address unknown since 1995.
Coun. of Student Personnel Assns. in Higher Education - Defunct.
Coun. on Students Travel [★8608]
Coun. on Students Travel [★IO]
Coun. for the Study of Mankind - Defunct.
Coun. on the Stud. of Religion [★9274]
Coun. of Supply Chain Mgt. Professionals [4018], 333 E Butterfield Rd., Ste. 140, Lombard, IL 60148, (630)574-0985
Coun. for Surface Mining and Reclamation Res. in Appalachia [★6114]
Coun. on Synthetic Fuels [★1677]
Coun. on Synthetic Fuels [★IO]
Council on Tall Buildings and Urban Habitat [IO], Chicago, IL, United States
Coun. on Tall Buildings and Urban Habitat [6474], Illinois Inst. of Tech., S.R. Crown Hall, 3360 S State St., Chicago, IL 60616-3850, (312)909-0253
Coun. of Teachers of Southeast Asian Languages [7990], PO Box 3798, Arlington, VA 22203-0798
Coun. of Teaching Hospitals [14879], c/o Assn. of Amer. Medical Colleges, 2450 N St. NW, Washington, DC 20037-1126, (202)828-0400
Coun. for Technological Advancement - Defunct.
Coun. of Technology Education Assns. - Defunct.
Coun. on Tech. Teacher Educ. [8543], c/o Intl. Tech. Educ. Assn., 1914 Assn. Dr., Reston, VA 20191, (703)860-2100
Coun. on Tech. Teacher Educ. [IO], Reston, VA, United States
Coun. for a TV Course in Humanities for Secondary Schools - Defunct.
Coun. for TV Development - Defunct.
Coun. of Textile and Fashion Indus. of Australia [IO], Melbourne, Australia

Reference to "IO" in place of a book number signifies that the association may be found in the 45th edition of International Organizations.

Coun. for Textile Recycling [3991], c/o Secondary Materials and Recycled Textiles Assn., 131 E Broad St., Ste. 206, Falls Church, VA 22046, (703)538-1000
Coun. for Tobacco Res. - U.S.A. - Defunct.
Coun. of Tree and Landscape Appraisers - Address unknown since 2001.
Coun. on Undergraduate Res. [9059], 734 15th St. NW, Ste. 550, Washington, DC 20005-1013, (202)783-4810
Coun. for Understanding Mental Illness - Defunct.
Coun. for the Understanding of Technology in Human Affairs - Defunct.
Coun. for Unified Res. and Education - Defunct.
Coun. on Union-Free Env. [3949], 825 W Bitters Rd., Ste. 103, San Antonio, TX 78216, (866)409-4283
Coun. of the United Textile Workers of Am. [24194]
Coun. of Univ. Institutes for Urban Affairs [★9287]
Coun. of Univ. Teaching Hospitals - Defunct.
Coun. for Urban Economic Development [★5812]
Coun. for Urban Economic Development [★IO]
Coun. of Urban Health Providers - Defunct.
Coun. of Vedic Astrology [21548], 854 Brock Ave., New Bedford, MA 02744, (508)990-0031
Coun. of Vehicle Assns. Classic Vehicle Advocate Gp. - Address unknown since 2007.
Coun. of Vietnam Veterans [★18786]
Coun. of Vocational Educators - Defunct.
Coun. of Volunteer Americans [18309], c/o Citizens' Investigative Commn., PO Box 1222, Sterling, VA 20167, (703)379-9188
Coun. for a Volunteer Military - Defunct.
Coun. of Women Chiropractors - Defunct.
Coun. of Women Citizens - Defunct.
Coun. for Women in Independent Schools - Defunct.
Coun. of Women's and Infants' Specialty Hospitals [14880], c/o Natl. Perinatal Info. Center, 144 Wayland Ave., Ste. 300, Providence, RI 02906, (401)274-0650
Coun. of Women's Organizations in Israel [IO], Jerusalem, Israel
Coun. of Writers Orgs. - Defunct.
Coun. of Writing Prog. Administrators [9333], c/o Dr. Linda Bergmann, Sec., Purdue Univ., English Dept., Heavilon Hall, West Lafayette, IN 47907-1356, (765)494-7268
Coun. of Young Israel Rabbis [★20197]
Coun. of Young Men's Hebrew and Kindred Associations [★12473]
Coun. of Yukon First Nations [IO], Whitehorse, YT, Canada
Councils of Catholic Educ; Natl. Assn. of Boards, Commissions, and [8056]
Councils for Soviet Jews; Union of [★17452]
Councils; Union of [★17452]
Counseil Canadien de droit Intl. [★IO]
Counsel; Amer. Coll. of Probate [★6183]
Counsel; Amer. Coll. of Trust and Estate [6183]
Counsel Assn; Amer. Corporate [★5614]
Counsel; Assn. of Life Insurance [5826]
Counsel; Assn. of Philanthropic [958]
Counsel for Children; Natl. Assn. of [11711]
Counsel; Intl. Assn. of Insurance [★5499]
Counsel; Natl. Org. of Bar [5953]
Counsel Trial Acad; Defense [★5499]
Counsel Trial Acad; Defense [★IO]
Counseling
  Acad. of Psychosomatic Medicine [16195]
  Access Point [11813]
  Addiction Res. and Treatment Corp. [13213]
  Al-Anon Family Gp. HQ, World Ser. Off. [13214]
  Albert Ellis Inst. [16197]
  Alcohol Res. Info. Ser. [13217]
  Alcoholics Anonymous World Services [13218]
  Alfred Adler Inst. [16117]
  Alive Alone [11511]
  Alliance for Children and Families [12136]
  Alliance Credit Counseling [11833]
  Alternative Family Proj. [11814]
  AMEND [12020]
  Amer. Acad. of Clinical Psychiatrists [16064]
  Amer. Acad. of Counseling Psychology [16118]
  Amer. Acad. of Medical Hypnoanalysts [14914]
  Amer. Acad. of Psychoanalysis and Dynamic Psychiatry [16101]

Amer. Acad. of Psychotherapists [16198]
Amer. Adoption Cong. [11234]
Amer. Amputee Found. [11916]
Amer. Art Therapy Assn. [16199]
Amer. Assn. of Christian Counselors [19862]
Amer. Assn. of Christian Counselors [IO]
Amer. Assn. of Directors of Psychiatric Residency Training [16067]
Amer. Assn. of LifeStyle Counselors [14053]
Amer. Assn. for Marriage and Family Therapy [16200]
Amer. Assn. of Pastoral Counselors [19863]
Amer. Assn. of Psychiatric Technicians [16069]
Amer. Assn. of Sexuality Educators, Counselors and Therapists [16398]
Amer. Assn. of State Counseling Boards [14054]
Amer. Bd. of Examiners in Pastoral Counseling [19864]
Amer. Bd. of Genetic Counseling [14492]
Amer. Bd. of Professional Psychology [16121]
Amer. Bd. of Vocational Experts [9299]
Amer. Coll. of Addiction Treatment Administrators [13219]
Amer. Coll. Counseling Assn. [8162]
American College Counseling Association [IO]
Amer. Coll. of Counselors [12137]
Amer. Coun. on Alcohol Problems [13220]
Amer. Coun. on Alcoholism [13221]
Amer. Coun. for Drug Educ. [13222]
Amer. Coun. of Hypnotist Examiners [14918]
Amer. Counseling Assn. [11815]
Amer. Dance Therapy Assn. [16203]
Amer. Family Therapy Acad. [11816]
Amer. Found. for Suicide Prevention [13287]
Amer. Gp. Psychotherapy Assn. [16204]
Amer. Hea. and Temperance Assn. [13303]
Amer. Mental Hea. Alliance [15188]
Amer. Mental Hea. Counselors Assn. [15189]
Amer. Mothers, Inc. [12139]
Amer. Music Therapy Assn. [16205]
Amer. Psychoanalytic Assn. [16102]
Amer. Psychological Assn. [16122]
Amer. Psychological Assn. - Addictions Div. [16123]
American Psychological Association Division 31 - State, Provincial, and Territorial Psychological Association Affairs [16124]
Amer. Psychological Assn. - Division of Family Psychology [16125]
Amer. Psychological Assn. Division of Independent Practice [16126]
Amer. Psychological Assn. - Div. of Intl. Psychology [16127]
Amer. Psychological Assn. - Div. of Trauma Psychology [16128]
Amer. Psychological Assn. - Hea. Psychology Div. [16130]
Amer. Psychological Assn. - Media Psychology Div. [16131]
Amer. Psychological Assn. - Psychology of Religion (Division 36) [16132]
Amer. Psychology-Law Soc. [16133]
Amer. Psychopathological Assn. [16190]
Amer. Psychosocial Oncology Soc. [15638]
Amer. Psychosomatic Soc. [16196]
Amer. Psychotherapy Assn. [16207]
Amer. Rehabilitation Counseling Assn. [16313]
Amer. School Counselor Assn. [8163]
American School Counselor Association [IO]
Amer. School Hea. Assn. [14718]
Amer. Schools Assn. [8164]
Amer. Soc. of Psychoanalytic Physicians [16104]
Amer. Soc. of Separated and Divorced Men [12005]
AMHS [11817]
Amputees in Motion, Intl. [11921]
Anxiety Disorders Assn. of Am. [12743]
Anxiety Disorders Special Interest Gp. [12744]
Anxiety and Phobia Treatment Center [12745]
Assn. for Advanced Training in the Behavioral Sciences [8878]
Assn. for Advancement of Psychoanalysis (of the Karen Horney Psychoanalytic Inst. and Center) [16105]
Assn. for the Advancement of Psychology [16136]

Assn. for the Advancement of Psychotherapy [16210]
Assn. for Assessment in Counseling and Educ. [9247]
Assn. of Behavioral Healthcare Mgt. [15191]
Assn. for Birth Psychology [16137]
Assn. of Black Psychologists [16138]
Assn. for Careers Educ. and Guidance [IO]
Assn. for Child Psychoanalysis [16106]
Assn. for Clinical Pastoral Educ. [19915]
Assn. for Counselling at Work [IO]
Assn. for Counselor Educ. and Supervision [8165]
Assn. for Counselors and Educators in Govt. [11818]
Assn. for Couples in Marriage Enrichment [12505]
Assn. for Death Educ. and Counseling [11909]
Assn. of Fraternity Advisors [24475]
Assn. for Gay, Lesbian, and Bisexual Issues in Counseling [12216]
Assn. of Graduate Careers Advisory Services [IO]
Assn. of Halfway House Alcoholism Programs of North Am. [13224]
Assn. for Humanistic Psychology [16140]
Assn. of Mormon Counselors and Psychotherapists [16212]
Assn. for Multicultural Counseling and Development [11819]
Assn. of Oncology Social Work [13199]
Assn. for Pet Loss and Bereavement [12706]
Assn. for Psychoanalytic Medicine [16107]
Assn. for Psychological Type Intl. [16143]
Assn. for Specialists in Gp. Work [11820]
Assn. for Spiritual, Ethical and Religious Values in Counseling [8166]
Assn. of State and Provincial Psychology Boards [16144]
Assn. of Traumatic Stress Specialists [11821]
Assn. of Traumatic Stress Specialists [IO]
Assn. for Univ. and Coll. Counseling Center Directors [IO]
Assn. for Univ. and Coll. Counseling Center Directors [8167]
Assn. for Women in Psychology [16145]
BACCHUS Network [13226]
Bereavement Services [12663]
Better Boys Found. [11675]
Black Mental Hea. Alliance [15193]
Bonus Families [12143]
Bridge Pastoral Found. [IO]
British Columbia School Counsellors' Assn. [IO]
Canadian Career Development Found. [IO]
Canadian Counselling Assn. [IO]
Canadian Univ. and Coll. Counselling Assn. [IO]
Cancer Info. Ser. [13807]
Career Planning and Adult Development Network [12070]
Catholic Parents Network [12664]
Center for Applications of Psychological Type [16146]
Center for Death Educ. and Bioethics [13314]
Center for Psychological and Spiritual Hea. [15194]
Center for Visionary Leadership [18002]
C.G. Jung Found. for Analytical Psychology [16147]
Chi Sigma Iota [1099]
Childhelp USA [11680]
Children of Alcoholics Found. [13228]
Children of the Americas [11574]
Children of the Night [12933]
Children's Defense Fund [11685]
Children's Grief Educ. Assn. [12265]
Christian Assn. for Psychological Stud. [16148]
Christian Chaplain Sers. [19745]
Christian Counsellors Assn. of Australia - New South Wales [IO]
Christian Counsellors Assn. of Australia - Queensland [IO]
Christian Counsellors Assn. of Australia - South Australia [IO]
Christian Counsellors Assn. of Australia - Victoria [IO]
Christian Counsellors Assn. of Australia - Western Australia [IO]
Christian Family Life [12146]

A star before a book entry number signifies that the name is not listed separately, but is mentioned within the entry.

Christian Family Renewal [19776]
Commn. on Rehabilitation Counselor Certification [11822]
Commn. on Religious Counseling and Healing [19445]
Community Guidance Ser. [16214]
Compassion in Dying Fed. [12130]
The Compassionate Friends [12666]
Concerned Persons for Adoption [11240]
Concerned United Birthparents [11241]
Concerns of Police Survivors [12752]
CONTACT USA [19865]
Corporate and Found. Relations [12075]
Coun. for Accreditation of Counseling and Related Educational Programs [8168]
Coun. on Career for Minorities [8047]
Coun. on Compulsive Gambling of New Jersey [12209]
Coun. for Sex Info. and Educ. [16400]
Counseling Assn. for Humanistic Educ. and Development [8527]
Counselling Assn. of South Australia [IO]
CRISTA Ministries [13166]
Damien Ministries [19866]
DateAble [11936]
Dementia Advocacy and Support Network Intl. [12638]
Do It Now Found. [13235]
Donors' Offspring [13298]
Drustvo Prijatelja Biblije [IO]
Druzya Svyashchennogo Pisaniya [IO]
Educ. and Enrichment Sect. of the Natl. Coun. on Family Relations [12151]
Employee Assistance Soc. of North Am. [11823]
Ethos Found. [13239]
European Forum for Student Guidance [IO]
Euthanasia Res. and Guidance Org. [12132]
Exodus Trust [16401]
Faces and Voices of Recovery [18688]
Fairview Pregnancy and Newborn Loss Information [12668]
Families Adopting Children Everywhere [11242]
Families Worldwide [13241]
Family Therapy Sect. of the Natl. Coun. on Family Relations [16612]
Feminism and Family Stud. Sect. of the Natl. Coun. on Family Relations [12156]
Found. for Sci. and Disability [11946]
Friendly Hand Found. [13243]
Gay Men's Hea. Crisis [13564]
Gift From Within [12768]
God's Love We Deliver [12283]
Good Tidings [19629]
Goodwill Indus. Intl. [11949]
Goodwill Indus. Volunteer Services [11950]
Gp. for the Advancement of Psychiatry [16084]
Hazelden Found. [13244]
Hea. Connection [13245]
Heartbeat [13288]
Hetrick-Martin Inst. [12234]
Hospice Educ. Inst. [14854]
House of Ruth [12029]
Inst. for the Advancement of Human Behavior [13735]
Inst. of Career Guidance [IO]
Inst. for the Development of Emotional and Life Skills/National Inst. of Relationship Enhancement [15201]
Inst. for Expressive Anal. [16217]
Inst. for Labor and Mental Health [15202]
Inst. on Psychiatric Services/American Psychiatric Assn. [16085]
Inter-Association Task Force on Alcohol and Other Substance Abuse Issues [13250]
Intl. Alliance of Holistic Lawyers [5498]
Intl. Assn. of Addictions and Offender Counselors [11824]
International Association of Addictions and Offender Counselors [IO]
Intl. Assn. of Biblical Counselors [IO]
Intl. Assn. of Biblical Counselors [19867]
Intl. Assn. for Cognitive Psychotherapy [16218]
Intl. Assn. of Counseling Services [8169]
Intl. Assn. of Counseling Services [IO]
Intl. Assn. for Educational and Vocational Guidance [IO]

Intl. Assn. of Integrative Coaches [11740]
Intl. Assn. for Marriage and Family Counselors [11825]
Intl. Assn. for Marriage and Family Counselors [IO]
Intl. Assn. of Medical Intuitives [15040]
Intl. Assn. of Pastoral Psychologists [16151]
Intl. Assn. for Regression Res. and Therapies [16617]
Intl. Assn. for Relational Psychoanalysis and Psychotherapy [16108]
Intl. Assn. for Relationship Res. [7571]
Intl. Assn. for Truancy and Dropout Prevention [8326]
Intl. Center for Attitudinal Healing [15206]
Intl. Commn. for the Prevention of Alcoholism and Drug Dependency [13251]
Intl. Comm. Against Mental Illness [15207]
Intl. Doctors in Alcoholics Anonymous [13252]
Intl. Expressive Arts Therapy Assn. [13712]
Intl. Hea. and Temperance Assn. [13304]
Intl. Mentoring Network Org. [11520]
Intl. Professional Surrogates Assn. [16403]
Intl. Psycho-Oncology Soc. [13834]
Intl. REST Investigators Soc. [16220]
Intl. Soc. for Adolescent Psychiatry and Psychology [16087]
Intl. Soc. for Dialogical Sci. [7544]
Intl. Soundex Reunion Registry [11248]
Intl. Transactional Anal. Assn. [16089]
Irish Assn. for Counselling and Psychotherapy [IO]
ISCO Careerscope [IO]
Islamic Correctional Reunion Assn. [20105]
Jean Piaget Soc.: Soc. for the Stud. of Knowledge and Development [16156]
Jewish Bd. of Family and Children's Services/ Youth Counseling League Div. [13492]
Jewish Guild for the Blind [16862]
Just One Break [11957]
Karen Horney Clinic [16109]
Last Harvest Ministries [12917]
Latin Am. Parents Assn. [11252]
Liberal Educ. for Adoptive Families [11253]
LIFE [20060]
Ligue pour la Lecture de la Bible - Brazzaville [IO]
Ligue pour la Lecture de la Bible - Burkina Faso [IO]
Ligue pour la Lecture de la Bible - Central African Republic [IO]
Ligue pour la Lecture de la Bible - Cote d'Ivoire [IO]
Ligue pour la Lecture de la Bible - Guinea [IO]
Ligue pour la Lecture de la Bible - Madagascar [IO]
Love in Action [19868]
Loved Ones and Drivers Support [13347]
ManKind Proj. [13021]
Men's Rsrc. Center [12357]
Mental Hea. Am. [15211]
Metanoia Ministries [19869]
Milton H. Erickson Found. [16221]
A Minor Consideration [11826]
NAADAC The Assn. for Addiction Professionals [16509]
Narcotic Educational Found. of Am. [13256]
Natl. Academic Advising Assn. [8170]
National Academic Advising Association [IO]
Natl. Action for Former Military Wives [12012]
Natl. Adoption Center [11254]
Natl. Alliance on Mental Illness [15214]
Natl. Amputation Found. [11965]
Natl. Assn. of Academic Advisors for Athletics [8171]
Natl. Assn. for the Advancement of Psychoanalysis [16110]
Natl. Assn. of Advisors for the Hea. Professions [8866]
Natl. Assn. for Children of Alcoholics [13261]
Natl. Assn. for Drama Therapy [16222]
Natl. Assn. on Drug Abuse Problems [13262]
Natl. Assn. of Forensic Counselors [5647]
Natl. Assn. of Lesbian/Gay Addiction Professionals [13263]
Natl. Assn. of Mental Hea. Planning and Advisory Councils [15216]

Natl. Assn. of Peer Programs [11827]
Natl. Assn. for Poetry Therapy [16223]
Natl. Assn. of Psychiatric Hea. Systems [16091]
Natl. Assn. for Res. and Therapy of Homosexuality [14434]
Natl. Assn. for Rural Mental Hea. [15217]
Natl. Assn. of School Psychologists [16160]
Natl. Assn. of State Mental Hea. Prog. Directors [15219]
Natl. Assn. of Therapeutic Wilderness Camps [23276]
Natl. Assn. for Visually Handicapped [16874]
Natl. Bd. for Certified Counselors and Affiliates [11828]
Natl. Career Development Assn. [12090]
Natl. Catholic Coun. on Alcoholism and Related Drug Problems [13266]
Natl. Center for Amer. Indian and Alaska Native Mental Hea. Res. [15220]
Natl. Center for Victims of Crime [13366]
Natl. Coalition Against Domestic Violence [12034]
Natl. Comm. for the Prevention of Alcoholism and Drug Dependency [13267]
Natl. Coun. for Adoption [11255]
Natl. Coun. on Alcoholism and Drug Dependence [13268]
Natl. Council for Single Adoptive Parents [11256]
Natl. Employment Counseling Assn. [12091]
Natl. Exchange Club Found. [11637]
Natl. Families in Action [13269]
Natl. Family Partnership [13270]
Natl. Marriage Encounter [12507]
Natl. MultiCultural Inst. [11829]
Natl. Network for Youth [12935]
Natl. Org. for People of Color Against Suicide [13289]
Natl. Org. for Victim Assistance [13369]
Natl. Psychological Assn. for Psychoanalysis [16111]
Natl. Rehabilitation Counseling Assn. [16331]
Natl. Religious Affairs Assn. [19872]
Natl. Runaway Switchboard [12936]
Natl. Soc. of Genetic Counselors [14506]
Natl. Temperance and Prohibition Coun. [13305]
Natl. Woman's Christian Temperance Union [13306]
New Zealand Christian Counsellors Assn. [IO]
Nigeria Scripture Union [IO]
North Amer. Coun. on Adoptable Children [11257]
North Amer. Soc. of Adlerian Psychology [16162]
The Nurturing Network [13434]
Obsessive-Compulsive Anonymous [12555]
Ontario Native Educ. Counselling Assn. [IO]
Ontario School Counsellor's Assn. [IO]
Org. for Attempters and Survivors of Suicide in Interfaith Services [13290]
Organized Adoption Search Info. Services [11259]
ORIGINS [11260]
Orphan Voyage [11261]
Our Little Bros. and Sisters [20380]
Outpost [19870]
Pact Training [11830]
Partnership for a Drug-Free Am. [13272]
Paul and Lisa Prog. [13082]
Phoenix House [13273]
Postgraduate Center for Mental Hea. [16227]
PRIDE Youth Programs [13276]
Psychohistory Forum [16113]
Psychology Soc. [16165]
Psychometric Soc. [16166]
Psychonomic Soc. [16167]
Psychotherapy Network [16228]
Rabbinic Center for Res. and Counseling [16229]
Radical Caucus in Psychiatry [16092]
Real Found. [13438]
Reclamation Inc. [12556]
Recovery, Inc. [16230]
Regeneration [19871]
Religion and Family Life Sect. of the Natl. Coun. on Family Relations [12165]
Sandplay Therapists of Am. [16635]
Scripture Union - Australia [IO]
Scripture Union - Benin [IO]
Scripture Union - Botswana [IO]
Scripture Union Burundi [IO]

Reference to "IO" in place of a book number signifies that the association may be found in the 45th edition of International Organizations.

Scripture Union - Cambodia [IO]
Scripture Union - Cameroon [IO]
Scripture Union - Canada [IO]
Scripture Union - Democratic Republic of Congo [IO]
Scripture Union - Egypt [IO]
Scripture Union England and Wales [IO]
Scripture Union Equatorial Guinea [IO]
Scripture Union in Fiji [IO]
Scripture Union - India [IO]
Scripture Union - Indonesia [IO]
Scripture Union - Israel [IO]
Scripture Union Japan [IO]
Scripture Union of Kenya [IO]
Scripture Union - Kyrgyzstan [IO]
Scripture Union of Lesotho [IO]
Scripture Union - Liberia [IO]
Scripture Union Lithuania [IO]
Scripture Union of Malawi [IO]
Scripture Union - Mongolia [IO]
Scripture Union - Namibia [IO]
Scripture Union - Nepal [IO]
Scripture Union - New Caledonia [IO]
Scripture Union New South Wales [IO]
Scripture Union in New Zealand [IO]
Scripture Union - Niger [IO]
Scripture Union Northern Ireland [IO]
Scripture Union - Pakistan [IO]
Scripture Union - Philippines [IO]
Scripture Union Poland [IO]
Scripture Union Romania [IO]
Scripture Union - Russia [IO]
Scripture Union Rwanda [IO]
Scripture Union - Samoa [IO]
Scripture Union Scotland [IO]
Scripture Union of Sierra Leone [IO]
Scripture Union Singapore [IO]
Scripture Union - Sri Lanka [IO]
Scripture Union - Sudan [IO]
Scripture Union - Swaziland [IO]
Scripture Union in Taiwan [IO]
Scripture Union of Tanzania [IO]
Scripture Union - Togo [IO]
Scripture Union - Tonga [IO]
Scripture Union - Uganda [IO]
Scripture Union - Vanuatu [IO]
Scripture Union Victoria [IO]
Scripture Union - Zambia [IO]
Seamen's Church Inst. of New York and New Jersey [19970]
Senior Action in a Gay Env. [12256]
September 11th Families' Assn. [13371]
Sex and Love Addicts Anonymous [13074]
Shanti [11831]
Sigmund Freud Archives [16115]
Social Psychiatry Res. Inst. [16094]
Social/Vocational Rehabilitation Clinic [16231]
Soc. of Behavioral Medicine [13740]
Soc. of Biological Psychiatry [16095]
Soc. of Clinical Child and Adolescent Psychology [16171]
Soc. of Consulting Psychology [16172]
Soc. for Indus. and Organizational Psychology [16173]
Soc. of Multivariate Experimental Psychology [16174]
Soc. for Pediatric Psychology [16175]
Soc. for Personality Assessment [16176]
Soc. of Professors of Child and Adolescent Psychiatry [16096]
Soc. for the Psychological Stud. of Men and Masculinity [16181]
Soc. for the Psychological Stud. of Social Issues [16182]
Soc. for Psychophysiological Res. [16183]
Soc. of St. Vincent de Paul Coun. of the U.S. [13190]
Soc. for Vocational Psychology [7551]
Stroke Awareness for Everyone [16495]
Stroke Clubs, Intl. [16496]
Suicide Prevention Action Network USA [13292]
Teaching-Family Assn. [12169]
Toughlove Intl. [12694]
Tragedy Assistance Prog. for Survivors [11503]
Uniao Biblica Mocambique [IO]

Union Biblica Argentina [IO]
Union Biblica Chilena [IO]
Union Biblica de Colombia [IO]
Union Biblica Ecuatorina [IO]
United Church of Christ Coalition for Lesbian, Gay, Bisexual and Transgender Concerns [20067]
United Fathers of Am. [12014]
U.S.A. Transactional Anal. Assn. [13743]
U.S. Psychiatric Rehabilitation Assn. [16336]
Victims of Choice [12930]
Village of Childhelp West [11661]
Violent Death Bereavement Soc. [11513]
VOICES in Action [13086]
Western Australia Scripture Union [IO]
William Glasser Inst. [16233]
William Wendt Center for Loss and Healing [13317]
Wives-Self-Help Found. [11832]
Women's Drug Res. Project [13285]
World Ability Fed. [11995]
World Assn. for Infant Mental Hea. [16098]
World Assn. for Social Psychiatry [16099]
World Fed. for Mental Hea. [15237]
Zero to Three: Natl. Center for Infants, Toddlers and Families [13944]
Counseling; Amer. Bd. of Genetic [14492]
Counseling; Amer. Bd. on Professional Standards in Vocational [★8169]
Counseling; Amer. Inst. of Employment [★1272]
Counseling Assn; Amer. Rehabilitation [16313]
Counseling; Assn. for Assessment in [★9247]
Counseling; Assn. for Death Educ. and [11909]
Counseling; Assn. for Gay, Lesbian, and Bisexual Issues in [12216]
Counseling Assn. for Humanistic Educ. and Development [8527], c/o Amer. Counseling Assn., PO Box 791006, Baltimore, MD 21279-1006, (703)823-9800
Counseling Assn; Natl. Employment [12091]
Counseling Assn; Natl. Rehabilitation [16331]
Counseling; Assn. for Religious and Value Issues in [★8166]
Counseling Center; Allied Youth and Family [13465]
Counseling Center; Amer. Coll. and Career [7911]
Counseling Center; Intl. [★11829]
Counseling Center; James Weldon Johnson Family and Children's [★12785]
Counseling Center; Multicultural Inst. of the Intl. [★11829]
Counseling and Development; Amer. Assn. for [★11815]
Counseling and Development; Assn. for Measurement and Evaluation in [★9247]
Counseling and Educ. to Stop Domestic Violence; Emerge: [12026]
Counseling; Forum for Death Educ. and [★11909]
Counseling and Human Development Found. [★11815]
Counseling; Intl. Assn. of Trauma [★11821]
Counseling League Div; Jewish Bd. of Family and Children's Services/Youth [13492]
Counseling; Natl. Assn. for Coll. Admission [7912]
Counseling Program; Readjustment [★21308]
Counseling Psychology; Acad. of [★16118]
Counseling Psychology; Amer. Acad. of [16118]
Counseling and Psychotherapy; Amer. Soc. for Philosophy [16209]
Counseling; Rabbinic Center for Res. and [16229]
Counseling Ser. on Domestic Violence; Emerge: A Men's [★12026]
Counseling Services; Amer. Bd. on [★8169]
Counselling Assn. of South Australia [IO], Kent Town, Australia
Counselling and Psychotherapy in Scotland [IO], Stirling, United Kingdom
Counsellors; Natl. Inst. of Mgt. [2508]
Counsellors and Psychotherapists Assn. of New South Wales [IO], Sydney, Australia
Counsellors' and Psychotherapists' Assn. of Victoria [IO], Brighton, Australia
Counselor Assn. - Address unknown since 1999.
Counselor Educators; Coun. of Rehabilitation [★16329]
Counselors; Acad. of Clinical Mental Hea. [★11828]

Counselors; Amer. Assn. of Marriage [★16200]
Counselors; Amer. Assn. of Marriage and Family [★16200]
Counselors; Amer. Assn. of Sex Educators and [★16398]
Counselors; Amer. Coll. of [12137]
Counselors; Amer. Soc. of Real Estate [★3308]
Counselors in APGA; Catholic [★8166]
Counselors Assn; Amer. Mental Hea. [15189]
Counselors Assn; Independent Educational [★7871]
Counselors and Family Therapists; Natl. Acad. of [★12137]
Counselors; Inst. of Certified Bus. [726]
Counselors; Natl. Assn. of [3318]
Counselors; Natl. Assn. of Alcoholism and Drug Abuse [★16509]
Counselors; Natl. Bd. for Certified [★11828]
Counselors; Natl. Soc. of Genetic [14506]
Counselors of Real Estate [3308], 430 N Michigan Ave., Chicago, IL 60611-4011, (312)329-8427
Counselors of Real Estate [IO], Chicago, IL, United States
Counselors; Soc. of Certified Insurance [8577]
Counselors and Therapists; Amer. Assn. of Sexuality Educators, [16398]
Counsels' Assn. of Accident and Hea. Counsels; Gen. [★5499]
Count Dracula Fan Club [★9639]
Count Dracula Fan Club [★24824]
Count Dracula Fan Club [★IO]
Count Dracula Soc. [10420]
Countdown 2001 [★8453]
Counted Thread Soc. of America - Defunct.
Counter Intelligence Corps Assn; Natl. [21164]
Counter-Terrorism Officers Assn; Intl. [18732]
Counterfeiting Coalition; Intl. Anti [17333]
CounterIntelligence Assn; Marine Corps [19224]
Counterpart Found. [★12426]
Counterpart Found. [★IO]
Counterpart Intl. [IO], Washington, DC, United States
Counterpart Intl. [12426], 1200 18th St. NW, Ste. 1100, Washington, DC 20036, (202)296-9676
Counterpart - U.S. Off. [17834], 1200 18th St. NW, Ste. 1100, Washington, DC 20036-2561, (202)296-9676
Counterpart - U.S. Off. [IO], Washington, DC, United States
Counterparts - Address unknown since 2002.
Counterterrorism and Security Professionals; Intl. Assn. for [18731]
Counties; Conf. of Executives of State Associations of [★5624]
Counties; Natl. Assn. of [5618]
Country; Amers. United for God and [17287]
Country Bound - Defunct.
Country Class Fan Club - Address unknown since 2002.
Country Coach Intl. [23012], PO Box 400, Junction City, OR 97448, (800)537-0622
Country Dance Soc. of Am. [★9873]
Country Dance and Song Soc. [9873], 132 Main St., PO Box 338, Haydenville, MA 01039-0338, (413)268-7426
Country Dance and Song Soc. of Am. [★9873]
Country Day School Headmasters Assn. of the U.S. - Defunct.
Country Edition Fan Club - Defunct.
Country Fire Fan Club - Address unknown since 1988.
Country Land and Bus. Assn. [IO], London, United Kingdom
Country Landowners Assn. [★IO]
Country Legends Assn. [10583], 942 89th Ave. W, No. 102, Duluth, MN 55808, (218)626-9044
Country Music
Acad. of Country Music [10518]
Americana Music Assn. [10555]
Annie Sims Intl. Fan Club [24842]
Art Greenhaw Official Intl. Fan Club [24843]
Austin Cody's Official Intl. Fan Club [24845]
Billy "Crash" Craddock Fan Club [24849]
Carla Riggs-Hall Intl. Fan Club [24855]
Chris Blair Fan Club [24802]
Chris LeDoux Intl. Fan Club [24861]

A star before a book entry number signifies that the name is not listed separately, but is mentioned within the entry.

Chris Young Fan Club **[24862]**
Circle Club - The Official Fan Club of the Grand Ole Opry **[24864]**
Clay Underwood Fan Club **[24865]**
Country Dance and Song Soc. **[9873]**
Country Legends Assn. **[10583]**
Country Music Assn. **[10584]**
Country Music Found. **[10585]**
Dolly Parton's Fan Club **[24877]**
Dollywood Found. **[24878]**
Donna Fargo Intl. Fan Club **[24879]**
Ethel Delaney Intl. Fan Club **[24886]**
Friends of Guy Clark **[24893]**
Friends of Ty Herndon Fan Club **[24896]**
Gary Morris Fan Club **[24897]**
Hank Williams Jr. Fan Club **[24906]**
Intl. Traditional Country Music Fan Club **[24914]**
Intl. Willie Nelson Fan Club **[24915]**
Jeannie Seely's Circle of Friends **[24917]**
Jim Hubbard Fan Club **[24920]**
Kelly Lang Fan Club **[24932]**
Lee's Familee **[24937]**
Linda Davis Fan Club **[24939]**
Marty Stuart Fan Club **[24945]**
Natl. Traditional Country Music Assn. **[10670]**
North Am. Country Music Associations, Intl. **[10674]**
Official Lane Brody and Eleni Global Fan Club **[24953]**
Pam Tillis Fan Club **[24956]**
Rustie Blue Intl. Fan Club **[24972]**
Sawyer Brown Intl. Fan Club **[24974]**
Shon Branham Fan Club **[24803]**
Tammy Wynette Intl. Fan Club **[24979]**
Tanya Tucker Fan Club **[24980]**
Ursuline Companions in Mission **[20408]**
Wynonna Intl. Fan Club **[24992]**
Country Music; Acad. of **[10518]**
Country Music Assn. **[10584]**, 1 Music Cir. S, Nashville, TN 37203-4312, (615)244-2840
Country Music Assn. of Australia **[IO]**, Tamworth, Australia
Country Music Assn; Natl. Traditional **[10670]**
Country Music Assn; Natl. Traditional **[★10670]**
Country Music Assn; Traditional **[★10670]**
Country Music Club; Cornhusker **[★10670]**
Country Music Disk Jockeys Assn. - Defunct.
Country Music Fan Club - Defunct.
Country Music Found. **[10585]**, 222 Fifth Ave. S, Nashville, TN 37203, (615)416-2001
Country Music Showcase Intl. **[10586]**, PO Box 368, Carlisle, IA 50047-0368, (515)989-3748
Country Owners Registry; Chrysler Town and **[21612]**
Country Party of Australia **[★IO]**
Country Pride Dance Club **[IO]**, Red Deer, AB, Canada
Country Radio Broadcasters **[557]**, 819 18th Ave. S, Nashville, TN 37203, (615)327-4487
Country Radio Broadcasters; Org. of **[★557]**
Country-Rock Music
Alabama Fan Club **[24838]**
Dolly Parton's Fan Club **[24877]**
Gram Parsons Found. **[24903]**
Lorrie Morgan Intl. Fan Club **[24940]**
Suzy Bogguss Fan Club **[24978]**
Trisha Yearwood Fan Club **[24988]**
Country Spirit Dance Soc. **[IO]**, Calgary, AB, Canada
Country-Western Music
Always Patsy Cline World Wide Fan Org. **[24840]**
Art Greenhaw Official Intl. Fan Club **[24843]**
Bob Homan Fan Club **[24852]**
Bonnie Lou Bishop Intl. Fan Club **[24853]**
Cecilia Lee Intl. Fan Club **[24856]**
Charley Pride Fan Club **[24857]**
Chet Atkins Appreciation Soc. **[24858]**
Country Dance and Song Soc. **[9873]**
Country Legends Assn. **[10583]**
Country Radio Broadcasters **[557]**
Danny Cooksey Fan Club **[24736]**
David Allan Coe Fan Club **[24870]**
George Strait Fan Club **[24901]**
Intl. Traditional Country Music Fan Club **[24914]**
Jana Jae Fan Club **[24916]**
Jerry Jeff Walker Fan Club **[24919]**

Jimmy Kish "The Flying Cowboy" Fan Club **[24922]**
Johnny Len Fan Club **[24928]**
Kitty Wells-Johnny Wright-Bobby Wright Intl. Fan Club **[24936]**
North Am. Country Music Associations, Intl. **[10674]**
Oak Ridge Boys Intl. Fan Club **[24952]**
Ray Price Intl. Fan Club **[24963]**
Razzy Bailey Fan Club **[24964]**
Ricky Skaggs Intl. Fan Club **[24968]**
Roy Rogers - Dale Evans Collectors Assn. **[24971]**
Tex Ritter Fan Club **[24982]**
Country and Western Music; Acad. of **[★10518]**
Country Women's Assn. of Australia **[IO]**, Sassafras, Australia
Country Women's Coun. U.S.A. - Defunct.
Countryside Alliance **[IO]**, London, United Kingdom
Countryside Coun. for Wales **[IO]**, Bangor, United Kingdom
Countrywomen's League Program Parade - Defunct.
County 4-H Club Agents; Natl. Assn. of **[★13495]**
County Agricultural Agents; Natl. Assn. of **[5438]**
County Behavioral Hea. Directors; Natl. Assn. of **[14708]**
County Building Officials; Assn. of Major City/ **[5547]**
County Chasers of America - Address unknown since 2006.
County and City Hea. Officials; Natl. Assn. of **[6217]**
County Club Agents; Natl. Assn. of **[★13495]**
County Community Development Directors; Natl. Assn. of **[★17225]**
County Community and Economic Development; Natl. Assn. for **[17225]**
County Development Coordinators; Natl. Conf. of **[★5622]**
County of Employment and Training Administrators; Natl. Assn. of **[★5618]**
County Engineers; Natl. Assn. of **[7029]**
County Government
Natl. Assn. of Black County Officials **[5617]**
Natl. Assn. of Counties **[5618]**
Natl. Assn. of County Civil Attorneys **[5619]**
Natl. Assn. of County Info. Officers **[5620]**
Natl. Assn. of County Recorders, Election Officials, and Clerks **[5621]**
Natl. Assn. of County Relations Officials **[5622]**
Natl. Assn. of County Surveyors **[5623]**
Natl. Assn. of Local Housing Finance Agencies **[5794]**
Natl. Black Caucus of Local Elected Officials **[6127]**
Natl. Coun. of County Assn. Executives **[5624]**
County Hea. Fac. Administrators; Natl. Assn. of **[15069]**
County Hea. Officers; Natl. Assn. of **[★6217]**
County Hea. Officials; Natl. Assn. of **[★6217]**
County Human Services Administrators; Natl. Assn. of **[★5618]**
County Intermediate Unit Superintendents (of NEA) **[★7882]**
County and Municipal Employees; Amer. Fed. of State, **[24069]**
County Off. Employees; Natl. Assn. of Farm Ser. Agency **[5779]**
County Officials; Natl. Assn. of **[★5618]**
County Park and Recreation Officials; Natl. Assn. of **[6155]**
County of Philadelphia; Carpenters' Company of the City and **[★10018]**
County Planners; Natl. Assn. of **[5589]**
County Planning Directors; Natl. Assn. of **[★5589]**
County and Prosecuting Attorneys; Natl. Assn. of **[★5668]**
County Recorders and Clerks; Natl. Assn. of **[★5621]**
County Training and Employment Professionals; Natl. Assn. of **[★5618]**
County Treasurers and Finance Officers; Natl. Assn. of **[6205]**
County Veterans Ser. Officers; Natl. Assn. of **[21309]**
County Welfare Directors; Natl. Assn. of **[★5618]**
Couple Counselling Scotland **[★IO]**
Couple to Couple League **[12636]**, PO Box 111184, Cincinnati, OH 45211-1184, (513)471-2000

Couples, Inc. - Address unknown since 1989.
Couples in Marriage Enrichment; Assn. for **[12505]**
Couples Natl. Network **[17650]**, PO Box 500699, Marathon, FL 33050-0699, (800)896-0717
Coupon Exchange Club **[17327]**
Coupon Professionals; Assn. of **[3399]**
Cour permanente d'arbitrage **[★IO]**
Courage **[IO]**, New York, NY, United States
Courage **[20052]**, c/o St. John the Baptist Church, 210 W 31st St., New York, NY 10001, (212)268-1010
Courage Stroke Network **[★13890]**
Courier Assn. of Am; Messenger **[★3573]**
Courier Assn. of the Americas; Messenger **[3573]**
Courier Conf. of Am; Air **[★3565]**
Courier and Logistics Assn; Canadian **[IO]**
Court Admin; Natl. Assn. for **[★5627]**
Court Administrative Officers; Natl. Conf. of **[★5625]**
Court Administrators; Natl. Assn. of Trial **[★5627]**
Court Administrators; Natl. Conf. of State **[★5625]**
Court Appointed Special Advocate Assn; Natl. **[11636]**
Court Appointed Special Advocates Assn. **[★11636]**
Court of Arbitration for Sport **[IO]**, Lausanne, Switzerland
Court Center; Natl. Youth **[18854]**
Court Clubs Assn; Natl. **[★3021]**
Court and Commercial Newspapers; Amer. **[3202]**
Court and Commercial Newspapers; Assoc. **[★3202]**
Court Employees
Amer. Guild of Court Videographers **[6019]**
Assn. of Legal Court Interpreters and Translators **[IO]**
Conf. of State Court Administrators **[5625]**
Fed. Circuit Bar Assn. **[5493]**
Fed. Court Clerks Assn. **[5626]**
John Marshall Found. **[10042]**
Natl. Assn. of County Recorders, Election Officials, and Clerks **[5621]**
Natl. Assn. for Court Mgt. **[5627]**
Natl. Assn. for Court Mgt. **[5627]**
Natl. Assn. of Hearing Officials **[5906]**
Natl. Assn. of Judiciary Interpreters and Translators **[5628]**
Natl. Conf. of Appellate Court Clerks **[5629]**
Natl. Court Reporters Assn. **[5630]**
Shorthand Reporters Assn. of Australia **[IO]**
Soc. for the Technological Advancement of Reporting **[5631]**
U.S. Court Reporters Assn. **[5632]**
Court Excellence; Coun. for **[5897]**
Court Interpreters and Translators Assn. **[★5628]**
Court Judges Assn; Natl. Amer. Indian **[5905]**
Court Judges; Natl. Conf. of Special **[★5911]**
Court Judges; Natl. Conf. of Specialized **[5911]**
Court Judges; Natl. Coun. of Juvenile **[★5912]**
Court Judges; Natl. Coun. of Juvenile and Family **[5912]**
Court Justice; Natl. Alliance for Family **[5904]**
Court of Last Resort - Defunct.
Court Professionals; Natl. Assn. of Drug **[6289]**
Court Prog. of the Amer. Bar Assn; Traffic **[6310]**
Court Services Assn; Natl. Juvenile **[5702]**
Courtiers Indenpendants en securite financiere **[★IO]**
Courtney Family Assn; Coatney/ **[20867]**
Courts; Assn. of Family and Conciliation **[5699]**
Courts Fund; Comm. for Modern **[★5901]**
Courts; Fund for Modern **[5901]**
Courts; Natl. Center for State **[5908]**
The Cousteau Soc. **[8385]**, 710 Settlers Landing Rd., Hampton, VA 23669-4035, (757)722-9300
Cousteau Soc. **[★8385]**
Cousteau Soc. **[★IO]**
The Cousteau Soc. **[IO]**, Hampton, VA, United States
Covenant Fellowship of Presbyterians **[★20476]**
Covenant House **[13481]**, 5 Penn Plz., New York, NY 10108, (212)727-4000
Covenant, the Sword and Arm of the Lord - Address unknown since 1997.
Covenant of Unitarian Universalist Pagans **[20459]**, PO Box 480157, Charlotte, NC 28269-5301, (866)646-3348
Covenant World Relief **[12848]**, c/o Jim Sundholm, Dir., Evangelical Covenant Church, 5101 N Francisco Ave., Chicago, IL 60625, (800)338-4332

Reference to "IO" in place of a book number signifies that the association may be found in the 45th edition of International Organizations.

Covenant World Relief [IO], Chicago, IL, United States
Covenant Young Adults - Defunct.
Coventry and Warwickshire Chamber of Commerce [IO], Coventry, United Kingdom
Cover Assn; Indus. Bag and [★2875]
Cover Club; Intl. Seapost [★22841]
Cover Collectors Circuit Club [22812], c/o Renate Thompson, Managing Dir., 241 Beachers Brook Ln., Cary, NC 27511
Cover Collectors Club - Defunct.
Cover Collectors Club; First Day [★22780]
Cover Crops Intl. CH [IO], Tegucigalpa, Honduras
Cover Soc; Amer. First Day [22781]
Cover Soc; Western [22890]
Cover Stud. Unit; John F. Kennedy First Day [22835]
Cover the Uninsured [14960], 1010 Wisconsin Ave. NW, Ste. 800, Washington, DC 20007, (202)572-2928
Covered Bridges; Natl. Soc. for the Preservation of [10049]
Covered Button Assn. of New York [★2836]
Covered Button and Buckle Assn. of New York [★2836]
Covered Threads Assn. - Defunct.
Covering Inst; Resilient Floor [665]
Covering Kids and Families [12271], c/o Southern Inst. on Children and Families, 500 Taylor St., Ste. 202, Columbia, SC 29201, (803)779-2607
Coverlet Guild of Am; Colonial [21998]
Covert Family Assn. [20871], c/o Diane Covert Siddons, Ed., 303 W Violet St., Tampa, FL 33603, (813)238-3816
Cow Horse Assn; Natl. Reined [22586]
Cow Observers Worldwide [22002], 240 Wahl Ave., Evans City, PA 16033
Cow Observers Worldwide [IO], Evans City, PA, United States
Coward Family Org. [20872]
Cowart Family - Defunct.
CowBelles; Amer. Natl. [★4240]
Cowboy Culture Assn; Amer. [9379]
Cowboy Hall of Fame and Western Heritage Center; Natl. [★9381]
Cowboy Mounted Shooting Assn. [23716], 14227 E Rock View Rd., Scottsdale, AZ 85262, (480)683-0485
Cowboy and Western Heritage Museum; Natl. [9381]
Cowboys Assn; Professional Rodeo [23694]
Cowboys Assn; Rodeo [★23694]
Cowboys Assn; Working Ranch [3294]
Cowboys for Christ [19792], c/o Ted K. Pressley, Founder/Pres., PO Box 7557, Fort Worth, TX 76111, (817)236-0023
Cowboys for Christ [IO], Fort Worth, TX, United States
Cowboys; Fellowship of Christian [19796]
Cowboys Turtle Assn. [★23694]
Cowles Charitable Trust [9564], PO Box 219, Rumson, NJ 07760, (732)936-9826
Cowles Family Assn. - Defunct.
Cowlitz Indians; Native Amer. Church of North Am. of the [19447]
Cowsills Fan Club [24869], c/o Robin Records, 135 St. Andrews Dr., Ste. 2, Rochester, NY 14626
Cowsills Fan Club [IO], Lexington, MS, United States
Cox Exchange - Defunct.
Cox and Mary Rue Family Assn; Joseph [20967]
CP Australia [IO], Adelaide, Australia
CPA Associates [★IO]
CPA Associates [★24]
CPA Associates Intl. [24], Meadows Off. Complex, 301 Rte. 17 N, Rutherford, NJ 07070, (201)804-8686
CPA Associates Intl. [IO], Rutherford, NJ, United States
CPA Associates Intl. Asia Pacific Region [IO], Hong Kong, People's Republic of China
CPA Associates Intl. Latin Am. [IO], Cuernavaca, Mexico
CPA Australia [IO], Melbourne, Australia
CPA Australia - Hong Kong China Div. [IO], Hong Kong, People's Republic of China

CPA Auto Dealer Consultants Assn. [25], PO Box 542055, Omaha, NE 68154, (402)964-3805
CPA Firms; Continental Assn. of [★5]
CPA Firms; Natl. Assoc. [43]
CPA Hea. Care Advisors Assn; Natl. [13530]
CPA Mfg. Services Assn. [26], One Valmont Plz., 4th Fl., Omaha, NE 68154-5214, (402)964-3805
CPA Practitioners; Natl. Conf. of [47]
CPA Soc. of Personal Financial Planners - Defunct.
CPAmerica Intl. [27], 11801 Res. Dr., Alachua, FL 32615, (386)418-4001
CPAmerica Intl. [IO], Alachua, FL, United States
CPAs; Amer. Assn. of Hispanic [★16]
CPA's; Amer. Associations of Spanish Speaking [★16]
CPAs/Consultants Assn; Constr. Indus. [21]
CPCU; Amer. Inst. for [2137]
CPCU Soc. [2160], 720 Providence Rd., Malvern, PA 19355-3402, (610)251-2727
CPExchange [7280], c/o IDEAlliance, 100 Daingerfield Rd., Alexandria, VA 22314, (703)837-1066
CPPA [★21610]
CPPA [★IO]
CPPS Volunteer Program - Defunct.
CPR Inst. for Dispute Resolution [★11488]
CPR Intl. Inst. for Conflict Prevention and Resolution [11488], 575 Lexington Ave., 21st Fl., New York, NY 10022, (212)949-6490
CPR Panels of Distinguished Neutrals [★11488]
CPRI-HOST - Defunct.
CPS User Group - Defunct.
Crab Apple - Defunct.
Crab Industry Assn; Natl. Blue [3495]
Cracker Jack Collectors Assn. [22003], c/o Deb Gunnerson, Membership Chair, 3225 Edward St. NE, St. Anthony, MN 55418
Cracker Manufacturers Assn; Biscuit and [450]
Craddock Fan Club; Billy "Crash" 24849
Craft Assn; Amer. Home Sewing and [★3784]
Craft Australia [IO], Barton, Australia
Craft Designers; Soc. of [1915]
Craft Designers; Soc. of Small [2593]
Craft Guild of Chefs [IO], Richmond, United Kingdom
Craft Guild; Leather [2417]
Craft and Hobby Assn. [1911], 319 E 54th St., Elmwood Park, NJ 07407, (201)794-1133
Craft Inst; Crayon, Water Color and [★1799]
Craft Materials Inst; Art and [★1799]
Craft Org. Development Assn. [1100], c/o Linda Van Trump, Managing Dir., PO Box 51, Onia, AR 72663, (870)746-4396
Craft Organization Development Association [IO], Onia, AR, United States
Craft Potters Assn. of Great Britain [IO], London, United Kingdom
Craft Sailors Assn; Patrol [21218]
Craft Yarn Coun. of Am. [22153], PO Box 9, Gastonia, NC 28053, (704)824-7838
Crafted with Pride in U.S.A. Coun. - Address unknown since 2006.

Crafts
Affiliated Woodcarvers [9533]
Aid to Artisans [12415]
Alliance for Amer. Quilts [9823]
Amer. Art Pottery Assn. [9411]
Amer. Arts and Crafts Alliance [9824]
Amer. Assn. of Woodturners [9825]
American Association of Woodturners [IO]
Amer. Bladesmith Soc. [9826]
Amer. Bunka Embroidery Assn. [22721]
Amer. Craft Coun. [9827]
Amer. Gourd Soc. [22489]
Amer. Needlepoint Guild [22148]
Amer. Quilt Study Group [9828]
Amer. Quilter's Soc. [22149]
Amer. Sewing Guild [22150]
Amer. Tapestry Alliance [9416]
The Applique Soc. [22151]
The Applique Soc. [IO]
Assn. for Craft Producers [IO]
Basketmakers' Assn. [IO]
Brazilian Dimensional Embroidery Intl. Guild [22987]
British Stickmakers Guild [IO]

Canadian Crafts Fed. [IO]
Caricature Carvers of Am. [9829]
Center for Wooden Boats [21869]
Chamber of Crafts of Luxembourg [IO]
Charted Designers Assn. [2833]
Colonial Coverlet Guild of Am. [21998]
Confed. of Turkish Tradesmen and Craftsmen [IO]
Contemporary Quilt Art Assn. [22152]
Cow Observers Worldwide [22002]
Craft Australia [IO]
Craft Organization Development Association [IO]
Craft Org. Development Assn. [1100]
Craft Potters Assn. of Great Britain [IO]
Craft Yarn Coun. of Am. [22153]
Crafts Coun. [IO]
Crochet Assn. Intl. [22154]
Crochet Guild of Am. [22722]
Cross Stitch Guild [IO]
Doll Artisan Guild [22394]
Doll Costumer's Guild [22395]
Elder Craftsmen [11285]
Embroiderers' Guild [IO]
Embroiderers' Guild of Am. [22155]
Enamelist Soc. [22156]
European Folk Art and Craft Fed. [IO]
Fed. of Crafts and Commerce [IO]
Firearms Engravers Guild of Am. [IO]
Firearms Engravers Guild of Am. [9830]
Florence Ceramics Collectors Soc. [22025]
Folk Art Soc. of Am. [9956]
Guild of Amer. Papercutters [22157]
Guild of Book Workers [9750]
Guild of Glass Engravers [IO]
Guild of Taxidermists [IO]
Handcrafted Soap Makers Guild [1155]
Handicraft Assn. of Nepal [IO]
Handweavers Guild of Am. [22158]
Homeworkers Organized for More Employment [12081]
Inst. of Amer. Indian Arts [10745]
Inter-Tribal Indian Ceremonial Assn. [10747]
Intl. Assn. of Duncan Certified Ceramic Teachers [21928]
Intl. Doll Makers Assn. [22397]
Intl. Guild of Candle Artisans [9831]
Intl. Guild of Candle Artisans [IO]
Intl. Guild of Glass Artists [299]
Intl. Guild of Miniature Artisans [22159]
International Guild of Miniature Artisans [IO]
Intl. Ivory Soc. [IO]
Intl. Ivory Soc. [9832]
Intl. Jewelry Design Guild [2368]
Intl. Machine Quilters Assn. [22160]
Intl. Machine Quilters Assn. [IO]
Intl. Old Lacers, Inc. [IO]
Intl. Old Lacers, Inc. [22161]
Intl. Quilt Assn. [22162]
International Quilt Association [IO]
Intl. Soc. of Folk Harpers and Craftsmen [10627]
Intl. Soc. of Glass Beadmakers [311]
Intl. String Figure Assn. [9833]
Intl. String Figure Assn. [IO]
Intl. Wildlife Carving Assn. [IO]
Intl. Wildlife Carving Assn. [22163]
Intl. Wood Collectors Soc. [23031]
Irish Woodturners' Guild [IO]
Italian Folk Art Fed. of Am. [10259]
Kit Collectors Intl. [22649]
Knifemakers' Guild [9834]
The Knitting Guild Assn. [22164]
Lace Guild [IO]
Lock Museum of Am. [9835]
McCoy Pottery Collectors' Soc. [21932]
Miniature Arms Collectors/Makers Soc. [21538]
Natl. Acad. of Needlearts [22165]
National Academy of Needlearts [IO]
Natl. Assn. of Artists and Crafters [301]
Natl. Assn. of Independent Artists [9513]
Natl. Assn. of Miniature Enthusiasts [22077]
Natl. Assn. of Wheat Weavers [22166]
National Association of Wheat Weavers [IO]
Natl. Basketry Org. [22167]
Natl. Coun. on Educ. for the Ceramic Arts [9836]
Natl. Fenton Glass Soc. [22564]
Natl. Guild of Decoupeurs [22168]

A star before a book entry number signifies that the name is not listed separately, but is mentioned within the entry.

Natl. Inst. of Amer. Doll Artists [22403]
Natl. Pig Carvers Assn. [22169]
Natl. Polymer Clay Guild [22579]
Natl. Quilting Assn. [22170]
Natl. Soc. of Arkansas Pottery Collectors [22088]
Natl. Wood Carvers Assn. [22171]
National Wood Carvers Association [IO]
New York Coun. of Motion Picture and TV Unions [24056]
North Am. Native Amer. (Indian) Info. and Trade Center [10752]
North Amer. Quilling Guild [21541]
Northwest Regional Spinners' Assn. [22172]
Origami USA [22771]
Pomegranate Guild of Judaic Needlework [9837]
Potters Coun. [9780]
Potters for Peace [9838]
Potters for Peace [IO]
Precious Metal Clay Guild [IO]
Precious Metal Clay Guild [8172]
Professional Knifemakers Assn. [9839]
Quilters' Guild of the British Isles [IO]
Quilters Hall of Fame [22173]
Quimper Club Intl. [21546]
Retailers of Art Glass and Supplies [1734]
Roycrofters-at-Large Assn. [9840]
Rural Crafts Assn. [IO]
Sewing Educator Alliance [9121]
Smocking Arts Guild of Am. [22174]
Soc. of Decorative Painters [22175]
Soc. of Designer Craftsmen [IO]
Soc. for Folk Arts Preservation [9963]
Soc. of North Amer. Goldsmiths [9841]
Soc. of Ornamental Turners [IO]
Solace Intl. [13439]
Swedish Soc. of Crafts and Design [IO]
Swiss Craft Found. [IO]
UNIMA-U.S.A., Amer. Center of the Union Internationale de la Marionnette [22916]
United Chainsaw Carvers Guild [9842]
United Fed. of Doll Clubs [22407]
U.S. Faceters Guild [1121]
Victorian Hairwork Soc. [22176]
Wales Craft Coun. [IO]
Ward Museum of Wildfowl Art, Salisbury Univ. [9529]
Wood Engravers Network [9843]
Wood Engravers Network [IO]
Wooden Canoe Heritage Assn. [21887]
World Org. of China Painters [22177]
World Org. of China Painters [IO]
Crafts Alumni Assn; California Coll. of Arts and [18882]
Crafts Assn; Indian Arts and [10743]
Crafts Assn; Southeastern Fabric, Notions and [3798]
Crafts Coun. [IO], London, United Kingdom
Crafts Coun; Amer. [★9827]
Crafts Movement at Roycroft; Found. for the Stud. of the Arts and [21530]
Crafts and Theatre Safety; Arts, [12950]
Craftsman Assn; Autobody [372]
Craftsmen and Artists; Assn. of Restorers and Coun. of [218]
Craftsmen; Brotherhood of Shoe and Allied [24063]
Craftsmen; Elder [11285]
Craftsmen; Intl. Union of Bricklayers and Allied [★24027]
Craftsmen's Coun; Amer. [★9827]
Craftsmen's Guild - Defunct.
Craftsworkers; Intl. Coun. of Employers of Bricklayers and Allied [★1029]
Craftsworkers; Intl. Union of Bricklayers and Allied [1029]
Craftworkers; Intl. Union of Bricklayers and Allied [24027]
Cranberries Official North American Fan Club - Defunct.
Cranberry Growers Assn; Amer. [4702]
Cranberry Inst. [4725], 3203-B Cranberry Hwy., East Wareham, MA 02538, (800)295-4132
Crandall Family Assn. [20873], PO Box 1472, Westerly, RI 02891
Crane Certification Assn. of Am. [942], PO Box 87907, Vancouver, WA 98687-7907, (360)834-3805

Crane Conservation Assn; Whooping [5392]
Crane Conservation Gp; Whooping [★5392]
Crane Found; Intl. [5327]
Crane Inst; Elec. Overhead [★2016]
Crane Mfrs. Assn. of Am. [2016], 8720 Red Oak Blvd., Ste. 201, Charlotte, NC 28217, (704)676-1190
Crane-Rogers Found. [★18837]
Crane-Rogers Found. [★IO]
Crane and Shovel Assn; Power [2058]
Crane Working Group; North Amer. [5353]
Cranes Coun; Mfrs. of Telescoping and Articulated [2041]
Cranial Acad. [15811], 8202 Clearvista Pkwy., No. 9-D, Indianapolis, IN 46256, (317)594-0411
Cranial Assn; Osteopathic [★15811]
Cranio-Facial Deformities; Debbie Fox Found. for Treatment of [★14061]
Cranio-Mandibular Orthopedics; Intl. Coll. of [15770]
Craniofacial Abnormalities
  Amer. Cleft Palate-Craniofacial Assn. [14055]
  Center for Craniofacial Development and Disorders [14056]
  Children's Craniofacial Assn. [14057]
  Cleft Palate Found. [14058]
  Craniofacial Found. of Am. [14059]
  Craniosynostosis and Positional Plagiocephaly Support [14060]
  FACES: The Natl. Craniofacial Assn. [14061]
  Forward Face [14062]
  Freeman-Sheldon Parent Support Gp. [14063]
  Freeman-Sheldon Parent Support Group [IO]
  Intl. Assn. of Oral and Maxillofacial Surgeons [15736]
  Let's Face It USA [14064]
  Let's Face It USA [IO]
  Natl. Found. for Facial Reconstruction [14065]
  Soc. for Craniofacial Morphometry [14066]
  Treacher Collins Found. [14067]
  Uplift Internationale [15737]
  World Craniofacial Found. [14068]
Craniofacial Assn; Amer. Cleft Palate- [14055]
Craniofacial Found. of Am. [14059], 975 E 3rd St., Box 269, Chattanooga, TN 37403, (423)778-9192
Craniofacial Foundations; Intl. [★14057]
Craniofacial Morphometry; Soc. for [14066]
Craniofacial Pain; Amer. Acad. of [15751]
Craniofacial Res; Friends of the Natl. Inst. of Dental and [14154]
Craniofacial Res; Natl. Inst. of Dental and [14180]
Craniofacially Handicapped; Natl. Assn. for the [★14061]
Craniomandibular Disorders; Amer. Acad. of [★14106]
Craniomandibular Orthopedics; Amer. Acad. of [★14106]
Craniopathic Soc; Intl. [★14013]
Craniosacral Therapy
  Biodynamic Craniosacral Therapy Assn. of North Am. [14069]
  Craniosacral Therapy Assn. of North Am. [IO]
CranioSacral Therapy Assn; Amer. [14822]
Craniosacral Therapy Assn. of Australia [IO], Adelaide, Australia
Craniosacral Therapy Assn. of North Am. [IO], Santa Fe, NM, United States
Craniosacral Therapy Assn. of North Am. [★14069]
Craniosacral Therapy Assn. of the UK [IO], London, United Kingdom
Craniosynostosis and Positional Plagiocephaly Support [14060], 6905 Xandu Ct., Fredericksburg, VA 22407-2580
Crape Myrtle Soc. of Am. [4976], PO Box 2758, McKinney, TX 75070-2758
Crape Myrtle Soc; Amer. [★4976]
Crappie Assn; Amer. [22449]
Crappie USA [★22449]
Crayon, Water Color and Craft Inst. [★1799]
Crazy Horse Memorial Found. [10739], 12151 Ave. of the Chiefs, Crazy Horse, SD 57730-9506, (605)673-4681
Crazy4Clay Gang [24819], PO Box 853, Independence, KY 41051, (859)356-0837
CRB Educational Found., Inc. [★9736]
CRC World Literature Ministries [★19832]

CRC World Literature Ministries [★IO]
Cream Draft Horse Assn; Amer. [4816]
Creameries Assn; Natl. [★4489]
Creameries Assn; Wisconsin [★4495]
Creamery Assn. [★4076]
CREATE [IO], Dublin, Ireland
Create A Smile Dental Found. [13318], 115 S Div. St., Ste. A, Carterville, IL 62918, (618)925-2140
Creation
  Access Res. Network [9095]
  Creation Health Found. [20547]
  Creation Res. Soc. [20548]
  Inst. for Creation Res. [20538]
  Reasons to Believe [20551]
Creation Health Found. [20547]
Creation Res; Inst. for [20538]
Creation Res. Soc. [20548], PO Box 8263, St. Joseph, MO 64508-8263
Creation Science Comm. - Defunct.
Creation Social Science and Humanities Soc. - Defunct.
Creative Activity for Everyone [★IO]
Creative Anachronism; Soc. for [10463]
Creative Artists Public Service Program - Defunct.
Creative Audio and Music Electronics Org. - Defunct.
Creative Business Consultants - Address unknown since 2002.
The Creative Coalition [18290], 1100 Ave. of the Americas, 3rd Fl., New York, NY 10036, (212)512-5876
Creative Commons [5613], Corporate HQ, 171 2nd St., Ste. 300, San Francisco, CA 94105-3808, (415)369-8481
Creative Education
  Amer. Fired Arts Alliance [9542]
  Creative Educ. Found. [8173]
  Natl. Center for Creativity [17356]
  Soc. of Amer. Mosaic Artists [9525]
Creative Educ. Found. [8173], 289 Bay Rd., Hadley, MA 01035, (413)559-6614
Creative Ethics Gp. [★10793]
Creative Ethics; Soc. for [★10793]
Creative Initiative [★18203]
Creative Leadership; Center for [2488]
Creative Materials Inst; Art and [1799]
Creative Music Found. [10587], PO Box 671, Woodstock, NY 12498, (845)679-8847
Creative Musicians; Assn. for the Advancement of [10558]
Creative Musicians Coalition [2827], PO Box 6205, Peoria, IL 61601-6205, (309)685-4843
Creative New Zealand [IO], Wellington, New Zealand
Creative Playthings Found. - Defunct.
Creative Resources Guild [18612], PO Box 3397, Santa Monica, CA 90408-3397, (310)828-0130
Creative Response to Conflict [★11684]
Creative Response to Conflict Prog; Children's [11684]
Creative Stud. Alumni Assn; Coll. for [18888]
Creative Stud. - Coll. of Art and Design Alumni Assn; Center for [★18888]
Creative Time [9565], 59 E 4th St. 6E, New York, NY 10003, (212)206-6674
Creative Tour Operators Assn. - Address unknown since 1995.
Creative Will [★15349]
Creative Youth of Novi Sad [IO], Novi Sad, Serbia
Creativity
  Amer. Creativity Assn. [10168]
  Assn. for Applied Poetry [16211]
  Catholic Fine Arts Soc. [9562]
  Found. for Philosophy of Creativity [10793]
  Innovation Network [2115]
  Renaissance Universal [IO]
  Well-Springs Found. [10179]
Creativity Assn; Amer. [10168]
Creativity; Found. for Philosophy of [10793]
The Creativity Movement [18798], PO Box 2002, East Peoria, IL 61611
The Creativity Movement [IO], Bloomington, IL, United States
Creativity; Natl. Center for [17356]
Creativity; Soc. for Philosophy of [★10793]
Credential Evaluation Services; Natl. Assn. of [8409]

Reference to "IO" in place of a book number signifies that the association may be found in the 45th edition of International Organizations.

Credentialing Agency for Lab. Personnel; Natl. [15145]
Credentialing Commn. [★15126]
Credentialing International/Board of Cardiovascular Tech; Cardiovascular [★13898]
Credentialing Intl; Cardiovascular [★13898]
Credentialing; Natl. Bd. for Cardiopulmonary [★13898]
Credentialing; Natl. Bd. for Cardiovascular and Pulmonary [★13898]
Credentialing Prog; CDA Natl. [★11526]
Credit
  Alliance Credit Counseling [11833]
  Allied Bd. of Trade [2249]
  Amer. Credit Card Collectors Soc. [17357]
  Amer. Money Mgt. Gp. [1454]
  Australian Inst. of Credit Mgt. [IO]
  Brazilian Assn. of Credit Card Companies and Services [IO]
  Canadian Credit Inst. Educational Found. [IO]
  Consumer Credit Counseling Services [17358]
  Consumer Credit Industry Association [2158]
  Consumer Data Indus. Assn. [1409]
  Credit Card Users of America [1410]
  Credit Professionals Intl. [1411]
  Credit Protection Assn. [IO]
  Credit Res. Found. [1412]
  Credit Union Executives Soc. [1106]
  Credit Union Natl. Assn. [1107]
  Defense Credit Union Coun. [1108]
  Educ. Credit Union Coun. [1109]
  Electronic Transactions Assn. [472]
  Forius Bus. Credit Resources [1422]
  Info. Technologies Credit Union Assn. [1110]
  Intl. Assn. of Financial Crimes Investigators [5881]
  Investment Trusts Assn. [IO]
  Irish Inst. of Credit Mgt. [IO]
  Jewelers Bd. of Trade [2371]
  Natl. Assn. of Credit Mgt. [1436]
  Natl. Assn. of Finance Institutions [IO]
  Natl. Assn. of Mortgage Planners [490]
  Natl. Fed. of Credit Guarantee Corporations [IO]
  Natl. Found. for Credit Counseling [2428]
  Network Branded Prepaid Card Assn. [1443]
  Print Alliance Credit Exchange [1444]
  Printing Indus. Credit Executives [1101]
  Soc. of Certified Credit Executives [1447]
Credit Administrators; Natl. Assn. of Consumer [5610]
Credit Assn; Amer. Petroleum [★1427]
Credit Assn; Broadcast Cable [552]
Credit Assn; Bus. Products [1405]
Credit Assn; Intl. Petroleum [★1427]
Credit Assn; Media [1432]
Credit Assn; Motion Picture and TV [1434]
Credit Assn; Natl. Chem. [1440]
Credit Assn; Natl. Radiator Core Mfg. [★1422]
Credit Assn; Natl. Radiator Mfg. [★1422]
Credit Bureaus; Assoc. [★1409]
Credit Card Collectors Soc; Amer. [17357]
Credit Card Investigators; Assn. of [★5881]
Credit Card Users of America [1410]
Credit Cards; Intl. Assn. of [★5881]
Credit Coun; Farm [474]
Credit Executives Assn; Advt. Media [1397]
Credit Executives; Soc. of Certified [1447]
Credit Inst. of Am; Retail [★2428]
Credit Inst. of Canada [IO], Toronto, ON, Canada
Credit Institutions; Pan-American Assn. of Educational [IO]
Credit Insurance Assn; Foreign [2164]
Credit Interchange Bur; Foreign [★2282]
Credit Mgt; Natl. Assn. of [1436]
Credit; Natl. Inst. of [★1436]
Credit Officers Group - Defunct.
Credit Professionals; CWI [★1411]
Credit Professionals Intl. [1411], 525 B N Laclede Sta. Rd., St. Louis, MO 63119, (314)961-0031
Credit Professionals Intl. [IO], St. Louis, MO, United States
Credit Protection Assn. [IO], London, United Kingdom
Credit Res. Found. [1412], 8840 Columbia 100 Pkwy., Columbia, MD 21045, (410)740-5499
Credit Risk; Robert Morris Associates/Association of Lending and [★498]

Credit Union Assn; Intl. Telephone [★1110]
Credit Union Examination; Natl. Inst. for State [★5633]
Credit Union Executives Soc. [1106], PO Box 14167, Madison, WI 53708-0167, (608)271-2664
Credit Union Mortgage Assn. and Amer. CU Housing Alliance; Amer. [★1103]
Credit Union Natl. Assn. [1107], PO Box 431, Madison, WI 53701-0431, (608)231-4000
Credit Union Presidents; Natl. Assn. of [★1112]
Credit Unions
  Amer. Assn. of Credit Union Leagues [1102]
  Amer. Credit Union Mortgage Assn. [1103]
  Asian Confed. of Credit Unions [IO]
  Assn. of British Credit Unions Limited [IO]
  Assn. of Credit Union Internal Auditors [1104]
  Assn. for Financial Tech. [61]
  Coun. of Gen. Motors Credit Unions [1105]
  Coun. of Mortgage Lenders [IO]
  Credit Union Executives Soc. [1106]
  Credit Union Natl. Assn. [1107]
  Defense Credit Union Coun. [1108]
  Educ. Credit Union Coun. [1109]
  Info. Technologies Credit Union Assn. [1110]
  LICU [1111]
  Natl. Assn. of Credit Union Chairmen [1112]
  Natl. Assn. of Credit Union Services Organizations [1113]
  Natl. Assn. of Credit Union Supervisory and Auditing Committees [1114]
  Natl. Assn. of Fed. Credit Unions [1115]
  Natl. Assn. of State Credit Union Supervisors [5633]
  Natl. Coun. of Postal Credit Unions [1116]
  Natl. Credit Union Mgt. Assn. [1117]
  Natl. Fed. of Community Development Credit Unions [1118]
  New Zealand Assn. of Credit Unions [IO]
  World Coun. of Credit Unions [IO]
  World Coun. of Credit Unions [1119]
Credit Unions; League of IBM Employees [★1111]
Credit Women - Intl. [★1411]
Credit Women - Intl. [★IO]
Credit Women's Breakfast Clubs of North Am. [★IO]
Credit Women's Breakfast Clubs of North Am. [★1411]
CREDO [19746], PO Box 788160, Twentynine Palms, CA 92278-8160, (760)830-4989
CREED - Address unknown since 2003.
Creek Indian Memorial Assn. [10740], Creek Coun. House Museum, Town Sq., 106 W 6th, Okmulgee, OK 74447, (918)756-2324
Creekmore Family Assn. - Address unknown since 2002.
Creeping Red Fescue Commn; Chewings Fescue and [4792]
Creepy Crawlers Fan Club - Address unknown since 2003.
Cremation
  Telophase Soc. [2792]
Cremation Assn. of Am. [★2777]
Cremation Assn. of North Am. [2777], 401 N Michigan Ave., Chicago, IL 60611, (312)245-1077
Cremation Fed; Intl. [IO]
Cremation Soc. of Great Britain [IO], Maidstone, United Kingdom
Creme d'Argent Rabbit Fed. - Address unknown since 2002.
Creme Horse Registry; Amer. White Horse and Amer. [4855]
Creo Soc. - Defunct.
Creole-Amer. Genealogical Soc. - Address unknown since 2003.
Creole Found. - Address unknown since 1995.
Crested Fowl Fanciers' Assn. - Address unknown since 2001.
Cretans' Assn. "Omonoia" [19085], 32-33 31st St., Astoria, NY 11106, (718)721-9172
Crew Members; USS Intrepid Assn. of Former [21225]
CREW Network [3309], 1201 Wakarusa Dr., Ste. C3, Lawrence, KS 66049, (785)832-1808
Crewcuts Fan Club - Address unknown since 1995.
Cri du Chat Syndrome Mutual Help Gp. [14448], c/o Dr. Robert F. Clarke, PhD, 10640 SW 129th Ct., Miami, FL 33186, (305)382-1952

Cri du Chat Syndrome Soc. [★16534]
Cribbage Bd. Collectors Soc. [22004], PO Box 170, Carolina, RI 02812, (401)364-7241
Cricket
  Afghanistan Cricket Fed. [IO]
  Argentine Cricket Assn. [IO]
  Assn. of Cricket Statisticians and Historians [IO]
  Assn. of Cricket Umpires and Scorers [IO]
  Australian Cricketers' Assn. [IO]
  Austrian Cricket Assn. [IO]
  Belgian Cricket Fed. [IO]
  British Indoor Cricket Assn. [IO]
  Canadian Cricket Assn. [IO]
  Chilean Cricket Assn. [IO]
  Cricket Assn. of Nepal [IO]
  Cricket Australia [IO]
  Cricket Scotland [IO]
  Croatia Cricket Bd. [IO]
  Danish Cricket Assn. [IO]
  England and Wales Cricket Bd. [IO]
  European Cricket Coun. [IO]
  Fed. Francaise de Baseball, Softball and Cricket [IO]
  Finnish Cricket Assn. [IO]
  German Cricket Fed. [IO]
  Gibraltar Cricket Assn. [IO]
  Hellenic Cricket Fed. [IO]
  Hong Kong Cricket Assn. [IO]
  Intl. Women's Cricket Coun. [IO]
  Irish Cricket Union [IO]
  Israel Cricket Assn. [IO]
  Italian Cricket Fed. [IO]
  Japan Cricket Assn. [IO]
  Kenya Cricket Assn. [IO]
  Korea Cricket Assn. [IO]
  Luxembourg Cricket Fed. [IO]
  Malaysian Cricket Assn. [IO]
  Malta Cricket Assn. [IO]
  Manitoba Cricket Assn. [IO]
  Norwegian Cricket Bd. [IO]
  Pakistan Cricket Bd. [IO]
  Papua New Guinea Cricket Bd. [IO]
  Philippines Cricket Assn. [IO]
  Royal Dutch Cricket Assn. [IO]
  Saudi Cricket Centre [IO]
  Singapore Cricket Assn. [IO]
  Spanish Cricket Assn. [IO]
  Sri Lanka Cricket [IO]
  Swiss Cricket Assn. [IO]
  Swiss Fed. of Cricket Umpires and Scorers [IO]
  Tanzania Cricket Assn. [IO]
  Tonga Cricket Assn. [IO]
  United Arab Emirates Cricket Bd. [IO]
  United Cricket Bd. of South Africa [IO]
  U.S.A. Cricket Assn. [23299]
  Vanuatu Cricket Assn. [IO]
Cricket Assn. of Nepal [IO], Kathmandu, Nepal
Cricket Australia [IO], Jolimont, Australia
Cricket Scotland [IO], Edinburgh, United Kingdom
Crigler-Najjar Assn. [14805], c/o Cory Mauck, Dir., 3134 Bayberry St., Wichita, KS 67226, (316)685-7477
Crime
  A. Philip Randolph Educal. Fund [17078]
  ABLE: Assn. for Better Living and Educ. Intl. [11756]
  Acad. of Criminal Justice Sciences [11850]
  Aid to Incarcerated Mothers [11851]
  Alberta Community Crime Prevention Assn. [IO]
  All of Us or None [17081]
  Alliance of Guardian Angels [11834]
  Alliance of Guardian Angels [IO]
  Alston Wilkes Veterans Home [11852]
  Amer. Assn. for Correctional and Forensic Psychology [11853]
  Amer. Correctional Assn. [11854]
  Amer. Criminal Justice Assn. (Lambda Alpha Epsilon) [11855]
  Amer. Jail Assn. [11856]
  Amer. Justice Inst. [11835]
  Amer. Soc. of Crime Lab. Directors [5754]
  Amer. Soc. of Criminology [11899]
  Amer. Soc. of Victimology [13360]
  Amer. Youth Work Center [13469]
  Anti-Child Pornography Org. [12766]

A star before a book entry number signifies that the name is not listed separately, but is mentioned within the entry.

Assn. of Certified Fraud Specialists [2085]
Assn. for Crime Scene Reconstruction [5634]
Assn. of Forensic DNA Analysts and Administrators [5756]
Assn. of Inspectors Gen. [5777]
Assn. on Programs for Female Offenders [11857]
Assn. of State Correctional Administrators [11858]
Aviation Crime Prevention Inst. [433]
Center for Neighborhood Enterprise [17208]
Center for Stud. in Criminal Justice [11859]
Coalition Against Insurance Fraud [2155]
Coalition for an Intl. Criminal Court [17361]
Commn. on Crime Prevention and Criminal Justice [IO]
Correctional Educ. Assn. [11862]
Corrections Tech. Assn. [1076]
Crime Prevention Coalition of Am. [5635]
Crime Stoppers Intl. [11836]
Crime Stoppers Intl. [IO]
Death Row Support Proj. [11863]
Families Against Mandatory Minimums Found. [11864]
Fight Crime: Invest in Kids [17057]
Fortune Soc. [11867]
Friends Outside [11868]
Genocide Watch [17660]
ICC Commercial Crime Services [IO]
ICC Intl. Maritime Bur. [IO]
Independence Inst. [17120]
Intl. Assn. of Asian Crime Investigators [5636]
Intl. Assn. of Asian Crime Investigators [IO]
International Association of Bloodstain Pattern Analysts [IO]
Intl. Assn. of Bloodstain Pattern Analysts [5637]
Intl. Assn. of Correctional Officers [11870]
Intl. Assn. of Correctional Training Personnel [11871]
Intl. Assn. for Counterterrorism and Security Professionals [18731]
Intl. Assn. of Crime Writers, North Amer. Br. [11175]
Intl. Assn. of Financial Crimes Investigators [5881]
Intl. Assn. of Reentry [17355]
Intl. Assn. for the Stud. of Organized Crime [11837]
Intl. Assn. for the Stud. of Organized Crime [IO]
Intl. Community Corrections Assn. [11872]
Intl. Counter-Terrorism Officers Assn. [18732]
Intl. Criminal Court Alliance [5654]
Intl. Homicide Investigators Assn. [5883]
Intl. Latino Gang Investigator's Assn. [5884]
Intl. Prison Ministry [11873]
Intl. Soc. of Crime Prevention Practitioners [11838]
Intl. Soc. of Crime Prevention Practitioners [IO]
Intl. Soc. of Social Defence [IO]
Intl. Utilities Revenue Protection Assn. [6338]
John Howard Assn. [11874]
Justice Res. and Statistics Assn. [11876]
Law Enforcement Thermographers' Assn. [5982]
London Club [11900]
Milton S. Eisenhower Found. [11839]
Mystery Writers of Am. [11181]
Natl. Alliance of Gang Investigators Associations [5638]
Natl. Assn. of Blacks in Criminal Justice [11877]
Natl. Assn. Citizens on Patrol [12970]
Natl. Assn. of Crime Commissions [11840]
Natl. Assn. of Crime Victim Compensation Boards [13364]
Natl. Assn. of Drug Court Professionals [6289]
Natl. Assn. for Justice Info. Systems [5648]
Natl. Assn. of Police Athletic Leagues [13496]
Natl. Assn. of Property Recovery Investigators [5886]
Natl. Assn. of State Sentencing Commissions [5650]
Natl. Assn. of Town Watch [11841]
Natl. Black on Black Love Campaign [11842]
Natl. Center on Institutions and Alternatives [11878]
Natl. Center for Juvenile Justice [11879]
Natl. Center for Victims of Crime [13366]
Natl. Coalition of Homicide Survivors [13368]
Natl. Correctional Indus. Assn. [11880]

Natl. Coun. on Crime and Delinquency [11843]
Natl. Crime Prevention Coun. [11844]
Natl. Crime Prevention Inst. [11845]
Natl. Crime Victim Bar Assn. [6349]
Natl. Criminal Justice Assn. [11881]
Natl. Insurance Crime Bur. [2224]
Natl. Juvenile Detention Assn. [11882]
Natl. Major Gang Task Force [5651]
Natl. Org. for Victim Assistance [13369]
Natl. Prison Proj. of the ACLU [11883]
Natl. Religious Affairs Assn. [19872]
Natl. Union of Law Enforcement Associations [24124]
Natl. Victims' Constitutional Amendment Network [18779]
North Amer. Assn. of Wardens and Superintendents [11884]
Osborne Assn. [11885]
Police Found. [6006]
Prison Fellowship Intl. [11887]
Prison Fellowship Ministries [11888]
Prison Ministry of Yokefellow's Intl. [11889]
Prisoners' Rights Union [11890]
Pups for Peace [12700]
Robert F. Kennedy Memorial [13513]
Safer Soc. Found. [11891]
Security on Campus [11846]
Sentencing Proj. [11893]
Stolen Horse Intl. [11461]
TIPS Prog. [11847]
USCCCN Natl. CH on Satanic Crime in Am. [11848]
Victim Support [IO]
Victims' Assistance Legal Org. [5639]
Victims of Crime and Leniency [13373]
Victims of Violence [IO]
Volunteers in Prevention, Probation, Prisons [11896]
We Care Prog. [11897]
WeTip [11849]
Witness Justice [18790]
Women's Prison Assn. [11898]
Youth Crime Watch of Am. [13519]
Crime Bur; Natl. Insurance [2224]
Crime Commissions; Natl. Assn. of Citizens [★11840]
Crime Data Center; National Computer [★2091]
Crime Data; Natl. Center for Computer [2091]
Crime and Delinquency; Natl. Coun. on [11843]
Crime-Free Am. - Address unknown since 2004.
Crime; Inst. for Reduction of [★9085]
Crime Investigation Assn; High Tech. [★5880]
Crime Lab. Directors; Amer. Soc. of [5754]
Crime and Leniency; Victims of [13373]
Crime Prevention Coalition [★11844]
Crime Prevention Coalition of Am. [5635], 1000 Connecticut Ave. NW, 13th Fl., Washington, DC 20036, (202)466-6272
Crime Prevention Coun; Natl. [11844]
Crime Prevention Inst; Aviation [433]
Crime Prevention; Inst. for Financial [★2084]
Crime Prevention Inst; Insurance [★2224]
Crime Stoppers Intl. [11836], 3100 Main St., Ste. 201, Kansas City, MO 64111, (800)850-7574
Crime Stoppers Intl. [IO], Kansas City, MO, United States
Crime Stoppers U.S.A. [★IO]
Crime Stoppers U.S.A. [★11836]
Crime Victim Compensation Boards; Natl. Assn. of [13364]
Crime; Vocational Found. Bur. of the Assn. for the Prevention of [★12103]
Crime Watch of Am; Youth [13519]
Crime Writers' Assn. [IO], Birmingham, United Kingdom
Crime Writers of Canada [IO], Toronto, ON, Canada
Criminal Cases; Natl. Assn. of Defense Lawyers in [★5656]
Criminal and Civil Trial Advocates Program; National Certification of Family Law, [★6333]
Criminal Defense; Natl. Coll. for [★5657]
Criminal Identification; Intl. Assn. for [★5763]
Criminal Investigators Assn; Fed. [★5653]
Criminal Justice
   Acad. of Criminal Justice Sciences [11850]

African Amer. Criminal Justice Soc. [17359]
Aid to Incarcerated Mothers [11851]
All of Us or None [17081]
Alston Wilkes Veterans Home [11852]
Amer. Assn. for Correctional and Forensic Psychology [11853]
Amer. Assn. for Justice [6328]
Amer. Correctional Assn. [11854]
Amer. Criminal Justice Assn. (Lambda Alpha Epsilon) [11855]
Amer. Jail Assn. [11856]
Amer. Soc. of Criminology [11899]
Amer. Soc. of Victimology [13360]
Amer. Youth Work Center [13469]
Asia Crime Prevention Found. [IO]
Assn. for Crime Scene Reconstruction [5634]
Assn. in Defence of the Wrongly Convicted [IO]
Assn. of Forensic DNA Analysts and Administrators [5756]
Assn. on Programs for Female Offenders [11857]
Assn. of State Correctional Administrators [11858]
Bahamas Crisis Centre [IO]
Canadian Assn. of Elizabeth Fry Societies [IO]
Canadian Criminal Justice Assn. [IO]
Center on Juvenile and Criminal Justice [5640]
Center for Stud. in Criminal Justice [11859]
Citizens United for Alternatives to the Death Penalty [5641]
Citizens United for Rehabilitation of Errants [11860]
Coalition for an Intl. Criminal Court [17361]
Comm. to End the Marion Lockdown [11861]
Correctional Educ. Assn. [11862]
Corrections Tech. Assn. [1076]
Criminal Justice Legal Found. [5642]
Death Row Support Proj. [11863]
European Inst. for Crime Prevention and Control Affiliated with the United Nations [IO]
Falun Data Info. Center [17757]
Families Against Mandatory Minimums Found. [11864]
Family Justice [11865]
Fathers Behind Bars [11866]
Fed. Law Enforcement Officers Assn. [5879]
Fellowship of Christian Peace Officers - U.S.A. [19798]
Fortune Soc. [11867]
Friends Outside [11868]
Gay Officers' Action League [12231]
Genocide Watch [17660]
Good News Jail and Prison Ministry [11869]
Good News Jail and Prison Ministry [IO]
Hispanic Amer. Police Command Officers Assn. [5970]
Howard League for Penal Reform [IO]
Innocence Proj. [5643]
Intl. Assn. of Asian Crime Investigators [5636]
Intl. Assn. of Bloodstain Pattern Analysts [5637]
Intl. Assn. of Correctional Officers [11870]
Intl. Assn. of Correctional Training Personnel [11871]
International Association of Correctional Training Personnel [IO]
Intl. Assn. of Financial Crimes Investigators [5881]
Intl. Assn. of Law Enforcement Planners [5644]
Intl. Assn. of Law Enforcement Planners [IO]
Intl. Assn. of Reentry [17355]
Intl. Assn. for the Stud. of Organized Crime [11837]
Intl. Community Corrections Assn. [11872]
Intl. Community Corrections Assn. [IO]
Intl. Criminal Court Alliance [5654]
Intl. Homicide Investigators Assn. [5883]
Intl. Latino Gang Investigator's Assn. [5884]
Intl. Law Enforcement Educators and Trainers Assn. [5978]
Intl. Prison Ministry [11873]
Intl. Prison Ministry [IO]
John Howard Assn. [11874]
Justice Fellowship [11875]
Justice Res. Assn. [5655]
Justice Res. and Statistics Assn. [11876]
Justice Stud. Assn. [13109]
Law Enforcement Assn. of Asian Pacifics [19201]
Life After Exoneration Prog. [17360]

Reference to "IO" in place of a book number signifies that the association may be found in the 45th edition of International Organizations.

London Club [11900]
Nacro [IO]
Natl. Alliance of Sentencing Advocates and Mitigation Specialists [5645]
Natl. Assn. of Asian Amer. Law Enforcement Commanders [5984]
Natl. Assn. of Blacks in Criminal Justice [11877]
Natl. Assn. of Drug Court Professionals [6289]
Natl. Assn. of Fed. Defenders [5646]
Natl. Assn. of Field Training Officers [5987]
Natl. Assn. of Forensic Counselors [5647]
Natl. Assn. for Justice Info. Systems [5648]
Natl. Assn. of Official Prison Visitors [IO]
Natl. Assn. of Probation Executives [5649]
Natl. Assn. of Probation Officers [IO]
Natl. Assn. of Property Recovery Investigators [5886]
Natl. Assn. of State Sentencing Commissions [5650]
Natl. Center on Institutions and Alternatives [11878]
Natl. Center for Juvenile Justice [11879]
Natl. Center for Victims of Crime [13366]
Natl. Correctional Indus. Assn. [11880]
Natl. Crime Prevention Inst. [11845]
Natl. Crime Victim Bar Assn. [6349]
Natl. Criminal Justice Assn. [11881]
Natl. Juvenile Detention Assn. [11882]
Natl. Major Gang Task Force [5651]
Natl. Org. of Fed. Employees Against Abuse and Retaliation [24078]
Natl. Prison Proj. of the ACLU [11883]
Natl. Religious Affairs Assn. [19872]
Natl. Union of Law Enforcement Associations [24124]
Natl. Victims' Constitutional Amendment Network [18779]
Natl. White Collar Crime Center of Canada [IO]
North Amer. Assn. of Wardens and Superintendents [IO]
North Amer. Assn. of Wardens and Superintendents [11884]
November Coalition [18690]
Osborne Assn. [11885]
Penal Reform Intl. [IO]
People of Faith Against the Death Penalty [17034]
Permanent European Conf. on Probation and Aftercare [IO]
Police Executive Res. Forum [6005]
Pretrial Justice Indus. [6034]
Prison-Ashram Proj. [11886]
Prison Fellowship Intl. [11887]
Prison Fellowship Intl. [IO]
Prison Fellowship Ministries [11888]
Prison Ministry of Yokefellow's Intl. [11889]
Prison Ministry of Yokefellow's Intl. [IO]
Prisoners' Friends' Assn. [IO]
Prisoners' Rights Union [11890]
Probation Boards' Assn. [IO]
Quakers Fostering Justice [IO]
Robert F. Kennedy Memorial [13513]
Safer Soc. Found. [11891]
Salvation Army - Caribbean Territory [IO]
SEARCH - The Natl. Consortium for Justice Info. and Statistics [11892]
Sentencing Proj. [11893]
Soc. for Police and Criminal Psychology [16177]
Soc. of Rehabilitation and Crime Prevention [IO]
Stop Prisoner Rape [11894]
United Nations Asia and Far East Inst. for the Prevention of Crime and the Treatment of Offenders [IO]
Vera Inst. of Justice [11895]
Victims' Assistance Legal Org. [5639]
Volunteers in Prevention, Probation, Prisons [11896]
We Care Prog. [11897]
WeTip [11849]
Women's Prison Assn. [11898]
Criminal Justice; Center for Stud. in [11859]
Criminal Justice; Commn. on Crime Prevention and [IO]
Criminal Justice; Inst. for the Advancement of [★13262]
Criminal Justice Legal Found. [5642], PO Box 1199, Sacramento, CA 95812, (916)446-0345

Criminal Justice; Natl. Assn. of Blacks in [11877]
Criminal Justice Planning Administrators; Natl. Conf. of State [★11881]
Criminal Justice Policy Found. [17959], 8730 Georgia Ave., Ste. 400, Silver Spring, MD 20910, (301)589-6020
Criminal Justice Sciences; Acad. of [11850]
Criminal Justice Sect; Amer. Bar Assn. [5922]
Criminal Justice Statistics Assn. [★11876]
Criminal Law
　Acad. of Criminal Justice Sciences [11850]
　Alston Wilkes Veterans Home [11852]
　Amer. Assn. for Correctional and Forensic Psychology [11853]
　Amer. Bar Assn. Criminal Justice Sect. [5922]
　Amer. Correctional Assn. [11854]
　Amer. Criminal Justice Assn. (Lambda Alpha Epsilon) [11855]
　Amer. Jail Assn. [11856]
　Amer. Prosecutors Res. Inst. [5481]
　Amer. Soc. of Criminology [11899]
　Americans for Effective Law Enforcement [5652]
　Assn. of Certified Fraud Specialists [2085]
　Assn. of Inspectors Gen. [5777]
　Assn. on Programs for Female Offenders [11857]
　Assn. of State Correctional Administrators [11858]
　Center for Stud. in Criminal Justice [11859]
　Coalition Against Insurance Fraud [2155]
　Coalition for an Intl. Criminal Court [17361]
　Coalition for an Intl. Criminal Court [IO]
　Correctional Educ. Assn. [11862]
　Criminal Law Soc. of Japan [IO]
　Family Justice [11865]
　Fed. Criminal Investigators Assn. [5653]
　Fed. Law Enforcement Officers Assn. [5879]
　Fortune Soc. [11867]
　Friends Outside [11868]
　Intl. Assn. of Cmpt. Investigative Specialists [8133]
　Intl. Assn. of Correctional Officers [11870]
　Intl. Assn. of Correctional Training Personnel [11871]
　Intl. Assn. of Financial Crimes Investigators [5881]
　Intl. Assn. for Identification [5763]
　Intl. Assn. of Penal Law - Austria [IO]
　Intl. Assn. of Penal Law - Switzerland [IO]
　Intl. Assn. of Reentry [17355]
　Intl. Community Corrections Assn. [11872]
　Intl. Criminal Court Alliance [5654]
　Intl. Criminal Law Network [IO]
　Intl. Narcotics Interdiction Assn. [5742]
　Intl. Utilities Revenue Protection Assn. [6338]
　John Howard Assn. [11874]
　Justice Res. Inst. [5655]
　Justice Res. and Statistics Assn. [11876]
　Justice Stud. Assn. [13109]
　Life After Exoneration Prog. [17360]
　London Club [11900]
　Natl. Amer. Indian Court Judges Assn. [5905]
　Natl. Assn. of Criminal Defense Lawyers [5656]
　Natl. Assn. of Fed. Defenders [5646]
　Natl. Assn. of Forensic Counselors [5647]
　Natl. Assn. of State Sentencing Commissions [5650]
　Natl. Center on Institutions and Alternatives [11878]
　Natl. Center for Juvenile Justice [11879]
　Natl. Correctional Indus. Assn. [11880]
　Natl. Criminal Defense Coll. [5657]
　Natl. Criminal Justice Assn. [11881]
　Natl. Juvenile Detention Assn. [11882]
　Natl. Major Gang Task Force [5651]
　Natl. Prison Proj. of the ACLU [11883]
　North Amer. Assn. of Wardens and Superintendents [11884]
　Osborne Assn. [11885]
　People of Faith Against the Death Penalty [17034]
　Prison Fellowship Intl. [11887]
　Prison Fellowship Ministries [11888]
　Prison Ministry of Yokefellow's Intl. [11889]
　Prisoners' Rights Union [11890]
　Safer Soc. Found. [11891]
　Victims' Assistance Legal Org. [5639]
　Volunteers in Prevention, Probation, Prisons [11896]

We Care Prog. [11897]
　Women's Prison Assn. [11898]
Criminal Law; Sect. of [★5922]
Criminal Law Soc. of Japan [IO], Tokyo, Japan
Criminal Psychology; Soc. for Police and [16177]
Criminalistics; Amer. Bd. of [5749]
Criminals to Justice; Ad Hoc Comm. to Bring Nazi War [★17719]
Criminology
　Amer. Soc. of Criminology [11899]
　Australian Inst. of Criminology [IO]
　British Soc. of Criminology [IO]
　Coun. of Intl. Investigators [2322]
　Intl. Assn. of Crime Analysts [5658]
　Intl. Assn. of Crime Analysts [IO]
　Intl. Center for Comparative Criminology [IO]
　Intl. Soc. of Crime Prevention Practitioners [11838]
　Intl. Soc. of Criminology [IO]
　Justice Stud. Assn. [13109]
　London Club [11900]
　Scandinavian Res. Coun. for Criminology [IO]
Criminology; Soc. for the Advancement of [★11899]
Crippled Children; Intl. Soc. for [★16333]
Crippled Children's Directors; Assn. of State and Territorial Maternal and Child Hea. and [★13947]
Cripples; Intl. Soc. for the Welfare of [★16333]
Crisis; Christians in [20555]
Crisis Comm; Population [★12758]
Crisis Intervention
　Albert Ellis Inst. [16197]
　Assn. of Gospel Rescue Missions [13155]
　Center for Psychological and Spiritual Hea. [15194]
　CONTACT USA [19865]
　Corporate Alliance to End Partner Violence [12025]
　Direct Aid Intl. [12849]
　Ethos Found. [13239]
　Girls and Boys Town [12934]
　Heartbeat [13288]
　House of Ruth [12029]
　Natl. Coalition Against Domestic Violence [12034]
　Natl. Domestic Violence Hotline [12036]
　Natl. Org. for Victim Assistance [13369]
　Natl. Tactical Officers Assn. [6175]
　Org. for Attempters and Survivors of Suicide in Interfaith Services [13290]
　Pact Training [11830]
　Suicide and Mental Hea. Assn. Intl. [15234]
　Suicide Prevention Action Network USA [13292]
　William Wendt Center for Loss and Healing [13317]
Crisis Intervention Counselor's Assn. - Address unknown since 1995.
Crisis Training; Performing Arts for [★11830]
Crisis; Women in [13443]
CrisisShield UK [IO], Tunbridge Wells, United Kingdom
Crispell Family Assn. [20874], PO Box 35, Tafton, PA 18464-0035
CRISTA Ministries [13166], 19303 Fremont Ave. N, Seattle, WA 98133, (206)546-7200
Cristina Found; Natl. [11969]
Critical Care
　Canadian Critical Care Soc. [IO]
　European Soc. of Intensive Care Medicine [IO]
　German Interdisciplinary Assn. of Critical Care Medicine [IO]
　Intensive Care Soc. [IO]
　Neurocritical Care Soc. [IO]
　Neurocritical Care Soc. [14070]
　Soc. of Critical Care Medicine [14071]
　Soc. of Critical Care Medicine [IO]
　Student Veterinary Emergency and Critical Care Soc. [16810]
Critical Care; NAMDRC: Physician Advocacy for Excellence in the Delivery of Pulmonary and [★15068]
Critical-Care Nurses; Amer. Assn. of [15433]
Critical Care Soc; Intl. Trauma Anesthesia and [13686]
Critical Care; Soc. of Neurosurgical Anesthesia and [15417]
Critical Care Technicians; Acad. of Veterinary Emergency and [16734]

A star before a book entry number signifies that the name is not listed separately, but is mentioned within the entry.

Critical Incident Stress Found; Intl. **[16491]**
Critical Issues Coun. - Defunct.
Critical Mass **[★18134]**
Critical Mass Energy Proj. of Public Citizen **[★18134]**
Critical Thinking Assn. - Defunct.
Critical Thinking; Assn. for Informal Logic and **[10785]**
Critical Thinking; Center for **[8179]**
Critical Will; Reaching **[17436]**
Critics Assn; Amer. Theatre **[11004]**
Critics Assn; Dance **[9875]**
Critics Assn; Music **[★10650]**
Critics Assn. of North Am; Music **[10650]**
Critics Circle; Natl. Book **[9753]**
Critics Circle; Outer **[11037]**
Critics Consensus - Defunct.
Critics Inst; Natl. **[★11036]**
Critics Inst; O'Neill **[11036]**
Critics - U.S. Sect; Intl. Assn. of Art **[9573]**
Crittenton Assn. of Amer; Florence **[★11572]**
Critter Companions - Address unknown since 2004.
Croatia Cricket Bd. **[IO]**, Zagreb, Croatia
Croatian
  CFU Junior Cultural Fed. **[9844]**
  Croatian Acad. of Am. **[19020]**
  Croatian Amer. Assn. **[17868]**
  Croatian Amer. Bar Assn. **[5489]**
  Croatian-American Chamber of Commerce **[24314]**
  Croatian-American Chamber of Commerce **[IO]**
  Croatian Catholic Union of U.S.A. and Canada **[19021]**
  Croatian Fraternal Union of Am. **[19022]**
  Croatian Philatelic Soc. **[22813]**
  Natl. Fed. of Croatian Americans **[17362]**
Croatian Acad. of Am. **[19020]**, PO Box 1767, Grand Central Sta., New York, NY 10163-1767
Croatian Acad. of Sciences and Arts **[IO]**, Zagreb, Croatia
Croatian Aeronautical Fed. **[IO]**, Zagreb, Croatia
Croatian Agricultural Engg. Soc. **[IO]**, Zagreb, Croatia
Croatian Amer. Assn. **[17868]**, c/o Daniella Sumera, Natl. Treas., 6607 W Archer Ave., Chicago, IL 60638
Croatian Amer. Bar Assn. **[5489]**, 1850 Whittier Ave., Unit E201, Costa Mesa, CA 92627
Croatian-American Chamber of Commerce **[24314]**, 50-52 49th St., Woodside, NY 11377, (718)937-4040
Croatian-American Chamber of Commerce **[IO]**, Woodside, NY, United States
Croatian Archery Alliance **[★IO]**
Croatian Archery Assn. **[IO]**, Zagreb, Croatia
Croatian Archery Fed. **[★IO]**
Croatian Article Numbering Assn. **[★IO]**
Croatian Assn. of the Blind **[IO]**, Zagreb, Croatia
Croatian Assn. of Consulting Engineers **[IO]**, Zagreb, Croatia
Croatian Assn. of Physiotherapists **[IO]**, Zagreb, Croatia
Croatian Assn. for the Treatment of Pain **[IO]**, Karlovac, Croatia
Croatian Assn. of Univ. Women **[IO]**, Zagreb, Croatia
Croatian Athletic Fed. **[IO]**, Zagreb, Croatia
Croatian Badminton Assn. **[IO]**, Zagreb, Croatia
Croatian Bar Assn. **[IO]**, Zagreb, Croatia
Croatian Baseball Assn. **[IO]**, Zagreb, Croatia
Croatian Bible Soc. **[IO]**, Zagreb, Croatia
Croatian Canoe Fed. **[IO]**, Zagreb, Croatia
Croatian Cardiac Soc. **[IO]**, Zagreb, Croatia
Croatian Catholic Union of the U.S.A. **[★19021]**
Croatian Catholic Union of U.S.A. and Canada **[19021]**, 1 E Old Ridge Rd., PO Box 602, Hobart, IN 46342-0602, (219)942-1191
Croatian Chess Fed. **[IO]**, Zagreb, Croatia
Croatian Composers Soc. **[IO]**, Zagreb, Croatia
Croatian Cycling Fed. **[IO]**, Zagreb, Croatia
Croatian Dance Sport Fed. **[IO]**, Zagreb, Croatia
Croatian Democracy Project - Address unknown since 2001.
Croatian Dental Soc. **[IO]**, Zagreb, Croatia
Croatian Dermatovenerological Soc. of the Croatian Medical Assn. **[IO]**, Zagreb, Croatia

Croatian Economic Assn. **[IO]**, Zagreb, Croatia
Croatian Entomological Soc. **[IO]**, Zagreb, Croatia
Croatian Fed. for EEG and Neurophysiology **[IO]**, Zagreb, Croatia
Croatian Football Fed. **[IO]**, Zagreb, Croatia
Croatian Fraternal Union of Am. **[19022]**, 100 Delaney Dr., Pittsburgh, PA 15235, (412)843-0380
Croatian Gas Assn. **[IO]**, Zagreb, Croatia
Croatian Genealogical Soc. - Defunct.
Croatian Hockey Fed. **[IO]**, Zagreb, Croatia
Croatian League Against Epilepsy **[IO]**, Zagreb, Croatia
Croatian League Against Rheumatism **[IO]**, Zagreb, Croatia
Croatian League of Illinois **[★19022]**
Croatian Lib. Assn. **[IO]**, Zagreb, Croatia
Croatian Mgt. Assn. **[★IO]**
Croatian Managers' and Entrepreneurs Assn. **[IO]**, Zagreb, Croatia
Croatian Medical Assn. **[IO]**, Zagreb, Croatia
Croatian Microscopy Soc. **[IO]**, Zagreb, Croatia
Croatian Mineralogical Assn. **[IO]**, Zagreb, Croatia
Croatian Natl. Cong. - Defunct.
Croatian Nuclear Soc. **[IO]**, Zagreb, Croatia
Croatian Olympic Comm. **[IO]**, Zagreb, Croatia
Croatian Operational Res. Soc. **[IO]**, Zagreb, Croatia
Croatian Orienteering Fed. **[IO]**, Zagreb, Croatia
Croatian Osteoporosis Soc. **[IO]**, Zagreb, Croatia
Croatian Peasant Party - Address unknown since 1999.
Croatian Pharmaceutical Soc. **[IO]**, Zagreb, Croatia
Croatian Pharmacological Soc. **[IO]**, Zagreb, Croatia
Croatian Philatelic Soc. **[22813]**, PO Box 696, Fritch, TX 79036-0696, (806)857-0129
Croatian Physical Soc. **[IO]**, Zagreb, Croatia
Croatian Physiological Soc. **[IO]**, Zagreb, Croatia
Croatian Red Cross **[IO]**, Zagreb, Croatia
Croatian Rock-n-Roll Assn. **[IO]**, Zagreb, Croatia
Croatian Sailing Fed. **[IO]**, Split, Croatia
Croatian Skating Fed. **[IO]**, Zagreb, Croatia
Croatian Soc. for Bird and Nature Protection **[IO]**, Zagreb, Croatia
Croatian Soc. of Chem. Engineers **[IO]**, Zagreb, Croatia
Croatian Soc. of Chemotherapy **[IO]**, Zagreb, Croatia
Croatian Soc. for Communications, Computing, Electronics, Measurement and Control **[IO]**, Zagreb, Croatia
Croatian Soc. for Electron Microscopy **[★IO]**
Croatian Soc. of Environmental Hea. **[IO]**, Zagreb, Croatia
Croatian Soc. for Hospice and P.C. **[IO]**, Zagreb, Croatia
Croatian Soc. of Hypertension **[IO]**, Split, Croatia
Croatian Soc. for Medical Informatics **[IO]**, Zagreb, Croatia
Croatian Soc; Natl. **[★19022]**
Croatian Soc. for Rheumatology **[IO]**, Zagreb, Croatia
Croatian Soc. for Soil Mechanics and Geotechnical Engg. **[IO]**, Zagreb, Croatia
Croatian Sports Fed. for the Disabled **[IO]**, Zagreb, Croatia
Croatian Sports Medicine Soc. **[IO]**, Zagreb, Croatia
Croatian Squash Assn. **[IO]**, Zagreb, Croatia
Croatian Taekwondo Fed. **[IO]**, Zagreb, Croatia
Croatian Tennis Assn. **[IO]**, Zagreb, Croatia
Croatian Union of Tenants **[IO]**, Zagreb, Croatia
Croatian Workers Assn. of America - Address unknown since 1999.
Croatian Youth Coun. **[IO]**, Zagreb, Croatia
Croatian Youth Hostel Assn. **[IO]**, Zagreb, Croatia
Crochet Assn. Intl. **[22154]**
Crochet Guild of Am. **[22722]**, 1100-H Brandywine Blvd., Zanesville, OH 43701-7303, (740)452-4541
Crockett Club; Boone and **[5301]**
Crohn's and Colitis Found. of Am. **[14414]**, 386 Park Ave. S, 17th Fl., New York, NY 10016-8804, (212)685-3440
Crohn's and Colitis Found. of Canada **[IO]**, Toronto, ON, Canada
Crohn's Disease; Natl. Assn. of Colitis and **[IO]**
Croissant Rouge Tunisien **[★IO]**
Cromwell Assn. **[IO]**, Sutton, United Kingdom

Cromwell, Oliver
  Cromwell Assn. **[IO]**
Crookston Alumni Assn; Univ. of Minnesota - **[18936]**
CROP **[★12842]**
CROP **[★IO]**
Crop Conservancy Garden and Seed Bank; Southwest Traditional **[★4429]**
Crop Consultants; Natl. Alliance of Independent **[4078]**
Crop-Hail Insurance Actuarial Assn. **[★2223]**
Crop Improvement Assn; Intl. **[★5436]**
Crop Insurance Agents of Am. - Defunct.
Crop Insurance Assn; Natl. **[★2223]**
Crop Insurance Res. Bur. **[2161]**, 10800 Farley, Ste. 330, Overland Park, KS 66210, (913)338-0470
Crop Insurance Services; Natl. **[2223]**
Crop Insurers; Amer. Assn. of **[2129]**
Crop Protection Assn. **[IO]**, Peterborough, United Kingdom
Crop Protection Assn; Amer. **[★807]**
Crop Quality Coun. - Defunct.
Crop Sci. Division of the Amer. Soc. of Agronomy **[★4099]**
Crop Sci. Division of the Amer. Soc. of Agronomy **[★IO]**
Crop Science Society of America **[IO]**, Madison, WI, United States
Crop Sci. Soc. of Am. **[4099]**, 677 S Segoe Rd., Madison, WI 53711, (608)273-8080
Crop Sci. Soc. of Japan **[IO]**, Tokyo, Japan
CropLife Am. **[807]**, 1156 15th St. NW, Washington, DC 20005, (202)296-1585
CropLife Australia **[IO]**, Canberra, Australia
Crops; Assn. for the Advancement of Indus. **[4110]**
Croquet
  All England Lawn Tennis and Croquet Club **[IO]**
  Amer. Roque and Croquet Assn. **[23090]**
  Australian Croquet Assn. **[IO]**
  Croquet Assn. **[IO]**
  Croquet Assn. Queensland **[IO]**
  Croquet Canada **[IO]**
  Croquet Fed. of Belgium **[IO]**
  Croquet Found. of Am. **[23300]**
  Croquet Victoria **[IO]**
  New Zealand Croquet Coun. **[IO]**
  Scottish Croquet Assn. **[IO]**
  South Australian Croquet Assn. **[IO]**
  South West Fed. of Croquet Clubs **[IO]**
  U.S. Croquet Assn. **[23301]**
  Welsh Croquet Assn. **[IO]**
  West Australian Croquet Assn. **[IO]**
Croquet Assn. **[IO]**, Cheltenham, United Kingdom
Croquet Assn; Amer. Roque and **[23090]**
Croquet Assn. Queensland **[IO]**, West End, Australia
Croquet Canada **[IO]**, Toronto, ON, Canada
Croquet Fed. of Belgium **[IO]**, Brussels, Belgium
Croquet Found. of Am. **[23300]**, 700 Florida Mango Rd., West Palm Beach, FL 33406-4461, (561)478-0760
Croquet Victoria **[IO]**, Niddrie, Australia
Crosby, Bing
  Bing's Friends and Collectors Soc. **[24851]**
  Intl. Crosby Circle **[24804]**
Crosier Heritage Assn. - Defunct.
Crosier Missions **[20325]**, 4332 N 24th St., Phoenix, AZ 85016-6259, (602)443-7100
Crosier Missions **[IO]**, Shoreview, MN, United States
Crosley Auto. Club **[21624]**, 307 Schaeffer Rd., Blandon, PA 19510
Cross; Armenian Red **[★18966]**
Cross Country Coaches Assn; Natl. Collegiate **[★23924]**
Cross Country Coaches Assn; U.S. **[23924]**
Cross Country Ski Areas of Am. **[★3660]**
Cross Country Ski Areas Assn. **[3660]**, 259 Bolton Rd., Winchester, NH 03470, (603)239-4341
Cross Country Ski Nova Scotia **[IO]**, Halifax, NS, Canada
Cross Country Skiers; Amer. **[23750]**
Cross Cultural Collaborative **[8177]**, 45 Auburn St., Brookline, MA 02446, (617)277-0482
Cross Cultural Collaborative **[IO]**, Brookline, MA, United States
Cross-Cultural Dance Resources **[IO]**, Flagstaff, AZ, United States

Reference to "IO" in place of a book number signifies that the association may be found in the 45th edition of International Organizations.

Cross-Cultural Dance Resources [9874], 518 S Agassiz St., Flagstaff, AZ 86001-5711, (928)774-8108

Cross Cultural Hea. Care Prog. [14626], 270 S Hanford St., Ste. 208, Seattle, WA 98134, (206)860-0329

Cross-Cultural Res; Soc. for [10230]

Cross-Cultural Shamanism Network [20444], PO Box 270, Williams, OR 97544, (541)846-1313

Cross-Cultural Solutions [11901], 2 Clinton Pl., New Rochelle, NY 10801, (914)632-0022

Cross-Examination Debate Assn. - Defunct.

Cross; Knights of the White [★19293]

Cross-Reference Dir. Publishers; Intl. Assn. of [3228]

Cross Stitch Guild [IO], Fairford, United Kingdom

Crossbowmen of the U.S.A., Inc; Natl. [★23054]

Crossbowmen of the U.S.A; The Natl. [23054]

Crosscurrents Intl. Inst. [17880], 7122 Hardin-Wapak Rd., Sidney, OH 45365, (937)492-0407

Crosscurrents Intl. Inst. [IO], Sidney, OH, United States

Crossdressers Intl. [IO], New York, NY, United States

Crossdressers Intl. [13089], 404 W 40th St., New York, NY 10018, (212)564-4847

Crossdressing
Crossdressers Intl. [13089]
Intl. Found. for Gender Educ. [13091]
Soc. for the Second Self [13102]

CrossRef [3220], 40 Salem St., Lynnfield, MA 01940, (781)295-0072

Crossroads [★12226]

Crossroads [★IO]

Crossroads Africa; Oper. [16932]

CrossSphere: the Global Assn. for Packaged Travel [★3930]

Crossword Fed; Amer. [22458]

Crossword Game Players; Scrabble [★22470]

Crossworld [20326], PO Box 306, Bala Cynwyd, PA 19004, (610)667-7660

Crossworld [IO], Bala Cynwyd, PA, United States

Crotty Family Org. - Defunct.

Crowl Name Assn. [20875], c/o A. Crowell, 1600 Brentworth Way, Reno, NV 89521

Crown and Bridge Prosthodontics; Amer. Acad. of [★14097]

Crown Cat Fanciers Fed. - Defunct.

Crown Victoria Assn. [21625], PO Box 6, Bryan, OH 43506-9141, (419)636-2475

Crowncap Collectors Soc. Intl. [22005], c/o Lance Wood, Treas., 4420 Running Pine, League City, TX 77573

Croydon Chamber of Commerce and Indus. [IO], Croydon, United Kingdom

CRRTS Program - Defunct.

CRU Inst. [8138], 2330 130th Ave. NE, Bldg. C, Ste. 102, Bellevue, WA 98005, (425)869-4041

Crucible Inst. - Defunct.

Cruelty to Animals; Amer. Soc. for the Prevention of [11350]

Cruelty to Animals; Irish Soc. for the Prevention of [IO]

Cruise Club of Am. [3914], PO Box 318, North Pembroke, MA 02358, (800)982-2276

Cruise Conf; Pacific [★3915]

Cruise Lines Intl. Assn. [3915], 910 SE 17th St., Ste. 400, Fort Lauderdale, FL 33316, (754)224-2200

Cruise Lines Intl. Assn. [IO], Fort Lauderdale, FL, United States

Cruise Lines; Intl. Coun. of [3923]

Cruise Only Agencies; Natl. Assn. of [★3928]

Cruise-Oriented Agencies; Natl. Assn. of [3928]

Cruiser Olympia Assn. [★21266]

Cruisermen's Assn. - Defunct.

Cruising Assn. [IO], London, United Kingdom

Cruising Assn; Seven Seas [23217]

Cruising Club of Am. [23166], 77 Churchills Ln., Milton, MA 02186-3522

Crusade to Abolish War and Armaments by World Law [18310]

Crusade Against Corruption - Defunct.

Crusade for the Ballot [★17154]

Crusade for a Cleaner Environment - Defunct.

Crusade for Decency - Address unknown since 1995.

Crusade for a More Fruitful Preaching and Hearing of the Word of God - Defunct.

Crusaders for Christ [20462], 585 W Orange Ave., El Centro, CA 92243, (760)337-9408

Cruse Bereavement Care Scotland [IO], Perth, United Kingdom

Crushed Stone Assn; Natl. [★3699]

Crusher and Portable Plant Assn. - Defunct.

Crushers' Assn; Interstate Cotton Seed [★2854]

The Crustacean Soc. [7863], PO Box 7065, Lawrence, KS 66044-7065, (785)843-1221

Cryo-Ophthalmology; Soc. for [★15666]

Cryobiology; Soc. for [6847]

Cryogenic Engg. Conf. [6843], c/o Dr. Jay C. Theilacker, Sec., PO Box 500, Batavia, IL 60510-0500

Cryogenic Soc. of Am. [6844], c/o Laurie Huget, Exec. Dir., Huget Advt., 218 Lake St., Oak Park, IL 60302-2609, (708)383-6220

Cryogenics
Amer. Type Culture Coll. [6567]
British Cryogenics Coun. [IO]
Cryogenic Engg. Conf. [6843]
Cryogenic Soc. of Am. [6844]
Cryonics Soc. of Canada [IO]
Immortalist Soc. [6845]
Intl. Cryogenic Materials Conf. [6846]
Intl. Inst. of Refrigeration [IO]
Life Extension Soc. [14074]
Soc. for Cryobiology [6847]
Soc. for Low Temperature Biology [IO]
World Transhumanist Assn. [7163]

Cryonics
Alcor Life Extension Found. [14072]
Alcor Life Extension Foundation [IO]
Amer. Cryonics Soc. [14073]
Cryonics Assn. of Australia [IO]
Cryonics Inst. [1120]
Immortalist Soc. [6845]
Life Extension Soc. [14074]

Cryonics Assn. [★6845]

Cryonics Assn. of Australia [IO], Hampton, Australia

Cryonics Inst. [1120], 24355 Sorrentino Ct., Clinton Township, MI 48035, (586)791-5961

Cryonics Soc; Bay Area [★14073]

Cryonics Soc. of Canada [IO], Toronto, ON, Canada

Cryonics Soc. of Michigan [★6845]

Cryptography
Amer. Cryptogram Assn. [22178]
Marine Corps Cryptologic Assn. [21174]

Cryptology
Amer. Cryptogram Assn. [22178]
Beale Cipher Assn. [6848]
Intl. Assn. for Cryptologic Res. [6849]
Intl. Assn. for Cryptologic Res. [IO]
Marine Corps Cryptologic Assn. [21174]
New York Cipher Soc. [6850]
U.S. Naval Cryptologic Veterans Assn. [21327]

Crystal Gayle Fan Club - Defunct.

Crystal Growth; Amer. Assn. for [6851]

Crystal Growth; Amer. Comm. for [★6851]

Crystal StarGate - Defunct.

Crystallographic Assn; Amer. [6852]

Crystallographic Assn; British [IO]

Crystallographic Soc. of Am. [★6852]

Crystallography
Amer. Assn. for Crystal Growth [6851]
Amer. Crystallographic Assn. [6852]
British Assn. of Crystal Growth [IO]
British Crystallographic Assn. [IO]
Egyptian Soc. of Crystallography and Applications [IO]
Intl. Liquid Crystal Soc. [IO]
Intl. Liquid Crystal Soc. [6853]
Intl. Union of Crystallography [IO]
Soc. of Crystallographers in Australia and New Zealand [IO]
U.S. Faceters Guild [1121]

C.S. Forester Soc. - Defunct.

C.S. Lewis Soc; New York [9696]

The CS Register [★21592]

CSA Fraternal Life [19026], 122 W 22nd St., Oak Brook, IL 60523, (800)543-3272

CSA Intl. [IO], Toronto, ON, Canada

CSA and U.S.A; Armies of Tennessee, [20722]

CSB [★6443]

CSB [★IO]

CSB Ministries [20640], PO Box 150, Wheaton, IL 60189, (630)424-1330

CSC Clearing Corp. - Defunct.

CSLR [★5841]

CSLR [★IO]

Csomagolasi es Anyagmozgatasi Orszagos Szovetseg [★IO]

CTAM - Cable and Telecommunications Assn. for Marketing [558], 201 N Union St., Ste. 440, Alexandria, VA 22314, (703)549-4200

CTAM, The Marketing Soc. for the Cable and Telecommunications Indus. [★558]

CTC, The Natl. Cyclists' Org. [IO], Guildford, United Kingdom

CTIA - The Wireless Assn. [3741], 1400 16th St. NW, Ste. 600, Washington, DC 20036, (202)785-0081

CTIA - The Wireless Assn. and Wireless Data Forum [★3741]

CTR for Dance Medicine [★16055]

CTSNet: Cardiothoracic Surgery Network [16643], 3108 Queeny Tower, St. Louis, MO 63110, (314)361-6084

CUAMM - Medici con l'Africa [★IO]

Cub Koda Fan Club - Defunct.

Cuba
Alpha-66 [17363]
Alpha-66 [IO]
Assn. for the Stud. of the Cuban Economy [8214]
Bay of Pigs Veterans Assn. [20717]
Center for Cuban Studies/Cuban Art Space [9845]
Cuban Amer. Natl. Coun. [13167]
Cuban Amer. Natl. Found. [17364]
Cuban Amer. Natl. Found. [IO]
Directorio Democratico Cubano [IO]
Directorio Democratico Cubano [17365]
Junta Civico-Militar Cubana [17366]
Movement for an Independent and Democratic Cuba [17367]
Movement for an Independent and Democratic Cuba [IO]
U.S.-Cuba Trade Assn. [2316]
Venceremos Brigade [17917]

Cuba Independiente y Democratica [★17367]

Cuba Independiente y Democratica [★IO]

Cuba Information Proj. - Defunct.

Cuba Poster Project - Address unknown since 2006.

Cuba Reconciliation Initiative; US- [17675]

Cuba Resource Center - Defunct.

Cuba Support Gp. - Ireland [IO], Dublin, Ireland

Cuban
Asociacion de Ingenieros Cubanos [7002]
Assn. for the Stud. of the Cuban Economy [8214]
Center for Cuban Studies/Cuban Art Space [9845]
Cuban Amer. Alliance Educ. Fund [19023]
Cuban Amer. Natl. Coun. [13167]
Cuban Amer. Veterans Assn. [21297]
Cuban Numismatic Assn. [22735]
Havana Silk Dog Assn. of Am. [22282]
U.S.-Cuba Trade Assn. [2316]

Cuban Amer. Alliance Educ. Fund [19023], PO Box 5113, San Luis Obispo, CA 93403, (805)627-1959

Cuban-Amer. Comm. - Address unknown since 2003.

Cuban Amer. Found. [★17364]

Cuban Amer. Found. [★IO]

Cuban Amer. Freedom Coalition [★IO]

Cuban Amer. Freedom Coalition [★17364]

Cuban Amer. Legal Defense and Education Fund - Address unknown since 1999.

Cuban Amer. Natl. Coun. [13167], 1223 SW 4th St., Miami, FL 33135, (305)642-3484

Cuban Amer. Natl. Found. [17364], 1312 SW 27th Ave., Miami, FL 33145, (305)592-7768

Cuban Amer. Natl. Found. [IO], Miami, FL, United States

Cuban Amer. Public Affairs Comm. [★IO]

Cuban Amer. Public Affairs Comm. [★17364]

Cuban Amer. Republican Women - Defunct.

Cuban Amer. Veterans Assn. [21297], PO Box 140305, Coral Gables, FL 33114-0305, (305)534-0372

Cuban Art Space; Center for Cuban Studies/ [9845]

A star before a book entry number signifies that the name is not listed separately, but is mentioned within the entry.

Cuban Assn. of Marfan Syndrome **[IO]**, Havana, Cuba
Cuban Assn. for Pattern Recognition **[IO]**, Havana, Cuba
Cuban Clinical Neurophysiology Soc. **[IO]**, Havana, Cuba
Cuban Democratic Directorate **[★IO]**
Cuban Democratic Directorate **[★17365]**
Cuban Freedom Comm. - Defunct.
Cuban League Against Epilepsy **[IO]**, Havana, Cuba
Cuban Municipalities in Exile - Address unknown since 1995.
Cuban Natl. Comm. for the Stud. of Hypertension **[IO]**, Havana, Cuba
Cuban Natl. Planning Coun. **[★13167]**
Cuban Numismatic Assn. **[22735]**, c/o Robert Freeman, Treas., 523 Meridian St., Tallahassee, FL 32301-1281, (727)531-7337
Cuban Numismatic Assn. **[IO]**, Tallahassee, FL, United States
Cuban Philatelic Soc. of America - Address unknown since 1994.
Cuban Representation of Exiles - Address unknown since 1999.
Cuban Soc. of Physiological Sciences **[IO]**, Havana, Cuba
Cuban Stud; Center for **[★9845]**
Cuban Studies/Cuban Art Space; Center for **[9845]**
Cuban Women's Club - Address unknown since 2000.
Cubanos; Asociacion de Ingenieros **[7002]**
Cuda Owners Club; Plymouth Barracuda/ **[21763]**
Cued Speech Association/Deaf Children's Literacy Proj; Natl. **[16452]**
Cuemakers Assn; Amer. **[518]**
CUES Financial Suppliers Forum **[2623]**, 5510 Res. Park Dr., Madison, WI 53711-5377, (608)271-2664
CUES Managers Soc. **[★1106]**
Cuisine Assn. of Am; Chefs de **[792]**
Cuisine Assn. of Am; Executive Chefs de **[★792]**
Culinaire Philanthropique; Societe **[19138]**
Culinarians - Defunct.
Culinarians' Home Foundation **[★19138]**
Culinary Arts
  Amer. Inst. of Wine and Food **[22568]**
  Amer. Personal and Private Chef Assn. **[791]**
  Black Culinarian Alliance **[1122]**
  Confrerie de la Chaine des Rotisseurs, Bailliage des U.S.A. **[22569]**
  Culinary Inst. of Canada **[IO]**
  The Culinary Trust **[IO]**
  The Culinary Trust **[8174]**
  Intl. Chili Soc. **[22571]**
  Les Dames d'Escoffier Intl. **[1123]**
  Res. Chefs Assn. **[1124]**
  Terlingua Intl. Chili Championship **[22574]**
  Vinegar Connoisseurs Intl. **[22575]**
Culinary Arts Club - Defunct.
Culinary Fed; Amer. **[790]**
Culinary Guild of Windsor **[IO]**, Windsor, ON, Canada
Culinary Inst. of Canada **[IO]**, Charlottetown, PE, Canada
Culinary Professionals Found; Intl. Assn. of **[★8174]**
The Culinary Trust **[8174]**, PO Box 273, New York, NY 10013, (646)224-6989
The Culinary Trust **[IO]**, Louisville, KY, United States
Culion Foundation **[★IO]**
Culion Foundation **[★15010]**
Culligan Dealers Assn. of North Am. **[1667]**, c/o JSJ Productions, Inc., 14101 Hwy. 290 W, Bldg. 1600B, Austin, TX 78737, (512)894-4106
Cullowhee Fan Club - Defunct.
Cult Awareness Network **[19873]**, 1680 N Vine St., Ste. 415, Los Angeles, CA 90028, (323)468-0567
Cult Awareness Network **[IO]**, Los Angeles, CA, United States
Cult Fan Club - Address unknown since 1999.
Cult of the Virgin - Address unknown since 2001.
Cults
  Christian Res. Inst. **[19785]**
  Cult Awareness Network **[19873]**
  Cult Awareness Network **[IO]**
  Free Minds, Inc. **[19874]**
  Intl. Cultic Stud. Assn. **[17368]**

  Jews for Judaism **[20500]**
  Personal Freedom Outreach **[19875]**
  Spiritual Counterfeits Proj. **[19876]**
  USCCCN Natl. CH on Satanic Crime in Am. **[11848]**
  Watchman Fellowship **[19877]**
Cultura; Istituto Italiano di **[10257]**
Cultural Affairs; Inst. of **[12350]**
Cultural Alliance; African Amer. **[9351]**
Cultural Alliance; Bi Women's **[12219]**
Cultural Arts in Progress **[9850]**, 1250 Dolington Rd., Yardley, PA 19067, (215)493-3124
Cultural Arts in Progress **[IO]**, Yardley, PA, United States
Cultural Assistance Center **[★9535]**
Cultural Assn. of Bengal **[9737]**, 143 Grymes Hill Rd., Staten Island, NY 10301, (718)815-1401
Cultural Assn., Inc; Tartan Educational and **[★19354]**
Cultural Assn; Pacific Islanders' **[10767]**
Cultural Assn. - U.S.A; Subud Intl. **[9600]**
Cultural Center; Chinese **[★9792]**
Cultural Center; East-West **[9619]**
Cultural Center; Indian Pueblo **[★18089]**
Cultural Center; Mexican Amer. **[20286]**
Cultural Center; Slovak-Amer. **[10970]**
Cultural Center; Swedish Museum and **[★10990]**
Cultural Center; Swedish Museum and **[★IO]**
Cultural Center; Turkish **[★19409]**
Cultural Centers
  Amer. Community Cultural Center Assn. **[9846]**
  Ethnic Cultural Preservation Coun. **[9847]**
  Grosse Pointe War Memorial Assn. **[21300]**
  John M. Olin Found. **[12047]**
  Schomburg Center for Res. in Black Culture **[9363]**
  World Heritage Alliance **[10077]**
Cultural and Community Center; Italian **[★19162]**
Cultural Conservancy **[10741]**, PO Box 29044, San Francisco, CA 94129-0044, (415)561-6594
Cultural Coun. Found. - Defunct.
Cultural Democracy; Alliance for **[9536]**
Cultural Educ; Amer. Coun. on Intl. Inter **[8651]**
Cultural Environments; Saving and Preserving Arts and **[9470]**
Cultural Exchange
  Africa-American Friendship Soc. **[18862]**
  AFS Intercultural Programmes - New Zealand **[IO]**
  AFS Intercultural Programs - Argentina **[IO]**
  AFS Intercultural Programs - Australia **[IO]**
  AFS Intercultural Programs - Austria **[IO]**
  AFS Intercultural Programs - Brazil **[IO]**
  AFS Intercultural Programs - Chile **[IO]**
  AFS Intercultural Programs - China **[IO]**
  AFS Intercultural Programs - Costa Rica **[IO]**
  AFS Intercultural Programs - Czech Republic **[IO]**
  AFS Intercultural Programs - Denmark **[IO]**
  AFS Intercultural Programs - Dominican Republic **[IO]**
  AFS Intercultural Programs - Ecuador **[IO]**
  AFS Intercultural Programs - Finland **[IO]**
  AFS Intercultural Programs - Germany **[IO]**
  AFS Intercultural Programs - Ghana **[IO]**
  AFS Intercultural Programs - Guatemala **[IO]**
  AFS Intercultural Programs - Honduras **[IO]**
  AFS Intercultural Programs - Hong Kong **[IO]**
  AFS Intercultural Programs - Hungary **[IO]**
  AFS Intercultural Programs - Iceland **[IO]**
  AFS Intercultural Programs - India **[IO]**
  AFS Intercultural Programs - Italy **[IO]**
  AFS Intercultural Programs - Latvia **[IO]**
  AFS Intercultural Programs - Malaysia **[IO]**
  AFS Intercultural Programs - Panama **[IO]**
  AFS Intercultural Programs - Peru **[IO]**
  AFS Intercultural Programs - Portugal **[IO]**
  AFS Intercultural Programs - Slovakia **[IO]**
  AFS Intercultural Programs - Spain **[IO]**
  AFS Intercultural Programs - Sweden **[IO]**
  AFS Intercultural Programs - Thailand **[IO]**
  AFS Intercultural Programs - Venezuela **[IO]**
  AFS Interculture South Africa **[IO]**
  AFS Intl. **[IO]**
  AFS Intl. **[8175]**
  AFS Norge **[IO]**
  Aga Khan Trust for Culture **[IO]**
  Amer. Bahraini Friendship Soc. **[19150]**

Amer. Inst. for Managing Diversity **[17369]**
Amer. Iranian Coun. **[17926]**
Amer. Portuguese Stud. Assn. **[9004]**
Amer. Russian Theatrical Alliance **[11001]**
American-Scandinavian Found. **[10942]**
Amer. Soc. for Muslim Advancement **[10245]**
Amer. Telugu Assn. **[9848]**
Asian/Pacific Amer. Heritage Assn. **[18972]**
Associates in Cultural Exchange **[8176]**
Assn. for the Advancement of Dutch-American Stud. **[9908]**
Assn. for Africanist Anthropology **[6408]**
Assn. of Cultural Executives **[IO]**
Assn. of Latina and Latino Anthropologists **[6410]**
Associazione Culturale Antonio Pedrotti **[IO]**
AZUR Development **[IO]**
Bhojpuri Assn. of North Am. **[10299]**
Bihar Assn. of North Am. **[10220]**
Brahman Samaj of North Am. **[9998]**
Brazilian-American Cultural Inst. **[9757]**
Bridges to Community **[13389]**
British Mexican Soc. **[IO]**
Butimar Productions **[9849]**
CEC ArtsLink **[17370]**
CEC ArtsLink **[IO]**
Center on Religion and Soc. **[20491]**
Champa Cultural Preservation Assn. of USA **[11082]**
Chinese-American Arts Coun. **[9608]**
Chinese Amer. Forum **[9786]**
Chinese School Assn. in the U.S. **[9090]**
Cladan Cultural Exchange Inst. of Australia **[IO]**
Coalition for Harmony of Races in the U.S. **[18198]**
Cross Cultural Collaborative **[8177]**
Cross Cultural Collaborative **[IO]**
Cultural Arts in Progress **[IO]**
Cultural Arts in Progress **[9850]**
Ecuadorian Experiment in Intl. Living **[IO]**
Egyptian Soc. for Intercultural Exchange **[IO]**
EIL Intercultural Learning **[IO]**
Ellis Island Medal of Honor Soc. **[19044]**
European Folklore Inst. **[IO]**
Fed. of Afrikaans Cultural Societies **[IO]**
Fed. of Jain Associations in North America **[20495]**
Finnish Cultural Found. **[IO]**
Franco-British Soc. **[IO]**
Friends of Malawi **[IO]**
Friends of Malawi **[9851]**
Getty Grant Prog. **[9569]**
Global Nomads Gp. **[9336]**
Global Routes **[9852]**
Globe Aware **[13393]**
Heaven On Earth **[IO]**
Hungarian Amer. Coalition **[12451]**
Hunterian Society **[IO]**
Imagine Canada **[IO]**
Indian Coun. for Cultural Relations **[IO]**
Indian and Northern Affairs Canada **[IO]**
Intl. Christian Technologists Assn. **[20282]**
Intl. Inst. for Promotion and Prestige **[IO]**
Intl. Print Triennial Soc. - Krakow **[IO]**
Intl. Soc. for Cultural and Activity Res. **[IO]**
Istanbul Found. for Culture and Arts **[IO]**
Japan Art History Forum **[9480]**
Japan Found. **[10264]**
Japan Info. Access Proj. **[10265]**
Japan Soc. **[10266]**
Jewel Heart **[19552]**
Joseph Campbell Found. **[9206]**
Kosciuszko Found. **[10879]**
Laotian Amer. Natl. Alliance **[19192]**
Laotian Amer. Soc. **[19193]**
Leuva Patidar Samaj of USA **[10221]**
Malaysian Cultural Gp. **[IO]**
Malaysian Danish Assn. **[IO]**
Maniilaq Assn. **[12627]**
Milan Cultural Assn. **[10222]**
My Travel Bug **[9279]**
Natl. Assn. of Asian Amer. Professionals **[9623]**
Natl. Assn. of Latino Arts and Culture **[9584]**
Natl. Coun. of Japanese Language Teachers **[9226]**
Natl. Ethnic Coalition of Organizations **[19046]**

Reference to "IO" in place of a book number signifies that the association may be found in the 45th edition of International Organizations.

Natl. Fed. of Croatian Americans [17362]
Natl. Initiative for a Networked Cultural Heritage [9858]
Natl. Iranian Amer. Coun. [19151]
Natl. MultiCultural Inst. [11829]
Nepali Amer. Friendship Assn. [19288]
North Amer. Assn. for Belarusian Stud. [9735]
North Amer. Assn. for the Stud. of Welsh Culture and History [11083]
North Amer. Dhrupad Assn. [10677]
North Amer. Sankethi Assn. [9802]
North Amer. Taiwan Stud. Assn. [9205]
Ogwashi-Uku Assn., USA [19291]
Panamerican/PanAfrican Assn. [17371]
Patidar Cultural Assn. of USA [10218]
Press Div., Taipei Economic and Cultural Off. in New York [9792]
Prog. of Academic Exchange [8628]
Punjabi-American Cultural Assn. [10223]
SENEVOLU [IO]
Sister Island Proj. [11788]
Slavic and East European Folklore Assn. [9962]
Slavic Heritage Coalition [10969]
Soc. for Indonesian-Americans [19116]
Student Org. of North Am. [9194]
Swiss-American Soc. for Cultural Relations [IO]
Tamizdat [9853]
Tree of Peace Soc. [9913]
UNESCO-ASCHBERG Bursaries for Artists Programme [IO]
United South and Eastern Tribes [12632]
U.S.-Japan Culture Center [10268]
United States-Japan Found. [19024]
United States-Japan Found. [IO]
USA Sanatan Sports and Cultural Assn. [23787]
Uttaranchal Assn. of North Am. [10219]
Wildflowers Inst. [9794]
World Assn. for Vedic Stud. [9854]
World Assn. for Vedic Stud. [IO]
World Council of Elders [IO]
World Coun. of Elders [9855]
Cultural Exchange; French Amer. [8560]
Cultural Exchange; Fulbright Assn. of Alumni of Intl. Educational and [★8613]
Cultural Exchange Soc. of America - Address unknown since 1999.
Cultural Exchange Soc; U.S. [★23861]
Cultural Fed; CFU Junior [9844]
Cultural Forum; Austrian [9625]
cultural informationser. [★8155]
Cultural Inst; Austrian [★9625]
Cultural Inst; Irish Amer. [10241]
Cultural Inst; Italian [★10257]
Cultural Inst. of Miami; Polish-American [★10876]
Cultural Integration Fellowship [9618], 360 Cumberland St., San Francisco, CA 94114, (415)626-2442
Cultural Laureate Found. - Address unknown since 1995.
Cultural Orientation Rsrc. Center [★10401]
Cultural Preservation Comm; Comanche Language and [10736]
Cultural Pride; Interracial-Inter [12162]
Cultural Relations; Coun. on Inter- [★10234]
Cultural Res; Soc. for Cross- [10230]
Cultural Resources
African Amer. Literature and Culture Soc. [8798]
Alliance of Natl. Heritage Areas [9856]
Assn. for Cultural Evolution [9857]
Bihar Assn. of North Am. [10220]
Blue Earth Alliance [10847]
China Times Cultural Found. [7984]
Cowles Charitable Trust [9564]
Cross-Cultural Solutions [11901]
Dene Cultural Inst. [IO]
European Forum of Heritage Associations [IO]
European Inst. of Cultural Routes [IO]
European Network of Cultural Admin. Training Centres [IO]
European Network of Natl. Heritage Organisations [IO]
Found. for the Advancement of Sephardic Stud. and Culture [19181]
Friends of Malawi [9851]
Historians of Eighteenth-Century Art and Architecture [9479]

Indigenous Peoples Coun. on Biocolonialism [12407]
Macedonian Arts Coun. [10437]
Natl. Initiative for a Networked Cultural Heritage [9858]
Navy and Marine Living History Assn. [21206]
North Amer. Dhrupad Assn. [10677]
Pew Charitable Trusts [13129]
Robert Sterling Clark Found. [11902]
Saving Antiquities for Everyone [9389]
Soc. for Conservation GIS [6831]
Soc. for Psychological Anthropology [7550]
Tamizdat [9853]
Vietnamese Nom Preservation Found. [10433]
Wordcraft Circle of Native Writers and Storytellers [9859]
Wordcraft Circle of Native Writers and Storytellers [IO]
Cultural Resources Assn; Amer. [9540]
Cultural Services and Educational Aid; Soc. for French Amer. [★8560]
Cultural Shamanism Network; Cross- [20444]
Cultural and Social Stud; Soc. For Iranian [★10238]
Cultural Soc; Acadian [21096]
Cultural Society; Gaelic [★11717]
Cultural Society; Gaelic [★IO]
Cultural Soc; Italian Amer. [19162]
Cultural Soc; Portuguese Historical and [19321]
Cultural Soc; San Francisco African Amer. Historical and [9362]
Cultural Stud; Inst. for Inter [10234]
Cultural Survival [10171], 215 Prospect St., Cambridge, MA 02139, (617)441-5400
Cultural Survival [IO], Cambridge, MA, United States
Cultural and Tech. Interchange Between East and West; Center for [★17882]
Cultural Travel Orgs. Intl. - Address unknown since 1994.
Cultural Union Brazil U.S. [IO], Paraiso, Brazil
Culture; Amer. Coun. for Polish [19301]
Culture and Animals Found. [11384], 3509 Eden Croft Dr., Raleigh, NC 27612, (919)782-3739
Culture and Arts Prog; Native Hawaiian [10884]
Culture Assn; Amer. [10886]
Culture Assn; Amer. Cowboy [9379]
Culture Assn; Chinese [9787]
Culture Assn; Popular [10888]
Culture Center; U.S.-Japan [10268]
Culture Coll; Amer. Type [6567]
Culture Collections; U.S. Fed. for [6603]
Culture; Cong. for Jewish [10278]
Culture and Educ; Intl. Sex Worker Found. for Art, [13092]
Culture and Educ; Sex Worker Found. for Art, [★13092]
Culture; Found. for the Arts, Religion and [★9599]
Culture Found; Polish Arts and [19307]
Culture Found. of San Francisco; Chinese [9788]
Culture, Hea., Env. and Safety; Beach Educ. Advocates for [10761]
Culture; Inst. for the Advanced Stud. of Black Family Life and [9359]
Culture; Inst. of Chinese [9791]
Culture; Omohundro Inst. of Early Amer. History and [10140]
Culture Res. Center; Amer. Indian [10731]
Culture; Soc. for the Arts, Religion and Contemporary [9599]
Culture Soc; Rural [19387]
Cultured Marble Inst. [★630]
Cultured Marble Inst. [★IO]
Cultured Pearl Assn. of America - Address unknown since 2005.
Cultures; The Assn. of Amer. [9554]
Cultures; Homowo African Arts and [9350]
Cultwatch Response - Defunct.
Gum Laude Soc. [24503], 23490 Caraway Lakes Dr., Bonita Springs, FL 34135, (239)390-3257
Cumann Bainistiocht Eolaiocht na h-Eireann [★IO]
Cumann Camogaiochta nan Gael [★IO]
Cumann Cheol Tire Eireann [★IO]
Cumann Corpoideachais na hEireann [★IO]
Cumann Geinealais na heireann [★IO]
Cumann Innealtoiri Comhairle na h Eirann [★IO]
Cumann Leabharfhoilsitheoiri Eireann [★IO]

Cumann Leabharlann na hEireann [★IO]
Cumann Liathroid Leadoige Na heireann [★IO]
Cumann Lucht Capaillini Chonamara [★IO]
Cumann Luthchleas Gael [★IO]
Cumann na Meanmhuinteori Eire [★IO]
Cumann Muinteoiri Eireann [★IO]
Cumann Peile na hEireann [★IO]
Cumann na Scoileanna Pobail agus Cuimsitheacha [★IO]
Cumann Tireolaiochta na hEireann [★IO]
Cumann Uaigheann Na Laochra Gael [★IO]
Cumbria and North Lancs Campaign for Nuclear Disarmament [IO], Carlisle, United Kingdom
CUMELA Nederland [IO], Nijkerk, Netherlands
Cummings Found; Nathan [13125]
CUMREC [8249], c/o EDUCAUSE, 4772 Walnut St., Ste. 206, Boulder, CO 80301-2538, (303)449-4430
Cumunn na Camanachd [★IO]
CUNA Intl. [★1107]
Cunha Philatelic Soc; St. Helena, Ascension, and Tristan da [22866]
Cunningham Soc. of Am; Clan [20823]
Cup; Kids to the [23504]
Cup and Mug Collectors of Am; Advt. [21956]
Cupid Collectors Club [22006], c/o Ted Lussem, Treas., 2919 John Patterson Rd., Des Moines, IA 50317
Cupido Pinnatus; Soc. of Tympanuchus [5383]
Curacao
Curacao Convention Bureau/Tourist Bd. [24362]
Curacao and Bonaire Tourist Boards [★24362]
Curacao Chamber of Commerce and Indus. [IO], Curacao, Netherlands Antilles
Curacao Convention Bureau/Tourist Bd. [24362], Curacao Tourism Corp., 3361 SW Third Ave., Ste. 201, Miami, FL 33145, (305)285-0511
Curacao Info. Center [★24362]
Curacao Tourist Bd. [★24362]
Curatio Intl. Found. [IO], Tbilisi, Georgia
Curators Incorporated; Independent [★9444]
Curb Agency; New York [★3507]
Curb Exchange; New York [★3507]
Curb Market Assn; New York [★3507]
Curb Market; New York [★3507]
Cure For Lymphoma Found. [★13840]
CURE Formaldehyde Poisoning Assn. [13324]
CURE Intl. [13975], 701 Bosler Ave., Lemoyne, PA 17043, (717)730-6706
CURE Intl. [IO], Lemoyne, PA, United States
Cure Res. Found. [13818], PO Box 3782, Westlake Village, CA 91359, (805)498-0185
CuresNow [15135], 10100 Santa Monica Blvd., Ste. 1300, Los Angeles, CA 90067
Curl des Sourds du Canada [★IO]
Curling
Canadian Curling Assn. [IO]
Canadian Firefighters Curling Assn. [IO]
Curling Club Hamburg e.V. [IO]
English Curling Assn. [IO]
Finnish Curling Assn. [IO]
Irish Curling Assn. [IO]
New Zealand Curling Assn. [IO]
Nova Scotia Curling Assn. [IO]
Southern Alberta Curling Assn. [IO]
U.S. Curling Assn. [23302]
U.S. Women's Curling Assn. [23303]
World Curling Fed. [IO]
Curling Assn; U.S. Men's [★23302]
Curling Assn; U.S. Women's [23303]
Curling Club Hamburg e.V. [IO], Hamburg, Germany
Curly-Coated Retriever Club of Am. [22252], c/o David Ferguson, Treas., 90 N Gunflint Lake Rd., Grand Marais, MN 55604, (218)388-0300
Curly Horse Org; Intl. [4898]
Curly Registry; Amer. Bashkir [4812]
Curly Sporthorse Intl. [4874], PO Box 129, Cross Anchor, SC 29331, (864)316-4672
Curly Sporthorse International [IO], Cross Anchor, SC, United States
Currency Dealers Assn; Professional [22753]
Current Evangelism Ministries [★19993]
Curriculum
Amer. Assn. of Teaching and Curriculum [9209]
Amer. Indian Res. and Development [8464]
Assn. for Core Texts and Courses [8776]

A star before a book entry number signifies that the name is not listed separately, but is mentioned within the entry.

Assn. for Supervision and Curriculum Development [8178]
Assn. for Supervision and Curriculum Development [IO]
Australian Curriculum Stud. Assn. [IO]
Canadian Assn. for Curriculum Stud. [IO]
Center for Critical Thinking [8179]
Coalition of Essential Schools [8180]
EPIE Inst. [8559]
Grace Contrino Abrams Peace Educ. Found. [8139]
High/Scope Educational Res. Found. [8181]
The Madison Proj. [8824]
Natl. Assn. of Supervisors and Administrators of Hea. Occupations Educ. [8870]
Qualifications and Curriculum Authority [IO]
World Coun. for Curriculum and Instruction [IO]
World Coun. for Curriculum and Instruction [8182]
Curriculum Development (of NEA); Dept. of Supervision and [★8178]
Curriculum Development; Soc. for [★8178]
Curriculum In Public Schools; Natl. Coun. On Bible [9052]
Curriculum Proj; Japanese Amer. [★8598]
Currier and Ives Dinnerware Collectors [22007], c/o Charles Burgess, Treas., 308 Jodi Dr., Brownstown, IN 47220, (812)358-4569
Cursillo Movement; Natl. [19685]
Curtis/Curtiss Soc. [20876], c/o Jennifer L. Seney, Membership Sec., 25605 Apple Blossom Ln., Wesley Chapel, FL 33544
Curtiss Soc; Curtis/ [20876]
Curved Dash Olds Owners Club - Address unknown since 1999.
CUSA: An Apostolate of the Sick and Disabled [19620], 4856 W 29th St., Cicero, IL 60804
Cushing Soc; Harvey [★15410]
Cushing's Support and Res. Found. [14352], 65 E India Row, Ste. 22B, Boston, MA 02110, (617)723-3674
Cushion Coun; Carpet [2253]
Cushman Club of Am. [22676], PO Box 661, Union Springs, AL 36089, (334)738-3874
Cushman Found. for Foraminiferal Res. [7428], c/o Jennifer Jett, Sec.-Treas., Smithsonian Inst., Washington, DC 20013-7012, (202)633-1333
CUSO - Canada [IO], Ottawa, ON, Canada
CUSO/Women Development Proj. [★IO]
Cuspidore Hitters Assn. Worldwide - Defunct.
Custer Battlefield Historical and Museum Assn. [10106], PO Box 902, Hardin, MT 59034-0902
Custer, George Armstrong
Little Bighorn History Alliance [11135]
Custody Action for Lesbian Mothers - Defunct.
Custody Assn; Joint [12011]
Custody Reform
Children's Rights Coun. [12007]
Custom Assn; Goodguys Rod and [21649]
Custom Clothing Guild of America - Defunct.
Custom Electronic Design Installation Assn. [3548], 7150 Winton Dr., Ste. 300, Indianapolis, IN 46268, (317)328-4336
Custom Gunmakers Guild; Amer. [1477]
Custom Legal Plans, LLC [6022], 139-30 Queens Blvd., Briarwood, NY 11435-2926, (718)526-6100
Custom Legal Plans, LLC [IO], Briarwood, NY, United States
Custom Roll Forming Inst. [2706], 6363 Oak Tree Blvd., Independence, OH 44131-2500, (216)901-8800
Custom Tailors and Designers Assn. of Am. [231], PO Box 41331, Cleveland, OH 44141, (440)526-8860
Customary Weight and Measure; Americans for [18679]
Customer Contact Assn. [IO], Glasgow, United Kingdom
Customer Contact Mgt. Assn. [IO], Melbourne, Australia
Customer Satisfaction Measurement Assn. [716], c/o The Benchmarking Network, 4606 FM 1960 W, Ste. 250, Houston, TX 77069-9949, (281)440-5044
Customer Ser. Assn; Intl. [3551]
Customs
Canadian Soc. of Customs Brokers [IO]

Customs Brokers and Freight Forwarders Assn. of Jamaica [IO]
Customs and Intl. Trade Bar Assn. [IO]
Customs and Intl. Trade Bar Assn. [5659]
Intl. Customs Tariffs Bur. [IO]
Italian Folk Art Fed. of Am. [10259]
World Customs Org. [IO]
Customs Bar; Assn. of the [★5659]
Customs Brokers Assn. of Jamaica [★IO]
Customs Brokers Assn; New York [★2309]
Customs Brokers and Forwarders Assn. of Am. [★2309]
Customs Brokers and Forwarders Assn. of Am; Natl. [2309]
Customs Brokers and Freight Forwarders Assn. of Jamaica [IO], Kingston, Jamaica
Customs Clerks Assn. of the Port of New York [★2309]
Customs Co-operation Coun. (CCC) [★IO]
Customs and Intl. Trade Bar Assn. [IO], New York, NY, United States
Customs and Intl. Trade Bar Assn. [5659], c/o Allison M. Baron, Esq., Membership Chair, 75 Broad St., 26th Fl., New York, NY 10004, (212)425-0055
Customs Ser. Assn; Natl. [★24080]
Cut Glass Assn; Amer. [22550]
Cutaneous Oncology; Amer. Coll. of Mohs Micrographic Surgery and [15636]
Cutlery and Allied Trades Res. Assn. [IO], Sheffield, United Kingdom
Cutlery Manufacturers Assn; Amer. [★3708]
Cutter and Chariot Racing Assn; World Championship [23281]
Cutter Collectors Club; Cookie [22000]
Cutting Die Inst. - Address unknown since 1999.
Cutting Fluid Mfrs. Assn. - Defunct.
Cutting Horse Assn; Amer. [23520]
Cutting Horse Assn; Natl. [4918]
Cutting Tool Inst; U.S. [2076]
Cutting Tool Mfrs. of Am. [★2076]
Cutting Tool Mfrs. Assn. [★2076]
CVJM - Gesamtverband [IO], Kassel, Germany
CWA; Printing, Publishing and Media Workers Sector of the [24086]
CWI: Credit Professionals [★1411]
CWI: Credit Professionals [★IO]
The Cybele Soc. - Address unknown since 1999.
CyberAngels [12452], PO Box 3171, Allentown, PA 18106, (610)377-2966
CyberKnife Soc. [16581], c/o Dianna Brogden, 1310 Chesapeake Terr., Sunnyvale, CA 94089, (408)716-4663
Cybernetics
Cybernetics Soc. [IO]
Cybernetics; Amer. Soc. for [6719]
Cybernetics Soc. [IO], Welwyn Garden City, United Kingdom
Cybernetics Soc; IEEE Systems, Man, and [6728]
The Cycad Soc. [4387], c/o Dr. Bart Schutzman, Univ. of Florida, Environmental Horticulture Dept., 1531 Fifield Hall, Gainesville, FL 32611-0670
The Cycad Soc. [IO], Gainesville, FL, United States
Cyclamen Soc. [IO], Sevenoaks, United Kingdom
Cycle
Inst. for Trans. and Development Policy [17840]
Cycle Assn; Amer. Historic Racing Motor [22665]
Cycle Assn; British Intl. Motor [★22673]
Cycle Assn; U.S. Bi [★23305]
Cycle Assn; Wheelchair Motor [23370]
Cycle Club; All-American Indian Motor [22663]
Cycle Club of Am; Antique Motor [22667]
Cycle Club; Ariel Owners' Motor [★22668]
Cycle Club; Knights of Life Motor [12968]
Cycle Club North Am; Ariel Motor [22668]
Cycle Fed. of Am; Bi [★23315]
Cycle Forum; Bi [★23304]
Cycle Heritage Found; Amer. Motor [23621]
Cycle Indus. Coun; Motor [2795]
Cycle Jobbers Assn. [★3640]
Cycle League; Natl. Bi [23313]
Cycle Owners; Vintage BMW Motor [22698]
Cycle Parts and Accessories Assn. - Defunct.
Cycle Polo Fed. of India [IO], Jaipur, India
Cycle Prdt. Suppliers Assn; Bi [3640]
Cycle Racing Assn. [IO], Gwangmyeong, Republic of Korea

Cycle Ride Directors' Assn. of Am; Bi [23308]
Cycle Safety Found; Motor [3447]
Cyclic Vomiting Syndrome Assn. [14415], 3585 Cedar Hill Rd. NW, Canal Winchester, OH 43110, (614)837-2586
Cyclic Vomiting Syndrome Assn. [★14415]
Cyclic Vomiting Syndrome Assn. [IO], Canal Winchester, OH, United States
Cyclic Vomiting Syndrome Assn. [★IO]
Cycling
Adventure Cycling Assn. [23304]
Am. Bikes [17022]
Amer. Bicycle Assn. [23305]
Amer. Bicycle Polo Assn. [23658]
Amer. Track Racing Assn. [23306]
Amer. Volkssport Assn. [23803]
Auto-Cycle Union - Motorcycling Great Britain [IO]
Bicycle Parking Proj. [23307]
Bicycle Ride Directors' Assn. of Am. [23308]
Bicycle Stamps Club [22796]
Bicycle Tasmania [IO]
Bikes Belong Coalition [21831]
British Cycle Speedway Commn. [IO]
British Cycling [IO]
Calgary BMX Assn. [IO]
Camping Women [23269]
Canadian Cycling Assn. [IO]
Croatian Cycling Fed. [IO]
CTC, The Natl. Cyclists' Org. [IO]
Cycle Racing Assn. [IO]
Cycling Ireland [IO]
Cycling Time Trials [IO]
European Cyclists' Fed. [IO]
Intl. Christian Cycling Club USA [IO]
Intl. Christian Cycling Club USA [23309]
Intl. Cycling Union [IO]
Intl. Fed. of Bike Messenger Associations [517]
Intl. Mountain Bicycling Assn. [23310]
International Mountain Bicycling Association [IO]
Intl. Unicycling Fed. [23311]
League of Amer. Bicyclists [23312]
Natl. Bicycle League [23313]
Natl. Bicycle Tour Directors Assn. [23314]
Natl. Center for Bicycling and Walking [23315]
Natl. Ethiopian Cycling Fed. [IO]
Randonneurs USA [23316]
Scottish Cyclists' Union [IO]
Tandem Club of Am. [23317]
Trans. Alternatives [7813]
Ultra Marathon Cycling Assn. [23318]
Ultra Marathon Cycling Association [IO]
Unicycling Soc. of Am. [23319]
U.S. Adventure Racing Assn. [23672]
U.S. Bicycle Polo Assn. [23660]
U.S. Cycling Fed. [23320]
U.S. Handcycling Fed. [23321]
The Wheelmen [23322]
Women's Mountain Bike and Tea Soc. [23323]
Cycling Assn; Natl. Off-Road Bi [★23320]
Cycling Assn; Ultra Marathon [23318]
Cycling Assn; U.S. Deaf [23365]
Cycling Australia [IO], Bass Hill, Australia
Cycling Ireland [IO], Dublin, Ireland
Cycling Parking Found; Bi [★23307]
Cycling Parking Proj; Bi [★23307]
Cycling Time Trials [★IO]
Cycling Time Trials [IO], Leigh, United Kingdom
Cyclist Assn; Amer. Motor [23622]
Cyclists; Assn. of Recovering Motor [13225]
Cyclone Montego Torino Registry [21626], 19 Glyn Dr., Newark, DE 19713-4016, (302)737-4252
Cyclone Torino Montego Registry [★21626]
Cykel Motor och Sportfackhandlarna [★IO]
Cylinder Grinders Assn; Natl. [★375]
Cylinder Mfrs. Assn. - Defunct.
Cymbidium Soc. of Am. [22508], c/o Clara Moura, Membership Sec., 1742 Grove Way, Castro Valley, CA 94546, (510)537-8923
Cymbidium Soc. of Am. [IO], Sacramento, CA, United States
Cymdeithas Bridwyr Merlod A Cobiau Cymreig Gwynedd [★IO]
Cymdeithas Gwartheg Duon Cymreig [★IO]
Cymdeithas Judo Cymru [★IO]
Cymdeithas Ysgolion Uwchradd Cymru [★IO]

Reference to "IO" in place of a book number signifies that the association may be found in the 45th edition of International Organizations.

Cymric Cat Club - Address unknown since 2001.
Cyngor Cefn Gwlad Cymru [★IO]
Cyngor Celfyddydau Cymru [★IO]
Cyngor Llyfrau Cymru [★IO]
CYO Fed; Natl. [★19688]
Cypress Mfrs. Assn; Southern [1621]
Cyprus
　Amer. Hellenic Inst. [24325]
　Cyprus Tourism Org. [24315]
Cyprus Advertisers Assn. [IO], Nicosia, Cyprus
Cyprus Airsports Fed. [IO], Nicosia, Cyprus
Cyprus Amateur Baseball Fed. [IO], Larnaca, Cyprus
Cyprus Amateur Judo, Taekwondo Fed. [IO], Nicosia, Cyprus
Cyprus Amateur Radio Soc. [IO], Limassol, Cyprus
Cyprus Assn. of Medical Physics and Biomedical Engg. [IO], Nicosia, Cyprus
Cyprus Assn. of Physiotherapists [IO], Nicosia, Cyprus
Cyprus Assn. of Professional Quantity Surveyors [IO], Nicosia, Cyprus
Cyprus Assn. of Sports Medicine [IO], Nicosia, Cyprus
Cyprus Badminton Fed. [IO], Nicosia, Cyprus
Cyprus Chamber of Commerce and Indus. [IO], Nicosia, Cyprus
Cyprus Clothing Indus. Assn. [IO], Latsia, Cyprus
Cyprus Clothing Manufacturers Assn. [★IO]
Cyprus Cmpt. Hardware and Software Suppliers Assn. [★IO]
Cyprus Cmpt. Soc. [IO], Nicosia, Cyprus
Cyprus Embassy Trade Center [IO], New York, NY, United States
Cyprus Embassy Trade Center [24273], 13 E 40th St., New York, NY 10016, (212)213-9100
Cyprus Employers' and Industrialists' Fed. [IO], Nicosia, Cyprus
Cyprus Family Planning Assn. [IO], Nicosia, Cyprus
Cyprus Football Assn. [IO], Nicosia, Cyprus
Cyprus Hotel Assn. [IO], Nicosia, Cyprus
Cyprus Ice Skating Fed. [IO], Nicosia, Cyprus
Cyprus Info. Tech. Enterprises Assn. [IO], Nicosia, Cyprus
Cyprus League against Rheumatism [IO], Nicosia, Cyprus
Cyprus Milk Indus. Org. [IO], Nicosia, Cyprus
Cyprus Multiple Sclerosis Assn. [IO], Nicosia, Cyprus
Cyprus Natl. Paralympic Comm. [IO], Nicosia, Cyprus
Cyprus Newspaper and Magazines Publishers Assn. [IO], Nicosia, Cyprus
Cyprus Olympic Comm. [IO], Nicosia, Cyprus
Cyprus Org. for Promotion of Quality [IO], Nicosia, Cyprus
Cyprus Orinthological Soc. [★IO]
Cyprus Orthodontic Soc. [IO], Limassol, Cyprus
Cyprus Professional Engineers Assn. [IO], Nicosia, Cyprus
Cyprus Ski Club [IO], Nicosia, Cyprus
Cyprus Soc. Against Osteoporosis and Myoskeletal Diseases [IO], Nicosia, Cyprus
Cyprus Soc. of Cardiology [IO], Nicosia, Cyprus
Cyprus Soc. of Chemotherapy and Infectious Diseases [IO], Nicosia, Cyprus
Cyprus Soc. of Dermatology and Venerology [IO], Nicosia, Cyprus
Cyprus Sport Org. [IO], Nicosia, Cyprus
Cyprus Squash Rackets Assn. [IO], Nicosia, Cyprus
Cyprus Tennis Fed. [IO], Nicosia, Cyprus
Cyprus Tourism Org. [IO], Nicosia, Cyprus
Cyprus Tourism Org. [24315], 13 E 40th St., New York, NY 10016, (212)683-5280
Cyprus Veterans Assn. World War II [IO], Nicosia, Cyprus
Cyprus Water Ski Fed. [IO], Limassol, Cyprus
Cyprus Weightlifting Fed. [IO], Limassol, Cyprus
Cyprus Yachting Assn. [IO], Limassol, Cyprus
Cyriac Elias Voluntary Assn. [IO], Kochi, India
Cyrus Spirit; Billy Ray [24850]
Cystic Fibrosis Assn. of Ireland [IO], Dublin, Ireland
Cystic Fibrosis Assn; Norwegian [IO]
Cystic Fibrosis Australia [IO], North Ryde, Australia
Cystic Fibrosis Australia - Australian Capital Territory [IO], Civic Square, Australia

Cystic Fibrosis Australia - Tasmania [IO], Hobart, Australia
Cystic Fibrosis Australia - Victoria [IO], Melbourne, Australia
Cystic Fibrosis Australia - Western Australia [IO], Nedlands, Australia
Cystic Fibrosis Found. [16358], 6931 Arlington Rd., Bethesda, MD 20814, (301)951-4422
Cystic Fibrosis Found; Canadian [IO]
Cystic Fibrosis Res. Found; Natl. [★16358]
Cystic Fibrosis Trust [IO], Bromley, United Kingdom
Cystic Fibrosis Worldwide [16359], c/o Ms. Christine Noke, Prog. Dir., 210 Park Ave., No. 267, Worcester, MA 01609, (508)733-6120
Cystinosia Found. of California [★15246]
Cystinosis Found. [15246], 604 Vernon St., Oakland, CA 94610, (559)222-7997
Cystinosis Res. Network [15247], 10 Pine Ave., Burlington, MA 01803, (781)229-6182
Cystitis Assn; Interstitial [16708]
Cytochrome C Oxidase Deficiency Parental Res. and Support Found. - Address unknown since 1999.
Cytogenetic Technologists; Assn. of [★6569]
Cytokine Res; Intl. Soc. for Interferon and [16351]
Cytokine Soc; Intl. [6580]
Cytology
　Amer. Soc. of Cytopathology [14075]
　Amer. Soc. for Cytotechnology [14076]
　British Soc. for Clinical Cytology [IO]
　European Tissue Culture Soc. [IO]
　European Tissue Repair Soc. [IO]
　Intl. Acad. of Cytology [IO]
　Intl. Cell Death Soc. [IO]
　Intl. Cell Death Soc. [6854]
　Intl. Fed. of Societies for Histochemistry and Cytochemistry [14077]
　Intl. Fed. of Societies for Histochemistry and Cytochemistry [IO]
　Intl. Soc. for Analytical Cytology [6583]
　Mitochondrial Medicine Soc. [14078]
　Natl. Assn. of Cytologist [IO]
　PanAmerican Soc. for Pigment Cell Res. [15111]
Cytology; Amer. Soc. of [★14075]
Cytology Center; Natl. Cancer [★15650]
Cytology Coun; Inter-Society [★14075]
Cytology Found. of Am; Cancer [★15650]
Cytology; Intl. Soc. for Experimental [★6581]
Cytology; Soc. for Analytical [★6583]
Cytometry Soc; Clinical [15865]
Cytopathology; Amer. Soc. of [14075]
Czech
　Amer. Fund for Czechoslovak Relief [12802]
　Amer. Sokol Educational and Physical Culture Org. [19025]
　CSA Fraternal Life [19026]
　Czech Catholic Union [19027]
　Czech Collector's Assn. [22008]
　Czech Heritage Found. [19028]
　Czech Heritage Preservation Soc. [10022]
　Czech-North Amer. Chamber of Commerce [24274]
　Czechoslovak Soc. of Arts and Sciences [9860]
　Czechoslovak Soc. of Arts and Sciences [IO]
　Intl. Assn. of Teachers of Czech [IO]
　Intl. Assn. of Teachers of Czech [9861]
　Natl. Alliance of Czech Catholics [19029]
　Slovak-Amer. Cultural Center [10970]
　Soc. for the History of Czechoslovak Jews [10289]
　Western Fraternal Life Assn. [19030]
Czech ACM SIGCHI [IO], Prague, Czech Republic
Czech Aikido Assn. - Aikikai of Czech Republic [IO], Prague, Czech Republic
Czech Amer. Natl. Alliance - Address unknown since 1995.
Czech Assn. for Branded Products [IO], Prague, Czech Republic
Czech Assn. of Consulting Engineers [IO], Prague, Czech Republic
Czech Assn. for Geoinformation [IO], Prague, Czech Republic
Czech Assn. of Geomorphologists [IO], Prague, Czech Republic
Czech Assn. of Occupational Therapists [IO], Prague, Czech Republic

Czech Assn. of Proj. Mgt. [IO], Brno, Czech Republic
Czech Badminton Fed. [IO], Prague, Czech Republic
Czech Banking Assn. [IO], Prague, Czech Republic
Czech Bar Assn. [IO], Prague, Czech Republic
Czech Baseball Fed. [IO], Prague, Czech Republic
Czech Benedictines [★19027]
Czech Biathlon Union [IO], Prague, Czech Republic
Czech Bible Soc. [IO], Prague, Czech Republic
Czech Bioclimatological Soc. [IO], Prague, Czech Republic
Czech Catholic Union [19027], 5349 Dolloff Rd., Cleveland, OH 44127, (216)341-0444
Czech Chem. Soc. [IO], Prague, Czech Republic
Czech Collector's Assn. [IO], Shawnee, OK, United States
Czech Collector's Assn. [22008], c/o Patti Ferguson, Dir. of Membership, 9 Mockingbird Ln., Shawnee, OK 74804
Czech Confed. of Commerce and Tourism [IO], Prague, Czech Republic
Czech Dance Sport Fed. [IO], Litomerice, Czech Republic
Czech Dental Chamber [IO], Prague, Czech Republic
Czech Figure Skating Assn. [IO], Prague, Czech Republic
Czech Fish Farmers' Assn. [IO], Ceske Budejovice, Czech Republic
Czech Floorball Union [IO], Prague, Czech Republic
Czech Franchise Assn. [IO], Prague, Czech Republic
Czech Gas Assn. [IO], Prague, Czech Republic
Czech Gynecological and Obstetrical Soc. [IO], Prague, Czech Republic
Czech Heritage Found. [19028]
Czech Heritage Preservation Soc. [10022], PO Box 199, Tyndall, SD 57066-0199
Czech Insurance Assn. [IO], Prague, Czech Republic
Czech Ladies and Men; Unity of [★19026]
Czech League Against Epilepsy [IO], Brno, Czech Republic
Czech League Against Rheumatism [IO], Prague, Czech Republic
Czech Medical Assn. of J.E. Purkyne [IO], Prague, Czech Republic
Czech Member Comm. of the World Energy Coun. [IO], Prague, Czech Republic
Czech Meteorological Soc. [IO], Prague, Czech Republic
Czech-Moravian Assn. of Plant Breeders and Seed Traders [IO], Prague, Czech Republic
Czech and Moravian Elecl. and Electronic Assn. [IO], Prague, Czech Republic
Czech-Moravian Psychological Soc. [IO], Prague, Czech Republic
Czech Multiple Sclerosis Soc. [IO], Prague, Czech Republic
Czech; North Amer. Assn. of Teachers of [★9861]
Czech-North Amer. Chamber of Commerce [24274], 2110 Powers Ferry Rd., Ste. 220, Atlanta, GA 30339, (678)533-7191
Czech Olympic Comm. [IO], Prague, Czech Republic
Czech Operational Res. Soc. [IO], Cheb, Czech Republic
Czech Orthodontic Soc. [IO], Prague, Czech Republic
Czech Osteoporosis League [IO], Prague, Czech Republic
Czech Pain Soc. [IO], Prague, Czech Republic
Czech Paralympic Comm. [IO], Prague, Czech Republic
Czech Physiological Soc. [IO], Prague, Czech Republic
Czech Publishers Assn. [IO], Prague, Czech Republic
Czech Radio Club [IO], Prague, Czech Republic
Czech Radiological Soc. [IO], Plzen, Czech Republic
Czech Republic Union of Tenants [IO], Prague, Czech Republic
Czech Rheumatological Soc. [IO], Prague, Czech Republic

A star before a book entry number signifies that the name is not listed separately, but is mentioned within the entry.

Czech Rosa Club **[IO]**, Prague, Czech Republic
Czech Sailing Assn. **[IO]**, Prague, Czech Republic
Czech Seed Trade Assn. **[IO]**, Prague, Czech Republic
Czech and Slovak Assn. of Canada **[IO]**, Toronto, ON, Canada
Czech and Slovak Solidarity Coun. - Address unknown since 2002.
Czech and Slovak-U.S. Bus. Coun. **[2302]**, c/o Chamber of Commerce of the U.S., 1615 H St. NW, Washington, DC 20062-2000, (202)659-6000
Czech and Slovak-U.S. Economic Coun. **[★2302]**
Czech Soc. of Cardiology **[IO]**, Brno, Czech Republic
Czech Soc. of Chemotherapy **[IO]**, Prague, Czech Republic
Czech Soc. for Clinical Neurophysiology **[IO]**, Prague, Czech Republic
Czech Soc. for Cybernetics and Informatics **[IO]**, Prague, Czech Republic
Czech Soc. for Experimental and Clinical Pharmacology and Toxicology **[IO]**, Plzen, Czech Republic
Czech Soc. of Geronology and Geriatrics **[★IO]**
Czech Soc. of Geronology and Geriatrics of the Czech Medical Assn. **[IO]**, Prague, Czech Republic
Czech Soc. of Hypertension **[IO]**, Prague, Czech Republic
Czech Soc. for Infectious Disease **[IO]**, Prague, Czech Republic
Czech Soc. for Mechanics **[IO]**, Prague, Czech Republic
Czech Soc. for Metabolic Skeletal Diseases **[IO]**, Hradec Kralove, Czech Republic
Czech Soc. of Sports Medicine **[IO]**, Brno, Czech Republic
Czech Speed Skating Fed. **[IO]**, Prague, Czech Republic
Czech Squash Assn. **[IO]**, Prague, Czech Republic
Czech Taekwondo Fed. WTF **[IO]**, Prague, Czech Republic
Czech Tenisova Asociace **[IO]**, Prague, Czech Republic
Czech Union of Inventors and Rationalizers **[IO]**, Prague, Czech Republic
Czech Village Assn. **[★19028]**
Czech Water Ski Fed. **[IO]**, Prague, Czech Republic
Czech World Union - Defunct.
Czech Youth Hostel Assn. **[IO]**, Prague, Czech Republic
Czechoslovak Biathlon Assn. **[★IO]**
Czechoslovak Chem. Soc. **[★IO]**
Czechoslovak Christian Democracy - Defunct.
Czechoslovak Genealogical Soc. **[★21113]**
Czechoslovak Genealogical Soc. **[★IO]**
Czechoslovak Genealogical Soc. Intl. **[IO]**, St. Paul, MN, United States
Czechoslovak Genealogical Soc. Intl. **[21113]**, PO Box 16225, St. Paul, MN 55116-0225, (763)595-7799
Czechoslovak Microscopy Soc. **[IO]**, Prague, Czech Republic
Czechoslovak Military Sports Assn. **[★IO]**
Czechoslovak Natl. Coun. of Am. - Defunct.
Czechoslovak Pattern Recognition Soc. **[IO]**, Prague, Czech Republic
Czechoslovak Rationalist Fed. of America - Address unknown since 1995.
Czechoslovak Relief; Amer. Fund for **[12802]**
Czechoslovak Soc. of Am. **[★19026]**
Czechoslovak Soc. of Arts and Sciences **[9860]**, c/o Dr. Karel Raska, Jr., Pres., 254 Easton Ave., New Brunswick, NJ 08901, (732)745-8504
Czechoslovak Soc. of Arts and Sciences **[IO]**, New Brunswick, NJ, United States
Czechoslovak Soc. of Arts and Sciences in Am. **[★IO]**
Czechoslovak Soc. of Arts and Sciences in Am. **[★9860]**
Czechoslovak-U.S. Economic Coun. **[★2302]**
Czechoslovak Workingmen's Assn. "Sokol" - Address unknown since 1995.
Czechoslovakia
    Amer. Fund for Czechoslovak Relief **[12802]**
    Czech Collector's Assn. **[22008]**

Czechoslovak Soc. of Arts and Sciences **[9860]**
    Slovak-Amer. Cultural Center **[10970]**
    Soc. for the History of Czechoslovak Jews **[10289]**
Czechoslovakian Jewish Aid Trust **[★IO]**
Czechosloval Refugees; Amer. Fund for **[★12802]**

D

Dachshund
    Dachshund Club of Am. **[22253]**
    Dachshund Rescue of North Am. **[11385]**
    North Amer. Teckel Club **[22329]**
Dachshund Club of Am. **[22253]**, c/o Marlies Noll, Sec., 31010 108th St., Princeton, MN 55371-4646, (763)389-4622
Dachshund Rescue of North Am. **[11385]**, 7821 Sabre Ct., Manassas, VA 20109
Dachverband der Osterreichischen Osteoporose-Selbsthilfegruppen **[IO]**, Graz, Austria
Dachverband Schweizer Lehrerinnen und Lehrer **[★IO]**
DACOR Bacon House Found. **[★5745]**
Dads Against Discrimination - Defunct.
Dads and Daughters **[12150]**, 2 W 1st St., Ste. 101, Duluth, MN 55802, (218)722-3942
Dads Rights **[12008]**, 3140 De La Cruz Blvd., Ste. 200, Santa Clara, CA 95054, (415)853-6877
Dads; Slowlane/Stay At Home **[18182]**
Daedalian Found. **[20649]**, PO Box 249, Universal City, TX 78148-0249, (210)945-2113
Daedalians; Order of **[20650]**
Daffodil Soc; Amer. **[22487]**
Dag Hammarskjold Found. **[IO]**, Uppsala, Sweden
Daguerreian Soc. **[10848]**, 3043 W Liberty Ave., Pittsburgh, PA 15216-2460, (412)221-0306
Dai Dong - Defunct.
Daily Money Managers; Amer. Assn. of **[1453]**
Daimler and Lanchester Owners' Club - England **[IO]**, Southampton, United Kingdom
Daimler and Lanchester Owners Club of North America - Defunct.
Dairies
    Amer. Assn. of Medical Milk Commissions **[16384]**
    Amer. Dairy Sci. Assn. **[4485]**
    Amer. Farm Bur. Fed. **[4642]**
    Amer. Goat Soc. **[4128]**
    Assn. of the Processed Cheese Indus. of the EU **[IO]**
    Belgian Confed. of the Dairy Indus. **[IO]**
    British Sheep Dairying Assn. **[IO]**
    Dairy Farmers of Canada **[IO]**
    Dairylea Cooperative **[4486]**
    Indian Dairy Assn. **[IO]**
    Intl. Milk Producers Assn. **[IO]**
    Intl. Milk Producers Assn. **[4487]**
    Natl. Assn. of Milk Bottle Collectors **[22076]**
    Natl. Conf. on Interstate Milk Shipments **[4493]**
    Natl. Dairy Shrine **[4488]**
    Natl. Milk Producers Fed. **[4489]**
    Pioneer Dairymen's Club of Am. **[4490]**
    Royal Assn. of British Dairy Farmers **[IO]**
    Stilton Cheese Makers' Assn. **[IO]**
    U.S. Dairy Export Coun. **[4491]**
Dairy Australia **[IO]**, Southbank, Australia
Dairy Cattle Assn; Purebred **[4288]**
Dairy Coun; Natl. **[★1132]**
Dairy Coun. - United Kingdom **[IO]**, London, United Kingdom
Dairy-Deli-Bakery Assn; Intl. **[1522]**
Dairy-Deli-Bakery Assn; Intl. **[★1522]**
Dairy Equip. Manufacturers; Natl. Assn. of Food and **[★1133]**
Dairy Farmers of Canada **[IO]**, Montreal, QC, Canada
Dairy Fed; U.S.A. Natl. Comm. of the Intl. **[★4487]**
Dairy and Food Indus. Supply Assn. **[★1133]**
Dairy and Food Indus. Supply Assn. **[★IO]**
Dairy Foods Assn; Wisconsin **[★4495]**
Dairy Goat Assn; Amer. **[4126]**
Dairy Herd Improvement Assn; Natl. **[4274]**
Dairy and Ice Cream Machinery and Supplies Assn. **[★1133]**
Dairy and Ice Cream Machinery and Supplies Assn. **[★IO]**

Dairy Indus. Supply Assn. **[★IO]**
Dairy Indus. Supply Assn. **[★1133]**
Dairy Indus. Assn. **[★IO]**
Dairy Mgt., Inc. **[1132]**, 10255 W Higgins Rd., Ste. 900, Rosemont, IL 60018-5616, (847)803-2000
Dairy and Milk Inspectors; Intl. Assn. of **[★5739]**
Dairy Products
    3-A Sanitary Standards Committees, Inc. **[1125]**
    All Star Dairy Assn. **[1126]**
    Allied Purchasing Company **[1127]**
    Amer. Assn. of Medical Milk Commissions **[16384]**
    Amer. Butter Inst. **[1128]**
    Amer. Cheese Soc. **[1129]**
    Amer. Dairy Goat Assn. **[4126]**
    Amer. Dairy Products Inst. **[1130]**
    Amer. Dairy Sci. Assn. **[4485]**
    Amer. Farm Bur. Fed. **[4642]**
    Amer. Grassfed Assn. **[2438]**
    Animal Agriculture Alliance **[1501]**
    Assn. of French Dairy Processors **[IO]**
    Belgische Confederatie van de Zuivelindustrie **[IO]**
    Bundesverband Molkereiprodukte eV **[IO]**
    Canadian Dairy Commn. **[IO]**
    Centre Natl. Interprofessionnel de l'Economie Laitiere **[IO]**
    Cheese of Choice Coalition **[4492]**
    Cheese Importers Assn. of Am. **[1131]**
    Cyprus Milk Indus. Org. **[IO]**
    Dairy Australia **[IO]**
    Dairy Coun. - United Kingdom **[IO]**
    Dairy Mgt., Inc. **[1132]**
    Dairy UK **[IO]**
    Danish Dairy Bd. **[IO]**
    Estonian Dairy Assn. **[IO]**
    European Dairy Assn. **[IO]**
    European Union of Dairy Trade **[IO]**
    Export Union for Milk Products **[IO]**
    Fed. of Swiss Milk Producers **[IO]**
    Food Processing Suppliers Assn. **[IO]**
    Food Processing Suppliers Assn. **[1133]**
    French Dairy Assn. **[IO]**
    German Dairy Assn. **[IO]**
    Ice Cream Alliance **[IO]**
    Intl. Cheese Coun. of Canada **[IO]**
    Intl. Dairy-Deli-Bakery Assn. **[1522]**
    Intl. Dairy Fed. **[IO]**
    Intl. Dairy Fed. - Canadian Natl. Comm. **[IO]**
    Intl. Dairy Foods Assn. **[IO]**
    Intl. Dairy Foods Assn. **[1134]**
    Intl. Milk Producers Assn. **[4487]**
    Irish Creamery Milk Suppliers' Assn. **[IO]**
    Irish Dairy Bd. **[IO]**
    Italian Assn. of Milk and Cheese Producers **[IO]**
    Japan Sheep Casing Importers' Assn. **[IO]**
    Korea Dairy Indus. Assn. **[IO]**
    Milk Indus. Center **[IO]**
    Milk Indus. Found. **[IO]**
    Milk Indus. Found. **[1135]**
    Natl. Assn. of Dairy Producers **[IO]**
    Natl. Assn. of Milk Bottle Collectors **[22076]**
    Natl. Assn. of Retailers and Wholesalers of Dairy Products **[IO]**
    Natl. Chamber of Milk Producers **[IO]**
    Natl. Cheese Inst. **[1136]**
    Natl. Conf. on Interstate Milk Shipments **[4493]**
    Natl. Dairy Coun. **[4494]**
    Natl. Dairy Coun. **[IO]**
    Natl. Dairy Shrine **[4488]**
    Natl. Fed. of the Dairy Indus. **[IO]**
    Natl. Fed. of Dairy Producers **[IO]**
    Natl. Ice Cream Retailers Assn. **[1137]**
    Natl. Milk Producers Fed. **[4489]**
    Natl. Yogurt Assn. **[1138]**
    Netherlands Natl. Comm. of the Intl. Dairy Fed. **[IO]**
    New Zealand Ice Cream Mfrs'. Assn. **[IO]**
    New Zealand Specialist Cheesemakers Assn. **[IO]**
    Panamerican Dairy Fed. **[IO]**
    Pioneer Dairymen's Club of Am. **[4490]**
    Purebred Dairy Cattle Assn. **[4288]**
    Quality Chekd Dairies **[1139]**
    Spanish Dairy Fed. **[IO]**
    Swedish Dairy Assn. **[IO]**
    United Dairy Industry Assn. **[1140]**
    Wisconsin Cheese Makers' Assn. **[1141]**

Reference to "IO" in place of a book number signifies that the association may be found in the 45th edition of International Organizations.

Wisconsin Dairy Products Assn. [4495]
Dairy Products Improvement Inst. - Defunct.
Dairy Remembrance Fund - Defunct.
Dairy Res. Found. - Address unknown since 2001.
Dairy Shrine [★4488]
Dairy Soc. Intl. - Defunct.
Dairy Suppliers Found. - Defunct.
Dairy UK [IO], London, United Kingdom
Dairy; United [★1127]
Dairylea Cooperative [4486], PO Box 4844,
  Syracuse, NY 13221-4844, (315)433-0100
Dairymen's League Cooperative Assn. [★4486]
Daiwa Anglo-Japanese Found. [IO], London, United
  Kingdom
Dakota Alumni Assn; Univ. of South [18937]
Dakota Women of All Red Nations - Defunct.
Dakshinayan [IO], New Delhi, India
Dalat Univ. Alumni Assn. - Defunct.
Dalcroze Soc. of America - Defunct.
Dale Chapp Fan Club - Defunct.
Dale Earnhardt Fan Club; Club E: The [25002]
Dale Evans Collectors Assn; Roy Rogers - [24971]
Dale Jarrett Fan Club [25003], 1915 Fairgrove
  Church Rd. SE, Newton, NC 28658, (828)464-
  8818
Dale and Keith Found. - Address unknown since
  2004.
Dale Midkiff Fan Assn. - Address unknown since
  2003.
Dales Pony Assn. of North Am. [4875], PO Box 585,
  New Portland, ME 04954, (207)628-6061
Dales Pony Association of North America [IO], New
  Portland, ME, United States
Dales Pony Soc. of Am. [4876], c/o Heather Loeber,
  Registrar/Treas., 32 Welsh Rd., Lebanon, NJ
  08833, (908)236-6087
Dalit Liberation Educ. Trust [IO], Chennai, India
Dalkon Shield Victims Educ. Assn; Intl. [16898]
Dallas Cotton Exchange - Address unknown since
  2002.
Dalmatian
  Dalmatian Club of Am. [22254]
Dalmatian Club of Am. [22254], c/o Mrs. Mary Wid-
  der, Membership Chair, 864 Ettin Ave., Simi Valley,
  CA 93065, (805)583-5914
Dalmo Giacometti Found. [IO], Brasilia, Brazil
Dalriada Celtic Heritage Trust [IO], Isle of Arran,
  United Kingdom
Dalton Floor Covering Market Assn. [★2250]
Dam Safety Officials; Assn. of State [6249]
Damage Appraisers Assn; Independent Automotive
  [281]
Damage Control Assn; Natl. Animal [5076]
Damascus Fraternity - Address unknown since 1995.
Dameron Family Assn. [20877], c/o John P.
  Dameron, Membership Dir./Treas., 1932 Orphan-
  age Rd., Danville, VA 24540
Dames of the Loyal Legion of the U.S.A. - Address
  unknown since 2002.
Dames of Malta - Address unknown since 1995.
Damfinos: The Intl. Buster Keaton Soc. [24797], c/o
  David B. Pearson, 317 Magnolia Dr., Picayune, MS
  39466
Damien-Dutton Soc. [★15008]
Damien-Dutton Soc. for Leprosy Aid [15008], 616
  Bedford Ave., Bellmore, NY 11710, (516)221-5829
Damien Found. - Belgium [IO], Brussels, Belgium
Damien Ministries [19866], PO Box 10202,
  Washington, DC 20018-0202, (202)526-3020
Damon Runyon Cancer Res. Found. [13819], 675
  3rd Ave., 25th Fl., New York, NY 10017, (212)455-
  0500
Damon Runyon Found. for Cancer Res. [★13819]
Damon Runyon Memorial Fund for Cancer Res.
  [★13819]
Damon Runyon - Walter Winchell Cancer Fund
  [★13819]
Damon Runyon - Walter Winchell Cancer Res. Fund
  [★13819]
Damp and Waterproof Workers Assn; United Slate,
  Tile and Composition Roofers, [★24033]
Dams; U.S. Comm. on Large [★7843]
Dams; U.S. Soc. on [7843]
Dan Gillis Fan Club - Defunct.
Dana Alliance for Brain Initiatives [15387], 745 Fifth
  Ave., Ste. 900, New York, NY 10151, (212)223-
  4040

Dana-Farber Cancer Inst. [13820], 44 Binney St.,
  Boston, MA 02115, (617)632-3000
Dana-Farber Cancer Inst. [IO], Boston, MA, United
  States
Dance
  African Heritage Center for African Dance and
    Music [9347]
  Albanian Dance Sport Fed. [IO]
  Alberta Ballet [IO]
  All India Dance Sport Fed. [IO]
  Amer. Alliance for Hea., Physical Educ.,
    Recreation and Dance [8979]
  Amer. Ballet Competition [9862]
  Amer. Bop Assn. [9863]
  Amer. Coll. Dance Festival Assn. [9864]
  Amer. Dance Festival [9865]
  Amer. Dance Guild [9866]
  Amer. Dance Therapy Assn. [16203]
  Amer. Fed. of Musicians of the U.S. and Canada
    [24149]
  Amer. Friends of the Paris Opera and Ballet
    [9543]
  Amer. Guild of Musical Artists [24150]
  Amer. Musicians Union [24152]
  American-Slovenian Polka Found. [10549]
  Amer. Soc. for Aesthetics [9545]
  Andorra DanceSport Fed. [IO]
  Armenian Dance Sport Fed. [IO]
  Art Resources in Collaboration [9867]
  Asian Amer. Arts Centre [9553]
  Asociacion Argentina de Baile Deportivo [IO]
  Asociacion Colombiana de Baille Deportivo [IO]
  Assn. of Performing Arts Presenters [7968]
  Assn. for the Preservation and Presentation of the
    Arts [9355]
  Associazione Compagnia Jazz Ballet [IO]
  Austrian DanceSport Fed. [IO]
  Ballet Theatre Found. [9868]
  Ballroom Dancers' Fed. Intl. [IO]
  Belarusian Dance Sport Fed. [IO]
  Belgian Dance Sport Fed. [IO]
  Benesh Inst. [IO]
  British Assn. of Teachers of Dancing [IO]
  British Ballet Org. [IO]
  British Dance Coun. [IO]
  Bulgarian Dance Sport Fed. [IO]
  Burlesque Historical Soc. [11009]
  Callerlab - Intl. Assn. of Square Dance Callers
    [9869]
  Callerlab - Intl. Assn. of Square Dance Callers
    [IO]
  Canadian Amateur Dancesport Assn. [IO]
  Canadian Dance Assembly [IO]
  Canadian Dance Teachers' Assn. [IO]
  Career Transition For Dancers [12071]
  Cecchetti Coun. of Am. [8183]
  Center for Sports and Osteopathic Medicine
    [16055]
  Chinese-American Arts Coun. [9608]
  Chinese DanceSport Fed. [IO]
  Chinese Taipei DanceSport Fed. [IO]
  Christian Dance Fellowship of Australia [IO]
  Comm. for Handicapable Dancers [9870]
  Cong. on Res. in Dance [9871]
  Cong. on Res. in Dance [IO]
  Connolly Dance Found. [9872]
  Cooperation Comm. for Folk Dance [IO]
  Country Dance and Song Soc. [9873]
  Country Pride Dance Club [IO]
  Country Spirit Dance Soc. [IO]
  Croatian Dance Sport Fed. [IO]
  Cross-Cultural Dance Resources [IO]
  Cross-Cultural Dance Resources [9874]
  Czech Dance Sport Fed. [IO]
  Dance Critics Assn. [9875]
  Dance/Drill Team Directors of Am. [9876]
  Dance Educators of Am. [8184]
  Dance Films Assn. [8185]
  Dance Heritage Coalition [9877]
  Dance Masters of Am. [8186]
  Dance Notation Bur. [9878]
  Dance Sport Assn. of the Azerbaijan Republic [IO]
  Dance Sport Assn. of Bosnia and Herzegovina
    [IO]
  Dance Sport Coun. of the Philippines [IO]

  Dance Sport Fed. of the Kyrgyz Republic [IO]
  Dance/U.S.A. [9879]
  Dancers Without Borders [9880]
  DanceSafe [12041]
  Dancesport Australia [IO]
  Danish Dance Sport Fed. [IO]
  Danish Jazz Fed. [IO]
  DC Dance Club [IO]
  Early Childhood Music and Movement Assn.
    [12618]
  English Amateur Dancesport Assn. [IO]
  Estonian Dance Sport Assn. [IO]
  Exotic Dancers League of Am. [9881]
  Federacao Portuguesa de Danca Desportiva [IO]
  Federacion Chilena de Baile Deportivo [IO]
  Fed. of Alpine and Schuhplattler Clubs in North
    Am. [9627]
  Fed. Camerounaise Des Danses Sportives et As-
    simile [IO]
  Fed. of Dance Sport South Africa [IO]
  Fed. Luxembourgeoise de Danse pour Amateurs
    [IO]
  Fed. Mexicana De Baile A.C. [IO]
  Financial Managers Soc. [1418]
  Finnish Dance Sport Assn. [IO]
  Folk Alliance [9955]
  Found. for Pacific Dance [9882]
  Foundation for Pacific Dance [IO]
  Gathering of Nations [10742]
  Georgian Natl. DanceSport Fed. [IO]
  German Dance Sport Fed. [IO]
  Hispanic Org. of Latin Actors [10001]
  Hong Kong DanceSport Assn. [IO]
  Hungarian Dancesport Assn. [IO]
  Icelandic Dance Sport Fed. [IO]
  Imperial Soc. of Teachers of Dancing [IO]
  Indonesian Amateur Dancesport Assn. [IO]
  Inst. for Expressive Anal. [16217]
  Interlochen Center for the Arts [9571]
  Intl. Acad. of Aquatic Art [23884]
  Intl. Assn. for Creative Dance [9883]
  Intl. Assn. for Creative Dance [IO]
  Intl. Assn. for Dance Medicine and Sci. [15170]
  Intl. Assn. for Gay/Lesbian Country Western Dance
    Clubs [9884]
  Intl. Assn. for Gay/Lesbian Country Western Dance
    Clubs [IO]
  Intl. Assn. of Gay Square Dance Clubs [IO]
  Intl. Assn. of Gay Square Dance Clubs [9885]
  Intl. Assn. of Round Dance Teachers [9886]
  Intl. Assn. of Round Dance Teachers [IO]
  Intl. Christian Dance Fellowship [IO]
  Intl. Coun. for Hea., Physical Educ., Recreation,
    Sport, and Dance [8981]
  Intl. Coun. of Kinetography Laban [9887]
  Intl. Coun. of Kinetography Laban [IO]
  Intl. Dance Coun. [IO]
  Intl. Dance Sport Fed. [IO]
  Intl. Dance Teachers' Assn. [IO]
  Intl. Fed. of Teachers of Dalcroze Eurhythmics
    [IO]
  Intl. Guild of Musicians in Dance [10774]
  Intl. Org. for the Transition of Professional Danc-
    ers [IO]
  Intl. Ski Dancing Assn. [23751]
  Intl. Tap Assn. [9888]
  Israel Dance Sport Assn. [IO]
  Israeli Dance Inst. [9889]
  ISTD Dance Examinations Bd. [IO]
  Italian Dance Sport Fed. [IO]
  Italian Folk Art Fed. of Am. [10259]
  Japan Dancesport Fed. [IO]
  Junior Shag Assn. [9890]
  Korean Fed. of DanceSport [IO]
  Laban/Bartenieff Inst. of Movement Stud. [9891]
  Laban Guild [IO]
  Latvian Dancesport Fed. [IO]
  Liechtensteiner Tanzsportverband [IO]
  Line Dance Assn. of Australia [IO]
  Line Dance Soc. Singapore [IO]
  Lithuanian Dancesport Fed. [IO]
  Lloyd Shaw Found. [8187]
  London Swing Dance Soc. [IO]
  Luxembourg Amateur Dance Fed. [IO]
  Macau DanceSport Fed. [IO]

A star before a book entry number signifies that the name is not listed separately, but is mentioned within the entry.

Macedonian Dance Assn. [IO]
Malta Dancesport Assn. [IO]
Middle Eastern Dance Assn. of New Zealand [IO]
Moldova Dance Sport Fed. [IO]
Monaco DanceSport Assn. Stade Louis II [IO]
Monash Dance Sport [IO]
Mongolian Dancesport Assn. [IO]
Morris Fed. [IO]
Movement Theatre Intl. [11025]
Natl. Assn. of Schools of Dance [8188]
Natl. Ballroom and Entertainment Assn. [1317]
Natl. Clogging Org. [9892]
Natl. Coun. of Secondary School Athletic Directors [8988]
Natl. Dance Assn. [9893]
Natl. Dance Coun. of Am. [8189]
Natl. Dance Educ. Assn. [23324]
Natl. Dance Inst. [8190]
Natl. Dance Teacher's Assn. [23325]
Natl. DanceSport Fed. of Greece [IO]
Natl. Fastdance Assn. [9894]
Natl. Found. for Advancement in the Arts [9587]
Natl. Performance Network [11031]
Natl. Square Dance Convention [9895]
Nederlandse Algemene Danssport Bond [IO]
NETA - Natl. Exercise Trainers Assn. [23037]
New Zealand Dancesport Assn. [IO]
NFHS Spirit Assn. [23295]
Norges Danseforbund [IO]
North Amer. Fed. of German Folk Dance Groups [9965]
Old Time Dance Soc. [IO]
Pakistan DanceSport Fed. [IO]
Performing Arts Resources [9593]
Polski Towarzystwo Taneczne [IO]
Professional Dance Teachers Assn. [8191]
Professional Dancers Fed. [23326]
Royal Acad. of Dance [9896]
Royal Acad. of Dance [IO]
Royal Scottish Country Dance Soc. [IO]
Royal Winnipeg Ballet Alumni Assn. [IO]
Sacred Dance Guild [IO]
Sacred Dance Guild [9897]
Sacred Dance Soc. [19878]
Scottish Dance Teacher's Alliance [IO]
Scottish Dancesport [IO]
Scottish Official Bd. of Highland Dancing [IO]
Singapore DanceSport Fed. [IO]
Slovak Dance Sport Fed. [IO]
Slovene Dance Sport Fed. [IO]
Soc. of Dance History Scholars [10154]
Spanish Assn. of Dance Sport and Competition Dancing [IO]
Sport Dance Fed. of the Republic of Kazakhstan [IO]
Swedish Dance Sport Fed. [IO]
Swiss DanceSport Assn. [IO]
Thailand Dance Sport Assn. [IO]
Thunderbird Amer. Indian Dancers [10754]
Turkish Gymnastic and DanceSport Fed. [IO]
Uganda Dance Sport Assn. [IO]
Ukrainian Dance Sport Assn. [IO]
United Dance Merchants of Am. [1142]
United Kingdom Dance and Drama Fed. [IO]
United Square Dancers of Am. [9898]
U.S. Competitive Aerobics Fed. [23038]
U.S. Natl. Inst. of Dance [9899]
U.S. Scottish Fiddling Revival [10716]
Univ. of Calgary Ballroom Dance Club [IO]
USA Dance [9900]
Welsh Amateur Dance Sport Assn. [IO]
World Cong. of Teachers of Dancing [8192]
World Dance Alliance [9901]
World Dance Alliance [IO]
World Dance Coun. [IO]
World Dance Coun. - Germany [IO]
World Swing Dance Coun. [IO]
World Swing Dance Coun. [9902]
Dance Alliance; North Amer. Folk Music and [★9955]
Dance Alliance; North Amer. Folk Music and Folk [22718]
Dance; Amer. Alliance for Hea., Physical Educ., Recreation and [8979]
Dance Assn; Eastern Regional [★9897]

Dance Assn; Pacific [★9882]
Dance; Comm. on Res. in [★9871]
Dance Critics Assn. [9875], PO Box 1882, Old Chelsea Sta., New York, NY 10011
Dance Div. (of AAHPER) [★9893]
Dance/Drill Team Directors of Am. [9876], 10604 Whispering Pines Dr., Frisco, TX 75034
Dance Educators of Am. [8184], PO Box 607, Pelham, NY 10803-0607, (914)636-3200
Dance Exercise Assn; IDEA: Intl. [★15965]
Dance Exercise Instructors Training Assn; NDEITA - Natl. [★23037]
Dance Festival; Amer. [★9865]
Dance Festival; Assn. for the Amer. [★9865]
Dance Films Assn. [8185], 48 W 21st St., No. 907, New York, NY 10010, (212)727-0764
Dance Films, Inc. [★8185]
Dance Found; Intl. Folk [★9592]
Dance Guild; Natl. [★9866]
Dance Heritage Coalition [9877], 1111 16th St. NW, Ste. 300, Washington, DC 20036, (202)223-8393
Dance History Scholars [★10154]
DANCE, Inc. [★16597]
Dance Magazine Found. - Defunct.
Dance Masters of Am. [8186], c/o Robert Mann, Exec. Sec., PO Box 610533, Bayside, NY 11361-0533, (718)225-4013
Dance Medicine; CTR for [★16055]
Dance Medicine and Sci; Intl. Assn. for [15170]
Dance-Movement Therapy Assn. of Australia [IO], Carlton South, Australia
Dance Notation Bur. [9878], 151 W 30th St., Ste. 202, New York, NY 10001-4007, (212)564-0985
Dance Orchestra Leaders of America - Defunct.
Dance Res. Found. - Address unknown since 1991.
Dance Soc. of Am; Country [★9873]
Dance Sport Assn. of the Azerbaijan Republic [IO], Baku, Azerbaijan
Dance Sport Assn. of Bosnia and Herzegovina [IO], Sarajevo, Bosnia-Hercegovina
Dance Sport Coun. of the Philippines [IO], Makati City, Philippines
Dance Sport Fed. of the Kyrgyz Republic [IO], Bishkek, Kirgizstan
Dance Teacher Organizations; Natl. Coun. of [★8189]
Dance Teachers Guild [★9866]
Dance Teachers Guild; Natl. [★9866]
Dance Teachers; Intl. Assn. of Round [★9886]
Dance Theater Workshop [9566], 219 W 19th St., New York, NY 10011, (212)691-6500
Dance Therapy Assn; Amer. [16203]
Dance Therapy Assn. of Australia [★IO]
Dance/U.S.A. [9879], 1111 16th St. NW, Ste. 300, Washington, DC 20036, (202)833-1717
Dancers; Career Transition For [12071]
Dancers for Disarmament - Defunct.
Dancers Fed; Professional [23326]
Dancers; Thunderbird Amer. Indian [10754]
Dancers Without Borders [9880]
DanceSafe [12041], 8100-M4 Wyoming Blvd. NE, No. 116, Albuquerque, NM 87113
DanceSafe [IO], Oakland, CA, United States
Dancesport Australia [IO], Ardross, Australia
Dancing; Foundation for the Promotion and Preservation of Square [★IO]
Dancing; Foundation for the Promotion and Preservation of Square [★9869]
Dancing for Life - Defunct.
Dancing, U.S. Br; Royal Acad. of [★9896]
Dandie Dinmont Terrier Club of Am. [22255], c/o Gail B. Isner, Sec., 151 Junaluska Dr., Woodstock, GA 30188-3135
Danforth Compton Fellowships; Dorthy [★8250]
Danforth Found. [8250], 211 N Broadway, Ste. 2390, 1 Metropolitan Sq., St. Louis, MO 63102, (314)588-1900
Danforth Prog. for School Bd. Members [★8250]
Dangerous Goods Advisory Coun. [3563], 1100 H St. NW, Ste. 740, Washington, DC 20005-5484, (202)289-4550
Daniel Boone and Frontier Families Res. Assn. [10107], c/o Ken Kamper, Historian, 1770 Little Bay Rd., Hermann, MO 65041, (573)943-6423
Daniel Cole Soc; Descendants of [20881]

Daniel McVicar Fan Club - Address unknown since 1994.
Danischer Handelsvertreterverband [★IO]
Danish
  Amer. Soc. of Danish Engineers [6993]
  Danish Amer. Chamber of Commerce [24316]
  Danish Amer. Heritage Soc. [9903]
  Danish Amer. Heritage Soc. [IO]
  Danish Brotherhood in Am. [19031]
  Danish Irish Soc. [IO]
  North Amer. Danish Warmblood Assn. [4930]
  Supreme Lodge of the Danish Sisterhood of Am. [19032]
Danish 4 H Clubs [★IO]
Danish Acad. of Tech. Sciences [IO], Lyngby, Denmark
Danish Acoustic Neuroma Assn. [IO], Lyngby, Denmark
Danish Actors' Assn. [IO], Frederiksberg, Denmark
Danish Afghan Hound Club [IO], Holme Olstrup, Denmark
Danish Agricultural Coun. [IO], Copenhagen, Denmark
Danish Agriculture [IO], Copenhagen, Denmark
Danish Aid and Relief Soc. - Defunct.
Danish Airtaxi Assn. [IO], Norresundby, Denmark
Danish Amateur Theatre Coun. [IO], Grasten, Denmark
Danish Amer. Chamber of Commerce [24316], 1 Dag Hammerskjold Plz., 885 2nd Ave., 18th Fl., New York, NY 10017, (212)705-4945
Danish Amer. Heritage Soc. [9903], 4105 Stone Brooke Rd., Ames, IA 50010, (515)232-7479
Danish Amer. Heritage Soc. [IO], Ames, IA, United States
Danish Amer. Trade Coun. [★24316]
Danish Amer. Women's Assn. - Defunct.
Danish Antiquarian Booksellers Assn. [IO], Stege, Denmark
Danish Arctic Inst. [IO], Copenhagen, Denmark
Danish Article Numbering Assn. [★IO]
Danish Assn. of Advt. and Relationship Agencies [IO], Copenhagen, Denmark
Danish Assn. of Commercial Agents and Exclusive Distributors [IO], Copenhagen, Denmark
Danish Assn. of Consulting Engineers [IO], Copenhagen, Denmark
Danish Assn. of Graduates in Forestry [IO], Copenhagen, Denmark
Danish Assn. of Graduates in Horticulture [IO], Copenhagen, Denmark
Danish Assn. for von Hippel-Lindau [IO], Roskilde, Denmark
Danish Assn. for Intl. Cooperation - Denmark [IO], Copenhagen, Denmark
Danish Assn. of Medical Imaging [IO], Tjele, Denmark
Danish Assn. of the Pharmaceutical Indus. [IO], Copenhagen, Denmark
Danish Assn. for Prdt. Modelling [IO], Lyngby, Denmark
Danish Assn. of Social Workers [IO], Copenhagen, Denmark
Danish Assn. of the Specialist Press [IO], Copenhagen, Denmark
Danish Assn. of Sports Medicine [IO], Farum, Denmark
Danish Assn. of State-Authorized Translators and Interpreters [IO], Copenhagen, Denmark
Danish Assn. of Univ. Women [IO], Copenhagen, Denmark
Danish Astronomical Assn. [IO], Rodovre, Denmark
Danish Athletic Fed. [IO], Brondby, Denmark
Danish Atlantic Treaty Assn. [IO], Copenhagen, Denmark
Danish Author's Assn. [★IO]
Danish Authors' Society/Danish Writers' Union [★IO]
Danish Auto. Dealers Assn. [IO], Taastrup, Denmark
Danish Auto. Sports Union [IO], Brondby, Denmark
Danish Bankers Assn. [IO], Copenhagen, Denmark
Danish Baseball Softball Fed. [IO], Brondby, Denmark
Danish Basketball Fed. [IO], Brondby, Denmark
Danish Bible Soc. [IO], Copenhagen, Denmark
Danish Bone Soc. [IO], Odense, Denmark

Danish Booksellers Assn. [IO], Copenhagen, Denmark

Danish Brain Injury Assn. [IO], Brondby, Denmark

Danish Brewers' Assn. [IO], Valby, Denmark

Danish Brotherhood in Am. [19031]

Danish Butchers' Assn. [IO], Odense, Denmark

Danish Cancer Soc. [IO], Copenhagen, Denmark

Danish Chamber of Commerce [IO], Copenhagen, Denmark

Danish Chem. Soc. [IO], Copenhagen, Denmark

Danish Confed. of Trade Unions [IO], Copenhagen, Denmark

Danish Constr. Assn. [IO], Copenhagen, Denmark

Danish Consumer Goods Suppliers' Assn. [IO], Copenhagen, Denmark

Danish Coun. of Ethics [IO], Copenhagen, Denmark

Danish Cricket Assn. [IO], Brondby, Denmark

Danish Dairy Bd. [IO], Arhus, Denmark

Danish Dance Sport Fed. [IO], Brondby, Denmark

Danish Deaf Assn. [IO], Copenhagen, Denmark

Danish Dental Assn. [IO], Copenhagen, Denmark

Danish Dental Mfrs. [IO], Copenhagen, Denmark

Danish Dermatological Soc. [IO], Roskilde, Denmark

Danish Designers [IO], Copenhagen, Denmark

Danish Economic Soc. [IO], Copenhagen, Denmark

Danish Engineers; Amer. Soc. of [6993]

Danish Epilepsy Soc. [IO], Dianalund, Denmark

Danish Family Farmers Assn. [★IO]

Danish Fed. of Graduates in Agricultural Sci., Economics, Forestry, Horticulture and Landscape Architecture [IO], Copenhagen, Denmark

Danish Fed. of Teachers of Tech. Educ. [IO], Copenhagen, Denmark

Danish Fencing Fed. [IO], Brondby, Denmark

Danish Fishermen's Assn. [IO], Fredericia, Denmark

Danish Floorball Fed. [IO], Brondby, Denmark

Danish Football Assn. [IO], Brondby, Denmark

Danish Foreign Policy Soc. [IO], Copenhagen, Denmark

Danish Forest Assn. [IO], Frederiksberg, Denmark

Danish Forest and Landscape Res. Inst. [IO], Hoersholm, Denmark

Danish Galloway Soc. [IO], Tollose, Denmark

Danish Gerontological Assn. [IO], Copenhagen, Denmark

Danish Gordon Setter Club [IO], Logumkloster, Denmark

Danish Gymnastics Fed. [IO], Brondby, Denmark

Danish Historical Assn. [IO], Copenhagen, Denmark

Danish Huntington Assn. [IO], Copenhagen, Denmark

Danish Hypertension Soc. [IO], Holbaek, Denmark

Danish Ice Cream Indus. [IO], Copenhagen, Denmark

Danish Import Promotion Off. for Products from Developing Countries [IO], Copenhagen, Denmark

Danish Inst. of Forest Tech. [★IO]

Danish Inst. for Intl. Stud. [IO], Copenhagen, Denmark

Danish Inst. Park Tech. [★IO]

Danish Insurance Assn. [IO], Copenhagen, Denmark

Danish Inventors Assn. [IO], Farum, Denmark

Danish Irish Soc. [IO], Copenhagen, Denmark

Danish Jazz Fed. [IO], Copenhagen, Denmark

Danish Jockey Club [IO], Charlottenlund, Denmark

Danish Kennel Club [IO], Solrod Strand, Denmark

Danish Lancia Register [IO], Humlebaek, Denmark

Danish Landscape Assn. [★IO]

Danish Lib. Assn. [IO], Copenhagen, Denmark

Danish Literature Centre [IO], Copenhagen, Denmark

Danish Livestock and Meat Bd. [IO], Copenhagen, Denmark

Danish Luncheon Club of New York [★24316]

Danish Magazine Publishers Assn. [IO], Copenhagen, Denmark

Danish Marfan Assn. [IO], Hillerod, Denmark

Danish Maritime [IO], Copenhagen, Denmark

Danish Marketing Forum [IO], Frederiksberg, Denmark

Danish Mathematical Soc. [IO], Copenhagen, Denmark

Danish Medical Assn. [IO], Copenhagen, Denmark

Danish Medical Soc. [IO], Copenhagen, Denmark

Danish Missionary Coun. [IO], Frederiksberg, Denmark

Danish Motel and Restaurant Assn. [★IO]

Danish Multiple Sclerosis Soc. [IO], Valby, Denmark

Danish Museums Assn. of Cultural History [IO], Niva, Denmark

Danish Music Lib. Assn. [IO], Alborg, Denmark

Danish Musicological Soc. [IO], Copenhagen, Denmark

Danish Natl. Fed. of Early Childhood Teachers and Youth Educators [IO], Copenhagen, Denmark

Danish Natl. Union of Upper Secondary School Teachers [IO], Copenhagen, Denmark

Danish Newspaper Publishers' Assn. [IO], Copenhagen, Denmark

Danish Nurses' Org. [IO], Copenhagen, Denmark

Danish Open Source Bus. Assn. [IO], Copenhagen, Denmark

Danish Operations Res. Soc. [IO], Lyngby, Denmark

Danish Ophthalmological Soc. [IO], Copenhagen, Denmark

Danish Optical Soc. [IO], Arhus, Denmark

Danish Org. of Youth with Rheumatism [IO], Arhus, Denmark

Danish Orienteering Fed. [IO], Brondby, Denmark

Danish Orthopedic Soc. [IO], Copenhagen, Denmark

Danish Pattern Recognition Soc. [IO], Lyngby, Denmark

Danish Petroleum Indus. Assn. [IO], Copenhagen, Denmark

Danish Physical Soc. [IO], Roskilde, Denmark

Danish Plastics Fed. [IO], Copenhagen, Denmark

Danish Pointer Club [IO], Ringe, Denmark

Danish Precast Concrete Fed. [IO], Copenhagen, Denmark

Danish Psychologists' Assn. [IO], Copenhagen, Denmark

Danish Publishers' Assn. [IO], Copenhagen, Denmark

Danish Ready-Mixed Concrete Assn. [IO], Copenhagen, Denmark

Danish Red Cross [IO], Copenhagen, Denmark

Danish Refugee Coun. [IO], Copenhagen, Denmark

Danish Retriever Club [★IO]

Danish Rheumatism Assn. [IO], Copenhagen, Denmark

Danish Rottweiler Club [IO], Hjorring, Denmark

Danish Sailing Assn. [IO], Brondby, Denmark

Danish Sailors and Firemen's Union, U.S. Br. - Defunct.

Danish Samoyed Club [IO], Odense, Denmark

Danish School Librarian Assn. [IO], Hojer, Denmark

Danish Schoolsport [IO], Nyborg, Denmark

Danish Sea Fishery Assn. [★IO]

Danish Seed Trade Assn. [IO], Roskilde, Denmark

Danish Shipowners' Assn. [IO], Copenhagen, Denmark

Danish Shooting Union [IO], Brondby, Denmark

Danish Skating Union [IO], Brondby, Denmark

Danish Slaughterhouses [IO], Copenhagen, Denmark

Danish Social-Liberal Party [IO], Copenhagen, Denmark

Danish Soc. of Agricultural Engg. [IO], Horsens, Denmark

Danish Soc. for Biochemistry and Molecular Biology [IO], Glostrup, Denmark

Danish Soc. for Biomedical Engg. [IO], Bagsvaerd, Denmark

Danish Soc. of Cardiology [IO], Copenhagen, Denmark

Danish Soc. of Clinical Neurophysiology [IO], Glostrup, Denmark

Danish Soc. of Engineers [IO], Copenhagen, Denmark

Danish Soc. of Food Sci. and Tech. [IO], Copenhagen, Denmark

Danish Soc. of Gastroenterology [IO], Odense, Denmark

Danish Soc. of Heating, Ventilating and Airconditioning Engineers [IO], Ballerup, Denmark

Danish Soc. for Jazz, Rock, and Folk Composers [IO], Copenhagen, Denmark

Danish Soc. for Medical Physics [IO], Copenhagen, Denmark

Danish Soc. for Nature Conservation [IO], Copenhagen, Denmark

Danish Soc. for Neuroscience [IO], Copenhagen, Denmark

Danish Soc. of Obstetrics and Gynaecology [IO], Hjorring, Denmark

Danish Soc. of Palliative Medicine [IO], Copenhagen, Denmark

Danish Soc. for Patient Safety [IO], Hvidovre, Denmark

Danish Soc. of Periodontology [IO], Arhus, Denmark

Danish Soc. of Pharmacology and Toxicology [IO], Arhus, Denmark

Danish Soc. of Rheumatology [IO], Copenhagen, Denmark

Danish Songwriters Guild [IO], Copenhagen, Denmark

Danish Squash Assn. [IO], Odense, Denmark

Danish Standards Assn. [IO], Charlottenlund, Denmark

Danish Taekwondo Fed. [IO], Olgod, Denmark

Danish Technological Inst. [IO], Taastrup, Denmark

Danish Terrier Club [IO], Hjorring, Denmark

Danish Textile Union [IO], Hellerup, Denmark

Danish Tourist Bd. [IO], Copenhagen, Denmark

Danish-UK Chamber of Commerce [IO], London, United Kingdom

Danish Union of Teachers [IO], Copenhagen, Denmark

Danish United Nations Assn. [IO], Copenhagen, Denmark

Danish Water Ski Fed. [IO], Brondby, Denmark

Danish Wind Indus. Assn. [IO], Copenhagen, Denmark

Danish Wine and Spirits' Assn. [IO], Copenhagen, Denmark

Danish Women's Soc. [IO], Copenhagen, Denmark

Danish Wound Healing Soc. [IO], Allerod, Denmark

Danish Writers Assn. [IO], Copenhagen, Denmark

Danish Young Farmers [IO], Arhus, Denmark

Danish Youth Assn. [★IO]

Danish Youth Coun. [IO], Copenhagen, Denmark

Danlos Natl. Found; Ehlers [16651]

Danmarks Automobilforhandler Forening [★IO]

Danmarks Basketball-Forbund [★IO]

Danmarks Biblioteksforening [★IO]

Danmarks Farmaceutiske Selskab [★IO]

Danmarks Fiskeindustri-Og Eksportforening [★IO]

Danmarks Fiskeriforening [★IO]

Danmarks Forskningsbiblioteksforening [★IO]

Danmarks Gymnastik Forbund [★IO]

Danmarks Idraets-Forbund [★IO]

Danmarks Jurist- og Okonomforbund [★IO]

Danmarks Laererforening [★IO]

Danmarks Naturfredningsforening [★IO]

Danmarks Rederiforening [★IO]

Danmarks Rejsebureau Forening [★IO]

Danmarks Skohandlerforening [★IO]

Danmarks Socialdemokratiske Ungdom [★IO]

Danmarks Turistrad [★IO]

Dannemiller Memorial Educational Found. [13683], 5711 Northwest Pkwy., San Antonio, TX 78249, (210)641-8311

Dannenmueller-Hoefler Family Assn. [20878], 1039 State Rd. W, Warrenton, MO 63383, (636)456-4610

Danny Cooksey Fan Club [24736]

Danny Found. [12959]

Danny Lineweaver Found. [★12959]

Danny Vann Fan Club - Address unknown since 2000.

Dansiprottasamband Islands [★IO]

Dansk Acusticusneurinom Forening [★IO]

Dansk Akustik Selskab [★IO]

Dansk Amater Teater Samvirke [★IO]

Dansk Annoncorforening [★IO]

Dansk Arbejdsgiverforening [★IO]

Dansk Atletik Forbund [★IO]

Dansk Automobil Sports Union [★IO]

Dansk Baseball Softball Forbund [★IO]

Dansk Boldspil-Union [★IO]

Dansk Byggeri [★IO]

Dansk Cardiologisk selskab [★IO]

Dansk Cricket-Forbund [★IO]

Dansk Dagligvareleverandor Forening [★IO]

Dansk Dermatologisk Selskab [★IO]

Dansk Dobermann Klub [IO], Lynge, Denmark

A star before a book entry number signifies that the name is not listed separately, but is mentioned within the entry.

Dansk Energiokonomisk Selskab [★IO]
Dansk Epilepsiforening [★IO]
Dansk Fabriksbetonforening [★IO]
Dansk Faegte-Forbund [★IO]
Dansk Fagpresse [★IO]
Dansk Farmaceutforening [★IO]
Dansk Floorball Union [★IO]
Dansk Flygtningehjaelp [★IO]
Dansk Forening til Fremme af Opfindelser [★IO]
Dansk Forfatterforening [★IO]
Dansk Frisbee Sport Union [IO], Copenhagen, Denmark
Dansk Frohandlerforening [★IO]
Dansk Fysisk Selskab [★IO]
Dansk Galop [★IO]
Dansk Gastroenterologisk Selskab [★IO]
Dansk Geologisk Forening [★IO]
Dansk Gerontologisk Selskab [★IO]
Dansk Gordon Setter Klub [★IO]
Dansk Hortonomforening [★IO]
Dansk Hypertensionsselskab [★IO]
Dansk Idraetsmedicinsk Selskab [★IO]
Dansk Industri [★IO]
Dansk Institut for Internationale Studier [★IO]
Dansk Irsk Selskab [★IO]
Dansk Isindustri [★IO]
Dansk Jordbrugsteknisk Forening [★IO]
Dansk Journalistforbund [IO], Copenhagen, Denmark
Dansk Kennel Klub [★IO]
Dansk Kulturhistorisk Museumsforening [★IO]
Dansk Kunst og Antikvitetshandler Union [IO], Copenhagen, Denmark
Dansk Kvindesamfund [★IO]
Dansk Lancia Register [★IO]
Dansk Landbrug [★IO]
Dansk Litteraturcenter [★IO]
Dansk Maganipresses Udgiverforening [★IO]
Dansk Matematisk Forening [★IO]
Dansk Medicinsk Selskab [★IO]
Dansk MedikoTeknisk Selskab [★IO]
Dansk Missionsrad [★IO]
Dansk Musikbiblioteks Forening [★IO]
Dansk Oftalmologisk Selskab [★IO]
Dansk Optisk Selskab [★IO]
Dansk Orienterings-Forbund [★IO]
Dansk Ortopaedisk Selskab [★IO]
Dansk Pointer Klub [★IO]
Dansk Presses Faellesindkobs-Forening [★IO]
Dansk Psykolog Forening [★IO]
Dansk Retriever Klub [IO], Odense, Denmark
Dansk Rode Kors [★IO]
Dansk Sejlunion [★IO]
Dansk Selskab for Medicinsk Fysik [★IO]
Dansk Selskab for Musikforskning [★IO]
Dansk Selskab for Neurovidenskab [★IO]
Dansk Selskab for Obstetrik og Gynaekologi [★IO]
Dansk Selskab for Operationsanalyse [★IO]
Dansk Selskab for Patientsikkerhed [★IO]
Dansk Selskab for Sarheling [★IO]
Dansk Skojte Union [★IO]
Dansk Skovforening [★IO]
Dansk Skuespillerforbund [★IO]
Dansk Skytte Union [★IO]
Dansk Socialradgiverforening [★IO]
Dansk Sportdanserforbund [★IO]
Dansk Squash Forbund [★IO]
Dansk Standard [★IO]
Dansk Sygeplejeraad [★IO]
Dansk Taekwondo Forbund [★IO]
Dansk Tandlaegeforening [★IO]
Dansk Teknisk Laererforbund [★IO]
Dansk Tennis Forbund [IO], Brondby, Denmark
Dansk Terrier Klub [★IO]
Dansk Textil and Beklaedning [★IO]
Dansk Textil Union [★IO]
Dansk Translatorforbund [★IO]
Dansk Ungdoms Faellesrad [★IO]
Dansk Vandski Forbund [★IO]
Dansk Yngling Klub [IO], Klampenborg, Denmark
Danske Antikvarboghandlerforening [★IO]
Danske Designere [★IO]
Danske Doves Landsforbund [★IO]
Danske Forstkandidaters Forening [★IO]
Danske Fysioterapeuter [★IO]

Danske Jazz, Beat og Folkemusik Autorer [★IO]
Danske Landbrugsskoler [★IO]
Danske Landskabsarkitekter [★IO]
Danske Malermestre [★IO]
Danske Maritime [★IO]
Danske Populaerautorer [★IO]
Danske Radiologers Org. [★IO]
Danske Reklame- og Relationsbureauers Branche-forening [★IO]
Danske Slagterier [★IO]
Danske Slagtermestres Landsforening [★IO]
Dante Alighieri Soc. of Southern California - Defunct.
Dante Soc. [★9644]
Dante Soc. of Am. [9644], PO Box 711, Framing-ham, MA 01701-0711
Danube Tourist Commn. [IO], Vienna, Austria
Danubian Psychiatric Assn. [IO], Linz, Austria
Danzig Study Group - Defunct.
Dao-Confucianism; Center for [★19879]
Daoist
    Center for Confucian Sci. [19879]
Daoist Sanctuary - Address unknown since 1994.
Daphne Centre for Applied Ecology [★IO]
Daphne Found. [★IO]
Daphne Institut Aplikovanej Ekologie [★IO]
Daphne Inst. of Applied Ecology [IO], Bratislava, Slovakia
D'Aquitaine Found; Natl. Blonde [★4215]
Dar Serca [★13961]
Dar Serca [★IO]
D.A.R.E. Am. [13234], PO Box 512090, Los Angeles, CA 90051-0090, (310)215-0575
Dark Leaf Tobacco Dealers and Exporters; Assn. of [3817]
Dark Shadows Clubs; World Fed. of [★25026]
Dark Shadows Fan Info. Ser. [★25026]
Dark Shadows Fan Info. Ser. [★IO]
Dark Shadows Official Fan Club [IO], Maplewood, NJ, United States
Dark Shadows Official Fan Club [25026], PO Box 92, Maplewood, NJ 07040
Dark Shadows; The World of [25046]
Dark Skies for Comet Halley - Defunct.
Darkness to Light [11590], 7 Radcliffe St., Ste. 200, Charleston, SC 29403, (843)965-5444
Darkride and Funhouse Enthusiasts [21511], PO Box 484, Vienna, OH 44473-0484
Darnall Family Assn. - Address unknown since 2006.
Darrell Shepherd Fan Club - Address unknown since 2000.
Dart
    Slant 6 Club of Am. [21784]
Dart Automotive Refurbishing Tech. Services [★21627]
Dart Swinger 340s Registry; 1970 [21558]
Dart/Valiant Slant 6 Club of Am. [★21784]
Dartmoor Pony Assn; Amer. [4817]
Dartmoor Sheep Breeders' Assn. [IO], Crediton, United Kingdom
Darts
    All India Darts Assn. [IO]
    Amer. Darters Assn. [23327]
    Amer. Darts Org. [23328]
    AMOA Natl. Dart Assn. [23329]
    AMOA National Dart Association [IO]
DARTS Club [21627], PO Box 9, Wethersfield, CT 06129-0009, (860)257-8434
Darul Vietii [★IO]
Darwin Found; Charles [★4401]
Darwin Found. for the Galapagos Islands; Charles [IO]
Darwin Found. for the Galapagos Isles; Charles [★4401]
Data Bank; Schaarschmidt Family Assn. and [21043]
Data Center for Collections of Microorganisms; World [★IO]
Data Center; National Climatic [★4590]
Data Center; National Computer Crime [★2091]
Data Center; National Geophysical [★4590]
Data Center; National Oceanographic [★4590]
Data Communication Dealers Assn. - Address unknown since 1991.
Data Commun; Special Interest Gp. on [★6750]
Data Consortium; Linguistic [2437]
Data Educ; Soc. of Independent and Private School [★8132]

Data Educators; Soc. for [★8132]
Data Indus. Assn; Consumer [1409]
Data and Info. Ser; Environmental [★4590]
Data Inst; Highway Loss [2168]
Data Interchange Standards Assn. [18680], 7600 Leesburg Pike, Ste. 430, Falls Church, VA 22043, (703)970-4480
Data Mgt. Assn; Insurance [2175]
Data Mgt. Assn. Intl. [7193], 19239 N Dale Mabry Hwy., No. 132, Lutz, FL 33548, (813)448-7786
Data Mgt. Assn. Intl. [IO], Bellevue, WA, United States
Data Network; National Materials Properties [★7319]
Data Processing
    Amer. Assn. of Electronic Reporters and Transcribers [3180]
    Amer. Medical Informatics Assn. [14079]
    AMIGOS Lib. Services [10325]
    Assn. for Pathology Informatics [15864]
    Assn. of Rehabilitation Programs in Cmpt. Tech. [11924]
    Blind Info. Tech. Specialists [16835]
    Brazilian Assn. of Software Companies [IO]
    Chamber of Software Businesses and Info. Services [IO]
    Colombian Chamber of Info. Tech. and Telecom-munications [IO]
    Govt. Mgt. Info. Sciences [5818]
    Hea. Indus. Bus. Communications Coun. [14080]
    Hungarian Assn. of IT Companies [IO]
    Info. Tech. Solution Provider Alliance [2102]
    Infrared Data Assn. [6855]
    Infrared Data Assn. [IO]
    Intl. Assn. for Info. and Data Quality [7197]
    Intl. Soc. for Ethics and Info. Tech. [7198]
    Israeli Assn. of Software Houses [IO]
    Ithaka [7200]
    Japan Embedded Systems Tech. Assn. [IO]
    Latinos in Info. Sciences and Tech. Assn. [7201]
    Mobile Data Assn. [IO]
    Natl. Assn. for Justice Info. Systems [5648]
    Natl. Assn. of Software and Ser. Companies [IO]
    Natl. Dental EDI Coun. [14176]
    Open Data Acquisition Assn. [891]
    Pakistan Software Houses Assn. [IO]
    Software Contractors' Guild [1143]
    Software Distributors' Assn. [IO]
    U.S. Prdt. Data Assn. [2112]
Data Processing Associates; Black [62]
Data Processing Assn; Textile [★3772]
Data Processing Auditors Assn; Electronic [★65]
Data Processing; Financial Mgt. for [★1430]
Data Processing Mgt. Assn. [★IO]
Data Processing and Mgt; Special Interest Group for Business [76]
Data Processing Org; Multi-Bank [★61]
Data Prog; Natl. Serials [10376]
Data Publishers Assn. [IO], London, United Kingdom
Data Ser; Environmental [★4590]
Data; Special Interest Gp. on Mgt. of [6750]
Data Systems; Soc. for Educational [★8132]
Data Users; Assn. of Public [7190]
Data Vaults; Natl. Assn. of Security and [★2109]
Database Management
    Intl. DB2 Users Gp. [6856]
    Open Data Acquisition Assn. [891]
    Quest Intl. Users Gp. [6857]
DataCenter [18412], 1904 Franklin St., Ste. 900, Oakland, CA 94612-2923, (510)835-4692
Dataworks Users Alliance [★6793]
Date-Able/HI [★11936]
Date-Able/HI [★IO]
Date Administrative Comm. [★4711]
Date Administrative Comm; California [4711]
Date Administrative Comm; California [★4711]
Date Commn; California [★4711]
Date Growers' Inst. - Defunct.
Date Nail Collectors Assn; Texas [22121]
Date Rape; Natl. CH on Marital and [12790]
DateAble [11936], 15520 Bald Eagle School Rd., Brandywine, MD 20613, (301)888-1177
DateAble [IO], Brandywine, MD, United States
Dateable Intl. [★IO]
Dateable Intl. [★11936]
Datsun Fairlady Registry - Defunct.

Reference to "IO" in place of a book number signifies that the association may be found in the 45th edition of International Organizations.

Datsun Owners Club - Defunct.
Daubenspeck-Doverspike Family Exchange [20879]
Daughters of the 17th Century; Natl. Soc. Colonial [20745]
Daughters of '98, Auxiliary United Spanish War Veterans; Natl. Fort [21267]
Daughters of 1812; Natl. Soc., U.S. [21355]
Daughters of America; Natl. Coun., [19132]
Daughters of the Amer. Colonists; Natl. Soc., [20746]
Daughters of the Amer. Revolution; Natl. Soc., [20675]
Daughters of the Americas; Catholic [18992]
Daughters with Breast Cancer; Mothers Supporting [13844]
Daughters of the British Empire in the U.S.A; Natl. Soc., [18985]
Daughters of the Cincinnati [20670], 122 E 58th St., New York, NY 10022, (212)319-6915
Daughters of Columbus [★18998]
Daughters of the Confederacy; United [20732]
Daughters; Dads and [12150]
Daughters of the Defenders of the Republic, U.S.A. - Address unknown since 1995.
Daughters of Early Amer. Witches; Assoc. [21358]
Daughters of the Elderly Bridging the Unknown Together - Defunct.
Daughters of Evrytania [19086], 121 Greenwich Rd., Ste. 212, Charlotte, NC 28211, (704)366-6571
Daughters of the Golden West; Native [18986]
Daughters of Hirsutism Assn. of America - Address unknown since 2001.
Daughters of Holland Dames; Soc. of [20759]
Daughters of Isabella, Intl. Circle [19000], PO Box 9585, New Haven, CT 06535, (203)865-2570
Daughters of Isabella, Intl. Circle [IO], New Haven, CT, United States
Daughters of Isabella, Natl. Circle [★IO]
Daughters of Isabella, Natl. Circle [★19000]
Daughters of Isabella, Supreme Circle [★19000]
Daughters of Isabella, Supreme Circle [★IO]
Daughters of the King [★19969]
Daughters of the King; Order of the [19969]
Daughters of Mokanna [19231], 126 Hilltop Cir., Elyria, OH 44035, (440)365-9536
Daughters of the Nile, Supreme Temple [19232], 13309 W Meeker Blvd., Sun City West, AZ 85375-3808
Daughters of Norway [★19293]
Daughters of Norway [★IO]
Daughters of Oregon Pioneers; Sons and [21257]
Daughters of Penelope [19087], 440 Whitehall Rd., Albany, NY 12208, (518)489-4442
Daughters of Penelope Foundation [★19087]
Daughters of Peter Claver; Junior [19002]
Daughters of Pioneer Rivermen; Sons and [21258]
Daughters of the Republic of Texas [21114], 510 E Anderson Ln., Austin, TX 78752, (512)339-1997
Daughters of Saint Paul - European Off. [IO], Rome, Italy
Daughters of Scotia [19353], 7595 Carter Rd., Sagamore Hills, OH 44067, (330)467-6387
Daughters and Sons United - Defunct.
Daughters of Union Veterans of the Civil War, 1861-1865 [20725], 503 S Walnut St., Springfield, IL 62704-1932, (217)544-0616
Daughters of the U.S.A; Children, Sons and [★11335]
Daughters of Utah Pioneers; Natl. Soc. [★21252]
Daughters of Veterans; Natl. Alliance [★20725]
Daughters of Zion [★20139]
Daughters of Zion [★IO]
Dave Durham Fan Club - Address unknown since 1999.
Davenport Family Fan Club - Defunct.
Daves Intl. - Address unknown since 1999.
David Allan Coe Fan Club [24870], 783 Rippling Creek, Nixa, MO 65714
David Ball Intl. Fan Club [24871], c/o Susan Collier, Public Relations Off., 6204 Jocelyn Hollow Rd., Nashville, TN 37205, (615)356-0375
David Birney Intl. Fan Club [24737], c/o Bret Adams, Ltd., Artists Agency, 488 W 44th St., New York, NY 10036, (212)265-5630
David Birney International Fan Club [IO], New York, NY, United States

David Cassidy Support Group - Address unknown since 1989.
David Copperfield Intl. Fan Club - Address unknown since 2001.
David Family Org. - Address unknown since 2007.
David Frizzell Fan Club - Address unknown since 1989.
David Heavener Fan Club - Address unknown since 1989.
David Hedison Fan Club - Defunct.
David Hutchinson and Agnus Nish Family Org. - Address unknown since 2003.
David Kirchner Fan Club - Defunct.
David and Lucile Packard Found. [11808], 300 Second St., Los Altos, CA 94022, (650)948-7658
David and Lucile Packard Found. [IO], Los Altos, CA, United States
David Selby Official Fan Club - Address unknown since 1999.
David Suzuki Found. [IO], Vancouver, BC, Canada
Davidson Soc; Clan [20825]
Davis Assn; Jefferson [11129]
Davis Dyslexia Assn. - UK [IO], Kent, United Kingdom
Davis Fan Club; Linda [24939]
Davis Foundations; Arthur Vining [12048]
Davis Memorial Assn; Sam [11149]
Davis Registry [21628], 6487 Munger Rd., Ypsilanti, MI 48197-9014, (734)434-5581
Davis Registry [IO], Ypsilanti, MI, United States
DaVita Patient Citizens [15291], 1155 15th St. NW, Ste. 1100, Washington, DC 20005, (866)877-4242
Dawkins Children's Project; Paul Andrew [★11690]
The Dawkins Project [11690]
Dawley Family Assn. - Defunct.
Dawn Bible Students Assn. [19517], 199 Railroad Ave., East Rutherford, NJ 07073, (888)440-DAWN
Dawson Family Org. - Address unknown since 2006.
Day Animal League; Doris [11387]
DAY Assn. - Defunct.
The Day Before Community Forums on Our Response to the Future - Defunct.
Day-Break Geriatric Massage Inst. [15026], c/o Sharon Puszko, PhD, Dir./Owner, 7434 King George Dr., Ste. A, Indianapolis, IN 46240, (317)722-9896
Day Care Assn; Natl. Child [★11534]
Day Care Coun. of America - Defunct.
Day Care Program; Get Set [★11539]
Day Care Programs; Comprehensive [11539]
Day of Prayer; Intl. Comm. for World [★20629]
Day Sailer Assn. [23167], c/o Patricia Skeen, Sec., 1936 Danebo Ave., Eugene, OR 97402-1135, (541)689-2190
Day School Administrators; Natl. Assn. of Hebrew [7901]
Day School PTAs; Natl. Assn. of Hebrew [8953]
Day Services Assn; Natl. Adult [11298]
Daycare; Natl. Assn. for Sick Child [11532]
Daycare Trust [IO], London, United Kingdom
Daylight Saving Time Coalition - Address unknown since 2006.
Daytime Apparel Inst. - Defunct.
Daytime Broadcasters Assn. [★569]
Daytonas Fan Club; Ronny and the [24970]
DB-Link [★16845]
DB-Link: The Natl. Info. CH On Children Who Are Deaf-Blind [16845], 345 N Monmouth Ave., Monmouth, OR 97361, (800)438-9376
DB - Panhard Registry [★21686]
DBA ESI - Defunct.
DBA - The Barge Assn. [IO], Rickmansworth, United Kingdom
DC Dance Club [IO], Calgary, AB, Canada
DC Feminists Against Pornography [17527]
DCCC [★22814]
DDA, Assn. of the DEC Marketplace - Address unknown since 2005.
De Havilland Moth Club [IO], Berkhamsted, United Kingdom
De Lange Syndrome Found; Cornelia [13754]
De Maatschappij der Nederlandse Letterkunde [★IO]
De Mertonvrienden in de Lage Landen [★IO]
De Montbrun Heritage Soc; Jacques Timothe Boucher Sieur [20741]

De Nederlandse Rozenvereniging [IO], Liempde, Netherlands
De Porres Guild; St. Martin [20389]
De Re Militari: The Soc. for Medieval Military History [10474], c/o Carroll Gillmor, Sec.-Treas., PO Box 784, Salt Lake City, UT 84111
De Sales; Secular Inst. of Saint Francis [19716]
De Vaux Registry - Defunct.
Deacon
 Concordia Deaconess Conf. [20213]
 Lutheran Deaconess Conf. [20220]
 Natl. Assn. of Diaconate Directors [19664]
 North Amer. Assn. for the Diaconate [19967]
Deaconess Assn; Lutheran [20213]
Deaconess Conf; Concordia [20213]
Deaconess Conf; Lutheran [20220]
Dead Composers Society - Address unknown since 2002.
Dead; Natl. Shrine to the Jewish War [★21312]
Deadline Club [3109], 15 Gramercy Park S, New York, NY 10003, (212)353-9598
Deaf
 Abused Deaf Women's Advocacy Services [11903]
 Acad. of Doctors of Audiology [14733]
 Acad. of Rehabilitative Audiology [14734]
 ADARA: Professionals Networking for Excellence in Ser. Delivery with Individuals who are Deaf or Hard of Hearing [14735]
 Alexander Graham Bell Assn. for the Deaf and Hard of Hearing [14736]
 Amer. Assn. of the Deaf-Blind [14737]
 Amer. Auditory Soc. [14738]
 Amer. Hearing Impaired Hockey Assn. [23337]
 Amer. Hearing Res. Found. [14740]
 Amer. Neurotology Soc. [16441]
 Amer. Sign Language Teachers Assn. [14741]
 Amer. Soc. for Deaf Children [14742]
 Amer. Speech Language Hearing Assn. [16442]
 Assn. of Late-Deafened Adults [14743]
 Audiology Awareness Campaign [13716]
 Better Hearing Inst. [14745]
 Children of Deaf Adults [14747]
 Christian Record Services [16842]
 Conf. of Educational Administrators of Schools and Programs for the Deaf [14749]
 Coun. of Amer. Instructors of the Deaf [14750]
 Coun. on Educ. of the Deaf [14751]
 Deaf Friends Intl. [11904]
 Deaf Friends Intl. [IO]
 Deaf History Intl. [14081]
 Deaf Women United [11905]
 Deafness Res. Found. [14753]
 Disabled Sports USA [23343]
 Dogs for the Deaf [14754]
 Elwyn [12383]
 Global Deaf Connection [12274]
 HEAR Center [14756]
 Hear Now [14757]
 Hearing Loss Assn. of Am. [14759]
 Helen Keller Natl. Center for Deaf-Blind Youths and Adults [14760]
 Help the Helpless [12405]
 House Ear Inst. [16446]
 Intl. Catholic Deaf Assn. - U.S. Sect. [19641]
 Intl. Hearing Dog, Inc. [14762]
 Intl. Hearing Soc. [14763]
 Intl. Lutheran Deaf Assn. [20217]
 John Tracy Clinic [14764]
 Model Secondary School for the Deaf [14766]
 Natl. Alliance of Black Interpreters [3854]
 Natl. Assn. of the Deaf [14767]
 Natl. Assn. of School Nurses for the Deaf [14768]
 Natl. Black Assn. for Speech-Language and Hearing [16448]
 Natl. Captioning Inst. [14769]
 Natl. Catholic Off. for the Deaf [19675]
 Natl. Cued Speech Association/Deaf Children's Literacy Proj. [16452]
 Natl. Deaf Educ. Network and CH [11906]
 Natl. Hearing Conservation Assn. [14772]
 Natl. Ser. Dog Center [14774]
 Natl. Student Speech Language Hearing Assn. [16453]
 NIDCD - Natl. Temporal Bone, Hearing and Balance Pathology Rsrc. Registry [15121]

A star before a book entry number signifies that the name is not listed separately, but is mentioned within the entry.

Oral Hearing-Impaired Sect. [14775]
Parents' Sect. of the Alexander Graham Bell Assn. for the Deaf and Hard of Hearing [14776]
Phone-TTY [14777]
Protestant Guild for Human Services [16884]
Rainbow Alliance of the Deaf [12255]
Registry of Interpreters for the Deaf [14778]
Ski for Light [23361]
Telecommunications for the Deaf and Hard of Hearing, Inc. [14780]
UK Coun. on Deafness [IO]
U.S.A. Deaf Basketball [23136]
U.S. Assn. for Blind Athletes [23363]
U.S. Flag Football for the Deaf [23367]
Univ. of Colorado Hea. Sciences Center Alumni Assn. [24494]
USA Deaf Sports Fed. [23369]
Wheelchair Sports, USA [23371]
Deaf Adults; Children of [14747]
Deaf Adults Sect; Oral [★14775]
Deaf Advocates; Natl. Black [17418]
Deaf Africans; Christian Mission for [★20318]
Deaf; Alexander Graham Bell Assn. for the [★14736]
Deaf; Amer. Assn. to Promote the Teaching of Speech to the [★14736]
Deaf; Amer. Athletic Assn. for the [★23369]
Deaf; Amer. Instructors of the [★14750]
Deaf Artists of America - Defunct.
Deaf Assn. of New Zealand [IO], Auckland, New Zealand
Deaf; Assn. of Superintendents and Principals of Amer. Schools for the [★14749]
Deaf Assn. - U.S. Sect; Intl. Catholic [19641]
Deaf-Blind; Amer. Assn. of the [14737]
Deaf-Blind; Amer. League for [★14737]
Deaf and Blind; Ephphatha Services for the [★20216]
Deaf-Blind Youths and Adults; Helen Keller Natl. Center for [14760]
Deaf in Bulgaria; Union of the [IO]
Deaf; Canadian Assn. of the [IO]
Deaf Charity; Commonwealth Soc. for [IO]
Deaf Children; Amer. Soc. for [14742]
Deaf Children; Signing Exact English Center for the Advancement of [14779]
Deaf Children's Literacy Proj. [★16452]
Deaf Children's Literacy Proj; Natl. Cued Speech Association/ [16452]
Deaf; Christian Mission for the [20318]
Deaf Communications Inst. - Defunct.
Deaf; Conf. of Church Workers Among the [★19954]
Deaf; Conf. of Educational Administrators Serving the [★14749]
Deaf; Conf. of Executives of Amer. Schools for the [★14749]
Deaf; Coun. of Amer. Instructors of the [14750]
Deaf; Coun. on Educ. of the [14751]
Deaf Cycling Assn; U.S. [23365]
Deaf; Dogs for the [14754]
Deaf Educ. Through Listening and Talking [IO], Peterborough, United Kingdom
Deaf; Episcopal Conf. of the [19954]
Deaf; European Union of the [IO]
Deaf Friends Intl. [IO], Hamilton, OH, United States
Deaf Friends Intl. [11904], PO Box 13192, Hamilton, OH 45013
Deaf and Hard of Hearing Entrepreneurs Coun. - Defunct.
Deaf and Hard of Hearing; Parents' Sect. of the Alexander Graham Bell Assn. for the [14776]
Deaf History Intl. [14081], c/o Mr. Ulf Hedberg, PO Box 298, Rockville, MD 20848
Deaf; Hong Kong Soc. for the [IO]
Deaf, Inc; Telecommunications for the [★14780]
Deaf; Intl. Assn. of Parents of the [★14742]
Deaf Missions - Defunct.
Deaf; Model Secondary School for the [14766]
Deaf; Natl. Assn. of the [14767]
Deaf; Natl. Catholic Off. for the [19675]
Deaf; Natl. Center on Employment of the [★12095]
Deaf; Natl. Fraternal Soc. of the [19134]
Deaf; Natl. Hea. Care Found. for the [★14752]
Deaf; Natl. Registry of Professional Interpreters and Translators for the [★14778]
Deaf Olympics [★23345]

Deaf Olympics [★IO]
Deaf; Parents' Sect. of the Alexander Graham Bell Assn. for the [★14776]
Deaf People; Natl. Assn. for [IO]
Deaf; Rainbow Alliance of the [12255]
Deaf-REACH [14752], 3521 12th St. NE, Washington, DC 20017, (202)832-6681
Deaf; Registry of Interpreters for the [14778]
Deaf; Singapore Assn. for the [IO]
Deaf Ski and Snowboard Assn; U.S. [23366]
Deaf Soc; Irish [IO]
Deaf Sports Assn; Canadian [IO]
Deaf Sports Australia [IO], East Melbourne, Australia
Deaf Sports Fed; USA [23369]
Deaf; Swedish Natl. Assn. of the [IO]
Deaf; Teletypewriters for the [★14780]
Deaf; U.S. Flag Football for the [23367]
Deaf; Volta Speech Assn. for the [★14736]
Deaf Women United [11905], PO Box 152795, Austin, TX 78715-2795
Deaf Women's Bowling Assn; Natl. [23352]
Deafblind Assn. [IO], Camberwell, Australia
Deafblind Intl. [IO], London, United Kingdom
Deafblind New Zealand [IO], Wellington, New Zealand
Deafblind Scotland [IO], Glasgow, United Kingdom
Deafblind UK [IO], Peterborough, United Kingdom
Deafchild Intl. [IO], Reading, United Kingdom
Deafened Adults; Assn. of Late- [14743]
Deafened People; Natl. Assn. of [IO]
Deafness and Other Commun. Disorders Info. CH; Natl. Inst. on [14773]
Deafness and Rehabilitation Assn; Amer. [★14735]
Deafness Res. Found. [14753], 641 Lexington Ave., 15th Fl., New York, NY 10022, (212)328-9480
Deafness Res. Found. Alliance [14753]
Deafpride - Address unknown since 1999.
Deal and the Rhondels Fan Club; Bill [24848]
Dealer Assn; Antiques and Collectibles [863]
Dealer Consultants Assn; CPA Auto [25]
Dealer Counsel; Natl. Assn. of [361]
Dealer Mgt. Assn. [717], 239 Drakeside Rd., Hampton, NH 03842, (603)926-8000
Dealers Alliance [412], Continental Plz., 401 Hackensack Ave., Hackensack, NJ 07601, (201)342-4542
Dealers of Am. and Allied Trades; Ser. Sta. [★2946]
Dealers of Am; Ser. Sta. [★2946]
Dealers; Amer. Assn. of Franchisees and [1665]
Dealers; Amer. Inst. of Kitchen [★2271]
Dealers Art Exchange - Address unknown since 1995.
Dealers Assn; Amer. Marinelife [5007]
Dealers Assn; Antique Tribal Art [296]
Dealers Assn; Ford, Lincoln, Mercury Minority [★413]
Dealers Assn; Ford Motor Minority [413]
Dealers Assn; Intl. Fine Print [309]
Dealers Assn; Intl. Milk [★1135]
Dealers Assn; Intl. Systems [★2847]
Dealers Assn; Intl. Vintage Poster [106]
Dealers Assn; Natl. Antique Doll [22402]
Dealers Assn; Natl. Electronic Ser. [★1224]
Dealers Assn; Natl. Emergency Equip. [14339]
Dealers Assn; Natl. Independent Flag [1488]
Dealers Assn; Natl. Off. Machine [★2844]
Dealers Assn; Natl. Typewriter and Off. Machine [★2844]
Dealers Assn; North Amer. Retail [1227]
Dealers Assn; Retail Print Music [2823]
Dealers Assn; Wireless [3765]
Dealers Intl; Assn. of Ser. and Cmpt. [897]
Dealers and Manufacturers Assn; Trophy [★441]
Dealers; Natl. Assn. of Fleet Resale [419]
Dealers; Natl. Assn. of Limited Edition [862]
Dealers; Pacific Northwest Pea Growers and [★4314]
Dealers Safety and Mobility Coun. - Defunct.
Dean Martin Collector's Club - Defunct.
Dean Martin Fan Center [24816], PO Box 660212, Arcadia, CA 91066-0212
Dean Reed U.S. Fan Club - Defunct.
Deans and Advisers of Men; Natl. Assn. of [★7904]
Deans of Am. Colleges of Veterinary Medicine; Assn. of [★9293]

Deans; Amer. Conf. of Academic [7885]
Deans and Directors; Assn. of Summer Sessions [★9199]
Death Commun. Res. Found; After [14903]
Death with Dignity Natl. Center [17109], 520 SW 6th Ave., Ste. 1030, Portland, OR 97204, (503)228-4415
Death and Dying
  Aiding Mothers and Fathers Experiencing Neonatal Death [11907]
  Amer. Inst. of Life Threatening Illness and Loss (Division of Found. of Thanatology) [11908]
  Amer. Soc. of Embalmers [2773]
  Assn. for Death Educ. and Counseling [11909]
  Assn. for Pet Loss and Bereavement [12706]
  Bereaved Parents of the USA [11512]
  Intl. Assn. of Obituarists [4062]
  Palliative Care Policy Center [14082]
  Rallying Points [14083]
  Sacred Dying Found. [11910]
  Violent Death Bereavement Soc. [11513]
Death Educ. and Bioethics; Center for [13314]
Death Educ. and Counseling; Assn. for [11909]
Death Educ. and Counseling; Forum for [★11909]
Death Educ. and Res; Center for [★13314]
Death Experience Res. Found; Near [14904]
Death and Immortality; Intl. Inst. for the Stud. of [★13315]
Death Penalty; Campaign to End the [17028]
Death Penalty; Citizens United for Alternatives to the [5641]
Death Penalty Info. Center [17030], 1101 Vermont Ave. NW, Ste. 701, Washington, DC 20005, (202)289-2275
Death Penalty; Natl. Coalition to Abolish the [17033]
Death Penalty; Natl. Coalition Against the [★17033]
Death Penalty; Proj. Hope to Abolish the [17035]
Death Rsrc. Center; Natl. SIDS/Infant [16526]
Death Row Support Proj. [11863], PO Box 600, Liberty Mills, IN 46946, (260)982-7480
Death Syndrome Alliance; Sudden Infant [★16525]
Death Syndrome Found; Natl. Sudden Infant [★16525]
Death Syndromes Found; Sudden Arrhythmia [14484]
Death and Taxes - Defunct.
Death Valley '49ers [4807], PO Box 338, Death Valley, CA 92328
Death With Dignity Educ. Center [★17109]
Death With Dignity Educ. Fund [★17109]
Death With Dignity Natl. Center [★17109]
Debaillon Louisiana Iris Soc; Mary Swords [★22542]
DeBakey Intl. Cardiovascular Soc; Michael E. [★13917]
DeBakey Intl. Surgical Soc; Michael E. [13917]
Debate Assn; Amer. [9151]
Debate Assn; Natl. Fed. Interscholastic Speech and [★9161]
Debate Leagues; Natl. Assn. of Urban [9155]
Debate and Theatre Assn; NFHS Speech, [9161]
Debates; Commn. on Presidential [18350]
Debbie Fox Found. [★14061]
Debbie Fox Found. for Treatment of Cranio-Facial Deformities [★14061]
Debbie Harry Collector's Soc. [24872], 124 S Locust Point Rd., Mechanicsburg, PA 17055-9709
Debbie Myers Intl. Fan Club [IO], Amherst, NS, Canada
Debbie Reynolds Fan Club; Friends of [24741]
Debby Boone Fan Club - Defunct.
Deborah Harry Appreciation Soc. - Address unknown since 1999.
DEBRA of Am. [★14200]
DEBRA European [IO], Crowthorne, United Kingdom
DEBRA Intl. [IO], Crowthorne, United Kingdom
DEBRA Ireland [IO], Dublin, Ireland
Debs Found; Eugene V. [10295]
Debt Buyers' Assn. [1146], 8201 Greensboro Dr., Ste. 300, McLean, VA 22102, (703)610-0224
Debt Collection
  ACA Intl. [1144]
  ACA Intl. [IO]
  Amer. Recovery Assn. [1145]
  Assn. of Trade and Forfaiting in the Americas [1404]

Reference to "IO" in place of a book number signifies that the association may be found in the 45th edition of International Organizations.

Debt Buyers' Assn. [1146]
Debtors Anonymous [13017]
Intl. Assn. of Commercial Collectors [1147]
Intl. Assn. of Commercial Collectors [IO]
Money Mgt. Intl. [12190]
State Debt Mgt. Network [6288]
Debt Crisis Network - Defunct.
Debt Mgt. Network; State [6288]
Debt Payment Club - Defunct.
Debtors Anonymous [13017], PO Box 920888,
Needham, MA 02492-0009, (781)453-2743
Debts AIDS Trade Africa [16928], 1400 Eye St. NW,
Ste. 600, Washington, DC 20005, (202)639-8010
Debts AIDS Trade Africa [IO], Washington, DC,
United States
DECA [★23918]
DECA, The Decathlon Assn. [23918], c/o Dr. Frank
Zarnowski, Founder/Exec. Dir., 58 2nd Ave., Em-
mitsburg, MD 21727-9169, (301)447-6122
Decade of the Brain Coalition [★15397]
A Decade of Study of the Constitution - Defunct.
Decalogue Soc. of Lawyers [5490], 39 S LaSalle St.,
Ste. 410, Chicago, IL 60603, (312)263-6493
Decathlon
DECA, The Decathlon Assn. [23918]
Decency; Americans for [17282]
Decency Assn; Amer. [17281]
Decency; Natl. Fed. for [★17162]
Decentralist Coalition - Defunct.
DECHEMA [IO], Frankfurt, Germany
Deciduous Tree Fruit Disease Workers - Address
unknown since 2001.
Decision Making; Comm. on Non-Market [★7527]
Decision Making; Soc. for Judgement and [8041]
Decision Making; Soc. for Medical [15180]
Decision Sciences
Alpha Iota Delta [24412]
Soc. for Judgement and Decision Making [8041]
Soc. for Medical Decision Making [15180]
Decision Sciences; Amer. Inst. for [★8021]
Decision Sciences Inst. [8021], Georgia State Univ.,
J. Mack Robinson Coll. of Bus., Univ. Plz., Atlanta,
GA 30303, (404)413-7710
Deck Inst; Steel [671]
Declaration of Atlantic Unity - Defunct.
Declaration Found. [5662], PO Box 1310, Herndon,
VA 20191
Declaration of Independence; Descendants of the
Signers of the [20671]
Declaration of Independence House and Library -
Address unknown since 1995.
Declaration of Independence Second Centennial
Commemorative Natl. Comm. - Address unknown
since 2004.
Deco Dealers Assn; Amer. Art [295]
Decorating Contractors of Am; Painting and [1057]
Decorating and Drywall Apprenticeship and
Manpower Training Fund; Intl. Joint Painting,
[★12082]
Decorating, and Drywall Apprenticeship and
Manpower Training Fund; Natl. Painting, [★12082]
Decorating, and Drywall Apprenticeship and Training
Comm; Natl. Joint Painting, [★12082]
Decorating Products Assn; Canadian [★2274]
Decorating Products Assn; Natl. [★2274]
Decoration; Historical Soc. of Early Amer. [9482]
Decoration; Soc. of Early Amer. [★9482]
Decorative Accessories Assn. of Am; Gift and
[★859]
Decorative Arts League; Antique and [★297]
Decorative Arts Trust [9567], 106 Bainbridge St.,
Philadelphia, PA 19147, (215)627-2859
Decorative Fabric Distributors; Natl. Assn. of [3793]
Decorative Fabrics Inst. - Defunct.
Decorative Furniture Mfrs. Assn. - Defunct.
Decorative Laminate Products Assn. - Defunct.
Decorative Painters; Soc. of [22175]
Decorative Window Coverings Assn. - Address
unknown since 2002.
Decorators; Amer. Inst. of [★2251]
Decorators Assn; Natl. Metal [★1775]
Decorators Club - Address unknown since 2003.
Decorators and Paperhangers of Am; Brotherhood of
Painters, [★12082]
Decorators; Soc. of Glass and Ceramic [1735]

Decoupeurs; Natl. Guild of [22168]
Decoy Assn; Amer. Fish [21960]
Decoy Collectors Assn; Midwest [22071]
Dedham Pottery Collectors Soc. [22009], c/o Jim
Kaufman, 248 Highland St., Dedham, MA 02026-
5833, (800)283-8070
Dedicated Otaku Anime Club [IO], Calgary, AB,
Canada
Dedicated Wooden Money Collectors [22736]
Dee Scofield Awareness Program - Defunct.
Deep Bed Farming Soc. - Address unknown since
1999.
Deep Found. Testing Professionals; Alliance of
[6650]
Deep Foundations Inst. [1013], 326 Lafayette Ave.,
Hawthorne, NJ 07506, (973)423-4030
Deep Foundations Institute [IO], Hawthorne, NJ,
United States
Deep Griha Soc. of Pune, India [IO], Pune, India
Deep Purple Appreciation Soc. [IO], Sheffield,
United Kingdom
Deep Purple Made in Italy Fan Club [IO], Turin, Italy
Deer
Deer Commn. for Scotland [IO]
North Amer. Deer Farmers Assn. [4654]
Whitetails Unlimited [5391]
Deer Commn. for Scotland [IO], Inverness, United
Kingdom
Deer Farmers Assn; North Amer. [4654]
Deer Soc; British [IO]
Deer Unlimited of America - Address unknown since
1999.
Deerfield; Historic [10034]
Deerhound
Scottish Deerhound Club of Am. [22356]
Deerhound Club of Am; Scottish [22356]
Defamation; Gay Lesbian Alliance Against [17652]
Defamation League; Christian Anti- [17102]
Defamation New York; Gay and Lesbian Alliance
Against [★17652]
Defamation; Resisting [17150]
Defence for Children Intl. - Bolivia [IO], Cocha-
bamba, Bolivia
Defence for Children Intl. - Canada [IO], Toronto,
ON, Canada
Defence for Children Intl. - Chile [IO], Santiago,
Chile
Defence for Children Intl. - Colombia [IO], Bogota,
Colombia
Defence for Children Intl. - Costa Rica [IO], San
Jose, Costa Rica
Defence for Children Intl. - Czech Republic [IO],
Prague, Czech Republic
Defence for Children Intl. - India [★IO]
Defence for Children Intl. - Lebanon [IO], Beirut,
Lebanon
Defence for Children Intl. - Netherlands [IO], Amster-
dam, Netherlands
Defence for Children Intl. - Palestine Sect. [IO],
Jerusalem, Israel
Defence for Children Intl. - Switzerland [IO],
Geneva, Switzerland
Defender Assn; Natl. Legal Aid and [6031]
Defender Investigator Assn; Natl. [5888]
Defenders of the Amer. Constitution - Address
unknown since 1995.
Defenders of Bataan and Corregidor; Amer. [21386]
Defenders of the Christian Faith [★19774]
Defenders of Furbearers [★5307]
Defenders; Gay and Lesbian Advocates and [17118]
Defenders of Property Rights [6188], 1350 Con-
necticut Ave. NW, Ste. 410, Washington, DC
20036, (202)822-6770
Defenders of Wildlife [5307], 1130 17th St. NW,
Washington, DC 20036, (800)385-9712
Defending Against Drugs and Social Disorder; MAD
DADS Men Against Destruction [12043]
Defensa de Ninas y Ninos Internacional - Seccion
Bolivia [★IO]
Defensa de los Ninos Internacional - Chile [★IO]
Defensa de los Ninos Internacional - Colombia
[★IO]
Defensa de los Ninos Internacional - Costa Rica
[★IO]
Defense
Aircraft Carrier Indus. Base Coalition [1148]

Alliance Defense Fund [17372]
Amer. Defense Inst. [17373]
Arms Control Association/Arms Control Today
[17422]
Assn. of Defense Trial Attorneys [5825]
Assn. of Old Crows [6908]
Atlantic Coun. of Canada [IO]
Atlantic Treaty Assn. [IO]
Australia Defence Assn. [IO]
British Amer. Security Info. Coun. [IO]
British Amer. Security Info. Coun. [17374]
Bus. Executives for Natl. Security [18587]
Campaign to Boycott SDI [18143]
Canadian Inst. of Strategic Stud. [IO]
Center for Defense Info. [17375]
Contract Services Assn. of Am. [1743]
Danish Atlantic Treaty Assn. [IO]
Defense Credit Union Coun. [1108]
Defense Forum Found. [17376]
Defense Mfrs. Assn. of Great Britain [IO]
Defense Orientation Conf. Assn. [18591]
Directed Energy Professional Soc. [6858]
Family Defense Coun. [17377]
German Atlantic Assn. [IO]
Inst. of Civil Defence and Disaster Stud. [IO]
Inst. for Defense Analyses [6256]
Inst. for Security Stud. [IO]
Inter-American Defense Bd. [IO]
Inter-American Defense Bd. [17378]
Intl. Assn. of Professional Protection Specialists
[13009]
Intl. Defense Equip. Exhibitors Assn. [1343]
Intl. Inst. for Strategic Stud. [IO]
Intl. Strategic Stud. Assn. [IO]
Intl. Strategic Stud. Assn. [17379]
Italian Atlantic Comm. [IO]
Jewish Inst. for Natl. Security Affairs [IO]
Jewish Inst. for Natl. Security Affairs [17380]
Leonard Peltier Defense Comm. [17381]
Leonard Peltier Defense Committee [IO]
Lincoln Inst. for Res. and Educ. [16940]
Marine Corps Aviation Reconnaissance Assn.
[6052]
Missile Defense Advocacy Alliance [17382]
Natl. Assn. of Criminal Defense Lawyers [5656]
Natl. Assn. of Fed. Defenders [5646]
Natl. Defense Indus. Assn. [6089]
Natl. Defense Trans. Assn. [6090]
Natl. Strategy Info. Center [17383]
NATO Parliamentary Assembly [IO]
Naval Submarine League [17384]
Netherlands Atlantic Assn. [IO]
North Atlantic Coun. [IO]
North Atlantic Treaty Org. [IO]
Patriots for the Defense of Am. [18186]
Proj. on Defense Alternatives [17385]
Red River Valley Fighter Pilots Assn. [21318]
Soldiers for the Truth [20683]
South African Aerospace Maritime and Defence
Indus. Assn. [IO]
State Guard Assn. of the U.S. [6105]
Submarine Indus. Base Coun. [1149]
U.S. Indus. Coalition [7637]
Western European Union [IO]
Women in Defense, a Natl. Security Org. [17386]
Defense Advisory Comm. on Women in the Services
[6075], 4000 Defense Pentagon, Rm. 2C548A,
Washington, DC 20301-4000, (703)697-2122
Defense of Am; Patriots for the [18186]
Defense Analyses; Inst. for [6256]
Defense Assn; The Amer. Civil [5559]
Defense Assn; Amer. Indian [★18092]
Defense Assn; Electronic [★6908]
Defense Assn; Men's [18039]
Defense Awareness; Civil [★18469]
Defense Budget Proj. [★18075]
Defense for Children Intl. - U.S.A. - Address
unknown since 2001.
Defense Coll; Natl. Criminal [5657]
Defense Comm; Dennis Brutus [★17740]
Defense and Corporate Counsel; Fed. of [5827]
Defense and Corporate Counsel Foundation;
Federation of [★5827]
Defense Coun. of Am; Serbian Natl. [19358]
Defense Coun. Found; Natl. [18465]

A star before a book entry number signifies that the name is not listed separately, but is mentioned within the entry.

Defense Coun; U.S. Civil [★5563]
Defense Counsel Trial Acad. [★5499]
Defense Counsel Trial Acad. [★IO]
Defense Credit Union Coun. [1108], 601 Pennsylvania Ave. NW, South Bldg., Ste. 600, Washington, DC 20004-2601, (202)638-3950
Defense Directors; Natl. Assn. of State Civil [★5565]
Defense and Educ. Fund; Asian Amer. Legal [17095]
Defense and Educ. Fund; Minority Bus. Enterprise Legal [2763]
Defense and Educ. Fund; NOW Legal [★17546]
Defense des Enfants - Intl. [★IO]
Defense des Enfants Intl. - Canada [★IO]
Defense des Enfants Intl. - Liban [★IO]
Defense; Environmental [4562]
Defense Equip. Exhibitors Assn; Intl. [1343]
Defense Force Assn. of the U.S; State [★6105]
Defense Forum Found. [17376], 3014 Castle Rd., Falls Church, VA 22044, (703)534-4313
Defense Found; Natl. [★20767]
Defense of Free Enterprise; Center for the [17625]
Defense Fund; Animal Legal [11351]
Defense Fund; Canine [11373]
Defense Fund; Children's [11685]
Defense Fund; Disability Rights Educ. and [11940]
Defense Fund; Free Enterprise Legal [17630]
Defense Fund; Sierra Club Legal [★5690]
Defense Indus. Assn; Natl. [6089]
Defense Intel Alumni Assn. [18892], PO Box 489, Hamilton, VA 20159, (571)426-0098
Defense Lawyers in Criminal Cases; Natl. Assn. of [★5656]
Defense Lawyers; Natl. Assn. of Criminal [5656]
Defense League/Citizen's Emergency Defense Sys; Christian-Patriots [17263]
Defense League; Workers' [17159]
Defense Mfrs. Assn. of Great Britain [IO], Surrey, United Kingdom
Defense; Natl. Assn. of Supervisors, Dept. of [★5708]
Defense; Natl. Coll. for Criminal [★5657]
Defense Org; Jewish [17948]
Defense Org. Youth Movement; Jewish [17949]
Defense Orientation Conf. Assn. [18591], 9271 Old Keene Mill Rd., Ste. 200, Burke, VA 22015-4202, (703)451-1200
Defense Preparedness Assn; Natl. [★6089]
Defense Res. Inst. [6042], 150 N Michigan Ave., Ste. 300, Chicago, IL 60601, (312)795-1101
Defense and Rsrc. Center; Natl. Child Abuse [13367]
Defense and Space Indus. Associations; Coun. of [147]
Defense Study Group; Coast [10473]
Defense Supply Assn. [★6064]
Defense Trans. Assn; Natl. [6090]
Defense Trial Attorneys; Assn. of [5825]
Defensive Pistol Assn; Intl. [23718]
Defensive Spray Mfrs; Assn. of [3544]
Deferred Compensation Administrators; Natl. Assn. of Govt. [★2340]
Deficiency Assn; Acid Maltase [13535]
Deficiency Found; Immune [14936]
Deficit Reduction Coalition - Defunct.
Defined Contribution Administrators; Natl. Assn. of Govt. [2340]
DeForest Kelley; Fans of Leonard Nimoy and [24739]
DeForest Pioneers - Defunct.
Deformities; Debbie Fox Found. for Treatment of Cranio-Facial [★14061]
Degenerative Diseases; Independent Citizens Res. Found. for the Study of [14263]
Degenerative Diseases Res. Found. - Address unknown since 1995.
Degree of Honor Protective Assn. [19121], 400 Robert St. N, Ste. 1600, St. Paul, MN 55101-2029, (651)228-7600
Degree of Pocahontas, Improved Order of Red Men [19327], 4521 Speight Ave., Waco, TX 76711-1708, (254)756-1221
Dehydrated and Convenience Foods Coun. - Defunct.
Deidre Hall Fan Club - Defunct.

DeKalb Families in Action [★13269]
Del Gray Fan Club - Address unknown since 1989.
Del Reeves Fan Club - Defunct.
Del Shannon Appreciation Soc. [24873], PO Box 44201, Tacoma, WA 98444-0201
Delage Owners Club and Register - Address unknown since 1995.
Delahaye Club of America - Address unknown since 2000.
Delaine and Merino Record Assn; Amer. [5182]
Delaine Merino Sheep Assn; Black Top and Natl. [5199]
Delancey St. Found. [13018], 600 Embarcadero, San Francisco, CA 94107, (415)957-9800
Delaney Intl. Fan Club; Ethel [24886]
Delaware Valley; Scottish Historic and Res. Soc. of [10955]
Delbert McClinton Intl. Fan Club [24874], PO Box 218248, Nashville, TN 37221
Delegation Catholique pour la Cooperation [IO], Paris, France
Delegation de la Commn. europeenne en Republique Democratique du Congo [★IO]
Delegation of the European Commn. to Guyana and Suriname [★IO]
Delegation of the European Commn. to Guyana, Suriname, Trinidad and Tobago, Aruba and the Netherlands Antilles [IO], Georgetown, Guyana
Delegation of the European Commn. - Jamaica [★IO]
Delegation of the European Commn. - Jamaica, Belize, The Bahamas, Turks and Caicos Islands and the Cayman Islands [IO], Kingston, Jamaica
Delegation of the Finnish Academies of Sci. and Letters [IO], Helsinki, Finland
Delegation for Friendship Among Women [17528], 1630 Edgecumbe Rd., St. Paul, MN 55116
Delegations; Hospitality Comm. for United Nations [17895]
Delhi Mgt. Assn. [IO], New Delhi, India
Deli Assn; Intl. Cheese and [★1522]
Deli-Bakery Assn; Intl. Dairy- [1522]
Deli-Bakery Assn; Intl. Dairy- [★1522]
Deli/Prepared Meats Comm. - Defunct.
Deli Seminar; Intl. Cheese and [★1522]
Delinquency; Natl. Coun. on Crime and [11843]
Delius Soc. [IO], London, United Kingdom
Deliver the Dream [13019], 3223 NW 10th Terr., Ste. 602, Fort Lauderdale, FL 33309, (954)564-3512
Delivery; Depression After [12667]
Delivery Ser; Telegraph [★1494]
DeLorean Club Intl. - Address unknown since 2003.
DeLorean Motor Club of America - Defunct.
DeLorean Owners Assn. [21629], c/o Tony Hilger, Pres., 7 Hydrangea St., Ladera Ranch, CA 92694, (818)576-9932
Delphi Found. [24451], 2020 Pennsylvania Ave. NW, No. 355, Washington, DC 20006-1811, (202)558-2295
Delphi Intl. Prog. of World Learning [17881], 1015 18th St. NW, Ste. 1000, Washington, DC 20036-5272, (202)898-0950
Delphi International Program of World Learning [IO], Washington, DC, United States
Delphinid Res; Inst. for [★7261]
Delphinium Soc. [IO], Chippenham, United Kingdom
Delta Chi Sigma - Address unknown since 1995.
Delta Delta Delta [24682], 2331 Brookhollow Plaza Dr., PO Box 5987, Arlington, TX 76005-5987, (817)633-8001
Delta Dental Plans Assn. [14687]
Delta Eagles [★21400]
Delta Epsilon Sigma [24504], c/o Tina McCready, Exec. Asst., 11300 NE 2nd Ave., Barry Univ., Miami Shores, FL 33161
Delta Gamma [24683], PO Box 21397, Columbus, OH 43221-0397, (614)481-8169
Delta Gamma [IO], Columbus, OH, United States
Delta Gamma Pi Multicultural Sorority [24704], 4000 Vestal Pkwy., Binghamton, NY 13045
Delta Hospice Soc. [IO], Delta, BC, Canada
Delta Houseboat Rental Assn. [3367]
Delta Kappa - Address unknown since 1995.
Delta Kappa Alpha - Defunct.
Delta Kappa Epsilon [24623], PO Box 8360, Ann Arbor, MI 48107, (734)302-4210

Delta Kappa Phi [24478], 9 Mt. Hope St., Lowell, MA 01854, (978)455-1978
Delta Lambda Phi [★24624]
Delta Lambda Phi Natl. Social Fraternity [24624], 2020 Pennsylvania Ave. NW, No. 355, Washington, DC 20006-1811, (202)558-2295
Delta Ministry of Mississippi - Defunct.
Delta Mu Delta Honor Soc. [24418], 9217 Broadway Ave., Brookfield, IL 60513-1251, (708)485-8494
Delta Nu Alpha Trans. Fraternity [24722], PO Box 596, Nolensville, TN 37135, (615)776-1935
Delta Omega [24582], c/o Allison Foster, Exec. Sec., 1101 15th St. NW, Ste. 910, Washington, DC 20005, (202)296-1099
Delta Omega [★24564]
Delta Omicron [24550], c/o Julie Hensley, Exec. Sec., 910 Church St., Jefferson City, TN 37760, (865)471-6155
Delta Org. [★4435]
Delta Org. [★IO]
Delta Phi [24625], PO Box 81521, Athens, GA 30608-1521, (706)552-1444
Delta Phi Alpha [24493], c/o Dr. John F. Reynolds, Sec.-Treas., Natl. German Honor Soc., Longwood Univ., Grainger Bldg. 306, 201 High St., Farmville, VA 23909, (434)395-2145
Delta Phi Delta [★24527]
Delta Phi Delta - Defunct.
Delta Phi Epsilon [24684], 16A Worthington Dr., Maryland Heights, MO 63043, (314)275-2626
Delta Phi Epsilon, Professional Foreign Ser. Fraternity [24472], 3401 Prospect St. NW, Washington, DC 20007, (202)337-9702
Delta Phi Epsilon Professional Foreign Ser. Sorority [24473], c/o Delta Phi Epsilon Professional Foreign Ser. Fraternity, 3401 Prospect St. NW, Washington, DC 20007
Delta Phi Omega Sorority [24705], c/o Delta Phi Omega Natl. Coun., 2900 Oak Tree Ave., Apt. No. 8103, Norman, OK 73072
Delta Phi Upsilon [24431], PO Box 8275, Houston, TX 77288-8275, (832)767-6239
Delta Pi Epsilon [24426], c/o Dr. Robert B. Mitchell, Exec. Dir., PO Box 4340, Little Rock, AR 72214, (501)219-1866
Delta Psi [24626], PO Box 876, Ithaca, NY 14851-0876, (607)533-9994
Delta Psi Kappa [24573], PO Box 90264, Indianapolis, IN 46290, (317)334-8720
Delta Psi Omega [24444], c/o James Fisher, Natl. Bus. Mgr./Ed., Wabash Coll., Theater Dept., Crawfordsville, IN 47933, (765)361-6394
Delta Res. and Educational Foundation [★24597]
Delta Sigma Chi - Address unknown since 1995.
Delta Sigma Chi Sorority [24706], 114-75 226th St., Cambria Heights, NY 11411, (866)439-6489
Delta Sigma Delta [24438], 296 15th Ave., Nekoosa, WI 54457, (715)325-6320
Delta Sigma Delta [IO], Nekoosa, WI, United States
Delta Sigma Epsilon [★24686]
Delta Sigma Pi [24627], 330 S Campus Ave., Oxford, OH 45056-0230, (513)523-1907
Delta Sigma Pi Leadership Foundation [★24627]
Delta Sigma Rho [★24719]
Delta Sigma Rho - Tau Kappa Alpha [24719], c/o Dr. Frank M. Thompson, Co-Dir., Univ. of Alabama, Dept. of Commun. Stud., PO Box 870172, Tuscaloosa, AL 35487-0172, (205)348-6010
Delta Sigma Theta [24597], 1707 New Hampshire Ave. NW, Washington, DC 20009, (202)986-2400
Delta Soc. [16611], 875 124th Ave. NE, Ste. 101, Bellevue, WA 98005, (425)679-5500
Delta Soc. Australia [IO], Sydney, Australia
Delta Tau Alpha - Address unknown since 1995.
Delta Tau Kappa - Address unknown since 1999.
Delta Tau Lambda Sorority [24707], PO Box 7714, Ann Arbor, MI 48107
Delta Teen-Lift [13341], c/o Delta Sigma Theta Sorority, Inc., 1707 New Hampshire Ave. NW, Washington, DC 20009, (202)986-2400
Delta Theta Phi [24527], 38640 Butternut Ridge Rd., Elyria, OH 44035, (440)458-4381
Delta Theta Tau - Address unknown since 1995.
Delta Upsilon [24628], PO Box 68942, Indianapolis, IN 46268-0942, (317)875-8900

Reference to "IO" in place of a book number signifies that the association may be found in the 45th edition of International Organizations.

Delta Upsilon **[IO]**, Indianapolis, IN, United States
Delta Vee - Defunct.
Delta Waterfowl Found. **[5308]**, PO Box 3128, Bismarck, ND 58502, (888)987-3695
Delta Xi Nu Multicultural Sorority **[24708]**, PO Box 701402, Dallas, TX 75370
Delta Xi Phi Multicultural Sorority **[24685]**, PO Box 5218, Chicago, IL 60680-5218
Delta Zeta **[24686]**, 202 E Church St., Oxford, OH 45056, (513)523-7597
Deltiologists of Am. **[22905]**, PO Box 8, Norwood, PA 19074, (610)485-8572
DEMA, The Assn. for Input Tech. and Mgt. **[★6787]**
Demand-Side Mgt. Society **[★6942]**
Demand-Side Mgt. Society **[★IO]**
Dement Family Assn. - Defunct.
Dementia Advocacy and Support Network Intl. **[12638]**, PO Box 1645, Mariposa, CA 95338
Dementia Advocacy and Support Network Intl. **[IO]**, Mariposa, CA, United States
Dementia; Alzheimer Scotland-Action on **[IO]**
Dementia and Alzheimer's Assn. Tasmania - Hobart **[IO]**, Hobart, Australia
Dementia and Alzheimer's Assn. Tasmania - Launceston **[IO]**, Launceston, Australia
Demeter Assn. **[4644]**, PO Box 1390, Philomath, OR 97370, (541)929-7148
Demi Moore Fan Club - Defunct.
Demilitarization for Democracy **[17427]**
Demir Celik Ureticileri Dernegi **[★IO]**
Democracy
  Afghans for Civil Soc. **[17079]**
  African-Americans for Democracy **[16936]**
  Alpha-66 **[17363]**
  Amer. Rights at Work **[17968]**
  Americans for Informed Democracy **[5660]**
  Americans for Religious Liberty **[17090]**
  America's Development Found. **[17387]**
  Artists for a New South Africa **[11911]**
  Artists for a New South Africa **[IO]**
  Assn. of America's Young Democratic Azerbaijanian Friends **[IO]**
  Assn. for Union Democracy **[24113]**
  BOSPO **[IO]**
  Center for the Study of Democratic Societies **[IO]**
  Center for the Stud. of Democratic Societies **[17388]**
  Citizens for Consumer Justice **[18641]**
  Coalition for Democracy in Iran **[17389]**
  Coun. for a Community of Democracies **[5661]**
  Coun. for a Community of Democracies **[IO]**
  Declaration Found. **[5662]**
  Demilitarization for Democracy **[17427]**
  Democracy for Am. **[18291]**
  Democracy Intl. **[18292]**
  Democracy Proj. **[17390]**
  Demos **[5663]**
  Free the Eagle **[17629]**
  German Historical Inst. **[10110]**
  Global Exchange **[17391]**
  Global Exchange **[IO]**
  Hate Free Zone **[17392]**
  Inst. on Religion and Democracy **[17393]**
  Inst. of Statehood and Democracy **[IO]**
  Inter-American Conf. of Ministers of Labor **[IO]**
  Inter-American Conf. of Ministers of Labor **[17394]**
  Intl. Assn. of Democratic Lawyers **[IO]**
  International People's Democratic Uhuru Movement **[IO]**
  Intl. People's Democratic Uhuru Movement **[17395]**
  Intl. Republican Inst. - USA **[17396]**
  Intl. Republican Inst. - USA **[IO]**
  Internews Network **[18027]**
  Iran Freedom Found. **[17925]**
  Israel Democracy Institute **[IO]**
  Konrad Adenauer Found. - Zimbabwe **[IO]**
  Movement for an Independent and Democratic Cuba **[17367]**
  Natl. Alliance for Civic Educ. **[8091]**
  Natl. Endowment for Democracy **[17397]**
  Natl. Voice **[17076]**
  No Peace Without Justice **[18227]**
  Partners for Democratic Change **[17844]**
  Patriots for the Defense of Am. **[18186]**

  People's Decade of Human Rights Educ. **[17782]**
  Preamble Center **[5664]**
  Reaching Critical Will **[17436]**
  ReclaimDemocracy.org **[17398]**
  Sam Adams Alliance **[17673]**
  Spirit of Am. **[18488]**
  Team and Workplace Excellence Forum **[7555]**
  Teamsters for a Democratic Union **[24199]**
  Union for Democratic Communications **[17196]**
  U.S. Copts Assn. **[10192]**
  U.S.-Vietnam Trade Coun. **[17010]**
  Vietnamese Professionals Soc. **[19429]**
  Young Koreans United **[12485]**
Democracy; Alliance for **[18386]**
Democracy; Alliance for Cultural **[9536]**
Democracy for Am. **[18291]**, PO Box 1717, Burlington, VT 05402, (802)651-3200
Democracy; Ashburn Inst. for Global Stud. in Federalism and **[18308]**
Democracy; Assn. for Union **[24113]**
Democracy; Campus Coalition for **[★8490]**
Democracy; Center for Moral **[★17090]**
Democracy; Center for the Stud. of **[IO]**
Democracy; Center for Voting and **[18348]**
Democracy Fund - Defunct.
Democracy; Inst. on Religion and **[17393]**
Democracy Intl. **[18292]**, 4802 Montgomery Ln., Ste. 200, Bethesda, MD 20814, (301)961-1660
Democracy Intl. **[IO]**, Bethesda, MD, United States
Democracy in the Middle East; Youth Comm. for Peace and **[★18073]**
Democracy; Natl. Endowment for **[17397]**
Democracy Now in Ulster - Address unknown since 2002.
Democracy Proj. **[17390]**, c/o Winfield J.C. Myers, Dir., Campus Watch, 1500 Walnut St., Ste. 1050, Philadelphia, PA 19102
Democracy and Tech; Center for **[17167]**
Democracy and Workers Rights Center **[IO]**, Palestine, Israel
Democrat Intl; Christian **[IO]**
Democrat Union; Intl. **[IO]**
Democrat Union; Intl. Young **[IO]**
Democrat Youth Community of Europe **[IO]**, Svendborg, Denmark
Democratiaid Rhyddfrydol Cymru **[★IO]**
Democratic Action; Americans for **[18009]**
Democratic Alternative - Address unknown since 1990.
Democratic Candidate Fund - Address unknown since 1989.
Democratic Chairmen; Assn. of State **[★17399]**
Democratic Chairs; Assn. of State **[17399]**
Democratic Change; Partners for **[17844]**
Democratic Club of Am; Young **[★17412]**
Democratic Communications; Union for **[17196]**
Democratic Congressional Campaign Comm. **[17402]**, 430 S Capitol St. SE, Washington, DC 20003, (202)863-1500
Democratic Coun. on Ethnic Americans - Defunct.
Democratic Dimensions; New **[17409]**
Democratic Educ; Inst. for **[★17091]**
Democratic Fed; Arab Amer. **[★17003]**
Democratic Forum; Natl. **[★18428]**
Democratic Governors Assn. **[6274]**, 1401 K St. NW, Ste. 200, Washington, DC 20005, (202)772-5600
Democratic Governors Conf. **[★6274]**
Democratic Inst; Natl. **[★17870]**
Democratic Leadership Coun. **[17403]**, 600 Pennsylvania Ave. SE, Ste. 400, Washington, DC 20003-4350, (202)546-0007
Democratic Majority; Fund for a **[★17401]**
Democratic Natl. Comm. **[17404]**, 430 S Capitol St. SE, Washington, DC 20003, (202)863-8000
Democratic Natl. Comm. - Dept. of Constituent Coordination - Defunct.
Democratic Nursing Org. of South Africa **[IO]**, Pretoria, Republic of South Africa
Democratic Officials; Natl. Assn. of Latino Appointed **[★17706]**
Democratic Party
  21st Century Democrats **[5665]**
  Arab Amer. Leadership Coun. **[17003]**
  Assn. of State Democratic Chairs **[17399]**
  Coll. Democrats of Am. **[17400]**

  Comm. for a Democratic Majority **[17401]**
  Congressional Automotive Caucus **[17255]**
  Congressional Human Rights Caucus **[17755]**
  Constitutional Rights Found. **[17291]**
  Democratic Congressional Campaign Comm. **[17402]**
  Democratic Governors Assn. **[6274]**
  Democratic Leadership Coun. **[17403]**
  Democratic Natl. Comm. **[17404]**
  Democratic Senatorial Campaign Comm. **[17405]**
  Democrats Abroad **[17406]**
  Democrats Abroad **[IO]**
  Democrats for Life of Am. **[18549]**
  EMILY's List **[18294]**
  Free Cong. Political Action Comm. **[17268]**
  Inst. on Religion and Democracy **[17393]**
  Natl. Comm. for an Effective Cong. **[17252]**
  Natl. Democratic Club **[17407]**
  Natl. Fed. of Democratic Women **[17408]**
  New Democratic Dimensions **[17409]**
  Senate Tourism Caucus **[17259]**
  U.S. Assn. of Former Members of Cong. **[17253]**
  Woman's Natl. Democratic Club **[17410]**
  Women's Leadership Forum **[17411]**
  Young Democrats of Am. **[17412]**
Democratic Party of Am; Social- **[★18335]**
Democratic Party Comm. Abroad **[★17406]**
Democratic Party Comm. Abroad **[★17406]**
Democratic Party Comm. Abroad **[★IO]**
Democratic Party Comm. Abroad **[★IO]**
Democratic Party of Hong Kong **[IO]**, Hong Kong, People's Republic of China
Democratic Party of Japan **[IO]**, Tokyo, Japan
Democratic Party of the Peoples of Europe - European Free Alliance **[IO]**, Brussels, Belgium
Democratic Policy Commn. - Defunct.
Democratic Political Party 66 **[★IO]**
Democratic Progressive Party **[IO]**, Taipei, Taiwan
Democratic Rally **[IO]**, Nicosia, Cyprus
Democratic Renewal; Center for **[17098]**
Democratic and Secular Humanism; Coun. for **[★20085]**
Democratic Senatorial Campaign Comm. **[17405]**, PO Box 96047, Washington, DC 20077, (202)224-2447
Democratic Socialism
  Committees of Correspondence for Democracy and Socialism **[5666]**
  Intl. People's Democratic Uhuru Movement **[17395]**
  Youth for Intl. Socialism **[18663]**
Democratic Socialist Fed. **[★18335]**
Democratic Socialist Fed. **[★18306]**
Democratic Socialist Fed; Socialist Party- **[★18306]**
Democratic Socialist Organizing Comm. **[★18652]**
Democratic Socialist Organizing Comm. Youth Sect. **[★18662]**
Democratic Socialists of Am. **[18652]**, 75 Maiden Ln., Ste. 505, New York, NY 10038, (212)727-8610
Democratic Socialists of Am; Religion and Socialism Commn. of the **[18657]**
Democratic Socialists of Am. - Youth Sect. **[★18662]**
Democratic Societies; Center for the Stud. of **[17388]**
Democratic Study Group - Defunct.
Democratic Union; Teamsters for a **[24199]**
Democratic Women; Natl. Fed. of **[17408]**
Democratica; Cuba Independiente y **[★17367]**
Democrats for the '90s - Defunct.
Democrats Abroad **[17406]**, 430 S Capitol St. SE, Washington, DC 20003, (202)488-5073
Democrats Abroad **[IO]**, Washington, DC, United States
Democrats of Am; Coll. **[17400]**
Democrats of Am; Coll. Young **[★17400]**
Democrats of Am; Young **[17412]**
Democrats; Coll. **[★17400]**
Democrats for Life of Am. **[18549]**, 601 Pennsylvania Ave. NW, South Bldg., Ste. 900, Washington, DC 20004, (202)220-3066
Democrats for Social Credit **[★IO]**
Democrats, U.S.A; Social **[18306]**
Demography
  Amer. Inst. for Managing Diversity **[17369]**
  Carrying Capacity Network **[6859]**

A star before a book entry number signifies that the name is not listed separately, but is mentioned within the entry.

Comm. for Intl. Cooperation in Natl. Res. in De-
mography [IO]
Economic and Social Res. Coun. [IO]
European Assn. for Population Stud. [IO]
Intl. Assn. of French Language Demographers
[IO]
Intl. Commn. for Historical Demography [IO]
Intl. Union for the Sci. Stud. of Population [IO]
Latin Amer. and Caribbean Demographic Centre
[IO]
Population Assn. of Am. [6860]
Population Reference Bur. [6861]
Population Reference Bur. [IO]
Soc. for the Stud. of Social Biology [6862]
Union for African Population Stud. [IO]
DeMolay Endowment Fund [★IO]
DeMolay Endowment Fund [★19235]
DeMolay Intl. [19375], 10200 NW Ambassador Dr.,
Kansas City, MO 64153, (816)891-8333
DeMolay Intl. [IO], Kansas City, MO, United States
DeMolay; International Supreme Coun. Order of
[★IO]
DeMolay; International Supreme Coun. Order of
[★19375]
DeMolay; Order of [★19375]
DeMolay Ser. and Leadership Center [★19375]
DeMolay Ser. and Leadership Center [★IO]
Demolition Assn; Natl. [1043]
Demolition Contractors; Natl. Assn. of [★1043]
Demonbreun Soc; Timothy [★20741]
Demonstration Coun; Natl. Home [★8513]
Demos [5663], 220 Fifth Ave., 5th Fl., New York, NY
10001, (212)633-1405
Demos [IO], Moscow, Russia
Den Almindelige Danske Legeforening [★IO]
Den Danske Boghandlerforening [★IO]
Den Danske Forlaeggerforening [★IO]
Den Danske Historiske Forening [★IO]
Den norske Forfatterforening [★IO]
Den Nasjonale Forskningsetiske Komite for Medisin
[★IO]
Den Norske Forleggerforening [★IO]
Den Norske Revisorforening [★IO]
Den Norske Tannlegeforening [★IO]
Den Norske Turistforening [★IO]
Den Norske Veterinaerforening [★IO]
Dena Kaye Fan Club - Address unknown since
1999.
Dendrochronology
Tree-Ring Soc. [7101]
Dene Cultural Inst. [IO], Hay River, NT, Canada
Denim Coun. - Defunct.
Denison Soc. [20880], PO Box 42, Mystic, CT
06355-0042, (860)536-9248
Denmark
Danish Amer. Chamber of Commerce [24316]
North Amer. Danish Warmblood Assn. [4930]
Scandinavian Tourist Boards [24372]
Denmark-America Found. [IO], Copenhagen,
Denmark
Denmark Cheese Assn. - Defunct.
Dennis Brutus Defense Comm. [★17740]
Dennis Miller Fan Club - Address unknown since
2001.
Dennis Wilson; Friends of [24892]
Denominational Bible Prophecy Stud. Assn; Non-
[19528]
Denominational Executives of Christian Education -
Address unknown since 2003.
Denominational Ministry Strategy [★20561]
Densa - Address unknown since 1991.
Dental Accreditation; Commission on [★14121]
Dental Anthropology Assn. [14150], c/o Edward F.
Harris, Ed., Univ. of Tennessee, Coll. of Dentistry,
870 Union Ave., Memphis, TN 38163
Dental Anxiety and Phobia Assn. [IO], London,
United Kingdom
Dental Assistants Assn; Certifying Bd. of the Amer.
[★14151]
Dental Assisting Natl. Bd. [14151], 444 N Michigan
Ave., Ste. 900, Chicago, IL 60611, (312)642-3368
Dental Assn; Auxiliary to the Amer. [★14092]
Dental Assn. Intl; Holistic [★14156]
Dental Assn; Interstate [★14175]
Dental Assn; Natl. [★14131]

Dental Assn; Natl. Medical and [19305]
Dental Assn. of South Africa [★IO]
Dental Assn; Southern [★14131]
Dental Assn; Student Amer. [★8194]
Dental Assn; Tri-State [★14175]
Dental Assn; Women's Auxiliary to the Amer.
[★14092]
Dental Ceramics; Amer. Soc. of [★14110]
Dental Chamber of Macedonia [IO], Skopje, Mace-
donia
Dental Chiefs; Amer. Assn. of Hosp. [★14116]
Dental Consultants; Amer. Assn. of [2130]
Dental Dealers of America [1858]
Dental Editors; Amer. Assn. of [3077]
Dental Educ; Amer. Fund for [★8196]
Dental Educ; Fund for [★8196]
Dental Examiners; Natl. Assn. of [★14112]
Dental Gold Inst. - Defunct.
Dental Gp. Mgt. Assn. [15065], 2525 E Arizona Bilt-
more Cir., Ste. 127, Phoenix, AZ 85016, (602)381-
8980
Dental Guidance Coun. for Cerebral Palsy - Defunct.
Dental Hea; Amer. Fund for [★8196]
Dental Hea. Found. [IO], Dublin, Ireland
Dental Hea. Intl. [IO], Athens, GA, United States
Dental Hea. Intl. [14152], 847 S Milledge Ave.,
Athens, GA 30605, (706)546-1716
Dental Hosp. Bus. Associates; Medical [40]
Dental Hygiene
Acad. of Dental Materials [14084]
Acad. of Dentistry Intl. [14085]
Acad. of Gen. Dentistry [14086]
Acad. for Implants and Transplants [14087]
Acad. of Operative Dentistry [14089]
Acad. of Oral Dynamics [14090]
Amer. Acad. of Dental Gp. Practice [14094]
Amer. Acad. of Dental Practice Admin. [14095]
Amer. Acad. of Esthetic Dentistry [14096]
Amer. Acad. of Fixed Prosthodontics [14097]
Amer. Acad. of Gnathologic Orthopedics [14098]
Amer. Acad. of the History of Dentistry [14100]
Amer. Acad. of Implant Dentistry [14101]
Amer. Acad. of Oral and Maxillofacial Radiology
[14104]
Amer. Acad. of Oral Medicine [14105]
Amer. Acad. of Orofacial Pain [14106]
Amer. Acad. of Orthodontics for the Gen.
Practitioner [14107]
Amer. Acad. of Pediatric Dentistry [14108]
Amer. Acad. of Periodontology [14109]
Amer. Acad. of Restorative Dentistry [14110]
Amer. Assn. for Community Dental Programs
[14111]
Amer. Assn. of Dental Examiners [14112]
Amer. Assn. for Dental Res. [14113]
Amer. Assn. of Endodontists [14114]
Amer. Assn. for Functional Orthodontics [14115]
Amer. Assn. of Hosp. Dentists [14116]
Amer. Assn. of Oral and Maxillofacial Surgeons
[15732]
Amer. Assn. of Orthodontists [14117]
Amer. Assn. of Public Hea. Dentistry [14118]
Amer. Assn. of Women Dentists [14119]
Amer. Bd. of Dental Public Hea. [14120]
Amer. Bd. of Endodontics [14121]
Amer. Bd. of Family Dentistry [14122]
Amer. Bd. of Oral and Maxillofacial Surgery
[15733]
Amer. Bd. of Orthodontics [14124]
Amer. Bd. of Periodontology [14125]
Amer. Bd. of Prosthodontics [14126]
Amer. Coll. of Dentists [14128]
Amer. Coll. of Prosthodontists [14129]
Amer. Dental Assistants Assn. [14130]
Amer. Dental Assn. [14131]
Amer. Dental Hygienists' Assn. [14132]
Amer. Dental Soc. of Anesthesiology [14133]
Amer. Endodontic Soc. [14134]
Amer. Equilibration Soc. [14135]
Amer. Inst. of Oral Biology [14137]
Amer. Orthodontic Soc. [14138]
Amer. Prosthodontic Soc. [14139]
Amer. Soc. for Dental Aesthetics [14140]
Amer. Soc. of Forensic Odontology [14142]
Amer. Soc. of Master Dental Technologists
[14143]

Amer. Soc. for the Stud. of Orthodontics [14144]
Assn. for Continuing Dental Educ. [8195]
Assn. for Dental Educ. in Europe [IO]
Assn. of State and Territorial Dental Directors
[14146]
Canadian Dental Assistants' Assn. [IO]
Canadian Dental Hygienists' Assn. [IO]
Canadian Dental Protective Assn. [IO]
Christian Dental Soc. [14147]
Consumers for Dental Choice [11912]
Delta Dental Plans Assn. [14687]
Dental Anthropology Assn. [14150]
Dental Assisting Natl. Bd. [14151]
Dental Gp. Mgt. Assn. [15065]
Dental Hea. Intl. [14152]
European Fed. of Periodontology [IO]
Flying Dentists Assn. [14153]
Holistic Dental Assn. [14156]
Hong Kong Dental Hygienists' Assn. [IO]
Intl. Acad. of Myodontics [14159]
Intl. Assn. for Dental Res. [14161]
Intl. Assn. for Orthodontics [14162]
Intl. Coll. of Dentists [14163]
Intl. Cong. of Oral Implantologists [14165]
Intl. Fed. of Denturists [IO]
Intl. Fed. of Esthetic Dentistry [14167]
Irish Soc. of Periodontology [IO]
Japanese Soc. for Dental Hea. [IO]
Kuwait Dental Assn. [IO]
Medicaid/SCHIP Dental Assn. [14168]
Medical Dental Hosp. Bus. Associates [40]
Natl. Assn. of Dental Assistants [14169]
Natl. Assn. of Dental Labs. [14170]
Natl. Assn. of Dental Plans [14962]
Natl. Bd. for Certification in Dental Lab. Tech.
[14172]
Natl. Dental Assn. [14175]
Natl. Dental EDI Coun. [14176]
Natl. Dental Hygienists' Assn. [14177]
Natl. Denturist Assn. [14178]
Natl. Found. of Dentistry for the Handicapped
[14179]
Natl. Oral Hea. Info. CH [14181]
New Zealand Dental Hygienists Assn. [IO]
Nordic Inst. of Dental Materials [IO]
Norwegian Dental Assn. [IO]
Orthodontic Education and Res. Found. [14183]
Pierre Fauchard Acad. [14184]
Serbian Amer. Medical and Dental Soc. [14185]
Sigma Phi Alpha [24441]
Dental Hygienists Assn. of Australia - Australian
Capital Territory Br. [IO], Canberra, Australia
Dental Hygienists Assn. of Australia - New South
Wales Br. [IO], Sydney, Australia
Dental Hygienists Assn. of Australia - Queensland
Br. [IO], Brisbane, Australia
Dental Hygienists Assn. of Australia - South Australia
Br. [IO], Adelaide, Australia
Dental Hygienists Assn. of Australia - Tasmania Br.
[IO], Sandy Bay, Australia
Dental Hygienists Assn. of Australia - Victoria Br.
[IO], Melbourne, Australia
Dental Hygienists Assn. of Australia - Western
Australia Br. [IO], Bentley, Australia
Dental Hypnosis; British Soc. of Medical and [IO]
Dental Labs. Assn. [IO], Nottingham, United
Kingdom
Dental Labs; Natl. Assn. of Certified [★14170]
Dental Laboratory Conf. - Defunct.
Dental Lab. Inst. of Amer. [★14170]
Dental Mfrs. of Am. [★1859]
The Dental and Medical Soc. for the Stud. of
Hypnosis [★IO]
Dental and Oral Hea. Therapists' Assn. of Queen-
sland [IO], Nundah, Australia
Dental Plans Assn; Delta [14687]
Dental Plans; Natl. Assn. of [14962]
Dental Practitioners Assn. [IO], London, United
Kingdom
Dental Radiology; Amer. Acad. of [★14104]
Dental Schools; Amer. Assn. [★8193]
Dental Ser. Plans; Natl. Assn. of [★14687]
Dental Services Programs; Donated [★14179]
Dental Soc; Amer. Veterinary [16778]
Dental Soc; Christian Medical and [★20238]

Dental Soc; Global Hea. Outreach of the Christian Medical and [★20238]
Dental Tennis Assn; U.S. [23911]
Dental Therapy and Hygiene Assn. Western Australia [IO], Como, Australia
Dental Trade Alliance [1859], 2300 Clarendon Blvd., Ste. 1003, Arlington, VA 22201, (703)379-7755
Dental Trade Assn; Amer. [★1859]
Dentalbranchforeningen [★IO]
Dentistry
    Acad. of Dental Materials [14084]
    Acad. of Dentistry Intl. [14085]
    Acad. of Dentistry Intl. [IO]
    Acad. of Gen. Dentistry [14086]
    Acad. for Implants and Transplants [14087]
    Acad. of Laser Dentistry [14088]
    Acad. of Operative Dentistry [14089]
    Acad. of Oral Dynamics [14090]
    Acad. of Osseointegration [14091]
    Adhesion Soc. [6661]
    Albanian Dental Assn. [IO]
    Albanian Orthodontic Soc. [IO]
    Alliance of the Amer. Dental Assn. [14092]
    Alpha Omega Intl. Dental Fraternity [24437]
    Alpha Omega Intl. Dental Fraternity [IO]
    Amer. Acad. of Cosmetic Dentistry [14093]
    Amer. Acad. of Cosmetic Surgery [14037]
    Amer. Acad. of Dental Gp. Practice [14094]
    Amer. Acad. of Dental Practice Admin. [14095]
    Amer. Acad. of Esthetic Dentistry [14096]
    Amer. Acad. of Fixed Prosthodontics [14097]
    Amer. Acad. of Gnathologic Orthopedics [14098]
    Amer. Acad. of Gold Foil Operators [14099]
    Amer. Acad. of the History of Dentistry [14100]
    Amer. Acad. of Implant Dentistry [14101]
    Amer. Acad. of Implant Prosthodontics [14102]
    Amer. Acad. of Maxillofacial Prosthetics [14103]
    Amer. Acad. of Oral and Maxillofacial Radiology [14104]
    Amer. Acad. of Oral Medicine [14105]
    Amer. Acad. of Orofacial Pain [14106]
    Amer. Acad. of Orthodontics for the Gen. Practitioner [14107]
    Amer. Acad. of Pediatric Dentistry [14108]
    Amer. Acad. of Periodontology [14109]
    Amer. Acad. of Restorative Dentistry [14110]
    Amer. Assn. for Community Dental Programs [14111]
    Amer. Assn. of Dental Consultants [2130]
    Amer. Assn. of Dental Examiners [14112]
    Amer. Assn. for Dental Res. [14113]
    Amer. Assn. of Endodontists [14114]
    Amer. Assn. for Functional Orthodontics [14115]
    Amer. Assn. for the History of Medicine [10082]
    Amer. Assn. of Hosp. Dentists [14116]
    Amer. Assn. of Oral and Maxillofacial Surgeons [15732]
    Amer. Assn. of Orthodontists [14117]
    Amer. Assn. of Public Hea. Dentistry [14118]
    Amer. Assn. of Women Dentists [14119]
    Amer. Bd. of Dental Public Hea. [14120]
    Amer. Bd. of Endodontics [14121]
    Amer. Bd. of Family Dentistry [14122]
    Amer. Bd. of Operative Dentistry [14123]
    Amer. Bd. of Oral and Maxillofacial Surgery [15733]
    Amer. Bd. of Orthodontics [14124]
    Amer. Bd. of Periodontology [14125]
    Amer. Bd. of Prosthodontics [14126]
    Amer. Central European Dental Inst. [14127]
    Amer. Central European Dental Inst. [IO]
    Amer. Cleft Palate-Craniofacial Assn. [14055]
    Amer. Coll. of Dentists [14128]
    Amer. Coll. of Oral and Maxillofacial Surgeons [15734]
    Amer. Coll. of Prosthodontists [14129]
    Amer. Dental Assistants Assn. [14130]
    Amer. Dental Assn. [14131]
    Amer. Dental Educ. Assn. [8193]
    Amer. Dental Educ. Assn. [IO]
    Amer. Dental Hygienists' Assn. [14132]
    Amer. Dental Soc. of Anesthesiology [14133]
    Amer. Endodontic Soc. [14134]
    Amer. Equilibration Soc. [14135]
    Amer. Fracture Assn. [15756]

Amer. Independent Dentist's Assn. [14136]
Amer. Inst. of Oral Biology [14137]
Amer. Medical Technologists [15127]
Amer. Orthodontic Soc. [14138]
Amer. Prosthodontic Soc. [14139]
Amer. Soc. of Clinical Hypnosis [14921]
Amer. Soc. of Clinical Hypnosis - Educ. and Res. Found. [14922]
Amer. Soc. for Dental Aesthetics [14140]
American Society for Dental Aesthetics [IO]
Amer. Soc. of Dentist Anesthesiologists [14141]
Amer. Soc. of Forensic Odontology [14142]
Amer. Soc. of Master Dental Technologists [14143]
Amer. Soc. of Maxillofacial Surgeons [15735]
Amer. Soc. for the Stud. of Orthodontics [14144]
Amer. Student Dental Assn. [8194]
Amer. Veterinary Dental Soc. [16778]
Andorran Coll. of Dentists [IO]
Armenian Assn. of Orthodontists [IO]
Asian Acad. of Aesthetic Dentistry [IO]
Asian Pacific Endodontic Confed. [IO]
Asociacion Dental Mexicana [IO]
Asociatia Nationala Romana de Ortodontie [IO]
Assn. of Canadian Faculties of Dentistry [IO]
Assn. for Continuing Dental Educ. [IO]
Assn. for Continuing Dental Educ. [8195]
Assn. Dentaire Francaise [IO]
Assn. of Dental Dealers in Europe [IO]
Assn. of German Dental Mfrs. [IO]
Assn. of Managed Care Dentists [14145]
Assn. of Military Surgeons of the U.S. [15263]
Assn. Orthodontique Francaise des Specialistres en Orthopedie Dento-Faciale [IO]
Assn. of Philippine Orthodontists [IO]
Assn. of State and Territorial Dental Directors [14146]
Australasian Soc. of Oral Medicine and Toxicology [IO]
Australian Capital Territory Dental Therapists' Assn. [IO]
Australian Dental Assn. [IO]
Australian Dental and Oral Hea. Therapists' Assn. [IO]
Australian Dental Therapists' Assn. - Northern Territory [IO]
Australian Soc. of Orthodontists [IO]
Baltic Orthodontic Assn. [IO]
Bangladesh Dental Soc. [IO]
Barbados Dental Assn. [IO]
Bay Area Physicians for Human Rights [12218]
Bermuda Dental Assn. [IO]
Brazilian Soc. of Aesthetic Dentistry [IO]
British Dental Assn. [IO]
British Dental Practice Managers' Assn. [IO]
British Dental Trade Assn. [IO]
British Endodontic Soc. [IO]
British Orthodontic Soc. [IO]
British Soc. of Dental Hygiene and Therapy [IO]
British Soc. for Dental and Maxillofacial Radiology [IO]
British Soc. for Dental Res. [IO]
British Soc. of Periodontology [IO]
British Soc. for Restorative Dentistry [IO]
British Soc. for the Stud. of Prosthetic Dentistry [IO]
Bulgarian Orthodontic Soc. [IO]
Bulgarian Sci. Dental Assn. [IO]
Canadian Acad. of Endodontics [IO]
Canadian Acad. of Periodontology [IO]
Canadian Assn. for Dental Res. [IO]
Canadian Assn. of Orthodontists [IO]
Canadian Assn. of Public Hea. Dentistry [IO]
Canadian Dental Assn. [IO]
Canadian Dental Therapists Assn. [IO]
Catholic Medical Assn. [15996]
Chinese Orthodontic Soc. [IO]
Christian Dental Soc. [14147]
Christian Medical and Dental Associations [20238]
Clinical Dental Technicians Assn. [IO]
Clinical Res. Associates [14148]
Coll. of Diplomates of the Amer. Bd. of Orthodontics [14149]
Commonwealth Dental Assn. [IO]
Confed. of Dental Employers [IO]

Consejo Gen. de Colegios Oficiales de Odontologos y Estomatologos de Espana [IO]
Consumers for Dental Choice [11912]
Croatian Dental Soc. [IO]
Cyprus Orthodontic Soc. [IO]
Czech Dental Chamber [IO]
Czech Orthodontic Soc. [IO]
Danish Dental Assn. [IO]
Danish Dental Mfrs. [IO]
Danish Soc. of Periodontology [IO]
Delta Dental Plans Assn. [14687]
Delta Sigma Delta [24438]
Delta Sigma Delta [IO]
Dental Anthropology Assn. [14150]
Dental Assisting Natl. Bd. [14151]
Dental Chamber of Macedonia [IO]
Dental Gp. Mgt. Assn. [15065]
Dental Hea. Found. [IO]
Dental Hea. Intl. [IO]
Dental Hea. Intl. [14152]
Dental Hygienists Assn. of Australia - Australian Capital Territory Br. [IO]
Dental Hygienists Assn. of Australia - New South Wales Br. [IO]
Dental Hygienists Assn. of Australia - Queensland Br. [IO]
Dental Hygienists Assn. of Australia - South Australia Br. [IO]
Dental Hygienists Assn. of Australia - Tasmania Br. [IO]
Dental Hygienists Assn. of Australia - Victoria Br. [IO]
Dental Hygienists Assn. of Australia - Western Australia Br. [IO]
Dental Labs. Assn. [IO]
Dental and Oral Hea. Therapists' Assn. of Queensland [IO]
Dental Practitioners Assn. [IO]
Dental Therapy and Hygiene Assn. Western Australia [IO]
Dental Trade Alliance [1859]
Dentists Assn. of Argentina [IO]
Denturist Assn. of British Columbia [IO]
Denturist Assn. of Canada [IO]
Denturist Assn. of Ontario [IO]
Dutch Dental Assn. [IO]
Egyptian Orthodontic Soc. [IO]
Estonian Dentistry Students' Assn. [IO]
European Acad. of Paediatric Dentistry [IO]
European Assn. for Dental Public Hea. [IO]
European Fed. of Orthodontic Specialists Associations [IO]
European Org. for Caries Res. [IO]
European Orthodontic Soc. [IO]
European Prosthodontic Assn. [IO]
European Union of Dentists [IO]
Faculty of Dental Surgery [IO]
FDI World Dental Fed. [IO]
Fed. of the European Dental Indus. [IO]
The Floating Hosp. [14882]
Flying Dentists Assn. [14153]
Friends of the Natl. Inst. of Dental and Craniofacial Res. [14154]
Gen. Dental Coun. [IO]
German Dental Assn. [IO]
Global Outreach Mission [12525]
Greek Orthodontic Soc. [IO]
Hea. Ministries [20241]
Hellenic Amer. Dental Soc. [1150]
Hispanic Dental Assn. [14155]
Holistic Dental Assn. [14156]
Hong Kong Assn. of Dental Surgery Assistants [IO]
Hong Kong Dental Assn. [IO]
Hong Kong Soc. of Oral Implantology [IO]
Hong Kong Soc. of Orthodontists [IO]
Hungarian Assn. of Pedodontics and Orthodontics [IO]
Icelandic Orthodontic Soc. [IO]
INDENT, Dutch Dental Assn. [IO]
Independent Assn. of German Dentists [IO]
Indian Dental Assn. [IO]
Indian Dental Assn., U.S.A. [14157]
Interchurch Medical Assistance [20242]
Intl. Acad. of Gnathology-American Sect. [14158]

A star before a book entry number signifies that the name is not listed separately, but is mentioned within the entry.

Intl. Acad. of Myodontics [14159]
Intl. Acad. of Myodontics [IO]
Intl. Acad. of Oral Medicine and Toxicology [IO]
Intl. Acad. of Oral Medicine and Toxicology
   [14160]
Intl. Acad. of Periodontology [IO]
Intl. Acad. for Sports Dentistry [16481]
Intl. Anesthesia Res. Soc. [13684]
Intl. Assn. for Dental Res. [14161]
Intl. Assn. for Dental Res. [IO]
Intl. Assn. of Dental Students [IO]
Intl. Assn. for Orthodontics [IO]
Intl. Assn. for Orthodontics [14162]
Intl. Assn. of Paediatric Dentistry [IO]
Intl. Coll. of Dentists [IO]
Intl. Coll. of Dentists [14163]
Intl. Coll. of Prosthodontists [14164]
Intl. Coll. of Prosthodontists [IO]
Intl. Cong. of Oral Implantologists [IO]
Intl. Cong. of Oral Implantologists [14165]
Intl. Dental Hea. Found. [14166]
Intl. Dental Hea. Found. [IO]
Intl. Fed. of Esthetic Dentistry [IO]
Intl. Fed. of Esthetic Dentistry [IO]
Intl. Fed. of Esthetic Dentistry [14167]
Intl. Medical and Dental Hypnotherapy Assn.
   [14924]
Intl. Org. for Forensic Odonto-Stomatology [IO]
Irish Dental Assn. [IO]
Italian Dental Indus. Assn. [IO]
Japan Assn. of Adult Orthodontics [IO]
Japanese Orthodontic Soc. [IO]
Jaw Joints and Allied Musculo-Skeletal Disorders
   Found. [15773]
Kazakhstan Stomatological Assn. [IO]
Korean Assn. of Orthodontics [IO]
Lebanese Orthodontic Soc. [IO]
Lithuanian Republic Chamber of Odontologists
   [IO]
Malaysian Dental Assn. [IO]
Malignant Hyperthermia Assn. of the U.S. [14464]
MAP Intl. [20243]
Medicaid/SCHIP Dental Assn. [14168]
Natl. Assn. of Dental Assistants [14169]
Natl. Assn. of Dental Labs. [14170]
Natl. Assn. of Residents and Interns [15175]
Natl. Assn. of Seventh-day Adventist Dentists
   [14171]
Natl. Assn. of VA Physicians and Dentists [16007]
Natl. Bd. for Certification in Dental Lab. Tech.
   [14172]
Natl. Bd. for Certification in Dental Tech. [14173]
Natl. Dental Assistants Assn. [14174]
Natl. Dental Assn. [14175]
Natl. Dental EDI Coun. [14176]
Natl. Dental Hygienists' Assn. [14177]
Natl. Denturist Assn. [14178]
Natl. Found. of Dentistry for the Handicapped
   [14179]
Natl. Inst. of Dental and Craniofacial Res. [14180]
Natl. Oral Hea. Info. CH [14181]
Nepal Dental Assn. [IO]
New South Wales Dental Therapists' Assn. [IO]
New Zealand Assn. of Orthodontics [IO]
New Zealand Dental Assn. [IO]
New Zealand Dental Therapists Assn. [IO]
North Amer. Sikh Medical and Dental Assn.
   [16416]
Omicron Kappa Upsilon [24439]
Oral Hea. Am. [8196]
Org. for Safety and Asepsis Procedures [14182]
Org. of Teachers of Oral Diagnosis [8197]
Orthodontic Education and Res. Found. [14183]
Orthodontic Soc. of Ireland [IO]
Pierre Fauchard Acad. [14184]
Polish Orthodontic Soc. [IO]
Portuguese Soc. of Stomatology and Dental
   Medicine [IO]
Psi Omega [24440]
Romanian Dental Assn. of Private Practitioners
   [IO]
Royal Australasian Coll. of Dental Surgeons [IO]
Royal Coll. of Dentists of Canada [IO]
Russian Assn. of Orthodontists [IO]
Saskatchewan Dental Therapists Assn. [IO]

Scandinavian Soc. for Prosthetic Dentistry [IO]
Serbian Amer. Medical and Dental Soc. [14185]
Sigma Phi Alpha [24441]
Singapore Dental Assn. [IO]
Slovak Chamber of Dentists [IO]
Slovak Orthodontic Soc. [IO]
Slovenian Orthodontic Soc. [IO]
Smile Alliance Intl. [11721]
Sociedad Colombiana de Ortodoncia [IO]
Sociedad Espanola de Ortodoncia [IO]
Sociedade Portuguesa de Ortopedia Dento Facial
   [IO]
Societe Luxembourgeoise d'Orthodontie [IO]
Soc. for Clinical and Experimental Hypnosis
   [14927]
Soc. for Executive Leadership in Academic
   Medicine Intl. [15179]
South African Dental Assn. [IO]
South Australia Dental Therapists' Assn. [IO]
Special Care Dentistry [14186]
Stomatological Soc. of Greece [IO]
Student Natl. Dental Assn. [8198]
Swedish Assn. of Orthodontists [IO]
Swedish Dental Trade Assn. [IO]
Swiss Orthodontic Soc. [IO]
Tasmania Dental Therapists' Assn. [IO]
Thai Assn. of Orthodontists [IO]
Turkish Dental Assn. [IO]
Turkish Orthodontic Soc. [IO]
Ukrainian Assn. of Orthodontists [IO]
Ukrainian Medical Assn. of North Am. [15182]
Union of Amer. Physicians and Dentists [24092]
Union of Denturists in Finland [IO]
U.S. Dental Tennis Assn. [23911]
Univ. of Colorado School of Dentistry Alumni
   Assn. [18932]
Victoria Dental Therapists' Assn. [IO]
Western Society of Periodontology [IO]
Western Soc. of Periodontology [14187]
World Fed. of Orthodontists [14188]
World Fed. of Orthodontists [IO]
World Medical Mission [20245]
Xi Psi Phi [24442]
Dentistry; Acad. for Sports [★16481]
Dentistry; Amer. Acad. for Plastics Res. in [★14084]
Dentistry; Amer. Soc. for Advancement of Anesthesia
   in [★13673]
Dentistry; Amer. Soc. for Geriatric [★14186]
Dentistry; Fed. of Special Care Organizations in
   [★14186]
Dentistry Overseas [★15778]
Dentistry Overseas [★IO]
Dentistry for Persons with Disabilities; Acad. of
   [★14186]
Dentistry; Soc. for the Advancement of Anaesthesia
   in [IO]
Dentists; Amer. Assn. of Hosp. [14116]
Dentists; Amer. Assn. of Hosp. [★14186]
Dentists; Amer. Assn. of Public Hea. [★14118]
Dentists; Amer. Soc. of Retired [19330]
Dentists; Assn. of Amer. Women [★14119]
Dentists Assn. of Argentina [IO], Buenos Aires,
   Argentina
Dentists for Life [18550], PO Box 1350, Stafford, VA
   22555, (540)659-4171
Dentists; Natl. Assn. of VA Physicians and [16007]
Dentists; Union of Amer. Physicians and [24092]
Dentures; Amer. Acad. of Implant [★14101]
Denturist Assn. of British Columbia [IO], Surrey, BC,
   Canada
Denturist Assn. of Canada [IO], Winnipeg, MB,
   Canada
Denturist Assn. of Ontario [IO], Mississauga, ON,
   Canada
Denver Heart to Heart Fan Club; John [★24909]
Denver; Hearts in Harmony - World Family of John
   [24909]
Denver; Partners in Harmony, World Family of John
   [★24909]
Denver Strikers Matchcover Club [22625], 219 Car-
   roll Ave., Cheyenne, WY 82009, (307)632-7374
Departement des Metiers de la Constr. - Bur. Cana-
   dien [★IO]
Dept. of Audiovisual Instruction [★8551]
Dept. of Bus. Educ. of the Natl. Educ. Assn.
   [★8036]

Dept. of Civil, Human and Women's Rights, AFL-CIO
   [17110], 815 16th St. NW, Washington, DC 20006,
   (202)637-5000
Dept. of Civil Rights, AFL-CIO [★17110]
Dept. of Defense; Natl. Assn. of Supervisors,
   [★5708]
Dept. of Elementary School Principals, NEA [★9014]
Dept. of Environmental and Drug-Induced Pathology
   [★15867]
Dept. of Environmental and Drug-Induced Pathology
   [★IO]
Department of Environmental and Toxicologic
   Pathology [IO], Washington, DC, United States
Dept. of Environmental and Toxicologic Pathology
   [15867], c/o Armed Forces Inst. of Pathology, 6825
   16th St. NW, Washington, DC 20306-6000,
   (202)782-2125
Dept. of History and Records Mgt. Services of the
   Presbyterian Church (U.S.A.) [★10891]
Dept. of Home Economics (of NEA) [★8418]
Dept. of Humanitarian Affairs - Geneva [★IO]
Dept. for Intl. Development [IO], London, United
   Kingdom
Dept. of Org. and Field Services, AFL-CIO - Address
   unknown since 1999.
Dept. for Professional Employees, AFL-CIO [24173],
   1025 Vermont Ave., Ste. 1030, Washington, DC
   20005, (202)638-0320
Dept. of Rural and Agricultural Educ. [★9069]
Dept. of Rural Educ. [★9069]
Dept. of School Nurses/NEA [★15501]
Dept. of School Superintendents of the Natl. Educ.
   Assn. [★7882]
Department of Social Development and World Peace
   [★19613]
Department of Social Development and World Peace
   [★IO]
Dept. of Socio-Economic Development - Caritas
   Ghana [IO], Accra, Ghana
Dept. of State Correspondents Assn. - Address
   unknown since 1999.
Dept. Store Union; Retail, Wholesale and [24182]
Dept. of Superintendents of the Natl. Educ. Assn.
   [★7882]
Dept. of Supervision and Curriculum Development
   (of NEA) [★8178]
Dept. of Supervision and Curriculum Development
   (of NEA) [★IO]
Dept. of Supervisors and Directors of Instruction (of
   NEA) [★IO]
Dept. of Supervisors and Directors of Instruction (of
   NEA) [★8178]
Dept. of Tourism and Hea. Resorts [★24363]
Dept. of United Church Women of the Natl. Coun. of
   Churches [★20618]
Dept. of Visual Instruction [★8551]
Dept. of Vocational Education - Defunct.
Department of Women's Ministries of the Advent.
   Christian Conference [★19443]
Departments of English in Amer. Colleges and
   Universities; Assn. of [★8374]
Departments of English; Assn. of [8374]
Departments of Foreign Languages; Assn. of [8728]
Dependence; Amer. Assn. for the Treatment of
   Opioid [16499]
Dependencies Philatelic Soc; Sta. Helena and
   [★22866]
Depew Family Assn. - Defunct.
Deportation Campaigns; Natl. Coalition of Anti- [IO]
Deposit Assn; The Amer. Safe [460]
Depreciation Professionals; Soc. of [52]
Depression After Delivery [12667], 91 E Somerset
   St., Ste. C, Raritan, NJ 08869, (908)541-9712
Depression Alliance [IO], London, United Kingdom
Depression Awareness; Families for [15198]
Depression and Bipolar Support Alliance [15196],
   730 N Franklin, Ste. 501, Chicago, IL 60610-7225,
   (312)642-0049
Depression; Depressives Anonymous: Recovery
   From [12547]
Depression Glass Assn; Natl. [22562]
Depression and Related Affective Disorders Assn.
   [15197], c/o Org. Guidance Gp., LLC, 11616 Bed-
   fordshire Ave., Potomac, MD 20854, (301)294-
   6266

Reference to "IO" in place of a book number signifies that the association may be found in the 45th edition of International Organizations.

Depressive and Depressive Assn; Manic [★15196]
Depressive Illness; Natl. Found. for [15225]
Depressive and Manic Depressive Assn; Natl. [★15196]
Depressives Anonymous: Recovery From Depression [12547]
Deputy Educators Against Narcotics - Defunct.
Deputy Sheriffs' Assn; Amer. [5961]
DERA Intl. [★5561]
Derby; Intl. Soap Box [23770]
Derby Rallies; Natl. [23771]
Derbyshire Chamber and Bus. Link [IO], Chesterfield, United Kingdom
Derbyshire Conservation Volunteers [IO], Derby, United Kingdom
Derbyshire England Red Cap Club of America - Defunct.
Derechos Iguales para la Mujer Argentina [★IO]
Derivatives Assn; Intl. Swaps and [2335]
Derleth Soc; August [9634]
Dermatitis; European Soc. of Contact [IO]
Dermatologic Surgery; Amer. Soc. for [14196]
Dermatological Retailers; Amer. Soc. of [86]
Dermatological Soc. of Iceland [IO], Kopavogur, Iceland
Dermatological Soc. of Malaysia [IO], Kuala Lumpur, Malaysia
Dermatological Soc. of Mauritius [IO], Port Louis, Mauritius
Dermatological Soc. of Singapore [IO], Singapore, Singapore
Dermatological Soc. of South Africa [IO], Johannesburg, Republic of South Africa
Dermatological Soc. of Thailand [IO], Bangkok, Thailand
Dermatology
  Accio Psoriasi [IO]
  Algerian Soc. of Dermatology [IO]
  Amer. Acad. of Dermatology [IO]
  Amer. Acad. of Dermatology [14189]
  Amer. Bd. of Dermatology [14190]
  Amer. Coll. of Veterinary Dermatology [16765]
  Amer. Contact Dermatitis Soc. [14191]
  Amer. Dermatological Assn. [14192]
  Amer. Hair Loss Coun. [14193]
  Amer. Osteopathic Coll. of Dermatology [14194]
  Amer. Skin Assn. [14195]
  Amer. Soc. for Dermatologic Surgery [14196]
  Amer. Soc. of Dermatology [14197]
  Amer. Soc. of Dermatopathology [14198]
  Argentine Soc. of Dermatology [IO]
  Argentinian Assn. of Dermatology [IO]
  Asian Dermatological Assn. [IO]
  Asociacion Guatemalteca de Dermatologia [IO]
  Assn. of Bangkok Alumni of Dermatology - Pakistan [IO]
  Assn. of Dermato-Venerologists of Latvia [IO]
  Assn. of Italian Clinical Dermatologists [IO]
  Assn. of Italian Hosp. Dermatologists [IO]
  Assn. Pour La Lutte Contre Le Psoriasis [IO]
  Associazione Nazionale per la tutela del Malato di Psoriasi e Vitiligine [IO]
  Australasian Coll. of Dermatologists [IO]
  Austrian Soc. of Dermatology and Venereology [IO]
  Brazilian Soc. of Dermatology [IO]
  British Assn. of Dermatologists [IO]
  British Photodermatology Gp. [IO]
  Canadian Dermatology Assn. [IO]
  Chilean Soc. of Dermatology and Venereology [IO]
  Chinese Dermatological Soc., Taipei [IO]
  Circulo Dermatologico del Peru [IO]
  Colombian Assn. of Dermatology [IO]
  Cote d'Ivoire Soc. of Dermatology and Venereology [IO]
  Croatian Dermatovenerological Soc. of the Croatian Medical Assn. [IO]
  Cyprus Soc. of Dermatology and Venerology [IO]
  Danish Dermatological Soc. [IO]
  Dermatological Soc. of Iceland [IO]
  Dermatological Soc. of Malaysia [IO]
  Dermatological Soc. of Mauritius [IO]
  Dermatological Soc. of Singapore [IO]
  Dermatological Soc. of South Africa [IO]
  Dermatological Soc. of Thailand [IO]
  Dermatology Found. [14199]
  Dermatology Nurses' Assn. [15476]
  Dermatovenereology Assn. of Turkey [IO]
  Dystrophic Epidermolysis Bullosa Res. Assn. of Am. [14200]
  Ecuadorian Soc. of Dermatology [IO]
  Eczema Assn. of Australasia [IO]
  European Acad. of Dermatology and Venereology [IO]
  European Nail Soc. [IO]
  European Soc. of Contact Dermatitis [IO]
  European Soc. for Dermatological Res. [IO]
  European Soc. for Dermatology and Psychiatry [IO]
  European Soc. for Laser Dermatology [IO]
  European Soc. for Photodynamic Therapy in Dermatology [IO]
  European Women's Dermatologic Soc. [IO]
  Finnish Psoriasis Assn. [IO]
  Found. for Ichthyosis and Related Skin Types [14201]
  French Soc. of Dermatology [IO]
  German Dermatological Soc. [IO]
  Hellenic Assn. of Dermatology and Venereology [IO]
  Hellenic Soc. for Dermatologic Surgery [IO]
  History of Dermatology Soc. [10115]
  Hong Kong Soc. of Dermatology and Venereology [IO]
  Hungarian Dermatological Soc. [IO]
  Ibero-Latin Amer. Coll. of Dermatology [IO]
  Indonesian Soc. of Dermatology and Venereology [IO]
  Intl. Acad. of Cosmetic Dermatology [IO]
  Intl. Acad. of Cosmetic Dermatology [14202]
  Intl. Fed. of Psoriasis Associations [14203]
  Intl. Fed. of Psoriasis Associations [IO]
  Intl. Found. for Dermatology [IO]
  Intl. Scleroderma Network [16387]
  Intl. Soc. for Biophysics and Imaging of the Skin [IO]
  Intl. Soc. for Dermatologic Surgery [IO]
  Intl. Soc. for Dermatologic Surgery [14204]
  Intl. Soc. of Dermatology [14205]
  Intl. Soc. of Dermatology [IO]
  Intl. Soc. of Veterinary Dermatopathology [16795]
  Irish Assn. of Dermatologists [IO]
  Irish Raynaud's and Scleroderma Soc. [IO]
  Israel Psoriasis Assn. [IO]
  Israel Soc. of Dermatology and Venereology [IO]
  Italian Soc. of Dermatology [IO]
  Italian Soc. of Surgical and Oncological Dermatology [IO]
  Japanese Dermatological Assn. [IO]
  Korean Dermatological Assn. [IO]
  Kuwait Soc. of Dermatologists [IO]
  Lebanese Dermatological Soc. [IO]
  Macedonian Dermatovenerologic Soc. [IO]
  Maltese Assn. of Dermatology and Venereology [IO]
  Medical Dermatology Soc. [14206]
  Mexican Acad. of Dermatology [IO]
  Mexican Soc. of Dermatologic Surgery and Oncology [IO]
  Mexican Soc. of Dermatology [IO]
  Moroccan Soc. of Dermatology [IO]
  Natl. Assn. for Pseudoxanthoma Elasticum [14207]
  Natl. Eczema Assn. [14208]
  Natl. Eczema Soc. [IO]
  Natl. Incontinentia Pigmenti Found. [14470]
  Natl. Psoriasis Foundation/USA [14209]
  Natl. Rosacea Soc. [14210]
  Natl. Vitiligo Found. [14211]
  Nevus Network [16545]
  New Zealand Dermatological Soc. [IO]
  North Amer. Clinical Dermatologic Soc. [IO]
  North Amer. Clinical Dermatologic Soc. [14212]
  Norwegian Dermatological Soc. [IO]
  Norwegian Psoriasis Assn. [IO]
  Norwegian Soc. of Dermatology [IO]
  Pacific Dermatologic Assn. [IO]
  Pacific Dermatologic Assn. [14213]
  Pakistan Assn. of Dermatologists [IO]
  Paraguayan Soc. of Dermatology [IO]
  Peruvian Soc. of Dermatology [IO]
  Philippine Dermatological Soc. [IO]
  Polish Assn. of Dermatology [IO]
  Portuguese Soc. of Dermatology and Venereology [IO]
  Psoriasis Assn. [IO]
  Psoriasis Assn. of Kenya [IO]
  Psoriasis Assn. of New Zealand [IO]
  Psoriasis Soc. of Canada [IO]
  Psoriasis Soc. of Lithuania [IO]
  Romanian Dermatological Soc. [IO]
  Salvadorian Soc. of Dermatology [IO]
  Saudi Soc. of Dermatology and Venereology [IO]
  Slovak Dermatovenereological Soc. [IO]
  Sociedad Venezolana de Dermatologia [IO]
  Soc. of Dermatologists, Venereologists and Leprologists of Nepal [IO]
  Soc. for Investigative Dermatology [14214]
  Soc. for Pediatric Dermatology [14215]
  Sri Lanka Assn. of Dermatologists [IO]
  Swedish Psoriasis Assn. [IO]
  Syrian Arab Soc. of Dermatology [IO]
  Tunisian Soc. of Dermatology and Venereology [IO]
  Turkish Soc. of Dermatology [IO]
  Turkish Soc. of Dermatopathology [IO]
  Ukrainian Assn. of Dermatologists, Venereologists and Cosmetologists [IO]
  Uruguayan Dermatological Soc. [IO]
  Women's Dermatologic Soc. [IO]
  Women's Dermatologic Soc. [14216]
Dermatology; Amer. Coll. of Veterinary [16765]
Dermatology Found. [14199], 1560 Sherman Ave., Ste. 870, Evanston, IL 60201-4808, (847)328-2256
Dermatology Nurses' Assn. [15476], E Holly Ave., PO Box 56, Pitman, NJ 08071-0056, (856)256-2330
Dermatology Physician Assistants; Soc. of [15978]
Dermatology Soc; History of [10115]
Dermatology and Syphilology; Amer. Acad. of [★14189]
Dermatopathology; Amer. Soc. of [14198]
Dermatovenereology Assn. of Turkey [IO], Izmir, Turkey
Derrick Clubs; Assn. of Desk and [2917]
Derrick Clubs of North Am; Assn. of Desk and [★2917]
Derricks Coun; Mfrs. of Aerial Devices and Digger- [2038]
Derrike Cope Fan Club [24783], c/o Ken Fleming, Pres., 750 Cartref Rd., Etters, PA 17319
Derwent Valley Horseriders Assn. [IO], Hobart, Australia
DES Action Canada [IO], Montreal, QC, Canada
DES Action, Natl. [★13821]
DES Action, U.S.A. [13821], 158 S Stanwood Rd., Columbus, OH 43209, (800)337-9288
DES Registry - Defunct.
DeSales Secular Inst. [★19716]
DeSales Secular Inst. [★IO]
Desalination and Environmental Assn; Intl. [★7831]
Desalting Assn; Amer. [★7824]
Desalting Assn; Southeast [5283]
Desarrollo; Banco Interamericano de [★17460]
Descendants of 1774 - Address unknown since 1994.
Descendants of the Ancient and Honorable Artillery Company; Natl. Soc. Women [20749]
Descendants; Assn. of Blauvelt [20785]
Descendants of the Colonial Clergy; Soc. of the [20760]
Descendants of Colonial Physicians and Chirurgiens; Order of [20752]
Descendants of Colonial Tavern Keepers; Flagon and Trencher - [20737]
Descendants of Daniel Cole Soc. [20881]
Descendants of Defenders of Baltimore; Assn. of [★21354]
Descendants of Early Quakers; Natl. Soc. [21134]
Descendants of Founders of New Jersey [20736], 816 Grove St., Point Pleasant Beach, NJ 08742
Descendants of the Illegitimate Sons and Daughters of the Kings of Britain - Address unknown since 1999.

A star before a book entry number signifies that the name is not listed separately, but is mentioned within the entry.

Descendants of Lords of the Maryland Manors; Natl. Soc. of [20747]

Descendants of the Loyalists and Patriots of the Amer. Revolution; Hereditary Order of [20673]

Descendants of Mexican War Veterans [21183], PO Box 830482, Richardson, TX 75083-0482

Descendants of the New Jersey Settlers - Defunct.

Descendants of Schwenkfeldian Exiles - Address unknown since 1995.

Descendants of the Schwenkfeldian Exiles; Soc. of the [21244]

Descendants of the Shoah [IO], Caulfield, Australia

Descendants of the Signers of the Declaration of Independence [20671], c/o Donald Crosset Ward, Pres. Gen., 15 Wards Way, Boyertown, PA 19512

Descendants; Soc. of Richmond County [21152]

Descendants of Washington's Army at Valley Forge; Soc. of the [20678]

Descendents of Richard Risley [★21035]

Descendents of Richard Risley [★IO]

Desenvolvimento; Banco Interamericano de [★17460]

Desert Alliance; Intl. Sonoran [4582]

Desert Bighorn Coun. - Address unknown since 1994.

Desert Botanical Garden [6633], 1201 N Galvin Pkwy., Phoenix, AZ 85008, (480)941-1225

Desert Experience; Lenten [★18161]

Desert Experience; Nevada [18161]

Desert Fishes Coun. [4388], PO Box 337, Bishop, CA 93515, (760)872-8751

Desert Fishes Coun. [IO], Bishop, CA, United States

Desert Fund; Turkhana [★12883]

Desert German Shorthaired Pointer Club [22256], c/o Doris Schoenfelder, Sec., 36633 N 21st St., Desert Hills, AZ 85086, (480)488-4687

Desert Lynx Cat Assn; Intl. [4207]

Desert Occupancy; Inst. for Sustainable [4510]

Desert Protective Coun. [4389], PO Box 3635, San Diego, CA 92163-1635, (619)342-5524

Desert Protective Coun. Foundation [★4389]

Desert Res. Inst; Chihuahuan [4374]

Desert Research; Jacob Blaustein Inst. for [★8673]

Desert Storm Veterans Assn. [21298], 2425 Wilson Blvd., Arlington, VA 22201, (703)604-6565

Desert Tortoise Coun. [5309], PO Box 3273, Beaumont, CA 92223

Desert Tortoise Preserve Comm. [4390], 4067 Mission Inn Ave., Riverside, CA 92501, (951)683-3872

Design
Accademia d'Arte e Design - Leonetto Cappiello [IO]
Amer. Assn. of Human Design Practitioners [1151]
Amer. Assn. of Webmasters [896]
Amer. Design Drafting Assn. [7152]
Amer. Floorcovering Alliance [2250]
Amer. Soc. of Furniture Designers [1691]
Amer. Soc. of Interior Designers [2251]
Amer. Tapestry Alliance [9416]
Aprovecho Res. Center [16993]
Architecture for Humanity [11761]
Assn. of Feng Shui Consultants [IO]
Assn. of Independent Commercial Producers [90]
Broadcast Designer's Assn. [554]
Bur. of European Designers Associations [IO]
Carpet Cushion Coun. [2253]
Carpet and Rug Inst. [2254]
Center for Design Planning [5588]
Contractors Co-Op Coun. [2256]
Coun. of Fashion Designers of Am. [230]
Design Bus. Assn. [IO]
Design Forum Finland [IO]
Design History Soc. [IO]
Design and Indus. Assn. [IO]
The Designer Cat Assn. [21906]
Designers Inst. of New Zealand [IO]
Ecological Landscaping Assn. [4989]
Environmental Design Res. Assn. [5464]
Faculty of Royal Designers for Indus. [IO]
Feng Shui Inst. of Am. [9904]
Feng Shui Soc. [IO]
Found. for Design Integrity [IO]
Found. for Design Integrity [1152]
German Design Coun. [IO]
Home Fashion Products Assn. [2258]

Inst. of Designers in Ireland [IO]

Interaction Design Assn. [IO]

Interaction Design Assn. [6863]

Interior Design Soc. [2260]

Intl. Assn. of Lighting Designers [2262]

Intl. Assn. of Webmasters and Designers [888]

Intl. Building Performance Simulation Assn. [6652]

Intl. Design Conf. in Aspen [9905]

Intl. Design Guild [2263]

Intl. Feng Shui Guild [9906]

Intl. Feng Shui Guild [IO]

Intl. Furnishings and Design Assn. [2264]

Intl. Guild of Glass Artists [299]

Intl. Jewelry Design Guild [2368]

Jute Carpet Backing Coun. and Burlap and Jute Assn. [2266]

Kitchen Cabinet Mfrs. Assn. [2267]

Natl. Assn. of Church Design Builders [831]

Natl. Assn. of Fashion and Accessory Designers [246]

Natl. Assn. of Scale Aeromodelers [22651]

Natl. Assn. of Visual Merchandisers [1153]

Natl. Coun. for Interior Design Qualification [2269]

Natl. Guild of Professional Paperhangers [2270]

Natl. Kitchen and Bath Assn. [2271]

Natl. Technical Services Assn. [7753]

Org. of Black Designers [9907]

Paint and Decorating Retailers Assn. [2274]

Planning and Visual Educ. Partnership [3426]

Proj. EverGreen [4991]

Set Decorators Soc. of Am. [2276]

Soc. of Boat and Yacht Designers [1154]

Soc. of Certified Kitchen Designers [2277]

Soc. for Design Admin. [6481]

Special Interest Gp. on Data Communications of the Assn. for Computing Machinery [6804]

U.S. Faceters Guild [1121]

Wallcoverings Assn. [2278]

Window Covering Mfrs. Assn. [2279]

Design Alliance; Rice [6479]

Design Alumni Assn; Center for Creative Stud. - Coll. of Art and [★18888]

Design; Amer. Inst. of Building [6464]

Design and Artists Copyright Soc. [IO], London, United Kingdom

Design; Assn. for Bridge Constr. and [6471]

Design; Assn. for the Mgt. of Org. [★2510]

Design Assn; Surface [3800]

Design Austria [IO], Vienna, Austria

Design Automation Consortium; Electronic [6911]

Design Automation; Special Interest Gp. for [6749]

Design; Beaux-Arts Inst. of [★7963]

Design-Build Inst. of Am. [617], 1100 H St. NW, Ste. 500, Washington, DC 20005-5476, (202)682-0110

Design Bus. Assn. [IO], London, United Kingdom

Design Coun. [IO], London, United Kingdom

Design and Drafting; Amer. Inst. for [★7152]

Design Drafting Assn; Amer. [7152]

Design and Drafting Mgt. Coun. - Defunct.

Design Educ. Assn; Indus. [★7180]

Design Educ. Foundation; Interior [★8585]

Design Educ. Res; Found. for Interior [★8584]

Design Educators Coun; Interior [8585]

Design Firms; Assn. of Professional [1806]

Design Forum Finland [IO], Helsinki, Finland

Design Forum; Org. [2510]

Design History Soc. [IO], Nottingham, United Kingdom

Design and Indus. Assn. [IO], Birmingham, United Kingdom

Design Indus. Found. for AIDS [★11328]

Design Indus. Found. Fighting AIDS [11328], 200 Lexington Ave., Ste. 1016, New York, NY 10016, (212)727-3100

Design Installation Assn; Custom Electronic [3548]

Design; Inst. for Urban [6475]

Design Intl. [★1811]

Design Intl. [★IO]

Design Intl; Women in [★1811]

Design Mgt. Inst. [1807], 29 Temple Pl., 2nd Fl., Boston, MA 02111-1350, (617)338-6380

Design and Mgt. Resources; Center for [★1807]

Design; Natl. Assn. of Schools of Art and [7978]

Design Off. Consortium [★IO]

Design Planning; Center for [5588]

Design Res. Assn; Environmental [5464]

Design; Soc. for Environmental Graphic [1809]

Design Soc; Interior [2260]

Design; Soc. for News [3163]

Design; Soc. of Newspaper [★3163]

Design and Tech. Assn. [IO], Warwick, United Kingdom

The Designer Cat Assn. [21906], c/o Nina Adkins, 916 CR 702, Cleburne, TX 76031

Designer Shoe Guild - Address unknown since 1995.

Designers of Am; Charted [★2833]

Designers of Am; Coun. of Fashion [230]

Designers; Amer. Inst. of Floral [1490]

Designers; Amer. Soc. of Bookplate Collectors and [21965]

Designers; Amer. Soc. of Furniture [1691]

Designers; Amer. Soc. of Interior [2251]

Designers and Art Directors Assn. of the U.K. [★IO]

Designers Assn. of Am; Custom Tailors and [231]

Designers Assn; Charted [2833]

Designers Assn. Intl; Broadcast [★554]

Designers Assn; United [★6464]

Designers Assn; Univ. and Coll. [8572]

Designers; Assn. of Univ. Interior [2252]

Designers; Coun. for Fed. Interior Designers; Inst. of Bus. [★2265]

Designers Guild; Professional Knitwear [★228]

Designers Inst; Indus. [★7180]

Designers Inst. of New Zealand [IO], Auckland, New Zealand

Designers; Intl. Assn. of Webmasters and [888]

Designers; Natl. Assn. of Clothing [★241]

Designers; Natl. Assn. of Fashion and Accessory [246]

Designers; Natl. Soc. of Interior [★2251]

Designers/Planners for Social Responsibility; Architects/ [18142]

Designers and Producers Assn; Exhibit [1337]

Designers Soc. of Am; Indus. [7180]

Designers; Soc. of Certified Kitchen [2277]

Designers; Soc. of Craft [1915]

Designers; Soc. of Environmental Graphic [★1809]

Designers; Soc. of Piping Engineers and [7045]

Designers; Soc. of Publication [1810]

Designers; Soc. of Small Craft [2593]

Designs for Change [9035], 814 S Western Ave., Chicago, IL 60612, (312)236-7252

Desiree Coleman Fan Club - Address unknown since 2006.

Desk and Derrick Clubs; Assn. of [2917]

Desk and Derrick Clubs of North Am; Assn. of [★2917]

Desk and Derrick Educational Trust [★2917]

Desk Owners Soc; Wooton [22131]

Desktop Publishing Applications Assn. - Address unknown since 1995.

DeSoto Club of Am. [21630], 403 S Thorton, Richmond, MO 64085, (816)470-3048

DeSoto Club; Buckeye [★21731]

DeSoto Club; Natl. [21731]

Despatch Assn. [IO], King's Lynn, United Kingdom

Destination Marketing Assn. Intl. [IO], Washington, DC, United States

Destination Marketing Assn. Intl. [2678], 2025 M St. NW, Ste. 500, Washington, DC 20036, (202)296-7888

Destiny Res. Found. - Defunct.

Destroyer Battalion Assn; 704th Tank [21383]

Destroyer Veterans; Tin Can Sailors - The Natl. Assn. of [21220]

Desuperheating Mfg; Assn. of Refrigerant and [1877]

Det Danske Bibelselskab [★IO]

Det Internationale Rehabiliteringsrad for Torturofre [★IO]

Det Kongelige Norske Videnskabers Selskabs [★IO]

Det Norske Bibelselskap [★IO]

Det Norske Selskab; Norwegian Club/ [19292]

Det Norske Videnskaps-Akademi [★IO]

Det Udenrigspolitiske Selskab [★IO]

Detachable Container Assn. - Defunct.

Detective Assn; U.S. Private Security and [★2323]

Detector Dog Assn; Natl. Narcotic [5997]

Detention Assn; Natl. Juvenile [11882]

Detergent
Assn. of Detergent Zeolite Producers [IO]

Reference to "IO" in place of a book number signifies that the association may be found in the 45th edition of International Organizations.

Dutch Assn. of Soap Mfrs. [IO]
Finnish Cosmetic, Toiletry and Detergent Assn. [IO]
German Cosmetic, Toiletry, Perfumery and Detergent Assn. [IO]
Handcrafted Soap Makers Guild [1155]
Intl. Assn. for Soaps, Detergents and Maintenance Products [IO]
Irish Cosmetics, Detergent and Allied Products Assn. [IO]
Japan Soap and Detergent Assn. [IO]
Natl. Assn. of Household Cleaning Products [IO]
Soap and Detergent Assn. [822]
Soaps and Detergents Indus. Assn. [IO]
UK Cleaning Products Indus. Assn. [IO]
Detergent Assn; Soap and [822]
Detoxification Assn; Natl. Acupuncture [16510]
Detroit; Afro-American Museum of [★9358]
Detroit Fast Food Workers' Union - Defunct.
Detroit Jazz Center - Defunct.
Detroit Tooling Assn. [★2073]
Detroit Waldhorn Soc. - Address unknown since 1995.
Detsky Fond Slovenskej Republiky [★IO]
Deustche Akademie fur Sprache und Dichtung [★IO]
Deutsch-Amerikanische Juristen-Vereinigung e.V. [★IO]
Deutsch-Amerikanischer National-Kongress [★19074]
Deutsch-Armenische Gesellschaft [★IO]
Deutsch-Australische Industrie- und Handelskammer [★IO]
Deutsch Bonnet; Les Amis de Panhard and [21686]
Deutsch Brasilianische Juristenvereinigung [★IO]
Deutsch-Britische Juristenvereinigung [★IO]
Deutsch-Britische Stiftung [★IO]
Deutsch-Chinesische Wirtschaftsvereinigung e.V. [★IO]
Deutsch-Indische Handelskammer [★IO]
Deutsch-Japanische Juristenvereinigung [★IO]
Deutsch-Namibische Gesellschafte e.V. [★IO]
Deutsche Akademie fur Psychoanalyse [★IO]
Deutsche Alzheimer Gesellschaft [IO], Berlin, Germany
Deutsche Arbeitsgemeinschaft Genealogischer Verbande [IO], Jena, Germany
Deutsche Arbeitsgemeinschaft fur Mustererkennung [IO], Freiburg, Germany
Deutsche Atlantische Gesellschaft [★IO]
Deutsche Bibelgesellschaft [★IO]
Deutsche Bunsen-Gesellschaft fur Physikalische Chemie [★IO]
Deutsche China-Gesellschaft [★IO]
Deutsche Dermatologische Gesellschaft [★IO]
Deutsche Forschungsgemeinschaft [★IO]
Deutsche Friedensgesellschaft - Vereinigte KriegsdienstgegnerInnen [★IO]
Deutsche Gartenbauwissenschaftliche Gesellschaft e.V. [★IO]
Deutsche Gemmologische Gesellschaft e.V. [★IO]
Deutsche Gesellschaft fur Amerikastudien [★IO]
Deutsche Gesellschaft fur Anaesthesiologie und Intensivmedizin [★IO]
Deutsche Gesellschaft fur Asienkunde e.V. [★IO]
Deutsche Gesellschaft fur Auswartige Politik [★IO]
Deutsche Gesellschaft fur Biomedizinische Technik im VDE [★IO]
Deutsche Gesellschaft fur Eisenbahngeschichte e.V. [★IO]
Deutsche Gesellschaft fur Endokrinologie [★IO]
Deutsche Gesellschaft fur Ernahrung [★IO]
Deutsche Gesellschaft fur Ernahrung e. V. [★IO]
Deutsche Gesellschaft fur Ernahrung e.V. [★IO]
Deutsche Gesellschaft fur Erziehungswissenschaft [★IO]
Deutsche Gesellschaft fur Experimentelle und Klinische Pharmakologie und Toxikologie e.v. [★IO]
Deutsche Gesellschaft fur Fettwissenschaft e.V. [★IO]
Deutsche Gesellschaft fur Gerontologie und Geriatrie [★IO]
Deutsche Gesellschaft fur Hamatologie und Onkologie e.V. [★IO]
Deutsche Gesellschaft fur Humangenetik [★IO]
Deutsche Gesellschaft fur Infektiologie [IO], Berlin, Germany

Deutsche Gesellschaft fur Informationswissenschaft u Informationspraxis [★IO]
Deutsche Gesellschaft fur Kinder- und Jugendmedizin [★IO]
Deutsche Gesellschaft fur Luft- und Raumfahrt - Lilienthal - Oberth e.V. [★IO]
Deutsche Gesellschaft fur Luft- und Raumfahrtmedizin [★IO]
Deutsche Gesellschaft fur Materialkunde [IO], Frankfurt am Main, Germany
Deutsche Gesellschaft fur Meeresforschung e.V. [★IO]
Deutsche Gesellschaft fur Moor- und Torfkunde e.V. [★IO]
Deutsche Gesellschaft fur Musiktherapie e.V. [★IO]
Deutsche Gesellschaft fur Muskelkranke [IO], Freiburg, Germany
Deutsche Gesellschaft fur Neurogenetik [★IO]
Deutsche Gesellschaft fur Online Forschung e.V. [★IO]
Deutsche Gesellschaft fur Ortung und Navigation e.V. [★IO]
Deutsche Gesellschaft fur Padiatrische Infektiologie [IO], Munich, Germany
Deutsche Gesellschaft fur Personalfuhrung e.V. [★IO]
Deutsche Gesellschaft fur Pharmazeutische Medizin [★IO]
Deutsche Gesellschaft fuer Philosphie e.V. [IO], Cologne, Germany
Deutsche Gesellschaft fur Photogrammetrie, Fernerkundung, und Geoinformation [★IO]
Deutsche Gesellschaft fur Physikalische Medizin und Rehabilitation [★IO]
Deutsche Gesellschaft fur Plastische und Wiederherstellungschirurgie e.V. [★IO]
Deutsche Gesellschaft fur Rheumatologie [IO], Berlin, Germany
Deutsche Gesellschaft fur Schlafforschung und Schlafmedizin e.V. [★IO]
Deutsche Gesellschaft fur Sexualforschung [★IO]
Deutsche Gesellschaft fur Sozialwissenschaftliche Sexualforschung e.V. [★IO]
Deutsche Gesellschaft fur Sprach- und Stimmheilkunde e.V. [★IO]
Deutsche Gesellschaft fur Tropenmedizin und Internationale Gesundheit [★IO]
Deutsche Gesellschaft fur Viszeralchirurgie e.V. [★IO]
Deutsche Gesellschaft fur Reproduktionsmedizin e.V. [★IO]
Deutsche Glastechnische Gesellschaft [★IO]
Deutsche Hausfrauengewerkscahft [★IO]
Deutsche Huntington Hilfe e.V. [★IO]
Deutsche Interdisziplinare Vereinigung fur Intensiv- und Notfallmedizin [★IO]
Deutsche Kakteen-Gesellschaft e.V. [★IO]
Deutsche Kautschuk-Gesellschaft e.V [★IO]
Deutsche Keramische Gesellschaft [★IO]
Deutsche Krankenhausgesellschaft [★IO]
Deutsche Landwirtschafts-Gesellschaft [★IO]
Deutsche Mathematiker Vereinigung [★IO]
Deutsche Mathematiker Vereinigung [★IO]
Deutsche Meteorologische Gesellschaft [★IO]
Deutsche Mineralogische Gesellschaft [IO], Bochum, Germany
Deutsche Motorrader Register [★22677]
Deutsche Multiple Sklerose Gesellschaft Bundesverband e.V. [IO], Hannover, Germany
Deutsche Ophthalmologische Gesellschaft Heidelberg e.V. [★IO]
Deutsche Physikalische Gesellschaft [★IO]
Deutsche Physiologische Gesellschaft [★IO]
Deutsche Physiologische Gesellschaft [IO], Hannover, Germany
Deutsche Phytomedizinische Gesellschaft e.V. [★IO]
Deutsche Public Relations Gesellschaft [★IO]
Deutsche Roemisch Katholisch Unterstuetzungs Gesellschaft von Minnesota [★18990]
Deutsche Statistische Gesellschaft [★IO]
Deutsche Taekwondo Union [IO], Furth, Germany
Deutsche Transpersonale Gesellschaft [★IO]
Deutsche Vereinigung zur Bekampfung der Viruskrankheiten [IO], Jena, Germany
Deutsche Vereinigung fur Datenschutz [★IO]

Deutsche Vereinigung fur Politische Wissenschaft [★IO]
Deutsche Welthungerhilfe [★IO]
Deutsche Yngling Klassenvereinigung e.V [IO], Stutensee, Germany
Deutschen Gesellschaft fur Geowissenshaften [★IO]
Deutschen Gesellschaft fur KatastrophenMedizin e.V. [★IO]
Deutschen Gesellschaft fur Sprachwissenschaft [★IO]
Deutschen Gesellschaft fur Zerstorungsfreie Prufung [★IO]
Deutschen Weinbauverband e.V. [★IO]
Deutscher Aero Club [★IO]
Deutscher Akademikerinnen Bund [IO], Berlin, Germany
Deutscher Akademischer Austausch Dienst [★8614]
Deutscher Akademischer Austauschdienst [★IO]
Deutscher Allgemeiner Sangerbund [IO], Hannover, Germany
Deutscher Alpenverein [★IO]
Deutscher Anwaltverein [★IO]
Deutscher Arbeitskreis fur Geomorphologie E.V. [IO], Bonn, Germany
Deutscher Asphaltverband [★IO]
Deutscher Badminton Verband [IO], Mulheim an der Ruhr, Germany
Deutscher Behindertensportverband [★IO]
Deutscher Beton- und Bautechnik-verein [★IO]
Deutscher Brauer-Bund [★IO]
Deutscher Cricket Bund [★IO]
Deutscher Direktmarketing Verband [★IO]
Deutscher Entwicklunsdiest Vietnam [★IO]
Deutscher Fleischer-Verband [IO], Frankfurt am Main, Germany
Deutscher Forstwirtschaftsrat e.V. [★IO]
Deutscher Franchise-Verband [★IO]
Deutscher Frauenring e.V. [IO], Berlin, Germany
Deutscher Fruchthandelsverband e.V. [★IO]
Deutscher Giessereiverband [★IO]
Deutscher Hausfrauen-Bund [IO], Bonn, Germany
Deutscher Holstein Verband e.V. [★IO]
Deutscher Hotel- und Gaststattenverband [★IO]
Deutscher Ingenieurinnenbund [★IO]
Deutscher Journalisten Verband [★IO]
Deutscher Journalisten-Verband e.V. [IO], Berlin, Germany
Deutscher Juristinnenbund [IO], Berlin, Germany
Deutscher Kaffee-Verband e.V. [★IO]
Deutscher Kalte- und Klimatechnischer Verein e.V. [★IO]
Deutscher Kunsthandelsverband E.V. [IO], Berlin, Germany
Deutscher Lehrerverband [★IO]
Deutscher Mieterbund [★IO]
Deutscher Museumsbund [★IO]
Deutscher Musikverlegerverband [★IO]
Deutscher Pelzverband e.V. [★IO]
Deutscher Rat fur Landespflege [★IO]
Deutscher Reisebuero und Reiseveranstalter Verband [★IO]
Deutscher Segler-Verband [IO], Hamburg, Germany
Deutscher Ski-Verband [★IO]
Deutscher Sportbund [★IO]
Deutscher Sportlehrerverband [IO], Dannewerk, Germany
Deutscher Squash Rackets Verband E.V. [IO], Bocholt, Germany
Deutscher Stahlbau-Verband [★IO]
Deutscher Steuerberaterverband [★IO]
Deutscher Tanzsportverband [★IO]
Deutscher Tennis Bund [IO], Hamburg, Germany
Deutscher Unihockey Bund [★IO]
Deutscher Verband fur Materialforschung und -prufung [IO], Berlin, Germany
Deutscher Verband fur Physiotherapie [★IO]
Deutscher Verband fur Schweissen und verwandte Verfahren [★IO]
Deutscher Verein fur Kunstwissenschaft e.V. [★IO]
Deutscher Verein fur Vermessungswesen e.V. [★IO]
Deutscher Volkshochschul-Verband [★IO]
Deutsches Atomforum [★IO]
Deutsches Historisches Institut [★10110]
Deutsches Jugendherbergswerk [★IO]
Deutsches Kunststoff-Institut [★IO]

A star before a book entry number signifies that the name is not listed separately, but is mentioned within the entry.

Deutsches Medikamenten-Hilfswerk, action medeor [★IO]

Deutsches Motorrad Register [22677], 8663 Grover Pl., Shreveport, LA 71115, (318)797-0803

Deutsches Nationales Kommitee des Weltenergier-ats [IO], Berlin, Germany

Deutsches Teppich-Forschungsinstitut [★IO]

Deutsches Tiefkuehlinstitut [IO], Cologne, Germany

Deutsches Weininstitut [★IO]

Deutsches Zentrum fur Altersfragen e.V. [★IO]

Deutsches Zentrum fuer Luft-und Raumfahrt e. V. [★IO]

Deutschsprachige Gesellschaft Fur Psychotrauma-tologie [IO], Munich, Germany

Developartners [★IO]

Developartners [★14871]

Developers; Assoc. Owners and [939]

Developers Assn; Natl. Rural Economic [18574]

Developers Council; United [★3323]

Developers; Natl. Alliance of Market [2641]

Developers; Natl. Assn. of Installation [★5811]

Developers; Natl. Assn. of Market [★2641]

Developing Countries Farm Radio Network [IO], Ot-tawa, ON, Canada

Developing Technologies [IO], London, United Kingdom

Development Agencies; Assn. of State Planning and [★5592]

Development Agencies; Coun. of State Community [6272]

Development Agencies; Natl. Assn. of State [5592]

Development Agencies; Natl. Assn. of State Economic [★5592]

Development Aid from People to People in Zimbabwe [IO], Harare, Zimbabwe

Development; Amer. Assn. for Counseling and [★11815]

Development; Amer. Soc. for Training and [★8018]

Development Assistance Comm. [IO], Paris, France

Development Assistance Gp. [★IO]

Development Assn; Amer. Land [★3298]

Development Assn; Amer. Resort [3298]

Development Assn; Amer. Resort and Residential [★3298]

Development Assn; Christian Community [20278]

Development Assn; Craft Org. [1100]

Development Assn; Intl. Cooperative [★4481]

Development; Assn. for Measurement and Evalua-tion in Counseling and [★9247]

Development Assn; Public Works and Economic [5595]

Development Assn./Resource Conservation and Recovery Act Project; Natl. Environmental [7835]

Development Bank of Southern Africa [IO], Midrand, Republic of South Africa

Development Banks
 Bretton Woods Comm. [17453]

Development Bd; Bermuda Trade [★24237]

Development Bond Issuers; Coun. of Indus. [★17458]

Development Companies; Natl. Assn. of [2427]

Development; Consortium for Sustainable Village-Based [★11793]

Development Coordinators; Natl. Conf. of County [★5622]

Development Coun; Natl. [17463]

Development Coun; Pacific Basin [17843]

Development; Coun. for Rural Housing and [★12310]

Development Councils; Natl. Assn. of Rsrc. Conservation and [4421]

Development; Counseling Assn. for Humanistic Educ. and [8527]

Development Educ. Assn. [IO], London, United Kingdom

Development; Engineers' Coun. for Professional [★6979]

Development; Env., and Security; Pacific Inst. for Stud. in [12120]

Development; Feminist Center for Human Growth and [13426]

Development Finance Agencies; Coun. of [17458]

Development; Found. for Child [11541]

Development Found; Guinea [16931]

Development Fund; Haitian [★11961]

Development Fund; Peace [18232]

Development Gp. [IO], Paris, France

Development Gp. for Alternative Policies [IO], Washington, DC, United States

Development Gp. for Alternative Policies [17835], 927 15th St. NW, 4th Fl., Washington, DC 20005, (202)898-1566

Development and Growth; Soc. for the Stud. of [★6595]

Development of Human Potential; Assn. for the [10181]

Development Innovations and Networks - Switzerland [IO], Geneva, Switzerland

Development Inst; African [16923]

Development Inst; First Nations [12625]

Development Intl. - Defunct.

Development; Jean Piaget Soc.: Soc. for the Stud. of Knowledge and [16156]

Development and Law Center; Natl. Economic [17464]

Development League; Professional [★5714]

Development League; Senior Executives Assn. Professional [5714]

Development; Life for Relief and [12867]

Development; Natl. Assembly for Social Policy and [★13400]

Development; Natl. Assn. for Govt. Training and [2904]

Development; Natl. Center for Amer. Indian Enterprise [12628]

Development; Natl. Coalition for Asian Pacific Amer. Community [11785]

Development; Natl. Inst. of Child Hea. and Human [13971]

Development Network; Career Planning and Adult [12070]

Development Network of Indigenous Voluntary As-sociations [IO], Kampala, Uganda

Development Network; Org. [2867]

Development Off; Intl. Rural [★17832]

Development Org; North Amer. YMCA [13461]

Development Org; Virginia Community [★11798]

Development Organizations; Natl. Assn. of [5590]

Development Organizations Res. Found; Natl. Assn. of [17226]

Development Planning Unit [IO], London, United Kingdom

Development Policy; Center for [★17613]

Development Policy; Intl. Center for [★17613]

Development and Population Activities; Centre for [12422]

Development Professionals; Natl. Assn. of Workforce [12088]

Development Promotion Gp. [IO], Chennai, India

Development Res. Coun; Intl. [★3305]

Development Res; Inst. for [★7918]

Development Rsrc. Centre [IO], Wellington, New Zealand

Development Rsrc. Coun; Human [12913]

Development; Seventh Generation Fund for Indian [18099]

Development of Space; Students for the Exploration and [7923]

Development Stud. Assn. [IO], Devon, United Kingdom

Development Stud. and Promotion Center [IO], Lima, Peru

Development and Training Assn; Natl. Staff [13180]

Development Trusts Assn. [IO], London, United Kingdom

Development; Women's World Org. for Rights, Literature and [18822]

Development, and World Reform; Parliamentarians Global Action for Disarmament, [★17433]

Developmental and Behavioral Pediatrics; Soc. for [15898]

Developmental Biology; Soc. for [6595]

Developmental Delay Registry [★13941]

Developmental Delay Resources [13941], 5801 Beacon St., Pittsburgh, PA 15217, (800)497-0944

Developmental Disabilities; Amer. Assn. of Univ. Af-filiated Programs for Persons With [★12563]

Developmental Disabilities Councils; Natl. Assn. of [★12575]

Developmental Disabilities and Mental Hea. Needs; NADD - An Assn. for Persons with [12552]

Developmental Disabilities; Natl. Assn. of Councils on [12575]

Developmental Disabilities; Natl. Conf. on [★12575]

Developmental Disabilities Nurses Assn. [15477], PO Box 536489, Orlando, FL 32853-6489, (407)835-0642

Developmental Disorders; Acad. of Learning and [12489]

Developmental Education
 Abhivyakti Media for Development [IO]
 A.L. Mailman Family Found. [11671]
 Amer. Assn. of Human Design Practitioners [1151]
 Amer. Cong. of Community Supports and Employ-ment Services [17206]
 Assn. of WORKSHOP WAY Consultants [9213]
 Children's Television Rsrc. and Educ. Center [11686]
 Lions-Quest [8199]
 Natl. Assn. for Developmental Educ. [8200]
 Natl. Parent Network on Disabilities [14245]
 Rural Inst. [11986]
 Staff and Educational Development Assn. [IO]
 STRIDE: Sports and Therapeutic Recreation Instruction/Developmental Educ. [8205]

Developmental Medicine; Amer. Acad. for Cerebral Palsy and [13934]

Developmental Treatment Assn; Neuro- [15399]

Developmentally Disabled; Amer. Assn. of Univ. Affili-ated Programs for the [★12563]

Developpement; Banque Interamericaine de [★17460]

Developpement Caritas Republique Democratique du Congo Democratic [IO], Kinshasa, Democratic Republic of the Congo

Devereux Natl. [13734], PO Box 638, Villanova, PA 19085, (800)345-1292

Device Assn; Smaller Mfrs. Medical [★3486]

DeviceNet Vendor Assn; Open [892]

Devices and Digger-Derricks Coun; Mfrs. of Aerial [2038]

Devil Dog Fleas; Military Order of the [21178]

Devil Pups [21172], 2815 Townsgate Rd., No. 325, Westlake Village, CA 91361-3097, (805)497-9810

Devils in Baggy Pants [★21378]

Devil's Brigade [★IO]

Devils Fan Club [25004], PO Box 504, East Ruther-ford, NJ 07073-0504, (201)768-9680

Devils Fan Club [★25004]

Devin Register - Defunct.

Devo Fan Club - Address unknown since 1988.

Devon Assn; North Amer. South [4284]

Devon Cattle Assn; Amer. Milking [4235]

Devon Cattle Club; Amer. [★4220]

Dewan Perniagaan Melayu Malaysia [★IO]

Dewan Perniagaan dan Perindustrian Antarabangsa Malaysia [★IO]

Dewey Soc; John [8272]

Dexter Cattle Assn; Amer. [4221]

Dexter Cattle Assn. of North Am; Purebred [4289]

Dexter Cattle Soc. New Zealand [IO], Te Puke, New Zealand

Dexter Club; Amer. Kerry and [★4221]

DFA of California [4726], 710 Striker Ave., Sacramento, CA 95834, (916)561-5900

DFK International/USA [28], c/o Jay Hauck, Exec. Dir., 1255 23rd St. NW, Ste. 200, Washington, DC 20037-1174, (202)452-1588

DG Soc. [★7151]

DG Soc. [★IO]

D.H. Lawrence Soc. of North Am. [IO], Alfred, NY, United States

D.H. Lawrence Soc. of North Am. [9645], c/o Julianne Newmark, Sec., New Mexico Tech, Humanities Dept., 801 Leroy Pl., Socorro, NM 87801, (505)835-5190

Dhaka Young Men's Christian Association [IO], Dhaka, Bangladesh

Dharma Realm Buddhist Assn. [19548], 1825 Murchison Dr., Burlingame, CA 94010-4504, (415)421-6117

dhg - Verband der Familienfrauen und -manner e.V. [★IO]

Dhoma e Tregtise dhe Industrise Korce [★IO]

Diabetes
 Amer. Assn. of Clinical Endocrinologists [14350]

Reference to "IO" in place of a book number signifies that the association may be found in the 45th edition of International Organizations.

Amer. Assn. of Diabetes Educators [14217]
Amer. Diabetes Assn. [14218]
Amer. Youth Understanding Diabetes Abroad [14219]
Amer. Youth Understanding Diabetes Abroad [IO]
Assn. malienne de Lutte contre le Diabete [IO]
Bahrain Diabetic Assn. [IO]
British Assn. of Retinal Screeners [IO]
Cameroon Diabetes Assn. [IO]
Canadian Diabetes Assn. [IO]
Canadian Diabetes Assn. - Barrie and District Br. [IO]
Canadian Diabetes Assn. - Belleville/Quinte Br. [IO]
Canadian Diabetes Assn. - Brantford Br. [IO]
Canadian Diabetes Assn. - Brockville/Tri-County Br. [IO]
Canadian Diabetes Assn. - Calgary and District Br. [IO]
Canadian Diabetes Assn. - Cambridge and District Br. [IO]
Canadian Diabetes Assn. - Cape Breton Br. [IO]
Canadian Diabetes Assn. - Chatham and District Br. [IO]
Canadian Diabetes Assn. - Cornwall and District Br. [IO]
Canadian Diabetes Assn. - Diabetes Educator Sect. [IO]
Canadian Diabetes Assn. - Durham Region Br. [IO]
Canadian Diabetes Assn. - Eastman District Region [IO]
Canadian Diabetes Assn. - Edmonton and District Br. [IO]
Canadian Diabetes Assn. - Elliot Lake/Blind River [IO]
Canadian Diabetes Assn. - Elmira and District Br. [IO]
Canadian Diabetes Assn. - Fredericton and District Br. [IO]
Canadian Diabetes Assn. - Grand Falls and District Br. [IO]
Canadian Diabetes Assn. - Greater Vancouver and District Br. [IO]
Canadian Diabetes Assn. - Guelph and South Wellington Br. [IO]
Canadian Diabetes Assn. - Haldimand/Norfolk Community Gp. [IO]
Canadian Diabetes Assn. - Hamilton and District Br. [IO]
Canadian Diabetes Assn. - Kawarthas Br. [IO]
Canadian Diabetes Assn. - Kelowna and District Br. [IO]
Canadian Diabetes Assn. - Kingston and District Br. [IO]
Canadian Diabetes Assn. - Kitchener-Waterloo Br. [IO]
Canadian Diabetes Assn. - Lakeshore Br. [IO]
Canadian Diabetes Assn. - Lethbridge and District Br. [IO]
Canadian Diabetes Assn. - Lindsay Br. [IO]
Canadian Diabetes Assn. - London Br. [IO]
Canadian Diabetes Assn. - Medicine Hat and District Br. [IO]
Canadian Diabetes Assn. - Midland/Penetanguish-ene Br. [IO]
Canadian Diabetes Assn. - Miramichi and District Br. [IO]
Canadian Diabetes Assn. - Moncton and District Br. [IO]
Canadian Diabetes Assn. - Nanaimo and District Br. [IO]
Canadian Diabetes Assn. - New Brunswick [IO]
Canadian Diabetes Assn. - Newfoundland and Labrador Region [IO]
Canadian Diabetes Assn. - Niagara Br. [IO]
Canadian Diabetes Assn. - North Bay and District Br. [IO]
Canadian Diabetes Assn. - North Perth/North Wellington Br. [IO]
Canadian Diabetes Assn. - Nova Scotia [IO]
Canadian Diabetes Assn. - Oakville Br. [IO]
Canadian Diabetes Assn. - Orangeville and District Br. [IO]
Canadian Diabetes Assn. - Ottawa and District Br. [IO]

Canadian Diabetes Assn. - Peel Region Br. [IO]
Canadian Diabetes Assn. - Pembroke and District Br. [IO]
Canadian Diabetes Assn. - Prince Edward Island [IO]
Canadian Diabetes Assn. - Prince George and District Br. [IO]
Canadian Diabetes Assn. - Red Deer and District Br. [IO]
Canadian Diabetes Assn. - Regina Br. [IO]
Canadian Diabetes Assn. - Sackville and District Br. [IO]
Canadian Diabetes Assn. - Sarnia and District Br. [IO]
Canadian Diabetes Assn. - Saskatoon Br. [IO]
Canadian Diabetes Assn. - Sault Ste. Marie and District Br. [IO]
Canadian Diabetes Assn. - Sect. de Bathurst [IO]
Canadian Diabetes Assn. - Sect. du Madawaska [IO]
Canadian Diabetes Assn. - South Parklands Br. [IO]
Canadian Diabetes Assn. - Sudbury and District Br. [IO]
Canadian Diabetes Assn. - Sussex and District Br. [IO]
Canadian Diabetes Assn. - Thunder Bay and District Br. [IO]
Canadian Diabetes Assn. - Timmins and District Br. [IO]
Canadian Diabetes Assn. - Toronto Br. [IO]
Canadian Diabetes Assn. - Victoria and District Br. [IO]
Canadian Diabetes Assn. - Westman Br. [IO]
Canadian Diabetes Assn. - Williams Lake and District Br. [IO]
Canadian Diabetes Assn. - Windsor and District Br. [IO]
Canadian Diabetes Assn. - Woodstock and District Br. [IO]
Canadian Diabetes Assn. - York Region Br. [IO]
Central Africa Diabetes Assn. [IO]
Chad Assn. for the Fight against Diabetes [IO]
Charles Ray III Diabetes Assn. [IO]
Charles Ray III Diabetes Assn. [14220]
City of Hope Natl. Medical Center [15102]
Diabetes Action Res. and Educ. Found. [14221]
Diabetes Ashburton [IO]
Diabetes Assn. of Nigeria [IO]
Diabetes Assn. of Sri Lanka [IO]
Diabetes Assn. of Zambia [IO]
Diabetes Assn. of Zanzibar [IO]
Diabetes Auckland [IO]
Diabetes Australia [IO]
Diabetes Australia - Australian Capital Territory [IO]
Diabetes Australia - New South Wales [IO]
Diabetes Australia - Northern Territory [IO]
Diabetes Australia - Queensland [IO]
Diabetes Australia - South Australia [IO]
Diabetes Australia - Tasmania [IO]
Diabetes Australia - Victoria [IO]
Diabetes Australia - Western Australia [IO]
Diabetes Buller [IO]
Diabetes Central Otago [IO]
Diabetes Christchurch [IO]
Diabetes Dannevirke [IO]
Diabetes Eastern Bay of Plenty [IO]
Diabetes Exercise and Sports Assn. [14222]
Diabetes Fed. of Ireland [IO]
Diabetes Gisborne [IO]
Diabetes Hawkes Bay [IO]
Diabetes Horowhenua [IO]
Diabetes Kapiti Coast [IO]
Diabetes Manawatu [IO]
Diabetes Marlborough [IO]
Diabetes Matamata [IO]
Diabetes Milton [IO]
Diabetes Nelson [IO]
Diabetes New Zealand [IO]
Diabetes North Otago [IO]
Diabetes Northland [IO]
Diabetes Otago [IO]
Diabetes Putaruru-Tirau [IO]
Diabetes Res. Assn. of Am. [14223]

Diabetes Res. Inst. Found. [14224]
Diabetes Rotorua [IO]
Diabetes South Africa [IO]
Diabetes South Canterbury [IO]
Diabetes South Otago [IO]
Diabetes South Taranaki [IO]
Diabetes South Waikato [IO]
Diabetes Southland [IO]
Diabetes Taranaki [IO]
Diabetes Taupo [IO]
Diabetes Tauranga [IO]
Diabetes UK [IO]
Diabetes Waikato [IO]
Diabetes Waimate [IO]
Diabetes Wairarapa [IO]
Diabetes Wakatipu [IO]
Diabetes Wanganui [IO]
Diabetes Wellington [IO]
Diabetes West Coast [IO]
Diabetic Soc. of Singapore [IO]
Ethiopian Diabetes Assn. [IO]
European Assn. for the Stud. of Diabetes [IO]
European Assn. for the Stud. of Diabetes Eye Complications Study Group [IO]
Finnish Diabetes Assn. [IO]
French Diabetes Assn. [IO]
French-Language Assn. for the Stud. of Diabetes and Metabolic Disorders [IO]
Gambia Diabetes Assn. [IO]
Ghana Diabetes Assn. [IO]
Guinean Assn. for the Educ. and Help to Diabetics [IO]
Immunology of Diabetes Soc. [14225]
Insulin-Free World Found. [14226]
Insulin-Free World Found. [IO]
Insulin for Life Australia [IO]
Intl. Diabetes Fed. [IO]
Intl. Soc. for Pediatric and Adolescent Diabetes [IO]
Irish Diabetes Assn. [IO]
Joslin Diabetes Center [14227]
Juvenile Diabetes Res. Found. [IO]
Juvenile Diabetes Res. Found. - Hellas [IO]
Juvenile Diabetes Res. Found. Intl. [IO]
Juvenile Diabetes Res. Found. Intl. [14228]
Kenya Diabetes Assn. [IO]
Latin Amer. Diabetes Assn. [IO]
Maltese Diabetes Assn. [IO]
MedicAlert Found. Intl. [14318]
Natl. Certification Bd. for Diabetes Educators [14229]
Natl. Diabetes Info. CH [14230]
Norwegian Diabetes Assn. [IO]
Philippine Diabetes Assn. [IO]
Scandinavian Soc. for the Stud. of Diabetes [IO]
Seva Found. [12443]
Soc. for Endocrinology, Metabolism and Diabetes of South Africa [IO]
Syndrome X Assn. [15259]
Taking Control of Your Diabetes [14231]
Uganda Diabetic Assn. [IO]
Diabetes Action Res. and Educ. Found. [14221], 426 C St. NE, Washington, DC 20002, (202)333-4520
Diabetes Ashburton [IO], Ashburton, New Zealand
Diabetes Assn. of Nigeria [IO], Lagos, Nigeria
Diabetes Assn. of Sri Lanka [IO], Rajagiriya, Sri Lanka
Diabetes Assn. of Zambia [IO], Lusaka, Zambia
Diabetes Assn. of Zanzibar [IO], Zanzibar, United Republic of Tanzania
Diabetes Auckland [IO], Auckland, New Zealand
Diabetes Australia [IO], Canberra, Australia
Diabetes Australia - Australian Capital Territory [IO], Weston, Australia
Diabetes Australia - New South Wales [IO], Sydney, Australia
Diabetes Australia - Northern Territory [IO], Casuarina, Australia
Diabetes Australia - Queensland [IO], Brisbane, Australia
Diabetes Australia - South Australia [IO], Hilton, Australia
Diabetes Australia - Tasmania [IO], Hobart, Australia
Diabetes Australia - Victoria [IO], Melbourne, Australia

A star before a book entry number signifies that the name is not listed separately, but is mentioned within the entry.

Diabetes Australia - Western Australia [IO], Subiaco, Australia
Diabetes Buller [IO], Westport, New Zealand
Diabetes Central Otago [IO], Cromwell, New Zealand
Diabetes Christchurch [IO], Christchurch, New Zealand
Diabetes Dannevirke [IO], Oamaru, New Zealand
Diabetes Eastern Bay of Plenty [IO], Wellington, New Zealand
Diabetes Exercise and Sports Assn. [14222], 8001 Montcastle Dr., Nashville, TN 37221, (800)898-4322
Diabetes Fed. of Ireland [IO], Dublin, Ireland
Diabetes Found. [★14227]
Diabetes Found; Joslin [★14227]
Diabetes Found; Juvenile [★14228]
Diabetes Gisborne [IO], Gisborne, New Zealand
Diabetes Hawkes Bay [IO], Napier, New Zealand
Diabetes Horowhenua [IO], Oamaru, New Zealand
Diabetes Kapiti Coast [IO], Paraparaumu, New Zealand
Diabetes Manawatu [IO], Palmerston North, New Zealand
Diabetes Marlborough [IO], Blenheim, New Zealand
Diabetes Matamata [IO], Matamata, New Zealand
Diabetes and Metabolism; Assn. of Prog. Directors in Endocrinology, [14351]
Diabetes Milton [IO], Milton, New Zealand
Diabetes Nelson [IO], Nelson, New Zealand
Diabetes New Zealand [IO], Wellington, New Zealand
Diabetes North Otago [IO], Oamaru, New Zealand
Diabetes Northland [IO], Whangarei, New Zealand
Diabetes Otago [IO], Dunedin, New Zealand
Diabetes Putaruru-Tirau [IO], Tirau, New Zealand
Diabetes Res. Assn. of Am. [14223], 10560 Wayzata Blvd., Ste. 19, Minnetonka, MN 55305, (612)730-2789
Diabetes Res. Found. - Hellas; Juvenile [IO]
Diabetes Res. Inst. Found. [14224], 200 S Park Rd., Hollywood, FL 33021, (954)964-4040
Diabetes Rotorua [IO], Rotorua, New Zealand
Diabetes South Africa [IO], Fontainebleau, Republic of South Africa
Diabetes South Canterbury [IO], Timaru, New Zealand
Diabetes South Otago [IO], Balclutha, New Zealand
Diabetes South Taranaki [IO], Opunake, New Zealand
Diabetes South Waikato [IO], Oamaru, New Zealand
Diabetes Southland [IO], Invercargill, New Zealand
Diabetes Taranaki [IO], New Plymouth, New Zealand
Diabetes Taupo [IO], Taupo, New Zealand
Diabetes Tauranga [IO], Tauranga, New Zealand
Diabetes UK [IO], London, United Kingdom
Diabetes Waikato [IO], Hamilton, New Zealand
Diabetes Waimate [IO], Waimate, New Zealand
Diabetes Wairarapa [IO], Featherston, New Zealand
Diabetes Wakatipu [IO], Queenstown, New Zealand
Diabetes Wanganui [IO], Wanganui, New Zealand
Diabetes Wellington [IO], Wellington, New Zealand
Diabetes West Coast [IO], Hokitika, New Zealand
Diabetesliitto [★IO]
Diabetic Soc. of Singapore [IO], Singapore, Singapore
Diaconate Directors; Natl. Assn. of [19664]
Diaconate Directors; Natl. Assn. of Permanent [★19664]
Diaconate; North Amer. Assn. for the [19967]
Diagnosis Assn; North Amer. Nursing [★15489]
Diagnosis; Org. of Teachers of Oral [8197]
Diagnostic Imaging; Coun. on [16288]
Diagnostic Imaging; European Assn. of Veterinary [IO]
Diagnostic and Interventional Nephrology; Amer. Soc. of [15287]
Diagnostic Mfrs; Assn. of Microbiological [★3482]
Diagnostic Marketing Assn. [2624], 10293 N Meridian St., Ste. 175, Indianapolis, IN 46290, (317)816-1640
Diagnostic Medical Sonography; Amer. Registry of [16437]
Diagnostic Medical Sonography; Joint Rev. Comm. on Educ. in [8837]

Diagnostic Medical Sonography; Soc. of [16438]
Diagnosticians; Amer. Assn. of Veterinary Lab. [16753]
Diagnostics Mfrs; Assn. of Medical [3482]
Diakonia of the Americas [★IO]
Diakonia of the Americas and Caribbean [IO], Penticton, BC, Canada
Dialect Soc; Amer. [10398]
Dialogue on Diversity [8888], 1000 Connecticut Ave. NW, Ste. 600, Washington, DC 20036, (703)631-0650
Dialogue Found. [20207], c/o Dialogue: A Jour. of Mormon Thought, PO Box 58423, Salt Lake City, UT 84158, (801)274-8210
Dialysis Assn; Kidney Transplant/ [16675]
Dialysis and Transplantation; North Amer. Soc. for [15295]
Diamond Assn. of Am; Indus. [★2026]
Diamond Assn; Indus. [2026]
Diamond and Colorstone Assn; Indian [2367]
Diamond Connection [IO], Witham, United Kingdom
Diamond Coun. of Am. [2360], 3212 W End Ave., Ste. 202, Nashville, TN 37203, (615)385-5301
Diamond Dealers Club [2361], 580 5th Ave., 47th St., New York, NY 10036, (212)869-9777
Diamond and Gemstone Remarketing Assn. - Defunct.
Diamond Industry Assn; Amer. [2355]
Diamond Mfrs. Assn. [★2362]
Diamond Mfrs. and Importers Assn. of Am. [2362], PO Box 5297, New York, NY 10185-5297, (212)944-2066
Diamond Rio Fan Club [24875], PO Box 2195, Hendersonville, TN 37077-2195
Diamond Setters Fraternal Guild - Defunct.
Diamond T Register [23023], PO Box 1657, St. Cloud, MN 56302-1657, (320)632-8664
Diamond T Register [IO], St. Cloud, MN, United States
Diamond Trade Assn. of America [★IO]
Diamond Trade Assn. of America [★2363]
Diamond Trade and Precious Stone Assn. of America [2363]
Diamond Trade and Precious Stone Assn. of America [IO], New York, NY, United States
Diamond Walnut Growers [5055], c/o Diamond Foods, Inc., 1050 S Diamond St., Stockton, CA 95205, (209)467-6000
Diamond Wheel Mfrs. Inst. [★2567]
Diamond Wheel Mfrs. Inst. [★2075]
Dian Fossey Fund [★5310]
Dian Fossey Fund [★IO]
Dian Fossey Gorilla Fund International [IO], Atlanta, GA, United States
Dian Fossey Gorilla Fund Intl. [5310], 800 Cherokee Ave. SE, Atlanta, GA 30315-1440, (404)624-5881
Di'anno Fan Club - Address unknown since 1990.
Dianthis Soc; North Amer. [★22507]
Dianthus Soc; Combined North Amer. Cottage Garden Soc. and North Amer. [22507]

Diaper
Diaper Ser. Accreditation Coun. [2386]
Natl. Assn. of Diaper Services [2389]

Diaper Ser. Accreditation Coun. [2386], 994 Old Eagle School Rd., Ste. 1019, Wayne, PA 19087-1802, (610)971-4850
Diaper Ser. Indus. Assn. [★2389]
Diaper Ser. Inst. of Am. [★2389]
Diaper Services; Natl. Assn. of [2389]
Diaphragmatic Hernia Res., Advocacy and Support; CHERUBS - Assn. of Congenital [13753]
Diazotype Coaters; Natl. Assn. of Blueprint and [★1800]
Dichtl Surname Org. - Address unknown since 2006.
Dick Curless Fan Club - Defunct.
Dick Damron Intl. Fan Club - Defunct.
Dick Family Assn. [20882]
Dickens Fellowship [IO], London, United Kingdom
Dickens Soc. [9646], Wilkes Univ., English Dept., 170 S Franklin St., Wilkes-Barre, PA 18766, (570)408-4533
Dicks of America - Address unknown since 2002.
DICOM Standards Comm. [7178], 1300 N 17th St., Ste. 1752, Rosslyn, VA 22209, (703)841-3285
Dictionaries and Lexicography; Soc. for the Stud. of [★9747]

Dictionary
Australasian Assn. for Lexicography [IO]
Dictionary Soc. of North Am. [9747]
European Assn. for Lexicography [IO]
Noah Webster House [10053]
Scottish Language Dictionaries [IO]

Dictionary Soc. of North Am. [9747], c/o Lisa Berglund, Exec. Sec., Buffalo State Coll., Dept. of English, Ketchum Hall 326, 1300 Elmwood Ave., Buffalo, NY 14222, (716)878-4049
DidiBahini [IO], Kathmandu, Nepal
Die Brangus Genootskap van Suid-Afrika [★IO]
Die Casting Assn; North Amer. [2054]
Die Casting Engineers; Soc. of [★2054]
Die Casting Fed. - Defunct.
Die Casting Inst; Amer. [★2054]
Die Casting Res. Found. [★2054]
Die Donau [★IO]
Die Geomorphologische Kommission der Oesterreichischen Geographischen Gesellschaft [★IO]
Die Mfrs. Assn; Natl. Tool and [★2031]
Die Misstofvereniging van Suid-Afrika [★IO]
Die and Mold Makers Guild; Tool, [★24100]
Die and Mold Makers; Intl. Union of Tool, [24100]
Die and Precision Machining Assn; Natl. Tool, [★2031]
Die Set Mfrs. Service Bur. - Defunct.
Die Sinkers Conf; Intl. [★24012]
Die Spitaler der Schweiz [★IO]
Die Stampers, and Engravers' Union of North Am; Intl. Plate Printers, [24085]
Die Suid-Afrikaanse Akademie vir Wetenskap en Kuns [★IO]
Die Suid-Afrikaanse Vereniging van Musiekonderwysers [★IO]
Diecast Exchange Club [22010]
Diecast Toy Collectors Assn. [★22997]
Diecast Toy Collectors Assn. [★IO]
Diecasting Development Coun. - Defunct.
Diecutters Assn; Diemakers and [★2029]
Diecutters; Natl. Assn. of Diemakers and [★2029]
Dielectrics and Elecl. Insulation Soc; IEEE [6902]
Diemakers and Diecutters Assn. [★2029]
Diemakers and Diecutters Assn. [★IO]
Diemakers and Diecutters; Natl. Assn. of [★2029]
Dierkundige Vereniging van Suidelike Afrika [★IO]
Diesel Automobile Assn. - Defunct.
Diesel Engine Mfrs. Assn. - Defunct.
Diesel Engineers and Users Assn. [★IO]
Dietary Foods Assn; Natl. [★3425]
Dietary Managers Assn. [15555], 406 Surrey Woods Dr., St. Charles, IL 60174, (630)587-6336
Dietary Support Coalition; Amer. Celiac Society/ [15543]
Dietetic Assn; Amer. [15546]
Dietetic Assn; Seventh-Day Adventist [15569]
Dietetic Products
Amer. Assn. of Nutritional Consultants [15540]
Amer. Bd. of Nutrition [15541]
Amer. Celiac Society/Dietary Support Coalition [15543]
Amer. Coll. of Nutrition [15544]
Amer. Coun. of Applied Clinical Nutrition [15545]
Amer. Dietetic Assn. [15546]
Amer. Soc. for Clinical Nutrition [15547]
Amer. Soc. for Nutrition [15548]
Amer. Soc. for Parenteral and Enteral Nutrition [15549]
Calorie Control Coun. [1505]
Community Systems Found. [15552]
Consultant Dietitians in Hea. Care Facilities [15554]
Dietary Managers Assn. [15555]
Food and Nutrition Bd. [15558]
Gluten Intolerance Gp. [15559]
Intl. and Amer. Associations of Clinical Nutritionists [15560]
Intl. Life Sciences Inst. - North Am. [15561]
Intl. Vitamin A Consultative Gp. [15564]
Nutrition for Optimal Hea. Assn. [15567]
Price-Pottenger Nutrition Found. [15568]
Seventh-Day Adventist Dietetic Assn. [15569]
Soc. for Nutrition Educ. [15570]
TOPS Club (Take Off Pounds Sensibly) [12649]
Weight Watchers Intl. [14603]

Reference to "IO" in place of a book number signifies that the association may be found in the 45th edition of International Organizations.

Dietetic Res; Canadian Found. for [IO]

Diethylenetriamine Producers Importers Alliance - Defunct.

Dieticians Special Interest Gp; Consultant [★15554]

Dietitians Assn. of Australia [IO], Deakin, Australia

Dietitians of Canada [IO], Toronto, ON, Canada

Dietitians; German Assn. of [IO]

Dietitians in Hea. Care Facilities; Consultant [15554]

Dietitians; Swedish Assn. of [IO]

Differently Abled Proud People Exercising Rights [12568]

Diffie Fan Club; Joe [24923]

Diffusion Coun; Air [1874]

Digestion and Motility Disorders Soc; Pediatric [15893]

Digestive Disease Natl. Coalition [14416], 507 Capitol Ct. NE, Ste. 200, Washington, DC 20002, (202)544-7497

Digestive Disease Organizations; Coalition of [★14416]

Digestive Diseases CH [★14422]

Digestive Diseases Educ. and Info. CH; Natl. [★14422]

Digestive Diseases Information Center - Defunct.

Digestive Diseases Info. CH; Natl. [14422]

Digestive Disorders Found. [★IO]

Digestive Hea. Found; Amer. [★14417]

Digestive Hea. and Nutrition; Found. for [14417]

Digger-Derricks Coun; Mfrs. of Aerial Devices and [2038]

Digit Fund [★5310]

Digit Fund [★IO]

Digital Cinema Soc. [IO], Studio City, CA, United States

Digital Cinema Soc. [1380], PO Box 1973, Studio City, CA 91614, (818)762-2214

Digital Distribution of Advt. for Publications [97], 1421 Prince St., Ste. 230, Alexandria, VA 22314, (425)707-2713

Digital Govt. Soc. of North Am. [7151], c/o Priscilla Rasmussen, 209 N Eighth St., Stroudsburg, PA 18360, (570)476-8006

Digital Govt. Soc. of North Am. [IO], Stroudsburg, PA, United States

Digital Graphic Imaging Technical Assn. - Address unknown since 2000.

Digital Imaging and Communications in Medicine [★7178]

Digital Media Assn. of Alberta [IO], Calgary, AB, Canada

Digital Media Device Assn. [7303], 14752 Beach Blvd., No. 103, La Mirada, CA 90638, (714)736-9774

Digital Printing and Imaging Assn. [1764], c/o Specialty Graphic Imaging Assn., 10015 Main St., Fairfax, VA 22031-3489, (703)385-1335

Digital Publishing Assn. - Address unknown since 2001.

Digital and Screen Printing Assn. [IO], Reigate, United Kingdom

Digital Special Interest Gp; Marklin [22635]

Digital TV Gp. [IO], London, United Kingdom

Digital Video Broadcasting [IO], Geneva, Switzerland

Digital Watch Assn. - Defunct.

Dignity After Death - Defunct.

Dignity in Dying [IO], London, United Kingdom

Dignity, Inc. [★20053]

Dignity Inst. of Tech. [★7594]

Dignity/USA [20053], PO Box 15373, Washington, DC 20003-0373, (202)861-0017

DIK Assn. [IO], Nacka, Sweden

Diller Fan Club [★24799]

Diller Fan Club; Natl. Phyllis [24799]

Dime Novel Club - Defunct.

Dimension Mfrs. Assn; Hardwood [★1656]

Dimokratikos Synagermos [★IO]

Dinah Shore Fan Club [24876], c/o Kay Daly, Pres., 3552 Fed. Ave., Los Angeles, CA 90066

Dinah Shore Memorial Fan Club [24738], c/o Kay Daly, Pres., 3552 Fed. Ave., Los Angeles, CA 90066

Dinah Shore Memorial Fan Club [★24876]

Dinajpur Young Men's Christian Association [IO], Dinajpur, Bangladesh

Dinghy Assn; U.S. Optimist [23230]

Dining Room Professionals; Fed. of [3393]

Dinner Theatre Inst; Amer. [1297]

Dinnerware Collectors; Currier and Ives [22007]

Dinnerware Matchers; Intl. Assn. of [1971]

Dinosaur Soc. [IO], Surbiton, United Kingdom

Dinshah Health Society [IO], Malaga, NJ, United States

Dinshah Hea. Soc. [13631], PO Box 707, Malaga, NJ 08328-0707, (856)692-4686

Diocesan Archivists; Assn. of Catholic [9399]

Diocesan Catholic Youth Councils; Natl. Fed. of [★19688]

Diocesan Ecumenical Officers; Natl. Assn. of [19901]

Diocesan Family Life Ministers; Natl. Assn. of Catholic [★20288]

Diocesan Guidance Councils; Natl. Conf. of [★8166]

Diocesan Liturgical Commissions; Fed. of [19623]

Diocesan Press; Natl. [★19953]

Diocesan Vocation Directors; Natl. Conf. of [19682]

Dip Galvanizers Assn; Amer. Hot [★850]

Diplomacy

    Amer. Acad. of Diplomacy [5744]

    Delta Phi Epsilon Professional Foreign Ser. Sorority [24473]

    Diplomacy Intl. [IO]

    Diplomats Without Borders [IO]

    Natl. Model United Nations [8661]

    Soc. for Historians of Amer. Foreign Relations [10156]

    Transnational Diplomatic Network [17874]

Diplomacy; Amer. Acad. of [5744]

Diplomacy Intl. [IO], Brussels, Belgium

Diplomacy; The Russian-American Center/Track Two Inst. for Citizen [17912]

Diplomas Nok Magyarorszagi Szovetsege [IO], Budapest, Hungary

Diplomates Sans Frontieres [★IO]

Diplomatic and Consular Officers, Retired [5745], 1801 F St. NW, Washington, DC 20006, (202)682-0500

Diplomats Without Borders [IO], Geneva, Switzerland

Direccion Nacional de Ciencia, Tecnologia e Innovacion [★IO]

Direct Aid Intl. [IO], Northfield, VT, United States

Direct Aid Intl. [12849], PO Box 394, Northfield, VT 05663

Direct Broadcast Satellite Assn. [★3754]

Direct Broadcast Satellite Assn. [★IO]

Direct Care Alliance [1868], c/o Paraprofessional Healthcare Inst., 349 E 149th St., 10th Fl., Bronx, NY 10451, (718)402-7766

Direct Instruction; Assn. for [8232]

Direct Link for the DisAbled - Defunct.

Direct Mail Advt. Assn. [★2625]

Direct Mail Educational Found. [★8816]

Direct Mail Fundraisers Assn. [★1685]

Direct Mail/Marketing Assn. [★2625]

Direct Mail/Marketing Educational Found. [★8816]

Direct Marketing Agencies; Assn. of [★2625]

Direct Marketing Assn. [2625], 1120 Ave. of the Americas, New York, NY 10036-6700, (212)768-7277

Direct Marketing Assn. [IO], London, United Kingdom

Direct Marketing Assn. Catalog Coun. [★1763]

Direct Marketing Assn. India [IO], New Delhi, India

Direct Marketing Assn; North Amer. Farmers' [5026]

Direct Marketing Assn. of Singapore [IO], Singapore, Singapore

Direct Marketing Assn. - United Kingdom [IO], London, United Kingdom

Direct Marketing Cmpt. Assn. [★2625]

Direct Marketing Computer Assn. - Defunct.

Direct Marketing Creative Guild - Address unknown since 1994.

Direct Marketing Credit Assn. - Address unknown since 1999.

Direct Marketing Educational Found. [8816], 1120 Ave. of the Americas, New York, NY 10036-6700, (212)768-7277

Direct Marketing Fundraisers Assn. [1685], 224 Seventh St., Garden City, NY 11530-5771, (516)746-6700

Direct Marketing Insurance Coun. [★2162]

Direct Marketing Insurance and Financial Services Coun. [2162], c/o Direct Marketing Assn., 1120 Ave. of the Americas, 13th Fl., New York, NY 10036-6700, (212)768-7277

Direct Marketing Intl; Women's [★2652]

Direct Marketing Minorities Opportunities - Defunct.

Direct Relief Found. [★12517]

Direct Relief Found. [★IO]

Direct Relief Intl. [IO], Santa Barbara, CA, United States

Direct Relief Intl. [12517], 27 S La Patera Ln., Santa Barbara, CA 93117, (805)964-4767

Direct Response Creative Assn. [★875]

Direct Sellers; Natl. Assn. of [★1684]

Direct Selling Assn. [3465], 1667 K St. NW, Ste. 1100, Washington, DC 20006, (202)452-8866

Direct Selling Assn. - Hungary [IO], Budapest, Hungary

Direct Selling Assn. of New Zealand [IO], Auckland, New Zealand

Direct Selling Assn. - South Africa [IO], Auckland Park, Republic of South Africa

Direct Selling Assn. - United Kingdom [IO], London, United Kingdom

Direct Selling Companies; Natl. Assn. of [★3465]

Direct Selling Educ. Found. [3466], 1667 K St. NW, Ste. 1100, Washington, DC 20006-1660, (202)452-8866

Direct Selling Education Foundation [IO], Washington, DC, United States

Directed Energy Professional Soc. [6858], 2600 Yale Blvd. SE, Ste. 139, Albuquerque, NM 87106, (505)998-4910

Direction Sports [13482]

Directional Crossing Contractors Assn. [1014]

Directorio Democratico Cubano [17365], PO Box 110235, Hialeah, FL 33011, (305)220-2713

Directorio Democratico Cubano [IO], Hialeah, FL, United States

Directorio Revolucionario Democratico Cubano [★IO]

Directorio Revolucionario Democratico Cubano [★17365]

Directors of Admin. and Gen. Ser. Officers; Natl. Assn. of State [★6278]

Directors and Administrators; Natl. Assn. of [★14574]

Directors of Agriculture; Natl. Assn. of Commissioners, Secretaries and [★5439]

Directors of Am; Advt. Funeral [★2790]

Directors; Amer. Assn. of Clinical [15986]

Directors; Amer. Assn. of Food Stamp [6261]

Directors; Amer. Soc. of Training [★8018]

Directors Assn; Amer. Choral [10531]

Directors Assn; Amer. Medical [15536]

Directors; Assn. of Art Museum [10494]

Directors; Assn. of Biomedical Communications [14030]

Directors Assn; Christian Instrumental [★20427]

Directors; Assn. of Family Medicine Residency [15059]

Directors Assn; Natl. Community Action Agency Executive [★12770]

Directors Association; National Head Start [★9006]

Directors; Assn. of Pediatric Prog. [8852]

Directors Assn; Public Housing Authorities [5798]

Directors Assn; Radio-Television News [581]

Directors; Assn. of Sci. Museum [10498]

Directors Assn; State Educational Tech. [9244]

Directors of Athletics; Natl. Assn. of Collegiate [23833]

Directors; Caucus for TV Producers, Writers, and [17165]

Directors and Choreographers Found; Stage [11044]

Directors and Choreographers; Soc. of Stage [24159]

Directors of Christian Education; Natl. Assn. of [★19937]

Directors Club; Art [9422]

Directors Club; Type [7156]

Directors Conf; Natl. Orientation [★7907]

Directors Conf; Orientation [★7907]

Directors of Educational Res; Natl. [★9053]

Directors Guild of Am. [24055], 7920 Sunset Blvd., Los Angeles, CA 90046, (310)289-2000

A star before a book entry number signifies that the name is not listed separately, but is mentioned within the entry.

Directors Guild of Am; Screen [★24055]

Directors Guild of Canada [IO], Toronto, ON, Canada

Directors Guild of Great Britain [IO], London, United Kingdom

Directors Guild; Radio and TV [★24055]

Directors Hall of Fame; Natl. High School Band [8926]

Directors of Hea. Promotion and Educ. [6215], 1101 5th St. NW, 3rd Fl., Washington, DC 20005, (202)659-2230

Directors Incorporated; Public Radio News [579]

Directors of Instruction (of NEA); Dept. of Supervisors and [★8178]

Directors of Instructional Res. in Large Cities - Address unknown since 1995.

Directors Intl. Guild; Screen [★24055]

Directors of Journalism Programs in Canadian Universities; Assn. of [IO]

Directors of Law Enforcement Standards and Training; Intl. Assn. of [5973]

Directors Local 161; Asst. [★24055]

Directors of Medical Educ; Assn. of Hosp. [★14873]

Directors and Medical Educators; Assn. of Osteopathic [15808]

Directors of Missions; Bd. of Trustees and [★19496]

Directors and Morticians Assn; Natl. Negro Funeral [★2789]

Directors; Natl. Assn. of County Community Development [★17225]

Directors; Natl. Assn. of Parish Catechetical [19932]

Directors' and Producers' Rights Soc. [IO], London, United Kingdom

Directors of Radiation Oncology Programs; Assn. for [3271]

Directors of Religious Life; National Assn. of Coll. and Univ. Chaplains and [★9168]

Directors; Soc. of Amer. Fight [9268]

Directors of Teacher Educ. and Certification; Natl. Assn. of State [9224]

Directors of Volunteer Services; Amer. Soc. of [13382]

Directors of YMCAs in the U.S; Assn. of Professional [★13460]

Directors, Young Men's Christian Associations in the U.S; Assn. of Professional [★13460]

Dir. Clearinghouse - Defunct.

Dir. and Database Publishers Assn. [★IO]

Dir. Marketing; Assn. of [2616]

Dir. Publishers; Assn. of [3208]

Dir. Publishers Assn. [★IO]

Dir. Publishers; Intl. Assn. of Cross-Reference [3228]

Disabilities
  Abilities! [11913]
  Academic Language Therapy Assn. [12488]
  Acad. of Doctors of Audiology [14733]
  Acad. on Mental Retardation [15238]
  Acad. of Rehabilitative Audiology [14734]
  Achilles Track Club [23331]
  Achromatopsia Network [16820]
  ADARA: Professionals Networking for Excellence in Ser. Delivery with Individuals who are Deaf or Hard of Hearing [14735]
  Adventures in Movement for the Handicapped [16597]
  Advocating Change Together [11914]
  Afghan Amputee Bicyclist for Rehabilitation and Recreation [IO]
  Alexander Graham Bell Assn. for the Deaf and Hard of Hearing [14736]
  AMBUCS [13034]
  Amer. Acad. for Cerebral Palsy and Developmental Medicine [13934]
  Amer. Acad. of Disability Evaluating Physicians [14033]
  Amer. Acad. of Orthotists and Prosthetists [15782]
  Amer. Acad. of Physical Medicine and Rehabilitation [16307]
  Amer. Amputee Found. [11916]
  Amer. Amputee Hockey Assn. [23799]
  Amer. Amputee Soccer Assn. [23773]
  Amer. Assn. of adaptedSPORTS Programs [23333]
  Amer. Assn. of the Deaf-Blind [14737]
  Amer. Assn. on Intellectual and Developmental Disabilities [15239]

Amer. Assn. of People with Disabilities [11917]
Amer. Assn. of Ser. Coordinators [1985]
Amer. Auditory Soc. [14738]
Amer. Blind Bowling Assn. [23334]
Amer. Blind Golf Assn. [23335]
Amer. Blind Skiing Found. [23336]
Amer. Bd. of Physical Medicine and Rehabilitation [16309]
Amer. Bd. of Professional Disability Consultants [6040]
Amer. Competition Opportunities for Riders with Disabilities [23330]
Amer. Cong. for Rehabilitation Medicine [16310]
Amer. Coun. of the Blind [16822]
Amer. Coun. of the Blind Enterprises and Services [16823]
Amer. Coun. of Blind Govt. Employees [16824]
Amer. Disability Assn. [11918]
Amer. Found. for the Blind [16826]
Amer. Hearing Aid Associates [14739]
Amer. Hearing Res. Found. [14740]
Amer. Hippotherapy Assn. [16600]
Amer. Israeli Lighthouse [16827]
Amer. Kinesiotherapy Assn. [16311]
Amer. Leprosy Missions [15007]
Amer. Medical Rehabilitation Providers Assn. [16312]
Amer. Network of Community Options and Resources [12560]
Amer. Neurotology Soc. [16441]
Amer. Occupational Therapy Assn. [16602]
Amer. Physical Therapy Assn. [16603]
Amer. Printing House for the Blind [16829]
Amer. Rehabilitation Counseling Assn. [16313]
Amer. Soc. for Deaf Children [14742]
Amer. Soc. of Handicapped Physicians [11919]
Amer. Speech Language Hearing Assn. [16442]
Amer. Wheelchair Bowling Assn. [23339]
Americans With Disabilities Act [11920]
Amputees in Motion, Intl. [11921]
Ankylosing Spondylitis Soc. in Hungary [IO]
Antigua and Barbuda Assn. of Persons with Disabilities [IO]
Arc of the U.S. [12561]
Assistance Dogs of Am., Inc. [11922]
Assistance Dogs Intl. [11923]
Assoc. Blind [16830]
Assoc. Services for the Blind [16831]
Assn. of Academic Physiatrists [16316]
Assn. for the Advancement of Blind and Retarded [16832]
Assn. of Assistive Tech. Act Programs [14237]
Assn. of Children's Prosthetic-Orthotic Clinics [15784]
Assn. of Disabled Amer. Golfers [23341]
Assn. for Educ. and Rehabilitation of the Blind and Visually Impaired [16833]
Assn. of Late-Deafened Adults [14743]
Assn. of Rehabilitation Programs in Cmpt. Tech. [11924]
Assn. of Univ. Centers on Disabilities [12563]
Attention Deficit Info. Network [15308]
Audiology Awareness Campaign [13716]
Autism Network Intl. [13719]
Autism Services Center [13722]
Better Hearing Inst. [14745]
Birth Defect Res. for Children [13752]
Blind Children's Fund [16834]
Blind Friends of Lesbian, Gay, Transgender and Bisexual People [12221]
Blind Info. Tech. Specialists [16835]
Blind Sailing Intl. [23151]
Blind Ser. Assn. [16836]
Blinded Veterans Assn. [16837]
B'nai B'rith Senior Citizens Housing Comm. [12469]
Braille Authority of North Am. [16838]
Braille Revival League [16839]
Brave Kids [13949]
Canadian Rehabilitation Coun. for the Disabled [IO]
Canine Assistants [11925]
Canine Companions for Independence [11926]
Canines for Disabled Kids [11927]
Carroll Center for the Blind [16840]

Center for Family Support [12566]
Center on Human Policy [11928]
Center for Workers with Disabilities [11929]
CFC Intl. [14435]
Challenge Aspen at Snowmass [23342]
Children of Deaf Adults [14747]
Children's Hemiplegia and Stroke Assn. [16493]
Christian Overcomers [11932]
Christian Record Services [16842]
CH on Disability Info. [11933]
Conf. of Educational Administrators of Schools and Programs for the Deaf [14749]
Consortium for Citizens with Disabilities [17416]
Continuing Care Accreditation Commn. [16318]
Coun. of Amer. Instructors of the Deaf [14750]
Coun. for Disability Rights [11935]
Coun. on Educ. of the Deaf [14751]
Coun. of Families with Visual Impairment [16844]
Coun. for Learning Disabilities [12490]
Coun. of Parent Attorneys and Advocates [9142]
Coun. on Quality and Leadership [12567]
Coun. of State Administrators of Vocational Rehabilitation [16320]
CUSA: An Apostolate of the Sick and Disabled [19620]
DateAble [11936]
Deaf History Intl. [14081]
Deafness Res. Found. [14753]
Disability Resources [11938]
Disability Rights Educ. and Defense Fund [11940]
Disabled and Alone/Life Services for the Handicapped [11941]
Disabled Amer. Veterans [20763]
Disabled Amer. Veterans Auxiliary [20764]
Disabled Birders Assn. [IO]
Disabled Collectors' Correspondence Club [22814]
Disabled Sports USA [23343]
Dog Assistance in Disability [IO]
Dogs for the Deaf [14754]
Easter Seals [11944]
Education-A-Must [12056]
European Acad. of Childhood Disability [IO]
European Disability Forum [IO]
Extensions for Independence [11945]
Fed. for Children with Special Needs [12569]
Fidelco Guide Dog Found. [16846]
First Signs [13942]
Fishing Has No Boundaries [23414]
Found. Fighting Blindness [16847]
Found. for Sci. and Disability [11946]
Free Wheelchair Mission [11947]
Friends of the Disabled Assn. [IO]
Friends of LADDERS [12491]
Global Applied Disability Res. and Info. Network [14240]
Global Deaf Connection [12274]
Goodwill Indus. Intl. [11949]
Goodwill Indus. Volunteer Services [11950]
Guide Dog Found. for the Blind [16849]
Guide Dog Users, Inc. [16850]
Guide Dogs of Am. [16851]
Guide Dogs for the Blind [16852]
Guiding Eyes for the Blind [16853]
Handicapped Scuba Assn. [23344]
Harvard Injury Control Res. Center [16690]
HEAR Center [14756]
Hear Now [14757]
Hearing Loss Assn. of Am. [14759]
Helen Keller Intl. [16854]
Helen Keller Natl. Center for Deaf-Blind Youths and Adults [14760]
Help Hospitalized Veterans [13351]
Helping Hands for the Blind [13379]
Hospitalized Veterans Writing Proj. [16321]
House Ear Inst. [16446]
Independent Visually Impaired Enterprisers [16855]
Indoor Sports Club [11951]
Institutes for the Achievement of Human Potential [11700]
Inter-American Conductive Educ. Assn. [9146]
Inter-National Assn. of Bus., Indus. and Rehabilitation [17417]
Intl. Assn. for Disability and Oral Hea. - Sweden [IO]

Reference to "IO" in place of a book number signifies that the association may be found in the 45th edition of International Organizations.

Intl. Assn. of Laryngectomees [11953]
Intl. Assn. of Rehabilitation Professionals [16322]
Intl. Child Amputee Network [11954]
Intl. Dalkon Shield Victims Educ. Assn. [16898]
Intl. Handicappers' Net [21502]
Intl. Hearing Dog, Inc. [14762]
Intl. Hearing Soc. [14763]
Intl. Lutheran Deaf Assn. [20217]
Intl. Post Polio Support Org. [16048]
Intl. Stuttering Assn. [16498]
Intl. Wheelchair Road Racers Club [23346]
InTouch Networks [16860]
JARC [12570]
JBI Intl. - Jewish Braille Inst. of Am. [16861]
Jewish Guild for the Blind [16862]
Job Accommodation Network [11955]
Joni and Friends [11956]
Just One Break [11957]
Kenya Programmes of Disabled Persons [IO]
Leader Dogs for the Blind [16864]
Learning Disabilities Assn. of Am. [12492]
Learning Disabilities Assn. of Peterborough [IO]
A Leg To Stand On [12659]
Lifespire [12572]
Little City Found. [12573]
Lutheran Braille Evangelism Assn. [16866]
Lutheran Braille Workers [16867]
MAB Community Services [16868]
Mail for Me Club [11621]
March of Dimes Birth Defects Found. [13756]
Mental Disability Rights Intl. [12574]
Mobility Intl. USA [11961]
Model Secondary School for the Deaf [14766]
MOVE Intl.: Mobility Opportunities Via Educ. - USA [11962]
MUMS Natl. Parent-to-Parent Network [16541]
NADD - An Assn. for Persons with Developmental Disabilities and Mental Hea. Needs [12552]
Natl. Ability Center [23347]
Natl. Accreditation Coun. for Agencies Serving the Blind and Visually Impaired [16870]
Natl. Adoption Center [11254]
Natl. Adult Day Services Assn. [11298]
Natl. Alliance for Accessible Golf [23348]
Natl. Alliance of Blind Students [16871]
Natl. Alliance for Direct Support Professionals [1986]
Natl. Alliance for Migrant and Seasonal Farmworker Vocational Rehabilitation [12591]
Natl. AMBUCS [11964]
Natl. Amputation Found. [11965]
Natl. Amputee Golf Assn. [23349]
Natl. Assn. of ADA Coordinators [11966]
Natl. Assn. for the Advancement of Orthotics and Prosthetics [15786]
Natl. Assn. of Blue Badge Holders [IO]
Natl. Assn. of Councils on Developmental Disabilities [12575]
Natl. Assn. of the Deaf [14767]
Natl. Assn. of Disability Evaluating Professionals [14575]
Natl. Assn. of Disability Examiners [14034]
Natl. Assn. of Disability Representatives [18648]
Natl. Assn. for the Educ. of African Amer. Children with Learning Disabilities [12493]
Natl. Assn. of Mental Hea. Planning and Advisory Councils [15216]
Natl. Assn. for Parents of Children With Visual Impairments [16873]
Natl. Assn. of the Physically Handicapped [11967]
Natl. Assn. for Recreational Equality [23836]
Natl. Assn. of Rehabilitation Instructors [16324]
Natl. Assn. of School Nurses for the Deaf [14768]
Natl. Assn. of Special Educ. Teachers [9148]
Natl. Assn. of State Directors of Developmental Disabilities Services [12576]
Natl. Assn. of State Directors of Special Educ. [9149]
Natl. Assn. of State Veterans Homes [13354]
Natl. Assn. for Visually Handicapped [16874]
Natl. Black Assn. for Speech-Language and Hearing [16448]
Natl. Braille Assn. [16875]
Natl. Braille Press [16876]
Natl. Captioning Inst. [14769]

Natl. Catholic Off. for the Deaf [19675]
Natl. Center for Learning Disabilities [12494]
Natl. Coun. on Independent Living [11968]
Natl. Coun. on Rehabilitation Educ. [16329]
Natl. Coun. for Support of Disability Issues [13212]
Natl. Disability Rights Network [11970]
Natl. Disability Sports Alliance [23353]
Natl. Dissemination Center for Children with Disabilities [11971]
Natl. Down Syndrome Cong. [12577]
Natl. Down Syndrome Soc. [12040]
Natl. Fed. of the Blind [16877]
Natl. Found. of Dentistry for the Handicapped [14179]
Natl. Fragile X Found. [14469]
Natl. Guardianship Assn. [1813]
Natl. Hearing Conservation Assn. [14772]
Natl. Indus. for the Blind [16878]
Natl. Inst. on Deafness and Other Commun. Disorders Info. CH [14773]
Natl. Inst. for Rehabilitation Engg. [11972]
Natl. Networker [12495]
Natl. Odd Shoe Exchange [11974]
Natl. Order of Trench Rats [20766]
Natl. Org. Caring for Kids [11638]
Natl. Org. of Nurses with Disabilities [15514]
Natl. Org. of Parents of Blind Children [16879]
Natl. Rehabilitation Assn. [16330]
Natl. Rehabilitation Info. Center [16332]
Natl. Ser. Dog Center [14774]
Natl. Special Needs Network Found. [14232]
Natl. Student Speech Language Hearing Assn. [16453]
Natl. Therapeutic Recreation Soc. [16628]
Natl. Veterans Services Fund [13356]
Natl. Wheelchair Basketball Assn. [23354]
Natl. Wheelchair Poolplayer Assn. [23355]
Natl. Wheelchair Softball Assn. [23356]
Networking Proj. for Young Adults with Disabilities [11975]
NISH [11976]
Nonverbal Learning Disorders Assn. [14998]
North Amer. Riding for the Handicapped Assn. [23357]
NRH Center for Hea. and Disability Res. [14233]
Oita Sports Assn. for the Disabled [IO]
One-Arm Dove Hunt Assn. [23358]
The One Shoe Crew [11977]
Opportunity Plus [11978]
Oral Hearing-Impaired Sect. [14775]
Paralyzed Veterans of Am. [20768]
Parents of Down Syndrome [12579]
Parents' Sect. of the Alexander Graham Bell Assn. for the Deaf and Hard of Hearing [14776]
Paws With a Cause [11979]
People First Intl. [12580]
People-to-People Comm. on Disability [11980]
People With Disabilities - Uganda [IO]
Phone-TTY [14777]
Physically Challenged Golf Assn. [23359]
Pilot Dogs [16881]
Pilot Parents of Southern Arizona [12581]
Post-Polio Hea. Intl. [11981]
Praying Hands Ranches [23360]
Prevent Blindness Am. [16882]
P.R.I.D.E. Found. - Promote Real Independence for the Disabled and Elderly [11982]
Proj. Magic [16634]
Protestant Guild for Human Services [16884]
REACH: Assn. for Children with Hand or Arm Deficiency [IO]
Rebuilding Together [12337]
Recording for the Blind and Dyslexic [16885]
Registry of Interpreters for the Deaf [14778]
Rehabilitation Engg. and Assistive Tech. Soc. of North Am. [11983]
Rehabilitation Intl. [16333]
Res. to Prevent Blindness [16886]
Res. and Training Center on Independent Living [11984]
Sahara Griha [IO]
School Nurse Achievement Prog. [15525]
Sect. for Long Term Care and Rehabilitation [14894]

Siblings for Significant Change [11987]
Sister Kenny Rehabilitation Inst. [16335]
Ski for Light [23361]
Societa Medica Italiana di Paraplegia [IO]
Soc. for Disability Stud. [11988]
Special Needs Advocate for Parents [11652]
Special Olympics [23362]
Special Recreation for disABLED Intl. [11989]
Spina Bifida Assn. of Am. [16458]
Spinal Cord Injuries Australia [IO]
Steps Charity Worldwide [IO]
STRIDE: Sports and Therapeutic Recreation Instruction/Developmental Educ. [8205]
Stroke Clubs, Intl. [16496]
Support Dogs, Inc. [11990]
Symbral Found. [12582]
Telecommunications for the Deaf and Hard of Hearing, Inc. [14780]
United Amputee Services Assn. [15080]
United Cerebral Palsy Associations [13935]
U.S.A. Deaf Basketball [23136]
U.S. Assn. for Blind Athletes [23363]
U.S. Blind Golf Assn. [23364]
U.S. Handcycling Fed. [23321]
U.S. Power Soccer Assn. [23783]
U.S. Psychiatric Rehabilitation Assn. [16336]
U.S. Quad Rugby Assn. [23705]
U.S. Soc. for Augmentative and Alternative Commun. [17198]
Universal Wheelchair Football Assn. [23368]
USA Deaf Sports Fed. [23369]
U.S.A. Toy Lib. Assn. [11548]
Veterans Educ. Proj. [13358]
VietNow Natl. [13359]
Vision World Wide [16890]
Visually Impaired Veterans of Am. [16891]
Vocational Evaluation and Career Assessment Professionals [16337]
VSA arts [11993]
Wheelchair Motorcycle Assn. [23370]
Wheelchair Sports, USA [23371]
Wheels for the World [11994]
World Ability Fed. [11995]
World Inst. on Disability [11996]
World Rehabilitation Fund [11997]
Xavier Soc. for the Blind [16892]
Young Adult Institute/National Inst. for People with Disabilities [12584]
Disabilities; Acad. of Dentistry for Persons with [★14186]
Disabilities; Accreditation Coun. on Services for People with [★12567]
Disabilities; Amer. Assn. of Univ. Affiliated Programs for Persons With Developmental [★12563]
Disabilities Assn. of Am; Learning [12492]
Disabilities; Assn. for Children and Adults with Learning [★12492]
Disabilities; Assn. for Children with Learning [★12492]
Disabilities; Assn. of Univ. Centers on [12563]
Disabilities; Coun. for Learning [12490]
Disabilities; Coun. on Quality and Leadership in Supports for People with [★12567]
Disabilities Councils; Natl. Assn. of Developmental [★12575]
Disabilities; Div. for Children with Learning [★12490]
Disabilities; Found. for Children with Learning [★12494]
Disabilities and Gifted Education; ERIC CH on [★9141]
Disabilities and Gifted Education; ERIC CH on [★11998]
Disabilities and Gifted Education; ERIC CH on [★IO]
Disabilities; Intl. Assn. for the Sci. Stud. of Intellectual [IO]
Disabilities; Ministry with Persons with [★20216]
Disabilities; Natl. Assn. of Councils on Developmental [12575]
Disabilities; Natl. Catholic Off. for Persons With [★19676]
Disabilities; Natl. Center for Learning [12494]
Disabilities; Natl. Conf. on Developmental [★12575]
Disabilities Nurses Assn; Developmental [15477]
Disabilities; Young Adult Institute/National Inst. for People with [12584]

A star before a book entry number signifies that the name is not listed separately, but is mentioned within the entry.

Disability Alliance [IO], London, United Kingdom
Disability Alliance Educ. and Res. Assn. [★IO]
Disability Australia [IO], Richmond, Australia
Disability Central [11937]
Disability Consultants; Amer. Bd. of Professional [6040]
Disability Coun; Natl. Bus. and [12089]
Disability Evaluating Physicians; Amer. Acad. of [14033]
Disability Evaluating Professionals; Natl. Assn. of [14575]
Disability Examiner Certification; Commission on [★14575]
Disability Examiners; Natl. Assn. of [14034]
Disability Fed. of Ireland [IO], Dublin, Ireland
Disability Insurance Training Coun. - Defunct.
Disability Intl. Found. [14239]
Disability Law; Amer. Bar Assn. - Commn. on Mental and Physical [5781]
Disability Legal Res. Services and Databases; Mental and Physical [★5781]
Disability Legal Rsrc. Center; Mental [★5781]
Disability Mgt. Employer Coalition [1259], 5173 Waring Rd., Ste. 134, San Diego, CA 92120-2705, (800)789-3632
Disability Ministries [20216], c/o Evangelical Lutheran Church in Am., 8765 W Higgins Rd., Chicago, IL 60631, (773)380-2700
Disability; Natl. Assn. on Alcohol, Drugs and [16512]
Disability; Natl. Catholic Partnership on [19676]
Disability; Natl. Challenge Comm. on [★17415]
Disability Resources [11938], 4 Glatter Ln., Centereach, NY 11720-1032, (631)585-0290
Disability Rights Center [11939], PO Box 2007, Augusta, ME 04338-2007, (207)626-2774
Disability Rights Clinical Legal Educ. Prog. [★11940]
Disability Rights Educ. and Defense Fund [11940], 2212 6th St., Berkeley, CA 94710, (510)644-2555
Disability Sport - England [★IO]
Disability Sport Events [IO], Manchester, United Kingdom
Disability Sport South Africa [IO], Bezuidenhout Valley, Republic of South Africa

Disabled
  Abilities! [11913]
  Academic Language Therapy Assn. [12488]
  Acad. of Doctors of Audiology [14733]
  Acad. on Mental Retardation [15238]
  Acad. of Rehabilitative Audiology [14734]
  Accessibility Equip. Manufacturers Assn. [1156]
  Achilles Track Club [23331]
  Achromatopsia Network [16820]
  Action on Disability and Development [IO]
  Adaptive Sports Assn. [23332]
  ADARA: Professionals Networking for Excellence in Ser. Delivery with Individuals who are Deaf or Hard of Hearing [14735]
  Adventures in Movement for the Handicapped [16597]
  Advocating Change Together [11914]
  Afghanistan Paralympic Comm. [IO]
  AFL-CIO Working for Am. Inst. [12065]
  African Sports Confed. of Disabled [IO]
  Agape Center [IO]
  Alberta Amputee Sport and Recreation Assn. [IO]
  Alexander Graham Bell Assn. for the Deaf and Hard of Hearing [14736]
  Algerian Sports Fed. for Disabled [IO]
  All-Russian Soc. for Disabled [IO]
  Alliance of Organisations of Disabled People Slovakia [IO]
  Alliance for Tech. Access [11915]
  AMBUCS [13034]
  Ambucs Rsrc. Center [14234]
  Amer. Acad. for Cerebral Palsy and Developmental Medicine [13934]
  Amer. Acad. of Disability Evaluating Physicians [14033]
  Amer. Acad. of Orthotists and Prosthetists [15782]
  Amer. Acad. of Physical Medicine and Rehabilitation [16307]
  Amer. Amputee Found. [11916]
  Amer. Amputee Hockey Assn. [23799]
  Amer. Amputee Soccer Assn. [23773]

Amer. Assn. of adaptedSPORTS Programs [23333]
Amer. Assn. of the Deaf-Blind [14737]
Amer. Assn. on Hea. and Disability [14235]
Amer. Assn. on Intellectual and Developmental Disabilities [15239]
Amer. Assn. of People with Disabilities [11917]
Amer. Assn. of Ser. Coordinators [1985]
Amer. Auditory Soc. [14738]
Amer. Blind Bowling Assn. [23334]
Amer. Blind Golf Assn. [23335]
Amer. Blind Skiing Found. [23336]
Amer. Bd. of Physical Medicine and Rehabilitation [16309]
Amer. Competition Opportunities for Riders with Disabilities [23330]
Amer. Cong. of Community Supports and Employment Services [17206]
Amer. Cong. of Rehabilitation Medicine [16310]
Amer. Coun. of the Blind [16822]
Amer. Coun. of the Blind Enterprises and Services [16823]
Amer. Coun. of Blind Govt. Employees [16824]
Amer. Disability Assn. [11918]
Amer. Disabled for Attendant Prog. Today [17413]
Amer. Found. for the Blind [16826]
Amer. Friends of ALYN Hosp. [12825]
Amer. Hearing Aid Associates [14739]
Amer. Hearing Impaired Hockey Assn. [23337]
Amer. Hearing Res. Found. [14740]
Amer. Hippotherapy Assn. [16600]
Amer. Israeli Lighthouse [16827]
Amer. Kinesiotherapy Assn. [16311]
Amer. Medical Rehabilitation Providers Assn. [16312]
Amer. Network of Community Options and Resources [12560]
Amer. Neurotology Soc. [16441]
Amer. Occupational Therapy Assn. [16602]
Amer. Physical Therapy Assn. [16603]
Amer. Polocrosse Assn. [23338]
Amer. Printing House for the Blind [16829]
Amer. Rehabilitation Counseling Assn. [16313]
Amer. Soc. for Deaf Children [14742]
Amer. Soc. of Handicapped Physicians [11919]
Amer. Speech Language Hearing Assn. [16442]
Amer. Wheelchair Bowling Assn. [23339]
Americans With Disabilities Act [11920]
America's Athletes with Disabilities [23340]
Amputee Coalition of Am. [14236]
Amputees in Motion, Intl. [11921]
APSE: The Network on Employment [17414]
Arc of the U.S. [12561]
L'Arche Australia [IO]
Armenian Natl. Paralympic Comm. [IO]
Asia Pacific Deaf Sports Confed. [IO]
Askio Disabled People Switzerland [IO]
Assistance Dogs of Am., Inc. [11922]
Assistance Dogs Australia [IO]
Assistance Dogs Intl. [IO]
Assistance Dogs Intl. [11923]
Associacao Portuguesa de Deficientes [IO]
Assoc. Blind [16830]
Assoc. Services for the Blind [16831]
Assn. of Academic Physiatrists [16316]
Assn. of Administrators of the Interstate Compact on Adoption and Medical Assistance [11236]
Assn. for the Advancement of Blind and Retarded [16832]
Assn. of Assistive Tech. Act Programs [14237]
Assn. for Children with a Disability [IO]
Assn. of Children's Prosthetic-Orthotic Clinics [15784]
Assn. of Disabled Amer. Golfers [23341]
Assn. of Disabled Professionals [IO]
Assn. for Educ. and Rehabilitation of the Blind and Visually Impaired [16833]
Assn. for Higher Educ. Access and Disability [IO]
Assn. on Higher Educ. and Disability [IO]
Assn. on Higher Educ. and Disability [8201]
Assn. of Late-Deafened Adults [14743]
Assn. for the Neurologically Disabled of Canada [IO]
Assn. of Organizations of Disabled People of Croatia [IO]

Assn. for Persons With Special Needs [IO]
Assn. of Rehabilitation Programs in Cmpt. Tech. [11924]
Assn. for Support of Social and Community Integration [IO]
Assn. of Univ. Centers on Disabilities [12563]
Assn. of Wheelchair Children [IO]
Associazione la Nostra Famiglia [IO]
Attention Deficit Info. Network [15308]
Audiology Awareness Campaign [13716]
Australian Athletes with a Disability [IO]
Australian Blind Sports Federations [IO]
Australian Fed. of Disability Organisations [IO]
Australian Paralympic Comm. [IO]
Australian Rehabilitation and Assistive Tech. Assn. [IO]
Austrian Paralympic Comm. [IO]
Autism Network Intl. [13719]
Autism Services Center [13722]
Bahrain Disabled Sports Fed. [IO]
Bangladesh Protibandhi Kallyan Somity [IO]
Barbados Natl. Org. For The Disabled [IO]
BC Wheelchair Sports Assn. [IO]
Belgian Paralympic Comm. [IO]
Bellwoods Centres for Community Living [IO]
Bethany Care Soc. [IO]
Better Hearing Inst. [14745]
Birth Defect Res. for Children [13752]
Black Lung Assn. [13323]
Blind Children's Fund [16834]
Blind Friends of Lesbian, Gay, Transgender and Bisexual People [12221]
Blind Info. Tech. Specialists [16835]
Blind Ser. Assn. [16836]
Blind Sport New Zealand [IO]
Blinded Veterans Assn. [16837]
B'nai B'rith Senior Citizens Housing Comm. [12469]
Braille Authority of North Am. [16838]
Braille Revival League [16839]
British Blind Sport [IO]
British Deaf Sports Coun. [IO]
British Disabled Angling Assn. [IO]
British Disabled Water Ski Assn. [IO]
British Dyslexia Assn. [IO]
British Inst. of Learning Disabilities [IO]
British Paralympic Assn. [IO]
British Soc. for Disability and Oral Hea. [IO]
Bulgarian Paralympic Comm. [IO]
Cambodian Disabled People's Org. [IO]
Cameroonian Paralympic Comm. [IO]
Canadian Amputee Sports Assn. [IO]
Canadian Assn. for Disabled Skiing [IO]
Canadian Assn. of Independent Living Centres [IO]
Canadian Cerebral Palsy Sports Assn. [IO]
Canadian Deaf Curling Assn. [IO]
Canadian Deaf Golf Assn. [IO]
Canadian Deaf Sports Assn. [IO]
Canadian Deafblind and Rubella Assn. [IO]
Canadian Found. for Physically Disabled Persons [IO]
Canadian Paralympic Comm. [IO]
Canadian Paraplegic Assn. [IO]
Canadian Wheelchair Sports Assn. [IO]
Canine Assistants [11925]
Canine Companions for Independence [11926]
Canines for Disabled Kids [11927]
Carers UK [IO]
Carnegie Hero Fund Commn. [13036]
Carroll Center for the Blind [16840]
Catholic Guardian Soc. [11564]
Center for Bio-Ethical Reform [18547]
Center for Family Support [12566]
Center on Human Policy [11928]
Center for Medicare Advocacy [14684]
Center for Workers with Disabilities [11929]
Centra Cam Vocational Training Assn. [IO]
Cerebral Palsy Intl. Sports and Recreation Assn. [IO]
CFC Intl. [14435]
Challenge Aspen at Snowmass [23342]
Challenge Intl. [17415]
Challenge Intl. [IO]
Challenged Am. [14238]

Reference to "IO" in place of a book number signifies that the association may be found in the 45th edition of International Organizations.

Challenged Conquistadors [11930]
Cheshire Ireland [IO]
Children of Deaf Adults [14747]
Children's Hemiplegia and Stroke Assn. [16493]
China Disabled Persons' Fed. [IO]
Chinese Taipei Paralympic Comm. [IO]
Chinese Taipei Sports Fed. for the Disabled [IO]
Christian Blind Mission Intl. [16841]
Christian Coun. on Persons with Disabilities [11931]
Christian Coun. on Persons with Disabilities [IO]
Christian Outreach to the Handicapped [IO]
Christian Overcomers [11932]
Christian Record Services [16842]
Christian Record Services [IO]
CH on Disability Info. [11933]
Cleft Lip and Palate Assn. [IO]
Comite Paralimpico Angolano [IO]
Comm. for Handicapable Dancers [9870]
Comm. on the Rehabilitation and Integration of People with Disabilities [IO]
Conf. of Educational Administrators of Schools and Programs for the Deaf [14749]
Consortium for Citizens with Disabilities [17416]
Continuing Care Accreditation Commn. [16318]
Coun. of Amer. Instructors of the Deaf [14750]
Coun. of Citizens With Low Vision Intl. [11934]
Coun. for Disability Rights [11935]
Coun. of Disabled People of Thailand [IO]
Coun. on Educ. of the Deaf [14751]
Coun. for Exceptional Children [9141]
Coun. of Families with Visual Impairment [16844]
Coun. for Learning Disabilities [12490]
Coun. of Parent Attorneys and Advocates [9142]
Coun. on Quality and Leadership [12567]
Coun. for the Registration of Schools Teaching Dyslexic Pupils [IO]
Coun. of State Administrators of Vocational Rehabilitation [16320]
Create A Smile Dental Found. [13318]
Croatian Sports Fed. for the Disabled [IO]
CURE Intl. [13975]
CUSA: An Apostolate of the Sick and Disabled [19620]
Cyprus Natl. Paralympic Comm. [IO]
Czech Paralympic Comm. [IO]
DateAble [IO]
DateAble [11936]
Deaf History Intl. [14081]
Deaf Sports Australia [IO]
Deafblind Intl. [IO]
Deafness Res. Found. [14753]
Developmental Delay Resources [13941]
Disability Alliance [IO]
Disability Australia [IO]
Disability Central [11937]
Disability Fed. of Ireland [IO]
Disability Intl. Found. [14239]
Disability Resources [11938]
Disability Rights Center [11939]
Disability Rights Educ. and Defense Fund [11940]
Disability Sport Events [IO]
Disability Sport South Africa [IO]
Disabled and Alone/Life Services for the Handicapped [11941]
Disabled Amer. Veterans [20763]
Disabled Amer. Veterans Auxiliary [20764]
Disabled Businesspersons Assn. [12076]
Disabled Collectors' Correspondence Club [22814]
Disabled Drivers' Assn. - England [IO]
Disabled Drivers' Assn. of Ireland [IO]
Disabled Living Found. [IO]
Disabled People's Assn. of Singapore [IO]
Disabled Peoples' Intl. [IO]
Disabled Peoples' Intl. - Europe [IO]
Disabled Peoples' Intl. - India [IO]
Disabled Peoples' Intl. - Jamaica [IO]
Disabled People's Intl. - Korea [IO]
Disabled Peoples' Intl. - North Am. and the Caribbean [IO]
Disabled Peoples' Intl. - Poland [IO]
Disabled Peoples' Intl. - Sweden [IO]
Disabled Persons Assembly New Zealand [IO]
Disabled Sports USA [23343]

DisAbled Women's Network Canada [IO]
Disabled Womyn's Educational Proj. [11942]
Div. on Visual Impairments [9145]
Dogs for the Deaf [14754]
Dominica Assn. of Disabled People [IO]
Dream Catchers, USA [11943]
Dutch Coun. of the Chronically Ill and Disabled [IO]
Dyslexia Action [IO]
Easter Seals [11944]
Education-A-Must [12056]
Elwyn [12383]
Enable - Ireland [IO]
English Natl. Assn. of Visually Handicapped Bowlers [IO]
Estonian Paralympic Comm. [IO]
European Paralympic Comm. [IO]
Extensions for Independence [11945]
Family Rsrc. Center on Disabilities [8202]
Fed. Centrafricaine Handisports [IO]
Fed. for Children with Special Needs [12569]
Fed. Malgache Handisport [IO]
Fed. Mauritanienne de Sport pour Handicapes [IO]
Fed. Nigerienne Sports pour Personnes Handicapes [IO]
Fed. Rwandaise Handisport [IO]
Fed. Sportive des Handicapes du Burundi [IO]
Fidelco Guide Dog Found. [16846]
Fiji Disabled Peoples Assn. [IO]
Fiji Islands Blind Sport Assn. [IO]
Finnish Paralympic Comm. [IO]
Fishing Has No Boundaries [23414]
Found. Fighting Blindness [16847]
Found. for Sci. and Disability [11946]
Free Wheelchair Mission [11947]
Free Wheelchair Mission [IO]
Freedom Is Not Free [12596]
Friends' Hea. Connection [22136]
Gambia Assn. of the Physically Disabled [IO]
Georgian Paralympic Comm. [IO]
Glenkirk [11948]
Global Applied Disability Res. and Info. Network [14240]
Global Applied Disability Res. and Info. Network [IO]
Global Deaf Connection [12274]
Goodwill Indus. Intl. [11949]
Goodwill Indus. Intl. [IO]
Goodwill Indus. of Venezuela [IO]
Goodwill Indus. Volunteer Services [11950]
Goodwill - The Amity Gp. [IO]
Great Britain Wheelchair Basketball Assn. [IO]
Grenada Natl. Coun. of the Disabled [IO]
Guide Dog Found. for the Blind [16849]
Guide Dog Users, Inc. [16850]
Guide Dogs of Am. [16851]
Guide Dogs for the Blind [16852]
Guiding Eyes for the Blind [16853]
Guinea Sports Fed. for Disabled [IO]
Guyana Coalition of Citizens with Disability [IO]
Handicap Intl. - Belgium [IO]
Handicap Intl. Canada [IO]
Handicap Intl. Denmark [IO]
Handicap Intl. - France [IO]
Handicap Intl. Germany [IO]
Handicap Intl. Luxembourg [IO]
Handicap Intl. Switzerland [IO]
Handicap Intl. - Thailand [IO]
Handicap Intl. - UK [IO]
Handicapped Scuba Association [IO]
Handicapped Scuba Assn. [23344]
Handicaps Welfare Assn. [IO]
Handidactis [IO]
Harrow Assn. of Disabled People [IO]
Harvard Injury Control Res. Center [16690]
HEAR Center [14756]
Hear Now [14757]
Hearing Loss Assn. of Am. [14759]
HEATH Rsrc. Center [8203]
Helen Keller Intl. [16854]
Helen Keller Natl. Center for Deaf-Blind Youths and Adults [14760]
Hellenic Paralympic Comm. [IO]
Help the Helpless [12405]

Help Hospitalized Veterans [13351]
Helping Hands for the Blind [13379]
Homes for Our Troops [21302]
Hong Kong Paralympic Comm. and Sports Assn. for the Physically Disabled [IO]
Hong Kong PHAB Assn. [IO]
Hong Kong Sports Assn. for the Physically Disabled [IO]
Hospitalized Veterans Writing Proj. [16321]
House Ear Inst. [16446]
Hungarian Paralympic Comm. [IO]
I CAN [IO]
Independent Visually Impaired Enterprisers [16855]
Indoor Sports Club [11951]
Inspiration Ministries [11952]
Institutes for the Achievement of Human Potential [11700]
Inter-American Conductive Educ. Assn. [9146]
Inter-National Assn. of Bus., Indus. and Rehabilitation [17417]
Intl. Assn. of Assistance Dog Partners [14241]
Intl. Assn. for Disability and Oral Hea. [14242]
Intl. Assn. for Disability and Oral Hea. [IO]
Intl. Assn. for Handicapped Divers [IO]
Intl. Assn. of Laryngectomees [IO]
Intl. Assn. of Laryngectomees [11953]
Intl. Assn. of Rehabilitation Professionals [16322]
Intl. Blind Sports Fed. [IO]
Intl. Blind Sports Fed. Europe [IO]
Intl. Blind Sports Fed. Oceania [IO]
International Child Amputee Network [IO]
Intl. Child Amputee Network [11954]
Intl. Comm. of Sports for the Deaf/DEAFLYMPICS [23345]
Intl. Comm. of Sports for the Deaf/DEAFLYMPICS [IO]
Intl. Dalkon Shield Victims Educ. Assn. [16898]
Intl. Fed. of Persons with Physical Disabilities [IO]
Intl. Handicappers' Net [21502]
Intl. Hearing Dog, Inc. [14762]
Intl. Hearing Soc. [14763]
Intl. Lutheran Deaf Assn. [20217]
Intl. Paralympic Comm. [IO]
Intl. Post Polio Support Org. [16048]
Intl. Sports Fed. for Persons with Intellectual Disability [IO]
Intl. Stuttering Assn. [16498]
Intl. Wheelchair and Amputee Sports Fed. [IO]
Intl. Wheelchair Road Racers Club [IO]
Intl. Wheelchair Road Racers Club [23346]
InTouch Networks [16860]
Iraqi Natl. Paralympic Comm. [IO]
Irish Wheelchair Assn. [IO]
Israel Sports Assn. for the Disabled [IO]
Italian Paralympic Comm. [IO]
ITEM Coalition [14690]
Jamaican Assn. for the Deaf [IO]
Japan Natl. Assembly of Disabled People's Intl. [IO]
Japanese Assn. on Disability and Difficulty [IO]
JARC [12570]
JBI Intl. - Jewish Braille Inst. of Am. [16861]
Jewish Guild for the Blind [16862]
Job Accommodation Network [11955]
Joint Coun. for the Physically and Mentally Disabled - Hong Kong [IO]
Joni and Friends [11956]
Just One Break [11957]
KDWB Variety Family Center [13964]
Kenya Disabled Development Soc. [IO]
Keren Or [16863]
Knowbility [11958]
Korea Polio Found. [IO]
Korea Sports Assn. for the Disabled [IO]
Kuwait Soc. for the Handicapped [IO]
Landmine Survivors Network [11959]
Lao Disabled People's Assn. [IO]
Latvian Paralympic Comm. [IO]
Leader Dogs for the Blind [16864]
Learning Disabilities Assn. of Am. [12492]
Learning Disabilities Assn. of Canada [IO]
Lebanese Coun. of Disabled People [IO]
Lebanese Paralympics Comm. [IO]
A Leg To Stand On [12659]

A star before a book entry number signifies that the name is not listed separately, but is mentioned within the entry.

Leonard Cheshire Intl. [IO]
Libyan Fed. of Sports for Disabled [IO]
Lifespire [12572]
Limbless Assn. [IO]
Lithuanian Paralympic Comm. [IO]
Little City Found. [12573]
Logan Community Resources [11960]
Lutheran Braille Evangelism Assn. [16866]
Lutheran Braille Workers [16867]
MAB Community Services [16868]
Mail for Me Club [11621]
Mali Fed. of Sport for the Disabled [IO]
March of Dimes Birth Defects Found. [13756]
Mental Disability Rights Intl. [12574]
Mobility Intl. USA [11961]
Mobility Intl. USA [IO]
Model Secondary School for the Deaf [14766]
Mongolia Fed. of Disabled Persons [IO]
MOVE International: Mobility Opportunities Via
    Education - USA [IO]
MOVE Intl.: Mobility Opportunities Via Educ. -
    USA [11962]
MUMS Natl. Parent-to-Parent Network [16541]
NADD - An Assn. for Persons with Developmental
    Disabilities and Mental Hea. Needs [12552]
Namibia Sports Fed. of the Disabled [IO]
NASEN [IO]
Natl. Ability Center [23347]
Natl. Accessible Apartment CH [11963]
Natl. Accreditation Coun. for Agencies Serving the
    Blind and Visually Impaired [16870]
Natl. Adoption Center [11254]
Natl. Adult Day Services Assn. [11298]
Natl. Alliance for Accessible Golf [23348]
Natl. Alliance of Blind Students [16871]
Natl. Alliance for Direct Support Professionals
    [1986]
Natl. Alliance for Migrant and Seasonal Farm-
    worker Vocational Rehabilitation [12591]
Natl. AMBUCS [11964]
Natl. Amputation Found. [11965]
Natl. Amputee Golf Assn. [23349]
Natl. Assn. of ADA Coordinators [11966]
Natl. Assn. for Adults with Special Learning Needs
    [8204]
Natl. Assn. for the Advancement of Orthotics and
    Prosthetics [15786]
Natl. Assn. of Councils on Developmental Dis-
    abilities [12575]
Natl. Assn. of the Deaf [14767]
Natl. Assn. of Disability Evaluating Professionals
    [14575]
Natl. Assn. of Disability Examiners [14034]
Natl. Assn. of Disability Representatives [18648]
Natl. Assn. for the Dually Diagnosed [14243]
Natl. Assn. for the Educ. of African Amer. Children
    with Learning Disabilities [12493]
Natl. Assn. for Parents of Children With Visual
    Impairments [16873]
Natl. Assn. of the Physically Handicapped [11967]
Natl. Assn. for Recreational Equality [23836]
Natl. Assn. of Rehabilitation Instructors [16324]
Natl. Assn. of School Nurses for the Deaf [14768]
Natl. Assn. of Societies for Care of the
    Handicapped [IO]
Natl. Assn. of State Directors of Developmental
    Disabilities Services [12576]
Natl. Assn. of State Veterans Homes [13354]
Natl. Assn. for Visually Handicapped [16874]
Natl. Beep Baseball Assn. [23350]
Natl. Black Assn. for Speech-Language and Hear-
    ing [16448]
Natl. Black Deaf Advocates [17418]
Natl. Braille Assn. [16875]
Natl. Braille Press [16876]
Natl. Bus. and Disability Coun. [12089]
Natl. Captioning Inst. [14769]
Natl. Catholic Off. for the Deaf [19675]
Natl. Center for the Dissemination of Disability
    Res. [14244]
Natl. Center for Learning Disabilities [12494]
Natl. Center for Therapeutic Riding [23351]
Natl. Coun. on Independent Living [11968]
Natl. Coun. on Rehabilitation Educ. [16329]
Natl. Coun. for Support of Disability Issues
    [13212]

Natl. Cristina Found. [11969]
National Cristina Foundation [IO]
Natl. Deaf Women's Bowling Assn. [23352]
Natl. Disability Rights Network [11970]
Natl. Disability Services [IO]
Natl. Disability Sports Alliance [23353]
Natl. Dissemination Center for Children with Dis-
    abilities [11971]
Natl. Down Syndrome Cong. [12577]
Natl. Down Syndrome Soc. [12040]
Natl. Educ. for Assistance Dog Services [14770]
Natl. Fed. of the Blind [16877]
Natl. Fed. of the Disabled Nepal [IO]
Natl. Fed. of Disabled Persons Associations [IO]
Natl. Found. of Dentistry for the Handicapped
    [14179]
Natl. Fragile X Found. [14469]
Natl. Hearing Conservation Assn. [14772]
Natl. Indus. for the Blind [16878]
Natl. Inst. on Deafness and Other Commun.
    Disorders Info. CH [14773]
Natl. Inst. for Rehabilitation Engg. [11972]
Natl. League of the Blind and Disabled [IO]
Natl. Network for the Disabled [11973]
Natl. Networker [12495]
Natl. Odd Shoe Exchange [11974]
National Odd Shoe Exchange [IO]
Natl. Order of Trench Rats [20766]
Natl. Org. Caring for Kids [11638]
Natl. Org. on Disability [17419]
Natl. Org. on Disability [IO]
Natl. Org. of Nurses with Disabilities [15514]
Natl. Org. of Parents of Blind Children [16879]
Natl. Paralympic Comm. Germany [IO]
Natl. Paralympic Comm. Islamic Republic of Iran
    [IO]
Natl. Paralympic Comm. of Turkey [IO]
Natl. Parent Network on Disabilities [14245]
Natl. Rehabilitation Assn. [16330]
Natl. Rehabilitation Info. Center [16332]
Natl. Ser. Dog Center [14774]
Natl. Soc. of Persons with disAbilities [IO]
Natl. Student Speech Language Hearing Assn.
    [16453]
Natl. Therapeutic Recreation Soc. [16628]
Natl. Union of Disabled Persons of Uganda [IO]
Natl. Veterans Services Fund [13356]
Natl. Wheelchair Basketball Assn. [23354]
Natl. Wheelchair Poolplayer Assn. [23355]
National Wheelchair Poolplayer Association [IO]
Natl. Wheelchair Softball Assn. [23356]
NEIGHBOURS [IO]
Netherlands Inst. for Care and Welfare [IO]
Netherlands Paralympic Comm. [IO]
Networking Proj. for Young Adults with Disabilities
    [11975]
New South Wales Wheelchair Sports Assn. [IO]
NISH [11976]
Nonverbal Learning Disorders Assn. [14998]
Nordic Cooperation on Disability [IO]
North Amer. Riding for the Handicapped Assn.
    [23357]
North Amer. Squirrel Assn. [22773]
Norwegian Dyslexia Assn. [IO]
Norwegian Fed. of Organisations of Disabled
    People [IO]
NRH Center for Hea. and Disability Res. [14233]
One-Arm Dove Hunt Assn. [23358]
The One Shoe Crew [11977]
Opening Door [3932]
Opportunity Plus [11978]
Oral Hearing-Impaired Sect. [14775]
PACER Center - Parent Advocacy Coalition for
    Educational Rights [14246]
Pan African Fed. of the Disabled [IO]
Paralympic Comm. of Azerbaijan Republic [IO]
Paralympic Comm. of Moldova [IO]
Paralympic Comm. of Moscow [IO]
Paralympic Comm. of the Republic of Belarus [IO]
Paralympic Comm. of Russia [IO]
Paralympic Comm. of Serbia and Montenegro [IO]
Paralympic Coun. of Ireland [IO]
Paralympics New Zealand [IO]
Paralyzed Veterans of Am. [20768]
Parents of Down Syndrome [12579]

Parents Helping Parents [12684]
Parents' Sect. of the Alexander Graham Bell
    Assn. for the Deaf and Hard of Hearing [14776]
Paws With a Cause [11979]
People First Intl. [12580]
People-to-People Comm. on Disability [11980]
Philippine Sports Assn. of the Differently Abled
    [IO]
Phone-TTY [14777]
Physical Disability Coun. of Australia [IO]
Physically Challenged Bowhunters of Am. [23549]
Physically Challenged Golf Assn. [23359]
Physically Challenged Golf Assn. [IO]
Pilot Dogs [16881]
Pilot Parents of Southern Arizona [12581]
Polish Paralympic Comm. [IO]
Post-Polio Hea. Intl. [IO]
Post-Polio Hea. Intl. [11981]
Praying Hands Ranches [23360]
Prevent Blindness Am. [16882]
P.R.I.D.E. Found. - Promote Real Independence
    for the Disabled and Elderly [11982]
Proj. Magic [16634]
Protestant Guild for Human Services [16884]
Rebuilding Together [12337]
Recording for the Blind and Dyslexic [16885]
Registry of Interpreters for the Deaf [14778]
Rehabilitation Engg. and Assistive Tech. Soc. of
    North Am. [11983]
Rehabilitation Intl. [16333]
Res. to Prevent Blindness [16886]
Res. and Training Center on Independent Living
    [11984]
Responsible Hospitality Inst. [11985]
Responsible Hospitality Inst. [IO]
Restricted Growth Assn. [IO]
Riding for the Disabled Assn. - Ireland [IO]
Riding for the Disabled Assn. of Singapore [IO]
Royal Assn. for Disability and Rehabilitation [IO]
Rural Inst. [11986]
Saudi Sports Fed. for Special Needs [IO]
School Nurse Achievement Prog. [15525]
Scottish Disability Sport [IO]
Sea to See Proj. [13760]
Sect. for Long Term Care and Rehabilitation
    [14894]
Siblings for Significant Change [11987]
Singapore Disability Sports Coun. [IO]
Sister Kenny Rehabilitation Inst. [16335]
Ski for Light [23361]
Ski for Light [IO]
Slovak Paralympic Comm. [IO]
Soc. for Accessible Travel and Hospitality [17420]
Soc. for Disability Stud. [11988]
Soc. of Teachers of the Alexander Technique [IO]
Southern Africa Fed. of the Disabled [IO]
Southern African Assn. for Learning and
    Educational Difficulties [IO]
Sozialverband Vdk Deutschland [IO]
Spanish Paralympic Comm. [IO]
Special Interest Gp. on Accessible Computing
    [6803]
Special Needs Advocate for Parents [11652]
Special Olympics [23362]
Special Olympics [IO]
Special Olympics Albania [IO]
Special Olympics Andorra [IO]
Special Olympics Armenia [IO]
Special Olympics Australia [IO]
Special Olympics Austria [IO]
Special Olympics Bangladesh [IO]
Special Olympics Belarus [IO]
Special Olympics Benin [IO]
Special Olympics Bolivia [IO]
Special Olympics Bosnia and Herzegovina [IO]
Special Olympics Botswana [IO]
Special Olympics Bulgaria [IO]
Special Olympics Burkina Faso [IO]
Special Olympics Cameroon [IO]
Special Olympics Canada [IO]
Special Olympics Chad [IO]
Special Olympics Costa Rica [IO]
Special Olympics Croatia [IO]
Special Olympics Cuba [IO]
Special Olympics Cyprus [IO]

Reference to "IO" in place of a book number signifies that the association may be found in the 45th edition of International Organizations.

Special Olympics Czech Republic [IO]
Special Olympics East Asia [IO]
Special Olympics Ecuador [IO]
Special Olympics El Salvador [IO]
Special Olympics Finland [IO]
Special Olympics Gambia [IO]
Special Olympics Germany [IO]
Special Olympics Ghana [IO]
Special Olympics Greece [IO]
Special Olympics Honduras [IO]
Special Olympics Iceland [IO]
Special Olympics Ireland [IO]
Special Olympics Italy [IO]
Special Olympics Japan [IO]
Special Olympics Kenya [IO]
Special Olympics Latvia [IO]
Special Olympics Lesotho [IO]
Special Olympics Malaysia [IO]
Special Olympics Moldova [IO]
Special Olympics Netherlands [IO]
Special Olympics Norway [IO]
Special Olympics Paraguay [IO]
Special Olympics Philippines [IO]
Special Olympics Poland [IO]
Special Olympics Portugal [IO]
Special Olympics Russia [IO]
Special Olympics Slovakia [IO]
Special Olympics Slovenia [IO]
Special Olympics Spain [IO]
Special Olympics Sweden [IO]
Special Olympics Switzerland [IO]
Special Olympics Thailand [IO]
Special Olympics Uganda [IO]
Special Olympics Uruguay [IO]
Special Olympics Uzbekistan [IO]
Special Recreation for disABLED Intl. [IO]
Special Recreation for disABLED Intl. [11989]
Spina Bifida Assn. of Am. [16458]
Sporting Wheelies and Disabled Sport and
    Recreation Assn. of Queensland [IO]
STRIDE: Sports and Therapeutic Recreation
    Instruction/Developmental Educ. [8205]
Stroke Clubs, Intl. [16496]
Support Dogs, Inc. [11990]
Support Dogs, Inc. [IO]
Swedish Assn. of Neurologically Disabled [IO]
Swimming/Natation Canada [IO]
Swiss Paralympic Comm. [IO]
Symbral Found. [12582]
TASH [11991]
Tech. Assistance Collaborative [13145]
Tee it up for the Troops [13357]
Telecommunications for the Deaf and Hard of
    Hearing, Inc. [14780]
THEO BC [IO]
UK Sports Assn. for People with Learning Dis-
    ability [IO]
United Amputee Services Assn. [15080]
United Cerebral Palsy Associations [13935]
United Kingdom's Disabled People's Coun. [IO]
U.S.A. Deaf Basketball [23136]
U.S. Assn. for Blind Athletes [23363]
U.S. Blind Golf Assn. [23364]
U.S. Deaf Cycling Assn. [23365]
U.S. Deaf Ski and Snowboard Assn. [23366]
U.S. Flag Football for the Deaf [23367]
U.S. Intl. Coun. on Disabilities [11992]
U.S. Intl. Coun. on Disabilities [IO]
U.S. Power Soccer Assn. [23783]
U.S. Psychiatric Rehabilitation Assn. [16336]
U.S. Quad Rugby Assn. [23705]
U.S. Soc. for Augmentative and Alternative
    Commun. [17198]
Universal Wheelchair Football Assn. [23368]
USA Deaf Sports Fed. [23369]
U.S.A. Toy Lib. Assn. [11548]
Vanuatu Sport Fed. Blind Disabled [IO]
Very Special Arts Bahamas [IO]
Veterans Educ. Proj. [13358]
Vietnam Assistance for the Handicapped - Ho Chi
    Minh City [IO]
VietNow Natl. [13359]
Vision World Wide [16890]
Visually Impaired Veterans of Am. [16891]
Vitalise [IO]

Vocational Evaluation and Career Assessment
    Professionals [16337]
VSA arts [11993]
VSA arts [IO]
VSA arts of Albania [IO]
VSA arts of Argentina [IO]
VSA arts of Brazil [IO]
VSA arts of Cyprus [IO]
Wheelchair Motorcycle Assn. [23370]
Wheelchair Sports Assn. of South Australia [IO]
Wheelchair Sports, USA [23371]
Wheelchair Sports Victoria [IO]
WheelPower - British Wheelchair Sport [IO]
Wheels for the World [IO]
Wheels for the World [11994]
Wilderness Inquiry [23274]
World Ability Fed. [11995]
World Ability Fed. [IO]
World Association of Persons with disAbilities [IO]
World Assn. of Persons with disAbilities [14247]
World Comm. on Disability [14248]
World Comm. on Disability [IO]
World Inst. on Disability [IO]
World Inst. on Disability [11996]
World Rehabilitation Fund [11997]
World Rehabilitation Fund [IO]
Xavier Soc. for the Blind [16892]
Yes I Can! Found. for Exceptional Children
    [11998]
Yes I Can! Foundation for Exceptional Children
    [IO]
Young Adult Institute/National Inst. for People with
    Disabilities [12584]
Disabled for Accessible Public Transit; Amer.
    [★17413]
Disabled in Action Natl. - Defunct.
Disabled Adults; Natl. Network of Learning [★12495]
Disabled and Alone/Life Services for the
    Handicapped [11941], 61 Broadway, Ste. 510,
    New York, NY 10006, (212)532-6740
Disabled; Amer. Assn. of Univ. Affiliated Programs
    for the Developmentally [★12563]
Disabled Amer. Veterans [20763], PO Box 14301,
    Cincinnati, OH 45250-0301, (859)441-7300
Disabled Amer. Veterans Auxiliary [20764], PO Box
    14301, Cincinnati, OH 45250-0301
Disabled; Assn. of Driver Educators for the [★8209]
Disabled Birders Assn. [IO], Essex, United Kingdom
Disabled Businesspersons Assn. [12076], San Diego
    State Univ. Interwork Indus., 3590 Camino del Rio
    N, San Diego, CA 92108-1716, (619)594-8805
Disabled Collectors' Correspondence Club [22814],
    c/o Glen Chisholm, Sec., 16878 Laramie Ave., Oak
    Forest, IL 60452-4428
Disabled; Commn. on the Mentally [★5781]
Disabled; Committee for Purchase From People
    Who Are Blind or Severely [★16878]
Disabled; CUSA: An Apostolate of the Sick and
    [19620]
Disabled Drivers' Assn. - England [IO], Norwich,
    United Kingdom
Disabled Drivers' Assn. of Ireland [IO], Claremorris,
    Ireland
Disabled; Intl. Soc. for Rehabilitation of the
    [★16333]
Disabled Journalists of America - Defunct.
Disabled Living Found. [IO], London, United
    Kingdom
Disabled Motorists Fed. [IO], Chester-Le-Street,
    United Kingdom
Disabled; Natl. Challenge Comm. of the [★17415]
Disabled; Natl. Legal Center for the Medically
    Dependent and [6032]
Disabled Officers Assn. - Defunct.
Disabled People's Assn. of Singapore [IO], Sin-
    gapore, Singapore
Disabled Peoples' Intl. [IO], Winnipeg, MB, Canada
Disabled Peoples' Intl. - Europe [IO], Lamezia
    Terme, Italy
Disabled Peoples' Intl. - India [IO], New Delhi, India
Disabled Peoples' Intl. - Jamaica [IO], Kingston,
    Jamaica
Disabled People's Intl. - Korea [IO], Seoul, Republic
    of Korea
Disabled Peoples' Intl. - North Am. and the Carib-
    bean [IO], St. Johns, Antigua-Barbuda

Disabled Peoples' Intl. - Poland [IO], Warsaw,
    Poland
Disabled Peoples' Intl. - Sweden [IO], Leksand,
    Sweden
Disabled Persons Assembly New Zealand [IO], Well-
    ington, New Zealand
Disabled Photographers' Soc. [IO], Richmond,
    United Kingdom
Disabled Sailors; Council of [★23155]
Disabled Ser. Assn; Regular and [★21319]
Disabled Ser. Assn; Regular and [★21320]
Disabled; Special Recreation for [★11989]
Disabled Sports USA [23343], 451 Hungerford Dr.,
    Ste. 100, Rockville, MD 20850, (301)217-0960
Disabled Veterans
    Blinded Amer. Veterans Found. [20762]
    Blinded Veterans Assn. [16837]
    Coalition to Salute America's Heroes [21294]
    Disabled Amer. Veterans [20763]
    Disabled Amer. Veterans Auxiliary [20764]
    Friends of Israel Disabled Veterans [21166]
    Gay, Lesbian, Bisexual, and Transgendered
        Disabled Veterans of Am. [20765]
    Help Hospitalized Veterans [13351]
    Homes for Our Troops [21302]
    Hospitalized Veterans Writing Proj. [16321]
    Iraq War Veterans Org. [21304]
    Natl. Assn. of State Veterans Homes [13354]
    Natl. Order of Trench Rats [20766]
    Natl. Veterans Services Fund [13356]
    The One Shoe Crew [11977]
    Oper. Appreciation [20767]
    Paralyzed Veterans of Am. [20768]
    Tee it up for the Troops [13357]
    Veterans Educ. Proj. [13358]
    VietNow Natl. [13359]
    Visually Impaired Veterans of Am. [16891]
Disabled Veterans; Friends of Israel [21166]
Disabled Veterans Keychain Tag and Chaffeur's
    Badge Collectors Newsl. [22011], c/o Dr. Edward
    H. Miles, Ed., 888 8th Ave., New York, NY 10019,
    (212)765-2660
Disabled War Veterans (Beit Halochem); Friends of
    Israel [★21166]
DisAbled Women's Network Canada [IO], Montreal,
    QC, Canada
Disabled Womyn's Educational Proj. [11942], PO
    Box 8773, Madison, WI 53708-8773, (608)256-
    8883
Disarm Educ. Fund [17428], 113 Univ. Pl., 8th Fl.,
    New York, NY 10003, (212)353-9800
Disarmament
    Abolition 2000 [17421]
    Abolition 2000 [IO]
    Agency for the Prohibition of Nuclear Weapons in
        Latin Am. and the Caribbean [IO]
    Architects and Engineers for Social Responsibility
        [IO]
    Archivio Disarmo [IO]
    Arms Control Association/Arms Control Today
        [17422]
    Cambridgeshire Area Campaign for Nuclear
        Disarmament [IO]
    Campaign Against Arms Trade [IO]
    Campaign for Nuclear Disarmament [IO]
    Canadian Assn. for Mine and Explosive Ordnance
        Security [IO]
    Canadian Disarmament Info. Ser. [IO]
    Canadian Landmine Found. [IO]
    Center for Economic Conversion [17423]
    Clear Path Intl. [17424]
    Clear Path Intl. [IO]
    Coalition to Oppose the Arms Trade [IO]
    Comm. of 100 in Finland [IO]
    Coun. for a Livable World [IO]
    Coun. for a Livable World [17425]
    Coun. for a Livable World Educ. Fund [17426]
    Coun. for a Livable World Educ. Fund [IO]
    Crusade to Abolish War and Armaments by World
        Law [18310]
    Cumbria and North Lancs Campaign for Nuclear
        Disarmament [IO]
    Demilitarization for Democracy [17427]
    Disarm Educ. Fund [17428]
    EarthAction Intl. [4554]

A star before a book entry number signifies that the name is not listed separately, but is mentioned within the entry.

East Midlands Campaign for Nuclear Disarmament [IO]
Economists for Peace and Security [IO]
Economists for Peace and Security [17429]
Greater Manchester and District Campaign for Nuclear Disarmament [IO]
Inst. for Defense and Disarmament Stud. [17430]
Intl. Assn. of Lawyers Against Nuclear Arms [IO]
Intl. Campaign to Ban Landmines [IO]
Intl. Campaign to Ban Landmines [17431]
Intl. Network of Engineers and Scientists Against Proliferation [IO]
Irish Campaign for Nuclear Disarmament [IO]
London Region Campaign for Nuclear Disarmament [IO]
Merseyside Campaign for Nuclear Disarmament [IO]
Mid Somerset Campaign for Nuclear Disarmament [IO]
NGO Comm. on Disarmament, Peace and Security [IO]
NGO Comm. on Disarmament, Peace and Security [17432]
Norwich Campaign for Nuclear Disarmament [IO]
Nuclear Control Inst. [18163]
Nuclear Free Philippines Coalition [IO]
Parliamentarians For Global Action [IO]
Parliamentarians For Global Action [17433]
Peace Action [18166]
Physicians Against Landmines [17434]
Proposition One Comm. [17435]
Reaching Critical Will [17436]
Scottish Campaign for Nuclear Disarmament [IO]
South West Region Campaign for Nuclear Disarmament [IO]
Southern Region Campaign for Nuclear Disarmament [IO]
Sussex Peace Alliance [IO]
Tyne and Wear Campaign for Nuclear Disarmament [IO]
West Midlands Campaign for Nuclear Disarmament [IO]
Yorkshire Campaign for Nuclear Disarmament [IO]
Young Koreans United [12485]
Disarmament and Arm Trade Campaign [★18167]
Disarmament, Development, and World Reform; Parliamentarians Global Action for [★17433]
Disarmament Issues Comm. - Defunct.
Disarmament; NGO Comm. on [★17432]
Disarmament; Non-Governmental Org. Comm. on [★17432]
Disarmament Resource Center - Defunct.
Disarmament Stud; Inst. for Defense and [17430]
Disarmament; Women's Action for Nuclear [★18175]
Disaster Aid
Action Against Hunger [11999]
Action Against Hunger [IO]
Adventist Community Services [20552]
Adventist Development and Relief Agency Intl. [12826]
Amer. Disaster Reserve [12000]
Amer. Red Cross Natl. HQ [12830]
Amer. Red Magen David for Israel - Amer. Friends of Magen David Adom [12832]
Amer. Rescue Dog Assn. [12889]
AmeriCares Found. [12833]
Assyrian Aid Soc. of Am. [11508]
CARE Intl. USA [12838]
Catholic Relief Services (U.S. Catholic Conf.) [12807]
Center for Intl. Disaster Info. [12001]
Center for Intl. Disaster Info. [IO]
Christian Reformed World Relief Comm. [12424]
Church World Ser. [12842]
Circle of Hea. Intl. [12268]
Coalition of 9/11 Families [13307]
Concern Am. [12845]
Convoy of Hope [12847]
Disaster Psychiatry Outreach [16083]
Disaster Volunteers of Ghana [IO]
Disasters Emergency Comm. [IO]
Doctors Worldwide [12851]
EMDR - Humanitarian Assistance Programs [12767]
Estonian Relief Comm. [12853]

Feed the Children [12854]
Food for the Hungry [12391]
GeoHazards Intl. [12633]
Grassroots Intl. [12428]
Humanitarian Medical Relief [12527]
Indian Muslim Relief Comm. of ISNA [12860]
Interaction/American Coun. for Voluntary Intl. Action [12433]
Intl. Disaster Recovery Assn. [7774]
Intl. Healthcare Safety Professional Certification Bd. [16379]
Intl. Relief Teams [12863]
Mapendo Intl. [12868]
Medical Teams Intl. [12869]
MediSend Intl. [12530]
Mennonite Disaster Ser. [12870]
Mir Pace Intl. [12872]
My Good Deed [13308]
Natl. Air Disaster Alliance [11510]
Natl. Assn. of Catastrophe Adjusters [2205]
Natl. Disaster Search Dog Found. [12892]
Natl. Relief Network [12873]
Natl. Ski Patrol Sys. [23753]
Natl. Voluntary Organizations Active in Disaster [12874]
Need [12875]
Oper. U.S.A. [12535]
Our Voices Together [13309]
OXFAM Am. [12438]
Planet Aid [13144]
Plenty Intl. [12878]
RedR Australia [IO]
RedR Eastern Africa [IO]
RedR India [IO]
RedR London - Intl. Hea. Exchange [IO]
Save the Children [11720]
September 11 Widows and Victims' Families Assn. [12002]
September's Mission [13310]
Tuesday's Children [12003]
U.S.A. for Africa [12882]
Windows of Hope Family Relief Fund [12004]
Windows of Hope Family Relief Fund [IO]
Wings of Hope [12883]
World Mercy Fund [12886]
World Rehabilitation Fund [11997]
World Trade Center Survivors' Network [13311]
WTC Families For Proper Burial [13312]
Disaster Emergency Response Assn. [5560], PO Box 797, Longmont, CO 80502, (970)532-3362
Disaster Mitigation Inst. [★IO]
Disaster; Natl. Voluntary Organizations Active in [12874]
Disaster Preparedness Center; Asian [IO]
Disaster Preparedness; Doctors for [14315]
Disaster Preparedness and Emergency Response Assn. [5561], PO Box 797, Longmont, CO 80502
Disaster Preparedness; Natl. Assn. of State Directors for [★5565]
Disaster Psychiatry Outreach [16083], 50 Broad St., No. 1714, New York, NY 10004, (212)598-9995
Disaster Recovery Inst. Intl. [★5562]
Disaster Ser; Friends [12856]
Disaster Ser; Mennonite [12870]
Disaster Volunteers of Ghana [IO], Ho, Ghana
Disasters Emergency Comm. [IO], London, United Kingdom
Disc Assn; Blue-ray [1207]
Disc Assn; Intl. Tape/ [★1370]
Disc Jockey Assn; Amer. [2796]
Disc Sports
Australian Flying Disc Assn. [IO]
Canadian Ultimate Players Assn. [IO]
European Flying Disc Fed. [IO]
Freestyle Players Assn. [IO]
Freestyle Players Assn. [23372]
Hong Kong Ultimate Players Assn. [IO]
Intl. Disc Dog Handlers' Assn. [23373]
New Zealand Flying Disc Assn. [IO]
Professional Disc Golf Assn. [IO]
Riders of the Wind, The Field Events Player's Assn. [IO]
Riders of the Wind, The Field Events Player's Assn. [23374]
Ultimate Players Assn. [23375]

U.S. Disc Sports [23376]
DISC Tax Assn; FSC/ [★2281]
Discalced Bros. of the Most Blessed Virgin Mary of Mount Carmel [IO], Rome, Italy
Disciple Directors; Natl. Fellowship of [★19842]
Disciple Nations Alliance [19847], 1220 E Washington St., Phoenix, AZ 85034, (480)609-7793
Disciples of Christ; Division of Higher Educ., Christian Church- [19854]
Disciples of Christ Historical Soc. [19853], 1101 19th Ave. S, Nashville, TN 37212-2109, (615)327-1444
Disciples of Christ; Social and Hea. Services of the Christian Church [★13177]
Disciples Ecumenical Consultative Coun. [19848], c/o Coun. on Christian Unity, PO Box 1986, Indianapolis, IN 46206-1986, (317)713-2586
Disciples Justice Action Network [19793], 1040 Harbor Dr., Annapolis, MD 21403, (410)212-7964
Disciples Peace Fellowship [18201], PO Box 1986, Indianapolis, IN 46206-1986, (317)357-3809
Discipline
Natl. Center for the Stud. of Corporal Punishment and Alternatives [8206]
Natl. Coalition to Abolish Corporal Punishment in Schools [8207]
Parents and Teachers Against Violence in Educ. [8208]
Discover Our Presidents - Address unknown since 2003.
Discovery Owners Assn., Inc. [22947], c/o Portia Williams, Membership Dir., PO Box 95, St. George, UT 84771-0095, (888)594-6818
Discrimination Comm; American-Arab Anti- [17082]
Discrimination; Coun. on Size and Weight [12644]
Discrimination; Intl. Org. for the Elimination of All Forms of Racial [IO]
Discus Study Group - Address unknown since 2003.
Discussion Club [17111]
Disease
A-T Medical Res. Found. [14436]
Acad. of Dentistry Intl. [14085]
Accelerated Cure Proj. for Multiple Sclerosis [15301]
Accreditation Coun. on Optometric Educ. [15710]
Acoustic Neuroma Assn. [15816]
African Assn. for the Stud. of Liver Diseases [IO]
Aicardi Syndrome Newsl. [14437]
Aid for AIDS [13547]
AIDS Empowerment and Treatment Intl. [13550]
Albinism World Alliance [15242]
Alliance for Childhood Cancer [13787]
Alliance for Lupus Res. [15013]
Alliance for Microbicide Development [13555]
ALSAC/Saint Jude Children's Res. Hosp. [13946]
Alstrom Syndrome - Canada [IO]
Alstrom Syndrome Intl. - United Kingdom [IO]
Amer. Acad. of Dermatology [14189]
Amer. Acad. of Neurological and Orthopaedic Surgeons [15409]
Amer. Acad. of Neurology [15376]
Amer. Acad. of Ophthalmology [15656]
Amer. Acad. of Optometry [15711]
Amer. Acad. of Oral and Maxillofacial Pathology [15852]
Amer. Acad. of Oral Medicine [14105]
Amer. Acad. of Otolaryngology - Head and Neck Surgery [15817]
Amer. Acad. of Periodontology [14109]
Amer. Aging Assn. [14507]
Amer. Assn. of Hosp. Podiatrists [16026]
Amer. Assn. of Kidney Patients [15283]
Amer. Assn. of Neurological Surgeons [15410]
Amer. Assn. of Neuropathologists [15853]
Amer. Assn. of Pathologists' Assistants [15854]
Amer. Assn. for Pediatric Ophthalmology and Strabismus [15660]
Amer. Assn. for the Stud. of Liver Diseases [14801]
Amer. Behcet's Disease Assn. [13746]
Amer. Bd. of Colon and Rectal Surgery [16059]
Amer. Bd. of Dermatology [14190]
Amer. Bd. of Neurological Surgery [15411]
Amer. Bd. of Ophthalmology [15661]
Amer. Bd. of Opticianry [15704]

Reference to "IO" in place of a book number signifies that the association may be found in the 45th edition of International Organizations.

Amer. Bd. of Oral and Maxillofacial Pathology [15855]
Amer. Bd. of Otolaryngology [15818]
Amer. Bd. of Pathology [15856]
Amer. Broncho-Esophagological Assn. [13778]
Amer. Clinical and Climatological Assn. [14018]
Amer. Coll. of Cardiology [13888]
Amer. Coll. of Epidemiology [14373]
Amer. Coll. of Gastroenterology [14405]
Amer. Coll. of Neuropsychopharmacology [15915]
Amer. Coll. of Obstetricians and Gynecologists [15584]
Amer. Coll. of Veterinary Pathologists [16769]
Amer. Fed. for Aging Res. [14508]
Amer. Fed. for Medical Res. [14019]
Amer. Found. for Aging Res. [14509]
Amer. Found. for AIDS Res. [13557]
Amer. Gastroenterological Assn. [14406]
Amer. Geriatrics Soc. [14510]
Amer. Gulf War Veterans Assn. [21281]
Amer. Head and Neck Soc. [15819]
Amer. Headache Soc. [14531]
Amer. Inst. of Stress [16487]
Amer. Kidney Fund [15284]
Amer. Liver Found. [14803]
Amer. Lung Assn. [16354]
Amer. Lyme Disease Found. [14249]
Amer. Nephrology Nurses' Assn. [15286]
Amer. Ophthalmological Soc. [15662]
Amer. Optometric Assn. [15712]
Amer. Optometric Found. [15713]
Amer. Optometric Student Assn. [15714]
Amer. Orthoptic Coun. [15663]
Amer. Osteopathic Coll. of Dermatology [14194]
Amer. Osteopathic Colleges of Ophthalmology and Otolaryngology-Head and Neck Surgery [15664]
Amer. Otological Soc. [15822]
Amer. Parkinson Disease Assn. [15304]
Amer. Partnership for Eosinophilic Disorders [14408]
Amer. Pathology Found. [15857]
Amer. Porphyria Found. [15243]
Amer. Prostate Soc. [16701]
Amer. Rhinologic Soc. [15823]
Amer. Sepsis Alliance [14946]
Amer. Soc. of Breast Disease [13772]
Amer. Soc. of Cataract and Refractive Surgery [15665]
Amer. Soc. for Clinical Investigation [14020]
Amer. Soc. for Clinical Pathology [15859]
Amer. Soc. of Colon and Rectal Surgeons [16060]
Amer. Soc. of Contemporary Medicine, Surgery, and Ophthalmology [15666]
Amer. Soc. for Dermatologic Surgery [14196]
Amer. Soc. of Diagnostic and Interventional Nephrology [15287]
Amer. Soc. of Echocardiography [13891]
Amer. Soc. for Gastrointestinal Endoscopy [14409]
Amer. Soc. of Interventional and Therapeutic Neuroradiology [16280]
Amer. Soc. for Investigative Pathology [15860]
Amer. Soc. of Nephrology [15288]
Amer. Soc. of Neuroradiology [16282]
Amer. Soc. for Stereotactic and Functional Neurosurgery [15412]
Amer. Syringomyelia Alliance Proj. [15305]
Amer. Urological Assn. Found. [16705]
Amer. Uveitis Soc. [15668]
Amer. Youth Understanding Diabetes Abroad [14219]
Amyloidosis Support Groups [14250]
Amyloidosis Support Network [14251]
Amyotrophic Lateral Sclerosis Assn. [15306]
Androgen Insensitivity Syndrome Support Gp. - USA [14441]
Angioma Alliance [15307]
Ankylosing Spondylitis Assn. of Ireland [IO]
Ankylosing Spondylitis Soc. in Italy [IO]
Archaeus Proj. [13625]
Armed Forces Inst. of Pathology [15261]
Asbestos Disease Awareness Org. [16655]
Asbestos Litigation Gp. [13321]
Asperger Syndrome Assn. of Ireland [IO]

Assn. of Asthma Educators [16355]
Assn. for the Bladder Exstrophy Community [14252]
Assn. for the Bladder Exstrophy Community [IO]
Assn. of Clinical Scientists [14022]
Assn. of Community Cancer Centers [13797]
Assn. for Eradication of Heart Attack [13894]
Assn. for Macular Diseases [15669]
Assn. of Nurses Endorsing Transplantation [15670]
Assn. of Pathology Chairs [15863]
Assn. for Professionals in Infection Control and Epidemiology [14947]
Assn. of Regulatory Boards of Optometry [15716]
Assn. for Res. in Vision and Ophthalmology [15672]
Assn. for Retinopathy of Prematurity and Related Diseases [15673]
Assn. of Schools and Colleges of Optometry [15717]
Assn. of Tech. Personnel in Ophthalmology [15674]
Assn. of Univ. Professors of Ophthalmology [15675]
Ataxia Telangiectasia Children's Proj. [14253]
Australian Addison's Disease Assn. [IO]
Autism Speaks [13724]
Avenues, Natl. Support Gp. for Arthrogryposis Multiplex Congenita [15309]
Benign Essential Blepharospasm Res. Found. [15311]
Better Vision Inst. [15678]
Bladder Cancer Advocacy Network [13799]
Brain Tumor Soc. [14254]
Brass Ring Soc. [11677]
Brave Kids [13949]
British Atherosclerosis Soc. [IO]
Cajal Club [15385]
Canadian Addison Soc. [IO]
Canadian Assn. for Clinical Microbiology and Infectious Diseases [IO]
Canadian Org. for Rare Disorders [IO]
Cancer Care [13803]
Cancer Info. Ser. [13807]
Cancer Prevention Coalition [13808]
Cancer Quality Alliance [13809]
Candlelighters Childhood Cancer Found. [13810]
Cardiovascular Credentialing Intl. [13898]
Care4Dystonia [15312]
Caring Voice Coalition [12712]
CCHS Family Network [14255]
Central Soc. for Clinical Res. [14023]
CFIDS Assn. of Am. [14256]
Charles Ray III Diabetes Assn. [14220]
Chem. Injury Info. Network [16656]
Child Neurology Soc. [15386]
Childhood Arthritis and Rheumatology Res. Alliance [16371]
Childhood Brain Tumor Found. [14257]
Children's Blood Found. [14786]
Children's Cause for Cancer Advocacy [13812]
Children's Eye Found. [15679]
Children's Leukemia Res. Assn. [13813]
Children's Liver Assn. for Support Services [14804]
Children's PKU Network [15245]
Children's Tumor Found. [15315]
Children's Wish Found. Intl. [11687]
Chromosome 9P Network [14443]
Chromosome 18 Registry and Res. Soc. [14444]
Chromosome Deletion Outreach [14445]
Chronic Granulomatous Disease Assn. [14258]
Chronic Granulomatous Disease Association [IO]
Chronic Syndrome Support Assn. [14259]
Churg Strauss Syndrome Assn. [13729]
City of Hope Natl. Medical Center [15102]
Coalition for the Advancement of Medical Res. [15103]
Coalition of Cancer Cooperative Groups [13814]
Coalition for Hemophilia B [14787]
Coffin-Lowry Syndrome Found. [14447]
Coll. of Amer. Pathologists [15866]
Coll. of Optometrists in Vision Development [15718]
Collegium Internationale Neuro-Psychopharmacologicum [15929]

Conf. of Res. Workers in Animal Diseases [16790]
Congenital Cardiac Anesthesia Soc. [13682]
Cong. of Lung Assn. Staff [16357]
Contact Lens Assn. of Ophthalmologists [15680]
Cooper Inst. [15962]
Cornea Res. Found. of Am. [15105]
Cornelia de Lange Syndrome Found. [13754]
Corporate Angel Network [13817]
Coun. on Arteriosclerosis, Thrombosis and Vascular Biology of the Amer. Heart Assn. [13902]
Crigler-Najjar Assn. [14805]
Crohn's and Colitis Found. of Am. [14414]
Crohn's and Colitis Found. of Canada [IO]
Cure Res. Found. [13818]
Cyclic Vomiting Syndrome Assn. [14415]
Cystic Fibrosis Found. [16358]
Cystic Fibrosis Worldwide [16359]
Cystinosis Found. [15246]
Cystinosis Res. Network [15247]
DaVita Patient Citizens [15291]
DEBRA Ireland [IO]
Dementia Advocacy and Support Network Intl. [12638]
Depression and Bipolar Support Alliance [15196]
Dermatology Found. [14199]
Diabetes Res. Assn. of Am. [14223]
Diabetes Res. Inst. Found. [14224]
Digestive Disease Natl. Coalition [14416]
Disease Mgt. Assn. of Am. [IO]
DMAA: The Care Continuum Alliance [14260]
Doris Duke Charitable Found. [13115]
Dutch Addison and Cushing Soc. [IO]
Dysautonomia Found. [15317]
Dysautonomia Youth Network of Am. [15318]
Dystonia Medical Res. Found. [15319]
Dystrophic Epidermolysis Bullosa Res. Assn. of Am. [14200]
Ear Found. [15825]
Ehlers Danlos Natl. Found. [16651]
Endometriosis Assn. [15599]
The Erythromelalgia Assn. [14261]
Esophageal Cancer Awareness Assn. [13822]
European Cystic Fibrosis Soc. [IO]
European Fed. of Hereditary Ataxias [IO]
European Org. for Rare Diseases [IO]
European Org. for Rare Disorders [IO]
European Soc. for Clinical Virology [IO]
European Soc. for Phenylketonuria and Allied Disorders [IO]
European Venous Forum [IO]
Evans Syndrome Res. and Support Gp. [14934]
Fabry Support and Info. Gp. [14262]
Facioscapulohumeral (FSH) Soc. [15320]
Fanconi Anemia Res. Fund [14450]
Fed. for Children with Special Needs [12569]
Fed. of Clinical Immunology Societies [14935]
Floating Harbor Syndrome Support Gp. of North Am. [14451]
Focus [15681]
FOD Family Support Gp. [15248]
Forbes Norris MDA/ALS Res. Center [15323]
Found. for Advancement in Cancer Therapy [13824]
Found. for Ichthyosis and Related Skin Types [14201]
Friedreich's Ataxia Res. Alliance [14403]
Friends of the Jose Carreras Intl. Leukemia Found. [13825]
Friends of Karen [11694]
Frontline Hepatitis Awareness [14806]
Gay Men's Hea. Crisis [13564]
Genetics Policy Inst. [14499]
Gerontological Soc. of Am. [14511]
Glaucoma Res. Found. [15683]
Global Bus. Coalition on HIV/AIDS [11329]
Global Org. for Lysosomal Diseases [IO]
Global and Regional Asperger Syndrome Partnership [15325]
Global Strategies for HIV Prevention [13566]
Haitian Coalition on AIDS [13567]
Heart Disease Res. Found. [13905]
Heart Rhythm Soc. [13907]
Hemochromatosis Info. Soc. [14800]

A star before a book entry number signifies that the name is not listed separately, but is mentioned within the entry.

Hemophilia Fed. of Am. [14789]
Hepatitis C Assn. [14807]
Hepatitis C Caring Ambassadors Prog. [14808]
Hepatitis Rsrc. Network [14810]
HHT Found. Intl. [14454]
Huntington's Disease Soc. of Am. [15329]
Hydrocephalus Assn. [15330]
Hypoparathyroidism Assn. [14356]
IDEA Hea. and Fitness Assn. [15965]
Immune Deficiency Found. [14936]
Incontinentia Pigmenti Intl. Found. [14455]
Independent Citizens Res. Found. for the Study of
    Degenerative Diseases [14263]
Infectious Diseases Soc. of Am. [14948]
Inflammation Res. Assn. [14264]
Inflammatory Skin Disease Inst. [14265]
Institut Pierre Richet [IO]
InterAmerican Heart Found. [13909]
Intl. Assn. for Chronic Fatigue Syndrome [14266]
Intl. Assn. for Comparative Res. on Leukemia and
    Related Diseases [15647]
Intl. Assn. of Ocular Surgeons [15684]
Intl. Assn. of Optometric Executives [15720]
Intl. Assn. for Paratuberculosis [16793]
Intl. Assn. for Res. on Epstein Barr Virus [IO]
Intl. Atherosclerosis Soc. [13910]
Intl. Bronchoesophagological Soc. [13779]
Intl. Bundle Br. Block Assn. [13911]
Intl. Children's Anophthalmia Network [16857]
Intl. Contact Dermatitis Res. Gp. [IO]
Intl. Coun. for the Control of Iodine Deficiency
    Disorders - Australia [IO]
Intl. Dental Hea. Found. [14166]
Intl. EECP Therapists Assn. [16619]
Intl. Eye Found. [15685]
Intl. Fed. of Marfan Syndrome Organizations
    [14456]
Intl. Fed. of Psoriasis Associations [14203]
Intl. Fed. for Spina Bifida and Hydrocephalus [IO]
Intl. Genetic Epidemiology Soc. [14376]
Intl. Leptospirosis Soc. [14950]
Intl. Lyme and Assoc. Diseases Soc. [14267]
Intl. Lyme and Assoc. Diseases Soc. [IO]
Intl. Org. of Multiple Sclerosis Nurses [15486]
Intl. Partnership for Microbicides [13572]
Intl. Pediatric Nephrology Assn. [15292]
Intl. Pemphigus Found. [14268]
Intl. Post Polio Support Org. [16048]
Intl. Prader-Willi Syndrome Org. [IO]
Intl. Refractive Surgery Club [15689]
Intl. Scleroderma Network [16387]
Intl. Skeletal Soc. [16289]
Intl. Soc. for Dermatologic Surgery [14204]
Intl. Soc. of Dermatology [14205]
Intl. Soc. for Disease Surveillance [14269]
Intl. Soc. for Disease Surveillance [IO]
Intl. Soc. for Infectious Diseases [14951]
Intl. Soc. on Metabolic Eye Disease [15691]
Intl. Soc. for Pharmacoepidemiology [15939]
Intl. Soc. for Plastination [15870]
Intl. Soc. for Stem Cell Res. [14503]
Intl. Trachoma Initiative [16858]
Intl. Treatment Preparedness Coalition [13573]
Intersociety Coun. for Pathology Info. [15871]
Intestinal Disease Found. [14421]
Irritable Bowel Info. and Support Assn. [IO]
Italian Assn. for Inflammatory Bowel Diseases [IO]
Japan Ankylosing Spondylitis Club [IO]
Jaw Joints and Allied Musculo-Skeletal Disorders
    Found. [15773]
Joint Commn. on Allied Hea. Personnel in
    Ophthalmology [15692]
Kennedy's Disease Assn. [15334]
LAM Found. [14270]
Latino Org. for Liver Awareness [14811]
Leukemia and Lymphoma Soc. [13837]
Lewy Body Dementia Assn. [15335]
LMBS Network [16539]
Lung Cancer Alliance [13839]
Lupus Found. of Am. [15014]
Lupus Info. Network [15015]
Lyme Disease Assn. [14271]
Lyme Disease Found. [14272]
Make-A-Wish Found. of Am. [11707]
Make Today Count [13841]

The Mastocytosis Soc. [14273]
Med Help Intl. [15042]
Medical Dermatology Soc. [14206]
Mended Hearts, Inc. [13916]
Meniere's Network [15826]
Mesothelioma Applied Res. Found. [14274]
Michael E. DeBakey Intl. Surgical Soc. [13917]
Millennium Promise [11485]
Mitochondria Res. Soc. [14275]
Mitochondria Research Society [IO]
Mitochondrial Medicine Soc. [14078]
Multiple Sclerosis Assn. of Am. [14276]
Multiple Sclerosis Found. [15338]
MUMS Natl. Parent-to-Parent Network [16541]
Myasthenia Gravis Found. of Am. [15340]
The Myositis Assn. [15341]
NAADAC The Assn. for Addiction Professionals
    [16509]
Nail Patella Syndrome Worldwide [14467]
Natl. Acad. of Opticianry [15707]
Natl. Adrenal Diseases Found. [14358]
Natl. Alliance for Autism Res. [13726]
Natl. Alliance for Thrombosis and Thrombophilia
    [13931]
Natl. Alopecia Areata Found. [16386]
Natl. Anemia Action Coun. [14794]
Natl. Assn. of Hepatitis Task Forces [14812]
Natl. Assn. on HIV Over Fifty [14952]
Natl. Assn. of Optometrists and Opticians [15721]
Natl. Assn. of People With AIDS [13578]
Natl. Assn. for Pseudoxanthoma Elasticum
    [14207]
Natl. Assn. of Vision Professionals [15693]
Natl. Ataxia Found. [15342]
Natl. Bd. of Examiners in Optometry [15722]
Natl. Brachial Plexus-Erb's Palsy Assn. [14277]
Natl. Chronic Fatigue Syndrome and Fibromyalgia
    Assn. [14278]
Natl. Coalition for Cancer Survivorship [13852]
Natl. Coalition for Res. in Neurological Disorders
    [15346]
Natl. Contact Lens Examiners [15723]
Natl. Digestive Diseases Info. CH [14422]
Natl. Dysautonomia Res. Found. [14279]
Natl. Eosinophilia-Myalgia Syndrome Network
    [16662]
Natl. Eye Res. Found. [15724]
Natl. Found. for Ectodermal Dysplasias [14468]
Natl. Found. for Infectious Diseases [14953]
Natl. Gaucher Found. [15252]
Natl. Headache Found. [14533]
Natl. Heartburn Alliance [14423]
Natl. Hemophilia Found. [14795]
Natl. Hepatitis C Advocacy Coun. [14813]
Natl. Hydrocephalus Found. [14280]
Natl. Incontinentia Pigmenti Found. [14470]
Natl. Infant Torticollis Assn. [14945]
Natl. Inst. of Electromedical Info. [14311]
Natl. Jewish Medical and Res. Center [16361]
Natl. Kidney Found. [15294]
Natl. Lung Cancer Partnership [13854]
Natl. Lymphedema Network [15018]
Natl. Meningitis Assn. [14281]
Natl. Multiple Sclerosis Soc. [15349]
Natl. Optometric Assn. [15725]
Natl. Org. for Albinism and Hypopigmentation
    [15255]
Natl. Org. for Rare Disorders [14282]
Natl. Parkinson Found. [15351]
Natl. Phlebotomy Assn. [14796]
Natl. Prostate Cancer Coalition [13856]
Natl. Reye's Syndrome Found. [16366]
Natl. Spasmodic Dysphonia Assn. [15352]
Natl. Spasmodic Torticollis Assn. [15353]
Natl. Special Needs Network Found. [14232]
Natl. Tay-Sachs and Allied Diseases Assn.
    [15354]
Natl. Tuberculosis Controllers Assn. [14283]
Natl. Viral Hepatitis Roundtable [14815]
NCI Alliance for Nanotechnology in Cancer
    [15110]
Neurocritical Care Soc. [14070]
Nevus Outreach [14284]
North Amer. Clinical Dermatologic Soc. [14212]
Norwegian Soc. for Virology [IO]

Ophthalmic Photographers' Soc. [15696]
OPP Concerned Sheep Breeders Soc. [16803]
Opticians Assn. of Am. [15709]
Optometric Extension Prog. Found. [15727]
Optometric Historical Soc. [15728]
ORBIS Intl. [15697]
Org. for Autism Res. [13728]
Outpatient Ophthalmic Surgery Soc. [15698]
Pacific Dermatologic Assn. [14213]
Paget Found. for Paget's Disease of Bone and
    Related Disorders [15256]
Pan-American Assn. of Ophthalmology [15699]
Pan Amer. Hea. Org. [14592]
Paratuberculosis Awareness and Res. Assn.
    [14425]
Parents of Kids with Infectious Diseases [14954]
Parkinson Alliance [15359]
Parkinson's Action Network [14285]
Parkinson's Disease Found. [15360]
Partnership for Prevention [14594]
PBCers Org. [14816]
Pediatric Cardiac Intensive Care Soc. [15892]
Pediatric Infectious Diseases Soc. [14955]
Pediatric Neurotransmitter Disease Assn. [15361]
Peripheral Arterial Disease Coalition [13922]
Pierre Robin Network [14473]
Pituitary Network Assn. [16022]
Polio Soc. [15362]
Post-Polio Hea. Intl. [11981]
Prader-Willi Found. [14474]
Pregnant With Cancer Network [13865]
Purine Res. Soc. [15258]
Radiology Mammography Intl. [13774]
Renal Physicians Assn. [15298]
Renal Support Network [15299]
Retinoblastoma Intl. [13869]
Roger Wyburn-Mason and Jack M. Blount Found.
    for the Eradication of Rheumatoid Disease
    [16375]
Scleroderma Found. [16389]
Scleroderma Res. Found. [16390]
Shingles Support Soc. [IO]
Shwachman-Diamond Syndrome Canada [IO]
Shy Drager Syndrome/Multiple Sys. Atrophy Sup-
    port Gp. [15364]
Sickle Cell Disease Assn. of Am. [14797]
Soc. for Clinical Trials [14028]
Soc. for Ear, Nose, and Throat Advances in
    Children [15827]
Soc. of Eye Surgeons [15703]
Soc. for Hematopathology [15874]
Soc. for Investigative Dermatology [14214]
Soc. for Leukocyte Biology [16365]
Soc. for Melanoma Res. [13875]
Soc. of Military Otolaryngologists - Head and
    Neck Surgeons [15267]
Soc. for Muscular Dystrophy Info. Intl. [IO]
Soc. for Pediatric Dermatology [14215]
Soc. for Progressive Supranuclear Palsy [14286]
Soc. of Univ. Otolaryngologists - Head and Neck
    Surgeons [15828]
Solidarity and Action Against the HIV Infection in
    India [16969]
South African Natl. Tuberculosis Assn. [IO]
South Amer. Commn. for the Control of Foot-and-
    Mouth Disease [IO]
A Special Wish Found. [11723]
Starlight Starbright Children's Found. [11724]
Student Soc. for Stem Cell Res. [15114]
Sturge-Weber Found. [15365]
Sudden Cardiac Arrest Assn. [13933]
Sunshine Found. [11726]
Support Org. for Trisomy 18, 13, and Related
    Disorders [14485]
Syndrome X Assn. [15259]
Take Charge! Cure Parkinson's [15366]
Taking Control of Your Diabetes [14231]
Task Force for Child Survival and Development
    [12542]
Thyroid Cancer Survivors' Assn. [16648]
Thyroid Soc. for Educ. and Res. [16650]
Tourette Syndrome Assn. [15367]
Transatlantic Partners Against AIDS [13586]
Transverse Myelitis Assn. [15368]
Tremor Action Network [15369]

Reference to "IO" in place of a book number signifies that the association may be found in the 45th edition of International Organizations.

Tuberous Sclerosis Alliance [15371]
Turner Syndrome Soc. of the U.S. [14486]
United Mitochondrial Disease Found. [16363]
U.S. Adult Cystic Fibrosis Assn. [16364]
U.S. Hereditary Angioedema Assn. [14487]
U.S.-Mexico Border Hea. Assn. [16256]
Us TOO Intl. [13879]
Vasculitis Found. [16552]
Venous Soc. of Am. [16732]
Vietnam Veteran Wives [21332]
Wildlife Disease Assn. [5398]
Williams Syndrome Assn. [14490]
A Wish With Wings [11728]
Women Alive Coalition [13588]
WomenHeart: Natl. Coalition for Women with Heart Disease [13929]
World Arnold Chiari Malformation Assn. [16556]
World Assn. of Veterinary Lab. Diagnosticians [16819]
World Fed. of Neurology Res. Gp. on Motor Neuron Diseases [15373]
World Muscle Soc. [IO]
World Parkinson Disease Assn. [IO]
World Soc. for Stereotactic and Functional Neurosurgery [15418]
Young Onset Parkinson's Assn. [15374]
Disease; Amer. Found. for the Prevention of Venereal [16409]
Disease Assn. of Am; Sickle Cell [14797]
Disease Assn; Amer. Parkinson [15304]
Disease; Assn. for Glycogen Storage [15244]
Disease Assn; Natl. Tuberculosis and Respiratory [★16354]
Disease Assn; Wildlife [5398]
Disease of Bone and Related Disorders; Paget Found. for Paget's [15256]
Disease Conf; Natl. Respiratory [★16357]
Disease; Families with Maple Syrup Urine [★15250]
Disease Found. of Am; Huntington [★15329]
Disease Found; Celiac [14412]
Disease Found; Graves' [★16647]
Disease Found; Hereditary [15328]
Disease Found; Intestinal [14421]
Disease Found; Natl. Addison's [★14358]
Disease Found; Natl. Graves' [16647]
Disease Found; Natl. Kidney [★15294]
Disease Found; Parkinson's [15360]
Disease; Found. for the Study of Wilson's [★15251]
Disease Found; United Mitochondrial [16363]
Disease Mgt. Assn. of Am. [★14260]
Disease Mgt. Assn. of Am. [IO], Washington, DC, United States
Disease; Natl. Assn. for Sickle Cell [★14797]
Disease; Natl. Center for the Study of Wilson's [15251]
Disease Natl. Coalition; Digestive [14416]
Disease Res. Found; Heart [13905]
Disease Resources; Intersociety Commn. for Heart [★13890]
Disease; Roger Wyburn-Mason and Jack M. Blount Found. for the Eradication of Rheumatoid [16375]
Disease Soc. of Am; Huntington's [15329]
Disease Support and Res. Assn; Batten [15310]
Diseases; Amer. Assn. for the Stud. of Liver [14801]
Diseases Assn; Amer. Autoimmune Related [14930]
Diseases Assn; Iron Overload [15249]
Diseases; Assn. for Macular [15669]
Diseases CH; Digestive [★14422]
Diseases; Conf. of Res. Workers in Animal [16790]
Diseases Educ. and Info. CH; Natl. Digestive [★14422]
Diseases Found; Natl. Adrenal [14358]
Diseases and Human Infertility; Intl. Soc. of Infectious [★16347]
Diseases Info. CH; Natl. Digestive [14422]
Diseases Info. CH; Natl. Inst. of Arthritis and Musculoskeletal and Skin [16372]
Diseases Info. CH; Natl. Kidney and Urologic [16710]
Diseases; Natl. Found. for Infectious [14953]
Diseases Soc. of Am; Infectious [14948]
Diseases; Women Organized to Respond to Life-Threatening [13589]
Disinfectant Manufacturers; Natl. Assn. Insecticide and [★806]

Disinfected Mail Stud. Circle [IO], London, United Kingdom
Dismantlers and Recyclers of Am; Automotive [★3988]
Disney Collectors Soc; Walt [22129]
Disneyana Enthusiasts; Natl. Fantasy Fan Club for [24791]
Disorder; Children and Adults With Attention Deficit [★15314]
Disorder; Children and Adults With Attention Deficit/Hyperactivity [15314]
Disorders; Amer. Acad. of Craniomandibular [★14106]
Disorders Anonymous; Dual [13237]
Disorders Assn; Dizziness and Balance [★15829]
Disorders Assn; Natl. Eating [14302]
Disorders Centers; Amer. Assn. of Sleep [★16418]
Disorders Centers; Assn. of Sleep [★16418]
Disorders; Children with Attention-Deficit [★15314]
Disorders of Chromosome 16 Found. [14449], c/o Rosalyn Gregg, 23 Lawrencia Dr., Lawrenceville, NJ 08648, (609)219-9449
Disorders of Chromosome 16 Foundation [IO], Vernon Hills, IL, United States
Disorders of the Corpus Callosum; Natl. Org. for [15350]
Disorders; Coun. for Children with Behavioral [9140]
Disorders Info. CH; Natl. Inst. on Deafness and Other Commun. [14773]
Disorders; Natl. Coalition for Res. in Neurological [15346]
Disorders; Natl. Org. for Rare [14282]
Disorders Soc; Pediatric Digestion and Motility [15893]
Disorganization; Natl. Study Group on Chronic [1979]
Dispatchers Dept. of the BLE; Amer. Train [24175]
Dispensing Audiologists; Acad. of [★14733]
Dispensing Equip. Assn; Intl. Beverage [507]
Dispensing Equip. Assn; Natl. Soda [★507]
Displaced Homemakers Network; Natl. [★18819]
Display Consortium; U.S. [3729]
Display Indus; Natl. Assn. of [2642]
Display Producers and Screen Printers Assn. [★IO]
Disposable Products
  Foodservice and Packaging Inst. [1157]
  Manufacturers Representatives of Am. [1158]
Disposables Assn. [★3785]
Disposables Assn; Intl. Nonwovens and [★3785]
Dispute Resolution; Amer. Bar Assn. Sect. of [5449]
Dispute Resolution; Amer. Bar Assn. Special Comm. on [★5449]
Dispute Resolution; Amer. Bar Assn. Standing Comm. on [★5449]
Dispute Resolution; CPR Inst. for [★11488]
Dispute Resolution; Soc. of Professionals in [★5450]
Dispute Settlement; Center for [5451]
Disputes; Amer. Bar Assn. Comm. on the Resolution of Minor [★5449]
Dissatisfied Parents Together [★13972]
Dissemin/Action - Defunct.
Dissemination Assn; Natl. [8291]
Dissemination Center for Children with Disabilities; Natl. [11971]
Dissociation; Intl. Soc. for the Stud. of Multiple Personalities and [★15210]
Distaff Foundation/Knollwood; Army [21192]
Distance Educ. Consortium; Amer. [8227]
Distance Educ. and Training Coun. [8517], 1601 18th St. NW, Washington, DC 20009, (202)234-5100
Distance Learning Assn; U.S. [8523]
Distance Running
  Assn. of Intl. Marathons and Road Races [IO]
  Lifelong Fitness Alliance [23920]
  New York Road Runners Club [23921]
  Road Runners Club of Am. [23923]
Distillate Burner Mfrs. Assn. - Defunct.
Distilled Spirits Assn. of New Zealand [IO], Auckland, New Zealand
Distilled Spirits Coun. of the U.S. [199], 1250 Eye St. NW, Ste. 400, Washington, DC 20005, (202)628-3544
Distilled Spirits Indus. Coun. of Australia [IO], South Melbourne, Australia

Distilled Spirits Inst. [★199]
Distillers Feed Res. Coun. [★1749]
Distillers Grains Tech. Coun. [1749], Univ. of Louisville, Lutz Hall, Rm. 435, Louisville, KY 40292, (502)852-1575
Distillery, Wine and Allied Workers Intl. Union [★24061]
Distillery Workers of Am. (AFL-CIO); Intl. Union of United Brewery, Flour, Cereal, Soft Drink and [★24020]
Distillery Workers; Canadian Brewery and [★24061]
Distinguished Americans; Horatio Alger Assn. of [20712]
Distinguished Flying Cross Soc. [20711], PO Box 530250, San Diego, CA 92153, (866)332-6332
Distributed Computing Indus. Assn. [899], 2838 Cox Neck Rd., Ste. 200, Chester, MD 21619, (410)476-7965
Distributing Assn; Photographic Merchandising and [★3007]
Distribution Assn; Amer. Commodity [4302]
Distribution Assn; Heavy Duty [357]
Distribution Assn; Off. Furniture [4025]
Distribution Bus. Mgt. Assn. [4019], 2938 Columbia Ave., Ste. 1102, Lancaster, PA 17603, (717)295-0033
Distribution Codes Inst. - Defunct.
Distribution Comm; Joint [★12464]
Distribution Contractors Assn. [24162], 101 W Renner Rd., Ste. 460, Richardson, TX 75082-2024, (972)680-0261
Distribution, Inc; Allied [3975]
Distribution and LTL Carriers Assn. [3564], 4218 Roanoke Rd., Ste. 200, Kansas City, MO 64111-4735, (816)753-0411
Distribution Mgt; Natl. Coun. of Physical [★4018]
Distribution Res. and Educ. Found. [4020], c/o Ron Schreiman, Exec. Dir., 1725 K St. NW, Ste. 300, Washington, DC 20006, (202)872-0885
Distribution Res. Soc; Food [7093]
Distributive Education
  Iota Lambda Sigma [24724]
Distributive Educ. Assn; Marketing and [★8818]
Distributive Educ. Clubs of Am. [8817], 1908 Assn. Dr., Reston, VA 20191, (703)860-5000
Distributive Educ. Local Supervisors; Natl. Assn. of [★8818]
Distributive Educ; Natl. Assn. of State Supervisors of [★8818]
Distributive Educ. Teachers; Natl. Assn. for [★8818]
Distributive Teacher Educ; Coun. for [★8818]
Distributors of Am; Motion Picture Producers and [★1389]
Distributors of Am; Retail Paint and Wallpaper [★2274]
Distributors Assn; Amer. Veterinary [2957]
Distributors Assn; Ceramic Tile [611]
Distributors Assn; Chem. Producers and [803]
Distributors Assn. of Constr. Equip; Natl. [★2000]
Distributors Assn. Educational Foundation; Wholesale [★3067]
Distributors Assn; Gases and Welding [2021]
Distributors Assn; Hea. Indus. [1860]
Distributors Assn; Independent Lab. [3483]
Distributors Assn; Independent Medical [1862]
Distributors Assn; Independent Turf and Ornamental [2394]
Distributors; Assn. of Ingersoll-Rand [2002]
Distributors Assn; Mech. Power Transmission Equip. [★2060]
Distributors Assn; Natl. Independent Poultry and Food [★1551]
Distributors Assn; Natl. Institutional Food [★1566]
Distributors Assn; Natl. Pyrotechnic [★3267]
Distributors Assn; Outdoor Power Equip. [★1293]
Distributors Assn; Pet Indus. [2964]
Distributors Assn; Photoimaging Mfrs. and [3007]
Distributors Assn; Post Card and Souvenir [3074]
Distributors Assn; Safety Equip. [3454]
Distributors Assn; Textile [3802]
Distributors Assn; Textile Fabric [★3802]
Distributors Assn; United Plastics [★3051]
Distributors Assn; Wholesale [3067]
Distributors Coun; Gen. Merchandise [4021]
Distributors; Independent Cosmetic Manufacturers and [1847]

A star before a book entry number signifies that the name is not listed separately, but is mentioned within the entry.

Distributors; Independent Sealing [4022]
Distributors Inst; Textile [★3802]
Distributors; Natl. Assn. of Elecl. [1190]
Distributors; Natl. Assn. of Plastics [★3051]
Distributors; Natl. Assn. of Plumbing Specialty [3063]
Distributors; Natl. Assn. of Sign Supply [4023]
Distributors; Natl. Assn. of Tobacco [★1500]
Distributors; Natl. Assn. of Uniform Manufacturers and [248]
Distributors; Natl. Assn. of Wholesaler- [4024]
Distributors; Natl. League of Wholesale Fresh Fruit and Vegetable [★4766]
Distributors; Natl. Radio Parts [★1223]
Distributors and Retailers of Am; Footwear [1597]
Distributors Secretaries of Am; Beer [★204]
Distributors and Suppliers; Assn. of Fund-Raising [1684]
District 1 of Marine Engineers Beneficial Association/ National Maritime Union and Professional Airways Systems Specialists [★24015]
District 925, AFL-CIO; SEIU, [23996]
District Attorneys
  Natl. Child Support Enforcement Assn. [5701]
  Natl. Coll. of District Attorneys [5667]
  Natl. District Attorneys Assn. [5668]
District Attorneys Assn. Found; Natl. [★5668]
District of Columbia Speleological Soc. [★7693]
District Courts Assn. [IO], Motherwell, United Kingdom
District Heating Assn; Intl. [★1888]
District Heating Assn; Natl. [★1888]
District Heating and Cooling Assn; Intl. [★1888]
Distripress - Assn. for the Promotion of the Intl. Press Distribution [IO], Zurich, Switzerland
Ditchley Found. [IO], Chipping Norton, United Kingdom
Ditchley Found; Amer. [17857]
Divadelni, Literarni, Audiovizualni Agentura [★IO]
Divadelni Ustav [★IO]
DIVAS of Lambda Fe Uson Sorority [24709], PO Box 339, East Setauket, NY 11733
Divco Club of Am. [22012], PO Box 1142, Kingston, WA 98346-1142
Divers Alert Network [23378], Peter B. Bennett Ctr., 6 W Colony Pl., Durham, NC 27705, (919)684-2948
Divers Reunited; U.S. Navy Salvage [21409]
Diversified Manufacturers Representatives; Natl. Assn. of [★2541]
Diversity
  All One Heart [17080]
Diversity Coun; Unity in [★17916]
Diversity; Dialogue on [8888]
Diversity in Hea. Mgt; Inst. for [14704]
Diversity Info. Resources [2761], 2105 Central Ave. NE, Minneapolis, MN 55418, (612)781-6819
Diversity World Org; Unity and [★17916]
Divided Spouses Coalition - Defunct.
Dividends From Space - Defunct.
Divine Science
  Divine Sci. Fed. Intl. [19880]
  Divine Sci. Fed. Intl. [IO]
  Divine Sci. Ministers Assn. [19881]
Divine Sci. Fed. Intl. [19880], 8084 Watson Rd., Ste. 236, St. Louis, MO 63119, (314)842-2335
Divine Sci. Fed. Intl. [IO], St. Louis, MO, United States
Divine Sci. Ministers Assn. [19881], 8847 Airline Hwy., Baton Rouge, LA 70815-4004, (225)924-3780
Divine Sci. Ministers Org. [★19881]
Diving
  Assn. of Commercial Diving Educators [23960]
  Assn. of Dive Prog. Administrators [23377]
  Assn. of Diving Contractors Intl. [1007]
  British Sub-Aqua Club [IO]
  Canadian Amateur Diving Assn. [IO]
  Divers Alert Network [23378]
  Diving Plongeon Canada [IO]
  Emirates Diving Assn. [IO]
  European Comm. of Professional Diving Instructors [IO]
  European Diving Tech. Comm. [IO]
  Found. for Aquatic Injury Prevention [12963]
  Handicapped Scuba Assn. [23344]

Historical Diving Soc. USA [23576]
  Inst. of Diving [23961]
  Intl. Assn. of Dive Rescue Specialists [23574]
  Intl. Assn. of Nitrox and Tech. Divers [23379]
  Intl. Assn. of Nitrox and Tech. Divers [IO]
  Intl. Underwater Spearfishing Assn. [23418]
  Natl. Assn. for Cave Diving [23962]
  Natl. Assn. of Underwater Instructors [23963]
  Natl. Swimming Pool Found. [3360]
  Professional Assn. of Diving Instructors [23964]
  Recreational Scuba Training Coun. [23965]
  Scottish Sub-Aqua Club [IO]
  Sub-Aqua Assn. [IO]
  Undersea and Hyperbaric Medical Soc. [16697]
  Underwater Soc. of Am. [23966]
  U.S. Apnea Assn. [23380]
  U.S. Apnea Assn. [IO]
  U.S. Aquatic Sports [23890]
  U.S. BASE Assn. [23647]
  U.S. Parachute Assn. [23648]
  U.S. Professional Diving Coaches Assn. [23381]
  USA Diving [23382]
  World Diving Coaches Assn. [23383]
Diving Contractors; Assn. of [★1007]
Diving Dentists Soc. - Defunct.
Diving Educators; Assn. of Commercial [23960]
Diving Equip. Manufacturers Assn. [★3642]
Diving Equip. Manufacturers Assn. [★IO]
Diving Equip. and Marketing Assn. [IO], San Diego, CA, United States
Diving Equip. and Marketing Assn. [3642], 3750 Convoy St., Ste. 310, San Diego, CA 92111-3741, (858)616-6408
Diving Historical Soc. Norway [IO], Bergen, Norway
Diving; Inst. of [23961]
Diving; Natl. Assn. for Cave [23962]
Diving Plongeon Canada [IO], Ottawa, ON, Canada
Diving Plungeon Canada [★IO]
Div. 54, APA [★IO]
Div. 54, APA [★16175]
Div. on Career Development of The Coun. for Exceptional Children [★9143]
Div. on Career Development and Transition [9143], c/o Coun. for Exceptional Children, PO Box 79026, Baltimore, MD 21279-0026, (888)232-7733
Div. on Career Development and Transition of the Coun. for Exceptional Children [★9143]
Division of Cataloging and Classification - of ALA [★10333]
Div. for Children with Learning Disabilities [★12490]
Division of Christian Social Concern [★19484]
Div. for Early Childhood of the Coun. for Exceptional Children [9144], 27 Ft. Missoula Rd., Ste. 2, Missoula, MT 59804, (406)543-0872
Division of Girl's and Women's Sports of the Amer. Assn. of Hea., Physical Educ., and Recreation [★8983]
Division of Hea. and Welfare Ministries of The United Methodist Church [★14602]
Division of Higher Educ., Christian Church-Disciples of Christ [19854], 11477 Olde Cabin Rd., Ste. 310, St. Louis, MO 63141-7137, (314)991-3000
Division of Homeland Ministries [★19856]
Division of Independent Practice; Amer. Psychological Assn. [16126]
Division of Intl. Affairs [★17832]
Division of Intl. Affairs [★IO]
Division of the Jewish Labor Comm; United Hebrew Trades - New York [24214]
Div. on Mental Retardation and Developmental Disabilities of the Coun. for Exceptional Children - Address unknown since 1999.
Div. Order Analysts; Natl. Assn. of [2934]
Division of Overseas Ministries [★19856]
Div. of Physical Chemistry - Address unknown since 1999.
Div. for Physically Handicapped [★11998]
Div. for Physically Handicapped [★9141]
Div. for Physically Handicapped [★IO]
Div. on Physically Handicapped, Homebound and Hospitalized [★IO]
Div. on Physically Handicapped, Homebound and Hospitalized [★9141]
Div. on Physically Handicapped, Homebound and Hospitalized [★11998]

Division of Psychotherapy; Amer. Psychological Assn. - [16206]
Div. de la Region de la Capitale nationale, Assn. canadienne pour les Nations Unies [★IO]
Div. for the Spanish Speaking [★12282]
Division of Specialty Vehicle Inst. of Am; ATV Safety Institute/ [12952]
Div. on Visual Handicaps [★9145]
Div. on Visual Impairments [9145], c/o Coun. for Exceptional Children, 1110 N Glebe Rd., Ste. 300, Arlington, VA 22201-5704, (703)620-3660
Div. for the Visually Handicapped [★9145]
Div. for Women in Medicine - Defunct.
Divorce
  Amer. Soc. of Separated and Divorced Men [12005]
  Bonus Families [12143]
  Child Support Resistance [12006]
  Children's Rights Coun. [12007]
  CoMamas Assn. [12148]
  Comm. for Mother and Child Rights [11689]
  Dads Rights [12008]
  Ex-Partners of Ser. Members for Equality [17437]
  Ex-Partners of Servicemembers for Equality [12009]
  Fathers for Equal Rights [12010]
  Intl. Assn. for Marriage and Family Counselors [11825]
  Joint Custody Assn. [12011]
  Kids Need Both Parents [17509]
  Natl. Action for Former Military Wives [12012]
  Natl. Assn. of Non-Custodial Moms [11538]
  Natl. Center for Mediation Educ. [5461]
  Natl. Men's Rsrc. Center [18044]
  North Amer. Conf. of Separated and Divorced Catholics [12013]
  Oper. Identity [11258]
  Parents Without Partners [12688]
  Single Booklovers [22142]
  Single Mothers By Choice [12692]
  Stepfamily Found. [12168]
  United Fathers of Am. [12014]
Divorce After 60 - Defunct.
Divorce Aid/Co-Parents - Defunct.
Divorce and Alimony Laws; Natl. Comm. for Fair [★18045]
Divorce Anonymous - Defunct.
Divorce Support - Address unknown since 2000.
Divorced Men; Am'.s Soc. of [★12005]
Divorced Parents X-Change - Address unknown since 2004.
Divorced and Separated Men; Aid to [★18039]
Divya Disha [IO], Secunderabad, India
Dixie Coun. of Authors and Journalists [★11172]
Diyalo Pariwar [IO], Narayangarh, Nepal
Dizziness and Balance Disorders Assn. [★IO]
Dizziness and Balance Disorders Assn. [★15829]
Django Reinhardt Appreciation Soc. - Defunct.
Django Reinhardt Soc. - Address unknown since 2002.
DKT Intl. - Vietnam [IO], Hanoi, Vietnam
DKW Club of Am. [21631], c/o Robert Paul, Membership Sec., 4406 Bridle Rd., Bartlesville, OK 74006, (918)333-5182
DM - Fagforening for hojtuddannede [IO], Frederiksberg, Denmark
DMA; Circulation Coun. of [2620]
DMA Gp. [★717]
DMA Nonprofit Fed. [317], 1615 L St. NW, Ste. 1100, Washington, DC 20036, (202)628-4380
DMAA Educational Found. [★8816]
DMAA: The Care Continuum Alliance [14260], 701 Pennsylvania Ave. NW, Ste. 700, Washington, DC 20004, (202)737-5980
DNA Analysts and Administrators; Assn. of Forensic [5756]
Do Do Club [★20651]
Do It Now Found. [13235], PO Box 27568, Tempe, AZ 85285-7568, (480)736-0599
Do It Yourself Aids
  Catholic Homesteading Movement [11742]
  Center for Self-Sufficiency [11743]
  Home Improvement Res. Inst. [1159]
Do-It-Yourself Res. Inst. [★1159]
Do Right Found. [20492], 991-C Lomas Santa Fe Dr., No. 413, Solana Beach, CA 92075

Reference to "IO" in place of a book number signifies that the association may be found in the 45th edition of International Organizations.

Do Something [17215], 24-32 Union Sq. E, 4th Fl., New York, NY 10003

Doane Family Assn. of Am. [20883], c/o Mrs. Eunice Brabec, Membership Chair, 461 Dellbrook Ave., South San Francisco, CA 94080

Doberman Pinscher
Doberman Pinscher Club of Am. [22257]
Natl. Conf. of Local Environmental Hea. Administrators [16246]
Natl. Rural Hea. Assn. [16248]
NSF Intl. [16249]
Public Citizen Hea. Res. Gp. [16250]
Soc. for Public Hea. Educ. [16254]
United Doberman Club [22369]
U.S.-Mexico Border Hea. Assn. [16256]
World Fed. of Public Hea. Associations [16258]

Doberman Pinscher Club of Am. [22257], c/o Lesley Reeves-Hunt, Membership Sec., 6400 Tripp Rd., China, MI 48054, (810)326-3792

Dobie Clan of North America [20884]

Doboku-Gakkai [★IO]

DOCARE Intl., N.F.P. [IO], East Dundee, IL, United States

DOCARE Intl., N.F.P. [12518], 430 King Ave., East Dundee, IL 60118, (847)836-8022

Docent Assn. [★9402]

DOCHAS, The Irish Assn. of Non-Governmental Development Organisations [IO], Dublin, Ireland

Dock Equip. Mfrs; Loading [2035]

Docs for Tots [13958], 2000 M St. NW, Ste. 201, Washington, DC 20036, (202)296-2131

Dr. to Dr. [12519], 1749 MLK Jr. Way, Berkeley, CA 94709, (510)548-5200

Dr. to Dr. [IO], Berkeley, CA, United States

Dr. Edward Bach Healing Soc. - Defunct.

Dr. James Naismith Basketball Found. [IO], Almonte, ON, Canada

Dr. John W. Tintera Memorial/Hypoglycemia Lay Group - Defunct.

Dr. Thomas A. Dooley Found. [★14982]

Dr. Thomas A. Dooley Found. [★IO]

Dr. Who Appreciation Soc. [★IO]

Dr. Who Info. Network [IO], Toronto, ON, Canada

Drs. for Artists [12520]

Doctors of Audiology; Natl. Assn. of Future [13718]

Doctors; Consortium of [12074]

Doctors for Developing Countries [IO], Turin, Italy

Doctors for Disaster Preparedness [14315], 1601 N Tucson Blvd., Ste. No. 9, Tucson, AZ 85716, (520)325-2680

Doctors for the Env. - Australia [IO], Adelaide, Australia

Doctors for the Env. - Switzerland [IO], Basel, Switzerland

Doctor's Exchange [★24740]

Doctors for Life Intl. [IO], Zimbali, Republic of South Africa

Doctors of Mercy; Flying [★12528]

Doctors Opposing Circumcision [11730], 2442 NW Market St., Ste. 42, Seattle, WA 98107-4137, (360)385-1882

Doctors Ought to Care [14554]

Doctors Without Borders - Australia [IO], Broadway, Australia

Doctors Without Borders - Canada [IO], Toronto, ON, Canada

Doctors Without Borders - France [IO], Paris, France

Doctors Without Borders USA [IO], New York, NY, United States

Doctors Without Borders USA [12850], 333 7th Ave., 2nd Fl., New York, NY 10001-5004, (212)679-6800

Doctors to the World [12522], PO Box 370167, Denver, CO 80237, (303)758-5405

Doctors of the World [12521], 80 Maiden Ln., Ste. 607, New York, NY 10038, (212)226-9890

Doctors to the World [IO], Denver, CO, United States

Doctors of the World [IO], New York, NY, United States

Doctors of the World UK [★IO]

Doctors Worldwide [IO], Stockport, United Kingdom

Doctors Worldwide [IO], Oakbrook Terrace, IL, United States

Doctors Worldwide [12851], 1S132 Summit Ave., No. 301, Oakbrook Terrace, IL 60181, (630)889-9513

Document Examiners; Amer. Soc. of Questioned [5755]

Document Examiners; Assn. of Forensic [5757]

Document Examiners; Independent Assn. of Questioned [5762]

Document Examiners; Natl. Assn. of [5765]

Document Mgt. Indus. Assn. [3679], 433 E Monroe Ave., Alexandria, VA 22301-1645, (703)836-6232

Document Systems Found; Electronic [2100]

Documentaristes du Canada [★IO]

Documentary Org. of Canada [IO], Toronto, ON, Canada

Documentation Center; Philosophy [10824]

Documentation Exchange [★17989]

Documentation Exchange [★IO]

Documentation Exchange; Human Rights [17989]

Documentation Inst; Amer. [★7188]

Documentation Technologies; Intl. Assn. for [729]

Dodge and Allied Family Surname Org. - Address unknown since 2003.

Dodge Ball Fed; Intl. [23821]

Dodge Bros. Club [21632], c/o Less Hoffman, PO Box 1648, Cambridge, OH 43725, (740)439-5102

Dodge Family Assn. [20885], 10105 W 17th Pl., Lakewood, CO 80215, (303)237-4947

Dodge Found; Geraldine R. [13119]

Dodge Pilothouse Era Truck Club of Am. [23024], 3778 Hoen Ave., Santa Rosa, CA 95405

Dodge Wayfarer Sportabout Registry - Defunct.

Dodgeball Assn; Natl. Amateur [23091]

Dodgson, Charles Lutwidge
Lewis Carroll Soc. of North Am. [9681]

Doe Network [12608], c/o Todd Matthews, 121 Short St., Livingston, TN 38570, (931)397-3893

Doe Network [IO], Livingston, TN, United States

Dog
Action for Singapore Dogs [IO]
Afghan Hound Club of Am. [22179]
African Wild Dog Conservancy [5288]
Agility Dog Assn. of Australia [IO]
Agility Dog Club of Queensland [IO]
Airedale Terrier Club of Am. [22180]
Akita Club of Am. [22181]
Akita Rescue Soc. of Am. [11341]
Alaskan Malamute Assistance League [11342]
Alaskan Malamute Club of Am. [22182]
All Amer. Premier Breeds Admin. [22183]
Amateur Field Trial Clubs of Am. [22184]
Amer. Assn. of Black Russian Terriers [22185]
Amer. Belgian Malinois Club [22186]
American Belgian Malinois Club [IO]
Amer. Bloodhound Club [22187]
Amer. Bouvier des Flandres Club [22188]
Amer. Boxer Club [22189]
Amer. Boxer Rescue Assn. [11346]
Amer. Brittany Club [22190]
Amer. Brussels Griffon Assn. [22191]
Amer. Bullmastiff Assn. [22192]
Amer. Canine Educ. Found. [22193]
Amer. Canine Sports Medicine Assn. [16761]
Amer. Cavalier King Charles Spaniel Club [22194]
Amer. Chesapeake Club [22195]
Amer. Dobermann Assn. [22196]
Amer. Dog Breeders Assn. [22197]
Amer. Dog Owner's Assn. [11347]
Amer. Dog Show Judges [22198]
Amer. Eskimo Dog Club of Am. [22199]
Amer. Fox Terrier Club [22200]
Amer. German Shepherd Rescue Assn. [11348]
Amer. Greyhound Track Operators Assn. [23391]
Amer. Heartworm Soc. [16772]
Amer. Kennel Club [22201]
Amer. Kuvasz Assn. [12015]
Amer. Lhasa Apso Club [22202]
Amer. Maltese Assn. [22203]
Amer. Manchester Terrier Club [22204]
Amer. Miniature Schnauzer Club [22205]
Amer. Pointer Club [22206]
Amer. Pomeranian Club [22207]
Amer. Rare Breed Assn. [4496]
Amer. Rescue Dog Assn. [12889]
Amer. Rottweiler Club [22208]
Amer. Sealyham Terrier Club [22209]
Amer. Shetland Sheepdog Assn. [22210]
Amer. Shih Tzu Club [22211]

Amer. Sighthound Field Assn. [22212]
Amer. Spaniel Club [22213]
Amer. Spaniel Club [IO]
Amer. Toy Fox Terrier Club [22214]
Amer. Water Spaniel Club [22215]
Amer. Water Spaniel Club [IO]
Amer. Whippet Club [22216]
Amer. White Shepherd Assn. [22217]
Amer. Working Collie Assn. [22218]
Amer. Working Dog Fed. [21516]
Amer. Working Malinois Assn. [21517]
Arizona Canine Acad. [22219]
Assistance Dogs of Am., Inc. [11922]
Assistance Dogs Intl. [11923]
Assoc. Services for the Blind [16831]
Assn. for Explosive Detection K-9s, Intl. [5964]
Assn. for People with Dogs Named Marty [22220]
Assn. of Pet Dog Trainers [IO]
Assn. of Pet Dog Trainers Australia [IO]
Assn. of Pet Dog Trainers - United Kingdom [IO]
Australian Cattle Dog Club of Am. [22221]
Australian Labradoodle Assn. [IO]
Australian Natl. Kennel Coun. [IO]
Australian Native Dog Conservation Soc. [IO]
Australian Shepherd Club of Am. [22222]
Australian Terrier Club of Am. [22223]
Authentic Hovawarts of North Am. [22224]
Basenji Club of Am. [22225]
Basset Hound Club of Am. [22226]
Bearded Collie Club of Am. [22227]
Belgian Sheepdog Club of Am. [22228]
Berger Picard Club of Am. [22229]
Bernese Mountain Dog Club of Am. [22230]
Bichon Frise Club of Am. [22231]
Black Russian Terrier Club of Am. [22232]
Blind Children's Fund [16834]
Blind Info. Tech. Specialists [16835]
Bluetick Breeders of Am. [22233]
Border Terrier Club of Am. [22234]
Borzoi Club of Am. [22235]
Boston Terrier Club of Am. [22236]
Boxer Club - Denmark [IO]
Bull Terrier Club of Am. [22237]
Bulldog Club of Am. Rescue Network [11372]
Cairn Terrier Club of Am. [22238]
Canaan Dog Club of Am. [22239]
Canadian Assn. of Professional Pet Dog Trainers [IO]
Canadian Kennel Club [IO]
Canine Assistants [11925]
Canine Assn. of Western Australia [IO]
Canine Cancer Awareness [16788]
Canine Companions for Independence [11926]
Canine Defense Fund [11373]
Canines for Disabled Kids [11927]
Cardigan Welsh Corgi Club of Am. [22240]
Caucasian Ovcharka Club of Am. [22241]
Cavalier King Charles Spaniel Club of Am. [22242]
Chihuahua Club of Am. [22243]
Chinese Shar-Pei Club of Am. [22244]
Chow Chow Club, Inc. [22245]
Club du Basset Hound [IO]
Club du Braque Francais [IO]
Club des Chiens Tibetains de France [IO]
Club des Epagneuls Nains Anglais [IO]
Clumber Spaniel Club of Am. [22246]
Cockapoo Club of Am. [22247]
Collie Club of Am. [22248]
Colonial Rottweiler Club [22249]
Continental Mi-Ki Assn. [22250]
CorgiAid [22251]
Curly-Coated Retriever Club of Am. [22252]
Dachshund Club of Am. [22253]
Dalmatian Club of Am. [22254]
Dandie Dinmont Terrier Club of Am. [22255]
Danish Afghan Hound Club [IO]
Danish Gordon Setter Club [IO]
Danish Kennel Club [IO]
Danish Pointer Club [IO]
Danish Rottweiler Club [IO]
Danish Samoyed Club [IO]
Danish Terrier Club [IO]
Dansk Dobermann Klub [IO]
Dansk Retriever Klub [IO]

A star before a book entry number signifies that the name is not listed separately, but is mentioned within the entry.

Desert German Shorthaired Pointer Club [22256]
Doberman Pinscher Club of Am. [22257]
Dog Scouts of Am. [12016]
Dog Writers' Assn. of Am. [3110]
Dogs for the Deaf [14754]
Dogs Deserve Better [12017]
Dogs New South Wales [IO]
Dogs on Stamps Stud. Unit [22815]
Dogue de Bordeaux Soc. of Am. [22258]
Echo Dogs White Shepherd Rescue [11388]
English Cocker Spaniel Club of Am. [22259]
English Setter Assn. of Am. [22260]
English Shepherd Club [22261]
English Springer Spaniel Field Trial Assn. [22262]
English Toy Spaniel Club of Am. [22263]
Epagneul Breton USA [22264]
Epagneul Breton USA [IO]
Estrela Mountain Dog Assn. of Am. [22265]
Fed. for the Amer. Staffordshire Terrier [21518]
Fidelco Guide Dog Found. [16846]
Field Spaniel Soc. of Am. [22266]
Finnish Kennel Club [IO]
Finnish Spitz Club of Am. [22267]
Flat-Coated Retriever Soc. of Am. [22268]
Fox Terrier Network [22269]
Fox Terrier Network [IO]
French Airedale Terrier and Various Terriers Club [IO]
French Brittany Gun Dog Assn. [22270]
French Bull Dog Club of Am. [22271]
German Shepherd Dog Club of Am. [22272]
German Shepherd Dog Club of Am. - Working Dog Assn. [22273]
German Shorthaired Pointer Club of Am. [22274]
German Wirehaired Pointer Club of Am. [22275]
Giant Schnauzer Club of Am. [22276]
Golden Retriever Club of Am. [22277]
Gordon Setter Club of Am. [22278]
Great Dane Club of Am. [22279]
Great Pyrenees Club of Am. [22280]
GREY2K USA [4800]
Greyhound Adoption Center [11401]
Greyhound Club of Am. [22281]
Greyhound Racing Assn. of Am. [23392]
Guide Dog Found. for the Blind [16849]
Guide Dog Users, Inc. [16850]
Guide Dogs of Am. [16851]
Guide Dogs for the Blind [16852]
Guiding Eyes for the Blind [16853]
Havana Silk Dog Assn. of Am. [22282]
Heart Bandits Amer. Eskimo Dog Rescue [12018]
Heart Bandits Amer. Eskimo Dog Rescue [IO]
Hearts United for Animals [11405]
Helen Keller Intl. [16854]
Helping Hands Rescue [11406]
Hovawart Club of Am. [22283]
Hungarian Pumi Club of Am. [22284]
Hunting Retriever Club [22285]
Icelandic Sheepdog Assn. of Am. [22286]
Independent Visually Impaired Enterprisers [16855]
Intl. Assn. of Assistance Dog Partners [14241]
Intl. Assn. of Canine Professionals [1161]
Intl. Assn. of Canine Professionals [IO]
Intl. Borzoi Coun. [IO]
Intl. Borzoi Coun. [22287]
Intl. Disc Dog Handlers' Assn. [23373]
Intl. Fed. of Kennel Clubs [IO]
Intl. Fed. of Sleddog Sports [23393]
Intl. French Brittany Club of Am. [22288]
Intl. French Brittany Club of Am. [IO]
Intl. Hearing Dog, Inc. [14762]
Intl. Kennel Club of Chicago [22289]
Intl. Kennel Soc. [22290]
Intl. Kennel Soc. [IO]
Intl. Police Work Dog Assn. [5979]
Intl. Seppala Assn. [22291]
Intl. Sheep Dog Soc. [IO]
Intl. Sled Dog Racing Assn. [23394]
Intl. Soc. of Animal License Collectors [22058]
Intl. Weight Pull Assn. [23384]
International Weight Pull Association [IO]
InTouch Networks [16860]
Irish Setter Club of Am. [22292]
Irish Terrier Club of Am. [22293]

Irish Water Spaniel Club of Am. [22294]
Irish Wolfhound Club of Am. [22295]
Italian Greyhound Club of Am. [22296]
Jack Russell Terrier Club of Am. [22297]
Japanese Akita Club of Am. [22298]
Japanese Chin Club of Am. [22299]
JBI Intl. - Jewish Braille Inst. of Am. [16861]
Jewish Guild for the Blind [16862]
Keeshond Club of Am. [22300]
Kennel Club [IO]
Kennel Club Boliviano [IO]
Komondor Club of Am. [22301]
Kuvasz Club of Am. [22302]
Ladies Kennel Assn. of Am. [22303]
Lakes Region Sled Dog Club [23395]
Leader Dogs for the Blind [16864]
Lutheran Braille Evangelism Assn. [16866]
Lutheran Braille Workers [16867]
MAB Community Services [16868]
Maremma Sheepdog Club of Am. [22304]
Mastiff and Bullmastiff Club in France [IO]
Mastiff Club of Am. [22305]
Miniature Australian Shepherd Club of Am. [22306]
Miniature Bull Terrier Club of Am. [22307]
Miniature Pinscher Club of Am. [22308]
Musical Dog Sport Assn. [23385]
Natl. Accreditation Coun. for Agencies Serving the Blind and Visually Impaired [16870]
Natl. Alliance of Blind Students [16871]
Natl. Amateur Retriever Club [22309]
Natl. Amer. Eskimo Dog Assn. [22310]
Natl. Amer. Pit Bull Terrier Assn. [22311]
Natl. Assn. of Dog Obedience Instructors [22312]
Natl. Assn. of Louisiana Catahoulas [22313]
Natl. Assn. for Parents of Children With Visual Impairments [16873]
Natl. Beagle Club of Am. [22314]
Natl. Bird Dog Challenge Assn. [22315]
Natl. Braille Assn. [16875]
Natl. Braille Press [16876]
Natl. Cesky Terrier Club of Am. [22316]
Natl. Disaster Search Dog Found. [12892]
Natl. Entlebucher Mountain Dog Assn. [22317]
Natl. Entlebucher Mountain Dog Assn. [IO]
Natl. Fed. of the Blind [16877]
Natl. Greyhound Adoption Prog. [11438]
Natl. Greyhound Assn. [22318]
Natl. Indus. for the Blind [16878]
Natl. Labrador Retriever Club [22319]
Natl. Narcotic Detector Dog Assn. [5997]
Natl. Pet Alliance [11441]
Natl. Retriever Club [23386]
Natl. Ser. Dog Center [14774]
Natl. Shiba Club of Am. [22320]
Natl. Toy Fox Terrier Assn. [22321]
Natl. War Dog Memorial Fund [21347]
New Zealand Kennel Club [IO]
Newfoundland Club of Am. [22322]
North Amer. Border Terrier Welfare [12019]
North Amer. Deutsch Kurzhaar Club [22323]
North Amer. Dog Agility Coun. [23387]
North Amer. Jack Russell Terrier Assn. [22324]
North Amer. Jack Russell Terrier Assn. [IO]
North Amer. Kai Assn. [22325]
North Amer. Llewellin Breeders Assn. [22326]
North Amer. Llewellin Breeders Assn. [IO]
North Amer. Ring Assn. [IO]
North Amer. Ring Assn. [22327]
North Amer. Sheep Dog Soc. [22328]
North Amer. Teckel Club [22329]
North Amer. Working Bouvier Assn. [22330]
Norwegian Elkhound Assn. of Am. [22331]
Norwegian Lundehund Assn. of Am. [22332]
Norwich and Norfolk Terrier Club [22333]
Old English Sheepdog Club of Am. [22334]
Orthopedic Found. for Animals [16805]
Otterhound Club of Am. [22335]
Papillon Club of Am. [22336]
Parson Russell Terrier Assn. of Am. [22337]
Patterdale Terrier Club of Am. [22338]
Paws With a Cause [11979]
Pekingese Club of Am. [22339]
Pembroke Welsh Corgi Club of Am. [22340]
Peruvian Inca Orchid Dog Club of Am. [22341]

Pet Savers Found. [11449]
Pilot Dogs [16881]
Pointer Club Francais [IO]
Polish Tatra Sheepdog Club of Am. [22342]
Poodle Club of Am. [22343]
Portuguese Podengo Club of Am. [22344]
Portuguese Water Dog Club of Am. [22345]
Positively Addictive Dog Sports [IO]
Prevent Blindness Am. [16882]
Professional Handlers Assn. [22346]
Protection Sports Assn. [23848]
Protestant Guild for Human Services [16884]
Pug Dog Club of Am. [22347]
Puli Club of Am. [22348]
Pups for Peace [12700]
Pyrenean Mastiff Club of Am. [22349]
Rassemblement des Amateurs de Levriers d'Irlande et d'Ecosse [IO]
Rat Terrier Club of Am. [22350]
Recording for the Blind and Dyslexic [16885]
Res. to Prevent Blindness [16886]
Retriever Club de France [IO]
Reunion des Amateurs de Fox Terriers [IO]
Rhodesian Ridgeback Club of the U.S. [22351]
Rhodesian Ridgeback Klubben [IO]
Rin Tin Tin Fan Club [25041]
Rough and Smooth Collie Training Assn. [IO]
Saint Bernard Club of Am. [22352]
Saluki Club of Am. [22353]
Samoyed Club of Am. [22354]
Schipperke Club of Am. [22355]
Scottish Deerhound Club of Am. [22356]
Scottish Terrier Club of Am. [22357]
Seeing Eye [16888]
Senior Conformation Judges Assn. [22358]
Siberian Husky Club of Am. [22359]
Silky Terrier Club of Am. [22360]
Skye Terrier Club of Am. [22361]
Spaniel Club Francais [IO]
Spanish Water Dog Assn. of Am. [22362]
Spinone Club of Am. [22363]
Spitz Dog Club [IO]
Staffordshire Terrier Club of Am. [22364]
Standard Schnauzer Club of Am. [22365]
Standard Schnauzer Club of America [IO]
SunCoast Fundogs Agility Club [IO]
Support Dogs, Inc. [11990]
Tasmanian Canine Assn. [IO]
Tattoo-a-Pet [11463]
Therapy Dogs Intl. [16638]
Tibetan Spaniel Club of Am. [22366]
Tibetan Terrier Club of Am. [22367]
Toy Fox Terrier Club of Canada [IO]
Treeing Walker Breeders and Fanciers Assn. [22368]
United Action for Animals [11468]
United Doberman Club [22369]
United Kennel Club [22370]
United Schutzhund Clubs of Am. [22371]
U.S. Border Collie Club [22372]
U.S. Boxer Assn. [22373]
U.S. Dog Agility Assn. [23388]
U.S. Kerry Blue Terrier Club [22374]
U.S. Lakeland Terrier Club [22375]
U.S. Mondioring Assn. [23389]
U.S. Neapolitan Mastiff Club [22376]
U.S. Rottweiler Club [22377]
U.S. War Dogs Assn. [20769]
U.S.A. Defenders of Greyhounds [11473]
Vietnam Dog Handler Assn. [21338]
Visually Impaired Veterans of Am. [16891]
Vizsla Club of Am. [22378]
Vizsla Club of France [IO]
WAAG Agility Dog Club [IO]
Weimaraner Club of Am. [22379]
Welsh Springer Spaniel Club of Am. [22380]
West Highland White Terrier Club of Am. [22381]
Westminster Kennel Club [22382]
White German Shepherd Dog Club of Am. [22383]
White German Shepherd Dog Club of Am. [IO]
Wirehaired Vizsla Club of Am. [22384]
Working Kelpie Coun. of Australia [IO]
Working Pit Bull Terrier Club of Am. [22385]
Working Riesenschnauzer Fed. [22386]

Reference to "IO" in place of a book number signifies that the association may be found in the 45th edition of International Organizations.

Working Riesenschnauzer Fed. [IO]
World Bulldog Alliance [22387]
World Canine Freestyle Org. [23390]
World Wide Kennel Club [22388]
World Wide Kennel Club [IO]
WTCARES [22389]
Xavier Soc. for the Blind [16892]
Yorkshire Terrier Club of Am. [22390]
Dog Assistance in Disability [IO], Rugeley, United Kingdom
Dog Assn; Intl. Bird [21452]
Dog Assn; North Amer. Police Work [6003]
Dog Center; Natl. Ser. [22390]
Dog Club; Laconia Sled [★23395]
Dog Club of New England; German Shepherd [★22272]
Dog Found. for the Blind; Guide [16849]
Dog Found; Fidelco Guide [16846]
Dog Groomers Assn. of Am; Natl. [2962]
Dog Guides Canada [IO], Oakville, ON, Canada
Dog Handlers' Assn; Intl. Disc [23373]
Dog Info; Natl. Center for Hearing [★14774]
Dog Judges Assn. of America - Defunct.
Dog League for the Blind; Leader [★16864]
Dog Owner's Assn; Amer. [11347]
Dog Owners League of America - Defunct.
Dog Prog; Hearing [★14774]
Dog Prog; Hearing Ear [★14770]
Dog Prog; New England Assistance [★14770]
Dog Proj; Hearing [★14774]

Dog Racing
Amer. Greyhound Track Operators Assn. [23391]
European Sled Dog Racing Assn. [IO]
GREY2K USA [4800]
Greyhound Adoption Center [11401]
Greyhound Racing Assn. of Am. [23392]
Intl. Fed. of Sleddog Sports [23393]
International Federation of Sleddog Sports [IO]
Intl. Sled Dog Racing Assn. [IO]
Intl. Sled Dog Racing Assn. [23394]
Lakes Region Sled Dog Club [23395]
Natl. Greyhound Adoption Prog. [11438]
U.S.A. Defenders of Greyhounds [11473]
Dog Registry; Natl. [11436]
Dog Rsrc. Center; Hearing [★14774]
Dog Scouts of Am. [12016], 5068 Nestel Rd., St. Helen, MI 48656, (989)389-2000
Dog Services; Natl. Educ. for Assistance [14770]
Dog Sports; Intl. Fed. of Sled [23393]
Dog Users; Coordinating Comm. of Guide [★16850]
Dog Users, Inc; Guide [16850]
Dog Users; Natl. Soc. of Guide [★16850]
Dog Writers' Assn. of Am. [3110], c/o Ms. Pat Santi, Sec., 173 Union Rd., Coatesville, PA 19320, (610)384-2436
Doga Dernegi [IO], Ankara, Turkey
Dogman and the Shepherds Fan Club - Address unknown since 1990.
Dogs of Am; Guide [16851]
Dogs of Am., Inc; Assistance [11922]
Dogs for the Blind; Leader [16864]
Dogs; Children Before [11682]
Dogs for the Deaf [14754], 10175 Wheeler Rd., Central Point, OR 97502, (541)826-9220
Dogs for Deaf and Disabled Americans [★14770]
Dogs Deserve Better [12017], PO Box 23, Tipton, PA 16684, (814)941-7447
Dogs for the Handicapped, Inc; Guide [★11922]
Dogs for the Handicapped; Support [★11990]
Dogs; Hearing [★14762]
Dogs, Inc; Support [11990]
Dogs New South Wales [IO], St. Marys, Australia
Dogs; Path-Finder Guide [★16864]
Dogs; Pilot [16881]
Dogs on Stamps Stud. Unit [22815]
Dogs Trust [IO], London, United Kingdom
Dogue de Bordeaux Soc. of Am. [22258], c/o Angie Reed, Recording Sec., 301 16th St. NW, Puyallup, WA 98371, (253)848-4901
Doheny Found; Carrie Estelle [13156]
Dohne Merino Breed Soc. of South Africa [IO], Stutterheim, Republic of South Africa
Dohne Merino Breeders' Org. of South Africa [★IO]
Doily Inst; Plate, Cup, Container, and [★1157]
Doing Things for Animals [11386], 59 S Bayles Ave., Port Washington, NY 11050-3728, (516)883-7767

Doirse Dochais [★17931]
Doirse Dochais [★IO]
Doitsu Kikai Kogyo Renmei - Nihon Daihyo Jimusho [★IO]
Dole Found. For Employment of People With Disabilities - Address unknown since 2000.
Doll Artisan Guild [22394], 118 Commerce Rd., PO Box 1113, Oneonta, NY 13820-5113, (607)432-4977
Doll Artisan Guild [IO], Oneonta, NY, United States
The Doll Center [★IO]
The Doll Center [★22394]
Doll Collectors of America - Defunct.
Doll Costumer's Guild [22395], PO Box 247, New Harmony, IN 47631, (812)682-3802
Doll Makers Assn; Intl. [★22397]
Doll Makers Assn. - Internationals; Intl. [★22397]
Doll Supply Mfrs. Assn. - Defunct.
Doll and Toy Collectors; Natl. [★22407]
Doll and Toy Workers of the U.S. and Canada; Intl. Union of [★24196]
Dollars and Sense; Economic Affairs Bureau/ [6879]
Dollars & Sense Magazine [★6879]

Dollhouses
Australian Miniature Enthusiasts Assn. [IO]
Cottage Indus. Miniaturists Trade Assn. [1162]

Dolls
Amy's Doll Lover's Club [22391]
Annalee Club [22392]
Cabbage Patch Kids Collectors Club [21982]
Chatty Cathy Collectors Club [22393]
Doll Artisan Guild [22394]
Doll Artisan Guild [IO]
Doll Costumer's Guild [22395]
Ginny Doll Club [22396]
Intl. Doll Makers Assn. [22397]
Intl. Doll Makers Assn. [IO]
Intl. Found. of Doll Makers [22398]
Intl. Rose O'Neill Club Found. [22399]
Intl. Rose O'Neill Club Found. [IO]
Lawton Collector's Guild [22400]
Lizzie High Soc. [22401]
Natl. Antique Doll Dealers Assn. [22402]
National Antique Doll Dealers Association [IO]
Natl. Assn. of Fashion and Accessory Designers [246]
Natl. Assn. of Wheat Weavers [22166]
Natl. Inst. of Amer. Doll Artists [22403]
Original Doll Artists Coun. of Am. [22404]
Original Paper Doll Artists Guild [22405]
Strawberry Shortcake Chat Gp. [22406]
United Fed. of Doll Clubs [22407]
Dolls, Toys, Playthings, Novelties and Allied Prdts. of the U.S. and Canada; Intl. Union of [★24196]
Dolly Parton Fan Club [★24878]
Dolly Parton's Fan Club [24877], 708 Dollywood Ln., Pigeon Forge, TN 37863
Dollywood Ambassadors [★24878]
Dollywood Ambassadors and Dollywood Found. [★24878]
Dollywood Found. [24878], 1020 Dollywood Ln., Pigeon Forge, TN 37863, (865)428-9890
Dolphin Alliance; Blue [5008]
Dolphin Circle - Address unknown since 2004.
Dolphin Res. Center [7261], 58901 Overseas Hwy., Grassy Key, FL 33050-6019, (305)289-1121
Dome Assn; Natl. [★2530]
Dome Comm. of the Home Mfrs. Coun. of NAHB [★2530]
Dome Comm; Natl. [★2530]
Dome Coun; Natl. [2530]
Dome Home Mfrs; Natl. Assn. of [★2530]
Domestic Appliance Ser. Assn. [IO], London, United Kingdom

Domestic Development
ABANTU for Development - Regional Off. for Eastern and Southern Africa [IO]
ActionAid - Brasil [IO]
ActionAid Intl. USA [11758]
ActionAid Intl. - Vietnam [IO]
ActionAid - Sierra Leone [IO]
ActionAid - United Kingdom [IO]
Adventist Development and Relief Agency - Vietnam [IO]
African Enterprise [IO]

Asociacion Andar Costa Rica [IO]
Asociacion Costarricense para Organizaciones de Desarrollo [IO]
Assn. for the Development of Microenterprise [IO]
Bariloche Found. [IO]
Cordaid [IO]
European Assn. for Info. on Local Development [IO]
Intl. Assn. of Character Cities [11781]
Joaquim Nabuco Found. [IO]
Natl. Coun. of Development Commun. [IO]
Private Sector Org. of Jamaica [IO]
Stefan Batory Found. [IO]
United Nations Development Prog. - Armenia [IO]
Domestic European Ferret Fanciers and Breeders Assn. of Minnesota - Defunct.
Domestic/Foreign Missionary Soc. of the Protestant Episcopal Church [20327], Episcopal Church Ctr., 815 2nd Ave., New York, NY 10017, (212)716-6000
Domestic/Foreign Missionary Soc. of the Protestant Episcopal Church [IO], New York, NY, United States
Domestic Policy Assn. [★18467]
Domestic Sea Food Producers Assn. of New England - Address unknown since 1995.
Domestic Service
Intl. Guild of Professional Butlers [24040]
Domestic Services
Intl. Guild of Professional Butlers [IO]
United Kingdom Housekeepers Assn. [IO]
Domestic Social Development; Office of [★IO]
Domestic Social Development; Office of [★19613]
Domestic Technologies [16994], PO Box 44, Evergreen, CO 80437-2043, (303)674-7700
Domestic Technologies [IO], Evergreen, CO, United States
Domestic Tech. Inst. [★IO]
Domestic Tech. Inst. [★16994]
Domestic Violence
AMEND [12020]
Amer. Women Overseas Domestic Violence Fund [12021]
Amer. Women Overseas Domestic Violence Fund [IO]
Asian and Pacific Islander Inst. on Domestic Violence [12022]
Batterers Anonymous - Beyond Abuse [12023]
Break the Cycle [12024]
Communities Against Violence Network [13374]
Corporate Alliance to End Partner Violence [12025]
Educ. Wife Assault [IO]
Emerge: Counseling and Educ. to Stop Domestic Violence [12026]
FaithTrust Inst. [12027]
Family Violence Prevention Fund [12028]
Femmes en Detresse [IO]
Glasgow Women's Aid [IO]
House of Ruth [12029]
Illusion Theater [12030]
Immigrant Women Services Ottawa [IO]
INCITE! Women of Color Against Violence [18788]
Leadership Coun. on Child Abuse and Interpersonal Violence [12031]
Love Our Children USA [11619]
Men's Rsrc. Center [12357]
Natl. Center for Assault Prevention [12032]
Natl. Center on Elder Abuse [12033]
Natl. CH on Marital and Date Rape [12790]
Natl. Coalition Against Domestic Violence [12034]
Natl. Coun. on Child Abuse and Family Violence [12035]
Natl. Domestic Violence Hotline [12036]
Natl. Latino Alliance for the Elimination of Domestic Violence [12037]
Natl. Network to End Domestic Violence [12038]
Natl. Network to End Violence Against Immigrant Women [13433]
Natl. Org. for Women's Shelters and Young Women's Shelters in Sweden [IO]
Native Amer. Community Bd. [12630]
NICRO Women's Support Centre [IO]
Pact Training [11830]

A star before a book entry number signifies that the name is not listed separately, but is mentioned within the entry.

People Opposing Women Abuse [IO]
Raising Voices [IO]
Refugee Coun. USA [18500]
Scottish Women's Aid [IO]
Stop Abuse for Everyone [12039]
Stop the Violence, Face The Music [13376]
Trinidad and Tobago Coalition Against Domestic Violence [IO]
Welsh Women's Aid - Cardiff Natl. Off. [IO]
Women in Crisis [13443]
Women and Men Against Sexual Harassment and Other Abuses [13088]
Women in Transition [13447]
Women's Support Proj. [IO]
WomensLaw.org [18823]
Domestic Violence; Emerge: A Men's Counseling Ser. on [★12026]
Domestic Water Tank Mfrs. Coun. - Defunct.
Domineck Allen Fan Club - Defunct.
Dominic; Maryknoll Sisters of Saint [20355]
Dominica Amateur Athletic Assn. [IO], Roseau, Dominica
Dominica Assn. of Disabled People [IO], Roseau, Dominica
Dominica Assn. of Teachers [IO], Roseau, Dominica
Dominica Employers' Fed. [IO], Roseau, Dominica
Dominica Lawn Tennis Assn. [IO], Roseau, Dominica
Dominica Natl. Development Corp. [IO], Roseau, Dominica
Dominica Taekwondo Fed. [IO], Roseau, Dominica
Dominican Assn. of Foreign Investment Enterprises [IO], Santo Domingo, Dominican Republic
Dominican Chamber of Commerce of the U.S. - Defunct.
Dominican Educational Assn. - Defunct.
Dominican Inst. of Genealogy - Address unknown since 2008.
Dominican Mission Found. [20328], PO Box 15367, San Francisco, CA 94115-0367, (415)931-2183

Dominican Republic
Batey Relief Alliance [12835]
Dominicans on Wall St. [1413]
Hermandad [17046]
Natl. Dog Groomers Assn. of Am. [2962]
Pet Food Inst. [2963]
Response-Ability [20386]
Restoration Proj. Intl. [12441]
Sister Island Proj. [11788]
Dominican Republic Bible Soc. [IO], Santo Domingo, Dominican Republic
Dominican Republic League Against Epilepsy [IO], Santo Domingo, Dominican Republic
Dominican Republic Study Group - Defunct.
Dominican Soc. of Cardiology [IO], Santo Domingo, Dominican Republic
Dominican Soc. of EEG and Clinical Neurophysiology [IO], Santo Domingo, Dominican Republic
Dominican Volunteers USA [20329], 7200 W Div. St., River Forest, IL 60305-1222, (708)524-5985
Dominicans on Wall St. [1413], 160 E 48th St., Apt. 2L, New York, NY 10017
Dominicans on Wall St. [IO], New York, NY, United States
Dominion Sports Services, Inc. [★23486]
Domino Players Assn. of Am. [22465]
Domra Assn. of Am; Balalaika and [10563]
Don DeLillo Soc. [11169], c/o Marni Gauthier, Sec., PO Box 2000, Cortland, NY 13045-0900
Don Winters and the Winters Brothers Fan Club - Defunct.
Don Youngblood and the Hoosier Beats Intl. Fan Club - Defunct.
DONA Intl. [15598], PO Box 626, Jasper, IN 47547-0626, (888)788-DONA
Donald W. Reynolds Found. [13903], 1701 Village Center Cir., Las Vegas, NV 89134, (702)804-6000
Donated Dental Services Programs [★14179]
Donavant Family Assn; Dunnavant/ [20889]
Doncaster Chamber [IO], Doncaster, United Kingdom
Dondino Fan Club - Address unknown since 1994.
Donee Gp. [★12732]
Donizetti Soc. [IO], Morden, United Kingdom
Donkey Assn; Natl. Miniature [5004]
Donkey Breed Soc. [IO], Edenbridge, United Kingdom

Donkey and Mule Soc; Amer. [4127]
Donkey and Mule Soc; Southwestern [21521]
Donkey Registry; Miniature [4137]
Donkey Sanctuary [IO], Sidmouth, United Kingdom
Donna Fargo Fan Club [★24879]
Donna Fargo Intl. Fan Club [24879], c/o Linda Cottingham, Coor., PO Box 210877, Nashville, TN 37221-0877, (615)662-9484
Donner Found; William H. [13880]
Donny Osmond Fan Club [★24880]
Donny Osmond Intl. Network [24880], 223 W Bulldog, No. 520, Provo, UT 84604
Donor Registry; Natl. Bone Marrow [★14292]
Donors
Amer. Assn. of Blood Banks [13761]
Amer. Assn. of Tissue Banks [16663]
Amer. Organ Transplant Assn. [16664]
Amer. Soc. for Apheresis [13706]
Amer. Soc. of Transplant Surgeons [16667]
America's Blood Centers [13762]
Assn. of Organ Procurement Organizations [14287]
Assn. of Small Foundations [18267]
Australia and New Zealand Organ Donation Registry [IO]
Bone Marrow Donors Worldwide [IO]
Center for Organ Recovery and Educ. [16670]
Coalition for Hemophilia B [14787]
Eye Bank Assn. of Am. [14288]
Eye Bank Assn. of India [IO]
Eye-Bank for Sight Restoration [14289]
Hemophilia Fed. of Am. [14789]
Intl. Assn. for Organ Donation [16671]
Intl. Liver Transplantation Soc. [16672]
Intl. Soc. for Heart and Lung Transplantation [16674]
Japan Donor Family Club [IO]
LifeBanc [14290]
The Living Bank Intl. [14291]
The Living Bank Intl. [IO]
Locks of Love [17055]
Natl. Bone Marrow Transplant Link [16676]
Natl. Coun. on Minority Educ. in Transplantation [16677]
Natl. Hemophilia Found. [14795]
Natl. Marrow Donor Prog. [14292]
National Marrow Donor Program [IO]
North Amer. Soc. for Dialysis and Transplantation [15295]
North Amer. Transplant Coordinators Org. [16681]
Transplant Recipients Intl. Org. [16682]
Transplant Speakers Intl. [16683]
United Kingdom Assn. for Milk Banking [IO]
United Network for Organ Sharing [16684]
USBloodDonors.org [13766]
Donors Interested in Catholic Activities; Foundations and [19625]
Donors' Offspring [13298]
Don't Waste Us - Address unknown since 1999.
Doody Memorabilia Collectors Club; Howdy [22038]
Doodyville Historical Soc. [★22038]
Dooley Found; Dr. Thomas A. [★14982]
Dooley Foundation/INTERMED [★14982]
Dooley Foundation/INTERMED [★IO]
Dooley Foundation/INTERMED U.S.A; Thomas A. [★14982]
Dooley Found; Thomas A. [★14982]
Door
Amer. Architectural Manufacturers Assn. [588]
Amer. Assn. of Automatic Door Mfrs. [1163]
Antique Doorknob Collectors of Am. [21971]
Assn. of Millwork Distributors [600]
Door and Hardware Inst. [1821]
Institutional Locksmiths' Assn. [1164]
Insulated Steel Door Inst. [628]
Intl. Door Assn. [631]
Natl. Fenestration Rating Coun. [648]
Screen Mfrs. Assn. [1833]
Steel Door Inst. [672]
Window and Door Manufacturers Assn. [686]
Door and Access Systems Mfrs. Assn. Intl. [2554], 1300 Sumner Ave., Cleveland, OH 44115-2851, (216)241-7333
Door and Access Systems Manufacturers Assn. Intl. [IO], Cleveland, OH, United States

Door Assn; Natl. Wood Window and [★686]
Door Export Company - Defunct.
Door and Frame Assn; Natl. Steel [★2719]
Door and Hardware Fed. [IO], Tamworth, United Kingdom
Door and Hardware Inst. [IO], Chantilly, VA, United States
Door and Hardware Inst. [1821], 14150 Newbrook Dr., Ste. 200, Chantilly, VA 20151, (703)222-2010
Door Inst; Insulated Steel [628]
Door Inst; Steel [672]
Door Jobbers Assn; Northern Sash and [★600]
Door Jobbers Assn; Southern Sash and [★600]
Door Manufacturers Assn; Natl. [★686]
Door Manufacturers Assn; Window and [686]
Door and Operator Dealers of Am. [★631]
Door and Operator Dealers of Am. [★IO]
Door and Operator Dealers Assn. [★IO]
Door and Operator Dealers Assn. [★631]
Door Operator and Remote Controls Mfrs. Assn. - Defunct.
Door and Shutter Mfrs. Assn. and Assn. of Building Hardware Mfrs. [★IO]
Door and Window Inst; Sliding Glass [★588]
Doorknob Collectors of Am; Antique [21971]
Doors Collectors Club [24881], c/o TDM Inc., PO Box 1441, Orem, UT 84059-1441, (801)224-7390
Doors of Hope [17931], PO Box 485, Ho Ho Kus, NJ 07423, (201)444-4786
Doors of Hope [IO], Ho Ho Kus, NJ, United States
Doorstop Collectors Club of America - Address unknown since 1999.
Doris Day Animal League [11387], 2100 L St. NW, Washington, DC 20037, (202)452-1100
Doris Day Collectors - Defunct.
Doris Duke Charitable Found. [13115], Off. of Grants Admin., 650 Fifth Ave., 19th Fl., New York, NY 10019, (212)974-7000
Dorothy L. Sayers Soc. [IO], Hassocks, United Kingdom
Dorper Sheep Breeders' Soc. of South Africa [IO], Middelburg, Republic of South Africa
Dorpers Skaaptelersgenootskap van Suid-Afrika [★IO]
Dorset Bus., The Chamber of Commerce and Indus. [IO], Poole, United Kingdom
Dorset Chamber of Commerce and Indus. [★IO]
Dorset Club; Continental [5202]
Dorset Horn and Poll Dorset Sheep Breeders Assn. [IO], London, United Kingdom
Dorset Natural History and Archaeological Soc. [IO], Dorchester, United Kingdom
Dorthy Danforth Compton Fellowships [★8250]
Dosimetrists; Amer. Assn. of Medical [15116]
Doty Soc; Pilgrim Edward [20756]
Double Dutch League; Amer. [23697]
Double Harvest [4088], 55 S Main St., Oberlin, OH 44074, (440)714-1694
Double Harvest [IO], Oberlin, OH, United States
Double Trouble in Recovery [12548], c/o Howie Vogle, PO Box 245055, Brooklyn, NY 11224, (718)373-2684
Doublespeak; Comm. on Public [17173]
Dougan-Theodorus Scowden Family Org; Neal [21010]
Douglas Barr Fan Club - Defunct.
Douglas Fir Export Company - Defunct.
Douglas Fir Plywood Assn. [★1637]
Douglas Soc. of North Am; Clan [20826]
Doulas of North Am. [★15598]
Dove Assn; Amer. [21839]
Dove Assn; Great Lakes [★21839]
Dove Hunt Assn; One-Arm [23358]
Dove; Soc. of the Ark and the [20758]
Dove Sportsman's Soc. [11515], PO Box 610, Edgefield, SC 29824, (803)637-5731
Dove Sportsman's Soc. [IO], Edgefield, SC, United States
Dovenschap [★IO]
Doverspike Family Exchange; Daubenspeck- [20879]
Doves Unlimited [★11515]
Doves Unlimited [★IO]
Dow Jones
Independent Assn. of Publishers' Employees [24174]

Reference to "IO" in place of a book number signifies that the association may be found in the 45th edition of International Organizations.

Encyclopedia of Associations, 46th Edition   3359

Dow Jones Employees Assn. [★24174]
Dow Jones Newspaper Fund [8711], PO Box 300, Princeton, NJ 08543-0300, (609)452-2820
Down Assn; Amer. [★2258]
Down Record Assn; Amer. Oxford [★5190]
Down Syndrome; Assn. for Children with [12562]
Down Syndrome Assn; Hong Kong [IO]
Down Syndrome Assn. - Singapore [IO], Singapore, Singapore
Down Syndrome Children; Parents of [★12579]
Down Syndrome Cong; Natl. [12577]
Down Syndrome Ireland [IO], Dublin, Ireland
Down Syndrome; Parents of [12579]
Down Syndrome; Parents of Children with [★12579]
Down Syndrome Soc; Natl. [12040]
Downed Bikers Assn. [12612], PO Box 21713, Oklahoma City, OK 73156, (405)789-5565
Downhill Battle [2803], c/o Nicholas Reville, Dir., 28 Monadnock Rd., Worcester, MA 01609, (508)963-7832

Down's Syndrome
Amer. Network of Community Options and Resources [12560]
Arc of the U.S. [12561]
Assn. for Children with Down Syndrome [12562]
Assn. of Univ. Centers on Disabilities [12563]
Calgary Down Syndrome Assn. [IO]
Canadian Down Syndrome Soc. [IO]
Center for Family Support [12566]
Coun. on Quality and Leadership [12567]
Down Syndrome Assn. - Singapore [IO]
Down Syndrome Ireland [IO]
Down's Syndrome Assn. [IO]
Down's Syndrome Fed. of India [IO]
European Down's Syndrome Assn. [IO]
Lifespire [12572]
Little City Found. [12573]
Michael Fund/International Found. for Genetic Res. [14466]
Natl. Assn. of Councils on Developmental Disabilities [12575]
Natl. Assn. of State Directors of Developmental Disabilities Services [12576]
Natl. Down Syndrome Cong. [12577]
Natl. Down Syndrome Soc. [12040]
Parents of Down Syndrome [12579]
People First Intl. [12580]
Symbral Found. [12582]
Young Adult Institute/National Inst. for People with Disabilities [12584]
Down's Syndrome Assn. [IO], Teddington, United Kingdom
Down's Syndrome Cong. [★12577]
Down's Syndrome Cong; Natl. [★12577]
Down's Syndrome Fed. of India [IO], Chennai, India
Downtown Development Found. - Defunct.
Downtown Executives Assn; Intl. [★732]
Downwinders [18150], 254 W 500 N, Malad City, ID 83252, (208)766-5649
Downwinders [IO], Malad City, ID, United States
Dowsers; Amer. Soc. of [7470]

Dowsing
Borderland Sciences Res. Found. [7471]
Canadian Soc. of Dowsers [IO]
Canadian Soc. of Questers [IO]
Doyle Holly Intl. Fan Club - Defunct.
Dozenal Soc. of Am. [7695], 472 Village Oaks Ln., Babylon, NY 11702-3123, (631)669-0273
The DPVOA [★IO]
Dr Pepper Bottlers Assn. [506], PO Box 906, Rowlett, TX 75030, (972)475-7397
Dracula Fan Club; Count [★24824]
Dracula Soc. [IO], London, United Kingdom
Dracula Soc; Count [10420]
Dracula Soc. - Great Britain [IO], London, United Kingdom

Draft
Center on Conscience and War [IO]
Center on Conscience and War [17438]
Central Comm. for Conscientious Objectors [17439]
Comm. Opposed to Militarism and the Draft [5669]
Draft Action - Defunct.
Draft Help - Defunct.

Draft Horse Assn; Amer. Cream [4816]
Draft Horse Assn; North Amer. Spotted [4938]
Draft Horse Corp. of Am; Belgian [4865]
Draft Horse and Mule Assn. of America - Address unknown since 1999.
Draft Horses; Amer. Assn. of Importers and Breeders of Belgian [★4865]
Draft; Natl. Coalition for a Just [★18041]
Drafting; Amer. Inst. for Design and [★7152]
Drafting Assn; Amer. Design [7152]
Draftsman; Assn. of Professional [★7152]
Drag Racers Assn; Midwest United [★23070]
Drag Racers Assn; United [★23070]
Drag Racing
Natl. Elec. Drag Racing Assn. [23396]
United Black Drag Racers Assn. [23397]
Drag Racing Assn; Amer. [★23071]
Drag Racing Assn; Amer. Motors [★23080]
Drag Racing Assn; Natl. Amer. Motors [★23080]
Drag Racing Assn; Professional [★23077]
Dragon Boat Assn; Pacific [21883]
Dragonfly Soc. of Am. [★7061]
Dragonfly Soc. of the Americas [7061], c/o Jerell J. Daigle, 2067 Little River Ln., Tallahassee, FL 32311-9400, (850)878-8787
Dragonfly Soc; British [IO]
Drainage and Flood Control; U.S. Comm. on Irrigation, [★7842]
Drainage Inst; Plumbing and [3065]
Drainage Mfrs. Assn; Plumbing and [★3065]
Drainage; U.S. Comm. on Irrigation and [7842]
Drainage; U.S. Natl. Comm., Intl. Commn. on Irrigation and [★7842]
Drake Exploration Soc. [IO], Burnham-on-Sea, United Kingdom
Drama; Amer. Soc. of Gp. Psychotherapy and Psycho [16208]
Drama Assn. of Wales [IO], Cardiff, United Kingdom
Drama Australia [★IO]
Drama Desk [11010], c/o Lester Schecter, 244 W 54th St., 9th Fl., New York, NY 10019, (212)586-2600
Drama; Inst. of Outdoor [11018]
Drama League [11011], 520 8th Ave., Ste. 320, New York, NY 10018, (212)244-9494
Drama, Sociometry, and Gp. Psychotherapy; Amer. Bd. of Examiners of Psycho [16201]
Drama Therapy; Natl. Assn. for [16222]
Drama Tree - Defunct.
Drama, Variety and Comedy; Soc. to Preserve and Encourage Radio [22930]
Dramatic, Artistic and Literary Rights Org. [IO], Braamfontein, Republic of South Africa
Dramatic Order Knights of Khorassan [19186], 110 N Wabash Ave., Marion, IN 46952-2614, (765)664-7925
Dramatic and Speech Arts; Natl. Assn. of [11026]
Dramatics
African Heritage Center for African Dance and Music [9347]
Alliance of Resident Theatres/New York [10997]
Alpha Psi Omega [24443]
Amer. Alliance for Theatre and Educ. [10998]
Amer. Conservatory Theater Found. [11000]
Amer. Guild of Variety Artists [24151]
Amer. Theatre Arts for Youth [11003]
Assn. of Theatrical Press Agents and Managers [24154]
Bernard Shaw Soc. [9636]
Chinese-American Arts Coun. [9608]
Delta Psi Omega [24444]
Drama Desk [11010]
Dramatists Guild of Am. [11012]
Episcopal Actors' Guild of Am. [11013]
Eugene O'Neill Memorial Theater Center [11014]
Inst. of Outdoor Drama [11018]
Intl. Alliance of Theatrical Stage Employees, Moving Picture Technicians, Artists and Allied Crafts of the U.S., Its Territories and Canada [24156]
Intl. Guild of Symphony, Opera and Ballet Musicians [24157]
Marlowe Lives! Assn. [9689]
Movement Theatre Intl. [11025]
Natl. Assn. for Drama Therapy [16222]
Natl. Theatre Conf. [11032]

Natl. Theatre Workshop of the Handicapped [11033]
New Dramatists [11034]
New England Theatre Conf. [11035]
New York Coun. of Motion Picture and TV Unions [24056]
Omega Theatre and the Omega Arts Network [9590]
O'Neill Critics Inst. [11036]
The Players [11038]
Puerto Rican Traveling Theatre Company [11040]
Soc. of Stage Directors and Choreographers [24159]
Southeastern Theatre Conf. [11043]
Theatre Communications Gp. [11047]
Theatre Guild [11049]
Theatre for Young Audiences/USA [11051]
Theta Alpha Phi [24721]
United Scenic Artists [24160]
Dramatist Guild [★11012]
Dramatists Centre [IO], Montreal, QC, Canada
Dramatists Comm; New [★11034]
Dramatists Guild of Am. [11012], 1501 Broadway, Ste. 701, New York, NY 10036, (212)398-9366
Dramatists; New [11034]
Dramaturgs of the Americas; Literary Managers and [11023]
Drapery Assn; Intl. [★2256]
Drapery Concessionaires; White Front [★2256]
Drapery Hardware Mfrs. Assn. - Defunct.
Draugas [★19213]
Draught Horse Soc. of North Am; Irish [4909]
Draught Proofing Advisory Assn. [IO], Haslemere, United Kingdom
Draughts Fed. of India [IO], Chandigarh, India
Draughts Fed. of Turkmenistan [IO], Balkanabat, Turkmenistan
The Drawing Center [9438], 35 Wooster St., New York, NY 10013, (212)219-2166
Drawing Soc. - Address unknown since 2002.
Drawings Assn; Master [9456]
Dread Zeppelin Fan Club - Address unknown since 1999.
Dream Catchers, USA [11943], c/o Nancy J. Copeland, Pres./CEO, PO Box 701, Killen, AL 35645, (256)272-0286
Dream Drama; Center for [★16425]
Dream Factory [11691], 200 W Broadway, Ste. 504, Louisville, KY 40202, (502)561-3001
Dreams; Assn. for the Stud. of [★16426]
Dreams; Intl. Assn. for the Stud. of [16426]
Dreamsharing Grassroots Network [★16425]
Dreamsharing Network; Community [16425]
Dreamsicles Club [22013], c/o Cast Art Indus., 1693 Rimpau Ave., Corona, CA 92881-3202, (909)371-3025
Dreco Inst; Art [9423]
Dredging Assn; Eastern [★2597]
Dredging Assn; Eastern [★IO]
Dredging Assn; Western [2596]
Dredging Assn; World [★2597]
Dredging Contractors of Am. [2576], 503 D St. NW, Ste. 150, Washington, DC 20001, (202)737-2674
Dredging Contractors; Natl. Assn. of [★2576]
Dredging Industry Size Standard Comm. [18293]
Dredging and Marine Constr. Companies; Amer. Assn. for Small [★2576]
Dress Contractors Assn; Popular Price [★244]
Dress Mfrs. Assn; Natl. [★225]
Dress Mfrs. Assn; United Popular [★244]
Dress Mfrs. Gp; Popular Priced [★225]
Dress for Success Worldwide [13424], 32 E 31st St., 7th Fl., New York, NY 10016, (212)532-1922
Dress for Success Worldwide [IO], New York, NY, United States
Dressage Canada [IO], Ottawa, ON, Canada
Dressage Fed; U.S. [23533]
Dressing Inst; Mayonnaise and Salad [★1502]
Dressing Manufacturers Assn; Mayonnaise and Salad [★1502]
Dressings and Sauces; Assn. for [1502]
Dreyfus Found; Camille and Henry [8237]
DRI Intl. [5562], 1400 Eye St. NW, Ste. 1050, Washington, DC 20005, (202)962-3979
Dried Fruit Assn. of California [★4726]

A star before a book entry number signifies that the name is not listed separately, but is mentioned within the entry.

Dried Fruit Assn. of New York [★1503]
Dried Fruit Export Assn; California [★4761]
Drifters, Inc. - Address unknown since 1994.
Drill Instructors Assn; U.S. Marine Corps [6109]
Drill Team Alliance; Intl. Equestrian [23527]
Drill Team Directors of Am; Dance/ [9876]
Drilled Shaft Contractors; Assn. of [★1000]
Drilling Assn; Concrete Sawing and [923]
Drilling Assn; Natl. [1044]
Drilling Contractors; Amer. Assn. of Oilwell [★2930]
Drilling Contractors Assn; Natl. [★1044]
Drilling Engg. Assn. [2922], c/o Morris Keene, Chm., Occidental Oil and Gas Corp., 5 Greenway Plz., Ste. 2400, Houston, TX 77046, (713)215-7118
Drilling Engineers; Amer. Assn. of [7460]
Drilling Fed; Intl. [★1044]
Drilling and Sawing Assn. [IO], Belper, United Kingdom
Drillsite Supervisors Assn. - Address unknown since 1994.
Drinker Lib. of Choral Music [10588], Free Lib. of Philadelphia, 1901 Vine St., Philadelphia, PA 19103, (215)686-5364
Drinkers Against Mad Mothers - Address unknown since 1991.
Drinking Straw Inst. - Defunct.
Drinking Water Administrators; Assn. of State [6211]
Drip Irrigation Assn; Intl. [★182]
Dripps-Drips Family Assn. - Address unknown since 2001.
Drive Canada [IO], Vancouver, BC, Canada
Drive-In Theatre Owners Assn; United [2794]
Drive Trans. Assn; Elec. [6517]
driveAWARE [12960], PO Box 2114, Warminster, PA 18974-2114, (877)343-1919
Driver Education
  ADED: The Assn. for Driver Rehabilitation Specialists [8209]
  ADED: The Association for Driver Rehabilitation Specialists [8209]
  Alfa Romeo Owners Club [21565]
  Amer. Driver and Traffic Safety Educ. Assn. [8210]
  driveAWARE [12960]
  Driving Instruction Register of Ireland [IO]
  Driving Instructors Assn. [IO]
  Driving School Assn. of the Americas [8211]
  Finnish Driving School Assn. [IO]
  Inst. of Advanced Motorists [IO]
  Motor Schools Assn. of Great Britain [IO]
  Natl. Truckdrivers Safety Assn. [2843]
  North Amer. Trans. Mgt. Inst. [8212]
  Parents Against Tired Truckers [12984]
Driver Educ. Assn; Amer. [★8210]
Driver Educators for the Disabled; Assn. of [★8209]
Driver Employer Coun. of Am. [3867], 1150 17th St. NW, Ste. 900, Washington, DC 20036, (202)842-3400
Driver Inst; Professional Truck [3889]
Driver Leasing Coun. of Am. [★3867]
Driver and Safety Educ. Assn; Amer. [★8210]
Drivers Assn; Independent Truckers and [3870]
Drivers Assn; Maryland Independent Truckers and [★3870]
Drivers Assn; Owner-Operator Independent [3888]
Drivers; Citizens Against Drug Impaired [13230]
Driver's Club; Studebaker [21790]
Drivers' Club; Subaru 360 [21792]
Drivers Intl. Union; Team [★24198]
Drivers; Mothers Against Drunk [★12969]
Drivers and Racers Assn; Natl. Amer. Motors [23080]
Drivers; Soc. of Professional [3893]
Drivers - U.S.A; Remove Intoxicated [★12987]
Driving; Boaters Against Drunk [12955]
Driving Instruction Register of Ireland [IO], Glasnevin, Ireland
Driving Instructors Assn. [IO], Croydon, United Kingdom
Driving; Mothers Against Drunk [12969]
Driving; Natl. Commn. Against Drunk [12973]
Driving; Recording Artists, Actors and Athletes Against Drunk [12986]
Driving School Assn. of the Americas [8211], 3090 E Gause Blvd., Ste. 425, Slidell, LA 70461, (985)643-7803

Driving Soc; Amer. [23491]
Drop Forging Assn. [★2708]
Drop-Outs Anonymous - Defunct.
Dropout Prevention Center/Network; Natl. [8330]
Dror [★20138]
Dror Labor Zionist Youth; Ichud Habonim [★20138]
Drown Found; Joseph [12051]
Drug Abuse
  Addiction Res. and Treatment Corp. [13213]
  Adult Children of Alcoholics World Ser. Org. [13012]
  Al-Anon Family Gp. HQ, World Ser. Off. [13214]
  Alcohol Res. Info. Ser. [13217]
  Alcoholics Anonymous World Services [13218]
  Allied Youth and Family Counseling Center [13465]
  Amer. Assn. for the Treatment of Opioid Dependence [16499]
  Amer. Coll. of Addiction Treatment Administrators [13219]
  Amer. Coun. on Alcohol Problems [13220]
  Amer. Coun. on Alcoholism [13221]
  Amer. Coun. for Drug Educ. [13222]
  Amer. Hea. and Temperance Assn. [13303]
  Amer. Osteopathic Acad. of Addiction Medicine [16500]
  Amer. Outreach Assn. [13223]
  Amer. Psychological Assn. - Addictions Div. [16123]
  Amer. Soc. of Addiction Medicine [16501]
  Assn. of Halfway House Alcoholism Programs of North Am. [13224]
  Assn. for Medical Educ. and Res. in Substance Abuse [8849]
  Assn. of Recovering Motorcyclists [13225]
  BACCHUS Network [13226]
  Because I Love You: The Parent Support Gp. [13293]
  Birth Defect Res. for Children [13752]
  Center for Substance Abuse Prevention [16502]
  Children of Alcoholics Found. [13228]
  Christian Addiction Rehabilitation Assn. [13229]
  DanceSafe [12041]
  DanceSafe [IO]
  Do It Now Found. [13235]
  Double Trouble in Recovery [12548]
  Drug and Alcohol Testing Indus. Assn. [13236]
  Ethos Found. [13239]
  Faces and Voices of Recovery [18688]
  Families Worldwide [13241]
  Friendly Hand Found. [13243]
  Harm Reduction Coalition [12042]
  Harm Reduction Coalition [IO]
  Hazelden Found. [13244]
  Hea. Connection [13245]
  Hearts and Minds Network [18730]
  Impaired Physician Prog. [13246]
  Inst. for the Advanced Stud. of Black Family Life and Culture [9359]
  Inst. for a Drug-Free Workplace [13247]
  Inst. on Global Drug Policy [13248]
  Inst. for Integral Development [13249]
  Inter-Association Task Force on Alcohol and Other Substance Abuse Issues [13250]
  Intl. Assn. of Addictions and Offender Counselors [11824]
  Intl. Coalition for Addiction Stud. Educ. [9197]
  Intl. Commn. for the Prevention of Alcoholism and Drug Dependency [13251]
  Intl. Doctors in Alcoholics Anonymous [13252]
  Intl. Harm Reduction Assn. [IO]
  Intl. Hea. and Temperance Assn. [13304]
  Intl. Latino Gang Investigator's Assn. [5884]
  Intl. Narcotics Interdiction Assn. [5742]
  Join Together [18689]
  Law Enforcement Against Prohibition [17999]
  Luz Social Services [13255]
  MAD DADS (Men Against Destruction - Defending Against Drugs and Social Disorder) [12043]
  March of Dimes Birth Defects Found. [13756]
  Milton S. Eisenhower Found. [11839]
  Mothers' Voices [13574]
  Musicians' Assistance Prog. [12619]
  Musicians' Assistance Prog. Alumni Assn. [12620]
  NAADAC The Assn. for Addiction Professionals [16509]

  Narcotic Educational Found. of Am. [13256]
  Narcotics Anonymous [13257]
  Natl. African Amer. Drug Policy Coalition [17440]
  Natl. Alliance of Advocates for Buprenorphine Treatment [16511]
  Natl. Alliance of Methadone Advocates [14293]
  Natl. Assn. of Addiction Treatment Providers [13259]
  Natl. Assn. for Children of Alcoholics [13261]
  Natl. Assn. on Drug Abuse Problems [13262]
  Natl. Assn. of Drug Court Professionals [6289]
  Natl. Assn. of Lesbian/Gay Addiction Professionals [13263]
  Natl. Assn. for Regulatory Admin. [15011]
  Natl. Black Alcoholism and Addiction Coun. [13265]
  Natl. Catholic Coun. on Alcoholism and Related Drug Problems [13266]
  Natl. Comm. for the Prevention of Alcoholism and Drug Dependency [13267]
  Natl. Coun. on Alcoholism and Drug Dependence [13268]
  Natl. Families in Action [13269]
  Natl. Family Partnership [13270]
  Natl. Gym Assn. [23654]
  Natl. Inst. on Drug Abuse [5670]
  Natl. Temperance and Prohibition Coun. [13305]
  Natl. Woman's Christian Temperance Union [13306]
  November Coalition [18690]
  Partnership for a Drug-Free Am. [13272]
  People Against Rape [13083]
  People Helping People [12385]
  Phoenix House [13273]
  Pill Addicts Anonymous [13274]
  Pills Anonymous [13275]
  PRIDE Youth Programs [13276]
  Remembering ADAM [13280]
  Res. Soc. on Alcoholism [16517]
  Secular Organizations for Sobriety [13281]
  SMART Recovery [16519]
  SmokeFree Educational Services [16434]
  Substance Abuse Librarians and Info. Specialists [10390]
  Substance Abuse Prog. Administrators Assn. [16521]
  VietNow Natl. [13359]
  Vocational Found., Inc. [12103]
  Women for Sobriety [13284]
  Women in Transition [13447]
  Women's Drug Res. Project [13285]
  World Archaeological Soc. [6460]
  Youth Organizations U.S.A. [13523]
Drug Abuse Coun. - Defunct.
Drug Abuse Counselors; Natl. Assn. of Alcoholism and [★16509]
Drug Abuse Directors; Natl. Assn. of State Alcohol and [13264]
Drug Abuse Problems; Natl. Assn. on [13262]
Drug Abuse Prog. Coordinators; Natl. Assn. of State [★13264]
Drug and Alcohol Testing Indus. Assn. [13236], 1325 G St. NW, Ste. 500, No. 5001, Washington, DC 20005, (800)355-1257
Drug-Anon Focus - Address unknown since 2000.
Drug, Chem. and Allied Trades Assn. [★2974]
Drug, Chem. and Allied Trades Sect. of the New York Bd. of Trade [★2974]
Drug, Chem. and Assoc. Technologies Assn. [2974], 1 Washington Blvd., Ste. 7, Robbinsville, NJ 08691-3162, (609)448-1000
Drug Conference; PRIDE World [★13276]
Drug Court Professionals; Natl. Assn. of [6289]
Drug Dependence; Natl. Coun. on Alcoholism and [13268]
Drug Dependencies; Amer. Medical Soc. on Alcoholism and Other [★16501]
Drug Dependency; Natl. Comm. for the Prevention of Alcoholism and [13267]
Drug Diversion Investigators; Natl. Assn. of [5986]
Drug Educ; Amer. Coun. for [13222]
Drug Educ; Parent Resources and Info. on [★13276]
Drug Enforcement Officers Assn; Natl. [5993]
Drug-Free Am; Media-Advertising Partnership for a [★13272]

Reference to "IO" in place of a book number signifies that the association may be found in the 45th edition of International Organizations.

Drug-Free Am; Partnership for a [13272]
Drug Free Kids: America's Challenge [18687], PO
  Box 60865, Washington, DC 20039, (301)681-
  7861
Drug-Free Workplace; Inst. for a [13247]
Drug-Free Youth; Natl. Fed. of Parents for [★13270]
Drug Impaired Drivers; Citizens Against [13230]
Drug-Induced Pathology; Dept. of Environmental and
  [★15867]
Drug Info. Assn. [15931], 800 Enterprise Rd., Ste.
  200, Horsham, PA 19044-3595, (215)442-6100
Drug Info. Assn. [IO], Horsham, PA, United States
Drug Info. Center [★13269]
Drug Info. Center; Families in Action [★13269]
Drug Info. Center; Families in Action Natl. [★13269]
Drug Law Inst; Food and [5738]
Drug Mfrs. Assn; Amer. [★2980]
Drug Mfrs. Assn; Nonprescription [★2973]
Drug Manufacturers Representatives; Natl. Assn. of
  [★2541]
Drug Marketing Associates; Chain [★2972]
Drug Officials; Assn. of Food and [5736]
Drug Officials of the U.S; Assn. of Food and
  [★5736]
Drug Peace Campaign [18022], PO Box 323,
  Middletown, CA 95461, (415)971-3573
Drug Policy
  Amer. Alliance for Medical Cannabis [15020]
  Amer. Outreach Assn. [13223]
  Canadian Found. for Drug Policy [IO]
  DanceSafe [12041]
  Drug Peace Campaign [18022]
  Drug Policy Alliance [17112]
  Drug Strategies [16503]
  Friends and Families of Cannabis Consumers
    [18023]
  Harm Reduction Coalition [12042]
  Inst. for a Drug-Free Workplace [13247]
  Inst. on Global Drug Policy [13248]
  Intl. Narcotic Enforcement Officers Assn. [5741]
  Intl. Narcotics Interdiction Assn. [5742]
  Law Enforcement Against Prohibition [17999]
  Natl. African Amer. Drug Policy Coalition [17440]
  Natl. Alliance for Model State Drug Laws [5671]
  Natl. Assn. of State Controlled Substances
    Authorities [5672]
  Natl. Inst. on Drug Abuse [5670]
  November Coalition [18690]
Drug Policy Alliance [17112], 925 15th St. NW, 2nd
  Fl., Washington, DC 20005, (202)216-0035
Drug Policy; Common Sense for [18436]
Drug Policy Found. [★17112]
Drug Problems Assn. of North Am; Alcohol and
  [13216]
Drug Problems; Natl. Catholic Coun. on Alcoholism
  and Related [13266]
Drug Problems; Natl. Clergy Coun. on Alcoholism
  and Related [★13266]
Drug Programs; Natl. Coun. for Prescription [2987]
Drug Rehabilitation
  Addiction Res. and Treatment Corp. [13213]
  Adult Children of Alcoholics World Ser. Org.
    [13012]
  Amer. Coll. of Addiction Treatment Administrators
    [13219]
  Amer. Coun. for Drug Educ. [13222]
  Amer. Osteopathic Acad. of Addiction Medicine
    [16500]
  Amer. Outreach Assn. [13223]
  Amer. Soc. of Addiction Medicine [16501]
  Assn. of Recovering Motorcyclists [13225]
  Center for Substance Abuse Prevention [16502]
  Do It Now Found. [13235]
  Double Trouble in Recovery [12548]
  Drug Strategies [16503]
  Faces and Voices of Recovery [18688]
  Hea. Connection [13245]
  Inst. for a Drug-Free Workplace [13247]
  Inst. on Global Drug Policy [13248]
  Inst. for Integral Development [13249]
  Intl. Assn. of Addictions and Offender Counselors
    [11824]
  Luz Social Services [13255]
  NAADAC The Assn. for Addiction Professionals
    [16509]

Narcotic Educational Found. of Am. [13256]
Narcotics Anonymous [13257]
Natl. African Amer. Drug Policy Coalition [17440]
Natl. Alliance of Advocates for Buprenorphine
  Treatment [16511]
Natl. Alliance of Methadone Advocates [14293]
National Alliance of Methadone Advocates [IO]
Natl. Assn. of Addiction Treatment Providers
  [13259]
Natl. Assn. on Drug Abuse Problems [13262]
Natl. Black Alcoholism and Addiction Coun.
  [13265]
Natl. Families in Action [13269]
Natl. Family Partnership [13270]
Partnership for a Drug-Free Am. [13272]
Phoenix House [13273]
Pill Addicts Anonymous [13274]
Pills Anonymous [13275]
PRIDE Youth Programs [13276]
Secular Organizations for Sobriety [13281]
Substance Abuse Prog. Administrators Assn.
  [16521]
Women for Sobriety [13284]
Women's Drug Res. Project [13285]
Drug Res. Project; Women's [13285]
Drug Stores; Affiliated [★2972]
Drug Stores; Affiliated/Associated [★2972]
Drug Stores; Assoc. Chain [★2972]
Drug Stores; Natl. Assn. of Chain [2985]
Drug Strategies [16503], 1616 P St. NW, Ste. 220,
  Washington, DC 20036, (202)289-9070
Drug Strategy Network; Natl. [17136]
Drug and Therapeutic Info. [★15940]
Drug Wholesalers Assn. [★2984]
Druggists' Assn; Natl. Wholesale [★2984]
Druggist's Guild of Saint James - Defunct.
Druggists; Natl. Assn. of Retail [★2986]
Drugless Practitioners; Amer. Assn. of [13615]
Drugs; Amer. Coun. on Marijuana and Other Psycho-
  active [★13222]
Drugs Anonymous [★13275]
Drugs and Disability; Natl. Assn. on Alcohol, [16512]
Drugs; Natl. Assn. of Athletes Against [13260]
Drugs; Natl. Episcopal Coalition on Alcohol and
  [★13279]
Drugs; Registry of Tissue Reactions to [★15867]
DrugScope [IO], London, United Kingdom
Druid Hill Park; Friends of [★4407]
Drum Assn; Natl. Barrel and [★994]
Drum Corps Intl. [10589], 470 S Irmen Dr., Addison,
  IL 60101, (630)628-7888
Drum Corps Intl. [IO], Addison, IL, United States
Drum Seiners Assn. - Defunct.
Drummers; Company of Fifers and [10580]
Drummond Soc. of North Am; Clan [20827]
Drums
  Company of Fifers and Drummers [10580]
  Drum Corps Intl. [10589]
  Percussion Marketing Coun. [1165]
  Percussive Arts Soc. [10686]
Drums No Guns [17591], PO Box 1455, New
  Haven, CT 06510, (203)467-7344
Drunk Drivers; Mothers Against [★12969]
Drunk Driving
  Boaters Against Drunk Driving [12955]
  Mothers Against Drunk Driving [12969]
  Natl. Assn. of State Alcohol and Drug Abuse
    Directors [13264]
  Natl. Commn. Against Drunk Driving [12973]
  Recording Artists, Actors and Athletes Against
    Drunk Driving [12986]
  RID - U.S.A. [12987]
  Students Against Destructive Decisions, Students
    Against Drunk Driving [12992]
Drunk Driving; Mothers Against [12969]
Drunk Driving; Natl. Commn. Against [12973]
Drunk Driving; Students Against Destructive Deci-
  sions, Students Against [12992]
Drustvo Hrvatskih Intelektualki [★IO]
Drustvo Inzenirjev in Tehnikov Papirnistva [★IO]
Drustvo matematikov, fizikov in astronomov Slov-
  enije [★IO]
Drustvo Prijatelja Biblije [IO], Zagreb, Croatia
Drustvo Slovenskih Pisateljev [★IO]
Drustvo fiziologa Srbije [★IO]

Drustvo Za Psiholosku Pomoc [★IO]
Drustvo Znanstvenih in Tehniskih Prevajalcev Slov-
  enije [★IO]
Druze Soc; Amer. [20095]
Druzya Svyashchennogo Pisaniya [IO], Minsk, Be-
  larus
Dry Bean Advisory Bd; California [4713]
Dry Bean Coun; Natl. [★4769]
Dry Cleaners Machinery Mfrs. Assn; Laundry and
  [★2407]
Dry Cleaning
  Intl. Drycleaners Cong. [2404]
  Intl. Fabricare Inst. [2405]
  Textile Care Allied Trades Assn. [2407]
Dry Color Manufacturers Assn. [★868]
Dry Dock Assn; Atlantic and Gulf Coasts [★2592]
Dry Milk; Amer. [★1130]
Dry Pea Marketing Coun. - Defunct.
Dry Salami Inst. - Defunct.
Dry Stone Walling Assn. of Great Britain [IO],
  Milnthorpe, United Kingdom
Drycleaning Inst. of Australia [IO], Brisbane,
  Australia
Drycleaning; Natl. Inst. of [★2405]
Drying Assn; New England Kiln [1610]
Drywall Apprenticeship and Manpower Training
  Fund; Intl. Joint Painting, Decorating and [★12082]
Drywall Apprenticeship and Manpower Training
  Fund; Natl. Painting, Decorating, and [★12082]
Drywall Apprenticeship and Training Comm; Natl.
  Joint Painting, Decorating, and [★12082]
DSA [★20887]
DSA; Religion and Socialism Comm. of [★18657]
DSL Forum [2099], 48377 Fremont Blvd., Ste. 117,
  Fremont, CA 94538, (510)492-4020
DTA [★IO]
DTC Assn. [IO], Hong Kong, People's Republic of
  China
DUAL [★6793]
Dual Disorders Anonymous [13237], PO Box
  681264, Schaumburg, IL 60168-1264, (847)490-
  9379
Dual Dr. Families - Defunct.
Dually Diagnosed; Natl. Assn. for the [14243]
Dually Diagnosed; Natl. Assn. for the [★12552]
Duane Eddy Circle [IO], Sheffield, United Kingdom
Duane Eddy Circle, U.S.A. - Address unknown since
  1995.
Dublin Chamber of Commerce [IO], Dublin, Ireland
Dublin City Bus. Assn. [IO], Dublin, Ireland
DuBois Family Assn. [20886], c/o Terry L. DuBois,
  Pres., 76715 McLeod Rd., Myakka City, FL 34251
Dubos Center for Human Environments; Rene
  [4602]
Dubos Forum; Rene [★4602]
Ducati Intl. Owners Club - Address unknown since
  1999.
Duck
  Callmakers and Collectors Assn. of Am. [21984]
  Midwest Decoy Collectors Assn. [22071]
  Natl. Duck Stamp Collectors Soc. [22850]
  Waterfowl U.S.A. [4465]
Duckpin Bowling Cong; Natl. [23253]
Ducks Unlimited [5311], 1 Waterfowl Way, Memphis,
  TN 38120, (901)758-3825
Ductile Iron Pipe Res. Assn. [3029], 245 Riverchase
  Pkwy. E, Ste. O, Birmingham, AL 35244, (205)402-
  8700
Ductile Iron Soc. [7313], 28938 Lorain Rd., Ste. 202,
  North Olmsted, OH 44070, (440)734-8040
Dude Ranchers' Assn. [1940], 1122 12th St., PO
  Box 2307, Cody, WY 82414, (307)587-2339
Dude Ranchers Assn; Montana Outfitters and
  [★23944]
Dudley Found. [13116], 609 N Shore Dr., Belling-
  ham, WA 98226-4414, (360)671-8251
Due Process of Law Fund - Defunct.
Duesenberg Club; Auburn-Cord- [21582]
Duisberg Soc; Carl [★8019]
Duke Charitable Found; Doris [13115]
Duke of Edinburgh's Award Intl. Assn. [IO], London,
  United Kingdom
Duke Ellington Jazz Soc. [★10590]
The Duke Ellington Soc. [10590], PO Box 31,
  Church St. Sta., New York, NY 10008-0031

A star before a book entry number signifies that the name is not listed separately, but is mentioned within the entry.

Duke Ellington Soc. - New York Chap; The [★10590]
The Duke Ellington Soc. - New York Chap. [★10590]
Dulcimer Assn; Southern Appalachian [10708]
Duluth Bd. of Trade - Defunct.
Dumaguete City Habitat for Humanity [IO], Dumaguete City, Philippines
Dummer Family in America - Address unknown since 2003.
Dunamis; Knights of [★13002]
Duncan Black Macdonald Center for the Stud. of Islam and Christian/Muslim Relations [★20100]
Duncan Black Macdonald Center for the Stud. of Islam and Christian/Muslim Relations [★IO]
Duncan Certified Ceramic Teachers; Intl. Assn. of [21928]
Duncan Glass Soc; Natl. [22563]
Duncan Surname Assn. [20887], 8080 N Illinois St., Indianapolis, IN 46260-2939
Dundee and Tayside Chamber of Commerce and Indus. [IO], Dundee, United Kingdom
Duneland Post Card Club - Defunct.
Dunlap Family Soc; Dunlop - [20888]
Dunlop - Dunlap Family Soc. [20888], c/o Mr. Peter Dunlop, Pres., PO Box 652, East Aurora, NY 14052, (716)655-2521
Dunn Fan Club; Brooks and [24854]
Dunnavant/Donavant Family Assn. [20889]
Dunya Enerji Konseyi Turk Milli Komitesi [★IO]
Duodecimal Soc. of Am. [★7695]
Dupin, Amandine
   George Sand Soc. [9653]
DuPont Fund; Jessie Ball [12727]
DuPont Workers; Intl. Brotherhood of [24034]
Durable Woods Inst. - Defunct.
Durango/Purgatory Adaptive Sports Assn. [★23332]
Durant Family Registry - Defunct.
Durant Owners Club - Defunct.
Durene Assn. of Amer. - Defunct.
Durex Abrasives Corp. - Defunct.
Duroc Swine Registry; United [5243]
Duroc Swine Registry; United [★5241]
Durrell Soc; Intl. Lawrence [9662]
Durrell Wildlife Conservation Trust [IO], Jersey, United Kingdom
Durum Growers Assn; U.S. [4318]
Durum Wheat Inst. [★2738]
Duster Class Yacht Racing Assn. - Defunct.
DUSTOFF Assn. [20700], PO Box 8091, San Antonio, TX 78208
Dutch
   Amer. Dutch Bantam Soc. [5103]
   Assn. for the Advancement of Dutch-American Stud. [9908]
   Association for the Advancement of Dutch-American Studies [IO]
   Assn. of Dutch Businessmen in Singapore [IO]
   Dutch Language Union [IO]
   Genealogical Soc. of Flemish Americans [21118]
   Holland Historical Trust [9909]
   Holland Historical Trust [IO]
   Holland Soc. of New York [20740]
   Intl. Assn. of Dutch Stud. [IO]
   Netherlands Bd. of Tourism and Conventions [24359]
   Netherlands Chamber of Commerce in the U.S. [24360]
   Royal Acad. of Dutch Language and Literature [IO]
   Soc. of Daughters of Holland Dames [20759]
Dutch Addison and Cushing Soc. [IO], Nijkerk, Netherlands
Dutch Alliance of Booksellers [IO], Bilthoven, Netherlands
Dutch-Amer. Historical Commn. - Address unknown since 1995.
Dutch Article Numbering Assn. [★IO]
Dutch Assn. of Abortion Doctors [IO], Geldrop, Netherlands
Dutch Assn. of Commun. Agencies [IO], Amsterdam, Netherlands
Dutch Assn. of Consulting Engineers [IO], The Hague, Netherlands
Dutch Assn. of Corporate Treasurers [IO], The Hague, Netherlands

Dutch Assn. of Cost Engineers [IO], Nijkerk, Netherlands
Dutch Assn. of Environmental Medicine [IO], Hertogenbosch, Netherlands
Dutch Assn. for Medical Records Admin. [IO], The Hague, Netherlands
Dutch Assn. of Paediatric Nurses [IO], Leiden, Netherlands
Dutch Assn. for Producers and Importers of Audio, Video and Multimedia [IO], Hilversum, Netherlands
Dutch Assn. of Psychiatric Nursing [IO], Utrecht, Netherlands
Dutch Assn. of Public Libraries; NBLC [IO]
Dutch Assn. of the Research-based Pharmaceutical Indus. [IO], The Hague, Netherlands
Dutch Assn. of Sign Language Interpreters [IO], Ugchelen, Netherlands
Dutch Assn. of Soap Mfrs. [IO], Zeist, Netherlands
Dutch Assn. of Subcontracting Indus. [IO], Zoetermeer, Netherlands
Dutch Bakery Center [IO], Wageningen, Netherlands
Dutch Belted Cattle Assn. of America - Address unknown since 1995.
Dutch Biscuit, Chocolate and Confectionery Indus. Assn. [IO], Rijswijk, Netherlands
Dutch Cancer Soc. [IO], Amsterdam, Netherlands
Dutch Corporate Finance Assn. [IO], Breda, Netherlands
Dutch Cosmetics Assn. [IO], Zeist, Netherlands
Dutch Coun. of the Chronically Ill and Disabled [IO], Utrecht, Netherlands
Dutch Dairy Bur. - Defunct.
Dutch Deaf Assn. [★IO]
Dutch Deafship [IO], Houten, Netherlands
Dutch Dental Assn. [IO], Nieuwegein, Netherlands
Dutch Don Johnson Fan Club [IO], Bodegraven, Netherlands
Dutch Family Heritage Soc. - Address unknown since 2002.
Dutch Fed. of Traders in Livestock [IO], Zoetermeer, Netherlands
Dutch Fish Prdt. Bd. [IO], Rijswijk, Netherlands
Dutch Flower Auctions Assn. [IO], Leiden, Netherlands
Dutch Flying Disc Assn. [IO], Utrecht, Netherlands
Dutch Friends of Jose Carreras [IO], Waalwijk, Netherlands
Dutch-Friesian Assn. of Am. [★4263]
Dutch Fruit Growers' Org. [IO], Zoetermeer, Netherlands
Dutch Gen. Alliance of Beauty Parlours [IO], Utrecht, Netherlands
Dutch Goatbreeders' Assn. [IO], Heerde, Netherlands
Dutch Intl. Fiscal Assn. Br. [IO], Amsterdam, Netherlands
Dutch Jewelry, Watch and Clock Makers' Br. [IO], Voorburg, Netherlands
Dutch Language Union [IO], The Hague, Netherlands
Dutch League Against Epilepsy [IO], Heemstede, Netherlands
Dutch Newspaper Publishers Assn. [IO], Amsterdam, Netherlands
Dutch Pharmacological Soc. [IO], Oss, Netherlands
Dutch Physiological Soc. [IO], Maastricht, Netherlands
Dutch Publishers' Assn. [IO], Amsterdam, Netherlands
Dutch Rabbit Club; Amer. [5133]
Dutch Soc. for Biomaterials and Tissue Engg. [IO], Amsterdam, Netherlands
Dutch Soc. for Calcium and Bone Metabolism [IO], Amsterdam, Netherlands
Dutch Soc. of Cardiology [★IO]
Dutch Soc. for Jewish Genealogy [IO], Amsterdam, Netherlands
Dutch Soc. for Microscopy [IO], Utrecht, Netherlands
Dutch Soc. of Psychosomatic Obstetrics and Gynaecology [IO], Arnhem, Netherlands
Dutch Soc. for Quality in Healthcare [IO], Utrecht, Netherlands
Dutch Soc. for Rheumatology [IO], Utrecht, Netherlands
Dutch Soft Drinks Assn. [IO], Rotterdam, Netherlands

Dutch Textile-Employers Assn. [IO], Zoetermeer, Netherlands
Dutch Textile Inst. [IO], Zeist, Netherlands
Dutch Tourette Syndrome Assn. [IO], Rhoon, Netherlands
Dutch Union of Tenants [IO], Amsterdam, Netherlands
Dutch Warmblood Studbook in North America [★4931]
Dutch Youth Assn. for Astronomy [IO], Utrecht, Netherlands
Dutton Soc; Damien- [★15008]
Dutton Soc. for Leprosy Aid; Damien- [15008]
Duty's in America [20890]
Duvall Descendants; Soc. of Mareen [21055]
DVD Assn. [7304], 2250 E Tropicana Ave., Ste. 19-435, Las Vegas, NV 89119, (702)948-0443
DVF [★20678]
Dvizhenje na ekologistite na Makedonija [★IO]
Dvorak Intl. [IO], Poultney, VT, United States
Dvorak Intl. [2846], PO Box 44, Poultney, VT 05764-0044, (802)287-2343
Dvorak Intl. Fed. [★2846]
Dvorak Intl. Fed. [★IO]
Dwarf Athletic Assn. of Am. [23063], 418 Willow Way, Lewisville, TX 75077, (972)317-8299
Dwarf Fruit Tree Assn. [★5257]
Dwarf Fruit Tree Assn. [★IO]
Dwarf Goat Assn; Nigerian [4788]
Dwarf Iris Soc. of Am. [22509], c/o Hugh Thurman, Pres., 521 Kickapoo Trail, Frankfort, KY 40601-1716
Dwarfism
   Alaskan Malamute Club of Am. [22182]
   Amer. Bonsai Soc. [22483]
   Billy Barty Found. [13104]
   Bonsai Clubs Intl. [22504]
   Little People of Am. [13105]
   Share and Care Cockayne Syndrome Network [14480]
Dwelling Sculpture Inst. - Defunct.
Dwight D. Eisenhower Philatelic and Historical Soc. - Defunct.
Dyckman/Dikeman/Dykeman Family Assn. - Address unknown since 1999.
Dye Mfrs. Operating Comm. of ETAD; U.S. [★5089]
Dyers Assn; Yarn [★3774]
Dyers' Company [IO], London, United Kingdom
Dyes
   Dyers' Company [IO]
   ETAD North Am. - Ecological and Toxicological Assn. of Dyes and Organic Pigments Mfrs. [5089]
   Natural Dyes Intl. [8213]
Dyes Environmental and Toxicology Org. [★IO]
Dyes Environmental and Toxicology Org. - Defunct.
Dyes and Organic Pigments Mfrs; ETAD North Am. - Ecological and Toxicological Assn. of [5089]
Dyfed Welsh Pony and Cob Assn. [IO], St. Clears, United Kingdom
Dying; Americans for Better Care of the [13313]
Dying; Compassion in [★12130]
Dying with Dignity [IO], Toronto, ON, Canada
Dying Found; Sacred [11910]
Dying Proj; Living/ [13316]
Dying With Dignity Victoria [IO], Melbourne, Australia
DYLEAGUE - Defunct.
Dymphna; League of St. [19650]
Dynamic Tom Jones Fan Club - Defunct.
Dynamic Youth Ministries [19831], 1333 Alger St. SE, PO Box 7259, Grand Rapids, MI 49507, (616)241-5616
Dynamics Intl. Gardening Assn. - Address unknown since 1999.
Dynasty Fan Club - Address unknown since 1989.
D'Youville Coll. Alumni Assn. [18893], 631 Niagara St., Buffalo, NY 14201-1084, (716)829-7806
Dysautonomia Found. [15317], 315 W 39th St., Ste. 701, New York, NY 10018, (212)279-1066
Dysautonomia Res. Found; Natl. [14279]
Dysautonomia Youth Network of Am. [15318], c/o Debra L. Dominelli, Pres./Exec. Dir., 1301 Greengate Ct., Waldorf, MD 20601, (301)705-6995
Dysleksiforbundet i Norge [★IO]
Dyslexia
   AVKO Dyslexia Res. Found. [9138]

Reference to "IO" in place of a book number signifies that the association may be found in the 45th edition of International Organizations.

Canadian Dyslexia Assn. [IO]
Davis Dyslexia Assn. - UK [IO]
Dyslexia Res. Inst. [14294]
Intl. Dyslexia Assn. [14295]
Intl. Dyslexia Assn. [IO]
Dyslexia Action [IO], Egham, United Kingdom
Dyslexia Assn; British [IO]
Dyslexia Assn; Canadian [IO]
Dyslexia Assn; Norwegian [IO]
Dyslexia Inst. [★IO]
Dyslexia Res. Found; AVKO [9138]
Dyslexia Res. Inst. [14294], 5746 Centerville Rd.,
  Tallahassee, FL 32309, (850)893-2216
Dyslexia Soc; Orton [★14295]
Dyslexic; Recording for the Blind and [16885]
Dyson Found. [12715], 25 Halcyon Rd., Millbrook,
  NY 12545-6137, (845)677-0644
Dysphonia Assn; Natl. Spasmodic [15352]
Dysphoria Assn; Natl. Harry Benjamin Gender
  [★13103]
Dysplasia Ossificans Progressiva Assn; Intl. Fibro
  [14457]
Dysplasia Soc. of Am; Fibromuscular [15322]
Dysplasias; Natl. Found. for Ectodermal [14468]
Dyspraxia Assn. of Ireland [IO], Leixlip, Ireland
Dyspraxia Found. County Durham [IO], Durham,
  United Kingdom
Dystonia Found. - Defunct.
Dystonia Medical Res. Found. [15319], 1 E Wacker
  Dr., Ste. 2430, Chicago, IL 60601-1905, (312)755-
  0198
Dystonia Soc. [IO], London, United Kingdom
Dystrophic Epidermolysis Bullosa Res. Assn. of Am.
  [14200], 5 W 36th St., Ste. 404, New York, NY
  10018, (212)868-1573
Dystrophic Epidermolysis Bullosa Res. Assn. -
  Europe [IO], Crowthorne, United Kingdom
Dystrophie Musculaire Canada [★IO]
Dystrophy Found; United Leuko [15372]
Dystrophy Syndrome Assn. of Am; Reflex
  Sympathetic [15363]
Dzieci Holocaustu w Polsce [★IO]

E

E-22 Class Assn; Intl. [★23184]
E. C. Brown Found. - Defunct.
E-Commerce
  Americans for Fair Electronic Commerce Transac-
    tions [17441]
  Assn. for Electronic Hea. Care Transactions
    [14618]
  Assn. Global View [8017]
  eMarketing Assn. [1166]
  eMarketing Assn. [IO]
  Independent Online Booksellers Assn. [530]
  Interactive Travel Services Assn. [3946]
  Internet Professional Publishers Assn. [1777]
  OASIS PKI Member Sect. [7780]
  WECAI Network [1167]
E. F. Schumacher Soc. [16995], 140 Jug End Rd.,
  Great Barrington, MA 01230, (413)528-1737
E. P. Impersonators Assn. Intl. - Address unknown
  since 1995.
E-quip Africa [12704], PO Box 3178, Willmar, MN
  56201-8178, (320)894-1680
E-quip Africa [IO], Willmar, MN, United States
EAA Antique/Classic Div. [★21442]
EAA Aviation Found. - Defunct.
EAA Ultralight Assn. [21441], EAA Aviation Ctr.,
  3000 Poberezny Rd., Oshkosh, WI 54902,
  (920)426-6527
EAA Vintage Aircraft Assn. [21442], EAA Aviation
  Center, PO Box 3086, Oshkosh, WI 54903-3086,
  (920)426-4800
EAA Warbirds of Am. [21443], EAA Aviation Center,
  PO Box 3086, Oshkosh, WI 54903-3086,
  (920)426-4874
EAGLE [★14602]
Eagle Forum [17267], PO Box 618, Alton, IL 62002,
  (618)462-5415
The Eagle Found. - Defunct.
Eagle; Free the [17629]
Eagle; Knights of the Golden [19128]
Eagle Scout Assn; Natl. [13002]

Eagles
  Grand Aerie, Fraternal Order of Eagles [19033]
Eagles; Legal [★5539]
Eagras Naisiunta Chumann Tionontaithe [★IO]
Eagras Um Chearta Cheolta [★IO]
EAN Argentina [IO], Buenos Aires, Argentina
EAN Austria GmbH [★IO]
EAN Azerbaijan [IO], Baku, Azerbaijan
EAN Bahrain [IO], Manama, Bahrain
EAN Belarus [IO], Minsk, Belarus
EAN Ceska Republika [★IO]
EAN Croatia [IO], Zagreb, Croatia
EAN Czech Republic [IO], Prague, Czech Republic
EAN Iceland [IO], Reykjavik, Iceland
EAN a Islandi [★IO]
EAN Lietuva [★IO]
EAN Lithuania [IO], Vilnius, Lithuania
EAN Malta [★IO]
EAN Malta [IO], Ta'Xbiex, Malta
EAN Mauritius [★IO]
EAPA [★13203]
EAPE/Campolo Ministries - Evangelical Assn. for the
  Promotion of Educ. [20330], PO Box 7238, St.
  Davids, PA 19087, (610)341-1722
EAPE/Campolo Ministries - Evangelical Assn. for the
  Promotion of Educ. [IO], St. Davids, PA, United
  States
Ear Dog Prog; Hearing [★14770]
Ear Found. [15825], PO Box 330867, Nashville, TN
  37203, (615)627-2724
Ear Hospitals; Amer. Assn. of Eye and [14859]
Ear Inst; House [16446]
Ear, Nose, and Throat Advances in Children; Soc.
  for [15827]
Ear Res. Inst. [★16446]
Earl Thomas Conley Fan Club - Address unknown
  since 1999.
Earl Warren Legal Training Prog. [8765], 99 Hudson
  St., Ste. 1600, New York, NY 10013, (212)965-
  2200
Early Amer. Coppers [22737], PO Box 15782,
  Cincinnati, OH 45215
Early Amer. Decoration; Historical Soc. of [9482]
Early Amer. Decoration; Soc. of [★9482]
Early Amer. History and Culture; Omohundro Inst. of
  [10140]
Early Amer. Indus. Assn. [9481], c/o Elton W. Hall,
  Exec. Dir., 167 Bakerville Rd., South Dartmouth,
  MA 02748-4198, (508)993-9578
Early Amer. Pattern Glass Soc. [22014], c/o Fred
  Phelps, Coor., PO Box 266, Colesburg, IA 52035-
  0266
Early Amer. Republic; Soc. for Historians of the
  [10157]
Early Amer. Soc. - Defunct.
Early Birds of Aviation - Defunct.
Early Childhood Assn. of North Am; Waldorf [9008]
Early Childhood Assn; Southern [11722]
Early Childhood Australia [IO], Watson, Australia
Early Childhood of the Coun. for Exceptional
  Children; Div. for [9144]
Early Childhood Directors Assn. - Address unknown
  since 2003.
Early Childhood Educ. U.S. Natl. Comm; World Org.
  for [8071]
Early Childhood Music and Movement Assn.
  [12618], 805 Mill Ave., Snohomish, WA 98290,
  (360)568-5635
Early Childhood Workforce; Natl. Center for the
  [★12072]
Early Day Gas Engine and Tractor Assn. [22410],
  c/o Larry Voris, Pres./Dir., 2340 S Luster Ave.,
  Springfield, MO 65804, (417)882-7195
Early English Text Soc. [IO], Oxford, United
  Kingdom
Early Ford V-8 Club of Am. [21633], PO Box 2222,
  Livermore, CA 94551-2222, (866)427-7583
Early Four Cylinder Chevrolet Club, Intl. - Defunct.
Early Hemi Assn. - Address unknown since 1999.
Early Interventionists; Amer. Assn. for Home-Based
  [17056]
Early Money is Like Yeast [★18294]
Early Music Am. [8909], 2366 Eastlake Ave. E, No.
  429, Seattle, WA 98102, (206)720-6270
Early Music Network [10591], PO Box 854, Atlanta,
  GA 30301, (770)638-7554

Early Settlers Assn. of the Western Reserve - Ad-
  dress unknown since 2002.
Early Sites Found. - Defunct.
Early Sites Res. Soc. [6444]
Early Six Mustang Registry - Defunct.
Early Typewriter Collectors Assn. [22015], c/o Rich
  Cincotta, PO Box 286, Southborough, MA 01772,
  (508)229-2064
Earnhardt Fan Club; Club E: The Dale [25002]
Ears for the Deaf [★11979]
Earth 2 Founds. - Address unknown since 2001.
Earth Action Group - Defunct.
Earth Awareness Found. - Defunct.
Earth Charter USA Campaign [4502], 2100 L St.
  NW, Washington, DC 20037, (202)778-6133
Earth Charter USA Campaign [IO], Washington, DC,
  United States
Earth Communications [★IO]
Earth Communications [★21500]
Earth Communications Off. [4547], 16815 Victory
  Blvd., No. 226, Van Nuys, CA 91406-5550,
  (818)787-9550
Earth Corps [★18861]
Earth Day 2000 [★4548]
Earth Day Canada [IO], Toronto, ON, Canada
Earth Day Network [4548], 1616 P St. NW, Ste. 340,
  Washington, DC 20036, (202)518-0044
Earth Day Resources [★4569]
Earth Ecology Found. [4503], 6120 W Tropicana,
  No. A16-303, Las Vegas, NV 89103, (702)340-
  3925
Earth Energy Soc. of Canada [IO], Ottawa, ON,
  Canada
Earth; For Mother [17813]
Earth Force [4549], 2120 W 33rd Ave., Denver, CO
  80211, (703)299-9400
Earth; Friends of the [4397]
Earth; Hollow [★12354]
Earth Island Inst. [4550], 300 Broadway, Ste. 28,
  San Francisco, CA 94133, (415)788-3666
Earth Island Inst. [IO], San Francisco, CA, United
  States
Earth; Kids for Saving [8390]
Earth Liberation Front [4551]
Earth Regeneration Soc. [4552], c/o Alden Bryant,
  Pres., 1442A Walnut St., No. 57, Berkeley, CA
  94709, (510)527-9716
Earth Repair Found. [IO], Katoomba, Australia
Earth Sci. Editors; Assn. of [3093]
Earth Sci. Teachers' Assn. [IO], Cumbria, United
  Kingdom
Earth Sci. Teachers Assn; Natl. [9111]
Earth Sciences
  Amer. Geological Inst. [7126]
  Assn. of Women Soil Scientists [7672]
  Chilean Assn. of Seismology and Earthquake
    Engg. [IO]
  Earth Communications Off. [4547]
  Earth Day Network [4548]
  Earth Soc. Found. [4553]
  Earth's Physical Features Stud. Unit [22816]
  European Network on Lateritic Weathering and
    Global Env. [IO]
  Geodetic Soc. of Japan [IO]
  Geoscience Info. Soc. [7142]
  German Geophysical Soc. [IO]
  The Green Life [4569]
  Inst. of Environmental Sciences and Tech. [7570]
  Intl. Assn. for the Advancement of Earth and
    Environmental Sciences [4511]
  Intl. Biogeography Soc. [7122]
  Natl. Registry of Environmental Professionals
    [4593]
  Sci. Comm. on Solar Terrestrial Physics [7508]
  Soc. of Independent Professional Earth Scientists
    [7135]
  U.S. Permafrost Assn. [7675]
Earth Sciences Soc; History of [10116]
Earth Scientists; Soc. of Independent Professional
  [7135]
Earth, Sea and Sky [IO], Weymouth, United
  Kingdom
Earth Ser. Corps; YMCA [18861]
Earth Share [8394], 7735 Old Georgetown Rd., Ste.
  900, Bethesda, MD 20814, (240)333-0300

A star before a book entry number signifies that the name is not listed separately, but is mentioned within the entry.

Earth Soc. Found. [4553], 238 E 58th St., Ste. 2400, New York, NY 10022

Earth Soc. Found. [IO], New York, NY, United States

Earth-Spirit [★IO]

Earth-Spirit [★14818]

Earth-Spirit, Inc. [★14818]

Earth-Spirit, Inc. [★IO]

Earth; Women's Voices for the [4616]

EarthAction Intl. [4554], 30 Cottage St., Amherst, MA 01002, (413)549-8118

EarthAction Intl. [IO], Amherst, MA, United States

EarthBank Assn. of North America - Address unknown since 1991.

EarthConnection - Defunct.

EarthEcho Intl. [4391], 888 16th St. NW, Ste. 800, Washington, DC 20006, (202)349-9828

EarthEcho Intl. [IO], Washington, DC, United States

Earthen Family Org. - Defunct.

Earthjustice [5690], 426 17th St., 6th Fl., Oakland, CA 94612-2820, (510)550-6700

Earthjustice [IO], Oakland, CA, United States

EarthLink [IO], Munich, Germany

Earthmind - Address unknown since 1999.

The Earthology Found. [★4503]

Earthology Found; The [★4503]

Earthquake and Civil Engg. Dynamics; Soc. for [IO]

Earthquake Engg; Natl. Info. Ser. for [7641]

Earthquake Engg. Res. Inst. [7638], 499 14th St., Ste. 320, Oakland, CA 94612-1934, (510)451-0905

Earthquake Engg. Soc; Australian [IO]

EarthRights Intl. - Asia [IO], Chiang Mai, Thailand

Earthrise [7103], 2151 Michelson Dr., Ste. 258, Irvine, CA 92612, (949)623-0980

Earthroots [IO], Toronto, ON, Canada

Earth's Physical Features Stud. Unit [22816], c/o Fred W. Klein, Sec.-Treas., 515 Magdalena Ave., Los Altos, CA 94024

EarthSave Canada [IO], Vancouver, BC, Canada

Earthsave Found. [★IO]

Earthsave Found. [★4504]

EarthSave Intl. [4504], PO Box 96, New York, NY 10108, (718)459-7503

EarthSave Intl. [IO], New York, NY, United States

EarthSharing [IO], Melbourne, Australia

Earthspirit Community [20445], PO Box 723, Williamsburg, MA 01096, (413)238-4240

Earthstewards Network [12344], Box 10697, Bainbridge Island, WA 98110, (206)842-7986

Earthstewards Network [IO], Bainbridge Island, WA, United States

Earthtrust [IO], Kailua, HI, United States

Earthtrust [5312], c/o Windward Environmental Center, 1118 Maunawili Rd., Kailua, HI 96734, (808)261-5339

EarthVoice [4555], 2100 L St. NW, Washington, DC 20037, (202)778-6146

Earthvote Intl. [★4554]

Earthvote Intl. [★IO]

Earthvote Network [★IO]

Earthvote Network [★4554]

Earthwatch [★IO]

Earthwatch Inst. [8413], 3 Clock Tower Pl., Ste. 100, Box 75, Maynard, MA 01754-0075, (978)461-0081

EarthWave Soc. [4556], 16151 Hwy., 377 S, Fort Worth, TX 76126, (817)443-3780

Earthwise Living Found. New Zealand [IO], Thames, New Zealand

Earthworks [6115], 1612 K St. NW, Ste. 808, Washington, DC 20006, (202)887-1872

East Africa Natural History Soc. [★IO]

East Africa Natural History Soc. [★IO]

East Africa Tourist Travel Assn. - Defunct.

The East African Assn. [★IO]

East African Wild Life Soc. [IO], Nairobi, Kenya

East African Youth Alliance [IO], Nairobi, Kenya

East Anglian Traditional Music Trust [IO], Stowmarket, United Kingdom

East Asia Christian Conf. [★IO]

East Asia Regional Coun. of Overseas Schools [IO], Laguna, Philippines

East Asian Economic Assn. - Hong Kong Off. [IO], Hong Kong, People's Republic of China

East Bay Fan Guild [★IO]

East Bay Fan Guild [★22021]

East Bay Workers in Child Care [★12072]

East Coast Marine Sci. Librarians [★10361]

East Coast Marine Sci. Librarians [★IO]

East Coast Migrant Hea. Proj. [★12586]

East Coast Music Assn. [IO], Charlottetown, PE, Canada

East Coast Timing Assn. [22920], c/o Joe Timney, Pres., 1081 Dexter Corner Rd., Townsend, DE 19734, (302)378-3013

East European Family History Assn. [★21112]

East European Family History Assn. [★IO]

East European Jewry; Center for Russian and [17946]

East European Languages; Amer. Assn. of Teachers of Slavic and [9125]

East European Law; Committee on Soviet and [★5475]

East Jerusalem YMCA [IO], East Jerusalem, Israel

East Lancashire Chamber of Commerce [IO], Accrington, United Kingdom

East Meets West Found. [IO], Oakland, CA, United States

East Meets West Found. [IO], Da Nang, Vietnam

East Meets West Found. [17836], PO Box 29292, Oakland, CA 94604, (510)763-7045

East Meets West - Vietnam [★IO]

East Midlands Campaign for Nuclear Disarmament [IO], Leicester, United Kingdom

East Midlands Welsh Pony and Cob Assn. [IO], Worksop, United Kingdom

East Relief; Near [★18068]

East Texas Big Thicket Assn. [★4367]

East Timor

East Timor and Indonesia Action Network/US [17442]

East Timor Action Network/US [★17442]

East Timor Human Rights Comm. - Defunct.

East Timor and Indonesia Action Network/US [17442], PO Box 21873, Brooklyn, NY 11202-1873, (212)596-7668

East Timor Project - Defunct.

East West Acad. of Healing Arts [15744], 117 Topaz Way, San Francisco, CA 94131, (415)285-9400

East-West Bridges for Peace - Defunct.

East-West Center [17882], 1601 East-West Rd., Honolulu, HI 96848, (808)944-7111

East-West Center [IO], Honolulu, HI, United States

East and West; Center for Cultural and Tech. Interchange Between [★17882]

East-West Cultural Center [9619], 12329 Marshall St., Culver City, CA 90230, (310)390-9083

East West Educ. Development Found. [12716], PO Box 701560, Dallas, TX 75370-1560, (214)265-8300

East West Educ. Development Found. [IO], Addison, TX, United States

East West News Bur. [★4066]

East-West Trade Coun. - Defunct.

East Wind Trade Associates - Defunct.

Easter Seal Home Service - Defunct.

Easter Seal Soc; Natl. [★11944]

Easter Seals [11944], 230 W Monroe St., Ste. 1800, Chicago, IL 60606, (312)726-6200

Easterling Family Genealogical Soc. [20891], 1124 Pearl Valley Rd., Wesson, MS 39191-9361, (601)894-2642

Eastern Acad. of Sexual Therapy [★16408]

Eastern Africa Assn. [IO], London, United Kingdom

Eastern Amputee Golf Association [IO], Bethlehem, PA, United States

Eastern Amputee Golf Assn. [23446], 2015 Amherst Dr., Bethlehem, PA 18015-5606, (610)867-9295

Eastern Apicultural Soc. [★4165]

Eastern Apicultural Soc. of North Am. [4165], c/o Loretta Surprenant, Sec., PO Box 300, Essex, NY 12936, (518)963-7593

Eastern Asia Soc. for Trans. Stud. [IO], Tokyo, Japan

Eastern Assn. of Mosquito Control Workers [★IO]

Eastern Assn. of Mosquito Control Workers [★5072]

Eastern Assn. of Rowing Colleges [23699], c/o Eastern Coll. Athletic Conf., 1311 Craigville Beach Rd., Centerville, MA 02632, (508)771-5060

Eastern Bird Banding Assn. [7417], c/o Don Mease, Treas., 2366 Springtown Hill Rd., Hellertown, PA 18055

Eastern Caribbean Central Bank [IO], Basseterre, St. Kitts and Nevis

Eastern Claims Conf. [2163], PO Box 2730, Stamford, CT 06906-0730, (203)352-3074

Eastern Coal Transportation Conf. - Address unknown since 1995.

Eastern Coast Breweriana Assn. [21830], c/o Larry Handy, VP, PO Box 1541, North Wales, PA 19454, (215)412-2344

Eastern Coll. Athletic Conf. [23484], PO Box 3, Centerville, MA 02632, (508)771-5060

Eastern Coll. Basketball Assn. - Address unknown since 2008.

Eastern Coll. Soccer Assn. [23776], PO Box 3, Centerville, MA 02632, (508)771-5060

Eastern Coll. Soccer Officials Bur. [★23776]

Eastern Collegiate Hockey Assn. [23485], c/o Marshall Stevenson, Commissioner, 18206 Bunker Hill Rd., Parkton, MD 21120-9435, (410)704-2963

Eastern Conf. of Rehabilitation Teachers of the Visually Handicapped - Defunct.

Eastern Connecticut Clam Diggers Assn. - Defunct.

Eastern Dark-Fired Tobacco Growers Assn. [5247]

Eastern Dredging Assn. [★2597]

Eastern Dredging Assn. [★IO]

Eastern Dry Cleaning and Laundry Machinery Distributors Assn. - Defunct.

Eastern Europe

Action for Post-Soviet Jewry [17443]

Action for Post-Soviet Jewry [IO]

Amer. St. Boniface Soc. [19568]

Amers. for Human Rights in Ukraine [17744]

Balalaika and Domra Assn. of Am. [10563]

Baltic Amer. Freedom League [17019]

Chicago Action for Jews in the Former Soviet Union [17444]

Chicago Action for Jews in the Former Soviet Union [IO]

Civil Soc. Intl. [IO]

Civil Soc. Intl. [17445]

Continental European Family History Assn. [21112]

Fed. of East European Family History Societies [19068]

Inst. for Democracy in Eastern Europe [17446]

Inst. for Democracy in Eastern Europe [IO]

Jamestown Found. [IO]

Jamestown Found. [17447]

Joint Baltic Amer. Natl. Comm. [17020]

Lithuanian Natl. Found. [18021]

Natl. Captive Nations Comm. [18088]

NCSJ: Advocates on Behalf of Jews in Russia, Ukraine, the Baltic States and Eurasia [17448]

NCSJ: Advocates on Behalf of Jews in Russia, Ukraine, the Baltic States and Eurasia [IO]

Raoul Wallenberg Committee of the United States [IO]

Raoul Wallenberg Comm. of the U.S. [17449]

Slavic and East European Folklore Assn. [9962]

Slavic Heritage Coalition [10969]

SMOLOSKYP, Ukrainian Info. Ser. [17450]

SMOLOSKYP, Ukrainian Info. Ser. [IO]

Student Struggle for Soviet Jewry [IO]

Student Struggle for Soviet Jewry [17451]

Tamizdat [9853]

Ukrainian Natl. Info. Ser. [18757]

Union of Councils for Jews in the Former Soviet Union [17452]

Union of Councils for Jews in the Former Soviet Union [IO]

Women's Assn. for the Defense of Four Freedoms for Ukraine [18759]

World Fed. of Free Latvians [17997]

Eastern European Bible Mission [★20372]

Eastern European Bible Mission [★IO]

Eastern Finance Assn. [1414], c/o David R. Lange, Exec. Dir., Auburn Montgomery, School of Bus., PO Box 244023, Montgomery, AL 36124-4023

Eastern Foresters; Assn. of [★4689]

Eastern Hockey League - Address unknown since 1995.

Eastern Intercollegiate Gymnastic League [23475], c/o Eastern Coll. Athletic Conf., 1311 Craigville Beach Rd., PO Box 3, Centerville, MA 02632, (508)771-5060

Reference to "IO" in place of a book number signifies that the association may be found in the 45th edition of International Organizations.

Eastern Lamp and Lighting Assn. - Defunct.
Eastern Marathon Swimming Assn. - Address unknown since 1995.
Eastern Mineral Law Found. [★6136]
Eastern Museum of Motor Racing [21634], PO Box 688, Mechanicsburg, PA 17055, (717)528-8279

Eastern Orthodox
Axios USA [20049]
Fellowship of Saint James [19800]
Fellowship of St. John the Divine [19882]
Macedonian Orthodox Youth Assn. of North Am. [19883]
Macedonian Orthodox Youth Assn. of North Am. [IO]
Orthodox People in Am. [19884]
Orthodox Theological Soc. in Am. [19885]
Standing Conf. of the Canonical Orthodox Bishops in the Americas [19886]
Standing Conf. of the Canonical Orthodox Bishops in the Americas [IO]
Eastern Packard Club [21635], PO Box 1259, Stratford, CT 06615, (203)374-7757
Eastern Police Bloodhound Assn. [★6000]
Eastern Professional River Outfitters Assn. [★23681]
Eastern Psychiatric Res. Assn. - Address unknown since 1995.
Eastern Railroad Assn. - Defunct.
Eastern Regional Dance Assn. [★9897]
Eastern Regional Dance Assn. [★IO]
Eastern Regional Org. for Public Admin. [IO], Quezon City, Philippines
Eastern Ski Assn. [★23760]
Eastern Ski Representatives Assn. [★3661]
Eastern Soccer Officials Bur. [★23776]
Eastern and Southern Africa Intl. Assn. for Schools of Social Work [★IO]
Eastern and Southern Africa Mgt. Inst. [IO], Arusha, United Republic of Tanzania
Eastern Star; Gen. Grand Chap., Order of the [19234]
Eastern States Blast Furnace and Coke Oven Assn. - Address unknown since 1994.
Eastern Surfing Assn. [23878], PO Box 625, Virginia Beach, VA 23451, (757)233-1790
Eastern Tribes; United South and [12632]
Eastern Water Polo Assn. [★23972]
Eastern Welsh Pony and Cob Assn. [IO], Newmarket, United Kingdom
Eastern Winter Sports Representatives Assn. [3661], 5142 State St., White Haven, PA 18661, (570)443-7180
Eastern Women's Amateur Basketball League of the AAU - Address unknown since 1991.
Easti Gerontoloogia ja Geriaatria Assotsiatsioon [★IO]
EastWest Inst. [IO], New York, NY, United States
EastWest Inst. [17823], 700 Broadway, 2nd Fl., New York, NY 10003, (212)824-4100
Easy Magic Cookery Coun. - Defunct.
Eating Disorder Rsrc. Centre of British Columbia [IO], Vancouver, BC, Canada

Eating Disorders
Acad. for Eating Disorders [14296]
Alliance for Eating Disorders Awareness [14297]
Anorexia Nervosa and Bulimia Assn. [IO]
Anorexia Nervosa and Related Eating Disorders [14298]
Assn. for Rehabilitation of Commun. and Oral Skills [IO]
Assn. for the Stud. of Obesity [IO]
BODYWHYS: The Eating Disorders Assn. of Ireland [IO]
Do It Now Found. [13235]
Eating Disorder Rsrc. Centre of British Columbia [IO]
Eating Disorders Assn. [IO]
Eating Disorders Assn. (Queensland) [IO]
Eating Disorders Coalition for Res., Policy and Action [14299]
European Coun. on Eating Disorders [IO]
Intl. Assn. of Eating Disorders Professionals [IO]
Intl. Assn. of Eating Disorders Professionals [14300]
Natl. Assn. to Advance Fat Acceptance [12647]
Natl. Assn. of Anorexia Nervosa and Assoc. Disorders [14301]

Natl. Eating Disorder Info. Centre [IO]
Natl. Eating Disorders Assn. [14302]
Niagara Network for Freedom from Weight Preoccupation and Eating Disorders [IO]
Obesity Action Coalition [15577]
Overeaters Anonymous World Ser. Off. [12648]
Soc. for the Stud. of Ingestive Behavior [13742]
Eating Disorders Assn. [IO], Norwich, United Kingdom
Eating Disorders Assn. (Queensland) [IO], Brisbane, Australia
Eating Disorders Awareness and Prevention, Inc. [★14302]
Eating Disorders Coalition for Res., Policy and Action [14299], 611 Pennsylvania Ave. SE, No. 423, Washington, DC 20003-4303, (202)543-9570
Eating Disorders; European Coun. on [IO]
Eating Disorders Org; Natl. [★14302]
Eau Claire Alumni Assn; Univ. of Wisconsin - [18940]
Ebenezer Center for Aging and Human Development [★11284]
Ebenezer Found. [★11284]
Ebenezer Soc. [11284], 2722 Park Ave. S, Minneapolis, MN 55407, (612)874-3460
Ebix Users Assn. [340]
eBusiness Assn. [98], PO Box 804, Adams Basin, NY 14410-0804, (585)234-1322
EC Dairy Trade Assn. [★IO]
EC Seed Crushers' and Oil Processors' Fed. [IO], Brussels, Belgium
Ecclesia Cantans - Defunct.
Ecclesiastical History Soc. [IO], Worthing, United Kingdom
e.centre [★IO]
Echo Dogs White Shepherd Rescue [11388], PO Box 240028, Ballwin, MO 63024
Echo Res. Inst. [IO], Markham, ON, Canada

Echocardiography
British Soc. of Echocardiography [IO]
Intl. Veterinary Ultrasound Soc. [16797]
Echocardiography; Amer. Soc. of [13891]
ECKANKAR [20493], PO Box 2000, Chanhassen, MN 55317-2000, (952)380-2222
ECMA Intl. [IO], Geneva, Switzerland
Eco-Animal Allies [11773]
Eco-friendly Nepal [IO], Kathmandu, Nepal
Eco-Justice Working Group [18613], c/o Natl. Coun. of Churches, 110 Maryland Ave. NE, Ste. 108, Washington, DC 20002, (202)544-2350
Eco-Spirit [4622], PO Box 239, Clarksburg, MD 20871, (866)709-0131
EcoBolivia USA - Address unknown since 2003.
Ecobrasil [IO], Rio de Janeiro, Brazil
EcoDesign Found. [★IO]
Ecoforestry Inst. - U.S. - Address unknown since 2004.
Ecoglasnost [★IO]
Ecoliteracy; Center for [4501]
EcoLogic Development Fund [4505], 25 Mt. Auburn St., Ste. 203, Harvard Sq., Cambridge, MA 02138, (617)441-6300
EcoLogic Development Fund [IO], Cambridge, MA, United States
Ecologic - Institut fur Internationale und Europaische Umweltpolitik [★IO]
Ecologic - Inst. for Intl. and European Environmental Policy [IO], Berlin, Germany
Ecologic; Intl. Soc. of Dermatology: Tropical, Geographic, and [★14205]
Ecological Agriculture Projects [IO], Ste.-Anne-de-Bellevue, QC, Canada
Ecological Farming Assn. [4100], 406 Main St., Ste. 313, Watsonville, CA 95076, (831)763-2111
Ecological Found; Thorne [★4523]
Ecological Landscaping Assn. [4989], 60 Thoreau St., No. 252, Concord, MA 01742-2456, (617)436-5838
Ecological Landscaping Assn. [IO], Concord, MA, United States
Ecological Restoration and Mgt; Soc. for [★4522]
Ecological Soc. of Am. [4506], 1707 H St. NW, Ste. 400, Washington, DC 20006, (202)833-8773
Ecological Soc. of Am; Comm. on Preservation of Natural Conditions [★4433]

Ecological Soc. of Australia [IO], Alice Springs, Australia
Ecological Soc. of Germany, Austria, and Switzerland [IO], Berlin, Germany
Ecological Soc. of Japan [IO], Kyoto, Japan
Ecological Soc. of Physicians [IO], Bremen, Germany
Ecological and Toxicological Assn. of Dyes and Organic Pigments Mfrs. [IO], Basel, Switzerland
Ecological and Toxicological Assn. of Dyes and Organic Pigments Mfrs; ETAD North Am. - [5089]
Ecological and Toxicological Assn. of the Dyestuffs Mfg. Indus. [★IO]
Ecologist Workshop [IO], Rosario, Argentina
Ecologists; Assn. of Applied Insect [★5073]
Ecologists; Assn. of Applied IPM [5073]
Ecologists; Soc. of Vector [★5079]
Ecologists Union [★4433]

Ecology
Africa Rainforest and River Conservation [4341]
African Blackwood Conservation Proj. [4342]
Albert Schweitzer Ecological Centre [IO]
Amer. Acad. of Environmental Medicine [14360]
Amer. Ecological Engg. Soc. [6864]
Amer. Land Conservancy [4348]
Amer. Marinelife Dealers Assn. [5007]
Arcosanti, A Proj. of the Cosanti Found. [4497]
Argentine Assn. of Ecology [IO]
Assn. for Arid Lands Stud. [4498]
Assn. of Ecosystem Res. Centers [4499]
Assn. of Heads of Outdoor Educ. Centres [IO]
Bamboo of The Americas [4365]
Blue Dolphin Alliance [5008]
British Ecological Soc. [IO]
Canadian Coun. on Ecological Areas [IO]
Canyonlands Field Inst. [4500]
Center for Ecoliteracy [4501]
Center for Respect of Life and Env. [4620]
Centre for Ecology and Hydrology [IO]
Centro Ecologico Akumal [IO]
Charles A. and Anne Morrow Lindbergh Found. [4539]
Children of the Earth United [4621]
Commonwealth Human Ecology Coun. [IO]
Compassionate Kids [8384]
ConservAmerica [4378]
Earth Charter USA Campaign [4502]
Earth Charter USA Campaign [IO]
Earth Ecology Found. [4503]
EarthEcho Intl. [4391]
EarthSave Intl. [4504]
EarthSave Intl. [IO]
EarthWave Soc. [4556]
Eco-Animal Allies [11773]
Eco-Spirit [4622]
EcoLogic Development Fund [4505]
EcoLogic Development Fund [IO]
Ecological Landscaping Assn. [4989]
Ecological Soc. of Am. [4506]
Ecological Soc. of Australia [IO]
Ecological Soc. of Germany, Austria, and Switzerland [IO]
Ecological Soc. of Japan [IO]
Ecologist Workshop [IO]
Environmental and Energy Stud. Inst. [4507]
European Soc. for Ecological Economics [IO]
Fed. of Alberta Naturalists [IO]
Field Naturalists Club of Victoria [IO]
Filipino Amer. Coalition for Environmental Solidarity [4634]
ForestEthics [4685]
Found. for Deep Ecology [4508]
Found. for Deep Ecology [IO]
French Ecological Soc. [IO]
Gaia Inst. [4509]
Galilee Restoration Proj. [IO]
Great Lakes Indian Fish and Wildlife Commn. [5323]
Human Ecology Action League [14364]
Inst. of Ecotechnics [IO]
Inst. for Sustainable Desert Occupancy [4510]
Intl. Assn. for the Advancement of Earth and Environmental Sciences [4511]
Intl. Assn. for Ecology [IO]
Intl. Biogeography Soc. [7122]

A star before a book entry number signifies that the name is not listed separately, but is mentioned within the entry.

Intl. Coun. for Human Ecology and Ethnology [4512]

Intl. Coun. for Human Ecology and Ethnology [IO]

Intl. Ecology Inst. [IO]

Intl. Found. of the High-Altitude Res. Stations Jungfraujoch and Gornergrat [IO]

Intl. Geosphere-Biosphere Programme [IO]

Intl. Humic Substances Soc. [7610]

Intl. Inst. for Baubiologie and Ecology [4513]

Intl. Soc. for Biological and Environmental Repositories [6585]

Intl. Soc. for Bioluminescence and Chemiluminescence [7612]

Intl. Soc. of Chem. Ecology [6550]

Intl. Soc. for Ecological Modelling [4514]

Intl. Soc. for Ecological Modelling [IO]

Intl. Soc. for Ecology and Culture [IO]

Intl. Soc. for Indus. Ecology [4580]

Intl. Soc. for Microbial Ecology [4515]

Intl. Soc. for Microbial Ecology [IO]

Intl. Sonoran Desert Alliance [4582]

Intl. Union of Radioecology [IO]

Italian Soc. of Ecology [IO]

Keeping Track [5335]

Media Ecology Assn. [8831]

Natl. Assn. of Exotic Pest Plant Councils [5077]

Natl. Coun. for Sci. and the Env. [7067]

Natl. Environmental Hea. Assn. [14367]

Natl. Network of Forest Practitioners [4692]

Natural Areas Assn. [4430]

New Zealand Ecological Soc. [IO]

NextGen Energy Coun. [6966]

North Amer. Benthological Soc. [4516]

North American Benthological Society [IO]

North Amer. Coalition for Christianity and Ecology [4517]

North Amer. Coalition on Religion and Ecology [4598]

North Amer. Hazardous Materials Mgt. Assn. [4806]

Pachamama Alliance [5163]

Pacific Shellfish Inst. [4182]

PACON Intl. [5011]

People-Plant Coun. [4518]

Pesticide Action Network North Am. Regional Center [13329]

Pesticide Action Network UK [IO]

Pitch-In Canada [IO]

Point Found. [4519]

Polish Assn. for Landscape Ecology [IO]

Rachel Carson Homestead Assn. [11143]

Reef Check [5012]

Reef Relief [5013]

ReefGuardian Intl. [5014]

Scottish Ecological Design Assn. [IO]

Sierra Club [4520]

Sierra Student Coalition [4521]

Soc. for Conservation GIS [6831]

Soc. for Ecological Restoration Intl. [4522]

Soc. of Grasslands Naturalists [IO]

Soc. for Marine Mammalogy [5017]

Soc. of Woman Geographers [7124]

Southern African Inst. of Ecologists and Environmental Scientists [IO]

Sustainable Travel Intl. [5252]

Swedish Soc. OIKOS [IO]

Tall Timbers Res. Sta. [4457]

Thorne Ecological Inst. [4523]

The True Nature Network [11465]

U.S. Soc. for Ecological Economics [6865]

U.S. Soc. for Ecological Economics [IO]

U.S. Tourist Coun. [4462]

Urban Ecology Australia [IO]

Vegetarian Rsrc. Gp. [11073]

Wallace Genetic Found. [4117]

Water Planet USA [5018]

Wild Farm Alliance [4661]

Wildfowl Trust of North Am. [5397]

Wildlands Proj. [4614]

Women's Voices for the Earth [4616]

World Environmental Org. [4475]

World Parks [4617]

World Preserve [4476]

Ecology Action Centre [IO], Halifax, NS, Canada

Ecology Action League; Human [14364]

Ecology Center Communications Coun. - Defunct.

Ecology Center Found. - Defunct.

Ecology Center of Southern California [★8386]

Ecology Center of Southern California [★IO]

Ecology; Daphne Inst. of Applied [IO]

Ecology and Environmental Mgt; Inst. of [IO]

Ecology and Ethnology; Intl. Commn. for Human [★4512]

Ecology; Intl. Coun. on Human [★4512]

Ecology; North Amer. Coalition on Religion and [4598]

Ecology; Soc. for Clinical [★14360]

Ecology; Soc. for Vector [5079]

Econometric Association [★7645]

Econometric Soc. [7705], New York Univ., Dept. of Economics, 19 W 4th St., 6th Fl., New York, NY 10012, (212)998-3820

Econometric Soc. [IO], New York, NY, United States

Economic Affairs Bureau/Dollars and Sense [6879], 29 Winter St., Boston, MA 02108, (617)447-2177

Economic Alternatives; Exploratory Proj. for [★18409]

Economic Assn; Amer. Farm [★6867]

Economic Assn; Catholic [★6873]

Economic Botany; Soc. for [6649]

Economic Chamber of the Czech Republic [IO], Prague, Czech Republic

Economic Civil Liberties Assn. - Defunct.

Economic Commn. for Asia and the Far East [★IO]

Economic Commn. for Latin Am. and the Caribbean [IO], Santiago, Chile

Economic Community of West African States [IO], Abuja, Nigeria

Economic Conversion; Center for [17423]

Economic Cooperation and Development; Org. for [6866]

Economic Coun; Czechoslovak-U.S. [★2302]

Economic Coun; Romanian-U.S. [★24370]

Economic Coun; U.S.-Korea [★24350]

Economic Coun; U.S. Yugoslav [★2292]

Economic Coun; U.S.A.-Republic of China [★2294]

Economic Crisis; Inst. for the Stud. of Labor and [★18448]

Economic and Cultural Off. in New York; Info. Div., Taipei [★9792]

Economic and Cultural Off. in New York; Press Div., Taipei [9792]

Economic Development

Action for Humanity - Uganda [IO]

African Development Bank [IO]

African Inst. for Economic Development and Planning [IO]

Alliance for Responsible Trade [3836]

Amer. Entrepreneurs for Economic Growth [695]

Amer. Intl. Chamber of Commerce [24247]

American-Russian Chamber of Commerce and Indus. [24261]

Argentine-American Chamber of Commerce [24227]

Armenian Amer. Chamber of Commerce [24263]

Ashoka: Innovators for the Public [12419]

Asia Pacific Mountain Network [IO]

Asia Pacific - USA Chamber of Commerce [24264]

Asian Development Bank [IO]

Asian Productivity Org. [IO]

Assn. of Development Financing Institutions in Asia and the Pacific [IO]

Assn. for the Stud. of the Cuban Economy [8214]

Australia Pacific Islands Bus. Coun. [IO]

Australian New Zealand - Amer. Chambers of Commerce [24248]

Bilateral US-Arab Chamber of Commerce [24226]

Bretton Woods Commn. [17453]

Bretton Woods Proj. [IO]

Bridging Nations [17861]

Bulgarian-American Chamber of Commerce [24243]

Bus. Alliance for Local Living Economies [887]

Bus. History Conf. [10098]

Bus. Leaders for Sensible Priorities [18387]

Cameroon-USA Chamber of Commerce [24249]

Canadian/American Border Trade Alliance [3838]

Canadian Executive Ser. Org. [IO]

Caribbean Development Bank [IO]

Center for New Community [17210]

Central Amer. Bank for Economic Integration [IO]

Centro De Investigacion y Accion Social [IO]

China Bus. Coun. for Sustainable Development [IO]

Citizens Network for Sustainable Development [11767]

Cliometric Soc. [17454]

Comm. for Economic Development [17455]

Comm. for Economic Development of Australia [IO]

Comm. for the Economic Growth of Israel [24337]

Community Ser. [17214]

Concord Coalition [17456]

Consultative Gp. to Assist the Poor [17833]

Corporate Coun. on Africa [169]

Corp. for Enterprise Development [17457]

Coun. of Development Finance Agencies [17458]

Coun. on Food, Agricultural and Rsrc. Economics [4524]

Counterpart Intl. [12426]

Croatian-American Chamber of Commerce [24314]

Cuban Amer. Natl. Coun. [13167]

Development Assistance Comm. [IO]

Dialogue on Diversity [8888]

East Meets West Found. [IO]

Eastern Africa Assn. [IO]

Economic Commn. for Latin Am. and the Caribbean [IO]

Economic and Social Coun. [IO]

Economic and Social Coun. [17459]

Emerging Markets Private Equity Assn. [1415]

Employment Policy Found. [12077]

Energy Future Coalition [6952]

Enterprise Development Intl. [12044]

Enterprise Development Intl. [IO]

Entrepreneurship Development Inst. of India [IO]

Estonian Amer. Chamber of Commerce and Indus. [24318]

Estonian Amer. Fund for Economic Educ. [8215]

Euro Inst. [IO]

European League for Economic Cooperation [IO]

European Travel Commn. [3916]

Fed. of Philippine Amer. Chambers of Commerce [24277]

Fed. of Southern Cooperatives Land Assistance Fund [12937]

First Nations Development Inst. [12625]

First Peoples Worldwide [10224]

Found. for Intl. Community Assistance [17217]

Found. of Occupational Development [IO]

Friedrich Naumann Found. [IO]

GALA: Globalization and Localization Association [IO]

GALA: Globalization and Localization Assn. [1168]

German Development Ser. - Vietnam [IO]

Ghana-USA Chamber of Commerce [24279]

Global Envision [12194]

Global Marshall Plan Initiative [IO]

Global Offset and Countertrade Assn. [2305]

Globe Found. of Canada [IO]

Green Innovations of Australia [IO]

Heritage Inst. [19271]

Hong Kong Chinese Enterprises Assn. [IO]

Hong Kong Economic Assn. [IO]

HOUR Money Network [17218]

Ijaw Natl. Alliance of the Americas [12639]

Inst. for Local Self-Reliance [11747]

Inst. of Natl. Affairs [IO]

Inst. of Policy Anal. and Res. [IO]

Inst. of Small Enterprise and Development [IO]

Institution of Economic Development [IO]

Inter-American Conf. of Ministers of Labor [17394]

Inter-American Development Bank [17460]

Inter-American Development Bank [IO]

Intl. Assn. for the Plant Protection Sciences [6397]

Intl. Assn. of Sci. and Tech. for Development [IO]

Intl. Coalition for Sustainable Production and Consumption [17222]

Intl. Cooperation for Development and Solidarity - Vietnam [IO]

Intl. Finance Corp. [IO]

Intl. Finance Corp. [17461]

Reference to "IO" in place of a book number signifies that the association may be found in the 45th edition of International Organizations.

Intl. Monetary Fund [17462]
Intl. Monetary Fund [IO]
Iraqi Amer. Chamber of Commerce and Indus. [24285]
Islamic Development Bank [IO]
Jamaica USA Chamber of Commerce [24287]
Japan External Trade Org. [24342]
Just Transition Alliance [24105]
JustAct: Youth Action for Global Justice [18853]
Latin Amer. Assn. of Development Financing Institutions [IO]
Latino Issues Forum [19098]
Leadership Development Network [17223]
Mario Santo Domingo Found. [IO]
Mercy-USA for Aid and Development [12871]
Mexican Amer. Unity Coun. [12277]
Milton S. Eisenhower Found. [11839]
More Than Money [17471]
Namibian Economic Policy Res. Unit [IO]
Natl. Assn. of Community Development Extension Professionals [11784]
Natl. Assn. of Development Organizations Res. Found. [17226]
Natl. Assn. of Regional Councils [6244]
Natl. Assn. of State Development Agencies [5592]
Natl. Black United Fed. of Charities [16943]
Natl. Collegiate Inventors and Innovators Alliance [7218]
Natl. Coun. of Asian Amer. Bus. Associations [774]
Natl. Development Coun. [17463]
Natl. Economic Development and Law Center [17464]
Natl. Organizers Alliance [13136]
Natl. Tribal Development Assn. [19280]
Neighborhood Funders Gp. [12734]
New Am. Alliance [1169]
New Mgt. Era [IO]
New Zealand Bus. Coun. for Sustainable Development [IO]
North America-Mongolia Bus. Coun. [2310]
North American-Bulgarian Chamber of Commerce [24291]
North America's SuperCorridor Coalition [3887]
One Earth One Justice [12437]
One Economy [7755]
Oper. HOPE, Inc. [11787]
Org. for Economic Cooperation and Development [6866]
Pakistan Chamber of Commerce USA [24364]
Parliamentarians For Global Action [17433]
Planeta Sustenable [IO]
PolicyLink [18276]
Polish Amer. Chamber of Commerce [24293]
Positive Futures Network [18839]
Proj. South: Inst. for the Elimination of Poverty and Genocide [17872]
Public Works and Economic Development Assn. [5595]
Regency Found. Networx [IO]
Rsrc. Generation [13137]
Russian-American Chamber of Commerce in the USA [24371]
Sales Exchange for Refugee Rehabilitation and Vocation [3846]
Scottish Coun. for Development and Indus. [IO]
Serbian-American Chamber of Commerce [24373]
Sierra Visions [12444]
Single Global Currency Assn. [17021]
Social Enterprise Alliance [3633]
Social Venture Network [764]
Soc. for the Development of Austrian Economics [6894]
Soc. of Govt. Economists [5674]
Soc. for Intl. Development [IO]
Solace Intl. [13439]
South Africa Partners [18666]
South African USA Chamber of Commerce [24295]
Structured Employment Economic Development Corp. [12045]
Surface Trans. Policy Proj. [18750]
Sustainable Harvest Intl. [4115]
SustainUS [13517]
Trinidad and Tobago/USA Chamber of Commerce [24298]

Turkish-American Chamber of Commerce and Indus. [24384]
TWIN [IO]
Umanotera, Slovenian Found. for Sustainable Development [IO]
United Nations Economic Commn. for Africa [IO]
United Nations Economic Commn. for Europe [IO]
United Nations Economic and Social Commn. for Asia and the Pacific [IO]
U.S. Hispanic Chamber of Commerce [24327]
U.S. Indian Amer. Chamber of Commerce [24331]
U.S. Natl. Comm. for Pacific Economic Cooperation [17465]
U.S. Natl. Comm. for Pacific Economic Cooperation [IO]
U.S. Women's Chamber of Commerce [24389]
Uruguayan Found. of Joint Cooperation and Development [IO]
U.S.A. - Bus. and Indus. Advisory Comm. to the OECD [17466]
USA Engage [17467]
Wales North Am. Bus. Chamber [24306]
The Waterfront Center [11794]
West Africa Bus. Assn. [IO]
William J. Clinton Found. [17855]
Windustry [7853]
Women's Intl. Coalition for Economic Justice [17475]
World Development Fed. [12449]
World Economic Forum [IO]
World Heritage Alliance [10077]
Economic Development Agencies; Natl. Assn. of State [★5592]
Economic Development Associates; Mennonite [20249]
Economic Development Assn; Public Works and [5595]
Economic Development Corp; Amer. Woman's [3604]
Economic Development Coun; Amer. [★5812]
Economic Development; Coun. for Urban [★5812]
Economic Development of Cuba; Institute for [★17367]
Economic Development of Cuba; Institute for [★IO]
Economic Development; Natl. Assn. for County Community and [17225]
Economic Dignity and Independence for Women; Justice, [18812]
Economic Education for Clergy - Address unknown since 1999.
Economic Educ; Found. for [18406]
Economic Educ; Joint Coun. in [★8217]
Economic Education League - Defunct.
Economic Education Project - Defunct.
Economic Entomologists and Entomological Society of America; Amer. Assn. of [★7062]
Economic Equality; Fellowship for Racial and [★18629]
Economic Freedom; Natl. Comm. for [★17296]
Economic Geologists; Soc. of [7134]
Economic Growth of Israel; Comm. for the [24337]
Economic History Assn. [8504], Santa Clara Univ., Dept. of Economics, 500 El Camino Real, Santa Clara, CA 95053-0385, (408)554-4348
Economic History Soc. [IO], Oxford, United Kingdom
Economic Inst. of Am; Korea [★17965]
Economic Integration
Andean Community - Gen. Secretariat [IO]
Benelux Economic Union [IO]
Bus. and Professional Women's Found. [11084]
Caribbean Community [IO]
Eastern Caribbean Central Bank [IO]
Economic Community of West African States [IO]
GALA: Globalization and Localization Assn. [1168]
Inst. for the Integration of Latin Am. and the Caribbean [IO]
Latin Amer. and Caribbean Economic Sys. [IO]
Org. for Economic Co-Operation and Development [IO]
PolicyLink [18276]
U.S. Natl. Comm. for Pacific Economic Cooperation [17465]
Economic Justice Inst. [6221], 975 Bascom Mall, Madison, WI 53706-1399, (608)262-9143
Economic Leadership Inst; Congressional [18438]

Economic Opportunity Off. Directors; Natl. Assn. for State [★6279]
Economic Options; Center for [12073]
Economic Outreach; Global [20341]
Economic Paleontologists and Mineralogists; Soc. of [★7432]
Economic Poisons Control Officials; Assn. of [★6170]
Economic Policy Inst. [18441], 1333 H St. NW, Ste. 300, East Tower, Washington, DC 20005-4707, (202)775-8810
Economic Policy Stud; Intl. Center for [★18408]
Economic Res. Coun. [IO], London, United Kingdom
Economic Res. Round Table - Address unknown since 1985.
Economic Round Table; Women's [18484]
Economic and Security Alternatives; Natl. Center for [18409]
Economic Security Proj. - Address unknown since 2008.
Economic and Social Coun. [17459], c/o Mr. Nikhil Seth, Dir., Off. for ECOSOC Support and Coordination, 1 UN Plz., New York, NY 10017, (212)963-1811
Economic and Social Coun. [IO], New York, NY, United States
Economic and Social History Soc. of Ireland [IO], Dublin, Ireland
Economic and Social Planning Assn; Natl. [★5593]
Economic and Social Res. Coun. [IO], Swindon, United Kingdom
Economic and Social Res. Found. [IO], Dar es Salaam, United Republic of Tanzania
Economic and Social Res. Inst. [IO], Dublin, Ireland
Economic Soc. of Australia [IO], St. Ives, Australia
Economic Soc. of Finland [IO], Helsinki, Finland
Economic Soc. of South Africa [IO], Lynnwood Ridge, Republic of South Africa
Economic Stud. Assn; North Amer. [★6890]
Economic Stud; Coun. for Social and [18440]
Economic Stud; Inst. for Socio [18458]
Economic Stud; Joint Center for Political and [7526]
Economic Success CH [12771], c/o The Finance Proj., 1401 New York Ave. NW, Ste. 800, Washington, DC 20005, (202)628-4200
Economic Summit of North Am; The Other [★6891]
Economic Survival; Coalition for [13160]
Economic Trends; Found. on [18615]
Economic Writers; Soc. of Amer. Bus. and [★3161]
Economics
50 Years is Enough: U.S. Network for Global Economic Justice [18829]
Acad. of Accounting Historians [10079]
Adam Smith Inst. [IO]
Africa Action [16918]
Africa News Ser. [16921]
African Economic Res. Consortium [IO]
Agricultural Economics Assn. of South Africa [IO]
All Indian Pueblo Coun. [18089]
Alliance for Responsible Trade [3836]
Am. Bus. Conf. [1170]
America-Georgia Bus. Coun. [2296]
Amer. Agricultural Economics Assn. [6867]
Amer. Agricultural Economics Assn. [IO]
Amer. Bankers Assn. [457]
Amer. Conservative Union [17261]
Amer. Coun. for Capital Formation [17347]
Amer. Coun. on Consumer Interests [17305]
Amer. Coun. for an Energy-Efficient Economy [6938]
Amer. Economic Assn. [6868]
Amer. Entrepreneurs for Economic Growth [695]
Amer. Freedom Center [18421]
Amer. Hellenic Inst. [24325]
Amer. Inst. for Economic Res. [6869]
Amer. Intl. Chamber of Commerce [24247]
Amer. League of Financial Institutions [459]
Amer. Mideast Bus. Associates [24357]
American-Russian Chamber of Commerce and Indus. [24261]
Amer. Soc. of Women Accountants [11]
Amer.-Southern Africa Chamber of Trade and Indus. [24375]
America's Future [17624]
Arab Community Center for Economic and Social Services [18952]

A star before a book entry number signifies that the name is not listed separately, but is mentioned within the entry.

Argentine-American Chamber of Commerce [24227]
Armenian Amer. Chamber of Commerce [24263]
The Asia Found. [17005]
Asia Pacific - USA Chamber of Commerce [24264]
Asian Indian Chamber of Commerce [24228]
Asociacion Argentina de Economia Politica [IO]
Assn. of Amer. Chambers of Commerce in Latin Am. [24352]
Assn. on Amer. Indian Affairs [18092]
Assn. of Caribbean Economists [IO]
Assn. for Comparative Economic Stud. [6870]
Assn. for Cultural Economics Intl. [6871]
Assn. for Cultural Economics Intl. [IO]
Assn. of Economic Sci. Institutions [IO]
Assn. of Environmental and Rsrc. Economists [4359]
Assn. of European Conjuncture Institutes [IO]
Assn. for Evolutionary Economics [6872]
Assn. for Global Bus. [8016]
Assn. of Norwegian Economists [IO]
Assn. for Social Economics [6873]
Assn. for the Stud. of the Cuban Economy [8214]
Assn. of Young Economists of Georgia [IO]
Athena Alliance [17468]
Atlantic Assn. of Applied Economists [IO]
Atlantic Coun. of the U.S. [17014]
Atlas Economic Res. Found. [6874]
Australia New Zealand Soc. for Ecological Economics [IO]
Australian New Zealand - Amer. Chambers of Commerce [24248]
Australian Property Inst. [IO]
Australian Trade Commn. [24229]
Austrian Economic Assn. [IO]
Austrian Inst. of Economic Res. [IO]
Austrian Press and Info. Ser. [24230]
Austrian Trade Commn. [24232]
Bangladesh Economic Assn. [IO]
Bionomics Inst. [1171]
Brazil-U.S. Bus. Coun. [24266]
Brazilian-American Chamber of Commerce [24239]
Brazilian Govt. Trade Bur. of the Consulate Gen. of Brazil in New York [24240]
Brazilian Inst. of Economics [IO]
Bridging Nations [17861]
British Inst. of Energy Economics [IO]
British Trade Off. at Consulate-General [24241]
Bulgarian-American Chamber of Commerce [24243]
Bus. Alliance for Local Living Economies [887]
Bus. History Conf. [10098]
Bus. Leadership South Africa [IO]
Bus. and Professional Women's Found. [11084]
Bus. Roundtable [18402]
Cameroon-USA Chamber of Commerce [24249]
Canadian Assn. for Bus. Economics [IO]
Canadian Economics Assn. [IO]
Canadian Found. for Economic Educ. [IO]
Caribbean Assn. of Home Economists [IO]
Center for the Defense of Free Enterprise [17625]
Center for Economic Conversion [17423]
Center for Economic and Policy Res. [17469]
Center for Economic and Social Justice [12046]
Center for Neighborhood Enterprise [17208]
Center for Popular Economics [6875]
Center on Urban Poverty and Community Development [18377]
Centre for Economic Policy Res. [IO]
Centre for Latin Amer. Monetary Stud. [IO]
Chile-U.S. Chamber of Commerce [24270]
China Fed. of Indus. Economics [IO]
Chinese Amer. Assn. of Commerce [24308]
Chinese Chamber of Commerce of Hawaii [24309]
Chinese Economists Soc. [6876]
Chinese Economists Soc. [IO]
Colegio De Doctores En Ciencias Economicas Y Contadores Del Uruguay [IO]
Colegio De Economistas Del Paraguay [IO]
Colombian Amer. Assn. [24312]
Colombian Govt. Trade Bur. [24271]
Commercial Off. of Spain [24376]

Comm. for Economic Development [17455]
Comm. for the Economic Growth of Israel [24337]
Comm. for a Responsible Fed. Budget [18405]
Comm. to Restore the Constitution [17290]
Comm. on the Status of Women in the Economics Profession [5673]
Community Ser. [17214]
The Conf. Bd. [6877]
The Conf. Bd. [IO]
Conf. of Bus. Economists [6878]
Consumers for World Trade [17325]
Consuming Indus. Trade Action Coalition [771]
Corp. for Enterprise Development [17457]
Coun. of the Americas [24353]
Coun. on Food, Agricultural and Rsrc. Economics [4524]
Croatian-American Chamber of Commerce [24314]
Croatian Economic Assn. [IO]
Cuban Amer. Natl. Coun. [13167]
Czech-North Amer. Chamber of Commerce [24274]
Czech and Slovak-U.S. Bus. Coun. [2302]
Danish Amer. Chamber of Commerce [24316]
Danish Economic Soc. [IO]
DataCenter [18412]
Development Gp. for Alternative Policies [17835]
Domestic Technologies [16994]
E. F. Schumacher Soc. [16995]
EarthSharing [IO]
East Asian Economic Assn. - Hong Kong Off. [IO]
Econometric Soc. [7705]
Economic Affairs Bureau/Dollars and Sense [6879]
Economic History Assn. [8504]
Economic Policy Inst. [18441]
Economic Res. Coun. [IO]
Economic and Social Res. Found. [IO]
Economic Soc. of Australia [IO]
Economic Soc. of Finland [IO]
Economic Soc. of South Africa [IO]
Economics Soc. of Calgary [IO]
Emerging Markets Private Equity Assn. [1415]
Employment Policy Found. [12077]
Environmental Entrepreneurs [4392]
Estonian Amer. Chamber of Commerce and Indus. [24318]
Estonian Amer. Fund for Economic Educ. [8215]
Estonian Amer. Fund for Economic Educ. [IO]
Estonian Economic Assn. [IO]
Ethiopian Economic Assn. [IO]
European Assn. for Comparative Economic Stud. [IO]
European Assn. for Evolutionary Political Economy [IO]
European Economic Assn. [IO]
European Historical Economics Soc. [IO]
European Network on Debt and Development [IO]
European Soc. for Population Economics [IO]
European Travel Commn. [3916]
Fed. of Philippine Amer. Chambers of Commerce [24277]
Finnish Amer. Chamber of Commerce [24319]
Fisher Inst. for Medical Res. [17628]
Found. for the Advancement of Monetary Educ. [8423]
Found. for Economic Educ. [18406]
Found. Francisco Marroquin [9910]
Found. Francisco Marroquin [IO]
Found. for Latin-American Economic Res. [IO]
Found. for Rational Economics and Educ. [17293]
Found. for Teaching Economics [8216]
French-American Chamber of Commerce [24320]
Fund for an OPEN Soc. [17819]
Georgia-USA Chamber of Commerce [24278]
German Amer. Chamber of Commerce [24323]
German Marshall Fund of the U.S. [17890]
Ghana-USA Chamber of Commerce [24279]
Global Envision [12194]
Global Interdependence Center [18835]
Gp. of Thirty [1172]
Guatemala News and Info. Bur. [17680]
Hellenic-American Chamber of Commerce [24326]
History of Economics Soc. [10117]

Hong Kong Trade Development Coun. [24329]
Honolulu Japanese Chamber of Commerce [24348]
Hungarian Economic Assn. [IO]
Hungarian Sci. Soc. of Energy Economics [IO]
IFO Inst. for Economic Res. [IO]
Independent Americans [17294]
Indian Economic Assn. [IO]
Innovation Norway - U.S. [24283]
INSEE Info Ser. [IO]
Inst. for Community Economics [17221]
Inst. of Consumer Financial Educ. [8424]
Inst. of Developing Economies, Japan External Trade Org. [IO]
Inst. of Economic Affairs [IO]
Inst. for Economic Anal. [6880]
Inst. for Food and Development Policy [17795]
Inst. for Intl. Economic Co-operation [IO]
Inst. for Intl. Economics [IO]
Inst. for SocioEconomic Stud. [18458]
Inst. on Taxation and Economic Policy [17470]
Inst. for World Economics of the Hungarian Acad. of Sciences [IO]
Intercollegiate Stud. Inst. [17271]
Intermediate Tech. Development Gp. of North Am. [16997]
Intl. Assn. of Agricultural Economists [6881]
Intl. Assn. of Agricultural Economists [IO]
Intl. Assn. for Energy Economics [6956]
Intl. Assn. for Feminist Economics - Europe [IO]
Intl. Assn. for Feminist Economics - USA [IO]
Intl. Assn. for Feminist Economics - USA [6882]
Intl. Assn. for Res. in Income and Wealth [18407]
Intl. Atlantic Economic Soc. [6883]
Intl. Atlantic Economic Soc. [IO]
Intl. Center for Monetary and Banking Stud. [IO]
Intl. Centre of Res. and Info. on Public and Cooperative Economy [IO]
Intl. Economic Assn. [IO]
Intl. Economics and Finance Soc. [6884]
Intl. Economics and Philosophy Soc. [IO]
Intl. Inst. of Public Finance [IO]
Intl. Joseph A. Schumpeter Soc. [IO]
Intl. Open Finance Assn. [17584]
Intl. Sci. Assn. for World Economy and World Economics [IO]
Intl. Soc. of Commodity Sci. and Tech. [IO]
Intl. Soc. for Ecological Economics [IO]
Intl. Soc. for Ecological Economics [1173]
Intl. Soc. for New Institutional Economics [6885]
Intl. Soc. for New Institutional Economics [IO]
Intl. Soc. of Statistical Sci. [7710]
Iraqi Amer. Chamber of Commerce and Indus. [24285]
Irish Economic Assn. [IO]
Irish Economic Assn. [IO]
Italy-America Chamber of Commerce [24339]
Jamaica USA Chamber of Commerce [24287]
Japan Bus. Fed. [IO]
Japan Economic Policy Assn. [IO]
Japan External Trade Org. [24342]
Japan Soc. of Political Economy [IO]
Japanese Chamber of Commerce and Industry of Hawaii [24345]
Japanese Soc. for the History of Economic Thought [IO]
John M. Olin Found. [12047]
Joint Center for Political and Economic Stud. [7526]
Jordan Info. Bur. [24349]
Junior Achievement [8028]
Just Transition Alliance [24105]
The Korea Soc. [24350]
Korea Trade Promotion Center [24351]
Korean Economic Assn. [IO]
Lambda Alpha Intl. [24445]
Latin Amer. and Caribbean Economic Assn. [IO]
Latin Amer. Venture Capital Assn. [1431]
Lincoln Inst. for Res. and Educ. [16940]
Local Initiatives Support Corp. [17224]
Malaysian Economic Assn. [IO]
Manhattan Inst. for Policy Res. [18408]
Media Access Proj. [17182]
Middle East Policy Coun. [18063]
More Than Money [17471]

Reference to "IO" in place of a book number signifies that the association may be found in the 45th edition of International Organizations.

Natl. Assn. for Bus. Economics [6886]
Natl. Assn. of Chamber Ambassadors [789]
Natl. Assn. of Community Development Extension Professionals [11784]
Natl. Assn. for County Community and Economic Development [17225]
Natl. Assn. of Cuban Economists [IO]
Natl. Assn. of Forensic Economics [6044]
Natl. Assn. of Latino Elected and Appointed Officials [17706]
Natl. Bur. of Economic Res. [6887]
Natl. Center for Economic and Security Alternatives [18409]
Natl. Center on Educ. and the Economy [8283]
Natl. Chamber Found. [18464]
Natl. Community Development Assn. [17228]
Natl. Cong. of Amer. Indians [18096]
Natl. Coun. of Applied Economic Res. [IO]
Natl. Coun. of Asian Amer. Bus. Associations [774]
Natl. Coun. on Economic Educ. [8217]
Natl. Development Coun. [17463]
Natl. Economic Assn. [6888]
Natl. Economic Development and Law Center [17464]
Natl. Economists Club [6889]
Natl. Fed. of Enterprise Agencies [IO]
Natl. Inst. of Economic and Social Res. [IO]
Natl. Rural Economic Developers Assn. [18574]
Natl. Schools Comm. for Economic Educ. [8218]
Natl. United States-Arab Chamber of Commerce [24290]
Native Amer. Indian Info. and Trade Center [24358]
Native Amer. Rights Fund [18098]
Netherlands Chamber of Commerce in the U.S. [24360]
Netherlands Economic Inst. [IO]
New Am. Alliance [1169]
New Economics Found. [IO]
New Zealand Inst. of Economic Res. [IO]
NextGen Energy Coun. [6966]
Nigerian Economic Soc. [IO]
North American-Bulgarian Chamber of Commerce [24291]
North American-Chilean Chamber of Commerce [24307]
North Amer. Economics and Finance Assn. [6890]
Norwegian Amer. Chamber of Commerce - New York City [24292]
Omicron Delta Epsilon [24446]
Org. for Professionals in Regulatory Affairs [IO]
Org. for Economic Cooperation and Development [6866]
The Other Economic Summit of the U.S. [6891]
Pacific Stud. Center [6892]
Pakistan Chamber of Commerce USA [24364]
Peace Development Fund [18232]
People's Rights Fund [17144]
Phi Chi Theta [24422]
Phi Gamma Nu [24423]
Philadelphia Soc. [18475]
Philippine-Amer. Chamber of Commerce [24365]
Polish Amer. Chamber of Commerce [24293]
Polish Economic Soc. [IO]
Polish-U.S. Bus. Coun. [24366]
Political Economy and Economic History Soc. [IO]
Private Enterprise Res. Center [17635]
Proj. South: Inst. for the Elimination of Poverty and Genocide [17872]
Public Citizen Litigation Gp. [17342]
Res. Center for Economic Growth and Bus. Development [IO]
Romanian-U.S. Bus. Coun. [24370]
Royal Economic Soc. [IO]
Royal Economic Soc. of Friends of Tenerife [IO]
Russian-American Chamber of Commerce [24294]
Russian-American Chamber of Commerce in the USA [24371]
Scottish Economic Soc. [IO]
Serbian-American Chamber of Commerce [24373]
Seventh Generation Fund for Indian Development [18099]
Sierra Visions [12444]

Single Global Currency Assn. [17021]
Social Sciences Services and Resources [7656]
Social Venture Network [764]
Societe Royale D'Economie Politique De Belgique [IO]
Soc. for the Advancement of Economic Theory [6893]
Soc. for the Advancement of Socio-Economics [17472]
Soc. of Bus. Economists [IO]
Soc. for the Development of Austrian Economics [6894]
Soc. for Energy Educ. [6972]
Soc. of Govt. Economists [5674]
South African USA Chamber of Commerce [24295]
Southern Economic Assn. [6895]
Spain-United States Chamber of Commerce [24296]
Spanish Economic Assn. [IO]
Students in Free Enterprise [17637]
Swedish-American Chambers of Commerce, USA [24297]
Swedish Trade Coun. [3847]
Swiss-American Bus. Coun. [2314]
Trinidad and Tobago/USA Chamber of Commerce [24298]
Tunisian Economic Assn. [IO]
Turkish-American Chamber of Commerce and Indus. [24384]
Ukrainian Engineers' Soc. of Am. [7050]
Union of Economists of Slovenia [IO]
Union for Radical Political Economics [6896]
United for a Fair Economy [17473]
U.S. Assn. for Energy Economics [6974]
U.S.-Bahrain Bus. Coun. [2315]
U.S. Bus. and Indus. Coun. [17639]
U.S. Bus. and Indus. Coun. Educational Found. [18638]
U.S. Chamber of Commerce [24301]
U.S.-Cuba Trade Assn. [2316]
U.S. Hispanic Chamber of Commerce [24327]
U.S. Indian Amer. Chamber of Commerce [24331]
United States-Indonesia Soc. [775]
U.S.-Kazakhstan Bus. Assn. [2317]
United States-Mexico Chamber of Commerce [24302]
U.S. Soc. for Ecological Economics [6865]
U.S. Women's Chamber of Commerce [24389]
U.S.A. - Bus. and Indus. Advisory Comm. to the OECD [17466]
USA Engage [17467]
Venezuelan Amer. Assn. of the U.S. [24386]
Verein Fur Socialpolitik [IO]
Wales North Am. Bus. Chamber [24306]
Western Economic Assn. Intl. [6897]
Western Economic Assn. Intl. [IO]
William E. Simon Found. [17474]
Women Involved in Farm Economics [16960]
Women Leaders Online [18817]
Women's Economic Round Table [18484]
Women's Intl. Coalition for Economic Justice [17475]
Women's Intl. Coalition for Economic Justice [IO]
World Inst. for Development Economics Res. of the United Nations Univ. [IO]
World Policy Inst. [17620]
Economics of Allergy; Joint Coun. of Socio [★13602]
Economics Assn; Amer. Home [★12285]
Economics Assn; Amer. Real Estate and Urban [9050]
Economics Assn; Amer. Rehabilitation [16314]
Economics Assn; Pacific Coast [★6897]
Economics and Bus. Educ. Assn. [IO], Burgess Hill, United Kingdom
Economics; Center for the Stud. of [18704]
Economics; Coun. for Ethics in [★714]
Economics of Distribution Found. - Address unknown since 1995.
Economics and Educ; Found. for Rational [17293]
Economics and Educ; Found. for Res. in [★17293]
Economics and the Env; Found. for Res. on [4396]
Economics and Govt; Robert Brookings Graduate School of [★18424]

Economics, Inc; Community [12308]
Economics; Indian Soc. of Agricultural [IO]
Economics; Inst. for Community [17221]
Economics; Inst. for Govt. Res; Inst. of [★18424]
Economics; Inst. for Medical Record [★15098]
Economics; Intl. Soc. of Statistical Sci. in [★7710]
Economics and Mgt. - Hong Kong Natl. Comm; Intl. Assn. of Students in [IO]
Economics and Mgt. Soc; Mineral [6139]
Economics; Natl. Assn. of Forensic [6044]
Economics News Broadcasters Assn. [★3164]
Economics and Outcomes Res; Intl. Soc. for Pharmaco [15938]
Economics Program; Personal [★457]
Economics Soc. of Calgary [IO], Calgary, AB, Canada
Economics Soc; Canadian Agricultural [IO]
Economics Soc; History of [10117]
Economics; Women Involved in Farm [16960]
Economie et Humanisme [★IO]
Economies; Assn. for the Stud. of Soviet-Type [★6870]
Economies; Coalition for Environmentally Responsible [4544]
Economiesuisse, The Swiss Bus. Fed. [IO], Zurich, Switzerland
Economiques et Commerciales; Assn. Internationale Des Etudiants en Sciences [★8012]
Economists Allied for Arms Reduction [★17429]
Economists Allied for Arms Reduction [★IO]
Economists; Assn. of Environmental and Rsrc. [4359]
Economists Club; Natl. [6889]
Economists; Conf. of Bus. [6878]
Economists; Intl. Conf. of Agricultural [★6881]
Economists; Natl. Assn. of Bus. [★6886]
Economists; Natl. Assn. of Forensic [★6044]
Economists' Natl. Comm. on Monetary Policy - Address unknown since 1995.
Economists; North Amer. Assn. of Fisheries [1485]
Economists for Peace and Security [17429], c/o The Levy Inst., PO Box 5000, Annandale-on-Hudson, NY 12504, (845)758-0917
Economists for Peace and Security [IO], Annandale-on-Hudson, NY, United States
Economists Soc; Chinese Young [★6876]
Economists; Soc. of Govt. [5674]
Economy; Amer. Coun. for an Energy-Efficient [6938]
Economy; Carnegie Forum on Educ. and the [★8283]
Economy and Humanism [IO], Lyon, France
Economy; Natl. Center on Educ. and the [8283]
Economy; United for a Fair [17473]
Ecopravo-Lviv [★IO]
ECORYS Nederland BV [★IO]
ECOSENS [IO], Bucharest, Romania
ECOSOC [★5801]
Ecosystem Alliance; Greater [★4546]
Ecosystem Alliance; Northwest [★4546]
Ecosystem Res. Centers; Assn. of [4499]
ECOTERRA Intl. [IO], Nairobi, Kenya
Ecotourism Australia [IO], Brisbane, Australia
Ecotourism Soc. [★IO]
Ecotourism Soc. [★3829]
EcoVentures Intl. [4623], 1519 Connecticut Ave. NW, Ste. 301, Washington, DC 20036, (202)667-0802
EcoVentures Intl. [IO], Washington, DC, United States
EcoVillage at Ithaca [4557], 100 Rachel Carson Way, Ithaca, NY 14850, (607)272-5149
ECRI [15136], 5200 Butler Pike, Plymouth Meeting, PA 19462-1298, (610)825-6000
ECRI [IO], Plymouth Meeting, PA, United States
Ectodermal Dysplasias; Natl. Found. for [14468]
ECU Inst. [★IO]
Ecuador
Assn. of Natl. Advertisers [91]
Earth Day Network [4548]
Ecuadorian-American Chamber of Commerce of Greater Miami [24317]
Gabriel Garcia Moreno Memorial Assn. [11117]
Global Vaccine Awareness League [14559]
Natl. Dance Coun. of Am. [8189]
Pachamama Alliance [5163]

A star before a book entry number signifies that the name is not listed separately, but is mentioned within the entry.

Volunteering Ecuador Org. [IO]
Ecuador Concerns Comm. - Defunct.
Ecuador Volunteer [IO], Quito, Ecuador
Ecuadorean
  Arab World and Islamic Resources and School
    Services [9393]
  Ecuadorean Amer. Assn. [19034]
  Gabriel Garcia Moreno Memorial Assn. [11117]
Ecuadorean Amer. Assn. [19034], 30 Vesey St., Ste.
  506, New York, NY 10007, (212)233-7776
Ecuadorian-American Chamber of Commerce of
  Greater Miami [24317], 1390 Brickell Ave., Ste.
  220, Miami, FL 33131, (305)539-0010
Ecuadorian-American Chamber of Commerce -
  Quito [IO], Quito, Ecuador
Ecuadorian Assn. of Newspaper Publishers [IO],
  Quito, Ecuador
Ecuadorian Bible Soc. [IO], Quito, Ecuador
Ecuadorian Broadcasting Assn. [IO], Quito, Ecuador
Ecuadorian Consulting Companies' Assn. [IO],
  Quito, Ecuador
Ecuadorian Electron Microscopy Soc. [IO], Guayaq-
  uil, Ecuador
Ecuadorian Experiment in Intl. Living [IO], Quito,
  Ecuador
Ecuadorian Hotel Fed. [IO], Quito, Ecuador
Ecuadorian League Against Epilepsy [IO], Cuenca,
  Ecuador
Ecuadorian Olympic Comm. [IO], Guayaquil,
  Ecuador
Ecuadorian Soc. of Dermatology [IO], Guayaquil,
  Ecuador
Ecuatorian Assn. of Exporters [IO], Quito, Ecuador
Ecumenical
  Amer. Coun. of Christian Churches [19761]
  Amer. and Foreign Christian Union [19762]
  Amer. Forum for Jewish-Christian Cooperation
    [19887]
  Amer. Forum for Jewish-Christian Cooperation
    [IO]
  Bishops' Comm. for Ecumenical and Interreligious
    Affairs [19584]
  Canadian Centre for Ecumenism [IO]
  Canadian Coun. of Christians and Jews [IO]
  Canadian Coun. of Churches [IO]
  Center for Christian/Jewish Understanding of
    Sacred Heart Univ. [19888]
  Christian Bus. Men's Comm. [19771]
  Christian Century Found. [19772]
  Christian Communications, Inc. [19774]
  Christian Holiness Partnership [19779]
  Church Women United [20618]
  Churches Together in Britain and Ireland [IO]
  Churches Uniting in Christ [19889]
  Commn. of the Churches on Intl. Affairs [20094]
  Commn. on Intl. Relations [IO]
  Cong. of Natl. Black Churches [19890]
  Coun. on Christian Unity [19891]
  Diakonia of the Americas and Caribbean [IO]
  Ecclesiastical History Soc. [IO]
  Ecumenical Assn. of Academies and Laity Centres
    in Europe [IO]
  Ecumenical Celebrations [19892]
  Ecumenical Network for Youth Action [IO]
  Ecumenical Theological Seminary [19924]
  European Contact Gp. - Ecumenical Network for
    Economic and Social Action [IO]
  Faith at Work [19893]
  Fellowship in Prayer [19894]
  Fellowship in Prayer [IO]
  Found. DIAKONIA World Fed. of Diaconal As-
    sociations and Diaconal Communities [IO]
  Graymoor Ecumenical and Interreligious Institute
    [IO]
  Graymoor Ecumenical and Interreligious Inst.
    [19895]
  Hong Kong Christian Coun. [IO]
  Inst. for Ecumenical Res. [IO]
  The Interchurch Center [19896]
  Intercontinental Church Soc. [IO]
  Interfaith Encounter Assn. [IO]
  Intl. Assn. of Ministers Wives and Ministers
    Widows [IO]
  Intl. Assn. of Ministers Wives and Ministers
    Widows [19897]

Intl. Coun. of Christians and Jews [IO]
Intl. Coun. of Community Churches [19850]
Intl. Prayer Fellowship [19898]
Intl. Prayer Fellowship [IO]
John La Farge Inst. [19645]
Koinonia Found. [19899]
Latin Amer. Coun. of Churches [IO]
Light to the Nations [IO]
Liturgical Conf. [IO]
Liturgical Conf. [19900]
Missionary Soc. of Saint Paul the Apostle [19663]
Nanzan Inst. for Religion and Culture [IO]
Natl. Assn. of Diocesan Ecumenical Officers
  [19901]
Natl. Assn. of Ecumenical and Interreligious Staff
  [19902]
Natl. Cathedral Assn. [19903]
Natl. Conf. for Community and Justice [19904]
Natl. Coun. of Churches of Christ in the U.S.A.
  [19905]
North Amer. Acad. of Ecumenists [19906]
Order of Saint Andrew the Apostle [20073]
Paulist Memorial Soc. [19699]
Pilgrim Adventure [IO]
Prayers for Life [19907]
Reformed Ecumenical Coun. [19908]
Reformed Ecumenical Coun. [IO]
Retreats Intl. [19710]
Searching Together Educational Ministries [19909]
Secretariat for Catholic-Jewish Relations [19910]
Seventh Day Baptist World Fed. [19497]
Societas Liturgica [19911]
Societas Liturgica [IO]
Tantur Ecumenical Inst. [IO]
U.S. Conf. for the World Coun. of Churches
  [19912]
World Alliance of Reformed Churches [IO]
World Cong. of Faiths [IO]
World Coun. of Churches [IO]
Ecumenical Affairs; Bishops' Commn. for [★19584]
Ecumenical Assn. of Academies and Laity Centres in
  Europe [IO], Brussels, Belgium
Ecumenical Assn. of Professors [★19906]
Ecumenical Celebrations [19892], c/o Church
  Women United, The Interchurch Center, 475
  Riverside Dr., New York, NY 10115, (212)870-2347
Ecumenical Comm. on the Andes - Defunct.
Ecumenical Consultative Coun; Disciples [19848]
Ecumenical Inst. [★12350]
Ecumenical Inst; Graymoor [★19895]
Ecumenical Inst. for Theological Stud. [★IO]
Ecumenical and Interreligious Affairs; Bishops'
  Comm. for [19584]
Ecumenical Migration Centre [IO], Collingwood,
  Australia
Ecumenical Network for Youth Action [IO], Prague,
  Czech Republic
Ecumenical Officers; Natl. Assn. of Diocesan
  [19901]
Ecumenical Prog. on Central Am. and the Caribbean
  [17987], 1470 Irving St. NW, Washington, DC
  20010, (202)332-0292
Ecumenical Prog. on Central Am. and the Caribbean
  [IO], Washington, DC, United States
Ecumenical Prog. for Inter Amer. Commun. and Ac-
  tion [★IO]
Ecumenical Prog. for Inter Amer. Commun. and Ac-
  tion [★17987]
Ecumenical Relations of the Episcopal Church;
  Standing Commn. on [19974]
Ecumenical Resource Consultants - Address
  unknown since 2000.
Ecumenical Soc. of the Blessed Virgin Mary (U.S.
  Br.) - Address unknown since 2002.
Ecumenical Theological Center [★19924]
Ecumenical Theological Seminary [19924], 2930
  Woodward Ave., Detroit, MI 48201, (313)831-5200
Ecumenical Voluntary Service - Defunct.
Ecumenical Women's Caucus; Evangelical and
  [19978]
Ecumenical Youth Coun. in Europe [IO], Brussels,
  Belgium
Ecumenists; North Amer. Acad. of [19906]
Eczema Assn. of Australasia [IO], Cleveland,
  Australia

Eczema Assn. for Sci. and Educ. [★14208]
Eczema Soc; Natl. [IO]
Ed Bruce Fan Club - Defunct.
Eddie Cantor Appreciation Soc. - Defunct.
Eddie Rabbitt Fan Club - Address unknown since
  1999.
Eddy Family Assn. [20892], c/o Elaine Darrah,
  Treas., 322-A Trescony St., Santa Cruz, CA 95060-
  4753
Eddy Raven Fan Club [24882], PO Box 2476, Hend-
  ersonville, TN 37077, (615)452-7878
Eden Found. [IO], Falkenberg, Sweden
Eden Intl. Fan Club; Barbara [★24731]
Eden's Official Fan Club; Barbara [24731]
Edexcel Intl. [IO], London, United Kingdom
Edexcel Intl. Found. [★IO]
Edgar Allan Poe Soc. of Baltimore [9647], c/o Mr.
  Jeffrey A. Savoye, Sec.-Treas., 1610 Dogwood Hill
  Rd., Towson, MD 21286-1506, (410)821-1285
Edgar Cayce Found. [★7443]
Edgar Cayce Found. [★IO]
Edge Collectors Assn; Amer. [22612]
Edge-ucate [12057], PO Box 126, Englewood, CO
  80151-0126
Edge-ucate [IO], Englewood, CO, United States
EDGES Group - Address unknown since 2001.
EDI Coun; Natl. Dental [14176]
Edible Oils; Inst. of Shortening and [2851]
Edinburgh Architectural Assn. [IO], Edinburgh,
  United Kingdom
Edinburgh Bibliographical Soc. [IO], Edinburgh,
  United Kingdom
Edinburgh Chamber of Commerce [IO], Edinburgh,
  United Kingdom
Edinburgh Geological Soc. [IO], Edinburgh, United
  Kingdom
Edinburgh Mathematical Soc. [IO], Edinburgh,
  United Kingdom
Edinburgh Ski Touring Club [IO], Edinburgh, United
  Kingdom
Edison Birthplace Assn. [11110], c/o Edison
  Birthplace Museum, PO Box 451, Milan, OH
  44846, (419)499-2135
Edison Elec. Inst. [3956], 701 Pennsylvania Ave.
  NW, Washington, DC 20004-2696, (202)508-5000
Edison Elec. Inst. [IO], Washington, DC, United
  States
Edison Illuminating Companies; Assn. of [3952]
Edison Memorial Youth Fund; Charles [★8747]
Edison Pioneers - Defunct.
Edison Welding Inst. [7848], 1250 Arthur E. Adams
  Dr., Columbus, OH 43221-3585, (614)688-5000
Edison Youth Fund; Charles [★8747]
Edith Stein Guild [19621]
Edition Bookbinders of New York - Defunct.
Editions; Comm. on Scholarly [11167]
Editorial Assn; Freelance [★3111]
Editorial Assn; Natl. Broadcast [★3136]
Editorial Cartoonists; Assn. of Amer. [3092]
Editorial Collective; Feminist Teacher [9318]
Editorial Coun. of the Religious Press [★3205]
Editorial Found; Natl. [★8715]
Editorial Freelancers Assn. [3111], 71 W 23rd St.,
  4th Fl., New York, NY 10010-4181, (212)929-5400
Editorial Photographers [2996], PO Box 591811,
  San Francisco, CA 94159-1811
Editorial Projects in Educ. [8251], 6935 Arlington,
  Ste. 100, Bethesda, MD 20814, (301)280-3100
Editorial Services
  Assn. of Art Editors [3207]
  Natl. Resume Writers' Assn. [4063]
  Public Safety Writers Assn. [4068]
Editorial Writers; Natl. Conf. of [3136]
Editors
  Amer. Assn. of Dental Editors [3077]
  Amer. Cinema Editors [1376]
  Amer. Medical Writers Assn. [3082]
  Amer. Soc. of Bus. Publication Editors [3084]
  Amer. Soc. of Healthcare Publication Editors
    [14613]
  Amer. Soc. of Magazine Editors [3085]
  Amer. Soc. of Newspaper Editors [3086]
  Assoc. Church Press [3205]
  Assoc. Press Managing Editors [3090]
  Assn. of Art Editors [3207]

Reference to "IO" in place of a book number signifies that the association may be found in the 45th edition of International Organizations.

Assn. of Capitol Reporters and Editors [6181]
Assn. of Earth Sci. Editors [3093]
Assn. for Women in Sports Media [3097]
Coll. Fraternity Editors Assn. [24447]
Coun. of Sci. Editors [3108]
Dog Writers' Assn. of Am. [3110]
Editorial Freelancers Assn. [3111]
Editorial Photographers [2996]
Evangelical Press Assn. [20004]
Gridiron Club of Washington, DC [3114]
Intl. Assn. of Bus. Communicators [879]
Intl. Assn. of Crime Writers, North Amer. Br. [11175]
Intl. Pentecostal Press Assn. [3122]
Intl. Press Inst., Amer. Comm. [3123]
Intl. Soc. of Weekly Newspaper Editors [3125]
Intl. Travel Writers and Editors Assn. [3926]
Military Reporters and Editors [6182]
Natl. Assn. of Black Journalists [3129]
Natl. Assn. of Real Estate Editors [3132]
Natl. Assn. of Women Writers [11183]
Natl. Fed. of Hispanic Owned Newspapers [3240]
Natl. Pan-Hellenic Editors Conf. [24448]
Natl. Writers Assn. [3146]
Overseas Press Club of Am. [3154]
Religion News Ser. [3158]
Religion Newswriters Assn. [3159]
Sisters in Crime [4069]
Soc. of Amer. Bus. Editors and Writers [3161]
Soc. of Amer. Travel Writers [3162]
Soc. for Tech. Commun. [886]
Special Interest Gp. on Design of Commun. [6823]
William Dean Howells Soc. [9724]
Women's Natl. Book Assn. [3174]
World Assn. of Medical Editors [14303]
World Assn. of Medical Editors [IO]
Editors; Amer. Assn. of Agricultural Coll. [★4098]
Editors; Amer. Assn. of Dental [3077]
Editors; Amer. Assn. of Indus. [★879]
Editors; Amer. Assn. of Sunday and Feature [3079]
Editors; Amer. Cinema [1376]
Editors; Amer. Soc. of Bus. Press [★3084]
Editors; Amer. Soc. of Bus. Publication [3084]
Editors; Amer. Soc. of Magazine [3085]
Editors; Amer. Soc. of Newspaper [3086]
Editors; Assoc. Press Managing [3090]
Editors' Assn; Amer. Agricultural [3076]
Editors' Assn. of Canada [IO], Toronto, ON, Canada
Editors; Assn. of Earth Sci. [3093]
Editors Assn; Fed. [★5583]
Editors; Conf. of Biological [★3108]
Editors Conf; Sorority [★24448]
Editors; Coun. of Biology [★3108]
Editors; Coun. of Sci. [3108]
Editors; Intl. Coun. of Indus. [★879]
Editors; Investigative Reporters and [3126]
Editors; Natl. Assn. of Real Estate [3132]
Editors; Natl. Conf. of Real Estate [★3132]
Editors Organizing Comm. and Writers' and Publishers' Alliance for Disarmament - Address unknown since 1994.
Editors and Public Relations Conf; CIO [★3229]
Editors; Soc. of Bus. Magazine [★3084]
Editors; Soc. of Tech. Writers and [★886]
Editors and Writers Assn; Newspaper Food [★3094]
Editors and Writers; Soc. of Amer. Bus. [3161]
Edlisfraedifelag Islands [★IO]
Edmondson Family Assn. - Defunct.
Edmonton Area Narcotics Anonymous [IO], Edmonton, AB, Canada
Edmonton Chamber of Commerce/World Trade Center Edmonton [IO], Edmonton, AB, Canada
Edmonton Epilepsy Assn. [IO], Edmonton, AB, Canada
Edna Hibel Soc. [10503], PO Box 9721, Coral Springs, FL 33075, (954)731-6699
Edna Josephson Inst. of Ethics; Joseph and [17505]
EDP Auditors Assn. [★65]
EDP Auditors Assn. [★IO]
EDP Coun; Automotive Manufacturers [★70]
EdPress - The Assn. of Educational Publishers [★9009]
Edsel Club [21636], 19296 Tuckaway Ct., Fort Myers, FL 33903-1244

Edsel Owner's Club [21637], c/o Lois Roth, 1740 NW 3rd St., Gresham, OR 97030, (503)492-0807
EDU Assn; Overseas [★24043]
Educate People - Protect Innocent Children - Defunct.
Educating for Justice [9126], 601 Bangs Ave., Ste. 601, Asbury Park, NJ 07712, (732)988-7322
Educating for Justice [IO], Asbury Park, NJ, United States
Education
A. Philip Randolph Educal. Fund [17078]
AACSB Intl. - Assn. to Advance Collegiate Schools of Bus. [8010]
ABLE: Assn. for Better Living and Educ. Intl. [11756]
Academic Travel Abroad [8588]
Acad. of Criminal Justice Sciences [11850]
Acad. for Educational Development [8219]
Acad. for Educational Development [IO]
Acad. of Intl. Bus. [8011]
Acad. of Legal Stud. in Bus. [8757]
Acad. of Mgt. [8805]
Acad. of Marketing Sci. [8814]
Acad. of Security Educators and Trainers [9119]
Accordionists and Teachers Guild, Intl. [8897]
Accrediting Coun. for Continuing Educ. and Training [8145]
Accrediting Coun. on Educ. in Journalism and Mass Communications [8703]
Accuracy in Academia [8352]
ACE Fellows Prog. [7881]
ACT [9246]
Action Coalition for Media Educ. [18026]
ACUO [8341]
ACUTA: The Assn. for Communications Tech. Professionals in Higher Educ. [8548]
Adult Christian Educ. Found. [19913]
Adult Higher Educ. Alliance [7915]
Adult Learning Australia [IO]
Advisory Centre for Educ. [IO]
Advisory Coun. for the Educ. of Romany and Other Travellers [IO]
AFNA Natl. Educ. and Res. Fund [8045]
African Educational Res. Network [8220]
African Educational Res. Network [IO]
African Language Teachers Assn. [9207]
AFS Intercultural Programs [8589]
Agency for Instructional Tech. [8549]
AIESEC - U.S. [8012]
Aikido Yoshokai Assn. of North Am. [7943]
Algemene Centrale der Openbare Diensten Sector Onderwijs [IO]
ALI-ABA Comm. on Continuing Professional Educ. [8758]
All India Primary Teachers Fed. [IO]
Alliance for Academic Internal Medicine [8586]
Alliance for Excellent Educ. [9118]
Alliance for Intl. Educational and Cultural Exchange [8591]
Alliance for a Media Literate Am. [8830]
Alliance for the Separation of School and State [8221]
Alpha Chi [24498]
Alpha Chi Sigma [24428]
Alpha Delta Kappa [24449]
Alpha Delta Kappa [IO]
Alpha Epsilon [24395]
Alpha Epsilon Delta [24541]
Alpha Gamma Rho [24396]
Alpha Iota Sorority [24413]
Alpha Kappa Delta [24701]
Alpha Kappa Psi [24414]
Alpha Mu Gamma Natl. [24525]
Alpha Omega Alpha Honor Medical Soc. [24542]
Alpha Omega Intl. Dental Fraternity [24437]
Alpha Phi Sigma Honorary Scholastic Society [24450]
Alpha Psi Lambda Natl. [24615]
Alpha Sigma Nu [24500]
Alpha Tau Delta [24559]
Alpha Zeta [24397]
Alpha Zeta Omega [24567]
Alston Wilkes Veterans Home [11852]
Alternative Educ. Rsrc. Org. [8222]
Amateur Movie Makers Assn. [22418]

Ambrose Monell Found. [13110]
Amer. Acad. of Advt. [7919]
Amer. Acad. of Kinesiology and Physical Educ. [8978]
Amer. Acad. for Liberal Educ. [8775]
Amer. Acad. of Ministry [19914]
Amer. Acad. of Religion [8223]
Amer. Acad. in Rome [IO]
Amer. Acad. of Teachers of Singing [8898]
Amer. Alliance for Hea., Physical Educ., Recreation and Dance [8979]
Amer. Assembly [18418]
Amer. Associates, Ben-Gurion Univ. of the Negev [8673]
Amer. Assn. for Adult and Continuing Educ. [8146]
Amer. Assn. for Affirmative Action [12066]
Amer. Assn. for Agricultural Educ. [7933]
Amer. Assn. for Career Educ. [8046]
Amer. Assn. for Chinese Stud. [8074]
Amer. Assn. of Christian Schools [7875]
Amer. Assn. of Classified School Employees [24041]
Amer. Assn. of Colleges of Nursing [8842]
Amer. Assn. of Colleges for Teacher Educ. [9208]
Amer. Assn. for Collegiate Independent Stud. [7944]
Amer. Assn. of Collegiate Registrars and Admissions Officers [7910]
Amer. Assn. of Community Colleges [8117]
Amer. Assn. for Correctional and Forensic Psychology [11853]
Amer. Assn. of Cosmetology Schools/Cosmetology Educators of Am. [8160]
Amer. Assn. of Dispensing Ophthalmologists [15658]
Amer. Assn. for Employment in Educ. [8994]
Amer. Assn. for Gifted Children [8463]
Amer. Assn. for Higher Educ. [8478]
Amer. Assn. of Human Design Practitioners [1151]
Amer. Assn. of Individual Investors [8422]
Amer. Assn. of Physics Teachers [8993]
Amer. Assn. of Presidents of Independent Colleges and Universities [8534]
Amer. Assn. of School Administrators [7882]
Amer. Assn. of School Personnel Administrators [7883]
Amer. Assn. of State Colleges and Universities [8096]
Amer. Assn. of Teachers of Arabic [7958]
Amer. Assn. of Teachers of French [8448]
Amer. Assn. of Teachers of German [8460]
Amer. Assn. of Teachers of Slavic and East European Languages [9125]
Amer. Assn. of Teachers of Spanish and Portuguese [8725]
Amer. Assn. of Teachers of Turkic Languages [9282]
Amer. Assn. of Teaching and Curriculum [9209]
Amer. Assn. for Ukrainian Stud. [8650]
Amer. Assn. of Univ. Administrators [7884]
Amer. Assn. of Univ. Professors [9022]
Amer. Assn. of Univ. Women [9311]
Amer. Assn. of Univ. Women Educational Found. [9312]
Amer. Assn. for Vocational Instructional Materials [9298]
Amer. Assn. for Women in Community Colleges [9313]
Amer. Bd. of Bioanalysis [7235]
Amer. Bd. of Funeral Ser. Educ. [8896]
Amer. Camp Assn. [23268]
Amer. Catholic Philosophical Assn. [8965]
Amer. Ceramic Soc. [6657]
Amer. Chem. Soc. [6664]
Amer. Classical League [8726]
Amer. Coll. and Career Counseling Center [7911]
Amer. Coll. of Musicians [8899]
Amer. Collegiate Retailing Assn. [8815]
Amer. Comm. for Shenkar Coll. [8674]
Amer. Conf. of Academic Deans [7885]
Amer. Correctional Assn. [11854]
Amer. Coun. for Constr. Educ. [8141]
Amer. Coun. on Educ. [8224]
Amer. Coun. on Intl. Intercultural Educ. [8651]

A star before a book entry number signifies that the name is not listed separately, but is mentioned within the entry.

Amer. Coun. on Rural Special Educ. [9137]
Amer. Coun. on Schools and Colls. [8225]
Amer. Coun. on the Teaching of Foreign Languages [8727]
Amer. Councils for Intl. Educ. [8226]
Amer. Councils for Intl. Educ. [IO]
Amer. Criminal Justice Assn. (Lambda Alpha Epsilon) [11855]
Amer. Debate Assn. [9151]
Amer. Dental Educ. Assn. [8193]
Amer. Distance Educ. Consortium [8227]
Amer. Driver and Traffic Safety Educ. Assn. [8210]
Amer. Educ. Finance Assn. [8342]
Amer. Educational Res. Assn. [9053]
Amer. Educational Stud. Assn. [8228]
Amer. Educational Stud. Assn. [IO]
Amer. Escrow Assn. [1398]
Amer. Fed. of School Administrators [7886]
Amer. Fed. of Teachers [24042]
Amer. Fired Arts Alliance [9542]
Amer. Forensic Assn. [9152]
Amer. Forum for Global Educ. [8593]
Amer. Friends of the Alliance Israelite Universelle [8675]
Amer. Hackney Horse Soc. [4820]
Amer. Hellenic Educational Progressive Assn. [19083]
Amer. History Forum and Civil War Educ. Assn. [8500]
Amer. Humanics [8743]
Amer. Hungarian Educators' Assn. [8533]
Amer. Indian Graduate Center [8426]
Amer. Indian Higher Educ. Consortium [8935]
Amer. Indian Inst. [10733]
Amer. Indian Res. and Development [8464]
Amer. Inst. of Biological Sciences [6560]
Amer. Inst. for Foreign Stud. [8652]
Amer. Inst. for Foreign Stud. Found. [8595]
Amer. Inst. of Indian Stud. [8541]
Amer. Inst. of Musical Stud. [8900]
Amer. Institutes for Res. [7560]
Amer. Institutes for Res. in the Behavioral Sciences [6523]
Amer. Jail Assn. [11856]
Amer. Labor Education Center [8720]
Amer. Literacy Coun. [8785]
Amer. Mathematical Assn. of Two-Year Colleges [8821]
Amer. Matthay Assn. [8901]
Amer. Medical Assn. Found. [8843]
Amer. Medical Student Assn. [8844]
Amer. Montessori Soc. [8891]
Amer. Morgan Horse Assn. [4831]
Amer. Overseas Schools Historical Soc. [10012]
Amer. Portuguese Stud. Assn. [9004]
Amer. Pre-Veterinary Medical Assn. [16774]
Amer. Press Inst. [8704]
Amer. Printing House for the Blind [16829]
Amer. Psychological Assn. of Graduate Students [16129]
Amer. Real Estate Soc. [9049]
Amer. Real Estate and Urban Economics Assn. [9050]
Amer. Recorder Teachers Assn. [8902]
Amer. Risk and Insurance Assn. [8574]
Amer. School Band Directors' Assn. [8903]
Amer. School Counselor Assn. [8163]
Amer. Schools Assn. [8164]
Amer. Shorin Kempo Karate Assn. [23581]
Amer. Soc. for Bioethics and Humanities [8845]
Amer. Soc. for Engg. Educ. [8366]
Amer. Soc. for Microbiology [6565]
Amer. Soc. for Muslim Advancement [10245]
Amer. Soc. for Technion-Israel Inst. of Tech. [8677]
Amer. Sports Inst. [8229]
Amer. String Teachers Assn. [8904]
Amer. Student Dental Assn. [8194]
Amer. Tech. Educ. Assn. [9228]
Amer. TeleEdCommunications Alliance [7766]
Amer. Textbook Coun. [9258]
Amer. Type Culture Coll. [6567]
Amer. Univ. in Moscow [8597]
Americanism Educational League [17623]

AMISTAD Am. [8502]
Anglican Assn. of Biblical Scholars [19449]
Anglo Danish Soc. [IO]
Anthroposophical Soc. in Canada [IO]
Anthroposophical Soc. in Great Britain [IO]
Appaloosa Horse Club [4857]
Approved Driving Instructors Natl. Joint Coun. [IO]
Aquatic Resources Educ. Assn. [7956]
Arab Bur. of Educ. for the Gulf States [IO]
Armenian Educational Found. [8343]
Armenian Natl. Educ. Comm. [7964]
Arnold Air Soc. [24546]
Arthur Vining Davis Foundations [12048]
Arts Educ. Partnership [7966]
ASA Intl. [8230]
ASA Intl. [IO]
Asia-Pacific Programme of Educational Innovation for Development [IO]
Asia and Pacific Regional Bur. for Educ. [IO]
Asian Amer. Curriculum Proj. [8598]
ASPECT Found. [8599]
ASPIRA Assn. [8231]
Assoc. Colleges of the Midwest [8097]
Assoc. Collegiate Press [8705]
Assoc. Schools of Constr. [8143]
Associates in Cultural Exchange [8176]
Assn. of Academic Hea. Centers [14546]
Assn. of Accredited Naturopathic Medical Colleges [8943]
Assn. for the Advancement of Computing in Educ. [9237]
Assn. for the Advancement of Intl. Educ. [8640]
Assn. for the Advancement of Sustainability in Higher Educ. [8479]
Assn. of African Stud. Programs [7928]
Assn. of Amer. Colleges and Universities [8098]
Assn. of Amer. Intl. Colleges and Universities [8641]
Assn. of Amer. Law Schools [8760]
Assn. of Amer. Medical Colleges [8846]
Assn. of Amer. Universities [8099]
Assn. of Amer. Univ. Presses [8550]
Assn. of Amer. Veterinary Medical Colleges [9293]
Assn. for Applied Interactive Multimedia [2666]
Assn. of Arts Admin. Educators [7967]
Assn. for Asian Stud. [7983]
Assn. for Assessment in Counseling and Educ. [9247]
Assn. of Asthma Educators [16355]
Assn. for the Behavioral Sciences and Medical Educ. [6527]
Assn. for Biblical Higher Educ. [8080]
The Assn. of Boarding Schools [9018]
Assn. for Borderlands Stud. [8653]
Assn. for Bus. Simulation and Experiential Learning [8015]
Assn. for Canadian Stud. in the U.S. [8043]
Assn. for Career and Tech. Educ. [9300]
Assn. for Career and Tech. Educ. Res. [9301]
Assn. of Catholic Colleges and Universities [8051]
Assn. of Catholic Institutes of Educ. [IO]
Assn. of Chairmen of Departments of Mechanics [8829]
Assn. for Childhood Educ. Intl. [8064]
Assn. of Christian Schools Intl. [8081]
Assn. of Classical and Christian Schools [9089]
Assn. for Clinical Pastoral Educ. [19915]
Assn. of Coll. Honor Societies [24501]
Assn. of Coll. Unions Intl. [9166]
Assn. of Coll. and Univ. Auditors [7888]
Assn. of Collegiate Schools of Architecture [7959]
Assn. of Collegiate Schools of Planning [9285]
Assn. for Commun. Admin. [9154]
Assn. for Community Based Education [8123]
Assn. for Community Coll. Trustees [8118]
Assn. of Community and Comprehensive Schools [IO]
Assn. of Community Tribal Schools [8936]
Assn. of Concerned African Scholars [16926]
Assn. for Continuing Dental Educ. [8195]
Assn. for Continuing Higher Educ. [8148]
Assn. for Continuing Legal Educ. [8762]
Assn. of Cooperative Educators [8156]
Assn. for Core Texts and Courses [8776]
Assn. for Counselor Educ. and Supervision [8165]

Assn. of Departments of English [8374]
Assn. of Departments of Foreign Languages [8728]
Assn. for the Development of Educ. in Africa [IO]
Assn. for Direct Instruction [8232]
Assn. for the Educ. of Children with Medical Needs [8072]
Assn. for Educ. in Journalism and Mass Commun. [8706]
Assn. for Educational Activity [IO]
Assn. for Educational Communications and Tech. [8551]
Assn. of Educational Psychologists [IO]
Assn. of Educational Publishers [9009]
Assn. of Environmental and Engg. Geologists [7130]
Assn. of Episcopal Colleges [8397]
Assn. for Experiential Educ. [8411]
Assn. of Fraternity Advisors [24475]
Assn. of Free Methodist Educational Institutions [8447]
Assn. for Gender Equity Leadership in Educ. [8399]
Assn. for Gen. and Liberal Stud. [8777]
Assn. for Gerontology Educ. in Social Work [8461]
Assn. for Gerontology in Higher Educ. [8462]
The Assn. for the Gifted [8465]
Assn. for Global Bus. [8016]
Assn. Global View [8017]
Assn. of Governing Boards of Universities and Colleges [7889]
Assn. of Graduate Liberal Stud. Programs [8778]
Assn. of Graduate Schools in Assn. of Amer. Universities [7890]
Assn. on Higher Educ. and Disability [8201]
Assn. for Intl. Agriculture and Rural Development [7935]
Assn. of Intl. Educ. Administrators [7891]
Assn. for Intl. Practical Training [8601]
Assn. of Jesuit Colleges and Universities [8052]
Assn. for Jewish Stud. [8684]
Assn. for Lib. and Info. Sci. Educ. [8782]
Assn. of Lutheran Secondary Schools [8801]
Assn. for Machine Translation in the Americas [7807]
Assn. for Media-Based Continuing Educ. for Engineers [8367]
Assn. for Medical Educ. and Res. in Substance Abuse [8849]
Assn. of Mercy Colleges [8053]
Assn. of Military Colleges and Schools of the U.S. [8883]
Assn. of Minority Hea. Professions Schools [8850]
Assn. Montessori International-U.S.A. [8892]
Assn. for Moral Educ. [8233]
Assn. of Nepal and Himalayan Stud. [8944]
Assn. for Non-Traditional Students in Higher Educ. [7916]
Assn. of NROTC Colleges and Universities [8884]
Assn. of Nutrition Departments and Programs [8947]
Assn. of Optometric Educators [8851]
Assn. of Orthodox Jewish Teachers [9210]
Assn. of Presbyterian Colleges and Universities [9005]
Assn. of Professional Schools of Intl. Affairs [8654]
Assn. for Professionals in Services for Adolescents [IO]
Assn. of Professors of Medicine [8853]
Assn. of Professors of Secondary and Higher Educ. [IO]
Assn. on Programs for Female Offenders [11857]
Assn. Promoting Educ. and Conservation in Amazonia [5294]
Assn. for the Promotion of Tourism to Africa [3826]
Assn. of Psychology Postdoctoral and Internship Centers [8854]
Assn. for Religion and Intellectual Life [19916]
Assn. for Sandwich Educ. and Training [IO]
Assn. of School Bus. Officials Intl. [7892]
Assn. of Schools of Journalism and Mass Commun. [7893]

Reference to "IO" in place of a book number signifies that the association may be found in the 45th edition of International Organizations.

Assn. of Secondary Teachers Ireland [IO]
Assn. for Skilled and Tech. Sciences [8542]
Assn. for the Social Sci. Stud. of Jewry [8685]
Assn. of Specialized and Professional Accreditors [1174]
Assn. of Specialty Professors [8587]
Assn. for Spiritual, Ethical and Religious Values in Counseling [8166]
Assn. of State Correctional Administrators [11858]
Assn. for the Stud. of Free Institutions [8481]
Assn. for the Stud. of Higher Educ. [8482]
Assn. for the Stud. of the Worldwide African Diaspora [7929]
Assn. for Supervision and Curriculum Development [8178]
Assn. for Surgical Educ. [8856]
Assn. of Teacher Educators [9212]
Assn. of Teachers of Japanese [8682]
Assn. of Teachers of Tech. Writing [9332]
Assn. for Tech. in Music Instruction [8905]
Assn. of Thai Professionals in Am. and Canada [19406]
Assn. for Theatre in Higher Educ. [9262]
Assn. of Theatre Movement Educators [9263]
Assn. of Theological Schools in the U.S. and Canada [9270]
Assn. of Univ. Architects [6472]
Assn. for Univ. and Coll. Counseling Center Directors [8167]
Assn. of Univ. Leaders for a Sustainable Future [8483]
Assn. of Univ. Programs in Hea. Admin. [8857]
Assn. of Univ. Res. Parks [9054]
Assn. of Univ. Summer Sessions [9199]
Assn. of Univ. Tech. Managers [5838]
Assn. for World Travel Exchange [8602]
Astronaut Scholars Honor Soc. [24584]
Athena Alliance [17468]
Augustinian Secondary Educational Assn. [8054]
Australian Coll. of Educators [IO]
Australian Educ. Union [IO]
Australian and New Zealand Stud. Assn. of North Amer. [8484]
Aviation Technician Educ. Coun. [7921]
Awake In Am. [18601]
Bahamas Union of Teachers [IO]
Barbados Secondary Teachers' Union [IO]
Barbados Union of Teachers [IO]
Belize Natl. Teachers' Union [IO]
Benjamin Franklin Educ. Found. [8234]
Bermuda Union of Teachers [IO]
Beta Alpha Psi [24391]
Beta Beta Beta [24408]
Beta Gamma Sigma [24415]
Beta Gamma Sigma Alumni [24416]
Beta Phi Mu [24532]
Beta Sigma Kappa [24562]
Bhojpuri Assn. of North Am. [10299]
Bibliographical Soc. of Australia and New Zealand [IO]
Big Picture Company [8353]
Bighelp for Educ. [IO]
Bishops' Comm. on Priestly Formation [19917]
Black Alliance for Educational Options [8322]
Boarding Schools Assn. [IO]
Books for the Barrios [IO]
Books for the Barrios [12049]
Books for a Better World [8235]
Books for a Better World [IO]
Boston Theological Inst. [9271]
Boys Town Jerusalem Found. of Am. [13473]
Brahman Samaj of North Am. [9998]
Braille Revival League [16839]
Brazilian Stud. Assn. [8604]
Breakthrough Collaborative [8236]
British Educational Communications and Tech. Agency [IO]
British Educational Res. Assn. [IO]
British Learning Assn. [IO]
British Schools and Universities Found. [8102]
British Universities North Am. Club [8606]
Broadcast Educ. Assn. [8001]
Broadcast Found. of College/University Students [8002]
Business-Higher Educ. Forum [8008]

Bus. Professionals of Am. [9302]
Cambridge in Am. [9284]
Camille and Henry Dreyfus Found. [8237]
Campus Compact [8238]
Campus Ministry Women [19918]
Canadian Alliance of Home Schoolers [IO]
Canadian Assn. for Distance Educ. [IO]
Canadian Assn. of Independent Schools [IO]
Canadian Assn. of Univ. Teachers [IO]
Canadian Coun. for the Advancement of Educ. [IO]
Canadian Coun. for Exceptional Children [IO]
Canadian Educ. Assn. [IO]
Canadian Educ. Centre Network [IO]
Canadian Educational Standards Inst. [IO]
Canadian Home and School Fed. [IO]
Canadian Soc. for the Stud. of Educ. [IO]
Canon Collins Educational Trust for Southern Africa [IO]
Career Coll. Assn. [9303]
Career Planning and Adult Development Network [12070]
Caribbean Stud. Assn. [8050]
Carnegie Corp. of New York [8239]
Carnegie Found. for the Advancement of Teaching [9214]
Carrie Estelle Doheny Found. [13156]
Catching the Dream [8427]
Catholic Acad. of Sciences in the U.S.A. [19919]
Catholic Biblical Assn. of Am. [9272]
Catholic Campus Ministry Assn. [19595]
Catholic Healthcare Audit Network [8240]
Catholic Negro-Amer. Mission Bd. [19601]
CDS Intl. [8019]
Cecchetti Coun. of Am. [8183]
Center for Aviation Res. and Educ. [5537]
Center for Commercial-Free Public Educ. [8241]
Center for Commun. [8003]
Center of Concern [17747]
Center for Consumer Affairs, Univ. of Wisconsin-Milwaukee [17313]
Center for Ecoliteracy [4501]
Center for Environmental Stud. [4538]
Center for Global Educ. [8662]
Center for Intl. Initiatives [8745]
Center for Investigation and Development of Educ. [IO]
Center for the Ministry of Teaching [19920]
Center for Occupational Res. and Development [8354]
Center for Philosophy, Law, Citizenship [18271]
Center for School Change [8242]
Center for Sci. in the Public Interest [17314]
Center for Social Stud. Educ. [9127]
Center for Stud. in Criminal Justice [11859]
Center for the Stud. of the Coll. Fraternity [24476]
Center for the Stud. of Democracy [IO]
Center for the Stud. of Human Rights [17750]
Central Agency for Jewish Educ. [19180]
Central and Eastern European Networking Assn. [IO]
Central Off. Executives Assn. of Natl. Pan-Hellenic Conf. [24477]
Central Org. for Jewish Educ. [8688]
Centre for Animation, Development, and Res. in Educ. [IO]
Challenged Conquistadors [11930]
CHALLENGES - Youth Action for Sustainable Development [IO]
Character Educ. Partnership [17476]
Chess in the Schools [21945]
Chi Eta Phi Sorority [24560]
Chicano Family Center [17701]
Children's Creative Response to Conflict Prog. [11684]
Children's Grief Educ. Assn. [12265]
China Times Cultural Found. [7984]
Chinese-Amer. Educational Found. [8428]
Chinese Historians in the U.S. [8503]
Chinese Language Assn. of Secondary-Elementary Schools [8075]
Chinese Language Teachers Assn. [8076]
Chinese School Assn. in the U.S. [9090]
Christian Bros. Conf. [19921]
Christian Coll. Consortium [8082]

Christian Educ. [IO]
Christian Educators Assn. Intl. [IO]
Christian Educators Assn. Intl. [19922]
Christian Educators Fellowship of the United Methodist Church [19923]
Christian Home Educators Assn. of California [8516]
Christian Literacy Associates [8788]
Christian Schools Intl. [8083]
Christian Teachers Fed. of Belgium [IO]
Citizens for Educational Freedom [8338]
Clean Islands Intl. [4541]
Clinical Legal Educ. Assn. [8763]
Close Up Found. [17071]
Coalition for the Advancement of Jewish Educ. [8689]
Coalition of Essential Schools [8180]
Coll. Band Directors Natl. Assn. [8906]
The Coll. Bd. [9248]
Coll. Consortium for Intl. Stud. [8103]
Coll. English Assn. [8375]
Coll. Language Assn. [8729]
Coll. Media Advisers [8708]
Coll. Music Soc. [8907]
Coll. Parents of Am. [8485]
Coll. Reading and Learning Assn. [9042]
Coll. Summit [8486]
Coll. Theology Soc. [9273]
Coll. and Univ. Professional Assn. for Human Resources [8962]
College-University Rsrc. Inst. [9055]
Columbia Scholastic Press Advisers Assn. [9010]
Columbia Scholastic Press Assn. [9011]
Commn. on Accreditation of Allied Hea. Educ. Programs [8832]
Comm. on Accreditation for Opthalmic Medical Personnel [8834]
Comm. on Capacity Building Sci. [9099]
Comm. for Educ. Funding [8345]
Comm. on Institutional Cooperation [8104]
Comm. on Public Doublespeak [17173]
Comm. for a Responsible Fed. Budget [18405]
The Comm. for Western Civilization [8243]
Common Destiny Alliance [8244]
Commonwealth of Learning [IO]
Communities in Schools [8323]
Community Coll. Baccalaureate Assn. [8119]
Community Coll. Journalism Assn. [8710]
Community Colleges for Intl. Development [8607]
Community Development Soc. [17213]
Community Ser. [17214]
Comparative and Intl. Educ. Soc. [8655]
Comprehensive Hea. Educ. Found. [8860]
Cmpt. Assisted Language Instruction Consortium [8553]
Cmpt. Sci. Teachers Assn. [8130]
Computers for Children [8137]
Concerned Educators Against Forced Unionism - A Special Proj. of the Natl. Right to Work Legal Defense Found. [17971]
Conf. on Christianity and Literature [8799]
Conf. on Coll. Composition and Commun. [8376]
Conf. on English Educ. [8377]
Consciousness-Based Educ. Assn. [9029]
Consortium for the Advancement of Private Higher Educ. [8105]
Consortium of Coll. and Univ. Media Centers [8554]
Consortium on Financing Higher Educ. [9057]
Consortium of Institutions for Development and Res. in Educ. in Europe [IO]
Consortium for North Amer. Higher Educ. Collaboration [8487]
Consortium for School Networking [8555]
Consumers Educ. and Protective Assn. [17323]
Consumers for World Trade [17325]
Cooperative Educ. and Internship Assn. [8157]
Cordell Hull Found. for Intl. Educ. [8656]
Corporate and Found. Relations [12075]
Correctional Educ. Assn. [11862]
Coun. on Accreditation of Nurse Anesthesia Educational Programs [8835]
Coun. of Administrators of Special Educ. [9139]
Coun. for Adult and Experiential Learning [8412]
Coun. for the Advancement of Standards in Higher Educ. [9177]

A star before a book entry number signifies that the name is not listed separately, but is mentioned within the entry.

Coun. for Advancement and Support of Educ. [8245]
Coun. for Agricultural Sci. and Tech. [7936]
Coun. for Aid to Educ. [8346]
Coun. for Amer. Private Educ. [9020]
Coun. on Career for Minorities [8047]
Coun. of Chief State School Officers [8246]
Coun. for Children with Behavioral Disorders [9140]
Coun. for Christian Colleges and Universities [8084]
Coun. of Christian Scholarly Societies [8085]
Coun. of Colleges of Arts and Sciences [7971]
Coun. for Educ. in the Commonwealth [IO]
Coun. of Educational Fac. Planners, Intl. [8335]
Coun. for Elementary Sci. Intl. [9100]
Coun. for European Stud. [8404]
Coun. on Governmental Relations [9058]
Coun. of Graduate Schools [8488]
Coun. of the Great City Schools [9289]
Coun. for Higher Educ. Accreditation [8247]
Coun. for Indian Educ. [8937]
Coun. for Interior Design Accreditation [8584]
Coun. on Intl. Educational Exchange - USA [8608]
Coun. on Intl. Exchange of Scholars/Institute of Intl. Educ. [8609]
Coun. on Islamic Educ. [8669]
Coun. for Jewish Educ. [8690]
Coun. for Learning Disabilities [12490]
Coun. on Library-Media Technicians [8783]
Coun. for a Livable World Educ. Fund [17426]
Coun. on Medical Educ. of the Amer. Medical Assn. [8836]
Coun. on Medical Student Educ. in Pediatrics [8861]
Coun. of Ministers of Educ., Canada [IO]
Coun. of Nordic Teachers' Unions [IO]
Coun. on Occupational Educ. [8248]
Coun. of Parent Attorneys and Advocates [9142]
Coun. for Res. in Music Educ. [8908]
Coun. for Rsrc. Development [8347]
Coun. on Sexual Orientation and Gender Expression [9132]
Coun. on Social Work Educ. [9133]
Coun. of Societies for the Stud. of Religion [9274]
Coun. for Spiritual and Ethical Educ. [8536]
Coun. for Standards in Human Ser. Educ. [9130]
Coun. on Standards for Intl. Educational Travel [8610]
Coun. of Teachers of Southeast Asian Languages [7990]
Coun. on Undergraduate Res. [9059]
Counseling Assn. for Humanistic Educ. and Development [8527]
Cowles Charitable Trust [9564]
Creative Educ. Found. [8173]
Cross Cultural Collaborative [8177]
The Culinary Trust [8174]
Cum Laude Soc. [24503]
CUMREC [8249]
Dance Educators of Am. [8184]
Dance Masters of Am. [8186]
Danforth Found. [8250]
Danish Fed. of Teachers of Tech. Educ. [IO]
Danish Natl. Fed. of Early Childhood Teachers and Youth Educators [IO]
Danish Natl. Union of Upper Secondary School Teachers [IO]
Danish Union of Teachers [IO]
Decision Sciences Inst. [8021]
Delphi Found. [24451]
Delta Epsilon Sigma [24504]
Delta Kappa Epsilon [24623]
Delta Lambda Phi Natl. Social Fraternity [24624]
Delta Mu Delta Honor Soc. [24418]
Delta Omega [24582]
Delta Omicron [24550]
Delta Phi Epsilon, Professional Foreign Ser. Fraternity [24472]
Delta Phi Epsilon Professional Foreign Ser. Sorority [24473]
Delta Phi Upsilon [24431]
Delta Pi Epsilon [24426]
Delta Psi Omega [24444]
Delta Sigma Delta [24438]

Delta Theta Phi [24527]
Design and Tech. Assn. [IO]
Designs for Change [9035]
Direct Marketing Educational Found. [8816]
Direction Sports [13482]
Distance Educ. and Training Coun. [8517]
Distributive Educ. Clubs of Am. [8817]
Div. on Career Development and Transition [9143]
Div. for Early Childhood of the Coun. for Exceptional Children [9144]
Division of Higher Educ., Christian Church-Disciples of Christ [19854]
DM - Fagforening for hojtuddannede [IO]
Dominica Assn. of Teachers [IO]
Dow Jones Newspaper Fund [8711]
Driving School Assn. of the Americas [8211]
E-quip Africa [12704]
EAPE/Campolo Ministries - Evangelical Assn. for the Promotion of Educ. [20330]
Earl Warren Legal Training Prog. [8765]
Earthwatch Inst. [8413]
Eco-Animal Allies [11773]
Ecumenical Theological Seminary [19924]
Edge-ucate [12057]
Editorial Projects in Educ. [8251]
Educating for Justice [9126]
Education-A-Must [12056]
The Educ. Coalition [8325]
Educ. Commn. of the States [8252]
Educ. Credit Union Coun. [1109]
Educ. and Culture Union [IO]
Educ. Development Center [IO]
Educ. Development Center [8253]
Educ. Pioneers [9178]
Educ. and Sci. Employees' Union of Russia [IO]
Educ. and Sci. Trade Union of Slovenia [IO]
Educ. Turnkey Inst. [8557]
Educ. Writers Assn. [3112]
Educational Communications [8386]
Educational Equity Center [8400]
Educational Found. for Women in Accounting [9316]
Educational Leadership Inst. [8746]
Educational Leadership Prog. [8779]
Educational Planning Inst. [8998]
Educational Records Bur. [9249]
Educational Res. Associates [8254]
Educational Res. Ser. [7895]
Educational Software Cooperative [6765]
Educational Testing Ser. [9250]
Educational Theatre Assn. [9264]
Educators Serving the Community [8318]
Educators for Social Responsibility [17883]
EDUCAUSE [8558]
EF Found. for Foreign Stud. [8611]
Egyptian Student Assn. in North Am. [9179]
Emotional Hea. Educ. Assn. [8255]
English Inst. [8378]
Environmental Careers Org. [8388]
Epsilon Pi Tau [24720]
Epsilon Sigma Phi [24436]
Equine Guided Educ. Assn. [8524]
ERIC CH on Languages and Linguistics [8730]
Estonian Amer. Fund for Economic Educ. [8215]
Estonian Educ. Personnel Union [IO]
Eta Phi Beta [24419]
Eta Sigma Alpha Natl. Home School Honor Soc. [8316]
Eta Sigma Phi, Natl. Classics Honorary Soc. [24433]
Ethnic Cultural Preservation Coun. [9847]
European Assn. for Res. on Learning and Instruction [IO]
European Centre for Strategic Mgt. of Universities [IO]
European Confed. of Upper Rhine Universities [IO]
European Coun. for Steiner Waldorf Educ. [IO]
European Educational Res. Assn. [IO]
European Inst. of Educ. and Social Policy [IO]
European Inst. of Postgraduate Stud. [IO]
European Soc. for Translation Stud. [IO]
European Univ. Continuing Educ. Network [IO]
Evangelical Lutheran Educ. Assn. [8802]
Evangelical Training Assn. [19925]

F. Scott Fitzgerald Soc. [9649]
Families, 4-H, and Nutrition [13483]
Families for Natural Living [8416]
Family, Career and Community Leaders of Am. [8417]
Farm-Based Educ. Assn. [7937]
Fe y Alegria - Colombia [IO]
Fe y Alegria - El Salvador [IO]
Fe y Alegria del Peru [IO]
Federacion de Ensenanza de Comisiones Obreras [IO]
Fed. Educ. Assn. [24043]
Fed. Govt. Distance Learning Assn. [8256]
Federated Coun. of Beth Jacob Schools [8691]
Fed. of Estonian Universitas [IO]
Fed. des Etablissements d'Enseignment Prives [IO]
Fed. of Galaxy Explorers [9136]
Fed. for Unified Sci. Educ. [9102]
Fellowship of Christian Released Time Ministries [19926]
The Feminist Press at the City Univ. of New York [9317]
Feminist Teacher Editorial Collective [9318]
First Book [8789]
Food and Drug Admin. Alumni Assn. [17606]
For Inspiration and Recognition of Sci. and Tech. [8319]
Fortune Soc. [11867]
Forum Intl.: Intl. Ecosystems Univ. [18833]
Found. for Accounting Educ. [31]
Found. for Amer. Christian Educ. [8086]
Found. for Amer. Communications [17177]
Found. for Educational Futures [318]
Found. for European Language and Educational Centres U.S.A. [8731]
Found. ICPR Junior Coll. [8022]
Found. for Independent Higher Educ. [8537]
Found. for Intl. Cooperation [8612]
Found. for Student Commun. [8023]
Found. for Teaching Economics [8216]
Found. for Women's Resources [9319]
Frank Lloyd Wright Assn. [7961]
French Amer. Cultural Exchange [8560]
Friends Assn. for Higher Educ. [8451]
Friends Coun. on Educ. [8452]
Friends Outside [11868]
Friends of South African Schools Fund [8257]
Fulbright Assn. [8613]
The Fund for Amer. Stud. [8747]
Fund for Constitutional Govt. [17669]
Future Bus. Leaders of Am. - Phi Beta Lambda [24420]
Future Problem Solving Prog. Intl. [8158]
G. Unger Vetlesen Found. [12719]
Gamma Iota Sigma [24520]
Gamma Sigma Delta [24398]
Gamma Theta Upsilon [24491]
Gen. Soc. of Mechanics and Tradesmen of the City of New York [9229]
George Lucas Educational Found. [8258]
Geraldine R. Dodge Found. [13119]
German Academic Exchange Ser. [8614]
German Teachers' Union [IO]
Gifts In Kind Intl. [12720]
Girls Educ. [IO]
Girls Inc. [13486]
Girls' Schools Assn. [IO]
Girlstart [8468]
Global Alliance for Justice Educ. [8766]
Global Alliance for Medical Educ. [8862]
Global Deaf Connection [12274]
Global Educ. Associates [17891]
Global Learning [8658]
Global Nomads Gp. [9336]
Global Outreach [8615]
Global Stud. Assn. North Am. [8583]
Golden Key Intl. Honour Soc. [24506]
Graduate Mgt. Admission Coun. [8807]
Graduate Record Examinations Bd. [9251]
Gravure Educ. Found. [8469]
Great Books Found. [9748]
Great Lakes Colleges Assn. [8106]
GreatSchools [8066]
Green Leaf Natl. Honor Soc. [24471]

Reference to "IO" in place of a book number signifies that the association may be found in the 45th edition of International Organizations.

The Green Life [4569]
Greenpeace U.S.A. [4571]
Grenada Union of Teachers [IO]
Gp. of Universities for the Advancement of Vietnamese Abroad [9296]
Guatemala News and Info. Bur. [17680]
Hands On Sci. Outreach [8067]
Harry S. Truman Scholarship Found. [8430]
Hea. Occupations Students of Am. [8863]
Hea. Sciences Consortium [8561]
Healthcare Educ. Assn. [8259]
Healthy Schools Network [4635]
HeartStrong [12232]
HEATH Rsrc. Center [8203]
Henry Luce Found. [12050]
High/Scope Educational Res. Found. [8181]
Higher Educ. Consortium for Urban Affairs [9286]
Higher Educ. Info. Tech. Alliance [8489]
Hindustan Bible Inst. [19927]
Hispanic Coun. for Reform and Educational Options [8260]
Hispanic Policy Development Proj. [17704]
Hispanic Scholarship Fund [8431]
History of Educ. Soc. [10118]
Holy Childhood Assn. [19632]
Home and School Inst. [8261]
Home School Legal Defense Assn. [8339]
Home Stud. Exchange [8518]
Honors Prog. Student Assn. of the Amer. Sociological Assn. [24702]
Horace Mann League of the U.S.A. [9036]
Hugh O'Brian Youth Leadership [8748]
Human Resources Res. Org. [6532]
Icelandic Pre-School Teachers Union [IO]
IEEE Educ. Soc. [8262]
IES, Inst. for the Intl. Educ. of Students [8405]
Incorporated Assn. of Preparatory Schools [IO]
Independent Educ. Union of Australia [IO]
Independent Educational Consultants Assn. [7871]
Independent Educational Services [1263]
Independent Schools Coun. [IO]
India Literacy Proj. [8790]
Indian Educators Fed. [8938]
Info. Network on Educ. in European [IO]
INROADS [8749]
Inst. for Advanced Stud. of World Religions [9275]
Inst. for the Advanced Stud. of Black Family Life and Culture [9359]
Inst. for Amer. Universities [8643]
Inst. for Axiomatic Knowledge and Educ. [7606]
Inst. of Catalan Stud. [IO]
Inst. for Chem. Educ. [8062]
Inst. for Childhood Resources [8068]
Inst. for Computers in Jewish Life [8562]
Inst. of Consumer Financial Educ. [8424]
Inst. for Development of Educational Activities [8263]
Inst. for Earth Educ. [8389]
Inst. for Educational Leadership [8264]
Inst. for Educational Services [8265]
Inst. of Intl. Educ. [8616]
Inst. for Learning Technologies [8355]
Inst. of Near Eastern and African Stud. [8266]
Inst. of Near Eastern and African Stud. [IO]
Inst. for Outdoor Learning [IO]
Inst. for People's Educ. and Action [8267]
Inst. for Public Relations [9031]
Inst. for Responsive Educ. [8408]
Inst. for Stud. in Amer. Music [8911]
Inst. for the Transfer of Tech. to Educ. [8563]
Instructional Systems Assn. [8564]
Instructional Tech. Coun. [8565]
Inter-American Conductive Educ. Assn. [9146]
Intercollegiate Broadcasting Sys. [8004]
Intercollegiate Stud. Inst. [17271]
Intercultural Development Res. Assn. [7998]
Interdisciplinary Biblical Res. Inst. [19928]
Interdisciplinary Environmental Assn. [4988]
InterExchange [8617]
Intermediate Tech. Development Gp. of North Am. [16997]
Intl. Accrediting Commn. for Real Estate and Appraisal Educ. and Training [3313]
Intl. Alliance in Ser. and Educ. [11748]

Intl. Alumni Assn. of Shri Mahavir Jain Vidyalaya [19346]
Intl. Assn. of Baptist Colleges and Universities [9276]
Intl. Assn. of Campus Law Enforcement Administrators [9084]
Intl. Assn. for Cmpt. Info. Systems [8132]
Intl. Assn. of Cmpt. Investigative Specialists [8133]
Intl. Assn. for Continuing Educ. and Training [8150]
Intl. Assn. of Correctional Officers [11870]
Intl. Assn. of Correctional Training Personnel [11871]
Intl. Assn. of Counseling Services [8169]
Intl. Assn. of Culinary Professionals [1582]
Intl. Assn. for Educational Assessment [IO]
Intl. Assn. for Game Educ. and Res. [8823]
Intl. Assn. for Intelligence Educ. [8581]
Intl. Assn. for Jazz Educ. [8912]
Intl. Assn. of Jesuit Bus. Schools [8026]
Intl. Assn. of Law Schools [8767]
Intl. Assn. for Learning Alternatives [7945]
Intl. Assn. for the Mgt. of Tech. [7740]
Intl. Assn. of Physical Educ. and Sport for Girls and Women [8980]
Intl. Assn. for Sci., Tech. and Soc. [7608]
Intl. Assn. for Statistical Educ. [IO]
Intl. Assn. for the Stud. of Sexuality, Culture and Soc. [9124]
Intl. Assn. for Truancy and Dropout Prevention [8326]
Intl. Baccalaureate Org. [IO]
Intl. Book Proj. [8620]
Intl. Boys' Schools Coalition [8268]
Intl. Boys' Schools Coalition [IO]
Intl. Bur. of Educ. [IO]
Intl. Center for the Health Sciences [8476]
Intl. Center of Photography [8972]
Intl. Coalition for Addiction Stud. Educ. [9197]
Intl. Community Corrections Assn. [11872]
Intl. Coordination Coun. of Educational Institutions Alumni [IO]
Intl. Coun. on Educ. for Teaching [9216]
Intl. Coun. of Fine Arts Deans [7973]
Intl. Coun. for Hea., Physical Educ., Recreation, Sport, and Dance [8981]
Intl. Coun. on Hotel, Restaurant, and Institutional Educ. [8525]
Intl. Educ. Res. Found. [8644]
Intl. Educ. and Rsrc. Network [8269]
Intl. Educ. and Rsrc. Network [IO]
Intl. Educator's Inst. [8645]
Intl. Fed. for Psychoanalytic Educ. [9028]
Intl. Graphic Arts Educ. Assn. [8470]
Intl. Initiatives of the Amer. Coun. on Educ. [8659]
Intl. Inst. of Catechetics and Pastoral Stud. [IO]
Intl. Inst. for Educational Planning [IO]
Intl. Labor History Assn. [5916]
Intl. Listening Assn. [8270]
Intl. Listening Assn. [IO]
Intl. Mentoring Network Org. [11520]
Intl. Nursing Coalition for Mass Casualty Educ. [8946]
Intl. Org. on Shape Memory and Superelastic Technologies [7317]
Intl. Public Debate Assn. [9041]
Intl. Reading Assn. [9043]
Intl. Res. and Exchanges Bd. [8621]
Intl. Schools Services [8647]
Intl. Soc. of Anglo-Saxonists [8379]
Intl. Soc. of Difference Equations [7292]
Intl. Soc. for Educational Planning [8999]
Intl. Soc. for Language Stud. [10302]
Intl. Soc. for Medical Publication Professionals [16259]
Intl. Soc. for the Scholarship of Teaching and Learning [9073]
Intl. Soc. for Tech. in Educ. [8134]
Intl. Tech. Educ. Assn. [9231]
Intl. Tech. Educ. Assn. - Coun. for Supervisors [9232]
Intl. Textile and Apparel Assn. [3791]
Intl. Univ. Consortium [8566]
Intl. Univ. Found. [8648]

Intl. Visual Literacy Assn. [8271]
Intl. Visual Literacy Assn. [IO]
Intl. Vocational Educ. and Training Assn. [9306]
Interstate Migrant Educ. Coun. [12588]
InterVarsity Link [9182]
Iota Beta Sigma [24410]
Iota Lambda Sigma [24724]
Iota Phi Lambda [24421]
Irish Assn. of Pastoral Care in Educ. [IO]
Irish Fed. of Univ. Teachers [IO]
Irish Natl. Teachers' Org. [IO]
Iroquois Stud. Assn. [10748]
Jack and Jill of Am. Found. [11703]
Jagannath Org. for Global Awareness [20527]
Jamaica Teachers' Assn. [IO]
Japan-America Student Conf. [8622]
Japan Art History Forum [9480]
Japan Intl. Christian Univ. Found. [19929]
Japan Intl. Christian Univ. Found. [IO]
Japanese Natl. Honor Soc. [24521]
Japanese Soc. for the Stud. of Educ. [IO]
Jefferson Educational Found. [17273]
Jesuit Assn. of Student Personnel Administrators [7896]
Jesuit Secondary Educ. Assn. [8055]
Jewish Educ. Ser. of North Am. [8692]
Jewish Educators Assembly [8693]
Jewish Student Press Ser. [8694]
John Dewey Soc. [8272]
John Howard Assn. [11874]
Joint Action in Community Ser. [11803]
Joint Info. Systems Comm. [IO]
Joint Rev. Comm. on Educ. in Diagnostic Medical Sonography [8837]
Joint Rev. Comm. on Educ. in Radiologic Tech. [8838]
Joseph Drown Found. [12051]
Journalism Assn. of Community Colleges [8712]
Journalism Educ. Assn. [8713]
Judge David L. Bazelon Center for Mental Hea. Law [17123]
Junior Achievement of Canada [IO]
Junior Engg. Tech. Soc. [8368]
Junior State of Am. [8750]
Junior Statesmen Found. [8751]
Just Think [18852]
Justice Res. and Statistics Assn. [11876]
Kappa Delta Epsilon [24452]
Kappa Delta Pi [24453]
Kappa Mu Epsilon [24537]
Kappa Omicron Nu [24496]
Kappa Pi Intl. Honorary Art Fraternity [24404]
Kappa Psi [24568]
Kappa Tau Alpha [24522]
Kennedy Center Alliance for Arts Educ. Network [7975]
Kids for a Clean Env. [4585]
Kids Universe, Inc. [8320]
Knowledge Alliance [9061]
Labor Union Cong. of Quebec [IO]
Labor and Working Class History Assn. [8723]
Lambda Alpha Intl. [24445]
Lambda Iota Tau [24533]
Lambda Kappa Sigma [24569]
LASPAU: Academic and Professional Programs for the Americas [8108]
Law School Admission Coun. [8768]
Law Student Div. [8769]
Law Students for Choice [18517]
Leadership Enterprise for a Diverse Am. [9183]
Leadership Inst. [8753]
League for Innovation in the Community Coll. [8120]
Learning First Alliance [8273]
Learning Resources Network [8151]
Learning and Teaching Scotland [IO]
LearnWell Resources [13142]
Lebanese Amer. Professional Soc. [19205]
Lewis J. Smith Assn. [8274]
Liaison Comm. on Medical Educ. [8839]
Lincoln Inst. for Res. and Educ. [16940]
Lisle Intercultural [8623]
Literacy and Evangelism Intl. [8791]
Literacy USA [8792]
Lithuanian Teachers' Union [IO]

A star before a book entry number signifies that the name is not listed separately, but is mentioned within the entry.

LOGOI [IO]
LOGOI [19930]
Lotus Outreach [13143]
Louis Finkelstein Inst. for Religious and Social Stud. at the Louis Stein Center [19931]
LULAC Natl. Educational Ser. Centers [8275]
Lutheran Educ. Assn. [8803]
Lutheran Educational Conf. of North Am. [8804]
The Madison Proj. [8824]
Maine Folklife Center [9959]
Makassed Found. of Am. [12730]
Malaysia/Singapore/Brunei Stud. Gp. of the Southeast Asia Coun. Assn. for Asian Stud. [7987]
Malta Union of Teachers [IO]
Mgt. Educ. Alliance [8029]
Manpower Educ. Inst. [8567]
Marketing Educ. Assn. [8818]
Maryknoll Mission Center of New England [8660]
Math/Science Network [8825]
MediSend Intl. [12530]
MENC: The Natl. Assn. for Music Educ. [8913]
Mennonite Educ. Agency [20250]
Metro Intl. Prog. Services of New York [8624]
Mid-Atlantic Equity Consortium [8276]
Middle Atlantic Planetarium Soc. [9105]
Middle States Assn. of Colleges and Schools [8277]
Midwifery Educ. Accreditation Coun. [8063]
Military Child Educ. Coalition [8886]
Minority Student Achievement Network [8401]
Modern Language Assn. of Am. [8735]
Montessori Accreditation Coun. for Teacher Educ. [8278]
Montessori Accreditation Coun. for Teacher Educ. [IO]
Montessori Educational Programs Intl. [8895]
Montessori Inst. of Am. [8279]
Moorhead Kennedy Gp. [8666]
Mortar Bd. [24509]
The Mountain Inst. [9960]
Mu Alpha Theta [24538]
Mu Beta Psi [24552]
Mu Phi Epsilon Intl. [24553]
Music Teachers Natl. Assn. [8918]
My Own Bus., Inc. [8030]
NACEL Open Door [8625]
NAFSA/Association of Intl. Educators [8445]
Natl. 4-H Coun. [13494]
Natl. Abstinence Educ. Assn. [9123]
Natl. Academic Advising Assn. [8170]
Natl. Acad. of Educ. [8280]
Natl. Accrediting Commn. of Cosmetology Arts and Sciences [7877]
Natl. Action Coun. for Minorities in Engg. [8369]
Natl. Adult Educ. Honor Soc. [24392]
Natl. Alliance of Black School Educators [9217]
Natl. Alliance for Civic Educ. [8091]
Natl. Alliance for Public Charter Schools [9037]
Natl. Alliance for Safe Schools [9085]
Natl. Alliance of State Sci. and Mathematics Coalitions [9106]
Natl. Alpha Lambda Delta [24510]
Natl. Architectural Accrediting Bd. [7962]
Natl. Art Educ. Assn. [7977]
Natl. Assessment of Educational Progress [9253]
Natl. Assn. for the Advancement of Caring Teachers [9218]
Natl. Assn. of Advisors for the Hea. Professions [8866]
Natl. Assn. of Agricultural Educators [7938]
Natl. Assn. for Alternative Certification [8360]
Natl. Assn. for Asian and Pacific Amer. Educ. [7988]
Natl. Assn. of Baptist Professors of Religion [9277]
Natl. Assn. for Beginning Teachers [9219]
Natl. Assn. for Bilingual Educ. [7999]
Natl. Assn. of Biology Teachers [8000]
Natl. Assn. of Blind Teachers [9220]
Natl. Assn. of Boards, Commissions, and Councils of Catholic Educ. [8056]
Natl. Assn. for Bus. Teacher Educ. [8032]
Natl. Assn. for Campus Activities [9169]
Natl. Assn. of Catholic Homes and Educators [8057]

Natl. Assn. of Catholic School Teachers [8058]
Natl. Assn. of Charter School Authorizers [8281]
Natl. Assn. for Chicana and Chicano Stud. [8498]
Natl. Assn. for Coll. Admission Counseling [7912]
Natl. Assn. of Coll. and Univ. Bus. Officers [7897]
Natl. Assn. of Coll. Wind and Percussion Instructors [8919]
Natl. Assn. of Colleges and Employers [8995]
Natl. Assn. of Comics Art Educators [8115]
Natl. Assn. for Community Coll. Entrepreneurship [8033]
Natl. Assn. of Community Coll. Teacher Educ. Programs [9221]
Natl. Assn. for Developmental Educ. [8200]
Natl. Assn. of Distance Educ. and Open Learning in South Africa [IO]
Natl. Assn. for the Educ. of African Amer. Children with Learning Disabilities [12493]
Natl. Assn. for the Educ. of Young Children [8069]
Natl. Assn. of Educational Off. Professionals [7898]
Natl. Assn. of Educational Procurement [7899]
Natl. Assn. of Elementary School Principals [9014]
Natl. Assn. of Episcopal Schools [8398]
Natl. Assn. for Equal Opportunity in Higher Educ. [8109]
Natl. Assn. for the Exchange of Indus. Resources [8336]
Natl. Assn. for Family and Community Educ. [8513]
Natl. Assn. of Fed. Educ. Prog. Administrators [7900]
Natl. Assn. of Federally Impacted Schools [8349]
Natl. Assn. of Fellowships Advisors [9080]
Natl. Assn. of Geoscience Teachers [8459]
Natl. Assn. of Geriatric Educ. Centers [14513]
Natl. Assn. for Gifted Children [8466]
Natl. Assn. of Hea. Educ. Centers [14675]
Natl. Assn. of Hea. Sci. Educ. Partnership [9107]
Natl. Assn. of Hebrew Day School PTAs [8953]
Natl. Assn. for Humanities Educ. [8531]
Natl. Assn. of Independent Colleges and Universities [8539]
Natl. Assn. of Independent Schools [8540]
Natl. Assn. of Indus. and Tech. Teacher Educators [8544]
Natl. Assn. of Indus. Tech. [8545]
Natl. Assn. for Industry-Education Cooperation [8048]
Natl. Assn. for Kinesiology and Physical Educ. in Higher Educ. [8984]
Natl. Assn. of the Knights of Scorpius, Honorary Leadership Soc. [24511]
Natl. Assn. for Legal Support of Alternative Schools [7946]
Natl. Assn. of Marine Labs. [7274]
Natl. Assn. of Maritime Educators [8813]
Natl. Assn. of Multicultural Engg. Prog. Advocates [8370]
Natl. Assn. for Neighborhood Schools [17820]
Natl. Assn. of Parish Catechetical Directors [19932]
Natl. Assn. for Pastoral Care in Educ. [IO]
Natl. Assn. of Pastoral Musicians [8920]
Natl. Assn. for Physical Educ. in Higher Educ. [8985]
Natl. Assn. for Practical Nurse Educ. and Ser. [8869]
Natl. Assn. for Primary Educ. [IO]
Natl. Assn. of Principals of Schools for Girls [9015]
Natl. Assn. of Private Special Educ. Centers [9147]
Natl. Assn. for Professional Development Schools [9091]
Natl. Assn. of Professors of Hebrew [8695]
Natl. Assn. of Pupil Services Administrators [7902]
Natl. Assn. for Res. in Sci. Teaching [9108]
Natl. Assn. of Scholars [8490]
Natl. Assn. of School Rsrc. Officers [9086]
Natl. Assn. of Schoolmasters and Union of Women Teachers [IO]
Natl. Assn. of Schools of Art and Design [7978]
Natl. Assn. of Schools, Colleges and Universities of the United Methodist Church [8879]

Natl. Assn. of Schools of Dance [8188]
Natl. Assn. of Schools of Music [8921]
Natl. Assn. of Schools of Theatre [9265]
Natl. Assn. of Secondary School Principals [9016]
Natl. Assn. of Self-Instructional Language Programs [8736]
Natl. Assn. for Single Sex Public Educ. [9038]
Natl. Assn. for Small Schools [IO]
Natl. Assn. of Special Educ. Teachers [9148]
Natl. Assn. of State Administrators and Supervisors of Private Schools [9021]
Natl. Assn. of State Boards of Educ. [9082]
Natl. Assn. of State Directors of Special Educ. [9149]
Natl. Assn. of State Directors of Teacher Educ. and Certification [9224]
Natl. Assn. of State Directors of Vocational Tech. Educ. Consortium [9307]
Natl. Assn. of State Educational Media Professionals [8568]
Natl. Assn. of State Universities and Land-Grant Colleges [8110]
Natl. Assn. of St. Schools [9337]
Natl. Assn. of Student Councils [9186]
Natl. Assn. of Student Personnel Administrators [7904]
Natl. Assn. of Students Against Violence Everywhere [18117]
Natl. Assn. for the Stud. and Performance of African-American Music [8922]
Natl. Assn. of Substance Abuse Trainers and Educators [9198]
Natl. Assn. of Supervisors and Administrators of Hea. Occupations Educ. [8870]
Natl. Assn. of Supervisors of Agricultural Educ. [7939]
Natl. Assn. of Supervisors of Bus. Educ. [8034]
Natl. Assn. of Teacher Educators for Family and Consumer Sciences [8515]
Natl. Assn. of Teachers' Agencies [1275]
Natl. Assn. of Teachers of Singing [8923]
Natl. Assn. for Tech Prep Leadership [9239]
Natl. Assn. of Temple Educators [20164]
Natl. Assn. of Test Directors [9254]
Natl. Assn. of Trade and Indus. Instructors [9233]
Natl. Assn. of Univ. Women [9320]
Natl. Assn. of Veterans Prog. Administrators [9292]
Natl. Assn. for Year-Round Educ. [8282]
Natl. Assn. of Youth Clubs [13498]
Natl. At-Risk Educ. Assn. [8327]
Natl. Automotive Technicians Educ. Found. [7992]
Natl. Aviation and Space Educ. Alliance [7994]
Natl. Beta Club [24592]
Natl. Black Graduate Student Assn. [18869]
Natl. Black Home Educators [8519]
Natl. Black Law Students Assn. [8771]
Natl. Block and Bridle Club [24401]
Natl. Broadcasting Soc. - Alpha Epsilon Rho [24411]
Natl. Bus. Educ. Assn. [8036]
Natl. Campus Ministry Assn. [19933]
Natl. Catholic Coll. Admission Assn. [19672]
Natl. Catholic Educational Assn. [8059]
Natl. Catholic Forensic League [9156]
Natl. Center for Community Educ. [8125]
Natl. Center on Educ. and the Economy [8283]
Natl. Center for Educ. Statistics [8284]
Natl. Center for Higher Educ. Mgt. Systems [7905]
Natl. Center for Homeless Educ. [12295]
Natl. Center on Institutions and Alternatives [11878]
Natl. Center for Juvenile Justice [11879]
Natl. Center for Res. on Evaluation, Standards, and Student Testing [8285]
Natl. Center for the Stud. of Collective Bargaining in Higher Educ. and the Professions [24036]
Natl. Center for the Stud. of Corporal Punishment and Alternatives [8206]
Natl. Chinese Honor Soc. [24432]
Natl. Christian Forensics and Communications Assn. [8521]
Natl. Circus Proj. [8286]
Natl. CH for Commuter Programs [9187]

Reference to "IO" in place of a book number signifies that the association may be found in the 45th edition of International Organizations.

Natl. CH for English Language Acquisition and Language Instruction Educational Programs [8287]
Natl. Coalition to Abolish Corporal Punishment in Schools [8207]
Natl. Coalition of Advocates for Students [8328]
Natl. Coalition of Alternative Community Schools [7948]
Natl. Coalition for Aviation Educ. [7995]
Natl. Coalition of Girls' Schools [8288]
Natl. Coalition for Literacy [8794]
Natl. Coalition for Tech. in Educ. and Training [9241]
Natl. Coalition of Title I/Chapter 1 Parents [8289]
Natl. Coalition for Women and Girls in Educ. [9321]
Natl. Collegiate Honors Coun. [8290]
Natl. Commn. for Cooperative Educ. [8159]
Natl. Comm. on the Educ. of Migrant Children (of the Natl. Child Labor Comm.) [12593]
Natl. Comm. for the Furtherance of Jewish Educ. [8696]
Natl. Commun. Assn. [9157]
Natl. Community Educ. Assn. [8126]
Natl. Confed. of Workers in Educ. [IO]
Natl. Conf. for Catechetical Leadership [19934]
Natl. Conf. on Student Leadership [9188]
Natl. Conf. of Yeshiva Principals [9017]
Natl. Cong. of Amer. Indians [18096]
Natl. Consortium of Arts and Letters for Historically Black Colls. and Universities [8111]
Natl. Correctional Indus. Assn. [11880]
Natl. Coun. of Churches, Educ. and Leadership Ministries Commn. [19935]
Natl. Coun. for Continuing Educ. and Training [8152]
Natl. Coun. on Economic Educ. [8217]
Natl. Coun. of Educ. Providers [8329]
Natl. Coun. for Geographic Educ. [8457]
Natl. Coun. for History Educ. [8508]
Natl. Coun. of Japanese Language Teachers [9226]
Natl. Coun. on Measurement in Educ. [9256]
Natl. Coun. on Minority Educ. in Transplantation [16677]
Natl. Coun. On Bible Curriculum In Public Schools [9052]
Natl. Coun. for Res. and Planning [8121]
Natl. Coun. of Secondary School Athletic Directors [8988]
Natl. Coun. for the Social Stud. [9128]
Natl. Coun. of State Directors of Community Colleges [8122]
Natl. Coun. of State Educ. Associations [7906]
Natl. Coun. of State Supervisors of Foreign Languages [8738]
Natl. Coun. on Student Development [9170]
Natl. Coun. of Supervisors of Mathematics [8826]
Natl. Coun. on Teacher Retirement [24044]
Natl. Coun. of Teachers of English [8380]
Natl. Coun. of Teachers of Mathematics [8827]
Natl. Coun. of Univ. Res. Administrators [9063]
Natl. Criminal Justice Assn. [11881]
Natl. Dance Inst. [8190]
Natl. Dissemination Assn. [8291]
Natl. Dissemination Center for Children with Disabilities [11971]
Natl. Dropout Prevention Center/Network [8330]
Natl. Earth Sci. Teachers Assn. [9111]
Natl. Educ. Assn. [24045]
Natl. Educ. Fed. [IO]
Natl. Educ., Hea. and Allied Workers' Union [IO]
Natl. Fed. of Modern Language Teachers Associations [8739]
Natl. Fed. of Professors [IO]
Natl. FFA Org. [7940]
Natl. Forensic Assn. [9158]
Natl. Forensic League [9159]
Natl. Found. for Educational Res. [IO]
Natl. Fraternity of Student Musicians [8924]
Natl. Geographic Soc. Educ. Found. [8458]
Natl. Guild of Community Schools of the Arts [7979]
Natl. Guild of Piano Teachers [8925]
Natl. Head Start Assn. [9006]

Natl. Hea. Policy Forum [17693]
Natl. High School Band Directors Hall of Fame [8926]
Natl. Hispanic Bus. Assn. [8039]
Natl. History Day [8510]
Natl. Home Educ. Res. Inst. [8522]
Natl. Honor Soc. [24512]
Natl. Humanities Inst. [8532]
Natl. Indian Educ. Assn. [8941]
Natl. Info. Center for Educational Media [8569]
Natl. Inst. of Ceramic Engineers [6658]
Natl. Interscholastic Athletic Administrators Assn. [8989]
Natl. Jewish Coalition for Literacy [8795]
Natl. Journalism Center [17634]
Natl. Junior Honor Soc. [24513]
Natl. Justice Found. of Am. [17298]
Natl. Juvenile Detention Assn. [11882]
Natl. Kappa Kappa Iota [24454]
Natl. Kindergarten Alliance [9007]
Natl. Liberty Museum [17723]
Natl. Marine Educators Assn. [8810]
Natl. Medical Fellowships [8871]
Natl. Middle Level Sci. Teachers' Assn. [9112]
Natl. Middle School Assn. [8881]
Natl. Native Amer. Law Students Assn. [8772]
Natl. Org. for Continuing Educ. of Roman Catholic Clergy [19936]
Natl. Org. of Forensic Social Work [8446]
Natl. Org. for Human Services [9131]
Natl. Org. of Nurses with Disabilities [15514]
Natl. Orientation Directors Assn. [7907]
Natl. Panhellenic Conf. [24485]
Natl. Parliamentary Debate Assn. [9160]
Natl. Partnership for Community Leadership [11805]
Natl. Pell Grant Coalition [8433]
Natl. Photography Instructors Assn. [8973]
Natl. Piano Found. [8927]
Natl. Portage Assn. [IO]
Natl. Postdoctoral Assn. [9064]
Natl. Prison Proj. of the ACLU [11883]
Natl. PTA - Natl. Cong. of Parents and Teachers [8954]
Natl. Ramah Commn. [8697]
Natl. Reading Conf. [9044]
Natl. Registration Center for Stud. Abroad [8626]
Natl. Registry of Environmental Professionals [4593]
Natl. Rsrc. Center for Paraprofessionals in Educ. and Related Services [9150]
Natl. Retired Teachers Assn., Division of AARP [9065]
Natl. Rural Educ. Advocacy Coalition [9068]
Natl. Rural Educ. Assn. [9069]
Natl. Scholarship Providers Assn. [9074]
Natl. Scholastic Press Assn. [9013]
Natl. School Boards Assn. [9083]
Natl. School Development Coun. [8292]
Natl. School Public Relations Assn. [9033]
Natl. Schools Comm. for Economic Educ. [8218]
Natl. Sci. Found. [7622]
Natl. Sci. Teachers Assn. [9114]
Natl. Service-Learning CH [9092]
Natl. Soc. for Experiential Educ. [8414]
Natl. Soc. for the Stud. of Educ. [8293]
Natl. Sorority of Phi Delta Kappa [24455]
Natl. Staff Development Coun. [7908]
Natl. Student Employment Assn. [8996]
Natl. Student Exchange [9172]
Natl. Student Nurses' Assn. [8873]
Natl. Teachers' Union [IO]
Natl. Tech Prep Network [8358]
Natl. Tech. Honor Soc. [24725]
Natl. Tertiary Educ. Union [IO]
Natl. Tutoring Assn. [9283]
Natl. Union of School Workers [IO]
Natl. Union of Teachers in Sweden [IO]
Natl. Union of the Teaching Profession [IO]
Natl. Urban Alliance for Effective Educ. [9291]
Natl. Urban League [17138]
Natl. Valedictorian Honor Soc. [24514]
Natl. Valedictorian Soc. [9077]
Natl. Vocational Technical Education Found. [9308]

Natl. Women's Hall of Fame [20716]
Natl. Women's Stud. Assn. [9323]
Natl. Writing Proj. [9334]
Natl. Youth Leadership Coun. [8754]
Natl. Youth and Student Peace Coalition [18226]
Native Financial Educ. Coalition [8442]
Native Forest Network [4428]
Natural Dyes Intl. [8213]
Natural Sci. Collections Alliance [6590]
Navajo Area School Bd. Assn. [8942]
NEA Found. for the Improvement of Educ. [8294]
NETWORK [8295]
New England Assn. of Schools and Colleges [8296]
New Leaders for New Schools [8755]
New Parents Network [8956]
New Zealand Coun. for Educational Res. [IO]
NFHS Music Assn. [8928]
Nieman Found. [8716]
Nigerian Women Leadership Coun. Intl. [12640]
Nonverbal Learning Disorders Assn. [14998]
Nordic Educational Res. Assn. [IO]
North Amer. Assn. for Belarusian Stud. [9735]
North Amer. Assn. of Commencement Officers [8492]
North Amer. Assn. of Educational Negotiators [24046]
North Amer. Assn. for Environmental Educ. [8393]
North Amer. Assn. of Jewish High Schools [8698]
North Amer. Assn. of Medical Educ. and Commun. Companies [8874]
North Amer. Assn. for the Stud. of Welsh Culture and History [11083]
North Amer. Assn. of Summer Sessions [9200]
North Amer. Assn. of Wardens and Superintendents [11884]
North Amer. Coalition for Christian Admissions Professionals [7914]
North Amer. Colleges and Teachers of Agriculture [7942]
North Amer. Coordinating Coun. on Japanese Lib. Resources [8781]
North Amer. Coun. of Automotive Teachers [7993]
North Amer. Coun. for Online Learning [7949]
North Amer. Interfraternal Found. [24486]
North-American Interfraternity Conf. [24487]
North Amer. Professors of Christian Educ. [8088]
North Amer. Reggio Emilia Alliance [11641]
North Amer. South Asian Law Student Assn. [8773]
North Amer. Students of Cooperation [9190]
North Amer. Sundial Soc. [9278]
North Amer. Taiwan Stud. Assn. [9205]
North Central Assn. of Colleges and Schools Commn. on Accreditation and School Improvement [8297]
North Central Conf. on Summer Schools [9201]
Northamerican Assn. of Masters in Psychology [9030]
Northeast Conf. on the Teaching of Foreign Languages [8742]
Northwest Assn. of Accredited Schools [8298]
Northwest Assn. of Accredited Schools [IO]
NTL Inst. for Applied Behavioral Sciences [8415]
Off. for the Advancement of Public Black Colleges of the Natl. Assn. of State Universities and Land-Grant Colleges [8112]
Off. of Women in Higher Educ., Amer. Coun. on Educ. [9324]
Omega Delta [24563]
Omicron Delta Epsilon [24446]
Omicron Delta Kappa Soc. [24515]
Omicron Kappa Upsilon [24439]
OMNI Learning Inst. [8299]
O'Neill Natl. Theater Inst. [9266]
Open and Distance Learning Quality Coun. [IO]
Open Door Educ. Found. [9242]
Oper. Crossroads Africa [16932]
Oper. Enterprise [8808]
Oral Hea. Am. [8196]
Order of the Coif [24516]
Org. of Swedish-Speaking Teachers in Finland [IO]
Org. of Amer. Kodaly Educators [8929]
Org. Development Network [2867]

A star before a book entry number signifies that the name is not listed separately, but is mentioned within the entry.

Org. for Equal Education of the Sexes [8402]
Org. of Professional Acting Coaches and Teachers [9267]
Organizational Behavior Teaching Soc. [6537]
Organizational Systems Res. Assn. [9234]
ORT Am. [12480]
Osborne Assn. [11885]
Our Voices Together [13309]
Outward Bound [9204]
Ozar Hatorah [20171]
PALTEX - Expanded Textbook and Instructional Materials Prog. [9261]
Parent Cooperative Preschools Intl. [8070]
Parents in Control [8340]
Parents for Public Schools [12052]
Parents' Rights Org. [7950]
Pathways to Coll. Network [8493]
Patidar Cultural Assn. of USA [10218]
Patriotic Educ. Inc. [8092]
Peer Hea. Exchange [9338]
PEO Intl. [9325]
People Helping People [12385]
People to People Intl. [17909]
Per Scholas [8300]
Permanent Intl. Altaistic Conf. [7989]
Pew Charitable Trusts [13129]
Pharmacy Technician Educators Coun. [8963]
Phelps-Stokes Fund [8301]
Phelps-Stokes Fund [IO]
Phi Alpha Delta [24528]
Phi Alpha Sigma [24543]
Phi Alpha Theta [24495]
Phi Beta [24405]
Phi Beta Delta [24517]
Phi Beta Kappa [24406]
Phi Chi Medical Fraternity [24544]
Phi Delta Chi [24570]
Phi Delta Epsilon Medical Fraternity [24540]
Phi Delta Gamma [24577]
Phi Delta Phi Intl. Legal Fraternity [24530]
Phi Kappa Phi [24518]
Phi Mu Alpha Sinfonia Fraternity and Found. Natl. HQ [24555]
Phi Sigma [24409]
Phi Sigma Iota [24526]
Phi Sigma Pi Natl. Honor Fraternity [24531]
Phi Theta Kappa, Intl. Honor Soc. [24456]
Phi Theta Kappa, Intl. Honor Soc. [IO]
Philosophy of Educ. Soc. [8969]
Phonics Inst. [9046]
Photo Imaging Educ. Assn. [8974]
Photographic Art and Sci. Found. [8975]
Pi Kappa Phi [24651]
Pi Lambda Theta [24457]
Pi Omicron Natl. Sorority [24601]
Pirchei Agudath Israel [8699]
Plan of Action for Challenging Times [8331]
PlanetRead [8796]
Playing for Keeps [11544]
Plymouth Rock Found. [8302]
Point Found. [4519]
Point-of-Purchase Advt. Intl. [115]
Polish-American-Jewish Alliance for Youth Action [13510]
Postsecondary Electronic Standards Coun. [9165]
Practising Law Inst. [8774]
Precious Metal Clay Guild [8172]
Prepare Tomorrow's Parents [13511]
Prison Fellowship Intl. [11887]
Prison Fellowship Ministries [11888]
Prison Ministry of Yokefellow's Intl. [11889]
Prisoners' Rights Union [11890]
Probe Ministries Intl. [8090]
ProEnglish [9912]
Professional Assn. of Christian Educators [19937]
Professional Association of Christian Educators [IO]
Professional Dance Teachers Assn. [8191]
Professional Fraternity Assn. [24488]
Professional and Organizational Development Network in Higher Educ. [8494]
Prog. of Academic Exchange [8628]
Progressive, Radically Inclusive Student Ministry [19938]
Proj. Food, Land and People [4525]

Proj. Human Aid [IO]
Proj. South: Inst. for the Elimination of Poverty and Genocide [17872]
ProLiteracy Worldwide [8797]
Psi Beta [24579]
Psi Omega [24440]
Public Educ. Center [18398]
Public Educ. Network [9040]
Public Leadership Educ. Network [9326]
Public Relations Student Soc. of Am. [9034]
Public Responsibility in Medicine and Res. [18585]
Quality Educ. for Minorities Network [8303]
Reading Is Fundamental [9047]
Reading Recovery Coun. of North Am. [9048]
Real Estate Educators Assn. [3338]
Regional Educ. Bd. of the Christian Bros. [8060]
Religious Commun. Assn. [8116]
Religious Educ. Assn.: An Assn. of Professors, Practitioners, and Researchers in Religious Educ. [19939]
Response-Ability [20386]
Restoration Proj. Intl. [12441]
River of Words [4186]
Rolling Readers [12502]
Room to Read [12053]
Room to Read [IO]
Safer Soc. Found. [11891]
Sallie Mae Fund [8434]
Salvadoran Amer. Medical Soc. [15092]
Sarawak Teachers' Union [IO]
Saving the Arts [9598]
Scandinavian Seminar [8630]
School Nutrition Assn. [9173]
School Sci. and Mathematics Assn. [9115]
School Social Work Assn. of Am. [9134]
Schwab Learning - A Prog. of the Charles Schwab Found. [12496]
Schweizerischer Verband des Personals Oeffentlicher Dienste [IO]
Scottish Coun. for Res. in Educ. [IO]
Scottish Parent-Teacher Coun. [IO]
Scottish Secondary Teachers' Assn. [IO]
Sea Educ. Assn. [8811]
SEAMEO Regional Centre for Educational Innovation and Tech. [IO]
Secondary Educ. Union [IO]
Secondary School Admission Test Bd. [9257]
Senior Executives Assn. Professional Development League [5714]
Senior Scholars [8153]
Sensus Educational Assn. [IO]
September's Mission [13310]
Sewing Educator Alliance [9121]
Sierra Student Coalition [4521]
Sigma Alpha Iota Intl. Music Fraternity [24557]
Sigma Alpha Lambda [24519]
Sigma Delta Chi Found. [24524]
Sigma Delta Epsilon, Graduate Women in Sci. [24587]
Sigma Kappa Found. [24697]
Sikh Amer. Legal Defense and Educ. Fund [18600]
Silver Wings [24549]
Singapore Malay Teachers' Union [IO]
SkillsUSA [8546]
Skolenes Landsforbund [IO]
Slavic and East European Folklore Assn. [9962]
Sloan Consortium [8304]
Social Policy Action Network [13138]
Social Sci. Educ. Consortium [9129]
Sociedad Honoraria Hispanica [8499]
Societe des Professeurs Francais et Francophones d'Amerique [8450]
Soc. for Academic Achievement [9078]
Soc. for Academic Continuing Medical Educ. [8875]
Soc. for the Advancement of Educ. [8305]
Soc. for the Advancement of Excellence in Educ. [IO]
Soc. for the Advancement of Games and Simulations in Educ. and Training [IO]
Soc. for Advancement of Mgt. [2515]
Soc. for the Advancement of Scandinavian Stud. [9070]

Soc. for Anthropology in Community Colleges [7954]
Soc. for Applied Anthropology [6427]
Soc. for Applied Learning Tech. [8571]
Soc. of Assistants Teaching in Preparatory Schools [IO]
Soc. of Building Sci. Educators [8363]
Soc. for Coll. and Univ. Planning [9000]
Soc. for Cross-Cultural Res. [10230]
Soc. for Educational Reconstruction [8306]
Soc. for Energy Educ. [6972]
Soc. for Executive Leadership in Academic Medicine Intl. [15179]
Soc. of Financial Examiners [6209]
Soc. for Gen. Music [8930]
Soc. for History Educ. [8511]
Soc. for Indus. and Applied Mathematics [7294]
Soc. for Intercultural Educ., Training and Res. U.S.A. [8667]
Soc. of Intl. Chinese in Educational Tech. [9236]
Soc. for Italian Historical Stud. [8681]
Soc. of Mfg. Engineers Educ. Found. [8373]
Soc. for Music Teacher Educ. [8931]
Soc. for Organizational Learning [2868]
Soc. for Philosophy of Religion [8970]
Soc. for Photographic Educ. [8976]
Soc. for the Preservation of English Language and Literature [8381]
Soc. of Professional Journalists [3164]
Soc. of Professors of Educ. [8307]
Soc. for the Promotion of Educ. and Awareness [IO]
Soc. for Social Work and Res. [9135]
Soc. of State Directors of Hea., Physical Educ. and Recreation [8992]
Soc. for the Stud. of Early China [8077]
Soc. for the Stud. of Early Modern Women [9331]
Soc. for the Stud. of Japanese Religions [20529]
Soc. for the Stud. of Peace, Conflict, and Violence: Peace Psychology Div. of the Amer. Psychological Assn. [16185]
Soc. for Values in Higher Educ. [19940]
Software in the Public Interest [6777]
Solace Intl. [13439]
Solomon Schechter Day School Assn. [8701]
South African Acad. for Sci. and Arts [IO]
Southeast Asian Ministers of Educ. Org. [IO]
Southeastern Regional Off. Natl. Scholarship Ser. and Fund for Negro Students [8435]
Southern Assn. of Colleges and Schools [8308]
Southern Educ. Found. [8309]
Southern Poverty Law Center [17155]
Space Found. [7922]
Spencer Found. [12054]
Sphinx Org. [10710]
StandardsWork [9094]
State Educational Tech. Directors Assn. [9244]
State Higher Educ. Executive Officers [9001]
Stelios M. Stelson Found. [8631]
STRIDE: Sports and Therapeutic Recreation Instruction/Developmental Educ. [8205]
Student African Amer. Brotherhood [19444]
Student Conservation Assn. [4455]
Student Environmental Action Coalition [4607]
Student Leadership Network [9193]
Student Org. of North Am. [9194]
Student Press Law Center [17194]
Student Veterinary Emergency and Critical Care Soc. [16810]
Students for America [17277]
Students for the Exploration and Development of Space [7923]
Supporting Our Sons [11547]
Suzuki Assn. of the Americas [8932]
Svenska Folkhogskolans Laraforbund [IO]
Swedish Assn. of School Principals and Directors of Educ. [IO]
Swedish Assn. of Univ. Teachers [IO]
Swedish Teachers' Union [IO]
Swiss Teachers Fed. [IO]
Syndicat des Enseignants [IO]
Syrian Stud. Assn. [8880]
Tamarind Inst. [8471]
Tanzania Teachers' Union [IO]
Tau Epsilon Rho Law Soc. [24529]

Reference to "IO" in place of a book number signifies that the association may be found in the 45th edition of International Organizations.

Teachers of English to Speakers of Other Languages [8382]
Teachers Insurance and Annuity Assn. [8579]
Teachers' Union of Hungary [IO]
Teachers' Union of Ireland [IO]
Teaching, Learning and Technology Group [IO]
Teaching, Learning and Tech. Gp. [6898]
Tech. Inst. for Music Educators [8933]
Tech. Mgt. Educ. Assn. [9245]
Tech. Student Assn. [8547]
Telluride Assn. [8310]
Theta Alpha Phi [24721]
Theta Psi [24566]
Theta Tau [24469]
Thomas B. Fordham Found. [17477]
Thunderbird Amer. Indian Dancers [10754]
TIAA-CREF [9066]
Touching Hearts [11267]
Trade Union of Educ. in Finland [IO]
Trade Union of Educ. - Germany [IO]
Triangle Coalition for Sci. and Tech. Educ. [9116]
Tripoli Rocketry Assn. [9117]
TTS Inst. [IO]
UIL-Scuola [IO]
Ulster Teachers' Union [IO]
UNESCO Inst. for Lifelong Learning [IO]
Union of Sci. and Educ. [IO]
United Bd. for Christian Higher Educ. in Asia [8649]
United Jewish Appeal - Fed. of Jewish Philanthropies of New York [12482]
United Negro Coll. Fund [8437]
U.S.-China Educ. Found. [8632]
U.S. Distance Learning Assn. [8523]
U.S. Soc. for Educ. Through Art [7980]
U.S. Student Assn. [9195]
United Synagogue of Conservative Judaism Commn. on Jewish Educ. [8702]
Univ. Aviation Assn. [7924]
Univ. and Coll. Designers Assn. [8572]
Univ. and Coll. Lecturers' Union [IO]
Univ. Continuing Educ. Assn. [8154]
Univ. Coun. for Educational Admin. [7909]
Univ. Film and Video Assn. [8420]
Univ. Film and Video Found. [8421]
Univ. Photographers Assn. of Am. [8977]
Univ. Professors for Academic Order [9026]
University/Resident Theatre Assn. [9269]
Up With People [8311]
Upsilon Pi Epsilon Assn. [24435]
Urban Affairs Assn. [9287]
Urban Superintendent's Assn. of Am. [9288]
U.S.A. Toy Lib. Assn. [11548]
Van Alen Inst.: Projects in Public Architecture [7963]
Van Andel Educ. Inst. [8312]
Visitor Stud. Assn. [9280]
Vocational Instructional Materials Sect. [8573]
Volunteers in Asia [13407]
Volunteers in Prevention, Probation, Prisons [11896]
Wallace-Reader's Digest Funds [12055]
Washington Journalism Center [8719]
Washington Workshops Found. [8093]
Waters Found. [8313]
WAVE [12105]
We Care Prog. [11897]
Welders Without Borders [7850]
Wellesley Centers for Women [9327]
Welsh Secondary Schools Assn. [IO]
Western Assn. of Schools and Colleges [8314]
Wilderness Classroom Org. [9951]
Wilderness Educ. Assn. [8952]
The Wilderness Soc. [4468]
Wildlife Info. Center [5400]
The Wildlife Soc. [5401]
Wimbum Cultural and Development Assn. in the U.S.A. [9344]
Winston Churchill Found. [8438]
Women Band Directors Intl. [8934]
Women Educators [9328]
Women and Mathematics Educ. [8828]
Women in Scholarly Publishing [3260]
Women's Coll. Coalition [9330]
Women's Prison Assn. [11898]

Woodrow Wilson Natl. Fellowship Found. [8439]
World Care [17478]
World Care [IO]
World Commun. Assn. [8005]
World Cong. of Teachers of Dancing [8192]
World Coun. for Curriculum and Instruction [8182]
World Educ. [7918]
World Heritage [8634]
World Learning [8635]
World Org. for Early Childhood Educ. U.S. Natl. Comm. [8071]
World Pen Pals [8636]
WorldTeach [8315]
Worldwide Univ. Consortium [8114]
Xi Psi Phi [24442]
Yale-China Assn. [8637]
Young Audiences [9603]
Youth Educ. in the Arts [9604]
Youth For Understanding USA [8639]
YouthBuild USA [13525]
Zarrow Families Found. [13197]
Education-A-Must [12056], PO Box 216, East Derry, NH 03041, (603)437-6286
Educ; AACSB-The Intl. Assn. for Mgt. [★8010]
Educ. and Accreditation; Comm. on Allied Hea. [★8832]
Educ; Accreditation Coun. for Continuing Medical [15151]
Educ; Accreditation Coun. on Optometric [15710]
Educ; Accrediting Commn. for Cosmetology [★7877]
Educ. Action Intl. [IO], London, United Kingdom
Education Activists; Natl. Coalition of [9039]
Educ; ACUTA: The Assn. for Communications Tech. Professionals in Higher [8548]
Educ; ACUTA: The Assn. for Telecommunication Professionals in Higher [★8548]
Educ. Administrators; Assn. of Continuing Legal [★8762]
Educ. for Adoptive Families; Liberal [11253]
Educ. and Advancement of Cambodian, Laotian, and Vietnamese Americans; Natl. Assn. for the [19424]
Educ; Advisory Coun. for Orthopedic Resident [★15752]
Educ. and Advocacy; Gender [13090]
Educ. Advocates for Culture, Hea., Env. and Safety; Beach [10761]
Educ., AFL-CIO; Comm. on Political [★18303]
Educ; Agricultural Communicators in [★4098]
Educ., and AIDS Leadership; Project Hea., [★13580]
Educ. on Alcoholism; Natl. Comm. for [★13268]
Educ; ALI-ABA Comm. on Continuing Professional [8758]
Educ; Alliance for Arts [★7975]

Education, Alternative

Adult Higher Educ. Alliance [7915]
Amer. Assn. for Collegiate Independent Stud. [7944]
Amer. Montessori Soc. [8891]
Assn. for Community Based Education [8123]
Assn. of Cooperative Educators [8156]
Assn. for Experiential Educ. [8411]
Assn. Montessori International-U.S.A. [8892]
Assn. for Non-Traditional Students in Higher Educ. [7916]
Black Alliance for Educational Options [8322]
Center for Global Educ. [8662]
Christian Home Educators Assn. of California [8516]
Commun. Inst. for Online Scholarship [6899]
Consciousness-Based Educ. Assn. [9029]
Cooperative Educ. and Internship Assn. [8157]
Coun. for Adult and Experiential Learning [8412]
Distance Educ. and Training Coun. [8517]
Equine Guided Educ. Assn. [8524]
Eta Sigma Alpha Natl. Home School Honor Soc. [8316]
Fed. Govt. Distance Learning Assn. [8256]
Hands On Sci. Outreach [8067]
High/Scope Educational Res. Found. [8181]
Hispanic Coun. for Reform and Educational Options [8260]
Home School Legal Defense Assn. [8339]
Home School Sports Network [23490]
Home Stud. Exchange [8518]

Intl. Assn. for Learning Alternatives [7945]
Natl. Assn. of Catholic Homes and Educators [8057]
Natl. Assn. of St. Schools [9337]
Natl. Black Home Educators [8519]
Natl. Christian Forensics and Communications Assn. [8521]
Natl. Home Educ. Res. Inst. [8522]
Natl. Soc. for Experiential Educ. [8414]
North Amer. Coun. for Online Learning [7949]
Educ; Am. Coun. on Educ., Off. of Minorities in Higher [★8889]
Educ; Amer. Acad. of Kinesiology and Physical [8978]
Educ; Amer. Acad. for Liberal [8775]
Educ; Amer. Acad. of Physical [★8978]
Educ; Amer. Alliance for Theatre and [10998]
Educ; Amer. Assn. for Adult and Continuing [8146]
Educ; Amer. Assn. for Advancement of Physical [★8979]
Educ; Amer. Assn. for Agricultural [7933]
Educ; Amer. Assn. for Cancer [13789]
Educ; Amer. Assn. for Career [8046]
Educ; Amer. Assn. of Colleges for Teacher [9208]
Educ; Amer. Assn. for Employment in [8994]
Educ; Amer. Assn. for Higher [8478]
Educ; Amer. Assn. for Jewish [★8692]
Educ; Amer. Assn. for Paralegal [8759]
Educ; Amer. Bd. of Funeral Ser. [8896]
Educ; Amer. Comm. for the Advancement of Torah [★8678]
Educ; Amer. Coun. for Constr. [8141]
Educ; Amer. Coun. for Drug [13222]
Educ; Amer. Coun. on Indus. Arts Teacher [★8543]
Educ; Amer. Coun. on Pharmaceutical [★15907]
Educ; Amer. Coun. on Rural Special [9137]
Educ; Amer. Forum for Global [8593]
Educ; Amer. Found. for Pharmaceutical [15916]
Educ; Amer. Fund for Dental [★8196]
Educ. of the Amer. Medical Assn; Coun. on Medical [8836]
Educ. of the Amer. Osteopathic Assn; Bur. of Professional [15810]
Educ. Application Network; Micro Cmpt. [★8557]
Educ. for Asian Pacifics; Leadership [9621]
Educ. and Assistance Fund; Fed. Employee [19264]
Educ. Assn; Amer. Driver and Traffic Safety [8210]
Educ. Assn; Amer. Lutheran [★8802]
Educ. Assn; Amer. Physical [★8979]
Educ. Assn; Amer. Sailing [★8811]
Educ; Assn. for the Behavioral Sciences and Medical [6527]
Educ; Assn. for Biblical Higher [8080]
Educ; Assn. of Black Women in Higher [9314]
Educ. Assn; Broadcast [8001]
Educ; Assn. for Career and Tech. [9300]
Educ. Assn; Catholic [★8059]
Educ. Assn; Childbirth Without Pain [★15607]
Educ. Assn; Christian Bros. [★8060]
Educ. Assn; Coll. and Univ. Dept. of the Natl. Catholic [★8051]
Education; Assn. for Community Based [8123]
Educ; Assn. for Continuing Higher [8148]
Educ; Assn. for Continuing Legal [8762]
Educ. Assn; Cooperative [★8157]
Educ. Assn; Correctional [11862]
Educ. Assn; Dept. of Superintendents of the Natl. [★7882]
Educ. Assn; Emotional [★8255]
Educ. Assn; Evangelical Lutheran [8802]
Educ; Assn. for Experiential [8411]
Educ. Assn; Family and Consumer Sciences [8418]
Educ; Assn. for Gender Equity Leadership in [8399]
Educ; Assn. for Gerontology in Higher [8462]
Educ; Assn. for Higher [★8478]
Educ; Assn. for Hosp. Medical [14873]
Educ. Assn; Hunter [★23545]
Educ. Assn; Indus. Design [★7180]
Educ. Assn; Intl. Graphic Arts [8470]
Educ. Assn; Intl. Hunter [23545]
Educ. Assn; Jesuit Secondary [8055]
Educ. Assn; Journalism [8713]
Educ. Assn; Lamaze Birth Without Pain [15607]

A star before a book entry number signifies that the name is not listed separately, but is mentioned within the entry.

Educ; Assn. for Lib. and Info. Sci. [8782]
Educ. Assn; Lutheran [8803]
Educ. Assn; Marketing [8818]
Educ. Assn; Marketing and Distributive [★8818]
Educ. Assn. for Men; Natl. Coll. Physical [★8985]
Educ. Assn; Natl. Art [7977]
Educ. Assn; Natl. Bus. [8036]
Educ. Assn; Natl. Christian School [★8081]
Educ. Assn; Natl. Community [8126]
Educ. Assn; Natl. Community School [★8126]
Educ. Assn; Natl. Dance [23324]
Educ. Assn; Natl. Graphic Arts [★8470]
Educ. Assn; Natl. Indian [8941]
Educ. Assn; Natl. Marine [★8810]
Educ. Assn; Natl. Rural [9069]
Educ. Assn; Natl. Univ. Continuing [★8154]
Educ; Assn. Off. [★9302]
Educ; Assn. of Private Enterprise [9019]
Educ. Assn; Rural [★9069]
Educ. Assn; Sea [8811]
Educ; Assn. of State and Territorial Directors of Public Hea. [★6215]
Educ. Assn; Student Natl. [★24045]
Educ; Assn. for the Stud. of Higher [8482]
Educ; Assn. for Theatre in Higher [9262]
Educ. Assn; United Bus. [★8036]
Educ. Assn; Univ. Continuing [8154]
Educ. Assn; Univ. Labor [8722]
Educ. Assn. of the U.S.A; Adult [★8146]
Educ. Assn; White Mountain [20567]
Educ. Assn; Wilderness [8952]
Educ. Associations; Natl. Coun. of State [7906]
Educ. Associations; Natl. Coun. of Urban [9290]
Educ. and Bioethics; Center for Death [13314]
Educ. Bd. of the Christian Bros; Regional [8060]
Educ; Bd. of Higher [★19854]
Educ. Bd; Independent Schools [★8540]
Educ. Bureau; Royal Arch [★19235]
Educ. Bureau; Royal Arch [★IO]
Educ. for Bus; Coun. for Professional [★8010]
Education Center; Amer. Labor [8720]
Educ; Center for Aviation Res. and [5537]
Educ. Center; Children's Television Rsrc. and [11686]
Educ. Center; Death With Dignity [★17109]
Educ; Center for Environmental [★4435]
Educ. Center; Holocaust Documentation and [17717]
Educ. Center; Norma Terris Humane [★11433]
Educ; Center for Organ Recovery and [16670]
Educ. Center; Public [18398]
Educ. Center of Quebec [★IO]
Educ; Center for Social Stud. [9127]
Educ; Center for U.N. Reform [18761]
Educ; Center for Vocational [★9304]
Educ. Centers; Natl. Assn. of Private Special [9147]
Educ; Central Agency for Jewish [19180]
Educ; Central Org. for Jewish [8688]
Educ. Centre for Women in Democracy [IO], Nairobi, Kenya
Educ. for the Ceramic Arts; Natl. Coun. on [9836]
Educ. and Certification; Natl. Assn. of State Directors of Teacher [9224]
Educ; CHA-Association for Horsemanship Safety and [★23523]
Educ., Christian Church-Disciples of Christ; Division of Higher [19854]
Educ. for Christian Life and Mission [★19935]
Educ. Clearinghouse; California Tobacco [★8556]
Educ. Clubs of Am; Distributive [8817]
The Educ. Coalition [8325], 31 Segovia, San Clemente, CA 92672, (949)369-3867
Educ; Coalition for Alternatives in Jewish [★8689]
Educ; Coalition on Urban Renewal and [18774]
Educ. of Coll. Women; Natl. Assn. for Physical [★8985]
Educ; Commn. on Gay/Lesbian Issues in Social work [★9132]
Education; Commission on Higher [★8277]
Educ. Commn. of the States [8252], 700 Broadway, Ste. 1200, Denver, CO 80203-3460, (303)299-3600
Educ; Comm. on Assessing the Progress of [★9253]
Educ. Comm. of the Christian Bros; Regional [★8060]
Education; Community for Religious Res. and [20537]

Educ; Concern for Hea. Options - Info., Care and [★12178]
Educ; Conf. on English [8377]
Educ. Conference; Frontiers in [★8366]
Educ. Conference; Frontiers in [★IO]
Educ., and Conservation; Jane Goodall Inst. for Wildlife Res., [5334]
Educ; Consortium for the Advancement of Private Higher [★8535]
Educ; Consortium for the Advancement of Private Higher [8105]
Educ. Consortium; Amer. Indian Higher [8935]
Educ; Consortium on Financing Higher [9057]
Educ. Consortium; Natl. Assn. of State Directors of Vocational Tech. [9307]
Educ. Consortium; Social Sci. [9129]
Education Cooperation; Natl. Assn. for Industry- [8048]
Educ; Coun. of Administrators of Special [9139]
Educ. Coun. for Amer. Private [9020]
Educ; Coun. on Anthropology and [6415]
Educ; Coun. for Art [7970]
Educ. Coun; Aviation Technician [7921]
Educ; Coun. on Chiropractic [13998]
Educ. Coun. of the Christian Bros; Natl. [★8060]
Educ. Coun. of the Christian Bros; Regional [★8060]
Educ. Coun; Continuing [★8145]
Educ; Coun. for Distributive Teacher [★8818]
Educ. Coun. of the Graphic Arts Indus. [★1770]
Educ; Coun. on Hea. Info. and [14553]
Educ; Coun. for Indian [8937]
Educ; Coun. Interstate Migrant [12588]
Educ; Coun. on Music Teacher [★8931]
Educ. Coun; NEA Higher [★24045]
Educ; Coun. for Noncollegiate Continuing [★8145]
Educ; Coun. on Optometric [★15710]
Educ; Coun. on Podiatric Medical [16042]
Educ; Coun. on Rehabilitation [16319]
Educ; Coun. for Sex Info. and [16400]
Educ; Coun. on Social Work [9133]
Educ; Coun. for Spiritual and Ethical [8536]
Educ; Coun. for Standards in Human Ser. [9130]
Educ. Coun. of the U.S; Sex Info. and [★16406]
Educ. Coun. of the U.S; Sexuality Info. and [16406]
Educ. and Counseling; Assn. for Death [11909]
Educ. and Counseling; Forum for Death [★11909]
Educ. Credit Union Coun. [1109], c/o Lorraine Zerfas, Exec. Dir., PO Box 7558, Spanish Fort, AL 36577, (251)626-3399
Education and Cultural Development Assn. - Defunct.
Educ. and Culture Union [IO], Berlin, Germany
Educ. Day Proj; Natl. Energy [★17497]
Educ. of the Deaf; Coun. on [14751]
Educ. Dealers; Natl. Assn. of Visual [★331]
Educ. and Defense Fund; Disability Rights [11940]
Educ; Dept. of Rural [★9069]
Educ; Dept. of Rural and Agricultural [★9069]
Educ. Development Center [8253], 55 Chapel St., Newton, MA 02458, (617)969-7100
Educ. Development Center [IO], Newton, MA, United States
Educ. and Development; Consortium on Peace Res., [★18233]
Educ. and Development; Counseling Assn. for Humanistic [8527]
Educ. Development Proj; Natl. Energy [17497]
Educ. in Diagnostic Medical Sonography; Joint Rev. Comm. on [8837]
Educ. Directors Soc; Insurance Company [★8578]
Educ. and the Economy; Carnegie Forum on [★8283]
Educ. Effort; Minority Engg. [★8369]
Educ. for Engineers; Assn. for Media-Based Continuing [8367]
Educ. and Enrichment Sect. [★12151]
Educ. and Enrichment Sect. of the Natl. Coun. on Family Relations [12151], 3989 Central Ave. NE, Ste. 550, Minneapolis, MN 55421, (763)781-9331
Educ; Evangelical Assn. for the Promotion of [★20330]
Education Excellence Partnership - Defunct.
Educ. Executive Officers; State Higher [9001]
Education Exploration Center - Defunct.
Educ; Exploratory Comm. on Assessing the Progress of [★9253]

Educ; Fed. for Unified Sci. [9102]
Educ. Forum; Business-Higher [8008]
Educ. Forum; Susan B. Anthony Women's Spirituality [★20628]
Educ; Found. for Accounting [31]
Educ; Found. for Accredited Chiropractic [★14004]
Educ; Found. for the Advancement of Chiropractic [8079]
Educ. Found; Aerospace [★6062]
Educ. Found; Alternatives to Abortion/Women's Hea. and [★12912]
Educ. Found; Amer. Canine [22193]
Educ; Found. for Amer. Christian [8086]
Educ. Found; Amer. Medical [★8843]
Educ. Found; Amer. Security Coun. [★16986]
Educ. Found. of Amer. Soc. of Plastic and Reconstructive Surgeons [★14051]
Educ. Found; The Conservative Caucus Res., Anal. and [17265]
Educ. Found; Cooking Advancement Res. and [★8174]
Educ; Found. for Cotton Res. and [★1091]
Educ. Found; Creative [8173]
Educ. Found; Direct Selling [3466]
Educ. Found; Distribution Res. and [4020]
Educ; Found. for Economic [18406]
Educ. Found; Exhibit Indus. [★1349]
Educ; Found; Free Cong. Res. and [18295]
Educ. Found; Gravure [8469]
Educ. Found; Hea. [16243]
Educ. Found; Hearth [1880]
Educ; Found. for Independent Higher [8537]
Educ. Found; Insurance [8575]
Educ. Foundation; Interior Design [★8585]
Educ. Found; Luso-American [10890]
Educ. Found; Motorcycle Indus. Coun. Safety and [★3447]
Educ. Found; Natl. Automotive Technicians [7992]
Educ. Found; Natl. Bowhunter [23053]
Educ. Found; Natl. Geographic Soc. [8458]
Educ. Found; Natl. Right to Work Legal Defense and [17983]
Educ. Found; Natl. Roofing [★8144]
Education Found; Natl. Vocational Technical [9308]
Educ. Found; Orthopaedic Res. and [8949]
Educ. Found; Pacific Northwest Ski [★23754]
Educ; Found. for Rational Economics and [17293]
Educ; Found. for Res. in Economics and [★17293]
Educ. Found; Soc. of Mfg. Engineers [8373]
Educ. Foundation; Solar Energy Res. and [★7679]
Educ. Found; Southern Public Admin. [6199]
Educ. Foundations; Natl. Assn. of Veterans' Res. and [6347]
Educ; Friends Assn. for Higher [8451]
Educ; Friends Coun. on [8452]
Educ. Fund; 9 to 5 Working Women [17513]
Educ. Fund; Amer. Canine [★22193]
Educ. Fund; Asian Amer. Legal Defense and [17095]
Educ. Fund; Chaine [★22569]
Educ. Fund for Dental [★8196]
Educ. Fund; Disarm [17428]
Educ. Fund; Herbert Lehman [★17130]
Educ. Fund; Lambda Legal Defense and [12241]
Educ. Fund; League of Women Voters [18459]
Educ. Fund; Minority Bus. Enterprise Legal Defense and [2763]
Educ. Fund; NOW Legal Defense and [★17546]
Educ. Fund; Peace Action [18167]
Educ. Fund; Peace Through Law [18236]
Educ. Fund for Podiatric Medical [16044]
Educ. Fund; Puerto Rican Legal Defense and [17149]
Educ. Fund; SANE/FREEZE [★18167]
Educ. Fund; Senior Conformation Judges Assn. [★22193]
Educ. Fund; TEI [★6304]
Educ. Fund; WAND [18174]
Educ. Fund; Women's Leadership Network, Natl. Student [★9195]
Educ. Fund; World Without War [★18259]
Educ. Funding Res. Coun. [8348], c/o Thompson Publishing Gp., Inc., Govt. Info. Services, 1725 K St. NW, Ste. 700, Washington, DC 20006, (202)872-4000
Educ. of Girls and Women; Assn. for the Promotion of the Mathematics [★8828]

Reference to "IO" in place of a book number signifies that the association may be found in the 45th edition of International Organizations.

Educ. in a Global Age; Amer. Forum: [★8593]
Educ; Global Perspectives in [★8593]
Educ. in Healthcare Info. Tech; Assn. for [15132]
Educ. in Human Rights Network [IO], Birmingham, United Kingdom
Educ; In Coun. on Hotel, Restaurant and Institutional [★8525]
Educ. Inc; Patriotic [8092]
Educ; Indian Amer. Forum for Political [18352]
Educ. Indus. Assn. [★3479]
Educ. Indus. Assn. [9215], c/o Steven Pines, Exec. Dir., 5909 Barbados Pl., Ste. 20, Rockville, MD 20852, (800)252-3280
Educ. and Indus; School Facilities Coun. of Architecture, [★7892]
Educ. Info. Center; Natl. Special [★11971]
Educ. and Info. CH; Natl. Digestive Diseases [★14422]
Educ; Inst. for Chem. [8062]
Educ; Inst. of Consumer Financial [8424]
Educ; Inst. for Democratic [★17091]
Educ. Inst; Investment [8425]
Educ. Inst; Manpower [8567]
Educ; Inst. for Responsive [8408]
Educ. Inst. for the Transfer of Tech. to [8563]
Educ. Inst; Women's Res. and [17580]
Educ. Institutions; Assn. of Teachers of [★8096]
Educ. Institutions of Metropolitan Districts; Natl. Assn. of Teacher [★9208]
Educ. Intl. [IO], Brussels, Belgium
Educ. Intl., Africa Regional Off. [IO], Lome, Togo
Educ. Intl., Asia-Pacific Regional Off. [IO], Kuala Lumpur, Malaysia
Educ; Intl. Assembly for Collegiate Bus. [8024]
Educ; Intl. Assn. for Computing in [★8134]
Educ. in Intl. Bus; Assn. for [★8011]
Educ. Intl. Coun. for Computers in [★8134]
Educ. Intl., Latin Am. Regional Off. [IO], San Jose, Costa Rica
Educ. Intl., North America-Caribbean Regional Off. [IO], Babonneau, St. Lucia
Educ; Intl. Sex Worker Found. for Art, Culture and [13092]
Educ. and Internship Assn; Cooperative [8157]
Education; Interstate Compact for [★8252]
Educ; Joint Coun. in Economic [★8217]
Educ; Joint Rev. Comm. for Respiratory Therapy [★16610]
Educ. for Journalism; Amer. Coun. on [★8703]
Educ. in Journalism; Assn. for [★8706]
Educ. in Journalism and Mass Commun; Assn. for [8706]
Educ. in Journalism and Mass Communications; Accrediting Coun. on [8703]
Educ; Keystone Center for Continuing [★7746]
Educ; Labor's League for Political [★18303]
Education Law
    Alliance for the Separation of School and State [8221]
    Center for Law and Educ. [5675]
    Coun. on Law in Higher Educ. [8317]
    Educ. Law Assn. [5676]
    Education Law Association [IO]
    European Assn. for Educ. Law and Policy [IO]
    Global Alliance for Justice Educ. [8766]
    Independence Inst. [17120]
    Intl. Assn. of Workforce Professionals [5679]
    Natl. Assn. of Coll. and Univ. Attorneys [5677]
    Natl. Assn. of State Workforce Agencies [5680]
    North Amer. South Asian Law Student Assn. [8773]
Educ. Law Assn. [5676], Mail Drop 0528, 300 Coll. Park, Dayton, OH 45469, (937)229-3589
Education Law Association [IO], Dayton, OH, United States
Educ. Leadership Assn; Natl. Sci. [9113]
Educ; Leadership Network for Intl. [★8659]
Educ; Leadership Network for Intl. [★IO]
Educ. and Legal Fund; Get Oil Out [★5092]
Educ; Liaison Comm. on Continuing Medical [★15151]
Educ; Liaison Comm. on Medical [8839]
Educ. and Licensure; Fed. for Accessible Nursing [15478]
Educ. in the Life Sciences; Coalition for [9098]

Educ; Lincoln Inst. for Res. and [16940]
Educ. Lobby; Taxpayers [★18717]
Educ. Local Supervisors; Natl. Assn. of Distributive [★8818]
Educ. Mgt. Systems; Natl. Center for Higher [7905]
Educ. in Maternal and Child Hea; Natl. Center for [13969]
Educ; MENC: The Natl. Assn. for Music [8913]
Educ; Mennonite Bd. of [★20250]
Educ. in the Middle East and North Africa; Soc. for Jewish Youth [★20171]
Educ. of Migrant Children (of the Natl. Child Labor Comm.); Natl. Comm. on the [12593]
Educ; Ministries in Public [★19938]
Educ. Ministries Team/United Ministries in Higher Educ; Higher [★19938]
Educ. for Minorities Proj; Quality [★8303]
Educ; Montana Coun. for Indian [★8937]
Educ; Narcotics [★13245]
Educ; Natl. Assn. for the Advancement of Humane [★11433]
Educ; Natl. Assn. for Asian and Pacific Amer. [7988]
Educ; Natl. Assn. for Bilingual [7999]
Educ; Natl. Assn. of Boards of [★8056]
Educ; Natl. Assn. of Boards, Commissions, and Councils of Catholic [8056]
Educ; Natl. Assn. for Bus. Teacher [8032]
Educ; Natl. Assn. of Colleges and Departments of [★9208]
Educ; Natl. Assn. for Developmental [8200]
Education; Natl. Assn. of Directors of Christian [19937]
Educ; Natl. Assn. for Equal Opportunity in Higher [8109]
Educ; Natl. Assn. for Family and Community [8513]
Educ; Natl. Assn. for Humane and Environmental [11433]
Educ; Natl. Assn. for Humanities [8531]
Educ; Natl. Assn. for Multicultural [8582]
Educ; Natl. Assn. for Nursery [★8069]
Educ; Natl. Assn. of Parish Coordinators/Directors of Religious [★19932]
Educ; Natl. Assn. for Physical Educ. in Higher [8985]
Educ; Natl. Assn. of Professors of Christian [★8088]
Educ; Natl. Assn. for Public Continuing Adult [★8146]
Educ; Natl. Assn. for Sport and Physical [8986]
Educ; Natl. Assn. for State Administrators of Hea. Occupations [★8870]
Educ; Natl. Assn. of State Aviation Officials Center for Aviation Res. and [★5537]
Educ; Natl. Assn. of State Boards of [9082]
Educ; Natl. Assn. of State Directors of Migrant [12592]
Educ; Natl. Assn. of State Directors of Special [9149]
Educ; Natl. Assn. of State Supervisors of Distributive [★8818]
Educ; Natl. Assn. of Supervisors and Administrators of Hea. Occupations [8870]
Educ; Natl. Assn. of Supervisors of Agricultural [7939]
Educ; Natl. Assn. of Supervisors of Bus. [8034]
Educ; Natl. Assn. of Supervisors of Bus. and Off. [★8034]
Educ; Natl. Center for Community [8125]
Education; National Center for ESL Literacy [★10401]
Educ; Natl. Center for Hea. [14582]
Educ; Natl. Center for Improving Sci. [9109]
Educ; Natl. Center for Mediation [5461]
Educ; Natl. Center for Res. in Vocational [★9304]
Educ; Natl. Center for Sci. [9110]
Educ; Natl. Center for the Stud. of Collective Bargaining in Higher [★24036]
Educ; Natl. Coalition for Consumer [17336]
Educ; Natl. Coalition for Sex Equity in [★8399]
Educ; Natl. Coalition for Women and Girls in [9321]
Educ; Natl. Commn. for Cooperative [8159]
Educ; Natl. Conf. of Directors of Religious [★19934]
Educ; Natl. Coun. for Accreditation of Teacher [7879]
Educ; Natl. Coun. for Bus. [★8036]
Educ; Natl. Coun. of Churches, Ministries in Christian [★19935]
Educ. of the Natl. Coun. of Churches; Professors and Res. Sect. of the Division of Christian [★19939]

Educ; Natl. Coun. on Community Services and Continuing [★8152]
Educ; Natl. Coun. on Economic [8217]
Educ; Natl. Coun. for Geographic [8457]
Educ; Natl. Coun. for History [8508]
Educ; Natl. Coun. on Hotel and Restaurant [★8525]
Educ; Natl. Coun. for Jewish [★8690]
Educ; Natl. Coun. on Measurement in [9256]
Educ; Natl. Coun. on Measurements Used in [★9256]
Educ; Natl. Coun. on Patient Info. and [15946]
Educ; Natl. Coun. of Primary [★8064]
Educ; Natl. Coun. on Rehabilitation [16329]
Educ; Natl. Coun. on Religion in Higher [★19940]
Educ. of the Natl. Educ. Assn; Dept. of Bus. [8036]
Educ; Natl. Found. for the Improvement of [★8294]
Educ; Natl. Herbart Soc. for the Sci. Stud. of [★8293]
Educ; Natl. Org. for Human Ser. [★9131]
Educ; Natl. Org. on Legal Problems of [★5676]
Educ; Natl. Schools Comm. for Economic [8218]
Educ; Natl. Soc. of Coll. Teachers of [★8307]
Educ; Natl. Soc. for Experiential [8414]
Educ; Natl. Soc. for Vocational [★9300]
Educ. Network; Conflict Resolution [★5450]
Educ. Network for Continuing Medical [15177]
Educ. Network and Exchange; Continuing Lib. [★10350]
Educ. Network and Exchange Round Table; Continuing Lib. [10350]
Educ. Network; Gay, Lesbian, and Straight [8456]
Educ. Network; Kennedy Center Alliance for Arts [7975]
Educ. Network; Public [9040]
Educ. Network; Public Leadership [9326]
Educ; North Amer. Assn. for Environmental [8393]
Educ; North Amer. Assn. of Professors of Christian [★8088]
Educ; North Amer. Professors of Christian [8088]
Educ. in Obstetrics and Gynecology; Coun. on Resident [15597]
Educ; Off. of Minorities in Higher [★8887]
Educ. Opportunity; Coun. on Legal [8764]
Educ; Parent Resources and Info. on Drug [★13276]
Educ; Parents Active for Vision [16880]
Educ; Parents and Teachers Against Violence in [8208]
Educ. of the Partially Seeing; Coun. for the [★9145]
Educ. for Peace in Iraq Center [17927], 611 Pennsylvania Ave. SE, No. 132, Washington, DC 20003, (202)543-6176
Educ. for the Physician Asst; Accreditation Rev. Commn. on [15972]
Educ. for Physician Assistants; Accreditation Rev. Comm. on [★15972]
Educ. Pioneers [9178], PO Box 28293, San Jose, CA 95159-8293, (408)315-3986
Educ; Police Assn. for Coll. [6004]
Education Policy Fellowship Program [★8264]
Educ. Practitioners and Provider; Assn. of [★9215]
Educ; Professional and Organizational Development Network in Higher [8494]
Educ. and the Professions; Natl. Center for the Stud. of Collective Bargaining in Higher [24036]
Educ. Prog. Administrators; Natl. Assn. of Fed. [7900]
Educ. Program; International Bowhunter [★23053]
Educ. Prog; National Geographic Soc. Geography [★7123]
Educ. Prog; Natl. Judicial [17964]
Educ. Prog. to Promote Equality for Women and Men in the Courts; Natl. Judicial [★17964]
Educ. Programs; Commn. on Accreditation of Allied Hea. [8832]
Educ. Programs; Comm. for Full Funding of [★8345]
Educ. Programs; Emergency Comm. for Full Funding of [★8345]
Educ. Programs; Natl. Assn. of Administrators of State and Fed. [★7900]
Educ. Project; International Cmpt. [★18763]
Educ. Project; International Cmpt. [★IO]
Educ. Proj; League of Rural Voters [★16955]
Educ. Proj; Southwest Voter Registration [18367]

A star before a book entry number signifies that the name is not listed separately, but is mentioned within the entry.

Educ. Proj; U.S./Guatemala Labor [★17978]
Educ. Proj; Veterans [13358]
Educ. for Public Admin; Coun. on Graduate [★6194]
Educ. for Public Hea; Coun. on [16242]
Educ. in Radiologic Tech; Joint Rev. Comm. on [8838]
Educ. and Recreation; Amer. Alliance for Hea., Physical [★8979]
Educ. and Recreation; Amer. Assn. for Hea., Physical [★8979]
Educ., Recreation and Dance; Amer. Alliance for Hea., Physical [8979]
Educ. and Recreation; School Hea. Division of Amer. Assn. for Hea., Physical [★16234]
Educ. and Recreation; Soc. of State Directors of Hea., Physical [8992]
Educ. and Related Services; Natl. Rsrc. Center for Paraprofessionals in [9150]
Educ. and Research; ASM Found. for [★7311]
Educ. and Research; ASM Found. for [★IO]
Educ. Res. Assn; Amer. Vocational [★9301]
Educ. and Res; Center for Death [★13314]
Educ. and Res; Coalition of Labor Union Women Center for [24204]
Educ. and Res. Coun; Warehousing [3984]
Educ. and Res. Found; Amer. Soc. of Clinical Hypnosis - [14922]
Educ. and Res. Foundation; ASRT [★15131]
Educ. Res. Foundation; Business [★8032]
Educ. and Res; Found. for Chiropractic [14004]
Educ. Res; Found. for Interior Design [★8584]
Educ. and Res. Foundation; Medical [★14549]
Educ. and Res. Found; NAED [2503]
Educ. and Res. Foundation; Naprapathic [★15276]
Educ. and Res. Foundation; National Judges [★5913]
Education and Res. Found; Operations Mgt. [7167]
Education and Res. Found; Orthodontic [14183]
Educ. and Res. Found; Wood Heating [★1880]
Educ. and Res. in Free Enterprise; Center for [★17635]
Educ. and Res. Fund; American Found. for Negro Affairs Natl. [★8045]
Educ. and Res. Inst. [★17634]
Educ. Res. Inst; Natl. Home [8522]
Educ. and Res; Natl. Center for Constr. [17632]
Educ. and Res. Proj; Labor [★24116]
Educ. and Res. in Substance Abuse; Assn. for Medical [8849]
Educ. Rsrc. Center; Inter-Hemispheric [★16976]
Educ. Rsrc. Center; Native Amer. Women Hea. [★12630]
Educ. Rsrc. Org; Hea. [13568]
Educ. Roundtable; Museum [10509]
Educ. Schools; Accrediting Bur. of Hea. [15124]
Educ., Sci. and Culture Trade Union for Slovenia [★IO]
Educ. and Sci. Employees' Union of Russia [IO], Moscow, Russia
Educ. and Sci. Trade Union of Slovenia [IO], Ljubljana, Slovenia
Educ. and Ser; Natl. Assn. for Practical Nurse [8869]
Educ. Ser. of North Am; Jewish [8692]
Educ. Services; AAF [★24393]
Educ. Services; Amer. Advt. Fed. [24393]
Educ; Sex Worker Found. for Art, Culture and [★13092]
Education of the Sexes; Org. for Equal [8402]
Educ. in Social Work Regulation; American Found. for Res. and Consumer [★13200]
Educ. Soc; Amer. Humane [★11429]
Educ. Soc; Amer. Peanut Res. and [5050]
Educ; Soc. for Automation in Bus. [★8132]
Educ; Soc. for Automation in Professional [★8132]
Educ. Soc; Comparative [★8655]
Educ; Soc. for Field Experience [★8414]
Educ; Soc. for History of [10118]
Educ; Soc. for History [8511]
Educ; Soc. of Independent and Private School Data [★8132]
Educ; Soc. for Info. Tech. and Teacher [9243]
Educ; Soc. for Music Teacher [8931]
Educ; Soc; Natl. Humane [11440]
Educ; Soc. for Nutrition [15570]
Educ. Soc; Philosophy of [8969]

Educ; Soc. for Photographic [8976]
Educ. Soc. of the Protestant Episcopal Church; Evangelical [★19955]
Educ; Soc. for Public Hea. [16254]
Educ; Soc. for Religion in Higher [★19940]
Educ; Soc. of State Directors of Physical and Hea. [★8992]
Education, Special
Amer. Coun. on Rural Special Educ. [9137]
Amer. Printing House for the Blind [16829]
Assn. for Direct Instruction [8232]
Braille Revival League [16839]
Coun. of Administrators of Special Educ. [9139]
Coun. for Learning Disabilities [12490]
Div. for Early Childhood of the Coun. for Exceptional Children [9144]
Education-A-Must [12056]
Educational Leadership Inst. [8746]
Friends of LADDERS [12491]
Inter-American Conductive Educ. Assn. [9146]
Model Secondary School for the Deaf [14766]
Natl. Assn. of Special Educ. Teachers [9148]
Natl. Assn. of State Directors of Special Educ. [9149]
Natl. Dissemination Center for Children with Disabilities [11971]
Rural Inst. [11986]
Educ; Special Interest Gp. on Cmpt. Sci. [8135]
Educ. Specialists; Circus [9796]
Educ. Statistics; Natl. Center for [★8284]
Educ. to Stop Domestic Violence; Emerge: Counseling and [12026]
Educ; Student Personnel Assn. for Teacher [★8527]
Educ. Studies; Center for [★9258]
Educ; Suntanning Assn. for [3364]
Educ. and Supervision; Assn. for Counselor [8165]
Educ. for the Surgical Technologist; Joint Rev. Comm. on [★15123]
Educ. in Surgical Tech; Accreditation Rev. Comm. on [15123]
Educ. Systems Exchange [8136], 1111 Torrey Pines Rd., La Jolla, CA 92037-4551, (858)454-9765
Educ. Task Force; Interstate Migrant [★12588]
Educ. Teachers; Natl. Assn. for Distributive [★8818]
Educ. Through Art; U.S. Soc. for [7980]
Educ. Through Art; U.S. Soc. for [★7980]
Educ. Through Auditory Res. Found; Hearing [★14756]
Educ. in the Total Env; Total [★4602]
Educ. and Training; Accrediting Coun. for Continuing [8145]
Educ., Training, and Advocacy; Multicultural [11625]
Educ. and Training Coun; Distance [8517]
Educ. and Training for Employment; Center on [9304]
Education and Training Found. [★20768]
Educ. and Training; Natl. Coun. for Continuing [8152]
Educ., Training and Res. Associates [8556], 4 Carbonero Way, Scotts Valley, CA 95066-4200, (831)438-4060
Educ., Training and Res; Intl. Soc. for Intercultural [★8667]
Educ., Training and Res; Soc. for Intercultural [★8667]
Educ; Triangle Coalition for Sci. and Tech. [9116]
Educ. Turnkey Inst. [8557], 256 N Washington St., Falls Church, VA 22046, (703)536-2310
Educ. Turnkey Systems [★8557]
Educ. Unit; Coun. on the Continuing [★8150]
Educ; United Ministries in [★19938]
Educ; United Ministries in Higher [★19938]
Educ. U.S. Natl. Comm; World Org. for Early Childhood [8071]
Educ; United Synagogue Commn. on Jewish [★8702]
Educ. - USA; MOVE Intl.: Mobility Opportunities Via [11962]
Education Voucher Inst. - Defunct.
Educ. and Welfare Assn; New Kuban [19019]
Educ. and Welfare Assn; Presbyterian Hea., [13184]
Educ. and Welfare Assn; United Presbyterian Hea., [★13184]
Educ. Wife Assault [IO], Toronto, ON, Canada
Educ; Women and Mathematics [8828]

Educ. in World Govt; Assn. for [★17620]
Educ. in World Law; Pierce Butler, Jr. Found. for [★18834]
Educ. in World Order; Fund for [★18834]
Educ. Writers Assn. [3112], 2122 P St. NW, Ste. 201, Washington, DC 20037, (202)452-9830
Educ. Writing; Natl. Coun. for the Advancement of [★3112]
Educ. of Young Children; Natl. Assn. for the [8069]
Education Youth
Big Picture Company [8353]
Boys Town Jerusalem Found. of Am. [13473]
Chinese School Assn. in the U.S. [9090]
Coun. for Children with Behavioral Disorders [9140]
CRU Inst. [8138]
Direction Sports [13482]
Div. for Early Childhood of the Coun. for Exceptional Children [9144]
Educators Serving the Community [8318]
Families, 4-H, and Nutrition [13483]
Fed. of Galaxy Explorers [9136]
For Inspiration and Recognition of Sci. and Tech. [8319]
Girls Inc. [13486]
Global Nomads Gp. [9336]
Global Outreach [8615]
Hands On Sci. Outreach [8067]
Help the Afghan Children [IO]
Help Afghan School Children Org [IO]
Home School Sports Network [23490]
Intl. Boys' Schools Coalition [8268]
Interstate Migrant Educ. Coun. [12588]
Just Think [18852]
Kids Universe, Inc. [8320]
Milton S. Eisenhower Found. [11839]
Natl. 4-H Coun. [13494]
Natl. Assn. for the Educ. of Young Children [8069]
Natl. Assn. of Youth Clubs [13498]
Natl. Coalition for Aviation Educ. [7995]
Natl. Coun. of Educ. Providers [8329]
Natl. Head Start Assn. [9006]
Natl. Rural Educ. Advocacy Coalition [9068]
Natl. Urban Alliance for Effective Educ. [9291]
Natl. Youth Rights Assn. [18855]
Parent Cooperative Preschools Intl. [8070]
Parents for Public Schools [12052]
Prepare Tomorrow's Parents [13511]
Safe Sitter [11537]
Waters Found. [8313]
WAVE [12105]
Young Audiences [9603]
Youth Educ. in the Arts [9604]
Educational Admin; Univ. Coun. for [7909]
Educational Administrators of Schools and Programs for the Deaf; Conf. of [14749]
Educational Administrators Serving the Deaf; Conf. of [★14749]
Educational Advocacy
Alliance for Excellent Educ. [9118]
Amer. Assn. of Teaching and Curriculum [9209]
Assn. for the Advancement of Sustainability in Higher Educ. [8479]
Assn. for Core Texts and Courses [8776]
A Better Chance [8321]
Black Alliance for Educational Options [8322]
Coll. Parents of Am. [8485]
Coll. Summit [8486]
Communities in Schools [8323]
Coun. for Opportunity in Educ. [8324]
Education-A-Must [12056]
The Educ. Coalition [8325]
Higher Educ. Info. Tech. Alliance [8489]
Inst. for Educational Services [8265]
Intl. Assn. for Truancy and Dropout Prevention [8326]
Intl. Assn. for Truancy and Dropout Prevention [IO]
Kids Universe, Inc. [8320]
Leadership Conf. Educ. Fund [8094]
Natl. Abstinence Educ. Assn. [9123]
Natl. Assn. for Professional Development Schools [9091]
Natl. Assn. for Single Sex Public Educ. [9038]
Natl. At-Risk Educ. Assn. [8327]

Reference to "IO" in place of a book number signifies that the association may be found in the 45th edition of International Organizations.

Natl. Coalition of Advocates for Students [8328]
Natl. Coun. of Educ. Providers [8329]
Natl. Coun. for Graduate Entrepreneurship [IO]
Natl. Coun. for Support of Disability Issues [13212]
Natl. Dropout Prevention Center/Network [8330]
Natl. Jewish Coalition for Literacy [8795]
Natl. Rural Educ. Advocacy Coalition [9068]
Natl. Urban Alliance for Effective Educ. [9291]
NETWORK [8295]
North Amer. Assn. of Jewish High Schools [8698]
Parents for Public Schools [12052]
Pathways to Coll. Network [8493]
Plan of Action for Challenging Times [8331]
Police Assn. for Coll. Educ. [6004]
Proj. Appleseed: The Natl. Campaign for Public School Improvement [8332]
Sloan Consortium [8304]
Sudan-American Found. for Educ. [8073]
Educational Aid; Soc. for French Amer. Cultural Services and [★8560]
Educational Assessment Guidelines Leading Toward Excellence [★14602]
Educational Assn; Augustinian Secondary [8054]
Educational Assn; Jesuit [★8052]
Educational Assn; Jesuit [★8055]
Educational Assn; Natl. Catholic [8059]
Educational Assn; Natl. Young Farmer [4653]
Educational Assn; Rural/Regional [★9069]
Educational Audiology Assn. [14755], 3030 W 81st Ave., Westminster, CO 80031, (800)460-7322
Educational Audiology Assn. [IO], Tampa, FL, United States
Educational Audiology Soc. [★IO]
Educational Audiology Soc. [★14755]
Educational Bridges Project - Address unknown since 1995.
Educational Broadcasting Corp. [9763], c/o Thirteen/WNET, 450 W 33rd St., New York, NY 10001, (212)560-1313
Educational Buyers Assn. [★7899]
Educational Buyers; Natl. Assn. of [★7899]
Educational Center; AAUW [★9312]
Educational Center for Applied Ekistics [10228], 1900 DeKalb Ave. NE, Atlanta, GA 30307, (404)378-2219
Educational Centre; Nelson Jack Edwards [★17158]
Educational Commn. for Foreign Medical Graduates [15997], 3624 Market St., Philadelphia, PA 19104-2685, (215)386-5900
Educational Commn. for Foreign Medical Graduates [IO], Philadelphia, PA, United States
Educational Commn. for Foreign Veterinary Graduates [★16779]
Educational Communication Assn. - Defunct.
Educational Communications [8386], PO Box 351419, Los Angeles, CA 90035-9119, (310)559-9160
Educational Communications [IO], Los Angeles, CA, United States
Educational Communications and Tech; Assn. for [8551]
Educational Concerns for Hunger Org. [12389], 17391 Durrance Rd., North Fort Myers, FL 33917, (239)543-3246
Educational Concerns for Hunger Org. [IO], North Fort Myers, FL, United States
Educational Conf. of North Am; Lutheran [8804]
Educational and Cooperative Union of Am; Farmers' [★4651]
Educational Coun; Ceramic [8061]
Educational Coun. for Foreign Medical Graduates [★15997]
Educational Coun. for Foreign Medical Graduates [★IO]
Educational Coun. - Natl. Assn. of Accredited Cosmetology Schools; Teachers' [★8160]
Educational Coun. - Natl. Assn. of Cosmetology Schools; Teachers' [★8160]
Educational Counselors Assn; Independent [★7871]
Educational Credentials; Center for Adult Learning and [★8406]
Educational and Cultural Assn., Inc; Tartan [★19354]
Educational and Cultural Exchange; Fulbright Assn. of Alumni of Intl. [★8613]

Educational Dealers and Suppliers Assn. Intl. - Defunct.
Educational Development Assn. [IO], Keighley, United Kingdom
Educational Development; Black Women Organized for [13421]
Educational Development; Copred Consortium: Peace Res. and [★18233]
Educational Development Corp. - Defunct.
Educational Development and Res; Coun. for [★9061]
Educational Equity Center [8400], 100 5th Ave., 8th Fl., New York, NY 10011, (212)243-1110
Educational Excellence; Texans for [★7998]
Educational Exchange; Liaison Gp. for Intl. [★8591]
Educational Exhibitors Assn. [1336], c/o VMS, Inc., 805 Airway Dr., Allegan, MI 49010-8516, (269)673-2200
Educational Exhibitors; Natl. Catholic [1347]
Educational Expeditions Intl. [★8413]
Educational Facilities
  APPA: The Assn. of Higher Educ. Facilities Officers [8333]
  APPA: The Association of Higher Education Facilities Officers [IO]
  Community Learning and Info. Network [IO]
  Community Learning and Info. Network [8334]
  Coun. of Educational Fac. Planners, Intl. [8335]
  Coun. of Educational Fac. Planners, Intl. [IO]
  Edge-ucate [12057]
  Natl. Assn. of Comics Art Educators [8115]
  Natl. Assn. for the Exchange of Indus. Resources [8336]
  Natl. Educational Telecommunications Assn. [8337]
  Room to Read [12053]
Educational Facilities Laboratories - Defunct.
Educational Fellowship; Oral Roberts Univ. [8089]
Educational Foundation; Alpha Kappa Lambda [★24612]
Educational Found. of Am. [12119], 35 Church Ln., Westport, CT 06880, (203)226-6498
Educational Found. of Am. [IO], Westport, CT, United States
Educational Found. of Am; Narcotic [13256]
Educational Found; Amer. Acad. of Medical Administrators Res. and [15046]
Educational Found; Amer. Assn. of Univ. Women [9312]
Educational Found; Amer. Water Ski [23975]
Educational Found. for the Apparel Indus. [★232]
Educational Found; ASID [★2251]
Educational Found; Belgian Amer. [9736]
Educational Found; British Amer. [8605]
Educational Found; Chimera [★13436]
Educational Found; Chinese-Amer. [8428]
Educational Found; College Stores Res. and [★3415]
Educational Found; Dannemiller Memorial [13683]
Educational Foundation; Delta Res. and [★24597]
Educational Found; Direct Marketing [8816]
Educational Found. for the Fashion Indus. [232], 7th Ave. at 27th St., Bldg. C, Rm. 204, New York, NY 10001, (212)217-7999
Educational Found. for Foreign Stud; EF [★8611]
Educational Found; Givat Haviva [18059]
Educational Found; INTACT [★11732]
Educational Found; Jefferson [17273]
Educational Found; Latin Amer. [8496]
Educational Found; Natl. Restaurant Assn. [1960]
Educational Found. of the Natl. Restaurant Assn. [★1960]
Educational Found; Natl. Tennis [★23903]
Educational Found; Natl. Vocational [★9308]
Educational Foundation; NATPE [★571]
Educational Foundation; NATPE [★IO]
Educational Found. for Nuclear Sci. [★7603]
Educational Found; Plastic Surgery [14051]
Educational Foundation; Professional Ski Instructors of Am. [★23755]
Educational Found. and School; Threefold [8529]
Educational Found; Sigma Phi Epsilon [★24660]
Educational Found; Tennis [★23903]
Educational Found; Theta Delta Chi [★24668]
Educational Found; Theta Delta Chi [★IO]

Educational Found; United Cerebral Palsy Res. and [★13935]
Educational Found; U.S. Bus. and Indus. Coun. [18638]
Educational Foundation; Wholesale Distributors Assn. [★3067]
Educational Found; Willa Cather Pioneer Memorial and [9722]
Educational Found. for Women in Accounting [9316], c/o Cynthia Hires, Admin., PO Box 1925, Southeastern, PA 19399-1925, (610)407-9229
Educational Found; Zeta Psi [★24671]
Educational Freedom
  Citizens for Educational Freedom [8338]
  Home School Legal Defense Assn. [8339]
  Parents in Control [8340]
Educational Freedom Found. - Address unknown since 2001.
Educal. Fund; A. Philip Randolph [17078]
Educational Fund to End Handgun Violence [★17592]
Educational Fund for Individual Rights - Defunct.
Educational Fund; Mexican Amer. Legal Defense and [17705]
Educational Fund; Natl. Assn. for the Advancement of Colored People Legal Defense and [17130]
Educational Fund; Natl. Student [★9196]
Educational Fund; Results [★17797]
Educational Fund; Results [★IO]
Educational Fund to Stop Gun Violence [17592], 1023 15th St. NW, Ste. 301, Washington, DC 20005-2602, (202)408-0061
Educational Funding
  ACUO [8341]
  Amer. Educ. Finance Assn. [8342]
  Armenian Educational Found. [8343]
  Bill Raskob Found. [17479]
  Coalition of Higher Educ. Assistance Organizations [8344]
  Comm. for Educ. Funding [8345]
  Coun. for Aid to Educ. [8346]
  Coun. for Rsrc. Development [8347]
  Edge-ucate [12057]
  Edge-ucate [IO]
  Educ. Funding Res. Coun. [8348]
  Henry M. Jackson Found. [17480]
  Natl. Assn. of Federally Impacted Schools [8349]
  Natl. Assn. of Student Financial Aid Administrators [8350]
  Natl. Coun. of Higher Educ. Loan Programs [8351]
  Room to Read [12053]
  Scottish Further Educ. Funding Coun. [IO]
  Van Andel Educ. Inst. [8312]
  William and Flora Hewlett Found. [13194]
Educational Funds; Nurses [15516]
Educational Futures; Found. for [318]
Educational Futures, Inc. - Address unknown since 2002.
Educational Gender Info. Ser; Amer. [★13090]
Educational Guidance Associates School and Coll. Advisory Center - Defunct.
Educational Guidance Center for the Mentally Retarded - Defunct.
Educational and Health Career Services - Defunct.
Educational Innovation; Inst. for [★8253]
Educational Inst; Roofing Indus. [1064]
Educational Inst. of Scotland [IO], Edinburgh, United Kingdom
Educational and Institutional Cooperative Service [★7899]
Educational Institutions; Assn. for Community Based [★8123]
Educational Institutions; Assn. of Free Methodist [8447]
Educational Institutions; Clearinghouse for Community Based Free Standing [★8123]
Educational Jewelry Mfrs. Assn. - Defunct.
Educational Leadership Inst. [8746]
Educational Leadership Prog. [8779], 15 E 91st St., Apt. 2B, New York, NY 10128, (917)330-0320
Educational Leadership Program [IO], New York, NY, United States
Educational League; Americanism [17623]
Educational Media Coun. - Defunct.

A star before a book entry number signifies that the name is not listed separately, but is mentioned within the entry.

Educational Media; Natl. Info. Center for [8569]
Educational Media Professionals; Natl. Assn. of State [8568]
Educational and Medical Aid; Restoring Hope through [★12881]
Educational Ministries; Searching Together [19909]
Educational Negotiators; Assn. of [★24046]
Educational Negotiators; Natl. Assn. of [★24046]
Educational Network; Alternative Religions [20457]
Educational Off. Personnel; Natl. Assn. of [★7898]
Educational Off. Professionals; Natl. Assn. of [7898]
Educational Opportunity Associations; Natl. Coun. of [★8324]
Educational Org; Basque [9732]
Educational Paperback Assn. [3221], c/o Marilyn Abel, Exec. Sec., PO Box 1399, East Hampton, NY 11937, (631)329-3315
Educational Personnel; Amer. Assn. of Examiners and Administrators of [★7883]
Educational and Physical Culture Org; Amer. Sokol [19025]
Educational Planning [★8999]
Educational Planning [★IO]
Educational Planning Inst. [8998]
Educational Planning; Intl. Soc. for [★8999]
Educational Policies Commn. - Defunct.
Educational Policy Center [★8321]
Educational Press Assn. of Am. [★9009]
Educational Products Info. Exchange Inst. [★8559]
Educational Professional Development Found; Natl. Vocational [★9308]
Educational Program Assn. of America - Defunct.
Educational Programmers and Systems Analysts; Soc. of [★8132]
Educational Programs; Coun. on Accreditation of Nurse Anesthesia [8835]
Educational Programs for the EMS Professions; Comm. on Accreditation for [8833]
Educational Programs for the EMT-Paramedic; Joint Rev. Comm. on [★8833]
Educational Programs; New Century Policies [18469]
Educational Programs in Surgical Tech; Accreditation Rev. Comm. for [★15123]
Educational Progress; Natl. Assessment of [★9253]
Educational Progress; Natl. Assessment of [9253]
Educational Progress, The Nation's Rpt. Card; Natl. Assessment of [★9253]
Educational Publishers; Assn. of [9009]
Educational Publishers; Classroom Publishers Assn. and Assn. of [★9009]
Educational Publishers Coun. [IO], London, United Kingdom
Educational Publishers; EdPress - The Assn. of [★9009]
Educational Radio and Assn. of Communications Technicians; Natl. Assn. of Bus. and [★3752]
Educational Records Bur. [9249], 220 E 42nd St., New York, NY 10017, (212)672-9800
Educational Records Bur. [IO], New York, NY, United States

Educational Reform
Accuracy in Academia [8352]
Alliance for the Separation of School and State [8221]
Big Picture Company [8353]
Center for Occupational Res. and Development [8354]
Center for School Change [8242]
The Educ. Coalition [8325]
Educ. Pioneers [9178]
Hispanic Coun. for Reform and Educational Options [8260]
Info. for School and Coll. Governors [IO]
Inst. for Learning Technologies [8355]
Intl. Assn. for Learning Alternatives [7945]
Intl. Movement Towards Educational Change [IO]
Natl. Acad. of Amer. Scholars [8356]
Natl. Alliance for Public Charter Schools [9037]
Natl. Center for Fair and Open Testing [9255]
Natl. Center for Res. on Evaluation, Standards, and Student Testing [8285]
Natl. Coun. of Educ. Providers [8329]
Natl. Paideia Center [8357]
Natl. Tech Prep Network [8358]

StandardsWork [9094]
Syndicat Gen. de l'Education Nationale [IO]
Teaching for Change [8359]
Thomas B. Fordham Found. [17477]
Educational Reptiles in Captivity Zoological Compound - Address unknown since 1989.
Educational Res. Analysts [9259], PO Box 7518, Longview, TX 75607-7518, (903)753-5993
Educational Res. Associates [8254], PO Box 8795, Portland, OR 97207-8795, (503)228-6345
Educational Res. Assn; Amer. [9053]
Educational Res. Assn. Women's Caucus; Amer. [★9328]
Educational Res. Coun. of America - Defunct.
Educational and Res. Found; Forging Indus. [7314]
Educational Res. Found; High/Scope [8181]
Educational Res. Found; Mfrs. Representatives [2539]
Educational Res. Ser. [7895], 1001 N Fairfax St., Ste. 500, Alexandria, VA 22314-1587, (703)243-2100
Educational Rsrc. Center; Parents [★12496]
Educational Resources and Services Found; Hysterectomy [15601]
Educational and Sci. Foundation; SFPE [★7082]
Educational Secretaries; Natl. Assn. of [★7898]
Educational Ser; Citizenship [★17072]
Educational Services [★8253]
Educational Services [★IO]
Educational Services; Independent [1263]
Educational Soc; Estonian [19042]
Educational Software Cooperative [6765], 127 The Ranch Rd., Del Valle, TX 78617
Educational Software Cooperative [IO], Del Valle, TX, United States
Educational Systems Corp. - Defunct.
Educational TV Media Assn. [★IO]
Educational TV; Natl. [★9763]
Educational Testing
ACT [9246]
Coun. on Career for Minorities [8047]
Educational Records Bur. [9249]
Educational Testing Ser. [9250]
Natl. Assessment of Educational Progress [9253]
Natl. Assn. of Test Directors [9254]
Natl. Center for Res. on Evaluation, Standards, and Student Testing [8285]
Natl. Coun. on Measurement in Educ. [9256]
Secondary School Admission Test Bd. [9257]
Educational Testing Ser. [9250], Rosedale Rd., Princeton, NJ 08541, (609)921-9000
Educational Theatre Assn. [9264], 2343 Auburn Ave., PO Box 632347, Cincinnati, OH 45219, (513)421-3900
Educational Travel Ltd. [★IO]
Educational Trust; Amer. [18049]
Educational Trust of the Amer. Hosp. Assn. [★14884]
Educational Trust; Chi Psi [★24622]
Educational Trust; Hea. Res. and [14884]
Educational Trust; Hosp. Res. and [★14884]
Educator Training Program; Childbirth [★15602]
Educators
Acad. of Mgt. [8805]
Action Coalition for Media Educ. [18026]
Adult Higher Educ. Alliance [7915]
African Language Teachers Assn. [9207]
Alliance for Academic Internal Medicine [8586]
Alliance for Excellent Educ. [9118]
Amateur Movie Makers Assn. [22418]
Amer. Acad. of Advt. [7919]
Amer. Alliance for Hea., Physical Educ., Recreation and Dance [8979]
Amer. Assn. of Colleges for Teacher Educ. [9208]
Amer. Assn. for Collegiate Independent Stud. [7944]
Amer. Assn. for Employment in Educ. [8994]
Amer. Assn. of Physics Teachers [8993]
Amer. Assn. of School Personnel Administrators [7883]
Amer. Assn. of Teachers of Arabic [7958]
Amer. Assn. of Teachers of German [8460]
Amer. Assn. of Teachers of Slavic and East European Languages [9125]
Amer. Assn. of Teachers of Spanish and Portuguese [8725]

Amer. Assn. of Teachers of Turkic Languages [9282]
Amer. Assn. of Teaching and Curriculum [9209]
Amer. Assn. of Univ. Professors [9022]
Amer. Assn. for Women in Community Colleges [9313]
Amer. Catholic Philosophical Assn. [8965]
Amer. Coun. on Rural Special Educ. [9137]
Amer. Distance Educ. Consortium [8227]
Amer. Educational Res. Assn. [9053]
Amer. Educational Stud. Assn. [8228]
Amer. History Forum and Civil War Educ. Assn. [8500]
Amer. Hungarian Educators' Assn. [8533]
Amer. Labor Education Center [8720]
Amer. Mathematical Assn. of Two-Year Colleges [8821]
Amer. Matthay Assn. [8901]
Amer. Mock Trial Assn. [9281]
Amer. Overseas Schools Historical Soc. [10012]
Amer. Real Estate Soc. [9049]
Amer. Real Estate and Urban Economics Assn. [9050]
Amer. Recorder Teachers Assn. [8902]
Amer. Risk and Insurance Assn. [8574]
Amer. School Band Directors' Assn. [8903]
Amer. Soc. for Bioethics and Humanities [8845]
Amer. Soc. of Women Accountants [11]
Amer. String Teachers Assn. [8904]
Amer. Teachers Assn. of the Martial Arts [23582]
Amer. Tech. Educ. Assn. [9228]
Amer. Textbook Coun. [9258]
Assn. for the Advancement of Intl. Educ. [8640]
Assn. for the Advancement of Sustainability in Higher Educ. [8479]
Assn. of Amer. Universities [8099]
Assn. of Arts Admin. Educators [7967]
Assn. for Asian Stud. [7983]
Assn. of Asthma Educators [16355]
Assn. for Bus. Simulation and Experiential Learning [8015]
Assn. for Canadian Stud. in the U.S. [8043]
Assn. for Career and Tech. Educ. [9300]
Assn. for Career and Tech. Educ. Res. [9301]
Assn. for Childhood Educ. Intl. [8064]
Assn. of Cooperative Educators [8156]
Assn. for Direct Instruction [8232]
Assn. for the Educ. of Children with Medical Needs [8072]
Assn. of Educational Publishers [9009]
Assn. for Gender Equity Leadership in Educ. [8399]
Assn. for Gerontology Educ. in Social Work [8461]
Assn. for Global Bus. [8016]
Assn. Global View [8017]
Assn. of Labor Assistants and Childbirth Educators [13977]
Assn. of Macintosh Trainers [6810]
Assn. Montessori International-U.S.A. [8892]
Assn. of Optometric Educators [8851]
Assn. of Orthodox Jewish Teachers [9210]
Assn. of Professional Humane Educators [12058]
Assn. of Professional Schools of Intl. Affairs [8654]
Assn. of Professors of Medicine [8853]
Assn. of Specialty Professors [8587]
Assn. of State Supervisors of Mathematics [8822]
Assn. for the Stud. of Higher Educ. [8482]
Assn. for the Stud. of the Worldwide African Diaspora [7929]
Assn. for Supervision and Curriculum Development [8178]
Assn. of Teacher Educators [9212]
Assn. for Tech. in Music Instruction [8905]
Assn. of Vision Educators [15677]
Assn. of Women Martial Arts Instructors [23585]
Big Picture Company [8353]
Carnegie Found. for the Advancement of Teaching [9214]
Center for Commun. [8003]
Center for Lifelong Learning [8406]
Center for Occupational Res. and Development [8354]
Central Eurasian Stud. Soc. [10233]

Reference to "IO" in place of a book number signifies that the association may be found in the 45th edition of International Organizations.

Children's Grief Educ. Assn. [12265]
Chinese Language Assn. of Secondary-Elementary Schools [8075]
Christian Home Educators Assn. of California [8516]
Clinical Legal Educ. Assn. [8763]
Coalition of Essential Schools [8180]
Coll. Art Assn. [7969]
Coll. Band Directors Natl. Assn. [8906]
Coll. Music Soc. [8907]
Columbia Scholastic Press Advisers Assn. [9010]
Comm. on Capacity Building Sci. [9099]
Comm. on Public Doublespeak [17173]
Comparative and Intl. Educ. Soc. [8655]
Cmpt. Sci. Teachers Assn. [8130]
Concerned Educators Against Forced Unionism - A Special Proj. of the Natl. Right to Work Legal Defense Found. [17971]
Conf. on English Leadership [1175]
Congressional Mgt. Found. [5599]
Consortium for North Amer. Higher Educ. Collaboration [8487]
Cooperative Educ. and Internship Assn. [8157]
Cordell Hull Found. for Intl. Educ. [8656]
Coun. of Administrators of Special Educ. [9139]
Coun. for the Advancement of Standards in Higher Educ. [9177]
Coun. for Aid to Educ. [8346]
Coun. of Chief State School Officers [8246]
Coun. of Educational Fac. Planners, Intl. [8335]
Coun. for Elementary Sci. Intl. [9100]
Coun. on Medical Student Educ. in Pediatrics [8861]
Coun. on Standards for Intl. Educational Travel [8610]
Dance Educators of Am. [8184]
Dance Masters of Am. [8186]
The Educ. Coalition [8325]
Educ. Development Center [8253]
Educ. Pioneers [9178]
Educational Planning Inst. [8998]
Educational Res. Ser. [7895]
Educational Theatre Assn. [9264]
Educators Serving the Community [8318]
Educators for Social Responsibility [17883]
Elderhostel, Inc. [8149]
Equine Guided Educ. Assn. [8524]
Eta Sigma Alpha Natl. Home School Honor Soc. [8316]
Farm-Based Educ. Assn. [7937]
Fed. for Unified Sci. Educ. [9102]
Feminist Teacher Editorial Collective [9318]
Girlstart [8468]
Global Alliance for Justice Educ. [8766]
HEATH Rsrc. Center [8203]
Home and School Inst. [8261]
Horace Mann League of the U.S.A. [9036]
Independent Educational Consultants Assn. [7871]
Indian Educators Fed. [8938]
Inst. for Chem. Educ. [8062]
Inst. for Earth Educ. [8389]
Inst. for Educational Leadership [8264]
Inst. for Responsive Educ. [8408]
Inter-American Conductive Educ. Assn. [9146]
Intl. Assn. for Intelligence Educ. [8581]
Intl. Assn. for Jazz Educ. [8912]
Intl. Assn. of Law Schools [8767]
Intl. Assn. for Learning Alternatives [7945]
Intl. Assn. for Truancy and Dropout Prevention [8326]
Intl. Center of Photography [8972]
Intl. Coalition for Addiction Stud. Educ. [9197]
Intl. Coun. on Educ. for Teaching [9216]
Intl. Educator's Inst. [8645]
Intl. Graphic Arts Educ. Assn. [8470]
Intl. Law Enforcement Educators and Trainers Assn. [5978]
Intl. Reading Assn. [9043]
Intl. Soc. for Educational Planning [8999]
Intl. Soc. for the Scholarship of Teaching and Learning [9073]
Intl. Textile and Apparel Assn. [3791]
Intl. Vocational Educ. and Training Assn. [9306]
Jewish Educators Assembly [8693]

Labor and Working Class History Assn. [8723]
Learning First Alliance [8273]
Learning Resources Network [8151]
Marketing Educ. Assn. [8818]
MENC: The Natl. Assn. for Music Educ. [8913]
Metro Intl. Prog. Services of New York [8624]
Middle Atlantic Planetarium Soc. [9105]
Modernist Stud. Assn. [8780]
Music Teachers Natl. Assn. [8918]
NAFSA/Association of Intl. Educators [8445]
Natl. Abstinence Educ. Assn. [9123]
Natl. Academic Advising Assn. [8170]
Natl. Alliance of Black School Educators [9217]
Natl. Alliance for Civic Educ. [8091]
Natl. Alliance for Safe Schools [9085]
Natl. Art Educ. Assn. [7977]
Natl. Assn. for the Advancement of Caring Teachers [9218]
Natl. Assn. of Agricultural Educators [7938]
Natl. Assn. for Alternative Certification [8360]
Natl. Assn. for Beginning Teachers [9219]
Natl. Assn. for Bilingual Educ. [7999]
Natl. Assn. of Biology Teachers [8000]
Natl. Assn. of Blind Teachers [9220]
Natl. Assn. for Bus. Teacher Educ. [8032]
Natl. Assn. of Catholic Homes and Educators [8057]
Natl. Assn. of Catholic School Teachers [8058]
Natl. Assn. for Chicana and Chicano Stud. [8498]
Natl. Assn. of Coll. Wind and Percussion Instructors [8919]
Natl. Assn. of Comics Art Educators [8115]
Natl. Assn. of Community Coll. Teacher Educ. Programs [9221]
Natl. Assn. for Developmental Educ. [8200]
Natl. Assn. for the Educ. of Young Children [8069]
Natl. Assn. of Elementary School Principals [9014]
Natl. Assn. for Equal Opportunity in Higher Educ. [8109]
Natl. Assn. of Fellowships Advisors [9080]
Natl. Assn. of Geoscience Teachers [8459]
Natl. Assn. for Girls and Women in Sport [8983]
Natl. Assn. of Hea. Educ. Centers [14675]
Natl. Assn. of Hea. Sci. Educ. Partnership [9107]
Natl. Assn. of Hebrew Day School PTAs [8953]
Natl. Assn. for Humanities Educ. [8531]
Natl. Assn. of Indus. and Tech. Teacher Educators [8544]
Natl. Assn. for Kinesiology and Physical Educ. in Higher Educ. [8984]
Natl. Assn. for Legal Support of Alternative Schools [7946]
Natl. Assn. of Maritime Educators [8813]
Natl. Assn. of Multicultural Educ. [8582]
Natl. Assn. of Pastoral Musicians [8920]
Natl. Assn. for Physical Educ. in Higher Educ. [8985]
Natl. Assn. of Principals of Schools for Girls [9015]
Natl. Assn. for Professional Development Schools [9091]
Natl. Assn. of Professors of Hebrew [8695]
Natl. Assn. for Res. in Sci. Teaching [9108]
Natl. Assn. of Scholars [8490]
Natl. Assn. for Secondary School Principals [9016]
Natl. Assn. for Single Sex Public Educ. [9038]
Natl. Assn. of Special Educ. Teachers [9148]
Natl. Assn. of State Directors of Special Educ. [9149]
Natl. Assn. of State Directors of Teacher Educ. and Certification [9224]
Natl. Assn. for the Stud. and Performance of African-American Music [8922]
Natl. Assn. of Supervisors and Administrators of Hea. Occupations Educ. [8870]
Natl. Assn. of Teachers of Singing [8923]
Natl. Assn. of Trade and Indus. Instructors [9233]
Natl. Aviation and Space Educ. Alliance [7994]
Natl. Black Home Educators [8519]
Natl. Bus. Educ. Assn. [8036]
Natl. Coalition for Aviation Educ. [7995]
Natl. Coalition for Tech. in Educ. and Training [9241]
Natl. Commun. Assn. [9157]

Natl. Coun. for Continuing Educ. and Training [8152]
Natl. Coun. on Economic Educ. [8217]
Natl. Coun. of Educ. Providers [8329]
Natl. Coun. for History Educ. [8508]
Natl. Coun. of Japanese Language Teachers [9226]
Natl. Coun. for the Social Stud. [9128]
Natl. Coun. of Supervisors of Mathematics [8826]
Natl. Coun. of Teachers of Mathematics [8827]
Natl. Coun. for Workforce Educ. [8361]
Natl. Earth Sci. Teachers Assn. [9111]
Natl. Fraternity of Student Musicians [8924]
Natl. Guild of Piano Teachers [8925]
Natl. High School Band Directors Hall of Fame [8926]
Natl. Kindergarten Alliance [9007]
Natl. Marine Educators Assn. [8810]
Natl. Middle Level Sci. Teachers' Assn. [9112]
Natl. Middle School Assn. [8881]
Natl. Photography Instructors Assn. [8973]
Natl. Piano Found. [8927]
Natl. PTA - Natl. Cong. of Parents and Teachers [8954]
Natl. Reading Conf. [9044]
Natl. Rsrc. Center for Paraprofessionals in Educ. and Related Services [9150]
Natl. Retired Teachers Assn., Division of AARP [9065]
Natl. Rural Educ. Assn. [9069]
Natl. Schools Comm. for Economic Educ. [8218]
Natl. Sci. Teachers Assn. [9114]
Natl. Service-Learning Partnership [9120]
Natl. Soc. for the Stud. of Educ. [8293]
Natl. Tech Prep Network [8358]
Natl. Urban Alliance for Effective Educ. [9291]
Natl. Women's Stud. Assn. [9323]
Nature and Environmental Writers - Coll. and Univ. Educators [8362]
NETWORK [8295]
New Leaders for New Schools [8755]
North Amer. Assn. of Jewish High Schools [8698]
North Amer. Assn. of Summer Sessions [9200]
North Amer. Colleges and Teachers of Agriculture [7942]
North Amer. Coun. of Automotive Teachers [7993]
North Amer. Professors of Christian Educ. [8088]
Off. of Women in Higher Educ., Amer. Coun. on Educ. [9324]
Oper. Crossroads Africa [16932]
Org. of Amer. Kodaly Educators [8929]
Organizational Systems Res. Assn. [9234]
Pharmacy Technician Educators Coun. [8963]
Philosophy of Educ. Soc. [8969]
Photo Imaging Educ. Assn. [8974]
Photographic Art and Sci. Found. [8975]
Probe Ministries Intl. [8090]
Professional Dance Teachers Assn. [8191]
Professional and Organizational Development Network in Higher Educ. [8494]
Proj. Food, Land and People [4525]
Reading Is Fundamental [9047]
Reading Recovery Coun. of North Am. [9048]
Religious Commun. Assn. [8116]
Sewing Educator Alliance [9121]
Social Sci. Educ. Consortium [9129]
Soc. for the Advancement of Educ. [8305]
Soc. for the Advancement of Scandinavian Stud. [9070]
Soc. for Anthropology in Community Colleges [7954]
Soc. of Building Sci. Educators [8363]
Soc. of Chinese Amer. Professors and Scientists [9024]
Soc. for Coll. and Univ. Planning [9000]
Soc. for Gen. Music [8930]
Soc. for History Educ. [8511]
Soc. for Music Teacher Educ. [8931]
Soc. for Philosophy of Religion [8970]
Soc. for Photographic Educ. [8976]
Soc. of Professors of Educ. [8307]
Soc. for Social Work and Res. [9135]
Student Photographic Soc. [10857]
Student Press Law Center [17194]
Suzuki Assn. of the Americas [8932]

A star before a book entry number signifies that the name is not listed separately, but is mentioned within the entry.

Teachers Insurance and Annuity Assn. [8579]
Teachers Resisting Unhealthy Children's Entertainment [11657]
Tech. Mgt. Educ. Assn. [9245]
Telluride Assn. [8310]
TIAA-CREF [9066]
U.S. Soc. for Educ. Through Art [7980]
Univ. Aviation Assn. [7924]
Univ. Film and Video Assn. [8420]
Univ. Professors for Academic Order [9026]
Van Alen Inst.: Projects in Public Architecture [7963]
Women Band Directors Intl. [8934]
Women Educators [9328]
World Antique Dealers Assn. [219]
World Commun. Assn. [8005]
World Cong. of Teachers of Dancing [8192]
Educators' Ad Hoc Comm. on Copyright Law - Defunct.
Educators to Africa - Defunct.
Educators Against Forced Unionism - A Special Proj. of the Natl. Right to Work Legal Defense Found; Concerned [17971]
Educators in Agriculture; Amer. Assn. of Teacher [★7933]
Educators Allied for a Safe Env; Concerned [18148]
Educators of Am; Dance [8184]
Educators; Amer. Assn. of Diabetes [14217]
Educators; Amer. Assn. of Housing [12303]
Educators; Amer. Soc. of Childbirth [15589]
Educators on the Americas; Network of [★8359]
Educators Assembly of Am. [★8693]
Educators Assembly of Am. [★IO]
Educators; Assn. of Arts Admin. [7967]
Educators Assn. of California; Christian Home [8516]
Educators Assn; Christian [★19922]
Educators; Assn. of Christian Church [19842]
Educators; Assn. of Clinical Pastoral [★19915]
Educators; Assn. of Commercial Diving [23960]
Educators; Assn. for Cmpt. [★8132]
Educators; Assn. of Leadership [8744]
Educators Assn; Liberal Religious [20599]
Educators Assn; Music and Entertainment Indus. [8916]
Educators Assn; Natl. Catholic Music [★8920]
Educators Assn; Natl. Marine [8810]
Educators Assn; Natl. Standards [7697]
Educators; Assn. of Optometric [8851]
Educators; Assn. of Osteopathic Directors and Medical [15808]
Educators Assn; Real Estate [3338]
Educators; Assn. of Teacher [9212]
Educators; Assn. of Theatre Movement [9263]
Educators Bed and Breakfast Club - Defunct.
Educators Coun; Interior Design [8585]
Educators; Coun. of Rehabilitation Counselor [★16329]
Educators and Counselors; Amer. Assn. of Sex [★16398]
Educators, Counselors and Therapists; Amer. Assn. of Sexuality [16398]
Educators for Family and Consumer Sciences; Natl. Assn. of Teacher [8515]
Educators Fellowship; Natl. [★19922]
Educators Fellowship of the United Methodist Church; Christian [19923]
Educators of Gifted Children; Assn. of [★8465]
Educators for Homebound and Hospitalized Children; Assn. of [★9141]
Educators for Homebound and Hospitalized Children; Assn. of [★11998]
Educators; Intl. Alliance of Healthcare [8475]
Educators; Intl. Assn. of Jazz [★8912]
Educators in Landscape Architecture; Coun. of [8724]
Educators; Natl. Alliance of Black School [9217]
Educators; Natl. Assn. of Agricultural [7938]
Educators; Natl. Assn. of EMS [8867]
Educators; Natl. Assn. of Independent Maritime [★8813]
Educators; Natl. Assn. of Indus. and Tech. Teacher [8544]
Educators; Natl. Assn. of Maritime [8813]
Educators; Natl. Assn. of Medical Minority [8868]
Educators; Natl. Assn. of Professional [9223]

Educators; Natl. Assn. of Small Bus. Intl. Trade [★8031]
Educators; Natl. Assn. of Substance Abuse Trainers and [9198]
Educators; Natl. Assn. of Temple [20164]
Educators; Natl. Certification Bd. for Diabetes [14229]
Educators Natl. Conf; Music [★8913]
Educators Natl. Conf; Natl. Black Music Caucus of the Music [★8922]
Educators; Natl. Coun. of BIA [★8938]
Educators; Natl. Org. of Human Ser. [★9131]
Educators; Org. of Amer. Kodaly [8929]
Educators in Private Practice; Assn. of [★9215]
Educators; Professional Assn. of Christian [19937]
Educators in Radiological Sciences; Assn. of [★9096]
Educators Serving the Community [8318], PO Box 2536, Laurel, MD 20709, (301)498-2899
Educators for Social Responsibility [17883], 23 Garden St., Cambridge, MA 02138, (617)492-1764
Educators; Soc. for Data [★8132]
Educators; Soc. of Insurance Trainers and [8578]
Educators; Soc. of Park and Recreation [6163]
Educators; Soc. of Public Hea. [★16254]
Educators; Soc. of Wine [23029]
Educators and Trainees; Acad. of Security [★9119]
Educators and Trainers; Acad. of Security [9119]
Educators; Women [9328]
EDUCAUSE [8558], 4772 Walnut St., Ste. 206, Boulder, CO 80301-2538, (303)449-4430
Edward Doty Soc; Pilgrim [20756]
Edward E. Ford Found. [13117], 66 Pearl St., Ste. 322, Portland, ME 04101, (207)774-2346
Edward E. Ford Found. [IO], Portland, ME, United States
Edward Mulhare's Founds. - Defunct.
Edwards Educational Centre; Nelson Jack [★17158]
Edwards Family Assn. - Defunct.
EEC Wheat Starch Manufacturers Assn. [★IO]
EEG and EP Technologists; Amer. Bd. of Registration of [14305]
EEG Soc. [★IO]
EEG Technologists; Amer. Bd. of Registration of [★14305]
EEI—Nuclear Div. [6969]
Eelam Tamils Assn. of America - Defunct.
EEMA [IO], Worcester, United Kingdom
Eesti Ajalehtede Liit [★IO]
Eesti Akadeemiliste Naiste Uhing [★IO]
Eesti Arstide Liit [★IO]
Eesti Ehitusmaterjalide Tootjate Liit [★IO]
Eesti Ekspedeerijate Assotsiatsioon [★IO]
Eesti Farmakoloogia Selts [★IO]
Eesti Fuusika Selts [★IO]
Eesti Hambaarstiuliopilaste Liit [★IO]
Eesti Haridustootajate Liit [★IO]
Eesti Hasartmangude Korraldajate Liit [★IO]
Eesti Hotellide Ja Restoranide Liit [★IO]
Eesti Infotehnoloogia Selts [★IO]
Eesti Infotehnoloogia ja Telekommunikatsiooni Liit [★IO]
Eesti Inimoiguste Instituut [★IO]
Eesti Jalgpalli Liit [★IO]
Eesti Kardioloogide Selts [★IO]
Eesti Kaubandus-Toostuskoda [★IO]
Eesti Kaupmeeste Liit [★IO]
Eesti Keemiatoostuse Liit [★IO]
Eesti Kergejoustikuliit [★IO]
Eesti Kiirabi Liit [★IO]
Eesti Kindlustusseltside Liit [★IO]
Eesti Kinnisvarafirmade Liit [★IO]
Eesti Kunstnike Liit [★IO]
Eesti Lennuspordi Foderatsioon [IO], Tallinn, Estonia
Eesti Lihaliit [★IO]
Eesti Maaturism [★IO]
Eesti Masinatoostuse Liit [★IO]
Eesti Noorte Naiste ja Meeste Kristlike Uhingute Liit [★IO]
Eesti Noorte Reumaliit [★IO]
Eesti Oelletootjate Liit [★IO]
Eesti Oliuhing [★IO]
Eesti Olumpiakomitee [★IO]
Eesti Orienteerumisliit [★IO]
Eesti Osteoporoosi Selts [★IO]

Eesti Pangaliit [★IO]
Eesti Paraolumpiakomitee [★IO]
Eesti Personalitoo Arendamise Uhing [★IO]
Eesti Piimaliit [★IO]
Eesti Psuhholoogide Liit [★IO]
Eesti Purjelaualiit [★IO]
Eesti Raadioamatooride Uhing [★IO]
Eesti Raamatukoguhoidjate Uhing [★IO]
Eesti Reformierakonna Peakontor [★IO]
Eesti Ringhaalingute Liit [★IO]
Eesti Roeiva- ja Tekstiililiit [★IO]
Eesti Roheline Liikumine [★IO]
Eesti Saalihoki Liit [★IO]
Eesti Seskuaaltervise Liit [★IO]
Eesti Skautide Uhing [★IO]
Eesti Squashifoderatsioon [★IO]
Eesti Sulgpalliliit [★IO]
Eesti Suurettevotjate Assotsiatsioon [★IO]
Eesti Teaduste Akadeemia [★IO]
Eesti Toiduainetoostuse Liit [★IO]
Eesti Tooandjate Keskliit [★IO]
Eesti Touloomakasvatajate Uhistu [★IO]
Eesti Turbaliit [★IO]
Eesti Turismifirmade Liit [★IO]
Eesti Turvaettevotete Liit [★IO]
Eesti Tuuleenergia Assotsiatsioon [★IO]
Eesti Uisuliit [★IO]
Eesti Uliopilaskondade Liit [★IO]
Eestimaa Looduse Fond [★IO]
E.F. Benson Soc. [IO], Rye, United Kingdom
EF Educational Found. for Foreign Stud. [★IO]
EF Educational Found. for Foreign Stud. [★8611]
EF Found. for Foreign Stud. [8611], One Educ. St., Cambridge, MA 02141, (800)44-SHARE
EF Found. for Foreign Stud. [IO], Cambridge, MA, United States
Effective Citizens Org. [★17354]
Effective Citizens Org. Found. [★18447]
Effective Cong; Natl. Comm. for an [17252]
Effective Govt. Comm. - Address unknown since 2007.
Efficiency Alliance; Northwest Energy [4528]
Efficiency Assn; World Energy [6978]
Efficiency and Renewable Energy Info. Center; Energy [6951]
Efficiency and Renewable Technologies; Center for Energy [4526]
Efficient Windows Collaborative [4029], c/o Nils Petermann, Res. Assoc., Alliance to Save Energy, 1850 M St. NW, Ste. 600, Washington, DC 20036, (202)530-2254
EFNARC [IO], Knowle, United Kingdom
The EFT Assn. [★471]
Egale Canada [IO], Ottawa, ON, Canada
Egalitarian Communities; Fed. of [11746]
Egbe Omo Yoruba: Natl. Assn. of Yoruba Descendants in North America [19289], 3840 Bladensburg Rd., Cottage City, MD 20722, (925)858-2565
Egbe Omo Yoruba: National Association of Yoruba Descendants in North America [IO], Cottage City, MD, United States
Egg Assn. Further Processors; United [5120]
Egg Assn; United [★5121]
Egg Bd; Amer. [5104]
Egg Bd; Chicago Butter and [★4324]
Egg CH, Inc. [5110], PO Box 817, Dover, NH 03821, (800)872-3324
Egg Cup Collectors' Corner [22016], c/o Dr. Joan M. George, 67 Stevens Ave., Old Bridge, NJ 08857
Egg Exchange of the City of New York; Butter, Cheese, and [★4333]
Egg Export Coun; U.S.A. Poultry and [5123]
Egg Natl. Bd; Poultry and [★5104]
Egg Nutrition Center [15556], 1900 L St. NW, Ste. 725, Washington, DC 20036, (202)833-8850
Egg Packaging Assn. [★1157]
Egg Processors Coun; Canadian Poultry and [IO]
Egg Producers' Assn; Swiss [IO]
Egg Producers; Spanish Assn. of [IO]
Egg Producers; United [5121]
Egypt
     Amer. Egyptian Cooperation Found. [17481]
     Amer. Egyptian Cooperation Found. [IO]
     Egyptian Arabian Horse Alliance [4877]

Reference to "IO" in place of a book number signifies that the association may be found in the 45th edition of International Organizations.

Egyptian Student Assn. in North Am. [9179]
Egyptians Relief Assn. [11774]
Historical Soc. of Jews from Egypt [10282]
Soc. for Coptic Archaeology (North Am.) [10153]
U.S. Copts Assn. [10192]
Egypt Exploration Fund [★IO]
Egypt Exploration Soc. [IO], London, United
Kingdom
Egypt Flying Disc Fed. [IO], Cairo, Egypt
Egypt; Historical Soc. of Jews from [10282]
Egypt-U.S. Business Coun. - Defunct.
Egyptian Amer. Chamber of Commerce - Defunct.
Egyptian Arabian Horse Alliance [4877], PO Box
262, Cleburne, TX 76033-0262
Egyptian Arabic Order Nobles of the Mystic Shrine;
Ancient [19227]
Egyptian Article Numbering Assn. [IO], Cairo, Egypt
Egyptian Assn. of Univ. Women [IO], Alexandria,
Egypt
Egyptian Athletic Fed. [IO], Cairo, Egypt
Egyptian Badminton Fed. [IO], Giza, Egypt
Egyptian Cmpt. Soc. [IO], Cairo, Egypt
Egyptian Exporters Assn. [IO], Giza, Egypt
Egyptian Family Planning Assn. [IO], Cairo, Egypt
Egyptian Fertility and Sterility Soc. [IO], Cairo, Egypt
Egyptian Gas Assn. [IO], Cairo, Egypt
Egyptian Gen. Company for Tourism and Hotels
[IO], Cairo, Egypt
Egyptian Geotechnical Soc. [IO], Giza, Egypt
Egyptian Hotel Assn. [IO], Giza, Egypt
Egyptian Hypertension Soc. [IO], Cairo, Egypt
Egyptian Medical Assn. [IO], Cairo, Egypt
Egyptian Natl. Gp. of IFPI [IO], Cairo, Egypt
Egyptian Nuclear Physics Assn. [IO], Cairo, Egypt
Egyptian Olympic Comm. [IO], Cairo, Egypt
Egyptian Ophthalmological Soc. [IO], Cairo, Egypt
Egyptian Order of Sciots; Ancient [19228]
Egyptian Org. for Human Rights [IO], Cairo, Egypt
Egyptian Orthodontic Soc. [IO], Alexandria, Egypt
Egyptian Orthopaedic Assn. [IO], Cairo, Egypt
Egyptian Osteoporosis Prevention Soc. [IO], Cairo,
Egypt
Egyptian Red Crescent Soc. [IO], Cairo, Egypt
Egyptian Seed Assn. [IO], Cairo, Egypt
Egyptian Soc. Against Epilepsy [IO], Cairo, Egypt
Egyptian Soc; Amer. [★24357]
Egyptian Soc. of Cardiology [IO], Alexandria, Egypt
Egyptian Soc. of Consulting Engineers [IO], Cairo,
Egypt
Egyptian Soc. of Crystallography and Applications
[IO], Cairo, Egypt
Egyptian Soc. of Gastrointestinal Endoscopy [IO],
Cairo, Egypt
Egyptian Soc. for Intercultural Exchange [IO], Giza,
Egypt
Egyptian Soc. of Nephrology [IO], Cairo, Egypt
The Egyptian Soc. of South Africa [IO], Cape Town,
Republic of South Africa
Egyptian Student Assn. in North Am. [IO], Raleigh,
NC, United States
Egyptian Student Assn. in North Am. [9179], c/o
Hatem Seliem, Pres., 1810 Crossroads Vista Dr.,
Apt. No. 202, Raleigh, NC 27606, (919)513-1222
Egyptian Taekwondo Fed. [IO], Cairo, Egypt
Egyptian Yachting and Water Ski Fed. [IO], Cairo,
Egypt
Egyptians Relief Assn. [11774], c/o Nadia Tadros,
Pres., 6121 Winnepeg Dr., Burke, VA 22015,
(703)503-8816
Egyptology
The Egyptian Soc. of South Africa [IO]
Soc. for the Stud. of Egyptian Antiquities [IO]
U.S. Copts Assn. [10192]
Egyptology Special Interest Group - Defunct.
eHealth Initiative [14627], 818 Connecticut Ave. NW,
Ste. 500, Washington, DC 20006, (202)624-3270
Ehlers Danlos Natl. Found. [16651], 3200 Wilshire
Blvd., Ste. 1601, South Tower, Los Angeles, CA
90010, (213)368-3800
EHS Hea. Care [★14821]
Eichelmann Clan Diggers Assn. - Defunct.
EIDD - Design for All Europe [IO], Bromma, Sweden
EIFS Indus. Members Assn. [618], 3000 Corporate
Center Dr., Ste. 270, Morrow, GA 30260, (770)968-
7945

Eight Sheet Outdoor Advt. Assn. [99], PO Box 2680,
Bremerton, WA 98310-0344, (360)377-9867
Eighteen Nineties Soc. [IO], High Wycombe, United
Kingdom
Eighteenth-Century Scottish Stud. Soc. [IO],
Newark, NJ, United States
Eighteenth-Century Scottish Stud. Soc. [8505], New
Jersey Inst. of Tech., Newark, NJ 07102-1982,
(973)596-3377
Eighteenth-Century Stud; Amer. Soc. for [10089]
Eighth Air Force Historical Soc. [21392], c/o Mamie
Kent, Mgr., PO Box 956, Pooler, GA 31322,
(912)748-8884
Eighth Armored Div. Assn. - Address unknown since
1995.
Eigse Eireann [★IO]
Eikon Gesellschaft der Freunde der Ikonenkunst e.v.
[IO], Recklinghausen, Germany
EIL Intercultural Learning [IO], Cork, Ireland
Eileen Davidson Fan Club - Address unknown since
2003.
Einstein Institution; Albert [18108]
Eire Philatelic Assn. [22817], c/o David J. Brennan,
Sec., PO Box 704, Bernardsville, NJ 07924-0704
EISCAT Sci. Assn. [IO], Kiruna, Sweden
Eiseman Center for Color Info. and Training [6707],
c/o Pantone, Inc., 590 Commerce Blvd., Carlstadt,
NJ 07072-3013, (201)935-5500
Eisenhower Birthplace Found; Mamie Doud [10044]
Eisenhower Exchange Fellowships [★17884]
Eisenhower Fellowships [17884], 256 S 16th St.,
Philadelphia, PA 19102, (215)546-1738
Eisenhower Found; Milton S. [11839]
Eisenhower Found. for the Prevention of Violence
[★11839]
Eisenhower Inst. [★18442]
Eisenhower Inst. [18392], 915 15th St. NW, 8th Fl.,
Washington, DC 20005-2311, (202)628-4444
Eisenhower Inst. [★IO]
Eisenhower/Jennings Randolph Intl. Public Works
Fellowship [★IO]
Eisenhower/Jennings Randolph Intl. Public Works
Fellowship [★18442]
Eisenhower World Affairs Inst. [18442], 915 15th St.
NW, 8th Fl., Washington, DC 20005, (202)628-
4444
Eisenhower World Affairs Inst. [IO], Washington, DC,
United States
Ekistics; Educational Center for Applied [10228]
EKJ (Emmett Kelly Jr.) Collectors' Soc. [22017], c/o
Flambro Imports, 1530 Ellsworth Indus. Dr.,
Atlanta, GA 30318-3752, (404)352-1381
Ekonomiska Samfundet i Finland [★IO]
El Bireh Palestine Soc. of the U.S.A. - Defunct.
El Cariso Publications [★20484]
El Congreso Nacional de Asuntos Colegiales -
Defunct.
El Dorado Winery Assn. [200], PO Box 1614, Plac-
erville, CA 95667, (916)966-5008
El Rescate [12809], 1501 W 8th St., Ste. 100, Los
Angeles, CA 90017, (213)387-3284
El Salvador
Assoc. Collectors of El Salvador [22794]
Christians for Peace in El Salvador [20322]
COAR Peace Mission [17482]
Comm. in Solidarity With the People of El
Salvador [17483]
Comm. in Solidarity With the People of El
Salvador [IO]
MADRE [12529]
Salvadoran Amer. Leadership and Educational
Fund [17484]
Salvadoran Amer. Medical Soc. [15092]
SHARE Found.: Building a New El Salvador
Today [17485]
SHARE Found.: Building a New El Salvador
Today [IO]
El Salvador; Assoc. Collectors of [22794]
El Salvador; Christians for Peace in [20322]
El Salvador Media Projects - Address unknown since
2003.
El Salvador; Religious Task Force on [★17052]
El Salvador Today; New [★17485]
El Salvador; U.S. Comm. in Solidarity With the
People of [★17483]

El Taller [IO], Tunis, Tunisia
El Toro Intl. Yacht Racing Assn. [23168], 1014 Hop-
per Ave., No. 419, Santa Rosa, CA 95403-1613,
(707)526-6621
Elainsuojeluliitto Animalia [★IO]
Elasmobranch Soc; Amer. [7278]
Elastic Braid Mfrs. Assn. [★3780]
Elastic Fabric Mfrs. Assn. of the Northern Textile
Assn. [★3780]
Elastic Fabric Mfrs. Coun. of the Natl. Textile Assn.
[3780], 6 Beacon St., Ste. 1125, Boston, MA
02108, (617)542-8220
Elastic Fabric Mfrs. Inst. [★3780]
Elastic Mfrs. Assn; Woven [★3780]
Elastric Fabric Mfrs. Coun. of the Natl. Textile Assn.
[★3780]
Elbe Alliance - Defunct.
Elbeetian Legion, LSA - Address unknown since
2004.
Elberton Granite Assn. [3693], PO Box 640, Elber-
ton, GA 30635, (706)283-2551
Elbow Surgeons; Amer. Shoulder and [16567]
ELCINA Electronic Indus. Assn. of India [IO], New
Delhi, India
Elder Abuse
Action on Elder Abuse [IO]
Intl. Network for the Prevention of Elder Abuse
[IO]
Natl. Assn. to Stop Guardian Abuse [12059]
Natl. Center on Elder Abuse [12033]
Natl. Comm. for the Prevention of Elder Abuse
[11308]
Natl. Coun. on Child Abuse and Family Violence
[12035]
Elder Brewster Soc. [20893], c/o Gregory E.
Thompson, Historian/Membership Chm., PO Box
355, Branford, CT 06405
Elder Craftsmen [11285], 307 7th Ave., Ste. 1401,
New York, NY 10001, (212)319-8128
Elder Hea. Care Rsrc. Center; Native [19282]
Elder Law Attorneys; Natl. Acad. of [6029]
Elder Rights Advocacy [IO], Melbourne, Australia
Elder Support Network [★12467]
Elderhostel Canada [★IO]
Elderhostel, Inc. [IO], Boston, MA, United States
Elderhostel, Inc. [8149], 11 Ave. de Lafayette,
Boston, MA 02111-1746, (617)426-7788
Elderly; AIDS Ser. Prog. for the [★12256]
Elderly; Center for Advocacy for the Rights and
Interests of the [11279]
Elderly; Commn. on Legal Problems of the [★5935]
Elderly; Found. Aiding the [17329]
Elderly; Legal Counsel for the [12497]
Elderly; Legal Sers. for the [12499]
Elderly; Little Bros. - Friends of the [11295]
Elderly; Natl. Assn. for Hispanic [19100]
Elderly; Natl. Soc. for Amer. Indian [19279]
Elderly Poor; Legal Sers. for the [★12499]
Elderly; P.R.I.D.E. Found. - Promote Real
Independence for the Disabled and [11982]
Elders; World Coun. of [9855]
Eldred Family Org. - Defunct.
Eleanor Assn. [★17529]
Eleanor Found. [17529], 325 W Huron St., Ste. 706,
Chicago, IL 60610, (312)337-7766
Eleanor Leff Jewish Women's Rsrc. Center [10280],
820 2nd Ave., 2nd Fl., New York, NY 10017-4504,
(212)687-5030
Eleanor Roosevelt Inst. [★11111]
Eleanor Roosevelt Inst; Franklin and [11111]
Eleanor Steber Music Found. - Defunct.
Eleanor Women's Found. [★17529]
Elected and Appointed Officials; Natl. Assn. of Latino
[17706]
Elected Local Officials; Hispanic [6122]
Elected Officials; Natl. Black Caucus of Local [6127]
Elected Officials; Natl. League of Spanish Speaking
[★6122]
Elected Spanish Speaking Officials [★6122]
Election Officials, and Clerks; Natl. Assn. of County
Recorders, [5621]
Elections
Asian Network for Free Elections [IO]
Asian Pacific Americans for Progress [17012]
Asian and Pacific Islander Amer. Vote [18345]

A star before a book entry number signifies that the name is not listed separately, but is mentioned within the entry.

Assn. of African Election Authorities [IO]
Assn. of Caribbean Electoral Organizations [5557]
Assn. of Central and Eastern European Election Officials [IO]
Citizens for Consumer Justice [18641]
Citizens for Legitimate Govt. [17663]
Democracy for Am. [18291]
Electoral Reform Soc. [IO]
Fair Elections Legal Network [5491]
Hall of Fame for Great Americans [11119]
Honest Ballot Assn. [17486]
Intl. Found. for Election Systems [17487]
League of Young Voters [18356]
Mobile Voter [18032]
Natl. Assn. of County Recorders, Election Officials, and Clerks [5621]
Natl. Assn. of State Election Directors [1176]
Open Debates [17488]
Open Voting Consortium [17489]
Open Voting Consortium [IO]
South Asian Amer. Voting Youth [18366]
Student Assn. for Voter Empowerment [17490]
UrgentCall.org [18173]
Voter Rights March [17491]
Elections Res. Center - Defunct.
Electoral Organizations; Assn. of Caribbean [5557]
Electoral Reform Soc. [IO], London, United Kingdom
Electoral Systems; Intl. Found. for [★17487]
Electra Class Yacht Racing Assn. - Defunct.
Electrapages Directory of Women's Organizations - Address unknown since 2004.
ELECTRI Intl. - The Found. for Elecl. Contraction [1179], 3 Bethesda Metro Ctr., Ste. 1100, Bethesda, MD 20814-6302, (301)215-4538
Elec. Auto Assn. [6516], 323 Los Altos Dr., Aptos, CA 95003-5248, (831)688-8669
Elec. Boat Assn. of Am. [★21872]
Elec. Boat Assn. of the Americas [21872]
Elec. Companies; Natl. Assn. of [★3956]
Elec. Consumers Info. Comm. [★17321]
Elec. Drag Racing Assn; Natl. [23396]
Elec. Drive Trans. Assn. [6517], 1101 Vermont Ave. NW, Ste. 401, Washington, DC 20005, (202)408-0774
Elec. Energy Assn. [★3956]
Elec. Energy Assn. [★IO]
Electric Fuse Mfrs. Guild - Defunct.
Elec. Generation Assn. [★6950]
Elec. Indus. Truck Assn. [★387]
Elec. Motors, Their Control and Application; SMMA - The Assn. for [★1198]
Elec. Overhead Crane Inst. [★2016]
Electric Photometry; Intl. Amateur-Professional Photo [6505]
Elec. Power Club [★1191]
Elec. Power Club [★IO]
Elec. Power Res. Inst. [IO], Palo Alto, CA, United States
Elec. Power Res. Inst. [★6953]
Elec. Power Res. Inst. [7531], 3420 Hillview Ave., Palo Alto, CA 94304, (650)855-2121
Elec. Power Supply Assn. [6950], 1401 New York Ave. NW, 11th Fl., Washington, DC 20005-2110, (202)628-8200
Elec. Railfans' Assn; Central [22933]
Elec. Railroaders' Assn. [10911], PO Box 3323, Grand Central Sta., New York, NY 10163-3323, (212)986-4482
Elec. Railway and Motor Coach Employees of Am; Amalgamated Assn. of St., [★24197]
Elec. Railway Soc. [IO], Sutton Coldfield, United Kingdom
Elec. Reliability Coun; Natl. [★1195]
Elec. Reliability Coun; North Amer. [1195]
Elec. Tool Inst. [★1831]
Elec. Utility Benchmarking Assn. [6901], 4606 FM 1960 W, Ste. 250, Houston, TX 77069-9949, (281)440-5044
Elec. Utilization Coun; Inter-Industry Farm [★6963]
Elec. Vehicle Assn. of the Americas [★6517]
Electric Vehicle Coun. - Defunct.
Elec. Wholesalers Assn; Natl. [★1190]
Electrical
 Action Comm. for Rural Electrification [1177]
 Amer. Public Power Assn. [6336]

Antique Fan Collectors Assn. [21533]
Assn. of Danish Energy Companies [IO]
Assn. of Elecl. Contractors - Ireland [IO]
Assn. of Mfrs. of Domestic Appliances [IO]
Assn. of Wholesale Elecl. Bulk Buyers [IO]
Bahamas Elecl. Workers' Union [IO]
BEAMA Capacitor Manufacturer's Assn. [IO]
BEAMA Installation [IO]
BEAMA Metering and Communications Assn. [IO]
BEAMA Transmission and Distribution Assn. [IO]
Belgian Electrotechnical Comm. [IO]
Brazilian Elecl. and Electronics Indus. Assn. [IO]
British Electrostatic Mfrs. Assn. [IO]
British Hydropower Assn. [IO]
Canadian Elecl. Contractors Assn. [IO]
Canadian Hydropower Assn. [IO]
Central Elec. Railfans' Assn. [22933]
Consumer Electronics Assn. TechHome Div. [1178]
ELECTRI Intl. - The Found. for Elecl. Contraction [1179]
Elec. Boat Assn. of the Americas [21872]
Elec. Railroaders' Assn. [10911]
Elecl. Apparatus Ser. Assn. [1180]
Electrical Apparatus Service Association [IO]
Elecl. Contractors Assn. [IO]
Elecl. Contractors Assn. of Finland [IO]
Elecl. Equip. Representatives Assn. [1181]
Elecl. Generating Systems Assn. [1182]
Elecl. Mfg. and Coil Winding Assn. [1183]
Electricity Consumers Rsrc. Coun. [1184]
Electricity Storage Assn. [3957]
Electroheat Mfrs. Assn. of BEAMA [IO]
Energy Telecommunications and Elecl. Assn. [1185]
European Comm. for Electrotechnical Standardization [IO]
Fabless Semiconductor Assn. [1215]
Fed. of Westinghouse Independent Salaried Unions [24047]
Finnish Elecl. Wholesalers Fed. [IO]
Hong Kong Elecl. Contractors' Assn. [IO]
IEC Sys. for Conformity Testing and Certification of Elecl. Equip. [IO]
Inst. of Elecl. and Electronics Engineers - USA [7015]
Intl. Assn. of Elecl. Inspectors [1186]
Intl. Assn. of Elecl. Inspectors [IO]
Intl. Assn. of Elecl. Inspectors - Japan Chap. [IO]
Intl. Assn. of Elecl. Inspectors - Korea Chap. [IO]
Intl. Assn. of Elecl. Inspectors - Mexico Chap. [IO]
Intl. Assn. of Elecl. Inspectors - Saudi Arabia Chap. [IO]
Intl. Brotherhood of Elecl. Workers [24048]
Intl. Cablemakers' Fed. [IO]
Intl. Coun. on Large Elec. Systems [IO]
Intl. Elecl. Testing Assn. [IO]
Intl. Elecl. Testing Assn. [1187]
Intl. League of Elecl. Associations [1188]
Intl. League of Elecl. Associations [IO]
Intl. Sign Assn. [IO]
Intl. Sign Assn. [1189]
Intl. Union of Electronic, Elecl., Salaried, Machine, and Furniture Workers [24049]
Japan Elec. Measuring Instruments Mfrs'. Assn. [IO]
Japan Elecl. Mfrs. Assn. [IO]
Joint Indus. Bd. of the Elecl. Indus. [1030]
Lighting Controls Assn. [2433]
Mid-Continent Railway Historical Soc. [22934]
NAED Educ. and Res. Found. [2503]
Natl. Assn. of Elecl. Distributors [1190]
Natl. Elecl. Contractors Coun. [1046]
Natl. Elecl. Manufacturers Assn. [1191]
National Electrical Manufacturers Association [IO]
Natl. Elecl. Manufacturers Representatives Assn. [1192]
Natl. Fed. of Wholesale Distributors of Elec. Materials [IO]
Natl. Inspection Coun. for Elecl. Installation Contracting [IO]
Natl. Regap Network [1193]
Natl. Rural Elec. Cooperative Assn. [1194]
Natl. Rural Elec. Cooperative Assn. [IO]
North Amer. Elec. Reliability Coun. [1195]

Org. for Nordic Elecl. Cooperation [IO]
Professional Elecl. Apparatus Recyclers League [1196]
Railroadiana Collectors Assn. Incorporated [22936]
Regional Integration Energy Commn. [IO]
Relay and Switch Indus. Assn. [1197]
Rotating Elecl. Machines Assn. [IO]
Scottish Joint Indus. Bd. for the Elecl. Contracting Indus. [IO]
SELECT [IO]
SMMA - The Motor and Motion Association [IO]
SMMA - The Motor and Motion Assn. [1198]
Swiss Electrotechnical Assn. [IO]
Union for the Coordination of Transmission of Electricity [IO]
Union of the Elec. Indus. - EURELECTRIC [IO]
United Elecl., Radio and Machine Workers of Am. [24050]
Wire and Cable Indus. Suppliers Assn. [1231]
Wiring Harness Manufacturer's Assn. [1199]
Women's Intl. Network of Utility Professionals [1200]
World Sign Associates [1201]
World Sign Associates [IO]
Electrical Apparatus Service Association [IO], St. Louis, MO, United States
Elecl. Apparatus Ser. Assn. [1180], 1331 Baur Blvd., St. Louis, MO 63132, (314)993-2220
Elecl. Assn; Petroleum Indus. [★1185]
Elecl. Commun. Commn; Inter-American [★3744]
Elecl. and Communications Assn. of Western Australia [IO], West Perth, Australia
Elecl. and Cmpt. Engg. Dept. Heads Assn. [7011], 300 W Adams, Ste. 1210, Chicago, IL 60606-5114, (312)559-3724
Elecl. Contracting; Academy of [★1045]
Elecl. Contracting Found. [★1179]
Elecl. Contractors of Am; Assoc. Independent [★1018]
Elecl. Contractors Assn. [IO], London, United Kingdom
Elecl. Contractors Assn. - England [★IO]
Elecl. Contractors Assn. of Finland [IO], Espoo, Finland
Elecl. Contractors Assn. of Hamilton [IO], Hamilton, ON, Canada
Elecl. Contractors Assn. of London [IO], Dorchester, ON, Canada
Elecl. Contractors Assn; Natl. [1045]
Elecl. Contractors Assn. of New Zealand [IO], Wellington, New Zealand
Elecl. Contractors Assn. of Northern Ontario [IO], Sudbury, ON, Canada
Elecl. Contractors Assn. of Ottawa [IO], Ottawa, ON, Canada
Elecl. Contractors Assn. of Quinte-St. Lawrence [IO], Kingston, ON, Canada
Elecl. Contractors Assn. of Sarnia [IO], Sarnia, ON, Canada
Elecl. Contractors Assn. of Saskatchewan [IO], Regina, SK, Canada
Elecl. Contractors Assn. of Scotland [★IO]
Elecl. Contractors Coun; Natl. [1046]
Elecl. Contractors; Independent [1018]
The Elecl. and Electronics Assn. of Malaysia [IO], Kuala Lumpur, Malaysia
Elecl. and Electronics Engineers; Inst. of [6926]
Elecl. and Electronics Engineers - USA; Inst. of [7015]
Electrical/Electronics Insulation Conf. - Address unknown since 1999.
Electrical Engineering
 Assn. of German Electrocial Engineers [IO]
 Chinese Soc. of Elecl. Engg. [IO]
 Elecl. Engg. and Allied Indus. Assn. [IO]
 Eta Kappa Nu [24459]
 IEEE Geoscience and Remote Sensing Soc. [7144]
 IEEE Indus. Applications Soc. [7183]
 Inst. of Elecl. and Electronics Engineers - Nigerian Sect. [IO]
 Inst. of Elecl. Engineers of Japan [IO]
 Italian Elecl. and Electronics Assn. [IO]
 Kappa Eta Kappa [24460]

Reference to "IO" in place of a book number signifies that the association may be found in the 45th edition of International Organizations.

Romanian EMC Assn. [IO]
Slovak Electrotechnical Comm. [IO]
South African Inst. of Elecl. Engineers [IO]
United Engg. Found. [7051]
Elecl. Engg. and Allied Indus. Assn. [IO], Johannesburg, Republic of South Africa
Elecl. Engg. Dept. Heads Assn; Natl. [★7011]
Elecl. Engineers; Amer. Inst. of [★6926]
Elecl. Equip. Representatives Assn. [1181], 638 W 39th St., Kansas City, MO 64111, (816)561-5323
Elecl. Generating Systems Assn. [1182], 1650 S Dixie Hwy., Ste. 500, Boca Raton, FL 33432-7462, (561)750-5575
Elecl. Generating Systems Marketing Assn. [★1182]
Electrical Historical Found. - Defunct.
Electrical Horology Soc. - Address unknown since 1999.
Electrical Housewares Distributors Assn. - Defunct.
Elecl. Indus; Joint Indus. Bd. of the [1030]
Electrical Industry Study Bd. - Defunct.
Elecl. Installation Equip. Mfrs'. Assn. [★IO]
Elecl. Insulation Assn. [IO], Stafford, United Kingdom
Elecl. Insulation Soc; IEEE [★6902]
Elecl. Insulation Soc; IEEE Dielectrics and [6902]
Elecl. Leagues; Intl. Assn. of [★1188]
Elecl. Manufacturers Assn; Consumer Products Division of the Natl. [★264]
Elecl. Mfg. and Coil Winding Assn. [1183], PO Box 278, Imperial Beach, CA 91933, (619)435-3629
Elecl. Overstress/Electrostatic Discharge Assn. [6910], 7900 Turin Rd., Bldg. 3, Rome, NY 13440-2069, (315)339-6937
Elecl. Protection Assn; Central Sta. [★3442]
Elecl., Radio and Machine Workers of Am; United [24050]
Elecl., Radio and Machine Workers; Intl. Union of [★24049]
Elecl., Salaried, Machine, and Furniture Workers; Intl. Union of Electronic, [24049]
Electrical Sensitivity Network - Defunct.
Elecl. Soc; Aerospace [6367]
Elecl. Soc; Aircraft [★6367]
Elecl. and Supplies; Assoc. Manufacturers of [★1191]
Elecl. Supply Jobbers Assn. [★1190]
Elecl., Tech., Salaried, Machine, and Furniture Workers; Intl. Union of Electronic, [★24049]
Elecl. Testing Assn; Natl. [★1187]
Elecl. Trade Coun. [★1046]
Elecl. Women's Roundtable [★1200]
Elecl. Workers; Intl. Brotherhood of [24048]
Electricity
Amer. Electrophoresis Soc. [6900]
Americans for Balanced Energy Choices [17495]
Coun. of European Energy Regulators [IO]
Edison Birthplace Assn. [11110]
Elec. Power Supply Assn. [6950]
Elec. Utility Benchmarking Assn. [6901]
Electricity Networks Assn. [IO]
Electricity Storage Assn. [3957]
EPRI [6953]
IEEE Dielectrics and Elecl. Insulation Soc. [6902]
IEEE Power Engg. Soc. [6903]
IEEE Solid-State Circuits Soc. [6904]
Insulated Cable Engineers Assn. [7017]
Lightning Strike and Elec. Shock Survivors Intl. [14304]
Lightning Strike and Elec. Shock Survivors Intl. [IO]
Natl. Assn. of Energy Ser. Companies [6960]
Natl. Food and Energy Coun. [6963]
Natl. Hydropower Assn. [6964]
Natl. Insulator Assn. [22408]
Nuclear Energy Inst. [6969]
Solar Elec. Power Assn. [7678]
Electricity Consumers Rsrc. Coun. [1184], 1333 H St. NW, West Tower, 8th Fl., Washington, DC 20005, (202)682-1730
Electricity Networks Assn. [IO], Wellington, New Zealand
Electricity Storage Assh. [IO], Morgan Hill, CA, United States
Electricity Storage Assn. [3957], 830 Claremont Dr., Morgan Hill, CA 95037, (614)716-1269
Electricity Supply Assn. of Australia [★IO]

Electrics, and Frequency Control Soc; IEEE Ultrasonics, Ferro [6366]
Electrification Coun. - Defunct.
Electrification Coun; Farm [★6963]
Electro-Acoustic Music in the U.S; Soc. for [10700]
Electro-Federation Canada [IO], Mississauga, ON, Canada
Electro-Optics Mfrs. Assn; Laser and [7246]
Electro-Optics Soc; IEEE Lasers and [6920]
Electro-Technical Coun. of Ireland [IO], Dublin, Ireland
Electrocardiology; Intl. Soc. for Computerized [13913]
Electrochemical Soc. [6680], 65 S Main St., Bldg. D, Pennington, NJ 08534-2839, (609)737-1902
Electrochemical Soc; Amer. [★6680]
Electrocoat Assn. [7730], PO Box 541083, Cincinnati, OH 45254-1083, (816)496-2308
Electrodiagnosis; Amer. Assn. of Electromyography and [★15303]
Electrodiagnostic Medicine; Amer. Assn. of Neuromuscular and [15303]
Electroencephalographic Technologists; Amer. Soc. of [★14307]
Electroencephalography
Amer. Bd. of Registration of EEG and EP Technologists [14305]
Amer. Clinical Neurophysiology Soc. [14306]
Amer. Soc. of Electroneurodiagnostic Technologists [14307]
Electrogists Intl. [★1045]
Electroheat Mfrs. Assn. of BEAMA [IO], London, United Kingdom
Electrologist Certification; International Bd. of [★14308]
Electrologists; Soc. of Clinical and Medical [★14310]
Electrology Assn; Amer. [14308]
Electrolysis
Amer. Electrology Assn. [14308]
Intl. Guild of Hair Removal Specialists [14309]
Intl. Guild of Hair Removal Specialists [IO]
Soc. for Clinical and Medical Hair Removal [14310]
Electrolysis Assn; Amer. [★14308]
Electrolysis Org; Natl. [★14310]
Electrolysis Soc. of Am. [★14310]
Electromagnetic Compatibility Soc; IEEE [6917]
Electromagnetic Energy Assn. - Address unknown since 2005.
Electromagnetics Soc; Applied Computational [6906]
Electromagnetics Soc; Bio [6555]
Electromagnetics Special Interest Gp; Bio [6556]
Electromedicine
Intl. Soc. for Computerized Electrocardiology [13913]
Natl. Inst. of Electromedical Info. [14311]
Electromyography and Electrodiagnosis; Amer. Assn. of [★15303]
Electron Device Engg. Coun; Joint [★1222]
Electron Devices Soc; IEEE [6918]
Electron Diffraction; Amer. Soc. for X-Ray and [★6852]
Electron Microscope Soc. of India [IO], New Delhi, India
Electron Microscopy Sect. of Moldova Republic [IO], Chisinau, Moldova
Electron Microscopy Soc. of Am. [★7335]
Electron Probe Anal. Soc. of Am. [★7334]
Electroneurodiagnostic Technologists; Amer. Soc. of [14307]
Electroneurophysiology Technologists; Canadian Assn. of [IO]
Electronic Appliance Guild [★IO]
Electronic Associations; Natl. [★1224]
Electronic Banking Economics Soc. - Address unknown since 2001.
Electronic Bible Soc. [19518], PO Box 701356, Dallas, TX 75370
Electronic Commerce; Aftermarket Coun. on [3835]
Electronic Commerce; Alliance Against Fraud in Telemarketing and [17302]
Electronic Commerce Assn. [★IO]
Electronic Commerce Assn. - Address unknown since 2008.
Electronic Commerce Coun. of Canada [★IO]

Electronic Communications Corp; Intl. BBSing and [3747]
Electronic Components Certification Bd. [1210], c/o Mr. Joe V. Chapman, Sec.-Treas., PO Box 9041, Midland, TX 79708, (432)697-9970
Electronic Components Indus'. Assn. [★IO]
Electronic Connector Study Group [★IO]
Electronic Connector Study Group [★6929]
Electronic Data Interchange Assn. - Address unknown since 1999.
Electronic Data Interchange Coun. of Canada [★IO]
Electronic Data Interchange; Workgroup for [1854]
Electronic Data Processing Auditors Assn. [★65]
Electronic Data Processing Auditors Assn. [★IO]
Electronic Defense Assn. [★6908]
Electronic Design Automation Consortium [6911], 111 W St. John St., Ste. 220, San Jose, CA 95113-1104, (408)287-3322
Electronic Design Installation Assn; Custom [3548]
Electronic Distribution Show and Conf. [1211], 222 S Riverside Plz., Ste. 2160, Chicago, IL 60606, (312)648-1140
Electronic Document Systems Found. [2100], 1845 Precinct Line Rd., Ste. 212, Hurst, TX 76054, (817)849-1145
Electronic, Elecl., Tech., Salaried, Machine, and Furniture Workers; Intl. Union of [★24049]
Electronic Engg. Comm; Airlines [6981]
Electronic Frontier Found. [7731], 454 Shotwell St., San Francisco, CA 94110-1914, (415)436-9333
Electronic Frontiers Australia [IO], North Adelaide, Australia
Electronic Funds Transfer Assn. [471], 11350 Random Hills Rd., Ste. 800, Fairfax, VA 22030, (703)934-6052
Electronic Funds Transfer Assn. [★471]
Electronic Govt. Directorate [IO], Islamabad, Pakistan
Electronic Hea. Care Transactions; Assn. for [14618]
Electronic Indus. Alliance [1212], 2500 Wilson Blvd., Arlington, VA 22201, (703)907-7500
Electronic Indus. Assn. [★1212]
Electronic Indus. Assn; Info. and Telecommunications Technologies Gp. of [★3759]
Electronic Indus. Assn. of Japan [★IO]
Electronic Indus. Assn. of Korea [IO], Seoul, Republic of Korea
Electronic Indus. Assn. of the Philippines [IO], Quezon City, Philippines
Electronic Indus. Fed. [IO], Halfway House, Republic of South Africa
Electronic Indus. Found. [★13126]
Electronic Industry Show Corp. - Defunct.
Electronic Keyboard Mfrs; Natl. Assn. of [★2808]
Electronic Library Assn. - Defunct.
Electronic Literature Org. [1202], Maryland Inst. for Tech. in the Humanities, B0131 McKeldin Lib., Univ. of Maryland, College Park, MD 20742, (301)314-6545
Electronic Manufacturers; Assn. of [★1212]
Electronic Media Rating Coun. [★566]
Electronic Messaging Assn. - Address unknown since 2005.
Electronic Money Coun. [★471]
Electronic Motion Control Assn. - Defunct.
Electronic MRO Distributors Assn. - Defunct.
Electronic Music Consortium - Address unknown since 2008.
Electronic Music Found. [10592], PO Box 8748, Albany, NY 12208, (518)434-4110
Electronic Networking Assn. - Defunct.
Electronic Organ Mfrs; Natl. Assn. of [★2808]
Electronic Payments Assn; NACHA: The [486]
Electronic Pest Control Assn. - Defunct.
Electronic Policy Network [★18460]
Electronic Power Res. Inst. [★7531]
Electronic Power Res. Inst. [★IO]
Electronic Privacy Info. Center [7194], 1718 Connecticut Ave. NW, Ste. 200, Washington, DC 20009, (202)483-1140
Electronic Products Manufacturers; Representatives of [★1213]
Electronic Publication Technology Group - Defunct.
Electronic Publishing
Educational Software Cooperative [6765]

A star before a book entry number signifies that the name is not listed separately, but is mentioned within the entry.

Electronic Bible Soc. [19518]
Electronic Literature Org. [1202]
  Internet Content Rating Assn. [12060]
  Internet Content Rating Assn. [IO]
  Macrocosm USA [3234]
Electronic Publishing Assn. [IO], Prague, Czech Republic
Electronic Publishing Special Interest Group - Address unknown since 2006.
Electronic Retailing Assn. [2626], 2000 N 14th St., Ste. 300, Arlington, VA 22201, (703)841-1751
Electronic Retailing Assn. [IO], Arlington, VA, United States
Electronic Revenue Commun. Advancement; Coun. for [3740]
Electronic Sales-Marketing Assn. - Defunct.
Electronic Security Distributors Assn. [IO], Benmore, Republic of South Africa
Electronic Ser. Dealers Assn; Natl. [★1224]
Electronic Servicers of Am; Natl. Assn. of TV and [★1224]
Electronic Technical Inst. - Defunct.
Electronic Tech. Services Assn. [★IO]
Electronic Transactions Assn. [IO], Washington, DC, United States
Electronic Transactions Assn. [472], 1101 16th St. NW, Ste. 402, Washington, DC 20036, (202)828-2635
Electronic Voice Phenomena; Amer. Assn. - [★7469]
Electronic Voice Phenomena; Amer. Assn. of [7469]
Electronically Published Internet Connection; EPIC - [22914]

Electronics
  1394 High Performance Serial Bus Trade Assn. [3720]
  AeA - Advancing the Bus. of Tech. [1203]
  AeA - Advancing the Bus. of Tech. [IO]
  Air Traffic Control Assn. [132]
  Airlines Electronic Engg. Comm. [6981]
  Amer. Quaternary Assn. [7359]
  Amer. Soc. of Test Engineers [7788]
  Americans for Fair Electronic Commerce Transactions [17441]
  Antenna Measurement Techniques Assn. [6905]
  Appliance and Electronic Indus. Assn. [IO]
  Applied Computational Electromagnetics Soc. [6906]
  Argentine Chamber of Elecl. Material Distributors [IO]
  Argentine Chamber of Electronics Indus. [IO]
  Armed Forces Communications and Electronics Assn. of Canada [IO]
  Asian Amer. MultiTechnology Assn. [1204]
  Assn. of the Austrian Elecl. and Electronics Indus. [IO]
  Assn. of Elecl. and Mech. Trades [IO]
  Association for Electronics Manufacturing of the Society of Manufacturing Engineers [IO]
  Assn. for Electronics Mfg. of the Soc. of Mfg. Engineers [6907]
  Assn. of the Electrotechnical Indus. of the Slovak Republic [IO]
  Assn. for Enterprise Integration [700]
  Assn. for High Tech. Distribution [1205]
  Assn. of Loudspeaker Mfrs. and Acoustics Intl. [1206]
  Assn. of Manufacturers and Importers of Elecl. Household Appliances [IO]
  Assn. of Old Crows [6908]
  Assn. Pour Le Commerce Et Les Services En Ligne [IO]
  Assn. of Suppliers of Electronic Instruments and Components [IO]
  Audio Engg. Soc. [6909]
  Australian Elecl. and Electronic Mfrs. Assn. [IO]
  Blue-ray Disc Association [IO]
  Blue-ray Disc Assn. [1207]
  British Audio-Visual Dealers Assn. [IO]
  British Electrostatic Control Assn. [IO]
  British Electrotechnical and Allied Mfrs'. Assn. [IO]
  British Electrotechnical Approvals Bd. [IO]
  British Fed. of Audio [IO]
  Canadian Electronic and Appliance Ser. Assn. [IO]
  Center for Electronic Packaging Res. [7425]
  China Audio Indus. Assn. [IO]

China Printed Circuit Assn. [IO]
Chinese American Semiconductor Professional Association [IO]
Chinese Amer. Semiconductor Professional Assn. [1208]
Chinese Inst. of Electronics [IO]
Collins Collectors Assn. [21499]
Consumer Electronics Assn. [1209]
COTREL [IO]
Czech and Moravian Elecl. and Electronic Assn. [IO]
ELCINA Electronic Indus. Assn. of India [IO]
Elecl. Insulation Assn. [IO]
Elecl. Overstress/Electrostatic Discharge Assn. [6910]
Electro-Technical Coun. of Ireland [IO]
Electronic Components Certification Bd. [1210]
Electronic Design Automation Consortium [6911]
Electronic Distribution Show and Conf. [1211]
Electronic Indus. Alliance [1212]
Electronic Indus. Assn. of Korea [IO]
Electronic Indus. Assn. of the Philippines [IO]
Electronic Indus. Fed. [IO]
Electronic Music Found. [10592]
Electronics and Elecl. Engg. Assn. of Slovenia [IO]
Electronics Indus. Assn. [IO]
Electronics Representatives Assn. [1213]
ETA Intl. - Electronics Technicians Assn., Intl. [1214]
ETA International - Electronics Technicians Association, International [IO]
European Assn. for Signal, Speech and Image Processing [IO]
European Electronic Chips and Systems Design Initiative [IO]
European Electronic Component Mfrs. Assn. [IO]
European Inst. of Printed Circuits [IO]
European Power Electronics and Drives Assn. [IO]
European Vending Assn. [IO]
Fabless Semiconductor Association [IO]
Fabless Semiconductor Assn. [1215]
Fed. Assn. of the Radio and Elecl. Trade [IO]
Fed. des Indus. Electriques, Electroniques et de Commun. [IO]
Fed. of Intl. Mech. Engg. and Electronics Indus. [IO]
Fed. of Westinghouse Independent Salaried Unions [24047]
French Assn. for Elecl. Equip., Automation and Related Services [IO]
Game Audio Network Guild [1715]
German Elecl. and Electronic Mfrs. Assn. [IO]
GS1 Canada [IO]
HAVi [6513]
Home Recording Rights Coalition [5844]
HomePlug Powerline Alliance [1216]
Hong Kong Electronic Indus. Assn. [IO]
Hong Kong and Kowloon Elec. Trade Assn. [IO]
Hong Kong and Kowloon Elecl. Appliances Merchants' Assn. [IO]
IEEE Aerospace and Electronics Systems Soc. [6912]
IEEE Antennas and Propagation Soc. [6913]
IEEE Broadcast Tech. Soc. [7768]
IEEE Circuits and Systems Soc. [6914]
IEEE Components, Packaging, and Mfg. Tech. Soc. [6915]
IEEE Cmpt. Soc. [6727]
IEEE Consumer Electronics Soc. [6916]
IEEE Dielectrics and Elecl. Insulation Soc. [6902]
IEEE Educ. Soc. [8262]
IEEE Electromagnetic Compatibility Soc. [6917]
IEEE Electron Devices Soc. [6918]
IEEE Engg. Mgt. Soc. [7014]
IEEE Indus. Electronics Soc. [6919]
IEEE Industrial Electronics Society [IO]
IEEE Indus. Applications Soc. [7183]
IEEE Info. Theory Gp. [7770]
IEEE Instrumentation and Measurement Soc. [7219]
IEEE Lasers and Electro-Optics Soc. [6920]
IEEE Lasers and Electro-Optics Society [IO]
IEEE Magnetics Soc. [6921]

IEEE Nuclear and Plasma Sciences Soc. [7386]
IEEE Power Electronics Soc. [6922]
IEEE Power Engg. Soc. [6903]
IEEE Professional Commun. Soc. [6923]
IEEE Reliability Soc. [6924]
IEEE Robotics and Automation Soc. [7582]
IEEE Solid-State Circuits Soc. [6904]
IEEE Systems, Man, and Cybernetics Soc. [6728]
IEEE Ultrasonics, Ferroelectrics, and Frequency Control Soc. [6366]
IEEE Vehicular Tech. Soc. [6925]
India Semiconductor Assn. [IO]
Indian Elecl. and Electronics Mfrs. Assn. [IO]
Industry Coalition on Technology Transfer [1217]
Inst. of Elecl. and Electronics Engineers [6926]
Inst. of Elecl. and Electronics Engineers - USA [7015]
Intellect [IO]
Intl. Assn. for Cryptologic Res. [6849]
Intl. Assn. of Electronics Recyclers [1218]
Intl. Assn. of Electronics Recyclers [IO]
Intl. Auto Sound Challenge Assn. [1219]
Intl. BBSing and Electronic Communications Corp. [3747]
Intl. Brotherhood of Elecl. Workers [24048]
Intl. Coordinating Comm. on Solid State Sensors and Actuators Res. [6927]
Intl. Coordinating Comm. on Solid State Sensors and Actuators Res. [IO]
Intl. DB2 Users Gp. [6856]
Intl. Electronics Mfg. Initiative [7265]
Intl. Engg. Consortium [6928]
Intl. Engg. Consortium [IO]
Intl. Inst. of Connector and Interconnection Tech. [IO]
Intl. Inst. of Connector and Interconnection Tech. [6929]
Intl. Microelectronic and Packaging Soc. [6930]
Intl. Microelectronic and Packaging Soc. [IO]
Intl. Photonics Commercialization Alliance [2862]
Intl. Soc. of Certified Electronics Technicians [1220]
Intl. Soc. of Certified Electronics Technicians [IO]
Intl. Union of Electronic, Elecl., Salaried, Machine, and Furniture Workers [24049]
IPC - Assn. Connecting Electronics Indus. [1221]
Israel Assn. of Electronics and Info. Indus. [IO]
Japan Electronic Products Importers Assn. [IO]
Japan Electronics and Info. Tech. Indus. Assn. [IO]
Japan Electronics Show Assn. [IO]
Japanese Elec. Wire and Cable Makers Assn. [IO]
Japanese Elecl., Electronic and Info. Union [IO]
JEDEC [1222]
Korea Elecl. Contractors' Assn. [IO]
Korea Elecl. Mfrs'. Co-operative [IO]
Korea Electronic Indus. Cooperative [IO]
Microelectronic Indus. Design Assn. - Ireland [IO]
Musical Instrument Technicians Assn., Intl. [2816]
Natl. Assn. of Commun. Systems Engineers [6715]
Natl. Assn. of Domestic Elecl. Appliance Manufactures [IO]
Natl. Chamber of Elec. Manufactures [IO]
Natl. Coalition for Electronics Educ. [8364]
Natl. Electronic Distributors Assn. [1223]
Natl. Electronics Ser. Dealers Assn. [1224]
Natl. Fed. of Electrotechnical and Electronic Indus. [IO]
Natl. Marine Electronics Assn. [2586]
Natl. Systems Contractors Assn. [1225]
New Zealand Photovoltaic Assn. [IO]
North America Chinese Semiconductor Association [IO]
North Am. Chinese Semiconductor Assn. [1226]
North Amer. Retail Dealers Assn. [1227]
Norwegian Electrotechnical Comm. [IO]
Optoelectronics Indus. Development Assn. [2861]
Pacific Stud. Center [6892]
Philippine Electronics and Telecommunications Fed. [IO]
Postsecondary Electronic Standards Coun. [9165]
Professional Ser. Assn. [3553]
Register of Elecl. Contractors of Ireland [IO]

Reference to "IO" in place of a book number signifies that the association may be found in the 45th edition of International Organizations.

SEMI Intl. **[IO]**
SEMI Intl. **[1228]**
Semiconductor Environmental, Safety and Hea. Assn. **[6931]**
Semiconductor Indus. Assn. **[1229]**
Small Domestic Elecl. Appliance Manufacturers' Assn. **[IO]**
Soc. for Electro-Acoustic Music in the U.S. **[10700]**
South African Electrotechnical Export Coun. **[IO]**
Spanish Fed. of Elecl. Appliances Retailers **[IO]**
Swedish Assn. of Suppliers of Elecl. Household Appliances **[IO]**
Swedish Electronics Retailers' Assn. **[IO]**
Swiss Tech. Distributors' Assn. **[IO]**
Taiwan Elec. and Electronic Mfrs'. Assn. **[IO]**
Turkish Electronics and Info. Indus. Assn. **[IO]**
Union Internationale de la Presse Electronique **[IO]**
United Elecl., Radio and Machine Workers of Am. **[24050]**
U.S. Display Consortium **[3729]**
Variable Electronic Components Inst. **[1230]**
Video Electronics Standards Assn. **[6932]**
Wi-Fi Alliance **[6829]**
Wire and Cable Indus. Suppliers Assn. **[1231]**
Xplor Intl. **[1798]**
Electronics Assn; Natl. Marine **[2586]**
Electronics Club - Defunct.
Electronics Conf; Natl. **[★6928]**
Electronics Coun; IEEE Power **[★6922]**
Electronics and Elecl. Engg. Assn. of Slovenia **[IO]**, Ljubljana, Slovenia
Electronics Engineers - USA; Inst. of Elecl. and **[7015]**
Electronics Indus. Fed. **[IO]**, Gauteng, Republic of South Africa
Electronics Indus. Assn. **[IO]**, Eastwood, Australia
Electronics Mfrs. Assn. of BC **[★IO]**
Electronics Mfrs. Assn. - Defunct.
Electronics Manufacturers Assn; West Coast **[★1203]**
Electronics Manufacturers Assn; Western **[★1203]**
Electronics Mfg. Initiative; Intl. **[7265]**
Electronics Mfg. Initiative; Natl. **[★7265]**
Electronics Representatives Assn. **[1213]**, 300 W Adams St., Ste. 617, Chicago, IL 60606, (312)527-3050
Electronics Technicians Assn., Intl; ETA Intl. - **[1214]**
Electronics TV Manufacturers Assn; Radio **[★1212]**
Electrophoresis Soc; Intl. **[★6900]**
Electrophysiology; North Amer. Soc. of Pacing and **[★13907]**
Electroplaters and Surface Finishers Soc; Metal Finishing Suppliers' Assn., Natl. Assn. of Metal Finishers and Amer. **[★1474]**
Electrostatic Discharge Assn; Elecl. Overstress/ **[6910]**
Electrotechnical Standardization; European Comm. for **[IO]**
Elektriska Hushaallsapparat Leverantoerer Foerening **[★IO]**
Elektroniikan Komponentti-ja Mittalaitetoimittajat **[★IO]**
ElektronikForbundet Svenska **[★IO]**
Elementary Education
Big Picture Company **[8353]**
Books for the Barrios **[12049]**
Chinese Language Assn. of Secondary-Elementary Schools **[8075]**
Christian Schools Intl. **[8083]**
The Coll. Bd. **[9248]**
Coun. for Elementary Sci. Intl. **[9100]**
Inst. for Learning Technologies **[8355]**
Natl. Assn. for the Educ. of Young Children **[8069]**
Natl. Assn. of Elementary School Principals **[9014]**
Natl. Assn. of Hebrew Day School PTAs **[8953]**
Natl. Assn. of Principals of Schools for Girls **[9015]**
Natl. Circus Proj. **[8286]**
Natl. Commun. Assn. **[9157]**
Natl. Coun. for Geographic Educ. **[8457]**
Natl. Coun. for History Educ. **[8508]**
Natl. Coun. for the Social Stud. **[9128]**

Natl. School Boards Assn. **[9083]**
Natl. Tutoring Assn. **[9283]**
Phonics Inst. **[9046]**
School Sci. and Mathematics Assn. **[9115]**
Elementary School Principals; Natl. Assn. of **[9014]**
Elementary School Principals, NEA; Dept. of **[★9014]**
Elementary Schools; Commission on **[★8277]**
Elementary Schools Press Assn; Natl. **[9012]**
Elementary Sci; Natl. Coun. for **[★9100]**
Elephant Care Intl. **[5313]**, 166 Limo View Ln., Hohenwald, TN 38462, (931)796-7102
Elephant Care Intl. **[IO]**, Hohenwald, TN, United States
Elephant Collectors Soc; Natl. **[22081]**
Elephant Interest Gp. **[★5314]**
Elephant Mgt. and Owners Assn. **[IO]**, Vaalwater, Republic of South Africa
Elephant Managers Assn. **[IO]**, Buffalo, NY, United States
Elephant Managers Assn. **[4158]**, c/o Daryl Hoffman, Exec. Dir., Buffalo Zoo, 300 Parkside Ave., Buffalo, NY 14214, (407)938-1988
Elephant Res. Found. **[5314]**
Elephant Sanctuary in Tennessee **[11389]**, PO Box 393, Hohenwald, TN 38462, (931)796-6500
Elevator Contractors; Natl. Assn. of **[1034]**
Elevator Escalator Safety Found. **[1232]**, 362 Pinehill Dr., Mobile, AL 36606-1715, (251)479-2199
Elevator Escalator Safety Found. of Canada **[IO]**, Mississauga, ON, Canada
Elevator Industries Assn. - Address unknown since 2003.
Elevator Mfg. Indus; Natl. **[★2049]**
Elevator and Processing Soc; Grain **[1750]**
Elevator Superintendents; Soc. of Grain **[★1750]**
Elevators
Elevator Escalator Safety Found. **[1232]**
European Elevator Assn. **[IO]**
Intl. Union of Elevator Constructors **[24099]**
Natl. Assn. of Vertical Trans. Professionals **[2048]**
Natl. Elevator Indus., Inc. **[2049]**
Eleventh Commandment Fellowship - Address unknown since 1999.
Elfquest Fan Club - Defunct.
Elgin Motorcar Owners Registry **[21638]**, 2226 E Apache Ln., Vincennes, IN 47591, (812)888-4172
Elgin Motorcar Owners Registry **[IO]**, Vincennes, IN, United States
Elijah Gillespie Family Org. - Address unknown since 2004.
Eliminate the Natl. Debt - Address unknown since 1994.
Elintarviketeollisuusliitto **[★IO]**
Elisabeth Kubler-Ross Center - Address unknown since 1999.
Elisabeth Sladen Information Network - Defunct.
Elite Coaches' Assn. for Women's Gymnastics; U.S. **[23297]**
Elizabeth Linington Soc. - Defunct.
Elizabethan Club of Yale Univ. **[10421]**, 459 Coll. St., New Haven, CT 06511, (203)432-0172
Elk Breeders Assn; North Amer. **[4028]**
Elk Found; Rocky Mountain **[5374]**
Elkhound Assn. of Am; Norwegian **[22331]**
Elks
Benevolent and Protective Order of Elks **[19035]**
Benevolent and Protective Order of Elks of Canada **[IO]**
Improved Benevolent Protective Order of Elks of the World **[IO]**
Improved Benevolent Protective Order of Elks of the World **[19036]**
Supreme Emblem Club of the U.S.A. **[19037]**
Elks Natl. Foundation **[★19035]**
Ella Baker Student Program **[★17097]**
Eller Family Assn. **[20894]**, c/o Thomas J. Eller, Pres., 1311 Masters Dr., Woodland Park, CO 80863
Ellington Jazz Soc; Duke **[★10590]**
Ellington Navigators Observers Assn. **[★20659]**
Ellington Soc. - New York Chap; The Duke **[★10590]**
Elliniki Aerathlitiki Omospondia **[IO]**, Glyfada, Greece
Elliniko Diktio Diaxeiriston Ergon **[★IO]**

Elliot Clan Soc. USA **[20895]**, c/o Evelyn M. Elliott, Treas., 2146 Deer Trail, Suwanee, GA 30024
Elliot Inst. **[16911]**, PO Box 7348, Springfield, IL 62791-7348, (217)525-8202
Elliot Inst. for Social Sciences Res. **[★16911]**
Ellis Family Genealogical Assn. - Defunct.
Ellis Inst; Albert **[16197]**
Ellis Island Found; Statue of Liberty - **[10066]**
Ellis Island Medal of Honor Soc. **[19044]**, c/o Natl. Ethnic Coalition of Organizations, 232 Madison Ave., Ste. 900, New York, NY 10016-2901, (212)755-1492
Elm Res. Inst. **[4682]**, 11 Kit St., Keene, NH 03431, (603)358-6198
Elmer Bird Intl. Fan Club - Address unknown since 2002.
Elms Unlimited **[★4682]**
Elmwood Inst. **[★4501]**
The Elongated Collectors **[22738]**, c/o Dave Bradley, PO Box 3182, Cocoa, FL 32924-3182, (321)302-6053
Elrod Fan Club; P.N. **[9702]**
Elsa Clubs of America - Defunct.
Elsa Wild Animal Appeal - U.S.A. - Address unknown since 2003.
Elsey Family Assn. - Defunct.
Elswick Family Assn. **[20896]**
Elton John AIDS Found. **[16963]**, PO Box 17139, Beverly Hills, CA 90209-3139
Elton Sawyer Fan Club **[25005]**
Elton Sawyer - Patty Moise Fan Club **[★25005]**
Elva Owners of America - Address unknown since 1999.
Elva Owners Club **[IO]**, Worthing, United Kingdom
Elves', Gnomes', and Little Men's Science Fiction, Chowder and Marching Soc. - Address unknown since 1999.
Elvira Fan Club **[24817]**, PO Box 38246, Hollywood, CA 90038
Elvira Fan Club **[IO]**, Hollywood, CA, United States
Elvis' Angels Fan Club **[24806]**, 10152 La Hwy. 1, Mooringsport, LA 71060-8948
Elvis Brothers Fan Club - Address unknown since 1989.
Elvis Costello Info. Ser. **[IO]**, Purmerend, Netherlands
Elvis Fan Club; TCB for **[24814]**
Elvis Fan Club; We Remember **[24815]**
Elvis Fever Fan Club **[24807]**
Elvis Forever TCB Fan Club **[24808]**
Elvis' Little Buddies **[★24815]**
Elvis Lives On Fan Club - Defunct.
Elvis Now Fan Club - Defunct.
Elvis Our Guardian AngEL, Elvis Presley Fan Club - Address unknown since 1994.
Elvis Presley
Asian Worldwide Elvis Fan Club **[24805]**
Elvis' Angels Fan Club **[24806]**
Elvis Fever Fan Club **[24807]**
Elvis Forever TCB Fan Club **[24808]**
Elvis Presley Memorial Soc. **[24809]**
Elvis Teddy Bears **[24810]**
Elvis - The Legend Continues Fan Club **[24811]**
ElvisNet Elvis Presley Fan Club **[24812]**
Presley-ites Fan Club Intl. **[24813]**
TCB for Elvis Fan Club **[24814]**
We Remember Elvis Fan Club **[24815]**
Elvis Presley Burning Love Fan Club - Address unknown since 2001.
Elvis Presley Circle City Fan Club - Address unknown since 1999.
Elvis Presley Fan Club; ElvisNet **[24812]**
Elvis Presley Memorial Soc. **[24809]**, 315 Cypress Glen Dr., Mount Juliet, TN 37122, (615)758-0913
Elvis Presley Tribute Fan Club - Defunct.
Elvis Special Photo Assn. - Address unknown since 2001.
Elvis Teddy Bears **[24810]**
Elvis - The Legend Continues Fan Club **[24811]**, c/o David Lewis, Pres., 4221 Crestview Dr., Chattanooga, TN 37415, (615)867-6722
Elvis, This One's for You Fan Club - Address unknown since 1994.
Elvis Worldwide Fan Club **[★24805]**
Elvis Worldwide Memorial Fan Club **[★24805]**

A star before a book entry number signifies that the name is not listed separately, but is mentioned within the entry.

Elvish Linguistic Fellowship [10402], c/o Carl F. Hostetter, Hd., 2509 Ambling Cir., Crofton, MD 21114
Elvish Linguistic Fellowship [IO], Crofton, MD, United States
Elvisly Yours [IO], Watford, United Kingdom
ElvisNet Elvis Presley Fan Club [24812]
Elwyn [12383], 111 Elwyn Rd., Elwyn, PA 19063, (610)891-2000
Ely-Chatelaine; Free Territory of [18351]
EM - The Employers' Org. of the Metal Trades in Europe [★IO]
Email
    Coalition Against Unsolicited Commercial Email [6933]
    Intl. Assn. of Messaging Professionals [6711]
    Privacy Rights CH [3176]
Emanuel Family Genealogy - Defunct.
Emanuel Found. for Hungarian Culture - Address unknown since 2006.
eMarketing Assn. [1166], 105 Franklin St., No. 16-129, Westerly, RI 02891, (401)315-2194
eMarketing Assn. [IO], Westerly, RI, United States
Emba Mink Breeders Assn. [★4129]
Embalming Chemical Mfrs. Assn. - Address unknown since 2003.
Embassy Guard Assn; Marine [21177]
Embassy Social Secretaries Assn. - Defunct.
Embedded Linux Consortium [6726], 3760 Cross Creek Rd., Santa Rosa, CA 95403, (707)576-0111
Emblem Club of the U.S.A; Supreme [19037]
Embossing Assn; Foil Stamping and [2707]
Embroiderers' Guild [IO], East Molesey, United Kingdom
Embroiderers' Guild of Am. [22155], 426 W Jefferson St., Louisville, KY 40202, (502)589-6956
Embroiderers' Guild of London, Amer. Br. [★22155]
Embroidery Coun. of Am. - Defunct.
Embroidery Inst; Schiffli [★3796]
Embroidery Mfrs. Assn; Schiffli Lace and [3797]
Embroidery Mfrs. Bur. [★3797]
Embroidery Mfrs. Promotion Bd. [★3796]
Embroidery Mfrs. Promotion Found; Schiffli [★3796]
Embroidery Mfrs. Promotion Fund; Schiffli [★3796]
Embroidery Mfrs. Promotion Fund; Schiffli [3796]
Embroidery Promotion Coun; Schiffli [★3796]
Embroidery-Stitchery-Textile Unit - Defunct.
Embroidery Trade Assn. [3781], 12300 Ford Rd., Ste. 135, Dallas, TX 75234, (888)628-2545
Embryo Transfer Assn; Amer. [4149]
Embryology; European Soc. of Human Reproduction and [IO]
EMDR Assn. of Australia [IO], Wyong, Australia
EMDR Europe [IO], Hertfordshire, United Kingdom
EMDR - Humanitarian Assistance Programs [IO], Hamden, CT, United States
EMDR - Humanitarian Assistance Programs [12767], PO Box 6505, Hamden, CT 06517, (203)288-4450
EMDR Intl. Assn. [16215], 5806 Mesa Dr., Ste. 360, Austin, TX 78731, (512)451-5200
EMDR Intl. Assn. [IO], Austin, TX, United States
EMDR Mexico [IO], Mexico City, Mexico
EMDR Network Japan [IO], Hyogo, Japan
EMDRIA Latinoamerica Asociacion Civil [IO], Buenos Aires, Argentina
Emerald Green Miniature Golf Assn. - Address unknown since 2003.
Emerald Isle Immigration Center [17804], 59-26 Woodside Ave., Woodside, NY 11377, (718)478-5502
Emerald Isle Immigration Center [IO], Woodside, NY, United States
Emerald Society of the Federal Law Enforcement Agencies [IO], Rochester, NY, United States
Emerald Soc. of the Fed. Law Enforcement Agencies [19199], PO Box 16413, Rochester, NY 14616-0413
Emerge: A Men's Counseling Ser. on Domestic Violence [★12026]
Emerge: Counseling and Educ. to Stop Domestic Violence [12026], 2464 Massachusetts Ave., Ste. 101, Cambridge, MA 02140-1645, (617)547-9879
Emerge: Counseling and Educ. to Stop Male Violence [★12026]
Emergency Aid
    Air Charity Network [14312]

All4Israel [12454]
Amer. Ambulance Assn. [14313]
Amer. Assn. for Accreditation of Ambulatory Surgery Facilities [16557]
Amer. Bd. of Emergency Medicine [14325]
Amer. Coll. of Emergency Physicians [14326]
Amer. Coll. of Osteopathic Emergency Physicians [14327]
Amer. Disaster Reserve [12000]
Amer. Osteopathic Bd. of Emergency Medicine [14328]
Amer. Red Cross Natl. HQ [12830]
Amer. Red Magen David for Israel - Amer. Friends of Magen David Adom [12832]
AmeriCares Found. [12833]
Assn. of Air Medical Services [14314]
Assn. of Air Medical Services [IO]
Batey Relief Alliance [12835]
CARE Intl. USA [12838]
Center for Intl. Disaster Info. [12001]
Center for Res. in Ambulatory Hea. Care Admin. [15064]
Christian Reformed World Relief Comm. [12424]
Church World Ser. [12842]
Commn. on Accreditation of Ambulance Services [13532]
Doctors for Disaster Preparedness [14315]
Emergency Medicine Found. [14331]
Emergency Medicine Residents' Assn. [14332]
Emergency Nurses Assn. [14333]
Estonian Relief Comm. [12853]
Fed. of Fire Chaplains [19747]
Grassroots Intl. [12428]
House of Ruth [12029]
Intl. Assn. of Dive Rescue Specialists [23574]
Intl. Assn. of Flight Paramedics [14334]
Intl. Fire Buff Associates [22421]
Intl. Healthcare Safety Professional Certification Bd. [16379]
Intl. Medical Corps [12862]
Intl. Police and Fire Chaplain's Assn. [19750]
Intl. Rescue and Emergency Care Assn. [14316]
Intl. Rescue and Emergency Care Assn. [IO]
Intl. Soc. of First Responders [IO]
Intl. Soc. of First Responders [14317]
Irish Assn. of the Sovereign Military Order of Malta [IO]
Islamic Amer. Relief Agency [12864]
Life for Relief and Development [12867]
Mapendo Intl. [12868]
MedicAlert Found. Intl. [14318]
MedicAlert Found. Intl. [IO]
MediSend Intl. [12530]
Mennonite Disaster Ser. [12870]
Miracle Flights for Kids [14319]
Natl. Academies of Emergency Dispatch [14348]
Natl. Assn. of Emergency Medical Technicians [14335]
Natl. Assn. of Emergency Vehicle Technicians [418]
Natl. Assn. of First Responders [14320]
Natl. Assn. for Search and Rescue [12891]
Natl. Assn. of State EMS Officials [14337]
Natl. Coalition Against Domestic Violence [12034]
Natl. Emergency Equip. Dealers Assn. [14339]
Natl. Emergency Number Assn. [14321]
Natl. EMS Pilots Assn. [14322]
Natl. Native Amer. EMS Assn. [14341]
Natl. Registry of Emergency Medical Technicians [14342]
Natl. Ski Patrol Sys. [23753]
Natl. Voluntary Organizations Active in Disaster [12874]
North Amer. Assn. for Ambulatory Urgent Care [13663]
Oper. U.S.A. [12535]
OXFAM Am. [12438]
Pan Amer. Hea. Org. [14592]
Plenty Intl. [12878]
Pontifical Mission for Palestine [12816]
Rapha Intl. [12539]
Refugees Intl. [12818]
Save the Children [11720]
Skyaid Org. [14349]
Soc. for Academic Emergency Medicine [14344]

Soc. for the Preservation and Appreciation of Antique Motor Fire Apparatus in Am. [22423]
State EMS Training Coordinators Coun. of NASEMSO [14345]
Travelers Aid Intl. [13191]
U.S. Homeland Emergency Response Org. [12893]
U.S. Lifesaving Assn. [12894]
U.S. Mine Rescue Assn. [12600]
Urgent Care Assn. of Am. [13665]
U.S.A. for Africa [12882]
Wings of Hope [12883]
World Mercy Fund [12886]
World Relief [19985]
Emergency Air Medical Services; Amer. Soc. of Hospital-Based [★14314]
Emergency Assoc. Communications Teams; Radio [★6254]
Emergency Assoc. Communications Teams; Radio [★IO]
Emergency Black Survival Fund [★12780]
Emergency Care Res. Inst. [★15136]
Emergency Care Res. Inst. [★IO]
Emergency Centers; Natl. Assn. of Freestanding [★13663]
Emergency Civil Liberties Comm; Natl. [★17097]
Emergency Coalition for Haitian Refugees; Natl. [★18499]
Emergency Coalition for U.S. Financial Support of the United Nations [18764], 110 Maryland Ave. NE, Ste. 409, Washington, DC 20002, (202)546-1572
Emergency Comm. for Amer. Trade [2303], 1211 Connecticut Ave. NW, Ste. 801, Washington, DC 20036, (202)659-5147
Emergency Comm. to Defend Constitutional Welfare Rights, U.S.A. [18443], c/o Mr. Martin J. Sawma, Exec. Dir./Intl. Rep., 3501 Westwood Dr., Rm. 4, Niagara Falls, NY 14305-3416, (716)297-7273
Emergency Comm. for Full Funding of Educ. Programs [★8345]
Emergency Comm. to Save America's Marine Resources - Defunct.
Emergency Comm. to Suspend Immigration - Defunct.
Emergency Conservation Comm. - Defunct.
Emergency Contraception; Intl. Consortium for [12183]
Emergency Coun. of Jewish Families - Address unknown since 1999.
Emergency and Critical Care Technicians; Acad. of Veterinary [16734]
Emergency Defense Sys; Christian-Patriots Defense League/Citizen's [17263]
Emergency Dept. Nurses Assn. [★14333]
Emergency Dept. Nurses Assn; Natl. [★14333]
Emergency Dept. Practice Mgt. Assn. [14330], 8405 Greensboro Dr., Ste. 800, McLean, VA 22102, (703)506-3292
Emergency Fund; Chaplains [★21193]
Emergency Fund; United Nations Intl. Children's [★11658]
Emergency Intl. - Address unknown since 1989.
Emergency Land Fund [★12937]
Emergency Lead-Zinc Producers Comm. [★2723]
Emergency Lighting Mfrs. Assn. - Defunct.
Emergency Mgt. Assn; Natl. [5565]
Emergency Mgt; Natl. Coordinating Coun. on [★5563]
Emergency Medical Technicians - Ambulance; Registry of [★14342]
Emergency Medicine
    Accreditation Assn. for Ambulatory Hea. Care [13661]
    Air Charity Network [14312]
    Ambulance Ser. Assn. [IO]
    Amer. Acad. of Emergency Medicine [14323]
    Amer. Ambulance Assn. [14313]
    Amer. Assn. for Accreditation of Ambulatory Surgery Facilities [16557]
    Amer. Assn. of Women Emergency Physicians [14324]
    Amer. Bd. of Emergency Medicine [14325]
    Amer. Burn Assn. [13781]
    Amer. Coll. of Emergency Physicians [14326]

Reference to "IO" in place of a book number signifies that the association may be found in the 45th edition of International Organizations.

Amer. Coll. of Osteopathic Emergency Physicians [14327]
Amer. Osteopathic Bd. of Emergency Medicine [14328]
Amer. Red Cross Natl. HQ [12830]
Amer. Red Magen David for Israel - Amer. Friends of Magen David Adom [12832]
AmeriCares Found. [12833]
Assn. of Air Medical Services [14314]
Assn. of Emergency Physicians [14329]
Assn. of Organ Procurement Organizations [14287]
Australasian Coll. for Emergency Medicine [IO]
British Assn. for Emergency Medicine [IO]
British Assn. for Immediate Care [IO]
CARE Intl. USA [12838]
Center for Res. in Ambulatory Hea. Care Admin. [15064]
Christian Reformed World Relief Comm. [12424]
Church World Ser. [12842]
Commn. on Accreditation of Ambulance Services [13532]
Comm. on Accreditation for Educational Programs for the EMS Professions [8833]
Committee on Accreditation of Medical Transport Systems [IO]
Emergency Dept. Practice Mgt. Assn. [14330]
Emergency Medicine Found. [14331]
Emergency Medicine Residents' Assn. [14332]
Emergency Nurses Assn. [14333]
Estonian Relief Comm. [12853]
European Aero-Medical Inst. [IO]
European Soc. for Emergency Medicine [IO]
Fed. of Fire Chaplains [19747]
German Soc. for Disaster Medicine [IO]
Grassroots Intl. [12428]
Indian Soc. of Critical Care Medicine [IO]
Intl. Assn. for Ambulatory Surgery [IO]
Intl. Assn. of Dive Rescue Specialists [23574]
Intl. Assn. of EMTs and Paramedics [24051]
Intl. Assn. of EMTs and Paramedics [IO]
Intl. Assn. of Flight Paramedics [14334]
Intl. Critical Incident Stress Found. [16491]
Intl. Fire Buff Associates [22421]
Intl. Medical Corps [12862]
Intl. Soc. of First Responders [14317]
MedicAlert Found. Intl. [14318]
Mennonite Disaster Ser. [12870]
Natl. Academies of Emergency Dispatch [14348]
Natl. Assn. of Emergency Medical Technicians [14335]
National Association of Emergency Medical Technicians [IO]
Natl. Assn. of EMS Physicians [14336]
Natl. Assn. of First Responders [14320]
Natl. Assn. of State EMS Officials [14337]
Natl. Burn Victim Found. [13784]
Natl. Collegiate EMS Found. [14338]
Natl. Emergency Equip. Dealers Assn. [14339]
Natl. Emergency Medicine Assn. [14340]
Natl. Heart Coun. [13918]
Natl. Native Amer. EMS Assn. [14341]
Natl. Registry of Emergency Medical Technicians [14342]
Natl. Ski Patrol Sys. [23753]
Natl. Voluntary Organizations Active in Disaster [12874]
Oper. U.S.A. [12535]
Pan Amer. Hea. Org. [14592]
Plenty Intl. [12878]
Residency Rev. Comm. for Emergency Medicine [14343]
Royal Flying Dr. Ser. of Australia [IO]
Skyaid Org. [14349]
Soc. for Academic Emergency Medicine [14344]
Soc. of Air Force Physicians [15264]
Soc. for the Preservation and Appreciation of Antique Motor Fire Apparatus in Am. [22423]
State EMS Training Coordinators Coun. of NASEMSO [14345]
Student Veterinary Emergency and Critical Care Soc. [16810]
Turkish Assn. of Trauma and Emergency Surgery [IO]
Urgent Care Assn. of Am. [13665]

U.S.A. for Africa [12882]
Wings of Hope [12883]
World Mercy Fund [12886]
World Relief [19985]
Emergency Medicine Found. [14331], PO Box 619911, Dallas, TX 75261-9911, (972)550-0911
Emergency Medicine Mgt. Assn. - Defunct.
Emergency Medicine Physician Assistants; Soc. of [15979]
Emergency Medicine Residents' Assn. [14332], 1125 Executive Cir., Irving, TX 75038-2522, (972)550-0920
Emergency Medicine; Soc. of Teachers of [★14344]
Emergency Medicine; Univ. Assn. for [★14344]
Emergency Money Soc. - Address unknown since 1995.
Emergency Natl. Coun. Against U.S. Intervention in Central America/the Caribbean - Defunct.
Emergency Nurses Assn. [14333], 915 Lee St., Des Plaines, IL 60016-6569, (847)460-4095
Emergency Planning Comm., IACP - Defunct.
Emergency Planning Soc. [IO], Cardiff, United Kingdom
Emergency Project for Equal Rights - Defunct.
Emergency Radiology; Amer. Soc. of [16278]
Emergency Relief; Army [18958]
Emergency Relief Response Fund [20562], PO Box 2300, Redlands, CA 92373, (909)793-2009
Emergency Rescue Comm. [★12812]
Emergency Rescue Comm. [★IO]
Emergency Response Assn; Disaster [5560]
Emergency Response Team; Amer. Lifesaving [★12894]
Emergency Services
　Accreditation Assn. for Ambulatory Hea. Care [13661]
　Air Charity Network [14312]
　All4Israel [12454]
　Amer. Ambulance Assn. [14313]
　Amer. Assn. for Accreditation of Ambulatory Surgery Facilities [16557]
　Amer. Bd. of Emergency Medicine [14325]
　Amer. Burn Assn. [13781]
　Amer. Coll. of Emergency Physicians [14326]
　Amer. Coll. of Osteopathic Emergency Physicians [14327]
　Amer. Disaster Reserve [12000]
　Amer. Osteopathic Bd. of Emergency Medicine [14328]
　Amer. Red Cross Natl. HQ [12830]
　Amer. Red Magen David for Israel - Amer. Friends of Magen David Adom [12832]
　AmeriCares Found. [12833]
　Assn. of Air Medical Services [14314]
　Canadian Emergency Preparedness Assn. [IO]
　CARE Intl. USA [12838]
　Center for Intl. Disaster Info. [12001]
　Center for Res. in Ambulatory Hea. Care Admin. [15064]
　Christian Reformed World Relief Comm. [12424]
　Church World Ser. [12842]
　Civil Air Patrol [5538]
　COMCARE Alliance [14346]
　Commn. on Accreditation of Ambulance Services [13532]
　Comm. on Accreditation of Medical Transport Systems [14347]
　Emergency Medicine Found. [14331]
　Emergency Medicine Residents' Assn. [14332]
　Emergency Nurses Assn. [14333]
　Estonian Relief Comm. [12853]
　Fed. Alliance For Safe Homes [12061]
　Fed. of Fire Chaplains [19747]
　Fire and Emergency Mfrs. and Services Assn. [12062]
　FireFlag/EMS [5773]
　Grassroots Intl. [12428]
　House of Ruth [12029]
　Intl. Assn. of Dive Rescue Specialists [23574]
　Intl. Assn. of EMTs and Paramedics [24051]
　Intl. Assn. of Fire Chiefs [5718]
　Intl. Assn. of Flight Paramedics [14334]
　Intl. Critical Incident Stress Found. [16491]
　Intl. Fire Buff Associates [22421]
　Intl. Medical Corps [12862]

Intl. Police and Fire Chaplain's Assn. [19750]
Intl. Soc. for Fire Ser. Instructors [5720]
Intl. Soc. of First Responders [14317]
Law Enforcement and Emergency Services Video Assn. [6350]
MedicAlert Found. Intl. [14318]
MediSend Intl. [12530]
Mennonite Disaster Ser. [12870]
Natl. Academies of Emergency Dispatch [14348]
Natl. Assn. of Emergency Medical Technicians [14335]
Natl. Assn. of Emergency Vehicle Technicians [418]
Natl. Assn. of First Responders [14320]
Natl. Assn. of State EMS Officials [14337]
Natl. Burn Victim Found. [13784]
Natl. Coalition Against Domestic Violence [12034]
Natl. Emergency Equip. Dealers Assn. [14339]
Natl. Memorial Inst. for the Prevention of Terrorism [18734]
Natl. Registry of Emergency Medical Technicians [14342]
Natl. Relief Network [12873]
Natl. Ski Patrol Sys. [23753]
Natl. Voluntary Organizations Active in Disaster [12874]
North Amer. Assn. for Ambulatory Urgent Care [13663]
Oper. U.S.A. [12535]
OXFAM Am. [12438]
Pan Amer. Hea. Org. [14592]
Plenty Intl. [12878]
Pontifical Mission for Palestine [12816]
Pups for Peace [12700]
Refugees Intl. [12818]
Save the Children [11720]
Skyaid Org. [14349]
Soc. for Academic Emergency Medicine [14344]
Soc. for the Preservation and Appreciation of Antique Motor Fire Apparatus in Am. [22423]
State EMS Training Coordinators Coun. of NASEMSO [14345]
Travelers Aid Intl. [13191]
U.S. Homeland Emergency Response Org. [12893]
Urgent Care Assn. of Am. [13665]
U.S.A. for Africa [12882]
Wings of Hope [12883]
World Mercy Fund [12886]
World Relief [19985]
Emergency Social Services Assn. [IO], New Westminster, BC, Canada
Emergency Task Force for Indochinese Refugees - Defunct.
Emergency Vehicle Owners and Operators Assn. [21639], c/o John Bujosa, Pres./Founder, PO Box 1149, Airway Heights, WA 99001-1149
Emerging Bus; Res. Inst. for Small and [3624]
Emerging Infections Network; Infectious Diseases Soc. of Am. [14949]
Emerging Markets Private Equity Assn. [1415], 1055 Thomas Jefferson St. NW, Ste. 240, Washington, DC 20007, (202)449-1155
Emerging Markets Private Equity Association [IO], Washington, DC, United States
Emerging Markets Traders Assn. [★IO]
Emerging Markets Traders Assn. [★3513]
Emerging Peoples; Found. for [★12426]
Emerson Coll. Alumni Assn. [18894], 120 Boylston St., Boston, MA 02116-4624, (617)824-8500
Emerson Memorial Assn; Ralph Waldo [9706]
Emerson Soc. - Defunct.
Emigration
Amer. Fund for Czechoslovak Relief [12802]
Emil Gilels Soc. - Defunct.
Emil Verban Memorial Soc. - Address unknown since 2001.
EMILY's List [18294], 1120 Connecticut Ave. NW, Ste. 1100, Washington, DC 20036-3949, (202)326-1400
EMILY'S List [IO], Malmesbury, United Kingdom
Emirates Body Building and Weightlifting Fed. [IO], Dubai, United Arab Emirates
Emirates Cardiac Soc. [IO], Abu Dhabi, United Arab Emirates

A star before a book entry number signifies that the name is not listed separately, but is mentioned within the entry.

Emirates Diving Assn. [IO], Dubai, United Arab Emir-
ates
Emirates Green Building Coun. [IO], Dubai, United
Arab Emirates
Emirates Philatelic Assn. [IO], Dubai, United Arab
Emirates
Emirates Physiotherapy Soc. [IO], Dubai, United
Arab Emirates
Emirates Racing Assn. [IO], Dubai, United Arab
Emirates
Emissary Found. - Defunct.
Emission Controls Assn; Mfrs. of [3072]
Emmett Kelly Jr. Collectors' Soc; EKJ [22017]
Emmett's Elite [22018], c/o Flambro Imports, 1530
Ellsworth Indus. Dr., Atlanta, GA 30318-3752,
(404)352-1381
Emmylou Harris Fan Club - Address unknown since
1989.
Emotional Educ. Assn. [★8255]
Emotional Health Anonymous - Address unknown
since 1994.
Emotional Hea. Educ. Assn. [8255], 1949 W Acacia
Bluffs Dr., Green Valley, AZ 85614, (520)398-5081
Emotional and Life Skills/National Inst. of Relation-
ship Enhancement; Inst. for the Development of
[15201]
Emotions Anonymous Intl. Ser. Center [12549], PO
Box 4245, 2233 Univ. Ave. W, Ste. 402, St. Paul,
MN 55104-0245, (651)647-9712
Emotions Anonymous Intl. Ser. Center [IO], St. Paul,
MN, United States
Emphysema Anonymous - Address unknown since
2003.
Emphysema Found; Natl. [13932]
Empire/Americans Against Bombing; Americans
Against World [18794]
Empire of Burravia [★11097]
Empire Forestry Assn. [★IO]
Empire Karakul Registry [★5186]
Empire State Tattoo Club of Am. [10993]
Employed Coun. Officers Assn. [★19902]
Employed Inst; Women [12109]
Employed Mothers at the Leading Edge; Formerly
[★12086]
Employed; Women [12108]
Employed Women; Federally [17531]
Employee Assistance Professionals Assn. [13203],
4350 N Fairfax Dr., Ste. 410, Arlington, VA 22203,
(703)387-1000

Employee Assistance Programs
AFL-CIO Working for Am. Inst. [12065]
Career Gear [12705]
Dress for Success Worldwide [13424]
Employee Assistance Professionals Assn. [13203]
Employee Assistance Soc. of North Am. [11823]
Inter-National Assn. of Bus., Indus. and
Rehabilitation [17417]
Structured Employment Economic Development
Corp. [12045]
Upwardly Global [3186]
Employee Assistance Soc. of North Am. [11823],
2001 Jefferson Davis Hwy., Ste. 1004, Arlington,
VA 22202-3617, (703)416-0060
Employee Benefit Assn; Fed. of [★1234]
Employee Benefit Plans; Coun. on [★1234]
Employee Benefit Res. Inst. [1235], 2121 K St. NW,
Ste. 600, Washington, DC 20037-1896, (202)659-
0670

Employee Benefits
AARP [12895]
Alliance for Worker Retirement Security [18544]
Amer. Assn. of State Compensation Insurance
Funds [2134]
Amer. Benefits Coun. [6169]
Amer. Cooperative Coun. on Compensation Tech.
[4059]
Amer. Soc. of Pension Professionals and Actuar-
ies [1233]
Canadian Pension and Benefits Inst. [IO]
Change to Win [24201]
Coun. on Employee Benefits [1234]
Employee Benefit Res. Inst. [1235]
Employee Services Mgt. Assn. [12796]
Employers Assn. [1236]
Employers Coun. on Flexible Compensation
[1237]

ERISA Indus. Comm. [1238]
Fund for Assuring an Independent Retirement
[5709]
Global Equity Org. [1239]
Global Equity Org. [IO]
Intl. Found. of Employee Benefit Plans [IO]
Intl. Found. of Employee Benefit Plans [1240]
Intl. Soc. of Certified Employee Benefit Specialists
[1241]
Intl. Soc. of Certified Employee Benefit Specialists
[IO]
Natl. Coordinating Comm. for Multiemployer Plans
[1242]
Natl. Employee Benefits Inst. [1243]
Natl. Inst. of Pension Administrators [1244]
New Ways to Work [12094]
Pension Res. Coun. [12702]
Pension Rights Center [12703]
Profit Sharing/401(k) Coun. of Am. [1279]
Profit Sharing/401(k) Educ. Found. [1280]
Residential Constr. Workers' Assn. [948]
Soc. of Professional Benefit Administrators [1245]
WEB - Worldwide Employee Benefits Network
[1246]
WEB - Worldwide Employee Benefits Network
[IO]
Workers Compensation Insurance Organizations
[2248]
Workplace Benefits Assn. [1247]
WorldatWork [1283]
Employee Benefits; Web Network of [★1246]
Employee Benefits; Working in [★1246]
Employee Educ. and Assistance Fund; Fed. [19264]
Employee Involvement Assn. [1260], PO Box 2307,
Dayton, OH 45401-2307, (937)586-3724
Employee Involvement Assn. [IO], Dayton, OH,
United States
Employee Organizations; Natl. Coun. of Naval Air
Stations [★6088]
Employee Ownership
ESOP Assn. [1248]
Global Equity Org. [1239]
ICA Gp. [1249]
Natl. Center for Employee Ownership [1250]
Employee Protection Agency; War Agencies
[★5776]
Employee Recognition; Natl. Assn. for [★17492]
Employee Recognition Prog. [1765], c/o Deena
Hower, 200 Deer Run Rd., Sewickley, PA 15143,
(800)910-4283
Employee Relations Professionals; Soc. of Fed.
Labor and [5919]
Employee Relations Prog; California Public [17969]
Employee Relocation Council/Worldwide ERC
[1261], 1717 Pennsylvania Ave. NW, Ste. 800,
Washington, DC 20006, (202)857-0857
Employee Relocation Real Estate Advisory Coun.
[★1261]
Employee Retirement Systems; Natl. Conf. on Public
[5570]
Employee Rights
Alliance for Sustainable Jobs and the Env.
[24053]
Alliance for Worker Freedom [24217]
Alliance for Worker Retirement Security [18544]
Amer. Assn. for Affirmative Action [12066]
The Amer. Cause [17642]
Amer. Inst. for Full Employment [12068]
Andolan - Organizing South Asian Workers
[24138]
A.W.A.R.E. - Amer. Workforce Alliance for
Responsible Economics [1258]
Equal Employment Advisory Coun. [12079]
FACE Intel - Former and Current Employees of
Intel [1262]
Freelancers Union [24218]
Global Workers Justice Alliance [18074]
Intl. Assn. of EMTs and Paramedics [24051]
Intl. Public Mgt. Assn. for Human Resources
[1267]
Lesbian, Bisexual, Gay and Transgendered United
Employees at AT&T [12242]
Natl. Alliance for Worker and Employer Rights
[24110]
Natl. Assn. for the Employment of Amers. [1269]

Natl. Assn. of Public Sector Equal Opportunity
Officers [1274]
Natl. Assn. of Social Workers Natl. Comm. on
Lesbian, Gay and Bisexual Issues [12245]
Natl. Day Laborer Organizing Network [24111]
Natl. Employment Counseling Assn. [12091]
Natl. Employment Law Proj. [12092]
Natl. Hire Amer. Citizens Soc. [1276]
North Amer. Alliance for Fair Employment [1277]
The Org. for the Rights of Amer. Workers [1278]
Recognition Professionals Intl. [17492]
Residential Constr. Workers' Assn. [948]
Save U.S. Jobs [1282]
Social Accountability Intl. [18828]
Verite [12063]
Verite [IO]
Wider Opportunities for Women [12106]
Workplace Benefits Assn. [1247]
Workplace Fairness [12064]
Employee Services Mgt. Assn. [12796], 568 Spring
Rd., Ste. D, Elmhurst, IL 60126-3896, (630)559-
0020
Employee Services and Recreation Assn; Natl.
[★12796]
Employee Share Ownership Plan Assn. [★IO]
Employee Union Information Center; Natl. [24076]
Employees, AFL-CIO; Dept. for Professional [24173]
Employees Against Abuse and Retaliation; Natl. Org.
of Fed. [24078]
Employees; Amer. Coun. of Blind Govt. [16824]
Employees; Amer. Fed. of Govt. [24068]
Employees; Amer. Fed. of State, County and
Municipal [24069]
Employees Assn; Civil Ser. [24073]
Employees Assn; Dow Jones [★24174]
Employees at AT0mp;T; Lesbian, Bisexual, Gay and
Transgendered United [12242]
Employees; Brotherhood of Railway, Airline and
Steamship Clerks, Freight Handlers, Express and
Sta. [★24180]
Employees; Brotherhood of Railway and Steamship
Clerks, Freight Handlers, Express and Sta.
[★24180]
Employees; Coun. of AFL-CIO Unions for Profes-
sional [24173]
Employees of Intel; FACE Intel - Former and Current
[1262]
Employees' Intl. Union; Building Ser. [★24189]
Employees Intl. Union; Off. [★23995]
Employees Intl. Union; Off. and Professional [23995]
Employees; Natl. Assn. of Farm Ser, Agency County
Off. [5779]
Employees; Natl. Assn. of Govt. [24075]
Employees; Natl. Assn. of Internal Revenue
[★24080]
Employees; Natl. Assn. of Part-Time and Temporary
[1271]
Employees; Natl. Assn. of Retired Civil [★5710]
Employees; Natl. Assn. of Retired Fed. [★5710]
Employees; Natl. Assn. of Retired and Veteran
Railway [3286]
Employees; Natl. Assn. of Retired and Veteran
Railway [★3286]
Employees; Natl. Fed. of Fed. [24077]
Employees Org; Natl. Weather Ser. [6357]
Employees Roundtable; Public [5572]
Employees and Technicians - Communications
Workers of Am; Natl. Assn. Broadcast [24024]
Employees Union; Natl. Treasury [24080]
Employees Union; Transportation-Communication
[★24180]
Employees of the U.S. Dept. of Agriculture; Org. of
Professional [5441]
Employees; United Transport Ser. [★24180]
Employees Veterans Assn; Fed. [6343]
Employees Veterans Assn; Fed. [★24075]
Employer Assn. Gp. [2555], c/o Natl. Assn. of Mfrs.,
1331 Pennsylvania Ave. NW, Washington, DC
20004, (202)637-3000
Employer Coalition; Disability Mgt. [1259]
Employer Coun. of Am; Driver [3867]
Employer Labor Relations Assn; Natl. Public [5918]
Employer Organizations; Natl. Assn. of Professional
[1273]

Reference to "IO" in place of a book number signifies that the association may be found in the 45th edition of International Organizations.

Employer Plans; Natl. Coordinating Comm. for Multi [1242]
Employer Support of the Guard and Reserve; Natl. Comm. for [6087]
Employers
 Aid to Artisans [12415]
 Amer. Assn. of State Compensation Insurance Funds [2134]
 The Amer. Cause [17642]
 Amer. Inst. for Full Employment [12068]
 Amer. Rights at Work [17968]
 Amer. Soc. of Employers [1251]
 Assn. of Civilian Technicians [24072]
 Assn. of Finnish Furniture and Joinery Indus. [IO]
 Assn. of Power Producers of Ontario [IO]
 A.W.A.R.E. - Amer. Workforce Alliance for Responsible Economics [1258]
 Bahamas Employers' Confed. [IO]
 Barbados Employers' Confed. [IO]
 Bermuda Employers' Coun. [IO]
 Compete Am. [8365]
 Confed. of Danish Employers [IO]
 Cyprus Employers' and Industrialists' Fed. [IO]
 Dominica Employers' Fed. [IO]
 Employers' Fed. of Ceylon [IO]
 Employers' and Manufacturers' Assn. [IO]
 Employers' and Mfrs'. Assn. (Northern) [IO]
 Employment Policy Found. [12077]
 Equal Employment Advisory Coun. [12079]
 Estonian Employers Confed. [IO]
 Fed. of Kenya Employers [IO]
 Gainsharing Inst. [13020]
 Hea. Employers Assn. of British Columbia [IO]
 Inst. for a Drug-Free Workplace [13247]
 Intl. Assn. of Employment Web Sites [1266]
 Jobs for America's Graduates [12084]
 Jobs for the Future [12085]
 Malta Employers' Assn. [IO]
 Mauritius Employers' Fed. [IO]
 Natl. Alliance for Worker and Employer Rights [24110]
 Natl. Assn. for Alternative Staffing [1268]
 Natl. Assn. for the Employment of Amers. [1269]
 Natl. Coun. of Agricultural Employers [4079]
 Natl. Employment Services Assn. [IO]
 Natl. Hire Amer. Citizens Soc. [1276]
 Natl. Job Corps Alumni Assn. [12093]
 Natl. Treasury Employees Union [24080]
 New Ways to Work [12094]
 Nigeria Employers' Consultative Assn. [IO]
 The Org. for the Rights of Amer. Workers [1278]
 Save U.S. Jobs [1282]
 Singapore Natl. Employers Fed. [IO]
 Spanish Confed. of Small and Medium-Sized Companies [IO]
 Workplace Benefits Assn. [1247]
Employers of Am. [3608], c/o Mr. Jim Collison, Pres., PO Box 1874, Mason City, IA 50402-1874, (641)424-3187
Employers of Am; Graphic Arts [24082]
Employers of Am; Graphic Arts Union [★24082]
Employers; Amer. Soc. of [1251]
Employers Assn. [1236], 3020 W Arrowood Rd., Charlotte, NC 28273, (704)522-8011
Employers Assn; BEST [3607]
Employers' Assn; Building Trades [609]
Employers Assn; Cement [920]
Employers Assn; Constr. [613]
Employers' Assn. of the Swedish Plate Works [IO], Stockholm, Sweden
Employers of Bricklayers and Allied Craftsworkers; Intl. Coun. of [★1029]
Employers' Consultative Assn. of Malawi [IO], Blantyre, Malawi
Employers' Consultative Assn. of Trinidad and Tobago [IO], Port of Spain, Trinidad and Tobago
Employers Coun. on Flexible Compensation [1237], 927 15th St. NW, Ste. 1000, Washington, DC 20005, (202)659-4300
Employers Coun; Residential Constr. [947]
Employers' Fed. of Ceylon [IO], Rajagiriya, Sri Lanka
Employers' Fed. of Hong Kong [IO], Hong Kong, People's Republic of China
Employers Forum on Age [IO], London, United Kingdom

Employers Gp. [2494], 1150 S Olive St., Ste. 2300, Los Angeles, CA 90015, (213)748-0421
Employers and Industrialists Fed. [IO], Nicosia, Cyprus
Employers; International Org. of [★IO]
Employers; International Org. of [★766]
Employers' Managed Hea. Care Assn. [★14682]
Employers' and Manufacturers' Assn. [IO], Wellington, New Zealand
Employers' and Mfrs'. Assn. (Northern) [IO], Auckland, New Zealand
Employers; Natl. Assn. of Colleges and [8995]
Employers; Natl. Assn. of Waterfront [2609]
Employers; Natl. Coun. of Agricultural [4079]
Employers for Traffic Safety; Network of [18746]
Employing Bookbinders of Amer. [★1761]
Employing Photo-Engravers Assn. of America - Defunct.
Employing Printers Assn. of America - Defunct.
Employment
 AARP [12895]
 Aboriginal Peoples Training and Employment Comm. [IO]
 ACCION Intl. [17205]
 AFL-CIO Working for Am. Inst. [12065]
 Aid to Artisans [12415]
 Alliance for Worker Freedom [24217]
 American-Arab Anti-Discrimination Comm. [17082]
 Amer. Assn. for Affirmative Action [12066]
 Amer. Assn. of State Compensation Insurance Funds [2134]
 Amer. Assn. of Working People [12067]
 Amer. Cong. of Community Supports and Employment Services [17206]
 Amer. Contract Compliance Assn. [17493]
 Amer. Coun. on Intl. Personnel [1252]
 Amer. Coun. on Intl. Personnel [IO]
 Amer. Inst. for Full Employment [IO]
 Amer. Inst. for Full Employment [12068]
 Amer. Payroll Assn. [1253]
 Amer. Rights at Work [17968]
 Amer. Staffing Assn. [1254]
 Andolan - Organizing South Asian Workers [24138]
 ASEAN Confed. of Employers [IO]
 Asian Resources [12069]
 Assn. of Canadian Search, Employment and Staffing Services [IO]
 Assn. of Career Mgt. Consulting Firms Intl. [IO]
 Assn. of Career Mgt. Consulting Firms Intl. [1255]
 Assn. of Civilian Technicians [24072]
 Assn. of Executive Search Consultants [1256]
 Assn. of Executive Search Consultants [IO]
 Assn. of Farmworker Opportunity Programs [12585]
 Assn. of Graduate Recruiters [IO]
 Assn. of Manpower Franchise Owners [1257]
 Assn. of Professional Recruiters of Canada [IO]
 Assn. for Public Ser. Excellence [IO]
 Assn. of Staff Physician Recruiters [15995]
 A.W.A.R.E. - Amer. Workforce Alliance for Responsible Economics [1258]
 Canadian Career Info. Assn. [IO]
 Canadian Payments Assn. [IO]
 Career Gear [12705]
 Career Planning and Adult Development Network [12070]
 Career Transition For Dancers [12071]
 Careers Res. and Advisory Centre [IO]
 Center for the Child Care Workforce, A Proj. of the Amer. Fed. of Teachers Educational Found. [12072]
 Center for Economic Options [12073]
 Center for Workers with Disabilities [11929]
 Compete Am. [8365]
 Consortium of Doctors [12074]
 Constr. Employers Assn. [613]
 Corporate and Found. Relations [12075]
 Disability Mgt. Employer Coalition [1259]
 Disabled Businesspersons Assn. [12076]
 Dress for Success Worldwide [13424]
 Employee Involvement Assn. [12060]
 Employee Involvement Assn. [IO]
 Employee Relocation Council/Worldwide ERC [1261]

Employers Forum on Age [IO]
Employment Policy Found. [12077]
Employment Support Center [12078]
Equal Employment Advisory Coun. [12079]
European Network of the Unemployed [IO]
Every Mother is a Working Mother Network [18810]
Experience Works [12080]
Experience Works [IO]
FACE Intel - Former and Current Employees of Intel [1262]
Farm Worker Hea. Services [12586]
Fed. of European Employers [IO]
Freelancers Union [24218]
Gainsharing Inst. [13020]
Global Applied Disability Res. and Info. Network [14240]
Global Workers Justice Alliance [18074]
Goodwill Indus. Intl. [11949]
Goodwill Indus. Volunteer Services [11950]
Grand Coun. of Hispanic Societies in Public Ser. [12275]
Green Cross Intl. [IO]
Hispanic Policy Development Proj. [17704]
Homeworkers Organized for More Employment [12081]
Hong Kong Inst. of Human Rsrc. Mgt. [IO]
HR Soc. [IO]
Independent Educational Services [1263]
Indus. Found. of Am. [1264]
Inst. for a Drug-Free Workplace [13247]
Inst. for Labor and Mental Health [15202]
Inter-National Assn. of Bus., Indus. and Rehabilitation [17417]
Intl. Assn. of Corporate and Professional Recruitment [1265]
International Association of Corporate and Professional Recruitment [IO]
Intl. Assn. of Employment Web Sites [IO]
Intl. Assn. of Employment Web Sites [1266]
Intl. Assn. of Indus. Accident Boards and Commissions [5678]
Intl. Assn. of Indus. Accident Boards and Commissions [IO]
Intl. Assn. of Workforce Professionals [IO]
Intl. Assn. of Workforce Professionals [5679]
Intl. Black Women for Wages for Housework [18811]
Intl. Public Mgt. Assn. for Human Resources [1267]
Intl. Public Mgt. Assn. for Human Resources [IO]
Intl. Union of Painters and Allied Trades/Joint Apprenticeship and Training Fund [IO]
Intl. Union of Painters and Allied Trades/Joint Apprenticeship and Training Fund [12082]
Job Accommodation Network [11955]
A Job is a Right Campaign [12083]
Jobs for America's Graduates [12084]
Jobs for the Future [12085]
Joint Action in Community Ser. [11803]
Just One Break [11957]
Lebanese Amer. Professional Soc. [19205]
Legal Immigrant Assn. [5808]
Lesbian, Bisexual, Gay and Transgendered United Employees at AT&T [12242]
Migrant Hea. Promotion [12590]
Mothers And More [12086]
Natl. Assn. for Alternative Staffing [1268]
Natl. Assn. for the Employment of Amers. [1269]
Natl. Assn. of Executive Recruiters [1270]
Natl. Assn. for Human Development [11303]
Natl. Assn. of Locum Tenens Org. [16004]
Natl. Assn. of Part-Time and Temporary Employees [1271]
Natl. Assn. of Personnel Services [1272]
Natl. Assn. of Professional Background Screeners [1983]
Natl. Assn. of Professional Employer Organizations [1273]
Natl. Assn. of Public Sector Equal Opportunity Officers [1274]
Natl. Assn. of Social Workers Natl. Comm. on Lesbian, Gay and Bisexual Issues [12245]
Natl. Assn. of State Directors of Migrant Educ. [12592]

A star before a book entry number signifies that the name is not listed separately, but is mentioned within the entry.

Natl. Assn. of State Workforce Agencies [5680]
Natl. Assn. of Teachers' Agencies [1275]
Natl. Assn. of Workforce Boards [12087]
Natl. Assn. of Workforce Development Professionals [12088]
Natl. Bus. and Disability Coun. [12089]
Natl. Career Development Assn. [12090]
Natl. Caucus and Center on Black Aged [11306]
Natl. Child Labor Comm. [13500]
Natl. Comm. on the Educ. of Migrant Children (of the Natl. Child Labor Comm.) [12593]
Natl. Economic Development and Law Center [17464]
Natl. Employment Counseling Assn. [12091]
Natl. Employment Law Proj. [12092]
Natl. Farm Worker Ministry [12594]
Natl. Found. for Unemployment Compensation and Workers Compensation [5681]
Natl. Hire Amer. Citizens Soc. [1276]
Natl. Indus. for the Blind [16878]
Natl. Job Corps Alumni Assn. [12093]
Natl. Soc. for Hispanic Professionals [1908]
Natl. Treasury Employees Union [24080]
Natl. Urban League [17138]
Natl. Youth Employment Coalition [13506]
New Ways to Work [12094]
NISH [11976]
North Amer. Alliance for Fair Employment [1277]
NRH Center for Hea. and Disability Res. [14233]
NTID's Center on Employment [12095]
The Nurturing Network [13434]
Ontario Assn. of Youth Employment Centres [IO]
Opportunities Industrialization Centers of Am. [12096]
The Org. for the Rights of Amer. Workers [1278]
Pension Res. Coun. [12702]
Pension Rights Center [12703]
POWER: People Organized to Win Employment Rights [17494]
Professional Assn. of Resume Writers and Career Coaches [12097]
Profit Sharing/401(k) Coun. of Am. [1279]
Profit Sharing/401(k) Educ. Found. [1280]
PUSH Commercial Div. [12098]
Recruiters Online Network [1281]
Recruiting and Staffing Focus Area [1984]
Recruitment and Employment Confed. [IO]
Rescue Amer. Jobs [17984]
Residential Constr. Workers' Assn. [948]
Save U.S. Jobs [1282]
Scottish Low Pay Unit [IO]
Senior Community Ser. Employment Prog. [12099]
SER - Jobs for Progress Natl. [12100]
Structured Employment Economic Development Corp. [12045]
Together, Inc. [12365]
Tradeswomen [12101]
Uglies Unlimited [12102]
U.S. Equal Employment Opportunity Commn. [5682]
Upwardly Global [3186]
Verite [12063]
Vocational Found., Inc. [12103]
W. E. Upjohn Inst. for Employment Res. [12104]
WAVE [12105]
Wider Opportunities for Women [12106]
Wildcat Ser. Corp. [12107]
Women Employed [12108]
Women Employed Inst. [12109]
Work Fairness [12110]
Workers Compensation Insurance Organizations [2248]
Workplace Benefits Assn. [1247]
WorldatWork [1283]
WorldatWork [IO]
Employment Administrators; Natl. Assn. of Student [★8996]
Employment Agencies; Natl. Assn. of [★1272]
Employment Agencies (Protective) Assn. [★1272]
Employment of Amers; Natl. Assn. for the [1269]
Employment Assn; Natl. [★1272]
Employment Assn; Natl. Student [8996]
Employment Bd; Natl. [★1272]
Employment; Center on Educ. and Training for [9304]

Employment Company; 70001—The Youth [12105]
Employment Counseling; Amer. Inst. of [★1272]
Employment of the Deaf; Natl. Center on [★12095]
Employment in Educ; Amer. Assn. for [8994]
Employment: Globalizing and Organizing; Women in Informal [13444]
Employment and Guidance Ser; Fed. [★12075]
Employment Inst; 70001 Training and [★12105]
Employment Lawyers Assn; Natl. [5520]
Employment Mgt. Assn. [★1984]
Employment Managers; Natl. Assn. of [★2481]
Employment; Natl. Found. for the Study of Equal [★12077]
Employment Policy Found. [12077]
Employment Policy; Natl. Found. for the Study of [★12077]
Employment Professionals; Natl. Assn. of County Training and [★5618]
Employment Proj; Natl. Women's [★17512]
Employment Rights; POWER: People Organized to Win [17494]
Employment Security Agencies; Interstate Conf. of [★5680]
Employment Services; Amer. Cong. of Community Supports and [17206]
Employment Services; Intl. Assn. of Public [★5679]
Employment Support Center [12078], 1556 Wisconsin Ave. NW, Washington, DC 20007, (202)628-2919
Employment and Training Administrators; Natl. Assn. of County of [★5618]
Employment and Training Service Center - Address unknown since 2001.
Employment; Women and [★12073]
Employment; Women Work! The Natl. Network for Women's [18819]
Empower Prog. [8945]
Empowerment Enterprizes - Defunct.
Empowerment Proj. [17174], 8218 Farrington Mill Rd., Chapel Hill, NC 27517, (919)928-0382
Empowerment; Simple Soc. Alliance for Human [18637]
Empowerment Soc. Intl. [11775], 4460 S Cobblestone St., Gilbert, AZ 85296
Empowerment Soc. of the U.S.A. [13425], PO Box 51, Oyster Bay, NY 11771, (516)922-7134
Emprender Found. [IO], Madrid, Spain
Empresa Brasileira de Pesquisa Agropecuaria [★IO]
Empresa Para Agroalimentacao e Cereais, S.A. [IO], Lisbon, Portugal
Empress Chinchilla Breeders Cooperative [4134], PO Box 318, Sixes, OR 97476, (541)332-3222
EMS Assn; Natl. Native Amer. [14341]
EMS Educators; Natl. Assn. of [8867]
EMS; FireFlag/ [5773]
EMS Pilots Assn; Natl. [14322]
EMS Professions; Comm. on Accreditation for Educational Programs for the [8833]
EMS/Science Commun. Network [5032], 1320 18th St. NW, Ste. 500, Washington, DC 20036, (202)463-6670
EMT-Paramedic; Joint Rev. Comm. on Educational Programs for the [★8833]
EMTA [3513], 360 Madison Ave., 18th Fl., New York, NY 10017, (646)637-9100
EMTA [IO], New York, NY, United States
Emu Assn; Amer. [4993]
Emulsion Manufacturers Assn; Asphalt [594]
Emulsion Polymers Inst. [6681], Lehigh Univ., Iacocca Hall, Rm. D-325, 111 Res. Dr., Bethlehem, PA 18015, (610)758-3590
Emulsion Polymers Liaison Program [★6681]
Emunah of Am. [12457], 7 Penn Plz., New York, NY 10001, (212)564-9045
Emunah Women of Am. [20136], 7 Penn Plz., New York, NY 10001, (212)564-9045
Emunah Women of Am. [IO], New York, NY, United States
Emunah Women of Canada [IO], Montreal, QC, Canada
En Foco [10849], 1738 Hone Ave., Bronx, NY 10461, (718)584-7718
Enable - Ireland [IO], Dublin, Ireland
ENABLE Scotland [IO], Glasgow, United Kingdom
Enabled Artists United - Defunct.

Enamel Guild: West - Address unknown since 1999.
Enamel Inst; Porcelain [662]
Enameled Utensil Mfrs. Coun. - Defunct.
Enameling
  British Soc. of Enamellers [IO]
  Cloisonne Collectors Club [21996]
  Enamelist Soc. [22156]
  Vitreous Enamel Services [IO]
Enamelist Soc. [22156], 6105 Bay Hill Cir., Jamesville, NY 13078
Enamelled Leather Mfrs. Assn; Patent and [★2416]
Encampment for Citizenship - Defunct.
ENCAMS [IO], Wigan, United Kingdom
Enchondroma Diseases; AAMED - The Amer. Assn. of Multiple [15749]
ENCOMPASS [6792], 401 N Michigan Ave., Ste. 2200, Chicago, IL 60611, (312)321-5151
Encompass Inst. - Defunct.
Encounter [IO], Bray, Ireland
Encounter - Defunct.
Encuentro con la Biblica Argentina [★IO]
End Child Prostitution, Child Pornography and Trafficking of Children for Sexual Purposes - New Zealand [IO], Auckland, New Zealand
End Child Prostitution, Pornography and Trafficking [IO], London, United Kingdom
End Homelessness Now [12289]
End Hunger Network [17793], PO Box 3032, Santa Monica, CA 90408-3032, (310)454-3716
End Notch Discrimination - Defunct.
End-of-Life Choices [12131], PO Box 101810, Denver, CO 80250-1810, (303)639-1202
End Poverty in America Soc. - Address unknown since 2000.
End Stage Renal Disease Program [★15298]
End Violence Against the Next Generation - Address unknown since 2001.
ENDA Caribe [IO], Santo Domingo, Dominican Republic
Endangered Arid-Land Rsrc. Clearing House; Native Seeds/Southwestern [★4429]
Endangered Cats; Intl. Soc. for [4209]
Endangered Language Fund [10300], 300 George St., Ste. 900, New Haven, CT 06511
Endangered Species Coalition [5315], PO Box 65195, Washington, DC 20035, (202)244-7138
Endangered Species Coalition; Grassroots [4154]
Endangered Wildlife Trust [IO], Johannesburg, Republic of South Africa
Enders Family Assn. [IO], Halifax, PA, United States
Enders Family Assn. [20897], c/o David Enders, Pres., 56 Marie Dr., Halifax, PA 17032, (717)362-8959
Ending Relationship Abuse Soc. of British Columbia [IO], Fort Langley, BC, Canada
Endocrine Fellows Found. [14353], 5959 W Century Blvd., Ste. 550, Los Angeles, CA 90045, (877)877-6515
Endocrine Nurses Soc. [14354], PO Box 211068, Milwaukee, WI 53221, (414)727-7422
Endocrine Soc. [14355], 8401 Connecticut Ave., Ste. 900, Chevy Chase, MD 20815-5817, (301)941-0200
Endocrine Soc. of Australia [IO], Sydney, Australia
Endocrinology
  Amer. Assn. of Clinical Endocrinologists [14350]
  Amer. Neuroendocrine Soc. [15035]
  Argentine Soc. of Endocrinology and Metabolism [IO]
  Asia and Oceania Thyroid Assn. [IO]
  Asia Pacific Paedeatric Endocrine Soc. [IO]
  Assn. of Prog. Directors in Endocrinology, Diabetes and Metabolism [14351]
  Bulgarian Soc. of Endocrinology [IO]
  Canadian Soc. of Endocrinology and Metabolism [IO]
  Cushing's Support and Res. Found. [14352]
  Endocrine Fellows Found. [14353]
  Endocrine Nurses Soc. [14354]
  Endocrine Soc. [14355]
  Endocrine Soc. of Australia [IO]
  European Soc. of Endocrinology [IO]
  European Soc. for Paediatric Endocrinology [IO]
  European Thyroid Assn. [IO]
  German Org. of Endocrinology [IO]

Reference to "IO" in place of a book number signifies that the association may be found in the 45th edition of International Organizations.

Hypoparathyroidism Assn. [IO]
Hypoparathyroidism Assn. [14356]
Intl. Assn. of Endocrine Surgeons [IO]
Intl. Hyperhidrosis Soc. [IO]
Intl. Hyperhidrosis Soc. [14357]
Intl. Soc. for Endocrinology [IO]
Intl. Soc. of Psychoneuroendocrinology [15108]
Natl. Adrenal Diseases Found. [14358]
Natl. Hormone and Pituitary Prog. [16021]
Netherlands Soc. for Endocrinology [IO]
Pediatric Endocrinology Nursing Soc. [15894]
Sociedad Chilena de Endocrinologia y Diabetes
  [IO]
Societa Italiana di Endocrinologia [IO]
Societa Italiana di Endocrinologia e Diabetologia
  Pediatrica [IO]
Soc. for Behavioral Neuroendocrinology [13741]
Soc. for Endocrinology [IO]
Soc. for Endocrinology, Metabolism and Diabetes
  of Southern Africa [IO]
Soc. of Endocrinology and Metabolism of Turkey
  [IO]
Soc. for the Stud. of Reproduction [16350]
Thyroid Cancer Survivors' Assn. [16648]
Women in Endocrinology [14359]
Endocrinology and Infertility; Soc. for Reproductive
  [16348]
Endocrinology; Intl. Soc. of Psychoneuro [15108]
Endocrinology and Metabolism; Assn. of Prog. Direc-
  tors in [★14351]
Endocrinology Nursing Soc; Pediatric [15894]
Endocrinology; Soc. for Behavioral Neuro [13741]
Endocrinology; Women in [14359]
Endodontic Soc; Amer. [14134]
Endodontics; Amer. Bd. of [14121]
Endodontists; Amer. Assn. of [14114]
Endometriosis Assn. [15599], 8585 N 76th Pl.,
  Milwaukee, WI 53223, (414)355-2200
Endometriosis Assn. [IO], Milwaukee, WI, United
  States
Endometriosis Found; New Zealand [IO]
Endometriosis Soc; Natl. [IO]
Endorsers Conf. for Veterans Affairs Chaplaincy -
  Defunct.
Endoscopic Sect. of the Gastroenterological Assn. of
  Thailand [IO], Bangkok, Thailand
Endoscopic Surgeons; Soc. of Amer. Gastrointestinal
  and [14428]
Endoscopy; Amer. Soc. for Gastrointestinal [14409]
Endoscopy Soc; Hong Kong Gynaecological [IO]
Endowment Fund; DeMolay [★IO]
Endowment Fund; DeMolay [★19235]
Endowment Fund; Shriners Hospitals for Children
  [★13973]
Endurance Horse Registry of America - Address
  unknown since 2005.
Endurance Ride Conf; Amer. [23933]
Energetic Healing Assn. [IO], Terrey Hills, Australia
Energia-alan Keskusliitto [★IO]
Energia Klub [★IO]
Energiagazdalkodasi Tudomanyos Egyesulet [★IO]
Energieforum Schweiz [IO], Bern, Switzerland
Energy
  African Energy Policy Res. Network - Kenya [IO]
  Agri-Energy Roundtable [17826]
  Alliance of Energy Suppliers [1284]
  Alliance to Save Energy [6934]
  Alternative Energy Resources Org. [6935]
  Amer. Assn. of Blacks in Energy [6936]
  Amer. Assn. for Fuel Cells [6937]
  Amer. Coun. for an Energy-Efficient Economy
    [6938]
  Amer. Coun. on Renewable Energy [6939]
  Amer. Exploration and Production Coun. [2914]
  Amer. Hydrogen Assn. [6940]
  Amer. Oil and Gas Historical Soc. [2915]
  Amer. Soc. of Gas Engineers [6941]
  Amer. Solar Energy Soc. [7676]
  Amer. Wind Energy Assn. [7852]
  Americans for Balanced Energy Choices [17495]
  Asian Energy Inst. [IO]
  Assn. of Desk and Derrick Clubs [2917]
  Assn. for Efficient Environmental Energy Systems
    [7138]
  Assn. of Energy Engineers [6942]

  Association of Energy Engineers [IO]
  Assn. of Energy Engineers, Bulgaria/Sofia [IO]
  Assn. of Energy Engineers, Poland/Czestochowa
    [IO]
  Assn. of Energy Engineers, Poland/Warsaw [IO]
  Assn. of Energy Engineers, West Georgia Chap.
    [IO]
  Assn. of Energy Services Professionals [IO]
  Assn. of Energy Services Professionals [6943]
  Assn. of Municipal Electricity Undertakings
    (Southern Africa) [IO]
  Assn. of Professional Energy Managers [6944]
  Assn. of State Energy Res. and Tech. Transfer
    Institutions [6945]
  Assn. for the Stud. of Peak Oil and Gas - USA
    [7461]
  Atomic Energy Coun. [IO]
  Australian Bus. Coun. for Sustainable Energy [IO]
  Australian Inst. of Energy [IO]
  Austrian Member Comm. of the World Energy
    Coun. [IO]
  Benelux Assn. for Energy Economics [IO]
  Bioenergy Assn. of New Zealand [IO]
  Biomass Energy Res. Assn. [6946]
  Bus. Coun. for Sustainable Energy [1285]
  Canadian Assn. of Energy Ser. Companies [IO]
  Canadian Assn. for Renewable Energies [IO]
  Canadian Energy Res. Inst. [IO]
  Canadian Energy Workers Assn. [IO]
  Canadian Inst. of Energy [IO]
  Canadian Inst. for Energy Training [IO]
  Center for Clean Air Policy [5083]
  Center for Energy Efficiency and Renewable
    Technologies [4526]
  Center for Energy Policy and Res. [6947]
  Center for Stud. of Responsive Law [17315]
  Circum-Pacific Coun. for Energy and Mineral
    Resources [7340]
  Citizens for Renewable Energy [IO]
  Clean Energy Gp. [6948]
  Clean Energy States Alliance [6949]
  Clean Fuels Development Coalition [5086]
  Clean Harbors Cooperative [3070]
  Comitetul Natl. Roman al Consiliului Mondial al
    Energiei [IO]
  Consortium for Energy Efficiency [1286]
  Consumer Energy Coun. of Am. Res. Found.
    [17496]
  Coun. of Energy Rsrc. Tribes [18093]
  Czech Member Comm. of the World Energy
    Coun. [IO]
  Deutsches Nationales Kommitee des Weltener-
    gierats [IO]
  Domestic Technologies [16994]
  Earth Energy Soc. of Canada [IO]
  Efficient Windows Collaborative [4029]
  Elec. Power Supply Assn. [6950]
  Electricity Storage Assn. [3957]
  Energieforum Schweiz [IO]
  Energy Bar Assn. [5683]
  Energy Club [IO]
  Energy Communities Alliance [4527]
  Energy Coun. of Canada [IO]
  Energy Efficiency and Renewable Energy Info.
    Center [6951]
  Energy Fed. of New Zealand [IO]
  Energy Forum of Finland [IO]
  Energy Frontiers Intl. [1677]
  Energy Future Coalition [6952]
  Energy Indus. Coun. [IO]
  Energy Mgt. Assn. of New Zealand [IO]
  Energy Networks Assn. [IO]
  Energy Probe Res. Found. [IO]
  Energy Retailers Assn. of Australia [IO]
  Energy Systems Trade Assn. [IO]
  Environmental Action Found. [4558]
  Environmental Bus. Coun. of New England [4560]
  EPRI [6953]
  European Alliance of Companies for Energy Ef-
    ficiency in Buildings [IO]
  European Assn. for the Promotion of Cogenera-
    tion [IO]
  European Biomass Indus. Assn. [IO]
  European Energy Forum [IO]
  European Fed. of Energy Traders [IO]

  European Forum for Renewable Energy Sources
    [IO]
  European Photovoltaic Indus. Assn. [IO]
  European Pure Plant Oil Assn. [IO]
  European Renewable Energy Coun. [IO]
  E.V.V.E. - European Assn. for the consumption-
    based billing of energy costs [IO]
  Finnish Energy Indus. Fed. [IO]
  Folkecenter for Renewable Energy [IO]
  FORATOM: Assn. of European Atomic Forums
    [IO]
  Fusion Power Associates [IO]
  Fusion Power Associates [6954]
  Georgian Chap. of the Assn. of Energy Engineers
    [IO]
  Geothermal Resources Coun. [7143]
  Gesellschaft fur Energieplanung und Systemanal-
    yse [IO]
  Green Empowerment [4335]
  HELIO Intl. [IO]
  IIEC-Asia [IO]
  Independence Plan for Neighborhood Councils
    [17219]
  Inst. for Energy and Environmental Res. [6955]
  Inst. of Public Utilities [3958]
  Inst. for Rsrc. and Security Stud. [18457]
  Intl. Assn. for Energy Economics [6956]
  Intl. Assn. for Energy Economics [IO]
  Intl. Assn. for Energy Economics - Austria [IO]
  Intl. Assn. for Energy Economics - Canada [IO]
  Intl. Assn. for Energy Economics - Czech
    Republic [IO]
  Intl. Assn. for Energy Economics - Denmark [IO]
  Intl. Assn. for Energy Economics - Finland [IO]
  Intl. Assn. for Energy Economics - France [IO]
  Intl. Assn. for Energy Economics - Germany [IO]
  Intl. Assn. for Energy Economics - Japan [IO]
  Intl. Assn. for Energy Economics - Korea [IO]
  Intl. Assn. for Energy Economics - Latvia [IO]
  Intl. Assn. for Energy Economics - Lithuania [IO]
  Intl. Assn. for Energy Economics - Mexico [IO]
  Intl. Assn. for Energy Economics - Oceania [IO]
  Intl. Assn. for Energy Economics - Poland [IO]
  Intl. Assn. for Energy Economics - Spain [IO]
  Intl. Assn. for Energy Economics - Sweden [IO]
  Intl. Assn. for Energy Economics - Switzerland
    [IO]
  Intl. Assn. for Energy Economics - Taiwan [IO]
  Intl. Assn. for Energy Economics - Turkey [IO]
  Intl. Assn. for Hydrogen Energy [IO]
  Intl. Assn. for Hydrogen Energy [6957]
  Intl. District Energy Assn. [1888]
  Intl. Energy Agency [IO]
  Intl. Energy Found. [IO]
  Intl. Fed. of Indus. Energy Consumers [IO]
  Intl. Input-Output Assn. [IO]
  International Institute for Energy Conservation [IO]
  Intl. Inst. for Energy Conservation [6958]
  Intl. Network for Sustainable Energy [IO]
  Intl. Utilities Revenue Protection Assn. [6338]
  Interstate Oil and Gas Compact Commn. [5684]
  Interstate Renewable Energy Coun. [6959]
  Iranian Assn. for Energy Economics [IO]
  Irish Bioenergy Assn. [IO]
  Italian Assn. of Energy Economists [IO]
  Italian Assn. for Hydrogen and Fuel Cells [IO]
  Korean Energy Forum [IO]
  Latin Amer. Energy Org. [IO]
  Major Energy Users Coun. [IO]
  Mexico/Monterrey Chap. of the Assn. of Energy
    Engineers [IO]
  Mineral Info. Inst. [7343]
  Natl. Alliance of Clean Energy Bus. Incubators
    [1287]
  Natl. Assn. of Energy Ser. Companies [6960]
  Natl. Assn. of State Energy Officials [5685]
  Natl. Center for Appropriate Tech. [16998]
  Natl. Energy Educ. Development Proj. [17497]
  Natl. Energy Found. [IO]
  Natl. Energy Mgt. Inst. [6961]
  Natl. Energy Marketers Assn. [1288]
  National Energy Marketers Association [IO]
  Natl. Energy Services Assn. [6962]
  Natl. Ethanol Vehicle Coalition [4776]
  Natl. Food and Energy Coun. [6963]

A star before a book entry number signifies that the name is not listed separately, but is mentioned within the entry.

Natl. Hydropower Assn. [6964]
Natl. Old Timers' Assn. of the Energy Indus. [6965]
Natl. Petroleum Coun. [5686]
Natural Resources Defense Coun. [4432]
Netherlands Bio-Energy Assn. [IO]
New Zealand Atomic Energy Advocacy Coun. [IO]
NextGen Energy Coun. [6966]
North Amer. Bd. of Certified Energy Practitioners [6967]
Northeast Sustainable Energy Assn. [6968]
Northwest Energy Efficiency Alliance [4528]
Norwegian Assn. for Energy Economics [IO]
Nuclear Energy Inst. [6969]
Paper, Allied-Indus., Chem. and Energy Workers Intl. Union [24211]
Planetary Assn. for Clean Energy [IO]
Process Gas Consumers Gp. [17340]
Proj. Underground [18079]
Redwood Alliance [17498]
Regional Energy Resources Info. Center [IO]
Renewable Energy Assn. [IO]
Renewable Energy Assn. of Swaziland [IO]
Renewable Energy Policy Proj. - Center For Renewable Energy and Sustainable Tech. [6970]
Renewable Fuels Assn. [6971]
Residential Energy Services Network [664]
Resource Policy Inst. [4603]
Scottish Enterprise Energy Team [IO]
Slovenski nacionalni komite Svetovnega ener-getskega sveta [IO]
Soc. for Energy Educ. [6972]
Solar Elec. Power Assn. [7678]
Solar Energy Indus. Assn. [7679]
Solar Energy Intl. [7680]
Southface Energy Inst. [6973]
Space Energy Assn. [6386]
Sri Aurobindo Soc. [IO]
Stove, Furnace, Energy, and Allied Appliance Workers Division of the Intl. Brotherhood of Boilermakers [24001]
Surface Trans. Policy Proj. [18750]
Sustainable Buildings Indus. Coun. [7682]
Swiss Assn. for Energy Economics [IO]
Turbine Inlet Cooling Assn. [7055]
Ukraine/Kiev Chap. of the Assn. of Energy Engineers [IO]
United Kingdom Hydrogen Assn. [IO]
U.S. Assn. for Energy Economics [6974]
U.S. Combined Heat and Power Assn. [7821]
U.S. Energy Assn. [6975]
U.S. Energy Assn. [IO]
US Fuel Cell Coun. [6976]
Utilities Ser. Alliance [3966]
Western Interstate Energy Board/WINB [18139]
Windustry [7853]
Women of Wind Energy [7854]
Women's Coun. on Energy and the Env. [6977]
World Coun. for Renewable Energy [IO]
World Energy Coun. Argentina Comm. [IO]
World Energy Coun. - England [IO]
World Energy Coun. Indian Member Comm. [IO]
World Energy Coun. Italian Natl. Comm. [IO]
World Energy Coun. Polish Member Comm. [IO]
World Energy Coun. Turkish Natl. Comm. [IO]
World Energy Efficiency Association [IO]
World Energy Efficiency Assn. [6978]
Energy Action [IO], Dublin, Ireland
Energy Action Educational Project of C/LEC - Defunct.
Energy, and Allied Appliance Workers Division of the Intl. Brotherhood of Boilermakers; Stove, Furnace, [24001]
Energy Assistance Directors' Assn; Natl. [1987]
Energy Assn. [IO], Ljubljana, Slovenia
Energy Assn; Amer. Solar [★7676]
Energy Assn; Amer. Wind [7852]
Energy Assn; Elec. [★3956]
Energy Assn; Space [6386]
Energy Awareness; U.S. Coun. for [★6969]
Energy Bar Assn. [5683], 1020-19th St. NW, Ste. 525, Washington, DC 20036, (202)223-5625
Energy Bar Assn; Fed. [★5683]
Energy Board/WINB; Western Interstate [18139]

Energy and Chem. Workers Union [★IO]
Energy Club [IO], Budapest, Hungary
Energy Communities Alliance [4527], 1101 Connecticut Ave. NW, Ste. 1000, Washington, DC 20036-4374, (202)828-2317
Energy Conservation Caucus - Defunct.
Energy Conservation Coalition - Address unknown since 1999.
Energy Conservation; Natl. Assn. of Professionals in [★6942]
Energy Consumers and Producers Assn. - Address unknown since 1994.
Energy Coun. of Canada [IO], Ottawa, ON, Canada
Energy Coun; Food and [★6963]
Energy Economics Educational Foundation [★6956]
Energy Economics Educational Foundation [★IO]
Energy, Economics and Environment Inst. - Defunct.
Energy Educ. Day Proj; Natl. [★17497]
Energy Efficiency and Renewable Energy Info. Center [6951], Dept. of Energy, Mail Stop EE-1, Washington, DC 20585, (202)586-9220
Energy Efficient Building Assn. [★619]
Energy Efficient Lighting Assn. - Defunct.
Energy and the Env; Fund for Renewable [★7677]
Energy and Env. Prog; Public Citizen's Critical Mass [18134]
Energy and Env. Proj; Public Citizen's Critical Mass [★18134]
Energy and Environmental Building Assn. [619], 6520 Edenvale Blvd., Ste. 112, Eden Prairie, MN 55346, (952)881-1098
Energy Fed. of New Zealand [IO], Wellington, New Zealand
Energy Forum of Finland [IO], Helsinki, Finland
Energy Found; Natl. [8392]
Energy Frontiers Intl. [1677], 1425 K St. NW, Ste. 350, Washington, DC 20005, (202)587-5780
Energy Frontiers Intl. [IO], Arlington, VA, United States
Energy Future Coalition [6952], 1800 Massachusetts Ave. NW, Ste. 400, Washington, DC 20036, (202)463-1947
Energy Indus. Assn; Solar [7679]
Energy Indus. Coun. [IO], London, United Kingdom
Energy Info. Ser; Nuclear [18131]
Energy Inquiry and Referral Ser; Conservation and Renewable [★6951]
Energy Inst. [IO], London, United Kingdom
Energy Inst; Wood [★1679]
Energy Law Inst. - Defunct.
Energy Liability Underwriters; Mutual Atomic [2201]
Energy Mgt. Assn. of New Zealand [IO], Wellington, New Zealand
Energy Mgt. and Controls Soc. [★IO]
Energy Mgt. and Controls Soc. [★6942]
Energy Mgt. Professionals; Total [★6942]
Energy in Man's Env. [★8392]
Energy and Mineral Law Found. [6136], 340 S Broadway, Ste. 101, Lexington, KY 40508, (859)231-0271
Energy Networks Assn. [IO], Barton, Australia
Energy; New Mexico People and [★16976]
Energy Policy Information Center - Defunct.
Energy Policy Project - Defunct.
Energy Policy Res. Found., Inc. [7462], 1031 31st St. NW, Washington, DC 20007-4401, (202)944-3339
Energy Probe Res. Found. [IO], Toronto, ON, Canada
Energy Producers; Natl. Independent [★6950]
Energy Professional Soc; Directed [6858]
Energy Psychology; Assn. for Comprehensive [16192]
Energy Res. and Educ. Foundation; Solar [★7679]
Energy Res. Gp. [IO], Dublin, Ireland
Energy Res. Inst. - Address unknown since 2004.
Energy Rsrc. Tribes; Coun. of [18093]
Energy Retailers Assn. of Australia [IO], St. Leonards, Australia
Energy Security Coun. [2089], 10701 Corporate Dr., Ste. 250, Stafford, TX 77477, (281)565-6677
Energy Ser. Companies; Assn. of [2918]
Energy Services Professionals; Assn. of [★6943]
Energy Soc; Amer. Sect. of the Intl. Solar [★7676]
Energy Soc; Amer. Solar [7676]

Energy Stud. Inst; Environmental and [4507]
Energy Supply Assn. of Australia [IO], Melbourne, Australia
Energy Systems Trade Assn. [IO], Benfleet, United Kingdom
Energy Telecommunications and Elecl. Assn. [1185], 5005 Royal Ln., Ste. 190, Irving, TX 75063, (888)503-8700
Energy Traffic Assn. [2923], 3303 Main St. Corridor, Houston, TX 77002-9321, (713)528-2868
Energy Workers Intl. Union; Paper, Allied-Indus., Chem. and [24211]
EnergyWatch [IO], London, United Kingdom
Enersol Associates [18665], 55 Middlesex St., Ste. 221, North Chelmsford, MA 01863, (978)251-1828
Enesco Precious Moments Collectors' Club - Address unknown since 1995.
Enfance; Fonds des Nations Unies pour l' [★11658]
Enfants and Developpement [IO], Paris, France
Enfants du Monde [IO], Marseille, France
Enfants Solidaires d'Afrique et du Monde [★IO]
Enfoprensa U.S.A. - Defunct.
Enforcement; Amer. Assn. of Code [5959]
Enforcement Assn; Natl. Child Support [5701]
Enforcement Officers Assn; Natl. Drug [5993]
Enforcement Officers Assn; Natl. Narcotic [★5741]
Enforcement Officers Assn; North Amer. Wildlife [5357]
Enforcement Officers; Natl. Assn. of School Safety and Law [9087]
Enforcement, and Regulation; Natl. CH on Licensure, [★6271]
Enforcement Services Assn. [IO], Bristol, United Kingdom
ENG Study Group [★16441]
Engelbert Humperdinck
FR-ENGE Intl. [24889]
Engelbert's Aquarians - Address unknown since 1999.
Engelbert's "Goils" [24883], c/o Dot Gillberg, Co-Pres., 22249 Berry Dr., Cleveland, OH 44116
Engelbert's Golden Eagles [24884]
The Engelettes - Defunct.
Engel's Angels in Humperdinck Heaven Fan Club [24885], 3024 4th Ave., Baltimore, MD 21234-3208, (410)767-4633
Engel's Angels in Humperdinck Heaven Fan Club [IO], Baltimore, MD, United States
Engender [IO], Edinburgh, United Kingdom
Engender; Scottish Women's Aid [★IO]
EngenderHealth [IO], New York, NY, United States
EngenderHealth [12180], 440 9th Ave., New York, NY 10001, (212)561-8000
Engenharia Sanitaria; Asociacao Interamericana de [★7589]
Enge's Entourage - Address unknown since 2001.
Enge's Flaming Hearts - Address unknown since 2004.
Engine and Boat Mfrs; Natl. Assn. of [★2587]
Engine Builders Assn; Tesla [679]
Engine Generator Set Manufacturers Assn. [★1182]
Engine Manufacturers Assn. [1291], 2 N LaSalle St., Ste. 2200, Chicago, IL 60602, (312)827-8700
Engine Mfrs. Assn; Marine [★2587]
Engine Rebuilders Assn; Production [★1295]
Engine Rebuilders Assn; Western [★1295]
Engine Res. Gp; British Stationary [★22977]
Engine Soc; Stationary [★22977]
Engine, Tractor, and Toy Assn; Antique [23001]
Engineer Assn; 107th [5467]
Engineer Assn; Army [5469]
Engineered Wood Assn; APA: The [1637]
Engineered Wood Res. Found. [★1646]
Engineered Wood Tech. Assn. [1646], c/o APA - The Engineered Wood Assn., 7011 S 19th St., Tacoma, WA 98466, (253)565-6600
Engineering
1394 High Performance Serial Bus Trade Assn. [3720]
AACE Intl. [6842]
ABET [6979]
Academic Automotive Assn. [IO]
ACEC Res. and Mgt. Found. [6980]
Acoustical Soc. of Am. [6364]
Adhesion Soc. [6661]

Reference to "IO" in place of a book number signifies that the association may be found in the 45th edition of International Organizations.

Advanced Transit Assn. [7808]
Advocates for Women in Sci., Engg., and Mathematics [7593]
Aerospace Dept. Chairman's Assn. [7920]
African Sci. Inst. [7594]
AIDIS-USA Sect. [7589]
Air Traffic Control Assn. [132]
Airlines Electronic Engg. Comm. [6981]
Albanian Assn. of Consulting Engineers [IO]
Alliance of Deep Found. Testing Professionals [6650]
Alliance for Sci. and Tech. Res. in Am. [7595]
Alpha Pi Mu [24458]
AME Assn. (Atlantic) [IO]
Amer. Acad. of Environmental Engineers [6982]
Amer. Assn. for Aerosol Res. [6662]
Amer. Assn. of Blacks in Energy [6936]
Amer. Assn. of Drilling Engineers [7460]
Amer. Assn. of Engg. Societies [6983]
Amer. Assn. of Professional Sales Engineers [3462]
Amer. Ceramic Soc. [6657]
Amer. Chem. Soc. [6664]
Amer. Concrete Inst. [6832]
Amer. Cong. on Surveying and Mapping [7717]
Amer. Coun. of Engg. Companies [6984]
Amer. Ecological Engg. Soc. [6864]
Amer. Engg. Alliance [6985]
Amer. Engg. Assn. [6986]
Amer. Filtration and Separations Soc. [7724]
Amer. Helicopter Soc. [139]
Amer. Indian Coun. of Architects and Engineers [6462]
Amer. Indian Sci. and Engg. Soc. [6987]
Amer. Inst. of Aeronautics and Astronautics [6369]
Amer. Inst. of Chem. Engineers [6665]
Amer. Inst. of Chemists [6666]
Amer. Inst. of Engineers [6988]
Amer. Lebanese Engg. Soc. [6989]
Amer. Nuclear Soc. [7385]
Amer. Oil Chemists' Soc. [6669]
Amer. Portuguese Engg. and Architecture Soc. [7530]
Amer. Railway Engg. and Maintenance of Way Assn. [3280]
Amer. Soc. of Agricultural and Biological Engineers [6990]
Amer. Soc. of Agricultural and Biological Engineers [IO]
Amer. Soc. of Certified Engg. Technicians [6991]
Amer. Soc. of Civil Engineers [6992]
Amer. Soc. for Composites [6651]
Amer. Soc. of Danish Engineers [6993]
Amer. Soc. for Engg. Educ. [8366]
Amer. Soc. for Engg. Educ. [IO]
Amer. Soc. for Engg. Mgt. [6994]
Amer. Soc. of Gas Engineers [6941]
Amer. Soc. for Healthcare Engg. of the Amer. Hosp. Assn. [14865]
Amer. Soc. of Heating, Refrigerating and Air-Conditioning Engineers [6995]
American Society of Heating, Refrigerating and Air-Conditioning Engineers [IO]
Amer. Soc. of Inventors [7226]
Amer. Soc. of Mech. Engineers [7298]
Amer. Soc. of Mech. Engineers Auxiliary [7299]
Amer. Soc. of Naval Engineers [7270]
Amer. Soc. for Nondestructive Testing [7787]
Amer. Soc. of Plumbing Engineers [6996]
Amer. Soc. for Precision Engg. [6997]
Amer. Soc. for Quality [7552]
Amer. Soc. of Safety Engineers [7586]
Amer. Soc. of Sanitary Engg. [7590]
Amer. Soc. of Swedish Engineers [6998]
Amer. Soc. of Test Engineers [7788]
Amer. Soc. for Testing and Materials [7789]
Amer. Soc. of Validation Engineers [1289]
Amer. Supplier Inst. [7725]
Amer. Underground Constr. Assn. [7715]
Amer. Water Resources Assn. [7827]
APEC - Automated Procedures for Engineering Consultants [6999]
Applied Tech. Coun. [7000]
Arab Amer. Assn. of Engineers and Architects [6467]

Architectural Engg. Inst. [6468]
Argentine Centre of Engg. [IO]
Army Engineer Assn. [5469]
ASEAN Fed. of Elecl. Engg. Contractors [IO]
ASFE [7137]
Asian Amer. Architects and Engineers [6470]
ASM Intl. [7311]
ASME Intl. Gas Turbine Inst. [7001]
ASME Intl. Gas Turbine Inst. [IO]
Asociacion Espanola de Consultores en Ingenieria [IO]
Asociacion Espanola de Ingenieria de Proyectos [IO]
Asociacion de Ingenieros Cubanos [7002]
Associacao Tecnica Brasil-Alemanha [IO]
Assn. of Australasian Diesel Specialists [IO]
Assn. of Chinese Scientists and Engineers - U.S.A. [6698]
Assn. of Conservation Engineers [4357]
Assn. for Consultancy and Engg. [IO]
Assn. of Consulting Chemists and Chem. Engineers [6672]
Assn. of Consulting Engineers Australia [IO]
Assn. of Consulting Engineers of Australia - Australian Capital Territory [IO]
Assn. of Consulting Engineers of Australia - New South Wales [IO]
Assn. of Consulting Engineers of Australia - Northern Territory [IO]
Assn. of Consulting Engineers of Australia - South Australia [IO]
Assn. of Consulting Engineers of Australia - Tasmania [IO]
Assn. of Consulting Engineers of Australia - Victoria [IO]
Assn. of Consulting Engineers Botswana [IO]
Assn. of Consulting Engineers of Canada [IO]
Assn. of Consulting Engineers of Ireland [IO]
Assn. of Consulting Engineers of Kenya [IO]
Assn. of Consulting Engineers Malaysia [IO]
Assn. of Consulting Engineers of Namibia [IO]
Assn. of Consulting Engineers New Zealand [IO]
Assn. of Consulting Engineers, Nigeria [IO]
Assn. of Consulting Engineers of Norway [IO]
Assn. of Consulting Engineers of Pakistan [IO]
Assn. of Consulting Engineers of Zambia [IO]
Assn. of Elecl., Electronics and Automation Societies in Finland [IO]
Assn. of Elecl. Engineers [IO]
Assn. for Electronics Mfg. of the Soc. of Mfg. Engineers [6907]
Assn. of Energy Engineers [6942]
Assn. of Energy Ser. Companies [2918]
Assn. of Engg. Graphics and Imaging Systems [1800]
Assn. of Environmental and Engg. Geologists [7130]
Assn. of Environmental Engg. and Sci. Professors [9023]
Assn. for Facilities Engg. [7003]
Assn. of Fed. Communications Consulting Engineers [7767]
Assn. for Finishing Processes of the Soc. of Mfg. Engineers [6703]
Assn. of German Engineers [IO]
Assn. of Ground Water Scientists and Engineers - A Division of Natl. Ground Water Assn. [7828]
Assn. of Hungarian Consulting Engineers and Architects [IO]
Assn. of Intl. Motion Engineers [IO]
Assn. of Intl. Motion Engineers [7004]
Assn. of Japanese Consulting Engineers [IO]
Assn. of Korean-Canadian Scientists and Engineers [IO]
Assn. of Licensed Aircraft Engineers [IO]
Assn. of Licensed Architects [290]
Assn. of Luxembourg Engineers, Architects and Industrialists [IO]
Assn. of Mgt., Consulting and Tech. for Constr. [IO]
Assn. for Media-Based Continuing Educ. for Engineers [8367]
Assn. of Municipal Engineers [IO]
Assn. of Muslim Scientists and Engineers [7005]
Assn. of Polish Engineers in Canada [IO]

Assn. of Professional Engineers, Scientists and Managers Australia [IO]
Assn. of Professional Model Makers [7006]
Assn. of South African Quantity Surveyors [IO]
Assn. of Swedish Engg. Indus. [IO]
Assn. of Tech. Lightning and Access Specialists [IO]
Assn. of Turkish Consulting Engineers and Architects [IO]
Assn. for Women Geoscientists [7139]
Assn. for Women in Sci. [7602]
Associazione Italiana di Ingegneria Agraria [IO]
Astronaut Scholars Honor Soc. [24584]
Audio Engg. Soc. - British Sect. [IO]
Australian Acad. of Technological Sciences and Engg. [IO]
Austrian Consultants Assn. [IO]
Austrian Natl. Soc. of Agricultural Engineers [IO]
Austrian Soc. of Automotive Engineers [IO]
Automotive Engineers and Technicians Assn. [IO]
AVS Sci. and Tech. Soc. [7822]
Bangladesh Assn. of Consulting Engineers [IO]
Belarusian Assn. of Consulting Engineers [IO]
Bioelectromagnetics Soc. [6555]
Biomedical Engg. Soc. [6607]
Bd. of Certified Prdt. Safety Mgt. [3441]
Brazilian Assn. of Automotive Engg. [IO]
Brazilian Assn. of Engg. Consultants [IO]
British Chem. Engg. Contractors Assn. [IO]
British Soc. for Strain Measurement [IO]
Building and Constr. Trades Dept. - AFL-CIO [24025]
Building Futures Coun. [606]
Bulgarian Assn. of Consulting Engineers and Architects [IO]
California Engg. Found. [7007]
Canadian Acad. of Engg. [IO]
Canadian Fed. of Engg. Students [IO]
Canadian Soc. for Chem. Engg. [IO]
Canadian Soc. for Civil Engg. [IO]
Canadian Soc. for Mech. Engg. [IO]
Canadian Soc. of Professional Engineers [IO]
Canadian Union of Operating Engineers and Gen. Workers [IO]
Chambre des Ingenieurs-Conseils de France [IO]
Chartered Institution of Building Services Engineers - England [IO]
China Engg. Cost Assn. [IO]
China Natl. Assn. of Engg. Consultants [IO]
Chinese Amer. Assn. of Engg. [7008]
Chinese Amer. Food Soc. [7092]
Chinese Hydraulic Engg. Soc. [IO]
Chinese Inst. of Engineers [IO]
Colombian Soc. of Engineers [IO]
Combustion Inst. [6709]
The Communications Network [IO]
Completion Engg. Assn. [7182]
Composites Mfg. Assn. of the Soc. of Mfg. Engineers [2552]
Computational Intelligence Soc. [7009]
Confed. Francaise d'Ingenierie Rurale et Agricole [IO]
Conf. of European Schools for Advanced Engg. Educ. and Res. [IO]
Conseil Natl. des Ingenieurs et des Scientifiques de France [IO]
Constr. Indus. Round Table [940]
Constr. Specifications Inst. [6836]
Consulting Engineers Assn. of India [IO]
Consulting Engineers Assn. of Thailand [IO]
Convention of Natl. Societies of Elecl. Engineers of Europe [IO]
CoreNet Global [3305]
Coun. for Chem. Res. [6679]
Coun. of Engg. and Sci. Soc. Executives [7010]
Coun. of Engineers and Scientists Organizations [7817]
Coun. on Forest Engg. [4681]
Coun. for the Regulation of Engg. in Nigeria [IO]
Coun. on Tall Buildings and Urban Habitat [6474]
Croatian Agricultural Engg. Soc. [IO]
Croatian Assn. of Consulting Engineers [IO]
Croatian Soc. of Chem. Engineers [IO]
Cryogenic Engg. Conf. [6843]
Cyprus Assn. of Professional Quantity Surveyors [IO]

A star before a book entry number signifies that the name is not listed separately, but is mentioned within the entry.

Cyprus Professional Engineers Assn. [IO]
Czech Assn. of Consulting Engineers [IO]
Czech Assn. of Proj. Mgt. [IO]
Danish Assn. of Consulting Engineers [IO]
Danish Soc. of Agricultural Engg. [IO]
Danish Soc. of Engineers [IO]
Danish Soc. of Heating, Ventilating and Airconditioning Engineers [IO]
Drilling Engg. Assn. [2922]
Ductile Iron Soc. [7313]
Dutch Assn. of Consulting Engineers [IO]
Dutch Assn. of Cost Engineers [IO]
Earthquake Engg. Res. Inst. [7638]
Egyptian Soc. of Consulting Engineers [IO]
Elecl. and Cmpt. Engg. Dept. Heads Assn. [7011]
Electrochemical Soc. [6680]
Engineering Coll. Magazines Associated [3222]
Engg. Consulting Firms Assn., Japan [IO]
Engg. Coun. (UK) [IO]
Engg. Employers' Fed. [IO]
Engg. Equip. and Materials Users Assn. [IO]
Engg. Export Promotion Coun. of India [2304]
Engg. Indus. Assn. - England [IO]
Engg. Inst. of Canada [IO]
Engg. Integrity Soc. [IO]
Engg. and Physical Sciences Res. Coun. [IO]
Engg. and Sci. Network on Thinking [7217]
Engg. Soc. of Detroit [7012]
Engg. Soc. of Detroit [IO]
Engg. Workforce Commn. [7013]
Engineers' Assn. of Chile [IO]
Engineers without Borders - India [IO]
Engineers Canada [IO]
Engineers' Company [IO]
Engineers Ireland [IO]
Engineers Without Borders (Canada) [IO]
Engineers Without Borders - USA [IO]
Engineers Without Borders - USA [12111]
Environmental and Engg. Geophysical Soc. [7140]
Environmental and Planning Engineers' Assn. [IO]
Eta Kappa Nu [24459]
European Assn. for Educ. in Elecl. and Info. Engg. [IO]
European Coun. of Civil Engineers [IO]
European Fed. of Engg. Consultancy Associations [IO]
European Fed. of Natl. Engg. Associations [IO]
European Soc. of Agricultural Engineers [IO]
European Soc. for Engg. Educ. [IO]
European Soc. for Engg. and Medicine [IO]
European Soc. for Precision Engg. and Nanotechnology [IO]
European Structural Integrity Soc. [IO]
Fed. of Estonian Engg. Indus. [IO]
Fed. of Materials Societies [7281]
Fiber Soc. [7078]
Finnish Assn. of Graduate Engineers [IO]
Finnish Assn. of Municipal Engg. [IO]
Finnish Soc. of Agricultural Engineers [IO]
For Inspiration and Recognition of Sci. and Tech. [8319]
French-speaking Proj. Mgt. Assn. [IO]
Gen. Assn. of Engineers in Romania [IO]
German Assn. of Consulting Engineers [IO]
German Assn. of Women Engineers [IO]
German Economic Engineers Assn. [IO]
Ghana Assn. of Consultants [IO]
Ghana Institution of Engineers [IO]
Gp. for Reference Guide on Costs - Venezuela [IO]
Hong Kong Inst. of Occupational and Environmental Hygiene [IO]
Hong Kong Institution of Engineers [IO]
Human Powered Vehicle Assn. [7811]
Hungarian Cost Engg. Club [IO]
The Hydrographic Soc. of Am. [7718]
IEEE Aerospace and Electronics Systems Soc. [6912]
IEEE Broadcast Tech. Soc. [7768]
IEEE Circuits and Systems Soc. [6914]
IEEE Components, Packaging, and Mfg. Tech. Soc. [6915]
IEEE Cmpt. Soc. [6727]
IEEE Consumer Electronics Soc. [6916]

IEEE Control Systems Soc. [6514]
IEEE Dielectrics and Elecl. Insulation Soc. [6902]
IEEE Educ. Soc. [8262]
IEEE Electromagnetic Compatibility Soc. [6917]
IEEE Electron Devices Soc. [6918]
IEEE Engg. Mgt. Soc. [7014]
IEEE Geoscience and Remote Sensing Soc. [7144]
IEEE Indus. Electronics Soc. [6919]
IEEE Indus. Applications Soc. [7183]
IEEE Info. Theory Gp. [7770]
IEEE Instrumentation and Measurement Soc. [7219]
IEEE Lasers and Electro-Optics Soc. [6920]
IEEE Magnetics Soc. [6921]
IEEE Nuclear and Plasma Sciences Soc. [7386]
IEEE Power Engg. Soc. [6903]
IEEE Professional Commun. Soc. [6923]
IEEE Solid-State Circuits Soc. [6904]
IEEE Vehicular Tech. Soc. [6925]
Illuminating Engg. Soc. of North Am. [7250]
Inst. of Domestic Heating and Environmental Engineers [IO]
Inst. of Elecl. and Electronics Engineers [6926]
Inst. of Elecl. and Electronics Engineers - USA [7015]
Inst. of Environmental Sciences and Tech. [7570]
Inst. of Explosives Engineers [IO]
Inst. of Healthcare Engg. and Estate Mgt. [IO]
Inst. of Indus. Engineers [7016]
Inst. of Indus. Engineers (Hong Kong) [IO]
Inst. of Noise Control Engg. [7382]
Inst. of Professional Engg. Technologists [IO]
Inst. of Trans. Engineers [7812]
Institution of Agricultural Engineers [IO]
Institution of Certificated Mech. and Elecl. Engineers, South Africa [IO]
Institution of Civil Engineers [IO]
Institution of Diagnostic Engineers [IO]
Institution of Diesel and Gas Turbine Engineers [IO]
Institution of Elecl. Engineers - England [IO]
Institution of Electronics and Telecommunication Engineers [IO]
Institution of Engg. Designers [IO]
Institution of Engineers Australia/Engineers Australia [IO]
Institution of Engineers - India [IO]
Institution of Engineers - Malaysia [IO]
Institution of Engineers, Pakistan [IO]
Institution of Engineers, Sri Lanka [IO]
Institution of Gas Engineers and Managers [IO]
Institution of Incorporated Engineers [IO]
Institution of Mech. Engineers [IO]
Institution of Municipal Engg. of Southern Africa [IO]
Institution of Nuclear Engineers [IO]
Institution of Professional Engineers New Zealand [IO]
Institution of Railway Signal Engineers [IO]
Institution of Structural Engineers [IO]
Instrument Contracting and Engg. Assn. [1020]
Insulated Cable Engineers Assn. [7017]
Intl. Alliance for Interoperability [7018]
International Alliance for Interoperability [IO]
Intl. Assn. for Bridge Maintenance and Safety [538]
Intl. Assn. for Bridge and Structural Engg. [IO]
Intl. Assn. for Cryptologic Res. [6849]
Intl. Assn. for Engg. Geology and the Env. [IO]
Intl. Assn. of Financial Engineers [1424]
Intl. Assn. for Great Lakes Res. [7239]
Intl. Assn. for Hydrogen Energy [6957]
Intl. Assn. of Knowledge Engineers [6485]
Intl. Assn. of Nanotechnology [7741]
Intl. Assn. for Radio, Telecommunications and Electromagnetics [7773]
Intl. Assn. for Sci., Tech. and Soc. [7608]
Intl. Commn. of Agricultural Engg. [IO]
Intl. Cost Engg. Coun. [IO]
Intl. Coun. for Engg. and Tech. [IO]
Intl. Coun. on Systems Engg. [IO]
Intl. Coun. on Systems Engg. [7019]
Intl. Coun. on Systems Engg. - South Africa [IO]
Intl. Cryogenic Engineering Committee [IO]

Intl. Cryogenic Materials Conf. [6846]
Intl. Dark-Sky Assn. [6506]
Intl. Engg. Consortium [6928]
Intl. Fed. of Automotive Engg. Societies [IO]
Intl. Fed. of Consulting Engineers [IO]
Intl. Fed. for Heat Treatment and Surface Engg. [IO]
Intl. Fed. of Municipal Engineers [IO]
Intl. Fed. of Professional and Tech. Engineers [24052]
Intl. Geosynthetics Soc. [6700]
Intl. Inst. of Connector and Interconnection Tech. [6929]
Intl. Microelectronic and Packaging Soc. [6930]
Intl. Network of Engineers and Scientists for Global Responsibility [IO]
Intl. Network on Participatory Irrigation Mgt. [7233]
Intl. Org. of Overhead Catenary Engineers [IO]
Intl. Org. on Shape Memory and Superelastic Technologies [7317]
Intl. Soc. of African Scientists [7611]
Intl. Soc. of Coating Sci. and Tech. [6705]
Intl. Soc. of Difference Equations [7292]
Intl. Soc. for Engg. Educ. [IO]
Intl. Soc. of Explosives Engineers [IO]
Intl. Soc. of Explosives Engineers [7020]
Intl. Soc. of India Chemists and Chem. Engineers [6685]
Intl. Soc. for Nanoscale Sci., Computation and Engg. [7614]
Intl. Soc. of Offshore and Polar Engineers [7021]
Intl. Soc. of Offshore and Polar Engineers [IO]
Intl. Soc. of Parametric Analysts [6734]
Intl. Soc. for Pharmaceutical Engg. [7468]
Intl. Soc. for Productivity Enhancement [7022]
International Society for Productivity Enhancement [IO]
Intl. Soc. of Soil Mechanics and Geotechnical Engg. [7147]
Intl. Systems Security Engg. Assn. [7023]
Intl. Systems Security Engg. Assn. [IO]
Intl. Union of Operating Engineers [24028]
Intl. Union for Physical and Engg. Sciences in Medicine [IO]
Intervention and Coiled Tubing Assn. [7512]
Iranian Soc. of Consulting Engineers [IO]
Irish Engg. Enterprises Fed. [IO]
Italian Assn. of Cost Mgt. [IO]
Japan Dam Found. [IO]
Japan Soc. of Cost and Proj. Engineers [IO]
JEDEC [1222]
Junior Engg. Tech. Soc. [8368]
Kappa Eta Kappa [24460]
Keramos [24461]
Korean-American Scientists and Engineers Assn. [7024]
Latvian Assn. of Consulting Engineers [IO]
Leonardo, The Intl. Soc. for the Arts, Sciences and Tech. [9610]
Liaison Gp. of the European Mech., Elecl., Electronic, and Metalworking Indus. [IO]
Lithuanian Assn. of Consulting Companies [IO]
Lithuanian Soc. of Agricultural Engineers [IO]
Machine Vision Assn. of the Soc. of Mfg. Engineers [7583]
Machining and Material Removal Community [7025]
Machining and Material Removal Community of the Soc. of Mfg. Engineers [7747]
Malayalee Engineers Assn. in North Am. [7026]
Mfg. Integration Tech. Gp. of the Soc. of Mfg. Engineers [6737]
Marine Bd. [7272]
Marine Corps Engineer Assn. [6142]
Marine Tech. Soc. [7273]
The Masonry Soc. [6837]
Materials Handling Engineers Assn. [IO]
Materials Handling and Mgt. Soc. [7282]
Materials Res. Soc. [7283]
Mauritius Assn. of Quantity Surveyors [IO]
Mexican Soc. of Economic, Financial and Cost Engg. [IO]
Mexican Soc. on Mechatronics [IO]
Miles Value Found. [7184]

Reference to "IO" in place of a book number signifies that the association may be found in the 45th edition of International Organizations.

Minerals Engg. Soc. [IO]
MTM Assn. for Standards and Res. [7165]
NACE Intl. - Brazil Sect. [IO]
NACE Intl. - Chile Sect. [IO]
NACE Intl. - Colombia Sect. [IO]
NACE Intl. - India Sect. [IO]
NACE Intl. - Israel Sect. [IO]
NACE Intl. - Italian Sect. [IO]
NACE Intl. - Kuwait Sect. [IO]
NACE Intl. - Mainland China Sect. [IO]
NACE Intl. - Mexico Sect. [IO]
NACE Intl. - Montreal Sect. [IO]
NACE Intl. - Oman Sect. [IO]
NACE Intl. - Pakistan Sect. [IO]
NACE Intl. - Peru Sect. [IO]
NACE Intl. - Qatar Sect. [IO]
NACE Intl. - Saskatchewan Sect. [IO]
NACE Intl. - Saudi Arabia Sect. [IO]
NACE Intl. - Singapore Sect. [IO]
NACE International: The Corrosion Society [IO]
NACE Intl.: The Corrosion Soc. [7027]
NACE Intl. - Toronto Sect. [IO]
NACE Intl. - Trinidad and Tobago Sect. [IO]
NACE Intl. - United Arab Emirates Sect. [IO]
NACE Intl. - United Kingdom Sect. [IO]
NACE Intl. - West Asia/Africa Region [IO]
NanoBusiness Alliance [7750]
Natl. Acad. of Engg. [7028]
Natl. Acad. of Sciences [7616]
Natl. Action Coun. for Minorities in Engg. [8369]
Natl. Alliance of State Sci. and Mathematics Coalitions [9106]
Natl. Assn. of Agricultural Engineers [IO]
Natl. Assn. of Chimney Engineers [IO]
Natl. Assn. of Commun. Systems Engineers [6715]
Natl. Assn. of Consulting Engineers of Slovenia [IO]
Natl. Assn. of Corrosion Engineers [6840]
Natl. Assn. of County Engineers [7029]
Natl. Assn. of Engg. Student Councils [7030]
Natl. Assn. of Indonesian Consultants [IO]
Natl. Assn. of Multicultural Engg. Prog. Advocates [8370]
Natl. Assn. of Power Engineers [7532]
Natl. Assn. of PreCollege Directors [8371]
Natl. Building Museum [6477]
Natl. Conf. on Fluid Power [7085]
Natl. Consortium for Graduate Degrees for Minorities in Engg. and Sci. [8372]
Natl. Coun. of Black Engineers and Scientists [7618]
Natl. Coun. of Examiners for Engg. and Surveying [7031]
Natl. Coun. of Structural Engineers Associations [7032]
Natl. Found. of Indian Engineers [IO]
Natl. Info. Ser. for Earthquake Engg. [7641]
Natl. Inst. of Building Sciences [6838]
Natl. Inst. of Ceramic Engineers [6658]
Natl. Inst. for Certification in Engg. Technologies [7033]
Natl. Inst. of Packaging, Handling and Logistics Engineers [7427]
Natl. One Coat Stucco Assn. [650]
Natl. Registry of Environmental Professionals [4593]
Natl. Res. Coun. [7621]
Natl. Restaurant Assn. Multi-Unit Architects, Engineers and Constr. Officers [1050]
Natl. Soc. of Black Engineers [7034]
Natl. Soc. of Professional Engineers [7035]
Natl. Standards Educators Assn. [7697]
Natl. Tech. Assn. [7752]
Natl. Technical Services Assn. [7753]
Netherlands Soc. of Agricultural Engineers [IO]
New Zealand Engg., Printing and Mfg. Union [IO]
New Zealand Heavy Engg. Res. Assn. [IO]
New Zealand Soc. for Sustainability Engg. and Sci. [IO]
Nigerian Soc. of Engineers [IO]
North Am. Taiwanese Engineers' Assn. [IO]
North Am. Taiwanese Engineers' Assn. [7036]
North Amer. Alliance of Chem. Engineers [6690]
North Amer. Computational Social and Org. Sciences [6740]

North Amer. Fuzzy Info. Processing Soc. [6741]
North Amer. Geosynthetics Soc. [6701]
North Amer. Mfg. Res. Institution of the Soc. of Mfg. Engineers [7266]
Norwegian Assn. of Municipal Engineers [IO]
Norwegian Proj. Mgt. Assn. [IO]
Norwegian Soc. of Agricultural Engg. [IO]
Norwegian Soc. of Engineers [IO]
Nuclear Info. and Records Mgt. Assn. [7389]
The Oceanography Soc. [7403]
Omega Chi Epsilon [24462]
Order of Architects and Consulting Engineers [IO]
Phi Alpha Epsilon [24463]
Phi Kappa Upsilon Fraternity [24464]
Pi Tau Sigma [24465]
Pi Tau Sigma [IO]
Plant Engg. and Maintenance Assn. of Canada [IO]
PM - Greece [IO]
Polish Soc. of Agricultural Engg. [IO]
Proj. Mgt. Assn. of Denmark [IO]
Proj. Mgt. Assn. of Finland [IO]
Proj. Mgt. Assn. of Iceland [IO]
Proj. Mgt. Assn. of Slovakia [IO]
Proj. Mgt. South Africa [IO]
Projekt Mgt. Austria [IO]
Railway Engineering-Maintenance Suppliers Assn. [3289]
Refrigerating Engineers and Technicians Assn. [7037]
Reliability Engg. and Mgt. Institute/Reliability Testing Inst. [7038]
Res. Coun. on Structural Connections [7712]
Road Engg. Assn. of Malaysia [IO]
Robotics Tech Gp. of the Soc. of Mfg. Engineers [7585]
Royal Acad. of Engg. [IO]
Royal Institution of Engineers in the Netherlands [IO]
Royal Swedish Acad. of Engg. Sciences [IO]
Rubber Div., Amer. Chem. Soc. [3433]
Russian Assn. of Bidders and Cost Engg. [IO]
Russian Assn. for Continuing Engg. Educ. [IO]
Russian Assn. of Engineers for Heating, Ventilation, Air-Conditioning, Heat Supply and Building Thermal Physics [IO]
SAVE Intl. [7185]
Sci. Soc. of Mech. Engg. [IO]
Scottish Engg. [IO]
Seismological Soc. of Am. [7642]
Sigma Gamma Tau [24466]
Silicon Valley Chinese Engineers Assn. [7039]
Silicon Valley Chinese Engineers Assn. [IO]
Slovenian Proj. Mgt. Assn. [IO]
Sociedad Espanola de Agroingenieria [IO]
Societe de Chimie Industrielle, Amer. Sect. [6693]
Societe Royale Belge des Electriciens [IO]
Soc. for the Advancement of Material and Process Engg. [7285]
Soc. of Allied Weight Engineers [7699]
Soc. of Automotive Engineers [7632]
Soc. of Automotive Engineers (Australasia) [IO]
Soc. of Automotive Engineers (Japan) [IO]
Soc. for Biological Engg. [6593]
Soc. of Cable Telecommunication Engineers [IO]
Soc. of Cable Telecommunications Engineers [7040]
Soc. of Consulting Marine Engineers and Ship Surveyors [IO]
Soc. for Earthquake and Civil Engg. Dynamics [IO]
Soc. of Elecl. and Mech. Engineers Serving Local Govt. [IO]
Soc. of Engg. Sci. [7041]
Soc. of Environmental Engineers [IO]
Soc. for Experimental Mechanics [7713]
Soc. of Hispanic Professional Engineers [7042]
Soc. for Imaging Sci. and Tech. [7497]
Soc. for Indus. and Applied Mathematics [7294]
Soc. for Indus. Microbiology [6599]
Soc. for Info. Display [6745]
Soc. of Mfg. Engineers [7268]
Soc. of Mfg. Engineers Educ. Found. [8373]
Soc. of Marine Port Engineers [3588]
Soc. for Marketing Professional Services [2649]

Soc. of Mexican Amer. Engineers and Scientists [7043]
Soc. of Motion Picture and TV Engineers [7044]
Soc. of Naval Architects and Marine Engineers [7368]
Soc. of Petrophysicists and Well Log Analysts [7466]
Soc. of Piping Engineers and Designers [7045]
Soc. of Plastics Engineers [7514]
Soc. of Professional Engineers [IO]
Soc. of Reliability Engineers [7046]
Soc. of Rheology [7579]
Soc. of Tribologists and Lubrication Engineers [7047]
Soc. of Tribologists and Lubrication Engineers [IO]
Soc. of Turkish Amer. Architects, Engineers and Scientists [IO]
Soc. of Turkish Amer. Architects, Engineers and Scientists [7048]
Soc. of Women Engineers [7049]
SOLE - The Intl. Soc. of Logistics [7186]
South African Assn. of Consulting Engineers [IO]
South African Coun. for the Proj. and Constr. Mgt. Professions [IO]
South African Reinforced Concrete Engineers' Assn. [IO]
South African Soc. for Professional Engineers [IO]
Special Interest Gp. on Data Communications of the Assn. for Computing Machinery [6804]
Special Interest Gp. for Design Automation [6749]
SPIE - The Intl. Soc. for Optical Engg. [7408]
Standards Engg. Soc. [7700]
Steel Erectors Assn. of Am. [6839]
Steel Truss and Component Assn. [2733]
Structural Stability Res. Coun. [7714]
Sustainable Buildings Indus. Coun. [7682]
Swedish Assn. of Engineers [IO]
Swedish Assn. of Graduate Engineers [IO]
Swedish Fed. of Consulting Engineers and Architects [IO]
Swedish Proj. Mgt. Soc. [IO]
Swedish Soc. of Agricultural Engineers [IO]
Swiss Acad. of Engg. Sciences [IO]
Swiss Assn. of Agricultural and Food Stuff Engineers [IO]
Swiss Assn. of Consulting Engineers [IO]
Systems Engg. Soc. of China [IO]
Tau Alpha Pi [24467]
Tau Beta Pi Assn. [24468]
Tech., Engg. and Elecl. Union [IO]
Theta Tau [24469]
Tilt-Up Concrete Assn. [1067]
Turbine Inlet Cooling Assn. [7055]
Turkish Amer. Scientists and Scholars Assn. [7636]
Uganda Assn. of Consulting Engineers [IO]
Ukrainian Engineers' Soc. of Am. [7050]
Union of Japanese Scientists and Engineers [IO]
United Engg. Found. [7051]
United Kingdom Assn. of Professional Engineers [IO]
U.S. Comm. on Irrigation and Drainage [7842]
U.S. Metric Assn. [7701]
U.S. Microscopic Welding Assn. [7849]
U.S. Permafrost Assn. [7675]
Utilities Ser. Alliance [3966]
Value Engg. Soc. Intl. [7052]
Value Engg. Soc. Intl. [IO]
Verband Osterreichischer Ingenieure [IO]
Verband Selbstandiger Ingenieure und Architekten [IO]
Vibration Inst. [7302]
Vietnam Engg. Consultant Assn. [IO]
Visual Indicators Coun. [7053]
Welders Without Borders [7850]
Welding Res. Coun. [7851]
Winston Churchill Found. [8438]
Wire Assn. Intl. [7323]
W.M. Keck Found. [15115]
Women in Sci. and Engg. [7635]
Women into Sci. and Engg. [IO]
Women's Engg. Soc. [IO]
World Assn. for Chinese Biomedical Engineers [6611]

A star before a book entry number signifies that the name is not listed separately, but is mentioned within the entry.

World Fed. of Engg. Organisations [IO]
World Sci. and Engg. Acad. and Soc. [IO]
World Sci. and Engg. Acad. and Soc. [7054]
Zentralverband Deutscher Ingenieure [IO]
Zimbabwe Assn. of Consulting Engineers [IO]
Zimbabwe Inst. of Engineers [IO]
Engg. Action Network; Genetic [6615]
Engg. of the Amer. Hosp. Assn; Amer. Soc. for Healthcare [14865]
Engg; Amer. Inst. of Wood [★7100]
Engg; Amer. Soc. for Hosp. [★14865]
Engg; Amer. Soc. of Inspectors of Plumbing and Sanitary [★7590]
Engg; Amer. Soc. of Sanitary [7590]
Engg. and Assistive Tech. Soc. of North Am; Rehabilitation [11983]
Engg. Assn; Instrument Contracting and [1020]
Engg. Bus; Res. Inst. for Small and [★3624]
Engg. Center for Hosp. Mgt. [★14885]
Engg. Center; Rehabilitation [★13126]
Engg. Coating Assn; Surface [6706]
Engineering Coll. Magazines Associated [3222]
Engg. Comm. on Oceanic Resources [★IO]
Engg. Conf; Cryogenic [6843]
Engg. Consortium; Natl. [★6928]
Engg. Constr. Indus. Assn. [IO], London, United Kingdom
Engineering Consultants, Inc; Automated Procedures for [★6999]
Engg. Consulting Firms Assn., Japan [IO], Tokyo, Japan
Engg. Contractors Assn. [1015], 8310 Florence Ave., Downey, CA 90240, (562)861-0929
Engg. Contractors' Assn; Underground [★1015]
Engg; Coun. on Forest [4681]
Engg. Coun. for Guidance; Natl. [★8368]
Engg. Coun; Joint Electron Device [★1222]
Engg. Coun. (UK) [IO], London, United Kingdom
Engg. Dept. Heads Assn; Natl. Elecl. [★7011]
Engg. Educ. Effort; Minority [★8369]
Engg. Employers' Fed. [IO], London, United Kingdom
Engg. and Env; Inter-American Assn. of Sanitary [★7589]
Engg. and Environmental Sciences; Inter-American Assn. of Sanitary [★7589]
Engg. Equip. and Materials Users Assn. [IO], London, United Kingdom
Engg. Examiners; Natl. Coun. of [★7031]
Engg. Examiners; Natl. Coun. of State Boards of [★7031]
Engg. Export Promotion Coun. [★2304]
Engg. Export Promotion Coun. [IO], Calcutta, India
Engg. Export Promotion Coun. of India [2304], Kensington Bus. Center, 1601 Feehanville Dr., Ste. 200, Mount Prospect, IL 60056, (312)236-2162
Engg. Firms Practicing in the Geosciences; ASFE/ The Assn. of [★7137]
Engg. Geologists; Assn. of Environmental and [7130]
Engg. Geophysical Soc; Environmental and [7140]
Engg. and Grading Contractors Assn. [★1015]
Engg. Gp; IRE Mgt. [★7014]
Engg. Indus. Assn. - England [IO], London, United Kingdom
Engg. Indus. Assn. [★IO]
Engg. Inst; Architectural [6468]
Engg. Inst. of Canada [IO], Kingston, ON, Canada
Engg. Institute; Materials [★IO]
Engg. Institute; Materials [★7311]
Engg., and Inst. of Medicine; Comm. on Human Rights of the U.S. Natl. Acad. of Sciences, Natl. Acad. of [★17753]
Engg; Inst. of Noise Control [7382]
Engg. Integrity Soc. [IO], Sheffield, United Kingdom
Engg; Inter-American Assn. of Sanitary [★7589]
Engg; Inter-American Assn. of Sanitary and Environmental [★7589]
Engg. and Maintenance Assn; Amer. Railway [★3280]
Engineering-Maintenance Suppliers Assn; Railway [3289]
Engg. and Maintenance of Way Assn; Amer. Railway [3280]
Engg. Manpower Commn. [★7013]

Engg. Ministries Intl. [19794], 130 E Kiowa St., No. 200, Colorado Springs, CO 80903-1722, (719)633-2078
Engg. Ministries Intl. [IO], Colorado Springs, CO, United States
Engg; Missionary [★20359]
Engg; Natl. Advisory Coun. for Minorities in [★8369]
Engg; Natl. Consortium for Graduate Degrees for Minorities in [★8372]
Engg; Natl. Consortium for Graduate Degrees for Minorities in Sci. and [★8372]
Engg. Natl. Info. Ser. for Earthquake [7641]
Engg. Natl. Inst. for Rehabilitation [11972]
Engg. and Physical Sciences Res. Coun. [IO], Swindon, United Kingdom
Engg. Professors; Assn. of Environmental [★9023]
Engg. Res. Inst; Earthquake [7638]
Engg. Res. Inst; Illuminating [★7251]
Engg. and Sci. Network on Thinking [7217], 154 Hamilton Blvd., Struthers, OH 44471-1446, (330)755-2710
Engg. and Sci. Professors; Assn. of Environmental [9023]
Engineering Societies Commn. on Energy - Defunct.
Engg. Soc; Abrasive [1989]
Engg. Soc. for the Advancement of Material and Process [7285]
Engg. Soc; Audio [6909]
Engg. Soc; Biomedical [6607]
Engg. Soc. of Detroit [7012], 2000 Town Ctr., Ste. 2610, Southfield, MI 48075, (248)353-0735
Engg. Soc. of Detroit [IO], Southfield, MI, United States
Engg. Soc. in Finland [★IO]
Engg. Soc; IEEE Oceanic [7397]
Engg. Soc; IEEE Power [6903]
Engg. Soc; Mexican-American [★7043]
Engg. Soc. of North Am; Illuminating [7250]
Engg. Soc. of Photographic [★7497]
Engg. Soc. of Photographic Scientists and [★7497]
Engg. Soc; Standards [7700]
Engg. Soc; United [★7051]
Engg; Special Interest Gp. on Software [6779]
Engg. Standards Comm; Amer. [★6267]
Engg. Students; Natl. Fund for Minority [★8369]
Engg. Technicians; Inst. for the Certification of [★7033]
Engg. and Technological Sciences; Coun. of Academies of [★9104]
Engg. Technologist Certification Inst. [★7033]
Engg. Training for Schools; Junior [★8368]
Engg. Trustees; United [★7051]
Engg; U.S. Natl. Soc. for the Intl. Soc. of Soil Mechanics and Found. [★7147]
Engg. and Vocational Agriculture; Amer. Assn. for Agricultural [★9298]
Engg. Workforce Commn. [7013], 1620 I St. NW, Ste. 210, Washington, DC 20006, (202)296-2237
Engineers - A Division of Natl. Ground Water Assn; Assn. of Ground Water Scientists and [7828]
Engineers in Am; Soc. of Ukrainian [★7050]
Engineers; Amer. Acad. of Environmental [6982]
Engineers; Amer. Acad. of Sanitary [★6982]
Engineers; Amer. Assn. of Cost [★6842]
Engineers; Amer. Fed. of Tech. [★24052]
Engineers; Amer. Indian Coun. of Architects and [6462]
Engineers; Amer. Inst. of [6988]
Engineers; Amer. Inst. of Chem. [6665]
Engineers; Amer. Inst. of Consulting [★6984]
Engineers; Amer. Inst. of Elecl. [★6926]
Engineers; Amer. Inst. of Indus. [★7016]
Engineers; Amer. Inst. of Mining and Metallurgical [★7346]
Engineers; Amer. Inst. of Mining, Metallurgical, and Petroleum [7346]
Engineers; Amer. Soc. of Aeronautical [★6520]
Engineers; Amer. Soc. of Civil [6992]
Engineers; Amer. Soc. of Danish [6993]
Engineers; Amer. Soc. of Gas [6941]
Engineers; Amer. Soc. Heating and Air-Conditioning [★6995]
Engineers; Amer. Soc. of Heating, Refrigerating and Air-Conditioning [6995]
Engineers; Amer. Soc. of Instrument [★7220]

Engineers; Amer. Soc. of Lubrication [★7047]
Engineers; Amer. Soc. of Mech. [7298]
Engineers; Amer. Soc. of Municipal [★6233]
Engineers; Amer. Soc. of Naval [7270]
Engineers; Amer. Soc. of Plumbing [6996]
Engineers; Amer. Soc. of Refrigerating [★6995]
Engineers; Amer. Soc. of Safety [7586]
Engineers; Amer. Soc. of Swedish [6998]
Engineers; Amer. Soc. of Test [7788]
Engineers; Amer. Soc. of Tool [★7268]
Engineers; Amer. Soc. of Tool and Mfg. [★7268]
Engineers and Architects Inst. - Defunct.
Engineers of the ASEIB; Roster of Certified [★6982]
Engineers; Asian Amer. Architects and [6470]
Engineers; Assoc. Soil and Found. [★7137]
Engineers Assn. in Am; Korean Scientists and [★7024]
Engineers' Assn. of Chile [IO], Santiago, Chile
Engineers; Assn. of Conservation [4357]
Engineers; Assn. of Consulting Chemists and Chem. [6672]
Engineers; Assn. of Consulting Mgt. [★2485]
Engineers; Assn. of Energy [6942]
Engineers; Assn. of Fed. Communications Consulting [7767]
Engineers Assn; Insulated Cable [7017]
Engineers Assn; Insulated Power Cable [★7017]
Engineers; Assn. for Media-Based Continuing Educ. for [8367]
Engineers; Assn. of Muslim Scientists and [7005]
Engineers; Assn. of Mutual Fire Insurance [★2178]
Engineers; Assn. of Mutual Insurance [★2178]
Engineers; Assn. of Soil and Found. [★7137]
Engineers Associations; Natl. Coun. of Structural [7032]
Engineers Auxiliary; Amer. Soc. of Mech. [7299]
Engineers' Beneficial Assn; Marine [7308]
Engineers Beneficial Association/National Maritime Union and Professional Airways Systems Specialists; District 1 of Marine [★24015]
Engineers without Borders - India [IO], Hyderabad, India
Engineers Canada [IO], Ottawa, ON, Canada
Engineers Club; India Chemists and Chem. [★6685]
Engineers Comm; Annular Bearing [★1991]
Engineers Comm; Roller Bearing [★1991]
Engineers' Company [IO], London, United Kingdom
Engineers; Conf. of Municipal Public Hea. [★16246]
Engineers; Conf. of State Utility Commn. [★6341]
Engineers; Conf. of Utility Commn. [★6341]
Engineers and Constr. Officers; Natl. Restaurant Assn. Multi-Unit Architects, [1050]
Engineers Coun; Consulting [★6984]
Engineers' Coun. - Defunct.
Engineers' Coun. for Professional Development [★6979]
Engineers and Designers; Soc. of Piping [7045]
Engineers; Grand Intl. Brotherhood of Locomotive [★24176]
Engineers' Historical Assn; Rough and Tumble [22979]
Engineers; Inst. of Environmental [★7570]
Engineers; Inst. of Indus. [7016]
Engineers; Inst. of Radio [★6926]
Engineers; Inst. of Trans. [7812]
Engineers; Inter-American Assn. of Sanitary [★7589]
Engineers; Intl. Brotherhood of Locomotive [★24176]
Engineers; Intl. Soc. of Pharmaceutical [★7468]
Engineers; Intl. Union of Operating [24028]
Engineers Intersociety Bd; Environmental [★6982]
Engineers Ireland [IO], Dublin, Ireland
Engineers Joint Coun. [★6983]
Engineers; Machining and Material Removal Community of the Soc. of Mfg. [7747]
Engineers and Managers Assn. [★IO]
Engineers and Managers Institute; Environmental [★IO]
Engineers and Managers Institute; Environmental [★6942]
Engineers; Mining Br., Amer. Inst. of Mining, Metallurgical and Petroleum [★7349]
Engineers; Natl. Acad. of Building Inspection [640]
Engineers; Natl. Assn. of Corrosion [★7027]
Engineers; Natl. Assn. of County [7029]

Reference to "IO" in place of a book number signifies that the association may be found in the 45th edition of International Organizations.

Encyclopedia of Associations, 46th Edition 3403

Engineers; Natl. Assn. of Power [7532]

Engineers; Natl. Assn. Practical Refrigerating [★7037]

Engineers; Natl. Assn. of Radio and Telecommunications [★7773]

Engineers; Natl. Inst. of Ceramic [6658]

Engineers; Natl. Inst. of Packaging, Handling and Logistics [7427]

Engineers; Natl. Org. of Black Chemists and Chem. [★6689]

Engineers; Natl. Org. for the Professional Advancement of Black Chemists and Chem. [6689]

Engineers; Natl. Soc. of Architectural [★6468]

Engineers; Natl. Soc. of Black [7034]

Engineers; Natl. Soc. of Professional [7035]

Engineers Res. Foundation; American Soc. of Plumbing [★6996]

Engineers and Scientists of America - Defunct.

Engineers and Scientists in Am; Soc. of Turkish Architects, [★7048]

Engineers and Scientists; Lesbian and Gay Assoc. [★7620]

Engineers and Scientists; Natl. Coun. of Black [7618]

Engineers and Scientists Organizations; Coun. of [7817]

Engineers and Scientists; Soc. of Mexican Amer. [7043]

Engineers for Social and Political Action; SESPA Scientists and [★7627]

Engineers for Social Responsibility [IO], Christchurch, New Zealand

Engineers; Soc. of Aerospace Material and Process [★7285]

Engineers; Soc. of Aircraft Material and Process [★7285]

Engineers; Soc. of Allied Weight [7699]

Engineers' Soc. of Am; Ukrainian [7050]

Engineers; Soc. of Auto. [★6520]

Engineers; Soc. of Broadcast [582]

Engineers; Soc. of Cable Telecommunications [7040]

Engineers; Soc. of Carbide [★7322]

Engineers; Soc. of Carbide and Tool [7322]

Engineers; Soc. of Die Casting [★2054]

Engineers; Soc. of Environmental [★7570]

Engineers; Soc. of Explosives [★7020]

Engineers; Soc. of Fire Protection [7082]

Engineers; Soc. of Flight Test [6385]

Engineers Soc; Gas Appliance [★6941]

Engineers; Soc. of Hispanic Professional [7042]

Engineers; Soc. of Indus. [★2515]

Engineers; Soc. of Mfg. [7268]

Engineers; Soc. of Marine Port [3588]

Engineers; Soc. of Mining [★7349]

Engineers; Soc. of Motion Picture and TV [7044]

Engineers; Soc. of Naval Architects and Marine [7368]

Engineers; Soc. of Photo-Optical Instrumentation [★7408]

Engineers; Soc. of Photographic Instrumentation [★7408]

Engineers; Soc. of Plastics [7514]

Engineers Soc; Refrigeration Ser. [1899]

Engineers; Soc. of Reliability [7046]

Engineers Soc; Standards [★7700]

Engineers; Soc. of Tractor [★6520]

Engineers; Soc. of Women [7049]

Engineers for a Sustainable World [11776], 935A Scott St., San Francisco, CA 94115, (415)796-2127

Engineers for a Sustainable World [IO], Ithaca, NY, United States

Engineers and Technicians Assn; Refrigerating [7037]

Engineers and Technicians; Slovenian Assn. of Pulp and Paper [IO]

Engineers - USA; Inst. of Elecl. and Electronics [7015]

Engineers Veterans Assn; 147th [21372]

Engineers Without Borders (Canada) [IO], Toronto, ON, Canada

Engineers Without Borders - USA [IO], Longmont, CO, United States

Engineers Without Borders - USA [12111], 1811 Lefthand Cir., Ste. A-1, Longmont, CO 80501, (303)772-2723

Engineers; Woman's Auxiliary to the Amer. Soc. of Mech. [★7299]

Engineers of World War II; Topographic [21407]

Enginemen; Brotherhood of Locomotive Firemen and [★24181]

Engines

Aircraft Engine Historical Soc. [9364]

Aircraft Fleet Recycling Assn. [12800]

Antique Engine, Tractor, and Toy Assn. [23001]

Antique Small Engine Collectors Club [22409]

Assn. of Diesel Specialists [1290]

Assn. of Diesel Specialists [IO]

Brazilian Machinery Builders' Assn. [IO]

Early Day Gas Engine and Tractor Assn. [22410]

Engine Manufacturers Assn. [1291]

European Assn. of Internal Combustion Engine Mfrs. [IO]

Fed. of Engine Re-Manufacturers [IO]

Intl. Stationary Steam Engine Soc. [22977]

Natl. Marine Mfrs. Assn. [2587]

Northwest Marine Trade Assn. [2589]

Northwest Steam Soc. [22978]

Outdoor Power Equip. Aftermarket Assn. [1292]

Outdoor Power Equipment Aftermarket Association [IO]

Outdoor Power Equip. and Engine Ser. Assn. [1293]

Outdoor Power Equip. Inst. [1294]

OX5 Aviation Pioneers [21469]

Pacific Coast Marine Firemen, Oilers, Watertenders and Wipers Assn. [24130]

Production Engine Remanufacturers Assn. [1295]

Retail Motor Indus. Org. [IO]

Rough and Tumble Engineers' Historical Assn. [22979]

Steamship Historical Soc. of Am. [22980]

Turbine Inlet Cooling Assn. [7055]

England Basketball [IO], Sheffield, United Kingdom

England Hockey [IO], Milton Keynes, United Kingdom

England Touch Assn. [IO], London, United Kingdom

England, U.S. Area; TVR Car Club of [★21802]

England and Wales Cricket Bd. [IO], London, United Kingdom

English

ACT Assn. for the Teaching of English [IO]

Assn. for Commun. Admin. [9154]

Assn. of Departments of English [8374]

Australian Assn. for the Teaching of English [IO]

Coll. English Assn. [8375]

Coll. Language Assn. [8729]

Comm. on Public Doublespeak [17173]

Conf. on Christianity and Literature [8799]

Conf. on Coll. Composition and Commun. [8376]

Conf. on English Educ. [8377]

Conf. on English Leadership [1175]

English Acad. of Southern Africa [IO]

English in Action [17885]

English Assn. [IO]

English First [9911]

English Inst. [8378]

English Place-Name Society/Institute for Name Stud. [IO]

English Speaking Bd. [IO]

English Speaking Union of the Commonwealth [IO]

English Teachers Assn. of NSW [IO]

English Teachers' Assn. of Queensland [IO]

English Teachers Assn. of Western Australia [IO]

European Soc. for the Stud. of English [IO]

Intl. Fed. for the Teaching of English [IO]

Intl. Soc. of Anglo-Saxonists [IO]

Intl. Soc. of Anglo-Saxonists [8379]

Modern Language Assn. of Am. [8735]

Natl. Coun. on Interpreting in Hea. Care [1851]

Natl. Coun. of Teachers of English [8380]

Natl. Writing Proj. [9334]

Netherlands Soc. for English Stud. [IO]

New Zealand Assn. for the Teaching of English [IO]

North Amer. Torquay Soc. [22094]

Phonics Inst. [9046]

Primary English Teaching Assn. [IO]

ProEnglish [9912]

ProLiteracy Worldwide [8797]

Queen's English Soc. [IO]

Richard III Soc., Amer. Br. [11145]

Sigma Tau Delta, the Intl. English Honor Soc. [24470]

Sigma Tau Delta, the Intl. English Honor Soc. [IO]

Soc. for the Preservation of English Language and Literature [8381]

South Australian English Teachers Assn. [IO]

Stonehenge Study Group [6459]

Swedish Translators in North Am. [11059]

Teachers of English to Speakers of Other Languages [8382]

Teachers of English to Speakers of Other Languages Aotearoa New Zealand [IO]

Teachers of English to Speakers of Other Languages - Arabia [IO]

Teachers of English to Speakers of Other Languages - France [IO]

Victorian Assn. for the Teaching of English [IO]

Volunteers in Asia [13407]

English Acad. of Southern Africa [IO], Wits, Republic of South Africa

English in Action [17885], 144 E 39th St., New York, NY 10016, (212)818-1200

English in Action; Greater New York Coun. for Foreign Students - [★17885]

English Amateur Dancesport Assn. [IO], Hook, United Kingdom

English in Amer. Colleges and Universities; Assn. of Departments of [★8374]

English Assn. [IO], Leicester, United Kingdom

English Assn; Coll. [8375]

English; Assn. of Departments of [8374]

English Assn. Sydney [IO], Sydney, Australia

English Bowling Assn. [IO], Worthing, United Kingdom

English Bridge Union [IO], Aylesbury, United Kingdom

English Centre of Intl. PEN [IO], London, United Kingdom

English Centre of Intl. PEN (Poets, Playwrights, Editors, Essayists, Novelists and their Translators) [IO], London, United Kingdom

English Chess Fed. [IO], Battle, United Kingdom

English Cocker Spaniel Club of Am. [22259], c/o Mrs. Kate D. Romanski, Corresponding Sec., PO Box 252, Hales Corners, WI 53130, (414)529-9714

English Curling Assn. [IO], Bedford, United Kingdom

English Draughts Assn. [IO], Ryde, United Kingdom

English Educ; Conf. on [8377]

English and European Ford Registry; North Amer. [21744]

English First [9911], 8001 Forbes Pl., Ste. 102, Springfield, VA 22151, (703)321-8818

English Folk Dance and Song Soc. [IO], London, United Kingdom

English Golf Union [IO], Woodhall Spa, United Kingdom

English Grand Lodge; Rosicrucian Order, AMORC [19336]

English Handbell Ringers; Amer. Guild of [10535]

English Hockey Assn. [★IO]

English and the Humanities; Soc. for Automation in [★8132]

English Indoor Bowling Assn. [IO], Melton Mowbray, United Kingdom

English Inst. [8378], The Carpenter Center, 24 Quincy St., Harvard Univ., Cambridge, MA 02138, (617)496-1006

English Lacrosse Assn. [IO], Manchester, United Kingdom

English Ladies' Golf Assn. [IO], Birmingham, United Kingdom

English Language Acquisition and Language Instruction Educational Programs; Natl. CH for [8287]

English Language Editors' Assn. [IO], Jerusalem, Israel

English Language and Literature; Soc. for the Preservation of [8381]

English Leadership; Conf. on [1175]

English Manufacturers Assn; Western and [★259]

English Mini-Basketball Assn. [★IO]

English Natl. Assn. of Visually Handicapped Bowlers [IO], Lowestoft, United Kingdom

English; Natl. Coun. of Teachers of [8380]

A star before a book entry number signifies that the name is not listed separately, but is mentioned within the entry.

English Nature [IO], Peterborough, United Kingdom

English Place-Name Society/Institute for Name Stud. [IO], Nottingham, United Kingdom

English Poetry and Song Soc. [IO], Hersham, United Kingdom

English Pool Assn. [IO], Norwich, United Kingdom

English Rose Doll Club - Defunct.

English Schools Football Assn. [IO], Stafford, United Kingdom

English Schools' Table Tennis Assn. [IO], Northwich, United Kingdom

English Setter
English Setter Assn. of Am. [22260]

English Setter Assn. of Am. [22260], 17842 W Club Vista Dr., Surprise, AZ 85374-2907, (623)556-4712

English Sheepdog Club of Am; Old [22334]

English Shepherd Club [22261], c/o Mary Peaslee, Pres., 551 Mayotte Rd., East Fairfield, VT 05448-9799

English Shepherd Club of Amer. [★22261]

English Ski Coun. [★IO]

English to Speakers of Other Languages; Teachers of [8382]

English-Speaking
English-Speaking Union of the U.S. [19038]
Intl. Assn. for Medical Assistance to Travellers [13343]
Volunteers in Asia [13407]

English Speaking Bd. [IO], Southport, United Kingdom

English Speaking Union of the Commonwealth [IO], London, United Kingdom

English-Speaking Union of the U.S. [19038], 144 E 39th St., New York, NY 10016, (212)818-1200

English Spot Rabbit Club; Amer. [5134]

English Springer Rescue Am. [11390], 2721 Walker Lee Dr., Los Alamitos, CA 90720-4935, (800)921-1047

English Springer Spaniel Field Trial Assn. [22262], c/o Aime Weniger, Membership Sec., 24452 Over-lake Dr., Lake Forest, CA 92630, (949)581-7510

English Table Tennis Assn. [IO], Hastings, United Kingdom

English Teachers Assn. of NSW [IO], Leichhardt, Australia

English Teachers' Assn. of Queensland [IO], Stafford, Australia

English Teachers Assn. of Western Australia [IO], Perth, Australia

English Text Soc; Renaissance [10932]

English Toy Spaniel
English Toy Spaniel Club of Am. [22263]

English Toy Spaniel Club of Am. [22263], c/o Michael Allen, Ed., 14531 Jefferson St., Midway City, CA 92655-1030, (714)893-0053

English Trade Assn; Western- [259]

English UK [IO], London, United Kingdom

English; U.S. [18307]

English Vineyards Assn. [★IQ]

English Westerners Soc. [IO], Kingston Upon Thames, United Kingdom

English Women's Bowling Assn. [IO], Royal Leam-ington Spa, United Kingdom

Engraved Stationery Mfrs. Assn. [3680], 305 Plus Park Blvd., Nashville, TN 37217-1005, (615)366-1094

Engraved Stationery Mfrs. Res. Institute [★3680]

Engravers; Natl. Assn. of Steel and Copper Plate [★3680]

Engravers' Union of North Am; Intl. Plate Printers, Die Stampers, and [24085]

Engraving
Amer. Plate Number Single Soc. [22787]
Amer. Soc. of Bookplate Collectors and Designers [21965]
Firearms Engravers Guild of Am. [9830]
Intl. Plate Printers, Die Stampers, and Engravers' Union of North Am. [24085]
U.S. Stamp Soc. [22888]
Wood Engravers Network [9843]

Enid Bd. of Trade - Defunct.

ENJOIN for Responsible Govt. - Defunct.

Enkosini Wildlife Sanctuary [IO], Lydenburg, Republic of South Africa

Enlisted Assn. of Natl. Guard of the U.S. [6076], 3133 Mt. Vernon Ave., Alexandria, VA 22305, (703)519-3846

Enlisted Assn; The Retired [21321]

Enlisted Personnel Benefit Assn; Armed Forces [★18959]

Enlisted Reserve Assn; Naval [6095]

Eno Found. for Highway Traffic Control [★7809]

Eno Found. for Trans. [★7809]

Eno Trans. Found. [7809], 1634 I St. NW, Ste. 500, Washington, DC 20006, (202)879-4700

Enologists; Amer. Soc. of [★5407]

Enology and Viticulture; Amer. Soc. for [5407]

Enology and Viticulture; South African Soc. for [IO]

Enough Is Enough [17923], 746 Walker Rd., Ste. 116, Great Falls, VA 22066, (888)744-0004

Enough Is Enough Club - Defunct.

Enrichment; Inst. for Professional [★7901]

Enrichment Sect; Educ. and [★12151]

Enrolled Agents; Assn. of [★6299]

Enrolled Agents; Natl. Assn. of [6299]

Ensign Class Assn. - Defunct.

Entanglement Network Coalition - Address unknown since 1999.

Entayant Inst. - Defunct.

Ente Nazionale Italiano di Unificazione [IO], Milan, Italy

Entente des Hopitaux Luxembourgeois [★IO]

Enteral Nutrition; Amer. Soc. for Parenteral and [15549]

Enteral Nutrition Coun. - Defunct.

Enteral Nutrition; Oley Found. for Home Parenteral and [14843]

Enterostomal Therapy; Intl. Assn. for [★15533]

Enterprise Am. [★17644]

Enterprise Assn; Amer. [★18420]

Enterprise Assn. of the U.S. - Address unknown since 2002.

Enterprise; Center for the Defense of Free [17625]

Enterprise; Center for Neighborhood [17208]

Enterprise Communications Assn. [877], 1901 Pennsylvania Ave. NW, 5th Fl., Washington, DC 20006, (202)467-4868

Enterprise Community Partners [12311], 10227 Win-copin Cir., Columbia, MD 21044, (800)624-4298

Enterprise Cmpt. Telephony Forum [878], c/o Com-TIA, 1815 S Meyers Rd., Ste. 300, Oakbrook Ter-race, IL 60181-5228, (510)608-5915

Enterprise Content Mgt. Assn; AIIM - The [2095]

Enterprise Development Assn. - Address unknown since 1989.

Enterprise Development; Corp. for [17457]

Enterprise Development; Found. for [★704]

Enterprise Development Intl. [12044], 7910 Wood-mont Ave., Ste. 800, Bethesda, MD 20814, (240)396-1146

Enterprise Development Intl. [IO], Bethesda, MD, United States

Enterprise Development; Natl. Center for Amer. Indian [12628]

Enterprise Found. [★12311]

Enterprise II Intl. - Address unknown since 1999.

Enterprise Inst. for Public Policy Res; Amer. [18420]

Enterprise Integration; Assn. for [700]

Enterprise Legal Defense and Educ. Fund; Minority Bus. [2763]

Enterprise; Natl. Center for Neighborhood [★17208]

Enterprise Networking Assn. - Defunct.

Enterprise; Oper. [8808]

Enterprise Opportunity; Assn. for [3605]

Enterprise Solutions Assn. Intl; Mfg. [7722]

Enterprise Wireless Alliance [3742], 8484 Westpark Dr., Ste. 630, McLean, VA 22102-3590, (703)528-5115

EnterpriseWorks - Benin [IO], Cotonou, Benin

EnterpriseWorks - Burkina Faso [IO], Ouagadougou, Burkina Faso

EnterpriseWorks - Ghana [IO], Accra, Ghana

EnterpriseWorks - Guinea [IO], Conakry, Guinea

EnterpriseWorks - Guinea-Bissau [IO], Bissau, Guinea-Bissau

EnterpriseWorks - Mali [IO], Bamako, Mali

EnterpriseWorks - Philippines [IO], Makati City, Philippines

EnterpriseWorks - Senegal [IO], Dakar, Senegal

EnterpriseWorks - Tanzania [IO], Mbeya, United Republic of Tanzania

EnterpriseWorks/VITA [IO], Washington, DC, United States

EnterpriseWorks/VITA [16996], 1825 Connecticut Ave. NW, Ste. 630, Washington, DC 20009, (202)293-4600

EnterpriseWorks Worldwide and Volunteers in Tech. Assistance [★16996]

EnterpriseWorks Worldwide and Volunteers in Tech. Assistance [★IO]

Entertainers
Actors' Fund of Am. [12112]
Alliance of Artists and Recording Companies [3346]
Amer. Youth Circus Org. [9795]
Annie Sims Intl. Fan Club [24842]
Asiatic Philharmonia Soc. [10557]
Assn. of Club Executives [1932]
Assn. of Gospel Rescue Missions [13155]
Bread and Roses [12113]
Circus Educ. Specialists [9796]
Circus Fans Assn. of Am. [9797]
Clowns of Am., Intl. [21951]
Coalition of Asian Pacifics in Entertainment [1300]
Coalition to Protect Animals in Entertainment [11378]
Connie Francis Intl. Fan Club [24867]
Country Legends Assn. [10583]
Country Music Showcase Intl. [10586]
Dean Martin Fan Center [24816]
Dinah Shore Memorial Fan Club [24738]
Elvira Fan Club [24817]
Elvira Fan Club [IO]
Entertainment Indus. Found. [12114]
Evangelical Lutheran Good Samaritan Soc. [13168]
Frankie Laine Soc. of Am. [24890]
Friars Club [11016]
Friends of Dennis Lee Fan Club [24780]
Gale Storm Appreciation Soc. [24744]
Global Alliance of Performers [10773]
Global Mobile Entertainers Assn. [1302]
Hosp. Audiences [11017]
Howdy Doody Memorabilia Collectors Club [22038]
Humor Stamp Club [22827]
Intl. Brotherhood of Magicians [22620]
Intl. Concert Alliance [10617]
Intl. Crosby Circle [24804]
Intl. Jugglers' Assn. [23557]
Intl. Platform Assn. [10901]
Intl. Shrine Clown Assn. [21952]
Joni James Intl. Fan Club [24818]
The Lambs [11019]
Magic Collectors' Assn. [22621]
Magic Youth Intl. [22622]
Magicians Without Borders [12503]
Michael Jackson Fan Club [24948]
Motion Picture and TV Fund [12115]
Natl. Benevolent Assn. of the Christian Church [13177]
Natl. Circus Preservation Soc. [9799]
Natl. Lum and Abner Soc. [22925]
Peter Sellers Appreciation Soc. [24767]
Presbyterian Hea., Educ. and Welfare Assn. [13184]
Rita Hayworth Fan Club [24769]
Salvation Army [13187]
Soc. of Amer. Magicians [22623]
Stars for Stripes [20770]
Sword Swallowers Assn. Intl. [10776]
Talent Managers Assn. [1325]
Texas Intl. Theatrical Arts Soc. [11045]
Theatre Authority [11046]
U.S. Sports Acrobatics [23035]
U.S.A. for Africa [12882]
Veterans Bedside Network [12116]
Volunteers of Am. [13192]
Women in Show Business for Children [13069]
World Clown Assn. [21953]
World Juggling Fed. [23558]

Entertainers for Kids; Athletes and [★13560]

Entertainment
Actors' Fund of Am. [12112]
Alliance of Artists and Recording Companies [3346]
Amer. Amusement Machine Assn. [1296]
American Amusement Machine Association [IO]

Amer. Dinner Theatre Inst. [1297]
Amer. Dog Show Judges [22198]
Amer. Soc. of Wedding Professionals [532]
Amer. Youth Circus Org. [9795]
Amusement Indus. Mfrs. and Suppliers Intl. [1298]
Amusement Indus. Manufacturers and Suppliers Intl. [IO]
Amusement and Music Operators Assn. [1299]
Asian Amer. Music Soc. [10556]
Asiatic Philharmonia Soc. [10557]
Assn. of Gospel Rescue Missions [13155]
Assn. of Scottish Games and Festivals [19348]
Bar Entertainment and Dance Assn. [IO]
Black Rock Coalition [17499]
Blue-ray Disc Assn. [1207]
Bread and Roses [12113]
British Amusement Catering Trade Assn. [IO]
British Assn. of Leisure Parks, Piers and Attractions [IO]
British Pyrotechnists Assn. [IO]
Canadian Picture Pioneers [IO]
China Assn. of Amusement Parks and Attractions [IO]
Circus Educ. Specialists [9796]
Circus Fans Assn. of Am. [9797]
Clowns of Am., Intl. [21951]
Clowns Without Borders - USA [11768]
Coalition of Asian Pacifics in Entertainment [1300]
Coalition to Protect Animals in Entertainment [11378]
Country Legends Assn. [10583]
Country Music Showcase Intl. [10586]
Darkride and Funhouse Enthusiasts [21511]
Digital Cinema Soc. [1380]
Entertainment Indus. Found. [12114]
Entertainment Services and Tech. Assn. [2556]
Entertainment Software Assn. [6766]
Evangelical Lutheran Good Samaritan Soc. [13168]
FilmAid Intl. [12811]
Friends of Dennis Lee Fan Club [24780]
Game Audio Network Guild [1715]
Game Mfr. Assn. [1301]
Game Manufacturer Association [IO]
Gartlan USA's Collectors' League [22028]
Glamour Photographers Intl. [2997]
Global Alliance of Performers [10773]
Global Mobile Entertainers Assn. [1302]
Global Mobile Entertainers Assn. [IO]
Hea. Jam [14674]
Hollywood Sign Trust [17710]
HomePlug Powerline Alliance [1216]
Hong Kong Digital Entertainment Assn. [IO]
Howdy Doody Memorabilia Collectors Club [22038]
Indian Assn. of Amusement Parks and Indus. [IO]
Inst. of Entertainment and Arts Mgt. [IO]
Intl. Artist Managers' Assn. [IO]
Intl. Assn. of Amusement Parks and Attractions [IO]
Intl. Assn. of Amusement Parks and Attractions [1303]
Intl. Assn. of Haunted Attractions [1304]
Intl. Assn. of Haunted Attractions [IO]
Intl. Assn. for the Leisure and Entertainment Indus. [IO]
Intl. Assn. for the Leisure and Entertainment Indus. [1305]
Intl. Brotherhood of Magicians [22620]
Intl. Concert Alliance [10617]
Intl. DJ Guild [2812]
Intl. Entertainment Buyers Assn. [1306]
Intl. Fed. of Festival Organizations [1307]
Intl. Fed. of Festival Organizations [IO]
Intl. Festivals and Events Assn. [IO]
Intl. Festivals and Events Assn. [1308]
Intl. Jugglers' Assn. [23557]
Intl. Laser Display Assn. [1309]
Intl. Laser Display Assn. [IO]
Intl. Recreational Go-Kart Assn. [IO]
Intl. Recreational Go-Kart Assn. [1310]
Intl. Shrine Clown Assn. [21952]
Intl. Special Events Soc. [1311]
International Special Events Society [IO]
Intl. Ticketing Assn. [IO]

Intl. Ticketing Assn. [1312]
Intl. Webcasting Assn. [2667]
The Lambs [11019]
Large Format Cinema Assn. [1387]
Live Performance Australia [IO]
Location Managers Guild of Am. [2522]
Magic Collectors' Assn. [22621]
Magic Youth Intl. [22622]
Magicians Without Borders [12503]
Media Action Network for Asian Americans [18029]
Media Res. Center [12511]
Mediascope [18031]
Michael Jackson Fan Club [24948]
A Minor Consideration [11826]
Motion Picture and TV Fund [12115]
Nashville Entertainment Assn. [9579]
Natl. Assn. of Black Female Executives in Music and Entertainment [12117]
Natl. Assn. of Casino Party Operators [1313]
Natl. Assn. of Concessionaires [1589]
Natl. Assn. of Mobile Entertainers [1314]
Natl. Assn. of Recording Merchandisers [3349]
Natl. Assn. of Rhythm and Blues Dee Jay's [10659]
Natl. Assn. of St. Entertainers [IO]
National Association of Theatre Owners [IO]
Natl. Assn. of Theatre Owners [1315]
Natl. Assn. of Ticket Brokers [1316]
Natl. Ballroom and Entertainment Assn. [1317]
Natl. Benevolent Assn. of the Christian Church [13177]
Natl. Caricaturist Network [1318]
Natl. Caves Assn. [1319]
Natl. Circus Preservation Soc. [9799]
Natl. Club Indus. Assn. of Am. [1320]
Natl. Club Indus. Assn. of Am. [IO]
Natl. Conf. of Personal Managers [174]
Natl. Entertainment Agents Coun. [IO]
Natl. Independent Concessionaires Assn. [1591]
Natl. Lum and Abner Soc. [22925]
Natl. New Play Network [11030]
Natl. Park Hospitality Assn. [1321]
New Violin Family Assn. [10672]
New Zealand Rodeo Cowboys Assn. [IO]
North Amer. Assn. of Ventriloquists [1322]
North Amer. Model Horse Shows Assn. [22587]
Oh Ji Ho Intl. Fan Club [24781]
Oper.: Take a Soldier to the Movies [11498]
Org. of Black Screenwriters [1323]
Org. of Black Screenwriters [IO]
Outdoor Amusement Bus. Assn. [1324]
Presbyterian Hea., Educ. and Welfare Assn. [13184]
Pro Players Assn. [13402]
Production Services Assn. [IO]
Recording Indus. Assn. of Am. [3350]
Salvation Army [13187]
Showmen's Guild of Great Britain [IO]
Showmen's League of Am. [19039]
Soc. of Amer. Magicians [22623]
Soc. of Independent Roundabout Proprietors [IO]
Soc. of Professional Audio Recording Services [3351]
Stars for Stripes [20770]
Swimming Pool and Allied Trades Assn. [IO]
Sword Swallowers Assn. Intl. [10776]
Syndicated Network TV Assn. [120]
Talent Managers Assn. [1325]
Teachers Resisting Unhealthy Children's Entertainment [11657]
Themed Entertainment Assn. [1326]
Themed Entertainment Assn. [IO]
Tournament of Roses Assn. [19040]
U.S. Online Disc Jockey Assn. [2825]
U.S. Sports Acrobatics [23035]
Variety Intl. - The Children's Charity [11660]
Veterans Bedside Network [12116]
Volunteers of Am. [13192]
Western Fairs Assn. [1327]
Women in Show Business for Children [13069]
Women in Toys [3834]
World Canine Freestyle Org. [23390]
World Clown Assn. [21953]
World Juggling Fed. [23558]

World Robotic Boxing Assn. [1328]
World Waterpark Assn. [1329]
World Waterpark Assn. [IO]
Entertainment Agents Assn. [★IO]
Entertainment Assn; Nashville [9579]
Entertainment Assn; World Airline [440]
Entertainment and Campus Activities Assn; Natl. [★9169]
Entertainment; Canadians Concerned About Violence in [IO]
Entertainment; Coalition to Protect Animals in [11378]
Entertainment Conf; Natl. [★9169]
Entertainment; Fellowship of Christians in the Arts, Media and [★20024]
Entertainment Indus. Coun. [13238], c/o Govt. Relations and Admin., 1760 Reston Pkwy., Ste. 415, Reston, VA 20190, (703)481-1414
Entertainment Indus. Educators Assn; Music and [8916]
Entertainment Indus. Found. [12114], 1201 W 5th St., Ste. T-700, Los Angeles, CA 90017, (213)240-3900
Entertainment Industry Referral and Assistance Center - Address unknown since 2001.
Entertainment Industry Support Comm. - Defunct.
Entertainment Law
  Black Entertainment and Sports Lawyers Assn. [5687]
  Intl. Assn. of Entertainment Lawyers - France [IO]
  Los Angeles Copyright Soc. [5854]
Entertainment Lawyers Assn; Black [★5687]
Entertainment and Leisure Software Publishers Assn. [IO], London, United Kingdom
Entertainment Managers Assn. - Defunct.
Entertainment Operators of Am. [★1317]
Entertainment Retailers; Professional Assn. of Comics [9523]
Entertainment Services and Tech. Assn. [2556], 875 6th Ave., Ste. 1005, New York, NY 10001, (212)244-1505
Entertainment Services and Technology Association [IO], New York, NY, United States
Entertainment Software Assn. [6766], 575 7th St. NW, Ste. 300, Washington, DC 20004, (202)223-2400
Enthronement Center; Natl. [19686]
Enthronement of the Sacred Heart in the Home [★19686]
Entomological Livestock Gp. [IO], Sheffield, United Kingdom
Entomological Soc. of Am. [7062], 10001 Derekwood Ln., Ste. 100, Lanham, MD 20706-4876, (301)731-4535
Entomological Soc. of Canada [IO], Ottawa, ON, Canada
Entomological Soc. of New Zealand [IO], Canterbury, New Zealand
Entomological Soc. of Southern Africa [IO], Hatfield, Republic of South Africa
Entomologiese Vereniging van Suidelike Afrika [★IO]
Entomologists; Amer. Registry of Professional [★7062]
Entomologists and Entomological Society of America; Amer. Assn. of Economic [★7062]
Entomology
  Acadian Entomological Soc. [IO]
  Acarological Soc. of Am. [IO]
  Acarological Soc. of Am. [7056]
  Amateur Entomologists' Soc. [IO]
  Amer. Mosquito Control Assn. [5072]
  Assn. of Applied IPM Ecologists [5073]
  Assn. of Indian Entomologists in North Am. [7057]
  Assn. of Indian Entomologists in North Am. [IO]
  Assn. of Natural Biocontrol Producers [5074]
  Assn. for Tropical Lepidoptera [7058]
  Australian Entomological Soc. [IO]
  Brazilian Soc. of Entomology [IO]
  British Dragonfly Soc. [IO]
  British Entomological and Natural History Soc. [IO]
  Coleopterists Soc. [7059]
  Coun. of Entomology Dept. Administrators [7060]
  Croatian Entomological Soc. [IO]
  Dragonfly Soc. of the Americas [7061]

A star before a book entry number signifies that the name is not listed separately, but is mentioned within the entry.

Entomological Livestock Gp. [IO]
Entomological Soc. of Am. [7062]
Entomological Soc. of Canada [IO]
Entomological Soc. of New Zealand [IO]
Entomological Soc. of Southern Africa [IO]
Estonian Naturalists' Soc. - Sect. of Entomology [IO]
European Assn. of Acarologists [IO]
European Assn. of Coleopterology [IO]
Flemish Entomological Soc. [IO]
Gazi Entomological Res. Soc. [IO]
Intl. Centre of Insect Physiology and Ecology [IO]
Intl. Union for the Stud. of Social Insects [IO]
Intl. Union for the Stud. of Social Insects [7063]
Japan Soc. of Medical Entomology and Zoology [IO]
Japanese Soc. of Applied Entomology and Zool-ogy [IO]
Natl. Assn. of Agriculture Employees [5437]
North Amer. Forensic Entomology Assn. [7064]
North Amer. Forensic Entomology Assn. [IO]
Orthopterists' Soc. [IO]
Orthopterists' Soc. [7065]
Philippine Assn. of Entomologists [IO]
Polish Entomological Soc. [IO]
Royal Entomological Soc. [IO]
Royal Entomological Soc. of Antwerp, Belgium [IO]
Sociedad Mexicana de Entomologia [IO]
Spanish Entomological Assn. [IO]
Systematic and Applied Acarology Soc. [IO]
Worldwide Dragonfly Assn. [IO]
Xerces Soc. [5405]
Young Entomologists' Soc. [7066]
Entomology Gp; Teen Intl. [★7066]
Entraide Missionnaire [IO], Montreal, QC, Canada
Entraineurs d'Athletisme; Assn. Intl. des [★23919]
Entrepreneurial Leadership Center [17627], Bellevue Univ., 1000 Galvin Rd. S, Bellevue, NE 68005, (402)557-7510
Entrepreneurial Leadership; Kauffman Center for [739]
Entrepreneurial Parents; Natl. Assn. of [12675]
Entrepreneurs Assn. of Slovakia [IO], Bratislava, Slovakia
Entrepreneurs de l'audiovisuel europeene [★IO]
Entrepreneurs of North Am; Org. of Pakistani [756]
Entrepreneurs' Org. [718], 500 Montgomery St., Ste. 500, Alexandria, VA 22314, (703)519-6700
Entrepreneurs' Org; Young [★718]
Entrepreneurs Workshop International [★5851]
Entrepreneurs Workshop International [★IO]
Entrepreneurship Development Inst. of India [IO], Gandhinagar, India
The Entrepreneurship Inst. [719], 3592 Corporate Dr., Ste. 101, Columbus, OH 43231, (614)895-1153
Entrepreneurship; Natl. Found. for Teaching [8038]
Entrepreneurship; U.S. Assn. for Small Bus. and [3632]
Enuresis Soc; Natl. [★15294]
Envelope Makers' and Mfg. Stationers' Assn. [IO], Royston, United Kingdom
Envelope Mfrs. of Am; Bur. of [★3681]
Envelope Mfrs. Assn. [3681], 500 Montgomery St., Ste. 550, Alexandria, VA 22314, (703)739-2200
Envelope Mfrs. Assn. of Am. [★3681]
Envelope Mfrs. Assn; Amer. [★3681]
Environ Found. Intl. [8387], 12035 Stonewick Pl., Glen Allen, VA 23059-7152, (804)360-9130
Environic Found. Intl. [IO], Chevy Chase, MD, United States

Environment
Acad. of Arts and Sciences of the Americas [18830]
Advocacy Inst. [12650]
African Amer. Environmentalist Assn. [4529]
African Blackwood Conservation Proj. [4342]
African Environmental Res. and Consulting Gp. [4530]
African Environmental Res. and Consulting Gp. [IO]
Air and Waste Mgt. Assn. [5081]
Aircraft Fleet Recycling Assn. [12800]
Airfields Env. Trust [IO]

Alaska Coalition [4343]
ALEPH: Alliance for Jewish Renewal [18141]
Alliance for Am. [11807]
Alliance for Community Trees [4678]
Alliance for Global Sustainability [IO]
Alliance for Intl. Reforestation [4344]
Alliance for Sustainable Jobs and the Env. [24053]
Alliance of Veterinarians for the Env. [4626]
Amazon Alliance [4531]
Amazon Alliance [IO]
Am. the Beautiful Fund [4532]
Amer. Acad. of Environmental Engineers [6982]
Amer. Acad. of Environmental Medicine [14360]
Amer. Acad. of Sanitarians [16383]
Amer. Coll. of Occupational and Environmental Medicine [15624]
Amer. Conf. of Governmental Indus. Hygienists [15625]
Amer. Conservation Assn. [4346]
Amer. Coun. on Sci. and Hea. [14539]
Amer. Decentralized Wastewater Assn. [4006]
Amer. Ecological Engg. Soc. [6864]
Amer. Farmland Trust [16951]
Amer. Indoor Air Quality Coun. [5082]
Amer. Industrial Health Coun. [15626]
Amer. Indus. Hygiene Assn. [15627]
American-Israel Environmental Coun. [10254]
Amer. Land Conservancy [4348]
Amer. Lands Alliance [4533]
Amer. Medical Fly Fishing Assn. [4349]
Amer. Plastics Coun. [3044]
Amer. Public Hea. Assn. [16236]
Amer. Public Info. on the Env. [17500]
Amer. Safe Climbing Assn. [21950]
Amer. Soc. for Environmental History [8383]
American Society for Environmental History [IO]
Amer. Soc. for Healthcare Environmental Services of the Amer. Hosp. Assn. [14866]
Americans for Balanced Energy Choices [17495]
Animals as Intermediaries [4157]
Aquaculture Intl. [4169]
Aquatic Animal Life Support Operators [7279]
Aquatic Resources Educ. Assn. [7956]
Architectural Heritage Found. [10014]
Assn. Ecosystem [IO]
Assn. for Environmental Educ., Russia [IO]
Assn. of Environmental Engg. and Sci. Professors [9023]
Assn. for the Environmental Hea. of Soils [5221]
Assn. of Environmental and Rsrc. Economists [4359]
Assn. for Forests, Development and Conservation [IO]
Assn. for Gnotobiotics Res. and Tech. [4534]
Assn. of Intl. Res. Initiatives for Environmental Stud. [IO]
Assn. of Lighting and Mercury Recyclers [5168]
Assn. of Natural Burial Grounds [IO]
Assn. of Professional Humane Educators [12058]
Assn. Promoting Educ. and Conservation in Ama-zonia [5294]
Assn. of Univ. Leaders for a Sustainable Future [8483]
Assn. of Women in Environmental Professions [4619]
Australian Life Cycle Assessment Soc. [IO]
Bangladesh Centre for Advanced Stud. [IO]
Bangladesh Unnayan Parishad [IO]
Barh Koh Env. and Sustainable Development Aid [IO]
Basel Action Network [18797]
Beldon Fund [4535]
Beyond Pesticides - Natl. Coalition Against the Misuse of Pesticides [13322]
Big Thicket Assn. [4367]
Big Thicket Natural Heritage Trust [4368]
Biopolitics Intl. Org. [IO]
Blue Earth Alliance [10847]
Boreal Songbird Initiative [5302]
Both ENDS [IO]
Canadian Assn. of Physicians for the Env. [IO]
Canyonlands Field Inst. [4500]
Caretakers of the Env. Intl. [IO]
Caretakers of the Env. Intl. - Cameroon [IO]

Caretakers of the Env. Intl. - Canada (Nova Scotia) [IO]
Caretakers of the Env. Intl. - Portugal [IO]
Caretakers of the Env. Intl. - Scotland [IO]
Caucasus Environmental NGO Network [IO]
Center for Alternative Mining Development Policy [4536]
Center for Environmental Info. [4537]
Center for Environmental Investigation and Plan-ning [IO]
Center for Environmental Stud. [4538]
Center For Hea., Env. and Justice [5266]
Change Design [IO]
Charles A. and Anne Morrow Lindbergh Found. [4539]
Children of the Earth United [4621]
Children's Hea. Environmental Coalition [13953]
Citizens Coal Coun. [4299]
Clean Beaches Coun. [4540]
Clean Calgary Assn. [IO]
Clean Energy Gp. [6948]
Clean Energy States Alliance [6949]
Clean Islands Intl. [4541]
Clean Islands Intl. [IO]
Clean Up Australia [IO]
Clean Up the World [IO]
Climate Inst. [4542]
Co-op Am. [1069]
Coalition to End Childhood Lead Poisoning [4543]
Coalition for Environmentally Responsible Economies [4544]
Coalition for Environmentally Safe Communities [12118]
Coast Alliance [4375]
The Coastal Soc. [7395]
Colong Found. for Wilderness [IO]
Commons, Open Spaces and Footpaths Preservation Soc. [IO]
Community Environmental Coun. [5267]
Compassionate Kids [8384]
Compassionate Kids [IO]
Concern [4545]
ConservAmerica [4378]
Conservation Intl. - USA [4381]
Conservation Northwest [4546]
Conservation Tech. Info. Center [4384]
Consumer Energy Coun. of Am. Res. Found. [17496]
Cornerstone Found. [IO]
CorpWatch [17756]
Coun. for Biotechnology Info. [6614]
Coun. for Environmental Educ. [IO]
The Cousteau Soc. [IO]
The Cousteau Soc. [8385]
Cultural Conservancy [10741]
David Suzuki Found. [IO]
Doris Duke Charitable Found. [13115]
Dudley Found. [13116]
Earth Communications Off. [4547]
Earth Day Network [4548]
Earth Force [4549]
Earth Island Inst. [4550]
Earth Island Inst. [IO]
Earth Liberation Front [4551]
Earth Regeneration Soc. [4552]
Earth Repair Found. [IO]
Earth Soc. Found. [IO]
Earth Soc. Found. [4553]
EarthAction Intl. [4554]
EarthAction Intl. [IO]
EarthEcho Intl. [4391]
EarthRights Intl. - Asia [IO]
EarthSave Canada [IO]
EarthSave Intl. [4504]
Earthtrust [5312]
EarthVoice [4555]
EarthWave Soc. [4556]
Eco-Animal Allies [11773]
Eco-Spirit [4622]
Ecological Landscaping Assn. [4989]
ECOSENS [IO]
ECOTERRA Intl. [IO]
EcoVentures Intl. [4623]
EcoVillage at Ithaca [4557]
Educational Communications [8386]

Reference to "IO" in place of a book number signifies that the association may be found in the 45th edition of International Organizations.

Educational Communications [IO]
Educational Found. of Am. [IO]
Educational Found. of Am. [12119]
EMS/Science Commun. Network [5032]
Energy Future Coalition [6952]
EnterpriseWorks/VITA [16996]
Environic Found. Intl. [8387]
Environic Found. Intl. [IO]
Env. Africa [IO]
Env. Bus. Australia [IO]
Env., Culture, Agriculture, Res. and Development Soc. in Nepal [IO]
Env. and Development in the Arab World [IO]
Env. and Development Gp. [IO]
Env. and Development Inst. [IO]
Env. and Natural Resources Found. [IO]
Env. Tobago [IO]
Environmental Action Found. [4558]
Environmental Alliance for Senior Involvement [11809]
Environmental Assessment Assn. [4559]
Environmental Bur. of Investigation [IO]
Environmental Bus. Coun. of New England [4560]
Environmental Camps for Conservation Awareness [IO]
Environmental Careers Org. [8388]
Environmental Conservation Org. [4561]
Environmental and Contamination Res. Center [7172]
Environmental Defence Soc. - New Zealand [IO]
Environmental Defender's Off. Network of Australia [IO]
Environmental Defense [4562]
Environmental Design Res. Assn. [5464]
Environmental and Energy Stud. Inst. [4507]
Environmental Entrepreneurs [4392]
Environmental Found. [IO]
Environmental Found. Bellona [IO]
Environmental Indus. Associations [3992]
Environmental Mgt. and Law Assn. - Hungary [IO]
Environmental Policy Center [5693]
Environmental Protection Assn. of Ghana [IO]
Environmental Risk Resources Assn. [4563]
Environmental Safety [5694]
Environmental Stud. Assn. of Canada [IO]
Environmental Stud. Gp. [IO]
Environmental Working Group [4564]
Eurasia Found. - Western NIS Regional Off. [IO]
European Assn. for Environmental Mgt. Educ. [IO]
European Assn. of Environmental and Rsrc. Economists [IO]
European Environmental Mutagen Soc. [IO]
European Fed. of Regional Energy and Environmental Agencies [IO]
European Soc. for Environmental History [IO]
Filipino Amer. Coalition for Environmental Solidarity [4634]
Floodplain Mgt. Assn. [5038]
Forest School Camps [IO]
Forest Stewardship Coun. - U.S. [4684]
ForestEthics [4685]
Forum Intl.: Intl. Ecosystems Univ. [18833]
Found. for Res. on Economics and the Env. [4396]
Friends of the Earth [4397]
Friends of the Everglades [4398]
Friends of the Trees Soc. [4400]
Fuller Found. [13118]
Gaia Inst. [4509]
Generation Green [17054]
George Wright Soc. [4565]
George Wright Society [IO]
Geraldine R. Dodge Found. [13119]
Gifts In Kind Intl. [12720]
Global Alliance for Incinerator Alternatives [5268]
Global Ecovillage Network Oceania/Asia [IO]
Global Environmental Mgt. Initiative [4628]
Global Green USA [4566]
Global Response [4567]
Global Response [IO]
Global Warming Intl. Center [IO]
Global Warming Intl. Center [4568]
Graduation Pledge Alliance [18617]
Grassland Heritage Found. [4404]
Green Action for Eco-Social Change [IO]

Green Cross Russia [IO]
Green Leaf Natl. Honor Soc. [24471]
The Green Life [4569]
Green Line [IO]
Green Meeting Indus. Coun. [2681]
Green Org. [IO]
Green Party of the U.S. [18325]
Green Seal [17331]
Green Step [IO]
Greening Australia [IO]
Greening Earth Soc. [4570]
Greenpeace Argentina [IO]
Greenpeace Australia Pacific [IO]
Greenpeace Belgium [IO]
Greenpeace Brazil [IO]
Greenpeace Canada [IO]
Greenpeace in Central and Eastern Europe [IO]
Greenpeace Chile [IO]
Greenpeace China [IO]
Greenpeace European Unit [IO]
Greenpeace France [IO]
Greenpeace Japan [IO]
Greenpeace Luxembourg [IO]
Greenpeace Mediterranean [IO]
Greenpeace Mexico [IO]
Greenpeace Netherlands [IO]
Greenpeace New Zealand [IO]
Greenpeace Nordic - Helsinki Off. [IO]
Greenpeace Russia [IO]
Greenpeace Slovakia [IO]
Greenpeace Spain [IO]
Greenpeace Sweden [IO]
Greenpeace Switzerland [IO]
Greenpeace UK [IO]
Greenpeace U.S.A. [IO]
Greenpeace U.S.A. [4571]
Groundwater Found. [5275]
Harmony Found. [IO]
Hastings Center [12125]
Hea. Care Without Harm [14634]
Healthy Building Network [4629]
Healthy Schools Network [4635]
Hearts and Minds Network [18730]
Henry M. Jackson Found. [17480]
Hikers Against Doo Doo [4572]
Household Hazardous Waste Proj. [5269]
Howard Gilman Found. [11504]
Hudson River Sloop Clearwater [10038]
Human Ecology Action League [14364]
Independence Plan for Neighborhood Councils [17219]
Independent Citizens Res. Found. for the Study of Degenerative Diseases [14263]
Indigenous Environmental Network [4624]
Indoor Air Quality Assn. [5093]
INFORM [18644]
Info. for Action [IO]
Inst. of Clean Air Companies [3071]
Inst. for Conservation Leadership [4573]
Inst. for Earth Educ. [8389]
Inst. for Earth Educ. [IO]
Inst. for European Environmental Policy [IO]
Inst. for Global Communications [7772]
Inst. of Global Env. and Soc. [4574]
Inst. of Global Env. and Soc. [IO]
Inst. for the Human Env. [4575]
Inst. of Professional Environmental Practice [4576]
Inst. of Professional Environmental Practice [IO]
Inst. for Rsrc. and Security Stud. [18457]
Inst. for Spiritual and Environmental Awareness [20572]
Inst. for Sustainable Desert Occupancy [4510]
Inst. for Tribal Environmental Professionals [19274]
Institution of Environmental Sciences [IO]
Interamerican Assn. for Environmental Defense [4630]
Interdisciplinary Environmental Assn. [4988]
Intermediate Tech. Development Gp. of North Am. [16997]
Intl. Arid Lands Consortium [4577]
Intl. Arid Lands Consortium [IO]
Intl. Assn. for the Advancement of Earth and Environmental Sciences [4511]

Intl. Assn. for the Plant Protection Sciences [6397]
Intl. Assn. for Soc. and Natural Resources [5039]
Intl. Assn. for the Stud. of Common Property [4410]
Intl. Biogeography Soc. [7122]
Intl. Bd. of Environmental Medicine [14365]
Intl. Center for the Solution of Environmental Problems [4578]
Intl. Center for the Solution of Environmental Problems [IO]
Intl. Centre for Conservation Educ. [IO]
Intl. Circle for the Promotion of Creation [IO]
Intl. Coalition for Children and the Env. [4636]
Intl. Compost Tea Coun. [5244]
Intl. Coun. for Local Environmental Initiatives [IO]
Intl. Coun. on Mining and Metals [IO]
Intl. Feng Shui Guild [9906]
The Intl. Found. [12434]
Intl. Humic Substances Soc. [7610]
Intl. League of Conservation Photographers [5080]
Intl. Lignin Inst. [IO]
Intl. Ozone Assn. [7109]
Intl. Ozone Assn. - EA3G [IO]
Intl. SeaKeepers Soc. [5010]
Intl. Ser. for the Acquisition of Agri-biotech Applications [6398]
Intl. Soc. for Biological and Environmental Repositories [6585]
Intl. Soc. for Bioluminescence and Chemiluminescence [7612]
Intl. Soc. of Doctors for the Env. [IO]
Intl. Soc. for Environmental Ethics [IO]
Intl. Soc. for Environmental Ethics [4579]
Intl. Soc. of Environmental Forensics [7098]
Intl. Soc. for Environmental Protection [IO]
Intl. Soc. of Indoor Air Quality and Climate [IO]
International Society for Industrial Ecology [IO]
Intl. Soc. for Indus. Ecology [4580]
Intl. Soc. for Reef Stud. [4581]
International Society for Reef Studies [IO]
Intl. Soc. of Regulatory Toxicology and Pharmacology [14570]
Intl. Sonoran Desert Alliance [4582]
International Sonoran Desert Alliance [IO]
Iranian Soc. of Environmentalists [IO]
Ittleson Found. [13122]
Japan Environmental Mgt. Assn. for Indus. [IO]
Japan for Sustainability [IO]
Jessie Smith Noyes Found. [4583]
Kathmandu Environmental Educ. Proj. [IO]
Keep Am. Beautiful [4584]
Keeping Track [5335]
Kids for a Clean Env. [4585]
Kids for Saving Earth [8390]
The Land Inst. [4647]
Latin Amer. Center of Social Ecology [IO]
Legacy Intl. [8665]
Legal Environmental Assistance Found. [4586]
Legambiente Campania [IO]
Low Impact Living Initiative [IO]
Media Access Proj. [17182]
Merck Family Fund [4587]
Midwest Center for Environmental Sci. and Public Policy [5095]
NAEM - Natl. Assn. for Environmental Mgt. [4588]
Natl. Assn. for Environmental Educ. [IO]
Natl. Assn. of Environmental Professionals [4589]
Natl. Assn. of Exotic Pest Plant Councils [5077]
Natl. Assn. for Humane and Environmental Educ. [11433]
Natl. Assn. of Regional Councils [6244]
Natl. Assn. of Univ. Fisheries and Wildlife Programs [8391]
Natl. Biosolids Partnership [5096]
Natl. Clean Cities [6399]
Natl. Collegiate Inventors and Innovators Alliance [7218]
Natl. Conf. of Local Environmental Hea. Administrators [16246]
Natl. Conservation District Employees Assn. [24209]
Natl. Coun. for Sci. and the Env. [7067]
Natl. Energy Found. [8392]

A star before a book entry number signifies that the name is not listed separately, but is mentioned within the entry.

Natl. Environmental Hea. Assn. [14367]
Natl. Environmental, Safety and Hea. Training Assn. [5097]
Natl. Environmental Satellite, Data, and Info. Ser. [4590]
Natl. Environmental Trust [4591]
Natl. Ethanol Vehicle Coalition [4776]
Natl. Forest Protection Alliance [4592]
Natl. Mitigation Banking Assn. [4425]
Natl. Network of Forest Practitioners [4692]
Natl. Registry of Environmental Professionals [4593]
Natl. Registry of Environmental Professionals [IO]
Natl. Religious Partnership for the Env. [19941]
Natl. Rural Hea. Assn. [16248]
Natl. Soc. of Environmental Consultants [3334]
Natl. Tree Soc. [4594]
Natl. Tribal Environmental Coun. [18097]
Natl. Whistleblower Center [12982]
Natl. Wildlife Fed. [4426]
Native Amer. Fish and Wildlife Soc. [4595]
Native Amer. Water Assn. [4012]
Native Habitat Org. [4596]
Nature and Environmental Writers - Coll. and Univ. Educators [8362]
Netherlands Soc. for Nature and Env. [IO]
Network for Environmental Policy Awareness [17501]
New Env. Assn. [4597]
New Zealand Assn. for Environmental Educ. [IO]
NextGen Energy Coun. [6966]
Nigeria Org. of Volunteers for the Preservation of the Env. [IO]
Nordic Soc. for Aerosol Res. [IO]
North Amer. Assn. for Environmental Educ. [8393]
North Amer. Coalition on Religion and Ecology [4598]
North Amer. Hazardous Materials Mgt. Assn. [4806]
North Amer. Weed Mgt. Assn. [4106]
Northwest Coalition for Alternatives to Pesticides [13328]
NSF Intl. [16249]
Occupational Knowledge Intl. [5099]
Ocean Res. and Conservation Assn. [4436]
Oilwatch Network [IO]
Open Space Inst. [4599]
Pachamama Alliance [5163]
Pacific Inst. for Stud. in Development, Env., and Security [12120]
PACON Intl. [5011]
Panos Inst. [12440]
Peace Rsrc. Proj. [18625]
People, Animals, Nature [13319]
People and Planet [IO]
People-Plant Coun. [4518]
People's Commn. on Env. and Development India [IO]
Peruvian Assn. for Conservation of Nature [IO]
Pesticide Action Network North Am. Regional Center [13329]
The Pesticide Stewardship Alliance [7068]
Pew Charitable Trusts [13129]
Planet 21 [IO]
Planet Aid [13144]
Planet Ark [IO]
Political Ecology Group [17502]
Political Economy Res. Center - The Center for Free Market Environmentalism [4600]
Pollution Probe [IO]
Preservation Inst. [13130]
Programa de las Naciones Unidas para el Medio Ambiente [IO]
Proj. EverGreen [4991]
Proj. Food, Land and People [4525]
Proj. Underground [18079]
Public Citizen Hea. Res. Gp. [16250]
Puerto Rico Water and Env. Assn. [5282]
Quebec-Labrador Foundation/Atlantic Center for the Env. [4601]
Quebec-Labrador Foundation/Atlantic Center for the Environment [IO]
Rachel Carson Coun. [13330]
Rainforest Relief [5164]
Recent Past Preservation Network [7162]

Reef Check [5012]
Reef Relief [5013]
ReefGuardian Intl. [5014]
Regional Environmental Centre for Central and Eastern Europe - Country Off. Lithuania [IO]
Rene Dubos Center for Human Environments [4602]
Renew Am. [4336]
Renew the Earth [7677]
Republicans for Environmental Protection [4444]
Resource Policy Inst. [4603]
River of Words [4186]
Rock the Earth [4604]
Rockefeller Family Fund [12737]
Royal Forest and Bird Protection Soc. of New Zealand [IO]
RuralScotland [IO]
Sacred Earth Network [IO]
Sacred Earth Network [4605]
Sahabat Alam Malaysia [IO]
Sahara and Sahel Observatory [IO]
Save Our Seas [4449]
Scenic Am. [4606]
Scherman Found. [13189]
Sci. Comm. on Problems of the Env. [IO]
SeaWeb [5015]
Shenandoah Natl. Park Assn. [10062]
Sierra Legal Defence Fund [IO]
Sierra Student Coalition [4521]
Singapore Env. Connecticut [IO]
SkyTruth [4637]
Soc. for Energy Educ. [6972]
Soc. for Environmental Graphic Design [1809]
Soc. of Environmental Understanding and Sustainability [5274]
Soc. for Marine Mammalogy [5017]
Soc. for Occupational and Environmental Hea. [15633]
Soc. for Philosophy in the Contemporary World [18274]
Soc. for Public Hea. Educ. [16254]
Socio-Ecological Union [IO]
Somali Environmental Protection and Anti-Desertification Org. [IO]
Southeast Desalting Assn. [5283]
Spill Control Assn. of Am. [3073]
Student Conservation Assn. [4455]
Student Environmental Action Coalition [4607]
Sustainable Obtainable Solutions [5129]
Sustainable Travel Intl. [5252]
Tall Timbers Land Conservancy [4456]
Tall Timbers Res. Sta. [4457]
Thailand Bus. Coun. for Sustainable Development [IO]
Theodore Roosevelt Conservation Partnership [4458]
Thoreau Inst. [4696]
Thorne Ecological Inst. [4523]
Thornton W. Burgess Soc. [4608]
Threshold [4609]
Tread Lightly! [5167]
Tree Musketeers [4459]
Tree of Peace Soc. [9913]
Trees, Water and People [4610]
Trees, Water and People [IO]
Tropical Flowering Tree Soc. [4986]
Turner Found. [4611]
Ukrainian Energy Brigades [IO]
United Kingdom-Ireland Controlled Release Soc. [IO]
United Nations Env. Programme - Kenya [IO]
United Nations Env. Programme - Regional Off. for Asia and the Pacific [IO]
United Nations Env. Programme - Regional Off. for Europe [IO]
United States-Asia Environmental Partnership [4612]
U.S. Comm. for the United Nations Env. Prog. [4613]
U.S.-Mexico Border Hea. Assn. [16256]
U.S. Soc. for Ecological Economics [6865]
West Coast Environmental Law [IO]
Western Gamebird Alliance [4466]
Wild Farm Alliance [4661]
Wilderness Medical Soc. [15184]

The Wilderness Soc. - Australia [IO]
Wilderness Volunteers [22774]
Wildlands Proj. [4614]
Wildlife and Env. Soc. of Southern Africa [IO]
Windstar Found. [4615]
Women's Coun. on Energy and the Env. [6977]
Women's Healthy Environments Network [IO]
Women's Voices for the Earth [4616]
World Assn. of Soil and Water Conservation [4473]
World Env. Center [4474]
World Environmental Org. [4475]
World Fed. of Public Hea. Associations [16258]
World Parks [4617]
World Parks [IO]
World Peace One [12367]
World Preserve [4476]
World Res. Found. [14604]
WorldWIDE Network, Women in Development and Environment [4618]
Young Naturalists' Circle [IO]
Zero Waste Alliance [5272]
Env. 2000 Found. [★IO]
Env. Africa [IO], Harare, Zimbabwe
Env. Assn; Puerto Rico Water and [5282]
Env; Assn. for the Stud. of Literature and [10414]
Env; Atlantic Center for the [★4601]
Environment Balance; Population- [12763]
Env. Bus. Australia [IO], Kingston, Australia
Env; Citizens for a Better [★5095]
Env; Concerned Educators Allied for a Safe [18148]
The Env. Coun. [IO], London, United Kingdom
Env., Culture, Agriculture, Res. and Development Soc. in Nepal [IO], Kathmandu, Nepal
Env. and Development in Action [IO], Ho Chi Minh City, Vietnam
Env. and Development Action in the Third World [IO], Dakar, Senegal
Env. and Development in the Arab World [IO], Tunis, Tunisia
Env. and Development Gp. [IO], Oxford, United Kingdom
Env. and Development Inst. [IO], Lima, Peru
Env; Energy in Man's [★8392]
Env. Fac; Global [★17851]
Env. Fac; Global [★IO]
Env; Found. for Res. on Economics and the [4396]
Env; Fund for Renewable Energy and the [★7677]
Env. and I [IO], Brest, Belarus
Env. Info; Center for Intl. [★4474]
Env; Inter-American Assn. of Sanitary Engg. and [★7589]
Env. and Justice; Center For Hea. [5266]
Env. Liaison Centre Intl. [IO], Nairobi, Kenya
Env. and Natural Resources Found. [IO], Buenos Aires, Argentina
Environment-People-Law [IO], Lviv, Ukraine
Env. Prog; Friends of the United Nations [★4613]
Env. Prog; Public Citizen's Critical Mass Energy and [18134]
Env. Proj; Public Citizen's Critical Mass Energy and [★18134]
Env; Rachel Carson Trust for the Living [★13330]
Env; Responsible Indus. for a Sound [2912]
Env. and Safety; Beach Educ. Advocates for Culture, Hea., [10761]
Env; Sculpture in the [17240]
Env. Testing Assn; Controlled [7790]
Env. Tobago [IO], Scarborough, Trinidad and Tobago
Env; Total Educ. in the Total [★4602]
Env; Women's Coun. on Energy and the [6977]
Environment; World Women in the [★4618]
Environmental Action [★4558]
Environmental Action Coalition - Defunct.
Environmental Action Found. [4558], 2300 Wilson Blvd., Ste. 400, Arlington, VA 22201, (703)837-5335
Environmental Action for Survival - Defunct.
Environmental Alert [IO], Kampala, Uganda
Environmental Alliance for Senior Involvement [11809], 5615 26th St. N, Arlington, VA 22207-1407, (703)241-4927
Environmental Assessment Assn. [4559], 1224 N Nokomis NE, Alexandria, MN 56308, (320)763-4320

Reference to "IO" in place of a book number signifies that the association may be found in the 45th edition of International Organizations.

Environmental Assn; Intl. Desalination and [★7831]
Environmental Awareness; Inst. for Spiritual and [20572]
Environmental Balancing Bur; Natl. [1895]
Environmental Bankers Assn. [473], 510 King St., Ste. 410, Alexandria, VA 22314, (703)549-0977
Environmental Building Assn; Energy and [619]
Environmental Bur. of Investigation [IO], Toronto, ON, Canada
Environmental Bus. Coun. of New England [4560], 18 Tremont St., Ste. 402, Boston, MA 02108, (617)725-0207
Environmental Camps for Conservation Awareness [IO], Kathmandu, Nepal
Environmental Careers Org. [IO], Calgary, AB, Canada
Environmental Careers Org. [8388], 30 Winter St., 6th Fl., Boston, MA 02108-4720, (617)426-4375
Environmental Clinics; Assn. of Occupational and [15629]
Environmental Coalition on Nuclear Power [18127], 433 Orlando Ave., State College, PA 16803, (814)237-3900
Environmental Commn. of Democratic Socialists of America - Defunct.
Environmental Communicators' Org. [IO], Hertford, United Kingdom
Environmental Conservation Org. [4561], PO Box 191, Hollow Rock, TN 38342, (731)986-0099
Environmental Consultants; Natl. Soc. of [3334]
Environmental and Contamination Res. Center [7172], U.S. Geological Survey, 4200 New Haven Rd., Columbia, MO 65201, (573)875-5399
Environmental Contractors Mgt. Assn. [IO], Hong Kong, People's Republic of China
Environmental Coun; Community [5267]
Environmental Coun; Natl. Tribal [18097]
Environmental Coun. of the States [4632], 444 N Capitol St. NW, Ste. 445, Washington, DC 20001, (202)624-3660
Environmental Crisis Fund [★4609]
Environmental Data and Info. Ser. [★4590]
Environmental Data Ser. [★4590]
Environmental Defence [IO], Toronto, ON, Canada
Environmental Defence Soc. - New Zealand [IO], Auckland, New Zealand
Environmental Defender's Off. Network of Australia [IO], Sydney, Australia
Environmental Defense [4562], 257 Park Ave. S, New York, NY 10010, (212)505-2100
Environmental Defense Fund [★4562]
Environmental Design Res. Assn. [5464], PO Box 7146, Edmond, OK 73083-7146, (405)330-4863
Environmental Development Action in the Third World [IO], Dakar, Senegal
Environmental Development Action in the Third World - Vietnam [★IO]
Environmental Development Assn./Ground Water Project; Natl. [★7835]
Environmental Development Assn./Resource Conservation and Recovery Act Project; Natl. [7835]
Environmental and Drug-Induced Pathology; Dept. of [★15867]

Environmental Education
The Adirondack Coun. [4340]
Alaska Coalition [4343]
Alliance for Intl. Reforestation [4344]
Alliance of Veterinarians for the Env. [4626]
Aquaculture Intl. [4169]
Aquatic Resources Educ. Assn. [7956]
Assn. of Lighting and Mercury Recyclers [5168]
Assn. Promoting Educ. and Conservation in Amazonia [5294]
Assn. of Univ. Leaders for a Sustainable Future [8483]
Assn. of Women in Environmental Professions [4619]
Beyond Pesticides - Natl. Coalition Against the Misuse of Pesticides [13322]
Big Thicket Assn. [4367]
Boreal Songbird Initiative [5302]
Center for Commun. Programs [12755]
Center for Energy Efficiency and Renewable Technologies [4526]

Center for Respect of Life and Env. [4620]
Children of the Earth United [4621]
Children of the Earth United [IO]
Community Environmental Coun. [5267]
Compassionate Kids [8384]
Concern [4545]
ConservAmerica [4378]
Earth Share [8394]
Eco-Spirit [4622]
EcoVentures Intl. [4623]
EcoVentures Intl. [IO]
Environmental Action Found. [4558]
Environmental Alliance for Senior Involvement [11809]
Environmental Defense [4562]
Environmental Policy Center [5693]
Forum Intl.: Intl. Ecosystems Univ. [18833]
Green Leaf Natl. Honor Soc. [24471]
Greenpeace U.S.A. [4571]
Indigenous Environmental Network [4624]
Interdisciplinary Environmental Assn. [4988]
Intl. Assn. for the Advancement of Earth and Environmental Sciences [4511]
Intl. Assn. for Soc. and Natural Resources [5039]
Intl. Center for the Solution of Environmental Problems [4578]
Intl. Coalition for Children and the Env. [4636]
Intl. Soc. of Environmental Forensics [7098]
Intl. Soc. for Reef Stud. [4581]
Keeping Track [5335]
Natl. Assn. for Humane and Environmental Educ. [11433]
Natl. Assn. of Marine Labs. [7274]
Natl. Environmental Educ. Found. [8395]
Natl. Environmental, Safety and Hea. Training Assn. [5097]
Natl. Mitigation Banking Assn. [4425]
Natl. Wildlife Fed. [4426]
Nature and Environmental Writers - Coll. and Univ. Educators [8362]
Negative Population Growth [12756]
Population Action Intl. [12758]
Population Commun. [12759]
Population Connection [12761]
Population Coun. [12762]
Population-Environment Balance [12763]
Population Inst. [12764]
Population Rsrc. Center [12765]
Rachel Carson Coun. [13330]
Rachel Carson Homestead Assn. [11143]
SkyTruth [4637]
Soc. of Building Sci. Educators [8363]
Soc. of Environmental Understanding and Sustainability [5274]
Student Conservation Assn. [4455]
Trips for Kids [8396]
Turner Found. [4611]
Wilderness Classroom Org. [8951]
Wilderness Educ. Assn. [8952]
William and Flora Hewlett Found. [13194]
World Preserve [4476]
Youth for Environmental Sanity [4625]
Environmental Educ; Center for [★4435]
Environmental Education Group - Defunct.
Environmental Educ; Natl. Assn. for Humane and [11433]
Environmental Educ. and Training Found; Natl. [★8395]
Environmental and Energy Study Conf. - Defunct.
Environmental and Energy Stud. Inst. [4507], 122 C St. NW, Ste. 630, Washington, DC 20001, (202)628-1400
Environmental and Engg. Geophysical Soc. [7140], 1720 S Bellaire, Ste. 110, Denver, CO 80222-4303, (303)531-7517
Environmental and Engineering Geophysical Society [IO], Denver, CO, United States
Environmental Engg; Inter-American Assn. of Sanitary and [★7589]
Environmental Engg. Professors; Assn. of [★9023]
Environmental Engg. and Sci. Professors; Assn. of [9023]
Environmental Engineers; Amer. Acad. of [6982]
Environmental Engineers; Inst. of [★7570]
Environmental Engineers Intersociety Bd. [★6982]

Environmental Engineers and Managers Institute [★6942]
Environmental Engineers and Managers Institute [★IO]
Environmental Engineers; Soc. of [★7570]
Environmental Entrepreneurs [4392], c/o Priscilla Bayley, Natural Resources Defense Coun., 40 W 20th St., New York, NY 10011, (212)727-4422
Environmental Equipment Inst. - Defunct.
Environmental Ethics; Forest Ser. Employees for [5126]
Environmental Found. [IO], Colombo, Sri Lanka
Environmental Found. Bellona [IO], Oslo, Norway
Environmental Fund [★12763]
Environmental Graphic Design; Soc. for [1809]
Environmental Graphic Designers; Soc. of [★1809]

Environmental Health
African Amer. Environmentalist Assn. [4529]
Air Barrier Assn. of Am. [587]
Alliance of Veterinarians for the Env. [4626]
Amer. Acad. of Environmental Medicine [14360]
Amer. Acad. of Environmental Medicine [IO]
Amer. Acad. of Sanitarians [16383]
Amer. Assn. of Pesticide Safety Educators [4627]
Amer. Coll. of Occupational and Environmental Medicine [15624]
Amer. Conf. of Governmental Indus. Hygienists [15625]
Amer. Coun. on Sci. and Hea. [14539]
Amer. Environmental Hea. Found. [14361]
Amer. Industrial Health Coun. [15626]
Amer. Indus. Hygiene Assn. [15627]
Amer. Osteopathic Coll. of Occupational and Preventive Medicine [15802]
Amer. Public Hea. Assn. [16236]
Argentine Assn. of Doctors for the Env. [IO]
Assn. for Env. and Public Hea. [IO]
Assn. for the Environmental Hea. of Soils [5221]
Assn. of Lighting and Mercury Recyclers [5168]
Assn. of Physicians for the Env. of Turkey [IO]
Assn. of Physicians and Medical Workers for Social Responsibility [IO]
Assn. Promoting Educ. and Conservation in Amazonia [5294]
Austrian Doctors for a Healthy Env. [IO]
Benevolent Org. for Development, Hea., and Insight [IO]
Boreal Songbird Initiative [5302]
Campus Safety, Hea. and Environmental Mgt. Assn. [4300]
Caribbean Environmental Hea. Inst. [IO]
Center for Health and the Global Environment [IO]
Center for Hea. and the Global Env. [14362]
Center Perzent - Karakalpak Center for Reproductive Hea. and Env. [IO]
Center for Respect of Life and Env. [4620]
Chartered Inst. of Environmental Hea. [IO]
Children of the Earth United [4621]
Children's Environmental Hea. Network [14363]
Citizens Coal Coun. [4299]
Clean Beaches Coun. [4540]
Clean Production Action [4631]
Coalition for Environmentally Safe Communities [12118]
Croatian Soc. of Environmental Hea. [IO]
Doctors for the Env. - Australia [IO]
Doctors for the Env. - Switzerland [IO]
Dutch Assn. of Environmental Medicine [IO]
EarthEcho Intl. [4391]
Ecological Soc. of Physicians [IO]
EcoVentures Intl. [4623]
Environmental Res. and Educ. Found. [4633]
Filipino Amer. Coalition for Environmental Solidarity [4634]
Food Alliance [4676]
Friends of Virgin Islands Natl. Park [5264]
Generation Green [17054]
Genetic Engg. Action Network [6615]
Global Alliance for Incinerator Alternatives [5268]
Global Environmental Mgt. Initiative [4628]
Global Green USA [4566]
Green Meeting Indus. Coun. [2681]
Healthy Building Network [4629]
Healthy Schools Network [4635]

A star before a book entry number signifies that the name is not listed separately, but is mentioned within the entry.

Human Ecology Action League [14364]
Indigenous Environmental Network [4624]
Indoor Air Quality Assn. [5093]
Interamerican Assn. for Environmental Defense [4630]
Interamerican Assn. for Environmental Defense [IO]
Interdisciplinary Environmental Assn. [4988]
Intl. Assn. of Medicine and Biology of Env. [IO]
Intl. Bd. of Environmental Medicine [IO]
Intl. Bd. of Environmental Medicine [14365]
Intl. Coalition for Children and the Env. [4636]
Intl. Programme on Chem. Safety [IO]
Intl. Soc. of Environmental Forensics [7098]
Intl. Soc. for Preservation of the Tropical Rainforest [5162]
Intl. Soc. of Regulatory Toxicology and Pharmacology [14570]
Iranian Assn. of Environmental Hea. [IO]
Irish Doctors Environmental Assn. [IO]
MEDACT [IO]
Mercury Policy Proj. [18745]
Natl. Assn. of Exotic Pest Plant Councils [5077]
Natl. Biosolids Partnership [5096]
Natl. Center for Environmental Hea. Strategies [14366]
Natl. Conf. of Local Environmental Hea. Administrators [16246]
Natl. Environmental Coalition of Native Americans [5037]
Natl. Environmental Hea. Assn. [14367]
Natl. Environmental Hea. Sci. and Protection Accreditation Coun. [14368]
Natl. Environmental Trust [4591]
Natl. Ethanol Vehicle Coalition [4776]
Natl. Network of Forest Practitioners [4692]
Natl. Religious Partnership for the Env. [19941]
Natl. Rural Hea. Assn. [16248]
NSF Intl. [16249]
Occupational Knowledge Intl. [5099]
Oil Companies' European Org. for Environmental and Hea. Protection [IO]
The Pesticide Stewardship Alliance [7068]
Protect All Children's Env. [14369]
Public Citizen Hea. Res. Gp. [16250]
REAP Intl. [12940]
Reef Relief [5013]
ReefGuardian Intl. [5014]
Renew Am. [4336]
Rock the Earth [4604]
Royal Environmental Hea. Inst. of Scotland [IO]
SkyTruth [4637]
Soc. of Environmental Toxicology and Chemistry [14370]
Soc. of Environmental Understanding and Sustainability [5274]
Soc. for Human Ecology [14371]
Soc. for Human Ecology [IO]
Soc. for Occupational and Environmental Hea. [15633]
Soc. for Public Hea. Educ. [16254]
Sustainable Obtainable Solutions [5129]
Swedish Doctors for the Env. [IO]
Towards Freedom [17503]
Trees, Water and People [4610]
U.S.-Mexico Border Hea. Assn. [16256]
Women's Voices for the Earth [4616]
World Fed. of Public Hea. Associations [16258]
World Parks [4617]
Youth for Environmental Sanity [4625]
Zero Waste Alliance [5272]
Environmental Hea. Accreditation Coun. [★14368]
Environmental Hea. Administrators; Conf. of Local [★16246]
Environmental Hea. Administrators; Natl. Conf. of Local [16246]
Environmental Hea. Assn. of New Jersey [★14366]
Environmental Health Network - Defunct.
Environmental, Hea. and Safety Coun; Silicones [821]
Environmental Hea. Sci. and Protection Accreditation Coun; Natl. [★14368]
Environmental Hea; Soc. for Occupational and [15633]
Environmental Hea. of Soils; Assn. for the [5221]

Environmental Indus. Commn. [IO], London, United Kingdom
Environmental Indus. Associations [3992], 4301 Connecticut Ave. NW, Ste. 300, Washington, DC 20008-2304, (202)244-4700
Environmental Industry Coun. - Address unknown since 2003.
Environmental Info. Assn. [620], 6935 Wisconsin Ave., Ste. 306, Chevy Chase, MD 20815-6112, (301)961-4999
Environmental Info. Assn; NAC - [★620]
Environmental Intern Programs; Center for [★8388]
Environmental Journalists; Soc. of [8718]
Environmental Law
Alliance for Sustainable Jobs and the Env. [24053]
Amer. Farmland Trust [16951]
Assn. of State and Interstate Water Pollution Control Administrators [5688]
Bangladesh Environmental Lawyers Assn. [IO]
Bellona Europe [IO]
Canadian Environmental Law Assn. [IO]
Canadian Inst. for Environmental Law and Policy [IO]
Canadian Inst. of Resources Law [IO]
Center for Intl. Environmental Law [IO]
Center for Intl. Environmental Law [5689]
Center for Respect of Life and Env. [4620]
Coalition for Environmentally Responsible Economies [4544]
Consumer Energy Coun. of Am. Res. Found. [17496]
Earthjustice [5690]
Earthjustice [IO]
Ecologic - Inst. for Intl. and European Environmental Policy [IO]
Energy Future Coalition [6952]
Environment-People-Law [IO]
Environmental Defense [4562]
Environmental Law Alliance Worldwide - U.S. [5691]
Environmental Law Alliance Worldwide - U.S. [IO]
Environmental Law Inst. [IO]
Environmental Law Inst. [5692]
Environmental and Natural Resources Law Center [IO]
Environmental Policy Center [5693]
Environmental Safety [5694]
Found. for Intl. Environmental Law and Development [IO]
Greenaction for Hea. and Environmental Justice [17699]
Harvard Environmental Law Soc. [5695]
Hastings Center [12125]
Independence Inst. [17120]
Interamerican Assn. for Environmental Defense [4630]
Intl. Coun. of Environmental Law [IO]
Intl. Soc. of Environmental Forensics [7098]
Midwest Center for Environmental Sci. and Public Policy [5095]
Natl. Assn. of Clean Air Agencies [5696]
Natl. Assn. of Environmental Law Societies [5697]
Natl. Assn. of Environmental Professionals [4589]
Natl. Endangered Species Act Reform Coalition [17504]
Natl. Environmental Trust [4591]
Republicans for Environmental Protection [4444]
Ruckus Soc. [18178]
United Kingdom Environmental Law Assn. [IO]
Environmental Law Alliance Worldwide - U.S. [IO], Eugene, OR, United States
Environmental Law Alliance Worldwide - U.S. [5691], 1877 Garden Ave., Eugene, OR 97403, (541)687-8454
Environmental Law Assn. [★IO]
Environmental Law Inst. [IO], Washington, DC, United States
Environmental Law Inst. [5692], 2000 L St. NW, Ste. 620, Washington, DC 20036, (202)939-3800
Environmental Leadership Prog. [★4460]
Environmental Mgt. Assn. [2463], c/o Bill Doetsch, Pres., PO Box 610548, Port Huron, MI 48061, (810)982-7271
Environmental Mgt. Assn. - Address unknown since 2003.

Environmental Mgt. and Law Assn. - Hungary [IO], Budapest, Hungary
Environmental Mgt; Natl. Assn. for [★4588]
Environmental Media Services [★5032]
Environmental Mediation Intl. - Defunct.
Environmental Medicine; Amer. Coll. of Occupational and [15624]
Environmental Monitoring Gp. [IO], Mowbray, Republic of South Africa
Environmental Mutagen Societies; Intl. Assn. of [6578]
Environmental Mutagen Soc. [6575], 1821 Michael Faraday Dr., Ste. 300, Reston, VA 20190, (703)438-8220
Environmental and Natural Resources Law Center [IO], San Jose, Costa Rica
Environmental Network; Evangelical [20003]
Environmental Network; Indigenous [4624]
Environmental Partners [★17331]
Environmental and Planning Engineers' Assn. [IO], Milan, Italy
Environmental Policy Center [5693], c/o Dept. of Environmental Hea., Univ. of Cincinnati, PO Box 670056, Cincinnati, OH 45267-0056, (513)558-5439
Environmental Policy Inst. [★4397]
Environmental Professionals; Natl. Assn. of Local Govt. [6125]
Environmental Project on Central America - Defunct.
Environmental Protection Assn. of Ghana [IO], Kumasi, Ghana
Environmental Protection Res. Found. [IO], Sangli, India
Environmental Public Advocacy Gp. [★IO]
Environmental Quality
African Amer. Environmentalist Assn. [4529]
Air Barrier Assn. of Am. [587]
Alliance for Community Trees [4678]
Alliance for Sustainable Jobs and the Env. [24053]
Am. the Beautiful Fund [4532]
Amer. Assn. for Fuel Cells [6937]
Amer. Decentralized Wastewater Assn. [4006]
Amer. Land Conservancy [4348]
Amer. Safe Climbing Assn. [21950]
The Antarctica Proj. [7517]
Aquaculture Certification Coun. [4168]
Aquatic Animal Life Support Operators [7279]
Aquatic Resources Educ. Assn. [7956]
Assn. for the Environmental Hea. of Soils [5221]
Assn. of Lighting and Mercury Recyclers [5168]
Basel Action Network [18797]
Big Thicket Natural Heritage Trust [4368]
Carrying Capacity Network [6859]
Center for a New Amer. Dream [17260]
Center for Respect of Life and Env. [4620]
Chem. Injury Info. Network [16656]
Clean Energy Gp. [6948]
Clean Energy States Alliance [6949]
Clean Islands Intl. [4541]
Clean Production Action [4631]
Clean Production Action [IO]
Coalition for Environmentally Safe Communities [12118]
Community Environmental Coun. [5267]
Conservation Intl. - USA [4381]
Coun. for Biotechnology Info. [6614]
Earth Liberation Front [4551]
Eco-Spirit [4622]
Ecological Landscaping Assn. [4989]
EcoVentures Intl. [4623]
Environmental Coun. of the States [4632]
Environmental Res. and Educ. Found. [4633]
Environmental Risk Resources Assn. [4563]
Environmental Working Group [4564]
European Christian Environmental Network [IO]
Filipino Amer. Coalition for Environmental Solidarity [4634]
German Soc. for Mining, Metallurgy, Rsrc. and Environmental Tech. [IO]
Get Oil Out! [5092]
Global Alliance for Incinerator Alternatives [5268]
Global Aquaculture Alliance [4173]
Global Green USA [4566]
Green Empowerment [4335]

Reference to "IO" in place of a book number signifies that the association may be found in the 45th edition of International Organizations.

Encyclopedia of Associations, 46th Edition

3411

Green Meeting Indus. Coun. [2681]
Greenpeace U.S.A. [4571]
Healthy Building Network [4629]
Healthy Schools Network [4635]
Holistic Mgt. Intl. [4408]
Indigenous Environmental Network [4624]
Indoor Air Quality Assn. [5093]
Inst. of Clean Air Companies [3071]
Interamerican Assn. for Environmental Defense [4630]
Intl. Assn. for the Advancement of Earth and Environmental Sciences [4511]
Intl. Coalition for Children and the Env. [4636]
Intl. Coalition for Children and the Env. [IO]
Intl. Rivers Network [7833]
Intl. Soc. for Indus. Ecology [4580]
Intl. Soc. for Preservation of the Tropical Rainforest [5162]
Just Transition Alliance [24105]
JustAct: Youth Action for Global Justice [18853]
Midwest Center for Environmental Sci. and Public Policy [5095]
Natl. Assn. of Black Scuba Divers [23711]
Natl. Assn. of Exotic Pest Plant Councils [5077]
Natl. Assn. of Mold Professionals [1330]
Natl. Clean Cities [6399]
Natl. Coun. for Sci. and the Env. [7067]
Natl. Network of Forest Practitioners [4692]
Natl. Org. of Remediators and Mold Inspectors [1331]
Natl. Wildlife Fed. [4426]
Native Amer. Water Assn. [4012]
Nature and Environmental Writers - Coll. and Univ. Educators [8362]
New Forests Proj. [12436]
North Amer. Hazardous Materials Mgt. Assn. [4806]
One Earth One Justice [12437]
Radical Philosophy Assn. [18273]
Rainforest Relief [5164]
REAP Intl. [12940]
Rene Dubos Center for Human Environments [4602]
Renew Am. [4336]
Rock the Earth [4604]
SkyTruth [4637]
Soc. of Environmental Understanding and Sustainability [5274]
Surface Trans. Policy Proj. [18750]
Sustainable Obtainable Solutions [5129]
Trees, Water and People [4610]
United States-Asia Environmental Partnership [4612]
US Fuel Cell Coun. [6976]
World Forestry Center [4701]
World Parks [4617]
World Preserve [4476]
Youth for Environmental Sanity [4625]
Zero Waste Alliance [5272]
Enval. Repercussions; Save Us From Formaldehyde [★13324]
Environmental Res. and Educ. Found. [4633], 901 N Pitt St., Ste. 270, Alexandria, VA 22314, (703)299-5139
Environmental Res. Found. [13599], PO Box 160, New Brunswick, NJ 08903-0160, (732)828-9995
Environmental Rsrc. [★4558]
Environmental and Rsrc. Economists; Assn. of [4359]
Environmental Responsibility Program - Defunct.
Environmental Rights Action [IO], Benin City, Nigeria
Environmental Risk Resources Assn. [4563], 4901 Pine Cone Cir., Middleton, WI 53562, (877)735-0800
Environmental Safety [5694], 1700 N Moore St., Ste. 2000, Arlington, VA 22209, (703)527-8300
Environmental Safety Coun; Amer. [★5694]
Environmental, Safety and Hea. Assn; Semiconductor [6931]
Environmental, Safety and Hea. Training Assn; Natl. [5097]
Environmental Sanitarians; Intl. Assn. of Milk, Food and [★5739]
Environmental Sanity; Youth for [4625]
Environmental Sciences; Inst. of [★7570]

Environmental Sciences; Inter-American Assn. of Sanitary Engg. and [★7589]
Environmental Sciences and Tech; Inst. of [7570]
Environmental Services of the Amer. Hosp. Assn; Amer. Soc. for Healthcare [14866]
Environmental Services Assn. [IO], London, United Kingdom
Environmental Stud. Assn. of Canada [IO], Waterloo, ON, Canada
Environmental Stud. Gp. [IO], Mexico City, Mexico
Environmental Stud. in Tel Aviv; CBI Center for [★IO]
Environmental Stud. in Tel Aviv; CBI Center for [★10254]
Environmental Systems Contractors Assn; Natl. [★1872]
Environmental Task Force [★4558]
Environmental and Tech. Assn. for the Paper Sack Indus. [IO], Glasgow, United Kingdom
Environmental Technologists; Fed. of [5090]
Environmental Tech; Alliance for [1632]
Environmental Tech. Coun. [3993], 734 15th St. NW, Ste. 720, Washington, DC 20005-1013, (202)783-0870
Environmental Technology Seminar - Address unknown since 1999.
Environmental Thrust - Defunct.
Environmental and Toxicologic Pathology; Dept. of [15867]
Environmental Training Assn; Natl. [★5097]
Environmental Transport Assn. [IO], Weybridge, United Kingdom
Environmental Working Group [4564], 1436 U St. NW, Ste. 100, Washington, DC 20009, (202)667-6982
Environmental Writers - Coll. and Univ. Educators; Nature and [8362]
Environmentalists for Full Employment - Defunct.
Environnement et developpement du tiers monde [★IO]
Environnement; Assn. Internationale de Societes s'Occupant des Agents Mutagenes Presents dans l' [★6578]
Environnement et Developpement du Tiers Monde [★IO]
Environnement Jeunesse [IO], Montreal, QC, Canada
Enzipan de Colombia [IO], Bogota, Colombia
Enzymology
  European Study Group on Lysosomal Diseases [IO]
EP Technologists; Amer. Bd. of Registration of EEG and [14305]
Epagneul Breton USA [22264], 288 Clayton St., Ste. 204, Denver, CO 80206
Epagneul Breton USA [IO], Denver, CO, United States
Ephemera
  Ephemera Soc. of Am. [22411]
  Natl. Assn. of Paper and Advt. Collectors [22412]
Ephemera Soc. [IO], Northwood, United Kingdom
Ephemera Soc. of Am. [22411], PO Box 95, Cazenovia, NY 13035-0095, (315)655-9139
Ephphatha Services [★20216]
Ephphatha Services for the Deaf and Blind [★20216]
Ephphatha Services - Div. for Services and Mission in Am. [★20216]
EPIC - Electronically Published Internet Connection [22914], c/o Barbara Woodward, Treas., PO Box 2278, Glen Rose, TX 76043
Epic Enterprises [★396]
Epicor Users Gp. [6793], PO Box 10368, Lancaster, PA 17605-0368, (717)209-7177
Epidemiologists of Am; Soc. of Healthcare [★14378]
Epidemiologists of Am; Soc. of Hosp. [★14378]
Epidemiologists; Conf. of State and Territorial [★14374]
Epidemiology
  Aeras Global TB Vaccine Found. [14372]
  Aeras Global TB Vaccine Foundation [IO]
  Amer. Coll. of Epidemiology [14373]
  Assn. for Professionals in Infection Control and Epidemiology [14947]
  British Infection Soc. [IO]

Certification Bd. of Infection Control and Epidemiology [14702]
  Community and Hosp. Infection Control Assn. - Canada [IO]
  Community Info. and Epidemiological Technologies [IO]
  Community Info. and Epidemiological Technologies [12121]
  Coun. of State and Territorial Epidemiologists [14374]
  Disinfected Mail Stud. Circle [IO]
  Dystrophic Epidermolysis Bullosa Res. Assn. - Europe [IO]
  Hong Kong Epidemiological Assn. [IO]
  Intl. Clinical Epidemiology Network [14375]
  Intl. Epidemiological Assn. [IO]
  Intl. Genetic Epidemiology Soc. [IO]
  Intl. Genetic Epidemiology Soc. [14376]
  Intl. Regional Org. of Plant Protection and Animal Hea. [IO]
  Intl. Soc. for Disease Surveillance [14269]
  Intl. Soc. for Pharmacoepidemiology [15939]
  Natl. Found. for Infectious Diseases [14953]
  Soc. for Epidemiologic Res. [14377]
  Soc. for Healthcare Epidemiology of Am. [14378]
Epidermolysis Bullosa Res. Assn. of Am; Dystrophic [14200]
EPIE Inst. [8559], PO Box 590, Hampton Bays, NY 11946-0509, (631)728-9100
Epigraphia; Sociedad de [★10130]
Epigraphic Soc. [6445], c/o Mr. Donal B. Buchanan, Sec.-Treas./Ed., 97 Village Post Rd., Danvers, MA 01923, (978)774-1275
Epigraphic Soc; Mexican [10130]
Epilepsi Cymru [★IO]
Epilepsie Canada [★IO]
Epilepsy
  Albanian League Against Epilepsy [IO]
  Algerian League Against Epilepsy [IO]
  Amer. Epilepsy Soc. [14379]
  Argentinean League Against Epilepsy [IO]
  Armenian Natl. League Against Epilepsy [IO]
  Asian and Oceanian Epilepsy Assn. [IO]
  Austrian League Against Epilepsy [IO]
  Azerbaijan League Against Epilepsy [IO]
  Belgian League Against Epilepsy [IO]
  Brainwave The Irish Epilepsy Assn. [IO]
  Brasilian League Against Epilepsy [IO]
  British Epilepsy Assn. [IO]
  Bulgarian Assn. Against Epilepsy [IO]
  Burkina Faso League Against Epilepsy [IO]
  Canadian League Against Epilepsy [IO]
  Colombian League Against Epilepsy [IO]
  Costa Rica Chap. of the ILAE [IO]
  Croatian League Against Epilepsy [IO]
  Cuban League Against Epilepsy [IO]
  Czech League Against Epilepsy [IO]
  Danish Epilepsy Soc. [IO]
  Dominican Republic League Against Epilepsy [IO]
  Dutch League Against Epilepsy [IO]
  Ecuadorian League Against Epilepsy [IO]
  Edmonton Epilepsy Assn. [IO]
  Egyptian Soc. Against Epilepsy [IO]
  Epilepsy Assn. of the Australian Capital Territory [IO]
  Epilepsy Assn. of Calgary [IO]
  Epilepsy Assn. - Central Alberta Off. [IO]
  Epilepsy Assn. of Nova Scotia [IO]
  Epilepsy Assn. of Pakistan [IO]
  Epilepsy Assn. of South Australia and Northern Territory [IO]
  Epilepsy Assn. of Tasmania - Burnie [IO]
  Epilepsy Assn. of Tasmania - Hobart [IO]
  Epilepsy Assn. of Tasmania - Launceston [IO]
  Epilepsy Assn. of Western Australia [IO]
  Epilepsy Australia - New South Wales [IO]
  Epilepsy Brampton [IO]
  Epilepsy Canada [IO]
  Epilepsy Care Gp. - Singapore [IO]
  Epilepsy Cornwall [IO]
  Epilepsy Durham Region [IO]
  Epilepsy Found. [14380]
  Epilepsy Huron-Perth-Bruce [IO]
  Epilepsy Kingston [IO]
  Epilepsy Mississauga [IO]

A star before a book entry number signifies that the name is not listed separately, but is mentioned within the entry.

Epilepsy New Zealand [IO]
Epilepsy New Zealand - Canterbury [IO]
Epilepsy New Zealand - North Shore and Rodney [IO]
Epilepsy New Zealand - Otago [IO]
Epilepsy New Zealand - Rotorua [IO]
Epilepsy New Zealand - South Canterbury [IO]
Epilepsy New Zealand - Southland Br. [IO]
Epilepsy New Zealand - Taranaki [IO]
Epilepsy New Zealand - Waikato [IO]
Epilepsy New Zealand - Wanganui [IO]
Epilepsy New Zealand - Wellington [IO]
Epilepsy Newfoundland and Labrador [IO]
Epilepsy Niagara [IO]
Epilepsy North Bay [IO]
Epilepsy Ontario [IO]
Epilepsy Ottawa-Carleton [IO]
Epilepsy Peterborough [IO]
Epilepsy Queensland Inc. [IO]
Epilepsy Regina [IO]
Epilepsy Saskatoon [IO]
Epilepsy Sault Ste. Marie [IO]
Epilepsy Scotland [IO]
Epilepsy Simcoe County [IO]
Epilepsy Soc. of Australia [IO]
Epilepsy Soc. of Cyprus [IO]
Epilepsy Soc. of Malta [IO]
Epilepsy Soc. of Thailand [IO]
Epilepsy South Africa [IO]
Epilepsy Sudbury/Manitoulin [IO]
Epilepsy Therapy Development Proj. [14381]
Epilepsy Toronto [IO]
Epilepsy Wales [IO]
Epilepsy Waterloo-Wellington [IO]
Epilepsy Windsor/Essex County [IO]
Epilepsy York Region [IO]
Epileptology Soc. of Chile [IO]
Esther A. and Joseph Klingenstein Fund [15106]
Estonian League Against Epilepsy [IO]
European Epilepsy Acad. [IO]
Finnish Epilepsy Soc. [IO]
Fraser Valley Epilepsy Soc. [IO]
French League Against Epilepsy [IO]
Georgian Soc. Against Epilepsy [IO]
German League Against Epilepsy [IO]
Greek League Against Epilepsy [IO]
Guatemala League Against Epilepsy [IO]
Honduran Epilepsy Soc. [IO]
Hong Kong Chap. of the ILAE [IO]
Hungarian Chap. of the ILAE [IO]
Indian Epilepsy Soc. [IO]
Indonesian Soc. Against Epilepsy [IO]
Intl. Bur. for Epilepsy [IO]
Intl. League Against Epilepsy [IO]
Intl. League Against Epilepsy of United Kingdom [IO]
Iraq Soc. Against Epilepsy [IO]
Irish Epilepsy League [IO]
Israel Chap. of the ILAE [IO]
Italian League Against Epilepsy [IO]
Jamaican Chap. of ILAE [IO]
Japan Epilepsy Soc. [IO]
Jordan Chap. of Epilepsy [IO]
Kazakhstan Natl. League Against Epilepsy [IO]
Kenya Soc. for Epilepsy [IO]
Korean Epilepsy Soc. [IO]
Kyrgyz League Against Epilepsy [IO]
Latvian League Against Epilepsy [IO]
League Against Epilepsy of Republic Macedonia [IO]
Lebanese League Against Epilepsy [IO]
Manitoba Epilepsy Assn. [IO]
Mexican League Against Epilepsy [IO]
Moldavian League Against Epilepsy [IO]
Mongolian Epilepsy Soc. [IO]
Morrocan League Against Epilepsy [IO]
Natl. Soc. for Epilepsy [IO]
Nepal Epilepsy Soc. [IO]
Nicaragua Chap. of the ILAE [IO]
Norwegian Epilepsy Assn. [IO]
Panama League Against Epilepsy [IO]
Paraguayan League Against Epilepsy [IO]
Parents Against Childhood Epilepsy [14382]
Peruvian League Against Epilepsy [IO]
Philippine League Against Epilepsy [IO]

Polish Assn. of People Suffering From Epilepsy [IO]
Portuguese League Against Epilepsy [IO]
Qatar League Against Epilepsy [IO]
Romania Soc. Against Epilepsy [IO]
Russian League Against Epilepsy [IO]
Saudi Chap. of Epilepsy [IO]
Senegal League Against Epilepsy [IO]
Slovak League Against Epilepsy [IO]
Slovenian League Against Epilepsy [IO]
Soc. of Epileptologists of Lithuania [IO]
Southern Alberta Epilepsy Assn. [IO]
Spanish League Against Epilepsy [IO]
Swedish Epilepsy Soc. [IO]
Swiss League Against Epilepsy [IO]
Syrian Chap. of Epilepsy [IO]
Taiwan Epilepsy Soc. [IO]
Tunisian Assn. Against Epilepsy [IO]
Turkish League Against Epilepsy [IO]
Ukrainian League Against Epilepsy [IO]
Uruguayan League Against Epilepsy [IO]
Venezuelean League Against Epilepsy [IO]
Epilepsy Action [★IO]
Epilepsy Action Scotland [★IO]
Epilepsy Assn. of the Australian Capital Territory [IO], Holder, Australia
Epilepsy Assn. of Calgary [IO], Calgary, AB, Canada
Epilepsy Assn. - Central Alberta Off. [IO], Red Deer, AB, Canada
Epilepsy Assn. of Nova Scotia [IO], Halifax, NS, Canada
Epilepsy Assn. of Pakistan [IO], Karachi, Pakistan
Epilepsy Assn. of Scotland [★IO]
Epilepsy Assn. of South Australia and Northern Territory [IO], Woodville, Australia
Epilepsy Assn. of Tasmania - Burnie [IO], Hobart, Australia
Epilepsy Assn. of Tasmania - Hobart [IO], Hobart, Australia
Epilepsy Assn. of Tasmania - Launceston [IO], Launceston, Australia
Epilepsy Assn. of Western Australia [IO], Nedlands, Australia
Epilepsy Australia - New South Wales [IO], Parramatta, Australia
Epilepsy Brampton [IO], Brampton, ON, Canada
Epilepsy Canada [IO], Toronto, ON, Canada
Epilepsy Care Gp. - Singapore [IO], Singapore, Singapore
Epilepsy Concern Service Group - Defunct.
Epilepsy Cornwall [IO], Cornwall, ON, Canada
Epilepsy Durham Region [IO], Whitby, ON, Canada
Epilepsy Found. [14380], 8301 Professional Pl., Landover, MD 20785-2223, (301)459-3700
Epilepsy Huron-Perth-Bruce [IO], Clinton, ON, Canada
Epilepsy; Intl. League Against [IO]
Epilepsy Kingston [IO], Kingston, ON, Canada
Epilepsy Mississauga [IO], Mississauga, ON, Canada
Epilepsy New Zealand [IO], Hamilton, New Zealand
Epilepsy New Zealand - Canterbury [IO], Christchurch, New Zealand
Epilepsy New Zealand - North Shore and Rodney [IO], North Shore City, New Zealand
Epilepsy New Zealand - Otago [IO], Dunedin, New Zealand
Epilepsy New Zealand - Rotorua [IO], Rotorua, New Zealand
Epilepsy New Zealand - South Canterbury [IO], Timaru, New Zealand
Epilepsy New Zealand - Southland Br. [IO], Invercargill, New Zealand
Epilepsy New Zealand - Taranaki [IO], New Plymouth, New Zealand
Epilepsy New Zealand - Waikato [IO], Hamilton, New Zealand
Epilepsy New Zealand - Wanganui [IO], Wanganui, New Zealand
Epilepsy New Zealand - Wellington [IO], Wellington, New Zealand
Epilepsy Newfoundland and Labrador [IO], St. John's, NL, Canada
Epilepsy Niagara [IO], Niagara Falls, ON, Canada
Epilepsy North Bay [IO], North Bay, ON, Canada

Epilepsy Ontario [IO], Thornhill, ON, Canada
Epilepsy Ottawa-Carleton [IO], Ottawa, ON, Canada
Epilepsy Peterborough [IO], Peterborough, ON, Canada
Epilepsy Queensland Inc. [IO], Coorparoo, Australia
Epilepsy Regina [IO], Regina, SK, Canada
Epilepsy Saskatoon [IO], Saskatoon, SK, Canada
Epilepsy Sault Ste. Marie [IO], Sault Ste. Marie, ON, Canada
Epilepsy Scotland [IO], Glasgow, United Kingdom
Epilepsy Simcoe County [IO], Barrie, ON, Canada
Epilepsy Soc. of Australia [IO], Parkville, Australia
Epilepsy Soc. of Cyprus [IO], Nicosia, Cyprus
Epilepsy Soc. of Malta [IO], Msida, Malta
Epilepsy Soc. of Thailand [IO], Bangkok, Thailand
Epilepsy South Africa [IO], Observatory, Republic of South Africa
Epilepsy Sudbury/Manitoulin [IO], Sudbury, ON, Canada
Epilepsy Therapy Development Proj. [14381], 11921 Freedom Dr., Ste. 730, Reston, VA 20190, (703)437-4250
Epilepsy Toronto [IO], Toronto, ON, Canada
Epilepsy Wales [IO], Cardiff, United Kingdom
Epilepsy Waterloo-Wellington [IO], Kitchener, ON, Canada
Epilepsy Windsor/Essex County [IO], Windsor, ON, Canada
Epilepsy York Region [IO], Richmond Hill, ON, Canada
Epileptology Soc. of Chile [IO], Santiago, Chile
Epiphyllum Soc. of Am. [22510], PO Box 1395, Monrovia, CA 91017-1395
Episcopal
Amer. Friends of the Anglican Centre in Rome [19451]
Anglican Soc. [19942]
Anglicans United [19943]
Assembly of Episcopal Healthcare Chaplains [19944]
Assoc. Parishes for Liturgy and Mission [19945]
Assn. of Anglican Musicians [20425]
Assn. of Episcopal Colleges [8397]
Assn. of Episcopal Colleges [IO]
Assn. of Member Episcopal Conferences in Eastern Africa [IO]
Brotherhood of Saint Andrew [19946]
Church Army [19947]
Church Pension Fund [19948]
Church Periodical Club [19949]
Commn. of the Bishops' Conferences of the European Community [IO]
Concerned Clergy and Laity of the Episcopal Church [19950]
Confraternity of the Blessed Sacrament [19951]
Episcopal Church Building Fund [19952]
Episcopal Communicators [19953]
Episcopal Conf. of the Deaf [19954]
Episcopal Evangelical Educ. Soc. [19955]
Episcopal Women's Caucus [19956]
Faith Alive [19957]
Fellowship of Saint Paul [19958]
Forward in Faith North Am. [19959]
Found. for Christian Theology [19960]
Foundation for Christian Theology [IO]
Global Teams [IO]
Global Teams [19961]
Historical Soc. of the Episcopal Church [19962]
Integrity [20058]
Intl. Order of St. Vincent [19963]
Intl. Order of St. Vincent [IO]
Living Church Found. [19964]
Natl. Assn. of Episcopal Schools [8398]
Natl. Episcopal Hea. Ministries [14584]
Natl. Guild of Churchmen [19965]
Natl. Network of Episcopal Clergy Associations [19966]
New Wineskins Missionary Network [20375]
North Amer. Assn. for the Diaconate [19967]
Off. of Black Ministries/Episcopal Church Center [19968]
Order of the Daughters of the King [19969]
Recovered Alcoholic Clergy Assn. [13278]
Seamen's Church Inst. of New York and New Jersey [19970]

Reference to "IO" in place of a book number signifies that the association may be found in the 45th edition of International Organizations.

Soc. of the Companions of the Holy Cross [19971]

Soc. for the Increase of the Ministry [20290]

Soc. for Promoting and Encouraging Arts and Knowledge of the Church [19972]

South Amer. Missionary Soc. - USA [20398]

Standing Commn. on Church Music [19973]

Standing Commn. on Ecumenical Relations of the Episcopal Church [19974]

Women's Missionary Soc., AME Church [20627]

Episcopal Actors' Guild of Am. [11013], Little Church Around the Corner, 1 E 29th St., New York, NY 10016-7405, (212)685-2927

Episcopal AIDS Coalition; Natl. [11332]

Episcopal Book Club [★19972]

Episcopal Center for Evangelism - Defunct.

Episcopal Church Building Fund [19952], 815 2nd Ave., New York, NY 10017, (212)716-6003

Episcopal Church Center; Off. of Black Ministries/ [19968]

Episcopal Church Missionary Community [★20375]

Episcopal Church; Women's Missionary Coun. of the Christian Methodist [20270]

Episcopal Churchpeople for a Free Southern Africa - Address unknown since 2001.

Episcopal Church's Presiding Bishop's Fund for World Relief [★12852]

Episcopal Church's Presiding Bishop's Fund for World Relief [★IO]

Episcopal Clergy Associations; Natl. Network of [19966]

Episcopal Colleges; Found. for [★8397]

Episcopal Colleges; Fund for [★8397]

Episcopal Commn. for Black Ministries [★19968]

Episcopal Communicators [19953], c/o Jennifer Martin, Membership Coor., 316 Lehman-Outlet Rd., Dallas, PA 18612

Episcopal Conf. of the Deaf [19954], c/o St. Hilda's Episcopal Church, 245 W Main St., Monmouth, OR 97361, (503)838-6087

Episcopal Coun. for Foreign Students and Other Visitors - Defunct.

Episcopal Coun. for Global Mission - Address unknown since 1999.

Episcopal Evangelical Educ. Soc. [19955], PO Box 20247, Alexandria, VA 22320, (703)807-1862

Episcopal Evangelical Fellowship [★19955]

Episcopal Guild for the Blind - Address unknown since 1990.

Episcopal Pacifist Fellowship [★18614]

Episcopal Peace Fellowship [18614], 637 S Dearborn St., Chicago, IL 60605-1839, (312)922-8628

Episcopal Radio-T.V. Found. - Address unknown since 1999.

Episcopal Relief and Development [12852], 815 2nd Ave., New York, NY 10017, (800)334-7626

Episcopal Relief and Development [IO], New York, NY, United States

Episcopal School Assn. [★8398]

Episcopal Schools; Natl. Assn. of [8398]

Episcopal Soc. for Cultural and Racial Unity - Defunct.

Episcopal Soc. for Ministry on Aging - Defunct.

Episcopal Synod of Am. [★19959]

Episcopal Women's Caucus [19956], 5665 S Cherokee Bend, New Era, MI 49446-8905

Episcopal World Mission [★19961]

Episcopal World Mission [★IO]

Episcopalian

Anglican Soc. [19942]

Anglican Use Assn. [19450]

Anglicans United [19943]

Assembly of Episcopal Healthcare Chaplains [19944]

Assoc. Parishes for Liturgy and Mission [19945]

Assn. of Anglican Musicians [20425]

Brotherhood of Saint Andrew [19946]

Church Army [19947]

Church Periodical Club [19949]

Confraternity of the Blessed Sacrament [19951]

Episcopal Actors' Guild of Am. [11013]

Episcopal Church Building Fund [19952]

Episcopal Evangelical Educ. Soc. [19955]

Episcopal Women's Caucus [19956]

Faith Alive [19957]

Fellowship of Saint Paul [19958]

Forward in Faith North Am. [19959]

Found. for Christian Theology [19960]

Global Teams [19961]

Historical Soc. of the Episcopal Church [19962]

Integrity [20058]

Intl. Order of St. Vincent [19963]

Living Church Found. [19964]

Natl. Episcopal AIDS Coalition [11332]

Natl. Guild of Churchmen [19965]

New Wineskins Missionary Network [20375]

North Amer. Assn. for the Diaconate [19967]

Seamen's Church Inst. of New York and New Jersey [19970]

Soc. of the Companions of the Holy Cross [19971]

South Amer. Missionary Soc. - USA [20398]

Standing Commn. on Ecumenical Relations of the Episcopal Church [19974]

Episcopalians for Life [★12905]

Episcopalians and Others for Responsible Social Action - Address unknown since 1995.

Episcopalians United [★19943]

Episcopalians United for Revelation, Renewal, and Reformation [★19943]

Epitestudomanyi Egyesulet [★IO]

Epping Forest Conservation Volunteers [IO], London, United Kingdom

EPRI [6953], 3420 Hillview Ave., Palo Alto, CA 94304, (650)855-2121

EPS Molders Assn. [3050], 1298 Cronson Blvd., Ste. 201, Crofton, MD 21114, (410)451-8341

Epsilon Eta Phi [★24422]

Epsilon; Kappa Sigma Alpha [★24463]

Epsilon Nu Eta - Address unknown since 2001.

Epsilon Pi Tau [24720], Bowling Green State Univ., 105 A Tech. Bldg., Bowling Green, OH 43403-0296, (419)372-2425

Epsilon Pi Tau [IO], Bowling Green, OH, United States

Epsilon Sigma Alpha [24598], 363 W Drake Rd., Fort Collins, CO 80526, (970)223-2824

Epsilon Sigma Phi [24436], c/o Linda D. Cook, Exec. Dir., PO Box 357340, Gainesville, FL 32635-7340, (352)378-6665

Epstein-Barr Virus Assn; Natl. Chronic [★14278]

Equal - Address unknown since 1995.

Equal Education

Assn. for Gender Equity Leadership in Educ. [8399]

Educational Equity Center [8400]

Gay, Lesbian, and Straight Educ. Network [8456]

Mid-Atlantic Equity Consortium [8276]

Minority Student Achievement Network [8401]

Org. for Equal Education of the Sexes [8402]

Quality Educ. for Minorities Network [8303]

Equal Employment Advisory Coun. [12079], 1015 15th St. NW, Ste. 1200, Washington, DC 20005, (202)789-8650

Equal Employment; Natl. Found. for the Study of [★12077]

Equal Justice Soc. [6258], 220 Sansome St., 14th Fl., San Francisco, CA 94104, (415)288-8700

Equal Justice Works [5898], c/o David Stern, CEO, 2120 L St. NW, Ste. 450, Washington, DC 20037-1541, (202)466-3686

Equal Opportunities Commn. - Northern Ireland [★IO]

Equal Opportunity; Center for [10216]

Equal Opportunity in Higher Educ; Natl. Assn. for [8109]

Equal Opportunity Officers; Natl. Assn. of Public Sector [1274]

Equal Partners in Faith [20494], c/o Washington Off. of the UUA, 2026 P St. NW, Washington, DC 20036, (202)296-4673

Equal Relationships Inst. [★17236]

Equal Rights Advocates [6222], 1663 Mission St., Ste. 250, San Francisco, CA 94103-2488, (415)621-0672

Equal Rights; Amer. Veterans for [12215]

Equal Rights for Argentine Women [IO], Buenos Aires, Argentina

Equal Rights Cong. - Defunct.

Equal Rights; Fathers for [12010]

Equal Rights for Women in Education - Defunct.

Equal Tax Soc; Thomas Jefferson [18720]

Equality Commn. for Northern Ireland [IO], Belfast, United Kingdom

Equality; Commn. for Women's [17522]

Equality; Cong. of Racial [16939]

Equality; Ex-Partners of Servicemembers for [12009]

Equality Exchange; Fathers Rights and [★12008]

Equality; Hispanas Organized for Political [17703]

Equality; Natl. Assn. for Recreational [23836]

Equality; Natl. Commn. for Women's [★17522]

Equality Now [18809], PO Box 20646, New York, NY 10023

Equality Now [IO], New York, NY, United States

Equality Now Intl; Men's [★18040]

Equality in Palestine; Search for Justice and [★18071]

Equality; Priests for [17568]

Equality; Proj. [17148]

Equatorial Guinea Badminton Fed. [IO], Malabo, Equatorial Guinea

Equatorial Guinea Tennis Fed. [IO], Malabo, Equatorial Guinea

Equestrian Alliance; Amer. [1923]

Equestrian Assn; Amer. Medical [★16474]

Equestrian Assn; Gladstone [23524]

Equestrian Association/Safe Riders Found; Amer. Medical [16474]

Equestrian Assn; U.S.A. [★23534]

Equestrian Club of Riyadh [IO], Riyadh, Saudi Arabia

Equestrian Drill Team Alliance; Intl. [23527]

Equestrian Fed; British [IO]

Equestrian Fed. of Ireland [IO], Kildare, Ireland

Equestrian Land Conservation Rsrc. [5130], 4037 Iron Works Pike, Ste. 120, Lexington, KY 40511, (859)455-8383

Equestrian Ministries Intl. [20082], PO Box 164, Wilmore, KY 40390, (859)858-3511

Equestrian Polo Assn; Collegiate [23659]

Equestrian Team; U.S. [★23534]

Equestrian Trade Assn; British [IO]

Equilibration Soc; Amer. [14135]

Equilibrium Fund - Defunct.

Equine Advocates [11391], c/o Susan Wagner, Pres./Founder, PO Box 354, Chatham, NY 12037-0354, (518)245-1599

Equine Art; Amer. Acad. of [9410]

Equine Assisted Growth and Learning Assn. [16216], PO Box 993, Santaquin, UT 84655, (801)754-0400

Equine Assisted Growth and Learning Association [IO], Santaquin, UT, United States

Equine Assn; Amer. [4819]

Equine Canada [IO], Ottawa, ON, Canada

Equine Guided Educ. Assn. [8524], PO Box 337, Valley Ford, CA 94972, (707)876-1908

Equine Practitioners; Amer. Assn. of [16742]

Equine Professionals; Intl. Assn. of [1925]

Equine Ranching Info. Coun; North Amer. [1926]

Equine Relief Programme; Horseaid [11408]

Equine Rescue; Front Range [4881]

Equine Rescue League [11392], PO Box 4366, Leesburg, VA 20177, (703)771-1240

Equine Veterinary Assn; British [IO]

Equip. Advertisers; Constr. [★82]

Equip. Advertisers and Public Relations Coun; Constr. [★82]

Equip. Aftermarket Assn; Outdoor Power [1292]

Equip. Appraisers; Assn. of Machinery and [277]

Equip. Appraisers Assn. of North Am. [279], 1270 State Rte. 30, Clinton, PA 15026, (800)790-1053

Equip. Appraisers Assn. of North Am. [IO], Clinton, PA, United States

Equip. Assn; Indus. Heating [1885]

Equip. Assn; for Info. Media and [328]

Equip. Assn; Intl. Beverage Dispensing [507]

Equip. Assn; Natl. Retail Farm [★185]

Equip. Assn; Natl. School Supply and [3479]

Equip. Assn; Natl. Time [3812]

Equip. Assn; Natl. Truck [395]

Equip. Claims Coun; Natl. Truck and Heavy [2228]

Equip. Companies; Natl. Affiliation of Durable Medical [★14670]

Equip. Dealers; Assn. of Independent Mailing [★2448]

A star before a book entry number signifies that the name is not listed separately, but is mentioned within the entry.

Equip. Dealers Assn; Midwest [4092]
Equip. Dealers Assn; Natl. Emergency [14339]
Equip. Dealers Assn; Natl. Farm and Power [★185]
Equip. Dealers Assn; North Amer. [185]
Equip. Distributors; Assoc. [2000]
Equip. Distributors Assn; Foodservice [1574]
Equip. Distributors Assn; Material Handling [2043]
Equip. Distributors Assn; Outdoor Power [★1293]
Equip. Distributors Assn; Safety [3454]
Equip. Distributors; Natl. Assn. of Fire [3448]
Equip. and Engine Ser. Assn; Outdoor Power [1293]
Equip. Exhibitors Assn; Intl. Defense [1343]
Equip. Indus; Food Ser. [★1574]
Equip. Inst; Outdoor Power [1294]
Equip. Inst; Petroleum [2941]
Equip. Inst; Safety [3455]
Equip. Inst; Trans. Safety [3458]
Equip. Inst; Truck Safety [★3458]
Equipment Interchange Assn. - Defunct.
Equip. Leasing Assn. [★3381]
Equip. Leasing Assn. [★IO]
Equip. Leasing Assn. [★IO]
Equip. Leasing Assn. of Am. [★IO]
Equip. Leasing Assn. of Am. [★3381]
Equip. Leasing Brokers; Natl. Assn. of [3382]
Equip. Leasing and Finance Assn. [3381], 1825 K
   St. NW, Ste. 900, Washington, DC 20006,
   (202)238-3400
Equip. Leasing and Finance Assn. [IO], Arlington,
   VA, United States
Equip. Maintenance Coun. [★IO]
Equip. Maintenance Coun. [★2442]
Equip. Managers Assn; Athletic [23805]
Equip. Managers Coun. of Am. [943], PO Box 794,
   South Amboy, NJ 08879-0794, (908)309-3905
Equip. Manufacturers Assn; Accessibility [1156]
Equip. Mfrs. Assn. Bus. [★904]
Equip. Mfrs. Assn; Cmpt. and Bus. [★904]
Equip. Mfrs. Assn; Converting [2012]
Equip. Mfrs. Assn; Conveyor [2013]
Equip. Mfrs; Assn. of Conveyor and Material
   Preparation [★2013]
Equip. Manufacturers Assn; Diving [★3642]
Equip. Manufacturers Assn; Farm [179]
Equip. Mfrs'. Assn; Fire [3443]
Equipment Mfrs. Assn; Food [1573]
Equip. Mfrs. Assn; Process [2063]
Equip. Manufacturers Assn; Water and Wastewater [2077]
Equip. Manufacturers Assn; Western Apparel and
   [★259]
Equip. Mfrs. Coun. [178], c/o Amer. Feed Indus.
   Assn., 1501 Wilson Blvd., Ste. 1100, Arlington, VA
   22209, (703)524-0810
Equip. Manufacturers Inst. [★177]
Equip. Manufacturers Inst. [★IO]
Equip. Mfrs. Inst; Off. [★904]
Equip. Mfrs. Intl; Assn. of Vacuum [★2006]
Equip. Mfrs; Loading Dock [2035]
Equip. Manufacturers; Natl. Assn. of Food and Dairy
   [★1133]
Equip. Mfrs; North Amer. Assn. of Food [1576]
Equip. Mfrs. Representatives Assn; Mech. [2540]
Equip. Market Assn; Specialty [397]
Equip. Materials Assn; Foundry [★2009]
Equip. and Materials Inst; Semiconductor [★1228]
Equip. and Materials Intl; Semiconductor [★1228]
Equip; Natl. Operating Comm. on Standards for
   Athletic [3451]
Equip. Needs; Christian Hospitals Overseas Secure
   [★12516]
Equip. Rental Assn; Production [2793]
Equip. Representatives Assn; Elecl. [1181]
Equip. Ser. Agencies of Am; Commercial Food
   [★1571]
Equip. Ser. Assn. [3549], c/o Kathleen A. DeMarco,
   Exec. Dir., PO Box 1420, Cherry Hill, NJ 08034,
   (856)489-0753
Equip. Ser. Assn; Commercial Food [1571]
Equip. Ser. Assn; United Fire [3460]
Equip. Services; Natl. Assn. for Medical [★14670]
Equip. Suppliers; Assn. of Independent Medical
   [★14670]
Equip. Suppliers Assn; Original [777]
Equip. Suppliers Assn; Petroleum [2942]

Equip. Suppliers; Natl. Assn. of Medical [★14670]
Equip. and Systems Assn; Natl. Independent Bank
   [★476]
Equip. Technicians; Natl. Assn. of Photographic
   [3004]
Equip. and Tool Inst. [383], 134 W Univ. Dr., Ste.
   206, Rochester, MI 48307, (248)656-5080
Equip. Trade Assn; Cleaning [2461]
Equip. Wholesalers Assn; Farm [180]
Equitable Reserve Assn. [19122], PO Box 448,
   Neenah, WI 54957-0448, (800)722-1574
Equitas - Centre Intl. d'education aux droits humains
   [★IO]
Equitas - Intl. Centre for Human Rights Educ. [IO],
   Montreal, QC, Canada
Equitoy [IO], Cranbrook, United Kingdom
Equity [IO], London, United Kingdom
Equity Asset Managers Assn. - Address unknown
   since 2004.
Equity Assn; Actors' [24148]
Equity Assn; Artists [★9511]
Equity Assn; Emerging Markets Private [1415]
Equity Assn; Natl. Artists [9511]
Equity Center; Educational [8400]
Equity Conversion; Natl. Center for Home [1470]
Equity in Educ; Natl. Coalition for Sex [★8399]
Equity Fights AIDS; Broadway Cares/ [11326]
Equity Leadership in Educ; Assn. for Gender [8399]
Equity Policy Center - Address unknown since 1999.
Equity Source Banks; Natl. Assn. of [488]
Equus Sanctuary [16983], PO Box 9, Ravendale,
   CA 96123, (530)931-0108
ERA Impact Project - Defunct.
Eradication of TV; Soc. for the [17193]
ERAmerica - Defunct.
Erasmus Student Network [IO], Brussels, Belgium
Erb's Palsy Assn. of Ireland [IO], Blackrock, Ireland
Erb's Palsy Assn; Natl. Brachial Plexus- [14277]
Ercoupe Owners Club [21444], c/o Skip Carden,
   Exec. Dir., 52 Hunters Ln., Timberlake, NC 27583-
   8781, (919)471-9492
Erectors Assn. of Am; Steel [6839]
Erectors Assn; Metal Building Contractors and
   [2528]
Erectors Assn; Natl. [★1056]
Erectors, Fabricators and Riggers; Natl. Coun. of
   [1042]
Erectors; Natl. Assn. of Tower [6653]
Eretz Natna Yevulah [★IO]
Ergonomic Res; Center for [7565]
Ergonomics
   Assn. of Canadian Ergonomists [IO]
   Center for Ergonomic Res. [7565]
   Ergonomics Soc. of South Africa [IO]
   Fed. of European Ergonomics Soc. [IO]
   Human Factors and Ergonomics Soc. [7164]
   Human Factors and Ergonomics Soc. of Australia
      [IO]
   Intl. Ergonomics Assn. [IO]
   Irish Ergonomics Soc. [IO]
   New Zealand Ergonomics Soc. [IO]
Ergonomics Soc. of Australia [★IO]
Ergonomics Soc. - England [IO], Loughborough,
   United Kingdom
Ergonomics Soc; Human Factors and [7164]
Ergonomics Soc. of South Africa [IO], Auckland
   Park, Republic of South Africa
Ergonomics Soc. - Sweden [IO], Lund, Sweden
Ergonomisallskapet, Sverige [★IO]
Eric Braeden Fan Club - Address unknown since
   2001.
ERIC Clearinghouse on Adult, Career, and
   Vocational Educ. - Defunct.
ERIC CH on Disabilities and Gifted Education
   [★9141]
ERIC CH on Disabilities and Gifted Education
   [★11998]
ERIC CH on Disabilities and Gifted Education [★IO]
ERIC CH on Languages and Linguistics [8730],
   4646 40th St. NW, Washington, DC 20016-1859,
   (202)362-0700
Erickson Found; Milton H. [16221]
Eric's Wasted Worldwide Repair Soc. - Address
   unknown since 1994.
Ericson Class Assn. - Address unknown since 2001.

Ericson Viking Ship; Leif [11134]
Ericsson Soc; John [11130]
Erika Slezak Official Fan Club - Address unknown
   since 1994.
Erikoishammasteknikkoliitto ry [★IO]
ERIS Roundtable for Independent Study [10792]
ERISA Indus. Comm. [1238], 1400 L St. NW, Ste.
   350, Washington, DC 20005, (202)789-1400
Eritrean Natl. Athletics Fed. [IO], Asmara, Eritrea
Eritrean Natl. Badminton Fed. [IO], Asmara, Eritrea
Eritrean Relief Comm. - Address unknown since
   2000.
Eritrean Students Union [★IO]
Eritrean Tennis Fed. [IO], Asmara, Eritrea
Ernest Bloch Soc. - Address unknown since 1999.
Ernest Fan Club - Defunct.
Ernest Tubb Fan Club - Defunct.
Ernst Bacon Soc. [10593], 8 Johnson Rd., Sharon,
   MA 02067
Erosion Control Tech. Coun. [5224], PO Box 18012,
   St. Paul, MN 55118, (651)554-1895
Erosion Control Tech. Coun. [IO], St. Paul, MN,
   United States
Errants; Citizens United for Rehabilitation of [11860]
Error Collectors of Am; Combined Organizations of
   Numismatic [22734]
Errors, Freaks and Oddities Collector's Club
   [22818], 7643 Sequoia Dr. N, Mobile, AL 36695-
   2809, (251)607-9253
Erskine Alumni Assn. [18895], c/o Erskine Colorado,
   2 Washington St., PO Box 608, Due West, SC
   29639, (864)379-2131
Erskine Registry [21640], 1144 Dockside Dr., Lutz,
   FL 33559, (813)948-1822
The Erythromelalgia Assn. [14261], 200 Old Castle
   Ln., Wallingford, PA 19086
ESA [18602], 6 E Lancaster Ave., Wynnewood, PA
   19096, (610)645-9390
ESA Intl. [★24598]
Esalen Inst. [10172], 55000 Hwy. 1, Big Sur, CA
   93920-9546, (831)667-3000
Escadrilles Canadiennes de Plaisance [★IO]
Escalator Safety Found; Elevator [1232]
Escalen Inst. Russian-American Exchange Center
   [★17912]
Escalen Inst. Russian-American Exchange Center
   [★IO]
Escalen Inst. Soviet-American Exchange Prog.
   [★IO]
Escalen Inst. Soviet-American Exchange Prog.
   [★17912]
Escape and Evasion Soc; Air Forces [20660]
Escapees [22948], 100 Rainbow Dr., Livingston, TX
   77351, (936)327-8873
Escarre Intl. Center for the Ethnic Minorities and Na-
   tions [IO], Barcelona, Spain
Eschaton Found.: Community Spirit Fund - Defunct.
Esclerosis Multiple Argentina [IO], Buenos Aires,
   Argentina
Escoffier Soc. of New York; Les Amis d' [1535]
Escoffier Soc. of Toronto [IO], Toronto, ON, Canada
Escort Carrier Sailors and Airmen Assn. [21185], c/o
   Ralph Magerkurth, Membership Chm., 13114 Blue
   Bonnet Dr., Sun City, AZ 85375, (623)584-4794
Escrow Assn; Amer. [1398]
ESEA Title I Parents; Natl. Coalition of [★8289]
ESIB - Natl. Unions of Students in Europe [IO],
   Brussels, Belgium
Eskimo
   Amer. Eskimo Dog Club of Am. [22199]
   Amer. Indian Higher Educ. Consortium [8935]
   Americans for Indian Opportunity [12624]
   Bur. of Catholic Indian Missions [19591]
   Maniilaq Assn. [12627]
   Natl. Amer. Eskimo Dog Assn. [22310]
   Natl. Center for Amer. Indian and Alaska Native
      Mental Hea. Res. [15220]
   Natl. Indian Hea. Bd. [12629]
   Tekakwitha Conf. Natl. Center [19727]
Eskimo Dog Assn; Natl. Amer. [22310]
Eskimo Dog Soc. of the Northwest Territories -
   Defunct.
Eskimo, Indian-
   Americans for Indian Opportunity [12624]
   Bur. of Catholic Indian Missions [19591]

Reference to "IO" in place of a book number signifies that the association may be found in the 45th edition of International Organizations.

Maniilaq Assn. **[12627]**

Natl. Center for Amer. Indian and Alaska Native Mental Hea. Res. **[15220]**

Natl. Indian Hea. Bd. **[12629]**

Esko-Graphics' Users; Assn. of **[6761]**

Eskridge Family Assn. **[20898]**, c/o Fran Markowski, Treas., 1931 Medallion Ct., Forest Hill, MD 21050-2761

ESOMAR: World Assn. of Opinion and Marketing Res. Professionals **[IO]**, Amsterdam, Netherlands

ESOP Assn. **[1248]**, 1726 M St. NW, Ste. 501, Washington, DC 20036, (202)293-2971

ESOP Assn. Canada **[IO]**, Thornhill, ON, Canada

ESOP Companies; Natl. Assn. of **[★1248]**

ESOP Coun. of Am. **[★1248]**

Esophageal Cancer Awareness Assn. **[13822]**, PO Box 3842, Ithaca, NY 14852-3842, (607)257-1141

Esophagological Assn; Amer. Broncho- **[13778]**

ESP Res. Associates Found. - Defunct.

Espaco t **[★IO]**

Espanola; Spanish Heritage-Herencia **[★8634]**

Esperanca **[14628]**, 1911 W Earll Dr., Phoenix, AZ 85015, (602)252-7772

Esperanca **[IO]**, Phoenix, AZ, United States

Esperantic Stud. Found. **[IO]**, Burnaby, BC, Canada

Esperantista; Internacia Katolika Unio **[★9915]**

Esperantlingva Verkista Asocio **[★IO]**

Esperanto

Amer. Assn. of Teachers of Esperanto **[8403]**

Canadian Esperanto Assn. **[IO]**

Center for Res. and Documentation on Intl. Language Problems **[IO]**

Esperantic Stud. Found. **[IO]**

Esperanto Cultural Centre **[IO]**

Esperanto League for North Am. **[9914]**

Esperanto Writers Assn. **[IO]**

Internacia Libro-Klubo Esperanta **[IO]**

Intl. Catholic Esperanto Assn. **[9915]**

Intl. Esperanto Inst. **[IO]**

Intl. League of Esperantist Teachers **[IO]**

Intl. Naturist Org. for Esperanto **[IO]**

Intl. Naturist Org. for Esperanto **[9916]**

Intl. Soc. of Friendship and Good Will **[9917]**

Intl. Soc. of Friendship and Good Will **[IO]**

Kristana Esperantista Ligo Internacia **[19812]**

Nationless Worldwide Assn. **[IO]**

Union for the Intl. Language Ido **[IO]**

Union des Travailleurs Esperantistes des Pays de Langue Francaise/Esperanto-Informations **[IO]**

Universal Esperanto Assn. **[IO]**

World Org. of Young Esperantists **[IO]**

Esperanto-Asocio de Skotlando **[★IO]**

Esperanto Assn. of North America - Defunct.

Esperanto Cultural Centre **[IO]**, La Chaux-de-Fonds, Switzerland

Esperanto Info. Center **[★9914]**

Esperanto Instructors; U.S. Soc. of **[★8403]**

Esperanto League for North Am. **[9914]**, PO Box 1129, El Cerrito, CA 94530, (510)653-0998

Esperanto Writers Assn. **[IO]**, Zagreb, Croatia

Espionage Controls and Countermeasures Assn; Bus. **[2086]**

Esport Escolar **[IO]**, Sant Julia de Loria, Andorra

Espression

Spiritual Frontiers Fellowship Intl. **[20579]**

ESPRIT **[IO]**, Brussels, Belgium

Esquel Gp. Found. - Brazil **[IO]**, Brasilia, Brazil

Essay-Proof Soc. - Address unknown since 1999.

Essence Soc; Flower **[14818]**

Essentia - Defunct.

Essential Info. **[17175]**, PO Box 19405, Washington, DC 20036, (202)387-8030

Essential Oil Assn. of the U.S.A. **[★1662]**

Essential Schools; Coalition of **[8180]**

Essex Chamber of Commerce **[IO]**, Colchester, United Kingdom

Essex Terraplane Historical Soc; Hudson **[21660]**

ESSI, Inc; LS **[★14304]**

Estate Counsel; Amer. Coll. of Trust and **[6183]**

Estate Editors; Natl. Conf. of Real **[★3132]**

Estate Management

Natl. Assn. of Financial and Estate Planning **[1437]**

Natl. Assn. of Senior Move Managers **[2523]**

Soc. of Trust and Estate Practitioners **[IO]**

Soc. of Trust and Estate Practitioners Ireland **[IO]**

Soc. of Trust and Estate Practitioners USA **[1332]**

Estate Planners and Councils; Natl. Assn. of **[1466]**

Estate Planning Attorneys; Amer. Acad. of **[5473]**

Estate Planning Attorneys; Natl. Network of **[5524]**

Estate Planning Councils; Natl. Assn. of **[★1466]**

Estate Professionals; Natl. Assn. of Hispanic Real **[3319]**

Estate Taxation; Amer. Coun. on Capital Gains and **[★17347]**

Esteem; Natl. Assn. for Self **[15218]**

Esther A. and Joseph Klingenstein Fund **[15106]**, c/o Mr. John Klingenstein, Pres., 787 7th Ave., 6th Fl., New York, NY 10019-6016, (212)492-6181

Esther Stevens Brazer Guild **[★9482]**

Esthetic Dentistry; Amer. Acad. of **[14096]**

Estimating and Anal; Soc. of Cost **[1448]**

Estimating Soc; Natl. **[★1448]**

Estimators; Amer. Soc. of Professional **[8142]**

Estimators Assn. of Am; Professional Constr. **[1061]**

Estonia

Assn. for the Advancement of Baltic Stud. **[9730]**

Estonian Amer. Chamber of Commerce and Indus. **[24318]**

Estonian Relief Comm. **[12853]**

Estonia Natl. Comm. of Geomorphology **[IO]**, Tallinn, Estonia

Estonia Physiological Soc. **[IO]**, Tartu, Estonia

Estonian

Estonian Amer. Chamber of Commerce and Indus. **[24318]**

Estonian Amer. Natl. Coun. **[19041]**

Estonian Educational Soc. **[19042]**

Estonian Relief Comm. **[12853]**

Estonian Acad. of Sciences **[IO]**, Tallinn, Estonia

Estonian Aid - Address unknown since 1990.

Estonian Amer. Chamber of Commerce and Indus. **[24318]**, c/o Krista Altok Tassa, Pres./Founder, 157-61 17th Ave., Whitestone, NY 11357, (718)747-3805

Estonian Amer. Fund for Economic Educ. **[8215]**, 4 Noyes Ct., Silver Spring, MD 20910, (301)587-9115

Estonian Amer. Fund for Economic Educ. **[IO]**, Silver Spring, MD, United States

Estonian Amer. Natl. Coun. **[19041]**, 9814 Hill St., Kensington, MD 20895, (301)587-8353

Estonian Artists' Assn. **[IO]**, Tallinn, Estonia

Estonian Assn. of Info. Tech. and Telecommunications **[IO]**, Tallinn, Estonia

Estonian Assn. for Personnel Development **[IO]**, Tallinn, Estonia

Estonian Assn. for Rheumatology **[IO]**, Tartu, Estonia

Estonian Assn. of Travel Agencies **[IO]**, Tallinn, Estonia

Estonian Assn. of Travel Agents **[★IO]**

Estonian Assn. of Univ. Women **[IO]**, Tartu, Estonia

Estonian Athletic Assn. **[IO]**, Tallinn, Estonia

Estonian Badminton Fed. **[IO]**, Tartu, Estonia

Estonian Banking Assn. **[IO]**, Tallinn, Estonia

Estonian Baseball and Softball Fed. **[IO]**, Keila, Estonia

Estonian Bible Soc. **[IO]**, Tallinn, Estonia

Estonian Bus. Assn. **[IO]**, Tallinn, Estonia

Estonian Chamber of Commerce and Indus. **[IO]**, Tallinn, Estonia

Estonian Clothing and Textile Assn. **[IO]**, Tallinn, Estonia

Estonian Clothing and Textiles Manufacturers' Assn. **[★IO]**

Estonian Dairy Assn. **[IO]**, Tallinn, Estonia

Estonian Dance Sport Assn. **[IO]**, Tallinn, Estonia

Estonian Dentistry Students' Assn. **[IO]**, Tartu, Estonia

Estonian Doctor's Assn. **[★IO]**

Estonian Draughts Fed. **[IO]**, Tallinn, Estonia

Estonian Economic Assn. **[IO]**, Tallinn, Estonia

Estonian Educ. Personnel Union **[IO]**, Tallinn, Estonia

Estonian Educational Soc. **[19042]**, Estonian House, 243 E 34th St., New York, NY 10016, (212)684-0336

Estonian Employers Confed. **[IO]**, Tallinn, Estonia

Estonian First Medical Aid Assn. **[★IO]**

Estonian Floorball Union **[IO]**, Tallinn, Estonia

Estonian Food Indus. Assn. **[★IO]**

Estonian Football Assn. **[IO]**, Tallinn, Estonia

Estonian Freight Forwarders Assn. **[IO]**, Tallinn, Estonia

Estonian Fund for Nature **[IO]**, Tartu, Estonia

Estonian Gambling Operator Assn. **[IO]**, Tallinn, Estonia

Estonian Geotechnical Soc. **[IO]**, Tallinn, Estonia

Estonian Gerontology and Geriatrics Assn. **[IO]**, Tartu, Estonia

Estonian Heart Assn. **[IO]**, Tallinn, Estonia

Estonian Hotel and Restaurant Assn. **[IO]**, Tallinn, Estonia

Estonian Info. Tech. Soc. **[IO]**, Tallinn, Estonia

Estonian Inst. **[IO]**, Tallinn, Estonia

Estonian Inst. of Human Rights **[IO]**, Tallinn, Estonia

Estonian Insurance Assn. **[IO]**, Tallinn, Estonia

Estonian League Against Epilepsy **[IO]**, Tallinn, Estonia

Estonian Learned Soc. of America - Defunct.

Estonian Liberal Democratic Party **[★IO]**

Estonian Librarians' Assn. **[IO]**, Tallinn, Estonia

Estonian Meat Assn. **[IO]**, Tallinn, Estonia

Estonian Medical Assn. **[IO]**, Tartu, Estonia

Estonian Music Center, U.S.A. - Defunct.

Estonian Naturalists' Soc. - Sect. of Entomology **[IO]**, Tartu, Estonia

Estonian Newspaper Assn. **[IO]**, Tallinn, Estonia

Estonian Oil Assn. **[IO]**, Tallinn, Estonia

Estonian Olympic Comm. **[IO]**, Tallinn, Estonia

Estonian Orienteering Fed. **[IO]**, Tallinn, Estonia

Estonian Osteoporosis Soc. **[IO]**, Tartu, Estonia

Estonian Pain Soc. **[IO]**, Tartu, Estonia

Estonian Paralympic Comm. **[IO]**, Tallinn, Estonia

Estonian Peat Assn. **[IO]**, Tallinn, Estonia

Estonian Physical Soc. **[IO]**, Tartu, Estonia

Estonian Physiotherapists Assn. **[IO]**, Tartu, Estonia

Estonian Press Coun. **[IO]**, Tallinn, Estonia

Estonian Progressive Soc. "Kiir" - Address unknown since 1995.

Estonian Radio Amateurs Union **[IO]**, Tallinn, Estonia

Estonian Reform Party **[IO]**, Tallinn, Estonia

Estonian Relief Comm. **[IO]**, New York, NY, United States

Estonian Relief Comm. **[12853]**, Estonian House, 243 E 34th St., New York, NY 10016, (212)685-7467

Estonian Rural Tourism Org. **[IO]**, Tallinn, Estonia

Estonian School Center, USA - Address unknown since 2007.

Estonian Schoolsport Union **[IO]**, Tallinn, Estonia

Estonian Scout Assn. **[IO]**, Tallinn, Estonia

Estonian Security Assn. **[IO]**, Tallinn, Estonia

Estonian Sexual Hea. Assn. **[IO]**, Tallinn, Estonia

Estonian Skating Union **[IO]**, Tallinn, Estonia

Estonian Soc. of Cardiology **[IO]**, Tartu, Estonia

Estonian Soc. of Clinical Neurophysiology **[IO]**, Tallinn, Estonia

Estonian Soc. of Gastrointestinal Endoscopy **[IO]**, Tallinn, Estonia

Estonian Soc. of Hypertension **[IO]**, Tartu, Estonia

Estonian Soc. of Merchants **[IO]**, Tallinn, Estonia

Estonian Soc. of Pharmacology **[IO]**, Tartu, Estonia

Estonian Sports Medicine Fed. **[IO]**, Tallinn, Estonia

Estonian Squash Fed. **[IO]**, Tallinn, Estonia

Estonian Student Assn. in the U.S.A. - Defunct.

Estonian Taekwondo Fed. **[IO]**, Tallinn, Estonia

Estonian Tenants Union **[IO]**, Tartu, Estonia

Estonian Tennis Assn. **[IO]**, Tallinn, Estonia

Estonian Traders Assn. **[★IO]**

Estonian Union of Banks **[★IO]**

Estonian Wind Power Assn. **[IO]**, Tallinn, Estonia

Estonian Windsurfers' Assn. **[★IO]**

Estonian Windsurfing Assn. **[IO]**, Tallinn, Estonia

Estonian Women's Clubs; Federated **[★18981]**

Estonian Youth Rheumatism Assn. **[IO]**, Tallinn, Estonia

Estrela Mountain Dog Assn. of Am. **[22265]**, c/o Cindy Martishius, Pres., 2681 Mt. Misery Rd., Leland, NC 28451, (910)371-9216

Estuaries; Restore America's **[5278]**

Estuarine and Brackish-Water Biological Assn. **[★IO]**

Estuarine and Brackish Water Sciences Assn. **[★IO]**

Estuarine and Coastal Sciences Assn. **[IO]**, Dublin, Ireland

---

A star before a book entry number signifies that the name is not listed separately, but is mentioned within the entry.

Estuarine Res. Fed. [7271], PO Box 510, Port Republic, MD 20676, (410)326-7467

Estuarine Res. Soc; Atlantic [★7271]

ETA Intl. - Electronics Technicians Assn., Intl. [1214], 5 Depot St., Greencastle, IN 46135, (765)653-8262

ETA International - Electronics Technicians Association, International [IO], Greencastle, IN, United States

Eta Kappa Nu [24459], 300 W Adams, Ste. 1210, Chicago, IL 60606-5114, (800)406-2590

Eta Mu Pi - Address unknown since 1995.

Eta Phi Beta [24419], 16815 James Couzens Fwy., Detroit, MI 48235, (313)862-0600

Eta Sigma Alpha Natl. Home School Honor Soc. [8316], 11665 Fuqua St., Ste. A-100, Houston, TX 77034, (281)922-0478

Eta Sigma Phi, Natl. Classics Honorary Soc. [24433], Dept. of Classics, Monmouth Coll., 700 E Broadway, Monmouth, IL 61462, (309)457-2371

ETAD North Am. - Ecological and Toxicological Assn. of Dyes and Organic Pigments Mfrs. [5089], 1850 M St. NW, Ste. 700, Washington, DC 20036, (202)721-4154

ETAD; U.S. Dye Mfrs. Operating Comm. of [★5089]

ETAD; U.S. Operating Comm. of [★5089]

Etaipeia Apxaion Ellhnikon Meleton [★IO]

Etch-A-Sketch Club [22994], c/o The Ohio Art Co., 1 Toy St., PO Box 111, Bryan, OH 43506-0111, (419)636-3141

Etched Circuit Soc. - Defunct.

Etchers; California Soc. of [★1762]

Etchers, Gravers, Lithographers and Woodcutters; Soc. of Amer. [★9992]

Etchers; Soc. of Amer. [★9992]

Etchers; Soc. of Brooklyn [★9992]

Etching and Fabricating Assn; Metal [★2720]

Etching Mfrs. Trade Assn; Amer. Metal [★2720]

Etchingham Family Tree [20899]

Eternal Artists Network [★9506]

Eternal Life [18551], 902 W Stephen Foster Ave., Bardstown, KY 40004, (800)842-2871

Eternally Elvis TCB - Address unknown since 2006.

Ethel Delaney Intl. Fan Club [24886], 301 Firestone Dr., Las Vegas, NV 89145

Ethernet Alliance; 10 Gigabit [7372]

Ethical Educ; Coun. for Spiritual and [8536]

Ethical Investment Assn. [IO], Sydney, Australia

Ethical Organizations; Coun. of [1333]

Ethical Soc; Washington [20087]

Ethical Treatment of Animals; People for the [11444]

Ethical Treatment of Animals; Psychologists for the [★11460]

Ethical Union; Amer. [20083]

Ethics

Amer. Bd. of Quality Assurance and Utilization Rev. Physicians [16260]

Amer. Bd. of Radiology [16272]

Amer. Coll. of Medical Quality [16261]

Amer. Ethical Union [20083]

Amer. Healthcare Radiology Administrators [16275]

Amer. Humanist Assn. [20084]

Amer. Inst. of Medical Ethics [12122]

Americans for the Enforcement of Attorney Ethics [12123]

Americans for the Enforcement of Judicial Ethics [12124]

AMHS [11817]

Applied Res. Ethics Natl. Assn. [15101]

Assn. for the Accreditation of Human Res. Protection Programs [11225]

Assn. for Christian Ethics [19574]

Australian Assn. for Professional and Applied Ethics [IO]

Better World J. L. Inst. [12142]

Canadian Centre for Ethics in Sport [IO]

Carnegie Coun. for Ethics in Intl. Affairs [20093]

Center for Applied Christian Ethics [19975]

Center for Medical Ethics and Mediation [5452]

Character Educ. Partnership [17476]

Coun. of Ethical Organizations [1333]

Coun. for Secular Humanism [20085]

Ethics Rsrc. Center [17072]

EthicsCentre CA [IO]

Found. for Ethics and Meaning [7069]

Hastings Center [12125]

Inst. for the Advancement of Philosophy for Children [10796]

Inst. for Global Ethics [7070]

Inst. for Global Ethics [IO]

Insurance Marketplace Standards Assn. [2180]

Intl. Network on Feminist Approaches to Bioethics [12126]

Intl. Network on Feminist Approaches to Bioethics [IO]

Intl. Soc. for Ethics and Info. Tech. [7198]

Joseph and Edna Josephson Inst. of Ethics [17505]

Joseph P. and Rose F. Kennedy Inst. of Ethics [17506]

Natl. Assn. for Healthcare Quality [16264]

Natl. Client Protection Org. [5949]

Natl. Legal and Policy Center [17671]

The Objectivist Center [10821]

Scientists Center for Animal Welfare [11456]

Soc. and Animals Forum [11460]

Soc. for Bus. Ethics [12127]

Society for Business Ethics [IO]

Soc. of Christian Ethics [12128]

Soc. for Veterinary Medical Ethics [16808]

Unitarian Universalist Assn. of Congregations [13135]

W. Maurice Young Centre for Applied Ethics [IO]

Washington Ethical Soc. [20087]

Ethics; Amer. Soc. of Christian [★12128]

Ethics; Amer. Soc. of Law, Medicine and [15002]

Ethics; Assn. for Christian [19574]

Ethics; Assn. for Practical and Professional [8967]

Ethics; Center for Bio [6557]

Ethics; Center for Bio [6558]

Ethics and Compliance Officer Assn. [720], 411 Waverley Oaks Rd., Ste. 324, Waltham, MA 02452-8420, (781)647-9333

Ethics in Economics; Coun. for [★714]

Ethics; Forest Ser. Employees for Environmental [5126]

Ethics Gp; Creative [★10793]

Ethics; Institute of [★19931]

Ethics Inst. [IO], Utrecht, Netherlands

Ethics Inst; Cmpt. [9056]

Ethics, Law and Public Policy; Newport Inst. for [18470]

Ethics Laws; Coun. on Governmental [6270]

Ethics, and the Life Sciences; Inst. of Soc., [★12125]

Ethics Natl. Assn; Applied Res. [15101]

Ethics Officer Assn. [★720]

Ethics; Outdoor [★4413]

Ethics and Public Policy Center [18444], 1015 15th St. NW, Ste. 900, Washington, DC 20005, (202)682-1200

Ethics and Religious Liberty Commn. of the Southern Baptist Convention [19487], 901 Commerce St., Ste. 550, Nashville, TN 37203, (615)244-2495

Ethics Rsrc. Center [17072], 1747 Pennsylvania Ave. NW, Ste. 400, Washington, DC 20006, (202)737-2258

Ethics and Social Policy; Center for Religion, [18609]

Ethics; Soc. for Creative [★10793]

Ethics in the U.S. and Canada; Amer. Soc. of Christian Social [★12128]

EthicsCentre CA [IO], Toronto, ON, Canada

Ethiek Instituut [★IO]

Ethington Family Org. - Defunct.

Ethiopia

Ethiopian North Amer. Hea. Professionals Assn. [14629]

Ethiopian

Ethiopian Community Mutual Assistance Assn. [19043]

Ethiopian Pharmacists Assn. in North Am. [15932]

Inst. of Ethiopian Stud. [IO]

Israel Assn. for Ethiopian Jews [IO]

Ethiopian Athletic Fed. [IO], Addis Ababa, Ethiopia

Ethiopian Badminton Fed. [IO], Addis Ababa, Ethiopia

Ethiopian Coffee Exporters' Assn. [IO], Addis Ababa, Ethiopia

Ethiopian Community Development Council [IO], Arlington, VA, United States

Ethiopian Community Development Coun. [12810], 901 S Highland St., Arlington, VA 22204, (703)685-0510

Ethiopian Community Mutual Assistance Assn. [19043], 552 Massachusetts Ave., Ste. 202, Cambridge, MA 02139, (617)492-4232

Ethiopian Diabetes Assn. [IO], Addis Ababa, Ethiopia

Ethiopian Economic Assn. [IO], Addis Ababa, Ethiopia

Ethiopian Evangelical Church Mekane Yesus [IO], Addis Ababa, Ethiopia

Ethiopian Free-Press Journalists Assn. [IO], Addis Ababa, Ethiopia

Ethiopian Info. Tech. Professionals Assn. [IO], Addis Ababa, Ethiopia

Ethiopian Medical Assn. [IO], Addis Ababa, Ethiopia

Ethiopian North Amer. Hea. Professionals Assn. [14629], 6632 Telegraph Rd., Box 150, Bloomfield Hills, MI 48301, (248)858-6974

Ethiopian Pharmacists Assn. in North Am. [15932], 13208 Bellevue St., Silver Spring, MD 20904, (202)806-4214

Ethiopian Pharmacists Assn. in North Am. [IO], Silver Spring, MD, United States

Ethiopian Philatelic Soc. - Address unknown since 1994.

Ethiopian Tennis Fed. [IO], Addis Ababa, Ethiopia

Ethiopian Trade Information - Defunct.

Ethiopian Weightlifting Fed. [IO], Addis Ababa, Ethiopia

Ethiopian World Taekwondo Fed. [IO], Addis Ababa, Ethiopia

Ethnic Affairs; Natl. Center for Urban [11753]

Ethnic Amer. Coalition (of Eastern Europeans) [★19360]

Ethnic Americans; Assn. of Multi [12141]

Ethnic Awareness Center - Defunct.

Ethnic Cultural Preservation Coun. [9847], 6500 S Pulaski Rd., Chicago, IL 60629, (773)582-5143

Ethnic Employees of the Library of Cong. - Address unknown since 2001.

Ethnic Equity; Am. Coun. on Educ., Center for Advancement of Racial and [8889]

Ethnic Found. - Address unknown since 1995.

Ethnic Heritage Center [★19369]

Ethnic Heritage Studies Clearinghouse - Defunct.

Ethnic Materials and Info. Exchange Round Table [★10354]

Ethnic Materials Info. Exchange Task Force (SRRT) [★10354]

Ethnic Millions Political Action Comm. - Address unknown since 1995.

Ethnic Minorities Development Assn. [IO], Blackburn, United Kingdom

Ethnic and Multicultural Info. Exchange [★10354]

Ethnic and Multicultural Info. Exchange Roundtable [10354], c/o Amer. Lib. Assn., 50 E Huron, Chicago, IL 60611, (312)280-4295

Ethnic Relations; Proj. on [17785]

Ethnic, Religious, Linguistic and Other Minorities; Intl. Fed. for the Protection of the Rights of [17768]

Ethnic Studies

Amer. Ethnological Soc. [6404]

Amer. Soc. for Ethnohistory [9918]

Assn. for the Stud. of African-American Life and History [9356]

Assn. for the Stud. of the Worldwide African Diaspora [7929]

Before Columbus Found. [10416]

Canadian Ethnic Stud. Assn. [IO]

Canadian Ethnocultural Coun. [IO]

Center for Migration Stud. of New York [10468]

Cultural Survival [10171]

Ellis Island Medal of Honor Soc. [19044]

Ethnic Cultural Preservation Coun. [9847]

Igorot Global Org. [10225]

Inter-University Prog. for Latino Res. [19045]

Intl. Centre for Ethnic Stud. [IO]

Interracial-Intercultural Pride [12162]

Natl. Assn. for Ethnic Stud. [9919]

Natl. Assn. of Hispanic and Latino Stud. [9920]

Natl. Assn. for Multicultural Educ. [8582]

Natl. Center for Urban Ethnic Affairs [11753]

Reference to "IO" in place of a book number signifies that the association may be found in the 45th edition of International Organizations.

Natl. Ethnic Coalition of Organizations [19046]
Natl. MultiCultural Inst. [11829]
Poverty and Race Res. Action Coun. [12781]
Proj. RACE [19047]
Slovenian Res. Center of Am. [10972]
Soc. for the Psychological Stud. of Ethnic Minority Issues [16179]
Soc. of Vertebrate Paleontology [7433]
Ethnic Stud; Natl. Assn. for [9919]
Ethnic Stud; Natl. Assn. of Interdisciplinary [★9919]
Ethnic United - Address unknown since 2000.
Ethnobiology; Soc. of [6596]
Ethnobotany Specialist Group - Defunct.
Ethnographic Film; Prog. in [★6436]
Ethnohistoric Conf; Amer. Indian [★9918]
Ethnohistory
Assn. for the Stud. of the Worldwide African Diaspora [7929]
Ethnohistory; Amer. Soc. for [9918]
Ethnological Soc; Amer. [6404]
Ethnology and Eugenics; Intl. Assn. for the Advancement of [★4512]
Ethnology; Intl. Commn. for Human Ecology and [★4512]
Ethnomusicology; Soc. for [10701]
Ethnoviolence; Center for the Applied Stud. of Prejudice and [★17146]
Ethnoviolence; Prejudice Institute/Center for the Applied Stud. of [17146]
Ethology; Amer. Soc. of Veterinary [★16780]
Ethology; Intl. Soc. for Applied [IO]
Ethos Found. [13239], 312 S Washington St., Ste. 3-A, Alexandria, VA 22314, (703)535-6800
Ethos Gp. - Infant, Child, Adolescent and Family Therapy Centers [★13239]
Ethylene Oxide Sterilization Assn. [808], PO Box 33361, Washington, DC 20033, (630)928-1758
Etling Clearinghouse - Address unknown since 2006.
Etruscan Found. [6446], PO Box 26, Fremont, MI 49412, (231)519-0675
Etudes d'Oiseaux Canada [★IO]
Etudes Tsiganes [★IO]
Etudiants en Sciences Economiques et Commerciales; Assn. Internationale Des [★8012]
Eucalyptus Improvement Assn. - Address unknown since 1999.
EUCARPIA [IO], Valencia, Spain
EUCC - The Coastal Union [IO], Leiden, Netherlands
Eucharistic Guard for Nocturnal Adoration - Defunct.
Eucharistic League; Priests [★19617]
Eucomed [IO], Woluwe-Saint-Pierre, Belgium
Eugene L. Garey Cancer Found. [★15650]
Eugene O'Neill Memorial Theater Center [11014], 305 Great Neck Rd., Waterford, CT 06385, (860)443-5378
Eugene O'Neill Memorial Theater Found. [★11014]
Eugene O'Neill Soc. [9648], PO Box 402, Danville, CA 94526, (925)828-0659
Eugene O'Neill Society [IO], Danville, CA, United States
Eugene V. Debs Found. [10295], PO Box 843, Terre Haute, IN 47808, (812)232-2163
Eugenics; Intl. Assn. for the Advancement of Ethnology and [★4512]
Eugenics Soc; Amer. [★6862]
Eugenics Special Interest Gp. [7114], PO Box 138, East Schodack, NY 12063-0138, (518)732-2390
Euler Soc. [10453], c/o Mary Ann McLoughlin, Treas., Dept. of Mathematics, Coll. of St. Rose, 432 Western Ave., Albany, NY 12203
EUR Network of EB Support Groups [★IO]
Eur-Roots Genealogy Club - Defunct.
Eurasia Found. - Western NIS Regional Off. [IO], Kiev, Ukraine
Eurasia; NCSJ: Advocates on Behalf of Jews in Russia, Ukraine, the Baltic States and [17448]
Eurasian Assn. of Youth Environmental Groups [★IO]
Eurasian and East European Res; Natl. Coun. for [10968]
EURATEX: European Apparel and Textile Org. [IO], Brussels, Belgium
EUREKA [IO], Brussels, Belgium
Eureka - Croatia [IO], Zagreb, Croatia

Eureka Secretariat AISBL [★IO]
Eureka Soc. [20634], PO Box 3117, Montrose, CO 81402-3117
Eureka - Ukraine [IO], Kiev, Ukraine
EURISOL, The UK Mineral Wool Assn. [IO], London, United Kingdom
Euro-Amer. Alliance - Address unknown since 2000.
Euro Amer. Cultural Exchange - Defunct.
Euro-American Women's Coun. [17530], 147-37 Beech Ave., Ste. 4A, Flushing, NY 11355, (718)321-3179
Euro Banking Assn. [IO], Paris, France
Euro-Children [IO], Antwerp, Belgium
Euro Chlor [IO], Brussels, Belgium
Euro Inst. [IO], Lyon, France
Euro-Mediterranean Human Rights Network [IO], Copenhagen, Denmark
Euro-Molders Assn. [★IO]
Euroavia - Assn. of European Aeronautical and Astronautical Students [★IO]
EUROAVIA - European Assn. of Aerospace Students [IO], Delft, Netherlands
Eurobike - Address unknown since 1991.
Eurocare: Advocacy for the Prevention of Alcohol Related Harm in Europe [IO], St. Ives, United Kingdom
Eurocentres Bus. Inst. [IO], London, United Kingdom
EUROCENTRES USA [★IO]
EUROCENTRES USA [★8731]
EUROCITIES Mobility Forum - ACCESS [IO], Brussels, Belgium
EUROCLIO: European Standing Conf. of History Teachers' Associations [IO], The Hague, Netherlands
EuroCommerce [IO], Brussels, Belgium
Eurofuel [IO], Brussels, Belgium
EuroHealthNet [IO], Brussels, Belgium
Euroheat and Power [IO], Brussels, Belgium
EUROMECH [★IO]
EUROMICRO [IO], St. Augustin, Germany
Euromissiles Working Group - Defunct.
Euromoulders [IO], Brussels, Belgium
Euronaid [IO], The Hague, Netherlands
Europa Cantat - European Fed. of Young Choirs [IO], Bonn, Germany
Europa Nostra Pan European Fed. for Heritage [IO], The Hague, Netherlands
Europa Study Unit - Address unknown since 1999.
Europaeische Evangelikale Akkreditieru [★IO]
Europai Folklor Intezet [★IO]
Europaische Akademie Otzenhausen [★IO]
Europaische Akademie fur stadtische Umwelt [★IO]
Europaische Akademie der Wissenschaften und Kunste [★IO]
Europaische Baptistische Foderation [★IO]
Europaische Baptistische Frauenunion [★IO]
Europaische Bausparkassenvereinigung [★IO]
Europaische Beratervereinigung [★IO]
Europaische Evangelische Allianz [★IO]
Europaische Foderation der Bergbau-, Chemie-, Und Energie Gewerkschaften [★IO]
Europaische Foderation fur Betriebessport [★IO]
Europaische Foderation fur Chemie-Ingenieur-Wesen [★IO]
Europaische Gesellschaft fur Herbologie [★IO]
Europaische Gesellschaft fur Schriftpsychologie und Schriftexpertise [★IO]
Europaische Go Fed. [★IO]
Europaische Kernenergie-Gesellschaft [★IO]
Europaische Marchengesellschaft [★IO]
Europaische Metall-Union [★IO]
Europaische Musikschul-Union [★IO]
Europaische Org. der Militarverbande [★IO]
Europaische Radsport Union [★IO]
Europaische Schulleitervereinigung [★IO]
Europaische Union Judischer Studenten [★IO]
Europaische Union der Musikwettbewerbe fur die Jugend [★IO]
Europaische Vereinigung der Allgemeinartze [★IO]
Europaische Vereinigung der Arzteverbande der besonderen Therapierichtungen [★IO]
Europaische Vereinigung der Erdgaswirtschaft [★IO]
Europaische Vereinigung der Industrie Flexibler Verpackung [★IO]
Europaische Vereinigung der Lack-, Druckfarben- und Kunstlerfarbenindustrie [★IO]

Europaische Vereinigung der Verbande der Reformwaren-Hersteller [★IO]
Europaische Zentrum fur Minderheitenfragen [★IO]
Europaischen Baptistischen Mission [★IO]
Europaischen Ombudsmann-Institut [★IO]
Europaischen Senioren Union [★IO]
Europaischer Fachverband der Arzneimittel-Hersteller [★IO]
Europaischer Sportschiffahrtsverband [★IO]
Europaischer Tabakwaren-Grosshandels-Verband [★IO]
Europaischer Verband der Binnenhafen [★IO]
Europaischer Verband der Lichtwerbung [★IO]
Europaischer Verband der Veranstaltungs-Centren [★IO]
Europaischer Wohnwagen-Verband [★IO]
Europaisches Collegium fur Bewusstseinsstudien [★IO]
Europaisches Institut fur postgraduale Bildung [★IO]
Europaisches Komitee Olhydraulik und Pneumatik [★IO]
Europaisches Medieninstitut [★IO]
Europaisches Patentamt [★IO]
Europalia Intl. [IO], Brussels, Belgium
Europe
Africa Faith and Justice Network [16920]
Amer. Assn. for the Advancement of Slavic Stud. [10966]
Amer. Central European Dental Inst. [14127]
Amer. Fed. of Jews From Central Europe [17944]
Balalaika and Domra Assn. of Am. [10563]
Basque Educational Org. [9732]
Central Eurasian Stud. Soc. [10233]
Centre for Development and Population Activities [12422]
Consultative Coun. of Jewish Organizations [17947]
Croatian Philatelic Soc. [22813]
Democratic Party of the Peoples of Europe - European Free Alliance [IO]
Ercoupe Owners Club [21444]
European-American Chamber of Commerce in the U.S. [24276]
European Democrat Students [IO]
European Evaluation Soc. [IO]
European Union - Delegation of the Commn. to the U.S. [IO]
European Union - Delegation of the Commn. to the U.S. [17507]
Found. for the Advancement of Sephardic Stud. and Culture [19181]
Human Rights Watch - Helsinki [17763]
Intl. Law Students Assn. [5868]
Natl. Coun. for Eurasian and East European Res. [10968]
New Hope Intl. [20372]
Ozar Hatorah [20171]
People-to-People Hea. Found. [14984]
Radio Free Europe/Radio Liberty [17191]
Soc. for the Anthropology of Europe [6423]
U.S. Assn. of Former Members of Cong. [17253]
Europe Air Sports [IO], Heemstede, Netherlands
Europe; Amer. Fed. of Jews From Central [17944]
Europe; Free [★17191]
Europe/Radio Liberty; Radio Free [17191]
European
Academia Europaea [IO]
Amer. Central European Dental Inst. [14127]
Assn. for Renaissance Martial Arts [8820]
Before Columbus Found. [10416]
Belgo-Canadian Assn. [IO]
Chinese Soc. for EU Stud. [IO]
Coun. for European Stud. [IO]
Coun. for European Stud. [8404]
Croatian Philatelic Soc. [22813]
Ercoupe Owners Club [21444]
Europalia Intl. [IO]
European/American Issues Forum [17113]
European Amer. Musical Alliance [10594]
European-American Unity and Rights Org. [17114]
European Found. Centre [IO]
European Travel Commn. [3916]
European Union - Delegation of the Commn. to the U.S. [17507]

Fed. Union of European Nationalities [IO]
Fed. of East European Family History Societies [19068]
Historians of German and Central European Art and Architecture [9921]
Historians of German and Central European Art and Architecture [IO]
IES, Inst. for the Intl. Educ. of Students [IO]
IES, Inst. for the Intl. Educ. of Students [8405]
Ligeia Assn. pour le Renouvellement de la Culture Artistique Europeenne [IO]
Mexican Epigraphic Soc. [10130]
New Hope Intl. [20372]
Slavic and East European Folklore Assn. [9962]
Slavic Heritage Coalition [10969]
Soc. for Austrian and Habsburg History [9628]
Univ. Assn. for Contemporary European Stud. [IO]
YIVO Inst. for Jewish Res. [10292]
European Acad. of Advanced Res. in Marketing [★IO]
European Acad. of Allergology and Clinical Immunology [IO], Stockholm, Sweden
European Acad. of Andrology [IO], Rome, Italy
European Acad. of Childhood Disability [IO], Brussels, Belgium
European Acad. of Dermatology and Venereology [IO], Brussels, Belgium
European Acad. of Design [IO], Lancaster, United Kingdom
European Acad. of Facial Plastic Surgery [IO], Milan, Italy
European Acad. For Aviation Safety [IO], Blagnac, France
European Acad. of Nutritional Sciences [IO], Lausanne, Switzerland
European Acad. Otzenhausen [IO], Nonnweiler, Germany
European Acad. of Paediatric Dentistry [IO], Dublin, Ireland
European Acad. of Sciences and Arts [IO], Salzburg, Austria
European Acad. of Teachers in Gen. Practice [IO], Ljubljana, Slovenia
European Acad. of the Urban Env. [IO], Berlin, Germany
European Accounting Assn. [IO], Brussels, Belgium
European Actuarial Consultative Gp. [IO], Oxford, United Kingdom
European Advt. Standards Alliance [IO], Brussels, Belgium
European Aero-Medical Inst. [IO], Filderstadt, Germany
European Aerosol Fed. [IO], Brussels, Belgium
European Aggregates Assn. [IO], Brussels, Belgium
European AIDS Clinical Soc. [IO], Paris, France
European AIDS Treatment Gp. [IO], Brussels, Belgium
European Airlines Res. Bur. [★IO]
European Alliance of Companies for Energy Efficiency in Buildings [IO], Brussels, Belgium
European Alliance Genetic Support Groups [★IO]
European Alliance of Neuromuscular Disorders Associations [IO], Gzira, Malta
European Alliance of News Agencies [IO], Stockholm, Sweden
European Alliance of Press Agencies [★IO]
European Aluminium Assn. [IO], Brussels, Belgium
European Aluminum Foil Assn. [IO], Dusseldorf, Germany
European Amateur Boxing Assn. [IO], Moscow, Russia
European - Amer. Bus. Coun. [IO], Washington, DC, United States
European - Amer. Bus. Coun. [24275], 1325 G St. NW, Ste. 500, Washington, DC 20005, (202)449-7705
European Amer. Chamber of Commerce (France) [IO], Paris, France
European-American Chamber of Commerce in the U.S. [24276], 12 E 49th St., 24th Fl., New York, NY 10017, (212)315-2196
European-American Chamber of Commerce in the U.S. [IO], New York, NY, United States
European-American Chamber of Commerce in Washington, DC [★IO]

European-American Chamber of Commerce in Washington, DC [★24275]
European American Constitution Heritage - Address unknown since 2004.
European/American Issues Forum [17113], c/o Lou Calabro, Pres., PMB 253, 1212H El Camino Real, San Bruno, CA 94066, (650)312-8284
European Amer. Musical Alliance [10594], 1160 Fifth Ave., Ste. 201, New York, NY 10029, (212)831-7424
European-American Unity and Rights Org. [17114], c/o David Duke, PhD, Pres., PO Box 188, Mandeville, LA 70470, (985)626-7714
European Anodisers' Assn. [★IO]
European Anti-poverty Network [IO], Brussels, Belgium
European Apparel and Textile Org. [IO], Brussels, Belgium
European Aquaculture Soc. [IO], Oostende, Belgium
European Arboricultural Coun. [IO], Bad Honnef, Germany
European Architectural Endoscopy Assn. [IO], Dresden, Germany
European Arenas Assn. [IO], Birmingham, United Kingdom
European Article Numbering Assn. [★IO]
European and Asian Stud; Inst. of [★7985]
European Asphalt Pavement Assn. [IO], Brussels, Belgium
European Aspirin Found. [IO], Haslemere, United Kingdom
European Assembly of Turkish Academics [IO], Stuttgart, Germany
European Assn. of Acarologists [IO], Vienna, Austria
European Assn. of Aerospace Indus. Standardisation [★IO]
European Assn. Against Violence Against Women at Work [IO], Paris, France
European Assn. of Agricultural Economists [IO], The Hague, Netherlands
European Assn. of Air Heater Manufacturers [IO], Menen, Belgium
European Assn. of Aluminum Aerosol Cans Mfrs. [★IO]
European Assn. for Amer. Stud. [IO], Paris, France
European Assn. for Animal Production [IO], Rome, Italy
European Assn. for Apitherapy [IO], Limoges, France
European Assn. for Aquatic Mammals [IO], St. Andrews, United Kingdom
European Assn. of Archaeologists [IO], Prague, Czech Republic
European Assn. of Architectural Educ. [IO], Leuven, Belgium
European Assn. of Artists' Managers [IO], Levallois Perret, France
European Assn. of Automotive Suppliers [IO], Brussels, Belgium
European Assn. for Aviation Psychology [IO], Hamburg, Germany
European Assn. for Banking and Financial History [IO], Frankfurt am Main, Germany
European Assn. for Banking History [★IO]
European Assn. for Battery, Hybrid and Fuel Cell Elec. Vehicles [IO], Brussels, Belgium
European Assn. for Behavioural and Cognitive Therapies [IO], Utrecht, Netherlands
European Assn. for Bioindustries [IO], Brussels, Belgium
European Assn. for Body Psychotherapy [IO], Amsterdam, Netherlands
European Assn. for Cancer Res. [IO], Nottingham, United Kingdom
European Assn. for Cardio-Thoracic Surgery [IO], Windsor, United Kingdom
European Assn. of Centres of Medical Ethics [IO], Maastricht, Netherlands
European Assn. of Chem. Distributors [IO], Brussels, Belgium
European Assn. for Chem. and Molecular Sciences [IO], London, United Kingdom
European Assn. of Chinese Stud. [IO], Cambridge, United Kingdom
European Assn. of Classification Societies [★IO]

European Assn. of Clinical Anatomy [IO], Graz, Austria
European Assn. for Coal and Lignite [IO], Brussels, Belgium
European Assn. of Coleopterology [IO], Barcelona, Spain
European Assn. for Commonwealth Literature and Language Stud. [IO], Aachen, Germany
European Assn. of Communications Agencies [IO], Brussels, Belgium
European Assn. for Comparative Economic Stud. [IO], Perugia, Italy
European Assn. for Cmpt. Assisted Language Learning [IO], Limerick, Ireland
European Assn. for Cmpt. Graphics [IO], Aire-la-Ville, Switzerland
European Assn. for Cmpt. Sci. Logic [IO], Bologna, Italy
European Assn. for the Conservation of the Geological Heritage [IO], Uppsala, Sweden
European Assn. of Conservatories [★IO]
European Assn. of Consultants to and about Not-for-Profit Organisations [IO], London, United Kingdom
European Assn. of Consultants to and about the Not-for-Profit Sector [★IO]
European Assn. of Cooperative Banks [IO], Brussels, Belgium
European Assn. of Craft, Small and Medium-Sized Enterprises [IO], Brussels, Belgium
European Assn. for Cranio-Maxillofacial Surgery [IO], Midhurst, United Kingdom
European Assn. for Dental Public Hea. [IO], Marburg, Germany
European Assn. of Dermato-Oncology [IO], Vienna, Austria
European Assn. of Development Agencies [IO], Brussels, Belgium
European Assn. of Development Res. and Training Institutes [IO], Bonn, Germany
European Assn. of Dir. and Database Publishers [IO], Brussels, Belgium
European Assn. Dir. Publishers [★IO]
European Assn. of Distance Learning [★IO]
European Assn. for Distance Learning [IO], Grootebroek, Netherlands
European Assn. of Distance Teaching Universities [IO], Heerlen, Netherlands
European Assn. of Earth Sci. Editors [★IO]
European Assn. for Earthquake Engg. [IO], Istanbul, Turkey
European Assn. for the Educ. of Adults [IO], Brussels, Belgium
European Assn. for Educ. in Elecl. and Info. Engg. [IO], Rennes, France
European Assn. for Educ. Law and Policy [IO], Antwerp, Belgium
European Assn. for Endoscopic Surgery and Other Interventional Techniques [IO], Veldhoven, Netherlands
European Assn. of Engravers and Flexographers [IO], Wiesbaden, Germany
European Assn. for Environmental Mgt. Educ. [IO], Varese, Italy
European Assn. of Environmental and Rsrc. Economists [IO], Venice, Italy
European Assn. of Establishments for Veterinary Educ. [IO], Zurich, Switzerland
European Assn. of Event Centers [IO], Bad Homburg, Germany
European Assn. for Evolutionary Political Economy [IO], Delft, Netherlands
European Assn. of Experimental Social Psychology [IO], Munster, Germany
European Assn. of Feldspar Producers [IO], Brussels, Belgium
European Assn. of Fibre Drum Mfrs. [IO], Uckfield, United Kingdom
European Assn. of Fish Pathologists [IO], Weymouth, United Kingdom
European Assn. of Fisheries Economists [IO], Frederiksberg, Denmark
European Assn. of Flexible Foam Block Mfrs. [★IO]
European Assn. of Flexible Polyurethane Foam Blocks Mfrs. [IO], Brussels, Belgium
European Assn. for Forensic Child and Adolescent Psychiatry, Psychology and other involved Professionals [IO], Manchester, United Kingdom

---

Reference to "IO" in place of a book number signifies that the association may be found in the 45th edition of International Organizations.

European Assn. for Geochemistry [IO], Grenoble, France

European Assn. of Geoscientists and Engineers [IO], Houten, Netherlands

European Assn. for Grain Legume Res. [IO], Paris, France

European Assn. for Hea. Info. and Libraries [IO], Utrecht, Netherlands

European Assn. for Higher Educ. in Biotechnology [IO], Genoa, Italy

European Assn. for the History of Medicine and Hea. [IO], Gottingen, Germany

European Assn. of Hosp. Pharmacists [IO], Niort, France

European Assn. of Hotel and Tourism Schools [IO], Diekirch, Luxembourg

European Assn. of Indus. Silica Producers [IO], Brussels, Belgium

European Assn. of Indus. of Branded Products [★IO]

European Assn. of Info. Dissemination Centres [★IO]

European Assn. for Info. on Local Development [IO], Brussels, Belgium

European Assn. of Info. Services [IO], Amersfoort, Netherlands

European Assn. for Institutional Res. [IO], Amsterdam, Netherlands

European Assn. of Internal Combustion Engine Mfrs. [IO], Frankfurt, Germany

European Assn. for Intl. Educ. [IO], Amsterdam, Netherlands

European Assn. for Investors in Non-listed Real Estate Vehicles [IO], Amsterdam, Netherlands

European Assn. for Japanese Stud. [IO], Frankfurt, Germany

European Assn. for Jewish Stud. [IO], Oxford, United Kingdom

European Assn. of Labour Economists [IO], Maastricht, Netherlands

European Assn. of Lawyers for Democracy and World Human Rights [IO], Dusseldorf, Germany

European Assn. for Lexicography [IO], Birmingham, United Kingdom

European Assn. of Linguists and Language Teachers [IO], Perros-Guirec, France

European Assn. of Machine Tool Merchants [IO], Brussels, Belgium

European Assn. for Machine Translation [IO], Geneva, Switzerland

European Assn. of Makers of Packaging Papers [IO], Darmstadt, Germany

European Assn. of Mfrs. of Aluminum Aerosol Cans [★IO]

European Assn. of Mfrs. of Moulded Polyurethane Parts for the Automotive Indus. [IO], Brussels, Belgium

European Assn. of Metals [IO], Brussels, Belgium

European Assn. for Microprocessing and Microprogramming [IO], St. Augustin, Germany

European Assn. of Microprocessing and Microprogramming [★IO]

European Assn. for Middle Eastern Stud. [IO], Mainz, Germany

European Assn. of Mining Indus. [★IO]

European Assn. of Mining Indus., Metals Ores and Indus. Minerals [IO], Brussels, Belgium

European Assn. of Museums of the History of Medical Sciences [IO], Paris, France

European Assn. of Music Academies [IO], Utrecht, Netherlands

European Assn. of Music Conservatories, Academies, and High Schools [IO], Utrecht, Netherlands

European Assn. of Natl. Organisations of Textile Retailers [IO], Brussels, Belgium

European Assn. of Natl. Productivity Centres [IO], Brussels, Belgium

European Assn. for NeuroOncology [IO], Kreischa, Germany

European Assn. of Neurosurgical Societies [IO], Southampton, United Kingdom

European Assn. of Nitrogen Mfrs. [★IO]

European Assn. of Nuclear Medicine [IO], Vienna, Austria

European Assn. of Organic Geochemists [IO], Paris, France

European Assn. for Osseointegration [IO], Brussels, Belgium

European Assn. for Palliative Care [IO], Milan, Italy

European Assn. for Passive Fire Protection [IO], Farnham, United Kingdom

European Assn. of Perinatal Medicine [IO], Lund, Sweden

European Assn. for Personality Psychology [IO], Bielefeld, Germany

European Assn. for Personnel Mgt. [IO], Dusseldorf, Germany

European Assn. of Pharmaceutical Full-Line Wholesalers [IO], Brussels, Belgium

European Assn. for Planned Giving [IO], Lenham, United Kingdom

European Assn. of Plastic Surgeons [IO], Gent, Belgium

European Assn. Poison Control Centres [★IO]

European Assn. of Poisons Centres and Clinical Toxicologists [IO], Zurich, Switzerland

European Assn. for Population Stud. [IO], The Hague, Netherlands

European Assn. for Potato Res. [IO], Zeist, Netherlands

European Assn. for Prdt. and Process Modelling in the Building Indus. [IO], Dresden, Germany

European Assn. of Professional Secretaries [IO], Bagsvaerd, Denmark

European Assn. for Professions in Biomedical Sci. [IO], Salzburg, Austria

European Assn. of Programmes in Hea. Services Stud. [★IO]

European Assn. for the Promotion of Cogeneration [IO], Brussels, Belgium

European Assn. for the Promotion of Poetry [IO], Gent, Belgium

European Assn. of Psychological Assessment [IO], Barcelona, Spain

European Assn. of Psychology and Law [IO], Erlangen, Germany

European Assn. for Psychotherapy [IO], Vienna, Austria

European Assn. of Pump Mfrs. [IO], Brussels, Belgium

European Assn. of Radiology [IO], Paris, France

European Assn. of Refrigeration Enterprises [★IO]

European Assn. of Remote Sensing Labs. [IO], Hannover, Germany

European Assn. for Renewable Energy [IO], Bonn, Germany

European Assn. for Res. on Adolescence [IO], Utrecht, Netherlands

European Assn. for Res. on Learning and Instruction [IO], Leuven, Belgium

European Assn. of Res. and Tech. Organisations [IO], Brussels, Belgium

European Assn. of the Rubber Indus. [★IO]

European Assn. of Schools and Colleges of Optometry [★IO]

European Assn. of Schools of Occupational Medicine [IO], Driebergen, Netherlands

European Assn. of Schools of Social Work [IO], Maastricht, Netherlands

European Assn. for the Sci. of Air Pollution [IO], Sofia, Bulgaria

European Assn. of Sci. Editors [IO], Reading, United Kingdom

European Assn. for the Self-Adhesive Tape Indus. [IO], The Hague, Netherlands

European Assn. of Senior Hosp. Physicians [IO], Brussels, Belgium

European Assn. of Ser. Providers for Persons with Disability [IO], Brussels, Belgium

European Assn. for Share Promotion [IO], Holte, Denmark

European Assn. for Signal Processing [★IO]

European Assn. for Signal, Speech and Image Processing [IO], Kessariani, Greece

European Assn. of Social Anthropologists [IO], Bremen, Germany

European Assn. for Southeast Asian Stud. [IO], Naples, Italy

European Assn. for Speech Signal and Image Processing [IO], Kessariani, Greece

European Assn. for Sport Mgt. [IO], Florence, Italy

European Assn. for the Streamlining of Energy Exchange [IO], Paris, France

European Assn. for Stud. on Nutrition and Child Development [IO], Paris, France

European Assn. for the Stud. of Diabetes [IO], Dusseldorf, Germany

European Assn. for the Stud. of Diabetes Eye Complications Study Group [IO], Rome, Italy

European Assn. for the Stud. of Religions [IO], Leeds, United Kingdom

European Assn. for Stud. of Safety Problems in Production and Use of Propellants [IO], Kilmacolm, United Kingdom

European Assn. of Teachers [IO], Strasbourg, France

European Assn. of Teachers - UK Sect. [IO], Shoeburyness, United Kingdom

European Assn. for Terminology [IO], Brussels, Belgium

European Assn. for Textile Polyolefins [IO], Brussels, Belgium

European Assn. for Theoretical Cmpt. Sci. [IO], Bratislava, Slovakia

European Assn. for the Trade in Jute and Related Products [IO], The Hague, Netherlands

European Assn. of Transactional Anal. [IO], Konstanz, Germany

European Assn. for the Transfer of Technologies, Innovation, and Indus. Info. [IO], Luxembourg, Luxembourg

European Assn. for the Treatment of Addiction - U.K. [IO], London, United Kingdom

European Assn. of Turkish Academics - Belgium [IO], Brussels, Belgium

European Assn. of Universities, Schools and Colleges of Optometry [IO], Bures-sur-Yvette, France

European Assn. of Urology [IO], Arnhem, Netherlands

European Assn. of Veterinary Anatomists [IO], Oslo, Norway

European Assn. of Veterinary Diagnostic Imaging [IO], Merelbeke, Belgium

European Assn. for Vision and Eye Res. [IO], Leuven, Belgium

European Assn. of Work and Organizational Psychology [IO], Liege, Belgium

European Assn. of Young Historians [IO], Louvain-la-Neuve, Belgium

European Assn. of Youth Orchestras [IO], Dedemsvaart, Netherlands

European Assn. for Zoological Nomenclature [IO], Bern, Switzerland

European Assn. of Zoos and Aquaria [IO], Amsterdam, Netherlands

European Astronomical Soc. [IO], Versoix, Switzerland

European Atherosclerosis Soc. [IO], Malmo, Sweden

European Athletic Assn. [IO], Lausanne, Switzerland

European Athletics Coaches Assn. [IO], Richmond, United Kingdom

European Atomic Forum [IO], Brussels, Belgium

European Audiovisual Entrepreneurs [IO], Bertrange, Luxembourg

European Auto. Mfrs. Assn. [IO], Brussels, Belgium

European Badminton Union [★IO]

European Baha'i Bus. Forum [IO], Chambery, France

European Bank of Frozen Blood of Rare Groups [IO], Amsterdam, Netherlands

European Banking Fed. [IO], Brussels, Belgium

European Baptist Fed. [IO], Prague, Czech Republic

European Baptist Mission [IO], Wustermark, Germany

European Baptist Press Ser. of the European Baptist Fed. [IO], Prague, Czech Republic

European Baptist Women's Union [IO], Bialystok, Poland

European Barge Union [IO], Rotterdam, Netherlands

European Battery Recycling Assn. [IO], Brussels, Belgium

European Beer Consumers' Union [IO], St. Albans, United Kingdom

European Behavioral Pharmacology Soc. [IO], Hamburg, Germany

A star before a book entry number signifies that the name is not listed separately, but is mentioned within the entry.

European Bentonite Producers Assn. [IO], Brussels, Belgium
European Biological Rhythms Soc. [IO], Guildford, United Kingdom
European Biomass Indus. Assn. [IO], Brussels, Belgium
European Biomedical Res. Assn. [IO], London, United Kingdom
European Biophysical Societies' Assn. [IO], Debrecen, Hungary
European Biosafety Assn. [IO], Aartselaar, Belgium
European Bitumen Assn. [IO], Brussels, Belgium
European Blind Union [IO], Paris, France
European Blue Cross Youth Assn. [IO], Uppsala, Sweden
European Bd. of Cardiovascular Perfusion [IO], Zurich, Switzerland
European Bd. and Coll. of Obstetrics and Gynaecology [IO], Newcastle upon Tyne, United Kingdom
European Bd. of Ophthalmology [IO], Edegem, Belgium
European Bd. of Plastic, Reconstructive and Aesthetic Surgery [IO], Toulouse, France
European Bd. of Urology [IO], Arnhem, Netherlands
European Bd. of Veterinary Specialization [IO], Limal, Belgium
European Boating Assn. [IO], Southampton, United Kingdom
European Booksellers Fed. [IO], Brussels, Belgium
European Borates Assn. [IO], Brussels, Belgium
European Botanical and Horticultural Libraries Gp. [IO], Richmond, United Kingdom
European Bowling Proprietors Assn. [IO], Norrkoping, Sweden
European Brain and Behaviour Soc. [IO], Rome, Italy
European Brain Coun. [IO], Brussels, Belgium
European Brain Injury Consortium [IO], Rotterdam, Netherlands
European Brain Injury Soc. [IO], Brussels, Belgium
European Brands Assn. [IO], Brussels, Belgium
European Brewery Convention [IO], Zoeterwoude, Netherlands
European Bridge League [IO], Milan, Italy
European Broadcasting Union [IO], Grand-Saconnex, Switzerland
European Brushware Fed. [IO], Tilburg, Netherlands
European Buddhist Union [IO], Nantes, France
European Building and Services Assn. [IO], Berlin, Germany
European Building Sites Assn. [★IO]
European Bur. for Conscientious Objection [IO], Brussels, Belgium
European Bur. for Lesser-Used Languages [IO], Dublin, Ireland
European Bur. of Lib., Info. and Documentation Associations [IO], The Hague, Netherlands
European Burns Assn. [IO], Beverwijk, Netherlands
European Bus. Angel Network [IO], Brussels, Belgium
European Bus. Aviation Assn. [IO], Tervuren, Belgium
European Bus. Club [★IO]
European Bus. Ethics Network [IO], Leuven, Belgium
European Bus. History Assn. [IO], Glasgow, United Kingdom
European Bus. and Innovation Centre Network [IO], Brussels, Belgium
European Bus. Network [★IO]
European Cable Communications Assn. [★IO]
European Calcified Tissue Soc. [IO], Bristol, United Kingdom
European Calcium Carbonate Assn. - Europe [IO], Brussels, Belgium
European Calcium Soc. [IO], Brussels, Belgium
European Canoe Assn. [IO], Nottingham, United Kingdom
European Car and Truck Rental Assn. [IO], Brussels, Belgium
European Caravan Fed. [IO], Frankfurt, Germany
European Carton Makers Assn. [IO], The Hague, Netherlands
European Casino Assn. [IO], Brussels, Belgium
European Catalysts Mfrs. Assn. [IO], Brussels, Belgium

European Catering Assn. Intl. [IO], Kingston Upon Thames, United Kingdom
European Cell Death Org. [IO], Gent, Belgium
European Cement Assn. [IO], Brussels, Belgium
European Center for Missing and Sexually Exploited Children [★IO]
European Center for Social Welfare Training and Res. [★IO]
European Centre for Development Policy Mgt. [IO], Maastricht, Netherlands
European Centre for Ecotoxicology and Toxicology of Chemicals [IO], Brussels, Belgium
European Centre of Enterprises with Public Participation and of Enterprises of Gen. Economic Interest [IO], Brussels, Belgium
European Centre for Higher Educ. [IO], Bucharest, Romania
European Centre for Medium-Range Weather Forecasts [IO], Reading, United Kingdom
European Centre for Minority Issues [IO], Flensburg, Germany
European Centre for Modern Language of the Coun. of Europe [IO], Graz, Austria
European Centre for Nature Conservation [IO], Tilburg, Netherlands
European Centre for Occupational Hea., Safety and the Env. [IO], Glasgow, United Kingdom
European Centre for Parliamentary Res. and Documentation [IO], Brussels, Belgium
European Centre for Population Stud. [★IO]
European Centre of Public Enterprises [★IO]
European Centre for Social Welfare Policy and Res. [IO], Vienna, Austria
European Centre for Strategic Mgt. of Universities [IO], Brussels, Belgium
European Centre of Stud. on Linear Alkylbenzene [IO], Brussels, Belgium
European Centre for Stud. of Sulfuric Acid [★IO]
European Ceramic Soc. [IO], Mons, Belgium
European Ceramic Tile Mfrs. Assn. [IO], Brussels, Belgium
European Cetacean Soc. [IO], La Rochelle, France
European Charcot Found. [IO], Nijmegen, Netherlands
European Chem. Indus. Coun. [IO], Brussels, Belgium
European Chem. Indus. Ecology and Toxicology Centre [★IO]
European Chem. Marketing and Strategy Assn. [IO], The Hague, Netherlands
European Chem. Soc. [IO], Louvain-la-Neuve, Belgium
European Chem. Transport Assn. [IO], Brussels, Belgium
European Chemoreception Res. Org. [IO], Cagliari, Italy
European Children's Network [IO], Brussels, Belgium
European Chilled Food Fed. [IO], Kettering, United Kingdom
European Chinese Soc. for Clinical Magnetic Resonance [IO], Freiburg, Germany
European Chips and Snacks Assn. [★IO]
European Chlorinated Solvent Assn. [IO], Brussels, Belgium
European Christian Environmental Network [IO], Brussels, Belgium
European Citric Acid Mfrs. Assn. [IO], Brussels, Belgium
European Civil Aviation Conf. [IO], Neuilly-sur-Seine, France
European Civil Ser. Fed. [IO], Brussels, Belgium
European Club for Paediatric Burns [IO], Cape Town, Republic of South Africa
European Club for Textile Polyolefins [★IO]
European Coal Combustion Products Assn. [IO], Essen, Germany
European Coalition to End Animal Experiments [IO], London, United Kingdom
European Coastal Assn. for Sci. and Tech. [IO], Cardiff, United Kingdom
European Cockpit Assn. [IO], Brussels, Belgium
European Coffee Fed. [IO], Amsterdam, Netherlands
European Coil Coating Assn. [IO], Brussels, Belgium
European Cold Storage and Logistics Assn. [IO], Brussels, Belgium

European Coll. of Hypnotherapy [IO], Crowborough, United Kingdom
European Coll. of Lab. Animal Medicine [IO], Utrecht, Netherlands
European Coll. of Neuropsychopharmacology [IO], Utrecht, Netherlands
European Coll. of Sport Sci. [IO], Cologne, Germany
European Coll. for the Stud. of Consciousness [IO], Gottingen, Germany
European Coll. of Veterinary Anaesthesia [IO], Thessaloniki, Greece
European Coll. of Veterinary Diagnostic Imaging [IO], Gent, Belgium
European Coll. of Veterinary Internal Medicine - Companion Animals [IO], Bearsden, United Kingdom
European Coll. of Veterinary Pathologists [IO], Ware, United Kingdom
European Coll. of Veterinary Surgeons [IO], Zurich, Switzerland
European Colloid and Interface Soc. [IO], Fribourg, Switzerland
European Colloquium of Independent Inspecting Organizations [★IO]
European Commn. - Barbados and Eastern Caribbean Delegation [IO], Christ Church, Barbados
European Commn. - Congo Delegation [IO], Kinshasa, Republic of the Congo
European Commn. - Kenya Delegation [IO], Nairobi, Kenya
European Commn. - Mozambique Delegation [IO], Maputo, Mozambique
European Commn. Off. of Press and Public Affairs [★IO]
European Commn. Off. of Press and Public Affairs [★17507]
European Commn. - Pacific Delegation [IO], Suva, Fiji
European Commn. on Preservation and Access [IO], Amsterdam, Netherlands
European Commn. - Suriname Off. [IO], Paramaribo, Suriname
European Commn. - Tanzania Delegation [IO], Dar es Salaam, United Republic of Tanzania
European Commn. - Togo Delegation [IO], Lome, Togo
European Commn. - Trinidad and Tobago Delegation [IO], Port of Spain, Trinidad and Tobago
European Comm. for the Advancement of Thermal Sciences and Heat Transfer [IO], Villeurbanne, France
European Comm. of the Amer. Chamber of Commerce in Belgium [★IO]
European Comm. of Associations of Mfrs. of Agricultural Machinery [IO], Paris, France
European Comm. of Associations of Manufacturers of Gears and Transmission Parts [IO], Frankfurt am Main, Germany
European Comm. for Banking Standards [IO], Brussels, Belgium
European Comm. for Building Tech. Equip. [★IO]
European Comm. for Catholic Educ. [IO], Brussels, Belgium
European Comm. for Electrotechnical Standardization [IO], Brussels, Belgium
European Comm. for External Quality Assessment Programmes in Lab. Medicine [IO], Brussels, Belgium
European Comm. of Indus. Furnace and Heating Equip. Associations [IO], Frankfurt, Germany
European Comm. of Machinery Mfrs. for the Plastics and Rubber Indus. [IO], Frankfurt, Germany
European Comm. of Mfrs. of Compressors, Vacuum Pumps, and Pneumatic Tools [IO], Brussels, Belgium
European Comm. of the Mfrs. of Fire Protection Equip. and Fire Fighting Vehicles [IO], Wurzburg, Germany
European Comm. of Professional Diving Instructors [IO], Antibes, France
European Comm. for Standardization [IO], Brussels, Belgium
European Comm. for the Stud. of Corrosion and Protection of Pipes [IO], Brussels, Belgium
European Comm. for the Stud. of Salt [★IO]

Reference to "IO" in place of a book number signifies that the association may be found in the 45th edition of International Organizations.

European Comm. for Sugar Manufacturers [IO], Brussels, Belgium

European Comm. for the Valve Indus. [IO], Brussels, Belgium

European Comm. for Young Farmers and 4H Clubs [★IO]

European Commodities Exchange [IO], Strasbourg, France

European Community of Consumer Cooperatives [IO], Brussels, Belgium

European Community Info. Ser. [★IO]

European Community Info. Ser. [★17507]

European Community Off. of Press and Public Affairs [★17507]

European Community Off. of Press and Public Affairs [★IO]

European Community Shipowners' Assn. [IO], Brussels, Belgium

European Community of Young Horticulturists [IO], Grunberg, Germany

European Community Youth Orchestra [★IO]

European Competitive Telecommunications Assn. [IO], Brussels, Belgium

European Cmpt. Driving License Found. [IO], Dublin, Ireland

European Confed. of Executives and Managerial Staff [IO], Brussels, Belgium

European Confed. of the Footwear Indus. [IO], Brussels, Belgium

European Confed. of Independent Trade Unions [IO], Brussels, Belgium

European Confed. of Independents [IO], Neunkirchen, Germany

European Confed. of Intl. Trading Houses Associations [IO], The Hague, Netherlands

European Confed. of Iron and Steel Indus. [IO], Brussels, Belgium

European Confed. of Junior Enterprises [IO], Brussels, Belgium

European Confed. of Medical Devices Associations [★IO]

European Confed. of Natl. Associations of Mfrs. of Insulated Wire and Cable [IO], Brussels, Belgium

European Confed. of Organizations for Testing, Inspection, Certification and Prevention [★IO]

European Confed. of Paint, Printing Ink and Artists' Colours Mfrs. [★IO]

European Confed. of Police [IO], Luxembourg, Luxembourg

European Confed. of Property Managers [IO], Brussels, Belgium

European Confed. of Pulp, Paper, and Bd. Indus. [★IO]

European Confed. of Real Estate Agents [IO], The Hague, Netherlands

European Confed. of Spirits Producers [★IO]

European Confed. of Upper Rhine Universities [IO], Strasbourg, France

European Confed. of Woodworking Indus. [IO], Brussels, Belgium

European Confed. of Workers' Cooperatives, Social Cooperatives and Social and Participative Enterprises [IO], Brussels, Belgium

European Conf. of Associations of Telecommunications Indus. [★IO]

European Conf. on Christian Educ. [IO], Lausanne, Switzerland

European Conf. of Conscripts Organisations [★IO]

European Conf. of Ministers of Transport [IO], Paris, France

European Conf. of Postal and Telecommunications Administrations [IO], Berlin, Germany

European Conf. of Promoters of New Music [IO], Amsterdam, Netherlands

European Conf. of Radio and Electronic Equip. Associations [★IO]

European Conservation Agriculture Fed. [IO], Brussels, Belgium

European Consortium for Agricultural Res. in the Tropics [IO], Paris, France

European Consortium for Communications Res. [IO], Brussels, Belgium

European Consortium of Innovative Universities [IO], Glasgow, United Kingdom

European Consortium for the Learning Org. [IO], Wavre, Belgium

European Consortium for Mathematics in Indus. [IO], Linz, Austria

European Consortium for Political Res. [IO], Colchester, United Kingdom

European Consortium of Social Professions with Educational and Social Stud. [IO], Koblenz, Germany

European Consortium for Sociological Res. [IO], Nijmegen, Netherlands

European Constr. Indus. Fed. [IO], Brussels, Belgium

European Constr. Inst. [IO], Loughborough, United Kingdom

European Consultants Unit [IO], Munich, Germany

European Consultation on Refugees and Exiles [★IO]

European Consumers Org. [IO], Brussels, Belgium

European Contact Gp. on Church and Indus. [★IO]

European Contact Gp. - Ecumenical Network for Economic and Social Action [IO], Prague, Czech Republic

European Contact Lens Soc. of Ophthalmologists [IO], Valmont, France

European Container Glass Fed. [IO], Brussels, Belgium

European Control Data User's Org. - Defunct.

European Convention for Constructional Steelwork [IO], Brussels, Belgium

European Cooperation in the Field of Sci. and Tech. Res. [IO], Brussels, Belgium

European Cooperation in Legal Metrology [IO], Vienna, Austria

European Coordinating Committee for Artificial Intelligence [IO], Vienna, Austria

European Copper Inst. [IO], Brussels, Belgium

European Cosmetic, Toiletry and Perfumery Assn. [IO], Brussels, Belgium

European Coun. for Agricultural Law [IO], Gent, Belgium

European Coun. of Amer. Chambers of Commerce [IO], Frankfurt am Main, Germany

European Coun. of Applied Sciences and Engg. [IO], Paris, France

European Coun. of Artists [IO], Copenhagen, Denmark

European Coun. for Cardiovascular Res. [IO], London, United Kingdom

European Coun. on Chiropractic Educ. [IO], Havant, United Kingdom

European Coun. of Civil Engineers [IO], Bratislava, Slovakia

European Coun. for Classical Homeopathy [IO], Norfolk, United Kingdom

European Coun. of Conscripts Organisations [IO], Stockholm, Sweden

European Coun. for Constr. Res., Development and Innovation [IO], Brussels, Belgium

European Coun. of Doctors for Plurality in Medicine [IO], Basel, Switzerland

European Coun. on Eating Disorders [IO], London, United Kingdom

European Coun. for Educ. by Correspondence [★IO]

European Coun. for High Ability [IO], Oxford, United Kingdom

European Coun. of Interior Architects [IO], Amsterdam, Netherlands

European Coun. of Intl. Schools [IO], Petersfield, United Kingdom

European Coun. of Legal Medicine [IO], Zurich, Switzerland

European Coun. of Natl. Associations of Independent Schools [IO], Copenhagen, Denmark

European Coun. for Non-Profit Organisations [IO], Brussels, Belgium

European Coun. of the Paint, Printing Ink and Artists' Colours Indus. [IO], Brussels, Belgium

European Coun. for Plasticisers and Intermediates [IO], Brussels, Belgium

European Coun. on Refugees and Exiles [IO], London, United Kingdom

European Coun. for Rural Law [IO], Gent, Belgium

European Coun. of Skeptical Organizations [IO], Rossdorf, Germany

European Coun. for Steiner Waldorf Educ. [IO], Forest Row, United Kingdom

European Coun. of Town Planners [IO], London, United Kingdom

European Coun. for the Village and Small Town [IO], Eastleigh, United Kingdom

European Coun. of Vinyl Manufacturers [IO], Brussels, Belgium

European Coun. for Voluntary Organisations [★IO]

European Coun. of Young Farmers [IO], Brussels, Belgium

European Cricket Coun. [IO], London, United Kingdom

European Crop Protection Assn. [IO], Brussels, Belgium

European Cultural Found. [IO], Amsterdam, Netherlands

European Culture Collections' Org. [IO], Genoa, Italy

European Cycling Union [IO], Erlenbach, Switzerland

European Cyclists' Fed. [IO], Bremen, Germany

European Cystic Fibrosis Soc. [IO], Karup, Denmark

European Dairy Assn. [IO], Brussels, Belgium

European Dehydrators Assn. [IO], Brussels, Belgium

European Democrat Students [IO], Brussels, Belgium

European Demolition Assn. [IO], Baarn, Netherlands

European Desalination Soc. [IO], L'Aquila, Italy

European Diagnostic Mfrs. Assn. [IO], Brussels, Belgium

European Dialysis and Transplant Nurses Association/European Renal Care Assn. [IO], Paris, France

European Direct Marketing Assn. [★IO]

European Direct Selling Fed. [★IO]

European Disability Forum [IO], Brussels, Belgium

European Disposables and Nonwovens Assn. [IO], Brussels, Belgium

European Distance Selling Trade Assn. [IO], Brussels, Belgium

European Diving Tech. Comm. [IO], Stavanger, Norway

European Down and Feather Assn. [IO], Mainz, Germany

European Down's Syndrome Assn. [IO], Pula, Croatia

European Dragon Boat Assn. [★IO]

European Dragon Boat Fed. [IO], Newport, United Kingdom

European Dystonia Fed. [IO], Helensburgh, United Kingdom

European Economic Assn. [IO], Coventry, United Kingdom

European Educational Res. Assn. [IO], Glasgow, United Kingdom

European Elec. Road Vehicle Assn. [★IO]

European Electronic Chips and Systems Design Initiative [IO], Gieres, France

European Electronic Component Mfrs. Assn. [IO], Brussels, Belgium

European Elevator Assn. [IO], Brussels, Belgium

European Employers' Comm. of Yeast Manufacturers [IO], Paris, France

European Energy Forum [IO], Brussels, Belgium

European Energy Found. [★IO]

European Environmental Bur. [IO], Brussels, Belgium

European Environmental Mutagen Soc. [IO], Lyon, France

European Epilepsy Acad. [IO], Bielefeld, Germany

European Evaluation Soc. [IO], Nijkerk, Netherlands

European Evangelical Accrediting Assn. [IO], Rome, Italy

European Evangelical Alliance [IO], London, United Kingdom

European Expedition Guild [IO], Paris, France

European Express Assn. [IO], Brussels, Belgium

European Eye Bank Assn. [IO], Venice, Italy

European Fac. Mgt. Network [IO], Naarden, Netherlands

European Fair Trade Assn. [IO], Schin op Geul, Netherlands

European Fairytale Assn. [IO], Rheine, Germany

European Family History Assn; East [★21112]

European Family History Societies; Fed. of East [★21112]

European Farmer Co-ordination [IO], Brussels, Belgium

A star before a book entry number signifies that the name is not listed separately, but is mentioned within the entry.

European Fed. of Accountants [IO], Brussels, Belgium

European Fed. of Accountants and Auditors for Small and Medium Sized Enterprises [IO], Brussels, Belgium

European Fed. Against Hunting [IO], Rome, Italy

European Fed. of Agents of Indus. in Indus. Property [IO], Basel, Switzerland

European Fed. of Amer. Football [IO], Frankfurt am Main, Germany

European Fed. of Amusement and Leisure Parks [IO], Brussels, Belgium

European Fed. of Animal Feed Additive Mfrs. [IO], Brussels, Belgium

European Fed. of Associations of Burned Persons [IO], Paris, France

European Fed. of Associations and Centres of Irish Stud. [IO], Preston, United Kingdom

European Fed. of Associations of Coffee Roasters [IO], Amsterdam, Netherlands

European Fed. of the Associations of Dietitians [IO], Emmerich, Germany

European Fed. of Associations of Families of Mentally Ill People [★IO]

European Fed. of Associations of Families of People with Mental Illness [IO], Leuven, Belgium

European Fed. of Associations of Hea. Prdt. Mfrs. [IO], Brussels, Belgium

European Fed. of Associations of Insulation Contractors [IO], Berlin, Germany

European Fed. of Associations of Lock and Builders' Hardware Manufacturers [IO], Solothurn, Switzerland

European Fed. of Associations of Market Res. Organisations [IO], The Hague, Netherlands

European Fed. of Associations of Particleboard Mfrs. [★IO]

European Fed. of Audiology Societies [IO], Riga, Latvia

European Fed. of Biotechnology [IO], Barcelona, Spain

European Fed. of Biotechnology - Germany [IO], Frankfurt, Germany

European Fed. of Building Societies [IO], Brussels, Belgium

European Fed. of Campingsite Organisations and Holiday Park Associations [IO], Gloucester, United Kingdom

European Fed. of Chem. Engg. [IO], Frankfurt, Germany

European Fed. of City Farms [IO], Sint-Martens-Lennik, Belgium

European Fed. of Clean Air and Environmental Protection Associations [IO], Delft, Netherlands

European Fed. of Cleaning Indus. [IO], Brussels, Belgium

European Fed. of Coin Machine Associations [★IO]

European Fed. for Company Sports [IO], Giessen, Germany

European Fed. of Compound Animal Feedingstuff Mfrs. [★IO]

European Fed. of Conf. Towns [IO], Brussels, Belgium

European Fed. of the Contact Lens Indus. [IO], Moerdijk, Netherlands

European Fed. of Corrosion [IO], Frankfurt am Main, Germany

European Fed. of Corrugated Bd. Mfrs. [IO], Brussels, Belgium

European Fed. of Critical Care Nursing Associations [IO], Munster, Germany

European Fed. of Cytology Societies [IO], Brussels, Belgium

European Fed. for Diaconia [IO], Brussels, Belgium

European Fed. of the Elderly [★IO]

European Fed. of Employees in Public Services [IO], Brussels, Belgium

European Fed. of Endocrine Societies [★IO]

European Fed. of Energy Traders [IO], Amsterdam, Netherlands

European Fed. of Engg. Consultancy Associations [IO], Brussels, Belgium

European Fed. for Experimental Morphology [IO], Bologna, Italy

European Fed. of Farm and Village Tourism [IO], Strasbourg, France

European Fed. of Financial Analysts Societies [IO], Dreieich, Germany

European Fed. for the Flexible Packaging Indus. [IO], The Hague, Netherlands

European Fed. of Food, Agriculture and Tourism Trade Unions [IO], Brussels, Belgium

European Fed. of Food Sci. and Tech. [IO], Wageningen, Netherlands

European Fed. of Found. Contractors [IO], Beckenham, United Kingdom

European Fed. of Frozen Food Products [IO], Paris, France

European Fed. of Geologists [IO], Brussels, Belgium

European Fed. of Green Parties [IO], Brussels, Belgium

European Fed. of Hereditary Ataxias [IO], Dunlavin, Ireland

European Fed. of Illuminated Signs [IO], Peterborough, United Kingdom

European Fed. of Immunological Societies [IO], Budapest, Hungary

European Fed. for Info. Tech. in Agriculture [IO], Aylesbury, United Kingdom

European Fed. of Inland Ports [IO], Brussels, Belgium

European Fed. of Insurance Intermediaries [IO], Brussels, Belgium

European Fed. for Intercultural Learning [IO], Brussels, Belgium

European Fed. of Internal Medicine [IO], Brighton, United Kingdom

European Fed. of Journalists [IO], Brussels, Belgium

European Fed. of Liberal, Democrat, and Reform Parties [★IO]

European Fed. of Liberal and Radical Youth [★IO]

European Fed. of Local Public Energy Distribution Companies [IO], Brussels, Belgium

European Fed. of Loss Adjusting Experts [IO], Rotterdam, Netherlands

European Fed. of Magazine Publishers [IO], Brussels, Belgium

European Fed. of Mgt. Consultancies Associations [IO], Brussels, Belgium

European Fed. of Marine Sci. and Tech. Societies [IO], Paris, France

European Fed. of Materials Handling and Storage Equip. [IO], Brussels, Belgium

European Fed. for Medical Informatics [IO], Munich, Germany

European Fed. for Medicinal Chemistry [IO], Vienna, Austria

European Fed. of Multiwall Paper Sack Mfrs. [IO], Paris, France

European Fed. of Museum and Tourist Railways [IO], Haaksbergen, Netherlands

European Fed. of Natl. Associations of Measurement, Testing and Analytical Labs. [IO], Paris, France

European Fed. of Natl. Associations of Orthopaedics and Traumatology [IO], Zurich, Switzerland

European Fed. of Natl. Associations of Specialist Repair Contractors [★IO]

European Fed. of Natl. Engg. Associations [IO], Brussels, Belgium

European Fed. of Natl. Organisations Working with the Homeless [IO], Brussels, Belgium

European Fed. of Neurological Societies [IO], Vienna, Austria

European Fed. of Older Persons [IO], Graz, Austria

European Fed. of Organizations for Medical Physics [IO], Udine, Italy

European Fed. of Orthodontic Specialists Associations [IO], Falun, Sweden

European Fed. of Paper Bag Mfrs. [★IO]

European Fed. of Parasitologists [IO], Geneva, Switzerland

European Fed. of the Parquet Indus. [IO], Brussels, Belgium

European Fed. of Periodontology [IO], Madrid, Spain

European Fed. of Pharmaceutical Indus. and Associations [IO], Brussels, Belgium

European Fed. for Pharmaceutical Sciences [IO], Stockholm, Sweden

European Fed. of the Plywood Indus. [IO], Brussels, Belgium

European Fed. for Primatology [IO], Zurich, Switzerland

European Fed. of Professional Florist Associations [IO], Ede, Netherlands

European Fed. for Psychoanalytic Psychotherapy [IO], Deurne, Belgium

European Fed. of Psychoanalytic Self-Psychology [IO], Munich, Germany

European Fed. of Psychology Students' Associations [IO], Brussels, Belgium

European Fed. of Public Ser. Unions [IO], Brussels, Belgium

European Fed. of Purchasing [★IO]

European Fed. of Regional Energy and Environmental Agencies [IO], Brussels, Belgium

European Fed. of Road Traffic Victims [IO], Geneva, Switzerland

European Fed. of Salaried Doctors [IO], Paris, France

European Fed. of Savings and Loan Institutions for Constr. [★IO]

European Fed. for the Sci. and Tech. of Lipids [IO], Frankfurt am Main, Germany

European Fed. of Sexology [IO], Sheffield, United Kingdom

European Fed. of Societies for Ultrasound in Medicine and Biology [IO], Bromley, United Kingdom

European Fed. of Statisticians in the Pharmaceutical Indus. [IO], Macclesfield, United Kingdom

European Fed. for Table and Ornamental Ware [IO], Brussels, Belgium

European Fed. of Therapeutic Communities [IO], Oosterzele, Belgium

European Fed. of the Trade in Dried Fruit, Edible Nuts, Preserved Food, Spices, Honey, and Similar Foodstuffs [IO], Brussels, Belgium

European Fed. of Trade Unions in the Food, Agriculture, and Tourism Sectors and Allied Branches [★IO]

European Fed. for Transport and Env. [IO], Brussels, Belgium

European Fed. of Waste Mgt. and Environmental Services [IO], Brussels, Belgium

European Fed. for Welding, Joining and Cutting [IO], Porto Salvo, Portugal

European Fed. for the Welfare of the Elderly [★IO]

European Fed. of Wooden Pallet and Packaging Mfrs. [IO], Tilburg, Netherlands

European Fed. of Youth Ser. Organisations [IO], Frankfurt am Main, Germany

European Feed Mfrs'. Fed. [IO], Brussels, Belgium

European Ferrous Recovery and Recycling Fed. [IO], Brussels, Belgium

European Fertilizer Mfrs. Assn. [IO], Brussels, Belgium

European Festivals Assn. [IO], Gent, Belgium

European Film Acad. [IO], Berlin, Germany

European Finance Assn. [IO], Brussels, Belgium

European Financial Mgt. and Marketing Assn. [IO], Paris, France

European Financial Marketing Assn. [★IO]

European Financial Planning Assn. [IO], Rotterdam, Netherlands

European Fire and Security Advisory Coun. [IO], Brussels, Belgium

European Fireworks Assn. [IO], Amsterdam, Netherlands

European Fishing Tackle Trade Assn. [IO], London, United Kingdom

European Flavour and Fragrance Assn. [IO], Brussels, Belgium

European Flexible Intermediate Bulk Container Assn. [IO], Dundee, United Kingdom

European Flexographic Tech. Assn. - (UK) [IO], Long Sutton, United Kingdom

European Flour Milling Assn. [IO], Brussels, Belgium

European Flying Disc Fed. [IO], Karlsruhe, Germany

European Folk Art and Craft Fed. [IO], Oslo, Norway

European Folklore Inst. [IO], Budapest, Hungary

European Food Emulsifiers Mfrs. Assn. [IO], Brussels, Belgium

European Food Info. Coun. [IO], Brussels, Belgium

European Food Law Assn. [IO], Brussels, Belgium

European Food Phosphates Producers' Assn. [IO], Brussels, Belgium

---

Reference to "IO" in place of a book number signifies that the association may be found in the 45th edition of International Organizations.

European Food Ser. and Packaging Assn. [IO], Brussels, Belgium

European Foodservice Equip. Distributors Assn. [IO], Caterham, United Kingdom

European Foot and Ankle Soc. [IO], Dun Laoghaire, Ireland

European Ford Registry; North Amer. English and [21744]

European Forest Genetic Resources Programme [IO], Rome, Italy

European Forest Inst. [IO], Joensuu, Finland

European Forum for Advanced Bus. Commun. [★IO]

European Forum for Electronic Bus. [★IO]

European Forum for Flexible Packaging [★IO]

European Forum for the Flexible Packaging Indus. [★IO]

European Forum for Good Clinical Practice [IO], Brussels, Belgium

European Forum of Heritage Associations [IO], Padua, Italy

European Forum for Renewable Energy Sources [IO], Brussels, Belgium

European Forum for Student Guidance [IO], Poitiers, France

European Forum for Urban Safety [IO], Paris, France

European Forum for Victim Services [IO], Utrecht, Netherlands

European Found. Centre [IO], Brussels, Belgium

European Found. for Chinese Music Res. [IO], Leiden, Netherlands

European Found. for the Improvement of Living and Working Conditions [IO], Loughlinstown, Ireland

European Found. for Landscape Architecture [IO], Brussels, Belgium

European Found. for Mgt. Development [IO], Brussels, Belgium

European Found. for Plant Pathology [IO], Wageningen, Netherlands

European Found. for Quality Mgt. [IO], Brussels, Belgium

European Found. for St. Children Worldwide [IO], Brussels, Belgium

European Free Trade Assn. [IO], Geneva, Switzerland

European Fresh Produce Importers Assn. [★IO]

European Fuel Oxygenates Assn. [IO], Brussels, Belgium

European Funds and Asset Mgt. Assn. [IO], Brussels, Belgium

European Fur Breeders Assn. [IO], Brussels, Belgium

European Furniture Mfrs. Fed. [IO], Brussels, Belgium

European Gaming and Amusement Fed. [IO], Brussels, Belgium

European Gaming and Betting Assn. [IO], Brussels, Belgium

European Garage Equip. Assn. [IO], Brussels, Belgium

European Gas Res. Gp. [★IO]

European Gay and Lesbian Sports Fed. [IO], Amsterdam, Netherlands

European Gen. Galvanizers Assn. [IO], Caterham, United Kingdom

European Generic Medicines Assn. [IO], Brussels, Belgium

European Genetic Alliances Network [IO], Soestdijk, Netherlands

European Genetics Found. [IO], Bologna, Italy

European Geophysical Soc. [★IO]

European Geosciences Union [IO], Strasbourg, France

European Glass Weavers Assn. [IO], Paris, France

European Glaucoma Soc. [IO], London, United Kingdom

European Glaziers Assn. [IO], De Rijp, Netherlands

European Go Fed. [IO], Vantaa, Finland

European Golf Assn. [IO], Epalinges, Switzerland

European Golf Course Owners Assn. [IO], Amsterdam, Netherlands

European Good Templar Youth Fed. [IO], Orebro, Sweden

European Greenways Assn. [IO], Namur, Belgium

European Gp. of Flat Glass Manufacturers [IO], Brussels, Belgium

European Gp. for Organizational Stud. [IO], Berlin, Germany

European Gp. of Public Admin. [IO], Brussels, Belgium

European Gp. for Rapid Viral Diagnosis [★IO]

The European Gp. of Valuers' Associations [IO], Brussels, Belgium

European Grouping of Societies of Authors and Composers [IO], Brussels, Belgium

European Guitar Teachers Assn. [IO], Denver, CO, United States

European Guitar Teachers Assn. [22576], c/o Jonathan Leathwood, Jour. Ed., 2363 S York St., No. 304, Denver, CO 80210

European Hair Res. Soc. [IO], Zurich, Switzerland

European Hea. Indus. Bus. Communications Coun. [IO], The Hague, Netherlands

European Hea. Mgt. Assn. [IO], Dublin, Ireland

European Hea. Managers Forum [IO], Seville, Spain

European Hea. Psychology Soc. [IO], Greifswald, Germany

European Hearing Instrument Mfrs. Assn. [IO], Villers-la-Ville, Belgium

European Heart and Lung Transplant Fed. [IO], Dublin, Ireland

European Heart Network [IO], Brussels, Belgium

European Helicopter Assn. [IO], Amsterdam, Netherlands

European Hematology Assn. [IO], Rotterdam, Netherlands

European Herbal Infusions Assn. [IO], Hamburg, Germany

European Herbal Practitioners Assn. [IO], London, United Kingdom

European Hernia Soc. [IO], Milan, Italy

European Herpetological Soc. [IO], Pisa, Italy

European Histamine Res. Soc. [IO], Stockholm, Sweden

European Historical Economics Soc. [IO], Oxford, United Kingdom

European Home Stud. Coun. [★IO]

European Home Systems Assn. [IO], Brussels, Belgium

European Hosp. and Healthcare Fed. [IO], Brussels, Belgium

European Hotel Managers Assn. [IO], Rome, Italy

European Human Rsrc. Forum [IO], Bristol, United Kingdom

European Humanist Fed. [IO], Brussels, Belgium

European Hydrogen Assn. [IO], Brussels, Belgium

European Ichthyological Soc. [IO], Lisbon, Portugal

European Indus. Fasteners Inst. [IO], West Bromwich, United Kingdom

European Indus. Minerals Assn. [IO], Brussels, Belgium

European Indus. Res. Mgt. Assn. [IO], Paris, France

European Indus. Assn. [IO], Brussels, Belgium

European Info. Assn. [IO], Mold, United Kingdom

European Info., Communications and Consumer Electronics Tech. Indus. Assn. [IO], Brussels, Belgium

European Inland Fisheries Advisory Commn. [IO], Rome, Italy

European Inst. for Advanced Stud. in Mgt. [IO], Brussels, Belgium

European Inst. for Cmpt. Anti-Virus Res. [IO], Munich, Germany

European Inst. for Crime Prevention and Control Affiliated with the United Nations [IO], Helsinki, Finland

European Inst. of Cultural Routes [IO], Luxembourg, Luxembourg

European Inst. for Design and Disability [★IO]

European Inst. of Educ. and Social Policy [IO], Paris, France

European Inst. of Golf Course Architects [IO], Chiddingfold, United Kingdom

European Inst. for the Media [IO], Dortmund, Germany

European Inst. of Postgraduate Stud. [IO], Dresden, Germany

European Inst. of Printed Circuits [IO], Maastricht, Netherlands

European Inst. of Public Admin. [IO], Maastricht, Netherlands

European Inst. of Purchasing Mgt. [IO], Archamps, France

European Inst. for Res. and Strategic Stud. in Telecommunications GmbH [IO], Heidelberg, Germany

European Inst. of Social Security [IO], Leuven, Belgium

European Insurance Coun. [IO], Paris, France

European Insurance Fed. [IO], Paris, France

European Intelligent Building Gp. [★IO]

European Intermodal Assn. [IO], Brussels, Belgium

European Intl. Bus. Acad. [IO], Brussels, Belgium

European Intl. Bus. Assn. [★IO]

European Internet Services Providers Assn. [IO], Brussels, Belgium

European Intestinal Transport Gp. [IO], Berlin, Germany

European Investment Casters' Fed. [IO], Redditch, United Kingdom

European Isocyanate and Polyol Producers Assn. [IO], Brussels, Belgium

European Isocyanate Producers Assn. [★IO]

European Jazz Fed. [★IO]

European Jazz Fed. [★10632]

European Jewry; Center for Russian and East [17946]

European Journalism Centre [IO], Maastricht, Netherlands

European Journalism Training Assn. [IO], Maastricht, Netherlands

European Judo Union [IO], Ta'Xbiex, Malta

European Juggling Assn. [IO], Stockholm, Sweden

European Landowners Org. [IO], Brussels, Belgium

European Landscape Contractors Assn. [IO], Bad Honnef, Germany

European Language Coun. [IO], Berlin, Germany

European Language Resources Assn. [IO], Paris, France

European Languages; Amer. Assn. of Teachers of Slavic and East [9125]

European Laryngological Soc. [IO], Taufkirchen, Germany

European Law; Committee on Soviet and East [★5475]

European Law Faculties Assn. [IO], Leuven, Belgium

European Law Students' Assn. [IO], Brussels, Belgium

European Lawyers' Union [IO], Rome, Italy

European Lead Stabilizers Assn. [★IO]

European League Against Rheumatism [IO], Kilchberg, Switzerland

European League for Economic Cooperation [IO], Brussels, Belgium

European League of Institutes of the Arts [IO], Amsterdam, Netherlands

European League of Societies for the Mentally Handicapped [★IO]

European League of Stuttering Associations [IO], Cologne, Germany

European Leisure and Recreation Assn. [IO], Diemen, Netherlands

European Liaison Comm. of Machine Tool Importers [IO], Bonn, Germany

European Liaison Comm. for Pulp and Paper [IO], Paris, France

European Liberal Democrat and Reform Party [IO], Brussels, Belgium

European Life Sci. Editors [★IO]

European Life Scientist Org. [IO], Sandhausen, Germany

European Lift Components Assn. [IO], Brussels, Belgium

European Lime Assn. [IO], Brussels, Belgium

European Liquefied Petroleum Gas Assn. [IO], Brussels, Belgium

European Livestock and Meat Trading Union [IO], Brussels, Belgium

European Logistics Assn. [IO], Brussels, Belgium

European Lotteries [IO], Lausanne, Switzerland

European Lupus Erythematosus Fed. [IO], Romford, United Kingdom

European Mail Order and Distance Selling Trade Assn. [★IO]

European Major Exhibition Centres Assn. [IO], Paris, France

A star before a book entry number signifies that the name is not listed separately, but is mentioned within the entry.

European Managed Futures Assn. [★IO]

European Mgt. Assistants [IO], Wels, Austria

European Mfrs. of Expanded Polystyrene [IO], Brussels, Belgium

European Mfrs. of Thermal and Elec. Locomotives [★IO]

European Marine Equip. Coun. [IO], Brussels, Belgium

European Maritime Pilots' Assn. [IO], Antwerp, Belgium

European Marketing Acad. [IO], Brussels, Belgium

European Marmoset Res. Gp. [IO], Zurich, Switzerland

European Mastic Asphalt Assn. [IO], Bern, Switzerland

European Materials Res. Soc. [IO], Strasbourg, France

European Mathematical Soc. [IO], Helsinki, Finland

European Mechanics Soc. [IO], Udine, Italy

European Medical Assn. [IO], Brussels, Belgium

European Medical Res. Councils [★IO]

European Medical Students' Assn. [IO], Brussels, Belgium

European Medical Tech. Indus. Assn. [★IO]

European Medical Writers Assn. [IO], Zug, Switzerland

European and Mediterranean Cereal Rusts Found. [IO], Rehovot, Israel

European and Mediterranean Network of the Social Sciences [IO], Valletta, Malta

European and Mediterranean Plant Protection Org. [IO], Paris, France

European-Mediterranean Seismological Centre [IO], Bruyeres-le-Chatel, France

European Membrane Soc. [IO], Toulouse, France

European Metal Trade and Recycling Fed. [IO], Brussels, Belgium

European Metal Union [IO], Brussels, Belgium

European Metallizers Assn. [IO], The Hague, Netherlands

European Metalworkers' Fed. [IO], Brussels, Belgium

European Meteorological Soc. [IO], Berlin, Germany

European Microbeam Anal. Soc. [IO], Antwerp, Belgium

European Microscopy Soc. [IO], Basel, Switzerland

European Mine, Chem., and Energy Workers' Fed. [IO], Brussels, Belgium

European Molecular Biology Lab. [IO], Heidelberg, Germany

European Molecular Biology Org. [IO], Heidelberg, Germany

European Money and Finance Forum [IO], Vienna, Austria

European Mortar Indus. Org. [IO], Duisburg, Germany

European Mortgage Fed. [IO], Brussels, Belgium

European Motorcycle Assn. - Defunct.

European Motorcycle Indus. Assn. [★IO]

European Movement [IO], London, United Kingdom

European Movement - Ireland [IO], Dublin, Ireland

European Multimedia Forum [IO], Brussels, Belgium

European Music Festival for Young People [IO], Neerpelt, Belgium

European Music Festival for the Youth [★IO]

European Music School Union [IO], Utrecht, Netherlands

European Music Therapy Confed. [IO], Schoten, Belgium

European Mutual Guarantee Assn. [IO], Brussels, Belgium

European Nail Soc. [IO], Brussels, Belgium

European Natural Gas Vehicle Assn. [IO], Hoofddorp, Netherlands

European Nature Heritage Fund [IO], Radolfzell, Germany

European Network Against Arms Trade [IO], Amsterdam, Netherlands

European Network Against Racism [IO], Brussels, Belgium

European Network of Building Res. Institutes [IO], Brussels, Belgium

European Network of Cancer Registries [IO], Lyon, France

European Network for Commun. Development [IO], St. Gallen, Switzerland

European Network of Cultural Admin. Training Centres [IO], Brussels, Belgium

European Network on Debt and Development [IO], Brussels, Belgium

European Network of Geography Teachers' Assn. [IO], Utrecht, Netherlands

European Network of Hea. Promoting Schools [IO], Copenhagen, Denmark

European Network of Hea. Promotion Agencies [★IO]

European Network for Housing Res. [IO], Gaule, Sweden

European Network of Info. Centres for the Performing Arts [IO], Brussels, Belgium

European Network on Lateritic Weathering and Global Env. [IO], Berlin, Germany

European Network on Law and Soc. [IO], Rieux-Minervois, France

European Network Male Prostitution [IO], Amsterdam, Netherlands

European Network of Natl. Heritage Organisations [IO], Bratislava, Slovakia

European Network of Policewomen [IO], Amersfoort, Netherlands

European Network for Sci. Res. Coordination in Organic Farming [IO], Barcelona, Spain

European Network for Smoking Prevention [IO], Brussels, Belgium

European Network of Sport Sci., Educ. and Employment [IO], Cologne, Germany

European Network on St. Children Worldwide [★IO]

European Network of the Unemployed [IO], Limoges, France

European Network for Workplace Hea. Promotion [IO], Essen, Germany

European Network on Young People and Tobacco [IO], Helsinki, Finland

European Neural Network Soc. [IO], Nijmegen, Netherlands

European Neuroendocrine Assn. [IO], Rotterdam, Netherlands

European Neurological Soc. [IO], Basel, Switzerland

European Newspaper Publishers' Assn. [IO], Brussels, Belgium

European Non-Governmental Sports Org. [IO], Belgrade, Serbia

European Nuclear Soc. [IO], Brussels, Belgium

European Nut Assn. [IO], Tilburg, Netherlands

European Oil Hydraulic and Pneumatic Comm. [IO], Frankfurt am Main, Germany

European Oleochemicals and Allied Products Gp. [IO], Brussels, Belgium

European Ombudsman Inst. [IO], Innsbruck, Austria

European Oncology Nursing Soc. [IO], Brussels, Belgium

European Operations Mgt. Assn. [IO], Brussels, Belgium

European Ophthalmic Pathology Soc. [IO], Helsinki, Finland

European Optical Soc. [IO], Hannover, Germany

European Org. for Civil Aviation Equip. [IO], Paris, France

European Org. for the Development and Constr. of Space Vehicle Launchers [★IO]

European Org. for the Exploitation of Meteorological Satellites [IO], Darmstadt, Germany

European Org. for Res. and Treatment of Cancer [IO], Brussels, Belgium

European Org. of Supreme Audit Institutions [IO], Madrid, Spain

European Org. for Tech. Approvals [IO], Brussels, Belgium

European Org. of Tomato Indus. [IO], Brussels, Belgium

European Org. for Caries Res. [IO], Amsterdam, Netherlands

European Org. of Military Associations [IO], Brussels, Belgium

European Org. for Nuclear Res. [IO], Geneva, Switzerland

European Org. for Packaging and the Env. [IO], Brussels, Belgium

European Org. for Quality [IO], Brussels, Belgium

European Org. for Quality Control [★IO]

European Org. for Rare Diseases [IO], Paris, France

European Org. for Rare Disorders [IO], Paris, France

European Ornithologists' Union [IO], Vienna, Austria

European Orthodontia Soc. [★IO]

European Orthodontic Soc. [IO], London, United Kingdom

European Ostomy Assn. [IO], Bonn, Germany

European Ozone Res. Coordinating Unit [IO], Cambridge, United Kingdom

European Paediatric Neurology Soc. [IO], Bolton, United Kingdom

European Palm Soc. [IO], Richmond, United Kingdom

European Pancreatic Club [IO], Greifswald, Germany

European Panel Fed. [IO], Brussels, Belgium

European Paralympic Comm. [IO], Rome, Italy

European Parking Assn. [IO], Cologne, Germany

European Parkinson's Disease Assn. [IO], Kent, United Kingdom

European Parliamentarians for Africa [IO], Amsterdam, Netherlands

European Passenger Train Timetable Conf. [★IO]

European Patent Off. [IO], Munich, Germany

European Peace Res. Assn. [IO], Helsinki, Finland

European Pentecostal Theological Assn. [IO], Linkoping, Sweden

European Peoples' Party [IO], Brussels, Belgium

European Perforators Assn. [IO], Goppingen, Germany

European Personal Construct Assn. [IO], Preston, United Kingdom

European Pet Food Indus. Fed. [IO], Brussels, Belgium

European Petrochemical Assn. [IO], Brussels, Belgium

European Petroleum Indus. Assn. [IO], Brussels, Belgium

European Pharmaceutical Students' Assn. [IO], Brussels, Belgium

European Phenolic Foam Assn. [IO], Aldershot, United Kingdom

European Photochemistry Assn. [IO], Tampere, Finland

European Photovoltaic Indus. Assn. [IO], Brussels, Belgium

European Physical Educ. Assn. [IO], Sint-Amandsberg, Belgium

European Physical Soc. [IO], Mulhouse, France

European Physics Educ. Network [IO], Gent, Belgium

European Piano Teachers Assn. [IO], London, United Kingdom

European Pineal and Biological Rhythm Soc. [★IO]

European Plastics Converters [IO], Brussels, Belgium

European Plastics Distributors Assn. [IO], Munich, Germany

European Platform for Dutch Educ. [IO], Alkmaar, Netherlands

European Pocket Billiard Fed. [IO], Brunssum, Netherlands

European Policy Forum [IO], London, United Kingdom

European Portable Battery Assn. [IO], Brussels, Belgium

European Powder Metallurgy Assn. [IO], Shrewsbury, United Kingdom

European Power Electronics and Drives Assn. [IO], Brussels, Belgium

European Power Tool Assn. [IO], Frankfurt am Main, Germany

European Powerlifting Fed. [IO], Halden, Norway

European Primary Aluminum Assn. [★IO]

European Prison Educ. Assn. [IO], Drammen, Norway

European Private Equity and Venture Capital Assn. [IO], Zaventem, Belgium

European Professional Women's Network [IO], Paris, France

European Prosthodontic Assn. [IO], Cardiff, United Kingdom

European Psychoanalytical Fed. [IO], Paris, France

European Public Hea. Alliance [IO], Brussels, Belgium

Reference to "IO" in place of a book number signifies that the association may be found in the 45th edition of International Organizations.

European Public Hea. Assn. **[IO]**, Utrecht, Netherlands

European Public Relations Confed. **[IO]**, London, United Kingdom

European Publishers Coun. **[IO]**, Brussels, Belgium

European Pultrusion Tech. Assn. **[IO]**, Frankfurt, Germany

European Pure Phosphoric Acid Producers' Assn. **[IO]**, Brussels, Belgium

European Pure Plant Oil Assn. **[IO]**, Agen, France

European Rare-Earth Actinide Soc. **[IO]**, Lausanne, Switzerland

European Real Estate Soc. **[IO]**, Helsinki, Finland

European Refractories Producers Fed. **[IO]**, Brussels, Belgium

European Regional Airlines Org. **[★IO]**

European Regional Sci. Assn. **[IO]**, Milan, Italy

European Regions Airline Assn. **[IO]**, Woking, United Kingdom

European Registration Plate Assn. **[IO]**, Taunton, United Kingdom

European Relocation Assn. **[IO]**, Diss, United Kingdom

European Renewable Energy Coun. **[IO]**, Brussels, Belgium

European Rental Assn. **[IO]**, Brussels, Belgium

European Res. Consortium for Informatics and Mathematics **[IO]**, Sophia Antipolis, France

European Res. Gp. on Military and Soc. **[IO]**, Bonn, Germany

European Res; Natl. Coun. for Eurasian and East **[10968]**

European Res; Natl. Coun. for Soviet and East **[★10968]**

European Res. Org. of Genital Infection and Neoplasia **[IO]**, Paris, France

European Reserve Noncommissioned Officers Assn. **[IO]**, Bonn, Germany

European Resin Mfrs'. Assn. **[IO]**, London, United Kingdom

European Rsrc. Centre for Alternatives in Higher Educ. **[IO]**, Utrecht, Netherlands

European Respiratory Soc. **[IO]**, Lausanne, Switzerland

European Rheumatoid Arthritis Surgical Soc. **[IO]**, Zurich, Switzerland

European Rhinologic Soc. **[IO]**, Tampere, Finland

European River-Sea-Transport Union **[IO]**, Berlin, Germany

European Road Riders Assn. - Defunct.

European Rotogravure Assn. **[IO]**, Munich, Germany

European Round Table of Industrialists **[IO]**, Brussels, Belgium

European Safety Fed. **[IO]**, Harelbeke, Belgium

European Sales and Marketing Assn. **[IO]**, High Wycombe, United Kingdom

European Salt Producers' Assn. **[IO]**, Brussels, Belgium

European Satellite Operators Assn. **[IO]**, Brussels, Belgium

European Savings Banks Gp. **[IO]**, Brussels, Belgium

European School Heads Assn. **[IO]**, Jyvaskyla, Finland

European Sci. Found. **[IO]**, Strasbourg, France

European Sci. Cooperative on Phytotherapy **[IO]**, Exeter, United Kingdom

European Sea Ports Org. **[IO]**, Brussels, Belgium

European Sealing Assn. **[IO]**, Tregarth, United Kingdom

European Secretariat of Mfrs. of Light Metal Packaging **[IO]**, Paris, France

European Seed Assn. **[IO]**, Brussels, Belgium

European Seismological Commn. **[IO]**, Edinburgh, United Kingdom

European Senior Citizens Union **[IO]**, Berlin, Germany

European Shippers' Coun. **[IO]**, Brussels, Belgium

European Slag Assn. **[IO]**, Duisburg, Germany

European Sled Dog Racing Assn. **[IO]**, Bromma, Sweden

European Sleep Res. Soc. **[IO]**, Madrid, Spain

European Small Hydropower Assn. **[IO]**, Brussels, Belgium

European Snacks Assn. **[IO]**, London, United Kingdom

European Social Action Network **[IO]**, Brussels, Belgium

European Social Network **[IO]**, Brighton, United Kingdom

European Soc. of Agricultural Engineers **[IO]**, Bedford, United Kingdom

European Soc. for Agronomy **[IO]**, Bologna, Italy

European Soc. of Anaesthesiology **[IO]**, Brussels, Belgium

European Soc. for Analytic Philosophy **[IO]**, Geneva, Switzerland

European Soc. for Animal Cell Tech. **[IO]**, Zurich, Switzerland

European Soc. for Artificial Organs - East European Off. **[IO]**, Warsaw, Poland

European Soc. of Assn. Executives **[IO]**, London, United Kingdom

European Soc. for Ballistocardiographic Res. **[★IO]**

European Soc. for Ballistocardiography and Cardiovascular Dynamics **[★IO]**

European Soc. of Biomaterials **[IO]**, London, United Kingdom

European Soc. of Biomechanics **[IO]**, Bologna, Italy

European Soc. for Biomedical Res. on Alcoholism **[IO]**, Vienna, Austria

European Soc. of Breast Imaging **[IO]**, Vienna, Austria

European Soc. of Cardiology **[IO]**, Sophia Antipolis, France

European Soc. for Cardiovascular Surgery **[IO]**, Brescia, Italy

European Soc. for Cataract and Refractive Surgeons **[IO]**, Dublin, Ireland

European Soc. for Central Asian Stud. **[IO]**, Leiden, Netherlands

European Soc. of Child and Adolescent Psychiatry **[IO]**, Modena, Italy

European Soc. of Clinical Microbiology and Infectious Diseases **[IO]**, Basel, Switzerland

European Soc. of Clinical Microbiology and Infectious Diseases - Switzerland **[IO]**, Basel, Switzerland

European Soc. of Clinical Pharmacy **[IO]**, Brussels, Belgium

European Soc. for Clinical Virology **[IO]**, Solna, Sweden

European Soc. for Cognitive Psychology **[IO]**, Copenhagen, Denmark

European Soc. for the Cognitive Sciences of Music **[IO]**, Liege, Belgium

European Soc. of Coloproctology **[IO]**, Edinburgh, United Kingdom

European Soc. of Comparative Physiology and Biochemistry **[IO]**, Liege, Belgium

European Soc. for Computing and Tech. in Anaesthesia and Intensive Care **[IO]**, Berlin, Germany

European Soc. of Contact Dermatitis **[IO]**, Barcelona, Spain

European Soc. of Contraception **[IO]**, Ternat, Belgium

European Soc. of Culture **[IO]**, Venice, Italy

European Soc. of Dermatological Res. **[IO]**, Geneva, Switzerland

European Soc. for Dermatology and Psychiatry **[IO]**, Brussels, Belgium

European Soc. for Developmental Psychology **[IO]**, Vienna, Austria

European Soc. of Domestic Animal Reproduction **[IO]**, Belfield, Ireland

European Soc. for Ecological Economics **[IO]**, Aberdeen, United Kingdom

European Soc. for Emergency Medicine **[IO]**, Novara, Italy

European Soc. of Endocrinology **[IO]**, Bristol, United Kingdom

European Soc. for Engg. Educ. **[IO]**, Brussels, Belgium

European Soc. for Engg. and Medicine **[IO]**, Groningen, Netherlands

European Soc. for Environmental History **[IO]**, Prague, Czech Republic

European Soc. for Evolutionary Biology **[IO]**, Leiden, Netherlands

European Soc. of Feline Medicine **[IO]**, Tisbury, United Kingdom

European Soc. of Gastrointestinal and Abdominal Radiology **[IO]**, Vienna, Austria

European Soc. of Gastrointestinal Endoscopy **[IO]**, Munich, Germany

European Soc. of Gene and Cell Therapy **[IO]**, Stockholm, Sweden

European Soc. of Gene Therapy **[★IO]**

European Soc. for Geography **[IO]**, Brussels, Belgium

European Soc. for Gynaecological Endoscopy **[IO]**, Ternat, Belgium

European Soc. of Gynaecological Oncology **[IO]**, Geneva, Switzerland

European Soc. of Gynecology **[IO]**, Paris, France

European Soc. for Haemapheresis and Haemotherapy **[IO]**, Vienna, Austria

European Soc. for Handwriting Psychology **[IO]**, Zurich, Switzerland

European Soc. of Head and Neck Radiology **[IO]**, Frankfurt, Germany

European Soc. of Human Genetics **[IO]**, Vienna, Austria

European Soc. of Human Reproduction and Embryology **[IO]**, Grimbergen, Belgium

European Soc. for Hyperthermic Oncology **[IO]**, Rotterdam, Netherlands

European Soc. for Immunodeficiencies **[IO]**, Freiburg, Germany

European Soc. of Intensive Care Medicine **[IO]**, Brussels, Belgium

European Soc. of Intravenous Anaesthesia **[IO]**, Zurich, Switzerland

European Soc. of Knee Surgery Sports Traumatology and Arthroscopy **[★IO]**

European Soc. for Lab. Animal Veterinarians **[IO]**, Fuellinsdorf, Switzerland

European Soc. for Laser Aesthetic Surgery **[IO]**, Athens, Greece

European Soc. for Laser Dermatology **[IO]**, Bassum, Germany

European Soc. for Magnetic Resonance in Medicine and Biology **[IO]**, Vienna, Austria

European Soc. for Mass Spectrometry **[IO]**, Edinburgh, United Kingdom

European Soc. of Mastology **[IO]**, Florence, Italy

European Soc. for Medical Oncology **[IO]**, Viganello-Lugano, Switzerland

European Soc. for Microcirculation **[IO]**, Berlin, Germany

European Soc. for Movement Anal. for Adults and Children **[IO]**, Headington, United Kingdom

European Soc. of Nematologists **[IO]**, Belfast, United Kingdom

European Soc. for Neurochemistry **[IO]**, Budapest, Hungary

European Soc. for Neurogastroenterology and Motility **[IO]**, Leuven, Belgium

European Soc. of Neuroradiology **[IO]**, Leuven, Belgium

European Soc. of Neurosonology and Cerebral Hemodynamics **[IO]**, Chemnitz, Germany

European Soc. of New Methods in Agricultural Res. **[IO]**, Brno, Czech Republic

European Soc. for Noninvasive Cardiovascular Dynamics **[IO]**, Ljubljana, Slovenia

European Soc. for Oceanists **[IO]**, Verona, Italy

European Soc. of Ophthalmic Plastic and Reconstructive Surgery **[IO]**, Munich, Germany

European Soc. for Oral Laser Applications **[★IO]**

European Soc. for Organ Transplantation **[IO]**, Groningen, Netherlands

European Soc. of Paediatric Allergy and Clinical Immunology **[IO]**, Berlin, Germany

European Soc. for Paediatric Endocrinology **[IO]**, Bristol, United Kingdom

European Soc. for Paediatric Infectious Diseases **[IO]**, Geneva, Switzerland

European Soc. of Paediatric and Neonatal Intensive Care **[IO]**, Geneva, Switzerland

European Soc. of Paediatric Radiology **[IO]**, Brussels, Belgium

European Soc. for Paediatric Res. **[IO]**, Geneva, Switzerland

European Soc. for Paediatric Urology **[IO]**, Leuven, Belgium

A star before a book entry number signifies that the name is not listed separately, but is mentioned within the entry.

European Soc. of Pathology **[IO]**, Ioannina, Greece

European Soc. for Pediatric Nephrology **[IO]**, Helsinki, Finland

European Soc. for Phenylketonuria and Allied Disorders **[IO]**, Aalter, Belgium

European Soc. for Philosophy and Psychology **[IO]**, Edinburgh, United Kingdom

European Soc. for Photobiology **[IO]**, Pisa, Italy

European Soc. for Photodynamic Therapy in Dermatology **[IO]**, Regensburg, Germany

European Soc. for Pigment Cell Res. **[IO]**, Rome, Italy

European Soc. for Population Economics **[IO]**, Bilbao, Spain

European Soc. for Precision Engg. and Nanotechnology **[IO]**, Bedford, United Kingdom

European Soc. for Primary Care Gastroenterology **[IO]**, Geldermalsen, Netherlands

European Soc. of Regulatory Affairs **[★IO]**

European Soc. of Reproductive and Development Immunology **[IO]**, Poznan, Poland

European Soc. for Res. on the Educ. of Adults **[IO]**, Leiden, Netherlands

European Soc. of Residents in Urology **[IO]**, Arnhem, Netherlands

European Soc. of Rheology **[IO]**, Berlin, Germany

European Soc. for Rural Sociology **[IO]**, Oxford, United Kingdom

European Soc. of Sonochemistry **[IO]**, Bath, United Kingdom

European Soc. of Sports Traumatology, Knee Surgery and Arthroscopy 2000 **[IO]**, Luxembourg, Luxembourg

European Soc. for Stereotactic and Functional Neurosurgery **[IO]**, Toulouse, France

European Soc. for the Stud. of Cognitive Systems **[IO]**, Groningen, Netherlands

European Soc. for the Stud. of English **[IO]**, Joensuu, Finland

European Soc. for the Stud. of Purine and Pyrimidine Metabolism in Man **[IO]**, Innsbruck, Austria

European Soc. for the Stud. of Sci. and Theology **[IO]**, Leiden, Netherlands

European Soc. for Surgery of Shoulder and Elbow **[IO]**, St. Genis Laval, France

European Soc. of Surgical Oncology **[IO]**, Brussels, Belgium

European Soc. for Surgical Res. **[IO]**, Gent, Belgium

European Soc. for Therapeutic Radiology and Oncology **[IO]**, Brussels, Belgium

European Soc. of Thoracic Imaging **[IO]**, Bern, Switzerland

European Soc. of Thoracic Surgeons **[IO]**, Exeter, United Kingdom

European Soc. of Toxicology **[★IO]**

European Soc. for Toxicology In Vitro **[IO]**, Utrecht, Netherlands

European Soc. for Translation Stud. **[IO]**, Leuven, Belgium

European Soc. for Traumatic Stress Stud. **[IO]**, Utrecht, Netherlands

European Soc. of Urogenital Radiology **[IO]**, Vienna, Austria

European Soc. for Vascular Surgery **[IO]**, Copenhagen, Denmark

European Soc. of Veterinary Cardiology **[IO]**, Geneva, Switzerland

European Soc. of Veterinary Clinical Ethology **[IO]**, Upton, United Kingdom

European Soc. of Veterinary Dermatology **[IO]**, Newton Abbot, United Kingdom

European Soc. of Veterinary Neurology **[IO]**, Milan, Italy

European Soc. of Veterinary Ophthalmology **[IO]**, Leominster, United Kingdom

European Soc. of Veterinary Orthopaedics and Traumatology **[IO]**, Cremona, Italy

European Soc. of Veterinary Pathology **[IO]**, Bologna, Italy

European Soc. of Veterinary Virology **[IO]**, Merelbeke, Belgium

European Soc. of Women in Theological Res. **[IO]**, Binningen, Switzerland

European Sociological Assn. **[IO]**, Paris, France

European Software Assn. **[IO]**, Brussels, Belgium

European Software Inst. **[IO]**, Bizkaia, Spain

European Solar Indus. Fed. **[IO]**, Brussels, Belgium

European Solar Thermal Indus. Fed. **[IO]**, Brussels, Belgium

European Southern Observatory **[IO]**, Garching bei Munchen, Germany

European Space Agency **[IO]**, Paris, France

European Space Res. Org. **[★IO]**

European Sponsorship Assn. **[IO]**, Surbiton, United Kingdom

European Sports Press Union **[IO]**, Vellinge, Sweden

European Squash Fed. **[IO]**, Hastings, United Kingdom

European Stabiliser Producers Assn. **[IO]**, Brussels, Belgium

European Stage Authors and Composers; Society of **[★9817]**

European Strabismological Assn. **[IO]**, Bologna, Italy

European String Teachers Assn. **[IO]**, Weston Turville, United Kingdom

European Structural Integrity Soc. **[IO]**, Turin, Italy

European Students of Indus. Engg. and Mgt. **[IO]**, Eindhoven, Netherlands

European Stud; Inst. for **[★8405]**

European Stud; Inst. of **[★7985]**

European Study Group on Lysosomal Diseases **[IO]**, Rotterdam, Netherlands

European Sulphuric Acid Assn. **[IO]**, Brussels, Belgium

European Sumo Union **[IO]**, Schilde, Belgium

European Sunglass Assn. **[IO]**, Freiburg, Germany

European Surf Indus. Mfrs. Assn. **[IO]**, Capbreton, France

European Surface Treatment on Aluminium **[IO]**, Zurich, Switzerland

European Surfing Fed. **[IO]**, Newquay, United Kingdom

European Surgical Trade Assn. **[IO]**, Venlo, Netherlands

European Suzuki Assn. **[IO]**, Colchester, United Kingdom

European Table Tennis Union **[IO]**, Wasserbillig, Luxembourg

European Taekwondo Union **[IO]**, Oldenzaal, Netherlands

European Taxpayers Assn. **[★IO]**

European Tech. Contractors Comm. for the Constr. Indus. **[IO]**, Brussels, Belgium

European Telecommunications Network Operators' Assn. **[IO]**, Brussels, Belgium

European Telecommunications and Professional Electronics Indus. **[★IO]**

European Telecommunications Satellite Org. **[IO]**, Paris, France

European Telecommunications Standards Inst. **[IO]**, Sophia Antipolis, France

European Tennis Assn. **[★IO]**

European Tennis Fed. - Tennis Europe **[IO]**, Basel, Switzerland

European Textile Finishers' Org. **[IO]**, Wageningen, Netherlands

European Textile Network **[IO]**, Hannover, Germany

European Textile Services Assn. **[IO]**, Brussels, Belgium

European Theological Libraries **[IO]**, Edinburgh, United Kingdom

European Thrombosis Res. Org. **[IO]**, Santa Maria Imbaro, Italy

European Thyroid Assn. **[IO]**, Regenstauf, Germany

European Tile and Brick Producers Fed. **[IO]**, Brussels, Belgium

European Tissue Culture Soc. **[IO]**, Heidelberg, Germany

European Tissue Repair Soc. **[IO]**, Oxford, United Kingdom

European Tobacco Products Wholesalers' Union **[★IO]**

European Tobacco Wholesalers Assn. **[IO]**, Cologne, Germany

European Toner and Inkjet Remanufacturers Assn. **[IO]**, Breda, Netherlands

European Tour Operators Assn. **[IO]**, London, United Kingdom

European Tourism Trade Fairs Assn. **[IO]**, Richmond, United Kingdom

European Trade Union Confed. **[IO]**, Brussels, Belgium

European Trade Union Inst. **[★IO]**

European Trade Union Inst. for Res., Educ. and Hea. and Safety **[IO]**, Brussels, Belgium

European Training Found. **[IO]**, Turin, Italy

European Training and Simulation Assn. **[IO]**, Warminster, United Kingdom

European Transmission Sys. Operators **[IO]**, Brussels, Belgium

European Transplant Coordinators Org. **[IO]**, Barcelona, Spain

European Transport Safety Coun. **[IO]**, Brussels, Belgium

European Transport Workers' Fed. **[IO]**, Brussels, Belgium

European Travel Agents and Tour Operators' Associations **[IO]**, Brussels, Belgium

European Travel Commn. **[IO]**, New York, NY, United States

European Travel Commn. **[3916]**, c/o Spring, O'Brien and Co., 50 W 23rd St., 11th Fl., New York, NY 10010

European Travel Commn. - Belgium **[IO]**, Brussels, Belgium

European Tropical Forest Res. Network **[IO]**, Wageningen, Netherlands

European Tube Mfrs. Assn. **[IO]**, Dusseldorf, Germany

European Tyre Recycling Assn. **[IO]**, Paris, France

European Tyre and Rim Tech. Org. **[IO]**, Brussels, Belgium

European Tyre and Rubber Mfrs'. Assn. **[IO]**, Brussels, Belgium

European Umbrella Org. for Geographic Info. **[IO]**, Lisbon, Portugal

European Underwater and BaroMedical Soc. **[IO]**, Essex, United Kingdom

European Union of Agreement **[IO]**, Watford, United Kingdom

European Union Choir **[IO]**, Brussels, Belgium

European Union of Coachbuilders **[IO]**, Brussels, Belgium

European Union for Coastal Conservation **[★IO]**

European Union of Dairy Trade **[IO]**, Brussels, Belgium

European Union of the Deaf **[IO]**, Brussels, Belgium

European Union - Delegation of the Commn. to the U.S. **[IO]**, Washington, DC, United States

European Union - Delegation of the Commn. to the U.S. **[17507]**, 2300 M St. NW, Washington, DC 20037, (202)862-9500

European Union of Dentists **[IO]**, London, United Kingdom

European Union of Developers and House Builders **[IO]**, Brussels, Belgium

European Union Fed. of Youth Hostel Associations **[IO]**, Brussels, Belgium

European Union of Gen. Practitioners **[IO]**, Lisbon, Portugal

European Union of Importers, Exporters, and Dealers in Dairy Prdt. **[★IO]**

European Union of Independent Home-Builders **[★IO]**

European Union of Independent Hospitals **[IO]**, Brussels, Belgium

European Union of Jewish Students **[IO]**, Brussels, Belgium

European Union of Medical Specialists **[IO]**, Brussels, Belgium

European Union of Music Competition for Youth **[IO]**, Munich, Germany

European Union of Music Schools **[★IO]**

European Union of Natl. Associations of Water Suppliers and Waste Water Services **[IO]**, Brussels, Belgium

European Union of the Natural Gas Indus. **[IO]**, Brussels, Belgium

European Union Off. of Press and Public Affairs **[★IO]**

European Union Off. of Press and Public Affairs **[★17507]**

European Union for Responsible Incineration and Treatment of Special Waste **[IO]**, London, United Kingdom

---

Reference to "IO" in place of a book number signifies that the association may be found in the 45th edition of International Organizations.

European Union of Sci. Journalists' Associations [IO], Budapest, Hungary
European Union of Tourist Officers [IO], Irvine, United Kingdom
European Union of Veterinary Practitioners [IO], Brussels, Belgium
European Union of Young Christian Democrats [★IO]
European Union Youth Orchestra [IO], London, United Kingdom
European Univ. Assn. [IO], Brussels, Belgium
European Univ. Center for Peace Stud. [IO], Stadtschlaining, Austria
European Univ. Continuing Educ. Network [IO], Barcelona, Spain
European Vegetable Protein Fed. [IO], Brussels, Belgium
European Vegetarian Union [IO], Neukirch, Switzerland
European Vending Assn. [IO], Brussels, Belgium
European Venous Forum [IO], Greenford, United Kingdom
European Venture Capital Assn. [★IO]
European Veterans Fencing Comm. [IO], Konstanz, Germany
European Veterinary Dental Coll. [IO], Gerrards Cross, United Kingdom
European Veterinary Dental Soc. [IO], Hastings, United Kingdom
European Veterinary Soc. for Small Animal Reproduction [IO], Budapest, Hungary
European Volcanological Assn. [IO], Paris, France
European Water Assn. [IO], Hennef, Germany
European Water Assn. [IO], Hennef, Germany
European Water Resources Assn. [IO], Athens, Greece
European Wax Fed. [IO], Brussels, Belgium
European Weed Res. Soc. [IO], Doorwerth, Netherlands
European Weightlifting Fed. [IO], San Marino, San Marino
European Welding Assn. [★IO]
European Whey Products Assn. [IO], Brussels, Belgium
European Wholesale and Intl. Trade Assn. [★IO]
European Wind Energy Assn. [IO], Brussels, Belgium
European Women in Mathematics [IO], Turku, Finland
European Women's Dermatologic Soc. [IO], Brugge, Belgium
European Women's Lobby [IO], Brussels, Belgium
European Women's Mgt. Development Asia/Pacific [IO], Hong Kong, People's Republic of China
European Women's Mgt. Development Austria [IO], Linz, Austria
European Women's Mgt. Development Belgium [IO], Brussels, Belgium
European Women's Mgt. Development Italy [IO], Parma, Italy
European Women's Mgt. Development Network [IO], Brussels, Belgium
European Women's Mgt. Development Sweden [IO], Stockholm, Sweden
European Women's Mgt. Development Switzerland [IO], Zurich, Switzerland
European Working Comm. of Natl. Associations of Officers in Resort and Tourist Organizations [★IO]
European Wound Mgt. Assn. [IO], Frederiksberg, Denmark
European Writers' Cong. [IO], Munich, Germany
European Writing Instrument Mfrs. Assn. [IO], Nuremberg, Germany
European Wrought Aluminum Assn. [★IO]
European Young Bar Assn. [IO], St. Albans, United Kingdom
European Youth Forest Action [IO], Amsterdam, Netherlands
European Youth Forum [IO], Brussels, Belgium
European Youth Found. [IO], Strasbourg, France
Europeans; Ethnic Amer. Coalition of Eastern [★19360]
Europeenne des Constructeurs de Material Aerospatial; Association [★154]
Europeenne des Constructeurs de Material Aerospatial; Association [★IO]

Europees Muziek festival voor de Jeugd [★IO]
Europees Platform voor het Nederlandse Onderwijs [★IO]
Europese Federatie van Het Overheidspersoneel [★IO]
Europese Federatie van Verenigingen Familieleden van de Psychisch Zieken [★IO]
Eurostep: European Solidarity Towards Equal Participation of People [IO], Brussels, Belgium
Eurotransplant Intl. Found. [IO], Leiden, Netherlands
Eurovision [★IO]
Eurovision [★20395]
Eurythmics Fan Club - Address unknown since 1999.
EuTeCer - European Tech. Ceramics Fed. [IO], Brussels, Belgium

Euthanasia
2nd Chance 4 Pets [11481]
Americans United for Life [12904]
Assn. for the Right to Die with Dignity [IO]
Baptists for Life [12907]
Citizens United Resisting Euthanasia [12129]
Compassion in Dying Fed. [12130]
Dignity in Dying [IO]
Doing Things for Animals [11386]
Dying With Dignity Victoria [IO]
End-of-Life Choices [12131]
Euthanasia Prevention Coalition [IO]
Euthanasia Prevention Coalition BC [IO]
Euthanasia Res. and Guidance Org. [12132]
EXIT [IO]
Human Life Found. [12914]
Intl. Task Force on Euthanasia and Assisted Suicide [12133]
Natl. Assn. of Pro-Life Nurses [18378]
Presbyterians Pro-Life [12926]
Priests for Life [18564]
Voluntary Euthanasia Soc. of New Zealand [IO]
Euthanasia Prevention Coalition [IO], London, ON, Canada
Euthanasia Prevention Coalition BC [IO], North Vancouver, BC, Canada
Euthanasia Res. and Guidance Org. [12132], 24829 Norris Ln., Junction City, OR 97448-9559, (541)998-1873
Euthanasia Task Force; Intl. Anti- [★12133]
Evaluating Professionals; Natl. Assn. of Disability [14575]

Evaluation
Amer. Evaluation Assn. [7071]
Center for Lifelong Learning [8406]
Commn. on Certification of Work Adjustment and Vocational Evaluation Specialists [8407]
Inst. for Responsive Educ. [8408]
Intl. Test and Evaluation Assn. [7791]
Natl. Assn. of Credential Evaluation Services [8409]
Natl. Coun. for Accreditation of Teacher Educ. [7879]
Natl. Stud. of School Evaluation [8410]
Evaluation and Career Assessment Professionals; Vocational [16337]
Evaluation in Counseling and Development; Assn. for Measurement and [★9247]
Evaluation in Guidance; Assn. for Measurement and [★9247]
Evaluation Network [★7071]
Evaluation Res. Soc. [★7071]
Evaluation and Res. Special Interest Group - Address unknown since 1991.
Evaluation Soc; European [IO]
Evaluation; Special Interest Gp. on Measurement and [6751]
Evaluation, Standards, and Student Testing; Natl. Center for Res. on [8285]
Evaluation Task Force - Defunct.
Evaluation and Work Adjustment Assn; Vocational [★16337]

Evangelical
Adopt-A-Church Intl. [19839]
Advancing Churches in Missions Commitment [20293]
Advancing Native Missions [19833]
Africa Inland Mission Intl. [20294]
African Amer. Lutheran Assn. [20211]

All Roads Ministry [19564]
All-Ukrainian Evangelical Baptist Fellowship [19469]
Amer. Tract Soc. [19987]
AMF Intl. [19988]
Apostleship of Prayer [19569]
Apostolate for Family Consecrations [19571]
Archconfraternity of the Holy Ghost [19573]
Assoc. Comm. of Friends on Indian Affairs [20039]
Assn. of Evangelicals in Africa [IO]
Assn. of Romanian Catholics of America [19579]
BCM Intl. [19508]
Bethany Intl. Missions [20304]
Bibles For The World [20305]
Biblical Ministries Worldwide [19991]
Billy Graham Evangelistic Assn. [19992]
Bread on the Waters [19993]
Bros. and Sisters in Christ [19767]
Bruderhof Communities [20481]
Campus Crusade for Christ Intl. [19994]
CBM Ministries [19995]
Center for the Evangelical United Brethren Heritage [19976]
Champions for Life Intl. [19996]
Child Evangelism Fellowship [19997]
Christ in Action Ministries [19999]
Christian Literature and Bible Center [20317]
Christian Motorcyclists Assn. [22674]
Christian Res. Inst. [19785]
Christian TV Mission [19536]
Church Army [19947]
Comm. on Missionary Evangelism [20001]
Commun. Commn. [19537]
Company of Saint Paul [19614]
Covenant World Relief [12848]
Cowboys for Christ [19792]
Crossworld [20326]
EAPE/Campolo Ministries - Evangelical Assn. for the Promotion of Educ. [20330]
Episcopal Evangelical Educ. Soc. [19955]
Equestrian Ministries Intl. [20082]
Ethiopian Evangelical Church Mekane Yesus [IO]
European Evangelical Accrediting Assn. [IO]
European Evangelical Alliance [IO]
Evangelical Assn. of the Caribbean [IO]
Evangelical Church Alliance [19977]
Evangelical Church Lib. Assn. [10355]
Evangelical Coun. for Financial Accountability [20002]
Evangelical and Ecumenical Women's Caucus [19978]
Evangelical and Ecumenical Women's Caucus [IO]
Evangelical Environmental Network [20003]
Evangelical Free Church of Am. - Intl. Mission [20333]
Evangelical Friends Intl. - North Amer. Region [20040]
Evangelical Missiological Soc. [20334]
Evangelical Philosophical Soc. [19979]
Evangelical Philosophical Society [IO]
Evangelical Press Assn. [20004]
Evangelical and Reformed Historical Soc. [20607]
Evangelical Social Action Commn. [20005]
Evangelical Theological Soc. [19980]
Evangelical Training Assn. [19925]
Evangelicals Concerned [20054]
Evangelism and Home Missions Assn. [20006]
Evangelistic Faith Missions [20336]
Fed. of Protestant Welfare Agencies [20482]
Fellowship of Christian Airline Personnel [20007]
Fellowship Intl. Mission [20338]
Forum for Scriptural Christianity [20262]
Friends of Israel Gospel Ministry [20010]
The Gideons Intl. [20011]
Hebrew Christian Fellowship [20012]
High School Evangelism Fellowship [20013]
Hindustan Bible Inst. [19927]
Independent Bd. for Presbyterian Foreign Missions [20467]
Inst. of Apostolic Oblates [19638]
Inst. for Biblical Res. [19519]
Interdisciplinary Biblical Res. Inst. [19928]
Intl. Assn. of Women Ministers [20619]

A star before a book entry number signifies that the name is not listed separately, but is mentioned within the entry.

Intl. Bd. of Jewish Missions [20014]
Intl. Coun. of Christian Churches [20015]
Intl. Fed. of Messianic Jews [20255]
Intl. Fed. of Rabbis [20144]
Intl. Fellowship of Evangelical Students [IO]
Intl. Students, Inc. [20017]
InterServe U.S.A. [20351]
Lay Carmelite Order of the Blessed Virgin Mary of Mount Carmel [19647]
Laymen's Home Missionary Movement [20018]
Life Action Revival Ministries [20020]
Life Outreach Intl. [20021]
Maryheart Crusaders [19657]
Media Associates Intl. [19981]
Media Associates Intl. [IO]
Mission to the World [20468]
Morris Cerullo World Evangelism [20025]
Natl. Apostolate for Inclusion Ministry [20026]
Natl. Assn. of Evangelicals [19982]
Natl. Cursillo Movement [19685]
Natl. Evangelization Teams [19687]
Natl. Ghost Ranch Found. [20469]
Natl. Religious Broadcasters [19539]
Natl. Religious Partnership for the Env. [19941]
Near East Archaeological Soc. [6451]
Paulist Memorial Soc. [19699]
Paulist Natl. Catholic Evangelization Assn. [19700]
Pentecostal Assemblies of the World [20463]
Pentecostal Charismatic Churches of North Am. [20464]
Pilots for Christ Intl. [20028]
Pocket Testament League [19529]
Presbyterian Evangelistic Fellowship [20471]
Presbyterian Lay Comm. [20472]
Presbyterian Men [20473]
Presbyterian-Reformed Ministries Intl. [20474]
Presbyterian Women [20475]
Revival Fires (Christian Evangelizers Assn.) [20031]
Rosedale Mennonite Missions [20253]
Saints Alive in Jesus [20032]
Samaritans Intl. [20392]
Seafarers and Intl. House [20232]
Secular Inst. of Saint Francis de Sales [19716]
Serra Intl. [19717]
Skinner Leadership Inst. [20033]
Soc. of Missionaries of Africa [19721]
Soc. for Pentecostal Stud. [20465]
STEER [20401]
Teen Challenge Intl. [20643]
Teen Missions Intl. [20402]
WEC Intl. [20034]
World Evangelical Alliance [19983]
World Evangelical Alliance [IO]
World Fellowship of Slavic Evangelical Christians [IO]
World Fellowship of Slavic Evangelical Christians [19984]
World Impact [20414]
World Mission Prayer League [20234]
World Relief [19985]
World Relief [IO]
World Team [20417]
Youth for Christ/U.S.A. [20645]
Youth Evangelism Assn. [20036]
Youth Ministry [20235]
The Evangelical Alliance Mission [20331], PO Box 969, Wheaton, IL 60189-0969, (630)653-5300
Evangelical Alliance of the United Kingdom [IO], London, United Kingdom
Evangelical Assn. of the Caribbean [IO], Christ Church, Barbados
Evangelical Assn. for the Promotion of Educ. [★IO]
Evangelical Assn. for the Promotion of Educ. [★20330]
Evangelical Baptist Fellowship; All-Ukrainian [19469]
Evangelical Christian Publishers Assn. [3223], 9633 S 48th St., Ste. 140, Phoenix, AZ 85044, (480)966-3998
Evangelical Christian Publishers Association [IO], Phoenix, AZ, United States
Evangelical Church Alliance [19977], 205 W Broadway St., PO Box 9, Bradley, IL 60915, (815)937-0720

Evangelical Church Lib. Assn. [10355], PO Box 353, Glen Ellyn, IL 60138, (630)375-7865
Evangelical Coun. for Financial Accountability [20002], 440 W Jubal Early Dr., Ste. 130, Winchester, VA 22601, (540)535-0103
Evangelical and Ecumenical Women's Caucus [19978], PO Box 78171, Indianapolis, IN 46278-0171
Evangelical and Ecumenical Women's Caucus [IO], Indianapolis, IN, United States
Evangelical Educ. Soc; Episcopal [19955]
Evangelical Educ. Soc. of the Protestant Episcopal Church [★19955]
Evangelical Environmental Network [20003], 4485 Tench Rd., Ste. 850, Suwanee, GA 30024, (678)541-0747
Evangelical Fellowship Commun. Commm; World [★19538]
Evangelical Fellowship; Episcopal [★19955]
Evangelical Fellowship of India Commn. on Relief [IO], New Delhi, India
Evangelical Fellowship of Mission Agencies [20332], 4201 N Peachtree Rd., Atlanta, GA 30341, (770)457-6677
Evangelical Fellowship; World [★19983]
Evangelical Foreign Missions Assn. [★20332]
Evangelical Free Church of Am. - Intl. Mission [20333], 901 E 78th St., Minneapolis, MN 55420-1334, (952)854-1300
Evangelical Free Church of Am. - Intl. Mission [IO], Minneapolis, MN, United States
Evangelical Free Church Mission [★IO]
Evangelical Free Church Mission [★20333]
Evangelical Friends Alliance [★20040]
Evangelical Friends Alliance [★IO]
Evangelical Friends; Assn. of [★20040]
Evangelical Friends Intl. [★20040]
Evangelical Friends Intl. [★IO]
Evangelical Friends Intl. - North Amer. Region [IO], Canton, OH, United States
Evangelical Friends Intl. - North Amer. Region [20040], c/o World Outreach Center, 5350 Broadmoor Cir. NW, Canton, OH 44709, (330)493-1660
Evangelical Literature Overseas [★19981]
Evangelical Literature Overseas [★IO]
Evangelical Lutheran Church; Assn. of [★20224]
Evangelical Lutheran Educ. Assn. [8802], 500 N Estrella Pkwy., Ste. B2, Box 601, Goodyear, AZ 85338, (623)925-1594
Evangelical Lutheran Good Samaritan Soc. [13168], PO Box 5038, Sioux Falls, SD 57117-5038, (605)362-3100
Evangelical Lutheran Sanatorium Assn. [★20233]
Evangelical Medical Aid Soc. [IO], Mississauga, ON, Canada
Evangelical Missiological Soc. [20334], PO Box 794, Wheaton, IL 60189, (630)752-7158
Evangelical Philosophical Soc. [19979], c/o Dr. R. Scott Smith, Sec.-Treas., Biola Univ., 13800 Biola Ave., La Mirada, CA 90639-0001, (562)906-4570
Evangelical Philosophical Society [IO], La Mirada, CA, United States
Evangelical Press Association [IO], Crystal, MN, United States
Evangelical Press Assn. [20004], PO Box 28129, Crystal, MN 55428, (763)535-4793
Evangelical and Reformed Church; Historical Soc. of the [★20607]
Evangelical and Reformed Historical Soc. [20607], 555 W James St., Lancaster, PA 17603, (717)290-8734
Evangelical and Reformed Historical Soc. and Archives of the United Church of Christ [★20607]
Evangelical and Reformed Historical Soc., United Church of Christ [★20607]
Evangelical and Reformed Historical Soc., United Church of Christ [★20607]
Evangelical Relief and Development Organizations; Assn. of [20486]
Evangelical Slovak Women's Union [★19219]
Evangelical Social Action Commn. [20005], c/o Natl. Assn. of Evangelicals, PO Box 23269, Washington, DC 20026, (202)789-1011
Evangelical Social Work Conf. [★13208]
Evangelical Teacher Training Assn. [★19925]

Evangelical Theological Soc. [19980], c/o Dr. James A. Borland, Sec.-Treas., 200 Russell Woods Dr., Lynchburg, VA 24502-3574, (434)237-5309
Evangelical Training Assn. [19925], PO Box 327, Wheaton, IL 60189, (630)384-6920
Evangelical Union; Slovak [★19219]
Evangelical United Brethren Church; Historical Soc. of the [★10467]
Evangelical United Brethren Heritage; Center for the [19976]
Evangelical Women's Caucus, Intl. [★19978]
Evangelical Women's Caucus, Intl. [★IO]
Evangelicals Concerned [20054], 311 E 72nd St., Ste. 1G, New York, NY 10021
Evangelicals for Social Action [★18602]
Evangelicals; World Relief Commn. of the Natl. Assn. of [★19985]
Evangelische Frauenarbeit in Deutschland [★IO]
Evangelischer Frauenbund der Schweiz [IO], Zurich, Switzerland
Evangelisches Missionswerk in Deutschland [★IO]

Evangelism
Aboriginal Evangelical Fellowship of Australia [IO]
Action Intl. Ministries [IO]
Action Intl. Ministries [19986]
Adopt-A-Church Intl. [19839]
Advancing Churches in Missions Commitment [20293]
Advancing Native Missions [19833]
Africa Inland Mission Intl. [20294]
All Roads Ministry [19564]
All-Ukrainian Evangelical Baptist Fellowship [19469]
Ambassadors of Mary [19565]
Amer. Tract Soc. [19987]
AMF Intl. [19988]
AMF Intl. [IO]
Apostleship of Prayer [19569]
Apostolate for Family Consecrations [19571]
Archconfraternity of the Holy Ghost [19573]
Artists in Christian Testimony [19989]
Artists in Christian Testimony [IO]
Assoc. Comm. of Friends on Indian Affairs [20039]
Assn. of Baptists for World Evangelism [19472]
Assn. of Marian Helpers [19576]
Assn. of Romanian Catholics of America [19579]
Athletes in Action [19990]
Athletes in Action [IO]
Avant Ministries [20303]
Baptist World Alliance [19482]
BCM Intl. [19508]
Berean Bible Soc. [19509]
Bethany Intl. Missions [20304]
Bibles For The World [20305]
Biblical Ministries Worldwide [19991]
Biblical Ministries Worldwide [IO]
Billy Graham Evangelistic Assn. [19992]
BLI [19512]
Bread on the Waters [19993]
Bros. and Sisters in Christ [19767]
Bruderhof Communities [20481]
Campus Crusade for Christ Intl. [19994]
Campus Crusade for Christ Intl. [IO]
Catholic Kolping Soc. of Am. [19599]
Catholic Pamphlet Soc. of the U.S. [19603]
Catholics United for the Faith [19606]
CBM Ministries [19995]
Center for the Evangelical United Brethren Heritage [19976]
Central Assn. of the Miraculous Medal [19609]
Champions for Life Intl. [19996]
Champions for Life International [IO]
Child Evangelism Fellowship [IO]
Child Evangelism Fellowship [19997]
Child Evangelism Fellowship of Canada [IO]
Chinese Coordination Centre of World Evangelism [IO]
Chosen People Ministries [19998]
Christ in Action Ministries [19999]
Christ in Action Ministries [IO]
Christ Truth Ministries [19514]
Christian Boaters Assn. [20000]
Christian Golfers' Assn. [23283]
Christian Literature and Bible Center [20317]

Reference to "IO" in place of a book number signifies that the association may be found in the 45th edition of International Organizations.

Christian Motorcyclists Assn. [22674]
Christian Pharmacists Fellowship Intl. [15928]
Christian TV Mission [19536]
Church Army [19947]
Comm. on Missionary Evangelism [20001]
Commun. Commn. [19537]
Company of Saint Paul [19614]
Conservative Baptist Assn. of Am. [19485]
Continental Baptist Missions [19486]
Cowboys for Christ [19792]
Crossworld [20326]
EAPE/Campolo Ministries - Evangelical Assn. for the Promotion of Educ. [20330]
Episcopal Evangelical Educ. Soc. [19955]
Equestrian Ministries Intl. [20082]
Evangelical Church Alliance [19977]
Evangelical Coun. for Financial Accountability [20002]
Evangelical and Ecumenical Women's Caucus [19978]
Evangelical Environmental Network [20003]
Evangelical Free Church of Am. - Intl. Mission [20333]
Evangelical Friends Intl. - North Amer. Region [20040]
Evangelical Missiological Soc. [20334]
Evangelical Press Assn. [20004]
Evangelical Press Association [IO]
Evangelical and Reformed Historical Soc. [20607]
Evangelical Social Action Commn. [20005]
Evangelical Theological Soc. [19980]
Evangelical Training Assn. [19925]
Evangelicals Concerned [20054]
Evangelism and Home Missions Assn. [20006]
Evangelistic Faith Missions [20336]
Fed. of Protestant Welfare Agencies [20482]
Fellowship of Associates of Medical Evangelism [20240]
Fellowship of Christian Airline Personnel [20007]
Fellowship of Christian Airline Personnel [IO]
Fellowship of Christian Athletes [20008]
Fellowship of Christian Peace Officers - U.S.A. [19798]
Fellowship Intl. Mission [20338]
First Fruit [20009]
Focolare Movement [19624]
Forum for Scriptural Christianity [20262]
Friends of Israel Gospel Ministry [20010]
The Gideons Intl. [20011]
The Gideons Intl. [IO]
Glenmary Res. Center [19628]
Hebrew Christian Fellowship [20012]
High School Evangelism Fellowship [20013]
Hindustan Bible Inst. [19927]
Holy Cross Foreign Mission Soc. [19633]
IFCA Intl. [19849]
Independent Bd. for Presbyterian Foreign Missions [20467]
Inst. of Apostolic Oblates [19638]
Inst. for Biblical Res. [19519]
Interdisciplinary Biblical Res. Inst. [19928]
Intl. Alliance of Messianic Congregations and Synagogues [20254]
Intl. Assn. of Women Ministers [20619]
Intl. Bible Students Assn. [19521]
Intl. Bd. of Jewish Missions [20014]
Intl. Bd. of Jewish Missions [IO]
Intl. Coun. of Christian Churches [IO]
Intl. Coun. of Christian Churches [20015]
Intl. Coun. of Iranian Christians [19809]
Intl. Fed. of Messianic Jews [20255]
Intl. Fed. of Rabbis [20144]
Intl. Messianic Jewish Alliance [20016]
Intl. Messianic Jewish Alliance [IO]
Intl. Students, Inc. [IO]
Intl. Students, Inc. [20017]
InterServe U.S.A. [20351]
Jesuit Volunteer Corps: Northwest [19644]
Jews for Jesus [20256]
Jews for Judaism [20500]
Lay Carmelite Order of the Blessed Virgin Mary of Mount Carmel [19647]
Laymen's Home Missionary Movement [20018]
Laymen's Home Missionary Movement [IO]
Lederer Messianic Ministries [20019]

Life Action Revival Ministries [20020]
Life Outreach Intl. [20021]
Literacy and Evangelism Intl. [8791]
Lithuanian Catholic Religious Aid [19653]
Luis Palau Assn. [20022]
Luis Palau Assn. [IO]
Maranatha Volunteers Intl. [IO]
Maranatha Volunteers Intl. [20023]
Maryheart Crusaders [19657]
Maryknoll Fathers and Bros. [19658]
Media Associates Intl. [19981]
Media Fellowship Intl. [20024]
Media Fellowship Intl. [IO]
Messianic Jewish Alliance of Am. [20257]
Messianic Jewish Movement Intl. [20258]
Militia of the Immaculata Movement [19660]
Mission to the World [20468]
Missions Door [19491]
Missions Intl. [IO]
Morris Cerullo World Evangelism [IO]
Morris Cerullo World Evangelism [20025]
Natl. Apostolate for Inclusion Ministry [20026]
Natl. Assn. of Evangelicals [19982]
Natl. Baptist Convention, U.S.A. [19493]
Natl. Christian Life Community of the U.S.A. [19680]
Natl. Cursillo Movement [19685]
Natl. Evangelization Teams [19687]
Natl. Ghost Ranch Found. [20469]
Natl. Religious Broadcasters [19539]
Natl. Ser. Committee/Chariscenter USA [19693]
The Navigators [19817]
North Amer. Assn. for the Catechumenate [19697]
Open Air Campaigners, U.S.A. [20027]
Overseas Missionary Fellowship Canada [IO]
Paraclete [20381]
Paulist Memorial Soc. [19699]
Paulist Natl. Catholic Evangelization Assn. [19700]
Pentecostal Assemblies of the World [20463]
Pentecostal Charismatic Churches of North Am. [20464]
Pilots for Christ Intl. [20028]
Pilots for Christ Intl. [IO]
Pocket Testament League [19529]
Presbyterian Evangelistic Fellowship [20471]
Presbyterian Lay Comm. [20472]
Presbyterian Men [20473]
Presbyterian-Reformed Ministries Intl. [20474]
Presbyterian Women [20475]
Pro Athletes Outreach [20029]
Pro Maria Comm. [19704]
Pro Sanctity Movement [19705]
Promise Keepers [19834]
Remnant Of Israel [20030]
Revival Fires (Christian Evangelizers Assn.) [20031]
Revival Fires (Christian Evangelizers Association) [IO]
Rosedale Mennonite Missions [20253]
Sacred Heart League [19711]
Saints Alive in Jesus [20032]
Samaritans Intl. [20392]
Seafarers and Intl. House [20232]
Searching Together Educational Ministries [19909]
Secular Inst. of Saint Francis de Sales [19716]
Serra Intl. [19717]
Seventh Day Baptist Missionary Soc. [19496]
Skinner Leadership Inst. [20033]
Soc. of Missionaries of Africa [19721]
Soc. for Pentecostal Stud. [20465]
Southern Baptist Historical Lib. and Archives [19499]
STEER [20401]
Swiss Alliance Mission [IO]
Teen Challenge Intl. [20643]
Teen Missions Intl. [20402]
Toward Tradition [20508]
Water Missions Intl. [13411]
WEC Intl. [20034]
WEC Intl. [IO]
Women Nationally Active for Christ [19502]
Word of Life Fellowship [20035]
World Convention of Churches of Christ [19857]
World Evangelical Alliance [19983]

World Fellowship of Slavic Evangelical Christians [19984]
World Impact [20414]
World Mission Prayer League [20234]
World Relief [19985]
World Team [20417]
WorldVenture [19503]
Youth for Christ/U.S.A. [20645]
Youth Evangelism Assn. [20036]
Youth Ministry [20235]
Evangelism Assn; Lutheran Braille [16866]
Evangelism; Fellowship of Associates of Medical [20240]
Evangelism Fellowship; High School [★20013]
Evangelism Fellowship Intl; Child [★19997]
Evangelism and Home Mission Commn. [★20006]
Evangelism and Home Missions Assn. [20006], c/o Natl. Assn. of Evangelicals, PO Box 23269, Washington, DC 20026-3269, (202)789-1011
Evangelism Intl; Literacy and [8791]
Evangelism and Missions Info. Ser. [20335], 500 Coll. Ave., Wheaton, IL 60187, (630)752-7158
Evangelism in the Orient; Assn. of Baptists for [★19472]
Evangelism; World [★20025]
Evangelistic Assn; Larry Jones [★12854]
Evangelistic Campaign; Latin Amer. [★20353]
Evangelistic Faith Missions [20336], PO Box 609, Bedford, IN 47421, (812)275-7531
Evangelistic Faith Missions [IO], Bedford, IN, United States
Evangelistic Fellowship; Presbyterian [20471]
Evangelistic Team; Luis Palau [★20022]
Evangelization
Advancing Churches in Missions Commitment [20293]
Africa Inland Mission Intl. [20294]
All Roads Ministry [19564]
Ambassadors of Mary [19565]
Amer. Tract Soc. [19987]
AMF Intl. [19988]
Apostleship of Prayer [19569]
Apostolate for Family Consecrations [19571]
Archconfraternity of the Holy Ghost [19573]
Assoc. Comm. of Friends on Indian Affairs [20039]
Assn. of Baptists for World Evangelism [19472]
Assn. of Marian Helpers [19576]
Assn. of Romanian Catholics of America [19579]
Athletes in Action [19990]
Aurora Ministries [20276]
Baptist World Alliance [19482]
BCM Intl. [19508]
Berean Bible Soc. [19509]
Bethany Intl. Missions [20304]
Bibles For The World [20305]
Biblical Ministries Worldwide [19991]
Billy Graham Evangelistic Assn. [19992]
BLI [19512]
Bread on the Waters [19993]
Bros. and Sisters in Christ [19767]
Bruderhof Communities [20481]
Campus Crusade for Christ Intl. [19994]
Catholic Kolping Soc. of Am. [19599]
Catholic Pamphlet Soc. of the U.S. [19603]
Catholics United for the Faith [19606]
CBM Ministries [19995]
Center for the Evangelical United Brethren Heritage [19976]
Central Assn. of the Miraculous Medal [19609]
Champions for Life Intl. [19996]
Child Evangelism Fellowship [19997]
Christ in Action Ministries [19999]
Christ Truth Ministries [19514]
Christian Literature and Bible Center [20317]
Christian Motorcyclists Assn. [22674]
Church Army [19947]
Comm. on Missionary Evangelism [20001]
Company of Saint Paul [19614]
Conservative Baptist Assn. of Am. [19485]
Continental Baptist Missions [19486]
Cowboys for Christ [19792]
Crossworld [20326]
EAPE/Campolo Ministries - Evangelical Assn. for the Promotion of Educ. [20330]

A star before a book entry number signifies that the name is not listed separately, but is mentioned within the entry.

Episcopal Evangelical Educ. Soc. [19955]
Evangelical Church Alliance [19977]
Evangelical Coun. for Financial Accountability [20002]
Evangelical and Ecumenical Women's Caucus [19978]
Evangelical Free Church of Am. - Intl. Mission [20333]
Evangelical Friends Intl. - North Amer. Region [20040]
Evangelical Missiological Soc. [20334]
Evangelical Press Assn. [20004]
Evangelical and Reformed Historical Soc. [20607]
Evangelical Social Action Commn. [20005]
Evangelical Theological Soc. [19980]
Evangelicals Concerned [20054]
Evangelism and Home Missions Assn. [20006]
Evangelistic Faith Missions [20336]
Fed. of Protestant Welfare Agencies [20482]
Fellowship of Christian Airline Personnel [20007]
Fellowship of Christian Athletes [20008]
Fellowship of Christian Peace Officers - U.S.A. [19798]
Fellowship Intl. Mission [20338]
Forum for Scriptural Christianity [20262]
Friends of Israel Gospel Ministry [20010]
The Gideons Intl. [20011]
Glenmary Res. Center [19628]
Hebrew Christian Fellowship [20012]
High School Evangelism Fellowship [20013]
Holy Cross Foreign Mission Soc. [19633]
IFCA Intl. [19849]
Independent Bd. for Presbyterian Foreign Missions [20467]
Inst. of Apostolic Oblates [19638]
Interdisciplinary Biblical Res. Inst. [19928]
Intl. Assn. of Women Ministers [20619]
Intl. Bd. of Jewish Missions [20014]
Intl. Coun. of Christian Churches [20015]
Intl. Fed. of Messianic Jews [20255]
Intl. Fed. of Rabbis [20144]
Intl. Students, Inc. [20017]
InterServe U.S.A. [20351]
Jesuit Volunteer Corps: Northwest [19644]
Lay Carmelite Order of the Blessed Virgin Mary of Mount Carmel [19647]
Laymen's Home Missionary Movement [20018]
Life Action Revival Ministries [20020]
Life Outreach Intl. [20021]
Lithuanian Catholic Religious Aid [19653]
Luis Palau Assn. [20022]
Maryheart Crusaders [19657]
Maryknoll Fathers and Bros. [19658]
Media Associates Intl. [19981]
Mission to the World [20468]
Missions Door [19491]
Missions Intl. [20037]
Morris Cerullo World Evangelism [20025]
Natl. Apostolate for Inclusion Ministry [20026]
Natl. Assn. of Evangelicals [19982]
Natl. Baptist Convention, U.S.A. [19493]
Natl. Christian Life Community of the U.S.A. [19680]
Natl. Cursillo Movement [19685]
Natl. Evangelization Teams [19687]
Natl. Ghost Ranch Found. [20469]
Natl. Ser. Committee/Chariscenter USA [19693]
The Navigators [19817]
North Amer. Assn. for the Catechumenate [19697]
Paulist Memorial Soc. [19699]
Paulist Natl. Catholic Evangelization Assn. [19700]
Pentecostal Assemblies of the World [20463]
Pentecostal Charismatic Churches of North Am. [20464]
Pilots for Christ Intl. [20028]
Pocket Testament League [19529]
Presbyterian Evangelistic Fellowship [20471]
Presbyterian Lay Comm. [20472]
Presbyterian Men [20473]
Presbyterian-Reformed Ministries Intl. [20474]
Presbyterian Women [20475]
Pro Athletes Outreach [20029]
Pro Maria Comm. [19704]
Pro Sanctity Movement [19705]

Revival Fires (Christian Evangelizers Assn.) [20031]
Rosedale Mennonite Missions [20253]
Sacred Heart League [19711]
Saints Alive in Jesus [20032]
Samaritans Intl. [20392]
Seafarers and Intl. House [20232]
Searching Together Educational Ministries [19909]
Secular Inst. of Saint Francis de Sales [19716]
Serra Intl. [19717]
Seventh Day Baptist Missionary Soc. [19496]
Skinner Leadership Inst. [20033]
Soc. of Missionaries of Africa [19721]
Soc. for Pentecostal Stud. [20465]
Southern Baptist Historical Lib. and Archives [19499]
STEER [20401]
Teen Challenge Intl. [20643]
Teen Missions Intl. [20402]
Water Missions Intl. [13411]
WEC Intl. [20034]
Women Nationally Active for Christ [19502]
World Evangelical Alliance [19983]
World Fellowship of Slavic Evangelical Christians [19984]
World Impact [20414]
World Mission Prayer League [20234]
World Relief [19985]
World Team [20417]
WorldVenture [19503]
Youth for Christ/U.S.A. [20645]
Youth Evangelism Assn. [20036]
Youth Ministry [20235]
Evangelization Assn; Paulist Natl. Catholic [19700]
Evangelization of the Greeks; Amer. Comm. for the [★20298]
Evangelization Soc. - Address unknown since 2002.
Evangelization Teams; Natl. [19687]
Evangelize China Fellowship [20337], 437 S Garfield Ave., Monterey Park, CA 91754, (626)288-8828
Evangelize China Fellowship [IO], Monterey Park, CA, United States
Evans Collectors Assn; Roy Rogers - Dale [24971]
Evans of Merthyr Tydil; John Morgan [20965]
Evans Scholars Foundation [★23471]
Evans Syndrome Res. and Support Gp. [14934], 1376 Presidential Hwy., Jefferson, NH 03583
Evans Syndrome Research and Support Group [IO], Jefferson, NH, United States
Evaporated Milk Assn. [★1130]
Evaporative Cooling Inst. [1879], MSC 3ECI - NMSU, PO Box 30001, Las Cruces, NM 88003-8001, (505)646-1846
Evasion Soc; Air Forces Escape and [20660]
Evelyn Scott Soc. [11170], c/o Dr. Tim Edwards, VP/Treas., Univ. of West Alabama, Dept. of Languages and Literature, Sta. 22, Livingston, AL 35470
Evelyn Waugh Soc. - Defunct.
Evening Student Assn. - Defunct.
The Event Services Assn. [IO], Chepstow, United Kingdom
Eventing Assn; U.S. [23535]
Events Indus. Alliance [IO], Berkhamsted, United Kingdom
Events Soc; Intl. Special [1311]
Everglades; Friends of the [4398]
Evergreen Agricultural Coun. - Defunct.
Evergreen Found. [★12226]
Evergreen Found. [★IO]
Evergreen Freedom Found. [6230], PO Box 552, Olympia, WA 98507, (360)956-3482
Evergreen Intl. [12226], 307 W 200 S, Ste. 4006, Salt Lake City, UT 84101, (801)363-3837
Evergreen Intl. [IO], Salt Lake City, UT, United States
Everly Bros. Intl. [IO], Gouda, Netherlands
Everly Brothers Intl. - Defunct.
Every Child By Two [13959], 666 11th St. NW, Ste. 202, Washington, DC 20001-4542, (202)783-7034
Every Mother is a Working Mother Network [18810], PO Box 86681, Los Angeles, CA 90086-0681, (323)292-7405
Every Person Influences Children [11540], 1000 Main St., Buffalo, NY 14202, (716)332-4100

Everyday Ayurveda [13606], PO Box 681, Cedar Ridge, CA 95924, (530)470-9789
Evidence; Intl. Assn. for Property and [5975]
Evidence Photographers Intl. Coun. [5759], 229 Peachtree St. NE, No. 2200, Atlanta, GA 30303, (404)614-6406
Evidence Photographers Intl. Coun. [IO], Honesdale, PA, United States
Evolution
Access Res. Network [9095]
Amer. Museum of Natural History [7357]
Amer. Teilhard Assn. [9632]
ERIS Roundtable for Independent Study [10792]
Evolutionary Anthropology Soc. [6416]
Human Behavior and Evolution Soc. [6531]
Inst. for Creation Res. [20538]
Inst. of Human Origins [7072]
Intl. Soc. for Phylogenetic Nomenclature [7116]
Intl. Soc. for the Stud. of the Origin of Life [IO]
Natl. Center for Sci. Educ. [9110]
Soc. for Molecular Biology and Evolution [6601]
Soc. for the Stud. of Evolution [7073]
Southern African Assn. of Geomorphologists [IO]
Evolution Soc; Human Behavior and [6531]
Evolutionary Anthropology Soc. [6416], c/o Amer. Anthropological Assn., 2200 Wilson Blvd., Ste. 600, Arlington, VA 22201-3357, (703)528-1902
Evolutionary Economics; Assn. for [6872]
Evrytania; Daughters of [19086]
Evrytanian Assn. of America - Address unknown since 2001.
E.V.V.E. - European Assn. for the consumption-based billing of energy costs [IO], Bonn, Germany
Ewing Marion Kaufman Found. [18846], 4801 Rockhill Rd., Kansas City, MO 64110-2046, (816)932-1000
Ewing Soc; James [★15655]
EWM Global Teams [★19961]
EWM Global Teams [★IO]
Ex-Masons for Jesus [19795], PO Box 28702, Las Vegas, NV 89126
Ex-Partners of Ser. Members for Equality [17437], PO Box 11191, Alexandria, VA 22312-0191, (703)941-5844
Ex-Partners of Servicemembers for Equality [12009], PO Box 11191, Alexandria, VA 22312-0191, (703)941-5844
Ex-Prisoners of War; Amer. [21262]
Ex-Students Assn; Angelo State Univ. [★18874]
Exam Comm., Amer. Assn. of Nurse Anesthetists [★15475]
Examination Bd. of Professional Home Inspectors [2118], 800 E Northwest Hwy., Ste. 700, Palatine, IL 60074, (847)298-7750
Examination Commn; Foreign Pharmacy Graduate [★15933]
Examination Comm; Foreign Pharmacy Graduate [15933]
Examination of Religion; Committee for the Sci. [★20085]
Examination of Religion; Committee for the Sci. [★IO]
Examinations Bd; Graduate Record [9251]
Examiner Certification; Commission on Disability [★14575]
Examiners and Administrators of Educational Personnel; Amer. Assn. of [★7883]
Examiners of Am; Natl. Assn. of Boards of Barbers [★1083]
Examiners; Amer. Assn. of Dental [14112]
Examiners; Amer. Bd. of Independent Medical [8877]
Examiners; Amer. Coun. of Hypnotist [14918]
Examiners Assn; Airline Medical [★13540]
Examiners; Assn. of Certified Public Accountant [★5428]
Examiners; Natl. Assn. of Certified Fraud [★2084]
Examiners; Natl. Assn. of Disability [14034]
Examiners; Natl. Bd. of Chiropractic [14010]
Examiners; Natl. Bd. of Osteopathic Medical [15812]
Examiners; Natl. Bd. of Podiatric Medical [16046]
Examiners; Natl. Bd. of Podiatry [★16046]
Examiners; Natl. Conf. of Bar [5950]
Examiners; Natl. Contact Lens [15723]
Examiners; Natl. Coun. of Engg. [★7031]
Examiners; Natl. Coun. of State Boards of Engg. [★7031]

Reference to "IO" in place of a book number signifies that the association may be found in the 45th edition of International Organizations.

Examiners of Nursing Home Administrators; Natl. Assn. of Boards of [★15538]

Examiners Nursing and Tech; Bd. of Nephrology [15290]

Examiners - Nursing and Tech; Bd. of Nephrology [★15290]

Examiners in Optometry; Natl. Bd. of [15722]

Examiners for Osteopathic Physicians and Surgeons; Natl. Bd. of [★15812]

Examiners in Pastoral Counseling; Amer. Bd. of [19864]

Examiners of Psychodrama, Sociometry, and Gp. Psychotherapy; Amer. Bd. of [16201]

Examiners Soc; Insurance Regulatory [2182]

Examining Boards of the U.S; Conf. of Funeral Ser. [★6120]

Examining Boards of the U.S; Intl. Conf. of Funeral Ser. [6120]

Excellence; Texans for Educational [★7998]

Excelsior Coll. Alumni Assn. [18896], Excelsior Coll., 7 Columbia Cir., Albany, NY 12203-5159, (518)464-8500

Exceptional Children; Coun. for [9141]

Exceptional Children; Found. for [★11998]

Exceptional Children; Natl. Assn. of Private Schools for [★9147]

Excess and Casualty Reinsurance Assn. - Defunct.

Exchange Accommodators; Fed. of [3717]

Exchange Assn; Intl. [★8591]

Exchange; Boston Intl. Found. for Medical [★15089]

Exchange Carrier Assn. [★3960]

Exchange Carrier Assn; Natl. [3960]

Exchange Center; Escalen Inst. Russian-American [★17912]

Exchange; Classical Music Lovers' [10578]

Exchange Club; Coupon [17327]

Exchange Club Found; Natl. [11637]

Exchange Club Found. for the Prevention of Child Abuse; Natl. [★11637]

Exchange Club; Natl. [13054]

Exchange Clubs of Am. [★13054]

Exchange Commn. Alumni; Assn. of Securities and [3508]

Exchange Commission; Securities and [★3508]

Exchange Fellowships; Eisenhower [★17884]

Exchange Gp. for Appropriate Tech. [IO], Brussels, Belgium

Exchange; Liaison Gp. for Intl. Educational [★8591]

Exchange Prog; Escalen Inst. Soviet-American [★17912]

Exchange of Students for Tech. Experience (U.S.); Intl. Assn. for the [★8601]

Exchanger Mfrs. Assn; Tubular [1902]

Exchanges; Intl. Assn. of Trade [★3841]

Exchanges; Natl. Assn. of Real Estate [★3328]

Exchanges; Natl. Assn. of Trade [3844]

Exchanges; Org. for Amer.-Soviet [★17905]

Exchangors; Natl. Coun. of [3331]

Excipients Coun; Intl. Pharmaceutical [★2977]

Exclusive Agent Associations; Coalition of [173]

Execution Alert Network; Natl. [★17033]

Executive Assistants; Hea. Care [64]

Executive Chef Assn. - Defunct.

Executive Chefs de Cuisine Assn. of Am. [★792]

Executive Coun. on Diplomacy - Address unknown since 2001.

Executive Directors Assn; Natl. Community Action Agency [★12770]

Executive Directors Assn; Natl. Guard [6092]

Executive Leadership Coun. [2762], 1001 N Fairfax St., Ste. 300, Alexandria, VA 22314, (703)706-5200

Executive Link in Washington - Defunct.

Executive Officers; State Higher Educ. [9001]

Executive Placement Comm; National [★19202]

Executive and Professional Women; The Intl. Alliance, An Assn. of [★728]

Executive Protection Institute [★3540]

Executive Protection Institute [★IO]

Executive Recruiters; Natl. Assn. of [1270]

Executive Res. Forum; Police [6005]

Executive Search Coun. - Defunct.

Executive Search Roundtable [7567], PO Box 3565, Grand Central Sta., New York, NY 10163, (212)439-4630

Executive Search Roundtable [IO], New York, NY, United States

Executive Secretaries and Administrative Assistants; Natl. Assn. of [72]

Executive Secretaries; Assn. of [★19902]

Executive Ser. Corps; Natl. [747]

Executive Staff; Assn. of Girl Scout [12996]

Executive Stewards and Caterers Assn. [★1584]

Executive Stewards and Caterers Assn. [★IO]

Executive Suite Assn. [★74]

Executive Suite Network [★74]

Executive Systems Corp. - Defunct.

Executive Women; Cosmetic [1842]

Executive Women in Govt. [5706], PO Box 1046, Laurel, MD 20725-1046, (301)725-3500

Executive Women Intl. [63], 515 S 700 E, Ste. 2A, Salt Lake City, UT 84102, (801)355-2800

Executive Women Intl. [IO], Salt Lake City, UT, United States

Executive Women Intl. - Calgary Chap. [IO], Calgary, AB, Canada

Executive Women's Coun. [4038], 425 6th Ave., Ste. 1860, Pittsburgh, PA 15219, (412)731-1500

Executive Women's Golf Assn. [23447], 300 Ave. of the Champions, Ste. 140, Palm Beach Gardens, FL 33418-3620, (561)691-0096

Executive Women's Networks; Natl. Alliance of Professional and [★728]

Executives of Am; State Beer Assn. of [★204]

Executives; Amer. Assn. of Airport [138]

Executives; Amer. Assn. of Commercial [★24251]

Executives; Amer. Assn. of Medical Soc. [15153]

Executives; Amer. Chamber of Commerce [24251]

Executives; Amer. Coll. of Medical Practice [15054]

Executives; Amer. Coll. of Physician [15056]

Executives; Amer. Inst. of Park [★6153]

Executives; Amer. Org. of Nurse [15454]

Executives of Amer. Schools for the Deaf; Conf. of [★14749]

Executives of the Arc; Natl. Conf. of [2506]

Executives Assn; Advt. Media Credit [1397]

Executives; Assn. of Cancer [13795]

Executives Assn; Christian Financial [★20511]

Executives; Assn. of Club [1932]

Executives; Assn. of Corporate Travel [3909]

Executives Assn; Fraternity [24479]

Executives Assn. of Great Britain [IO], Beaconsfield, United Kingdom

Executives; Assn. of Hispanic Fed. [★5711]

Executives Assn; Loss [2197]

Executives; Assn. of Master of Business Administration [702]

Executives Assn; Medical Soc. [★15153]

Executives Assn. of Natl. Pan-Hellenic Conf; Central Off. [24477]

Executives Assn. Professional Development League; Senior [5714]

Executives Assn; Senior [5713]

Executives; Assn. of Travel Marketing [3912]

Executives; Automotive Trade Assn. [349]

Executives Club; Radio [★563]

Executives; Coll. of Healthcare Info. Mgt. [2098]

Executives; Coll. of Osteopathic Healthcare [14876]

Executives in Corporate Real Estate; Intl. Assn. of Attorneys and [3314]

Executives Coun; Assn. Chief [698]

Executives; Coun. of Protocol [2677]

Executives; Food Indus. Assn. [3405]

Executives Inst; Tax [6304]

Executives; Intl. Builders Exchange [1024]

Executives; Intl. Org. of Black Security [3533]

Executives; Intl. Soc. of Facilities [2467]

Executives; Natl. Assn. of Bar [5948]

Executives; Natl. Assn. of Catering [1951]

Executives; Natl. Assn. for Female [742]

Executives; Natl. Assn. of Hea. Services [14577]

Executives; Natl. Assn. of Minority Media [882]

Executives; Natl. Assn. of State Personnel [6280]

Executives; Natl. Assn. of Women Law Enforcement [5989]

Executives; Natl. Conf. of Bar [★5948]

Executives; Natl. Coun. of County Assn. [5624]

Executives; Natl. Fellowship of Child Care [13501]

Executives; Natl. Org. of Black Law Enforcement [5999]

Executives for Natl. Security; Bus. [18587]

Executives; Natl. Soc. of Fund Raising [★12197]

Executives of North Am; Nursery Assn. [★5047]

Executives of North Am; Nursery and Landscape Assn. [5047]

Executives; North Amer. Assn. of Synagogue [20517]

Executives; Nursery Assn. [★5047]

Executives Org; Chief [712]

Executives in Public Relations; Women [3197]

Executives Res. Found; Financial [1417]

Executives' Secretaries [★63]

Executives' Secretaries [★IO]

Executives; Soc. of Assn. Optometric [★15720]

Executives; Soc. of Certified Credit [1447]

Executives Soc; Credit Union [1106]

Executives; Soc. of Incentive Travel [★3935]

Executives Soc; Licensing [5853]

Executives Soc. of NAPSA; Young [★266]

Executives; Soc. of Recreation [3363]

Executives of State Associations of Counties; Conf. of [★5624]

Exer-Safety Assn. [★15963]

Exer-Safety Assn; Intl. [★15963]

Exercise; Amer. Coun. on [15958]

Exercise Assn; Aquatic [23652]

Exercise Assn; IDEA: Intl. Dance [★15965]

Exercise Instructors Training Assn; NDEITA - Natl. Dance [★23037]

Exercise Physiologists; Amer. Soc. of [16019]

Exercise Safety Assn. [15963], PO Box 547916, Orlando, FL 32854-7916, (407)246-5090

Exercise and Sports Assn; Diabetes [14222]

Exercise Trainers Assn; NETA - Natl. [23037]

Exhaust Systems Professional Assn. - Defunct.

Exhibit Designers and Producers Assn. [1337], 1100 Johnson Ferry Rd., Ste. 300, Atlanta, GA 30342, (404)303-7310

Exhibit Indus. Educ. Found. [★1349]

Exhibition Assn. of South Africa [★IO]

Exhibition Assn. of Southern Africa [IO], Midrand, Republic of South Africa

Exhibition and Event Assn. of Australasia [IO], Frenchs Forest, Australia

Exhibition Fed. of Ukraine [IO], Kiev, Ukraine

Exhibition Services Assn. Holland [IO], Breukelen, Netherlands

Exhibition Services and Contractors Assn. [★2679]

Exhibitions Found; Intl. [★9426]

Exhibitor Appointed Contractor Assn. [1338], 2214 NW 5th St., Bend, OR 97701, (541)317-8768

Exhibitors

Amer. Veterinary Exhibitors Assn. [1334]

Assn. of British Professional Conf. Organisers [IO]

Assn. for Conferences and Events [IO]

Assn. of Event Organisers [IO]

Assn. of the German Trade Fair Indus. [IO]

Assn. of the Hungarian Exhibition and Fair Organisers [IO]

Assn. of Intl. Trade Fairs of Am. [IO]

Assn. of Show and Agricultural Organisations [IO]

Assn. of Trade Fair and Exhibition Organisers of the Czech Republic [IO]

British Arts Festivals Assn. [IO]

British Assn. of Conf. Destinations [IO]

British Exhibition Contractors Assn. [IO]

Canadian Assn. of Exposition Mgt. [IO]

Canadian Assn. of Fairs and Exhibitions [IO]

Canadian Natl. Exhibition [IO]

Caribou Carnival Assn. [IO]

Center for Exhibition Indus. Res. [1335]

Educational Exhibitors Assn. [1336]

European Fed. of Conf. Towns [IO]

European Major Exhibition Centres Assn. [IO]

European Tourism Trade Fairs Assn. [IO]

The Event Services Assn. [IO]

Events Indus. Alliance [IO]

Exhibit Designers and Producers Assn. [1337]

Exhibition Assn. of Southern Africa [IO]

Exhibition and Event Assn. of Australasia [IO]

Exhibition Fed. of Ukraine [IO]

Exhibition Services Assn. Holland [IO]

Exhibitor Appointed Contractor Assn. [1338]

Exposition Operations Soc. [1339]

Fair and Exhibition Assn. [IO]

Fairground Soc. [IO]

Flanders-Brussels Convention Bur. [IO]

A star before a book entry number signifies that the name is not listed separately, but is mentioned within the entry.

French Trade Fairs and Exhibitions [IO]
Goodguys Rod and Custom Assn. [21649]
Healthcare Convention and Exhibitors Assn. [1340]
Hong Kong Exhibition and Convention Indus. Assn. [IO]
Intl. Assn. of Butterfly Exhibitions [IO]
Intl. Assn. of Butterfly Exhibitions [1341]
Intl. Assn. for Modular Exhibitry [1342]
Intl. Defense Equip. Exhibitors Assn. [1343]
International Defense Equipment Exhibitors Association [IO]
Intl. Exhibition Logistics Associates [IO]
Intl. Fed. of Boat Show Organisers [IO]
Intl. Fed. of Exhibition and Event Services [IO]
Intl. Sport Show Producers Assn. [1344]
Intl. Trade Exhibitions in France [1345]
Intl. Trade Exhibitions in France [IO]
Lions-Quest [8199]
Mexican Assn. of Fair, Exhibition, and Convention Professionals [IO]
Natl. Assn. of Consumer Shows [1346]
Natl. Catholic Educational Exhibitors [1347]
Natl. Convention Assn. [2688]
Natl. Independent Concessionaires Assn. [1591]
Natl. Outdoor Events Assn. [IO]
Natl. Show Pig Assn. [22982]
New Zealand Assn. of Events Professionals [IO]
Polish Trade Fair Corp. [IO]
Russian Union of Exhibitions and Fairs [IO]
Singapore Assn. of Convention and Exhibition Organisers and Suppliers [IO]
Soc. of Independent Show Organizers [1348]
Soc. for Voluntary Control of Trade Fair and Exhibition Statistics [IO]
Spotted Saddle Horse Breeders' and Exhibitors' Assn. [4955]
Trade Exhibition Assn. (Thai) [IO]
Trade Show Exhibitors Assn. [1349]
Union of Intl. Fairs [IO]
World Council for Venue Management [IO]
World Coun. for Venue Mgt. [1350]
Exhibitors Assn; Hea. Care [★1340]
Exhibitors Assn; Healthcare Convention and [1340]
Exhibitors Assn; Intl. [★1349]
Exhibitors Assn; Medical [★1340]
Exhibitors Assn; Natl. Trade Show [★1349]
Exhibitors; Soc. of Parrot Breeders and [21860]
Exile Fan Club - Defunct.
Exiled Cuban Dental Affairs Comm. - Defunct.
Existential Philosophy; Soc. for Phenomenology and [10834]
Existentialism
    Intl. Soc. for Phenomenological Stud. [10805]
    Karl Jaspers Soc. of North Am. [10808]
    Merleau-Ponty Circle [10811]
    Soc. for Existential Anal. [IO]
    Soc. for Phenomenology and Existential Philosophy [10834]
EXIT [IO], Edinburgh, United Kingdom
Exmoor Horn Sheep Breeders Soc. [IO], Barnstaple, United Kingdom
Exocrine Found; Children's [★16358]
Exodontists; Amer. Soc. of [★15732]
Exodus Intl. [20055], PO Box 540119, Orlando, FL 32854, (407)599-6872
Exodus Trust [16401]
Exotic Bird Rescue [11393], 317 H. Goodpasture Island Rd., Eugene, OR 97401, (541)461-4333
Exotic Bird Soc. of Am. [21846], 9724 5th Ave., Orlando, FL 32824-8423, (407)855-3367
Exotic Dancers League of Am. [9881], c/o Burlesque Hall of Fame, PO Box 1437, Las Vegas, NV 89125
Exotic Pathology Soc. [IO], Paris, France
Exotic Wildlife Assn. [5316], 105 Henderson Br. Rd. W, Ingram, TX 78025, (830)367-7761
Expanded Metal Mfrs. Assn. - Defunct.
Expanded Shale Clay and Slate Inst. [621], 2225 Murray Holladay Rd., Ste. 102, Salt Lake City, UT 84117, (801)272-7070
Expanded Shale Inst. [★621]
Expanded Textbook and Instructional Materials Prog; PALTEX - [9261]
Expanding and Specialty Paper Products Inst. - Defunct.

Expansion Anchor Mfrs. Inst. - Defunct.
Expansion Joint Mfrs. Assn. [3030], 25 N Broadway, Tarrytown, NY 10591, (914)332-0040
Expansionist Party of the U.S. [18324], 295 Smith St., Newark, NJ 07106-2517, (973)416-6151
Expansionist Party of the U.S. [IO], Newark, NJ, United States
Expediting Mgt. Assn. [IO], Calgary, AB, Canada
Experience Works [IO], Arlington, VA, United States
Experience Works [12080], 2200 Clarendon Blvd., Ste. 1000, Arlington, VA 22201, (703)522-7272
Experiential Education
    Assn. for Experiential Educ. [8411]
    Coun. for Adult and Experiential Learning [8412]
    Earthwatch Inst. [8413]
    Feathered Pipe Found. [12345]
    Natl. Soc. for Experiential Educ. [8414]
    NTL Inst. for Applied Behavioral Sciences [8415]
    NTL Institute for Applied Behavioral Sciences [IO]
Experiential Educ; Assn. for [8411]
Experiential Educ; Center for [★8388]
Experiential Educ; Natl. Soc. for [8414]
Experiential Learning; Assn. for Bus. Simulation and [8015]
Experiential Learning; Coun. for the Advancement of [★8412]
Experiment in Intl. Living [★8635]
Experiment in Intl. Living [★IO]
Experiment in Intl. Living - Ireland [★IO]
Experiment in Intl. Living/School for Intl. Training [★IO]
Experiment in Intl. Living/School for Intl. Training [★8635]
Experimental Aircraft Assn. [6373], EAA Aviation Center, PO Box 3086, Oshkosh, WI 54903-3086, (920)426-4800
Experimental Ballistics Associates - Defunct.
Experimental Biology; Fed. of Amer. Societies for [6576]
Experimental Biology and Medicine; Soc. for [6597]
Experimental Cities, Inc. [17236], PO Box 731, Pacific Palisades, CA 90272-0731, (323)935-4585
Experimental Hematology; Intl. Soc. for [14792]
Experimental Hypnosis; Soc. for Clinical and [14927]
Experimental Mechanics; Soc. for [7713]
Experimental Neuro Therapeutics; Amer. Soc. for [15379]
Experimental Pathology; Amer. Soc. for [★15860]
Experimental Psychology Soc. [IO], Bristol, United Kingdom
Experimental Psychology; Soc. of Multivariate [16174]
Experimental Res. Soc. - Defunct.
Experimental Test Pilots; Soc. of [6384]
Experimental Therapeutics; Amer. Soc. for Pharmacology and [15925]
Experimental Yacht Soc. - Defunct.
Experimento de Convivencia Internacional [★IO]
Experiments in Art and Tech. [9439], c/o Dr. Billy Kluver, Co-Founder/Pres., 69 Apple Tree Rd., Berkeley Heights, NJ 07922, (212)285-1690
Expert Group on Monetary Issues - Defunct.
Expert Witness Assn; Forensic [5760]
Experts; Amer. Bd. of Vocational [9299]
Exploited Children; Commn. on Missing and [11586]
Exploited Children; Natl. Center for Missing and [11630]
Explomet - Address unknown since 1991.
Exploration
    Amer. Alpine Club [7074]
    Australian Soc. of Exploration Geophysicists [IO]
    Christopher Columbus Philatelic Soc. [22805]
    Circumnavigators Club [7075]
    Explorers Club [7076]
    Explorers Club [IO]
    Frederick A. Cook Soc. [11112]
    Inst. for the Stud. of Amer. Cultures [10746]
    Intl. Soc. for a Complete Earth [12354]
    Leif Ericson Viking Ship [11134]
    Lewis and Clark Trail Heritage Found. [10128]
    Oceanic Soc. Expeditions [23016]
    Polynesian Voyaging Soc. [22775]
    Prince Henry Sinclair Soc. of the U.S. [9922]
    Soc. for the History of Discoveries [10158]
    South Amer. Explorers [3937]

Exploration and Development of Space; Students for the [7923]
Exploration Geo-physicists; Soc. of [7149]
Exploration Geophysicists; Canadian Soc. of [IO]
Exploration of Human Potential; Natl. Center for the [★14826]
Exploration; Soc. for Mining, Metallurgy, and [7349]
Exploratory Comm. on Assessing the Progress of Educ. [★9253]
Exploratory Project on the Conditions of Peace - Defunct.
Exploratory Proj. for Economic Alternatives [★18409]
Explorers Club [7076], 46 E 70th St., New York, NY 10021, (212)628-8383
Explorers Club [IO], New York, NY, United States
Explorers Club; South Amer. [★3937]
Explorers - Defunct.
Explorers Res. Corp. - Defunct.
Explorers; Soc. of [★10826]
Explosive Distributors Assn. - Defunct.
Explosive Waste Contractors; Natl. Assn. of Ordnance and [1038]
Explosives
    Assn. for Explosive Detection K-9s, Intl. [5964]
    European Fireworks Assn. [IO]
    Fed. of European Explosive Mfrs. [IO]
    Inst. of Makers of Explosives [1351]
    Intl. Assn. of Bomb Technicians and Investigators [7077]
    Intl. Assn. of Bomb Technicians and Investigators [IO]
    Japan Explosives Soc. [IO]
    Natl. Fire Protection Assn. [12975]
    Natl. Fireworks Assn. [1352]
Explosives Engineers; Soc. of [★7020]
Expo Collectors - Historians Org. - Address unknown since 1994.
Expo West Trade Assn. - Address unknown since 2003.
Export Advt. Assn. [★104]
Export Advt. Assn. [★IO]
Export Assn; California Dried Fruit [★4761]
Export Assn; Phosphate Chemicals [817]
Export Assn; U.S. Soda Ash [★1725]
Export Companies; Natl. Assn. of [2307]
Export Coun; Amer. Hardwood [1603]
Export Coun. of Norway [★24283]
Export Coun. of Norway [★IO]
Export Coun; U.S.A. Poultry and Egg [5123]
Export Credit Insurance Org. [IO], Athens, Greece
Export Development, Assn; U.S. Rice [★4321]
Export Industrial Parks
    World Economic Processing Zones Assn. [3849]
Export Inst. of the U.S. [3840], 6901 W 84th St., Ste. 317, Minneapolis, MN 55438, (952)943-1505
Export Inst. of the U.S. [IO], Minneapolis, MN, United States
Export Managers Club of Chicago [★IO]
Export Managers Club of Chicago [★2284]
Export Marketing Group - Defunct.
Export Packers Assn. of New York - Defunct.
Export Processing Zones Assn; World [★3849]
Export Promotion Coun. of India; Engg. [2304]
Export Task Force - Address unknown since 2003.
Export Trade Coun; Hardwood [★1603]
Export-Union fur Milchprodukte [★IO]
Export Union for Milk Products [IO], Bonn, Germany
Exporters; Assn. of Dark Leaf Tobacco Dealers and [3817]
Exporters Assn; Natl. Lumber [★1603]
Exporters' Assn. of Northern Greece [IO], Thessaloniki, Greece
Exporters Assn; Pacific Lumber [1616]
Exporters Assn; Small Bus. [★2313]
Exporters Assn. of the U.S; Coal [841]
Exporters Assn. of the U.S; Small Bus. [2313]
Exporters and Importers; Amer. Assn. of [2297]
Exporters; Northwest Fruit [4752]
Exposition and Conf. Coun. - Defunct.
Exposition Mgt. Assn. - Defunct.
Exposition Managers; Natl. Assn. of [★2682]
Exposition Nationale Canadienne [★IO]
Exposition Operations Soc. [1339], c/o Stephen A. Schuldenfrei, Pres., PO Box 949, Framingham, MA 01701-0949, (508)544-1527

Reference to "IO" in place of a book number signifies that the association may be found in the 45th edition of International Organizations.

Exposition Ser. Contractors Assn. [2679], 2340 E Trinity Mills Rd., Ste. 100, Carrollton, TX 75006, (469)574-0698

Express Carriers Assn. - Defunct.

Express Delivery and Logistics Assn. [3565], 14 W Third St., No. 200, Kansas City, MO 64105, (816)221-0254

Express and Sta. Employees; Brotherhood of Railway, Airline and Steamship Clerks, Freight Handlers, [★24180]

Express and Sta. Employees; Brotherhood of Railway and Steamship Clerks, Freight Handlers, [★24180]

Expression; Amer. Soc. of Psychopathology of [16191]

Expression Found; Freedom of [17116]

Expressive Anal; Center for [★16217]

Expressive Anal; Inst. for [16217]

Expressive Psychotherapy; Center for [★16217]

Extension 4-H Agents; Natl. Assn. of [13495]

Extension Assn; Natl. Univ. [★8154]

Extension Professionals; Natl. Assn. of Community Development [11784]

Extension Prog. Found; Optometric [15727]

Extension Soc. Volunteers - Defunct.

Extensions for Independence [11945], 555 Saturn Blvd., No. B-368, San Diego, CA 92154, (619)618-2154

Exterior Insulation Manufacturers Assn. [★618]

Exterminators and Fumigators; Natl. Assn. of [★2910]

External Representation of the Ukrainian Helsinki Group - Address unknown since 2001.

External Wall Insulation Assn. [★IO]

Extra-Corporeal Tech; Amer. Soc. of [15129]

Extra Miler Club [23013], PO Box 31, Annandale, VA 22003-0031

Extra Milers [★23013]

Extracorporeal Circulation Technicians; Amer. Soc. of [★15129]

Extract Manufacturers Assn. of the U.S; Flavor and [1509]

Extract Manufacturers Assn. of the U.S; Flavoring [★1509]

Extractive Metallurgy Inst. - Address unknown since 2004.

Extremism; Inst. for Prevention and Control of Violence and [★17146]

Extropy Inst. - Defunct.

Extruders Coun; Aluminum [2693]

Eye Acquisition; Consortium of Registered Nurses for [★15670]

Eye Bank Assn. of Am. [14288], 1015 18th St. NW, Ste. 1010, Washington, DC 20036, (202)775-4999

Eye Bank Assn. of India [IO], Hyderabad, India

Eye-Bank for Sight Restoration [14289], 120 Wall St., 3rd Fl., New York, NY 10005-3902, (212)742-9000

Eye Care - Address unknown since 1999.

Eye Care Found; Children's [★15679]

Eye Care Proj; Natl. [★15701]

Eye and Ear Hospitals; Amer. Assn. of [14859]

Eye Level Gallery Soc. [IO], Halifax, NS, Canada

Eye Movement Desensitization and Reprocessing Assn. of Canada [IO], Toronto, ON, Canada

Eye Res. - Defunct.

Eye Res. Found; Natl. [15724]

Eye; Seeing [16888]

Eye Surgeons; Amer. Coll. of [16564]

Eye Surgeons; Soc. of [15703]

Eyecare Info. Ser. [★IO]

EyeCare Prog; Seniors [15701]

Eyecare; Soc. for Excellence in [15702]

Eyecare Trust [IO], Aylesbury, United Kingdom

Eyes for the Blind; Guiding [16853]

Eyes for the Needy; New [12533]

Eyes Right - Address unknown since 1995.

Eymard League - Defunct.

Ezra Pound Soc. - Address unknown since 2002.

Ezrat Nashim - Defunct.

F

F-4 Phantom II Soc. [21445], 3053 Rancho Vista Blvd., Ste. H-102, Palmdale, CA 93551

F-4 Phantom II Society [IO], Palmdale, CA, United States

F. Marion Crawford Memorial Soc. - Address unknown since 2001.

F. Scott Fitzgerald Soc. [9649], c/o Prof. Ruth Prigozy, Exec. Dir., 107 Hofstra Univ., Hempstead, NY 11549

F. Scott Fitzgerald Society [IO], Hempstead, NY, United States

Fabless Semiconductor Association [IO], Dallas, TX, United States

Fabless Semiconductor Assn. [1215], 3 Lincoln Center, 5430 LBJ Freeway, Ste. 280, Dallas, TX 75240, (972)866-7579

Fabric Belting Mfrs. Assn; Woven [★3792]

Fabric Distributors Assn; Textile [★3802]

Fabric Distributors; Natl. Assn. of Decorative [3793]

Fabric Distributors; Natl. Assn. of Upholstery [★3793]

Fabric Laminators Assn. - Defunct.

Fabric Mfrs. Coun. of the Natl. Textile Assn; Elastic [3780]

Fabric Mfrs. Inst; Elastic [★3780]

Fabric, Notions and Crafts Assn; Southeastern [3798]

Fabric Salesmen's Assn. [3782]

Fabric Salesmen's Guild [★3782]

Fabric Show; Southeastern [★3798]

Fabricants de produits allmentaires du Canada [★IO]

Fabricating Assn; Metal Etching and [★2720]

Fabricating Machinery Assn. [★2017]

Fabricating Machinery Assn. [★IO]

Fabricating Mfrs. Assn. [★IO]

Fabricating Mfrs. Assn. [★2017]

Fabrication Assn; Fiberglass [★589]

Fabrication Inst; Pipe [3036]

Fabricators; Assoc. Wire Rope [2001]

Fabricators Assn; Composites [★589]

Fabricators Assn; Gasket [2022]

Fabricators Assn; Wire [1840]

Fabricators Coun; Copper and Brass [2704]

Fabricators and Mfrs. Assn., Intl. [2017], 833 Featherstone Rd., Rockford, IL 61107-6301, (815)399-8775

Fabricators and Mfrs. Assn., Intl. [IO], Rockford, IL, United States

Fabricators; Natl. Assn. of Pipe [3031]

Fabricators and Riggers; Natl. Coun. of Erectors, [1042]

Fabrics and Film Assn; Chem. [3048]

Fabrics Indus; INDA, Assn. of the Nonwoven [3785]

Fabrics Inst; Narrow [3792]

Fabrics; Natl. Assn. of Finishers of Textile [★3772]

Fabry Disease; Intl. Center for [16537]

Fabry Support and Info. Gp. [14262], PO Box 510, Concordia, MO 64020, (660)463-1355

Fabulous Fifties Ford Club of America - Defunct.

Fabulous Thunderbirds Fan Club - Address unknown since 1995.

FACCT Found. for Accountability - Defunct.

Face Brick Assn; Amer. [★604]

Face; Forward [14062]

FACE Intel - Former and Current Employees of Intel [1262], 7349 Cross Dr., Citrus Heights, CA 95610

Face the Music Fan Club [24887], c/o Katrina Walker, Pres., PO Box 6061-572, Sherman Oaks, CA 91413

Face The Music; Stop the Violence, [13376]

Facel Vega Owners Club - Defunct.

FACES: The Natl. Craniofacial Assn. [14061], PO Box 11082, Chattanooga, TN 37401, (800)332-2373

Faces and Voices of Recovery [18688], 1010 Vermont Ave., No. 708, Washington, DC 20005, (202)737-0690

Faceters Guild; U.S. [1121]

FACETS U.S.A. - Defunct.

Fachverband der Audiovisions- und Filmindustrie Osterreichs [★IO]

Fachverband der Bekleidungsindustrie Osterreichs [★IO]

Fachverband Biomedizinische Technik [★IO]

Fachverband der Chemischen Industrie Oesterreichs [★IO]

Fachverband Dampfkessel-, Behaelter- und Rohrleitungsbau e.V. [★IO]

Fachverband der Elektro- und Elektronikindustrie [★IO]

Fachverband der Fahrzeugindustrie Osterreichs [★IO]

Fachverband Gastronomie [★IO]

Fachverband der Gewurzindustrie e.V. [★IO]

Fachverband der Hotellerie [★IO]

Fachverband der Lederverarbeitenden Industrie [★IO]

Fachverband Maschinen and Metallwaren Industrie [★IO]

Fachverband Messe-und Ausstellungsbau [★IO]

Fachverband fur Multimediale Informationsverarbeitung [★IO]

Fachverband der Papier und Pappe verarbeitenden Industrie [★IO]

Fachverband der Reisebueros [★IO]

Fachverband der Textilindustrie Oesterreichs [★IO]

Facial Assn; Amer. Cleft Palate-Cranio [14055]

Facial Assn; Children's Cranio [14057]

Facial Deformities; Debbie Fox Found. for Treatment of Cranio- [★14061]

Facial Foundations; Intl. Cranio [★14057]

Facial Pain; Amer. Acad. of Head, Neck and [★15751]

Facial Plastic and Reconstructive Surgery; Amer. Acad. of [14038]

Facial Plastic and Reconstructive Surgery; Amer. Bd. of [16562]

Facial Plastic Surgery; Amer. Soc. of [★14038]

Facial Prosthetics; Amer. Acad. of Maxillo [14103]

Facial Reconstruction; Natl. Found. for [14065]

Facial Res; Friends of the Natl. Inst. of Dental and Cranio [14154]

Facilities Administrators; Natl. Assn. of State [6195]

Facilities Coun; Fed. [5707]

Facilities Engg; Assn. for [7003]

Facilities Executives; Intl. Soc. of [2467]

Facilities Officers; APPA: The Assn. of Higher Educ. [8333]

Fac. Licensure and Certification Directors; Assn. of Hea. [★6210]

Fac. Mgt. Assn; Natl. [★3188]

Facility Managers and Planners; Org. of [★7167]

Facing History and Ourselves [★10108]

Facing History and Ourselves [★IO]

Facing History and Ourselves Natl. Found. [IO], Brookline, MA, United States

Facing History and Ourselves Natl. Found. [10108], 16 Hurd Rd., Brookline, MA 02445, (617)232-1595

Facing Our Risk of Cancer Empowered [13823], 16057 Tampa Palms Blvd. W, PMB No. 373, Tampa, FL 33647, (954)255-8732

Facing Tile Inst. - Defunct.

Facioscapulohumeral (FSH) Soc. [15320], 3 Westwood Rd., Lexington, MA 02420, (781)860-0501

Facsimile Assn; Amer. [3732]

Facsimile Text Soc. - Defunct.

Fact, Inc [★4997]

Factories Marketing Assn. of the South; Furniture [★1701]

Factors and Discounters Assn. [IO], Richmond, United Kingdom

Factory Inspectors; Intl. Assn. of [★5917]

Facts Are Facts Intelligence Service - Defunct.

Facts and Logic About the Middle East [18057], PO Box 590359, San Francisco, CA 94159, (415)356-7801

Facultad Latinoamericana de Estudios Teologicos [★19930]

Facultad Latinoamericana de Estudios Teologicos [★IO]

Faculty of Actuaries [IO], Edinburgh, United Kingdom

Faculty of Advocates [IO], Edinburgh, United Kingdom

Faculty; Assn. of Black Nursing [8848]

Faculty of Astrological Stud. [IO], London, United Kingdom

Faculty of Building [★IO]

Faculty of Dental Surgery [IO], London, United Kingdom

Faculty Exchange
League for the Exchange of Commonwealth Teachers [IO]

A star before a book entry number signifies that the name is not listed separately, but is mentioned within the entry.

U.S. Comm. for Sci. Cooperation With Vietnam [8633]
Faculty of Homeopathy [IO], Luton, United Kingdom
Faculty for Human Rights in El Salvador and Central America - Defunct.
Faculty of Occupational Medicine [IO], London, United Kingdom
Faculty of Public Hea. Medicine [IO], London, United Kingdom
Faculty of Radiologists [★IO]
Faculty of Royal Designers for Indus. [IO], London, United Kingdom
Fagan Family Assn. [20900]
Fagazdasagi Orszagos Szakmai Szovetseg [★IO]
FAI - The World Air Sports Fed. [★IO]
Fainting Goat Assn; Amer. Tennessee [4781]
Fainting Goat Assn; Intl. [4784]
Fair Agencies
   Natl. Independent Concessionaires Assn. [1591]
Fair Budget Action Campaign - Defunct.
Fair Campaign Practices Comm. - Address unknown since 1994.
Fair Chance - Defunct.
Fair Competition; Alliance for [★3613]
Fair Competition; Bus. Coalition for [★3621]
Fair Competition; Natl. Alliance for [3613]
Fair Competition; Natl. Center for [3621]
F.A.I.R. - Defunct.
Fair Economy; United for a [17473]
Fair Elections Legal Network [5491], 1730 Rhode Island Ave. NW, Ste. 712, Washington, DC 20036, (202)331-0114
Fair Electronic Commerce Transactions; Americans for [17441]
Fair Employment; North Amer. Alliance for [1277]
Fair and Exhibition Assn. [IO], Rheda-Wiedenbruck, Germany
Fair Housing Alliance; Natl. [17733]
Fair and Open Testing; Natl. Center for [9255]
Fair Organ Preservation Soc. [IO], Chorleywood, United Kingdom
Fair Play for Children Assn. [IO], Bognor Regis, United Kingdom
Fair Tax Education Fund - Address unknown since 1991.
Fair Tax Found. - Defunct.
Fair-Witness Project - Defunct.
Fairchild Club [21446], 7645 Echo Point Rd., Cannon Falls, MN 55009, (507)263-2414
Fairground Soc. [IO], Telford, United Kingdom
Fairlane Club of Am. [21641], 340 Clicktown Rd., Church Hill, TN 37642, (423)245-6678
Fairness and Accuracy in Reporting [17176], 112 W 27th St., New York, NY 10001, (212)633-6700
Fairness Everywhere; Natl. Org. Taunting Safety and [22599]
Fairness Fund [★17653]
Fairness in Media - Address unknown since 1994.
Fairness; Turkish Amer. Alliance for [19410]
Fairs Assn; Western [1327]
Fairs and Salons of France [IO], Paris, France
FairTest [★9255]
Fairview Pregnancy and Newborn Loss Information [12668]
Fairy Lamp Club [22019], c/o James L. Sapp, PO Box 438, Pine, CO 80470-0438
Fairy Tale-Folklore Study Unit - Defunct.
Faith Alive [19957], 431 Richmond Pl. NE, Albuquerque, NM 87106, (505)255-3233
Faith, Churches and Ministers; Intl. Convention of [★19807]
Faith; Defenders of the Christian [★19774]
Faith Development; Center for [★20534]
Faith; Equal Partners in [20494]
Faith and Family; Women for [19739]
Faith and Freedom Intl. [★13169]
Faith Generation - Defunct.
Faith and History; Conf. on [20079]
Faith and Joy - Venezuela [IO], Caracas, Venezuela
Faith and Justice Network; Africa [16920]
Faith and Moral Development; Center for Res. in [20534]
Faith North Am; Forward in [19959]
Faith; Soc. for the Propagation of the [19723]
Faith and Tech; Servants in [17001]

Faith at Work [19893], 106 E Broad St., Ste. B, Falls Church, VA 22046-4501, (703)237-3426
FaithTrust Inst. [12027], 2400 N 45th St., No. 101, Seattle, WA 98103, (206)634-1903
FaithWorks Intl. [11777], 3121 Middletown Rd., Ste. 9D, Bronx, NY 10461, (347)293-5460
FaithWorks Intl. [IO], Bronx, NY, United States
Falcon Club of Am. [21642], PO Box 113, Jacksonville, AR 72078-0113, (501)982-9721
Falconry
   North Amer. Falconers Assn. [23398]
   Soc. for the Preservation of Birds of Prey [5382]
Falcons of Am; Polish [19310]
Falkland Islands Philatelic Study Group [IO], Camberley, United Kingdom
Falklands Conservation [IO], Stanley, Falkland Islands
Fallen Angels Intl. - Address unknown since 2003.
False Claims Act Legal Center; Taxpayers Against Fraud, The [18719]
False Memory Syndrome Found. [16150], 1955 Locust St., Philadelphia, PA 19103-5766, (215)940-1040
Falun Data Info. Center [17757], 331 W 57th St., PMB 409, New York, NY 10019, (646)533-6147
Falun Gong; Friends of [17061]
Famagusta Chamber of Commerce and Indus. [IO], Limassol, Cyprus
Fame; Assn. of Executive Directors of Halls of [★23827]
Fame; Assn. of Sports Museums and Halls of [★23827]
Famiglia X1/9 - Defunct.
FAMILIA Ancestral Res. Assn. [19067], PO Box 10359, Westminster, CA 92685-0359, (714)687-0390
FAMILIA Ancestral Res. Assn. [IO], Westminster, CA, United States
Familial Ovarian Cancer Registry; Gilda Radner [13826]
Familiares y Amigos de Enfermos de la Neurona Motora [IO], Mexico City, Mexico
Families
   9/11 Families for a Secure Am. [18728]
   AASK - Adopt a Special Kid [11226]
   Ackerman Inst. for the Family [12134]
   Adopt Am. Network [11227]
   Adoptee-Birthparent Support Network [11228]
   Adoption Identity Movement [11229]
   Adoption Info. Services [11230]
   Adoption Roots and Rights [IO]
   Adoptions Together [11231]
   Advocates for Fair Family Support [12135]
   Ahern Clan Assn. [19048]
   Aid to Incarcerated Mothers [11851]
   AIDS Alliance for Children, Youth and Families [13548]
   A.L. Mailman Family Found. [11671]
   Alan Guttmacher Inst. [12175]
   Albert Ellis Inst. [16197]
   Alliance for Children and Families [12136]
   Alliance for Children and Families [IO]
   Alternative Family Proj. [11814]
   Am. World Adoption Assn. [11233]
   Amer. Acad. of Family Physicians [14383]
   Amer. Acad. of Fertility Care Professionals [12634]
   Amer. Agri-Women [16948]
   Amer. Agri-Women Rsrc. Center [16949]
   Amer. Agriculture Movement [16950]
   Amer. Assn. of Family and Consumer Sciences [12285]
   Amer. Assn. for Marriage and Family Therapy [16200]
   Amer. Assn. of Ser. Coordinators [1985]
   Amer. Bd. of Family Medicine [14384]
   American-Canadian Genealogical Soc. [21098]
   Amer. Center for Law and Justice [12901]
   Amer. Coll. of Counselors [12137]
   Amer. Coll. of Domiciliary Midwives [15583]
   Amer. Coll. of Heraldry [21099]
   Amer. Coll. of Osteopathic Family Physicians [15793]
   Amer. Decency Assn. [17281]
   Amer. Family Communiversity [12138]

   Amer. Family Rights Assn. [17508]
   Amer. Family Therapy Acad. [11816]
   Amer. Fathers Coalition [12660]
   American-French Genealogical Soc. [21101]
   Amer. Heraldry Soc. [21102]
   Amer. Mothers, Inc. [12139]
   Amer. Osteopathic Bd. of Family Physicians [15799]
   Amer. Psychological Assn. - Division of Family Psychology [16125]
   Amer. Soc. of Genealogists [21103]
   America's Angel [12140]
   Angelman Syndrome Found. [16528]
   Archconfraternity of Christian Mothers [19572]
   Ark-La-Tex Genealogical Assn. [21104]
   Assn. of Children's Museums [10495]
   Assn. of Family Practice Administrators [15060]
   Assn. of Family Practice Physician Assistants [14698]
   Assn. of the German Nobility in North Am. [21105]
   Assn. for Interdisciplinary Res. in Values and Social Change [12906]
   Assn. of Jewish Family and Children's Agencies [12467]
   Assn. of Maternal and Child Hea. Programs [13947]
   Assn. of MultiEthnic Americans [12141]
   Assn. for the Restoration of the Church and Home [19844]
   Attachment Parenting Intl. [12662]
   Augustan Soc. [21107]
   Australian Camp Connect Assn. [IO]
   Australian Family Assn. [IO]
   Bereaved Parents of the USA [11512]
   Better World J. L. Inst. [12142]
   Billings Ovulation Method Assn. - USA [12635]
   Black Americans for Life [12909]
   Bonus Families [12143]
   Brinton Assn. of Am. [21110]
   Call to Renewal [18376]
   Campaign for Working Families [18286]
   Catholic Family Services of Regina [IO]
   Catholic Family Services Windsor-Essex County [IO]
   Catholic Kolping Soc. of Am. [19599]
   Catholics United for Life [12910]
   Center for Assessment and Policy Development [18636]
   Center for Work and the Family [12144]
   Centro de Apoyo al Nino de la Calle de Oaxaca [IO]
   Chicano Family Center [17701]
   Child Family Hea. Intl. [11551]
   Child and Family Policy Center [12145]
   Child-Friendly Initiative [11678]
   Child Trends [11679]
   Child Welfare Inst. [11571]
   Children in Scotland [IO]
   Christian Action Network [19770]
   Christian Family Life [12146]
   Christian Family Movement [12147]
   Christian Family Renewal [19776]
   Christian Sports Intl. [23298]
   CityMatch [13957]
   Clan Arthur Assn., USA [19349]
   Clan Brown Soc. [20818]
   Clan Craig Assn. of Am. [19350]
   Clan Ewing in Am. [19351]
   Clan MacAlpine Soc. [19049]
   Clan MacKinnon Soc. [19050]
   Clan McAlister of Am. [19051]
   Clan Phail Soc. in North America [19052]
   Clanwilliam Inst. [IO]
   Coalition of 9/11 Families [13307]
   Coffee Kids [11769]
   CoMamas Assn. [12148]
   Commn. on Accreditation for Marriage and Family Therapy Educ. [8819]
   Concerns of Police Survivors [12752]
   Confed. of Family Organisations in the European Union [IO]
   Conservative Majority for Citizen's Rights [17266]
   Coun. on Accreditation [13164]
   Coun. on Contemporary Families [12149]
   Couple to Couple League [12636]

Reference to "IO" in place of a book number signifies that the association may be found in the 45th edition of International Organizations.

Covering Kids and Families [12271]
Dads and Daughters [12150]
David and Lucile Packard Found. [11808]
Deliver the Dream [13019]
Doe Network [12608]
Domestic Technologies [16994]
Educ. and Enrichment Sect. of the Natl. Coun. on Family Relations [12151]
EngenderHealth [12180]
Enough Is Enough [17923]
Fairview Pregnancy and Newborn Loss Information [12668]
Families Against Internet Censorship [17039]
Families Against Mandatory Minimums Found. [11864]
Families with Children from China [11243]
Families Like Mine [17651]
Families for Natural Living [8416]
Families Need Fathers [IO]
Families for Private Adoption [11244]
Families and Work Inst. [12152]
Families Worldwide [13241]
Family of the Americas Found. [12637]
Family Campers and RVers [23271]
Family, Career and Community Leaders of Am. [8417]
Family and Church History Dept. of the Church of Jesus Christ of Latter-Day Saints [21115]
Family and Consumer Sciences Educ. Assn. [8418]
Family Coun. on Drug Awareness [13242]
Family Educ. Trust [IO]
Family Fed. of Finland [IO]
Family Hea. Care Assn. of Am. [24090]
Family Hea. Intl. [12181]
Family and Hea. Sect. of the Natl. Coun. on Family Relations [14385]
Family Justice [11865]
Family Learning Assn. [8419]
Family Literacy Alliance [18020]
Family Mediation Canada [IO]
Family Mediation Scotland [IO]
Family Res. Coun. [12153]
Family Rosary [19622]
Family Support Am. [12154]
Family Supports [12155]
Family Supports [IO]
Family Therapy Sect. of the Natl. Coun. on Family Relations [16612]
Family Violence Prevention Fund [12028]
Father Matters [18180]
Fatty Oxidation Disorders (FOD) Family Support Gp. [16532]
Fed. of East European Family History Societies [19068]
Fed. of Genealogical Societies [21116]
Fellowship of Christian Peace Officers - U.S.A. [19798]
Feminism and Family Stud. Sect. of the Natl. Coun. on Family Relations [12156]
FG Syndrome Family Alliance [16533]
Five P Minus Soc. [16534]
Focus on the Chinese Family [20496]
Focus on the Family [12157]
Focus on the Family - Canada [IO]
Foster Family-Based Treatment Assn. [11593]
Foster Parents Plan [IO]
Fostering Network [IO]
Found. for Child Development [11541]
FRAXA Res. Found. [16535]
Free Cong. Res. and Educ. Found. [18295]
Friends in Adoption [11245]
Fuller Found. [13118]
Genealogical Inst. [21117]
Global Family [13140]
Grantmakers for Children, Youth, and Families [12723]
Great Dads [12672]
Healthy Teen Network [12182]
Hebrew Immigrant Aid Soc. [12471]
Herbalife Family Found. [11599]
Holistic Moms Network [12673]
Home-Start North and Mid Beds [IO]
Hunters Helping Hunters [22604]
IAB Partners [1464]

Independence Plan for Neighborhood Councils [17219]
Inst. for Amer. Values [12158]
Inst. in Basic Life Principles [13489]
Inter-American Children's Inst. [IO]
Intl. Assn. for the Leisure and Entertainment Indus. [1305]
Intl. Assn. for Marriage and Family Counselors [11825]
Intl. Center for Positive Psychotherapy, Transcultural Family Therapy and Psychosomatic Medicine [IO]
Intl. Comm. for the Rescue of KAL 007 Survivors [18541]
Intl. Family Recreation Assn. [12798]
Intl. Fed. of Family Associations of Missing Persons from Armed Conflicts [12609]
Intl. Planned Parenthood Fed., Western Hemisphere Region [12184]
Intl. Sect. of the Natl. Coun. on Family Relations [12159]
Intl. Sect. of the Natl. Coun. on Family Relations [IO]
Intl. Soc. for British Genealogy and Family History [21123]
Intl. Soc. Daughters of Utah Pioneers [21252]
Interracial Family Alliance of Houston [12160]
Interracial Family Circle [12161]
Interracial-Intercultural Pride [12162]
Jewish Bd. of Family and Children's Services/Youth Counseling League Div. [13492]
Jews for Morality [20154]
Johannes Schwalm Historical Assn. [21128]
Karl Kuebel Found. for Child and Family [IO]
Kids Need Both Parents [17509]
Kids With Food Allergies [13603]
Kidsave Intl. [11251]
KIDSCOPE [11518]
Kin Canada [IO]
Labor Proj. for Working Families [24117]
Loved Ones and Drivers Support [13347]
Luz Social Services [13255]
Mediators Inst. Ireland [IO]
Mental Res. Inst. [13737]
Mir Pace Intl. [12872]
Morgan Family Club [19053]
Mothers Against Munchausen Syndrome by Proxy Allegations [13968]
Mothers And More [12086]
Mothers' Union Australia [IO]
Mothers' Union - England [IO]
MUMS Natl. Parent-to-Parent Network [16541]
Myotubular Myopathy Rsrc. Gp. [16542]
Natl. Abortion Fed. [11223]
Natl. African-American RV'ers Assn. [22958]
Natl. Alliance for Caregiving [12163]
Natl. Alliance of Families for the Return of America's Missing Servicemen [21263]
Natl. Assn. for Family and Child Care [12171]
Natl. Assn. of Mothers' Centers [12676]
Natl. Assn. of Non-Custodial Moms [11538]
Natl. Assn. for Parents of Children With Visual Impairments [16873]
Natl. Assn. of Public Child Welfare Administrators [11629]
Natl. Black United Fed. of Charities [16943]
Natl. Center for Educ. in Maternal and Child Hea. [13969]
Natl. Commn. on Human Life, Reproduction and Rhythm [16008]
Natl. Coun. on Family Relations [12164]
Natl. Enthronement Center [19686]
Natl. Family Planning and Reproductive Hea. Assn. [12185]
Natl. Fatherhood Initiative [17510]
Natl. Genealogical Soc. [21133]
Natl. Infertility Network Exchange [12678]
Natl. Partnership for Community Leadership [11805]
Natl. Right to Life Comm. [12923]
Natl. Soc. of Madison Family Descendants [21135]
Natl. Soc. of the Sons of Utah Pioneers [21254]
Natl. Tots and Teens [13503]
Native Amer. Fatherhood and Families Assn. [12681]

New England Historic Genealogical Soc. [21136]
New York Genealogical and Biographical Soc. [21137]
North Amer. Family Campers Assn. [23273]
Org. of Parents Through Surrogacy [13299]
Parents' Action For Children [12682]
Parents of Kids with Infectious Diseases [14954]
Parents Rights Coalition [12687]
Partners in Foster Care [12193]
Pathfinder Intl. [12186]
Paul and Lisa Prog. [13082]
Pennsylvania German Soc. [21243]
Pilgrim Soc. [21249]
Pilgrims of the U.S. [21250]
Plan Netherlands [IO]
Plan - United Kingdom [IO]
Planned Parenthood Fed. of Am. [12187]
Polish Genealogical Soc. of Am. [21142]
Postgraduate Center for Mental Hea. [16227]
Presbyterians Pro-Life [12926]
Psychotherapy Network [16228]
Rabbinic Center for Res. and Counseling [16229]
Rainier Soc. [21145]
Reach the Children [11649]
Relate [IO]
Relate Scotland [IO]
Relationships Australia [IO]
Religion and Family Life Sect. of the Natl. Coun. on Family Relations [IO]
Religion and Family Life Sect. of the Natl. Coun. on Family Relations [12165]
Robert Bruce Bradley Family Org. [21036]
Sacred Space Inst. [13101]
Saint Nicholas Soc. of the City of New York [21148]
Save a Family Plan [12166]
Save a Family Plan [IO]
Savoie Acadian Cultural and Historical Soc. [21149]
Scripps Assn. of Families [8113]
Secretariat for Family, Laity, Women, and Youth [12167]
September 11th Families' Assn. [13371]
Single and Custodial Fathers Network [12691]
Slowlane/Stay At Home Dads [18182]
Soc. of Blessed Gianna Beretta Molla [20038]
Soc. of Blessed Gianna Beretta Molla [IO]
Soc. of California Pioneers [21255]
Soc. of Indiana Pioneers [21256]
Soc. of Teachers of Family Medicine [14387]
Sons and Daughters of Oregon Pioneers [21257]
Sons and Daughters of Pioneer Rivermen [21258]
Southeast Inst. for Gp. and Family Therapy [18629]
Stepfamily Found. [12168]
Stop Abuse for Everyone [12039]
Teaching-Family Assn. [12169]
Tuesday's Children [12003]
TV-Turnoff Network [12170]
Twins Found. [12616]
United Fathers of Am. [12014]
United Jewish Appeal - Fed. of Jewish Philanthropies of New York [12482]
U.S. Coalition for Life [12929]
United We Serve [21203]
Vesterheim Genealogical Center and Naeseth Lib. [21155]
VOICES in Action [13086]
We Are Family [17659]
Well Spouse Assn. [16553]
WishKids Intl. [11665]
Wives-Self-Help Found. [11832]
Women Exploited by Abortion [12932]
Women Involved in Farm Economics [16960]
World Jewish Genealogy Org. [21158]
WTC Families For Proper Burial [13312]
Families, 4-H, and Nutrition [13483], Cooperative State Res. Educ. and Extension Ser., 1400 Independence Ave. SW, Stop 2225, Washington, DC 20250-2225, (202)720-2908
Families in Action [★13269]
Families in Action Drug Info. Center [★13269]
Families in Action; Natl. [13269]
Families in Action Natl. Drug Info. Center [★13269]
Families Adopting Children Everywhere [11242], PO Box 28058, Baltimore, MD 21239, (410)488-2656

A star before a book entry number signifies that the name is not listed separately, but is mentioned within the entry.

Families of Adults Afflicted with Asperger's Syndrome [16531], PO Box 514, Centerville, MA 02632, (508)790-1930

Families Against Internet Censorship [17039], 2135 Wickes Rd., Colorado Springs, CO 80919, (719)548-4989

Families Against Mandatory Minimums Found. [11864], 1612 K St. NW, Ste. 700, Washington, DC 20006, (202)822-6700

Families Against Substance Abuse; Natl. Asian Pacific Amer. [13258]

Families of Am; Presidential [21143]

Families Anonymous [13240], PO Box 3475, Culver City, CA 90231-3475, (310)815-8010

Families Anonymous [IO], Culver City, CA, United States

Families; Campaign for Working [18286]

Families with Children from China [11243], c/o Susan Caughman, 255 W 90th St., 11C, New York, NY 10024

Families and Children; Coun. on Accreditation of Services for [★13164]

Families for Children's Mental Hea; Fed. of [12550]

Families; Covering Kids and [12271]

Families for Depression Awareness [15198], 395 Totten Pond Rd., Ste. 404, Waltham, MA 02451, (781)890-0220

Families, and Friends of Lesbians and Gays; Parents, [12253]

Families; Grantmakers for Children, Youth, and [12723]

Families; Hazelden Center for Youth and [★13244]

Families; Liberal Educ. for Adoptive [11253]

Families Like Mine [17651], 51 Church St., Boston, MA 02116, (617)482-3593

Families with Maple Syrup Urine Disease [★15250]

Families of Massachusetts; Hereditary Order of the First [20739]

Families of Minnesota; Natl. Soc. - First [21253]

Families; Natl. Center for Infants, Toddlers and [★13944]

Families; Natl. Coalition for the Protection of Children and [18374]

Families; Natl. Partnership for Women and [17561]

Families for Natural Living [8416], PO Box 3653, Williamsburg, VA 23187-3653, (757)566-9630

Families Need Fathers [IO], London, United Kingdom

Families for Prayer - Defunct.

Families for Private Adoption [11244], PO Box 6375, Washington, DC 20015-0375, (202)722-0338

Families of September 11 [18729], 1560 Broadway, Ste. 305, New York, NY 10036-1518, (212)575-1878

Families of S.M.A. [15321], PO Box 196, Libertyville, IL 60048-0196, (847)367-7620

Families and TV; Natl. Coun. for [17186]

Families U.S.A. Found. [11286], 1201 New York Ave. NW, Ste. 1100, Washington, DC 20005-6100, (202)628-3030

Families USA; Natl. Assn. of Minority Political [18357]

Families with Visual Impairment; Coun. of [16844]

Families and Work Inst. [12152], 267 5th Ave., 2nd Fl., New York, NY 10016, (212)465-2044

Families Worldwide [13241], 5248 Pinemont Dr., Ste. C-190, Salt Lake City, UT 84123, (801)268-6461

Families Worldwide [IO], Salt Lake City, UT, United States

Families; Zero to Three: Natl. Center for Infants, Toddlers and [13944]

Family Action for the Seriously Emotionally Disturbed - Defunct.

Family Alliance; Interracial [★12160]

Family Alliance; VHL [14489]

Family America - Defunct.

Family of Am; Purcell [21028]

Family of the Americas [★12637]

Family of the Americas Found. [12637], PO Box 1170, Dunkirk, MD 20754, (301)627-3346

Family Assn. of Am. [★12136]

Family Assn. of Am. [★IO]

Family Assn; Amer. [17162]

Family Assn; Flippin [20902]

Family Assn; Grinnell [20923]

Family Assn; IDB [19436]

Family Assn; Natl. Military [21198]

Family Business; Center for [709]

Family Bus. Coun; Natl. [748]

Family Campers Assn; North Amer. [23273]

Family Campers and RVers [23271], 4804 Transit Rd., Bldg. 2, Depew, NY 14043, (716)668-6242

Family Camping Fed. of America - Defunct.

Family Cancer Home; Holy [★19027]

Family Care Intl. [16402], 588 Broadway, Ste. 503, New York, NY 10012, (212)941-5300

Family Care Intl. [IO], New York, NY, United States

Family Care Intl. - Bolivia [IO], La Paz, Bolivia

Family Care Intl. - Burkina Faso [IO], Ouagadougou, Burkina Faso

Family Care Intl. - Dominican Republic [IO], Santo Domingo, Dominican Republic

Family Care Intl. - Ecuador [IO], Quito, Ecuador

Family Care Intl. - Kenya [IO], Nairobi, Kenya

Family Care Intl. - Mali [IO], Bamako, Mali

Family Care Intl. - Niger [IO], Niamey, Niger

Family Care Intl. - Tanzania [IO], Dar es Salaam, United Republic of Tanzania

Family, Career and Community Leaders of Am. [8417], 281 Park Ave. S, New York, NY 10010-6102, (212)358-1250

Family Cause [★12138]

Family Center; Chicano [17701]

Family Center; KDWB Variety [13964]

Family and Child Stud. Center [★12155]

Family and Child Stud. Center [★IO]

Family and Children's Agencies; Assn. of Jewish [12467]

Family and Children's Counseling Center; James Weldon Johnson [★12785]

Family and Church History Dept. of the Church of Jesus Christ of Latter-Day Saints [21115], c/o Family History Lib., 35 NW Temple St., Salt Lake City, UT 84150-3400, (801)240-2584

Family and Church History Dept. of the Church of Jesus Christ of Latter-Day Saints [IO], Salt Lake City, UT, United States

Family Circle of PenDelfin [22020], c/o Susan Beard, 230 Spring St. NW, Ste. 1238, Atlanta, GA 30303, (800)872-4876

Family Communion Crusade - Defunct.

Family and Community Educ; Natl. Assn. for [8513]

Family Community Leadership Program [★8513]

Family Consecrations; Apostolate for [19571]

Family and Consumer Sciences; Amer. Assn. of [12285]

Family and Consumer Sciences Educ. Assn. [8418], Dept. of Family & Consumer Sci., Central Washington Univ., 400 E 8th Univ. Way, Ellensburg, WA 98926-7565, (509)963-2766

Family and Consumer Sciences; Natl. Assn. of Teacher Educators for [8515]

Family and Consumer Sciences; Natl. Extension Assn. of [5612]

Family and Consumer Services; Natl. Extension Assn. of [★5612]

Family Coun. on Drug Awareness [13242], c/o Mikki Norris, PO Box 1716, El Cerrito, CA 94530, (510)215-8326

Family Coun. on Drug Awareness [IO], El Cerrito, CA, United States

Family Counseling Center; Allied Youth and [13465]

Family Counselors; Amer. Assn. of Marriage and [★16200]

Family Court Judges; Natl. Coun. of Juvenile and [5912]

Family Defense Coun. [17377], PO Box 310478, Jamaica, NY 11431-0478

Family Education and Information Coun. - Defunct.

Family Educ. Trust [IO], Twickenham, United Kingdom

Family Farm Coalition; Natl. [16956]

Family Farm Coalition; Natl. Save the [★16956]

Family Farm Defenders [4645], PO Box 1772, Madison, WI 53701, (608)260-0900

Family Farm Movement - Address unknown since 1995.

Family Fed. of Finland [IO], Helsinki, Finland

Family Firm Inst. [IO], Boston, MA, United States

Family Firm Inst. [3609], 200 Lincoln St., Ste. 201, Boston, MA 02111, (617)482-3045

Family; Focus on the Chinese [20496]

Family Found; Ludwick [17646]

Family and Freedom Resource Center - Defunct.

Family Fund; Merck [4587]

Family Hea. Care Assn. of Am. [24090], c/o James Mark Reynolds, Sr., Pres., PO Box 222, Jamestown, NC 27282, (336)987-0108

Family Hea. Intl. [12181], PO Box 13950, Research Triangle Park, NC 27709, (919)544-7040

Family Hea. Intl. [IO], Research Triangle Park, NC, United States

Family Hea. Intl. - Bangladesh [IO], Dhaka, Bangladesh

Family Hea. Intl. - Burundi [IO], Bujumbura, Burundi

Family Hea. Intl. - Cambodia [IO], Phnom Penh, Cambodia

Family Hea. Intl. - Cote d' Ivore [IO], Abidjan, Cote d'Ivoire

Family Hea. Intl. - Dominican Republic [IO], Santo Domingo, Dominican Republic

Family Hea. Intl. - Egypt [IO], Cairo, Egypt

Family Hea. Intl. - Eritrea [IO], Asmara, Eritrea

Family Hea. Intl. - Ethiopia [IO], Addis Ababa, Ethiopia

Family Hea. Intl. - Ghana [IO], Accra, Ghana

Family Hea. Intl. - Guatemala [IO], Guatemala City, Guatemala

Family Hea. Intl. - Guinea [IO], Conakry, Guinea

Family Hea. Intl. - Guyana [IO], Georgetown, Guyana

Family Hea. Intl. - Haiti [IO], Port-au-Prince, Haiti

Family Hea. Intl. - India [IO], New Delhi, India

Family Hea. Intl. - Indonesia [IO], Jakarta, Indonesia

Family Hea. Intl. - Jordan [IO], Amman, Jordan

Family Hea. Intl. - Kenya [IO], Nairobi, Kenya

Family Hea. Intl. - Laos [IO], Vientiane, Lao People's Democratic Republic

Family Hea. Intl. - Malawi [IO], Lilongwe, Malawi

Family Hea. Intl. - Mozambique [IO], Maputo, Mozambique

Family Hea. Intl. - Namibia [IO], Windhoek, Namibia

Family Hea. Intl. - Nepal [IO], Kathmandu, Nepal

Family Hea. Intl. - Nigeria [IO], Abuja, Nigeria

Family Hea. Intl. - People's Republic of China [IO], Beijing, People's Republic of China

Family Hea. Intl. - Philippines [IO], Manila, Philippines

Family Hea. Intl. - Senegal [IO], Dakar, Senegal

Family Hea. Intl. - South Africa [IO], Pretoria, Republic of South Africa

Family Hea. Intl. - Thailand [IO], Bangkok, Thailand

Family Hea. Intl. - Vietnam [IO], Hanoi, Vietnam

Family Hea. Options Kenya [IO], Nairobi, Kenya

Family and Hea. Sect. [★14385]

Family and Hea. Sect. of the Natl. Coun. on Family Relations [14385], c/o B. Jan McCulloch, Sect. Sec.-Treas., 290D McNeal Hall, 1985 Buford Ave., St. Paul, MN 55108-6134, (612)624-1208

Family History Assn; East European [★21112]

Family History Dept. of the Church of Jesus Christ of Latter-day Saints [★21115]

Family History Dept. of the Church of Jesus Christ of Latter-day Saints [★IO]

Family History Forum; Irish [9974]

Family History Societies; Fed. of East European [★21112]

Family History Soc; Irish [★21125]

Family and Home Network [12669], PO Box 545, Merrifield, VA 22116, (703)352-1072

Family of Humanists [10195], PO Box 4153, Salem, OR 97302

Family Inst. [★12134]

Family Inst; Nathan W. Ackerman [★12134]

Family Inst; Puerto Rican [12281]

Family Justice [11865], 625 Broadway, 8th Fl., New York, NY 10012, (212)475-1500

Family Law

Amer. Acad. of Matrimonial Lawyers [5698]

Amer. Family Rights Assn. [17508]

Assn. of Family and Conciliation Courts [5699]

Family Justice [11865]

Intl. Commn. on Civil Status [IO]

Joint Custody Assn. [12011]

Reference to "IO" in place of a book number signifies that the association may be found in the 45th edition of International Organizations.

Natl. Alliance for Family Court Justice [5904]
Natl. Amer. Indian Court Judges Assn. [5905]
Natl. Assn. for Family and Child Care [12171]
Natl. Bd. of Trial Advocacy [6333]
Natl. Center for Youth Law [5700]
Natl. Child Support Enforcement Assn. [5701]
Natl. Cong. for Fathers and Children [12172]
Natl. Juvenile Court Services Assn. [5702]
Natl. Law Center for Children and Families [5703]
Parents Rights Coalition [12687]
Resolution - first for family law [IO]
Family Law Coun. - Address unknown since 1999.
Family Law Res. Found. [★12138]
Family Learning Assn. [8419], 3925 Hagan St., No. 101, Bloomington, IN 47401, (812)323-9862
Family Liaison Action Group - Address unknown since 1987.
Family Life Achievement Center [★11647]
Family Life Achievement Center [★IO]
Family Life Assn. of Swaziland [IO], Manzini, Swaziland
Family Life Bur. [★12167]
Family Life Coalition - Defunct.
Family Life and Culture; Inst. for the Advanced Stud. of Black [9359]
Family Life Div., U.S. Catholic Conf. [★12167]
Family Life Info. Exchange [★12757]
Family Life Insurance; Catholic [18993]
Family Life Ministers; Natl. Assn. of Catholic [20288]
Family Life Ministers; Natl. Assn. of Catholic Diocesan [★20288]
Family Life Ministry, U.S. Catholic Conf. [★12167]
Family Life Mission [IO], Kehl, Germany
Family Life; Natl. Alliance for [★12137]
Family Life; Natl. Catholic Conf. on [★12167]
Family Life and Population Program/Church World Service - Defunct.
Family Life; Secretariat on Laity and [★12167]
Family Life Sect; Religion and [★12165]
Family Literacy Alliance [18020], 325 W Main St., Ste. 300, Louisville, KY 40202-4237, (502)584-1133
Family Literacy; Barbara Bush Found. for [8786]
Family Mediation Canada [IO], Waterloo, ON, Canada
Family Mediation Manitoba [IO], Winnipeg, MB, Canada
Family Mediation Scotland [IO], Edinburgh, United Kingdom
Family Mediators; Acad. of [★5450]
Family Medicine
Amer. Acad. of Family Physicians [14383]
Amer. Bd. of Family Dentistry [14122]
Amer. Bd. of Family Medicine [14384]
Amer. Coll. of Domiciliary Midwives [15583]
Amer. Coll. of Osteopathic Family Physicians [15793]
Amer. Osteopathic Bd. of Family Physicians [15799]
Assn. of Family Practice Administrators [15060]
Assn. of Family Practice Physician Assistants [14698]
CityMatch [13957]
Coll. of Family Physicians of Canada - Ontario Chap. [IO]
Families Worldwide [13241]
Family and Hea. Sect. of the Natl. Coun. on Family Relations [14385]
The Floating Hosp. [14882]
Interstate Postgraduate Medical Assn. of North Am. [14386]
North Amer. Primary Care Res. Gp. [13664]
Royal Coll. of Gen. Practitioners [IO]
Soc. of Teachers of Family Medicine [14387]
World Org. of Family Doctors [IO]
Family Medicine Residency Directors; Assn. of [15059]
Family Motor Coach Assn. [22949], 8291 Clough Pike, Cincinnati, OH 45244, (513)474-3622
Family Name Societies
A.D. Johnson Family Assn. [20771]
Adam Hawkes Family Assn. [20772]
Adam Wise Family Assn. [20773]
Addington Assn. [20774]
Ahern Clan Assn. [19048]

Alden Kindred of Am. [20775]
Alderson Cousins [20776]
Alford Amer. Family Assn. [20777]
Allison Family Assn. [20778]
Allton, Alton, Aulton Family Assn. [20779]
Amer. Clan Gregor Soc. [20780]
Andlauer Family Assn. [20781]
Anneke Jans and Everardus Bogardus Descendants Assn. [20782]
Ansley Family Assn. [20783]
Archer Assn. [20784]
Assn. of Blauvelt Descendants [20785]
Association of Blauvelt Descendants [IO]
Assn. of the German Nobility in North Am. [21105]
Aurand - Aurant - Aurandt Family Assn. [20786]
Austin Families Genealogical Soc. [20787]
Baker Family Intl. [20788]
Baker Family Intl. [IO]
Ballew Family Assn. of Am. [20789]
Barney Family Historical Assn. [20790]
Bater Surname Org. [20791]
Beall Family Assn. [20792]
Bell Family Assn. of the U.S. [20793]
Bigelow Soc. [20794]
Bigelow Soc. [IO]
Blackburn Family Assn. [20795]
Blair Soc. for Genealogical Res. [20796]
Blair Society for Genealogical Research [IO]
Blencowe Families Assn. [20797]
Bloss-Pyles-Ross-Sellards Family [20798]
Blunden Family History Assn. [20799]
B'Man Family Assn. [20800]
Boggess Family Assn. [20801]
Bolling Family Assn. [20802]
Bondurant Family Assn. [20803]
Boone Soc. [20804]
Boone Soc. [IO]
Boyt/e - Boyet/t/e Assn. [20805]
Brainard-Brainerd-Braynard Family Assn. [20806]
Brancheau-Branchaud Family Assn. [20807]
Brantley Assn. of Am. [20808]
Brinton Assn. of Am. [21110]
Britenburg Surname Org. [20809]
Brough/Wilson/Willson Family Org. [20810]
Bunker Family Assn. of Am. [20811]
Bunker Family Assn. of Am. [IO]
Burleson Family Assn. [20812]
Cahill Cooperative Ancestors [20813]
Caton Family Assn. [20814]
Champe Surname Org. [20815]
Chapman Family Assn. [20816]
Chartier Family Assn. [20817]
Chartier Family Assn. [IO]
Clan Arthur Assn., USA [19349]
Clan Brown Soc. [20818]
Clan Campbell Soc., North Am. [20819]
Clan Carmichael U.S.A. [20820]
Clan Chisholm Soc. - U.S. Br. [20821]
Clan Colquhoun Soc. of North Am. [20822]
Clan Craig Assn. of Am. [19350]
Clan Cunningham Soc. of Am. [20823]
Clan Currie Soc. [20824]
Clan Currie Soc. [IO]
Clan Davidson Soc. [20825]
Clan Douglas Soc. of North Am. [20826]
Clan Drummond Soc. of North Am. [20827]
Clan Ewing in Am. [19351]
Clan Forrester Soc. [20828]
Clan Graham Soc. [20829]
Clan Guthrie USA [20830]
Clan Hamilton Soc. [20831]
Clan Hunter Assn. USA [20832]
Clan Irwin Assn. [20833]
Clan Johnston(e) in Am. [20834]
Clan Johnston(e) in America [IO]
Clan Keith Soc. [20835]
Clan Leslie Soc. Intl. [20836]
Clan MacAlpine Soc. [19049]
Clan MacDuff Soc. of Am. [20837]
Clan MacIntyre Assn. [20838]
Clan MacIntyre Assn. [20839]
Clan MacKay Soc. [20840]
Clan MacKenzie Soc. in the Americas [20841]
Clan MacKinnon Soc. [19050]
Clan Mackintosh of North Am. [20842]

Clan MacLennan Assn., U.S.A. [20843]
Clan Macneil Assn. of Am. [20844]
Clan Macpherson Assn. [20845]
Clan Macpherson Association [IO]
Clan MacRae Soc. of North Am. [20846]
Clan Maitland Soc. of North Am. [20847]
Clan Matheson Soc. [20848]
Clan Maxwell Soc. of the USA [20849]
Clan McAlister of Am. [19051]
Clan McLaren Assn. of North America [20850]
Clan Menzies Soc., North Amer. Br. [20851]
Clan Moffat Soc. [20852]
Clan Moncreiffe Soc. of North Am. [20853]
Clan Moncreiffe Soc. of North Am. [IO]
Clan Montgomery Society International [IO]
Clan Montgomery Soc. Intl. [20854]
Clan Munro Assn. [20855]
Clan Napier in North America [20856]
Clan Phail Soc. in North America [19052]
Clan Pollock [20857]
Clan Ramsey Assn. of North Am. [20858]
Clan Rose Soc. of Am. [20859]
Clan Ross Assn. of the U.S. [20860]
Clan Scott Soc. [20861]
Clan Shaw Soc. [20862]
Clan Sinclair Assn. U.S.A. [20863]
Clan Sutherland Soc. of North Am. [20864]
Clan Young [20865]
Cloud Family Assn. [20866]
Coatney/Courtney Family Assn. [20867]
Cogswell Family Assn. [20868]
Corbin Res. [20869]
Corson/Colson Family History Assn. [20870]
Covert Family Assn. [20871]
Coward Family Org. [20872]
Crandall Family Assn. [20873]
Crispell Family Assn. [20874]
Crowl Name Assn. [20875]
Curtis/Curtiss Soc. [20876]
Dameron Family Assn. [20877]
Dannenmueller-Hoefler Family Assn. [20878]
Daubenspeck-Doverspike Family Exchange [20879]
Denison Soc. [20880]
Descendants of Daniel Cole Soc. [20881]
Dick Family Assn. [20882]
Doane Family Assn. of Am. [20883]
Dobie Clan of North America [20884]
Dodge Family Assn. [20885]
DuBois Family Assn. [20886]
Duncan Surname Assn. [20887]
Dunlop - Dunlap Family Soc. [20888]
Dunnavant/Donavant Family Assn. [20889]
Duty's in America [20890]
Easterling Family Genealogical Soc. [20891]
Eddy Family Assn. [20892]
Elder Brewster Soc. [20893]
Eller Family Assn. [20894]
Elliot Clan Soc. USA [20895]
Elswick Family Assn. [20896]
Enders Family Assn. [20897]
Enders Family Assn. [IO]
Eskridge Family Assn. [20898]
Etchingham Family Tree [20899]
Fagan Family Assn. [20900]
Fed. of East European Family History Societies [19068]
Fed. of Genealogical Societies [21116]
Felton Family Assn. [20901]
Flippin Family Assn. [20902]
Forby Family Historical Soc. [20903]
Fretz Family Assn. [20904]
Friend Family Assn. of Am. [20905]
Frisbie - Frisbee Family Assn. of Am. [20906]
Fullam Family Org. [20907]
Fuller Soc. [20908]
Fuqua(y) Family Assn. [20909]
Gafford Family Assn. of Am. [20910]
Gaylord Family Org. [20911]
George McCleave Family Org. [20912]
Germroth Family Assn. Intl. [20913]
Geshkewich Surname Org. [20914]
Gideon Family Assn. [20915]
Gilstrap Family Assn. [20916]
Goff/Gough Family Assn. [20917]

A star before a book entry number signifies that the name is not listed separately, but is mentioned within the entry.

Goodenow Family Assn. [20918]
Goodwin Family Org. [20919]
Gottscheer Heritage and Genealogy Assn. [9978]
Graves Family Assn. [20920]
Graves Family Assn. [IO]
Grawunder and Graffunder Connection [20921]
Griesemer Family Assn. [20922]
Grinnell Family Assn. [20923]
Groberg - Holbrook Genealogical Org. [20924]
Grover Family Org. [20925]
Hamilton Natl. Genealogical Soc. [20926]
Hans/Henry Segrist Family Org. [20927]
Harden - Hardin - Harding Family Assn. [20928]
Harrison Family Assn. [20929]
Hartshorn Family Assn. [20930]
Hartshorn Family Assn. [IO]
Hasbrouck Family Assn. [20931]
Hathaway Family Assn. [20932]
Haviland Family Org. [20933]
Hawkins Assn. [20934]
Haymore Family Org. [20935]
Hazelbaker Families [20936]
Heald Family Assn. [20937]
Heiney Family Tree [20938]
Henlein/Heinlein Family Assn. [20939]
Higdon Family Assn. [20940]
Hinman Family Assn. [20941]
Hoefler Family Assn. [20942]
Holloway - Ralston Family Assn. [20943]
Honaker Family Assn. [20944]
House of Boyd Soc. [20945]
House of Boyd Soc. [IO]
Hoyt Family Assn. [20946]
Hubbell Family Historical Soc. [20947]
The Hubbell Family Historical Soc. [IO]
Hudson Family Assn. [20948]
Huebotter Family Org. [20949]
Innes Clan Soc. [20950]
Innes Clan Society [IO]
Intl. Assn. of Clan MacInnes [20951]
Intl. Assn. of the Skubinna Family [20952]
Intl. Assn. of the Skubinna Family [IO]
Intl. Molyneux Family Assn. [20953]
Intl. Soc. for British Genealogy and Family History
    [21123]
Intl. Soc. Daughters of Utah Pioneers [21252]
Isaac Garrison Family Assn. [20954]
Jacob Hochstetler Family Assn. [20955]
James Happy Family Org. [20956]
James Leonard Williams Family Org. [20957]
James Redman Miller Family Org. [20958]
Johann Frederick Mouser Family Org. [20959]
Johannes Schwalm Historical Assn. [21128]
John Bosher Family Org. [20960]
John Carver Family Org. [20961]
John Clough Genealogical Soc. [20962]
John Libby Family Assn. [20963]
John More Assn. [20964]
John Morgan Evans of Merthyr Tydil [20965]
John Thomas Martin Family Org. [20966]
Joseph Cox and Mary Rue Family Assn. [20967]
Joseph Goodbrake Montgomery Family Org.
    [20968]
Judkins Family Assn. [20969]
Junkins Family Assn. [20970]
Kelsey Kindred of Am. [20971]
Kerr Family Assn. of North Am. [20972]
Kerr Family Assn. of North Am. [IO]
Kershner Family Assn. [20973]
Kilts Family Assn. [20974]
Kjaerulf Family Assn. [20975]
Kump Family Assn. [20976]
Lasher Family Assn. [20977]
Lillard Family Assn. [20978]
Littlefield Family Newsl. [20979]
Litzenberger-Litzenberg Assn. [20980]
Locke Surname Org. [20981]
Lorin Elias Bassett Family Org. [20982]
Lucky Mee Family Assn. [20983]
Luther Family Assn. [20984]
Lybarger Memorial Assn. [20985]
MacCartney Clan Soc. [20986]
MacFaddien Family Soc. [20987]
MacLellan Clan in Am. [20988]
MacThomas North Am. [20989]

Magny Families Assn. [20990]
Marley Family Assn. [20991]
Maxfield Family Org. [20992]
Maybee Soc. [20993]
Mazur Surname Org. [20994]
McAdams Historical Soc. [20995]
McCune Family Assn. [20996]
McCurdy Family Assn. [20997]
McGregor Family Assn. [20998]
Meader Family Assn. [20999]
Merier-Gourley-Roark Family Org. [21000]
Miles Merwin Assn. [21001]
Milliron - Millison - Muhleisen Family Exchange
    [21002]
Moody Family Assn. [21003]
Morgan Family Club [19053]
Morse Soc. [21131]
Mumpower Family Assn. [21004]
Murray Clan Soc. North Am. [21005]
Natl. Aldrich Family Assn. [21006]
Natl. Assn. of Lively Families [21007]
Natl. Assn. of the Van Valkenburg Family [21008]
Natl. Genealogical Soc. [21133]
Natl. Grigsby Family Soc. [21009]
Natl. Soc. of Madison Family Descendants
    [21135]
Natl. Soc. of the Sons of Utah Pioneers [21254]
Neal Dougan-Theodorus Scowden Family Org.
    [21010]
Nesbitt-Nisbet Soc.: A Worldwide Clan Soc.
    [21011]
Nesbitt-Nisbet Soc.: A Worldwide Clan Soc. [IO]
New England Historic Genealogical Soc. [21136]
New York Genealogical and Biographical Soc.
    [21137]
Nims Family Assn. [21012]
Nixon Family Assn. [21013]
Norvell Family Org. [21014]
Oblinger/Oplinger Family Assn. [21015]
O'Hare Family Assn. [21016]
Ouderkerk Family Genealogical Assn. [21017]
Owen Family Assn. [21018]
Owsley Family Historical Soc. [21019]
Paisley Family Soc. [21020]
Parke Soc. [21021]
Pellien/Jaeger/Loretan/Steiner/Ross Soc. [21022]
Pennsylvania German Soc. [21243]
Pierre Chastain Family Assn. [21023]
Pilgrim Soc. [21249]
Pilgrims of the U.S. [21250]
Platt Family Assn. [21024]
Polish Genealogical Soc. of Am. [21142]
Pontius Family Assn. [21025]
Prall Family Assn. [21026]
Premm Family Assn. [21027]
Purcell Family of Am. [21028]
Rader Assn. [21029]
Rainier Soc. [21145]
Ralph Shepard Family Org. [21030]
Reed-Reid CH [21031]
Reynolds Family Assn. [21032]
Rich Family Assn. [21033]
Rickey Family Assn. [21034]
Risley Family Assn. [21035]
Risley Family Assn. [IO]
Robert Bruce Bradley Family Org. [21036]
Rockafellow Family Assn. [21037]
Ronald Lee Shankland Family Org. [21038]
Rose Family Assn. [21039]
Runkle Family Assn. [21040]
Saint Nicholas Soc. of the City of New York
    [21148]
Saleeby-Saliba Family Assn. [21041]
Sapp Family Assn. [21042]
Savoie Acadian Cultural and Historical Soc.
    [21149]
Schaarschmidt Family Assn. and Data Bank
    [21043]
Schreckengost Family Exchange [21044]
Scruggs Family Assn. [21045]
Sears Family Assn. [21046]
Seeley Genealogical Soc. [21047]
Shafer Family Assn. [21048]
Shanks Family Assn. [21049]
Shirley Family Assn. [21050]

Skinner Surname Org. [21051]
Smith-Hedrick Family Assn. [21052]
Snodgrass Clan Soc. [21053]
Soc. of California Pioneers [21255]
Soc. of the Hawley Family [21054]
Soc. of Indiana Pioneers [21256]
Soc. of Mareen Duvall Descendants [21055]
Soc. of Stukely Westcott Descendants of Am.
    [21056]
Sons and Daughters of Oregon Pioneers [21257]
Sons and Daughters of Pioneer Rivermen [21258]
Southern Bean Assn. [21057]
Sparks Family Assn. [21058]
Spencer Historical and Genealogical Soc. [21153]
Spurlock Family Assn. [21059]
Steere Family Assn. [21060]
Stires Family Assn. [21061]
Stovall Family Assn. [21062]
Streeter Family Assn. [21063]
Strong Family Assn. of Am. [21064]
Studebaker Family Natl. Assn. [21065]
Sumner Family Assn. [21066]
Sumner Family Assn. [IO]
Tackett Family Assn. [21067]
Taft Family Assn. [21068]
Templin Family Assn. [21069]
Tevebaugh - Teverbaugh Surname Org. [21070]
Thomas Minor Soc. [21071]
Tripp Family Assn. [21072]
Turnbull Clan Assn. [21073]
Urbain Baudreau Graveline Genealogical Assn.
    [21074]
Van Voorhees Assn. [21075]
Vawter - Vauter - Vaughter(s) Family Assn.
    [21076]
Veitch Historical Soc. [21077]
Vesterheim Genealogical Center and Naeseth Lib.
    [21155]
Waltermire Family Assn. [21078]
Wardner Family Historical Assn. [21079]
Wefel Family Assn. [21080]
Wells Family Res. Assn. [21081]
Wells Family Res. Assn. [IO]
Wert Family History Assn. [21082]
Wilkerson/Wilkinson Clearinghouse [21083]
William Burrup Family Org. [21084]
William Geddes Family Org. [21085]
William Jacob Heckman Family Org. [21086]
William Kindel Family Org. [21087]
Wingfield Family Soc. [21088]
Wingfield Family Soc. [IO]
Woenne/Wonne/Winne Family Assn. [21089]
Wolfensberger Family Assn. [21090]
World Jewish Genealogy Org. [21158]
Young Surname Org. [21091]
Zang Family Org. [21092]
Zartman Assn. of Am. [21093]
Family Network; Treacher Collins [★14067]
Family Nursing; Frontier School of Midwifery and
    [★15479]
Family Partnership; Natl. [13270]
Family Physicians; Amer. Coll. of Osteopathic
    [15793]
Family Physicians; Amer. Osteopathic Bd. of [15799]
Family Physicians; Uniformed Services Acad. of
    [15268]
Family Planning
Advocates for Youth [12173]
Advocates for Youth [IO]
Advocates for Youth's Media Proj. [12174]
Alan Guttmacher Inst. [12175]
Amer. Acad. of Fertility Care Professionals
    [12634]
Amer. Center for Law and Justice [12901]
Amer. Life League [12902]
Amer. Victims of Abortion [12903]
Antigua Planned Parenthood Assn. [IO]
Asian-Pacific Rsrc. and Res. Centre for Women
    [IO]
Asociacion Argentina de Proteccion Familiar [IO]
Asociacion Chilena de Proteccion de la Familia
    [IO]
Asociacion Civil de Planificacion Familiar [IO]
Asociacion Dominicana Pro-Bienestar de la Fa-
    milia [IO]

Reference to "IO" in place of a book number signifies that the association may be found in the 45th edition of International Organizations.

Asociacion Pro-Bienestar de la Familia Colombi-
ana [IO]
Asociacion Pro-Bienestar de la Familia Ecuatori-
ana [IO]
Asociacion Pro Bienestar de la Familia de
Guatemala [IO]
Asociacion Pro-Bienestar de la Familia Nicara-
guense [IO]
Asociacion Puertorriquena Pro-Bienestar de la
Familia [IO]
Asociacion Puertorriquena Pro-Bienestar de la
Familia [12176]
Assn. Algerienne pour la Planification Familiale
[IO]
Assn. Centrafricaine pour le Bien-Etre Familial
[IO]
Assn. Djiboutienne pour l'Equilibre et la Promotion
de la Famille [IO]
Assn. for Interdisciplinary Res. in Values and
Social Change [12906]
Assn. Ivoirienne pour le Bien-Etre Familial [IO]
Assn. for Population/Family Planning Libraries
and Info. Centers-International [10336]
Assn. pour la Promotion de la Famille Haitienne
[IO]
Assn. of Reproductive Hea. Professionals [12177]
Bahrain Family Planning Assn. [IO]
Barbados Family Planning Assn. [IO]
Belize Family Life Assn. [IO]
BEMFAM (Sociedade Civil Bem-Estar Familiar no
Brazil) [IO]
Billings Ovulation Method Assn. - USA [12635]
Black Americans for Life [12909]
Canadian Fed. for Sexual Hea. [IO]
Caribbean Family Planning Affiliation [IO]
Catholics United for Life [12910]
Center for Commun. Programs [12755]
Center for Reproductive and Family Hea. [IO]
Centre for African Family Stud. [IO]
Centre for Development and Population Activities
[12422]
Centre for Development and Population Activities
- Egypt [IO]
Centre for Development and Population Activities
- Nigeria [IO]
Centro de Investigacion, Educacion y Servicios
[IO]
Centro Paraguayo de Estudios de Poblacion [IO]
Child Trends [11679]
China Family Planning Assn. [IO]
CHOICE [12178]
Clayton Fund [12179]
Community Systems Found. [15552]
Cook Islands Family Welfare Assn. [IO]
Costa Rican Demographic Assn. [IO]
Couple to Couple League [12636]
Cyprus Family Planning Assn. [IO]
Egyptian Family Planning Assn. [IO]
EngenderHealth [IO]
EngenderHealth [12180]
Estonian Sexual Hea. Assn. [IO]
Family of the Americas Found. [12637]
Family Hea. Intl. [IO]
Family Hea. Intl. [12181]
Family Hea. Intl. - Bangladesh [IO]
Family Hea. Intl. - Burundi [IO]
Family Hea. Intl. - Cambodia [IO]
Family Hea. Intl. - Cote d' Ivore [IO]
Family Hea. Intl. - Dominican Republic [IO]
Family Hea. Intl. - Egypt [IO]
Family Hea. Intl. - Eritrea [IO]
Family Hea. Intl. - Ethiopia [IO]
Family Hea. Intl. - Ghana [IO]
Family Hea. Intl. - Guatemala [IO]
Family Hea. Intl. - Guinea [IO]
Family Hea. Intl. - Guyana [IO]
Family Hea. Intl. - Haiti [IO]
Family Hea. Intl. - India [IO]
Family Hea. Intl. - Indonesia [IO]
Family Hea. Intl. - Jordan [IO]
Family Hea. Intl. - Kenya [IO]
Family Hea. Intl. - Laos [IO]
Family Hea. Intl. - Malawi [IO]
Family Hea. Intl. - Mozambique [IO]
Family Hea. Intl. - Namibia [IO]

Family Hea. Intl. - Nepal [IO]
Family Hea. Intl. - Nigeria [IO]
Family Hea. Intl. - People's Republic of China [IO]
Family Hea. Intl. - Philippines [IO]
Family Hea. Intl. - Senegal [IO]
Family Hea. Intl. - South Africa [IO]
Family Hea. Intl. - Thailand [IO]
Family Hea. Intl. - Vietnam [IO]
Family Hea. Options Kenya [IO]
Family Life Assn. of Swaziland [IO]
Family Planning Assn. of Bangladesh [IO]
Family Planning Assn. of Greece [IO]
Family Planning Assn. of Hong Kong [IO]
Family Planning Assn. of India [IO]
Family Planning Assn. of Iran [IO]
Family Planning Assn. of Moldova [IO]
Family Planning Assn. of New Zealand [IO]
Family Planning Assn. Of Nepal [IO]
Family Planning Assn. Of Pakistan [IO]
Family Planning Assn. of Sri Lanka [IO]
Family Planning Assn. of Trinidad and Tobago
[IO]
Family Planning Assn. of the United Kingdom [IO]
Family Planning Assn. of Western Australia [IO]
Family Planning Org. of the Philippines [IO]
Family Planning and Sexual Hea. Assn. [IO]
Famplan Jamaica [IO]
Fed. of Family Planning Associations of Malaysia
[IO]
Fed. Laique de Centres de Planning Familial [IO]
Fertile Hope [14390]
For Family and Hea. Armenian Assn. [IO]
Found. for the Promotion of Responsible Parent-
hood - Aruba [IO]
FPA [IO]
Freedom from Hunger [12394]
Healthy Teen Network [12182]
Heartbeat Intl. [12912]
Indonesian Planned Parenthood Assn. [IO]
Instituto Peruano de Paternidad Responsible [IO]
International Consortium for Emergency
Contraception [IO]
Intl. Consortium for Emergency Contraception
[12183]
Intl. Planned Parenthood Fed. - Africa Regional
Off. [IO]
Intl. Planned Parenthood Fed. - East and South
East Asia and Oceania Regional Off. [IO]
Intl. Planned Parenthood Fed. European Network
[IO]
Intl. Planned Parenthood Fed. - United Kingdom
[IO]
Intl. Planned Parenthood Fed., Western
Hemisphere Region [IO]
Intl. Planned Parenthood Fed., Western
Hemisphere Region [12184]
Iraqi Reproductive Hea. and Family Planning
Assn. [IO]
Irish Family Planning Assn. [IO]
Israel Family Planning Assn. [IO]
Japanese Org. for Intl. Cooperation in Family
Planning [IO]
Jordanian Assn. for Family Planning and Protec-
tion [IO]
La Asociacion Pro-Bienestar de la Familia
Colombia [IO]
Latvia's Assn. for Family Planning and Sexual
Hea. Assn. [IO]
Lebanon Family Planning Assn. [IO]
Liberty Godparent Home [12918]
Marie Stopes Intl. - United Kingdom [IO]
Marie Stopes Intl. - Vietnam [IO]
Mexican Found. for Family Planning [IO]
Mongolian Family Welfare Assn. [IO]
Mouvement Francais pour le Planning Familial
[IO]
Natl. Assn. of Ovulation Method Instructors UK
[IO]
Natl. Assn. of the Ovulation Method of Ireland [IO]
Natl. Family Planning and Reproductive Hea.
Assn. [12185]
Natl. Infertility Network Exchange [12678]
Natl. Life Center [12922]
Natl. Right to Life Comm. [12923]
Native Amer. Community Bd. [12630]

Natural Fertility New Zealand [IO]
Negative Population Growth [12756]
The Nurturing Network [13434]
Off. of Population Affairs CH [12757]
Osterreichische Gesellschaft fur Familienplanung
[IO]
Palestinian Family Planning and Protection Assn.
[IO]
Panamanian Assn. for Planned Parenthood [IO]
Pathfinder Intl. [IO]
Pathfinder Intl. [12186]
Pathfinder Intl. - Brazil [IO]
Planned Parenthood Assn. of Sierra Leone [IO]
Planned Parenthood Assn. of South Africa [IO]
Planned Parenthood Assn. of Thailand [IO]
Planned Parenthood Edmonton [IO]
Planned Parenthood Fed. of Am. [12187]
Planned Parenthood Fed. of Nigeria [IO]
Population Action Intl. [12758]
Population Commun. [12759]
Population Communications Intl. [12760]
Population Connection [12761]
Population Coun. [12762]
Population-Environment Balance [12763]
Population Inst. [12764]
Population Rsrc. Center [12765]
Presbyterian Hunger Prog. [12397]
Presbyterians Pro-Life [12926]
Pro Familia: Deutsche Gesellschaft fur Familien-
planung, Sexualpadagogik und Sexualberatung
[IO]
Pro Familia Hungarian Sci. Soc. [IO]
Pro-Life Alliance of Gays and Lesbians [12927]
Reproductive and Family Hea. Assn. of Fiji [IO]
Russian Family Planning Assn. [IO]
Sabah Family Planning Assn. [IO]
St. Lucia Planned Parenthood Assn. [IO]
Salvadoran Demographic Assn. [IO]
Samoa Family Hea. Assn. [IO]
Sexual Hea. and Family Planning Australia - Intl.
Prog. [IO]
Singapore Planned Parenthood Assn. [IO]
Slovak Family Planning Assn. [IO]
Societatea de Educatie Contraceptiva si Sexuala
[IO]
Soc. for Hea. Educ. [IO]
Stichting Lobi [IO]
Swedish Assn. for Sexuality Educ. [IO]
Swiss Found. for Sexual and Reproductive Hea.
[IO]
Syrian Family Planning Assn. [IO]
Tonga Family Hea. Assn. [IO]
U.S. Coalition for Life [12929]
Uruguayan Family Planning Assn. [IO]
Uzbek Assn. on Reproductive Hea. [IO]
Vanuatu Family Hea. Assn. [IO]
Women Exploited by Abortion [12932]
WOOMB Philippines [IO]
WOOMB Tanzania [IO]
Family Planning; Amer. Acad. of Natural [★12634]
Family Planning Assn. [★IO]
Family Planning Assn. of Bangladesh [IO], Dhaka,
Bangladesh
Family Planning Assn. of Estonia [★IO]
Family Planning Assn. of Greece [IO], Athens,
Greece
Family Planning Assn. of Hong Kong [IO], Hong
Kong, People's Republic of China
Family Planning Assn. of India [IO], Bombay, India
Family Planning Assn. of Iran [IO], Tehran, Iran
Family Planning Assn. of Kenya [★IO]
Family Planning Assn. of Moldova [IO], Chisinau,
Moldova
Family Planning Assn. of New Zealand [IO], Welling-
ton, New Zealand
Family Planning Assn. Of Nepal [IO], Kathmandu,
Nepal
Family Planning Assn. Of Pakistan [IO], Lahore,
Pakistan
Family Planning Assn. of Singapore [★IO]
Family Planning Assn. of Sri Lanka [IO], Colombo,
Sri Lanka
Family Planning Assn. of Trinidad and Tobago [IO],
Port of Spain, Trinidad and Tobago
Family Planning Assn. of the United Kingdom [IO],
London, United Kingdom

A star before a book entry number signifies that the name is not listed separately, but is mentioned within the entry.

Family Planning Assn. of Western Australia [IO], Perth, Australia
Family Planning Australia [★IO]
Family Planning Coun. of Nigeria [★IO]
Family Planning Fed. of Australia [★IO]
Family Planning Forum; Natl. [★12185]
Family Planning; Friends of [★18521]
Family Planning Org. of the Philippines [IO], Quezon City, Philippines
Family Planning Prog. Development; Center for [★12175]
Family Planning and Sexual Hea. Assn. [IO], Vilnius, Lithuania
Family Planning; Voters for Choice/Friends of [18521]
Family Practice Administrators; Assn. of [15060]
Family Pride Coalition [12227], PO Box 65327, Washington, DC 20035-5327, (202)331-5015
Family Promise [12290], 71 Summit Ave., Summit, NJ 07901, (908)273-1100
Family and Property; Amer. Soc. for the Defense of Tradition, [★19763]
Family Protection League of U.S.A. - Defunct.
Family Psychology; Amer. Psychological Assn. - Division of [16125]
Family Records Assn; Amer. [21100]
Family Recreation Assn; Intl. [12798]
Family Relations; Family and Hea. Sect. of the Natl. Coun. on [14385]
Family Relations Family Therapy Sect; Natl. Coun. on [★16612]
Family Relations; Family Therapy Sect. of the Natl. Coun. on [16612]
Family Relations Feminism and Family Stud. Sect; Natl. Coun. of [★12156]
Family Relations; Natl. Conf. of [★12164]
Family Renewal; Christian [19776]
Family Res. Coun. [12153], 801 G St. NW, Washington, DC 20001, (202)393-2100
Family Res. Coun. of Am. [★12153]
Family Res. Gp. [★12153]
Family Res. Inst. [17688], PO Box 62640, Colorado Springs, CO 80962-2640, (303)681-3113
Family Rsrc. Center on Disabilities [8202], 20 E Jackson Blvd., Rm. 300, Chicago, IL 60604, (312)939-3513
Family Rsrc. Coalition of Am. [★12154]
Family Rosary [19622], 518 Washington St., North Easton, MA 02356-1202, (508)238-4095
Family Rosary Crusade [★19622]
Family Security Coalition [★1464]
Family Ser. Assn. of Am. [★12136]
Family Ser. Assn. of Am. [★IO]
Family Ser. Charities of Am; Women, Children and [12207]
Family Ser. Units [★IO]
Family Setzekorn Assn. - Address unknown since 2004.
Family Stability; Assn. for the Advancement of [★12138]
Family Support Am. [12154], 307 W 200 S, Ste. 2004, Salt Lake City, UT 84101, (877)338-3722
Family Support; Center for [12566]
Family Support Enforcement Assn; Natl. Reciprocal and [★5701]
Family Support Gp; FOD [15248]
Family Support Gp; Maple Syrup Urine [15250]
Family Support Gp; MSUD [★15250]
Family Supports [12155], c/o Charles B. Hennon, Assoc. Dir., Center for Human Development, Learning, and Tech., 101D McGuffey Hall, Miami Univ., Oxford, OH 45056, (513)529-2323
Family Supports [IO], Oxford, OH, United States
Family Therapists; Natl. Acad. of Counselors and [★12137]
Family Therapy Acad; Amer. [11816]
Family Therapy; Ackerman Inst. for [★12134]
Family Therapy; Amer. Assn. for Marriage and [16200]
Family Therapy Assn; Amer. [★11816]
Family Therapy Educ; Commn. on Accreditation for Marriage and [8819]
Family Therapy Network [★16228]
Family Therapy Sect. of the Natl. Coun. on Family Relations [16612], 3989 Central Ave. NE, No. 550, Minneapolis, MN 55421, (248)370-3069

Family Therapy; Southeast Inst. for Gp. and [18629]
Family Ties - Address unknown since 2004.
Family Violence; Natl. Coun. on Child Abuse and [12035]
Family Violence Prevention Fund [12028], 383 Rhode Island St., Ste. 304, San Francisco, CA 94103-5133, (415)252-8900
Family Voices [13960], 2340 Alamo SE, Ste. 102, Albuquerque, NM 87106, (505)872-4774
Family; We Are [17659]
Family Welfare Assn. of Am. [★12136]
Family Welfare Assn. of Am. [★IO]
Family; Women for Faith and [19739]
Family and Youth Concern [★IO]
Famous Fone Friends [11692]
Famous Personalities' Business Card Collectors of America - Defunct.
Famplan Jamaica [IO], St. Ann, Jamaica
Fan Assn. of North Am. [IO], Brentwood, NH, United States
Fan Assn. of North Am. [22021], c/o Ms. Linda S. Rousseau, Public Relations Chair, 90 Prescott Rd., Brentwood, NH 03833, (603)772-4534
Fan Circle Intl. [IO], Norwich, United Kingdom
Fan Club; Abbott and Costello [★24795]
Fan Club; Abbott and Costello Intl. [24795]
Fan Club; Abbott and Costello Official [24796]
Fan Club; Air Supply [24837]
Fan Club; Alabama [24838]
Fan Club; Aldo Ray [24726]
Fan Club of Am; Cliff Richard [24866]
Fan Club; Amer. Bandstand [25024]
Fan Club; Andrea McArdle [24728]
Fan Club; Atlanta Flames [24996]
Fan Club; Beach Boys [24846]
Fan Club; Betty White [24732]
Fan Club; Billy "Crash" Craddock 24849
Fan Club; Bob Homan [24852]
Fan Club; Bonnie Lou Bishop [★24853]
Fan Club; Bonnie Lou Bishop Intl. [24853]
Fan Club; Bruce Boxleitner's Official [24734]
Fan Club; Carla Riggs-Hall Intl. [24855]
Fan Club; Cecilia Lee [★24856]
Fan Club; Cecilia Lee Intl. [24856]
Fan Club; Charley Pride [24857]
Fan Club; Chicago [24859]
Fan Club; Chris LeDoux Intl. [24861]
Fan Club; Club E: The Dale Earnhardt [25002]
Fan Club; Connie Francis Intl. [24867]
Fan Club; Connie Stevens [24868]
Fan Club; Cowsills [24869]
Fan Club; Danny Cooksey [24736]
Fan Club; David Allan Coe [24870]
Fan Club; David Birney Intl. [24737]
Fan Club; Devils [25004]
Fan Club; Diamond Rio [24875]
Fan Club; Dinah Shore [24876]
Fan Club for Disneyana Enthusiasts; Natl. Fantasy [24791]
Fan Club; Donna Fargo Intl. [24879]
Fan Club; Elvira [24817]
Fan Club; Elvis Forever TCB [24808]
Fan Club; Elvis Worldwide [★24805]
Fan Club; Engel's Angels in Humperdinck Heaven [24885]
Fan Club; Ethel Delaney Intl. [24886]
Fan Club; Flight Patrol [25027]
Fan Club; Florence Ballard [24888]
Fan Club; Friends of Debbie Reynolds [24741]
Fan Club; Friends of Hopalong Cassidy [24742]
Fan Club; Galaxy Patrol [25029]
Fan Club; Gary Morris [24897]
Fan Club; Gene Pitney [★24898]
Fan Club; Gene Pitney Intl. [24898]
Fan Club; George Strait [24901]
Fan Club; Gilligan's Island [25030]
Fan Club; Good Day Sunshine; Beatles [24786]
Fan Club; Grand Ole Opry [★24864]
Fan Club of the Grand Ole Opry; Circle Club - The Official [24864]
Fan Club; Guiding Light [25031]
Fan Club; Hank Williams Intl. [24905]
Fan Club; Hank Williams Jr. [24906]
Fan Club; Hank Williams, Sr. Intl. [★24905]
Fan Club; Harry Connick, Jr. [24907]

Fan Club; Helen Forrest [24910]
Fan Club, Inc; ZZ Top Intl. [24993]
Fan Club Intl; Presley-ites [24813]
Fan Club; Intl. Sybil Jason [24746]
Fan Club; Intl. Willie Nelson [24915]
Fan Club; Jana Jae [24916]
Fan Club; Jane Powell [24747]
Fan Club; Jeff Carson Intl. [24918]
Fan Club; Jerry Jeff Walker [24919]
Fan Club; Jimmy Kish "The Flying Cowboy" 24922
Fan Club; John Denver Heart to Heart [★24909]
Fan Club; Johnny Len [24928]
Fan Club; Jon-Erik Hexum [24749]
Fan Club; Joni James Intl. [24818]
Fan Club; KISS Rocks [24935]
Fan Club; Kitty Wells/Johnny Wright [★24936]
Fan Club; Kitty Wells-Johnny Wright-Bobby Wright Intl. [24936]
Fan Club; Laura Hendler [24751]
Fan Club; Lesley Gore [24938]
Fan Club; Leslie Charleson [24752]
Fan Club; Linda Gray's Official [24753]
Fan Club; Lindsay Wagner's Official [24754]
Fan Club; Lou Christie Intl. [24941]
Fan Club; Magic of Bewitched [25034]
Fan Club; Mamie Van Doren [24757]
Fan Club; Mark Slade [24758]
Fan Club; Martin Van Buren [11136]
Fan Club; Martina McBride [24944]
Fan Club; Marty Stuart [24945]
Fan Club; Mary Jo Cattlett [24759]
Fan Club; Mary Wilson [★24954]
Fan Club; Mel Tillis [24946]
Fan Club/Michele Lee Online; Michele Lee [24761]
Fan Club; Norma Zimmer Natl. [24950]
Fan Club; North Amer. Toyah [24951]
Fan Club; Official Betty Boop [24792]
Fan Club; Official Gilligan's Island [25038]
Fan Club; Official Gumby [24793]
Fan Club; Official Intl. Michael York [24763]
Fan Club; Official Lane Brody and Eleni Global [24953]
Fan Club; Official Mary Wilson Message Bd. and [24954]
Fan Club; Once Upon A Time The Prisoner [25040]
Fan Club; Pat Compton [24957]
Fan Club; Peter Breck [24766]
Fan Club; Philadelphia Flyers [25011]
Fan Club; Princess Kitty [24778]
Fan Club; Razzy Bailey [24964]
Fan Club; Ricky Skaggs Intl. [24968]
Fan Club; Robert Redford [24770]
Fan Club; Sawyer Brown [★24974]
Fan Club; Sawyer Brown Intl. [24974]
Fan Club; Skidrow Joe [24773]
Fan Club; Star Trek: The Official [25016]
Fan Club; Stefanie Powers' Official [24774]
Fan Club; Supremes Intl. [★24954]
Fan Club; Tammy Wynette Intl. [24979]
Fan Club; Tanya Tucker [24980]
Fan Club; TCB for Elvis [24814]
Fan Club; Tex Ritter [24982]
Fan Club; T.G. Sheppard Intl. [24983]
Fan Club (The Original); Gilligan's Island [★25038]
Fan Club; Three Stooges [24800]
Fan Club; Tom Jones "Tom Terrific" 24986
Fan Club; Tom Mix Intl. [24775]
Fan Club (U.S.); Sharon Gless [24771]
Fan Club and Walt Kelly Soc; Pogo [24794]
Fan Club; Washington Capitals [25014]
Fan Club; W.C. Fields [24801]
Fan Club; We Remember Elvis [24815]
Fan Club; Young and the Restless [25047]
Fan Clubs
Abbott and Costello Official Fan Club [24796]
af2 Natl. Fan Club [24829]
Air, Sea, and Space Club [25023]
Annie Sims Intl. Fan Club [24842]
Art Greenhaw Official Intl. Fan Club [24843]
Austin Cody's Official Intl. Fan Club [24845]
Barbara Bain Intl. [24730]
Barbara Eden's Official Fan Club [24731]
Beatles Connection [24785]
Beatles Fans Unite [24787]
Beyond the Rainbow [24733]

Reference to "IO" in place of a book number signifies that the association may be found in the 45th edition of International Organizations.

Branscombe Richmond Fan Club [24779]
Cassie Edwards Intl. Fan Club [24782]
Chet Atkins Appreciation Soc. [24858]
Chris Young Fan Club [24862]
Chuck Negron Fan Club [24863]
Clay Underwood Fan Club [24865]
Club E: The Dale Earnhardt Fan Club [25002]
Conrad Veidt Soc. [24735]
Cowsills Fan Club [24869]
Crazy4Clay Gang [24819]
Damfinos: The Intl. Buster Keaton Soc. [24797]
Dean Martin Fan Center [24816]
Debbie Harry Collector's Soc. [24872]
Delbert McClinton Intl. Fan Club [24874]
Derrike Cope Fan Club [24783]
Diamond Rio Fan Club [24875]
Doors Collectors Club [24881]
Elvira Fan Club [24817]
ElvisNet Elvis Presley Fan Club [24812]
Flight Patrol Fan Club [25027]
Frankie Laine Soc. of Am. [24890]
Friends of Ty Herndon Fan Club [24896]
F.U.G.I.T.I.V.E.S. [25028]
Galaxy Patrol Fan Club [25029]
Gilligan's Island Fan Club [25030]
The Grascals Fan Club [24904]
Guiding Light Fan Club [25031]
Hank Williams Intl. Fan Club [24905]
Heart of Texas Country Music Assn. [24908]
Hearts in Harmony - World Family of John Denver [24909]
Intl. Fan Club Org. [24912]
Intl. Jack Benny Fan Club [24798]
Intl. Sybil Jason Fan Club [24746]
Intl. Traditional Country Music Fan Club [24914]
Jane Powell Fan Club [24747]
Jeannie Seely's Circle of Friends [24917]
Jeff Carson Intl. Fan Club [24918]
Jim Hubbard Fan Club [24920]
Joe Diffie Fan Club [24923]
Johnnie Ray Intl. Fan Club [24927]
Johnny Benson Fan Club [24784]
Jon-Erik Hexum Fan Club [24749]
Joni James Intl. Fan Club [24818]
Julio - Am. Fan Club [24834]
Keith Bulluck Fan Club [24830]
Kelly Lang Fan Club [24932]
Kevin Sorbo's Official Fan Club [24820]
Lee's Familee [24937]
Little Mouse Club [22413]
Little Mouse Club [IO]
Lone Ranger Fan Club [25032]
Magic of Bewitched Fan Club [25034]
Magnum Memorabilia [25035]
Martina McBride Fan Club [24944]
Mel Tillis Fan Club [24946]
Michael Crawford Intl. Fan Assn. [24760]
Michael Jackson Fan Club [24948]
Michele Lee Fan Club/Michele Lee Online [24761]
Motion Picture Sound Editors [1371]
Natl. Lum and Abner Soc. [22925]
Natl. Pat Boone Fan Club [24949]
Nick Mancuso Fan Network [24762]
Official Betty Boop Fan Club [24792]
Official Gilligan's Island Fan Club [25038]
Official Intl. Michael York Fan Club [24763]
Official Julio Iglesias Intl. Fan Club [24835]
Official Robert Newman Fan Club [24765]
Oh Ji Ho Intl. Fan Club [24781]
Once Upon A Time (The Prisoner Fan Club) [25040]
Original Four Aces and Al Alberts Archv. [24955]
Pat Shea Intl. Fan Club [24958]
Perry Como Circle [24960]
Peter Sellers Appreciation Soc. [24767]
Ray Price Intl. Fan Club [24963]
REG - The Intl. Roger Waters Fan Club [24965]
Richard Burgi Fan Club [24768]
Rustie Blue Intl. Fan Club [24972]
Sawyer Brown Intl. Fan Club [24974]
Shatner and Friends Intl. [24772]
Six of One Club: The Prisoner Appreciation Soc. [25043]
Stefanie Powers' Official Fan Club [24774]
Surfun: The Official Jan and Dean Fan Club [24977]

T.G. Sheppard Intl. Fan Club [24983]
Three Dog Night Fan Club [24984]
Tom Mix Intl. Fan Club [24775]
United Network Command [25045]
Young and the Restless Fan Club [25047]
Fan Clubs; Natl. Assn. of Pat Boone [★24949]
Fan Collectors Assn; Amer. [★21533]
Fan Collectors Assn; Antique [21533]
Fan Info. Ser; Dark Shadows [★25026]
Fan Makers' Company [IO], London, United Kingdom
Fan Manufacturers Assn; Power [★1876]
Fan Manufacturers; Natl. Assn. of [★1876]
Fan Tek [10943], 1610 Lee Rd., Fort Washington, MD 20744, (301)292-5231
Fanciers Club; Ferret [22416]
Fanconi Anemia Res. Fund [14450], 1801 Willamette St., Ste. 200, Eugene, OR 97401, (541)687-4658
Fanconi's Anemia Support Gp. [★14450]
Fancy Rat and Mouse Assn; Amer. [22704]
Fanderson [IO], Bradford, United Kingdom
Fannish Alliance; Lost in Space [25033]
Fans of Abner - Address unknown since 1999.
Fans Against Indian Racism - Address unknown since 1990.
Fans Assn. of Am; Circus [9797]
Fans and Friends of Ray Price [★24963]
Fans of General Hospital - Address unknown since 2001.
Fans of Leonard Nimoy and DeForest Kelley [24739], 383 Yellow Pine Dr., Bailey, CO 80421-1871, (303)816-0083
Fans of Oz [25048], c/o Vampire Empire, 29 Washington Sq. W, PHN, Ste. C, New York, NY 10011-9180
Fans of Oz [IO], New York, NY, United States

Fantasy
Acad. of Sci. Fiction, Fantasy, and Horror Films [9925]
August Derleth Soc. [9634]
Fan Tek [10943]
Intl. Assn. for the Fantastic in the Arts [10945]
Intl. Fantasy Gaming Soc. [22467]
Krystonia Collector's Club [22064]
Mythopoeic Soc. [10427]
Natl. Fantasy Fan Fed. [10946]
Parallax Soc. [10947]
Strategy Gaming Soc. [22475]
Fantasy Artists; Assn. of Sci. Fiction and [307]
Fantasy Assn. - Defunct.
Fantasy Fan Club for Disneyana Enthusiasts; Natl. [24791]
Fantasy, and Horror Films; Acad. of Sci. Fiction, [9925]
Fantasy Writers of Am; Sci. Fiction and [11193]
FAO/ECE Agriculture and Timber Div. [★IO]
FAO/ECE Timber Sect. [IO], Geneva, Switzerland
Far Beyond the Stars [24740], c/o Gayle Stever, Club Coor., PO Box 11261, Scottsdale, AZ 85271-1261
Far East-America Coun. of Commerce and Industry - Defunct.
Far East Auto Owners Assn. - Address unknown since 2002.
Far East Conf. - Defunct.
Far East Merchants Assn. - Defunct.
Far Eastern Assn. [★7983]
Far Eastern Assn. [★IO]
Far and Wide Tape Club - Address unknown since 1995.
Faraday Soc. [★IO]
Farband; Yiddisher Kultur [10291]
Farbard Labor Zionist Order [★19174]
Fargo Fan Club; Donna [★24879]
Fargo Intl. Fan Club; Donna [24879]
Farm and Agricultural Museums; Assn. for Living History, [10497]
Farm Aid [16953], 11 Ward St., Ste. 200, Somerville, MA 02143, (617)354-2922
Farm Animal Care Trust [★4997]
Farm Animal Task Force [★11394]
Farm Assn; Historical [★10147]
Farm-Based Educ. Assn. [7937], Minuteman Natl. Historic Park, 174 Liberty St., Concord, MA 01742, (978)318-7827

Farm; Bright Futures [4867]
Farm Broadcasters; Natl. Assn. of [★570]
Farm Brokers; Inst. of [★3342]
Farm Bur. [★4642]
Farm Bur. Found. for Agriculture; Amer. [4095]
Farm-City Comm; Natl. [★4649]
Farm Coalition; Natl. Family [16956]
Farm Coalition; Natl. Save the Family [★16956]
Farm Credit Coun. [474], 50 F St. NW, Ste. 900, Washington, DC 20001-1530, (202)626-8710
Farm Crisis Comm. - Defunct.
Farm Directors; Natl. Assn. of Radio [★570]
Farm Directors; Natl. Assn. of Television-Radio [★570]
Farm Economic Assn; Amer. [★6867]
Farm Economics; Women Involved in [16960]
Farm Elec. Utilization Coun; Inter-Industry [★6963]
Farm Electrification Coun. [★6963]

Farm Equipment
Aerial Agricultural Assn. of Australia [IO]
Amer. Rainwater Catchment Systems Assn. [7825]
Assn. of Equip. Mfrs. - Canada [IO]
Farm Tractor and Machinery Trade Assn. [IO]
Intl. Harvester Collectors [23003]
Intl. Rainwater Catchment Systems Assn. [7832]
Intl. Ser. for the Acquisition of Agri-biotech Applications [6398]
Japan Farm Machinery Manufacturers Assn. [IO]
Mexican Assn. of Farm Equip. Distributors [IO]
Midwest Equip. Dealers Assn. [4092]
PIMA - Agricultural Manufacturers of Canada [IO]
Rough and Tumble Engineers' Historical Assn. [22979]
Self Help Intl. [12442]
Two-Cylinder Club [23005]
Farm Equip. Appraisers; Amer. Soc. of [273]
Farm Equip. Assn; Natl. Retail [★185]
Farm Equip. Manufacturers Assn. [179], 1000 Executive Pkwy., Ste. 100, St. Louis, MO 63141-6369, (314)878-2304
Farm Equip. Manufacturers Assn; Allied [★179]
Farm Equip. Wholesalers Assn. [180], PO Box 1347, Iowa City, IA 52244, (319)354-5156
Farm Equipment Wholesalers Association [IO], Iowa City, IA, United States
FARM (Farm Animal Reform Movement) [11394], 10101 Ashburton Ln., Bethesda, MD 20817, (301)530-1737
Farm Found. [4101], 1301 W 22nd St., Ste. 615, Oak Brook, IL 60523, (630)571-9393
Farm Labor Coalition - Address unknown since 1990.
Farm Labor Organizing Comm. [23997], 1221 Broadway St., Toledo, OH 43609, (419)243-3456
Farm Labor Res. Comm. - Defunct.
Farm Labor Res. Proj. [23998], 1221 Broadway St., Toledo, OH 43609, (419)243-3456
Farm and Land Brokers; Natl. Inst. of [★3342]
Farm and Land Inst. [★3342]
Farm Law Inst. - Defunct.

Farm Management
Agricultural Personnel Mgt. Assn. [4638]
Amer. Farmland Trust [16951]
Amer. Soc. of Farm Managers and Rural Appraisers [274]
Aprovecho Res. Center [16993]
Educational Concerns for Hunger Org. [12389]
EnterpriseWorks/VITA [16996]
Farm-Based Educ. Assn. [7937]
FARMS Intl. [12427]
Food Alliance [4676]
Global Aquaculture Alliance [4173]
Independent Professional Seedsmen Assn. [187]
Natl. Farm and Ranch Bus. Mgt. Educ. Assn. [4639]
North Amer. Farmers' Direct Marketing Assn. [5026]
Northwest Farm Managers Assn. [4640]
Rural Advancement Found. Intl. - USA [4108]
Wild Farm Alliance [4661]
Women Involved in Farm Economics [16960]
Farm Mgt. Assn; Amer. [★6867]
Farm Managers; Amer. Soc. of [★274]
Farm Managers and Rural Appraisers; Amer. Soc. of [274]

A star before a book entry number signifies that the name is not listed separately, but is mentioned within the entry.

Farm and Power Equip. Dealers Assn; Natl. [★185]
Farm Publications Reports - Defunct.
Farm; Quiet Valley Living Historical [10147]
Farm Safety 4 Just Kids [12961], 11304 Aurora Ave., Urbandale, IA 50322, (515)331-6506
Farm Sanctuary [11395], PO Box 150, Watkins Glen, NY 14891, (607)583-2225
Farm Ser. Agency County Off. Employees; Natl. Assn. of [5779]
Farm Show Coun; North Amer. [4114]
Farm Store Merchandising Assn. - Defunct.
Farm; Takoma Urban [★4105]
Farm Tractor and Machinery Trade Assn. [IO], Naas, Ireland
Farm Underwriters Assn. - Defunct.
Farm/Water Alliance - Defunct.
Farm Worker Hea. Services [12586], 1221 Massachusetts Ave. NW, Ste. 5, Washington, DC 20005, (202)347-7377
Farm Worker Ministry; Natl. [12594]
Farm Workers of Am; United [23999]
Farm Workers Assn; Natl. [★23999]
Farm Workers Organizing Comm; United [★23999]
Farmer Cooperatives; Natl. Coun. of [4483]
Farmer Soc; Philip Jose [9700]
Farmers and Agriculturists Assn; Black [4111]
Farmers of Am; Catfish [4170]
Farmers of Am; Future [★7940]
Farmers of Am; New [★7940]
Farmers Assistance Relief Mission - Defunct.
Farmers Assn; Forest [★4683]
Farmers Assn. of Iceland [IO], Reykjavik, Iceland
Farmers Assn; Natl. Flying [★4646]
Farmers Assn; U.S. [16958]
Farmers Development Agency [IO], Chickballapur, India
Farmers' Direct Marketing Assn; North Amer. [5026]
Farmers' Educational and Cooperative Union of Am. [★4651]
Farmers' Legal Action Gp. [6023], 360 N Robert St., Ste. 500, St. Paul, MN 55101-1589, (651)223-5400
Farmers-to-Coops Assn. - Defunct.
Farmers Union Intl. Assn. Corp. [★4481]
Farmers Union Intl. Assn. Corp. [★IO]
Farmers and World Affairs - Defunct.
FarmFolk/CityFolk Soc. [IO], Vancouver, BC, Canada
Farmhouse [24629], 11020 NW Ambassador Dr., Ste. 330, Kansas City, MO 64153, (816)891-9445
Farming
  Agri-Club Natl. Togo [IO]
  Agricultural Groups Concerned About Resources and the Env. [IO]
  Agricultural Producers Union [IO]
  Alley Farming Network for Tropical Africa [IO]
  Alliance for Sustainability [4641]
  Amer. Agri-Women [16948]
  Amer. Agricultural Editors' Assn. [3076]
  Amer. Agriculture Movement [16950]
  Amer. Assn. of Crop Insurers [2129]
  Amer. Farm Bur. Fed. [4642]
  Amer. Farm Bur. Found. for Agriculture [4095]
  Amer. Farmland Trust [16951]
  Amer. Forage and Grassland Coun. [5165]
  Amer. Pastured Poultry Producers Assn. [5106]
  Amer. Soc. of Agricultural Appraisers [271]
  Animal Rights Coalition [11356]
  Animal Traction Network for Eastern and Southern Africa [IO]
  Aprovecho Res. Center [16993]
  Assn. for the Advancement of Indus. Crops [4110]
  Assn. of Equip. Manufacturers [177]
  Assn. of Farmworker Opportunity Programs [12585]
  Assn. for Living History, Farm and Agricultural Museums [10497]
  Bio-Dynamic Agricultural Assn. [IO]
  Biodynamic Agriculture Australia [IO]
  Biodynamic Farming and Gardening Assn. [4643]
  Biological Farmers of Australia [IO]
  Canadian Assn. of Farm Advisors [IO]
  Canadian Organic Growers [IO]
  Canadian Plowing Org. [IO]
  Catfish Farmers of Am. [4170]
  Center for Farm Hea. and Safety [12188]

Central Union of Swedish-Speaking Agricultural Producers in Finland [IO]
Chem. Producers and Distributors Assn. [803]
City Farmer Soc. [IO]
Coalition for a Competitive Food and Agricultural Sys. [4075]
Coalition to Protect Animals in Entertainment [11378]
Conservation Farmers Inc. [IO]
Consultative Gp. on Intl. Agricultural Res. [12425]
Cow Observers Worldwide [22002]
Crop Insurance Res. Bur. [2161]
Crop Sci. Soc. of Japan [IO]
Danish Agriculture [IO]
Demeter Assn. [4644]
Eden Found. [IO]
Educational Concerns for Hunger Org. [12389]
EnterpriseWorks/VITA [16996]
European Coun. of Young Farmers [IO]
European Farmer Co-ordination [IO]
Family Farm Defenders [4645]
Farm-Based Educ. Assn. [7937]
Farm Equip. Manufacturers Assn. [179]
Farm Equip. Wholesalers Assn. [180]
FARM (Farm Animal Reform Movement) [11394]
Farm Found. [4101]
Farm Labor Organizing Comm. [23997]
Farm Safety 4 Just Kids [12961]
Farm Sanctuary [11395]
Farm Worker Hea. Services [12586]
Farmers Development Agency [IO]
Farmers' Legal Action Gp. [6023]
FarmFolk/CityFolk Soc. [IO]
Farmland Indus. [4482]
FARMS Intl. [12427]
Federated Farmers of New Zealand [IO]
Fed. of City Farms and Community Gardens [IO]
Fertilizer Indus. Round Table [1364]
Food Alliance [4676]
Genetic Engg. Action Network [6615]
Hooved Animal Humane Soc. [11407]
Humane Farming Assn. [11411]
ILEIA: Centre for Info. on Low External Input and Sustainable Agriculture [IO]
Independent Professional Seedsmen Assn. [187]
Intl. Fed. of Agricultural Producers [IO]
Intl. Flying Farmers [IO]
Intl. Flying Farmers [4646]
Intl. Network on Participatory Irrigation Mgt. [7233]
Intl. Silo Assn. [181]
Intl. Soc. for Cow Protection [4155]
Intl. Trade Coun. [2285]
Interstate Migrant Educ. Coun. [12588]
Irrigation Assn. [182]
The Land Inst. [4647]
Land Loss Fund [12486]
Livestock Publications Coun. [3233]
Migrant Hea. Promotion [12590]
Natl. Alliance for Migrant and Seasonal Farmworker Vocational Rehabilitation [12591]
Natl. Assn. of Farm Broadcasting [570]
Natl. Assn. of Farmers' Market Nutrition Programs [4648]
Natl. Assn. of State Directors of Migrant Educ. [12592]
Natl. Black Farmers Assn. [12189]
Natl. Catholic Rural Life Conf. [19677]
Natl. Center for Farmworker Hea. [14581]
Natl. Comm. on the Educ. of Migrant Children (of the Natl. Child Labor Comm.) [12593]
Natl. Cottonseed Products Assn. [2854]
Natl. Coun. on Agricultural Life and Labor Res. Fund [12322]
Natl. Coun. of Farmer Cooperatives [4483]
Natl. Crop Insurance Services [2223]
Natl. Farm-City Coun. [4649]
Natl. Farm Worker Ministry [12594]
Natl. Farmers Org. [4650]
Natl. Farmers Union [4651]
Natl. Grange [4652]
Natl. Inst. for Farm Safety [12976]
Natl. Young Farmer Educational Assn. [4653]
North Amer. Bramble Growers Res. Found. [1675]
North Amer. Deer Farmers Assn. [4654]

North Amer. Farmers' Direct Marketing Assn. [5026]
Northwest Farm Managers Assn. [4640]
Organic Crop Improvement Assn. [4655]
Organic Crop Improvement Assn. [IO]
Organic Exchange [2864]
Organic Growers and Buyers Assn. [5070]
People Food and Land Found. [4656]
Pesticide Action Network North Am. Regional Center [13329]
Professional Farmers of Am. [4657]
Quiet Valley Living Historical Farm [10147]
Rice Millers' Assn. [2739]
Rough and Tumble Engineers' Historical Assn. [22979]
Royal Highland Educ. Trust [IO]
Rural Advancement Found. Intl. - USA [4108]
Rural Restoration Adopt [4658]
Rural Women New Zealand [IO]
Scottish for Crop Res. Inst. [IO]
Self Help Intl. [12442]
Senior Gleaners [12398]
Soc. of Ploughmen [IO]
South African Women's Agricultural Union [IO]
Student/Farmworker Alliance [24054]
Sustain: The Alliance for Better Food and Farming [IO]
Sustainable Harvest Intl. [4115]
Tenant Farmers' Assn. [IO]
True Food Network [4677]
United Activists for Animal Rights [11469]
United Producers [5030]
U.S. Animal Hea. Assn. [16811]
U.S. Farmers Assn. [16958]
Universal Proutist Farmers Fed. [4659]
U.S.A. Plowing Org. [4660]
Victorian Farmers Fed. [IO]
Viva! USA [11484]
Western Australian Farmers Fed. [IO]
Wild Farm Alliance [4661]
Windstar Found. [4615]
Women's Food and Farming Union [IO]
World Ploughing Org. [IO]
Farming Assn; Ecological [4100]
Farming Assn; Humane [11411]
Farming; Joint Comm. on Grassland [★5165]
Farmland Indus. [4482]
Farmland Trust; Amer. [16951]
Farms and Agricultural Museums; Assn. for Living Historical [★10497]
Farms Assn; Florida Tropical Fish [4172]
FARMS, Inc. [★12427]
FARMS, Inc. [★IO]
FARMS Intl. [IO], Knife River, MN, United States
FARMS Intl. [12427], PO Box 270, Knife River, MN 55609-0270, (218)834-2676
Farmworker Hea; Natl. Center for [14581]
Farmworker Housing Coalition - Defunct.
Farmworker Justice Fund [12587], 1126 16th St. NW, Ste. 270, Washington, DC 20036, (202)293-5420
Farmworker Opportunity Programs; Assn. of [12585]
Faroe Islands Amateur Theatre Coun. [IO], Torshavn, Faroe Islands
Faron Young Fan Club - Address unknown since 1989.
Farriers
  Brotherhood of Working Farriers Assn. [1353]
  Guild of Professional Farriers [1354]
  Sisterhood of Shoers [1355]
  World Farriers Assn. [1356]
  World Farriers Assn. [IO]
Farrier's Assn; Amer. [522]
Farriers' Company [★IO]
Farsarotul; Soc. [18971]
Fasciitis Found; Natl. Necrotizing [16543]
Fascist Union; United [18315]
Fashion
  Amer. Cloak and Suit Mfrs. Assn. [223]
  Associated Corset and Brassiere Mfrs. [227]
  Chamber of Commerce of the Apparel Indus. [24269]
  Clothing Mfrs. Assn. of the U.S.A. [229]
  Coun. of Fashion Designers of Am. [230]
  Educational Found. for the Fashion Indus. [232]

Reference to "IO" in place of a book number signifies that the association may be found in the 45th edition of International Organizations.

Fashion Exports New York [233]
Fashion Outreach [235]
Fur Info. Coun. of Am. [236]
Glamour Photographers Intl. [2997]
Greater Blouse, Skirt and Undergarment Assn. [237]
The Hosiery Assn. [239]
Infant and Juvenile Mfrs. Assn. [240]
Intl. Jewelry Design Guild [2368]
Intl. Wooden Bow Tie Club [243]
Ladies Apparel Contractors Assn. [244]
Natl. Assn. of Blouse Mfrs. [245]
Natl. Assn. of Fashion and Accessory Designers [246]
Natl. Fashion Accessories Assn. [250]
Neckwear Assn. of America [252]
New York Coat and Suit Assn. [253]
New York Skirt and Sportswear Assn. [254]
Org. of Black Designers [9907]
Young Menswear Assn. [262]
Fashion Accessories Assn; Natl. [250]
Fashion Accessories Shippers Assn. [★250]
Fashion and Accessory Designers; Natl. Assn. of [246]
Fashion Assn. [★221]
Fashion Coordination Inst. - Defunct.
Fashion and Costume Jewelry Club; Vintage [22128]
Fashion Designers of Am; Coun. of [230]
Fashion Exports New York [233], c/o New York Fashion Intl., 275 7th Ave., 9th Fl., New York, NY 10001, (212)366-6160
Fashion Exports New York [IO], New York, NY, United States
Fashion Footwear Materials Assn. - Defunct.
Fashion Gp. Intl. [234], 8 W 40th St., 7th Fl., New York, NY 10018, (212)302-5511
Fashion Gp. Intl. [IO], New York, NY, United States
Fashion and Image Consultants; Assn. of [★957]
Fashion Indus; Educational Found. for the [232]
Fashion Inst. of Tech. [★232]
Fashion Jewelry Assn. of America - Address unknown since 2004.
Fashion Originators Guild of America - Defunct.
Fashion Outreach [235]
Fashion Products Assn; Home [2258]
Fashions League; Home [★2264]
Fashions League; Natl. Home [★2264]
Fast-Draw Assn; World [23733]
Fast for Famine Relief - Defunct.
Fast Food Association; National Soft Serve and [★1958]
Fast Food Association; United Soft Serve and [★1958]
Fastbreak Syndicate - Address unknown since 1994.
Fastener Distributors Assn; Natl. [1828]
Fastener Engg. and Res. Assn. [IO], West Bromwich, United Kingdom
Fasteners Distributors Assn; Specialty Tools and [2069]
Fasteners Inst; Indus. [1823]
Fasteners Res. Coun. - Defunct.
Fastpitch Assn; North Amer. [23793]
Fastpitch Coaches Assn; Natl. [23840]
Fat Acceptance; Natl. Assn. to Advance [12647]
Fat Americans; Natl. Assn. to Aid [★12647]
Fat Lip Readers Theater - Defunct.
Fat Res; Intl. Soc. for [7405]
Fatal Light Awareness Prog. [IO], Toronto, ON, Canada
Father Judge Apostolic Center - Defunct.
Father Marquette Tercentenary Commn. - Defunct.
Father Matters [18180], PO Box 13575, Tempe, AZ 85284-3575, (888)648-0718
Father Moriarty Asylum Project - Defunct.
Fatherhood Initiative; Natl. [17510]
Fatherhood Proj. [12670], c/o Families and Work Inst., 267 5th Ave., 2nd Fl., New York, NY 10016, (212)465-2044
Fathering; Natl. Center for [18181]
Fathers of Am; United [12014]
Fathers Are Forever - Defunct.
Fathers Behind Bars [11866], 525 Superior St., Niles, MI 49120-3338, (269)684-5715
Fathers and Children; Natl. Cong. for [12172]
Fathers Coalition; Amer. [12660]

Fathers Coalition; Gay [★12227]
Fathers Coalition Intl; Gay [★12227]
Father's Day Comm; Natl. [18674]
Father's Day Coun. [★18671]
Father's Day/Mother's Day Coun. [18671], 47 W 34th St., Ste. 534, New York, NY 10001, (212)594-5977
Fathers for Equal Rights [12010], 701 Commerce St., Ste. 302, Dallas, TX 75202, (214)953-2233
Fathers Experiencing Neonatal Death; Aiding Mothers and [11907]
Fathers Hotline; Men/ [★18038]
Fathers at Large - Address unknown since 1995.
The Fathers' Network [★18044]
Fathers Network - Defunct.
Fathers Rsrc. Center; Men and [18038]
Father's Rights of America - Address unknown since 1989.
Fathers Rights and Equality Exchange [★12008]
Fathers; Slovene Franciscan [19718]
Fatigue Syndrome; Amer. Assn. for Chronic [★14266]
Fatigue Syndrome Assn; Natl. Chronic [★14278]
Fatigue Syndrome and Fibromyalgia Assn; Natl. Chronic [14278]
Fatigue Syndrome, Fibromyalgia, and Orthostatic Intolerance; Pediatric Network for Chronic [15895]
Fatigue Syndrome; Intl. Assn. for Chronic [14266]
Fatima Campaign; America Needs [★19763]
Fatima, U.S.A; Blue Army of Our Lady of [19589]
Fats and Proteins Res. Found. [2850], c/o Sergio Nates, PhD, Pres./Dir. of Tech. Services, 801 N Fairfax St., Ste. 205, Alexandria, VA 22314-1776, (703)683-2914
Fats and Proteins Research Foundation [IO], Alexandria, VA, United States
Fatty Acid Producers Assn; Glycerine and [★822]
Fatty Acid Producers' Coun. [★822]
Fatty Oxidation Disorders (FOD) Family Support Gp. [16532], c/o Deb Lee Gould, MEd, Dir., 2041 Tomahawk, Okemos, MI 48864, (517)381-1940
Fauchard Acad; Pierre [14184]
Fauna and Flora Intl. [IO], Cambridge, United Kingdom
Fauna and Flora Preservation Soc. [★IO]
Fauna Found. [IO], Chambly, QC, Canada
Fawcett Soc. [IO], London, United Kingdom
Fax
    Amer. Facsimile Assn. [3732]
FCC Chapitre Montreal [IO], Boucherville, QC, Canada
FCIB-NACM Corp. [IO], Columbia, MD, United States
FCIB-NACM Corp. [2282], 8840 Columbia 100 Pkwy., Columbia, MD 21045-2158, (410)423-1840
FDI World Dental Fed. [IO], Ferney-Voltaire, France
FDR and Democratic Political Items Collectors - Defunct.
FDR Natl. Centennial Comm. - Defunct.
Fe y Alegria [★IO]
Fe y Alegria - Colombia [IO], Bogota, Colombia
Fe y Alegria - El Salvador [IO], San Salvador, El Salvador
Fe y Alegria del Peru [IO], Lima, Peru
FEAR [★5577]
Fear; Freedom From [15199]
Fearing Surname Org. - Defunct.
Feather and Down Assn. - Defunct.
Feathered Pipe Found. [12345], PO Box 1682, Helena, MT 59624, (406)442-8196
Feathers in the Wind - Intl. Led Zeppelin Fan Club - Defunct.
Feature Editors; Amer. Assn. of Sunday and [3079]
Feature Proj; Independent [1381]
February Group - Address unknown since 1988.
FED des associations de fonctionnaires internationaux [★IO]
Fed Andorrana de Tennis St. Antoni [IO], Andorra la Vella, Andorra
FEDAPT - Defunct.
Federacao Angolana de Andebol [IO], Luanda, Angola
Federacao Angolana de Atletismo [IO], Luanda, Angola
Federacao Angolana de Tenis [IO], Luanda, Angola

Federacao Angolana de Vela [IO], Luanda, Angola
Federacao de Atletismo da Guinea-Bissau [IO], Bissau, Guinea-Bissau
Federacao Brasileira de Albergues da Juventude [★IO]
Federacao Brasileira de Vela e Motor [IO], Rio de Janeiro, Brazil
Federacao Cabo Verdiana de Tenis [IO], Praia, Cape Verde
Federacao Iberoamericana de Acustica [★IO]
Federacao Mocambicana de Atletismo [IO], Maputo, Mozambique
Federacao Mocambicana de Badminton [IO], Beira, Mozambique
Federacao Mocambicana de Tenis [IO], Maputo, Mozambique
Federacao Mundial de Jovens Lideres e Empreendedores [★IO]
Federacao Nacional dos Professores [★IO]
Federacao Paulista de Aikido [IO], Sao Paulo, Brazil
Federacao Portuguesa de Aikido [IO], Carcavelos, Portugal
Federacao Portuguesa de Atletismo [IO], Linda-a-Velha, Portugal
Federacao Portuguesa de Badminton [IO], Caldas da Rainha, Portugal
Federacao Portuguesa de Danca Desportiva [IO], Lisbon, Portugal
Federacao Portuguesa de Futebol [★IO]
Federacao Portuguesa de Orientacao [★IO]
Federacao Portuguesa de Taekwondo [IO], Lisbon, Portugal
Federacao Portuguesa de Tenis [IO], Linda-a-Velha, Portugal
Federacion Andorrana de Vela [IO], Encamp, Andorra
Federacio d'Associacions de Veins d'Habitatge Social de Catalunya [★IO]
Federacion Aerea de Chile [IO], Santiago, Chile
Federacion Argentina de Beisbol [IO], Cordoba, Argentina
Federacion Argentina de Industrias Textiles [★IO]
Federacion Argentina de Medicina del Deporte [IO], Buenos Aires, Argentina
Federacion Argentina de Musica Electroacustica [IO], Buenos Aires, Argentina
Federacion Argentina de Yachting [IO], Buenos Aires, Argentina
Federacion de Asociaciones Molturadores y Refinadores de Aceites Vegetales del Reino de Espana [IO], Madrid, Spain
Federacion de Asociaciones de Productores Audiovisuales Espanoles [★IO]
Federacion Atletica de Chile [IO], Santiago, Chile
Federacion de Badminton de Chile [IO], Santiago, Chile
Federacion de Badminton de la Republica Argentina [IO], San Fernando, Argentina
Federacion de Beisbol de Chile [★IO]
Federacion Boliviana de Beisbol y Softbol [IO], Cochabamba, Bolivia
Federacion Boliviana De Tennis [IO], La Paz, Bolivia
Federacion Boliviana de Medicina Deportiva [IO], La Paz, Bolivia
Federacion Boliviana de Taekwondo [IO], Santa Cruz, Bolivia
Federacion Chilena de Baile Deportivo [IO], Santiago, Chile
Federacion Chilena de Handball [IO], Santiago, Chile
Federacion Chilena de Squash [★IO]
Federacion Chilena de Taekwondo [IO], Santiago, Chile
Federacion Colombiana de ACJs - YMCA [★IO]
Federacion Colombiana de Albergues Juveniles [★IO]
Federacion Colombiana de Deportes Aereos [IO], Bogota, Colombia
Federacion Colombiana de Squash [IO], Bogota, Colombia
Federacion Colombiana de Taekwondo [IO], Bogota, Colombia
Federacion Colombiana de Tenis [IO], Bogota, Colombia
Federacion Colombiana de Vela [IO], Bogota, Colombia

A star before a book entry number signifies that the name is not listed separately, but is mentioned within the entry.

Federacion Costarricense de Beisbol Aficionado **[IO]**, San Jose, Costa Rica

Federacion Costarricense de Tenis **[IO]**, San Jose, Costa Rica

Federacion Cuban de Taekwondo **[IO]**, Havana, Cuba

Federacion Cubana de Badminton **[IO]**, Havana, Cuba

Federacion Cubana de Beisbol **[IO]**, Havana, Cuba

Federacion Cubana de Medicina del Deporte **[IO]**, Havana, Cuba

Federacion Cubana de Tenis De Ocampo **[IO]**, Havana, Cuba

Federacion del Deporte de Orientacion de la Republica Argentina **[IO]**, Buenos Aires, Argentina

Federacion Deportiva Chilena de Aikido - Aikikai Chile **[IO]**, Santiago, Chile

Federacion Deportiva Peruana de Taekwondo **[IO]**, Lima, Peru

Federacion Dominicana de Asociaciones de Atletismo **[IO]**, Santo Domingo, Dominican Republic

Federacion Dominicana de Juego de Damas **[IO]**, Santiago, Dominican Republic

Federacion Dominicana Republica de Squash **[IO]**, Santo Domingo, Dominican Republic

Federacion Dominicana de Taekwondo **[IO]**, Santo Domingo, Dominican Republic

Federacion Dominicana de Tenis **[IO]**, Santo Domingo, Dominican Republic

Federacion Dominicana de Vela **[IO]**, Santo Domingo, Dominican Republic

Federacion Ecuatoguineana de Tenis **[★IO]**

Federacion Ecuatoriana de Badminton **[IO]**, Guayaquil, Ecuador

Federacion Ecuatoriana de Beisbol **[IO]**, Guayaquil, Ecuador

Federacion Ecuatoriana De Fisoterepia **[IO]**, Quito, Ecuador

Federacion Ecuatoriana De Squash **[IO]**, Guayaquil, Ecuador

Federacion Ecuatoriana de Exportadores **[★IO]**

Federacion Ecuatoriana de Medicina Deportiva **[IO]**, Quito, Ecuador

Federacion Ecuatoriana de Taekwondo **[IO]**, Guayaquil, Ecuador

Federacion Ecuatoriana de Tenis **[IO]**, Guayaquil, Ecuador

Federacion Ecuatoriana de Yachting **[IO]**, Guayaquil, Ecuador

Federacion Empresarial de la Industria Quimica Espanola **[IO]**, Madrid, Spain

Federacion de Ensenanza de Comisiones Obreras **[IO]**, Madrid, Spain

Federacion Equatiguineana de Taekwondo **[IO]**, Malabo, Equatorial Guinea

Federacion Espanola de Asociaciones del Dulce **[★IO]**

Federacion Espanola de Asociaciones de Espina Bifida e Hidrocefalia **[IO]**, Madrid, Spain

Federacion Espanola de Badminton **[IO]**, Madrid, Spain

Federacion Espanola de Comerciantes de Electrodomesticos **[★IO]**

Federacion Espanola de Empresas de la Confeccion **[★IO]**

Federacion Espanola de Industrias de la Alimentacion y Bebidas **[★IO]**

Federacion Espanola de Medicina del Deporte **[IO]**, Pamplona, Spain

Federacion Espanola de Taekwondo **[IO]**, Alicante, Spain

Federacion Espanola del Vino **[★IO]**

Federacion Espeleologica de Am. Latina y el Caribe **[★IO]**

Federacion Estudiantil Hispanoamericana - Address unknown since 1995.

Federacion de Gremios de Editores de Espana **[★IO]**

Federacion Hondurena de Beisbol Aficionado **[IO]**, Tegucigalpa, Honduras

Federacion Hondurena de Tenis **[IO]**, Tegucigalpa, Honduras

Federacion Hotelera del Ecuador **[★IO]**

Federacion Ibero-Latinoamericana de Cirugia Plastica y Reconstructiva **[★IO]**

Federacion Iberoamericana de Bolsas **[★IO]**

Federacion Iberoamericana del World Coun. for Gifted and Talented Children **[★IO]**

Federacion de la Industria Licorista Argentina **[★IO]**

Federacion de Industrias del Calzado Espanol **[★IO]**

Federacion Interamericana de Empresas de Seguros **[★IO]**

Federacion Interamericana de Touring y Automovil Clubes **[★IO]**

Federacion Internacional de actores **[★IO]**

Federacion Internacional de Asociaciones de Estudiantes de Medicina **[★IO]**

Federacion Internacional de Asociaciones de Profesores de Ciencias **[★IO]**

Federacion Internacional de Asociaciones Vexilologicas **[★IO]**

Federacion Internacional de Asociaciones Vexilologicas **[★11075]**

Federacion Internacional de Estudios Sobre Am. Latina y el Caribe **[★IO]**

Federacion Internacional de Hospitales **[★IO]**

Federacion Internacional de Patologia Cervical y Colposcopia **[★IO]**

Federacion Internacional de Pelota Vasca **[★IO]**

Federacion Internacional de Sociedades Psicoanaliticas **[★IO]**

Federacion Internacional de Trabajadores Sociales **[★IO]**

Federacion Intl. de Juventudes Liberales y Radicales **[★IO]**

Federacion Latinoamericana de Asociaciones de Familiares de Detenidos-Desaparecidos **[★IO]**

Federacion Latinoamericana de Bancos **[★IO]**

Federacion Latinoamericana de Ciudades, Municipios y Asociaciones **[IO]**, Quito, Ecuador

Federacion Latinoamericana de la Industria Farmaceutica **[★IO]**

Federacion Latinoamericana de Sociedades de Obesidad **[★IO]**

Federacion Medica Colombiana **[IO]**, Bogota, Colombia

Federacion Medica Venezolana **[IO]**, Caracas, Venezuela

Federacion Mexicana de Aeronautica **[IO]**, Mexico City, Mexico

Federacion Mexicana de Aikido **[IO]**, Mexico City, Mexico

Federacion Mexicana de Atletismo **[IO]**, Mexico City, Mexico

Federacion Mexicana de Beisbol **[IO]**, Mexico City, Mexico

Federacion Mexicana de Tenis **[IO]**, Mexico City, Mexico

Federacion Mexicana de Vela **[IO]**, Mexico City, Mexico

Federacion Mondiale des Organizationes des Femmes Ukrainiennes **[★IO]**

Federacion Mundial de Medicos que Respectan la Vida Humana **[★IO]**

Federacion Nacional de Arroceros **[★IO]**

Federacion Nacional de Asociaciones de la Industria de Conservas Vegetales **[★IO]**

Federacion Nacional de Badminton de Guatemala **[IO]**, Guatemala City, Guatemala

Federacion Nacional de Badminton de Honduras **[IO]**, Tegucigalpa, Honduras

Federacion Nacional de Beisbol de Guatemala **[IO]**, Guatemala City, Guatemala

Federacion Nacional de Cafeteros de Columbia **[★IO]**

Federacion Nacional de Comerciantes **[★IO]**

Federacion Nacional de Cultivadores de Cereales y Leguminosas **[IO]**, Bogota, Colombia

Federacion Nacional de Cultivadores de Cereales y Leguminosas **[★IO]**

Federacion Nacional de Cultivadores de Palma de Aceite **[★IO]**

Federacion Nacional de Empresas de Publicidad **[★IO]**

Federacion Nacional de Industrias Lacteas **[★IO]**

Federacion Nacional Taekwondo de Guatemala **[IO]**, Guatemala City, Guatemala

Federacion Nacional de Taekwondo de Honduras **[IO]**, Tegucigalpa, Honduras

Federacion Nautica de Cuba **[IO]**, Havana, Cuba

Federacion Nicaraguense de Atletismo **[IO]**, Managua, Nicaragua

Federacion Nicaraguense de Beisbol Asociada **[IO]**, Managua, Nicaragua

Federacion Nicaraguense de Taekwondo **[IO]**, Managua, Nicaragua

Federacion Nicaraguense de Tenis **[IO]**, Managua, Nicaragua

Federacion Panamena de Atletismo **[IO]**, Panama City, Panama

Federacion Panamena de Beisbol Aficionado **[IO]**, Panama City, Panama

Federacion Panamena de Tenis **[IO]**, Panama City, Panama

Federacion Panamericana de Consultores **[★IO]**

Federacion Panamericana de Lecheria **[★IO]**

Federacion Paraguaya de Atletismo **[IO]**, Asuncion, Paraguay

Federacion Paraguaya de Halterofilia **[IO]**, Lambare, Paraguay

Federacion Peruana de Atletismo **[IO]**, Lima, Peru

Federacion Peruana de Squash **[IO]**, Lima, Peru

Federacion Peruana de Vela **[★IO]**

Federacion Salvadorena de Badminton **[IO]**, San Salvador, El Salvador

Federacion Salvadorena de Beisbol **[IO]**, San Salvador, El Salvador

Federacion Salvadorena De Squash **[IO]**, San Salvador, El Salvador

Federacion Salvadorena de Paracaidismo y Aerodeportes **[IO]**, San Salvador, El Salvador

Federacion Salvadorena de Taekwondo **[IO]**, San Salvador, El Salvador

Federacion Salvadorena de Tenis **[IO]**, San Salvador, El Salvador

Federacion de Sociedades Hispanas - Defunct.

Federacion de Squash de Mexico, A.C. **[IO]**, Mexico City, Mexico

Federacion de Tenis de Chile **[IO]**, Santiago, Chile

Federacion de Tenis de Peru **[IO]**, Lima, Peru

Federacion Uruguaya de Aikido - Aikikai Uruguay **[IO]**, Montevideo, Uruguay

Federacion Uruguaya de Pesas **[IO]**, Montevideo, Uruguay

Federacion Uruguaya de Squash **[IO]**, Montevideo, Uruguay

Federacion Uruguaya de Taekwondo **[IO]**, Montevideo, Uruguay

Federacion Venezolana de Atletismo **[IO]**, Caracas, Venezuela

Federacion Venezolana de Beisbol **[IO]**, Caracas, Venezuela

Federacion Venezolana de Squash **[IO]**, Caracas, Venezuela

Federacion Venezolana de Tenis **[IO]**, Caracas, Venezuela

Federacion Venezolana de Terapeutas Ocupacionales **[IO]**, Caracas, Venezuela

Federacion Venezolana de Vela **[IO]**, Caracas, Venezuela

Fed. Administrative Law Judges Conf. **[5899]**, 2020 Pennsylvania Ave. NW, PMB 260, Washington, DC 20006, (202)675-3065

Fed. Alliance For Safe Homes **[12061]**, 1427 E Piedmont Dr., Ste. 2, Tallahassee, FL 32308, (877)221-SAFE

Fed. Assn. of Artists of the Fine Arts **[IO]**, Bonn, Germany

Fed. Assn. of the Chem. Trade **[IO]**, Vienna, Austria

Fed. Assn. of Dealers of Furniture and Interior Products **[IO]**, Vienna, Austria

Fed. Assn. of the Gem, Stone and Diamond Indus. **[IO]**, Idar-Oberstein, Germany

Fed. Assn. of German Newspaper Publishers **[IO]**, Berlin, Germany

Fed. Assn. of the German Spirits Indus. and Importers **[IO]**, Bonn, Germany

Fed. Assn. of Leather Goods, Toys and Fitness Equip. **[IO]**, Vienna, Austria

Federal Assn. of Mgt. Analysts - Defunct.

Fed. Assn. of the Radio and Elecl. Trade **[IO]**, Vienna, Austria

Fed. Assn. of Teachers of Dancing **[IO]**, Kings Langley, Australia

Fed. Assn. of the Textile Trade **[IO]**, Vienna, Austria

Reference to "IO" in place of a book number signifies that the association may be found in the 45th edition of International Organizations.

Fed. Aviation Employees; Natl. Black Coalition of [5541]

Federal Aviation Science and Technological Assn. - Defunct.

Fed. Bakers' Assn. [IO], Vienna, Austria

Fed. Bar Assn. [5492], 2011 Crystal Dr., Ste. 400, Arlington, VA 22202, (703)682-7000

Fed. Bar Assn; Found. of the [5937]

Fed. Budget; Comm. for a Responsible [18405]

Fed. Bur. of Investigation Agents Assn. [5968], PO Box 250, New Rochelle, NY 10801, (914)235-7580

Fed. Bur. of Investigation; Soc. of Former Special Agents of the [19202]

Fed. Butchers' Assn. [IO], Vienna, Austria

Fed. Chamber of Architects, Germany [IO], Berlin, Germany

Fed. Circuit Bar Assn. [5493], 1620 I St. NW, Ste. 900, Washington, DC 20006, (202)466-3923

Fed. Communications Bar Assn. [5580], 1020 19th St. NW, Ste. 325, Washington, DC 20036-6101, (202)293-4000

Fed. Communications Consulting Engineers; Assn. of [7767]

Fed. Confectionery Assn. [IO], Vienna, Austria

Fed. Consumer Info. Center Prog. [5817], 1800 F St. NW, Rm. G-142, Washington, DC 20405, (202)501-1794

Fed. Coun. of Australian Apiarists' Assn. [IO], Maryborough, Australia

Fed. Court Clerks Assn. [5626], c/o Sheryl L. Loesch, Pres., U.S. District Ct. - Middle District of Florida, 80 N Hughey Ave., Rm. 300, Orlando, FL 32801, (407)835-4222

Fed. Credit Unions; Natl. Assn. of [1115]

Fed. Criminal Investigators Assn. [5653], PO Box 23400, Washington, DC 20026, (630)969-8537

Fed. Criminal Investigators Assn. [★5653]

Federal Dental Services Officers' Assn. - Defunct.

Federal Design Coun. - Defunct.

Fed. Editors Assn. [★5583]

Fed. Educ. Assn. [24043], 1201 16th St. NW, Ste. 117, Washington, DC 20036, (202)822-7850

Fed. Educ. Prog. Administrators; Natl. Assn. of [7900]

Fed. Educ. Programs; Natl. Assn. of Administrators of State and [★7900]

Federal Education Project - Defunct.

Federal Emergency Volunteers Assn. - Address unknown since 2002.

Fed. Employee Educ. and Assistance Fund [19264], 8441 W Bowles Ave., Ste. 200, Littleton, CO 80123-9501, (303)933-7580

Federal Employees Coordinating Comm. - Defunct.

Fed. Employees; Natl. Alliance of Postal and [24167]

Fed. Employees; Natl. Fed. of [24077]

Fed. Employees Veterans Assn. [6343], PO Box 183, Merion Station, PA 19066

Fed. Employees Veterans Assn. [★24075]

Fed. Energy Bar Assn. [★5683]

Federal Excise Tax Coun. - Defunct.

Federal Executive and Professional Assn. - Defunct.

Fed. Facilities Coun. [5707], c/o Natl. Res. Coun., 500 5th St. NW, Washington, DC 20001, (202)334-3374

Federal Field Comm. for Development Planning in Alaska - Defunct.

Federal Fire Coun. - Defunct.

Fed. Food Retailing Assn. [IO], Vienna, Austria

Federal Government

Advisory Coun. on Historic Preservation [10007]
Air Mail Pioneers [21425]
Amer. Fed. of Govt. Employees [24068]
Amer. Fed. of State, County and Municipal Employees [24069]
Amer. Foreign Ser. Assn. [24070]
Amer. Postal Workers Union [24166]
Amer. Soc. of Access Professionals [5814]
Armed Forces Stamp Exchange Club [22793]
Asian Amer. Govt. Executives Network [5704]
Asian Amer. Govt. Executives Network [IO]
Associates of the Amer. Foreign Ser. Worldwide [24071]
Assn. of Civilian Technicians [24072]
Civil Ser. Employees Assn. [24073]
Coun. for Excellence in Govt. [5705]

Defense Credit Union Coun. [1108]
Diplomatic and Consular Officers, Retired [5745]
Executive Women in Govt. [5706]
Fed. Circuit Bar Assn. [5493]
Fed. Employees Veterans Assn. [6343]
Fed. Facilities Coun. [5707]
Fed. Govt. Distance Learning Assn. [8256]
Fed. Lib. and Info. Center Comm. [10356]
Fed. Managers Assn. [5708]
Fed. Physicians Assn. [15998]
Fund for Assuring an Independent Retirement [5709]
Logistics Mgt. Inst. [5607]
Natl. Active and Retired Fed. Employees Assn. [5710]
Natl. Alliance of Postal and Fed. Employees [24167]
Natl. Assn. of Fed. Veterinarians [16799]
Natl. Assn. of Govt. Employees [24075]
Natl. Assn. of Hispanic Fed. Executives [5711]
Natl. Assn. of Letter Carriers of the U.S.A. [24168]
Natl. Assn. of Postal Supervisors [24169]
Natl. Conf. of Fed. Trial Judges [5910]
Natl. Fed. of Fed. Employees [24077]
Natl. League of Postmasters of the U.S. [24170]
Natl. Legal and Policy Center [17671]
Natl. Org. of Fed. Employees Against Abuse and Retaliation [24078]
Natl. Org. of Legal Services Workers, UAW Local 2320 [24079]
Natl. Postal Mail Handlers Union [24171]
Natl. Priorities Proj. [17511]
Natl. Rural Letter Carriers' Assn. [24172]
Natl. Treasury Employees Union [24080]
NLRB Professional Assn. [24081]
Professional Managers Assn. [5712]
Senior Executives Assn. [5713]
Senior Executives Assn. Professional Development League [5714]
Southern Governors' Assn. [6287]

Fed. Govt. Accountants Assn. [★5426]

Fed. Govt. Distance Learning Assn. [8256], c/o Dee Olsen, Treas., 13894 Bently Cir., Fort Myers, FL 33912

Fed. Govt; Natl. Assn. of Supervisors; [★5708]

Fed. Govt; Soc. for History in the [10159]

Fed. Hispanic Law Enforcement Officers Assn. [5969], c/o Tom Allison, VP/Legal Advisor, 4445 Summer Oak Dr., Tampa, FL 33618, (813)390-7532

Fed. Hispanic Law Enforcement Officers Assn. [IO], Tampa, FL, United States

Fed. Info. Center Prog. [★5817]

Fed. Info. Resources Mgt; Assn. for [5815]

Fed. Interior Designers; Inst. of Bus. Designers, Coun. for [★2265]

Fed. Investigators Assn. [★5653]

Federal and Judicial Appointments Project - Defunct.

Fed. Labor and Employee Relations Professionals; Soc. of [5919]

Fed. Labor Relations Professionals; Soc. of [★5919]

Fed. Law Enforcement Agencies; Emerald Soc. of the [19199]

Fed. Law Enforcement Officers Assn. [5879], PO Box 326, Lewisberry, PA 17339, (717)938-2300

Federal Lesbians and Gays - Address unknown since 2006.

Federal Librarians Assn. - Defunct.

Federal Librarians Round Table - Defunct.

Fed. Lib. Comm. [★10356]

Fed. Lib. and Info. Center Comm. [10356], c/o The Lib. of Cong., 101 Independence Ave. SE, Adams Bldg., Rm. 217, Washington, DC 20540-4935, (202)707-4800

Federal Licensed Officers Assn. - Address unknown since 1995.

Fed. Managers Assn. [5708], 1641 Prince St., Alexandria, VA 22314-2818, (703)683-8700

Federal Music Soc. - Defunct.

Fed. Natl. Assn. of the German Brick Indus. [★IO]

Fed. Natl. Assn. of the German Brick and Tile Indus. [IO], Bonn, Germany

Fed. Physicians Assn. [15998], 12427 Hedges Run Dr., Ste. 104, Lake Ridge, VA 22192, (703)323-9888

Fed. Plant Quarantine Inspectors Natl. Assn. [★5437]

Fed. Power Bar Assn. [★5683]

Federal Probation and Pretrial Officers Assn. - Address unknown since 1995.

Fed. Prog. Administrators; Natl. Assn. of [★7900]

Federal Publishers Comm. [5581]

Federal Radiation Coun. - Defunct.

Federal Relations; Office of State- [★6283]

Federal Reserve

Liberty Services [17666]

Fed. Reserve Act and the Internal Revenue Code; Natl. Org. for the Repeal of the [★17666]

Federal Reserve Act; Natl. Comm. to Repeal the [18410]

Fed. Ser. Campaign for Natl. Hea. Agencies; Natl. Comm. of the [★12200]

Fed. Services; Gower [★6141]

Fed. Services; Gower [★IO]

Federal Services Podiatric Medical Assn. - Address unknown since 1990.

Fed. Statistics; Coun. of Professional Associations on [5816]

Federal Statistics Users' Conf. - Defunct.

Fed. Superannuates Natl. Assn. [IO], Ottawa, ON, Canada

Federal Timber Purchasing Assn. - Defunct.

Fed. Trial Examiners Conf. [★5899]

Fed. Trial Judges; Natl. Conf. of [5910]

Fed. Union [★18308]

Fed. Union [★IO]

Fed. Union of European Nationalities [IO], Flensburg, Germany

Fed. Veterinarians; Natl. Assn. of [16799]

Federal Water Quality Assn. - Address unknown since 1990.

Federal Women's Interagency Bd. - Address unknown since 1995.

Federal Women's Program - Defunct.

Federalism and Democracy; Ashburn Inst. for Global Stud. in [18308]

Federalist Caucus - Defunct.

Federalist Soc. for Law and Public Policy Stud. [5900], 1015 18th St. NW, Ste. 425, Washington, DC 20036, (202)822-8138

Federally Donated Food Program [★4302]

Federally Employed Women [17531], 1666 K St. NW, Ste. 440, Washington, DC 20006, (202)898-0994

Federally Impacted Schools; Natl. Assn. of [8349]

Federally Licensed Firearms Dealers; Natl. Assn. of [1478]

Federasi Aero Sport Indonesia [IO], Jakarta, Indonesia

Federasie van Afrikaanse Kultuurvereniginge [★IO]

Federated Ambulatory Surgery Assn. [16582], 1012 Cameron St., Alexandria, VA 22314, (703)836-8808

Federated Coun. of Beth Jacob Schools [8691]

Federated Coun. of Israel Institutions - Address unknown since 2003.

Federated Craft; Natl. [19244]

Federated Employers [★2494]

Federated Estonian Women's Clubs [★18981]

Federated Estonian Women's Clubs [★IO]

Federated Farmers of New Zealand [IO], Wellington, New Zealand

Federated Farmers of New Zealand - Women's Div. [★IO]

Federated Fishing Boats of New England and New York - Address unknown since 1995.

Federated Funeral Directors of Am. [2778], PO Box 19244, Springfield, IL 62794-9244, (217)525-1712

Federated Hospitality Assn. of South Africa [IO], Bryanston, Republic of South Africa

Federated Mountain Clubs of New Zealand [IO], Wellington, New Zealand

Federated Norwegian Lutheran Young People's Societies of America [★20225]

Federated Pecan Growers' Assns. of the U.S. - Defunct.

Federated Russian Orthodox Clubs [★20542]

Federated States of Micronesia Athletic Assn. [IO], Palikir, Federated States of Micronesia

Federated States of Micronesia Lawn Tennis Assn. [IO], Palikir, Federated States of Micronesia

A star before a book entry number signifies that the name is not listed separately, but is mentioned within the entry.

Federated States of Micronesia Natl. Olympic Comm. **[IO]**, Palikir, Federated States of Micronesia

Federated States of Micronesia Weightlifting Assn. **[IO]**, Palikir, Federated States of Micronesia

Federated Women in Timber - Address unknown since 2002.

Federated Women's Institutes of Canada **[IO]**, St. George, ON, Canada

Federated Workers Union **[★IO]**

Federatia de Aeromodelism din Republica Moldova **[IO]**, Chisinau, Moldova

Federatia de Atletism din Republica Moldova **[IO]**, Chisinau, Moldova

Federatia Educatiei Nationale **[★IO]**

Federatia Romana de Atletism **[IO]**, Bucharest, Romania

Federatia Romana de Badminton **[★IO]**

Federatia Romana de Baseball si Softbol **[★IO]**

Federatia Romana de Patinaj **[★IO]**

Federatia Romana de Taekwondo **[★IO]**

Federatia Romana de Tennis **[IO]**, Bucharest, Romania

Federatia YMCA Romania **[★IO]**

Federatie van het Belgisch Vlees **[IO]**, Brussels, Belgium

Federatie van de Belgische Magazines **[★IO]**

Federatie Filmbelangen **[★IO]**

Federatie Nederlandse Gehandicaptenraad **[★IO]**

Federatie van Organisaties in het Bibliotheek-, Informatie-, en Documentatiewezen **[★IO]**

Federatie van Ouders van Dove Kinderen **[IO]**, Utrecht, Netherlands

Fed. europeenne de biotechnologie **[★IO]**

Fed. des societes africaines de biochimie et de biologie moleculaire **[★IO]**

Fed. canadienne des societes de biologie **[★IO]**

Fed. for Accessible Nursing Educ. and Licensure **[15478]**, PO Box 1418, Lewisburg, WV 24901, (304)645-4357

Fed. of Active Retirement Assn. **[IO]**, Dublin, Ireland

Fed. Aeronautique Internationale **[IO]**, Lausanne, Switzerland

Fed. Aeronautique Luxembourgeoise **[IO]**, Luxembourg, Luxembourg

Fed. of Aerospace Enterprises in Ireland **[IO]**, Dublin, Ireland

Fed. of African Natl. Insurance Companies **[IO]**, Dakar, Senegal

Fed. of African Societies of Biochemistry and Molecular Biology **[IO]**, Cape Town, Republic of South Africa

Fed. of Afrikaans Cultural Societies **[IO]**, Brooklyn, Republic of South Africa

Fed. Against Copyright Theft **[IO]**, London, United Kingdom

Fed. Against Software Theft **[IO]**, Maidenhead, United Kingdom

Fed. Albanaise de Handball **[IO]**, Tirana, Albania

Fed. of Alberta Naturalists **[IO]**, Edmonton, AB, Canada

Fed. Algerienne du Sport Scolaire **[IO]**, Algiers, Algeria

Fed. Algerienne de Voile **[IO]**, Algiers, Algeria

Federation of Alpine and Schuhplattler Clubs in North America **[IO]**, Pewaukee, WI, United States

Fed. of Alpine and Schuhplattler Clubs in North Am. **[9627]**, N21 W26682 Cattail Ct., Pewaukee, WI 53072, (262)695-2112

Fed. for Amer. Afghan Action - Address unknown since 1995.

Fed. of Amer. Aquarium Societies **[7173]**, c/o Pat Smith, Membership Chm., 109 Bucknell Rd., West Sayville, NY 11796, (217)359-6707

Fed. of Amer. Arab Orgs. - Address unknown since 1985.

Fed. of Amer. Consumers and Travelers **[13342]**, PO Box 104, Edwardsville, IL 62025, (618)656-0454

Fed. of Amer. Controlled Shipping - Address unknown since 2003.

Fed. of Amer. Cultural and Language Communities - Address unknown since 1995.

Fed. of Amer. Hea. Systems **[★14881]**

Fed. of Amer. Hospitals **[14881]**, 801 Pennsylvania Ave. NW, Ste. 245, Washington, DC 20004-2604, (202)624-1500

Fed. for Amer. Immigration Reform **[17805]**, 1666 Connecticut Ave. NW, Ste. 400, Washington, DC 20009, (202)328-7004

Federation for American Immigration Reform **[IO]**, Washington, DC, United States

Fed. of Amer. Scientists **[18445]**, 1717 K St. NW, Ste. 209, Washington, DC 20036, (202)546-3300

Federation of Amer. Scientists Fund **[★18445]**

Fed. of Amer. Societies for Experimental Biology **[6576]**, 9650 Rockville Pike, Bethesda, MD 20814, (301)634-7000

Fed. for the Amer. Staffordshire Terrier **[21518]**, c/o Leri Hanson, 619 W 35th St., Long Beach, CA 90806, (562)427-2259

Fed. of Amer. Women's Clubs in Europe **[★IO]**

Fed. of Amer. Women's Clubs Overseas **[IO]**, Lyngby, Denmark

Fed. of Amer. Zionists **[★20201]**

Fed. of Analytical Chemistry and Spectroscopy Societies **[6682]**, PO Box 24379, Santa Fe, NM 87502, (505)820-1648

Fed. Andorrana de Taekwondo **[IO]**, Andorra la Vella, Andorra

Fed. of Animal Sci. Societies **[4151]**, 1111 N Dunlap Ave., Savoy, IL 61874, (217)356-3182

Fed. of Apparel Mfrs. - Address unknown since 1994.

Fed. des Architectes Suisses **[★IO]**

Fed. of Argentine Textile Indus. **[IO]**, Buenos Aires, Argentina

Fed. of Army Wives **[★IO]**

Fed. of Artistic Roller Skating **[IO]**, Thatcham, United Kingdom

Fed. of ASEAN Shipowners' Associations **[IO]**, Singapore, Singapore

Fed. of Asian Chem. Societies **[IO]**, Seoul, Republic of Korea

Fed. of Asian and Oceanian Biochemists and Molecular Biologists **[IO]**, Tokyo, Japan

Fed. of Asian, Pacific and African Risk Mgt. Organisations **[IO]**, Brisbane, Australia

Fed. of Asian Sci. Academies and Societies - Malaysia **[IO]**, Kuala Lumpur, Malaysia

Fed. des Associations de Chasse et Conservation de la Faune Sauvage de l'U.E. **[★IO]**

Fed. des Associations Europeennes des Constructeurs de Fenetres et de Facades **[★IO]**

Fed. des Associations Europeennes et Internationales etablies en Belgique **[★IO]**

Fed. des Associations Europeennes de Mousse de Polyurethane Rigide **[★IO]**

Fed. of Associations of Former Intl. Civil Servants **[IO]**, Geneva, Switzerland

Fed. of Associations of Ghanaian Exporters **[IO]**, Accra, Ghana

Fed. of Associations of Hea. Regulatory Boards **[★14555]**

Fed. of Associations for Hunting and Conservation of the E.U. **[IO]**, Brussels, Belgium

Fed. of Associations of Periodical Publishers in the EC **[★IO]**

Fed. of Associations of Regulatory Boards **[14555]**, 1603 Orrington Ave., Ste. 2080, Evanston, IL 60201, (847)328-7909

Fed. of the Associations of Technicians of the Paint, Varnish, Enamel, and Printing Ink Indus. of Continental Europe **[IO]**, Paris, France

Fed. of Astronomical and Geophysical Data Anal. Services **[IO]**, Copenhagen, Denmark

Fed. of Astronomical Societies **[IO]**, Birmingham, United Kingdom

Fed. of AT&T Global Information Solutions User Groups - Address unknown since 1999.

Fed. of Atomic Scientists **[★18445]**

Fed. des Auberges de Jeunesse de l'Union Europeenne **[★IO]**

Fed. of Australia-Japan Societies **[IO]**, Royal Exchange, Australia

Fed. of Australian Astrologers **[IO]**, Waterford, Australia

Fed. of Australian Commercial TV Stations **[★IO]**

Fed. of Australian Radio Broadcasters **[★IO]**

Fed. of Australian Sci. and Technological Societies **[IO]**, Canberra, Australia

Fed. of Automated Coding Technologies - Defunct.

Fed. of Auto. Distributors **[IO]**, Paris, France

Fed. of Bakers **[IO]**, London, United Kingdom

Fed. Bancaire de l'Union Europeenne **[★IO]**

Fed. of Bangladesh Chambers of Commerce and Indus. **[IO]**, Dhaka, Bangladesh

Fed. of Bankers Associations of Japan **[★IO]**

Fed. of Baseball of Chile **[IO]**, Santiago, Chile

Fed. of Baseball Malaysia **[IO]**, Kuala Lumpur, Malaysia

Fed. Baseball Softball Ukraine **[IO]**, Kiev, Ukraine

Fed. of BC Writers **[IO]**, Vancouver, BC, Canada

Fed. of Behavioral, Psychological, and Cognitive Sciences **[6530]**, 750 1st St. NE, 9th Fl., Washington, DC 20002, (202)336-5920

Fed. Belge des entreprises de distribution **[★IO]**

Fed. Belge des Exploitants d'Autobus et d'Autocars et des Organisateurs de Voyages **[★IO]**

Fed. Belge des Femmes Diplomees des Universites **[★IO]**

Fed. Belge de la Franchise **[★IO]**

Fed. Belge de l'Industrie de la Chaussure **[★IO]**

Fed. Belge des Magazines **[IO]**, Brussels, Belgium

Fed. Belge de Musique Electroacoustique **[IO]**, Brussels, Belgium

Fed. Belge des Negociants en Combustibles et Carburants **[★IO]**

Fed. Belge des Psychologues **[★IO]**

Fed. Belge de Tir aux Clays **[★IO]**

Fed. Belge de la Viande **[★IO]**

Fed. of Belgian Chambers of Commerce Abroad **[★IO]**

Fed. of the Belgian Chem. Indus. **[IO]**, Brussels, Belgium

Fed. of the Belgian Textile Indus. **[IO]**, Brussels, Belgium

Fed. Beninoise d'Athletisme Amateur **[IO]**, Cotonou, Benin

Fed. Beninoise de Lawn Tennis **[IO]**, Cotonou, Benin

Fed. Beninoise de Taekwondo **[IO]**, Cotonou, Benin

Fed. des Brasseurs Luxembourgeois **[IO]**, Luxembourg, Luxembourg

Fed. of British Artists **[IO]**, London, United Kingdom

Fed. of British Detectives **[★IO]**

Fed. of British Engineers' Tool Manufacturers **[IO]**, Sheffield, United Kingdom

Fed. of British Hand Tool Mfrs. **[IO]**, Sheffield, United Kingdom

Fed. of British Historic Vehicle Clubs **[IO]**, Taunton, United Kingdom

Fed. of Buddhist Women's Associations; Buddhist Churches of Am. **[19543]**

Fed. of Bulgarian Alpine Clubs **[IO]**, Sofia, Bulgaria

Fed. Burkinabe De Tennis **[IO]**, Ouagadougou, Burkina Faso

Fed. Burkinabe de Handball **[IO]**, Ouagadougou, Burkina Faso

Fed. Burkinabe du Jeu de Dames **[IO]**, Ouagadougou, Burkina Faso

Fed. Burkinabe de Taekwondo **[IO]**, Ouagadougou, Burkina Faso

Fed. Burundaise de Handball **[IO]**, Bujumbura, Burundi

Fed. of Cambodian Assns. in North America - Defunct.

Fed. Camerounaise Des Danses Sportives et Assimile **[IO]**, Yaounde, Cameroon

Fed. Camerounaise de Handball **[IO]**, Yaounde, Cameroon

Fed. Camerounaise de Jeu de Dames **[IO]**, Yaounde, Cameroon

Fed. Camerounaise de Taekwondo **[IO]**, Yaounde, Cameroon

Fed. Camerounaise de Tennis **[IO]**, Yaounde, Cameroon

Fed. of Canadian Archers **[IO]**, Ottawa, ON, Canada

Fed. of Canadian Music Festivals **[IO]**, Winnipeg, MB, Canada

Fed. of Canadian Naturalists **[★IO]**

Fed. Canadienne pour la sante sexuelle **[★IO]**

Fed. Canadienne des Amis de Musees **[★IO]**

Fed. Canadienne des Archers **[★IO]**

Fed. Canadienne des Associations Foyer-Ecole **[★IO]**

Fed. Canadienne de Ballon sur Glace **[★IO]**

Fed. Canadienne de Baton Sportif **[★IO]**

Reference to "IO" in place of a book number signifies that the association may be found in the 45th edition of International Organizations.

Fed. Canadienne du Civisme [★IO]
Fed. Canadienne de Course d'Orientation [★IO]
Fed. Canadienne Des Doyens Des Ecoles D'Administration [★IO]
Fed. Canadienne d'Escrime [★IO]
Fed. Canadienne des Dix-Quilles [★IO]
Fed. Canadienne des Enseignantes et des Enseignants [★IO]
Fed. Canadienne des Epiciers Independants [★IO]
Fed. Canadienne des Etudiantes et Etudiants [★IO]
Fed. Canadienne de la Faune [★IO]
Fed. Canadienne des Femmes Diplomees des Universites [★IO]
Fed. Canadienne des Gemmes et des Mineraux [★IO]
Fed. Canadienne de Handball Olympique [★IO]
Fed. Canadienne des Infirmieres et Infirmiers en Sante Mentale [★IO]
Fed. Canadienne des Jeunes Ligues [★IO]
Fed. Canadienne de Kendo [★IO]
Fed. Canadienne de l'Entreprise Independante [★IO]
Fed. Canadienne des Metiers d'Art [★IO]
Fed. Canadienne du Mouton [★IO]
Fed. Canadienne Nationale des Syndicats Independants [★IO]
Fed. Canadienne des Professeurs de Musique [★IO]
Fed. Canadienne des Sci. Humanies et Sociales [★IO]
Fed. Canadienne des Services de Garde a l'Enfance [★IO]
Fed. Canadienne du Sport Scolaire [★IO]
Fed. Canadienne des Syndicats d'Infirmieres et Infirmiers [★IO]
Fed. of Cash Grain Commn. Merchants Assns. - Defunct.
Fed. of Catholic Scouts [IO], Brussels, Belgium
Fed. Catholique des Scouts [★IO]
Fed. Centrafricaine Taekwondo [IO], Bangui, Central African Republic
Fed. Centrafricaine de Handball [IO], Bangui, Central African Republic
Fed. Centrafricaine Handisports [IO], Bangui, Central African Republic
Fed. Centrafricaine de Tennis [IO], Bangui, Central African Republic
Fed. of Chambers of Commerce and Indus. of Belgium [IO], Brussels, Belgium
Fed. of Chambers of Commerce and Indus. of Sri Lanka [IO], Colombo, Sri Lanka
Fed. des Chambres de Commerce et D'Industrie de Belgique [★IO]
Fed. for Children with Special Needs [12569], 1135 Tremont St., Ste. 420, Boston, MA 02120, (617)236-7210
Fed. of Children's Book Groups [IO], Leeds, United Kingdom
Fed. of Chinese Amer. and Chinese Canadian Medical Societies [IO], San Francisco, CA, United States
Fed. of Chinese Amer. and Chinese Canadian Medical Societies [13985], c/o Chinese Hosp., 835 Jackson St., Ste. 304, San Francisco, CA 94133, (415)421-4240
Fed. of Chiropractic Licensing Boards [14000], 5401 W 10th St., Ste. 101, Greeley, CO 80634-4400, (970)356-3500
Federation of Chiropractic Licensing Boards [IO], Greeley, CO, United States
Fed. of City Farms and Community Gardens [IO], Bristol, United Kingdom
Fed. of Citywide Block Assns. - Defunct.
Fed. of Clinical Immunology Societies [14935], 11950 W Lake Park Dr., Ste. 320, Milwaukee, WI 53224, (414)359-1670
Fed. of Clothing Designers and Executives [IO], London, United Kingdom
Fed. of Cocoa Commerce [IO], London, United Kingdom
Fed. of Coffee Organisations [IO], Mexico City, Mexico
Fed. du Commerce des Cacaos [★IO]
Fed. of Commercial Audio Visual Libraries Intl. [★IO]
Fed. of Commun. Services [IO], Beckenham, United Kingdom

Fed. Comorienne d'Halterophilie [IO], Moroni, Comoros
Fed. of Computer Users in the Medical Sciences - Address unknown since 1990.
Fed. Congolaise d'Athletisme [IO], Brazzaville, Republic of the Congo
Fed. Congolaise Democratique de Lawn Tennis [IO], Kinshasa, Democratic Republic of the Congo
Fed. Congolaise de Handball [IO], Brazzaville, Republic of the Congo
Fed. Congolaise de Lawn Tennis [IO], Brazzaville, Democratic Republic of the Congo
Fed. Congolaise de Taekwondo [IO], Brazzaville, Republic of the Congo
Fed. for Constitutional Govt. - Defunct.
Fed. Constr. Coun. [★5707]
Fed. for Continuing Educ. in Tertiary Institutions [IO], Hong Kong, People's Republic of China
Fed. Coun. - Defunct.
Fed. of Crafts and Commerce [IO], Waterlooville, United Kingdom
Fed. Culinaire Canadienne [★IO]
Fed. Culinaire Canadienne Saskatoon Br. [★IO]
Fed. Cynologique Internationale [★IO]
Fed. of Dance Sport South Africa [IO], Durban, Republic of South Africa
Fed. of Danish Architects [IO], Copenhagen, Denmark
Fed. of Danish Investment Associations [IO], Copenhagen, Denmark
Fed. of Danish Painting Contractors [IO], Copenhagen, Denmark
Fed. of Danish Textile and Clothing [IO], Herning, Denmark
Fed. d'Associations de Techniciens des Indus. des Peintures, Vernis, Emaux et Encres d'Imprimerie de l'Europe Continentale [★IO]
Fed. d'Athletisme du Burundi [IO], Bujumbura, Burundi
Fed. d'Athletisme Mauritanie [IO], Nouakchott, Mauritania
Fed. of Defense and Corporate Counsel [5827], 11812 N 56th St., Tampa, FL 33617, (813)983-0022
Federation of Defense and Corporate Counsel Foundation [★5827]
Fed. of Dental Diagnostic Sciences - Defunct.
Fed. Des Grandes Tours Du Monde [★IO]
Fed. Des Minerais, Mineraux Industriels Et Metaux Non Ferreux [IO], Paris, France
Fed. of Digestive Disease Societies - Defunct.
Fed. of Dining Room Professionals [3393], 1417 Sadler Rd., No. 100, Fernandina Beach, FL 32034, (904)491-6690
Federation of Dining Room Professionals [IO], Fernandina Beach, FL, United States
Fed. of Diocesan Liturgical Commissions [19623], 415 Michigan Ave. NE, Ste. 70, Washington, DC 20017, (202)635-6990
Fed. of Distribution Companies [IO], Milan, Italy
Fed. of Distribution and Retailing Companies [IO], Paris, France
Fed. Djiboutienne de Tennis [IO], Djibouti, Djibouti
Fed. of Drug and Alcohol Professionals [IO], London, United Kingdom
Fed. of East European Family History Societies [★IO]
Fed. of East European Family History Societies [★21112]
Fed. of East European Family History Societies [19068], PO Box 510898, Salt Lake City, UT 84151-0898
Fed. of Eastern Stars - Address unknown since 2001.
Fed. of Eastern Stars of the World - Address unknown since 2001.
Fed. des Editeurs Europeens [★IO]
Fed. of Egalitarian Communities [11746], c/o FEC Sec., 2 Dancing Rabbit Ln., Rutledge, MO 63563, (206)324-6822
Fed. des Eglises Evangeliques Baptistes de France [IO], Paris, France
Fed. of Egyptian Chambers of Commerce [IO], Cairo, Egypt
Fed. of Employee Benefit Assn. [★1234]

Fed. des Employeurs Europeens [★IO]
Fed. Employment and Guidance Ser. [★12075]
Fed. of Engine Re-Manufacturers [IO], Plymouth, United Kingdom
Fed. des Entreprises du Commerce et de la Distribution [★IO]
Fed. des Entreprises Industrielles et Commerciales Internationales de la Mecanique et de l'Electronique [★IO]
Fed. of Environmental Citizens Organisations [★IO]
Fed. of Environmental Technologists [5090], 9451 N 107th St., Milwaukee, WI 53224, (414)354-0070
Fed. of Environmental Trade Associations [IO], Reading, United Kingdom
Fed. Equestre Internationale [★IO]
Fed. of the Estonian Chem. Indus. [IO], Tallinn, Estonia
Fed. of Estonian Engg. Indus. [IO], Tallinn, Estonia
Fed. of Estonian Student Unions [IO], Tallinn, Estonia
Fed. of Estonian Universitas [IO], Tallinn, Estonia
Fed. des Etablissements d'Enseignment Prives [IO], Montreal, QC, Canada
Fed. des Etudiant(e)s Francophones [IO], Brussels, Belgium
Fed. des Etudiants et des Etudiantes en Medecine du Canada [★IO]
Fed. of Euro-Asian Stock Exchanges [IO], Istanbul, Turkey
Fed. of European Accountants [★IO]
Fed. of European Aquaculture Producers [IO], Boncelles, Belgium
Fed. of European Associations of Paediatric Anaesthesia [IO], Warsaw, Poland
Fed. of European Biochemical Societies [IO], Copenhagen, Denmark
Fed. of European Cancer Societies [IO], Brussels, Belgium
Fed. of European Chem. Societies - England [★IO]
Fed. of European Companion Animal Veterinary Associations [IO], Oslo, Norway
Fed. of the European Cutlery, Flatware, Holloware, and Cookware Indus. [IO], Solingen, Germany
Fed. of the European Cutlery and Flatware Indus. [★IO]
Fed. of the European Dental Indus. [IO], Cologne, Germany
Fed. of European Direct and Interactive Marketing [IO], Brussels, Belgium
Fed. of European Direct Marketing [★IO]
Fed. of European Direct Selling Associations [IO], Brussels, Belgium
Fed. of European Employers [IO], London, United Kingdom
Fed. of European Ergonomics Soc. [IO], Bedford, United Kingdom
Fed. of European Explosive Mfrs. [IO], Brussels, Belgium
Fed. of European Food Additives, Food Enzymes and Food Cultures Indus. [IO], Brussels, Belgium
Fed. of European Food Additives and Food Enzymes Indus. [★IO]
Fed. of European Heating and Air Conditioning Associations [IO], Brussels, Belgium
Fed. of European and Intl. Associations Established in Belgium [IO], Brussels, Belgium
Fed. of European Lab. Animal Sci. Associations [IO], Tamworth, United Kingdom
Fed. of European Materials Societies [IO], London, United Kingdom
Fed. of European Microbiological Societies [IO], Delft, Netherlands
Fed. of European Neuroscience Societies - Milan [IO], Kuopio, Finland
Fed. of European Nurses in Diabetes [IO], London, United Kingdom
Fed. of European Pharmacological Societies [IO], Manchester, United Kingdom
Fed. of European Philatelic Associations [IO], Lisbon, Portugal
Fed. of European Physiological Societies [IO], Copenhagen, Denmark
Fed. of European Physiological Societies [IO], Maastricht, Netherlands
Fed. of European Private Port Operators [IO], Brussels, Belgium

A star before a book entry number signifies that the name is not listed separately, but is mentioned within the entry.

Fed. of European Producers of Abrasives [IO], Paris, France

Fed. of European Professional Photographers [IO], Rome, Italy

Fed. of European Publishers [IO], Brussels, Belgium

Fed. of European Rigid Polyurethane Foam Associations [IO], Brussels, Belgium

Fed. of European Risk Mgt. Associations [IO], Brussels, Belgium

Fed. of European Rope, Twine and Netting Indus. [IO], Paris, France

Fed. of European Securities Exchanges [IO], Brussels, Belgium

Fed. of European Societies of Plant Biology [IO], Heraklion, Greece

Fed. of European Societies of Plant Physiology [★IO]

Fed. of European Societies for Surgery of the Hand [IO], Barcelona, Spain

Fed. of European Societies of Toxicology [★IO]

Fed. of European Societies for Tropical Medicine and Intl. Hea. [IO], Hamburg, Germany

Fed. of the European Sporting Goods Indus. [IO], Brussels, Belgium

Fed. of European Wholesale and Intl. Trade Associations [★IO]

Fed. of European Window and Curtain Wall Mfrs. Associations [IO], Milan, Italy

Fed. of European Window Mfr. Associations [★IO]

Fed. Europeenae de la Diaconie [★IO]

Fed. Europeene des Associations de Fabricants de Serrures et de Ferrures [★IO]

Fed. Europeene des Associations de Specialistes en Orthodontie [★IO]

Fed. Europeene de Baseball [★IO]

Fed. Europeene des Indus. de Colles et Adhesifs [★IO]

Fed. Europeene pour l'Art Populaire et l'Artisanat [★IO]

Fed. Europeene de l'Industrie des Aliments pour Animaux Familiers [★IO]

Fed. Europeene de la Recuperation et du Recyclage des Ferrailles [★IO]

Fed. Europeene des Unions Professionnelles d'Experts en Dammages apres Incendie et Risques Divers [★IO]

Fed. Europeenne des Activites du Dechet et de l'Environnement [★IO]

Fed. Europeenne des Aerosols [★IO]

Fed. Europeenne des Associations de Conseils en Org. [★IO]

Fed. Europeenne des Associations de Dieteticiens [★IO]

Fed. Europeenne des Associations de l'Industrie Pharmaceutique [★IO]

Fed. Europeenne des Associations de Torrefacteurs de Cafe [★IO]

Fed. Europeenne des Associations de Vente Directe [★IO]

Fed. Europeenne des Chemins de Fer Touristique et Historiques [★IO]

Fed. Europeenne du Commerce Chimique [★IO]

Fed. Europeenne du Commerce de Produits Surgeles [★IO]

Fed. Europeenne de la Corrosion [★IO]

Fed. Europeenne de la Coutellerie, Orfevrerie, Couverts de Table et Articles Culinaires [★IO]

Fed. Europeenne des Cyclistes [★IO]

Fed. Europeenne d'Associations Nationales d'Ingenieurs [★IO]

Fed. Europeenne d'Associations Nationales Travaillant avec les Sans-Abri [★IO]

Fed. Europeenne d'Editeurs de Periodiques [★IO]

Fed. Europeenne Des Associations De Brules [★IO]

Fed. Europeenne des Fabricants de Carton Ondule [★IO]

Fed. Europeenne des Fabricants d'Adjuvants pour la Nutrition Animale [★IO]

Fed. Europeenne des Fabricants d'Aliments Composes [★IO]

Fed. Europeenne des Fabricants de Palettes et Emballages en Bois [★IO]

Fed. Europeenne des Fabricants de Produits Abrasifs [★IO]

Fed. Europeenne des Fabricants des Tuiles et de Briques [★IO]

Fed. Europeenne des Geologues [★IO]

Fed. Europeenne des Greffes du Coeur et du Poumon [★IO]

Fed. Europeenne des Indus. de Ficellerie Corderie et Filets [★IO]

Fed. Europeenne des Jeunes Chorales [★IO]

Fed. Europeenne des Jeunesse Bons Templiers [★IO]

Fed. Europeenne de l'Industrie du Contreplaque [★IO]

Fed. Europeenne des Mandataires de l'Industrie en Propriete Industrielle [★IO]

Fed. Europeenne de la Manutention [★IO]

Fed. Europeenne des Medecins Salaries [★IO]

Fed. Europeenne des Metallurgistes [★IO]

Fed. Europeenne des Personnes Agees [★IO]

Fed. Europeenne de Psychanalyse [★IO]

Fed. Europeenne des Societes de Cytologie [★IO]

Fed. Europeenne des Syndicats d'Entreprises d'Isolation [★IO]

Fed. Europeenne pour le Transport et l'Environment [★IO]

Fed. Europeenne des Unions Professionnelles de Fleuristes [★IO]

Fed. Europeenne du Verre d'Emballage [★IO]

Fed. Europeenne des Victimes de la Route [★IO]

Fed. Europeenne de Zootechnie [★IO]

Fed. of Exchange Accommodators [3717], 100 N 20th St., 4th Fl., Philadelphia, PA 19103-1443, (215)320-3881

Fed. des Experts Comptables Europeens [★IO]

Fed. of Families for Children's Mental Hea. [12550], 9605 Medical Center Dr., Ste. 280, Rockville, MD 20850, (240)403-1901

Fed. of Family History Societies [IO], Coventry, United Kingdom

Fed. of Family Planning Associations of Malaysia [IO], Petaling Jaya, Malaysia

Fed. Feminine Franco-Americaine [★19063]

Fed. of Feminist Women's Health Centers - Address unknown since 2001.

Fed. des Femmes Chinoises [★IO]

Fed. of Field Sports Associations of the EU [★IO]

Fed. of Finnish Commerce and Trade [IO], Helsinki, Finland

Fed. of Finnish Fisheries Associations [IO], Helsinki, Finland

Fed. of Finnish Fisheries Associations [IO], Helsinki, Finland

Fed. of Finnish Insurance Companies [IO], Helsinki, Finland

Fed. of Finnish Textile and Clothing Indus. [IO], Tampere, Finland

Fed. of Fire Chaplains [19747], 185 County Rd., No. 1602, Clifton, TX 76634, (254)622-8514

Fed. of Floorball of Russia [IO], Moscow, Russia

Fed. of Fly Fishermen [★IO]

Fed. of Fly Fishermen [★23413]

Fed. of Fly Fishers [23413], 215 E Lewis St., Livingston, MT 59047, (406)222-9369

Federation of Fly Fishers [IO], Livingston, MT, United States

Fed. Flying Disc France [IO], Versailles, France

Fed. de la Fonction Publique Europeenne [★IO]

Fed. of Food Indus. [IO], Brussels, Belgium

Fed. of Former Jewish Fighters - Address unknown since 2006.

Fed. Francaise Amateur de Mineralogie et Paleontologie [★IO]

Fed. Francaise de Baseball, Softball and Cricket [IO], Paris, France

Fed. Francaise du Batiment [★IO]

Fed. Francaise de Course d'Orientation [★IO]

Fed. Francaise de la Couture, du Pret-a-Porter des Couturiers et des Createurs de Mode [★IO]

Fed. Francaise d'Aikido, d'Aikibudo et Affinitaires [IO], Paris, France

Fed. Francaise de la Franchise [★IO]

Fed. Francaise des Indus. Jouet et Puericulture [★IO]

Fed. Francaise des Indus. Lainiere et Cotonniere [★IO]

Fed. Francaise des Indus. du Sport et des Loisirs [★IO]

Fed. Francaise de la Lingerie et du Balneaire [★IO]

Fed. Francaise des Masseurs Kinesitherapeutes Reeducateurs [IO], Paris, France

Fed. Francaise des Mouvements et Services Feminins [IO], Paris, France

Fed. Francaise du Pret-a-Porter Feminin [★IO]

Fed. Francaise des Societes d'Assurances [★IO]

Fed. Francaise des Spiritueux [★IO]

Fed. Francaise du Sport Auto. [IO], Paris, France

Fed. Francaise de Squash [IO], St. Maur des Fosses, France

Fed. Francaise de Taekwondo et Disciplines Associees [IO], Lyon, France

Fed. Francaise de Tennis [IO], Paris, France

Fed. Francaise de Voile [IO], Paris, France

Fed. Francaise de Voile [★IO]

Fed. of Franco-Amer. Genealogical and Historical Societies - Defunct.

Fed. Francophone Belge pour le Planning Familial et l'Education Sexuelle [★IO]

Fed. of Freight Forwarders' Assn. in India [IO], Bombay, India

Fed. of French Amer. Women [19063]

Fed. of French Ladies' Fashion [IO], Paris, France

Fed. of French Maltsters [IO], Paris, France

Fed. of French War Veterans [21416], Grand Central Sta., New York, NY 10017, (212)213-0812

Fed. Gabonaise d'Athletisme [IO], Libreville, Gabon

Fed. Gabonaise du Sport Scolaire [IO], Libreville, Gabon

Fed. Gabonaise de Taekwondo [IO], Libreville, Gabon

Fed. Gabonaise de Tennis [IO], Libreville, Gabon

Fed. of Galaxy Explorers [9136], 12609 Springloch Ct., Silver Spring, MD 20904, (877)761-1266

Fed. for the Gardening Trades [IO], Paris, France

Fed. of Gay Games [IO], San Francisco, CA, United States

Fed. of Gay Games [23818], 584 Castro St., Ste. 343, San Francisco, CA 94114, (415)695-0222

Fed. of Genealogical Societies [21116], PO Box 200940, Austin, TX 78720-0940, (512)336-2731

Fed. of German Catholic Youth [IO], Dusseldorf, Germany

Fed. of the German Export Trade [IO], Berlin, Germany

Fed. of German Indus. [IO], Berlin, Germany

Fed. of German Indus. [★IO]

Fed. of German Indus. [★762]

Fed. of German Landscape Architects [IO], Berlin, Germany

Fed. of the German Motor Indus. [★IO]

Fed. of Ghana Indus. [★IO]

Fed. of the Glass Indus. [IO], Brussels, Belgium

Fed. of Govt. Info. Processing Councils [★5813]

Fed. of Greek Indus. [IO], Athens, Greece

Fed. Guineenne de Taekwondo [IO], Conakry, Guinea

Fed. Haitienne du Jeu de Dames [IO], Port-au-Prince, Haiti

Fed. Haitienne de Tennis [IO], Port-au-Prince, Haiti

Fed. of Hellenic Amer. Societies of Greater New York - Address unknown since 1995.

Fed. of Hellenic Food Indus. [IO], Neo Psychiko, Greece

Fed. of Hellenic Info. Tech. and Communications Enterprises [IO], Athens, Greece

Fed. of Hellenic Info. Tech. Enterprises [★IO]

Fed. of High Frequency Welders [★IO]

Fed. of Hispanic Societies - Defunct.

Fed. of Historical Bottle Collectors [21888], c/o June Lowry, Bus. Mgr., 401 Johnston Ct., Raymore, MO 64083, (816)318-0160

Fed. of Home Economics Teachers [IO], Helsinki, Finland

Fed. of Homemakers - Address unknown since 1989.

Fed. of Hong Kong Indus. [IO], Hong Kong, People's Republic of China

Fed. of Hong Kong Watch Trades and Indus. [IO], Hong Kong, People's Republic of China

Fed. of Hotel and Restaurant Associations of India [IO], New Delhi, India

Fed. of Huguenot Societies [★21163]

Fed. of Hungarian Former Political Prisoners - Address unknown since 1995.

Reference to "IO" in place of a book number signifies that the association may be found in the 45th edition of International Organizations.

Fed. of Hungarian Medical Societies [★IO]
Fed. Hypothecaire Europeenne [★IO]
Fed. of Icelandic Indus. [IO], Reykjavik, Iceland
Fed. of Icelandic Landscape Architects [IO], Reykjavik, Iceland
Fed. of Icelandic Trade [IO], Reykjavik, Iceland
The Fed. of Image Consultants [IO], Haslemere, United Kingdom
Fed. of Immunological Societies of Asia-Oceania [IO], Bangkok, Thailand
Fed. of Independent Advice Centres [★IO]
Fed. of India Assns. of the U.S. and Canada - Address unknown since 1995.
Fed. of Indian Chambers of Commerce and Indus. [IO], New Delhi, India
Fed. of Indian Export Organisations [IO], New Delhi, India
Fed. des Industriels Luxembourgeois [★IO]
Fed. des Indus. Agro-Alimentaires Luxembourgeoises [★IO]
Fed. des Indus. Chimiques de Belgique [★IO]
Fed. des Indus. et Commerces Utilisateurs des Basses Temperatures, Congelation, Surgeles, Glaces [IO], Paris, France
Fed. des Indus. Electriques, Electroniques et de Commun. [IO], Paris, France
Fed. des Indus. des Equipements pour Vehicules [★IO]
Fed. des Indus. de la Parfumerie [★IO]
Fed. des Indus. des Peintures, Encres, Couleurs, Colles et Adhesifs [★IO]
Fed. of Indus. Products Systems and Services for Constr. [★IO]
Fed. of Indus. Products Systems and Services for Constr. [IO], Rome, Italy
Fed. des Indus. Transformatrices de Papier et Carton [★IO]
Fed. of Info. and Advice Centres [★IO]
Fed. of Information Users - Defunct.
Fed. of Inline Speed Skating [IO], Birmingham, United Kingdom
Fed. of Institutes Caring for Protestant Children [★20482]
Fed. of Insurance and Corporate Counsel [★5827]
Fed. of Insurance Counsel [★5827]
Fed. of Intl. Associations Established in Belgium [★IO]
Fed. Intl. des Associations pour l'Education des Travailleurs [★IO]
Fed. of Intl. Bandy [IO], Katrineholm, Sweden
Fed. of Intl. Civil Servants' Associations [IO], Geneva, Switzerland
Fed. of Intl. Country Air Personalities - Defunct.
Fed. Intl. de Genetique [★IO]
Fed. Intl. des Indus. Textiles [★IO]
Fed. of Intl. Mech. Engg. and Electronics Indus. [IO], Paris, France
Fed. of Intl. Poetry Assns. - Address unknown since 2001.
Fed. of Intl. Polo [23819], 9663 Santa Monica Blvd., PMB 848, Beverly Hills, CA 90210
Fed. of Intl. Polo [IO], Beverly Hills, CA, United States
Fed. Intl. de Sauvetage Aquatique [★IO]
Fed. of Intl. Trade Associations [IO], Reston, VA, United States
Fed. of Intl. Trade Associations [2283], 1900 Campus Commons Dr., Ste. 340, Reston, VA 20191, (703)620-1588
Fed. Intl. Trampoline Technical Comm. - Defunct.
Fed. Intl. Triathlon [★IO]
Fed. of Intl. Youth Travel Organisations [IO], Copenhagen, Denmark
Fed. Internationale des Architectes d'Interieur [★IO]
Fed. Internationale des Architectes Paysagistes [★IO]
Fed. Internationale des Archives du Film [★IO]
Fed. Internationale des Armateurs [★IO]
Fed. Internationale des Associations Contre la Lepre [★IO]
Fed. Internationale des Associations de Controleurs du Trafic Aerien [★IO]
Fed. Internationale des Associations d'Apiculture [★IO]
Fed. Internationale des Associations d'Etudes Classiques [★IO]

Fed. Internationale des Associations d'Inventeurs [★IO]
Fed. Internationale des Associations de l'Electronique de Securite du Trafic Aerien [★IO]
Fed. Internationale des Associations de Medecins Catholiques [★IO]
Fed. Internationale des Associations Medicales Catholiques [★IO]
Fed. Internationale des Associations de Patrons de Navires [★IO]
Fed. Internationale des Associations de Pilotes de Ligne [★IO]
Fed. Internationale des Associations de Producteurs de Film [★IO]
Fed. Internationale des Associations de Thanatologues [★IO]
Fed. Internationale des Associations de Transitaires et Assimilies [★IO]
Fed. Internationale des Auberges de Jeunesse [★IO]
Fed. Internationale des Autorites Hippiques de Courses au Galop [★IO]
Fed. Internationale de Basketball [★IO]
Fed. Internationale de Bobsleigh et de Tobogganing [IO], Milan, Italy
Fed. Internationale des Bureaux d'Extraits de Presse [★IO]
Fed. Internationale des Bureaux de Justification de la Diffusion [★IO]
Fed. Internationale de Camping et de Caravanning [★IO]
Fed. Internationale des Centres d'Entrainement aux Methodes d'Education Active [★IO]
Fed. Internationale des Chambres Syndicales de Negociants en Timbres-Poste [★IO]
Fed. Internationale des Chasseurs de Sons [★IO]
Fed. Internationale de Chimie Clinique [★IO]
Fed. Internationale de Chiropratique du Sport [★IO]
Fed. Internationale des Corps et Associations Consulaires [★IO]
Fed. Internationale de Cremation [★IO]
Fed. Internationale de la Croix-Bleu [★IO]
Fed. Internationale des Culturistes [★IO]
Fed. Internationale d'Astronautique [★IO]
Fed. Internationale d'Education Physique [★IO]
Fed. Internationale des Demenageurs Internationaux [★IO]
Fed. Internationale d'Eutonie Gerda Alexander [★IO]
Fed. Internationale d'Ingegnerie Municipal [★IO]
Fed. Internationale des Echecs [★IO]
Fed. Internationale des Enseignants de Rythmique [★IO]
Fed. Internationale des Enterprises de Nettoyage [★IO]
Fed. Internationale des Experts en Auto. [★IO]
Fed. Internationale des Fabricants des Papiers Gommes [★IO]
Fed. Internationale des Femmes Diplomees des Universites [★IO]
Fed. Internationale de Football Assn. [IO], Zurich, Switzerland
Fed. Internationale de Football Assn. [★IO]
Fed. Internationale de Genie Medical et Biologique [★IO]
Fed. Internationale des Geometres [★IO]
Fed. Internationale des Grossistes, Importateurs, et Exportateurs en Fourniture Automobiles [★IO]
Fed. Internationale de Gymnastique [★IO]
Fed. Internationale de Gynecologie et d'Obstetrique [★IO]
Fed. Internationale de Gynecologie Infantile et Juvenile [★IO]
Fed. Internationale de Handball [★IO]
Fed. Internationale de Hockey [★IO]
Fed. Internationale des Indus. Consommatrices d'Energie [★IO]
Fed. Internationale des Ingenieurs Conseils [★IO]
Fed. Internationale des Jeunesses Musicales [★IO]
Fed. Internationale des Journalistes [★IO]
Fed. Internationale de Judo [★IO]
Fed. Internationale de Laiterie [★IO]
Fed. Internationale des Langues et Litteratures Modernes [★IO]
Fed. Internationale de l'art Photographique [★IO]
Fed. Internationale de l'Art Photographique [IO], Paris, France

Fed. Internationale de l'Automobile [★IO]
Fed. Internationale de l'Esthetique-Cosmetique [★IO]
Fed. Internationale pour l'Habitation, l'Urbanisme et l'Amenagement des Territoires [★IO]
Fed. Internationale des Ligues des Droits de l'Homme [★IO]
Fed. Internationale de l'Industrie du Medicament [★IO]
Fed. Internationale de Luge de Course [★IO]
Fed. Internationale des Luttes Associees [★IO]
Fed. Internationale des Maisons de l'Europe [★IO]
Fed. Internationale de Medecine Manuelle [★IO]
Fed. Internationale de Medecine du Sport [★IO]
Fed. Internationale de Motocyclisme [★IO]
Fed. Internationale des Mouvements Catholiques d'Action Paroissiales [★IO]
Fed. Internationale des Mouvements d'Adultes Ruraux Catholiques [★IO]
Fed. Internationale des Mouvements d'Agriculture Biologique [★IO]
Fed. Internationale des Mouvements d'Ecole Moderne [★IO]
Fed. Internationale des Musiciens [★IO]
Fed. Internationale de Natation Amateur [★IO]
Fed. Internationale de Natation Amateur [IO], Lausanne, Switzerland
Fed. Internationale de Navigabilite Aerospatiale [★IO]
Fed. Internationale de Neurophysiologie Clinique [★IO]
Fed. Internationale des Organisations de Donneurs de Sang [★IO]
Fed. Internationale des Organisations Syndicales du Personnel des Transports [★IO]
Fed. Internationale des Organisations de Travailleurs de la Metallurgie [★IO]
Fed. Internationale des Organizations de Festivals [★IO]
Fed. Internationale des Organizations de Festivals [★1307]
Fed. Internationale des Ouvriers du Transport [★IO]
Fed. Internationale des P.E.N. Clubs [★IO]
Fed. Internationale du Personnel des Services Publics [★IO]
Fed. Internationale des Personnes Handicapees Physiques [★IO]
Fed. Internationale de Petanque et Jeu Provencal [★IO]
Fed. Internationale des Petits Freres des Pauvres [★IO]
Fed. Internationale Pharmaceutique [★IO]
Fed. Internationale de Philatelie [★IO]
Fed. Internationale pour la Planification Familiale [★IO]
Fed. Internationale Pour La Recherche En Histoire Des Femmes [★IO]
Fed. Internationale de la Presse Periodique [★IO]
Fed. Internationale des Producteurs Agricoles [★IO]
Fed. Internationale des Producteurs de Jus de Fruits [★IO]
Fed. Internationale des Professeurs de Francais [★IO]
Fed. Internationale des Professions Immobilieres [★IO]
Fed. Internationale des Quilleurs [★IO]
Fed. Internationale pour la Recherche Theatrale [★IO]
Fed. Internationale des Services des Espaces Verts et de la Recreation [★IO]
Fed. Internationale de Ski [★IO]
Fed. Internationale des Societes d'Aviron [★IO]
Fed. Internationale des Societes d'Ingenieurs des Techniques de l' Auto. [★IO]
Fed. Internationale des Societes Oto-Rhino-Laryngologiques [★IO]
Fed. Internationale du Sport Universitaire [★IO]
Fed. Internationale de Tennis [★IO]
Fed. Internationale de Tennis de Table [★IO]
Fed. Internationale de Tir a l'Arc [★IO]
Fed. Internationale des Traducteurs [★IO]
Fed. Internationale pour le Traitement de l'Information [★IO]
Fed. Internationale des Travailleurs du Batiment et du Bois [★IO]

A star before a book entry number signifies that the name is not listed separately, but is mentioned within the entry.

Fed. Internationale des Travailleurs du Textile, de l'Habillement et du Cuir [★IO]

Fed. Internationale des Universites Catholiques . [★IO]

Fed. Internationale du Vieillissement [★IO]

Fed. Internationale des Vins et Spiritueux [★IO]

Fed. Internationale de Volleyball [★IO]

Fed. of Investment Clubs - Defunct.

Fed. of Iraqi Associations in Sweden [IO], Stockholm, Sweden

Fed. of Irish Beekeepers Associations [IO], Enfield, Ireland

Fed. of Irish Cyclists [★IO]

Fed. of Irish Employers [★IO]

Fed. of Irish Film Societies [★IO]

Fed. of Islamic Associations in the U.S. and Canada [IO], Redford, MI, United States

Fed. of Islamic Associations in the U.S. and Canada [20098], 25231 5 Mile Rd., Redford, MI 48239, (313)534-3295

Fed. of Israeli Chambers of Commerce [IO], Tel Aviv, Israel

Fed. of the Italian Associations of Mech. and Engg. Indus. [IO], Milan, Italy

Fed. Italian Flying Disc [IO], Milan, Italy

Fed. Ivoirienne d'Athletisme [IO], Abidjan, Cote d'Ivoire

Fed. Ivoirienne de Taekwondo [IO], Abidjan, Cote d'Ivoire

Fed. Ivoirienne de Tennis [IO], Abidjan, Cote d'Ivoire

Fed. of Jain Associations in North America [20495], PO Box 700, Getzville, NY 14068, (716)636-5342

Fed. des Jeux du Commonwealth [★IO]

Fed. of Jewish Charities in Brooklyn [★12482]

Fed. of Jewish Men's Clubs [20137], 475 Riverside Dr., Ste. 832, New York, NY 10115-0022, (212)749-8100

Fed. of Jewish Philanthropies of Greater New York [★12482]

Fed. of Jewish Philanthropies of New York; United Jewish Appeal - [12482]

Fed. of Jewish Student Orgs. - Defunct.

Fed. of Jewish Women's Orgs. - Defunct.

Fed. of Kenya Employers [IO], Nairobi, Kenya

Fed. of Korea Aeronautics [IO], Seoul, Republic of Korea

Fed. of Korean Trade Unions [IO], Seoul, Republic of Korea

Fed. Lainiere Internationale [★IO]

Fed. Laique de Centres de Planning Familial [IO], Brussels, Belgium

Fed. of Latin Amer. Societies of Obesity [IO], Buenos Aires, Argentina

Fed. of Lawyers, Economists, Sys. Managers, Human Rsrc. Managers, and Other Social Scientists [IO], Stockholm, Sweden

Fed. of Leather Guilds [★2413]

Fed. de l'Habillement [★IO]

Fed. Libanaise de Badminton [IO], Beirut, Lebanon

Fed. Libanaise d'Athletisme [IO], Jounieh, Lebanon

Fed. Libanaise de Tennis [IO], Beirut, Lebanon

Fed. Libanaise de Yachting [IO], Jounieh, Lebanon

Fed. of Liberal and Democratic Parties in the European Community [★IO]

Fed. Life Insurance of Am. [19123], 6011 S 27th St., Greenfield, WI 53221-4804, (414)281-6281

Fed. de l'industrie horlogere suisse [★IO]

Fed. de l'Industrie Alimentaire [★IO]

Fed. de l'Industrie du Beton [IO], Brussels, Belgium

Fed. de l'Industrie Dentaire en Europe [★IO]

Fed. de l'Industrie Europeenne de la Constr. [★IO]

Fed. de l'Industrie de l'Huilerie de la CE [★IO]

Fed. de l'Industrie du Verre [★IO]

Fed. of Lutheran Clubs - Address unknown since 1995.

Fed. Lutherienne Mondiale [★IO]

Fed. of Luxembourg Food Indus. [IO], Luxembourg, Luxembourg

Fed. of Luxembourg Industrialists [IO], Luxembourg, Luxembourg

Fed. Luxembourgeoise des Arts Martiaux-Aikido [IO], Strassen, Luxembourg

Fed. Luxembourgeoise de Badminton [★IO]

Fed. Luxembourgeoise de Danse pour Amateurs [★IO]

Fed. Luxembourgeoise de Danse pour Amateurs [IO], Hautcharage, Luxembourg

Fed. Luxembourgeoise d'Athletisme [IO], Luxembourg, Luxembourg

Fed. Luxembourgeoise des Editeurs de Livres [IO], Luxembourg, Luxembourg

Fed. Luxembourgeoise des Editeurs de Livres [★IO]

Fed. Luxembourgeoise de Tennis [IO], Esch-sur-Alzette, Luxembourg

Fed. Luxembourgoise de Cricket [★IO]

Fed. Malagasy de Badminton [IO], Antananarivo, Madagascar

Fed. Malagasy d'Athletisme [IO], Antananarivo, Madagascar

Fed. of Malaysian Consumers Associations [IO], Petaling Jaya, Malaysia

Fed. of Malaysian Mfrs. [IO], Kuala Lumpur, Malaysia

Fed. Malgache Handisport [IO], Antananarivo, Madagascar

Fed. Malgache de Tennis [IO], Antananarivo, Madagascar

Fed. Malienne de Base-Ball et de Softball [IO], Bamako, Mali

Fed. Malienne d'Athletisme Amateur [IO], Bamako, Mali

Fed. Malienne du Jeu de Dames [IO], Bamako, Mali

Fed. Malienne de Taekwondo [IO], Bamako, Mali

Fed. Malienne de Tennis [IO], Bamako, Mali

Fed. of Mfrs. of Constr. Equip. and Cranes [★IO]

Fed. Maritime du Canada [★IO]

Fed. of Masons of the World [19233]

Fed. of Master Builders [IO], London, United Kingdom

Fed. of Materials Societies [7281], 910 17th St. NW, Ste. 800, Washington, DC 20006, (202)296-9282

Fed. du Materiel pour l'Automobile [IO], Brussels, Belgium

Fed. Mauritanienne de Sport pour Handicapes [IO], Nouakchott, Mauritania

Fed. Mauritanienne de Tennis [IO], Nouakchott, Mauritania

Fed. of McGuffey Societies - Address unknown since 1995.

Fed. of Mech. Engg. of the Slovak Republic [IO], Bratislava, Slovakia

Fed. of Medical Societies of Hong Kong [IO], Hong Kong, People's Republic of China

Fed. of Mental Health Centers - Defunct.

Fed. of Metal Detector and Archaeological Clubs [22578], 184 Grange Rd., McClellandtown, PA 15458, (724)439-1380

Fed. Mexicana De Baile A.C. [IO], Mexico City, Mexico

Fed. of Mineral and Non-Ferrous Metal Indus. [★IO]

Fed. of Modern Painters and Sculptors [9502], c/o Anneli Arms, 113 Greene St., New York, NY 10012, (212)966-4864

Fed. Mondiale des Anciens Combattants [★IO]

Fed. Mondiale des Annonceurs [★IO]

Fed. Mondiale des Concours Internationaux de Musique [★IO]

Fed. Mondiale des Employes [★IO]

Fed. Mondiale des Ergotherapeutes [★IO]

Fed. Mondiale du Jeu de Dames [★IO]

Fed. Mondiale de Karate [★IO]

Fed. Mondiale pour l'Enseignement de la Medicine [★IO]

Fed. Mondiale de l'Hemophilie [★IO]

Fed. Mondiale des Missions Islamiques [★IO]

Fed. Mondiale des Organisations d'Ingenieurs [★IO]

Fed. Mondiale des Societes d'Anesthesiologistes [★IO]

Fed. Mondiale des Travailleurs Scientifiques [★IO]

Fed. Monegasque d'Athletisme [IO], Monaco, Monaco

Fed. Monegasque De Squash Rackets [IO], Monaco, Monaco

Fed. Monegasque de Lawn Tennis [★IO]

Fed. of Motion Picture Couns. - Defunct.

Fed. of Mutual Fire Insurance Companies - Defunct.

Fed. of Natl. Assns. - Defunct.

Fed. of Natl. Associations of Shipbrokers and Agents [IO], London, United Kingdom

Fed. of Natl. Educ. and Res. Unions [IO], Paris, France

Fed. of Natl. Electrolysis Assns. - Defunct.

Fed. of Natl. Orgs. for Recreation - Defunct.

Fed. Nationale de la Coiffure Francaise [★IO]

Fed. Nationale des Cooperatives Laitieres [★IO]

Fed. Nationale des Femmes Canadiennes-Francaises [★IO]

Fed. Nationale Hogroise [IO], Budapest, Hungary

Fed. Nationale des Hoteliers, Restaurateurs et Cafetiers de Luxembourg [★IO]

Fed. Nationale des Indus. des Peintures, Vernis, Encres d'Imprimerie et Couleurs Fines [★IO]

Fed. Nationale de l'Industrie Hoteliere [★IO]

Fed. Nationale de l'Industrie Laitiere [★IO]

Fed. Nationale des Metiers de la Jardinerie [★IO]

Fed. Nationale de la Presse d'Information Specialisee [★IO]

Fed. Nationale de la Presse d'Information Specialisee [★IO]

Fed. Nationale des Producteurs de Lait [★IO]

Fed. Nationale des Producteurs de Legumes [★IO]

Fed. Nationale des Producteurs de Plants de Pommes de Terre [★IO]

Fed. of Natural Medicine Users in North America - Address unknown since 2007.

Fed. Naturiste Internationale [★IO]

Fed. Nautique du Canada [★IO]

Fed. of Nepalese Chambers of Commerce and Indus. [IO], Kathmandu, Nepal

Fed. of Netherlands Indus. and the Netherlands Christian Fed. of Employers [★IO]

Fed. Nigerienne d'Athletisme [IO], Niamey, Niger

Fed. Nigerienne Sports pour Personnes Handicapes [IO], Niamey, Niger

Fed. Nigerienne de Taekwondo [IO], Niamey, Niger

Fed. Nigerienne de Tennis [IO], Niamey, Niger

Fed. of Norwegian Indus. [IO], Oslo, Norway

Fed. of Norwegian Mfg. Indus. and Fed. of Norwegian Process Indus. [★IO]

Fed. of Nova Scotian Heritage [IO], Halifax, NS, Canada

Fed. of Nurses and Hea. Professionals [★24087]

Fed. of Obstetric and Gynecological Societies of India [IO], Bombay, India

Fed. Oceanienne d' Halterophile [★IO]

Fed. of Oils, Seeds, and Fats Associations [IO], London, United Kingdom

Fed. of Ontario Naturalists [★IO]

Fed. of Ophthalmic and Dispensing Opticians [★IO]

Fed. of Ophthalmic and Dispensing Opticians [IO], London, United Kingdom

Fed. of Organizations in the Field of Libraries, Info. and Documentation [IO], The Hague, Netherlands

Fed. of Orgs. for Professional Women - Address unknown since 2006.

Fed. of Orthodontic Assns. - Defunct.

Fed. of Outdoor Recreationists - Defunct.

Fed. of Overseas Property Developers, Agents and Consultants [IO], Hove, United Kingdom

Fed. of Paint and Varnish Production Clubs [★IO]

Fed. of Paint and Varnish Production Clubs [★6704]

Fed. of Paints, Inks, Glues and Adhesives Indus. [IO], Paris, France

Fed. of Pakistan Chambers of Commerce and Indus. [IO], Karachi, Pakistan

Fed. of the Paper and Bd. Converting Indus. [IO], Brussels, Belgium

Fed. of Partial Hospitalization Stud. Groups [★16080]

Fed. of Patients and Consumer Organisations in the Netherlands [IO], Utretch, Netherlands

Fed. of Pediatric Organizations [15887], 3723 Haven Rd., MS 3705-190, Menlo Park, CA 94025, (650)839-1933

Fed. of Petanque U.S.A. [23649], c/o Frank Pipal, Sec., PO Box 180, Kenwood, CA 95452, (707)833-2020

Fed. of Petanque of U.S.A. [★23649]

Fed. of Petroleum Suppliers [IO], Knutsford, United Kingdom

Fed. of Pharmaceutical Mfrs'. Associations of Japan [IO], Tokyo, Japan

Fed. of Philippine Amer. Chambers of Commerce [24277], Philippine Consulate Bldg., Stes. 700-701, 447 Sutter St., San Francisco, CA 94108-0000, (415)398-3043

Reference to "IO" in place of a book number signifies that the association may be found in the 45th edition of International Organizations.

Fed. of Piling Specialists [IO], Beckenham, United Kingdom

Fed. of Plastering and Drywall Contractors [IO], London, United Kingdom

Fed. de la Plasturgie [★IO]

Fed. of Podiatric Medical Boards [16043], 6551 Malta Dr., Boynton Beach, FL 33437, (561)752-3735

Fed. of Podiatry Boards [★16043]

Fed. of Podiatry Medical Boards [★16043]

Fed. of Police, Security and Correction Officers - Defunct.

Fed. of Polish Americans [10877], 2000 L St. NW, Ste. 200, Washington, DC 20036

Fed. of Polish Americans [IO], Washington, DC, United States

Fed. of Polish Jews in the U.S. [★19302]

Fed. of Postal Police Officers - Defunct.

Fed. of Pre-University Educ. Trade Unions of Romania [IO]

Fed. de la Presse Periodique de Belgique [★IO]

Fed. of the Printing Indus. in Finland [IO], Helsinki, Finland

Fed. of Private Residents' Associations [IO], Colchester, United Kingdom

Fed. of Professional Associations [IO], Hayes, United Kingdom

Fed. of Professional Writers of America - Address unknown since 1995.

Fed. for Progress - Defunct.

Fed. des Proprietaires de lots boises du N-B [★IO]

Fed. of Prosthodontic Orgs. - Defunct.

Fed. of Protestant Welfare Agencies [20482], 281 Park Ave. S, New York, NY 10010, (212)777-4800

Fed. of Reconstructionist Congregations and Fellowships [★20151]

Fed. Reconstructionist Congregations and Havurot [★20151]

Fed. of Recorded Music Societies [IO], Stoke-On-Trent, United Kingdom

Fed. for the Repair and Protection of Structures [★IO]

Fed. of the Retail Licensed Trade [IO], Belfast, United Kingdom

Fed. of Retail Merchants - Defunct.

Fed. of Rose Societies of South Africa [IO], Pretoria, Republic of South Africa

Fed. Royal Marocaine de Badminton [IO], Casablanca, Morocco

Fed. Royale Belge de Tennis [★IO]

Fed. Royale Belge du Yachting [IO], Antwerp, Belgium

Fed. Royale de l'Industrie des Eaux et des Boissons Rafraichissantes [★IO]

Fed. Royale Marocaine d'Athletisme [IO], Rabat, Morocco

Fed. Royale Marocaine de Judo Aikido et AMA [IO], Casablanca, Morocco

Fed. Royale Marocaine du Sport Scolaire [IO], Rabat, Morocco

Fed. Royale Marocaine de Taekwondo [IO], Rabat, Morocco

Fed. Royale Marocaine de Tennis [IO], Casablanca, Morocco

Fed. Royale Marocaine de Yachting a Voile [IO], Rabat, Morocco

Fed. of Russian Charitable Orgs. of U.S.A. - Defunct.

Fed. Rwandaise d'Athletisme [IO], Kigali, Rwanda

Fed. Rwandaise Handisport [IO], Kigali, Rwanda

Fed. Rwandaise de Tennis [IO], Kigali, Rwanda

Fed. of Scandinavian Societies of Obstetrics and Gynecology [★IO]

Fed. of Sci. and Tech. Unions in Bulgaria [IO], Sofia, Bulgaria

Fed. Senegalaise d'Athletisme [IO], Dakar, Senegal

Fed. Senegalaise de Taekwondo [IO], Dakar, Senegal

Fed. Senegalaise de Tennis [IO], Dakar, Senegal

Fed. of Sewage and Indus. Wastes Associations [★IO]

Fed. of Sewage and Indus. Wastes Associations [★5101]

Fed. of Sewage Works Associations [★5101]

Fed. of Sewage Works Associations [★IO]

Fed. Sioniste Canadienne [★IO]

Fed. of Small Businesses [IO], Blackpool, United Kingdom

Fed. des Societes d'Assurances de Droit Natl. Africaines [★IO]

Fed. des Societes d'Histoire du Quebec [★IO]

Fed. des Societes Nationales des Ingenieurs Ecectriciens de L'Europe [★IO]

Fed. of Societies for Coatings Tech. [IO], Blue Bell, PA, United States

Fed. of Societies for Coatings Tech. [6704], 492 Norristown Rd., Blue Bell, PA 19422-2350, (610)940-0777

Fed. of Societies for Paint Tech. [★6704]

Fed. of Societies for Paint Tech. [★IO]

Fed. of Southern Cooperatives [★12937]

Fed. of Southern Cooperatives Land Assistance Fund [12937], 2769 Church St., East Point, GA 30344, (404)765-0991

Fed. of Spanish Audiovisual Producer Associations [IO], Madrid, Spain

Fed. of Spanish Footwear Indus. [IO], Madrid, Spain

Fed. of Spanish Publishers' Associations [IO], Madrid, Spain

Fed. of Special Care Organizations in Dentistry [★14186]

Fed. of Sporting Billiards of Ukraine [★IO]

Fed. Sportive des Handicapes du Burundi [IO], Bujumbura, Burundi

Fed. of Sports and Play Associations [IO], Kenilworth, United Kingdom

Fed. de Squash Luxembourgeoise [IO], Luxembourg, Luxembourg

Fed. of State Associations of Independent Colleges and Universities [★8539]

Fed. of State Humanities Councils [10198], 1600 Wilson Blvd., Ste. 902, Arlington, VA 22209, (703)908-9700

Fed. of State Medical Boards of the U.S. [15165], PO Box 619850, Dallas, TX 75261-9850, (817)868-4000

Federation of State Medical Boards of the United States [IO], Dallas, TX, United States

Fed. of State and Municipal Employees [IO], Reykjavik, Iceland

Fed. of State Physician Hea. Programs [15999], c/o Vickie Grosso, Amer. Medical Assn., 515 N State St., Chicago, IL 60610, (312)464-4574

Fed. of Sterea Hellas - Address unknown since 1995.

Fed. of Straight Chiropractic Organizations [★14001]

Fed. of Straight Chiropractors and Organizations [14001], 2276 Wassergass Rd., Hellertown, PA 18055, (610)838-3030

Fed. Suisse de Basketball Amateur [★IO]

Fed. Suisse des Familles Monoparentales [IO], Bern, Switzerland

Fed. Suisse des Femmes Protestantes [★IO]

Fed. Suisse des Journalistes [★IO]

Fed. Suisse de Musique Electroacoustique [IO], Geneva, Switzerland

Fed. for the Support of Jewish Philanthropic Societies of New York [★12482]

Fed. de Surf des Neiges du Canada [★IO]

Fed. of Swedish Farmers [IO], Stockholm, Sweden

Fed. of Swiss Architects [IO], Basel, Switzerland

Fed. of Swiss Employers' Organizations [★IO]

Fed. of Swiss Importers and Wholesalers [IO], Basel, Switzerland

Fed. of Swiss Milk Producers [IO], Bern, Switzerland

Fed. of the Swiss Watch Indus. [IO], Bienne, Switzerland

Fed. of the Swiss Watch Indus. [IO], Tokyo, Japan

Fed. Syndicale Europeenne des Services Publics [★IO]

Fed. Syndicale Mondiale [★IO]

Fed. des Syndicats de la Distribution Auto. [★IO]

Fed. des Syndicats Generaux de l'Education Nationale et de la Recherche publique [★IO]

Fed. of Syrian Chambers of Commerce [IO], Damascus, Syrian Arab Republic

Fed. of Taekwondo of the Republic of Moldova [IO], Chisinau, Moldova

Fed. of Tax Administrators [6292], 444 N Capitol St. NW, Ste. 348, Washington, DC 20001, (202)624-5890

Fed. Tchadienne de Handball [IO], N'Djamena, Chad

Fed. Tchadienne de Taekwondo [IO], N'Djamena, Chad

Fed. of Tech. and Sci. Societies, Hungary [IO], Budapest, Hungary

Fed. de Tennis du Burundi [IO], Bujumbura, Burundi

Fed. de Tennis de la Guinee-Bissau [IO], Bissau, Guinea-Bissau

Fed. de Tennis de Vanuatu [IO], Port Vila, Vanuatu

Fed. canadienne des sciences de la Terre [★IO]

Fed. of Thai Indus. [IO], Bangkok, Thailand

Fed. Togolaise de Badminton [IO], Lome, Togo

Fed. Togolaise de Base-ball et Soft-ball [IO], Lome, Togo

Fed. Togolaise d'Athletisme [IO], Lome, Togo

Fed. Togolaise de Taekwondo [IO], Lome, Togo

Fed. of Tour Operators [IO], Haywards Heath, United Kingdom

Fed. of Trainers and Training Programs in Psychodrama - Defunct.

Fed. of Travel Agencies [★IO]

Fed. Truck Associations of Am. [★3863]

Fed. Tunisienne de Baseball et Softball [IO], Tunis, Tunisia

Fed. Tunisienne d'Athletisme [IO], Tunis, Tunisia

Fed. of Turkish Amer. Associations [19409], 821 UN Plz., 2nd Fl., New York, NY 10017, (212)682-7688

Fed. of Turkish-American Societies [★19409]

Fed. of Ukrainian Student Orgs. of America - Address unknown since 1995.

Fed. Unie des Auberges de Jeunesse [★IO]

Fed. for Unified Sci. Educ. [9102], Ctr. for Unified Sci., 6529 Sunbury Rd., Westerville, OH 43082, (614)895-2252

Fed. of United Arab Emirates Chambers of Commerce and Indus. [IO], Abu Dhabi, United Arab Emirates

Fed; Universal Proutist Intellectual [★18627]

Fed. of Univ. Women (Russia) [IO], St. Petersburg, Russia

Fed. of Veterinarians of Europe [IO], Brussels, Belgium

Fed. Vietnamienne du Canada [★IO]

Federation of Volunteer Firefighters' Associations [★5723]

Fed. W/O TV [★18725]

Fed. of Western Outdoor Clubs - Address unknown since 2003.

Fed. of Westinghouse Independent Salaried Unions [24047]

Fed. Without TV [18725], 6282 12th St. N, No. 105, Oakdale, MN 55128

Fed. of Woman's Exchanges [13040]

Fed. of Women Lawyers', Judicial Screening Panel - Defunct.

Fed. of Women Shareholders in Amer. Business - Address unknown since 1988.

Fed. of Worker Writers and Community Publishers [IO], Stoke-On-Trent, United Kingdom

Fed. of Workers' Singing Societies of the U.S.A. - Defunct.

Federative van Belgische Fabrikanten van Vetten en Olien [IO], Brussels, Belgium

Federauto [IO], Brussels, Belgium

Federazione Alzheimer Italia [IO], Milan, Italy

Federazione Associazioni Imprese Distribuzione [★IO]

Federazione Associazioni Italiane Spina Bifida e Idrocefalo [IO], Milan, Italy

Federazione delle Associazioni Nazionali della Industria Meccanica Varia ed Affine [★IO]

Federazione CEMAT [IO], Rome, Italy

Federazione Cricket Italiana [★IO]

Federazione Industria Musicale Italiana [IO], Milan, Italy

Federazione Industrie Prodotti Impianti e Servizi per le Costruzioni [★IO]

Federazione Italiana delle Acque Minerali e delle Bevande Analcooliche [★IO]

Federazione Italiana Amici della Bicicletta [★IO]

Federazione Italiana della Associazione Christiane dei Giovani [★IO]

Federazione Italiana di Atletica Leggera [IO], Rome, Italy

Federazione Italiana Badminton [IO], Rome, Italy

A star before a book entry number signifies that the name is not listed separately, but is mentioned within the entry.

Federazione Italiana Danza Sportiva [★IO]
Federazione Italiana dell'Industria Alimentare [★IO]
Federazione Italiana Dettaglianti dell'Alimentazione [★IO]
Federazione Italiana Editori Giornali [★IO]
Federazione Italiana di Elettrotecnica, Elettronica, Automazione, Informatica e Telecomunicazioni [★IO]
Federazione Italiana Flying Disc [★IO]
Federazione Italiana Giuoco Squash [★IO]
Federazione Italiana Industriali, Produttori, Esportatori ed Importatori di Vini, Acquaviti, Liquori, Sciroppi, Aceti Affini [★IO]
Federazione Italiana delle Industrie del Legno, del Sughero, del Mobile e dell'Arridamento [★IO]
Federazione Italiana Laureate e Diplomate di Istituti Superiori [★IO]
Federazione Italiana Mercanti d'Arte [IO], Milan, Italy
Federazione Italiana Tabaccai [★IO]
Federazione Italiana Taekwondo [IO], Rome, Italy
Federazione Italiana Tennis [IO], Rome, Italy
Federazione Italiana Unihockey Floorball [★IO]
Federazione Italiana Vela [★IO]
Federazione Nazionale Commercianti Calzature [★IO]
Federazione Nazionale Commercianti Mobili [★IO]
Federazione Nazionale del Commercio Oleario [★IO]
Federazione Nazionale Del Commercio Vinicolo [★IO]
Federazione Nazionale dell'Industria Chimica [★IO]
Federazione Nazionale Grossisti Distributori Materiale Elettrico [★IO]
Federazione Nazionale Grossisti Orafi Gioiellieri Argentieri [★IO]
Federazione Nazionale delle Impresa di Pesca [★IO]
Federazione Nazionale Imprese Elettrotecniche ed Elettroniche [★IO]
Federazione Nazionale Industria dei Viaggi e del Turismo [★IO]
Federazione Nazionale Orafi Gioiellieri Fabbricanti [★IO]
Federazione Nazionale Profumieri Italiani [★IO]
Federazione Nazionale Rivenditori Specialisti di Pneumatici [★IO]
Federazione Nazionale della Stampa Italiana [IO], Rome, Italy
Federazione Ordini Farmacisti Italiani [★IO]
Federazione Radio Televisioni [★IO]
Federazione Sammarinese [IO], Serravalle, San Marino
Federazione Sammarinese Atletica Leggera [IO], Serravalle, San Marino
Federazione Sammarinese Tennis [★IO]
Fedevela El Portal de la vela Chilena [IO], Santiago, Chile
Fee Appraisers; Natl. Assn. of Independent [284]
Feed
  Amer. Feed Indus. Assn. [1357]
  Animal Feed Mfrs. Assn. [IO]
  Animal Nutrition Assn. of Canada [IO]
  Australian Fodder Indus. Assn. [IO]
  Chamber of Petfood Mfrs. [IO]
  CLFMA of India [IO]
  European Dehydrators Assn. [IO]
  European Fed. of Animal Feed Additive Mfrs. [IO]
  European Feed Mfrs'. Fed. [IO]
  Feed Microscopy Div. [4662]
  Grain and Feed Trade Assn. [IO]
  Inorganic Feed Phosphates/CEFIC Sector Gp. [IO]
  Intl. Feed Indus. Fed. [IO]
  Irish Grain and Feed Assn. [IO]
  Natl. Alfalfa and Forage Alliance [1358]
  Natl. Assn. of Pet Food and Animal Feed Manufacturers and Producers [IO]
  Natl. Barley Foods Coun. [1751]
  Natl. Barley Growers Assn. [4663]
  Natl. Grain and Feed Assn. [1359]
  Natl. Hay Assn. [1360]
  Natl. Lamb Feeders Assn. [5206]
  Pacific Northwest Grain and Feed Assn. [4314]
  Pet Food Assn. of Canada [IO]
  Portuguese Assn. of Animal Feed Mfrs. [IO]

  Soc. of Feed Technologists [IO]
  U.S. Grains Coun. [IO]
  U.S. Grains Coun. [4664]
  Venezuelan Assn. of Concentrated Animal Food Mfrs. [IO]
  Wild Bird Feeding Indus. [1361]
Feed Assn; Natl. Mineral [★1357]
Feed Assn; Pacific Northwest Grain and [4314]
Feed Assn; Washington [★4314]
Feed the Children [12854], PO Box 36, Oklahoma City, OK 73101-0036, (405)942-0228
Feed the Children [IO], Oklahoma City, OK, United States
Feed Control Officials; Assn. of Amer. [5432]
Feed Dealers Natl. Assn; Grain and [★1359]
Feed Grains Coun; U.S. [★4664]
Feed Indus. Assn; Amer. [★1357]
Feed Ingredients Assn; Natl. [★1357]
Feed Manufacturers Assn; Amer. [★1357]
Feed Manufacturers Assn; Midwest [★1357]
Feed Microscopy Div. [4662], c/o Amer. Oil Chemists' Soc., 2710 S Boulder, Urbana, IL 61802-6996, (217)359-2344
Feed Res. Coun; Distillers [★1749]
Feedback Certification Inst. of Am; Bio [13750]
Feeders; Amer. Collectors of Infant [21959]
Feeders Assn; Natl. Lamb [5206]
Feeding Hungry Children Intl. [12390], PO Box 2300, Redlands, CA 92373-0761, (909)793-2009
Feeding Hungry Children Intl. [IO], Redlands, CA, United States
Feingold Assn. of the U.S. [15557], 554 E Main St., No. 301, Riverhead, NY 11901, (631)369-9340
Felag bokasafns-og upplysingafraeda [★IO]
Felag Heyrnarlausra [★IO]
Felag Islenska Leikskolakennara [★IO]
Felag Islenskra Hjukrunarfraedinga [★IO]
Felag Islenskra Landslagsarkitekta [★IO]
Felag Islenskra Storkaupmanna [★IO]
Felag Islenzkra Bifreidaeigenda [★IO]
Felag Islenzkra Haskolakvenna [IO], Reykjavik, Iceland
Feldenkrais - Fed. Austria [IO], Vienna, Austria
Feldenkrais-Gilde Deutschland e.V. [IO], Munich, Germany
Feldenkrais Guild of North Am. [IO], Portland, OR, United States
Feldenkrais Guild of North Am. [10182], 5436 N Albina Ave., Portland, OR 97217, (503)221-6612
Feldenkrais Verband Osterreich [★IO]
Felicidades Wildlife Found. - Address unknown since 2003.
Feline Advisory Bur. [IO], Salisbury, United Kingdom
Feline and Canine Friends - Defunct.
Feline Control Coun. of Victoria [IO], Bayswater North, Australia
Feline Control Coun. of Western Australia [IO], Cannington, Australia
Feline Hea. Center; Cornell [16791]
Feline Practitioners; Amer. Assn. of [16744]
Felines; Friends of Feral [21908]
Fell Pony Soc. [IO], Cumbria, United Kingdom
Fell Pony Society and Conservancy of the Americas [IO], West Liberty, KY, United States
Fell Pony Soc. and Conservancy of the Americas [4878], c/o Victoria Tollman, Sec.-Treas., 10844 Hwy. 172, West Liberty, KY 41472
Fell Pony Soc. of North Am. [4879], c/o Lisa Lindholm, Gen. Sec., 2626 Diane Ln., Hibbing, MN 55746, (218)263-5217
Fell Pony Society of North America [IO], Rainier, WA, United States
Fellows of the American Bar Foundation [IO], Chicago, IL, United States
Fellows of the Amer. Bar Found. [5494], 750 N Lake Shore Dr., Chicago, IL 60611-4403, (312)988-6596
Fellows in Amer. Studies - Address unknown since 1995.
Fellows Prog; ACE [7881]
Fellowship of Amer. Baptist Musicians [20430], 1600 Tall Tree Dr., Trenton, MI 48183-1860, (317)635-3552
Fellowship of Artists for Cultural Evangelism - Address unknown since 2002.
Fellowship of Associates of Medical Evangelism [20240], 4545 Southeastern Ave., PO Box 33548, Indianapolis, IN 46203, (317)358-2480

Fellowship; The Augustine [★13074]
Fellowship of Australian Writers NSW [IO], Rozelle, Australia
Fellowship of Catholic Scholars [9777], c/o Dr. J. Brian Benestad, VP/Ed., PO Box 495, Notre Dame, IN 46556, (574)631-5825
Fellowship of Christian Airline Personnel [20007], 136 Providence Rd., Fayetteville, GA 30215, (770)461-9320
Fellowship of Christian Airline Personnel [IO], Fayetteville, GA, United States
Fellowship of Christian Athletes [20008], 8701 Leeds Rd., Kansas City, MO 64129, (816)921-0909
Fellowship of Christian Cowboys [19796], PO Box 3010, Colorado Springs, CO 80934, (719)630-7636
Fellowship of Christian Firefighters, Intl. [5715], PO Box 901, Fort Collins, CO 80522-0901, (800)322-9848
Fellowship of Christian Firefighters, Intl. [IO], Fort Collins, CO, United States
Fellowship of Christian Magicians [19797], 7739 Everest Ct. N, Maple Grove, MN 55311-1815, (763)494-5655
Fellowship; Christian Military [19782]
Fellowship of Christian Musicians [★20427]
Fellowship of Christian Peace Officers [★19798]
Fellowship of Christian Peace Officers - U.S.A. [19798], PO Box 3686, Chattanooga, TN 37404-0686, (423)622-1234
Fellowship of Christian Policemen [★19798]
Fellowship of Christian Racers - Defunct.
Fellowship of Christian Released Time Ministries [19926], 5722 Lime Ave., Long Beach, CA 90805, (562)428-7733
Fellowship; Christian Servicemen [★19782]
Fellowship of Christians in the Arts, Media and Entertainment [★20024]
Fellowship of Christians in the Arts, Media and Entertainment [★IO]
Fellowship Church Movement; Unity [20068]
Fellowship Club [★13244]
Fellowship of Companies for Christ Intl. [19799], c/o ChristWork, PO Box 270784, Oklahoma City, OK 73137-0784, (405)917-1681
Fellowship of Companies for Christ Intl. [IO], Oklahoma City, OK, United States
Fellowship of Concern - Address unknown since 1995.
Fellowship of Concerned Churchmen [19454], PO Box 427, Morrow, GA 30260, (770)961-4200
Fellowship of Concerned Churchmen [IO], Jonesboro, GA, United States
Fellowship of Conservative Southern Baptists - Address unknown since 2004.
Fellowship of Fire Chaplains [★19747]
Fellowship Found; Woodrow Wilson Natl. [8439]
Fellowship of the Golden Rule - Address unknown since 1988.
Fellowship for Intentional Community [17216], RR 1, Box 156-W, Rutledge, MO 63563-9720, (660)883-5545
Fellowship; Inter Varsity Christian [20347]
Fellowship of Intl. Communities [★17216]
Fellowship Intl. Mission [20338], 555 S 24th St., Allentown, PA 18104-6666, (610)435-9099
Fellowship Intl. Mission [IO], Allentown, PA, United States
Fellowship of Makers and Researchers of Historical Instruments [IO], London, United Kingdom
Fellowship of Missions [20339], 140 Jacqueline Dr., Berea, OH 44017-2730, (440)243-0156
Fellowship of Navajo Christian Missions - Address unknown since 1995.
Fellowship; Oral Roberts Univ. Educational [8089]
Fellowship of Orthodox Christians in Am. [20542], 10 Downs Dr., Wilkes-Barre, PA 18705, (570)825-3158
Fellowship in Prayer [19894], 291 Witherspoon St., Princeton, NJ 08542-3227, (609)924-6863
Fellowship in Prayer [IO], Princeton, NJ, United States
Fellowship; Presbyterian Evangelistic [20471]
Fellowship Program; Congressional [★7521]
Fellowship Program; Julius A. Thomas [★8047]
Fellowship for Racial and Economic Equality [★18629]

Reference to "IO" in place of a book number signifies that the association may be found in the 45th edition of International Organizations.

Fellowship of Reconciliation; North Manchester [★18723]

Fellowship of Reconciliation Task Force on Latin Am. and Caribbean [17988], PO Box 271, Nyack, NY 10960, (845)358-4601

Fellowship of Reconciliation Task Force on Latin Am. and Caribbean [IO], Nyack, NY, United States

Fellowship of Reconciliation - USA [IO], Nyack, NY, United States

Fellowship of Reconciliation - USA [18202], 521 N Broadway, Nyack, NY 10960, (845)358-4601

Fellowship of Religious Humanists - Address unknown since 1999.

Fellowship of Religious Journalists - Defunct.

Fellowship of Saint James [19800], PO Box 410788, Chicago, IL 60641, (773)481-1090

Fellowship of St. John the Divine [19882], c/o Antiochian Orthodox Christian Archdiocese, PO Box 5238, Englewood, NJ 07631-5238, (201)871-1355

Fellowship of St. Nicholas [IO], St. Leonards-on-Sea, United Kingdom

Fellowship of Saint Paul [19958], c/o The Soc. of Saint Paul, St. Paul's Cathedral, 2728 Sixth Ave., San Diego, CA 92103, (619)298-7261

Fellowship Soc; Intl. [★1474]

Fellowship for Spiritual Understanding - Defunct.

Fellowship of United Methodist Musicians [★20261]

Fellowship of United Methodists in Music and Worship Arts [20261], PO Box 24787, Nashville, TN 37202-4787, (615)749-6875

Fellowship of United Methodists in Worship, and Other Arts [★20261]

Fellowship of the White Boar [★11145]

Fellowship of World Citizens - Defunct.

Fellowships; Eisenhower [17884]

Fellowships; Eisenhower Exchange [★17884]

Fellowships; Natl. Medical [8871]

Felt Mfrs. Coun. - Defunct.

Felton Family Assn. [20901], PO Box 253, West Boylston, MA 01583

Female Europeans of Medium and Small Enterprises [IO], Brussels, Belgium

Female Executives; Natl. Assn. for [742]

Female Offenders; Assn. on Programs for [11857]

Females in Info. Tech. and Telecommunications [IO], Deakin West, Australia

FEMCONSULT [IO], The Hague, Netherlands

Feminism

9 to 5, Natl. Assn. of Working Women [17512]

9 to 5 Working Women Educ. Fund [17513]

Action for Development [IO]

Afghan Women's Network [IO]

African Women's Economic Policy Network [IO]

Akina Mama wa Afrika [IO]

ALA Social Responsibilities Round Table Feminist Task Force [17514]

All China Women's Fed. [IO]

All Pakistan Women's Assn. [IO]

Alliance for Women's Equality [13455]

Amer. Civil Liberties Union [17084]

Amer. Civil Liberties Union Found. [17085]

Asia Gender and Trade Network [IO]

Asia-Japan Women's Rsrc. Center [IO]

Assn. for the Advancement of Feminism [IO]

Babiker Badri Sci. Assn. for Women's Stud. [IO]

Biblioteca de Mujeres [IO]

Black Women in Church and Soc. [20617]

Bus. and Professional Women/USA [17515]

Campus Ministry Women [19918]

Canadian Women's Found. [IO]

Caribbean Assn. for Feminist Res. and Action [IO]

Caribbean Gender and Trade Network [IO]

Center for Amer. Women and Politics [17516]

Center for Community Solutions [17517]

Center for Women Policy Stud. [17518]

CH on Women's Issues [17519]

Coalition for Women's Appointments [17520]

Commn. on the Status of Women [17521]

Commn. on the Status of Women [IO]

Commn. for Women's Equality [17522]

Comm. on the Elimination of Discrimination Against Women [17523]

Comm. on the Elimination of Discrimination Against Women [IO]

Comm. on South Asian Women [IO]

Comm. on South Asian Women [17524]

Comm. on the Status of Women in Sociology [9923]

Commonwealth Countries League [IO]

Conf. for Catholic Lesbians [20051]

Congressional Caucus for Women's Issues [17525]

Coordinating Coun. for Women in History [17526]

Coun. of Women's Organizations in Israel [IO]

Danish Women's Soc. [IO]

DC Feminists Against Pornography [17527]

Delegation for Friendship Among Women [17528]

Deutscher Frauenring e.V. [IO]

Eleanor Found. [17529]

Empowerment Soc. of the U.S.A. [13425]

Engender [IO]

Equal Rights for Argentine Women [IO]

Equality Commn. for Northern Ireland [IO]

Euro-American Women's Coun. [17530]

European Women's Lobby [IO]

Evangelical and Ecumenical Women's Caucus [19978]

Every Mother is a Working Mother Network [18810]

Fawcett Soc. [IO]

Federally Employed Women [17531]

Feminism and Family Stud. Sect. of the Natl. Coun. on Family Relations [12156]

Feminist Center for Human Growth and Development [13426]

Feminist Dalit Org. [IO]

Feminist Intl. Radio Endeavour [IO]

Feminist Majority Found. [17532]

Feminists Concerned for Better Feminist Leadership [17533]

Feminists for Free Expression [17534]

Fredrika - Bremer - Assn. [IO]

Fundacion Puntos de Encuentro [IO]

Gaia Intl. Women's Center [IO]

Gender Action [18825]

Gender and Trade in Africa [IO]

Gen. Commn. on the Status and Role of Women [17535]

Global Fund for Women [17536]

Global Fund for Women [IO]

Guam Women's Club [17537]

INCITE! Women of Color Against Violence [18788]

Inst. of Women Today [17538]

Inst. for Women's Policy Res. [17539]

Inst. for Women's Stud. in the Arab World [IO]

Inter-American Commn. of Women [IO]

Inter-American Commn. of Women [17540]

Intl. Alliance of Women [IO]

Intl. Alliance of Women [IO]

Intl. Assn. for Women of Color Day [IO]

Intl. Assn. for Women of Color Day [17541]

Intl. Black Women for Wages for Housework [18811]

Intl. Black Women's Cong. [17542]

International Black Women's Congress [IO]

Intl. Center for Res. on Women [IO]

Intl. Center for Res. on Women [17543]

Intl. Coun. of Women [IO]

Intl. Gender and Trade Network - Central Asia [IO]

Intl. Gender and Trade Network - Europe [IO]

Intl. Info. Centre and Archives for the Women's Movement [IO]

Intl. Network on Feminist Approaches to Bioethics [12126]

Intl. Rebecca West Soc. [11178]

Intl. Women's Anthropology Conf. [6420]

Intl. Women's Forum [13429]

Intl. Women's Tribune Centre/Women, Ink [17544]

Intl. Women's Tribune Centre/Women, Ink [IO]

Isis International-Manila [IO]

ISIS - Women's Intl. Cross-Cultural Exchange [IO]

Israel Women's Network [IO]

Know, Inc. [17545]

Latin Am. Gender and Trade Network [IO]

Latin Amer. and Caribbean Comm. for the Defense of Women's Rights [IO]

Legal Momentum: Advancing Women's Rights [17546]

Lesotho Natl. Coun. of Women [IO]

Lucy Stone League [IO]

Lucy Stone League [17547]

MANA, A Natl. Latina Org. [17548]

Mothers And More [12086]

Ms. Found. for Women [17549]

Natl. Action Comm. on the Status of Women [IO]

Natl. Assembly of Women [IO]

Natl. Assn. of Commissions for Women [17550]

Natl. Black Women's Consciousness Raising Assn. [17551]

Natl. Coalition of 100 Black Women [17552]

Natl. Comm. on Pay Equity [17553]

Natl. Conf. of Puerto Rican Women [17554]

Natl. Coun. of Negro Women [17555]

Natl. Coun. for Res. on Women [17556]

Natl. Coun. of Women of Australia [IO]

Natl. Coun. of Women of Canada [IO]

Natl. Coun. of Women of Finland [IO]

Natl. Coun. of Women of New Zealand [IO]

Natl. Coun. of Women of Switzerland [IO]

Natl. Coun. of Women of Thailand [IO]

Natl. Coun. of Women of the U.S. [17557]

Natl. Coun. of Women's Organizations [17558]

Natl. Fed. of French-Canadian Women [IO]

Natl. Hook-Up of Black Women [17559]

Natl. Inst. of Womanhood [13432]

Natl. Network to End Violence Against Immigrant Women [13433]

Natl. Org. for Women [17560]

Natl. Partnership for Women and Families [17561]

Natl. Union of Tunisian Women [IO]

Natl. Woman's Party [17562]

Natl. Women's Conf. [17563]

Natl. Women's Conf. Center [17564]

Natl. Women's Law Center [17565]

Natl. Women's Political Caucus [17566]

Nederlandse Vereniging Van Huisvrouwen [IO]

Netherlands Assn. for Women's Interests, Women's Work and Equal Citizenship [IO]

Netherlands Coun. of Women [IO]

Network of NGOs of Trinidad and Tobago for the Advancement of Women [IO]

Older Women's League [13435]

Org. of Chinese Amer. Women [17567]

Pacific Gender and Trade Network [IO]

Pan-Pacific and South-East Asia Women's Assn. [IO]

Priests for Equality [17568]

Radical Women [17569]

Rights of Women [IO]

Roma Women Assn. in Romania [IO]

St. Joan's Intl. Alliance U.S. Sect. [IO]

St. Joan's Intl. Alliance U.S. Sect. [17570]

Semillas - Sociedad Mexicana Pro Derechos de la Mujer, AC [IO]

SisterSong Women of Color Reproductive Hea. Collective [18826]

Socialist Intl. Women [IO]

Soc. for the Stud. of Early Modern Women [9331]

Sociologists for Women in Soc. [9924]

Sociologists for Women in Soc. [IO]

SOS Sexisme [IO]

Step Up Women's Network [13440]

Thai Assn. of Univ. Women [IO]

Tibetan Women's Assn. [IO]

Truth Missionaries Chap. of Positive Accord [20585]

UNIFEM Natl. Comm. Japan [IO]

UNIFEM New Zealand [IO]

United Nations Development Fund for Women [IO]

United Nations Development Fund for Women [17571]

Univ. Women's Assn. - Singapore [IO]

Veteran Feminists of Am. [17572]

VIEW Clubs of Australia [IO]

Vrouwen Overleg Komitee [IO]

The Woman Activist [17573]

The Woman Activist Fund [17574]

Women in Bio [6618]

Women in Crisis [13443]

Women and Philanthropy [17575]

Women in Transition [13447]

Women of Wind Energy [7854]

A star before a book entry number signifies that the name is not listed separately, but is mentioned within the entry.

Women's Action Alliance [IO]
Women's Action Gp. [IO]
Women's Alliance for Theology, Ethics and Ritual [20626]
Women's Assn. of Romania [IO]
Women's Campaign Fund [17576]
Women's Env. and Development Org. [17577]
Women's Env. and Development Org. [IO]
Women's Infoteka [IO]
Women's Innovation Projects East-West [IO]
Women's Intl. Coalition for Economic Justice [17475]
Women's Intl. Network [17578]
Women's Intl. Network [IO]
Women's Law Proj. [17579]
Women's Legal Educ. and Action Fund [IO]
Women's Natl. Commn. [IO]
Women's Ordination Conf. [19740]
Women's Res. and Educ. Inst. [17580]
Women's Rights Comm. [17581]
Women's Rights Proj. [17582]
Women's Services Worldwide [13453]
Women's Spirituality Forum [20628]
Women's Union of Russia [IO]
Working Women's Forum (India) [IO]
Zimbabwe Women's Rsrc. Centre and Network [IO]
Feminism; Assn. for the Advancement of [IO]
Feminism and Family Stud. Sect. of the Natl. Coun. on Family Relations [12156], 3989 Central Ave. NE, Ste. 550, Minneapolis, MN 55421, (763)781-9331
Feminism and Family Stud. Sect; Natl. Coun. of Family Relations [★12156]
Feminism; Soc. for Analytical [10829]
Feminist Alliance Against Rape - Defunct.
Feminist Approaches to Bioethics; Network on [★12126]
Feminist Business and Professional Network - Address unknown since 1995.
Feminist Center for Human Growth and Development [13426], c/o Charlotte Schwab, PhD, Exec. Dir., 14719C Canalview Dr., Delray Beach, FL 33484, (561)638-4757
Feminist Collective; Iris Films/Iris [11086]
Feminist Dalit Org. [IO], Lalitpur, Nepal
Feminist Educ. and Res. in Europe; Assn. of Institutions for [IO]
Feminist Forums - Address unknown since 1995.
Feminist Intl. Radio Endeavour [IO], Ciudad Colon, Costa Rica
Feminist Karate Union [★23561]
Feminist Karate Union [23561], 1426 S Jackson St., Seattle, WA 98144, (206)325-3878
Feminist Karate Union/Alternatives to Fear [★23561]
Feminist Majority Found. [17532], 1600 Wilson Blvd., Ste. 801, Arlington, VA 22209, (703)522-2214
Feminist Majority; Fund for the [★17532]
The Feminist Press at the City Univ. of New York [9317], c/o The Graduate Center, CUNY, 365 5th Ave., Ste. 5406, New York, NY 10016, (212)817-7915
Feminist Radio Network - Defunct.
Feminist Resources on Energy and Ecology - Defunct.
Feminist Teacher Editorial Collective [9318], c/o Gail Cohee, Sarah Doyle Women's Center, Brown Univ., Box 1829, Providence, RI 02912
Feminist Women's Health Center/Women's Choice Clinic - Defunct.
Feminist Writers Guild [★11198]
Feminist Writers' Guild - Defunct.
Feministas Unidas [10000], c/o Candyce Leonard, Treas./Membership Recorder, Wake Forest Univ., PO Box 7332, Winston-Salem, NC 27109
Feminists for Animal Rights [11396], PO Box 41355, Tucson, AZ 85717-1355, (520)825-6852
Feminists; Assn. of Libertarian [18013]
Feminists on Children's Media - Defunct.
Feminists Concerned for Better Feminist Leadership [17533]
Feminists Fighting Pornography - Address unknown since 1999.
Feminists for Free Expression [17534], 2525 Times Square Sta., New York, NY 10108-2525, (718)651-1232

Feminists for Life of Am. [18552], PO Box 20685, Alexandria, VA 22320, (703)836-3354
Feminists on the March - Address unknown since 2007.
Femme Developpement Entreprise en Afrique [IO], Dakar, Senegal
Femmes en Detresse [IO], Luxembourg, Luxembourg
Femmes sous Lois Musulmanes Reseau [★IO]
Fence Indus. Assn; Intl. [★938]
Fencers League of Amer; Amateur [★23402]
Fencing
    Assn. for Historical Fencing [23399]
    Association for Historical Fencing [IO]
    Assn. for Renaissance Martial Arts [8820]
    British Fencing Assn. [IO]
    Canadian Fencing Fed. [IO]
    Chain Link Fence Manufacturers Inst. [1362]
    Christian Fencers Assn. [23400]
    Danish Fencing Fed. [IO]
    European Veterans Fencing Comm. [IO]
    Intercollegiate Fencing Assn. [23401]
    Qatar Fencing Fed. [IO]
    U.S. Acad. of European Fencing [22414]
    U.S. Fencing Assn. [23402]
    U.S. Fencing Coaches Assn. [23403]
Fencing Coaches Assn. of Am; Natl. [★23403]
Fencing Coaches Assn; U.S. [23403]
Fencing Contractors Assn. [IO], Monmouth, United Kingdom
Fenestration Rating Coun; Natl. [648]
Feng Shui Inst. of Am. [9904], 7547 Bruns Ct., Canal Winchester, OH 43110, (614)837-8370
Feng Shui Soc. [IO], London, United Kingdom
Fenton Art Glass Collectors of Am. [22552], PO Box 384, Williamstown, WV 26187-0384, (304)375-6196
Fenton Glass Soc; Natl. [22564]
Fenway Community Hea. [14430], 7 Haviland St., Boston, MA 02115-2608, (617)267-0900
Feral Cat Friends [21907], 8255 White Oak Rd., Garner, NC 27529, (919)662-5365
Feral Felines; Friends of [21908]
Ferdinand; Friends of Old St. [19626]
Ferenc Liszt Soc.; Budapest [IO], Budapest, Hungary
Feres Project Found. - Address unknown since 2003.
FeRFA Resin Flooring Assn. [IO], Farnham, United Kingdom
Ferguson Family Org. - Defunct.
Fern Found; Hardy [4977]
Fern Soc; Amer. [6623]
Ferrari Club of Am. [21643], PO Box 720597, Atlanta, GA 30358, (800)328-0444
Ferrari Data Bank - Defunct.
Ferrari Owners Club [21644], 18000 Studebakers Rd., Ste. 700, Cerritos, CA 90703, (562)467-6957
Ferret
    Alberta Ferret Soc. [IO]
    Amer. Ferret Assn. [22415]
    Ferret Aid Soc. [IO]
    Ferret Fanciers Club [22416]
    Natl. Ferret Welfare Soc. [IO]
    NSW Ferret Welfare Soc. [IO]
    Support Our Shelters [11462]
Ferret Aid Soc. [IO], Mississauga, ON, Canada
Ferret Blood Donor Program [★22416]
Ferret Fanciers Club [22416]
The Ferroalloys Assn. [★2734]
Ferroelectrics, and Frequency Control Soc; IEEE Ultrasonics, [6366]
Ferrous Founders' Soc; Non- [2053]
Ferrous Metals Producers Comm; Non- [2723]
Ferrous Scrap Consumers Coalition - Defunct.
Ferry/Ferrie Family History Assn. - Address unknown since 2007.
Fertile Hope [14390], PO Box 624, New York, NY 10014, (888)994-HOPE
Fertiliser Assn. of India [IO], New Delhi, India
Fertiliser Assn. of Ireland [IO], Dublin, Ireland
Fertiliser Mfrs'. Assn. [★IO]
Fertiliser Soc. - England [★IO]
Fertility
    Alan Guttmacher Inst. [12175]

    Amer. Acad. of Fertility Care Professionals [12634]
    Amer. Fertility Assn. [14388]
    Amer. Pregnancy Assn. [15588]
    Amer. Soc. for Reproductive Medicine [14389]
    American Society for Reproductive Medicine [IO]
    Assn. of Reproductive Hea. Professionals [12177]
    Billings Ovulation Method Assn. - USA [12635]
    Center for the Stud. of Multiple Birth [15272]
    Couple to Couple League [12636]
    Donors' Offspring [13298]
    EngenderHealth [12180]
    Family of the Americas Found. [12637]
    Family Hea. Intl. [12181]
    Fertile Hope [14390]
    Fertility Res. Found. [14391]
    Healthy Teen Network [12182]
    Intl. Coun. on Infertility Info. Dissemination [14392]
    International Council on Infertility Information Dissemination [IO]
    Intl. Planned Parenthood Fed., Western Hemisphere Region [12184]
    Maternal Life Intl. [16341]
    Natl. Abortion Fed. [11223]
    Natl. Family Planning and Reproductive Hea. Assn. [12185]
    Natl. Infertility Network Exchange [12678]
    Off. of Population Affairs CH [12757]
    Pathfinder Intl. [12186]
    Planned Parenthood Fed. of Am. [12187]
    Reproductive Toxicology Center [14393]
    Reproductive Toxicology Center [IO]
    Resolve, The Natl. Infertility Assn. [14394]
    Soc. for Assisted Reproductive Tech. [16346]
    Soc. for the Stud. of Reproduction [16350]
    Turner Syndrome Soc. of the U.S. [14486]
Fertility and Andrology Soc; Canadian [IO]
Fertility Care Professionals; Amer. Acad. of [12634]
Fertility Inst; New York [★14391]
Fertility; Intl. Soc. of Infectious Diseases and Human In [★16347]
Fertility Res. Found. [14391], 877 Park Ave., New York, NY 10021, (212)744-5500
Fertility Res. Found; New York [★14391]
Fertility Res. Prog; Intl. [★12181]
Fertility Soc; Amer. [★14389]
Fertility Soc. of Australia [IO], Melbourne, Australia
Fertility Soc; British [IO]
Fertilizer
    Agricultural Indus. Confed. [IO]
    Agricultural Retailers Assn. [1363]
    Arab Fertilizer Assn. [IO]
    Assn. of Amer. Plant Food Control Officials [5433]
    Assn. of Fertilizer and Phosphate Chemists [6673]
    Canadian Fertilizer Inst. [IO]
    Canadian Sphagnum Peat Moss Assn. [IO]
    Chem. Producers and Distributors Assn. [803]
    Compost Tea Indus. Assn. [186]
    Composting Coun. of Canada [IO]
    European Fertilizer Mfrs. Assn. [IO]
    Fertiliser Assn. of India [IO]
    Fertiliser Assn. of Ireland [IO]
    Fertilizer Indus. Round Table [1364]
    The Fertilizer Inst. [1365]
    Fertilizer Soc. of South Africa [IO]
    Finnish Peatland Soc. [IO]
    German Soc. for Bog and Peat Res. [IO]
    IFDC - An Intl. Center for Soil Fertility and Agricultural Development [IO]
    IFDC - An Intl. Center for Soil Fertility and Agricultural Development [4665]
    Intl. Fertiliser Soc. - England [IO]
    Intl. Fertilizer Indus. Assn. [IO]
    Intl. Peat Soc. [IO]
    Intl. Potash Inst. [IO]
    John Innes Mfrs. Assn. [IO]
    Natl. Assn. for the Diffusion of Fertilizers [IO]
    North Amer. Horticultural Supply Assn. [4984]
    Peat Soc. of Belarus [IO]
    Peat Soc. of Czech Republic [IO]
    Peat Soc. of Latvia [IO]
    Peat Soc. of Lithuania [IO]
    Peat Soc. of Netherlands [IO]

Reference to "IO" in place of a book number signifies that the association may be found in the 45th edition of International Organizations.

Peat Soc. of Poland [IO]
Peat Soc. of Russia [IO]
Peat Soc. of Ukraine [IO]
Fertilizer Control Officials; Assn. of Amer. [★5433]
Fertilizer Dealers Assn. - Defunct.
Fertilizer Development Center - USA; Intl. [★4665]
Fertilizer Indus. Round Table [1364], c/o Ms. Peggy
  Long, 1701 S Highland Ave., Baltimore, MD 21224,
  (410)276-4466
The Fertilizer Inst. [1365], Union Center Plz., 820
  1st St. NE, Ste. 430, Washington, DC 20002,
  (202)962-0490
Fertilizer; Korean Soc. of Soil Sci. and [IO]
Fertilizer Soc. of South Africa [IO], Lynnwood Ridge,
  Republic of South Africa
Fertilizer Solutions Assn; Natl. [★1363]
Fescue and Creeping Red Fescue Commn; Chew-
  ings [4792]
Festival; Amer. Dance [★9865]
Festival Comm; Scott Joplin Ragtime [★10694]
Festival of Microtonal Music; Amer. [10533]
Festivals; Assn. of Scottish Games and [19348]
Fetal Alcohol Syndrome; Natl. Org. on [16515]
Fetal Urology; Soc. for [16713]
FFA; Natl. [★7940]
FFA Org; Natl. [7940]
Ffederasiwn Cerddoriaeth Amatur Cymru [★IO]
FG Syndrome Family Alliance [IO], Corvallis, OR,
  United States
FG Syndrome Family Alliance [16533], 946 NW
  Circle Blvd., No. 290, Corvallis, OR 97330,
  (617)577-9050
FIABCI - Andorra [IO], Andorra la Vella, Andorra
FIABCI - Argentina [IO], Buenos Aires, Argentina
FIABCI - Australia [IO], Deakin West, Australia
FIABCI - Austria [IO], Vienna, Austria
FIABCI - Brazil [IO], Sao Paulo, Brazil
FIABCI - Bulgaria [IO], Sofia, Bulgaria
FIABCI - Canada [IO], Oakville, ON, Canada
FIABCI - Colombia [IO], Bogota, Colombia
FIABCI - Costa Rica [IO], San Jose, Costa Rica
FIABCI - Cyprus [IO], Nicosia, Cyprus
FIABCI - Czech Republic [IO], Prague, Czech
  Republic
FIABCI - Dominican Republic [IO], Santo Domingo,
  Dominican Republic
FIABCI - Finland [IO], Helsinki, Finland
FIABCI - Georgia [IO], Tbilisi, Georgia
FIABCI - German Chap. [IO], Hamburg, Germany
FIABCI - Greece [IO], Athens, Greece
FIABCI - Hungary [IO], Budapest, Hungary
FIABCI - Indonesia [IO], Jakarta, Indonesia
FIABCI - Ireland [IO], Dublin, Ireland
FIABCI - Israel [IO], Jerusalem, Israel
FIABCI - Italy [IO], Milan, Italy
FIABCI - Japan [IO], Tokyo, Japan
FIABCI - Korea [IO], Seoul, Republic of Korea
FIABCI - Latvia [IO], Riga, Latvia
FIABCI - Luxembourg [IO], Luxembourg,
  Luxembourg
FIABCI - Malaysia [IO], Kuala Lumpur, Malaysia
FIABCI - Mexico [IO], Mexico City, Mexico
FIABCI - Monaco [IO], Monte Carlo, Monaco
FIABCI - Netherlands [IO], Nieuwegein, Netherlands
FIABCI - Nigeria [IO], Lagos, Nigeria
FIABCI - Norway [IO], Oslo, Norway
FIABCI - Panama [IO], Panama City, Panama
FIABCI - Philippines Intl. [IO], Quezon City, Philip-
  pines
FIABCI - Portugal [IO], Lisbon, Portugal
FIABCI - Russia [IO], Moscow, Russia
FIABCI - Singapore [IO], Singapore, Singapore
FIABCI - Slovenia [IO], Ljubljana, Slovenia
FIABCI - Spain [IO], Madrid, Spain
FIABCI - Sweden [IO], Stockholm, Sweden
FIABCI - Switzerland [IO], Fribourg, Switzerland
FIABCI - Taiwan [IO], Taipei, Taiwan
FIABCI - Thailand [IO], Bangkok, Thailand
FIABCI - Turkey [IO], Istanbul, Turkey
FIABCI - United Kingdom [IO], London, United
  Kingdom
FIABCI - Uruguay [IO], Montevideo, Uruguay
FIABCI-U.S.A. - U.S. Chap., Intl. Real Estate Fed.
  [3310], 2000 N 15th St., Arlington, VA 22201,
  (703)524-4279

Fianna Fail [IO], Dublin, Ireland
Fiat 600/600D Exchange Club - Defunct.
Fiat Club of America - Defunct.
Fiat Drivers Intl. - Defunct.
FIBA Oceania [IO], Toormina, Australia
Fiber Assn; Mid Atlantic [310]
Fiber Economics Bur. [1366], 1530 Wilson Blvd.,
  Ste. 690, Arlington, VA 22209, (703)875-0432
Fiber Economics Bur. [IO], Arlington, VA, United
  States
Fiber, Fabric and Apparel Coalition for Trade - Ad-
  dress unknown since 1999.
Fiber Fuels Inst. [★1683]
Fiber Mfrs. Assn; Amer. [3769]
Fiber Optic Assn. [9238], 1119 S Mission Rd., Ste.
  355, Fallbrook, CA 92028, (760)451-3655
Fiber Optic Assn. [IO], Fallbrook, CA, United States
Fiber Producers Credit Assn. - Address unknown
  since 2003.
Fiber Soc. [7078], North Carolina State Univ., Coll.
  of Textiles, Raleigh, NC 27695-8301, (919)513-
  0143
Fiber Soc; Indus. [★7078]
Fiberboard Assn; Amer. [590]
Fiberglass Fabrication Assn. [★589]
Fiberglass Reinforced Panel Assn. - Defunct.
Fiberglass Tank and Pipe Inst. [979], 11150 S Wil-
  crest Dr., Ste. 101, Houston, TX 77099-4343,
  (281)568-4100
Fibers
  Artificial and Synthetic Fibers Manufacturers'
    Assn. [IO]
  Assn. of Federchimica [IO]
  Coir Bd. of India [IO]
  Complex Weavers [308]
  Fiber Economics Bur. [1366]
  Fiber Economics Bur. [IO]
  Fiber Soc. [7078]
  Friends of Fiber Art Intl. [9441]
  Intl. Food and Agribusiness Mgt. Assn. [1524]
  Korea Chem. Fibers Assn. [IO]
  Mid Atlantic Fiber Assn. [310]
  North Amer. Indus. Hemp Coun. [7079]
  Plastic Optical Fiber Trade Org. [2863]
  Refractory Ceramic Fibers Coalition [788]
Fibers and By-Products Assn; Textile [3803]
Fibonacci Assn. [IO], Halifax, NS, Canada
Fibre Box Assn. [2887], 25 NW Point Blvd., Ste.
  510, Elk Grove Village, IL 60007, (847)364-9600
Fibre Can and Tube Assn; Natl. [★976]
Fibre Channel Associates [★3743]
Fibre Channel Indus. Assn. [3743], PO Box 29920,
  San Francisco, CA 94129-0920, (415)561-6270
Fibre Drum Mfrs. Assn. - Defunct.
Fibreoptic Indus. Assn. [IO], Buntingford, United
  Kingdom
Fibrodysplasia Ossificans Progressiva Assn; Intl.
  [14457]
FibroHugs: Support for Fibromyalgia [IO], Regina,
  SK, Canada
Fibrohugs.com [★IO]
Fibromatosis Found; Natl. Neuro [★15315]
Fibromatosis; Neuro [14471]
Fibromuscular Dysplasia Soc. of Am. [15322], 20325
  Center Ridge Rd., Ste. 620, Rocky River, OH
  44116, (330)653-8416
Fibromyalgia
  Amer. Fibromyalgia Syndrome Assn. [14395]
  Chronic Syndrome Support Assn. [14259]
  FibroHugs: Support for Fibromyalgia [IO]
  Fibromyalgia Network [IO]
  Fibromyalgia Network [14396]
  Natl. Fibromyalgia Assn. [14397]
  Natl. Fibromyalgia Partnership [14398]
Fibromyalgia Alliance of Am. - Defunct.
Fibromyalgia Assn. of Greater Washington [★14398]
Fibromyalgia Assn; Natl. Chronic Fatigue Syndrome
  and [14278]
Fibromyalgia Assn. U.S.A. - Address unknown since
  2006.
Fibromyalgia Network [14396], PO Box 31750,
  Tucson, AZ 85751-1750, (520)290-5508
Fibromyalgia Network [IO], Tucson, AZ, United
  States
Fibromyalgia, and Orthostatic Intolerance; Pediatric
  Network for Chronic Fatigue Syndrome, [15895]

Fibromyalgia Patients' Assn; Norwegian [IO]
Fibromyalgia Res. Assn; Natl. [15347]
Fibrosis Res. Found; Natl. Cystic [★16358]
Fibrositis
  Fibromyalgia Network [14396]
  Natl. Fibromyalgia Partnership [14398]
Fichte Soc; North Amer. [10815]
Fiction
  Amer. Christian Fiction Writers [11156]
  Arthur Miller Soc. [11159]
  August Derleth Soc. [9634]
  Bread Loaf Writers Conf. [11163]
  Broad Universe [23034]
  Carson McCullers Soc. [11164]
  Catharine Maria Sedgwick Soc. [11165]
  Cormac McCarthy Soc. [11168]
  Don DeLillo Soc. [11169]
  Evelyn Scott Soc. [11170]
  Friends of Freddy [24821]
  Intl. Assn. of Crime Writers, North Amer. Br.
    [11175]
  Intl. Assn. of Media Tie-in Writers [11176]
  Intl. Frankenstein Soc. [24822]
  Intl. Frankenstein Soc. [IO]
  Intl. Rebecca West Soc. [11178]
  Intl. Thriller Writers [11179]
  Jack London Res. Center [9669]
  Mystery Readers Intl. [24823]
  Natl. Alliance of Short Fiction Authors [11182]
  Philip Roth Soc. [11187]
  Susan Glaspell Soc. [11197]
  Thornton Wilder Soc. [11200]
  The Vampire Empire [24824]
Fiction and Fantasy Artists; Assn. of Sci. [307]
Fiction and Fantasy Writers of Am; Sci. [11193]
Fiction Films; Acad. of Horror Films and Sci.
  [★9925]
Fiction Rev; Intl. [IO]
Fiddle Assn. of Am; Hardanger [10606]
Fiddlers' Assn; Natl. Oldtime [10665]
Fiddling Revival; U.S. Scottish [10716]
FIDE Inversion y Exportaciones [★IO]
Fidelco Breeder's Found. [★16846]
Fidelco Found. [★16846]
Fidelco Guide Dog Found. [16846], 103 Old Iron
  Ore Rd., Bloomfield, CT 06002, (860)243-5200
Fidelity; Inst. of High [★1212]
Fiduciaries; Natl. Coun. of Real Estate Investment
  [2344]
Field Archery Assn; Natl. [23055]
Field Artillery Assn; U.S. [★6071]
Field Experience Educ; Soc. for [★8414]
Field Guides Assn. of South Africa [IO], Cresta,
  Republic of South Africa
Field Hockey
  Atlantic Coast Conf. [23806]
  Big East Conf. [23807]
  Big Ten Conf. [23808]
  Coun. of Ivy Gp. Presidents [23817]
  Eastern Collegiate Hockey Assn. [23485]
  Intl. Hockey Fed. [IO]
  Natl. Assn. of Intercollegiate Athletics [23835]
  Natl. Christian Coll. Athletic Assn. [23837]
  Natl. Collegiate Athletic Assn. [23838]
  Natl. Field Hockey Coaches Assn. [23404]
  Natl. Junior Coll. Athletic Assn. [23843]
  Pacific 10 Conf. [23847]
  Southeastern Conf. [23851]
  Southern Conf. [23852]
  U.S. Collegiate Athletic Assn. [23859]
  U.S. Collegiate Sports Coun. [23860]
  U.S. Field Hockey Assn. [23405]
Field Hockey Assn. of Am. [★23405]
Field Hockey Assn; U.S.A. [★23405]
Field Hockey Canada [IO], Ottawa, ON, Canada
Field Hockey; U.S.A. [★23405]
Field Managers' Assn; Fraternal [2165]
Field Marketing Services Assn. [★3418]
Field Marketing Services Assn. - Defunct.
Field Naturalists Club of Victoria [IO], Blackburn,
  Australia
Field Ornithologists; Assn. of [7413]
Field Selling Assn; Natl. [3471]
Field Ser; Amer. [★8589]
Field Ser. Managers, Intl; Assn. of [★3545]

A star before a book entry number signifies that the name is not listed separately, but is mentioned within the entry.

Field Spaniel Soc. of Am. [22266], 351 E Kerley Corners Rd., Tivoli, NY 12583, (845)756-2595

Field Stations; Org. of Inland Biological [★6591]

Field Stud. Coun. [IO], Shrewsbury, United Kingdom

Field Trial Assn; English Springer Spaniel [22262]

Field Trial Clubs of Am; Amateur [22184]

Field in Trust [IO], London, United Kingdom

Field; U.S.A. Track and [23926]

Fielding Steele and Jane Brooks Descendants Org. - Defunct.

Fields Fan Club; W.C. [24801]

Fields Jarvis Family Org. - Defunct.

Fiero Owners Club of Am. [21645], 1598 S Anaheim Blvd., Unit B, Anaheim, CA 92805-6230, (714)917-2007

Fiesta Collectors Club [22022], PO Box 471, Valley City, OH 44280

Fife Chamber of Commerce and Enterprise [IO], Kirkcaldy, United Kingdom

Fife Chamber of Commerce and Indus. [★IO]

Fifers and Drummers; Company of [10580]

Fifinella; Order of [★21413]

Fifth Div; Soc. of the [21187]

Fifty Caliber Shooters Assn. [22973], PO Box 111, Monroe, UT 84754-0111, (435)527-9245

Fifty Caliber Shooters Assn. [IO], Monroe, UT, United States

Fifty Plus Financial Network [1460], c/o Amer. Money Mgt. Gp., 5755 N Point Pkwy., Ste. 57, Alpharetta, GA 30022-1145, (678)297-9500

Fifty-Plus Fitness Assn. [★23920]

Fifty-Plus Lifelong Fitness [★23920]

Fifty-Plus Runners Assn. [★23920]

Fifty-Six Fifty-Seven Lincoln Registry [★21773]

Fifty-Six Fifty-Seven Lincoln Registry [★IO]

Fig Advisory Bd; California [4714]

Fig Advisory Bd; California Dried [★4714]

Fig Growers; Valley [4772]

Fig Inst; California [4715]

Fight to Advance the Nation's Sports - Defunct.

Fight Against Animal Cruelty in Europe [IO], Southport, United Kingdom

Fight Against Child Exploitation [IO], Bangkok, Thailand

Fight Crime: Invest in Kids [17057], 1212 New York Ave. NW, Ste. 300, Washington, DC 20005, (202)776-0027

Fight Directors; Soc. of Amer. [9268]

Fighter Aces Assn; Amer. [20647]

Fighter Assn; 1st [21414]

Fighter Pilots Assn; Red River Valley [21318]

Fighter Squadron Assn., 359th Fighter Gp; 369th [20654]

Fighter Squadron Headhunters' Assn; 80th [5442]

Fighting Robot Assn. [IO], Daventry, United Kingdom

Figlie de San Paolo [★IO]

Figural Bottle Assn. - Defunct.

Figural Bottle Opener Collectors Club [22023], c/o Charles Reynolds, Pres., 2836 Monroe St., Falls Church, VA 22042, (703)533-1322

Figural Cast Iron Collector's Club [22417], 2833 Quaker Valley Rd., New Paris, PA 15554

Figure Skating Assn; U.S. [23744]

Figure Skating Fed. of the Republic of Uzbekistan [IO], Tashkent, Uzbekistan

Figure Skating Fed. of Russia [IO], Moscow, Russia

Figure Skating Union; Intl. Gay [23736]

Figure and Speed Skating Assn. of Thailand [IO], Bangkok, Thailand

Figures Collectors Club [22024], c/o Colleen Lewis, 11174 Hunts Corners Rd., Clarence, NY 14031-2035, (716)741-8399

Figurines

Beyond the Pond.International Frog Collectors Club [21977]

EKJ (Emmett Kelly Jr.) Collectors' Soc. [22017]

Emmett's Elite [22018]

Family Circle of PenDelfin [22020]

Figural Cast Iron Collector's Club [22417]

GI Joe Collectors' Club [22996]

Hummel Collectors Club [22040]

Little Elegance Memories of Yesterday [22065]

Lladro Soc. [21930]

Fiji Badminton Assn. [IO], Suva, Fiji

Fiji Disabled Peoples Assn. [IO], Suva, Fiji

Fiji Employers' Fed. [IO], Suva, Fiji

Fiji Hotel Assn. [★IO]

Fiji Islands Baseball Assn. [IO], Suva, Fiji

Fiji Islands Blind Sport Assn. [IO], Suva, Fiji

Fiji Islands Hotel and Tourism Assn. [IO], Suva, Fiji

Fiji Law Soc. [IO], Suva, Fiji

Fiji Medical Assn. [IO], Suva, Fiji

Fiji Natl. Training and Coun. [★IO]

Fiji Optometric Assn. [IO], Suva, Fiji

Fiji Physiotherapy Assn. [IO], Suva, Fiji

Fiji Taekwondo Assn. [IO], Suva, Fiji

Fiji Tennis Assn. [IO], Lautoka, Fiji

Fiji Touch Assn. [IO], Suva, Fiji

Fiji Visitors' Bur. [IO], Nadi, Fiji

Fiji Weightlifting Fed. [IO], Suva, Fiji

Fiji Women's Crisis Centre [IO], Suva, Fiji

Fiji Yachting Assn. [IO], Lautoka, Fiji

Fikambanana Kristiana hoan'ny Zatovovavy eto Madagasikara [★IO]

Filbert/Hazelnut Inst. - Defunct.

File Mfrs. Assn. - Defunct.

Filene Center [★9602]

Filers; Natl. Assn. of Form 1099 [18711]

Filipinas Americas Sci. and Art Found. [9609], 1209 Park Ave., New York, NY 10128, (212)427-6930

Filipinas Americas Sci. and Art Found. [IO], New York, NY, United States

Filipino Amer. Coalition for Environmental Solidarity [4634], 1808 Fifth St., Berkeley, CA 94710, (510)549-1808

Filipino Amer. Medical Inc. [14722], PO Box 161, New York, NY 10101, (212)582-3304

Filipino Amer. Medical Inc. [IO], New York, NY, United States

Filipino American National Historical Society [IO], Seattle, WA, United States

Filipino Amer. Natl. Historical Soc. [10779], 810 18th Ave., Rm. 100, Seattle, WA 98122, (206)322-0203

Filipino Amer. Political Assn. - Defunct.

Filipino Chamber of Commerce of Honolulu - Address unknown since 1995.

Filipino Shipowners Assn. [IO], Manila, Philippines

Filipino Student Assn. - Defunct.

Filipinos for Affirmative Action [18270], 310 8th St., Ste. 306, Oakland, CA 94607, (510)465-9876

Fillmore, Last of the Whigs; Soc. for the Preservation and Enhancement of the Recognition of Millard [22601]

Film

Abbott and Costello Intl. Fan Club [24795]

Acad. of Sci. Fiction, Fantasy, and Horror Films [9925]

access Cinema [IO]

African Amer. Cinema Soc. [9926]

Aldo Ray Fan Club [24726]

Alliance for Community Media [17161]

Alliance for Inclusion in the Arts [10996]

Amateur Movie Makers Assn. [22418]

Amer. Film Inst. [9927]

Amer. Guild of Variety Artists [24151]

Amer. Russian Theatrical Alliance [11001]

Amer. Screenwriters Assn. [4060]

Amer. Soc. for Aesthetics [9545]

Amer. Theatre Arts for Youth [11003]

Animators Unite [9388]

Anthology Film Archives [9928]

Armenian Film Found. [9405]

Art Directors Guild [9929]

Asian Cinema Stud. Soc. [7981]

Asian CineVision [9930]

Assn. of Canadian Film Craftspeople [IO]

Assn. of Cinema and Video Labs. [1367]

Assn. of Commercial Stock Image Licensors [1378]

Assn. of Film Commissioners Intl. [IO]

Assn. of Film Commissioners Intl. [1368]

Assn. of Independent Video and Filmmakers [9931]

Assn. for Micrography, Image and Info. Mgt. [IO]

Association of Moving Image Archivists [IO]

Assn. of Moving Image Archivists [9932]

Assn. of Polish Filmmakers [IO]

Assn. Quebecoise des Critiques de Cinema [IO]

Atlantic Film Festival Assn. [IO]

Australian Cinematographers Soc. [IO]

Australian Film Inst. [IO]

Auto. Film Club of Am. [344]

Black Filmmaker Found. [9933]

British Bd. of Film Classification [IO]

British Fantasy Soc. [IO]

British Fed. of Film Societies [IO]

British Film Inst. [IO]

British Soc. of Cinematographers [IO]

Butimar Productions [9849]

Canadian Film Centre [IO]

Canadian Film Inst. [IO]

Canadian Film and TV Production Assn. [IO]

Canadian Filmmakers Distribution Centre [IO]

Canadian Soc. of Cinematographers [IO]

Center for Independent Documentary [9934]

Centre of Films for Children and Young People in Germany [IO]

Children's Film Soc., India [IO]

Coalition of Asian Pacifics in Entertainment [1300]

Construction and Agricultural Film Mfrs. Assn. [1369]

Coun. on Intl. Nontheatrical Events [9935]

Coun. on Intl. Nontheatrical Events [IO]

Dance Films Assn. [8185]

Digital Cinema Soc. [1380]

Directors Guild of Am. [24055]

Directors Guild of Canada [IO]

Directors Guild of Great Britain [IO]

Documentary Org. of Canada [IO]

Far Beyond the Stars [24740]

Film Advisory Bd. [9936]

Film Arts Found. [9937]

Film Music Soc. [10595]

Film and TV Inst. of Western Australia [IO]

Film/Video Arts [9938]

FilmAid Intl. [12811]

Godzilla Soc. of North Am. [IO]

Golden Raspberry Award Found. [22419]

Hispanic Org. of Latin Actors [10001]

Historians Film Committee/Film and History Magazine [9939]

Indian Motion Picture Producers' Assn. [IO]

Inst. of the Amer. Musical [10610]

Intl. Alliance of Theatrical Stage Employees, Moving Picture Technicians, Artists and Allied Crafts of the U.S., Its Territories and Canada [24156]

Intl. Animated Film Assn. - Canada [IO]

Intl. Assn. for the Fantastic in the Arts [10945]

Intl. Assn. of Media Tie-in Writers [11176]

Intl. Centre of Films for Children and Young People [IO]

Intl. Coun. of the Museum of Modern Art [9448]

Intl. Crosby Circle [24804]

Intl. Fed. of Film Archives [IO]

Intl. Film Seminars [IO]

Intl. Film Seminars [9940]

Intl. Guild of Symphony, Opera and Ballet Musicians [24157]

Intl. Network of Somewhere in Time Enthusiasts [IO]

Intl. Network of Somewhere in Time Enthusiasts [24825]

Intl. Recording Media Assn. [1370]

Intl. Recording Media Assn. [IO]

Intl. Thriller Writers [11179]

Intl. Union of Non-Professional Cinema [IO]

Japanese Soc. of Cinematographers [IO]

Large Format Cinema Assn. [1387]

Location Managers Guild of Am. [2522]

Lone Ranger Fan Club [25032]

Mamie Van Doren Fan Club [24757]

Media Fellowship Intl. [20024]

Michael Crawford Intl. Fan Assn. [24760]

Motion Picture Sound Editors [1371]

Motion Picture and TV Fund [12115]

Natl. Acad. of TV Arts and Sciences [567]

Natl. Alliance for Media Arts and Culture [9580]

Natl. Assn. of Latino Independent Producers [1390]

Natl. Bd. of Rev. of Motion Pictures [9941]

Natl. Center for Film and Video Preservation [9942]

Natl. Center for Jewish Film [9943]

Natl. Fantasy Fan Club for Disneyana Enthusiasts [24791]

Reference to "IO" in place of a book number signifies that the association may be found in the 45th edition of International Organizations.

Natl. Film Bd. of Canada [IO]
New York Coun. of Motion Picture and TV Unions [24056]
The Official Austin Powers Collector's Club [24826]
Official Robert Newman Fan Club [24765]
Oh Ji Ho Intl. Fan Club [24781]
Old Time Western Film Club [24827]
Org. of Black Screenwriters [1323]
Outfest [9944]
Pacific Islanders in Communications [10455]
Peter Sellers Appreciation Soc. [24767]
Quickdraw Animation Soc. [IO]
Richard Burgi Fan Club [24768]
Rita Hayworth Fan Club [24769]
Robert Redford Fan Club [24770]
San Francisco Camerawork [9945]
Satellite Video Exchange Soc. [IO]
Scottish Screen [IO]
Screen Actors Guild [24158]
SIGNIS [IO]
Soc. for Cinema and Media Stud. [9946]
Soc. for Cinephiles/Cinecon [9947]
Sons of the Desert [24828]
Sons of the Desert [IO]
Sundance Inst. [9948]
Swedish Fed. of Film and Video Amateurs [IO]
Swedish Film Inst. [IO]
Talent Managers Assn. [1325]
Three Stooges Fan Club [24800]
Transylvania Soc. of Dracula [IO]
Univ. Film and Video Assn. [8420]
Univ. Film and Video Found. [8421]
U.S.A. Film Festival [9949]
Visual Stud. Workshop [9950]
Women in Animation [1372]
Women in Film and TV - United Kingdom [IO]
Women in Film and Video [1373]
Women Make Movies [11094]
World Chap. of Disneyana Enthusiasts [22132]
Writers Guild of Am., East [24220]
Writers Guild of Am., West [24221]
Film Advisory Bd. [9936], c/o Janet Stokes, Chair/CEO, 263 W Olive Ave., No. 377, Burbank, CA 91502, (323)461-6541
Film Artistes Assn. [IO], London, United Kingdom
Film Artistes Assn. [★IO]
Film Arts Found. [9937], 145 9th St., Ste. 101, San Francisco, CA 94103, (415)552-8760
Film Assn; Chem. Fabrics and [3048]
Film Assn; Plastic Coatings and [★3048]
Film Assn; Univ. [★8420]
Film and Bag Fed. [980], c/o Soc. of the Plastics Indus., Inc., 1667 K St. NW, Ste. 1000, Washington, DC 20006, (202)974-5218
Film Center; Anthropology [6407]
Film Center; Anthropology [★6407]
Film Center Found; Anthropology [★6407]
Film Center; Japan [★10266]
Film Center; Japan [★IO]
Film Centers; Consortium of Univ. [★8554]
Film Club [★9938]
Film Coalition - Defunct.
Film Commn; Broadcasting and [★19537]
Film Commn; Protestant [★19537]
Film Commissioners; Assn. of [★1368]
Film Comm; Historians [★9939]
Film Critics' Circle of the Foreign Language Press of New York - Address unknown since 1995.
Film Culture Non-Profit on Corp. - Address unknown since 1990.
Film Distribution Center; Youth [★9938]
Film Distributors' Assn. [IO], London, United Kingdom
Film Found; Univ. [★8421]
Film Foundation; Women in [★1396]
Film Fund - Defunct.
Film and History Magazine; Historians Film Committee/ [9939]
Film Industry
Acad. of Canadian Cinema and TV [IO]
Acad. of Motion Picture Arts and Sciences [1374]
Acad. of Sci. Fiction, Fantasy, and Horror Films [9925]
Advanced Media Workflow Assn. [3721]

African Amer. Cinema Soc. [9926]
Alliance for Community Media [17161]
Alliance of Motion Picture and TV Producers [1375]
Amateur Movie Makers Assn. [22418]
Amer. Cinema Editors [1376]
Amer. Film Inst. [9927]
Amer. Screenwriters Assn. [4060]
Amer. Soc. of Cinematographers [1377]
Armenian Film Found. [9405]
Art Directors Guild [9929]
Asian CineVision [9930]
Assn. of Audiovisual and Film Indus. of Austria [IO]
Assn. of Commercial Stock Image Licensors [1378]
Assn. of Intl. Collective Mgt. of Audiovisual Works [IO]
Assn. of Motion Picture Sound [IO]
Australian Screen Directors Assn. [IO]
Australian Screen Editors Guild [IO]
Auto. Film Club of Am. [344]
Black Stuntmen's Assn. [1379]
British Acad. of Film and TV Arts [IO]
British Acad. of Film and TV Arts - Scotland [IO]
British Video Assn. [IO]
Canadian Motion Picture Distribution Assn. [IO]
Celtic Film and TV Festival [IO]
Coalition of Asian Pacifics in Entertainment [1300]
Digital Cinema Soc. [1380]
Digital Cinema Soc. [IO]
Directors' and Producers' Rights Soc. [IO]
European Film Acad. [IO]
Fed. of Spanish Audiovisual Producer Associations [IO]
Film Distributors' Assn. [IO]
Golden Raspberry Award Found. [22419]
IMAGO - European Fed. of Cinematographers [IO]
Independent Feature Proj. [1381]
Independent Film and TV Alliance [1382]
Independent Film and Television Alliance [IO]
Independent Media Arts Alliance [IO]
Indian Soc. of Cinematographers [IO]
Intl. Animated Film Assn. [IO]
Intl. Animated Film Soc., ASIFA - Hollywood [1383]
Intl. Assn. of Audio Visual Communicators [1384]
Intl. Assn. of Audio Visual Communicators [IO]
Intl. Documentary Assn. [IO]
Intl. Documentary Assn. [1385]
Intl. Motion Picture and Lecturers Assn. [1386]
Intl. Motion Picture and Lecturers Assn. [IO]
Intl. Newsreel and News Film Assn. [IO]
Intl. TV Assn. Deutschland [IO]
Intl. TV Assn. - Japan [IO]
Intl. TV Assn. - New Zealand [IO]
Intl. Video Fed. [IO]
Large Format Cinema Assn. [1387]
Location Managers Guild of Am. [2522]
Media Communications Assn. - Denmark [IO]
Media Communications Assn. Intl. [IO]
Media Communications Assn. Intl. [1388]
Motion Picture Assn. of Am. [1389]
Motion Picture and TV Fund [12115]
Motion Picture Theatre Associations of Canada [IO]
Natl. Assn. of Latino Independent Producers [1390]
Natl. Assn. of Video Distributors [1391]
Natl. Bd. of Rev. of Motion Pictures [9941]
Natl. TV and Video Assn. of South Africa [IO]
Netherlands Fed. of Film Professionals [IO]
New Producers Alliance [IO]
New York Coun. of Motion Picture and TV Unions [24056]
New Zealand Film Commn. [IO]
Org. of Black Screenwriters [1323]
Producers Guild of Am. [1392]
Screen Producers Assn. of Australia [IO]
Set Decorators Soc. of Am. [2276]
Stuntmen's Assn. of Motion Pictures [1393]
Stuntwomen's Assn. of Motion Pictures [1394]
Sundance Inst. [9948]
Talent Managers Assn. [1325]

Wedding and Event Videographers Assn. Intl. [1395]
Wedding and Event Videographers Assn. Intl. [IO]
Women in Film [1396]
Film Inst. Alumni Assn. Writers Workshop; Amer. [★11203]
Film Inst; Anthropology [★6407]
Film Lecturers Assn. [★1386]
Film Lecturers Assn. [★IO]
Film-Makers' Cinematheque [★9928]
Film Music Soc. [10595], 1516 S Bundy Dr., Ste. 305, Los Angeles, CA 90025, (310)820-1909
Film Music; Soc. for the Preservation of [★10595]
Film Producers of Am; Info. [★1384]
Film Producers Assn; Indus. [★1384]
Film Producers Assn. of New York - Defunct.
Film Producers Assn; Univ. [★8420]
Film; Prog. in Ethnographic [★6436]
Film Sense - Address unknown since 1995.
Film Stud. Assn. of Canada [IO], Toronto, ON, Canada
Film and TV Archives Advisory Comm. [★IO]
Film and TV Archives Advisory Comm. [★9932]
Film and TV Coordinating Comm. - Defunct.
Film and TV Inst. of Western Australia [IO], Fremantle, Australia
Film/Video Arts [9938], 270 W 96th St., New York, NY 10025, (212)941-8787
Film and Video Communicators; IFPA [★1384]
FilmAid Intl. [12811], 24 E 23rd St., 4th Fl., New York, NY 10010, (212)529-1088
FilmAid Intl. [IO], New York, NY, United States
Filmmaker Found; Black [9933]
Filmmakers; Assn. of Independent Video and [9931]
Filmmakers Found; Young [★9938]
Filmmakers United Against Apartheid - Address unknown since 1988.
Films Assn; Dance [8185]
Films, Inc; Dance [★8185]
Films; Iris [★11086]
Films/Iris Feminist Collective; Iris [11086]
Films and Sci. Fiction Films; Acad. of Horror [★9925]
Fils de la Charite [★IO]
Filter Inst; Air [★1873]
Filter Manufacturers Coun. [384], PO Box 13966, Research Triangle Park, NC 27709-3966, (919)549-4800
Filter Manufacturers Coun. [IO], Research Triangle Park, NC, United States
Filter Manufacturers Coun; Automotive [★384]
Filtration
Filtration Soc. [IO]
Filtration Assn; Natl. Air [1894]
Filtration and Separations Soc; Amer. [7724]
Filtration Soc. [IO], Coleorton, United Kingdom
FIMITIC [★IO]
Finance
ACA Intl. [1144]
ACI - Financial Markets Assn. [IO]
Advt. Media Credit Executives Assn. [1397]
African Venture Capital Assn. [IO]
Alliance Credit Counseling [11833]
Alliance of Merger and Acquisition Advisors [54]
Alliance in Support of Independent Res. [3390]
Amer. Assn. of Individual Investors [8422]
Amer. Assn. for Long-Term Care Insurance [2132]
Amer. Bankers Assn. [457]
Amer. Coun. of State Savings Supervisors [458]
Amer. Economic Assn. [6868]
Amer. Escrow Assn. [1398]
Amer. Finance Assn. [1399]
Amer. Inst. for Economic Res. [6869]
Amer. League of Financial Institutions [459]
Amer. Money Mgt. Gp. [1454]
Amer. Recovery Assn. [1145]
Amer. Savings Educ. Coun. [8440]
Amer. Soc. of Tax Problem Solvers [6290]
Amer. Soc. of Tax Professionals [10]
Amer. Woman's Economic Development Corp. [3604]
Anguilla Financial Services Assn. [IO]
Arab Bankers Assn. of North Am. [462]
Asia Pacific Loan Market Assn. [IO]
Asian Clearing Union [IO]

A star before a book entry number signifies that the name is not listed separately, but is mentioned within the entry.

Asian Financial Soc. [1400]
Asset Managers Forum [1401]
Asset Managers Forum [IO]
Associacao Brasileira de Private Equity and
    Venture Capital [IO]
Assn. of African Amer. Financial Advisors [1455]
Assn. of Canadian Pension Mgt. [IO]
Assn. of Certified Anti-Money Laundering Special-
    ists [463]
Assn. of Certified Fraud Specialists [2085]
Assn. of Certified Treasury Managers [IO]
Assn. of Chinese Finance Professionals [1402]
Assn. for Comparative Economic Stud. [6870]
Assn. of Corporate Treasurers [IO]
Assn. of Corporate Treasurers (Singapore) [IO]
Assn. of Corporate Treasurers of Southern Africa
    [IO]
Assn. for Evolutionary Economics [6872]
Assn. of Finance and Insurance Professionals
    [2146]
Assn. for Financial Professionals [1403]
Assn. for Financial Tech. [61]
Assn. of Fund-Raising Distributors and Suppliers
    [1684]
Assn. of Govt. Accountants [5426]
Assn. of PVO Financial Managers [1458]
Assn. of Trade and Forfaiting in the Americas
    [1404]
Assn. of Trade and Forfaiting in the Americas [IO]
Australian Venture Capital Assn. Limited [IO]
British Cheque Cashers Assn. [IO]
British Venture Capital Assn. [IO]
Broadcast Cable Financial Mgt. Assn. [553]
Bus. Products Credit Assn. [1405]
Canada's Venture Capital and Private Equity
    Assn. [IO]
Canadian/American Border Trade Alliance [3838]
Canadian Capital Markets Assn. [IO]
Canadian Finance and Leasing Assn. [IO]
Center for Financial Freedom and Accuracy in
    Financial Reporting [18404]
Center for Popular Economics [6875]
Center for Venture Res. [2330]
Certified Financial Planner Bd. of Standards
    [1459]
CFA Inst. [2331]
Chartered Alternative Investment Analyst Assn.
    [2332]
Check Payment Systems Assn. [3678]
Chicago Stock Exchange [3510]
China Venture Capital Assn. [IO]
Chinese Finance Assn. [1406]
Clearpoint Financial Solutions [1407]
Coalition Against Insurance Fraud [2155]
Commercial Finance Assn. [2423]
Community Financial Services Assn. [1408]
The Conf. Bd. [6877]
Conf. on Consumer Finance Law [5608]
Consumer Bankers Assn. [470]
Consumer Credit Trade Assn. [IO]
Consumer Data Indus. Assn. [1409]
Controllers Coun. [22]
Corporate Coun. on Africa [169]
Coun. of Gen. Motors Credit Unions [1105]
Credit Card Users of America [1410]
Credit Professionals Intl. [1411]
Credit Professionals Intl. [IO]
Credit Res. Found. [1412]
CUES Financial Suppliers Forum [2623]
Debtors Anonymous [13017]
Direct Marketing Fundraisers Assn. [1685]
Dominicans on Wall St. [1413]
Dominicans on Wall St. [IO]
Dutch Assn. of Corporate Treasurers [IO]
Dutch Corporate Finance Assn. [IO]
Eastern Finance Assn. [1414]
Emerging Markets Private Equity Assn. [1415]
Emerging Markets Private Equity Association [IO]
European Fed. of Financial Analysts Societies
    [IO]
European Finance Assn. [IO]
European Financial Mgt. and Marketing Assn. [IO]
European Money and Finance Forum [IO]
European Org. of Supreme Audit Institutions [IO]
Factors and Discounters Assn. [IO]

Fed. of Euro-Asian Stock Exchanges [IO]
Finance and Leasing Assn. [IO]
Finance Proj. [17583]
Financial Accounting Standards Bd. [29]
Financial Executives Intl. [1416]
Financial Executives Intl. [IO]
Financial Executives Res. Found. [1417]
Financial Managers Soc. [1418]
Financial Markets Assn. [1419]
Financial Markets Assn. - U.S.A. [475]
Financial Planning Assn. [1420]
Financial Planning Assn. [IO]
Financial Planning Assn. of Australia [IO]
Financial Services Tech. Consortium [7732]
Financial Women's Assn. of New York [1421]
FINEX [1710]
Forius Bus. Credit Resources [1422]
Found. for the Advancement of Monetary Educ.
    [8423]
Gender Action [18825]
Giving Inst. [1686]
Global Assn. of Risk Professionals [1423]
Global Assn. of Risk Professionals [IO]
Global Equity Org. [1239]
Govt. Finance Officers Assn. of U.S. and Canada
    [6204]
The Grantsmanship Center [1687]
Gp. of Thirty [1172]
Gp. Underwriters Assn. of Am. [2167]
Healthcare Financial Mgt. Assn. [15066]
Hong Kong Venture Capital Assn. [IO]
Hospitality Asset Managers Assn. [1942]
Hungarian Venture Capital and Private Equity
    Assn. [IO]
Indian Venture Capital Assn. [IO]
Info. Technologies Credit Union Assn. [1110]
Insol Intl. [IO]
Insolvency Aid Soc. [IO]
Inst. of Certified Bus. Counselors [726]
Inst. of Consumer Financial Educ. [8424]
Inst. of Credit Mgt. [IO]
Inst. for Economic Anal. [6880]
Inst. of Financial Planning [IO]
Inst. of Licensed Trade Stock Auditors [IO]
Intl. Assn. of Commercial Collectors [1147]
Intl. Assn. of Financial Engineers [1424]
Intl. Assn. of Financial Executives Institutes [IO]
Intl. Assn. of Registered Financial Consultants
    [IO]
Intl. Assn. of Registered Financial Consultants
    [1425]
Intl. Assn. for Res. in Income and Wealth [18407]
Intl. Atlantic Economic Soc. [6883]
Intl. Bond and Share Soc. [22046]
Intl. Consortium on Governmental Financial Mgt.
    [1426]
Intl. Consortium on Governmental Financial Mgt.
    [IO]
Intl. Economics and Finance Soc. [6884]
Intl. Energy Credit Assn. [1427]
Intl. Energy Credit Assn. [IO]
Intl. Financial Services Assn. [483]
Intl. Network of Alternative Financial Institution
    [IO]
Intl. Newspaper Financial Executives [IO]
Intl. Newspaper Financial Executives [1428]
Intl. Open Finance Assn. [17584]
Intl. Open Finance Assn. [IO]
Intl. Soc. of Financiers [IO]
Intl. Soc. of Financiers [1429]
Investment Educ. Inst. [8425]
Investment Mgt. Consultants Assn. [2336]
Israel Venture Assn. [IO]
I.T. Financial Mgt. Assn. [1430]
Italian Private Equity and Venture Capital Assn.
    [IO]
Japan Securities Dealers' Assn. [IO]
Japanese Soc. of Certified Pension Actuaries [IO]
Latin Amer. Venture Capital Assn. [1431]
Latvian Venture Capital and Private Equity Assn.
    [IO]
LICU [1111]
Life Insurance Settlement Assn. [2193]
Loan Syndications and Trading Assn. [484]
Local Initiatives Support Corp. [17224]

London Investment Banking Assn. [IO]
Malaysian Venture Capital Assn. [IO]
Media Credit Assn. [1432]
Medical Banking Proj. [1433]
Money Mgt. Intl. [12190]
Motion Picture and TV Credit Assn. [1434]
NASD [3517]
Natl. Aboriginal Capital Corp. Assn. [IO]
Natl. African-American Insurance Assn. [2202]
Natl. Assn. of Christian Financial Consultants
    [1465]
Natl. Assn. of Commercial Finance Brokers [IO]
Natl. Assn. of Corporate Treasurers [1435]
Natl. Assn. of Credit Mgt. [1436]
Natl. Assn. of Credit Union Chairmen [1112]
Natl. Assn. of Development Companies [2427]
Natl. Assn. of Fed. Credit Unions [1115]
Natl. Assn. of Financial and Estate Planning
    [1437]
Natl. Assn. of Financial Services [IO]
Natl. Assn. of Govt. Defined Contribution
    Administrators [2340]
Natl. Assn. of Investors Corp. [2342]
Natl. Assn. of Mortgage Brokers [489]
Natl. Assn. of Mortgage Planners [490]
Natl. Assn. of Payment Professionals [1438]
Natl. Assn. of Payment Professionals [IO]
Natl. Assn. of Personal Financial Advisors [1468]
Natl. Assn. of Purchasing Card Professionals
    [3264]
Natl. Assn. of Purchasing and Payables [3265]
Natl. Assn. of Real Estate Companies [3325]
Natl. Assn. of Responsible Loan Officers [1978]
Natl. Assn. of Settlement Purchasers [1439]
Natl. Assn. of State Auditors, Comptrollers, and
    Treasurers [6206]
Natl. Assn. of State Credit Union Supervisors
    [5633]
Natl. Bur. of Economic Res. [6887]
Natl. Chem. Credit Assn. [1440]
Natl. Coun. of Hea. Facilities Finance Authorities
    [1850]
Natl. Credit Union Mgt. Assn. [1117]
Natl. Economic Development and Law Center
    [17464]
Natl. Economists Club [6889]
Natl. Fed. of Community Development Credit
    Unions [1118]
Natl. Found. for Credit Counseling [2428]
Natl. Grants Mgt. Assn. [2507]
Natl. Home Equity Mortgage Assn. [494]
Natl. Introducing Brokers Assn. [1714]
Natl. Reverse Mortgage Lenders Assn. [2430]
Natl. Rural Utilities Cooperative Finance Corp.
    [1441]
Native Amer. Finance Officers Assn. [1442]
Native Financial Educ. Coalition [8442]
Network Branded Prepaid Card Assn. [1443]
New York Financial Writers' Assn. [3148]
North Amer. Economics and Finance Assn. [6890]
Norwegian Soc. of Financial Analysts [IO]
The Other Economic Summit of the U.S. [6891]
Polish Private Equity Assn. [IO]
Print Alliance Credit Exchange [1444]
Private Equity CFO Assn. [1445]
Professional Accounting Soc. of Am. [1]
Professional Scripophily Trade Assn. [761]
Professional Women Controllers [1446]
Property Coun. of Australia [IO]
Real Estate Services Providers Coun. [3341]
Rural Innovation Network, India [IO]
Russian Venture Capital Assn. [IO]
Securities and Insurance Licensing Assn. [2236]
Shareholders Res. Alliance [3391]
Singapore Venture Capital and Private Equity
    Assn. [IO]
Single Global Currency Assn. [17021]
Slovak Venture Capital Assn. [IO]
Smart Card Alliance [7761]
Soc. of Certified Credit Executives [1447]
Soc. of Cost Estimating and Anal. [1448]
Soc. of Financial Examiners [6209]
Soc. of Financial Ser. Professionals [2240]
Soc. of Intl. Treasurers [IO]
Soc. of Medical Banking Excellence [1449]

Reference to "IO" in place of a book number signifies that the association may be found in the 45th edition of International Organizations.

Soc. of Quantitative Analysts [1450]
Soc. of Registered Professional Adjusters [2242]
Soc. of Trust and Estate Practitioners USA [1332]
South African Venture Capital Assn. [IO]
Southern Economic Assn. [6895]
Strategic Account Mgt. Assn. [2650]
Structured Employment Economic Development Corp. [12045]
Thai Venture Capital Assn. [IO]
Treasury Mgt. Assn. of Canada [IO]
Union of Finance Personnel in Europe [IO]
Value Engg. Soc. Intl. [7052]
Viatical and Life Settlement Assn. of Am. [1472]
Weather Risk Mgt. Assn. [4015]
Western Payments Alliance [1451]
Women in Housing and Finance [1452]
Women in Insurance and Financial Services [2247]
World Coun. of Credit Unions [1119]
Finance and Accounting; Assn. of Latino Professionals in [16]
Finance Adjusters; Natl. [493]
Finance Advisors; Natl. Assn. of Independent Public [1467]
Finance Agencies; Assn. of Local Housing [★5794]
Finance Agencies; Coun. of Development [17458]
Finance Agencies; Natl. Assn. of Local Housing [5794]
Finance Assn; Amer. Educ. [8342]
Finance Assn; Appalachian [★1414]
Finance Assn; Commercial [2423]
Finance; Assn. for Governmental Leasing and [6202]
Finance Assn; Insurance Premium [2181]
Finance Assn; Natl. Aircraft [2425]
Finance Assn; Natl. Automotive [421]
Finance Assn; Natl. Commercial [★2423]
Finance Assn; Natl. Consumer [★2422]
Finance Attorneys; Assn. of Commercial [5485]
Finance Authorities; Natl. Coun. of Hea. Facilities [1850]
Finance Benchmarking Consortium; Accounting and [690]
Finance Companies of New York; Assn. of Commercial [★2423]
Finance Conf; Natl. Commercial [★2423]
Finance Coun; Natl. Accounting and [3876]
Finance Houses Assn. [★IO]
Finance and Insurance Professionals; Assn. of [2146]
Finance Law; Conf. on Consumer [5608]
Finance Law; Conf. on Personal [★5608]
Finance and Leasing Assn. [IO], London, United Kingdom
Finance Officers Assn. of U.S. and Canada; Municipal [★6204]
Finance Officers; Natl. Assn. of County Treasurers and [6205]
Finance Proj. [17583], 1401 New York Ave. NW, Ste. 800, Washington, DC 20005, (202)628-4200
Finance Sector Union of Australia [IO], Melbourne, Australia
Finance; Women in Banking and [IO]
Financial Accountability; Evangelical Coun. for [20002]
Financial Accounting Found. [★5427]
Financial Accounting Standards Bd. [29], 401 Merritt 7, PO Box 5116, Norwalk, CT 06856-5116, (203)847-0700
Financial Advertisers Assn. [★2611]
Financial Advisors; Natl. Assn. of Insurance and [2212]
Financial Aid
Adopt-A-Church Intl. [19839]
Adopt a Dr. [12750]
Amer. Comm. for Shaare Zedek Hosp. in Jerusalem [12455]
Amer. Indian Graduate Center [8426]
Amer. Jewish Joint Distribution Comm. [12464]
Asian Aid Org. [IO]
The Blue Card [12468]
Bread for the Journey Intl. [12711]
Canadian Assn. of Student Financial Aid Administrators [IO]
Canadian Payday Loan Assn. [IO]
Catching the Dream [8427]

Chinese-Amer. Educational Found. [8428]
Coll. Savings Plans Network [8429]
Community Development Finance Assn. [IO]
Conf. on Jewish Material Claims Against Germany [12470]
Consultative Gp. to Assist the Poor [17833]
Coun. on Legal Educ. Opportunity [8764]
Debts AIDS Trade Africa [16928]
Downed Bikers Assn. [12612]
Emergency Relief Response Fund [20562]
Harry S. Truman Scholarship Found. [8430]
Hispanic Scholarship Fund [8431]
Hunters Helping Hunters [22604]
I Have a Dream Found. [13487]
INROADS [8749]
Jewish Philanthropic Fund of 1933 [12475]
Jubilee USA Network [17585]
Jubilee USA Network [IO]
Natl. Assn. of Student Loan Administrators [8432]
Natl. Assn. of Unemployment Insurance Appellate Boards [5831]
Natl. Consortium for Graduate Degrees for Minorities in Engg. and Sci. [8372]
Natl. Pell Grant Coalition [8433]
New Am. Alliance [1169]
North Amer. YMCA Development Org. [13461]
Nurses Educational Funds [15516]
Nurses' House [15518]
Pathways to Coll. Network [8493]
Sallie Mae Fund [8434]
Southeastern Regional Off. Natl. Scholarship Ser. and Fund for Negro Students [8435]
Structured Employment Economic Development Corp. [12045]
Students Helping St. Kids Intl. [11725]
Thanks to Scandinavia [8436]
Thanks to Scandinavia [IO]
United Negro Coll. Fund [8437]
Value Engg. Soc. Intl. [7052]
Winston Churchill Found. [8438]
Woodrow Wilson Natl. Fellowship Found. [8439]
Financial Aid Administrators; Natl. Assn. of Student [8350]
Financial Analysts Fed. [★2331]
Financial Analysts Fed. [★IO]
Financial Analysts; Inst. of Chartered [★2331]
Financial Assn. of New York; Young Women's [★1421]
Financial Crime Prevention; Inst. for [★2084]
Financial Crimes; Intl. Assn. of [★5881]
Financial and Estate Planning; Natl. Assn. of [1437]
Financial Examiners; Soc. of [6209]
Financial Executives Assn; Christian [★20511]
Financial Executives Inst. [★1416]
Financial Executives Inst. [★IO]
Financial Executives Inst. of Australia [★IO]
Financial Executives Intl. [IO], Florham Park, NJ, United States
Financial Executives Intl. [1416], 200 Campus Dr., Florham Park, NJ 07932-0674, (973)765-1000
Financial Executives Intl. of Australia [IO], Sydney, Australia
Financial Executives Res. Found. [1417], 200 Campus Dr., Florham Park, NJ 07932-0674, (973)765-1000
Financial Freedom and Accuracy in Financial Reporting; Center for [18404]
Financial Guaranty Insurers; Assn. of [2147]
Financial History; Museum of Amer. [★10508]
Financial Institutions; Amer. League of [459]
Financial Institutions Insurance Assn. [★2151]
Financial Institutions Marketing Assn. - Defunct.
Financial Instrument Exchange [★1710]
Financial Mgt. Assn; Broadcast [★553]
Financial Mgt. Assn; Broadcast Cable [553]
Financial Mgt. Assn; Constr. [1012]
Financial Mgt. Assn; Healthcare [15066]
Financial Mgt. Assn; Hosp. [★15066]
Financial Mgt. Assn. Intl. [8441], Univ. of South Florida, Coll. of Bus. Admin., 4202 E Fowler Ave., BSN 3331, Tampa, FL 33620-5500, (813)974-2084
Financial Mgt. Assn. Intl. [IO], Tampa, FL, United States
Financial Mgt. Assn; I.T. [1430]
Financial Mgt. Assn; Public Telecommunications [★578]

Financial Mgt. for Data Processing [★1430]
Financial Mgt; Inst. of Broadcasting [★553]
Financial Managers Soc. [1418], 100 W Monroe, Ste. 810, Chicago, IL 60603, (312)578-1300
Financial Managers Soc. for Savings Institutions [★1418]
Financial Marketing Assn. - Defunct.
Financial Markets Assn. [1419], c/o Carlene Crnkovich, Sec., U.S. Bancorp Center, 800 Nicollet Mall, Minneapolis, MN 55402, (212)645-5111
Financial Markets Assn. - U.S.A. [475], c/o Peter Wadkins, Pres., PO Box 156, Parlin, NJ 08859, (212)645-5111
Financial Officers of Savings Institutions; Natl. Soc. of Controllers and [★1418]
Financial Operations Assn. - Defunct.
Financial Planners; Intl. Bd. of Standards and Practices for Certified [★1459]
Financial Planning
AARP [12895]
Alliance Credit Counseling [11833]
Alliance of Merger and Acquisition Advisors [54]
Amer. Assn. of Daily Money Managers [1453]
Amer. Assn. for Long-Term Care Insurance [2132]
Amer. Escrow Assn. [1398]
Amer. Money Mgt. Gp. [1454]
Amer. Savings Educ. Coun. [8440]
Assn. of African Amer. Financial Advisors [1455]
Assn. of Chinese Finance Professionals [1402]
Assn. for Comparative Economic Stud. [6870]
Assn. of Financial Advisers [IO]
Assn. for Financial Counseling and Planning Educ. [1456]
Assn. for Financial Professionals [1403]
Assn. of Independent Trust Companies [1457]
Assn. of PVO Financial Managers [1458]
Assn. of PVO Financial Managers [IO]
Canadian Assn. of Gift Planners [IO]
Canadian Assn. of Insolvency and Restructuring Professionals [IO]
Canadian Inst. of Financial Planning [IO]
Certified Financial Planner Bd. of Standards [1459]
Chartered Alternative Investment Analyst Assn. [2332]
Commercial Finance Assn. [2423]
Consumer Credit Counseling Services [17358]
Debtors Anonymous [13017]
European Financial Planning Assn. [IO]
Fifty Plus Financial Network [1460]
Finance Proj. [17583]
Financial Mgt. Assn. Intl. [8441]
Financial Mgt. Assn. Intl. [IO]
Financial Planning Assn. [1420]
Financial Planning Assn. of Bermuda [IO]
Financial Planning Assn. of Malaysia [IO]
Financial Planning Assn. of Singapore [IO]
Financial Services and Banking Benchmarking Assn. [721]
Financial Services Tech. Network [1461]
Fixed Income Analysts Soc. [1462]
Forum for Investor Advice [1463]
Global Assn. of Risk Professionals [1423]
Healthcare Financial Mgt. Assn. [15066]
IAB Partners [1464]
Intl. Assn. of Financial Engineers [1424]
Intl. Bond and Share Soc. [22046]
I.T. Financial Mgt. Assn. [1430]
Life Insurance Settlement Assn. [2193]
Money Advice Scotland [IO]
Money Mgt. Intl. [12190]
Natl. Assn. of Christian Financial Consultants [1465]
Natl. Assn. of Corporate Treasurers [1435]
Natl. Assn. of Estate Planners and Councils [1466]
Natl. Assn. of Independent Public Finance Advisors [1467]
Natl. Assn. of Mortgage Planners [490]
Natl. Assn. of Personal Financial Advisors [1468]
Natl. Assn. of Purchasing Card Professionals [3264]
Natl. Assn. of Responsible Loan Officers [1978]
Natl. Assn. of Stock Plan Professionals [1469]
Natl. Center for Home Equity Conversion [1470]

A star before a book entry number signifies that the name is not listed separately, but is mentioned within the entry.

Natl. Home Equity Mortgage Assn. [494]
Natl. Priorities Proj. [17511]
Native Financial Educ. Coalition [8442]
North Amer. YMCA Development Org. [13461]
Registered Financial Planners Inst. [1471]
Savers and Investors League [18699]
Shareholders Res. Alliance [3391]
Soc. of Trust and Estate Practitioners USA [1332]
Structured Employment Economic Development Corp. [12045]
Viatical and Life Settlement Assn. of Am. [1472]
Workplace Benefits Assn. [1247]
Financial Planning Assn. [1420], 4100 E Mississippi Ave., Ste. 400, Denver, CO 80246-3053, (303)759-4910
Financial Planning Assn. [IO], Denver, CO, United States
Financial Planning Assn. [★IO]
Financial Planning Assn. of Australia [IO], West Melbourne, Australia
Financial Planning Assn. of Bermuda [IO], Hamilton, Bermuda
Financial Planning Assn. of Malaysia [IO], Kuala Lumpur, Malaysia
Financial Planning Assn. of Singapore [IO], Singapore, Singapore
Financial Planning; Intl. Assn. for [★1420]
Financial Products Standards Bd. - Address unknown since 2003.
Financial Professionals; Assn. for [1403]
Financial Public Relations Assn. [★2611]
Financial Relations Soc. - Defunct.
Financial Reporting; Center for Financial Freedom and Accuracy in [18404]
Financial and Security Products Assn. [476], 5300 Sequoia NW, Ste. 205, Albuquerque, NM 87120, (505)839-7958
Financial Ser. Professionals; Soc. of [2240]
Financial Services Assn; Amer. [2422]
Financial Services Assn; Community [1408]
Financial Services Assn; Intl. [483]
Financial Services; Assn. for Mgt. Info. in [464]
Financial Services Authority [IO], London, United Kingdom
Financial Services and Banking Benchmarking Assn. [721], 4606 FM 1960 W, Ste. 250, Houston, TX 77069-9949, (281)440-5044
Financial Services Coalition; Urban [499]
Financial Services Coun; Direct Marketing Insurance and [2162]
Financial Services Inst. of Australasia - South Australia and Northern Territory [IO], Adelaide, Australia
Financial Services Round Table [477], 1001 Pennsylvania Ave. NW, Ste. 500 S, Washington, DC 20004, (202)289-4322
Financial Services Tech. Consortium [7732], 44 Wall St., 12th Fl., New York, NY 10005, (212)461-7116
Financial Services Tech. Network [1461], 8 S Michigan Ave., Ste. 1000, Chicago, IL 60603, (312)782-4951
Financial Services Volunteer Corps [17837], 800 3rd Ave., 11th Fl., New York, NY 10022, (212)771-1400
Financial Services Volunteer Corps [IO], New York, NY, United States
Financial Services; Women in Insurance and [2247]
Financial Soc; Asian [1400]
Financial Stationers Assn. [★3678]
Financial Suppliers Assn. [★2623]
Financial Suppliers Forum [★2623]
Financial Tech; Assn. for [61]
Financial Women Intl. [478], 1027 W Roselawn Ave., Roseville, MN 55113, (651)487-7632
Financial Women Intl. [IO], Roseville, MN, United States
Financial Women's Assn. of New York [1421], 215 Park Ave. S, Ste. 1713, New York, NY 10003, (212)533-2141
Financial Writers' Assn; New York [3148]
Financing Higher Educ; Consortium on [9057]
Financing Organizations; Natl. Assn. of Church and Institutional [2426]
Finansraadet [★IO]
Finch Club of America; Toledo Bird Assn., Zebra [21862]

Finch Soc; Canary and [4195]
Finch and Softbill Soc; Natl. [21854]
Find the Children [11591], 2656 29th St., Ste. 203, Santa Monica, CA 90405, (916)323-7449
Find Your Feet [IO], London, United Kingdom
Findhorn Found. [IO], Forres, United Kingdom
Findik ve Mamuelleri Ihracatcilari Birligi [★IO]
Finding Our Own Ways - Defunct.
Findings Mfrs. Assn; Metal [2379]
Fine Art Dealers; Natl. Assn. of [★298]
Fine Art Trade Guild [IO], London, United Kingdom
Fine Arts Assn. of Finland [IO], Helsinki, Finland
Fine Arts Found. - Defunct.
Fine Arts Philatelists [22819], 19 Ramsey Rd., Great Neck, NY 11023, (516)466-6073
Fine Arts Philatelists [IO], Great Neck, NY, United States
Fine Arts Soc; Amer. [★9496]
Fine Arts; Soc. for Automation in [★8132]
Fine Arts Soc; Catholic [9562]
Fine Arts Unit of Amer. Topical Assn. [★22819]
Fine Arts Unit of Amer. Topical Assn. [★IO]
Fine Craftsmen and Artisans; Guild of [306]
Fine Hardwood Veneer Assn. [★1649]
Fine Hardwood Veneer Association/American Walnut Manufacturers Assn. [★1635]
Fine Hardwoods Amer. Walnut Assn. [★1635]
Fine Particle Soc. - Address unknown since 2000.
FINEX [1710], c/o New York Bd. of Trade (NYBOT), One North End Ave., New York, NY 10282-1101, (212)748-4094
Finger Lakes Wine Growers Assn. [5413], PO Box 222, Hammondsport, NY 14840, (607)569-6133
Fingerprint Soc. [IO], Leicester, United Kingdom
Finish Power Coun. [★IO]
Finishers and Amer. Electroplaters and Surface Finishers Soc; Metal Finishing Suppliers' Assn., Natl. Assn. of Metal [★1474]
Finishers, Shopworkers, and Granite Cutters Intl. Union; Tile, Marble, Terrazzo, [★24032]
Finishers Soc; Metal Finishing Suppliers' Assn., Natl. Assn. of Metal Finishers and Amer. Electroplaters and Surface [★1474]
Finishers of Textile Fabrics; Natl. Assn. of [★3772]
Finishing
    Assn. for Finishing Processes of the Soc. of Mfg. Engineers [6703]
    Indus. Fabrics Assn. Intl. [3787]
    Mass Finishing Job Shops Assn. [1473]
    Natl. Assn. for Surface Finishing [1474]
Finishing Contractors Assn. [622], 8150 Leesburg Pike, Ste. 1210, Vienna, VA 22182, (703)448-9001
Finkelstein Inst. for Religious and Social Stud. at the Louis Stein Center; Louis [19931]
Finland
    Finnish Amer. Chamber of Commerce [24319]
    Finnish Amer. Historical Archives [9951]
    Human Rights Watch - Helsinki [17763]
    Scandinavian Tourist Boards [24372]
    Yrjo Kilpinen Soc. of North Am. [9820]
Finland ACM SIGCHI [IO], Espoo, Finland
Finland Aikikai [IO], Helsinki, Finland
Finland-Israel Trade Assn. [IO], Helsinki, Finland
Finlandia Found. [★19054]
Finlandia Found. Natl. [19054], 470 W Walnut St., Pasadena, CA 91103-3562, (626)795-2081
Finlands svenska forfattareforening [★IO]
Finlands Svenska Lararforbund [★IO]
Finlands Veterinarforbund [★IO]
Finn Assn; U.S.A. [23238]
Finn Church Aid [IO], Helsinki, Finland
Finnish
    Finlandia Found. Natl. [19054]
    Finnish Amer. Chamber of Commerce [24319]
    Finnish Amer. Historical Archives [9951]
    Finnish American Historical Archives [IO]
    Finnish-American Historical Soc. of the West [19055]
    Finnish and Amer. Women's Network [17586]
    Intl. Order of Runeberg [9952]
    Intl. Order of Runeberg [IO]
    League of Finnish-American Societies [IO]
    Yrjo Kilpinen Soc. of North Am. [9820]
Finnish 4H Fed. [IO], Helsinki, Finland
Finnish Academies of Tech. [IO], Helsinki, Finland

Finnish Airline Pilots Assn. [IO], Helsinki, Finland
Finnish Amateur Musicians' Assn. [IO], Helsinki, Finland
Finnish Amateur Radio League [IO], Helsinki, Finland
Finnish Amateur Theatre Coun. [★IO]
Finnish Amer. Chamber of Commerce [24319], 866 UN Plz., Ste. 250, New York, NY 10017, (212)821-0225
Finnish Amer. Historical Archives [9951], c/o Gary Kaunonen, Archivist, Finlandia Univ., 601 Quincy St., Hancock, MI 49930, (906)487-7347
Finnish American Historical Archives [IO], Hancock, MI, United States
Finnish-American Historical Soc. of the West [19055], PO Box 5522, Portland, OR 97228-5522
Finnish Amer. League for Democracy - Address unknown since 2001.
Finnish-American Soc. [★IO]
Finnish and Amer. Women's Network [17586], PO Box 20342, New York, NY 10011
Finnish Asphalt Assn. [IO], Helsinki, Finland
Finnish Assn. of Advt. Agencies [★IO]
Finnish Assn. of Civil Engineers [IO], Helsinki, Finland
Finnish Assn. of Consulting Firms [IO], Espoo, Finland
Finnish Assn. of Designers Ornamo [IO], Helsinki, Finland
Finnish Assn. of Graduate Engineers [IO], Helsinki, Finland
Finnish Assn. of Landscape Architects [IO], Helsinki, Finland
Finnish Assn. of Marketing Commun. Agencies [IO], Helsinki, Finland
Finnish Assn. for Mental Hea. [IO], Helsinki, Finland
Finnish Assn. of Municipal Engg. [IO], Helsinki, Finland
Finnish Assn. of Palliative Care [IO], Tampere, Finland
Finnish Assn. of Physiotherapists [IO], Helsinki, Finland
Finnish Astronautical Soc. [IO], Helsinki, Finland
Finnish Badminton Assn. [IO], Helsinki, Finland
Finnish Bakery Assn. [IO], Helsinki, Finland
Finnish Bankers' Assn. [IO], Helsinki, Finland
Finnish Bar Assn. [IO], Helsinki, Finland
Finnish Benevolent and Aid Assn. of Am. and Swedish-Finnish Temperance Assn; Swedish- [★9952]
Finnish Biathlon Assn. [IO], Helsinki, Finland
Finnish Bible Soc. [IO], Helsinki, Finland
Finnish Billiard Fed. [IO], Helsinki, Finland
Finnish Biochemical Soc. [IO], Helsinki, Finland
Finnish Book Publishers Assn. [IO], Helsinki, Finland
Finnish Book Publishers' Assn. [★IO]
Finnish Booksellers' Assn. [IO], Helsinki, Finland
Finnish Cardiac Soc. [IO], Helsinki, Finland
Finnish Central Fed. of the Visually Handicapped [★IO]
Finnish Central Org. for Motor Trades and Repairs [IO], Helsinki, Finland
Finnish Centre of AITA/IATA [IO], Helsinki, Finland
Finnish Chem. Indus. Employers' Assn. [★IO]
Finnish Comm. for UNICEF [IO], Helsinki, Finland
Finnish Confed. of Salaried Employees [IO], Helsinki, Finland
Finnish Constr. Trade Union [IO], Helsinki, Finland
Finnish Cosmetic, Toiletry and Detergent Assn. [IO], Helsinki, Finland
Finnish Cricket Assn. [IO], Kerava, Finland
Finnish Cultural Found. [IO], Helsinki, Finland
Finnish Curling Assn. [IO], Vantaa, Finland
Finnish Dance Sport Assn. [IO], Helsinki, Finland
Finnish Diabetes Assn. [IO], Tampere, Finland
Finnish Direct Marketing Assn. [IO], Helsinki, Finland
Finnish Dramatists' Union [IO], Helsinki, Finland
Finnish Driving School Assn. [IO], Helsinki, Finland
Finnish Egyptological Soc. [IO], Helsinki, Finland
Finnish Elecl. Wholesalers Fed. [IO], Helsinki, Finland
Finnish Electrotechnical Standards Assn. [★IO]
Finnish Energy Indus. Fed. [IO], Helsinki, Finland
Finnish Epilepsy Soc. [IO], Tampere, Finland
Finnish Fed. of the Brewing and Soft Drink Indus. [IO], Helsinki, Finland

Reference to "IO" in place of a book number signifies that the association may be found in the 45th edition of International Organizations.

Encyclopedia of Associations, 46th Edition | 3461

Finnish Fed. of Petrol Retailers [IO], Helsinki, Finland
Finnish Fed. of Univ. Women [IO], Helsinki, Finland
Finnish Fed. of the Visually Impaired [IO], Helsinki, Finland
Finnish Fish Farmers' Assn. [IO], Jyvaskyla, Finland
Finnish Floorball Fed. [IO], Helsinki, Finland
Finnish Flying Disc Assn. [IO], Helsinki, Finland
Finnish Folk High School Assn. [IO], Helsinki, Finland
Finnish Food and Drink Indus'. Fed. [IO], Helsinki, Finland
Finnish Food Marketing Assn. [IO], Helsinki, Finland
Finnish Food Workers' Union [IO], Helsinki, Finland
Finnish Forest Indus. Fed. [IO], Helsinki, Finland
Finnish Found. for Share Promotion [IO], Helsinki, Finland
Finnish Franchising Assn. [IO], Lohja, Finland
Finnish Fur Breeders' Assn. [IO], Vantaa, Finland
Finnish Geodetic Inst. [IO], Masala, Finland
Finnish Gynecological Assn. [IO], Turku, Finland
Finnish Heart Assn. [IO], Helsinki, Finland
Finnish Historical Soc. [IO], Helsinki, Finland
Finnish Huntington Assn. [IO], Turku, Finland
Finnish Hydraulics and Pneumatics Assn. [IO], Tampere, Finland
Finnish Hypertension Soc. [IO], Tampere, Finland
Finnish Info. Processing Assn. [IO], Espoo, Finland
Finnish Kennel Club [IO], Espoo, Finland
Finnish League for Human Rights [IO], Helsinki, Finland
Finnish Lib. Assn. [IO], Helsinki, Finland
Finnish Literature Info. Centre [IO], Helsinki, Finland
Finnish Marfan Assn. [IO], Helsinki, Finland
Finnish Marketing Assn. [IO], Helsinki, Finland
Finnish Medical Assn. [IO], Helsinki, Finland
Finnish Medical Students' Intl. Comm. [IO], Helsinki, Finland
Finnish MS Soc. [IO], Masku, Finland
Finnish Museums Assn. [IO], Helsinki, Finland
Finnish Music Publishers' Assn. [IO], Helsinki, Finland
Finnish Musicians Union [IO], Helsinki, Finland
Finnish Natural Stone Assn. [IO], Helsinki, Finland
Finnish Newspapers Assn. [IO], Helsinki, Finland
Finnish Oil and Gas Fed. [IO], Helsinki, Finland
Finnish Oil Millers' Assn. [IO], Helsinki, Finland
Finnish Olympic Comm. [IO], Helsinki, Finland
Finnish Operations Res. Soc. [IO], Helsinki, Finland
Finnish Osteoporosis Soc. [IO], Vantaa, Finland
Finnish Painters' Union [IO], Helsinki, Finland
Finnish Paper Engineers' Assn. [IO], Helsinki, Finland
Finnish Paralympic Comm. [IO], Helsinki, Finland
Finnish Parkinson's Disease Assn., Huntington Disease Br. [IO], Turku, Finland
Finnish Peatland Soc. [IO], Helsinki, Finland
Finnish Pharmacological Soc. [IO], Tampere, Finland
Finnish Physical Soc. [IO], Helsinki, Finland
Finnish Physiological Soc. [IO], Helsinki, Finland
Finnish Plastics Assn. [IO], Helsinki, Finland
Finnish Population and Family Welfare Fed. [★IO]
Finnish Port Assn. [IO], Helsinki, Finland
Finnish Psoriasis Assn. [IO], Helsinki, Finland
Finnish Red Cross [IO], Helsinki, Finland
Finnish Refugee Coun. [IO], Helsinki, Finland
Finnish Rheumatism Assn. [IO], Helsinki, Finland
Finnish Rose Soc. [IO], Hameenkyro, Finland
Finnish School Sport Fed. [IO], Helsinki, Finland
Finnish Seamen's Union [IO], Helsinki, Finland
Finnish Shipowners' Assn. [IO], Helsinki, Finland
Finnish Shooting Sport Fed. [IO], Helsinki, Finland
Finnish Social Democratic Party [IO], Helsinki, Finland
Finnish Social and Hea. Informatics Assn. [IO], Kuopio, Finland
Finnish Soc. of Agricultural Engineers [IO], Vihti, Finland
Finnish Soc. of Anaesthesiologists [IO], Kuopio, Finland
Finnish Soc. of Automation [IO], Helsinki, Finland
Finnish Soc. of Gastroenterology [IO], Helsinki, Finland
Finnish Soc. of Rheumatology [IO], Helsinki, Finland
Finnish Soc. of Sciences and Letters [IO], Helsinki, Finland

Finnish Soc. of Sports Medicine [IO], Jyvaskyla, Finland
Finnish Spitz Club of Am. [22267], c/o Jill Kapirin, Membership Chair, 17177 Superior St., Northridge, CA 91325, (818)882-2171
Finnish Sports Fed. [IO], Helsinki, Finland
Finnish Squash Assn. [IO], Helsinki, Finland
Finnish Taekwondo Fed. [IO], Helsinki, Finland
Finnish Tennis Assn. [IO], Helsinki, Finland
Finnish Tourist Bd. [IO], Helsinki, Finland
Finnish Transport Workers' Union [IO], Helsinki, Finland
Finnish United Nations Assn. [IO], Helsinki, Finland
Finnish Veterinary Assn. [IO], Helsinki, Finland
Finnish War Veterans in America - Address unknown since 1995.
Finnish Watchmaker Assn. [IO], Espoo, Finland
Finnish Water Ski Sports Fed. [IO], Lempaala, Finland
Finnish White Ribbon Union [IO], Helsinki, Finland
Finnish Wind Power Assn. [IO], Halli, Finland
Finnish Wood and Allied Workers' Union [IO], Helsinki, Finland
Finnish Workers' Educational Assn. of Manhattan - Defunct.
Finnish Writers' Assn. [★IO]
Finnish Yachting Assn. [IO], Espoo, Finland
Finnish Youth Co-Operation Allianssi [IO], Helsinki, Finland
Finnish Youth Hostel Assn. [IO], Helsinki, Finland
Finno-Ugrian Soc. [IO], Helsinki, Finland
Finnsheep Breeders Assn; Amer. [5184]
FINPRO: Finnish Bus. Solutions Worldwide [IO], Helsinki, Finland
FinSec, Finance and Info. Union [IO], Wellington, New Zealand
Finska Kennelklubben [★IO]
Finska Pappesingeniorsforeningen [★IO]
Finska Vetenskaps-Societeten-Societas Scientiarum Fennica [★IO]
FIOCES [IO], Ivrea, Italy
Fiqh Comm; Islamic Soc. of North America [★20099]
Fiqh Coun. of North America [20099], PO Box 1250, Falls Church, VA 22041, (703)575-7737
Fir and Hemlock Door Assn. - Defunct.
Fir Plywood Assn; Douglas [★1637]
Firan Owners Assn. - Address unknown since 2003.
Fire Alarm Assn; Automatic [3439]
Fire Alarm Assn; Natl. Burglar and [3538]
Fire Apparatus Mfrs. Assn. - Defunct.
Fire Brigades Union [IO], Kingston Upon Thames, United Kingdom
Fire Chaplains; Fellowship of [★19747]
Fire Collectors Club - Address unknown since 2002.
Fire Contractors Fed. [★IO]
Fire Control Assn; Natl. Automatic Sprinkler and [★3449]
Fire Dept. Safety Officers Assn. [6250], 30 Main St., Ste. 6, PO Box 149, Ashland, MA 01721-0149, (508)881-3114
Fire and Emergency Mgt; Alliance for [★5720]
Fire and Emergency Mfrs. and Services Assn. [12062], PO Box 147, Lynnfield, MA 01940-0147, (781)334-2771
Fire Equip. Distributors; Natl. Assn. of [3448]
Fire Equip. Mfrs'. Assn. [3443], 1300 Sumner Ave., Cleveland, OH 44115, (216)241-7333
Fire Equip. Ser. Assn; United [3460]
Fire Extinguishing Trades Assn. [IO], Kingston Upon Thames, United Kingdom
Fire Fighters Assn; Natl. Police and [★5962]
Fire Fighting
Assn. of Principal Fire Officers [IO]
Assn. for Specialist Fire Protection [IO]
Canadian Assn. of Fire Chiefs [IO]
European Assn. for Passive Fire Protection [IO]
European Comm. of the Mfrs. of Fire Protection Equip. and Fire Fighting Vehicles [IO]
Fed. of Fire Chaplains [19747]
Fellowship of Christian Firefighters, Intl. [5715]
Fellowship of Christian Firefighters, Intl. [IO]
Fire Brigades Union [IO]
Fire Equip. Mfrs'. Assn. [3443]
Fire Extinguishing Trades Assn. [IO]

Fire Mark Circle of the Americas [22420]
FireFlag/EMS [5773]
Intl. Assn. of Arson Investigators [5716]
Intl. Assn. of Arson Investigators [IO]
Intl. Assn. of Black Professional Fire Fighters [IO]
Intl. Assn. of Black Professional Fire Fighters [5717]
Intl. Assn. of Fire Chiefs [5718]
Intl. Assn. of Fire Chiefs [IO]
Intl. Assn. of Fire Fighters [24057]
Intl. Assn. of Wildland Fire [4686]
Intl. Fire Buff Associates [22421]
Intl. Fire Buff Associates [IO]
Intl. Fire Chiefs' Assn. of Asia [IO]
Intl. Fire Marshals Assn. [IO]
Intl. Fire Marshals Assn. [5719]
Intl. Police and Fire Chaplain's Assn. [19750]
Intl. Soc. for Fire Ser. Instructors [5720]
Intl. Soc. for Fire Ser. Instructors [IO]
Natl. Assn. of Fire Equip. Distributors [3448]
Natl. Assn. of Hispanic Firefighters [5721]
Natl. Assn. of Hosp. Fire Officers [IO]
Natl. Assn. of State Fire Marshals [5722]
Natl. Conf. of Firemen and Oilers [24058]
Natl. Emergency Equip. Dealers Assn. [14339]
Natl. Fire Protection Assn. [12975]
Natl. Fire Sprinkler Assn. [3449]
Natl. Fireproofing Contractors Assn. [1476]
Natl. Historical Fire Found. [22422]
Natl. Volunteer Fire Coun. [5723]
New Zealand Professional Firefighters Union [IO]
Soc. of Fire Protection Engineers [7082]
Soc. for the Preservation and Appreciation of Antique Motor Fire Apparatus in Am. [22423]
United Fire Equip. Ser. Assn. [3460]
United Firefighters' Union of Australia, Queensland Br. [IO]
Women in the Fire Ser. [5724]
Fire Fighting Vehicle Mfrs. Assn. [IO], Guildford, United Kingdom
Fire Indus. Confed. [IO], Kingston Upon Thames, United Kingdom
Fire Insurance Engineers; Assn. of Mutual [★2178]
Fire Investigators; Natl. Assn. of [2206]
Fire Mark Circle of the Americas [22420], c/o Dave Oldham, Sec., 1113 Grant Ct., Taylorville, IL 62568-9351, (217)824-5308
Fire Marshals Assn. of North Am. [★5719]
Fire Marshals Assn. of North Am. [★IO]
Fire Philatelic Group - Address unknown since 1999.
Fire Professionals of Am; Intl. Union, Security, Police and [24187]
Fire Protection
Amer. Fire Safety Coun. [799]
Automatic Fire Alarm Assn. [3439]
British Approvals for Fire Equip. [IO]
British Automatic Fire Sprinkler Assn. [IO]
British Fire Protection Systems Assn. [IO]
Canadian Fire Alarm Assn. [IO]
Canadian Fire Safety Assn. [IO]
Central Sta. Alarm Assn. [3442]
Coalition for Fire-Safe Cigarettes [12191]
European Fire and Security Advisory Coun. [IO]
Fire Equip. Mfrs'. Assn. [3443]
Fire Indus. Confed. [IO]
Fire Protection Assn. Australia [IO]
Fire Protection Assn. - England [IO]
Fire Protection Assn. of Southern Africa [IO]
Fire and Risk Sciences [IO]
Fire Suppression Systems Assn. [3444]
Institution of Fire Engineers - England [IO]
Institution of Fire Engineers in South Africa [IO]
Intl. Assn. of Fire Chiefs [5718]
Intl. Assn. of Fire Fighters [24057]
Intl. Assn. for Fire Safety Sci. [7080]
Intl. Assn. for Fire Safety Sci. [IO]
Intl. Assn. of Wildland Fire [4686]
Intl. Fire Buff Associates [22421]
Intl. Fire Marshals Assn. [5719]
Intl. FireStop Coun. [7081]
Intl. FireStop Coun. [IO]
Intl. Healthcare Safety Professional Certification Bd. [16379]
Intl. Kitchen Exhaust Cleaning Assn. [1475]
Intl. Soc. for Fire Ser. Instructors [5720]

A star before a book entry number signifies that the name is not listed separately, but is mentioned within the entry.

Natl. Assn. of Fire Equip. Distributors [3448]
Natl. Assn. of Fire Investigators [2206]
Natl. Burglar and Fire Alarm Assn. [3538]
Natl. Fire Indus. Assn. [IO]
Natl. Fire Protection Assn. [12975]
Natl. Fire Sprinkler Assn. [3449]
Natl. Fireproofing Contractors Assn. [1476]
Natl. Historical Fire Found. [22422]
Refractory Ceramic Fibers Coalition [788]
Soc. of Fire Protection Engineers [7082]
Soc. for the Preservation and Appreciation of
   Antique Motor Fire Apparatus in Am. [22423]
United Fire Equip. Ser. Assn. [3460]
U.S. Homeland Emergency Response Org.
   [12893]
Fire Protection Assn. Australia [IO], Box Hill,
   Australia
Fire Protection Assn. - England [IO], Moreton-in-
   Marsh, United Kingdom
Fire Protection Assn; Natl. [12975]
Fire Protection Assn. of Southern Africa [IO], Impala
   Park, Republic of South Africa
Fire Protection Engineers; Soc. of [7082]
Fire Res. Inst. [★4686]
Fire Res. Inst. [★IO]
Fire Res. Sta. [★IO]
Fire Retardant Chemicals Assn. [★799]
Fire and Risk Sciences [IO], Watford, United
   Kingdom
Fire Safety Coun; Amer. [799]
Fire Sprinkler Assn; Amer. [3437]
Fire Sprinkler Assn; Natl. [3449]
Fire Suppression Systems Assn. [3444], 5024-R
   Campbell Blvd., Baltimore, MD 21236-5943,
   (410)931-8100
Fire Suppression; Women in [★5724]
Fire Underwriters; Natl. Bd. of [★2139]
Firearm and Security Trainers Mgt. Assn. - Defunct.
Firearms
   Amateur Trapshooting Assn. [23713]
   Amer. Airgun Field Target Assn. [22976]
   Amer. Custom Gunmakers Guild [1477]
   Amer. Single Shot Rifle Assn. [23714]
   Amer. Sons of Liberty [17087]
   Antique Reloading Tool Collector's Assn. [22424]
   Armed Females of Am. [17587]
   Assn. of Firearm and Tool Mark Examiners [7083]
   Assn. of Ohio Longrifle Collectors [22425]
   Brady Campaign to Prevent Gun Violence [17588]
   Brady Center to Prevent Gun Violence [17589]
   Browning Collectors Assn. [22426]
   Browning Collectors Association [IO]
   Citizens Comm. for the Right to Keep and Bear
      Arms [17105]
   Coalition to Stop Gun Violence [17590]
   Common Sense about Kids and Guns [8443]
   Cowboy Mounted Shooting Assn. [23716]
   Dream Catchers, USA [11943]
   Drums No Guns [17591]
   Educational Fund to Stop Gun Violence [17592]
   European Network Against Arms Trade [IO]
   Fifty Caliber Shooters Assn. [22973]
   Firearms Engravers Guild of Am. [9830]
   Firearms Res. and Identification Assn. [17593]
   German Gun Collectors' Assn. [22029]
   Glock Collectors Assn. [22427]
   Guitars Not Guns [18114]
   Gun Owners of Am. [5725]
   Gun Owners Found. [5726]
   Gun Trade Assn. [IO]
   Guns Save Lives [17594]
   Handgun Safety and Educ. Coun. [17684]
   HELP Network [17595]
   HELP Network [IO]
   High Standard Collectors' Assn. [22428]
   Hunter's Shooting Assn. [23543]
   Intl. Action Network on Small Arms [IO]
   Intl. Assn. of Law Enforcement Firearms Instruc-
      tors [5974]
   Intl. Benchrest Shooters [23717]
   Intl. Defensive Pistol Assn. [23718]
   Intl. Handgun Metallic Silhouette Assn. [23719]
   Join Together [18689]
   L.C. Smith Collectors Assn. [22429]
   Million Mom March [17596]

   Miniature Arms Collectors/Makers Soc. [21538]
   Muzzle Loaders Assn. of Great Britain [IO]
   Natl. Assn. of Federally Licensed Firearms Deal-
      ers [1478]
   Natl. Assn. of Firearms Retailers [1479]
   Natl. Assn. of Shooting Ranges [3599]
   Natl. Automatic Pistol Collectors Assn. [21539]
   Natl. Firearms Act Trade and Collectors Assn.
      [1480]
   Natl. Hunters Assn. [23547]
   Natl. Mossberg Collectors Assn. [22430]
   Natl. Muzzle Loading Rifle Assn. [23722]
   Natl. Reloading Mfrs. Assn. [1481]
   Natl. Rifle Assn. of Am. [23723]
   Natl. Rifle Assn. of New Zealand [IO]
   Natl. Sporting Clays Assn. [23726]
   North Amer. Hunting Club [23548]
   North-South Skirmish Assn. [23727]
   One-Arm Dove Hunt Assn. [23358]
   Peoples Rights Org. [17145]
   Permanent Intl. Commn. for the Proof of Small-
      Arms [IO]
   St. Gabriel Possenti Soc. [17597]
   Second Amendment Comm. [5727]
   Second Amendment Found. [17152]
   Second Amendment Sisters [17598]
   Silent March: Amers. Against Violence [17599]
   Sporting Arms and Ammunitions Mfrs. Inst. [1482]
   Sportsmen's Assn. for Firearms Educ. [17600]
   Student Pledge Against Gun Violence [17601]
   Students for the Second Amendment [17602]
   Thompson Collectors Assn. [22431]
   Thompson Collectors Assn. [IO]
   U.S. Helice Assn. [23729]
   U.S. Practical Shooting. Assn. [23730]
   U.S. Revolver Assn. [23731]
   Violence Policy Center [18789]
   Weatherby Collectors Assn. [22432]
   Winchester Arms Collectors Assn. [21540]
   World Fast-Draw Assn. [23733]
Firearms Engravers Guild of Am. [9830], 1452 Ivan-
   hoe Rd., Ludington, MI 49431, (231)843-4895
Firearms Engravers Guild of Am. [IO], Ludington, MI,
   United States
Firearms Litigation CH [★17592]
Firearms Lobby of Am. [★17105]
Firearms Ownership; Jews for the Preservation of
   [17122]
Firearms Policy Proj. [★18789]
Firearms Res. and Identification Assn. [17593], PO
   Box 620, Wrightwood, CA 92397-0620, (760)249-
   6837
Firebird Club; Natl. [★21732]
Firebird and T/A Club; Natl. [21732]
Firefighters' Associations; Federation of Volunteer
   [★5723]
FireFlag/EMS [5773], 208 W 13th St., New York, NY
   10011, (917)885-0127
Firemen and Enginemen; Brotherhood of Locomotive
   [★24181]
Firemen; Intl. Brotherhood of Stationary [★24058]
Firemen and Oilers; Natl. Conf. of [24058]
Firemen, Oilers, Watertenders and Wipers Assn;
   Pacific Coast Marine [24130]
Firemen's Insurance Assn; Police and [19136]
Firemen's Union; Marine [★24130]
Firemen's Union; Pacific Coast Marine [★24130]
Fireplace Assn; Natl. [IO]
Fireplace Inst. [★1679]
Firestop Contractors Intl. Assn. [944], 4415 W Harri-
   son St., No. 322a, Hillside, IL 60162, (708)202-
   1108
Firestop Contractors Intl. Assn. [IO], Hillside, IL,
   United States
Fireworks Assn; Natl. [1352]
Firm Fan Club - Defunct.
First Advertising Agency Network - Defunct.
First Air Commando Assn. - Address unknown since
   2002.
First Amendment Cong. - Defunct.
First Amendment Consumer and Trade Soc. - Ad-
   dress unknown since 1999.
First Amendment Found. [17115], 3321 12th St. NE,
   Washington, DC 20017, (202)529-4225
First Amendment Lawyers Assn. [5605], c/o Wayne
   Giampietro, Gen. Counselor, 121 S Wilke Rd., No.
   500, Arlington Heights, IL 60005, (847)590-8700

First Amendment Legal Fund; Omega [17140]
First Amendment Press - Address unknown since
   2007.
First Amendment Proj. [18393], 1736 Franklin St.,
   9th Fl., Oakland, CA 94612, (510)208-7744
First Amendment Res. Inst. - Defunct.
First Amendment Rights
   The Creative Coalition [18290]
   Feminists for Free Expression [17534]
   First Amendment Proj. [18393]
   Media Coalition [17126]
   Natl. Comm. Against Repressive Legislation
      [17134]
   Student Press Law Center [17194]
First Book [8789], 1319 F St. NW, Ste. 1000,
   Washington, DC 20004-1155, (202)393-1222
First Candle/SIDS Alliance [16525], 1314 Bedford
   Ave., Ste. 210, Baltimore, MD 21208, (410)653-
   8226
First Catholic Slovak Ladies Assn. [19361], 24950
   Chagrin Blvd., Beachwood, OH 44122-5634,
   (216)464-8015
First Catholic Slovak Union of the U.S.A. and
   Canada [19362], 6611 Rockside Rd.,
   Independence, OH 44131, (216)642-9406
First Cavalry Div. Assn. - Address unknown since
   1995.
First Chair of America - Defunct.
First Church of the Doors - Address unknown since
   1999.
First Czechoslovak Philatelic Club of North America -
   Defunct.
First Day Cover Collectors Club [★22780]
First Day Cover Collectors Club - Defunct.
First Day Cover Soc; Amer. [22781]
First Day Cover Stud. Unit; John F. Kennedy [22835]
First-Day School Gen. Conf. [★20042]
First Families of Georgia 1733-1797 - Address
   unknown since 2003.
First Families of Minnesota; Natl. Soc. - [21253]
First Fandom - Address unknown since 2003.
First Flight Soc. [21447], PO Box 1903, Kitty Hawk,
   NC 27949, (252)441-1903
First Foundations [13169], c/o Dick Jensen, Pres.,
   PO Box 991, Travelers Rest, SC 29690, (864)834-
   2300
First Fruit [20009], 14 Corporate Plz., Newport
   Beach, CA 92660, (949)720-3774
First Hungarian Literary Soc. [19105], 323 E 79th
   St., New York, NY 10021, (212)288-5002
First Infantry Div; Soc. of the [20706]
First Ladies of Am; Hereditary Order of the Families
   of the Presidents and [21261]
First Marine Aviation Force Veterans Assn. [★6080]
First Nations Development Inst. [12625], 703 3rd
   Ave., Ste. B, Longmont, CO 80501, (303)774-7836
First Nations Financial Proj. [★12625]
First Nations Natl. Building Officers Assn. [IO], Sh-
   annonville, ON, Canada
First Peoples Worldwide [IO], Fredericksburg, VA,
   United States
First Peoples Worldwide [10224], 3307 Bourbon St.,
   Fredericksburg, VA 22408, (540)899-6545
First Person Plural [IO], Wolverhampton, United
   Kingdom
First Responders; Amer. Assn. of [★14320]
First Ser. Special Force Memorial Trust [★IO]
First Signs [13942], PO Box 358, Merrimac, MA
   01860, (978)346-4380
First Soc. of Whale Watchers - Defunct.
First Special Service Force Association [IO], Moneta,
   VA, United States
First Special Ser. Force Assn. - Defunct.
First Steps to Freedom [IO], Newquay, United
   Kingdom
First Sunday [12671]
First Zen Inst. of Am. [19549], 113 E 30th St., New
   York, NY 10016, (212)686-2520
FISA [1572], 1207 Sunset Dr., Greensboro, NC
   27408, (336)274-6311
Fiscal Policy Coun. - Address unknown since 1995.
Fiscal Stud. Prog. [6275], Rockefeller Inst. of Govt.,
   411 State St., Albany, NY 12203-1003, (518)443-
   5285
Fischoff Natl. Chamber Music Assn. [10596], Univ.
   of Notre Dame, 303 Brownson Hall, Notre Dame,
   IN 46556, (574)631-0984

Reference to "IO" in place of a book number signifies that the association may be found in the 45th edition of International Organizations.

Fish

Alternative Aquaculture Assn. [4167]
Amer. Carp Soc. [22448]
Amer. Casting Assn. [23406]
Amer. Cichlid Assn. [22433]
Amer. Crappie Assn. [22449]
Amer. Elasmobranch Soc. [7278]
Amer. Fisheries Soc. [7169]
Amer. Inst. of Fishery Res. Biologists [7170]
Amer. Killifish Assn. [22434]
Amer. Livebearer Assn. [22435]
Amer. Livebearer Assn. [IO]
Amer. Medical Fly Fishing Assn. [4349]
Amer. Soc. of Ichthyologists and Herpetologists [7158]
Apistogramma Study Group [22436]
Apistogramma Study Group [IO]
Aquaculture Intl. [4169]
Aquatic Res. Inst. [7171]
Assoc. Koi Clubs of Am. [22437]
Associated Koi Clubs of America [IO]
Assn. of Conservation Engineers [4357]
Assn. of Fish and Wildlife Agencies [4360]
Assn. of Northwest Steelheaders [23409]
Assn. for Professional Observers [4667]
Atlantic Flyway Coun. [5295]
Atlantic States Marine Fisheries Commn. [5729]
Australia New Guinea Fishes Assn. [IO]
Bass Anglers Sportsman Soc. [23410]
The Billfish Found. [5298]
Bonefish and Tarpon Unlimited [4987]
Bowfishing Assn. of Am. [23411]
Breeder's Registry [22438]
British Killifish Assn. [IO]
Carp Anglers Gp. [22450]
The Catfish Inst. [4171]
Desert Fishes Coun. [4388]
Fed. of Fly Fishers [23413]
FishAmerica Found. [4393]
Future Fisherman Found. [23415]
Goldfish Soc. of Am. [22439]
Goldfish Society of America [IO]
Great Lakes Sport Fishing Coun. [23416]
Gulf and Caribbean Fisheries Inst. [4668]
Hawaiian Intl. Billfish Tournament [22440]
Hawaiian Intl. Billfish Tournament [IO]
Inter-American Tropical Tuna Commn. [5730]
Intl. Assn. of Astacology [7174]
Intl. Betta Cong. [22441]
Intl. Betta Cong. [IO]
Intl. Bonefishing Soc. [22452]
Intl. Fancy Guppy Assn. [22442]
Intl. Fancy Guppy Assn. [IO]
Intl. Fellowship of Fishing Rotarians [22453]
Intl. Game Fish Assn. [23417]
Intl. Inst. of Fisheries Economics and Trade [1484]
Intl. Oceanographic Found. [7399]
Intl. Pacific Halibut Commn. [5731]
Intl. Women Fly Fishers [22443]
Intl. Women Fly Fishers [IO]
Intl. Women's Fishing Assn. [23419]
Maine Lobstermen's Assn. [3492]
Marine Aquarium Coun. [4175]
Marine Aquarium Societies of North Am. [4176]
Marine Fish Conservation Network [4419]
Middle Atlantic Fisheries Assn. [3493]
Midwest Assn. of Fish and Wildlife Agencies [5339]
Molluscan Shellfish Inst. [3494]
Natl. Blue Crab Industry Assn. [3495]
Natl. Fisheries Inst. [3496]
Natl. Military Fish and Wildlife Assn. [5342]
Natl. Org. for Rivers [23683]
Natl. Ornamental Goldfish Growers Assn. [4181]
Natl. Shrimp Indus. Assn. [3498]
Natl. Teen Anglers [22454]
Native Amer. Fish and Wildlife Soc. [4595]
New England Fisheries Development Assn. [3499]
North Amer. Fish Breeders Guild [22444]
North American Fish Breeders Guild [IO]
North Amer. Fishing Club [23421]
North Amer. Native Fishes Assn. [7175]
Northwest Fisheries Assn. [3500]
Ocean Futures Soc. [5280]

Org. of Wildlife Planners [5360]
Pacific Coast Cichlid Assn. [22445]
Pacific Coast Fed. of Fishermen's Associations [4669]
Pacific Coast Shellfish Growers Assn. [3501]
Pacific Fishery Mgt. Coun. [5732]
Pacific Ocean Res. Found. [7176]
Pacific Seafood Processors Assn. [3502]
Pacific States Marine Fisheries Commn. [5733]
Rainbowfish Study Group of North Am. [22446]
Rainbowfish Study Group of North Am. [IO]
Recreational Fishing Alliance [17603]
Reel Recovery [11519]
Rocky Mountain Cichlid Assn. [22447]
Salmon Unlimited [23422]
Seafood Choices Alliance [3503]
Shark Res. Inst. [5019]
Shore Fishing and Casting Club Intl. [23423]
Soc. for the Protection of Old Fishes [7177]
Southeastern Assn. of Fish and Wildlife Agencies [5734]
Southeastern Fisheries Assn. [3504]
Striped Bass Growers Assn. [4670]
Theodore Roosevelt Conservation Partnership [4458]
Trout Unlimited [5387]
United Fly Tyers [23424]
U.S. Aquaculture Soc. [4183]
U.S. Shore Angling Assn. [23425]
U.S. Sportsmen's Alliance [23550]
U.S. Trout Farmers Assn. [4184]
U.S. Tuna Found. [3506]
Western Assn. of Fish and Wildlife Agencies [5735]
Women's Fisheries Network [4671]
Fish Biology; Australian Soc. for [IO]
Fish Commissioners; Natl. Assn. of Shell [★7255]
Fish Commissioners; Southeastern Assn. of Game and [★5734]
Fish Commissioners; Western Assn. of State Game and [★5735]
Fish, and Conservation Commissioners; Intl. Assn. of Game, [★4360]
Fish Decoy Assn; Amer. [21960]
Fish Exchange; New England [4330]
Fish Farmers of Am; Cat [4170]
Fish Farms Assn; Florida Tropical [4172]
Fish Found; The Bill [5298]
Fish and Game Commissioners; Assn. of Midwest [★5339]
Fish Growers Assn; Natl. Ornamental Gold [4181]
Fish Growers Assn; Pacific Coast Shell [3501]
Fish Inst; The Cat [4171]
Fish Inst; Pacific Shell [4182]
Fish and Lobster Assn; Atlantic Offshore [★5728]
Fish Meal and Oil Assn; Natl. [2855]
Fish Pesticide Res. Lab. [★7172]
Fish Soc. of Am; Gold [22439]
Fish Soc; Native [5347]
Fish and Wildlife Agencies; Assn. of Midwest [★5339]
Fish and Wildlife Agencies; Midwest Assn. of [5339]
Fish and Wildlife Assn; Natl. Military [5342]
Fish and Wildlife Commn; Great Lakes Indian [5323]
Fish and Wildlife Commissioners; Assn. of Midwest [★5339]
Fish and Wildlife Reference Service - Defunct.
FishAmerica Found. [4393], 225 Reinekers Ln., Ste. 420, Alexandria, VA 22314, (703)519-9691
Fisher Inst. [★17628]
Fisher Inst. for Medical Res. [17628], PO Box 530689, Grand Prairie, TX 75051, (972)660-3219
Fisher-Price Collector's Club [22995], 1442 N Ogden, Mesa, AZ 85205
Fisher-Price Collector's Club [IO], Mesa, AZ, United States
The Fisherfolk [★19790]
Fisheries Assn; Middle Atlantic [3493]
Fisheries Assn; Northwest [3500]
Fisheries; Assn. of Pacific [★3502]
Fisheries Assn; Southeastern [3504]
Fisheries Commn; Atlantic States Marine [5729]
Fisheries Commn; Pacific Marine [★5733]
Fisheries Commn; Pacific States Marine [5733]
Fisheries Commissioners; Natl. Assn. of [★7255]

Fisheries Comm. of the Org. for Economic Co-Operation and Development [IO], Paris, France
Fisheries Contaminant Res. Center; Natl. [★7172]
Fisheries Development Assn; New England [3499]
Fisheries Development Found; New England [★3499]
Fisheries Economists; North Amer. Assn. of [1485]
Fisheries Inst; Gulf and Caribbean [4668]
Fisheries Inst; Natl. [3496]
Fisheries Network; Women's [4671]
Fisheries and Oceans Canada [IO], Ottawa, ON, Canada
Fisheries Res. Lab; Columbia Natl. [★7172]
Fisheries and Wildlife Prog. Administrators; Assn. of Univ. [★8391]
Fisheries and Wildlife Programs; Natl. Assn. of Univ. [8391]
Fisherman's Clean Water Action Proj. [★5087]
Fishermen; Fed. of Fly [★23413]
Fishermen's Assn; Atlantic Offshore [★5728]
Fishermen's Associations; Pacific Coast Fed. of [4669]
Fishers; Fed. of Fly [23413]
Fishery Comm. for Eastern Central Atlantic [IO], Accra, Ghana
Fishery Coun. - Defunct.
Fishery Mgt. Coun; Pacific [5732]
Fishery Res. Biologists; Amer. Inst. of [7170]
Fishery Res. Found; Sport [★23408]
Fishes; Soc. for the Protection of Old [7177]
Fishhook Intl. - Address unknown since 2002.

Fishing

Amateur Fisherman's Assn. of the Northern Territory [IO]
Amer. Carp Soc. [22448]
Amer. Casting Assn. [23406]
Amer. Crappie Assn. [22449]
Amer. Fish Decoy Assn. [21960]
Amer. League of Anglers and Boaters [23407]
Amer. Medical Fly Fishing Assn. [4349]
Amer. Sportfishing Assn. [23408]
Amer. Tilapia Assn. [4666]
Angling Trades Assn. [IO]
Asian Fisheries Soc. [IO]
Assn. of Fish and Wildlife Agencies [4360]
Assn. of Northwest Steelheaders [23409]
Assn. of Northwest Steelheaders [IO]
Assn. for Professional Observers [4667]
Atlantic Offshore Lobstermen's Assn. [5728]
Atlantic Salmon Fed. [IO]
Atlantic States Marine Fisheries Commn. [5729]
Australian Natl. Sportfishing Assn. [IO]
Australian Natl. Sportfishing Assn. [IO]
Australian Natl. Sportfishing Assn. - NT Br. [IO]
Australian Natl. Sportfishing Assn. - Victoria [IO]
Australian Natl. Sportfishing Assn. - Western Australia [IO]
Bass Anglers Sportsman Soc. [23410]
Bermuda Anglers Club [IO]
Big Salmon River Angling Assn. [IO]
Bluewater Sportfishing Club [IO]
Bonefish and Tarpon Unlimited [4987]
Bowfishing Assn. of Am. [23411]
Bray Sea Anglers [IO]
Brotherhood of the Jungle Cock [23412]
Canadian Casting Fed. [IO]
Carp Anglers Gp. [22450]
The Catfish Inst. [4171]
Cobequid Salmon Assn. [IO]
Comm. on Marine Fisheries [IO]
Dream Catchers, USA [11943]
European Inland Fisheries Advisory Commn. [IO]
Federation of Fly Fishers [IO]
Fed. of Fly Fishers [23413]
FishAmerica Found. [4393]
Fisheries Comm. of the Org. for Economic Co-Operation and Development [IO]
Fishery Comm. for Eastern Central Atlantic [IO]
Fishing Has No Boundaries [23414]
Flydressers' Guild [IO]
Future Fisherman Found. [23415]
Gen. Fisheries Commn. for the Mediterranean [IO]
Great Lakes Sport Fishing Coun. [23416]
Gulf and Caribbean Fisheries Inst. [4668]
Hawaiian Intl. Billfish Tournament [22440]

A star before a book entry number signifies that the name is not listed separately, but is mentioned within the entry.

Howth Sea Angling Club [IO]
Inter-American Tropical Tuna Commn. [IO]
Inter-American Tropical Tuna Commn. [5730]
Intl. Assn. of Fly Fishing Veterinarians [22451]
International Association of Fly Fishing Veterinarians [IO]
Intl. Baltic Sea Fishery Commn. [IO]
International Bonefishing Society [IO]
Intl. Bonefishing Soc. [22452]
Intl. Commn. for the Conservation of Atlantic Tunas [IO]
Intl. Fellowship of Fishing Rotarians [IO]
Intl. Fellowship of Fishing Rotarians [22453]
Intl. Fly Fishing Assn. [IO]
Intl. Game Fish Assn. [IO]
Intl. Game Fish Assn. [23417]
Intl. Inst. of Fisheries Economics and Trade [1484]
Intl. Pacific Halibut Commn. [5731]
Intl. Pacific Halibut Commn. [IO]
Intl. Sport Show Producers Assn. [1344]
Intl. Underwater Spearfishing Assn. [23418]
International Underwater Spearfishing Association [IO]
Intl. Women's Fishing Assn. [IO]
Intl. Women's Fishing Assn. [23419]
Maine Lobstermen's Assn. [3492]
Marine Aquarium Coun. [4175]
Marine Stewardship Coun. [5171]
Meduxnekeag River Assn. [IO]
Middle Atlantic Fisheries Assn. [3493]
Molluscan Shellfish Inst. [3494]
Moncton Fish and Game Assn. [IO]
Nashwaak Watershed Assn. Inc. [IO]
Natl. Assn. of Sporting Goods Wholesalers [3644]
Natl. Blue Crab Industry Assn. [3495]
Natl. Fed. of Anglers [IO]
Natl. Fed. of Sea Anglers [IO]
Natl. Fisheries Inst. [3496]
Natl. Fishing Lure Collectors Club [22082]
Natl. Org. for Rivers [23683]
Natl. Ornamental Goldfish Growers Assn. [4181]
Natl. Professional Anglers' Assn. [23420]
Natl. Shrimp Indus. Assn. [3498]
Natl. Teen Anglers [22454]
Nepisiguit Salmon Assn. [IO]
New Brunswick Coun. of the Atlantic Salmon Fed. [IO]
New Brunswick Wildlife Fed. [IO]
New England Fisheries Development Assn. [3499]
North Amer. Fishing Club [23421]
North Amer. Squirrel Assn. [22773]
North Atlantic Salmon Conservation Org. [IO]
North-East Atlantic Fisheries Commn. [IO]
North Pacific Anadromous Fish Commn. [IO]
Northwest Atlantic Fisheries Org. [IO]
Northwest Fisheries Assn. [3500]
Nova Scotia Salmon Assn. [IO]
Old Reel Collectors Assn. [22099]
Pacific Coast Fed. of Fishermen's Associations [4669]
Pacific Coast Shellfish Growers Assn. [3501]
Pacific Fishery Mgt. Coun. [5732]
Pacific Salmon Commn. [IO]
Pacific Seafood Processors Assn. [3502]
Pacific States Marine Fisheries Commn. [5733]
Professional Anglers Assn. [IO]
Recreational Fishing Alliance [17603]
Rederscentrale [IO]
Reel Recovery [11519]
Sackville Rivers Assn. [IO]
St. Croix Intl. Atlantic Salmon Assn. [IO]
Saint John River Salmon Anglers Assn. [IO]
Salmon Preservation Assn. for the Waters of Newfoundland [IO]
Salmon and Trout Assn. [IO]
Salmon Unlimited [23422]
Salmonid Assn. of Eastern Newfoundland [IO]
Scottish Anglers Natl. Assn. [IO]
Scottish Fed. of Sea Anglers [IO]
Seafood Choices Alliance [3503]
Shore Fishing and Casting Club Intl. [23423]
Southeastern Assn. of Fish and Wildlife Agencies [5734]
Southeastern Fisheries Assn. [3504]

Specialist Anglers' Alliance [IO]
The Steamboaters [4454]
Striped Bass Growers Assn. [4670]
Theodore Roosevelt Conservation Partnership [4458]
Trout Unlimited [5387]
United Fly Tyers [23424]
United Fly Tyers [IO]
U.S. Aquaculture Soc. [4183]
U.S. Freshwater Prawn and Shrimp Growers Assn. [3505]
U.S. Shore Angling Assn. [23425]
U.S. Sportsmen's Alliance [23550]
U.S. Tuna Found. [3506]
Warrington Anglers Assn. [IO]
Western Assn. of Fish and Wildlife Agencies [5735]
Western Central Atlantic Fishery Commn. [IO]
Women's Fisheries Network [4671]
Fishing Assn; Amer. Medical Fly [4349]
Fishing Assn; Intl. Spin [★23417]
Fishing Club; North Amer. [23421]
Fishing Coun; Great Lakes Sport [23416]
Fishing Has No Boundaries [23414], PO Box 175, Hayward, WI 54843, (800)243-3462

Fishing Industries
Alternative Aquaculture Assn. [4167]
Amer. Carp Soc. [22448]
Amer. Crappie Assn. [22449]
Amer. Sportfishing Assn. [23408]
Amer. Tilapia Assn. [4666]
Amer. Wildlands [4354]
Aquaculture Certification Coun. [4168]
Assn. of Danish Fish Processing Indus. and Exporters [IO]
Assn. of Fish and Wildlife Agencies [4360]
Assn. for Professional Observers [4667]
At-sea Processors Assn. [1483]
Atlantic Offshore Lobstermen's Assn. [5728]
Australian Barramundi Farmers Assn. [IO]
Australian Seafood Indus. Coun. [IO]
BC Salmon Farmers Assn. [IO]
Bonefish and Tarpon Unlimited [4987]
Bowfishing Assn. of Am. [23411]
British Trout Assn. [IO]
Canadian Coun. of Professional Fish Harvesters [IO]
Carp Anglers Gp. [22450]
Chilean Salmon Indus. Assn. [IO]
Chilean Salmon and Trout Farmers' Assn. [IO]
Czech Fish Farmers' Assn. [IO]
Danish Fishermen's Assn. [IO]
Dutch Fish Prdt. Bd. [IO]
European Assn. of Fish Pathologists [IO]
European Assn. of Fisheries Economists [IO]
Fed. of Finnish Fisheries Associations [IO]
Fed. of Finnish Fisheries Associations [IO]
Finnish Fish Farmers' Assn. [IO]
FishAmerica Found. [4393]
Fisheries and Oceans Canada [IO]
Global Aquaculture Alliance [4173]
Gulf and Caribbean Fisheries Inst. [4668]
IFA Aquaculture [IO]
Inst. of Fisheries Mgt. [IO]
Intl. Game Fish Assn. [23417]
Intl. Inst. of Fisheries Economics and Trade [1484]
Intl. Inst. of Fisheries Economics and Trade [IO]
Irish Fish Producers Org. [IO]
Irish Salmon Growers' Assn. [IO]
Irish South and West Fish Producers Org. [IO]
Japan Fisheries Assn. [IO]
Japanese Soc. of Fisheries Sci. [IO]
Maine Lobstermen's Assn. [3492]
Marine Stewardship Coun. [5171]
Marine Stewardship Coun. [IO]
Middle Atlantic Fisheries Assn. [3493]
Molluscan Shellfish Inst. [3494]
Natl. Assn. of State Aquaculture Coordinators [4180]
Natl. Blue Crab Industry Assn. [3495]
Natl. Chamber of the Fish Indus. [IO]
Natl. Chamber of Fisheries [IO]
Natl. Fed. of Fish Friers [IO]
Natl. Fed. of Fishing Companies [IO]

Natl. Fed. of Fishmongers [IO]
Natl. Fisheries Inst. [3496]
Natl. Shrimp Indus. Assn. [3498]
Native Fish Australia [IO]
New England Fisheries Development Assn. [3499]
New Zealand Native Freshwater Fish Soc. [IO]
New Zealand Professional Fishing Guides Assn. [IO]
New Zealand Seafood Indus. Coun. [IO]
North Amer. Assn. of Fisheries Economists [1485]
Northwest Fisheries Assn. [3500]
Norwegian Fishermen's Sales Org. for Pelagic Fish [IO]
Norwegian Raw Fish Org. [IO]
Norwegian Seafood Assn. [IO]
Norwegian Seafood Export Coun. [IO]
Norwegian Seafood Export Coun. [1486]
Norwegian Seafood Fed. [IO]
Ornamental Aquatic Trade Assn. [IO]
Pacific Coast Fed. of Fishermen's Associations [4669]
Pacific Coast Shellfish Growers Assn. [3501]
Pacific Seafood Processors Assn. [3502]
Philippine Tropical Fish Exporters Assn. [IO]
Recreational Fishing Alliance [17603]
Scottish Fishermen's Fed. [IO]
Shellfish Assn. of Great Britain [IO]
Shore Fishing and Casting Club Intl. [23423]
Southeastern Fisheries Assn. [3504]
Striped Bass Growers Assn. [4670]
U.S. Aquaculture Soc. [4183]
U.S. Freshwater Prawn and Shrimp Growers Assn. [3505]
U.S. Sportsmen's Alliance [23550]
U.S. Tuna Found. [3506]
Women's Fisheries Network [4671]
WorldFish Center [IO]
Fishing Lure Collectors Club; Natl. [22082]
Fishing Trade Assn; Amer. Fly- [3635]
Fiskeri-og Havbruksnaeringens Landsforening [★IO]
Fitness; Amer. Chiropractic Assn. Coun. on Sports Injuries and Physical [13989]
Fitness Assn; Alternative Hea. and [10522]
Fitness Assn. of Am; Aerobics and [15956]
Fitness; Assn. of Hosp. Hea. and [★15966]
Fitness Assn; IDEA Hea. and [15965]
Fitness Assn; Medical [15966]
Fitness Assn; Natl. [★3670]
Fitness Assn; U.S. Water [23657]
Fitness Indus. Assn. [IO], London, United Kingdom
Fitness Indus. Suppliers Assn. - North Am. [IO], San Diego, CA, United States
Fitness Indus. Suppliers Assn. - North Am. [3020], 3525 Del Mar Heights Rd., Box 381, San Diego, CA 92130, (858)509-0034
The Fitness League [IO], Sunningdale, United Kingdom
Fitness for Life [15964]
Fitness; Natl. Assn. for Hea. and [15967]
Fitness and Nutrition; Amer. Coun. for [15959]
Fitness Professionals; African-Amer. Assn. of [15957]
Fitness Professionals; IDEA: The Assn. for [★15965]
Fitness Source; IDEA, The Hea. and [★15965]
Fitness and Sport; Natl. Assn. of Governor's Councils on Physical [★15967]
Fitness Trade Assn. [★3670]
Fitness; Truth in [15970]
Fittings Assn; Amer. Pipe [3025]
Fittings Assn; Plastic Pipe and [3037]
Fittings Indus; Mfrs. Standardization Soc. of the Valve and [2040]
Fittings Mfrs. Assn; Pipe [★3025]
Fitzgerald Soc; F. Scott [9649]
Fitzgerald's Fancys: Rat and Mouse Info. [22705], 210 La Verne Ave., Long Beach, CA 90803, (562)439-2002
Fiume Study Group - Defunct.
Five Civilized Tribes Found. - Defunct.
Five P Minus Soc. [16534], PO Box 268, Lakewood, CA 90714, (562)804-4506
Five Years Meeting of Friends [★20044]
Five Years Meeting of Friends [★IO]
Fixed Income Analysts Soc. [1462], 244 Fifth Ave., Ste. L230, New York, NY 10001, (212)726-8100

Reference to "IO" in place of a book number signifies that the association may be found in the 45th edition of International Organizations.

Fixed Prosthodontics; Amer. Acad. of [14097]
The Fixer - Defunct.
Fixture Manufacturers; Natl. Assn. of Store [644]
Fixtures Mfrs. and Dealers - Address unknown since 1995.
The Fixx Fan Club - Address unknown since 1989.
FJ U.S. [23169], c/o Rebecca Wyatt, Sec.-Treas., 6572 Margaret Dr., Westerville, OH 43082, (614)865-0145
Fjolis [IO], Reykjavik, Iceland
Fjord Horse Registry; Norwegian [4939]
Flag
    Citizens Flag Alliance [17300]
    Flag Mfrs. Assn. of Am. [1487]
    Flag Res. Center [11074]
    Intl. Fed. of Vexillological Associations [11075]
    Natl. Flag Day Found. [21094]
    Natl. Flag Found. [11076]
    Natl. Independent Flag Dealers Assn. [1488]
    North Amer. Vexillological Assn. [11077]
    Patriotic Order Sons of Am. [21242]
    Star-Spangled Banner Flag House Assn. [21095]
    U.S. Flag Football League [23440]
    U.S. Flag Found. [11078]
Flag Alliance; Citizens [17300]
Flag Berth Operators; Trans-Atlantic Amer. Flag Liner Operators/Trans-Pacific Amer. [3592]
Flag Cancel Soc. [★22839]
Flag Football for the Deaf; U.S. [23367]
Flag Football League; U.S. [23440]
Flag Found; Natl. [11076]
Flag Found; U.S. [11078]
Flag Inst. [IO], York, United Kingdom
Flag Liner Operators/Trans-Pacific Amer. Flag Berth Operators; Trans-Atlantic Amer. [3592]
Flag Mfrs. Assn. of Am. [1487], 15000 Commerce Pkwy., Ste. C, Mount Laurel, NJ 08054, (856)439-0500
Flag Plaza Found. [★11076]
Flag Res. Center [11074], c/o Dr. Whitney Smith, Dir., PO Box 580, Winchester, MA 01890-0880, (781)729-9410
Flag and Touch Football League; U.S. [23441]
Flagon and Trencher [★20737]
Flagon and Trencher - Descendants of Colonial Tavern Keepers [20737], c/o James Raywalt, Pres./Registrar, 1716 Bigley Ave., Charleston, WV 25302-3938
Flaherty Found; Robert [★9940]
Flair Bartenders' Assn. [201], 104 E Fairview Ave., No. 283, Meridian, ID 83642-1733, (208)888-3146
Flamenco Network - Address unknown since 2002.
Flames Fan Club; Atlanta [24996]
Flammability Comm; Furniture [★1708]
Flanders-Brussels Convention Bur. [IO], Brussels, Belgium
Flat-Coated Retriever Soc. of Am. [22268], c/o Joan Dever, Membership Sec., 13208 Mandarin Rd., Jacksonville, FL 32223-1746, (904)268-0325
Flat Earth Res. Soc; Intl. [7145]
Flat Earthers [★7145]
Flat Glass Coun. [★IO]
Flat Glass Jobbers Assn. [★1728]
Flat Glass Marketing Assn. [★1728]
Flat Roofing Alliance [IO], Haywards Heath, United Kingdom
Flat Roofing Contractors Advisory Bd. [★IO]
Flat Tax Found. - Defunct.
Flat Trackers Assn; White Plate [23629]
Flattie Yacht Racing Assn; Intl. [★23172]
Flatware Importers Assn. - Defunct.
Flavor Chemists; Soc. of [6696]
Flavor and Extract Manufacturers Assn. of the U.S. [1509], 1620 I St. NW, Ste. 925, Washington, DC 20006, (202)293-5800
Flavor and Fragrance Commerce; Women in [4051]
Flavoring Extract Manufacturers Assn. of the U.S. [★1509]
Flavorings
    Chem. Sources Assn. [1660]
Flavors and Food-Ingredient Systems; Natl. Assn. of [1539]
Flavors and Syrups; Natl. Assn. of Fruits, [★1539]
Flavour Mfrs. Assn. of Canada [IO], Don Mills, ON, Canada

Flax Development Comm. - Defunct.
Flax Inst. of the U.S. - Defunct.
Fleet Administrators; Natl. Assn. of [362]
Fleet Administrators; Natl. Conf. of State [6322]
Fleet Air Arm Officers Assn. [IO], London, United Kingdom
Fleet and Leasing Assn; Automotive [406]
Fleet Resale Dealers; Natl. Assn. of [419]
Fleet Reserve Assn. [21211], 125 N West St., Alexandria, VA 22314-2709, (703)683-1400
Fleet Specialists and National Wheel and Rim Assn; Council of [★382]
Fleet Tug Sailors; Natl. Assn. of [21213]
Fleming, Ian
    The Official Austin Powers Collector's Club [24826]
Flemish Entomological Soc. [IO], Antwerp, Belgium
Flemish Giant Rabbit Breeders; Natl. Fed. of [5151]
Flemish Org. for Assistance in Development - Belgium [IO], Leuven, Belgium
Flemish Watersports Assn. [IO], Antwerp, Belgium
Fletchers' Company [IO], London, United Kingdom
Fleuroselect [★IO]
FLEUROSELECT [IO], Noordwijk, Netherlands
Flexible Compensation; Employers Coun. on [1237]
Flexible Intermediate Bulk Container Assn. [981], PO Box 24792, Minneapolis, MN 55424, (866)600-8880
Flexible Intermediate Bulk Container Assn. [IO], Minneapolis, MN, United States
Flexible Metal Connector Inst. - Defunct.
Flexible Packaging Assn. [2875], 971 Corporate Blvd., Ste. 403, Linthicum, MD 21090-2253, (410)694-0800
Flexible Packaging Assn; Natl. [★2875]
Flexible Packaging Europe [IO], Dusseldorf, Germany
Flexible Polyurethane Foam Mfrs. Assn. [★3057]
Flexicore Mfrs. Assn. - Defunct.
Flexographic Tech. Assn. [1766], 900 Marconi Ave., Ronkonkoma, NY 11779-7212, (631)737-6020
Flexographic Technical Association [IO], Ronkonkoma, NY, United States
Flickinger Found. for Amer. Studies - Address unknown since 1995.
Flight Acad. for Youth; Summer [★164]
Flight Attendant Volunteer Corps - Address unknown since 1995.
Flight Attendants of Am; Black [18866]
Flight Attendants; Assn. of [★24009]
Flight Attendants; Assn. of Professional [24010]
Flight Attendants - CWA; Assn. of [24009]
Flight Attendants and Related Services Assn. [IO], Auckland, New Zealand
Flight Attendants; Union of [★24011]
Flight Engineers' Intl. Assn. - Address unknown since 2002.
Flight Equip. Assn; Space and [★6383]
Flight Equip. Assn; Survival and [★6383]
Flight Freedoms Found. - Defunct.
Flight Instructors; Natl. Assn. of [161]
Flight Nurses Assn; Natl. [★15427]
Flight Paramedics Assn; Natl. [★14334]
Flight Patrol Fan Club [25027]
Flight Safety Found. [148], 601 Madison St., Ste. 300, Alexandria, VA 22314-1756, (703)739-6700
Flight Safety Found. [IO], Alexandria, VA, United States
Flight Soc; First [21447]
Flight Surgeon-Pilots; Intl. Assn. of Military [13541]
Flight Surgeons; Soc. of U.S. Air Force [13543]
Flight Surgeons; Soc. of U.S. Naval [13544]
Flight Test Engineers; Soc. of [6385]
Flint/Glass Workers Conf; USWA [24067]
Flint Glass Workers of North Am; Amer. [★24067]
Flippin Family Assn. [20902], 12206 Brisbane Ave., Dallas, TX 75234-6528, (972)241-2739
Floatation Tank Assn. - Address unknown since 2003.
Floating Harbor Syndrome Support Gp. of North Am. [14451], 160 Guild St. NE, Grand Rapids, MI 49505
Floating Harbor Syndrome Support Gp. of North Am. [IO], Grand Rapids, MI, United States
The Floating Hosp. [14882], PO Box 3391, New York, NY 10163-3391, (212)514-7440

Floating Hosp; St. John's Guild - The [★14882]
Flock Assn; Amer. [3770]
Flood Control; U.S. Comm. on Irrigation, Drainage and [★7842]
Flood Mgt. Agencies; Natl. Assn. of Urban [★6140]
Flood and Storm Water Mgt. Agencies; Natl. Assn. of [6140]
Floodplain Mgt. Assn. [5038], PO Box 712080, Santee, CA 92072-2080, (619)204-4380
Floodplain Managers; Assn. of State [4362]
Floor Covering Coun. - Address unknown since 2005.
Floor Covering Distributors Coun. - Defunct.
Floor Covering Distributors; Natl. Assn. of [★657]
Floor Covering Installation Contractors Assn. [1016], 7439 Millwood Dr., West Bloomfield, MI 48322, (248)661-5015
Floor Covering Inst; Resilient [665]
Floor Covering Market Assn; Dalton [★2250]
Floor Installation Assn. of North Am. [623], PO Box 5505, Granbury, TX 76049, (817)326-2615
Floor Installation Association of North America [IO], Granbury, TX, United States
Floor Safety Inst; Natl. [3450]
Floor Truck Manufacturers Assn; Caster and [★2028]
Floor and Vacuum Machinery Mfrs. Assn. - Defunct.
Floorball Assn; U.S. [23093]
Floorball Fed. of India [IO], Lucknow, India
Floorball Zveza Slovenije [★IO]
Floorcovering Alliance; Amer. [2250]
Floorcovering Assn; Amer. [★3431]
Floorcovering Installers Assn; Intl. Certified [1025]
Flooring Assn; Natl. Wood [655]
Flooring Indus; Southern Oak [★656]
Flooring Mfrs. Assn; Bridge Grid [605]
Flooring Manufacturers Assn; Maple [635]
Flooring Manufacturers Assn; Natl. Oak [★656]
Flooring Manufacturers Assn; NOFMA: The Wood [656]
Flooring Manufacturers of U.S; Oak [★656]
Flora Neotropica Org. [★6645]
Flora Neotropica Org. [★IO]
Flora North America Program - Defunct.
Flora Soc; Arizona Cactus and Native [★6633]
Floral Commentators International; Professional [★1493]
Floral Coun; Fresh Produce and [1514]
Floral Designers; Amer. Inst. of [1490]
Floral Indus. Assn; Amer. [1489]
Floral Marketing Assn. - Defunct.
Florence Ballard Fan Club [24888], PO Box 360502, Los Angeles, CA 90036
Florence Ballard Fan Club [IO], Los Angeles, CA, United States
Florence Ceramics Collectors Soc. [22025], c/o Jay Houser, Pres., 1000 S Orange Grove Blvd., No. 7, Pasadena, CA 91101
Florence Collectors Club - Address unknown since 2002.
Florence Crittenton Assn. of Amer. [★11572]
Floresta U.S.A. [17838], 4903 Morena Blvd., Ste. 1215, San Diego, CA 92117, (858)274-3718
Floresta U.S.A. [IO], San Diego, CA, United States
Floriculture; American Acad. of [★1493]
Floriculture; SAF - The Center for Commercial [★1493]
Florida Bible Coll. Alumni Assn. - Address unknown since 2000.
Florida Citrus Commission [★4729]
Florida Citrus Commn. [★4729]
Florida Citrus Mutual [4727], PO Box 89, Lakeland, FL 33802, (863)682-1111
Florida Citrus Nurserymen's Assn. [4728], PO Box 12852, Fort Pierce, FL 34979-2852, (941)658-3400
Florida Citrus Packers - Address unknown since 1999.
Florida Commercial Fisheries Assn. - Address unknown since 1995.
Florida Dept. of Citrus [4729], PO Box 148, Lakeland, FL 33802-0148, (863)499-2500
Florida Express Fruit Shippers Assn. [★4731]
Florida Foliage Assn. - Defunct.
Florida Fruit and Vegetable Assn. [4730], PO Box 948153, Maitland, FL 32794-8153, (321)214-5200

A star before a book entry number signifies that the name is not listed separately, but is mentioned within the entry.

Florida Gift Fruit Shippers Assn. **[4731]**, 5500 W Concord Ave., Orlando, FL 32808, (407)295-1491

Florida Holocaust Memorial Center; Southeastern **[★17717]**

Florida Keys Wild Bird Rehabilitation Center **[5317]**, 93600 Overseas Hwy., Tavernier, FL 33070, (305)852-4486

Florida Lychee Growers Assn. **[4732]**

Florida Mango Forum - Address unknown since 1999.

Florida Marine Aquarium Soc. - Address unknown since 1995.

Florida Space Coast Writers Conf. **[★11196]**

Florida Tomato Comm. **[4733]**, 800 Trafalgar Ct., Ste. 300, Maitland, FL 32751-7135, (407)660-1949

Florida Tomato Exchange **[★4733]**

Florida Trail Assn. **[23939]**, 5415 SW 13th St., Gainesville, FL 32608, (352)378-8823

Florida Tropical Fish Farms Assn. **[4172]**, PO Box 1519, Winter Haven, FL 33882, (863)293-5710

Florists
  Amer. Floral Indus. Assn. **[1489]**
  Amer. Inst. of Floral Designers **[1490]**
  Assn. of Specialty Cut Flower Growers **[1491]**
  Associazione Italiana Fioristi **[IO]**
  British Dried Flowers Assn. **[IO]**
  Colombian Assn. of Flower Exporters **[IO]**
  European Fed. of Professional Florist Associations **[IO]**
  Flowers Canada **[IO]**
  Intl. Freeze-Dry Floral Assn. **[IO]**
  Intl. Freeze-Dry Floral Assn. **[1492]**
  Italian Florists Natl. Assn. **[IO]**
  Soc. of Amer. Florists **[1493]**
  Soc. of Floristry **[IO]**
  Teleflora **[1494]**
  Terrarium Assn. **[22548]**
  Wholesale Florist and Florist Supplier Assn. **[1495]**
  Zambia Export Growers' Assn. **[IO]**

Florists of Am; Wholesale Commn. **[★1495]**

Florists and Ornamental Horticulturists; Soc. of Amer. **[★1493]**

Florists and Seedsmen; Amer. Assn. of Nurserymen, **[★5042]**

Flotation Healthcare Found. - Address unknown since 1999.

Flour Advisory Bur. **[IO]**, London, United Kingdom

Flour, Cereal, Soft Drink and Distillery Workers of Am. (AFL-CIO); Intl. Union of United Brewery, **[★24020]**

Flour and Corn Meal Prog; Self-Rising **[★1520]**

Flour Distributors; Natl. Assn. of **[1540]**

Flour Inst; Self-Rising **[★1520]**

Flour Inst; Wheat **[★2738]**

Flour Millers Assn. of Japan **[IO]**, Tokyo, Japan

Flour Millers Export Assn. - Address unknown since 1995.

Flow Blue Intl. Collectors Club **[22026]**, c/o Jim Swan, Membership Chm., PO Box 442464, Lawrence, KS 66044

Flow Blue International Collectors Club **[IO]**, Lawrence, KS, United States

Flower Arranging
  Amer. Inst. of Floral Designers **[1490]**
  Soc. of Amer. Florists **[1493]**
  Teleflora **[1494]**

Flower Center; Lady Bird Johnson Wild **[6642]**

Flower Coun. of Holland **[IO]**, Leiden, Netherlands

Flower Essence Society **[IO]**, Nevada City, CA, United States

Flower Essence Soc. **[14818]**, PO Box 459, Nevada City, CA 95959, (530)265-9163

Flower Importers Assn; Amer. **[★1489]**

Flower Preservation Soc; New England Wild **[★4434]**

Flower Soc; New England Wild **[4434]**

Flowerbulb Wholesalers Assn; North Amer. **[4983]**

Flowers
  African Violet Soc. of Am. **[22480]**
  All-America Gladiolus Selections **[22481]**
  All-America Rose Selections **[4972]**
  Amer. Begonia Soc. **[22482]**
  Amer. Boxwood Soc. **[22484]**
  Amer. Brugmansia and Datura Soc. **[22455]**
  Amer. Clematis Soc. **[4672]**
  Amer. Community Gardening Assn. **[22486]**
  Amer. Daffodil Soc. **[22487]**
  Amer. Fuchsia Soc. **[22488]**
  Amer. Gourd Soc. **[22489]**
  Amer. Hemerocallis Soc. **[22490]**
  Amer. Hibiscus Soc. **[22491]**
  Amer. Horticultural Soc. **[22492]**
  Amer. Hosta Soc. **[22493]**
  Amer. Inst. of Floral Designers **[1490]**
  Amer. Iris Soc. **[22495]**
  Amer. Ivy Soc. **[22496]**
  Amer. Penstemon Soc. **[22497]**
  Amer. Peony Soc. **[22498]**
  Amer. Primrose Soc. **[22499]**
  Amer. Rhododendron Soc. **[22500]**
  Amer. Rose Soc. **[22501]**
  Aril Soc. Intl. **[22502]**
  Australian Flower Export Coun. **[IO]**
  Australian Rhododendron Soc. **[IO]**
  British Orchid Growers Assn. **[IO]**
  British Pelargonium and Geranium Soc. **[IO]**
  Bromeliad Soc. Intl. **[22505]**
  Cactus and Succulent Soc. of Am. **[22506]**
  Canadian Iris Soc. **[IO]**
  Costa Rican Assn. of Flower Growers **[IO]**
  Cyclamen Soc. **[IO]**
  Cymbidium Soc. of Am. **[22508]**
  Dutch Flower Auctions Assn. **[IO]**
  Epiphyllum Soc. of Am. **[22510]**
  Flower Coun. of Holland **[IO]**
  Flower Essence Soc. **[14818]**
  Garden Club of Am. **[22511]**
  Garden Conservancy **[4402]**
  Garden Writers Assn. **[22512]**
  The Gardeners of Am. **[22513]**
  Gesneriad Hybridizers Assn. **[22514]**
  Gesneriad Soc. **[22515]**
  Heritage Rose Found. **[22516]**
  Heritage Roses Gp. **[22517]**
  Holly Soc. of Am. **[5256]**
  Indoor Gardening Soc. of Am. **[22519]**
  Intl. Aroid Soc. **[22520]**
  Intl. Carnivorous Plant Soc. **[22521]**
  Intl. Clematis Soc. **[IO]**
  Intl. Cut Flower Growers Assn. **[4980]**
  Intl. Freeze-Dry Floral Assn. **[1492]**
  Intl. Lilac Soc. **[22522]**
  Intl. Oleander Soc. **[22523]**
  Median Iris Soc. **[22525]**
  Natl. Chrysanthemum Soc. **[22526]**
  Natl. Clay Pot Mfrs. **[183]**
  Natl. Fuchsia Soc. **[22527]**
  Natl. Garden Clubs **[22528]**
  Natl. Gardening Assn. **[22529]**
  Natl. Sunflower Assn. **[4312]**
  New England Wild Flower Soc. **[4434]**
  New Zealand Flower Exporters Assn. **[IO]**
  North Amer. Flowerbulb Wholesalers Assn. **[4983]**
  North Amer. Fruit Explorers **[22531]**
  North Amer. Gladiolus Coun. **[22532]**
  North Amer. Heather Soc. **[22533]**
  North Amer. Lily Soc. **[22534]**
  North Amer. Rock Garden Soc. **[22535]**
  Pacific Orchid Soc. of Hawaii **[22536]**
  Passiflora Soc. Intl. **[4673]**
  People-Plant Coun. **[4518]**
  Perennial Plant Assn. **[4985]**
  Plumeria Soc. of Am. **[22537]**
  Reblooming Iris Soc. **[22538]**
  Rose Bowl Collectors **[22112]**
  Rose Hybridizers Assn. **[22539]**
  Seed Savers Exchange **[22540]**
  Soc. of Amer. Florists **[1493]**
  Soc. for Japanese Irises **[22541]**
  Soc. for Louisiana Irises **[22542]**
  Soc. for Pacific Coast Native Iris **[22543]**
  Soc. for Siberian Irises **[22544]**
  Species Iris Gp. of North Am. **[22545]**
  Tall Bearded Iris Soc. **[22547]**
  Teleflora **[1494]**
  Terrarium Assn. **[22548]**
  Tropical Flowering Tree Soc. **[4986]**
  Violet Soc. **[IO]**
  World Wide Essence Soc. **[14833]**

Flowers Canada **[IO]**, Ottawa, ON, Canada

Flowers and Plants Assn. **[IO]**, London, United Kingdom

Flue-Cured Tobacco Cooperative Stabilization Corp. **[5248]**, 1304 Annapolis Dr., Raleigh, NC 27608, (919)821-4560

Flue-Cured Tobacco Growers Assn. - Address unknown since 1995.

Flugmalafelag Islands **[IO]**, Reykjavik, Iceland

Fluid Controls Inst. **[2018]**, 1300 Sumner Ave., Cleveland, OH 44115, (216)241-7333

Fluid Power
  British Fluid Power Assn. **[IO]**
  Intl. Assn. of Hydraulic Engg. and Res. **[IO]**
  Intl. Assn. for Hydromagnetic Phenomena and Applications **[IO]**
  Intl. Fluid Power Soc. **[7084]**
  Italian Assn. of Mfg. and Trading Companies in Fluid Power Equip. and Components **[IO]**
  Japan Fluid Power Assn. **[IO]**
  Natl. Conf. on Fluid Power **[7085]**
  WaterJet Tech. Assn. **[7086]**

Fluid Power Consultants Intl. - Defunct.

Fluid Power Distributors Assn. **[2019]**, PO Box 1420, Cherry Hill, NJ 08034-0054, (856)424-8998

Fluid Power Soc. **[★7084]**

Fluid Sealing Assn. **[2020]**, 994 Old Eagle School Rd., No. 1019, Wayne, PA 19087, (610)971-4850

Fluid Specialty Mfrs; Natl. Assn. of Steam and **[★2018]**

Fluorescent Lighting Assn. - Defunct.

Fluorescent Mineral Soc. **[7342]**, PO Box 572694, Tarzana, CA 91357-2694

Fluorescent Mineral Soc. **[IO]**, Tarzana, CA, United States

Fluoridation; Natl. Comm. Against **[★14587]**

Fluoridation Soc; British **[IO]**

Flute Assn; Intl. Native Amer. **[10622]**

Flute Assn; Natl. **[10663]**

Flxible Historic Assn. - Defunct.

Fly Fishermen; Fed. of **[★23413]**

Fly Fishers; Fed. of **[23413]**

Fly Fishing Assn; Amer. Medical **[4349]**

Fly-Fishing Trade Assn; Amer. **[3635]**

Fly Fishing Veterinarians; Intl. Assn. of **[22451]**

Fly-Inn Club; Intl. B and B **[21451]**

Fly Rodders of Am; Salt Water **[★23417]**

Fly Tyers; United **[23424]**

Fly Without Fear **[12746]**, 36 Meadow Rue Ln., East Northport, NY 11731, (516)829-2900

Flydressers' Guild **[IO]**, Oxford, United Kingdom

Flyers Fan Club; Philadelphia **[25011]**

FlygTekniska Foreningen **[★IO]**

Flying Accountants - Defunct.

Flying Adjusters; Organized **[2229]**

Flying Apache Assn. **[21448]**

Flying Architects Assn. - Defunct.

Flying Assn; Natl. Intercollegiate **[21466]**

Flying Chiropractors Assn. **[14002]**, 2001 Bridgeway St., Sausalito, CA 94965, (415)332-4304

Flying Club; Natl. Intercollegiate **[★21466]**

Flying Cowboy" Fan Club; Jimmy Kish "The 24922

Flying Dentists Assn. **[14153]**, 10032 Wind Hill Dr., Greenville, IN 47124-9673, (812)923-2100

Flying Disc Collectors Assn. - Address unknown since 1989.

Flying Disc Fed. of India **[IO]**, Ahmedabad, India

Flying Doctors of Am. **[IO]**, Cartersville, GA, United States

Flying Doctors of Am. **[12523]**, 15 Medical Dr., Cartersville, GA 30121, (770)386-5221

Flying Doctors of Mercy **[★12528]**

Flying Doctors of Mercy **[★IO]**

Flying Doctors Ser. **[★IO]**

Flying Eagle and Indian Head Cent Collectors Soc. - Address unknown since 2003.

Flying Farmers Assn; Natl. **[★4646]**

Flying Fifteen Intl. **[IO]**, Perth, Australia

Flying Funeral Directors of America **[2779]**

Flying Octogenarians; United **[21485]**

Flying Optometrists Assn. of America - Defunct.

Flying Padres **[★19667]**

Flying Pharmacists of America - Defunct.

Flying Physicians Assn. **[13731]**, PO Box 677427, Orlando, FL 32867, (407)568-0655

Reference to "IO" in place of a book number signifies that the association may be found in the 45th edition of International Organizations.

Flying Psychologists - Defunct.
Flying Scot Sailing Assn. [23170], 1 Windsor Cove, Ste. 305, Columbia, SC 29223, (803)252-5646
Flying Senior Citizens of U.S.A. - Defunct.
Flying Tigers of the 14th Air Force Assn. [21393], 4801 Courthouse St., Ste. 220, PO Box 934236, Williamsburg, VA 23188, (757)229-4631
Flying Tigers Assn. - Address unknown since 1995.
Flying Veterinarians Assn. - Defunct.
Flyway Coun; Atlantic [5295]
FN-forbundet [★IO]
F.O.A.L. Assn; Arabian [11365]
Foam Assn; Polyurethane [3057]
Foam Mfrs. Assn; Flexible Polyurethane [★3057]
FOCAL Intl. [IO], South Harrow, United Kingdom
Foco; En [10849]
Focolare Movement [19624], PO Box 496, New York, NY 10021
Focolare Movement [IO], New York, NY, United States
Focolare Movement - Italy [IO], Rocca di Papa, Italy
Focus [15681]
Focus 2000 [★18992]
Focus on the Chinese Family [20496], 750 Terrado Plz., No. 123, Covina, CA 91723, (626)974-5881
Focus on the Family [12157], 8605 Explorer Dr., Colorado Springs, CO 80920, (719)531-5181
Focus on the Family - Canada [IO], Vancouver, BC, Canada
Focus on the Global South [IO], Bangkok, Thailand
Focus Intl. - Kenya [IO], Nairobi, Kenya
Focus; United [★8299]
FOD Family Support Gp. [15248], c/o Deb Lee Gould, MEd, Dir., 2041 Tomahawk, Okemos, MI 48864, (517)381-1940
FOD Family Support Group [IO], Okemos, MI, United States
Foderalistische Union Europaischer Volksgruppen [★IO]
Foderation Der Europaischen Parkett Industrie [★IO]
FOG Intl. Computer Users Group - Address unknown since 2000.
Foggy River Boys Fan Club - Defunct.
Foil Container Manufacturers Assn; Aluminum [971]
Foil Operators; Amer. Acad. of Gold [14099]
Foil Stamping and Embossing Assn. [2707], 2150 SW Westport Dr., Ste. 101, Topeka, KS 66614, (785)271-5816
Foires Salons and Congres de France [★IO]
Foires et Salons de France [★IO]
Fokker Verein - Defunct.
Folding Paper Box Assn. of Am. [★2877]
Folio; Baptist Women in Ministry/ [19481]
Folk
  Amer. Folklore Soc. [9953]
  Amer. Hungarian Folklore Centrum [10213]
  Baidarka Historical Soc. [9954]
  British Columbia Folklore Soc. [IO]
  Center for Southern Folklore [9376]
  English Folk Dance and Song Soc. [IO]
  Folk Alliance [IO]
  Folk Alliance [9955]
  Folk Art Soc. of Am. [9956]
  Folk Arts Network [IO]
  FolkArts England [IO]
  Folklore Canada Intl. [IO]
  Folklore Soc. [IO]
  Folkus [IO]
  Hardanger Fiddle Assn. of Am. [10606]
  Independent Scholars of Asia [9957]
  Independent Scholars of Asia [IO]
  Intl. Coun. of Organizations for Folklore Festivals and Folk Art [IO]
  Intl. Soc. for Folk Narrative Res. [IO]
  Italian Folk Art Fed. of Am. [10259]
  Jargon Soc. [9958]
  Maine Folklife Center [9959]
  Mariposa Folk Found. [IO]
  Mariposa In The Schools [IO]
  The Mountain Inst. [9960]
  Natl. Assn. of Black Storytellers [10981]
  Natl. Coun. for the Traditional Arts [9961]
  Native Hawaiian Culture and Arts Prog. [10884]
  North Amer. Fed. of German Folk Dance Groups [9965]

  North Amer. Fed. of German Folk Dance Groups [IO]
  Saving and Preserving Arts and Cultural Environments [9470]
  Slavic and East European Folklore Assn. [9962]
  Slavic and East European Folklore Assn. [IO]
  Soc. for Folk Arts Preservation [9963]
  Soc. for Folk Life Stud. [IO]
  South East Folk Arts Network [IO]
  Southern Counties Folk Fed. [IO]
  Tennessee Folklore Soc. [9964]
  World Folk Music Assn. [10725]
Folk Alliance [9955], 510 S Main St., 1st Fl., Memphis, TN 38103, (901)522-1170
Folk Alliance [★22718]
Folk Alliance [IO], Memphis, TN, United States
Folk Art Fed. of Am; Italian [10259]
Folk Art Soc. of Am. [9956], PO Box 17041, Richmond, VA 23226-7041, (804)285-4532
Folk Arts Network [IO], Matlock, United Kingdom
Folk Coll. Assn. of Am. [★8267]
Folk Dance
  Calgary Recreational Intl. Folkdance Club [IO]
  Country Dance and Song Soc. [9873]
  Folk Alliance [9955]
  Lloyd Shaw Found. [8187]
  North Amer. Fed. of German Folk Dance Groups [9965]
Folk Dance Found; Intl. [★9592]
Folk Educ. Assn. of Am. [★8267]
Folk Festival Assn; Natl. [★9961]
Folk Heritage Inst. [10772], PO Box 141, Glenville, PA 17329, (717)235-4235
Folk Law
  Commn. on Legal Pluralism [IO]
Folk Music
  Americana Music Assn. [10555]
  Christchurch Folk Music Club [IO]
  Country Dance and Song Soc. [9873]
  Folk Alliance [9955]
  John Gary Intl. Fan Club [24925]
  Natl. Traditional Country Music Assn. [10670]
  World Folk Music Assn. [10725]
Folk Music and Dance Alliance; North Amer. [★9955]
Folk Music; Friends of [★10725]
Folk Music; Friends of [★IO]
Folk Music Soc. of Ireland [IO], Dublin, Ireland
Folk-Rock Music
  Kingston Korner [24934]
Folk-School Assn. of Am. [★8267]
FolkArts England [IO], Matlock, United Kingdom
Folkbildningsradet [★IO]
Folkecenter for Renewable Energy [IO], Hurup Thy, Denmark
Folkecenter for Vedvarende Energi [★IO]
Folkkampanjen Mot KarnKraft-Karnvapen [★IO]
Folklore Canada Intl. [IO], Montreal, QC, Canada
Folklore; Center for Southern [9376]
Folklore Centrum; Amer. Hungarian [10213]
Folklore Soc. [IO], London, United Kingdom
Folklore Soc; Pennsylvania German [★21243]
Folklore Soc; Tennessee [9964]
Folklore Stud. Gp; Asian [★9957]
Folkus [IO], Fleetwood, United Kingdom
FoMoCo Owners Club [21646]
Fondacioni Shoqeria e Hapur per Shqiperine [★IO]
Fondation canadienne de recherche sur le cancer de la prostate [★IO]
Fondation canadienne de la fibrose kystique [★IO]
Fondation canadienne des etudes ukrainiennes [★IO]
Fondation Aga Khan [★IO]
Fondation Aga Khan Canada [★IO]
Fondation Asie Pacifique du Canada [★IO]
Fondation du Basket-Ball Dr. James Naismith [★IO]
Fondation Bonderjnstichting [★IO]
Fondation Canada Ouest [★IO]
Fondation Canada-Scandinavie [★IO]
Fondation Canadiene du Foie [★IO]
Fondation Canadienne des tumeurs cerebrales [★IO]
Fondation Canadienne pour les Ameriques [★IO]
Fondation Canadienne du Cancer du Sein [★IO]
Fondation Canadienne des Champs de Bataille [★IO]

Fondation Canadienne d'Ergotherapie [★IO]
Fondation Canadienne pour le Developpement de Carriere [★IO]
Fondation Canadienne des Femmes [★IO]
Fondation Canadienne Pour La Securite dans les Ascenseurs et escaliers mechaniques [★IO]
Fondation Canadienne de la Recherche en Dietetique [★IO]
Fondation Canadienne Reves d'Enfants [★IO]
Fondation Canado-Palestinienne du Quebec [★IO]
Fondation Damien [★IO]
Fondation Europeene Charcot [★IO]
Fondation Europeene pour l'Architecture du Paysage [★IO]
Fondation Europeenne de la Culture [★IO]
Fondation Europeenne pour le Developpement du Mgt. [★IO]
Fondation Fauna [★IO]
Fondation Frontiere [★IO]
Fondation des Infirmieres et Infirmiers du Canada [★IO]
Fondation Internationale Lelio Basso pour le Droit et la Liberation des Peuples [★IO]
Fondation Internationale pour la Sauvegarde de la Faune [★IO]
Fondation canadienne un Monde de Reves [★IO]
Fondation Natl. des Realisations autochtones [★IO]
Fondation Recherche Medicale [★IO]
Fondation de Recherches sur les Blessures de la Route [★IO]
Fondation Scolaire de l'Institut Canadien du Credit [★IO]
Fondation du Scoutisme Mondial [★IO]
Fondation canadienne de recherche sur le SIDA [★IO]
Fondazione Africana per la Medicina e la Ricerca [★IO]
Fondazione Giovanni Agnelli [★IO]
Fondo Ecuatoriano Populorum Progressio [IO], Quito, Ecuador
Fondo Nacional de las Artes [★IO]
Fondo de Poblacion de las Naciones Unidas [★IO]
Fondo de Poblacion de las Naciones Unidas [★IO]
Fondo de Poblacion de las Naciones Unidas Costa Rica [★IO]
Fondo de Poblacion de las Naciones Unidas - Republica Dominicana [★IO]
Fondos Internacionales de Indemnizacion de Danos Debidos a la Contaminacion por Hidrocarburos [★IO]
Fonds Canadien pour la paix [★IO]
Fonds Europeen pour la Jeunesse [★IO]
Fonds zur Forderung der Wissenschaftlichen Forschung [★IO]
Fonds Mondial pour la Nature [★IO]
Fonds des Nations Unies pour l'Enfance [★IO]
Fonds des Nations Unies pour l'Enfance [★11658]
Fonds des Nations Unies pour la Population Benin [★IO]
Fonetic English Spelling Assn. - Defunct.
Food
  3-A Sanitary Standards Committees, Inc. [1125]
  AACC Intl. [6660]
  Advanced Foods and Materials Network [IO]
  All Food Importers Assn. [IO]
  All Star Dairy Assn. [1126]
  Alliance for Better Foods [4674]
  Allied Purchasing Company [1127]
  Allied Trades of the Baking Indus. [443]
  Almond Bd. of California [5048]
  Amer. Assn. of Candy Technologists [7087]
  Amer. Assn. of Food Hygiene Veterinarians [16745]
  Amer. Assn. of Food Stamp Directors [6261]
  Amer. Assn. of Meat Processors [2656]
  Amer. Assn. of Nutritional Consultants [15540]
  Amer. Bakers Assn. [444]
  Amer. Beekeeping Fed. [502]
  Amer. Bd. of Nutrition [15541]
  Amer. Butter Inst. [1128]
  Amer. Celiac Society/Dietary Support Coalition [15543]
  Amer. Cheese Soc. [1129]
  Amer. Coll. of Nutrition [15544]
  Amer. Commodity Distribution Assn. [4302]

A star before a book entry number signifies that the name is not listed separately, but is mentioned within the entry.

Amer. Coun. of Applied Clinical Nutrition [15545]
Amer. Coun. for Fitness and Nutrition [15959]
Amer. Coun. on Sci. and Hea. [14539]
Amer. Culinary Fed. [790]
Amer. Dairy Products Inst. [1130]
Amer. Dietetic Assn. [15546]
Amer. Frozen Food Inst. [1496]
Amer. Grassfed Assn. [2438]
Amer. Inst. of Baking [445]
Amer. Inst. of Food Distribution [1497]
Amer. Inst. of Food Distribution [IO]
Amer. Inst. of Wine and Food [22568]
Amer. Meat Inst. [2658]
Amer. Meat Sci. Assn. [7088]
Amer. Mushroom Inst. [4703]
Amer. Peanut Coun. [5049]
Amer. Peanut Res. and Educ. Soc. [5050]
Amer. Soc. for Clinical Nutrition [15547]
Amer. Soc. for Healthcare Food Ser. Administrators [14867]
Amer. Soc. for Nutrition [15548]
Amer. Soc. for Parenteral and Enteral Nutrition [15549]
Amer. Soc. of Sugar Beet Technologists [7089]
Amer. Soc. of Sugar Cane Technologists [3700]
Amer. Spice Trade Assn. [1498]
Amer. Sugar Alliance [1499]
Amer. Sugar Cane League of the U.S.A. [5225]
Amer. Sugarbeet Growers Assn. [5226]
Amer. Union of Pizza Delivery Drivers [24062]
Amer. Wholesale Marketers Assn. [1500]
America's Second Harvest [12388]
Animal Agriculture Alliance [1501]
Apple Processors Assn. [1673]
Aprovecho Res. Center [16993]
Arab Fed. for Food Indus. [IO]
Arab Fed. for Food Indus. - Jordan [IO]
Asia Pacific Network for Food Anal. [IO]
Asian Food Info. Centre [IO]
Assn. of Cereal Starch Producers in the EU [IO]
Assn. of Convenience Stores [IO]
Assn. of Correctional Food Ser. Affiliates [1577]
Assn. for Dressings and Sauces [1502]
Assn. of Dutch Fruit and Vegetable Exporters [IO]
Assn. of the Estonian Food Indus. [IO]
Assn. of Food Indus. [IO]
Assn. of Food Indus. [1503]
Assn. of Food Journalists [3094]
Assn. of Fruit and Vegetable Inspection and Standardization Agencies [1674]
Assn. of the Indus. of Juices and Nectars from Fruits and Vegetables of the European Union [IO]
Assn. of Italian Flour and Pasta Indus. [IO]
Assn. of Mfrs. and Formulators of Enzyme Products [IO]
Assn. of Nutrition Departments and Programs [8947]
Assn. of Pizza Delivery Drivers [1579]
Assn. for the Stud. of Food and Soc. [7090]
Australasian Meat Indus. Employees' Union [IO]
Australian Food and Grocery Coun. [IO]
Australian Inst. of Food Sci. and Tech. [IO]
Austrian Milling Assn. [IO]
Bakers, Food and Allied Workers' Union - United Kingdom [IO]
Baking Indus. Sanitation Standards Comm. [448]
Beef Improvement Fed. [7091]
Beet Sugar Development Found. [5227]
Belgian Assn. of Baby and Dietetic Food [IO]
BEMA, The Baking Indus. Suppliers Assn. [449]
Biscuit and Cracker Manufacturers Assn. [450]
Black Culinarian Alliance [1122]
Brazilian Food Indus. Assn. [IO]
Breakfast Cereal Manufacturers of Canada [IO]
British Frozen Food Fed. [IO]
British Sandwich Assn. [IO]
British Soc. of Flavourists [IO]
Broker Mgt. Coun. [1937]
Bundesforschungsanstalt fur Ernahrung und Lebensmittel [IO]
California Avocado Commn. [4707]
California Avocado Soc. [4708]
California Canning Peach Assn. [4709]
California Cling Peach Bd. [4710]

California Date Administrative Comm. [4711]
California Dried Plum Bd. [4712]
California Dry Bean Advisory Bd. [4713]
California Fig Advisory Bd. [4714]
California Fig Inst. [4715]
California Grape and Tree Fruit League [4716]
California Kiwifruit Commn. [4717]
California Macadamia Soc. [5053]
California Melon Res. Bd. [4718]
California Olive Assn. [1504]
California Pistachio Commn. [5054]
California Rare Fruit Growers [4719]
California Strawberry Commn. [4720]
California Table Grape Commn. [4721]
Calorie Control Coun. [1505]
Campaign to Label Genetically Engineered Foods [17604]
Campden and Chorleywood Food Res. Assn. [IO]
Canadian Coun. of Grocery Distributors [IO]
Canadian Fed. of Independent Grocers [IO]
Canadian Food Exporters Assn. [IO]
Canadian Hea. Food Assn. [IO]
Canadian Inst. of Food Sci. and Tech. [IO]
Canadian Snack Food Assn. [IO]
Canadian Spice Assn. [IO]
Catholic Inst. of the Food Indus. [19598]
Center for Food Safety [4675]
Center for Sci. in the Public Interest [17314]
Center for Veterinary Medicine [16789]
Central Off. for Bus. and Trade in Food [IO]
Chamber of Food Indus. [IO]
Cheese Importers Assn. of Am. [1131]
Chefs de Cuisine Assn. of Am. [792]
Chem. Sources Assn. [1660]
Chilled Food Assn. [IO]
Chinese Amer. Food Soc. [7092]
Chinese Inst. of Food Sci. and Tech. [IO]
Chocolate Mfrs. Assn. of the U.S.A. [1506]
CIES, Food Bus. Forum [3404]
Coalition for a Competitive Food and Agricultural Sys. [4075]
Cocoa Merchants' Assn. of Am. [1507]
Cocoa Producers' Alliance [IO]
Cocoa Res. Inst. of Ghana [IO]
Cold Storage and Distribution Fed. [IO]
Commercial Food Equip. Ser. Assn. [1571]
Community Food Security Coalition [1577]
Community Food Security Coalition [12192]
Community Systems Found. [15552]
Comparative Nutrition Soc. [15553]
Compassionate Cooks [13350]
Concord Grape Assn. [4724]
Confectionery Mfrs. Assn. of Canada [IO]
Confed. of the Food and Drink Indus. of the EU [IO]
Confrerie de la Chaine des Rotisseurs, Bailliage des U.S.A. [22569]
Consultative Gp. on Intl. Agricultural Res. [12425]
Consumer Goods Coun. of South Africa [IO]
Convenience Caterers and Food Mfrs. Assn. [1938]
Cooperative Grocers' Info. Network [1072]
Corn Refiners Assn. [1508]
Coun. for Biotechnology Info. [6614]
Coun. on Food, Agricultural and Rsrc. Economics [4524]
Coupon Exchange Club [17327]
Craft Guild of Chefs [IO]
Dairy Mgt., Inc. [1132]
Danish Soc. of Food Sci. and Tech. [IO]
Deutsches Tiefkuehlinstitut [IO]
DFA of California [4726]
Diamond Walnut Growers [5055]
Dietary Managers Assn. [15555]
Domestic Technologies [16994]
Egg CH, Inc. [5110]
Empresa Para Agroalimentacao e Cereais, S.A. [IO]
Environmental Working Group [4564]
Enzipan de Colombia [IO]
European Chilled Food Fed. [IO]
European Fed. of Food, Agriculture and Tourism Trade Unions [IO]
European Fed. of Food Sci. and Tech. [IO]
European Fed. of Frozen Food Products [IO]

European Fed. of the Trade in Dried Fruit, Edible Nuts, Preserved Food, Spices, Honey, and Similar Foodstuffs [IO]
European Food Emulsifiers Mfrs. Assn. [IO]
European Sales and Marketing Assn. [IO]
European Snacks Assn. [IO]
European Vegetable Protein Fed. [IO]
European Whey Products Assn. [IO]
Family Farm Defenders [4645]
FARMS Intl. [12427]
Fats and Proteins Res. Found. [2850]
Fed. Food Retailing Assn. [IO]
Fed. of European Food Additives, Food Enzymes and Food Cultures Indus. [IO]
Fed. of Food Indus. [IO]
Fed. of Hellenic Food Indus. [IO]
Fed. des Indus. et Commerces Utilisateurs des Basses Temperatures, Congelation, Surgeles, Glaces [IO]
Fed. of Luxembourg Food Indus. [IO]
Finnish Food and Drink Indus'. Fed. [IO]
Finnish Food Marketing Assn. [IO]
Finnish Food Workers' Union [IO]
Flavor and Extract Manufacturers Assn. of the U.S. [1509]
Flavour Mfrs. Assn. of Canada [IO]
Florida Citrus Mutual [4727]
Florida Citrus Nurserymen's Assn. [4728]
Florida Dept. of Citrus [4729]
Florida Gift Fruit Shippers Assn. [4731]
Florida Lychee Growers Assn. [4732]
Florida Tomato Comm. [4733]
Flour Millers Assn. of Japan [IO]
Food Additives and Ingredients Assn. [IO]
Food Additives Manufacturers' and Traders' Assn. [IO]
Food and Agriculture Org. of the United Nations [IO]
Food Alliance [4676]
Food Beverage Canada [IO]
Food and Beverage Importers Assn. [IO]
Food and Consumer Products of Canada [IO]
Food Distribution Res. Soc. [7093]
Food and Drink Fed. - England [IO]
Food and Drink Indus. Ireland [IO]
Food and Drug Law Inst. [5738]
Food Equipment Mfrs. Assn. [1573]
Food Importers' Assn. [IO]
Food Indus. Assn. Executives [3405]
Food Ingredient Distributors Assn. [1510]
Food Inst. [1511]
Food Inst. [IO]
Food for Life Global [12855]
Food Marketing Inst. [3406]
Food and Nutrition Bd. [15558]
Food Processing Suppliers Assn. [1133]
Food Processors of Canada [IO]
Food Providers of Am. [12392]
Food Res. and Action Center [12393]
Food Sci. and Nutrition Network for Africa [IO]
Food Shippers Assn. of North Am. [1512]
Foodservice Equip. Distributors Assn. [1574]
Foodservice Gp. [3467]
Foodservice and Packaging Inst. [1157]
Foodservice Sales and Marketing Assn. [1581]
Fresh Produce Assn. of the Americas [1513]
Fresh Produce Exporters' Assn. of Kenya [IO]
Fresh Produce and Floral Coun. [1514]
Frozen Potato Products Inst. [1515]
Fruit Trade Assn. Netherlands [IO]
Future Harvest [4089]
Gelatine Mfrs. of Europe [IO]
Genetic Engg. Action Network [6615]
Georgia Peanut Commn. [5056]
German Fed. for Food Law and Food Sci. [IO]
German Fruit Trade Assn. [IO]
German Sweets Export Assn. [IO]
Gingerbread [IO]
The Glutamate Assn. - U.S. [1516]
Gluten Intolerance Gp. [15559]
Granotec Chile [IO]
Greek Food and Wine Inst. [IO]
Greek Food and Wine Inst. [1517]
Grenada Co-operative Nutmeg Assn. [IO]
Grocery Mfrs. Association/Food Products Assn. [1518]

Reference to "IO" in place of a book number signifies that the association may be found in the 45th edition of International Organizations.

Guard Soc. [1519]
Guild of Fine Food Retailers [IO]
Guyana Rice Producers' Assn. [IO]
Hea. Food Manufactures Assn. [IO]
Home Baking Assn. [1520]
Home Orchard Soc. [4734]
Honey Assn. [IO]
Hosp. Caterers Assn. [IO]
ICC - Austria [IO]
ICC - Finland [IO]
ICC - Polska [IO]
ICC - Russia [IO]
Idaho Potato Commn. [4735]
Independent Bakers Assn. [452]
Independent Professional Seedsmen Assn. [187]
Inst. of Food Sci. and Tech. - UK [IO]
Inst. of Food Technologists [7094]
Inst. of Grocery Distribution [IO]
Intl. Aloe Sci. Coun. [1863]
Intl. and Amer. Associations of Clinical Nutrition-
    ists [15560]
Intl. Assn. for Cereal Sci. and Tech. [IO]
Intl. Assn. for Food Protection [5739]
Intl. Assn. of People Who Dine Over the Kitchen
    Sink [22594]
Intl. Banana Assn. [4736]
Intl. Castor Oil Assn. [2852]
Intl. Chili Soc. [22571]
Intl. Cocoa Org. [IO]
Intl. Commn. for Agricultural and Food Indus. [IO]
Intl. Commn. on Microbiological Specifications for
    Foods [IO]
Intl. Commn. of Sugar Tech. [IO]
Intl. Commn. for Uniform Methods of Sugar Anal.
    [IO]
Intl. Confectionery Assn. [IO]
Intl. Coun. of Grocery Mfrs. Associations [IO]
Intl. Coun. of Grocery Mfrs. Associations [1521]
Intl. Dairy-Deli-Bakery Assn. [IO]
International Dairy-Deli-Bakery Association [IO]
Intl. Dairy Foods Assn. [1134]
Intl. Fed. of Competitive Eating [23822]
Intl. Food Additives Coun. [1523]
Intl. Food Additives Coun. [IO]
Intl. Food and Agribusiness Mgt. Assn. [IO]
Intl. Food and Agribusiness Mgt. Assn. [1524]
Intl. Food Info. Coun. [1525]
Intl. Food Info. Ser. (IFIS Publishing) [IO]
Intl. Food Policy Res. Inst. [17796]
Intl. Food Safety Coun. [17605]
Intl. Food Safety Coun. [IO]
Intl. Food, Wine and Travel Writers Assn. [3118]
Intl. Foodservice Editorial Coun. [3119]
Intl. Foodservice Mfrs. Assn. [1526]
Intl. Foodservice Mfrs. Assn. [IO]
Intl. Frozen Food Assn. [IO]
Intl. Frozen Food Assn. [1527]
Intl. Glutamate Tech. Comm. [1528]
International Glutamate Technical Committee [IO]
Intl. Gold and Silver Plate Soc. [18977]
Intl. Grains Coun. [IO]
International Hydrolyzed Protein Council [IO]
Intl. Hydrolyzed Protein Coun. [1529]
Intl. Inst. for Beet Res. [IO]
Intl. Jelly and Preserve Assn. [IO]
Intl. Jelly and Preserve Assn. [1530]
Intl. Life Sciences Inst. - North Am. [15561]
Intl. Maillard Reaction Soc. [6683]
Intl. Maple Syrup Inst. [1531]
Intl. Maple Syrup Inst. [IO]
Intl. Natural Sausage Casing Assn. [2659]
Intl. Org. of the Flavor Indus. [IO]
Intl. Pepper Community [IO]
Intl. Soc. of Citriculture [4737]
Intl. Soc. of Lyophilization - Freeze Drying [6616]
Intl. Soc. of Sports Nutrition [15562]
Intl. Tech. Caramel Assn. [1532]
Intl. Tech. Caramel Assn. [IO]
Intl. Union of Food, Agricultural, Hotel, Restaurant,
    Catering, Tobacco, and Allied Workers' Associa-
    tions [IO]
Intl. Union of Food Sci. and Tech. [IO]
Intl. Vitamin A Consultative Gp. [15564]
Intl. Wheat Gluten Assn. [1533]
Intl. Wheat Gluten Assn. [IO]

Islamic Food and Nutrition Coun. of Am. [2353]
Italian Food Indus. Fed. [IO]
Italian Food Retailers' Fed. [IO]
Italian Frozen Food Inst. [IO]
Italian Pasta Makers' Union [IO]
Italian Rice Millers Assn. [IO]
Italian Wine and Food Inst. [1534]
James Beard Found. [11125]
Japan Maillard Reaction Soc. [IO]
Joint Labor Mgt. Comm. of the Retail Food Indus.
    [24059]
Kazakh Agrarian Expertise [IO]
Kids With Food Allergies [13603]
Kitchen Gardeners Intl. [9966]
Kitchen Gardeners Intl. [IO]
Leafy Greens Coun. [4738]
Leatherhead Food Intl. [IO]
Les Amis d'Escoffier Society of New York [IO]
Les Amis d'Escoffier Soc. of New York [1535]
Maine Lobstermen's Assn. [3492]
Malaysian Cocoa Bd. [IO]
Malaysian Cocoa Mfrs'. Gp. [IO]
Malaysian Food Mfg. Gp. [IO]
Malaysian Pepper Bd. [IO]
M&M's Collectors Club [22067]
Mfrs'. Agents for the Foodservice Indus. [1575]
MARINALG Intl., World Assn. of Seaweed Proces-
    sors [IO]
McDonald's Collectors Club [22070]
McDonald's Hispanic Operators Assn. [3395]
Meals4Israel [12459]
Meat Importers Coun. of Am. [2660]
Meat Indus. Suppliers Assn. [2661]
Meds and Food for Kids [11622]
Mexican Amer. Grocers Assn. [1536]
Michigan Apple Comm. [4739]
Michigan Assn. of Cherry Producers [4740]
Middle Atlantic Fisheries Assn. [3493]
Milk Indus. Found. [1135]
Milling and Baking Division of AACC Intl. [7095]
Molluscan Shellfish Inst. [3494]
Namibian Chef Assn. [IO]
Natl. Alliance for Food Safety and Security [1537]
Natl. Assn. of Catering Executives [1951]
Natl. Assn. of Chewing Gum Mfrs. [1538]
Natl. Assn. of Cocoa Exporters [IO]
Natl. Assn. of Convenience Stores [3416]
Natl. Assn. of Farmers' Market Nutrition Programs
    [4648]
Natl. Assn. of Flavors and Food-Ingredient
    Systems [1539]
Natl. Assn. of Flour Distributors [1540]
Natl. Assn. of Food Indus. [IO]
Natl. Assn. of Food Products Retailers and
    Manufacturers [IO]
Natl. Assn. of the German Food Indus. [IO]
Natl. Assn. of Margarine Mfrs. [2853]
Natl. Assn. of Pizzeria Operators [1953]
Natl. Assn. of Produce Market Managers [5022]
Natl. Assn. of Retail Grocers and Supermarkets of
    New Zealand [IO]
Natl. Assn. for the Specialty Food Trade [1541]
Natl. Automatic Merchandising Assn. [3971]
Natl. Barbecue Assn. [1542]
Natl. Barley Foods Coun. [1751]
Natl. Black McDonald's Operators Assn. [1955]
Natl. Blue Crab Industry Assn. [3495]
Natl. Bulk Vendors Assn. [3972]
Natl. Cattlemen's Beef Assn. [5023]
Natl. Center for Food Safety and Tech. [1543]
Natl. Chamber of the Restaurant and Seasoned
    Food Indus. [IO]
Natl. Cheese Inst. [1136]
Natl. Cherry Growers and Indus. Found. [4741]
Natl. Confectioners Assn. of the U.S. [1544]
Natl. Confectionery Sales Assn. [3419]
Natl. Cooperative Grocers Assn. [1074]
Natl. Corn Growers Assn. [4310]
Natl. Cottonseed Products Assn. [2854]
Natl. Coun. of Chain Restaurants [1957]
Natl. Country Ham Assn. [1545]
Natl. Fish Meal and Oil Assn. [2855]
Natl. Fisheries Inst. [3496]
Natl. Food and Energy Coun. [6963]
Natl. Frozen Dessert and Fast Food Assn. [1958]

Natl. Frozen Pizza Inst. [1546]
Natl. Frozen and Refrigerated Foods Assn. [1547]
Natl. Grocers Assn. [3421]
Natl. Honey Bd. [1548]
Natl. Honey Packers and Dealers Assn. [1549]
Natl. Ice Cream Retailers Assn. [1137]
Natl. Independent Concessionaires Assn. [1591]
Natl. Inst. for Sci., Law and Public Policy [4105]
Natl. Meat Assn. [2662]
Natl. Mushroom Growers' Assn. [4742]
Natl. Onion Assn. [4743]
Natl. Pasta Assn. [1550]
Natl. Peanut Festival Assn. [5058]
Natl. Pecan Shellers Assn. [5059]
Natl. Piggly Wiggly Operators Assn. [3422]
Natl. Potato Coun. [4746]
Natl. Poultry and Food Distributors Assn. [1551]
Natl. Renderers Assn. [2858]
Natl. Restaurant Assn. [1959]
Natl. Restaurant Assn. Educational Found. [1960]
Natl. Restaurant Assn. Quality Assurance Study
    Group [16385]
Natl. Rice Growers' Assn. [IO]
Natl. Rice Producers' Assn. [IO]
Natl. Seafood Educators [3497]
Natl. Seasoning Mfrs. Assn. [1552]
Natl. Shrimp Indus. Assn. [3498]
Natl. Sugar Ingredient Marketing Assn. [1553]
Natl. Sweet Sorghum Producers and Processors
    Assn. [871]
Natl. Yogurt Assn. [1138]
Network of Ingredient Marketing Specialists
    [1554]
New England Fisheries Development Assn. [3499]
New Jersey Asparagus Indus. Coun. [4748]
New Zealand Dairy Workers' Union [IO]
New Zealand Inst. of Food Sci. and Tech. [IO]
Nordic Comm. on Food Anal. [IO]
North Amer. Assn. of Food Equip. Mfrs. [1576]
North Amer. Assn. of Subway Franchisees [1670]
North Amer. Meat Processors Assn. [2663]
North Amer. Natural Casing Assn. [1555]
North Amer. Natural Casing Assn. [IO]
North Amer. Olive Oil Assn. [2859]
Northern Ireland Food and Drink Assn. [IO]
Northwest Fisheries Assn. [3500]
Nutrition for Optimal Hea. Assn. [15567]
OK Kosher Certification [20169]
Organic Consumers Assn. [5069]
Organic Food Fed. [IO]
Org. of European Indus. Transforming Fruit and
    Vegetables [IO]
OXFAM Am. [12438]
Pacific Coast Shellfish Growers Assn. [3501]
Pacific Seafood Processors Assn. [3502]
Panamanian Food Retailers and Distributors
    Assn. [IO]
Partnership for Food Safety Educ. [14399]
Peanut Advisory Bd. [5060]
Peanut and Tree Nut Processors Assn. [1556]
People Food and Land Found. [4656]
Pickle Packers Intl. [1557]
Pickle Packers Intl. [IO]
Pizza, Pasta and Italian Food Assn. [IO]
PMCA: An Intl. Assn. of Confectioners [IO]
PMCA: An Intl. Assn. of Confectioners [1558]
Popcorn Inst. [1559]
Potato Assn. of Am. [4757]
Price-Pottenger Nutrition Found. [15568]
Produce Marketing Assn. [5028]
Proj. Food, Land and People [4525]
Provision Trade Fed. [IO]
Quality Bakers of Am. Cooperative [453]
Quality Chekd Dairies [1139]
Red River Valley Sugarbeet Growers Assn. [5229]
Refrigerated Foods Assn. [1560]
Res. Associates of Am. [24060]
Res. Chefs Assn. [1124]
Res. and Development Associates for Military
    Food and Packaging Systems [7096]
Retail Confectioners Intl. [1561]
Retail Confectioners Intl. [IO]
Retailer's Bakery Assn. [454]
Rice Assn. [IO]
Scottish Food and Drink Fed. [IO]

A star before a book entry number signifies that the name is not listed separately, but is mentioned within the entry.

Scottish Grocers' Fed. [IO]
Senior Gleaners [12398]
Shelf-Stable Food Processors Assn. [2664]
Singapore Inst. of Food Sci. and Tech. [IO]
Slow Food Intl. [IO]
Snack Food Assn. [1562]
Soc. of Chemists and Technologists of Macedonia [IO]
Soc. of Flavor Chemists [6696]
Soc. of Food Hygiene Tech. [IO]
Soc. for Foodservice Mgt. [1594]
Soc. of Wine Educators [23029]
South African Assn. for Food Sci. and Tech. [IO]
South African Soc. for Enology and Viticulture [IO]
Southeastern Fisheries Assn. [3504]
Soy Protein Coun. [1563]
Spanish Food and Drink Indus. Fed. [IO]
Specialty Crop Trade Coun. [4761]
Spice Indus. Assn. [IO]
Spices Bd. India [IO]
State Public Interest Res. Groups' Campaign on Genetically Engineered Foods [4779]
Sudanese Standard and Metrology Org. [IO]
Sugar Assn. [1564]
Sugar Indus. Technologists [7097]
Sugar Indus. Technologists [IO]
Sunkist Growers [4763]
Sunsweet Growers [4764]
Sustainable Harvest Intl. [4115]
Swedish Frozen Food Assn. [IO]
Swiss Food Retailers' Assn. [IO]
Syndicat Natl. des Fabricants de Bouillons et Potages [IO]
Taiwan Frozen Seafood Indus. Assn. [IO]
Terlingua Intl. Chili Championship [22574]
Thai Food Processors' Assn. [IO]
Thai Frozen Foods Assn. [IO]
Thai Tapioca Trade Assn. [IO]
Tomato Genetics Cooperative [4765]
Tortilla Indus. Assn. [1565]
Tortilla Indus. Assn. [IO]
True Food Network [4677]
UniPro Foodservice [1566]
United Dairy Industry Assn. [1140]
United Food and Commercial Workers Intl. Union [24061]
U.S. Apple Assn. [4768]
U.S. Beet Sugar Assn. [1567]
U.S. Canola Assn. [1568]
U.S. Dry Bean Coun. [4769]
U.S. Freshwater Prawn and Shrimp Growers Assn. [3505]
U.S. Meat Export Fed. [2665]
U.S. Natl. Comm. for World Food Day [12401]
U.S. Potato Bd. [4770]
U.S. Tuna Found. [3506]
U.S.A. Harvest [12402]
U.S.A. Rice Fed. [1754]
Valley Fig Growers [4772]
Vegan Action [11071]
Venezuelan Assn. of Pasta Mfrs. [IO]
Venezuelan Food Indus. Assn. [IO]
Verein ICC - Schweiz [IO]
Vermont Maple Indus. Coun. [1569]
Vinegar Inst. [1570]
Washington State Apple Commn. [4773]
White Goods Suppliers' Assn. [IO]
Wild Blueberry Assn. of North Am. [4775]
Wisconsin Cheese Makers' Assn. [1141]
Women Chefs and Restaurateurs [794]
Women Grocers of Am. [3430]
Worshipful Company of Grocers [IO]
Food Additives Indus. Assn. [★IO]
Food Additives and Ingredients Assn. [IO], Maidstone, United Kingdom
Food Additives Manufacturers' and Traders' Assn. [IO], Barcelona, Spain
Food and Agriculture Org. of the United Nations [IO], Rome, Italy
Food and Agriculture Org. of the United Nations - Regional Off. for Europe [IO], Rome, Italy
Food and Agriculture Org. of the United Nations - Regional Off. for Latin Am. and the Caribbean [IO], Santiago, Chile
Food and Agriculture Org. of the United Nations - Trinidad and Tobago [IO], Port of Spain, Trinidad and Tobago

Food Aid Comm. [IO], London, United Kingdom
Food Allergy and Anaphylaxis Network [13600], 11781 Lee Jackson Hwy., Ste. 160, Fairfax, VA 22033-3309, (703)691-3179
Food Allergy Network [★13600]
Food Alliance [4676], 1829 NE Alberta, Ste. 5, Portland, OR 97211, (503)493-1066
Food Alliance; Organic [★5027]
Food and Allied Ser. Trades Dept. (of AFL-CIO) [★24060]
Food; Amer. Inst. of Wine and [22568]
Food Animal Concerns Trust [4997], PO Box 14599, Chicago, IL 60614, (773)525-4952
Food Assn; Natl. Frozen [★1547]
Food Assn; Natl. Frozen Dessert and Fast [1958]
Food Assn; Potato Chip/Snack [★1562]
Food Association; United Soft Serve and Fast [★1958]
Food Bank; Free Store/ [12773]
Food Bank Network; Second Harvest, The Natl. [★12388]
Food Beverage Canada [IO], Edmonton, AB, Canada
Food and Beverage Importers Assn. [IO], Sydney, Australia
Food and Beverage Trades Dept. (of AFL-CIO) [★24060]
Food Brokers Assn. [★1503]
Food Bus. Forum [★3404]
Food Bus. Forum [★IO]
Food Chains; Natl. Assn. of [★3406]
Food; Coalition for Non-Violent [11377]
Food and Consumer Products of Canada [IO], Toronto, ON, Canada
Food and Consumer Products Mfrs. of Canada [★IO]
Food Control Officials; Assn. of Amer. Plant [5433]
Food Corps, U.S.A. - Address unknown since 2002.
Food and Dairy Equip. Manufacturers; Natl. Assn. of [★1133]
Food Distribution Res. Soc. [7093], c/o Denise Mainville, Membership VP, 315 Hutcheson Hall, Blacksburg, VA 24061, (540)231-5774
Food Distributors of Am; Cooperative [★3421]
Food Distributors; Assn. of [★1503]
Food Distributors Assn; Natl. Frozen [★1547]
Food Distributors Assn; Natl. Independent Poultry and [★1551]
Food Distributors Assn; Natl. Institutional [★1566]
Food Distributors Assn; Natl. Wholesale Frozen [★1547]
Food Distributors Intl. - Defunct.
Food and Drink Fed. - England [IO], London, United Kingdom
Food and Drink Indus. Ireland [IO], Dublin, Ireland
Food and Drug Admin. Alumni Assn. [17606], 5600 Fishers Ln., Rm. 11-101, Rockville, MD 20857
Food and Drug Law Inst. [5738], 1155 15 St. NW, Ste. 800, Washington, DC 20005-4903, (202)371-1420
Food and Drug Officials of the U.S; Assn. of [★5736]

Food and Drugs
Apple Products Res. and Educ. Coun. [4705]
Assn. of Food and Drug Officials [5736]
Assn. of Tech. and Supervisory Professionals [5737]
Comm. of Experts on Cosmetic Products [IO]
Comm. of Experts on Flavouring Substances [IO]
Comm. of Experts on the Legal Classification of Medicines as Regards Their Supply [IO]
Comm. of Experts on Materials Coming into Contact with Food [IO]
Comm. of Experts on Nutrition, Food Safety and Consumer Hea. [IO]
Comm. of Experts on Pharmaceutical Questions [IO]
Coun. for Biotechnology Info. [6614]
European Aspirin Found. [IO]
Food and Drug Admin. Alumni Assn. [17606]
Food and Drug Law Inst. [5738]
Hea. Action Intl. Asia-Pacific [IO]
Intl. Assn. for Food Protection [IO]
Intl. Assn. for Food Protection [5739]
Intl. Assn. of Milk Control Agencies [5740]

Intl. Assn. of Milk Control Agencies [IO]
Intl. Narcotic Enforcement Officers Assn. [IO]
Intl. Narcotic Enforcement Officers Assn. [5741]
Intl. Narcotics Control Bd. [IO]
Intl. Narcotics Interdiction Assn. [IO]
Intl. Narcotics Interdiction Assn. [5742]
Intl. Wild Rice Exchange [4307]
Joint FAO-WHO Codex Alimentarius Commn. [IO]
Local Authorities Coordinators of Regulatory Services [IO]
Marine Stewardship Coun. [5171]
Natl. Coordinating Coun. for Medication Error Reporting and Prevention [14653]
Natl. Peach Coun. [4744]
North Amer. Blueberry Coun. [4749]
Org. of Professional Employees of the U.S. Dept. of Agriculture [5441]
People Food and Land Found. [4656]
Pineapple Growers Assn. of Hawaii [4756]
Raisin Administrative Comm. [4758]
Raisin Bargaining Assn. [4759]
Rare Fruit Coun. Intl. [4760]
Sun-Maid Growers of California [4762]
Food Editors Club Deutschland [IO], Munich, Germany
Food Editors and Writers Assn; Newspaper [★3094]
Food and Energy Coun. [★6963]
Food and Energy Coun; Natl. [6963]
Food and Environmental Sanitarians; Intl. Assn. of Milk, [★5739]
Food Equipment
Catering Equip. Distributors Assn. of Great Britain [IO]
Catering Equip. Suppliers Assn. [IO]
Commercial Food Equip. Ser. Assn. [1571]
European Foodservice Equip. Distributors Assn. [IO]
FISA [1572]
Food Equipment Mfrs. Assn. [1573]
Foodservice Equip. Distributors Assn. [1574]
Intl. Assn. of Used Equip. Dealers [3052]
Mfrs'. Agents for the Foodservice Indus. [1575]
North Amer. Assn. of Food Equip. Mfrs. [1576]
Partnership for Food Safety Educ. [14399]
United Egg Assn. Further Processors [5120]
Food Equipment Mfrs. Assn. [1573]
Food Equip. Ser. Agencies of Am; Commercial [★1571]
Food and Fertilizer Tech. Center for the Asian and Pacific Region [IO], Taipei, Taiwan
Food First [★IO]
Food First [★17795]
Food for the Hungry [12391], 1224 E Washington St., Phoenix, AZ 85034-1102, (480)998-3100
Food for the Hungry - UK [IO], Southampton, United Kingdom
Food Importers' Assn. [IO], Istanbul, Turkey
Food-In Corp. - Defunct.
Food Indus. Suppliers Assn. [★1572]
Food Indus. Supply Assn; Dairy and [★1133]
Food Indus. Assn. Executives [3405], PO Box 2510, Flemington, NJ 08822, (908)782-7833
Food Indus; Catholic Inst. of the [19598]
Food Industry Club of Florida - Defunct.
Food Indus. Sanitarians; Assn. of [★2463]
Food Ingredient Distributors Assn. [1510], 4646 W Jefferson, Ste. 200, Fort Wayne, IN 46804, (260)432-3033
Food Inst. [1511], 1 Broadway, Elmwood Park, NJ 07407, (201)791-5570
Food Inst. [IO], Elmwood Park, NJ, United States
Food Inst. of Canada [★IO]
Food Inst; Pet [2963]
Food Journalists; Assn. of [3094]
Food and Land Found; People [4656]
Food Law Inst. [★5738]
Food for Life Global [12855], PO Box 59037, Potomac, MD 20859, (301)987-5883
Food for Life Global [IO], Potomac, MD, United States
Food Mfrs. of Am; Institutional [★1526]
Food Marketing Inst. [3406], 2345 Crystal Dr., Ste. 800, Arlington, VA 22202-4801, (202)452-8444
Food Merchandisers of America - Address unknown since 1995.

Reference to "IO" in place of a book number signifies that the association may be found in the 45th edition of International Organizations.

Food and Nutrition Bd. **[15558]**, c/o Inst. of Medicine, 500 5th St. NW, Washington, DC 20001, (202)334-2352
Food and Nutrition; Soc. for the Anthropology of **[6424]**
Food Packaging Coun. - Address unknown since 1995.
Food Packers; Natl. Assn. of Frozen **[★1496]**
Food for Peace - Defunct.
Food for the Poor **[12772]**, 6401 Lyons Rd., Dept. 9662, Coconut Creek, FL 33073, (954)427-2222
Food for the Poor **[IO]**, Coconut Creek, FL, United States
Food Processing Suppliers Assn. **[IO]**, McLean, VA, United States
Food Processing Suppliers Assn. **[1133]**, 1451 Dolley Madison Blvd., Ste. 200, McLean, VA 22101-3850, (703)761-2600
Food Processors of Canada **[IO]**, Ottawa, ON, Canada
Food Processors Inst. - Defunct.
Food Providers of Am. **[12392]**, PO Box 83775, Phoenix, AZ 85071, (602)241-2873
Food Res. and Action Center **[12393]**, 1875 Connecticut Ave. NW, Ste. 540, Washington, DC 20009-5728, (202)986-2200
Food Safety Consortium **[5031]**, Univ. of Arkansas, 110 Agriculture Bldg., Fayetteville, AR 72701, (479)575-5647
Food Safety Coun. - Defunct.
Food Sanitarians; Intl. Assn. of Milk and **[★5739]**
Food Sci. and Nutrition Network for Africa **[IO]**, Addis Ababa, Ethiopia
Food Scientists and Technologists in Am; Assn. of Chinese **[★7092]**
Food Seasoning Mfrs; Natl. Assn. of Meat and **[★1552]**
Food Service
  Allied Trades of the Baking Indus. **[443]**
  Amer. Bakers Assn. **[444]**
  American Correctional Food Service Association **[IO]**
  Amer. Inst. of Baking **[445]**
  Amer. Inst. of Wine and Food **[22568]**
  Amer. Soc. for Healthcare Food Ser. Administrators **[14867]**
  Amer. Union of Pizza Delivery Drivers **[24062]**
  Amer. Wholesale Marketers Assn. **[1500]**
  Assn. of Correctional Food Ser. Affiliates **[1577]**
  Association of Correctional Food Service Affiliates **[1578]**
  Assn. of Pizza Delivery Drivers **[1579]**
  Baking Indus. Sanitation Standards Comm. **[448]**
  BEMA, The Baking Indus. Suppliers Assn. **[449]**
  Biscuit and Cracker Manufacturers Assn. **[450]**
  Black Culinarian Alliance **[1122]**
  Catholic Inst. of the Food Indus. **[19598]**
  Confrerie de la Chaine des Rotisseurs, Bailliage des U.S.A. **[22569]**
  Convenience Caterers and Food Mfrs. Assn. **[1938]**
  Cooperative Grocers' Info. Network **[1072]**
  Coun. of Hotel and Restaurant Trainers **[1939]**
  Coun. of Independent Restaurants of Am. **[1580]**
  Coun. of Intl. Restaurant Real Estate Brokers **[3392]**
  Egg CH, Inc. **[5110]**
  European Catering Assn. Intl. **[IO]**
  Food Ingredient Distributors Assn. **[1510]**
  Foodservice Consultants Soc. Intl. **[963]**
  Foodservice Equip. Distributors Assn. **[1574]**
  Foodservice Sales and Marketing Assn. **[1581]**
  Independent Bakers Assn. **[452]**
  Inst. of Food Technologists **[7094]**
  Intl. Assn. of Culinary Professionals **[1582]**
  Intl. Assn. of Culinary Professionals **[IO]**
  Intl. Chili Soc. **[22571]**
  International Flight Service Association **[1583]**
  International Flight Service Association **[IO]**
  Intl. Food Safety Coun. **[17605]**
  Intl. Food Ser. Executives Assn. **[1584]**
  Intl. Food Ser. Executives Assn. **[IO]**
  International Foodservice Distributors Association **[IO]**
  Intl. Foodservice Distributors Assn. **[1585]**

Intl. Foodservice Editorial Coun. **[3119]**
Intl. Foodservice Mfrs. Assn. **[1526]**
Intl. Frozen Food Assn. **[1527]**
Intl. Soc. of Lyophilization - Freeze Drying **[6616]**
Intl. Travel Catering Assn. **[IO]**
Joint Labor Mgt. Comm. of the Retail Food Indus. **[24059]**
Local Authority Caterers Assn. **[IO]**
Mfrs'. Agents for the Foodservice Indus. **[1575]**
Multicultural Foodservice and Hospitality Alliance **[1586]**
Natl. Alliance for Food Safety and Security **[1537]**
Natl. Assn. of Catering Executives **[1951]**
Natl. Assn. of Church Food Ser. **[1587]**
Natl. Assn. of Coll. and Univ. Food Services **[1588]**
Natl. Assn. of Concessionaires **[1589]**
Natl. Assn. of Flour Distributors **[1540]**
Natl. Assn. of Pizzeria Operators **[1953]**
Natl. Assn. for the Specialty Food Trade **[1541]**
Natl. Automatic Merchandising Assn. **[3971]**
Natl. Black McDonald's Operators Assn. **[1955]**
Natl. Cooperative Grocers Assn. **[1074]**
Natl. Coun. of Chain Restaurants **[1957]**
Natl. Food Ser. Mgt. Inst. **[1590]**
Natl. Frozen Dessert and Fast Food Assn. **[1958]**
Natl. Frozen Pizza Inst. **[1546]**
Natl. Frozen and Refrigerated Foods Assn. **[1547]**
Natl. Grocers Assn. **[3421]**
Natl. Honey Bd. **[1548]**
Natl. Independent Concessionaires Assn. **[1591]**
Natl. Restaurant Assn. **[1959]**
Natl. Restaurant Assn. Educational Found. **[1960]**
Natl. Restaurant Assn. Multi-Unit Architects, Engineers and Constr. Officers **[1050]**
Natl. Soc. for Healthcare Foodservice Mgt. **[1592]**
Nationwide Caterers Assn. **[IO]**
North Amer. Assn. of Subway Franchisees **[1670]**
Partnership for Food Safety Educ. **[14399]**
Quality Bakers of Am. Cooperative **[453]**
Res. Associates of Am. **[24060]**
Res. and Development Associates for Military Food and Packaging Systems **[7096]**
Retail Confectioners Intl. **[1561]**
Retailer's Bakery Assn. **[454]**
Roundtable for Women in Foodservice **[1593]**
Soc. for Foodservice Mgt. **[1594]**
Soc. of Wine Educators **[23029]**
Terlingua Intl. Chili Championship **[22574]**
Tortilla Indus. Assn. **[1565]**
Tourism, Hotels and Restaurants Assn. **[IO]**
UniPro Foodservice **[1566]**
UNITE HERE **[24095]**
United Egg Assn. Further Processors **[5120]**
United Food and Commercial Workers Intl. Union **[24061]**
Women Chefs and Restaurateurs **[794]**
Women Grocers of Am. **[3430]**
Women's Foodservice Forum **[1595]**
Food Ser. Administrators; Amer. Soc. for Healthcare **[14867]**
Food Ser. Assn; Amer. School **[★9173]**
Food Ser. Assn; Inflight **[★1583]**
Food Service Brokers of America - Defunct.
Food Ser. Equip. Indus. **[★1574]**
Food Ser. Executives Assn. **[★1584]**
Food Ser. Executives Assn. **[★IO]**
Food Ser. Foundation; School **[★9173]**
Food Ser. Indus; Marketing Agents for **[★1575]**
Food Service Marketing Inst. - Defunct.
Food Ser. Soc; Hosp., Institution and Educational **[★15555]**
Food and Shelter; Comm. for **[★12294]**
Food and Shelter; Natl. Citizens Comm. for **[★12294]**
Food Shippers Assn. of North Am. **[1512]**, 13240 Northup Way, No. 14, Bellevue, WA 98005, (425)649-0555
Food Stamp Directors; Amer. Assn. of **[6261]**
Food for Survival Prog. **[★12780]**
Food Transporters Conf; Agricultural and **[3856]**
Food Tray Assn. - Defunct.
Food Tray and Bd. Assn. **[★1157]**
Food USA; Slow **[9971]**
Food and Water **[17328]**, PO Box 543, Montpelier, VT 05601, (802)229-6222

Food and Water Irradiation; Natl. Coalition to Stop **[★17328]**
FoodFirst Info. and Action Network **[IO]**, Heidelberg, Germany
Foods Action Communications Team; Frozen **[★1496]**
Foods; Alliance for Better **[4674]**
Foods Assn; Natl. Dietary **[★3425]**
Foods Assn; National Nutritional **[★3425]**
Foods Assn; Wisconsin Dairy **[★4495]**
Foods Coun; Wheat **[1755]**
Foodservice Companies; ComSource Independent **[★1566]**
Foodservice Companies; North Amer. **[★1566]**
Foodservice Consultants Soc. Intl. **[963]**, 455 S 4th St., Ste. 650, Louisville, KY 40202, (502)583-3783
Foodservice Consultants Soc. Intl. **[IO]**, Louisville, KY, United States
Foodservice Distributors Assn; Intl. **[1585]**
Foodservice Equip. Distributors Assn. **[1574]**, 2250 Point Blvd., Ste. 200, Elgin, IL 60123-7887, (224)293-6500
Foodservice Gp. **[3467]**, 630 Village Trace, Bldg. 15, Ste. A, Marietta, GA 30067, (770)989-0049
Foodservice Gp. **[IO]**, Marietta, GA, United States
Foodservice Indus; Natl. Inst. for the **[★1960]**
Foodservice and Lodging Inst. **[★1957]**
Foodservice Mgt; Soc. for **[1594]**
Foodservice Marketing Associates; Natl. **[★3467]**
Foodservice Org. of Distributors **[★1547]**
FoodService Packaging Assn. **[IO]**, Oxon, United Kingdom
Foodservice and Packaging Inst. **[1157]**, 150 S Washington St., Ste. 204, Falls Church, VA 22046, (703)538-2800
Foodservice Sales and Marketing Assn. **[1581]**, 9192 Red Br. Rd., Ste. 200, Columbia, MD 21045, (410)715-6672
Foosball Assn; Valley Intl. **[1717]**
Foot and Ankle Orthopedics and Medicine; Amer. Coll. of **[16032]**
Foot and Ankle Pediatrics; Amer. Coll. of **[16033]**
Foot and Ankle Soc; Amer. Orthopaedic **[15758]**
Foot and Ankle Surgeons; Amer. Coll. of **[16034]**
Foot Orthopedists; Amer. CLG of **[★16032]**
Foot Surgeons; Amer. Coll. of **[★16034]**
Footbag
  World Footbag Assn. **[23426]**
  World Footbag Assn. **[IO]**
Footbag Players Assn; Natl. Hacky Sack **[★23426]**
Football
  af2 Natl. Fan Club **[24829]**
  Afghanistan Football Fed. **[IO]**
  Amer. Football Coaches Assn. **[23427]**
  Amer. Youth Football **[23428]**
  Atlantic Coast Conf. **[23806]**
  Australian Football Assn. of North Am. **[23429]**
  Australian Football Assn. of North Am. **[IO]**
  Australian Professional Footballers' Assn. **[IO]**
  Big East Conf. **[23807]**
  Big Ten Conf. **[23808]**
  Canadian Football League **[IO]**
  Canadian Junior Football League **[IO]**
  Coun. of Ivy Gp. Presidents **[23817]**
  Croatian Football Fed. **[IO]**
  Eastern Collegiate Hockey Assn. **[23485]**
  European Fed. of Amer. Football **[IO]**
  Fed. Internationale de Football Assn. **[IO]**
  Football Assn. of Wales **[IO]**
  Football Canada **[IO]**
  Football Fed. of Belize **[IO]**
  Football Writers Assn. of Am. **[23430]**
  Intl. Fed. of Amer. Football **[IO]**
  Intl. Fed. of Football History and Statistics **[IO]**
  Keith Bulluck Fan Club **[24830]**
  Natl. Assn. of Intercollegiate Athletics **[23835]**
  Natl. Christian Coll. Athletic Assn. **[23837]**
  Natl. Collegiate Athletic Assn. **[23841]**
  Natl. Football Found. and Coll. Hall of Fame **[23431]**
  Natl. Football League **[23432]**
  Natl. Football League Alumni **[23433]**
  Natl. Football League Players Assn. **[23434]**
  Natl. Junior Coll. Athletic Assn. **[23843]**
  North Amer. Football League **[23435]**

A star before a book entry number signifies that the name is not listed separately, but is mentioned within the entry.

North Amer. Football League [IO]
North Amer. Sports Fed. [23065]
Pacific 10 Conf. [23847]
Pop Warner Football [23436]
Professional Football Athletic Trainers Soc. [23437]
Professional Football Researchers Assn. [23438]
Professional Football Writers of Am. [23439]
Scottish Amateur Football Assn. [IO]
Scottish Women's Football Assn. [IO]
Southeastern Conf. [23851]
Southern Conf. [23852]
U.S. Collegiate Athletic Assn. [23859]
U.S. Collegiate Sports Coun. [23860]
U.S. Flag Football for the Deaf [23367]
U.S. Flag Football League [23440]
U.S. Flag and Touch Football League [23441]
U.S. Football Alliance [23442]
Universal Wheelchair Football Assn. [23368]
Valley Intl. Foosball Assn. [1717]
Football Assn; Cyprus [IO]
Football Assn. of the Czech Republic [IO], Prague, Czech Republic
Football Assn; Danish [IO]
Football Assn. of England [IO], London, United Kingdom
Football Assn; Estonian [IO]
Football Assn. of Iceland [IO], Reykjavik, Iceland
Football Assn. of Ireland [IO], Dublin, Ireland
Football Assn; Malta [IO]
Football Assn. of Moldova [IO], Chisinau, Moldova
Football Assn; Norwegian [IO]
Football Assn; Polish [IO]
Football Assn; Scottish [IO]
Football Assn; U.S. Soccer [★23786]
Football Assn. of Wales [IO], Cardiff, United Kingdom
Football Associations; Union of European [IO]
Football Canada [IO], Ottawa, ON, Canada
Football Coaches Assn; Canadian Univ. [IO]
Football Coaches Found. - Defunct.
Football Commissioners; Natl. Assn. of [★23815]
Football Confed; African [IO]
Football Confed; Asian [IO]
Football Conf; American [★23432]
Football Conf; National [★23432]
Football for the Deaf; U.S. Flag [23367]
Football Fed. of Armenia [IO], Yerevan, Armenia
Football Fed. Australia [IO], Sydney, Australia
Football Fed. of Belize [IO], Belize City, Belize
Football Fed; Latvian [IO]
Football Fed; Portuguese [IO]
Football Fed. of Ukraine [IO], Kiev, Ukraine
Football Hall of Fame and Museum; Canadian [IO]
Football Hall of Shame - Defunct.
Football League Alumni, Inc; Natl. [★23433]
Football League; American [★23432]
Football League Players Assn; Amer. [★23434]
Football; Pop Warner Junior League [★23436]
Football Shrine and Hall of Fame; Natl. [★23431]
Football Union; Midwest Rugby [★23706]
Football Union of Russia [IO], Moscow, Russia
Football Union; U.S. Rugby [23706]
Football Writers Assn. of Am. [23430], c/o Steve Richardson, Exec. Dir., 18652 Vista Del Sol Dr., Dallas, TX 75287-4021, (972)713-6198
Footboard; Brotherhood of the [★24176]
Footprint Assn; Intl. [5977]
FootSteps: Down Syndrome Ireland [★IO]
Footwear
    Assn. of Danish Shoe Retailers [IO]
    Belgian Fed. of the Footwear Indus. [IO]
    Boot and Shoe Mfrs'. Assn. [IO]
    Boot and Shoe Travelers Assn. of New York [1596]
    British Footwear Assn. [IO]
    Brotherhood of Shoe and Allied Craftsmen [24063]
    Canadian Assn. of Footwear Importers [IO]
    Chamber of the Footwear Indus. in the State of Guanajuato [IO]
    Cordwainers' Company [IO]
    European Confed. of the Footwear Indus. [IO]
    Fed. of Spanish Footwear Indus. [IO]
    Footwear Distributors and Retailers of Am. [1597]

Hellenic Assn. of Footwear Manufacturers and Exporters [IO]
    Independent Footwear Retailers' Assn. [IO]
    Indian Footwear Components Mfrs. Assn. [IO]
    Intl. Union of Shoe Indus. Technicians [IO]
    Korean Footwear Indus. Assn. [IO]
    MultiService Assn. [IO]
    Natl. Assn. of Footwear Suppliers [IO]
    Natl. Assn. of Italian Shoe Mfrs. [IO]
    Natl. Assn. of Suppliers for the Footwear and Leather Indus. [IO]
    Natl. Fed. of Shoe Traders [IO]
    Natl. Footwear Assn. of Russia [IO]
    Natl. Shoe Retailers Assn. [1598]
    Pakistan Footwear Mfrs. Assn. [IO]
    Pedorthic Footwear Assn. [1599]
    Portuguese Footwear, Components, Leather Goods Manufacturer's Assn. [IO]
    SATRA Tech. Centre [IO]
    Shoe Ser. Inst. of Am. [1600]
    Soc. of Shoe Fitters [IO]
    Taiwan Footwear Mfrs. Assn. [IO]
    Textile Clothing and Footwear Union of Australia [IO]
    Two/Ten Footwear Found. [1601]
    United Shoe Retailers Assn. [1602]
Footwear and Accessories Coun. - Defunct.
Footwear Assn; Amer. Apparel and [221]
Footwear Caucus - Defunct.
Footwear Coun. - Defunct.
Footwear Distributors and Retailers of Am. [1597], 1319 F St., Ste. 700, Washington, DC 20004, (202)737-5660
Footwear Indus. of Am. [★221]
Footwear Manufacturers Assn; Amer. Apparel and [★221]
Footwear Retailers of Am. [★1597]
Footwear Retailers of Am; Volume [★1597]
Footwear Retailers Assn; Volume [★1597]
For Family and Hea. Armenian Assn. [IO], Yerevan, Armenia
For the Heart Elvis Presley Fan Club - Address unknown since 2001.
For Inspiration and Recognition of Sci. and Tech. [8319], 200 Bedford St., Manchester, NH 03101, (603)666-3906
For the Love of Horses [17729], 7371 Sterrettania Rd., Fairview, PA 16415, (814)474-5382
For Mother Earth [17813], c/o Mark Stansbery, 1101 Bryden Rd., Columbus, OH 43205, (614)252-9255
For Mother Earth Intl. [★IO]
For Our Children's Unpaid Support - Defunct.
For Responsive Media: Citizens Commun. Center [★17171]
Forage and Grassland Coun; Amer. [5165]
Foragers of Am. [★1846]
Foragers Cosmetic Indus. Associates [1846], 135 E 55th St., 4th Fl., New York, NY 10022-9625, (212)759-1991
Foraminiferal Res; Cushman Found. for [7428]
An Foras um Cheannacht agus Bainistocht Abhar [★IO]
Foras Oiliuna agus Forbartha Eireann [★IO]
FORATOM: Assn. of European Atomic Forums [IO], Brussels, Belgium
Forbes Norris MDA/ALS Res. Center [15323], 2324 Sacramento St., Ste. 150, San Francisco, CA 94115, (415)600-3604
Forbes Norris Res. Center; ALS [★15323]
Forbrugerraadet [★IO]
Forbundet Blodarsjuka i Sverige [★IO]
Forbundet Djurens Ratt [★IO]
Forbundet for Jurister, Samhallsvetare, Ochekomomer [★IO]
Forbundet Sveriges Arbetsterapeuter [★IO]
Forby Family Historical Soc. [20903], 5521 Colorow Dr., Morrison, CO 80465, (303)697-2721
Force 5 Class Assn. [23171], c/o David S. Costanzo, Sec., 110 Baldwin Brook Rd., Canterbury, CT 06331-1805
Force Recon Assn. [21212], PO Box 783, Angels Camp, CA 95222, (209)607-6961
Forced Unionism - A Special Proj. of the Natl. Right to Work Legal Defense Found; Concerned Educators Against [17971]

Forces Veterans Assn; PBR [21348]
Ford
    71 429 Mustang Registry [21551]
    66,67,68 High Country Special Mustang Registry [21561]
    Boss 302 Registry [21595]
    Boss 429 Owners Dir. [21596]
    Classic Thunderbird Club Intl. [21617]
    Cobra Owners Club of Am. [21619]
    Crown Victoria Assn. [21625]
    Cyclone Montego Torino Registry [21626]
    Early Ford V-8 Club of Am. [21633]
    Edsel Club [21636]
    Fairlane Club of Am. [21641]
    Falcon Club of Am. [21642]
    FoMoCo Owners Club [21646]
    Ford Galaxie Club of Am. [21647]
    Heartland Vintage Thunderbird Club of Am. [21654]
    Model A Ford Cabriolet Club [21709]
    Model A Ford Club of Am. [21710]
    Model "A" Restorers Club [21712]
    Model "T" Ford Club of Am. [21713]
    Model "T" Ford Club Intl. [21714]
    Mustang Club of Am. [21722]
    Mustang Owners Club Intl. [21724]
    United Ford Owners [21804]
    Vintage Thunderbird Club Intl. [21812]
Ford Aerosports Club - Address unknown since 2000.
Ford Cabriolet Club; Model A [21709]
Ford Club of Am; Model A [21710]
Ford Club of Am; Model "T" 21713
Ford Dealers Alliance [★412]
Ford Found. [18394], 320 E 43rd St., New York, NY 10017, (212)573-5000
Ford Found. [IO], New York, NY, United States
Ford Found; Model A [21711]
Ford Galaxie Club of Am. [21647], PO Box 429, Valley Springs, AR 72682-0429, (870)743-9757
Ford, Lincoln, Mercury Minority Dealers Assn. [★413]
Ford Madox Ford Soc. [IO], Milton Keynes, United Kingdom
Ford Mercury Club of America - Defunct.
Ford Motor Minority Dealers Assn. [413], 16000 W 9 Mile Rd., Ste. 603, Southfield, MI 48075, (248)557-2500
Ford Motorsports Assn. - Defunct.
Ford Owners; United [21804]
Ford Registry; North Amer. English and European [21744]
Ford Sidevalve Owners Club - Defunct.
Ford V-8 Club of Am; Early [21633]
Forderkeis fur Internationales Wettbewerbsrecht [IO], Bad Homburg, Germany
Fordham Found; Thomas B. [17477]
Fords; LOVE [21692]
Ford's Theatre Soc. [11015], 511 10th St. NW, Washington, DC 20004, (202)638-2941
Fordson Tractor Club - Defunct.
Forecourt Equip. Fed. [IO], London, United Kingdom
Foreign Affairs Agencies USA; Gays and Lesbians in [24074]
Foreign Affairs; Citizens Network for [17866]
Foreign Affairs; Gays and Lesbians in [★24074]
Foreign Affairs Recreation Assn. - Address unknown since 2002.
Foreign Bankers; Inst. of [★481]
Foreign Banks' Assn. [IO], Bangkok, Thailand
Foreign Banks and Securities Houses Assn. [★IO]
Foreign Bases Proj. [17609], 48 Duffield St., Brooklyn, NY 11201, (718)596-7668
Foreign Bondholders Protective Coun. - Address unknown since 2002.
Foreign Car Haters Club of America - Address unknown since 1999.
The Foreign Christian Missionary Soc. [★19856]
Foreign Christian Missionary Soc; The [★19856]
Foreign Christian Union; Amer. and [19762]
Foreign Commerce Club of New York - Address unknown since 2002.
Foreign Correspondents' Club, Hong Kong [IO], Hong Kong, People's Republic of China
Foreign Correspondents' Club of Japan [IO], Tokyo, Japan

Reference to "IO" in place of a book number signifies that the association may be found in the 45th edition of International Organizations.

Foreign Credit Insurance Assn. [2164], 125 Park Ave., 14th Fl., New York, NY 10017, (212)885-1500
Foreign Credit Interchange Bur. [★2282]
Foreign Credit Interchange Bur. [★IO]
Foreign and Domestic Teachers' Bur. - Defunct.
Foreign Exchange Brokers of New York City - Address unknown since 1995.
Foreign Executive Women [IO], Tokyo, Japan
Foreign Freight Forwarders and Brokers Assn; New York [★3582]
Foreign Freight Forwarders and Brokers Assn; New York/New Jersey [3582]
Foreign Investors Assn. of Albania [IO], Tirana, Albania
Foreign Investors' Chamber of Commerce and Indus. [IO], Dhaka, Bangladesh
Foreign Investors in U.S. Real Estate; Assn. of [★2328]
Foreign Journalists; Center for [★3117]
Foreign Language Center; Natl. [8740]
Foreign Language and Intl. Stud; Natl. Coun. on [★8593]
Foreign Languages; Amer. Coun. on the Teaching of [8727]
Foreign Languages; Assn. of Departments of [8728]
Foreign Languages; Natl. Coun. of State Supervisors of [8738]
Foreign Languages; Northeast Conf. on the Teaching of [8742]
Foreign Law Assn; Amer. [5864]
Foreign Media Representatives Assn. - Defunct.
Foreign Medical Graduates; Educational Coun. for [★15997]
Foreign Medical Graduates; Natl. Assn. of [★14973]
Foreign Mission Assn. of North Am; Interdenominational [★20349]
Foreign Mission Bd. [★20350]
Foreign Mission Bd. [★IO]
Foreign Mission Commn. [★19535]
Foreign Mission Soc; Amer. Baptist [★19483]
Foreign Mission Soc; Holy Cross [19633]
Foreign Mission Soc; Woman's Amer. Baptist [★19483]
Foreign Missions Assn; Interdenominational [20349]
Foreign Missions; Gen. Convention of the Baptist Denomination in the U.S. for [★19483]
Foreign Missions; Independent Bd. for Presbyterian [20467]
Foreign Nursing Schools; Commn. on Graduates of [15473]
Foreign Orgs.' Employees Union - Address unknown since 1995.
Foreign Pharmacy Graduate Examination Commn. [★15933]
Foreign Pharmacy Graduate Examination Comm. [15933], c/o Carmen A. Catizone, MS, Exec. Dir./ Sec., Natl. Assn. of Boards of Pharmacy, 1600 Feehanville Dr., Mount Prospect, IL 60056, (847)391-4406

Foreign Policy
Amer. Acad. of Diplomacy [5744]
The Amer. Cause [17642]
Amer. Inst. for Contemporary German Stud. [9976]
Americans for Informed Democracy [5660]
Asian Speakers' Bur. [17607]
A.W.A.R.E. - Amer. Workforce Alliance for Responsible Economics [1258]
Bulgarian Natl. Front [17027]
Captive Nations Comm. [16988]
Carnegie Endowment for Intl. Peace [17863]
Christians' Israel Public Action Campaign [17936]
CitizensLobby.com [18435]
Coalition for Democracy in Iran [17389]
Comm. for Economic Development [17455]
Comm. on US/Latin Amer. Relations [19194]
Consumers for World Trade [17325]
Coun. on Foreign Relations [17608]
DataCenter [18412]
Eisenhower World Affairs Inst. [18442]
Families of September 11 [18729]
Foreign Bases Proj. [17609]
Foreign Policy Assn. [17610]
Foreign Policy Assn. [IO]

Foreign Policy in Focus [17611]
Foreign Policy Res. Inst. [5743]
Foreign Policy Res. Inst. [IO]
Found. for Rational Economics and Educ. [17293]
High Frontier Org. [18686]
Hispanic Coun. on Intl. Relations [17869]
Inst. for Foreign Policy Anal. [17612]
Intl. Center [17613]
Intl. Center [IO]
Jefferson Educational Found. [17273]
Jewish Comm. on the Middle East [18060]
Jewish Peace Lobby [17614]
Jewish Peace Lobby [IO]
A Jewish Voice for Peace [19184]
Middle East Policy Coun. [18063]
Natl. Assn. for the Employment of Amers. [1269]
Natl. Comm. on Amer. Foreign Policy [17615]
Natl. Comm. on Amer. Foreign Policy [IO]
Natl. Comm. on United States-China Relations [17064]
Natl. Coun. on U.S.-Arab Relations [18066]
Natl. Defense Coun. Found. [18465]
Natl. Hire Amer. Citizens Soc. [1276]
Network 20/20 [18004]
Nixon Center [17616]
The Org. for the Rights of Amer. Workers [1278]
Palestine Liberation Org. [18069]
Save U.S. Jobs [1282]
Secretary's Open Forum [17617]
State Dept. Watch [17618]
U.S.-Asia Inst. [17009]
U.S. Border Control [17810]
U.S.-Vietnam Trade Coun. [17010]
UrgentCall.org [18173]
William Penn House [17619]
Win Without War [18124]
World Policy Inst. [17620]
World Policy Inst. [IO]
Young Koreans United [12485]
Foreign Policy Assn. [17610], 470 Park Ave. S, New York, NY 10016, (212)481-8100
Foreign Policy Assn. [IO], New York, NY, United States
Foreign Policy Clearing House - Defunct.
Foreign Policy in Focus [17611], 1112 16th St. NW, Ste. 600, Washington, DC 20036, (202)234-9382
Foreign Policy Res. Inst. [5743], 1528 Walnut St., Ste. 610, Philadelphia, PA 19102, (215)732-3774
Foreign Policy Res. Inst. [IO], Philadelphia, PA, United States
Foreign Press Assn. [IO], New York, NY, United States
Foreign Press Assn. [3113], c/o Suzanne Adams, Exec. Dir., 333 E 46th St., Ste. 1K, New York, NY 10017-7425, (212)370-1054
Foreign Press Assn; Hollywood [3115]
Foreign Press Assn. - Israel [IO], Tel Aviv, Israel
Foreign Press Assn. in London [IO], London, United Kingdom
Foreign Press Center [★IO]
Foreign Press Center Japan [IO], Tokyo, Japan
Foreign Press in Japan [IO], Tokyo, Japan
Foreign Relations; Soc. for Historians of Amer. [10156]

Foreign Service
Amer. Acad. of Diplomacy [5744]
Amer. Foreign Ser. Assn. [24070]
Associates of the Amer. Foreign Ser. Worldwide [24071]
Delta Phi Epsilon, Professional Foreign Ser. Fraternity [24472]
Delta Phi Epsilon Professional Foreign Ser. Sorority [24473]
Diplomatic and Consular Officers, Retired [5745]
Intl. Fed. of Consular Corps and Associations [IO]
Foreign Ser. Assn; Amer. [24070]
Foreign Ser. Club [★24070]
Foreign Ser. Fraternity; Delta Phi Epsilon, Professional [24472]
Foreign Ser. Officers Assn; Retired [★5745]
Foreign Ser. Protective Assn; Amer. [19118]
Foreign Ser. Sorority; Delta Phi Epsilon Professional [24473]
Foreign Services Res. Inst. - Defunct.
Foreign Student Advisors; Natl. Assn. of [★8445]

Foreign Student Affairs; Natl. Assn. for [★8445]
Foreign Student Service Coun. - Address unknown since 2003.
Foreign Students
AYUSA Intl. [8444]
AYUSA Intl. [IO]
NAFSA/Association of Intl. Educators [IO]
NAFSA/Association of Intl. Educators [8445]
Soc. for Educational Visits and Exchanges in Canada [IO]
Foreign Students -English in Action; Greater New York Coun. for [★17885]
Foreign Stud; Amer. Inst. for [8652]
Foreign Stud; EF Educational Found. for [★8611]
Foreign Stud. Found; Amer. Inst. for [8595]
Foreign Stud. Scholarship Found; Amer. Inst. for [★8595]
Foreign Trade
The Amer. Cause [17642]
A.W.A.R.E. - Amer. Workforce Alliance for Responsible Economics [1258]
Foreign Credit Insurance Assn. [2164]
Mfrs. for Fair Trade [2538]
Natl. Assn. for the Employment of Amers. [1269]
Natl. Hire Amer. Citizens Soc. [1276]
The Org. for the Rights of Amer. Workers [1278]
Save U.S. Jobs [1282]
Foreign Trade; Bankers' Assn. for [★469]
Foreign Trade Law; Inst. for Intl. and [★5867]
Foreign-Trade Zones; Natl. Assn. of [2308]
Foreign Veterinary Graduates; Educational Commn. for [★16779]
Foreign Wars of the U.S; Ladies Auxiliary to the Veterans of [21307]
Foreign Wars of the U.S; Military Order of [21236]
Foreign Wars of the U.S; Veterans of [21331]
Foreman of Naval Shore Establishments; Natl. Assn. of Master Mechanics and [★6085]
Foreman's Assn. of America - Defunct.
Foremanship Found. - Defunct.
Foremen; Natl. Assn. of [★2509]
Foremen's Associations; Intl. Railway Gen. [★3283]
Foreningen for Dansk Projektledelse [★IO]
Foreningen af Danske Civiloekonomer [★IO]
Foreningen af Fabrikanter og Importorer af Elektriske Husholdningsapparater [★IO]
Foreningen Jordbruksteknikerna [★IO]
Foreningen Kvindelige Akademikere [★IO]
Foreningen for Miljo og folkesundhed [★IO]
Foreningen Nordiska Pappershistoriker [★IO]
Foreningen for Open Source Leverandorer i Danmark [★IO]
Foreningen for Produktmodellering i Danmark [★IO]
Foreningen af Radgivende Ingeniorer [★IO]
Foreningen Svensk Dentalhandel [★IO]
Foreningen Svenska Kompositorer av Popularmusik [★IO]
Foreningen Svenska Verktygs-och Verktygsmaskin-tillverkare [★IO]
Foreningen Svenska Verktygs-och Verktygsmaskin-tillverkare [★IO]
Foreningen Svenskt Orgelbyggeri [★IO]
Foreningen af Unge med Gigt [★IO]
Foreningen af Von Hippel-Lindau Patienter [★IO]
Forensic Accountants Soc. of North Am. [30], 4248 Park Glen Rd., Minneapolis, MN 55416, (952)928-4668
Forensic Assn; Amer. [9152]
Forensic Assn; Natl. [9158]
Forensic Chiropractors; Natl. Board of [14011]
Forensic Economics; Natl. Assn. of [6044]
Forensic Economists; Natl. Assn. of [★6044]
Forensic Examiners; Amer. Bd. of [★5751]
Forensic Expert Witness Assn. [5760], 2549 Eastbluff Dr., No. 497, Newport Beach, CA 92660, (949)640-9903
Forensic Geologists; Amer. Soc. of [7128]
Forensic and Indus. Chiropractic Consultants; Acad. of [830]
Forensic League; Natl. [9159]
Forensic League; Natl. Catholic [9156]
Forensic Medicine
Amer. Bd. of Forensic Anthropology [14400]
Amer. Bd. of Forensic Odontology [14401]
Amer. Forensic Nurses [15449]

A star before a book entry number signifies that the name is not listed separately, but is mentioned within the entry.

Amer. Rehabilitation Economics Assn. [16314]
Assn. of Forensic DNA Analysts and Administrators [5756]
British Assn. in Forensic Medicine [IO]
European Coun. of Legal Medicine [IO]
Intl. Soc. for Forensic Genetics [IO]
Japanese Soc. of Legal Medicine [IO]
Natl. Board of Forensic Chiropractors [14011]
Forensic Medicine; British Assn. in [IO]
Forensic Odontology; Amer. Soc. of [14142]
Forensic Psychology; Amer. Assn. for Correctional and [11853]
Forensic Sci. Soc. [IO], Harrogate, United Kingdom

Forensic Sciences
Amer. Acad. of Forensic Psychology [5746]
Amer. Acad. of Forensic Sciences [5747]
Amer. Assn. of Police Polygraphists [5748]
Amer. Bd. of Criminalistics [5749]
Amer. Bd. of Forensic Anthropology [14400]
Amer. Bd. of Forensic Document Examiners [5750]
Amer. Coll. of Forensic Examiners Intl. [5751]
Amer. Coll. of Forensic Examiners Intl. [IO]
Amer. Coll. of Forensic Psychiatry [5752]
Amer. Coll. of Forensic Psychology [14402]
Amer. Polygraph Assn. [5753]
Amer. Rehabilitation Economics Assn. [16314]
Amer. Soc. of Crime Lab. Directors [5754]
Amer. Soc. of Questioned Document Examiners [5755]
Assn. of Forensic DNA Analysts and Administrators [5756]
Association of Forensic DNA Analysts and Administrators [IO]
Association of Forensic Document Examiners [IO]
Assn. of Forensic Document Examiners [5757]
Assn. of Forensic Quality Assurance Managers [5758]
Assn. of Forensic Quality Assurance Managers [IO]
British Acad. of Forensic Sciences [IO]
Canadian Soc. for Clinical Investigation [IO]
Canadian Soc. of Forensic Sci. [IO]
Evidence Photographers Intl. Coun. [IO]
Evidence Photographers Intl. Coun. [5759]
Fingerprint Soc. [IO]
Forensic Expert Witness Assn. [5760]
Forensic Sci. Soc. [IO]
Forensic Sciences Found. [5761]
Independent Assn. of Questioned Document Examiners [5762]
Intl. Assn. of Cmpt. Investigative Specialists [8133]
Intl. Assn. for Identification [5763]
Intl. Assn. for Identification [IO]
Intl. Assn. for Identification - Great Britain [IO]
Intl. Assn. for Identification - New Zealand [IO]
Intl. Assn. for Identification - Russia [IO]
Intl. Assn. for Identification - Switzerland [IO]
Intl. Soc. of Environmental Forensics [IO]
Intl. Soc. of Environmental Forensics [7098]
Intl. Soc. of Stress Analysts [5764]
Intl. Soc. of Stress Analysts [IO]
Natl. Assn. of Document Examiners [5765]
Natl. Assn. of Forensic Counselors [5647]
Natl. Board of Forensic Chiropractors [14011]
Natl. Forensic Center [5766]
North Amer. Forensic Entomology Assn. [7064]
Soc. of Forensic Toxicologists [5767]
Swedish Forensic Sci. Assn. [IO]
Forensic Sciences Found. [5761], 410 N 21st St., Colorado Springs, CO 80904, (719)636-1100
Forensic Toxicology; American Bd. of [★5767]

Forensics
Amer. Acad. of Forensic Psychology [5746]
Amer. Bd. of Forensic Anthropology [14400]
Amer. Coll. of Forensic Psychology [14402]
Amer. Forensic Assn. [9152]
Amer. Forensic Nurses [15449]
Amer. Rehabilitation Economics Assn. [16314]
Amer. Soc. of Forensic Odontology [14142]
Amer. Soc. of Questioned Document Examiners [5755]
Assn. of Forensic Quality Assurance Managers [5758]

Delta Sigma Rho - Tau Kappa Alpha [24719]
Evidence Photographers Intl. Coun. [5759]
Independent Assn. of Questioned Document Examiners [5762]
Intl. Assn. of Bloodstain Pattern Analysts [5637]
Intl. Assn. of Cmpt. Investigative Specialists [8133]
Intl. Assn. for Identification [5763]
Intl. Public Debate Assn. [9041]
Intl. Soc. of Environmental Forensics [7098]
Law Enforcement and Emergency Services Video Assn. [6350]
Natl. Assn. of Forensic Accountants [46]
Natl. Assn. of Forensic Counselors [5647]
Natl. Assn. of Forensic Economics [6044]
Natl. Christian Forensics and Communications Assn. [8521]
Natl. Forensic Center [5766]
Natl. Org. of Forensic Social Work [8446]
NFHS Speech, Debate and Theatre Assn. [9161]
North Amer. Forensic Entomology Assn. [7064]
Foresight Inst. [7733], PO Box 61058, Palo Alto, CA 94306, (650)289-0860
Forest Action Gp; Big Island Rain [4366]
Forest Action Network [IO], Bella Coola, BC, Canada
Forest Alliance; New York Rain [★4442]
Forest Cat Breed Coun; Norwegian [21914]
Forest Coun; Native [4427]
Forest Ecosystem Rescue Network - Address unknown since 2001.
Forest Engg; Coun. on [4681]
Forest, Farm and Community Tree Network - Defunct.
Forest Farmers Assn. [★4683]
Forest Found; Natl. [4424]
Forest Found; Tropical [4698]
Forest Genetics Res. Found. - Defunct.
Forest Gold Products [IO], Maple Ridge, BC, Canada
Forest Guild [4394], PO Box 519, Santa Fe, NM 87504-0519, (505)983-8992
Forest History Found. [★10109]
Forest History Found; Amer. [★10109]
Forest History Soc. [10109], 701 William Vickers Ave., Durham, NC 27701-3162, (919)682-9319

Forest Industries
Amer. Hardwood Export Coun. [1603]
Amer. Loggers Coun. [1604]
Architectural Woodwork Mfrs. Assn. of Canada [IO]
Assn. of Western Pulp and Paper Workers [24064]
Assn. of Woodturners of Great Britain [IO]
British Woodworking Fed. [IO]
California Forestry Assn. [1605]
Canadian Inst. of Treated Wood [IO]
Canadian Lumbermen's Assn. [IO]
Canadian Wood Coun. [IO]
Canadian Wood Preservers Bur. [IO]
Composite Lumber Mfrs. Assn. [1642]
Cork Indus. Fed. [IO]
Cork Quality Coun. [1645]
Coun. on Forest Engg. [4681]
Coun. of Forest Indus. - Canada [IO]
Coun. of Forest Indus. - UK [IO]
European Confed. of Woodworking Indus. [IO]
European Fed. of the Plywood Indus. [IO]
European Panel Fed. [IO]
Forest Indus. Telecommunications [1606]
Forest Indus. Suppliers and Logging Assn. [IO]
Forest Landowners Tax Coun. [6293]
Forest Resources Assn. [1607]
Forest Stewardship Coun. - U.S. [4684]
German Timber Trade Fed. [IO]
Glued Laminated Timber Assn. [IO]
Hungarian Fed. of Forestry and Wood Indus. [IO]
Intermountain Forest Assn. [1608]
Intl. Wood Products Assn. [1609]
Intl. Wood Products Assn. [IO]
Malaysian Timber Coun. [IO]
Metropolitan Tree Improvement Alliance [5260]
Natl. Assn. of Forest Indus. [IO]
Natl. Assn. of State Foresters [4689]
Natl. Coun. for Air and Stream Improvement [4690]

Native Forest Network [4428]
New England Kiln Drying Assn. [1610]
North Amer. Wholesale Lumber Assn. [1611]
Northeastern Loggers Assn. [1612]
Northwest Forestry Assn. [1613]
Northwestern Lumber Assn. [1614]
Pacific Logging Cong. [1615]
Pacific Logging Cong. [IO]
Pacific Lumber Exporters Association [IO]
Pacific Lumber Exporters Assn. [1616]
Pacific Lumber Inspection Bur. [1617]
Pacific Lumber Inspection Bur. [IO]
Redwood Inspection Ser. [1618]
Res. Inst. of Chem. Processing and Utilization of Forest Products [IO]
Res. Inst. of the Wood Indus. [IO]
Scottish Timber Trade Assn. [IO]
Soc. of Amer. Foresters [4695]
Soc. of Wood Engravers [IO]
Softwood Export Coun. [IO]
Softwood Export Coun. [1619]
Southeastern Lumber Mfrs. Assn. [1620]
Southern Cypress Mfrs. Assn. [1621]
Southern Forest Products Assn. [1622]
Southern Pine Inspection Bur. [1623]
Southern Pressure Treaters' Assn. [1624]
Timber Framers Guild [1625]
Timber Framers Guild [IO]
Timber Products Mfrs. [1626]
Timber Res. and Development Assn. [IO]
Timber Trade Fed. [IO]
Washington Forest Protection Assn. [1627]
West Coast Lumber Inspection Bur. [1628]
Western Building Material Assn. [1629]
Western Forestry and Conservation Assn. [4700]
Western Hardwood Assn. [1630]
Western Red Cedar Lumber Assn. [IO]
Western Wood Products Assn. [1631]
World Forest Inst. [1658]
Forest Industries Coun. on Taxation - Address unknown since 2003.
Forest Indus. Development Coun. [IO], Edinburgh, United Kingdom
Forest Indus. Radio Communications [★1606]
Forest Indus. Telecommunications [1606], 1565 Oak St., Eugene, OR 97401, (541)485-8441
Forest Indus. Assn; Intermountain [★1608]
Forest Indus. Coun; Idaho [★1608]
Forest Indus. Suppliers and Logging Assn. [IO], Edmonton, AB, Canada
Forest Inst; World [1658]
Forest Landowners Assn. [4683], 900 Circle Pkwy., Ste. 205, Atlanta, GA 30339, (404)325-2954
Forest Landowners Tax Coun. [6293], PO Box 784, Alexandria, VA 22313-0784, (703)549-0747
Forest Network Australia; Native [IO]
Forest Network; Native [4428]
Forest Operations Inst. [★IO]

Forest Owners
Forest Landowners Tax Coun. [6293]
Natl. Woodland Owners Assn. [4693]
Redwood Region Logging Conf. [4694]
Forest and Paper Assn; Amer. [4679]
Forest Peoples Programme [IO], Moreton-in-Marsh, United Kingdom
Forest Prdt. Res. Soc. [★IO]
Forest Prdt. Res. Soc. [★7099]

Forest Products
Alberta Forest Products Assn. [IO]
Alliance for Environmental Tech. [1632]
Amer. Forest and Paper Assn. [4679]
Amer. Inst. of Timber Constr. [1633]
Amer. Loggers Coun. [1604]
Amer. Lumber Standard Comm. [1634]
American Lumber Standard Committee [IO]
Amer. Walnut Manufacturers Assn. [1635]
Amer. Wood-Preservers' Assn. [1636]
APA: The Engineered Wood Assn. [1637]
Appalachian Hardwood Manufacturers, Inc. [1638]
Assn. of Consulting Foresters of Am. [4680]
California Redwood Assn. [1639]
Canadian Hardwood Plywood and Veneer Assn. [IO]
Canadian Plywood Assn. [IO]
Cedar Shake and Shingle Bur. [IO]

Reference to "IO" in place of a book number signifies that the association may be found in the 45th edition of International Organizations.

Cedar Shake and Shingle Bur. [1640]
Coalition for Fair Lumber Imports [1641]
Composite Lumber Mfrs. Assn. [1642]
Composite Panel Assn. [1643]
Composite Panel Assn. [IO]
Cork Inst. of Am. [1644]
Cork Quality Coun. [1645]
Coun. on Forest Engg. [4681]
Engineered Wood Tech. Assn. [1646]
Forest Landowners Assn. [4683]
Hardwood Distributor's Assn. [1647]
Hardwood Mfrs. Assn. [1648]
Hardwood Plywood and Veneer Assn. [1649]
Intl. Soc. of Tropical Foresters [4687]
Lignin Inst. [1650]
Lignin Inst. [IO]
Malaysian Wood Indus. Assn. [IO]
Mulch and Soil Coun. [1651]
Natl. Assn. of State Foresters [4689]
Natl. Hardwood Lumber Assn. [1652]
Natl. Hardwood Lumber Assn. [IO]
Natl. Lumber and Building Material Dealers Assn.
  [1653]
New Brunswick Fed. of Woodlot Owners [IO]
New Zealand Timber Indus. Fed. [IO]
Northeastern Lumber Mfrs. Assn. [1654]
Northeastern Retail Lumber Assn. [1655]
Rainforest Relief [5164]
UK Forest Products Assn. [IO]
Wood Component Mfrs. Assn. [1656]
Wood Products Mfrs. Assn. [1657]
Forest Products Assn. of Canada [IO], Ottawa, ON,
  Canada
Forest Products History Found. of Minnesota Histori-
  cal Soc. [★10109]
Forest Products Safety Conf. [12962]
Forest Products Safety Conf; Western [★12962]
Forest Products Soc. [7099], 2801 Marshall Ct.,
  Madison, WI 53705-2295, (608)231-1361
Forest Products Soc. [IO], Madison, WI, United
  States
Forest Products Traffic Assn. - Defunct.
Forest Products Wholesalers Assn. - Defunct.
Forest Protection Alliance; Natl. [4592]
Forest Protective Assn; California [★1605]
Forest Rangers and Rangerettes [★18997]
Forest Recreation Assn; Natl. [3358]
Forest Rsrc. Coun; Inland [★1608]
Forest Rsrc. Gp; Tropical [IO]
Forest Resources Assn. [1607], 600 Jefferson Plz.,
  Ste. 350, Rockville, MD 20852-1157, (301)838-
  9385
Forest School Camps [IO], Stroud, United Kingdom
Forest Ser. Employees for Environmental Ethics
  [5126], PO Box 11615, Eugene, OR 97440-3815,
  (541)484-2692
Forest Ser. Volunteers Prog; U.S. Dept. of
  Agriculture - [4699]
Forest Stewardship Coun. - U.S. [4684], 1155 30th
  St. NW, Ste. 300, Washington, DC 20007,
  (202)342-0413
Forest Trust [★4394]
Forestation Center of the Ams. - Address unknown
  since 2008.
Forester Sisters Fan Club - Address unknown since
  2001.
Foresters of Am; Assn. of Consulting [4680]
Foresters; Assn. of Eastern [★4689]
Foresters; Catholic Assn. of [18991]
Foresters; Catholic Order of [18997]
Foresters; Massachusetts Catholic Order of
  [★18991]
Foresters; Natl. Assn. of State [4689]
Foresters; Natl. Catholic Soc. of [19007]
Foresters; Soc. of Amer. [4695]
Foresters; Women's Catholic Order of [★19007]
ForestEthics [4685], One Haight St., Ste. B, San
  Francisco, CA 94102, (415)863-4563
Forestry
  African Blackwood Conservation Proj. [4342]
  African Network for Agriculture, Agroforestry and
    Natural Resources Educ. [IO]
  Alliance for Community Trees [4678]
  Alliance for Intl. Reforestation [4344]
  The Amer. Chestnut Found. [6622]

Amer. Forest and Paper Assn. [4679]
Amer. Forests [4347]
Amer. Lands Alliance [4533]
Amer. Loggers Coun. [1604]
Amer. Resources Gp. [4350]
Amer. Wildlands [4354]
Arboricultural Assn. [IO]
Asia-Pacific Assn. of Forestry Res. Institutions
  [IO]
Asia-Pacific Forestry Commn. [IO]
Assoc. Equip. Distributors [2000]
Assn. of Consulting Foresters of Am. [4680]
Assn. of Foresters and Wood Technologists [IO]
Assn. for Temperate Agroforestry [4119]
Bolivian Forestry Assn. [IO]
Boreal Songbird Initiative [5302]
British Wood Preserving and Damp-Proofing
  Assn. [IO]
Camp Fire Conservation Fund [4370]
Canadian Forestry Assn. [IO]
Canadian Inst. of Forestry [IO]
Chinese Acad. of Forestry [IO]
Chinese Soc. of Forestry [IO]
COFORD: Natl. Coun. for Forest Res. and
  Development [IO]
Commonwealth Forestry Assn. [IO]
Confed. of European Forest Owners [IO]
Coun. on Forest Engg. [4681]
Coun. of Forest Indus. Canada [IO]
Danish Assn. of Graduates in Forestry [IO]
Danish Forest Assn. [IO]
Danish Forest and Landscape Res. Inst. [IO]
Elm Res. Inst. [4682]
European Forest Genetic Resources Programme
  [IO]
European Forest Inst. [IO]
European Tropical Forest Res. Network [IO]
FAO/ECE Timber Sect. [IO]
Finnish Forest Indus. Fed. [IO]
Forest Guild [4394]
Forest Indus. Development Coun. [IO]
Forest Landowners Assn. [4683]
Forest Landowners Tax Coun. [6293]
Forest Products Soc. [7099]
Forest Products Soc. [IO]
Forest Resources Assn. [1607]
Forest Stewardship Coun. - U.S. [4684]
ForestEthics [4685]
Forestry Assn. of Botswana [IO]
Forestry Conservation Communications Assn.
  [4395]
Forestry Res. Inst. of Sweden [IO]
Forestry and Timber Assn. [IO]
German Forestry Coun. [IO]
Inst. of Chartered Foresters [IO]
Inst. for Commercial Forestry Res. [IO]
Inst. of Wood Sci. [IO]
Intl. Assn. for Mediterranean Forests [IO]
Intl. Assn. of Wildland Fire [IO]
Intl. Assn. of Wildland Fire [4686]
Intl. Assn. of Wood Anatomists [IO]
Intl. Res. Gp. on Wood Preservation [IO]
Intl. Soc. of Tropical Foresters [IO]
Intl. Soc. of Tropical Foresters [4687]
Intl. Tech. Tropical Timber Assn. [IO]
Intl. Tree Found. [IO]
Intl. Union of Forest Res. Organizations [IO]
Irish Timber Growers' Assn. [IO]
Izaak Walton League of Am. [4413]
Izaak Walton League of Am. Endowment [4414]
Japan Forest Tech. Assn. [IO]
Japan Wood Res. Soc. [IO]
Latin Amer. Forestry Inst. [IO]
Live Oak Soc. [4688]
Los Algarrobos - Assn. for Sustainable Develop-
  ment [IO]
Malaysian Panel-Products Manufacturers' Assn.
  [IO]
Natl. Assn. of State Foresters [4689]
Natl. Coun. for Air and Stream Improvement
  [4690]
Natl. Coun. on Private Forests [4691]
Natl. Forest Recreation Assn. [3358]
Natl. Network of Forest Practitioners [4692]
Natl. Woodland Owners Assn. [4693]

Native Forest Coun. [4427]
Native Forest Network [4428]
New Zealand Forest Owners Assn. [IO]
New Zealand Inst. of Forestry [IO]
Nordic Forest Res. Cooperation Comm. [IO]
Nordic Wood Preservation Coun. [IO]
Pachamama Alliance [5163]
Rainforest Action Network [4441]
Rainforest Relief [5164]
Redwood Region Logging Conf. [4694]
Res. Inst. of Forestry, Policy and Info. [IO]
Res. Inst. - Subtropical Forestry [IO]
Royal Forestry Soc. [IO]
Royal Scottish Forestry Soc. [IO]
Save America's Forests [4448]
Soc. of Amer. Foresters [4695]
Soc. of Wood Sci. and Tech. [7100]
South African Inst. of Forestry [IO]
Southern African Inst. of Forestry [IO]
Swiss Forestry Soc. [IO]
Thoreau Inst. [4696]
Timber Decking Assn. [IO]
Tree-Ring Soc. [7101]
Trees for Tomorrow [4697]
Trees, Water and People [4610]
Tropical Flowering Tree Soc. [4986]
Tropical Forest Found. [4698]
U.S. Dept. of Agriculture - Forest Ser. Volunteers
  Prog. [4699]
Western European Inst. for Wood Preservation
  [IO]
Western Forestry and Conservation Assn. [IO]
Western Forestry and Conservation Assn. [4700]
World Agroforestry Centre [IO]
World Forest Institute [IO]
World Forest Inst. [1658]
World Forestry Center [4701]
World Forestry Center [IO]
Forestry Assn; Amer. [★4347]
Forestry Assn. of Botswana [IO], Gaborone,
  Botswana
Forestry Assn; Indus. [★1613]
Forestry Center; Western [★4701]
Forestry Conservation Communications Assn.
  [4395], PO Box 3217, Gettysburg, PA 17325,
  (717)388-1505
Forestry, Mining and Energy Union; Constr., [IO]
Forestry Res. Inst. of Sweden [IO], Uppsala,
  Sweden
Forestry Services; Intermountain [★1608]
Forestry and Timber Assn. [IO], Edinburgh, United
  Kingdom
Forests; Amer. [4347]
Forests Fund; New [★12436]
Forests; Natl. Coun. on Private [4691]
Forests Proj; New [12436]
Forests; Save America's [4448]
Forex Assn. of North Am. [★475]
Forex Club of North Am. [★475]
Forex U.S.A. [★475]
Forfeiture Endangers Amer. Rights [5577], 20 Sun-
  nyside Ave., Ste. A-419, Mill Valley, CA 94941,
  (415)389-8551
Forgers and Helpers; Intl. Brotherhood of Boilermak-
  ers, Iron Ship Builders, Blacksmiths, [24021]
Forging Assn; Drop [★2708]
Forging Indus. Assn. [2708], Landmark Off. Towers,
  25 Prospect Ave. W, Ste. 300, Cleveland, OH
  44115, (216)781-6260
Forging Indus. Educational and Res. Found. [7314],
  25 Prospect Ave. W, Ste. 300, Cleveland, OH
  44115, (216)781-5040
Forgiveness Alliance; Worldwide [8959]
Forius Bus. Credit Resources [1422], PO Box
  59149, Minneapolis, MN 55459-0149, (612)341-
  9600
Fork Lift Truck Assn. [IO], Alton, United Kingdom
ForLIFE - Defunct.
Form 1099 Filers; Natl. Assn. of [18711]
Form Assn; Insulating Concrete [925]
Formaldehyde Enval. Repercussions; Save Us From
  [★13324]
Formaldehyde Inst. - Defunct.
Formaldehyde Poisoning Assn; Citizens United to
  Reduce Emissions of [★13324]

A star before a book entry number signifies that the name is not listed separately, but is mentioned within the entry.

Formaldehyde Poisoning Assn; CURE [13324]
Formaldehyde Task Force Fund - Defunct.
Formalwear Assn; Amer. [★242]
Formalwear Assn; Intl. [242]
Formed Steel Tube Inst. [★997]
Formed Steel Tube Inst. [★IO]
Former Agents of the U.S. Secret Ser; Assn. of [5877]
Former and Current Employees of Intel; FACE Intel - [1262]
Former Members of Cong. [★17253]
Former Members of Cong; U.S. Assn. of [17253]
Former Mental Patients; Recovery, Inc., The Assn. of Nervous and [★16230]
Former Soviet Political Prisoners; Amer. Assn. of [★17766]
Former Special Agents of the Fed. Bur. of Investigation; Soc. of [19202]
Former Stewardesses Clubs - Address unknown since 1997.
Formerly Employed Mothers at the Leading Edge [★12086]
Formers of the 12th Armored Division - Address unknown since 2001.
Forming Inst; Scaffolding, Shoring and [670]
Formosan Assn. for Human Rights [18692], c/o Ms. Pearl Wang, Pres., 22 Aberdeen Crossing, The Woodlands, TX 77381, (281)367-1138
Formosan Assn. for Public Affairs [18693], 552 7th St. SE, Washington, DC 20003, (202)547-3686
Formosan Assn. for Public Affairs [IO], Washington, DC, United States
Forms Mgt. Assn; Bus. [3677]
Forms Manufacturers Credit Interchange [★1444]
Formula Coun; Infant [★2387]
Formula Coun; Intl. [2387]
FORMULA Inc. [12408]
Formula One Spectators Assn. - Defunct.
Foroige, Natl. Youth Development Org. [IO], Dublin, Ireland
Forrest Fan Club; Helen [24910]
Forrester Genealogical Assn. [★20828]
Forrester Soc; Clan [20828]
Forschungsinstitut der Vereinigung der Osterreichischen Zementindustrie [★IO]
Forsikringsforeningen [★IO]
Forskerparkforeningen [★IO]
Forskningscentret for Skov Landskab [★IO]
Forskningsradet for miljo, areella naringar och samhallsbyggande [★IO]
Forsvars- og Sikkerhetsindustriens forening [★IO]
Forsyth County Defense League [★18804]
Fort Greene Park; Friends of [★4407]
Fort McHenry-Living Classrooms; Patriots of [10057]
Fort Worth Grain and Cotton Exchange [★4325]
Fort Worth Grain Exchange [4325]
Fortean Soc. [★7477]
Fortean Soc. [★IO]
FORTH Interest Gp. [7535], c/o John Rible, Treas., 317 California St., Santa Cruz, CA 95060-4215, (831)458-0399
Fortress Study Group [IO], King's Lynn, United Kingdom
Fortune Soc. [11867], 53 W 23rd St., 8th Fl., New York, NY 10010, (212)691-7554
Forty and Eight [20667], 777 N Meridian St., Rm. 204, Indianapolis, IN 46204, (317)634-1804
Forty-Sixers; Adirondack [23930]
Forty Upward Network - Defunct.
The FORUM [12346]
Forum for the Advancement of Students in Science and Technology - Defunct.
Forum for the Advancement of Toxicology - Defunct.
Forum for African Women Educationalists [IO], Nairobi, Kenya
Forum-Asia: Asian Forum for Human Rights and Development [IO], Bangkok, Thailand
Forum for Bioteknologi [★IO]
Forum for the Built Env. [IO], Nottingham, United Kingdom
Forum Christian Fellowship of Light [★12346]
Forum for Databehandling i Helsesektoren [★IO]
Forum for Death Educ. and Counseling [★11909]
Forum on Debt and Development [IO], The Hague, Netherlands

Forum des Eglises Canadiennes pour les Ministeres Mondiaux [★IO]
Forum of the European Nuclear Indus. [★IO]
Forum Europeen des Associations pour le Patrimoine [★IO]
Forum Europeen de la Jeunesse [★IO]
Forum Europeen de l'Energie [★IO]
Forum Europeen de l'Orientation Academique [★IO]
Forum for Health Care Planning - Address unknown since 2004.
Forum Inst. - Defunct.
Forum Intl. - Defunct.
Forum Intl.: Intl. Ecosystems Univ. [18833], 91 Gregory Ln., No. 21, Pleasant Hill, CA 94523, (925)946-1500
Forum Intl.: Intl. Ecosystems Univ. [IO], Pleasant Hill, CA, United States
Forum for Investor Advice [1463], PO Box 3216, Mercerville, NJ 08619
Forum on Long Term Care - Defunct.
Forum Maritime Intl. des Compagnies Petrolieres [★IO]
Forum for Medical Affairs - Address unknown since 2003.
Forum of Natl. Dance Orgs. - Defunct.
Forum of Regional Associations of Grantmakers [12717], 1111 19th St. NW, Ste. 650, Washington, DC 20036, (202)467-1120
Forum on Res. Mgt. [★6530]
Forum for Scriptural Christianity [20262], c/o DBA Good News Magazine, 308 E Main St., PO Box 150, Wilmore, KY 40390, (859)858-4661
Forum for State Hea. Policy Leadership [17689], 444 N Capitol St. NW, Ste. 515, Washington, DC 20001, (202)624-5400
Forum du Tiers Monde [★IO]
Forum du Tiers Monde [★IO]
Forum Train Europe [IO], Bern, Switzerland
Forum for U.S.-Soviet Dialogue - Address unknown since 1994.
Forum for Women in Bridge - Defunct.
Forum for Women Business Owners - Defunct.
Forums Inst; Natl. Issues [18467]
Forums; Natl. Issues [★18467]
Forward America - Defunct.
Forward Face [14062], 317 E 34th St., Ste. 901A, New York, NY 10016, (212)684-5860
Forward in Faith North Am. [19959], PO Box 210248, Bedford, TX 76095-7248, (800)225-3661
Forwarders Assn. of Am; Air Freight [★145]
Forwarders Assn. of Am; Customs Brokers and [★2309]
Forwarders Assn. of Am; Household Goods [3567]
Forwarders Assn. of Am; Natl. Customs Brokers and [2309]
Forwarders and Brokers Assn; New York Foreign Freight [★3582]
Forwarders and Brokers Assn; New York/New Jersey Foreign Freight [3582]
FOSFA Intl. [IO], London, United Kingdom
Fossil Fuels Policy Action Institute [★17234]
The Fossils - Address unknown since 2005.
Foster Business - Address unknown since 1995.
Foster Care Alumni of Am. [11592], 118 S Royal St., 2nd Fl., Alexandria, VA 22314, (703)299-6767
Foster Care Assn. (NSW) [IO], Westmead, Australia
Foster Family-Based Treatment Assn. [11593], 294 Union St., Hackensack, NJ 07601, (201)343-2246
Foster Grandparent Prog. [11693], c/o Florida Senior Programs, Inc., 7400 Laurel Hill Oaks Cir., Orlando, FL 32818, (407)298-4180
Foster Parent Assn; Natl. [12677]

Foster Parents

Action for Child Protection [11553]
Adopt Am. Network [11227]
Adoptee-Birthparent Support Network [11228]
Adoption Info. Services [11230]
Adoptions Together [11231]
Alberta Foster Parent Assn. [IO]
Assn. of Administrators of the Interstate Compact on Adoption and Medical Assistance [11236]
Assn. of Administrators of the Interstate Compact on the Placement of Children [11559]
Child Welfare Inst. [11571]
Childreach, U.S. Member of Plan Intl. [11681]

Foster Care Alumni of Am. [11592]
Foster Care Assn. (NSW) [IO]
Foster Grandparent Prog. [11693]
Friends in Adoption [11245]
Healing the Children [11697]
Holt Intl. Children's Services [11698]
Indian Youth of Am. [12626]
Intl. Aid Serving Kids [11603]
Interracial Family Circle [12161]
Kidsave Intl. [11251]
Korean Foster Care Assn. [IO]
Lutheran Immigration and Refugee Ser. [12815]
Mothers Without Borders [11626]
Natl. Assn. of Former Foster Care Children of Am. [11626]
Natl. Center for Lesbian Rights [12246]
Natl. Foster Parent Assn. [12677]
Orphan Found. of Am. [11715]
Partners in Foster Care [12193]

Foster Parents Assn. - Defunct.
Foster Parents Plan [IO], Toronto, ON, Canada
Foster Parents Plan of Belgium [IO], Gent, Belgium
Foster Parents Plan of Germany [IO], Hamburg, Germany
Foster Parents Plan - U.S.A. [★IO]
Foster Parents Plan - U.S.A. [★11681]
Fostering Network [IO], London, United Kingdom
Fostering of Ophthalmic Care for Underserved Sectors; Interprofessional [16859]
Fostoria Glass Collectors [22553], PO Box 1625, Orange, CA 92856
Fostoria Glass Soc. of Am. [22554], PO Box 826, Moundsville, WV 26041, (304)845-9188
Found. for Academic Standards and Tradition - Address unknown since 2008.
Found. for Accounting Educ. [31], 3 Park Ave., 18th Fl., New York, NY 10016-5991, (212)719-8300
Found. for Accredited Chiropractic Educ. [★14004]
Found. for the Advancement of Artists - Defunct.
Found. for Advancement in Cancer Therapy [13824], PO Box 1242, Old Chelsea Sta., New York, NY 10113, (212)741-2790
Found. for the Advancement of Chiropractic Educ. [8079], PO Box 1052, Levittown, PA 19058, (800)397-9722
Found. for the Advancement of Chiropractic Tenets and Sci. [14003], c/o Intl. Chiropractors Assn., 1110 N Glebe Rd., Ste. 650, Arlington, VA 22201, (703)528-5000
Found. for the Advancement of Hispanic Amers. - Address unknown since 2004.
Found. for the Advancement of Monetary Educ. [8423], PO Box 625, FDR Sta., New York, NY 10150-0625, (212)818-1206
Found. for the Advancement of Sephardic Stud. and Culture [19181], c/o Robert Bedford, Exec. VP, 34 W 15th St., 3rd Fl., New York, NY 10011
Found. for Advances in Medicine and Sci. [14025], PO Box 485, Mahwah, NJ 07430-0485, (201)828-9150
Found. Against Trafficking in Women [IO], Amersfoort, Netherlands
Found. for Aging Res. - Defunct.
Found. Aid to South-East-Asia [★IO]
Found. Aiding the Elderly [17329], PO Box 254849, Sacramento, CA 95865-4849, (916)481-8558
Found. for Alternative Cancer Therapies [★13824]
Found. of America - Address unknown since 2005.
Found. for Amer. Agriculture - Defunct.
Found. of the Amer. Bd. of Trial Advocates [5495], Bryan Tower, Ste. 3000, 2001 Bryan St., Dallas, TX 75201, (214)871-7523
Found. for Amer.-Chinese Cultural Exchanges - Defunct.
Found. for Amer. Christian Educ. [8086], PO Box 9588, Chesapeake, VA 23321-9588, (757)488-6601
Found. of Amer. Coll. of Health Care Administrators - Defunct.
Found. for Amer. Communications [17177], 85 S Grand Ave., Pasadena, CA 91105, (626)584-0010
Found. of the Amer. Economic Coun. - Address unknown since 1995.
Foundation of the Amer. Subcontractors Assn. (FASA) [★1003]

Reference to "IO" in place of a book number signifies that the association may be found in the 45th edition of International Organizations.

Found. for America's Sexually Exploited Children - Defunct.

Found. for Anglican Traditions - Defunct.

Found. for Aquatic Injury Prevention [12963], c/o Ronald R. Gilbert, Chm., 11230 White Lake Rd., Fenton, MI 48430, (800)342-0330

Found. for the Arts of Peace - Defunct.

Found. for the Arts, Religion and Culture [★9599]

Found. for Australian Literary Stud. [IO], Townsville, Australia

Found. Beefmaster Assn. - Address unknown since 2003.

Found. for Better Living - Address unknown since 1991.

Found. for Biomedical Res. [13696], 818 Connecticut Ave. NW, Ste. 900, Washington, DC 20006, (202)457-0654

Found. for Blood Irradiation - Address unknown since 2004.

Found. for Books to China - Address unknown since 1999.

Found. Center [12653], 79 5th Ave., New York, NY 10003-3076, (212)620-4230

Found. for Character Education - Address unknown since 1995.

Found. for Child Development [11541], 145 E 32nd St., 14th Fl., New York, NY 10016-6055, (212)213-8337

Found. for Child Mental Welfare - Defunct.

Found. for Children with Learning Disabilities [★12494]

Found. for the Children's Oncology Gp. [★13850]

Found. for Chiropractic Educ. and Res. [14004], PO Box 400, Norwalk, IA 50211-0400, (515)981-9888

Found. for a Christian Civilization [★19763]

Found. for Christian Living [★19825]

Found. for Christian Psychic Res. - Defunct.

Found. for Christian Theology [19960], c/o The Christian Challenge, 1215 Independence Ave. SE, Washington, DC 20003, (202)547-5409

Foundation for Christian Theology [IO], Washington, DC, United States

Found. Comm. for Aid to South Vietnam [★IO]

Found. for the Community of Artists - Address unknown since 1995.

Found. for Community Encouragement - Defunct.

Found. of Compassionate Amer. Samaritans [20340], PO Box 428760, Cincinnati, OH 45242, (513)621-5300

Found. of Compassionate Amer. Samaritans [IO], Cincinnati, OH, United States

Found. for Cooperative Housing [★12309]

Found. for Cotton Res. and Educ. [★1091]

Found. for a Course in Miracles [20571], 41397 Buecking Dr., Temecula, CA 92590-5668, (951)296-6261

Found. for Credit Education - Defunct.

Found. for Cure - Defunct.

Found. for Deep Ecology [4508], Bldg. 1062, Ft. Cronkhite, Sausalito, CA 94965, (415)229-9339

Found. for Deep Ecology [IO], Sausalito, CA, United States

Found. for Depression and Manic Depression - Defunct.

Found. for Design Integrity [1152], 1950 N Main St., PO Box 139, Salinas, CA 93906, (650)326-1867

Found. for Design Integrity [IO], Salinas, CA, United States

Found. for Development Cooperation [IO], Brisbane, Australia

Found. for Development of Needy Communities - Uganda [IO], Mbale, Uganda

Found. DIAKONIA World Fed. of Diaconal Associations and Diaconal Communities [IO], Dusseldorf, Germany

Found. for Digestive Hea. and Nutrition [14417], 4930 Del Ray Ave., Bethesda, MD 20814-3015, (301)222-4002

Found. EARTH - Address unknown since 2006.

Found. for Economic Educ. [18406], 30 S Broadway, Irvington, NY 10533, (914)591-7230

Found. on Economic Trends [18615], 4520 E West Hwy., Ste. 600, Bethesda, MD 20814, (301)656-6272

Found. for Educational Futures [318], PO Box 6381, New York, NY 10150-6381, (800)285-1310

Foundation for Educational Futures [IO], New York, NY, United States

Found. for Elective Mutism, Inc. [★15233]

Found. for Emerging Peoples [★12426]

Found. for Emerging Peoples [★IO]

Found. Engineers; Assoc. Soil and [★7137]

Found. Engineers; Assn. of Soil and [★7137]

Found. for Enterprise Development [★704]

Found. for Episcopal Colleges [★8397]

Found. for Episcopal Colleges [★IO]

Found. for Ethics and Meaning [7069], 5445 Mariner St., Ste. 314, Tampa, FL 33609, (888)LETS-CARE

Found. for Ethnic Dance - Address unknown since 1995.

Found. for European Language and Educational Centres [IO], Zurich, Switzerland

Found. for European Language and Educational Centres U.S.A. [IO], Alexandria, VA, United States

Found. for European Language and Educational Centres U.S.A. [8731], 101 N Union St., Ste. 300, Alexandria, VA 22314, (703)684-1494

Found. Europeenne [★IO]

Found. for Exceptional Children [★IO]

Found. for Exceptional Children [★11998]

Found. for Exceptional Children; Yes I Can! [11998]

Found. Faith of God - Address unknown since 1986.

Found. of the Fed. Bar Assn. [5937], 2011 Crystal Dr., Ste. 400, Arlington, VA 22202, (703)682-7000

Found. Fed. for the Organizations in the Field of Lib., Info. and Documentation Services [★IO]

Found. for Field Res. - Defunct.

Found. Fighting Blindness [16847], 11435 Cronhill Dr., Owings Mills, MD 21117-2220, (410)568-0150

Found. for Financial Institutions Res. - Defunct.

Found. for Fire Safety - Defunct.

Found. for Fluency - Address unknown since 2001.

Found. for Foreign Affairs - Defunct.

Found. Francisco Marroquin [9910], c/o Mrs. Rosa Gutierrez, Admin. Mgr., PO Box 2422, Stuart, FL 34995-2422, (772)286-6450

Found. Francisco Marroquin [IO], Stuart, FL, United States

Found. for Fundamental Res. on Matter [IO], Utrecht, Netherlands

Found. for a Future - Defunct.

Found. for Future Generations - Address unknown since 1995.

Found. for Gifted and Creative Children - Defunct.

Found. for Glaucoma Res. [★15683]

Found. for Global Broadcasting - Address unknown since 2002.

Found. for Global Community [18203], 251 High St., Ste. B, Palo Alto, CA 94301, (650)328-7756

Found. for Grandparenting [12262], 108 Farnham Rd., Ojai, CA 93023

Found. for Hand Res. and Educ. [14526], c/o Indiana Hand Center, PO Box 80434, Indianapolis, IN 46280-0434, (317)875-9105

Found. for Hand Surgical Res; Indiana [★14526]

Found. for Handgun Educ. [★17592]

Found. for Hea. [14556], 337 East Ave., Watertown, NY 13601-3829, (315)782-6664

Found. for Homeopathic Res. - Defunct.

Found. for Hospice and Homecare - Defunct.

Found. for Hosp. Art [13708], 120 Stonemist Ct., Roswell, GA 30076, (770)645-1717

Found. for Human Ecological Health - Defunct.

Found. for Human Rights and Democracy in China - Address unknown since 1994.

Found. of Human Understanding [10465], PO Box 1000, Grants Pass, OR 97528, (541)956-6700

Found. for Ichthyosis and Related Skin Types [14201], 1364 Welsh Rd., North Wales, PA 19454, (215)619-0670

Found. ICPR Junior Coll. [8022]

Found. ICPR Junior Coll. [IO], San Juan, PR, United States

Found. for Ileitis and Colitis [★14414]

Found. for Illinois Archaeology [★6442]

Found. to Improve Television - Address unknown since 2002.

Found. for Independent Higher Educ. [8537], 1920 N St. NW, Ste. 210, Washington, DC 20036, (202)367-0333

Found. Info-Turk [IO], Brussels, Belgium

Found. for Informed Medical Decision Making [15137], 40 Court St., Ste. 200, Boston, MA 02108, (617)367-2000

Found. for Innovation in Medicine [15166], 411 North Ave. E, Cranford, NJ 07016, (908)272-2967

Found. for Instrumentation and Res. - Defunct.

Found. for Interior Design Educ. Res. [★8584]

Found. for Intl. Child Health - Address unknown since 1995.

Found. for Intl. Community Assistance [17217], 1101 14th St. NW, Ste. 1100, Washington, DC 20005, (202)682-1510

Found. for Intl. Community Assistance [IO], Washington, DC, United States

Found. for Intl. Cooperation [IO], Park Ridge, IL, United States

Found. for Intl. Cooperation [8612], 1237 S Western Ave., Park Ridge, IL 60068, (847)518-0934

Found. for Intl. Economic Policy - Address unknown since 1995.

Found. for Intl. Environmental Law and Development [IO], London, United Kingdom

Found. for Intl. Human Relations - Address unknown since 1999.

Found. for Intl. Meetings [2680], c/o Intl. Meeting Network Solutions, 1110 N Glebe Rd., Ste. 580, Arlington, VA 22201, (703)908-0707

Found. for Intl. Meetings [IO], Arlington, VA, United States

Found. for Intl. Trade Res. - Address unknown since 1995.

Found. for Investment and Development of Exports [IO], Tegucigalpa, Honduras

Found. for the Jewish Natl. Fund [★20150]

Found. for Latin Amer. Anthropological Res. - Defunct.

Found. for Latin-American Economic Res. [IO], Buenos Aires, Argentina

Found. of Law and Soc. - Defunct.

Found. Lib. Center [★12653]

Found. of Light and Metaphysical Education - Defunct.

Found. for Medical Technology - Defunct.

Found. for MicroBiology [★6605]

Found. for Middle East Peace [18058], 1761 N St. NW, Washington, DC 20036, (202)835-3650

Foundation for Middle East Peace [IO], Washington, DC, United States

Found. for Mideast Communication - Address unknown since 1999.

Found. for Moral Restoration [18372], PO Box 1009, Ashburn, VA 20146-1009, (703)724-4141

Found. of Motion Picture Pioneers - Defunct.

Found. for Nager and Miller Syndromes [14452], c/o DeDe Van Quill, Dir., 13210 SE 342nd St., Auburn, WA 98092, (253)333-1483

Found. for Natl. Progress [18446], 222 Sutter St., Ste. 600, San Francisco, CA 94108, (415)321-1700

Foundation of the Natl. Student Nurses' Assn. in memory of Frances Tompkins [★8873]

Found. for the New Freeman - Defunct.

Found. for Non-Lethal Warfare - Defunct.

Found. for North Amer. Wild Sheep [5318], 720 Allen Ave., Cody, WY 82414-3402, (307)527-6261

Found. of Occupational Development [IO], Chennai, India

Found. for Osteopathic Health Services - Address unknown since 1999.

Found. for Pacific Dance [9882]

Foundation for Pacific Dance [IO], Littleton, CO, United States

Found. for Pavement Preservation [945], 8613 Cross Park Dr., Austin, TX 78754, (866)862-4587

Found. for P.E.A.C.E. [18204], PO Box 9151, Asheville, NC 28815, (828)296-0194

Found. for P.E.A.C.E. [IO], Asheville, NC, United States

Found. for Peace - Spain [IO], Barcelona, Spain

Found. for a Peaceful Env. Among Communities Everywhere [★IO]

Found. for a Peaceful Env. Among Communities Everywhere [★18204]

Found. for People and Community Development [IO], Boroko, Papua New Guinea

A star before a book entry number signifies that the name is not listed separately, but is mentioned within the entry.

Found. for the Peoples of the South Pacific [★IO]

Found. for the Peoples of the South Pacific [★12426]

Found. for the Peoples of the South Pacific - Fiji [★IO]

Found. for the Peoples of the South Pacific - Kiribati [IO], Tarawa, Kiribati

Found. for Pet Provided Therapy; Love on a Leash - The [16623]

Found. of Pharmacists and Corporate America for AIDS Education - Address unknown since 1999.

Found. for Philosophy of Creativity [10793], c/o Dr. Larry Cobb, Exec. Dir., 250 Slippery Rock Rd., Slippery Rock, PA 16057, (724)794-2938

Found. for Physical Therapy [16613], c/o Amer. Physical Therapy Assn., 1111 N Fairfax St., Alexandria, VA 22314-1488, (703)684-2782

Found. for Preservation of America's Architectural Heritage - Defunct.

Found. for the Preservation of Antique and Contemporary Cup Plates - Defunct.

Found. for Preservation of the Archeological Heritage - Address unknown since 1990.

Found. for the Preservation of the Mahayana Tradition [19550], 1632 SE 11th Ave., Portland, OR 97214-4702, (503)808-1588

Found. for the President's Private Sector Survey on Cost Control - Defunct.

Found. for the Private Sector - Address unknown since 1999.

Found. for the Promotion of Finnish Music [IO], Helsinki, Finland

Foundation for the Promotion and Preservation of Square Dancing [★IO]

Foundation for the Promotion and Preservation of Square Dancing [★9869]

Found. for the Promotion of Responsible Parenthood - Aruba [IO], San Nicolas, Aruba

Found. for Public Affairs [18447], 2033 K St. NW, Ste. 700, Washington, DC 20006, (202)872-1790

Found. for Public Relations Res. and Educ. [★9031]

Found. for Rational Economics and Educ. [17293], PO Box 1776, Lake Jackson, TX 77566, (409)265-3034

Found. of Real Estate Appraisers [280], 4907 Morena Blvd., No. 1415, San Diego, CA 92117, (800)882-4410

Found. for Reformation Res. [★10930]

Found. for Religious Action in the Social and Civil Order - Address unknown since 1999.

Found. for Res. in the Afro-Amer. Creative Arts - Address unknown since 1999.

Found. for Res. Development [★IO]

Found. for Res. in Economics and Educ. [★17293]

Found. for Res. on Economics and the Env. [4396], 662 Ferguson Rd., Bozeman, MT 59718, (406)585-1776

Found. for Res. on Human Behavior - Defunct.

Found. for Res. on the Nature of Man [★7452]

Found. for Res. and Sustainable Development [IO], Madurai, India

Found. for Revitalization of Local Hea. Traditions [IO], Bangalore, India

Found. for Safer Athletic Field Environments [23064], c/o Sports Turf Managers Assn., 805 New Hampshire St., Ste. E, Lawrence, KS 66044-2774, (800)323-3875

Found. for Savings Institutions - Defunct.

Found. for Sci. and Disability [11946], c/o Dr. E.C. Keller, Jr., Treas./Newsletter Ed., West Virginia Univ., Biology Dept., Morgantown, WV 26506-6057, (304)293-5201

Found. for Sci. and the Handicapped [★11946]

Found. for Sci. and Indus. Res. at the Norwegian Inst. of Tech. [IO], Trondheim, Norway

Found. for Shamanic Stud. [20446], PO Box 1939, Mill Valley, CA 94942, (415)380-8282

Found. for the peoples of the South Pacific - Papua New Guinea [★IO]

Found. for Student Commun. [8023], 48 Univ. Pl., Rm. 305, Princeton, NJ 08540-5116, (609)258-1111

Found. for Stud. and Res. on Women [IO], Buenos Aires, Argentina

Found. for the Stud. of Women's Literature [IO], Bremen, Germany

Found. for the Stud. of the Arts and Crafts Movement at Roycroft [21530], 46 Walnut St., East Aurora, NY 14052, (716)652-3333

Found. for the Study of Cycles - Address unknown since 2003.

Found. for the Stud. of Independent Social Ideas [18010], 310 Riverside Dr., Ste. 2008, New York, NY 10025, (212)316-3120

Found. for the Stud. of Infant Deaths [IO], London, United Kingdom

Found. for the Stud. of Presidential and Congressional Terms [★17295]

Found. for the Study of Primitive Culture - Defunct.

Found. for the Study of Wilson's Disease [★15251]

Found. for the Support of Intl. Medical Training [14977], c/o Intl. Assn. for Medical Assistance to Travellers, 1623 Military Rd., No. 279, Niagara Falls, NY 14304-1745, (716)754-4883

Found. for the Support of Intl. Medical Training [IO], Niagara Falls, NY, United States

Found. for Teaching Economics [8216], 260 Russell Blvd., Ste. B, Davis, CA 95616-3839, (530)757-4630

Found. Testing Professionals; Alliance of Deep [6650]

Found. of Thanatology [★11908]

Found. of Thanatology; Amer. Inst. of Life Threatening Illness and Loss Division of [11908]

Found. for Theological Education in Southeast Asia - Address unknown since 1995.

Found. for Traditional Values [18505], c/o Student Statesmanship Inst., PO Box 80108, Lansing, MI 48908, (517)321-6233

Found. of the Twelve Apostles - Address unknown since 2004.

Found. VONK Projects [★IO]

Found. of the Wall and Ceiling Indus. [624], c/o Assn. of the Wall and Ceiling Indus., 513 W Broad St., Ste. 210, Falls Church, VA 22046, (703)538-1600

Found. for Wild Life Argentina [IO], Buenos Aires, Argentina

Found. for Women Judges [★5907]

Found. for Women's Equality [IO], Buenos Aires, Argentina

Found. for Women's Hea. Res. and Development [IO], London, United Kingdom

Found. for Women's Resources [9319], 3800 Parry Ave., Dallas, TX 75226, (214)421-5566

Found. for World Literacy - Defunct.

Found. for Young Australians [IO], Melbourne, Australia

Found. for Youth and Student Affairs - Defunct.

Foundations Assn; Concrete [1011]

Foundations; Coun. on [12652]

Foundations and Donors Interested in Catholic Activities [19625], 1350 Connecticut Ave. NW, Ste. 825, Washington, DC 20036, (202)223-3550

Foundations; First [13169]

Foundations Inst; Deep [1013]

Foundations; Natl. Coun. on Community [★12652]

Foundations and Trusts for Community Welfare; Natl. Comm. on [★12652]

Founder's Corporation; Theta Delta Chi [★24668]

Founder's Corporation; Theta Delta Chi [★IO]

Founders and Friends of Norwich, Connecticut; Soc. of the [10063]

Founders of Manakin in the Colony of Virginia; Huguenot Soc. of the [21162]

Founders of New Jersey; Descendants of [20736]

Founders of Norwich, Connecticut; Soc. of the [★10063]

Founders and Patriots of Am; Order of the [20755]

Foundries

  CAEF - The European Foundry Assn. [IO]

  CEMAFON: European Comm. Material Products for Foundries [IO]

  China Foundry Assn. [IO]

  Fabless Semiconductor Assn. [1215]

  German Foundry Assn. [IO]

  Inst. of British Foundrymen [IO]

  Inst. of Cast Metals Engineers [IO]

  Swedish Foundry Assn. [IO]

  Taiwan Foundry Soc. [IO]

Foundry Educational Found. - Defunct.

Foundry Equip. Materials Assn. [★2009]

Foundry Equip. and Supplies Assn. [IO], West Midlands, United Kingdom

Foundry Soc; Amer. [9227]

Foundry Supply Mfrs. Gp. [★2009]

Foundrymen's Assn; Amer. [★9227]

Fountain Pen and Mech. Pencil Mfrs. Assn. [★3688]

Fountain Soc. [IO], Dorking, United Kingdom

Four Aces and Al Alberts Archv; Original [24955]

Four Counties Brain Injury Assn. [IO], Peterborough, ON, Canada

Four Cylinder Club of America - Address unknown since 1995.

Four Freedoms for Ukraine; Women's Assn. for the Defense of [18759]

Four-One-One - Address unknown since 2002.

Four Sigma Soc. - Defunct.

Four-Wheel Drive Associations; United [21805]

Fourdrinier Wire Cloth Export Assn. - Defunct.

Fourdrinier Wire Coun. [★2056]

Fourth Armored Div. Assn. [20701], c/o Richard C. Schenker, Sec., 760 Crestview Dr., Sharpsville, PA 16150-8332

Fourth Freedom Forum [18112], 803 N Main St., Goshen, IN 46528, (574)534-3402

Fourth Freedom Forum [IO], Goshen, IN, United States

Fourth World Documentation Proj. [IO], Olympia, WA, United States

Fourth World Documentation Proj. [17814], c/o Center for World Indigenous Stud., Chief George Manuel Memorial Lib., Fourth World Documentation, 1001 Cooper Point Rd. SW, Ste. 140, PMB 214, Olympia, WA 98502-1107, (360)586-0656

Fowl Art, Salisbury Univ; Ward Museum of Wild [9529]

Fowl Breeders Assn; Guinea [4196]

Fox Found; Debbie [★14061]

Fox Found. for Treatment of Cranio-Facial Deformities; Debbie [★14061]

Fox Terrier Assn; Natl. Toy [22321]

Fox Terrier Club; Amer. [22200]

Fox Terrier Club; Amer. Toy [22214]

Fox Terrier Network [22269], c/o Phyllis Nash, Treas., 1237 Monte Vista Dr., Riverside, CA 92507, (951)672-2008

Fox Terrier Network [IO], Menifee, CA, United States

Fox Trotting Horse Breed Assn; Missouri [4913]

Foxhounds Assn. of Am; Masters of [23546]

Foxhounds Assn; Amer. Masters of [★23546]

FPA [IO], London, United Kingdom

FR-ENGE [★24889]

FR-ENGE [★IO]

FR-ENGE Intl. [IO], Pittsford, NY, United States

FR-ENGE Intl. [24889], c/o Marion E. Scowcroft, Pres., 124 Bradford Rd., Pittsford, NY 14534

Fracture Assn; Amer. [15756]

Fracture Assn; Amer. Ambulatory [★15756]

Fractured Atlas [9503], 248 W 35th St., Ste. 1202, New York, NY 10001; (212)277-8020

Fragile X Found; Natl. [14469]

Fragile X Soc. [IO], Great Dunmow, United Kingdom

Fragrance Assn; Cosmetic, Toiletry and [1845]

Fragrance Commerce; Women in Flavor and [4051]

Fragrance Found. [1661], 145 E 32nd St., New York, NY 10016-6002, (212)725-2755

Fragrance Found. [IO], New York, NY, United States

Fragrance Materials Assn. of the U.S. [1662], 1620 I St. NW, Ste. 925, Washington, DC 20006, (202)293-5800

Fragrance Res. Fund [★1664]

Fragrance Res. Fund [★IO]

Fragrances

  Amer. Soc. of Perfumers [1659]

  Aromatherapy Trade Coun. [IO]

  British Fragrance Assn. [IO]

  Canadian Cosmetic, Toiletry and Fragrance Assn. [IO]

  Chem. Sources Assn. [1660]

  Cosmetic, Toiletry and Fragrance Assn. [1845]

  Cosmetic, Toiletry, and Perfumery Assn. - England [IO]

  European Cosmetic, Toiletry and Perfumery Assn. [IO]

  European Flavour and Fragrance Assn. [IO]

Reference to "IO" in place of a book number signifies that the association may be found in the 45th edition of International Organizations.

Fragrance Found. [IO]
Fragrance Found. [1661]
Fragrance Materials Assn. of the U.S. [1662]
French Fed. of Fragrance, Cosmetics, and
Toiletries [IO]
Intl. Fed. of Essential Oils and Aroma Trades [IO]
Intl. Fragrance Assn. [IO]
Res. Inst. for Fragrance Materials [1663]
Sense of Smell Inst. [1664]
Sense of Smell Institute [IO]
Frame Assn; Natl. Steel Door and [★2719]
Frame Builders Assn; Natl. [1047]
Frame Relay Forum [★6714]
Frame Relay Forum [★IO]
Frame Screen Mfrs. Assn. [★IO]
Frame Screen Mfrs. Assn. [★1833]
Frame Stud; Intl. Inst. for [9991]
Framers Assn; Professional Picture [9467]
Framers Guild; Timber [1625]
Framing Manufacturers Assn; Metal [639]
Framingham State Coll; Alumni Assn., [18871]
Fran Lee Found. - Address unknown since 2004.
Franc-Dollar Comm. - Defunct.
Francais d'Amerique; Club [8449]
Francais et Francophones d'Amerique; Societe des
Professeurs [8450]
Francaise; French Inst. Alliance [9968]
Francaise de New York; Alliance [★9968]
Francaises; Friends of Vieilles Maisons [★10024]
France
American-Canadian Genealogical Soc. [21098]
American-French Genealogical Soc. [21101]
Amer. Friends of the Paris Opera and Ballet
[9543]
Assn. pour le Retablissement des Institutions et
Oeuvres Israelites en France [20121]
Conf. Gp. on French Politics and Soc. [17621]
Conference Group on French Politics and Society
[IO]
Dogue de Bordeaux Soc. of Am. [22258]
Fed. of French War Veterans [21416]
France and Colonies Philatelic Soc. [22820]
French-American Chamber of Commerce [24320]
French Heritage Soc. [10024]
Friends of French Art [10026]
Inter-American Tropical Tuna Commn. [5730]
Intl. Trade Exhibitions in France [1345]
Napoleonic Historical Soc. [11139]
U.S. Br. of the Intl. Comm. for the Defense of the
Breton Language [9758]
France-America Liberty Fund - Defunct.
France Amerique Latine [★IO]
France; Assn. pour le Retablissement des Institu-
tions et Oeuvres Israelites en [20121]
France and Colonies Gp. [★22820]
France and Colonies Gp. [★IO]
France and Colonies Philatelic Soc. [IO], Westfield,
NJ, United States
France and Colonies Philatelic Soc. [22820], c/o
Joel L. Bromberg, PO Box 102, Brooklyn, NY
11209-0102, (908)233-9318
France Latin Am. [IO], Paris, France
France-Louisiane/Franco-Americaine - Vivre
l'heritage Franceil aus Etats-Unis [IO], Paris,
France
France-United States Assn. [IO], Paris, France
Francena Purchase Applied Honors Society [IO],
Grand Rapids, MI, United States
Francena Purchase Applied Honors Soc. [17018],
PO Box 88304, Kentwood, MI 49518, (616)285-
5568
Francena Purchase Applied Liberal Stud. Soc.
[9180], PO Box 88304, Kentwood, MI 49518,
(616)285-5568
Francena Purchase Applied Liberal Stud. Soc. [IO],
Grand Rapids, MI, United States
Frances Tompkins; Foundation of the Natl. Student
Nurses' Assn. in memory of [★8873]
Franceschetti-Klein Syndrome
Treacher Collins Found. [14067]
Franchise of Amers. Needing Sports - Address
unknown since 2002.
Franchise Assn. of Greece [IO], Athens, Greece
Franchise Assn; Natl. [★1669]
Franchise Assn. of Southern Africa [IO], Bedford-
view, Republic of South Africa

Franchise Consultants Intl. Assn. - Address unknown
since 2006.
Franchise Coun. of Australia [IO], Malvern East,
Australia
Franchise Owners; Assn. of Manpower [1257]
Franchisees; Assn. for Car and Truck Rental
Independents and [★3376]
Franchising
Amer. Assn. of Franchisees and Dealers [1665]
Amer. Franchisee Assn. [1666]
Argentine Franchising Assn. [IO]
Belgian Franchise Fed. [IO]
Brazilian Franchising Assn. [IO]
British Franchise Assn. [IO]
Canadian Alliance of Franchise Operators [IO]
Canadian Franchise Assn. [IO]
China Chain Store and Franchise Assn. [IO]
Culligan Dealers Assn. of North Am. [1667]
Czech Franchise Assn. [IO]
Finnish Franchising Assn. [IO]
Franchise Assn. of Greece [IO]
Franchise Assn. of Southern Africa [IO]
Franchise Coun. of Australia [IO]
Franchising Assn. of India [IO]
Franchising and Licensing Assn. (Singapore) [IO]
French Franchise Fed. [IO]
German Franchise Assn. [IO]
Hong Kong Franchise Assn. [IO]
Hungarian Franchise Assn. [IO]
IAHI, The Owners' Assn. [1946]
Intl. Franchise Assn. [1668]
Intl. Franchise Assn. [IO]
Irish Franchise Assn. [IO]
Italian Franchising Assn. [IO]
Malaysian Franchise Assn. [IO]
McDonald's Hispanic Operators Assn. [3395]
Natl. Assn. of Equity Source Banks [488]
Natl. Franchisee Assn. [1669]
Natl. Franchisee Assn. [IO]
Netherlands Franchise Assn. [IO]
New Zealand Franchise Assn. [IO]
North Amer. Assn. of Subway Franchisees [1670]
Swedish Franchise Assn. [IO]
Swiss Franchise Assn. [IO]
Taiwan Chain Store and Franchise Assn. [IO]
Women in Franchising [1671]
World Franchise Coun. [IO]
Franchising Assn. of India [IO], Bombay, India
Franchising and Licensing Assn. (Singapore) [IO],
Singapore, Singapore
Francis Bacon Found. [9650], 100 Corson St.,
Pasadena, CA 91103
Francis Brett Young Soc. [IO], Halesowen, United
Kingdom
Francis Grose Soc. - Defunct.
Francis Intl. Fan Club; Connie [24867]
Francis de Sales; Secular Inst. of Saint [19716]
Francis Thompson Soc. [★IO]
Franciscan Educational Conf. - Defunct.
Franciscan Fathers; Slovene [19718]
Franciscan History; Acad. of Amer. [19560]
Franciscan Vocation Conf. - Defunct.
Franciscans (Province of Saint Joseph); Capuchin-
[19594]
Franck Goddio Soc. [IO], Geneva, Switzerland
Franco-Argentina Chamber of Commerce and Indus.
[IO], Buenos Aires, Argentina
Franco-British Chamber of Commerce and Indus.
[IO], Paris, France
Franco-British Lawyers Soc. [IO], London, United
Kingdom
Franco-British Soc. [IO], London, United Kingdom
Franco-Peruvian Chamber of Commerce and Indus.
[IO], Lima, Peru
Francophones d'Amerique; Societe des Professeurs
Francais et [8450]
Frank Center; Amer. Friends of the Anne [★17713]
Frank Center U.S.A; Anne [17713]
Frank Lloyd Wright Assn. [7961], Taliesin W, PO Box
4430, Scottsdale, AZ 85261-4430, (480)860-2700
Frank Lloyd Wright Found. [★7961]
Frank Lloyd Wright Newsl. - Address unknown since
1990.
Frank Lloyd Wright Preservation Trust [10023], 931
Chicago Ave., Oak Park, IL 60302, (708)848-1976

Frank London Brown Historical Assn. - Address
unknown since 1995.
Frank Porter Graham Center - Defunct.
Frankie Laine Soc. of Am. [24890], c/o Vicki Lock-
ridge, Pres., N Torrance Sta., PO Box 7996, Tor-
rance, CA 90504
Frankie Valli and The Four Seasons Fan Club -
Defunct.
Franklin Book Programs - Defunct.
Franklin Club; H.H. [21656]
Franklin D. Roosevelt Four Freedoms Found.
[★11111]
Franklin D. Roosevelt Philatelic Soc. - Address
unknown since 1999.
Franklin Educ. Found; Benjamin [8234]
Franklin and Eleanor Roosevelt Inst. [11111], 4079
Albany Post Rd., Hyde Park, NY 12538, (845)486-
1150
Franklin; Friends of [11114]
Franklin Furnace Archv. [9440], 80 Arts - The James
E. Davis Arts Bldg., 80 Hanson Pl., No. 301,
Brooklyn, NY 11217-1506, (718)398-7255
Franklin Literary and Medical Soc; Benjamin [14549]
Franklin Mint Collectors Soc. - Address unknown
since 2003.
Frankoma Family Collectors Assn. [22027], c/o Ms.
Donna Frank, Sec., 1300 Luker Ln., Sapulpa, OK
74066-6024, (918)224-6610
Frantz Fanon Inst. - Address unknown since 1995.
Franz Rosenzweig Soc. - Defunct.
Fraser Valley Epilepsy Soc. [IO], Abbotsford, BC,
Canada
The Frat [★19134]
Fratelli delle Scuole Cristiane [★IO]
Fraternal Actuarial Assn. - Defunct.
Fraternal Assn; Aircraft Mechanics [24006]
Fraternal Assn. of Steel Haulers - Defunct.
Fraternal Assn; William Penn [★19144]
Fraternal Brotherhood of Gamma Epsilon Theta -
Address unknown since 1985.
Fraternal Cong. of Am; Natl. [19133]
Fraternal Cong; Natl. [★19133]
Fraternal Fed. Scholarship Comm; Luso-American
[★10890]
Fraternal Field Managers' Assn. [2165], c/o Eugene
McBride, Sec.-Treas., PO Box 100, Temple, TX
76503-0100, (254)773-1575
Fraternal Insurance Company; Amer. [★19146]
Fraternal Insurance Counsellors Assn. [★2207]
Fraternal Life Assn; Western [19030]
Fraternal Life; CSA [19026]
Fraternal Life Insurance Soc; Sloga [★19022]
Fraternal Life; WSA [19148]
Fraternal and Military Club Managers Assn. -
Defunct.
Fraternal Order of Air Mail Pilots - Defunct.
Fraternal Order of Eagles; Grand Aerie, [19033]
Fraternal Order of Eagles, Ladies Auxiliaries - Ad-
dress unknown since 1995.
Fraternal Order Orioles [19298], 716 Maryland Ave.
SW, Canton, OH 44710
Fraternal Order of Police Auxiliary [★5995]
Fraternal Order of Police, Grand Lodge [19200], 710
Marriott Dr., Nashville, TN 37214, (615)399-0900
Fraternal Union; Amer. [19119]
Fraternitas Rosae Crucis [★19335]
Fraternite Blanche Universelle [★IO]
Fraternite Mondiale des Bouddhistes [★IO]
Fraternite Saint Pie X [★IO]
Fraternities of Am; Assoc. [★19133]
Fraternities of Am; Lutheran [19217]
Fraternities, Service
Alpha Chi [24498]
Alpha Chi Sigma [24428]
Alpha Delta Kappa [24449]
Alpha Epsilon [24395]
Alpha Epsilon Delta [24541]
Alpha Gamma Rho [24396]
Alpha Iota Omicron [24611]
Alpha Iota Sorority [24413]
Alpha Kappa Delta [24701]
Alpha Kappa Psi [24414]
Alpha Mu Gamma Natl. [24525]
Alpha Omega Alpha Honor Medical Soc. [24542]
Alpha Omega Intl. Dental Fraternity [24437]

A star before a book entry number signifies that the name is not listed separately, but is mentioned within the entry.

Alpha Phi Alpha Fraternity [24590]
Alpha Phi Omega Natl. Ser. Fraternity [24591]
Alpha Psi Lambda Natl. [24615]
Alpha Sigma Nu [24500]
Alpha Tau Delta [24559]
Alpha Zeta [24397]
Alpha Zeta Omega [24567]
Arnold Air Soc. [24546]
Assn. of Coll. Honor Societies [24501]
Assn. of Fraternity Advisors [24475]
Beta Alpha Psi [24391]
Beta Beta Beta [24408]
Beta Chi Theta Natl. Fraternity [24618]
Beta Gamma Sigma [24415]
Beta Gamma Sigma Alumni [24416]
Beta Phi Mu [24532]
Beta Sigma Kappa [24562]
Center for the Stud. of the Coll. Fraternity [24476]
Central Off. Executives Assn. of Natl. Pan-
  Hellenic Conf. [24477]
Chi Eta Phi Sorority [24560]
Cum Laude Soc. [24503]
Delphi Found. [24451]
Delta Epsilon Sigma [24504]
Delta Kappa Epsilon [24623]
Delta Lambda Phi Natl. Social Fraternity [24624]
Delta Mu Delta Honor Soc. [24418]
Delta Omega [24582]
Delta Omicron [24550]
Delta Phi Epsilon, Professional Foreign Ser.
  Fraternity [24472]
Delta Phi Epsilon Professional Foreign Ser. Soror-
  ity [24473]
Delta Phi Upsilon [24431]
Delta Pi Epsilon [24426]
Delta Psi Omega [24444]
Delta Sigma Delta [24438]
Delta Theta Phi [24527]
Epsilon Pi Tau [24720]
Epsilon Sigma Phi [24436]
Eta Phi Beta [24419]
Eta Sigma Phi, Natl. Classics Honorary Soc.
  [24433]
Fraternity Executives Assn. [24479]
Future Bus. Leaders of Am. - Phi Beta Lambda
  [24420]
Gamma Iota Sigma [24520]
Gamma Sigma Delta [24398]
Gamma Theta Upsilon [24491]
Gay Officers' Action League [12231]
Golden Key Intl. Honour Soc. [24506]
Honors Prog. Student Assn. of the Amer.
  Sociological Assn. [24702]
Iota Beta Sigma [24410]
Iota Nu Delta Fraternity [24631]
Iota Phi Lambda [24421]
Kappa Delta Epsilon [24452]
Kappa Delta Pi [24453]
Kappa Mu Epsilon [24537]
Kappa Omicron Nu [24496]
Kappa Pi Intl. Honorary Art Fraternity [24404]
Kappa Psi [24568]
Kappa Tau Alpha [24522]
Lambda Alpha Intl. [24445]
Lambda Iota Tau [24533]
Lambda Kappa Sigma [24569]
Mortar Bd. [24509]
Mu Alpha Theta [24538]
Mu Beta Psi [24552]
Mu Phi Epsilon Intl. [24553]
Natl. Alpha Lambda Delta [24510]
Natl. Assn. of the Knights of Scorpius, Honorary
  Leadership Soc. [24511]
Natl. Beta Club [24592]
Natl. Block and Bridle Club [24401]
Natl. Broadcasting Soc. - Alpha Epsilon Rho
  [24411]
Natl. Kappa Kappa Iota [24454]
Natl. Pan-Hellenic Editors Conf. [24448]
Natl. Panhellenic Conf. [24485]
Natl. Sorority of Phi Delta Kappa [24455]
Natl. Tech. Honor Soc. [24725]
Natl. Valedictorian Honor Soc. [24514]
North Amer. Interfraternal Found. [24486]
North-American Interfraternity Conf. [24487]

Omega Delta [24563]
Omicron Delta Epsilon [24446]
Omicron Delta Kappa Soc. [24515]
Omicron Kappa Upsilon [24439]
Order of the Coif [24516]
Phi Alpha Delta [24528]
Phi Alpha Sigma [24543]
Phi Alpha Theta [24495]
Phi Beta [24405]
Phi Beta Delta [24517]
Phi Beta Kappa [24406]
Phi Beta Sigma Fraternity [24593]
Phi Chi Medical Fraternity [24544]
Phi Delta Chi [24570]
Phi Delta Epsilon Medical Fraternity [24540]
Phi Delta Gamma [24577]
Phi Delta Phi Intl. Legal Fraternity [24530]
Phi Kappa Phi [24518]
Phi Mu Alpha Sinfonia Fraternity and Found. Natl.
  HQ [24555]
Phi Sigma [24409]
Phi Sigma Iota [24526]
Phi Sigma Pi Natl. Honor Fraternity [24531]
Pi Kappa Phi [24651]
Pi Omicron Natl. Sorority [24601]
Professional Fraternity Assn. [24488]
Psi Beta [24579]
Psi Omega [24440]
Psi Sigma Phi Multicultural Fraternity [24594]
Sigma Alpha Iota Intl. Music Fraternity [24557]
Sigma Beta Rho Fraternity [24656]
Sigma Delta Chi Found. [24524]
Sigma Delta Epsilon, Graduate Women in Sci.
  [24587]
Silver Wings [24549]
Soc. of Professional Journalists [3164]
Tau Epsilon Rho Law Soc. [24529]
Theta Alpha Phi [24721]
Theta Psi [24566]
Theta Tau [24469]
Upsilon Pi Epsilon Assn. [24435]
Xi Psi Phi [24442]

Fraternities, Social
Acacia [24605]
Alpha Chi [24498]
Alpha Chi Rho [24606]
Alpha Chi Sigma [24428]
Alpha Delta Gamma [24607]
Alpha Delta Kappa [24449]
Alpha Delta Phi [24608]
Alpha Delta Pi [24609]
Alpha Epsilon [24395]
Alpha Epsilon Delta [24541]
Alpha Epsilon Pi [24610]
Alpha Gamma Rho [24396]
Alpha Iota Omicron [24611]
Alpha Iota Sorority [24413]
Alpha Kappa Delta [24701]
Alpha Kappa Lambda [24612]
Alpha Kappa Psi [24414]
Alpha Lambda Tau Intl. Social Fraternity [24613]
Alpha Mu Gamma Natl. [24525]
Alpha Omega Alpha Honor Medical Soc. [24542]
Alpha Omega Intl. Dental Fraternity [24437]
Alpha Phi Delta [24614]
Alpha Phi Intl. Fraternity [24677]
Alpha Psi Lambda Natl. [24615]
Alpha Sigma Nu [24500]
Alpha Sigma Phi [24616]
Alpha Tau Delta [24559]
Alpha Tau Omega [24617]
Alpha Zeta [24397]
Alpha Zeta Omega [24567]
Arnold Air Soc. [24546]
Assn. of Coll. Honor Societies [24501]
Assn. of Fraternity Advisors [24475]
Beta Alpha Psi [24391]
Beta Beta Beta [24408]
Beta Chi Theta Natl. Fraternity [24618]
Beta Gamma Sigma [24415]
Beta Gamma Sigma Alumni [24416]
Beta Phi Mu [24532]
Beta Sigma Kappa [24562]
Beta Sigma Psi Natl. Lutheran Fraternity [24619]
Beta Theta Pi [24620]

Center for the Stud. of the Coll. Fraternity [24476]
Central Off. Executives Assn. of Natl. Pan-
  Hellenic Conf. [24477]
Chi Eta Phi Sorority [24560]
Chi Phi [24621]
Chi Psi [24622]
Cum Laude Soc. [24503]
Delphi Found. [24451]
Delta Epsilon Sigma [24504]
Delta Kappa Epsilon [24623]
Delta Lambda Phi Natl. Social Fraternity [24624]
Delta Mu Delta Honor Soc. [24418]
Delta Omega [24582]
Delta Omicron [24550]
Delta Phi [24625]
Delta Phi Epsilon, Professional Foreign Ser.
  Fraternity [24472]
Delta Phi Epsilon Professional Foreign Ser. Soror-
  ity [24473]
Delta Phi Upsilon [24431]
Delta Pi Epsilon [24426]
Delta Psi [24626]
Delta Psi Omega [24444]
Delta Sigma Delta [24438]
Delta Sigma Pi [24627]
Delta Theta Phi [24527]
Delta Upsilon [24628]
Epsilon Pi Tau [24720]
Epsilon Sigma Phi [24436]
Eta Phi Beta [24419]
Eta Sigma Phi, Natl. Classics Honorary Soc.
  [24433]
Farmhouse [24629]
Fraternity Executives Assn. [24479]
Future Bus. Leaders of Am. - Phi Beta Lambda
  [24420]
Gamma Iota Sigma [24520]
Gamma Sigma Delta [24398]
Gamma Theta Upsilon [24491]
Gay Officers' Action League [12231]
Golden Key Intl. Honour Soc. [24506]
Groove Phi Groove, Social Fellowship [24630]
Hard Hat Brotherhood [19257]
Honors Prog. Student Assn. of the Amer.
  Sociological Assn. [24702]
Iota Beta Sigma [24410]
Iota Nu Delta Fraternity [24631]
Iota Phi Lambda [24421]
Kappa Alpha Order [24632]
Kappa Alpha Psi Fraternity [24633]
Kappa Alpha Soc. [24634]
Kappa Delta Epsilon [24452]
Kappa Delta Pi [24453]
Kappa Delta Rho [24635]
Kappa Mu Epsilon [24537]
Kappa Omicron Nu [24496]
Kappa Pi Intl. Honorary Art Fraternity [24404]
Kappa Psi [24568]
Kappa Sigma [24636]
Kappa Tau Alpha [24522]
Lambda Alpha Intl. [24445]
Lambda Chi Alpha [24637]
Lambda Iota Tau [24533]
Lambda Kappa Sigma [24569]
Mortar Bd. [24509]
Mu Alpha Theta [24538]
Mu Beta Psi [24552]
Mu Phi Epsilon Intl. [24553]
Natl. Alpha Lambda Delta [24510]
Natl. Assn. of the Knights of Scorpius, Honorary
  Leadership Soc. [24511]
Natl. Beta Club [24592]
Natl. Block and Bridle Club [24401]
Natl. Broadcasting Soc. - Alpha Epsilon Rho
  [24411]
Natl. Kappa Kappa Iota [24454]
Natl. Pan-Hellenic Editors Conf. [24448]
Natl. Panhellenic Conf. [24485]
Natl. Sorority of Phi Delta Kappa [24455]
Natl. Tech. Honor Soc. [24725]
Natl. Valedictorian Honor Soc. [24514]
North Amer. Interfraternal Found. [24486]
North-American Interfraternity Conf. [24487]
Omega Delta [24563]
Omega Gamma Delta [24638]

Reference to "IO" in place of a book number signifies that the association may be found in the 45th edition of International Organizations.

Omega Psi Phi Fraternity [24639]
Omicron Delta Epsilon [24446]
Omicron Delta Kappa Soc. [24515]
Omicron Kappa Upsilon [24439]
Order of the Coif [24516]
Phi Alpha Delta [24528]
Phi Alpha Sigma [24543]
Phi Alpha Theta [24495]
Phi Beta [24405]
Phi Beta Delta [24517]
Phi Beta Kappa [24406]
Phi Chi Medical Fraternity [24544]
Phi Delta Chi [24570]
Phi Delta Epsilon Medical Fraternity [24540]
Phi Delta Gamma [24577]
Phi Delta Phi Intl. Legal Fraternity [24530]
Phi Delta Theta Intl. Fraternity [24640]
Phi Gamma Delta [24641]
Phi Kappa Phi [24518]
Phi Kappa Sigma [24642]
Phi Kappa Tau [24643]
Phi Kappa Theta Natl. [24644]
Phi Mu Alpha Sinfonia Fraternity and Found. Natl.
    HQ [24555]
Phi Mu Delta [24645]
Phi Sigma [24409]
Phi Sigma Iota [24526]
Phi Sigma Kappa [24646]
Phi Sigma Nu Native Amer. Fraternity [24647]
Phi Sigma Pi Natl. Honor Fraternity [24531]
Pi Beta Phi [24648]
Pi Delta Psi Fraternity [24649]
Pi Kappa Alpha [24650]
Pi Kappa Phi [24651]
Pi Lambda Phi Fraternity [24652]
Pi Omicron Natl. Sorority [24601]
Professional Fraternity Assn. [24488]
Psi Beta [24579]
Psi Omega [24440]
Psi Sigma Phi Multicultural Fraternity [24594]
Psi Upsilon [24653]
Sigma Alpha Epsilon [24654]
Sigma Alpha Iota Intl. Music Fraternity [24557]
Sigma Alpha Mu [24655]
Sigma Beta Rho Fraternity [24656]
Sigma Chi Intl. Fraternity [24657]
Sigma Delta Chi Found. [24524]
Sigma Delta Epsilon, Graduate Women in Sci.
    [24587]
Sigma Nu Fraternity [24658]
Sigma Phi Beta Fraternity [24659]
Sigma Phi Epsilon [24660]
Sigma Phi Soc. [24661]
Sigma Pi Fraternity, Intl. [24662]
Sigma Pi Phi Fraternity [24663]
Sigma Tau Gamma [24664]
Silver Wings [24549]
Soc. of Professional Journalists [3164]
Tau Epsilon Phi [24665]
Tau Epsilon Rho Law Soc. [24529]
Tau Kappa Epsilon [24666]
Theta Alpha Phi [24721]
Theta Chi Fraternity [24667]
Theta Delta Chi [24668]
Theta Psi [24566]
Theta Tau [24469]
Theta Xi [24669]
Upsilon Pi Epsilon Assn. [24435]
Xi Psi Phi [24442]
Zeta Beta Tau [24670]
Zeta Psi Fraternity of North Am. [24671]
Fraternities and Sororities
Alpha Iota Omicron [24611]
Alpha Pi Sigma [24474]
Alpha Rho Lambda Sorority [24703]
Assn. of Fraternity Advisors [24475]
Center for the Stud. of the Coll. Fraternity [24476]
Central Off. Executives Assn. of Natl. Pan-
    Hellenic Conf. [24477]
Chi Sigma Iota [1099]
Delta Gamma Pi Multicultural Sorority [24704]
Delta Kappa Phi [24478]
Delta Phi Omega Sorority [24705]
Delta Sigma Chi Sorority [24706]
Delta Tau Lambda Sorority [24707]

Delta Xi Nu Multicultural Sorority [24708]
Delta Xi Phi Multicultural Sorority [24685]
DIVAS of Lambda Fe Uson Sorority [24709]
Fraternity Executives Assn. [24479]
Future Bus. Leaders of Am. - Phi Beta Lambda
    [24420]
Gamma Alpha Omega Sorority [24599]
Gamma Delta Pi [24710]
Gamma Gamma Chi Sorority [24711]
Gay Officers' Action League [12231]
Intl. Guild of Nobles [19056]
Iota Nu Delta Fraternity [24631]
Kappa Phi Gamma Sorority [24712]
Kappa Psi Kappa Fraternity [24480]
Lambda Pi Alumni Assn. [24481]
Lambda Psi Delta Sorority [24713]
Lambda Theta Phi [24482]
Legionarios del Trabajo in America [19057]
Mid-American Greek Coun. Assn. [24483]
Moose Intl. [19058]
Moose Intl. [IO]
Natl. Assn. of Latino Fraternal Organizations
    [19059]
Natl. Pan-Hellenic Coun. [24484]
Natl. Pan-Hellenic Editors Conf. [24448]
Natl. Panhellenic Conf. [24485]
North Amer. Interfraternal Found. [24486]
North-American Interfraternity Conf. [24487]
Phi Sigma Nu Native Amer. Fraternity [24647]
Pi Delta Psi Fraternity [24649]
Professional Fraternity Assn. [24488]
Psi Sigma Phi Multicultural Fraternity [24594]
Sigma Alpha Lambda [24519]
Sigma Lambda Alpha Sorority [24714]
Sigma Lambda Gamma Natl. Sorority [24715]
Sigma Phi Beta Fraternity [24659]
Theta Chi Omega Multicultural Sorority [24716]
Zeta Beta Tau Fraternity [24489]
Zeta Chi Phi Multicultural Sorority [24717]
Fraternity Conf; Natl. Inter [★24487]
Fraternity Conf; North-American Inter [24487]
Fraternity Conf; Professional Inter- [★24488]
Fraternity; Delta Lambda Phi Natl. Social [24624]
Fraternity; Delta Nu Alpha Trans. [24722]
Fraternity; Delta Phi Epsilon, Professional Foreign
    Ser. [24472]
Fraternity Editors Assn; Coll. [24447]
Fraternity Executives Assn. [24479], c/o Sydney N.
    Dunn, Admin., 1750 Royalton Dr., Carmel, IN
    46032
Fraternity Found; Natl. Inter [★24486]
Fraternity of North Am; Zeta Psi [24671]
Fraternity of Original Descendants - Address
    unknown since 1995.
Fraternity; Phi Chi Medical [24544]
Fraternity; Phi Kappa Upsilon [24464]
Fraternity of Recording Executives - Address
    unknown since 1994.
Fraternity Secretaries Assn; Coll. [★24479]
Fraternity; Sigma Chi Intl. [24657]
Fraternity of Student Musicians; Natl. [8924]
Fraternity of the Wooden Leg - Defunct.
Fraters van O.L. Vrouw, Moeder van Barmhartigheid
    [★IO]
Fratres Presentationis Mariae [★IO]
Fraud Assn; Natl. Hea. Care Anti- [14963]
Fraud Control Assn; Communications [2087]
Fraud Examiners; Natl. Assn. of Certified [★2084]
Fraud Info. Center/Internet Fraud Watch; Natl.
    [17339]
Fraud; Natl. Coun. Against Hea. [★17692]
Fraud in Telemarketing and Electronic Commerce;
    Alliance Against [17302]
Frauen fur den Frieden Schweiz [★IO]
Fraunhofer-Gesellschaft zur Forderung der An-
    gewandten Forschung [IO], Munich, Germany
Fraunhofer-Information Centre for Regional Planning
    and Building Constr. [IO], Stuttgart, Germany
Fraunhofer-Informationszentrum RAUM und BAU
    [★IO]
Frawley Family History Assn. - Address unknown
    since 2006.
FRAXA, the Fragile X Res. Found. [★16535]
FRAXA Res. Found. [16535], 45 Pleasant St., New-
    buryport, MA 01950, (978)462-1866

Fred Bear Sports Club - Defunct.
Fred Hollows Found. - Australia [IO], Enfield,
    Australia
Fred Hollows Found. - Vietnam [IO], Da Nang,
    Vietnam
Fred Soc. - Address unknown since 1989.
Freddy Fender Fan Club - Address unknown since
    1989.
Freddy; Friends of [24821]
Frederick A. Cook Soc. [11112], c/o Russell W. Gib-
    bons, Exec. Dir./Ed., 207 Grandview Dr. S,
    Pittsburgh, PA 15215, (412)782-0171
Frederick Chopin Soc. [IO], Warsaw, Poland
Frederick Douglass Memorial and Historical Assn. -
    Address unknown since 2003.
Frederick Law Olmsted Assn. - Defunct.
Frederick Wilhelm Haury Family Org. - Address
    unknown since 2007.
Fredericton Northwest Constr. Assn. [IO], Frederic-
    ton, NB, Canada
Fredrika - Bremer - Assn. [IO], Stockholm, Sweden
Fredrika - Bremer - Forbundet [★IO]
Fred's Fan Club - Burstein's Buffalos - Defunct.
Free African Liberation Org.-African Liberation Move-
    ment - Address unknown since 2006.
Free Albania Org. - Address unknown since 1999.
Free Asia Found. - Address unknown since 1994.
Free Asia League - Address unknown since 1995.
Free Beaches Coalition [★10762]
Free Beaches Documentation Center [★10763]
Free Beaches Info. Center [★10763]
Free Burial Assn; Hebrew [20141]
Free Burma Coalition [17007], PO Box 9573,
    Berkeley, CA 94709, (510)685-4170
Free Burma Coalition [IO], Berkeley, CA, United
    States
Free Cambodia - Defunct.
Free Clinic Found. of Am; Natl. [14585]
Free Community Papers; Assn. of [88]
Free Community Papers; Midwest [3236]
Free Cong; Comm. for the Survival of a [★17268]
Free Cong. Found. [11810], 717 2nd St. NE,
    Washington, DC 20002, (202)546-3000
Free Cong. Political Action Comm. [17268], 717 2nd
    St. NE, Washington, DC 20002, (202)546-3000
Free Cong. Res. and Educ. Found. [18295], c/o
    Free Cong. Found., 717 2nd St. NE, Washington,
    DC 20002, (202)546-3000
Free Cuba PAC - Address unknown since 1995.
Free Cuba Patriotic Movement - Address unknown
    since 1995.
Free Democratic Party [IO], Berlin, Germany
Free Democratic Party of Switzerland [IO], Bern,
    Switzerland
Free the Eagle [17629], 3902 Pender Spring Dr.,
    Fairfax, VA 22033, (703)385-0600
Free Enterprise
    Alliance for Responsible Trade [3836]
    Amer. Agri-Women Rsrc. Center [16949]
    Amer. Bus. Conf. [17622]
    Amer. Citizenship Center [17067]
    Americanism Educational League [17623]
    America's Future [17624]
    Antitrust Coalition for Consumer Choice in Hea.
       Care [14615]
    Associacion Espanola para la Defensa de la Com-
       petencia [IO]
    Assn. pour l'etude du droit de la Concurrence [IO]
    Assn. for the Stud. of the Cuban Economy [8214]
    Assn. Suisse d'Etude de la Concurrence [IO]
    Associazione Italiana per la Tutela della Concor-
       renza [IO]
    Center for the Defense of Free Enterprise [17625]
    Center for Democracy and Free Enterprise [IO]
    Comm. to Support the Antitrust Laws [17626]
    Competition Law Assn. [IO]
    Competition Law Assn., Poland [IO]
    Corp. for Enterprise Development [17457]
    Entrepreneurial Leadership Center [17627]
    European Free Trade Assn. [IO]
    Fisher Inst. for Medical Res. [17628]
    Forderkeis fur Internationales Wettbewerbsrecht
       [IO]
    Found. for Economic Educ. [18406]
    Free the Eagle [17629]

A star before a book entry number signifies that the name is not listed separately, but is mentioned within the entry.

Free Enterprise Legal Defense Fund [17630]
Free Market Found. [IO]
French Assn. of Stud. of Competition [IO]
Global Envision [IO]
Global Envision [12194]
The Heritage Found. [17631]
Hungarian Assn. of Competition Law [IO]
Intl. League of Competition Law [IO]
Intl. League of Competition Law, Austria [IO]
Intl. League for Competition Law, Brazil [IO]
Intl. League for Competition Law, Czech Republic
   [IO]
Intl. League for Competition Law, Japan [IO]
Intl. League for Competition Law, Nordic
   Countries [IO]
Mfrs. for Fair Trade [2538]
Natl. Center for Constr. Educ. and Res. [17632]
Natl. Coun. for Public-Private Partnerships
   [17633]
Natl. Journalism Center [17634]
Natl. Org. Taunting Safety and Fairness
   Everywhere [22599]
Pacific Res. Inst. for Public Policy [18474]
Private Enterprise Res. Center [17635]
Professional Services Coun. [17636]
Students in Free Enterprise [17637]
United Savers Assn. [17638]
U.S. Bus. and Indus. Coun. [17639]
Vereniging voor Mededingingsrecht [IO]
William E. Simon Found. [17474]
Free Enterprise Awards Assn. - Address unknown
   since 1995.
Free Enterprise; Center for Educ. and Res. in
   [★17635]
Free Enterprise Legal Defense Fund [17630], c/o
   Center for the Defense of Free Enterprise, Liberty
   Park, 12500 NE 10th Pl., Bellevue, WA 98005,
   (425)455-5038
Free Europe [★17191]
Free Europe/Radio Liberty; Radio [17191]
Free Expression
   Amer. Civil Liberties Union [17084]
   Amer. Civil Liberties Union Found. [17085]
   Amer. Freedom Alliance [18507]
   Americans for Religious Liberty [17090]
   Beacon for Freedom of Expression [IO]
   Center For Inquiry [17643]
   Freedom of Info. Center [18413]
   Freedom of Info. CH [18414]
   Freemuse [IO]
   Internews Network [18027]
   IP Justice [5852]
   PEN Amer. Center [11185]
   PEN Center U.S.A. [11186]
   Writers-in-Exile Center, Amer. Br., Intl. PEN Club
      [11202]
Free the Fathers [17060], PO Box 85, Signal
   Mountain, TN 37377, (423)634-0644
Free the Grapes! [16971], 2700 Napa Valley
   Corporate Dr., Ste. H, Napa, CA 94558, (707)254-
   1107
Free Kids: America's Challenge; Drug [18687]
Free Lance Finders Network - Address unknown
   since 1991.
Free Learning Exchange - Defunct.
Free Lebanon; U.S. Comm. for a [18006]
Free Loan Assn; Jewish [20148]
Free Market Found. [IO], Sandton, Republic of
   South Africa
Free-Masonry (Northern Masonic Jurisdiction);
   Supreme Coun., Ancient Accepted Scottish Rite of
   [19252]
Free Men - Defunct.
Free Men; Natl. Coalition of [18043]
Free Methodist
   Assn. of Free Methodist Educational Institutions
      [8447]
Free Methodist Educational Institutions; Assn. of
   [8447]
Free Minds, Inc. [19874], PO Box 3818, Manhattan
   Beach, CA 90266, (310)545-7831
Free Muslims Coalition [18084], 2560 Virginia Ave.
   NW, Ste. 171, Washington, DC 20037, (202)776-
   7190
Free Muslims Coalition [IO], Washington, DC, United
   States

Free Nation Found. [★5768]
Free Nation Found. - Critical Institutions [5768], 111
   W Corbin St., Hillsborough, NC 27278
Free Nations Assn; League of [★17610]
Free Our Parks and Forests - Address unknown
   since 2006.
Free Press Assn. - Address unknown since 2001.
Free Radical Biology and Medicine; Soc. for [6613]
Free the Slaves [12371], 1012 14th St. NW, Ste.
   600, Washington, DC 20005, (202)638-1865
Free Software Found. [6767], 51 Franklin St., 5th
   Fl., Boston, MA 02110-1301, (617)542-5942
Free Software Foundation [IO], Boston, MA, United
   States
Free Sons of Israel [19182]
Free Sons of Israel; Independent Order [★19182]
Free South Africa Movement - Address unknown
   since 1999.
Free Southern Theatre - Defunct.
Free Speech Movement - Defunct.
Free Speech TV [18726], PO Box 44099, Denver,
   CO 80201, (303)442-8445
Free Speech Union - Defunct.
Free Store [★12773]
Free Store/Food Bank [12773], 1250 Tennessee
   Ave., Cincinnati, OH 45229, (513)482-4500
Free Territory of Ely-Chatelaine [18351], Royal Post
   FTEC, PO Box 7075, Laguna Niguel, CA 92607
Free The Children [IO], Toronto, ON, Canada
Free Thought Assn. - Address unknown since 1990.
Free Throwers [★23247]
Free Throwers Boomerang Soc. [23247], c/o The
   Jungle Gym Adventure Center, 320 London Rd.,
   Ste. 101, Delaware, OH 43015, (740)363-8332
Free Tibet Campaign [IO], London, United Kingdom
Free TV Australia [IO], Mosman, Australia
Free Univ. Network [★8151]
Free Wallenberg Comm. - Defunct.
Free Wheelchair Mission [11947], 9341 Irvine Blvd.,
   Irvine, CA 92618, (949)273-8470
Free Wheelchair Mission [IO], Irvine, CA, United
   States
Free Will Baptist Church; Master's Men of the
   [★19490]
Free Will Baptist Press Assn. - Defunct.
Free Will Baptists; Master's Men of the Natl. Assn. of
   [19490]
Free Will Baptists; Natl. Assn. of [19492]
FREE World Govt., Earthbank - Address unknown
   since 2006.
Freedom
   Action Without Borders/Idealist.org [17640]
   Action Without Borders/Idealist.org [IO]
   Africa Action [16918]
   Alliance for Worker Freedom [24217]
   Amer. Booksellers Found. for Free Expression
      [17641]
   The Amer. Cause [17642]
   Amer. Civil Liberties Union [17084]
   Amer. Civil Liberties Union Found. [17085]
   Amer. Freedom Alliance [18507]
   Amer. Freedom Center [18421]
   Amer. Soc. of Access Professionals [5814]
   Americans for Religious Liberty [17090]
   Americans United for Israel [19157]
   Canadian Journalists for Free Expression [IO]
   Center For Inquiry [17643]
   Free Nation Found. - Critical Institutions [5768]
   Freedom of Expression Found. [17116]
   Freedom House - Ukraine [IO]
   Freedoms Found. at Valley Forge [17644]
   Golden Rule Found. [10186]
   The Heritage Found. [17631]
   Historians Against the War [18795]
   Hungarian Freedom Fighters Fed. U.S.A. [17791]
   Intl. League for Human Rights [17769]
   Intl. People's Democratic Uhuru Movement
      [17395]
   IP Justice [5852]
   Natl. Coalition Against Censorship [17042]
   Natl. Juneteenth Observance Found. [16945]
   Spirit of Am. [18488]
   Toward Freedom [17645]
   Toward Freedom [IO]
Freedom and Accuracy in Financial Reporting;
   Center for Financial [18404]

Freedom to Advertise Coalition - Defunct.
Freedom Alliance [9369], 22570 Markey Ct., Ste.
   240, Dulles, VA 20166, (703)444-7940
Freedom in the Americas; Coalition for Jobs, Peace,
   and [★18463]
Freedom of Choice in Medicine; Comm. for [13628]
Freedom; Citizens for Educational [8338]
Freedom Coalition; Cuban Amer. [★17364]
Freedom; Comm. for Religious [★18511]
The Freedom Coun. - Defunct.
Freedom Eternally; Living in [★20060]
Freedom of Expression Found. [17116], UTC 106,
   California State Univ., Long Beach, CA 90840-
   2801, (562)985-4313
Freedom of Faith: A Christian Comm. for Religious
   Rights - Defunct.
Freedom Fed. - Defunct.
Freedom Fighters Fed. U.S.A; Hungarian [17791]
Freedom Forum [17117], 1101 Wilson Blvd.,
   Arlington, VA 22209, (703)528-0800
Freedom Forum [IO], Arlington, VA, United States
Freedom Found. [IO], Bangalore, India
Freedom Found; Citizens [★19873]
Freedom Found; Evergreen [6230]
Freedom Found; Future of [17270]
Freedom Found; Intl. [17272]
Freedom From Fear [15199], 308 Seaview Ave.,
   Staten Island, NY 10305, (718)351-1717
Freedom From Religion Found. [19837], PO Box
   750, Madison, WI 53701, (608)256-8900
Freedom; Frontiers of [5602]
Freedom Fund - Defunct.
Freedom Fund for Librarians; Natl. [★17040]
Freedom House [17269], 1301 Connecticut Ave.
   NW, 6th Fl., Washington, DC 20036, (202)296-
   5101
Freedom House [IO], Washington, DC, United
   States
Freedom House/National Forum Found. [★IO]
Freedom House/National Forum Found. [★17269]
Freedom House - Ukraine [IO], Kiev, Ukraine
Freedom from Hunger [12394], 1644 DaVinci Ct.,
   Davis, CA 95616, (530)758-6200
Freedom from Hunger Found. [★12394]
Freedom from Hunger Found; Amer. [★12394]
Freedom from Hunger Found; Meals for Millions/
   [★12394]
Freedom of Info. Center [18413], Univ. of Missouri-
   Columbia, 133 Neff Annex, Columbia, MO 65211-
   0012, (573)882-4856
Freedom of Info. CH [18414], Public Citizen Litiga-
   tion Gp., 1600 20th St. NW, Washington, DC
   20009, (202)588-7783
Freedom of Info. Coalition; Natl. [5822]
Freedom Institutes; Christian [★8302]
Freedom Is Not Free [12596], 11578 Sorrento Valley
   Rd., Ste. 30, San Diego, CA 92121, (858)847-9999
Freedom Leadership Found. - Defunct.
Freedom League - Address unknown since 1991.
Freedom; Media Coalition/Americans for
   Constitutional [★17126]
Freedom Movement; Natl. Socialist Amer. Workers
   [★18802]
Freedom; Natl. Comm. for Amish Religious [19448]
Freedom Network; Women's [13449]
Freedom Org. for the Right to Enjoy Smoking
   Tobacco [IO], London, United Kingdom
Freedom Outreach; Personal [19875]
Freedom Party; Peace and [18330]
Freedom; Political Action Comm. of Young
   Americans for [★17261]
Freedom of the Press; Reporters Comm. for [17192]
Freedom of the Press; Women's Inst. for [17200]
Freedom to Publish; Comm. on Intl. [★17041]
Freedom to Read Found. [17040], 50 E Huron St.,
   Chicago, IL 60611, (312)280-4226
Freedom Road Socialist Org. [6264], PO Box 1386,
   Stuyvesant Sta., New York, NY 10009
Freedom Scholarship Program; James Monroe
   [★11128]
Freedom Socialist Party [18653], Natl. Off., 4710
   Univ. Way NE, Ste. 100, Seattle, WA 98105,
   (206)985-4621
Freedom; Stockholders for World [★17351]
Freedom of Thought Found. [18616]

Reference to "IO" in place of a book number signifies that the association may be found in the 45th edition of International Organizations.

Freedom Through Christ Prison Ministry [★22141]
Freedom Through Truth Found. - Defunct.
Freedom; Towards [17503]
Freedom to Travel Campaign - Defunct.
Freedom Union [IO], Warsaw, Poland
Freedom Writers [★IO]
Freedom Writers [★17746]
Freedom; Young Americans for [17279]
Freedoms Found. [★17644]
Freedoms Found. at Valley Forge [17644], PO Box
706, Valley Forge, PA 19482-0706, (610)933-8825
Freedoms for Ukraine; Women's Assn. for the
Defense of Four [18759]
FreedomWorks [18296], 601 Pennsylvania Ave. NW,
North Bldg., Ste. 700, Washington, DC 20004,
(202)783-3870
Freelance
Copywriter's Coun. of Am. [875]
Working Today [1672]
Freelance Editorial Assn. [★3111]
Freelance Network - Defunct.
Freelancers Assn; Editorial [3111]
Freelancers Union [24218], 45 Main St., Ste. 710,
Brooklyn, NY 11201, (718)222-1099
Freeland League [★20157]
Freeman-Sheldon Parent Support Gp. [14063], 509
Northmont Way, Salt Lake City, UT 84103,
(801)364-7060
Freeman-Sheldon Parent Support Group [IO], Salt
Lake City, UT, United States
Freemasonry - Southern Jurisdiction; Supreme
Coun. 33rd Degree, Ancient and Accepted Scottish
Rite of [19251]
Freemasonry - Southern Masonic Jurisdiction;
Supreme Coun. 33rd Degree, Ancient and Ac-
cepted Scottish Rite of [★19251]
Freemen Inst. [★17297]
Freemuse [IO], Copenhagen, Denmark
Freestanding Ambulatory Surgery Assn. [★16582]
Freestanding Ambulatory Surgical Care; Soc. for the
Advancement of [★16582]
Freestanding Emergency Centers; Natl. Assn. of
[★13663]
Freestyle Players Assn. [23372], 864 Grand Ave.,
Box 475, San Diego, CA 92109, (800)321-8833
Freestyle Players Assn. [IO], San Diego, CA, United
States
Freethinkers of America - Address unknown since
1995.
Freeze Campaign; Nuclear Weapons [★18166]
FREEZE Educ. Fund; SANE/ [★18167]
Freezers Assn; California [★1496]
Freie Demokratische Partei [★IO]
Freier Verband Deutscher Zahnarzte [★IO]
Freight Assn. of Am; Air [★145]
Freight Assn; Amer. Highway [★3863]
Freight Car Historians; Soc. of [10922]
Freight Carriers Assn. of Canada [IO], Fort Erie, ON,
Canada
Freight Carriers Assn; Motor [★3898]
Freight Claim Coun., Inc; Shippers Natl. [★3595]
Freight Conf; Amer. West African [★3597]
Freight Forwarders Assn. of Am; Air [★145]
Freight Forwarders Assn; Canadian Intl. [IO]
Freight Forwarders and Brokers Assn; New York
Foreign [★3582]
Freight Forwarders and Brokers Assn; New York/
New Jersey Foreign [3582]
Freight Forwarders Inst. - Defunct.
Freight Forwarders Tariff Bur. - Defunct.
Freight Handlers, Express and Sta. Employees;
Brotherhood of Railway, Airline and Steamship
Clerks, [★24180]
Freight Handlers, Express and Sta. Employees;
Brotherhood of Railway and Steamship Clerks,
[★24180]
Freight Handlers, Express and Sta. Employees; Car-
men Division of the Brotherhood of Railway, Airline
and Steamship Clerks, [★24179]
Freight Traffic Assn; Natl. Motor [3577]
Freight Transport Assn. [IO], Tunbridge Wells,
United Kingdom
Freight Trans. Consultants Assn. [3566], c/o William
J. Augello, Esq., Exec. Dir./Gen. Counsel, 8683 W
Sahara Ave., Ste. 240, Las Vegas, NV 89117

Freighter Travel Club of America - Defunct.
Freisinnig-Demokratische Partei der Schweiz [★IO]
French
ACA Assurance [19060]
Academie Francaise [IO]
Alliance of France [IO]
Amer. Assn. of Teachers of French [IO]
Amer. Assn. of Teachers of French [8448]
American-Canadian Genealogical Soc. [21098]
American-French Genealogical Soc. [21101]
Amer. Friends of Lafayette [11102]
Amer. Friends of the Paris Opera and Ballet
[9543]
Amer. Maritain Assn. [10782]
Amer. Soc. of the French Legion of Honor [19061]
American Society of the French Order of Merit
[9967]
Amer. Teilhard Assn. [9632]
Assn. Francaise du Froid [IO]
Assn. for French Language Stud. [IO]
Assn. for Learning Languages en Famille [IO]
Assn. for the Stud. of Modern and Contemporary
France [IO]
Basque Educational Org. [9732]
Berger Picard Club of Am. [22229]
Bondurant Family Assn. [20803]
Club Francais d'Amerique [8449]
Comm. of French Speaking Societies [19062]
Coun. of French Life in Am. [IO]
Dogue de Bordeaux Soc. of Am. [22258]
Fed. of French Amer. Women [19063]
Fed. of French War Veterans [21416]
France and Colonies Philatelic Soc. [22820]
France-Louisiane/Franco-Americaine - Vivre
l'heritage Franceil aus Etats-Unis [IO]
France-United States Assn. [IO]
French Activities Centre [IO]
French-American Aid for Children [19064]
French-American Found. [17886]
French Bull Dog Club of Am. [22271]
French/Canadian/Metis Genealogical Soc. [20720]
French Heritage Soc. [10024]
French Inst. Alliance Francaise [9968]
French-speaking Cultural Assn. [IO]
Friends of French Art [10026]
Gabriel Marcel Soc. [10794]
George Sand Assn. [9652]
Huguenot Soc. of the Founders of Manakin in the
Colony of Virginia [21162]
Intl. Assn. for Medical Assistance to Travellers
[13343]
Intl. Coun. of the French Language [IO]
Les Amis de Panhard and Deutsch Bonnet
[21686]
Napoleonic Age Philatelists [22849]
North Amer. Levinas Soc. [10817]
Order of the Noble Companions of the Swan
[9969]
Order of the Noble Companions of the Swan [IO]
Pi Delta Phi [24490]
Quimper Club Intl. [21546]
Savoie Acadian Cultural and Historical Soc.
[21149]
Societe des Gens de Lettres [IO]
Societe des Professeurs Francais et Francoph-
ones d'Amerique [8450]
Soc. for French Historical Stud. [10155]
Soc. for French Stud. [IO]
Union Saint-Jean-Baptiste [19065]
W. T. Bandy Center for Baudelaire and Modern
French Stud. [9720]
French Acad. of Sciences [IO], Paris, France
French Activities Centre [IO], Penetanguishene, ON,
Canada
French Agricultural Res. Centre for Intl. Development
[IO], Paris, France
French Airedale Terrier and Various Terriers Club
[IO], Nantes, France
French Alpine Club [IO], Paris, France
French Amateur Fed. of Mineralogy and Paleontol-
ogy [IO], Boulogne, France
French Am. History Inst. [IO], Outremont, QC,
Canada
French-American Aid for Children [19064], 111 W
58th St., Ste. LL, New York, NY 10019, (212)486-
9593

French-Amer. Atlantique Assn. - Defunct.
French-American Chamber of Commerce [24320],
122 E 42nd St., Ste. 2015, New York, NY 10168,
(212)867-0123
French - Amer. Chamber of Commerce [★IO]
French-American Chamber of Commerce in the U.S.
[★24320]
French-Amer. Comm. for the Statue of Liberty -
Defunct.
French Amer. Cultural Exchange [8560], 972 5th
Ave., New York, NY 10021, (212)439-1449
French Amer. Cultural Services and Educational Aid;
Soc. for [★8560]
French-American Found. [17886], 28 W 44th St.,
Ste. 1420, New York, NY 10036, (212)829-8800
French-American Found. [IO], New York, NY, United
States
French Art; Friends of [10026]
French Article Numbering Assn. [IO], Issy-les-
Moulineaux, France
French Assn. of Amateurs in Micromineralogy [IO],
Carry le Rouet, France
French Assn. of Banks [IO], Paris, France
French Assn. for Commerce and Electronic Trade
[★IO]
French Assn. for Elecl. Equip., Automation and
Related Services [IO], Paris, France
French Assn. for Info. Commun. Tech. Development
[IO], Neuilly-sur-Seine, France
French Assn. of Landscape Contractors [IO], Paris,
France
French Assn. for Pattern Recognition and Interpreta-
tion [IO], Mont-Saint-Aignan, France
French Assn. for Plant Protection [IO], Alfortville,
France
French Assn. for Quality Assurance in Pathology
[IO], Strasbourg, France
French Assn. for Res. on South-East Asia [IO],
Paris, France
French Assn. for Standardization [IO], St.-Denis,
France
French Assn. of Stud. of Competition [IO], Paris,
France
French Assn. of Variable Star Observers [IO], Stras-
bourg, France
French Brittany Gun Dog Assn. [22270], c/o Robert
Olson, Sec., 12423 Carriage Stone Dr., Fishers, IN
46037
French Bull Dog Club of Am. [22271], c/o Pat Kosi-
nar, 2108 Inverness Dr., Lawrence, KS 66047-
1959
French Bulldog
French Bull Dog Club of Am. [22271]
French Canadian Assn. for the Advancement of the
Sciences [IO], Montreal, QC, Canada
French-Canadian Genealogical Soc. [IO], Montreal,
QC, Canada
French/Canadian/Metis Genealogical Soc. [IO],
Golden Valley, MN, United States
French/Canadian/Metis Genealogical Soc. [20720],
c/o Minnesota Genealogical Soc., 5768 Olson
Memorial Hwy., Golden Valley, MN 55422-5014
French Ceramic Soc. [IO], Paris, France
French Chamber of Commerce in Great Britain [IO],
London, United Kingdom
French Chamber of Commerce in the U.S. [★24320]
French Chem. Soc. [IO], Paris, France
French Club of Am. [★8449]
French Comm. Against Hypertension [IO], Paris,
France
French Confed. of the Paper, Cardboard and Cel-
lulose Indus. [IO], Paris, France
French Dairy Assn. [IO], Paris, France
French Democratic Union of Labour [IO], Paris,
France
French Diabetes Assn. [IO], Paris, France
French Ecological Soc. [IO], Sete, France
French Engineers in the U.S. - Address unknown
since 1990.
French Family Assn. - Defunct.
French Fed. of Building [IO], Paris, France
French Fed. of Cotton and Wool Indus. [IO], Clichy,
France
French Fed. of Fragrance, Cosmetics, and Toiletries
[IO], Paris, France

A star before a book entry number signifies that the name is not listed separately, but is mentioned within the entry.

French Fed. of Haute Couture and Ready-to-Wear and Fashion Designers **[IO]**, Paris, France

French Fed. of Insurance Companies **[IO]**, Paris, France

French Fed. of Lingerie and Swimwear **[IO]**, Paris, France

French Fed. of Spirits **[IO]**, Paris, France

French Fed. of the Sporting Goods Indus. **[IO]**, Levallois Perret, France

French Fed. of Toy Indus. **[IO]**, Paris, France

French Floorball Assn. **[IO]**, Levallois Perret, France

French Found. for Medical Res. **[IO]**, Paris, France

French Franchise Fed. **[IO]**, Paris, France

French Genealogical Soc; American- **[21101]**

French Heritage Center; Northwest Territory, Canadian and **[★20720]**

French Heritage Soc. **[10024]**, 14 E 60th St., Ste. 605, New York, NY 10022, (212)759-6846

French Historical Stud; Soc. for **[10155]**

French Honor Soc; Natl. **[★24490]**

French Inst. Alliance Francaise **[9968]**, 22 E 60th St., New York, NY 10022, (212)355-6100

French Inst. of Intl. Relations **[IO]**, Paris, France

French Inst. of Pondicherry **[IO]**, Pondicherry, India

French Inst. of Social History **[IO]**, Paris, France

French Inst. in the U.S. **[★9968]**

French Justice and Peace Commn. **[IO]**, Paris, France

French-Language Assn. for the Stud. of Diabetes and Metabolic Disorders **[IO]**, Paris, France

French Language Press Assn. **[IO]**, Ottawa, ON, Canada

French League Against Epilepsy **[IO]**, Paris, France

French League for Animal Rights **[IO]**, Paris, France

French Medical Gastronomical Soc. - Defunct.

French Natl. Shipowners Assn. **[IO]**, Paris, France

French Optics Mfrs. Assn. **[IO]**, Paris, France

French Orchid Soc. **[IO]**, Paris, France

French Org. of the Long QT Syndrome **[IO]**, Le Bou-lou, France

French Orienteering Fed. **[IO]**, Paris, France

French Petroleum Inst. **[IO]**, Rueil-Malmaison, France

French Pharmaceutical Distribution Assn. **[IO]**, Paris, France

French Pharmacology Soc. **[IO]**, Nancy, France

French Physical Soc. **[IO]**, Paris, France

French Plastic Packaging Manufacturer's Trade Assn. **[IO]**, Paris, France

French Refrigeration Assn. **[IO]**, Paris, France

French Road Union **[IO]**, Paris, France

French Sailing Fed. **[IO]**, Paris, France

French Soc. of Agricultural Economics **[IO]**, Paris, France

French Soc. of Anesthesia and Intensive Care **[IO]**, Paris, France

French Soc. of Authors, Composers and Publishers - Address unknown since 1995.

French Soc. of Automotive Engineers **[IO]**, Suresnes, France

French Soc. of Cardiology **[IO]**, Paris, France

French Soc. of Dermatology **[IO]**, Paris, France

French Soc. of Digestive Endoscopy **[IO]**, Paris, France

French Soc. of Genetics **[IO]**, Versailles, France

French Soc. of Geriatrics and Gerontology **[IO]**, Paris, France

French Soc. of Gerontology **[★IO]**

French Soc. for Metallurgy and Materials **[IO]**, Paris, France

French Soc. of Musicology **[IO]**, Paris, France

French Soc. of Orthopedic and Osteopathic Manual Medicine **[IO]**, Nice, France

French Soc. of Overseas History **[IO]**, St.-Denis, France

French Soc. of Psychosomatic Obstetrics and Gynaecology **[IO]**, Paris, France

French Soc. for Trenchless Tech. **[IO]**, Paris, France

French Soc. for Vitamins and Biofactors **[IO]**, Paris, France

French-speaking Cultural Assn. **[IO]**, Penetanguishene, ON, Canada

French-speaking Intl. Assn. of Elder **[IO]**, Quebec, QC, Canada

French-speaking Proj. Mgt. Assn. **[IO]**, Paris, France

French Speaking Societies; Comm. of **[19062]**

French-Speaking Universities Agency - Caribbean Off. **[IO]**, Port-au-Prince, Haiti

French-Speaking Univ. Agency **[IO]**, Montreal, QC, Canada

French Specialised Periodical Publishers Fed. **[IO]**, Paris, France

French Trade Fairs and Exhibitions **[IO]**, Paris, France

French Union of Petroleum Indus. **[IO]**, Paris, France

French Vacuum Soc. **[IO]**, Paris, France

French Vehicle Equip. Indus. Assn. **[IO]**, Suresnes, France

French War Veterans; Fed. of **[21416]**

French Young Men's Christian Association **[IO]**, Paris, France

French Youth Assn. **[IO]**, Saskatoon, SK, Canada

French Youth Hostels Fed. **[IO]**, Paris, France

Frequency Advisory Comm; Manufacturers Radio **[565]**

Frequency Control Soc; IEEE Ultrasonics, Ferroelectrics, and **[6366]**

Frequency Coordination Sys. Assn. **[IO]**, Ottawa, ON, Canada

Frequent Bus. Travellers Club **[IO]**, North Sydney, Australia

Freres de la Charite **[★IO]**

Freres Maristes des Ecoles **[★IO]**

Freres de Saint Gabriel **[★IO]**

Fresh Fruit and Vegetable Assn. and International Fresh-Cut Produce Assn; United **[★4766]**

Fresh Fruit-Vegetables Exporters' Union **[IO]**, Istanbul, Turkey

Fresh Garlic Assn. - Defunct.

Fresh Lifelines for Youth **[13484]**, 120 W Mission St., San Jose, CA 95110, (408)263-2630

Fresh Produce Assn. of the Americas **[1513]**, PO Box 848, Nogales, AZ 85628-0848, (520)287-2707

Fresh Produce Assn; United **[4766]**

Fresh Produce Consortium - UK **[IO]**, Peterborough, United Kingdom

Fresh Produce Exporters' Assn. of Kenya **[IO]**, Nairobi, Kenya

Fresh Produce and Floral Coun. **[1514]**, 16700 Valley View Ave., Ste. 130, La Mirada, CA 90638, (714)739-0177

Fresh Water Fish Wholesalers Assn. - Address unknown since 1995.

Freshfel Europe **[IO]**, Brussels, Belgium

Freshwater Biological Assn. **[IO]**, Cumbria, United Kingdom

Freshwater Institute **[★4380]**

Freshwater Mollusk Conservation Soc. **[5034]**, c/o Steve Ahlstedt, Pres., US Geological Survey, 1820 Midpark Dr., Knoxville, TN 37921

Freshwater Sciences Soc; New Zealand **[IO]**

Freshwater Soc. **[5091]**, 2500 Shadywood Rd., Excelsior, MN 55331, (952)471-9773

Fretted Instrument Guild of Am. **[10597]**, 2501 Saddleback Dr., Edmond, OK 73034

Fretz Family Assn. **[20904]**, 572 Kohlers Hill Rd., Lenhartsville, PA 19534, (610)756-6697

Freud Archives; Sigmund **[16115]**

Freunde Nepals **[★IO]**

Friars Club **[11016]**, 57 E 55th St., New York, NY 10022, (212)751-7272

Friars Natl. Assn. **[★11016]**

Friction Materials Standards Inst. **[385]**, 23 Woodland Rd., Ste. B-3, Madison, CT 06443, (203)245-8425

Friedl Expert Comm. - Defunct.

Friedreich's Ataxia

Friedreich's Ataxia Res. Alliance **[14403]**

Friedreich's Ataxia Group in America - Defunct.

Friedreich's Ataxia Res. Alliance **[14403]**, PO Box 1537, Springfield, VA 22151, (703)426-1576

Friedreichs Ataxia Soc. of Ireland **[IO]**, Dublin, Ireland

Friedrich Ebert Found. - Jordan **[IO]**, Amman, Jordan

Friedrich Naumann Found. **[IO]**, Harare, Zimbabwe

Friedrich Naumann Found. - Africa Regional Off. **[IO]**, Parklands, Republic of South Africa

Friend Family Assn. of Am. **[20905]**, PO Box 96, Friendsville, MD 21531, (301)746-4220

Friend Finders Intl. - Defunct.

Friendly Contacts Associates - Defunct.

Friendly Hand Found. **[13243]**, 347 S Normandie Ave., Los Angeles, CA 90020, (213)389-9964

Friendly House **[★13243]**

Friendly Peersuasion - Address unknown since 1999.

Friendly Sons of St. Patrick in the City of New York; Soc. of the **[19155]**

Friends

Assoc. Comm. of Friends on Indian Affairs **[20039]**

Canadian Friends Ser. Comm. **[IO]**

Evangelical Friends Intl. - North Amer. Region **[IO]**

Evangelical Friends Intl. - North Amer. Region **[20040]**

Friends Assn. for Higher Educ. **[8451]**

Friends Comm. on Natl. Legislation **[20041]**

Friends Coun. on Educ. **[8452]**

Friends Gen. Conf. **[20042]**

Friends Historical Assn. **[20043]**

Friends Historical Association **[IO]**

Friends United Meeting **[IO]**

Friends United Meeting **[20044]**

Friends World Comm. for Consultation - United Kingdom **[IO]**

Wider Quaker Fellowship **[20045]**

Friends of the Abraham Lincoln Museum **[11113]**, c/o Abraham Lincoln Museum, Lincoln Memorial Univ., 6965 Cumberland Gap Pkwy., Harrogate, TN 37752, (423)869-6235

Friends of ADIR - Defunct.

Friends in Adoption **[11245]**, 44 South St., PO Box 1228, Middletown Springs, VT 05757-1228, (802)235-2373

Friends of Africa in America - Defunct.

Friends of Alfred E. Packer in the Nation's Capitol - Defunct.

Friends Alliance; Evangelical **[★20040]**

Friends of the Alliance Israelite Universelle; Amer. **[8675]**

Friends of the Alliance Israelite Universelle; Canadian **[★17947]**

Friends of the Alliance Israelite Universelle; Canadian **[★IO]**

Friends of Amer. Art in Religion - Defunct.

Friends of the Amer. Museum in Britain/Halcyon Found. **[9370]**, 100 Park Ave., 20th Fl., New York, NY 10017, (212)370-0198

Friends of the Amer. Museum in Britain/Halcyon Found. **[IO]**, New York, NY, United States

Friends of Amer. Writers **[11171]**, 506 Rose Ave., Des Plaines, IL 60016, (847)827-8339

Friends of Animals **[11397]**, 777 Post Rd., Ste. 205, Darien, CT 06820, (203)656-1522

Friends of Ann Jillian - Address unknown since 1995.

Friends of Appropriate Technology - Defunct.

Friends of ARCC **[★19578]**

Friends Around the World - Address unknown since 2006.

Friends of Asian Elephants **[IO]**, Bangkok, Thailand

Friends; Assn. of Evangelical **[★20040]**

Friends Assn. for Higher Educ. **[8451]**, 1501 Cherry St., Philadelphia, PA 19102, (215)241-7116

Friends Association; National Head Start **[★9006]**

Friends of Astrology **[6493]**, 208 Rosewood Ct., Westmont, IL 60559-1577

Friends of the Australian Koala Found. **[5319]**, c/o Nolan Lehr Gp., 224 W 29th St., 15th Fl., New York, NY 10001, (212)967-8200

Friends of Beethoven in Am. **[★9803]**

Friends of Beth Hatefutsoth; Amer. **[10253]**

Friends of Bezalel Acad. of Arts **[10255]**, 501 5th Ave., Ste. 909, New York, NY 10017-6107, (212)687-0542

Friends of Bobby Vee - Address unknown since 2001.

Friends of Boys Town Jerusalem; Amer. **[★13473]**

Friends of Brain Tumor Res. **[★15344]**

Friends of Br. Brook Park **[★4407]**

Friends of Buckminster Fuller Found. **[★11104]**

Friends of Buddhism - Defunct.

Friends and Buddies of the Hour Glass Assn. **[21299]**, c/o Ms. Mary Jean Wise, 3001 Richmond Ave., Mattoon, IL 61938-2349, (217)234-6534

Reference to "IO" in place of a book number signifies that the association may be found in the 45th edition of International Organizations.

Friends of Cadwalader Park [★4407]

Friends of Cambridge Univ; Amer. [★9284]

Friends of Canadian Broadcasting [IO], Toronto, ON, Canada

Friends of the Cassidys [24891], c/o Cheryl Corwin, Pres., 1647 Crystal Downs St., Banning, CA 92220, (562)493-0718

Friends of Cast Iron Architecture [10025]

Friends of Celiac Disease Res. - Address unknown since 2008.

Friends of Central Park [★4407]

Friends of the Children [11594], 44 NE Morris, Ste. 2000, Portland, OR 97212-3015, (503)281-6633

Friends of Christ in India [20090], c/o Greenfield Hill Congregational Church, 1045 Old Acad. Rd., Fairfield, CT 06824, (203)259-5596

Friends of Clara Barton - Defunct.

Friends Comm. on Natl. Legislation [20041], 245 2nd St. NE, Washington, DC 20002-5761, (202)547-6000

Friends Comm. on War Tax Concerns - Defunct.

Friends of Community - Defunct.

Friends; The Compassionate [12666]

Friends of the Conservative Party - Defunct.

Friends Coordinating Comm. on Peace - Defunct.

Friends Coun. on Educ. [8452], 1507 Cherry St., Philadelphia, PA 19102, (215)241-7245

Friends of Country Music - Defunct.

Friends of Creation Spirituality - Address unknown since 1999.

Friends of Cyprus - Defunct.

Friends of David Cassidy - Defunct.

Friends of Debbie Reynolds Fan Club [24741], 5713 Rosario Blvd., North Highlands, CA 95660, (916)331-0247

Friends of Dennis Lee Fan Club [24780], PO Box 15557, West Palm Beach, FL 33416

Friends of Dennis Wilson [24892]

Friends of the Disabled Assn. [IO], Beirut, Lebanon

Friends Disaster Ser. [12856], 33937 US Rte. 30, Lisbon, OH 44432, (330)429-4292

Friends of Dr. Who - Address unknown since 1999.

Friends of Druid Hill Park [★4407]

Friends of the Earth [4397], 1717 Massachusetts Ave. NW, Ste. 600, Washington, DC 20036-2002, (202)783-7400

Friends of the Earth - Argentina [IO], Santa Fe, Argentina

Friends of the Earth - Australia [IO], Fitzroy, Australia

Friends of the Earth Austria [IO], Vienna, Austria

Friends of the Earth - Brazil [IO], Porto Alegre, Brazil

Friends of the Earth Cameroon [IO], Yaounde, Cameroon

Friends of the Earth Costa Rica [IO], San Jose, Costa Rica

Friends of the Earth Croatia [IO], Zagreb, Croatia

Friends of the Earth Curacao [IO], Curacao, Netherlands Antilles

Friends of the Earth - Cyprus [IO], Limassol, Cyprus

Friends of the Earth - Czech Republic [IO], Brno, Czech Republic

Friends of the Earth El Salvador [IO], San Salvador, El Salvador

Friends of the Earth - England, Wales, and Northern Ireland [IO], London, United Kingdom

Friends of the Earth Estonia [IO], Tartu, Estonia

Friends of the Earth - Europe [IO], Brussels, Belgium

Friends of the Earth Finland [IO], Turku, Finland

Friends of the Earth Flanders and Brussels [IO], Gent, Belgium

Friends of the Earth - France [IO], Montreuil, France

Friends of the Earth Georgia [IO], Tbilisi, Georgia

Friends of the Earth - Ghana [IO], Accra, Ghana

Friends of the Earth - Grenada [IO], St. George's, Grenada

Friends of the Earth Haiti [IO], Port-au-Prince, Haiti

Friends of the Earth - Hong Kong [IO], Hong Kong, People's Republic of China

Friends of the Earth Hungary [IO], Budapest, Hungary

Friends of the Earth Indonesia [IO], Jakarta, Indonesia

Friends of the Earth Intl. [IO], Amsterdam, Netherlands

Friends of the Earth - Ireland [IO], Dublin, Ireland

Friends of the Earth - Italy [IO], Rome, Italy

Friends of the Earth - Japan [IO], Tokyo, Japan

Friends of the Earth Latvia [IO], Riga, Latvia

Friends of the Earth Luxembourg [IO], Luxembourg, Luxembourg

Friends of the Earth - Macedonia [IO], Skopje, Macedonia

Friends of the Earth - Malaysia [IO], Penang, Malaysia

Friends of the Earth Malta [IO], Valletta, Malta

Friends of the Earth Mauritius/Maudesco [IO], Port Louis, Mauritius

Friends of the Earth Middle East - Amman [IO], Amman, Jordan

Friends of the Earth - Netherlands [IO], Amsterdam, Netherlands

Friends of the Earth - New Zealand [IO], Auckland, New Zealand

Friends of the Earth Nicaragua [IO], Managua, Nicaragua

Friends of the Earth - Papua New Guinea [IO], Boroko, Papua New Guinea

Friends of the Earth Peru [IO], Magdalena, Peru

Friends of the Earth Philippines [IO], Quezon City, Philippines

Friends of the Earth - Scotland [IO], Edinburgh, United Kingdom

Friends of the Earth - Sierra Leone [IO], Freetown, Sierra Leone

Friends of the Earth Slovakia [IO], Banska Bystrica, Slovakia

Friends of the Earth - Spain [IO], Madrid, Spain

Friends of the Earth Sweden [IO], Goteborg, Sweden

Friends of the Earth - Switzerland [IO], Basel, Switzerland

Friends of the Earth - Togo [IO], Lome, Togo

Friends of the Earth - Uruguay [IO], Montevideo, Uruguay

Friends for Education - Address unknown since 1995.

Friends Educ. Conf. [★20042]

Friends of the Elderly; Little Bros. - [11295]

Friends of the Env. [★IO]

Friends of Env. and Development Assn. [IO], Cairo, Egypt

Friends of the Everglades [4398], 7800 Red Rd., Ste. 215K, Miami, FL 33143, (305)669-0858

Friends of Eye Res. - Defunct.

Friends of Falun Gong [17061], 24 W Railroad Ave., PMB No. 124, Tenafly, NJ 07670, (866)343-7436

Friends of Falun Gong Europe [IO], Harrow, United Kingdom

Friends and Families of Cannabis Consumers [18023], PO Box 1716, El Cerrito, CA 94530, (510)215-8326

Friends of Families - Defunct.

Friends of Family Planning [★18521]

Friends of Family Planning; Voters for Choice/ [18521]

Friends; Famous Fone [11692]

Friends of the FBI - Address unknown since 1999.

Friends; Feral Cat [21907]

Friends of Feral Felines [21908], PO Box 473385, Charlotte, NC 28247, (704)348-1578

Friends of Fiber Art Intl. [9441], Box 468, Western Springs, IL 60558, (708)246-9466

Friends of the Filipino People - Address unknown since 1995.

Friends; Five Years Meeting of [★20044]

Friends of Folk Music [★10725]

Friends of Folk Music [★IO]

Friends of Fort Greene Park [★4407]

Friends of Frank Ashmore - Defunct.

Friends of Franklin [11114], PO Box 40048, Philadelphia, PA 19106, (856)833-1771

Friends of Freddy [24821], PO Box 912, Greenbelt, MD 20768-0912, (301)345-2774

Friends of Free Asia - Defunct.

Friends of Free China - Defunct.

Friends for Free Enterprise - Address unknown since 2004.

Friends of French Art [10026]

Friends Gen. Conf. [20042], 1216 Arch St., No. 2B, Philadelphia, PA 19107, (215)561-1700

Friends of George Sand [★9652]

Friends of Gracious [IO], Tokushima, Japan

Friends of Guy Clark [24893], PO Box 1, Yorkville, CA 95494-0001, (707)894-5446

Friends of Haiti [★17682]

Friends of Haitian Refugees - Defunct.

Friends' Hea. Connection [22136], PO Box 114, New Brunswick, NJ 08903, (732)418-1811

Friends of Hibakusha [18128], 1765 Sutter St., No. 2, San Francisco, CA 94115, (415)567-7599

Friends of Hibakusha [IO], San Francisco, CA, United States

Friends Historical Association [IO], Haverford, PA, United States

Friends Historical Assn. [20043], Haverford Coll. Lib., 370 Lancaster Ave., Haverford, PA 19041-1392, (610)896-1161

Friends of Historical Pharmacy - Defunct.

Friends Historical Soc. of Philadelphia [★20043]

Friends Historical Soc. of Philadelphia [★IO]

Friends of the Hop Marketing Order - Defunct.

Friends of Hopalong Cassidy Fan Club [24742], 6310 Friendship Dr., New Concord, OH 43762-9708

Friends of Hopalong Cassidy Fan Club [IO], New Concord, OH, United States

Friends of IBBY [★9756]

Friends of the IDF - Address unknown since 2005.

Friends-in-Art of Amer. Coun. of the Blind [9504], c/o Amer. Coun. of the Blind, 1155 15th St. NW, Ste. 1004, Washington, DC 20005, (202)467-5081

Friends of India Comm. - Defunct.

Friends of India Soc. Intl. [19112], PO Box 73327, Houston, TX 77273-3327, (281)494-1909

Friends of India Soc. Intl. [IO], Houston, TX, United States

Friends of Intl. Education - Address unknown since 2001.

Friends Intl; Evangelical [★20040]

Friends of Iracambi [★IO]

Friends of Israel Disabled Veterans [21166], 1133 Broadway, Ste. 232, New York, NY 10010, (212)689-3220

Friends of Israel Disabled War Veterans (Beit Halochem) [★21166]

Friends of Israel Gospel Ministry [20010], PO Box 908, Bellmawr, NJ 08099, (800)257-7843

Friends of Israel Missionary and Relief SOC [★20010]

Friends of the Israel Museum; Amer. [10491]

Friends of Jack Gilbert/The John Gilbert Appreciation Soc. - Address unknown since 2001.

Friends of Jackie Wilson - Address unknown since 2001.

Friends for Jamaica - Defunct.

Friends of James Rogers - Address unknown since 2001.

Friends of Jerusalem (Amer. Neturei Karta) - Address unknown since 2002.

Friends of John Beradino - Defunct.

Friends of Johnny Mathis - Defunct.

Friends of the Jose Carreras Intl. Leukemia Found. [13825], PO Box 19024, Seattle, WA 98109-1024, (206)667-7108

Friends of the Jose Carreras International Leukemia Foundation [IO], Seattle, WA, United States

Friends of Josh Groban Fan Club [24994], PO Box 8639, Emeryville, CA 94608

Friends of Julio [★24894]

Friends of Julio Intl. [24894], 28 Farmington Ave., Longmeadow, MA 01106-1433

Friends of Karen [11694], PO Box 190, Purdys, NY 10578-0190, (914)277-4547

Friends of Kate Smith [★24930]

Friends of Kate Smith [★IO]

Friends of the Kennedy Center [9568], c/o John F. Kennedy Center for the Performing Arts, 2700 F St. NW, Washington, DC 20566, (202)416-8301

Friends of Kristoffer Tabori - Defunct.

Friends of LADDERS [12491], PO Box 920025, Needham, MA 02492, (781)449-6074

Friends of Lafayette; Amer. [11102]

Friends of Lainie Kazan [24743]

Friends of the Land [★4413]

Friends for Lesbian, Gay, Bisexual, Transgender, and Queer Concerns [20056], c/o Sue Sierra, Treas., 1314 Wright St., Ann Arbor, MI 48105

A star before a book entry number signifies that the name is not listed separately, but is mentioned within the entry.

Friends for Lesbian, Gay, Bisexual, Transgender, and Queer Concerns [IO], Ann Arbor, MI, United States

Friends of Lesbians and Gays; Parents and [★12253]

Friends of Lesbians and Gays; Parents, Families, and [12253]

Friends of Libraries for Blind and Physically Handicapped Individuals in North America [10357]

Friends of Libraries U.S.A. [10358], 1420 Walnut St., Ste. 450, Philadelphia, PA 19102, (215)790-1674

Friends for Life - Defunct.

Friends of Lindenwald [10027], PO Box 64, Kinderhook, NY 12106, (518)758-2249

Friends of Literature - Defunct.

Friends of the Louvre Museum [IO], Paris, France

Friends of Lulu [22134], 83 Russell St., Ste. 3R, Brooklyn, NY 11222

Friends of Malawi [9851], c/o Lance Cole, Treas., 7940 SW 11th, Portland, OR 97219

Friends of Malawi [IO], Portland, OR, United States

Friends of Micronesia - Defunct.

Friends of Morocco [19261], PO Box 2579, Washington, DC 20013-2579, (703)660-9292

Friends of Morocco [IO], Washington, DC, United States

Friends of the Natl. Arboretum [6634], 3501 New York Ave. NE, Washington, DC 20002-1958, (202)544-8733

Friends of the Natl. Inst. of Dental and Craniofacial Res. [14154], 1901 Pennsylvania Ave. NW, Ste. 607, Washington, DC 20006, (202)223-0667

Friends of the Natl. Libraries [IO], London, United Kingdom

Friends of the Natl. Lib. of Medicine [15167], 2810 M St. NW, Washington, DC 20002, (202)719-8094

Friends of the Natl. Parks at Gettysburg [10028], PO Box 4622, Gettysburg, PA 17325, (717)334-0772

Friends of Natl. Public Radio - Defunct.

Friends of the Natl. Zoo [7858], PO Box 37012, Washington, DC 20013-7012, (202)633-4271

Friends of the Nemaiah Valley [IO], Victoria, BC, Canada

Friends of Nepal Assn. [IO], Rotenburg, Germany

Friends of New Zealand [★2318]

Friends of Nicaraguan Culture - Address unknown since 1989.

Friends of Nigeria [19290], 1203 Cambria Ct., Iowa City, IA 52246, (319)351-3375

Friends of Nigeria [IO], Iowa City, IA, United States

Friends of Norwich, Connecticut; Soc. of the Founders and [10063]

Friends of Old St. Ferdinand [19626], PO Box 222, Florissant, MO 63031, (314)837-2110

Friends of Old-Time Radio [22924], PO Box 4321, Hamden, CT 06514, (203)248-2887

Friends of the Outdoors [IO], Cheticamp, NS, Canada

Friends Outside [11868], PO Box 4085, Stockton, CA 95204, (209)938-0727

Friends of Palestinian Prisoners - Address unknown since 1995.

Friends of Patrick Henry [11115], PO Box 1776, Hanford, CA 93232, (559)582-8534

Friends of Paul Overstreet [24895], PO Box 320, Pegram, TN 37143, (615)952-3999

Friends Peace and Intl. Relations Coun. [★IO]

Friends of Peace Now [★IO]

Friends of Peace Now [★17935]

Friends of Peace Pilgrim [11116], PO Box 2207, Shelton, CT 06484-1207, (203)926-1581

Friends of Peace Pilgrim [IO], Copperopolis, CA, United States

Friends of Peace Relief Work [★IO]

Friends of the Peaceful Alternatives - Defunct.

Friends of Photography - Defunct.

Friends Prog. [★13317]

Friends of Prospect Park [★4407]

Friends of the Pyrenees [IO], Ariege, France

Friends of R. Emery - Address unknown since 1989.

Friends of Radio for Peace Intl. [21500], PO Box 3165, Newberg, OR 97132

Friends of Radio for Peace Intl. [IO], Newberg, OR, United States

Friends Religious Conf. [★20042]

Friends; Religious Soc. of [★18206]

Friends; Religious Soc. of [★IO]

Friends of Rhodesia Comm. - Address unknown since 1995.

Friends of Richard III [★11145]

Friends of the River [4399], 915 20th St., Sacramento, CA 95811, (916)442-3155

Friends of the River Foundation [★4399]

Friends of Robert Frost [10860], c/o Robert Frost Stone House Museum, 121 Historic Rte. 7A, Shaftsbury, VT 05262, (802)447-6200

Friends of Rwanda Assn. [11595], c/o Mathilde Mukantabana, Pres., PO Box 1311, Elk Grove, CA 95759-1311, (916)683-3356

Friends of Rwanda Assn. [IO], Elk Grove, CA, United States

Friends of Sabeel - North Am. [IO], Portland, OR, United States

Friends of Sabeel - North Am. [18205], PO Box 9186, Portland, OR.97207, (503)653-6625

Friends of St. Luke's Hosp. [IO], Dublin, Ireland

Friends of the Sea Lion Marine Mammal Center [★5361]

Friends of the Sea Otter [5320], 93 Via Ventura, Monterey, CA 93940, (831)373-2747

Friends Ser. Comm; Mississippi Surveillance Proj. of the Amer. [★17093]

Friends Ser. Coun. [★IO]

Friends of the Shakers [10963], c/o The Shaker Soc., 707 Shaker Rd., New Gloucester, ME 04260, (207)926-4597

Friends of Shaun Cassidy Fan Club [★24891]

Friends of Sherlock Holmes - Address unknown since 2006.

Friends of Solidarity - Address unknown since 1999.

Friends of South African Schools Fund [8257], c/o C. Sean Day, 15 E Putnam Ave., No. 245, Greenwich, CT 06830-5424, (203)422-2402

Friends Support Group for Moscow Trust - Defunct.

Friends of the Tango - Defunct.

Friends of Tara - Defunct.

Friends of the Tel Aviv Univ; Amer. [★8679]

Friends of Temperance [IO], Helsinki, Finland

Friends of Terra Cotta [10029], c/o Susan Tunick, Pres., 771 W End Ave., No. 10E, New York, NY 10025, (212)932-1750

Friends of The Hebrew Univ; Amer. [8676]

Friends: The Natl. Assn. of Young People Who Stutter [16445], c/o Lee Caggiano, 38 S Oyster Bay Rd., Syosset, NY 11791, (866)866-8335

Friends of the Third World [12774], 611 W Wayne St., Fort Wayne, IN 46802-2167, (260)422-6821

Friends of the Third World [IO], Fort Wayne, IN, United States

Friends of Thomas More [IO], Angers, France

Friends of Togo [IO], Washington, DC, United States

Friends of Togo [17887], PO Box 9436, Washington, DC 20016

Friends of Tom and Colin Baker - Defunct.

Friends of the Trees Soc. [4400], PO Box 4469, Bellingham, WA 98227, (360)927-1274

Friends of Ty Herndon Fan Club [24896], c/o Jackson Dance Music, LLC, PO Box 70688, Richmond, VA 23255-0688

Friends Union for Philanthropic Labor [★20042]

Friends United Meeting [20044], 101 Quaker Hill Dr., Richmond, IN 47374-1926, (765)962-7573

Friends United Meeting [IO], Richmond, IN, United States

Friends of the United Nations [18765], 1507 Stanford St., No. 5, Santa Monica, CA 90404, (310)453-1360

Friends of the United Nations Env. Prog. [★4613]

Friends of the U.S. of Latin America - Defunct.

Friends of the U.S. Natl. Arboretum [★6634]

Friends United Through Astronomy - Defunct.

Friends of the Valley Railroad [10912], PO Box 452, 1 Railroad Ave., Essex, CT 06426, (860)767-0103

Friends of the Vatican Lib; Amer. [10318]

Friends Vegetarian Soc. of North America - Defunct.

Friends of Vic and Sade - Defunct.

Friends of Vieilles Maisons Francaises [★10024]

Friends of the Vietnam Veterans Memorial - Defunct.

Friends of Virgin Islands Natl. Park [5264], PO Box 811, St. John, VI 00831, (340)779-4940

Friends of VISTA - Defunct.

Friends of Waycross Express - Defunct.

Friends of the Western Buddhist Order [19551], c/o Aryaloka Buddhist Centre, 14 Heartwood Cir., Newmarket, NH 03857, (603)659-5456

Friends of the Western Buddhist Order [IO], London, United Kingdom

Friends of the Wilderness - Defunct.

Friends of Workshop Way - Defunct.

Friends World Comm. for Consultation [18206], c/o Margaret Fraser, Exec. Sec., 1506 Race St., Philadelphia, PA 19102, (215)241-7250

Friends World Comm. for Consultation [IO], Philadelphia, PA, United States

Friends World Comm. for Consultation - United Kingdom [IO], London, United Kingdom

Friends of the World Coun. of Churches - Defunct.

Friends of Yesh Gvul - Address unknown since 1999.

Friends for Youth [13485], 1741 Broadway, Redwood City, CA 94063, (650)368-4444

Friendship; Ambassadors for [★17888]

Friendship Ambassadors Found. [17888], 299 Greenwich Ave., Greenwich, CT 06830, (203)542-0652

Friendship Ambassadors Found. [IO], Greenwich, CT, United States

Friendship Assn. of Chinese Students and Scholars - Address unknown since 1995.

Friendship Assn; U.S.-China Peoples [17066]

Friendship Club - Defunct.

Friendship Force Intl. [17889], 34 Peachtree St., Ste. 2250, Atlanta, GA 30303, (404)522-9490

Friendship Force Intl. [IO], Atlanta, GA, United States

Friendship Found; Intl. [★8631]

Friendship Found; World Relief [★13171]

Friendship League; America-Israel [10252]

Friendship Proj. for Northern Ireland; Children's [13478]

Friendship Soc; Hungarian/American [19106]

Friendshipment - Defunct.

Friesian Assn. of Am; Holstein- [★4263]

Friesian Horse Assn. of North Am. [4880], 4037 Iron Works Pkwy., Ste. 160, Lexington, KY 40511-8483, (859)455-7430

Friesian Horse Assn. of North Am. [IO], Lexington, KY, United States

Friesian Horse Soc. [IO], Armstrong, BC, Canada

Friesian Soc; Beef [★4270]

Frisbee Family Assn. of Am; Frisbie - [20906]

Frisbees

Austrian Frisbee-Sport Fed. [IO]

Beach Ultimate Gp. Portugal [IO]

Belgian Flying Disc Fed. [IO]

Belgian Wallonia-Brussels Discgolf Assn. [IO]

British Disc Golf Assn. [IO]

Chinese Taipei Flying Disc Assn. [IO]

Dansk Frisbee Sport Union [IO]

Dutch Flying Disc Assn. [IO]

Egypt Flying Disc Fed. [IO]

Fed. Flying Disc France [IO]

Fed. Italian Flying Disc [IO]

Finnish Flying Disc Assn. [IO]

Flying Disc Fed. of India [IO]

Irish Flying Disc Assn. [IO]

Israel Flying Disc Assn. [IO]

Japan Flying Disc Assn. [IO]

Latvian Flying Disc Fed. [IO]

Lithuanian Flying Disc Fed. [IO]

Pakistan Flying Disc Fed. [IO]

Riders of the Wind, The Field Events Player's Assn. [23374]

Russian Flying Disc Fed. [IO]

Slovak Assn. of Frisbee [IO]

Swedish Frisbeesport Fed. [IO]

Tallinn Frisbee Club [IO]

UK Ultimate Assn. [IO]

Ultimate Players Assn. [23375]

U.S. Disc Sports [23376]

Frisbie - Frisbee Family Assn. of Am. [20906], 1211 Dewey Ave., Evanston, IL 60202, (641)568-3234

Frisco and Pacific Assn; Wabash, [10927]

Frog Collectors Club; Beyond the Pond.International [21977]

Frog Collectors Club; Frog Pond - [★21977]
Frog Pond - Frog Collectors Club [★21977]
Front Assn. - U.S. Br; Western [10485]
Front Line [IO], Dublin, Ireland
Front Range Equine Rescue [4881], PO Box 307, Larkspur, CO 80118
Front Striker Bulletin [★21963]
Frontenac Club - Defunct.
Frontier [★IO]
Frontier Families Res. Assn; Daniel Boone and [10107]
Frontier Found; Electronic [7731]
Frontier; Museum Assn. of the Amer. [★10132]
Frontier Nursing Ser. [15479], 132 FNS Dr., Wendover, KY 41775, (606)672-2317
Frontier School of Midwifery and Family Nursing [★15479]
Frontier Soc. for Environmental Exploration - United Kingdom [★IO]
Frontiers of Am. [★IO]
Frontiers of Am. [★11778]
Frontiers in Educ. Conference [★8366]
Frontiers in Educ. Conference [★IO]
Frontiers Found. [IO], Toronto, ON, Canada
Frontiers of Freedom [5602], PO Box 69, Oakton, VA 22124, (703)246-0110
Frontiers Intl. [11778], 6301 Crittenden St., Philadelphia, PA 19138, (414)445-7661
Frontiers Intl. [IO], Philadelphia, PA, United States
Frontlash - Address unknown since 2003.
Frontline Hepatitis Awareness [14806], 701 W Elizabeth St., No. 54, Monroe, WA 98272, (360)805-1700
Frost; Friends of Robert [10860]
Frost Insulators and Asbestos Workers; Intl. Assn. of Heat and [24093]
Frozen Dessert and Fast Food Assn; Natl. [1958]
Frozen Food Assn; Natl. [★1547]
Frozen Food Distributors Assn; Natl. [★1547]
Frozen Food Distributors Assn; Natl. Wholesale [★1547]
Frozen Food Inst; Amer. [1496]
Frozen Food Locker Inst. [★2656]
Frozen Food Packers; Natl. Assn. of [★1496]
Frozen Foods Action Communications Team [★1496]
Frozen Onion Ring Packers Coun. [★1496]
Frozen Pea Coun. - Defunct.
Frozen Pizza Inst; Natl. [1546]
Frozen Potato Products Inst. [1515], 2000 Corporate Ridge, Ste. 1000, McLean, VA 22102, (703)821-0770
Frozen and Refrigerated Foods Assn; Natl. [1547]
Frozen Vegetable Coun. - Defunct.
Frugal Brugal Soc. - Defunct.
Frugi Venta [★IO]
Frugi Venta: Groenten en Fruit Handelsplatform Nederland [★IO]
Fruit Assn. of California; Dried [★4726]
Fruit Assn; California Grape and Tree [★4716]
Fruit Assn. of New York; Dried [★1503]
Fruit Coun; Rare [★4760]
Fruit Explorers; North Amer. [22531]
Fruit Growers Exchange; California [★4763]
Fruit Jobbers Assn; Western [★4766]
Fruit Shippers Assn; Florida Express [★4731]
Fruit Shippers Assn; Florida Gift [4731]
Fruit Testing Assn. Nursery - Defunct.
Fruit Trade Assn. Netherlands [IO], The Hague, Netherlands
Fruit Tree Assn; Dwarf [★5257]
Fruit Tree Assn; Intl. Dwarf [★5257]
Fruit and Vegetable Distributors; Natl. League of Wholesale Fresh [★4766]
Fruit and Vegetable Shippers Assn; Amer. [★4766]
Fruit Wine and Cider Makers of New Zealand [IO], New Plymouth, New Zealand
Fruitarian Network - Address unknown since 1989.
Fruitarian Worldwide Network [IO], Trinity Beach, Australia
Fruition Project - Defunct.
Fruits, Flavors and Syrups; Natl. Assn. of [★1539]
Fruits and Vegetables
   Amer. Cranberry Growers Assn. [4702]
   Amer. Mushroom Inst. [4703]

Amer. Pomological Soc. [4704]
Apple and Pear Growers Assn. of South Australia [IO]
Apple Processors Assn. [1673]
Apple Products Res. and Educ. Coun. [4705]
Apricot Producers of California [4706]
Asian Cassava Res. Network [IO]
Asian and Pacific Coconut Community [IO]
Asian Vegetable Res. and Development Center [IO]
Asparagus Growers Assn. [IO]
Assn. of Danish Fruit and Vegetables Indus. [IO]
Assn. of Fruit and Vegetable Inspection and Standardization Agencies [1674]
Assn. of Fruit and Vegetable Retailers [IO]
Assn. of Fruit and Vegetable Wholesalers [IO]
Assn. for the Improvement in Production and Utilisation of Banana [IO]
Australian Banana Growers' Coun. [IO]
Australian Chamber of Fruit and Vegetable Indus. [IO]
Australian Citrus Growers [IO]
Australian Dried Fruits Assn. [IO]
Australian Mushroom Growers Assn. [IO]
Australian Olive Assn. [IO]
Australian Vegetables and Potato Growers' Fed. [IO]
Ball Collectors Club [22551]
Belize Citrus Growers Assn. [IO]
Brazilian Assn. for Citrus Exporters [IO]
Brazilian Assn. of Vegetable Oil Indus. [IO]
British Assn. of Green Crop Driers [IO]
British Leafy Salads Assn. [IO]
Burnett Valley Olive Growers Assn. [IO]
California Avocado Commn. [4707]
California Avocado Soc. [4708]
California Canning Peach Assn. [4709]
California Cling Peach Bd. [4710]
California Date Administrative Comm. [4711]
California Dried Plum Bd. [4712]
California Dry Bean Advisory Bd. [4713]
California Fig Advisory Bd. [4714]
California Fig Inst. [4715]
California Grape and Tree Fruit League [4716]
California Kiwifruit Commn. [4717]
California Melon Res. Bd. [4718]
California Rare Fruit Growers [4719]
California Strawberry Commn. [4720]
California Table Grape Commn. [4721]
Canadian Mushroom Growers' Assn. [IO]
Caribbean Banana Exporters Assn. [IO]
Caribbean Fruit Network [IO]
Central Victorian Olive Growers Assn. [IO]
Central West Olive Growers Assn. [IO]
Cherry Central Cooperative [4722]
Cherry Marketing Inst. [4723]
Citrus Marketing Bd. of Israel [IO]
Co-operative Citrus Growers' Assn. of Trinidad and Tobago [IO]
Concord Grape Assn. [4724]
Cranberry Inst. [4725]
Czech Seed Trade Assn. [IO]
Danish Seed Trade Assn. [IO]
DFA of California [4726]
Dutch Fruit Growers' Org. [IO]
European Assn. for Potato Res. [IO]
European Org. of Tomato Indus. [IO]
Florida Citrus Mutual [4727]
Florida Citrus Nurserymen's Assn. [4728]
Florida Dept. of Citrus [4729]
Florida Fruit and Vegetable Assn. [4730]
Florida Gift Fruit Shippers Assn. [4731]
Florida Lychee Growers Assn. [4732]
Florida Tomato Comm. [4733]
Fresh Fruit-Vegetables Exporters' Union [IO]
Fresh Produce Consortium - UK [IO]
Fuellers' Company [IO]
Geelong and District Olive Assn. [IO]
Gippsland Olive Growers Assn. [IO]
Goulbourn Strathbogie Olive Growers Assn. [IO]
Great Southern Olive Assn. [IO]
Gunnedah Olive Growers Assn. [IO]
Home Orchard Soc. [4734]
Hunter Olive Assn. [IO]
Idaho Potato Commn. [4735]

Inglewood Region Olive Co-operative [IO]
International Banana Association [IO]
Intl. Banana Assn. [4736]
Intl. Banana Club [22596]
Intl. Connoisseurs of Green and Red Chile [22572]
Intl. Gen. Produce Assn. [IO]
Intl. Jelly and Preserve Assn. [1530]
Intl. Org. of Citrus Virologists [6638]
Intl. Potato Center [IO]
Intl. Pulse Trade and Indus. Confed. [IO]
International Society of Citriculture [IO]
Intl. Soc. of Citriculture [4737]
Intl. Soc. for Mushroom Sci. [IO]
Inverell and District Olive Growers Assn. [IO]
Jordan Exporters and Producers Assn. of Fruit and Vegetables [IO]
Juice Products Assn. [510]
Kolan Olive Growers Assn. [IO]
Leafy Greens Coun. [4738]
The Leek Growers Assn. [IO]
Maize Assn. of Australia [IO]
Malaysian Pineapple Indus. Bd. [IO]
Margaret River Olive Indus. Assn. [IO]
Michigan Apple Comm. [4739]
Michigan Assn. of Cherry Producers [4740]
Mid North Coast Olive Assn. [IO]
Midwest Olive Assn. [IO]
Moore River Olive Assn. [IO]
Mornington Peninsula Olive Assn. [IO]
Mudgee Olives Assn. [IO]
Mushroom Growers Assn. [IO]
Natl. Assn. of Exporters and Importers of Fruit, Vegetables and Citrus Fruits [IO]
Natl. Assn. of Farmers' Market Nutrition Programs [4648]
Natl. Assn. of Flavors and Food-Ingredient Systems [1539]
Natl. Assn. of Preserved Vegetable Indus. [IO]
Natl. Assn. of Produce Market Managers [5022]
Natl. Assn. of Retail Grocers of Australia [IO]
Natl. Cherry Growers and Indus. Found. [4741]
Natl. Dried Fruit Trade Assn. [IO]
Natl. Fed. of Preserved Vegetable Indus. Associations [IO]
Natl. Fed. of Seed Potato Growers [IO]
Natl. Fed. of Vegetable Producers [IO]
Natl. Interprofessional Off. of Fruit, Vegetables and Horticulture [IO]
Natl. Mushroom Growers' Assn. [4742]
Natl. Onion Assn. [4743]
Natl. Peach Coun. [4744]
Natl. Peach Partners [4745]
Natl. Potato Coun. [4746]
Natl. Union of Olive Growers Associations [IO]
Natl. Vegetable Soc. [IO]
Natl. Watermelon Assn. [4747]
New Jersey Asparagus Indus. Coun. [4748]
New York Wine/Grape Found. [5417]
New Zealand Avocado Growers Assn. [IO]
New Zealand Fruitgrowers' Fed. [IO]
New Zealand Vegetable and Potato Growers' Fed. [IO]
North Amer. Blueberry Coun. [4749]
North Amer. Bramble Growers Res. Found. [1675]
North Amer. Farmers' Direct Marketing Assn. [5026]
North Amer. Fruit Explorers [22531]
North Amer. Strawberry Growers Assn. [4750]
North American Strawberry Growers Association [IO]
Northwest Cherry Growers [4751]
Northwest Fruit Exporters [4752]
Northwest Horticultural Coun. [4753]
Olive Assn. Midnorth South Australia [IO]
Olive Producers (North East Victoria) [IO]
Olives South Australia [IO]
Paw Paw Found. [4754]
Pear Bur. Northwest [4755]
Peel Olive Assn. [IO]
Phylloxera and Grape Indus. Bd. of South Australia [IO]
Pineapple Growers Assn. of Hawaii [4756]
Potato Assn. of Am. [4757]
Processed Vegetable Growers Assn. [IO]

A star before a book entry number signifies that the name is not listed separately, but is mentioned within the entry.

Produce Marketing Assn. [5028]
Queensland Olive Coun. [IO]
Raisin Administrative Comm. [4758]
Raisin Bargaining Assn. [4759]
Rare Fruit Coun. Intl. [4760]
Rare Fruit Coun. Intl. [IO]
Res. and Breeding Inst. of Pomology Holovousy [IO]
Riverina Olive Growers Assn. [IO]
Seed Savers Exchange [22540]
Singapore Fruits and Vegetables Importers and Exporters Assn. [IO]
South African Avocado Growers' Assn. [IO]
South East Queensland Olive Assn. [IO]
South West Olive Assn. [IO]
Southern Flinders Olive Growers Assn. [IO]
Spanish Exporters and Mfrs. of Table Olives Assn. [IO]
Specialty Crop Trade Coun. [4761]
Summerland Olives [IO]
Sun-Maid Growers of California [4762]
Sunkist Growers [4763]
Sunsweet Growers [4764]
Swan-Avon Olive Assn. [IO]
Tamworth and District Olive Growers Assn. [IO]
Tasmanian Olive Coun. [IO]
Tomato Genetics Cooperative [IO]
Tomato Genetics Cooperative [4765]
Union of Czech and Moravian Producer Co-Operatives [IO]
United Fresh Produce Assn. [4766]
United Kingdom Vineyards Assn. [IO]
United Soybean Bd. [4767]
U.S. Apple Assn. [4768]
U.S. Apple Association [IO]
U.S. Dry Bean Coun. [4769]
U.S. Potato Bd. [4770]
U.S. Sweet Potato Coun. [4771]
Valley Fig Growers [4772]
Victorian Olive Coun. [IO]
Washington State Apple Commn. [4773]
West Australian Olive Coun. [IO]
Western Growers Assn. [4774]
Western Olive Assn. [IO]
Western Victorian Olive Assn. [IO]
Wild Blueberry Association of North America [IO]
Wild Blueberry Assn. of North Am. [4775]
World Apple and Pear Assn. [IO]
World Processing Tomato Coun. [IO]
York and Districts Olive Assn. [IO]
ZESPRI Intl. [IO]

Fry Glass Soc; H.C. [22556]
FSC/DISC Tax Assn. [★2281]
FSC/DISC Tax Assn. [★IO]
FSC/DISC Tax Club [★IO]
FSC/DISC Tax Club [★2281]
FSC Rural Training and Res. Center [★12937]
FSU - Investing in Families [IO], London, United Kingdom
FTD Assn. - Defunct.
Fuchsia Soc; Amer. [22488]
Fuchsia Soc; Natl. [22527]
Fudan Museum Found. [10504], 4206 73rd Terr. E, Sarasota, FL 34243-5112, (941)351-8208
Fudan Museum Found. [IO], Sarasota, FL, United States

Fuel
  Amer. Coal Found. [837]
  Amer. Gas Assn. [1676]
  Amer. Public Gas Assn. [3951]
  Assn. of Diesel Specialists [1290]
  Assn. of State Energy Res. and Tech. Transfer Institutions [6945]
  Assn. for the Stud. of Peak Oil and Gas - USA [7461]
  Belgium Fed. of Fuel Suppliers [IO]
  Biomass Energy Res. Assn. [6946]
  Canadian Energy Pipeline Assn. [IO]
  Canadian Oil Heat Assn. [IO]
  Canadian Renewable Fuels Assn. [IO]
  Croatian Gas Assn. [IO]
  Czech Gas Assn. [IO]
  Egyptian Gas Assn. [IO]
  Energy Frontiers Intl. [IO]
  Energy Frontiers Intl. [1677]

  Eurofuel [IO]
  European Natural Gas Vehicle Assn. [IO]
  European Union of the Natural Gas Indus. [IO]
  Gas Appliance Manufacturers Assn. [265]
  Gas Assn. of Bosnia and Herzegovina [IO]
  Gas Assn. of Serbia and Montenegro [IO]
  Gas Forum [IO]
  Gas Tech. Inst. [1678]
  Hearth, Patio and Barbeque Assn. [1679]
  Indonesian Gas Assn. [IO]
  Intl. Gas Union [IO]
  Interstate Natural Gas Assn. of Am. [1680]
  Lithuanian Gas Assn. [IO]
  Malaysian Gas Assn. [IO]
  Natl. Clean Cities [6399]
  Natl. Ethanol Vehicle Coalition [4776]
  Natl. Propane Gas Assn. [1681]
  Natural Gas Supply Assn. [1682]
  Natural Gas Vehicle Assn. [IO]
  Nigerian Gas Assn. [IO]
  Paraffin Safety Assn. of Southern Africa [IO]
  Pellet Fuels Inst. [1683]
  Renewable Fuels Assn. [6971]
  Rushlight Club [10396]
  Solid Fuel Assn. [IO]
  Southern African Biofuels Assn. [IO]
  Spanish Gas Assn. [IO]
  Swedish Gas Assn. [IO]
  US Fuel Cell Coun. [6976]
Fuel Cell Inst. - Defunct.
Fuel Cells; Amer. Assn. for [6937]
Fuel Inst; Natl. Oil [★2943]
Fuel Oxygenates Assn; European [IO]
Fuellers' Company [IO], London, United Kingdom
Fuels Assn; Renewable [6971]
Fuels Development Coalition; Clean [5086]
Fuels Inst; Fiber [★1683]
Fuels Production; Natl. Coun. of Synthetic [★1677]
Fuels Res. Coun. - Defunct.
Fueraz Armadas de Liberacion Nacional Puertor-riquena - Address unknown since 1997.
Fuerza Unida - Address unknown since 1999.
F.U.G.I.T.I.V.E.S. [25028]
Fulbright Assn. [8613], 666 11th St. NW, Ste. 525, Washington, DC 20001, (202)347-5543
Fulbright Assn. [IO], Washington, DC, United States
Fulbright Assn. of Alumni of Intl. Educational and Cultural Exchange [★IO]
Fulbright Assn. of Alumni of Intl. Educational and Cultural Exchange [★8613]
Fulbright Assn. of Uzbekistan [IO], Tashkent, Uzbeki-stan
Fuld Hea. Trust; Helene [15480]
Fulfillment Mgt. Assn. [3224], 60 E 42nd St., Ste. 1166, New York, NY 10165, (303)604-7362
Fulfillment Ser. Assn; Mailing and [108]
Full Circle Associates - Defunct.
Full Employment Action Coun. - Defunct.
Full Gospel Bus. Men's Fellowship Intl. [19801], 3 Holland, Irvine, CA 92618, (949)461-0100
Full Gospel Bus. Men's Fellowship Intl. [IO], Irvine, CA, United States
Full Gospel Evangelistic Assn. - Address unknown since 2003.
Full Gospel Student Fellowship - Address unknown since 2002.
Full Gospel Women Clergy; Assn. of [20275]
Full Straps Roosevelt Dime Club - Defunct.
Fullam Family Org. [20907]
Fuller Evangelistic Assn. - Address unknown since 1999.
Fuller Found. [13118], c/o John T. Bottomley, Exec. Dir., PO Box 479, Rye Beach, NH 03871, (603)964-6998
Fuller Found; Friends of Buckminster [★11104]
Fuller Inst; Buckminster [11104]
Fuller Soc. [20908], c/o John Hoffman, 42 Sugar Maple Ln., Tinton Falls, NJ 07724-2716
Fully Informed Jury Assn. [17960], PO Box 5570, Helena, MT 59604-5570, (406)442-7800
Fumigators; Natl. Assn. of Exterminators and [★2910]
Function Point Users Gp; Intl. [734]
Functional Jaw Stud. Club; Northern Virginia [★14115]

Functional Orthodontics; Amer. Assn. for [14115]
Functional Orthodontists; Amer. Assn. of [★14115]
Fund for the Advancement of Education - Defunct.
Fund for the Advancement of Music Education - Defunct.
Fund for an Amer. Renaissance - Address unknown since 1989.
The Fund for Amer. Stud. [8747], 1706 New Hampshire Ave. NW, Washington, DC 20009, (202)986-0384
The Fund for Amer. Stud. [IO], Washington, DC, United States
Fund for America's Future - Defunct.
Fund for Animals [11398], 200 W 57th St., New York, NY 10019, (212)246-2096
Fund for Artists' Colonies - Defunct.
Fund for Assuring an Independent Retirement [5709], c/o Natl. Assn. of Letter Carriers, 100 Indiana Ave. NW, Ste. 813, Washington, DC 20001-2144, (202)393-4695
Fund for a Conservative Majority - Defunct.
Fund for Constitutional Govt. [17669], 122 Maryland Ave. NE, Washington, DC 20002, (202)546-3799
Fund for Dance - Address unknown since 2001.
Fund for a Democratic Majority [★17401]
Fund for Dental Educ. [★8196]
Fund for Education in Economics - Address unknown since 1995.
Fund for Educ. in World Order [★18834]
Fund for Episcopal Colleges [★8397]
Fund for Episcopal Colleges [★IO]
Fund for the Feminist Majority [★17532]
Fund of Funds Assn. [★2333]
Fund of Funds Assn. [★IO]
Fund for Horses [IO], Houston, TX, United States
Fund for Horses [4159], 1918 Restridge Dr., Houston, TX 77055, (713)650-1973
Fund for Human Dignity - Address unknown since 1995.
Fund for Human Rights [★17159]
Fund for Integrative Biomedical Res. - Defunct.
Fund for Investigative Journalism [17178], PO Box 60184, Washington, DC 20039-0184, (202)362-0260
Fund for Labor Defense - Address unknown since 2002.
Fund for Lesbian and Gay Scholarships - Address unknown since 2004.
Fund for Librarians; Natl. Freedom [★17040]
Fund for Life - Defunct.
Fund for Modern Courts [5901], 351 W 54th St., New York, NY 10019, (212)541-6741
Fund for Multinational Mgt. Education - Address unknown since 1999.
Fund for New Leadership - Defunct.
Fund for New Priorities in Am. [18297], 171 Madison Ave., New York, NY 10016, (212)685-8848
Fund for Objective News Reporting [17179], 1 Mas-sachusetts Ave. NW, Ste. 600, Washington, DC 20001, (202)216-0600
Fund for Open Information and Accountability - Defunct.
Fund for an OPEN Soc. [17819], The Map Bldg., 515 Valley St., Ste. 170, Maplewood, NJ 07040, (973)821-4198
Fund for Peace [18834], 1701 K St. NW, 11th Fl., Washington, DC 20006, (202)223-7940
Fund for Peaceful Atomic Development - Defunct.
Fund for Podiatric Medical Educ. [16044], c/o Amer. Podiatric Medical Assn., 9312 Old Georgetown Rd., Bethesda, MD 20814, (301)581-9200
Fund Raisers and Direct Sellers; Assn. of [★1684]
Fund Raisers; Natl. Assn. of Prdt. [★1684]
Fund Raisers; Natl. Soc. of [★12197]
Fund Raising Executives; Natl. Soc. of [★12197]
Fund for the Relief of Russian Writers and Scientists in Exile - Address unknown since 1999.
Fund for Renewable Energy and the Env. [★7677]
Fund for Renewable Energy and the Env. [★IO]
Fund for a Republican Majority - Defunct.
Fund to Restore an Educated Electorate - Defunct.
Fund for Special Operations [★17460]
Fund for Special Operations [★IO]
Fund for Stockowners Rights [17351], c/o Carl Ol-son, Chm., PO Box 65398, Washington, DC 20035

Reference to "IO" in place of a book number signifies that the association may be found in the 45th edition of International Organizations.

Fund for Theological Education - Defunct.
Fund; Tibet [11055]
Fund for UFO Res. [7474], PO Box 7501, Alexandria, VA 22307
Fundacao Brasileira para a Conservacao da Natureza [★IO]
Fundacao Dalmo Giacometti [★IO]
Fundacao de Estudos do Mar [★IO]
Fundacao Grupo Esquel Brasil [★IO]
Fundacao Joaquim Nabuco [★IO]
Fundacao Pro-TAMAR [IO], Salvador, Brazil
Fundacio per la Pau [★IO]
Fundacion mujeres en igualdad [★IO]
Fundacion Acindar [★IO]
Fundacion Alfa-1 de Puerto Rico [IO], Bayamon, PR, United States
Fundacion Alfa-1 de Puerto Rico [16360], 2000 Carr. 8177, Ste. 26, PMB 318, Guaynabo, PR 00966-3762, (787)743-0268
Fundacion Alzheimer Espana [IO], Madrid, Spain
Fundacion Ambiente y Recursos Naturales [★IO]
Fundacion Anisa [★IO]
Fundacion Antidrogas de El Salvador [IO], San Salvador, El Salvador
Fundacion Arias para la Paz y el Progreso Humano [★IO]
Fundacion de Asistencia Sicopedagogica para Ninos, Adolescentes y Adultos con Retardo Mental [IO], Guayaquil, Ecuador
Fundacion Augusto Cesar Sandino [★IO]
Fundacion Bariloche [★IO]
Fundacion Boliviana para el Desarrollo de la Mujer [IO], Santa Cruz, Bolivia
Fundacion Braille del Uruguay [★IO]
Fundacion Centro de Investigacion y Accion Social [★IO]
Fundacion Charles Darwin para las Islas Galapagos [★IO]
Fundacion para el Desarrollo Agropecuario [★IO]
Fundacion para el Desarrollo en Justicia y Paz [IO], Buenos Aires, Argentina
Fundacion Emprender [★IO]
Fundacion Eugenio Espejo [IO], Guayaquil, Ecuador
Fundacion Golondrinas [★IO]
Fundacion Hondurena de Investigacion Agricola [★IO]
Fundacion ICPR Junior Coll. [★IO]
Fundacion ICPR Junior Coll. [★8022]
Fundacion Internacional Josep Carreras [★IO]
Fundacion para la Inversion y Desarrollo de Exportaciones [★IO]
Fundacion de Investigaciones Economicas Latinoamericanas [★IO]
Fundacion Juconi [IO], Puebla, Mexico
Fundacion Mario Santo Domingo [★IO]
Fundacion Mbong [★IO]
Fundacion Mexicana para la Planeacion Familiar [★IO]
Fundacion Nacional de Parques Zoologicos y Acuarios [★IO]
Fundacion Natura Colombia [IO], Bogota, Colombia
Fundacion Nuestros Jovenes [★IO]
Fundacion Operacion Sonrisa Panama [★IO]
Fundacion Paniamor [IO], San Jose, Costa Rica
Fundacion Para El Desarrollo Comunitario [★IO]
Fundacion Para Estudio e Investigacion de la Mujer [★IO]
Fundacion Puntos de Encuentro [IO], Managua, Nicaragua
Fundacion Sabiduria del Corazon [★IO]
Fundacion SARTAWI [IO], La Paz, Bolivia
Fundacion Uruguaya de Cooperacion y Desarrollo Solidarios [★IO]
Fundacion Vida Silvestre Argentina [★IO]
Fundacion de Viviendas Hogar de Cristo [★IO]
Fundacja Pogranicze [★IO]
Fundacja Stefana Batorego [★IO]
Fundamental Ministerial Assn. [★19977]
Fundamentalism
  Toward Tradition [20508]
Fundamentalists Anonymous - Address unknown since 1999.
Fundatia Biblia Pentru Toti din Romania [★IO]
Fundatia pentru o Societate Deschisa - Romania [★IO]

Funders' Collaborative on Youth Organizing [12718], 183 Madison Ave., Ste. 919, New York, NY 10016, (212)725-3386
Funders Comm. for Citizenship Participation - Address unknown since 1999.
Funders Gp; Neighborhood [12734]
Fundesarrollo [IO], Barranquilla, Colombia
Funding; Ad Hoc Gp. for Medical Res. [17686]
Funding Res. Coun; Educ. [8348]
Fundraising
  Alliance for Communities in Action [12416]
  ALSAC/Saint Jude Children's Res. Hosp. [13946]
  Amer. Charities for Reasonable Fundraising Regulation [12195]
  Amer. Friends of the Anglican Centre in Rome [19451]
  Amer. German Shepherd Rescue Assn. [11348]
  Amer. Inst. of Philanthropy [12709]
  America's Charities [12196]
  Amyloidosis Support Groups [14250]
  Assn. of Fund-Raising Distributors and Suppliers [1684]
  Assn. of Fundraising Professional Edmonton and Area Chap. [IO]
  Assn. of Fundraising Professionals [12197]
  Assn. of Fundraising Professionals Manitoba Chap. [IO]
  Assn. of Fundraising Professionals Nova Scotia [IO]
  Assn. of Fundraising Professionals - Ottawa Chap. [IO]
  Assn. for Healthcare Philanthropy [14871]
  Assn. for Intl. Medical Study [12834]
  Assn. of Professional Researchers for Advancement [12198]
  Assumption Guild [19580]
  Better World Chorus [12617]
  Bike and Build [11514]
  Bread for the Journey Intl. [12711]
  Broadway Cares/Equity Fights AIDS [11326]
  CASE Matching Gifts CH [12199]
  Christmas Seal and Charity Stamp Soc. [21993]
  Comm. to Encourage Corporate Philanthropy [12714]
  Community Hea. Charities [12200]
  Coun. for Advancement and Support of Educ. [8245]
  Coun. on Foundations [12652]
  Direct Marketing Fundraisers Assn. [1685]
  Entertainment Indus. Found. [12114]
  European Assn. for Planned Giving [IO]
  FACES: The Natl. Craniofacial Assn. [14061]
  Found. Center [12653]
  Giving Inst. [1686]
  Grantmakers in the Arts [12722]
  Grantmakers for Children, Youth, and Families [12723]
  Grantmakers Without Borders [12724]
  The Grantsmanship Center [1687]
  Hearing Found. of Canada [IO]
  Help Darfur Now [12259]
  Hunters Helping Hunters [22604]
  Independent Charities of Am. [1688]
  Intl. Found. for Terror Act Victims [12942]
  Intl. Open Finance Assn. [17584]
  Intimate Apparel Square Club [12201]
  Islamic Relief USA [12865]
  Lewa Wildlife Conservancy (USA) [5337]
  Ludwick Family Found. [17646]
  Meals4Israel [12459]
  Natl. Assn. of State Charity Officials [5769]
  Natl. Black United Fund [12656]
  Natl. Comm. on Planned Giving [1689]
  Natl. Found. for Transplants [16678]
  Natl. Network of Grantmakers [12202]
  North Amer. YMCA Development Org. [13461]
  North Star Fund [12657]
  Parents Against Childhood Epilepsy [14382]
  Parkinson Alliance [15359]
  PBCers Org. [14816]
  PEF Israel Endowment Funds [12461]
  Philanthropy Roundtable [12735]
  Social Enterprise Alliance [3633]
  Sports Charities USA [23854]
  Students Helping St. Kids Intl. [11725]

  Support Our Shelters [11462]
  TelecomPioneers [12203]
  United Black Fund [12204]
  United Charity Institutions of Jerusalem [12462]
  United Jewish Appeal - Fed. of Jewish Philanthropies of New York [12482]
  United Jewish Communities [12483]
  United Way of Am. [12205]
  United Way of Canada - Centraide Canada [IO]
  United Way Intl. [IO]
  United Way Intl. [12206]
  U.S.A. for Africa [12882]
  WISH List [5770]
  Women, Children and Family Ser. Charities of Am. [12207]
  Women's Funding Network [13450]
Funds Transfer Assn; Electronic [471]
Fundza [IO], Mbabane, Swaziland
Funeral
  Amer. Soc. of Embalmers [2773]
  Assoc. Funeral Directors Intl. [2774]
  Casket and Funeral Supply Assn. of Am. [2775]
  Catholic Cemetery Conf. [2776]
  Cremation Assn. of North Am. [2777]
  Federated Funeral Directors of Am. [2778]
  Flying Funeral Directors of America [2779]
  Funeral Consumers Alliance [2780]
  Funeral Ser. Consumer Assistance Prog. [17330]
  Hebrew Free Burial Assn. [20141]
  Intl. Cemetery and Funeral Assn. [2781]
  Intl. Order of the Golden Rule [2783]
  Jewish Funeral Directors of Am. [2784]
  Natl. Funeral Directors Assn. [2788]
  Natl. Funeral Directors and Morticians Assn. [2789]
  Preferred Funeral Directors Intl. [2790]
  WTC Families For Proper Burial [13312]
Funeral Consumers Alliance [2780], 33 Patchen Rd., South Burlington, VT 05403, (802)865-8300
Funeral Directors of Am; Advt. [★2790]
Funeral Directors of Am; Federated [2778]
Funeral Directors of America; Flying [2779]
Funeral Directors of Am; Jewish [2784]
Funeral Directors Assn; Natl. [2788]
Funeral Directors Assn. of New Zealand [IO], Wellington, New Zealand
Funeral Directors Intl; Assoc. [2774]
Funeral Directors and Morticians Assn; Natl. [2789]
Funeral Directors and Morticians Assn; Natl. Negro [★2789]
Funeral Directors; Natl. Assn. of [IO]
Funeral Directors; Natl. Soc. of Allied and Independent [IO]
Funeral Directors Ser; Assoc. [★2774]
Funeral Directors Ser. Intl; Assoc. [★2774]
Funeral Furnishing Mfrs. Assn. [IO], Solihull, United Kingdom
Funeral Home Public Service Group Intl. - Defunct.
Funeral Homes; Selected Independent [2791]
Funeral and Memorial Societies of Am. [★2780]
Funeral and Memorial Societies; Continental Assn. of [★2780]
Funeral Plans; Natl. Assn. for Pre-Paid [IO]
Funeral Ser. Assn. of Canada [IO], Aurora, ON, Canada
Funeral Ser. Consumer Assistance Prog. [17330], 13625 Bishop Dr., Brookfield, WI 53005-6607, (877)402-5900
Funeral Ser. Educ; Amer. Bd. of [8896]
Funeral Ser. Examining Boards of the U.S; Conf. of [★6120]
Funeral Ser. Examining Boards of the U.S; Intl. Conf. of [6120]
Funeral Supply Assn. of Am; Casket and [2775]
Fungi
  Intl. Mycological Assn. [7351]
  Medical Mycological Soc. of the Americas [15275]
  Nordic Lichen Soc. [IO]
Fungi; People to People Comm. on [★7353]
Fungicide Assn; Agricultural Insecticide and [★807]
Fungicide Manufacturers Assn; Agricultural Insecticides and [★807]
Funk Aircraft Owners Assn. [21449], c/o Thad Shelnutt; Treas., 2836 California Ave., Carmichael, CA 95608, (916)971-3452

A star before a book entry number signifies that the name is not listed separately, but is mentioned within the entry.

Funksjonshemmeds Fellesorganisasjon [★IO]
Funny Car Series; Amer. [23070]
Fuqua(y) Family Assn. [20909]
Fur-Bearer Defenders [★IO]
Fur Brokers Assn. of America - Defunct.
Fur Buyers Assn., Coat and Suit Industry - Address unknown since 1995.
Fur Commn. U.S.A. [11399], 826 Orange Ave., PMB 506, Coronado, CA 92118-2619, (619)575-0139
Fur Coun. of Canada [IO], Montreal, QC, Canada
Fur Dressers Guild - Address unknown since 1995.
Fur Finland [IO], Vantaa, Finland
Fur Free Alliance [IO], Washington, DC, United States
Fur Free Alliance [4153], c/o Andrea Cimino, 2100 L St. NW, Washington, DC 20037, (301)258-3109
Fur Free Am; Campaign for a [★11358]
Fur and Hemlock Assn. - Defunct.
Fur Industrialists and Businessmen Assn. [IO], Istanbul, Turkey
Fur Indus; Amer. [★236]
Fur Info. Coun. of Am. [236], 8424 A Santa Monica Blvd., No. 860, West Hollywood, CA 90069, (323)782-1700
Fur Inst. of Canada [IO], Ottawa, ON, Canada
Fur Sheep Registry; Amer. Karakul [★5186]
Fur Sheep Registry; Karakul [★5186]
Fur Takers of Am. [5250], c/o Ramona Plueger, Membership Coor., 17453 130th Ave., Monticello, IA 52310
Fur Wholesalers Assn. of America - Address unknown since 1990.
Furbearers; Defenders of [★5307]
Furnace, Energy, and Allied Appliance Workers Division of the Intl. Brotherhood of Boilermakers; Stove, [24001]
Furnace Mfrs. Assn; Indus. [★1885]
Furnishing Indus. Assn. of Australia [IO], Newington, Australia
Furnishings Assn; Natl. Home [1703]
Furnishings Assn; Western Home [1709]
Furnishings Forum; Contract [★1698]
Furnishings Intl. Assn; Home [1697]
Furnishings Market Authority; Intl. Home [1701]
Furnishings Marketing Assn; Intl. Home [★1701]
Furnishings Representatives Assn; Natl. Home [★1702]
Furnishings Suppliers; Assn. of Woodworking and [4058]

Furniture
  Amer. Home Furnishings Alliance [1690]
  Amer. Soc. of Furniture Designers [1691]
  Assn. for Development and Innovation of the Furniture Indus. [IO]
  Assn. of Master Upholsterers and Soft Furnishers [IO]
  Baby Products Assn. [IO]
  Brazilian Assn. of Furniture Indus. [IO]
  British Furniture Mfrs. [IO]
  Bus. and Institutional Furniture Manufacturer's Assn. [1692]
  Canadian Kitchen Cabinet Assn. [IO]
  Cast Iron Seat Collectors Assn. [22607]
  Casual Furniture Retailers [1693]
  Central Alliance of Furniture Mfrs. [IO]
  Chamber of Furniture Indus. of the Philippines [IO]
  Chamber of Furniture Mfrs. [IO]
  Contemporary Design Gp. [1694]
  European Down and Feather Assn. [IO]
  European Furniture Mfrs. Fed. [IO]
  Fed. Assn. of Dealers of Furniture and Interior Products [IO]
  Found. for Design Integrity [1152]
  Furnishing Indus. Assn. of Australia [IO]
  Furniture Indus. Res. Assn. [IO]
  Furniture Soc. [1695]
  Furniture and Wood Products Assn. of Ghana [IO]
  Futon Assn. Intl. [IO]
  Futon Assn. Intl. [1696]
  Hardwood Coun. [4056]
  Home Furnishings Intl. Assn. [1697]
  Independent Off. Products and Furniture Dealers Assn. [1698]
  Indonesian Furniture Indus. and Handicraft Assn. [IO]

Inst. of Inspection, Cleaning and Restoration Certification [2259]
Intl. Development Assn. of the Furniture Indus. of Japan [IO]
Intl. Furnishings and Design Assn. [2264]
Intl. Furniture Rental Assn. [1699]
Intl. Furniture Rental Assn. [IO]
Intl. Furniture Suppliers Assn. [IO]
Intl. Furniture Suppliers Assn. [1700]
Intl. Home Furnishings Market Authority [1701]
Intl. Home Furnishings Representatives Assn. [1702]
Intl. Home Furnishings Representatives Assn. [IO]
Intl. Union of Electronic, Elecl., Salaried, Machine, and Furniture Workers [24049]
Italian Fed. of the Wool, Cork, Furniture and Furnishing Indus. [IO]
Korea Fed. of Furniture Indus. Cooperatives [IO]
Leisure and Outdoor Furniture Assn. [IO]
Malaysian Furniture Indus. Coun. [IO]
Natl. Bed Fed. [IO]
Natl. Fed. of Furniture Traders [IO]
National Home Furnishings Association [IO]
Natl. Home Furnishings Assn. [1703]
Off. Furniture Recyclers Forum [1704]
Set Decorators Soc. of Am. [2276]
Singapore Furniture Assn. [IO]
Singapore Furniture Indus. Coun. [IO]
Soc. of Amer. Period Furniture Makers [9970]
Soft Furnishing Indus. Assn. of Australia [IO]
Soft Furnishing Indus. Assn. of Australia - New South Wales [IO]
Soft Furnishing Indus. Assn. of Australia - Queensland [IO]
Soft Furnishing Indus. Assn. of Australia - South Australia [IO]
Soft Furnishing Indus. Assn. of Australia - Tasmania [IO]
Soft Furnishing Indus. Assn. of Australia - Victoria [IO]
Soft Furnishing Indus. Assn. of Australia - Western Australia [IO]
Specialty Sleep Assn. [1705]
Summer and Casual Furniture Mfrs. Assn. [1706]
Swedish Furniture Indus. Assn. [IO]
Swedish Furniture Retailers' Assn. [IO]
Thai Furniture Indus. Assn. [IO]
Unfinished Furniture Assn. [1707]
United Furniture Workers Insurance Fund [24065]
Upholstered Furniture Action Coun. [1708]
Western Home Furnishings Assn. [1709]
Wooton Desk Owners Soc. [22131]
Furniture Assn; Natl. Retail [★1703]
Furniture Assn; Natl. Wholesale [★1700]
Furniture and Bedding Spring Inst. - Defunct.
Furniture Club of America - Defunct.
Furniture Dealers Alliance; Off. [★1698]
Furniture Distribution Assn; Off. [4025]
Furniture Factories Marketing Assn. of the South [★1701]
Furniture Flammability Comm. [★1708]
Furniture Forum; Budget [★1704]
Furniture Forum; Retail Off. [★1704]
Furniture History Soc. [IO], Haywards Heath, United Kingdom
Furniture Industry Consumer Advisory Panel - Address unknown since 2003.
Furniture Indus. Res. Assn. [IO], Stevenage, United Kingdom
Furniture Law Officials; Intl. Assn. of Bedding and [5823]
Furniture Mfrs. Alliance - Defunct.
Furniture Mfrs. Assn; Southern [★1690]
Furniture Mfrs; Natl. Assn. of [★1690]
Furniture Market; Southern [★1701]
Furniture Removers; Intl. Fed. of Intl. [IO]
Furniture Rental Assn. of Am. [★IO]
Furniture Rental Assn. of Am. [★1699]
Furniture Restorers Assn; British Antique [IO]
Furniture Salesmen's Assn; Natl. Wholesale [★1702]
Furniture Soc. [1695], 111 Grovewood Rd., Asheville, NC 28804, (828)255-1949
Furniture Traffic Conf; Natl. [★3570]
Furniture and Wood Products Assn. of Ghana [IO], Accra, Ghana

Furniture Workers of Am; United [★24065]
Furniture Workers Div., IUE [★24065]
Furniture Workers; Intl. Union of Electronic, Elecl., Salaried, Machine, and [24049]
Furniture Workers; Intl. Union of Electronic, Elecl., Tech., Salaried, Machine, and [★24049]
Further Poultry Processors Assn. of Canada [IO], Ottawa, ON, Canada
Furtwangler Soc. of Am; Wilhelm [9819]
Furuseth Found. for Maritime Res; Andrew [★3593]
Fusaliers - Defunct.
Fusion Bonded Coaters Assn. [★612]
Fusion Energy Found. - Address unknown since 1988.
Fusion Power Associates [6954], 2 Professional Dr., Ste. 249, Gaithersburg, MD 20879, (301)258-0545
Fusion Power Associates [IO], Gaithersburg, MD, United States
Fussballverband der Tschechischen Republik [★IO]
Futon Assn. Intl. [IO], Orlando, FL, United States
Futon Assn. Intl. [1696], 10705-7 Rocket Blvd., Orlando, FL 32824, (407)447-1706
Futon Assn. of North Am. [★1696]
Futon Assn. of North Am. [★IO]
Futsal Fed; U.S. [23862]
Future
  Assn. of Professional Futurists [7102]
  Assn. of Professional Futurists [IO]
  Earthrise [7103]
  Futuribles Intl. [IO]
  Institute for Alternative Futures [IO]
  Inst. for Alternative Futures [7104]
  Inst. for the Future [7105]
  Inst. for the Future [IO]
  Intl. Inst. of Forecasters [IO]
  Intl. Inst. of Forecasters [7106]
  Millennium Inst. [17647]
  Prog. for Res. and Documentation for a Sustainable Soc. [IO]
  Schiller Center [8453]
  World Future Soc. [7107]
  World Future Soc. [IO]
  World Transhumanist Assn. [7163]
Future 500 [1711], 335 Powell St., 14th Fl., San Francisco, CA 94102, (415)294-7775
Future Advancement of Camping - Defunct.
Future Bus. Leaders of Am. - Phi Beta Lambda [24420], 1912 Assn. Dr., Reston, VA 20191-1591, (703)860-3334
FUTURE - Defunct.
Future Engineers of America - Address unknown since 1995.
Future Farmers of Am. [★7940]
Future Farmers of Am. [★IO]
Future Fisherman Found. [23415], c/o Amer. Sportfishing Assn., 225 Reinekers Ln., Ste. 420, Alexandria, VA 22314-2875, (703)519-9691
Future of Freedom Found. [17270], 11350 Random Hills Rd., Ste. 800, Fairfax, VA 22030, (703)934-6101
Future Generations - Defunct.
Future Harvest [4089]
Future Harvest [IO], Alexandria, VA, United States
Future Homemakers of Amer. [★8417]
Future Horsemen of America - Address unknown since 1995.
Future Journalists of America - Address unknown since 2002.
Future of Man; Amer. Teilhard Assn. for the [★9632]
Future of Music Coalition [10598], 1325 13th St. NW, No. 34, Washington, DC 20005, (202)518-4117
Future Nepal [IO], Kathmandu, Nepal
Future Physicians Clubs - Defunct.
Future Problem Solving Prog. [★8158]
Future Problem Solving Prog. [★IO]
Future Problem Solving Prog. [IO], Melbourne, FL, United States
Future Problem Solving Prog. Intl. [8158], 2015 Grant Pl., Melbourne, FL 32901, (321)768-0074
Future Scientists of America - Defunct.
FutureChurch [19627], 17307 Madison Ave., Lakewood, OH 44107, (216)228-0869
Futures
  Assn. of Professional Futurists [7102]

Reference to "IO" in place of a book number signifies that the association may be found in the 45th edition of International Organizations.

CME Group [4324]
FINEX [1710]
Future 500 [1711]
Futures Indus. Assn. [1712]
Kansas City Bd. of Trade [4327]
Natl. Futures Assn. [1713]
Natl. Introducing Brokers Assn. [1714]
Futures for Children [11695], 9600 Tennyson St. NE, Albuquerque, NM 87122-2282, (505)821-2828
Futures Group - Address unknown since 1995.
Futures Indus. Assn. [1712], 2001 Pennsylvania Ave. NW, Ste. 600, Washington, DC 20006, (202)466-5460
Futures Information Network - Defunct.
Futures and Options Assn. [IO], London, United Kingdom
Futuribles Intl. [IO], Paris, France
Futurist Soc; Libertarian [18016]
Futurities of Am; Barrel [23495]
Futurliner; GM [21648]
Fuzzy Info. Processing Soc; North Amer. [6741]
Fuzzy Lop Rabbit Club; Amer. [22918]
Fylde Tramway Soc. [IO], Oldham, United Kingdom

G

G-4 Children's Coalition - Defunct.
G-Cat Class Assn. - Address unknown since 1987.
G. I. Joe Special Forces - Address unknown since 1994.
G-Jo Inst. [15745], PO Box 1460, Columbus, NC 28722-1460, (828)863-4660
G. Unger Vetlesen Found. [12719], One Rockefeller Plz., Ste. 301, New York, NY 10020-2002, (212)586-0700
G. Unger Vetlesen Foundation [IO], New York, NY, United States
Gabler Family Assn. - Defunct.
Gablers; The Mel [★9259]
Gabriel Garcia Moreno Memorial Assn. [11117], PO Box 826, Prentiss, MS 39474, (601)792-5708
Gabriel Garcia Moreno Memorial Association [IO], Prentiss, MS, United States
Gabriel Guild - Defunct.
Gabriel Marcel Soc. [10794], c/o Prof. Brendan Sweetman, PhD, Pres., Rockhurst Univ., 1100 Rockhurst Rd., Kansas City, MO 64110-2561, (816)501-4681
Gabriel Richard Inst. - Defunct.
Gabungan Komputer Nasional Malaysia [★IO]
Gabungan Persatuan-Persatuan Pengguna Malaysia [★IO]
Gabungan Perusahaan Karet Indonesia [★IO]
Gaddafi Charity Found. [★IO]
Gaddafi Intl. Found. for Charity Associations [IO], Tripoli, Libyan Arab Jamahiriya
Gadsden Purchase Refund Group - Defunct.
Gaelic Athletic Assn. [IO], Dublin, Ireland
Gaelic Cultural Society [★IO]
Gaelic Cultural Society [★11717]
Gafford Family of Am. Assn. [★20910]
Gafford Family Assn. of Am. [20910], PO Box 1416, Oxford, MS 38655, (662)234-7602
Gaia Inst. [4509], 440 City Island Ave., Bronx, NY 10464, (718)885-1906
Gaia Intl. Women's Center [IO], Moscow, Russia
Gaillimhe in Aghaidh an Chogaidh [★IO]
Gainsharing Inst. [13020], 937 N Ashland Ave., Chicago, IL 60622, (773)661-9070
Gait and Clinical Movement Anal. Soc. [14557], c/o Sahar Hassani, MS, Shriners Hosp. for Children, 2211 N Oak Park Ave., Chicago, IL 60707-3392, (773)385-5457
Gaited Horse Intl. Assn. [4882], c/o Whispering Pine Press, Inc., PO Box 1469, Spokane Valley, WA 99037-1469, (509)927-0404
GALA Choruses [★10599]
GALA: Globalization and Localization Assn. [1168], 23 Main St., Andover, MA 01810, (206)329-2596
GALA: Globalization and Localization Association [IO], Andover, MA, United States
GALA Performing Arts [★10599]
Galactic Empire - Address unknown since 1999.
Galactic Hitchhiker's Guild - Address unknown since 1995.

Galactosemic Children; Parents of [15257]
Galapagos Conservancy [4401], 407 N Washington St., Ste. 105, Falls Church, VA 22046-3436, (703)538-6833
Galapagos Islands; Charles Darwin Found. for the [IO]
Galapagos Isles; Charles Darwin Found. for the [★4401]
Galaxie Club of Am; Ford [21647]
Galaxy Patrol Fan Club [25029]
GalaxyGoo [8065], 4104 24th St., No. 349, San Francisco, CA 94114
Gale Storm Appreciation Soc. [24744], c/o Richard A. Bullis, Pres., 6119 3rd Ave. S, St. Petersburg, FL 33707, (727)381-1056
Galiceno Horse Breeders Assn. [4883]
Galilee Restoration Proj. [IO], Tzefat, Israel
Galilee Soc. [IO], Shefa-'Amr, Israel
Gallaudet Coll. Alumni Assn. [★18897]
Gallaudet Univ. Alumni Assn. [18897], PO Box 90974, Washington, DC 20090, (202)651-5060
Galleries; Assn. of Coll. and Univ. Museums and [10496]
Galleries Assn; Visual Artists and [5861]
Gallery of Living Catholic Authors - Defunct.
Gallipoli Soc. in the U.S.A. - Address unknown since 1995.
GalloSuisse - Assn. des producteurs d'oeufs suisses [★IO]
Galloway Breeders' Assn; Amer. [4222]
Galloway Cattle and Beef Marketing Assn. [IO], Hall, Australia
Galloway Cattle Breeders' Assn; Amer. Belted [★4256]
Galloway Cattle Soc. of America - Address unknown since 1995.
Galloway Cattle Soc. of Great Britain and Ireland [IO], Castle Douglas, United Kingdom
Galloway Foreningen Danmark [★IO]
Galloway Performance Intl. [★4222]
Galloway Soc; Belted [4256]
Gallups Island Radio Assn. - Defunct.
Galpin Soc. [IO], St. Albans, United Kingdom
Galvanized Ware Mfrs. Coun. - Defunct.
Galvanizers Assn. [IO], Sutton Coldfield, United Kingdom
Galvanizers Assn; Amer. [850]
Galvanizers Assn; Amer. Hot Dip [★850]
Galveston Cotton Exchange and Bd. of Trade - Address unknown since 2003.
Galveston Maritime Assn. [★2595]
Galway Alliance Against War [IO], Galway, Ireland
Galway Chamber of Commerce and Indus. [IO], Galway, Ireland
Gam-Anon Intl. Ser. Off. [IO], Whitestone, NY, United States
Gam-Anon Intl. Ser. Off. [12210], PO Box 157, Whitestone, NY 11357, (718)352-1671
GAMA Intl. [2166], 2901 Telestar Ct., Ste. 140, Falls Church, VA 22042-1205, (703)770-8184
GAMA Intl. [IO], Falls Church, VA, United States
Gambia Assn. of the Physically Disabled [IO], Banjul, Gambia
Gambia Athletics Assn. [IO], Banjul, Gambia
Gambia Chamber of Commerce and Indus. [IO], Serrekunda, Gambia
Gambia Diabetes Assn. [IO], Banjul, Gambia
Gambia Lawn Tennis Assn. [IO], Serrekunda, Gambia
Gambia Natl. Olympic Comm. [IO], Bakau, Gambia
Gambia Women's Finance Assn. [IO], Banjul, Gambia
Gambia YMCAs [IO], Banjul, Gambia
Gambica Assn. for the Instrumentation, Control and Automation Indus. in the United Kingdom [★IO]
GAMBICA, Assn. for Instrumentation, Control, Automation and Lab. Tech. [IO], London, United Kingdom
Gamblers Anonymous [12211], PO Box 17173, Los Angeles, CA 90017, (213)386-8789

Gambling
Alcohol Res. Info. Ser. [13217]
Amer. Greyhound Track Operators Assn. [23391]
Asia Pacific Lottery Assn. [IO]
Assn. of Problem Gambling Ser. Administrators [12208]

Australian Casino Assn. [IO]
British Casino Assn. [IO]
Casino Assn. of South Africa [IO]
Casino Chip and Gaming Token Collectors Club [21989]
Casino Operators Assn. of the UK [IO]
Coun. on Compulsive Gambling of New Jersey [12209]
Estonian Gambling Operator Assn. [IO]
European Casino Assn. [IO]
European Gaming and Betting Assn. [IO]
Gam-Anon Intl. Ser. Off. [IO]
Gam-Anon Intl. Ser. Off. [12210]
Gamblers Anonymous [12211]
Interactive Gaming Coun. [IO]
Intl. Sled Dog Racing Assn. [23394]
Lakes Region Sled Dog Club [23395]
Natl. Assn. for Gambling Stud. [IO]
Natl. Coalition Against Legalized Gambling [17648]
Natl. Coun. on Problem Gambling [12212]
Natl. Indian Gaming Assn. [5771]
Natl. Poker Assn. [22900]
New Hope Found. [13271]
North Amer. Gaming Regulators Assn. [5772]
U.S. Poker Assn. [22901]
World Poker Assn. [22902]
Gambling Chip Collectors Assn. - Address unknown since 2000.
Gambling; Natl. Coun. on Compulsive [★12212]
Gambling; Natl. Coun. on Problem [12212]
Gambling of New Jersey; Coun. on Compulsive [12209]
Game Audio Network Guild [1715], PO Box 507, San Juan Capistrano, CA 92693-0507, (949)340-3557
Game Birds in Am; More [★5311]
Game Breeders and Shooting Preserve Assn; North Amer. [★4144]
Game Collectors Assn; Amer. [★22460]
Game Commissioners; Assn. of Midwest Fish and [★5339]
Game Commissioners and Wardens; Natl. Assn. of [★4360]
Game Conservancy Trust [IO], Fordingbridge, United Kingdom
Game Conservation Intl. - Address unknown since 2001.
Game Developers' Assn. of Australia [IO], Melbourne, Australia
Game and Fish Commissioners; Southeastern Assn. of [★5734]
Game and Fish Commissioners; Western Assn. of State [★5735]
Game, Fish, and Conservation Commissioners; Intl. Assn. of [★4360]
Game Mfr. Assn. [1301], 280 N High St., Ste. 230, Columbus, OH 43215, (614)255-4500
Game Manufacturer Association [IO], Columbus, OH, United States
Game Players; Scrabble Crossword [★22470]
Game Protective Assn; Amer. [★5308]
Gamebird Assn; North Amer. [4144]
Gamefish Res. Found; Pacific [★7176]
Gamers Intl. [22478], c/o Maj. Pete Panzeri, Dir., 8230 Golf Green Cir., Houston, TX 77036, (713)774-3373
Games
All Ser. Postal Chess Club [21941]
Amer. Autoduel Assn. [22456]
Amer. Bridge Assn. [21891]
Amer. Bridge Teachers' Assn. [21892]
Amer. Checker Fed. [22457]
Amer. Checker Fed. [IO]
Amer. Contract Bridge League [21893]
Amer. Crossword Fed. [22458]
Amer. CueSports Alliance [23144]
Amer. Darters Assn. [23327]
Amer. Darts Org. [23328]
Amer. Go Assn. [22459]
Amer. Greyhound Track Operators Assn. [23391]
Amer. Intl. Shuffleboard [23734]
Amer. Postal Chess Tournaments [21943]
Amer. Roque and Croquet Assn. [23090]
Amer. Sports Org. [23993]

A star before a book entry number signifies that the name is not listed separately, but is mentioned within the entry.

Amer. Trans. Bowling Assn. [23249]
Armenian Draughts Fed. [IO]
Asociacion Panamena de Juego de Damas [IO]
Assn. of Game and Puzzle Collectors [22460]
Assn. of Problem Gambling Ser. Administrators [12208]
Australian Draughts Fed. [IO]
Azerbaijan Draughts Fed. [IO]
Belarus Draughts Fed. [IO]
Boardgame Players Assn. [22461]
Bowlers to Veterans Link [23250]
Casino Chip and Gaming Token Collectors Club [21989]
Chess Collectors Intl. [21944]
Chess in the Schools [21945]
Chicago Playing Card Collectors [21992]
Collegiate Assn. of Table Top Gamers [22462]
Comm. for the Advancement of Role-Playing Games [22463]
Comm. for the Game [22464]
Correspondence Chess League of Am. [21946]
Cribbage Bd. Collectors Soc. [22004]
Croquet Found. of Am. [23300]
Domino Players Assn. of Am. [22465]
Draughts Fed. of India [IO]
Draughts Fed. of Turkmenistan [IO]
English Draughts Assn. [IO]
Estonian Draughts Fed. [IO]
European Go Fed. [IO]
Fan Tek [10943]
Federacion Dominicana de Juego de Damas [IO]
Fed. Burkinabe du Jeu de Dames [IO]
Fed. Camerounaise de Jeu de Dames [IO]
Fed. Haitienne du Jeu de Dames [IO]
Fed. Malienne du Jeu de Dames [IO]
Game Audio Network Guild [1715]
Game Mfr. Assn. [1301]
Gamers Intl. [22478]
Golf Collectors Soc. [22031]
Grenada Draughts Assn. [IO]
Hong Kong Soc. of Wargamers [IO]
Horror Writers Assn. [11174]
Intl. Backgammon Assn. [22466]
Intl. Dodge Ball Fed. [23821]
Intl. Fantasy Gaming Soc. [22467]
Intl. Fantasy Gaming Soc. [IO]
Intl. Fed. of Competitive Eating [23822]
Intl. Jugglers' Assn. [23557]
Intl. Laser Tag Assn. [1716]
Intl. Mental Game Coaching Assn. [23289]
Intl. Shuffleboard Assn. [23735]
Intl. Sled Dog Racing Assn. [23394]
Israeli Draughts Fed. [IO]
Lakes Region Sled Dog Club [23395]
Lithuanian Draughts Fed. [IO]
Mongolian Fed. of Draughts [IO]
Mounted Games Across Am. [23830]
Natl. 42 Players Assn. [22899]
Natl. Amateur Dodgeball Assn. [23091]
The Natl. Bowling Assn. [23252]
Natl. Duckpin Bowling Cong. [23253]
Natl. Horseshoe Pitchers Assn. of Am. [23540]
Natl. Mah Jongg League [22468]
Natl. Marble Club of America [22084]
Natl. Paddleball Assn. [23092]
Natl. Poker Assn. [22900]
Natl. Puzzlers' League [22469]
Natl. Scrabble Assn. [22470]
Natl. Token Collectors Assn. [21954]
North Amer. Confed. of the Red Dragon [22479]
North Amer. Soc. of Ancient and Medieval Wargamers [22471]
North Amer. Stone Skipping Assn. [22939]
North Amer. Tiddlywinks Assn. [22472]
Othello Assn. Singapore [IO]
Pinball Owner's Assn. [IO]
Polish Draughts Fed. [IO]
Professional Bowlers Assn. of Am. [23254]
Puzzle Buffs Intl. [22473]
Role Playing Game Assn. Network [22474]
Strategy Gaming Soc. [22475]
Trinidad and Tobago Draughts Assn. [IO]
Uganda Amateur Draughts Assn. [IO]
Ukrainian Draughts Fed. [IO]
U.S. Airsoft Corps [23620]

U.S. Bocce Fed. [23241]
U.S. Boomerang Assn. [23248]
U.S. Bowling Cong. [23255]
U.S. Carrom Assn. [22476]
U.S. Chess Fed. [21948]
U.S. Croquet Assn. [23301]
U.S. Disc Sports [23376]
U.S. Floorball Assn. [23093]
U.S. Othello Assn. [22477]
U.S. Poker Assn. [22901]
U.S. Professional Poolplayers Assn. [23147]
U.S. ProMiniGolf Assn. [23469]
U.S. Snooker Assn. [23148]
Valley Intl. Foosball Assn. [1717]
Valley International Foosball Association [IO]
World Confed. of Billiard Sports [23150]
World Draughts - Checkers - Fed. [IO]
World Juggling Fed. [23558]
World Poker Assn. [22902]
World Rock Paper Scissors Soc. [IO]
World Sport Stacking Assn. [23868]
Games Assn; Natl. Senior [23655]
Games and Festivals; Assn. of Scottish [19348]
Gamewardens of Vietnam Assn. [21345], c/o John W. Woody, Pres., PO Box 701786, San Antonio, TX 78270, (866)220-7477

Gaming
Amer. Gaming Assn. [1718]
Assn. of Problem Gambling Ser. Administrators [12208]
Australasian Gaming Machine Mfrs. Assn. [IO]
Boardgame Players Assn. [22461]
Callmakers and Collectors Assn. of Am. [21984]
Casino Chip and Gaming Token Collectors Club [21989]
Collegiate Assn. of Table Top Gamers [22462]
Fan Tek [10943]
Game Audio Network Guild [1715]
Gamers Intl. [22478]
Gaming Standards Assn. [1719]
Gaming Standards Assn. [IO]
Intl. Fantasy Gaming Soc. [22467]
Intl. Simulation and Gaming Assn. [8454]
Intl. Simulation and Gaming Assn. [IO]
Natl. 42 Players Assn. [22899]
Natl. Indian Gaming Assn. [5771]
Natl. Poker Assn. [22900]
Natl. Token Collectors Assn. [21954]
North Amer. Confed. of the Red Dragon [22479]
North Amer. Simulation and Gaming Assn. [8455]
North Amer. Soc. of Ancient and Medieval Wargamers [22471]
Soc. for Advancement of Games and Simulation in Educ. and Training [IO]
Southeastern Assn. of Fish and Wildlife Agencies [5734]
Strategy Gaming Soc. [22475]
U.S. Airsoft Corps [23620]
U.S. Poker Assn. [22901]
World Poker Assn. [22902]
Gaming Assn; Amer. [1718]
Gaming Assn; Natl. Indian [5771]
Gaming Coun; Natl. [★8455]
Gaming Regulators Assn; North Amer. [5772]
Gaming Standards Assn. [1719], 48377 Fremont Blvd., Ste. 117, Fremont, CA 94538, (510)492-4060
Gaming Standards Assn. [IO], Fremont, CA, United States
Gaming Token Collectors Club; Casino Chip and [21989]
Gamma Alpha - Address unknown since 2002.
Gamma Alpha Omega Sorority [24599], PO Box 427, Tempe, AZ 85280
Gamma Alpha Rho [★24466]
Gamma Beta Phi Soc. [24505], 78A Mitchell Rd., Oak Ridge, TN 37830, (865)483-6212
Gamma Delta [★20227]
Gamma Delta Pi [24710], 1203 Rebecca Ln., No. 124, Norman, OK 73072, (405)329-0805
Gamma Eta Gamma - Address unknown since 1995.
Gamma Gamma Chi Sorority [24711], PO Box 15283, Alexandria, VA 22309, (703)780-7611
Gamma Iota Sigma [24520], 17 S High St., Ste. 200, Columbus, OH 43215, (614)221-1900

Gamma Iota Sigma [IO], Columbus, OH, United States
Gamma Omega Phi - Address unknown since 1995.
Gamma Phi Beta [24687], 12737 E Euclid Dr., Centennial, CO 80111, (303)799-1874
Gamma Phi Beta [IO], Centennial, CO, United States
Gamma Phi Delta - Address unknown since 1995.
Gamma Pi Epsilon [★24500]
Gamma Pi Epsilon [★IO]
Gamma Sigma Delta [IO], Baton Rouge, LA, United States
Gamma Sigma Delta [24398], c/o Steven A. Henning, Pres., Agricultural Economics and Agribusiness, 101 Ag. Admin. Bldg., Louisiana State Univ., Baton Rouge, LA 70803-5604, (225)578-2718
Gamma Sigma Epsilon - Address unknown since 2002.
Gamma Sigma Sigma [24600], PO Box 248, Rindge, NH 03461
Gamma Theta Upsilon [24491], c/o Lawrence Handley, Exec. Sec., 700 Cajundome Blvd., Lafayette, LA 70506, (337)266-8691
Gamper Method
Midwest Parentcraft Center [15609]
Gandhi Memorial Intl. Found. - Address unknown since 2001.
Gandhi Peace Center - Defunct.
Gandhi Soc. for Human Rights - Address unknown since 1995.
Gang Investigator's Assn; Intl. Latino [5884]
Gang Investigators Associations; Natl. Alliance of [5638]
GANU Assn. of U.S. and Canada; Natl. Gymanfa [★19432]
Gap Media Project - Address unknown since 2007.
Gar Hold/Darriel Coun. - Address unknown since 1999.
Gar Wood Soc. [21873], c/o The Antique Boat Museum, 750 Mary St., Clayton, NY 13624, (315)686-4104
Gar Wood Soc. [IO], Clayton, NY, United States
Garage Door Coun. - Defunct.
Garage Equip. Assn. [IO], Daventry, United Kingdom
Garden Bur; Natl. [4982]
Garden Centers of Am. [5043], PO Box 2945, LaGrange, GA 30241, (706)298-0287
Garden Centre Assn. [IO], Reading, United Kingdom
Garden Club of Am. [22511], 14 E 60th St., 3rd Fl., New York, NY 10022-7147, (212)753-8287
Garden Clubs of Am; Men's [★22513]
Garden Clubs; Natl. Coun. of State [★22528]
Garden Conservancy [4402], PO Box 219, Cold Spring, NY 10516, (845)265-2029
Garden Coun. - Address unknown since 2003.
Garden Design Soc. of New Zealand [IO], Auckland, New Zealand
Garden Distributors Assn; Lawn and [★2395]
Garden Foundation; Natl. Peace [18225]
Garden History Soc. [IO], London, United Kingdom
Garden Horticultural Indus. Assn; Intl. [★4975]
Garden Industry of America - Defunct.
Garden Indus. Mfrs. Assn. [IO], Birmingham, United Kingdom
Garden Marketing and Distribution Assn; Lawn and [2395]
Garden; Natl. Peace [★18225]
Garden Organic [★IO]
Garden Project; Peace [★18225]
Garden Seed Assn. - Defunct.
Garden and Seed Bank; Southwest Traditional Crop Conservancy [★4429]
Garden Soc; Amer. Rock [★22535]
Garden Supply Dealers Natl. - Defunct.
Garden Writers Assn. [22512], 10210 Leatherleaf Ct., Manassas, VA 20111, (703)257-1032
Garden Writers Assn. of Am. [★22512]
The Gardeners of Am. [22513], PO Box 241, Johnston, IA 50131-6245, (515)278-0295
The Gardeners of America/Men's Garden Clubs of Am. [4778], PO Box 241, Johnston, IA 50131-6245, (515)278-0295
Gardeners; Natl. Assn. of [★4803]
GARDENEX: Fed. of Garden and Leisure Mfrs. [IO], Brasted, United Kingdom

---

Reference to "IO" in place of a book number signifies that the association may be found in the 45th edition of International Organizations.

Gardenia Soc. of America - Address unknown since 2000.

Gardening

African Violet Soc. of Am. [22480]
African Violet Soc. of Canada [IO]
All-America Gladiolus Selections [22481]
All-America Rose Selections [4972]
Alpine Garden Soc. [IO]
Amateur Rose Breeders Assn. [IO]
Amer. Begonia Soc. [22482]
Amer. Bonsai Soc. [22483]
Amer. Boxwood Soc. [22484]
Amer. Brugmansia and Datura Soc. [22455]
Amer. Camellia Soc. [22485]
Amer. Community Gardening Assn. [22486]
Amer. Daffodil Soc. [22487]
American Daffodil Society [IO]
Amer. Fuchsia Soc. [22488]
Amer. Gourd Soc. [22489]
Amer. Hemerocallis Soc. [22490]
Amer. Herb Assn. [6624]
Amer. Hibiscus Soc. [22491]
American Hibiscus Society [IO]
Amer. Horticultural Soc. [22492]
Amer. Hosta Soc. [22493]
Amer. Hydrangea Soc. [22494]
Amer. Iris Soc. [22495]
American Iris Society [IO]
Amer. Ivy Soc. [IO]
Amer. Ivy Soc. [22496]
Amer. Nursery and Landscape Assn. [5042]
Amer. Penstemon Soc. [22497]
Amer. Peony Soc. [22498]
Amer. Primrose Soc. [22499]
Amer. Public Gardens Assn. [4973]
Amer. Rhododendron Soc. [22500]
Amer. Rose Soc. [22501]
Aquatic Gardeners Assn. [4777]
Aquatic Gardeners Assn. [IO]
Aril Soc. Intl. [22502]
Asociacion Chilena de la Rosa [IO]
Asociacion Espanola de la Rosa [IO]
Associazione Italiana della Rosa [IO]
Australian Lavender Indus. [IO]
Australian Plants Soc. - New South Wales Region [IO]
Azalea Soc. of Am. [22503]
Biodynamic Farming and Gardening Assn. [4643]
Bonsai Clubs Intl. [22504]
Bonsai Clubs Intl. [IO]
British Clematis Soc. [IO]
British and European Geranium Soc. [IO]
British Hosta and Hemerocallis Soc. [IO]
British Iris Soc. [IO]
Bromeliad Soc. Intl. [IO]
Bromeliad Soc. Intl. [22505]
Cactus and Succulent Soc. of Am. [22506]
Canadian Rose Soc. [IO]
China Rose Soc. [IO]
Combined North Amer. Cottage Garden Soc. and North Amer. Dianthus Soc. [22507]
Compost Tea Indus. Assn. [186]
Cottage Garden Soc. [IO]
Cymbidium Soc. of Am. [IO]
Cymbidium Soc. of Am. [22508]
Czech Rosa Club [IO]
De Nederlandse Rozenvereniging [IO]
Delphinium Soc. [IO]
Dwarf Iris Soc. of Am. [22509]
Epiphyllum Soc. of Am. [22510]
Fed. of Rose Societies of South Africa [IO]
Finnish Rose Soc. [IO]
French Orchid Soc. [IO]
Garden Centers of Am. [5043]
Garden Club of Am. [22511]
Garden Conservancy [4402]
Garden Writers Assn. [22512]
The Gardeners of Am. [22513]
The Gardeners of America/Men's Garden Clubs of Am. [4778]
Gesneriad Hybridizers Assn. [22514]
Gesneriad Soc. [22515]
Gesneriad Soc. [IO]
Good Gardeners Assn. [IO]
Hardy Plant Soc. [IO]

Heather Soc. [IO]
Hellenic Rose Soc. [IO]
Herb Soc. of Am. [6636]
Heritage Rose Found. [22516]
Heritage Roses Gp. [22517]
Hobby Greenhouse Assn. [22518]
Ikebana Intl. [IO]
Indoor Gardening Soc. of Am. [22519]
InterAmerican Soc. for Tropical Horticulture [4979]
Intl. Aroid Soc. [22520]
Intl. Aroid Soc. [IO]
Intl. Camellia Soc. [IO]
International Carnivorous Plant Society [IO]
Intl. Carnivorous Plant Soc. [22521]
Intl. Lilac Soc. [22522]
International Lilac Society [IO]
Intl. Oleander Soc. [IO]
Intl. Oleander Soc. [22523]
Intl. Soc. for Plant Pathology [IO]
International Waterlily and Water Gardening Society [IO]
Intl. Waterlily and Water Gardening Soc. [22524]
Japan Rose Soc. [IO]
Kitchen Gardeners Intl. [9966]
Lawn and Garden Dealers Assn. [1720]
Lawn and Garden Marketing and Distribution Assn. [2395]
Les Amis de la Rose Luxembourg [IO]
Median Iris Soc. [22525]
Natl. Auricula and Primula Soc. [IO]
Natl. Begonia Soc. [IO]
Natl. Chrysanthemum Soc. [IO]
Natl. Chrysanthemum Soc. [22526]
Natl. Fuchsia Soc. [22527]
Natl. Garden Bur. [4982]
Natl. Garden Clubs [22528]
Natl. Gardening Assn. [22529]
Natl. Gardens Scheme [IO]
Natl. Greenhouse Manufacturers Assn. [184]
Natl. Junior Horticultural Assn. [22530]
Natl. Landscape Assn. [2396]
Natl. Soc. of Allotment and Leisure Gardeners [IO]
New Zealand Bonsai Assn. [IO]
North Amer. Fruit Explorers [22531]
North Amer. Gladiolus Coun. [22532]
North Amer. Heather Soc. [22533]
North Amer. Heather Soc. [IO]
North American Lily Society [IO]
North Amer. Lily Soc. [22534]
North Amer. Rock Garden Soc. [22535]
North American Rock Garden Society [IO]
Norwegian Rose Soc. [IO]
Osterreichische Rosenfreunde in der Osterreichischen Gartenbau-Gessellschaft [IO]
Pacific Orchid Soc. of Hawaii [22536]
Pakistan Natl. Rose Soc. [IO]
Passiflora Soc. Intl. [4673]
People Food and Land Found. [4656]
Plumeria Soc. of Am. [22537]
Polish Soc. of Rose Fanciers [IO]
Professional Gardeners Guild [IO]
Professional Landcare Network [2398]
Proj. EverGreen [4991]
Reblooming Iris Soc. [22538]
Rhododendron Species Found. [6648]
Rose Hybridizers Assn. [22539]
Rose Hybridizers Association [IO]
Rose Soc. of Argentina [IO]
Royal Horticultural Soc. of Ireland [IO]
Royal Natl. Rose Soc. [IO]
Scottish Rock Garden Club [IO]
Seed Savers Exchange [22540]
Singapore Penjing and Stone Appreciation Soc. [IO]
Societe Francaise des Roses 'Les Amis des Roses' [IO]
Soc. for Japanese Irises [22541]
Soc. for Louisiana Irises [22542]
Soc. for Pacific Coast Native Iris [22543]
Society for Pacific Coast Native Iris [IO]
Soc. for Siberian Irises [22544]
Species Iris Gp. of North Am. [22545]
Spuria Iris Soc. [22546]
Spuria Iris Society [IO]

Succulent Soc. of South Africa [IO]
Tall Bearded Iris Soc. [IO]
Tall Bearded Iris Soc. [22547]
Terrarium Assn. [22548]
Uruguayan Rose Assn. [IO]

Gardening Assn; Biodynamic Farming and [4643]
Gardening Assn; Mailorder [3413]
Gardening From The Heart [★22513]
Gardening; Gardens For All, the Natl. Assn. for [★22529]
Gardening Soc. of Am; Indoor Light [★22519]
Gardens for All [★22529]
Gardens and Arboreta; Amer. Assn. of Botanical [★4973]
Gardens and Arboretums; Amer. Assn. of Botanical [★4973]
Gardens For All, the Natl. Assn. for Gardening [★22529]
Gardens; Natl. Coun. for the Conservation of Plants and [IO]
Gardner Registry - Address unknown since 1999.
Garey Cancer Found; Eugene L. [★15650]
Garin Arava - Address unknown since 1999.
Garin Yarden - Young Kibbutz Movement [★17937]
Garland, Judy
Beyond the Rainbow [24733]
Garment Assn; Merchants Ladies [★253]
Garment Assn. of Nepal [IO], Kathmandu, Nepal
Garment Manufacturers Assn; Pacific Coast [★221]
Garment Manufacturers Assn; Southern [★221]
Garment Network; Seamless [★18200]
Garment Workers of Am; United [★24061]
Garner Family History Assn. - Address unknown since 2007.
Garrison Family Assn; Isaac [20954]
Garter; Loyal Escorts of the Green [21173]
Gartlan USA's Collectors' League [22028], 560 Stokes Rd., Ste. 23 - No. 397, Medford, NJ 08055-2905, (609)953-0606
Gary Intl. Fan Club; John [24925]
Gary Memorial Fan Club; John [★24925]
Gary Morris Fan Club [24897], c/o Gary Morris Productions, PO Box 187, Chromo, CO 81128, (970)264-6791
Gary's Web Intl. [24745], c/o Polaris Public Relations, 431 S Fairfax Ave., Los Angeles, CA 90036
Gas Appliance Engineers Soc. [★6941]
Gas Appliance and Equip. Manufacturers; Assn. of [★265]
Gas Appliance Manufacturers Assn. [265], 2107 Wilson Blvd., Ste. 600, Arlington, VA 22201-3042, (703)525-7060
Gas Appliance Mfrs. Assn. of Australia [IO], Melbourne, Australia
Gas Assn; Independent Natural [★1680]
Gas Assn. of Am; Interstate Natural [1680]
Gas Assn; Amer. [1676]
Gas Assn; Amer. Public [3951]
Gas Assn. of Bosnia and Herzegovina [IO], Sarajevo, Bosnia-Hercegovina
Gas Assn; Liquefied Petroleum [★1681]
Gas Assn; Mid-Continent Oil and [★2950]
Gas Assn; Natl. Propane [1681]
Gas Assn. of New Zealand [IO], Wellington, New Zealand
Gas Assn. of Serbia and Montenegro [IO], Belgrade, Serbia
Gas Assn; U.S. Oil and [2950]
Gas Assn; Western Oil and [★2951]
Gas Associations; Liaison Comm. of Cooperating Oil and [2933]
Gas Chlorinators; Natl. Assn. of [★825]
Gas Cleaning Inst; Indus. [★3071]
Gas Compact Commn; Interstate Oil and [5684]
Gas Consumers Coun. [★IO]
Gas Consumers Gp; Process [17340]
Gas Coun; Natl. LP- [★1681]
Gas Engine and Tractor Assn; Early Day [22410]
Gas Engineers; Amer. Soc. of [6941]
Gas Forum [IO], London, United Kingdom
Gas Infrastructure Europe [IO], Brussels, Belgium
Gas Inst; Compressed Air and [2010]
Gas Inst. and Natl. Commercial Gas Assn. [★1676]
Gas Mfrs. Assn; Compressed [★1721]
Gas Processors Assn. [2924], 6526 E 60th St., Tulsa, OK 74145-9202, (918)493-3872

A star before a book entry number signifies that the name is not listed separately, but is mentioned within the entry.

Gas Processors Suppliers Assn. [2925], 6526 E 60th St., Tulsa, OK 74145-9202, (918)493-3872
Gas Res. Inst. [★1678]
Gas Stop Inst; Brass [★3066]
Gas Supply Assn; Natural [1682]
Gas Supply Comm; Natural [★1682]
Gas Tech. Inst. [1678], 1700 S Mt. Prospect Rd., Des Plaines, IL 60018-1804, (847)768-0500
Gas Tech; Inst. of [★1678]
Gas Turbine Div. [★7001]
Gas Turbine Div. [★IO]
Gas Turbine Inst; Intl. [★7001]
Gas Vent Inst. - Defunct.
Gases
Aerosol Soc. [IO]
All India Indus. Gases Mfrs. Assn. [IO]
Amer. Assn. of Radon Scientists and Technologists [7108]
Amer. Exploration and Production Coun. [2914]
Amer. Oil and Gas Historical Soc. [2915]
Assn. for the Stud. of Peak Oil and Gas - USA [7461]
Australian Gas Assn. [IO]
British Compressed Air Soc. [IO]
British Compressed Gases Assn. [IO]
Canadian Hydrogen Assn. [IO]
Completion Engg. Assn. [7182]
Compressed Gas Assn. [1721]
Coun. for Registered Gas Installers [IO]
Distribution Contractors Assn. [24162]
European Assn. for the Streamlining of Energy Exchange [IO]
European Hydrogen Assn. [IO]
Gas Assn. of New Zealand [IO]
Gas Infrastructure Europe [IO]
Gasification Technologies Council [IO]
Gasification Technologies Coun. [1722]
GERG - European Gas Res. Gp. [IO]
Intl. Oxygen Mfrs. Assn. [IO]
Intl. Oxygen Mfrs. Assn. [1723]
Intl. Ozone Assn. [7109]
Intl. Ozone Assn. [IO]
Interstate Oil and Gas Compact Commn. [5684]
Irish LP Gas Assn. [IO]
Japan Gas Assn. [IO]
LP Gas Assn. [IO]
Methanol Inst. [7110]
Natl. Home Oxygen Patients Assn. [14404]
Natl. Petroleum Coun. [5686]
Process Gas Consumers Gp. [17340]
Propane Gas Assn. of Canada [IO]
Soc. of British Gas Indus. [IO]
Swimming Pool Water Treatment Professionals [825]
United Kingdom Onshore Operators Gp. [IO]
Gases and Welding Distributors Assn. [2021], 100 N 20th St., 4th Fl., Philadelphia, PA 19103, (215)564-3484
Gasification Technologies Coun. [1722], 4301 N Fairfax Dr., Ste. 300, Arlington, VA 22203, (703)276-0110
Gasification Technologies Council [IO], Arlington, VA, United States
Gasket Cutters Assn. [IO], St. Albans, United Kingdom
Gasket Fabricators Assn. [2022], 994 Old Eagle School Rd., Ste. 1019, Wayne, PA 19087, (610)971-4850
Gasohol U.S.A. - Defunct.
Gasoline and Automotive Ser. Dealers Assn. [414], 78 Harvard Ave., Ste. 260, Stamford, CT 06902, (203)327-4773
Gasoline Marketers of Am; Soc. of Independent [2947]
Gasoline Merchants [★414]
Gasoline Pump Mfrs. Assn. [2926]
GaSp Network - Defunct.
Gastro-Intestinal Res. Found. [14418], 70 E Lake St., Ste. 1015, Chicago, IL 60601, (312)332-1350
Gastroenterological Assn; Natl. [★14405]
Gastroenterological and Digestive Endoscopy Soc. of Sri Lanka [IO], Colombo, Sri Lanka
Gastroenterological Soc. of Australia [IO], Sydney, Australia
Gastroenterological Soc. of Singapore [IO], Singapore, Singapore

Gastroenterology
Amer. Coll. of Gastroenterology [14405]
Amer. Gastroenterological Assn. [14406]
Amer. Neurogastroenterology and Motility Soc. [14407]
Amer. Partnership for Eosinophilic Disorders [14408]
Amer. Soc. for Gastrointestinal Endoscopy [14409]
Argentine Soc. of Gastroenterology [IO]
Asian Pacific Soc. for Digestive Endoscopy [IO]
Asian Pan-Pacific Soc. for Paediatric Gastroenterology Hepatology and Nutrition [IO]
Assn. of Coloproctology of Great Britain and Ireland [IO]
Association of Gastrointestinal Motility Disorders [IO]
Assn. of Gastrointestinal Motility Disorders [14410]
Assn. of Natl., European and Mediterranean Societies of Gastroenterology [IO]
Assn. of Upper Gastrointestinal Surgeons [IO]
Bockus Intl. Soc. of Gastroenterology [IO]
Bockus Intl. Soc. of Gastroenterology [14411]
British Soc. of Gastroenterology [IO]
Canadian Assn. for Enterostomal Therapy [IO]
Canadian Assn. of Gastroenterology [IO]
Canadian Celiac Assn. [IO]
Celiac Disease Found. [14412]
Celiac Sprue Association/United States of Am. [14413]
Certifying Bd. of Gastroenterology Nurses and Associates [15472]
CORE [IO]
Crohn's and Colitis Found. of Am. [14414]
Cyclic Vomiting Syndrome Assn. [14415]
Cyclic Vomiting Syndrome Assn. [IO]
Danish Soc. of Gastroenterology [IO]
Digestive Disease Natl. Coalition [14416]
European Intestinal Transport Gp. [IO]
European Soc. of Coloproctology [IO]
European Soc. of Gastrointestinal and Abdominal Radiology [IO]
European Soc. of Gastrointestinal Endoscopy [IO]
European Soc. for Neurogastroenterology and Motility [IO]
European Soc. for Primary Care Gastroenterology [IO]
Found. for Digestive Hea. and Nutrition [14417]
Gastro-Intestinal Res. Found. [14418]
Gastroenterological Soc. of Australia [IO]
Hong Kong Soc. of Gastroenterology [IO]
Indian Assn. of Gastrointestinal Endosurgeons [IO]
International Foundation for Functional Gastrointestinal Disorders [IO]
Intl. Found. for Functional Gastrointestinal Disorders [14419]
Intl. Soc. for Digestive Surgery [14420]
Intl. Soc. for Digestive Surgery [IO]
Intl. Soc. of Gastroenterological Carcinogenesis [IO]
Intestinal Disease Found. [14421]
Japan Gastroenterological Endoscopy Soc. [IO]
Life Raft Gp. [13838]
Natl. Assn. of Colitis and Crohn's Disease [IO]
Natl. Digestive Diseases Info. CH [14422]
Natl. Heartburn Alliance [14423]
North Amer. Soc. for Pediatric Gastroenterology, Hepatology and Nutrition [14424]
Paratuberculosis Awareness and Res. Assn. [14425]
Paratuberculosis Awareness and Res. Assn. [IO]
Pediatric/Adolescent Gastroesophageal Reflux Association [IO]
Pediatric/Adolescent Gastroesophageal Reflux Assn. [14426]
Pull-thru Network [14427]
Scandinavian Assn. for Gastrointestinal Motility [IO]
Sociedad Chilena de Gastroenterologia [IO]
Society of American Gastrointestinal and Endoscopic Surgeons [IO]
Soc. of Amer. Gastrointestinal and Endoscopic Surgeons [14428]

Soc. of Gastroenterology Nurses and Associates [14429]
United European Gastroenterology Fed. [IO]
World Gastroenterology Org. [IO]
World Soc. of the Abdominal Compartment Syndrome [IO]
Gastroenterology; North Amer. Soc. for Pediatric [★14424]
Gastroenterology Nurses and Associates; Certifying Bd. of [15472]
Gastroenterology Res. Group - Defunct.
Gastroenterology; Soc. for the Advancement of [★14405]
Gastroesophageal Reflux Assn; Pediatric/Adolescent [14426]
Gastrointestinal Assistants; Soc. of [★14429]
Gastrointestinal Disorders; Intl. Found. for Functional [14419]
Gastrointestinal and Endoscopic Surgeons; Soc. of Amer. [14428]
Gastrointestinal Endoscopy; Amer. Soc. for [14409]
Gastrointestinal Motility Disorders; Assn. of [14410]
Gastrointestinal Pathology Soc. - Address unknown since 1999.
Gastrointestinal Radiologists; Soc. of [16298]
Gastronomy
Slow Food USA [9971]
Slow Food USA [IO]
Gastroscopic Club; Amer. [★14409]
Gastroscopic Soc; Amer. [★14409]
Gates Found; Bill and Melinda [12273]
Gateway Intl. Center [IO], Kanagawa, Japan
Gathering of Nations [10742], 3301 Coors Blvd. NW, Ste. R300, Albuquerque, NM 87120-1229, (505)836-2810
Gaucher Disease Registry [★15252]
Gaucher Found; Natl. [15252]
Gauchers Assn. [IO], Gloucester, United Kingdom
Gaudeamus Found. [IO], Amsterdam, Netherlands
Gauge and Tool Makers' Assn. [IO], Princes Risborough, United Kingdom
Gauss Scientific Soc. - Defunct.
Gauverband Nordamerika [★9627]
Gauverband Nordamerika [★IO]
Gavel Clubs [10898], c/o Toastmasters Intl., PO Box 9052, Mission Viejo, CA 92690-9052, (949)858-8255
Gay AA - Address unknown since 2001.
Gay Academic Union - Defunct.
Gay Activists Alliance - Defunct.
Gay Addiction Professionals; Natl. Assn. of Lesbian/ [13263]
Gay Alcoholism Professionals; Natl. Assn. of [★13263]
Gay Amer. Indians - Address unknown since 1989.
Gay Anthropologists; Soc. of Lesbian and [6432]
Gay Art Found; Leslie-Lohman [9455]
Gay Asian Pacific Alliance [12228], PO Box 421884, San Francisco, CA 94142-1884
Gay Asian Pacific Support Network [12229], PO Box 461104, Los Angeles, CA 90046-1104, (213)368-6488
Gay Assoc. Engineers and Scientists; Lesbian and [★7620]
Gay Band Assn; Lesbian and [10638]
Gay Bands of Am; Lesbian and [★10638]
Gay and Bisexual Issues; Soc. for the Psychological Stud. of Lesbian, [16180]
Gay and Bisexual Returned Peace Corps Volunteers; Lesbian, [★18260]
Gay, Bisexual and Transgender US Peace Corps Alumni; Lesbian, [18260]
Gay Bowling Org; Intl. [23251]
Gay Caucus of Members of the Amer. Psychiatric Assn. [★12217]
Gay Caucus; United Church of Christ [★20067]
Gay Christian Movement [★IO]
Gay Community News Prisoner Project - Address unknown since 2003.
Gay Concerns; Affirmation: United Methodists for Lesbian/ [★20047]
Gay Concerns; Brethren/Mennonite Coun. for [★20050]
Gay Concerns; Brethren/Mennonite Coun. for Lesbian and [★20050]

Reference to "IO" in place of a book number signifies that the association may be found in the 45th edition of International Organizations.

Gay Concerns; Presbyterians for Lesbian and [★20063]
Gay Concerns; Unitarian Universalists for Lesbian and [★20059]
Gay Concerns; United Church Coalition for Lesbian/ [★20067]
Gay Episcopal Forum - Defunct.
Gay Fathers Coalition [★12227]
Gay Fathers Coalition Intl. [★12227]
Gay Games [★23818]
Gay Games [★IO]
Gay HIV Strategies [IO], Dublin, Ireland
Gay Issues; Natl. Assn. of Social Workers Comm. on Lesbian and [★12245]
Gay Issues; Natl. Assn. of Social Workers- Natl. Comm. on Lesbian and [★12245]
Gay Issues; Soc. for the Psychological Stud. of Lesbian and [★16180]
Gay Issues; Task Force on Lesbian/ [★9132]
Gay Journalists Assn; Natl. Lesbian and [3138]
Gay Law Assn; Natl. Lesbian and [5523]
Gay Lawyers Assn; Natl. Lesbian and [★5523]
Gay/Lesbian
   Affirm United [IO]
   Affirmation/Gay and Lesbian Mormons [20046]
   Affirmation: United Methodists for Lesbian, Gay and Bisexual Concerns [20047]
   African Asian Latina Lesbians United [17649]
   Alberta Rockies Gay Rodeo Assn. [IO]
   All Out Arts [9534]
   Alliance for Full-Acceptance [12213]
   Alpha Lambda Tau Intl. Social Fraternity [24613]
   Alternative Family Proj. [11814]
   Amer. Baptists Concerned [20048]
   Amer. Civil Liberties Union [17084]
   Amer. Civil Liberties Union Found. [17085]
   Amer. Lib. Association/Gay, Lesbian, Bisexual and Transgendered Round Table [12214]
   Amer. Veterans for Equal Rights [12215]
   And Justice for All [18639]
   Arcus Found. [18266]
   Assn. of Gay and Lesbian Armenians France [IO]
   Assn. for Gay, Lesbian, and Bisexual Issues in Counseling [12216]
   Assn. of Gay and Lesbian Psychiatrists [12217]
   Assn. of Welcoming and Affirming Baptists [19476]
   Axios USA [20049]
   Bay Area Physicians for Human Rights [12218]
   Bi Without Borders [17024]
   Bi Women's Cultural Alliance [12219]
   BiNet USA [12220]
   Blind Friends of Lesbian, Gay, Transgender and Bisexual People [12221]
   Brethren/Mennonite Coun. for Lesbian, Gay, Bisexual and Transgender Interest [20050]
   Catholic Parents Network [12664]
   Center for Lesbian and Gay Stud. [12222]
   COLAGE [12223]
   Columbia Queer Alliance [12224]
   Community United Against Violence [12225]
   Conf. for Catholic Lesbians [20051]
   Coun. on Sexual Orientation and Gender Expression [9132]
   Couples Natl. Network [17650]
   Courage [20052]
   Courage [IO]
   Delphi Found. [24451]
   Dignity/USA [20053]
   Disabled Womyn's Educational Proj. [11942]
   Egale Canada [IO]
   Evangelicals Concerned [20054]
   Evergreen Intl. [12226]
   Evergreen Intl. [IO]
   Exodus Intl. [20055]
   Families Like Mine [17651]
   Family Pride Coalition [12227]
   Fed. of Gay Games [23818]
   Fenway Community Hea. [14430]
   FireFlag/EMS [5773]
   Friends for Lesbian, Gay, Bisexual, Transgender, and Queer Concerns [20056]
   Friends for Lesbian, Gay, Bisexual, Transgender, and Queer Concerns [IO]
   Gay Asian Pacific Alliance [12228]

Gay Asian Pacific Support Network [12229]
Gay HIV Strategies [IO]
Gay and Lesbian Adolescent Social Services [18847]
Gay and Lesbian Advocates and Defenders [17118]
Gay, Lesbian and Affirming Disciples Alliance [20057]
Gay Lesbian Alliance Against Defamation [17652]
Gay and Lesbian Assn. of Choruses [10599]
Gay, Lesbian, Bisexual, Transgender Historical Soc. [10078]
Gay, Lesbian, Bisexual, and Transgender Natl. Hotline [12230]
Gay, Lesbian, Bisexual, and Transgendered Disabled Veterans of Am. [20765]
Gay and Lesbian Community Services Assn. [IO]
Gay and Lesbian Intl. Sport Assn. [IO]
Gay and Lesbian Medical Assn. [14431]
Gay, Lesbian, and Straight Educ. Network [8456]
Gay and Lesbian Tennis Alliance [23901]
Gay and Lesbian Underwater Gp. [IO]
Gay Men's Hea. Crisis [13564]
Gay Officers' Action League [12231]
Gay Police Assn. [IO]
Gaylactic Network [10944]
Golden Threads [22137]
HeartStrong [12232]
Heritage of Pride [12233]
Hetrick-Martin Inst. [12234]
Homosexual Info. Center [12235]
Homosexuals Anonymous Fellowship Services [12236]
Human Rights Campaign [17653]
Immigration Equality [12237]
Integrity [20058]
Interfaith Working Group [12887]
Intl. Assn. of Gay/Lesbian Country Western Dance Clubs [9884]
Intl. Assn. of Gay and Lesbian Martial Artists [23588]
Intl. Assn. of Lesbian and Gay Judges [5903]
Intl. Fed. of Black Prides [12238]
Intl. Gay Bowling Org. [23251]
Intl. Gay Figure Skating Union [23736]
International Gay Figure Skating Union [IO]
Intl. Gay and Lesbian Aquatics [23885]
Intl. Gay and Lesbian Football Assn. [23777]
Intl. Gay and Lesbian Human Rights Commn. [12239]
Intl. Gay and Lesbian Human Rights Commn. [IO]
Intl. Gay and Lesbian Travel Assn. [3924]
Intl. Lesbian and Gay Assn. [IO]
InterPride [IO]
InterPride [12240]
Interweave Continental (Unitarian Universalists for Lesbian, Gay, Bisexual and Transgender Concerns) [20059]
Lambda Amateur Radio Club [21504]
Lambda Legal Defense and Educ. Fund [12241]
Lesbian, Bisexual, Gay and Transgendered United Employees at AT&T [12242]
Lesbian and Gay Band Assn. [10638]
Lesbian, Gay, Bisexual, and Transgender People in Medicine [12243]
Lesbian Hea. Fund [14432]
Lesbian Health Fund [IO]
Lesbian Herstory Educational Found. [11088]
Lesbian Rsrc. Center [12244]
Lesbians in the Visual Arts [9454]
Leslie-Lohman Gay Art Found. [9455]
LIFE [20060]
Log Cabin Republicans [18523]
Love in Action [19868]
Lutherans Concerned/North Am. [20061]
Marriage Equality USA [12506]
Mautner Proj. for Lesbian Hea. [14433]
Men's Rsrc. Center [12357]
Metanoia Ministries [19869]
Metropolitan Community Churches [20062]
More Light Presbyterians for Lesbian, Gay, Bisexual and Transgender Concerns [20063]
Natl. Assn. of Lesbian/Gay Addiction Professionals [13263]
Natl. Assn. of Lesbian, Gay, Bisexual and Transgender Community Centers [11804]

Natl. Assn. for Res. and Therapy of Homosexuality [14434]
Natl. Assn. of Social Workers Natl. Comm. on Lesbian, Gay and Bisexual Issues [12245]
Natl. Black Justice Coalition [18643]
Natl. Center for Lesbian Rights [12246]
Natl. Coalition for LGBT Hea. [12247]
Natl. Coming Out Day [12248]
Natl. Gay and Lesbian Chamber of Commerce [24321]
Natl. Gay and Lesbian Task Force [12249]
Natl. Gay/Lesbian Travel Desk [24322]
Natl. Gay Pilot's Assn. [439]
Natl. Latina/o Lesbian, Gay, Bisexual, and Transgender Org. [9972]
Natl. Lesbian and Gay Law Assn. [5523]
Natl. Org. of Gay and Lesbian Scientists and Tech. Professionals [7620]
Natl. Youth Advocacy Coalition [13505]
New Dawn [22140]
New Ways Ministry [20064]
NOLOSE - The Natl. Org. for Lesbians of Size [12250]
North Amer. Man/Boy Love Assn. [13099]
Old Lesbians Organizing for Change [11317]
ONE, Inc. [12251]
Outfest [9944]
Outpost [19870]
OutProud [12252]
Parents, Families, and Friends of Lesbians and Gays [12253]
Parents and Friends of Ex-Gays and Gays [12254]
Partners Task Force for Gay and Lesbian Couples [17654]
Presbyterian Parents of Gays and Lesbians [17655]
Pro-Life Alliance of Gays and Lesbians [12927]
Proj. YES [9339]
Queer Nation [17656]
Racial Justice 911 [18493]
Rainbow Alliance of the Deaf [12255]
Rainbow Rsrc. Centre: Serving Manitoba's Gay, Lesbian, Bisexual, Transgendered, and Two-Spirited Communities [IO]
Reconciling Ministries Network [20065]
Regeneration [19871]
Sailing and Cruising Assn. [IO]
Scouting For All [13006]
Senior Action in a Gay Env. [12256]
Seventh Day Adventist Kinship Intl. [20066]
Seventh Day Adventist Kinship International [IO]
Soc. for the Psychological Stud. of Lesbian, Gay and Bisexual Issues [16180]
Soulforce [17657]
Stop Abuse for Everyone [12039]
Sydney Underwater Buddies [IO]
Tangent Gp. [12257]
Triangle Club [13283]
Trikone [12258]
Two Spirited People of the First Nations [IO]
An Uncommon Legacy Found. [17658]
United Church of Christ Coalition for Lesbian, Gay, Bisexual and Transgender Concerns [20067]
Unity Fellowship Church Movement [20068]
We Are Family [17659]
Wett Ones [IO]
Wishing Well [22146]
World Cong. of Gay, Lesbian, Bisexual, and Transgender Jews [20069]
World Cong. of Gay, Lesbian, Bisexual, and Transgender Jews [IO]
Gay and Lesbian Adolescent Social Services [18847], 650 N Robertson Blvd., West Hollywood, CA 90069, (310)358-8727
Gay and Lesbian Advocates and Defenders [17118], 30 Winter St., Ste. 800, Boston, MA 02108, (617)426-1350
Gay, Lesbian and Affirming Disciples Alliance [20057], PO Box 44400, Indianapolis, IN 46244-0400, (317)634-9297
Gay Lesbian Alliance Against Defamation [17652], 5455 Wilshire Blvd., Ste. 1500, Los Angeles, CA 90036, (323)933-2240

A star before a book entry number signifies that the name is not listed separately, but is mentioned within the entry.

Gay and Lesbian Alliance Against Defamation New York [★17652]

Gay and Lesbian Alliance; Columbia [★12224]

Gay and Lesbian Alumni/ae Assn; Northeastern [★18913]

Gay and Lesbian Alumni/ae Associations; Network of [18913]

Gay and Lesbian Assn. of Choruses [10599], PO Box 99998, Pittsburgh, PA 15233, (412)999-4489

Gay and Lesbian Atheists - Defunct.

Gay, Lesbian, and Bisexual Caucus of the Amer. Psychiatric Assn. [★12217]

Gay, Lesbian, and Bisexual Members of the Amer. Psychiatric Assn; Caucus of [★12217]

Gay, Lesbian, Bisexual, Transgender Historical Soc. [10078], 657 Mission St., No. 300, San Francisco, CA 94105, (415)777-5455

Gay, Lesbian, Bisexual, and Transgender Natl. Hotline [12230], PMB No. 296, 2261 Market St., San Francisco, CA 94114, (415)355-0003

Gay, Lesbian, Bisexual, and Transgendered Disabled Veterans of Am. [20765], c/o Sgt. Sharon F. Daugherty, II, 3124 Scranton St., Aurora, CO 80011

Gay, Lesbian, Bisexual and Transgendered Round Table; Amer. Lib. Association/ [12214]

Gay, Lesbian, and Bisexual Veterans of Am. [★12215]

Gay and Lesbian Coalition Intl. [★12227]

Gay and Lesbian Community Services Assn. [IO], Calgary, AB, Canada

Gay and Lesbian Democrats of America - Defunct.

Gay and Lesbian History Stamp Club - Address unknown since 2001.

Gay and Lesbian Intl. Sport Assn. [IO], St. Catharines, ON, Canada

Gay/Lesbian Issues in Social work Educ; Commn. on [★9132]

Gay and Lesbian Legal Issues, Assn. of Amer. Law Schools; Sect. on [★8761]

Gay and Lesbian Media Coalition [★9944]

Gay and Lesbian Medical Assn. [14431], 459 Fulton St., Ste. 107, San Francisco, CA 94102, (415)255-4547

Gay and Lesbian Mormons; Affirmation/ [20046]

Gay and Lesbian Press Assn. - Defunct.

Gay and Lesbian Scientists and Tech. Professionals; Natl. Org. of [7620]

Gay, Lesbian, and Straight Educ. Network [8456], 90 Broad St., 2nd Fl., New York, NY 10004, (212)727-0135

Gay/Lesbian Straight Teachers Network [★8456]

Gay and Lesbian Task Force [★12214]

Gay and Lesbian Tennis Alliance [23901], 5510 Curdy Rd., Howell, MI 48855

Gay and Lesbian Tennis Alliance [IO], Howell, MI, United States

Gay and Lesbian Travel Assn; Intl. [3924]

Gay and Lesbian Underwater Gp. [IO], London, United Kingdom

Gay and Lesbian Vegetarians - Defunct.

Gay Liberation; Task Force on [★12214]

Gay Media Task Force - Address unknown since 2006.

Gay Men's Hea. Crisis [13564], 119 W 24th St., The Tisch Bldg., New York, NY 10011-1913, (212)367-1000

Gay Nurses' Alliance - Defunct.

Gay Officers' Action League [12231], PO Box 1774, New York, NY 10113, (212)NY1-GOAL

Gay Parents Legal and Res. Group - Defunct.

Gay People in Christian Science - Defunct.

Gay People at Columbia [★12224]

Gay People; Lutherans Concerned for [★20061]

Gay People in Medicine [★12243]

Gay People in Medicine; Lesbian and [★12243]

Gay Police Assn. [IO], London, United Kingdom

Gay Pride Coordinators; Intl. Assn. of Lesbian/ [★12240]

Gay Task Force of ALA [★12214]

Gay Task Force; Natl. [★12249]

Gay Theatre Alliance - Defunct.

Gay West Community Network Toronto [IO], Toronto, ON, Canada

Gay Women's Alliance [★12244]

Gay Youth; Inst. for the Protection of Lesbian and [★12234]

Gaylactic Network [10944]

Gaylactic Network [IO], Washington, DC, United States

Gaylord Family Org. [20911], c/o Barry C. Wood, 1910 S Church St., Lodi, CA 95240, (209)366-2773

Gays Against Abortion [★12927]

Gays Everywhere; Children of Lesbians and [★12223]

Gays and Lesbians in Foreign Affairs [★24074]

Gays and Lesbians in Foreign Affairs Agencies USA [24074], PO Box 18774, Washington, DC 20036-8774, (202)232-1588

Gays and Lesbians; Pro-Life Alliance of [12927]

Gays; Parents and Friends of Lesbians and [★12253]

Gazelle Hounds
Saluki Club of Am. [22353]

Gazette Intl. Networking Inst. [★11981]

Gazette Intl. Networking Inst. [★IO]

Gazi Entomological Res. Soc. [IO], Ankara, Turkey

GDF [★16849]

GE Stockholders' Alliance for a Sustainable Nuclear-Free Future - Defunct.

Geary 18 Intl. Yacht Racing Assn. [23172], PO Box 4763, Federal Way, WA 98063, (253)946-2619

GEBECOMA [★IO]

Gebhardt-Heriot Found. for All Cats - Defunct.

Geburtshilfe und Gynakologie FMH [★IO]

Geddes Family Org; William [21085]

Geekcorps [3724], 901 15th St. NW, Ste. 1010, Washington, DC 20005, (202)326-0280

Geeks Without Borders [11806], 1121 Bailey Hill Rd., No. 8, Eugene, OR 97402, (541)359-1658

Geeks Without Borders [IO], Eugene, OR, United States

Geelona Hospice Care Assn. [IO], Geelong, Australia

Geelong Chamber of Commerce [IO], Geelong, Australia

Geelong and District Olive Assn. [IO], Torquay, Australia

Geelong Waterski Club [IO], Geelong, Australia

Gelatin Mfrs. Inst. of America - Address unknown since 1994.

Gelatine Mfrs. of Europe [IO], Brussels, Belgium

Gelbray Assn. [★IO]

Gelbray Assn. [★4262]

Gelbray Intl. [4262], Rte. 1, Box 273C, Madill, OK 73446, (580)223-5771

Gelbray Intl. [IO], Madill, OK, United States

Gelbvieh Assn; Amer. [4223]

Geluidstichting - Noise Found. [★IO]

Gem and Jewelry Export Promotion Coun. [IO], Bombay, India

Gem and Lapidary Dealers Assn. [2364], PO Box 2391, Tucson, AZ 85702-2391, (520)792-9431

Gem and Mineral Fed. of Canada [IO], Winfield, BC, Canada

Gem Soc; Amer. [2356]

Gem Trade Assn; Amer. [2357]

Gemmological Assn. of Australia [IO], Unley, Australia

Gemmological Assn. and Gem Testing Lab. of Great Britain [IO], London, United Kingdom

Gemological Inst. of Am. [2365], 5345 Armada Dr., The Robert Mouawad Campus, Carlsbad, CA 92008, (760)603-4000

Gemological Inst. of Am. Alumni Assn. [19173], The Robert Mouawad Campus, 5345 Armada Dr., Carlsbad, CA 92008, (760)603-4135

Gemological Inst. of Am.: Alumni Assn. [IO], Carlsbad, CA, United States

Gemologists Assn; Accredited [2354]

Gemology
Jeweler's Advisory Gp. [2369]
U.S. Faceters Guild [1121]

Gems and Aces [★10947]

Gems and Aces [★IO]

Gems of Hope [IO], Toronto, ON, Canada

Gems, Minerals and Jewelry Stud. Unit [22821], c/o George G. Young, Sec.-Treas., PO Box 632, Tewksbury, MA 01876, (978)851-8283

Gemstone Assn; Intl. Colored [3695]

Gen Art [9442], 133 W 25th St., 6th Fl., New York, NY 10001, (212)255-7300

GEN Movement [★19624]

GEN Movement [★IO]

Gencod EAN France [★IO]

Gender Action [18825], 1875 Connecticut Ave. NW, Ste. 1012, Washington, DC 20009, (202)587-5242

Gender Dysphoria Assn; Natl. Harry Benjamin [★13103]

Gender Educ. and Advocacy [13090], PO Box 33724, Decatur, GA 30033-0724

Gender Educ; Intl. Found. for [13091]

Gender Equity Leadership in Educ; Assn. for [8399]

Gender Info. Ser; Amer. Educational [★13090]

Gender and Sci. and Tech. Assn. [IO], Brighton, United Kingdom

Gender and Trade in Africa [IO], Johannesburg, Republic of South Africa

Gene Autry Intl. Fan Club - Address unknown since 1989.

Gene Pitney Fan Club [★24898]

Gene Pitney Intl. Fan Club [24898], 6201 - 39th Ave., Kenosha, WI 53142

Gene Stratton Porter Memorial Soc. [9651], 1205 Pleasant Point, Box 639, Rome City, IN 46784-9644, (260)854-3790

Gene Summers Intl. Fan Club [24899], 222 Tulane St., Garland, TX 75043-2239

Gene Summers Intl. Fan Club [IO], Garland, TX, United States

Genealogical Assn; Forrester [★20828]

Genealogical Assn. of Nova Scotia [IO], Halifax, NS, Canada

Genealogical Assn; Urbain Baudreau Graveline [21074]

Genealogical Center; Vesterheim [★21155]

Genealogical and Heraldic Inst. of America - Address unknown since 1995.

Genealogical and Heraldic Soc. [★IO]

Genealogical and Heraldry Soc. ADLER [IO], Vienna, Austria

Genealogical and Historical Assn; Acadian [★21098]

Genealogical and Historical Assn. of New Hampshire; Acadian [★21098]

Genealogical Inst. [21117], c/o Arlene H. Eakle, PhD, Founder/Pres., PO Box 129, Tremonton, UT 84337, (800)377-6058

Genealogical Org; Groberg - Holbrook [20924]

Genealogical Res; Blair Soc. for [20796]

Genealogical Societies; Assn. of Jewish [★21122]

Genealogical Soc; Afro-American Historical and [9353]

Genealogical Soc. of Am; Italian [10260]

Genealogical Soc. in Am; Russian Historical and [★21147]

Genealogical Soc; Austin Families [20787]

Genealogical Soc; Austins of Am. [★20787]

Genealogical Soc. of the Church of Jesus Christ of Latter-day Saints [★21115]

Genealogical Soc. of the Church of Jesus Christ of Latter-day Saints [★IO]

Genealogical Soc; Czechoslovak [★21113]

Genealogical Soc; Easterling Family [20891]

Genealogical Soc. of Flemish Americans [21118], 18740 13 Mile Rd., Roseville, MI 48066, (810)776-9579

Genealogical Soc. of Flemish Americans [IO], Roseville, MI, United States

Genealogical Soc. Intl; Irish [21125]

Genealogical Soc. of Ireland [IO], Dun Laoghaire, Ireland

Genealogical Soc; Polish [★21142]

Genealogical Soc; Progenitor [★21146]

Genealogical Soc; Seeley [21047]

Genealogical Soc. of South Africa [IO], Houghton, Republic of South Africa

Genealogical Soc. of Utah [★IO]

Genealogical Soc. of Utah [★21115]

Genealogical Speakers Guild [10899], PO Box 38314, Olmsted Falls, OH 44138-0314

Genealogists; Amer. Soc. of [21103]

Genealogists; Bd. for Certification of [21109]

Genealogists; Soc. of [IO]

Genealogy
Acadian Cultural Soc. [21096]

Reference to "IO" in place of a book number signifies that the association may be found in the 45th edition of International Organizations.

Encyclopedia of Associations, 46th Edition

3497

A.D. Johnson Family Assn. [20771]
Adam Hawkes Family Assn. [20772]
Adoption Identity Movement [11229]
Afro-American Historical and Genealogical Soc.
    [9353]
Ahern Clan Assn. [19048]
Alberta Family Histories Soc. [IO]
Alford Amer. Family Assn. [20777]
ALMA Soc. - Adoptees' Liberty Movement Assn.
    [11232]
Amer. Biographical Inst. Res. Assn. [21097]
American-Canadian Genealogical Soc. [21098]
American-Canadian Genealogical Soc. [IO]
Amer. Coll. of Heraldry [21099]
Amer. Family Records Assn. [21100]
American-French Genealogical Soc. [21101]
Amer. Heraldry Soc. [21102]
Amer. Legion Auxiliary [21189]
American/Schleswig-Holstein Heritage Soc.
    [19066]
Amer. Soc. of Genealogists [21103]
American Society of Genealogists [IO]
Andlauer Family Assn. [20781]
Ark-La-Tex Genealogical Assn. [21104]
Assn. of Genealogists and Researchers in
    Archives [IO]
Assn. of the German Nobility in North Am. [21105]
Assn. Houde Intl. [21106]
Assn. Houde Intl. [IO]
Assn. of Professional Genealogists in Ireland [IO]
Augustan Soc. [IO]
Augustan Soc. [21107]
Austin Families Genealogical Soc. [20787]
Australasian Fed. of Family History Organisations
    [IO]
Australian Inst. of Genealogical Stud. [IO]
Auxiliary to Sons of Union Veterans of the Civil
    War [20723]
Baker Family Intl. [20788]
Barney Family Historical Assn. [20790]
Baronial Order of Magna Charta and the Military
    Order of Crusades [10096]
Bell Family Assn. of the U.S. [20793]
Bishop Hill Heritage Assn. [21108]
Blackburn Family Assn. [20795]
Bloss-Pyles-Ross-Sellards Family [20798]
B'Man Family Assn. [20800]
Bd. for Certification of Genealogists [21109]
Bondurant Family Assn. [20803]
Brantley Assn. of Am. [20808]
Brinton Assn. of Am. [21110]
Burleson Family Assn. [20812]
Cahill Cooperative Ancestors [20813]
Canadian Assn. of Professional Heritage Consult-
    ants [IO]
Canadian Soc. of Mayflower Descendants [IO]
Catholic Family History Soc. [IO]
Catholic War Veterans Auxiliary of the U.S.A.
    [21194]
Children of the Confederacy [20724]
Clan Anderson Soc. [10953]
Clan Arthur Assn., USA [19349]
Clan Brown Soc. [20818]
Clan Chisholm Soc. [IO]
Clan Chisholm Soc., Australia [IO]
Clan Chisholm Soc., Canada [IO]
Clan Chisholm Soc., New Zealand [IO]
Clan Chisholm Soc., Nova Scotia [IO]
Clan Chisholm Soc., United Kingdom [IO]
Clan Craig Assn. of Am. [19350]
Clan Cunningham Soc. of Am. [20823]
Clan Donald Canada [IO]
Clan Douglas Soc. of North Am. [20826]
Clan Drummond Soc. of North Am. [20827]
Clan Ewing in Am. [19351]
Clan Farquharson Assn. of Canada [IO]
Clan Fergusson Soc. of North Am. [IO]
Clan Fergusson Soc. of North Am. [21111]
Clan Forsyth Soc. of Canada [IO]
Clan Fraser Soc. of Canada [IO]
Clan Guthrie USA [20830]
Clan Hamilton Soc. [20831]
Clan Hunter Assn. [IO]
Clan Hunter Assn. USA [20832]
Clan Irwin Assn. [20833]

Clan Keith Soc. [20835]
Clan MacAlpine Soc. [19049]
Clan MacGillivray Soc. - Australia [IO]
Clan MacIntyre Assn. [20838]
Clan MacIntyre Soc. [20839]
Clan Mackay Assn. of Canada [IO]
Clan MacKenzie Soc. in the Americas [20841]
Clan Mackenzie Soc. in the Americas - Canada
    [IO]
Clan MacKinnon Soc. [19050]
Clan MacLennan Assn., U.S.A. [20843]
Clan MacLennan, Central Ontario Br. [IO]
Clan MacNeil in Canada [IO]
Clan Macpherson Assn. [20845]
Clan Matheson Soc. [20848]
Clan Maxwell Soc. of the USA [20849]
Clan McAlister of Am. [19051]
Clan McLaren Assn. of North America [20850]
Clan Menzies Soc., North Amer. Br. [20851]
Clan Moffat Soc. [20852]
Clan Moncreiffe Soc. of North Am. [20853]
Clan Munro Assn. [20855]
Clan Munro Assn. of Canada [IO]
Clan Napier in North America [20856]
Clan Phail Soc. in North America [19052]
Clan Pollock [20857]
Clan Ramsey Assn. of North Am. [20858]
Clan Ross Assn. of Canada [IO]
Clan Ross Assn. of the U.S. [20860]
Clan Scott Soc. [20861]
Clan Shaw Soc. [20862]
Clan Sinclair Assn. of Canada [IO]
Clan Sutherland Soc. of North Am. [20864]
Cloud Family Assn. [20866]
Cogswell Family Assn. [20868]
Colonial Order of the Acorn [20735]
Continental European Family History Assn.
    [21112]
Continental European Family History Assn. [IO]
Czechoslovak Genealogical Soc. Intl. [IO]
Czechoslovak Genealogical Soc. Intl. [21113]
Daniel Boone and Frontier Families Res. Assn.
    [10107]
Dannenmueller-Hoefler Family Assn. [20878]
Daughters of the Cincinnati [20670]
Daughters of the Republic of Texas [21114]
Daughters of Union Veterans of the Civil War,
    1861-1865 [20725]
Denison Soc. [20880]
Descendants of the Signers of the Declaration of
    Independence [20671]
Deutsche Arbeitsgemeinschaft Genealogischer
    Verbande [IO]
Doane Family Assn. of Am. [20883]
Dodge Family Assn. [20885]
DuBois Family Assn. [20886]
Duncan Surname Assn. [20887]
Dunlop - Dunlap Family Soc. [20888]
Dutch Soc. for Jewish Genealogy [IO]
Duty's in America [20890]
Eller Family Assn. [20894]
Elliot Clan Soc. USA [20895]
FAMILIA Ancestral Res. Assn. [19067]
FAMILIA Ancestral Res. Assn. [IO]
Family and Church History Dept. of the Church of
    Jesus Christ of Latter-Day Saints [IO]
Family and Church History Dept. of the Church of
    Jesus Christ of Latter-Day Saints [21115]
Fed. of East European Family History Societies
    [19068]
Fed. of Family History Societies [IO]
Fed. of French War Veterans [21416]
Fed. of Genealogical Societies [21116]
Felton Family Assn. [20901]
Flagon and Trencher - Descendants of Colonial
    Tavern Keepers [20737]
French-Canadian Genealogical Soc. [IO]
French/Canadian/Metis Genealogical Soc. [20720]
Fuqua(y) Family Assn. [20909]
Gaylord Family Org. [20911]
Genealogical Assn. of Nova Scotia [IO]
Genealogical and Heraldry Soc. ADLER [IO]
Genealogical Inst. [21117]
Genealogical Soc. of Flemish Americans [21118]
Genealogical Soc. of Flemish Americans [IO]

Genealogical Soc. of Ireland [IO]
Genealogical Soc. of South Africa [IO]
Genealogical Speakers Guild [10899]
Gen. Soc. of Colonial Wars [20738]
Gen. Soc. of Mayflower Descendants [21247]
Gen. Soc., Sons of the Revolution [20672]
Gen. Soc. of the War of 1812 [21354]
George McCleave Family Org. [20912]
German Genealogical Soc. of Am. [21119]
German Genealogical Soc. of Am. [IO]
German Res. Assn. [21120]
Geshkewich Surname Org. [20914]
Gilstrap Family Assn. [20916]
Goff/Gough Family Assn. [20917]
Gosselin Family Assn. [IO]
Gottscheer Heritage and Genealogy Assn. [9978]
Graves Family Assn. [20920]
Griesemer Family Assn. [20922]
Grinnell Family Assn. [20923]
Grover Family Org. [20925]
Harden - Hardin - Harding Family Assn. [20928]
Harrison Family Assn. [20929]
Hathaway Family Assn. [20932]
Haviland Family Org. [20933]
Hawkins Assn. [20934]
Haymore Family Org. [20935]
Heald Family Assn. [20937]
Heiney Family Tree [20938]
Heraldry Soc. of England [IO]
Heraldry Soc. of Scotland [IO]
Hereditary Order of Descendants of the Loyalists
    and Patriots of the Amer. Revolution [20673]
Hispanic Genealogical Soc. [9973]
Hoefler Family Assn. [20942]
Holland Soc. of New York [20740]
Holloway - Ralston Family Assn. [20943]
Hood's Texas Brigade Assn. [20726]
House of Boyd Soc. [20945]
Hoyt Family Assn. [20946]
Hudson Family Assn. [20948]
Huebotter Family Org. [20949]
Immigrant Genealogical Soc. [21121]
Immigrant Genealogical Soc. [IO]
Inst. of Heraldic and Genealogical Stud. [IO]
Intl. Assn. of Jewish Genealogical Societies [IO]
Intl. Assn. of Jewish Genealogical Societies
    [21122]
Intl. Assn. of the Skubinna Family [20952]
Intl. Molyneux Family Assn. [20953]
Intl. Soc. for British Genealogy and Family History
    [21123]
Intl. Soc. for British Genealogy and Family History
    [IO]
Intl. Soc. Daughters of Utah Pioneers [21252]
Intl. Soundex Reunion Registry [11248]
The Irish Ancestral Res. Assn. [19069]
The Irish Ancestral Res. Assn. [IO]
Irish Family History Forum [9974]
Irish Genealogical Found. [21124]
Irish Genealogical Found. [IO]
Irish Genealogical Res. Soc. [IO]
Irish Genealogical Soc. Intl. [21125]
Israel Genealogical Soc. [IO]
Italian Genealogical Gp. [21126]
Italian Genealogical Soc. of Am. [10260]
Jacob Hochstetler Family Assn. [20955]
Jamestowne Soc. [20742]
Jardine Clan Soc. [IO]
Jewish Genealogical Soc. [21127]
Jewish War Veterans of the U.S.A. - Natl. Ladies
    Auxiliary [21196]
Johann Frederick Mouser Family Org. [20959]
Johannes Schwalm Historical Assn. [21128]
John Carver Family Org. [20961]
John Clough Genealogical Soc. [20962]
Joseph Goodbrake Montgomery Family Org.
    [20968]
Junkins Family Assn. [20970]
Kerr Family Assn. of North.Am. [20972]
Kershner Family Assn. [20973]
Knowles/Knoles/Noles Family Assn. [21129]
Ladies Auxiliary, Military Order of the Purple
    Heart, U.S.A. [20713]
Lancaster Mennonite Historical Soc. [21130]
Lancaster Mennonite Historical Society [IO]

A star before a book entry number signifies that the name is not listed separately, but is mentioned within the entry.

Lillard Family Assn. [20978]
Locke Surname Org. [20981]
Los Californianos [20719]
Luther Family Assn. [20984]
Lybarger Memorial Assn. [20985]
MacCartney Clan Soc. [20986]
MacFaddien Family Soc. [20987]
Magny Families Assn. [20990]
Maxfield Family Org. [20992]
Maybee Soc. [20993]
Mazur Surname Org. [20994]
McAdams Historical Soc. [20995]
McCune Family Assn. [20996]
McGregor Family Assn. [20998]
Meader Family Assn. [20999]
Merier-Gourley-Roark Family Org. [21000]
Miles Merwin Assn. [21001]
Military Order of the Loyal Legion of the U.S. [20728]
Moody Family Assn. [21003]
Morgan Family Club [19053]
Morse Soc. [21131]
Mt. Marty Coll. Alumni Assn. [24399]
Mountain Press Res. Center [21132]
Murray Clan Soc. North Am. [21005]
Natl. Aldrich Family Assn. [21006]
Natl. Assn. of Lively Families [21007]
Natl. Genealogical Soc. [21133]
Natl. Soc. of the Children of the Amer. Revolution [20674]
Natl. Soc. of the Colonial Dames of Am. [20743]
Natl. Soc. Colonial Dames XVII Century [20744]
Natl. Soc., Daughters of the Amer. Colonists [20746]
Natl. Soc., Daughters of the Amer. Revolution [20675]
Natl. Soc. Descendants of Early Quakers [21134]
Natl. Soc. of Madison Family Descendants [21135]
Natl. Soc., Sons of the Amer. Revolution [20676]
Natl. Soc. of the Sons of Utah Pioneers [21254]
Natl. Soc., U.S. Daughters of 1812 [21355]
Natl. Soc. Women Descendants of the Ancient and Honorable Artillery Company [20749]
Neal Dougan-Theodorus Scowden Family Org. [21010]
Nesbitt-Nisbet Soc.: A Worldwide Clan Soc. [21011]
New Canaan Historical Soc. [10137]
New England Historic Genealogical Soc. [21136]
New York Genealogical and Biographical Soc. [21137]
New Zealand Soc. of Genealogists [IO]
New Zealand Soc. of Genealogists - Auckland Br. [IO]
New Zealand Soc. of Genealogists - Cambridge Br. [IO]
New Zealand Soc. of Genealogists - Coromandel [IO]
New Zealand Soc. of Genealogists - Far North [IO]
New Zealand Soc. of Genealogists - Hamilton Br. [IO]
New Zealand Soc. of Genealogists - Hibiscus Coast Br. [IO]
New Zealand Soc. of Genealogists - Howick Br. [IO]
New Zealand Soc. of Genealogists - Matamata Br. [IO]
New Zealand Soc. of Genealogists - North Shore Br. [IO]
New Zealand Soc. of Genealogists - Northern Wairoa Br. [IO]
New Zealand Soc. of Genealogists - Onehunga Br. [IO]
New Zealand Soc. of Genealogists - Papakura Br. [IO]
New Zealand Soc. of Genealogists - Rotorua Br. [IO]
New Zealand Soc. of Genealogists - St. Johns Br. [IO]
New Zealand Soc. of Genealogists - Taupo Br. [IO]
New Zealand Soc. of Genealogists - Tauranga Br. [IO]

New Zealand Soc. of Genealogists - Waitakere Br. [IO]
New Zealand Soc. of Genealogists - Wanganui Br. [IO]
New Zealand Soc. of Genealogists - Wellsford Br. [IO]
New Zealand Soc. of Genealogists - Whakatane Br. [IO]
New Zealand Soc. of Genealogists - Whangarei Br. [IO]
North of Ireland Family History Soc. [IO]
Northwest Territory Genealogical Soc. [IO]
Norwegian Genealogical Soc. [IO]
O'Dochartaigh Clann Assn. [IO]
O'Hare Family Assn. [21016]
Ohio Genealogical Soc. [21138]
Orangeburgh German Swiss Genealogical Soc. [21139]
Order of Americans of Armorial Ancestry [20750]
Order of the Founders and Patriots of Am. [20755]
Orphan Train Heritage Soc. of Am. [21140]
Ouderkerk Family Genealogical Assn. [21017]
Ouellette Family Assn. of Am. [IO]
Paisley Family Soc. [21020]
Palatines to Am.: Researching German-Speaking Ancestry [21141]
Palatines to Am.: Researching German-Speaking Ancestry [IO]
Pan Amer. Indian Assn. [10753]
Parke Soc. [21021]
Pellien/Jaeger/Loretan/Steiner/Ross Soc. [21022]
Pennsylvania German Soc. [21243]
Pierre Chastain Family Assn. [21023]
Pilgrim Edward Doty Soc. [20756]
Pilgrim Soc. [21249]
Pilgrims of the U.S. [21250]
Platt Family Assn. [21024]
Polish Genealogical Soc. of Am. [21142]
Polish Genealogical Soc. of Am. [IO]
Prall Family Assn. [21026]
Premm Family Assn. [21027]
Presidential Families of Am. [21143]
Puerto Rican Hispanic Genealogical Soc. [9975]
Purcell Family of Am. [21028]
Pursuing Our Italian Names Together [21144]
Pursuing Our Italian Names Together [IO]
Rainier Soc. [21145]
Ralph Shepard Family Org. [21030]
Reynolds Family Assn. [21032]
Robert Bruce Bradley Family Org. [21036]
Rockafellow Family Assn. [21037]
Ron Bremer Seminars [21146]
Ron Bremer Seminars [IO]
Ronald Lee Shankland Family Org. [21038]
Rose Family Assn. [21039]
Royal Heraldry Soc. of Canada [IO]
Runkle Family Assn. [21040]
Russian Nobility Assn. in Am. [21147]
Saint Nicholas Soc. of the City of New York [21148]
Saleeby-Saliba Family Assn. [21041]
Savoie Acadian Cultural and Historical Soc. [21149]
Scotch-Irish Found. [21150]
Scotch-Irish Found. [IO]
Scotch-Irish Soc. of the U.S.A. [21151]
Scottish Genealogy Soc. [IO]
Smith-Hedrick Family Assn. [21052]
Snodgrass Clan Soc. [21053]
Societas Heraldica Scandinavica [IO]
Societe de genealogie et d'archives de Rimouski [IO]
Soc. of the Ark and the Dove [20758]
Soc. of Australian Genealogists [IO]
Soc. of California Pioneers [21255]
Soc. of the Cincinnati [20677]
Soc. of Daughters of Holland Dames [20759]
Soc. of the Descendants of the Colonial Clergy [20760]
Soc. of the Descendants of Washington's Army at Valley Forge [20678]
Soc. of Genealogists [IO]
Soc. of Indiana Pioneers [21256]
Soc. of Mareen Duvall Descendants [21055]

Soc. of Richmond County Descendants [21152]
Soc. of Stukely Westcott Descendants of Am. [21056]
Sons of the Amer. Legion [21201]
Sons of Confederate Veterans [20730]
Sons and Daughters of Oregon Pioneers [21257]
Sons and Daughters of Pioneer Rivermen [21258]
Sons of Union Veterans of the Civil War [20731]
Southern Bean Assn. [21057]
Sparks Family Assn. [21058]
Spencer Historical and Genealogical Soc. [21153]
Steere Family Assn. [21060]
Stovall Family Assn. [21062]
Studebaker Family Natl. Assn. [21065]
Swedish Amer. Museum Assn. of Chicago [10990]
Swiss Heraldry Soc. [IO]
Taft Family Assn. [21068]
Templin Family Assn. [21069]
Tevebaugh - Teverbaugh Surname Org. [21070]
Tripp Family Assn. [21072]
Ulster Historical Found. [IO]
Ulster-Scots Soc. of Am. [21154]
United Daughters of the Confederacy [20732]
Vawter - Vauter - Vaughter(s) Family Assn. [21076]
Veitch Historical Soc. [21077]
Venezuelan Inst. of Genealogy [IO]
Vesterheim Genealogical Center and Naeseth Lib. [21155]
Wardner Family Historical Assn. [21079]
Wefel Family Assn. [21080]
Welsh-American Genealogical Soc. [21156]
William Burrup Family Org. [21084]
William Geddes Family Org. [21085]
William Jacob Heckman Family Org. [21086]
William Kindel Family Org. [21087]
World Chamberlain Genealogical Soc. [21157]
World Jewish Genealogy Org. [21158]
World Jewish Genealogy Org. [IO]
York County Genealogical Soc. [21159]
Young Surname Org. [21091]
Zang Family Org. [21092]
Genealogy Club of America - Defunct.
Genealogy Copy Ser. [★21117]
Genealogy Res. Inst. [★21146]
Genealogy Res. Inst. [★IO]
Gen. Agents; Amer. Assn. of Managing [2133]
Gen. Agents and Managers Assn. [★2166]
Gen. Agents and Managers Assn. [★IO]
Gen. Agents and Managers Conf. of NALU [★IO]
Gen. Agents and Managers Conf. of NALU [★2166]
Gen. Anthropology Division of the Amer. Anthropological Assn. [6417], c/o Karl G. Heider, Pres., Univ. of South Carolina, Dept. of Anthropology, Columbia, SC 29208, (703)528-1902
Gen. Arbitration Coun. of the Textile and Apparel Indus. [5453], c/o Amer. Arbitration Assn., 335 Madison Ave., 10th Fl., New York, NY 10017-4605, (212)716-5800
Gen. Arbitration Coun. of the Textile Indus. [★5453]
Gen. Assembly Binding Women for Reforms, Integrity, Equality, Leadership, and Action [IO], Manila, Philippines
Gen. Assembly of Intl. Sports Federations [★IO]
General Assembly to Stop the Powerline - Address unknown since 2002.
Gen. Assn. of Engineers in Romania [IO], Bucharest, Romania
Gen. Assn. of Gen. Baptists [19488], 100 Stinson Dr., Poplar Bluff, MO 63901, (573)785-7746
Gen. Assn. of Intl. Sports Federations [IO], Monte Carlo, Monaco
Gen. Assn. of Regular Baptist Churches [19489], 1300 N Meacham Rd., Schaumburg, IL 60173-4806, (847)843-1600
Gen. Assn. of Romanian Engineers [★IO]
General Automation Users Group Exchange - Defunct.
Gen. Aviation Manufacturers Assn. [149], 1400 K St. NW, Ste. 801, Washington, DC 20005, (202)393-1500
Gen. Aviation Mfrs. and Traders Assn. [★IO]
Gen. Bd. of Church and Soc. of the United Methodist Church [20263], 100 Maryland Ave. NE, Washington, DC 20002, (202)488-5629

Reference to "IO" in place of a book number signifies that the association may be found in the 45th edition of International Organizations.

Gen. Building Contractors Assn. [625], 36 S 18th St., PO Box 15959, Philadelphia, PA 19103-0959, (215)568-7015

Gen. Chiropractic Coun. [IO], London, United Kingdom

Gen. Commn. on Archives and History of the United Methodist Church [10467], PO Box 127, Madison, NJ 07940, (973)408-3189

Gen. Commn. on the Status and Role of Women [17535], 77 W Washington St., Ste. 1009, Chicago, IL 60602, (312)346-4900

General Conf. of Grand Courts Heroines of Jericho, Prince Hall Affiliation, U.S.A. - Address unknown since 1995.

General Constituency Sect. for Small or Rural Hospitals - Address unknown since 1999.

Gen. Contractors Assn. of Ottawa [IO], Ottawa, ON, Canada

Gen. Convention of the Baptist Denomination in the U.S. for Foreign Missions [★IO]

Gen. Convention of the Baptist Denomination in the U.S. for Foreign Missions [★19483]

General Coun. of the Assemblies of God [★20643]

General Coun. of the Assemblies of God [★IO]

Gen. Coun. of the Bar [IO], London, United Kingdom

Gen. Coun. of the Bar of Northern Ireland [IO], Belfast, United Kingdom

Gen. Coun. of British Shipping [★IO]

Gen. Coun. of Cooperating Baptist Missions [★19480]

Gen. Coun. and Register of Naturopaths [IO], Somerset, United Kingdom

Gen. Counsels' Assn. of Accident and Hea. Counsels [★IO]

Gen. Counsels' Assn. of Accident and Hea. Counsels [★5499]

Gen. Dental Coun. [IO], London, United Kingdom

Gen. Dental Practitioners Assn. [★IO]

General Educational Development Inst. - Address unknown since 1994.

Gen. Egyptian Book Org. [IO], Cairo, Egypt

General Electric
Corporate Accountability Intl. [18149]

Gen. Fed. of Milk Cooperatives (CFMC) [★IO]

Gen. Fed. of Trade Unions [IO], London, United Kingdom

Gen. Fed. of Women's Clubs [IO], Washington, DC, United States

Gen. Fed. of Women's Clubs [19435], 1734 N St. NW, Washington, DC 20036-2990, (202)347-3168

Gen. Fisheries Commn. for the Mediterranean [IO], Rome, Italy

General Grand Chapter, Order of the Eastern Star [IO], Washington, DC, United States

Gen. Grand Chap., Order of the Eastern Star [19234], 1618 New Hampshire Ave. NW, Washington, DC 20009-2549, (202)667-4737

Gen. Grand Chap. of Royal Arch Masons Intl. [19235], PO Box 489, Danville, KY 40423-0489, (859)236-0757

Gen. Grand Chap. of Royal Arch Masons Intl. [IO], Danville, KY, United States

General Headquarters/Army Forces in the Pacific - Defunct.

General Hosp. Sect; Public- [★14895]

Gen. Hypnotherapy Register [IO], Lymington, United Kingdom

General Improvement Contractors Assn. - Address unknown since 1995.

Gen. Insurance Assn. of Japan [IO], Tokyo, Japan

Gen. Insurance Assn. of Singapore [IO], Singapore, Singapore

Gen. Internal Medicine; Soc. of [14970]

Gen. and Liberal Stud; Assn. for [8777]

Gen. Medical Coun. [IO], London, United Kingdom

Gen. Merchandise Distributors Coun. [4021], 1275 Lake Plaza Dr., Colorado Springs, CO 80906, (719)576-4260

General Milk Sales - Defunct.

Gen. Motors Credit Unions; Coun. of [1105]

Gen. Optical Coun. [IO], London, United Kingdom

Gen. Osteopathic Coun. [IO], London, United Kingdom

General Passenger Comm.-Eastern Railroads - Defunct.

Gen. Practice; Amer. Osteopathic Bd. of [★15799]

Gen. Practice of Pharmacy; Acad. of [★15918]

Gen. Practice Sect. of APhA [★15918]

Gen. Practitioner; Amer. Acad. of Orthodontics for the [14107]

General Pulaski Heritage Found. - Defunct.

Gen. Retailers and Traders Union [IO], Valletta, Malta

Gen. Semantics; Inst. of [10962]

Gen. Ser. Consumer Arbitration Prog. [★17330]

Gen. Ser. Employees Union Local 73 [24097], 1165 N Clark St., Ste. 500, Chicago, IL 60610, (312)787-5868

Gen. Soc. of Colonial Wars [20738], Univ. of Baltimore Special Collections, 1420 Maryland Ave., Baltimore, MD 21201

Gen. Soc. of Mayflower Descendants [21247], PO Box 3297, Plymouth, MA 02361-3297, (508)746-3188

General Society of Mayflower Descendants [IO], Plymouth, MA, United States

Gen. Soc. of Mechanics and Tradesmen [★9229]

Gen. Soc. of Mechanics and Tradesmen of the City of New York [9229], 20 W 44th St., New York, NY 10036, (212)840-1840

Gen. Soc., Sons of the Revolution [20672], 108 S Liberty St., Independence, MO 64050, (816)254-1776

Gen. Soc. of the War of 1812 [21354], c/o Mr. Timothy C. Harris, VP Gen., 6184 Stinson Blvd. NE, Fridley, MN 55432-5835

Gen. Surgeons; Amer. Soc. of [16571]

Gen. Teaching Coun. for Scotland [IO], Edinburgh, United Kingdom

General Union Democratic Students and Patriotic Afghan - Address unknown since 1985.

Gen. Union of Eritrean Students [★IO]

Gen. Union of Romanian Manufacturers [IO], Bucharest, Romania

Gen. Union of Workers [IO], Madrid, Spain

General Whale - Defunct.

Gen. Workers' Union [IO], Valletta, Malta

Generating Systems Assn; Elecl. [1182]

The Generation After [17119]

Generation Green [17054], PO Box 7027, Evanston, IL 60201, (800)652-0827

GenerationEngage [18848], 2800 Calvert St. NW, Washington, DC 20008, (202)465-4807

Generations [IO], Montreal, QC, Canada

Generations for Life [★IO]

Generations for Life [★18565]

Generations United [13170], 1331 H St. NW, Ste. 900, Washington, DC 20005, (202)289-3979

Generative Linguistics in the Old World [IO], Utrecht, Netherlands

Generic Horse Assn; Intl. [4899]

Generic Pharmaceutical Assn. [2975], 2300 Clarendon Blvd., Ste. 400, Arlington, VA 22201, (703)647-2480

Generic Pharmaceutical Indus. Assn. [★2975]

Genesis Expeditions [IO], Ensenada, Mexico

Genesis Fac. [★IO]

Genesis Fac. Found. [IO], West Vancouver, BC, Canada

Genesis Info. [24900]

Genesis Inst. [20549], 10220 N Nevada, Ste. 280, Spokane, WA 99218, (509)467-7913

Genesis Project - Address unknown since 2002.

Genetic Alliance [16536], 4301 Connecticut Ave. NW, Ste. 404, Washington, DC 20008, (202)966-5557

Genetic Defects
A-T Medical Res. Found. [14436]
Amer. Coll. of Medical Genetics [14494]
Amer. Hemochromatosis Soc. [14543]
CFC Intl. [14435]
Children's PKU Network [15245]
Cornelia de Lange Syndrome Found. [13754]
Friedreich's Ataxia Res. Alliance [14403]
Hemochromatosis Info. Soc. [14800]
Intl. Assn. of Sickle Cell Nurses And Physician Assistants [14706]
MUMS Natl. Parent-to-Parent Network [16541]
Nail Patella Syndrome Worldwide [14467]
Nevus Network [16545]

Prader-Willi Found. [14474]
PRISMS: Parents and Researchers Interested In Smith-Magenis Syndrome [14476]
Progressive Osseous Heteroplasia Assn. [14477]
Prune Belly Syndrome Network [14478]
Pull-thru Network [14427]
Purine Res. Soc. [15258]
Genetic Disorders
A-T Medical Res. Found. [14436]
Aicardi Syndrome Newsl. [14437]
Aicardi Syndrome Newsl. [IO]
Alagille Syndrome Alliance [14438]
Alpha-1 Assn. [16353]
Alpha 1 Found. [14439]
Alstrom Syndrome Intl. [14440]
Alstrom Syndrome Intl. [IO]
Amer. Coll. of Medical Genetics [14494]
Amer. Hemochromatosis Soc. [14543]
Androgen Insensitivity Syndrome Support Gp. - USA [14441]
Angelman Syndrome Assn. [IO]
Angelman Syndrome Found. [16528]
Asociacion de Afectados Sindrome de Marfan [IO]
Assn. Francaise du Syndrome de Marfan [IO]
Assn. for Glycogen Storage Disease [15244]
Assn. for Multiple Endocrine Neoplasia Disorders [IO]
Beckwith-Wiedemann Support Network [14442]
Canadian Ehlers Danlos Assn. [IO]
Canadian Genetic Diseases Network [IO]
Canadian Marfan Assn. [IO]
Canadian Porphyria Found. [IO]
Celiac Sprue Association/United States of Am. [14413]
Charcot-Marie-Tooth Assn. [15313]
Children's PKU Network [15245]
Chromosome 9P Network [14443]
Chromosome 9P Network [IO]
Chromosome 18 Registry and Res. Soc. [IO]
Chromosome 18 Registry and Res. Soc. [14444]
Chromosome Deletion Outreach [14445]
Chromosome Deletion Outreach [IO]
Coalition For Heritable Disorders Of Connective Tissue [14446]
Coffin-Lowry Syndrome Found. [14447]
Cornelia de Lange Syndrome Found. [13754]
Cri du Chat Syndrome Mutual Help Gp. [14448]
Cuban Assn. of Marfan Syndrome [IO]
Cystic Fibrosis Assn. of Ireland [IO]
Cystic Fibrosis Worldwide [16359]
Cystinosis Found. [15246]
Cystinosis Res. Network [15247]
Danish Assn. for von Hippel-Lindau [IO]
Danish Marfan Assn. [IO]
Disorders of Chromosome 16 Foundation [IO]
Disorders of Chromosome 16 Found. [14449]
Dysautonomia Found. [15317]
Ehlers Danlos Natl. Found. [16651]
Fabry Support and Info. Gp. [14262]
Fanconi Anemia Res. Fund [14450]
Fatty Oxidation Disorders (FOD) Family Support Gp. [16532]
FG Syndrome Family Alliance [16533]
Finnish Marfan Assn. [IO]
Five P Minus Soc. [16534]
Floating Harbor Syndrome Support Gp. of North Am. [14451]
Floating Harbor Syndrome Support Gp. of North Am. [IO]
Found. for Nager and Miller Syndromes [14452]
FRAXA Res. Found. [16535]
Friedreich's Ataxia Res. Alliance [14403]
Gauchers Assn. [IO]
Genetic Alliance [16536]
Genetic and Inherited Disorders Org. [IO]
Genetic Interest Gp. [IO]
Greek Assn. of the Marfan Syndrome [IO]
Hemochromatosis Info. Soc. [14800]
Hermansky-Pudlak Syndrome Network [14453]
Hermansky-Pudlak Syndrome Network [IO]
HHT Found. Intl. [IO]
HHT Found. Intl. [14454]
Huntington's Disease Assn. of Ireland [IO]
Incontinentia Pigmenti Intl. Found. [IO]
Incontinentia Pigmenti Intl. Found. [14455]

A star before a book entry number signifies that the name is not listed separately, but is mentioned within the entry.

Intl. Assn. of Sickle Cell Nurses And Physician Assistants [14706]
Intl. Fed. of Marfan Syndrome Organizations [14456]
Intl. Fed. of Marfan Syndrome Organizations [IO]
Intl. Fibrodysplasia Ossificans Progressiva Assn. [14457]
Intl. Huntington Assn. [IO]
International Society for Mannosidosis and Related Diseases [IO]
Intl. Soc. for Mannosidosis and Related Diseases [14458]
Irish Assn. for Spina Bifida and Hydrocephalus [IO]
Joubert Syndrome Found. and Related Cerebellar Disorders [14459]
Kennedy's Disease Assn. [15334]
Late-Onset Tay-Sachs Found. [14460]
Laurence-Moon-Bardet-Biedl Syndrome Network [14461]
Lowe Syndrome Assn. [14462]
Make Early Diagnosis to Prevent Early Death [14463]
Make Early Diagnosis to Prevent Early Death [IO]
Malignant Hyperthermia Assn. of the U.S. [14464]
Marfan Argentina [IO]
Marfan Assn. UK [IO]
Marfan Brasil [IO]
Marfan Hilfe (Deutschland) e.V. [IO]
MHE Coalition [14465]
Michael Fund/International Found. for Genetic Res. [14466]
Michael Fund/International Found. for Genetic Res. [IO]
MUMS Natl. Parent-to-Parent Network [16541]
Myotubular Myopathy Rsrc. Gp. [16542]
Nail Patella Syndrome Worldwide [14467]
Natl. Ataxia Found. [15342]
Natl. Found. for Ectodermal Dysplasias [14468]
Natl. Fragile X Found. [14469]
Natl. Incontinentia Pigmenti Found. [14470]
Natl. Marfan Found. [16652]
Natl. Niemann Pick Disease Found. [15254]
Neurofibromatosis [14471]
Organic Acidemia Assn. [14472]
Parkinson's Action Network [14285]
Pediatric Neurotransmitter Disease Assn. [15361]
Pierre Robin Network [14473]
Prader-Willi Found. [14474]
Prader-Willi Syndrome Assn. - South Africa [IO]
Prader-Willi Syndrome Assn. (U.S.A.) [14475]
PRISMS: Parents and Researchers Interested In Smith-Magenis Syndrome [14476]
PRISMS: Parents and Researchers Interested In Smith-Magenis Syndrome [IO]
Progressive Osseous Heteroplasia Assn. [14477]
Prune Belly Syndrome Network [14478]
Prune Belly Syndrome Network [IO]
Purine Res. Soc. [15258]
PXE Intl. [14479]
Share and Care Cockayne Syndrome Network [14480]
Shwachman Diamond Am. [14481]
Slovak Marfan Assn. [IO]
Sotos Syndrome Support Assn. [IO]
Sotos Syndrome Support Assn. [14482]
South African Marfan Syndrome Org. [IO]
Spondylitis Assn. of Am. [16377]
Stickler Involved People [14483]
Stickler Involved People [IO]
Sudden Arrhythmia Death Syndromes Found. [14484]
Support Org. For Trisomy 13/18 and Related Disorders - UK [IO]
Support Org. for Trisomy 13/18 Ireland [IO]
Support Org. for Trisomy 18, 13, and Related Disorders [14485]
Swedish Marfan Assn. [IO]
Take Charge! Cure Parkinson's [15366]
Treacher Collins Found. [14067]
Turner Syndrome Soc. of the U.S. [14486]
Turner's Syndrome Soc. [IO]
U.S. Adult Cystic Fibrosis Assn. [16364]
U.S. Hereditary Angioedema Assn. [14487]
Velo-Cardio-Facial Syndrome [14488]

Velo-Cardio-Facial Syndrome [IO]
VHL Family Alliance [14489]
Williams Syndrome Assn. [14490]
Xeroderma Pigmentosum Soc. [14491]
Genetic Engg. Action Network [6615], c/o Stephanie Weisenbach, Natl. Coor., PO Box 194, Mechanicsville, IA 52306, (563)432-6735
Genetic Found; Wallace [4117]
Genetic and Inherited Disorders Org. [IO], Dublin, Ireland
Genetic Interest Gp. [IO], London, United Kingdom
Genetic Resources Programme; Intl. [★4108]
Genetic Support Groups; Alliance of [★16536]
Genetic Support Groups; Alliance of [★15246]
Genetic Technologists; Assn. of [6569]
Genetic Toxicology Assn. [7802], c/o Leon Stankowski, Treas., Covance Labs., 9200 Leesburg Pike, Vienna, VA 22182, (302)366-6322
Genetically Engineered Foods; Campaign to Label [17604]
Genetically Engineered Foods; State Public Interest Res. Groups' Campaign on [4779]
Genetics
Alliance for Better Foods [4674]
Amer. Assn. of Immunologists [14929]
Amer. Bd. of Genetic Counseling [14492]
Amer. Bd. of Medical Genetics [14493]
Amer. Coll. of Medical Genetics [14494]
Amer. Genetic Assn. [7111]
Amer. Hemochromatosis Soc. [14543]
Amer. Inst. for Medical and Biological Engg. [7112]
Amer. Soc. of Gene Therapy [14495]
American Society of Gene Therapy [IO]
Amer. Soc. for Genomic Medicine [IO]
Amer. Soc. for Genomic Medicine [14496]
Amer. Soc. of Human Genetics [7113]
Americans to Ban Cloning [17089]
Androgen Insensitivity Syndrome Support Gp. - USA [14441]
Argentine Soc. of Medical Genetics [IO]
Assn. of Professors of Human and Medical Genetics [14497]
Behavior Genetics Assn. [14498]
Behavior Genetics Assn. [IO]
Belgian Soc. of Human Genetics [IO]
Brazilian Genetics Soc. [IO]
British Soc. for Human Genetics [IO]
Canadian Assn. of Genetic Counsellors [IO]
Canadian Coll. of Medical Geneticists [IO]
Center for Bioethics [6558]
Center for Bioethics [6557]
Clinical Genetics Soc. [IO]
Coalition for the Advancement of Medical Res. [15103]
Coalition for Genetic Fairness [17107]
Comm. for the Advancement of Stem Cell Res. [18542]
Cornelia de Lange Syndrome Found. [13754]
Dysautonomia Found. [15317]
Environmental Mutagen Soc. [6575]
Eugenics Special Interest Gp. [7114]
European Genetics Found. [IO]
European Soc. of Human Genetics [IO]
Floating Harbor Syndrome Support Gp. of North Am. [14451]
French Soc. of Genetics [IO]
Genetic Engg. Action Network [6615]
Genetics Policy Inst. [14499]
Genetics Policy Institute [IO]
Genetics Soc. [IO]
Genetics Soc. of Am. [7115]
Genetics Soc. of Australasia [IO]
Genetics Soc. of Canada [IO]
Genetics Soc. of Japan [IO]
German Soc. of Human Genetics [IO]
Hong Kong Soc. of Medical Genetics [IO]
Human Biology Assn. [6577]
Human Genetics Soc. of Australasia [IO]
Human Genetics Soc. of Australasia - New South Wales Br. [IO]
Human Genetics Soc. of Australasia - Queensland Br. [IO]
Human Genome Org. [IO]
Human Genome Variation Soc. [IO]

Intl. Centre for Genetic Engg. and Biotechnology [IO]
Intl. Fed. of Human Genetics Societies [IO]
Intl. Fed. of Human Genetics Societies [14500]
Intl. Fed. of Marfan Syndrome Organizations [14456]
Intl. Genetic Epidemiology Soc. [14376]
Intl. Genetics Fed. [IO]
Intl. Soc. for Biosafety Res. [6586]
Intl. Soc. of Nurses in Genetics [14501]
International Society of Nurses in Genetics [IO]
Intl. Soc. for Phylogenetic Nomenclature [IO]
Intl. Soc. for Phylogenetic Nomenclature [7116]
Intl. Soc. of Psychiatric Genetics [14502]
Intl. Soc. of Psychiatric Genetics [IO]
International Society for Stem Cell Research [IO]
Intl. Soc. for Stem Cell Res. [14503]
Irish Soc. of Human Genetics [IO]
Israeli Soc. of Gene Therapy [IO]
Middle East Genetics Assn. [IO]
Middle East Genetics Assn. [7117]
Mountain States Genetics Network [14504]
Natl. Coalition for Hea. Professional Educ. in Genetics [14505]
Natl. Coun. on Gene Resources [7118]
Natl. Soc. of Genetic Counselors [14506]
PRISMS: Parents and Researchers Interested In Smith-Magenis Syndrome [14476]
Progressive Osseous Heteroplasia Assn. [14477]
Proteome Soc. [7119]
Proteome Soc. [IO]
Prune Belly Syndrome Network [14478]
Sociedad de Genetica de Chile [IO]
Soc. for Molecular Biology and Evolution [6601]
Soc. for the Stud. of Social Biology [6862]
Southern African Soc. of Human Genetics [IO]
State Public Interest Res. Groups' Campaign on Genetically Engineered Foods [4779]
Student Soc. for Stem Cell Res. [15114]
Systematics Assn. [IO]
Tomato Genetics Cooperative [4765]
True Food Network [4677]
U.S. Human Proteome Org. [6604]
Washington State Apple Commn. [4773]
Genetics; Comm. for Responsible [★18584]
Genetics Cooperative; Tomato [4765]
Genetics; Coun. for Responsible [18584]
Genetics Fed; Intl. [IO]
Genetics, Paleontology and Systematics of Natl. Res. Coun; Comm. on Common Problems of [★7073]
Genetics Policy Inst. [14499], 11924 Forest Hill Blvd., Ste. 22, Wellington, FL 33414-6208, (888)238-1423
Genetics Policy Institute [IO], Wellington, FL, United States
Genetics Soc. [IO], Midlothian, United Kingdom
Genetics Soc. of Am. [7115], 9650 Rockville Pike, Bethesda, MD 20814-3998, (301)634-7300
Genetics Soc. of Australasia [IO], Melbourne, Australia
Genetics Soc. of Australia [★IO]
Genetics Soc. of Canada [IO], Aulac, NB, Canada
Genetics Soc. of Japan [IO], Mishima, Japan
Geneva Assn. [★IO]
Geneva Executives Club - Address unknown since 2001.
Geneva Infant Feeding Assn. [IO], Geneva, Switzerland
Geneva Initiative on Psychiatry [★IO]
Genital Integrity; Intl. Coalition for [11731]
Genito-Urinary Nurses Assn. [IO], London, United Kingdom
Genito-Urinary Surgeons; Amer. Assn. of [16699]
Genocide
Armenian Amer. Soc. for Stud. on Stress and Genocide [15190]
Genocide Watch [17660]
Genocide Watch [IO]
Help Darfur Now [IO]
Help Darfur Now [12259]
Inst. for the Stud. of Genocide [17764]
Intl. Assn. of Genocide Scholars [17661]
Intl. Assn. of Genocide Scholars [IO]
Soc. for the Philosophical Stud. of Genocide and the Holocaust [10835]

Reference to "IO" in place of a book number signifies that the association may be found in the 45th edition of International Organizations.

Genocide Watch **[17660]**, PO Box 809, Washington, DC 20044, (703)448-0222

Genocide Watch **[IO]**, Washington, DC, United States

Gensuibaku Kinshi Nihon Kyogikai Gensuikyo **[★IO]**

Geo and Chevy Club **[★21608]**

Geo Club **[★21608]**

Geo Club; Chevy and **[21608]**

Geo-physicists; Soc. of Exploration **[7149]**

Geochemical Soc. **[7141]**, Washington Univ., E&PS Bldg., Rm. 334, One Brookings Dr., CB 1169, St. Louis, MO 63130-4899, (314)935-4131

Geochemistry; Intl. Assn. of **[IO]**

Geochemists; European Assn. of Organic **[IO]**

GeoCosmic Res; Natl. Coun. for **[6841]**

Geode Rsrc., Conservation, and Development **[4077]**, 308 N 3rd St., Burlington, IA 52601, (319)752-6395

Geodeettinen Laitos **[★IO]**

Geodesy and Geophysics; Sect. of Physical Oceanography of the Intl. Union of **[★7398]**

Geodetic Soc. of Japan **[IO]**, Tokyo, Japan

Geodetic Surveying; Amer. Assn. for **[7716]**

GeoForschungsZentrum **[IO]**, Potsdam, Germany

GeoForum **[IO]**, Honefoss, Norway

Geografiska Sallskapet i Finland **[★IO]**

Geographic, and Ecologic; Intl. Soc. of Dermatology: Tropical, **[★14205]**

Geographic Info. Soc; Cartography and **[6654]**

Geographic Soc. Geography Educ. Prog; National **[★7123]**

Geographic Soc. of Lima **[IO]**, Lima, Peru

Geographical Assn. of England **[IO]**, Sheffield, United Kingdom

Geographical Org. of Finland **[IO]**, Helsinki, Finland

Geographical Scientist Prog; Visiting **[★24491]**

Geographical Soc. of China **[IO]**, Beijing, People's Republic of China

Geographical Soc. of Ireland **[IO]**, Belfield, Ireland

Geography

Amer. Friends of the Hakluyt Soc. **[10410]**

Amer. Geographical Soc. **[7120]**

Argentine Soc. of Geographical Stud. **[IO]**

Asociacion Espanola de Sistemas de Informacion Geografica **[IO]**

Assn. of Amer. Geographers **[7121]**

Assn. for Geographic Info. **[IO]**

Assn. of Japanese Geographers **[IO]**

Assn. for Mexican Cave Stud. **[7691]**

Australian Geography Teachers Assn. **[IO]**

Austrian Umbrella Org. for Geographic Info. **[IO]**

Canadian Assn. of Geographers **[IO]**

Czech Assn. for Geoinformation **[IO]**

Earth's Physical Features Stud. Unit **[22816]**

European Network of Geography Teachers' Assn. **[IO]**

European Soc. for Geography **[IO]**

European Umbrella Org. for Geographic Info. **[IO]**

Gamma Theta Upsilon **[24491]**

Geographic Soc. of Lima **[IO]**

Geographical Assn. of England **[IO]**

Geographical Org. of Finland **[IO]**

Geographical Soc. of China **[IO]**

Geographical Soc. of Ireland **[IO]**

Hellenic Geographic Info. Soc. **[IO]**

Hungarian Assn. for Geo-Information **[IO]**

Inst. of Australian Geographers **[IO]**

Intl. Biogeography Soc. **[7122]**

Intl. Boundaries Res. Unit **[IO]**

Intl. Geographical Union - Commn. on Geographical Educ. **[IO]**

Irish Org. for Geographic Info. **[IO]**

London Topographical Soc. **[IO]**

Military Geographic Inst. **[IO]**

Natl. Acad. of Geography **[IO]**

Natl. Coun. for Geographic Educ. **[8457]**

Natl. Geographic Soc. **[7123]**

Natl. Geographic Soc. Educ. Found. **[8458]**

New Zealand Geographical Soc. **[IO]**

Pan Amer. Inst. of Geography and History **[IO]**

Polish Geographical Soc. **[IO]**

Royal Canadian Geographical Soc. **[IO]**

Royal Danish Geographical Soc. **[IO]**

Royal Dutch Geographical Soc. **[IO]**

Royal Geographical Soc. with the Inst. of British Geographers **[IO]**

Royal Geographical Soc. of Queensland **[IO]**

Royal Physiographical Soc. of Lund **[IO]**

Royal Scottish Geographical Soc. **[IO]**

Social Sciences Services and Resources **[7656]**

Sociedade de Geografia de Lisboa **[IO]**

Soc. for Conservation GIS **[6831]**

Soc. for the History of Discoveries **[10158]**

Soc. of South African Geographers **[IO]**

Soc. of Woman Geographers **[IO]**

Soc. of Woman Geographers **[7124]**

Swiss Org. for Geographic Info. **[IO]**

Tokyo Geographical Soc. **[IO]**

Vernacular Architecture Forum **[6482]**

Volcanological Soc. of Japan **[IO]**

Geography Educ. Prog; National Geographic Soc. **[★7123]**

Geography; Swedish Soc. for Anthropology and **[IO]**

Geography Teachers; Natl. Coun. of **[★8457]**

GeoHazards Intl. **[12633]**, 200 Town and Country Village, Palo Alto, CA 94301, (650)614-9050

GeoHazards Intl. **[IO]**, Palo Alto, CA, United States

Geologica Belgica **[★IO]**

Geological Assn. of Canada **[IO]**, St. John's, NL, Canada

Geological Scientists; Assn. of Professional **[★7127]**

Geological Soc. of Am. **[7132]**, PO Box 9140, Boulder, CO 80301-9140, (303)357-1000

Geological Soc. of Australia **[IO]**, Sydney, Australia

Geological Soc. of China **[IO]**, Beijing, People's Republic of China

Geological Soc. of Denmark **[IO]**, Copenhagen, Denmark

Geological Soc. of England **[★IO]**

Geological Soc. of France **[IO]**, Paris, France

Geological Soc. of Glasgow **[IO]**, Glasgow, United Kingdom

Geological Soc. of Japan **[IO]**, Tokyo, Japan

Geological Soc. of London **[IO]**, London, United Kingdom

Geological Soc. of Malaysia **[IO]**, Kuala Lumpur, Malaysia

Geological Soc. of New Zealand **[IO]**, Te Awamutu, New Zealand

Geological Soc. of South Africa **[IO]**, Marshalltown, Republic of South Africa

Geological Soc. of Spain **[IO]**, Salamanca, Spain

Geological Soc. of Sweden **[IO]**, Jonkoping, Sweden

Geological Soc. of Turkey **[★IO]**

Geological Soc. of the United Kingdom **[★IO]**

Geologiska Foreningen **[★IO]**

Geologists' Assn. **[IO]**, London, United Kingdom

Geologists; Southwest Assn. of Petroleum **[★7125]**

Geology

Aberdeen Formation Evaluation Soc. **[IO]**

Aberdeen Geological Soc. **[IO]**

Amer. Assn. of Petroleum Geologists **[7125]**

Amer. Geological Inst. **[7126]**

Amer. Inst. of Professional Geologists **[7127]**

Amer. Soc. of Forensic Geologists **[7128]**

Argentine Acad. of Geophysicists and Geodesists **[IO]**

Asociacion Argentina de Sedimentologia **[IO]**

Assn. of Amer. State Geologists **[7129]**

Assn. of Applied Geochemists **[IO]**

Assn. of Environmental and Engg. Geologists **[7130]**

Assn. of European Geological Societies **[IO]**

Assn. Francaise pour l'Etude des Sols **[IO]**

Assn. for the Geological Collaboration in Japan **[IO]**

Assn. of Ground Water Scientists and Engineers - A Division of Natl. Ground Water Assn. **[7828]**

Australasian Quaternary Assn. **[IO]**

Australian Mineral Found. **[IO]**

Belgian Geological Soc. **[IO]**

British Geological Survey **[IO]**

British Geophysical Assn. **[IO]**

Bulgarian Geological Soc. **[IO]**

Canadian Geophysical Union **[IO]**

Canadian Soc. of Petroleum Geologists **[IO]**

Central Canadian Fed. of Mineralogical Societies **[IO]**

Chamber of Geological Engineers of Turkey **[IO]**

Chinese Geophysical Soc. **[IO]**

Computer Oriented Geological Soc. **[7131]**

Coun. on Undergraduate Res. **[9059]**

Cushman Found. for Foraminiferal Res. **[7428]**

Earth's Physical Features Stud. Unit **[22816]**

Edinburgh Geological Soc. **[IO]**

European Assn. for the Conservation of the Geological Heritage **[IO]**

European Fed. of Geologists **[IO]**

French Amateur Fed. of Mineralogy and Paleontology **[IO]**

Geochemical Soc. **[7141]**

Geological Assn. of Canada **[IO]**

Geological Soc. of Am. **[7132]**

Geological Soc. of Australia **[IO]**

Geological Soc. of China **[IO]**

Geological Soc. of Denmark **[IO]**

Geological Soc. of France **[IO]**

Geological Soc. of Glasgow **[IO]**

Geological Soc. of Japan **[IO]**

Geological Soc. of London **[IO]**

Geological Soc. of Malaysia **[IO]**

Geological Soc. of New Zealand **[IO]**

Geological Soc. of South Africa **[IO]**

Geological Soc. of Spain **[IO]**

Geological Soc. of Sweden **[IO]**

Geologists' Assn. **[IO]**

Geoscience Australia **[IO]**

Geoscience Info. Soc. **[7142]**

German Geological Soc. **[IO]**

Gold Prospectors Assn. of Am. **[22913]**

History of Earth Sciences Soc. **[10116]**

Hungarian Geological Soc. **[IO]**

Inst. of Geologists of Ireland **[IO]**

Intl. Assn. for Mathematical Geology **[IO]**

Intl. Assn. of Sedimentologists **[IO]**

Intl. Commn. on the History of the Geological Sciences **[IO]**

Intl. Comm. for Coal and Organic Petrology **[IO]**

Intl. Res. Training Center on Erosion and Sedimentation **[IO]**

Intl. Sand Collectors Soc. **[22056]**

Intl. Soc. for Rock Mechanics **[IO]**

Intl. Union of Geological Sciences **[IO]**

Intl. Union for Quaternary Res. **[IO]**

Irish Assn. for Economic Geology **[IO]**

Israel Geological Soc. **[IO]**

Italian Geological Soc. **[IO]**

Italian Soc. for Environmental Geology **[IO]**

Japanese Assn. of Mineralogists, Petrologists and Economic Geologists **[IO]**

Manchester Geological Assn. **[IO]**

Natl. Assn. of Geoscience Teachers **[8459]**

Natl. Assn. of State Boards of Geology **[7133]**

Natl. Ground Water Assn. **[4011]**

Natl. Speleological Soc. **[7693]**

New England Antiquities Res. Assn. **[6452]**

Norwegian Formation Evaluation Soc. **[IO]**

Paleontological Res. Institution/Museum of the Earth **[7429]**

Polish Geological Soc. **[IO]**

Quaternary Res. Assn. **[IO]**

Sigma Gamma Epsilon **[24492]**

Sociedad Geologica Mexicana **[IO]**

Soc. of Economic Geologists **[7134]**

Soc. of Exploration Geo-physicists **[7149]**

Soc. of Exploration Geophysicists of Japan **[IO]**

Soc. of Independent Professional Earth Scientists **[7135]**

Soc. for Sedimentary Geology **[7432]**

Soc. of Woman Geographers **[7124]**

South African Assn. for Geotechnology **[IO]**

South African Geophysical Assn. **[IO]**

Stonehenge Study Group **[6459]**

Surtsey Res. Soc. **[IO]**

U.S. Permafrost Assn. **[7675]**

Geology; Soc. for Sedimentary **[7432]**

Geology Teachers; Assn. of **[★8459]**

Geology Teachers; Assn. of Coll. **[★8459]**

Geomatics; Indian Soc. of **[IO]**

Geomatics Indus. Assn. of Canada **[IO]**, Ottawa, ON, Canada

Geomatics and Landmanagement; Swiss Assn. of **[IO]**

Geomorfolosko drustvo Slovenije **[IO]**, Postojna, Slovenia

Geomorphological Soc. of Slovenia **[★IO]**

A star before a book entry number signifies that the name is not listed separately, but is mentioned within the entry.

Geophysical Assn. of Ireland [IO], Galway, Ireland
Geophysical Data Center; National [★4590]
Geophysical Soc; Environmental and Engg. [7140]
Geophysical Soc; German [IO]
Geophysical Union; Amer. [7136]
Geophysical Year; Antarctic Prog. of the Intl.
  [★7518]
Geophysicists; Soc. of Petroleum [★7149]
Geophysics; Sect. of Physical Oceanography of the
  Intl. Union of Geodesy and [★7398]
Georganne LaPiere Fan Club - Defunct.
George C. Marshall Found. [11118], c/o VMI Parade,
  PO Drawer 1600, Lexington, VA 24450, (540)463-
  7103
George Hamilton IV and Friends - Defunct.
George, Henry
  Common Ground - U.S.A. [18707]
  Coun. of Georgist Organizations [18708]
George Inst. - New York; Henry [18710]
George Jones Country Fan Club - Address unknown
  since 1989.
George Khoury Assn. of Baseball Leagues [23109],
  5400 Meramec Bottom Rd., St. Louis, MO 63128,
  (314)849-8900
George Lucas Educational Found. [8258], PO Box
  3494, San Rafael, CA 94912, (415)662-1600
George MacDonald Soc. [IO], Forest Row, United
  Kingdom
George McCleave Family Org. [20912]
George Merritt Descendants Assn. - Defunct.
George Michael Intl. Fan Club - Defunct.
George Sand Assn. [9652], c/o Annabelle M. Rea,
  Pres., Occidental Coll., Spanish and French Liter-
  ary Stud., 1600 Campus Rd., Los Angeles, CA
  90041, (818)244-0487
George Sand Soc. [9653], c/o Linda E. Odenborg,
  Chair, PO Box 1333, Portland, OR 97207,
  (360)693-4785
George Smith Patton, Jr. Historical Soc. [★11141]
George Strait Fan Club [24901], PO Box 2119,
  Hendersonville, TN 37077, (615)824-7176
George Wadsworth Family Org. - Address unknown
  since 2004.
George Wright Soc. [4565], PO Box 65, Hancock,
  MI 49930-0065, (906)487-9722
George Wright Society [IO], Hancock, MI, United
  States
Georgia
  America-Georgia Bus. Coun. [2296]
    Georgia-USA Chamber of Commerce [24278]
Georgia Peanut Commn. [5056], PO Box 967, 110 E
  4th St., Tifton, GA 31794, (229)386-3470
Georgia Satellites Intl. Fan Club - Address unknown
  since 1995.
Georgia-USA Chamber of Commerce [24278], 5
  River Rd., Ste. 21, Wilton, CT 06897, (203)563-
  9430
Georgia Writers [★11172]
Georgia Writers Assn. and Young Georgia Writers
  [11172], Kennesaw State Univ., English Dept.
  Bldg., No. 2701, 1000 Chastain Rd., Kennesaw,
  GA 30144, (770)420-4736
Georgian
  America-Georgia Bus. Coun. [2296]
    Georgia-USA Chamber of Commerce [24278]
    Georgian Assn. in the U.S.A. [19070]
Georgian Acad. of Sciences [IO], Tbilisi, Georgia
Georgian Aeronautical Fed. [IO], Tbilisi, Georgia
Georgian Assn. of Cardiology [IO], Tbilisi, Georgia
Georgian Assn. of Sports Medicine [IO], Tbilisi,
  Georgia
Georgian Assn. in the U.S.A. [19070], 2300 M St.
  NW, Ste. 800, Washington, DC 20037, (217)698-
  7071
Georgian Badminton Fed. [IO], Tbilisi, Georgia
Georgian Bay Elecl. Contractors Assn. [IO], Toronto,
  ON, Canada
Georgian Chap. of the Assn. of Energy Engineers
  [IO], Tbilisi, Georgia
Georgian Figure Skating Assn. [IO], Tbilisi, Georgia
Georgian Floorball Assn. [IO], Kutaisi, Georgia
Georgian Gerontology and Geriatrics Soc. [IO],
  Tbilisi, Georgia
Georgian Medical Assn. [IO], Tbilisi, Georgia
Georgian Natl. Alliance [★19070]

Georgian Natl. DanceSport Fed. [IO], Tbilisi,
  Georgia
Georgian Paralympic Comm. [IO], Tbilisi, Georgia
Georgian Soc. Against Epilepsy [IO], Tbilisi, Georgia
Georgian Soc. of Paediatric Chemotherapy [IO],
  Tbilisi, Georgia
Georgian Soc. of Parasitologists [IO], Tbilisi,
  Georgia
Georgian Taekwondo Fed. [IO], Tbilisi, Georgia
Georgian Tennis Fed. [IO], Tbilisi, Georgia
Georgie Boy Owners' Club [22950], PO Box 198,
  Osceola, IN 46561-0198, (574)258-0571
Georgist Organizations; Coun. of [18708]
Georgist Registry [★18708]
Georgist Registry - Address unknown since 1999.
Geosat Comm. - Address unknown since 2007.
Geoscience
  Amer. Geophysical Union [7136]
  ASFE [7137]
  Asian Soc. for Environmental Geotechnology [IO]
  Asociacion Boliviana de Ingenieria Geotecnica
    [IO]
  Asociacion Costarricense de Geotecnia [IO]
  Assocazione Italiana di Geologia Applicata e Am-
    bientale [IO]
  Associacao Portuguesa de Geomorfologos [IO]
  Assn. for Efficient Environmental Energy Systems
    [7138]
  Assn. of Geomorphologists of Ukraine [IO]
  Assn. of Geotechnical and Geoenvironmental
    Specialists [IO]
  Assn. of Hungarian Geophysicists [IO]
  Assn. of Korean Geomorphologists [IO]
  Assn. of Polish Geomorphologists [IO]
  Assn. of Professional Engineers, Geologists and
    Geophysicists of Alberta [IO]
  Assn. of Slovak Geomorphologists [IO]
  Assn. Tunisienne de Mecanique des Sols [IO]
  Assn. for Women Geoscientists [7139]
  Australian Geomechanics Soc. [IO]
  Australian Geoscience Coun. [IO]
  Australian Geoscience Info. Assn. [IO]
  Australian Inst. of Geoscientists [IO]
  Austrian Commn. on Geomorphology [IO]
  Balkan Geophysical Soc. [IO]
  Brazilian Geomorphological Union [IO]
  Brazilian Geophysical Soc. [IO]
  Brazilian Soc. for Soil Mechanics and Geotechni-
    cal Engg. [IO]
  British Geotechnical Assn. [IO]
  British Soc. for Geomorphology [IO]
  Bulgarian Geophysical Soc. [IO]
  Canadian Fed. of Earth Sciences [IO]
  Canadian Geomorphological Res. Gp. [IO]
  Canadian Geotechnical Soc. [IO]
  Canadian Soc. of Exploration Geophysicists [IO]
  Canadian Well Logging Soc. [IO]
  Centre for Tech. Geosciences [IO]
  Chamber of Geophysical Engineers [IO]
  Croatian Soc. for Soil Mechanics and Geotechni-
    cal Engg. [IO]
  Czech Assn. of Geomorphologists [IO]
  Deutscher Arbeitskreis fur Geomorphologie E.V.
    [IO]
  Egyptian Geotechnical Soc. [IO]
  Environmental and Engineering Geophysical
    Society [IO]
  Environmental and Engg. Geophysical Soc.
    [7140]
  Estonia Natl. Comm. of Geomorphology [IO]
  Estonian Geotechnical Soc. [IO]
  European Assn. for Geochemistry [IO]
  European Assn. of Geoscientists and Engineers
    [IO]
  European Assn. of Organic Geochemists [IO]
  European Geosciences Union [IO]
  Finnish Geodetic Inst. [IO]
  Geochemical Soc. [7141]
  GeoForschungsZentrum [IO]
  GeoForum [IO]
  Geomorfolosko drustvo Slovenije [IO]
  Geophysical Assn. of Ireland [IO]
  Geoscience Info. Soc. [7142]
  Geotechnical Soc. of Ireland [IO]
  Geothermal Resources Coun. [7143]

Ghana Geotechnical Soc. [IO]
Groupe Francais de Geomorphologie [IO]
Hong Kong Geotechnical Soc. [IO]
Icelandic Geotechnical Soc. [IO]
IEEE Geoscience and Remote Sensing Soc.
  [7144]
Indian Geotechnical Soc. [IO]
Indonesian Soc. for Geotechnical Engg. [IO]
Intl. Assn. of Geochemistry [IO]
Intl. Assn. of Geodesy [IO]
Intl. Assn. of Geomagnetism and Aeronomy [IO]
Intl. Assn. of Geomorphologists [IO]
Intl. Center for Earth Tides [IO]
Intl. Centre for Training and Exchanges in the
  Geosciences [IO]
Intl. Flat Earth Res. Soc. [7145]
Intl. Geothermal Assn. [IO]
Intl. Landslide Res. Gp. [IO]
Intl. Landslide Res. Gp. [7146]
Intl. Soc. of Soil Mechanics and Geotechnical
  Engg. [7147]
Intl. Soc. of Soil Mechanics and Geotechnical
  Engg. [IO]
Intl. Union of Geodesy and Geophysics [IO]
Iranian Geotechnical Subcomm. [IO]
Japanese Geotechnical Soc. [IO]
Kazakhstan Geotechnical Soc. [IO]
Kenyan Geotechnical Soc. [IO]
Korean Geotechnical Soc. [IO]
Lithuanian Geotechnical Soc. [IO]
Macedonian Geotechnical Soc. [IO]
Meteoritical Soc. [7148]
Nepal Geotechnical Soc. [IO]
New Zealand Geotechnical Soc. [IO]
Nigerian Geotechnical Assn. [IO]
Norwegian Assn. of Geomorphologists [IO]
Pakistan Geotechnical Engg. Soc. [IO]
Polish Geotechnical Soc. [IO]
Quaternary and Geomorphological Assn. of
  Vietnam [IO]
Slovenian Geotechnical Soc. [IO]
Sociedad Chilena de Geotecnica [IO]
Sociedad Espanola de Geomorfologia [IO]
Sociedad Mexicana de Geomorfologia [IO]
Sociedad Peruana de Geotecnia [IO]
Sociedade Brasileira de Geologia Nucleo de Mi-
  nas Gerais [IO]
Soc. of Exploration Geo-physicists [7149]
Soc. of Geomagnetism and Earth, Planetary and
  Space Sci. [IO]
Southeast Asian Geotechnical Soc. [IO]
Sri Lankan Geotechnical Soc. [IO]
Swedish Res. Gp. in Geomorphology [IO]
Swiss Geomorphological Soc. [IO]
U.S. Permafrost Assn. [7675]
Vietnamese Geotechnical Soc. [IO]
Working Group on Applied Physical Geography
  [IO]
Geoscience Australia [IO], Canberra, Australia
Geoscience Info. Soc. [7142], c/o Andrea Twiss-
  Brooks, Sec., Univ. of Chicago, John Crerar
  Library, 5730 S Ellis Ave., Chicago, IL 60637,
  (773)702-8777
Geoscience Teachers; Natl. Assn. of [8459]
Geosciences; ASFE/The Assn. of Engg. Firms
  Practicing in the [★7137]
Geosciences Div; Seafloor [7404]
Geosciences Union; European [IO]
Geoscientists; Assn. of Women [★7139]
Geospatial Info. Soc; ASPRS - The Imaging and
  [7495]
Geospatial Info. and Tech. Assn. [900], 14456 E
  Evans Ave., Aurora, CO 80014, (303)337-0513
Geosynthetics Soc; Intl. [6700]
Geotechnical Soc; Canadian [IO]
Geotechnical Soc. of the Hong Kong Special
  Administrative Region of China [★IO]
Geotechnical Soc. of Ireland [IO], Dublin, Ireland
Geotechnical Soc; Southeast Asian [IO]
Geotechnology; Asian Soc. for Environmental [IO]
Geothermal Resources Coun. [7143], PO Box 1350,
  Davis, CA 95617, (530)758-2360
Gepipari Tudomanyos Egyesulet [★IO]
Geraldine R. Dodge Found. [13119], 163 Madison
  Ave., PO Box 1239, Morristown, NJ 07962-1239,
  (973)540-8442

Reference to "IO" in place of a book number signifies that the association may be found in the 45th edition of International Organizations.

Geranium Soc; British and European **[IO]**
Gerda Lissner Found. **[10765]**, 135 E 55th St., New York, NY 10022, (212)826-6100
GERG - European Gas Res. Gp. **[IO]**, Brussels, Belgium
Geriatric Cardiology; Coun. on **[★13927]**
Geriatric Cardiology; Soc. of **[13927]**
Geriatric Care Managers; Natl. Assn. of Professional **[15539]**
Geriatric Dentistry; Amer. Soc. for **[★14186]**
Geriatric Massage Inst; Day-Break **[15026]**
Geriatric Pharmacy; Commn. for Certification in **[15930]**
Geriatric Psychiatry; Amer. Assn. for **[16068]**
Geriatric Soc. of India **[IO]**, New Delhi, India
Geriatrics; Albanian Assn. of Gerontology and **[IO]**
Geriatrics Soc; Amer. **[14510]**
German
 Alliance of the Danube Swabians of Canada **[IO]**
 Amer. Aid Soc. of German Descendants **[IO]**
 Amer. Aid Soc. of German Descendants **[19071]**
 Amer. Assn. of Teachers of German **[8460]**
 Amer. Coun. on Germany **[19072]**
 Amer. Coun. on Germany **[IO]**
 Amer. Historical Soc. of Germans From Russia **[IO]**
 Amer. Historical Soc. of Germans From Russia **[19073]**
 Amer. Inst. for Contemporary German Stud. **[9976]**
 Amer. Inst. for Contemporary German Stud. **[IO]**
 American/Schleswig-Holstein Heritage Soc. **[19066]**
 Assn. of the German Nobility in North Am. **[21105]**
 BMW Car Club of Am. **[21591]**
 BMW Vintage Car Club of Am. **[21593]**
 Delta Phi Alpha **[24493]**
 Deutsches Motorrad Register **[22677]**
 German Agricultural Marketing Bd. - CMA **[5020]**
 German-American Natl. Cong. **[19074]**
 German Colonies Collectors Gp. **[22822]**
 German Convention Bur. **[24324]**
 German Gun Collectors' Assn. **[22029]**
 German Historical Inst. **[10110]**
 German Professional Women's Assn. **[4039]**
 German Soc. of the City of New York **[19075]**
 German Soc. of Pennsylvania **[19076]**
 German-Texan Heritage Soc. **[19077]**
 German-Texan Heritage Soc. **[IO]**
 Germans From Russia Heritage Soc. **[IO]**
 Germans From Russia Heritage Soc. **[19078]**
 Germany Philatelic Soc. **[22823]**
 Goethe-Institut Inter Nationes **[9977]**
 Goethe-Institut Inter Nationes **[IO]**
 Goethe Inst. - German Cultural Centre **[IO]**
 Goethe Inst. for Promoting the Stud. of the German Language Abroad and for Intl. Cultural Cooperation **[IO]**
 Gottscheer Heritage and Genealogy Assn. **[9978]**
 Historians of German and Central European Art and Architecture **[9921]**
 Hovawart Club of Am. **[22283]**
 Hummel Collectors Club **[22040]**
 Intl. Brecht Soc. **[9661]**
 Intl. Soc. for Hildegard Von Bingen Stud. **[11124]**
 Johannes Schwalm Historical Assn. **[21128]**
 Leibniz Soc. of North Am. **[10809]**
 Leo Baeck Inst. **[10284]**
 Liederkranz Found. **[10640]**
 North Amer. Auto Union Register **[21743]**
 North Amer. Fed. of German Folk Dance Groups **[9965]**
 North Amer. Fichte Soc. **[10815]**
 North Amer. Kant Soc. **[10816]**
 North Amer. Singers Assn. **[10680]**
 NSU Enthusiasts U.S.A. **[21746]**
 Opel Motorsports Club **[21752]**
 Pennsylvania German Soc. **[21243]**
 Raissa Tselentis Memorial Johann Sebastian Bach Intl. Competitions **[10690]**
 Res. Found. for Jewish Immigration **[10469]**
 Rometsch Registry **[21775]**
 Russian Zone Handoverprint Stud. and Res. Gp. **[22864]**
 Schlaraffia Nordamerika **[19079]**

 Soc. for German-American Stud. **[9979]**
 Soc. for the History of the Germans in Maryland **[9980]**
 Steuben Soc. of Am. **[19080]**
 Vintage Volkswagen Club of Am. **[21814]**
 Volkswagen Club of Am. **[21815]**
German Academic Exchange Ser. **[8614]**, 871 United Nations Plz., New York, NY 10017, (212)758-3223
German Academic Exchange Ser. **[IO]**, New York, NY, United States
German Acad. of Language and Poetry **[IO]**, Darmstadt, Germany
German Acad. for Psychoanalysis **[IO]**, Berlin, Germany
German Adult Educ. Assn. **[IO]**, Bonn, Germany
German Aero Club **[IO]**, Braunschweig, Germany
German Aerospace Center **[IO]**, Cologne, Germany
German Aerospace Indus. Assn. **[IO]**, Berlin, Germany
German Agricultural Marketing Bd. - CMA **[5020]**, 1800 Diagonal Rd., Ste. 210, Alexandria, VA 22314, (703)739-8900
German Agricultural Soc. **[IO]**, Frankfurt, Germany
German Agro Action - Germany **[IO]**, Bonn, Germany
German Alpine Assn. **[IO]**, Munich, Germany
German; Amer. Assn. of Teachers of **[8460]**
German Amer. Business Assn. - Defunct.
German Amer. Chamber of Commerce **[24323]**, 75 Broad St., 21st Fl., New York, NY 10004-2415, (212)974-8830
German-American Football Assn. **[★23775]**
German-Amer. Genealogy Club - Defunct.
German-Amer. Information and Education Assn. - Defunct.
German-American Lawyers Assn. **[IO]**, Bonn, Germany
German-American Natl. Cong. **[19074]**, 4740 N Western Ave., Chicago, IL 60625-2097, (773)275-1100
German Amer. Natl. Public Affairs - Address unknown since 2007.
German-American Stud; Soc. for **[9979]**
German Amer. World Soc. - Address unknown since 2004.
German Appropriate Tech. Exchange **[IO]**, Eschborn, Germany
German-Armenian Soc. **[IO]**, Cologne, Germany
German Asphalt Assn. **[IO]**, Bonn, Germany
German Assn. for Amer. Stud. **[IO]**, Potsdam, Germany
German Assn. for Asian Stud. **[IO]**, Hamburg, Germany
German Assn. of Biomedical Engg. **[IO]**, Frankfurt am Main, Germany
German Assn. of the Bread and Pastry Indus. **[IO]**, Dusseldorf, Germany
German Assn. of Consulting Engineers **[IO]**, Berlin, Germany
German Assn. of Dietitians **[IO]**, Dusseldorf, Germany
German Assn. of Land Surveyors **[IO]**, Wuppertal, Germany
German Assn. of Market and Social Researchers **[IO]**, Berlin, Germany
German Assn. of Medical Device Indus. **[★IO]**
German Assn. for Music Therapy **[IO]**, Berlin, Germany
German Assn. of Patent Engineers and Patent Assessors **[★IO]**
German Assn. for Personnel Mgt. **[IO]**, Dusseldorf, Germany
German Assn. of Pharmaceutical Medicine **[IO]**, Munich, Germany
German Assn. for Physiotherapy **[IO]**, Cologne, Germany
German Assn. for Railroad-History **[IO]**, Werl, Germany
German Assn. of Self-Employed Midwives **[IO]**, Frankfurt, Germany
German Assn. of Sport Psychology **[IO]**, Munich, Germany
German Assn. of Surveying **[IO]**, Vogtsburg im Kaiserstuhl, Germany

German Assn. of Tax Advisers **[IO]**, Berlin, Germany
German Assn. for Water, Wastewater and Waste **[IO]**, Hennef, Germany
German Assn. of Women Engineers **[IO]**, Darmstadt, Germany
German Assn. of Women and Men Working in the Home **[IO]**, Worms, Germany
German Atlantic Assn. **[IO]**, Bonn, Germany
German Atomic Forum **[IO]**, Berlin, Germany
German-Australian Chamber of Indus. and Commerce **[IO]**, Sydney, Australia
German Bar Assn. **[IO]**, Berlin, Germany
German Bible Soc. **[IO]**, Stuttgart, Germany
German - Brazilian Lawyers Assn. **[IO]**, Frankfurt am Main, Germany
German Brewers Union **[IO]**, Berlin, Germany
German-British Chamber of Indus. and Commerce **[IO]**, London, United Kingdom
German Bunsen Soc. for Physical Chemistry **[IO]**, Frankfurt am Main, Germany
German Bus. Assn. - Singapore **[★IO]**
German Bus. Aviation Assn. **[IO]**, Berlin, Germany
German Cactus Soc. **[IO]**, Pforzheim, Germany
German Cardiac Soc. **[IO]**, Dusseldorf, Germany
German Carpet Res. Inst. **[IO]**, Aachen, Germany
German Cement Works Assn. **[IO]**, Dusseldorf, Germany
German Centre of Gerontology **[IO]**, Berlin, Germany
German Centre Singapore **[IO]**, Singapore, Singapore
German Ceramic Soc. **[IO]**, Cologne, Germany
German Chap. of the ACM **[IO]**, Munich, Germany
German Chem. Soc. **[IO]**, Frankfurt am Main, Germany
German China Assn. **[IO]**, Karlsruhe, Germany
German-Chinese Bus. Assn. **[IO]**, Cologne, Germany
German-Chinese Friendship Assn. **[IO]**, Berlin, Germany
German Civil Ser. Fed. **[IO]**, Berlin, Germany
German Coffee Assn. **[IO]**, Hamburg, Germany
German Colonies Collectors Gp. **[IO]**, Stevens Point, WI, United States
German Colonies Collectors Gp. **[22822]**, c/o J.D. Manville, Sec.-Treas., PO Box 845, Stevens Point, WI 54481-0845
German Convention Bur. **[24324]**, 122 E 42nd St., Ste. 2000, New York, NY 10168-0072, (212)661-4582
German Convention Bur. **[IO]**, Frankfurt am Main, Germany
German Cosmetic, Toiletry, Perfumery and Detergent Assn. **[IO]**, Frankfurt am Main, Germany
German Coun. on Foreign Relations **[IO]**, Berlin, Germany
German Coun. for Land Stewardship **[IO]**, Bonn, Germany
German Coun. for Public Relations **[IO]**, Berlin, Germany
German Cricket Fed. **[IO]**, Passau, Germany
German Dairy Assn. **[IO]**, Bonn, Germany
German Dance Sport Fed. **[IO]**, Frankfurt am Main, Germany
German Data Protection Org. **[IO]**, Bonn, Germany
German Dental Assn. **[IO]**, Cologne, Germany
German Dermatological Soc. **[IO]**, Berlin, Germany
German Design Coun. **[IO]**, Frankfurt am Main, Germany
German Development Ser. - Vietnam **[IO]**, Hanoi, Vietnam
German Direct Marketing Assn. **[IO]**, Wiesbaden, Germany
German Directors Guild **[IO]**, Munich, Germany
German Economic Engineers Assn. **[IO]**, Berlin, Germany
German Educational Res. Assn. **[IO]**, Berlin, Germany
German Elecl. and Electronic Mfrs. Assn. **[IO]**, Frankfurt am Main, Germany
German Fed. Bar **[IO]**, Berlin, Germany
German Fed. for Food Law and Food Sci. **[IO]**, Bonn, Germany
German Fed. of Livestock, Meat and Wholesale Foreign Trade; German Assn. of Abbattoirs **[★IO]**

A star before a book entry number signifies that the name is not listed separately, but is mentioned within the entry.

German Fed. for Motor Trades and Repairs [IO], Bonn, Germany

German Fed. of Rural Youth [IO], Berlin, Germany

German Fed. of Sports Medicine and Prevention [IO], Freiburg, Germany

German Floorball Assn. [IO], Pinneberg, Germany

German Folklore Soc; Pennsylvania [★21243]

German Forestry Coun. [IO], Bonn, Germany

German Foundry Assn. [IO], Dusseldorf, Germany

German Franchise Assn. [IO], Berlin, Germany

German Fruit Trade Assn. [IO], Bonn, Germany

German Fur Assn. [IO], Frankfurt, Germany

German Gemmological Assn. [IO], Idar-Oberstein, Germany

German Genealogical Soc. of Am. [IO], Burbank, CA, United States

German Genealogical Soc. of Am. [21119], c/o Southern California Genealogical Soc., 417 Irving Dr., Burbank, CA 91504-2408, (818)843-7247

German Geological Soc. [IO], Hannover, Germany

German Geophysical Soc. [IO], Potsdam, Germany

German Gun Collectors' Association [IO], Meriden, NH, United States

German Gun Collectors' Assn. [22029], PO Box 385, Meriden, NH 03770, (603)469-3438

German Gymnastics Fed. - Orienteering Dept. [IO], Frankfurt, Germany

German Historical Inst. [10110], 1607 New Hampshire Ave. NW, Washington, DC 20009-2562, (202)387-3355

German History Soc. [IO], London, United Kingdom

German Holstein Assn. [IO], Bonn, Germany

German Hosp. Assn. [★IO]

German Hosp. Fed. [IO], Berlin, Germany

German Hotels and Restaurants Assn. [IO], Berlin, Germany

German Huntington Help [IO], Duisburg, Germany

German Indus; Fed. of [★762]

German Indus. Assn. - UK Chap. [★IO]

German Indus. UK [IO], London, United Kingdom

German Informatics Soc. [IO], Bonn, Germany

German Inst. for Intl. and Security Affairs [IO], Berlin, Germany

German Inst. of Navigation [IO], Bonn, Germany

German Inst. for Polymers [IO], Darmstadt, Germany

German Interdisciplinary Assn. of Critical Care Medicine [IO], Hamburg, Germany

German Interior Architects Assn. [IO], Bonn, Germany

German - Japanese Jurists Assn. [IO], Hamburg, Germany

German-Japanese Soc. for Social Sciences [IO], Konstanz, Germany

German Journalists' Fed. [IO], Berlin, Germany

German Language Club - Address unknown since 1991.

German Language Soc. [IO], Wiesbaden, Germany

German League Against Epilepsy [IO], Kehl, Germany

German Machine Tool Builders' Assn. [IO], Frankfurt am Main, Germany

German Machinery and Plant Mfrs. Assn. - Japan Liaison Off. [IO], Tokyo, Japan

German Marshall Fund of the U.S. [IO], Washington, DC, United States

German Marshall Fund of the U.S. [17890], 1744 R St. NW, Washington, DC 20009, (202)745-3950

German Mathematical Assn. [IO], Berlin, Germany

German Meat Assn. [IO], Bonn, Germany

German Medical Aid Org., Action Medeor [IO], Tonisvorst, Germany

German Medical Assn. [IO], Berlin, Germany

German Medical Tech. Assn. [IO], Berlin, Germany

German Medical Welfare Org., Action Medeor [★IO]

German Metal Dealers Assn. [IO], Berlin, Germany

German Meteorological Soc. [IO], Berlin, Germany

German Mining Assn. [IO], Berlin, Germany

German MPS Soc. [IO], Aschaffenburg, Germany

German Museums Assn. [IO], Berlin, Germany

German-Namibian Soc. [IO], Gottingen, Germany

German Natl. Mathematical Soc. [IO], Berlin, Germany

German Natl. Tourist Bd. [IO], New York, NY, United States

German Natl. Tourist Bd. [3917], German Natl. Tourist Off., 122 E 42nd St., 52nd Fl., New York, NY 10168-0072, (212)661-7200

German Neuroscience Soc. [IO], Berlin, Germany

German Nobility in North Am; Assn. of the [21105]

German Nutrition Soc. [IO], Bonn, Germany

German Ophthalmological Soc. [IO], Munich, Germany

German Order of Harugari - Address unknown since 2005.

German Org. of Endocrinology [IO], Munich, Germany

German Org. of Nutrition [IO], Bonn, Germany

German Org. of Victims of War and Military Ser., Disabled People and Pensioners [★IO]

German Ornithologists' Soc. [IO], Wilhelmshaven, Germany

German Peace Soc. - United War Resisters [IO], Velbert, Germany

German PennState Alumni Chap. [IO], Kiel, Germany

German-Peruvian Chamber of Commerce and Indus. [IO], Lima, Peru

German Physical Soc. [IO], Bad Honnef, Germany

German Phytomedical Soc. [IO], Braunschweig, Germany

German Pointer

Desert German Shorthaired Pointer Club [22256]

German Shorthaired Pointer Club of Am. [22274]

German Wirehaired Pointer Club of Am. [22275]

German Political Sci. Assn. [IO], Osnabruck, Germany

German Politics Assn. [17662], c/o Jonathan Olsen, Sec.-Treas., Univ. of Wisconsin-Parkside, Dept. of Political Sci., Kenosha, WI 53141-2000, (262)595-2377

German Prefab. Constr. Assn. [IO], Bad Honnef, Germany

German Printing and Media Indus. Fed. [IO], Wiesbaden, Germany

German Professional Women's Assn. [4039], PO Box 476, Lake Orion, MI 48361-0476

German Publishers and Booksellers Assn. [IO], Frankfurt am Main, Germany

German Pulp and Paper Assn. [IO], Bonn, Germany

German Pulp and Paper Chemists and Engineers Assn. [IO], Darmstadt, Germany

German Res. Assn. [21120], PO Box 711600, San Diego, CA 92171-1600

German Res. Found. [IO], Bonn, Germany

German Retailers Import Trade Assn. [IO], Cologne, Germany

German Shepherd

Amer. German Shepherd Rescue Assn. [11348]

Amer. Rescue Dog Assn. [12889]

Amer. White Shepherd Assn. [22217]

Echo Dogs White Shepherd Rescue [11388]

Fidelco Guide Dog Found. [16846]

German Shepherd Dog Club of Am. [22272]

German Shepherd Dog Club of Am. - Working Dog Assn. [22273]

Support Dogs, Inc. [11990]

United Schutzhund Clubs of Am. [22371]

White German Shepherd Dog Club of Am. [22383]

German Shepherd Dog Club of Am. [22272], c/o Sharon Allbright, Corresponding Sec., PO Box 429, Applegate, CA 95703, (530)878-2826

German Shepherd Dog Club of Am. - Working Dog Assn. [22273], c/o Joy Schultz, Recorder/Admin., 732 Lindley Blvd., DeLand, FL 32724, (386)736-2486

German Shepherd Dog Club of New England [★22272]

German Shipbuilding and Ocean Indus. Assn. [IO], Hamburg, Germany

German Shipowners' Assn. [IO], Hamburg, Germany

German Shipsupplier Assn. [IO], Hamburg, Germany

German Shoe Indus. Assn. [IO], Offenbach, Germany

German Shoe Indus. Assn. [★IO]

German Shorthaired Pointer Club of Am. [22274], c/o Charlie Blackbourn, Pres., 200 Goede Rd., Edgerton, WI 53534, (608)884-4342

German Ski Fed. [IO], Planegg, Germany

German Sleep Soc. [IO], Schwalmstadt, Germany

German Soc. for Aeronautics and Astronautics [IO], Bonn, Germany

German Soc. of Anaesthesiology and Intensive Care Medicine [IO], Nuremberg, Germany

German Soc. of Aviation and Space Medicine [IO], Cologne, Germany

German Soc. for Biochemistry and Molecular Biology [IO], Frankfurt am Main, Germany

German Soc. for Bog and Peat Res. [IO], Hannover, Germany

German Soc. of Cinematographers [IO], Munich, Germany

German Soc. of the City of New York [19075]

German Soc. of Concert Choirs [★IO]

German Soc. for Concrete and Constr. Tech. [IO], Berlin, Germany

German Soc. for Disaster Medicine [IO], Munich, Germany

German Soc. for Documentation [IO], Frankfurt am Main, Germany

German Soc. for Documentation [★IO]

German Soc. for Experimental and Clinical Pharmacology and Toxicology [IO], Dusseldorf, Germany

German Soc. for Fat Sci. [IO], Frankfurt am Main, Germany

German Soc. of Gerontology and Geriatrics [IO], Cologne, Germany

German Soc. of Glass Tech. [IO], Offenbach, Germany

German Soc. for Hematology and Oncology [IO], Rostock, Germany

German Soc. for Horticultural Sci. [IO], Hannover, Germany

German Soc. of Human Genetics [IO], Munich, Germany

German Soc. of Hypertension [IO], Heidelberg, Germany

German Soc. for Info. Sci. and Practice [IO], Frankfurt am Main, Germany

German Soc. for Linguistics [IO], Braunschweig, Germany

German Soc. for Marine Res. [IO], Hamburg, Germany

German Soc. for Medicinal Plant Res. [★IO]

German Soc. for Mining, Metallurgy, Rsrc. and Environmental Tech. [IO], Clausthal-Zellerfeld, Germany

German Soc. of Neurogenetics [IO], Tuebingen, Germany

German Soc. for Non-Destructive Testing [IO], Berlin, Germany

German Soc. of Nutrition [IO], Bonn, Germany

German Soc. for Online Res. [IO], Hurth, Germany

German Soc. of Operations Res. [IO], Bochum, Germany

German Soc. of Pediatrics and Adolescent Medicine [IO], Berlin, Germany

German Soc. of Pennsylvania [19076], 611 Spring Garden St., Philadelphia, PA 19123-3505, (215)627-2332

German Soc. for Photogrammetry and Remote Sensing [IO], Munster, Germany

German Soc. for Physical Medicine and Rehabilitation [IO], Jena, Germany

German Soc. of Physiology [IO], Rostock, Germany

German Soc. of Plastic and Reconstructive Surgery [IO], Rotenburg, Germany

German Soc. of Refrigeration and Airconditioning [IO], Stuttgart, Germany

German Soc. of Reproductive Medicine [IO], Regensburg, Germany

German Soc. of School Music Educators [IO], Mainz, Germany

German Soc. for Sex Res. [IO], Hamburg, Germany

German Soc. for Social Sci. Sexuality Res. [IO], Dusseldorf, Germany

German Soc. of Speech, Language, and Voice-Pathology [IO], Lubeck, Germany

German Soc. of Visceral Surgery [IO], Berlin, Germany

German Sports Confed. [IO], Frankfurt, Germany

German State Archaeologists' Assn. [IO], Bonn, Germany

Reference to "IO" in place of a book number signifies that the association may be found in the 45th edition of International Organizations.

German Statistical Soc. [IO], Cologne, Germany
German Steel Constr. Assn. [IO], Dusseldorf, Germany
German Susswarenexportforderung [★IO]
German Sweets Export Assn. [IO], Bonn, Germany
German Swiss Genealogical Soc; Orangeburgh [21139]
German Teachers' Union [IO], Bonn, Germany
German Tenants' Union [IO], Berlin, Germany
German-Texan Heritage Soc. [IO], Austin, TX, United States
German-Texan Heritage Soc. [19077], 507 E 10th St., PO Box 684171, Austin, TX 78768-4171, (512)482-0927
German Timber Trade Fed. [IO], Wiesbaden, Germany
German Transpersonal Assn. [IO], Berlin, Germany
German Venture Capital Assn. [IO], Berlin, Germany
German Welding Soc. [IO], Dusseldorf, Germany
German WindEnergy Assn. [IO], Osnabruck, Germany
German Wine Inst. [IO], Mainz, Germany
German Winegrowers Assn. [IO], Bonn, Germany
German Wirehaired Pointer Club of Am. [22275], c/o Sue Mueller, Treas., W12203 870th Ave., River Falls, WI 54022
German Youth Hostel Assn. [IO], Detmold, Germany
Germanistic Soc. of America - Address unknown since 1995.
Germanium Res. Comm. - Defunct.
Germanna Colonies in Virginia; Memorial Found. of the [10045]
Germanna Found. [★10045]
Germans From Russia Heritage Soc. [19078], 1125 W Turnpike Ave., Bismarck, ND 58501-8115, (701)223-6167
Germans From Russia Heritage Soc. [IO], Bismarck, ND, United States
Germans from Russia; North Dakota Historical Soc. of [★19078]
Germany
  Alpine Tourist Commn. [24223]
  Amer. Inst. for Contemporary German Stud. [9976]
  Assn. of the German Nobility in North Am. [21105]
  BMW Car Club of Am. [21591]
  BMW Vintage Car Club of Am. [21593]
  Conf. on Jewish Material Claims Against Germany [12470]
  Deutsches Motorrad Register [22677]
  German Academic Exchange Ser. [8614]
  German Amer. Chamber of Commerce [24323]
  German Colonies Collectors Gp. [22822]
  German Convention Bur. [24324]
  German Politics Assn. [17662]
  German Professional Women's Assn. [4039]
  Germany Philatelic Soc. [22823]
  Goethe-Institut Inter Nationes [9977]
  Hof Reunion Assn. [20682]
  Hovawart Club of Am. [22283]
  Hummel Collectors Club [22040]
  North Amer. Auto Union Register [21743]
  North Amer. Fed. of German Folk Dance Groups [9965]
  NSU Enthusiasts U.S.A. [21746]
  Opel Motorsports Club [21752]
  Pennsylvania German Soc. [21243]
  Representative of German Indus. and Trade [762]
  Rometsch Registry [21775]
  Russian Zone Handoverprint Stud. and Res. Gp. [22864]
  Soc. for German-American Stud. [9979]
  Soc. for the History of the Germans in Maryland [9980]
  Third Reich Study Group [22882]
  Vintage Volkswagen Club of Am. [21814]
  Volkswagen Club of Am. [21815]
  World Fed. of Bergen-Belsen Associations [17726]
Germany; Conf. on Jewish Material Claims Against [12470]
Germany Philatelic Soc. [22823], PO Box 6547, Chesterfield, MO 63006-6547
Germany Philatelic Soc. [IO], Chesterfield, MO, United States

Germroth Family Assn. Intl. [20913]
Gerontological & Geriatric Soc. of the USSR [★IO]
Gerontological Assn. of Malaysia [IO], Selangor, Malaysia
Gerontological Assn. of Slovenia [IO], Ljubljana, Slovenia
Gerontological Soc. [★14511]
Gerontological Soc. of Am. [14511], 1220 L St. NW, Ste. 901, Washington, DC 20005, (202)842-1275
Gerontological Soc. of the Russian Acad. of Sciences [IO], St. Petersburg, Russia
Gerontological Soc. of Serbia [IO], Belgrade, Serbia
Gerontological Soc. of Singapore [IO], Singapore, Singapore
Gerontological Soc; Western [★11275]
Gerontology
  Aging in Am. [11271]
  Albanian Assn. of Gerontology and Geriatrics [IO]
  Alberta Assn. on Gerontology [IO]
  Alliance for Aging Res. [11272]
  Amer. Aging Assn. [14507]
  American Aging Association [IO]
  Amer. Assn. of Homes and Services for the Aging [11273]
  Amer. Assn. for Intl. Aging [11274]
  Amer. Bd. of Psychiatry and Neurology [16071]
  Amer. Coll. of Hea. Care Administrators [15535]
  Amer. Fed. for Aging Res. [14508]
  Amer. Found. for Aging Res. [14509]
  Amer. Geriatrics Soc. [14510]
  Amer. Hea. Care Assn. [14540]
  Amer. Medical Directors Assn. [15536]
  Amer. Podiatric Circulatory Soc. [16036]
  Amer. Senior Fitness Assn. [15961]
  Amer. Soc. on Aging [11275]
  Assn. of Brethren Caregivers [11276]
  Assn. for Gerontology Educ. in Social Work [8461]
  Assn. for Gerontology in Higher Educ. [8462]
  Assn. of Gerontology India [IO]
  Assn. of Jewish Aging Services [11277]
  Assn. Luxemburgeoise de Gerontologie et Geriatrie [IO]
  Australian Assn. of Gerontology [IO]
  Austrian Soc. for Geriatrics and Gerontology [IO]
  Belgian Soc. of Gerontology and Geriatrics [IO]
  British Geriatrics Soc. [IO]
  British Soc. for Res. on Ageing [IO]
  Brookdale Found. [12260]
  Bulgarian Assn. on Aging [IO]
  Canadian Assn. of Gerontology [IO]
  Canadian Geriatrics Soc. [IO]
  The Center for Social Gerontology [11280]
  Center for the Stud. of Aging of Albany [11281]
  Children of Aging Parents [11282]
  Czech Soc. of Geronology and Geriatrics of the Czech Medical Assn. [IO]
  Danish Gerontological Assn. [IO]
  Elder Craftsmen [11285]
  Estonian Gerontology and Geriatrics Assn. [IO]
  Families U.S.A. Found. [11286]
  French Soc. of Geriatrics and Gerontology [IO]
  Georgian Gerontology and Geriatrics Soc. [IO]
  Geriatric Soc. of India [IO]
  German Centre of Gerontology [IO]
  German Soc. of Gerontology and Geriatrics [IO]
  Gerontological Assn. of Malaysia [IO]
  Gerontological Assn. of Slovenia [IO]
  Gerontological Soc. of Am. [14511]
  Gerontological Soc. of the Russian Acad. of Sciences [IO]
  Gerontological Soc. of Serbia [IO]
  Gerontological Soc. of Singapore [IO]
  Gray Panthers [11287]
  Harvard Injury Control Res. Center [16690]
  Hea. Promotion Inst. [11288]
  Hellenic Assn. of Gerontology and Geriatrics [IO]
  Hong Kong Assn. of Gerontology [IO]
  Hungarian Gerontological Assn. [IO]
  Inst. of Gerontology [IO]
  Intl. Assn. of Gerontology European Region [IO]
  Intl. Assn. of Gerontology and Geriatrics [IO]
  Intl. Assn. of Homes and Services for the Ageing [11289]
  Intl. Inst. on Ageing [IO]

Intl. Menopause Soc. [IO]
Intl. Psychogeriatric Assn. [IO]
Intl. Psychogeriatric Assn. [14512]
Intl. Soc. for Aging and Physical Activity [13545]
Irish Gerontological Soc. [IO]
Italian Soc. of Gerontology and Geriatrics [IO]
Japan Geriatrics Soc. [IO]
Japan Gerontological Soc. [IO]
Jewish Assn. for Services for the Aged [11290]
Leadership Coun. of Aging Organizations [11293]
Legal Counsel for the Elderly [12497]
Legal Sers. for the Elderly [12499]
Maltese Assn. of Gerontology and Geriatrics [IO]
Mature Market Rsrc. Center [11296]
Natl. Acad. for Teaching and Learning About Aging [11297]
Natl. Adult Day Services Assn. [11298]
Natl. Alliance of Senior Citizens [11299]
Natl. Asian Pacific Center on Aging [11300]
Natl. Assn. of Area Agencies on Aging [11301]
Natl. Assn. of County Aging Programs [11302]
Natl. Assn. of Geriatric Educ. Centers [14513]
Natl. Assn. of Hea. Care Assistants [14514]
Natl. Assn. for Human Development [11303]
Natl. Assn. of Senior Companion Proj. Directors [11304]
Natl. Assn. of State Units on Aging [11305]
Natl. Bd. for Certified Counselors and Affiliates [11828]
Natl. Caucus and Center on Black Aged [11306]
Natl. Coalition on Rural Aging [11307]
Natl. Coun. on the Aging [11309]
Natl. Gerontological Nursing Assn. [14515]
Natl. Hispanic Coun. on Aging [11310]
Natl. Inst. on Aging [14516]
Natl. Inst. of Senior Housing [12328]
Natl. Interfaith Coalition on Aging [11314]
Natl. Meals on Wheels Found. [11315]
Natl. Osteoporosis Soc. [IO]
Natl. Senior Citizens Law Center [11316]
Native Elder Hea. Care Rsrc. Center [19282]
Netherlands Soc. of Gerontology [IO]
New England Gerontological Assn. [14517]
New Zealand Assn. of Gerontology [IO]
Nordic Gerontological Fed. [IO]
Norwegian Gerontological Soc. [IO]
Osteoporosis Canada [IO]
Osteoporosis Canada - Ottawa Chap. [IO]
Osteoporosis Soc. of Canada - British Columbia Div. [IO]
Osteoporosis Soc. of Canada - Hamilton Chap. [IO]
Osteoporosis Soc. of Canada - Kelowna Chap. [IO]
Osteoporosis Soc. of Canada - London and Thames Valley Chap. [IO]
Osteoporosis Soc. of Canada - Manitoba Chap. [IO]
Osteoporosis Soc. of Canada - New Brunswick Chap. [IO]
Osteoporosis Soc. of Canada - Niagara Chap. [IO]
Osteoporosis Soc. of Canada - North Shore Chap. [IO]
Osteoporosis Soc. of Canada - Nova Scotia Chap. [IO]
Osteoporosis Soc. of Canada - Peterborough Chap. [IO]
Osteoporosis Soc. of Canada - Quebec City Chap. [IO]
Osteoporosis Soc. of Canada - Regina Chap. [IO]
Osteoporosis Soc. of Canada - Saskatoon Chap. [IO]
Osteoporosis Soc. of Canada - Sudbury Chap. [IO]
Osteoporosis Soc. of Canada - Toronto Chap. [IO]
Philippine Assn. of Gerontology [IO]
Polish Soc. of Gerontology [IO]
Slovak Soc. of Gerontology and Geriatrics [IO]
Sociedad Espanola de Geriatria y Gerontologia [IO]
Swedish Gerontological Soc. [IO]
Swedish Soc. for Geriatric Medicine and Gerontology [IO]
Swiss Soc. of Gerontology [IO]

A star before a book entry number signifies that the name is not listed separately, but is mentioned within the entry.

Ukrainian Gerontology and Geriatrics Soc. [IO]
United Seniors Assn. [11322]
Gerontology; The Center for Social [11280]
Gerontology in Higher Educ; Assn. for [8462]
Gerontology; Intl. Center for Social [★11280]
Gerontolosko Drustvo Srbije [★IO]
Gerontolosko drustvo Slovenije [★IO]
Gerson Inst. [13632], 1572 Second Ave., San Diego, CA 92101, (619)685-5353
Gertrude Stein Philately Soc. - Defunct.
Gertrudis Assn; Natl. Junior Santa [4277]
Gesamtverband Deutscher Holzhandel [★IO]
Gesamtverband Deutscher Musikfachgeschafte [★IO]
Gesamtverband der Textilindustrie in der Bundesrepublik Deutschland [★IO]
Geschaftsstelle des Deutscher Sportaztebund [★IO]
Geselleschaft fur deutsche Sprache [★IO]
Gesellschaft fur Aerosolforschung [★IO]
Gesellschaft fur Arzneipflanzenforschung [★IO]
Gesellschaft fuer Bedrohte Volker [★IO]
Gesellschaft fur Bergbau, Metallurgie, Rohstoff- und Umwelttechnik [★IO]
Gesellschaft fur Bergbau, Metallurgie, Rohstoff-und Umwelttechnik e.V. [★IO]
Gesellschaft fur Biochemie und Molekularbiologie e.V. [★IO]
Gesellschaft fur Chemische Technik und Biotechnologie [★IO]
Gesellschaft fur Deutsch-Chinesische Freundschaft Berlin [★IO]
Gesellschaft Deutscher Chemiker [★IO]
Gesellschaft fur Energieplanung und Systemanalyse [IO], Munster, Germany
Gesellschaft zur Forderung der Literatur aus Afrika, Asien und Lateinamerika [★IO]
Gesellschaft zur Freiwilligen Kontrolle von Messe- und Ausstellungszahlen [★IO]
Gesellschaft fuer Informatik [★IO]
Gesellschaft fuer Mukopolysaccharidosen e.V. [★IO]
Gesellschaft fuer Neonatologie und Padiatrische Intensivmedizin [★IO]
Gesellschaft fur Oekologie [★IO]
Gesellschaft fur Operations Res. e.V. [★IO]
Gesellschaft fur Selbstspielende Musikinstrumente e.V. [★IO]
Gesellschaft fuer Versuchstierkunde [★IO]
Gesellschaft fur die Volksmusik in der Schweiz [★IO]
Gesellschaft fur Wirbelsaulenforschung [★IO]
Gesellschaft zur Wissenschaftlichen Untersuchung von Parawissenschaften [★IO]
Gesellscraft fur Terminologie and Wissenstransfer [★IO]
GesherCity [19183], c/o Adam Courtney, Dir., 520 8th Ave., 4th Fl., New York, NY 10010, (212)786-5108
Geshkewich Surname Org. [20914]
Gesneriad Hybridizers Assn. [22514], 1122 E Pike St., Seattle, WA 98122-3916
Gesneriad Res. Found. - Address unknown since 2005.
Gesneriad Soc. [22515], 1122 E Pike St., PMB 637, Seattle, WA 98122-3916
Gesneriad Soc. [IO], Seattle, WA, United States
Gesneriad Soc. Intl. - Address unknown since 1995.
Gesselschaft fur bedrohte Sprachen [★IO]
Gestalt Australia and New Zealand [IO], Sydney, Australia
Gestalt Community [★10180]
Gestalt Inst. for Multiple Psychotherapy - Defunct.
Gestalt Therapy; Assn. for the Advancement of [16135]
Gestation; Center for Stud. of Multiple [★15272]
GESTAUTOR [IO], Lisbon, Portugal
Get Oil Out! [5092], c/o Environmental Defense Center, Santa Barbara Off., 906 Garden St., Santa Barbara, CA 93101, (805)963-1622
Get Oil Out Educ. and Legal Fund [★5092]
Get Set Day Care Program [★11539]
Get Set Pre-Kindergarten Program [★11539]
Getty Grant Prog. [9569], 1200 Getty Center Dr., Ste. 800, Los Angeles, CA 90049-1697, (310)440-7300
Getty Grant Prog. [IO], Los Angeles, CA, United States

Gettysburg Battlefield Preservation Assn. - Defunct.
Gettysburg Coll. [★18442]
Gettysburg Coll. [★IO]
Gettysburg; Friends of the Natl. Parks at [10028]
Gewerkschaft Erziehung und Wissenschaft [★IO]
Gewerkschaft Hotel, Gastgewerbe, Personlicher Dienst [★IO]
Geya - Intl. Women Forum [★IO]
GFWC-CARE Program - Defunct.
GFWC Hands Up Program - Defunct.
GH Questionnaire Club - Defunct.
Ghana
Cross Cultural Collaborative [8177]
E-quip Africa [12704]
Ghana-USA Chamber of Commerce [24279]
Gonja Assn. of North Am. [11779]
Self-Help Initiative for Sustainable Development [IO]
Ghana Acad. of Arts and Sciences [IO], Accra, Ghana
Ghana Acad. of Learning [★IO]
Ghana Assn. of Consultants [IO], Accra, Ghana
Ghana Assn. of Physiotherapists [IO], Accra, Ghana
Ghana Athletic Assn. [IO], Accra, Ghana
Ghana Baseball and Softball Assn. [IO], Accra, Ghana
Ghana Chamber of Mines [IO], Accra, Ghana
Ghana Cocoa Marketing Bd. [IO], Accra, Ghana
Ghana Diabetes Assn. [IO], Accra, Ghana
Ghana Employers Assn. [IO], Accra, Ghana
Ghana Export Promotion Coun. [IO], Accra, Ghana
Ghana Furniture Producers Assn. [IO]
Ghana Geotechnical Soc. [IO], Kumasi, Ghana
Ghana Institution of Engineers [IO], Accra, Ghana
Ghana Mfrs. Assn. [★IO]
Ghana Medical Assn. [IO], Accra, Ghana
Ghana Natl. Chamber of Commerce and Indus. [IO], Accra, Ghana
Ghana Red Cross Soc. [IO], Accra, Ghana
Ghana Soc. of Hypertension and Cardiology [IO], Accra, Ghana
Ghana Squash Assn. [IO], Accra, Ghana
Ghana Taekwondo Assn. [IO], Accra, Ghana
Ghana Tennis Assn. [IO], Accra, Ghana
Ghana Timber Export Development Bd. [IO], Takoradi, Ghana
Ghana-USA Chamber of Commerce [24279], 200 E Randolph St., Ste. 2200, Chicago, IL 60601, (708)331-3277
Ghana Wildlife Soc. [IO], Accra, Ghana
Ghaqda Biblika Maltija [★IO]
Ghaqda Maltija Kontra id-Dijabete [★IO]
Ghetto Resistance Org; Warsaw [20191]
Ghorfet el Monchekat el Fondokia [★IO]
Ghost Club [IO], St. Leonards-on-Sea, United Kingdom
Ghost Ranch Found; Natl. [20469]
Ghost Res. Soc. [7475], PO Box 205, Oak Lawn, IL 60454-0205, (708)425-5163
Ghost Soc; Amer. [7438]
Ghost Trackers Club [★7475]
GI Alliance - Defunct.
GI Forum [★21280]
GI Forum of U.S; Amer. [21280]
GI Joe Collectors' Club [22996], 225 Cattle Baron Parc, Fort Worth, TX 76108, (817)448-9863
Giacometti Found. of Brazil [★IO]
Giant Chinchilla Rabbit Assn. - Defunct.
Giant Club; Amer. Checkered [★5132]
Giant Scale Warbirds Assn. [22644], PO Box 4469, Columbus, GA 31914-0469
Giant Scale Warbirds Association [IO], Columbus, GA, United States
Giant Schnauzer Club of Am. [22276], c/o Tami Stoller, Sec., 5301 Finney Rd., Salida, CA 95368, (209)545-3231
Gibb Family Friendship Club - Address unknown since 1994.
Gibraltar Amateur Radio Soc. [IO], Gibraltar, United Kingdom
Gibraltar Badminton Fed. [IO], Gibraltar, Gibraltar
Gibraltar Cricket Assn. [IO], Vineyards, Gibraltar
Gibraltar Squash Assn. [IO], Gibraltar, Gibraltar
Gibraltar Taxi Assn. [IO], Gibraltar, Gibraltar
Gibran Centennial Found; Kahlil [★11132]

Gibran Memorial Found; Kahlil [11132]
Gideon Averill Descendants Org. - Defunct.
Gideon Family Assn. [20915], 160 W Dunedin Rd., Columbus, OH 43214, (614)263-4232
The Gideons Intl. [20011], PO Box 140800, Nashville, TN 37214-0800, (615)564-5000
The Gideons Intl. [IO], Nashville, TN, United States
Gift Associates Interchange Network [3710], c/o ABC-Amega, Inc., 1100 Main St., Buffalo, NY 14209-2356, (716)887-9508
Gift Assn. of Am. [859], 115 Rolling Hills Rd., Johnstown, PA 15905-5225, (814)288-1460
Gift and Collectibles Guild [860], PO Box A3294, Chicago, IL 60690, (312)236-3930
Gift and Decorative Accessories Assn. of Am. [★859]
Gift From Within [12768], 16 Cobb Hill Rd., Camden, ME 04843, (207)236-8858
Gift Fruit Shippers Assn; Florida [4731]
Gift from the Heart Found. [13961], 2653 N Narragansett Ave., Chicago, IL 60639, (773)237-4800
Gift from the Heart Found. [IO], Chicago, IL, United States
Gift of Life Intl. [IO], Great Neck, NY, United States
Gift of Life Intl. [12524], 475 Northern Blvd., Ste. 25, Great Neck, NY 11021, (516)504-0830
Gift Manufacturers' and Wholesale Traders' Assn. [IO], Madrid, Spain
Gift Novelty Trade Assn; Souvenir and [★861]
Gift Packaging and Greeting Card Assn. of Canada [IO], Toronto, ON, Canada
Gift Retailers, Mfrs. and Reps Assn. - Defunct.
Gift Wrappings and Tyings Assn. - Defunct.
Gifted
Amer. Assn. for Gifted Children [8463]
Amer. Indian Res. and Development [8464]
Amer. Mensa [9981]
The Assn. for the Gifted [8465]
Australian Mensa [IO]
European Coun. for High Ability [IO]
Hollingworth Center for Highly Gifted Children [9982]
Iberamerican Fed. of the World Coun. for Gifted and Talented Children [IO]
Intl. Soc. for Philosophical Enquiry [IO]
Intl. Soc. for Philosophical Enquiry [9983]
INTERTEL [9984]
Lewis M. Terman Soc. [9985]
Mega Soc. [9986]
Mensa Intl. [IO]
Mensa South Africa [IO]
Natl. Assn. for Gifted Children [IO]
Natl. Assn. for Gifted Children [8466]
Natl. Valedictorian Soc. [9077]
New Zealand Assn. for Gifted Children [IO]
Prometheus Soc. [9987]
Triple Nine Soc. [9988]
World Coun. for Gifted and Talented Children [8467]
World Coun. for Gifted and Talented Children [IO]
Gifted Advocacy Information Network - Defunct.
Gifted; The Assn. for the [8465]
Gifted Children; Assn. of Educators of [★8465]
Gifted Children; Natl. Assn. for [8466]
Gifted Children's Pen Pals Intl. - Defunct.
Gifted Education; ERIC CH on Disabilities and [★9141]
Gifted Education; ERIC CH on Disabilities and [★11998]
Gifted Education; ERIC CH on Disabilities and [★IO]
Giftmakers Guild; Collectibles and [★860]
Gifts
Anheuser-Busch Collectors Club [21967]
Gift Associates Interchange Network [3710]
Gift Assn. of Am. [859]
Gift Manufacturers' and Wholesale Traders' Assn. [IO]
Intl. Inflatable Products and Games Assn. [861]
Mexican Assn. of Gifts, Decorative Goods and Folk Art Producers [IO]
Natl. Specialty Gift Assn. [1724]
Natl. Tabletop and Giftware Assn. [3711]
New Zealand Gift Trade Assn. [IO]
North Amer. Celtic Buyers Assn. [784]
Taiwan Gift and Houseware Exporters Assn. [IO]

Reference to "IO" in place of a book number signifies that the association may be found in the 45th edition of International Organizations.

Gifts In Kind [★12720]
Gifts In Kind Intl. [12720], 333 N Fairfax St., Alexandria, VA 22314, (703)836-2121
Gifts in Kind of Am. [★12720]
Giftware Associate Interchange Network [★3710]
Giftware Assn. [IO], Birmingham, United Kingdom
Giftware Assn; Natl. Tabletop and [3711]
Giftware Manufacturers Credit Interchange [★3710]
Gilbert Heritage Soc; A.C. [22992]

Gilbert and Sullivan
Jack Point Preservation Soc. [9811]
Midwestern Gilbert and Sullivan Soc. [9813]

Gilbert and Sullivan Soc. [9809], Community Church of New York, 40 E 35th St., New York, NY 10016, (212)757-5804
Gilbert and Sullivan Soc. [IO], Sanderstead, United Kingdom
Gilbert and Sullivan Soc; Midwestern [9813]
Gilberth. Haws and Hannah Whitcomb Family Org. - Address unknown since 2004.
Gilda Radner Familial Ovarian Cancer Registry [13826], Roswell Park Cancer Inst., Elm & Carlton Sts., Buffalo, NY 14263-0001, (716)845-4503
Gilda Radner Familial Ovarian Cancer Registry [IO], Buffalo, NY, United States
Gilda's Club [13827], 322 8th Ave., Ste. 1402, New York, NY 10001, (917)305-1200
Gildea Family History Assn. - Address unknown since 2006.
Gill Fan Club; Vince [24989]
Gilles de la Tourette Syndrome Assn. [★15367]
Gillespie Clan - Defunct.
Gillie - Gilley Family Org. - Defunct.
Gilligan's Island Fan Club [★25038]
Gilligan's Island Fan Club [25030], 12429 Dormouse Rd., San Diego, CA 92129
Gilligan's Island Fan Club; Official [25038]
Gilligan's Island Fan Club; Original [★25038]
Gilligan's Island Fan Club (The Original) [★25038]
Gilman Found; Howard [11504]
Gilstrap Family Assn. [20916], c/o Marcus D. Gilstrap, 1921 N Harrison, San Angelo, TX 76901-1335, (915)949-0792
Gin Rectifiers and Distillers Assn. [★IO]
Gin and Vodka Assn. of Great Britain [IO], Salisbury, United Kingdom
Ginger Alden "Lady Superstar" Fan Club - Defunct.
Ginger Lynn Fan Club - Defunct.
Ginger Rogers: The Star Fan Club - Defunct.
Gingerbread [IO], London, United Kingdom
Ginners' Assn; Natl. Cotton [1096]
Ginners Assn; Southern Cotton [1098]
Ginny Doll Club [22396], PO Box 338, Oakdale, CA 95361, (209)848-0300
Ginseng Res. Inst. [★1905]
Ginseng Res. Inst. of Am. [1905], c/o Ginseng Bd. of Wisconsin, 555 N 72nd Ave., Ste. 2, Wausau, WI 54401, (715)845-7300
Giovanni Agnelli Found. [IO], Turin, Italy
Gippsland Olive Growers Assn. [IO], Heyfield, Australia
Giraffe Heroes Proj. [10185], PO Box 759, Langley, WA 98260, (360)221-7989
Giraffe Soc. - Defunct.
Girl Friends [19376]
Girl Guides Assn. [★IO]
Girl Guides Assn. - Australia [★IO]
Girl Guides Assn. of Kiribati [IO], Tarawa, Kiribati
Girl Guides Assn. - Malaysia [IO], Kuala Lumpur, Malaysia
Girl Guides Assn. of New Zealand [★IO]
Girl Guides Assn. - South Africa [IO], Randburg, Republic of South Africa
Girl Guides of Canada [IO], Toronto, ON, Canada
Girl Guides Singapore [IO], Singapore, Singapore
Girl Guiding Scotland [IO], Edinburgh, United Kingdom
Girl Pioneers; Lutheran [20221]
Girl Scout Comm; Natl. Jewish [13004]
Girl Scout Comm. of the Synagogue Coun. of Amer; Natl. Jewish [★13004]
Girl Scout Executive Staff; Assn. of [12996]
Girl Scout Executives; Natl. Assn. of [★12996]
Girl Scout Professional Workers; Assn. of [★12996]
Girl Scouts of the U.S.A. [12998], 420 5th Ave., New York, NY 10018-2798, (212)852-8000

Girl from U.N.C.L.E.
U.N.C.L.E. HQ [25044]

Girlguiding UK [IO], London, United Kingdom
Girlie Matchcover Club - Address unknown since 2002.

Girls
About-Face [13415]
Alliance for Women's Equality [13455]
Amer. Legion Auxiliary Girls Nation [17068]
Assn. of Albanian Girls and Women [18382]
Assn. of Girl Scout Executive Staff [12996]
Captive Daughters [18383]
Educational Equity Center [8400]
Empower Prog. [8945]
Girl Scouts of the U.S.A. [12998]
Girls Inc. [13486]
Girlstart [8468]
Helping Our Teen Girls in Real Life Situations [12261]
Lutheran Girl Pioneers [20221]
Natl. Assn. of Principals of Schools for Girls [9015]
Natl. Campaign to Prevent Teen Pregnancy [13499]
Natl. Coalition of Girls' Schools [8288]
Natl. Coalition for Women and Girls in Educ. [9321]
Natl. Jewish Girl Scout Comm. [13004]
Ophelia Proj. [13509]
Professional Assn. of Volleyball Officials [23875]
Sheclimbs [23285]
Solace Intl. [13439]
Step Up Women's Network [13440]
Wellesley Centers for Women [9327]
Women's Alliance for Peace and Human Rights in Afghanistan [12380]
Women's Learning Partnership for Rights, Development, and Peace [13452]

Girls and Boys Town [12934], 14100 Crawford St., Boys Town, NE 68010, (402)498-1300
Girls' Brigade Australia [IO], Blacktown, Australia
Girls' Brigade Australia - New South Wales [IO], Sydney, Australia
Girls' Brigade Australia - Queensland [IO], Mansfield, Australia
Girls' Brigade Australia - South Australia [IO], North Adelaide, Australia
Girls' Brigade Australia - Victoria [IO], Rangeview, Australia
Girls' Brigade Australia - Western Australia [IO], Belmont, Australia
Girls' Brigade - England and Wales [IO], Didcot, United Kingdom
Girls' Brigade Intl. Coun. [IO], Glasgow, United Kingdom
Girls' Brigade New Zealand [IO], Auckland, New Zealand
Girls' Brigade Northern Ireland [IO], Antrim, United Kingdom
Girls' Brigade Scotland [IO], Glasgow, United Kingdom
Girls' Brigade Singapore [IO], Singapore, Singapore
Girls; Camp Fire Boys and [★13475]
Girls' Club; Theta Rho [13518]
Girls Clubs of Am. [★13486]
Girls Clubs of Am; Boys and [13471]
Girls Clubs; Natl. Assn. of [★13498]
Girls Educ. [IO], Bangalore, India
Girls in Educ; Natl. Coalition for Women and [9321]
Girls Friday of Show Business [★13069]
Girls Friendly Soc. - United Kingdom - GFS Platform [IO], London, United Kingdom
Girls' Friendly Soc. of the U.S.A. - Address unknown since 1997.
Girls' Guild [★20642]
Girls Inc. [13486], 120 Wall St., New York, NY 10005-3902, (212)509-2000
Girls Nation; Amer. Legion Auxiliary [17068]
Girls; Natl. Assn. of Principals of Schools for [9015]
Girls; Pioneer [★20642]
Girls' Prout [★18633]
Girls Rodeo Assn. [★23696]
Girls' Schools Assn. [IO], Leicester, United Kingdom
Girls' Schools; Natl. Coalition of [8288]
Girls State [★17068]

Girls' Town of Rome [★13474]
Girls and Women; Assn. for the Promotion of the Mathematics Educ. of [★8828]
Girls and Women in Sport; Natl. Assn. for [8983]
Girl's and Women's Sports of the Amer. Assn. of Hea., Physical Educ., and Recreation; Division of [★8983]
Girlstart [8468], 1400 W Anderson Ln., Austin, TX 78757, (512)916-4775
Girth and Mirth - Defunct.
Givat Haviva Educational Found. [18059], 114 W 26th St., Ste. 1001, New York, NY 10001, (212)989-9272
Givat Haviva Educational Foundation [IO], New York, NY, United States
Give Kids the World [★IO]
Give Kids the World [★11696]
Give Kids the World Found. [★11696]
Give Kids the World Found. [★IO]
Give Kids the World Trust [★IO]
Give Kids the World Trust [★11696]
Give Kids the World Village [11696], 210 S Bass Rd., Kissimmee, FL 34746-6034, (407)396-1114
Give Kids the World Village [IO], Kissimmee, FL, United States
Give2TheTroops [12597], PO Box 445, Canton, CT 06019-0445, (888)876-6775
Giving Alliance; BBB Wise [17309]
Giving Children Hope [11596], 8332 Commonwealth Ave., Buena Park, CA 90621, (714)523-4454
Giving Children Hope [IO], Buena Park, CA, United States
Giving Inst. [1686], 4700 W Lake Ave., Glenview, IL 60025, (847)375-4709
Giving; Natl. Comm. on Planned [1689]
Giving U.S.A. Found. [12721], 4700 W Lake Ave., Glenview, IL 60025, (847)375-4709
Glaciological Soc. [★IO]
Gladiolus Coun; North Amer. [22532]
Gladiolus Selections; All-America [22481]
Gladstone Equestrian Assn. [23524], PO Box 119, Gladstone, NJ 07934, (908)470-0500
Glamour Photographers Intl. [2997], PO Box 84374, San Diego, CA 92138, (619)575-0100
Glamour Photographers Intl. [IO], San Diego, CA, United States
Glas Owners Club - Address unknown since 2001.
Glasgow Archaeological Soc. [IO], Glasgow, United Kingdom
Glasgow Chamber of Commerce [IO], Glasgow, United Kingdom
Glasgow Mathematical Assn. [IO], Glasgow, United Kingdom
Glasgow Natural History Soc. [IO], Glasgow, United Kingdom
Glasgow Women's Aid [IO], Glasgow, United Kingdom

Glass
Amer. Carnival Glass Assn. [22549]
Amer. Collectors of Infant Feeders [21959]
Amer. Cookie Jar Assn. [22577]
Amer. Cut Glass Assn. [22550]
Amer. Natural Soda Ash Corp. [1725]
Amer. Precision Optics Mfrs. Assn. [3480]
Amer. Sci. Glassblowers Soc. [3481]
Antique and Art Glass Salt Shaker Collectors Soc. [21968]
Art Alliance for Contemporary Glass [9421]
Art Glass Assn. [1726]
Art Glass Assn. [IO]
Assn. of the Glass and Ceramics Indus. of the Czech Republic [IO]
Assn. of Stained Glass Lamp Artists [2392]
Australian Glass and Glazing Assn. [IO]
Ball Collectors Club [22551]
Brazilian Assn. of the Automated Glass Indus. [IO]
British Glass [IO]
British Soc. of Sci. Glassblowers [IO]
Coalition for Auto Glass Safety and Public Awareness [1727]
Container Recycling Alliance [4479]
Contemporary Glass Soc. [IO]
Egg Cup Collectors' Corner [22016]
European Container Glass Fed. [IO]
European Glaziers Assn. [IO]

A star before a book entry number signifies that the name is not listed separately, but is mentioned within the entry.

European Gp. of Flat Glass Manufacturers [IO]
European Refractories Producers Fed. [IO]
Fed. of the Glass Indus. [IO]
Fenton Art Glass Collectors of Am. [22552]
Fostoria Glass Collectors [22553]
Fostoria Glass Soc. of Am. [22554]
German Soc. of Glass Tech. [IO]
Glass Art Soc. [22555]
Glass Assn. of North Am. [1728]
Glass and Glazing Fed. [IO]
Glass Inst. [IO]
Glass Mfg. Indus. Coun. [1729]
Glass Molders, Pottery, Plastics, and Allied Workers Intl. Union [24066]
Glass Tech. Inst. [7150]
H.C. Fry Glass Soc. [22556]
Heart of America Carnival Glass Assn. [22557]
Heisey Collectors of America/National Heisey Glass Museum [22558]
Homer Laughlin China Collectors Assn. [22036]
Independent Glass Assn. [1730]
Indian Refractory Makers Assn. [IO]
Insulating Glass Certification Coun. [1731]
Insulating Glass Mfrs. Alliance [IO]
Intl. Carnival Glass Assn. [IO]
Intl. Carnival Glass Assn. [22559]
Intl. Chinese Snuff Bottle Soc. [21890]
Intl. Collectors Guild [22051]
Intl. Commn. on Glass [IO]
Intl. Guild of Glass Artists [299]
Intl. Soc. of Glass Beadmakers [311]
M. T. Bottle Collectors Assn. [22066]
Natl. Amer. Glass Club [22560]
Natl. Assn. of the Glass Indus. [IO]
Natl. Assn. of Glass Manufacturers [IO]
Natl. Assn. of Milk Bottle Collectors [22076]
Natl. Cambridge Collectors [22561]
Natl. Depression Glass Assn. [22562]
Natl. Duncan Glass Soc. [22563]
Natl. Fenton Glass Soc. [22564]
Natl. Glass Assn. [1732]
Natl. Imperial Glass Collectors Soc. [22565]
Natl. Insulation Assn. [IO]
Natl. Milk Glass Collectors Soc. [22566]
Natl. Toothpick Holder Collectors' Soc. [22089]
Promotional Glass Collectors Assn. [22109]
Protective Glazing Coun. [1733]
Res. Assn. of the German Glass Indus. [IO]
Retailers of Art Glass and Supplies [IO]
Retailers of Art Glass and Supplies [1734]
Rose Bowl Collectors [22112]
Scandinavian Soc. of Glass Tech. [IO]
Soc. of Glass and Ceramic Decorators [1735]
Soc. of Glass Tech. [IO]
Soc. of Tobacco Jar Collectors [21936]
Stained Glass Assn. of Am. [1736]
Standing Comm. of the European Glass Indus. [IO]
Thermal Insulation Contractors Assn. [IO]
Tiffin Glass Collectors Club [22567]
Treasures for Little Children [23000]
USWA Flint/Glass Workers Conf. [24067]
Vaseline Glass Collectors, Inc. [22127]
Whisky Pitcher Collectors Assn. of Am. [22130]
Worshipful Company of Glaziers' and Painters of Glass [IO]

Glass Art Soc. [22555], 3131 Western Ave., Ste. 414, Seattle, WA 98121, (206)382-1305
Glass Assn; Laminators Safety [★1728]
Glass Assn. of North Am. [1728], 2945 SW Wanamaker Dr., Ste. A, Topeka, KS 66614-5321, (785)271-0208
Glass Club; Natl. Early Amer. [★22560]
Glass Collectors Soc; Imperial [★22565]
Glass Container Industry Corp. - Defunct.
Glass Container Manufacturers Inst. [★982]
Glass Crafts of America - Defunct.
Glass Dealers Assn; Natl. [★1732]
Glass Dealers Assn; Natl. Auto and Flat [★1732]
Glass Door and Window Inst; Sliding [★588]
Glass Engravers; Guild of [IO]
Glass and Glazing Fed. [IO], London, United Kingdom
Glass and Glazing Fed. Conservatory Assn. [★IO]
Glass Industry Air Quality Group - Defunct.

Glass Inst. [IO], Paris, France
Glass Jobbers Assn; Flat [★1728]
Glass Knife Collectors Club - Defunct.
Glass Lamp Artists; Assn. of Stained [2392]
Glass Mfrs. Assn; Natl. Ornamental [★1736]
Glass Mfrs. Fed. [★IO]
Glass Mfg. Indus. Coun. [1729], 735 Ceramic Pl., Ste. 101, Westerville, OH 43081, (614)818-9423
Glass Marketing Assn; Flat [★1728]
Glass Ministries; Bill [★19996]
Glass Molders, Pottery, Plastics, and Allied Workers Intl. Union [24066], 608 E Baltimore Pike, PO Box 607, Media, PA 19063-0607, (610)565-5051
Glass Packaging Inst. [982], 700 N Fairfax St., Ste. 510, Alexandria, VA 22314, (703)684-6359
Glass and Pottery Mfrs; Assoc. [3709]
Glass Salt Shaker Collectors Soc; Antique and Art [21968]
Glass-Steagall Act Stud. Comm. [★3523]
Glass Suppliers Assn; Art [★1726]
Glass Tech. Inst. [7150], 12653 Portada Pl., San Diego, CA 92130, (858)481-1277
Glass Tempering Assn. [★1728]
Glass Workers of North Am; Amer. Flint [★24067]
Glassblowers Soc; Amer. Sci. [3481]
Glasser Inst; William [16233]
Glaucoma Assn. [★IO]
Glaucoma Assn; Intl. [IO]
The Glaucoma Found. [15682], 80 Maiden Ln., Ste. 1206, New York, NY 10038, (212)285-0080
Glaucoma Res. Found. [15683], 251 Post St., Ste. 600, San Francisco, CA 94108, (415)986-3162
Glaucoma Res; Found. for [★15683]
Glaucoma Soc. of the Intl. Cong. of Ophthalmology - Address unknown since 2001.
Glazing Assn; Protective [★1733]
Glazing Certification Coun; Safety [668]
Glazing Coun; Protective [1733]
Glazing Indus. Code Comm. [626], 2945 SW Wanamaker Dr., Ste. A, Topeka, KS 66614-5321, (785)271-0208
Glazounov Soc. - Defunct.
Gleaner Life Insurance Soc. [19124], 5200 W U.S. Hwy. 223, PO Box 1894, Adrian, MI 49221-7894, (517)263-2244
Gleaners; Ancient Order of [★19124]
Gleaners; Senior [12398]
Glen Campbell Fan Club - Address unknown since 1995.
Glencoe Social Trail Riders [IO], Glencoe, Australia
Glenkirk [11948], 3504 Commercial Ave., Northbrook, IL 60062, (847)272-5111
Glenmary Home Missioners [★19628]
Glenmary Res. Center [19628], 1312 5th Ave. N., Nashville, TN 37208, (615)256-1905
Glenn Miller Birthplace Soc. [24902], 107 E Main St., PO Box 61, Clarinda, IA 51632, (712)542-2461
Gless as Cagney Fan Club; Sharon [★24771]
Gless Fan Club (U.S.); Sharon [24771]
Glider Assn; Southern California Hang [★23044]
Glider Club; Peninsula Hang [★23044]
Glider Infantry Assn; 325th [21374]
Gliding Assn; Natl. [★23043]
Gliding Assn; U.S. Hang [★23044]
Gliding Horse and Pony Registry [4884]
Global Access Proj; Hea. [11331]
Global Action for Disarmament, Development, and World Reform; Parliamentarians [★17433]
Global Action and Information Network - Defunct.
Global Action Intl. [12857], PO Box 717, Carlsbad, CA 92018-0717, (760)438-3979
Global Action Intl. [IO], Carlsbad, CA, United States
Global Action to Prevent War [IO], New York, NY, United States
Global Action to Prevent War [18113], 675 Third Ave., Ste. 315, New York, NY 10017, (212)818-1815
Global Action Proj. [18849], 4 W 37th St., 2nd Fl., New York, NY 10018, (212)594-9577
Global Action Proj. [IO], New York, NY, United States
Global Advt. Lawyers Alliance [IO], New York, NY, United States
Global Advt. Lawyers Alliance [5938], 599 Lexington Ave., 28th Fl., New York, NY 10022, (212)549-0343

Global Age; Amer. Forum: Educ. in a [★8593]
Global AIDS Alliance [13565], 1413 K St. NW, 4th Fl., Washington, DC 20005, (202)789-0432
Global AIDS Campaign; Student [13585]
Global Alliance for Africa [16929], 703 W Monroe, Chicago, IL 60661, (312)382-0607
Global Alliance Against Traffic in Women [IO], Bangkok, Thailand
Global Alliance for Incinerator Alternatives [5268], 1442A Walnut St., No. 20, Berkeley, CA 94709, (510)883-9490
Global Alliance for Intelligent Arts [9443], 795 S State St. 75, Ukiah, CA 95482, (413)374-6531
Global Alliance for Intelligent Arts [IO], Ukiah, CA, United States
Global Alliance for Justice Educ. [IO], Nashville, TN, United States
Global Alliance for Justice Educ. [8766], c/o Frank Bloch, Vanderbilt Univ. Law School, 131 21st Ave. S, Nashville, TN 37203-1181, (615)322-4964
Global Alliance for Medical Educ. [8862], c/o Celene Chasen, Membership Chair, Off. of Continuing Medical Educ., Baylor Coll. of Medicine, 1709 Dryden Rd., Ste. 1218, Houston, TX 77030-2404, (713)798-4024
Global Alliance for Medical Educ. [IO], Houston, TX, United States
Global Alliance of Mental Illness Advocacy Networks [IO], Staten Island, NY, United States
Global Alliance of Mental Illness Advocacy Networks [15200], 308 Seaview Ave., Staten Island, NY 10305, (718)351-1717
Global Alliance of Natl. Baton Twirling and Majorette Associations [23141], PO Box 266, Janesville, WI 53547-0266, (608)757-0939
Global Alliance of Performers [10773], 19924 Aurora Ave. N, Ste. 101, Seattle, WA 98133, (206)264-5072
Global Alliance of Performers [IO], Seattle, WA, United States
Global Alliance for Preserving the History of WWII in Asia [IO], Cupertino, CA, United States
Global Alliance for Preserving the History of WWII in Asia [13459], PO Box 1323, San Carlos, CA 94070-7323
Global Alliance for Sugar Trade Reform and Liberalisation [IO], Brisbane, Australia
Global Alliance for Transnational Educ. [IO], Englewood, CO, United States
Global Alliance for Transnational Educ. [8657], 9697 E Mineral Ave., Englewood, CO 80112, (303)784-8368
Global Alliance for Women's Hea. [16897], 777 UN Plz., 7th Fl., New York, NY 10017, (212)286-0424
Global Alliance for Women's Hea. [IO], New York, NY, United States
Global Anti-Incinerator Alliance [★5268]
Global Applied Disability Res. and Info. Network [14240], c/o Susanne M. Buyere, Chair, Cornell Univ., School of Indus. and Labor Relations, 201 ILR Extension Bldg., Ithaca, NY 14853-3901, (607)255-7727
Global Applied Disability Res. and Info. Network [IO], Ithaca, NY, United States
Global Aquaculture Alliance [IO], St. Louis, MO, United States
Global Aquaculture Alliance [4173], 5661 Telegraph Rd., Ste. 3A, St. Louis, MO 63129, (314)293-5500
Global Assn. for Interpersonal Neurobiology Stud. [7375], PO Box 3605, Santa Monica, CA 90408, (949)645-0828
Global Assn. for Interpersonal Neurobiology Stud. [IO], Santa Monica, CA, United States
Global Assn. for Packaged Travel; CrossSphere: the [★3930]
Global Assn. of Risk Professionals [1423], 111 Town Square Pl., Ste. 1215, Jersey City, NJ 07310, (201)719-7210
Global Assn. of Risk Professionals [IO], Jersey City, NJ, United States
Global Assn. of Virtual Assistants - Address unknown since 2004.
Global Autism Proj. [13725], 6910 Roosevelt Way NE, No. 201, Seattle, WA 98115, (206)850-9265
Global Autism Proj. [IO], Seattle, WA, United States

Reference to "IO" in place of a book number signifies that the association may be found in the 45th edition of International Organizations.

Global Bus. Coalition on HIV/AIDS **[IO]**, New York, NY, United States

Global Bus. Coalition on HIV/AIDS **[11329]**, One Liberty Plz., 165 Broadway, 36th Fl., New York, NY 10006, (212)584-1600

Global Bus. and Tech. Assn. **[778]**, PO Box 2686, Huntington Station, NY 11746, (516)876-3408

Global Bus. and Tech. Assn. **[IO]**, Huntington Station, NY, United States

Global Cities Proj. **[★5693]**

Global Climate Coalition - Defunct.

Global Coalition for Africa **[16930]**, 1818 H St., Rm. H2-200, Washington, DC 20433, (202)458-4338

Global Coalition for Africa **[IO]**, Washington, DC, United States

Global Comm. of Parliamentarians on Population and Development - Address unknown since 2005.

Global Community; Found. for **[18203]**

Global Competitiveness Coun. - Defunct.

Global Cong. of the World's Religions - Address unknown since 2004.

Global Cooperative Soc. - Address unknown since 2002.

Global Coral Reef Alliance **[4403]**, c/o Dr. Thomas J. Goreau, Pres., 37 Pleasant St., Cambridge, MA 02139, (617)864-4226

Global Deaf Connection **[12274]**, 2901 38th Ave. S, Minneapolis, MN 55406, (612)724-8565

Global Deaf Connection **[IO]**, Minneapolis, MN, United States

Global Economic Outreach **[IO]**, Wilmington, NC, United States

Global Economic Outreach **[20341]**, PO Box 12778, Wilmington, NC 28405

Global Ecovillage Network **[★6235]**

Global Ecovillage Network **[★IO]**

Global Ecovillage Network Oceania/Asia **[IO]**, Conondale, Australia

Global Educ.; Amer. Forum for **[8593]**

Global Educ. Associates **[17891]**, 475 Riverside Dr., No. 1850, New York, NY 10115, (212)870-3290

Global Educ. Associates **[IO]**, New York, NY, United States

Global Env; Center for Hea. and the **[14362]**

Global Env. Fac. **[★17851]**

Global Env. Fac. **[★IO]**

Global Environmental Mgt. Initiative **[4628]**, 1155 15th St. NW, Ste. 500, Washington, DC 20005, (202)296-7449

Global Envision **[12194]**, c/o Mercy Corps, 3015 SW, 1st Ave., Portland, OR 97201

Global Envision **[IO]**, Portland, OR, United States

Global Equity Gauge Alliance **[IO]**, Durban, Republic of South Africa

Global Equity Org. **[IO]**, Orange, CA, United States

Global Equity Org. **[1239]**, 1442 E Lincoln Ave., No. 487, Orange, CA 92865, (714)630-2908

Global Exchange **[17391]**, 2017 Mission St., No. 303, San Francisco, CA 94110, (415)255-7296

Global Exchange **[IO]**, San Francisco, CA, United States

Global Family **[IO]**, Santa Barbara, CA, United States

Global Family **[13140]**, PO Box 90710, Santa Barbara, CA 93190, (805)892-2864

Global Fund for Women **[17536]**, 1375 Sutter St., Ste. 400, San Francisco, CA 94109, (415)202-7640

Global Fund for Women **[IO]**, San Francisco, CA, United States

Global Futures Found. **[★1711]**

Global Gecko Assn. **[5169]**, c/o Leann Christenson, Membership Sec., 1155 Cameron Cove Cir., Leeds, AL 35094

Global Green USA **[4566]**, 2218 Main St., 2nd Fl., Santa Monica, CA 90405, (310)581-2700

Global Harmony Found. **[IO]**, Lausanne, Switzerland

Global Healing **[IO]**, Orinda, CA, United States

Global Healing **[12450]**, PO Box 2166, Orinda, CA 94563, (925)327-7889

Global Hea. Action **[14978]**, 1902 Clairmont Rd., Decatur, GA 30033, (404)634-5748

Global Hea. Action **[IO]**, Decatur, GA, United States

Global Hea. Coun. **[IO]**, Washington, DC, United States

Global Hea. Coun. **[14979]**, 1111 19th St. NW, Ste. 1120, Washington, DC 20036, (202)833-5900

Global Hea. Info. Network; SATELLIFE **[14663]**

Global Hea. Ministries **[14630]**, 7831 Hickory St. NE, Minneapolis, MN 55432-2500, (763)586-9590

Global Hea. Ministries **[IO]**, Minneapolis, MN, United States

Global Hea. Outreach of the Christian Medical and Dental Soc. **[★IO]**

Global Hea. Outreach of the Christian Medical and Dental Soc. **[★20238]**

Global Ideas Bank **[IO]**, London, United Kingdom

Global Initiative on Psychiatry **[IO]**, Hilversum, Netherlands

Global Interdependence Center **[18835]**, Univ. of Pennsylvania, 3701 Chestnut St., Philadelphia, PA 19104, (215)898-9453

Global Issues Rsrc. Center **[18151]**, East 1, Cuyahoga Community Coll., 4250 Richmond Rd., Cleveland, OH 44122, (216)987-2224

Global Jewish Assistance and Relief Network **[12372]**, 666 5th Ave., Ste. 246, New York, NY 10103, (212)868-3636

Global Jewish Assistance and Relief Network **[IO]**, New York, NY, United States

Global Justice; JustAct: Youth Action for **[18853]**

Global Lawyers and Physicians **[14558]**, c/o Dept. of Hea. Law, Bioethics and Human Rights, Boston Univ. of Public Hea., 715 Albany St., Boston, MA 02118, (617)638-4626

Global Lawyers and Physicians **[IO]**, Boston, MA, United States

Global Learning **[8658]**, 22 Mary Ann Dr., Brick, NJ 08723, (732)528-0016

Global Lottery Collectors Soc. **[22030]**, c/o George Beilke, Sec.-Treas., 1532 E 59th Pl., Tulsa, OK 74105-8008

Global Lung Cancer Coalition **[IO]**, Glasgow, United Kingdom

Global Majority **[IO]**, Monterey, CA, United States

Global Majority **[17249]**, 479 Pacific St., Ste. 5C, Monterey, CA 93940, (831)372-5518

Global March Against Child Labor **[IO]**, New Delhi, India

Global Marshall Plan Initiative **[IO]**, Hamburg, Germany

Global Militarization and Repression Study Group - Defunct.

Global Mission Ser. **[★13391]**

Global MissionAir **[20487]**, 214 Bel Air Dr., Yakima, WA 98908-3304, (509)966-7398

Global MissionAir **[IO]**, Yakima, WA, United States

Global Mobile Entertainers Assn. **[IO]**, Johnson City, NY, United States

Global Mobile Entertainers Assn. **[1302]**, 121 N Baldwin St., Johnson City, NY 13790, (607)729-1485

Global Movement for Children **[IO]**, Barcelona, Spain

Global Network **[★18152]**

Global Network Against Weapons and Nuclear Power in Space **[18152]**, c/o Bruce K. Gagnon, Sec./Coor., PO Box 652, Brunswick, ME 04011, (207)443-9502

Global Network for Environmental Monitoring - Defunct.

Global Neuro Rescue **[15324]**, 5539 Riverton Ave., North Hollywood, CA 91601, (818)516-6346

Global Neuro Rescue **[IO]**, North Hollywood, CA, United States

Global Nomads Gp. **[9336]**, 381 Broadway, 4th Fl., New York, NY 10013, (212)529-0377

Global Nomads Intl. **[17892]**, PO Box 8066, Reston, VA 20191, (703)993-2899

Global Nomads Intl. **[IO]**, Reston, VA, United States

Global Ocean Floor Anal. and Res. Center **[★7404]**

Global Offset and Countertrade Assn. **[2305]**, 818 Connecticut Ave. NW, 12th Fl., Washington, DC 20006, (202)887-9011

Global Options **[18448]**, PO Box 40601, San Francisco, CA 94140, (415)550-1703

Global Options **[IO]**, San Francisco, CA, United States

Global Org. for Lysosomal Diseases **[IO]**, Chalfont St. Giles, United Kingdom

Global Org. for Multi-Vendor Integration Protocol **[18681]**, 3220 N St. NW, Ste. 360, Washington, DC 20007, (903)769-3717

Global Org. of People of Indian Origin **[19113]**, PO Box 1413, Stamford, CT 06904, (818)708-3885

Global Outreach **[8615]**, 1920 Lee Blvd., North Mankato, MN 56003, (612)333-2353

Global Outreach **[IO]**, North Mankato, MN, United States

Global Outreach Mission **[IO]**, Buffalo, NY, United States

Global Outreach Mission **[12525]**, PO Box 2010, Buffalo, NY 14231*2010, (716)688-5048

Global Perioperative Res. Org. **[14026]**, PO Box 17969, Durham, NC 27715, (866)536-0568

Global Perspectives in Educ. **[★8593]**

Global Policy Forum **[17839]**, 777 UN Plz., Ste. 3D, New York, NY 10017, (212)557-3161

Global Polio Eradication Initiative **[IO]**, Geneva, Switzerland

Global Providence Found. - Defunct.

Global and Regional Asperger Syndrome Partnership **[15325]**, 666 Broadway, 8th Fl., New York, NY 10012, (646)242-4003

Global and Regional Asperger Syndrome Partnership **[IO]**, New York, NY, United States

Global Response **[IO]**, Boulder, CO, United States

Global Response **[4567]**, PO Box 7490, Boulder, CO 80306-7490, (303)444-0306

Global Rights **[17758]**, 1200 18th St. NW, Ste. 602, Washington, DC 20036, (202)822-4600

Global Rights **[IO]**, Washington, DC, United States

Global Routes **[9852]**, 1 Short St., Northampton, MA 01060, (413)585-8895

Global Security Inst. **[18153]**, GSB Bldg., Ste. 400, One Belmont Ave., Bala Cynwyd, PA 19004, (610)668-5488

Global Security Inst. **[IO]**, Bala Cynwyd, PA, United States

Global Security; SANE/FREEZE: Campaign for **[★18166]**

Global Ser. Corps **[13392]**, 300 Broadway, Ste. 28, San Francisco, CA 94133-3312, (415)788-3666

Global Ser. Corps **[IO]**, San Francisco, CA, United States

Global Solutions; Citizens for **[18762]**

Global Spatial Data Infrastructure Assn. **[7734]**, 946 Great Plain Ave., PMB 194, Needham, MA 02492-3030, (508)720-0325

Global Spatial Data Infrastructure Assn. **[IO]**, Orono, ME, United States

Global Strategies for HIV Prevention **[IO]**, San Rafael, CA, United States

Global Strategies for HIV Prevention **[13566]**, 104 Dominican Dr., San Rafael, CA 94901, (415)451-1814

Global Student Response - Address unknown since 2004.

Global Stud. Assn. North Am. **[8583]**, c/o Jerry Harris, Sec., 1250 N Wood St., Chicago, IL 60622

Global Stud. Assn. North Am. **[IO]**, Chicago, IL, United States

Global Stud. Center **[★17647]**

Global Stud. in Federalism and Democracy; Ashburn Inst. for **[18308]**

Global Tape Recording Exchange - Address unknown since 1995.

Global Teams **[19961]**, PO Box 490, Forest City, NC 28043, (828)248-1377

Global Teams **[IO]**, Forest City, NC, United States

Global Tomorrow Coalition - Address unknown since 1999.

Global Univ. **[19802]**, 1211 S Glenstone Ave., Springfield, MO 65804-0315, (417)862-9533

Global Univ. **[IO]**, Springfield, MO, United States

Global Vaccine Awareness League **[14559]**, 25422 Trabuco Rd., Ste. 105-230, Lake Forest, CA 92630-2797

Global Village Inst. **[6235]**, PO Box 90, Summertown, TN 38483-0090, (931)964-4474

Global Village Inst. **[★6235]**

Global Village Inst. **[IO]**, Summertown, TN, United States

Global Village Inst. **[★IO]**

Global Vision Intl. **[IO]**, St. Albans, United Kingdom

Global Vision for Peace **[18207]**, 5419 Hollywood Blvd., Ste. C208, Los Angeles, CA 90027

Global Visions **[★18612]**

A star before a book entry number signifies that the name is not listed separately, but is mentioned within the entry.

Global Volunteer Network [IO], Lower Hutt, New Zealand

Global Volunteers [IO], St. Paul, MN, United States

Global Volunteers [17893], 375 E Little Canada Rd., St. Paul, MN 55117-1628, (651)407-6100

Global Warming Intl. Center [4568], PO Box 50303, Palo Alto, CA 94303-0303, (630)910-1551

Global Warming Intl. Center [IO], Palo Alto, CA, United States

Global Wind Energy Coun. [IO], Brussels, Belgium

Global Witness [IO], London, United Kingdom

Global Women of African Heritage - Address unknown since 2000.

Global Work Prog. [★5875]

Global Work Prog. [★IO]

Global Workers Justice Alliance [IO], New York, NY, United States

Global Workers Justice Alliance [18074], 113 Univ. Pl., 8th Fl., New York, NY 10003, (917)238-0979

Global Youth Action Network [18850], 307 W 38th St., Ste. 1805, New York, NY 10018, (212)661-6111

Global Youth Action Network [IO], New York, NY, United States

Global Youth Connect [IO], Kingston, NY, United States

Global Youth Connect [18851], 15 Gage St., Kingston, NY 12401, (845)338-2220

Globalization and Localization Assn; GALA: [1168]

GlobalPlatform [7735], 1515 Cordilleras Rd., Redwood City, CA 94062

GlobalSecurity.org [18208], 300 N Washington St., Ste. B-100, Alexandria, VA 22314, (703)548-2700

Globe Aware [13393], 7232 Fisher Rd., Dallas, TX 75214-1917, (214)823-0083

Globe Aware [IO], Dallas, TX, United States

Globe Found. of Canada [IO], Vancouver, BC, Canada

Globetrotters' Club [IO], London, United Kingdom

Glock Collectors Assn. [22427], PO Box 1063, Maryland Heights, MO 63043, (314)878-2061

Gloria Dei Press - Address unknown since 1999.

Gloria Loring Fan Club - Defunct.

Glosa Educ. Org. [IO], Richmond, United Kingdom

Glosa Intl. Language Network [★IO]

Gloster Breeders Assn; Intl. [21849]

Gloster Breeders; United [21863]

Gloucester Fisheries Assn. - Address unknown since 1995.

Gloucester Master Mariners Assn. - Address unknown since 1995.

Glove Guild of Britain [★IO]

Glove Inst; Work [★2030]

Glove Mfrs. Assn; Work [★2030]

Glove Mfrs; Natl. Assn. of Cotton Cloth [★2030]

Glove Shippers Assn. - Address unknown since 2006.

Glovebox Soc; Amer. [7384]

Gloxina Soc; Amer. [★22515]

Gluckstal Colonies Res. Assn. [10111], 611 Esplanade, Redondo Beach, CA 90277-4130, (310)540-1872

Glued Laminated Timber Assn. [IO], High Wycombe, United Kingdom

The Glutamate Assn. - U.S. [1516], PO Box 14266, Washington, DC 20044-4266, (202)783-6135

Glutamate Mfrs. Technical Comm. - Defunct.

Glutamate Tech. Comm; Intl. [1528]

Glutaric Acidemia; Intl. Org. of [15332]

Gluten Intolerance Gp. [15559], 31214 124th Ave. SE, Auburn, WA 98092-3667, (253)833-6655

Gluten Intolerance Gp. [★15559]

Gluten Intolerance Gp. of North Am. [★15559]

Glycerine and Fatty Acid Producers Assn. [★822]

Glycerine and Oleochemicals Assn. [★822]

Glycerine Producers Assn. [★822]

Glycogen Storage Disease; Assn. for [15244]

GM Futurliner [21648], c/o Don M. Mayton, Proj. Dir., 4521 Majestic Vue, Zeeland, MI 49464, (616)875-3058

GM Futurliner [IO], Zeeland, MI, United States

GMB [IO], London, United Kingdom

GMC Intl. Truck Club; Chevy [21609]

GMC Truck Assn; Natl. Chevy/ [★21609]

Gnathologic Orthopedics; Amer. Acad. of [14098]

Gnathology-American Sect; Intl. Acad. of [14158]

Gnotobiotics Res. and Tech; Assn. for [4534]

GNU Proj. [★6767]

GNU Proj. [★IO]

Go Assn; Amer. [22459]

Go Go's Fan Club - Defunct.

GOAL [IO], Dun Laoghaire, Ireland

Goals 2000 Arts Educ. Partnership [★7966]

Goat Assn; Amer. Dairy [4126]

Goat Assn; Natl. Pygmy [4142]

Goat Breeder's Assn; Amer. Angora [4122]

Goat Practitioners; Amer. Assn. of Sheep and [★16749]

Goat Soc; Amer. [4128]

Goat Veterinary Soc. [IO], Newent, United Kingdom

Goats

  Alpines Intl. [4121]

  Amer. Angora Goat Breeder's Assn. [4122]

  Amer. Kiko Goat Assn. [4780]

  Amer. Tennessee Fainting Goat Assn. [4781]

  Boer Goat Breeders Assn. of Australia [IO]

  Colored Angora Goat Breeders Assn. [4782]

  Intl. Boer Goat Assn. [4783]

  Intl. Boer Goat Assn. [IO]

  International Fainting Goat Association [IO]

  Intl. Fainting Goat Assn. [4784]

  Intl. Goat Assn. [4785]

  Intl. Goat Assn. [IO]

  Intl. Nubian Breeders Assn. [4135]

  Kinder Goat Breeders Assn. [4786]

  Natl. Pygmy Goat Assn. [4142]

  Natl. Saanen Breeders Assn. [4143]

  Natl. Toggenburg Club [4787]

  New Zealand Dairy Goat Breeders Assn. [IO]

  Nigerian Dwarf Goat Assn. [4788]

  Oberhasli Breeders of Am. [4146]

  U.S. Boer Goat Assn. [4789]

God Bless Am. Found; Kate Smith/ [★24930]

God and Country; Amers. United for [17287]

God; General Coun. of the Assemblies of [★20643]

God; General Coun. of the Assemblies of [★IO]

God Inst; Word of [★19690]

God; Natl. Inst. for the Word of [19690]

Goddess

  Circle Sanctuary [20570]

Goddess - Intl; Re-Formed Congregation of the [20623]

Godolphin Soc. [10906], c/o Natl. Museum of Racing and Hall of Fame, 191 Union Ave., Saratoga Springs, NY 12866-3566, (518)584-0400

Godparent Home; Liberty [12918]

Godparent Ministry; Liberty [★12918]

God's Child Proj. [11597], PO Box 1573, Bismarck, ND 58504, (701)255-7956

God's Children; Rainbows for All [★11718]

God's Love We Deliver [12283], 166 Ave. of the Americas, New York, NY 10013, (212)294-8100

Godzilla: Asian and Pacific Islander Art Network - Address unknown since 1999.

Godzilla Soc. of North Am. [IO], Steinbach, MB, Canada

Goebel Collectors' Club [★21933]

Goebel Collectors Club; Intl. [★22040]

Goethe Institut [★9977]

Goethe-Institut [★IO]

Goethe Institut [★IO]

Goethe-Institut Inter Nationes [IO], New York, NY, United States

Goethe-Institut Inter Nationes [9977], 1014 5th Ave., New York, NY 10028, (212)439-8700

Goethe Institut Internationes [★IO]

Goethe Inst. - German Cultural Centre [IO], Hong Kong, People's Republic of China

Goethe Inst. for Promoting the Stud. of the German Language Abroad and for Intl. Cultural Cooperation [IO], Munich, Germany

Goethe Soc. of North Am. [9654], c/o Prof. Astrida Tantillo, Exec. Sec./Ed., Dept. of Germanic Stud., Univ. of Illinois at Chicago, 601 S Morgan St., Chicago, IL 60607, (312)413-2374

Goff/Gough Family Assn. [20917], c/o Allen S. Goff, Pres., 2125 Davis Rd., Waynesboro, VA 22980, (540)942-3188

Goiter; Amer. Assn. for the Stud. of [★16646]

Goiter Assn; Amer. [★16646]

Gold Bondholders Protective Coun. - Defunct.

The Gold Coast Chamber of Mines [★IO]

Gold Filled Assn. - Defunct.

Gold Foil Operators; Amer. Acad. of [14099]

Gold Inst. - Defunct.

Gold Prospectors Assn. of Am. [22913], PO Box 891509, Temecula, CA 92589, (951)699-4749

Gold and Silver Plate Soc; Intl. [18977]

Gold and Silver Wyre Drawers' Company [IO], Wiltshire, United Kingdom

Gold Star Mothers; Amer. [21188]

Gold Star Owners Club - Address unknown since 2008.

Gold Star Parents for Amnesty - Defunct.

Gold Star Wives of Am. [21195], PO Box 361986, Birmingham, AL 35236, (888)751-6350

Gold Star Wives of World War II [★21195]

Gold Wing Road Riders Assn. [22678], 21423 N 11th Ave., Phoenix, AZ 85027, (623)581-2500

Golden Age; Catholic [19597]

Golden Age Found; Catholic [★19597]

Golden Amer. Saddlebred Horse Assn. - Address unknown since 2002.

Golden Companions [★23018]

Golden Eagle; Knights of the [19128]

Golden Eagle; Order of the [★21320]

Golden Gloves Assn. of America - Address unknown since 2001.

Golden Glow of Christmas Past [22975], c/o Robert W. Dalluge, 6401 Winsdale St., Golden Valley, MN 55427

Golden Glow of Christmas Past [IO], Golden Valley, MN, United States

Golden Key Intl. Honour Soc. [24506], 621 North Ave. NE, Ste. C-100, Atlanta, GA 30308, (404)377-2400

Golden Key Natl. Honor Soc. [★24506]

Golden Lion Tamarin Conservation Program [★5321]

Golden Lion Tamarin Mgt. Comm. [5321]

Golden Lions [★21371]

Golden Lions [★IO]

Golden Memories of Elvis Fan Club - Address unknown since 1995.

Golden Raspberry Award Found. [22419], PO Box 835, Artesia, CA 90702-0835

Golden Retriever Club of Am. [22277], c/o Jolene Carey, Admin. Asst., PO Box 20434, Oklahoma City, OK 73156, (850)877-4817

Golden Ring Coun. of Senior Citizens Clubs - Defunct.

Golden Rule Found. [10186], PO Box 658, Camden, ME 04843, (207)236-4104

Golden Rule Found. [IO], Camden, ME, United States

Golden Rule; Intl. Order of the [2783]

Golden Threads [22137], PO Box 1688, Demorest, GA 30535-1688, (706)776-3959

Golden Threads [IO], Demorest, GA, United States

Golden West; Native Daughters of the [18986]

Golden West; Native Sons of the [18987]

Goldfish Growers Assn; Natl. Ornamental [4181]

Goldfish Soc. of Am. [22439], PO Box 551373, Fort Lauderdale, FL 33355, (954)423-0663

Goldfish Society of America [IO], Fort Lauderdale, FL, United States

Goldsmiths' Company [IO], London, United Kingdom

Goldsmiths; Soc. of North Amer. [9841]

Goldwing Flyers Club - Defunct.

Golf

  Alberta Golf Assn. [IO]

  All-Amer. Collegiate Golf Found. [23443]

  Amer. Blind Golf Assn. [23335]

  Amer. Junior Golf Assn. [23444]

  Amer. Recreational Golf Assn. [3636]

  Amer. Singles Golf Assn. [13106]

  Amer. Soc. of Golf Course Architects [6465]

  Assn. of Disabled Amer. Golfers [23341]

  Assn. of Golf Club Secretaries [IO]

  Atlantic Coast Conf. [23806]

  Austrian Golf Assn. [IO]

  Big East Conf. [23807]

  Big Ten Conf. [23808]

  Canadian Professional Golfers' Assn. [IO]

  Chinese-American Golf Assn. [23445]

Reference to "IO" in place of a book number signifies that the association may be found in the 45th edition of International Organizations.

Christian Golfers' Assn. [23283]
Club Managers Assn. of Am. [833]
Coun. of Ivy Gp. Presidents [23817]
Eastern Amputee Golf Assn. [23446]
Eastern Amputee Golf Association [IO]
Eastern Collegiate Hockey Assn. [23485]
English Golf Union [IO]
English Ladies' Golf Assn. [IO]
European Golf Assn. [IO]
European Golf Course Owners Assn. [IO]
Executive Women's Golf Assn. [23447]
Golf Coaches Assn. of Am. [23448]
Golf Collectors Soc. [22031]
Golf Course Builders Assn. of Am. [3662]
Golf Course Superintendents Assn. of Ireland [IO]
Golf Tournament Assn. of Am. [23449]
Golf Writers Assn. of Am. [23450]
Golfing Union of Ireland [IO]
Gp. Fore Golf Found. [23451]
Intl. Assn. of Golf Administrators [1737]
Intl. Assn. of Golf Tour Operators [IO]
Intl. Golf Associates [IO]
Intl. Golf Associates [23452]
Intl. Golf Fed. [23453]
Intl. Golf Fed. [IO]
Irish Ladies Golf Union [IO]
Ladies' Golf Union [IO]
Ladies Professional Golf Assn. [23454]
Malaysian Golf Assn. [IO]
Multicultural Golf Assn. of Am. [23455]
Natl. Advt. Golf Assn. [23456]
Natl. Alliance for Accessible Golf [23348]
Natl. Amputee Golf Assn. [23349]
Natl. Assn. of Golf Tournament Directors [23457]
Natl. Assn. of Intercollegiate Athletics [23835]
Natl. Assn. of Left-Handed Golfers [23458]
Natl. Assn. of Public Golf Courses [IO]
Natl. Christian Coll. Athletic Assn. [23837]
Natl. Collegiate Athletic Assn. [23838]
Natl. Golf Found. [3669]
Natl. Junior Coll. Athletic Assn. [23843]
Natl. Pan-American Junior Golf Assn. [23459]
Natl. Senior Golf Assn. [23460]
New Zealand Golf [IO]
Pacific 10 Conf. [23847]
PGA TOUR Tournaments Assn. [23461]
Physically Challenged Golf Assn. [23359]
Pitch and Putt Union of Ireland [IO]
Polish Amer. Golf Assn. [23462]
Professional Golf Teachers Assn. of Am. [23463]
Professional Golf Teachers Assn. of Am. [IO]
Professional Golfers' Assn. of Am. [23464]
Professional Golfers' Assn. - England [IO]
Professional Golfers' Associations of Europe [IO]
Professional Putters Assn. [23465]
Puerto Rico Golf Assn. [23466]
Royal and Ancient Golf Club [IO]
Royal and Ancient Golf Club of St. Andrews [IO]
Royal Canadian Golf Assn. [IO]
Scottish Golf Union [IO]
Scottish Ladies Golfing Assn. [IO]
Southeastern Conf. [23851]
Southern Conf. [23852]
Swiss Golf Assn. [IO]
Thailand Golf Assn. [IO]
UAE Golf Assn. [IO]
U.S. Blind Golf Assn. [23364]
U.S. Collegiate Athletic Assn. [23859]
U.S. Collegiate Sports Coun. [23860]
U.S. Golf Assn. [23467]
U.S. Golf Teachers Fed. [23468]
U.S. ProMiniGolf Assn. [23469]
USGA Green Sect. [23470]
Western Golf Assn. [23471]
Womens Golf New Zealand [IO]
World Senior Golf Fed. [IO]
World Senior Golf Fed. [23472]
Golf Assn. of Am; Minority [★23455]
Golf Assn. of Am; Multicultural [23455]
Golf Assn; Amer. Recreational [3636]
Golf Assn; Amer. Singles [13106]
Golf Assn; Intl. [★23452]
Golf Assn; Natl. Amputee [23349]
Golf Assn; U.S. Blind [23364]
Golf Assn. of the U.S; Miniature [23829]

Golf Assn; Women's Professional [★23454]
Golf Clubs' Advisory Assn; Natl. [IO]
Golf Coach Educators; Natl. Assn. of [★23291]
Golf Coaches Assn. of Am. [23448], 1225 W Main St., Ste. 110, Norman, OK 73069, (405)329-4222
Golf Coaches Assn; NCAA [★23448]
Golf Coaches and Educators; Natl. Assn. of [23291]
Golf Collectors Soc. [22031], PO Box 2386, Florence, OR 97439, (904)400-3400
Golf Collectors Soc. [IO], Ponte Vedra Beach, FL, United States
Golf Coun; World Amateur [★23453]
Golf Course Architects; Amer. Soc. of [6465]
Golf Course Builders of Am. [★3662]
Golf Course Builders Assn. [★3662]
Golf Course Builders Assn. of Am. [3662], 727 O St., Lincoln, NE 68508, (402)476-4444
Golf Course Constructors; British Assn. of [IO]
Golf Course Owners Assn; Natl. [3668]
Golf Course Superintendents Assn. of Am. [3663], 1421 Res. Park Dr., Lawrence, KS 66049-3859, (785)841-2240
Golf Course Superintendents Assn. of Ireland [IO], Banbridge, United Kingdom
Golf Found; Natl. [3669]
Golf Goods Assn; Japan [IO]
Golf Greenkeepers Assn; British and Intl. [IO]
Golf Management; National Inst. of [★3669]
Golf Products and Components Assn. - Defunct.
Golf Range Assn. of Am. [3664], c/o Mr. Steve J. di Costanzo, Founder/Pres., PO Box 240, Georgetown, CT 06829, (203)938-2720
Golf Sponsors; Amer. [★23461]
Golf Sponsors Assn; Intl. [★23461]
Golf Superintendents Assn; Canadian [IO]
Golf Tour; Women's Professional [★23451]
Golf Tournament Assn. of Am. [23449], PO Box 47405, Phoenix, AZ 85068, (602)667-3250
Golf Tournaments Assn; Professional [★23461]
Golf Writers Assn. of Am. [23450], c/o Melanie Hauser, Sec.-Treas., 10210 Greentree Rd., Houston, TX 77042-1232, (713)782-6664
Golfing Union of Ireland [IO], Kildare, Ireland
Goliath
    Borgward Owners' Club [21594]
Golondrinas Found. [IO], Quito, Ecuador
Golvbranschens Riksorganisation [★IO]
Gompers Stamp Club; Samuel [22867]
Gone With the Wind
    Gone With the Wind Soc. [24831]
Gone With the Wind Soc. [24831], c/o Herb Bridges, PO Box 192, Sharpsburg, GA 30277, (770)253-4934
Gonja Assn. of North Am. [11779], PO Box 403, Lithonia, GA 30058
Gonja Assn. of North Am. [IO], Lithonia, GA, United States
Gonstead Clinical Stud. Soc. [14005], 900 17th Ave., Santa Cruz, CA 95062, (888)556-4277
Good Amer. Helping Hands - Address unknown since 1995.
Good Bears of the World [13041], PO Box 13097, Toledo, OH 43613, (419)531-5365
Good Bears of the World [IO], Toledo, OH, United States
Good Faith - Address unknown since 2001.
Good Fellows (Old Newsboys) [13042], PO Box 44444, Detroit, MI 48244-0444, (586)775-6139
Good Gardeners Assn. [IO], Wooton-Under-Edge, United Kingdom
Good Gay Poets - Defunct.
Good Life Times - Address unknown since 1994.
Good Neighbors Intl. [IO], Seoul, Republic of Korea
Good News [★20262]
Good News Jail and Prison Ministry [★11869]
Good News Jail and Prison Ministry [11869], PO Box 9760, Richmond, VA 23228-0760, (804)553-4090
Good News Jail and Prison Ministry [★IO]
Good News Jail and Prison Ministry [IO], Richmond, VA, United States
Good News Mission [★IO]
Good News Mission [★11869]
Good Outdoor Manners Assn. - Defunct.
Good Sam Recreational Vehicle Club [22951], PO Box 6888, Englewood, CO 80155-6888, (800)234-3450

Good Samaritan Coalition - Defunct.
Good Samaritan Soc; Evangelical Lutheran [13168]
Good Shepherd Volunteers [13394], 337 E 17th St., New York, NY 10003, (212)475-4245
Good Templars
    European Good Templar Youth Fed. [IO]
    Natl. Coun. of the U.S., Intl. Org. of Good Templars [19081]
Good Tidings [19629], PO Box 283, Canadensis, PA 18325-0283, (570)595-2705
Good Water, America - Defunct.
Goodall Inst. for Wildlife Res., Educ., and Conservation; Jane [5334]
Goodenow Family Assn. [20918], 163 Landham Rd., Sudbury, MA 01776-3156
Goodguys Rod and Custom Assn. [21649], PO Box 9132, Pleasanton, CA 94566, (925)838-9876
Goodwill Indus. of Am. [★11949]
Goodwill Indus. of Am. [★IO]
Goodwill Indus. Intl. [IO], Rockville, MD, United States
Goodwill Indus. Intl. [11949], 15810 Indianola Dr., Rockville, MD 20855, (301)530-6500
Goodwill Indus; Natl. Assn. of [★11949]
Goodwill Indus; Natl. Auxiliary of [★11950]
Goodwill Indus; Natl. Women's Auxiliary to the [★11950]
Goodwill Indus. of Venezuela [IO], Caracas, Venezuela
Goodwill Indus. Volunteer Services [11950], c/o Goodwill Indus. Intl. Inc., 15810 Indianola Dr., Rockville, MD 20855, (800)741-0186
Goodwill; Men of [★17739]
Goodwill - The Amity Gp. [IO], Hamilton, ON, Canada
Goodwin Family Org. [20919], 39 Lost Trail Rd., Roswell, NM 88201-9509, (505)625-0961
Goolsby General Exchange - Defunct.
Goose and Gander, Soc. for the Preservation of First Wives and First Husbands - Defunct.
G.O.P. Women's Political Action League - Defunct.
Gordon Inst. for Music Learning [8910], c/o Jennifer McDonel, Exec. Dir., PO Box 528, Lebanon, OH 45036-0528, (513)932-0765
Gordon Setter
    Gordon Setter Club of Am. [22278]
Gordon Setter Club of Am. [22278], c/o Denise Dunham-Schiele, Membership Chair, 1259 Grace Ct., Downers Grove, IL 60516, (630)971-0861
Gore Fan Club; Lesley [24938]
Goree Inst. [IO], Ile de Goree, Senegal
Gorham Collectors' Guild - Defunct.
Gorilla Found. [7533], PO Box 620530, Woodside, CA 94062, (650)216-6450
Gorilla Fund Intl; Dian Fossey [5310]
Gospel
    Advancing Native Missions [19833]
    Affirmation/Gay and Lesbian Mormons [20046]
    Africa Inland Mission Intl. [20294]
    All-Ukrainian Evangelical Baptist Fellowship [19469]
    Amer. Coun. of Christian Churches [19761]
    Amer. and Foreign Christian Union [19762]
    AMG Intl. [20298]
    Armenian Missionary Assn. of Am. [19459]
    Assoc. Comm. of Friends on Indian Affairs [20039]
    Assn. of Baptists for World Evangelism [19472]
    Assn. of Contemplative Sisters [20563]
    Assn. of Life-Giving Churches [19843]
    Assn. of Southern Baptist Campus Ministers [19474]
    Baptist World Alliance [19482]
    BCM Intl. [19508]
    Berean Bible Soc. [19509]
    Bible League [19510]
    Biblical Ministries Worldwide [19991]
    BLI [19512]
    Bread on the Waters [19993]
    Bruderhof Communities [20481]
    Campus Crusade for Christ Intl. [19994]
    Catholic Pamphlet Soc. of the U.S. [19603]
    Catholics United for the Faith [19606]
    Child Evangelism Fellowship [19997]
    Chinese Christian Mission [20313]

A star before a book entry number signifies that the name is not listed separately, but is mentioned within the entry.

Christ in Action Ministries [19999]
Christ for the Nations [20314]
Christ Truth Ministries [19514]
Christian Boaters Assn. [20000]
Christian Bus. Men's Comm. [19771]
Christian Century Found. [19772]
Christian Chiropractors Assn. [19773]
Christian Communications, Inc. [19774]
Christian Holiness Partnership [19779]
Christian Literature and Bible Center [20317]
Christian Media Assn. [20237]
Christian Ser. Club [19515]
Christian TV Mission [19536]
Comm. on Missionary Evangelism [20001]
Commun. Commn. [19537]
Community of Celebration [19790]
Concordia Gospel Outreach [20214]
Conservative Baptist Assn. of Am. [19485]
Cowboys for Christ [19792]
Dawn Bible Students Assn. [19517]
Episcopal Evangelical Educ. Soc. [19955]
Evangelical Free Church of Am. - Intl. Mission [20333]
Fed. of Protestant Welfare Agencies [20482]
Fellowship of Christian Airline Personnel [20007]
Fellowship of Christian Magicians [19797]
Focolare Movement [19624]
Forward in Faith North Am. [19959]
Friends of Israel Gospel Ministry [20010]
Full Gospel Bus. Men's Fellowship Intl. [19801]
The Gideons Intl. [20011]
Glenmary Res. Center [19628]
Global MissionAir [20487]
Gospel Music Workshop of Am. [10601]
High School Evangelism Fellowship [20013]
Independent Bd. for Presbyterian Foreign Missions [20467]
Inst. for Biblical Res. [19519]
Inst. on Religious Life [19639]
Intl. Assn. of Biblical Counselors [19867]
Intl. Bible Soc. [19520]
Intl. Bible Students Assn. [19521]
Intl. Bd. of Jewish Missions [20014]
Intl. Org. for Septuagint and Cognate Stud. [19522]
Intl. Soc. of Bible Collectors [19523]
Intl. Students, Inc. [20017]
Lay Mission-Helpers Assn. [19648]
Laymen's Home Missionary Movement [20018]
Lithuanian Catholic Religious Aid [19653]
Lutheran Student Movement - U.S.A. [20227]
The Mailbox Club [19525]
Medical Missions Response [20246]
Mission to Haiti [12267]
Mission to the World [20468]
Missionary Gospel Fellowship [20363]
Missions Intl. [20037]
Narramore Christian Found. [19815]
Natl. Coun. On Bible Curriculum In Public Schools [9052]
Natl. Cursillo Movement [19685]
Natl. Evangelization Teams [19687]
Natl. Ghost Ranch Found. [20469]
Natl. Religious Broadcasters [19539]
Non-Denominational Bible Prophecy Stud. Assn. [19528]
ORACLE Religious Assn. [20070]
Pan Amer. Coun. for the Preservation of the Hellenic Orthodox Church and the Hellenic Language [20074]
Paulist Memorial Soc. [19699]
Paulist Natl. Catholic Evangelization Assn. [19700]
Pentecostal Assemblies of the World [20463]
Pentecostal Charismatic Churches of North Am. [20464]
Personal Freedom Outreach [19875]
Pilots for Christ Intl. [20028]
Pocket Testament League [19529]
Presbyterian Lay Comm. [20472]
Presbyterian Men [20473]
Presbyterian-Reformed Ministries Intl. [20474]
Presbyterian Women [20475]
Pro Maria Comm. [19704]
Revival Fires (Christian Evangelizers Assn.) [20031]

Sacred Heart League [19711]
Samaritans Intl. [20392]
Seventh Day Baptist Missionary Soc. [19496]
Slavic Gospel Assn. [20395]
Soc. of Biblical Literature [19530]
Soc. for Pentecostal Stud. [20465]
South Amer. Missionary Soc. - USA [20398]
Tyndale Soc. [20530]
WEC Intl. [20034]
World Mission Prayer League [20234]
World Team [20417]
WorldVenture [19503]
Wycliffe Bible Translators [19531]
Gospel Assn. for the Blind [16848], PO Box 1162, Bunnell, FL 32110, (904)586-5885
Gospel Bottle Crusade; Maranatha [★19993]
Gospel Crusade; Navajo [★20405]
Gospel Fellowship; Missionary [20363]
Gospel of Life Disciples; Agape: [19562]
Gospel Light Intl. [★20342]
Gospel Light Intl. [★IO]
Gospel Literature Intl. [IO], Ontario, CA, United States
Gospel Literature Intl. [20342], PO Box 4060, Ontario, CA 91761-1003, (909)481-5222
Gospel Ministry; Friends of Israel [20010]
Gospel Mission; Spanish World [★20399]
Gospel Missionary Union [★20303]
Gospel Music
  Country Legends Assn. [10583]
  Gospel Music Assn. [10600]
  Gospel Music Workshop of Am. [10601]
  Media in Ministry Assn. [20285]
  North Am. Country Music Associations, Intl. [10674]
  Rhythm and Blues Rock and Roll Soc., Inc. [10692]
Gospel Music Assn. [10600], 1205 Div. St., Nashville, TN 37203, (615)242-0303
Gospel Music Assn. Canada [IO], St. Davids, ON, Canada
Gospel Music Workshop of Am. [10601], PO Box 38842, Detroit, MI 48238, (313)491-9980
Gospel Outreach; Orient Crusades- [★20377]
Gospel Recordings [20343], 41823 Enterprise Cir. N, Temecula, CA 92590-5614, (951)719-1650
Gospel Truth Assn. - Defunct.
Gospelrama Gospel Expo - Address unknown since 1995.
Gospodarska Zbornica Slovenije [★IO]
Gosselin Family Assn. [IO], Ile d'Orleans, QC, Canada
Goteborgs Ornitologiska Forening [★IO]
Gothenburg Ornithological Soc. [IO], Vastra Frolunda, Sweden
Gothic Literature
  Bram Stoker Memorial Assn. [9639]
  Count Dracula Soc. [10420]
  Lord Ruthven Assembly Intl. Conf. on the Fantastic in the Arts [10426]
  Peale Center for Christian Living [19825]
  The Vampire Empire [24824]
Gotland Breeders' Soc; Swedish [4957]
Gotland-Russ Assn. of North Am. [4885], 811 Carpenter Hill Rd., Medford, OR 97501, (541)535-6756
Gottfried-Wilhelm-Leibniz-Gesellschaft [★IO]
Gottlieb Found; Adolph and Esther [9486]
Gottscheer Heritage and Genealogy Assn. [9978], PO Box 725, Louisville, CO 80027-0725
Goudy Soc. - Defunct.
Gough Family Assn; Goff/ [20917]
Goulbourn Strathbogie Olive Growers Assn. [IO], Euroa, Australia
Gould League [IO], Moorabbin, Australia
Gourd Soc. of Am. [★22489]
Gourd Soc; Amer. [22489]
Gourley-Roark Family Org; Merier- [21000]
Gourmet; Single [19388]
Gourmet Society; Vegetarian [★15745]
Gourmets
  Amer. Inst. of Wine and Food [22568]
  Confrerie de la Chaine des Rotisseurs, Bailliage des U.S.A. [22569]
  Intl. Barbeque Cookers Assn. [22570]

  Intl. Chili Soc. [22571]
  Intl. Chili Soc. [IO]
  Intl. Connoisseurs of Green and Red Chile [22572]
  Intl. Wine and Food Soc. - London [IO]
  James Beard Found. [11125]
  Kansas City Barbeque Soc. [22573]
  Kansas City Barbeque Society [IO]
  Natl. Govt. Publishing Assn. [1781]
  Natl. Specialty Gift Assn. [1724]
  Terlingua Intl. Chili Championship [22574]
  Terlingua Intl. Chili Championship [IO]
  Vinegar Connoisseurs Intl. [IO]
  Vinegar Connoisseurs Intl. [22575]
  World Alliance of Gourmet Robustas [1738]
  World Alliance of Gourmet Robustas [IO]
Governance Inst. [2495], 6333 Greenwich Dr., Ste. 200, San Diego, CA 92122, (858)909-0811
Governing Boards of Universities and Colleges; Assn. of [7889]
Governing Bodies Assn. [★IO]
Government
  Aaron Burr Accord [11097]
  Air Mail Pioneers [21425]
  Amer. Agriculture Movement [16950]
  Amer. Assn. of State Ser. Commissions [6189]
  Amer. Coun. of Blind Govt. Employees [16824]
  Amer. Fed. of Govt. Employees [24068]
  Amer. Fed. of State, County and Municipal Employees [24069]
  Amer. Foreign Ser. Assn. [24070]
  Amer. Inst. of Parliamentarians [10770]
  Amer. Legion Auxiliary Girls Nation [17068]
  Amer. Postal Workers Union [24166]
  Americans for Indian Opportunity [12624]
  Americans for Informed Democracy [5660]
  America's Future [17624]
  Armed Forces Stamp Exchange Club [22793]
  Asian Amer. Govt. Executives Network [5704]
  Associates of the Amer. Foreign Ser. Worldwide [24071]
  Assn. of Capitol Reporters and Editors [6181]
  Assn. of Civilian Technicians [24072]
  Assn. of Govt. Marketing Assistance Specialists [1740]
  Assn. of Inspectors Gen. [5777]
  Assn. of Pacific Island Legislatures [5774]
  Assn. of Pacific Island Legislatures [IO]
  Canada Employment and Immigration Union [IO]
  Center for Defense Info. [17375]
  Center for Mgt. Effectiveness [2489]
  Center for Reflective Community Practice [17211]
  Center for the Stud. of the Presidency [17069]
  Christians in Govt. [19516]
  Citizens Against Govt. Waste [17668]
  Citizens' Commn. on Civil Rights [17104]
  Citizens for Legitimate Govt. [17663]
  Citizens United [17664]
  Civil Ser. Employees Assn. [24073]
  Close Up Found. [17071]
  Coalition for Democracy in Iran [17389]
  Coalition for Women's Appointments [17520]
  Comm. on the Constitutional Sys. [17289]
  Comm. of the Regions [IO]
  Congressional Automotive Caucus [17255]
  The Conservative Caucus [17264]
  The Conservative Caucus Res., Anal. and Educ. Found. [17265]
  Conservative Majority for Citizen's Rights [17266]
  Coun. for Excellence in Govt. [5705]
  Coun. for Govt. Reform [17665]
  Coun. on Governmental Ethics Laws [6270]
  Coun. of Protocol Executives [2677]
  Demilitarization for Democracy [17427]
  Digital Govt. Soc. of North Am. [7151]
  Digital Govt. Soc. of North Am. [IO]
  Fed. Lib. and Info. Center Comm. [10356]
  Fed. Physicians Assn. [15998]
  Finance Proj. [17583]
  Financial Services Tech. Consortium [7732]
  Fisher Inst. for Medical Res. [17628]
  Forum for State Hea. Policy Leadership [17689]
  Free Cong. Political Action Comm. [17268]
  Free the Eagle [17629]
  Free Enterprise Legal Defense Fund [17630]

Reference to "IO" in place of a book number signifies that the association may be found in the 45th edition of International Organizations.

Fund for Constitutional Govt. [17669]
GenerationEngage [18848]
Govt. Accountability Proj. [17670]
Govt. Finance Officers Assn. of U.S. and Canada [6204]
Governmental Accounting Standards Bd. [5427]
Harry S. Truman Scholarship Found. [8430]
The Heritage Found. [17631]
Hispanic Elected Local Officials [6122]
Independent Americans [17294]
Inst. for Defense Analyses [6256]
Inter-American Defense Bd. [17378]
Intl. Assn. of Clerks, Recorders, Election Officials and Treasurers [5775]
Intl. Assn. of Clerks, Recorders, Election Officials and Treasurers [IO]
Intl. Assn. of Professional Bureaucrats [22595]
Intl. Assn. of Protocol Consultants [965]
James Buchanan Found. for the Preservation of Wheatland [11126]
James K. Polk Memorial Assn. [11127]
Jefferson Educational Found. [17273]
Judson Welliver Soc. [10127]
Liberty Amendment Comm. of the U.S.A. [17296]
Liberty Services [17666]
Logistics Mgt. Inst. [5607]
Martin Van Buren Fan Club [11136]
A Matter of Justice Coalition [6012]
Military Reporters and Editors [6182]
Movement for an Independent and Democratic Cuba [17367]
Natl. Alliance of Postal and Fed. Employees [24167]
Natl. Archives and Records Admin. Volunteer Assn. [9402]
Natl. Assn. of Fed. Veterinarians [16799]
Natl. Assn. of Govt. Archives and Records Administrators [5820]
Natl. Assn. of Govt. Employees [24075]
Natl. Assn. for Hea. and Fitness [15967]
Natl. Assn. of Letter Carriers of the U.S.A. [24168]
Natl. Assn. of Parliamentarians [10771]
Natl. Assn. of Postal Supervisors [24169]
Natl. Assn. of State Chief Info. Officers [5821]
Natl. Assn. of Volunteer Programs in Local Govt. [6352]
Natl. Black Republican Assn. [18524]
Natl. Bd. of Boiler and Pressure Vessel Inspectors [5824]
Natl. Center for Policy Anal. [18462]
Natl. Comm. Against Repressive Legislation [17134]
Natl. Comm. for an Effective Cong. [17252]
Natl. Conf. of CPA Practitioners [47]
Natl. Cong. of Patriotic Organizations [18185]
Natl. Consumers League [17338]
Natl. Coun. for Intl. Visitors [17903]
Natl. Coun. of Investigation and Security Services [3539]
Natl. Court Reporters Assn. [5630]
Natl. Fed. of Fed. Employees [24077]
Natl. Hea. Policy Forum [17693]
Natl. Inst. of Governmental Purchasing [6239]
Natl. Justice Found. of Am. [17298]
Natl. League of Postmasters of the U.S. [24170]
Natl. Legal and Policy Center [17671]
Natl. Org. of Fed. Employees Against Abuse and Retaliation [24078]
Natl. Org. of Legal Services Workers, UAW Local 2320 [24079]
Natl. Org. Taunting Safety and Fairness Everywhere [22599]
Natl. Postal Mail Handlers Union [24171]
Natl. Retail Sales Tax Alliance [18696]
Natl. Rural Letter Carriers' Assn. [24172]
Natl. Treasury Employees Union [24080]
Natl. Women's Hall of Fame [20716]
Natl. Workforce Assn. [1739]
NLRB Professional Assn. [24081]
North Amer. Gaming Regulators Assn. [5772]
OMB Watch [17672]
Open Debates [17488]
Philadelphia Soc. [18475]
Planning Assistance [17846]

Pres. Benjamin Harrison Found. [11142]
Presidential Prayer Team [20210]
Professional Services Coun. [17636]
Professional and Tech. Consultants Assn. [969]
Proj. on Govt. Oversight [18077]
Proj. RACE [19047]
Public Citizen [17341]
Public Citizen's Cong. Watch [17343]
Ronald Reagan Home Preservation Found. [11147]
Sam Adams Alliance [17673]
Senate Tourism Caucus [17259]
Seventh Generation Fund for Indian Development [18099]
Soc. for Advancement of Mgt. [2515]
Soc. of Govt. Economists [5674]
Soc. of Govt. Meeting Professionals [2691]
Soc. for History in the Fed. Govt. [10159]
Soc. for Info. Mgt. [2516]
Taxpayers for Common Sense [18700]
Transnational Diplomatic Network [17874]
U.S. Assn. of Former Members of Cong. [17253]
U.S. Chamber of Commerce [24301]
Universities Space Res. Assn. [6392]
Vera Inst. of Justice [11895]
Washington Workshops Found. [8093]
Women in Govt. [6133]
Worldwide Assurance for Employees of Public Agencies [5776]
Worldwide Assurance for Employees of Public Agencies [IO]
Young America's Found. [17280]
Govt; Acad. for State and Local [18417]

Government Accountability
9/11 CitizensWatch [18727]
Assn. of Inspectors Gen. [5777]
Center for Public Integrity [17667]
Citizens Against Govt. Waste [17668]
Citizens for Consumer Justice [18641]
Citizens for Sensible Safeguards [17106]
Coun. for a Community of Democracies [5661]
Fund for Constitutional Govt. [17669]
Govt. Accountability Proj. [17670]
Natl. Legal and Policy Center [17671]
Natl. Retail Sales Tax Alliance [18696]
OMB Watch [17672]
Owen M. Kupferschmid Holocaust and Human Rights Proj. [17781]
Sam Adams Alliance [17673]
Special Interest Gp. on Mgt. Info. Systems [6824]
Third Millennium: Advocates for the Future [17674]
Govt. Accountability Proj. [17670], 1612 K St. NW, Ste. 1100, Washington, DC 20006, (202)408-0034
Govt. Accountants; Assn. of [5426]
Govt. Accountants Assn; Fed. [★5426]
Government; Advocates for Self- [18012]
Government Advocates; Self- [★18012]
Govt. Affairs Coun. Found; State [★1746]
Govt. Affairs Found. - Defunct.
Govt; Americans Against Union Control of [17979]
Govt. Archives and Records Administrators; Natl. Assn. of [5820]
Govt. Assn; Better [18282]
Govt; Assn. for Educ. in World [★17620]
Govt. Auditors; Assn. of Local [5429]
Govt. Burden; Stockholders Against the [★17351]
Govt; Center for Excellence in [★5705]
Govt. Center; Local [★6131]
Govt; Christians in [19516]
Govt. Communicators; Natl. Assn. of [5583]
Govt. Contract Mgt. Assn. of Am. [★1744]
Government Contracts
Assn. of Govt. Marketing Assistance Specialists [1740]
Coalition for Govt. Procurement [1741]
Coalition for Prompt Pay [1742]
Contract Services Assn. of Am. [1743]
Natl. Contract Mgt. Assn. [1744]
Natl. Property Mgt. Assn. [3190]
Govt; Coun. for Excellence in [5705]
Govt. Deferred Compensation Administrators; Natl. Assn. of [★2340]
Govt. Defined Contribution Administrators; Natl. Assn. of [2340]

Govt. Economists; Soc. of [5674]
Government Employees
Air Mail Pioneers [21425]
Akademikerforbundet SSR [IO]
All-Japan Prefectural and Municipal Workers' Union [IO]
Amer. Assn. of Port Authorities [IO]
Amer. Assn. of Port Authorities [5778]
Amer. Assn. of State Ser. Commissions [6189]
Amer. Coun. of Blind Govt. Employees [16824]
Amer. Fed. of Govt. Employees [24068]
Amer. Fed. of State, County and Municipal Employees [24069]
Amer. Foreign Ser. Assn. [24070]
Amer. Helicopter Soc. [139]
Amer. Postal Workers Union [24166]
AMICUS: Commun. Managers Assn. [IO]
Armed Forces Stamp Exchange Club [22793]
Asian Amer. Govt. Executives Network [5704]
Associates of the Amer. Foreign Ser. Worldwide [24071]
Associates of the Amer. Foreign Ser. Worldwide [IO]
Assn. of Civilian Technicians [24072]
Assn. of Electoral Administrators [IO]
Assn. of First Div. Civil Servants [IO]
Assn. of Veterans Affairs Anesthesiologists [13681]
Bermuda Public Services Union [IO]
British Assn. of Former United Nations Civil Servants [IO]
Canadian Union of Public Employees [IO]
Christians in Govt. [19516]
Civil Ser. Employees Assn. [24073]
Coalition for Women's Appointments [17520]
Defense Intel Alumni Assn. [18892]
European Fed. of Public Ser. Unions [IO]
Fed. Physicians Assn. [15998]
Fed. of State and Municipal Employees [IO]
Gays and Lesbians in Foreign Affairs Agencies USA [24074]
German Civil Ser. Fed. [IO]
Intl. Assn. of Professional Bureaucrats [22595]
Intl. Fed. of Employees in Public Ser. [IO]
Natl. Active and Retired Fed. Employees Assn. [5710]
Natl. Alliance of Postal and Fed. Employees [24167]
Natl. Assn. of Civilian Conservation Corps Alumni [19082]
Natl. Assn. of Farm Ser. Agency County Off. Employees [5779]
Natl. Assn. of Fed. Veterinarians [16799]
Natl. Assn. of Govt. Employees [24075]
Natl. Assn. of Letter Carriers of the U.S.A. [24168]
Natl. Assn. of Postal Supervisors [24169]
Natl. Employee Union Information Center [24076]
Natl. Fed. of Fed. Employees [24077]
Natl. League of Postmasters of the U.S. [24170]
Natl. Legal and Policy Center [17671]
Natl. Org. of Fed. Employees Against Abuse and Retaliation [24078]
Natl. Org. of Legal Services Workers, UAW Local 2320 [24079]
Natl. Postal Mail Handlers Union [24171]
Natl. Rural Letter Carriers' Assn. [24172]
Natl. Treasury Employees Union [24080]
Natl. Union of Public and Gen. Employees [IO]
Natl. Workforce Assn. [1739]
New Zealand Public Ser. Assn. [IO]
NLRB Professional Assn. [24081]
Northern Ireland Public Ser. Alliance [IO]
Professional Assn. of Foreign Ser. Officers [IO]
Public and Commercial Services Union [IO]
Public Ser. Alliance of Canada [IO]
Public Services Intl. [IO]
Union of Civil Servants [IO]
Women in Govt. Relations [17676]
Women in Govt. Relations LEADER Found. [17677]
Govt. Employees; Amer. Coun. of Blind [16824]
Govt; Executive Women in [5706]
Govt. Finance Officers Assn. of U.S. and Canada [6204], 203 N LaSalle St., Ste. 2700, Chicago, IL 60601-1216, (312)977-9700

A star before a book entry number signifies that the name is not listed separately, but is mentioned within the entry.

Govt. Finance Officers Assn. of U.S. and Canada [IO], Chicago, IL, United States
Govt. Guaranteed Lenders; Natl. Assn. of [6039]
Govt. Info. Org. [★5583]
Govt. Info. Processing Councils; Fed. of [★5813]
Govt; Inst. for Intl. [★17620]
Govt. of Israel Economic Mission - Address unknown since 1999.
Govt. Mgt. Info. Sciences [5818], PO Box 365, Bayville, NJ 08721, (973)632-0470
Govt. Meeting Professionals; Soc. of [2691]
Govt; Natl. Assn. of Supervisors, Fed. [★5708]
Govt; Natl. Org. of Blacks in [5571]
Govt. Officials in Indus. of the U.S. and Canada; Assn. of [★5917]
Govt. Oversight; Proj. on [18077]
Govt. Procurement; Coalition for Common Sense in [★1741]
Govt. Public Relations Assn. - Defunct.
Government Relations
  Affiliated Tribes of Northwest Indians [18948]
  Amer. Comm. for Peace in Chechnya [18189]
  Assn. of Natl. Advertisers [91]
  Coun. for a Community of Democracies [5661]
  Inst. for Foreign Policy Anal. [17612]
  Natl. Assn. of County Relations Officials [5622]
  Natl. Soc. of Compliance Professionals [1745]
  State Govt. Affairs Coun. [1746]
  Student Assn. for Voter Empowerment [17490]
  US-Cuba Reconciliation Initiative [17675]
  US-Cuba Reconciliation Initiative [IO]
  Veterans for Common Sense [21330]
  Women in Govt. Relations [17676]
  Women in Govt. Relations LEADER Found. [17677]
Govt. Res; Inst. of Economics, Inst. for [★18424]
Govt; Robert Brookings Graduate School of Economics and [★18424]
Govt. Service Contractors Assn. - Defunct.
Govt. Ser. Urologists; Soc. of [16714]
Govt; Soc. for History in the Fed. [10159]
Govt; Soc. of Travel Agents in [★6327]
Govt. Tourism Off; Mexican [★24356]
Govt. Tourist Off; Bonaire [24361]
Govt. Travel Professionals; Soc. of [6327]
Govt; Women in Municipal [6134]
Govt. of World Citizens; World Ser. Authority of the World [★18318]
Governmental Accounting Standards Bd. [5427], PO Box 5116, Norwalk, CT 06856-5116, (203)847-0700
Governmental Affairs Coun; State [★1746]
Governmental Affairs Inst. [★17902]
Governmental Appraisers; Assn. of [★272]
Governmental Ethics Laws; Coun. on [6270]
Governmental Hea. Policy Proj; Inter [★17689]
Governmental Indus. Hygienists; Amer. Conf. of [15625]
Governmental Indus. Hygienists; Natl. Conf. of [★15625]
Governmental Labor Officials; Assn. of [★5917]
Governmental Labor Officials; Intl. Assn. of [★5917]
Governmental Labor Officials; Natl. Assn. of [5917]
Governmental Leasing and Finance; Assn. for [6202]
Governmental Refuse Coll. and Disposal Assn. [★6355]
Governmental Relations; Coun. on [9058]
Governmental Relations Officials; Coun. of Inter [★5622]
Governmental Res. Assn. [18449], PO Box 292300, Birmingham, AL 35229, (205)726-2482
Governmental Res; Center for [18427]
Governmental Restraint; Citizens for [17288]
Governments; Coun. of State [6273]
Governor William Bradford Compact [21248], c/o Mrs. L.W. Pogue, Historian, 5204 Kenwood Ave., Chevy Chase, MD 20815-6604
Governors Assn; Democratic [6274]
Governors Assn; Natl. [6284]
Governors Assn; Natl. Lieutenant [6285]
Governors Assn; Republican [6286]
Governors' Assn; Southern [6287]
Governors' Conf. [★6284]
Governors Conf; Democratic [★6274]
Governors' Conf; Natl. [★6284]

Governors' Conf; Southern [★6287]
Governors Highway Safety Assn. [6317], 750 1st St. NE, Ste. 720, Washington, DC 20002-8002, (202)789-0942
Governors' Highway Safety Representatives; Natl. Assn. of [★6317]
Governors; Natl. Conf. of Lieutenant [★6285]
Governors State Univ. Energy Group - Defunct.
Gower Fed. Services [★6141]
Gower Fed. Services [★IO]
GP-14 Class Assn. of North America - Address unknown since 1991.
GPz Owners of America - Defunct.
Graafinen Teollisuus ry [★IO]
Grace and Compassion Benedictines [IO], Brighton, United Kingdom
Grace Contrino Abrams Peace Educ. Found. [8139], 1900 Biscayne Blvd., Miami, FL 33132-1025, (305)576-5075
Grace of God Movement for the Women of the World - Address unknown since 2004.
Graceland News Fan Club - Defunct.
Grading Contractors Assn; Engg. and [★1015]
Gradualist Way to Peace Found. for Res. and Education - Defunct.
Graduate Admissions Assistance Center - Defunct.
Graduate Admissions Professionals; Natl. Assn. of [7913]
Graduate Admissions Professionals; New England Assn. of [★7913]
Graduate Bus. Admission Coun. [★8807]
Graduate Bus. Admission Coun. [★IO]
Graduate Center; Amer. Indian [8426]
Graduate Degrees for Minorities in Engg. and Sci; Natl. Consortium for [8372]
Graduate Educ. for Public Admin; Coun. on [★6194]
Graduate Examination Commn; Foreign Pharmacy [★15933]
Graduate Examination Comm; Foreign Pharmacy [15933]
Graduate Fellowships for Black Americans - Defunct.
Graduate Fellowships for Mexican Americans, Native Americans and Puerto-Ricans - Defunct.
Graduate Liberal Stud. Programs; Assn. of [8778]
Graduate Mgt. Admission Coun. [8807], 1600 Tysons Blvd., Ste. 1400, McLean, VA 22102, (703)749-0131
Graduate Mgt. Admission Coun. [IO], McLean, VA, United States
Graduate Mgt. Admission Search Service [★IO]
Graduate Mgt. Admission Search Service [★8807]
Graduate Mgt. Assn. of Australia [IO], Melbourne, Australia
Graduate Medical Educ; Accreditation Coun. for [7872]
Graduate Pain Res. Found. [★15136]
Graduate Pain Res. Found. [★IO]
Graduate Record Examinations Bd. [9251], c/o Educational Testing Ser., PO Box 6000, Princeton, NJ 08541-6000, (609)771-7670
Graduate Schools in Assn. of Amer. Universities; Assn. of [7890]
Graduate Schools; Coun. of [8488]
Graduate Schools in the U.S; Coun. of [★8488]
Graduate Student Assn; Natl. Black [18869]
Graduate Stud; Maritime Inst. of Tech. and [★24128]
Graduate Stud. in Bus. for Negros; Consortium for [★8806]
Graduate Women in Bus. [★745]
Graduate Women in Sci; Sigma Delta Epsilon, [24587]
Graduates; Assn. of [8882]
Graduates; Assn. of Arab-American Univ. [18953]
Graduates; Educational Coun. for Foreign Medical [★15997]
Graduates of Italian Medical Schools - Defunct.
Graduates; Jobs for America's [12084]
Graduates; Natl. Assn. of Foreign Medical [★14973]
Graduates of the U.S. Air Force Acad; Assn. of [18875]
Graduation Pledge Alliance [18617], Manchester Coll., 604 E Coll. Ave., North Manchester, IN 46962, (260)982-5346
Graduation Pledge Alliance [IO], North Manchester, IN, United States

Graffunder Connection; Grawunder and [20921]
GRAFIA - Assn. of Professional Graphic Designers in Finland [IO], Helsinki, Finland
Graham Bond Appreciators Org. - Defunct.
Graham Bros. Truck and Bus Club [21894]
Graham Evangelistic Assn; Billy [19992]
Graham Family Assn. - Defunct.
Graham Found. [293], 4 W Burton Pl., Chicago, IL 60610-1416, (312)787-4071
Graham Owners Club Intl. [21650], c/o Gloria Reid, Treas., 3240 Shawn Way, Hayward, CA 94541, (510)886-7599
Graham Owners Club Intl. [IO], Hayward, CA, United States
Graham Soc; Clan [20829]
Grail Intl. Student Center - Defunct.
Grail Movement [★19630]
Grail Movement; International [★19630]
Grailville [19630], 932 O'Bannonville Rd., Loveland, OH 45140-9740, (513)683-2340
Grain
  Amer. Assn. of Grain Inspection and Weighing Agencies [1747]
  Amer. Celiac Society/Dietary Support Coalition [15543]
  Canada Grains Coun. [IO]
  Canadian Intl. Grains Inst. [IO]
  Canadian Wheat Bd. [IO]
  Commodity Markets Coun. [1748]
  Distillers Grains Tech. Coun. [1749]
  Equip. Mfrs. Coun. [178]
  European Assn. for Grain Legume Res. [IO]
  Gluten Intolerance Gp. [15559]
  Grain Elevator and Processing Soc. [1750]
  Grain and Feed Comm. of the EU [IO]
  Grains Coun. of Australia [IO]
  Kamut Assn. of North Am. [4308]
  Natl. Barley Foods Coun. [1751]
  Natl. Barley Growers Assn. [4663]
  Natl. Fed. of Grain Growers [IO]
  Natl. Sorghum Producers [4311]
  North Amer. Export Grain Assn. [1752]
  North Amer. Export Grain Assn. [IO]
  North Amer. Millers' Assn. [2738]
  Rice Millers' Assn. [2739]
  Ricegrowers' Assn. of Australia [IO]
  Trans., Elevator and Grain Merchants Assn. [1753]
  U.S. Grains Coun. [4664]
  U.S. Rice Producers Assn. [4790]
  U.S.A. Rice Fed. [1754]
  Wheat Export Trade Educ. Comm. [4791]
  Wheat Foods Coun. [1755]
Grain Cooperatives; Natl. Fed. of [★4483]
Grain and Cotton Exchange; Fort Worth [★4325]
Grain Dealers; Pacific Northwest [★4314]
Grain Elevator and Processing Soc. [1750], PO Box 15026, Minneapolis, MN 55415-0026, (612)339-4625
Grain Elevator Superintendents; Soc. of [★1750]
Grain Equipment Mfrs. Coun. - Defunct.
Grain Exchange; Fort Worth [4325]
Grain Exchange; Minneapolis [4329]
Grain and Feed Assn; Natl. [1359]
Grain and Feed Assn; Pacific Northwest [4314]
Grain and Feed Comm. of the EU [IO], Brussels, Belgium
Grain and Feed Dealers Natl. Assn. [★1359]
Grain and Feed Trade Assn. [IO], London, United Kingdom
Grain Millers Intl. Union; Bakery, Confectionery, Tobacco Workers and [24017]
Grain Milling Fed. [IO], Pretoria, Republic of South Africa
Grain Sorghum Producers; Natl. [★4311]
Grainger Lib. Soc; Percy [★9810]
Grainger Soc. [★IO]
Grains Coun. of Australia [IO], Kingston, Australia
Gram Parsons Found. [24903], c/o Gram's Place, 3109 N Ola Ave., Tampa, FL 33603, (813)221-0596
Gram Parsons Memorial Found. [★24903]
GRAMMY Found. [10602], 3402 Pico Blvd., Santa Monica, CA 90405, (310)392-3777
Grand Aerie, Fraternal Order of Eagles [19033], 1623 Gateway Cir. S, Grove City, OH 43123, (614)883-2200

Reference to "IO" in place of a book number signifies that the association may be found in the 45th edition of International Organizations.

Grand Amer. Road Racing Assn. [23068], 1801 W Intl. Speedway Blvd., Daytona Beach, FL 32114-1243, (386)947-6681
Grand Army of the Republic; Ladies of the [20727]
Grand Bahama Chamber of Commerce [IO], Grand Bahama, Bahamas
Grand Bahamas Assn. of Administrative Professionals [IO], Freeport, Bahamas
Grand Coun. of Hispanic Societies in Public Ser. [12275]
Grand-Dad's Day Coun. - Defunct.
Grand Duchy of Luxembourg Chamber of Commerce [IO], Luxembourg, Luxembourg
Grand Intl. Brotherhood of Locomotive Engineers [★IO]
Grand Intl. Brotherhood of Locomotive Engineers [★24176]
Grand Jury Project - Defunct.
Grand League of Amer. Horseshoe Pitchers [★23540]
Grand Lodge; Fraternal Order of Police, [19200]
Grand Lodge of Ladies Auxiliaries to Order of Scottish Clans - Address unknown since 1995.
Grand Lodge, Ladies Auxiliary, Fraternal Order of Police - Address unknown since 1995.
Grand Lodge Order of the Sons of Hermann in Texas [19125], c/o Mary Beam, Grand VP/Sec.-Treas., PO Box 1941, San Antonio, TX 78297-1941, (210)226-9261
Grand Natl. Archery Soc. [IO], Newport, United Kingdom
Grand Natl. Racing Assn. - Address unknown since 2001.
Grand Ole Opry; Circle Club - The Official Fan Club of the [24864]
Grand Ole Opry Fan Club [★24864]
Grand Order of Pachyderms [★18359]
Grand Rapids Area Furniture Mfrs. Assn. - Address unknown since 2005.
Grand Rapids Furniture Market Assn. - Defunct.
Grand United Order of Odd Fellows [19294]
Grande Prairie Constr. Assn. [IO], Grande Prairie, AB, Canada
Grandmother Clubs of Am; Natl. Fed. of [19383]
Grandmothers for Peace [★18154]
Grandmothers for Peace [★IO]
Grandmothers for Peace Intl. [IO], Elk Grove, CA, United States
Grandmothers for Peace Intl. [18154], PO Box 580788, Elk Grove, CA 95758, (916)685-1130
Grandparent Prog; Foster [11693]
Grandparents
   Found. for Grandparenting [12262]
   Grandparents as Parents [12263]
   Grandparents Rights Org. [12264]
   Grandparents United for Children's Rights [17058]
Grandparents Anonymous - Address unknown since 2004.
Grandparents Assn. of America - Address unknown since 1988.
Grandparents'/Children's Rights - Defunct.
Grandparents as Parents [12263], 22048 Sherman Way, Ste. 217, Canoga Park, CA 91303, (818)264-0880
Grandparents Raising Grandchildren - Address unknown since 2001.
Grandparents Rights Org. [12264], 100 W Long Lake Rd., Ste. 250, Bloomfield Hills, MI 48304, (248)646-7177
Grandparents United for Children's Rights [17058], c/o Ethel Dunn, Exec. Dir., 137 Larkin St., Madison, WI 53705-5115, (608)238-8751
Grandsons of Forty-Niners - Address unknown since 1995.
Grange-Farm Film Found. - Defunct.
Grange; Natl. [4652]
Granite Assn; Amer. [★2772].
Granite Assn; Barre [3691]
Granite Assn; Elberton [3693]
Granite Cutters Intl. Union; Tile, Marble, Terrazzo, Finishers, Shopworkers, and [★24032]
Granite Grit Inst. of America - Defunct.
Granite Producers; Natl. Assn. of Amer. [★2772]
Granite Quarries Assn; Natl. Building [3697]
Graniteware Assn; Amer. [★22083]

Graniteware Soc; Natl. [22083]
Granotec Chile [IO], Santiago, Chile
Grant-A-Wish Found. [★11674]
Grant Assn; Sea [7276]
Grant Assn; Ulysses S. [11154]
Grant Coalition; Natl. Pell [8433]
Grant Found; William T. [11549]
Grant/Lee Assn. - Address unknown since 2004.
Grant Professionals; Amer. Assn. of [12708]
Grant Prog. Institutions; Assn. of Sea [★7276]
Grant Program; National Sea [★7276]
Grantmakers in the Arts [12722], 604 W Galer St., Seattle, WA 98119-3253, (206)624-2312
Grantmakers for Children and Youth [★12723]
Grantmakers for Children, Youth, and Families [12723], 8757 Georgia Ave., Ste. 540, Silver Spring, MD 20910, (301)589-4293
Grantmakers; Forum of Regional Associations of [12717]
Grantmakers in Hea. [15954], 1100 Connecticut Ave. NW, Ste. 1200, Washington, DC 20036, (202)452-8331
Grantmakers; Natl. Network of [12202]
Grantmakers Without Borders [12724], PO Box 181282, Boston, MA 02118, (617)794-2253
Grantmakers Without Borders [IO], Boston, MA, United States
Grants; Ad Hoc Coalition on Block [★13161]
Grants and Human Needs; Coalition on Block [★13161]
Grants Mgt. Assn; Natl. [2507]
The Grantsmanship Center [1687], PO Box 17220, Los Angeles, CA 90017, (213)482-9860
Granulomatosis Support Gp. Intl; Wegener's [★16552]
Granulomatous Disease Assn; Chronic [14258]
Grape Assn; Amer. Concord [★4724]
Grape Assn; Concord [4724]
Grape Commn; California Table [4721]
Grape Coun; Concord [★4724]
Grape Found; New York Wine/ [5417]
Grape Growers Assn; Napa Valley [★5415]
Grape Growers Assn; Sonoma County [5421]
Grape Growers; California Assn. of Wine [5412]
Grape Growers; New York State Wine [★5417]
Grape and Tree Fruit Assn; California [★4716]
Grape and Tree Fruit League; California [4716]
Graphic Artists Guild [9505], 32 Broadway, Ste. 1114, New York, NY 10004-1612, (212)791-3400
Graphic Artists Guild [IO], New York, NY, United States
Graphic Artists Guild; Natl. [★9505]
Graphic Arts
   Advt. Production Club of New York [1756]
   Amer. Artists Professional League [9489]
   Amer. Design Drafting Assn. [7152]
   Amer. Historical Print Collectors Soc. [21523]
   Amer. Inst. of Graphic Arts [1757]
   Amer. Print Alliance [9544]
   Amer. Printing History Assn. [9989]
   Amer. Typecasting Fellowship [9990]
   American Typecasting Fellowship [IO]
   Animators Unite [9388]
   Apparel Graphics Inst. [224]
   Art and Creative Materials Inst. [1799]
   Assn. for Engg. Graphics and Imaging Systems [1800]
   Assn. for Graphic Arts Training [1758]
   Assn. of Graphic Communications [1759]
   Assn. of Illustrators [IO]
   Assn. of Medical Illustrators [13707]
   Benjamin Franklin Educ. Found. [8234]
   Binding Indus. Assn. Intl. [1760]
   Binding Indus. Assn. Intl. [IO]
   Book Manufacturers' Inst. [1761]
   British Design and Art Direction [IO]
   British Printing Indus. Fed. [IO]
   California Soc. of Printmakers [1762]
   Canadian Printing Indus. Assn. [IO]
   Cartoonists Northwest [9561]
   Catalog and Multichannel Marketing Coun. [1763]
   Comics Creators Guild [IO]
   Cupid Collectors Club [22006]
   Digital Printing and Imaging Assn. [1764]
   Digital and Screen Printing Assn. [IO]

   Employee Recognition Prog. [1765]
   European Assn. of Engravers and Flexographers [IO]
   European Flexographic Tech. Assn. - (UK) [IO]
   Flexographic Technical Association [IO]
   Flexographic Tech. Assn. [1766]
   German Printing and Media Indus. Fed. [IO]
   Graphic Artists Guild [9505]
   Graphic Arts Educ. and Res. Found. [1767]
   Graphic Arts Employers of Am. [24082]
   Graphic Arts Sales Found. [1768]
   Graphic Arts Tech. Found. [1769]
   Graphic Communications Conf. of the Intl. Brotherhood of Teamsters [24083]
   Graphic Communications Coun. [1770]
   Gravure Assn. of Am. [1771]
   Gravure Educ. Found. [8469]
   Guild of Natural Sci. Illustrators [7153]
   Gutenberg Soc.: Intl. Assn. for Past and Present History of the Art of Printing [IO]
   Heidelberg Digital Imaging Assn. [1772]
   Hong Kong Soc. of Illustrators [IO]
   IDEAlliance - Intl. Digital Enterprise Alliance [IO]
   IDEAlliance - Intl. Digital Enterprise Alliance [1773]
   Intl. Allied Printing Trades Assn. [24084]
   Intl. Artists Network [9506]
   Intl. Assn. of Printing House Craftsmen [1774]
   Intl. Assn. of Printing House Craftsmen [IO]
   Intl. Comic Arts Assn. [9447]
   Intl. Confed. for Printing and Allied Indus. [IO]
   International Graphic Arts Education Association [IO]
   Intl. Graphic Arts Educ. Assn. [8470]
   Intl. Inst. for Frame Stud. [9991]
   Intl. Metal Decorators Assn. [1775]
   Intl. Plate Printers, Die Stampers, and Engravers' Union of North Am. [24085]
   Intl. Publishing Mgt. Assn. [1776]
   Intl. Publishing Mgt. Assn. [IO]
   Intl. Reprographic Assn. [1801]
   Intl. Thermographers Assn. [2889]
   Intl. Vintage Poster Dealers Assn. [106]
   Internet Professional Publishers Assn. [1777]
   IPA The Assn. of Graphic Solutions Providers [7154]
   Israel Assn. of Illustrators [IO]
   Japan Assn. of Graphic Arts Tech. [IO]
   Label Printing Indus. of Am. [3684]
   Law Enforcement Thermographers' Assn. [5982]
   Lib. Binding Inst. [1778]
   Lib. Binding Inst. [IO]
   Natl. Art Materials Trade Assn. [1802]
   Natl. Assn. of Litho Clubs [1779]
   Natl. Assn. for Printing Leadership [1780]
   Natl. Catalog Managers Assn. [3134]
   Natl. Govt. Publishing Assn. [1781]
   North Amer. Cartographic Info. Soc. [6656]
   North Amer. Graphic Arts Suppliers Assn. [1804]
   NPES - The Assn. for Suppliers of Printing, Publishing and Converting Technologies [1782]
   Pacific Printing and Imaging Assn. [1783]
   Packaging and Label Gravure Assn. Global [1784]
   Packaging and Label Gravure Association Global [IO]
   Photo Imaging Educ. Assn. [8974]
   PrintImage Intl. [1785]
   PrintImage Intl. [IO]
   Printing Brokerage/Buyers Association [IO]
   Printing Brokerage/Buyers Assn. [1786]
   Printing Equip. and Supply Dealers' Assn. [IO]
   Printing and Graphic Communs. Assn. [1787]
   Printing Historical Soc. [IO]
   Printing Indus. of Am. [1788]
   Printing, Publishing and Media Workers Sector of the CWA [24086]
   Rank and File [IO]
   The Rock Poster Soc. [9469]
   Scottish Print Employers Fed. [IO]
   Screen Printers' Assn. of India [IO]
   Screen Printing Technical Foundation [IO]
   Screen Printing Tech. Found. [1789]
   Soc. of Amer. Graphic Artists [9992]
   Soc. for Calligraphy [11213]
   Soc. for Ser. Professionals in Printing [1790]

A star before a book entry number signifies that the name is not listed separately, but is mentioned within the entry.

Soc. of Typographic Aficionados [1791]
Specialty Graphic Imaging Assn. [1792]
Specialty Graphic Imaging Assn. [IO]
Tamarind Inst. [8471]
Tech. Assn. of the Graphic Arts [7155]
Typophiles [9993]
Vesalius Trust [8472]
Waterless Printing Assn. [1793]
Web Offset Assn. [1794]
Web Printing Assn. [1795]
Women in Production [1796]
Worldwide Printing Thermographers Assn. [1797]
Worldwide Printing Thermographers Assn. [IO]
Xplor Intl. [IO]
Xplor Intl. [1798]
Graphic Arts Advertisers and Exhibitors Coun. - Defunct.
Graphic Arts Assn. Executives - Defunct.
Graphic Arts Consultants; Assn. of [★1788]
Graphic Arts Coun. of North America - Defunct.
Graphic Arts Dealers Assn; Natl. [★1804]
Graphic Arts Educ. Assn; Natl. [★8470]
Graphic Arts Educ. and Res. Found. [1767], 1899 Preston White Dr., Reston, VA 20191, (703)264-7200
Graphic Arts Employers of Am. [24082], c/o Printing Indus. of America/Graphic Arts Tech. Found., 200 Deer Run Rd., Sewickley, PA 15143, (412)741-6860
Graphic Arts Equipment and Supply Dealers Assn. - Address unknown since 2004.
Graphic Arts Guild; Natl. [★8470]
Graphic Arts Intl. Union [★24083]
Graphic Arts Marketing Information Service - Defunct.

Graphic Arts Products
Amer. Historical Print Collectors Soc. [21523]
Apparel Graphics Inst. [224]
Art and Creative Materials Inst. [1799]
Assn. for Engg. Graphics and Imaging Systems [1800]
Gravure Assn. of Am. [1771]
Intl. Reprographic Assn. [1801]
Intl. Reprographic Assn. [IO]
Intl. Thermographers Assn. [2889]
Natl. Art Materials Trade Assn. [1802]
National Art Materials Trade Association [IO]
Natl. Assn. of Printing Ink Mfrs. [1803]
North Amer. Graphic Arts Suppliers Assn. [1804]
NPES - The Assn. for Suppliers of Printing, Publishing and Converting Technologies [1782]
Soc. of Typographic Aficionados [1791]
Graphic Arts Professionals Educational Found. - Defunct.
Graphic Arts Res. Found. - Address unknown since 2002.
Graphic Arts Sales Found. [1768], 113 E Evans St., West Chester, PA 19380, (610)431-9780
Graphic Arts Spray Mfrs. - Defunct.
Graphic Arts Suppliers Assn. [★1804]
Graphic Arts Suppliers Assn; North Amer. [1804]
Graphic Arts Tech. Found. [1769], 200 Deer Run Rd., Sewickley, PA 15143-2600, (800)910-GATF
Graphic Arts Union Employers of Am. [★24082]
Graphic Communications Assn. [★1773]
Graphic Communications Assn. [★IO]
Graphic Communications Career Center [★1770]
Graphic Communications Conf. of the Intl. Brotherhood of Teamsters [24083], 1900 L St. NW, Washington, DC 20036, (202)462-1400
Graphic Communications Coun. [1770], c/o Carol Hurlburt, Admin., 1899 Preston White Dr., Reston, VA 20191-4367, (703)648-1768
Graphic Communications Intl. Union [★24083]

Graphic Design
Alliance Graphique Internationale [IO]
Amalgamated Printers' Association [IO]
Amalgamated Printers' Assn. [1805]
Amer. Soc. of Picture Professionals [2993]
Amer. Typecasting Fellowship [9990]
Animators Unite [9388]
Assoc. Designers of Canada [IO]
Assn. of Dutch Designers [IO]
Assn. of Law Costs Draftsmen [IO]
Assn. of Medical Illustrators [13707]

Assn. of Professional Design Firms [1806]
Australian Graphic Design Assn. [IO]
CAD Soc. [6764]
Chartered Soc. of Designers [IO]
Design Austria [IO]
Design Mgt. Inst. [1807]
GRAFIA - Assn. of Professional Graphic Designers in Finland [IO]
Graphic Artists Guild [9505]
Graphic Arts Employers of Am. [24082]
Graphic Communications Conf. of the Intl. Brotherhood of Teamsters [24083]
Intl. Allied Printing Trades Assn. [24084]
Intl. Coun. of Graphic Design Associations [IO]
Intl. Soc. of Typographic Designers [IO]
Intl. Vintage Poster Dealers Assn. [106]
Natl. Assn. of Photoshop Professionals [1808]
National Association of Photoshop Professionals [IO]
Org. of Black Designers [9907]
Packaging and Label Gravure Assn. Global [1784]
Photo Imaging Educ. Assn. [8974]
Printing and Graphics Indus. Assn. of Alberta [IO]
The Rock Poster Soc. [9469]
Soc. for Environmental Graphic Design [1809]
Soc. of Graphic Designers of Canada [IO]
Soc. of Publication Designers [1810]
Soc. of Typographic Aficionados [1791]
Swiss Graphic Designers [IO]
Tech. Assn. of the Graphic Arts [7155]
Urban Art Intl. [1811]
Urban Art Intl. [IO]
Graphic Design; Soc. for Environmental [1809]
Graphic Designers; Soc. of Environmental [★1809]
Graphic and Prdt. Identification Mfrs; Natl. Assn. of [2720]
Graphic Products Assn. [2837], c/o Veda Communications Co., 4709 N El Capitan Ave., Ste. 103, Fresno, CA 93722, (559)276-8494

Graphics
Amer. Design Drafting Assn. [7152]
Assn. of Medical Illustrators [13707]
CAD Soc. [6764]
Graphic Arts Employers of Am. [24082]
Graphic Communications Conf. of the Intl. Brotherhood of Teamsters [24083]
Graphics Philately Assn. [22824]
Guild of Natural Sci. Illustrators [7153]
Intl. Allied Printing Trades Assn. [24084]
Intl. Plate Printers, Die Stampers, and Engravers' Union of North Am. [24085]
Intl. Sign Assn. [1189]
Intl. Vintage Poster Dealers Assn. [106]
IPA The Assn. of Graphic Solutions Providers [7154]
IPA The Association of Graphic Solutions Providers [IO]
Natl. Assn. of Photoshop Professionals [1808]
Packaging and Label Gravure Assn. Global [1784]
Photo Imaging Educ. Assn. [8974]
Printing and Graphic Communs. Assn. [1787]
The Rock Poster Soc. [9469]
Soc. of Typographic Aficionados [1791]
Tech. Assn. of the Graphic Arts [7155]
Tech. Assn. of the Graphic Arts [IO]
Type Directors Club [7156]
Graphics Assn; Natl. Cmpt. [★894]
Graphics; Center for the Stud. of Political [9434]
Graphics Communications Union; Intl. Printing and [★24083]
Graphics Inst; Apparel [224]
Graphics Philately Assn. [22824], c/o Bruce L. Johnson, Sec., 115 Raintree Dr., Zionsville, IN 46077-2012, (317)733-9737
Graphics Preparatory Assn. [★7154]
Graphics Preparatory Assn. [★IO]
Grapho Anal; Amer. Inst. of [★11210]
Graphological Societies; Coun. of [11209]
Graphological Soc; Intl. [11211]
Graphologists; Amer. Soc. of Professional [1812]

Graphology
Amer. Assn. of Handwriting Analysts [11205]
Amer. Handwriting Anal. Found. [11206]
Amer. Soc. of Professional Graphologists [1812]
British Inst. of Graphologists [IO]

Coun. of Graphological Societies [11209]
Intl. Graphoanalysis Soc. [11210]
Intl. Graphological Soc. [11211]
Intl. Graphology Assn. [IO]
Natl. Assn. of Document Examiners [5765]
Natl. Soc. for Graphology [11212]
Graphology; Natl. Soc. for [11212]
The Grascals Fan Club [24904], c/o Susie French, Pres., PO Box 148326, Nashville, TN 37214-8326

Grass
Amer. Forage and Grassland Coun. [5165]
Chewings Fescue and Creeping Red Fescue Commn. [4792]
Grassland Heritage Found. [4404]
Intl. Turf Producers Found. [4793]
Intl. Turf Producers Found. [IO]
Irish Grassland Assn. [IO]
Lawn Inst. [IO]
Lawn Inst. [4794]
Manhattan Ryegrass Growers Assn. [4795]
O.J. Noer Res. Found. [4796]
Oregon Highland Bentgrass Commn. [4797]
Oregon Ryegrass Growers Seed Commn. [4798]
Turfgrass Producers Intl. [4799]
Turfgrass Producers Intl. [IO]
Grass Roots Assn. - Address unknown since 1995.
Grassland Coun; Amer. [★5165]
Grassland Coun; Amer. Forage and [5165]
Grassland Farming; Joint Comm. on [★5165]
Grassland Heritage Found. [4404], PO Box 394, Shawnee Mission, KS 66201, (913)262-3506
Grassland Res. Found. - Address unknown since 1995.
Grassland Soc. of Southern Africa [IO], Pietermaritzburg, Republic of South Africa
Grassroot Soccer [11330], 2456 Christian St., Ste. 102, White River Junction, VT 05001, (802)295-2004
Grassroots Citizens Dispute Resolution Clearinghouse - Defunct.
Grassroots Endangered Species Coalition [4154], PO Box 423, Battle Ground, WA 98604, (206)687-2505
Grassroots Intl. [12428], 179 Boylston St., 4th Fl., Boston, MA 02130, (617)524-1400
Grassroots Intl. [IO], Boston, MA, United States
Grassroots Organisations Operating Together in Sisterhood [★IO]
Grateful Hearts [★13243]
Gravel Assn; Natl. Stone, Sand and [3699]
Graveline Genealogical Assn; Urbain Baudreau [21074]
Gravely Tractor Club of Am. [23002], c/o Jim Cherry, Registrar, 1569 Shadyside Rd., West Chester, PA 19380, (610)518-1028
Gravers, Lithographers and Woodcutters; Soc. of Amer. Etchers, [★9992]
Graves' Disease Found. [★16647]
Graves' Disease Found; Natl. [16647]
Graves Family Assn. [20920], 20 Binney Cir., Wrentham, MA 02093, (508)384-8084
Graves Family Assn. [IO], Wrentham, MA, United States
Graves - Merritt J. and James Bodine Family Assn. - Defunct.
Gravestone Stud; Assn. for [10015]
Gravitation; Intl. Soc. for Gen. Relativity and [IO]
Gravitational and Space Biology Student Assn; Amer. Soc. for [6563]

Gravity
Amer. Soc. for Gravitational and Space Biology Student Assn. [6563]
Intl. Commn. on Gen. Relativity and Gravitation [IO]
Intl. Gravity Sports Assn. [23823]
Gravity Sports Assn; Intl. [23823]
Gravure Assn. of Am. [1771], 1200-A Scottsville Rd., Rochester, NY 14624, (585)436-2150
Gravure Assn. Global; Packaging and Label [1784]
Gravure Educ. Found. [8469], 1200-A Scottsville Rd., Rochester, NY 14624, (585)436-2150
Gravure Res. Inst. [★1771]
Gravure Tech. Inst. [★1771]
Grawunder Connection [★20921]
Grawunder and Graffunder Connection [20921], 13108 Penn Ave., Burnsville, MN 55337, (952)890-3240

Reference to "IO" in place of a book number signifies that the association may be found in the 45th edition of International Organizations.

Encyclopedia of Associations, 46th Edition

3517

Gray Iron Res. Inst. [★2033]

Gray Line Sightseeing Assn. [3868], c/o Gray Line Worldwide, 1835 Gaylord St., Denver, CO 80206, (303)394-6920

Gray Panthers [11287], 1612 K St. NW, Ste. 300, Washington, DC 20006, (202)737-6637

Gray Panthers Proj. Fund [★11287]

Graymoor Ecumenical Inst. [★19895]

Graymoor Ecumenical Inst. [★IO]

Graymoor Ecumenical and Interreligious Institute [IO], Garrison, NY, United States

Graymoor Ecumenical and Interreligious Inst. [19895], c/o Mrs. Veronica Sullivan, Bus. Mgr., PO Box 300, Garrison, NY 10524-0300, (845)424-2109

Grays Harbor Historical Seaport Authority [8812], 712 Hagara St., PO Box 2019, Aberdeen, WA 98520, (800)200-5239

Gray's Official Fan Club; Linda [24753]

Grayson Found. [★4886]

Grayson-Jockey Club Res. Found. [4886], 821 Corporate Dr., Lexington, KY 40503, (859)224-2850

Grease Inst; Natl. Lubricating [2937]

Grease Inst. Res. Fund; National Lubricating [★2937]

Great Amer. Candy Bar Club - Defunct.

Great Amer. Station Wagon Owner's Assn. - Defunct.

Great Amer. Truck Racing - Address unknown since 2001.

Great Americans; Hall of Fame for [11119]

Great Ape Proj. [11400], 806A NW 51st St., Seattle, WA 98107, (206)579-5975

Great Ape Proj. [IO], Seattle, WA, United States

Great Atlantic Radio Conspiracy - Defunct.

Great Bear Found. [5322], PO Box 9383, Missoula, MT 59807-9383, (406)829-9378

Great Books Found. [9748], 35 E Wacker Dr., Ste. 400, Chicago, IL 60601-2205, (800)222-5870

Great Britain Collectors Club [22032], c/o Tim Burgess, Pres., 3547 Windmill Way, Concord, CA 94518

Great Britain Collectors Club [IO], Davie, FL, United States

Great Britain Correspondence Club [★IO]

Great Britain Correspondence Club [★22032]

Great Britain Floorball Fed. [IO], Basingstoke, United Kingdom

Great Britain Target Shooting Fed. [IO], Brookwood, United Kingdom

Great Britain Wheelchair Basketball Assn. [IO], Loughborough, United Kingdom

Great City Schools; Coun. of the [9289]

Great Coun. of U.S. Improved Order of Red Men [19328], 4521 Speight Ave., Waco, TX 76711-1708, (254)756-1221

Great Dads [12672], PO Box 7537, Fairfax Station, VA 22039, (703)830-7500

Great Dane
Great Dane Club of Am. [22279]

Great Dane Club of Am. [22279], c/o Mrs. Linda Ridder, Pres., 2933 Archer Ln., Springfield, OH 45503-1284

Great Lakes
Citizens for Alternatives to Chem. Contamination [5084]
Coastal States Org. [7396]
Great Lakes Colleges Assn. [8106]
Great Lakes Historical Soc. [10438]
Great Lakes Lighthouse Keepers Assn. [10030]
Great Lakes Maritime Inst. [10439]
Intl. Assn. for Great Lakes Res. [7239]
Intl. Ship Masters' Assn. [2579]
Lake Carriers' Assn. [2606]
Propeller Club of the U.S. [3586]

Great Lakes Booksellers Assn. [3225], PO Box 901, 208 Franklin St., Grand Haven, MI 49417, (616)847-2460

Great Lakes Cherry Producers Marketing Cooperative - Defunct.

Great Lakes Club - Address unknown since 2004.

Great Lakes Colleges Assn. [8106], 535 W William St., Ste. 301, Ann Arbor, MI 48103, (734)661-2350

Great Lakes Commn. [6137], Eisenhower Corporate Park, 2805 S Indus. Hwy., Ste. 100, Ann Arbor, MI 48104-6791, (734)971-9135

Great Lakes Dove Assn. [★21839]

Great Lakes Historical Soc. [10438], c/o Inland Seas Maritime Museum, PO Box 435, Vermilion, OH 44089-0435, (440)967-3467

Great Lakes Indian Fish and Wildlife Commn. [5323], PO Box 9, Odanah, WI 54861, (715)682-6619

Great Lakes Lighthouse Keepers Assn. [10030], PO Box 219, Mackinaw City, MI 49701-0219, (231)436-5580

Great Lakes Maritime Inst. [10439], PO Box 1990, Dearborn, MI 48121, (313)852-4051

Great Lakes Mink Assn. [★4129]

Great Lakes - Saint Lawrence Assn. - Defunct.

Great Lakes Seaplane Assn. - Defunct.

Great Lakes Ship Owners Assn. - Defunct.

Great Lakes Sport Fishing Coun. [23416], PO Box 297, Elmhurst, IL 60126-0297, (630)941-1351

Great Lakes Sugar Beet Growers Assn. - Defunct.

Great Lakes United [4405], Buffalo State Coll., Cassety Hall, 1300 Elmwood Ave., Buffalo, NY 14222, (716)886-0142

Great Peace March for Global Nuclear Disarmament - Defunct.

Great Plains
Inst. of the Great Plains [9994]

Great Plains Agricultural Coun. - Address unknown since 2001.

Great Plains Historical Assn. [★9994]

Great Plains Wheat [★4319]

Great Plains Wheat [★IO]

Great Pyrenees
Great Pyrenees Club of Am. [22280]

Great Pyrenees Club of Am. [22280], c/o Daniel Hodel, Sec., 12700 E Ave. NW, Cedar Rapids, IA 52405-9014, (319)446-7580

Great Southern Olive Assn. [IO], Mount Barker, Australia

Great Swamp Res. Inst. - Defunct.

Great War Assn. [10475], c/o Rob Zienta, Pres., 4601 Embassy Cir., No. 203, Owings Mills, MD 21117, (443)394-7605

Great Water Holt - Address unknown since 1990.

Great Whales Found. - Address unknown since 2007.

Greater Blouse and Skirt Contractors Assn. [★237]

Greater Blouse, Skirt and Undergarment Assn. [237], 1359 Broadway, Ste. 1814, New York, NY 10018, (212)563-5052

Greater Clothing Contractors Assn. - Defunct.

Greater Ecosystem Alliance [★4546]

Greater London Indus. Archaeology Soc. [IO], Orpington, United Kingdom

Greater Manchester and District Campaign for Nuclear Disarmament [IO], Manchester, United Kingdom

Greater New York Coalition for Soviet Jewry - Address unknown since 2004.

Greater New York Comm. Opposed to Fluoridation - Address unknown since 1995.

Greater New York Coun. for Foreign Students - Defunct.

Greater New York Coun. for Foreign Students -English in Action [★17885]

Greater New York Fund/United Way [★12479]

Greater North Amer. Aviculturist and Cage Bird Judges Assn. [★21845]

Greater North Amer. Color-Bred Judge Assn. [★21845]

Greater St. Louis Amateur Baseball Hall of Fame - Address unknown since 1999.

Greater Siamese Cat Club - Address unknown since 1995.

Greater Super Six Club - Defunct.

Greater Vancouver Alliance for Arts and Culture [IO], Vancouver, BC, Canada

Greater Vancouver Professional Theatre Alliance [IO], Vancouver, BC, Canada

Greater Washington, DC Assn. of Professionals Practicing the Transcendental Meditation Program - Address unknown since 2003.

Greater Yellowstone Coalition [4406], PO Box 1874, Bozeman, MT 59771, (406)586-1593

GreatSchools [8066], 301 Howard St., Ste. 1440, San Francisco, CA 94105, (415)977-0700

Greece
Amer. Hellenic Inst. [24325]
Found. for the Advancement of Sephardic Stud. and Culture [19181]
Greek Amer. Chamber of Commerce [24280]
Hellenic-American Chamber of Commerce [24326]
Hellenic Amer. Natl. Coun. [9995]
Hellenic Philatelic Soc. of Am. [22826]
Soc. for the Preservation of the Greek Heritage [9997]

Greek
Alpha Chi [24498]
Alpha Chi Sigma [24428]
Alpha Delta Kappa [24449]
Alpha Epsilon [24395]
Alpha Epsilon Delta [24541]
Alpha Gamma Rho [24396]
Alpha Iota Sorority [24413]
Alpha Kappa Delta [24701]
Alpha Kappa Psi [24414]
Alpha Mu Gamma Natl. [24525]
Alpha Omega Alpha Honor Medical Soc. [24542]
Alpha Omega Intl. Dental Fraternity [24437]
Alpha Psi Lambda Natl. [24615]
Alpha Sigma Nu [24500]
Alpha Tau Delta [24559]
Alpha Zeta [24397]
Alpha Zeta Omega [24567]
Amer. Comm. to Advance the Study of Petroglyphs and Pictographs [6437]
Amer. Hellenic Educational Progressive Assn. [19083]
Amer. Hellenic Inst. [24325]
Amer. Inst. for Patristic and Byzantine Stud. [9770]
Amer. Soc. of Greek and Latin Epigraphy [11207]
Arnold Air Soc. [24546]
Assn. of Coll. Honor Societies [24501]
Assn. of Fraternity Advisors [24475]
Australasian Hellenic Educational Progressive Assn. [IO]
Beta Alpha Psi [24391]
Beta Beta Beta [24408]
Beta Gamma Sigma [24415]
Beta Gamma Sigma Alumni [24416]
Beta Phi Mu [24532]
Beta Sigma Kappa [24562]
Center for the Stud. of the Coll. Fraternity [24476]
Central Off. Executives Assn. of Natl. Pan-Hellenic Conf. [24477]
Chi Eta Phi Sorority [24560]
Chian Fed. of Am. [19084]
Cretans' Assn. "Omonoia" [19085]
Cum Laude Soc. [24503]
Daughters of Evrytania [19086]
Daughters of Penelope [19087]
Delphi Found. [24451]
Delta Epsilon Sigma [24504]
Delta Kappa Epsilon [24623]
Delta Lambda Phi Natl. Social Fraternity [24624]
Delta Mu Delta Honor Soc. [24418]
Delta Omega [24582]
Delta Omicron [24550]
Delta Phi Epsilon, Professional Foreign Ser. Fraternity [24472]
Delta Phi Epsilon Professional Foreign Ser. Sorority [24473]
Delta Phi Upsilon [24431]
Delta Pi Epsilon [24426]
Delta Psi Omega [24444]
Delta Sigma Delta [24438]
Delta Theta Phi [24527]
Epsilon Pi Tau [24720]
Epsilon Sigma Phi [24436]
Eta Phi Beta [24419]
Eta Sigma Phi, Natl. Classics Honorary Soc. [24433]
Fraternity Executives Assn. [24479]
Future Bus. Leaders of Am. - Phi Beta Lambda [24420]
Gamma Iota Sigma [24520]
Gamma Sigma Delta [24398]
Gamma Theta Upsilon [24491]
Golden Key Intl. Honour Soc. [24506]

A star before a book entry number signifies that the name is not listed separately, but is mentioned within the entry.

Greek Amer. Chamber of Commerce [24280]
Greek Catholic Union of the U.S.A. [19088]
Greek Food and Wine Inst. [1517]
Greek Natl. Tourist Org. [3869]
Hellenic-American Chamber of Commerce [24326]
Hellenic Amer. Natl. Coun. [9995]
Hellenic Philatelic Soc. of Am. [22826]
Honors Prog. Student Assn. of the Amer. Sociological Assn. [24702]
Intl. Org. for Septuagint and Cognate Stud. [19522]
Iota Beta Sigma [24410]
Iota Phi Lambda [24421]
Kappa Delta Epsilon [24452]
Kappa Delta Pi [24453]
Kappa Mu Epsilon [24537]
Kappa Omicron Nu [24496]
Kappa Pi Intl. Honorary Art Fraternity [24404]
Kappa Psi [24568]
Kappa Tau Alpha [24522]
Lambda Alpha Intl. [24445]
Lambda Iota Tau [24533]
Lambda Kappa Sigma [24569]
Maids of Athena [19089]
Mid-American Greek Coun. Assn. [24483]
Modern Greek Stud. Assn. [9996]
Modern Greek Stud. Assn. [IO]
Mortar Bd. [24509]
Mu Alpha Theta [24538]
Mu Beta Psi [24552]
Mu Phi Epsilon Intl. [24553]
Natl. Alpha Lambda Delta [24510]
Natl. Assn. of the Knights of Scorpius, Honorary Leadership Soc. [24511]
Natl. Beta Club [24592]
Natl. Block and Bridle Club [24401]
Natl. Broadcasting Soc. - Alpha Epsilon Rho [24411]
Natl. Comm. for Latin and Greek [9800]
Natl. Honor Soc. [24512]
Natl. Junior Honor Soc. [24513]
Natl. Kappa Kappa Iota [24454]
Natl. Pan-Hellenic Editors Conf. [24448]
Natl. Panhellenic Conf. [24485]
Natl. Sorority of Phi Delta Kappa [24455]
Natl. Tech. Honor Soc. [24725]
Natl. Valedictorian Honor Soc. [24514]
North Amer. Interfraternal Found. [24486]
North-American Interfraternity Conf. [24487]
Omega Delta [24563]
Omicron Delta Epsilon [24446]
Omicron Delta Kappa Soc. [24515]
Omicron Kappa Upsilon [24439]
Order of the Coif [24516]
Pan Arcadian Fed. of Am. [19090]
Pan-Dodecanesian Assn. of Am. "Xanthos O Philikos" [19091]
Phi Alpha Delta [24528]
Phi Alpha Sigma [24543]
Phi Alpha Theta [24495]
Phi Beta [24405]
Phi Beta Delta [24517]
Phi Beta Kappa [24406]
Phi Chi Medical Fraternity [24544]
Phi Delta Chi [24570]
Phi Delta Epsilon Medical Fraternity [24540]
Phi Delta Gamma [24577]
Phi Delta Phi Intl. Legal Fraternity [24530]
Phi Kappa Phi [24518]
Phi Mu Alpha Sinfonia Fraternity and Found. Natl. HQ [24555]
Phi Sigma [24409]
Phi Sigma Iota [24526]
Phi Sigma Pi Natl. Honor Fraternity [24531]
Pi Kappa Phi [24651]
Pi Omicron Natl. Sorority [24601]
Professional Fraternity Assn. [24488]
Psi Beta [24579]
Psi Omega [24440]
Sigma Alpha Iota Intl. Music Fraternity [24557]
Sigma Delta Chi Found. [24524]
Sigma Delta Epsilon, Graduate Women in Sci. [24587]
Silver Wings [24549]

Soc. of Kastorians "Omonoia" [19092]
Soc. for the Preservation of the Greek Heritage [9997]
Soc. of Professional Journalists [3164]
Sons of Pericles [19093]
Tau Epsilon Rho Law Soc. [24529]
Theta Alpha Phi [24721]
Theta Psi [24566]
Theta Tau [24469]
Trireme Trust U.S.A. [10483]
United Hellenic Amer. Cong. [19094]
United Hellenic Voters of Am. [19095]
Upsilon Pi Epsilon Assn. [24435]
World Coun. of Hellenes Abroad [19096]
World Council of Hellenes Abroad [IO]
Xi Psi Phi [24442]
Greek Alzheimer's Assn. [IO], Thessaloniki, Greece
Greek Amer. Chamber of Commerce [24280], PO Box 58217, Philadelphia, PA 19102-8217
Greek-Amer. Counselor Center of Greece in U.S.A. - Defunct.
Greek Animal Rescue [IO], London, United Kingdom
Greek Assn. of Indus. and Processors of Olive Oil [IO], Athens, Greece
Greek Assn. of the Marfan Syndrome [IO], Athens, Greece
Greek Bible Soc. [IO], Athens, Greece
Greek Catholic Union of the U.S.A. [19088], 5400 Tuscarawas Rd., Beaver, PA 15009, (412)495-3400
Greek Collecting Soc. for Literary Works [IO], Athens, Greece
Greek Dietetic Assn. [IO], Athens, Greece
Greek Fed. of Customs Brokers Associations [IO], Piraeus, Greece
Greek Food and Wine Inst. [IO], Long Island City, NY, United States
Greek Food and Wine Inst. [1517], 34-80 48th St., Long Island City, NY 11101, (718)729-5277
Greek Hea. Informatics Assn. [IO], Athens, Greece
Greek League Against Epilepsy [IO], Athens, Greece
Greek Multiple Sclerosis Soc. [IO], Thessaloniki, Greece
Greek; Natl. Comm. for Latin and [9800]
Greek; Natl. Coordinating Off. for Latin and [★9800]
Greek Natl. Tourism Org. [★3869]
Greek Natl. Tourism Org. [★IO]
Greek Natl. Tourist Org. [★IO]
Greek Natl. Tourist Org. [IO], New York, NY, United States
Greek Natl. Tourist Org. [3869], Olympic Tower, 645 5th Ave., Ste. 903, New York, NY 10022, (212)421-5777
Greek Natl. Tourist Org. [★3869]
Greek Olympic Soc. [23635], 555 N High St., Columbus, OH 43215, (614)224-9020
Greek Olympic Soc. [IO], Columbus, OH, United States
Greek Orthodontic Soc. [IO], Athens, Greece
Greek Orthodox
  Greek Orthodox Ladies Philoptochos Soc. [20071]
  Greek Orthodox Young Adult League [20072]
  Natl. Forum of Greek Orthodox Church Musicians [20434]
  Order of Saint Andrew the Apostle [20073]
  Pan Amer. Coun. for the Preservation of the Hellenic Orthodox Church and the Hellenic Language [20074]
  Saint Photios Found. [20075]
Greek Orthodox Church Musicians; Natl. Forum of [20434]
Greek Orthodox Ladies Philoptochos Soc. [20071], 345 E 74th St., New York, NY 10021-3701, (212)744-4390
Greek Orthodox Young Adult League [20072], 83 St. Basil Rd., Garrison, NY 10524, (646)519-6180
Greek Orthodox Youth of Am. [★20072]
Greek Philosophy; Soc. for Ancient [10830]
Greek Seed Trade Assn. [IO], Athens, Greece
Greek Squash Rackets Fed. [IO], Athens, Greece
Greeks; Amer. Comm. for the Evangelization of the [★20298]
Greeks; Amer. Mission to [★20298]
Green Action for Eco-Social Change [IO], Tel Aviv, Israel

Green Balkans Fed. [IO], Plovdiv, Bulgaria
Green Book of Ireland [IO], Ballsbridge, Ireland
Green Circle Program - Defunct.
Green Coffee Assn. of New Orleans - Address unknown since 1999.
Green Committees of Correspondence [★18325]
Green Cross Intl. [IO], Geneva, Switzerland
Green Cross Russia [IO], Moscow, Russia
Green Destiny [IO], Hyderabad, India
Green Dossier [IO], Kiev, Ukraine
Green Educ. and Info. Network [★8477]
Green Empowerment [4335], 140 SW Yamhill St., Portland, OR 97204, (503)284-5774
Green Empowerment [IO], Portland, OR, United States
Green Garter; Loyal Escorts of the [21173]
Green Hotels Assn. [1941], PO Box 420212, Houston, TX 77242-0212, (713)789-8889
Green Hotels Association [IO], Houston, TX, United States
Green Innovations of Australia [IO], Melbourne, Australia
Green Leaf Natl. Honor Soc. [24471], c/o Environmental Stud. Prog., Univ. of Southern California, Sci. Bldg., Rm. 160, Los Angeles, CA 90089-0740, (213)740-7770
Green Library - Address unknown since 1999.
Green Lib. - Sweden [IO], Lund, Sweden
The Green Life [4569], 29 Temple Pl., Boston, MA 02111, (617)426-2502
Green Line [IO], Beirut, Lebanon
Green Meeting Indus. Coun. [2681], 6220 NE Glisan, Portland, OR 97213, (503)731-8971
Green Mountain Textile Overseers Assn. - Address unknown since 1995.
Green Movement; Amer. [★18325]
Green Network; U.S. [★18325]
Green Olive Trade Assn. - Defunct.
Green Org. [IO], Northampton, United Kingdom
Green Panthers! - Address unknown since 2006.
Green Party [★18325]
Green Party of Aotearoa - New Zealand [IO], Wellington, New Zealand
Green Party - Taiwan [IO], Taipei, Taiwan
Green Party of the U.S. [18325], PO Box 57065, Washington, DC 20037, (202)319-7191
Green Restaurant Association [5170], 89 South St., Ste. LL02, Boston, MA 02111, (858)452-7378
Green Seal [17331], 1001 Connecticut Ave. NW, Ste. 827, Washington, DC 20036-5525, (202)872-6400
Green Sect; USGA [23470]
Green Space [IO], Reading, United Kingdom
Green Step [IO], Sirajganj, Bangladesh
Green Step, Bangladesh [IO], Sirajganj, Bangladesh
Green Thumb [★IO]
Green Thumb [★12080]
Green Tourism Assn. [IO], Toronto, ON, Canada
Green USA; Global [4566]
Green Warriors of Norway [IO], Bergen, Norway
Green World [IO], Sosnovy Bor, Russia
Green World Center [IO], Sutton, QC, Canada
Greenaction for Hea. and Environmental Justice [17699], 1095 Market St., Ste. 712, San Francisco, CA 94103, (415)248-5010
Greenaway Soc; Kate [22063]
Greenback Party - Address unknown since 1995.
Greener Pastures Equine Sanctuary - Address unknown since 2007.
Greener Pastures Inst. [12312], c/o William L. Seavey, Dir., PO Box 2916, Orcutt, CA 93457, (800)688-6352
Greenhouse Action - Address unknown since 1994.
Greenhouse Assn; Hobby [22518]
Greenhouse Crisis Found. - Defunct.
Greenhouse Manufacturers Assn; Natl. [184]
Greenhouse Suppliers Assn. - Address unknown since 1994.
Greening Australia [IO], Yarralumla, Australia
Greening Earth Soc. [4570]
Greenkeeping Superintendents Assn; Natl. [★3663]
Greenland Badminton Fed. [IO], Ilulissat, Greenland
Greenland Union of Tenants [IO], Maniitsoq, Greenland
GreenLife Soc., North Am. Chap. - Address unknown since 2001.

Reference to "IO" in place of a book number signifies that the association may be found in the 45th edition of International Organizations.

GreenNet [IO], London, United Kingdom
Greenpeace Argentina [IO], Buenos Aires, Argentina
Greenpeace Australia Pacific [IO], Sydney, Australia
Greenpeace Belgium [IO], Brussels, Belgium
Greenpeace Brazil [IO], Sao Paulo, Brazil
Greenpeace Canada [IO], Toronto, ON, Canada
Greenpeace in Central and Eastern Europe [IO], Vienna, Austria
Greenpeace Chile [IO], Santiago, Chile
Greenpeace China [IO], Hong Kong, People's Republic of China
Greenpeace European Unit [IO], Brussels, Belgium
Greenpeace France [IO], Paris, France
Greenpeace Japan [IO], Tokyo, Japan
Greenpeace Luxembourg [IO], Esch-sur-Alzette, Luxembourg
Greenpeace Mediterranean [IO], Balzan, Malta
Greenpeace Mexico [IO], Mexico City, Mexico
Greenpeace Netherlands [IO], Amsterdam, Netherlands
Greenpeace Netherlands [★IO]
Greenpeace New Zealand [IO], Auckland, New Zealand
Greenpeace Nordic - Helsinki Off. [IO], Helsinki, Finland
Greenpeace Russia [IO], Moscow, Russia
Greenpeace Slovakia [IO], Bratislava, Slovakia
Greenpeace Spain [IO], Madrid, Spain
Greenpeace Sweden [IO], Stockholm, Sweden
Greenpeace Switzerland [IO], Zurich, Switzerland
Greenpeace UK [IO], London, United Kingdom
Greenpeace U.S.A. [IO], Washington, DC, United States
Greenpeace U.S.A. [4571], 702 H St. NW, Washington, DC 20001, (202)462-1177
Greenpeace in Zentral Osteuropa [★IO]
Greens Clearinghouse [★18325]
Greens Coun; Leafy [4738]
Greensboro Civil Rights Fund - Defunct.
Greensward Found. [4407], PO Box 610, New York, NY 10021, (212)625-8733
Greentown Glass Collectors' Assn. - Defunct.
Greenway Family Assn. - Defunct.
Greenways; American [★4380]
Greenwood Cotton Exchange [4326]
Greeting Card Assn. [3682], 1156 15th St. NW, Ste. 900, Washington, DC 20005, (202)393-1778
Greeting Card Assn. [IO], London, United Kingdom
Greeting Card Publishers; Natl. Assn. of [★3682]
Gregor Soc; Amer. Clan [20780]

Grenada
    Grenada Bd. of Tourism [24253]
Grenada Athletic Assn. [IO], St. George's, Grenada
Grenada Bd. of Tourism [24253], PO Box 1668, Lake Worth, FL 33460, (561)588-8176
Grenada Bd. of Tourism [★24253]
Grenada Chamber of Indus. and Commerce [IO], St. George's, Grenada
Grenada Co-operative Nutmeg Assn. [IO], St. George's, Grenada
Grenada Draughts Assn. [IO], St. Patrick's, Grenada
Grenada Hotel and Tourism Assn. [IO], St. George's, Grenada
Grenada Natl. Coun. of the Disabled [IO], St. George's, Grenada
Grenada Tennis Assn. [IO], St. George's, Grenada
Grenada Union of Teachers [IO], St. George's, Grenada
Gresham Family Org. - Address unknown since 1994.
Grey Assn; Amer. Murray [4239]
Grey Nuns - Defunct.
GREY2K USA [4800], PO Box 442117, Somerville, MA 02144, (866)247-3925

Greyhound
    American-European Greyhound Alliance [17678]
    American-European Greyhound Alliance [IO]
    Amer. Greyhound Track Operators Assn. [23391]
    Continental Greyhound Racing Confed. [IO]
    GREY2K USA [4800]
    Greyhound Adoption Center [11401]
    Greyhound Awareness League [IO]
    Greyhound Club of Am. [22281]
    Greyhound Friends [11402]
    Greyhound Racing Assn. of Am. [23392]

    Greyhounds in NEED [IO]
    Irish Greyhound Bd. [IO]
    Natl. Greyhound Adoption Prog. [11438]
    Natl. Greyhound Assn. [22318]
    Retired Greyhound Trust [IO]
    U.S.A. Defenders of Greyhounds [11473]
Greyhound Adoption Center [11401], PO Box 2433, La Mesa, CA 91943-2433, (877)478-8364
Greyhound Adoption Prog; Natl. [11438]
Greyhound Assn; Natl. [22318]
Greyhound Awareness League [IO], Glasgow, United Kingdom
Greyhound Club of Am. [22281], c/o Bill Hempel, Pres., 1543 Oslo Ct., Livermore, CA 94550, (972)475-5843
Greyhound Club of Am; Italian [22296]
Greyhound Friends [11402], 167 Saddle Hill Rd., Hopkinton, MA 01748, (508)435-5969
Greyhound Pets of Am. [★11401]
Greyhound Racing Assn. of Am. [23392], 110 W 9th St., No. 813, Wilmington, DE 19801, (717)664-5089
Greyhound Track Operators Assn; Amer. [23391]
Greyhound Trust [★IO]
Greyhounds As Pets; Retired [★11473]
Greyhounds in NEED [IO], Wraysbury, United Kingdom
Greyhounds; U.S.A. Defenders of [11473]
Grey's West Soc; Zane [9728]
Gridiron Club of Washington, DC [3114]

Grief
    AARP Grief and Loss Prog. [13414]
    Aiding Mothers and Fathers Experiencing Neonatal Death [11907]
    Assn. for Death Educ. and Counseling [11909]
    Bereaved Parents of the USA [11512]
    Center for Death Educ. and Bioethics [13314]
    Children's Grief Educ. Assn. [12265]
    GriefNet [13294]
    Twinless Twins Support Gp. Intl. [12615]
    UNITE [12695]
    Violent Death Bereavement Soc. [11513]
Grief and Loss Prog; AARP [13414]
GriefNet [13294], PO Box 3272, Ann Arbor, MI 48106-3272
Griesemer Family Assn. [20922], PO Box 814, Lompoc, CA 93438-0814, (805)736-9637
Griffith Show Rerun Watchers Club; The Andy [25025]
Grigori Rasputin Soc. - Address unknown since 1995.
Grigsby Family Soc; Natl. [21009]
Grinders Assn; Natl. Cylinder [★375]
Grinding Wheel Inst. [★2567]
Grinnell Family Assn. [20923], c/o Mr. F. Hugh Grinnell, Pres., 10290 N Alder Spring Dr., Oro Valley, AZ 85737, (520)797-3055
Griswold and Cast Iron Cookware Assn. [22588], c/o Peggy Knapp, Sec., 223 Summit Cir., Lakeville, PA 18438, (570)226-4988
Gritchenko Foundation [★11065]
Gritchenko Foundation [★IO]
GRITS [★IO]
Grizzly Found; Yellowstone [5406]
Groberg - Holbrook Genealogical Org. [20924], 1605 S Woodruff, Idaho Falls, ID 83404, (208)522-3185
Grocers of Am; Women [3430]
Grocers Assn; Mexican Amer. [1536]
Grocers Assn; Natl. [3421]
Grocers Secretaries Assn; Natl. Retail [★3405]
Grocers of the U.S; Natl. Assn. of Retail [★3421]
Grocery Mfrs. of Am. and Food Products Assn. [★1518]
Grocery Mfrs. Association/Food Products Assn. [1518], 1305 I St. NW, Ste. 300, Washington, DC 20037, (202)337-9400
Grocery Mfrs. Assn. of South Africa [★IO]
Grocery Mfrs. Associations; Intl. Assembly of [★1521]
Grocery Prdt. Code Coun; Uniform [★337]
Grocery Products Manufactures of Canada [★IO]
Grolier Club [9749], c/o Mr. Eric Holzenberg, Dir., 47 E 60th St., New York, NY 10022, (212)838-6690
Grondkundevereniging van Suid-Afrika [★IO]
Gronlands Badminton Forbund [★IO]

Groomers Assn. of Am; Natl. Dog [2962]
Groomers; Intl. Professional [2960]
Groove Phi Groove, Social Fellowship [24630], PO Box 8337, Silver Spring, MD 20907
Groovy Mondays [IO], Toronto, ON, Canada
Gross Natl. Waste Product Forum - Defunct.
Grosse Pointe War Memorial Assn. [21300], 32 Lake Shore Dr., Grosse Pointe Farms, MI 48236, (313)881-7511
Ground Saucer Watch - Address unknown since 1999.
Ground Source Heat Pump Assn; Intl. [1889]
Ground Trans. Assn; Airline [★3858]
Ground Trans. Assn; Airport [3858]
Ground - U.S.A; Common [18707]
Ground Water Assn; Natl. [4011]
Ground Water Coun. - Defunct.
Ground Water Inst. - Defunct.
Ground Water Project; Natl. Environmental Development Assn./ [★7835]
Ground Water Protection Coun. [3994], 13308 N MacArthur Blvd., Oklahoma City, OK 73142, (405)516-4972
Ground Water Scientists and Engineers - A Division of Natl. Ground Water Assn; Assn. of [7828]
Ground Water Tech. Division of the Natl. Water Well Assn. [★7828]
Ground Water Trust; Amer. [4007]
Ground Zero - Address unknown since 2002.
Ground Zero - Defunct.
Ground Zero Pairing Proj. [17894], 7135 SW 36th Ave., Portland, OR 97219, (503)245-3403
Ground Zero Resource Center - Defunct.

Grounds Management
    Natl. Inst. on Park and Grounds Mgt. [4801]
    Natl. Roadside Vegetation Mgt. Assn. [4802]
    Professional Grounds Mgt. Soc. [4803]
Groundswell Inc. of Minnesota [16954]
Groundwater Found. [5275], PO Box 22558, Lincoln, NE 68542-2558, (402)434-2740
Groundwater Mgt. Caucus [7829], PO Box 905, Colby, KS 67701-0905, (785)462-3915
Groundwater Mgt. Districts Assn. [5276], c/o Wayne Bossert, Sec.-Treas., PO Box 905, Colby, KS 67701-0905, (913)462-3915
Groundwater Mgt. Districts Assn. [★7829]
Groundwork for a Just World [18618], c/o Barbara Beesley, 11224 Kercheval St., Detroit, MI 48218, (313)822-2005
Groundwork for a Just World [IO], Detroit, MI, United States
Group 7 - Defunct.
Gp. for the Advancement of Psychiatry [16084], PO Box 570218, Dallas, TX 75357-0218, (972)613-3044
Group for Advertising Progress - Address unknown since 1995.
Group Against Smokers' Pollution - Address unknown since 2004.
Group-Analytic Soc. [IO], London, United Kingdom
Group of Ancient Drama - Address unknown since 1995.
Gp. B Strep Assn. [13962], PO Box 16515, Chapel Hill, NC 27516
Gp. for Community Guidance Centers [★16214]
Gp. for Environmental Monitoring [IO], Johannesburg, Republic of South Africa
Gp. and Family Therapy; Southeast Inst. for [18629]
Gp. Fore Golf Found. [23451], 1259 El Camino Real, Ste. 153, Menlo Park, CA 94025, (650)327-5207
Gp. Harmony Assn; United in [10715]
Gp. Leaders; Natl. Post Off. Mail Handlers, Watchmen, Messengers, and [★24171]
Gp. Mgt. Assn; Dental [15065]
Gp. Mgt. Assn; Medical [15067]
Gp. Practice; Amer. Acad. of Dental [14094]
Gp. Practice Assn; Amer. [★14717]
Gp. Processes; Center for the Stud. of [7648]
Gp. Proj. for Holocaust Survivors and Their Children [17716], 211 W 56th St., Ste. 7K, New York, NY 10019, (212)724-2161
Group Project for Holocaust Survivors and Their Children [IO], New York, NY, United States
Gp. for the Psychohistorical Stud. of Film - Address unknown since 2007.

A star before a book entry number signifies that the name is not listed separately, but is mentioned within the entry.

Gp. Psychotherapy; Amer. Bd. of Examiners of Psychodrama, Sociometry, and [16201]
Gp. Psychotherapy Assn; Amer. [16204]
Gp. Psychotherapy and Psychodrama; Amer. Soc. of [16208]
Group Purchasing Assn. - Address unknown since 2004.
Gp. for Reference Guide on Costs - Venezuela [IO], Caracas, Venezuela
Gp. of Samanway - Japan [IO], Chiba, Japan
Gp. of Thirty [1172], 1726 M St., Ste. 200, Washington, DC 20036, (202)331-2472
Gp. Ultra Van - Defunct.
Gp. Underwriters Assn. of Am. [2167], c/o Curt Zepeda, Treas., PO Box 581933, Minneapolis, MN 55458-1933, (612)342-3558
Gp. of Universities for the Advancement of Vietnamese Abroad [9296], Univ. of Washington, Southeast Asian Ctr., JSIS Box 353650, Seattle, WA 98195-3560, (206)543-9606
Gp. for the Use of Psychology in History [10112], c/o Charles B. Strozier, Exec. Off., John Jay Coll., CUNY, 555 W 57th St., Ste. 601, New York, NY 10019, (212)237-8432
Gp. of Volunteers of Italian Switzerland [IO], Arbedo, Switzerland
Gp. Work; Assn. for Specialists in [11820]
Groupe Canadien d'Oncologie Urologique [★IO]
Groupe Consultatif Actuariel Europeen [★IO]
Groupe Consultatif Intl. de Recherche sur le Colza [★IO]
Groupe canadien d'etude des parlements [★IO]
Groupe d'Etude Intl. du Plomb et du Zinc [★IO]
Groupe Developpement [★IO]
Groupe Europeen d'Administration Publique [★IO]
Groupe Europeen Des Experts Immobiliers [★IO]
Groupe Europeen des Femmes Diplomees des Universites [★IO]
Groupe Europeen de Recherches Gazieres [★IO]
Groupe Femmes pour l'Abolition des Mutilations Sexuelles [★IO]
Groupe Francais de Geomorphologie [IO], Paris, France
Groupe Intl. d'Etudes du Caoutchouc [★IO]
Groupe Intl. de Recherches sur la Preservation du Bois [★IO]
Groupe de Recherche et d'Echanges Technologiques [★IO]
Groupe de Recherche et d'Echanges Technologiques [★IO]
Groupe Socialiste au Parlement Europeen [★IO]
Groupe Suisse de l'Assn. Internationale de Droit Penal [★IO]
Groupement international des fabricants de revetements muraux [★IO]
Groupement des Annonceurs du Maroc [IO], Casablanca, Morocco
Groupement des Associations Meunieres de l'Union Europèenne [★IO]
Groupement Embalpack [★IO]
Groupement Europeen des Banques Cooperatives [★IO]
Groupement Europeen des Producteurs de Verre Plat [★IO]
Groupement Europeen des Produits Oleochimiques and Associes [★IO]
Groupement Europeen des Societies D'Auteurs et Compositeurs [★IO]
Groupement des Femmes d'Affaires du Cameroun [IO], Douala, Cameroon
Groupement des Femmes d'Affaires de la Guinee [IO], Conakry, Guinea
Groupement des Indus. Francaises Aeronautiques et Spatiales [★IO]
Groupement des Indus. Francaises de l'Optique [★IO]
Groupement des Indus. de l'Equipment Electrique, du Controle-Commande et des Services Associes [★IO]
Groupement des Indus. de Materiels d'Equipment Electrique et de l'Electronique Industrielle Associee [★IO]
Groupement Intl. d'Editeurs Scientifiques, Techniques et Medicaux [★IO]
Groupement Intl. d'Etiquetage pour l'Entretien des Textiles [★IO]

Groupement Intl. de la Repartition Pharmaceutique [★IO]
Groupement Interprofessionnel des Fabricants d'Appareils d'Equipement Menager [★IO]
Groupement Pharmaceutique de l'Union Europeene [★IO]
Groupo de Estados de Africa, del Caribe y del Pacifico [★IO]
Grouse Soc. of Am; Ruffed [★5376]
Grouse Soc. of North Am; Ruffed [★5376]
Grouse Soc; Ruffed [5376]
Grover Family Org. [20925]
Growers Assn. and; Louisiana Sugar Planters Assn., Amer. Cane [★5225]
Growers Assn. of Hawaii; Pineapple [4756]
Growers Assn; Monterey County Vintners and [5414]
Growers Assn; Natl. Barley [4663]
Growers Assn; Pacific Coast Shellfish [3501]
Growers Assn; Western [4774]
Growers Assn; Wild Rice [★4307]
Growers and Buyers Assn; Mountain State Organic [5068]
Growers and Buyers Assn; Organic [5070]
Growers and Dealers; Pacific Northwest Pea [★4314]
Growers Network; Amer. Willow [5255]
Growers; Northwest Cherry [4751]
Growers Protective Assn; Western [★4774]
Growers Res. Found; North Amer. Bramble [1675]
Growers; Valley Fig [4772]
Growing Companies; Coun. of [715]
Growing Healthy [★14582]
Growth and Development; Feminist Center for Human [13426]
Growth Found; Human [16020]
Growth Soc; Bioelectrical Repair and [★6554]
Growth; Soc. for the Stud. of Development and [★6595]
Grupa Tacaiochta Cuba - Eire [★IO]
Grupo de Artistas Latino Americanos - Defunct.
Grupo de Estudios Ambientales [★IO]
Grupo Internacional de Trabajo sobre Asuntos Indigenas [★IO]
Grupo Multidisciplinario Para la Atencion a Pacientes y Familiares con Diagnostico de Enfermedad de Huntington [IO], Havana, Cuba
Grupo OFC Guia Referencial de Costos [★IO]
Grupo Parlamentar do Partido Social-Democrata [★IO]
Grupo Parlamentario InterAmericano Sobre Poblacion y Desarrollo [★IO]
Grupo Parlamentario InterAmericano Sobre Poblacion y Desarrollo [★12432]
Grupo Pro Derechos Reproductivos - Address unknown since 2004.
Grupo Tortura Nunca Mais/RJ [IO], Rio de Janeiro, Brazil
Gruppo Autonomo di Volontariato Civile in Italia [IO], Bologna, Italy
Gruppo Esponenti Italiani [19161], PO Box 789, New York, NY 10150, (212)867-2772
Gruppo Volontari della Svizzera Italiana [★IO]
GS Club of Am; Buick [21600]
GS Intl.-BMW - Address unknown since 1999.
GS1 [IO], Brussels, Belgium
GS1 Austria GmbH [IO], Vienna, Austria
GS1 Canada [IO], Toronto, ON, Canada
GS1 Chile [IO], Santiago, Chile
GS1 Denmark [IO], Copenhagen, Denmark
GS1 Hong Kong [IO], Hong Kong, People's Republic of China
GS1 Ireland [IO], Dublin, Ireland
GS1 Macedonia [IO], Skopje, Macedonia
GS1 Malta [IO], Ta'Xbiex, Malta
GS1 Mauritius [IO], Port Louis, Mauritius
GS1 Nederland [IO], Amsterdam, Netherlands
GS1 Philippines [IO], Pasig City, Philippines
GS1 Republica Dominicana [IO], Santo Domingo, Dominican Republic
GS1 South Africa [IO], Craighall, Republic of South Africa
GS1 Tunisia [IO], Tunis, Tunisia
GS1 UK [IO], London, United Kingdom
GS1 Ukraine [IO], Kiev, Ukraine
GS1 Uruguay [IO], Montevideo, Uruguay

GS1 US [337], Princeton Pike Corporate Ctr., 1009 Lenox Dr., Ste. 202, Lawrenceville, NJ 08648, (609)620-0200
GSM Assn. [IO], London, United Kingdom
GTO Assn. of Am. [21651], PO Box 455, Timnath, CO 80547-0455, (970)221-0754
GTO Intl; The Judge [21678]
GTO and Judge Convertible Registry; 1971 [21559]
Guadalupe Cave Survey [★7692]
Guam Bar Assn. [6024], 120 West O'Brien Dr., Guam Judicial Ctr., 2nd Fl., Hagatna, GU 96910, (671)475-3396
Guam Chamber of Commerce [24246], Ada Plaza Ctr., 173 Aspinall Ave., Ste. 101, Hagatna, GU 96910, (671)472-6311
Guam Chamber of Commerce [IO], Hagatna, GU, United States
Guam Lytico and Bodig Assn. [IO], Hagatna, GU, United States
Guam Lytico and Bodig Assn. [14560], PO Box 1458, Hagatna, GU 96932, (671)477-2293
Guam Natl. Olympic Comm. [23636], PO Box 21809, Barrigada, GU 96921, (671)647-4662
Guam Racquetball Fed. [23675], PO Box 315619, Tamuning, GU 96931-3519, (671)472-1819
Guam Racquetball Fed. [IO], Tamuning, GU, United States
Guam Stamp Club and Western Pacific Philatelic Collectors - Defunct.
Guam Symphony Soc. [10603], PO Box 4069, Hagatna, GU 96932, (671)477-1959
Guam Women's Club [17537]
Guaranty Associations; Natl. Org. of Life and Hea. Insurance [1852]
Guard Assn; Marine Embassy [21177]
Guard Assn. of the U.S; Natl. [6091]
Guard Assn. of the U.S; State [6105]
Guard Combat Veterans Assn; Coast [21295]
Guard of Honor of the Immaculate Heart of Mary - Defunct.
Guard and Reserve; Natl. Comm. for Employer Support of the [6087]
Guard Soc. [1519], c/o Food Processing Machinery Assn., 1451 Dolley Madison Blvd., Ste. 200, McLean, VA 22101, (703)761-2600
Guard Soc; Old [★1519]
Guard Soc; Young [★1519]
Guardian Angels [★11834]
Guardian Angels [★IO]
Guardian Angels; Alliance of [★11834]
Guardian Assn. of Pinellas County [12266], PO Box 1826, Pinellas Park, FL 33780, (727)323-9380
Guardian Assn. of Pinellas County [★12266]
Guardian Soc; Catholic [11564]
Guardians
    Guardian Assn. of Pinellas County [12266]
    Missing Pet Partnership [12707]
    Natl. Assn. to Stop Guardian Abuse [12059]
    Natl. Guardianship Assn. [1813]
    Patriotic Pets [11442]
    Professional Bodyguard Assn. [IO]
Guardians of Amer. Rights and Demands - Defunct.
Guardians of Hydrocephalus Res. Found. [15326], 2618 Ave. Z, Brooklyn, NY 11235-2037, (718)743-4473
Guards Union of Am; Intl. [24185]
Guards and Watchmen; Intl. Union of [★24186]
Guatemala
    Alliance for Intl. Reforestation [4344]
    God's Child Proj. [11597]
    Guatemala Human Rights Commission/U.S.A. [17679]
    Guatemala News and Info. Bur. [17680]
    Hermandad [17046]
    Network in Solidarity With the People of Guatemala [17681]
    Only a Child [11643]
    Orphan Resources Intl. [11644]
    Rights Action/Guatemala Partners [12819]
    Seva Found. [12443]
Guatemala Hea. Rights Support Proj. [★12819]
Guatemala Human Rights Commission/U.S.A. [17679], 3321 12th St. NE, Washington, DC 20017, (202)529-6599
Guatemala Labor Educ. Proj; U.S./ [★17978]

Reference to "IO" in place of a book number signifies that the association may be found in the 45th edition of International Organizations.

Guatemala League Against Epilepsy [IO], Guatemala City, Guatemala

Guatemala News and Info. Bur. [17680], 3181 Mission St., Box 12, San Francisco, CA 94110, (415)826-3593

Guatemala; PEACE for [★12819]

Guatemala Res. Project - Defunct.

Guatemala Solidarity Comm. - Address unknown since 2003.

Guatemalan Banks' Assn. [IO], Guatemala City, Guatemala

Guatemalan Managers' Assn. [IO], Guatemala City, Guatemala

Guatemalan Olympic Comm. [IO], Guatemala City, Guatemala

Guernsey Assn; Amer. [4224]

Guernsey Cattle Club; Amer. [★4224]

Guernsey Chamber of Commerce [IO], Guernsey, United Kingdom

Guernsey Indoor Bowling Assn. [IO], Guernsey, United Kingdom

Guest House Accommodation of South Africa [IO], Cape Town, Republic of South Africa

Guidance Assn; Amer. Personnel and [★11815]

Guidance; Assn. for Measurement and Evaluation in [★9247]

Guidance Assn; Natl. Vocational [★12090]

Guidance Centers; Gp. for Community [★16214]

Guidance Conf; Natl. Catholic [★8166]

Guidance Councils; Natl. Conf. of Catholic [★8166]

Guidance Councils; Natl. Conf. of Diocesan [★8166]

Guidance; Natl. Engg. Coun. for [★8368]

Guidance Org; Euthanasia Res. and [12132]

Guidance Ser; Community [16214]

Guidance Ser; Fed. Employment and [★12075]

Guidance and Workshop Center; Vocational [★24603]

Guide Assn. Scotland [★IO]

Guide Assn. UK [★IO]

Guide Dog Found. [★16849]

Guide Dog Found. for the Blind [16849], 371 E Jericho Tpke., Smithtown, NY 11787-2976, (631)930-9000

Guide Dog Found; Fidelco [16846]

Guide Dog Users, Inc. [16850], 14311 Astrodome Dr., Silver Spring, MD 20906, (301)598-5771

Guide Dogs of Am. [16851], 13445 Glenoaks Blvd., Sylmar, CA 91342, (818)362-5834

Guide Dogs for the Blind [16852], PO Box 151200, San Rafael, CA 94915-1200, (415)499-4000

Guide Dogs for the Blind [IO], San Rafael, CA, United States

Guide Dogs for the Blind Assn. [IO], Reading, United Kingdom

Guide Dogs for the Handicapped, Inc. [★11922]

Guide Dogs; Path-Finder [★16864]

GUIDE Intl. Corp. - Address unknown since 2003.

Guided Vehicle Systems Sect. of the Material Handling Inst; Automatic [2005]

Guideline CH; Natl. [14654]

Guides Assn; Montana Outfitters and [23944]

Guides Australia [IO], Strawberry Hills, Australia

Guides Australia - Queensland [IO], Brisbane, Australia

Guides Australia - South Australia [IO], Adelaide, Australia

Guides Australia - Tasmania [IO], Battery Point, Australia

Guides Australia - Victoria [IO], South Melbourne, Australia

Guides Australia - Western Australia [IO], Perth, Australia

Guides du Canada [★IO]

Guides New Zealand [IO], Christchurch, New Zealand

Guides et Scouts d'Europe - France [IO], Chateau Landon, France

Guiding Eyes for the Blind [IO], Yorktown Heights, NY, United States

Guiding Eyes for the Blind [16853], 611 Granite Springs Rd., Yorktown Heights, NY 10598, (914)245-4024

Guiding Light Fan Club [25031], c/o Mindi Schulman, Pres., PO Box 455, Lynbrook, NY 11563-0455

The Guild [★24157]

Guild of Agricultural Journalists [IO], Crowborough, United Kingdom

Guild of Agricultural Journalists of Ireland [IO], Dublin, Ireland

Guild of Air Pilots and Air Navigators [IO], London, United Kingdom

Guild of Air Traffic Control Officers [IO], Bingham, United Kingdom

Guild of Amer. Funeral Directors - Defunct.

Guild of Amer. Luthiers [2804], 8222 S Park Ave., Tacoma, WA 98408-5226, (253)472-7853

Guild of American Luthiers [IO], Tacoma, WA, United States

Guild of Amer. Papercutters [22157], PO Box 512, Godley, TX 76044

Guild of Antique Dealers and Restorers [IO], Shrewsbury, United Kingdom

Guild of Architectural Ironmongers [IO], London, United Kingdom

Guild of Aviation Artists [IO], Farnborough, United Kingdom

Guild of Book Workers [IO], New York, NY, United States

Guild of Book Workers [9750], 521 5th Ave., New York, NY 10175-0038, (212)292-4444

Guild of British Butlers [★IO]

Guild of British Camera Technicians [IO], Greenford, United Kingdom

Guild of Bus. Travel Agents [★IO]

Guild of Carillonneurs in North America [IO], Gladwyne, PA, United States

Guild of Carillonneurs in North Am. [10604], PO Box 221, Gladwyne, PA 19035-0221

Guild of Catholic Lawyers [19631]

Guild of Church Musicians [IO], Surrey, United Kingdom

Guild CPO [★2883]

Guild of Drama Adjudicators [IO], Hertford, United Kingdom

Guild of Editors [★IO]

Guild of Experienced Motorists [IO], Forest Row, United Kingdom

Guild of Film Production Accountants and Financial Administrators [★IO]

Guild of Film Production Executives [★IO]

Guild of Fine Craftsmen and Artisans [306], c/o Leland R.S. Torrence, 17 Vernon Ct., Woodbridge, CT 06525, (203)397-8505

Guild of Fine Food Retailers [IO], Gillingham, United Kingdom

Guild of Food Writers [IO], Beckenham, United Kingdom

Guild of Glass Engravers [IO], London, United Kingdom

Guild of Guide Lecturers [★IO]

Guild of Incorporated Surveyors [IO], Oldham, United Kingdom

Guild of the Infant Saviour - Defunct.

Guild of Intl. Butler Administrators and Personal Assistants [IO], London, United Kingdom

Guild of Intl. Professional Toastmasters [IO], London, United Kingdom

Guild of Intl. Songwriters and Composers [IO], Penzance, United Kingdom

Guild of Investment and Financial Analysts [IO], Moscow, Russia

Guild of Italian Amer. Actors [24155], Canal Street Sta., PO Box 123, New York, NY 10013-0123, (212)420-6590

Guild of Master Craftsmen [IO], Lewes, United Kingdom

Guild of Motoring Writers [IO], Bournemouth, United Kingdom

Guild of Natural Sci. Illustrators [7153], PO Box 652, Ben Franklin Sta., Washington, DC 20044-0652, (301)309-1514

Guild of Philippine Jewellers [IO], Makati City, Philippines

Guild of Prescription Opticians of Am. [★15709]

Guild of Press Publishers [IO], Moscow, Russia

Guild of Professional Drycleaners - Defunct.

Guild of Professional Farriers [1354], 2020 Pennsylvania Ave. NW, No. 800, Washington, DC 20006, (301)898-6990

Guild of Professional Paperhangers [★2270]

Guild of Professional Translators - Defunct.

Guild for the Promotion of Welsh Music [★IO]

Guild of Psychotherapists [IO], London, United Kingdom

Guild of Railway Artists [IO], Minehead, United Kingdom

Guild of Recording Producers, Directors and Engineers [★IO]

Guild of Registered Tourist Guides [IO], London, United Kingdom

Guild of Saint Apollonia - Address unknown since 1995.

Guild of Saint Ives - Address unknown since 2007.

Guild of St. Vincent [★19963]

Guild of St. Vincent [★IO]

Guild for Structural Integration [13633], PO Box 1559, Boulder, CO 80306, (303)447-0122

Guild of Surveyors [★IO]

Guild of Taxi Drivers [★24180]

Guild of Taxidermists [IO], Glasgow, United Kingdom

Guild of TV Cameramen [IO], Bristol, United Kingdom

Guild of Temple Musicians [20431], c/o Bruce Shewitz, 13940 Cedar Rd., No. 115, University Heights, OH 44118-3204

Guild of Traditional Butlers - Address unknown since 1999.

Guild of Travel Mgt. Companies [IO], London, United Kingdom

Guild of Vision Mixers [IO], High Wycombe, United Kingdom

Guilde Canadienne des Medias [★IO]

Guilde Europeenne du Raid [★IO]

Guilde de la Marine Marchande du Canada [★IO]

GuildHE [IO], London, United Kingdom

Guilds Intl; Media [2668]

Guillain-Barre Syndrome Found. Intl. [15327], 104 1/2 Forrest Ave., Narberth, PA 19072, (610)667-0131

Guillain-Barre Syndrome Found. Intl. [IO], Wynnewood, PA, United States

Guillian-Barre Syndrome Support Gp. [★IO]

Guillian-Barre Syndrome Support Gp. [★15327]

Guillian-Barre Syndrome Support Gp. Intl. [★15327]

Guillian-Barre Syndrome Support Gp. Intl. [★IO]

Guinea Development Foundation [IO], New York, NY, United States

Guinea Development Found. [16931], 140 W End Ave., Ste. 17G, New York, NY 10023

Guinea Fowl Breeders Assn. [4196], c/o Phyllis Bender, Sec.-Treas., 4 Coach Ln., Westport, CT 06880

Guinea Fowl Intl. Assn. [4197], PO Box 367, Paradise, TX 76073

Guinea Sports Fed. for Disabled [IO], Conakry, Guinea

Guinean Assn. for the Educ. and Help to Diabetics [IO], Conakry, Guinea

Guitar

Chet Atkins Appreciation Soc. [24858]

European Guitar Teachers Assn. [22576]

European Guitar Teachers Assn. [IO]

Gram Parsons Found. [24903]

Guitar Found. of Am. [10605]

Guitars Not Guns [18114]

Intl. Steel Guitar Convention [10629]

Pedal Steel Guitar Assn. [10685]

Guitar and Accessories Marketing Assn. [2805], PO Box 757, New York, NY 10033, (212)795-3630

Guitar and Accessories Music Marketing Assn. [★2805]

Guitar and Accessory Mfrs. Assn. [★2805]

Guitar Assn; Pedal Steel [10685]

Guitar Convention; Annual Steel [★10629]

Guitar Found. of Am. [10605], PO Box 4909, Garden Grove, CA 92842, (909)624-7730

Guitarists; Amer. Guild of Banjoists, Mandolinists and [★10536]

Guitars Not Guns [18114], PO Box 9602, San Jose, CA 95157, (408)251-5775

Gulf and Caribbean Fisheries Inst. [4668], c/o Florida Fish and Wildlife Conservation Commn., Marine Res. Inst., 2796 Overseas Hwy., Ste. 119, Marathon, FL 33050, (305)289-2330

A star before a book entry number signifies that the name is not listed separately, but is mentioned within the entry.

Gulf Coast Allergy Study Group [★13604]
Gulf Coast Conservation Assn. [★4376]
Gulf Coasts Dry Dock Assn; Atlantic and [★2592]
Gulf-European Freight Assn. - Defunct.
Gulf Maritime Assn; West [2595]
Gulf Offshore Marine Ser. Assn. [★2590]
Gulf Oil Wholesale Marketers Assn. [★2920]
Gulf Org. for Indus. Consulting [IO], Doha, Qatar
Gulf War Rsrc. Center; Natl. [21311]
Gulf War Veterans Assn; Amer. [21281]
Gulf War Veterans Coalition; Natl. Vietnam and [18781]
Gulf Yachting Assn. [21874], c/o Janet Miller-Schmidt, Sec.-Treas., 2777 Lakeshore Dr., Mandeville, LA 70448, (985)624-8152
Gulfcoast Pulpwood Assn. - Address unknown since 1995.
Gull Wing Gp. Intl. [21652], 776 Cessna Ave., Chico, CA 95928-9571, (530)345-6701
Gull Wing Gp. Intl. [IO], Chico, CA, United States
Gullwing Gp. [★IO]
Gullwing Gp. [★21652]
Gum Mfrs; Natl. Assn. of Chewing [1538]
Gumby Fan Club; Official [24793]
Gummed Industries Assn. - Address unknown since 1994.
Gun Collectors' Assn; German [22029]
Gun Control; Hand [★17588]
Gun Control; Women Against [17685]
Gun Field Target Assn; Amer. Air [22976]
Gun Owners Action Comm. - Address unknown since 2006.
Gun Owners of Am. [5725], 8001 Forbes Pl., Ste. 102, Springfield, VA 22151, (703)321-8585
Gun Owners Found. [5726], 8001 Forbes Pl., Ste. 102, Springfield, VA 22151, (703)321-8585
Gun Trade Assn. [IO], Tewkesbury, United Kingdom
Gun Violence; Brady Campaign to Prevent [17588]
Gun Violence; Brady Center to Prevent [17589]
Gun Violence; Center to Prevent Hand [★17589]
Gun Violence; Coalition to Stop [17590]
Gun Violence; Educational Fund to Stop [17592]
Gun Violence; Student Pledge Against [17601]
Gun Violence; Women Against [18791]
Gungywamp Complex [★10031]
Gungywamp Soc. [10031], PO Box 592, Colchester, CT 06415-0592
Gunilla Hutton Fan Club - Address unknown since 1999.
Gunite Contractors Assn. [★1017]
Gunite/Shotcrete Assn. [★1017]
Gunite/Shotcrete Contractors Assn. [1017]
Gunmakers Guild; Amer. Custom [1477]
Gunnedah Olive Growers Assn. [IO], Gunnedah, Australia
Guns; Drums No [17591]
Guns Save Lives [17594]
Guppy Assn; Amer. [★22442]
Gurion Inst. and Archives; Ben- [★8673]
Gurion Univ. of the Negev; Amer. Associates, Ben- [8673]
Gustave Weigel Soc. - Defunct.
Gutenberg-Gesellschaft: Internationale Vereinigung fuer Geschichte und Gegenwart der Druckkunst [★IO]
Gutenberg Soc.: Intl. Assn. for Past and Present History of the Art of Printing [IO], Mainz, Germany
Guthrie USA; Clan [20830]
Guttmacher Inst; Alan [12175]
Guy Clark; Friends of [24893]
Guyana Badminton Assn. [IO], Demerara, Guyana
Guyana Coalition of Citizens with Disability [IO], Georgetown, Guyana
Guyana Lawn Tennis Assn. [IO], Georgetown, Guyana
Guyana Manufacturers' Assn. [IO], Georgetown, Guyana
Guyana Red Cross Soc. [IO], Georgetown, Guyana
Guyana Republican Party - Address unknown since 2003.
Guyana Responsible Parenthood Assn. [IO], Georgetown, Guyana
Guyana Rice Producers' Assn. [IO], Georgetown, Guyana
Guyana Squash Assn. [IO], Georgetown, Guyana

GWEN Project - Defunct.
Gwent Area Welsh Pony and Cob Assn. [IO], Ebbw Vale, United Kingdom
GWTW Collectors Club - Defunct.
Gwynedd Welsh Pony and Cob Breeders' Assn. [IO], Pwllheli, United Kingdom
Gym Affiliates; Universal [★3665]
Gym Assn; Natl. [23654]
Gymanfa GANU Assn. of U.S. and Canada; Natl. [★19432]
Gymnasieskolernes Laererforening [★IO]
Gymnastic Clubs; U.S. Assn. of Independent [3673]
Gymnastic Union; Amer. [★23802]
Gymnastic Union Sokol of the U.S.A; Slovak [★19367]
Gymnastics
    Amer. Gp. Gymnastics Assn. [23473]
    British Gymnastics [IO]
    Coll. Gymnastics Assn. [23474]
    Danish Gymnastics Fed. [IO]
    Eastern Intercollegiate Gymnastic League [23475]
    Intl. Gymnastic Fed. [IO]
    Intl. Vaulting Club [23968]
    Natl. Assn. of Collegiate Gymnastics Coaches/Women [23476]
    Natl. Assn. of Women's Gymnastic's Judges [23477]
    Natl. Gymnastics Judges Assn. [23478]
    Scottish Gymnastics Assn. [IO]
    U.S. Assn. of Independent Gymnastic Clubs [3673]
    USA Gymnastics [23479]
Gymnastics Assn; Coll. [23474]
Gymnastics Assn; Collegiate [★23474]
Gymnastics Coaches/Women; Natl. Assn. of Collegiate [23476]
Gymnastics Fed. - Orienteering Dept; German [IO]
Gymnastics Fed; U.S. [★23479]
Gymnastics; U.S. Elite Coaches' Assn. for Women's [23297]
Gymnastics; USA [23479]
Gynaecological Cancer Soc. [IO], Kenmore, Australia
Gynecologic Investigation; Soc. for [15618]
Gynecologic Laparoscopists; Amer. Assn. of [15581]
Gynecologic and Neonatal Nursing Specialties; Natl. Certification Corp. for the Obstetric, [15506]
Gynecologic Oncologists of Canada; Soc. of [IO]
Gynecologic Oncologists; Soc. of [15654]
Gynecologic Oncology Gp. [15646], 4 Penn Ctr., 1600 JFK Blvd., Ste. 1020, Philadelphia, PA 19103, (215)854-0770
Gynecologic Surgery Soc. [15600], 2440 M St. NW, Ste. 801, Washington, DC 20037-1474, (202)293-5205
Gynecological Laparoscopists; Amer. Assn. of [★15581]
Gynecological and Obstetrical Soc; Amer. [15587]
Gynecological Soc; Amer. [★15587]
Gynecologists; Amer. Assn. of Obstetricians and [★15587]
Gynecologists; Amer. Assn. of Pro Life Obstetricians and [18545]
Gynecologists; Amer. Coll. of Obstetricians and [15584]
Gynecologists; Amer. Coll. of Osteopathic Obstetricians and [15585]
Gynecologists; Nurses Assn. of the Amer. Coll. of Obstetricians and [★15470]
Gynecology; Amer. Acad. of Obstetrics and [★15584]
Gynecology; Amer. Bd. of Obstetrics and [15582]
Gynecology; Coun. on Resident Educ. in Obstetrics and [15597]
Gynecology; Intl. Fed. of Pediatric and Adolescent [IO]
Gynecology and Obstetrics; Assn. of Professors of [15592]
Gynecology and Obstetrics; Intl. Fed. of [IO]
Gynendra Ratna Tulabhar [★IO]
Gypsum, and Allied Workers Div; Cement, Lime, [24038]
Gypsum Assn. [2741], 810 1st St. NE, Ste. 510, Washington, DC 20002, (202)289-5440
Gypsum Products Development Assn. [IO], London, United Kingdom

Gypsy
    Gypsy Lore Soc. [10940]
    Roma Natl. Cong. [19334]
Gypsy Lore Soc. [10940], c/o Sheila Salo, Treas., 5607 Greenleaf Rd., Cheverly, MD 20785, (301)341-1261
Gypsy Lore Soc. [IO], Cheverly, MD, United States
Gypsy Lore Soc., North Amer. Chap. [★IO]
Gypsy Lore Soc., North Amer. Chap. [10940]
Gypsy Moth Coun; Natl. [★5078]
Gypsy Moth Mgt. Bd; Natl. [5078]
Gypsy Moths - Defunct.
Gypsy Stud. [IO], Paris, France
Gypsy Vanner Horse Soc. [4887], PO Box 507, Willington, CT 06279, (352)250-8908
Gyro Intl. [13043], 1019 Mentor Ave., PO Box 489, Painesville, OH 44077-0489, (440)352-2501
Gyro Intl. [IO], Painesville, OH, United States

H

H. M. 10th Foot in Am. [★9373]
Haagudah Lemilchama Besartan Beyisrael [★IO]
Haagudah Letichnun Vepituach Sherutim Lemaan Hazaken Beyisrael [★IO]
Haagudah Letoldot Hadoar Shel Eretz Yisrael [★IO]
Haagudah Lezechuyot Haezrach Beyisrael [★IO]
Haberdashers' Company [IO], London, United Kingdom
Habitat; Coun. on Tall Buildings and Urban [6474]
Habitat Coun; Wildlife [4470]
Habitat Enhancement Coun; Wildlife [★4470]
Habitat Faunique Canada [★IO]
Habitat for Horses [11403], PO Box 213, Hitchcock, TX 77563, (409)935-0277
Habitat para la Humanidad Argentina [★IO]
Habitat para la Humanidad de Costa Rica [★IO]
Habitat para la Humanidad El Salvador [★IO]
Habitat para la Humanidad Mexico [★IO]
Habitat para a Humanidade Brasil [★IO]
Habitat for Humanity [★IO]
Habitat for Humanity [★12313]
Habitat for Humanity - Afghanistan [IO], Mazar-i-Sharif, Afghanistan
Habitat for Humanity - Antigua and Barbuda [IO], St. Johns, Antigua-Barbuda
Habitat for Humanity - Argentina [IO], Buenos Aires, Argentina
Habitat for Humanity - Armenia [IO], Yerevan, Armenia
Habitat for Humanity - Australia [IO], Parramatta, Australia
Habitat for Humanity Australia (Adelaide) [IO], Adelaide, Australia
Habitat for Humanity - Banbury [IO], Banbury, United Kingdom
Habitat for Humanity - Bangladesh [IO], Dhaka, Bangladesh
Habitat for Humanity - Belize [IO], Belize City, Belize
Habitat for Humanity - Bermuda [IO], Hamilton, Bermuda
Habitat for Humanity - Bicol [IO], Naga City, Philippines
Habitat for Humanity - Birmingham [IO], Birmingham, United Kingdom
Habitat for Humanity - Bolivia [IO], Cochabamba, Bolivia
Habitat for Humanity - Botswana [IO], Gaborone, Botswana
Habitat for Humanity - Braga [IO], Braga, Portugal
Habitat for Humanity - Brampton [IO], Brampton, ON, Canada
Habitat for Humanity - Brandon [IO], Brandon, MB, Canada
Habitat for Humanity - Brant [IO], Brantford, ON, Canada
Habitat for Humanity - Brazil [IO], Recife, Brazil
Habitat for Humanity - Brooks [IO], Brooks, AB, Canada
Habitat for Humanity - Bulgaria [IO], Sofia, Bulgaria
Habitat for Humanity - Cabot [IO], St. John's, NL, Canada
Habitat for Humanity - Calgary [IO], Calgary, AB, Canada
Habitat for Humanity - Cambodia [IO], Phnom Penh, Cambodia

Reference to "IO" in place of a book number signifies that the association may be found in the 45th edition of International Organizations.

Habitat for Humanity - Cameroon [IO], Yaounde, Cameroon

Habitat for Humanity - Camrose Region [IO], Camrose, AB, Canada

Habitat for Humanity - Canada [IO], Waterloo, ON, Canada

Habitat for Humanity - Cayman Islands [IO], George Town, Cayman Islands

Habitat for Humanity - Central Plains [IO], Tarlac City, Philippines

Habitat for Humanity - Chile [IO], Santiago, Chile

Habitat for Humanity - China [IO], Kunming, People's Republic of China

Habitat for Humanity - Christchurch [IO], Christchurch, New Zealand

Habitat for Humanity - Colombia [IO], Bogota, Colombia

Habitat for Humanity - Comox Valley [IO], Courtenay, BC, Canada

Habitat for Humanity - Costa Rica [IO], San Jose, Costa Rica

Habitat for Humanity - Cote d'Ivoire [IO], Abidjan, Cote d'Ivoire

Habitat for Humanity - Democratic Republic of Congo [IO], Kinshasa, Democratic Republic of the Congo

Habitat for Humanity - Dominican Republic [IO], Santo Domingo, Dominican Republic

Habitat for Humanity, Dufferin-Caledon [IO], Orangeville, ON, Canada

Habitat for Humanity - Dunedin [IO], Dunedin, New Zealand

Habitat for Humanity - Eastbourne [IO], Eastbourne, United Kingdom

Habitat for Humanity - Ecuador [IO], Quito, Ecuador

Habitat for Humanity - Edmonton [IO], Edmonton, AB, Canada

Habitat for Humanity - Egypt [IO], Cairo, Egypt

Habitat for Humanity - El Salvador [IO], San Salvador, El Salvador

Habitat for Humanity - Ethiopia [IO], Addis Ababa, Ethiopia

Habitat for Humanity - Fiji [IO], Suva, Fiji

Habitat for Humanity - Franklin [IO], Pukekohe, New Zealand

Habitat for Humanity - Fredericton Area [IO], Fredericton, NB, Canada

Habitat for Humanity - Gdansk [IO], Gdansk, Poland

Habitat for Humanity - Gen. Santos City [IO], General Santos City, Philippines

Habitat for Humanity - Germany [IO], Cologne, Germany

Habitat for Humanity - Ghana [IO], Accra, Ghana

Habitat for Humanity - Gliwice [IO], Gliwice, Poland

Habitat for Humanity - Great Britain [IO], Banbury, United Kingdom

Habitat for Humanity - Greater Kingston and Frontenac [IO], Kingston, ON, Canada

Habitat for Humanity - Greater Metro Manila [IO], Makati City, Philippines

Habitat for Humanity - Greater Vancouver [IO], Vancouver, BC, Canada

Habitat for Humanity - Grey/Bruce [IO], Owen Sound, ON, Canada

Habitat for Humanity - Guangdong [IO], Guangzhou, People's Republic of China

Habitat for Humanity - Guangxi [IO], Nanning, People's Republic of China

Habitat for Humanity - Guatemala [IO], Quetzaltenango, Guatemala

Habitat for Humanity - Guyana [IO], Georgetown, Guyana

Habitat for Humanity - Gympie [IO], Gympie, Australia

Habitat for Humanity - Haiti [IO], Petionville, Haiti

Habitat for Humanity - Halifax/Dartmouth [IO], Dartmouth, NS, Canada

Habitat for Humanity - Halton [IO], Burlington, ON, Canada

Habitat for Humanity - Hamilton [IO], Hamilton, ON, Canada

Habitat for Humanity - Honduras [IO], San Pedro Sula, Honduras

Habitat for Humanity - Huronia [IO], Barrie, ON, Canada

Habitat for Humanity - Hutt Valley [IO], Lower Hutt, New Zealand

Habitat for Humanity - India [IO], Bangalore, India

Habitat for Humanity - Indonesia [IO], Jakarta, Indonesia

Habitat for Humanity Intl. [IO], Americus, GA, United States

Habitat for Humanity Intl. [12313], 121 Habitat St., Americus, GA 31709-3498, (229)924-6935

Habitat for Humanity - Invercargill [IO], Invercargill, New Zealand

Habitat for Humanity - Ireland [IO], Dublin, Ireland

Habitat for Humanity - Jamaica [IO], Kingston, Jamaica

Habitat for Humanity - Japan [IO], Tokyo, Japan

Habitat for Humanity - Jordan [IO], Amman, Jordan

Habitat for Humanity - Kamloops [IO], Kamloops, BC, Canada

Habitat for Humanity - Kelowna [IO], Kelowna, BC, Canada

Habitat for Humanity - Kenya [IO], Nairobi, Kenya

Habitat for Humanity - Korea [IO], Seoul, Republic of Korea

Habitat for Humanity - Kyrgyzstan [IO], Bishkek, Kirgizstan

Habitat for Humanity - Lebanon [IO], Beirut, Lebanon

Habitat for Humanity - Lesotho [IO], Maseru, Lesotho

Habitat for Humanity - Lethbridge [IO], Lethbridge, AB, Canada

Habitat for Humanity - London [IO], London, ON, Canada

Habitat for Humanity - Macedonia [IO], Skopje, Macedonia

Habitat for Humanity - Madagascar [IO], Antananarivo, Madagascar

Habitat for Humanity - Malawi [IO], Blantyre, Malawi

Habitat for Humanity Malaysia [IO], Kuching, Malaysia

Habitat for Humanity - Manukau [IO], Manukau City, New Zealand

Habitat for Humanity - Medicine Hat [IO], Medicine Hat, AB, Canada

Habitat for Humanity - Mexico [IO], Mexico City, Mexico

Habitat for Humanity - Moncton Area [IO], Moncton, NB, Canada

Habitat for Humanity - Mongolia [IO], Ulan Bator, Mongolia

Habitat for Humanity - Montreal [IO], Montreal, QC, Canada

Habitat for Humanity - Mozambique [IO], Maputo, Mozambique

Habitat for Humanity - Muskoka [IO], Gravenhurst, ON, Canada

Habitat for Humanity - Nanaimo [IO], Nanaimo, BC, Canada

Habitat for Humanity - Natl. Capital Region [IO], Ottawa, ON, Canada

Habitat for Humanity - Negros Occidental [IO], Talisay City, Philippines

Habitat for Humanity - Nelson [IO], Nelson, New Zealand

Habitat for Humanity - Netherlands [IO], Haarlem, Netherlands

Habitat for Humanity - New Zealand [IO], Auckland, New Zealand

Habitat for Humanity - Niagara [IO], St. Catharines, ON, Canada

Habitat for Humanity - Nicaragua [IO], Managua, Nicaragua

Habitat for Humanity - Nigeria [IO], Abuja, Nigeria

Habitat for Humanity - North Durham [IO], Uxbridge, ON, Canada

Habitat for Humanity - North Taranaki [IO], New Plymouth, New Zealand

Habitat for Humanity - Northern Ireland [IO], Belfast, United Kingdom

Habitat for Humanity - Northland [IO], Whangarei, New Zealand

Habitat for Humanity - On the Border [IO], Lloydminster, SK, Canada

Habitat for Humanity - Pakistan [IO], Islamabad, Pakistan

Habitat for Humanity - Palmerston North [IO], Porirua, New Zealand

Habitat for Humanity - Panama [IO], Panama City, Panama

Habitat for Humanity - Paraguay [IO], Asuncion, Paraguay

Habitat for Humanity - Peterborough and District [IO], Peterborough, ON, Canada

Habitat for Humanity Philippines [IO], Makati City, Philippines

Habitat for Humanity - Poland [IO], Warsaw, Poland

Habitat for Humanity - Porirua [IO], Porirua, New Zealand

Habitat for Humanity - Portugal [IO], Braga, Portugal

Habitat for Humanity - Prince Albert [IO], Prince Albert, SK, Canada

Habitat for Humanity - Prince Edward/Hastings [IO], Belleville, ON, Canada

Habitat for Humanity - Prince George [IO], Prince George, BC, Canada

Habitat for Humanity - Queens [IO], Charlottetown, PE, Canada

Habitat for Humanity - Red Deer Region [IO], Red Deer, AB, Canada

Habitat for Humanity - Regina [IO], Regina, SK, Canada

Habitat for Humanity - Romania [IO], Beius, Romania

Habitat for Humanity - Rotorua [IO], Rotorua, New Zealand

Habitat for Humanity - Russia [IO], Ulan-Ude, Russia

Habitat for Humanity - Saint John Region [IO], St. John, NB, Canada

Habitat for Humanity - Samoa [IO], Apia, Western Samoa

Habitat for Humanity - Sarnia/Lambton [IO], Sarnia, ON, Canada

Habitat for Humanity - Saskatoon [IO], Saskatoon, SK, Canada

Habitat for Humanity - Sault Ste. Marie and Area [IO], Sault Ste. Marie, ON, Canada

Habitat for Humanity - Senegal [IO], Dakar, Senegal

Habitat for Humanity - Singapore [IO], Singapore, Singapore

Habitat for Humanity - Slovakia [IO], Kosice, Slovakia

Habitat for Humanity - Solomon Islands [IO], Honiara, Solomon Islands

Habitat for Humanity - South Africa [IO], Marshalltown, Republic of South Africa

Habitat for Humanity - South Australia [★IO]

Habitat for Humanity - South Peace Soc. [IO], Grande Prairie, AB, Canada

Habitat for Humanity - Sri Lanka [IO], Colombo, Sri Lanka

Habitat for Humanity - Stratford/Perth [IO], Stratford, ON, Canada

Habitat for Humanity - Sudbury District [IO], Sudbury, ON, Canada

Habitat for Humanity - Sunshine Coast [IO], Sechelt, BC, Canada

Habitat for Humanity - Suriname [IO], Paramaribo, Suriname

Habitat for Humanity - Tajikistan [IO], Dushanbe, Tajikistan

Habitat for Humanity - Tanzania [IO], Dar es Salaam, United Republic of Tanzania

Habitat for Humanity - Tauranga [IO], Tauranga, New Zealand

Habitat for Humanity - Thailand [IO], Bangkok, Thailand

Habitat for Humanity - The Pas [IO], The Pas, MB, Canada

Habitat for Humanity - Thousand Islands [IO], Brockville, ON, Canada

Habitat for Humanity - Thunder Bay [IO], Thunder Bay, ON, Canada

Habitat for Humanity - Toronto [IO], Toronto, ON, Canada

Habitat for Humanity - Turkey [IO], Istanbul, Turkey

Habitat for Humanity - Uganda [IO], Kampala, Uganda

Habitat for Humanity - Upper Fraser Valley [IO], Abbotsford, BC, Canada

A star before a book entry number signifies that the name is not listed separately, but is mentioned within the entry.

Habitat for Humanity - Vanuatu [IO], Port Vila, Vanuatu
Habitat for Humanity - Victoria, Australia [IO], Ringwood, Australia
Habitat for Humanity - Vietnam [IO], Ho Chi Minh City, Vietnam
Habitat for Humanity - Waikato [IO], Hamilton, New Zealand
Habitat for Humanity - Waitakere [IO], Auckland, New Zealand
Habitat for Humanity - Waterloo Region [IO], Waterloo, ON, Canada
Habitat for Humanity - Wellington County [IO], Guelph, ON, Canada
Habitat for Humanity - West Kootenay [IO], Nelson, BC, Canada
Habitat for Humanity - Western Australia [IO], Perth, Australia
Habitat for Humanity - Windsor Essex [IO], Windsor, ON, Canada
Habitat for Humanity - Winnipeg [IO], Winnipeg, MB, Canada
Habitat for Humanity - Wood Buffalo [IO], Fort Mc-Murray, AB, Canada
Habitat for Humanity - York Region [IO], Newmarket, ON, Canada
Habitat for Humanity - Yukon Soc. [IO], Whitehorse, YT, Canada
Habitat for Humanity - Zambia [IO], Lusaka, Zambia
Habitat pour l'humanite Canada [★IO]
Habitat pour L'Humanite - Haiti [★IO]
Habitat pour l'humanite Montreal [★IO]
Habitat pour l'Humanite - Region de la Capitale Nationale [★IO]
Habitat Org; Native [4596]
Habonim Dror Labor Zionist Youth [★20138]
Habonim Dror Labor Zionist Youth; Ichud [★20138]
Habonim Dror North Am. [20138], 114 W 26 St., Ste. 1004, New York, NY 10001, (212)255-1796
Habonim Labor Zionist Youth; Ichud [★20138]
Habsburg History; Soc. for Austrian and [9628]
Hachevrah Hayisraelit Lechimia [★IO]
Hack and Band Saw Mfrs. Assn. of Am. [★1830]
Hack Saw Assn. and Metal Cutting Band [★1830]
Hackeysack
    World Footbag Assn. [23426]
Hackney Horse Soc; Amer. [4820]
Hacky Sack Footbag Players Assn; Natl. [★23426]
Hadassah; Junior [★20198]
Hadassah, The Women's Zionist Org. of Am. [20139], 50 W 58th St., New York, NY 10019, (212)355-7900
Hadassah, The Women's Zionist Org. of Am. [IO], New York, NY, United States
Hadassah WIZO Org. of Canada [IO], Montreal, QC, Canada
Hadati, Bnei Akiva; Hashomer [★20178]
Haematology Soc. of Australia and New Zealand [IO], Sydney, Australia
Haemophilia Soc. [IO], London, United Kingdom
Haemostasis; Intl. Soc. on Thrombosis and [★14793]
Haflinger Assn. of Am. [★4821]
Haflinger Breeders Org. [4888], PO Box 205, Conesville, OH 43811-0205, (740)622-3091
Haflinger Registry; Amer. [4821]
Haflinger Registry North Am. [★4821]
Hagan History Soc. - Defunct.
Hagdud Haivri League - Defunct.
Hagiography Soc. [20526], c/o Sherry L. Reames, Univ. of Wisconsin, Dept. of English, 600 N Park St., Madison, WI 53706, (608)262-7836
Hague Conf. on Private Intl. Law [IO], The Hague, Netherlands
Hague Ser. Convention [★6184]
Hahnemann Therapeutic Soc. - Defunct.
Hai Meditation Assn; Supreme Master Ching [19557]
Hai-Stiftung [★IO]
Haigud L'Sport Hanivut Belsrael [★IO]
Haiku Soc. of Am. [10861], c/o Lane Parker, Sec., 578 3rd Ave., San Francisco, CA 94118-3903
Haiku Soc; Yuki Teikei [10874]
Haines Family Org. - Defunct.
Hair
    Amer. Bd. of Hair Restoration Surgery [14518]

Amer. Hair Loss Assn. [14519]
    Amer. Soc. of Hair Restoration Surgery [14520]
    Amer. Soc. of Hair Restoration Surgery [IO]
    Antique Comb Collectors Club Intl. [21970]
    European Hair Res. Soc. [IO]
    Intl. Soc. of Hair Restoration Surgery [14521]
    Natl. Alopecia Areata Found. [16386]
Hair Intl./Associated Master Barbers and Beauticians of America [1079]
Hair Loss Coun; Amer. [14193]
Hair Removal; Soc. for Clinical and Medical [14310]
Hair Sys. Culture League; Natl. [★1084]
Hairdressers; Assn. of Cosmetologists and [1078]
Hairdressers and Cosmetologists Assn; Natl. [★1085]
Hairdressing Coun. [IO], Croydon, United Kingdom
Hairenik Assn. [18970], 80 Bigelow Ave., Watertown, MA 02472, (617)926-3974
Hairwork Soc; Victorian [22176]
Haiti
    Found. of Compassionate Amer. Samaritans [20340]
    Haiti Philatelic Soc. [22825]
    Haiti Support Network [17682]
    Haitian Stud. Assn. [17683]
    Intl. Child Care U.S.A. [11701]
    Meds and Food for Kids [11622]
    Mission to Haiti [12267]
    Mission to Haiti [IO]
    Natl. Assn. for the Advancement of Haitian Descendents [19097]
    Natl. Haitian Soc. [17817]
    Restoration Proj. Intl. [12441]
    RHEMA Intl. [12881]
Haiti; Friends of [★17682]
Haiti Overseas - Address unknown since 2003.
Haiti Philatelic Soc. [22825], c/o Mr. Ubaldo Deltoro, Sec.-Treas., 5709 Marble Archway, Alexandria, VA 22315-4013, (703)922-9531
Haiti Support Network [17682], c/o Intl. Action Center, 39 W 14th St., Rm. 206, New York, NY 10011, (212)633-6646
Haiti Survive [★IO]
Haitian Amer. Assn. Against Cancer [13828], 225 NE 34th St., Ste. 208, Miami, FL 33137, (305)572-1825
Haitian Amer. Assn. - Defunct.
Haitian-American Chamber of Commerce and Indus. [IO], Delmas, Haiti
Haitian Bible Soc. [IO], Port-au-Prince, Haiti
Haitian and Co-Arts Assn. - Address unknown since 2003.
Haitian Coalition on AIDS [13567], c/o Haitian Centers Coun., 10 St. Pauls Pl. - Wing B, 5th Fl., Brooklyn, NY 11226, (718)940-5200
Haitian Development Fund [★11961]
Haitian Development Fund [★IO]
Haitian Medical Assn. Abroad [★15159]
Haitian Patriotic Union - Address unknown since 1999.
Haitian Physicians Abroad; Assn. of [15159]
Haitian Refugee Center - Address unknown since 2008.
Haitian Refugee Project - Defunct.
Haitian Refugees; Natl. Emergency Coalition for [★18499]
Haitian Rights; Natl. Coalition for [18499]
Haitian Stud. Assn. [17683], c/o Univ. of Massachusetts Boston, 100 Morrissey Blvd., McCormack Hall Rm. 2-211, Boston, MA 02125-3393, (617)287-7138
Haitian Unity Coun. - Defunct.
Haitien de Liberation; Mouvement [★17682]
Hajji Baba Club - Address unknown since 2006.
Hakluyt Soc; Amer. Friends of the [10410]
Hakluyt Soc. - Australia [IO], Canberra, Australia
Hakluyt Soc. - England [IO], London, United Kingdom
Hale Inst; Nathan [17822]
Hales Family History Soc. - Defunct.
Half Mile Dirt Track Racing Exhibition Assn. - Defunct.
Half Saddlebred Registry of Am. [4889], 4083 Iron Works Pkwy., Lexington, KY 40511-8462, (859)259-2742

Halferty Family Registry - Defunct.
Halfway House Alcoholism Programs of North Am; Assn. of [13224]
Halfway House Assn; Intl. [★11872]
Halibut Assn. of North America - Address unknown since 1999.
Hall of Fame; Automotive [345]
Hall of Fame; Cooperative [★1073]
Hall of Fame Found; Natl. Black Coll. Alumni [18911]
Hall of Fame Found; Natl. Inventors [★5855]
Hall of Fame for Great Americans [11119], c/o Bronx Community Coll., Univ. Ave. at W 181st St., Bronx, NY 10453, (718)289-5161
Hall of Fame Museum; Intl. Boxing [23261]
Hall of Fame; Naismith Memorial Basketball [23132]
Hall of Fame; Natl. Football Found. and Coll. [23431]
Hall of Fame; Natl. Football Shrine and [★23431]
Hall of Fame; Natl. High School Band and Choral Directors [★8926]
Hall of Fame; Natl. High School Band Directors [8926]
Hall of Fame; National Judo [★23555]
Hall of Fame; Natl. Tennis Found. and [★23903]
Hall of Fame; Natl. Women's [20716]
Hall of Fame; Water Ski Museum [★23975]
Hall of Fame and Western Heritage Center; Natl. Cowboy [★9381]
Hall of Fame; Women's [★20716]
Hallam Assn. - Defunct.
Hallervorden-Spatz Syndrome Assn. [★15355]
Hallgatoi Onkormanyzatok Orszagos Konferenciaja [IO], Budapest, Hungary
Hallmark Soc. [IO], Victoria, BC, Canada
Halls of Fame; Assn. of Executive Directors of [★23827]
Halls of Fame; Assn. of Sports Museums and [★23827]
HALO USA [17245], 850 7th Ave., Ste. 506, New York, NY 10019-5230, (212)581-0099
HALO USA [IO], New York, NY, United States
Halogenated Solvents Indus. Alliance [809], 1300 Wilson Blvd., Arlington, VA 22209, (703)741-5780
Halogenated Solvents Industry Alliance - Applications Coun. - Defunct.
HALT - Americans for Legal Reform [★17961]
HALT. - An Org. of Americans for Legal Reform [17961], 1612 K St. NW, Ste. 510, Washington, DC 20006, (202)887-8255
HALT - Help Abolish Legal Tyranny [★17961]
Ham Assn; Natl. Country [1545]
The Hamill Exchange - Address unknown since 2001.
Hamilton Acoustic Music Club [IO], Hamilton, New Zealand
Hamilton District Soc. of Chefs and Cooks [IO], Hamilton, ON, Canada
Hamilton Natl. Genealogical Soc. [20926], 116 W Vine St., Vicksburg, MI 49097
Hamilton Soc; Clan [20831]
Hamiltonian Party; Natl. [18328]
Hamiltonian Soc. - Defunct.
Hamizrachi; Women's Org. of Hapoel [★20136]
Hamizrachi Women's Org; Hapoel [★20136]
Hammered Aluminum Collectors Assn. [22033], PO Box 1346, Weatherford, TX 76086, (817)594-4680
Hamoked: Center for the Defence of the Individual [IO], Jerusalem, Israel
Hamor, Hamour [★20935]
Hampshire Conservation Volunteers [IO], Romsey, United Kingdom
Hampshire Sheep Assn; Amer. [5185]
Hampshire Swine Registry [★5241]
Hampton One-Design Class Racing Assn. [23173], c/o Charles H. McCoy, Jr., Treas., 1721 Cloncurry Rd., Norfolk, VA 23505, (757)423-3109
Hamro Jivan Child Care House [IO], Kathmandu, Nepal
Hamster Fanciers; Rat, Mouse, and [22708]
Hand
    Amer. Assn. for Hand Surgery [14522]
    Amer. Found. for Surgery of the Hand [14523]
    Amer. Soc. of Hand Therapists [14524]
    Amer. Soc. for Surgery of the Hand [14525]
    Assn. of Independent Manufacturers'/Representatives [2534]

Reference to "IO" in place of a book number signifies that the association may be found in the 45th edition of International Organizations.

Found. for Hand Res. and Educ. [14526]
Intl. Fed. of Societies for Surgery of the Hand [14527]
Intl. Fed. of Societies for Surgery of the Hand [IO]
Northwest Regional Spinners' Assn. [22172]
Hand Knitting Assn. - Defunct.
Hand Protection Assn; Intl. [★2030]
Hand Surgical Res; Indiana Found. for [★14526]
Hand Tools Inst. [1822], 25 N Broadway, Tarrytown, NY 10591, (914)332-0040
Handbag Assn; Natl. [★250]
Handball
Afghanistan Handball Fed. [IO]
Armenian Handball Fed. [IO]
Asian Handball Fed. [IO]
Assn. Chinoise de Handball [IO]
Bahrain Handball Assn. [IO]
Bangladesh Handball Fed. [IO]
Bulgarian Handball Fed. [IO]
Canadian Team Handball Fed. [IO]
Federacao Angolana de Andebol [IO]
Federacion Chilena de Handball [IO]
Fed. Albanaise de Handball [IO]
Fed. Burkinabe de Handball [IO]
Fed. Burundaise de Handball [IO]
Fed. Camerounaise de Handball [IO]
Fed. Centrafricaine de Handball [IO]
Fed. Congolaise de Handball [IO]
Fed. Tchadienne de Handball [IO]
Handball Assn. of Barbados [IO]
Handball Fed. of Azerbaijan [IO]
Handball Fed. of Belarus [IO]
Handball Fed. of Bosnia and Herzegovina [IO]
Intl. Fed. of Basque Pelota [IO]
Intl. Handball Fed. [IO]
Irish Handball Coun. [IO]
Malta Handball Assn. [IO]
U.S. Handball Assn. [23480]
Handball Assn. of Barbados [IO], St. Michael, Barbados
Handball Fed. of Azerbaijan [IO], Baku, Azerbaijan
Handball Fed. of Belarus [IO], Minsk, Belarus
Handball Fed. of Bosnia and Herzegovina [IO], Sarajevo, Bosnia-Hercegovina
Handball Fed; U.S. Team [★23096]
Handball; U.S.A Team [23096]
Handball Ringers; Amer. Guild of English [10535]
Handbell Ringers of Great Britain [IO], Sheffield, United Kingdom
Handclasp; Proj. [17911]
Handcrafted Soap Makers Guild [1155], 3416 Primm Ln., Birmingham, AL 35216, (205)823-5517
Handel Soc; Amer. [9806]
Handgun Control [★17588]
Handgun Educ; Found. for [★17592]
Handgun Info. Center [★17589]
Handgun Safety and Educ. Coun. [17684]
Handgun Violence; Center to Prevent [★17589]
Handgun Violence; Educational Fund to End [★17592]
Handguns
Armed Females of Am. [17587]
Cowboy Mounted Shooting Assn. [23716]
Fifty Caliber Shooters Assn. [22973]
Guitars Not Guns [18114]
Handgun Safety and Educ. Coun. [17684]
Natl. Assn. of Firearms Retailers [1479]
Natl. Assn. of Shooting Ranges [3599]
Natl. Firearms Act Trade and Collectors Assn. [1480]
Peoples Rights Org. [17145]
Sportsmen's Assn. for Firearms Educ. [17600]
U.S. Airsoft Corps [23620]
U.S. Helice Assn. [23729]
Women Against Gun Control [17685]
Women Against Gun Control [IO]
Handguns; Natl. Coalition to Ban [★17590]
Handguns; Natl. Coun. to Control [★17588]
Handicap Intl. - Belgium [IO], Brussels, Belgium
Handicap Intl. Canada [IO], Montreal, QC, Canada
Handicap Intl. Denmark [IO], Copenhagen, Denmark
Handicap Intl. - France [IO], Lyon, France
Handicap Intl. Germany [IO], Munich, Germany
Handicap Intl. Luxembourg [IO], Luxembourg, Luxembourg

Handicap Intl. Switzerland [IO], Geneva, Switzerland
Handicap Intl. - Thailand [IO], Bangkok, Thailand
Handicap Intl. - UK [IO], Surrey, United Kingdom
Handicap Introductions [★IO]
Handicap Introductions [★11936]
Handicapable Dancers; Comm. for [9870]
Handicapped
Abilities! [11913]
Acad. of Doctors of Audiology [14733]
Acad. of Rehabilitative Audiology [14734]
Achilles Track Club [23331]
Achromatopsia Network [16820]
ADARA: Professionals Networking for Excellence in Ser. Delivery with Individuals who are Deaf or Hard of Hearing [14735]
Adventures in Movement for the Handicapped [16597]
Advocating Change Together [11914]
Alexander Graham Bell Assn. for the Deaf and Hard of Hearing [14736]
Alliance for Tech. Access [11915]
Amer. Acad. for Cerebral Palsy and Developmental Medicine [13934]
Amer. Acad. of Disability Evaluating Physicians [14033]
Amer. Acad. of Orthotists and Prosthetists [15782]
Amer. Acad. of Physical Medicine and Rehabilitation [16307]
Amer. Amputee Found. [11916]
Amer. Amputee Hockey Assn. [23799]
Amer. Amputee Soccer Assn. [23773]
Amer. Assn. of the Deaf-Blind [14737]
Amer. Assn. on Hea. and Disability [14235]
Amer. Assn. of People with Disabilities [11917]
Amer. Auditory Soc. [14738]
Amer. Blind Bowling Assn. [23334]
Amer. Blind Golf Assn. [23335]
Amer. Blind Skiing Found. [23336]
Amer. Bd. of Physical Medicine and Rehabilitation [16309]
Amer. Competition Opportunities for Riders with Disabilities [23330]
Amer. Cong. of Rehabilitation Medicine [16310]
Amer. Coun. of the Blind [16822]
Amer. Coun. of the Blind Enterprises and Services [16823]
Amer. Coun. of Blind Govt. Employees [16824]
Amer. Disability Assn. [11918]
Amer. Found. for the Blind [16826]
Amer. Friends of ALYN Hosp. [12825]
Amer. Hearing Res. Found. [14740]
Amer. Israeli Lighthouse [16827]
Amer. Kinesiotherapy Assn. [16311]
Amer. Medical Rehabilitation Providers Assn. [16312]
Amer. Occupational Therapy Assn. [16602]
Amer. Physical Therapy Assn. [16603]
Amer. Printing House for the Blind [16829]
Amer. Rehabilitation Counseling Assn. [16313]
Amer. Sailing Assn. Found. [23155]
Amer. Soc. for Deaf Children [14742]
Amer. Soc. of Handicapped Physicians [11919]
Amer. Wheelchair Bowling Assn. [23339]
Americans With Disabilities Act [11920]
Amputees in Motion, Intl. [11921]
Assistance Dogs of Am., Inc. [11922]
Assistance Dogs Intl. [11923]
Assoc. Blind [16830]
Assoc. Services for the Blind [16831]
Assn. of Academic Physiatrists [16316]
Assn. for the Advancement of Blind and Retarded [16832]
Assn. of Assistive Tech. Act Programs [14237]
Assn. of Children's Prosthetic-Orthotic Clinics [15784]
Assn. of Disabled Amer. Golfers [23341]
Assn. for Educ. and Rehabilitation of the Blind and Visually Impaired [16833]
Assn. of Late-Deafened Adults [14743]
Assn. of Rehabilitation Programs in Cmpt. Tech. [11924]
Attention Deficit Info. Network [15308]
Autism Network Intl. [13719]
Better Hearing Inst. [14745]
Birth Defect Res. for Children [13752]

Blind Info. Tech. Specialists [16835]
Blind Sailing Intl. [23151]
Blind Ser. Assn. [16836]
Blinded Veterans Assn. [16837]
B'nai B'rith Senior Citizens Housing Comm. [12469]
Braille Authority of North Am. [16838]
Braille Revival League [16839]
Canine Assistants [11925]
Canine Companions for Independence [11926]
Canines for Disabled Kids [11927]
Carroll Center for the Blind [16840]
Center on Human Policy [11932]
Challenge Aspen at Snowmass [23342]
Children of Deaf Adults [14747]
Christian Overcomers [11932]
Christian Record Services [16842]
CH on Disability Info. [11933]
Coleman Found. [13162]
Conf. of Educational Administrators of Schools and Programs for the Deaf [14749]
Continuing Care Accreditation Commn. [16318]
Coun. of Amer. Instructors of the Deaf [14750]
Coun. on Educ. of the Deaf [14751]
Coun. of Families with Visual Impairment [16844]
Coun. of State Administrators of Vocational Rehabilitation [16320]
CUSA: An Apostolate of the Sick and Disabled [19620]
DateAble [11936]
Deafness Res. Found. [14753]
Disability Intl. Found. [14239]
Disability Ministries [20216]
Disability Resources [11938]
Disability Rights Educ. and Defense Fund [11940]
Disabled and Alone/Life Services for the Handicapped [11941]
Disabled Amer. Veterans [20763]
Disabled Amer. Veterans Auxiliary [20764]
Disabled Collectors' Correspondence Club [22814]
Disabled Sports USA [23343]
Dogs for the Deaf [14754]
Easter Seals [11944]
Eastern Amputee Golf Assn. [23446]
Extensions for Independence [11945]
Fidelco Guide Dog Found. [16846]
Fishing Has No Boundaries [23414]
Found. Fighting Blindness [16847]
Found. for Sci. and Disability [11946]
Free Wheelchair Mission [11947]
Freedom Is Not Free [12596]
Friends of Libraries for Blind and Physically Handicapped Individuals in North America [10357]
Global Deaf Connection [12274]
Goodwill Indus. Intl. [11949]
Goodwill Indus. Volunteer Services [11950]
Guide Dog Found. for the Blind [16849]
Guide Dog Users, Inc. [16850]
Guide Dogs of Am. [16851]
Guide Dogs for the Blind [16852]
Guiding Eyes for the Blind [16853]
Handicapped Scuba Assn. [23344]
HEAR Center [14756]
Hear Now [14757]
Hearing Loss Assn. of Am. [14759]
Helen Keller Intl. [16854]
Helen Keller Natl. Center for Deaf-Blind Youths and Adults [14760]
Help the Helpless [12405]
Help Hospitalized Veterans [13351]
Helping Hands for the Blind [13379]
Homes for Our Troops [21302]
Hospitalized Veterans Writing Proj. [16321]
Independent Visually Impaired Enterprisers [16855]
Indoor Sports Club [11951]
Inter-American Conductive Educ. Assn. [9146]
Intl. Assn. of Rehabilitation Professionals [16322]
Intl. Child Amputee Network [11954]
Intl. Handicappers' Net [21502]
Intl. Hearing Dog, Inc. [14762]
Intl. Hearing Soc. [14763]
Intl. Lutheran Deaf Assn. [20217]

A star before a book entry number signifies that the name is not listed separately, but is mentioned within the entry.

Intl. Post Polio Support Org. [16048]
Intl. Wheelchair Aviators [21457]
Intl. Wheelchair Road Racers Club [23346]
InTouch Networks [16860]
JBI Intl. - Jewish Braille Inst. of Am. [16861]
Jewish Guild for the Blind [16862]
Job Accommodation Network [11955]
Just One Break [11957]
Leader Dogs for the Blind [16864]
A Leg To Stand On [12659]
Lutheran Braille Evangelism Assn. [16866]
Lutheran Braille Workers [16867]
MAB Community Services [16868]
Mail for Me Club [11621]
March of Dimes Birth Defects Found. [13756]
Mobility Intl. USA [11961]
Model Secondary School for the Deaf [14766]
MOVE Intl.: Mobility Opportunities Via Educ. -
    USA [11962]
MUMS Natl. Parent-to-Parent Network [16541]
NADD - An Assn. for Persons with Developmental
    Disabilities and Mental Hea. Needs [12552]
Natl. Ability Center [23347]
Natl. Accreditation Coun. for Agencies Serving the
    Blind and Visually Impaired [16870]
Natl. Alliance for Accessible Golf [23348]
Natl. Alliance of Blind Students [16871]
Natl. AMBUCS [11964]
Natl. Amputation Found. [11965]
Natl. Amputee Golf Assn. [23349]
Natl. Assn. of ADA Coordinators [11966]
Natl. Assn. for the Advancement of Orthotics and
    Prosthetics [15786]
Natl. Assn. of the Deaf [14767]
Natl. Assn. of Disability Evaluating Professionals
    [14575]
Natl. Assn. for Parents of Children With Visual
    Impairments [16873]
Natl. Assn. of the Physically Handicapped [11967]
Natl. Assn. of Rehabilitation Instructors [16324]
Natl. Assn. of School Nurses for the Deaf [14768]
Natl. Assn. of State Veterans Homes [13354]
Natl. Assn. for Visually Handicapped [16874]
Natl. Black Assn. for Speech-Language and Hear-
    ing [16448]
Natl. Braille Assn. [16875]
Natl. Braille Press [16876]
Natl. Captioning Inst. [14769]
Natl. Catholic Off. for the Deaf [19675]
Natl. Catholic Partnership on Disability [19676]
Natl. Coun. on Independent Living [11968]
Natl. Coun. on Rehabilitation Educ. [16329]
Natl. Disability Rights Network [11970]
Natl. Disability Sports Alliance [23353]
Natl. Dissemination Center for Children with Dis-
    abilities [11971]
Natl. Fed. of the Blind [16877]
Natl. Found. of Dentistry for the Handicapped
    [14179]
Natl. Hearing Conservation Assn. [14772]
Natl. Indus. for the Blind [16878]
Natl. Inst. on Deafness and Other Commun.
    Disorders Info. CH [14773]
Natl. Inst. for Rehabilitation Engg. [11972]
Natl. Odd Shoe Exchange [11974]
Natl. Order of Trench Rats [20766]
Natl. Org. Caring for Kids [11638]
Natl. Org. of Nurses with Disabilities [15514]
Natl. Org. of Parents of Blind Children [16879]
Natl. Rehabilitation Assn. [16330]
Natl. Rehabilitation Info. Center [16332]
Natl. Ser. Dog Center [14774]
Natl. Theatre Workshop of the Handicapped
    [11033]
Natl. Therapeutic Recreation Soc. [16628]
Natl. Veterans Services Fund [13356]
Natl. Wheelchair Basketball Assn. [23354]
Natl. Wheelchair Poolplayer Assn. [23355]
Natl. Wheelchair Softball Assn. [23356]
Networking Proj. for Young Adults with Disabilities
    [11975]
NISH [11976]
North Amer. Riding for the Handicapped Assn.
    [23357]
North Amer. Squirrel Assn. [22773]

NTID's Center on Employment [12095]
One-Arm Dove Hunt Assn. [23358]
The One Shoe Crew [11977]
Opportunity Plus [11978]
Oral Hearing-Impaired Sect. [14775]
Paralyzed Veterans of Am. [20768]
Parents' Sect. of the Alexander Graham Bell
    Assn. for the Deaf and Hard of Hearing [14776]
Paws With a Cause [11979]
People-to-People Comm. on Disability [11980]
Peter Burwash Intl. Special Tennis Programs
    [23908]
Phone-TTY [14777]
Physically Challenged Golf Assn. [23359]
Pilot Dogs [16881]
Post-Polio Hea. Intl. [11981]
Praying Hands Ranches [23360]
Prevent Blindness Am. [16882]
P.R.I.D.E. Found. - Promote Real Independence
    for the Disabled and Elderly [11982]
Proj. Magic [16634]
Protestant Guild for Human Services [16884]
Rebuilding Together [12337]
Recording for the Blind and Dyslexic [16885]
Registry of Interpreters for the Deaf [14778]
Rehabilitation Engg. and Assistive Tech. Soc. of
    North Am. [11983]
Rehabilitation Intl. [16333]
Res. to Prevent Blindness [16886]
Res. and Training Center on Independent Living
    [11984]
School Nurse Achievement Prog. [15525]
Sect. for Long Term Care and Rehabilitation
    [14894]
Siblings for Significant Change [11987]
Sister Kenny Rehabilitation Inst. [16335]
Skating Assn. for the Blind and Handicapped
    [23740]
Ski for Light [23361]
Soc. for Disability Stud. [11988]
Special Olympics [23362]
Special Recreation for disABLED Intl. [11989]
Spina Bifida Assn. of Am. [16458]
Support Dogs, Inc. [11990]
Tee it up for the Troops [13357]
Telecommunications for the Deaf and Hard of
    Hearing, Inc. [14780]
United Cerebral Palsy Associations [13935]
U.S. Assn. for Blind Athletes [23363]
U.S. Blind Golf Assn. [23364]
U.S. Power Soccer Assn. [23783]
U.S. Quad Rugby Assn. [23705]
Universal Wheelchair Football Assn. [23368]
USA Deaf Sports Fed. [23369]
Veterans Educ. Proj. [13358]
Visually Impaired Veterans of Am. [16891]
Vocational Evaluation and Career Assessment
    Professionals [16337]
VSA arts [11993]
Wheelchair Motorcycle Assn. [23370]
Wheelchair Sports, USA [23371]
World Ability Fed. [11995]
World Inst. on Disability [11996]
World Rehabilitation Fund [11997]
Xavier Soc. for the Blind [16892]
Handicapped; Adventures in Movement for the
    [16597]
Handicapped Aid Program - U.S.A. - Address
    unknown since 2006.
Handicapped Artists of America - Defunct.
Handicapped; Assn. for Educ. of the Visually
    [★16833]
Handicapped Assn; North Amer. Riding for the
    [23357]
Handicapped; The Assn. for the Severely [★11991]
Handicapped; Bibles for the Blind and Visually
    [19511]
Handicapped Boaters Assn. - Defunct.
Handicapped; Carleton E. Morse Radio Programs for
    the Blind and [★22929]
Handicapped Children and Youth; Natl. Info. Center
    for [★11971]
Handicapped Children and Youth; Parents Campaign
    for [★11971]
Handicapped; Christian League for the [★11952]

Handicapped; CH on the [★11933]
Handicapped; Disabled and Alone/Life Services for
    the [11941]
Handicapped; Div. for Physically [★9141]
Handicapped; Div. for Physically [★11998]
Handicapped; Div. for the Visually [★9145]
The Handicapped and Elderly Travelers Assn. -
    Defunct.
Handicapped; Found. for Sci. and the [★11946]
Handicapped - Ho Chi Minh City; Vietnam As-
    sistance for the [IO]
Handicapped, Homebound and Hospitalized; Div. on
    Physically [★9141]
Handicapped, Homebound and Hospitalized; Div. on
    Physically [★11998]
Handicapped, Inc; Guide Dogs for the [★11922]
Handicapped Individuals in North America; Friends
    of Libraries for Blind and Physically [10357]
Handicapped; Natl. Accreditation Coun. for Agencies
    Serving the Blind and Visually [★16870]
Handicapped; Natl. Aid to Visually [★16874]
Handicapped; Natl. Assn. for the Craniofacially
    [★14061]
Handicapped; Natl. Assn. of the Physically [11967]
Handicapped; Natl. Assn. for Visually [★16874]
Handicapped; Natl. Found. of Dentistry for the
    [14179]
Handicapped; Natl. Indus. for the Severely [★11976]
Handicapped; Natl. Info. Center for the [★11971]
Handicapped; Natl. Theatre Workshop of the [11033]
Handicapped Organized Women [★11978]
Handicapped; People-to-People Comm. for the
    [★11980]
Handicapped Physicians; Amer. Soc. of [11919]
Handicapped Radio Amateurs; Intl. Order of
    [★21502]
Handicapped Scuba Assn. [23344], 1104 El Prado,
    San Clemente, CA 92672-4637, (949)498-4540
Handicapped Scuba Association [IO], San Clem-
    ente, CA, United States
Handicapped; Skating Assn. for the Blind and
    [23740]
Handicapped; Special Interest Comm. for Computers
    and the Physically [★6803]
Handicapped; Special Interest Gp. for Computers
    and the Physically [★6803]
Handicapped Sports; Natl. [★23343]
Handicapped Sports and Recreation Assn; Natl.
    [★23343]
Handicapped; Support Dogs for the [★11990]
Handicapped Travel Club [22952], c/o Roland
    Winters, Jr., Pres., 604 Twilight St., Placentia, CA
    92870, (714)524-2700
Handicappers' Net; Intl. [21502]
Handicaps; Assn. for Persons with Severe [★11991]
Handicaps; Natl. Info. Center for Children and Youth
    with [★11971]
Handicaps Welfare Assn. [IO], Singapore, Singapore
Handicraft Assn. of Nepal [IO], Kathmandu, Nepal
Handidactis [IO], Scarborough, ON, Canada
Handkerchief Industry Assn. - Defunct.
Handlers' Assn; Intl. Disc Dog [23373]
Handlers Assn; Professional [22346]
Handlers, Watchmen, Messengers, and Gp. Lead-
    ers; Natl. Post Off. Mail [★24171]
Handling and Logistics Engineers; Natl. Inst. of
    Packaging, [7427]
Handloom Export Promotion Coun. [IO], Chennai,
    India
Handoverprint Stud. and Res. Gp; Russian Zone
    [22864]
Hands Across America - Defunct.
Hands for Help Nepal [IO], Kathmandu, Nepal
Hands of Mercy [12291], PO Box 320735, Cocoa
    Beach, FL 32932-0735, (321)799-9445
Hands Off Russian Comm. [★IO]
Hands On Sci. Outreach [IO], Silver Spring, MD,
    United States
Hands On Sci. Outreach [8067], 12118 Heritage
    Park Cir., Silver Spring, MD 20906, (301)929-2330
HandsNet [12641], PO Box 90477, San Jose, CA
    95109
Handsplit Red Cedar Shake Assn. [★1640]
Handsplit Red Cedar Shake Assn. [★IO]
Handsplit Shake Bur; Red Cedar Shingle and
    [★1640]

Reference to "IO" in place of a book number signifies that the association may be found in the 45th edition of International Organizations.

Handweavers Guild of Am. **[22158]**, 1255 Buford Hwy., Ste. 211, Suwanee, GA 30024, (678)730-0010

Handwriting Anal. Found; Amer. **[11206]**

Handwriting Analysts; Amer. Assn. of **[11205]**

Handwriting Analysts, Intl. - Address unknown since 2002.

Handwriting Found. - Address unknown since 1995.

Handy-Cap Horizons - Defunct.

Hanen Centre **[IO]**, Toronto, ON, Canada

Haney Family Assn. - Address unknown since 2003.

Hang Glider Assn. - Defunct.

Hang Glider Assn; Southern California **[★23044]**

Hang Glider Club; Peninsula **[★23044]**

Hang Glider Mfrs. Assn. of America - Defunct.

Hang Gliding
Soaring Soc. of Am. **[23043]**
U.S. Hang Gliding and Paragliding Assn. **[23044]**
U.S. Powered Paragliding Assn. **[23643]**

Hang Gliding Assn; U.S. **[★23044]**

Hangar and Industrial Door Technical Coun. - Defunct.

Hank Snow Fan Club - Defunct.

Hank Williams Appreciation Intl. Fan Club - Address unknown since 1989.

Hank Williams Intl. Fan Club **[24905]**, c/o Mary H. Wallace, Pres., PO Box 280, Georgiana, AL 36033, (334)376-9821

Hank Williams Jr. Fan Club **[24906]**, PO Box 1849, Madison, TN 37116, (615)865-8671

Hank Williams, Sr. Intl. Fan Club **[★24905]**

Hankes Found. **[10301]**, 1768 Colfax Ave. S, Minneapolis, MN 55403, (612)374-2453

Hanley-Hazelden Center **[★13244]**

Hanoverian Soc; Amer. **[4823]**

Hans Christian Andersen Soc. of Copenhagen **[IO]**, Hillerod, Denmark

Hans/Henry Segrist Family Org. **[20927]**, 145 New Haven Dr., Urbana, OH 43078, (937)653-6500

Hansard Soc. **[IO]**, London, United Kingdom

Hansen's Disease
Amer. Leprosy Missions **[15007]**
Damien-Dutton Soc. for Leprosy Aid **[15008]**
Intl. Christian Leprosy Mission **[15009]**
Leonard Wood Memorial - Amer. Leprosy Found. **[15010]**

Hanuman Found. **[12347]**, 223 N Guadalupe St., Box 269, Santa Fe, NM 87501-1850, (505)982-1176

Hapki Hae; U.S. **[23606]**

Hapoel Hamizrachi; Women's Org. of **[★20136]**

Hapoel Hamizrachi Women's Org. **[★20136]**

Hapoel Hamizrachi Women's Org. **[★IO]**

Happiness Advancement; Assn. for **[18046]**

Happiness Baby Club - Address unknown since 1999.

Happiness of Womanhood - Defunct.

Happy Family Org; James **[20956]**

Happy Hours Brotherhood - Defunct.

Happy Household Pet Cat Club **[21909]**, c/o Dorothy Lewis, Treas., 14508 Chester Ave., Saratoga, CA 95070

Hapsburg Monarchy; U.S. Comm. to Promote Stud. of the History of the **[★9628]**

Harbor History Associates; Pearl **[10144]**

Harbors Cooperative; Clean **[3070]**

Harbour Lights Collectors Soc. **[22034]**, PO Box 459, West Kennebunk, ME 04094-0459, (800)365-1219

Hard Fibres Assn. - Defunct.

Hard Hat Brotherhood **[19257]**, 8449 Parkridge Dr., Dexter, MI 48130, (734)846-2283

Hard Hatted Women **[4040]**, 3043 Superior Ave., Cleveland, OH 44114, (216)861-6500

Hard of Hearing; League for the **[14765]**

Hardanger Fiddle Assn. of Am. **[10606]**, PO Box 23046, Minneapolis, MN 55423-0046

Hardboard Assn; Amer. **[★1643]**

Harden - Hardin - Harding Family Assn. **[20928]**, 2500 Winningham Rd., Crewe, VA 23930, (434)645-8595

Hardin - Harding Family Assn; Harden - **[20928]**

Harding Family Assn; Harden - Hardin - **[20928]**

Hardware
Aircraft Locknut Mfrs. Assn. **[1814]**

Amer. Hardware Mfrs. Assn. **[1815]**
Amer. Ladder Inst. **[1816]**
Amer. Metal Detector Mfrs. Assn. **[1817]**
Antique Doorknob Collectors of Am. **[21971]**
Assoc. Locksmiths of Am. **[1818]**
Assn. of Building Hardware Mfrs. **[IO]**
British Hardware Fed. **[IO]**
British Hardware and Housewares Mfrs'. Assn. **[IO]**
Builders Hardware Mfrs. Assn. **[1819]**
Canadian Hardware and Housewares Mfrs. Assn. **[IO]**
Cold Formed Parts and Machine Inst. **[1820]**
CompactFlash Assn. **[6723]**
Door and Hardware Inst. **[1821]**
Door and Hardware Inst. **[IO]**
European Confed. of Natl. Associations of Mfrs. of Insulated Wire and Cable **[IO]**
European Fed. of Associations of Lock and Builders' Hardware Manufacturers **[IO]**
Fed. of British Hand Tool Mfrs. **[IO]**
Hand Tools Inst. **[1822]**
Indus. Fasteners Inst. **[1823]**
Inst. of Spring Tech. **[IO]**
Intl. Fed. of Hardware and Housewares Associations **[IO]**
Intl. Magnetics Assn. **[IO]**
Intl. Magnetics Assn. **[1824]**
Intl. Saw and Knife Assn. **[2390]**
Intl. Staple, Nail and Tool Assn. **[1825]**
Intl. Staple, Nail and Tool Assn. **[IO]**
Intl. Wire and Machinery Assn. **[IO]**
Irish Hardware and Building Materials Assn. **[IO]**
Lighter Assn. **[1826]**
Member Insurance Assn. **[1827]**
MultiMediaCard Assn. **[7305]**
Natl. Fastener Distributors Assn. **[1828]**
North Amer. Retail Hardware Assn. **[1829]**
North Amer. Sawing Assn. **[1830]**
Power Tool Inst. **[1831]**
Precision Machined Products Assn. **[1832]**
Screen Mfrs. Assn. **[1833]**
Screen Manufacturers Association **[IO]**
SD Card Assn. **[6743]**
Security Hardware Distributors Assn. **[1834]**
Software in the Public Interest **[6777]**
Specialty Tools and Fasteners Distributors Assn. **[2069]**
Spring Mfrs. Inst. **[1835]**
Taiwan Hand Tool Mfrs'. Assn. **[IO]**
The Transformer Assn. **[IO]**
The Transformer Assn. **[1836]**
U.S. Hardware Indus. Assn. **[1837]**
Valve Mfrs. Assn. of Am. **[1838]**
Valve Repair Coun. **[1839]**
Wire and Cable Indus. Suppliers Assn. **[1231]**
Wire Fabricators Assn. **[1840]**
Wire Fabricators Association **[IO]**

Hardware Affiliated Representatives - Defunct.

Hardware Assn. **[★1837]**

Hardware Assn; Natl. Builders' **[★1821]**

Hardware Consultants; Amer. Soc. of Architectural **[★1821]**

Hardware Mfrs. Statistical Assn. **[★1819]**

Hardwood Assn; Northwest **[★1630]**

Hardwood Assn; Western **[1630]**

Hardwood Coun. **[4056]**, PO Box 525, Oakmont, PA 15139

Hardwood Coun. **[IO]**, Oakmont, PA, United States

Hardwood Dimension Mfrs. Assn. **[★1656]**

Hardwood Distributor's Assn. **[1647]**, c/o Heidler Hardwood Lumber, Co., 2559 S Damen Ave., Chicago, IL 60608, (773)847-7444

Hardwood Export Coun; Amer. **[1603]**

Hardwood Export Trade Coun. **[★1603]**

Hardwood Lumber Mfrs. Assn; Southern **[★1648]**

Hardwood Mfrs. Assn. **[1648]**, 400 Penn Center Blvd., Ste. 530, Pittsburgh, PA 15235, (412)829-0770

Hardwood Manufacturers, Inc; Appalachian **[1638]**

Hardwood Mfrs. Inst. **[★1648]**

Hardwood Plywood Assn. of Am; Imported **[★1609]**

Hardwood Plywood Assn; Imported **[★1609]**

Hardwood Plywood Inst. **[★1649]**

Hardwood Plywood Mfrs. Assn. **[★1649]**

Hardwood Plywood and Veneer Assn. **[1649]**, 1825 Michael Faraday Dr., PO Box 2789, Reston, VA 20195-0789, (703)435-2900

Hardwood Producers; Southern **[★1648]**

Hardwood Products Assn; Imported **[★1609]**

Hardwood Products Assn; Intl. **[★1609]**

Hardwood Res. Coun. **[★1652]**

Hardwood Res. Coun. **[★IO]**

Hardwood Veneer Assn; Fine **[★1649]**

Hardwoods Amer. Walnut Assn; Fine **[★1635]**

Hardy Fern Found. **[4977]**, PO Box 3797, Federal Way, WA 98063-3797

Hardy Plant Soc. **[IO]**, Pershore, United Kingdom

Hare Club; Amer. Belgian **[5131]**

Haribon Found. **[IO]**, Quezon City, Philippines

Harlequin Rabbit Club; Amer. **[5136]**

Harless Family Assn. - Address unknown since 2006.

Harley Hummer Club **[22679]**, c/o Brent Dugan, 13 Sylvan Rd., High Bridge, NJ 08829-1716

Harley Owners Gp. **[22680]**, PO Box 453, Milwaukee, WI 53201, (414)343-4056

Harlow Conservation Volunteers **[IO]**, Harlow, United Kingdom

Harm Reduction Coalition **[IO]**, New York, NY, United States

Harm Reduction Coalition **[12042]**, 22 W 27th St., 5th Fl., New York, NY 10001, (212)213-6376

Harmelink Family Assn. - Address unknown since 1995.

Harmonica; Soc. for the Preservation and Advancement of the **[10703]**

Harmonie Associates **[10032]**, c/o Pennsylvania Historical and Museum Commn., Old Economy Village, 270 16th St., Ambridge, PA 15003-2225, (724)266-1803

Harmonious Human Being; Inst. for the Development of the **[12351]**

Harmony Assn; United in Gp. **[10715]**

Harmony Found. **[10607]**, 225 W Washington St., Ste. 2330, Chicago, IL 60606, (312)701-1001

Harmony Found. **[IO]**, Victoria, BC, Canada

Harmony House for Cats **[11404]**, PO Box 18098, Chicago, IL 60618-0098, (773)463-6667

Harmony of Races in the U.S; Coalition for **[18198]**

Harness and Allied Trades Assn; Saddle, **[2419]**

Harness Horse Youth Found. **[23496]**, 16575 Carey Rd., Westfield, IN 46074, (317)867-5877

Harness Horsemen Intl. **[23497]**

Harness Manufacturer's Assn; Wiring **[1199]**

Harness Racing Communications **[★23519]**

Harness Racing Museum and Hall of Fame **[23498]**, PO Box 590, Goshen, NY 10924, (845)294-6330

Harness Tracks of Am. **[23499]**, 4640 E Sunrise Dr., Ste. 200, Tucson, AZ 85718-4576, (520)529-2525

Harness Tracks Security - Defunct.

Harness Writers' Assn; U.S. **[3170]**

Harold Inst. - Defunct.

Harp Renaissance Soc. - Defunct.

Harp Soc. of Am; Scottish **[10695]**

Harp Soc; Amer. **[10538]**

Harp Soc; Historical **[10609]**

Harriet Beecher Stowe Center **[9655]**, 77 Forest St., Hartford, CT 06105, (860)522-9258

Harriet Beecher Stowe Soc. **[11173]**, c/o Nancy Lusignan Schultz, Treas., Dept. of English, Salem State Coll., 352 Lafayette St., Salem, MA 01970-5333

Harris, Joel Chandler
A-T Medical Res. Found. **[14436]**
Uncle Remus Museum **[9717]**

Harris Tweed Authority **[IO]**, Stornoway, United Kingdom

Harrison Family Assn. **[20929]**

Harrison Fisher Soc. - Address unknown since 2002.

Harrison Found; Pres. Benjamin **[11142]**

Harrow Assn. of Disabled People **[IO]**, Harrow, United Kingdom

Harry Benjamin Gender Dysphoria Assn; Natl. **[★13103]**

Harry Benjamin Intl. Gender Dysphoria Assn. **[★13103]**

Harry Benjamin Intl. Gender Dysphoria Assn. **[★IO]**

Harry Collector's Soc; Debbie **[24872]**

Harry Connick, Jr. Fan Club **[24907]**, 323 Broadway, Cambridge, MA 02139, (617)868-5858

A star before a book entry number signifies that the name is not listed separately, but is mentioned within the entry.

Harry Connick, Jr. Fan Club [IO], Cambridge, MA, United States

Harry Lundberg School of Seamanship; Seafarers/ [★24132]

Harry S. Truman Lib. Inst. for Natl. and Intl. Affairs [11120], 500 W U.S. Hwy. 24, Independence, MO 64050, (816)268-8248

Harry S. Truman Lib. Inst. for Natl. and Intl. Affairs [IO], Independence, MO, United States

Harry S. Truman Scholarship Found. [8430], 712 Jackson Pl. NW, Washington, DC 20006, (202)395-4831

Harry Singer Found. [18450], PO Box 223159, Carmel, CA 93923, (831)625-4223

Harry Stephen Keeler Soc. [9656], c/o Richard Polt, Ed., 4745 Winton Rd., Cincinnati, OH 45232, (513)591-1226

Harry Stephen Keeler Society [IO], Cincinnati, OH, United States

Hart Family Fan Club - Address unknown since 1989.

Hartford Found; John A. [11291]

Hartford Seminary [20100], 77 Sherman St., Hartford, CT 06105-2260, (860)509-9500

Hartford Seminary [IO], Hartford, CT, United States

Hartford Whalers Booster Club [25006], PO Box 273, Hartford, CT 06141, (860)225-0265

Harting Family Assn. - Defunct.

Hartlepool Special Needs Support Gp. [IO], Hartlepool, United Kingdom

Hartshorn Family Assn. [IO], Conover, NC, United States

Hartshorn Family Assn. [20930], 1204 4th St. Dr. SE, Conover, NC 28613, (828)464-4981

Hartz Club of Am. [22772], c/o Bob Buckles, Sec.-Treas., 9324 Paramount Blvd., Downey, CA 90240, (562)927-6247

Harvard Environmental Law Soc. [5695], 1563 Massachusetts Ave., Harvard Law School, Pound Hall, Cambridge, MA 02138

Harvard Film Soc. - Address unknown since 2002.

Harvard Injury Control Res. Center [16690], Harvard School of Public Hea., 677 Huntington Ave., 3rd Fl., Boston, MA 02115, (617)432-3420

Harvest [20280], PO Box 2670, Phoenix, AZ 85002, (602)258-1083

Harvest [IO], Phoenix, AZ, United States

Harvest; America's Second [12388]

Harvest Found. [★20280]

Harvest Found. [★IO]

Harvest; Future [4089]

Harvest Help [IO], Telford, United Kingdom

Harvest Intl; Sustainable [4115]

Harvest; Second [★12388]

Harvest; U.S.A. [12402]

Harvey Cushing Soc. [★15410]

Harvey Cushing Soc. [★IO]

Harvey Soc. [15168], c/o Marie Filbin, PhD, Sec., City Univ. of New York, Hunter Coll., 695 Park Ave., New York, NY 10065, (212)772-5270

Hasbrouck Family Assn. [20931], PO Box 176, New Paltz, NY 12561, (845)255-3223

Hashbrown Soc. of Am. Network - Address unknown since 2001.

Hashem; Tzivos [10290]

Hashomer [★20140]

Hashomer Hadati, Bnei Akiva [★20178]

Hashomer Hatzair Socialist Zionist Youth Movement [★20140]

Hashomer Hatzair Zionist Youth Movement [20140], 114 W 26th St., No. 1001, New York, NY 10001-0012, (212)627-2830

Hashomer Hatzair Zionist Youth Org. [★20140]

Haskins Soc; Charles Homer [10459]

Haskins Soc. for Viking, Anglo-Saxon, Anglo-Norman, and Angevin History [★10459]

Haskins Soc. for Viking, Anglo-Saxon, Anglo-Norman, and Angevin History [★IO]

Hasroun Men's and St. Laba Ladies Charity Societies; United [19732]

HASTI Friends of the Elephants - Defunct.

Hastings Center [12125], 21 Malcolm Gordon Rd., Garrison, NY 10524-4125, (845)424-4040

Hat Block and Die Makers Assn. - Defunct.

Hat Coun. - Address unknown since 1995.

Hat Inst. - Address unknown since 1995.

Hate Free Zone [17392], 1227 S Weller St., Ste. A, Seattle, WA 98144, (206)723-2203

Hatefutsoth; Amer. Friends of Beth [10253]

Hathaway Family Assn. [20932], 2231 Riverside Ave., Somerset, MA 02726-4104

Hatpin Soc; Amer. [21961]

Hatpins and Hatpin Holders; Intl. Collector's Club of [22050]

Hatters' Fur Cutters Assn. of America - Defunct.

Hatters Machinery and Equipment Assn. - Defunct.

Hatton Heritage Assn. - Address unknown since 2001.

Hatz Club - Address unknown since 2002.

Hatzaad Harishon - Defunct.

Hatzair Zionist Youth Movement; Hashomer [20140]

Haunt Hunters - Defunct.

Hauntings; Amer. Assn. for Critical Sci. Investigation into Claimed [7437]

Hauptverband der Deutschen Schuhindustrie [★IO]

Hauptverband des Osterreichischen Buchhandels [★IO]

Haut Commissariat des Nations Unies pour les Refugies [★IO]

Havana Rabbit Breeders Assn. [5145], c/o Julia Rittenour, Sec.-Treas., 5554 Old State Rd., Whittemore, MI 48770, (989)387-5095

Havana Silk Dog Assn. of Am. [22282], PO Box 237, Goochland, VA 23063

Havergal Brian Soc. [IO], Watford, United Kingdom

HAVi [6513], 40994 Encyclopedia Cir., Fremont, CA 94538, (510)979-1394

Haviland Collectors Intl. Found. [21927], PO Box 271383, Fort Collins, CO 80527

Haviland Family Org. [20933], 19662 Westover Ave., Rocky River, OH 44116-4037, (440)331-6444

Having Fun With Elvis - Defunct.

Haviva Educational Found; Givat [18059]

Havurah Comm; Natl. [20168]

Havurah Coordinating Comm; Natl. [★20168]

Hawaii Agriculture Res. Center [5228], 99-193 Aiea Heights Dr., Ste. 300, Aiea, HI 96701-3911, (808)487-5561

Hawaii; Chinese Chamber of Commerce of [24309]

Hawaii Heptachlor Res. and Educ. Found. [13325], c/o Sherry P. Broder, Esq., Attorney-at-Law, 841 Bishop St., Ste. 800, Honolulu, HI 96813, (808)589-2963

Hawaii; Japanese Chamber of Commerce and Industry of [24345]

Hawaii; Pacific Orchid Soc. of [22536]

Hawaii Surfing Assn. - Defunct.

Hawaiian Affairs; Inst. for the Advancement of [10883]

Hawaiian Culture and Arts Prog; Native [10884]

Hawaiian Intl. Billfish Assn. [★22440]

Hawaiian Intl. Billfish Assn. [★IO]

Hawaiian Intl. Billfish Tournament [IO], Kailua-Kona, HI, United States

Hawaiian Intl. Billfish Tournament [22440], PO Box 29638, Honolulu, HI 96820, (808)836-3422

Hawaiian Sugar Planters' Assn. [★5228]

HAWK Fed. [★9359]

Hawk Migration Assn. of North Am. [7418], c/o John Weeks, Membership Sec., 51 Pheasant Run, North Granby, CT 06060

Hawk Mountain Sanctuary [5324], 1700 Hawk Mountain Rd., Kempton, PA 19529, (610)756-6961

Hawk and Owl Trust [IO], Taunton, United Kingdom

Hawkes Bay Br. of the Royal Soc. of New Zealand [IO], Hastings, New Zealand

Hawkes Family Assn; Adam [20772]

Hawkfarm One Design Assn. - Address unknown since 2001.

Hawkins Assn. [20934], PO Box 2392, Setauket, NY 11733

Hawkwatch Intl. [7419], 1800 S West Temple, No. 226, Salt Lake City, UT 84115-5801, (801)484-6808

Hawkwatch Intl. [IO], Salt Lake City, UT, United States

Hawley Family; Soc. of the [21054]

Hawley Soc. [★21054]

Hawthorne Soc; Nathaniel [9694]

Hay Assn; Natl. [1360]

Hay Fever Prevention Soc. - Address unknown since 1995.

Hayes Fan Network; Wade [24990]

Hayes Lib. and Museum; Rutherford B. [★11148]

Hayes Presidential Center; Rutherford B. [11148]

Haymore Family Org. [20935], 437 Pimlico Dr., St. George, UT 84790, (435)656-4485

Haynes-Apperson Owners Club [21653]

Hayworth Fan Club; Rita [24769]

Hazard Control Mgt; Bd. of Certified [3440]

Hazard Control Manager Certification Bd; Intl. [★3440]

Hazardous Articles; Conf. on Safe Trans. of [3562]

Hazardous Articles; Coun. on the Safe Trans. of [★3562]

Hazardous Material

Acad. of Certified Hazardous Materials Managers [4804]

Bd. of Certified Hazard Control Mgt. [3440]

Conf. on Safe Trans. of Hazardous Articles [3562]

Dangerous Goods Advisory Coun. [3563]

Environmental Tech. Coun. [3993]

Hazardous Materials Training and Res. Inst. [7157]

Inst. of Hazardous Materials Mgt. [4805]

Intl. Campaign to Ban Landmines [17431]

Intl. Healthcare Safety Professional Certification Bd. [16379]

Intl. Inst. for Baubiologie and Ecology [4513]

Military Toxics Proj. [5033]

Mine Warfare Assn. [18592]

Natl. Assn. of Mold Professionals [1330]

Natl. Org. of Remediators and Mold Inspectors [1331]

Natl. Registry of Environmental Professionals [4593]

North Amer. Hazardous Materials Mgt. Assn. [4806]

Occupational Knowledge Intl. [5099]

Sheet Metal Occupational Hea. Inst. Trust [12991]

Hazardous Materials Advisory Comm. [★3563]

Hazardous Materials Advisory Coun. [★3563]

Hazardous Materials Control Resources Inst. - Address unknown since 2003.

Hazardous Materials Training and Res. Inst. [7157], PO Box 2068, Cedar Rapids, IA 52406, (319)398-5678

Hazardous Waste Fed. - Defunct.

Hazardous Waste Proj; Household [5269]

Hazardous Waste Services Assn. - Defunct.

Hazardous Waste Treatment Coun. [★3993]

Hazardous Wastes

Assn. of Lighting and Mercury Recyclers [5168]

Assn. of State and Territorial Solid Waste Mgt. Officials [6353]

Clean Production Action [4631]

Concerned Citizens for Nuclear Safety [18147]

Downwinders [18150]

Global Alliance for Incinerator Alternatives [5268]

Intl. Healthcare Safety Professional Certification Bd. [16379]

Mine Warfare Assn. [18592]

Natl. Registry of Environmental Professionals [4593]

Natl. Solid Wastes Mgt. Assn. [3579]

Natl. Waste Prevention Coalition [4001]

North Amer. Hazardous Materials Mgt. Assn. [4806]

The Pesticide Stewardship Alliance [7068]

Zero Waste Alliance [5272]

Hazards Res. and Applications Info. Center; Natural [7355]

Hazelbaker Families [20936], PO Box 450154, Grove, OK 74345-0154, (918)786-2360

Hazelden Center for Youth and Families [★13244]

Hazelden Found. [13244], PO Box 11-C03, Center City, MN 55012-0011, (651)213-4200

Hazelden Found. Center [★13244]

Hazelden Renewal Center [★13244]

Hazelnut and Products Exporters Union [IO], Istanbul, Turkey

Hazen Family Assn. - Defunct.

HB Tract Assn. - Address unknown since 1999.

H.C. Andersen-Samfundet i Kobenhavn [★IO]

H.C. Fry Glass Soc. [22556], PO Box 41, Beaver, PA 15009

Reference to "IO" in place of a book number signifies that the association may be found in the 45th edition of International Organizations.

HCJB World Radio [20344], PO Box 39800, Colorado Springs, CO 80949-9800, (719)590-9800
HCJB World Radio [IO], Colorado Springs, CO, United States
Head Injured Soc. of Western Australia [IO], Applecross, Australia
Head Injury
Acoustic Neuroma Assn. [15816]
Amer. Acad. of Otolaryngology - Head and Neck Surgery [15817]
Amer. Bd. of Otolaryngology [15818]
Amer. Head and Neck Soc. [15819]
Amer. Headache Soc. [14531]
Amer. Otological Soc. [15822]
Amer. Rhinologic Soc. [15823]
Assn. for the Rehabilitation of the Brain Injured [IO]
Brain Injury Assn. of Am. [14528]
Brain Injury Assn. of Nova Scotia [IO]
Brain Injury Rsrc. Center [16317]
Campbell River Head Injury Support Soc. [IO]
Coma Recovery Assn. [14029]
Comox Valley Head Injury Soc. [IO]
Ear Found. [15825]
European Brain Injury Consortium [IO]
Found. for Advances in Medicine and Sci. [14025]
Head Injured Soc. of Western Australia [IO]
Head Injury Assn. of Durham Region [IO]
Head Injury Assn. of Fort Erie and District [IO]
Head Injury Soc. of New Zealand [IO]
Headway Ireland - Natl. Assn. for Acquired Brain Injury [IO]
Headway - The Brain Injury Assn. [IO]
Manitoba Brain Injury Assn. [IO]
Natl. Assn. of State Head Injury Administrators [14529]
Natl. Guardianship Assn. [1813]
Natl. Headache Found. [14533]
Natl. Org. for Disorders of the Corpus Callosum [15350]
NBIA Disorders Assn. [15355]
Ryan's Reach [16550]
Soc. for Ear, Nose, and Throat Advances in Children [15827]
Soc. of Military Otolaryngologists - Head and Neck Surgeons [15267]
Soc. of Otorhinolaryngology and Head/Neck Nurses [15526]
Soc. of Univ. Otolaryngologists - Head and Neck Surgeons [15828]
Southland Head Injury Soc. [IO]
Vancouver Island Head Injury Soc. [IO]
Waikato Head Injury Soc. [IO]
World Org. for Human Potential [11550]
Head Injury Assn. of Durham Region [IO], Oshawa, ON, Canada
Head Injury Assn. of Fort Erie and District [IO], Fort Erie, ON, Canada
Head Injury Assn. of Ottawa Valley [IO], Ottawa, ON, Canada
Head Injury Hotline [★16317]
Head Injury Soc. of New Zealand [IO], Hamilton, New Zealand
"Head of the Monkees" Fan Club - Defunct.
Head, Neck and Facial Pain; Amer. Acad. of [★15751]
Head/Neck Nurses; Soc. of Otorhinolaryngology and [15526]
Head and Neck Soc; Amer. [15819]
Head and Neck Surgeons; Amer. Soc. of [★15819]
Head and Neck Surgeons; Soc. of [★15819]
Head and Neck Surgeons; Soc. of Military Otolaryngologists - [15267]
Head and Neck Surgeons; Soc. of Univ. Otolaryngologists - [15828]
Head and Neck Surgery; Amer. Acad. of Otolaryngology - [15817]
Head and Neck Surgery; Amer. Soc. for [★15819]
Head Start [★12588]
Head Start Assn; Natl. [9006]
Head Start Directors Association; National [★9006]
Head Start Friends Association; National [★9006]
Head Start Parent Association; National [★9006]
Head Start Staff Association; National [★9006]
Headache
Amer. Coun. for Headache Educ. [14530]

Amer. Headache Soc. [14531]
British Assn. for the Stud. of Headache [IO]
Headache Soc. of Singapore [IO]
Intl. Headache Soc. [IO]
Migraine Assn. of Ireland [IO]
Migraine Awareness Gp.: A Natl. Understanding for "Migraineurs" [14532]
Natl. Headache Found. [14533]
Headache Soc. of Singapore [IO], Singapore, Singapore
The Headhunters [★5442]
Headhunters' Assn; 80th Fighter Squadron [5442]
Headmasters Assn. - Address unknown since 2000.
Headmasters' Conf. [★IO]
Headmasters' and Headmistresses' Conf. [IO], Leicester, United Kingdom
HQ 310th Command Assn. [20702], PO Box 203, Vienna, VA 22183-0203, (540)297-5511
HQ for Ghost Investigations [★7445]
HQ for Ghost Investigations [★IO]
Headteachers' Assn. of Scotland [IO], Glasgow, United Kingdom
Headway Ireland - Natl. Assn. for Acquired Brain Injury [IO], Dublin, Ireland
Headway - The Brain Injury Assn. [IO], Nottingham, United Kingdom
Headway Victoria [IO], Northcote, Australia
Headwear Info. Bur. [238], 302 W 12th St., PHC, New York, NY 10014, (212)627-8333
Headwear Inst. of America - Address unknown since 1994.
Headwest [★IO]
Heal the Children [★11697]
Heald Family Assn. [20937]
Healers Assn; Sound [13653]
Healers League of the Natl. Spiritualist Assn. of Churches [20449], c/o Rev. E. Ann Otzelberger, Pres., 4332 Woodlynne Ln., Orlando, FL 32812
Healers Professional Associates Intl; Nurse [14831]
Healers Professional Associates; Nurse [★14831]
Healey Club of Am; Austin- [21584]
Healing Arts; Amer. Assn. of Oriental [★15024]
Healing Arts; East West Acad. of [15744]
Healing; Center for Attitudinal [★15206]
Healing Center; Jewish [★10287]
Healing the Children [11697], PO Box 9065, Spokane, WA 99209-9065, (509)327-4281
Healing; Commn. on Hea. and [★20241]
Healing; Commn. on Religious Counseling and [19445]
Healing the Culture [12788], PO Box 82842, Kenmore, WA 98028, (425)481-6563
Healing Hands Intl. [13141], 455 McNally Dr., Nashville, TN 37211, (615)832-2000
Healing Hands Intl. [IO], Nashville, TN, United States
Healing; Intl. Alliance for Animal Therapy and [13703]
Healing Ministries; Hea. and [★20241]
Healing Res. Trust [★IO]
Healing Touch Assn. of Canada [IO], Calgary, AB, Canada
Healing Touch Intl. [IO], Lakewood, CO, United States
Healing Touch Intl. [14631], 445 Union Blvd., Ste. 105, Lakewood, CO 80228, (303)989-7982
Healing Waters Intl. [13410], 534 Commons Dr., Golden, CO 80401, (303)526-7278
Healing Waters Intl. [IO], Golden, CO, United States
Health
AARP Pharmacy Services [2983]
Academic Orthopaedic Soc. [15750]
Acad. of Ambulatory Foot and Ankle Surgery [16023]
Acad. of Dental Materials [14084]
Acad. of Dentistry Intl. [14085]
Acad. of Gen. Dentistry [14086]
Acad. of Hea. Sciences [14534]
Acad. for Implants and Transplants [14087]
Acad. of Managed Care Providers [14677]
Acad. on Mental Retardation [15238]
Acad. of Operative Dentistry [14089]
Acad. of Oral Dynamics [14090]
Acad. of Osseointegration [14091]
Acad. of Pharmaceutical Res. and Sci. [15906]

Acad. of Psychosomatic Medicine [16195]
Acad. of Scientific Hypnotherapy [14913]
AcademyHealth [14535]
Accelerated Cure Proj. for Multiple Sclerosis [15301]
Accreditation Assn. for Ambulatory Hea. Care [13661]
Accreditation Commn. for Acupuncture and Oriental Medicine [15739]
Accreditation Coun. on Optometric Educ. [15710]
Accreditation Coun. for Pharmacy Educ. [15907]
Accreditation Rev. Commn. on Educ. for the Physician Asst. [15972]
Accreditation Rev. Comm. on Educ. in Surgical Tech. [15123]
Acoustic Neuroma Assn. [15816]
Action for Healthy Kids [13945]
Action on Smoking and Hea. [16431]
Actions for Intl. Solidarity - France [IO]
Acupuncturists Without Borders [13536]
Ad Hoc Gp. for Medical Res. Funding [17686]
Addiction Res. and Treatment Corp. [13213]
Adolescent Scoliosis Soc. of North Am. [16392]
Adopt a Dr. [12750]
Adult Congenital Heart Assn. [13884]
Adventist Development and Relief Agency Intl. [12826]
Advocacy Inst. [12650]
Advocate Hea. Care [14821]
Advocates for the Amer. Osteopathic Assn. [15789]
Advocates for Youth [12173]
Aerobics and Fitness Assn. of Am. [15956]
Aerospace Medical Assn. [13538]
Aesculapian Club [15982]
African-Amer. Assn. of Fitness Professionals [15957]
African Hea. For Empowerment and Development [IO]
African Medical and Res. Found. [14971]
African Medical and Res. Found. - Italy [IO]
African Medical and Res. Found. - Tanzania [IO]
AFT Healthcare [24087]
Aging in Am. [11271]
AHEAD-INC., African Hea. Educ. and Development [14536]
Aicardi Syndrome Newsl. [14437]
Aid for AIDS [13547]
Aid for Intl. Medicine [14972]
AIDS Clinical Trials Gp. [13549]
AIDS Empowerment and Treatment Intl. [13550]
AIDS Treatment Activists Coalition [11324]
Air and Surface Transport Nurses Assn. [15427]
Airlines Medical Directors Assn. [13539]
Al-Anon Family Gp. HQ, World Ser. Off. [13214]
Albert Ellis Inst. [16197]
Albinism World Alliance [15242]
Alcohol Res. Info. Ser. [13217]
Alcoholics Anonymous World Services [13218]
Alcor Life Extension Found. [14072]
All Indian Pueblo Coun. [18089]
Allergy and Asthma Network Mothers of Asthmatics [16352]
Alliance for Academic Internal Medicine [8586]
Alliance for Advancing Nonprofit Hea. Care [14606]
Alliance for Aging Res. [11272]
Alliance of Cardiovascular Professionals [13885]
Alliance for Childhood Cancer [13787]
Alliance for Eating Disorders Awareness [14297]
Alliance for Hea. Reform [17687]
Alliance for Lupus Res. [15013]
Alliance for Microbicide Development [13555]
Alliance of Minority Medical Associations [14607]
Alliance for the Prudent Use of Antibiotics [15908]
Alliance of State Pain Initiatives [15830]
Alliance of Veterinarians for the Env. [4626]
Alpha Epsilon Delta [24541]
Alpha Omega Alpha Honor Medical Soc. [24542]
Alpha Tau Delta [24559]
Alpha Zeta Omega [24567]
ALSAC/Saint Jude Children's Res. Hosp. [13946]
Alternative Hea. Professionals Assn. [13610]
Ambulatory Pediatric Assn. [15879]
Am. on the Move Found. [14537]

A star before a book entry number signifies that the name is not listed separately, but is mentioned within the entry.

Amer. Acad. of Allergy, Asthma and Immunology [13592]
Amer. Acad. of Alternative Medicine [13612]
Amer. Acad. of Ambulatory Care Nursing [15428]
Amer. Acad. for Cerebral Palsy and Developmental Medicine [13934]
Amer. Acad. of Child and Adolescent Psychiatry [16063]
Amer. Acad. of Clinical Psychiatrists [16064]
Amer. Acad. of Clinical Toxicology [16657]
Amer. Acad. of Cosmetic Surgery [14037]
Amer. Acad. of Craniofacial Pain [15751]
Amer. Acad. of Dental Gp. Practice [14094]
Amer. Acad. of Dental Practice Admin. [14095]
Amer. Acad. of Dermatology [14189]
Amer. Acad. of Disability Evaluating Physicians [14033]
Amer. Acad. of Environmental Medicine [14360]
Amer. Acad. of Esthetic Dentistry [14096]
Amer. Acad. of Facial Plastic and Reconstructive Surgery [14038]
Amer. Acad. of Family Physicians [14383]
Amer. Acad. of Fixed Prosthodontics [14097]
Amer. Acad. of Gnathologic Orthopedics [14098]
Amer. Acad. of the History of Dentistry [14100]
Amer. Acad. of HIV Medicine [13556]
Amer. Acad. of Implant Dentistry [14101]
Amer. Acad. of Medical Administrators [15045]
Amer. Acad. of Medical Administrators Res. and Educational Found. [15046]
Amer. Acad. of Medical Hypnoanalysts [14914]
Amer. Acad. of Neurological and Orthopaedic Surgeons [15409]
Amer. Acad. of Neurology [15376]
Amer. Acad. of Nurse Practitioners [15429]
Amer. Acad. of Nursing [15430]
Amer. Acad. of Ophthalmology [15656]
Amer. Acad. of Optometry [15711]
Amer. Acad. of Oral and Maxillofacial Pathology [15852]
Amer. Acad. of Oral and Maxillofacial Radiology [14104]
Amer. Acad. of Oral Medicine [14105]
Amer. Acad. of Orofacial Pain [14106]
Amer. Acad. of Orthodontics for the Gen. Practitioner [14107]
Amer. Acad. of Orthopaedic Manual Physical Therapists [15971]
Amer. Acad. of Orthopaedic Surgeons [15752]
Amer. Acad. of Orthotists and Prosthetists [15782]
Amer. Acad. of Osteopathy [15790]
Amer. Acad. of Otolaryngic Allergy and Found. [13593]
Amer. Acad. of Otolaryngology - Head and Neck Surgery [15817]
Amer. Acad. of Pediatric Dentistry [14108]
Amer. Acad. of Pediatrics [15880]
Amer. Acad. of Periodontology [14109]
Amer. Acad. of Physical Medicine and Rehabilitation [16307]
Amer. Acad. of Physician Assistants [15973]
Amer. Acad. of Podiatric Sports Medicine [16471]
Amer. Acad. of Psychoanalysis and Dynamic Psychiatry [16101]
Amer. Acad. of Psychotherapists [16198]
Amer. Acad. of Restorative Dentistry [14110]
Amer. Acad. of Sanitarians [16383]
Amer. Acad. of Sleep Medicine [16418]
Amer. Acad. of Somnology [16419]
Amer. Acad. of Sports Physicians [16472]
Amer. Acad. of Tropical Medicine [16692]
Amer. Acad. of Veterinary and Comparative Toxicology [16736]
Amer. Acad. of Veterinary Pharmacology and Therapeutics [16738]
Amer. Acupuncture Assn. [15741]
Amer. Aging Assn. [14507]
Amer. Alliance for Medical Cannabis [15020]
Amer. Alternative Medical Assn. [13613]
Amer. Ambulance Assn. [14313]
Amer. Animal Hosp. Assn. [16739]
Amer. Apitherapy Soc. [13614]
Amer. Art Therapy Assn. [16199]
Amer. Assembly for Men in Nursing [15431]
Amer. Assisted Living Nurses Assn. [15432]

Amer. Assn. for Accreditation of Ambulatory Surgery Facilities [16557]
Amer. Assn. of Ambulatory Surgery Centers [16558]
Amer. Assn. of Avian Pathologists [16740]
Amer. Assn. of Bioanalysts Bd. of Registry [15126]
Amer. Assn. of Birth Centers [15580]
Amer. Assn. of Blood Banks [13761]
Amer. Assn. of Bovine Practitioners [16741]
Amer. Assn. for Cancer Educ. [13789]
Amer. Assn. of Cardiovascular and Pulmonary Rehabilitation [13886]
Amer. Assn. of Caregiving Youth [13466]
Amer. Assn. of Certified Allergists [13594]
Amer. Assn. of Clinical Endocrinologists [14350]
Amer. Assn. of Colleges of Osteopathic Medicine [15791]
Amer. Assn. of Colleges of Pharmacy [15909]
Amer. Assn. of Colleges of Podiatric Medicine [16025]
Amer. Assn. of Community Psychiatrists [16066]
Amer. Assn. for Continuity of Care [14836]
Amer. Assn. of Critical-Care Nurses [15433]
Amer. Assn. of Dental Examiners [14112]
Amer. Assn. for Dental Res. [14113]
Amer. Assn. of Diabetes Educators [14217]
Amer. Assn. of Directors of Psychiatric Residency Training [16067]
Amer. Assn. of Dispensing Ophthalmologists [15658]
Amer. Assn. of Endodontists [14114]
Amer. Assn. of Equine Veterinary Technicians [16743]
Amer. Assn. of Eye and Ear Hospitals [14859]
Amer. Assn. of Food Hygiene Veterinarians [16745]
Amer. Assn. for Functional Orthodontics [14115]
Amer. Assn. of Genito-Urinary Surgeons [16699]
Amer. Assn. of Gynecologic Laparoscopists [15581]
Amer. Assn. for Hand Surgery [14522]
Amer. Assn. on Hea. and Disability [14235]
Amer. Assn. for Hea. Educ. [16234]
Amer. Assn. of Heart Failure Nurses [15434]
Amer. Assn. for the History of Nursing [10083]
Amer. Assn. of Homes and Services for the Aging [11273]
Amer. Assn. of Hosp. Dentists [14116]
Amer. Assn. of Hosp. Podiatrists [16026]
Amer. Assn. of Housecall Veterinarians [16746]
Amer. Assn. of Human-Animal Bond Veterinarians [13702]
Amer. Assn. of Immunologists [14929]
Amer. Assn. of Integrated Healthcare Delivery Systems [15048]
Amer. Assn. on Intellectual and Developmental Disabilities [15239]
Amer. Assn. for Intl. Aging [11274]
Amer. Assn. of Kidney Patients [15283]
Amer. Assn. for Klinefelter Syndrome Info. and Support [14538]
Amer. Assn. of Legal Nurse Consultants [14999]
Amer. Assn. of LifeStyle Counselors [14053]
Amer. Assn. of Managed Care Nurses [15435]
Amer. Assn. for Marriage and Family Therapy [16200]
Amer. Assn. of Medical Assistants [15081]
Amer. Assn. for Medical Chronobiology and Chronotherapeutics [13751]
Amer. Assn. of Medical Milk Commissions [16384]
Amer. Assn. of Medical Soc. Executives [15153]
Amer. Assn. of Mental Hea. Professionals in Corrections [15186]
Amer. Assn. of Neurological Surgeons [15410]
Amer. Assn. of Neuromuscular and Electrodiagnostic Medicine [15303]
Amer. Assn. of Neuropathologists [15853]
Amer. Assn. of Neuroscience Nurses [15436]
Amer. Assn. of Nurse Anesthetists [15437]
Amer. Assn. of Nurse Attorneys [15000]
Amer. Assn. of Nurse Life Care Planners [15438]
Amer. Assn. of Nutritional Consultants [15540]
Amer. Assn. of Occupational Hea. Nurses [15439]
Amer. Assn. of Off. Nurses [15440]

Amer. Assn. for Ophthalmic Standardized Echography [15659]
Amer. Assn. of Oral and Maxillofacial Surgeons [15732]
Amer. Assn. of Oriental Medicine [15742]
Amer. Assn. of Orthodontists [14117]
Amer. Assn. of Orthopedic Medicine [15753]
Amer. Assn. of Pathologists' Assistants [15854]
Amer. Assn. for Pediatric Ophthalmology and Strabismus [15660]
Amer. Assn. of Pesticide Safety Educators [4627]
Amer. Assn. of Physician Offices and Labs. [14990]
Amer. Assn. of Physician Specialists [15792]
Amer. Assn. of Plastic Surgeons [14040]
Amer. Assn. of Poison Control Centers [16658]
Amer. Assn. of Preferred Provider Organizations [14680]
Amer. Assn. of Professional Hypnotherapists [14915]
Amer. Assn. of Psychiatric Administrators [14861]
Amer. Assn. of Public Hea. Dentistry [14118]
Amer. Assn. of Public Hea. Veterinarians [16747]
Amer. Assn. for Respiratory Care [16599]
Amer. Assn. of Small Ruminant Practitioners [16749]
Amer. Assn. of Spinal Cord Injury Nurses [15441]
Amer. Assn. of Spinal Cord Injury Psychologists and Social Workers [16459]
Amer. Assn. for the Stud. of Liver Diseases [14801]
Amer. Assn. for the Surgery of Trauma [16687]
Amer. Assn. of Swine Veterinarians [16750]
Amer. Assn. for Tech. in Psychiatry [16070]
Amer. Assn. for Thoracic Surgery [16640]
Amer. Assn. of Tissue Banks [16663]
Amer. Assn. of Veterinary Lab. Diagnosticians [16753]
Amer. Assn. of Veterinary Parasitologists [16754]
Amer. Assn. of Veterinary State Boards [16755]
Amer. Assn. of Wildlife Veterinarians [16756]
Amer. Assn. of Women Dentists [14119]
Amer. Assn. of Zoo Veterinarians [16757]
Amer. Athletic Trainers Assn. and Certification Bd. [23953]
Amer. Autonomic Soc. [15406]
Amer. Behcet's Disease Assn. [13746]
Amer. Bd. of Abdominal Surgery [16561]
Amer. Bd. of Anesthesiology [13671]
Amer. Bd. of Cardiovascular Perfusion [13887]
American Bd. of Clinical Metal Toxicology [16659]
Amer. Bd. of Colon and Rectal Surgery [16059]
Amer. Bd. of Dental Public Hea. [14120]
Amer. Bd. of Dermatology [14190]
Amer. Bd. of Emergency Medicine [14325]
Amer. Bd. of Endodontics [14121]
Amer. Bd. of Family Dentistry [14122]
Amer. Bd. of Family Medicine [14384]
Amer. Bd. of Genetic Counseling [14492]
Amer. Bd. of Hea. Physics [16015]
Amer. Bd. of Indus. Hygiene [15623]
Amer. Bd. of Internal Medicine [14965]
Amer. Bd. of Medical Psychotherapists and Psychodiagnosticians [16202]
Amer. Bd. of Medical Specialties [15117]
Amer. Bd. of Neurological Surgery [15411]
Amer. Bd. of Nuclear Medicine [15419]
Amer. Bd. of Nutrition [15541]
Amer. Bd. of Obstetrics and Gynecology [15582]
Amer. Bd. for Occupational Hea. Nurses [15445]
Amer. Bd. of Ophthalmology [15661]
Amer. Bd. of Opticianry [15704]
Amer. Bd. of Oral and Maxillofacial Pathology [15855]
Amer. Bd. of Oral and Maxillofacial Surgery [15733]
Amer. Bd. of Orthodontics [14124]
Amer. Bd. of Orthopaedic Surgery [15755]
Amer. Bd. of Otolaryngology [15818]
Amer. Bd. of Pathology [15856]
Amer. Bd. of Pediatrics [15881]
Amer. Bd. of Periodontology [14125]
Amer. Bd. of Physical Medicine and Rehabilitation [16309]
Amer. Bd. of Plastic Surgery [14041]

Reference to "IO" in place of a book number signifies that the association may be found in the 45th edition of International Organizations.

Amer. Bd. of Podiatric Orthopedics and Primary Podiatric Medicine [16030]
Amer. Bd. of Podiatric Surgery [16031]
Amer. Bd. of Preventive Medicine [16050]
Amer. Bd. of Professional Disability Consultants [6040]
Amer. Bd. of Prosthodontics [14126]
Amer. Bd. of Psychiatry and Neurology [16071]
Amer. Bd. of Psychological Hypnosis [14917]
Amer. Bd. of Quality Assurance and Utilization Rev. Physicians [16260]
Amer. Bd. of Radiology [16272]
Amer. Bd. of Surgery [16563]
Amer. Bd. of Thoracic Surgery [16641]
Amer. Bd. of Urology [16700]
Amer. Bd. of Veterinary Specialties [16759]
Amer. Bd. of Veterinary Toxicology [16760]
Amer. Broncho-Esophagological Assn. [13778]
Amer. Burn Assn. [13781]
Amer. Case Mgt. Assn. [15051]
Amer. Celiac Society/Dietary Support Coalition [15543]
Amer. Central European Dental Inst. [14127]
Amer. Chiropractic Assn. [13988]
Amer. Chiropractic Registry of Radiologic Technologists [16273]
Amer. Chronic Pain Assn. [15834]
Amer. Cleft Palate-Craniofacial Assn. [14055]
Amer. Clinical and Climatological Assn. [14018]
Amer. Clinical Lab. Assn. [14991]
Amer. Clinical Neurophysiology Soc. [14306]
Amer. Coll. for Advancement in Medicine [16051]
Amer. Coll. of Allergy, Asthma and Immunology [13596]
Amer. Coll. of Angiology [16719]
Amer. Coll. of Apothecaries [15912]
Amer. Coll. of Cardiology [13888]
Amer. Coll. of Cardiovascular Administrators [15052]
Amer. Coll. of Chest Physicians [13889]
Amer. Coll. of Clinical Pharmacology [15913]
Amer. Coll. of Clinical Pharmacy [15914]
Amer. Coll. of Dentists [14128]
Amer. Coll. of Domiciliary Midwives [15583]
Amer. Coll. of Emergency Physicians [14326]
Amer. Coll. of Epidemiology [14373]
Amer. Coll. of Foot and Ankle Orthopedics and Medicine [16032]
Amer. Coll. of Foot and Ankle Pediatrics [16033]
Amer. Coll. of Foot and Ankle Surgeons [16034]
Amer. Coll. of Gastroenterology [14405]
Amer. Coll. Hea. Assn. [14714]
Amer. Coll. of Hea. Care Administrators [15535]
Amer. Coll. of Hea. Plan Mgt. [15053]
Amer. Coll. of Healthcare Executives [14862]
Amer. Coll. of Intl. Physicians [14973]
Amer. Coll. of Legal Medicine [15001]
Amer. Coll. of Medical Genetics [14494]
Amer. Coll. of Medical Practice Executives [15054]
Amer. Coll. of Medical Quality [16261]
Amer. Coll. of Medical Toxicology [16660]
Amer. Coll. of Mental Hea. Admin. [15187]
Amer. Coll. of Mohs Micrographic Surgery and Cutaneous Oncology [15636]
Amer. Coll. of Neuropsychopharmacology [15915]
Amer. Coll. of Nuclear Medicine [15421]
Amer. Coll. of Nuclear Physicians [15422]
Amer. Coll. of Nurse-Midwives [15447]
Amer. Coll. of Nutrition [15544]
Amer. Coll. of Obstetricians and Gynecologists [15584]
Amer. Coll. of Occupational and Environmental Medicine [15624]
Amer. Coll. of Oral and Maxillofacial Surgeons [15734]
Amer. Coll. of Osteopathic Emergency Physicians [14327]
Amer. Coll. of Osteopathic Family Physicians [15793]
Amer. Coll. of Osteopathic Internists [15794]
Amer. Coll. of Osteopathic Obstetricians and Gynecologists [15585]
Amer. Coll. of Osteopathic Pediatricians [15795]
Amer. Coll. of Osteopathic Surgeons [15797]

Amer. Coll. of Physician Executives [15056]
Amer. Coll. of Physicians-American Soc. of Internal Medicine [14966]
Amer. Coll. of Preventive Medicine [16052]
Amer. Coll. of Prosthodontists [14129]
Amer. Coll. of Radiation Oncology [16267]
Amer. Coll. of Radiology [16274]
Amer. Coll. of Rheumatology [16367]
Amer. Coll. of Sports Medicine [16473]
Amer. Coll. of Surgeons [15565]
Amer. Coll. of Theriogenologists [16763]
Amer. Coll. of Veterinary Anesthesiologists [16764]
Amer. Coll. of Veterinary Dermatology [16765]
Amer. Coll. of Veterinary Internal Medicine [16767]
Amer. Coll. of Veterinary Ophthalmologists [16768]
Amer. Coll. of Veterinary Pathologists [16769]
Amer. Coll. of Veterinary Radiology [16770]
Amer. Coll. of Veterinary Surgeons [16771]
Amer. Comm. for KEEP [12418]
Amer. Comm. for Shaare Zedek Hosp. in Jerusalem [12455]
Amer. Conf. of Governmental Indus. Hygienists [15625]
Amer. Cong. of Rehabilitation Medicine [16310]
Amer. Correctional Hea. Services Assn. [14715]
Amer. Coun. on Alcohol Problems [13220]
Amer. Coun. on Alcoholism [13221]
Amer. Coun. of Applied Clinical Nutrition [15545]
Amer. Coun. for Drug Educ. [13222]
Amer. Coun. on Exercise [15958]
Amer. Coun. for Fitness and Nutrition [15959]
Amer. Coun. of Hypnotist Examiners [14918]
Amer. Coun. on Sci. and Hea. [14539]
Amer. Cryonics Soc. [14073]
Amer. Dance Therapy Assn. [16203]
Amer. Dental Assistants Assn. [14130]
Amer. Dental Assn. [14131]
Amer. Dental Hygienists' Assn. [14132]
Amer. Dental Soc. of Anesthesiology [14133]
Amer. Diabetes Assn. [14218]
Amer. Dietetic Assn. [15546]
Amer. Electrology Assn. [14308]
Amer. Endodontic Soc. [14134]
Amer. Epilepsy Soc. [14379]
Amer. Equilibration Soc. [14135]
Amer. Fed. for Aging Res. [14508]
Amer. Fed. for Medical Res. [14019]
Amer. Found. for Aging Res. [14509]
Amer. Found. for AIDS Res. [13557]
Amer. Found. for Maternal and Child Health [15586]
Amer. Found. for Pharmaceutical Educ. [15916]
Amer. Found. for the Prevention of Venereal Disease [16409]
Amer. Fracture Assn. [15756]
Amer. Gastroenterological Assn. [14406]
Amer. Geriatrics Soc. [14510]
Amer. Gp. Psychotherapy Assn. [16204]
Amer. Guild of Hypnotherapists [14919]
Amer. Gynecological and Obstetrical Soc. [15587]
Amer. Head and Neck Soc. [15819]
Amer. Headache Soc. [14531]
Amer. Hea. Assistance Found. [15100]
Amer. Hea. Care Assn. [14540]
Amer. Hea. Decisions [14541]
Amer. Hea. Info. Mgt. Assn. [15097]
Amer. Hea. Planning Assn. [14542]
Amer. Hea. and Temperance Assn. [13303]
Amer. Healthcare Radiology Administrators [16275]
Amer. Hearing Aid Associates [14739]
Amer. Heartworm Soc. [16772]
Amer. Hemochromatosis Soc. [14543]
Amer. Herbalists Guild [14817]
Amer. Hippotherapy Assn. [16600]
Amer. Holistic Nurses' Assn. [14825]
Amer. Holistic Veterinary Medical Assn. [16773]
Amer. Horticultural Therapy Assn. [16601]
Amer. Industrial Health Coun. [15626]
Amer. Indus. Hygiene Assn. [15627]
Amer. Inst. of the History of Pharmacy [15917]
Amer. Inst. of Homeopathy [14845]

Amer. Inst. of Medical Ethics [12122]
Amer. Inst. of Oral Biology [14137]
Amer. Inst. for Preventive Medicine [16053]
Amer. Inst. of Stress [16487]
American Institute for Teen AIDS Prevention [13558]
Amer. Inst. of Ultrasound in Medicine [16436]
Amer. Institutes for Res. [7560]
Amer. Integrative Medical Assn. [15034]
Amer. Jewish Joint Distribution Comm. [12464]
Amer. Juvenile Arthritis Org. [16368]
Amer. Kidney Fund [15284]
Amer. Kinesiotherapy Assn. [16311]
Amer. Laryngological, Rhinological and Otological Soc. [15821]
Amer. Latex Allergy Assn. [13597]
Amer. Licensed Practical Nurses Assn. [15450]
Amer. Liver Found. [14803]
Amer. Lung Assn. [16354]
Amer. Lyme Disease Found. [14249]
Amer. Manual Medicine Assn. [13618]
Amer. Massage Therapy Assn. [15022]
Amer. Medical Assn. [15155]
Amer. Medical Assn. Alliance [15156]
Amer. Medical Athletic Assn. [23650]
Amer. Medical Directors Assn. [15536]
Amer. Medical Gp. Assn. [14717]
Amer. Medical Informatics Assn. [14079]
Amer. Medical Rehabilitation Providers Assn. [16312]
Amer. Medical Technologists [15127]
Amer. Medical Women's Assn. [14696]
Amer. Mental Hea. Alliance [15188]
Amer. Mental Hea. Counselors Assn. [15189]
Amer. Music Therapy Assn. [16205]
Amer. Naprapathic Assn. [15276]
Amer. Nephrology Nurses' Assn. [15286]
Amer. Neuroendocrine Soc. [15035]
Amer. Nordic Walking Assn. [15960]
Amer. Nurses Assn. [15451]
Amer. Nurses Found. [15452]
Amer. Nystagmus Network [16828]
Amer. Occupational Therapy Assn. [16602]
Amer. Ophthalmological Soc. [15662]
Amer. Optometric Assn. [15712]
Amer. Optometric Found. [15713]
Amer. Optometric Student Assn. [15714]
Amer. Organ Transplant Assn. [16664]
Amer. Org. for Bodywork Therapies of Asia [15024]
Amer. Org. of Nurse Executives [15454]
Amer. Orthodontic Soc. [14138]
Amer. Orthopaedic Assn. [15757]
Amer. Orthopaedic Foot and Ankle Soc. [15758]
Amer. Orthopaedic Soc. for Sports Medicine [16476]
Amer. Orthoptic Coun. [15663]
Amer. Osler Soc. [15157]
Amer. Osteopathic Acad. of Addiction Medicine [16500]
Amer. Osteopathic Acad. of Orthopedics [15759]
Amer. Osteopathic Acad. of Sports Medicine [16477]
Amer. Osteopathic Assn. [15798]
Amer. Osteopathic Bd. of Emergency Medicine [14328]
Amer. Osteopathic Bd. of Family Physicians [15799]
Amer. Osteopathic Bd. of Pediatrics [15800]
Amer. Osteopathic Coll. of Anesthesiologists [13672]
Amer. Osteopathic Coll. of Dermatology [14194]
Amer. Osteopathic Coll. of Occupational and Preventive Medicine [15802]
Amer. Osteopathic Coll. of Physical Medicine and Rehabilitation [15805]
Amer. Osteopathic Coll. of Radiology [16276]
Amer. Osteopathic Colleges of Ophthalmology and Otolaryngology-Head and Neck Surgery [15664]
Amer. Osteopathic Found. [15806]
Amer. Otological Soc. [15822]
Amer. Paraplegia Soc. [16460]
Amer. Parkinson Disease Assn. [15304]

A star before a book entry number signifies that the name is not listed separately, but is mentioned within the entry.

Amer. Partnership for Eosinophilic Disorders [14408]
Amer. Pathology Found. [15857]
Amer. Pediatric Soc. [15882]
Amer. Pharmacists Assn. - Acad. of Pharmacy Practice and Mgt. [15918]
Amer. Pharmacists Assn. Acad. of Student Pharmacists [15919]
Amer. Physical Therapy Assn. [16603]
Amer. Physicians Fellowship for Medicine in Israel [12456]
Amer. Podiatric Circulatory Soc. [16036]
Amer. Podiatric Medical Assn. [16037]
Amer. Podiatric Medical Students' Assn. [16038]
Amer. Podiatric Medical Writers Assn. [16039]
Amer. Porphyria Found. [15243]
Amer. Pre-Veterinary Medical Assn. [16774]
Amer. Pregnancy Assn. [15588]
Amer. Professional Wound Care Assn. [16688]
Amer. Prostate Soc. [16701]
Amer. Prosthodontic Soc. [14139]
Amer. Psychiatric Assn. [16076]
Amer. Psychiatric Assn. Alliance [16077]
Amer. Psychoanalytic Assn. [16102]
Amer. Psychological Assn. Division of Independent Practice [16126]
Amer. Psychological Assn. - Hea. Psychology Div. [16130]
Amer. Psychopathological Assn. [16190]
Amer. Psychosocial Oncology Soc. [15638]
Amer. Psychosomatic Soc. [16196]
Amer. Psychotherapy Assn. [16207]
Amer. Public Hea. Assn. [16236]
Amer. Qigong Assn. [13620]
Amer. Radiological Nurses Assn. [15457]
Amer. Radium Soc. [15639]
Amer. Registry of Diagnostic Medical Sonography [16437]
Amer. Registry of Medical Assistants [15082]
Amer. Registry of Pathology [15858]
Amer. Registry of Radiologic Technologists [15128]
Amer. Rehabilitation Counseling Assn. [16313]
Amer. Rehabilitation Economics Assn. [16314]
Amer. Rhinologic Soc. [15823]
Amer. Roentgen Ray Soc. [16277]
Amer. Running Assn. [23651]
Amer. School Hea. Assn. [14718]
Amer. Senior Fitness Assn. [15961]
Amer. Sepsis Alliance [14946]
Amer. Shoulder and Elbow Surgeons [16567]
Amer. Social Hea. Assn. [16410]
Amer. Soc. of Abdominal Surgeons [16568]
Amer. Soc. for Adolescent Psychiatry [16078]
Amer. Soc. for the Advancement of Pharmaco-therapy [16134]
Amer. Soc. for Aesthetic Plastic Surgery [14042]
Amer. Soc. on Aging [11275]
Amer. Soc. of Anesthesiologists [13674]
Amer. Soc. for Apheresis [13706]
Amer. Soc. of Bariatric Physicians [15575]
Amer. Soc. for Bone and Mineral Res. [15787]
Amer. Soc. of Breast Disease [13772]
Amer. Soc. of Breast Surgeons [16570]
Amer. Soc. of Cataract and Refractive Surgery [15665]
Amer. Soc. of Childbirth Educators [15589]
Amer. Soc. of Clinical Hypnosis [14921]
Amer. Soc. of Clinical Hypnosis - Educ. and Res. Found. [14922]
Amer. Soc. for Clinical Investigation [14020]
Amer. Soc. for Clinical Lab. Sci. [14992]
Amer. Soc. for Clinical Nutrition [15547]
Amer. Soc. of Clinical Oncology [15640]
Amer. Soc. for Clinical Pathology [15859]
Amer. Soc. for Clinical Pharmacology and Therapeutics [15920]
Amer. Soc. of Colon and Rectal Surgeons [16060]
Amer. Soc. for Colposcopy and Cervical Pathology [15590]
Amer. Soc. of Consultant Pharmacists [15922]
Amer. Soc. of Contemporary Medicine, Surgery, and Ophthalmology [15666]
Amer. Soc. of Cytopathology [14075]
Amer. Soc. for Cytotechnology [14076]

Amer. Soc. for Dental Aesthetics [14140]
Amer. Soc. for Dermatologic Surgery [14196]
Amer. Soc. of Diagnostic and Interventional Nephrology [15287]
Amer. Soc. of Directors of Volunteer Services [13382]
Amer. Soc. of Echocardiography [13891]
Amer. Soc. of Electroneurodiagnostic Technologists [14307]
Amer. Soc. of Exercise Physiologists [16019]
Amer. Soc. of Extra-Corporeal Tech. [15129]
Amer. Soc. of Forensic Odontology [14142]
Amer. Soc. for Gastrointestinal Endoscopy [14409]
Amer. Soc. of Hand Therapists [14524]
Amer. Soc. of Hea. Sys. Pharmacists [15923]
Amer. Soc. for Healthcare Central Ser. Professionals [14864]
Amer. Soc. for Healthcare Engg. of the Amer. Hosp. Assn. [14865]
Amer. Soc. for Healthcare Environmental Services of the Amer. Hosp. Assn. [14866]
Amer. Soc. for Healthcare Food Ser. Administrators [14867]
Amer. Soc. for Healthcare Risk Mgt. [14869]
Amer. Soc. of Hematology [14783]
Amer. Soc. for Histocompatibility and Immunogenetics [14931]
Amer. Soc. of Interventional Pain Physicians [15837]
Amer. Soc. of Interventional and Therapeutic Neuroradiology [16280]
Amer. Soc. for Investigative Pathology [15860]
Amer. Soc. for Laser Medicine and Surgery [14997]
Amer. Soc. of Law, Medicine and Ethics [15002]
Amer. Soc. of Lipo-Suction Surgery [16572]
Amer. Soc. of Master Dental Technologists [14143]
Amer. Soc. of Maxillofacial Surgeons [15735]
Amer. Soc. for Mohs Surgery [15641]
Amer. Soc. of Nephrology [15288]
Amer. Soc. for Neural Transplantation and Repair [15380]
Amer. Soc. of Neuroimaging [16281]
Amer. Soc. of Neurophysiological Monitoring [15381]
Amer. Soc. of Neuroradiology [16282]
Amer. Soc. for Nutrition [15548]
Amer. Soc. of Ophthalmic Administrators [15058]
Amer. Soc. of Ophthalmic Registered Nurses [15458]
Amer. Soc. for Ophthalmic Ultrasonography [15667]
Amer. Soc. of Pain Educators [15838]
Amer. Soc. for Parenteral and Enteral Nutrition [15549]
Amer. Soc. of Pharmacognosy [15924]
Amer. Soc. for Pharmacology and Experimental Therapeutics [15925]
Amer. Soc. for Pharmacy Law [15003]
Amer. Soc. of Plastic Surgeons and Plastic Surgery Educ. Found. [14045]
Amer. Soc. of Plastic Surgical Nurses [15461]
Amer. Soc. of Podiatric Medical Assistants [16040]
Amer. Soc. of Psychoanalytic Physicians [16104]
Amer. Soc. of Radiologic Technologists [15131]
Amer. Soc. for Reconstructive Microsurgery [16573]
Amer. Soc. of Regional Anesthesia and Pain Medicine [13676]
Amer. Soc. for Reproductive Medicine [14389]
Amer. Soc. of Safety Engineers [7586]
Amer. Soc. for Stereotactic and Functional Neurosurgery [15412]
Amer. Soc. for the Stud. of Orthodontics [14144]
Amer. Soc. for Surgery of the Hand [14525]
Amer. Soc. for Therapeutic Radiology and Oncology [16285]
Amer. Soc. of Transplant Surgeons [16667]
Amer. Soc. of Tropical Medicine and Hygiene [16693]
Amer. Soc. of Veterinary Ophthalmology [16775]
Amer. Spa and Hea. Resort Assn. [3352]

Amer. Spinal Injury Assn. [16461]
Amer. Sudden Infant Death Syndrome Inst. [16523]
Amer. Surgical Assn. [16575]
Amer. Syringomyelia Alliance Proj. [15305]
Amer. Tai Chi Assn. [16593]
Amer. Thoracic Soc. [16642]
Amer. Trauma Soc. [16689]
Amer. Turners [23802]
Amer. Urological Assn. [16704]
Amer. Urological Assn. Found. [16705]
Amer. Uveitis Soc. [15668]
Amer. Veterinary Dental Soc. [16778]
Amer. Veterinary Medical Assn. [16779]
Amer. Veterinary Soc. of Animal Behavior [16780]
Amer. Youth Understanding Diabetes Abroad [14219]
America's Blood Centers [13762]
America's Hea. Together [14614]
Amigos de las Americas [13384]
Amyloidosis Support Groups [14250]
Amyloidosis Support Network [14251]
Amyotrophic Lateral Sclerosis Assn. [15306]
Ananda Yoga Teachers Assn. [11217]
Androgen Insensitivity Syndrome Support Gp. - USA [14441]
Anesthesia Awareness Campaign [13677]
Anesthesia History Assn. [13678]
Anesthesia Patient Safety Found. [13679]
Aneurysm Outreach Inc. [14544]
Angioma Alliance [15307]
Animals as Intermediaries [4157]
Antitrust Coalition for Consumer Choice in Hea. Care [14615]
Archaeus Proj. [13625]
Archivists and Librarians in the History of the Hea. Sciences [10326]
Armed Forces Inst. of Pathology [15261]
Army Distaff Foundation/Knollwood [21192]
Army Nurse Corps Assn. [15262]
Arthritis Found. [16369]
Arthroscopy Assn. of North Am. [15762]
Arts in Therapy Network [13709]
The Arts We Need [13710]
Asbestos Disease Awareness Org. [16655]
ASEAN Inst. for Hea. Development [IO]
Ashoka: Innovators for the Public [12419]
ASHP Found. [15926]
Asian Amer./Pacific Islander Nurses Assn. [15463]
Asian and Pacific Islander Amer. Hea. Forum [14545]
Asociacion Puertorriquena Pro-Bienestar de la Familia [12176]
Assembly of Episcopal Healthcare Chaplains [19944]
Assoc. Hea. Found. [18983]
Assn. of Academic Hea. Centers [14546]
Assn. of Academic Physiatrists [16316]
Assn. for Academic Surgery [16576]
Assn. for Advancement of Psychoanalysis (of the Karen Horney Psychoanalytic Inst. and Center) [16105]
Assn. for the Advancement of Psychotherapy [16210]
Assn. for the Advancement of Wound Care [14547]
Assn. for Ambulatory Behavioral Healthcare [16080]
Assn. of Amer. Cancer Institutes [13794]
Assn. on Amer. Indian Affairs [18092]
Assn. of Amer. Physicians and Surgeons [15990]
Assn. for Applied Poetry [16211]
Assn. for Applied Psychophysiology and Biofeedback [13749]
Assn. for Applied and Therapeutic Humor [16605]
Assn. of Assistive Tech. Act Programs [14237]
Assn. of Asthma Educators [16355]
Assn. for Behavioral Hea. and Wellness [24088]
Assn. of Behavioral Healthcare Mgt. [15191]
Assn. of Biomedical Communications Directors [14030]
Assn. for the Bladder Exstrophy Community [14252]
Assn. of Bone and Joint Surgeons [15763]
Assn. of Brethren Caregivers [11276]

Reference to "IO" in place of a book number signifies that the association may be found in the 45th edition of International Organizations.

Assn. of Camp Nurses [15464]
Assn. for Child Hea. [IO]
Assn. of Child Neurology Nurses [15465]
Assn. for Child Psychoanalysis [16106]
Assn. for Childbirth at Home, Intl. [15591]
Assn. of Children's Prosthetic-Orthotic Clinics [15784]
Assn. of Chinese Amer. Physicians [15991]
Assn. of Chiropractic Colleges [13993]
Assn. of Clinical Scientists [14022]
Assn. for Community Affiliated Plans [14617]
Assn. of Community Cancer Centers [13797]
Assn. of Community Hea. Improvement [16238]
Assn. for Continuing Dental Educ. [8195]
Assn. of Doctors for the Env. - ISDE Italy [IO]
Assn. for the Educ. of Children with Medical Needs [8072]
Assn. for Electronic Hea. Care Transactions [14618]
Assn. for Eradication of Heart Attack [13894]
Assn. of Family Practice Administrators [15060]
Assn. of Family Practice Physician Assistants [14698]
Assn. of Freestanding Radiation Oncology Centers [16268]
Assn. of Hea. Fac. Survey Agencies [6210]
Assn. for Healthcare Documentation Integrity [15084]
Assn. for Healthcare Philanthropy [14871]
Assn. for Healthcare Rsrc. and Materials Mgt. [14872]
Assn. of Himalayan Yoga Meditation Societies [11218]
Assn. for Hosp. Medical Educ. [14873]
Assn. for Integrative Hea. Care Practitioners [15037]
Assn. of Intl. Hea. Researchers [IO]
Assn. of Intl. Hea. Researchers [14548]
Assn. of Jewish Aging Services [11277]
Assn. for Macular Diseases [15669]
Assn. of Maternal and Child Hea. Programs [13947]
Assn. of Medical Illustrators [13707]
Assn. of Medical Lab. Immunologists [14932]
Assn. of Medical School Pediatric Dept. Chairs [15884]
Assn. of Medicine and Psychiatry [16081]
Assn. of Military Osteopathic Physicians and Surgeons [15807]
Assn. of Military Surgeons of the U.S. [15263]
Assn. of Needle-Free Injection Mfrs. [2549]
Assn. of Nurses in AIDS Care [13559]
Assn. of Nurses Endorsing Transplantation [15670]
Assn. of Nutrition Departments and Programs [8947]
Assn. of Nutrition Services Agencies [14720]
Assn. for Ocular Pharmacology and Therapeutics [15671]
Assn. of Organ Procurement Organizations [14287]
Assn. of Osteopathic State Executive Directors [15809]
Assn. of Otolaryngology Administrators [15062]
Assn. of Pakistani Physicians of North Am. [15993]
Assn. of Pathology Chairs [15863]
Assn. for Pathology Informatics [15864]
Assn. of Pediatric Hematology/Oncology Nurses [15467]
Assn. of Pediatric Oncology Social Workers [15885]
Assn. of Pediatric Therapists [16606]
Assn. of PeriOperative Registered Nurses [15468]
Assn. of Physician Assistants in Cardiovascular Surgery [13895]
Assn. for Prevention Teaching and Res. [16054]
Assn. for Professionals in Infection Control and Epidemiology [14947]
Assn. of Professors of Cardiology [13896]
Assn. of Professors of Gynecology and Obstetrics [15592]
Assn. of Prog. Directors in Internal Medicine [14967]
Assn. of Prog. Directors in Vascular Surgery [16578]

Assn. Promoting Educ. and Conservation in Amazonia [5294]
Assn. for Psychoanalytic Medicine [16107]
Assn. of Regulatory Boards of Optometry [15716]
Assn. of Rehabilitation Nurses [15469]
Assn. of Reproductive Hea. Professionals [12177]
Assn. for Res. of Childhood Cancer [13798]
Assn. for Res. in Vision and Ophthalmology [15672]
Assn. for Retinopathy of Prematurity and Related Diseases [15673]
Assn. of Rheumatology Hea. Professionals [16370]
Assn. of Schools and Colleges of Optometry [15717]
Assn. of Schools of Public Hea. [16240]
Assn. of Shelter Veterinarians [16784]
Assn. of SIDS and Infant Mortality Programs [16524]
Assn. of Specialty Professors [8587]
Assn. of Staff Physician Recruiters [15995]
Assn. of State and Territorial Dental Directors [14146]
Assn. of State and Territorial Hea. Officials [6212]
Assn. of State and Territorial Local Hea. Liaison Officials [12524]
Assn. of Surgical Technologists [15133]
Assn. of Tech. Personnel in Ophthalmology [15674]
Assn. for Therapeutic Eurythmy in North Am. [16608]
Assn. for the Treatment of Tobacco Use and Dependence [16653]
Assn. of Univ. Anesthesiologists [13680]
Assn. of Univ. Professors of Ophthalmology [15675]
Assn. of Univ. Radiologists [16286]
Assn. of Veterans Affairs Ophthalmologists [15676]
Assn. of Veterinary Hematology and Transfusion Medicine [16785]
Assn. of Vision Educators [15677]
Assn. for Women Veterinarians [16786]
Assn. of Women's Hea., Obstetric and Neonatal Nurses [15470]
Assyrian Medical Soc. [13715]
Asthma and Allergy Found. of Am. [13598]
Asthma Found. of New South Wales [IO]
Audiology Awareness Campaign [13716]
Australian Coll. of Rural and Remote Medicine [IO]
Australian Coun. on Healthcare Standards [IO]
Australian Coun. on Safety and Quality in Hea. Care [IO]
Autism Speaks [13724]
Auxiliary to the Natl. Medical Assn. [15161]
Avenues, Natl. Support Gp. for Arthrogryposis Multiplex Congenita [15309]
Awake In Am. [18601]
BACCHUS Network [13226]
Bangladesh Medical Assn. of North Am. [15162]
Batey Relief Alliance [12835]
Bay Area Physicians for Human Rights [12218]
Behavior Genetics Assn. [14498]
Benign Essential Blepharospasm Res. Found. [15311]
Benjamin Franklin Literary and Medical Soc. [14549]
Better Sleep Coun. [16424]
Better Vision Inst. [15678]
Beverly Found. [11278]
BIO Ventures for Global Hea. [14975]
BioCommunications Assn. [14031]
BiOptic Driving Network - USA [15705]
Birth Defect Res. for Children [13752]
Bladder Cancer Advocacy Network [13799]
Blue Cross and Blue Shield Assn. [14959]
BoardSource [12651]
Brain Injury Assn. of Am. [14528]
Brave Kids [13949]
British Andrology Soc. [IO]
British Assn. of Skin Camouflage [IO]
British Pain Soc. [IO]
Brother's Brother Found. [12837]
Bur. of Professional Educ. of the Amer. Osteopathic Assn. [15810]

Burns United Support Groups [13782]
C/SEC [15593]
C3: Colorectal Cancer Coalition [13802]
Cable Positive [11327]
Caffeine Awareness Alliance [13747]
Cajal Club [15385]
Campaign For Our Children [13476]
Canadians for Hea. Res. [IO]
Cancer Care [13803]
Cancer Control Soc. [13804]
Cancer Fed. [13805]
Cancer Info. Ser. [13807]
Cancer Prevention Coalition [13808]
Cancer Quality Alliance [13809]
Candlelighters Childhood Cancer Found. [13810]
Canine Cancer Awareness [16788]
Cardiovascular Credentialing Intl. [13898]
Care4Dystonia [15312]
Caritas Puerto Rico [12839]
Catholic Guardian Soc. [11564]
Catholic Hea. Assn. of Canada [IO]
Catholic Hea. Assn. of the U.S. [14874]
Catholic Medical Assn. [15996]
Catholic Medical Mission Bd. [12515]
CCHS Family Network [14255]
CDC Natl. Prevention Info. Network [13563]
Center For Hea., Env. and Justice [5266]
Center for Humane Options in Childbirth Experiences [15594]
Center for Medical Consumers [14550]
Center for Organ Recovery and Educ. [16670]
Center for Professional Well-Being [14700]
Center for Psychological and Spiritual Hea. [15194]
Center for Res. in Ambulatory Hea. Care Admin. [15064]
The Center for Social Gerontology [11280]
Center for Sports and Osteopathic Medicine [16055]
Center for the Stud. of Aging of Albany [11281]
Center for the Stud. of Multiple Birth [15272]
Center for the Well Being of Hea. Professionals [14701]
Central Amer. Hea. Inst. [IO]
Central Soc. for Clinical Res. [14023]
Certification Bd. for Music Therapists [16213]
Certification Bd. for Urologic Nurses and Associates [16706]
CFC Intl. [14435]
CFIDS Assn. of Am. [14256]
Charles Ray III Diabetes Assn. [14220]
Chem. Injury Info. Network [16656]
Chemotherapy Found. [15644]
Chi Eta Phi Sorority [24560]
Child Family Hea. Intl. [11551]
Child Life Coun. [13951]
Child Neurology Soc. [15386]
Childbirth Connection [15595]
Childhood Arthritis and Rheumatology Res. Alliance [16371]
Children and Adults With Attention Deficit/Hyperactivity Disorder [15314]
Children of Aging Parents [11282]
Children of Alcoholics Found. [13228]
Children's Blood Found. [14786]
Children's Cause for Cancer Advocacy [13812]
Children's Craniofacial Assn. [14057]
Children's Eye Found. [15679]
Children's Hea. Environmental Coalition [13953]
Children's Hea. Fund [13954]
Children's Hemiplegia and Stroke Assn. [16493]
Children's Hospice Intl. [14853]
Children's Leukemia Res. Assn. [13813]
Children's Liver Assn. for Support Services [14804]
Children's PKU Network [15245]
Children's Tumor Found. [15315]
Children's Wish Found. Intl. [11687]
China Medical Bd. of New York [14976]
Chinese Amer. Medical Soc. [15163]
CHOICE [12178]
Christian Chiropractors Assn. [19773]
Christian Connections for Intl. Hea. [IO]
Christian Connections for Intl. Hea. [14551]
Christian Dental Soc. [14147]

A star before a book entry number signifies that the name is not listed separately, but is mentioned within the entry.

Christian Hea. Assn. of Kenya [IO]
Christian Medical and Dental Associations [20238]
Christopher and Dana Reeve Found. [16463]
Chromosome 9P Network [14443]
Chromosome 18 Registry and Res. Soc. [14444]
Chronic Syndrome Support Assn. [14259]
Churg Strauss Syndrome Assn. [13729]
Circle of Hea. Intl. [IO]
Circle of Hea. Intl. [12268]
Citizens Alliance for VD Awareness [16411]
City of Hope Natl. Medical Center [15102]
CityMatch [13957]
Civil Aviation Medical Assn. [13540]
Clinical Lab. Mgt. Assn. [14993]
Clinical and Lab. Standards Inst. [14994]
Clinical Ligand Assay Soc. [14995]
Coalition of Cancer Cooperative Groups [13814]
Coalition for Healthcare Commun. [14622]
Coalition for Hemophilia B [14787]
Coffin-Lowry Syndrome Found. [14447]
Coll. of Amer. Pathologists [15866]
Coll. of Optometrists in Vision Development [15718]
Coll. of Osteopathic Healthcare Executives [14876]
Collegium Internationale Neuro-Psychopharmacologicum [15929]
Colorectal Cancer Network [13815]
Coma Recovery Assn. [14029]
Commn. on Graduates of Foreign Nursing Schools [15473]
Commn. on Opticianry Accreditation [15706]
Comm. on Accreditation for Respiratory Care [16610]
Comm. for the Advancement of Stem Cell Res. [18542]
Comm. for Freedom of Choice in Medicine [13628]
Comm. of Interns and Residents [24089]
Comm. for the Promotion of Medical Res. [15104]
Comm. to Reduce Infection Deaths [14877]
Community Dreamsharing Network [16425]
Community Guidance Ser. [16214]
Community Hea. Charities [12200]
Community Systems Found. [15552]
Comparative Nutrition Soc. [15553]
Compassionate Cooks [13350]
Competency and Credentialing Inst. [14878]
Complementary Alternative Medical Assn. [13629]
Computerized Medical Imaging Soc. [16287]
Concern Am. [12845]
Conf. of Res. Workers in Animal Diseases [16790]
Congenital Cardiac Anesthesia Soc. [13682]
Congenital Heart Defects Awareness [13900]
Congenital Heart Info. Network [13901]
Cong. of Lung Assn. Staff [16357]
Connective Tissue Oncology Soc. [15645]
Conservative Orthopedics Intl. Assn. [15767]
Consultant Dietitians in Hea. Care Facilities [15554]
Consumer Healthcare Prdt. Assn. [2973]
Consumers for Dental Choice [11912]
Consumers' Hea. Forum of Australia [IO]
Contact Lens Assn. of Ophthalmologists [15680]
Continuing Care Accreditation Commn. [16318]
Cooper Inst. [15962]
Cornelia de Lange Syndrome Found. [13754]
Corporate Angel Network [13817]
Coun. on Accreditation [13164]
Coun. for Accreditation in Occupational Hearing Conservation [15632]
Coun. for Affordable Quality Healthcare [14625]
Coun. on Arteriosclerosis, Thrombosis and Vascular Biology of the Amer. Heart Assn. [13902]
Coun. on Certification of Hea., Environmental and Safety Technologists [14552]
Coun. on Certification of Nurse Anesthetists [15475]
Coun. on Chiropractic Educ. [13998]
Coun. on Chiropractic Orthopedics [15768]
Coun. of Colleges of Acupuncture and Oriental Medicine [15743]
Coun. on Compulsive Gambling of New Jersey [12209]

Coun. on Diagnostic Imaging [16288]
Coun. on Educ. for Public Hea. [16242]
Coun. on Hea. Info. and Educ. [14553]
Coun. on Hea. Res. for Development [IO]
Coun. of Medical Specialty Societies [15120]
Coun. for the Natl. Register of Hea. Ser. Providers in Psychology [16149]
Coun. of Pediatric Subspecialties [15886]
Coun. on Podiatric Medical Educ. [16042]
Coun. on Resident Educ. in Obstetrics and Gynecology [15597]
Coun. of State Administrators of Vocational Rehabilitation [16320]
Coun. of State and Territorial Epidemiologists [14374]
Coun. of Teaching Hospitals [14879]
Coun. of Women's and Infants' Specialty Hospitals [14880]
Cranial Acad. [15811]
Crigler-Najjar Assn. [14805]
Crohn's and Colitis Found. of Am. [14414]
CTSNet: Cardiothoracic Surgery Network [16643]
CURE Formaldehyde Poisoning Assn. [13324]
Cure Res. Found. [13818]
CyberKnife Soc. [16581]
Cyclic Vomiting Syndrome Assn. [14415]
Cystic Fibrosis Found. [16358]
Cystic Fibrosis Worldwide [16359]
Cystinosis Found. [15246]
Cystinosis Res. Network [15247]
Damon Runyon Cancer Res. Found. [13819]
Dana Alliance for Brain Initiatives [15387]
DanceSafe [12041]
Dannemiller Memorial Educational Found. [13683]
DaVita Patient Citizens [15291]
Delta Dental Plans Assn. [14687]
Delta Omega [24582]
Delta Psi Kappa [24573]
Dental Assisting Natl. Bd. [14151]
Dental Gp. Mgt. Assn. [15065]
Dental Hea. Intl. [14152]
Depression and Bipolar Support Alliance [15196]
Dermatology Found. [14199]
Dermatology Nurses' Assn. [15476]
DES Action, U.S.A. [13821]
Diabetes Res. Assn. of Am. [14223]
Diabetes Res. Inst. Found. [14224]
Dietary Managers Assn. [15555]
Digestive Disease Natl. Coalition [14416]
Direct Relief Intl. [12517]
Do It Now Found. [13235]
DOCARE Intl., N.F.P. [12518]
Docs for Tots [13958]
Drs. for Artists [12520]
Doctors Ought to Care [14554]
Drug Info. Assn. [15931]
Dysautonomia Found. [15317]
Dysautonomia Youth Network of Am. [15318]
Dystonia Medical Res. Found. [15319]
Dystrophic Epidermolysis Bullosa Res. Assn. of Am. [14200]
Ear Found. [15825]
EarthSave Intl. [4504]
Eating Disorders Coalition for Res., Policy and Action [14299]
ECRI [15136]
Educational Commn. for Foreign Medical Graduates [15997]
Ehlers Danlos Natl. Found. [16651]
Elder Craftsmen [11285]
EMDR - Humanitarian Assistance Programs [12767]
EMDR Intl. Assn. [16215]
Emergency Medicine Found. [14331]
Emergency Medicine Residents' Assn. [14332]
Emergency Nurses Assn. [14333]
Employee Services Mgt. Assn. [12796]
Endocrine Soc. [14355]
Endometriosis Assn. [15599]
Energetic Healing Assn. [IO]
EngenderHealth [12180]
Environmental Res. Found. [13599]
Epilepsy Found. [14380]
Epilepsy Therapy Development Proj. [14381]
Equine Assisted Growth and Learning Assn. [16216]

Esophageal Cancer Awareness Assn. [13822]
Ethiopian Pharmacists Assn. in North Am. [15932]
EuroHealthNet [IO]
European Dystonia Fed. [IO]
European Food Info. Coun. [IO]
European Genetic Alliances Network [IO]
European Hea. Mgt. Assn. [IO]
Everyday Ayurveda [13606]
Exercise Safety Assn. [15963]
Eye Bank Assn. of Am. [14288]
Eye-Bank for Sight Restoration [14289]
Fabry Support and Info. Gp. [14262]
FACES: The Natl. Craniofacial Assn. [14061]
Facing Our Risk of Cancer Empowered [13823]
Facioscapulohumeral (FSH) Soc. [15320]
Families for Depression Awareness [15198]
Families U.S.A. Found. [11286]
Family Hea. Intl. [12181]
Family and Hea. Sect. of the Natl. Coun. on Family Relations [14385]
Family Res. Inst. [17688]
Family Violence Prevention Fund [12028]
Famous Fone Friends [11692]
Fanconi Anemia Res. Fund [14450]
Farm Worker Hea. Services [12586]
Feathered Pipe Found. [12345]
Fed. Physicians Assn. [15998]
Federated Ambulatory Surgery Assn. [16582]
Fed. for Accessible Nursing Educ. and Licensure [15478]
Fed. of Amer. Hospitals [14881]
Fed. of Associations of Regulatory Boards [14555]
Fed. for Children with Special Needs [12569]
Fed. of Chinese Amer. and Chinese Canadian Medical Societies [13985]
Fed. of Clinical Immunology Societies [14935]
Fed. of Pediatric Organizations [15887]
Fed. of Podiatric Medical Boards [16043]
Fed. of State Medical Boards of the U.S. [15165]
Fed. of State Physician Hea. Programs [15999]
Fed. of Straight Chiropractors and Organizations [14001]
Feed the Children [12854]
Feldenkrais Guild of North Am. [10182]
Fertile Hope [14390]
Fertility Res. Found. [14391]
Fibromuscular Dysplasia Soc. of Am. [15322]
Filipino Amer. Medical Inc. [14722]
First Candle/SIDS Alliance [16525]
Fitness Indus. Suppliers Assn. - North Am. [3020]
Floating Harbor Syndrome Support Gp. of North Am. [14451]
The Floating Hosp. [14882]
Flower Essence Soc. [14818]
Flying Chiropractors Assn. [14002]
Flying Dentists Assn. [14153]
Flying Physicians Assn. [13731]
Focus [15681]
FOD Family Support Gp. [15248]
Food and Drug Admin. Alumni Assn. [17606]
Food and Nutrition Bd. [15558]
Forbes Norris MDA/ALS Res. Center [15323]
Foreign Pharmacy Graduate Examination Comm. [15933]
Forum for State Hea. Policy Leadership [17689]
Found. for Advancement in Cancer Therapy [13824]
Found. for the Advancement of Chiropractic Tenets and Sci. [14003]
Found. for Chiropractic Educ. and Res. [14004]
Found. for Hea. [14556]
Found. for Ichthyosis and Related Skin Types [14201]
Found. for Informed Medical Decision Making [15137]
Found. for Innovation in Medicine [15166]
Found. for Shamanic Stud. [20446]
Found. for the Support of Intl. Medical Training [14977]
Fragile X Soc. [IO]
Friedreich's Ataxia Res. Alliance [14403]
Friendly Hand Found. [13243]
Friends of the Jose Carreras Intl. Leukemia Found. [13825]

Reference to "IO" in place of a book number signifies that the association may be found in the 45th edition of International Organizations.

Friends of Karen [11694]
Frontier Nursing Ser. [15479]
Frontline Hepatitis Awareness [14806]
Gait and Clinical Movement Anal. Soc. [14557]
Galilee Soc. [IO]
Gay and Lesbian Medical Assn. [14431]
Gay Men's Hea. Crisis [13564]
Generations United [13170]
Genetic Engg. Action Network [6615]
Gerontological Soc. of Am. [14511]
Gift of Life Intl. [12524]
The Glaucoma Found. [15682]
Glaucoma Res. Found. [15683]
Global AIDS Alliance [13565]
Global Alliance for Medical Educ. [8862]
Global Alliance of Mental Illness Advocacy
    Networks [15200]
Global Applied Disability Res. and Info. Network
    [14240]
Global Autism Proj. [13725]
Global Bus. Coalition on HIV/AIDS [11329]
Global Healing [12450]
Global Hea. Coun. [14979]
Global Lawyers and Physicians [IO]
Global Lawyers and Physicians [14558]
Global Neuro Rescue [15324]
Global and Regional Asperger Syndrome Partner-
    ship [15325]
Global Vaccine Awareness League [14559]
Gluten Intolerance Gp. [15559]
God's Child Proj. [11597]
God's Love We Deliver [12283]
Gray Panthers [11287]
Gp. for the Advancement of Psychiatry [16084]
Guam Lytico and Bodig Assn. [14560]
Guam Lytico and Bodig Assn. [IO]
Guardians of Hydrocephalus Res. Found. [15326]
Haitian Coalition on AIDS [13567]
Harm Reduction Coalition [12042]
Harvard Injury Control Res. Center [16690]
Harvey Soc. [15168]
Hastings Center [12125]
Hazelden Found. [13244]
Healing Waters Intl. [13410]
Hea. Acad. [14883]
Hea. Action Intl. Africa [IO]
Hea. Action Intl. Latin Am. [IO]
Hea. Connection [13245]
Hea. and Development Intl. [IO]
Hea. and Development Intl. [14561]
Hea. Educ. Coun. [14562]
Hea. Educ. Found. [16243]
Hea. Educ. Rsrc. Org. [13568]
Hea. for Humanity [14563]
Hea. Indus. Representatives Assn. [2627]
Hea. Info. Rsrc. Center [14564]
Hea. Jam [14674]
Hea. Ministries [20241]
Hea. Ministries Assn. [16339]
Hea. Physics Soc. [16017]
Hea. Promotion Inst. [11288]
Hea. Promotion Inst. [14565]
Hea. Res. and Educational Trust [14884]
Hea. Sci. Communications Assn. [14032]
Hea. Volunteers Overseas [12526]
Healthcare Distribution Mgt. Assn. [2984]
Healthcare Financial Mgt. Assn. [15066]
Healthcare Info. and Mgt. Systems Soc. [14885]
Healthcare Laundry Accreditation Coun. [2403]
Healthy Building Network [4629]
Healthy Teen Network [12182]
Heart Disease Res. Found. [13905]
Heart Failure Soc. of Am. [13906]
Heart Rhythm Soc. [13907]
HELLP Syndrome Soc. [14906]
HELP - Inst. for Body Chemistry [14928]
Helping Our Teen Girls in Real Life Situations
    [12261]
Hemochromatosis Found. [14799]
Hemochromatosis Info. Soc. [14800]
Hemophilia Fed. of Am. [14789]
Hepatitis C Assn. [14807]
Hepatitis C Caring Ambassadors Prog. [14808]
Hepatitis C Coun. of Victoria [IO]
Hepatitis C Soc. of Canada [IO]

Hepatitis Rsrc. Network [14810]
Herbalists Without Borders [13634]
Hereditary Colon Cancer Assn. [13829]
Herpes Rsrc. Center - Amer. Social Hea. Assn.
    [16412]
Hesperian Found. [14980]
HHT Found. Intl. [14454]
Himalayan Intl. Inst. of Yoga Sci. and Philosophy
    of the U.S.A. [12348]
Hispanic Dental Assn. [14155]
Hispanic Neuropsychological Soc. [15388]
History of Dermatology Soc. [10115]
Holistic Dental Assn. [14156]
Homeopathic Nurses Assn. [14846]
Hospice Educ. Inst. [14854]
Hospice and Palliative Nurses Assn. [15482]
Hospitalized Veterans Writing Proj. [16321]
Howard Gilman Found. [11504]
Human Ecology Action League [14364]
Human Growth Found. [16020]
Humanity Intl. [12859]
Huntington's Disease Soc. of Am. [15329]
Hydrocephalus Assn. [15330]
Hypoparathyroidism Assn. [14356]
Hysterectomy Educational Resources and
    Services Found. [15601]
IDEA Hea. and Fitness Assn. [15965]
Imagine World Hea. [IO]
Imagine World Hea. [14566]
Immune Deficiency Found. [14936]
Immunology of Diabetes Soc. [14225]
Impaired Physician Prog. [13246]
Incurably Ill for Animal Res. [13697]
Independence Plan for Neighborhood Councils
    [17219]
Independent Citizens Res. Found. for the Study of
    Degenerative Diseases [14263]
Infectious Diseases Soc. of Am. [14948]
Informed Homebirth/Informed Birth and Parenting
    [15602]
Infusion Nurses Soc. [16614]
Inst. for the Advancement of Human Behavior
    [13735]
Inst. for the Development of Emotional and Life
    Skills/National Inst. of Relationship Enhance-
    ment [15201]
Inst. for Expressive Anal. [16217]
Inst. of HeartMath [10174]
Inst. for Integral Development [13249]
Inst. for Labor and Mental Health [15202]
Inst. on Psychiatric Services/American Psychiatric
    Assn. [16085]
Inst. for Traditional Medicine and Preventive Hea.
    Care [13635]
Inter-American Conductive Educ. Assn. [9146]
Inter-Association Task Force on Alcohol and Other
    Substance Abuse Issues [13250]
Interamerican Coll. of Physicians and Surgeons
    [16000]
InterAmerican Heart Found. [13909]
Interchurch Medical Assistance [20242]
Intercontinental Fed. of Behavioral Optometry
    [15719]
Intercultural Cancer Coun. [13830]
Intermed Intl. [14982]
Intl. Acad. for Child Brain Development [15389]
Intl. Acad. of Gnathology-American Sect. [14158]
Intl. Acad. of Health Care Professionals [14705]
Intl. Acad. of Myodontics [14159]
Intl. Acad. for Sports Dentistry [16481]
Intl. Alliance for Child and Adolescent Mental Hea.
    and Schools [15204]
Intl. Alliance in Ser. and Educ. [11748]
Intl. and Amer. Associations of Clinical Nutrition-
    ists [15560]
Intl. Anesthesia Res. Soc. [13684]
Intl. Assn. for Aquatic Animal Medicine [16792]
Intl. Assn. of Cancer Victors and Friends [13831]
Intl. Assn. for Cognitive Psychotherapy [16218]
Intl. Assn. for Colon Hydrotherapy [14567]
International Association for Colon Hydrotherapy
    [IO]
Intl. Assn. for Comparative Res. on Leukemia and
    Related Diseases [15647]
Intl. Assn. of Coroners and Medical Examiners
    [15093]

Intl. Assn. for Dental Res. [14161]
Intl. Assn. of Flight Paramedics [14334]
Intl. Assn. of Healthcare Central Ser. Materiel Mgt.
    [14886]
Intl. Assn. for Healthcare Security and Safety
    [14887]
Intl. Assn. of Homes and Services for the Ageing
    [11289]
Intl. Assn. of Human-Animal Interaction Organiza-
    tions [16615]
Intl. Assn. of Hygienic Physicians [15278]
Intl. Assn. for Medical Assistance to Travellers
    [13343]
Intl. Assn. of Medical Equip. Remarketers and
    Servicers [15139]
Intl. Assn. of Medical Intuitives [15040]
Intl. Assn. for Medicinal Compliance [15041]
Intl. Assn. of Military Flight Surgeon-Pilots [13541]
Intl. Assn. of Ocular Surgeons [15684]
Intl. Assn. of Optometric Executives [15720]
Intl. Assn. of Oral and Maxillofacial Surgeons
    [15736]
Intl. Assn. for Organ Donation [16671]
Intl. Assn. of Orofacial Myology [15869]
Intl. Assn. for Orthodontics [14162]
Intl. Assn. for Oxygen Therapy [16616]
Intl. Assn. for Paratuberculosis [16793]
Intl. Assn. of Pediatric Lab. Medicine [15888]
Intl. Assn. of Rehabilitation Professionals [16322]
Intl. Assn. of Reiki Professionals [13637]
Intl. Assn. for Relational Psychoanalysis and
    Psychotherapy [16108]
Intl. Assn. of Sickle Cell Nurses And Physician
    Assistants [14706]
Intl. Assn. of Structural Integrators [13638]
Intl. Assn. for the Stud. of Pain [15841]
Intl. Atherosclerosis Soc. [13910]
Intl. Behavioral Neuroscience Soc. [15408]
Intl. Bd. of Environmental Medicine [14365]
Intl. Bronchoesophagological Soc. [13779]
Intl. Bundle Br. Block Assn. [13911]
Intl. Center for Attitudinal Healing [15206]
Intl. Cesarean Awareness Network [15604]
Intl. Childbirth Educ. Assn. [15605]
Intl. Children's Anophthalmia Network [16857]
Intl. Chiropractors Assn. [14008]
Intl. Coll. of Dentists [14163]
Intl. Coll. for Hea. Cooperation in Developing
    Countries - Italy [IO]
Intl. Coll. of Surgeons [16583]
Intl. Commn. for the Prevention of Alcoholism and
    Drug Dependency [13251]
Intl. Comm. Against Mental Illness [15207]
Intl. Complement Soc. [14938]
Intl. Cong. of Oral Implantologists [14165]
Intl. Consumer Prdt. Hea. and Safety Org. [3178]
Intl. Correspondence Soc. of Allergists and Clini-
    cal Immunologists [13601]
Intl. Cytokine Soc. [6580]
Intl. Dalkon Shield Victims Educ. Assn. [16898]
Intl. Dental Hea. Found. [14166]
Intl. Doctors in Alcoholics Anonymous [13252]
Intl. EECP Therapists Assn. [16619]
Intl. Embryo Transfer Soc. [16794]
Intl. Expressive Arts Therapy Assn. [13712]
Intl. Eye Found. [15685]
Intl. Fed. of Esthetic Dentistry [14167]
Intl. Fed. of Foot and Ankle Societies [16045]
Intl. Fed. of Marfan Syndrome Organizations
    [14456]
Intl. Fed. of Martial Arts and Oriental Medicine
    [15021]
Intl. Fed. of Ophthalmological Societies [15686]
Intl. Fed. of Psoriasis Associations [14203]
Intl. Fed. for Psychoanalytic Educ. [9028]
The Intl. Found. [12434]
Intl. Found. for Homeopathy [14849]
Intl. Functional Elecl. Stimulation Soc. [15390]
Intl. Genetic Epidemiology Soc. [14376]
Intl. Guild of Hair Removal Specialists [14309]
Intl. Hea. Evaluation Assn. [IO]
Intl. Hea. Evaluation Assn. [14568]
Intl. Hea. Org., India [IO]
Intl. Hea. and Temperance Assn. [13304]
Intl. Healthcare Safety Professional Certification
    Bd. [16379]

A star before a book entry number signifies that the name is not listed separately, but is mentioned within the entry.

Intl. Hyperhidrosis Soc. [14357]
Intl. Inst. for Baubiologie and Ecology [4513]
Intl. Leptospirosis Soc. [14950]
Intl. Life Sciences Inst. - North Am. [15561]
Intl. Liver Transplantation Soc. [16672]
Intl. Lyme and Assoc. Diseases Soc. [14267]
Intl. Maritime Hea. Assn. [IO]
Intl. Medical Corps [12862]
Intl. Medical and Dental Hypnotherapy Assn.
  [14924]
Intl. Medical Equip. Collaborative [IO]
Intl. Medical Equip. Collaborative [14569]
Intl. Medical Spa Assn. [1870]
Intl. Medical Volunteers Assn. [15075]
Intl. Mental Game Coaching Assn. [23289]
Intl. Mobile Hea. Assn. [14724]
Intl. Order of Saint Luke the Physician [20499]
Intl. Org. of Glutaric Acidemia [15332]
Intl. Org. of Multiple Sclerosis Nurses [15486]
Intl. Partnership for Microbicides [13572]
Intl. Pediatric Hypertension Assn. [14907]
Intl. Pediatric Nephrology Assn. [15292]
Intl. Pediatric Transplant Assn. [16673]
Intl. Perimetric Soc. [15688]
Intl. Planned Parenthood Fed., Western
  Hemisphere Region [12184]
Intl. Post Polio Support Org. [16048]
Intl. Premature Ovarian Failure Assn. [15606]
Intl. Psycho-Oncology Soc. [13834]
Intl. RadioSurgery Assn. [16269]
Intl. Refractive Surgery Club [15689]
Intl. Relief Friendship Found. [13171]
Intl. REST Investigators Soc. [16220]
Intl. Scleroderma Network [16387]
Intl. Sharps Injury Prevention Soc. [16380]
Intl. Skeletal Soc. [16289]
Intl. Soc. for Aging and Physical Activity [13545]
Intl. Soc. for Anaesthetic Pharmacology [13685]
Intl. Soc. of Arthroscopy, Knee Surgery and Ortho-
  paedic Sports Medicine [15771]
Intl. Soc. for Behavioral Nutrition and Physical
  Activity [13745]
Intl. Soc. for Clinical Densitometry [15788]
Intl. Soc. for Complementary Medicine Res.
  [13639]
Intl. Soc. for Cmpt. Assisted Orthopaedic Surgery
  [15772]
Intl. Soc. of Cosmetic and Laser Surgeons
  [14048]
Intl. Soc. for Dermatologic Surgery [14204]
Intl. Soc. of Dermatology [14205]
Intl. Soc. of Disease Surveillance [14269]
Intl. Soc. of First Responders [14317]
Intl. Soc. for Heart and Lung Transplantation
  [16674]
Intl. Soc. for Imaging in the Eye [15690]
Intl. Soc. for Infectious Diseases [14951]
Intl. Soc. of Lymphology [15016]
Intl. Soc. on Metabolic Eye Disease [15691]
Intl. Soc. of Oncology Pharmacy Practitioners
  [15937]
Intl. Soc. for Pharmacoepidemiology [15939]
Intl. Soc. for Plastination [15870]
Intl. Soc. for the Psychological Treatments of the
  Schizophrenias and Other Psychoses - USA
  [15209]
Intl. Soc. of Regulatory Toxicology and
  Pharmacology [14570]
International Society of Regulatory Toxicology and
  Pharmacology [IO]
Intl. Soc. of Sports Nutrition [15562]
Intl. Soc. for the Stud. of Trauma and Dissociation
  [15210]
Intl. Soc. for the Stud. of Women's Sexual Hea.
  [16404]
Intl. Soc. on Thrombosis and Haemostasis
  [14793]
Intl. Soc. for Traumatic Stress Stud. [16489]
Intl. Soc. of Travel Medicine [15172]
Intl. Soc. for Vascular Surgery [16584]
Intl. Soc. of Veterinary Dermatopathology [16795]
Intl. Stillbirth Alliance [13982]
Intl. Stuttering Assn. [16498]
Intl. Trachoma Initiative [16858]
Intl. Transactional Anal. Assn. [16089]

Intl. Treatment Preparedness Coalition [13573]
Intl. Union Against Sexually Transmitted Infec-
  tions, Regional Off. for North Am. [16414]
Intl. Union for Hea. Promotion and Educ. [IO]
Intl. Veterinary Acupuncture Soc. [16796]
Intl. Veterinary Ultrasound Soc. [16797]
Intl. Vitamin A Consultative Gp. [15564]
Intl. Yan Xin Qigong Assn. [13640]
Intersociety Coun. for Pathology Info. [15871]
Interstate Postgraduate Medical Assn. of North
  Am. [14386]
Interstitial Cystitis Assn. [16708]
Iraqi Medical Sciences Assn. [14987]
Islamic Medical Assn. of North Am. [16003]
Islamic Org. for Medical Sciences [IO]
ITEM Coalition [14690]
Japan Overseas Christian Medical Cooperative
  Ser. [IO]
JARC [12570]
Jaw Joints and Allied Musculo-Skeletal Disorders
  Found. [15773]
Jewish Assn. for Services for the Aged [11290]
Jin Shin Do Found. for Bodymind Acupressure
  [15746]
Joint Commn. on Accreditation of Healthcare
  Organizations [14888]
Joint Commn. on Allied Hea. Personnel in
  Ophthalmology [15692]
Joint Commn. on Sports Medicine and Sci.
  [16483]
Joint Coun. of Allergy, Asthma and Immunology
  [13602]
Josiah Macy, Jr. Found. [14571]
Juvenile Diabetes Res. Found. Intl. [14228]
Kappa Psi [24568]
Karen Horney Clinic [16109]
Kennedy's Disease Assn. [15334]
Kids With Food Allergies [13603]
Kids With Heart Natl. Assn. for Children's Heart
  Disorders [13915]
KIDSCOPE [11518]
Korean-American Medical Assn. [15174]
Lalmba Assn. [12866]
Lamaze Birth Without Pain Educ. Assn. [15607]
Lambda Kappa Sigma [24569]
Largely Positive [18177]
Latino Org. for Liver Awareness [14811]
Leadership Coun. of Aging Organizations [11293]
Legal Counsel for the Elderly [12497]
Legal Sers. for the Elderly [12499]
Lesbian, Gay, Bisexual, and Transgender People
  in Medicine [12243]
Leukemia and Lymphoma Soc. [13837]
Lewy Body Dementia Assn. [15335]
Life Extension Soc. [14074]
Life Res. Inst. [14572]
LifeBanc [14290]
Lifegain Inst. [14573]
Little Hearts [13966]
The Living Bank Intl. [14291]
LMBS Network [16539]
Lung Cancer Alliance [13839]
Lupus Found. of Am. [15014]
Lupus Info. Network [15015]
Lyme Disease Assn. [14271]
Lyme Disease Found. [14272]
Lymphoma Assn. [IO]
Macro Soc. [10184]
Macular Disease Soc. [IO]
Mail for Me Club [11621]
Make-A-Wish Found. of Am. [11707]
Make Today Count [13841]
Malignant Hyperthermia Assn. of the U.S. [14464]
Maniilaq Assn. [12627]
MAP Intl. [20243]
MAP Intl. - Eastern Africa Off. [IO]
March of Dimes Birth Defects Found. [13756]
Marijuana Policy Proj. [18024]
Mature Market Rsrc. Center [11296]
Medicaid/SCHIP Dental Assn. [14168]
Medical Equip. and Tech. Assn. [7306]
Medical Gp. Mgt. Assn. [15067]
Medical Image Perception Soc. [15140]
Medical Letter [15940]
Medical Missions Response [20246]

Medical Records Inst. [15098]
Medical Res. Modernization Comm. [15109]
Medical Spa Soc. [1871]
Medical Subjects Unit [22843]
MedicAlert Found. Intl. [14318]
Medicare Rights Center [17690]
Medicus Mundi Intl. [IO]
MediSend Intl. [12530]
Meds and Food for Kids [11622]
Mended Hearts, Inc. [13916]
Meniere's Network [15826]
Mental Hea. Am. [15211]
Mental Hea. Workers Without Borders [15212]
Mental Res. Inst. [13737]
Michael E. DeBakey Intl. Surgical Soc. [13917]
Midwifery Educ. Accreditation Coun. [8063]
Midwives Alliance of North Am. [15610]
Milton H. Erickson Found. [16221]
Mission Doctors Assn. [12532]
Mitochondrial Medicine Soc. [14078]
Mothers' Voices [13574]
Multiple Sclerosis Found. [15338]
Musculoskeletal Ultrasound Soc. [16696]
Museum of Menstruation and Women's Hea.
  [15611]
Myasthenia Gravis Assn. [IO]
Myasthenia Gravis Found. of Am. [15340]
The Myositis Assn. [15341]
Nail Patella Syndrome Worldwide [14467]
NAMM Found. Res. Div. [10653]
NANDA Intl. [15489]
Narcotic Educational Found. of Am. [13256]
NARSAD: Mental Hea. Res. Assn. [15213]
Natl. Abandoned Infants Assistance Rsrc. Center
  [12412]
Natl. Aboriginal Hea. Org. [IO]
Natl. Abortion Fed. [11223]
Natl. Abstinence Educ. Assn. [9123]
Natl. Acad. of Neuropsychology [16158]
Natl. Acad. of Opticianry [15707]
Natl. Acad. for Teaching and Learning About Ag-
  ing [11297]
Natl. Accrediting Agency for Clinical Lab. Sciences
  [15141]
Natl. Adrenal Diseases Found. [14358]
Natl. Adult Day Services Assn. [11298]
Natl. AIDS Fund [13576]
Natl. Alliance of Advocates for Buprenorphine
  Treatment [16511]
Natl. Alliance for Autism Res. [13726]
Natl. Alliance for Eye and Vision Res. [16872]
Natl. Alliance for Food Safety and Security [1537]
Natl. Alliance for Hea. Info. Tech. [15142]
Natl. Alliance for Hispanic Hea. [13176]
Natl. Alliance for Infusion Therapy [14839]
Natl. Alliance of Medical Researchers and Teach-
  ing Physicians [15143]
Natl. Alliance on Mental Illness [15214]
Natl. Alliance of Primary Care Informatics [14956]
Natl. Alliance of Senior Citizens [11299]
Natl. Alliance of State Pharmacy Associations
  [15943]
Natl. Alliance for Thrombosis and Thrombophilia
  [13931]
Natl. Alopecia Areata Found. [16386]
Natl. Amer. Arab Nurses Assn. [15490]
Natl. Anemia Action Coun. [14794]
Natl. Asian Amer. Pacific Islander Mental Hea.
  Assn. [15215]
Natl. Asian Pacific Center on Aging [11300]
Natl. Assn. of Addiction Treatment Providers
  [13259]
Natl. Assn. for the Advancement of Orthotics and
  Prosthetics [15786]
Natl. Assn. for the Advancement of
  Psychoanalysis [16110]
Natl. Assn. of Alternative Benefits Consultants
  [1867]
Natl. Assn. of Area Agencies on Aging [11301]
Natl. Assn. of Boards of Examiners of Long Term
  Care Administrators [15538]
Natl. Assn. of Boards of Pharmacy [15944]
Natl. Assn. of Chain Drug Stores [2985]
Natl. Assn. for Children of Alcoholics [13261]
Natl. Assn. for Children's Behavioral Hea. [16090]

Reference to "IO" in place of a book number signifies that the association may be found in the 45th edition of International Organizations.

Natl. Assn. of Community Hea. Centers [14574]
Natl. Assn. for Continence [16709]
Natl. Assn. of County and City Hea. Officials [6217]
Natl. Assn. of County Hea. Fac. Administrators [15069]
Natl. Assn. of Dental Assistants [14169]
Natl. Assn. of Dental Labs. [14170]
Natl. Assn. for Direct Care Workers of Color [14709]
Natl. Assn. of Disability Evaluating Professionals [14575]
Natl. Assn. for Drama Therapy [16222]
Natl. Assn. on Drug Abuse Problems [13262]
Natl. Assn. of Emergency Medical Technicians [14335]
Natl. Assn. of Fed. Veterinarians [16799]
Natl. Assn. of First Responders [14320]
Natl. Assn. of Free Clinics [14727]
Natl. Assn. of Geriatric Educ. Centers [14513]
Natl. Assn. of Hea. Care Assistants [14514]
Natl. Assn. of Hea. Data Organizations [14576]
Natl. Assn. of Hea. Educ. Centers [14675]
Natl. Assn. for Hea. and Fitness [15967]
Natl. Assn. of Hea. Sci. Educ. Partnership [9107]
Natl. Assn. of Hea. Services Executives [14577]
Natl. Assn. of Hea. Unit Coordinators [14578]
Natl. Assn. for Healthcare Quality [16264]
Natl. Assn. for Healthcare Recruitment [15070]
Natl. Assn. of Healthcare Transport Mgt. [14579]
Natl. Assn. of Hepatitis Task Forces [14812]
Natl. Assn. of Hispanic Nurses [15494]
Natl. Assn. for Home Care and Hospice [14840]
Natl. Assn. of Hosp. Hospitality Houses [14891]
Natl. Assn. for Human Development [11303]
Natl. Assn. of Lesbian/Gay Addiction Professionals [13263]
Natl. Assn. of Locum Tenens Org. [16004]
Natl. Assn. of Medical Examiners [15094]
Natl. Assn. Medical Staff Services [15071]
Natl. Assn. of Myofascial Trigger Point Therapists [16624]
Natl. Assn. of Nurse Practitioners in Women's Hea. [15497]
Natl. Assn. of Optometrists and Opticians [15721]
Natl. Assn. of Orthopaedic Nurses [15498]
Natl. Assn. of People With AIDS [13578]
Natl. Assn. of Physician Nurses [15500]
Natl. Assn. of Physician Recruiters [16006]
Natl. Assn. for Poetry Therapy [16223]
Natl. Assn. for Premenstrual Syndrome [IO]
Natl. Assn. for Proton Therapy [15649]
Natl. Assn. for Pseudoxanthoma Elasticum [14207]
Natl. Assn. of Psychiatric Hea. Systems [16091]
Natl. Assn. of Public Hospitals and Hea. Systems [14892]
Natl. Assn. of Rehabilitation Instructors [16324]
Natl. Assn. of Rehabilitation Providers and Agencies [16326]
Natl. Assn. of Residents and Interns [15175]
Natl. Assn. of Rural Hea. Clinics [16245]
Natl. Assn. for Rural Mental Hea. [15217]
Natl. Assn. of School Nurses [15501]
Natl. Assn. of School Nurses for the Deaf [14768]
Natl. Assn. of Senior Companion Proj. Directors [11304]
Natl. Assn. of Specialty Hea. Organizations [14650]
Natl. Assn. of State Comprehensive Hea. Insurance Plans [14691]
Natl. Assn. of State EMS Officials [14337]
Natl. Assn. of State Head Injury Administrators [14529]
Natl. Assn. of State Mental Hea. Prog. Directors [15219]
Natl. Assn. of State Units on Aging [11305]
Natl. Assn. of Subacute and Post-Acute Care [14728]
Natl. Assn. of VA Physicians and Dentists [16007]
Natl. Assn. of Vietnamese Nurses [15504]
Natl. Assn. of Vision Professionals [15693]
Natl. Ataxia Found. [15342]
Natl. Athletic Trainers' Assn. [23954]
Natl. Attention Deficit Disorder Assn. [15343]

Natl. Ayurvedic Medical Assn. [13642]
Natl. Black Alcoholism and Addiction Coun. [13265]
Natl. Black Nurses Assn. [15505]
Natl. Bd. for Certification in Dental Lab. Tech. [14172]
Natl. Bd. for Certification in Dental Tech. [14173]
Natl. Bd. for Certification in Occupational Therapy [16625]
Natl. Bd. for Certification of Orthopaedic Technologists [15774]
Natl. Bd. of Examiners in Optometry [15722]
Natl. Bd. of Medical Examiners [15095]
Natl. Bd. of Osteopathic Medical Examiners [15812]
Natl. Bd. of Podiatric Medical Examiners [16046]
Natl. Bd. for Respiratory Care [16626]
Natl. Bone Marrow Transplant Link [16676]
Natl. Burn Victim Found. [13784]
Natl. Bus. Coalition on Hea. [14580]
Natl. Catholic Coun. on Alcoholism and Related Drug Problems [13266]
Natl. Catholic Pharmacists Guild of the U.S. [15945]
Natl. Caucus and Center on Black Aged [11306]
Natl. Center for Amer. Indian and Alaska Native Mental Hea. Res. [15220]
Natl. Center for Educ. in Maternal and Child Hea. [13969]
Natl. Center for Farmworker Hea. [14581]
Natl. Center for Hea. Educ. [14582]
Natl. Certification Commn. for Acupuncture and Oriental Medicine [15747]
Natl. Chronic Pain Soc. [15845]
Natl. Coalition for Adult Immunization [14583]
Natl. Coalition for Cancer Res. [17691]
Natl. Coalition for Cancer Survivorship [13852]
Natl. Coalition of Creative Arts Therapies Associations [16224]
Natl. Coalition of Ethnic Minority Nurse Associations [15507]
Natl. Coalition for LGBT Hea. [12247]
Natl. Coalition for Promoting Physical Activity [23653]
Natl. Coalition for Res. in Neurological Disorders [15346]
Natl. Coalition on Rural Aging [11307]
Natl. Commn. on Certification of Physician Assistants [15975]
Natl. Commn. on Correctional Hea. Care [14729]
Natl. Comm. for the Prevention of Alcoholism and Drug Dependency [13267]
Natl. Comm. for Quality Assurance [16265]
Natl. Community Pharmacists Assn. [2986]
Natl. Conf. of Local Environmental Hea. Administrators [16246]
Natl. Consortium on Hea. Sci. and Tech. Educ. [8473]
Natl. Contact Lens Examiners [15723]
Natl. Coordinating Coun. for Medication Error Reporting and Prevention [14653]
Natl. Coun. Against Hea. Fraud [17692]
Natl. Coun. on the Aging [11309]
Natl. Coun. on Alcoholism and Drug Dependence [13268]
Natl. Coun. for Community Behavioral Healthcare [15223]
Natl. Coun. on Interpreting in Hea. Care [1851]
Natl. Coun. on Minority Educ. in Transplantation [16677]
Natl. Coun. on Patient Info. and Educ. [15946]
Natl. Coun. for Prescription Drug Programs [2987]
Natl. Coun. on Rehabilitation Educ. [16329]
Natl. Coun. of State Boards of Nursing [15508]
Natl. Coun. on Strength and Fitness [23955]
Natl. Coun. for Therapeutic Recreation Certification [16627]
Natl. Coun. of Urban Indian Hea. [15277]
Natl. Coun. on Women's Hea. [16904]
Natl. Credentialing Agency for Lab. Personnel [15145]
Natl. Dental Assistants Assn. [14174]
Natl. Dental Assn. [14175]
Natl. Dental Hygienists' Assn. [14177]
Natl. Denturist Assn. [14178]

Natl. Digestive Diseases Info. CH [14422]
Natl. Educ. Alliance for Borderline Personality Disorder [15224]
Natl. Environmental Hea. Assn. [14367]
Natl. Eosinophilia-Myalgia Syndrome Network [16662]
Natl. Episcopal Hea. Ministries [14584]
Natl. Eye Res. Found. [15724]
Natl. Families in Action [13269]
Natl. Family Partnership [13270]
Natl. Family Planning and Reproductive Hea. Assn. [12185]
Natl. Fed. of Licensed Practical Nurses [15509]
Natl. Fitness Therapy Assn. [15968]
Natl. Found. for Brain Res. [15397]
Natl. Found. of Dentistry for the Handicapped [14179]
Natl. Found. for Depressive Illness [15225]
Natl. Found. for Ectodermal Dysplasias [14468]
Natl. Found. for Facial Reconstruction [14065]
Natl. Found. for Infectious Diseases [14953]
Natl. Fragile X Found. [14469]
Natl. Free Clinic Found. of Am. [14585]
Natl. Gaucher Found. [15252]
Natl. Gym Assn. [23654]
Natl. Headache Found. [14533]
Natl. Hea. Assn. [15279]
Natl. Hea. Care Anti-Fraud Assn. [14963]
Natl. Hea. Club Assn. [3670]
Natl. Hea. Coun. [14586]
Natl. Hea. Fed. [14587]
Natl. Hea. Info. Center [14588]
Natl. Hea. Policy Forum [17693]
Natl. Healthy Start Assn. [15613]
Natl. Heartburn Alliance [14423]
Natl. Hemophilia Found. [14795]
Natl. Hepatitis C Advocacy Coun. [14813]
Natl. Home Infusion Assn. [15043]
Natl. Home Oxygen Patients Assn. [14404]
Natl. Hospice and Palliative Care Org. [14856]
Natl. Indian Hea. Bd. [12629]
Natl. Infant Torticollis Assn. [14945]
Natl. Initiative for Children's Healthcare Quality [13970]
Natl. Inst. of Electromedical Info. [14311]
Natl. Inst. for Jewish Hospice [14857]
Natl. Inst. of Senior Housing [12328]
Natl. Interfaith Coalition on Aging [11314]
Natl. Jewish Medical and Res. Center [16361]
Natl. Kidney Found. [15294]
Natl. Labor Alliance of Hea. Care Coalitions [24091]
Natl. Latina Hea. Network [14589]
Natl. Latino Behavioral Hea. Assn. [15227]
Natl. Latino Coun. on Alcohol and Tobacco Prevention [12269]
Natl. League for Nursing [15510]
Natl. Lung Cancer Partnership [13854]
Natl. Lymphedema Network [15018]
Natl. Marfan Found. [16652]
Natl. Meals on Wheels Found. [11315]
Natl. Medical Assn. [15176]
Natl. Meningitis Assn. [14281]
Natl. Minority AIDS Coun. [13580]
Natl. Minority Hea. Assn. [14590]
Natl. MIS User Gp. [7207]
Natl. Multiple Sclerosis Soc. [15349]
Natl. Optometric Assn. [15725]
Natl. Org. for Albinism and Hypopigmentation [15255]
Natl. Org. of Alternative Programs [16382]
Natl. Org. for Associate Degree Nursing [15512]
Natl. Org. Caring for Kids [11638]
Natl. Org. of Circumcision Info. Rsrc. Centers [11732]
Natl. Org. for Competency Assurance [14591]
Natl. Org. for Disorders of the Corpus Callosum [15350]
Natl. Org. For Empowering Caregivers [13295]
Natl. Org. of Nurses with Disabilities [15514]
Natl. Osteoporosis Found. [15775]
Natl. Pain Educ. Coun. [15846]
Natl. Parkinson Found. [15351]
Natl. Perinatal Assn. [15900]
Natl. Pharmaceutical Assn. [15947]

A star before a book entry number signifies that the name is not listed separately, but is mentioned within the entry.

Natl. Pharmaceutical Coun. [2978]
Natl. Phlebotomy Assn. [14796]
Natl. Physicians Alliance [16009]
Natl. Podiatric Medical Assn. [16047]
Natl. Prison Hospice Assn. [14858]
Natl. Private Duty Assn. [14842]
Natl. Prostate Cancer Coalition [13856]
Natl. Psychological Assn. for Psychoanalysis
  [16111]
Natl. Qigong (Chi Kung) Assn. [13644]
Natl. Registry of Emergency Medical Technicians
  [14342]
Natl. Rehabilitation Assn. [16330]
Natl. Rehabilitation Counseling Assn. [16331]
Natl. Rehabilitation Info. Center [16332]
Natl. Remotivation Therapy Org. [16226]
Natl. Rsrc. Center for Hea. and Safety in Child
  Care and Early Educ. [11536]
Natl. Reye's Syndrome Found. [16366]
Natl. Rural Hea. Assn. [16248]
Natl. Safe Workplace Institute/SafeSpaces.com
  [12978]
Natl. Scoliosis Found. [16393]
Natl. Senior Citizens Law Center [11316]
Natl. Senior Games Assn. [23655]
Natl. SIDS/Infant Death Rsrc. Center [16526]
Natl. Soc. of Genetic Counselors [14506]
Natl. Soc. for Histotechnology [15146]
Natl. Spasmodic Dysphonia Assn. [15352]
Natl. Spasmodic Torticollis Assn. [15353]
Natl. Spinal Cord Injury Assn. [16468]
Natl. Strength and Conditioning Assn. [23957]
Natl. Stroke Assn. [16494]
Natl. Tay-Sachs and Allied Diseases Assn.
  [15354]
Natl. Temperance and Prohibition Coun. [13305]
Natl. Therapeutic Recreation Soc. [16628]
Natl. Tuberculosis Controllers Assn. [14283]
Natl. Urban League [17138]
Natl. Vaccine Info. Center [13972]
Natl. Viral Hepatitis Roundtable [14815]
Natl. Voluntary Organizations Active in Disaster
  [12874]
Natl. Wellness Inst. [16057]
Natl. Whistleblower Center [12982]
Natl. Woman's Christian Temperance Union
  [13306]
Natl. Women's Hea. Network [16906]
Native Amer. Community Bd. [12630]
NBIA Disorders Assn. [15355]
NEA Hea. Info. Network [8474]
Need [12875]
Neuro-Optometric Rehabilitation Assn., Intl.
  [15300]
Neuroblastoma Children's Cancer Soc. [13858]
Neurocritical Care Soc. [14070]
Neurofibromatosis [14471]
Neurosurgeons to Preserve Hea. Care Access
  [15414]
Neurosurgery Intl. [15415]
NIDCD - Natl. Temporal Bone, Hearing and Bal-
  ance Pathology Rsrc. Registry [15121]
Nigerian Women Leadership Coun. Intl. [12640]
NMC [16802]
Nonverbal Learning Disorders Assn. [14998]
Nordic Assn. for Andrology [IO]
North Amer. Alliance for the Advancement of Na-
  tive Peoples [12631]
North Amer. Assn. for Ambulatory Urgent Care
  [13663]
North Amer. Assn. of Medical Educ. and Commun.
  Companies [8874]
North Amer. Assn. for the Stud. of Obesity
  [15576]
North Amer. Clinical Dermatologic Soc. [14212]
North Amer. Menopause Soc. [15614]
North Amer. Sikh Medical and Dental Assn.
  [16416]
North Amer. Soc. for Dialysis and Transplantation
  [15295]
North Amer. Soc. of Obstetric Medicine [15615]
North Amer. Soc. for Pediatric Gastroenterology,
  Hepatology and Nutrition [14424]
North Amer. Soc. for Pediatric Medicine [15891]
North Amer. Soc. for the Stud. of Hypertension in
  Pregnancy [16342]

North Amer. Specialized Coagulation Lab. Assn.
  [14996]
North Amer. Tang Shou Tao Assn. [13645]
North Amer. Transplant Coordinators Org. [16681]
North Amer. Vascular Biology Org. [16728]
North Amer. Vodder Assn. of Lymphatic Therapy
  [15019]
North Amer. Yoga Fed. [11219]
NSF Intl. [16249]
Nuclear Medicine Tech. Certification Bd. [15423]
Nurses Educational Funds [15516]
Nurses for a Healthier Tomorrow [15517]
Nurses' House [15518]
Nurses Org. of Veterans Affairs [15519]
The Nurturing Network [13434]
Nutrition for Optimal Hea. Assn. [15567]
Obesity Action Coalition [15577]
Occupational Knowledge Intl. [5099]
Off. of Population Affairs CH [12757]
Ohashi Inst. [15748]
Oncology Nursing Soc. [15521]
Oper. Smile [12534]
Ophthalmic Photographers' Soc. [15696]
OPP Concerned Sheep Breeders Soc. [16803]
Opticians Assn. of Am. [15709]
Options for Animals Intl. [16804]
Optometric Extension Prog. Found. [15727]
Optometric Historical Soc. [15728]
ORBIS Intl. [15697]
Organic Acidemia Assn. [14472]
Org. for Autism Res. [13728]
Orthodontic Education and Res. Found. [14183]
Orthopaedic Res. Soc. [15776]
Orthopaedic Sect., Amer. Physical Therapy Assn.
  [16630]
Osteogenesis Imperfecta Found. [15779]
Osteopathic Intl. Alliance [15813]
Outpatient Ophthalmic Surgery Soc. [15698]
Pacific Dermatologic Assn. [14213]
Paget Found. for Paget's Disease of Bone and
  Related Disorders [15256]
Pain Mgt. and Sclerotherapy [15814]
Pan-American Allergy Soc. [13604]
Pan-American Assn. of Ophthalmology [15699]
Pan Amer. Hea. and Educ. Found. [12536]
Pan Amer. Hea. Org. [IO]
Pan Amer. Hea. Org. [14592]
Pan Amer. Sanitary Bur. [14593]
Pan Amer. Sanitary Bur. [IO]
Pancreatic Cancer Action Network [15851]
Paratuberculosis Awareness and Res. Assn.
  [14425]
Parents Against Childhood Epilepsy [14382]
Parents of Infants and Children with Kernicterus
  [15358]
Parents of Kids with Infectious Diseases [14954]
Parkinson Alliance [15359]
Parkinson's Disease Found. [15360]
Parkinson's Disease Soc. of the United Kingdom
  [IO]
Partners in Hea. [IO]
Partners in Hea. [12270]
Partnership for Prevention [14594]
Pathfinder Intl. [12186]
Patience T'ai Chi Assn. [23897]
PBCers Org. [14816]
PDA [2979]
PE4life [8991]
Pediatric Cardiac Intensive Care Soc. [15892]
Pediatric Infectious Diseases Soc. [14955]
Pediatric Keratoplasty Assn. [15700]
Pediatric Neurotransmitter Disease Assn. [15361]
Pediatric Nursing Certification Bd. [15522]
Pediatric Orthopedic Soc. of North Am. [15780]
Peer Hea. Exchange [9338]
People-Animals-Love [16632]
People-to-People Hea. Found. [14984]
People's Medical Soc. [17694]
Performing Arts Medicine Assn. [16164]
Perfusion Prog. Directors' Coun. [13921]
Peripheral Arterial Disease Coalition [13922]
Peruvian Heart Assn. [13923]
Pharmaceutical Care Mgt. Assn. [2988]
Pharmaceutical and Healthcare Sciences Soc.
  [IO]

Pharmaceutical Res. and Manufacturers of Am.
  [2980]
Pharmacy Technician Educators Coun. [8963]
Phi Alpha Sigma [24543]
Phi Chi Medical Fraternity [24544]
Phi Delta Chi [24570]
Phi Delta Epsilon Medical Fraternity [24540]
Phi Epsilon Kappa [24574]
Philippine Nurses Assn. of Am. [2840]
Phoenix House [13273]
Physician Asst. Educ. Assn. [15976]
Physicians Comm. for Responsible Medicine
  [14595]
Pierre Fauchard Acad. [14184]
Pierre Robin Network [14473]
Pituitary Network Assn. [16022]
Planetree [14596]
Planned Parenthood Fed. of Am. [12187]
Plastic Surgery Educational Found. [14051]
Plastic Surgery Res. Coun. [14052]
Platelet Disorder Support Assn. [13730]
Polio Soc. [15362]
Postgraduate Center for Mental Hea. [16227]
Prader-Willi Found. [14474]
Prader-Willi Syndrome Assn. (U.S.A.) [14475]
Pre-Eclampsia Soc. [IO]
Pregnant With Cancer Network [13865]
Premier Advocacy [14597]
Price-Pottenger Nutrition Found. [15568]
PRIDE Youth Programs [13276]
PRISMS: Parents and Researchers Interested In
  Smith-Magenis Syndrome [14476]
Private Practice Section/American Physical
  Therapy Assn. [16633]
Professional Women in Healthcare [4045]
Prog. for Appropriate Tech. in Hea. [17000]
Progressive Osseous Heteroplasia Assn. [14477]
Proj. HOPE [14598]
Proj. HOPE [IO]
Proj. Inform [13583]
Proj. Magic [16634]
Prune Belly Syndrome Network [14478]
PSRC of Am. [16266]
Psychohistory Forum [16113]
Psychotherapy Network [16228]
Public Citizen Hea. Res. Gp. [16250]
Public Hea. Leadership Soc. [16252]
Public Hosp. Pharmacy Coalition [15949]
Public Responsibility in Medicine and Res.
  [18585]
Pull-thru Network [14427]
Purine Res. Soc. [15258]
QiGong Res. Soc. [13647]
R.A. Bloch Cancer Found. [13867]
Rabbinic Center for Res. and Counseling [16229]
The Radiance Technique Intl. Assn. [13648]
Radiation and Public Hea. Proj. [16270]
Radiation Therapy Oncology Gp. [15653]
Radical Caucus in Psychiatry [16092]
Radiological Soc. of North Am. [16293]
Radiology Bus. Mgt. Assn. [15074]
Radiology Mammography Intl. [13774]
Radix Inst. [13649]
Recovery, Inc. [16230]
Reel Recovery [11519]
Refugee Relief Intl. [12540]
Regulatory Affairs Professionals Soc. [IO]
Regulatory Affairs Professionals Soc. [14599]
Rehabilitation Intl. [16333]
Rehabilitation Tech. Assn. [16334]
Reiki Alliance [13651]
Renal Pathology Soc. [15872]
Renal Physicians Assn. [15298]
Renal Support Network [15299]
Resolve, The Natl. Infertility Assn. [14394]
Retinoblastoma Intl. [13869]
Riders for Hea. [15271]
Roger Wyburn-Mason and Jack M. Blount Found.
  for the Eradication of Rheumatoid Disease
  [16375]
Rolf Inst. of Structural Integration [13652]
Rose Kushner Breast Cancer Advisory Center
  [13870]
Royal Soc. of Medicine Found. [15178]
Safety Pharmacology Soc. [15950]

Reference to "IO" in place of a book number signifies that the association may be found in the 45th edition of International Organizations.

Sahid Khudiram Pathagar [IO]
Salvadoran Amer. Medical Soc. [15092]
San Francisco AIDS Found. [13584]
Schizophrenia Intl. Res. Soc. [15232]
School Nurse Achievement Prog. [15525]
Scleroderma Found. [16389]
Scleroderma Res. Found. [16390]
Scleroderma Support Gp. [16391]
Scoliosis Assn., Inc. [16394]
Scoliosis Res. Soc. [16395]
Sect. for Long Term Care and Rehabilitation [14894]
Sect. for Metropolitan Hospitals [14895]
Selective Mutism Found. [15233]
Serbian Amer. Medical and Dental Soc. [14185]
Serendipity Assn. [14832]
Seventh-Day Adventist Dietetic Assn. [15569]
Sexual Medicine Soc. of North Am. [16405]
Shape Up Am. [15969]
Sharsheret [13872]
Sheet Metal Occupational Hea. Inst. Trust [12991]
Shriners Hospitals for Children [13973]
Shy Drager Syndrome/Multiple Sys. Atrophy Support Gp. [15364]
Sickle Cell Disease Assn. of Am. [14797]
Sigmund Freud Archives [16115]
Simon Found. for Continence [16711]
Sino-American Pharmaceutical Professionals Assn. [15951]
Sister Kenny Rehabilitation Inst. [16335]
SisterSong Women of Color Reproductive Hea. Collective [18826]
Skin Cancer Found. [13874]
Sleep Res. Soc. [16429]
Smile Alliance Intl. [11721]
SmokeFree Educational Services [16434]
Smokenders [16435]
Social Psychiatry Res. Inst. [16094]
Social/Vocational Rehabilitation Clinic [16231]
Soc. for Academic Emergency Medicine [14344]
Soc. for Acupuncture Res. [13537]
Soc. for the Advancement of Blood Mgt. [14798]
Soc. for the Advancement of Women's Imaging [16294]
Soc. of Air Force Physicians [15264]
Soc. of Amer. Gastrointestinal and Endoscopic Surgeons [14428]
Soc. for the Anal. of African-American Public Hea. Issues [16253]
Soc. for Assisted Reproductive Tech. [16346]
Soc. of Behavioral Medicine [13740]
Soc. of Biological Psychiatry [16095]
Soc. of Cardiovascular Anesthesiologists [13689]
Soc. of Clinical Child and Adolescent Psychology [16171]
Soc. for Clinical and Experimental Hypnosis [14927]
Soc. for Clinical and Medical Hair Removal [14310]
Soc. of Clinical Res. Associates [14027]
Soc. for Clinical Trials [14028]
Soc. of Consulting Psychology [16172]
Soc. of Correctional Physicians [16011]
Soc. of Critical Care Medicine [14071]
Soc. of Diagnostic Medical Sonography [16438]
Soc. for Ear, Nose, and Throat Advances in Children [15827]
Soc. for Epidemiologic Res. [14377]
Soc. of Eye Surgeons [15703]
Soc. of Gastroenterology Nurses and Associates [14429]
Soc. of Govt. Ser. Urologists [16714]
Soc. for Gynecologic Investigation [15618]
Soc. of Gynecologic Oncologists [15654]
Soc. for Healthcare Consumer Advocacy of the Amer. Hosp. Assn. [15005]
Soc. for Healthcare Strategy and Market Development of the Amer. Hosp. Assn. [14896]
Soc. for Hematopathology [15874]
Soc. for Human Performance in Extreme Environments [6540]
Soc. of Interventional Pain Mgt. Surgery Centers [16588]
Soc. of Interventional Radiology [16300]
Soc. of Invasive Cardiovascular Professionals [13928]

Soc. for Investigative Dermatology [14214]
Soc. of Jewish Sci. [20202]
Soc. for Leukocyte Biology [16365]
Soc. for Male Reproduction and Urology [16343]
Soc. of Medical Consultants to the Armed Forces [15265]
Soc. of Medical Friends of Wine [23028]
Soc. of Medical Jurisprudence [15006]
Soc. for Melanoma Res. [13875]
Soc. for Menstrual Cycle Res. [15619]
Soc. of Military Orthopaedic Surgeons [15266]
Soc. of Military Otolaryngologists - Head and Neck Surgeons [15267]
Soc. of Nuclear Medicine [15424]
Soc. of Nuclear Medicine Technologist Sect. [15425]
Soc. for Nutrition Educ. [15570]
Soc. for Obstetric Anesthesia and Perinatology [15903]
Soc. for Occupational and Environmental Hea. [15633]
Soc. of Otorhinolaryngology and Head/Neck Nurses [15526]
Soc. for Pediatric Dermatology [14215]
Soc. of Pediatric Nurses [15527]
Soc. for Pediatric Psychology [16175]
Soc. for Pediatric Radiology [16301]
Soc. for Pediatric Res. [15899]
Soc. for Pediatric Urology [16715]
Soc. of Primary Care Policy Fellows [14664]
Soc. of Professors of Child and Adolescent Psychiatry [16096]
Soc. for the Psychological Stud. of Lesbian, Gay and Bisexual Issues [16180]
Soc. for the Psychological Stud. of Men and Masculinity [16181]
Soc. for Public Hea. Educ. [16254]
Soc. for Radiation Oncology Administrators [16302]
Soc. of Reproductive Surgeons [16349]
Soc. for Sex Therapy and Res. [16408]
Soc. for Simulation in Healthcare [15148]
Soc. for Social Work Leadership in Hea. Care [13209]
Soc. for the Stud. of Male Reproduction [16344]
Soc. for the Stud. of Reproduction [16350]
Soc. of Surgical Oncology [15655]
Soc. of Teachers of Family Medicine [14387]
Soc. for Theriogenology [16806]
Soc. of Thoracic Radiology [16305]
Soc. of Thoracic Surgeons [16644]
Soc. of Toxicologic Pathology [15876]
Soc. of Univ. Otolaryngologists - Head and Neck Surgeons [15828]
Soc. of Univ. Surgeons [16591]
Soc. of Univ. Urologists [16716]
Soc. for Vascular Surgery [16730]
Soc. for Vascular Ultrasound [16731]
Soc. for Women's Hea. Res. [16910]
Solidarity and Action Against the HIV Infection in India [16969]
Spina Bifida Assn. of Am. [16458]
Spinal Cord Soc. [16469]
Spirit of Women Hosp. Network [14898]
Spondylitis Assn. of Am. [16377]
Starlight Starbright Children's Found. [11724]
State EMS Training Coordinators Coun. of NASEMSO [14345]
Stratis Hea. [14600]
Stroke Awareness for Everyone [16495]
Stroke Clubs, Intl. [16496]
Student Global AIDS Campaign [13585]
Student Soc. for Stem Cell Res. [15114]
Student Veterinary Emergency and Critical Care Soc. [16810]
Sturge-Weber Found. [15365]
Sudden Cardiac Arrest Assn. [13933]
Suicide and Mental Hea. Assn. Intl. [15234]
Sun Safety Alliance [13876]
Support Org. for Trisomy 18, 13, and Related Disorders [14485]
Support for People with Oral and Head and Neck Cancer [13877]
SurfAid Intl. [11791]
Swiss Soc. for Hea. Policy [IO]

Sword Swallowers Assn. Intl. [10776]
Syndrome X Assn. [15259]
Take Charge! Cure Parkinson's [15366]
Taking Control of Your Diabetes [14231]
Task Force for Child Survival and Development [12542]
Tear Film and Ocular Surface Soc. [15729]
Tel-Med [14601]
Thai Physicians Assn. of Am. [16012]
Thalidomide Soc. [IO]
Therapy Dogs Intl. [16638]
Theta Psi [24566]
Thoracic Surgery Residents Assn. [16645]
Tissue Engg. Soc. Intl. [6610]
TOPS Club (Take Off Pounds Sensibly) [12649]
Tourette Syndrome Assn. [15367]
Tourette Syndrome (UK) Assn. [IO]
Transatlantic Partners Against AIDS [13586]
Transplant Recipients Intl. Org. [16682]
Transplant Speakers Intl. [16683]
Treatment Action Gp. [13587]
Treatment and Res. Advancements Assn. for Personality Disorder [15235]
Tremor Action Network [15369]
Trinity Medical Center [14900]
Trust for America's Hea. [16255]
Truth in Fitness [15970]
Tuberous Sclerosis Alliance [15371]
Tuberous Sclerosis Assn. [IO]
Turner Syndrome Soc. of the U.S. [14486]
Ukrainian Medical Assn. of North Am. [15182]
Undersea and Hyperbaric Medical Soc. [16697]
Union of Amer. Physicians and Dentists [24092]
Unite for Sight [13381]
United Black Fund [12204]
United Brachial Plexus Network [15403]
United Cerebral Palsy Associations [13935]
United Methodist Assn. of Hea. and Welfare Ministries [14602]
United Network for Organ Sharing [16684]
U.S. Adult Cystic Fibrosis Assn. [16364]
U.S. Animal Hea. Assn. [16811]
U.S. Dental Tennis Assn. [23911]
U.S. Hapki Hae [23606]
U.S. Hereditary Angioedema Assn. [14487]
U.S. Medical Massage Assn. [15033]
U.S.-Mexico Border Hea. Assn. [16256]
U.S. Pharmacopeia [15953]
U.S. Psychiatric Rehabilitation Assn. [16336]
U.S. Sports Chiropractic Fed. [23282]
U.S. Trager Assn. [13656]
Univ. of Colorado Hea. Sciences Center Alumni Assn. [24494]
Us TOO Intl. [13879]
USAF Medical Ser. Corps Assn. [13590]
Vasculitis Found. [16552]
Vegan Action [11071]
Vegetarian Awareness Network [11072]
Vegetarian Rsrc. Gp. [11073]
Venous Soc. of Am. [16732]
Veterinary Botanical Medicine Assn. [16812]
Veterinary Orthopedic Soc. [16816]
VHA [14901]
VietNow Natl. [13359]
Vision World Wide [16890]
Visiting Nurse Associations of Am. [15532]
Vitamin Angel Alliance [15571]
Vitamin Soc. of Japan [IO]
Vocational Evaluation and Career Assessment Professionals [16337]
Voice Found. [16457]
Volunteer Trustees of Not-for-Profit Hospitals [14902]
Water Advocates [9310]
Waterbirth Intl. [13984]
Weight-Control Info. Network [15578]
Weight Watchers Intl. [IO]
Weight Watchers Intl. [14603]
Wellness Associates [16058]
Wemos [IO]
Western Surgical Assn. [16592]
Western Veterinary Conf. [16817]
Wilbur Hot Springs Hea. Sanctuary [10180]
Wilderness Medical Soc. [15184]
William Glasser Inst. [16233]

A star before a book entry number signifies that the name is not listed separately, but is mentioned within the entry.

Williams Syndrome Assn. [14490]
WishKids Intl. [11665]
Women Alive Coalition [13588]
Women in Neurotrauma Res. [15404]
WomenHeart: Natl. Coalition for Women with Heart Disease [13929]
Women's Auxiliary of the ICA [14016]
Women's Drug Res. Project [13285]
World Allergy Org. [13605]
World Assn. for the Advancement of Veterinary Parasitology [16818]
World Assn. of Cultural Psychiatry [16097]
World Assn. for Infant Mental Hea. [16098]
World Assn. for Psychosocial Rehabilitation - U.S. Br. [16338]
World Assn. of Sleep Medicine [16430]
World Assn. for Social Psychiatry [16099]
World Assn. of Veterinary Lab. Diagnosticians [16819]
World Coun. for Cardiovascular and Pulmonary Rehabilitation [13930]
World Fed. for Mental Hea. [15237]
World Fed. of Neurology Res. Gp. on Motor Neuron Diseases [15373]
World Fed. of Neuroradiological Societies [16306]
World Fed. of Public Hea. Associations [16258]
World Hea. Org. [IO]
World Hea. Org. - Regional Off. for the Eastern Mediterranean [IO]
World Hea. Org. - Regional Off. for Europe [IO]
World Hea. Org. - Regional Off. for South-East Asia [IO]
World Hea. Org. - Regional Off. for the Western Pacific [IO]
World Hea. Org. - Zimbabwe [IO]
World Homecare and Hospice Org. [14844]
World Medical Mission [20245]
World Medical Relief [12544]
World Res. Found. [IO]
World Res. Found. [14604]
World Soc. for Stereotactic and Functional Neurosurgery [15418]
World Spine Soc. [15405]
World Sports Medicine Assn. of Registered Therapists [16486]
World Tech. Volunteers [13196]
Wound, Ostomy and Continence Nurses Soc.: An Assn. of E.T. Nurses [15533]
Young Onset Parkinson's Assn. [15374]
Young Survival Coalition [13883]
Zero to Three: Natl. Center for Infants, Toddlers and Families [13944]
Hea. Acad. [14883], c/o Public Relations Soc. of Am., 33 Maiden Ln., 11th Fl., New York, NY 10038-5150, (212)460-1461
Hea. Accreditation Coun; Environmental [★14368]
Hea. Action Intl. [IO], Amsterdam, Netherlands
Hea. Action Intl. Africa [IO], Nairobi, Kenya
Hea. Action Intl. Asia-Pacific [IO], Colombo, Sri Lanka
Hea; Action on Smoking and [16431]
Hea. Admin; Amer. Coll. of Mental [15187]
Hea. Admin; Assn. of Univ. Programs in [8857]
Hea. Administrators; Conf. of Local Environmental [★16246]
Hea. Administrators; Natl. Conf. of Local Environmental [16246]
Hea. Affairs; Center for [★14984]
Hea. Affairs; Center for [★IO]
Hea. Agencies Comm. for the Combined Fed. Campaign; Natl. [★12200]
Hea. Agencies/Community Hea. Services; Coun. of Home [★14840]
Hea. Agencies; Natl. Comm. of the Fed. Ser. Campaign for Natl. [★12200]
Hea. Alliance; Black Mental [15193]
Hea; Amer. Bd. of Preventive Medicine and Public [★16050]
Health; Amer. Found. for Maternal and Child [15586]
Hea. Assistance Found; Amer. [15100]
Hea. Assoc. Representatives [★2627]
Hea. Assn; Amer. Public [16236]
Hea. Assn; Amer. Rural [★16248]
Hea. Assn; Amer. Social [16410]

Hea. Assn; Amer. Student [★14714]
Hea. Assn; Herpes Rsrc. Center - Amer. Social [16412]
Hea. Assn; HPV Support Prog. - Amer. Social [16413]
Hea. Assn; Mental [★15211]
Hea. Assn; Natl. [15279]
Hea. Assn; Natl. Environmental [14367]
Hea. Assn; Natl. Family Planning and Reproductive [12185]
Hea. Assn; Natl. Mental [★15211]
Hea. Assn; Natl. Rural [16248]
Hea. Assn. of New Jersey; Environmental [★14366]
Hea. Assn; Nutrition for Optimal [15567]
Hea; Assn. for Pre- and Perinatal Psychology and [13979]
Hea; Assn. of Schools of Public [16240]
Hea. Assn; Touch for [★13654]
Hea. Assn; U.S. Animal [16811]
Hea. Assn. of the U.S; Catholic [14874]
Hea. Assn; United States-Mexico Border [★16256]

Health and Beauty Products

Amer. Hea. and Beauty Aids Inst. [1841]
Cosmetic Executive Women [1842]
Cosmetic Indus. Buyers and Suppliers [1843]
Cosmetic Ingredient Rev. [1844]
Cosmetic, Toiletry and Fragrance Assn. [1845]
Drug, Chem. and Assoc. Technologies Assn. [2974]
Foragers Cosmetic Indus. Associates [1846]
Fragrance Found. [1661]
Fragrance Materials Assn. of the U.S. [1662]
History of Dermatology Soc. [10115]
Independent Cosmetic Manufacturers and Distributors [1847]
NAGMR [2541]
Natl. Beauty Culturists' League [1084]
Professional Beauty Assn. [1086]
World Intl. Nail and Beauty Assn. [1088]
Hea. Benefits Coalition for Affordable Choice and Quality [14688]
Hea. Bd; Natl. Indian [12629]
Hea. Book Collective; Boston Women's [★16909]
Hea. Bur; Chiropractic [★14008]

Health Care

A-T Medical Res. Found. [14436]
Academic Orthopaedic Soc. [15750]
Acad. of Ambulatory Foot and Ankle Surgery [16023]
Acad. of Dental Materials [14084]
Acad. of Dentistry Intl. [14085]
Acad. of Gen. Dentistry [14086]
Acad. for Implants and Transplants [14087]
Acad. of Managed Care Providers [14677]
Acad. on Mental Retardation [15238]
Acad. of Operative Dentistry [14089]
Acad. of Oral Dynamics [14090]
Acad. of Osseointegration [14091]
Acad. of Pharmaceutical Res. and Sci. [15906]
Acad. of Scientific Hypnotherapy [14913]
AcademyHealth [14535]
Accelerated Cure Proj. for Multiple Sclerosis [15301]
Access Proj. [14605]
Accreditation Assn. for Ambulatory Hea. Care [13661]
Accreditation Commn. for Acupuncture and Oriental Medicine [15739]
Accreditation Coun. on Optometric Educ. [15710]
Accreditation Coun. for Pharmacy Educ. [15907]
Accreditation Rev. Commn. on Educ. for the Physician Asst. [15972]
Accreditation Rev. Commn. on Educ. in Surgical Tech. [15123]
Acoustic Neuroma Assn. [15816]
Action for Healthy Kids [13945]
Action on Smoking and Hea. [16431]
Acupuncturists Without Borders [13536]
Addiction Res. and Treatment Corp. [13213]
Adolescent Scoliosis Soc. of North Am. [16392]
Adopt a Dr. [12750]
Adult Congenital Heart Assn. [13884]
Adventist Development and Relief Agency Intl. [12826]
Advocacy Inst. [12650]

Advocate Hea. Care [14821]
Advocates for the Amer. Osteopathic Assn. [15789]
Advocates for Youth [12173]
Aerospace Medical Assn. [13538]
Aesculapian Club [15982]
African-Amer. Assn. of Fitness Professionals [15957]
African Amer. Post Traumatic Stress Disorder Assn. [21276]
African Medical and Res. Found. [14971]
AFT Healthcare [24087]
Aging in Am. [11271]
Aicardi Syndrome Newsl. [14437]
Aid for AIDS [13547]
Aid for Intl. Medicine [14972]
AIDS Clinical Trials Gp. [13549]
AIDS Empowerment and Treatment Intl. [13550]
AIDS Treatment Activists Coalition [11324]
Air and Surface Transport Nurses Assn. [15427]
Airlines Medical Directors Assn. [13539]
Alan Guttmacher Inst. [12175]
Albinism World Alliance [15242]
Alcor Life Extension Found. [14072]
Allergy and Asthma Network Mothers of Asthmatics [16352]
Alliance for Academic Internal Medicine [8586]
Alliance for Advancing Nonprofit Hea. Care [14606]
Alliance for Aging Res. [11272]
Alliance of Cardiovascular Professionals [13885]
Alliance for Childhood Cancer [13787]
Alliance for Healthcare Strategy and Marketing [2612]
Alliance for Lupus Res. [15013]
Alliance of Minority Medical Associations [14607]
Alliance for the Prudent Use of Antibiotics [15908]
Alliance of State Pain Initiatives [15830]
Alpha Epsilon Delta [24541]
Alpha Omega Alpha Honor Medical Soc. [24542]
Alpha Tau Delta [24559]
Alpha Zeta Omega [24567]
ALSAC/Saint Jude Children's Res. Hosp. [13946]
Alternative Hea. Professionals Assn. [13610]
Ambulatory Pediatric Assn. [15879]
Amer. Acad. of Allergy, Asthma and Immunology [13592]
Amer. Acad. of Alternative Medicine [13612]
Amer. Acad. of Ambulatory Care Nursing [15428]
Amer. Acad. for Cerebral Palsy and Developmental Medicine [13934]
Amer. Acad. of Clinical Toxicology [16657]
Amer. Acad. of Cosmetic Surgery [14037]
Amer. Acad. for Craniofacial Pain [15751]
Amer. Acad. of Dental Gp. Practice [14094]
Amer. Acad. of Dental Practice Admin. [14095]
Amer. Acad. of Dermatology [14189]
Amer. Acad. of Disability Evaluating Physicians [14033]
Amer. Acad. of Environmental Medicine [14360]
Amer. Acad. of Esthetic Dentistry [14096]
Amer. Acad. of Facial Plastic and Reconstructive Surgery [14038]
Amer. Acad. of Family Physicians [14383]
Amer. Acad. of Fixed Prosthodontics [14097]
Amer. Acad. of Gnathologic Orthopedics [14098]
Amer. Acad. of the History of Dentistry [14100]
Amer. Acad. of HIV Medicine [13556]
Amer. Acad. of Implant Dentistry [14101]
Amer. Acad. of Medical Administrators [15045]
Amer. Acad. of Medical Administrators Res. and Educational Found. [15046]
Amer. Acad. of Medical Hypnoanalysts [14914]
Amer. Acad. of Neurological and Orthopaedic Surgeons [15409]
Amer. Acad. of Neurology [15376]
Amer. Acad. of Nurse Practitioners [15429]
Amer. Acad. of Nursing [15430]
Amer. Acad. of Ophthalmology [15656]
Amer. Acad. of Optometry [15711]
Amer. Acad. of Oral and Maxillofacial Pathology [15852]
Amer. Acad. of Oral and Maxillofacial Radiology [14104]
Amer. Acad. of Oral Medicine [14105]

Reference to "IO" in place of a book number signifies that the association may be found in the 45th edition of International Organizations.

Amer. Acad. of Orofacial Pain [14106]
Amer. Acad. of Orthodontics for the Gen. Practitioner [14107]
Amer. Acad. of Orthopaedic Manual Physical Therapists [15971]
Amer. Acad. of Orthopaedic Surgeons [15752]
Amer. Acad. of Orthotists and Prosthetists [15782]
Amer. Acad. of Osteopathy [15790]
Amer. Acad. of Otolaryngic Allergy and Found. [13593]
Amer. Acad. of Otolaryngology - Head and Neck Surgery [15817]
Amer. Acad. of Pediatric Dentistry [14108]
Amer. Acad. of Pediatrics [15880]
Amer. Acad. of Periodontology [14109]
Amer. Acad. of Physical Medicine and Rehabilitation [16307]
Amer. Acad. of Physician Assistants [15973]
Amer. Acad. of Restorative Dentistry [14110]
Amer. Acad. of Sleep Medicine [16418]
Amer. Acad. of Somnology [16419]
Amer. Acad. of Tropical Medicine [16692]
Amer. Acad. of Veterinary and Comparative Toxicology [16736]
Amer. Acad. of Veterinary Pharmacology and Therapeutics [16738]
Amer. Acupuncture Assn. [15741]
Amer. Aging Assn. [14507]
Amer. Alliance for Medical Cannabis [15020]
Amer. Alternative Medical Assn. [13613]
Amer. Ambulance Assn. [14313]
Amer. Animal Hosp. Assn. [16739]
Amer. Apitherapy Soc. [13614]
Amer. Assembly for Men in Nursing [15431]
Amer. Assisted Living Nurses Assn. [15432]
Amer. Assn. for Accreditation of Ambulatory Surgery Facilities [16557]
Amer. Assn. of Ambulatory Surgery Centers [16558]
Amer. Assn. of Avian Pathologists [16740]
Amer. Assn. of Bioanalysts Bd. of Registry [15126]
Amer. Assn. of Birth Centers [15580]
Amer. Assn. of Blood Banks [13761]
Amer. Assn. of Bovine Practitioners [16741]
Amer. Assn. for Cancer Educ. [13789]
Amer. Assn. of Cardiovascular and Pulmonary Rehabilitation [13886]
Amer. Assn. of Caregiving Youth [13466]
Amer. Assn. of Certified Allergists [13594]
Amer. Assn. of Clinical Directors [15986]
Amer. Assn. of Clinical Endocrinologists [14350]
Amer. Assn. of Colleges of Osteopathic Medicine [15791]
Amer. Assn. of Colleges of Pharmacy [15909]
Amer. Assn. of Colleges of Podiatric Medicine [16025]
Amer. Assn. of Critical-Care Nurses [15433]
Amer. Assn. of Dental Examiners [14112]
Amer. Assn. for Dental Res. [14113]
Amer. Assn. of Diabetes Educators [14217]
Amer. Assn. of Dispensing Ophthalmologists [15658]
Amer. Assn. of Endodontists [14114]
Amer. Assn. of Eye and Ear Hospitals [14859]
Amer. Assn. for Functional Orthodontics [14115]
Amer. Assn. of Genito-Urinary Surgeons [16699]
Amer. Assn. of Gynecologic Laparoscopists [15581]
Amer. Assn. for Hand Surgery [14522]
Amer. Assn. on Hea. and Disability [14235]
Amer. Assn. for Hea. Educ. [16234]
Amer. Assn. of Heart Failure Nurses [15434]
Amer. Assn. for the History of Nursing [10083]
Amer. Assn. of Homes and Services for the Aging [11273]
Amer. Assn. of Hosp. Dentists [14116]
Amer. Assn. of Hosp. Podiatrists [16026]
Amer. Assn. of Human-Animal Bond Veterinarians [13702]
Amer. Assn. of Immunologists [14929]
Amer. Assn. of Integrated Healthcare Delivery Systems [15048]
Amer. Assn. on Intellectual and Developmental Disabilities [15239]

Amer. Assn. for Intl. Aging [11274]
Amer. Assn. of Kidney Patients [15283]
Amer. Assn. of LifeStyle Counselors [14053]
Amer. Assn. of Managed Care Nurses [15435]
Amer. Assn. of Medical Assistants [15081]
Amer. Assn. of Medical Audit Specialists [15049]
Amer. Assn. for Medical Chronobiology and Chronotherapeutics [13751]
Amer. Assn. of Medical Milk Commissions [16384]
Amer. Assn. of Medical Soc. Executives [15153]
Amer. Assn. of Mental Hea. Professionals in Corrections [15186]
Amer. Assn. of Neurological Surgeons [15410]
Amer. Assn. of Neuromuscular and Electrodiagnostic Medicine [15303]
Amer. Assn. of Neuropathologists [15853]
Amer. Assn. of Neuroscience Nurses [15436]
Amer. Assn. of Nurse Anesthetists [15437]
Amer. Assn. of Nurse Assessment Coordinators [14608]
Amer. Assn. of Nurse Attorneys [15000]
Amer. Assn. of Nurse Life Care Planners [15438]
Amer. Assn. of Nutritional Consultants [15540]
Amer. Assn. of Occupational Hea. Nurses [15439]
Amer. Assn. for Ophthalmic Standardized Echography [15659]
Amer. Assn. of Oral and Maxillofacial Surgeons [15732]
Amer. Assn. of Oriental Medicine [15742]
Amer. Assn. of Orthodontists [14117]
Amer. Assn. of Orthopedic Medicine [15753]
Amer. Assn. of Pathologists' Assistants [15854]
Amer. Assn. for Pediatric Ophthalmology and Strabismus [15660]
Amer. Assn. of Physician Offices and Labs. [14990]
Amer. Assn. of Physician Specialists [15792]
Amer. Assn. of Plastic Surgeons [14040]
Amer. Assn. of Poison Control Centers [16658]
Amer. Assn. of Preferred Provider Organizations [14680]
Amer. Assn. of Professional Hypnotherapists [14915]
Amer. Assn. of Psychiatric Administrators [14861]
Amer. Assn. of Public Hea. Dentistry [14118]
Amer. Assn. of Public Hea. Veterinarians [16747]
Amer. Assn. for Respiratory Care [16599]
Amer. Assn. of Small Ruminant Practitioners [16749]
Amer. Assn. of Spinal Cord Injury Nurses [15441]
Amer. Assn. of Spinal Cord Injury Psychologists and Social Workers [16459]
Amer. Assn. for the Stud. of Liver Diseases [14801]
Amer. Assn. for the Surgery of Trauma [16687]
Amer. Assn. of Swine Veterinarians [16750]
Amer. Assn. for Tech. in Psychiatry [16070]
Amer. Assn. for Thoracic Surgery [16640]
Amer. Assn. of Tissue Banks [16663]
Amer. Assn. of Veterinary Lab. Diagnosticians [16753]
Amer. Assn. of Veterinary Parasitologists [16754]
Amer. Assn. of Veterinary State Boards [16755]
Amer. Assn. of Wildlife Veterinarians [16756]
Amer. Assn. of Women Dentists [14119]
Amer. Assn. of Zoo Veterinarians [16757]
Amer. Athletic Trainers Assn. and Certification Bd. [23953]
Amer. Autonomic Soc. [15406]
Amer. Behcet's Disease Assn. [13746]
Amer. Bd. of Abdominal Surgery [16561]
Amer. Bd. of Anesthesiology [13671]
Amer. Bd. of Cardiovascular Perfusion [13887]
American Bd. of Clinical Metal Toxicology [16659]
Amer. Bd. of Colon and Rectal Surgery [16059]
Amer. Bd. of Dental Public Hea. [14120]
Amer. Bd. of Dermatology [14190]
Amer. Bd. of Emergency Medicine [14325]
Amer. Bd. of Endodontics [14121]
Amer. Bd. of Family Dentistry [14122]
Amer. Bd. of Family Medicine [14384]
Amer. Bd. of Genetic Counseling [14492]
Amer. Bd. of Indus. Hygiene [15623]
Amer. Bd. of Internal Medicine [14965]
Amer. Bd. of Medical Specialties [15117]

Amer. Bd. of Neurological Surgery [15411]
Amer. Bd. of Nuclear Medicine [15419]
Amer. Bd. of Nutrition [15541]
Amer. Bd. of Obstetrics and Gynecology [15582]
Amer. Bd. for Occupational Hea. Nurses [15445]
Amer. Bd. of Ophthalmology [15661]
Amer. Bd. of Opticianry [15704]
Amer. Bd. of Oral and Maxillofacial Pathology [15855]
Amer. Bd. of Oral and Maxillofacial Surgery [15733]
Amer. Bd. of Orthodontics [14124]
Amer. Bd. of Orthopaedic Surgery [15755]
Amer. Bd. of Otolaryngology [15818]
Amer. Bd. of Pathology [15856]
Amer. Bd. of Pediatrics [15881]
Amer. Bd. of Periodontology [14125]
Amer. Bd. of Physical Medicine and Rehabilitation [16309]
Amer. Bd. of Plastic Surgery [14041]
Amer. Bd. of Podiatric Orthopedics and Primary Podiatric Medicine [16030]
Amer. Bd. of Podiatric Surgery [16031]
Amer. Bd. of Preventive Medicine [16050]
Amer. Bd. of Prosthodontics [14126]
Amer. Bd. of Psychological Hypnosis [14917]
Amer. Bd. of Quality Assurance and Utilization Rev. Physicians [16260]
Amer. Bd. of Radiology [16272]
Amer. Bd. of Surgery [16563]
Amer. Bd. of Thoracic Surgery [16641]
Amer. Bd. of Urology [16700]
Amer. Bd. of Veterinary Specialties [16759]
Amer. Bd. of Veterinary Toxicology [16760]
Amer. Broncho-Esophagological Assn. [13778]
Amer. Burn Assn. [13781]
Amer. Case Mgt. Assn. [15051]
Amer. Celiac Society/Dietary Support Coalition [15543]
Amer. Chiropractic Assn. [13988]
Amer. Chiropractic Coll. of Radiology [13990]
Amer. Chiropractic Registry of Radiologic Technologists [16273]
Amer. Chronic Pain Assn. [15834]
Amer. Cleft Palate-Craniofacial Assn. [14055]
Amer. Clinical and Climatological Assn. [14018]
Amer. Clinical Lab. Assn. [14991]
Amer. Clinical Neurophysiology Soc. [14306]
Amer. Coll. for Advancement in Medicine [16051]
Amer. Coll. of Allergy, Asthma and Immunology [13596]
Amer. Coll. of Angiology [16719]
Amer. Coll. of Apothecaries [15912]
Amer. Coll. of Cardiology [13888]
Amer. Coll. of Cardiovascular Administrators [15052]
Amer. Coll. of Chest Physicians [13889]
Amer. Coll. of Clinical Pharmacology [15913]
Amer. Coll. of Clinical Pharmacy [15914]
Amer. Coll. of Contingency Planners [14609]
Amer. Coll. of Dentists [14128]
Amer. Coll. of Domiciliary Midwives [15583]
Amer. Coll. of Emergency Physicians [14326]
Amer. Coll. of Epidemiology [14373]
Amer. Coll. of Foot and Ankle Orthopedics and Medicine [16032]
Amer. Coll. of Foot and Ankle Pediatrics [16033]
Amer. Coll. of Foot and Ankle Surgeons [16034]
Amer. Coll. of Gastroenterology [14405]
Amer. Coll. Hea. Assn. [14714]
Amer. Coll. of Hea. Care Administrators [15535]
Amer. Coll. of Hea. Plan Mgt. [15053]
Amer. Coll. of Healthcare Architects [14610]
Amer. Coll. of Healthcare Architects [IO]
Amer. Coll. of Healthcare Executives [14862]
Amer. Coll. of Healthcare Info. Administrators [14611]
Amer. Coll. of Intl. Physicians [14973]
Amer. Coll. of Legal Medicine [15001]
Amer. Coll. of Medical Genetics [14494]
Amer. Coll. of Medical Practice Executives [15054]
Amer. Coll. of Medical Quality [16261]
Amer. Coll. of Medical Toxicology [16660]
Amer. Coll. of Mohs Micrographic Surgery and Cutaneous Oncology [15636]

A star before a book entry number signifies that the name is not listed separately, but is mentioned within the entry.

Amer. Coll. of Neuropsychopharmacology [15915]
Amer. Coll. of Nuclear Medicine [15421]
Amer. Coll. of Nuclear Physicians [15422]
Amer. Coll. of Nurse-Midwives [15447]
Amer. Coll. of Nutrition [15544]
Amer. Coll. of Obstetricians and Gynecologists [15584]
Amer. Coll. of Occupational and Environmental Medicine [15624]
Amer. Coll. of Oral and Maxillofacial Surgeons [15734]
Amer. Coll. of Osteopathic Emergency Physicians [14327]
Amer. Coll. of Osteopathic Family Physicians [15793]
Amer. Coll. of Osteopathic Internists [15794]
Amer. Coll. of Osteopathic Obstetricians and Gynecologists [15585]
Amer. Coll. of Osteopathic Pediatricians [15795]
Amer. Coll. of Osteopathic Surgeons [15797]
Amer. Coll. of Physician Executives [15056]
Amer. Coll. of Physicians-American Soc. of Internal Medicine [14966]
Amer. Coll. of Preventive Medicine [16052]
Amer. Coll. of Prosthodontists [14129]
Amer. Coll. of Radiation Oncology [16267]
Amer. Coll. of Radiology [16274]
Amer. Coll. of Rheumatology [16367]
Amer. Coll. of Surgeons [16565]
Amer. Coll. of Theriogenologists [16763]
Amer. Coll. of Veterinary Anesthesiologists [16764]
Amer. Coll. of Veterinary Dermatology [16765]
Amer. Coll. of Veterinary Internal Medicine [16767]
Amer. Coll. of Veterinary Ophthalmologists [16768]
Amer. Coll. of Veterinary Pathologists [16769]
Amer. Coll. of Veterinary Radiology [16770]
Amer. Coll. of Veterinary Surgeons [16771]
Amer. Comm. for Shaare Zedek Hosp. in Jerusalem [12455]
Amer. Conf. of Governmental Indus. Hygienists [15625]
Amer. Cong. of Rehabilitation Medicine [16310]
Amer. Correctional Hea. Services Assn. [14715]
Amer. Coun. of Applied Clinical Nutrition [15545]
Amer. Coun. for Drug Educ. [13222]
Amer. Coun. on Exercise [15958]
Amer. Coun. of Hypnotist Examiners [14918]
Amer. Coun. on Sci. and Hea. [14539]
Amer. Cryonics Soc. [14073]
Amer. Dental Assistants Assn. [14130]
Amer. Dental Assn. [14131]
Amer. Dental Hygienists' Assn. [14132]
Amer. Dental Soc. of Anesthesiology [14133]
Amer. Diabetes Assn. [14218]
Amer. Dietetic Assn. [15546]
Amer. Disabled for Attendant Prog. Today [17413]
Amer. Electrology Assn. [14308]
Amer. Endodontic Soc. [14134]
Amer. Epilepsy Soc. [14379]
Amer. Equilibration Soc. [14135]
Amer. Fed. for Aging Res. [14508]
Amer. Fed. for Medical Res. [14019]
Amer. Found. for Aging Res. [14509]
Amer. Found. for AIDS Res. [13557]
Amer. Found. for Maternal and Child Health [15586]
Amer. Found. for Pharmaceutical Educ. [15916]
Amer. Found. for the Prevention of Venereal Disease [16409]
Amer. Fracture Assn. [15756]
Amer. Gastroenterological Assn. [14406]
Amer. Geriatrics Soc. [14510]
Amer. Guild of Hypnotherapists [14919]
Amer. Gynecological and Obstetrical Soc. [15587]
Amer. Hair Loss Assn. [14519]
Amer. Head and Neck Soc. [15819]
Amer. Headache Soc. [14531]
Amer. Hea. Assistance Found. [15100]
Amer. Hea. Decisions [14541]
Amer. Hea. Info. Mgt. Assn. [15097]
Amer. Hea. Planning Assn. [14542]
Amer. Hea. Quality Assn. [16262]

Amer. Healthcare Radiology Administrators [16275]
Amer. Hearing Aid Associates [14739]
Amer. Heartworm Soc. [16772]
Amer. Hemochromatosis Soc. [14543]
Amer. Herbalists Guild [14817]
Amer. Hippotherapy Assn. [16600]
Amer. Holistic Nurses' Assn. [14825]
Amer. Holistic Veterinary Medical Assn. [16773]
Amer. Horticultural Therapy Assn. [16601]
Amer. Industrial Health Coun. [15626]
Amer. Indus. Hygiene Assn. [15627]
Amer. Inst. of the History of Pharmacy [15917]
Amer. Inst. of Homeopathy [14845]
Amer. Inst. of Medical Ethics [12122]
Amer. Inst. of Oral Biology [14137]
Amer. Inst. for Preventive Medicine [16053]
Amer. Inst. of Stress [16487]
American Institute for Teen AIDS Prevention [13558]
Amer. Inst. of Ultrasound in Medicine [16436]
Amer. Institutes for Res. in the Behavioral Sciences [6523]
Amer. Integrative Medical Assn. [15034]
Amer. Juvenile Arthritis Org. [16368]
Amer. Kidney Fund [15284]
Amer. Kinesiotherapy Assn. [16311]
Amer. Laryngological, Rhinological and Otological Soc. [15821]
Amer. Latex Allergy Assn. [13597]
Amer. Licensed Practical Nurses Assn. [15450]
Amer. Liver Found. [14803]
Amer. Lung Assn. [16354]
Amer. Lyme Disease Found. [14249]
Amer. Manual Medicine Assn. [13618]
Amer. Massage Therapy Assn. [15022]
Amer. Medical Assn. [15155]
Amer. Medical Assn. Alliance [15156]
Amer. Medical Athletic Assn. [23650]
Amer. Medical Directors Assn. [15536]
Amer. Medical Informatics Assn. [14079]
Amer. Medical Rehabilitation Providers Assn. [16312]
Amer. Medical Technologists [15127]
Amer. Medical Women's Assn. [14696]
Amer. Mental Hea. Alliance [15188]
Amer. Mental Hea. Counselors Assn. [15189]
Amer. Naprapathic Assn. [15276]
Amer. Nephrology Nurses' Assn. [15286]
Amer. Nordic Walking Assn. [15960]
Amer. Nurses Assn. [15451]
Amer. Nurses Found. [15452]
Amer. Nutraceutical Assn. [14612]
Amer. Nystagmus Network [16828]
Amer. Occupational Therapy Assn. [16602]
Amer. Ophthalmological Soc. [15662]
Amer. Optometric Assn. [15712]
Amer. Optometric Found. [15713]
Amer. Optometric Student Assn. [15714]
Amer. Organ Transplant Assn. [16664]
Amer. Org. for Bodywork Therapies of Asia [15024]
Amer. Org. of Nurse Executives [15454]
Amer. Orthodontic Soc. [14138]
Amer. Orthopaedic Assn. [15757]
Amer. Orthopaedic Foot and Ankle Soc. [15758]
Amer. Orthoptic Coun. [15663]
Amer. Osler Soc. [15157]
Amer. Osteopathic Acad. of Orthopedics [15759]
Amer. Osteopathic Assn. [15798]
Amer. Osteopathic Bd. of Emergency Medicine [14328]
Amer. Osteopathic Bd. of Family Physicians [15799]
Amer. Osteopathic Bd. of Pediatrics [15800]
Amer. Osteopathic Coll. of Anesthesiologists [13672]
Amer. Osteopathic Coll. of Dermatology [14194]
Amer. Osteopathic Coll. of Occupational and Preventive Medicine [15802]
Amer. Osteopathic Coll. of Physical Medicine and Rehabilitation [15805]
Amer. Osteopathic Coll. of Radiology [16276]
Amer. Osteopathic Colleges of Ophthalmology and Otolaryngology-Head and Neck Surgery [15664]

Amer. Osteopathic Found. [15806]
Amer. Otological Soc. [15822]
Amer. Pain Soc. [15836]
Amer. Paraplegia Soc. [16460]
Amer. Parkinson Disease Assn. [15304]
Amer. Partnership for Eosinophilic Disorders [14408]
Amer. Pathology Found. [15857]
Amer. Pediatric Soc. [15882]
Amer. Pharmacists Assn. - Acad. of Pharmacy Practice and Mgt. [15918]
Amer. Pharmacists Assn. Acad. of Student Pharmacists [15919]
Amer. Physical Therapy Assn. [16603]
Amer. Physicians Fellowship for Medicine in Israel [12456]
Amer. Podiatric Circulatory Soc. [16036]
Amer. Podiatric Medical Assn. [16037]
Amer. Podiatric Medical Students' Assn. [16038]
Amer. Podiatric Medical Writers Assn. [16039]
Amer. Porphyria Found. [15243]
Amer. Pre-Veterinary Medical Assn. [16774]
Amer. Pregnancy Assn. [15588]
Amer. Professional Wound Care Assn. [16688]
Amer. Prostate Soc. [16701]
Amer. Prosthodontic Soc. [14139]
Amer. Psychological Assn. - Hea. Psychology Div. [16130]
Amer. Psychosocial Oncology Soc. [15638]
Amer. Public Hea. Assn. [16236]
Amer. Qigong Assn. [13620]
Amer. Radiological Nurses Assn. [15457]
Amer. Radium Soc. [15639]
Amer. Registry of Diagnostic Medical Sonography [16437]
Amer. Registry of Medical Assistants [15082]
Amer. Registry of Pathology [15858]
Amer. Registry of Radiologic Technologists [15128]
Amer. Rehabilitation Counseling Assn. [16313]
Amer. Rehabilitation Economics Assn. [16314]
Amer. Rhinologic Soc. [15823]
Amer. Roentgen Ray Soc. [16277]
Amer. Running Assn. [23651]
Amer. School Hea. Assn. [14718]
Amer. Senior Fitness Assn. [15961]
Amer. Sepsis Alliance [14946]
Amer. Shoulder and Elbow Surgeons [16567]
Amer. Social Hea. Assn. [16410]
Amer. Soc. of Abdominal Surgeons [16568]
Amer. Soc. for the Advancement of Pharmacotherapy [16134]
Amer. Soc. for Aesthetic Plastic Surgery [14042]
Amer. Soc. on Aging [11275]
Amer. Soc. of Anesthesiologists [13674]
Amer. Soc. for Apheresis [13706]
Amer. Soc. of Bariatric Physicians [15575]
Amer. Soc. of Breast Disease [13772]
Amer. Soc. of Cataract and Refractive Surgery [15665]
Amer. Soc. of Childbirth Educators [15589]
Amer. Soc. of Clinical Hypnosis [14921]
Amer. Soc. of Clinical Hypnosis - Educ. and Res. Found. [14922]
Amer. Soc. for Clinical Investigation [14020]
Amer. Soc. for Clinical Lab. Sci. [14992]
Amer. Soc. for Clinical Nutrition [15547]
Amer. Soc. of Clinical Oncology [15640]
Amer. Soc. for Clinical Pathology [15859]
Amer. Soc. for Clinical Pharmacology and Therapeutics [15920]
Amer. Soc. of Colon and Rectal Surgeons [16060]
Amer. Soc. for Colposcopy and Cervical Pathology [15590]
Amer. Soc. of Consultant Pharmacists [15922]
Amer. Soc. of Contemporary Medicine, Surgery, and Ophthalmology [15666]
Amer. Soc. of Cytopathology [14075]
Amer. Soc. for Cytotechnology [14076]
Amer. Soc. for Dental Aesthetics [14140]
Amer. Soc. for Dermatologic Surgery [14196]
Amer. Soc. of Diagnostic and Interventional Nephrology [15287]
Amer. Soc. of Directors of Volunteer Services [13382]

Reference to "IO" in place of a book number signifies that the association may be found in the 45th edition of International Organizations.

Amer. Soc. of Echocardiography [13891]
Amer. Soc. of Electroneurodiagnostic Technologists [14307]
Amer. Soc. of Exercise Physiologists [16019]
Amer. Soc. of Extra-Corporeal Tech. [15129]
Amer. Soc. of Forensic Odontology [14142]
Amer. Soc. for Gastrointestinal Endoscopy [14409]
Amer. Soc. of Hand Therapists [14524]
Amer. Soc. of Hea. Sys. Pharmacists [15923]
Amer. Soc. for Healthcare Central Ser. Professionals [14864]
Amer. Soc. for Healthcare Engg. of the Amer. Hosp. Assn. [14865]
Amer. Soc. for Healthcare Environmental Services of the Amer. Hosp. Assn. [14866]
Amer. Soc. for Healthcare Food Ser. Administrators [14867]
Amer. Soc. of Healthcare Publication Editors [14613]
Amer. Soc. for Healthcare Risk Mgt. [14869]
Amer. Soc. of Hematology [14783]
Amer. Soc. for Histocompatibility and Immunogenetics [14931]
Amer. Soc. of Interventional Pain Physicians [15837]
Amer. Soc. of Interventional and Therapeutic Neuroradiology [16280]
Amer. Soc. for Investigative Pathology [15860]
Amer. Soc. for Laser Medicine and Surgery [14997]
Amer. Soc. of Law, Medicine and Ethics [15002]
Amer. Soc. of Lipo-Suction Surgery [16572]
Amer. Soc. of Master Dental Technologists [14143]
Amer. Soc. of Maxillofacial Surgeons [15735]
Amer. Soc. for Mohs Surgery [15641]
Amer. Soc. of Nephrology [15288]
Amer. Soc. for Neural Transplantation and Repair [15380]
Amer. Soc. of Neuroimaging [16281]
Amer. Soc. of Neuroradiology [16282]
Amer. Soc. for Nutrition [15548]
Amer. Soc. of Ophthalmic Administrators [15058]
Amer. Soc. of Ophthalmic Registered Nurses [15458]
Amer. Soc. for Ophthalmic Ultrasonography [15667]
Amer. Soc. for Parenteral and Enteral Nutrition [15549]
Amer. Soc. of Pharmacognosy [15924]
Amer. Soc. for Pharmacology and Experimental Therapeutics [15925]
Amer. Soc. for Pharmacy Law [15003]
Amer. Soc. of Plastic Surgeons and Plastic Surgery Educ. Found. [14045]
Amer. Soc. of Plastic Surgical Nurses [15461]
Amer. Soc. of Podiatric Medical Assistants [16040]
Amer. Soc. of Radiologic Technologists [15131]
Amer. Soc. of Regional Anesthesia and Pain Medicine [13676]
Amer. Soc. for Reproductive Medicine [14389]
Amer. Soc. for Stereotactic and Functional Neurosurgery [15412]
Amer. Soc. for the Stud. of Orthodontics [14144]
Amer. Soc. for Surgery of the Hand [14525]
Amer. Soc. for Therapeutic Radiology and Oncology [16285]
Amer. Soc. of Transplant Surgeons [16667]
Amer. Soc. of Tropical Medicine and Hygiene [16693]
Amer. Soc. of Veterinary Ophthalmology [16775]
Amer. Spinal Injury Assn. [16461]
Amer. Sudden Infant Death Syndrome Inst. [16523]
Amer. Surgical Assn. [16575]
Amer. Syringomyelia Alliance Proj. [15305]
Amer. Thoracic Soc. [16642]
Amer. Trauma Soc. [16689]
Amer. Turners [23802]
Amer. Urological Assn. [16704]
Amer. Urological Assn. Found. [16705]
Amer. Uveitis Soc. [15668]
Amer. Veterinary Dental Soc. [16778]

Amer. Veterinary Medical Assn. [16779]
Amer. Veterinary Soc. of Animal Behavior [16780]
Amer. Youth Understanding Diabetes Abroad [14219]
America's Blood Centers [13762]
America's Hea. Together [14614]
Amyloidosis Support Groups [14250]
Amyloidosis Support Network [14251]
Amyotrophic Lateral Sclerosis Assn. [15306]
Ananda Yoga Teachers Assn. [11217]
Androgen Insensitivity Syndrome Support Gp. - USA [14441]
Anesthesia Awareness Campaign [13677]
Angioma Alliance [15307]
Animals as Intermediaries [4157]
Antitrust Coalition for Consumer Choice in Hea. Care [14615]
Archaeus Proj. [13625]
Armed Forces Inst. of Pathology [15261]
Army Distaff Foundation/Knollwood [21192]
Army Nurse Corps Assn. [15262]
Arthritis Found. [16369]
Arthroscopy Assn. of North Am. [15762]
Arthur Vining Davis Foundations [12048]
Arts in Therapy Network [13709]
The Arts We Need [13710]
Asbestos Disease Awareness Org. [16655]
Ashoka: Innovators for the Public [12419]
ASHP Found. [15926]
Asian Amer./Pacific Islander Nurses Assn. [15463]
Assembly of Episcopal Healthcare Chaplains [19944]
Assn. of Academic Hea. Centers [14546]
Assn. of Academic Physiatrists [16316]
Assn. for Academic Surgery [16576]
Assn. for Ambulatory Behavioral Healthcare [16080]
Assn. of Amer. Cancer Institutes [13794]
Assn. of Amer. Indian Physicians [15989]
Assn. of Amer. Physicians and Surgeons [15990]
Assn. for Applied Poetry [16211]
Assn. for Applied Psychophysiology and Biofeedback [13749]
Assn. for Applied and Therapeutic Humor [16605]
Assn. of Assistive Tech. Act Programs [14237]
Assn. of Asthma Educators [16355]
Assn. for Behavioral Hea. and Wellness [24088]
Assn. of Behavioral Healthcare Mgt. [15191]
Assn. for Benchmarking in Hea. Care [1848]
Assn. for the Bladder Exstrophy Community [14252]
Assn. of Bone and Joint Surgeons [15763]
Assn. of Brethren Caregivers [11276]
Assn. of Camp Nurses [15464]
Assn. for Childbirth at Home, Intl. [15591]
Assn. of Children's Prosthetic-Orthotic Clinics [15784]
Assn. of Chinese Amer. Physicians [15991]
Assn. of Chiropractic Colleges [13993]
Assn. of Clinical Scientists [14022]
Assn. of Clinicians for the Underserved [14616]
Assn. for Community Affiliated Plans [14617]
Assn. of Community Cancer Centers [13797]
Assn. for Community Hea. Improvement [16238]
Assn. for Continuing Dental Educ. [8195]
Assn. of Danish Pharmacists [IO]
Assn. for the Educ. of Children with Medical Needs [8072]
Assn. for Electronic Hea. Care Transactions [14618]
Assn. for Eradication of Heart Attack [13894]
Assn. of Family Practice Administrators [15060]
Assn. of Family Practice Physician Assistants [14698]
Assn. of Hea. Care Journalists [3095]
Assn. for Healthcare Documentation Integrity [15084]
Assn. for Healthcare Philanthropy [14871]
Assn. of Healthcare Philanthropy Canada [IO]
Assn. for Healthcare Rsrc. and Materials Mgt. [14872]
Assn. of Himalayan Yoga Meditation Societies [11218]
Assn. for Hosp. Medical Educ. [14873]
Assn. for Integrative Hea. Care Practitioners [15037]

Assn. of Intl. Hea. Researchers [14548]
Assn. of Jewish Aging Services [11277]
Assn. for Macular Diseases [15669]
Assn. of Maternal and Child Hea. Programs [13947]
Assn. of Medical Directors of Info. Systems [14957]
Assn. of Medical Illustrators [13707]
Assn. of Medical Lab. Immunologists [14932]
Assn. of Medical School Pediatric Dept. Chairs [15884]
Assn. of Medicine and Psychiatry [16081]
Assn. of Military Surgeons of the U.S. [15263]
Assn. of Needle-Free Injection Mfrs. [2549]
Assn. of Nurse Advocates for Childbirth Solutions [13978]
Assn. of Nurses in AIDS Care [13559]
Assn. of Nurses Endorsing Transplantation [15670]
Assn. of Nutrition Departments and Programs [8947]
Assn. for Ocular Pharmacology and Therapeutics [15671]
Assn. of Osteopathic State Executive Directors [15809]
Assn. of Otolaryngology Administrators [15062]
Assn. of Pakistani Physicians of North Am. [15993]
Assn. of Pathology Chairs [15863]
Assn. for Pathology Informatics [15864]
Assn. of Pediatric Hematology/Oncology Nurses [15467]
Assn. of Pediatric Oncology Social Workers [15885]
Assn. of Pediatric Therapists [16606]
Assn. of PeriOperative Registered Nurses [15468]
Assn. of Physician Assistants in Cardiovascular Surgery [13895]
Assn. for Prevention Teaching and Res. [16054]
Assn. for Professionals in Infection Control and Epidemiology [14947]
Assn. of Professors of Cardiology [13896]
Assn. of Professors of Gynecology and Obstetrics [15592]
Assn. of Prog. Directors in Internal Medicine [14967]
Assn. of Prog. Directors in Vascular Surgery [16578]
Assn. Promoting Educ. and Conservation in Amazonia [5294]
Assn. of Regulatory Boards of Optometry [15716]
Assn. of Rehabilitation Nurses [15469]
Assn. of Reproductive Hea. Professionals [12177]
Assn. for Res. of Childhood Cancer [13798]
Assn. for Res. in Vision and Ophthalmology [15672]
Assn. for Retinopathy of Prematurity and Related Diseases [15673]
Assn. of Rheumatology Hea. Professionals [16370]
Assn. of Schools and Colleges of Optometry [15717]
Assn. of Schools of Public Hea. [16240]
Assn. of Shelter Veterinarians [16784]
Assn. of SIDS and Infant Mortality Programs [16524]
Assn. of Specialty Professors [8587]
Assn. of Staff Physician Recruiters [15995]
Assn. of State and Territorial Dental Directors [14146]
Assn. of State and Territorial Local Hea. Liaison Officials [6213]
Assn. of Surgical Technologists [15133]
Assn. of Tech. Personnel in Ophthalmology [15674]
Assn. for Therapeutic Eurythmy in North Am. [16608]
Assn. for the Treatment of Tobacco Use and Dependence [16653]
Assn. of Univ. Anesthesiologists [13680]
Assn. of Univ. Professors of Ophthalmology [15675]
Assn. of Univ. Radiologists [16286]
Assn. of Veterans Affairs Anesthesiologists [13681]

A star before a book entry number signifies that the name is not listed separately, but is mentioned within the entry.

Assn. of Veterans Affairs Ophthalmologists [15676]
Assn. of Veterinary Hematology and Transfusion Medicine [16785]
Assn. for Women Veterinarians [16786]
Assn. of Women's Hea., Obstetric and Neonatal Nurses [15470]
Assyrian Medical Soc. [13715]
Asthma and Allergy Found. of Am. [13598]
Australian Assn. of Practice Managers [IO]
Australian Women's Hea. Network [IO]
Autism Speaks [13724]
Auxiliary to the Natl. Medical Assn. [15161]
Avenues, Natl. Support Gp. for Arthrogryposis Multiplex Congenita [15309]
Awake In Am. [18601]
Bangladesh Medical Assn. of North Am. [15162]
Batey Relief Alliance [12835]
Bay Area Physicians for Human Rights [12218]
Behavior Genetics Assn. [14498]
Benign Essential Blepharospasm Res. Found. [15311]
Benjamin Franklin Literary and Medical Soc. [14549]
Better Sleep Coun. [16424]
Better Vision Inst. [15678]
Beverly Found. [11278]
BIO Ventures for Global Hea. [14975]
BioCommunications Assn. [14031]
BiOptic Driving Network - USA [15705]
Birth Defect Res. for Children [13752]
Bladder Cancer Advocacy Network [13799]
Blue Cross and Blue Shield Assn. [14959]
BoardSource [12651]
Brain Injury Assn. of Am. [14528]
Brave Kids [13949]
British Healthcare Bus. Intelligence Assn. [IO]
Brother's Brother Found. [12837]
Bur. of Professional Educ. of the Amer. Osteopathic Assn. [15810]
Burns United Support Groups [13782]
C/SEC [15593]
C3: Colorectal Cancer Coalition [13802]
Cajal Club [15385]
Cancer Care [13803]
Cancer Control Soc. [13804]
Cancer Fed. [13805]
Cancer Info. Ser. [13807]
Cancer Prevention Coalition [13808]
Cancer Quality Alliance [13809]
Candlelighters Childhood Cancer Found. [13810]
Cardiovascular Credentialing Intl. [13898]
Care4Dystonia [15312]
Catholic Guardian Soc. [11564]
Catholic Hea. Assn. of the U.S. [14874]
Catholic Medical Assn. [15996]
Catholic Medical Mission Bd. [12515]
CCHS Family Network [14255]
CDC Natl. Prevention Info. Network [13563]
Center for Bioethics [6557]
Center for Bioethics [6558]
Center for Hea. Design [14619]
Center for Humane Options in Childbirth Experiences [15594]
Center for Medical Consumers [14550]
Center for Medicare Advocacy [14684]
Center for Organ Recovery and Educ. [16670]
Center for Patient Advocacy [14620]
Center for Professional Well-Being [14700]
Center for Res. in Ambulatory Hea. Care Admin. [15064]
The Center for Social Gerontology [11280]
Center for Sports and Osteopathic Medicine [16055]
Center for the Stud. of Multiple Birth [15272]
Center for Studying Hea. Sys. Change [14621]
Center for the Well Being of Hea. Professionals [14701]
Central Soc. for Clinical Res. [14023]
Certification Bd. for Music Therapists [16213]
Certification Bd. for Urologic Nurses and Associates [16706]
CFC Intl. [14435]
CFIDS Assn. of Am. [14256]
Charles Ray III Diabetes Assn. [14220]

Chem. Injury Info. Network [16656]
Chemotherapy Found. [15644]
Chi Eta Phi Sorority [24560]
Child Family Hea. Intl. [11551]
Child Life Coun. [13951]
Child Neurology Soc. [15386]
Childbirth Connection [15595]
Childhood Arthritis and Rheumatology Res. Alliance [16371]
Children and Adults With Attention Deficit/ Hyperactivity Disorder [15314]
Children of Aging Parents [11282]
Children's Blood Found. [14786]
Children's Cause for Cancer Advocacy [13812]
Children's Craniofacial Assn. [14057]
Children's Eye Found. [15679]
Children's Hea. Fund [13954]
Children's Hemiplegia and Stroke Assn. [16493]
Children's Hospice Intl. [14853]
Children's Leukemia Res. Assn. [13813]
Children's Liver Assn. for Support Services [14804]
Children's PKU Network [15245]
Children's Tumor Found. [15315]
Children's Wish Found. Intl. [11687]
China Medical Bd. of New York [14976]
Chinese Amer. Medical Soc. [15163]
CHOICE [12178]
Christian Chiropractors Assn. [19773]
Christian Dental Soc. [14147]
Christian Medical and Dental Associations [20238]
Christopher and Dana Reeve Found. [16463]
Chromosome 9P Network [14443]
Chromosome 18 Registry and Res. Soc. [14444]
Chronic Syndrome Support Assn. [14259]
Churg Strauss Syndrome Assn. [13729]
Circle of Hea. Intl. [12268]
Citizen Advocacy Center [17695]
Citizens Alliance for VD Awareness [16411]
Citizens for Consumer Justice [18641]
Citizens' Coun. on Hea. Care [17696]
City of Hope Natl. Medical Center [15102]
CityMatch [13957]
Civil Aviation Medical Assn. [13540]
Clinical Lab. Mgt. Assn. [14993]
Clinical and Lab. Standards Inst. [14994]
Clinical Ligand Assay Soc. [14995]
Coalition of Cancer Cooperative Groups [13814]
Coalition for Healthcare Commun. [14622]
Coalition for Healthcare eStandards [14623]
Coalition for Hemophilia B [14787]
Coalition for Improving Maternity Services [15596]
Cochrane Collaboration [IO]
Coffin-Lowry Syndrome Found. [14447]
Coll. of Amer. Pathologists [15866]
Coll. of Optometrists in Vision Development [15718]
Coll. of Osteopathic Healthcare Executives [14876]
Collegium Internationale Neuro- Psychopharmacologicum [15929]
Colorectal Cancer Network [13815]
Coma Recovery Assn. [14029]
Commn. on Graduates of Foreign Nursing Schools [15473]
Commn. on Opticianry Accreditation [15706]
Comm. on Accreditation for Respiratory Care [16610]
Comm. for Freedom of Choice in Medicine [13628]
Comm. of Interns and Residents [24089]
Comm. for the Promotion of Medical Res. [15104]
Comm. to Reduce Infection Deaths [14877]
Community-Campus Partnerships For Hea. [11744]
Community Systems Found. [15552]
Community Voices [11745]
Comparative Nutrition Soc. [15553]
Competency and Credentialing Inst. [14878]
Complementary Alternative Medical Assn. [13629]
Computerized Medical Imaging Soc. [16287]
Concern Am. [12845]
Conf. of Res. Workers in Animal Diseases [16790]
Congenital Cardiac Anesthesia Soc. [13682]

Congenital Heart Defects Awareness [13900]
Congenital Heart Info. Network [13901]
Cong. of Lung Assn. Staff [16357]
Connective Tissue Oncology Soc. [15645]
Conservative Orthopedics Intl. Assn. [15767]
Consultant Dietitians in Hea. Care Facilities [15554]
Consumer Coalition for Quality Hea. Care [14624]
Consumers for Dental Choice [11912]
Contact Lens Assn. of Ophthalmologists [15680]
Continuing Care Accreditation Commn. [16318]
Cooper Inst. [15962]
Cornelia de Lange Syndrome Found. [13754]
Corporate Angel Network [13817]
Coun. on Accreditation [13164]
Coun. for Affordable Quality Healthcare [14625]
Coun. on Arteriosclerosis, Thrombosis and Vascular Biology of the Amer. Heart Assn. [13902]
Coun. on Certification of Nurse Anesthetists [15475]
Coun. on Chiropractic Educ. [13998]
Coun. on Chiropractic Orthopedics [15768]
Coun. of Colleges of Acupuncture and Oriental Medicine [15743]
Coun. on Compulsive Gambling of New Jersey [12209]
Coun. on Diagnostic Imaging [16288]
Coun. on Educ. for Public Hea. [16242]
Coun. on Hea. Info. and Educ. [14553]
Coun. of Medical Specialty Societies [15120]
Coun. for the Natl. Register of Hea. Ser. Providers in Psychology [16149]
Coun. of Pediatric Subspecialties [15886]
Coun. on Podiatric Medical Educ. [16042]
Coun. on Resident Educ. in Obstetrics and Gynecology [15597]
Coun. for Responsible Telemedicine [16596]
Coun. of State Administrators of Vocational Rehabilitation [16320]
Coun. of State and Territorial Epidemiologists [14374]
Coun. of Teaching Hospitals [14879]
Coun. of Women's and Infants' Specialty Hospitals [14880]
Cover the Uninsured [14960]
Covering Kids and Families [12271]
Cranial Acad. [15811]
Crigler-Najjar Assn. [14805]
Crohn's and Colitis Found. of Am. [14414]
Cross Cultural Hea. Care Prog. [14626]
CTSNet: Cardiothoracic Surgery Network [16643]
CURE Formaldehyde Poisoning Assn. [13324]
CURE Intl. [13975]
Cure Res. Found. [13818]
CyberKnife Soc. [16581]
Cyclic Vomiting Syndrome Assn. [14415]
Cystic Fibrosis Found. [16358]
Cystic Fibrosis Worldwide [16359]
Cystinosis Found. [15246]
Cystinosis Res. Network [15247]
Damon Runyon Cancer Res. Found. [13819]
Dana Alliance for Brain Initiatives [15387]
DanceSafe [12041]
Danish Soc. for Patient Safety [IO]
Danish Wound Healing Soc. [IO]
Dannemiller Memorial Educational Found. [13683]
DaVita Patient Citizens [15291]
Delta Dental Plans Assn. [14687]
Delta Omega [24582]
Dental Assisting Natl. Bd. [14151]
Dental Gp. Mgt. Assn. [15065]
Dental Hea. Intl. [14152]
Depression and Bipolar Support Alliance [15196]
Dermatology Found. [14199]
Dermatology Nurses' Assn. [15476]
DES Action, U.S.A. [13821]
Diabetes Res. Assn. of Am. [14223]
Diabetes Res. Inst. Found. [14224]
Dietary Managers Assn. [15555]
Digestive Disease Natl. Coalition [14416]
Direct Care Alliance [1868]
Direct Relief Intl. [12517]
DMA Nonprofit Fed. [317]
Do It Now Found. [13235]

Reference to "IO" in place of a book number signifies that the association may be found in the 45th edition of International Organizations.

DOCARE Intl., N.F.P. [12518]
Docs for Tots [13958]
Dr. to Dr. [12519]
Drs. for Artists [12520]
Doctors Ought to Care [14554]
Drug Info. Assn. [15931]
Dutch Soc. for Quality in Healthcare [IO]
Dysautonomia Found. [15317]
Dysautonomia Youth Network of Am. [15318]
Dystonia Medical Res. Found. [15319]
Dystrophic Epidermolysis Bullosa Res. Assn. of Am. [14200]
Ear Found. [15825]
ECRI [15136]
Educational Commn. for Foreign Medical Graduates [15997]
eHealth Initiative [14627]
Ehlers Danlos Natl. Found. [16651]
Elder Craftsmen [11285]
EMDR - Humanitarian Assistance Programs [12767]
EMDR Intl. Assn. [16215]
Emergency Medicine Found. [14331]
Emergency Medicine Residents' Assn. [14332]
Emergency Nurses Assn. [14333]
Employee Services Mgt. Assn. [12796]
Endocrine Nurses Soc. [14354]
Endocrine Soc. [14355]
Endometriosis Assn. [15599]
EngenderHealth [12180]
Environmental Res. Found. [13599]
Epilepsy Found. [14380]
Epilepsy Therapy Development Proj. [14381]
Esophageal Cancer Awareness Assn. [13822]
Esperanca [14628]
Esperanca [IO]
Ethiopian North Amer. Hea. Professionals Assn. [14629]
Ethiopian Pharmacists Assn. in North Am. [15932]
European Hea. Indus. Bus. Communications Coun. [IO]
European Hea. Managers Forum [IO]
Everyday Ayurveda [13606]
Exercise Safety Assn. [15963]
Eye Bank Assn. of Am. [14288]
Eye-Bank for Sight Restoration [14289]
Fabry Support and Info. Gp. [14262]
FACES: The Natl. Craniofacial Assn. [14061]
Facing Our Risk of Cancer Empowered [13823]
Facioscapulohumeral (FSH) Soc. [15320]
Families for Depression Awareness [15198]
Families U.S.A. Found. [11286]
Family Hea. Care Assn. of Am. [24090]
Family Hea. Intl. [12181]
Family and Hea. Sect. of the Natl. Coun. on Family Relations [14385]
Family Violence Prevention Fund [12028]
Famous Fone Friends [11692]
Fanconi Anemia Res. Fund [14450]
Farm Worker Hea. Services [12586]
Feathered Pipe Found. [12345]
Fed. Physicians Assn. [15998]
Federated Ambulatory Surgery Assn. [16582]
Fed. for Accessible Nursing Educ. and Licensure [15478]
Fed. of Amer. Hospitals [14881]
Fed. of Associations of Regulatory Boards [14555]
Fed. for Children with Special Needs [12569]
Fed. of Chinese Amer. and Chinese Canadian Medical Societies [13985]
Fed. of Clinical Immunology Societies [14935]
Fed. of Patients and Consumer Organisations in the Netherlands [IO]
Fed. of Pediatric Organizations [15887]
Fed. of Podiatric Medical Boards [16043]
Fed. of State Medical Boards of the U.S. [15165]
Fed. of State Physician Hea. Programs [15999]
Fed. of Straight Chiropractors and Organizations [14001]
Feed the Children [12854]
Fertile Hope [14390]
Fertility Res. Found. [14391]
Fibromuscular Dysplasia Soc. of Am. [15322]
First Candle/SIDS Alliance [16525]

Floating Harbor Syndrome Support Gp. of North Am. [14451]
The Floating Hosp. [14882]
Flower Essence Soc. [14818]
Flying Chiropractors Assn. [14002]
Flying Dentists Assn. [14153]
Flying Physicians Assn. [13731]
Focus [15681]
FOD Family Support Gp. [15248]
Food and Nutrition Bd. [15558]
Forbes Norris MDA/ALS Res. Center [15323]
Foreign Pharmacy Graduate Examination Comm. [15933]
Found. for Advancement in Cancer Therapy [13824]
Found. for the Advancement of Chiropractic Tenets and Sci. [14003]
Found. for Chiropractic Educ. and Res. [14004]
Found. for Hea. [14556]
Found. for Ichthyosis and Related Skin Types [14201]
Found. for Informed Medical Decision Making [15137]
Found. for Innovation in Medicine [15166]
Found. for Shamanic Stud. [20446]
Found. for the Support of Intl. Medical Training [14977]
Friedreich's Ataxia Res. Alliance [14403]
Friends of the Jose Carreras Intl. Leukemia Found. [13825]
Friends of Karen [11694]
Frontier Nursing Ser. [15479]
Frontline Hepatitis Awareness [14806]
Gay and Lesbian Medical Assn. [14431]
Gay Men's Hea. Crisis [13564]
Generations United [13170]
Genetic Engg. Action Network [6615]
Gerontological Soc. of Am. [14511]
Gift of Life Intl. [12524]
The Glaucoma Found. [15682]
Glaucoma Res. Found. [15683]
Global Alliance for Medical Educ. [8862]
Global Alliance of Mental Illness Advocacy Networks [15200]
Global Applied Disability Res. and Info. Network [14240]
Global Autism Proj. [13725]
Global Bus. Coalition on HIV/AIDS [11329]
Global Equity Gauge Alliance [IO]
Global Healing [12450]
Global Hea. Coun. [14979]
Global Hea. Ministries [14630]
Global Hea. Ministries [IO]
Global Neuro Rescue [15324]
Global Perioperative Res. Org. [14026]
Global and Regional Asperger Syndrome Partnership [15325]
Gluten Intolerance Gp. [15559]
God's Child Proj. [11597]
God's Love We Deliver [12283]
Gray Panthers [11287]
Guardians of Hydrocephalus Res. Found. [15326]
Haitian Coalition on AIDS [13567]
Harm Reduction Coalition [12042]
Harvard Injury Control Res. Center [16690]
Harvey Soc. [15168]
Hastings Center [12125]
Healing Touch Intl. [14631]
Healing Touch Intl. [IO]
Hea. Acad. [14883]
Hea. Benefits Coalition for Affordable Choice and Quality [14688]
Hea. Care Compliance Assn. [14632]
Hea. Care eBusiness Collaborative [14633]
Hea. Care Without Harm [14634]
Hea. Coalition on Liability and Access [14635]
Hea. Connection [13245]
Hea. Educ. Coun. [14562]
Hea. Educ. Found. [16243]
Hea. Educ. Rsrc. Org. [13568]
Hea. for Humanity [14563]
Hea. Info. Rsrc. Center [14564]
Hea. Jam [14674]
Hea. Level Seven [14636]
Hea. Ministries [20241]

Hea. Promotion Inst. [11288]
Hea. Promotion Inst. [14565]
Hea. Res. and Educational Trust [14884]
Hea. Sci. Communications Assn. [14032]
Hea. Services Union of Australia [IO]
Hea. Tech. Center [15138]
Hea. Volunteers Overseas [12526]
Healthcare Convention and Exhibitors Assn. [1340]
Healthcare Financial Mgt. Assn. [15066]
Healthcare Info. and Mgt. Systems Soc. [14885]
Healthcare Laundry Accreditation Coun. [2403]
HealthCare Ministries [20076]
Healthcare Quality Certification Bd. [13533]
Healthy Teen Network [12182]
Heart Care Intl. [13904]
Heart Disease Res. Found. [13905]
Heart Failure Soc. of Am. [13906]
Heart Rhythm Soc. [13907]
HELLP Syndrome Soc. [14906]
HELP - Inst. for Body Chemistry [14928]
Hemochromatosis Found. [14799]
Hemochromatosis Info. Soc. [14800]
Hemophilia Fed. of Am. [14789]
Hepatitis C Assn. [14807]
Hepatitis C Caring Ambassadors Prog. [14808]
Hepatitis Rsrc. Network [14810]
Hereditary Colon Cancer Assn. [13829]
Herpes Rsrc. Center - Amer. Social Hea. Assn. [16412]
Hesperian Found. [14980]
HHT Found. Intl. [14454]
Himalayan Intl. Inst. of Yoga Sci. and Philosophy of the U.S.A. [12348]
Hispanic Dental Assn. [14155]
Hispanic Neuropsychological Soc. [15388]
History of Dermatology Soc. [10115]
Holistic Dental Assn. [14156]
Homeopathic Nurses Assn. [14846]
Hospice Educ. Inst. [14854]
Hospice and Palliative Nurses Assn. [15482]
Hospitalized Veterans Writing Proj. [16321]
Human Ecology Action League [14364]
Human Growth Found. [16020]
Humanity Intl. [12859]
Huntington's Disease Soc. of Am. [15329]
Hydrocephalus Assn. [15330]
Hypoparathyroidism Assn. [14356]
Hysterectomy Educational Resources and Services Found. [15601]
IDEA Hea. and Fitness Assn. [15965]
Immune Deficiency Found. [14936]
Immunology of Diabetes Soc. [14225]
Impaired Physician Prog. [13246]
Incurably Ill for Animal Res. [13697]
Independence Inst. [17120]
Independent Citizens Res. Found. for the Study of Degenerative Diseases [14263]
Infectious Diseases Soc. of Am. [14948]
Informed Homebirth/Informed Birth and Parenting [15602]
Infusion Nurses Soc. [16614]
Inst. for the Advancement of Human Behavior [13735]
Inst. for the Development of Emotional and Life Skills/National Inst. of Relationship Enhancement [15201]
Inst. for Healthcare Improvement [14637]
Inst. for Integral Development [13249]
Inst. for Labor and Mental Health [15202]
Inst. for Safe Medication Practices [14638]
Insulin-Free World Found. [14226]
Inter-American Conductive Educ. Assn. [9146]
Interamerican Coll. of Physicians and Surgeons [16000]
InterAmerican Heart Found. [13909]
Interchurch Medical Assistance [20242]
Intercontinental Fed. of Behavioral Optometry [15719]
Intercultural Cancer Coun. [13830]
Intermed Intl. [14982]
Intl. Acad. of Health Care Professionals [14705]
Intl. Acad. of Myodontics [14159]
Intl. Alliance for Child and Adolescent Mental Hea. and Schools [15204]

A star before a book entry number signifies that the name is not listed separately, but is mentioned within the entry.

Intl. Alliance of Patients' Organizations [IO]
Intl. and Amer. Associations of Clinical Nutritionists [15560]
Intl. Anesthesia Res. Soc. [13684]
Intl. Arts Medicine Assn. [7972]
Intl. Assn. for Aquatic Animal Medicine [16792]
Intl. Assn. of Cancer Victors and Friends [13831]
Intl. Assn. for Cognitive Psychotherapy [16218]
Intl. Assn. for Colon Hydrotherapy [14567]
Intl. Assn. for Comparative Res. on Leukemia and Related Diseases [15647]
Intl. Assn. of Coroners and Medical Examiners [15093]
Intl. Assn. for Dental Res. [14161]
Intl. Assn. of Flight Paramedics [14334]
Intl. Assn. of Healthcare Central Ser. Materiel Mgt. [14886]
Intl. Assn. of Healthcare Practitioners [14639]
Intl. Assn. of Healthcare Practitioners [IO]
Intl. Assn. for Healthcare Security and Safety [14887]
Intl. Assn. of Homes and Services for the Ageing [11289]
Intl. Assn. for Hospice and Palliative Care [14838]
Intl. Assn. of Human-Animal Interaction Organizations [16615]
Intl. Assn. for Human Caring [14640]
International Association for Human Caring [IO]
Intl. Assn. of Hygienic Physicians [15278]
Intl. Assn. for Medical Assistance to Travellers [13343]
Intl. Assn. of Medical Equip. Remarketers and Servicers [15139]
Intl. Assn. of Medical Intuitives [15040]
Intl. Assn. for Medicinal Compliance [15041]
Intl. Assn. of Ocular Surgeons [15684]
Intl. Assn. of Optometric Executives [15720]
Intl. Assn. of Oral and Maxillofacial Surgeons [15736]
Intl. Assn. for Organ Donation [16671]
Intl. Assn. of Orofacial Myology [15869]
Intl. Assn. for Orthodontics [14162]
Intl. Assn. for Oxygen Therapy [16616]
Intl. Assn. for Paratuberculosis [16793]
Intl. Assn. of Pediatric Lab. Medicine [15888]
Intl. Assn. of Rehabilitation Professionals [16322]
Intl. Assn. of Reiki Professionals [13637]
Intl. Assn. for Relational Psychoanalysis and Psychotherapy [16108]
Intl. Assn. of Sickle Cell Nurses And Physician Assistants [14706]
Intl. Assn. of Structural Integrators [13638]
Intl. Assn. for the Stud. of Pain [15841]
Intl. Assn. of Transpersonal Therapists and Physicians [15205]
Intl. Atherosclerosis Soc. [13910]
Intl. Behavioral Neuroscience Soc. [15408]
Intl. Bd. of Environmental Medicine [14365]
Intl. Bronchoesophagological Soc. [13779]
Intl. Bundle Br. Block Assn. [13911]
Intl. Center for Attitudinal Healing [15206]
Intl. Cesarean Awareness Network [15604]
Intl. Childbirth Educ. Assn. [15605]
Intl. Children's Anophthalmia Network [16857]
Intl. Chiropractors Assn. [14008]
Intl. Coll. of Dentists [14163]
Intl. Coll. of Surgeons [16583]
Intl. Comm. Against Mental Illness [15207]
Intl. Cong. of Oral Implantologists [14165]
Intl. Consumer Prdt. Hea. and Safety Org. [3178]
Intl. Correspondence Soc. of Allergists and Clinical Immunologists [13601]
Intl. Coun. on Infertility Info. Dissemination [14392]
Intl. Cytokine Soc. [6580]
Intl. EECP Therapists Assn. [16619]
Intl. Embryo Transfer Soc. [16794]
Intl. Expressive Arts Therapy Assn. [13712]
Intl. Eye Found. [15685]
Intl. Fed. of Esthetic Dentistry [14167]
Intl. Fed. of Foot and Ankle Societies [16045]
Intl. Fed. of Marfan Syndrome Organizations [14456]
Intl. Fed. of Martial Arts and Oriental Medicine [15021]

Intl. Fed. of Ophthalmological Societies [15686]
Intl. Fed. of Psoriasis Associations [14203]
Intl. Fed. for Psychoanalytic Educ. [9028]
Intl. Found. for Homeopathy [14849]
Intl. Functional Elecl. Stimulation Soc. [15390]
Intl. Genetic Epidemiology Soc. [14376]
Intl. Guild of Hair Removal Specialists [14309]
Intl. Hea. Evaluation Assn. [14568]
Intl. Healthcare Safety Professional Certification Bd. [16379]
Intl. Hyperhidrosis Soc. [14357]
Intl. Leptospirosis Soc. [14950]
Intl. Life Sciences Inst. - North Am. [15561]
Intl. Liver Transplantation Soc. [16672]
Intl. Lyme and Assoc. Diseases Soc. [14267]
Intl. Medical Corps [12862]
Intl. Medical and Dental Hypnotherapy Assn. [14924]
Intl. Medical Equip. Collaborative [14569]
Intl. Medical Spa Assn. [1870]
Intl. Medical Volunteers Assn. [15075]
Intl. Mobile Hea. Assn. [14724]
Intl. Org. of Glutaric Acidemia [15332]
Intl. Org. of Multiple Sclerosis Nurses [15486]
Intl. Pediatric Hypertension Assn. [14907]
Intl. Pediatric Nephrology Assn. [15292]
Intl. Pediatric Transplant Assn. [16673]
Intl. Perimetric Soc. [15688]
Intl. Planned Parenthood Fed., Western Hemisphere Region [12184]
Intl. Post Polio Support Org. [16048]
Intl. Premature Ovarian Failure Assn. [15606]
Intl. Psycho-Oncology Soc. [13834]
Intl. RadioSurgery Assn. [16269]
Intl. Refractive Surgery Club [15689]
Intl. Relief Friendship Found. [13171]
Intl. Scleroderma Network [16387]
Intl. Sharps Injury Prevention Soc. [16380]
Intl. Skeletal Soc. [16289]
Intl. Soc. for Aging and Physical Activity [13545]
Intl. Soc. of Arthroscopy, Knee Surgery and Orthopaedic Sports Medicine [15771]
Intl. Soc. for Behavioral Nutrition and Physical Activity [13745]
Intl. Soc. for Biological Therapy of Cancer [13835]
Intl. Soc. for Clinical Densitometry [15788]
Intl. Soc. for Complementary Medicine Res. [13639]
Intl. Soc. for Cmpt. Assisted Orthopaedic Surgery [15772]
Intl. Soc. of Cosmetic and Laser Surgeons [14048]
Intl. Soc. for Dermatologic Surgery [14204]
Intl. Soc. of Dermatology [14205]
Intl. Soc. for Disease Surveillance [14269]
Intl. Soc. for Equity in Hea. [IO]
Intl. Soc. of First Responders [14317]
Intl. Soc. for Heart and Lung Transplantation [16674]
Intl. Soc. for Imaging in the Eye [15690]
Intl. Soc. for Infectious Diseases [14951]
Intl. Soc. of Lymphology [15016]
Intl. Soc. on Metabolic Eye Disease [15691]
Intl. Soc. of Mine Safety Professionals [15270]
Intl. Soc. of Oncology Pharmacy Practitioners [15937]
Intl. Soc. for Pharmacoepidemiology [15939]
Intl. Soc. for the Psychological Treatments of the Schizophrenias and Other Psychoses - USA [15209]
Intl. Soc. for Quality in Healthcare [IO]
Intl. Soc. of Regulatory Toxicology and Pharmacology [14570]
Intl. Soc. of Sports Nutrition [15562]
Intl. Soc. for the Stud. of Women's Sexual Hea. [16404]
Intl. Soc. on Thrombosis and Haemostasis [14793]
Intl. Soc. for Traumatic Stress Stud. [16489]
Intl. Soc. of Travel Medicine [15172]
Intl. Soc. for Vascular Surgery [16584]
Intl. Soc. of Veterinary Dermatopathology [16795]
Intl. Stillbirth Alliance [13982]
Intl. Stuttering Assn. [16498]
Intl. Treatment Preparedness Coalition [13573]

Intl. Union Against Sexually Transmitted Infections, Regional Off. for North Am. [16414]
Intl. Veterinary Acupuncture Soc. [16796]
Intl. Veterinary Ultrasound Soc. [16797]
Intl. Vitamin A Consultative Gp. [15564]
Intl. Yan Xin Qigong Assn. [13640]
Intersociety Coun. for Pathology Info. [15871]
Interstate Postgraduate Medical Assn. of North Am. [14386]
Interstitial Cystitis Assn. [16708]
Iranian Amer. Medical Assn. [15173]
Iraqi Medical Sciences Assn. [14987]
Irish Soc. for Quality and Safety in Healthcare [IO]
Islamic Medical Assn. of North Am. [16003]
ITEM Coalition [14690]
Jacobs Inst. of Women's Hea. [14641]
JARC [12570]
Jaw Joints and Allied Musculo-Skeletal Disorders Found. [15773]
Jewish Assn. for Services for the Aged [11290]
Jin Shin Do Found. for Bodymind Acupressure [15746]
John A. Hartford Found. [11291]
Joint Commn. on Accreditation of Healthcare Organizations [14888]
Joint Commn. on Allied Hea. Personnel in Ophthalmology [15692]
Joint Coun. of Allergy, Asthma and Immunology [13602]
Juvenile Diabetes Res. Found. Intl. [14228]
Kaiser Family Found. [14642]
Kaiser Family Found. [IO]
Kappa Psi [24568]
Kennedy's Disease Assn. [15334]
Kids With Food Allergies [13603]
Kids With Heart Natl. Assn. for Children's Heart Disorders [13915]
Korean-American Medical Assn. [15174]
Lalmba Assn. [12866]
Lamaze Birth Without Pain Educ. Assn. [15607]
Lambda Kappa Sigma [24569]
Leadership Coun. of Aging Organizations [11293]
Leapfrog Gp. [14643]
Legal Counsel for the Elderly [12497]
Legal Sers. for the Elderly [12499]
Leukemia and Lymphoma Soc. [13837]
Lewy Body Dementia Assn. [15335]
LifeBanc [14290]
Lifegain Inst. [14573]
The Living Bank Intl. [14291]
LMBS Network [16539]
Long-term Conditions Alliance [IO]
Lung Cancer Alliance [13839]
Lupus Found. of Am. [15014]
Lupus Info. Network [15015]
Lyme Disease Assn. [14271]
Lyme Disease Found. [14272]
Make-A-Wish Found. of Am. [11707]
Make Today Count [13841]
Malaysian Soc. for Quality in Hea. [IO]
Malignant Hyperthermia Assn. of the U.S. [14464]
Maniilaq Assn. [12627]
MAP Intl. [20243]
March of Dimes Birth Defects Found. [13756]
Marijuana Policy Proj. [18024]
Maternal Life Intl. [16341]
Mature Market Rsrc. Center [11296]
Med Help Intl. [15042]
Medicaid/SCHIP Dental Assn. [14168]
Medical Benevolence Found. [14725]
Medical Equip. and Tech. Assn. [7306]
Medical Gp. Mgt. Assn. [15067]
Medical Image Perception Soc. [15140]
Medical Letter [15940]
Medical Missions Response [20246]
Medical Outcomes Trust [14644]
Medical Records Inst. [15098]
Medical Res. Modernization Comm. [15109]
Medical Spa Soc. [1871]
Medical Subjects Unit [22843]
Medical Wings Intl. [14645]
Medical Wings Intl. [IO]
MedicAlert Found. Intl. [14318]
MediSend Intl. [12530]

Reference to "IO" in place of a book number signifies that the association may be found in the 45th edition of International Organizations.

Meds and Food for Kids [11622]
MedShare Intl. [12531]
Mended Hearts, Inc. [13916]
Meniere's Network [15826]
Mental Hea. Am. [15211]
Mental Hea. Corporations of Am. [13736]
Mental Hea. Workers Without Borders [15212]
Mental Res. Inst. [13737]
Mercy-USA for Aid and Development [12871]
Michael E. DeBakey Intl. Surgical Soc. [13917]
Midwifery Educ. Accreditation Coun. [8063]
Midwives Alliance of North Am. [15610]
Mission Doctors Assn. [12532]
Mitochondrial Medicine Soc. [14078]
Mobile Healthcare Alliance [14646]
Mothers' Voices [13574]
Movement Disorder Soc. [14647]
Movement Disorder Soc. [IO]
Multiple Sclerosis Found. [15338]
Musculoskeletal Ultrasound Soc. [16696]
Myasthenia Gravis Found. of Am. [15340]
The Myositis Assn. [15341]
Nail Patella Syndrome Worldwide [14467]
NANDA Intl. [15489]
Narcotic Educational Found. of Am. [13256]
Natl. Abandoned Infants Assistance Rsrc. Center [12412]
Natl. Abortion Fed. [11223]
Natl. Academies of Practice [14648]
Natl. Acad. of Clinical Biochemistry [13748]
Natl. Acad. of Neuropsychology [16158]
Natl. Acad. of Opticianry [15707]
Natl. Acad. for State Hea. Policy [14649]
Natl. Acad. for Teaching and Learning About Aging [11297]
Natl. Accrediting Agency for Clinical Lab. Sciences [15141]
Natl. Adrenal Diseases Found. [14358]
Natl. Adult Day Services Assn. [11298]
Natl. AIDS Fund [13576]
Natl. Alliance of Advocates for Buprenorphine Treatment [16511]
Natl. Alliance for Caregiving [12163]
Natl. Alliance for Eye and Vision Res. [16872]
Natl. Alliance for Hea. Info. Tech. [15142]
Natl. Alliance for Infusion Therapy [14839]
Natl. Alliance of Medical Researchers and Teaching Physicians [15143]
Natl. Alliance of Medicare Set-Aside Professionals [17697]
Natl. Alliance on Mental Illness [15214]
Natl. Alliance of Primary Care Informatics [14956]
Natl. Alliance of Senior Citizens [11299]
Natl. Alliance of State Pharmacy Associations [15943]
Natl. Alliance for Thrombosis and Thrombophilia [13931]
Natl. Alopecia Areata Found. [16386]
Natl. Amer. Arab Nurses Assn. [15490]
Natl. Anemia Action Coun. [14794]
Natl. Asian Amer. Pacific Islander Mental Hea. Assn. [15215]
Natl. Asian Pacific Center on Aging [11300]
Natl. Assn. of Addiction Treatment Providers [13259]
Natl. Assn. for the Advancement of Orthotics and Prosthetics [15786]
Natl. Assn. of Alternative Benefits Consultants [1867]
Natl. Assn. of Area Agencies on Aging [11301]
Natl. Assn. of Boards of Examiners of Long Term Care Administrators [15538]
Natl. Assn. of Boards of Pharmacy [15944]
Natl. Assn. of Catholic Nurses - USA [15491]
Natl. Assn. for Children's Behavioral Hea. [16090]
Natl. Assn. of Community Hea. Centers [14574]
Natl. Assn. for Continence [16709]
Natl. Assn. of County Hea. Fac. Administrators [15069]
Natl. Assn. of Dental Assistants [14169]
Natl. Assn. of Dental Labs. [14170]
Natl. Assn. for Direct Care Workers of Color [14709]
Natl. Assn. of Disability Evaluating Professionals [14575]

Natl. Assn. on Drug Abuse Problems [13262]
Natl. Assn. of Emergency Medical Technicians [14335]
Natl. Assn. of Fed. Veterinarians [16799]
Natl. Assn. of First Responders [14320]
Natl. Assn. of Free Clinics [14727]
Natl. Assn. of Geriatric Educ. Centers [14513]
Natl. Assn. of Hea. Care Assistants [14514]
Natl. Assn. of Hea. Educ. Centers [14675]
Natl. Assn. of Hea. Unit Coordinators [14578]
Natl. Assn. for Healthcare Quality [16264]
Natl. Assn. for Healthcare Recruitment [15070]
Natl. Assn. of Healthcare Transport Mgt. [14579]
Natl. Assn. of Hepatitis Task Forces [14812]
Natl. Assn. of Hispanic Nurses [15494]
Natl. Assn. for Home Care and Hospice [14840]
Natl. Assn. of Hosp. Hospitality Houses [14891]
Natl. Assn. for Human Development [11303]
Natl. Assn. of Locum Tenens Org. [16004]
Natl. Assn. of Medical Examiners [15094]
Natl. Assn. Medical Staff Services [15071]
Natl. Assn. of Myofascial Trigger Point Therapists [16624]
Natl. Assn. of Nurse Practitioners in Women's Hea. [15497]
Natl. Assn. of Optometrists and Opticians [15721]
Natl. Assn. of Orthopaedic Nurses [15498]
Natl. Assn. of People With AIDS [13578]
Natl. Assn. of Physician Nurses [15500]
Natl. Assn. of Physician Recruiters [16006]
Natl. Assn. for Proton Therapy [15649]
Natl. Assn. for Pseudoxanthoma Elasticum [14207]
Natl. Assn. of Public Hospitals and Hea. Systems [14892]
Natl. Assn. of Rehabilitation Instructors [16324]
Natl. Assn. of Rehabilitation Providers and Agencies [16326]
Natl. Assn. of Residents and Interns [15175]
Natl. Assn. of Rural Hea. Clinics [16245]
Natl. Assn. for Rural Mental Hea. [15217]
Natl. Assn. of School Nurses [15501]
Natl. Assn. of School Nurses for the Deaf [14768]
Natl. Assn. of Senior Companion Proj. Directors [11304]
Natl. Assn. of Specialty Hea. Organizations [14650]
Natl. Assn. of State EMS Officials [14337]
Natl. Assn. of State Head Injury Administrators [14529]
Natl. Assn. of State Mental Hea. Prog. Directors [15219]
Natl. Assn. of State Units on Aging [11305]
Natl. Assn. of Subacute and Post-Acute Care [14728]
Natl. Assn. for the Support of Long Term Care [14651]
Natl. Assn. of VA Physicians and Dentists [16007]
Natl. Assn. of Vietnamese Nurses [15504]
Natl. Assn. of Vision Professionals [15693]
Natl. Ataxia Found. [15342]
Natl. Athletic Trainers' Assn. [23954]
Natl. Attention Deficit Disorder Assn. [15343]
Natl. Black Alcoholism and Addiction Coun. [13265]
Natl. Black Nurses Assn. [15505]
Natl. Bd. for Certification in Dental Lab. Tech. [14172]
Natl. Bd. for Certification in Dental Tech. [14173]
Natl. Bd. for Certification in Occupational Therapy [16625]
Natl. Bd. for Certification of Orthopaedic Technologists [15774]
Natl. Bd. of Examiners in Optometry [15722]
Natl. Bd. of Medical Examiners [15095]
Natl. Bd. of Osteopathic Medical Examiners [15812]
Natl. Bd. of Podiatric Medical Examiners [16046]
Natl. Bd. for Respiratory Care [16626]
Natl. Burn Victim Found. [13784]
Natl. Catholic Pharmacists Guild of the U.S. [15945]
Natl. Caucus and Center on Black Aged [11306]
Natl. Center for Assisted Living [14652]
Natl. Center for Educ. in Maternal and Child Hea. [13969]

Natl. Center for Farmworker Hea. [14581]
Natl. Center for Hea. Educ. [14582]
Natl. Certification Commn. for Acupuncture and Oriental Medicine [15747]
Natl. Certification Coun. for Activity Professionals [1849]
Natl. Chronic Pain Soc. [15845]
Natl. Coalition for Cancer Survivorship [13852]
Natl. Coalition of Creative Arts Therapies Associations [16224]
Natl. Coalition of Ethnic Minority Nurse Associations [15507]
Natl. Coalition on Hea. Care [17698]
Natl. Coalition for LGBT Hea. [12247]
Natl. Coalition for Res. in Neurological Disorders [15346]
Natl. Coalition on Rural Aging [11307]
Natl. Commn. on Certification of Physician Assistants [15975]
Natl. Commn. on Correctional Hea. Care [14729]
Natl. Comm. for Quality Assurance [16265]
Natl. Conf. of Local Environmental Hea. Administrators [16246]
Natl. Contact Lens Examiners [15723]
Natl. Coordinating Coun. for Medication Error Reporting and Prevention [14653]
Natl. Coun. on the Aging [11309]
Natl. Coun. for Community Behavioral Healthcare [15223]
Natl. Coun. of Hea. Facilities Finance Authorities [1850]
Natl. Coun. on Interpreting in Hea. Care [1851]
Natl. Coun. on Minority Educ. in Transplantation [16677]
Natl. Coun. on Patient Info. and Educ. [15946]
Natl. Coun. on Rehabilitation Educ. [16329]
Natl. Coun. of State Boards of Nursing [15508]
Natl. Coun. for Therapeutic Recreation Certification [16627]
Natl. Coun. of Urban Indian Hea. [15277]
Natl. Coun. on Women's Hea. [16904]
Natl. Credentialing Agency for Lab. Personnel [15145]
Natl. Dental Assistants Assn. [14174]
Natl. Dental Assn. [14175]
Natl. Dental Hygienists' Assn. [14177]
Natl. Denturist Assn. [14178]
Natl. Digestive Diseases Info. CH [14422]
Natl. Educ. Alliance for Borderline Personality Disorder [15224]
Natl. Environmental Hea. Assn. [14367]
Natl. Eosinophilia-Myalgia Syndrome Network [16662]
Natl. Eye Rés. Found. [15724]
Natl. Families in Action [13269]
Natl. Family Partnership [13270]
Natl. Family Planning and Reproductive Hea. Assn. [12185]
Natl. Fed. of Licensed Practical Nurses [15509]
Natl. Fitness Therapy Assn. [15968]
Natl. Found. for Brain Res. [15397]
Natl. Found. of Dentistry for the Handicapped [14179]
Natl. Found. for Depressive Illness [15225]
Natl. Found. for Ectodermal Dysplasias [14468]
Natl. Found. for Facial Reconstruction [14065]
Natl. Found. for Infectious Diseases [14953]
Natl. Fragile X Found. [14469]
Natl. Free Clinic Found. of Am. [14585]
Natl. Gaucher Found. [15252]
Natl. Guideline CH [14654]
Natl. Headache Found. [14533]
Natl. Hea. Assn. [15279]
Natl. Hea. Care Anti-Fraud Assn. [14963]
Natl. Hea. Coun. [14586]
Natl. Hea. Fed. [14587]
Natl. Hea. Info. Center [14588]
Natl. Healthcare Collectors Assn. [1869]
Natl. Healthy Start Assn. [15613]
Natl. Heartburn Alliance [14423]
Natl. Hemophilia Found. [14795]
Natl. Hepatitis C Advocacy Coun. [14813]
Natl. Home Infusion Assn. [15043]
Natl. Home Oxygen Patients Assn. [14404]
Natl. Hospice and Palliative Care Org. [14856]

A star before a book entry number signifies that the name is not listed separately, but is mentioned within the entry.

Natl. Indian Hea. Bd. [12629]
Natl. Infant Torticollis Assn. [14945]
Natl. Initiative for Children's Healthcare Quality [13970]
Natl. Inst. of Electromedical Info. [14311]
Natl. Inst. for Hea. Care Mgt. Res. and Educational Found. [14655]
Natl. Inst. for Jewish Hospice [14857]
Natl. Inst. of Senior Housing [12328]
Natl. Interfaith Coalition on Aging [11314]
Natl. Jewish Medical and Res. Center [16361]
Natl. Kidney Found. [15294]
Natl. Labor Alliance of Hea. Care Coalitions [24091]
Natl. Latina Hea. Network [14589]
Natl. Latino Behavioral Hea. Assn. [15227]
Natl. League for Nursing [15510]
Natl. Lung Cancer Partnership [13854]
Natl. Lymphedema Network [15018]
Natl. Marfan Found. [16652]
Natl. Meals on Wheels Found. [11315]
Natl. Medical Assn. [15176]
Natl. Meningitis Assn. [14281]
Natl. Minority AIDS Coun. [13580]
Natl. MIS User Gp. [7207]
Natl. Multiple Sclerosis Soc. [15349]
Natl. Nurses in Bus. Assn. [752]
Natl. Optometric Assn. [15725]
Natl. Org. for Albinism and Hypopigmentation [15255]
Natl. Org. of Alternative Programs [16382]
Natl. Org. for Associate Degree Nursing [15512]
Natl. Org. Caring for Kids [11638]
Natl. Org. of Circumcision Info. Rsrc. Centers [11732]
Natl. Org. for Competency Assurance [14591]
Natl. Org. for Disorders of the Corpus Callosum [15350]
Natl. Org. For Empowering Caregivers [13295]
Natl. Org. of Life and Hea. Insurance Guaranty Associations [1852]
Natl. Org. of Nurses with Disabilities [15514]
Natl. Osteoporosis Found. [15775]
Natl. PACE Assn. [12272]
Natl. Pain Educ. Coun. [15846]
Natl. Parent Network on Disabilities [14245]
Natl. Parkinson Found. [15351]
Natl. Patient Safety Found. [14656]
Natl. Perinatal Assn. [15900]
Natl. Pharmaceutical Assn. [15947]
Natl. Phlebotomy Assn. [14796]
Natl. Physicians Alliance [16009]
Natl. Podiatric Medical Assn. [16047]
Natl. Postdoctoral Assn. [9064]
Natl. Pressure Ulcer Advisory Panel [14657]
Natl. Prison Hospice Assn. [14858]
Natl. Private Duty Assn. [14842]
Natl. Prostate Cancer Coalition [13856]
Natl. Qigong (Chi Kung) Assn. [13644]
Natl. Quality Forum [14658]
Natl. Registry of Emergency Medical Technicians [14342]
Natl. Rehabilitation Assn. [16330]
Natl. Rehabilitation Info. Center [16332]
Natl. Rsrc. Center for Hea. and Safety in Child Care and Early Educ. [11536]
Natl. Reye's Syndrome Found. [16366]
Natl. Rural Hea. Assn. [16248]
Natl. Scoliosis Found. [16393]
Natl. Senior Citizens Law Center [11316]
Natl. Senior Games Assn. [23655]
Natl. SIDS/Infant Death Rsrc. Center [16526]
Natl. Soc. of Certified Healthcare Bus. Consultants [14711]
Natl. Soc. of Genetic Counselors [14506]
Natl. Soc. for Histotechnology [15146]
Natl. Spasmodic Dysphonia Assn. [15352]
Natl. Spasmodic Torticollis Assn. [15353]
Natl. Spinal Cord Injury Assn. [16468]
Natl. Strength and Conditioning Assn. [23957]
Natl. Stroke Assn. [16494]
Natl. Tay-Sachs and Allied Diseases Assn. [15354]
Natl. Therapeutic Recreation Soc. [16628]
Natl. Tuberculosis Controllers Assn. [14283]

Natl. Vaccine Info. Center [13972]
Natl. Viral Hepatitis Roundtable [14815]
Natl. Voluntary Organizations Active in Disaster [12874]
Natl. Wellness Inst. [16057]
Natl. Women's Hea. Network [16906]
Native Amer. Community Bd. [12630]
NBIA Disorders Assn. [15355]
Need [12875]
Neuro-Optometric Rehabilitation Assn., Intl. [15300]
Neuroblastoma Children's Cancer Soc. [13858]
Neurocritical Care Soc. [14070]
Neurofibromatosis [14471]
Neurosurgeons to Preserve Hea. Care Access [15414]
Neurosurgery Intl. [15415]
New Zealand Continence Assn. [IO]
NIDCD - Natl. Temporal Bone, Hearing and Balance Pathology Rsrc. Registry [15121]
NMC [16802]
Nonverbal Learning Disorders Assn. [14998]
North Amer. Alliance for the Advancement of Native Peoples [12631]
North Amer. Assn. for Ambulatory Urgent Care [13663]
North Amer. Assn. of Medical Educ. and Commun. Companies [8874]
North Amer. Assn. for the Stud. of Obesity [15576]
North Amer. Clinical Dermatologic Soc. [14212]
North Amer. Menopause Soc. [15614]
North Amer. Sikh Medical and Dental Assn. [16416]
North Amer. Soc. for Dialysis and Transplantation [15295]
North Amer. Soc. of Obstetric Medicine [15615]
North Amer. Soc. for Pediatric Gastroenterology, Hepatology and Nutrition [14424]
North Amer. Specialized Coagulation Lab. Assn. [14996]
North Amer. Tang Shou Tao Assn. [13645]
North Amer. Transplant Coordinators Org. [16681]
North Amer. Vodder Assn. of Lymphatic Therapy [15019]
North Amer. Yoga Fed. [11219]
Norwegian Soc. for Quality in Healthcare [IO]
NRH Center for Hea. and Disability Res. [14233]
NSF Intl. [16249]
Nuclear Medicine Tech. Certification Bd. [15423]
Nurses Educational Funds [15516]
Nurses for a Healthier Tomorrow [15517]
Nurses' House [15518]
Nurses Org. of Veterans Affairs [15519]
The Nurturing Network [13434]
Nutrition for Optimal Hea. Assn. [15567]
Obesity Action Coalition [15577]
Occupational Knowledge Intl. [5099]
Off. of Population Affairs CH [12757]
Ohashi Inst. [15748]
Oncology Nursing Soc. [15521]
Oper. Smile [12534]
Ophthalmic Photographers' Soc. [15696]
OPP Concerned Sheep Breeders Soc. [16803]
Opticians Assn. of Am. [15709]
Optometric Extension Prog. Found. [15727]
Optometric Historical Soc. [15728]
ORBIS Intl. [15697]
Organic Acidemia Assn. [14472]
Org. for Autism Res. [13728]
Orthodontic Education and Res. Found. [14183]
Orthopaedic Res. Soc. [15776]
Orthopaedic Sect., Amer. Physical Therapy Assn. [16630]
Osteogenesis Imperfecta Found. [15779]
Osteopathic Intl. Alliance [15813]
Outpatient Ophthalmic Surgery Soc. [15698]
Pacific Dermatologic Assn. [14213]
Paget Found. for Paget's Disease of Bone and Related Disorders [15256]
Pain Mgt. and Sclerotherapy [15814]
Pan-American Allergy Soc. [13604]
Pan-American Assn. of Ophthalmology [15699]
Pan Amer. Hea. and Educ. Found. [12536]
Pan Amer. Hea. Org. [14592]

Pancreatic Cancer Action Network [15851]
Paraprofessional Healthcare Inst. [1853]
Paratuberculosis Awareness and Res. Assn. [14425]
Parents Against Childhood Epilepsy [14382]
Parents of Infants and Children with Kernicterus [15358]
Parents of Kids with Infectious Diseases [14954]
Parkinson Alliance [15359]
Parkinson's Disease Found. [15360]
Partners in Hea. [12270]
Partnership for Patient Safety [14659]
Pathfinder Intl. [12186]
Patient Advocate Found. [14660]
Patient Safety Inst. [14661]
PBCers Org. [14816]
PE4life [8991]
Pediatric Cardiac Intensive Care Soc. [15892]
Pediatric Infectious Diseases Soc. [14955]
Pediatric Keratoplasty Assn. [15700]
Pediatric Neurotransmitter Disease Assn. [15361]
Pediatric Nursing Certification Bd. [15522]
Pediatric Orthopedic Soc. of North Am. [15780]
People-Animals-Love [16632]
People-to-People Hea. Found. [14984]
People's Medical Soc. [17694]
Performing Arts Medicine Assn. [16164]
Perfusion Prog. Directors' Coun. [13921]
Peripheral Arterial Disease Coalition [13922]
Permanent Working Group of European Junior Doctors [IO]
Peruvian Heart Assn. [13923]
Pharmacy Technician Educators Coun. [8963]
Phi Alpha Sigma [24543]
Phi Chi Medical Fraternity [24544]
Phi Delta Chi [24570]
Phi Delta Epsilon Medical Fraternity [24540]
Phi Epsilon Kappa [24574]
Philippine Nurses Assn. of Am. [2840]
Phoenix House [13273]
Physician Asst. Educ. Assn. [15976]
Physicians for Peace [15078]
Pierre Fauchard Acad. [14184]
Pierre Robin Network [14473]
Pituitary Network Assn. [16022]
Planned Parenthood Fed. of Am. [12187]
Plastic Surgery Educational Found. [14051]
Plastic Surgery Res. Coun. [14052]
Platelet Disorder Support Assn. [13730]
Polio Soc. [15362]
Prader-Willi Found. [14474]
Prader-Willi Syndrome Assn. (U.S.A.) [14475]
Pregnant With Cancer Network [13865]
Premier Advocacy [14597]
Price-Pottenger Nutrition Found. [15568]
PRIDE Youth Programs [13276]
PRISMS: Parents and Researchers Interested In Smith-Magenis Syndrome [14476]
Private Practice Section/American Physical Therapy Assn. [16633]
Professional Women in Healthcare [4045]
Prog. for Appropriate Tech. in Hea. [17000]
Progressive Osseous Heteroplasia Assn. [14477]
Proj. Inform [13583]
Proj. Magic [16634]
Prune Belly Syndrome Network [14478]
PSRC of Am. [16266]
Public Citizen Hea. Res. Gp. [16250]
Public Hea. Leadership Soc. [16252]
Public Hosp. Pharmacy Coalition [15949]
Pull-thru Network [14427]
P.U.L.S.E. [14662]
Purine Res. Soc. [15258]
QiGong Res. Soc. [13647]
R.A. Bloch Cancer Found. [13867]
The Radiance Technique Intl. Assn. [13648]
Radiation and Public Hea. Proj. [16270]
Radiation Therapy Oncology Gp. [15653]
Radiological Soc. of North Am. [16293]
Radiology Bus. Mgt. Assn. [15074]
Radiology Mammography Intl. [13774]
Reel Recovery [11519]
Refugee Relief Intl. [12540]
Regulatory Affairs Professionals Soc. [14599]
Rehabilitation Intl. [16333]

Reference to "IO" in place of a book number signifies that the association may be found in the 45th edition of International Organizations.

Rehabilitation Tech. Assn. [16334]
Reiki Alliance [13651]
Renal Pathology Soc. [15872]
Renal Physicians Assn. [15298]
Renal Support Network [15299]
Resolve, The Natl. Infertility Assn. [14394]
Retinoblastoma Intl. [13869]
Riders for Hea. [15271]
Roger Wyburn-Mason and Jack M. Blount Found. for the Eradication of Rheumatoid Disease [16375]
Rolf Inst. of Structural Integration [13652]
Rose Kushner Breast Cancer Advisory Center [13870]
Royal Soc. of Medicine Found. [15178]
Russian Amer. Medical Assn. [16378]
Safety Pharmacology Soc. [15950]
Salvadoran Amer. Medical Soc. [15092]
San Francisco AIDS Found. [13584]
SATELLIFE Global Hea. Info. Network [14663]
SATELLIFE Global Health Information Network [IO]
Schizophrenia Intl. Res. Soc. [15232]
School Nurse Achievement Prog. [15525]
Scleroderma Found. [16389]
Scleroderma Res. Found. [16390]
Scleroderma Support Gp. [16391]
Scoliosis Assn., Inc. [16394]
Scoliosis Res. Soc. [16395]
Scottsdale Inst. [14713]
Sea to See Proj. [13760]
Sect. for Long Term Care and Rehabilitation [14894]
Sect. for Metropolitan Hospitals [14895]
Serbian Amer. Medical and Dental Soc. [14185]
Serendipity Assn. [14832]
Seventh-Day Adventist Dietetic Assn. [15569]
Sexual Medicine Soc. of North Am. [16405]
Shape Up Am. [15969]
Sharsheret [13872]
Shriners Hospitals for Children [13973]
Shy Drager Syndrome/Multiple Sys. Atrophy Support Gp. [15364]
Sickle Cell Disease Assn. of Am. [14797]
Simon Found. for Continence [16711]
Sino-American Pharmaceutical Professionals Assn. [15951]
Sister Kenny Rehabilitation Inst. [16335]
SisterSong Women of Color Reproductive Hea. Collective [18826]
Skin Cancer Found. [13874]
Sleep Res. Soc. [16429]
Smile Alliance Intl. [11721]
Smokenders [16435]
Soc. for Academic Continuing Medical Educ. [8875]
Soc. for Academic Emergency Medicine [14344]
Soc. for Acupuncture Res. [13537]
Soc. for the Advancement of Blood Mgt. [14798]
Soc. for the Advancement of Women's Imaging [16294]
Soc. of Air Force Physicians [15264]
Soc. of Amer. Gastrointestinal and Endoscopic Surgeons [14428]
Soc. for Applied Anthropology [6427]
Soc. for the Arts in Healthcare [13714]
Soc. for Assisted Reproductive Tech. [16346]
Soc. of Behavioral Medicine [13740]
Soc. of Cardiovascular Anesthesiologists [13689]
Soc. of Chest Pain Centers and Providers [15849]
Soc. of Clinical Child and Adolescent Psychology [16171]
Soc. for Clinical and Experimental Hypnosis [14927]
Soc. for Clinical and Medical Hair Removal [14310]
Soc. of Clinical Res. Associates [14027]
Soc. for Clinical Trials [14028]
Soc. of Consulting Psychology [16172]
Soc. of Correctional Physicians [16011]
Soc. of Critical Care Medicine [14071]
Soc. of Diagnostic Medical Sonography [16438]
Soc. for Ear, Nose, and Throat Advances in Children [15827]
Soc. for Epidemiologic Res. [14377]

Soc. of Eye Surgeons [15703]
Soc. of Gastroenterology Nurses and Associates [14429]
Soc. of Govt. Ser. Urologists [16714]
Soc. for Gynecologic Investigation [15618]
Soc. of Gynecologic Oncologists [15654]
Soc. for Healthcare Consumer Advocacy of the Amer. Hosp. Assn. [15005]
Soc. for Healthcare Strategy and Market Development of the Amer. Hosp. Assn. [14896]
Soc. for Hematopathology [15874]
Soc. of Interventional Pain Mgt. Surgery Centers [16588]
Soc. of Interventional Radiology [16300]
Soc. of Invasive Cardiovascular Professionals [13928]
Soc. for Investigative Dermatology [14214]
Soc. for Leukocyte Biology [16365]
Soc. for Male Reproduction and Urology [16343]
Soc. of Medical Banking Excellence [1449]
Soc. of Medical Consultants to the Armed Forces [15265]
Soc. of Medical Friends of Wine [23028]
Soc. of Medical Jurisprudence [15006]
Soc. for Melanoma Res. [13875]
Soc. for Menstrual Cycle Res. [15619]
Soc. of Military Orthopaedic Surgeons [15266]
Soc. of Military Otolaryngologists - Head and Neck Surgeons [15267]
Soc. of Nuclear Medicine [15424]
Soc. of Nuclear Medicine Technologist Sect. [15425]
Soc. for Nutrition Educ. [15570]
Soc. for Obstetric Anesthesia and Perinatology [15903]
Soc. for Occupational and Environmental Hea. [15633]
Soc. of Otorhinolaryngology and Head/Neck Nurses [15526]
Soc. for Pediatric Dermatology [14215]
Soc. of Pediatric Nurses [15527]
Soc. for Pediatric Radiology [16301]
Soc. for Pediatric Res. [15899]
Soc. for Pediatric Urology [16715]
Soc. of Pharmaceutical and Biotech Trainers [3475]
Soc. of Primary Care Policy Fellows [14664]
Soc. for Public Hea. Educ. [16254]
Soc. for Radiation Oncology Administrators [16302]
Soc. of Reproductive Surgeons [16349]
Soc. for Sex Therapy and Res. [16408]
Soc. for Simulation in Healthcare [15148]
Soc. for Social Work Leadership in Hea. Care [13209]
Soc. for the Stud. of Male Reproduction [16344]
Soc. for the Stud. of Reproduction [16350]
Soc. of Surgical Oncology [15655]
Soc. of Teachers of Family Medicine [14387]
Soc. for Tech. in Anesthesia [13692]
Soc. for Theriogenology [16806]
Soc. of Thoracic Radiology [16305]
Soc. of Thoracic Surgeons [16644]
Soc. of Toxicologic Pathology [15876]
Soc. of Univ. Otolaryngologists - Head and Neck Surgeons [15828]
Soc. of Univ. Surgeons [16591]
Soc. of Univ. Urologists [16716]
Soc. for Vascular Surgery [16730]
Soc. for Vascular Ultrasound [16731]
Solidarity and Action Against the HIV Infection in India [16969]
Special Needs Advocate for Parents [11652]
Spinal Cord Soc. [16469]
Spirit of Women Hosp. Network [14898]
Spondylitis Assn. of Am. [16377]
Starlight Starbright Children's Found. [11724]
State EMS Training Coordinators Coun. of NASEMSO [14345]
Stratis Hea. [14600]
Stroke Awareness for Everyone [16495]
Stroke Clubs, Intl. [16496]
Student Veterinary Emergency and Critical Care Soc. [16810]
Sturge-Weber Found. [15365]

Sudden Cardiac Arrest Assn. [13933]
Sun Safety Alliance [13876]
Support Org. for Trisomy 18, 13, and Related Disorders [14485]
Support for People with Oral and Head and Neck Cancer [13877]
Swedish Assn. of Registered Physiotherapists [IO]
Swedish Dental Assn. [IO]
Swedish Medical Assn. [IO]
Swedish Psychological Assn. [IO]
Sword Swallowers Assn. Intl. [10776]
Syndrome X Assn. [15259]
Take Charge! Cure Parkinson's [15366]
Taking Control of Your Diabetes [14231]
Task Force for Child Survival and Development [12542]
Tear Film and Ocular Surface Soc. [15729]
TECH, Tech. Exchange for Christian Healthcare [20244]
Tel-Med [14601]
Therapy Dogs Intl. [16638]
Theta Psi [24566]
Thoracic Surgery Residents Assn. [16645]
Tissue Engg. Soc. Intl. [6610]
TOPS Club (Take Off Pounds Sensibly) [12649]
Tourette Syndrome Assn. [15367]
Transatlantic Partners Against AIDS [13586]
Transplant Recipients Intl. Org. [16682]
Transplant Speakers Intl. [16683]
Treatment Action Gp. [13587]
Treatment and Res. Advancements Assn. for Personality Disorder [15235]
Tremor Action Network [15369]
Trinity Hea. Intl. [14731]
Trinity Medical Center [14900]
Trust for America's Hea. [16255]
Truth in Fitness [15970]
Tuberous Sclerosis Alliance [15371]
Turner Syndrome Soc. of the U.S. [14486]
UK eHealth Assn. [IO]
Ukrainian Medical Assn. of North Am. [15182]
Undersea and Hyperbaric Medical Soc. [16697]
Union of Amer. Physicians and Dentists [24092]
Unite for Sight [13381]
United Black Fund [12204]
United Brachial Plexus Network [15403]
United Cerebral Palsy Associations [13935]
United Methodist Assn. of Hea. and Welfare Ministries [14602]
United Network for Organ Sharing [16684]
U.S. Adult Cystic Fibrosis Assn. [16364]
U.S. Animal Hea. Assn. [16811]
U.S. Hereditary Angioedema Assn. [14487]
U.S. Medical Massage Assn. [15033]
U.S. Pharmacopeia [15953]
U.S. Sports Chiropractic Fed. [23282]
Urgent Care Assn. of Am. [13665]
Us TOO Intl. [13879]
USAF Medical Ser. Corps Assn. [13590]
Vasculitis Found. [16552]
Venous Soc. of Am. [16732]
Veterinary Botanical Medicine Assn. [16812]
Veterinary Orthopedic Soc. [16816]
VHA [14901]
VietNow Natl. [13359]
Vision World Wide [16890]
Visiting Nurse Associations of Am. [15532]
Vitamin Angel Alliance [15571]
Vocational Evaluation and Career Assessment Professionals [16337]
Voice Found. [16457]
Volunteer Trustees of Not-for-Profit Hospitals [14902]
Volunteers in Hea. Care [14665]
Water Advocates [9310]
Waterbirth Intl. [13984]
Weight Watchers Intl. [14603]
Wellness Associates [16058]
Wellstart Intl. [14666]
Western Surgical Assn. [16592]
Western Veterinary Conf. [16817]
Wilderness Medical Soc. [15184]
Williams Syndrome Assn. [14490]
WishKids Intl. [11665]
Women Alive Coalition [13588]

A star before a book entry number signifies that the name is not listed separately, but is mentioned within the entry.

Women in Hea. Care Mgt. **[14667]**
Women in Neurotrauma Res. **[15404]**
WomenHeart: Natl. Coalition for Women with Heart Disease **[13929]**
Women's Auxiliary of the ICA **[14016]**
Women's Drug Res. Project **[13285]**
Workgroup for Electronic Data Interchange **[1854]**
World Allergy Org. **[13605]**
World Assn. for Psychosocial Rehabilitation - U.S. Br. **[16338]**
World Assn. of Sleep Medicine **[16430]**
World Assn. of Veterinary Lab. Diagnosticians **[16819]**
World Coun. for Cardiovascular and Pulmonary Rehabilitation **[13930]**
World Fed. for Mental Hea. **[15237]**
World Fed. of Neurology Res. Gp. on Motor Neuron Diseases **[15373]**
World Fed. of Neuroradiological Societies **[16306]**
World Fed. of Public Hea. Associations **[16258]**
World Homecare and Hospice Org. **[14844]**
World Medical Mission **[20245]**
World Medical Relief **[12544]**
World Soc. for Stereotactic and Functional Neuro-surgery **[15418]**
World Spine Soc. **[15405]**
World Sports Medicine Assn. of Registered Therapists **[16486]**
Wound Healing Soc. **[14668]**
Wound, Ostomy and Continence Nurses Soc.: An Assn. of E.T. Nurses **[15533]**
Young Onset Parkinson's Assn. **[15374]**
Zero to Three: Natl. Center for Infants, Toddlers and Families **[13944]**
Hea. Care; Accreditation Assn. for Ambulatory **[13661]**
Hea. Care Admin; Center for Res. in Ambulatory **[15064]**
Hea. Care Administrators; Amer. Coll. of **[15535]**
Hea. Care Advisors Assn; Natl. CPA **[13530]**
Hea. Care; Advocate **[14821]**
Hea. Care Anti-Fraud Assn; Natl. **[14963]**
Hea. Care Assn; Am. Individual and Gp. Home **[★12291]**
Hea. Care; Assn. for Benchmarking in **[1848]**
Hea. Care Assn; Natl. Rural **[★16248]**
Hea. Care Compliance Assn. **[14632]**, 6500 Barrie Rd., Ste. 250, Minneapolis, MN 55435, (952)988-8373
Hea. Care eBusiness Collaborative **[14633]**, 1405 N Pierce St., Ste. 100, Little Rock, AR 72207-5378, (501)661-9408
Health Care Education Group - Defunct.
Hea. Care; EHS **[★14821]**
Hea. Care Executive Assistants **[64]**, 1 N Franklin, Chicago, IL 60606, (312)422-3702
Hea. Care Exhibitors Assn. **[★1340]**
Hea. Care Facilities; Consultant Dietitians in **[15554]**
Hea. Care Found. for the Deaf; Natl. **[★14752]**
Health Care for the Homeless Program - Defunct.
Hea. Care Info; Center for Medical Consumers and **[★14550]**
Hea. Care Liability Alliance **[★14635]**
Hea. Care Off. Mgt; Professional Assn. of **[15073]**
Hea. Care Off. Managers; Professional Assn. of **[★15073]**
Health Care Products
Advanced Medical Tech. Assn. **[14669]**
Allied Beauty Assn. **[IO]**
Amer. Assn. for Homecare **[14670]**
Amer. Coun. for Fitness and Nutrition **[15959]**
Amer. Nutraceutical Assn. **[14612]**
Amer. Orthotic and Prosthetic Assn. **[1855]**
Amer. Soc. of Dermatological Retailers **[86]**
Assn. of British Healthcare Indus. **[IO]**
Assn. of Hea. Food Mfrs. **[IO]**
Assn. for Healthcare Rsrc. and Materials Mgt. **[14872]**
Assn. of Needle-Free Injection Mfrs. **[2549]**
BIO Ventures for Global Hea. **[14975]**
British Herb Trade Assn. **[IO]**
British Herbal Medicine Assn. **[IO]**
Center for Biologics Evaluation and Res. **[14671]**
China Assn. for Medical Devices Indus. **[IO]**
Coalition for Healthcare Commun. **[14622]**

Contact Lens Mfrs. Assn. **[1856]**
Contact Lens Mfrs. Assn. **[IO]**
Contact Lens Soc. of Am. **[1857]**
Dental Dealers of America **[1858]**
Dental Trade Alliance **[1859]**
European Disposables and Nonwovens Assn. **[IO]**
European Fed. of Associations of Hea. Prdt. Mfrs. **[IO]**
European Herbal Infusions Assn. **[IO]**
German Medical Tech. Assn. **[IO]**
Hea. Indus. Distributors Assn. **[1860]**
Hea. Indus. Gp. Purchasing Assn. **[14672]**
Hea. Level Seven **[14636]**
Healthcare Mfrs. Marketing Coun. **[14673]**
Hearing Indus. Assn. **[1861]**
Independent Medical Distributors Assn. **[1862]**
Intl. Aloe Sci. Coun. **[1863]**
Intl. Aloe Sci. Coun. **[IO]**
Intl. Sharps Injury Prevention Soc. **[16380]**
Irish Medical Devices Assn. **[IO]**
Medical Equip. and Tech. Assn. **[7306]**
Medical Indus. Assn. of Australia **[IO]**
Natl. Alliance for the Primary Prevention of Sharps Injuries **[16381]**
Natl. Home Oxygen Patients Assn. **[14404]**
Optical Labs. Assn. **[1864]**
Optical Laboratories Association **[IO]**
Orthopedic Surgical Mfrs. Assn. **[1865]**
Partnership for Quality Medical Donations **[12537]**
Professional Women in Healthcare **[4045]**
Prog. for Appropriate Tech. in Hea. **[17000]**
United Plant Savers **[13655]**
Vision Coun. of Am. **[1866]**
Hea. Care Professionals; Intl. Assn. of Physicians and **[16002]**
Hea. Care Providers; Amer. Acad. of **[★15302]**
Hea. Care Quality Measurement and Reporting; Natl. Forum for **[★14658]**
Health Care Resource Mgt. Soc. - Defunct.
Hea. Care; Soc. for Social Work Admin. in **[★13209]**
Hea. Care; Soc. for Social Work Leadership in **[13209]**
Health Care for Survival Program **[★12780]**
Hea. Care Without Harm **[14634]**, c/o Colleen Funk-houser, 1901 N Moore St., Ste. 509, Arlington, VA 22209, (703)243-0056
Health Careers Program; National **[★8231]**
Hea; Center for Psychological and Spiritual **[15194]**
Hea. Centers; Natl. Assn. of Neighborhood **[★14574]**
Hea. Centers; Natl. Coun. of **[★14540]**
Hea. Club Assn; Natl. **[3670]**
Hea. Coalition on Liability and Access **[14635]**, PO Box 19008, Washington, DC 20036-9008, (202)293-4255
Hea. Coalition; Natl. Women's **[★16899]**
Hea; Community-Campus Partnerships For **[11744]**
Health Conf. for Business and Industry - Defunct.
Hea. Connection **[13245]**, 55 W Oak Ridge Dr., Hag-erstown, MD 21740, (301)393-3290
Hea. Connection; Friends' **[22136]**
Hea. Consultants; Intl. **[★14575]**
Hea. Consumers' Self-Help CH; Natl. Mental **[12553]**
Hea. Corp; Kotzebue Area **[★12627]**
Hea. Corp; Kotzebue Area **[★12627]**
Health Coun; Amer. Industrial **[15626]**
Hea; Coun. on Educ. for Public **[16242]**
Hea. Coun; Silicones **[★821]**
Hea. Counselors; Acad. of Clinical Mental **[★11828]**
Hea. Counselors Assn; Amer. Mental **[15189]**
Hea. Counsels; Gen. Counsels' Assn. of Accident and **[★5499]**
Hea. and Crippled Children's Directors; Assn. of State and Territorial Maternal and Child **[★13947]**
Hea. Crisis; Gay Men's **[13564]**
Hea. Dentists; Amer. Assn. of Public **[★14118]**
Hea. and Development Intl. **[14561]**, c/o Michael Pa-jonk, Deputy Exec. Dir., 1001 Wenonah, Oak Park, IL 60304, (708)386-3688
Hea. and Development Intl. **[IO]**, Oak Park, IL, United States
Hea. Division of Amer. Assn. for Hea., Physical Educ. and Recreation; School **[★16234]**
Hea. Division of Prog. for the Introduction and Adaptation of Contraceptive Tech. **[★17000]**

Hea. Division of Prog. for the Introduction and Adaptation of Contraceptive Tech. **[★IO]**
Health Education
Amer. Acad. of Orthopaedic Manual Physical Therapists **[15971]**
Amer. Alliance for Hea., Physical Educ., Recreation and Dance **[8979]**
Amer. Alliance for Medical Cannabis **[15020]**
Amer. Assn. of Colleges of Nursing **[8842]**
Amer. Assn. for Hea. Educ. **[16234]**
Amer. Fertility Assn. **[14388]**
Amer. Hea. Decisions **[14541]**
Amer. Indoor Air Quality Coun. **[5082]**
Amer. Nutraceutical Assn. **[14612]**
Amer. School Hea. Assn. **[14718]**
Amer. Soc. for Bioethics and Humanities **[8845]**
Amer. Soc. of Pain Educators **[15838]**
Assn. of Academic Hea. Centers **[14546]**
Assn. of Asthma Educators **[16355]**
Assn. of Black Nursing Faculty **[8848]**
Assn. for Hosp. Medical Educ. **[14873]**
Assn. for Medical Educ. and Res. in Substance Abuse **[8849]**
Assn. of Minority Hea. Professions Schools **[8850]**
Assn. of Nutrition Departments and Programs **[8947]**
Assn. of Optometric Educators **[8851]**
Assn. of Professors of Gynecology and Obstetrics **[15592]**
Assn. of Schools of Public Hea. **[16240]**
Assn. for Surgical Educ. **[8856]**
Assn. of Univ. Programs in Hea. Admin. **[8857]**
Assyrian Medical Soc. **[13715]**
Australian Coun. for Hea., Physical Educ. and Recreation **[IO]**
Bill and Melinda Gates Found. **[12273]**
Black Women of Essence **[11269]**
Center for Medical Consumers **[14550]**
Center for Professional Well-Being **[14700]**
Children's Cross Connection Intl. **[11552]**
Commn. on Accreditation of Allied Hea. Educ. Programs **[8832]**
Comm. on Accreditation for Opthalmic Medical Personnel **[8834]**
Comprehensive Hea. Educ. Found. **[8860]**
Consortium of Institutes of Higher Educ. in Hea. and Rehabilitation in Europe **[IO]**
Consumer Hea. Educ. Coun. **[14685]**
Coun. on Accreditation of Nurse Anesthesia Educational Programs **[8835]**
Coun. on Educ. for Public Hea. **[16242]**
Coun. on Hea. Info. and Educ. **[14553]**
Coun. of Teaching Hospitals **[14879]**
DanceSafe **[12041]**
DEBRA Intl. **[IO]**
Diabetes Action Res. and Educ. Found. **[14221]**
Doctors Ought to Care **[14554]**
Doctors Worldwide **[12851]**
Facing Our Risk of Cancer Empowered **[13823]**
Fed. for Accessible Nursing Educ. and Licensure **[15478]**
Fed. of Associations of Regulatory Boards **[14555]**
Fed. of State Physician Hea. Programs **[15999]**
The Floating Hosp. **[14882]**
Hea. Educ. Found. **[16243]**
Hea. Jam **[14674]**
Healthcare Convention and Exhibitors Assn. **[1340]**
Intl. Alliance for Child and Adolescent Mental Hea. and Schools **[15204]**
Intl. Alliance of Healthcare Educators **[8475]**
Intl. Assn. for Human Caring **[14640]**
Intl. Assn. for Medicinal Compliance **[15041]**
Intl. Center for the Health Sciences **[8476]**
Intl. Center for the Health Sciences **[IO]**
Intl. Childbirth Educ. Assn. **[15605]**
Intl. Coalition for Addiction Stud. Educ. **[9197]**
Intl. Coun. for Hea., Physical Educ., Recreation, Sport, and Dance **[8981]**
Intl. Coun. on Infertility Info. Dissemination **[14392]**
Intl. Fed. for Psychoanalytic Educ. **[9028]**
Intl. Nursing Coalition for Mass Casualty Educ. **[8946]**

Reference to "IO" in place of a book number signifies that the association may be found in the 45th edition of International Organizations.

Joint Rev. Comm. on Educ. in Diagnostic Medical Sonography [8837]
Kaiser Family Found. [14642]
Midwifery Educ. Accreditation Coun. [8063]
Minority Hea. Professions Found. [18080]
Mothers' Voices [13574]
Natl. Abstinence Educ. Assn. [9123]
Natl. Acad. for State Hea. Policy [14649]
Natl. Assn. of Advisors for the Hea. Professions [8866]
Natl. Assn. of Geriatric Educ. Centers [14513]
Natl. Assn. for Girls and Women in Sport [8983]
Natl. Assn. of Hea. Educ. Centers [14675]
Natl. Assn. of Hea. Sci. Educ. Partnership [9107]
Natl. Assn. for Kinesiology and Physical Educ. in Higher Educ. [8984]
Natl. Assn. for Practical Nurse Educ. and Ser. [8869]
Natl. Assn. of School Nurses for the Deaf [14768]
Natl. Assn. for Sport and Physical Educ. [8986]
Natl. Assn. of Supervisors and Administrators of Hea. Occupations Educ. [8870]
Natl. Center for Hea. Educ. [14582]
Natl. Conf. of Local Environmental Hea. Administrators [16246]
Natl. Coun. of Athletic Training [8987]
Natl. Coun. on Minority Educ. in Transplantation [16677]
Natl. Educ. Alliance for Borderline Personality Disorder [15224]
Natl. Hea. Info. Center [14588]
Natl. Inst. for Hea. Care Mgt. Res. and Educational Found. [14655]
Natl. Latina Hea. Network [14589]
Natl. Pain Educ. Coun. [15846]
Natl. Rural Hea. Assn. [16248]
NSF Intl. [16249]
Nurses Educational Funds [15516]
OMNI Learning Inst. [8299]
PE4life [8991]
Pharmacy Technician Educators Coun. [8963]
Phi Epsilon Kappa [24574]
Public Citizen Hea. Res. Gp. [16250]
SATELLIFE Global Hea. Info. Network [14663]
Sea to See Proj. [13760]
Soc. of Hea. Educ. and Hea. Promotion Specialists [IO]
Soc. for Public Hea. Educ. [16254]
Soc. of State Directors of Hea., Physical Educ. and Recreation [8992]
Student Global AIDS Campaign [13585]
Sun Safety Alliance [13876]
Tel-Med [14601]
TOPS Club (Take Off Pounds Sensibly) [12649]
Weight Watchers Intl. [14603]
World Fed. of Public Hea. Associations [16258]
Young Survival Coalition [13883]
Hea. Educ. and Accreditation; Comm. on Allied [★8832]
Hea., Educ., and AIDS Leadership; Project [★13580]
Hea. Educ; Amer. Assn. for [16234]
Hea. Educ. Assn; Emotional [8255]
Hea. Educ; Assn. of State and Territorial Directors of Hea. Promotion and Public [★6215]
Hea. Educ; Assn. of State and Territorial Directors of Public [★6215]
Hea. Educ; Conf. of State and Territorial Directors of Public [★6215]
Hea. Educ. Coun. [14562], 3950 Indus. Blvd., Ste. 600, West Sacramento, CA 95691-6509, (916)556-3344
Hea. Educ. Found. [16243], 2600 Virginia Ave. NW, Ste. 502, Washington, DC 20037, (202)338-3501
Hea. and Educ. Found; Alternatives to Abortion/Women's [★12912]
Hea. Educ. Found; Comprehensive [8860]
Health Education Media Assn. - Defunct.
Hea. Educ. Programs; Commn. on Accreditation of Allied [8832]
Hea. Educ. Res. Coun. [★14582]
Hea. Educ. Rsrc. Center; Native Amer. Women [★12630]
Hea. Educ. Rsrc. Org. [13568], 1734 Maryland Ave., Baltimore, MD 21201, (410)685-1180

Health and Education Resources - Defunct.
Hea. Educ. Schools; Accrediting Bur. of [15124]
Hea. Educ; Soc. for Public [16254]
Hea. Educ; Soc. of State Directors of Physical and [★8992]
Hea., Educ. and Welfare Assn; Presbyterian [13184]
Hea., Educ. and Welfare Assn; United Presbyterian [★13184]
Hea. Educators; Soc. of Public [★16254]
Hea. Employers Assn. of British Columbia [IO], Vancouver, BC, Canada
Health and Energy Inst. - Defunct.
Hea. Engineers; Conf. of Municipal Public [★16246]
Hea., Env. and Justice; Center For [5266]
Hea., Env. and Safety; Beach Educ. Advocates for Culture, [10761]
Hea. Fac. Administrators; Natl. Assn. of County [15069]
Hea. Fac. Licensure and Certification Directors; Assn. of [★6210]
Hea. Fac. Survey Agencies; Assn. of [6210]
Hea; Fenway Community [14430]
Health First Intl. - Address unknown since 2003.
Hea. and Fitness Assn; Alternative [10522]
Hea. and Fitness; Assn. of Hosp. [★15966]
Hea. and Fitness Assn; IDEA [15965]
Hea. and Fitness; Natl. Assn. for [15967]
Hea. and Fitness Source; IDEA, The [★15965]

Health Food
Compassionate Cooks [13350]
Herb Res. Found. [6635]
Kitchen Gardeners Intl. [9966]
Vegan Action [11071]
Vegetarian Awareness Network [11072]
Weston A. Price Found. [15572]
Hea. Food Manufactures Assn. [IO], Surrey, United Kingdom
Hea. Found; Animal [16781]
Hea. Found; Assoc. [18983]
Health Found; Creation [20547]
Hea. Found; Intl. Child [★13950]
Hea. Found; Natl. Mental [★15211]
Hea. Fraud; California Coun. Against [★17692]
Hea. Fraud; Natl. Coun. Against [★17692]
Hea. Freedom; Amer. Assn. for [16049]
Hea. Fund; Children's [13954]
Hea. Fund; Lesbian [14432]
Hea. Global Access Proj. [11331], 429 W 127th St., 2nd Fl., New York, NY 10027, (212)937-5283
Health for Haiti Found. - Address unknown since 1999.
Hea. and Healing; Commn. on [★20241]
Hea. and Healing Ministries [★20241]
Hea. and Human Development; Natl. Inst. of Child [13971]
Hea. and Human Ser. Organizations; Natl. Assembly of [★13400]
Hea. and Human Services; Coun. for [★13165]
Hea. and Human Services Ministries, United Church of Christ; Coun. for [13165]
Hea. and Human Services Organizations; Natl. Coalition of Hispanic [★13176]
Hea. and Human Values; Soc. for [★8845]
Hea. for Humanity [14563], 415 Linden Ave., Ste. B, Wilmette, IL 60091, (847)425-7900
Hea. Imperative; Black Women's [16895]
Hea. Indus. Assn. [★14669]
Hea. Indus. Bar Code Coun. [★14080]
Hea. Indus. Bus. Communications Coun. [14080], 2525 E Arizona Biltmore Cir., Ste. 127, Phoenix, AZ 85016, (602)381-1091
Hea. Indus. Distributors Assn. [1860], 310 Montgomery St., Alexandria, VA 22314-1516, (703)549-4432
Hea. Indus. Gp. Purchasing Assn. [14672], 2025 M St. NW, Ste. 800, Washington, DC 20036, (202)367-1162
Hea. Indus. Mfrs. Assn. [★14669]
Hea. Indus. Representatives Assn. [2627], 7315 E 5th Ave., Denver, CO 80230, (303)756-8115
Hea. Informatics New Zealand [IO], Auckland, New Zealand
Hea. Info. Center; ODPHP [★14588]
Hea. Info. CH; Natl. [★14588]
Health Information Coun. - Defunct.

Hea. Info. Mgt. Assn; Amer. [15097]
Hea. Info. Network [★8474]
Hea. Info. Network; NEA [8474]
Hea. Info. Off; Midwest Migrant [★12590]
Hea. Info. Rsrc. Center [14564], 1850 W Winchester Rd., Ste. 213, Libertyville, IL 60048, (847)816-8660
Hea. Initiatives; Inst. for Mental [15203]
Hea; INSA, The Intl. Ser. Assn. for [★14978]
Hea. Inst; Animal [2970]
Hea. Institute; Children's Better [★14549]
Health; Inst. for Labor and Mental [15202]
Hea. Inst; Sheet Metal Occupational [★12991]
Hea. Inst. Trust; Sheet Metal Occupational [12991]
Hea. Insurance Advisors; Assn. of [14958]
Health Insurance Assn. of Am. - Defunct.
Hea. Insurance Services; Alternative [★13609]
Hea; Intl. Assn. for Infant Mental [16098]
Hea; Intl. Medical Services for [★14981]
Hea. Internet Ethics; Hi-Ethics - [14676]
Hea. Jam [14674], 221 E 122nd St., 5th Fl., New York, NY 10035, (212)722-7987
Hea., Justice and the Media; Leadership Coun. for Mental [★12031]
Hea. Kinesiology Assn; Touch for [13654]

Health Law
Amer. Acad. of Psychiatry and the Law [5780]
Amer. Bar Assn. - Commn. on Mental and Physical Disability Law [5781]
Amer. Hea. Lawyers Assn. [5782]
Center for Patient Advocacy [14620]
Global Lawyers and Physicians [14558]
Greenaction for Hea. and Environmental Justice [17699]
Hea. Coalition on Liability and Access [14635]
Hea. Law Sect. - Amer. Bar Assn. [5783]
Hi-Ethics - Hea. Internet Ethics [14676]
Inst. for Hea. Policy Solutions [14689]
Intl. Acad. of Legal Medicine [IO]
Natl. Hea. Law Prog. [5784]
Victims of Chiropractic [14015]
Hea. Law; Judge David L. Bazelon Center for Mental [17123]
Hea. Law Proj; Mental [★17123]
Hea. Law Sect. - Amer. Bar Assn. [5783], c/o Amer. Bar Assn., 321 N Clark St., Chicago, IL 60610, (312)988-5548
Hea. Level Seven [14636], 3300 Washtenaw Ave., Ste. 227, Ann Arbor, MI 48104, (734)677-7777
Health Media Education - Defunct.
Hea. Ministries [20241], Bd. for Human Care Ministries, 1333 S Kirkwood Rd., St. Louis, MO 63122-7295, (314)996-1382
Hea. Ministries Assn. [16339], 295 W Crossville Rd., Ste. 130, Roswell, GA 30075, (770)640-9955
Hea; Natl. Alliance for Hispanic [13969]
Hea; Natl. Assn. of Local Boards of [16244]
Hea; Natl. Assn. for Mental [★15211]
Hea; Natl. Assn. of Nurse Practitioners in Reproductive [★15497]
Hea; Natl. Assn. of Nurse Practitioners in Women's [15497]
Hea; Natl. Assn. of Professionals in Women's [★16903]
Hea; Natl. Assn. for Rural Mental [15217]
Hea; Natl. Assn. for Women's [16903]
Hea; Natl. Center for Educ. in Maternal and Child [13969]
Hea; Natl. Coun. for Intl. [★14979]
Hea; Natl. Coun. on Women's [16904]
Health; National Inst. of Safety and [★9101]
Hea. Network; Natl. Women's [16906]
Health News Inst. - Defunct.
Hea. Nurses; Amer. Assn. of Occupational [15439]
Hea. Nurses; Amer. Bd. for Occupational [15445]
Hea., Obstetric and Neonatal Nurses; Assn. of Women's [15470]
Hea. Occupations Educ; Natl. Assn. for State Administrators of [★8870]
Hea. Occupations Educ; Natl. Assn. of Supervisors and Administrators of [8870]
Hea. Occupations Students of Am. [8863], 6021 Morriss Rd., Ste. 111, Flower Mound, TX 75028, (800)321-HOSA
Hea. Officers; Assn. of State and Territorial [★6212]
Hea. Officers; Natl. Assn. of County [★6217]

A star before a book entry number signifies that the name is not listed separately, but is mentioned within the entry.

Hea. Officials; Assn. of State and Territorial [6212]
Hea. Officials; Natl. Assembly of Chief Livestock [★16811]
Hea. Officials; Natl. Assn. of County [★6217]
Hea. Officials; Natl. Assn. of County and City [6217]
Hea. Optimizing Inst. [14826], PO Box 1233, Del Mar, CA 92014, (858)481-7751
Hea. Options - Info., Care and Educ; Concern for [★12178]
Hea. Organizations; Coalition of Spanish Speaking Mental [★13176]
Health and Personal Care Distribution Conference - Address unknown since 2006.
Hea. Personnel in Ophthalmology; Amer. Assn. of Certified Allied [★15674]
Hea. Personnel in Ophthalmology; Joint Commn. on Allied [15692]
Hea., Physical Educ. and Recreation; Amer. Alliance for [★8979]
Hea., Physical Educ. and Recreation; Amer. Assn. for [★8979]
Hea., Physical Educ., Recreation and Dance; Amer. Alliance for [8979]
Hea., Physical Educ., and Recreation; Division of Girl's and Women's Sports of the Amer. Assn. of [★8983]
Hea., Physical Educ. and Recreation; Recreation Division of the Amer. Alliance for [★12793]
Hea., Physical Educ. and Recreation; School Hea. Division of Amer. Assn. for [★16234]
Hea., Physical Educ. and Recreation; Soc. of State Directors of [8992]
Hea. Physicians; Amer. Assn. of Public [16235]
Hea. Physics; Amer. Bd. of [16015]
Hea. Physics Soc. [16017], 1313 Dolley Madison Blvd., Ste. 402, McLean, VA 22101, (703)790-1745
Hea. Planning; Amer. Assn. for Comprehensive [★14542]

Health Plans
Acad. of Managed Care Providers [14677]
Alliance of Community Hea. Plans [14678]
Amer. Acad. of Insurance Medicine [IO]
Amer. Accreditation Healthcare Commn. [14679]
Amer. Assn. of Integrated Healthcare Delivery Systems [15048]
Amer. Assn. of Preferred Provider Organizations [14680]
Amer. Bd. of Managed Care Nursing [15442]
Amer. Coll. of Managed Care Medicine [14681]
Amer. Coll. of Managed Care Medicine [IO]
Amer. Horseman Alliance [1924]
America's Hea. Insurance Plans [14682]
Antitrust Coalition for Consumer Choice in Hea. Care [14615]
Assn. of Clinicians for the Underserved [14616]
Assn. for Community Affiliated Plans [14617]
Biotech Medical Mgt. Assn. [14683]
Blue Cross and Blue Shield Assn. [14959]
Canadian Assn. of Blue Cross Plans [IO]
Center for Medicare Advocacy [14684]
Citizens' Coun. on Hea. Care [17696]
Community Voices [11745]
Consumer Hea. Educ. Coun. [14685]
Coun. for Affordable Hea. Insurance [14686]
Coun. for Affordable Quality Healthcare [14625]
Covering Kids and Families [12271]
Delta Dental Plans Assn. [14687]
Hea. Benefits Coalition for Affordable Choice and Quality [14688]
Inst. for Hea. Policy Solutions [14689]
Intl. Hea. Evaluation Assn. [14568]
Intl. Medical Volunteers Assn. [15075]
ITEM Coalition [14690]
Life Insurance Settlement Assn. [2193]
Natl. Alliance of Medicare Set-Aside Professionals [17697]
Natl. Assn. of Alternative Benefits Consultants [1867]
Natl. Assn. of Specialty Hea. Organizations [14650]
Natl. Assn. of State Comprehensive Hea. Insurance Plans [14691]
Natl. Assn. of State Medicaid Directors [14692]
Natl. Center for Farmworker Hea. [14581]
Natl. Comm. for Quality Assurance [16265]

Natl. Dental EDI Coun. [14176]
Natl. Hea. Care Anti-Fraud Assn. [14963]
Physicians for a Natl. Hea. Prog. [18313]
Sect. for Metropolitan Hospitals [14895]
Stratis Hea. [14600]
Women in Managed Care [14693]
Women in Managed Care [IO]
Health Policy Advisory Center - Defunct.
Health Policy Coun. - Defunct.
Hea. Policy Solutions; Inst. for [14689]
Hea; Postgraduate Center for Mental [16227]
Hea. Practitioners Intl; Assoc. Professional Massage Therapists and Allied [★15025]
Hea. and Preventive Medicine; Amer. Osteopathic Acad. of Public [★15802]
Hea. in Prisons Proj. [IO], London, United Kingdom
Hea. Prdt. Wholesalers' and Manufacturers' Assn. in Finland [IO], Helsinki, Finland
Hea. Products Assn. of Southern Africa [IO], Johannesburg, Republic of South Africa

Health Professionals
Academic Orthopaedic Soc. [15750]
Acad. of Managed Care Providers [14677]
Acad. on Mental Retardation [15238]
Acad. of Osseointegration [14091]
Acad. of Scientific Hypnotherapy [14913]
AcademyHealth [14535]
Accelerated Cure Proj. for Multiple Sclerosis [15301]
Accreditation Commn. for Acupuncture and Oriental Medicine [15739]
Accreditation Coun. on Optometric Educ. [15710]
Accreditation Rev. Commn. on Educ. for the Physician Asst. [15972]
Accreditation Rev. Comm. on Educ, in Surgical Tech. [15123]
Acupuncturists Without Borders [13536]
Adopt a Dr. [12750]
Aesculapian Club [15982]
African-Amer. Assn. of Fitness Professionals [15957]
African Medical and Res. Found. [14971]
AFT Healthcare [24087]
Aid for Intl. Medicine [14972]
Air and Surface Transport Nurses Assn. [15427]
Airlines Medical Directors Assn. [13539]
Alisa Ann Ruch Burn Found. [13780]
Alliance for Aging Res. [11272]
Alliance of Cardiovascular Professionals [13885]
Alliance of Minority Medical Associations [14607]
Alliance of State Pain Initiatives [15830]
Alternative Hea. Professionals Assn. [13610]
Amer. Acad. of Alternative Medicine [13612]
Amer. Acad. of Ambulatory Care Nursing [15428]
Amer. Acad. of Disability Evaluating Physicians [14033]
Amer. Acad. of Environmental Medicine [14360]
Amer. Acad. of Family Physicians [14383]
Amer. Acad. of HIV Medicine [13556]
Amer. Acad. of Medical Administrators [15045]
Amer. Acad. of Medical Administrators Res. and Educational Found. [15046]
Amer. Acad. of Neurological and Orthopaedic Surgeons [15409]
Amer. Acad. of Neurology [15376]
Amer. Acad. of Nurse Practitioners [15429]
Amer. Acad. of Nursing [15430]
Amer. Acad. of Ophthalmology [15656]
Amer. Acad. of Optometry [15711]
Amer. Acad. of Orthopaedic Manual Physical Therapists [15971]
Amer. Acad. of Orthopaedic Surgeons [15752]
Amer. Acad. of Osteopathy [15790]
Amer. Acad. of Professional Coders [14694]
Amer. Acad. of Tropical Medicine [16692]
Amer. Assembly for Men in Nursing [15431]
Amer. Assisted Living Nurses Assn. [15432]
Amer. Assn. of Ambulatory Surgery Centers [16558]
Amer. Assn. of Bioanalysts Bd. of Registry [15126]
Amer. Assn. of Birth Centers [15580]
Amer. Assn. of Clinical Directors [15986]
Amer. Assn. of Colleges of Osteopathic Medicine [15791]

Amer. Assn. of Critical-Care Nurses [15433]
Amer. Assn. of Dispensing Ophthalmologists [15658]
Amer. Assn. of Gynecologic Laparoscopists [15581]
Amer. Assn. for Hand Surgery [14522]
Amer. Assn. of Heart Failure Nurses [15434]
Amer. Assn. for the History of Nursing [10083]
Amer. Assn. of Immunologists [14929]
Amer. Assn. on Intellectual and Developmental Disabilities [15239]
Amer. Assn. of Kidney Patients [15283]
Amer. Assn. of Legal Nurse Consultants [14999]
Amer. Assn. of LifeStyle Counselors [14053]
Amer. Assn. of Managed Care Nurses [15435]
Amer. Assn. of Medical Assistants [15081]
Amer. Assn. of Medical Audit Specialists [15049]
Amer. Assn. for Medical Chronobiology and Chronotherapeutics [13751]
Amer. Assn. of Medical Rev. Officers [14695]
Amer. Assn. of Medical Soc. Executives [15153]
Amer. Assn. of Neurological Surgeons [15410]
Amer. Assn. of Neuromuscular and Electrodiagnostic Medicine [15303]
Amer. Assn. of Neuropathologists [15853]
Amer. Assn. of Neuroscience Nurses [15436]
Amer. Assn. of Nurse Anesthetists [15437]
Amer. Assn. of Nurse Assessment Coordinators [14608]
Amer. Assn. of Nurse Attorneys [15000]
Amer. Assn. of Nurse Life Care Planners [15438]
Amer. Assn. of Nutritional Consultants [15540]
Amer. Assn. of Occupational Hea. Nurses [15439]
Amer. Assn. of Off. Nurses [15440]
Amer. Assn. of Oriental Medicine [15742]
Amer. Assn. of Orthopedic Medicine [15753]
Amer. Assn. for Pediatric Ophthalmology and Strabismus [15660]
Amer. Assn. of Physician Offices and Labs. [14990]
Amer. Assn. of Physician Specialists [15792]
Amer. Assn. of Professional Hypnotherapists [14915]
Amer. Assn. of Psychiatric Administrators [14861]
Amer. Assn. of Spinal Cord Injury Nurses [15441]
Amer. Assn. for the Stud. of Liver Diseases [14801]
Amer. Bd. of Family Dentistry [14122]
Amer. Bd. of Genetic Counseling [14492]
Amer. Bd. of Indus. Hygiene [15623]
Amer. Bd. of Internal Medicine [14965]
Amer. Bd. of Medical Specialties [15117]
Amer. Bd. of Neurological Surgery [15411]
Amer. Bd. of Nuclear Medicine [15419]
Amer. Bd. of Nutrition [15541]
Amer. Bd. of Obstetrics and Gynecology [15582]
Amer. Bd. of Ophthalmology [15661]
Amer. Bd. of Opticianry [15704]
Amer. Bd. of Orthopaedic Surgery [15755]
Amer. Bd. of Psychological Hypnosis [14917]
Amer. Bd. of Quality Assurance and Utilization Rev. Physicians [16260]
Amer. Bd. of Radiology [16272]
Amer. Bd. of Surgery [16563]
Amer. Case Mgt. Assn. [15051]
Amer. Celiac Society/Dietary Support Coalition [15543]
Amer. Central European Dental Inst. [14127]
Amer. Clinical Lab. Assn. [14991]
Amer. Coll. of Cardiology [13888]
Amer. Coll. of Cardiovascular Administrators [15052]
Amer. Coll. of Domiciliary Midwives [15583]
Amer. Coll. of Epidemiology [14373]
Amer. Coll. of Gastroenterology [14405]
Amer. Coll. Hea. Assn. [14714]
Amer. Coll. of Hea. Care Administrators [15535]
Amer. Coll. of Hea. Plan Mgt. [15053]
Amer. Coll. of Healthcare Executives [14862]
Amer. Coll. of Intl. Physicians [14973]
Amer. Coll. of Legal Medicine [15001]
Amer. Coll. of Medical Practice Executives [15054]
Amer. Coll. of Medical Quality [16261]
Amer. Coll. of Mental Hea. Admin. [15187]

Reference to "IO" in place of a book number signifies that the association may be found in the 45th edition of International Organizations.

Amer. Coll. of Neuropsychopharmacology [15915]
Amer. Coll. of Nuclear Medicine [15421]
Amer. Coll. of Nuclear Physicians [15422]
Amer. Coll. of Nurse-Midwives [15447]
Amer. Coll. of Nutrition [15544]
Amer. Coll. of Obstetricians and Gynecologists [15584]
Amer. Coll. of Occupational and Environmental Medicine [15624]
Amer. Coll. of Oral and Maxillofacial Surgeons [15734]
Amer. Coll. of Osteopathic Family Physicians [15793]
Amer. Coll. of Osteopathic Internists [15794]
Amer. Coll. of Osteopathic Obstetricians and Gynecologists [15585]
Amer. Coll. of Osteopathic Pediatricians [15795]
Amer. Coll. of Osteopathic Surgeons [15797]
Amer. Coll. of Physician Executives [15056]
Amer. Coll. of Physicians-American Soc. of Internal Medicine [14966]
Amer. Coll. of Surgeons [16565]
Amer. Conf. of Governmental Indus. Hygienists [15625]
Amer. Coun. of Applied Clinical Nutrition [15545]
Amer. Coun. on Sci. and Hea. [14539]
Amer. Dietetic Assn. [15546]
Amer. Epilepsy Soc. [14379]
Amer. Found. for Maternal and Child Health [15586]
Amer. Fracture Assn. [15756]
Amer. Gastroenterological Assn. [14406]
Amer. Guild of Hypnotherapists [14919]
Amer. Gynecological and Obstetrical Soc. [15587]
Amer. Head and Neck Soc. [15819]
Amer. Headache Soc. [14531]
Amer. Hea. Care Assn. [14540]
Amer. Hea. Planning Assn. [14542]
Amer. Holistic Nurses' Assn. [14825]
Amer. Industrial Health Coun. [15626]
Amer. Indus. Hygiene Assn. [15627]
Amer. Inst. of Homeopathy [14845]
Amer. Integrative Medical Assn. [15034]
Amer. Kidney Fund [15284]
Amer. Laryngological, Rhinological and Otological Soc. [15821]
Amer. Licensed Practical Nurses Assn. [15450]
Amer. Liver Found. [14803]
Amer. Manual Medicine Assn. [13618]
Amer. Massage Therapy Assn. [15022]
Amer. Medical Assn. [15155]
Amer. Medical Assn. Alliance [15156]
Amer. Medical Athletic Assn. [23650]
Amer. Medical Directors Assn. [15536]
Amer. Medical Technologists [15127]
Amer. Medical Tennis Assn. [23898]
Amer. Medical Women's Assn. [14696]
Amer. Mental Hea. Alliance [15188]
Amer. Mental Hea. Counselors Assn. [15189]
Amer. Naprapathic Assn. [15276]
Amer. Nephrology Nurses' Assn. [15286]
Amer. Neuroendocrine Soc. [15035]
Amer. Nurses Assn. [15451]
Amer. Nurses Found. [15452]
Amer. Ophthalmological Soc. [15662]
Amer. Optometric Assn. [15712]
Amer. Optometric Found. [15713]
Amer. Optometric Student Assn. [15714]
Amer. Org. of Nurse Executives [15454]
Amer. Orthopaedic Assn. [15757]
Amer. Orthopaedic Foot and Ankle Soc. [15758]
Amer. Orthoptic Coun. [15663]
Amer. Osler Soc. [15157]
Amer. Osteopathic Acad. of Orthopedics [15759]
Amer. Osteopathic Assn. [15798]
Amer. Osteopathic Bd. of Family Physicians [15799]
Amer. Osteopathic Bd. of Pediatrics [15800]
Amer. Osteopathic Coll. of Physical Medicine and Rehabilitation [15805]
Amer. Osteopathic Colleges of Ophthalmology and Otolaryngology-Head and Neck Surgery [15664]
Amer. Parkinson Disease Assn. [15304]
Amer. Partnership for Eosinophilic Disorders [14408]

Amer. Professional Practice Assn. [14697]
Amer. Professional Wound Care Assn. [16688]
Amer. Psychiatric Assn. Alliance [16077]
Amer. Psychological Assn. Division of Independent Practice [16126]
Amer. Psychological Assn. - Div. of Intl. Psychology [16127]
Amer. Psychosocial Oncology Soc. [15638]
Amer. Radiological Nurses Assn. [15457]
Amer. Registry of Radiologic Technologists [15128]
Amer. Senior Fitness Assn. [15961]
Amer. Shoulder and Elbow Surgeons [16567]
Amer. Soc. on Aging [11275]
Amer. Soc. of Breast Surgeons [16570]
Amer. Soc. of Cataract and Refractive Surgery [15665]
Amer. Soc. of Childbirth Educators [15589]
Amer. Soc. of Clinical Hypnosis [14921]
Amer. Soc. of Clinical Hypnosis - Educ. and Res. Found. [14922]
Amer. Soc. for Clinical Lab. Sci. [14992]
Amer. Soc. for Clinical Nutrition [15547]
Amer. Soc. for Colposcopy and Cervical Pathology [15590]
Amer. Soc. of Contemporary Medicine, Surgery, and Ophthalmology [15666]
Amer. Soc. of Diagnostic and Interventional Nephrology [15287]
Amer. Soc. of Echocardiography [13891]
Amer. Soc. of Exercise Physiologists [16019]
Amer. Soc. of Extra-Corporeal Tech. [15129]
Amer. Soc. for Gastrointestinal Endoscopy [14409]
Amer. Soc. of Hand Therapists [14524]
Amer. Soc. for Healthcare Central Ser. Professionals [14864]
Amer. Soc. for Healthcare Engg. of the Amer. Hosp. Assn. [14865]
Amer. Soc. for Healthcare Risk Mgt. [14869]
Amer. Soc. for Histocompatibility and Immunogenetics [14931]
Amer. Soc. of Interventional Pain Physicians [15837]
Amer. Soc. for Laser Medicine and Surgery [14997]
Amer. Soc. of Law, Medicine and Ethics [15002]
Amer. Soc. of Maxillofacial Surgeons [15735]
Amer. Soc. for Mohs Histotechnology [15130]
Amer. Soc. for Mohs Surgery [15641]
Amer. Soc. of Nephrology [15288]
Amer. Soc. of Neurophysiological Monitoring [15381]
Amer. Soc. of Neuroradiology [16282]
Amer. Soc. for Nutrition [15548]
Amer. Soc. of Ophthalmic Registered Nurses [15458]
Amer. Soc. for Ophthalmic Ultrasonography [15667]
Amer. Soc. of Pain Educators [15838]
Amer. Soc. for Parenteral and Enteral Nutrition [15549]
Amer. Soc. for Pharmacy Law [15003]
Amer. Soc. of Plastic Surgical Nurses [15461]
Amer. Soc. of Radiologic Technologists [15131]
Amer. Soc. for Reconstructive Microsurgery [16573]
Amer. Soc. for Reproductive Medicine [14389]
Amer. Soc. for Stereotactic and Functional Neurosurgery [15412]
Amer. Soc. for Surgery of the Hand [14525]
Amer. Surgical Assn. [16575]
Amyloidosis Support Network [14251]
Amyotrophic Lateral Sclerosis Assn. [15306]
Anesthesia Awareness Campaign [13677]
Anesthesia History Assn. [13678]
Antitrust Coalition for Consumer Choice in Hea. Care [14615]
Army Nurse Corps Assn. [15262]
Arthroscopy Assn. of North Am. [15762]
Asian Amer./Pacific Islander Nurses Assn. [15463]
Assn. of Academic Hea. Centers [14546]
Assn. for Academic Surgery [16576]
Assn. of Amer. Physicians and Surgeons [15990]
Assn. of Asthma Educators [16355]

Assn. for Behavioral Hea. and Wellness [24088]
Assn. of Behavioral Healthcare Mgt. [15191]
Assn. of Bone and Joint Surgeons [15763]
Assn. of Brethren Caregivers [11276]
Assn. of Camp Nurses [15464]
Assn. of Child Neurology Nurses [15465]
Assn. for Childbirth at Home, Intl. [15591]
Assn. of Chinese Amer. Physicians [15991]
Assn. of Clinicians for the Underserved [14616]
Assn. for Community Hea. Improvement [16238]
Assn. for the Educ. of Children with Medical Needs [8072]
Assn. of Family Practice Administrators [15060]
Assn. of Family Practice Physician Assistants [14698]
Assn. of Hea. Care Journalists [3095]
Assn. for Healthcare Documentation Integrity [15084]
Assn. for Healthcare Philanthropy [14871]
Assn. for Healthcare Rsrc. and Materials Mgt. [14872]
Assn. of Hispanic Healthcare Executives [14699]
Assn. for Hosp. Medical Educ. [14873]
Assn. for Integrative Hea. Care Practitioners [15037]
Assn. of Jewish Aging Services [11277]
Assn. for Macular Diseases [15669]
Assn. of Medical Directors of Info. Systems [14957]
Assn. of Medical Illustrators [13707]
Assn. of Medical Lab. Immunologists [14932]
Assn. of Medicine and Psychiatry [16081]
Assn. of Military Surgeons of the U.S. [15263]
Assn. of Minority Hea. Professions Schools [8850]
Assn. of Nurses in AIDS Care [13559]
Assn. of Nurses Endorsing Transplantation [15670]
Assn. of Ocular Pharmacology and Therapeutics [15671]
Assn. of Osteopathic State Executive Directors [15809]
Assn. of Otolaryngology Administrators [15062]
Assn. of Pakistani Physicians of North Am. [15993]
Assn. for Pathology Informatics [15864]
Assn. of Pediatric Hematology/Oncology Nurses [15467]
Assn. of Pediatric Therapists [16606]
Assn. of PeriOperative Registered Nurses [15468]
Assn. for Professionals in Infection Control and Epidemiology [14947]
Assn. of Professors of Gynecology and Obstetrics [15592]
Assn. of Professors of Human and Medical Genetics [14497]
Assn. of Prog. Directors in Internal Medicine [14967]
Assn. of Prog. Directors in Vascular Surgery [16578]
Assn. of Regulatory Boards of Optometry [15716]
Assn. of Rehabilitation Nurses [15469]
Assn. of Reproductive Hea. Professionals [12177]
Assn. for Res. in Vision and Ophthalmology [15672]
Assn. of Salaried Medical Specialists [IO]
Assn. of Schools and Colleges of Optometry [15717]
Assn. of Staff Physician Recruiters [15995]
Assn. of State and Provincial Psychology Boards [16144]
Assn. of State and Territorial Local Hea. Liaison Officials [6213]
Assn. of Tech. Personnel in Ophthalmology [15674]
Assn. for Therapeutic Eurythmy in North Am. [16608]
Assn. of Univ. Professors of Ophthalmology [15675]
Assn. of Veterans Affairs Anesthesiologists [13681]
Assn. of Veterans Affairs Ophthalmologists [15676]
Assn. of Veterinary Hematology and Transfusion Medicine [16785]
Assn. of Vision Educators [15677]

A star before a book entry number signifies that the name is not listed separately, but is mentioned within the entry.

Assn. of Women's Hea., Obstetric and Neonatal Nurses [15470]
Assyrian Medical Soc. [13715]
Australian Rural Nurses and Midwives [IO]
Australian Salaried Medical Officers' Fed. [IO]
Auxiliary to the Natl. Medical Assn. [15161]
Avenues, Natl. Support Gp. for Arthrogryposis Multiplex Congenita [15309]
Behavior Genetics Assn. [14498]
Benign Essential Blepharospasm Res. Found. [15311]
Benjamin Franklin Literary and Medical Soc. [14549]
Better Vision Inst. [15678]
Brain Injury Assn. of Am. [14528]
C/SEC [15593]
Cajal Club [15385]
Cancer Prevention Coalition [13808]
Cardiovascular Credentialing Intl. [13898]
Catholic Hea. Assn. of the U.S. [14874]
CDC Natl. Prevention Info. Network [13563]
Center for Humane Options in Childbirth Experiences [15594]
Center for Medical Consumers [14550]
Center for Professional Well-Being [14700]
The Center for Social Gerontology [11280]
Center for the Well Being of Hea. Professionals [14701]
Certification Bd. of Infection Control and Epidemiology [14702]
Certification Bd. for Urologic Nurses and Associates [16706]
Child Neurology Soc. [15386]
Childbirth Connection [15595]
Childhood Arthritis and Rheumatology Res. Alliance [16371]
Children of Aging Parents [11282]
Children's Eye Found. [15679]
Children's Hospice Intl. [14853]
Children's Tumor Found. [15315]
Citizen Advocacy Center [17695]
Civil Aviation Medical Assn. [13540]
Clinical Lab. Mgt. Assn. [14993]
Clinical and Lab. Standards Inst. [14994]
Clinical Ligand Assay Soc. [14995]
Coalition for Healthcare Commun. [14622]
Coll. of Optometrists in Vision Development [15718]
Coll. of Osteopathic Healthcare Executives [14876]
Collegium Internationale Neuro-Psychopharmacologicum [15929]
Commn. for Case Manager Certification [14703]
Commn. on Graduates of Foreign Nursing Schools [15473]
Comm. of Interns and Residents [24089]
Community Systems Found. [15552]
Comparative Nutrition Soc. [15553]
Competency and Credentialing Inst. [14878]
Congenital Cardiac Anesthesia Soc. [13682]
Congenital Heart Info. Network [13901]
Conservative Orthopedics Intl. Assn. [15767]
Consumer Coalition for Quality Hea. Care [14624]
Contact Lens Assn. of Ophthalmologists [15680]
Cornelia de Lange Syndrome Found. [13754]
Coun. on Arteriosclerosis, Thrombosis and Vascular Biology of the Amer. Heart Assn. [13902]
Coun. on Certification of Nurse Anesthetists [15475]
Coun. on Chiropractic Orthopedics [15768]
Coun. of Colleges of Acupuncture and Oriental Medicine [15743]
Coun. on Hea. Info. and Educ. [14553]
Coun. of Medical Specialty Societies [15120]
Coun. of Pediatric Subspecialties [15886]
Coun. on Resident Educ. in Obstetrics and Gynecology [15597]
Coun. of State and Territorial Epidemiologists [14374]
Coun. of Teaching Hospitals [14879]
Coun. of Women's and Infants' Specialty Hospitals [14880]
Crohn's and Colitis Found. of Am. [14414]
CTSNet: Cardiothoracic Surgery Network [16643]

Cure Res. Found. [13818]
CyberKnife Soc. [16581]
Dermatology Nurses' Assn. [15476]
Dietary Managers Assn. [15555]
Digestive Disease Natl. Coalition [14416]
Direct Care Alliance [1868]
Docs for Tots [13958]
Dr. to Dr. [12519]
Doctors Ought to Care [14554]
Dysautonomia Found. [15317]
Dystonia Medical Res. Found. [15319]
Educational Commn. for Foreign Medical Graduates [15997]
Elder Craftsmen [11285]
EMDR - Humanitarian Assistance Programs [12767]
EMDR Intl. Assn. [16215]
Endometriosis Assn. [15599]
Epilepsy Found. [14380]
Ethiopian Pharmacists Assn. in North Am. [15932]
Fed. Physicians Assn. [15998]
Federated Ambulatory Surgery Assn. [16582]
Fed. for Accessible Nursing Educ. and Licensure [15478]
Fed. of Amer. Hospitals [14881]
Fed. of Associations of Regulatory Boards [14555]
Fed. of Chinese Amer. and Chinese Canadian Medical Societies [13985]
Fed. of Pediatric Organizations [15887]
Fed. of Podiatric Medical Boards [16043]
Fed. of State Physician Hea. Programs [15999]
Fertility Res. Found. [14391]
Filipino Amer. Medical Inc. [14722]
First Signs [13942]
The Floating Hosp. [14882]
Flower Essence Soc. [14818]
Flying Physicians Assn. [13731]
Focus [15681]
Food and Nutrition Bd. [15558]
Forbes Norris MDA/ALS Res. Center [15323]
Found. for Innovation in Medicine [15166]
Found. for the Support of Intl. Medical Training [14977]
Frontier Nursing Ser. [15479]
Gay and Lesbian Medical Assn. [14431]
Glaucoma Res. Found. [15683]
Global Alliance for Medical Educ. [8862]
Global Hea. Coun. [14979]
Gluten Intolerance Gp. [15559]
Gray Panthers [11287]
Harvey Soc. [15168]
Hea. Acad. [14883]
Hea. Care Without Harm [14634]
Hea. for Humanity [14563]
Hea. Indus. Representatives Assn. [2627]
Hea. Res. and Educational Trust [14884]
Healthcare Info. and Mgt. Systems Soc. [14885]
Healthcare Quality Certification Bd. [13533]
Heart Disease Res. Found. [13905]
Heart Failure Soc. of Am. [13906]
Heart Rhythm Soc. [13907]
Hemochromatosis Found. [14799]
Hepatitis Rsrc. Network [14810]
Hesperian Found. [14980]
Hispanic Neuropsychological Soc. [15388]
Homeopathic Nurses Assn. [14846]
Human Ecology Action League [14364]
Huntington's Disease Soc. of Am. [15329]
Immunology of Diabetes Soc. [14225]
Informed Homebirth/Informed Birth and Parenting [15602]
Inst. for the Advancement of Human Behavior [13735]
Inst. for the Development of Emotional and Life Skills/National Inst. of Relationship Enhancement [15201]
Inst. for Diversity in Hea. Mgt. [14704]
Inst. for Labor and Mental Health [15202]
Interamerican Coll. of Physicians and Surgeons [16000]
InterAmerican Heart Found. [13909]
Intercontinental Fed. of Behavioral Optometry [15719]
Intermed Intl. [14982]

Intl. Acad. of Health Care Professionals [14705]
Intl. and Amer. Associations of Clinical Nutritionists [15560]
Intl. Assn. of Coroners and Medical Examiners [15093]
Intl. Assn. of Healthcare Central Ser. Materiel Mgt. [14886]
Intl. Assn. for Healthcare Security and Safety [14887]
Intl. Assn. of Homes and Services for the Ageing [11289]
Intl. Assn. for Human Caring [14640]
Intl. Assn. of Medical Intuitives [15040]
Intl. Assn. of Ocular Surgeons [15684]
Intl. Assn. of Optometric Executives [15720]
Intl. Assn. of Orofacial Myology [15869]
Intl. Assn. of Pediatric Lab. Medicine [15888]
Intl. Assn. of Physicians and Hea. Care Professionals [16002]
Intl. Assn. of Reiki Professionals [13637]
Intl. Assn. of Sickle Cell Nurses And Physician Assistants [14706]
Intl. Assn. of Sickle Cell Nurses And Physician Assistants [IO]
Intl. Assn. of Structural Integrators [13638]
Intl. Assn. of Transpersonal Therapists and Physicians [15205]
Intl. Bundle Br. Block Assn. [13911]
Intl. Center for Attitudinal Healing [15206]
Intl. Cesarean Awareness Network [15604]
Intl. Childbirth Educ. Assn. [15605]
Intl. Children's Anophthalmia Network [16857]
Intl. Coll. of Surgeons [16583]
Intl. Comm. Against Mental Illness [15207]
Intl. Critical Incident Stress Found. [16491]
Intl. Dental Hea. Found. [14166]
Intl. EECP Therapists Assn. [16619]
Intl. Eye Found. [15685]
Intl. Fed. of Esthetic Dentistry [14167]
Intl. Fed. of Marfan Syndrome Organizations [14456]
Intl. Fed. of Martial Arts and Oriental Medicine [15021]
Intl. Found. for Homeopathy [14849]
Intl. Functional Elecl. Stimulation Soc. [15390]
Intl. Genetic Epidemiology Soc. [14376]
Intl. Hea. Evaluation Assn. [14568]
Intl. Hyperhidrosis Soc. [14357]
Intl. Life Sciences Inst. - North Am. [15561]
Intl. Lyme and Assoc. Diseases Soc. [14267]
Intl. Medical Equip. Collaborative [14569]
Intl. Mobile Hea. Assn. [14724]
Intl. Org. of Multiple Sclerosis Nurses [15486]
Intl. Pediatric Hypertension Assn. [14907]
Intl. Pediatric Transplant Assn. [16673]
Intl. Refractive Surgery Club [15689]
Intl. Sharps Injury Prevention Soc. [16380]
Intl. Soc. of Arthroscopy, Knee Surgery and Orthopaedic Sports Medicine [15771]
Intl. Soc. for Clinical Densitometry [15788]
Intl. Soc. for Cmpt. Assisted Orthopaedic Surgery [15772]
Intl. Soc. of Cosmetic and Laser Surgeons [14048]
Intl. Soc. for Disease Surveillance [14269]
Intl. Soc. for Imaging in the Eye [15690]
Intl. Soc. for Infectious Diseases [14951]
Intl. Soc. on Metabolic Eye Disease [15691]
Intl. Soc. of Oncology Pharmacy Practitioners [15937]
Intl. Soc. for Pharmacoepidemiology [15939]
Intl. Soc. for the Psychological Treatments of the Schizophrenias and Other Psychoses - USA [15209]
Intl. Soc. of Travel Medicine [15172]
Intl. Trachoma Initiative [16858]
Intl. Vitamin A Consultative Gp. [15564]
Interstate Postgraduate Medical Assn. of North Am. [14386]
The IPA Assn. of Am. [3022]
Iranian Amer. Medical Assn. [15173]
Iraqi Medical Sciences Assn. [14987]
Islamic Medical Assn. of North Am. [16003]
Jewish Assn. for Services for the Aged [11290]
Joint Commn. on Accreditation of Healthcare Organizations [14888]

Reference to "IO" in place of a book number signifies that the association may be found in the 45th edition of International Organizations.

Joint Commn. on Allied Hea. Personnel in Ophthalmology [15692]
Kennedy's Disease Assn. [15334]
Korean-American Medical Assn. [15174]
Lamaze Birth Without Pain Educ. Assn. [15607]
Leadership Coun. of Aging Organizations [11293]
Legal Counsel for the Elderly [12497]
Legal Sers. for the Elderly [12499]
Lesbian, Gay, Bisexual, and Transgender People in Medicine [12243]
Lewy Body Dementia Assn. [15335]
Lupus Found. of Am. [15014]
Malignant Hyperthermia Assn. of the U.S. [14464]
Medicaid/SCHIP Dental Assn. [14168]
Medical Benevolence Found. [14725]
Medical Image Perception Soc. [15140]
Medical Wings Intl. [14645]
MedicAlert Found. Intl. [14318]
Mended Hearts, Inc. [13916]
Mental Hea. Am. [15211]
Michael E. DeBakey Intl. Surgical Soc. [13917]
Midwifery Educ. Accreditation Coun. [8063]
Midwives Alliance of North Am. [15610]
Myasthenia Gravis Found. of Am. [15340]
NANDA Intl. [15489]
Natl. Academies of Practice [14648]
Natl. Acad. of Opticiany [15707]
Natl. Accrediting Agency for Clinical Lab. Sciences [15141]
Natl. Adult Day Services Assn. [11298]
Natl. Alliance for Caregiving [12163]
Natl. Alliance for Hea. Info. Tech. [15142]
Natl. Alliance of Medical Researchers and Teaching Physicians [15143]
Natl. Alliance of Medicare Set-Aside Professionals [17697]
Natl. Alliance on Mental Illness [15214]
Natl. Alliance of Senior Citizens [11299]
Natl. Amer. Arab Nurses Assn. [15490]
Natl. Arab Amer. Medical Assn. [14707]
Natl. Asian Pacific Center on Aging [11300]
Natl. Assn. of Area Agencies on Aging [11301]
Natl. Assn. of Community Hea. Centers [14574]
Natl. Assn. of County Behavioral Hea. Directors [14708]
Natl. Assn. of County Hea. Fac. Administrators [15069]
Natl. Assn. for Direct Care Workers of Color [14709]
Natl. Assn. of Emergency Medical Technicians [14335]
Natl. Assn. of Free Clinics [14727]
Natl. Assn. of Geriatric Educ. Centers [14513]
Natl. Assn. of Hea. Care Assistants [14514]
Natl. Assn. of Hea. Educ. Centers [14675]
Natl. Assn. of Hea. Unit Coordinators [14578]
Natl. Assn. for Healthcare Quality [16264]
Natl. Assn. for Healthcare Recruitment [15070]
Natl. Assn. of Hepatitis Task Forces [14812]
Natl. Assn. of Hispanic Nurses [15494]
Natl. Assn. for Home Care and Hospice [14840]
Natl. Assn. for Human Development [11303]
Natl. Assn. of Locum Tenens Org. [16004]
Natl. Assn. of Medical Examiners [15094]
Natl. Assn. of Myofascial Trigger Point Therapists [16624]
Natl. Assn. of Optometrists and Opticians [15721]
Natl. Assn. of Orthopaedic Nurses [15498]
Natl. Assn. of Physician Nurses [15500]
Natl. Assn. of Physician Recruiters [16006]
Natl. Assn. of Public Hospitals and Hea. Systems [14892]
Natl. Assn. of Residents and Interns [15175]
Natl. Assn. for Rural Mental Hea. [15217]
Natl. Assn. of School Nurses [15501]
Natl. Assn. of School Nurses for the Deaf [14768]
Natl. Assn. of State Mental Hea. Prog. Directors [15219]
Natl. Assn. of State Units on Aging [11305]
Natl. Assn. of Subacute and Post-Acute Care [14728]
Natl. Assn. of Supervisors and Administrators of Hea. Occupations Educ. [8870]
Natl. Assn. of VA Physicians and Dentists [16007]
Natl. Assn. of Vietnamese Nurses [15504]

Natl. Assn. of Vision Professionals [15693]
Natl. Ataxia Found. [15342]
Natl. Ayurvedic Medical Assn. [13642]
Natl. Black Assn. for Speech-Language and Hearing [16448]
Natl. Black Nurses Assn. [15505]
Natl. Bd. of Examiners in Optometry [15722]
Natl. Bd. of Medical Examiners [15095]
Natl. Caucus and Center on Black Aged [11306]
Natl. Center for Assisted Living [14652]
Natl. Certification Commn. for Acupuncture and Oriental Medicine [15747]
Natl. Coalition of Ethnic Minority Nurse Associations [15507]
Natl. Coalition for Res. in Neurological Disorders [15346]
Natl. Coalition on Rural Aging [11307]
Natl. Contact Lens Examiners [15723]
Natl. Coordinating Coun. for Medication Error Reporting and Prevention [14653]
Natl. Coun. on the Aging [11309]
Natl. Coun. for Community Behavioral Healthcare [15223]
Natl. Coun. for the Professional Development of Nursing and Midwifery [IO]
Natl. Coun. of State Boards of Nursing [15508]
Natl. Credentialing Agency for Lab. Personnel [15145]
Natl. Dental Assistants Assn. [14174]
Natl. Digestive Diseases Info. CH [14422]
Natl. Environmental Hea. Assn. [14367]
Natl. Eosinophilia-Myalgia Syndrome Network [16662]
Natl. Eye Res. Found. [15724]
Natl. Fed. of Licensed Practical Nurses [15509]
Natl. Fitness Therapy Assn. [15968]
Natl. Found. for Ectodermal Dysplasias [14468]
Natl. Found. for Infectious Diseases [14953]
Natl. Gaucher Found. [15252]
Natl. Headache Found. [14533]
Natl. Hea. Assn. [15279]
Natl. Hea. Coun. [14586]
Natl. Hea. Fed. [14587]
Natl. Hea. Info. Center [14588]
Natl. Hea. Law Prog. [5784]
Natl. Healthcare Collectors Assn. [1869]
Natl. Hospice and Palliative Care Org. [14856]
Natl. Inst. of Senior Housing [12328]
Natl. Interfaith Coalition on Aging [11314]
Natl. Kidney Found. [15294]
Natl. League for Nursing [15510]
Natl. Lung Cancer Partnership [13854]
Natl. Marfan Found. [16652]
Natl. Meals on Wheels Found. [11315]
Natl. Medical Assn. [15176]
Natl. Multiple Sclerosis Soc. [15349]
Natl. Optometric Assn. [15725]
Natl. Org. of Alternative Programs [16382]
Natl. Org. for Associate Degree Nursing [15512]
Natl. Org. for Competency Assurance [14591]
Natl. Org. For Empowering Caregivers [13295]
Natl. Org. of Nurses with Disabilities [15514]
Natl. Pain Educ. Coun. [15846]
Natl. Parkinson Found. [15351]
Natl. Perinatal Assn. [15900]
Natl. Physicians Alliance [16009]
Natl. Postdoctoral Assn. [9064]
Natl. Private Duty Assn. [14842]
Natl. Rural Recruitment and Retention Network [14710]
Natl. Scoliosis Found. [16393]
Natl. Senior Citizens Law Center [11316]
Natl. Soc. of Certified Healthcare Bus. Consultants [14711]
Natl. Soc. of Genetic Counselors [14506]
Natl. Soc. for Histotechnology [15146]
Natl. Spasmodic Torticollis Assn. [15353]
Natl. Tay-Sachs and Allied Diseases Assn. [15354]
Natl. Viral Hepatitis Roundtable [14815]
Neuro-Optometric Rehabilitation Assn., Intl. [15300]
Neurocritical Care Soc. [14070]
Neurosurgeons to Preserve Hea. Care Access [15414]

Neurosurgery Intl. [15415]
North Amer. Assn. of Medical Educ. and Commun. Companies [8874]
North Amer. Sikh Medical and Dental Assn. [16416]
North Amer. Soc. of Obstetric Medicine [15615]
North Amer. Soc. for Pediatric Gastroenterology, Hepatology and Nutrition [14424]
North Amer. Taiwanese Medical Assn. [14712]
North Amer. Vodder Assn. of Lymphatic Therapy [15019]
Nuclear Medicine Tech. Certification Bd. [15423]
Nurses Educational Funds [15516]
Nurses for a Healthier Tomorrow [15517]
Nurses' House [15518]
Nurses Org. of Veterans Affairs [15519]
Nutrition for Optimal Hea. Assn. [15567]
Ohashi Inst. [15748]
Oncology Nursing Soc. [15521]
Ophthalmic Photographers' Soc. [15696]
Opticians Assn. of Am. [15709]
Optometric Extension Prog. Found. [15727]
Optometric Historical Soc. [15728]
ORBIS Intl. [15697]
Orthopaedic Res. Soc. [15776]
Osteopathic Intl. Alliance [15813]
Outpatient Ophthalmic Surgery Soc. [15698]
Pain Mgt. and Sclerotherapy [15814]
Pan-American Assn. of Ophthalmology [15699]
Paraprofessional Healthcare Inst. [1853]
Parents of Kids with Infectious Diseases [14954]
Parkinson Alliance [15359]
Parkinson's Disease Found. [15360]
Pediatric Cardiac Intensive Care Soc. [15892]
Pediatric Infectious Diseases Soc. [14955]
Pediatric Nursing Certification Bd. [15522]
Pediatric Pharmacy Advocacy Gp. [15896]
People-to-People Hea. Found. [14984]
Perfusion Prog. Directors' Coun. [13921]
Peripheral Arterial Disease Coalition [13922]
Philippine Nurses Assn. of Am. [2840]
Physicians for Peace [15078]
Physicians for Social Responsibility [18169]
Premier Advocacy [14597]
Price-Pottenger Nutrition Found. [15568]
PSRC of Am. [16266]
Public Hea. Leadership Soc. [16252]
Public Responsibility in Medicine and Res. [18585]
Radiation and Public Hea. Proj. [16270]
Ray Helfer Soc. [13976]
Regulatory Affairs Professionals Soc. [14599]
Renal Physicians Assn. [15298]
Resolve, The Natl. Infertility Assn. [14394]
Russian Amer. Medical Assn. [16378]
School Nurse Achievement Prog. [15525]
Scoliosis Assn., Inc. [16394]
Scoliosis Res. Soc. [16395]
Scottsdale Inst. [14713]
Sect. for Long Term Care and Rehabilitation [14894]
Sect. for Metropolitan Hospitals [14895]
Serbian Amer. Medical and Dental Soc. [14185]
Sexual Medicine Soc. of North Am. [16405]
Soc. for the Advancement of Women's Imaging [16294]
Soc. of Air Force Physicians [15264]
Soc. of Amer. Gastrointestinal and Endoscopic Surgeons [14428]
Soc. for the Anal. of African-American Public Hea. Issues [16253]
Soc. of Behavioral Medicine [13740]
Soc. for Clinical and Experimental Hypnosis [14927]
Soc. of Clinical Res. Associates [14027]
Soc. of Correctional Physicians [16011]
Soc. of Critical Care Medicine [14071]
Soc. for Epidemiologic Res. [14377]
Soc. of Eye Surgeons [15703]
Soc. of Gastroenterology Nurses and Associates [14429]
Soc. for Gynecologic Investigation [15618]
Soc. for Healthcare Consumer Advocacy of the Amer. Hosp. Assn. [15005]
Soc. for Healthcare Strategy and Market Development of the Amer. Hosp. Assn. [14896]

A star before a book entry number signifies that the name is not listed separately, but is mentioned within the entry.

Soc. of Interventional Pain Mgt. Surgery Centers [16588]
Soc. of Medical Consultants to the Armed Forces [15265]
Soc. of Medical Jurisprudence [15006]
Soc. for Melanoma Res. [13875]
Soc. for Menstrual Cycle Res. [15619]
Soc. of Military Orthopaedic Surgeons [15266]
Soc. of Nuclear Medicine [15424]
Soc. of Nuclear Medicine Technologist Sect. [15425]
Soc. for Obstetric Anesthesia and Perinatology [15903]
Soc. for Occupational and Environmental Hea. [15633]
Soc. of Otorhinolaryngology and Head/Neck Nurses [15526]
Soc. of Pediatric Nurses [15527]
Soc. of Primary Care Policy Fellows [14664]
Soc. for the Psychological Stud. of Men and Masculinity [16181]
Soc. of Teachers of Family Medicine [14387]
Soc. for Tech. in Anesthesia [13692]
Soc. of Univ. Surgeons [16591]
Spirit of Women Hosp. Network [14898]
Student Veterinary Emergency and Critical Care Soc. [16810]
Support Org. for Trisomy 18, 13, and Related Disorders [14485]
Tear Film and Ocular Surface Soc. [15729]
Tel-Med [14601]
Thoracic Surgery Residents Assn. [16645]
Tissue Engg. Soc. Intl. [6610]
Tourette Syndrome Assn. [15367]
Tremor Action Network [15369]
Trinity Hea. Intl. [14731]
Trinity Medical Center [14900]
Trust for America's Hea. [16255]
Tuberous Sclerosis Alliance [15371]
Ukrainian Medical Assn. of North Am. [15182]
Union of Amer. Physicians and Dentists [24092]
United Methodist Assn. of Hea. and Welfare Ministries [14602]
U.S. Dental Tennis Assn. [23911]
U.S. Hereditary Angioedema Assn. [14487]
Urgent Care Assn. of Am. [13665]
Visiting Nurse Associations of Am. [15532]
Volunteer Trustees of Not-for-Profit Hospitals [14902]
Western Surgical Assn. [16592]
Women in Hea. Care Mgt. [14667]
Women in Neurotrauma Res. [15404]
World Fed. for Mental Hea. [15237]
World Fed. of Neurology Res. Gp. on Motor Neuron Diseases [15373]
World Homecare and Hospice Org. [14844]
World Soc. for Stereotactic and Functional Neuro-surgery [15418]
World Spine Soc. [15405]
Zero to Three: Natl. Center for Infants, Toddlers and Families [13944]
Hea. Professionals; Assn. of Reproductive [12177]
Hea. Professionals; Assn. of Rheumatology [16370]
Hea. Professionals; Center for the Well-Being of [★14700]
Hea. Professionals and Consumers; Natl. Coalition of Mental [15221]
Hea. Professionals; Fed. of Nurses and [★24087]
Hea. Professionals Found; Minority [★18080]
Hea. Professions; Amer. Soc. of Allied [★8855]
Hea. Professions Assn; Arthritis [★16370]
Hea. Professions; Assn. of Schools of Allied [8855]
Hea. Professions Found; Minority [18080]
Hea. Professions; Natl. Assn. of Advisors for the [8866]
Hea. Professions Schools; Assn. of Minority [8850]
Hea. Professions Schools; Hispanic-Serving [8864]
Hea. Professions Schools; Natl. Assn. of Hispanic-Serving [★8864]
Hea. Prog. Directors; Natl. Assn. of State Mental [15219]
Hea. Prog; Physicians for a Natl. [18313]
Hea. Programs; Assn. of Maternal and Child [13947]
Hea. Proj; Black Women's [★16895]
Hea. Proj; East Coast Migrant [★12586]

Hea. Proj; Natl. Black Women's [★16895]
Hea. Promotion and Aging; Natl. Center for [★11288]
Hea. Promotion; Assn. for Worksite [★16473]
Hea. Promotion Inst. [11288], c/o Natl. Coun. on Aging, 1901 L St. NW, 4th Fl., Washington, DC 20036, (202)479-1200
Hea. Promotion Inst. [14565]
Hea. Promotion; Migrant [12590]
Hea. and Psychiatric Services; Special Constituency Sect. for Mental [★16093]
Hea. Quality Assn; Amer. [16262]
Health and Radiation Projects [★17345]
Hea. Regulatory Boards; Fed. of Associations of [★14555]
Hea. and Rehabilitative Lib. Services [★10340]
Hea. Res. Bd. [IO], Dublin, Ireland
Hea. Res; CIIT Centers for [7801]
Hea. Res. Coun. of New Zealand [IO], Auckland, New Zealand
Hea. Res. and Educational Trust [14884], c/o Amer. Hosp. Assn., 1 N Franklin, Ste. 2800, Chicago, IL 60606, (312)422-2600
Hea. Res. Gp; Public Citizen [16250]
Hea. Res; Melpomene Inst. for Women's [★16900]
Hea. Res; Natl. Center for Amer. Indian and Alaska Native Mental [15220]
Hea. Res; Soc. for the Advancement of Women's [★16910]
Hea. Res; Soc. for Women's [16910]
Hea. Resort Assn; Amer. Spa and [3352]
Hea. Resorts; Dept. of Tourism and [★24363]
Hea. Rsrc. Center; Natl. Women's [16907]
Hea. Rights Support Proj; Guatemala [★12819]
Hea. and Safety; Center for Farm [12188]
Hea. and Safety Coun; Silicones Environmental, [821]
Hea. and Safety Org; Intl. Consumer Prdt. [3178]
Hea. Sanctuary; Wilbur Hot Springs [10180]
Hea. Sci. Communications Assn. [14032], 39 Wedgewood Dr., Ste. A, Jewett City, CT 06351-2420, (860)376-5915
Hea. Sci. and Protection Accreditation Coun; Natl. Environmental [★14368]
Hea. Sciences; Archivists and Librarians in the History of the [10326]
Hea. Sciences Assn. of Alberta [IO], Edmonton, AB, Canada
Hea. Sciences; Assn. of Librarians in the History of the [★10326]
Hea. Sciences Consortium [8561], 300 Silver Cedar Ct., Chapel Hill, NC 27514-1696, (919)942-8731
Hea. Sect. [★14883]
Hea. Sect; Family and [★14385]
Hea. Sect. of the Natl. Coun. on Family Relations; Family and [14385]
Health Security Action Coun. - Address unknown since 2000.
Hea. Ser. Clinical Soc; U.S. Public [★6214]
Hea. Ser; Commissioned Officers Assn. of the U.S. Public [6214]
Hea. Ser. Providers in Psychology; Coun. for the Natl. Register of [16149]
Hea. Ser. Providers in Psychology; Natl. Register of [16161]

Health Services
AcademyHealth [14535]
Action Hea. - Nigeria [IO]
Adopt a Dr. [12750]
Afghan Hea. and Development Services [IO]
Aid for AIDS [13547]
Alliance for Advancing Nonprofit Hea. Care [14606]
Alliance of Minority Medical Associations [14607]
Alliance of State Pain Initiatives [15830]
Amer. Acad. of Orthopaedic Manual Physical Therapists [15971]
Amer. Assisted Living Nurses Assn. [15432]
Amer. Assn. of Caregiving Youth [13466]
Amer. Assn. of Mental Hea. Professionals in Corrections [15186]
Amer. Assn. of Nurse Life Care Planners [15438]
Amer. Coll. Hea. Assn. [14714]
Amer. Correctional Hea. Services Assn. [14715]
Amer. Integrative Medical Assn. [15034]

Amer. Intl. Hea. Alliance [14716]
Amer. Intl. Hea. Alliance [IO]
Amer. Medical Gp. Assn. [14717]
Amer. School Hea. Assn. [14718]
Amer. Soc. of Directors of Volunteer Services [13382]
Amer. Soc. of Pain Educators [15838]
Amer. Spa and Hea. Resort Assn. [3352]
America's Hea. Together [14614]
Amyloidosis Support Network [14251]
Angel Flight West [12512]
Antitrust Coalition for Consumer Choice in Hea. Care [14615]
Assoc. Medical Services [IO]
Assn. of Asian Pacific Community Hea. Organizations [14719]
Assn. for Benchmarking in Hea. Care [1848]
Assn. for Integrative Hea. Care Practitioners [15037]
Assn. of Nutrition Services Agencies [14720]
Assn. Promoting Educ. and Conservation in Amazonia [5294]
Assyrian Medical Soc. [13715]
Australian Coll. of Hea. Ser. Executives [IO]
Blessings Intl. [12514]
Blue Cross and Blue Shield Assn. [14959]
Britain - Nepal Medical Trust [IO]
Canadian Assn. for Community Care [IO]
Canadian Assn. for Hea. Services and Policy Res. [IO]
Canadian Assn. for School Hea. [IO]
Canadian Coll. of Hea. Ser. Executives [IO]
Canadian Coun. on Hea. Services Accreditation [IO]
Canadian Hea. Coalition [IO]
Canadian Soc. for Intl. Hea. [IO]
Cancer Quality Alliance [13809]
Carers Assn. [IO]
Carers Assn. of South Australia [IO]
Carers Australia [IO]
Carers Australian Capital Territory [IO]
Carers New South Wales [IO]
Carers Queensland [IO]
Carers Queensland - Brisbane North and Sunshine Coast [IO]
Carers Queensland - Brisbane South and Gold Coast [IO]
Carers Queensland - Brisbane West [IO]
Carers Queensland - Central Queensland [IO]
Carers Queensland - Darling Downs/South West Queensland [IO]
Carers Queensland - Far North Queensland [IO]
Carers Queensland - Mackay [IO]
Carers Queensland - North Queensland [IO]
Carers Queensland - Toowoomba/Ipswich [IO]
Carers Queensland - Wide Bay [IO]
Carers Tasmania [IO]
Carers Victoria [IO]
Carers Western Australia [IO]
Center for Patient Advocacy [14620]
Center for Res. in Ambulatory Hea. Care Admin. [15064]
Children's Cross Connection Intl. [11552]
Christian Connections for Intl. Hea. [14551]
Citizen Advocacy Center [17695]
Citizens for Consumer Justice [18641]
Clinical Directors Network [14721]
Coalition for Improving Maternity Services [15596]
Comm. to Reduce Infection Deaths [14877]
Community Hea. Charities [12200]
Coun. for Hea. and Human Services Ministries, United Church of Christ [13165]
Coun. for Hea. Ser. Accreditation of South Africa [IO]
Coun. for the Natl. Register of Hea. Ser. Providers in Psychology [16149]
Coun. of Women's and Infants' Specialty Hospitals [14880]
Covering Kids and Families [12271]
DKT Intl. - Vietnam [IO]
Doctors of the World [12521]
European Assn. for Palliative Care [IO]
European Assn. of Ser. Providers for Persons with Disability [IO]
Family Care Intl. - Bolivia [IO]

Reference to "IO" in place of a book number signifies that the association may be found in the 45th edition of International Organizations.

Family Care Intl. - Burkina Faso [IO]
Family Care Intl. - Dominican Republic [IO]
Family Care Intl. - Ecuador [IO]
Family Care Intl. - Kenya [IO]
Family Care Intl. - Mali [IO]
Family Care Intl. - Niger [IO]
Family Care Intl. - Tanzania [IO]
Fenway Community Hea. [14430]
Filipino Amer. Medical Inc. [14722]
Filipino Amer. Medical Inc. [IO]
Global Bus. Coalition on HIV/AIDS [11329]
Global Healing [12450]
Harm Reduction Coalition [12042]
Hea. Care Without Harm [14634]
Hea. Educ. Coun. [14562]
Hea. for Humanity [14563]
Hea. Level Seven [14636]
Hea. in Prisons Proj. [IO]
Hea. Sci. Communications Assn. [14032]
Hea. Sciences Assn. of Alberta [IO]
Hea. Systems Trust - South Africa [IO]
Healthcare Leadership Coun. [14723]
Hong Kong Coll. of Hea. Services Executives [IO]
Inst. for Diversity in Hea. Mgt. [14704]
Inst. of Healthcare Mgt. - United Kingdom [IO]
Intercultural Cancer Coun. [13830]
Intl. Alliance in Ser. and Educ. [11748]
Intl. Assn. of Healthcare Practitioners [14639]
Intl. Assn. of Homes and Services for the Ageing [11289]
Intl. Assn. for Hospice and Palliative Care [14838]
Intl. Assn. of Sickle Cell Nurses And Physician Assistants [14706]
Intl. Child Care - Canada [IO]
Intl. Fed. of Hea. Plans [IO]
Intl. Medical Spa Assn. [IO]
Intl. Medical Spa Assn. [1870]
Intl. Mobile Hea. Assn. [14724]
Intl. Mobile Hea. Assn. [IO]
ITEM Coalition [14690]
Lotus Outreach [13143]
Makassed Found. of Am. [12730]
Map Intl. - Latin Am. Off. [IO]
Medical Benevolence Found. [14725]
Medical Officers of Schools Assn. [IO]
Medical Spa Soc. [1871]
Microsoft Healthcare Users Gp. [14726]
Minority Hea. Professions Found. [18080]
Morning Bird Social Welfare Org. [IO]
Muscular Dystrophy Assn. [IO]
Muscular Dystrophy Canada [IO]
Natl. Acad. for State Hea. Policy [14649]
Natl. Alliance of Medicare Set-Aside Professionals [17697]
Natl. Alliance of Primary Care Informatics [14956]
Natl. Assn. of Alternative Benefits Consultants [1867]
Natl. Assn. for Direct Care Workers of Color [14709]
Natl. Assn. of Free Clinics [14727]
Natl. Assn. of Healthcare Transport Mgt. [14579]
Natl. Assn. of Locum Tenens Org. [16004]
Natl. Assn. of Primary Care [IO]
Natl. Assn. of Private Ambulance Services [IO]
Natl. Assn. of Rural Hea. Clinics [16245]
Natl. Assn. of School Nurses for the Deaf [14768]
Natl. Assn. of Specialty Hea. Organizations [14650]
Natl. Assn. of State Comprehensive Hea. Insurance Plans [14691]
Natl. Assn. of State Head Injury Administrators [14529]
Natl. Assn. of Subacute and Post-Acute Care [14728]
Natl. Assn. for the Support of Long Term Care [14651]
Natl. Bone Marrow Transplant Link [16676]
Natl. Commn. on Correctional Hea. Care [14729]
Natl. Coun. on Interpreting in Hea. Care [1851]
Natl. Coun. of Urban Indian Hea. [15277]
Natl. Fitness Therapy Assn. [15968]
Natl. Hea. Care for the Homeless Coun. [14730]
Natl. Initiative for Children's Healthcare Quality [13970]
Natl. Inst. for Hea. Care Mgt. Res. and Educational Found. [14655]

Natl. Labor Alliance of Hea. Care Coalitions [24091]
Natl. Org. For Empowering Caregivers [13295]
Natl. Private Duty Assn. [14842]
Natl. Quality Forum [14658]
Natl. Rural Recruitment and Retention Network [14710]
New Zealand Guidelines Gp. [IO]
Off. of Hea. Economics [IO]
Oper. Smile - Australia [IO]
Oper. Smile - Bolivia [IO]
Oper. Smile - Colombia [IO]
Oper. Smile - Ecuador [IO]
Oper. Smile - Hangzhou [IO]
Oper. Smile - Honduras [IO]
Oper. Smile - Hong Kong [IO]
Oper. Smile - India [IO]
Oper. Smile Intl. - Vietnam [IO]
Oper. Smile - Ireland [IO]
Oper. Smile - Italy [IO]
Oper. Smile - Jordan [IO]
Oper. Smile - Mission in Kenya [IO]
Oper. Smile - Morocco [IO]
Oper. Smile - Nicaragua [IO]
Oper. Smile - Panama [IO]
Oper. Smile - Peru [IO]
Oper. Smile - Philippines [IO]
Oper. Smile - Russia [IO]
Oper. Smile - Thailand [IO]
Oper. Smile - United Kingdom [IO]
Oper. Smile - Venezuela [IO]
Pan Amer. Hea. Org. [14592]
Partnership for Prevention [14594]
Partnership for Quality Medical Donations [12537]
Patient Advocate Found. [14660]
Physicians for a Natl. Hea. Prog. [18313]
Physicians for Peace [15078]
Public Responsibility in Medicine and Res. [18585]
Soc. of Correctional Physicians [16011]
Soc. of Primary Care Policy Fellows [14664]
Spirit of Women Hosp. Network [14898]
Tech. Assistance Collaborative [13145]
Transatlantic Partners Against AIDS [13586]
Transverse Myelitis Assn. [15368]
Trinity Hea. Intl. [14731]
Urgent Care Assn. of Am. [13665]
USAF Medical Ser. Corps Assn. [13590]
Weight-Control Info. Network [15578]
Wellness Councils of Am. [14732]
Hea. Services of the Christian Church (Disciples of Christ); Social and [★13177]
Hea. Services; Farm Worker [12586]
Hea. Services Res; Assn. for [★14535]
Hea. Services Union of Australia [IO], Carlton South, Australia
Hea. and Social Welfare Organizations; Natl. Assembly of Natl. [★13400]
Hea. Soc; Dinshah [13631]
Hea; Soc. for Occupational and Environmental [15633]
Hea. Specialties; Assn. of Mental [★11817]
Hea. Statistics; Amer. Assn. for Vital Records and Public [★6218]
Hea. Statistics; Assn. for Vital Records and [★6218]
Hea. Statistics and Info. Systems; Natl. Assn. for Public [6218]
Hea. Strategies; Natl. Center for Environmental [14366]
Hea. Sys; Lutheran Gen. [★14821]
Hea. Sys. Pharmacists; Amer. Soc. of [15923]
Hea. Systems; Assoc. [★14597]
Hea. Systems; Fed. of Amer. [★14881]
Hea. Systems; Natl. Assn. of Public Hospitals and [14892]
Hea. Systems Trust - South Africa [IO], Durban, Republic of South Africa
Hea. Tech. Center [15138], 524 2nd St., 2nd Fl., San Francisco, CA 94107, (415)537-6978
Hea. and Temperance Assn; Amer. [13303]
Hea. and Temperance Soc; Amer. [★13303]
Hea. Training Assn; Natl. Environmental, Safety and [5097]
Hea. Trust; Helene Fuld [15480]
Hea. Underwriters; Intl. Assn. of [★2208]

Hea. Underwriters; Intl. Assn. of Accident and [★2208]
Hea. Underwriters; Natl. Assn. of [2208]
Hea. Underwriters; Natl. Assn. of Accident and [★2208]
Hea. Unit Clerks-Coordinators; Natl. Assn. of [★14578]
Hea. Veterinarians; Amer. Assn. of Public [16747]
Hea. Veterinarians; Assn. of State Public [★16747]
Hea. Veterinarians; Assn. of State and Territorial Public [★16747]
Hea. Veterinarians; Natl. Assn. of State Public [★16747]
Hea. Veterinarians; Natl. Assn. of State and Territorial Public [★16747]
Hea. Volunteers Overseas [12526], 1900 L St. NW, Ste. 310, Washington, DC 20036, (202)296-0928
Hea. Volunteers Overseas [IO], Washington, DC, United States
Hea. and Welfare Assn; Natl. Presbyterian [★13184]
Hea., Welfare and Pension Plans; Natl. Found. of [★1240]
Hea. and Welfare Services [★20552]
Hea. and Welfare Services, United Church of Christ; Coun. for [★13165]
Hea. Workers Without Borders; Mental [15212]
Hea. and World Peace; Serendipity Assn. for Res. and Implementation of Holistic [★14832]
Healthcare Access Mgt; Natl. Assn. of [14890]
Healthcare; Alliance for Alternatives in [13609]
Healthcare Attorneys; Amer. Acad. of [★5782]
Healthcare Audit Network [★8240]
Healthcare Billing and Mgt. Assn. [15169], 1540 S Coast Hwy., Ste. 203, Laguna Beach, CA 92651, (877)640-4262
Healthcare Central Ser. Professionals; Amer. Soc. for [14864]
HealthCare Chaplaincy [16340], 315 E 62nd St., 4th Fl., New York, NY 10021-7767, (212)644-1111
Healthcare Chaplains; Assembly of Episcopal [19944]
HealthCare Compliance Packaging Coun. [15934], 131 E Broad St., Ste. 206, Falls Church, VA 22046, (703)538-4030
Healthcare Consultants; Amer. Assn. of [14860]
Healthcare Consumer Advocacy of the Amer. Hosp. Assn; Soc. for [15005]
Healthcare Convention and Exhibitors Assn. [1340], 1100 Johnson Ferry Rd., Ste. 300, Atlanta, GA 30342, (404)252-3663
Healthcare Coun; Natl. Community Mental [★15223]
Healthcare Delivery Systems; Amer. Assn. of Integrated [15048]
Healthcare Distribution Mgt. Assn. [2984], 901 N Glebe Rd., Ste. 1000, Arlington, VA 22203, (703)787-0000
Healthcare Educ. Assn. [8259], PO Box 388, Florissant, MO 63032-0388, (888)298-3861
Healthcare Engg. of the Amer. Hosp. Assn; Amer. Soc. for [14865]
Healthcare Environmental Services of the Amer. Hosp. Assn; Amer. Soc. for [14866]
Healthcare Epidemiologists of Am; Soc. of [★14378]
Healthcare Epidemiology of Am; Soc. for [14378]
Healthcare Executives; Amer. Coll. of [14862]
Healthcare Executives; Assn. of Hispanic [14699]
Healthcare Executives; Coll. of Osteopathic [14876]
Healthcare Financial Mgt. Assn. [15066], 2 Westbrook Corporate Ctr., Ste. 700, Westchester, IL 60154, (708)531-9600
Healthcare Financial Mgt. Assn. [IO], Bristol, United Kingdom
Healthcare Financing Study Group - Defunct.
Healthcare Food Ser. Administrators; Amer. Soc. for [14867]
Healthcare Foodservice Mgt; Natl. Soc. for [1592]
The Healthcare Forum - Address unknown since 2001.
Healthcare Forum - Address unknown since 2004.
Healthcare Human Resources Admin; Amer. Soc. for [14868]
Healthcare Informatics Soc. of Ireland [IO], Dublin, Ireland
Healthcare Info. Mgt. Executives; Coll. of [2098]
Healthcare Info. and Mgt. Systems Soc. [14885], 230 E Ohio St., Ste. 500, Chicago, IL 60611-3270, (312)664-4467

A star before a book entry number signifies that the name is not listed separately, but is mentioned within the entry.

Healthcare Information Systems Sharing Group - Address unknown since 1995.
Healthcare Info. Tech; Assn. for Educ. in [15132]
Healthcare Inst; Amer. [★14597]
Healthcare Internal Audit Gp. [★15061]
Healthcare Internal Auditors; Assn. of [15061]
Healthcare Is a Legal Duty; Children's [15004]
Healthcare Laundry Accreditation Coun. [2403], c/o Chris Isely, Exec. Dir., 2123 McDaniel Ave., Evanston, IL 60201-2126, (847)328-3700
Healthcare Leadership Coun. [14723], 1001 Pennsylvania Ave. NW, Ste. 550 S, Washington, DC 20004-2505, (202)452-8700
Healthcare Mfrs. Marketing Coun. [14673], 1 Rebecca Ln., Savannah, GA 31411, (912)598-1607
Healthcare Marketing and Communications Coun. [100], 1525 Valley Center Pkwy., Ste. 150, Bethlehem, PA 18017, (610)868-8299
HealthCare Ministries [20076], 521 W Lynn St., Springfield, MO 65802, (417)866-6311
Healthcare; Natl. Coun. for Community Behavioral [15223]
Healthcare Nurses Assn; Home [15481]
Healthcare Organizations; Assn. of Managed [★14680]
Healthcare Organizations; Joint Commn. on Accreditation of [14888]
Healthcare People Mgt. Assn. [IO], Richmond, United Kingdom
Healthcare Planning and Marketing of the Amer. Hosp. Assn; Soc. for [★14896]
Healthcare Prdt. Assn; Consumer [2973]
Healthcare Quality Certification Bd. [13533], PO Box 19604, Lenexa, KS 66285-9604, (913)895-4609
Healthcare Quality; Natl. Assn. for [16264]
Healthcare Radiology Administrators; Amer. [16275]
Healthcare Recruiters; Natl. Assn. of [★15070]
Healthcare Recruitment; Natl. Assn. for [15070]
Healthcare Rsrc. and Materials Mgt; Assn. for [14872]
Healthcare Risk Mgt; Amer. Soc. for [14869]
Healthcare Strategy and Market Development of the Amer. Hosp. Assn; Soc. for [14896]
Healthcare Strategy and Marketing; Alliance for [2612]
Healthcare Systems; United [★14597]
HealthFare U.S.A. - Defunct.
Healthlink Worldwide [IO], London, United Kingdom
HealthRight - Defunct.
HEALTHsports, Inc. [★23361]
HEALTHsports, Inc. [★IO]
Healthy America - Defunct.
Healthy Building Network [4629], 927 15th St. NW, 4th Fl., Washington, DC 20005, (202)898-1610
Healthy Cities Found; Intl. [13349]
Healthy Homes; Alliance for [13320]
Healthy House Inst. - Defunct.
Healthy Korean Americans; Coalition for [14988]
Healthy Mothers, Healthy Babies [★15612]
Healthy Schools Network [4635], 110 Maryland Ave. NE, Ste. 505, Washington, DC 20002, (202)543-7555
Healthy Teen Network [12182], 509 2nd St. NE, Washington, DC 20002, (202)547-8814
HEAR Center [14756], 301 E Del Mar Blvd., Pasadena, CA 91101, (626)796-2016
Hear Now [14757], c/o The Starkey Hearing Found., 6700 Washington Ave. S, Eden Prairie, MN 55344-3405, (800)648-4327
Hear O Israel - Address unknown since 1995.
Hearing Aid Audiologists; Soc. of [★14763]
Hearing Aid Indus. Conf. [★1861]
Hearing Aid Soc; Natl. [★14763]
Hearing; Amer. Assn. for the Hard of [★16442]
Hearing; Amer. Fed. of Organizations for the Hard of [★16442]
Hearing; Amer. Soc. for the Hard of [★16442]
Hearing Assn; Amer. Speech Language [16442]
Hearing Assn; Natl. Student Speech and [★16453]
Hearing Assn; Natl. Student Speech Language [16453]
Hearing Assn. New Zealand [IO], Palmerston North, New Zealand
Hearing Assn; Student Jour. Gp. of the Amer. Speech and [★16453]

Hearing Concern [IO], London, United Kingdom
Hearing Concern, British Assn. of the Hard of Hearing [★IO]
Hearing Conservation; Coun. for Accreditation in Occupational [15632]
Hearing Dog Info; Natl. Center for [★14774]
Hearing Dog Prog. [★14774]
Hearing Dog Proj. [★14774]
Hearing Dog Rsrc. Center [★14774]
Hearing Dogs [★14762]
Hearing Dogs [★IO]
Hearing Ear Dog Prog. [★14770]
Hearing Educ. and Awareness for Rockers [16056], 1405 Lyon St., San Francisco, CA 94115, (415)409-3277
Hearing Educ. Through Auditory Res. Found. [★14756]
Hearing, Educational Aid and Res. Found. - Defunct.
Hearing Found. of Canada [IO], Toronto, ON, Canada

Hearing Impaired
Acad. of Doctors of Audiology [14733]
Acad. of Rehabilitative Audiology [14734]
ADARA: Professionals Networking for Excellence in Ser. Delivery with Individuals who are Deaf or Hard of Hearing [14735]
Advisory Coun. for Children with Impaired Hearing [IO]
Alexander Graham Bell Assn. for the Deaf and Hard of Hearing [IO]
Alexander Graham Bell Assn. for the Deaf and Hard of Hearing [14736]
Amer. Assn. of the Deaf-Blind [14737]
Amer. Assn. of Eye and Ear Hospitals [14859]
Amer. Auditory Soc. [14738]
Amer. Hearing Aid Associates [14739]
Amer. Hearing Res. Found. [14740]
Amer. Neurotology Soc. [16441]
Amer. Otological Soc. [15822]
Amer. Sign Language Teachers Assn. [14741]
Amer. Soc. for Deaf Children [14742]
Amer. Speech Language Hearing Assn. [16442]
Asia-Pacific Implant Centre [IO]
Assn. of the Deaf in Israel [IO]
Assn. of Late-Deafened Adults [14743]
Assn. of Medical Professionals with Hearing Losses [14744]
Association of Medical Professionals with Hearing Losses [IO]
Assn. of Sign Language Interpreters [IO]
Assn. of Teachers of Lipreading to Adults [IO]
Audiology Awareness Campaign [13716]
Australian Assn. of the Deaf [IO]
Australian Sign Language Interpreters Assn. [IO]
Better Hearing Australia [IO]
Better Hearing Inst. [14745]
British Assn. of Audiological Physicians [IO]
British Assn. of Teachers of the Deaf [IO]
British Deaf Assn. [IO]
British Soc. of Audiology [IO]
British Soc. of Hearing Aid Audiologists [IO]
Canadian Assn. of the Deaf [IO]
Canadian Cultural Soc. of The Deaf [IO]
Canadian Hard of Hearing Assn. [IO]
Canadian Hard of Hearing Assn. - Alberni Valley Br. [IO]
Canadian Hard of Hearing Assn. - BC Parents' Br. [IO]
Canadian Hard of Hearing Assn. - British Columbia Chap. [IO]
Canadian Hard of Hearing Assn. - Calgary Br. [IO]
Canadian Hard of Hearing Assn. - Edmonton Br. [IO]
Canadian Hard of Hearing Assn. - Fredericton Br. [IO]
Canadian Hard of Hearing Assn. - Kamloops Br. [IO]
Canadian Hard of Hearing Assn. - Kelowna Br. [IO]
Canadian Hard of Hearing Assn. - Lethbridge Br. [IO]
Canadian Hard of Hearing Assn. - Manitoba Chap. [IO]
Canadian Hard of Hearing Assn. - Moncton Br. [IO]

Canadian Hard of Hearing Assn. - Nanaimo Br. [IO]
Canadian Hard of Hearing Assn. - New Brunswick Chap. [IO]
Canadian Hard of Hearing Assn. - Newfoundland and Labrador Chap. [IO]
Canadian Hard of Hearing Assn. - North Shore Br. [IO]
Canadian Hard of Hearing Assn. - Ontario Chap. [IO]
Canadian Hard of Hearing Assn. - Orillia and District Br. [IO]
Canadian Hard of Hearing Assn. - Outaouais Br. [IO]
Canadian Hard of Hearing Assn. - Prince George Br. [IO]
Canadian Hard of Hearing Assn. - Quebec Chap. [IO]
Canadian Hard of Hearing Assn. - Regina and District Br. [IO]
Canadian Hard of Hearing Assn. - Saskatoon Br. [IO]
Canadian Hard of Hearing Assn. - Sudbury Br. [IO]
Canadian Hard of Hearing Assn. - Vancouver Br. [IO]
Canadian Hard of Hearing Assn. - Victoria Br. [IO]
Canadian Hard of Hearing Assn. - Yellowknife Br. [IO]
Canadian Hearing Soc. [IO]
Canadian Natl. Soc. of the Deaf-Blind [IO]
Centre for Deaf Stud. [IO]
Child Aid [IO]
Child Aid [14746]
Children of Deaf Adults [14747]
Christian Mission for the Deaf [20318]
Christian Record Services [16842]
Cochlear Implant Assn., Inc. [14748]
Cochlear Implant Assn., Inc. [IO]
Commonwealth Soc. for Deaf Charity [IO]
Conf. of Educational Administrators of Schools and Programs for the Deaf [14749]
CORAL [IO]
Coun. for Accreditation in Occupational Hearing Conservation [15632]
Coun. for the Advancement of Commun. with Deaf People [IO]
Coun. of Amer. Instructors of the Deaf [14750]
Coun. on Educ. of the Deaf [14751]
Danish Deaf Assn. [IO]
DB-Link: The Natl. Info. CH On Children Who Are Deaf-Blind [16845]
Deaf Assn. of New Zealand [IO]
Deaf Educ. Through Listening and Talking [IO]
Deaf Friends Intl. [11904]
Deaf History Intl. [14081]
Deaf-REACH [14752]
Deafblind Assn. [IO]
Deafblind New Zealand [IO]
Deafblind Scotland [IO]
Deafblind UK [IO]
Deafchild Intl. [IO]
Deafness Res. Found. [14753]
Disabled Sports USA [23343]
Dog Guides Canada [IO]
Dogs for the Deaf [14754]
Dutch Assn. of Sign Language Interpreters [IO]
Dutch Deafship [IO]
Ear Found. [15825]
Educational Audiology Assn. [14755]
Educational Audiology Assn. [IO]
European Hearing Instrument Mfrs. Assn. [IO]
European Union of the Deaf [IO]
Federatie van Ouders van Dove Kinderen [IO]
Global Deaf Connection [IO]
Global Deaf Connection [12274]
HEAR Center [14756]
Hear Now [14757]
Hearing Assn. New Zealand [IO]
Hearing Concern [IO]
Hearing Educ. and Awareness for Rockers [16056]
Hearing Instrument Manufacturers' Software Assn. [14758]
Hearing Loss Assn. of Am. [14759]

Reference to "IO" in place of a book number signifies that the association may be found in the 45th edition of International Organizations.

Helen Keller Natl. Center for Deaf-Blind Youths and Adults [14760]
HIKE Fund [14761]
Hong Kong Soc. for the Deaf [IO]
House Ear Inst. [16446]
Icelandic Assn. of the Deaf [IO]
Intl. Catholic Deaf Assn. - U.S. Sect. [19641]
Intl. Comm. of Sports for the Deaf/DEAFLYMPICS [23345]
Intl. Fed. of Hard of Hearing People [IO]
Intl. Fed. of Hard of Hearing Young People [IO]
Intl. Hearing Dog, Inc. [IO]
Intl. Hearing Dog, Inc. [14762]
Intl. Hearing Soc. [14763]
Intl. Hearing Soc. [IO]
Intl. Lutheran Deaf Assn. [20217]
Intl. Soc. for Oral Laser Applications [IO]
Intervenor Org. of Ontario [IO]
Irish Deaf Soc. [IO]
Irish Hard of Hearing Assn. [IO]
John Tracy Clinic [14764]
Kingston Hard of Hearing Club [IO]
League for the Hard of Hearing [14765]
Military Audiology Assn. [13717]
Model Secondary School for the Deaf [14766]
Natl. Assn. of the Deaf [14767]
Natl. Assn. for Deaf People [IO]
Natl. Assn. of Deafened People [IO]
Natl. Assn. of School Nurses for the Deaf [14768]
Natl. Black Assn. for Speech-Language and Hearing [16448]
Natl. Black Deaf Advocates [17418]
Natl. Captioning Inst. [14769]
Natl. Catholic Off. for the Deaf [19675]
Natl. Cochlear Implant Users Assn. [IO]
Natl. Deaf Children's Soc. [IO]
Natl. Deaf Educ. Network and CH [11906]
Natl. Educ. for Assistance Dog Services [14770]
Natl. Family Assn. for Deaf-Blind [14771]
Natl. Hearing Conservation Assn. [14772]
Natl. Inst. on Deafness and Other Commun. Disorders Info. CH [14773]
Natl. Ser. Dog Center [14774]
Natl. Student Speech Language Hearing Assn. [16453]
New Zealand Audiological Soc. [IO]
New Zealand Sign Language Tutors Assn. [IO]
NIDCD - Natl. Temporal Bone, Hearing and Balance Pathology Rsrc. Registry [15121]
Nordic Audiological Soc. [IO]
Oral Hearing-Impaired Sect. [IO]
Oral Hearing-Impaired Sect. [14775]
Parents' Sect. of the Alexander Graham Bell Assn. for the Deaf and Hard of Hearing [14776]
Phone-TTY [14777]
Protestant Guild for Human Services [16884]
Registry of Interpreters for the Deaf [14778]
Royal Assn. for Deaf People [IO]
Royal Inst. for Deaf and Blind Children [IO]
Royal Natl. Inst. for Deaf People [IO]
Scottish Assn. of Sign Language Interpreters [IO]
Scottish Coun. on Deafness [IO]
SENSE [IO]
Sign Language Interpreters Assn. of New Zealand [IO]
Signing Exact English Center for the Advancement of Deaf Children [14779]
Singapore Assn. for the Deaf [IO]
Ski for Light [23361]
Swedish Natl. Assn. of the Deaf [IO]
Telecommunications for the Deaf and Hard of Hearing, Inc. [14780]
Toronto Hard of Hearing Br. [IO]
TRIPOD [14781]
Union of the Deaf in Bulgaria [IO]
U.S.A. Deaf Basketball [23136]
U.S. Assn. for Blind Athletes [23363]
U.S. Flag Football for the Deaf [23367]
USA Deaf Sports Fed. [23369]
Verbond der Vlaamse Tandartsen [IO]
Wheelchair Sports, USA [23371]
World Fed. of the Deaf [IO]
Hearing Impaired Hockey Assn.; Amer. [23337]
Hearing Impaired Kids Endowment Fund [★14761]
Hearing Impaired Prog; Community Housing for the [★14752]

Hearing Impaired; Stan Mikita Hockey School for the [★23337]
Hearing Indus. Assn. [1861], 515 King St., Ste. 420, Alexandria, VA 22314, (703)684-5744
Hearing Instrument Manufacturers' Software Assn. [14758], 2550 Univ. Ave. W, Ste. 241N, St. Paul, MN 55114, (651)644-2921
Hearing Instruments Stud; International Inst. for [★14763]
Hearing Instruments Stud; International Inst. for [★IO]
Hearing Loss Assn. of Am. [14759], 7910 Woodmont Ave., Ste. 1200, Bethesda, MD 20814, (301)657-2248
Hearing; Natl. Black Assn. for Speech-Language and [16448]
Hearing Officials; Natl. Assn. of [5906]
Hearing Soc; Amer. [★16442]
Hearing, Speech and
  Acad. of Doctors of Audiology [14733]
  Amer. Auditory Soc. [14738]
  Amer. Hearing Aid Associates [14739]
  Amer. Neurotology Soc. [16441]
  Amer. Speech Language Hearing Assn. [16442]
  Amer. Tinnitus Assn. [16443]
  Assn. of Late-Deafened Adults [14743]
  Coun. for Accreditation in Occupational Hearing Conservation [15632]
  Hearing Indus. Assn. [1861]
  House Ear Inst. [16446]
  Intl. Catholic Deaf Assn. - U.S. Sect. [19641]
  Military Audiology Assn. [13717]
  Natl. Black Assn. for Speech-Language and Hearing [16448]
  Natl. Catholic Off. for the Deaf [19675]
  Natl. Hearing Conservation Assn. [14772]
  Natl. Inst. on Deafness and Other Commun. Disorders Info. CH [14773]
  Natl. Student Speech Language Hearing Assn. [16453]
  U.S.A. Deaf Basketball [23136]
  USA Deaf Sports Fed. [23369]
  VOICES Assn. [13211]
Hearing and Speech Action; Natl. Assn. for [★16442]
Hearing and Speech Agencies; Natl. Assn. of [★16442]
Hearst Found. [13120], 90 New Montgomery St., Ste. 1212, San Francisco, CA 94105, (415)908-4500
Hearst Memorial Morab Registry [★4947]
Hearst Memorial Morab Registry [★IO]
Heart of Africa Mission [★IO]
Heart of Africa Mission [★20034]
Heart of America Carnival Glass Assn. [22557]
Heart of Am. Northwest [18395], 1314 56th St. NE, Ste. 100, Seattle, WA 98105, (206)382-1014
Heart of America Walking Horse Assn. - Address unknown since 1994.
Heart Assn; Amer. [13890]
Heart Assn; Coun. on Arteriosclerosis, Thrombosis and Vascular Biology of the Amer. [13902]
Heart Assn. of Thailand [IO], Bangkok, Thailand
Heart Bandits Amer. Eskimo Dog Rescue [IO], Fresno, CA, United States
Heart Bandits Amer. Eskimo Dog Rescue [12018], PO Box 4322, Fresno, CA 93744-4322, (559)787-2459
Heart Care Intl. [13904], 139 E Putnam Ave., Greenwich, CT 06830, (203)552-5343
Heart Care Intl. [IO], Greenwich, CT, United States
Heart Coun; Natl. [13918]
Heart Disease
  Adult Congenital Heart Assn. [13884]
  Amer. Assn. of Heart Failure Nurses [15434]
  Amer. Coll. of Cardiology [13888]
  Amer. Soc. of Echocardiography [13891]
  Assn. for Eradication of Heart Attack [13894]
  Cardiovascular Credentialing Intl. [13898]
  Congenital Cardiac Anesthesia Soc. [13682]
  Congenital Heart Defects Awareness [13900]
  Congenital Heart Info. Network [13901]
  Coun. on Arteriosclerosis, Thrombosis and Vascular Biology of the Amer. Heart Assn. [13902]

Fibromuscular Dysplasia Soc. of Am. [15322]
French Org. of the Long QT Syndrome [IO]
Gift of Life Intl. [12524]
Heart Disease Res. Found. [13905]
Heart Failure Soc. of Am. [13906]
Heart Rhythm Soc. [13907]
Hypertrophic Cardiomyopathy Assn. [14782]
Hypertrophic Cardiomyopathy Association [IO]
InterAmerican Heart Found. [13909]
Intl. Bundle Br. Block Assn. [13911]
Intl. EECP Therapists Assn. [16619]
Kids With Heart Natl. Assn. for Children's Heart Disorders [13915]
Make Early Diagnosis to Prevent Early Death [14463]
Mended Hearts, Inc. [13916]
Michael E. DeBakey Intl. Surgical Soc. [13917]
Pediatric Cardiac Intensive Care Soc. [15892]
Peruvian Heart Assn. [13923]
Soc. for Women's Hea. Res. [16910]
Stickler Involved People [14483]
Sudden Cardiac Arrest Assn. [13933]
Velo-Cardio-Facial Syndrome [14488]
WomenHeart: Natl. Coalition for Women with Heart Disease [13929]
Heart Disease Res. Found. [13905]
Heart Disease Resources; Intersociety Commn. for [★13890]
Heart of the Earth Survival School [★18090]
Heart Failure Soc. of Am. [13906], c/o Cheryl Yano, Exec. Dir., Court Intl. - Ste. 240 S, 2550 Univ. Ave. W, St. Paul, MN 55114, (651)642-1633
Heart Fan Club - Address unknown since 1999.
Heart Found. of Australia [IO], Deakin, Australia
Heart Found; InterAmerican [13909]
Heart Fund; Children's [★13899]
Heart to Heart Intl. [12858], 401 S Claiborne, Ste. 302, Olathe, KS 66062, (913)764-5200
Heart to Heart Intl. [IO], Olathe, KS, United States
Heart House Learning Center [★13888]
Heart and Lung Found. - Defunct.
Heart and Lung Transplantation Registry; International [★16674]
Heart and Lung Transplantation Registry; International [★IO]
Heart Res; Natl. [★13918]
Heart Rhythm Soc. [13907], 1400 K St. NW, Ste. 500, Washington, DC 20005, (202)464-3400
Heart Rhythm Soc. [IO], Washington, DC, United States
Heart of Romania's Children Found. [11598], 103 S Aurora Dr., Apopka, FL 32712, (407)814-9095
Heart Savers Assn; Natl. [13919]
Heart and Stroke Found. of Canada [IO], Ottawa, ON, Canada
Heart of Texas Country Music Assn. [24908], c/o Mr. Tracy Pitcox, 1701 S Bridge St., Brady, TX 76825, (325)597-1895
Heart Transplantation; Intl. Soc. for [★16674]
Heartbeat [13288], PO Box 16985, Colorado Springs, CO 80935, (719)596-2575
Heartbeat Intl. [12912], 665 E Dublin-Granville, Ste. 440, Columbus, OH 43229-3245, (614)885-7577
Heartbeat Intl. [IO], Columbus, OH, United States
Heartbeat/Survivors After Suicide [★13288]
Hearth Educ. Found. [1880], Dept. 4045, Washington, DC 20042-4045, (703)524-8030
Hearth, Patio & Barbecue Assn. [★1679]
Hearth, Patio and Barbeque Assn. [1679], 1901 N Moore St., Ste. 600, Arlington, VA 22209, (703)522-0086
Heartland Conservation Soc. [IO], Camberley, United Kingdom
Heartland Doulton Collectors - Defunct.
Heartland Inst. [13121], 19 S LaSalle St., Ste. 903, Chicago, IL 60603, (312)377-4000
Heartland Vintage Thunderbird Club of Am. [21654]
Heartlife - Address unknown since 1990.
Heartline/Natl. Assn. of Older Americans - Address unknown since 1995.
HeartLink; Children's [13899]
HeartMath; Inst. of [10174]
Hearts Club; Mended [★13916]
Hearts in Harmony - World Family of John Denver [24909]

A star before a book entry number signifies that the name is not listed separately, but is mentioned within the entry.

Hearts, Inc; Mended [13916]
Hearts and Minds Network [18730], 3074 Broadway, New York, NY 10027, (212)280-0333
Hearts and Minds; Proj.: [12538]
Hearts United for Animals [11405], Box 286, Auburn, NE 68305, (402)274-3679
HeartStrong [12232], PO Box 2051, Seattle, WA 98111, (206)388-3894
Heartworm Soc; Amer. [16772]
Heat Exchange Inst. [1881], 1300 Sumner Ave., Cleveland, OH 44115-2851, (216)241-7333
Heat Inst. of Am; Oil [★2943]
Heat and Power Assn; U.S. Combined [7821]
Heater Assn; Indus. Unit [★1876]
HEATH Rsrc. Center [8203], George Washington Univ., 2134 G St. NW, Washington, DC 20037-2704, (202)973-0904
Heather Soc. [IO], Wisbech, United Kingdom
Heather's Soc; Pacific Northwest [★22533]
Heather's Teddy Bear Org. [22035], c/o Arlene Marie Wood, CEO/Pres., 16 Oakdale Rd., Terryville, CT 06786, (860)585-1735
Heating and Air Conditioning Assn; Manufacturers Members of the Natl. Warm Air [★1873]
Heating and Air Conditioning Assn; Natl. Warm Air [★1872]
Heating and Air-Conditioning Engineers; Amer. Soc. [★6995]
Heating, Airconditioning and Refrigeration Distributors Intl. [1882], 1389 Dublin Rd., Columbus, OH 43215-1084, (614)488-1835
Heating, Airconditioning and Refrigeration Distributors Intl. [IO], Columbus, OH, United States
Heating Alliance; Wood [★1679]
Heating Assn; Hydronic Radiant [★1884]
Heating Assn; Intl. District [★1888]
Heating Assn; Natl. District [★1888]

Heating and Cooling
Air Conditioning Contractors of Am. [1872]
Air Conditioning Equip. Manufacturers' Assn. [IO]
Air Conditioning and Mech. Contractors Assn. - Australian Capital Territory [IO]
Air Conditioning and Mech. Contractors Assn. - New South Wales [IO]
Air Conditioning and Mech. Contractors Assn. - Queensland [IO]
Air Conditioning and Mech. Contractors Assn. - South Australia [IO]
Air Conditioning and Mech. Contractors Assn. - Western Australia [IO]
Air Conditioning and Refrigeration European Assn. [IO]
Air-Conditioning and Refrigeration Inst. [1873]
Air Conditioning and Refrigeration Mfrs'. Assn. [IO]
Air Diffusion Coun. [1874]
Air Distribution Inst. [1875]
Air Movement and Control Assn. Intl. [1876]
Air Movement and Control Assn. Intl. [IO]
Amer. Soc. of Heating, Refrigerating and Air-Conditioning Engineers [6995]
Amer. Supply Assn. [3061]
Assn. of European Refrigeration Compressor and Controls Mfrs. [IO]
Assn. of Plumbing and Heating Contractors [IO]
Assn. of Refrigerant and Desuperheating Mfg. [1877]
British Refrigeration Assn. [IO]
Canadian Heat Exchanger and Vessel Mfrs. Assn. [IO]
Canadian Inst. of Plumbing and Heating [IO]
Commercial Refrigerator Mfrs. Div. [1878]
Euroheat and Power [IO]
European Assn. of Air Heater Manufacturers [IO]
European Cold Storage and Logistics Assn. [IO]
European Comm. of Indus. Furnace and Heating Equip. Associations [IO]
Evaporative Cooling Inst. [1879]
Fed. of Environmental Trade Associations [IO]
Fed. of European Heating and Air Conditioning Associations [IO]
German Soc. of Refrigeration and Airconditioning [IO]
Hearth Educ. Found. [1880]
Heat Exchange Inst. [1881]

Heating, Airconditioning and Refrigeration Distributors Intl. [1882]
Heating, Airconditioning and Refrigeration Distributors Intl. [IO]
Heating, Refrigeration and Air Conditioning Inst. of Canada [IO]
Heating, Ventilating and Air Conditioning Mfrs'. Assn. [IO]
Heating and Ventilating Contractors' Assn. [IO]
Home Ventilating Inst. [1883]
Hong Kong Air-Conditioning and Refrigeration Assn. [IO]
Hydronics Inst. Division of GAMA [1884]
Indus. Heating Equip. Assn. [1885]
Inst. of Refrigeration [IO]
Intl. Assn. for Cold Storage Constr. [IO]
Intl. Assn. for Cold Storage Constr. [1886]
Intl. Assn. of Heat and Frost Insulators and Asbestos Workers [24093]
Intl. Assn. of Refrigerated Warehouses [3978]
Intl. Compressor Remanufacturers Assn. [1887]
Intl. Compressor Remanufacturers Assn. [IO]
Intl. District Energy Assn. [IO]
Intl. District Energy Assn. [1888]
Intl. Ground Source Heat Pump Assn. [1889]
International Ground Source Heat Pump Association [IO]
Intl. Inst. of Ammonia Refrigeration [IO]
Intl. Inst. of Ammonia Refrigeration [1890]
Intl. Packaged Ice Assn. [1891]
Intl. Union for Electricity Applications [IO]
Japan Soc. of Refrigerating and Air Conditioning Engineers [IO]
Masonry Heater Assn. of North Am. [1892]
Mobile Air Conditioning Soc. Worldwide [1893]
Mobile Air Conditioning Soc. Worldwide [IO]
Natl. Air Filtration Assn. [1894]
Natl. Environmental Balancing Bur. [1895]
Natl. Kerosene Heater Assn. [1896]
Natl. Standard Plumbing Code Comm. [5553]
North Amer. Technician Excellence [1897]
North Central Wholesalers Assn. [3064]
Radiant Panel Assn. [1898]
Refrigerating Engineers and Technicians Assn. [7037]
Refrigeration Ser. Engineers Soc. [1899]
Refrigeration Service Engineers Society [IO]
Sheet Metal and Air Conditioning Contractors' Natl. Assn. [1900]
Sheet Metal Industry Promotion Plan [1065]
Soc. of Heating, Airconditioning and Sanitary Engineers of Japan [IO]
Steamfitting Indus. Promotion Fund [1901]
Stove, Furnace, Energy, and Allied Appliance Workers Division of the Intl. Brotherhood of Boilermakers [24001]
Swedish Heating Boilers and Burners Assn. [IO]
Tubular Exchanger Mfrs. Assn. [1902]
Used Oil Mgt. Assn. [1903]
Wholesale Distributors Assn. [3067]
World Food Logistics Org. [3985]
Heating and Cooling Assn; Intl. District [★1888]
Heating-Cooling Contractors Assn; Plumbing- [1059]
Heating-Cooling Contractors; Natl. Assn. of Plumbing- [★1059]
Heating-Cooling Coun; Better [★1884]
Heating and Cooling; Natl. Solar [★6951]
Heating Educ. and Res. Found; Wood [★1880]
Heating and Piping and Air Conditioning Contractors Natl. Assn. [★1033]
Heating and Piping Contractors Natl. Assn. [★1033]
Heating, Refrigerating and Air-Conditioning Engineers; Amer. Soc. of [6995]
Heating, Refrigeration and Air Conditioning Inst. of Canada [IO], Mississauga, ON, Canada
Heating, Refrigeration, and Airconditioning Wholesalers Assn; Northamerican [★1882]
Heating, Ventilating and Air Conditioning Mfrs'. Assn. [IO], Reading, United Kingdom
Heating and Ventilating Contractors' Assn. [IO], London, United Kingdom
Heaven On Earth [IO], Mont-Saint-Aignan, France
Heavy-Duty Bus. Forum [356], 10 Lab. Dr., PO Box 13966, Research Triangle Park, NC 27709-3966, (919)406-8808

Heavy Duty Distribution Assn. [357], 4600 East-West Hwy., Ste. 300, Bethesda, MD 20814, (301)654-6664
Heavy Duty Mfrs. Assn. [2557], 10 Lab. Dr., PO Box 13966, Research Triangle Park, NC 27709-3966, (919)549-4800
Heavy Duty Representatives Assn. [386], 4015 Marks Rd., Ste. 2B, Medina, OH 44256-8316, (330)725-7160
Heavy-Duty Truck Mfrs. Assn. - Defunct.
Heavy Equip. Claims Coun; Natl. Truck and [2228]
Heavy Metal Music
KISS Rocks Fan Club [24935]
Heavy Specialized Carriers Conf. [★3589]
Heavy Specialized Carriers Conf. [★IO]
Heavy Specialized Carriers Sect. - Local Cartage Natl. Conf. [★IO]
Heavy Specialized Carriers Sect. - Local Cartage Natl. Conf. [★3589]
Hebe Haven Yacht Club [IO], Hong Kong, People's Republic of China
Hebe Soc. [IO], Macclesfield, United Kingdom
Hebrew
Central Agency for Jewish Educ. [19180]
Edith Stein Guild [19621]
Jewish Book Coun. [9751]
Natl. Assn. of Hebrew Day School PTAs [8953]
Hebrew Actors Union - Address unknown since 2002.
Hebrew Christian Alliance of Am. [★20257]
Hebrew Christian Alliance; Intl. [★20016]
Hebrew Christian Fellowship [20012], PO Box 177, Dresher, PA 19025-0177, (215)887-3447
Hebrew Congregations; Religious Action Center of the Union of Amer. [★17954]
Hebrew Culture Found. - Defunct.
Hebrew Day School Administrators; Natl. Assn. of [7901]
Hebrew Day School PTAs; Natl. Assn. of [8953]
Hebrew Free Burial Assn. [20141], 224 W 35th St., Rm. 300, New York, NY 10001, (212)239-1662
Hebrew Free Loan [★20148]
Hebrew Immigrant Aid Soc. [12471], 333 7th Ave., 16th Fl., New York, NY 10001, (212)967-4100
Hebrew Immigrant Aid Soc. [IO], New York, NY, United States
Hebrew and Kindred Associations; Coun. of Young Men's [★12473]
Hebrew Literacy Campaign [★20137]
Hebrew Lutheran Mission; Salem [★20019]
Hebrew Master Bakers Assn. - Defunct.
Hebrew Mission; Chicago [★19988]
Hebrew; Natl. Assn. of Professors of [8695]
Hebrew Religious Protective Assn. of Greater New York - Address unknown since 1995.
Hebrew Schools Prog. for Adult Stud. [★20172]
Hebrew Sheltering and Immigrant Aid Soc. [★12471]
Hebrew Sheltering and Immigrant Aid Soc. [★IO]
Hebrew Trades Division of the Jewish Labor Comm; United [★24214]
Hebrew Trades - New York Division of the Jewish Labor Comm; United [24214]
Hebrew Univ; Amer. Friends of The [8676]
Hebrew Writers Assn. in Israel [IO], Jerusalem, Israel
Hechalutz Orgs. of America - Defunct.
Heckman Family Org; William Jacob [21086]
Hector Kobbekaduwa Agrarian Res. and Training Inst. [IO], Colombo, Sri Lanka
Hedge Fund Assn. [IO], Aventura, FL, United States
Hedge Fund Assn. [2333], 2875 NE 191st St., Ste. 900, Aventura, FL 33180, (202)478-2000
Hedgehog Club; Intl. [★11417]
Hedonic Soc. of Am. [10758]
Hedrick Family Assn; Smith- [21052]
Hegel Soc. of Am. [9657], c/o Philosophy Documentation Center, PO Box 7147, Charlottesville, VA 22906-7147, (804)220-3300
Heidelberg Digital Imaging Assn. [1772], One Barney Rd., Ste. 232, Clifton Park, NY 12065, (518)373-1225
Heifer Proj. Intl. [12429], 1 World Ave., Little Rock, AR 72202, (800)422-0474
Heifer Proj. Intl. [IO], Little Rock, AR, United States
Heifers for Relief [★IO]

Reference to "IO" in place of a book number signifies that the association may be found in the 45th edition of International Organizations.

Heifers for Relief [★12429]
Heiney Family Tree [20938]
Heinkel-Messerschmitt-Isetta Club - Defunct.
Heinlein Family Assn; Henlein/ [20939]
Heinline CH [★20939]
Heirs, Inc. [17332], PO Box 292, Villanova, PA 19085, (610)525-4442
Heisey Collectors of America/National Heisey Glass Museum [22558], 169 W Church St., Newark, OH 43055, (740)345-2932
Helen Cornelius Fan Club - Defunct.
Helen Forrest Fan Club [24910]
Helen Keller Intl. [★16854]
Helen Keller Intl. [16854], 352 Park Ave. S, 12th Fl., New York, NY 10010, (212)532-0544
Helen Keller Intl. [IO], New York, NY, United States
Helen Keller Intl. [★IO]
Helen Keller Intl. - Asia-Pacific Regional Off. [IO], Phnom Penh, Cambodia
Helen Keller Intl. - Bangladesh [IO], Dhaka, Bangladesh
Helen Keller Intl. - Burkina Faso [IO], Ouagadougou, Burkina Faso
Helen Keller Intl. - Cambodia [IO], Phnom Penh, Cambodia
Helen Keller Intl. - Cameroon [IO], Yaounde, Cameroon
Helen Keller Intl. - China [IO], Guangzhou, People's Republic of China
Helen Keller Intl. - Cote d'Ivoire [IO], Abidjan, Cote d'Ivoire
Helen Keller Intl. - Europe [IO], Paris, France
Helen Keller Intl. - Guinea [IO], Conakry, Guinea
Helen Keller Intl. - Indonesia [IO], Jakarta, Indonesia
Helen Keller Intl. - Mali [IO], Bamako, Mali
Helen Keller Intl. - Mexico [IO], Chihuahua, Mexico
Helen Keller Intl. - Morocco [IO], Rabat, Morocco
Helen Keller Intl. - Mozambique [IO], Maputo, Mozambique
Helen Keller Intl. - Nepal [IO], Kathmandu, Nepal
Helen Keller Intl. - Niger [IO], Niamey, Niger
Helen Keller Intl. - Nigeria [IO], Jos, Nigeria
Helen Keller Intl. - Philippines [IO], Manila, Philippines
Helen Keller Intl. - Sierra Leone [IO], Freetown, Sierra Leone
Helen Keller Intl. - Tanzania [IO], Dar es Salaam, United Republic of Tanzania
Helen Keller Intl. - Vietnam [IO], Hanoi, Vietnam
Helen Keller Natl. Center for Deaf-Blind Youths and Adults [14760], 141 Middle Neck Rd., Sands Point, NY 11050-1218, (516)944-8900
Helen Keller Worldwide [★16854]
Helen Keller Worldwide [★IO]
Helen Suzman Found. [IO], Houghton, Republic of South Africa
Helena, Ascension, and Tristan da Cunha Philatelic Soc; St. [22866]
Helena and Dependencies Philatelic Soc; Sta. [★22866]
Helene Fuld Hea. Trust [15480], HSBC Bank USA, 452 Fifth Ave., 13th Fl., New York, NY 10018-2706, (212)525-2418
Helical Washer Inst. - Defunct.
Heliconia Soc. Intl. [4978], c/o Raymond F. Baker, 3860 Manoa Rd., Honolulu, HI 96822-1180, (808)988-0455
Heliconia Soc. Intl. [IO], Honolulu, HI, United States
Helicopter
　　Aerospace Indus. Assn. of Am. [130]
　　Amer. Helicopter Soc. [139]
　　Combat Helicopter Pilots Assn. [20648]
　　Helicopter Club of America [21450]
　　Helicopter Club of Great Britain [IO]
　　Helicopter Found. Intl. [151]
　　Intl. R/C Helicopter Assn. [22647]
　　Popular Rotorcraft Assn. [21471]
　　Twirly Birds [21484]
　　Whirly-Girls - Intl. Women Helicopter Pilots [21487]
Helicopter Advisory Bd; British [IO]
Helicopter Assn. of Am. [★IO]
Helicopter Assn. of Am. [★150]
Helicopter Assn. of Great Britain [★IO]
Helicopter Assn. Intl. [IO], Alexandria, VA, United States

Helicopter Assn. Intl. [150], 1635 Prince St., Alexandria, VA 22314-2818, (703)683-4646
Helicopter Assn; Intl. R/C [22647]
Helicopter Club of America [21450]
Helicopter Club of Great Britain [IO], Banbury, United Kingdom
Helicopter Found. Intl. [IO], Alexandria, VA, United States
Helicopter Found; Intl. [★151]
Helicopter Found. Intl. [151], 1635 Prince St., Alexandria, VA 22314-2818, (703)683-4646
Helicopter Loggers Assn. - Defunct.
Helicopter Pilots Assn; Vietnam [21351]
Helicopter Safety Advisory Conf. [152], c/o Joseph Gross, Treas., BHP Billiton Petroleum, Inc., 1360 Post Oak Blvd., Ste. 150, Houston, TX 77056-3020, (713)499-5452
HELIO Intl. [IO], Paris, France
Helium Soc. [★6844]
Hellenes Abroad; World Coun. of [19096]
Hellenic Advertisers Assn. [IO], Athens, Greece
Hellenic Aerosol Assn. [IO], Athens, Greece
Hellenic Amateur Baseball Fed. [IO], Athens, Greece
Hellenic Amer. Bankers Assn. [479], PO Box 7244, New York, NY 10150, (212)421-1057
Hellenic-American Chamber of Commerce [24326], 960 Ave. of the Americas, Ste. 1008, Atlantic Bank Bldg., New York, NY 10001-2112, (212)629-6380
Hellenic Amer. Cong; United [19094]
Hellenic Amer. Dental Soc. [1150], PO Box 4803, Oak Brook, IL 60523-4803, (847)698-1180
Hellenic Amer. Natl. Coun. [9995], 2155 W 80th St., Chicago, IL 60620, (773)994-2222
Hellenic Assn. of Dermatology and Venereology [IO], Athens, Greece
Hellenic Assn. of Footwear Manufacturers and Exporters [IO], Neo Psychiko, Greece
Hellenic Assn. for Geronontoolgy and Geriatrics [★IO]
Hellenic Assn. of Gerontology and Geriatrics [IO], Athens, Greece
Hellenic Assn. of Pharmaceutical Companies [IO], Athens, Greece
Hellenic Assn. of Professional Cong. Organisers [IO], Athens, Greece
Hellenic Assn. of Travel and Tourist Agencies [IO], Athens, Greece
Hellenic Badminton Fed. [IO], Athens, Greece
Hellenic Billiard Fed. [IO], Athens, Greece
Hellenic Cardiological Soc. [IO], Athens, Greece
Hellenic Chamber of Hotels [IO], Athens, Greece
Hellenic Cricket Fed. [IO], Corfu, Greece
Hellenic Fertility and Sterility Soc. [IO], Athens, Greece
Hellenic Found. for European and Foreign Policy [IO], Athens, Greece
Hellenic Geographic Info. Soc. [IO], Athens, Greece
Hellenic Ice Sports Fed. [IO], Athens, Greece
Hellenic Inst; Amer. [24325]
Hellenic Language; Pan Amer. Coun. for the Preservation of the Hellenic Orthodox Church and the [20074]
Hellenic League Against Rheumatism [IO], Athens, Greece
Hellenic Olympic Comm. [IO], Athens, Greece
Hellenic Operational Res. Soc. [IO], Pireaus, Greece
Hellenic Orthodox Church and the Hellenic Language; Pan Amer. Coun. for the Preservation of the [20074]
Hellenic Pain Soc. [IO], Athens, Greece
Hellenic Paralympic Comm. [IO], Athens, Greece
Hellenic Philatelic Soc. of Am. [22826]
Hellenic Physical Soc. [IO], Athens, Greece
Hellenic Professional Yacht Owners Assn. [IO], Piraeus, Greece
Hellenic Radiological Soc. [IO], Athens, Greece
Hellenic Rose Soc. [IO], Piraeus, Greece
Hellenic Soc. for Chemotherapy [IO], Athens, Greece
Hellenic Soc. for Dermatologic Surgery [IO], Athens, Greece
Hellenic Soc. of Dermatology and Venereology [★IO]
Hellenic Soc. of Hypertension [IO], Athens, Greece
Hellenic Soc. for Infectious Diseases [IO], Athens, Greece

Hellenic Soc. for Microbiology [IO], Athens, Greece
Hellenic Soc. for Photogrammetry and Remote Sensing [IO], Athens, Greece
Hellenic Soc. of Physiology [IO], Athens, Greece
Hellenic Soc. of Rheology [IO], Nicosia, Cyprus
Hellenic Soc. for Rheumatology [IO], Athens, Greece
Hellenic Stud; Amer. Soc. for Neo- [★9770]
Hellenic Tennis Fed. [IO], Athens, Greece
Hellenic Voters of Am; United [19095]
Hellenic Voters of Illinois; United [★19095]
Hellenic Weightlifting Fed. [IO], Athens, Greece
HELLP Syndrome Soc. [IO], Bethany, WV, United States
HELLP Syndrome Soc. [14906], PO Box 44, Bethany, WV 26032
Hell's Angels Bomb Gp. [★21373]
Helmet Comm., Washington Area Bicyclist Assn. [★12954]
Helmet Safety Inst; Bicycle [12954]
HELP - Address unknown since 2000.
Help the Afghan Children [IO], Kabul, Afghanistan
Help Afghan School Children Org [IO], Vienna, Austria
Help the Aged [IO], Ottawa, ON, Canada
Help the Aged [★11274]
Help Alopecia Intl. Res. - Defunct.
Help Assn; Southern Mutual [11790]
Help Belma Campaign - Address unknown since 2003.
Help the Bolivian Children - Address unknown since 1999.
Help Darfur Now [12259], PO Box 5062, Basking Ridge, NJ 07920-5062, (908)647-4198
Help Darfur Now [IO], Basking Ridge, NJ, United States
Help Desk Inst. [3550], 102 S Tejon, Ste. 1200, Colorado Springs, CO 80903, (719)268-0174
Help Found; Wives-Self- [11832]
Help the Helpless [12405], PO Box 270308, Vadnais Heights, MN 55127, (651)762-8857
Help Hospitalized Veterans [13351], 36585 Penfield Ln., Winchester, CA 92596, (951)926-4500
Help for Incontinent People [★16709]
Help for Incontinent People [★IO]
HELP - Inst. for Body Chemistry [14928], 6 Mellon Terr., Pittsburgh, PA 15206, (412)441-2909
HELP, Intl. - Defunct.
Help Liberia Found. [IO], Nawojowa, Poland
HELP Network [IO], Chicago, IL, United States
HELP Network [17595], c/o Children's Memorial Hosp., 2300 Children's Plz., No. 88, Chicago, IL 60614, (773)880-3993
Help Offering Parents Empowerment; Team H.O.P.E [12606]
Help-One Women's Org. [IO], Iganga, Uganda
Help Our Wolves Live - Defunct.
Help Save America for Our Kids' Future - Address unknown since 1994.
Help Us Make a Nation - Address unknown since 1989.
HELP USA [12292], 5 Hanover Sq., 17th Fl., New York, NY 10004, (212)400-7000
HelpAge Intl. [IO], London, United Kingdom
HelpAge Intl. - Africa Regional Development Centre [IO], Nairobi, Kenya
HelpAge Intl. - Caribbean Regional Development Centre [IO], Kingston, Jamaica
HelpAge Intl. - EU Off. (Brussels) [IO], Brussels, Belgium
HelpAge Intl. - Latin Am. Regional Development Centre [IO], La Paz, Bolivia
HelpArgentina [IO], Buenos Aires, Argentina
Helpers Assn; Natl. Peer [★11827]
Helpers of God's Precious Infants [18553], c/o The Monastery of the Precious Blood, 5300 Ft. Hamilton Pkwy., Brooklyn, NY 11219, (718)853-2789
Helpful Soc. [★19263]
Helping Hands for the Blind [13379], 20734-C Devonshire St., Chatsworth, CA 91311, (818)341-8217
Helping Hands Rescue [11406], PO Box 1975, Lewiston, ID 83501, (208)746-2777
Helping Hands Rescue [IO], Lewiston, ID, United States
Helping Other Parents in Normal Grieving - Address unknown since 2004.

A star before a book entry number signifies that the name is not listed separately, but is mentioned within the entry.

Helping Our Teen Girls in Real Life Situations
[12261], 3645 Marketplace Blvd., Ste. 130-190,
Atlanta, GA 30344, (404)495-3542
Helping Parents; Parents [12684]
Helps Intl. Ministries [20345], 573 Fairview Rd.,
Asheville, NC 28803, (828)277-3812
Helps Intl. Ministries [IO], Asheville, NC, United
States
Helsinki Commn. - Baltic Marine Env. Protection
Commn. [IO], Helsinki, Finland
Helsinki Found. for Human Rights [IO], Warsaw,
Poland
Helsinki Guarantees for Ukraine Comm. - Defunct.
Helsinki Inst. for Crime Prevention and Control, Affili-
ated with the United Nations [★IO]
Helsinki Watch [★IO]
Helsinki Watch [★17763]
Helsinki Watch; U.S. [★17763]
Helsinska Fundacja Praw Czloweka [★IO]
HELVETAS - Bhutan [IO], Thimphu, Bhutan
HELVETAS - Mali [IO], Bamako, Mali
HELVETAS - Philippines [IO], Palawan, Philippines
Helvetas - Swiss Assn. for Intl. Cooperation [IO],
Zurich, Switzerland
Helvetia Assn. of North America - Defunct.
Helvetia Philatelic Soc. [★22782]
Helvetia Philatelic Soc. [★IO]
Hematology
Amer. Assn. of Blood Banks [13761]
American Bd. of Clinical Metal Toxicology [16659]
Amer. Soc. for Apheresis [13706]
Amer. Soc. of Hematology [14783]
Amer. Soc. of Pediatric Hematology/Oncology
[14784]
Aplastic Anemia and MDS Intl. Found. [14785]
Aplastic Anemia and MDS International Founda-
tion [IO]
Aplastic Anemia and Myelodysplasia Assn. of
Canada [IO]
Argentine Soc. of Hematology [IO]
Assn. of Veterinary Hematology and Transfusion
Medicine [16785]
British Soc. for Haematology [IO]
Canadian Hematology Soc. [IO]
Canadian Hemochromatosis Soc. [IO]
Canadian Hemophilia Soc. [IO]
Children's Blood Found. [14786]
Coalition for Hemophilia B [14787]
Cooley's Anemia Found. [14788]
European Hematology Assn. [IO]
European Soc. for Haemapheresis and Haemo-
therapy [IO]
German Soc. for Hematology and Oncology [IO]
Haematology Soc. of Australia and New Zealand
[IO]
Haemophilia Soc. [IO]
Hemochromatosis Info. Soc. [14800]
Hemophilia Fed. of Am. [14789]
Hemophilia Fed. India [IO]
HHT Found. Intl. [14454]
Histiocytosis Assn. of Am. [14790]
Hong Kong Assn. of Blood Transfusion and Hae-
matology [IO]
Intl. Soc. of Blood Purification [IO]
Intl. Soc. of Blood Purification [14791]
Intl. Soc. for Clinical Haemorheology [IO]
International Society for Experimental Hematology
[IO]
Intl. Soc. for Experimental Hematology [14792]
Intl. Soc. of Haematology - European and African
Div. [IO]
Intl. Soc. on Thrombosis and Haemostasis [IO]
Intl. Soc. on Thrombosis and Haemostasis
[14793]
Irish Haemophilia Soc. [IO]
Italian Assn. of Pediatric Hematology and Oncol-
ogy [IO]
Japanese Soc. of Hematology [IO]
Natl. Anemia Action Coun. [14794]
Natl. Eosinophilia-Myalgia Syndrome Network
[16662]
Natl. Hemophilia Found. [14795]
Natl. Phlebotomy Assn. [14796]
North Amer. Specialized Coagulation Lab. Assn.
[14996]

Sickle Cell Disease Assn. of Am. [14797]
Soc. for the Advancement of Blood Mgt. [14798]
Soc. for the Advancement of Blood Mgt. [IO]
Soc. for Hematopathology [15874]
Swedish Hemophilia Soc. [IO]
World Fed. of Hemophilia [IO]
Hematology; Amer. Soc. of [14783]
Hematopathology; Soc. for [15874]
Hemerocallis Soc; Amer. [22490]
Hemi-Sync
The Monroe Inst. [7378]
Hemingway, Ernest
Hemingway Found. and Soc. [9658]
Hemingway Found. and Soc. [9658], c/o Susan F.
Beegel, Ed., 14 Terhune Dr., Phippsburg, ME
04562, (207)389-2839
Hemispheric Affairs; Coun. on [16975]
Hemispheric Cong. of Latin Chambers of Commerce
[24281], c/o Latin Chamber of Commerce of USA,
1417 W Flagler St., Miami, FL 33135, (305)642-
3870
Hemispheric Cong. of Latin Chambers of Commerce
[IO], Miami, FL, United States
Hemlock Soc. [★12131]
Hemlock Soc. U.S.A. [★12131]
Hemochromatosis
Hemochromatosis Found. [14799]
Hemochromatosis Info. Soc. [14800]
Iron Overload Diseases Assn. [15249]
Hemochromatosis Found. [14799]
Hemochromatosis Info. Soc. [14800], 3017 Princ-
eton Dr., Plano, TX 75075, (214)893-6960
Hemochromatosis Research Found. [★14799]
Hemochromatosis Soc; Canadian [IO]
Hemodialysis; Natl. Assn. of Patients on [★15283]
Hemodialysis and Transplantation; Natl. Assn. of
Patients on [★15283]
Hemophilia Fed. of Am. [14789], 1405 W Pinhook
Rd., Ste. 101, Lafayette, LA 70503, (337)261-9787
Hemophilia Fed. India [IO], New Delhi, India
Hemophilia Found. [★14795]
Hemophilia Found; Natl. [14795]
Hemophilia Res. - Defunct.
Hemophilia Soc; Canadian [IO]
Hemophilia Soc; Swedish [IO]
Hemophilia; World Fed. of [IO]
Hemp; Bus. Alliance for Commerce in [18283]
Hemp Coun; North Amer. Indus. [7079]
Hemp Indus. Assn. [3783], PO Box 1571, Brattle-
boro, VT 05302, (707)874-3648
Hemp Indus. Assn. [IO], Occidental, CA, United
States
Hendler Fan Club; Laura [24751]
Hendrix Info. Mgt. Inst; Jimi [24921]
Henlein/Heinlein Family Assn. [20939], c/o Enid I.
Beihold, Founder, 11502 Grace Terr., Indianapolis,
IN 46236, (317)823-2376
Henry A. Wallace Inst. for Alternative Agriculture -
Address unknown since 2004.
Henry Clay Memorial Found. [11121], 120 Sycamore
Rd., Lexington, KY 40502, (859)266-8581
Henry Doubleday Res. Assn. [IO], Coventry, United
Kingdom
Henry; Friends of Patrick [11115]
Henry George Inst. - New York [18710], 121 E 30th
St., New York, NY 10016, (212)889-8020
Henry Hazlitt Foundation - Defunct.
Henry Irving Aficionados [★24727]
Henry Irving; Amer. Friends of [24727]
Henry J. Perahia Funds for the Needy Committee
[★20179]
Henry L. Stimson Center [17824], 1111 19th St. NW,
Ste. 1200, Washington, DC 20036, (202)223-5956
Henry Luce Found. [12050], 111 W 50th St., Ste.
4601, New York, NY 10020, (212)489-7700
Henry M. Jackson Found. [17480], 1001 4th Ave.,
Ste. 3117, Seattle, WA 98154-1101, (206)682-8565
Henry Nyberg Soc. [21655], 17822 Chicago Ave.,
Lansing, IL 60438, (708)474-3416
Henry Nyberg Soc. [IO], Lansing, IL, United States
Henry Segrist Family Org; Hans/ [20927]
Henry Sinclair Soc. of the U.S; Prince [9922]
Henry Williamson Soc. [IO], Cambridge, United
Kingdom
Hepatitis C Assn. [14807], 1351 Cooper Rd., Scotch
Plains, NJ 07076-2844, (866)437-4377

Hepatitis C Caring Ambassadors Prog. [14808], PO
Box 1748, Oregon City, OR 97045, (503)632-9032
Hepatitis C Coalition; Natl. [14814]
Hepatitis C Coun. of Victoria [IO], Brunswick,
Australia
Hepatitis C Soc. of Canada [IO], Hamilton, ON,
Canada
Hepatitis Found. Intl. [IO], Silver Spring, MD, United
States
Hepatitis Found. Intl. [14809], 504 Blick Dr., Silver
Spring, MD 20904-2901, (301)622-4200
Hepatitis Rsrc. Network [14810], 400 E Pioneer
Ave., Ste. 102, Puyallup, WA 98372, (253)435-
4582
Hepato-Biliary Pancreatic Assn; Intl. [★14802]
Hepato-Pancreato-Biliary Assn; Intl. [★14802]
Hepatology
Amer. Assn. for the Stud. of Liver Diseases
[14801]
Amer. Hepato-Pancreato-Biliary Assn. [14802]
Amer. Hepato-Pancreato-Biliary Assn. [IO]
Amer. Liver Found. [14803]
Belgian Assn. for the Stud. of the Liver [IO]
Canadian Liver Found. [IO]
Children's Liver Assn. for Support Services
[14804]
Crigler-Najjar Assn. [14805]
Frontline Hepatitis Awareness [14806]
Hepatitis C Assn. [14807]
Hepatitis C Caring Ambassadors Prog. [14808]
Hepatitis Found. Intl. [14809]
Hepatitis Found. Intl. [IO]
Hepatitis Rsrc. Network [14810]
Intl. Assn. for the Stud. of the Liver [IO]
Latino Org. for Liver Awareness [14811]
Natl. Assn. of Hepatitis Task Forces [14812]
Natl. Hepatitis C Advocacy Coun. [14813]
Natl. Hepatitis C Coalition [14814]
Natl. Viral Hepatitis Roundtable [14815]
Parents of Kids with Infectious Diseases [14954]
PBCers Org. [14816]
Heptachlor Res. and Educ. Found; Hawaii [13325]
Heptagonal Games Assn. - Defunct.
Heraldisch-Genealogische Gesellschaft [★IO]
Heraldisk Selskab [★IO]
Heraldry; Amer. Coll. of [21099]
Heraldry Soc. of England [IO], Guildford, United
Kingdom
Heraldry Soc. of Scotland [IO], Edinburgh, United
Kingdom
Heraldry Soc. of the U.S.A. - Address unknown
since 1999.
Herb Assn; Amer. [6624]
Herb Assn. of South Africa [IO], Rivonia, Republic of
South Africa
Herb Growers and Marketers Assn; Intl. [★1907]
Herb Growing and Marketing Network [1906], PO
Box 245, Silver Spring, PA 17575-0245, (717)393-
3295
Herb Res. Found. [6635], 4140 15th St., Boulder,
CO 80304, (303)449-2265
Herb Soc. [IO], Banbury, United Kingdom
Herb Soc. of Am. [6636], 9019 Kirtland Chardon
Rd., Kirtland, OH 44094, (440)256-0514
Herb Soc. of Victoria [IO], Camberwell, Australia
Herb Soc. of Western Australia [IO], Como, Australia
Herb Trade Assn. - Defunct.
Herbal Medicine Assn; British [IO]
Herbal Medicine Res; Tang Center for [14986]
Herbalife Family Found. [11599], c/o Joan Kardash-
ian, Exec. Dir., 1800 Century E, Los Angeles,
CA 90067-1501, (310)410-9600
Herbalife Family Found. [IO], Los Angeles, CA,
United States
Herbalism
Amer. Herbalists Guild [14817]
Flower Essence Soc. [14818]
Flower Essence Society [IO]
Herbalists Without Borders [13634]
Intl. Herb Assn. [1907]
North Amer. Coll. of Botanical Medicine [14819]
Veterinary Botanical Medicine Assn. [16812]
Herbalists; Natl. Inst. of Medical [IO]
Herbalists Without Borders [IO], State College, PA,
United States

Reference to "IO" in place of a book number signifies that the association may be found in the 45th edition of International Organizations.

Encyclopedia of Associations, 46th Edition

3563

Herbalists Without Borders [13634], 153 S Allen St., State College, PA 16801
Herbart Soc. for the Sci. Stud. of Educ; Natl. [★8293]
Herbert Hoover Birthplace Found. [★11122]
Herbert Hoover Presidential Lib. Assn. [11122], PO Box 696, West Branch, IA 52358, (319)643-5327
Herbert Lehman Educ. Fund [★17130]
Herbert's Standard Plate Number Single Catalogue [★22787]
Herbs
  Amer. Herb Assn. [6624]
  Amer. Herbal Products Assn. [1904]
  Australian Ginseng Growers Assn. [IO]
  British Columbia Herb Growers Assn. [IO]
  Ginseng Res. Inst. of Am. [1905]
  Hebe Soc. [IO]
  Herb Growing and Marketing Network [1906]
  Herb Res. Found. [6635]
  Herb Soc. [IO]
  Herb Soc. of Am. [6636]
  Herb Soc. of Victoria [IO]
  Herb Soc. of Western Australia [IO]
  Herbalists Without Borders [13634]
  Indian Pepper and Spice Trade Assn. [IO]
  Inst. for Traditional Medicine and Preventive Hea. Care [13635]
  Intl. Herb Assn. [1907]
  Intl. Herb Assn. [IO]
  Natl. Herbalists Assn. of Australia [IO]
  Organic Growers of Australia [IO]
  Queensland Herb Soc. [IO]
  United Plant Savers [13655]
  Veterinary Botanical Medicine Assn. [16812]
Hercules Intl. - Elton John Fan Club [IO], Munich, Germany
Hereditary Colon Cancer Assn. [13829], 3601 N 4th Ave., Ste. 201, Sioux Falls, SD 57104, (800)264-6783
Hereditary Disease Found. [15328], 3960 Broadway, 6th Fl., New York, NY 10032, (212)928-2121
Hereditary Order of Armigerous Augustans - Address unknown since 1999.
Hereditary Order of the Descendants of Colonial Governors - Address unknown since 2001.
Hereditary Order of Descendants of the Loyalists and Patriots of the Amer. Revolution [20673], c/o James Raywalt, Registrar Gen., 300 N Hill Rd., Sutton, WV 26601, (304)765-0321
Hereditary Order of the Families of the Presidents and First Ladies of Am. [21261], 1716 Bigley Ave., Charleston, WV 25302-3938
Hereditary Order of the First Families of Massachusetts [20739]
Hereford Assn; Amer. [4225]
Hereford Assn; Amer. Black [4214]
Hereford Assn; Amer. Junior [★4276]
Hereford Assn; Natl. Junior [4276]
Hereford Hog Record Assn; Natl. [5236]
Herefords Australia Ltd. [IO], Armidale, Australia
Herencia Espanola; Spanish Heritage- [★8634]
Herens Assn; Amer. [4226]
Heritable Disorders Of Connective Tissue; Coalition For [14446]
Heritage Areas; Alliance of Natl. [9856]
Heritage Assn; Asian/Pacific Amer. [18972]
Heritage Assn; Bishop Hill [21108]
Heritage Assn. Intl; Amer. [★8590]
Heritage Assn; Melungeon [18950]
Heritage Assn; Spanish [8634]
Heritage Canada Found. [IO], Ottawa, ON, Canada
Heritage Center; Christian [17285]
Heritage Center; Natl. Cowboy Hall of Fame and Western [★9381]
Heritage Center; Northwest Territory, Canadian and French [★20720]
Heritage Conservation Network [10033], 1557 North St., Boulder, CO 80304, (303)444-0128
Heritage Conservation Network [IO], Boulder, CO, United States
Heritage Coun; Asian Pacific Amer. [18973]
Heritage Coun; Indian [10744]
Heritage Education and Review Org. - Defunct.
The Heritage Found. [17631], 214 Massachusetts Ave. NE, Washington, DC 20002-4999, (202)546-4400

Heritage Found. [★10034]
Heritage Found; Amer. Motorcycle [23621]
Heritage Found; Architectural [10014]
Heritage Found; Chem. [10101]
Heritage Found; Czech [19028]
Heritage Found; Labor [9578]
Heritage Found; Marine Corps [10477]
Heritage Inst. [19271], PO Box 860, Clinton, WA 98236-0860, (360)341-3020
Heritage Inst. of Ellis Island - Address unknown since 2007.
Heritage Inst; Folk [10772]
Heritage Preservation Assn. [20721], PO Box 356, Mansfield, GA 30055, (404)435-5184
Heritage Preservation Soc; Czech [10022]
Heritage of Pride [12233], 154 Christopher St., Ste. 1D, New York, NY 10014, (212)807-7433
Heritage Railway Assn. [IO], Potters Bar, United Kingdom
Heritage Rsrc. Bank [★17631]
Heritage Rose Found. [22516], PO Box 831414, Richardson, TX 75083
Heritage Roses Gp. [22517], c/o Beverly Dobson, Sec., 916 Union St., No. 302, Alameda, CA 94501
Heritage Soc. of Am; Orphan Train [21140]
Heritage Soc; American/Schleswig-Holstein [19066]
Heritage Soc; Cornish Amer. [9759]
Heritage Soc; Jacques Timothe Boucher Sieur de Montbrun [20741]
Heritage Soc; Rural Cultural [★19387]
Heritage Trail Found; Lincoln [23943]
Heritage Trails Fund [23940]
Heritage Trust; Big Thicket Natural [4368]
Heritage U.S.A; Scottish [19356]
Hermanas de San Jose del Sagrado Corazon [★IO]
Hermandad [IO], Long Beach, NY, United States
Hermandad [17046], 430 Shore Rd., Apt. 6D, Long Beach, NY 11561, (516)431-6602
Hermania: The Herman's Hermits Fan Club - Address unknown since 1991.
Hermanitas Project [★17548]
Hermann in Texas; Grand Lodge Order of the Sons of [19125]
Hermanos - Defunct.
Hermanos; Nuestros Pequenos [★20380]
Hermansky-Pudlak Syndrome Network [14453], 1 South Rd., Oyster Bay, NY 11771-1905, (516)922-3440
Hermansky-Pudlak Syndrome Network [IO], Oyster Bay, NY, United States
Hermetic Rebuilders Assn; Independent [★1887]
Hermitage Assn; Ladies' [11133]
Hernia Res., Advocacy and Support; CHERUBS - Assn. of Congenital Diaphragmatic [13753]
Hernia Soc; Amer. [16566]
Herniologists; Amer. Osteopathic Soc. of [★15814]
Herniologists; Central States Osteopathic [★15814]
HERO [★13568]
Hero Fund Commn; Carnegie [13036]
Heroes of '76 [19236], c/o Natl. Sojourners, Inc., 8301 E Boulevard Dr., Alexandria, VA 22308-1399, (703)765-5000
Herpes Network - Defunct.
Herpes Rsrc. Center - Amer. Social Hea. Assn. [16412], PO Box 13827, Research Triangle Park, NC 27709, (919)361-8400
Herpes Viruses Assn. [IO], London, United Kingdom
Herpetological Assn. of Africa [IO], Cape Town, Republic of South Africa
Herpetological Soc; Ohio [★7160]
Herpetologists' League [7159], c/o Dr. Lora Smith, Treas., Joseph W. Jones Ecological, Research Center, Rte. 2, Box 2324, Newton, GA 39870, (229)734-4706
Herpetology
  Amer. Soc. of Ichthyologists and Herpetologists [7158]
  British Herpetological Soc. [IO]
  Desert Tortoise Coun. [5309]
  European Herpetological Soc. [IO]
  Global Gecko Assn. [5169]
  Herpetological Assn. of Africa [IO]
  Herpetologists' League [7159]
  Soc. for Northwestern Vertebrate Biology [7364]
  Soc. for the Stud. of Amphibians and Reptiles [7160]

Stockholm Herpetological Soc. [IO]
TortoiseAid Intl. [5385]
HERS Found. [★15601]
HERS Found. [★IO]
Herstigte Nasionale Party van Suid Afrika [★IO]
Hertfordshire Chamber of Commerce and Indus. [IO], Hatfield, United Kingdom
Hesperian Found. [IO], Berkeley, CA, United States
Hesperian Found. [14980], 1919 Addison St., Ste. 304, Berkeley, CA 94704, (510)845-1447
Het Nederlandse Rodekruis [★IO]
Heterocera Sumatrana Soc. [IO], Gottingen, Germany
Heteroplasia Assn; Progressive Osseous [14477]
Hetrick-Martin Inst. [12234], 740 Broadway, 8th Fl., New York, NY 10003, (212)674-2400
Hewlett Found; William and Flora [13194]
Hewlett-Packard Computing Professionals; The Intl. Assn. of [★6795]
Hexum Fan Club; Jon-Erik [24749]
H.G. Wells Soc. [IO], London, United Kingdom
H.H. Franklin Club [21656], Cazenovia Coll., Cazenovia, NY 13035
HHT Found. Intl. [14454], PO Box 329, Monkton, MD 21111, (410)357-9932
HHT Found. Intl. [IO], Monkton, MD, United States
Hi-Ethics - Hea. Internet Ethics [14676]
HIAS [★12471]
HIAS [★IO]
HIAS Ser; United [★12471]
Hiawatha Baptist Mission [★19486]
Hibel Soc; Edna [10503]
Hibernians in Am; Ancient Order of [19152]
Hibiscus Soc; Amer. [22491]
Hickory Handle Assn. - Defunct.
Hid Islenska Bokmenntafelag [★IO]
HIDA Educational Foundation [★1860]
Hidden Child Foundation [★17715]
Hide Assn; Natl. [★2421]
Hide, Skin and Leather Assn; U.S. [2421]
Hide, Skin and Leather Merchants; Amer. Assn. of [★2421]
Hiep Hoi Doanh Nghiep Phan Mem Viet Nam [★IO]
Hieronymus - Address unknown since 2001.
Higdon Family Assn. [20940], c/o Charles P. Higdon, Treas., 112 Blossom Ln., Clinton, TN 37716
High Blood Pressure
  Intl. Pediatric Hypertension Assn. [14907]
  Natl. Hypertension Assn. [14910]
High Coun. for Private Enterprise [IO], Managua, Nicaragua
High Fidelity; Inst. of [★1212]
High Flight - Address unknown since 1999.
High Frontier [6374], 500 N Washington St., Alexandria, VA 22314-2314, (703)535-8774
High Frontier Org. [18686], 500 N Washington St., Alexandria, VA 22314-2314, (703)535-8774
High Plains Genealogical Soc. - Defunct.
High School Associations; Natl. Fed. of State [23841]
High School Athletic Associations; Natl. Fed. of State [★23841]
High School Athletic Coaches Assn; Natl. [23292]
High School Band and Choral Directors Hall of Fame; Natl. [★8926]
High School Band Directors Hall of Fame; Natl. [8926]
High School Band Inst; Natl. [★8926]
High School Evangelism Fellowship [★20013]
High School Evangelism Fellowship [20013], 1 Maple St., Allendale, NJ 07401, (888)281-4887
High School Geography Project - Defunct.
High School Journalism; Natl. Assn. of Supervisors and Teachers of [★8713]
High School and Junior Coll. Mathematics Club; Natl. [★24538]
High School Rodeo Assn; Natl. [23690]
High School Student Information Center - Address unknown since 1995.
High School Young Christian Students - Address unknown since 2001.
High Schools and Inst; Amer. Assn. of Tech. [★9228]
High/Scope Educational Res. Found. [8181], 600 N River St., Ypsilanti, MI 48198, (734)485-2000

A star before a book entry number signifies that the name is not listed separately, but is mentioned within the entry.

High Speed Ground Trans. Assn. [7810], 1666 K St. NW, Ste. 1100, Washington, DC 20006-1215, (202)261-6020
High Speed Rail/Magnetic Levitation Assn. - Defunct.
High Standard Collectors' Assn. [22428], PO Box 1578, Decatur, IL 62525
High Tech Distribution; Assn. for [★1205]
High Tech Distributors; Assn. of [★1205]
High Tech. Consortium - Defunct.
High Tech. Crime Investigation Assn. [★5880]
High Tech. Crime Investigation Assn. [★IO]
High Tech. Crime Investigation Assn. Intl. [IO], Roseville, CA, United States
High Tech. Crime Investigation Assn. Intl. [5880], c/o Carol Hutchings, Exec. Sec., 4021 Woodcreek Oaks Blvd., Ste. 156, PMB 209, Roseville, CA 95747, (916)408-1751
High Tech. Distribution; Assn. for [1205]
High Technology Professionals for Peace - Defunct.
High Twelve Intl. [19237], 2029 Washington Ave., Ste. 105, Evansville, IN 47714, (812)422-9770
High Twelve Intl. [IO], Evansville, IN, United States
Highamerica Balloon Club [23099]

Higher Education
Acad. of Security Educators and Trainers [9119]
ACE Fellows Prog. [7881]
ACUO [8341]
ACUTA: The Assn. for Communications Tech. Professionals in Higher Educ. [8548]
Adult Higher Educ. Alliance [7915]
ALI-ABA Comm. on Continuing Professional Educ. [8758]
Alliance for Higher Educ. [8477]
Amer. Acad. of Advt. [7919]
Amer. Assn. of Colleges for Teacher Educ. [9208]
Amer. Assn. for Collegiate Independent Stud. [7944]
Amer. Assn. of Collegiate Registrars and Admissions Officers [7910]
Amer. Assn. of Community Colleges [8117]
Amer. Assn. for Employment in Educ. [8994]
Amer. Assn. for Higher Educ. [8478]
Amer. Assn. of Univ. Women [9311]
Amer. Assn. of Univ. Women Educational Found. [9312]
Amer. Coll. and Career Counseling Center [7911]
Amer. Debate Assn. [9151]
Amer. Educ. Finance Assn. [8342]
Amer. Forensic Assn. [9152]
Amer. Indian Higher Educ. Consortium [8935]
Amer. Soc. for Engg. Educ. [8366]
Amer. Soc. for Technion-Israel Inst. of Tech. [8677]
Amer. TeleEdCommunications Alliance [7766]
Asia Pacific Higher Educ. Res. Network [IO]
Assoc. Colleges of the Midwest [8097]
Assn. of Advanced Rabbinical and Talmudic Schools [8683]
Assn. for the Advancement of Sustainability in Higher Educ. [8479]
Assn. for the Advancement of Sustainability in Higher Educ. [IO]
Assn. of African Stud. Programs [7928]
Assn. of Amer. Colleges and Universities [8098]
Assn. of Amer. Intl. Colleges and Universities [8641]
Assn. of Amer. Veterinary Medical Colleges [9293]
Assn. of Coll. and Univ. Auditors [7888]
Assn. of Collegiate Schools of Architecture [7959]
Assn. of Collegiate Schools of Planning [9285]
Assn. of Community Coll. Trustees [8118]
Assn. for Consortium Leadership [8480]
Assn. for Continuing Higher Educ. [8148]
Assn. for Gerontology in Higher Educ. [8462]
Assn. of Graduate Liberal Stud. Programs [8778]
Assn. of Graduate Schools in Assn. of Amer. Universities [7890]
Assn. for Higher Educ. and Development [IO]
Assn. on Higher Educ. and Disability [8201]
Assn. for Lib. and Info. Sci. Educ. [8782]
Assn. for Media-Based Continuing Educ. for Engineers [8367]
Assn. for Non-Traditional Students in Higher Educ. [7916]
Assn. of NROTC Colleges and Universities [8884]

Assn. of Nutrition Departments and Programs [8947]
Assn. of Presbyterian Colleges and Universities [9005]
Assn. of Southeast Asian Institutions of Higher Learning [IO]
Assn. for the Stud. of Free Institutions [8481]
Assn. for the Stud. of Higher Educ. [8482]
Assn. for Tertiary Educ. Mgt. [IO]
Assn. for Theatre in Higher Educ. [9262]
Assn. of Univ. Leaders for a Sustainable Future [8483]
Assn. of Univ. Leaders for a Sustainable Future [IO]
Assn. of Univ. Res. Parks [9054]
Assn. of Univ. Summer Sessions [9199]
Australian Coun. for Private Educ. and Training [IO]
Australian Higher Educ. Indus. Assn. [IO]
Australian and New Zealand Stud. Assn. of North Amer. [IO]
Australian and New Zealand Stud. Assn. of North Amer. [8484]
British Universities North Am. Club [8606]
Business-Higher Educ. Forum [8008]
Bus. Professionals of Am. [9302]
Campus Safety, Hea. and Environmental Mgt. Assn. [4300]
Canadian Assn. for Graduate Stud. [IO]
Canadian Soc. for the Stud. of Higher Educ. [IO]
Career Coll. Assn. [9303]
Catching the Dream [8427]
Center for Advancement of Racial and Ethnic Equity [8887]
Chinese-Amer. Educational Found. [8428]
The Coll. Bd. [9248]
Coll. Consortium for Intl. Stud. [8103]
Coll. English Assn. [8375]
Coll. Parents of Am. [8485]
Coll. Summit [8486]
Coll. and Univ. Professional Assn. for Human Resources [8962]
Community Coll. Baccalaureate Assn. [8119]
Community Colleges for Intl. Development [8607]
Comparative and Intl. Educ. Soc. [8655]
Compete Am. [8365]
Confed. of European Union Rectors' Conferences [IO]
Consortium of Coll. and Univ. Media Centers [8554]
Consortium on Financing Higher Educ. [9057]
Consortium for North Amer. Higher Educ. Collaboration [8487]
Consortium for North Amer. Higher Educ. Collaboration [IO]
Coun. for Adult and Experiential Learning [8412]
Coun. for the Advancement of Standards in Higher Educ. [9177]
Coun. for Christian Colleges and Universities [8084]
Coun. of Christian Scholarly Societies [8085]
Coun. for European Stud. [8404]
Coun. of Graduate Schools [8488]
Coun. for Rsrc. Development [8347]
Coun. on Undergraduate Res. [9059]
Educ. Pioneers [9178]
European Assn. for Higher Educ. in Biotechnology [IO]
European Centre for Higher Educ. [IO]
Found. ICPR Junior Coll. [8022]
Found. for Independent Higher Educ. [8537]
Friends Assn. for Higher Educ. [8451]
Graduate Mgt. Admission Coun. [8807]
Graduate Record Examinations Bd. [9251]
Great Lakes Colleges Assn. [8106]
Higher Educ. Consortium for Urban Affairs [9286]
Higher Educ. Funding Coun. for England [IO]
Higher Educ. Info. Tech. Alliance [8489]
Higher Educ. Res. and Development Soc. of Australasia [IO]
Higher Educ. South Africa [IO]
Higher Educ. and Training Awards Coun. [IO]
IES, Inst. for the Intl. Educ. of Students [8405]
Inst. for Amer. Universities [8643]
Inter-American Org. for Higher Educ. [IO]

Intl. Coalition of Lib. Consortia [8784]
Intl. Coun. of Fine Arts Deans [7973]
Intl. Soc. for Educational Planning [8999]
Intl. Soc. for the Scholarship of Teaching and Learning [9073]
Intl. Univ. Consortium [8566]
Ithaka [7200]
Jesuit Assn. of Student Personnel Administrators [7896]
Joint Rev. Comm. on Educ. in Diagnostic Medical Sonography [8837]
LASPAU: Academic and Professional Programs for the Americas [8108]
Latin Amer. Inst. for Advanced Stud. [IO]
League for Innovation in the Community Coll. [8120]
Lutheran Educational Conf. of North Am. [8804]
Metro Intl. Prog. Services of New York [8624]
Natl. Academic Advising Assn. [8170]
Natl. Acad. of Educ. [8280]
Natl. Assn. of Baptist Professors of Religion [9277]
Natl. Assn. for Campus Activities [9169]
Natl. Assn. for Chicana and Chicano Stud. [8498]
Natl. Assn. of Colleges and Employers [8995]
Natl. Assn. of Community Coll. Teacher Educ. Programs [9221]
Natl. Assn. of Fellowships Advisors [9080]
Natl. Assn. of Geoscience Teachers [8459]
Natl. Assn. of Independent Colleges and Universities [8539]
Natl. Assn. for Kinesiology and Physical Educ. in Higher Educ. [8984]
Natl. Assn. of Multicultural Engg. Prog. Advocates [8370]
Natl. Assn. for Professional Development Schools [9091]
Natl. Assn. of Scholars [8490]
Natl. Assn. of Schools of Theatre [9265]
Natl. Assn. of State Universities and Land-Grant Colleges [8110]
Natl. Assn. of Student Personnel Administrators [7904]
Natl. Assn. of Substance Abuse Trainers and Educators [9198]
Natl. Assn. of Univ. Women [9320]
Natl. Assn. of Veterans Prog. Administrators [9292]
Natl. Center for Higher Educ. Mgt. Systems [7905]
Natl. CH for Commuter Programs [9187]
Natl. Coalition of Independent Scholars [8491]
Natl. Collegiate Inventors and Innovators Alliance [7218]
Natl. Conf. on Student Leadership [9188]
Natl. Consortium of Arts and Letters for Historically Black Colls. and Universities [8111]
Natl. Coun. for Continuing Educ. and Training [8152]
Natl. Coun. for Res. and Planning [8121]
Natl. Coun. of State Directors of Community Colleges [8122]
Natl. Coun. on Student Development [9170]
Natl. Hispanic Bus. Assn. [8039]
Natl. Parliamentary Debate Assn. [9160]
Natl. Reading Conf. [9044]
Natl. Registration Center for Stud. Abroad [8626]
Natl. Rsrc. Center for Paraprofessionals in Educ. and Related Services [9150]
Natl. Soc. of Leadership and Success [9189]
Natl. Student Employment Assn. [8996]
Natl. Tutoring Assn. [9283]
Natl. Writing Proj. [9334]
Netherlands Org. for Intl. Cooperation in Higher Educ. [IO]
North Amer. Assn. of Commencement Officers [8492]
North Amer. Professors of Christian Educ. [8088]
Northamerican Assn. of Masters in Psychology [9030]
Off. of Women in Higher Educ., Amer. Coun. on Educ. [9324]
O'Neill Natl. Theater Inst. [9266]
Pathways to Coll. Network [8493]
Peer Hea. Exchange [9338]

Reference to "IO" in place of a book number signifies that the association may be found in the 45th edition of International Organizations.

PEO Intl. [9325]
Philosophy of Educ. Soc. [8969]
Photo Imaging Educ. Assn. [8974]
Postsecondary Electronic Standards Coun. [9165]
Professional and Organizational Development Network in Higher Educ. [8494]
Professional and Organizational Development Network in Higher Education [IO]
Public Leadership Educ. Network [9326]
Sallie Mae Fund [8434]
Scottish Further and Higher Educ. Funding Coun. [IO]
Second Nature [8495]
Senior Scholars [8153]
Soc. of Building Sci. Educators [8363]
Soc. for Coll. and Univ. Planning [9000]
Soc. for Philosophy of Religion [8970]
Soc. for Res. into Higher Educ. [8970]
State Higher Educ. Executive Officers [9001]
Students for the Exploration and Development of Space [7923]
Teachers of English to Speakers of Other Languages [8382]
Tech. Mgt. Educ. Assn. [9245]
Tel Aviv Univ.: Amer. Coun. [8679]
U.S. Student Assn. [9195]
Univ. and Coll. Designers Assn. [8572]
Univ. Continuing Educ. Assn. [8154]
Univ. Professors for Academic Order [9026]
University/Resident Theatre Assn. [9269]
Women Educators [9328]
Women's Coll. Coalition [9330]
World Cong. of Teachers of Dancing [8192]
Worldwide Univ. Consortium [8114]
Higher Educ; ACUTA: The Assn. for Communications Tech. Professionals in [8548]
Higher Educ. Admin; Natl. Identification Prog. for the Advancement in [★9324]
Higher Education Administration Referral Service - Defunct.
Higher Educ; Amer. Assn. for [8478]
Higher Educ. Assistance Organizations; Coalition of [8344]
Higher Educ; Assn. for [★8478]
Higher Educ; Assn. of Black Women in [9314]
Higher Educ; Assn. for Continuing [8148]
Higher Educ; Assn. for Gerontology in [8462]
Higher Educ., Christian Church-Disciples of Christ; Division of [19854]
Higher Education; Commission on [★8277]
Higher Educ; Consortium for the Advancement of Private [8105]
Higher Educ. Consortium; Amer. Indian [8935]
Higher Educ; Consortium on Financing [9057]
Higher Educ. Consortium for Urban Affairs [9286], 2233 Univ. Ave. W, Ste. 210, Wright Bldg., St. Paul, MN 55114, (651)646-8832
Higher Educ. Consortium for Urban Affairs [IO], St. Paul, MN, United States
Higher Educ. Coun; NEA [★24045]
Higher Educ. Executive Officers; State [9001]
Higher Educ. Facilities Officers; APPA: The Assn. of [8333]
Higher Educ. Forum; Business- [8008]
Higher Educ; Found. for Independent [8537]
Higher Educ; Friends Assn. for [8451]
Higher Educ. Funding Coun. for England [IO], Bristol, United Kingdom
Higher Education and the Handicapped - Defunct.
Higher Educ. Info. Tech. Alliance [8489], c/o Hilary Goldmann, Coor., 1307 New York Ave. NW, 4th Fl., Washington, DC 20036, (202)478-6086
Higher Educ. Loan Programs; Natl. Coun. of [8351]
Higher Educ. Mgt. Systems; Natl. Center for [7905]
Higher Educ. Ministries Team/United Ministries in Higher Educ. [★19938]
Higher Educ; Natl. Assn. for Equal Opportunity in [8109]
Higher Educ; Natl. Assn. for Physical Educ. in [8985]
Higher Educ; Natl. Coun. on Religion in [★19940]
Higher Education Panel - Defunct.
Higher Educ; Professional and Organizational Development Network in [8494]
Higher Educ. and the Professions; Natl. Center for the Stud. of Collective Bargaining in [24036]

Higher Educ. Res. and Development Soc. of Australasia [IO], Milperra, Australia
Higher Educ. Resource Services/New England - Address unknown since 2002.
Higher Educ; Soc. for Religion in [★19940]
Higher Educ; Soc. for Values in [19940]
Higher Educ. South Africa [IO], Pretoria, Republic of South Africa
Higher Educ. and Training Awards Coun. [IO], Dublin, Ireland
Higher Educ; United Ministries in [★19938]
The Higher We Fly John Denver Appreciation Soc. - Address unknown since 2000.
Highland Bentgrass Commn; Oregon [4797]
Highland Cattle Assn; Amer. [4227]
Highland Cattle Soc. [IO], Thornhill, United Kingdom
Highland Railway Soc. [IO], Templecombe, United Kingdom
Highlander Class Intl. Assn. [23174], c/o Bryan Hollingsworth, Exec. Sec.-Treas., 410 Holiday Rd., Lexington, KY 40502
Highpointers Club [23014], c/o Mr. R. Craig Noland, Membership Chm., PO Box 6364, Sevierville, TN 37864-6364
Highway Advertisers; Amer. Coun. of [85]
Highway Assn; Lincoln [10043]
Highway and Auto Safety; Advocates for [12944]
Highway Freight Assn; Amer. [★3863]
Highway Info. Found; Better [★6313]
Highway Loss Data Inst. [2168], 1005 N Glebe Rd., Ste. 700, Arlington, VA 22201, (703)247-1600
Highway Officials; Amer. Assn. of State [★6312]
Highway Post Off. Soc; Natl. [★22848]
Highway Proj; Amer. [10010]
Highway Res. Bd. [★7814]
Highway Res. Program; National Cooperative [★6312]
Highway Safety Association; American Insurance [★12964]
Highway Safety Assn; Governors [6317]
Highway Safety; Insurance Inst. for [12964]
Highway Safety Leaders; Natl. Assn. of Women [12971]
Highway Safety; Natl. Conf. on St. and [★6309]
Highway Safety Representatives; Natl. Assn. of Governors' [★6317]
Highway Sign Assn; Amer. [★85]
Highway Sign Support Assn. - Address unknown since 2002.
Highway and Traffic Technicians Assn. [★IO]
Highway and Trans. Officials; Amer. Assn. of State [6312]
Highway Users Alliance; Amer. [12949]
Highways
AAA Found. for Traffic Safety [12943]
Alfa Romeo Owners Club [21565]
Alliance for a New Trans. Charter [6311]
Amer. Assn. of State Highway and Trans. Officials [6312]
Amer. Highway Proj. [10010]
Amer. Highway Users Alliance [12949]
Amer. Traffic Safety Services Assn. [3438]
Americans for Trans. Mobility [6315]
Asphalt Emulsion Manufacturers Assn. [594]
Asphalt Pavement Alliance [596]
Asphalt Recycling and Reclaiming Assn. [3987]
Assn. for the Advancement of Automotive Medicine [12951]
Assn. of Modified Asphalt Producers [601]
Center for Auto Safety [12956]
Citizens for Reliable and Safe Highways [18577]
Citizens for Roadside Safety [12957]
Governors Highway Safety Assn. [6317]
Highway Loss Data Inst. [2168]
Insurance Inst. for Highway Safety [12964]
Inter-Amer. Safety Coun. [12965]
Intl. Road Fed. [3874]
Intl. Trans. Mgt. Assn. [6319]
Mothers Against Drunk Driving [12969]
Motorist Info. and Services Assn. [13344]
Natl. Assn. of Professional Accident Reconstructionists [6252]
Natl. Assn. of Women Highway Safety Leaders [12971]
Natl. Commn. Against Drunk Driving [12973]

Natl. Motorists Assn. [13340]
Natl. Safety Coun. [12979]
Natl. Transit Benefit Assn. [6324]
Natl. Truckdrivers Safety Assn. [2843]
North America's SuperCorridor Coalition [3887]
Oper. Lifesaver [12983]
Road Emulsion Assn. Limited [IO]
School and Community Safety Soc. of Am. of the Amer. Assn. for Active Lifestyles and Fitness [12989]
Students Against Destructive Decisions, Students Against Drunk Driving [12992]
Traffic Records Comm. [12993]
HIKE Fund [14761], c/o Mrs. Shirley R. Terrill, Bd. Sec., 10115 Cherryhill Pl., Spring Hill, FL 34608-7116, (352)688-2579
Hikers Against Doo Doo [4572], c/o Trionics Intl., Inc., 66 Upper Oak Point Rd., Winterport, ME 04496
Hikers Assn; Natl. Campers and [★23271]
Hiking
Adirondack Forty-Sixers [23930]
Adirondack Mountain Club [23931]
Adirondack Trail Improvement Soc. [23932]
Amer. Canyoneering Assn. [21949]
Amer. Endurance Ride Conf. [23933]
Amer. Hiking Soc. [23934]
Amer. Mountain Guides Assn. [23284]
Amer. Trails [23935]
Appalachian Mountain Club [23936]
Appalachian Trail Conservancy [23937]
Camping Women [23269]
Continental Divide Trail Soc. [23938]
Florida Trail Assn. [23939]
Hawk Mountain Sanctuary [5324]
Intercollegiate Outing Club Assn. [23941]
IOCALUM [23942]
Light Living Library [23272]
Lincoln Heritage Trail Found. [23943]
Montana Outfitters and Guides Assn. [23944]
Mountaineers [23945]
New England Trails Conf. [23948]
North Amer. Trail Ride Conf. [23949]
North Country Trail Assn. [23950]
Quetzaltrekkers Guatemala [IO]
Quetzaltrekkers - Nicaragua [IO]
Rails-to-Trails Conservancy [23952]
U.S. Orienteering Fed. [23641]
U.S. Ski Mountaineering Assn. [23759]
Hiking Fed. of Southern Africa [★IO]
Hiking Soc; Amer. [23934]
Hiking South Africa [IO], Centurion, Republic of South Africa
Hilfswerk der Evangelischen Kirchen Schweiz [IO], Zurich, Switzerland
Hillbilly Hits Fan Club [★24908]
Hillel: The Found. for Jewish Campus Life [20142], c/o Charles and Lynn Schusterman Intl. Center, Arthur and Rochelle Belfer Bldg., 800 8th St. NW, Washington, DC 20001-3724, (202)449-6500
Hilton Found; Conrad N. [13163]
HIMAL Assn. [IO], Lalitpur, Nepal
Himalayan Inst. Teachers Association [★IO]
Himalayan Inst. Teachers Association [★12348]
Himalayan Intl. Inst. of Yoga Sci. and Philosophy of the U.S.A. [12348], 952 Bethany Tpke., Honesdale, PA 18431-4194, (570)253-5551
Himalayan Intl. Inst. of Yoga Sci. and Philosophy of the U.S.A. [IO], Honesdale, PA, United States
Himalayan Rabbit Assn; Amer. [5137]
Hinckley Pilot 35 Assn. - Address unknown since 2001.
Hindenberg Soc. - Defunct.
Hinduism
Amer. Hindu Assn. [20077]
Ananda Marga Pracarka Samgha - Berlin Sector [IO]
Brahman Samaj of North Am. [IO]
Brahman Samaj of North Am. [9998]
Soc. for Hindu-Christian Stud. [20528]
Hindustan Bible Inst. [19927], HBI Ministries Intl., PO Box 584, Forest, VA 24551, (434)525-5847
Hineni [10281], 232 W End Ave., New York, NY 10023, (212)496-1660
Hineni [IO], New York, NY, United States

A star before a book entry number signifies that the name is not listed separately, but is mentioned within the entry.

Hineni World Heritage Center [★IO]
Hineni World Heritage Center [★10281]
Hinman Family Assn. [20941], c/o Joan Hinman, Sec.-Treas., 46 Main St., Stamford, NY 12167
Hip-Hop Assn. [10887], PO Box 1181, New York, NY 10035, (212)500-5970
Hip and Knee Surgeons; Amer. Assn. of [16559]
Hip Soc. [15769], c/o Karen V. Andersen, Exec. Dir., 951 Old County Rd., No. 182, Belmont, CA 94002, (650)525-1074
Hippotherapy Assn; Amer. [16600]
Hire Assn. Europe [IO], Birmingham, United Kingdom
Hire Indus. Assn. of New Zealand [IO], Auckland, New Zealand
Hirkozlesi es Informatikai Tudomanyos Egyesulet [★IO]
Hirkozlesi es Informatikai Tudomanyos Egyesulet [★IO]

Hiroshima
   Nevada Desert Experience [18161]
Hiroshima and Nagasaki; Comm. for U.S. Veterans of [★13353]
Hiroshima Peace Center Associates - Defunct.
The Hirschfeld Centre [★17773]
The Hirschfeld Centre [★IO]
Hirschsprung's Disease Soc; Amer. Pseudo-Obstruction and [★14419]
Hispanas Organized for Political Equality [17703], 634 S Spring St., Ste. 920, Los Angeles, CA 90014, (213)622-0606

Hispanic
   African Asian Latina Lesbians United [17649]
   Alpha Psi Lambda Natl. [24615]
   Alpha Rho Lambda Sorority [24703]
   Amer. GI Forum of U.S. [21280]
   ASPIRA Assn. [8231]
   Assn. for the Advancement of Mexican Americans [11763]
   Assn. of Hispanic Arts [9999]
   Assn. of Hispanic Arts [IO]
   Assn. of Latina and Latino Anthropologists [6410]
   Bilingual Found. of the Arts [11007]
   Center for U.S.-Mexican Stud. [17700]
   Center for U.S.-Mexican Stud. [IO]
   Chicano Family Center [IO]
   Chicano Family Center [17701]
   Congressional Hispanic Caucus [17702]
   Coun. on Career for Minorities [8047]
   Delta Tau Lambda Sorority [24707]
   DIVAS of Lambda Fe Uson Sorority [24709]
   En Foco [10849]
   Farm Labor Organizing Comm. [23997]
   Fed. Hispanic Law Enforcement Officers Assn. [5969]
   Feministas Unidas [10000]
   Gamma Alpha Omega Sorority [24599]
   Grand Coun. of Hispanic Societies in Public Ser. [12275]
   Hispanas Organized for Political Equality [17703]
   Hispanic Amer. Police Command Officers Assn. [5970]
   Hispanic Amer. Veterans Assn. [21301]
   Hispanic Coun. on Intl. Relations [17869]
   Hispanic Coun. for Reform and Educational Options [8260]
   Hispanic Dental Assn. [14155]
   Hispanic Elected Local Officials [6122]
   Hispanic Marketing and Commun. Assn. [2628]
   Hispanic Natl. Bar Assn. [5496]
   Hispanic Neuropsychological Soc. [15388]
   Hispanic Org. of Latin Actors [10001]
   Hispanic Policy Development Proj. [17704]
   Hispanic Policy Development Project [IO]
   Hispanic Professional Women's Assn. [4041]
   Hispanic Public Relations Assn. [17180]
   Hispanic Scholarship Fund [8431]
   Hispanic Soc. of Am. [10002]
   Hispanic Soc. of Am. [IO]
   Hispanic Women's Corp. [10003]
   INROADS [8749]
   Instituto Nacional Hispano de Liturgia [19640]
   Intl. Assn. of Hispanic Meeting Professionals [2684]
   Intl. Assn. of Hispanists [IO]

Intl. Latino Gang Investigator's Assn. [5884]
Intl. Manuel Ponce Soc. [10621]
Labor Coun. for Latin Amer. Advancement [24094]
Latin Amer. Art Song Alliance [10636]
Latin Amer. Educational Found. [8496]
Latin Amer. Venture Capital Assn. [1431]
Latino Issues Forum [19098]
Latino Org. for Liver Awareness [14811]
Latinos in Info. Sciences and Tech. Assn. [7201]
Lawyers for One Am. [6028]
Leadership Enterprise for a Diverse Am. [9183]
League of United Latin Amer. Citizens [19099]
LULAC Natl. Educational Ser. Centers [8275]
Mgt. Educ. Alliance [8029]
Mexican Amer. Cultural Center [20286]
Mexican Amer. Legal Defense and Educational Fund [17705]
Mexican American Legal Defense and Educational Fund [IO]
Mexican Amer. Music Assn. [10647]
Mexican-American Opportunity Found. [12276]
Mexican Amer. Unity Coun. [12277]
Minority Student Achievement Network [8401]
Mujeres Activas en Letras Y Cambio Social [8497]
Natl. Alliance for Hispanic Hea. [13176]
Natl. Assn. for Chicana and Chicano Stud. [8498]
Natl. Assn. for Hispanic Elderly [19100]
Natl. Assn. of Hispanic Journalists [3130]
Natl. Assn. of Hispanic and Latino Stud. [9920]
Natl. Assn. of Hispanic Nurses [15494]
Natl. Assn. of Hispanic Priests of the USA [19665]
Natl. Assn. of Latina Leaders [2411]
Natl. Assn. of Latino Arts and Culture [9584]
Natl. Assn. of Latino Elected and Appointed Officials [17706]
Natl. Assn. of Latino Fraternal Organizations [19059]
Natl. Assn. of Latino Independent Producers [1390]
Natl. Assn. of PreCollege Directors [8371]
Natl. Assn. of Puerto Rican Hispanic Social Workers [13205]
Natl. Center for Neurogenic Commun. Disorders [16449]
Natl. Community for Latino Leadership [19203]
Natl. Coun. of La Raza [12278]
National Council of La Raza [IO]
Natl. Fed. of Hispanic Owned Newspapers [3240]
Natl. Hispana Leadership Inst. [17707]
Natl. Hispanic Bus. Assn. [8039]
Natl. Hispanic Coun. on Aging [11310]
Natl. Hispanic Employee Assn. [12279]
Natl. Hispanic Found. for the Arts [19101]
Natl. Hispanic Inst. [10004]
Natl. Hispanic Leadership Agenda [17708]
Natl. Hispanic Medical Assn. [14820]
Natl. Image [19102]
Natl. Latina Hea. Network [14589]
Natl. Latino Alliance for the Elimination of Domestic Violence [12037]
Natl. Latino Behavioral Hea. Assn. [15227]
Natl. Latino Coun. on Alcohol and Tobacco Prevention [12269]
Natl. Latino Officers Assn. [5921]
Natl. Org. for Mexican Amer. Rights [17709]
Natl. Puerto Rican Forum [12280]
Natl. Soc. of Hispanic MBAs [754]
Natl. Soc. of Hispanic Physicists [7505]
Natl. Soc. for Hispanic Professionals [1908]
New Am. Alliance [1169]
Puerto Rican Family Inst. [12281]
Quality Educ. for Minorities Network [8303]
Rainbow/PUSH Coalition [13185]
Secretariat for Hispanic Affairs, U.S. Conf. of Catholic Bishops [12282]
SER - Jobs for Progress Natl. [12100]
Sigma Lambda Alpha Sorority [24714]
Sociedad Honoraria Hispanica [8499]
Soc. of Hispanic Professional Engineers [7042]
Southwest Voter Registration Educ. Proj. [18367]
Spanish Colonial Arts Soc. [10005]
Sphinx Org. [10710]
U.S. Hispanic Chamber of Commerce [24327]
UNITY: Journalists of Color [3172]

Hispanic Advt. Agencies; Assn. of [89]
Hispanic Affairs/National Conf. of Catholic Bishops; Secretariat for [★12282]
Hispanic Amer. Geriatrics Soc. - Defunct.
Hispanic-Amer. Inst. - Defunct.
Hispanic Amer. Ministries Task Force of JSAC - Defunct.
Hispanic Amer. Police Command Officers Assn. [5970], 6450 NW Loop 410, PMB 1546, San Antonio, TX 78238-1986, (210)431-7349
Hispanic Amer. Veterans Assn. [21301]
Hispanic Assembly of the U.S; Republican Natl. [18535]
Hispanic Assn. of Colleges and Universities [8107], 8415 Datapoint Dr., Ste. 400, San Antonio, TX 78229, (210)692-3805
Hispanic Assn. on Corporate Responsibility [17352], 1444 I St. NW, Ste. 850, Washington, DC 20005, (202)835-9672
Hispanic Coalition for Economic Recovery - Defunct.
Hispanic Coalition for Free America - Defunct.
Hispanic Computing Assn. - Address unknown since 1995.
Hispanic Corporate Coun; Natl. [750]
Hispanic Coun. on Aging; Natl. [11310]
Hispanic Coun. on Intl. Relations [17869]
Hispanic Coun. on Intl. Relations [IO], Washington, DC, United States
Hispanic Coun. for Reform and Educational Options [8260], 2600 Virginia Ave. NW, Ste. 408, Washington, DC 20037, (202)625-6766
Hispanic CPAs; Amer. Assn. of [★16]
Hispanic Dental Assn. [14155], 3085 Stevenson Dr., Ste. 200, Springfield, IL 62703, (217)529-6517
Hispanic Designers - Address unknown since 2006.
Hispanic Educ. Found. [★21280]
Hispanic Elected Local Officials [6122], c/o Natl. League of Cities, 1301 Pennsylvania Ave. NW, Ste. 550, Washington, DC 20004, (202)626-3000
Hispanic Energy Forum - Defunct.
Hispanic Fed. Executives; Natl. Assn. of [5711]
Hispanic Fed. Executives; Assn. of [★5711]
Hispanic Firefighters; Natl. Assn. of [5721]
Hispanic Found. - Address unknown since 1987.
Hispanic Genealogical Soc. [9973], PO Box 231271, Houston, TX 77223-1271
Hispanic Genealogical Soc; Puerto Rican [9975]
Hispanic Hea. and Human Services Organizations; Natl. Coalition of [★13176]
Hispanic Hea; Natl. Alliance for [13176]
Hispanic Higher Education Coalition - Defunct.
Hispanic Inst. for the Performing Arts - Defunct.
Hispanic Inst. in the U.S. [★10004]
Hispanic Journalists; Natl. Assn. of [3130]
Hispanic and Latino Stud; Natl. Assn. of [9920]
Hispanic Marketing and Commun. Assn. [2628], PO Box 565891, Miami, FL 33256-5891, (305)648-2848
Hispanic Marketing and Commun. Assn. [IO], Miami, FL, United States
Hispanic MBAs; Natl. Soc. of [754]
Hispanic Media Coalition; Natl. [17187]
Hispanic Natl. Bar Assn. [5496], 1101 Connecticut Ave. NW, Ste. 1000, Washington, DC 20036, (202)223-4777
Hispanic Neuropsychological Soc. [15388], c/o Leo Shea, PhD, Treas., 151 E 31st St., No. 22C, New York, NY 10016
Hispanic Nurses; Natl. Assn. of [15494]
Hispanic Operators Assn; McDonald's [3395]
Hispanic Org. of Latin Actors [10001], 107 Suffolk St., Ste. 302, New York, NY 10002, (212)253-1015
Hispanic Org. of Latin Actors [★10001]
Hispanic Org. of Professionals and Executives - Defunct.
Hispanic Owned Newspapers; Natl. Fed. of [3240]
Hispanic Police; Assn. of Retired [6171]
Hispanic Policy Development Proj. [17704], 122 E 42nd St., 42nd Fl., New York, NY 10168, (646)723-0750
Hispanic Policy Development Project [IO], New York, NY, United States
Hispanic Professional Engineers; Soc. of [7042]
Hispanic Professional Women's Assn. [4041], 700 12th St., Ste. 700, Washington, DC 20005, (202)250-0887

Reference to "IO" in place of a book number signifies that the association may be found in the 45th edition of International Organizations.

Hispanic Public Relations Assn. [17180], PO Box 86760, Los Angeles, CA 90086-0760, (310)473-2031
Hispanic Publications; Natl. Assn. of [3237]
Hispanic Publications; Natl. Fed. of [★3240]
Hispanic Res. Center - Defunct.
Hispanic Scholarship Fund [8431], 55 2nd St., Ste. 1500, San Francisco, CA 94105, (877)473-4636
Hispanic-Serving Hea. Professions Schools [8864], 1120 Connecticut Ave. NW, Ste. 261, Washington, DC 20036, (202)293-2701
Hispanic-Serving Hea. Professions Schools; Natl. Assn. of [★8864]
Hispanic Social Workers; Natl. Assn. of Puerto Rican [13205]
Hispanic Soc. of Am. [10002], 613 W 155th St., New York, NY 10032, (212)926-2234
Hispanic Soc. of Am. [IO], New York, NY, United States
Hispanic Women's Corp. [10003], 4545 N 36th St., Ste. 108, Phoenix, AZ 85018-3473, (602)954-7995
Hispanics; National Commn. on Secondary Schooling for [★17704]
Hispanics; National Commn. on Secondary Schooling for [★IO]
Hispano de Liturgia; Instituto Nacional [19640]
Hispano-Suiza Soc. - Address unknown since 1994.
Hispanos; Instituto Nacional de Liturgia Para [★19640]
Histadrut Campaign; Israel [★12460]
Histadrut Development Found; Amer. [★12458]
Histadruth Ivrith of America - Defunct.
Histamine Res. Soc. of North America - Address unknown since 1994.
Histiocytosis Assn. of Am. [14790], 332 N Broadway, Pitman, NJ 08071, (856)589-6606
Histiocytosis-X Assn. of Am. [★14790]
Histochemical Soc. [13938], PO Box 85630, Univ. Sta., Seattle, WA 98145-1630, (206)616-5278
Histocompatibility and Immunogenetics; Amer. Soc. for [14931]
Historians Against the War [18795], PO Box 442154, Somerville, MA 02144
Historians of Amer. Communism [8506], c/o Daniel Leab, Gen. Sec., PO Box 1216, Washington, CT 06793, (860)868-7408
Historians Anonymous - Defunct.
Historians of British Art [9478], c/o Anne Helmreich, 10900 Euclid Ave., Cleveland, OH 44106
Historians; Company of Military [22629]
Historians; Company of Military Collectors and [★22629]
Historians of the Early Amer. Republic; Soc. for [10157]
Historians of Eighteenth-Century Art and Architecture [9479], 2507 Foxwood Dr., Chapel Hill, NC 27514
Historians Film Comm. [★9939]
Historians Film Committee/Film and History Magazine [9939], c/o Peter C. Rollins, Ed.-in-Chief, Popular Culture Center, RR 3, Box 80, Cleveland, OK 74020-0515, (918)243-7637
Historians of German and Central European Art and Architecture [9921], c/o Rose-Carol Washton Long, Treas., Prog. in Art History, CUNY Graduate Center, 365 Fifth Ave., New York, NY 10016-4309
Historians of German and Central European Art and Architecture [IO], New York, NY, United States
Historians; Intl. Assn. of Paper [IO]
Historians Org; Mid-Atlantic Radical [★10129]
Historians; Soc. of Ancient Military [10481]
Historians; Soc. of Automotive [21785]
Historians; Soc. of Freight Car [10922]
Historic Amer. Theatres; League of [11021]
Historic and Artistic Works—American Gp; Intl. Inst. for Conservation of [10011]
Historic Art's Arthur Szyk Soc. [★9497]
Historic Brass Soc. [10608], 148 W 23rd St., No. 5F, New York, NY 10011, (212)627-3820
Historic Commands of the Amer. Revolution - Address unknown since 1990.
Historic Commercial Vehicle Soc. [IO], Tonbridge, United Kingdom
Historic Communal Societies Assn; Natl. [★10020]
Historic Deerfield [10034], PO Box 321, Deerfield, MA 01342, (413)774-5581

Historic Genealogical Soc; New England [21136]
Historic Hawaii Found. [5785], 680 Iwilei Rd., Ste. No. 690, Honolulu, HI 96817, (808)523-2900
Historic House Assn. of Am. [★10051]
Historic Houses Assn. [IO], London, United Kingdom
Historic Huguenot St. [★21161]
Historic Military Commands; Centennial Legion of [21240]
Historic Monument Soc; Amer. [★2785]
Historic Motor Sports Assn. [21657], 2029 Verdugo Blvd., No. 1010, Montrose, CA 91020, (818)249-3515
Historic Naval Ships Assn. [10440], PO Box 401, Smithfield, VA 23431-0401, (757)356-9422
Historic Naval Ships Association [IO], Smithfield, VA, United States
Historic Naval Ships Assn. of North Am. [★IO]
Historic Naval Ships Assn. of North Am. [★10440]
Historic New England [10035], 141 Cambridge St., Boston, MA 02114, (617)227-3956
Historic Peace Churches EUR Continuation Comm. [★IO]

Historic Preservation

1904 World's Fair Soc. [23033]
1965-66 Full Size Chevrolet Club [21557]
Abarth Register, U.S.A. [21562]
Abraham Lincoln Natl. Cemetery Support Comm. [21160]
Accokeek Found. [10006]
Advisory Coun. on Historic Preservation [10007]
Aeronca Lovers Club [21423]
Aerostar Owners Assn. [21424]
Airflow Club of Am. [21563]
Alfa Romeo Owners Club [21565]
Alliance of Natl. Heritage Areas [9856]
AMC Rambler Club [21567]
Amer. Antiquarian Soc. [10008]
Amer. Austin/Bantam Club [21568]
Amer. Bugatti Club [21569]
Amer. Canal Soc. [9772]
Amer. Civil War Assn. [10087]
Amer. Friends of St. David's Cathedral [10009]
Amer. Guild of Town Criers [10896]
Amer. Heraldry Soc. [21102]
Amer. Highway Proj. [10010]
Amer. Historic Inns [1909]
Amer. Historical Assn. [10088]
Amer. History Forum and Civil War Educ. Assn. [8500]
Amer. Inst. for Conservation of Historic and Artistic Works [10011]
American Institute for Conservation of Historic and Artistic Works [IO]
Amer. Lancia Club [21573]
Amer. MGB Assn. [21574]
Amer. MGC Register [21575]
Amer. Motors Owners Assn. [21576]
Amer. Oil and Gas Historical Soc. [2915]
Amer. Overseas Schools Historical Soc. [10012]
Amer. Photographic Historical Soc. [10843]
Amer. Soc. for Jewish Heritage in Poland [10273]
Amer. Sta. Wagon Owners Assn. [21577]
Amer. Yankee Assn. [21429]
Ancient Monuments Soc. [IO]
Anguilla Natl. Trust [IO]
Anonymous Arts Recovery Soc. [10956]
Antique Airplane Assn. [21430]
Antique Auto Racing Assn. [21578]
Antique Auto. Club of Am. [21579]
Antique Barbed Wire Soc. [21969]
Antique Studebaker Club [21580]
APVA Preservation Virginia [10013]
Architectural Heritage Found. [10014]
Architectural Heritage Soc. of Scotland [IO]
Asia and West Pacific Network for Urban Conservation [IO]
Assn. of Amer. Military Uniform Collectors [22628]
Assn. for Gravestone Stud. [10015]
Assn. for Heritage Interpretation [IO]
Assn. for Indus. Archaeology [IO]
Assn. of Moving Image Archivists [9932]
Assn. of Ohio Longrifle Collectors [22425]
Assn. for Preservation Tech. Intl. [10016]
Assn. for Preservation Tech. Intl. [IO]
Assn. of Railway Museums [10908]

Assn. of Significant Cemeteries in Europe [IO]
Assn. for Stud. in the Conservation of Historic Buildings [IO]
Athra Kadisha: The Soc. for the Preservation of Jewish Holy Sites [10274]
Austin Bantam Soc. [21583]
Austin-Healey Sports and Touring Club [21586]
Barbados Natl. Trust [IO]
Barbara Pym Soc. [9635]
Bellanca-Champion Club [21431]
Berkeley Exchange [21590]
Bird Airplane Club [21432]
Blackburn Family Assn. [20795]
BMW Car Club of Am. [21591]
BMW Vintage Car Club of Am. [21593]
Boss 429 Owners Dir. [21596]
Bricklin Intl. Owners Club [21598]
Bridge Line Historical Soc. [22932]
Brinton Assn. of Am. [21110]
British Assn. for Cemeteries in South Asia [IO]
British Assn. of Paintings Conservator-Restorers [IO]
British Columbia Historical Fed. [IO]
Browning Collectors Assn. [22426]
Buffalo Bill Historical Center [11105]
Buick Club of Am. [21599]
Buick GS Club of Am. [21600]
Cadillac-LaSalle Club [21602]
Canadian Assn. of Professional Conservators [IO]
Canadian Museum of Nature [IO]
Canadian Railroad Historical Assn. [IO]
Canadiana.org [IO]
Capitol Hill Restoration Soc. [10017]
Captain Eddie Premier Gala [11108]
Cardinal Club [21433]
Carpenters' Company [10018]
Carriage Assn. of Am. [21987]
Center for Jewish History [19179]
Center for Wooden Boats [21869]
Central Elec. Railfans' Assn. [22933]
Cessna Owner Org. [21435]
Cessna Pilots Assn. [21436]
Charles Rennie Mackintosh Soc. [IO]
Cherokee Pilots' Assn. [21437]
Chesapeake and Ohio Historical Soc. [10910]
Chevrolet Nomad Assn. [21607]
Chris Craft Antique Boat Club [21870]
Chrysler 300 Club Intl. [21611]
Chrysler Town and Country Owners Registry [21612]
The Churches Conservation Trust [IO]
Citroen Quarterly Car Club [21613]
Civil War Preservation Trust [10019]
Civil War Round Table Associates [10102]
Civil War Soc. [10103]
Classic Chevy Intl. [21615]
Classic Jaguar Assn. [21616]
Classic Thunderbird Club Intl. [21617]
Club Du Vieux Manoir [IO]
Coast Defense Study Group [10473]
Cobbett Assn. for Chamber Music Res. [10579]
Cobra Owners Club of Am. [21619]
Combat Helicopter Pilots Assn. [20648]
Communal Stud. Assn. [10020]
Company of Military Historians [22629]
The Conservation Fund [4380]
Contemporary Historical Vehicle Assn. [21620]
Corben Club [21440]
Corvair Soc. of Am. [21622]
Coun. of the Alleghenies [9365]
Coun. on America's Military Past [10021]
Crosley Auto. Club [21624]
Crown Victoria Assn. [21625]
Cushman Club of Am. [22676]
Czech Heritage Preservation Soc. [10022]
Dance Heritage Coalition [9877]
De Re Militari: The Soc. for Medieval Military History [10474]
Death Valley '49ers [4807]
Decorative Arts Trust [9567]
Denison Soc. [20880]
DeSoto Club of Am. [21630]
Dodge Bros. Club [21632]
Dodge Pilothouse Era Truck Club of Am. [23024]
EAA Vintage Aircraft Assn. [21442]

A star before a book entry number signifies that the name is not listed separately, but is mentioned within the entry.

EAA Warbirds of Am. [21443]
Early Amer. Indus. Assn. [9481]
Early Ford V-8 Club of Am. [21633]
Early Music Network [10591]
Edsel Club [21636]
Emergency Vehicle Owners and Operators Assn. [21639]
Ercoupe Owners Club [21444]
Ernst Bacon Soc. [10593]
Erskine Registry [21640]
Eskridge Family Assn. [20898]
Europa Nostra Pan European Fed. for Heritage [IO]
European Greenways Assn. [IO]
F-4 Phantom II Soc. [21445]
Fairchild Club [21446]
Fairlane Club of Am. [21641]
Ferrari Owners Club [21644]
First Flight Soc. [21447]
Flying Apache Assn. [21448]
Folk Art Soc. of Am. [9956]
Ford Galaxie Club of Am. [21647]
Fountain Soc. [IO]
Frank Lloyd Wright Preservation Trust [10023]
French Heritage Soc. [10024]
Friends of Cast Iron Architecture [10025]
Friends of French Art [10026]
Friends of Lindenwald [10027]
Friends of the Natl. Parks at Gettysburg [10028]
Friends of Terra Cotta [10029]
Funk Aircraft Owners Assn. [21449]
Gamers Intl. [22478]
Garden Conservancy [4402]
Gene Stratton Porter Memorial Soc. [9651]
German Gun Collectors' Assn. [22029]
Graham Bros. Truck and Bus Club [21894]
Graham Owners Club Intl. [21650]
Gravely Tractor Club of Am. [23002]
Great Lakes Historical Soc. [10438]
Great Lakes Lighthouse Keepers Assn. [10030]
Gull Wing Gp. Intl. [21652]
Gungywamp Soc. [10031]
Hallmark Soc. [IO]
Harmonie Associates [10032]
Hasbrouck Family Assn. [20931]
Haynes-Apperson Owners Club [21653]
Helicopter Club of America [21450]
Herbert Hoover Presidential Lib. Assn. [11122]
Heritage Canada Found. [IO]
Heritage Conservation Network [IO]
Heritage Conservation Network [10033]
Heritage Railway Assn. [IO]
H.H. Franklin Club [21656]
Historic Deerfield [10034]
Historic Hawaii Found. [5785]
Historic Houses Assn. [IO]
Historic Motor Sports Assn. [21657]
Historic New England [10035]
Historic Pullman Found. [10036]
Historic Winslow House Assn. [10037]
Historical Diving Soc. USA [23576]
Historical Manuscripts Commn. [IO]
Historical Soc. of the United Methodist Church [10113]
Hollywood Sign Trust [17710]
Hoover Historical Center [21534]
Horseless Carriage Club of Am. [21658]
Hudson-Essex-Terraplane Club [21659]
Hudson Essex Terraplane Historical Soc. [21660]
Hudson River Sloop Clearwater [10038]
Hull Pottery Assn. [22039]
Hurst/Olds Club of Am. [21661]
Intl. 190SL Gp. [21663]
Intl. Amphicar Owners Club [21664]
Intl. B and B Fly-Inn Club [21451]
Intl. Bird Dog Assn. [21452]
Intl. Bus Collectors Club [21895]
Intl. Camaro Club [21665]
Intl. Catacomb Soc. [10039]
International Catacomb Society [IO]
Intl. Centre for the Stud. of the Preservation and Restoration of Cultural Property [IO]
Intl. Cessna 120/140 Assn. [21453]
The Intl. Cessna 170 Assn. [21454]
Intl. Comm. for Documentation of the Intl. Coun. of Museums [IO]

Intl. Coun. of Air Shows [21455]
Intl. Coun. on Monuments and Sites [IO]
Intl. Edsel Club [21666]
Intl. Fire Buff Associates [22421]
Intl. Garden Club [10040]
Intl. Garden Club [IO]
Intl. King Midget Car Club [21667]
Intl. Kodak Historical Soc. [10850]
The Intl. Molinological Soc. [IO]
Intl. Mustang Bullitt Owners Club [21669]
Intl. Photographic Historical Org. [10851]
Intl. Pietenpol Assn. [21456]
Intl. Soc. for Vehicle Preservation [21670]
Intl. Stationary Steam Engine Soc. [22977]
Intl. Time Capsule Soc. [10041]
International Time Capsule Society [IO]
Interstate Club [21458]
Irish Georgian Soc. [IO]
Iso and Bizzarrini Owners Club [21672]
Italian Car Registry [21673]
Jaguar Clubs of North Am. [21674]
James Buchanan Found. for the Preservation of Wheatland [11126]
Jensen Healey Preservation Soc. [21675]
Jewett Owners Club [21676]
Jew's Harp Guild [10634]
John Marshall Found. [10042]
Jordan Register [21677]
Kaiser-Frazer Owners Club Intl. [21680]
Kissel Kar Klub [21682]
Kustom Kemps of Am. [21683]
Lamborghini Club Am. [21684]
Late Great Chevrolet Assn. [21685]
League of Historic Amer. Theatres [11021]
Les Amis de Panhard and Deutsch Bonnet [21686]
Lighter-Than-Air Soc. [21460]
Lincoln and Continental Owners Club [21687]
Lincoln Highway Assn. [10043]
Lincoln Owners' Club [21688]
London Vintage Taxi Assn. - Amer. Sect. [21690]
Lotus, Ltd. [21691]
Luscombe Endowment [21461]
Lybarger Memorial Assn. [20985]
Macbride Museum Soc. [IO]
Mai Wah Soc. [9622]
Mamie Doud Eisenhower Birthplace Found. [10044]
Man Will Never Fly Memorial Soc. Internationale [22598]
Manorial Soc. of Great Britain [IO]
MAPS Air Museum - Military Aviation Preservation Soc. [9342]
Marine Corps Engineer Assn. [6142]
Marmon Club [21694]
Martin Van Buren Fan Club [11136]
Maverick/Comet Club Intl. [21697]
Memorial Found. of the Germanna Colonies in Virginia [10045]
Mercedes-Benz Club of Am. [21699]
Metropolitan Owners Club of North Am. [21701]
Mid-Continent Railway Historical Soc. [22934]
Midstates Jeepster Assn. [21705]
Midwest Archives Conf. [9401]
Midwest Sunbeam Registry [21706]
Milestone Car Soc. [21707]
Military Vehicle Preservation Assn. [22630]
Mini Car Club, U.S.A. [21708]
Missionary Church Historical Soc. [19851]
Model A Ford Cabriolet Club [21709]
Model A Ford Club of Am. [21710]
Model "A" Restorers Club [21712]
Model "T" Ford Club of Am. [21713]
Model "T" Ford Club Intl. [21714]
Monocoupe Club [21462]
Morgan Car Club [21717]
Morgan Plus Four Club [21718]
Morris Minor Registry [21720]
Motor Bus Soc. [21896]
Mount Rushmore Natl. Memorial Soc. [10046]
Muntz Jet Registry [21721]
Nash Car Club of Am. [21725]
Natl. 210 Owners Assn. [21463]
Natl. Aeronca Assn. [21464]
Natl. Alliance of Preservation Commissions [5786]

Natl. Amusement Park Historical Assn. [21512]
Natl. Antique Oldsmobile Club [21726]
Natl. Archives and Records Admin. Volunteer Assn. [9402]
Natl. Assn. of Auto. Museums [10511]
Natl. Assn. for Outlaw and Lawman History [9380]
Natl. Assn. of Tribal Historic Preservation Officers [10047]
Natl. Automotive and Truck Museum of U.S. [10512]
Natl. Capital Historical Museum of Trans. [10133]
Natl. Carousel Assn. [21897]
Natl. Center for the Amer. Revolution [10134]
Natl. Center for Preservation Tech. and Training [7161]
Natl. Conf. of State Historic Preservation Officers [5787]
Natl. Corvette Owners Assn. [21728]
Natl. Corvette Restorers Soc. [21729]
Natl. Coun. of Corvette Clubs [21730]
Natl. DeSoto Club [21731]
Natl. Firebird and T/A Club [21732]
Natl. Historic Route 66 Fed. [24328]
Natl. Indian Wars Assn. [9371]
Natl. Intercollegiate Flying Assn. [21466]
Natl. Main St. Center [17237]
Natl. Mossberg Collectors Assn. [22430]
Natl. Museum of Racing and Hall of Fame [23508]
Natl. Old Timers Auto Racing Club [21737]
Natl. Preservation Inst. [10048]
Natl. Register of Prominent Americans and Intl. Notables [11140]
Natl. Soc. of Madison Family Descendants [21135]
Natl. Soc. for the Preservation of Covered Bridges [10049]
Natl. Stinson Club [21467]
Natl. St. Rod Assn. [21738]
Natl. Temple Hill Assn. [10050]
Natl. Trust [IO]
Natl. Trust of Australia [IO]
Natl. Trust, Central Volunteering Team [IO]
Natl. Trust for Historic Preservation [10051]
Natl. Trust Main St. Center [17231]
Natl. Trust for Scotland [IO]
Natl. Woodie Club [21739]
Natl. World War II Glider Pilots Assn. [21468]
Navy and Marine Living History Assn. [21206]
Nevis Historical and Conservation Soc. [IO]
New England M.G. "T" Register Limited [21740]
New Zealand Historic Places Trust [IO]
Newport Restoration Found. [10052]
Nikon Historical Soc. [10854]
Nineteen Thirty-Two Buick Registry [21741]
Noah Webster House [10053]
North Amer. Araucanian Royalist Soc. [10054]
North Amer. Mini Moke Registry [21745]
North Amer. Soc. of Ancient and Medieval War-gamers [22471]
North Amer. Sundial Soc. [9278]
North Amer. Victorian Stud. Assn. [11079]
North Amer. Voyageur Coun. [10055]
North-South Skirmish Assn. [23727]
NSU Enthusiasts U.S.A. [21746]
Oakland-Pontiac Enthusiast Org. [21748]
Old Reel Collectors Assn. [22099]
Oldsmobile Club of Am. [21749]
Opel Motorsports Club [21752]
Order of the Indian Wars [10479]
Orders and Medals Soc. of Am. [22631]
Oregon-California Trails Assn. [10056]
Org. of Bricklin Owners [21753]
OX5 Aviation Pioneers [21469]
Packard Auto. Classics [21755]
Packards Intl. Motor Car Club [21758]
Pantera Intl. [21759]
Patriots of Fort McHenry-Living Classrooms [10057]
Penobscot Marine Museum [10445]
Philip Boileau Collectors' Soc. [21542]
The Photographic Historical Soc. [10855]
Pierce-Arrow Soc. [21761]
Pine Creek Railroad [22935]
Plymouth Barracuda/Cuda Owners Club [21763]

Reference to "IO" in place of a book number signifies that the association may be found in the 45th edition of International Organizations.

Plymouth Owners Club [21764]
Police History Soc. [IO]
Pontiac-Oakland Club Intl. [21766]
Pony Express Historical Assn. [10145]
Popular Rotorcraft Assn. [21471]
Porsche Club of Am. [21767]
Porterfield Airplane Club [21472]
Preservation Action [10058]
Preservation Volunteers [10059]
Pres. Benjamin Harrison Found. [11142]
Professional Car Soc. [21768]
Professional Scripophily Trade Assn. [761]
Quebec Fed. of Historical Societies [IO]
The Questers [21532]
Quilters Hall of Fame [22173]
Railroadiana Collectors Assn. Incorporated
  [22936]
Railway Preservation Soc. of Ireland [IO]
Rainier Soc. [21145]
Ranching Heritage Assn. [10148]
Rearwin Club [21474]
Recent Past Preservation Network [7162]
Red Earth [19285]
Renault Owners Club of North Am. [21769]
REO Club of Am. [21770]
Rickenbacker Automobile Club of America [21771]
Road Race Lincoln Register [21773]
Rodeo Historical Soc. [9382]
Rolls-Royce Owners' Club [21774]
Rometsch Registry [21775]
Royal Historical Soc. of Queensland [IO]
Royal Oak Found. [10060]
Saab Club of North Am. [21778]
Sabra Automobile Connection [21779]
San Francisco African Amer. Historical and
  Cultural Soc. [9362]
Save the Battlefield Coalition [10061]
Saving Antiquities for Everyone [9389]
Saving and Preserving Arts and Cultural Environ-
  ments [9470]
Saxon Owners Registry [21781]
Scottish Soc. for Conservation and Restoration
  [IO]
Scottish Urban Archaeological Trust [IO]
Shelby Amer. Auto. Club [21782]
Shenandoah Natl. Park Assn. [10062]
Short Wing Piper Club [21475]
Silver Wings Fraternity [21476]
Soc. of Amer. Archivists [9403]
Soc. of Antiquaries of Newcastle-upon-Tyne [IO]
Soc. of Antique Modelers [21477]
Soc. of Architectural Historians [10150]
Soc. of Automotive Historians [21785]
Soc. for Commercial Archeology [9485]
Soc. of the Founders and Friends of Norwich,
  Connecticut [10063]
Soc. for the History of Tech. [10160]
Soc. for Military History [10482]
Soc. for the Preservation and Appreciation of
  Antique Motor Fire Apparatus in Am. [22423]
Soc. for the Preservation of Natural History Col-
  lections [10064]
Soc. for the Preservation of Old Mills [10065]
Soc. for the Protection of Ancient Buildings [IO]
Soo Line Historical and Tech. Soc. [10923]
Spohr Soc. of Great Britain [IO]
Sports Car Club of Am. [21787]
Stampe Club Intl. [21479]
Stangl Fulper Collectors Club [22117]
Statue of Liberty - Ellis Island Found. [10066]
Steam Auto. Club of Am. [21789]
Stearman Restorers Assn. [21480]
Studebaker Driver's Club [21790]
Stutz Club [21791]
Subaru 360 Drivers' Club [21792]
Superstition Mountain Historical Soc. [9383]
Surratt Soc. [10067]
Surveyors Historical Soc. [10162]
Swedish Assn. for the Protection of Ancient Monu-
  ments [IO]
Swift Museum Found. [21481]
Tangier Amer. Legation Museum Soc. [10068]
Terminal Railroad Assn. Historical and Tech. Soc.
  [10925]
Theatre Historical Soc. of Am. [11050]

The Thomas Hardy Assn. [9712]
Thomas Jefferson's Poplar Forest [10069]
Thompson Collectors Assn. [22431]
Titanic Historical Soc. [10447]
Titanic Intl. Soc. [10448]
Topolino Register of North Am. [21797]
Touro Synagogue Found. [10070]
Traditions for Tomorrow [IO]
Trail of Tears Assn. [11057]
Travel Air Club [21482]
Tribal Preservation Prog. [10755]
Triumph Register of Am. [21800]
Tucker Auto. Club of Am. [21801]
TVR Car Club North Am. [21802]
Twin Bonanza Assn. [21483]
Two-Cylinder Club [23005]
Ulster-Scots Soc. of Am. [21154]
Union of European Historic Houses Associations
  [IO]
United Flying Octogenarians [21485]
United Four-Wheel Drive Associations [21805]
United Kingdom Inst. for Conservation of Historic
  and Artistic Works [IO]
U.S. Classic Racing Assn. [22694]
U.S. Historical Soc. [10071]
U.S. Life-Saving Ser. Heritage Assn. [10072]
U.S. Lighthouse Soc. [10073]
U.S. Natl. Comm. of the Intl. Coun. on Monu-
  ments and Sites [10074]
U.S. Natl. Comm. of the Intl. Coun. on Monu-
  ments and Sites [IO]
U.S. Ultralight Assn. [21486]
Uttaranchal Assn. of North Am. [10219]
Veteran Feminists of Am. [17572]
Veteran Motor Car Club of Am. [21808]
Victorian Homeowner's Assn. and Old House Lov-
  ers [10075]
Victorian Soc. in Am. [11081]
Vietnamese Nom Preservation Found. [10433]
Vintage Chevrolet Club of Am. [21809]
Vintage Drivers Club of Am. [21810]
Vintage Locomotive Soc. [IO]
Vintage Thunderbird Club Intl. [21812]
Vintage Triumph Register [21813]
Vintage Volkswagen Club of Am. [21814]
Volkswagen Club of Am. [21815]
Volvo Club of Am. [21816]
Walden Woods Proj. [10076]
Walter Burley Griffin Soc. of Am. [9398]
Weatherby Collectors Assn. [22432]
Whirly-Girls - Intl. Women Helicopter Pilots
  [21487]
William H. Whitsitt Baptist Heritage Soc. [19500]
Wills Sainte Claire Museum [21817]
Willys Overland Jeepster Club [21818]
Willys-Overland-Knight Registry [21819]
Winged Warriors/National B-Body Owners Assn.
  [21820]
Wooden Canoe Heritage Assn. [21887]
Woodrow Wilson Presidential Lib. Found. [11155]
World Airline Historical Soc. [21488]
World Atlatl Assn. [22611]
World Coun. of Elders [9855]
World Heritage Alliance [10077]
World Heritage Alliance [IO]
World Heritage Centre [IO]
World War I Aeroplanes [21490]
Worldwide Camaro Club [21821]
Yukon Historical and Museums Assn. [IO]
Historic Pullman Found. [10036], 614 E 113th St.,
  Chicago, IL 60628, (773)785-8181
Historic Racing Motorcycle Assn; Amer. [22665]
Historic and Res. Soc. of Delaware Valley; Scottish
  [10955]
Historic and Res. Soc; Scottish [★10955]
Historic Sites and Buildings; Natl. Coun. for
  [★10051]
Historic Sites Officials; Assn. of [★10084]
Historic Winslow House Assn. [10037], 634 Care-
  swell St., Marshfield, MA 02050-5623, (781)837-
  5753
Historical Anomalies; Center for the Stud. of Natural
  and [7862]
Historical Archives; Finnish Amer. [9951]
Historical Assn. [IO], London, United Kingdom

Historical Assn; Acadian Genealogical and [★21098]
Historical Assn; Adirondack [9340]
Historical Assn; Friends [20043]
Historical Assn; Great Plains [★9994]
Historical Assn; Johannes Schwalm [21128]
Historical Assn; John Pelham [11131]
Historical Assn; Mississippi Valley [★10142]
Historical Assn; Natl. Amusement Park [21512]
Historical Assn. of New Hampshire; Acadian
  Genealogical and [★21098]
Historical Assn; Norwegian-American [10759]
Historical Assn; Presbyterian [★10891]
Historical Assn; Public Archives Commn. of the
  Amer. [★9403]
Historical Assn; Rough and Tumble Engineers'
  [22979]
Historical Assn; Southern [9378]
Historical Assn; Thomas Paine Natl. [11153]
Historical Bottle Collectors; Fed. of [21888]
Historical Bottle Collectors Guild - Defunct.
Historical Center; Hoover [21534]
Historical Commn. of the Polish Inst. of Arts and Sci-
  ences in Am; Polish Amer. [★10880]
Historical Commn., Southern Baptist Convention
  [★19499]
Historical Comm. of the Mennonite Church [★20248]
Historical Conf; Lutheran [20222]
Historical and Cultural Soc; Portuguese [19321]
Historical and Cultural Soc; San Francisco African
  Amer. [9362]
Historical Diving Soc. [IO], Reigate, United Kingdom
Historical Diving Soc. Canada [IO], North Vancouver,
  BC, Canada
Historical Diving Soc. Germany [IO], Herzogenrath,
  Germany
Historical Diving Soc. Italia [IO], Ravenna, Italy
Historical Diving Soc. Mexico [IO], Mexico City,
  Mexico
Historical Diving Soc. South Africa [IO], Cape Town,
  Republic of South Africa
Historical Diving Soc. USA [23576], PO Box 2837,
  Santa Maria, CA 93457, (805)934-1660
Historical Farm Assn. [★10147]
Historical Farms and Agricultural Museums; Assn. for
  Living [★10497]
Historical Fencing; Assn. for [23399]
Historical Fire Found; Natl. [22422]
Historical Found; Air Force [10470]
Historical Found; Army [10471]
Historical Found; Marine Corps [★10477]
Historical Found; Mosquito [★20663]
Historical Found; Naval [10478]
Historical Found; Netherlands Pioneer and [★9909]
Historical and Genealogical Soc; Afro-American
  [9353]
Historical and Genealogical Soc. in Am; Russian
  [★21147]
Historical and Genealogical Soc; Spencer [21153]
Historical Harp Soc. [10609], c/o Anne Humphrey,
  Proj. Chair, 631 N 3rd Ave., St. Charles, IL 60174
Historical Inst; Concordia [20215]
Historical Keyboard Soc; Southeastern [22720]
Historical Lib. and Archives; Southern Baptist
  [19499]
Historical Manuscripts Commn. [IO], London, United
  Kingdom
Historical Metallurgy Soc. [IO], Swansea, United
  Kingdom
Historical Model Railway Soc. [IO], Ripley, United
  Kingdom
Historical Motion Picture Milestones Assn. - Address
  unknown since 1995.
Historical Museum; Amer. Swedish [10987]
Historical Org; Intl. Photographic [10851]
Historical Print Collectors Soc; Amer. [21523]
Historical Publications and Records Commission;
  National [★11129]
Historical Radio Soc. of Australia [IO], Melbourne,
  Australia
Historical Reenactment
  Fan Tek [10943]
  Gamers Intl. [22478]
  Great War Assn. [10475]
  H.M. 10th Regiment of Foot, Amer. Contingent
    [9373]

A star before a book entry number signifies that the name is not listed separately, but is mentioned within the entry.

Natl. Center for the Amer. Revolution [10134]
North Amer. Voyageur Coun. [10055]
North-South Skirmish Assn. [23727]
Northwest Schooner Soc. [21882]
Polynesian Voyaging Soc. [22775]
Strategy Gaming Soc. [22475]
Historical Rev; Inst. for [17711]
Historical Revisionism
Inst. for Historical Rev. [17711]
Historical Seaport Authority; Grays Harbor [8812]
Historical Societies
Amer. Oil and Gas Historical Soc. [2915]
Filipino Amer. Natl. Historical Soc. [10779]
Gay, Lesbian, Bisexual, Transgender Historical Soc. [10078]
Natl. Indian Wars Assn. [9371]
World Heritage Alliance [10077]
Historical Societies; Assn. of Methodist [★10467]
Historical Societies; Coun. of [★10084]
Historical Soc. of Am; Steamship [22980]
Historical Soc. of Am; Theatre [11050]
Historical Soc. of Am; Zeiss [22133]
Historical Soc; Amer. Aviation [21426]
Historical Soc; Amer. Baptist [19470]
Historical Soc; Amer. Hungarian Lib. and [10215]
Historical Soc; Amer. Italian [★10261]
Historical Soc; Amer. Photographic [10843]
Historical Soc; Amer. Steamship [★22980]
Historical Soc; Amer. Truck [23021]
Historical Soc; Anthracite Railroads [10907]
Historical Soc; Augustana [19343]
Historical Soc; B-26 Marauder [21389]
Historical Soc; Baidarka [9954]
Historical Soc; Baltimore and Ohio Railroad [10909]
Historical Soc; Bridge Line [22932]
Historical Soc; Burlesque [11009]
Historical Soc; Cherokee Natl. [10735]
Historical Soc; Chesapeake and Ohio [10910]
Historical Soc; Church [★19962]
Historical Soc; Circus [9798]
Historical Soc; Columbia [★10114]
Historical Soc; Congregational Christian [19860]
Historical Soc; Disciples of Christ [19853]
Historical Soc. of Early Amer. Decoration [9482], c/o Ann Stewart, Admin. Asst., PO Box 30, The Farmer's Museum, Cooperstown, NY 13326, (607)547-5667
Historical Soc; Eighth Air Force [21392]
Historical Soc. of the Episcopal Church [19962], PO Box 2098, Manchaca, TX 78652-2098, (617)996-9272
Historical Soc; Evangelical and Reformed [20607]
Historical Soc. of the Evangelical and Reformed Church [★20607]
Historical Soc. of the Evangelical United Brethren Church [★10467]
Historical Soc; Filipino Amer. Natl. [10779]
Historical Soc; Great Lakes [10438]
Historical Soc; Hudson Essex Terraplane [21660]
Historical Soc; Huguenot [21161]
Historical Soc. Inc; Abigail Adams [11099]
Historical Soc; Intl. Kodak [10850]
Historical Soc; Intl. Methodist [★20273]
Historical Soc. of Jews from Egypt [10282], PO Box 230445, Brooklyn, NY 11223
Historical Soc; Lancaster Mennonite [21130]
Historical Soc; Lancaster (Pennsylvania) Railway and Locomotive [★10915]
Historical Soc; McAdams [20995]
Historical Soc; Mid-Continent Railway [22934]
Historical Soc; Moravian [20423]
Historical Soc. Museum; Afro-American [9354]
Historical Soc; Natl. Auto Racing [23082]
Historical Soc; Natl. Japanese Amer. [10267]
Historical Soc; Nikon [10854]
Historical Soc; Ontario and Western Railway [10916]
Historical Soc; Optometric [15728]
Historical Soc; Organ [10683]
Historical Soc; Partisan Prohibition [22103]
Historical Soc; The Photographic [10855]
Historical Soc; Presbyterian [10891]
Historical Soc; Presbyterian [★10891]
Historical Soc; Railroad Sta. [10920]
Historical Soc; Railway and Locomotive [10921]
Historical Soc. of the Reformed Church in the U.S. [★20607]

Historical Soc; Rodeo [9382]
Historical Soc; St. Louis Railway [★10926]
Historical Soc; Seventh Day Baptist [19495]
Historical Soc; Spokane, Portland and Seattle Railway [10924]
Historical Soc; Superstition Mountain [9383]
Historical Soc; Swedish-American [10989]
Historical Soc; Swedish Pioneer [★10989]
Historical Soc; Titanic [10447]
Historical Soc; Unitarian [★20601]
Historical Soc; Unitarian Universalist [20601]
Historical Soc. of the United Lutheran Church in America - Defunct.
Historical Soc. of the United Methodist Church [10113], c/o Bill Bakeman, 1178 County Rd. B.W., Roseville, MN 55113-4301
Historical Soc; Universalist [★20601]
Historical Soc; Valley Forge [9375]
Historical Soc; Veitch [21077]
Historical Soc. of Washington, DC [10114], Mt. Vernon Sq., 801 K St. NW, Washington, DC 20001, (202)383-1850
Historical Soc. of the West; Finnish-American [19055]
Historical Stud; Soc. for Italian [8681]
Historical and Tech. Soc; Soo Line [10923]
Historical and Tech. Soc; Terminal Railroad Assn. [10925]
Historical Trust; Holland [9909]
Historical Union; Intl. Methodist [★20273]
Historical Union; Methodist [★20273]
Historical Vehicle Assn; Contemporary [21620]
History
1904 World's Fair Soc. [23033]
1965-66 Full Size Chevrolet Club [21557]
Aaron Burr Assn. [11098]
Abarth Register, U.S.A. [21562]
Abigail Adams Historical Soc. Inc. [11099]
Abingdon Pottery Club [21522]
Abraham Lincoln Natl. Cemetery Support Comm. [21160]
A.C. Gilbert Heritage Soc. [22992]
Academia Nacional de la Historia de la Republica Argentina [IO]
Acad. of Accounting Historians [10079]
Acad. of Amer. Franciscan History [19560]
Accokeek Found. [10006]
Adirondack Historical Assn. [9340]
Advisory Coun. on Historic Preservation [10007]
African Amer. Cultural Alliance [9351]
African Amer. Museums Assn. [10488]
Afro-American Historical Soc. Museum [9354]
Agricultural History Soc. [10080]
Ahern Clan Assn. [19048]
Air-Britain Historians [IO]
Air Force Historical Found. [10470]
Aircraft Engine Historical Soc. [9364]
Airflow Club of Am. [21563]
Alfa Romeo Owners Club [21565]
AMC Rambler Club [21567]
Amer. Acad. of the History of Dentistry [14100]
Amer. Acad. of Res. Historians of Medieval Spain [10081]
Amer. Assn. for the History of Medicine [10082]
Amer. Assn. for the History of Nursing [10083]
Amer. Assn. for State and Local History [10084]
Amer. Austin/Bantam Club [21568]
Amer. Aviation Historical Soc. [21426]
Amer. Baptist Historical Soc. [19470]
American-Canadian Genealogical Soc. [21098]
Amer. Catholic Historical Assn. [10085]
Amer. Catholic Historical Soc. [10086]
American Catholic Historical Society [IO]
Amer. Civil War Assn. [10087]
American-French Genealogical Soc. [21101]
Amer. Friends of Lafayette [11102]
Amer. Heraldry Soc. [21102]
Amer. Historic Inns [1909]
Amer. Historical Assn. [10088]
Amer. History Forum and Civil War Educ. Assn. [8500]
Amer. Inst. for Contemporary German Stud. [9976]
Amer. Inst. of the History of Pharmacy [15917]

Amer. Jewish Historical Soc. [10272]
Amer. Journalism Historians Assn. [8501]
Amer. Lancia Club [21573]
Amer. MGB Assn. [21574]
Amer. MGC Register [21575]
Amer. Motors Owners Assn. [21576]
Amer. Museum of Natural History [7357]
Amer. Numismatic Assn. [22724]
Amer. Numismatic Soc. [22725]
Amer. Oil and Gas Historical Soc. [2915]
Amer. Overseas Schools Historical Soc. [10012]
Amer. Philatelic Res. Lib. [22784]
Amer. Philatelic Soc. [22785]
Amer. Photographic Historical Soc. [10843]
Amer. Printing History Assn. [9989]
Amer. Racing Pigeon Union [22894]
Amer. Revolution Round Table [9372]
American-Slovenian Polka Found. [10549]
Amer. Soc. of Camera Collectors [10844]
Amer. Soc. of Church History [10078]
American Society of Church History [IO]
Amer. Soc. for Eighteenth-Century Stud. [10089]
Amer. Soc. for Ethnohistory [9918]
Amer. Soc. of Genealogists [21103]
Amer. Soc. of Greek and Latin Epigraphy [11207]
Amer. Soc. for Jewish Heritage in Poland [10273]
Amer. Soc. for Legal History [10090]
Amer. Spelean Historical Assn. [10091]
Amer. Stud. Assn. [9367]
Amer. Tax Token Soc. [22727]
Amer. Theatre and Drama Soc. [11005]
Amer. Truck Historical Soc. [23021]
Amer. Wooden Money Guild [22728]
AMISTAD Am. [8502]
Ancient Coin Collectors Guild [22729]
Ancient Egypt and Middle East Soc. [IO]
Anesthesia History Assn. [13678]
Antique Airplane Assn. [21430]
Antique Auto Racing Assn. [21578]
Antique Auto. Club of Am. [21579]
Antique Studebaker Club [21580]
Antique Wireless Assn. [22923]
Appalachian Stud. Assn. [9391]
Arabian Horse Historians Assn. [10092]
Archaeological Conservancy [6439]
Archives of Amer. Art [9419]
Archivists and Librarians in the History of the Hea. Sciences [10326]
Ark-La-Tex Genealogical Assn. [21104]
Armies of Tennessee, CSA and U.S.A. [20722]
Army Historical Found. [10471]
Assoc. Daughters of Early Amer. Witches [21358]
Assn. of Amer. Military Uniform Collectors [22628]
Assn. of Ancient Historians [10093]
Assn. for the Bibliography of History [10094]
Assn. of the German Nobility in North Am. [21105]
Assn. of Historians of Nineteenth-Century Art [9431]
Assn. of History and Computing (UK Br.) [IO]
Assn. of North Amer. Radio Clubs [21498]
Assn. of Ohio Longrifle Collectors [22425]
Assn. of Personal Historians [10095]
Assn. for Renaissance Martial Arts [8820]
Assn. for Res. in Modern History [IO]
Assn. for the Stud. of African-American Life and History [9356]
Assn. for the Stud. and Preservation of Roman Mosaics [IO]
Assn. for the Stud. of the Worldwide African Diaspora [7929]
Athenaeum of Philadelphia [10342]
Augustan Reprint Soc. [10415]
Augustan Soc. [21107]
Austin Bantam Soc. [21583]
Austin-Healey Sports and Touring Club [21586]
Australian Capital Territory History Teachers Assn. [IO]
Bahamas Historical Soc. [IO]
Baidarka Historical Soc. [9954]
Baronial Order of Magna Charta and the Military Order of Crusades [10096]
Baronial Order of Magna Charta and the Military Order of Crusades [IO]
Berkeley Exchange [21590]
Black History Month Assn. [IO]

Reference to "IO" in place of a book number signifies that the association may be found in the 45th edition of International Organizations.

Black Holocaust Soc. [16938]
Black Military History Inst. of Am. [10472]
BMW Car Club of Am. [21591]
BMW Vintage Car Club of Am. [21593]
Bohemia Ragtime Soc. [10568]
Boss 429 Owners Dir. [21596]
Bostonian Soc. [10097]
Brazilian Inst. of History and Geography [IO]
Bricklin Intl. Owners Club [21598]
Bridge Line Historical Soc. [22932]
Brinton Assn. of Am. [21110]
British Agricultural History Soc. [IO]
British Assn. for Local History [IO]
British Soc. for Eighteenth Century Stud. [IO]
British Soc. for the History of Mathematics [IO]
British Soc. for the History of Medicine [IO]
British Soc. for the History of Sci. [IO]
British Soc. of Sports History [IO]
British Sundial Soc. [IO]
Browning Collectors Assn. [22426]
Buick Club of Am. [21599]
Buick GS Club of Am. [21600]
Bus History Assn. [IO]
Bus. History Conf. [10098]
Cadillac-LaSalle Club [21602]
Canada's Natl. History Soc. [IO]
Canadian Assn. for the History of Nursing [IO]
Canadian Aviation Historical Soc. [IO]
Canadian Comm. on Labour History [IO]
Canadian Friends Historical Assn. [IO]
Canadian Heritage Info. Network [IO]
Canadian Historical Assn. [IO]
Canadian Immigration Historical Soc. [IO]
Canadian Oral History Assn. [IO]
Canadian Soc. for 18th Century Stud. [IO]
Canadian Soc. of Church History [IO]
Canadian Soc. of the History of the Catholic
  Church - French Sect. [IO]
Canterbury Historical Assn. [IO]
Capitol Hill Restoration Soc. [10017]
Carpenters' Company [10018]
Carriage Assn. of Am. [21987]
Centennial Legion of Historic Military Commands
  [21240]
Center for Jewish History [19179]
Center for Socialist History [10099]
Central Elec. Railfans' Assn. [22933]
Centre for Intl. Historical Stud. [IO]
Charles Babbage Inst. for the History of Info.
  Tech. [10100]
Charles H. Wright Museum of African Amer. His-
  tory [9358]
Chem. Heritage Found. [10101]
Cherokee Natl. Historical Soc. [10735]
Cherokee Pilots' Assn. [21437]
Chess Collectors Intl. [21944]
Chevrolet Nomad Assn. [21607]
Chilean Acad. of History [IO]
Chinese Historians in the U.S. [IO]
Chinese Historians in the U.S. [8503]
Chinese Historical Soc. of Am. [9789]
Chrysler 300 Club Intl. [21611]
Chrysler Town and Country Owners Registry
  [21612]
Churchill Soc. London [IO]
Citroen Quarterly Car Club [21613]
Civil War Round Table Associates [10102]
Civil War Soc. [10103]
Civil War Token Soc. [22732]
CLAL: Natl. Jewish Center for Learning and
  Leadership [20132]
Clan MacAlpine Soc. [19049]
Clan MacKinnon Soc. [19050]
Clan McAlister of Am. [19051]
Clan Phail Soc. in North America [19052]
Classic Chevy Intl. [21615]
Classic Jaguar Assn. [21616]
Classic Thunderbird Club Intl. [21617]
Coast Defense Study Group [10473]
Cobbett Assn. for Chamber Music Res. [10579]
Cobra Owners Club of Am. [21619]
Colonial Coin Collectors Club [22733]
Colonial Order of the Acorn [20735]
Colonial Soc. of Massachusetts [10104]
Combat Helicopter Pilots Assn. [20648]

Combined Organizations of Numismatic Error Col-
  lectors of Am. [22734]
Communal Stud. Assn. [10020]
Company of Military Historians [22629]
Concordia Historical Inst. [20215]
Confederate Memorial Assn. [9368]
Confederate Memorial Literary Soc. [10105]
Conf. on Asian History [9617]
Conf. on Faith and History [20079]
Contemporary Historical Vehicle Assn. [21620]
Corvair Soc. of Am. [21622]
Crosley Auto. Club [21624]
Crown Victoria Assn. [21625]
Cuban Numismatic Assn. [22735]
Custer Battlefield Historical and Museum Assn.
  [10106]
Daguerreian Soc. [10848]
Dance Heritage Coalition [9877]
Daniel Boone and Frontier Families Res. Assn.
  [10107]
Danish Amer. Heritage Soc. [9903]
Danish Historical Assn. [IO]
De Re Militari: The Soc. for Medieval Military His-
  tory [10474]
Deaf History Intl. [14081]
Dedicated Wooden Money Collectors [22736]
DeSoto Club of Am. [21630]
Diamond T Register [23023]
Disciples of Christ Historical Soc. [19853]
Distinguished Flying Cross Soc. [20711]
Dodge Bros. Club [21632]
Dodge Pilothouse Era Truck Club of Am. [23024]
Drake Exploration Soc. [IO]
EAA Vintage Aircraft Assn. [21442]
EAA Warbirds of Am. [21443]
Early Amer. Coppers [22737]
Early Amer. Indus. Assn. [9481]
Early Ford V-8 Club of Am. [21633]
Early Music Network [10591]
Economic History Assn. [8504]
Economic History Soc. [IO]
Economic and Social History Soc. of Ireland [IO]
Edsel Club [21636]
Eighteenth-Century Scottish Stud. Soc. [8505]
Eighteenth-Century Scottish Stud. Soc. [IO]
Elec. Railroaders' Assn. [10911]
Emergency Vehicle Owners and Operators Assn.
  [21639]
Epigraphic Soc. [6445]
Ernst Bacon Soc. [10593]
Erskine Registry [21640]
Euler Soc. [10453]
EUROCLIO: European Standing Conf. of History
  Teachers' Associations [IO]
European Assn. of Young Historians [IO]
F-4 Phantom II Soc. [21445]
Facing History and Ourselves Natl. Found.
  [10108]
Facing History and Ourselves Natl. Found. [IO]
Fairlane Club of Am. [21641]
Family and Church History Dept. of the Church of
  Jesus Christ of Latter-Day Saints [21115]
Fed. of East European Family History Societies
  [19068]
Fed. of Genealogical Societies [21116]
Fed. of Nova Scotian Heritage [IO]
Ferrari Owners Club [21644]
Filipino Amer. Natl. Historical Soc. [10779]
Finnish Amer. Historical Archives [9951]
Finnish Historical Soc. [IO]
First Flight Soc. [21447]
Flag Res. Center [11074]
Flagon and Trencher - Descendants of Colonial
  Tavern Keepers [20737]
Ford Galaxie Club of Am. [21647]
Forest History Soc. [10109]
Francis Brett Young Soc. [IO]
French Am. History Inst. [IO]
French Heritage Soc. [10024]
French Inst. of Social History [IO]
French Soc. of Overseas History [IO]
Friends of the Amer. Museum in Britain/Halcyon
  Found. [9370]
Funk Aircraft Owners Assn. [21449]
Garden History Soc. [IO]

Gay, Lesbian, Bisexual, Transgender Historical
  Soc. [10078]
Gene Stratton Porter Memorial Soc. [9651]
Genealogical Inst. [21117]
Gen. Soc. of Colonial Wars [20738]
Gen. Soc. of Mayflower Descendants [21247]
German Genealogical Soc. of Am. [21119]
German Historical Inst. [10110]
German History Soc. [IO]
Glasgow Natural History Soc. [IO]
Gluckstal Colonies Res. Assn. [10111]
Gottscheer Heritage and Genealogy Assn. [9978]
Graham Bros. Truck and Bus Club [21894]
Graham Owners Club Intl. [21650]
Gravely Tractor Club of Am. [23002]
Great Lakes Historical Soc. [10438]
Great Lakes Maritime Inst. [10439]
Great War Assn. [10475]
Gp. for the Use of Psychology in History [10112]
Gull Wing Gp. Intl. [21652]
Hagiography Soc. [20526]
Harmonie Associates [10032]
Harriet Beecher Stowe Center [9655]
Haynes-Apperson Owners Club [21653]
Helicopter Club of America [21450]
Henry Williamson Soc. [IO]
Heritage Conservation Network [10033]
H.H. Franklin Club [21656]
Historians of Amer. Communism [8506]
Historians of British Art [9478]
Historians of Eighteenth-Century Art and
  Architecture [9479]
Historic Motor Sports Assn. [21657]
Historic New England [10035]
Historical Assn. [IO]
Historical Diving Soc. USA [23576]
Historical Soc. of Early Amer. Decoration [9482]
Historical Soc. of the United Methodist Church
  [10113]
Historical Soc. of Washington, DC [10114]
History of Dermatology Soc. [10115]
History of Earth Sciences Soc. [10116]
History of Economics Soc. [10117]
History of Educ. Soc. [10118]
History of Sci. Soc. [10119]
History of Sci. Soc. [IO]
History Teachers Assn. of Australia [IO]
History Teachers Assn. of Australia - New South
  Wales [IO]
History Teachers Assn. of Victoria [IO]
History Teachers Assn. of Western Australia [IO]
H.M. 10th Regiment of Foot, Amer. Contingent
  [9373]
Hof Reunion Assn. [20682]
Holland Soc. of New York [20740]
Hoover Historical Center [21534]
HOPOS - The Intl. Soc. for the History of
  Philosophy of Sci. [9103]
Horseless Carriage Club of Am. [21658]
Hudson-Essex-Terraplane Club [21659]
Huguenot Historical Soc. [21161]
Huguenot Soc. of the Founders of Manakin in the
  Colony of Virginia [21162]
Hurst/Olds Club of Am. [21661]
IEEE Soc. Social Implications of Tech. [7737]
Igorot Global Org. [10225]
Illinois Central Railroad Historical Soc. [10120]
Immigration and Ethnic History Soc. [10121]
Immigration and Ethnic History Soc. [IO]
Indian Heritage Coun. [10744]
Indian Military Historical Soc. [IO]
Indochina Center [10122]
Indus. Heritage Assn. of Ireland [IO]
Inn Sign Soc. [IO]
Inst. for Axiomatic Knowledge and Educ. [7606]
Inst. of Outdoor Drama [11018]
Inst. for Psychohistory [10123]
Inst. for the Stud. of Amer. Cultures [10746]
Inst. of Turkish Stud. [11061]
Intl. 190SL Gp. [21663]
Intl. Anchoritic Soc. [10460]
Intl. Assn. for the History of Glass [10124]
Intl. Assn. for the History of Glass [IO]
Intl. Assn. for the History of Religions [IO]
Intl. Assn. of Labour History Institutions [IO]

A star before a book entry number signifies that the name is not listed separately, but is mentioned within the entry.

Intl. Bank Note Soc. [22739]
Intl. Bird Dog Assn. [21452]
Intl. Black Writers and Artists [11177]
Intl. Brick Collectors' Assn. [22048]
Intl. Bus Collectors Club [21895]
Intl. Camaro Club [21665]
Intl. Cessna 120/140 Assn. [21453]
The Intl. Cessna 170 Assn. [21454]
Intl. Churchill Soc. - Canada [IO]
Intl. Commn. for the History of Representative and
   Parliamentary Institutions [IO]
Intl. Commn. for the History of Towns [IO]
Intl. Comm. for Historical Metrology [IO]
Intl. Comm. for the History of the Second World
   War [IO]
Intl. Comm. for the History of Tech. [IO]
Intl. Conf. of Labour and Social History [IO]
Intl. Coun. of Air Shows [21455]
Intl. Economic History Assn. [IO]
Intl. Edsel Club [21666]
Intl. Fed. of Amer. Homing Pigeon Fanciers
   [22895]
Intl. Fed. of Vexillological Associations [11075]
Intl. Fire Buff Associates [22421]
Intl. Handicappers' Net [21502]
Intl. Inst. for Frame Stud. [9991]
Intl. Inst. of Social History [IO]
Intl. Kodak Historical Soc. [10850]
Intl. Photographic Historical Org. [10851]
Intl. Pietenpol Assn. [21456]
Intl. Planning History Soc. [IO]
Intl. Psychohistorical Assn. [IO]
Intl. Psychohistorical Assn. [10125]
Intl. Radio Club of Am. [21503]
Intl. Skiing History Assn. [10965]
Intl. Soc. for British Genealogy and Family History
   [21123]
Intl. Soc. for the Comparative Stud. of Civilizations
   [7652]
Intl. Soc. Daughters of Utah Pioneers [21252]
Intl. Soc. for Eighteenth-Century Stud. [IO]
Intl. Soc. for History Didactics [IO]
Intl. Soc. for the History of the Neurosciences
   [7376]
Intl. Soc. for the History, Philosophy, and Social
   Stud. of Biology [8507]
Intl. Soc. for the History, Philosophy, and Social
   Stud. of Biology [IO]
Intl. Soc. for the History of Physical Educ. and
   Sport [IO]
International Society for Intellectual History [IO]
Intl. Soc. for Intellectual History [10126]
Intl. Soc. for the Stud. of Pilgrimage Art [9451]
Intl. Soc. for Vehicle Preservation [21670]
Intl. Stationary Steam Engine Soc. [22977]
Intl. Theodore Dreiser Soc. [9664]
Intl. Time Capsule Soc. [10041]
Intl. Union of the History and Philosophy of Sci.
   [IO]
Irish Family History Soc. [IO]
Irish Special Interest Gp. of Mensa [10244]
Iso and Bizzarrini Owners Club [21672]
Italian Car Registry [21673]
Jaguar Clubs of North Am. [21674]
James Buchanan Found. for the Preservation of
   Wheatland [11126]
James K. Polk Memorial Assn. [11127]
Jamestowne Soc. [20742]
Jefferson Legacy Found. [9002]
Jerome K. Jerome Soc. [IO]
Jewett Owners Club [21676]
Jew's Harp Guild [10634]
Johannes Schwalm Historical Assn. [21128]
John Clare Soc. [IO]
John F. Kennedy First Day Cover Stud. Unit
   [22835]
John Hampden Soc. [IO]
John Marshall Found. [10042]
Jordan Register [21677]
Jozef Pilsudski Inst. of Am. for Res. in the Modern
   History of Poland [10878]
Judson Welliver Soc. [10127]
Judson Welliver Society [IO]
Kaiser-Frazer Owners Club Intl. [21680]
Karg-Elert Archv. [IO]

Kilvert Soc. [IO]
Kissel Kar Klub [21682]
Kustom Kemps of Am. [21683]
La Societe Guernesiaise [IO]
Labor and Working Class History Assn. [8723]
Lamborghini Club Am. [21684]
Late Great Chevrolet Assn. [21685]
Latin Amer. Paper Money Soc. [22741]
Les Amis de Panhard and Deutsch Bonnet
   [21686]
Lewis and Clark Trail Heritage Found. [10128]
Lexington Gp. in Trans. History [10913]
Liberty Seated Collectors Club [22742]
Lighter-Than-Air Soc. [21460]
Lincoln and Continental Owners Club [21687]
Lincoln Owners' Club [21688]
Lithuanian Numismatic Assn. [22743]
Lollard Soc. [20524]
London Natural History Soc. [IO]
London Record Soc. [IO]
London Vintage Taxi Assn. - Amer. Sect. [21690]
Longwave Club of Am. [21505]
Lotus, Ltd. [21691]
Love Token Soc. [22744]
Lutheran Historical Conf. [20222]
Mai Wah Soc. [9622]
Mamie Doud Eisenhower Birthplace Found.
   [10044]
Man Will Never Fly Memorial Soc. Internationale
   [22598]
Manuscript Soc. [22068]
MAPS Air Museum - Military Aviation Preservation
   Soc. [9342]
MARHO: The Radical Historians' Org. [10129]
Marine Corps Engineer Assn. [6142]
Marine Corps Heritage Found. [10477]
Marlowe Soc. [IO]
Marmon Club [21694]
Martin Van Buren Fan Club [11136]
Medal Collectors of Am. [22745]
Mediterranean Stud. Assn. [10466]
Mennonite Church USA Historical Comm. [20248]
Mennonite Educ. Agency [20250]
Mercedes-Benz Club of Am. [21699]
Metropolitan Owners Club of North Am. [21701]
Mexican Epigraphic Soc. [10130]
Mid-Continent Railway Historical Soc. [22934]
Midstates Jeepster Assn. [21705]
Midwest Sunbeam Registry [21706]
Milestone Car Soc. [21707]
Military Postal History Soc. [22847]
Military Vehicle Preservation Assn. [22630]
Mini Car Club, U.S.A. [21708]
Mining History Assn. [10131]
Mobile Post Off. Soc. [22848]
Model A Ford Cabriolet Club [21709]
Model A Ford Club of Am. [21710]
Model "A" Restorers Club [21712]
Model "T" Ford Club of Am. [21713]
Model "T" Ford Club Intl. [21714]
Moravian Historical Soc. [20423]
Morgan Car Club [21717]
Morgan Plus Four Club [21718]
Mormon History Assn. [20208]
Morris Minor Registry [21720]
Motor Bus Soc. [21896]
Mozart Soc. of Am. [9814]
Muntz Jet Registry [21721]
Museum of African Amer. History [9360]
Museum of the Fur Trade [10132]
Museum of the Fur Trade [IO]
Mystic Seaport [10441]
Nash Car Club of Am. [21725]
Natl. Acad. of History [IO]
Natl. Amusement Park Historical Assn. [21512]
Natl. Antique Oldsmobile Club [21726]
Natl. Assn. for Armenian Stud. and Res. [9406]
Natl. Assn. of Auto. Museums [10511]
Natl. Assn. of Mining History Organisations [IO]
Natl. Assn. for Outlaw and Lawman History [9380]
Natl. Auto Racing Historical Soc. [23082]
Natl. Automotive and Truck Museum of U.S.
   [10512]
Natl. Black Herstory Task Force [11089]
Natl. Capital Historical Museum of Trans. [10133]

Natl. Carousel Assn. [21897]
Natl. Center of Afro-American Artists [9361]
Natl. Center for the Amer. Revolution [10134]
Natl. Coalition for History [10135]
Natl. Collectors Assn. of Die Doubling [22746]
Natl. Corvette Owners Assn. [21728]
Natl. Corvette Restorers Soc. [21729]
Natl. Coun. of Corvette Clubs [21730]
Natl. Coun. for History Educ. [8508]
Natl. Coun. on Public History [10136]
Natl. DeSoto Club [21731]
Natl. Firebird and T/A Club [21732]
Natl. Flag Found. [11076]
Natl. Genealogical Soc. [21133]
Natl. Historical Fire Found. [22422]
Natl. History Club [8509]
Natl. History Day [8510]
Natl. Huguenot Soc. [21163]
Natl. Indian Wars Assn. [9371]
Natl. Intercollegiate Flying Assn. [21466]
Natl. Mossberg Collectors Assn. [22430]
Natl. Museum of Racing and Hall of Fame
   [23508]
Natl. Old Timers Auto Racing Club [21737]
Natl. Soc. of the Colonial Dames of Am. [20743]
Natl. Soc. Colonial Dames XVII Century [20744]
Natl. Soc., Daughters of the Amer. Colonists
   [20746]
Natl. Soc. - First Families of Minnesota [21253]
Natl. Soc. of Madison Family Descendants
   [21135]
Natl. Soc. of the Sons of Utah Pioneers [21254]
Natl. Stereoscopic Assn. [10853]
Natl. St. Rod Assn. [21738]
Natl. Trust for Historic Preservation [10051]
Natl. Women's History Proj. [11090]
Natl. Woodie Club [21739]
Natl. World War II Glider Pilots Assn. [21468]
Native Hawaiian Culture and Arts Prog. [10884]
Natural Law Soc. [10813]
Nature Kenya [IO]
Naval Historical Found. [10478]
Navy and Marine Living History Assn. [21206]
Negro Leagues Baseball Museum [23123]
Nepal and Tibet Philatelic Stud. Circle [22852]
Netherlands Economic History Archv. [IO]
New Canaan Historical Soc. [10137]
New England Historic Genealogical Soc. [21136]
New England M.G. "T" Register Limited [21740]
New York Genealogical and Biographical Soc.
   [21137]
New Zealand Historical Assn. [IO]
Newcomen Soc. for the Stud. of the History of
   Engg. and Tech. [IO]
Newcomen Soc. of the U.S. [10138]
Newport Restoration Found. [10052]
Nikon Historical Soc. [10854]
Nineteen Thirty-Two Buick Registry [21741]
Noah Webster House [10053]
North Amer. Assn. for the Stud. of Welsh Culture
   and History [11083]
North Amer. Collectors [22747]
North Amer. Conf. on British Stud. [9760]
North Amer. Levinas Soc. [10817]
North Amer. Mini Moke Registry [21745]
North Amer. Radio Archives [22926]
North Amer. Shortwave Assn. [21507]
North Amer. Soc. of Ancient and Medieval War-
   gamers [22471]
North Amer. Soc. for Oceanic History [10443]
North Amer. Soc. for Sport History [10139]
North Amer. Sundial Soc. [9278]
North Amer. Vexillological Assn. [11077]
North Amer. Victorian Stud. Assn. [11079]
North-South Skirmish Assn. [23727]
Northwest Steam Soc. [22978]
Norwegian-American Historical Assn. [10759]
Norwegian Heraldic Assn. [IO]
Norwegian Inst. of Local History [IO]
NSU Enthusiasts U.S.A. [21746]
Numismatic Literary Guild [22749]
Numismatics Intl. [22750]
Oakland-Pontiac Enthusiast Org. [21748]
Oldsmobile Club of Am. [21749]
Omnibus Soc. [IO]

Reference to "IO" in place of a book number signifies that the association may be found in the 45th edition of International Organizations.

Omohundro Inst. of Early Amer. History and Culture [10140]
On the Lighter Side, Intl. Lighter Collectors [22100]
Opel Motorsports Club [21752]
Optometric Historical Soc. [15728]
Oral History Assn. [10141]
Oral History Soc. [IO]
Order of Americans of Armorial Ancestry [20750]
Order of the Indian Wars [10479]
Orders and Medals Soc. of Am. [22631]
Org. of Amer. Historians [10142]
Org. of Bricklin Owners [21753]
Org. for the History of Canada [IO]
Org. of World Heritage Cities [IO]
Original Hobo Nickel Soc. [22752]
Oughtred Soc. [22101]
OX5 Aviation Pioneers [21469]
Pacific Railroad Soc. [10917]
Packard Auto. Classics [21755]
Packards Intl. Motor Car Club [21758]
Pantera Intl. [21759]
Patriots of Fort McHenry-Living Classrooms [10057]
Peace History Soc. [10143]
Pearl Harbor History Associates [10144]
Pennsylvania German Soc. [21243]
Penobscot Marine Museum [10445]
Phi Alpha Theta [24495]
Philippine Amer. Writers and Artists [11188]
The Photographic Historical Soc. [10855]
Pierce-Arrow Soc. [21761]
Pilgrim Soc. [21249]
Pilgrims of the U.S. [21250]
Plymouth Barracuda/Cuda Owners Club [21763]
Plymouth Owners Club [21764]
Polish Amer. Historical Assn. [10880]
Polish-American-Jewish Alliance for Youth Action [13510]
Polish Genealogical Soc. of Am. [21142]
Polish Underground Movement (1939-1945) Stud. Trust [IO]
Polonus Philatelic Soc. [22857]
Pontiac-Oakland Club Intl. [21766]
Pony Express Historical Assn. [10145]
Popular Rotorcraft Assn. [21471]
Porsche Club of Am. [21767]
Portuguese Acad. of History [IO]
Portuguese Historical and Cultural Soc. [19321]
Post Mark Collectors Club [22858]
Postal Commemorative Soc. [22859]
Postal History Soc. [22860]
Postcard History Soc. [22909]
Precancel Stamp Soc. [22861]
Prehistoric Soc. [IO]
Presbyterian Historical Soc. [10891]
Preservation Volunteers [10059]
Pres. Benjamin Harrison Found. [11142]
Prince Henry Sinclair Soc. of the U.S. [9922]
Professional Car Soc. [21768]
Professional Numismatists Guild [22754]
Professional Scripophily Trade Assn. [761]
Psychohistory Forum [16113]
Public Works Historical Soc. [10146]
Quarter Century Wireless Assn. [21509]
Queensland History Teachers Assn. [IO]
The Questers [21532]
Quiet Valley Living Historical Farm [10147]
Quilters Hall of Fame [22173]
Radio Club of Am. [22928]
Radio Collectors of Am. [22929]
Railroadiana Collectors Assn. Incorporated [22936]
Rainier Soc. [21145]
Ranching Heritage Assn. [10148]
Real Sociedad Espanola de Historia Natural [IO]
REO Club of Am. [21770]
Richard the III Found. [11144]
Richard III Soc. of Canada [IO]
Rickenbacker Automobile Club of America [21771]
Rider Haggard Soc. [IO]
Road Race Lincoln Register [21773]
Robert H. Smith Intl. Center for Jefferson Stud. [9003]
Rolls-Royce Owners' Club [21774]

Romany Soc. [IO]
Rometsch Registry [21775]
Rossica Soc. of Russian Philately [22862]
Rotary on Stamps Fellowship [22863]
Rough and Tumble Engineers' Historical Assn. [22979]
Royal Acad. of Letters, History and Antiquities [IO]
Royal Australian Historical Soc. [IO]
Royal Bath and West of England Soc. [IO]
Royal Historical Soc. - United Kingdom [IO]
Royal Historical Soc. of Victoria [IO]
Royal Soc. of New South Wales [IO]
Royal Soc. of Western Australia [IO]
Royal Western Australian Historical Soc. [IO]
Russian Zone Handoverprint Stud. and Res. Gp. [22864]
Ryukyu Philatelic Specialist Soc. [22865]
Saab Club of North Am. [21778]
Sabra Automobile Connection [21779]
St. Helena, Ascension, and Tristan da Cunha Philatelic Soc. [22866]
Saint Nicholas Soc. of the City of New York [21148]
Samuel Gompers Stamp Club [22867]
San Francisco African Amer. Historical and Cultural Soc. [9362]
SATS/EAF Assn. [21179]
Save the Battlefield Coalition [10061]
Savoie Acadian Cultural and Historical Soc. [21149]
Saxon Owners Registry [21781]
Scandinavian Collectors Club [22868]
Schubert Soc. of the USA [9816]
Scottish Assn. of Family History Societies [IO]
Scottish Church History Soc. [IO]
Scottish Historic and Res. Soc. of Delaware Valley [10955]
Scottish History Soc. [IO]
Scottish Military Historical Soc. [IO]
Scottish Railway Preservation Soc. [IO]
Scouts on Stamps Soc. Intl. [22869]
Seventh Day Baptist Historical Soc. [19495]
Sharkhunters Intl. [10480]
Shelby Amer. Auto. Club [21782]
Shenandoah Natl. Park Assn. [10062]
Ships on Stamps Unit [22870]
Silver Wings Fraternity [21476]
Sir Arthur Sullivan Soc. [IO]
Social History Soc. [IO]
Social Sciences Services and Resources [7656]
Social Welfare History Gp. [10149]
Sociedad Mexicana de Historia Natural [IO]
Soc. for Amer. Baseball Res. [23126]
Soc. of Antique Modelers [21477]
Soc. of Archer-Antiquaries [IO]
Soc. of Architectural Historians [10150]
Soc. for Armenian Stud. [9407]
Soc. of Army Historical Res. [IO]
Soc. of Australasian Specialists/Oceania [22871]
Soc. for Austrian and Habsburg History [9628]
Soc. of Automotive Historians [21785]
Soc. of California Pioneers [21255]
Soc. of Civil War Historians [10151]
Soc. for the Comparative Stud. of Soc. and History [10152]
Soc. for Coptic Archaeology (North Am.) [10153]
Soc. of Dance History Scholars [10154]
Soc. of the Founders and Friends of Norwich, Connecticut [10063]
Soc. of Freight Car Historians [10922]
Soc. for French Historical Stud. [10155]
Soc. for Historians of Amer. Foreign Relations [10156]
Soc. for Historians of the Early Amer. Republic [10157]
Soc. for Historical Archaeology [6457]
Soc. for the History of Czechoslovak Jews [10289]
Soc. for the History of Discoveries [10158]
Soc. for the History of Discoveries [IO]
Soc. for History Educ. [8511]
Soc. for History in the Fed. Govt. [10159]
Soc. for the History of Psychology [7548]
Soc. for the History of Tech. [10160]
Soc. for Hungarian Philately [22873]

Soc. of Indiana Pioneers [21256]
Soc. for Indus. Archeology [6458]
Soc. of Israel Philatelists [22874]
Soc. of Lincoln Cent Collectors [22756]
Soc. for Lincolnshire History and Archaeology [IO]
Soc. for Military History [10482]
Soc. of Paper Money Collectors [22757]
Soc. for the Preservation and Appreciation of Antique Motor Fire Apparatus in Am. [22423]
Soc. of Ration Token Collectors [22759]
Soc. for Romanian Stud. [10939]
Soc. for the Sci. Stud. of Religion [20506]
Soc. for the Social History of Medicine [IO]
Soc. for the Stud. of Early Modern Women [9331]
Soc. for the Stud. of Japanese Religions [20529]
Soc. for the Stud. of Labour History [IO]
Soc. for Thai Philately [22875]
Soc. of U.S. Pattern Collectors [22761]
Sons and Daughters of Oregon Pioneers [21257]
Sons and Daughters of Pioneer Rivermen [21258]
Soo Line Historical and Tech. Soc. [10923]
South St. Seaport Museum [10446]
Southern Historical Assn. [9378]
Souvenir Napoleonien [IO]
Space Topic Stud. Unit [22876]
Sports Car Club of Am. [21787]
Sports Philatelists Intl. [22877]
Stair Soc. [IO]
Stamps on Stamps Collectors Club [22878]
Stamps for the Wounded [22879]
State Revenue Soc. [22880]
Statue of Liberty Club [22118]
Statue of Liberty - Ellis Island Found. [10066]
Steam Auto. Club of Am. [21789]
Steamship Historical Soc. of Am. [22980]
Studebaker Driver's Club [21790]
Stutz Club [21791]
Subaru 360 Drivers' Club [21792]
Supreme Court Historical Soc. [10161]
Surratt Soc. [10067]
Surveyors Historical Soc. [10162]
Swift Museum Found. [21481]
Syrian Stud. Assn. [8880]
Tasmanian History Teachers Assn. [IO]
TE Lawrence Soc. [IO]
Telecommunications Heritage Gp. [IO]
Telephone Collectors Intl. [22986]
Terminal Railroad Assn. Historical and Tech. Soc. [10925]
Thomas Jefferson's Poplar Forest [10069]
Thomas Lovell Beddoes Soc. [IO]
Thompson Collectors Assn. [22431]
Titanic Historical Soc. [10447]
Titanic Intl. Soc. [10448]
Token and Medal Soc. [22763]
Topolino Register of North Am. [21797]
Toxicological History Soc. [7805]
Treasury Historical Assn. [10163]
Trireme Trust U.S.A. [10483]
Triumph Register of Am. [21800]
Tucker Auto. Club of Am. [21801]
Turner Soc. [IO]
TVR Car Club North Am. [21802]
Tyndale Soc. [20530]
Ukrainian Philatelic and Numismatic Soc. [22883]
Ulster Folk and Transport Museum [IO]
Ulster-Scots Soc. of Am. [21154]
Unitarian Universalist Historical Soc. [20601]
United Four-Wheel Drive Associations [21805]
United Nations Philatelists, Inc. [22884]
United Postal Stationery Soc. [22885]
U.S. Cancellation Club [22886]
U.S. Capitol Historical Soc. [10164]
U.S. Cavalry Assn. and Memorial Res. Lib. [10484]
U.S. Classic Racing Assn. [22694]
U.S. Flag Found. [11078]
U.S. Life-Saving Ser. Heritage Assn. [10072]
U.S. Mexican Numismatic Assn. [22765]
U.S. Natl. Comm. for Byzantine Stud. [9771]
Universal Ship Cancellation Soc. [22889]
Unrecognised States Numismatic Soc. [22766]
USMC Vietnam Tankers Assn. [21337]
Uttaranchal Assn. of North Am. [10219]
Valley Forge Historical Soc. [9375]

A star before a book entry number signifies that the name is not listed separately, but is mentioned within the entry.

Veitch Historical Soc. **[21077]**
Vernacular Architecture Forum **[6482]**
Vesterheim Genealogical Center and Naeseth Lib.
  [21155]
Veteran Feminists of Am. **[17572]**
Veteran Motor Car Club of Am. **[21808]**
Victorian Homeowner's Assn. and Old House Lovers **[10075]**
Vietnam Era Seabees **[21339]**
Vietnamese Nom Preservation Found. **[10433]**
Vintage Chevrolet Club of Am. **[21809]**
Vintage Drivers Club of Am. **[21810]**
Vintage Radio and Phonograph Soc. **[22931]**
Vintage Sailplane Assn. **[23045]**
Vintage Thunderbird Club Intl. **[21812]**
Vintage Triumph Register **[21813]**
Vintage Volkswagen Club of Am. **[21814]**
Volkswagen Club of Am. **[21815]**
Volvo Club of Am. **[21816]**
Walter Burley Griffin Soc. of Am. **[9398]**
Weatherby Collectors Assn. **[22432]**
Western Cover Soc. **[22890]**
Western History Assn. **[9384]**
Westerners Intl. **[9385]**
Westerners Intl. **[IO]**
Whirly-Girls - Intl. Women Helicopter Pilots
  [21487]
White House Historical Assn. **[10165]**
White Owners Register **[23026]**
Wilkie Collins Soc. **[IO]**
William Barnes Soc. **[IO]**
William H. Whitsitt Baptist Heritage Soc. **[19500]**
William Herschel Soc. **[IO]**
Wills Sainte Claire Museum **[21817]**
Willys Overland Jeepster Club **[21818]**
Willys-Overland-Knight Registry **[21819]**
Winged Warriors/National B-Body Owners Assn.
  [21820]
Women Writing the West **[4071]**
Women's Classical Caucus **[9801]**
Women's History Network **[11095]**
Wooden Canoe Heritage Assn. **[21887]**
World Airline Historical Soc. **[21488]**
World Assn. for Vedic Stud. **[9854]**
World Heritage Alliance **[10077]**
World History Assn. **[10166]**
World History Assn. **[IO]**
World Internet Numismatic Soc. **[22768]**
World Jewish Genealogy Org. **[21158]**
World Methodist Historical Soc. **[20273]**
World Proof Numismatic Assn. **[22769]**
World War I Aeroplanes **[21490]**
World War Two Stud. Assn. **[10167]**
World War Two Stud. Assn. **[IO]**
Worldwide Camaro Club **[21821]**
Worldwide Television-FM DX Assn. **[21510]**
Young Numismatists of Am. **[22770]**
Zeppelin Collectors Club **[22892]**
History; Acad. of Amer. Franciscan **[19560]**
History; Amer. Museum of Natural **[7357]**
History; Amer. Museum of Negro **[★9360]**
History; Amer. Soc. for Environmental **[8383]**
History; Amer. Soc. for Ethno **[9918]**
History Assn; Amer. Printing **[9989]**
History Assn; Big Bend Natural **[7361]**
History Assn; Mormon **[20208]**
History Assn; Shenandoah Natural **[★10062]**
History Assn; Social Sci. **[7654]**
History; Assn. for the Stud. of Negro Life and
  [★9356]
History Assn; Wert Family **[21082]**
History Assn; Western **[9384]**
History Assn; Yosemite Natural **[★7367]**
History of Authorship, Reading and Publishing; Soc.
  for the **[9754]**
History Buffs Home Page **[★22092]**
History; Center for Military **[★10471]**
History of Chiropractic; Assn. for the **[13994]**
History Collections; Soc. for the Preservation of
  Natural **[10064]**
History; Conf. on Asian **[9617]**
History; Conf. on Latin Amer. **[10310]**
History; Coordinating Coun. for Women in **[17526]**
History of Dentistry; Amer. Acad. of the **[14100]**
History of Dermatology Soc. **[10115]**, 1760 Market
  St., No. 301, Philadelphia, PA 19103-4106,
  (215)563-8333

History of Earth Sciences Soc. **[10116]**, c/o Emma
  Rainforth, Treas., Ramapo Coll. of New Jersey,
  505 Ramapo Valley Rd., Mahwah, NJ 07430
History of Economics Soc. **[10117]**, c/o Neil B. Niman, Treas., Univ. of New Hampshire, McConnell
  Hall, 15 Coll. Rd., Durham, NH 03824, (603)862-
  3336
History of Educ. Soc. **[10118]**, c/o History of Educ.
  Quarterly, Univ. of Illinois at Urbana - Champaign,
  Educational Policy Stud., 360 Educ. Bldg., MC-
  708, 1310 S Sixth St., Champaign, IL 61820,
  (213)333-2446
History, Farm and Agricultural Museums; Assn. for
  Living **[10497]**
History Forum; Irish Family **[9974]**
History Forum; Psycho **[16113]**
History Found; Amer. Military **[★10482]**
History of the Germans in Maryland; Soc. for the
  [9980]
History of the Hapsburg Monarchy; U.S. Comm. to
  Promote Stud. of the **[★9628]**
History Inst. of Am; Black Military **[10472]**
History; Inst. for Psycho **[10123]**
History; Lexington Gp. in Trans. **[10913]**
History Magazine; Historians Film Committee/Film
  and **[9939]**
History; Museum of African Amer. **[9360]**
History; Museum of Amer. Financial **[★10508]**
History; Natl. Assn. for Outlaw and Lawman **[9380]**
History; Natl. Coordinating Comm. for the Promotion
  of **[★10135]**
History; Natl. Museum of Amer. Jewish Military
  [21312]
History Network; Women's **[11095]**
History and Ourselves; Facing **[★10108]**
History of Pharmacy; Amer. Inst. of the **[15917]**
History of Poland; Institute for Res. in Modern
  [★10878]
History of Poland; Institute for Res. in Modern **[★IO]**
History of Poland; Jozef Pilsudski Inst. of Am. for
  Res. in the Modern **[10878]**
History and Records Mgt. Services of the
  Presbyterian Church (U.S.A.); Dept. of **[★10891]**
History Scholars; Dance **[★10154]**
History in Schools; Bradley Commn. on **[★8508]**
History of Sci. Soc. **[10119]**, PO Box 117360,
  Gainesville, FL 32611-7360, (352)392-1677
History of Sci. Soc. **[IO]**, Gainesville, FL, United
  States
History of Sci. Soc. of Japan **[IO]**, Tokyo, Japan
History of the Second World War; Amer. Comm. on
  the **[★10167]**
History of Social Welfare; Comm. on the **[★10149]**
History Societies; Fed. of East European Family
  [★21112]
History; Soc. for Austrian and Habsburg **[9628]**
History Soc; Immigration and **[★10121]**
History Soc; Irish Family **[★21125]**
History; Soc. for Military **[10482]**
History Soc; Postal **[22860]**
History Soc; Postcard **[22909]**
History Soc; Toxicological **[7805]**
History Teachers' Natl. **[★8511]**
History Teachers Assn. of Australia **[IO]**, Perth,
  Australia
History Teachers Assn. of Australia - New South
  Wales **[IO]**, Sydney, Australia
History Teachers Assn. of Victoria **[IO]**, Fitzroy,
  Australia
History Teachers Assn. of Western Australia **[IO]**,
  Nedlands, Australia
History of the United Methodist Church; Gen.
  Commn. on Archives and **[10467]**
History Week Proj; Natl. Women's **[★11090]**
Histotechnology; Natl. Soc. for **[15146]**
Histradut Golden Jubilee Comm. - Defunct.
Hitchhikers for America - Address unknown since
  1995.
HitchHikers of Am. Intl. **[22953]**, PO Box 180, Osceola, IN 46561, (574)258-0571
HIV/AIDS Assn. of Zambia **[IO]**, London, United
  Kingdom
HIV/AIDS Prevention Grants Prog. **[16964]**, c/o U.S.
  Conf. of Mayors, 1620 I St. NW, Washington, DC
  20006, (202)293-7330

HIV/AIDS Prog. **[★16964]**
HIV/AIDS Treatment Info. Ser. **[★13554]**
HIV Information Exchange and Support Group -
  Defunct.
HIV Medicine Assn. **[13569]**, 1300 Wilson Blvd., Ste.
  300, Arlington, VA 22209, (703)299-1215
HIV Medicine; Australasian Soc. for **[IO]**
HIV Over Fifty; Natl. Assn. on **[14952]**
HIV Pharmacy Assn. **[IO]**, Langley, United Kingdom
HIV Prevention; Global Strategies for **[13566]**
HIV Rsrc. Center; Natl. Pediatric and Family **[13581]**
HIV Strategies; Gay **[IO]**
HivNorge **[★IO]**
HivNorway **[IO]**, Oslo, Norway
Hjalparstarf Kirkjunnar **[★IO]**
Hjartasjukdomafelag Islenskra Laekna **[★IO]**
Hjerneskadeforeningen **[★IO]**
H.M. 10th Regiment of Foot, Amer. Contingent
  [9373], 61 Ivan St., Lexington, MA 02420-1422,
  (781)862-2586
HMI Ministries **[20597]**, PO Box 8451, Grand
  Rapids, MI 49518-8451, (616)455-5760
The HMO Gp. **[★14678]**
Hmong Natl. Development **[17815]**, 1112 16th St.
  NW, Ste. 110, Washington, DC 20036, (202)463-
  2118
Hnuti Duha **[★IO]**
Hnuti Pro zivot CR **[★IO]**
Hoard/Hord Clearinghouse - Defunct.
Hobbies
  Amer. Assn. of Riding Schools **[22582]**
  Amer. Assn. of Spanish Timbrado Breeders
    [21834]
  Amer. Cichlid Assn. **[22433]**
  Amer. Cookie Jar Assn. **[22577]**
  Amer. Hydrangea Soc. **[22494]**
  Amer. Lands Access Assn. **[22937]**
  Amer. Model Yachting Assn. **[22642]**
  Antique Barbed Wire Soc. **[21969]**
  Antique Reloading Tool Collector's Assn. **[22424]**
  Authentic Artifact Collectors Assn. **[21543]**
  Boardgame Players Assn. **[22461]**
  Bullseye Cancel Collectors' Club **[22798]**
  Canadian Corkscrew Collectors Club **[21985]**
  Canadian Craft and Hobby Assn. **[IO]**
  Challenge Coin Assn. **[22731]**
  Collegiate Assn. of Table Top Gamers **[22462]**
  Collins Collectors Assn. **[21499]**
  Combined North Amer. Cottage Garden Soc. and
    North Amer. Dianthus Soc. **[22507]**
  Cribbage Bd. Collectors Soc. **[22004]**
  Crochet Guild of Am. **[22722]**
  Elec. Boat Assn. of the Americas **[21872]**
  The Elongated Collectors **[22738]**
  Fed. of Metal Detector and Archaeological Clubs
    [22578]
  Fifty Caliber Shooters Assn. **[22973]**
  Figural Cast Iron Collector's Club **[22417]**
  Gamers Intl. **[22478]**
  Giant Scale Warbirds Assn. **[22644]**
  Golden Glow of Christmas Past **[22975]**
  Intl. Assn. of Duncan Certified Ceramic Teachers
    [21928]
  Intl. Assn. of R.S. Prussia Collectors **[22043]**
  Intl. Assn. of Silver Art Collectors **[22044]**
  Intl. Autograph Collectors Club and Dealers Alliance **[22045]**
  Intl. Bird Dog Assn. **[21452]**
  Intl. Match Safe Assn. **[22053]**
  Intl. Meteorite Collectors Assn. **[22981]**
  Intl. Miniature Aircraft Assn. **[22938]**
  Intl. Modena Club **[22896]**
  Intl. Plastic Modelers Society/United States Br.
    [22646]
  Intl. Scale Soaring Assn. **[22648]**
  Intl. String Figure Assn. **[9833]**
  L.C. Smith Collectors Assn. **[22429]**
  M&M's Collectors Club **[22067]**
  Metal Boat Soc. **[526]**
  Natl. 42 Players Assn. **[22899]**
  Natl. Antique Doll Dealers Assn. **[22402]**
  Natl. Polymer Clay Guild **[22579]**
  Natl. Retail Hobby Stores Assn. **[753]**
  Natl. Stamp Dealers Assn. **[22851]**
  Natl. Token Collectors Assn. **[21954]**

Reference to "IO" in place of a book number signifies that the association may be found in the 45th edition of International Organizations.

North Amer. Confed. of the Red Dragon [22479]
North Amer. Model Horse Shows Assn. [22587]
North Amer. Soc. of Ancient and Medieval War-
gamers [22471]
North Amer. Steam Boat Assn. [21881]
North Amer. Stone Skipping Assn. [22939]
Pacific Coast Cichlid Assn. [22445]
Pen Collectors of Am. [22105]
Precious Metal Clay Guild [8172]
Precision Aerobatics Model Pilots Assn. [21473]
Promotional Glass Collectors Assn. [22109]
Role Playing Game Assn. Network [22474]
Scale Ship Modelers Assn. of North Am. [22656]
Scale Warbird Racing Assn. [22657]
Strategy Gaming Soc. [22475]
Thompson Collectors Assn. [22431]
Toy Stitchers Intl., Inc. [22998]
Toyota Territory Off-Roaders Assn. [22965]
Tugboat Enthusiasts Soc. of the Americas [21886]
United League Toy Representatives Associations
[3833]
US Scale Masters Assn. [22660]
Vaseline Glass Collectors, Inc. [22127]
Weatherby Collectors Assn. [22432]
Women in Toys [3834]
World Miniature Warbird Assn. [22662]
Hobbies to Enjoy Soc. - Defunct.
Hobbit Assn; Amer. [9631]
Hobby Assn; Craft and [1911]
Hobby Club; World Airline [★21488]
Hobby Clubs of America - Address unknown since
1995.
Hobby Greenhouse Assn. [22518], 2049 Baughman
Rd., Jeannette, PA 15644
Hobby Greenhouse Owners Assn. of America -
Defunct.
Hobby Guild of America - Address unknown since
1995.
Hobby Horse Brigade of the Legion of Guardsmen -
Address unknown since 1995.
Hobby Indus. Assn. [★1911]
Hobby Indus. Assn. of Am. [★1911]
Hobby Supplies
Amer. Stamp Dealers Assn. [1910]
Collins Collectors Assn. [21499]
Craft and Hobby Assn. [1911]
Intl. Plastic Modelers Society/United States Br.
[22646]
Model Railroad Indus. Assn. [1912]
Natl. Plastercraft Assn. [1913]
Natl. Retail Hobby Stores Assn. [753]
Radio Control Hobby Trade Assn. [1914]
Soc. of Craft Designers [1915]
Strategy Gaming Soc. [22475]
Track Owners Assn. [1916]
Track Owners Assn. [IO]
Hobbyists; Musical Box [★22717]
Hobie 33 Class Assn. - Defunct.
Hobie Class Assn. [★23186]
Hobie Class Assn. [★IO]
Hochstetler Family Assn; Jacob [20955]
Hocker Intl. Fed. - Address unknown since 2001.
Hockey
African Hockey Fed. [IO]
Amer. Amputee Hockey Assn. [23799]
Amer. Hockey Coaches Assn. [23481]
Amer. Hockey League [23482]
Amer. Hockey League [IO]
Asian Hockey Fed. [IO]
Atlanta Flames Fan Club [24996]
Austrian Ice Hockey Fed. [IO]
Blackhawk Standbys, Inc. [24997]
Blueliners [24998]
British Inline Puck Hockey Assn. [IO]
British Inline Skater Hockey Assn. [IO]
Buffalo Sabres Booster Club [25000]
Bulgarian Ice Hockey Fed. [IO]
Canadian Adult Recreational Hockey Assn. [IO]
Canadian Hockey League [IO]
Central Collegiate Hockey Assn. [23483]
Cleveland Hockey Booster Club [25001]
Croatian Hockey Fed. [IO]
Devils Fan Club [25004]
Eastern Coll. Athletic Conf. [23484]
Eastern Collegiate Hockey Assn. [23485]

England Hockey [IO]
Field Hockey Canada [IO]
Hartford Whalers Booster Club [25006]
Hockey Canada [IO]
Hockey North Am. [23486]
Ice Hockey UK [IO]
Intl. Ice Hockey Fed. [IO]
Los Angeles Kings Booster Club [25007]
Natl. Collegiate Roller Hockey Assn. [23487]
Natl. Field Hockey Coaches Assn. [23404]
Natl. Hockey League Booster Clubs Assn. [25008]
Natl. Roller Hockey Assn. of England [IO]
New York Islanders Booster Club [25009]
New York Rangers Fan Club [25010]
Philadelphia Flyers Fan Club [25011]
Pittsburgh Penguins Booster Club [25012]
Professional Hockey Writers' Assn. [3156]
Red Wing For'em Club [25013]
Scottish Hockey Union [IO]
Soc. for Intl. Hockey Res. [IO]
U.S. Broomball Assn. [23858]
U.S. Field Hockey Assn. [23405]
USA Broomball [23095]
USA Hockey [23488]
Washington Capitals Fan Club [25014]
Western Collegiate Hockey Assn. [23489]
Hockey Assn. [★IO]
Hockey Assn. of Am; Field [★23405]
Hockey Assn; Amer. Hearing Impaired [23337]
Hockey Assn; Canadian Ball [IO]
Hockey Assn; Eastern Collegiate [23485]
Hockey Assn; Intercollegiate Ice [★23484]
Hockey Assn; U.S. Field [23405]
Hockey Assn; U.S.A. Field [★23405]
Hockey Booster Club; Cleveland [25001]
Hockey sur gazon Canada [★IO]
Hockey Canada [IO], Calgary, AB, Canada
Hockey League Booster Clubs Assn; Natl. [25008]
Hockey League Players' Assn; Natl. [IO]
Hockey North Am. [23486], PO Box 78, Sterling, VA
20167-0078, (703)430-8100
Hockey School for the Hearing Impaired; Stan Mikita
[★23337]
Hockey; U.S.A. Field [★23405]
Hockey Writers' Assn; Professional [3156]
Hodgkins Disease and Lymphoma Org. - Defunct.
Hoefler Family Assn. [20942], 1039 Hwy. W, Warren-
ton, MO 63383, (636)456-4610
Hoefler Family Assn; Dannenmueller- [20878]
Hof Reunion Assn. [20682], 6855 S River Rd.,
Geneva, OH 44041-9348, (440)466-5867
Hog Record Assn; Natl. Hereford [5236]
Hogan Software
HUG Intl. - HTE Users' Gp. [6794]
Hogan's Heroes Fan Club - Defunct.
Hogar de Cristo Housing Found. [IO], Santiago,
Chile
Hoge Raad voor Diamant [★IO]
Hogg Family Genealogical Soc. - Defunct.
Hoggatt - Hockett Family Assn. - Defunct.
Hohenzollern Soc. - Defunct.
Hoi Chur thap do Viet Nam [★IO]
Hoist Mfrs. Assn. [★2023]
Hoist Mfrs. Inst. [2023], 8720 Red Oak Blvd., Ste.
201, Charlotte, NC 28217-3992, (704)676-1190
Hola Kumba Ya! - Address unknown since 1999.
Holbrook Genealogical Org; Groberg - [20924]
HOLD; Project [★13223]
Holder Collectors' Soc; Toothpick [★22089]
Holding Companies; Assn. of Bank [★477]
Holding Companies; Assn. of Registered Bank
[★477]
Holiday Accommodation Parks Assn. of New
Zealand [IO], Paraparaumu, New Zealand
Holiday Assn; African Amer. [22974]
Holiday Happenings Ornament Collectors Club -
Defunct.
Holiday Hosp. Proj. [★13395]
Holiday Inst. of Yonkers [18672]
Holiday Proj. [13395], 21 Eagle St., Iselin, NJ
08830, (732)231-6725
Holiday Rambler Recreational Vehicle Club [22954],
PO Box 587, 600 E Wabash, Wakarusa, IN 46573,
(574)862-7330
Holiday Service [★22580]

Holiday Trav-L-Park Assn; Best [3354]
Holidays for Humanity - Defunct.
Holiness Partnership; Christian [19779]
Holistic Dental Assn. [14156], PO Box 151444, San
Diego, CA 92175, (619)923-3120
Holistic Dental Assn. Intl. [★14156]
Holistic Hea. and World Peace; Serendipity Assn. for
Res. and Implementation of [★14832]
Holistic Life Found. [★12345]
Holistic Mgt; Allan Savory Center for [★4408]
Holistic Mgt; Center for [★4408]
Holistic Mgt. Intl. [4408], 1010 Tijeras Ave. NW,
Albuquerque, NM 87102, (505)842-5252
Holistic Medical Assn; Amer. [14824]
Holistic Medical Assn; Amer. Veterinary [★16773]
Holistic Medicine
Advocate Hea. Care [14821]
Alliance for Alternatives in Healthcare [13609]
Amer. Acad. of Alternative Medicine [13612]
Amer. CranioSacral Therapy Assn. [14822]
Amer. Holistic Hea. Assn. [14823]
Amer. Holistic Medical Assn. [14824]
Amer. Holistic Nurses' Assn. [14825]
Amer. Holistic Veterinary Medical Assn. [16773]
Amer. Inst. of Homeopathy [14845]
Ananda Yoga Teachers Assn. [11217]
Assn. of Himalayan Yoga Meditation Societies
[11218]
Assn. of Holistic Biodynamic Massage Therapists
[IO]
Assn. of Natural Medicine Pharmacists [15282]
Craniosacral Therapy Assn. of Australia [IO]
East West Acad. of Healing Arts [15744]
Flower Essence Soc. [14818]
Friends of Falun Gong [17061]
Hea. Optimizing Inst. [14826]
Himalayan Intl. Inst. of Yoga Sci. and Philosophy
of the U.S.A. [12348]
Holistic Dental Assn. [14156]
Intl. Assn. of Medical Intuitives [15040]
Intl. Center for Reiki Training [22969]
Intl. Coll. of Applied Kinesiology - U.S.A. [14827]
International College of Applied Kinesiology -
U.S.A. [IO]
Intl. Found. for Homeopathy [14849]
Kundalini Res. Network [14828]
Life Resources Inst. [14829]
Mandala Soc. [12356]
Natl. Assn. for Holistic Aromatherapy [14830]
North Amer. Yoga Fed. [11219]
Nurse Healers Professional Associates Intl.
[14831]
Serendipity Assn. [14832]
Veterinary Inst. of Integrative Medicine [16815]
Wilbur Hot Springs Hea. Sanctuary [10180]
World Wide Essence Soc. [14833]
World Wide Essence Soc. [IO]
Yoga Alliance [11220]
Zero Balancing Hea. Assn. [14834]
Holistic Moms Network [12673], PO Box 408, Cald-
well, NJ 07006, (877)465-6667
Holistic Veterinary Medical Assn; Amer. [16773]
Holland Comm. on Southern Africa [★IO]
Holland Dames; Soc. of Daughters of [20759]
Holland Historical Trust [9909], 31 W 10th St., Hol-
land, MI 49423, (616)394-1362
Holland Historical Trust [IO], Holland, MI, United
States
Holland Lop Rabbit Specialty Club [5146], 2633
Seven Eleven Rd., Chesapeake, VA 23322,
(757)421-9607
Holland Soc. of Arts and Sciences [IO], Haarlem,
Netherlands
Holland Soc. of New York [20740], 122 E 58th St.,
New York, NY 10022, (212)758-1675
Holland's Opus Found; Mr. [8914]
Hollingworth Center for Highly Gifted Children
[9982], 827 Central Ave., No. 282, Dover, NH
03820-2506, (207)655-3767
Hollow Earth [★12354]
Hollow Earth [★IO]
Hollow Metal Door and Buck Assn. - Address
unknown since 2003.
Holloway - Ralston Family Assn. [20943], 7650 Fair-
view Rd., Tillamook, OR 97141, (503)842-6036

A star before a book entry number signifies that the name is not listed separately, but is mentioned within the entry.

Holly Dunn Fan Club - Address unknown since 1995.
Holly Soc. of Am. [5256], c/o Rondalyn Reeser, Sec., PO Box 803, 309 Buck St., Millville, NJ 08332-0803, (856)825-4300
Hollywood Chap. of Natl. Acad. of TV Arts and Sciences [★542]
Hollywood Comedy Club - Address unknown since 1991.
Hollywood Foreign Press Assn. [3115], 646 N Robertson Blvd., West Hollywood, CA 90069, (310)657-1731
Hollywood Radio and TV Soc. [559], 13701 Riverside Dr., Ste. 205, Sherman Oaks, CA 91423, (818)789-1182
Hollywood Sign Trust [17710], PO Box 480314, Los Angeles, CA 90048, (323)939-1191
Hollywood Studio Collectors Club - Address unknown since 1995.
Hollywood Women's Political Comm. - Address unknown since 2001.
Holmes-Greatorex Family Org. - Defunct.
Holmes, Sherlock
Baker St. Irregulars [10964]
Holocaust
AMCHA, the Natl. Israeli Centre for Psychosocial Support of Holocaust Survivors and the Second Generation [IO]
Amer. Gathering of Jewish Holocaust Survivors [17712]
Anne Frank Center U.S.A. [17713]
Anne Frank Center U.S.A. [IO]
Anne Frank - Fonds [IO]
Anne Frank House [IO]
Anti-Defamation League [17091]
Assn. of Holocaust Organizations [17714]
Assn. of Holocaust Organizations [IO]
The Blue Card [12468]
Braun Holocaust Inst. [17715]
Children of the Holocaust Assn. in Poland [IO]
Conf. on Jewish Material Claims Against Germany [12470]
Descendants of the Shoah [IO]
Facing History and Ourselves Natl. Found. [10108]
Found. for the Advancement of Sephardic Stud. and Culture [19181]
Gp. Proj. for Holocaust Survivors and Their Children [17716]
Group Project for Holocaust Survivors and Their Children [IO]
Holocaust Centre of Toronto [IO]
Holocaust Documentation and Educ. Center [17717]
Holocaust Rsrc. Center [17718]
Holocaust Survivors and Friends in Pursuit of Justice [17719]
Inst. for Historical Rev. [17711]
Intl. Network of Children of Jewish Holocaust Survivors [17720]
Intl. Network of Children of Jewish Holocaust Survivors [IO]
Jewish Found. for the Righteous [IO]
Jewish Found. for the Righteous [17721]
Jewish Philanthropic Fund of 1933 [12475]
Masada the Holocaust Survivors Org. [17722]
Masada the Holocaust Survivors Org. [IO]
National Liberty Museum [IO]
Natl. Liberty Museum [17723]
Simon Wiesenthal Center [17724]
Simon Wiesenthal Center [IO]
Soc. for the Philosophical Stud. of Genocide and the Holocaust [10835]
Thanks to Scandinavia [8436]
U.S. Holocaust Memorial Coun. [17725]
Warsaw Ghetto Resistance Org. [20191]
World Fed. of Bergen-Belsen Associations [17726]
World Fed. of Bergen-Belsen Associations [IO]
Yad Vashem, The Holocaust Martyrs' and Heroes' Remembrance Authority [IO]
Holocaust; Center for Stud. on the [★17715]
Holocaust Centre of Toronto [IO], Toronto, ON, Canada
Holocaust Documentation and Educ. Center [17717], 2031 Harrison St., Hollywood, FL 33020, (954)929-5690

Holocaust/Human Rights Res. Proj. [★17781]
Holocaust/Human Rights Res. Proj. [★IO]
Holocaust Information Network - Defunct.
Holocaust Memorial Center; Southeastern Florida [★17717]
Holocaust; Natl. Inst. on the [★17723]
Holocaust Oral History Project - Address unknown since 2003.
Holocaust; President's Commn. on the [★17725]
Holocaust Rsrc. Center [17718], Kean Univ. Lib., 2nd Fl., Union, NJ 07083, (908)737-4660
Holocaust Soc; Black [16938]
Holocaust Stud; Braun Center for [★17715]
Holocaust Stud; Intl. Center for [★17715]
Holocaust Survivors Assn., U.S.A. [★17119]
Holocaust Survivors of Auschwitz - Address unknown since 1999.
Holocaust Survivors and Friends in Pursuit of Justice [17719], 800 New Loudon Rd., Ste. 400, Latham, NY 12110, (518)785-0035
Holocaust Survivors Memorial Found. - Address unknown since 2001.
Holotropic Breathwork Intl; Assn. for [13626]
Holstein Assn. of Am. [★4263]
Holstein Assn. USA [4263], 1 Holstein Pl., Brattleboro, VT 05302-0808, (802)254-4551
Holstein Cattle Breeders' Assn. of the Czech Republic [IO], Prague, Czech Republic
Holstein-Friesian Assn. of Am. [★4263]
Holstein Heritage Soc; American/Schleswig- [19066]
Holstein Horse Assn; Amer. [★4824]
Holstein Junior Prog. [4264], c/o Holstein Assn. USA, Inc., 1 Holstein Pl., Brattleboro, VT 05302-0808, (802)254-4551
Holsteiner Horse Assn; Amer. [4824]
Holsteiner Horses; Amer. Assn. of Breeders of [★4824]
Holt Adoption Prog. and Holt Children's Services [★11698]
Holt Adoption Prog. and Holt Children's Services [★IO]
Holt Intl. Children's Services [IO], Eugene, OR, United States
Holt Intl. Children's Services [11698], 1195 City View, PO Box 2880, Eugene, OR 97402, (541)687-2202
Holy Childhood Assn. [19632], 366 5th Ave., New York, NY 10001, (212)563-8700
Holy Cross Foreign Mission Soc. [19633], c/o Holy Cross Mission Center, PO Box 543, Notre Dame, IN 46556, (574)631-5477
Holy Cross; Soc. of the Companions of the [19971]
Holy Face Assn. [19634], PO Box 821, Champlain, NY 12919-0821, (514)747-0357
Holy Face Assn. [IO], Montreal, QC, Canada
Holy Family Cancer Home [★19027]
Holy Ghost; Archconfraternity of the [19573]
Holy Innocents Reparation Comm. [18554]
Holy Land Christian Mission [★20312]
Holy Land Christian Mission [★IO]
Holy Land Christian Mission Intl. [★IO]
Holy Land Christian Mission Intl. [★20312]
Holy Land State Comm. - Address unknown since 1989.
Holy Name Soc. - Defunct.
Holy Name Soc; Natl. Assn. of the [19666]
Holy Sepulchre of Jerusalem; Religious and Military Order of Knights of the [19008]
Holy Shroud Guild [19635], PO Box 993, Canandaigua, NY 14424, (716)394-2606
Holy Sites; Athra Kadisha: The Soc. for the Preservation of Jewish [10274]
Holy Spirit Stud. Centre [IO], Hong Kong, People's Republic of China
Holyearth Found. - Defunct.
Homan Fan Club; Bob [24852]
Home
African Amer. Alliance for Homeownership [1975]
Amer. Clipper Owners Club [22942]
Amer. Historic Inns [1909]
Amer. Homeowners Grassroots Alliance [17727]
Assn. for the Restoration of the Church and Home [19844]
Community Associations Inst. [17212]
Discovery Owners Assn., Inc. [22947]

Escapees [22948]
European Home Systems Assn. [IO]
Family Motor Coach Assn. [22949]
Fed. Alliance For Safe Homes [12061]
Good Sam Recreational Vehicle Club [22951]
Homelink Intl. [22580]
Homeowners Against Deficient Dwellings [12314]
Intl. Assn. of Home Staging Professionals [2261]
Interval Intl. [22581]
Jayco Travel Club [22955]
Loners on Wheels [22957]
Natl. Assn. of Mold Professionals [1330]
Natl. Assn. of Trailer Owners [22959]
Natl. Org. of Remediators and Mold Inspectors [1331]
NeighborWorks Am. [12335]
RV Mfrs'. Clubs Assn. [22961]
SunnyTravelers [22963]
Victorian Homeowner's Assn. and Old House Lovers [10075]
Wally Byam Caravan Club Intl. [22967]
Winnebago-Itasca Travelers [22968]
Home Administrators; Amer. Coll. of Nursing [★15535]
Home Appliance Manufacturers; Assn. of [264]
Home Assn; Bide-A-Wee [11371]
Home Automation Assn. [★1178]
Home Baking Assn. [1520], 2931 SW Gainsboro Rd., Topeka, KS 66614-4413, (785)478-3283
Home Based Business
Amer. Assn. of Home Based Businesses [1917]
Amer. Historic Inns [1909]
Amer. Home Bus. Assn. [1918]
Catholic Homesteading Movement [11742]
Center for Self-Sufficiency [11743]
Fed. of Egalitarian Communities [11746]
Home Office Assn. of Am. [1919]
Homeworkers Organized for More Employment [12081]
Mothers' Home Bus. Network [1920]
Natl. Assn. of At-Home Mothers [12674]
Natl. Assn. of Home Based Businesses [1921]
Natl. Work at Home Mom Assn. [1922]
Natl. Work at Home Mom Assn. [IO]
SOHO Am. [3630]
Solace Intl. [13439]
Home Based Businesses; Amer. Assn. of [1917]
Home-Based Early Interventionists; Amer. Assn. for [17056]
Home-Based Working Moms [722], c/o Lesley Spencer Pyle, Founder/Pres., PO Box 1628, Spring, TX 77383-1628, (281)350-4495
Home Bible League; World [★19510]
Home Birth Assn. of Ireland [IO], Bray, Ireland
Home Brewing
Brewmeisters Anonymous [21829]
Home Builders Assn. of North Am; Log [1031]
Home Builders Inst. [627], 1201 15th St. NW, 6th Fl., Washington, DC 20005, (202)371-0600
Home Builders; Natl. Assn. of [1035]
Home Builders of the U.S; Natl. Assn. of [★1035]
Home Care
ACT Hospice Palliative Care Soc. [IO]
Amer. Acad. of Home Care Physicians [14835]
Amer. Assn. for Continuity of Care [14836]
Asia Pacific Hospice Palliative Care Network [IO]
Assn. for Childbirth at Home, Intl. [15591]
Assn. Congolaise Accompagner [IO]
Assn. Izida [IO]
Assn. of Jewish Aging Services [11277]
Australasian Palliative Link Intl. [IO]
Australian and New Zealand Soc. of Palliative Medicine [IO]
British Columbia Hospice Palliative Care Assn. [IO]
Canadian Home Care Assn. [IO]
Carers Northern Ireland [IO]
Center for Humane Options in Childbirth Experiences [15594]
Children's Hospice Intl. [14853]
Croatian Soc. for Hospice and P.C. [IO]
Danish Soc. of Palliative Medicine [IO]
Delta Hospice Soc. [IO]
Finnish Assn. of Palliative Care [IO]
Geelona Hospice Care Assn. [IO]

Reference to "IO" in place of a book number signifies that the association may be found in the 45th edition of International Organizations.

God's Love We Deliver [12283]
Home Healthcare Nurses Assn. [15481]
Hong Kong Soc. of Palliative Medicine [IO]
Hospice Assn. of Am. [14837]
Hungarian Hospice Assn. [IO]
Informed Homebirth/Informed Birth and Parenting [15602]
Intl. Assn. for Hospice and Palliative Care [14838]
Intl. Assn. for Hospice and Palliative Care [IO]
Lithuanian Soc. of Palliative Care [IO]
Little Bros. - Friends of the Elderly [11295]
Meals on Wheels Assn. of Am. [12284]
Natl. Adult Day Services Assn. [11298]
Natl. Alliance for Infusion Therapy [14839]
Natl. Assn. for Home Care and Hospice [14840]
Natl. Assn. of Mold Professionals [1330]
Natl. Coun. on the Aging [11309]
Natl. Family Caregivers Assn. [14841]
Natl. Home Infusion Assn. [15043]
Natl. Hospice and Palliative Care Org. [14856]
Natl. Meals on Wheels Found. [11315]
Natl. Org. of Remediators and Mold Inspectors [1331]
Natl. Palliative Care Nursing Org. [IO]
Natl. Private Duty Assn. [14842]
Newfoundland and Labrador Palliative Care Assn. [IO]
Nordic Assn. for Palliative Care [IO]
Oley Found. for Home Parenteral and Enteral Nutrition [14843]
Palliative Care Assn. of Alberta [IO]
Palliative Care Assn. of NSW [IO]
Palliative Care Victoria [IO]
P.R.I.D.E. Found. - Promote Real Independence for the Disabled and Elderly [11982]
Saskatchewan Palliative Care Assn. [IO]
United Kingdom Home Care Assn. [IO]
World Homecare and Hospice Org. [IO]
World Homecare and Hospice Org. [14844]
Home Center Inst. [3407], c/o North Amer. Retail Hardware Assn., 5822 W 74th St., Indianapolis, IN 46278-1787, (317)290-0338
Home Counties Welsh Pony and Cob Assn. [IO], Windsor, United Kingdom
Home Dads; Slowlane/Stay At [18182]
Home Delivered and Congregate Meal Providers; Natl. Assn. of [★12284]
Home Demonstration Agents' Assn; Natl. [★5612]
Home Demonstration Coun; Natl. [★8513]
Home Economics
Amer. Assn. of Family and Consumer Sciences [12285]
Canadian Assn. for Res. in Home Economics [IO]
Fed. of Home Economics Teachers [IO]
Hong Kong Home Economics Assn. [IO]
Intl. Fed. for Home Economics - USA [IO]
Intl. Fed. for Home Economics - USA [8512]
Kappa Omicron Nu [24496]
Natl. Assn. for Family and Community Educ. [8513]
Natl. Assn. of State Administrators for Family Consumer Sciences [8514]
Natl. Assn. of Teacher Educators for Family and Consumer Sciences [8515]
Phi Upsilon Omicron [24497]
Home Economics Assn; Amer. [★12285]
Home Economics Assn. of Seventh-day Adventists - Defunct.
Home Economics Educ. Assn. [★8418]
Home Economics; Natl. Assn. of State Supervisors of Vocational [★8514]
Home Economics; Natl. Assn. of Teacher Educators for [★8515]
Home Economics; Natl. Assn. of Teacher Educators for Vocational [★8515]
Home Economics Supervisors; Natl. Assn. of [★8514]
Home Economists in Business - Address unknown since 2003.
Home Educ. Assn. [IO], Stanmore, Australia
Home Education Resource Center - Defunct.
Home Energy Rating Systems Coun. - Defunct.
Home Equity Conversion; Natl. Center for [1470]
Home Exchange
Homelink Intl. [22580]

Interval Intl. [22581]
Interval Intl. [IO]
Home Executives Natl. Networking Assn. - Address unknown since 2003.
Home Fashion Products Assn. [2258], 355 Lexington Ave., New York, NY 10017-6603, (212)297-2155
Home Fashions League [★2264]
Home Fashions League [★IO]
Home Fashions League; Natl. [★2264]
Home and Foreign Mission Soc; Woman's [19443]
Home Front Campaign [★11672]
Home Front Campaign [★IO]
Home Furnishings Assn; Natl. [1703]
Home Furnishings Industry Comm. - Defunct.
Home Furnishings Intl. Assn. [1697], PO Box 420807, Dallas, TX 75342, (214)741-7632
Home Furnishings Market Authority; Intl. [1701]
Home Furnishings Marketing Assn; Intl. [★1701]
Home Furnishings Representatives Assn; Natl. [★1702]
Home and Garden Show Executives Intl. - Defunct.
Home Hea. Agencies/Community Hea. Services; Coun. of [★14840]
Home Hea. Agencies; Natl. Assn. of [★14840]
Home Hea. Care Assn; Am. Individual and Gp. [★12291]
Home Health Services and Staffing Assn. - Address unknown since 2002.
Home Healthcare Nurses Assn. [15481], PO Box 91486, Washington, DC 20090, (202)547-7424
Home Improvement Coun; Natl. [★643]
Home Improvement Dealers Assn. of America - Defunct.
Home Improvement Lenders Assn. - Defunct.
Home Improvement Products Assn. - Defunct.
Home Improvement Res. Inst. [1159], 3922 Coconut Palm Dr., 3rd Fl., Tampa, FL 33619, (813)627-6750
Home Inspectors; Amer. Soc. of [592]
Home Inspectors; Examination Bd. of Professional [2118]
Home Inspectors; Housing Inspection Foundation/ Association of [★2119]
Home Inspectors; Natl. Assn. of Certified [2121]
Home Laundering Consultative Coun. [IO], London, United Kingdom
Home Laundry Manufacturers Assn; Amer. [★264]
Home Lighting Assn; Amer. [★2431]
Home Mfrs. Assn. [★2524]
Home Mfrs. Assn; Mobile [★2527]
Home Mfrs. Coun. of NAHB; Dome Comm. of the [★2530]
Home Mfrs. Councils of NAHB [★2524]
Home Mfrs. Inst; Prefab. [★2524]
Home Mfrs; Natl. Assn. of [★2524]
Home Mfrs; Natl. Assn. of Dome [★2530]
Home Mission Soc; Amer. Baptist [★19484]
Home Mission Soc; Woman's Amer. Baptist [★19484]
Home Missionary Movement; Laymen's [20018]
Home Missions Assn; Evangelism and [20006]
Home Missions Fellowship; Natl. [★20301]
Home; Mothers at [★12669]
Home Office Assn. of Am. [1919]
Home Off. Life Underwriters Assn. [★2148]
Home Off. Life Underwriters Assn. [★IO]
Home Off. Products Assn; School and [2849]
Home Off. Underwriters; Assn. of [2148]
Home Orchard Soc. [4734], PO Box 230192, Tigard, OR 97281-0192, (503)293-1468
Home Oriented Maternity Experience - Defunct.
Home Owners Found; Natl. Mobile/Manufactured [★12323]
Home Owners; Natl. Found. of Manufactured [12323]
Home Ownership Made Easy Assn. - Defunct.
Home Products Safety Coun. - Defunct.
Home Recording Rights Coalition [5844], PO Box 14267, Washington, DC 20044-4267, (202)628-9212
Home Rental Managers; Assn. of Vacation [★3344]
Home Repair
Home Improvement Res. Inst. [1159]
Homeowners Against Deficient Dwellings [12314]
Homes for Our Troops [21302]

Natl. Assn. of Mold Professionals [1330]
Natl. Org. of Remediators and Mold Inspectors [1331]
NeighborWorks Am. [12335]
Victorian Homeowner's Assn. and Old House Lovers [10075]
Home Safety Coun. - Defunct.
Home Safety; Inst. for Bus. and [2171]
Home Safety and Security Professionals; Intl. Assn. of [3527]
Home and School Inst. [8261], MegaSkills Educ. Center, 1500 Massachusetts Ave. NW, Washington, DC 20005, (202)466-3633
Home School Legal Defense Assn. [8339], PO Box 3000, Purcellville, VA 20134-9000, (540)338-5600
Home School Sports Network [23490], PO Box 69, Linden, VA 22642, (540)636-3713
Home Schooling Inst. - Defunct.
Home Sewing Assn. [3784], PO Box 1312, Monroeville, PA 15146, (412)372-5950
Home Sewing Assn; Natl. [★3784]
Home Sewing and Craft Assn; Amer. [★3784]
Home-Start North and Mid Beds [IO], Bedford, United Kingdom
Home Study
Assn. of British Correspondence Colleges [IO]
Catholic Homesteading Movement [11742]
Christian Home Educators Assn. of California [8516]
Distance Educ. and Training Coun. [8517]
European Assn. for Distance Learning [IO]
Home Educ. Assn. [IO]
Home School Legal Defense Assn. [8339]
Home School Sports Network [23490]
Home Stud. Exchange [8518]
Home Stud. Exchange [IO]
Intl. Soc. for Educative Communities [IO] Mentalphysics [20503]
Natl. Assn. of Catholic Homes and Educators [8057]
Natl. Assn. for Legal Support of Alternative Schools [7946]
Natl. Black Home Educators [8519]
Natl. Challenged Homeschoolers Assoc. Network [8520]
Natl. Christian Forensics and Communications Assn. [8521]
Natl. Home Educ. Res. Inst. [8522]
National Home Education Research Institute [IO]
Parents' Rights Org. [7950]
U.S. Distance Learning Assn. [8523]
Home Stud. Exchange [8518], PO Box 289, Torreon, NM 87061-0289, (505)847-2909
Home Stud. Exchange [IO], Torreon, NM, United States
Home for Unwanted and Lost Animals [IO], Milton Keynes, United Kingdom
Home Ventilating Inst. [★1883]
Home Ventilating Inst. [1883], 1000 N Rand Rd., Ste. 214, Wauconda, IL 60084, (847)526-2010
Home Ventilating Inst. Division of the Air Movement Control Assn. [★1883]
Home Wine and Beer Trade Assn. [202], c/o Dee Roberson, Exec. Dir., PO Box 1373, Valrico, FL 33595, (813)685-4261
Home Wine and Beer Trade Association [IO], Valrico, FL, United States
Home and Workshop Writers; Natl. Assn. of [3131]
Homebirth/Informed Birth and Parenting; Informed [15602]
Homebound and Hospitalized Children; Assn. of Educators for [★11998]
Homebound and Hospitalized Children; Assn. of Educators for [★9141]
Homebound and Hospitalized; Div. on Physically Handicapped, [★11998]
Homebound and Hospitalized; Div. on Physically Handicapped, [★9141]
Homebound Programs; Natl. Assn. of Sheltered Workshops and [★16312]
Homebrewers Assn; Am. [191]
Homefront Hugs USA [13352], 1449 Tiger Lake Dr., Gulf Breeze, FL 32563, (412)498-3855
Homeland Ministries; Division of [★19856]
Homeless
Amer. Bar Assn. Commn. on Homelessness and Poverty [12286]

A star before a book entry number signifies that the name is not listed separately, but is mentioned within the entry.

Amer. Rescue Team Intl. **[12287]**
America's Second Harvest **[12388]**
Australian Fed. of Homelessness Organisations
[IO]
Children of the Americas **[11574]**
Children of the Night **[12933]**
Circle of Friends for Amer. Veterans **[21293]**
CityTeam Ministries **[12844]**
Community for Creative Non-Violence **[12288]**
Coun. to Homeless Persons **[IO]**
End Homelessness Now **[12289]**
European Fed. of Natl. Organisations Working
with the Homeless **[IO]**
Family Promise **[12290]**
Hands of Mercy **[12291]**
HELP USA **[12292]**
Homeless Children Intl. **[20080]**
Homeless Children Intl. **[IO]**
Homeless Children Intl. - Kenya **[IO]**
Homeless Children Intl. - Thailand **[IO]**
Homeless Children Intl. - United Kingdom **[IO]**
Inst. for Children and Poverty **[11602]**
Kindness in Suffering **[11616]**
Lotus Outreach **[13143]**
Manna House **[12293]**
Mothers Without Borders **[11624]**
Natl. Alliance to End Homelessness **[12294]**
Natl. Center for Homeless Educ. **[12295]**
Natl. Coalition for the Homeless **[12296]**
Natl. Coalition for Homeless Veterans **[21310]**
Natl. Law Center on Homelessness and Poverty
[12297]
Natl. Network for Youth **[12935]**
Natl. Rsrc. Center on Homelessness and Mental
Illness **[12298]**
Natl, Runaway Switchboard **[12936]**
Natl. Student Campaign Against Hunger and
Homelessness **[12396]**
North Amer. St. Newspaper Assn. **[18102]**
Only a Child **[11643]**
Orphan Found. of Am. **[11715]**
Orphan Resources Intl. **[11644]**
Outpost for Hope **[12610]**
People Helping People **[12385]**
Proj. Renewal **[13277]**
ReREAD **[12299]**
Scottish Coun. for Single Homeless **[IO]**
Seva Found. **[12443]**
Smile Alliance Intl. **[11721]**
Tatry Housing Org. **[12300]**
Tatry Housing Org. **[IO]**
Tech. Assistance Collaborative **[13145]**
Travelers Aid Intl. **[13191]**
Windward Found. **[13195]**
Work Fairness **[12110]**
Homeless Children Intl. **[20080]**, PO Box 416, Re-
idville, SC 29375-0416
Homeless Children Intl. **[IO]**, Reidville, SC, United
States
Homeless Children Intl. - Kenya **[IO]**, Nairobi, Kenya
Homeless Children Intl. - Thailand **[IO]**, Chiang Mai,
Thailand
Homeless Children Intl. - United Kingdom **[IO]**, Wor-
thing, United Kingdom
Homeless Coun; Natl. Hea. Care for the **[14730]**
Homeless Proj; Amer. Bar Assn. Representation of
the **[★12286]**
Homeless Veterans; Natl. Coalition for **[21310]**
Homelessness Info. Exchange **[★12296]**
Homelessness; Natl. Student Campaign Against
Hunger and **[12396]**
Homelink International **[★22580]**
Homelink Intl. **[22580]**, c/o Karl Costabel, Exec. Off.,
2937 NW 9th Terr., Wilton Manors, FL 33311,
(954)566-2687
HomeLink Intl. Canada **[IO]**, North Vancouver, BC,
Canada
Homemakers of Am; New **[★8417]**
Homemakers of Amer; Future **[★8417]**
Homemakers Coun; Natl. Extension **[★8513]**
Homemakers Equal Rights Assn. - Defunct.
Homemakers Network; Natl. Displaced **[★18819]**
Homeopathic Assn; British **[IO]**
Homeopathic Coun. for Res. and Education -
Defunct.

Homeopathic Medical Coun. of Canada **[IO]**, Tor-
onto, ON, Canada
Homeopathic Nurses Assn. **[IO]**, Silver Spring, MD,
United States
Homeopathic Nurses Assn. **[14846]**, c/o Margaret
Easter, Sec.-Treas., 8403 Tahona Dr., Silver
Spring, MD 20903, (866)240-0495
Homeopathic Pharmacopoeia of the U.S. **[14847]**,
PO Box 2221, Southeastern, PA 19399-2221,
(610)575-0955
Homeopaths Without Borders **[14848]**, c/o Joe Lil-
lard, Treas., 33 Fairfax St., Berkeley Springs, WV
25411, (304)258-2541
Homeopathy
Alliance for Alternatives in Healthcare **[13609]**
Alliance of Registered Homeopaths **[IO]**
Amer. Inst. of Homeopathy **[14845]**
Australian Homoeopathic Assn. **[IO]**
British Assn. of Homoeopathic Veterinary
Surgeons **[IO]**
European Coun. for Classical Homeopathy **[IO]**
Holistic Moms Network **[12673]**
Homeopathic Medical Coun. of Canada **[IO]**
Homeopathic Nurses Assn. **[IO]**
Homeopathic Nurses Assn. **[14846]**
Homeopathic Pharmacopoeia of the U.S. **[14847]**
Homeopaths Without Borders **[14848]**
Homoeopathic Medical Assn. **[IO]**
Homoeopathic Medical Assn. of India **[IO]**
Indian Homoeopathic Medical Assn. **[IO]**
Intl. Found. for Homeopathy **[14849]**
Intl. Homeopathic Medical League **[IO]**
Iranian Homeopathic Assn. **[IO]**
Irish Soc. of Homeopaths **[IO]**
Natl. Center for Homeopathy **[14850]**
North Amer. Soc. of Homeopaths **[14851]**
Homeopathy; Faculty of **[IO]**
Homeopathy; Intl. Found. for the Promotion of
[★14849]
Homeowners Against Deficient Dwellings **[12314]**,
c/o Nancy Seats, Pres., 410 S Geyer Rd., Kirk-
wood, MO 63122, (314)909-1667
Homeowners Assn; Amer. **[2458]**
Homeowners Assn; Natl. **[12324]**
Homeowner's Assn. and Old House Lovers;
Victorian **[10075]**
Homeowners Found; Amer. **[3296]**
Homeowners' Rsrc. Center; Amer. **[17743]**
Homeowner's Rights Org. - Address unknown since
1999.
HomePlug Powerline Alliance **[1216]**, 2400 Camino
Ramon, Ste. 375, San Ramon, CA 94583,
(925)275-6630
Homer Haskins Soc; Charles **[10459]**
Homer Laughlin China Collectors Assn. **[22036]**, PO
Box 721, North Platte, NE 69103-0721
Homer Laughlin China Collectors Association **[IO]**,
North Platte, NE, United States
Homes; Alliance for Healthy **[13320]**
Homes for Boys; Natl. Assn. of **[★13501]**
Homes for Children; Natl. Assn. of **[★12136]**
Homes Coun; Amer. Log **[★2525]**
Homes Coun; Log **[2525]**
Homes and Hospitals; Assn. of Baptist **[★19471]**
Homes and Hospitals Assn; Church of the Brethren
[★11276]
Homes and Older Adult Ministries; Bd. of Brethren
[★11276]
Homes and Older Adult Ministries; Brethren
[★11276]
Homes for Our Troops **[21302]**, 37 Main St., Taun-
ton, MA 02780, (508)823-3300
Homes for Scotland **[IO]**, Edinburgh, United
Kingdom
Homes and Services for the Aging; Amer. Assn. of
[11273]
Homesteaders Assn. - Defunct.
Homesteading Assistance Bd; Urban **[12339]**
Homesteading Movement; Catholic **[11742]**
HomeSupport Canada **[★IO]**
Homeworkers Organized for More Employment
[12081], PO Box 10, Orland, ME 04472, (207)469-
7961
Homicide Investigators Assn; Intl. **[5883]**
Homiletics
Acad. of Homiletics **[20081]**

Homiletics; Amer. Acad. of **[★20081]**
Homoeopathic Medical Assn. **[IO]**, Gravesend,
United Kingdom
Homoeopathic Medical Assn. of India **[IO]**, Kanpur,
India
Homophile Effort for Legal Protection - Defunct.
Homophile League; Student **[★12224]**
Homosexual Info. Center **[12235]**, c/o Tangent Gp.,
PO Box 310, Bell, CA 90201, (585)880-0831
Homosexual Men and Women in Alcoholics
Anonymous; Intl. Advisory Coun. for **[★13283]**
Homosexuality; Natl. Assn. for Res. and Therapy of
[14434]
Homosexuality; Natl. Assn. for the Res. and Treat-
ment of **[★14434]**
Homosexuals Anonymous Fellowship Services
[12236], PO Box 7881, Reading, PA 19603-7881,
(610)779-2500
Homowo African Arts and Cultures **[9350]**, 4839 NE
Martin Luther King Blvd., Ste. 209, Portland, OR
97211, (503)288-3025
Homowo Found. for African Arts and Cultures
[★9350]
Honaker Family Assn. **[20944]**, PO Box 3636,
Alexandria, VA 22302-0636, (703)751-7321
Honda
Gold Wing Road Riders Assn. **[22678]**
Intl. CBX Owners Assn. **[22683]**
S2000 Club of Am. **[21777]**
Honda 750 Riders of America - Address unknown
since 1985.
Honda Car Club - Defunct.
Honda Sport Touring Assn. **[22681]**, 4040 E 82nd
St., Ste. C9, PMB 331, Indianapolis, IN 46250-
4209, (317)890-8858
Honda V-4 Sport Touring Assn. **[★22681]**
Hondacar Intl. - Defunct.
Honduran Agricultural Res. Found. **[IO]**, San Pedro
Sula, Honduras
Honduran Amer. Chamber of Commerce - Teg-
ucigalpa **[IO]**, Tegucigalpa, Honduras
Honduran Assn. of Banking Institutions **[IO]**, Teg-
ucigalpa, Honduras
Honduran Assn. of Sugar Producers **[IO]**, Teg-
ucigalpa, Honduras
Honduran Epilepsy Soc. **[IO]**, Tegucigalpa, Honduras
Honduran Mfrs. Assn. **[IO]**, San Pedro Sula,
Honduras
Honduran Private Enterprise Coun. **[IO]**, Teg-
ucigalpa, Honduras
Honduran Wood Indus. Assn. **[IO]**, Tegucigalpa,
Honduras
Honduras
Hermandad **[17046]**
Honduras Documentation Center **[IO]**
Honduras Outreach, Inc. **[IO]**
Honduras Outreach, Inc. **[17728]**
Intermed Intl. **[14982]**
Honduras Documentation Center **[IO]**, Tegucigalpa,
Honduras
Honduras Educ. Proj; Nicaragua- **[★8662]**
Honduras Information Center - Address unknown
since 1991.
Honduras Outreach, Inc. **[17728]**, 150 E Ponce De
Leon Ave., Ste. 270, Decatur, GA 30030-2547,
(404)378-0919
Honduras Outreach, Inc. **[IO]**, Decatur, GA, United
States
Honduras Popular Support Group - Address
unknown since 2002.
Honduras Squash Assn. **[IO]**, Tegucigalpa, Honduras
Honest Ballot Assn. **[17486]**, 272-30 Grand Central
Pkwy., Floral Park, NY 11005, (800)541-1851
Honey Assn. **[IO]**, Hamburg, Germany
Honey Assn. of Germany **[★IO]**
Honey Bd; Natl. **[1548]**
Honey Defense Fund **[★502]**
Honey Industry Coun. of America - Defunct.
Honey Packers and Dealers Assn; Natl. **[1549]**
Honey Producers Assn; Amer. **[4163]**
Honey Producers Marketing Assn; Mid-U.S. **[4166]**
Honeybees - Defunct.
Hong Chi Assn. **[IO]**, Hong Kong, People's Republic
of China
Hong Kong
China Stamp Soc. **[22803]**

Reference to "IO" in place of a book number signifies that the association may be found in the 45th edition of International Organizations.

Encyclopedia of Associations, 46th Edition

3579

Hong Kong Trade Development Coun. [24329]
Natl. Comm. on United States-China Relations
[17064]
Hong Kong ACM SIGGRAPH [IO], Hong Kong,
People's Republic of China
Hong Kong Advertisers Assn. [IO], Hong Kong,
People's Republic of China
Hong Kong Aikido Assn. [IO], Hong Kong, People's
Republic of China
Hong Kong Air-Conditioning and Refrigeration Assn.
[IO], Hong Kong, People's Republic of China
Hong Kong Alzheimer's Disease Assn. [IO], Hong
Kong, People's Republic of China
Hong Kong Alzheimer's Disease and Brain Failure
Assn. [★IO]
Hong Kong Amateur Athletic Assn. [IO], Hong Kong,
People's Republic of China
Hong Kong Amateur Basketball Assn. [★IO]
Hong Kong Amateur Karatedo Assn. [IO], Hong
Kong, People's Republic of China
Hong Kong Amateur Radio Transmitting Soc. [IO],
Hong Kong, People's Republic of China
Hong Kong Anti-Cancer Soc. [IO], Hong Kong,
People's Republic of China
Hong Kong Article Numbering Assn. [★IO]
Hong Kong Arts Festival Soc. [IO], Hong Kong,
People's Republic of China
Hong Kong Assn. of Accounting Technicians [★IO]
Hong Kong Assn. for Applied Linguistics [IO], Hong
Kong, People's Republic of China
Hong Kong Assn. of Banks [IO], Hong Kong,
People's Republic of China
Hong Kong Assn. of Blood Transfusion and Haema-
tology [IO], Hong Kong, People's Republic of
China
Hong Kong Assn. of Certification Labs. [IO], Hong
Kong, People's Republic of China
Hong Kong Assn. for Cmpt. Educ. [IO], Hong Kong,
People's Republic of China
Hong Kong Assn. of Critical Care Nurses [IO], Hong
Kong, People's Republic of China
Hong Kong Assn. of Dental Surgery Assistants [IO],
Hong Kong, People's Republic of China
Hong Kong Assn. of Freight Forwarding and
Logistics [IO], Hong Kong, People's Republic of
China
Hong Kong Assn. of Gerontology [IO], Hong Kong,
People's Republic of China
The Hong Kong Assn. for Mentally Handicapped
Children and Young Persons [★IO]
Hong Kong Assn. of the Pharmaceutical Indus. [IO],
Hong Kong, People's Republic of China
Hong Kong Assn. of Property Mgt. Companies [IO],
Hong Kong, People's Republic of China
Hong Kong Assn. of Registered Tour Coordinators
[IO], Hong Kong, People's Republic of China
Hong Kong Assn. of Rehabilitation Medicine [IO],
Hong Kong, People's Republic of China
Hong Kong Assn. of Secretaries and Administrative
Professionals [IO], Hong Kong, People's Republic
of China
Hong Kong Assn. of Speech Therapists [IO], Hong
Kong, People's Republic of China
Hong Kong Assn. of Sports Medicine and Sports
Sci. [IO], Hong Kong, People's Republic of China
Hong Kong Assn. of Textile Bleachers, Dyers, Print-
ers and Finishers [IO], Hong Kong, People's
Republic of China
Hong Kong Assn. of Travel Agents [IO], Hong Kong,
People's Republic of China
Hong Kong Assn. of Univ. Women [IO], Hong Kong,
People's Republic of China
Hong Kong Auto. Assn. [IO], Hong Kong, People's
Republic of China
Hong Kong Aviation Club [IO], Hong Kong, People's
Republic of China
Hong Kong Badminton Assn. [IO], Hong Kong,
People's Republic of China
Hong Kong Bar Assn. [IO], Hong Kong, People's
Republic of China
Hong Kong Basketball Assn. [IO], Hong Kong,
People's Republic of China
Hong Kong Bible Soc. [IO], Hong Kong, People's
Republic of China
Hong Kong Bioethics Assn. [IO], Hong Kong,
People's Republic of China

Hong Kong Buddhist Assn. [IO], Hong Kong,
People's Republic of China
Hong Kong Call Centre Assn. [IO], Hong Kong,
People's Republic of China
Hong Kong Cancer Chemotherapy Soc. [IO], Hong
Kong, People's Republic of China
Hong Kong Chap. of the ILAE [IO], Hong Kong,
People's Republic of China
Hong Kong Chefs Assn. [IO], Hong Kong, People's
Republic of China
Hong Kong Chinese Enterprises Assn. [IO], Hong
Kong, People's Republic of China
Hong Kong Chinese Medical Assn. [★IO]
Hong Kong Chinese Textile Mills Assn. [IO], Hong
Kong, People's Republic of China
Hong Kong Christian Coun. [IO], Hong Kong,
People's Republic of China
Hong Kong Christian Inst. [IO], Hong Kong, People's
Republic of China
Hong Kong Christian Ser. [IO], Hong Kong, People's
Republic of China
Hong Kong Coalition of AIDS Ser. Organizations
[IO], Hong Kong, People's Republic of China
Hong Kong Coll. of Cardiology [IO], Hong Kong,
People's Republic of China
Hong Kong Coll. of Hea. Services Executives [IO],
Hong Kong, People's Republic of China
Hong Kong Coll. of Obstetricians and Gynaecolo-
gists [IO], Hong Kong, People's Republic of China
Hong Kong Coll. of Radiologists [IO], Hong Kong,
People's Republic of China
Hong Kong Comm. for UNICEF [IO], Hong Kong,
People's Republic of China
Hong Kong Cmpt. Soc. [IO], Hong Kong, People's
Republic of China
Hong Kong Confed. of Trade Unions [IO], Hong
Kong, People's Republic of China
Hong Kong Constr. Assn. [IO], Hong Kong, People's
Republic of China
Hong Kong Coun. of Social Ser. [IO], Hong Kong,
People's Republic of China
Hong Kong Cricket Assn. [IO], Hong Kong, People's
Republic of China
Hong Kong DanceSport Assn. [IO], Hong Kong,
People's Republic of China
Hong Kong Democratic Found. [IO], Hong Kong,
People's Republic of China
Hong Kong Dental Assn. [IO], Hong Kong, People's
Republic of China
Hong Kong Dental Hygienists' Assn. [IO], Hong
Kong, People's Republic of China
Hong Kong Digital Entertainment Assn. [IO], Hong
Kong, People's Republic of China
Hong Kong Discharged Prisoners' Aid Soc. [★IO]
Hong Kong Distance Runners Club [IO], Hong Kong,
People's Republic of China
Hong Kong Down Syndrome Assn. [IO], Hong Kong,
People's Republic of China
Hong Kong Dragon Boat Assn. [IO], Hong Kong,
People's Republic of China
Hong Kong Economic Assn. [IO], Hong Kong,
People's Republic of China
Hong Kong Elecl. Contractors' Assn. [IO], Hong
Kong, People's Republic of China
Hong Kong Electronic Indus. Assn. [IO], Hong Kong,
People's Republic of China
Hong Kong Epidemiological Assn. [IO], Hong Kong,
People's Republic of China
Hong Kong Equestrian Fed. [IO], Hong Kong,
People's Republic of China
Hong Kong Exchanges and Clearing [IO], Hong
Kong, People's Republic of China
Hong Kong Exhibition and Convention Indus. Assn.
[IO], Hong Kong, People's Republic of China
Hong Kong Exhibition and Convention Organisers
and Suppliers Assn. [★IO]
Hong Kong Exporters' Assn. [IO], Hong Kong,
People's Republic of China
Hong Kong Fashion Designers Assn. [IO], Hong
Kong, People's Republic of China
Hong Kong Fed. of Insurers [IO], Hong Kong,
People's Republic of China
Hong Kong Fed. of Trade Unions [IO], Hong Kong,
People's Republic of China
Hong Kong Film Awards Assn. [IO], Kowloon,
People's Republic of China

Hong Kong Found. for the Sci. of Creative Intel-
ligence [IO], Hong Kong, People's Republic of
China
Hong Kong Franchise Assn. [IO], Hong Kong,
People's Republic of China
Hong Kong Fur Fed. [IO], Hong Kong, People's
Republic of China
Hong Kong Futures Exchange [★IO]
Hong Kong Garment Mfrs. Assn. [IO], Hong Kong,
People's Republic of China
Hong Kong Gemstone Mfrs'. Assn. [IO], Hong Kong,
People's Republic of China
Hong Kong Gen. Chamber of Commerce [IO], Hong
Kong, People's Republic of China
Hong Kong Geotechnical Soc. [IO], Hong Kong,
People's Republic of China
Hong Kong Gynaecological Endoscopy Soc. [IO],
Hong Kong, People's Republic of China
Hong Kong Hide and Leather Traders' Assn. [IO],
Hong Kong, People's Republic of China
Hong Kong Home Economics Assn. [IO], Hong
Kong, People's Republic of China
Hong Kong Horse Soc. [★IO]
Hong Kong Hotels Assn. [IO], Hong Kong, People's
Republic of China
Hong Kong Housing Soc. [IO], Hong Kong, People's
Republic of China
Hong Kong Info. Tech. Fed. [IO], Hong Kong,
People's Republic of China
Hong Kong Inst. of Accredited Accounting Techni-
cians [IO], Hong Kong, People's Republic of China
Hong Kong Inst. of Architects [IO], Hong Kong,
People's Republic of China
Hong Kong Inst. of Certified Public Accountants [IO],
Hong Kong, People's Republic of China
Hong Kong Inst. of Company Secretaries [IO], Hong
Kong, People's Republic of China
Hong Kong Inst. of Human Rsrc. Mgt. [IO], Hong
Kong, People's Republic of China
Hong Kong Inst. of Landscape Architects [IO], Hong
Kong, People's Republic of China
Hong Kong Inst. of Occupational and Environmental
Hygiene [IO], Hong Kong, People's Republic of
China
Hong Kong Inst. of Professional Photographers [IO],
Hong Kong, People's Republic of China
Hong Kong Inst. of Real Estate [IO], Hong Kong,
People's Republic of China
Hong Kong Inst. of Surveyors [IO], Hong Kong,
People's Republic of China
Hong Kong Institution of Engineers [IO], Hong Kong,
People's Republic of China
Hong Kong Interior Design Assn. [IO], Hong Kong,
People's Republic of China
Hong Kong Invention Assn. [IO], Hong Kong,
People's Republic of China
Hong Kong Jade and Stone Manufacturers Assn.
[IO], Hong Kong, People's Republic of China
Hong Kong Jewelers' and Goldsmiths' Assn. [IO],
Hong Kong, People's Republic of China
Hong Kong Jewellery and Jade Mfrs. Assn. [IO],
Hong Kong, People's Republic of China
Hong Kong Jewelry Mfrs. Assn. [IO], Hong Kong,
People's Republic of China
Hong Kong Journalists Assn. [IO], Hong Kong,
People's Republic of China
Hong Kong and Kowloon Elec. Trade Assn. [IO],
Hong Kong, People's Republic of China
Hong Kong and Kowloon Elecl. Appliances
Merchants' Assn. [IO], Hong Kong, People's
Republic of China
Hong Kong Lacrosse Assn. [IO], Hong Kong,
People's Republic of China
Hong Kong Ladies Road Runners Club [IO], Hong
Kong, People's Republic of China
Hong Kong Lawn Bowls Assn. [IO], Hong Kong,
People's Republic of China
Hong Kong Lib. Assn. [IO], Hong Kong, People's
Republic of China
Hong Kong Mgt. Assn. [IO], Hong Kong, People's
Republic of China
Hong Kong Mathematical Soc. [IO], Hong Kong,
People's Republic of China
Hong Kong Medical Assn. [IO], Hong Kong, People's
Republic of China

A star before a book entry number signifies that the name is not listed separately, but is mentioned within the entry.

Hong Kong Metal Finishing Soc. [IO], Hong Kong, People's Republic of China

Hong Kong Mountaineering Union [IO], Hong Kong, People's Republic of China

Hong Kong Museum of Medical Sciences Soc. [IO], Hong Kong, People's Republic of China

Hong Kong Netball Assn. [IO], Hong Kong, People's Republic of China

Hong Kong Network on Religion and Peace [IO], Hong Kong, People's Republic of China

Hong Kong - New Zealand Bus. Assn. [IO], Auckland, New Zealand

Hong Kong Occupational Therapy Assn. [IO], Hong Kong, People's Republic of China

Hong Kong Optical Mfrs. Assn. [IO], Hong Kong, People's Republic of China

Hong Kong Orienteering Club [IO], Hong Kong, People's Republic of China

Hong Kong Packaging Inst. [IO], Hong Kong, People's Republic of China

Hong Kong Paediatric Haematology and Oncology Study Group [IO], Hong Kong, People's Republic of China

Hong Kong Paralympic Comm. and Sports Assn. for the Physically Disabled [IO], Hong Kong, People's Republic of China

Hong Kong PHAB Assn. [IO], Hong Kong, People's Republic of China

Hong Kong Pharmacology Soc. [IO], Hong Kong, People's Republic of China

Hong Kong Philharmonic Soc. [IO], Hong Kong, People's Republic of China

Hong Kong Plastics Mfrs. Assn. [IO], Hong Kong, People's Republic of China

Hong Kong Political Sci. Assn. [IO], Hong Kong, People's Republic of China

Hong Kong Printers' Assn. [IO], Hong Kong, People's Republic of China

Hong Kong Productivity Coun. [IO], Hong Kong, People's Republic of China

Hong Kong Psychological Soc. [IO], Hong Kong, People's Republic of China

Hong Kong Public Admin. Assn. [IO], Hong Kong, People's Republic of China

Hong Kong Quality Circles Assn. [★IO]

Hong Kong Quality Mgt. Assn. [IO], Hong Kong, People's Republic of China

Hong Kong Red Cross [IO], Hong Kong, People's Republic of China

Hong Kong Reprographic Rights Licensing Soc. [IO], Hong Kong, People's Republic of China

Hong Kong Retail Mgt. Assn. [IO], Hong Kong, People's Republic of China

Hong Kong Sailing Fed. [IO], Hong Kong, People's Republic of China

Hong Kong Schools Music and Speech Assn. [IO], Hong Kong, People's Republic of China

Hong Kong Securities Inst. [IO], Hong Kong, People's Republic of China

Hong Kong Sex Educ. Assn. [IO], Hong Kong, People's Republic of China

Hong Kong Shipowners Assn. [IO], Hong Kong, People's Republic of China

Hong Kong Sinfonietta [IO], Hong Kong, People's Republic of China

Hong Kong Skating Union [IO], Hong Kong, People's Republic of China

Hong Kong Soc. of Accountants [★IO]

Hong Kong Soc. of Certified Prosthetist-Orthotists [IO], Hong Kong, People's Republic of China

Hong Kong Soc. of Clinical Chemistry [IO], Hong Kong, People's Republic of China

Hong Kong Soc. for Colposcopy and Cervical Pathology [IO], Hong Kong, People's Republic of China

Hong Kong Soc. for the Deaf [IO], Hong Kong, People's Republic of China

Hong Kong Soc. of Dermatology and Venereology [IO], Hong Kong, People's Republic of China

Hong Kong Soc. of Digestive Endoscopy [IO], Hong Kong, People's Republic of China

Hong Kong Soc. of Gastroenterology [IO], Hong Kong, People's Republic of China

Hong Kong Soc. of Hea. Services Executives [★IO]

Hong Kong Soc. of Illustrators [IO], Hong Kong, People's Republic of China

Hong Kong Soc. for Infectious Diseases [IO], Hong Kong, People's Republic of China

Hong Kong Soc. of Medical Genetics [IO], Hong Kong, People's Republic of China

Hong Kong Soc. of Medical Informatics [IO], Hong Kong, People's Republic of China

Hong Kong Soc. for Microbiology and Infection [IO], Hong Kong, People's Republic of China

Hong Kong Soc. of Minimal Access Surgery [IO], Hong Kong, People's Republic of China

Hong Kong Soc. for Multimedia and Image Computing [IO], Hong Kong, People's Republic of China

Hong Kong Soc. of Nephrology [IO], Hong Kong, People's Republic of China

Hong Kong Soc. for Nursing Educ. [IO], Hong Kong, People's Republic of China

Hong Kong Soc. of Oral Implantology [IO], Hong Kong, People's Republic of China

Hong Kong Soc. of Orthodontists [IO], Hong Kong, People's Republic of China

Hong Kong Soc. of Palliative Medicine [IO], Hong Kong, People's Republic of China

Hong Kong Soc. of Professional Optometrists [IO], Hong Kong, People's Republic of China

Hong Kong Soc. for the Protection of Children [IO], Hong Kong, People's Republic of China

Hong Kong Soc. for Quality of Life [IO], Hong Kong, People's Republic of China

Hong Kong Soc. for Rehabilitation [IO], Hong Kong, People's Republic of China

Hong Kong Soc. of Rheumatology [IO], Hong Kong, People's Republic of China

Hong Kong Soc. of Transplantation [IO], Hong Kong, People's Republic of China

Hong Kong Soc. of Wargamers [IO], Hong Kong, People's Republic of China

Hong Kong Softball Assn. [IO], Hong Kong, People's Republic of China

Hong Kong Sports Assn. for the Physically Disabled [★IO]

Hong Kong Sports Assn. for the Physically Disabled [IO], Hong Kong, People's Republic of China

Hong Kong Surgical Laser Assn. [IO], Hong Kong, People's Republic of China

Hong Kong Taekwondo Assn. [IO], Hong Kong, People's Republic of China

Hong Kong Telemedicine Assn. [IO], Hong Kong, People's Republic of China

Hong Kong Tennis Assn. [IO], Hong Kong, People's Republic of China

Hong Kong Tenpin Bowling Cong. [IO], Hong Kong, People's Republic of China

Hong Kong Thoracic Soc. [IO], Hong Kong, People's Republic of China

Hong Kong Touch and Tag Rugby Assn. [IO], Hong Kong, People's Republic of China

Hong Kong Tourism Bd. [IO], London, United Kingdom

Hong Kong Tourism Bd. [IO], Hong Kong, People's Republic of China

Hong Kong Toys Coun. [IO], Hong Kong, People's Republic of China

Hong Kong Trade Development Coun. [IO], Hong Kong, People's Republic of China

Hong Kong Trade Development Coun. [24329], 219 E 46th St., New York, NY 10017, (212)838-8688

Hong Kong Trade Development Coun. - London Off. [IO], London, United Kingdom

Hong Kong Tuberculosis, Chest and Heart Diseases Assn. [IO], Hong Kong, People's Republic of China

Hong Kong Ultimate Players Assn. [IO], Hong Kong, People's Republic of China

Hong Kong Underwater Assn. [IO], Hong Kong, People's Republic of China

Hong Kong Urological Assn. [IO], Hong Kong, People's Republic of China

Hong Kong Venture Capital Assn. [IO], Hong Kong, People's Republic of China

Hong Kong Veterinary Assn. [IO], Hong Kong, People's Republic of China

Hong Kong Watch Mfrs. Assn. Ltd. [IO], Hong Kong, People's Republic of China

Hong Kong Water Ski Assn. [IO], Hong Kong, People's Republic of China

Hong Kong Wine Soc. [IO], Hong Kong, People's Republic of China

Hong Kong Women Professionals and Entrepreneurs Assn. [IO], Hong Kong, People's Republic of China

Hong Kong Wushu Union [IO], Hong Kong, People's Republic of China

Hong Kong Youth Hostels Assn. [IO], Hong Kong, People's Republic of China

Hong Kong's Women in Publishing Soc. [IO], Hong Kong, People's Republic of China

Honig-Verband [★IO]

Honolulu Japanese Chamber of Commerce [24348], 2454 S Beretania St., Ste. 201, Honolulu, HI 96826, (808)949-5531

Honor Am. [★21094]

Honor the Earth [19272], 2104 Stevens Ave. S, Minneapolis, MN 55404, (612)879-7529

Honor Societies

Alpha Beta Gamma Intl. [24425]

Alpha Chi [24498]

Alpha Chi Sigma [24428]

Alpha Delta Kappa [24449]

Alpha Epsilon [24395]

Alpha Epsilon Delta [24541]

Alpha Gamma Rho [24396]

Alpha Iota Sorority [24413]

Alpha Kappa Delta [24701]

Alpha Kappa Mu [24499]

Alpha Kappa Psi [24414]

Alpha Mu Gamma Natl. [24525]

Alpha Omega Alpha Honor Medical Soc. [24542]

Alpha Omega Intl. Dental Fraternity [24437]

Alpha Phi Sigma Honorary Scholastic Society [24450]

Alpha Psi Lambda Natl. [24615]

Alpha Psi Omega [24443]

Alpha Sigma Nu [24500]

Alpha Sigma Nu [IO]

Alpha Tau Delta [24559]

Alpha Zeta [24397]

Alpha Zeta Omega [24567]

Arnold Air Soc. [24546]

Assn. of Coll. Honor Societies [24501]

Assn. of Fraternity Advisors [24475]

Astronaut Scholars Honor Soc. [24584]

Beta Alpha Psi [24391]

Beta Beta Beta [24408]

Beta Gamma Sigma [24415]

Beta Gamma Sigma Alumni [24416]

Beta Phi Mu [24532]

Beta Sigma Kappa [24562]

Blue Key Honor Soc. [24502]

Center for the Stud. of the Coll. Fraternity [24476]

Central Off. Executives Assn. of Natl. Pan-Hellenic Conf. [24477]

Chi Eta Phi Sorority [24560]

Cum Laude Soc. [24503]

Delphi Found. [24451]

Delta Epsilon Sigma [24504]

Delta Kappa Epsilon [24623]

Delta Lambda Phi Natl. Social Fraternity [24624]

Delta Mu Delta Honor Soc. [24418]

Delta Omega [24582]

Delta Omicron [24550]

Delta Phi Epsilon, Professional Foreign Ser. Fraternity [24472]

Delta Phi Epsilon Professional Foreign Ser. Sorority [24473]

Delta Phi Upsilon [24431]

Delta Pi Epsilon [24426]

Delta Psi Omega [24444]

Delta Sigma Delta [24438]

Delta Sigma Rho - Tau Kappa Alpha [24719]

Delta Theta Phi [24527]

Epsilon Pi Tau [24720]

Epsilon Sigma Phi [24436]

Eta Phi Beta [24419]

Eta Sigma Alpha Natl. Home School Honor Soc. [8316]

Eta Sigma Phi, Natl. Classics Honorary Soc. [24433]

Fraternity Executives Assn. [24479]

Future Bus. Leaders of Am. - Phi Beta Lambda [24420]

Gamma Beta Phi Soc. [24505]

Gamma Iota Sigma [24520]

Reference to "IO" in place of a book number signifies that the association may be found in the 45th edition of International Organizations.

Gamma Sigma Delta [24398]
Gamma Theta Upsilon [24491]
Golden Key Intl. Honour Soc. [24506]
Green Leaf Natl. Honor Soc. [24471]
Honors Prog. Student Assn. of the Amer.
  Sociological Assn. [24702]
Intercollegiate Knights [24507]
Iota Beta Sigma [24410]
Iota Phi Lambda [24421]
Japanese Natl. Honor Soc. [24521]
Kappa Delta Epsilon [24452]
Kappa Delta Pi [24453]
Kappa Gamma Pi [24508]
Kappa Mu Epsilon [24537]
Kappa Omicron Nu [24496]
Kappa Pi Intl. Honorary Art Fraternity [24404]
Kappa Psi [24568]
Kappa Tau Alpha [24522]
Lambda Alpha [24402]
Lambda Alpha Intl. [24445]
Lambda Iota Tau [24533]
Lambda Kappa Sigma [24569]
Mortar Bd. [24509]
Mu Alpha Theta [24538]
Mu Beta Psi [24552]
Mu Phi Epsilon Intl. [24553]
Natl. Adult Educ. Honor Soc. [24392]
Natl. Alpha Lambda Delta [24510]
Natl. Assn. of the Knights of Scorpius, Honorary
  Leadership Soc. [24511]
Natl. Beta Club [24592]
Natl. Block and Bridle Club [24401]
Natl. Broadcasting Soc. - Alpha Epsilon Rho
  [24411]
Natl. Chinese Honor Soc. [24432]
Natl. Honor Soc. [24512]
Natl. Junior Honor Soc. [24513]
Natl. Kappa Kappa Iota [24454]
Natl. Pan-Hellenic Editors Conf. [24448]
Natl. Panhellenic Conf. [24485]
Natl. Soc. of Pershing Rifles [24547]
Natl. Soc. of Scabbard and Blade [24548]
Natl. Sorority of Phi Delta Kappa [24455]
Natl. Tech. Honor Soc. [24725]
Natl. Valedictorian Honor Soc. [24514]
North Amer. Interfraternal Found. [24486]
North-American Interfraternity Conf. [24487]
Omega Delta [24563]
Omicron Delta Epsilon [24446]
Omicron Delta Kappa Soc. [24515]
Omicron Kappa Upsilon [24439]
Order of the Coif [24516]
Phi Alpha Delta [24528]
Phi Alpha Epsilon [24463]
Phi Alpha Sigma [24543]
Phi Alpha Theta [24495]
Phi Beta [24405]
Phi Beta Delta [24517]
Phi Beta Kappa [24406]
Phi Chi Medical Fraternity [24544]
Phi Delta Chi [24570]
Phi Delta Epsilon Medical Fraternity [24540]
Phi Delta Gamma [24577]
Phi Delta Phi Intl. Legal Fraternity [24530]
Phi Kappa Phi [24518]
Phi Mu Alpha Sinfonia Fraternity and Found. Natl.
  HQ [24555]
Phi Sigma [24409]
Phi Sigma Iota [24526]
Phi Sigma Pi Natl. Honor Fraternity [24531]
Phi Sigma Tau [24572]
Phi Theta Kappa, Intl. Honor Soc. [24456]
Phi Theta Pi [24424]
Phi Upsilon Omicron [24497]
Phi Zeta [24723]
Pi Delta Phi [24490]
Pi Gamma Mu [24672]
Pi Kappa Lambda [24556]
Pi Kappa Phi [24651]
Pi Lambda Theta [24457]
Pi Mu Epsilon [24539]
Pi Omega Pi [24427]
Pi Omicron Natl. Sorority [24601]
Pi Sigma Alpha [24576]
Pi Tau Sigma [24465]

Professional Fraternity Assn. [24488]
Psi Beta [24579]
Psi Chi, the Natl. Honor Soc. in Psychology
  [24580]
Psi Omega [24440]
Quill and Scroll Soc. [24523]
Rho Chi - Alpha Beta Chap. [24571]
Sigma Alpha Iota Intl. Music Fraternity [24557]
Sigma Alpha Lambda [24519]
Sigma Delta Chi Found. [24524]
Sigma Delta Epsilon, Graduate Women in Sci.
  [24587]
Sigma Delta Pi [24718]
Sigma Gamma Epsilon [24492]
Sigma Gamma Tau [24466]
Sigma Iota Epsilon [24534]
Sigma Phi Alpha [24441]
Sigma Pi Sigma [24575]
Sigma Sigma Phi [24565]
Sigma Tau Delta, the Intl. English Honor Soc.
  [24470]
Sigma Theta Tau Intl. [24561]
Sigma Xi, The Sci. Res. Soc. [24588]
Sigma Zeta [24589]
Silver Wings [24549]
Soc. of Professional Journalists [3164]
Tau Alpha Pi [24467]
Tau Beta Pi Assn. [24468]
Tau Beta Sigma [24558]
Tau Epsilon Rho Law Soc. [24529]
Tau Sigma Delta [24403]
Theta Alpha Phi [24721]
Theta Chi Beta [24583]
Theta Psi [24566]
Theta Tau [24469]
Upsilon Pi Epsilon Assn. [24435]
Xi Psi Phi [24442]
Honor Societies; Assn. of Coll. [★24470]
Honor Soc; Natl. Social Sci. [★24672]
Honor Soc; Natl. Tech. [24725]
Honor Soc; Natl. Vocational-Technical [★24725]
Honor Student Association; Christian [★8089]
Honorable Artillery Company of Massachusetts;
  Ancient and [21191]
Honorable Order of the Blue Goose, Intl. [19126],
  c/o Terrence M. Maloney, Grand Wielder, 12940
  Walnut Rd., Elm Grove, WI 53122, (414)221-0341
Honorable Order of the Blue Goose, Intl. [IO], Elm
  Grove, WI, United States
Honoraria Hispanica; Sociedad [8499]
Honors Coun; Natl. Collegiate [8290]
Honors Inst. [★24456]
Honors Inst. [★IO]
Honors Prog. Student Assn. of the Amer. Sociologi-
  cal Assn. [24702], c/o Univ. of Wisconsin-Parkside,
  PO Box 2000, Kenosha, WI 53141-2000,
  (202)383-9005
Honors Soc; Francena Purchase Applied [17018]
Honour Soc; Golden Key Intl. [24506]
Honourable Company of Master Mariners [IO],
  London, United Kingdom
Hoo-Hoo
  Hoo-Hoo Intl. [19103]
Hoo-Hoo Intl. [19103], c/o Beth Thomas, Exec. Sec.,
  PO Box 118, Gurdon, AR 71743, (870)353-4997
Hoo-Hoo; Intl. Order of [★19103]
Hood's Texas Brigade Assn. [20726], PO Box 619,
  Hillsboro, TX 76645, (254)582-2555
Hoofdbedrijschap Detailhandel [★IO]
Hook Lifters Sect. of the Material Handling Inst;
  Below/ [★2042]
Hooved Animal Humane Soc. [11407], 10804 McCo-
  nnell Rd., Woodstock, IL 60098, (815)337-5563
Hoover Historical Center [21534], Walsh Univ., 1875
  E Maple St., North Canton, OH 44720-3331,
  (330)499-0287
Hoover Institution [★18836]
Hoover Institution on War, Revolution and Peace
  [18836], 434 Galvez Mall, Stanford Univ., Stanford,
  CA 94305-6010, (650)723-1754
Hoover Presidential Lib. Assn; Herbert [11122]
Hop Growers of Am. [4305], PO Box 9218, Yakima,
  WA 98909, (509)248-7043
HOP Study Group [★22864]
Hopalong Cassidy Fan Club; Friends of [24742]

HOPE [IO], Heeslingen-Sassenholz, Germany
Hope Acad. International [★IO]
Hope Acad. International [★12881]
Hope for African Children Initiative [IO], Nairobi,
  Kenya
Hope After Rape [IO], Kampala, Uganda
HOPE for Children [IO], Hemel Hempstead, United
  Kingdom
Hope through Educational and Medical Aid; Restor-
  ing [★12881]
Hope Found; New [13271]
Hope Intl. [13427], 227 Granite Run Dr., Ste. 102,
  Lancaster, PA 17601, (717)464-3220
Hope Intl. [IO], Kokomo, IN, United States
Hope Intl. Univ. Alumni Assn. [18898], 2500 E Nut-
  wood Ave., Fullerton, CA 92831, (714)879-3901
Hope; Kids at [11705]
Hope Natl. Medical Center; City of [15102]
Hope Network; Rainbow Celebration of [15297]
Hope; Plant Seeds of [★19135]
HOPE Worldwide - Afghanistan [IO], Kabul,
  Afghanistan
HOPE Worldwide - Africa [IO], Johannesburg,
  Republic of South Africa
HOPE Worldwide - Australia [IO], North Epping,
  Australia
HOPE Worldwide - Brazil [IO], Sao Paulo, Brazil
HOPE Worldwide - Canada [IO], Toronto, ON,
  Canada
HOPE Worldwide - Caribbean [IO], Kingston,
  Jamaica
HOPE Worldwide - Germany [IO], Berlin, Germany
HOPE Worldwide - Indonesia [IO], Jakarta,
  Indonesia
HOPE Worldwide - Malaysia [IO], Kuala Lumpur,
  Malaysia
HOPE Worldwide - Papua New Guinea [IO], Boroko,
  Papua New Guinea
Hopelessly Devoted - Olivia Newton-John Fan Club -
  Address unknown since 2002.
Hopkins Center for Alternatives to Animal Testing;
  Johns [11423]
HOPOS - The Intl. Soc. for the History of Philosophy
  of Sci. [9103], 222 Cockefair Hall, Dept. of
  Philosophy, Univ. of Missouri, 5100 Rockhill Rd.,
  Kansas City, MO 64110-2499, (816)235-1331
Horace Mann Bond Center for Equal Education -
  Defunct.
Horace Mann League of the U.S.A. [9036], c/o Dr.
  Jack McKay, Exec. Dir., 61D N Chandler Ct., Port
  Ludlow, WA 98365, (360)437-1186
Horatio Alger Assn. of Distinguished Americans
  [20712], 99 Canal Center Plz., Alexandria, VA
  22314, (703)684-9444
Horatio Alger Awards Comm. [★20712]
Horatio Alger Newsboy Club [★9659]
Horatio Alger Soc. [9659], PO Box 70361,
  Richmond, VA 23255
Horizons of Friendship [IO], Cobourg, ON, Canada
Hormone and Pituitary Prog; Natl. [16021]
Horn Relief [IO], Nairobi, Kenya
Horn and Steam Whistle Enthusiasts; Air [★22037]
Horn and Whistle Enthusiasts Gp. [22037], c/o Mr.
  Eric C. Larson, Publisher/Webmaster, 2 Abell Ave.,
  Ipswich, MA 01938
Horned Order's Magickal Existence - Address
  unknown since 2004.
Hornets Booster Club; Pittsburgh [★25012]
Horney Clinic; Karen [16109]
Horney Psychoanalytic Clinic; Karen [★16109]
Horney Psychoanalytic Inst. and Center; Assn. for
  Advancement of Psychoanalysis of the Karen
  [16105]
Horological Assn. of Amer; United [★2359]
Horological Inst. [★2359]
Horror Films; Acad. of Sci. Fiction, Fantasy, and
  [9925]
Horror Films and Sci. Fiction Films; Acad. of
  [★9925]
Horror Writers of Am. [★11174]
Horror Writers Assn. [11174], 244 5th Ave., Ste.
  2767, New York, NY 10001-7604
Horse of the Americas Registry - Defunct.
Horse Assn. of Am; Amer. Cream Draft [★4816]
Horse Assn; Amer. Holstein [★4824]

A star before a book entry number signifies that the name is not listed separately, but is mentioned within the entry.

Horse Assn; Amer. Junior Quarter [★4839]
Horse Assn; Amer. Paint Quarter [★4834]
Horse Assn; Amer. Paint Stock [★4834]
Horse Assn; Amer. Saddlebred Pleasure [★4842]
Horse Assn; Intl. Amer. Saddlebred Pleasure [★4842]
Horse Assn; Intl. Peruvian Paso [★4934]
Horse Assn; North Amer. Single-Footed [★4937]
Horse Breeders' Assn. of Am; Tennessee Walking [★4959]
Horse Breeders Assn; Amer. Saddle [★4842]
Horse Cavalry Assn; U.S. [★10484]
Horse Club; Morgan [★4831]
Horse Club; Race [★4922]
Horse Club Registry of Am; Arabian [★4858]

Horse Driving
Amer. Assn. for Horsemanship Safety [12946]
Amer. Collegiate Horsemen's Assn. [4814]
Amer. Driving Soc. [23491]
Amer. Equestrian Alliance [1923]
Amer. Equestrian Trade Assn. [4818]
Amer. Horseman Alliance [1924]
Amer. Riding Instructors Assn. [22583]
Carriage Assn. of Am. [21987]
Carriage Operators of North Am. [783]
Centered Riding [22584]
Cowboy Mounted Shooting Assn. [23716]
Drive Canada [IO]
Equestrian Land Conservation Rsrc. [5130]
Equestrian Ministries Intl. [20082]
Horse Lovers United [17730], PO Box 2744, Salisbury, MD 21802-2744, (410)749-3599
Horse Museum; Trotting [★23498]
Horse Organized Assistance; Wild [5394]
Horse Prog; Adopt-A- [★4868]
Horse Protection Assn; Amer. [5291]
Horse Protection League [4890], PO Box 741089, Arvada, CO 80006, (303)216-0141
Horse Publications; Amer. [3203]

Horse Racing
Amer. Barrel Racing Assn. [23492]
Amer. Cmpt. Barrel Racing Assn. [23493]
Arabian Jockey Club [23494]
Asian Racing Fed. [IO]
Barrel Futurities of Am. [23495]
Danish Jockey Club [IO]
Emirates Racing Assn. [IO]
Equestrian Club of Riyadh [IO]
Harness Horse Youth Found. [23496]
Harness Horsemen Intl. [23497]
Harness Racing Museum and Hall of Fame [23498]
Harness Tracks of Am. [23499]
Horse Racing Ireland [IO]
Hyderabad Race Club [IO]
International Barrel Racing Association [IO]
Intl. Barrel Racing Assn. [23500]
Intl. Fed. of Horseracing Authorities [IO]
Intl. Trotting and Pacing Assn. [IO]
Intl. Trotting and Pacing Assn. [23501]
Japan Assn. for Intl. Horse Racing [IO]
Japan Racing Assn. [IO]
Jockey Club [IO]
The Jockey Club [23502]
Jockey Club Argentina [IO]
Jockey Club of Canada [IO]
Jockey Club Czech Republic [IO]
Jockey Club Royal de Belgique [IO]
Jockey Club of Turkey [IO]
Jockeys' Guild [23503]
Kids to the Cup [23504]
Korea Racing Assn. [IO]
Macau Jockey Club [IO]
Mauritius Turf Club [IO]
Natl. Assn. of Off-Track Betting [23505]
Natl. Barrel Horse Assn. [23506]
Natl. Christian Barrel Racers Assn. [23507]
Natl. Horsemen's Benevolent and Protective Assn. [12301]
Natl. Horseracing [IO]
Natl. Horseracing Authority of Southern Africa [IO]
Natl. Museum of Racing and Hall of Fame [23508]
Natl. Steeplechase Assn. [23509]
Natl. Thoroughbred Racing Assn. [23510]

Natl. Trainers Fed. [IO]
Natl. Turf Writers Assn. [3145]
New Zealand Thoroughbred Racing [IO]
Norsk Jockey Club [IO]
North Amer. Pt-to-Pt Assn. [23511]
North Amer. Thoroughbred Soc. [23538]
Oregon Horsemen's Benevolent Protective Assn. [23512]
Penang Turf Club [IO]
Racecourse Assn. [IO]
Racehorse Owners Assn. of Great Britain [IO]
Royal Western India Turf Club [IO]
Singapore Turf Club [IO]
Slovakian Turf Club [IO]
Slovenian Turf Club [IO]
Standardbred Owners Assn. [23513]
Thoroughbred Adoption and Retirement Assn. [12302]
Thoroughbred Club of Am. [23514]
Thoroughbred Owners and Breeders Assn. [23515]
Thoroughbred Racing Associations [23516]
Thoroughbred Racing Protective Bur. [23517]
U.S. Harness Writers' Assn. [3170]
U.S. Team Penning Assn. [23518]
United States Team Penning Association [IO]
U.S. Trotting Assn. [23519]
World Championship Cutter and Chariot Racing Assn. [23281]
Horse Racing Ireland [IO], Kill, Ireland
Horse Registry of Am; Akhal-Teke Sport [★4808]
Horse Registry; Amer. Peruvian Paso [★4934]
Horse Registry; Intl. Buckskin [★4896]
Horse Registry; Intl. Miniature [★4830]
Horse Shows Assn; Amer. [★23534]
Horse Soc; Amer. Hackney [4820]
Horse Soc. - Pony Club; British [★23537]
Horse Trainers Assn; Walking [★4967]
Horseaid Equine Relief Programme [11408]

Horseback Riding
Albany Natural Trail Riders [IO]
Amer. Assn. for Horsemanship Safety [12946]
Amer. Assn. of Riding Schools [22582]
Amer. Barrel Racing Assn. [23492]
Amer. Collegiate Horsemen's Assn. [4814]
Amer. Competition Opportunities for Riders with Disabilities [23330]
Amer. Cmpt. Barrel Racing Assn. [23493]
Amer. Cutting Horse Assn. [23520]
Amer. Endurance Ride Conf. [23933]
Amer. Equestrian Alliance [1923]
Amer. Equestrian Trade Assn. [4818]
Amer. Hippotherapy Assn. [16600]
Amer. Horse Trials Found. [23521]
Amer. Horseman Alliance [1924]
Amer. Junior Rodeo Assn. [23684]
Amer. Medical Equestrian Association/Safe Riders Found. [16474]
Amer. Riding Instructors Assn. [22583]
Arabian Professional and Amateur Horseman's Assn. [4862]
Assn. of British Riding Schools [IO]
Australian Horse Alliance [IO]
Australian Trail Horse Riders Assn. [IO]
Australian Trail Horse Riders Assn. - New South Wales Br. [IO]
Australian Trail Horse Riders Assn. - Queensland [IO]
Australian Trail Horse Riders Assn. - South Australian Br. [IO]
Australian Trail Horse Riders Assn. - Victoria Br. [IO]
Back Country Horsemen of Am. [23522]
Barrel Futurities of Am. [23495]
British Equestrian Fed. [IO]
British Show Jumping Assn. [IO]
Canadian Long Distance Riding Assn. [IO]
Canadian Therapeutic Riding Assn. [IO]
Centered Riding [22584]
CHA - Certified Horsemanship Assn. [23523]
Cowboy Mounted Shooting Assn. [23716]
Derwent Valley Horseriders Assn. [IO]
Equestrian Fed. of Ireland [IO]
Equestrian Land Conservation Rsrc. [5130]
Equestrian Ministries Intl. [20082]

Fed. of Intl. Polo [23819]
Gaited Horse Intl. Assn. [4882]
Gladstone Equestrian Assn. [23524]
Glencoe Social Trail Riders [IO]
Harness Horse Youth Found. [23496]
Heritage Trails Fund [23940]
Horsemanship Safety Assn. [23525]
Icelandic Horse Trekkers [4893]
Intercollegiate Horse Show Assn. [23526]
Intl. Barrel Racing Assn. [23500]
Intl. Equestrian Drill Team Alliance [23527]
Intl. Fed. for Equestrian Sports [IO]
Intl. Jumper Futurity [23528]
Intl. Professional Rodeo Assn. [23686]
Intl. Side Saddle Org. [23529]
Intl. Sport Horses of Color [4905]
Intl. Vaulting Club [23968]
Melbourne Trail Horse Riders Club [IO]
Mounted Games Across Am. [23830]
Natl. Assn. of Competitive Mounted Orienteering [23640]
Natl. Center for Therapeutic Riding [23351]
Natl. Christian Barrel Racers Assn. [23507]
Natl. Finals Rodeo Comm. [23689]
Natl. High School Rodeo Assn. [23690]
Natl. Hunter Jumper Assn. [23530]
Natl. Hunter/Jumper Coun. [23531]
Natl. Intercollegiate Rodeo Assn. [23691]
Natl. Little Britches Rodeo Assn. [23692]
Natl. Reined Cow Horse Assn. [22586]
Natl. Steeplechase Assn. [23509]
Natl. Trail Ride Assn. [23946]
New Zealand Mounted Games Assn. [IO]
North Amer. Pt-to-Pt Assn. [23511]
North Amer. Riding for the Handicapped Assn. [23357]
North Amer. Single-footing Horse Assn. [4937]
North Amer. Thoroughbred Soc. [23538]
North Amer. Trail Ride Conf. [23949]
Northern Trail Horse Riders Club [IO]
Norwegian Fjord Horse Registry [4939]
Oregon Horsemen's Benevolent Protective Assn. [23512]
Pacific Riding for the Disabled Assn. [IO]
Pony Club Australia [IO]
Praying Hands Ranches [23360]
Professional Armed Forces Rodeo Assn. [23693]
Professional Rodeo Cowboys Assn. [23694]
Ride and Tie Assn. [23849]
Riverland and Mallee Trail Horse Riders' Club [IO]
Scottish Equestrian Assn. [IO]
Side Saddle Assn. [IO]
Trail Riders of Today [23532]
U.S. Calf Ropers Assn. [23695]
U.S. Dressage Fed. [23533]
U.S. Equestrian Fed. [23534]
U.S. Eventing Assn. [23535]
U.S. Hunter Jumper Assn. [23536]
U.S. Polo Assn. [23661]
U.S. Pony Clubs [23537]
U.S. Team Penning Assn. [23518]
WA Horse Trekkers Club [IO]
Western Saddle Clubs Assn. [4971]
Wild Horses of Am. Registry [5395]
Women's Professional Rodeo Assn. [23696]
Horseback Writers and Artists, Intl. - Address unknown since 2001.
Horseless Carriage Club of Am. [21658], PO Box 62, Bakersfield, CA 93302, (661)321-0539
Horsemanship Assn; Camp [★23523]
Horsemanship Safety Assn. [23525], c/o Ted Marthe, 5304 Reeve Rd., Mazomanie, WI 53560, (608)767-2593
Horsemanship Safety and Educ; CHA-Association for [★23523]
Horsemen's Assn; United Professional [4961]
Horsemen's Benevolent and Protective Assn; Natl. [12301]

Horses
Ada Cole Rescue Stables [IO]
Akhal-Teke Assn. of Am. [4808]
Alberta Equestrian Fed. [IO]
Alberta Standardbred Horse Assn. [IO]
Amer. Acad. of Equine Art [9410]
Amer. Appaloosa Assn. Worldwide [4809]

Reference to "IO" in place of a book number signifies that the association may be found in the 45th edition of International Organizations.

American Appaloosa Association Worldwide [IO]
Amer. Assn. of Equine Practitioners [16742]
Amer. Assn. of Equine Veterinary Technicians [16743]
Amer. Assn. for Horsemanship Safety [12946]
Amer. Assn. of Owners and Breeders of Peruvian Paso Horses [4810]
Amer. Assn. of Riding Schools [22582]
Amer. Azteca Horse Intl. Assn. [4811]
American Azteca Horse International Association [IO]
Amer. Barrel Racing Assn. [23492]
Amer. Bashkir Curly Registry [4812]
Amer. Buckskin Registry Assn. [4813]
Amer. Collegiate Horsemen's Assn. [4814]
Amer. Competition Opportunities for Riders with Disabilities [23330]
Amer. Cmpt. Barrel Racing Assn. [23493]
Amer. Connemara Pony Soc. [4815]
Amer. Cream Draft Horse Assn. [4816]
Amer. Dartmoor Pony Assn. [4817]
Amer. Driving Soc. [23491]
Amer. Endurance Ride Conf. [23933]
Amer. Equestrian Alliance [1923]
Amer. Equestrian Trade Assn. [4818]
Amer. Equine Assn. [4819]
Amer. Farrier's Assn. [522]
Amer. Hackney Horse Soc. [4820]
Amer. Haflinger Registry [4821]
Amer. Half-Quarter Horse Registry [4822]
Amer. Hanoverian Soc. [4823]
Amer. Hippotherapy Assn. [16600]
Amer. Holsteiner Horse Assn. [4824]
Amer. Horse Coun. [4825]
Amer. Horse Defense Fund [4826]
Amer. Horse Publications [3203]
Amer. Horse Trials Found. [23521]
Amer. Horseman Alliance [1924]
Amer. Indian Horse Registry [4827]
Amer. Junior Paint Horse Assn. [4828]
Amer. Junior Rodeo Assn. [23684]
Amer. Kerry Bog Pony Soc. [4829]
American Kerry Bog Pony Society [IO]
Amer. Miniature Horse Assn. [4830]
Amer. Morgan Horse Assn. [4831]
Amer. Mustang Assn. [4832]
Amer. Mustang and Burro Assn. [4833]
Amer. Paint Horse Assn. [4834]
Amer. Part-Blooded Horse Registry [4835]
Amer. Paso Fino Horse Assn. [4836]
Amer. Pinto Arabian Registry [4837]
Amer. Quarter Horse Assn. [4838]
Amer. Quarter Horse Youth Assn. [4839]
Amer. Quarter Pony Assn. [4840]
Amer. Ranch Horse Assn. [4841]
Amer. Riding Instructors Assn. [22583]
Amer. Saddlebred Horse Assn. [4842]
Amer. Saddlebred Sporthorse Assn. [4843]
Amer. Shagya Arabian Verband [4844]
Amer. Shetland Pony Club/American Miniature Horse Registry [4845]
Amer. Shire Horse Assn. [4846]
Amer. Suffolk Horse Assn. [4847]
Amer. Sulphur Horse Assn. [22585]
American Sulphur Horse Association [IO]
American Trakehner Association [IO]
Amer. Trakehner Assn. [4848]
Amer. Trote and Trocha Assn. [4849]
Amer. Walking Pony Assn. [4850]
Amer. Warmblood Registry [4851]
Amer. Warmblood Soc. [4852]
Amer. Warmblood and Sport Horse Guild [4853]
Amer. Welara Pony Soc. [4854]
American Welara Pony Society [IO]
Amer. White Horse and Amer. Creme Horse Registry [4855]
Amer. Youth Horse Coun. [4856]
Animal Hea. Found. [16781]
Appaloosa Horse Assn. of New Zealand [IO]
Appaloosa Horse Club [IO]
Appaloosa Horse Club [4857]
Appaloosa Horse Club of Canada [IO]
Arab Horse Soc. [IO]
Arabian Horse Assn. [4858]
Arabian Horse Breeders Alliance [4859]

Arabian Horse Breeders Alliance [IO]
Arabian Horse Owners Found. [4860]
Arabian Horse Trust [4861]
Arabian Jockey Club [23494]
Arabian Professional and Amateur Horseman's Assn. [4862]
Auckland Miniature Horse Club [IO]
Australian Stock Horse Soc. [IO]
Avon and Border Counties Welsh Pony and Cob Assn. [IO]
Azteca Horse Registry of Am. [4863]
Back in the Saddle Horse Adoption [4864]
Barrel Futurities of Am. [23495]
Bay of Plenty Miniature Horse Club [IO]
Belgian Draft Horse Corp. of Am. [4865]
Blazer Horse Assn. [4866]
Brecon and Borders Welsh Pony and Cob Breeders Assn. [IO]
Bright Futures Farm [4867]
British Appaloosa Soc. [IO]
British Driving Soc. [IO]
British Equestrian Trade Assn. [IO]
British Harness Racing Club [IO]
British Horse Soc. [IO]
British Palomino Soc. [IO]
British Show Pony Soc. [IO]
Bur. of Land Mgt. Natl. Wild Horse and Burro Prog. [4868]
Canadian Arabian Horse Registry [IO]
Canadian Belgian Horse Assn. [IO]
Canadian Cutting Horse Assn. [IO]
Canadian Dressage Owners and Riders Assn. [IO]
Canadian Fjord Horse Assn. [IO]
Canadian Hackney Soc. [IO]
Canadian Haflinger Assn. [IO]
Canadian Icelandic Horse Fed. [IO]
Canadian Morgan Horse Assn. [IO]
Canadian Palomino Horse Assn. [IO]
Canadian Pinto Horse Assn. [IO]
Canadian Pony Club [IO]
Canadian Quarter Horse Assn. [IO]
Canadian Shire Horse Assn. [IO]
Canadian Sport Horse Assn. [IO]
Canadian Thoroughbred Horse Soc. [IO]
Canadian Trakehner Horse Soc. [IO]
Canadian Western Horse Assn. [IO]
Carmarthenshire Welsh Pony and Cob Assn. [IO]
Carriage Assn. of Am. [21987]
Carriage Operators of North Am. [783]
Caspian Breed Soc. (UK) [IO]
Caspian Horse Soc. of the Americas [4869]
Catholic Homesteading Movement [11742]
Centered Riding [22584]
Ceredigion Welsh Pony and Cob Assn. [IO]
CHA - Certified Horsemanship Assn. [23523]
Champagne Horse Breeders' and Owners' Assn. [4870]
Cleveland Bay Horse Soc. of Australasia [IO]
Cleveland Bay Horse Soc. of North Am. [4871]
Clwyd Welsh Pony and Cob Assn. [IO]
Clydesdale Breeders of the U.S.A. [4872]
Collegiate Equestrian Polo Assn. [23659]
Colorado Ranger Horse Assn. [4873]
Connemara Pony Breeders Soc. [IO]
Cowboy Mounted Shooting Assn. [23716]
Cowboys for Christ [19792]
CSA Intl. [IO]
Curly Sporthorse International [IO]
Curly Sporthorse Intl. [4874]
Dales Pony Assn. of North Am. [4875]
Dales Pony Association of North America [IO]
Dales Pony Soc. of Am. [4876]
Dressage Canada [IO]
Dyfed Welsh Pony and Cob Assn. [IO]
East Midlands Welsh Pony and Cob Assn. [IO]
Eastern Welsh Pony and Cob Assn. [IO]
Egyptian Arabian Horse Alliance [4877]
Equestrian Land Conservation Rsrc. [5130]
Equestrian Ministries Intl. [20082]
Equine Assisted Growth and Learning Assn. [16216]
Equine Canada [IO]
Equine Guided Educ. Assn. [8524]
Equine Rescue League [11392]

Fell Pony Soc. [IO]
Fell Pony Society and Conservancy of the Americas [IO]
Fell Pony Soc. and Conservancy of the Americas [4878]
Fell Pony Soc. of North Am. [4879]
Fell Pony Society of North America [IO]
For the Love of Horses [17729]
Friesian Horse Assn. of North Am. [4880]
Friesian Horse Assn. of North Am. [IO]
Friesian Horse Soc. [IO]
Front Range Equine Rescue [4881]
Fund for Horses [4159]
Gaited Horse Intl. Assn. [4882]
Galiceno Horse Breeders Assn. [4883]
Gladstone Equestrian Assn. [23524]
Gliding Horse and Pony Registry [4884]
Gotland-Russ Assn. of North Am. [4885]
Grayson-Jockey Club Res. Found. [4886]
Guild of Professional Farriers [1354]
Gwent Area Welsh Pony and Cob Assn. [IO]
Gwynedd Welsh Pony and Cob Breeders' Assn. [IO]
Gypsy Vanner Horse Soc. [4887]
Habitat for Horses [11403]
Haflinger Breeders Org. [4888]
Half Saddlebred Registry of Am. [4889]
Harness Horse Youth Found. [23496]
Harness Horsemen Intl. [23497]
Harness Racing Museum and Hall of Fame [23498]
Harness Tracks of Am. [23499]
Heritage Trails Fund [23940]
Home Counties Welsh Pony and Cob Assn. [IO]
Hong Kong Equestrian Fed. [IO]
Horse Lovers United [17730]
Horse Protection League [4890]
Horseaid Equine Relief Programme [11408]
Horsemanship Safety Assn. [23525]
Hungarian Horse Assn. of Am. [4891]
Iberian Sport Horse and Warmblood Registry [4892]
Icelandic Horse Trekkers [4893]
Intercollegiate Horse Show Assn. [23526]
Intl. Andalusian and Lusitano Horse Assn. [4894]
International Andalusian and Lusitano Horse Association [IO]
International Arabian Horse Association [IO]
Intl. Arabian Horse Assn. [4895]
Intl. Assn. of Equine Professionals [1925]
Intl. Barrel Racing Assn. [23500]
Intl. Buckskin Horse Assn. [4896]
International Buckskin Horse Association [IO]
International Colored Appaloosa Association [IO]
Intl. Colored Appaloosa Assn. [4897]
Intl. Curly Horse Org. [4898]
International Curly Horse Organization [IO]
Intl. Fed. of Registered Equine Massage Therapists [IO]
Intl. Generic Horse Assn. [4899]
Intl. League for the Protection of Horses [IO]
International Morab Breeders' Association [IO]
Intl. Morab Breeders' Assn. [4900]
Intl. Morab Registry [4901]
Intl. Pedigree Assignment and Bloodline Res. Assn. [4902]
Intl. Pedigree Assignment and Bloodline Res. Assn. [IO]
Intl. Professional Rodeo Assn. [23686]
Intl. Quarab Horse Assn. [4903]
International Quarab Horse Association [IO]
Intl. Quarter Pony Assn. [4904]
Intl. Side Saddle Org. [23529]
Intl. Sport Horses of Color [4905]
Intl. Sporthorse Registry [4906]
Intl. Spotted Horse Registry Assn. [4907]
International Spotted Horse Registry Association [IO]
Intl. Trotting and Pacing Assn. [23501]
Intl. Vaulting Club [23968]
Intl. Warlander Soc. and Registry [4908]
International Warlander Society and Registry [IO]
Irish Draught Horse Soc. [IO]
Irish Draught Horse Society of North America [IO]
Irish Draught Horse Soc. of North Am. [4909]

A star before a book entry number signifies that the name is not listed separately, but is mentioned within the entry.

The Jockey Club [23502]
Jockeys' Guild [23503]
Kiger Mesteno Assn. [4910]
Lancashire Welsh Pony and Cob Assn. [IO]
Lipizzan Assn. of North Am. [4911]
Lippitt Morgan Breeders Assn. [4912]
Lusitano Breed Soc. of Great Britain [IO]
Mainland Miniature Horse Club [IO]
Miniature Horse Assn. of Australia [IO]
Miniature Horse Club of Southland [IO]
Missouri Fox Trotting Horse Breed Assn. [4913]
Morab Breeders Consortium [4914]
Morgan Single-Footing Horse Found. [4915]
Mountain Pleasure Horse Assn. [4916]
Mounted Games Across Am. [23830]
Mounted Games Assn. of Ireland [IO]
Natl. Assn. of Off-Track Betting [23505]
Natl. Chincoteague Pony Assn. [4917]
Natl. Christian Barrel Racers Assn. [23507]
Natl. Cutting Horse Assn. [4918]
Natl. Finals Rodeo Comm. [23689]
Natl. High School Rodeo Assn. [23690]
Natl. Horse Protection Coalition [11439]
Natl. Horse Show Commn. [4919]
Natl. Hunter Jumper Assn. [23530]
Natl. Intercollegiate Rodeo Assn. [23691]
Natl. Little Britches Rodeo Assn. [23692]
Natl. Morgan Reining Horse Assn. [4920]
Natl. Museum of Racing and Hall of Fame
    [23508]
Natl. Mustang Assn. [4921]
Natl. Pony Soc. [IO]
Natl. Quarter Horse Registry [4922]
Natl. Quarter Pony Assn. [4923]
Natl. Reined Cow Horse Assn. [22586]
Natl. Reining Horse Assn. [4924]
National Reining Horse Association [IO]
Natl. Show Horse Registry [4925]
Natl. Snaffle Bit Assn. [4926]
Natl. Spotted Saddle Horse Assn. [4927]
Natl. Steeplechase Assn. [23509]
Natl. Thoroughbred Racing Assn. [23510]
Natl. Trail Ride Assn. [23946]
Natl. Walking Horse Assn. [4928]
New Forest Pony Assn. and Registry [4929]
New Forest Pony Breeding and Cattle Soc. [IO]
New Zealand Miniature Horse Assn. [IO]
North Amer. Danish Warmblood Assn. [IO]
North Amer. Danish Warmblood Assn. [4930]
North Amer. Dept. of the Royal Warmblood
    Studbook of the Netherlands [4931]
North Amer. Equine Ranching Info. Coun. [1926]
North Amer. Horsemen's Assn. [4932]
North Amer. Model Horse Shows Assn. [22587]
North Amer. Mustang Assn. and Registry [4933]
North Amer. Peruvian Horse Assn. [4934]
North Amer. Peruvian Horse Assn. [IO]
North Amer. Pt-to-Pt Assn. [23511]
North Amer. Riding for the Handicapped Assn.
    [23357]
North Amer. Selle Francais Assn. [4935]
North Amer. Shagya-Arabian Soc. [4936]
North Amer. Single-footing Horse Assn. [4937]
North Amer. Spotted Draft Horse Assn. [4938]
North American Spotted Draft Horse Association
    [IO]
North Amer. Thoroughbred Soc. [23538]
North Amer. Trail Ride Conf. [23949]
North Eastern Counties Welsh Pony and Cob
    Assn. [IO]
Northland Miniature Horse Club [IO]
Norwegian Fjord Horse Registry [4939]
Nova Scotia Equestrian Fed. [IO]
Oldenburg Registry N.A. [4940]
Oregon Horsemen's Benevolent Protective Assn.
    [23512]
Palomino Horse Assn. [4941]
Palomino Horse Breeders of Am. [4942]
Paso Fino Horse Assn. [4943]
Paso Fino Horse Assn. [IO]
Peruvian Horse Assn. of Canada [IO]
Pinto Horse Assn. of Am. [4944]
Ponies Assn. - UK [IO]
Pony of the Americas Club [4945]
Pony Club [IO]

Praying Hands Ranches [23360]
Professional Armed Forces Rodeo Assn. [23693]
Professional Rodeo Cowboys Assn. [23694]
Pure Puerto Rican Paso Fino Fed. of Am. [4946]
Purebred Morab Horse Association/Registry
    [4947]
Purebred Morab Horse Association/Registry [IO]
Racking Horse Breeders' Assn. of Am. [4948]
Ranching Heritage Assn. [10148]
ReRun [17731]
Ride and Tie Assn. [23849]
Rocky Mountain Horse Assn. [4949]
Saddle, Harness and Allied Trades Assn. [2419]
Saskatchewan Horse Fed. [IO]
Scottish and Northern Welsh Pony and Cob Assn.
    [IO]
Scottish Welsh Pony and Cob Assn. [IO]
Severn Valley Welsh Pony and Cob Assn. [IO]
Show Horse Alliance [4950]
Sisterhood of Shoers [1355]
South Eastern Welsh Pony and Cob Assn. [IO]
South Western Assn. of WPCS [IO]
Southern Counties Welsh Pony and Cob Assn.
    [IO]
Southwest Spanish Mustang Assn. [4951]
Spanish-Barb Breeders Assn. [4952]
Spanish Mustang Registry [4953]
Spanish-Norman Horse Registry [4954]
Sport Horse Owners and Breeders Assn. [23539]
Spotted Saddle Horse Breeders' and Exhibitors'
    Assn. [4955]
Standardbred Owners Assn. [23513]
Standardbred Retirement Found. [4956]
Stolen Horse Intl. [11461]
Swedish Gotland Breeders' Soc. [4957]
Swedish Warmblood Assn. of North Am. [4958]
Tennessee Walking Horse Breeders' and Exhibi-
    tors' Assn. [4959]
Tennessee Walking Horse Breeders' and Exhibi-
    tors' Association [IO]
Thoroughbred Adoption and Retirement Assn.
    [12302]
Thoroughbred Breeders' Assn. [IO]
Thoroughbred Club of Am. [23514]
Thoroughbred Owners and Breeders Assn.
    [23515]
Thoroughbred Racing Associations [23516]
Thoroughbred Racing Protective Bur. [23517]
Tiger Horse Assn. [4960]
United Pegasus Found. [17732]
United Professional Horsemen's Assn. [4961]
U.S. Calf Ropers Assn. [23695]
U.S. Cavalry Assn. and Memorial Res. Lib.
    [10484]
U.S. Dressage Fed. [23533]
U.S. Equestrian Fed. [23534]
U.S. Eventing Assn. [23535]
U.S. Hunter Jumper Assn. [23536]
U.S. Icelandic Horse Cong. [4962]
U.S. Lipizzan Registry [4963]
U.S. Peruvian Horse Assn. [4964]
U.S. Polo Assn. [23661]
U.S. Pony Clubs [23537]
U.S. Team Penning Assn. [23518]
U.S. Trotting Assn. [23519]
Universal Perkehner Soc. [22602]
Verband Hannoverscher Warmblutzuechter [IO]
Walkaloosa Horse Assn. [IO]
Walkaloosa Horse Assn. [4965]
Walking Horse Owners' Assn. [4966]
Walking Horse Trainers Assn. [4967]
Warmblood Breeders of North Am. [4968]
Welsh Pony and Cob Soc. [IO]
Welsh Pony and Cob Soc. of Am. [4969]
Western Intl. Walking Horse Assn. [4970]
Western Intl. Walking Horse Assn. [IO]
Western Saddle Clubs Assn. [4971]
Wild Horse Organized Assistance [5394]
Wild Horse Sanctuary [11477]
Wild Horses of Am. Registry [5395]
Women's Professional Rodeo Assn. [23696]
World Arabian Horse Org. [IO]
World Championship Cutter and Chariot Racing
    Assn. [23281]
World Farriers Assn. [1356]

Horses of Am. Registry; Wild [★5330]
Horses of Am. Registry; Wild [5395]
Horses; Amer. Assn. of Breeders of Holsteiner
    [★4824]
Horses; Amer. Assn. of Importers and Breeders of
    Belgian Draft [★4865]
Horseshoe Canada Assn. [IO], River Heights, SK,
    Canada
Horseshoe Pitchers; Grand League of Amer.
    [★23540]
Horseshoe and Quoit Pitchers; Natl. Assn. of
    [★23540]

Horseshoes
    Artist-Blacksmith's Assn. of North Am. [523]
    Horseshoe Canada Assn. [IO]
    Natl. Horseshoe Pitchers Assn. of Am. [23540]
Horticultural Assn; Natl. Junior [22530]
Horticultural Coun; Northwest [4753]
Horticultural Dealers Assn. [★4983]
Horticultural Indus. Assn; Intl. Garden [★4975]
Horticultural Libraries; Coun. on Botanical and
    [10352]
Horticultural Res. Inst. [5044], 1000 Vermont Ave.
    NW, Ste. 300, Washington, DC 20005-4914,
    (202)789-2900
Horticultural Sci; Amer. Soc. for [6627]
Horticultural Soc; Amer. [22492]
Horticultural Therapy Assn; Amer. [16601]
Horticultural Trades Assn. [IO], Reading, United
    Kingdom

Horticulture
    African Violet Soc. of Am. [22480]
    Agri-Horticultural Soc. of India [IO]
    Agricultural Res. Trust [IO]
    All-America Gladiolus Selections [22481]
    All-America Rose Selections [4972]
    Amer. Begonia Soc. [22482]
    Amer. Bonsai Soc. [22483]
    Amer. Boxwood Soc. [22484]
    Amer. Brugmansia and Datura Soc. [22455]
    The Amer. Chestnut Found. [6622]
    Amer. Community Gardening Assn. [22486]
    Amer. Daffodil Soc. [22487]
    Amer. Fern Soc. [6623]
    Amer. Fuchsia Soc. [22488]
    Amer. Gourd Soc. [22489]
    Amer. Hemerocallis Soc. [22490]
    Amer. Hibiscus Soc. [22491]
    Amer. Horticultural Soc. [22492]
    Amer. Horticultural Therapy Assn. [16601]
    Amer. Hosta Soc. [22493]
    Amer. Iris Soc. [22495]
    Amer. Ivy Soc. [22496]
    Amer. Orchid Soc. [6625]
    Amer. Penstemon Soc. [22497]
    Amer. Peony Soc. [22498]
    Amer. Phytopathological Soc. [6626]
    Amer. Primrose Soc. [22499]
    Amer. Public Gardens Assn. [4973]
    Amer. Rhododendron Soc. [22500]
    Amer. Rose Soc. [22501]
    Amer. Soc. for Horticultural Sci. [6627]
    Amer. Soc. of Plant Biologists [6628]
    Amer. Soc. of Plant Taxonomists [6629]
    Amer. Soc. for Plasticulture [4097]
    Aril Soc. Intl. [22502]
    Assn. of Zoological Horticulture [4974]
    Australasian Plant Soc. [IO]
    Bonsai Clubs Intl. [22504]
    Bonsai and Orchid Assn. [4975]
    Bonsai and Orchid Assn. [IO]
    Botanical Soc. of Am. [6632]
    British Bedding and Pot Plant Assn. [IO]
    British Christmas Tree Growers Assn. [IO]
    British Soc. of Plant Breeders [IO]
    Bromeliad Soc. Intl. [22505]
    Cactus and Succulent Soc. of Am. [22506]
    Canadian Horticultural Coun. [IO]
    Canadian Nursery Landscape Assn. [IO]
    Canadian Ornamental Plant Found. [IO]
    Commercial Horticultural Assn. [IO]
    Coun. on Botanical and Horticultural Libraries
        [10352]
    Crape Myrtle Soc. of Am. [4976]
    Cymbidium Soc. of Am. [22508]

Reference to "IO" in place of a book number signifies that the association may be found in the 45th edition of International Organizations.

Danish Assn. of Graduates in Horticulture [IO]
Desert Botanical Garden [6633]
Epiphyllum Soc. of Am. [22510]
European Community of Young Horticulturists [IO]
Fed. for the Gardening Trades [IO]
Flowers and Plants Assn. [IO]
French Assn. for Plant Protection [IO]
Garden Club of Am. [22511]
Garden Conservancy [4402]
Garden Writers Assn. [22512]
The Gardeners of Am. [22513]
German Cactus Soc. [IO]
German Soc. for Horticultural Sci. [IO]
Gesneriad Hybridizers Assn. [22514]
Gesneriad Soc. [22515]
Hardy Fern Found. [4977]
Heliconia Soc. Intl. [4978]
Heliconia Soc. Intl. [IO]
Heritage Roses Gp. [22517]
Hobby Greenhouse Assn. [22518]
Horticultural Res. Inst. [5044]
Horticultural Trades Assn. [IO]
Independent Turf and Ornamental Distributors
    Assn. [2394]
Indian Phytopathological Soc. [IO]
Indoor Gardening Soc. of Am. [22519]
Inst. of Horticulture [IO]
InterAmerican Soc. for Tropical Horticulture [4979]
Intl. Aroid Soc. [22520]
Intl. Asclepiad Soc. [IO]
Intl. Assn. of Horticultural Producers [IO]
Intl. Assn. for the Plant Protection Sciences
    [6397]
Intl. Bulb Soc. [6637]
Intl. Carnivorous Plant Soc. [22521]
Intl. Cut Flower Growers Assn. [4980]
Intl. Cut Flower Growers Assn. [IO]
Intl. Lilac Soc. [22522]
Intl. Oleander Soc. [22523]
Intl. Org. of Citrus Virologists [6638]
Intl. Palm Soc. [6640]
Intl. Plant Propagators Soc. [4981]
International Plant Propagators Society [IO]
Interstate Professional Applicators Assn. [2909]
Irish Farmers' Assn. [IO]
Magnolia Soc. Intl. [6643]
Median Iris Soc. [22525]
Natl. Auricula and Primula Soc. Midland and West
    Sect. [IO]
Natl. Chrysanthemum Soc. [22526]
Natl. Fuchsia Soc. [22527]
Natl. Garden Bur. [4982]
Natl. Garden Clubs [22528]
Natl. Gardening Assn. [22529]
Natl. Junior Horticultural Assn. [22530]
New England Wild Flower Soc. [4434]
New York State Turf and Landscape Assn. [2397]
New Zealand Inst. of Agricultural and Horticultural
    Sci. [IO]
New Zealand Plant Protection Soc. [IO]
North Amer. Flowerbulb Wholesalers Assn. [4983]
North Amer. Fruit Explorers [22531]
North Amer. Gladiolus Coun. [22532]
North Amer. Heather Soc. [22533]
North Amer. Horticultural Supply Assn. [4984]
North Amer. Lily Soc. [22534]
North Amer. Native Plant Soc. [IO]
North Amer. Plant Protection Org. [IO]
North Amer. Rock Garden Soc. [22535]
Northwest Horticultural Coun. [4753]
Nursery and Garden Indus. Australia [IO]
Org. for Flora Neotropica [6645]
Pacific Orchid Soc. of Hawaii [22536]
Passiflora Soc. Intl. [4673]
Paw Paw Found. [4754]
Perennial Plant Assn. [4985]
Plumeria Soc. of Am. [22537]
Reblooming Iris Soc. [22538]
Rhododendron Species Found. [6648]
Rose Hybridizers Assn. [22539]
Royal Horticultural Soc. [IO]
Seed Savers Exchange [22540]
Soc. for Economic Botany [6649]
Soc. for Japanese Irises [22541]
Soc. for Louisiana Irises [22542]

Soc. for Pacific Coast Native Iris [22543]
Soc. for Siberian Irises [22544]
Species Iris Gp. of North Am. [22545]
Tall Bearded Iris Soc. [22547]
Terrarium Assn. [22548]
Thrive [IO]
Tropical Flowering Tree Soc. [IO]
Tropical Flowering Tree Soc. [4986]
Horticulture Awareness Assn. - Address unknown
    since 1995.
Horticulturists; Soc. of Amer. Florists and
    Ornamental [★1493]
Horton Family Assn. - Defunct.
Hose and Accessories Distribution; Natl. Assn. of
    [2047]
Hosei-shi Gakkai [★IO]
Hoshasen Eikyo Kenkyu-sho [★IO]
The Hosiery Assn. [239], 7421 Carmel Executive
    Park, Ste. 200, Charlotte, NC 28226, (704)365-
    0913
Hosiery Manufacturers; Natl. Assn. of [★239]
Hosiery Wholesalers Natl. Assn. - Address unknown
    since 1995.

Hospice
Acute Long Term Hosp. Assn. [14852]
Assn. of Children's Hospices [IO]
Canadian Hospice Palliative Care Assn. [IO]
Children's Hospice Intl. [IO]
Children's Hospice Intl. [14853]
Hospice Assn. of Ontario [IO]
Hospice Educ. Inst. [IO]
Hospice Educ. Inst. [14854]
Hospice Found. of Am. [14855]
Hospice New Zealand [IO]
Hospice and Palliative Nurses Assn. [15482]
Medical Dental Hosp. Bus. Associates [40]
Natl. Assn. for Home Care and Hospice [14840]
Natl. Coun. for Palliative Care [IO]
Natl. Hospice and Palliative Care Org. [14856]
Natl. Inst. for Jewish Hospice [14857]
Natl. Prison Hospice Assn. [14858]
Nova Scotia Hospice Palliative Care Assn. [IO]
Rallying Points [14083]
World Homecare and Hospice Org. [14844]
Hospice Assn. of Am. [14837], 228 Seventh St. SE,
    Washington, DC 20003, (202)546-4759
Hospice Assn. of Ontario [IO], Toronto, ON, Canada
Hospice Educ. Inst. [IO], Machiasport, ME, United
    States
Hospice Educ. Inst. [14854], 3 Unity Sq., PO Box
    98, Machiasport, ME 04655-0098, (207)255-8800
Hospice Found. of Am. [14855], 1621 Connecticut
    Ave. NW, Ste. 300, Washington, DC 20009,
    (800)854-3402
Hospice New Zealand [IO], Wellington, New Zealand
Hospice Nurses Assn. [★15482]
Hospice Org; Natl. [★14856]
Hospice and Palliative Medicine; Amer. Acad. of
    [15985]
Hospice and Palliative Nurses Assn. [15482], One
    Penn Ctr. W, Ste. 229, Pittsburgh, PA 15276,
    (412)787-9301

Hospital
Acute Long Term Hosp. Assn. [14852]
Adelaide Hosp. Soc. [IO]
Alliance for Healthcare Strategy and Marketing
    [2612]
Amer. Animal Hosp. Assn. [16739]
Amer. Assn. of Blood Banks [13761]
Amer. Assn. of Eye and Ear Hospitals [14859]
American Association of Eye and Ear Hospitals
    [IO]
Amer. Assn. of Healthcare Consultants [14860]
Amer. Assn. of Hosp. Dentists [14116]
Amer. Assn. of Hosp. Podiatrists [16026]
Amer. Assn. of Psychiatric Administrators [14861]
Amer. Baptist Homes and Hospitals Assn. [19471]
Amer. Case Mgt. Assn. [15051]
Amer. Coll. of Healthcare Executives [14862]
Amer. Comm. for Shaare Zedek Hosp. in Jerusa-
    lem [12455]
Amer. Hosp. Assn. [14863]
Amer. Soc. of Directors of Volunteer Services
    [13382]
Amer. Soc. of Hea. Sys. Pharmacists [15923]

Amer. Soc. for Healthcare Central Ser. Profes-
    sionals [14864]
Amer. Soc. for Healthcare Engg. of the Amer.
    Hosp. Assn. [14865]
Amer. Soc. for Healthcare Environmental Services
    of the Amer. Hosp. Assn. [14866]
American Society for Healthcare Environmental
    Services of the American Hospital Association
    [IO]
Amer. Soc. for Healthcare Food Ser. Administra-
    tors [14867]
Amer. Soc. for Healthcare Human Resources
    Admin. [14868]
Amer. Soc. for Healthcare Risk Mgt. [14869]
Amer. Women's Hospitals Ser. Comm. of AMWA
    [14870]
Asian Hosp. Fed. [IO]
Assembly of Episcopal Healthcare Chaplains
    [19944]
Assn. of Canadian Academic Healthcare
    Organizations [IO]
Assn. for Healthcare Philanthropy [IO]
Assn. for Healthcare Philanthropy [14871]
Assn. for Healthcare Rsrc. and Materials Mgt.
    [14872]
Assn. for Hosp. Medical Educ. [14873]
Assn. of Private Hospitals of Malaysia [IO]
Assn. of Psychology Postdoctoral and Internship
    Centers [8854]
Australian Private Hospitals Assn. [IO]
Canadian Healthcare Assn. [IO]
Canadian Healthcare Engg. Soc. [IO]
Catholic Hea. Assn. of the U.S. [14874]
Center to Advance Palliative Care [14875]
Coll. of Osteopathic Healthcare Executives
    [14876]
Comm. to Reduce Infection Deaths [14877]
Community Hospitals Assn. [IO]
Competency and Credentialing Inst. [14878]
Coun. of Teaching Hospitals [14879]
Coun. of Women's and Infants' Specialty
    Hospitals [14880]
European Hosp. and Healthcare Fed. [IO]
Fed. of Amer. Hospitals [14881]
The Floating Hosp. [14882]
Friends of St. Luke's Hosp. [IO]
German Hosp. Fed. [IO]
Hea. Acad. [14883]
Hea. Res. and Educational Trust [14884]
Healthcare Financial Mgt. Assn. [15066]
Healthcare Info. and Mgt. Systems Soc. [14885]
Healthcare Laundry Accreditation Coun. [2403]
Hosp. Audiences [11017]
Hosp. Consultants and Specialists Assn. [IO]
Hosp. Infection Soc. [IO]
Hosp. Org. of Pedagogues in Europe [IO]
Intl. Assn. of Healthcare Central Ser. Materiel Mgt.
    [IO]
Intl. Assn. of Healthcare Central Ser. Materiel Mgt.
    [14886]
Intl. Assn. for Healthcare Security and Safety
    [14887]
Intl. Assn. for Healthcare Security and Safety [IO]
Intl. Hea. Evaluation Assn. [14568]
Intl. Healthcare Safety Professional Certification
    Bd. [16379]
Intl. Hosp. Fed. [IO]
Joint Commn. on Accreditation of Healthcare
    Organizations [14888]
Natl. Assn. of Children's Hospitals and Related
    Institutions [14889]
Natl. Assn. of Healthcare Access Mgt. [14890]
Natl. Assn. of Healthcare Transport Mgt. [14579]
Natl. Assn. of Hosp. Hospitality Houses [14891]
Natl. Assn. of Public Hospitals and Hea. Systems
    [14892]
Natl. Assn. of Urban Hospitals [14893]
Natl. Healthcare Collectors Assn. [1869]
Premier Advocacy [14597]
Public Hosp. Pharmacy Coalition [15949]
Reclamation Inc. [12556]
Sect. for Long Term Care and Rehabilitation
    [14894]
Sect. for Metropolitan Hospitals [14895]
Shriners Hospitals for Children [13973]

A star before a book entry number signifies that the name is not listed separately, but is mentioned within the entry.

Soc. for Healthcare Strategy and Market Development of the Amer. Hosp. Assn. [14896]
Soc. of Hosp. Medicine [14897]
Spirit of Women Hosp. Network [14898]
Sustainable Hospitals Proj. [14899]
Swiss Hosp. Assn. [IO]
Trinity Medical Center [14900]
United Methodist Assn. of Hea. and Welfare Ministries [14602]
VHA [14901]
Volunteer Trustees of Not-for-Profit Hospitals [14902]
Hosp. Acad. [★14883]
Hosp. Accountants; Amer. Assn. of [★15066]
Hosp. Admin; Assn. of Univ: Programs in [★8857]
Hosp. Administrators; Amer. Coll. of [★14862]
Hosp. Administrators; Amer. Coll. of Osteopathic [★14876]
Hosp. Admitting Managers; Natl. Assn. of [★14890]
Hosp; ALSAC/Saint Jude Children's Res. [13946]
Hosp; Amer. Friends of ALYN [12825]
Hosp. Art; Found. for [13708]
Hosp. Assn; Amer. Animal [16739]
Hosp. Assn; Amer. Small and Rural [★16248]
Hosp. Assn; Catholic [★14874]
Hosp. Assn; Chaplains Assn. of the Amer. Protestant [★19744]
Hosp. Assn; Educational Trust of the Amer. [★14884]
Hosp. Assn; Natl. Soc. of Patient Representatives of the Amer. [★15005]
Hosp. Assn. of U.S. and Canada; Catholic [★14874]
Hosp. Attorneys; Amer. Acad. of [★5782]
Hosp. Attorneys; Amer. Soc. of [★5782]
Hosp. Attorneys; Soc. of [★5782]
Hosp. Audiences [11017], 548 Broadway, 3rd Fl., New York, NY 10012, (212)575-7676
Hospital-Based Emergency Air Medical Services; Amer. Soc. of [★14314]
Hospital-Based Massage Network [15027], c/o Info. for People, PO Box 1038, Olympia, WA 98507-1038, (360)754-9799
Hospital Bur. - Address unknown since 1995.
Hospital Bur. Res. Inst. - Defunct.
Hosp. Bus. Associates; Medical Dental [40]
Hosp. Caterers Assn. [IO], Stoke-On-Trent, United Kingdom
Hosp. Central Ser. Mgt; Intl. Assn. of [★14886]
Hosp. Central Ser. Personnel; Natl. Assn. of [★14886]
Hosp. Consultants; Amer. Assn. of [★14860]
Hosp. Consultants and Specialists Assn. [IO], Basingstoke, United Kingdom
Hosp. Dental Chiefs; Amer. Assn. of [★14116]
Hosp. Dentists; Amer. Assn. of [★14186]
Hosp. Dentists; Amer. Assn. of [14116]
Hosp. Development; Natl. Assn. for [★14871]
Hosp. Directors of Medical Educ; Assn. of [★14873]
Hosp. Engg; Amer. Soc. for [★14865]
Hosp. Epidemiologists of Am; Soc. of [★14378]
Hosp. Financial Mgt. Assn. [★15066]
Hosp. Food Ser. Administrators; Amer. Soc. for [★14867]
Hosp. Hea. and Fitness; Assn. of [★15966]
Hosp. Infection Soc. [IO], London, United Kingdom
Hosp., Institution and Educational Food Ser. Soc. [★15555]
Hosp. in Jerusalem; Amer. Comm. for Shaare Zedek [12455]
Hosp. Mgt. Engg; Center for [★14885]
Hosp. Mgt. Systems Soc. [★14885]
Hosp. Managers Assn; Veterinary [16814]
Hosp. Marketing and Public Relations; Amer. Soc. for [★14896]
Hosp. Materials Mgt; Amer. Soc. for [★14872]
Hosp. Nursing Ser. Administrators; Amer. Soc. for [★15454]
Hosp. Org. of Pedagogues in Europe [IO], Brussels, Belgium
Hosp. Pharmacists Res. and Educ. Found; Amer. Soc. of [★15926]
Hosp. Podiatrists; Amer. Assn. of [16026]
Hosp. Proj; Holiday [★13395]
Hosp. Public Relations; Amer. Soc. for [★14896]
Hosp. Purchasing Agents; Amer. Soc. for [★14872]

Hospital Purchasing Agents Assn. of Greater New York - Address unknown since 1995.
Hosp. Purchasing and Materials Mgt; Amer. Soc. for [★14872]
Hosp. Radio and TV Guild; Veterans [★12116]
Hosp. Radiology Administrators; Amer. [★16275]
Hospital Reading Soc. - Defunct.
Hosp. and Res. Center; Natl. Jewish [★16361]
Hosp. Res. and Educational Trust [★14884]
Hosp; St. John's Guild - The Floating [★14882]
Hosp. and Sanitaria; Natl. Coun. of Chiropractic [★13988]
Hosp. Sect. of the Amer. Recreation Soc. [★16628]
Hosp. Sect; Public-General [★14895]
Hosp. Security; Intl. Assn. for [★14887]
Hosp. Superintendents of U.S. and Canada; Assn. of [★14863]
Hosp; Trauma Found. at San Francisco Gen. [16691]
Hospitality Alliance; Multicultural Foodservice and [1586]
Hospitality Asset Managers Assn. [1942], c/o Stephanie Roy, Coor., PO Box 381, North Scituate, MA 02060, (781)544-7330
Hospitality Assn. of Namibia [IO], Windhoek, Namibia
Hospitality Assn; Natl. Park [1321]
Hospitality Assn. of New Zealand [IO], Wellington, New Zealand
Hospitality Assn. of Northern Ireland [★IO]
Hospitality Comm. for United Nations Delegations [17895], PO Box 1201, New York, NY 10164, (212)963-8753
Hospitality Financial and Tech. Professionals [32], 11709 Boulder Ln., Ste. 110, Austin, TX 78726-1832, (512)249-5333
Hospitality Financial and Tech. Professionals [IO], Austin, TX, United States
Hospitality Houses; Natl. Assn. of Hosp. [14891]
Hospitality Industries
  Amer. Hotel and Lodging Assn. [1927]
  Amer. Hotel and Lodging Educational Found. [1928]
  Amer. Resort Development Assn. [3298]
  Amer. Soc. of Travel Agents [3907]
  Amer. Travel Inns [1929]
  Arab Hotel Assn. [IO]
  Asian Amer. Hotel Owners Assn. [IO]
  Asian Amer. Hotel Owners Assn. [1930]
  Asociacion Mexicana de Hoteles y Moteles [IO]
  Assoc. Luxury Hotels Intl. [1931]
  Assn. of Club Executives [1932]
  Assn. for Convention Marketing Executives [1933]
  Assn. of the Hotel, Restaurant, and Tourism Indus. in Denmark [IO]
  Assn. of Meeting Professionals [1934]
  Assn. of Tourist Hotels of the Republic of Argentina [IO]
  Association for Wedding Professionals International [IO]
  Assn. for Wedding Professionals Intl. [1935]
  Australian Bartenders Guild [IO]
  Australian Hotels Assn. (NSW) [IO]
  Australian Hotels Assn. (South Australian Br.) [IO]
  Australian Hotels Assn. (Tasmania) [IO]
  Australian Hotels Assn. (Victoria Br.) [IO]
  Austrian Hotels' Assn. [IO]
  Austrian Soc. for Applied Res. in Tourism [IO]
  Bed and Breakfast League/Sweet Dreams and Toast [1936]
  Black Culinarian Alliance [1122]
  Brazilian Hotels' Assn. [IO]
  British Holiday and Home Parks Assn. [IO]
  British Hospitality Assn. [IO]
  British Inst. of Innkeeping [IO]
  British Resorts and Destinations Assn. [IO]
  Broker Mgt. Coun. [1937]
  Canadian Resort Development Assn. [IO]
  Canadian Restaurant and Foodservices Assn. [IO]
  Caribbean Hotel Assn. [3913]
  Caribbean Soc. of Hotel Assn. Executives [24330]
  Caribbean Soc. of Hotel Assn. Executives [IO]
  Chilean Hotels' Assn. [IO]
  Commercial Food Equip. Ser. Assn. [1571]
  Confed. of Natl. Associations of Hotels, Restaurants, Cafes and Similar Establishments [IO]

  Convenience Caterers and Food Mfrs. Assn. [1938]
  Coun. of Hotel and Restaurant Trainers [1939]
  Coun. of Intl. Restaurant Real Estate Brokers [3392]
  Cyprus Hotel Assn. [IO]
  Dude Ranchers' Assn. [1940]
  Ecuadorian Hotel Fed. [IO]
  Egyptian Hotel Assn. [IO]
  Estonian Hotel and Restaurant Assn. [IO]
  European Hotel Managers Assn. [IO]
  Federated Hospitality Assn. of South Africa [IO]
  Fed. of Hotel and Restaurant Associations of India [IO]
  Fiji Islands Hotel and Tourism Assn. [IO]
  Flair Bartenders' Assn. [201]
  German Hotels and Restaurants Assn. [IO]
  Green Book of Ireland [IO]
  Green Hotels Association [IO]
  Green Hotels Assn. [1941]
  Green Meeting Indus. Coun. [2681]
  Grenada Hotel and Tourism Assn. [IO]
  Guest House Accommodation of South Africa [IO]
  Hellenic Chamber of Hotels [IO]
  Holiday Accommodation Parks Assn. of New Zealand [IO]
  Hong Kong Hotels Assn. [IO]
  Hospitality Asset Managers Assn. [1942]
  Hospitality Assn. of Namibia [IO]
  Hospitality Assn. of New Zealand [IO]
  Hospitality Inst. of Tech. and Mgt. [1943]
  Hospitality Sales and Marketing Assn. Intl. [1944]
  Hospitality Sales and Marketing Assn. Intl. [IO]
  Hotel Assn. of Canada [IO]
  Hotel Assn. of Hungary [IO]
  Hotel Assn. of India [IO]
  Hotel Assn. Nepal [IO]
  Hotel Brokers Intl. [3311]
  Hotel and Catering Assn. of Zambia [IO]
  Hotel and Catering Intl. Mgt. Assn. [IO]
  Hotel Electronic Distribution Network Assn. [1945]
  Hotel and Restaurant Assn. of the Philippines [IO]
  Hotel, Restaurant and Personal Services Workers Union [IO]
  Hotels, Restaurants and Cafes in Europe [IO]
  IAHI, The Owners' Assn. [IO]
  IAHI, The Owners' Assn. [1946]
  Innholders' Company [IO]
  Intl. Assn. of Conf. Center Administrators [IO]
  Intl. Assn. of Conf. Center Administrators [1947]
  Intl. Assn. of Hispanic Meeting Professionals [2684]
  Intl. Assn. of Tour Managers [IO]
  Intl. Assn. of Tour Managers - North Amer. Region [3922]
  Intl. Coun. on Hotel, Restaurant, and Institutional Educ. [8525]
  Intl. Food, Wine and Travel Writers Assn. [3118]
  Intl. Galapagos Tour Operators Assn. [24383]
  Intl. Gay and Lesbian Travel Assn. [3924]
  Intl. Guild of Professional Butlers [24040]
  Intl. Hotel and Restaurant Assn. [IO]
  Intl. Soc. of Hospitality Purchasers [IO]
  Intl. Soc. of Hospitality Purchasers [1948]
  Irish Hospitality Inst. [IO]
  Irish Hotels Fed. [IO]
  Israel Hotel Assn. [IO]
  Israel Hotel Managers Assn. [IO]
  Jamaica Hotel and Tourist Assn. [IO]
  Jordan Hotel Assn. [IO]
  Kenya Assn. of Hotelkeepers and Caterers [IO]
  Leading Spas of Canada [IO]
  Les Clefs d'Or U.S.A. [1949]
  Liquor, Hospitality and Miscellaneous Workers' Union [IO]
  Luxembourg Fed. of Hotels, Restaurants and Coffee Shops [IO]
  Malaysia Budget Hotel Assn. [IO]
  Malaysian Assn. of Hotels [IO]
  Malta Hotels and Restaurants Assn. [IO]
  Natl. Assn. of Black Hotel Owners, Operators and Developers [1950]
  Natl. Assn. of Catering Executives [1951]
  National Association of Catering Executives [IO]
  Natl. Assn. of Condo Hotel Owners [1952]

Reference to "IO" in place of a book number signifies that the association may be found in the 45th edition of International Organizations.

Natl. Assn. of the Hotel Indus. [IO]
Natl. Assn. of Pizzeria Operators [1953]
Natl. Bed-and-Breakfast Assn. [1954]
Natl. Black McDonald's Operators Assn. [1955]
Natl. Concierge Assn. [1956]
Natl. Coun. of Chain Restaurants [1957]
Natl. Forest Recreation Assn. [3358]
Natl. Frozen Dessert and Fast Food Assn. [1958]
Natl. Hotels' and Restaurants' Assn. - Dominican
   Republic [IO]
Natl. Restaurant Assn. [1959]
Natl. Restaurant Assn. Educational Found. [1960]
Natl. Ski Areas Assn. [1961]
Native Tourism Alliance [24381]
North Amer. Meat Processors Assn. [2663]
Northern Ireland Hotels Fed. [IO]
Norwegian Hospitality Assn. [IO]
Org. for Timeshare in Europe [IO]
Portuguese Hotel Assn. [IO]
Professional Assn. of Innkeepers Intl. [IO]
Professional Assn. of Innkeepers Intl. [1962]
Recreation Managers' Assn. of Great Britain [IO]
Resort and Commercial Recreation Assn. [3361]
Resort Hotel Assn. [1963]
Restaurant Assn. [IO]
Restaurant and Catering New South Wales [IO]
Restaurants Assn. of Ireland [IO]
Saint Croix Hotel and Tourism Assn. [IO]
Saint Croix Hotel and Tourism Assn. [1964]
St. Maarten Hospitality and Trade Assn. [IO]
Scottish Licensed Trade Assn. [IO]
Select Registry, Distinguished Inns of North Am.
   [1965]
Singapore Hotel Assn. [IO]
Small Luxury Hotels of the World [1966]
Soc. of Incentive and Travel Executives [3935]
Spanish Hotel Fed. [IO]
Student and Youth Travel Assn. [3938]
Swedish Hotel and Restaurant Assn. [IO]
Thai Vacation Ownership Assn. [IO]
UK Inbound [IO]
UNITE HERE [24095]
United Kingdom Bartenders Guild [IO]
U.S. Tour Operators Assn. [3943]
Waiters Assn. [1967]
The Hospitality and Info. Ser. [17896]
Hospitality Info. Tech. Assn. [6717], c/o Corliss
   Rodgers, Sec.-Treas., 450 S Quinn St., No. 8,
   Mesa, AZ 85206, (928)523-0393
Hospitality Inst. of Tech. and Mgt. [1943], c/o Dr. O.
   Peter Snyder, Jr., Pres., 670 Transfer Rd., Ste.
   21A, St. Paul, MN 55114, (651)646-7077
Hospitality Network; Natl. Interfaith [★12290]
Hospitality Sales and Marketing Assn. [IO], Bendorf-
   Sayn, Germany
Hospitality Sales and Marketing Assn. Intl. [IO],
   McLean, VA, United States
Hospitality Sales and Marketing Assn. Intl. [1944],
   8201 Greensboro Dr., Ste. 300, McLean, VA
   22102, (703)610-9024
Hospitalization Study Group; Partial [★16080]
Hospitalization Stud. Groups; Fed. of Partial
   [★16080]
Hospitalized Children; Assn. of Educators for Home-
   bound and [★9141]
Hospitalized Children; Assn. of Educators for Home-
   bound and [★11998]
Hospitalized; Div. on Physically Handicapped, Home-
   bound and [★9141]
Hospitalized; Div. on Physically Handicapped, Home-
   bound and [★11998]
Hospitalized Veterans; Help [13351]
Hospitalized Veterans Writing Proj. [16321], 5920
   Nall, Rm. 105, Mission, KS 66202-3456, (913)432-
   1214
Hospitaller Order of St. John Knights - Defunct.
Hospitals of Am; Voluntary [★14901]
Hospitals Assn; Amer. Baptist Homes and [19471]
Hospitals; Assn. of Baptist Homes and [★19471]
Hospitals Assn; Church of the Brethren Homes and
   [★11276]
Hospitals; Assn. of Medical Superintendents of
   Mental [★14861]
Hospitals; Center for Urban [★14895]
Hospitals for Children Endowment Fund; Shriners
   [★13973]

Hospitals for Children; Shriners [13973]
Hospitals and Homes of The Methodist Church; Bd.
   of [★14602]
Hospitals; Joint Commn. on Accreditation of
   [★14888]
Hospitals; Natl. Assn. of Private Psychiatric
   [★16091]
Hospitals; Natl. Assn. of Public [★14892]
Hospitals Overseas Secure Equip. Needs; Christian
   [★12516]
Hospitals Proj; Sustainable [14899]
Hospitals and Services; Center for Rehabilitation
   [★14894]
Hosta Soc; Amer. [22493]
Hostage Bracelet Comm. - Defunct.
Hostage Exchange Found; Peace [★17370]
Hostages
   No Greater Love [13370]
   Pact Training [11830]
Hostel Assn; Finnish Youth [IO]
Hostel Assn; German Youth [IO]
Hostel Assn; Irish Youth [IO]
Hostel Fed; Intl. Youth [IO]
Hostel; Inter [8618]
Hostelling Ecuador [IO], Guayaquil, Ecuador
Hostelling International-American Youth Hostels [IO],
   Silver Spring, MD, United States
Hostelling International-American Youth Hostels
   [12797], 8401 Colesville Rd., Ste. 600, Silver
   Spring, MD 20910, (301)495-1240
Hostelling Intl. Argentina [IO], Buenos Aires,
   Argentina
Hostelling Intl. Bolivia [IO], Sucre, Bolivia
Hostelling Intl. Brazil [IO], Rio de Janeiro, Brazil
Hostelling Intl. - Canada [IO], Ottawa, ON, Canada
Hostelling Intl. Chile [IO], Santiago, Chile
Hostelling Intl. Colombia [IO], Bogota, Colombia
Hostelling Intl. Costa Rica [IO], San Jose, Costa
   Rica
Hostelling Intl. Finland [★IO]
Hostelling Intl. Iceland [IO], Reykjavik, Iceland
Hostelling Intl. Mexico [IO], Mexico City, Mexico
Hostelling Intl. Northern Island [IO], Belfast, United
   Kingdom
Hostelling Intl. Norway [IO], Oslo, Norway
Hostelling Intl. Slovenia [IO], Maribor, Slovenia
Hostels; Amer. Youth [★12797]
Hostels Assn. of India; Youth [IO]
Hostels Assn; Kenya Youth [IO]
Hostess Assn; Armed Forces [6068]
Hostess Assn; Army [★6068]
Hot Dip Galvanizers Assn; Amer. [★850]
Hot Dip Galvanizers Assn. of Southern Africa [IO],
   Edenvale, Republic of South Africa
Hot Melt Equipment Mfrs. Assn. - Defunct.
Hot Rod Assn; Intl. [23077]
Hot Rod Assn; Natl. [23083]
Hot Springs Hea. Sanctuary; Wilbur [10180]
Hot Tubs
   Assn. of Pool and Spa Professionals [3353]
   Wood Tank Mfrs. Assn. [3366]
Hotel Assn; Amer. [★1927]
Hotel Assn. of Canada [IO], Ottawa, ON, Canada
Hotel Assn. of Hungary [IO], Budapest, Hungary
Hotel Assn. of India [IO], New Delhi, India
Hotel Assn. Nepal [IO], Kathmandu, Nepal
Hotel Assn; Resort [1963]
Hotel Brokers Intl. [3311], 1420 NW Vivion Rd., Ste.
   111, Kansas City, MO 64118, (816)505-4315
Hotel Brokers Intl. [IO], Kansas City, MO, United
   States
Hotel and Catering Assn. of Zambia [IO], Lusaka,
   Zambia
Hotel and Catering Intl. Mgt. Assn. [IO], Sutton,
   United Kingdom
Hotel Coun. of the Caribbean Travel Assn; Carib-
   bean [★3913]
Hotel Credit Managers Assn. - Defunct.
Hotel Electronic Distribution Assn. [★1945]
Hotel Electronic Distribution Network Assn. [1945],
   1156-15th St. NW, Ste. 900, Washington, DC
   20005, (202)785-3232
Hotel Employees and Restaurant Employees Intl.
   Union and Union of Needletrades, Indus. and
   Textile Employees [★24095]

Hotel Found; Amer. [★1928]
Hotel and Lodging Assn; Amer. [1927]
Hotel and Lodging Educational Found; Amer. [1928]
Hotel Management
   Amer. Historic Inns [1909]
   Assoc. Luxury Hotels Intl. [1931]
   European Assn. of Hotel and Tourism Schools
      [IO]
   Hospitality Asset Managers Assn. [1942]
   Intl. Coun. on Hotel, Restaurant, and Institutional
      Educ. [8525]
   Intl. Coun. on Hotel, Restaurant, and Institutional
      Educ. [IO]
   Natl. Assn. of Black Hotel Owners, Operators and
      Developers [1950]
   Natl. Assn. of Condo Hotel Owners [1952]
   Resort Hotel Assn. [1963]
   UNITE HERE [24095]
Hotel and Motel Assn; Amer. [★1927]
Hotel Motel Brokers of Am. [★3311]
Hotel Motel Brokers of Am. [★IO]
Hotel and Motel Brokers; Amer. [★3311]
Hotel-Motel Greeters Intl. - Address unknown since
   1994.
Hotel and Restaurant Assn. of the Philippines [IO],
   Makati City, Philippines
Hotel and Restaurant Educ; Natl. Coun. on [★8525]
Hotel and Restaurant Employees and Bartenders
   Intl. Union [★24095]
Hotel, Restaurant and Institutional Educ; In Coun. on
   [★8525]
Hotel and Restaurant Meat Purveyors; Natl. Assn. of
   [★2663]
Hotel, Restaurant and Personal Services Workers
   Union [IO], Vienna, Austria
Hotel and Restaurant Trainers; Coun. of [1939]
Hotel-, Restaurant- og Turisterhvervets Arbejdsgiver-
   forening [★IO]
Hotels Assn; Green [1941]
Hotels Assn; Small Luxury [★1966]
Hotels Intl; Assoc. Luxury [1931]
Hotels, Restaurants and Cafes in Europe [IO], Brus-
   sels, Belgium
Hotels; Small Luxury [★1966]
Hotels of the World; Small Luxury [1966]
Hotline; Gay, Lesbian, Bisexual, and Transgender
   Natl. [12230]
Hotline; Natl. Autism [★13722]
Hotline; Natl. Domestic Violence [12036]
Hotot Rabbit Breeders Intl. [5147], c/o Laurie Staley-
   Jones, Sec.-Treas., 51 S Olive Church Rd.,
   Paragon, IN 46166
Hotot Rabbit Breeders International [IO], Choudrant,
   LA, United States
Houdini Historical Center/Outagamie County Histori-
   cal Soc. [11123], 330 E Coll. Ave., Appleton, WI
   54911-5715, (920)733-8445
Hound
   Afghan Hound Club of Am. [22179]
   Basset Hound Club of Am. [22226]
   Natl. Beagle Club of Am. [22314]
   Norwegian Elkhound Assn. of Am. [22331]
   Treeing Walker Breeders and Fanciers Assn.
      [22368]
Hour Glass Assn; Friends and Buddies of the
   [21299]
HOUR Money Network [17218], PO Box 6731, Ith-
   aca, NY 14851, (607)272-3738
House Assn. of Am; Historic [★10051]
House Assn. of North Am; Log [★1031]
House of Boyd Soc. [20945], c/o Lauren M. Boyd,
   Pres., 6 Sylvia Cir., Novato, CA 94947-2025
House of Boyd Soc. [IO], Novato, CA, United States
House Builder's Assn. of North Am; Log [★1031]
House Builders Fed. [IO], London, United Kingdom
House Democratic Res. Org. - Defunct.
House Ear Inst. [16446], 2100 W 3rd St., Los
   Angeles, CA 90057, (213)483-4431
House Leadership Fund - Defunct.
House Rabbit Network [11409], PO Box 2602,
   Woburn, MA 01888-1102, (781)431-1211
House Rabbit Soc. [11410], 148 Broadway,
   Richmond, CA 94804, (510)970-7575
House of Ruth [12029], 5 Thomas Cir. NW,
   Washington, DC 20005, (202)667-7001

A star before a book entry number signifies that the name is not listed separately, but is mentioned within the entry.

House Wednesday Group - Address unknown since 2003.
Houseboat Assn. of America - Defunct.
Houseboat Rental Assn; Delta [3367]
Housecall Veterinarians; Amer. Assn. of [16746]
Household Brigade Assn. - Address unknown since 1995.
Household Goods Carriers' Bur. [★3559]
Household Goods Carriers' Bur. [★IO]
Household Goods Forwarders Association of America [IO], Alexandria, VA, United States
Household Goods Forwarders Assn. of Am. [3567], 5904 Richmond Hwy., Ste. 404, Alexandria, VA 22303-1864, (703)317-9950
Household Hazardous Waste Proj. [5269], c/o Off. of Waste Mgt., Univ. of Missouri Extension, Columbia, MO 65211, (573)882-5011
Housekeepers Assn; United Kingdom [IO]

Housewares
Amer. Brush Mfrs. Assn. [1968]
Amer. Innerspring Manufacturers [1969]
Assn. of Mfrs. of Household Appliances [IO]
Assn. of Suppliers of Household Appliances in the Netherlands [IO]
Canadian Brush Mfrs. Assn. [IO]
Cookware Mfrs. Assn. [1970]
European Brushware Fed. [IO]
Griswold and Cast Iron Cookware Assn. [22588]
Home Furnishings Intl. Assn. [1697]
Intl. Assn. of Dinnerware Matchers [1971]
International Association of Dinnerware Matchers [IO]
Intl. Housewares Assn. [IO]
Intl. Housewares Assn. [1972]
Intl. Housewares Representatives Assn. [1973]
Intl. Housewares Representatives Assn. [IO]
Intl. Sleep Products Assn. [IO]
Intl. Sleep Products Assn. [1974]
Japan Elec. Lamp Mfrs. Assn. [IO]
Kitchen, Bathroom, Bedroom Specialists Assn. [IO]
Kitchen Cabinet Mfrs. Assn. [2267]
Lighting Assn. [IO]
Lighting Indus. Fed. [IO]
Microwave Technologies Assn. [IO]
Natl. Fireplace Assn. [IO]
Natl. Inst. of Carpet and Floorlayers [IO]
Natl. Kitchen and Bath Assn. [2271]
Natl. Union of Domestic Appliances and Gen. Operatives [IO]
Small Elecl. Appliance Marketing Assn. [IO]
Soc. of Certified Kitchen Designers [2277]
Taiwan Gas Appliance Manufacturers' Assn. [IO]
Housewares Mfrs. Assn; Natl. [★1972]
Housework Campaign; Wages for [★13428]
Housework; Intl. Black Women for Wages for [18811]

Housing
Adsum for Women and Children [IO]
African Amer. Alliance for Homeownership [1975]
Alberta Senior Citizens' Housing Assn. [IO]
Amer. Assn. of Code Enforcement [5959]
Amer. Assn. of Homes and Services for the Aging [11273]
Amer. Assn. of Housing Educators [12303]
Amer. Assn. for Intl. Aging [11274]
Amer. Assn. of Ser. Coordinators [1985]
Amer. Clipper Owners Club [22942]
Amer. Homeowners' Rsrc. Center [17743]
Amer. Seniors Housing Assn. [12304]
Amer. Soc. of Roommate Services [12305]
Army Distaff Foundation/Knollwood [21192]
Asian Coalition for Housing Rights [IO]
Asociacion de Inquilinos del Ecuador [IO]
Assisted Living Fed. of Am. [12306]
Associacao dos Inquilinos Lisbonenses [IO]
Associacao dos Inquilinos do Norte de Portugal [IO]
Assn. for Settlements and Housing Activities [IO]
Assn. Solidarite Defense Droits de Locataires [IO]
Assn. of Tenants - BIHUSS-Saravejo [IO]
Assn. of Tenants of the Slovak Republic [IO]
Assn. of Tenants of Slovenia [IO]
Bike and Build [11514]
B'nai B'rith Senior Citizens Housing Comm. [12469]

Builders Without Borders [12307]
Builders Without Borders [IO]
Canadian Housing and Renewal Assn. [IO]
Cara Irish Housing Assn. [IO]
Center for Neighborhood Enterprise [17208]
Central Union of Tenants [IO]
Centro Experimental de la Vivienda Economica [IO]
Chartered Inst. of Housing [IO]
Cluid Housing Assn. - North East [IO]
Coalition for Economic Survival [13160]
Community Associations Inst. [17212]
Community Economics, Inc. [12308]
Community Housing Fed. of Australia [IO]
Community Trans. Assn. of Am. [11772]
Confed. Nationale du Logement [IO]
Cooperative Housing Found. [12309]
Coun. for Affordable and Rural Housing [12310]
Coun. of Large Public Housing Authorities [5788]
Croatian Union of Tenants [IO]
Czech Republic Union of Tenants [IO]
Deaf-REACH [14752]
Discovery Owners Assn., Inc. [22947]
Doctors for Life Intl. [IO]
Dumaguete City Habitat for Humanity [IO]
Dutch Union of Tenants [IO]
Enterprise Community Partners [12311]
Escapees [22948]
Estonian Tenants Union [IO]
European Network for Housing Res. [IO]
FaithWorks Intl. [11777]
Family Justice [11865]
Family Motor Coach Assn. [22949]
Fed. of Private Residents' Associations [IO]
Found. of Real Estate Appraisers [280]
Fund for an OPEN Soc. [17819]
German Tenants' Union [IO]
Good Sam Recreational Vehicle Club [22951]
Gray Panthers [11287]
Greener Pastures Inst. [12312]
Greenland Union of Tenants [IO]
Habitat for Humanity - Afghanistan [IO]
Habitat for Humanity - Antigua and Barbuda [IO]
Habitat for Humanity - Argentina [IO]
Habitat for Humanity - Armenia [IO]
Habitat for Humanity - Australia [IO]
Habitat for Humanity Australia (Adelaide) [IO]
Habitat for Humanity - Banbury [IO]
Habitat for Humanity - Bangladesh [IO]
Habitat for Humanity - Belize [IO]
Habitat for Humanity - Bermuda [IO]
Habitat for Humanity - Bicol [IO]
Habitat for Humanity - Birmingham [IO]
Habitat for Humanity - Bolivia [IO]
Habitat for Humanity - Botswana [IO]
Habitat for Humanity - Braga [IO]
Habitat for Humanity - Brampton [IO]
Habitat for Humanity - Brandon [IO]
Habitat for Humanity - Brant [IO]
Habitat for Humanity - Brazil [IO]
Habitat for Humanity - Brooks [IO]
Habitat for Humanity - Bulgaria [IO]
Habitat for Humanity - Cabot [IO]
Habitat for Humanity - Calgary [IO]
Habitat for Humanity - Cambodia [IO]
Habitat for Humanity - Cameroon [IO]
Habitat for Humanity - Camrose Region [IO]
Habitat for Humanity - Canada [IO]
Habitat for Humanity - Cayman Islands [IO]
Habitat for Humanity - Central Plains [IO]
Habitat for Humanity - Chile [IO]
Habitat for Humanity - China [IO]
Habitat for Humanity - Christchurch [IO]
Habitat for Humanity - Colombia [IO]
Habitat for Humanity - Comox Valley [IO]
Habitat for Humanity - Costa Rica [IO]
Habitat for Humanity - Cote d'Ivoire [IO]
Habitat for Humanity - Democratic Republic of Congo [IO]
Habitat for Humanity - Dominican Republic [IO]
Habitat for Humanity, Dufferin-Caledon [IO]
Habitat for Humanity - Dunedin [IO]
Habitat for Humanity - Eastbourne [IO]
Habitat for Humanity - Ecuador [IO]
Habitat for Humanity - Edmonton [IO]

Habitat for Humanity - Egypt [IO]
Habitat for Humanity - El Salvador [IO]
Habitat for Humanity - Ethiopia [IO]
Habitat for Humanity - Fiji [IO]
Habitat for Humanity - Franklin [IO]
Habitat for Humanity - Fredericton Area [IO]
Habitat for Humanity - Gdansk [IO]
Habitat for Humanity - Gen. Santos City [IO]
Habitat for Humanity - Germany [IO]
Habitat for Humanity - Ghana [IO]
Habitat for Humanity - Gliwice [IO]
Habitat for Humanity - Great Britain [IO]
Habitat for Humanity - Greater Kingston and Frontenac [IO]
Habitat for Humanity - Greater Metro Manila [IO]
Habitat for Humanity - Greater Vancouver [IO]
Habitat for Humanity - Grey/Bruce [IO]
Habitat for Humanity - Guangdong [IO]
Habitat for Humanity - Guangxi [IO]
Habitat for Humanity - Guatemala [IO]
Habitat for Humanity - Guyana [IO]
Habitat for Humanity - Gympie [IO]
Habitat for Humanity - Haiti [IO]
Habitat for Humanity - Halifax/Dartmouth [IO]
Habitat for Humanity - Halton [IO]
Habitat for Humanity - Hamilton [IO]
Habitat for Humanity - Honduras [IO]
Habitat for Humanity - Huronia [IO]
Habitat for Humanity - Hutt Valley [IO]
Habitat for Humanity - India [IO]
Habitat for Humanity - Indonesia [IO]
Habitat for Humanity Intl. [IO]
Habitat for Humanity Intl. [12313]
Habitat for Humanity - Invercargill [IO]
Habitat for Humanity - Ireland [IO]
Habitat for Humanity - Jamaica [IO]
Habitat for Humanity - Japan [IO]
Habitat for Humanity - Jordan [IO]
Habitat for Humanity - Kamloops [IO]
Habitat for Humanity - Kelowna [IO]
Habitat for Humanity - Kenya [IO]
Habitat for Humanity - Korea [IO]
Habitat for Humanity - Kyrgyzstan [IO]
Habitat for Humanity - Lebanon [IO]
Habitat for Humanity - Lesotho [IO]
Habitat for Humanity - Lethbridge [IO]
Habitat for Humanity - London [IO]
Habitat for Humanity - Macedonia [IO]
Habitat for Humanity - Madagascar [IO]
Habitat for Humanity - Malawi [IO]
Habitat for Humanity Malaysia [IO]
Habitat for Humanity - Manukau [IO]
Habitat for Humanity - Medicine Hat [IO]
Habitat for Humanity - Mexico [IO]
Habitat for Humanity - Moncton Area [IO]
Habitat for Humanity - Mongolia [IO]
Habitat for Humanity - Montreal [IO]
Habitat for Humanity - Mozambique [IO]
Habitat for Humanity - Muskoka [IO]
Habitat for Humanity - Nanaimo [IO]
Habitat for Humanity - Natl. Capital Region [IO]
Habitat for Humanity - Negros Occidental [IO]
Habitat for Humanity - Nelson [IO]
Habitat for Humanity - Netherlands [IO]
Habitat for Humanity - New Zealand [IO]
Habitat for Humanity - Niagara [IO]
Habitat for Humanity - Nicaragua [IO]
Habitat for Humanity - Nigeria [IO]
Habitat for Humanity - North Durham [IO]
Habitat for Humanity - North Taranaki [IO]
Habitat for Humanity - Northern Ireland [IO]
Habitat for Humanity - Northland [IO]
Habitat for Humanity - On the Border [IO]
Habitat for Humanity - Pakistan [IO]
Habitat for Humanity - Palmerston North [IO]
Habitat for Humanity - Panama [IO]
Habitat for Humanity - Paraguay [IO]
Habitat for Humanity - Peterborough and District [IO]
Habitat for Humanity Philippines [IO]
Habitat for Humanity - Poland [IO]
Habitat for Humanity - Porirua [IO]
Habitat for Humanity - Portugal [IO]
Habitat for Humanity - Prince Albert [IO]
Habitat for Humanity - Prince Edward/Hastings [IO]

Reference to "IO" in place of a book number signifies that the association may be found in the 45th edition of International Organizations.

Habitat for Humanity - Prince George [IO]
Habitat for Humanity - Queens [IO]
Habitat for Humanity - Red Deer Region [IO]
Habitat for Humanity - Regina [IO]
Habitat for Humanity - Romania [IO]
Habitat for Humanity - Rotorua [IO]
Habitat for Humanity - Russia [IO]
Habitat for Humanity - Saint John Region [IO]
Habitat for Humanity - Samoa [IO]
Habitat for Humanity - Sarnia/Lambton [IO]
Habitat for Humanity - Saskatoon [IO]
Habitat for Humanity - Sault Ste. Marie and Area
    [IO]
Habitat for Humanity - Senegal [IO]
Habitat for Humanity - Singapore [IO]
Habitat for Humanity - Slovakia [IO]
Habitat for Humanity - Solomon Islands [IO]
Habitat for Humanity - South Africa [IO]
Habitat for Humanity - South Peace Soc. [IO]
Habitat for Humanity - Sri Lanka [IO]
Habitat for Humanity - Stratford/Perth [IO]
Habitat for Humanity - Sudbury District [IO]
Habitat for Humanity - Sunshine Coast [IO]
Habitat for Humanity - Suriname [IO]
Habitat for Humanity - Tajikistan [IO]
Habitat for Humanity - Tanzania [IO]
Habitat for Humanity - Tauranga [IO]
Habitat for Humanity - Thailand [IO]
Habitat for Humanity - The Pas [IO]
Habitat for Humanity - Thousand Islands [IO]
Habitat for Humanity - Thunder Bay [IO]
Habitat for Humanity - Toronto [IO]
Habitat for Humanity - Turkey [IO]
Habitat for Humanity - Uganda [IO]
Habitat for Humanity - Upper Fraser Valley [IO]
Habitat for Humanity - Vanuatu [IO]
Habitat for Humanity - Victoria, Australia [IO]
Habitat for Humanity - Vietnam [IO]
Habitat for Humanity - Waikato [IO]
Habitat for Humanity - Waitakere [IO]
Habitat for Humanity - Waterloo Region [IO]
Habitat for Humanity - Wellington County [IO]
Habitat for Humanity - West Kootenay [IO]
Habitat for Humanity - Western Australia [IO]
Habitat for Humanity - Windsor Essex [IO]
Habitat for Humanity - Winnipeg [IO]
Habitat for Humanity - Wood Buffalo [IO]
Habitat for Humanity - York Region [IO]
Habitat for Humanity - Yukon Soc. [IO]
Habitat for Humanity - Zambia [IO]
Hogar de Cristo Housing Found. [IO]
Home Center Inst. [3407]
Homelink Intl. [22580]
Homeowners Against Deficient Dwellings [12314]
Homes for Our Troops [21302]
Hong Kong Housing Soc. [IO]
Housing Assistance Coun. [12315]
Housing Inspection Found. [2119]
Housing Statistics Users Gp. [5789]
Hungarian Tenants Assn. [IO]
Independence Plan for Neighborhood Councils
    [17219]
Indian Fed. of Tenants Coun. [IO]
Inst. for Community Economics [17221]
Inst. for Responsible Housing Preservation [5790]
Intl. Assn. of Homes and Services for the Ageing
    [11289]
Intl. Assn. for Housing Sci. [12316]
Intl. Assn. for Housing Sci. [IO]
Intl. Fed. for Housing and Planning [IO]
Intl. Union of Tenants [IO]
Interval Intl. [22581]
Irish Natl. Assn. of Tenants [IO]
Jamaica Assn. of Villas and Apartments [IO]
Japanese Tenants Assn. [IO]
Jayco Travel Club [22955]
Joint Action in Community Ser. [11803]
Latvia Tenants Soc. of Liepaja [IO]
League of Homeowners' Associations - Habitat
    [IO]
Log Home Builders Assn. of North Am. [1031]
Loners on Wheels [22957]
Manufactured Housing Assn. for Regulatory
    Reform [2526]
Manufactured Housing Res. Alliance [1976]

McAuley Institute [12317]
Mietervereinigung Osterreichs [IO]
Modular Building Systems Coun. [2529]
Natl. Accessible Apartment CH [11963]
Natl. Affordable Housing Mgt. Assn. [1977]
Natl. Affordable Housing Network [12318]
Natl. AIDS Housing Coalition [12319]
Natl. Alliance to End Homelessness [12294]
Natl. Alliance of HUD Tenants [18514]
Natl. Amer. Indian Housing Coun. [5791]
Natl. Apartment Assn. [3317]
Natl. Assn. of Certified Home Inspectors [2121]
Natl. Assn. for County Community and Economic
    Development [17225]
Natl. Assn. of Housing Cooperatives [12320]
Natl. Assn. of Housing Info. Managers [5792]
Natl. Assn. of Housing and Redevelopment Of-
    ficials [5793]
Natl. Assn. of Local Housing Finance Agencies
    [5794]
Natl. Assn. of Responsible Loan Officers [1978]
Natl. Assn. of Senior Move Managers [2523]
Natl. Assn. of Trailer Owners [22959]
Natl. Caucus and Center on Black Aged [11306]
Natl. Center for Housing Mgt. [12321]
Natl. Coalition for the Homeless [12296]
Natl. Community Development Assn. [17228]
Natl. Coun. on Agricultural Life and Labor Res.
    Fund [12322]
Natl. Coun. on Independent Living [11968]
Natl. Coun. of State Housing Agencies [5795]
Natl. Economic Development and Law Center
    [17464]
Natl. Fair Housing Alliance [17733]
Natl. Found. of Manufactured Home Owners
    [12323]
Natl. Homeowners Assn. [12324]
Natl. House Buyers Assn. [IO]
Natl. Housing Conf. [12325]
Natl. Housing Inst. [12326]
Natl. Housing Law Proj. [5796]
Natl. Housing and Rehabilitation Assn. [12327]
Natl. Inst. of Senior Housing [12328]
Natl. Leased Housing Assn. [12329]
Natl. Low Income Housing Coalition [12330]
Natl. Multi Housing Coun. [3332]
Natl. Neighborhood Coalition [17230]
Natl. Org. of African Americans in Housing
    [12331]
Natl. Rsrc. Center on Homelessness and Mental
    Illness [12298]
Natl. Retail Tenants Assn. [3383]
Natl. Rural Housing Coalition [12332]
Natl. Shared Housing Rsrc. Center [12333]
Natl. Town Builders' Assn. [654]
Natl. Union of Tenants of Nigeria [IO]
Natl. Urban League [17138]
Neighborhood Housing Services of Am. [12334]
NeighborWorks Am. [12335]
Nepal Habitat for Humanity [IO]
Northern Ireland Fed. of Housing Associations
    [IO]
NSW Fed. of Housing Associations [IO]
Panelized Building Systems Coun. [2531]
Pannellinios Syllogos Epikiaston [IO]
Polish Assn. of Tenants [IO]
Professional Housing Mgt. Assn. [5797]
Provincial Tenant's Rights Action Coalition - British
    Colombia [IO]
Public Housing Authorities Directors Assn. [5798]
Real Estate Services Providers Coun. [3341]
Rebuilding Alliance [12336]
Rebuilding Alliance [IO]
Rebuilding Together [12337]
Res. and Training Center on Independent Living
    [11984]
Residential Constr. Employers Coun. [947]
Residential Energy Services Network [664]
Rooftops Canada [IO]
ROOMatRTPI [IO]
RV Mfrs'. Clubs Assn. [22961]
Scottish Churches Housing Action [IO]
Scottish Fed. of Housing Associations [IO]
Sindacato Unitario Nazionale Inquilini ed Asseg-
    natari [IO]

Social Housing Neighbourhood Fed. of Catalonia
    [IO]
Southwark Habitat for Humanity [IO]
SunnyTravelers [22963]
Swedish Union of Tenants [IO]
Swiss Assn. of Tenants [IO]
Syndicat des Locataires - Huurdersbond [IO]
Tech. Assistance Collaborative [13145]
Tenant Assn. in Bergen [IO]
Tenant Participation Advisory Ser. [IO]
Tenants Advice Ser. [IO]
Tenants Org. of Denmark [IO]
Tenants Org. - Norway [IO]
Tenants Union of Australia Capital Territory [IO]
Tenants Union of New South Wales [IO]
Tenants' Union of Queensland [IO]
Tenants Union of Victoria [IO]
Teton Club Intl. [22632]
Tile Partners for Humanity [12338]
Tile Partners for Humanity [IO]
Union for Protection of Tenants MakeDom [IO]
Urban Homesteading Assistance Bd. [12339]
Victoria Habitat for Humanity [IO]
Wally Byam Caravan Club Intl. [22967]
Winnebago-Itasca Travelers [22968]
World Floor Covering Assn. [3431]
World Orphans [11667]
Housing Agencies; Coun. of State [★5795]
Housing for the Aging; North Amer. Assn. of Jewish
    Homes and [★11277]
Housing Alliance; Rural [★11772]
Housing Assistance Coun. [12315], 1025 Vermont
    Ave. NW, Ste. 606, Washington, DC 20005,
    (202)842-8600
Housing Assn; Sect. 23 Leased [★12329]
Housing Center Coun; Natl. [★647]
Housing Coalition; Ad Hoc Low Income [★12330]
Housing Comm; B'nai B'rith Intl. Senior Citizens
    [★12469]
Housing Comm; B'nai B'rith Senior Citizens [12469]
Housing Communities Assn; Western Manufactured
    [2532]
Housing Conf. to Improve Instruction [★12303]
Housing Conf; Natl. Public [★12325]
Housing Corp; NAACP Natl. [★17129]
Housing Coun; Natl. Multi [3332]
Housing Coun; Natl. Rental [★3332]
Housing and Development; Coun. for Rural
    [★12310]
Housing Endowment; Natl. [649]
Housing Fed; Natl. Manufactured [★2527]
Housing Finance Agencies; Assn. of Local [★5794]
Housing and Finance; Women in [1452]
Housing; Found. for Cooperative [★12309]
Housing for the Hearing Impaired Prog; Community
    [★14752]
Housing Indus; Natl. Coun. of the [647]
Housing Industry; National Coun. of the Multifamily
    [★1035]
Housing Inspection Found. [2119], 21640 N 23rd
    Dr., Ste. C-2, Phoenix, AZ 85027, (623)580-4646
Housing Inspection Foundation/Association of Home
    Inspectors [★2119]
Housing Inst; Manufactured [2527]
Housing Inst; Southeastern Manufactured [★2527]
Housing Investment; Sponsors of Open [★17819]
Housing Lenders; Natl. Assn. of Affordable [487]
Housing Officials; Natl. Assn. of [★5793]
Housing Rehabilitation Assn; Natl. [★12327]
Housing Res. Group - Defunct.
Housing Rsrc. Center; Natl. Shared [★12333]
Housing Rsrc. Center; Shared [★12333]
Housing Statistics Users Gp. [5789], c/o Natl. Assn.
    of Home Builders, 1201 15th St. NW, Washington,
    DC 20005, (202)266-2398
Housing Tax Credit Coalition; Affordable [586]
Housman Soc. [IO], Bromsgrove, United Kingdom
Houston Cotton Exchange and Bd. of Trade -
    Defunct.
Houston Maritime Assn. [★2595]
Hovawart Club of Am. [22283], c/o Christina Ferraro,
    Treas., 2370 Main St., Bethlehem, NH 03574
Hoverclub of Am. [★22589]
Hovercraft
    Hovercraft Club of Am. [22589]

A star before a book entry number signifies that the name is not listed separately, but is mentioned within the entry.

Hovercraft Club of Great Britain **[IO]**
Hovercraft Assn; Amer. **[★22589]**
Hovercraft Club of Am. **[22589]**, PO Box 908, Foley, AL 36536-0908, (251)946-3800
Hovercraft Club of Great Britain **[IO]**, Bolton, United Kingdom
HOW **[★11978]**
Howard Assn; John **[11874]**
Howard Center **[★20491]**
Howard Gilman Found. **[11504]**, 111 W 50th St., New York, NY 10020, (212)307-1073
Howard Gilman Foundation **[IO]**, New York, NY, United States
Howard Hughes Medical Institute **[IO]**, Chevy Chase, MD, United States
Howard Hughes Medical Inst. **[15107]**, 4000 Jones Bridge Rd., Chevy Chase, MD 20815-6720, (301)215-8500
Howard Jarvis Taxpayers Assn. **[18695]**, 621 S Westmoreland Ave., Ste. 202, Los Angeles, CA 90005, (213)384-9656
Howard League for Penal Reform **[IO]**, London, United Kingdom
Howdy Doody Memorabilia Collectors Club **[22038]**, c/o Jeff Judson, Founder/Newsletter Ed., 8 Hunt Ct., Flemington, NJ 08822, (908)782-1159
Howth Sea Angling Club **[IO]**, Howth, Ireland
Hoya Soc. Intl. - Address unknown since 1991.
Hoyres Hovedorganisasjon **[★IO]**
Hoyt Axton Fan Club - Defunct.
Hoyt Family Assn. **[20946]**, 360 Watson Rd., Paducah, KY 42003-8978
HPV Support Prog. - Amer. Social Hea. Assn. **[16413]**, PO Box 13827, Research Triangle Park, NC 27709, (919)361-8400
HQ V Corps Veterans Assn. - Address unknown since 2002.
HR Policy Assn. **[17972]**, 1015 15th St. NW, Ste. 1200, Washington, DC 20005-2605, (202)789-8670
HR Soc. **[IO]**, Burnham-on-Crouch, United Kingdom
Hroswitha Club - Address unknown since 1999.
Hrvatska udruga fizioterapeuta **[★IO]**
Hrvatska Odvjetnieka Komora **[★IO]**
Hrvatski klizacki savez **[★IO]**
Hrvatski orijentacijski savez **[★IO]**
Hrvatski Atletski Savez **[★IO]**
Hrvatski Badmintonski Savez **[★IO]**
Hrvatski Baseball Savez **[★IO]**
Hrvatski Biciklisticki Savez **[★IO]**
Hrvatski Crveni Kriz **[★IO]**
Hrvatski Ferijalni i Hostelski Savez **[★IO]**
Hrvatski Hokejski Savez **[★IO]**
Hrvatski Jedrilicarski Savez **[★IO]**
Hrvatski Kajakaski Savez **[★IO]**
Hrvatski Nogometni Savez **[★IO]**
Hrvatski Olimpijski Odbor **[★IO]**
Hrvatski Rock'n'Roll Savez **[★IO]**
Hrvatski Sahovski Savez **[★IO]**
Hrvatski Savez Mladeskih Udruga **[★IO]**
Hrvatski Savez Slijepih **[★IO]**
Hrvatski Sportski Plesni Savez **[★IO]**
Hrvatski Sportski Savez Invalida **[★IO]**
Hrvatski Squash Savez **[★IO]**
Hrvatski Strelicarski Savez **[★IO]**
Hrvatski Taekwondo Savez **[★IO]**
Hrvatski Teniski Savez **[★IO]**
Hrvatski Zrakoplovni Savez **[★IO]**
Hrvatsko fizikalno drustvo **[★IO]**
Hrvatsko drustvo za medicinsku informatiku **[★IO]**
Hrvatsko mikroskopijsko drustvo **[★IO]**
Hrvatsko drustvo za zdravstvenu ekologiju **[★IO]**
Hrvatsko Drustvo Farmakologa **[★IO]**
Hrvatsko Drustvo Kemijskih Inzenjera i Tehnologa **[★IO]**
Hrvatsko Drustvo Skladatelja **[★IO]**
Hrvatsko Drustvo za Zastitu Ptica i Prirode **[★IO]**
Hrvatsko Entomolosko Drustvo **[★IO]**
Hrvatsko Farmaceutsko Drustvo **[★IO]**
Hrvatsko Kardiolosko Drustvo **[★IO]**
Hrvatsko Stomatolosko Drustvo **[★IO]**
HSIA Water Work Group - Defunct.
HSP Academy **[★16379]**
HSP Academy **[★IO]**
HSUS Animal Control Acad. **[★11412]**
HTE Users' Gp; HUG Intl. - **[6794]**

HTML Writers Guild **[901]**, 119 E Union St., Ste. F, Pasadena, CA 91103
Huang Hsing Found. (USA) - Address unknown since 2007.
Hubbell Family Historical Soc. **[20947]**, 5601 Brisbane Dr., Chapel Hill, NC 27514, (515)243-3586
The Hubbell Family Historical Soc. **[IO]**, Chapel Hill, NC, United States
Hubcappers - Address unknown since 2001.
Hububat-Bakliyat-Yagli ve Mamuelleri Ihracatcilari Birligi **[★IO]**
HUD Tenants; Natl. Alliance of **[18514]**
Hudson-Essex-Terraplane Club **[21659]**, PO Box 8412, Wichita, KS 67208-0412, (316)744-1363
Hudson-Essex-Terraplane Club **[IO]**, Wichita, KS, United States
Hudson Essex Terraplane Historical Soc. **[21660]**, c/o Ms. Sue Figert Meyer, Pres., 342 Mass Ave., No. 500, Indianapolis, IN 46204, (317)257-1175
Hudson Family Assn. **[20948]**, c/o Nancy Fredenberg, Membership Sec.-Treas., 2600 Cobre Valle Ln., Plano, TX 75023, (469)241-1161
Hudson Inst. **[18451]**, 1015 15th St. NW, 6th Fl., Washington, DC 20005, (202)974-2400
Hudson River Region Wine Coun. - Address unknown since 2003.
Hudson River Sloop Clearwater **[10038]**, 112 Market St., Poughkeepsie, NY 12601, (845)454-7673
Hudson River Sloop Restoration, Inc. **[★10038]**
Huebotter Family Org. **[20949]**
Huettentechnische Vereinigung der Deutschen Glasindustrie **[★IO]**
HUG **[★6794]**
Hug-A-Tree and Survive **[11600]**, c/o Don Abney, ABCANTRA Canine Training, PO Box 248, Abita Springs, LA 70420, (985)892-6773
Hug Club - Address unknown since 1995.
HUG Intl. - HTE Users' Gp. **[6794]**, c/o Tino Anthony, Pres., PO Box 490630, Leesburg, FL 34749-0630, (352)728-9703
Hug-Laf-Luv - Defunct.
Hug Teva - Defunct.
Hugh Moore Fund - Defunct.
Hugh O'Brian Youth Found. **[★8748]**
Hugh O'Brian Youth Found. Alumni Association **[★8748]**
Hugh O'Brian Youth Leadership **[8748]**, 10880 Wilshire Blvd., Ste. 410, Los Angeles, CA 90024, (310)474-4370
Hughes Medical Inst; Howard **[15107]**
Hughes Soc; Langston **[9678]**
Huguenot
   Huguenot Historical Soc. **[21161]**
   Huguenot Soc. of the Founders of Manakin in the Colony of Virginia **[21162]**
   Huguenot Soc. of Great Britain and Ireland **[IO]**
   Natl. Huguenot Soc. **[21163]**
Huguenot Historical Soc. **[21161]**, 18 Broadhead Ave., New Paltz, NY 12561-1403, (845)255-1660
Huguenot Societies; Fed. of **[★21163]**
Huguenot Soc. of the Founders of Manakin in the Colony of Virginia **[21162]**, c/o Dr. Ann Woodlief, Natl. Librarian, Natl. HQ, 981 Huguenot Trail, Midlothian, VA 23113, (804)794-5702
Huguenot Soc. of Great Britain **[★IO]**
Huguenot Soc. of Great Britain and Ireland **[IO]**, London, United Kingdom
Huileries de France **[IO]**, Paris, France
Hull and Humber Chamber of Commerce, Indus. and Shipping **[IO]**, Hull, United Kingdom
Hull Insurance Syndicate; Amer. **[2136]**
Hull Pottery Assn. **[22039]**, c/o Nancy Ankeney, Membership Chair, 4201 Brentwood Dr., Columbia, MO 65203, (573)445-6583
Human Anatomy and Physiology Soc. **[7951]**, c/o Shanan Molnar, PO Box 2945, LaGrange, GA 30241-2945, (800)448-4277
Human-Animal Bond Assn. of Canada **[IO]**, Nepean, ON, Canada
Human Appeal Intl. **[IO]**, Manchester, United Kingdom
Human Appeal Intl. - United Arab Emirates **[IO]**, Ajman, United Arab Emirates
Human Assistance and Development Intl. **[IO]**, Culver City, CA, United States

Human Assistance and Development Intl. **[20437]**, PO Box 4598, Culver City, CA 90231
Human Behavior and Evolution Soc. **[6531]**, Univ. of Nebraska, Center for Great Plains Stud., 1155 Q St., Lincoln, NE 68588-0214, (402)472-6240
Human Behavior; Inst. for the Advancement of **[13735]**
Human Biology Assn. **[6577]**, c/o Dr. Gillian Ice, Sec.-Treas., Ohio Univ. Coll. of Osteopathic Medicine, Dept. of Social Medicine, 309 Grosvenor Hall, Athens, OH 45701, (740)593-2128
Human Caring; Intl. Assn. for **[14640]**
Human and Civil Rights Organizations of Am. **[11738]**, 10 Chestnut St., Salem, MA 01970-3131, (978)744-2608
Human Communities in Space; Center for the Studies of **[★6387]**
Human-Companion Animal Bond; Intl. Soc. for the Stud. of the **[★16615]**
Human Concern Intl. **[IO]**, Ottawa, ON, Canada
Human Development
   Aloha Intl. **[IO]**
   Aloha Intl. **[12340]**
   Amer. Assn. of Human Design Practitioners **[1151]**
   Amer. Coll. of Counselors **[12137]**
   Amer. Creativity Assn. **[10168]**
   Amer. Men's Stud. Assn. **[12341]**
   Arica Inst. **[10169]**
   Arica Inst. **[IO]**
   Asia Partnership for Human Development **[IO]**
   Assn. of Camphill Communities **[IO]**
   Assn. for the Development of Human Potential **[10181]**
   Assn. for Neuro-Linguistic Programming **[IO]**
   Assn. for Transpersonal Psychology **[10170]**
   Be Somebody, Be Yourself Inst. **[12342]**
   Chartered Inst. of Personnel and Development **[IO]**
   Citizens Network for Sustainable Development **[11767]**
   Consciousness Res. and Training Project **[12343]**
   Conversations for the 21st Century - Sydney NSW **[IO]**
   Cultural Survival **[IO]**
   Cultural Survival **[10171]**
   Earthstewards Network **[12344]**
   Earthstewards Network **[IO]**
   Empowerment Soc. Intl. **[11775]**
   Env. and Development Action in the Third World **[IO]**
   Equine Guided Educ. Assn. **[8524]**
   Esalen Inst. **[10172]**
   Feathered Pipe Found. **[12345]**
   The FORUM **[12346]**
   Hanuman Found. **[12347]**
   Hedonic Soc. of Am. **[10758]**
   Himalayan Intl. Inst. of Yoga Sci. and Philosophy of the U.S.A. **[12348]**
   Himalayan Intl. Inst. of Yoga Sci. and Philosophy of the U.S.A. **[IO]**
   Human Assistance and Development Intl. **[20437]**
   Human Relations Area Files **[10187]**
   HUNA Res. **[12349]**
   HUNA Research **[IO]**
   Huna Res. Assn. **[IO]**
   Inner Peace Movement **[10173]**
   Inst. of Cultural Affairs **[12350]**
   Inst. of Cultural Affairs Brazil **[IO]**
   Inst. of Cultural Affairs Chile **[IO]**
   Inst. of Cultural Affairs Cote D'Ivoire **[IO]**
   Inst. of Cultural Affairs Egypt **[IO]**
   Inst. of Cultural Affairs Ghana **[IO]**
   Inst. of Cultural Affairs Guatemala **[IO]**
   Inst. of Cultural Affairs India **[IO]**
   Inst. of Cultural Affairs Kenya **[IO]**
   Inst. of Cultural Affairs Malaysia **[IO]**
   Inst. of Cultural Affairs Nepal **[IO]**
   Inst. of Cultural Affairs Nigeria **[IO]**
   Inst. of Cultural Affairs Peru **[IO]**
   Inst. of Cultural Affairs Taiwan **[IO]**
   Inst. of Cultural Affairs Tanzania **[IO]**
   Inst. of Cultural Affairs Uganda **[IO]**
   Inst. of Cultural Affairs - United Kingdom **[IO]**
   Inst. of Cultural Affairs Zambia **[IO]**
   Inst. for the Development of the Harmonious Human Being **[12351]**

Reference to "IO" in place of a book number signifies that the association may be found in the 45th edition of International Organizations.

Inst. of HeartMath [10174]
Inst. for Individual and World Peace [12352]
Inst. for Individual and World Peace [IO]
Inst. for the Stud. of Human Knowledge [10175]
Inst. for Theological Encounter With Sci. and
Tech. [12353]
Intl. Center for Reiki Training [22969]
Intl. Coun. for Human Ecology and Ethnology
[4512]
Intl. Imagery Assn. [10183]
Intl. Inst. of Integral Human Sciences [IO]
Intl. Inst. of Rural Reconstruction, U.S. Chap.
[12938]
Intl. Soc. for a Complete Earth [12354]
Intl. Soc. for a Complete Earth [IO]
Involvement and Participation Assn. [IO]
Jean Piaget Soc.: Soc. for the Stud. of Knowledge
and Development [16156]
Krishnamurti Found. of Am. [12355]
Lama Found. [10176]
Learning Light Found. [10177]
Mandala Soc. [12356]
Men's Rsrc. Center [12357]
MOVE Intl.: Mobility Opportunities Via Educ. -
USA [11962]
Natl. Alliance to Nurture the Aged and the Youth
[12358]
Natl. Assn. of Barbados Organizations [9731]
Natl. Economic and Social Rights Initiative
[17778]
Natl. Forum API [IO]
Natl. Inst. of Child Hea. and Human Development
[13971]
Natl. Marriage Encounter [12507]
Natl. Organizations for Youth Safety [13502]
Natl. Soc. of High School Scholars [9076]
Natl. Study Group on Chronic Disorganization
[1979]
New Civilization Network [12359]
New Road Map Found. [12360]
New World [IO]
NOWZUWAN [IO]
People, Animals, Nature [13319]
Percy Grainger Soc. [IO]
Quartus Found. for Spiritual Res. [12361]
Rajagiri Outreach Ser. Soc. [IO]
Sacred Passage and the Way of Nature Fellow-
ship [IO]
Sacred Passage and the Way of Nature Fellow-
ship [12362]
School of Living [10178]
Secret Soc. of Happy People [10212]
Simply Love Found. [10191]
Soc. for Human Performance in Extreme Environ-
ments [6540]
Somatics Soc. [12363]
South Asia Partnership Canada [IO]
SustainUS [13517]
Teleos Inst. [12364]
Together, Inc. [12365]
Tuesday's Children [12003]
Unarius Acad. of Sci. [12366]
Unarius Acad. of Sci. [IO]
Venture Scotland [IO]
Well-Springs Found. [10179]
Wilbur Hot Springs Hea. Sanctuary [10180]
World Peace One [12367]
World Peace One [IO]
World Transhumanist Assn. [IO]
World Transhumanist Assn. [7163]
World Vision [20488]
World Volunteers [IO]
Human Development; Campaign for [★12713]
Human Development; Catholic Campaign for
[12713]
Human Development; Ebenezer Center for Aging
and [★11284]
Human Development; Natl. Assn. for [11303]
Human Development Rsrc. Coun. [12913], 5415
Sugarloaf Pkwy., Ste. 2201, Lawrenceville, GA
30043, (770)513-0060
Human Dignity Coalition [★18603]
Human/Dolphin Found. - Address unknown since
1999.
Human Ecology Action League [14364], PO Box
29629, Atlanta, GA 30359-0629, (404)248-1898

Human Ecology and Ethnology; Intl. Commn. for
[★4512]
Human Ecology Fund - Defunct.
Human Ecology; Intl. Coun. on [★4512]
Human Economy Center and Society for Human
Economy - Address unknown since 2003.
Human Engineering
Ergonomics Soc. - England [IO]
Ergonomics Soc. - Sweden [IO]
Human Factors and Ergonomics Soc. [7164]
Intl. Assn. for Time Use Res. [IO]
MTM Assn. for Standards and Res. [7165]
Natl. Assn. of Professional Organizers [7166]
Natl. Study Group on Chronic Disorganization
[1979]
Operations Mgt. Education and Res. Found.
[7167]
Proj. on Tech., Work and Character [7168]
Human Environment Center - Address unknown
since 2003.
Human Env; Inst. for the [4575]
Human Environmental League for Preservation - Ne-
pal [IO], Kathmandu, Nepal
Human Environments; Rene Dubos Center for
[4602]
Human Factors and Ergonomics Soc. [7164], PO
Box 1369, Santa Monica, CA 90406-1369,
(310)394-1811
Human Factors and Ergonomics Soc. of Australia
[IO], Baulkham Hills, Australia
Human Factors Soc. [★7164]
Human Genetics; Amer. Soc. of [7113]
Human Genetics Soc. of Australasia [IO], Alexandra,
Australia
Human Genetics Soc. of Australasia - New South
Wales Br. [IO], Sydney, Australia
Human Genetics Soc. of Australasia - Queensland
Br. [IO], Brisbane, Australia
Human Genome Org. [IO], London, United Kingdom
Human Genome Variation Soc. [IO], Fitzroy,
Australia
Human Growth [★16020]
Human Growth and Development; Feminist Center
for [13426]
Human Growth Found. [16020], 997 Glen Cove
Ave., Ste. 5, Glen Head, NY 11545-1584,
(516)671-4041
Human Infertility; Intl. Soc. of Infectious Diseases
and [★16347]
Human Interaction; Special Interest Gp. on Cmpt.
and [6542]
Human Lactation Center [12409], 666 Sturges Hwy.,
Westport, CT 06880, (203)259-5995
Human Lactation Center [IO], Westport, CT, United
States
Human Life Amendment; Natl. Comm. for a [18557]
Human Life Center - Defunct.
Human Life Found. [12914], 215 Lexington Ave.,
New York, NY 10016
Human Life Intl. [12915], 4 Family Life Ln., Front
Royal, VA 22630, (540)635-7884
Human Life Intl. [IO], Front Royal, VA, United States
Human Life Intl. - Argentina [IO], Buenos Aires,
Argentina
Human Life Intl. - Austria [IO], Vienna, Austria
Human Life Intl. - Belarus [IO], Mogilev, Belarus
Human Life Intl. - Belgium [IO], Mechelen, Belgium
Human Life Intl. - Bolivia [IO], Cochabamba, Bolivia
Human Life Intl. - Brazil [IO], Brasilia, Brazil
Human Life Intl. - Cameroon [IO], Douala, Cam-
eroon
Human Life Intl. - Chile [IO], Santiago, Chile
Human Life Intl. - Colombia [IO], Bogota, Colombia
Human Life Intl. - Costa Rica [IO], San Jose, Costa
Rica
Human Life Intl. - Croatia [IO], Pozega, Croatia
Human Life Intl. - Czech Republic [★IO]
Human Life Intl. - El Salvador [IO], La Libertad, El
Salvador
Human Life Intl. - Germany [IO], Essen, Germany
Human Life Intl. - Hong Kong [IO], Hong Kong,
People's Republic of China
Human Life Intl. - Hungary [IO], Budapest, Hungary
Human Life Intl. - India [IO], Bangalore, India
Human Life Intl. - Ireland [IO], Dublin, Ireland

Human Life Intl. - Italy [IO], Rome, Italy
Human Life Intl. - Japan [IO], Kochi, Japan
Human Life Intl. - Kenya [IO], Nyeri, Kenya
Human Life Intl. - Latvia [IO], Riga, Latvia
Human Life Intl. - Lithuania [IO], Kaunas, Lithuania
Human Life Intl. - Malaysia [IO], Sarawak, Malaysia
Human Life Intl. - Mexico [IO], Mexico City, Mexico
Human Life Intl. - Nicaragua [IO], Managua,
Nicaragua
Human Life Intl. - Nigeria [IO], Ijebu Ode, Nigeria
Human Life Intl. - Panama [IO], Panama City,
Panama
Human Life Intl. - Paraguay [IO], Asuncion,
Paraguay
Human Life Intl. - Peru [IO], Lima, Peru
Human Life Intl. - Philippines [IO], Quezon City,
Philippines
Human Life Intl. - Poland [IO], Gdansk, Poland
Human Life Intl. - Puerto Rico [IO], Guaynabo, PR,
United States
Human Life Intl. - Romania [IO], Timisoara, Romania
Human Life Intl. - Russia [IO], Moscow, Russia
Human Life Intl. - Singapore [IO], Singapore, Sin-
gapore
Human Life Intl. - South Africa [IO], Milnerton,
Republic of South Africa
Human Life Intl. - South Korea [IO], Daegu,
Republic of Korea
Human Life Intl. - Spain [IO], Madrid, Spain
Human Life Intl. - Switzerland [IO], Zug, Switzerland
Human Life Intl. - Tanzania [IO], Dar es Salaam,
United Republic of Tanzania
Human Life Intl. - Ukraine [IO], Lviv, Ukraine
Human Life Intl. - Uruguay [IO], Montevideo,
Uruguay
Human Life Intl. - Venezuela [IO], La Guaira,
Venezuela
Human Life Intl. - Zimbabwe [IO], Harare, Zimbabwe
Human Life Issues
After Death Commun. Res. Found. [14903]
Americans to Ban Cloning [17089]
Americans United for Life [12904]
Anglicans for Life [12905]
Cryonics Inst. [1120]
Healing the Culture [12788]
Human Life Found. [12914]
Human Life Intl. [12915]
Intl. Soc. for Phenomenological Stud. [10805]
Intl. Soc. for Phenomenology and the Sciences of
Life [10807]
Intl. Task Force on Euthanasia and Assisted
Suicide [12133]
Lutherans For Life [12921]
Natl. Assn. of Barbados Organizations [9731]
Natl. Assn. of Pro-Life Nurses [18378]
Natl. Org. for People of Color Against Suicide
[13289]
Near Death Experience Res. Found. [14904]
Rocky Mountain Inst. [18101]
Sacred Dying Found. [11910]
Simple Soc. Alliance for Human Empowerment
[18637]
Southern Center for Human Rights [17036]
Suicide and Mental Hea. Assn. Intl. [15234]
Torture Abolition and Survivors Support Coalition
Intl. [17786]
World Org. for Human Rights USA [12381]
Human Life and Natural Family Planning Found. -
Defunct.
Human Life, Reproduction and Rhythm; Natl.
Commn. on [16008]
Human Milk and Lactation; Intl. Soc. for Res. in
[13776]
Human Needs; Coalition on [13161]
Human Needs; Coalition on Block Grants and
[★13161]
Human Origins; Inst. of [7072]
Human Papillomavirus
HPV Support Prog. - Amer. Social Hea. Assn.
[16413]
Human Policy; Center on [11928]
Human Potential
Amer. Institutes for Res. [7560]
Asociacion Feldenkrais Argentina [IO]
Assn. for the Development of Human Potential
[10181]

A star before a book entry number signifies that the name is not listed separately, but is mentioned within the entry.

Consciousness Res. and Training Project [12343]
Earthstewards Network [12344]
Feldenkrais - Fed. Austria [IO]
Feldenkrais-Gilde Deutschland e.V. [IO]
Feldenkrais Guild of North Am. [IO]
Feldenkrais Guild of North Am. [10182]
The FORUM [12346]
Glenkirk [11948]
Inner Peace Movement [10173]
Intl. High IQ Soc. [19149]
Intl. Imagery Assn. [10183]
Intl. Imagery Assn. [IO]
Israeli Feldenkrais Qualified Practitioners Assn.
   [IO]
Macro Soc. [10184]
Natl. Soc. of High School Scholars [9076]
Soc. for Human Performance in Extreme Environ-
   ments [6540]
World Transhumanist Assn. [7163]
Human Potential; Institutes for the Achievement of
   [11700]
Human Potential; Natl. Center for the Exploration of
   [★14826]
Human Powered Vehicle Assn. [7811], PO Box
   1307, San Luis Obispo, CA 93406-1307, (805)772-
   5888
Human Powered Vehicle Assn. [IO], San Luis
   Obispo, CA, United States
Human Productivity Inst. - Defunct.
Human Relations
   Amer. Commun. Assn. [6710]
   Giraffe Heroes Proj. [10185]
   Global Assn. for Interpersonal Neurobiology Stud.
      [7375]
   Golden Rule Found. [10186]
   Golden Rule Found. [IO]
   Human Relations Area Files [10187]
   Initiatives of Change [17734]
   Initiatives of Change [IO]
   Inst. of HeartMath [10174]
   Inst. for the Stud. of Human Knowledge [10175]
   Intl. Assn. of Protocol Consultants [965]
   Intl. Laughter Soc. [10188]
   Intl. Laughter Soc. [IO]
   Intl. Org. for the Stud. of Gp. Tensions [IO]
   Intl. Org. for the Stud. of Gp. Tensions [10189]
   Intl. Peace Acad. [17735]
   Intl. Peace Acad. [IO]
   Interns for Peace [IO]
   Interns for Peace [17736]
   Joygerms Unlimited [10190]
   Joygerms Unlimited [IO]
   Lucis Trust [IO]
   Lucis Trust [17737]
   Lutheran Human Relations Assn. [20223]
   New Dimensions Radio [17738]
   New Dimensions Radio [IO]
   Secret Soc. of Happy People [10212]
   Simple Soc. Alliance for Human Empowerment
      [18637]
   Simply Love Found. [10191]
   Soc. of Afghan Professionals [9343]
   Tavistock Inst. [IO]
   Triangles [IO]
   World Goodwill - Commonwealth [IO]
   World Goodwill - USA [IO]
   World Goodwill - USA [17739]
Human Relations Area Files [10187], 755 Prospect
   St., New Haven, CT 06511-1225, (203)764-9401
Human Relations Assn. of Am; Lutheran [★20223]
Human Relations Assn; Lutheran [20223]
Human Rsrc. Certification Inst. [2902], 1800 Duke
   St., Alexandria, VA 22314, (703)548-3440
Human Rsrc. Certification Institute [★2908]
Human Rsrc. Mgt; Hong Kong Inst. of [IO]
Human Rsrc. Mgt; Soc. for [2908]
Human Rsrc. Planning Soc. [2496], 317 Madison
   Ave., Ste. 1509, New York, NY 10017, (212)490-
   6387
Human Rsrc. Systems Professionals; Assn. of [★67]
Human Resources
   Agricultural Personnel Mgt. Assn. [4638]
   The Amer. Cause [17642]
   Amer. Inst. for Full Employment [12068]
   Assn. for the Advancement of Policy, Res. and
      Development in the Third World [17828]

Assn. of Staff Physician Recruiters [15995]
Australian Human Rsrc. Inst. [IO]
A.W.A.R.E. - Amer. Workforce Alliance for
   Responsible Economics [1258]
Cable and Telecommunications Human
   Resources Assn. [1980]
Coll. and Univ. Professional Assn. for Human
   Resources [8962]
Employers Gp. [2494]
Environmental Careers Org. [IO]
Estonian Assn. for Personnel Development [IO]
European Human Rsrc. Forum [IO]
FACE Intel - Former and Current Employees of
   Intel [1262]
Healthcare People Mgt. Assn. [IO]
Human Rsrc. Certification Inst. [2902]
Human Rsrc. Planning Soc. [2496]
Human Resources Assn. of Calgary [IO]
Human Resources Outsourcing Assn. [1981]
Info. and Communications Tech. Coun. [IO]
Info. Tech. Contract and Recruitment Assn. [IO]
Instructional Systems Assn. [8564]
Intl. Assn. of Corporate and Professional Recruit-
   ment [1265]
Intl. Assn. of Employment Web Sites [1266]
Intl. Assn. for Human Rsrc. Info. Mgt. [67]
Marine Corps Recruiters Assn. [5799]
Natl. Alliance for Direct Support Professionals
   [1986]
Natl. Assn. of African Americans in Human
   Resources [1982]
Natl. Assn. for Alternative Staffing [1268]
Natl. Assn. for the Employment of Amers. [1269]
Natl. Assn. of Locum Tenens Org. [16004]
Natl. Assn. of Personnel Services [1272]
Natl. Assn. of Professional Background Screeners
   [1983]
Natl. Assn. of Public Sector Equal Opportunity
   Officers [1274]
Natl. Cong. of Amer. Indians [18096]
Natl. Hire Amer. Citizens Soc. [1276]
Natl. Human Resources Assn. [2905]
Natl. Study Group on Chronic Disorganization
   [1979]
North Amer. Alliance for Fair Employment [1277]
The Org. for the Rights of Amer. Workers [1278]
Recruiting and Staffing Focus Area [1984]
Save U.S. Jobs [1282]
Seventh Generation Fund for Indian Development
   [18099]
SHRM Global Forum [2907]
Soc. for Human Rsrc. Mgt. [2908]
Human Resources Admin; Amer. Soc. for Healthcare
   [14868]
Human Resources Assn. of Calgary [IO], Calgary,
   AB, Canada
Human Resources Assn; Natl. [2905]
Human Resources Benchmarking Assn. [723], c/o
   The Benchmarking Network, 4606 FM 1960 W,
   Ste. 250, Houston, TX 77069-9949, (281)440-5044
Human Resources Center [★11913]
Human Resources; Coll. and Univ. Professional
   Assn. for [8962]
Human Resources Inst. [★14573]
Human Resources Mgt. and Organizational
   Behavior; Assn. of [★6528]
Human Resources; Natl. Assn. of African Americans
   in [1982]
Human Resources Network; Black [2901]
Human Resources Outsourcing Assn. [1981], 601
   Pennsylvania Ave. NW, Ste. 900, Washington, DC
   20004, (202)220-3165
Human Resources Res. Org. [6532], 66 Canal
   Center Plz., Ste. 400, Alexandria, VA 22314,
   (703)549-3611
Human Resources Social Welfare Soc. [IO], Char-
   sadda, Pakistan
Human Rights
   Accio dels Cristians per l'Abolicio de la Tortura
      [IO]
   Action des Chretiens pour l'Abolition de la Torture
      - Belgium [IO]
   Action des Chretiens pour L'Abolition de la Torture
      - Luxembourg [IO]
   Action des Chretiens pour l'Abolition de la Torture
      - Switzerland [IO]

ActionAid [IO]
ADECOM Network [IO]
Advisory Comm. on Equal Opportunities for
   Women and Men [IO]
Advocacy Comm. for Human Experimentation
   Survivors and Mind Control [IO]
Advocates Intl. [17998]
Advocating Change Together [11914]
Afghan Women's Assn. Intl. [13416]
Afghans for Civil Soc. [17079]
Africa Network [17740]
African Centre for Democracy and Human Rights
   Stud. [IO]
African Commn. on Human and Peoples' Rights
   [IO]
African Gender Inst. [IO]
Al-Haq [IO]
Albanian Amer. Civic League [16970]
All of Us or None [17081]
Alliance for Am. [11807]
Alliance for Full Acceptance [12213]
Alliance for Human Res. Protection [17741]
Alliance for Women's Equality [13455]
Alliance for Worker Freedom [24217]
Amer. Assn. for the Intl. Commn. of Jurists
   [17742]
Amer. Assn. for the Intl. Commn. of Jurists [IO]
Amer. Comm. for Peace in Chechnya [18189]
Amer. Constitution Soc. for Law and Policy [5603]
Amer. Family Rights Assn. [17508]
Amer. Freedom Alliance [18507]
Amer. Homeowners' Rsrc. Center [17743]
Amer. Rights at Work [17968]
Amer. Soc. of Intl. Law [5866]
Amers. for Human Rights in Ukraine [17744]
Amers. for Human Rights in Ukraine [IO]
America's Development Found. [17387]
Amnesty Intl. - Algeria [IO]
Amnesty Intl. - Argentina [IO]
Amnesty Intl. - Aruba [IO]
Amnesty Intl. Asia Pacific [IO]
Amnesty Intl. Australia - NSW Br. [IO]
Amnesty Intl. - Austria [IO]
Amnesty Intl. - Bahamas [IO]
Amnesty Intl. - Barbados [IO]
Amnesty Intl. - Belgium [IO]
Amnesty Intl. - Benin [IO]
Amnesty Intl. - Bermuda [IO]
Amnesty Intl. - Burkina Faso [IO]
Amnesty Intl. - Canadian Sect. [IO]
Amnesty Intl. - Chile [IO]
Amnesty Intl. - Cote d'Ivoire [IO]
Amnesty Intl. - Croatia [IO]
Amnesty Intl. - Czech Republic [IO]
Amnesty Intl. Danish Sect. [IO]
Amnesty Intl. European Union Assn. [IO]
Amnesty Intl. - Faroe Islands [IO]
Amnesty Intl., Finnish Sect. [IO]
Amnesty Intl. France [IO]
Amnesty Intl. - Gambia [IO]
Amnesty Intl. - Ghana [IO]
Amnesty Intl. - Grenada [IO]
Amnesty Intl. - Guyana [IO]
Amnesty Intl. Hong Kong [IO]
Amnesty Intl. - Hungary [IO]
Amnesty Intl. - Icelandic Sect. [IO]
Amnesty Intl. - Intl. Secretariat [IO]
Amnesty Intl. - Ireland [IO]
Amnesty Intl. Israel Sect. [IO]
Amnesty Intl. - Italy [IO]
Amnesty Intl. - Jamaica [IO]
Amnesty Intl. Japan [IO]
Amnesty Intl. Luxembourg [IO]
Amnesty Intl. Malaysia [IO]
Amnesty Intl. - Mali [IO]
Amnesty Intl. Mexican Sect. [IO]
Amnesty Intl. - Mongolia [IO]
Amnesty Intl. New Zealand Sect. [IO]
Amnesty Intl. - Norway [IO]
Amnesty Intl. - Pakistan [IO]
Amnesty Intl. - Paraguay [IO]
Amnesty Intl. - Peru [IO]
Amnesty Intl. - Philippines [IO]
Amnesty Intl. - Poland [IO]
Amnesty Intl. - Puerto Rico [IO]

Reference to "IO" in place of a book number signifies that the association may be found in the 45th edition of International Organizations.

Amnesty Intl. - Puerto Rico [17745]
Amnesty Intl. - Russia [IO]
Amnesty Intl. - Senegal [IO]
Amnesty Intl. - Sierra Leone [IO]
Amnesty Intl. - South Africa [IO]
Amnesty Intl. - South Korean Sect. [IO]
Amnesty Intl. - Spain [IO]
Amnesty Intl. - Swiss Sect. [IO]
Amnesty Intl. - Taiwan [IO]
Amnesty Intl. - Thailand [IO]
Amnesty Intl. - Tunisia [IO]
Amnesty Intl. - Turkey [IO]
Amnesty Intl. - Ukraine [IO]
Amnesty Intl. - United Kingdom [IO]
Amnesty Intl. - United Kingdom Scottish Off. [IO]
Amnesty Intl. of the U.S.A. [IO]
Amnesty Intl. of the U.S.A. [17746]
Amnesty Intl. - Zambia [IO]
Amnesty Intl. - Zimbabwe [17747]
Amnesty for Women [IO]
Andean Commn. of Jurists [IO]
Andean Info. Network [IO]
Ansar Burney Welfare Trust Intl. [IO]
Arab Assn. for Human Rights [IO]
Arab Org. for Human Rights [IO]
Arcus Found. [18266]
Armed Females of Am. [17587]
Artists for a New South Africa [11911]
Asia Am. Initiative [11762]
Asian Fed. Against Involuntary Disappearances
  [IO]
Asian Human Rights Commn. [IO]
Asian Women's Human Rights Coun. [IO]
Assn. of Albanian Girls and Women [18382]
Assn. of Human Rights and Torture Defenders -
  Cameroon [IO]
Assn. for the Prevention of Torture [IO]
Assn. for Progressive Communications [17163]
August 13 Working Comm. [IO]
Australian Lawyers for Human Rights [IO]
Axis of Justice [18640]
Bastard Nation: The Adoptee Rights Org. [11237]
Bilateral Safety Corridor Coalition [12368]
British Inst. of Human Rights [IO]
Burma Action Ireland [IO]
Call to Renewal [18376]
Campaign to End the Death Penalty [17028]
Canada-Asia Working Group [IO]
Canada Tibet Comm. [IO]
Canadian Centre for Victims of Torture [IO]
Canadian Coalition Against the Death Penalty [IO]
Canadian Lawyers for Intl. Human Rights [IO]
Captive Daughters [18383]
Center for Civil and Human Rights [12369]
Center of Concern [17747]
Center of Concern [IO]
Center for Intl. Policy [IO]
Center for Intl. Policy [17748]
Center for Religious Freedom, Freedom House
  [17749]
Center for Religious Freedom, Freedom House
  [IO]
Center for the Stud. of Human Rights [17750]
Centre for Human Rights Res. and Development
  [IO]
Child Relief and You Am. [11569]
Children's Rights Div. - Human Rights Watch
  [11583]
Children's Watch Intl. [11585]
Chin Human Rights Org. [IO]
Christian Action for the Abolition of Torture -
  France [IO]
Citizens Equal Rights Alliance [5800]
Coalition to Abolish Slavery and Trafficking
  [12370]
Coalition Against Trafficking in Women [17751]
Coalition Against Trafficking in Women [IO]
Coalition for Democracy in Iran [17389]
Coalition of Immokalee Workers [13458]
COLAGE [12223]
Commn. Justice and Peace, Netherlands [IO]
Commn. Luxembourgeoise - Justice et Paix [IO]
Comm. of Concerned Scientists [17752]
Comm. on Human Rights [17753]
Comm. for Humanitarian Assistance to Iranian
  Refugees [12808]

Comm. of Ministers [IO]
Commonwealth Human Rights Initiative [IO]
Community United Against Violence [12225]
Concerned Citizens for Racially Free Am. [17754]
Congressional Human Rights Caucus [17755]
CorpWatch [17756]
CorpWatch [IO]
Coun. for a Community of Democracies [5661]
Coun. for Disability Rights [11935]
Dancers Without Borders [9880]
Disability Rights Educ. and Defense Fund [11940]
Discussion Club [17111]
Educ. in Human Rights Network [IO]
Egyptian Org. for Human Rights [IO]
Entraide Missionnaire [IO]
Equitas - Intl. Centre for Human Rights Educ. [IO]
Estonian Inst. of Human Rights [IO]
Euro-Mediterranean Human Rights Network [IO]
European-American Unity and Rights Org.
  [17114]
European Assn. of Lawyers for Democracy and
  World Human Rights [IO]
European Centre for Minority Issues [IO]
Falun Data Info. Center [17757]
Finnish League for Human Rights [IO]
Forum-Asia: Asian Forum for Human Rights and
  Development [IO]
France Latin Am. [IO]
Free the Fathers [17060]
Free the Slaves [12371]
Free Tibet Campaign [IO]
French Justice and Peace Commn. [IO]
Friends of Falun Gong Europe [IO]
Front Line [IO]
Gay, Lesbian, and Straight Educ. Network [8456]
Gender Action [18825]
Genocide Watch [17660]
Global Initiative on Psychiatry [IO]
Global Jewish Assistance and Relief Network [IO]
Global Jewish Assistance and Relief Network
  [12372]
Global Lawyers and Physicians [14558]
Global Rights [17758]
Global Rights [IO]
Global Witness [IO]
Global Workers Justice Alliance [18074]
Global Youth Connect [18851]
Golden Rule Found. [10186]
Good Neighbors Intl. [IO]
Grupo Tortura Nunca Mais/RJ [IO]
Guatemala Human Rights Commission/U.S.A.
  [17679]
Guatemala News and Info. Bur. [17680]
Hamoked: Center for the Defence of the Individual
  [IO]
Hate Free Zone [17392]
Hearts and Minds Network [18730]
Helsinki Found. for Human Rights [IO]
Henry M. Jackson Found. [17480]
Heritage of Pride [12233]
Human Appeal Intl. - United Arab Emirates [IO]
Human and Civil Rights Organizations of Am.
  [11738]
Human Rights Advocates [5801]
Human Rights Assn. of Swaziland [IO]
Human Rights in China [12373]
Human Rights Comm. [IO]
Human Rights First [IO]
Human Rights First [17759]
Human Rights Info. and Documentation Systems
  Intl. [IO]
Human Rights Internet [IO]
Human Rights Monitor [IO]
Human Rights and Peace Campaign Intl. Network
  - Nepal [IO]
Human Rights Res. and Educ. Centre [IO]
Human Rights Rsrc. Center [17760]
Human Rights Watch [17761]
Human Rights Watch [IO]
Human Rights Watch Asia [IO]
Human Rights Watch Asia [17762]
Human Rights Watch - Helsinki [17763]
Human Rights Watch - Helsinki [IO]
Human Rights for Women [IO]
Hungarian Amer. Coalition [12451]

Huquqalinsan.org [12374]
Immigration Equality [12237]
INCITE! Women of Color Against Violence
  [18788]
Indonesia Human Rights Campaign [IO]
Inst. for Global Communications [7772]
Inst. for Humane Stud. [12375]
Inst. for the Stud. of Genocide [17764]
Inst. for the Stud. of Genocide [IO]
Instituto Interamericano de Derechos Humanos -
  Programa Mujer y Derechos Humanos [IO]
Inter-American Commn. on Human Rights [IO]
Inter-American Commn. on Human Rights [17765]
Inter-American Conf. of Ministers of Labor [17394]
Inter-American Inst. of Human Rights [IO]
Interights, the Intl. Centre for the Legal Protection
  of Human Rights [IO]
Intl. Assn. of Former Soviet Political Prisoners and
  Victims of the Communist Regime [IO]
Intl. Assn. of Former Soviet Political Prisoners and
  Victims of the Communist Regime [17766]
Intl. Assn. of Genocide Scholars [17661]
Intl. Assn. for Human Rights of the Kurds [IO]
Intl. Assn. of Official Human Rights Agencies [IO]
Intl. Assn. of Official Human Rights Agencies
  [5802]
Intl. Campaign for Tibet [18738]
Intl. Center for Transitional Justice [17767]
Intl. Center for Transitional Justice [IO]
Intl. Commn. of Jurists - Canadian Sect. [IO]
Intl. Commn. of Jurists - Switzerland [IO]
Intl. Fed. of ACAT (Action by Christians for the
  Abolition of Torture) [IO]
Intl. Fed. for Human Rights Leagues [IO]
International Federation for the Protection of the
  Rights of Ethnic, Religious, Linguistic and Other
  Minorities [IO]
Intl. Fed. for the Protection of the Rights of Ethnic,
  Religious, Linguistic and Other Minorities
  [17768]
Intl. Gay and Lesbian Human Rights Commn.
  [12239]
Intl. Helsinki Fed. for Human Rights [IO]
Intl. Human Rights Assn. of Amer. Minorities [IO]
Intl. Indian Treaty Coun. [17816]
Intl. Inst. of Human Rights [IO]
Intl. Inst. of Humanitarian Law [IO]
Intl. Justice and Human Rights, Natl. Coun. of
  Churches of Christ USA [IO]
Intl. Justice and Human Rights, Natl. Coun. of
  Churches of Christ USA [12376]
Intl. Justice Mission [5803]
Intl. Justice Mission [IO]
Intl. League for Human Rights [IO]
Intl. League for Human Rights [17769]
Intl. People's Democratic Uhuru Movement
  [17395]
Intl. Possibilities Unlimited [18642]
Intl. Senior Lawyers Proj. [5502]
Intl. Ser. for Human Rights - Switzerland [IO]
Intl. Soc. for Human Rights - Germany [IO]
Intl. Women's Rights Action Watch [IO]
Intl. Women's Rights Action Watch [17770]
InterPride [12240]
Iranian Refugees' Alliance [12813]
Irish Natl. Caucus [17933]
Jacob Blaustein Inst. for the Advancement of Hu-
  man Rights [17771]
Jews Against the Occupation [17952]
June 4th Found. [17063]
Justice and Peace Commn. of the Hong Kong
  Catholic Diocese [IO]
Kenyan Sect. of the Intl. Commn. of Jurists [IO]
Kurdish Human Rights Proj. [IO]
Laogai Res. Found. [IO]
Laogai Res. Found. [17772]
Leadership Conf. Educ. Fund [8094]
Life After Exoneration Prog. [17360]
Love146 [11620]
Magnus Hirschfeld Center for Human Rights
  [17773]
Magnus Hirschfeld Center for Human Rights [IO]
Marangopoulos Found. for Human Rights [IO]
A Matter of Justice Coalition [6012]
Mbong Found., Intl. [IO]

A star before a book entry number signifies that the name is not listed separately, but is mentioned within the entry.

Medical Rehabilitation Center for Torture Victims [IO]
Meiklejohn Civil Liberties Inst. [5804]
Men Stopping Violence [12643]
Mental Disability Rights Intl. [12574]
Mexican Commn. for the Defense and Promotion of Human Rights [IO]
Middle East Children's Alliance [IO]
Middle East Children's Alliance [17774]
Mind Justice [17775]
Mind Justice [IO]
MindFreedom Intl. [17776]
Mission for Est. of Human Rights in Iran [17777]
Mission for Est. of Human Rights in Iran [IO]
Natl. Action Network [17127]
Natl. Alliance for Worker and Employer Rights [24110]
Natl. Assn. of Barbados Organizations [9731]
Natl. Assn. of Black Citizens Action [16942]
Natl. Assn. of Fed. Defenders [5646]
Natl. Assn. to Protect Children [11628]
Natl. Assn. to Stop Guardian Abuse [12059]
Natl. Coming Out Day [12248]
Natl. Economic and Social Rights Initiative [17778]
Natl. Immigration Forum [17806]
Natl. Legal Sanctuary for Community Advancement [6015]
Natl. Mobilization Against Sweatshops [17975]
Natl. Network to End Violence Against Immigrant Women [13433]
Natl. Org. of Fed. Employees Against Abuse and Retaliation [24078]
Natl. Org. for Men Against Sexism [17779]
Natl. Youth Rights Assn. [18855]
Netherlands Comm. of Jurists for Human Rights [IO]
Netherlands Helsinki Comm. [IO]
Network in Solidarity With the People of Guatemala [17681]
No Peace Without Justice [18227]
Off. of the High Commissioner for Human Rights [IO]
OneWorld Intl. Found. [IO]
OneWorld Intl. Found. [17780]
Org. for Defending Victims of Violence [IO]
Osterreichische Kommission Iustitia Et Pax [IO]
OutProud [12252]
Owen M. Kupferschmid Holocaust and Human Rights Proj. [17781]
Owen M. Kupferschmid Holocaust and Human Rights Proj. [IO]
PACT [12439]
Partners for Peace [18230]
Peace and Justice Ser. in Argentina [IO]
People for the Amer. Way [17143]
People of Faith Against the Death Penalty [17034]
People's Decade of Human Rights Educ. [17782]
People's Decade of Human Rights Educ. [IO]
Peruvian Inst. for Educ. in Human Rights and Peace [IO]
Physicians for Human Rights [IO]
Physicians for Human Rights [17783]
Physicians for Human Rights - Israel [IO]
Physicians for Human Rights (UK) [IO]
Polaris Proj. Combating Trafficking of Women and Children [17784]
Proj. on Ethnic Relations [17785]
Protection Proj. [12377]
Racial Justice 911 [18493]
Rainbow/PUSH Coalition [13185]
Raoul Wallenberg Comm. of the U.S. [17449]
Rebuilding Alliance [12336]
REDRESS [IO]
Refugee Coun. USA [18500]
Religious Task Force on Central Am. and Mexico [17052]
Ruckus Soc. [18178]
Saharan People's Support Comm. [16933]
Samuel Rubin Found. [13188]
Scherman Found. [13189]
Scholars for Peace in the Middle East [18070]
Schweizerische Nationalkommission Justitia et Pax [IO]
Sikh Amer. Legal Defense and Educ. Fund [18600]

Simon Wiesenthal Center [17724]
SisterSong Women of Color Reproductive Hea. Collective [18826]
SMOLOSKYP, Ukrainian Info. Ser. [17450]
Social Accountability Intl. [18828]
Soc. of Saint Stephen [20523]
Soc. for Threatened Peoples [IO]
Sociologists Without Borders [18664]
Soulforce [17657]
Southern Africa Res. and Documentation Centre [IO]
Southern African Catholic Bishops' Conf. - Justice and Peace [IO]
Southern Center for Human Rights [17036]
Starthrowers [18603]
Susila Dharma Intl. [IO]
Torture Abolition and Survivors Support Coalition Intl. [IO]
Torture Abolition and Survivors Support Coalition Intl. [17786]
Uglies Unlimited [12102]
Ukrainian Legal Found. [IO]
Unitarian Universalist Ser. Comm. [20603]
Unitarian Universalist Women's Fed. [20604]
U.S. Copts Assn. [10192]
U.S. Copts Association [IO]
U.S. Coun. for Human Rights in the Balkans [17787]
U.S.-Tibet Comm. [18741]
Uyghur Amer. Assn. [17788]
Uyghur Amer. Assn. [IO]
Verite [12063]
Vietnam Human Rights Network [12378]
Vietnam Human Rights Network [IO]
Voices in the Wilderness [18253]
Wal-Mart Alliance for Reform Now [24107]
Wal-Mart Workers Assn. [24109]
Washington Off. on Latin Am. [17995]
Watchlist on Children and Armed Conflict [11664]
WITNESS [17789]
Women for Afghan Women [12379]
Women for Afghan Women [IO]
Women's Alliance for Peace and Human Rights in Afghanistan [IO]
Women's Alliance for Peace and Human Rights in Afghanistan [12380]
Women's Learning Partnership for Rights, Development, and Peace [13452]
Women's World Org. for Rights, Literature and Development [18822]
Workers' Defense League [17159]
World Org. Against Torture [IO]
World Org. for Human Rights USA [IO]
World Org. for Human Rights USA [12381]
Young Koreans United [12485]
Youth for Human Rights Intl. [12382]
Youth for Human Rights Intl. [IO]
Human Rights Advocates [5801], PO Box 5675, Berkeley, CA 94705
Human Rights Advocates Intl. - Address unknown since 2003.
Human Rights; Amer. Assn. of Physicians for [★14431]
Human Rights; Amer. Comm. for [★17783]
Human Rights Assn. of Swaziland [IO], Mbabane, Swaziland
Human Rights; Bay Area Physicians for [12218]
Human Rights Campaign [17653], 1640 Rhode Island Ave. NW, Washington, DC 20036-3278, (202)628-4160
Human Rights Campaign Fund's Mobilization Proj. [★17653]
Human Rights in Central Am; Natl. Labor Comm. in Support of Worker and [★17049]
Human Rights in China [12373], 350 Fifth Ave., Ste. 3311, New York, NY 10118, (212)239-4495
Human Rights; Commn. on Peace and [★18242]
Human Rights Commission/U.S.A; Guatemala [17679]
Human Rights Comm. [IO], Geneva, Switzerland
Human Rights Documentation Exchange [IO], Austin, TX, United States
Human Rights Documentation Exchange [17989], PO Box 2327, Austin, TX 78768, (512)476-9841
Human Rights Educ. Radio Listener Clubs [IO], Kathmandu, Nepal

Human Rights First [IO], New York, NY, United States
Human Rights First [17759], 333 7th Ave., 13th Fl., New York, NY 10001-5108, (212)845-5200
Human Rights; Formosan Assn. for [18692]
Human Rights; Fund for [★17159]
Human Rights Info. and Documentation Systems Intl. [IO], Versoix, Switzerland
Human Rights and Intl. Affairs [★IO]
Human Rights and Intl. Affairs [★12376]
Human Rights Intl. - Defunct.
Human Rights Internet [IO], Ottawa, ON, Canada
Human Rights INTERNET [★IO]
Human Rights in Korea; North Amer. Coalition for [★17966]
Human Rights; Lawyers Comm. for Intl. [★17759]
Human Rights Monitor [IO], Tehran, Iran
Human Rights; Natl. Labor Comm. for Worker and [17049]
Human Rights and Peace Campaign Intl. Network - Nepal [IO], Kathmandu, Nepal
Human Rights Political Action Comm. - Defunct.
Human Rights Proj; Indigenous Affairs and [★17993]
Human Rights Proj; Indigenous Affairs and [★IO]
Human Rights and Race Relations Centre [IO], Toronto, ON, Canada
Human Rights Res. and Educ. Centre [IO], Ottawa, ON, Canada
Human Rights Res. Proj; Holocaust/ [★17781]
Human Rights Rsrc. Center [17760], Univ. of Minnesota Law School, Mondale Hall, 229 19th Ave. S, Ste. N-120, Minneapolis, MN 55455, (612)626-0041
Human Rights Soc. of Uzbekistan - Address unknown since 2001.
Human Rights; Southern Center for [17036]
Human Rights of the U.S. Natl. Acad. of Sciences; Comm. on [★17753]
Human Rights Watch [17761], 350 5th Ave., 34th Fl., New York, NY 10118-3299, (212)290-4700
Human Rights Watch [IO], New York, NY, United States
Human Rights Watch Asia [IO], New York, NY, United States
Human Rights Watch Asia [17762], 350 5th Ave., 34th Fl., New York, NY 10118-3299, (212)290-4700
Human Rights Watch - Helsinki [17763], 350 5th Ave., 34th Fl., New York, NY 10118-3299, (212)290-4700
Human Rights Watch - Helsinki [IO], New York, NY, United States
Human Rights for Women [IO], Tuebingen, Germany
Human Rights for Women - Defunct.
Human Sciences; Assn. for Commun. Excellence in Agriculture, Natural Resources, and Life and [4098]
Human Sciences Res. Coun. [IO], Pretoria, Republic of South Africa
Human SERVE - Address unknown since 2006.
Human Ser. Administrators; Natl. Coun. of Local Public [13178]
Human Ser. Administrators; Natl. Coun. of State [13179]
Human Ser. Educ; Coun. for Standards in [9130]
Human Ser. Educ; Natl. Org. for [★9131]
Human Ser. Organizations; Natl. Assembly of Hea. and [★13400]
Human Service Personnel Assn. - Defunct.

Human Services
Actors' Fund of Am. [12112]
Afghan Women's Assn. Intl. [13416]
Amer. Assn. of Ser. Coordinators [1985]
Amer. Coll. of Counselors [12137]
Amer. Public Human Services Assn. [13151]
Amer. Public Human Services Assn. - Info. Systems Mgt. [13152]
Assn. for Applied Poetry [16211]
Assn. for Humanistic Psychology [16140]
Assn. of Social Work Boards [13200]
Assyrian Aid Soc. of Am. [11508]
Batey Relief Alliance [12835]
Clinical Social Work Fed. [13201]
Coalition on Human Needs [13161]
Coun. for Hea. and Human Services Ministries, United Church of Christ [13165]

Reference to "IO" in place of a book number signifies that the association may be found in the 45th edition of International Organizations.

Coun. of Intl. Programs USA [13202]
Coun. for Standards in Human Ser. Educ. [9130]
Counterpart Intl. [12426]
CRISTA Ministries [13166]
Cuban Amer. Natl. Coun. [13167]
Deaf Friends Intl. [11904]
Dress for Success Worldwide [13424]
Elwyn [12383]
FaithTrust Inst. [12027]
Fed. of Protestant Welfare Agencies [20482]
Free Wheelchair Mission [11947]
Friars Club [11016]
Gifts In Kind Intl. [12720]
Giraffe Heroes Proj. [10185]
Glenkirk [11948]
HandsNet [12641]
Healing Hands Intl. [13141]
Helping Hands for the Blind [13379]
Hosp. Audiences [11017]
Illusion Theater [12030]
Israel Humanitarian Found. [12458]
Joygerms Unlimited [10190]
Little Bros. - Friends of the Elderly [11295]
Malawi Proj. [11266]
Maniilaq Assn. [12627]
Mapendo Intl. [12868]
Mexican-American Opportunity Found. [12276]
Mission to Haiti [12267]
Natl. Alliance for Direct Support Professionals [1986]
Natl. Alliance for Hispanic Hea. [13176]
Natl. Assn. of Disability Representatives [18648]
Natl. Assn. of Planning Councils [18275]
Natl. Assn. for Regulatory Admin. [15011]
Natl. Assn. of Social Workers [13206]
Natl. Coun. of Local Public Human Ser. Administrators [13178]
Natl. Coun. of State Human Ser. Administrators [13179]
Natl. Energy Assistance Directors' Assn. [1987]
Natl. Latina Hea. Network [14589]
Natl. Network for Social Work Managers [13207]
Natl. Org. for Human Services [9131]
Network of Iranian Amer. Soc. [13507]
North Amer. Assn. of Christians in Social Work [13208]
Off. of Population Affairs CH [12757]
Opportunity International-USA [12384]
Pact Training [11830]
People Helping People [12385]
Pew Charitable Trusts [13129]
Rapha Intl. [12539]
Samuel H. Kress Found. [13132]
Tech. Assistance Collaborative [13145]
Theatre Authority [11046]
Tomas Rivera Policy Inst. [19196]
United Black Fund [12204]
U.S. Conf. of City Human Services Officials [6263]
U.S.A. Harvest [12402]
Volunteers of Am. [13192]
Welfare Res., Inc. [13193]
Human Services Administrators; Natl. Assn. of County [★5618]
Human Services Assembly; Natl. [13400]
Human Services Assn; Amer. Public [13151]
Human Services; Coun. for Hea. and [★13165]
Human Services Forum - Defunct.
Human Services Ministries, United Church of Christ; Coun. for Hea. and [13165]
Human Services; Natl. Commun. Coun. for [★3195]
Human Services Officials; U.S. Conf. of City [6263]
Human Services Organizations; Natl. Coalition of Hispanic Hea. and [★13176]
Human Support Services [IO], Lagos, Nigeria
Human Understanding; Found. of [10465]
Human Values; Soc. for Hea. and [★8845]
Human Writes [IO], Nottingham, United Kingdom
Humane Assn; Amer. [13149]
Humane Assn. Children's Services; Amer. [11556]
Humane Educ. Center; Norma Terris [★11433]
Humane Educ; Natl. Assn. for the Advancement of [★11433]
Humane Educ. Soc; Amer. [★11429]
Humane Educ. Soc; Natl. [11440]

Humane Educators; Assn. of Professional [12058]
Humane and Environmental Educ; Natl. Assn. for [11433]
Humane Farming Assn. [11411], PO Box 3577, San Rafael, CA 94912, (415)771-2253
Humane Options in Childbirth Experiences; Center for [15594]
Humane Slaughter Assn. [IO], Wheathampstead, United Kingdom
Humane Societies; Assoc. [11366]
Humane Societies of New Jersey; Assoc. [★11366]
Humane Soc. Animal Shelter; Women's [11479]
Humane Soc. of Dominica [IO], Roseau, Dominica
Humane Soc; Hooved Animal [11407]
Humane Soc. Intl. - Australia [IO], Avalon, Australia
Humane Soc. of the U.S. [11412], 2100 L St. NW, Washington, DC 20037, (202)452-1100
Humane Stud; Inst. for [12375]
HumanHorizons.Net [IO], Victoria, BC, Canada
Humanics; Amer. [8743]
Humanics Found; Amer. [★8743]

Humanism
Alliance of Secular Humanist Societies [10193]
Amer. Ethical Union [20083]
Amer. Humanist Assn. [20084]
Aspen Inst. [10194]
British Humanist Assn. [IO]
Center For Inquiry [17643]
Coun. for Secular Humanism [20085]
Council for Secular Humanism [IO]
Economy and Humanism [IO]
European Humanist Fed. [IO]
Family of Humanists [10195]
Freedom From Religion Found. [19837]
Humanist Assn. of Ireland [IO]
International Federation of Secular Humanistic Jews [IO]
Intl. Fed. of Secular Humanistic Jews [20086]
Intl. Humanist and Ethical Union [IO]
Natl. Secular Soc. [IO]
New Zealand Assn. of Rationalists and Humanists [IO]
Secular Student Alliance [17790]
Washington Ethical Soc. [20087]
World Transhumanist Assn. [7163]
Humanism; Academy of [★20085]
Humanism; Academy of [★IO]
Humanist Assn. of Ireland [IO], Dublin, Ireland
Humanist Inst. for Development Co-operation [IO], The Hague, Netherlands
Humanist Movement of Iranian People - Address unknown since 1985.
Humanist Sociology; Assn. for [7660]
Humanist Youth - Defunct.

Humanistic Education
Assn. of Waldorf Schools of North Am. [8526]
Assn. of Waldorf Schools of North Am. [IO]
Counseling Assn. for Humanistic Educ. and Development [8527]
Gp. for the Use of Psychology in History [10112]
Inst. for Humanist Stud. [8528]
Natl. Humanities Inst. [8532]
Secular Student Alliance [17790]
Threefold Educational Found. and School [8529]
Humanistic Educ. and Development; Counseling Assn. for [8527]
Humanistic Inst. for Cooperation with Developing Countries [IO], Harare, Zimbabwe
Humanistic Judaism; Intl. Fed. for Secular [★20086]
Humanistic Psychology; Amer. Assn. for [★16140]
Humanistic Psychology; Assn. for [16140]
Humanistic Rabbis; Assn. of [20120]
Humanistic Stud; Aspen Inst. for [★10194]
Humanists; Family of [10195]
Humanitarian Assistance Project for Independent Agricultural Development in Nicaragua - Defunct.
Humanitarian Assistance for the Women and Children of Afghanistan [IO], Peshawar, Pakistan
Humanitarian Assn. of Jewish Women [IO], Baku, Azerbaijan
Humanitarian Found; Israel [12458]
Humanitarian Law Proj. - Intl. Educ. Development [18498], 8124 W 3rd St., Ste. 105, Los Angeles, CA 90048, (323)836-6316
Humanitarian Law Proj. - Intl. Educ. Development [IO], Los Angeles, CA, United States

Humanitarian League; Natl. [★11471]
Humanitarian Medical Relief [12527]
Humanitarian Proj. for the Physically Challenged Child; National [★19231]
Humanitarian Rehabilitation Org. For The Poor And Needy [IO], Tiko, Cameroon
Humanitarians; United [11471]
Humanitas Intl. Human Rights Comm. - Defunct.
Humanite Soc. of America - Address unknown since 1995.

Humanities
African Amer. Literature and Culture Soc. [8798]
Alexandria Soc. and Educal. Found. [8161]
Amer. Acad. of Arts and Letters [10196]
Amer. Coun. of Learned Societies [10197]
Assn. for Political and Legal Anthropology [6411]
Assn. of Senior Anthropologists [6412]
Assn. for the Stud. of Persianate Societies [8668]
Australian Acad. of the Humanities [IO]
Bavarian Acad. of Sciences and Humanities [IO]
Benjamin Franklin Literary and Medical Soc. [14549]
British Acad. [IO]
Community Coll. Humanities Assn. [8530]
Consortium of Humanities Centers and Institutes [12386]
Consortium of Humanities Centers and Institutes [IO]
Ethnic Cultural Preservation Coun. [9847]
Fed. of State Humanities Councils [10198]
Gp. for the Use of Psychology in History [10112]
Intl. Soc. for Phenomenological Stud. [10805]
Intl. Soc. for Phenomenology and the Sciences of Life [10807]
Joseph Drown Found. [12051]
Mediterranean Stud. Assn. [10466]
Modern Humanities Res. Assn. [IO]
Natl. Assn. for Humanities Educ. [8531]
Natl. Endowment for the Humanities [5805]
Natl. Humanities Alliance [10199]
Natl. Humanities Center [10200]
Natl. Humanities Inst. [8532]
Natl. Initiative for a Networked Cultural Heritage [9858]
Natl. Soc. of Arts and Letters [10201]
Natl. Women's Hall of Fame [20716]
Omega Theatre and the Omega Arts Network [9590]
Renaissance Artists and Writers Assn. [10202]
Soc. for the Anthropology of Religion [6426]
Soc. for Evolutionary Anal. in Law [6539]
Soc. for the Humanities [10203]
Soc. for Urban, Natl. and Transnational/Global Anthropology [6435]
Southern Humanities Coun. [10204]
Wilbur Found. [10205]
Woodrow Wilson Intl. Center for Scholars [10206]
Woodrow Wilson Intl. Center for Scholars [IO]
World Acad. of Art and Sci. [9612]
Humanities; Amer. Soc. for Bioethics and [8845]
Humanities Conf; Southern [★10204]
Humanities Councils; Natl. Fed. of State [★10198]
Humanities and Social Sciences Fed. of Canada [★IO]
Humanities; Soc. for Automation in English and the [★8132]
Humanity; Habitat for [★12313]
Humanity Intl. [12859], PO Box 8222, Gaithersburg, MD 20898, (800)HUMANITY
Humanity Intl. [IO], Gaithersburg, MD, United States
Humanity/International; Volunteer Optometric Services to [★12543]
Humanity; People United to Serve [★13185]
Humanity; Tile Partners for [12338]
Humanity United in Giving Internationally [11699], 1335 Cypress Dr., Richardson, TX 75080, (972)690-1484
Humanity United in Giving Internationally [IO], Richardson, TX, United States
Humans Against Rabbit Exploitation - Address unknown since 1994.
Hume Soc. [IO], Akureyri, Iceland
Humility of Mary Ser. [IO], Rocky River, OH, United States
Humility of Mary Ser. [19636], c/o Sister's of Humility of Mary, 20015 Detroit Rd., Rocky River, OH 44116, (440)333-5373

A star before a book entry number signifies that the name is not listed separately, but is mentioned within the entry.

Hummel Club; M.I. **[21933]**
Hummel Collectors Club **[22040]**, 1261 Univ. Dr., Yardley, PA 19067-2857, (215)493-6204
Hummels
 M.I. Hummel Club **[21933]**
Hummer Club; Harley **[22679]**
Hummingbird Soc. **[4198]**, 6560 Hwy. 179, Ste. 204, Sedona, AZ 86351, (928)284-2251
Humor
 Absurd Special Interest Gp. **[22590]**
 Amer. Humor Stud. Assn. **[10207]**
 Assn. for Applied and Therapeutic Humor **[16605]**
 Benevolent and Loyal Order of Pessimists **[22591]**
 Burlington Liars Club **[22592]**
 Clowns of Am., Intl. **[21951]**
 Clowns Without Borders - USA **[11768]**
 Humor Helps! **[10208]**
 HUMOR Proj. **[10209]**
 Humor Stamp Club **[22827]**
 Inst. of Totally Useless Skills **[22593]**
 Intl. Assn. of People Who Dine Over the Kitchen Sink **[22594]**
 Intl. Assn. of People Who Dine Over the Kitchen Sink **[IO]**
 International Association of Professional Bureaucrats **[IO]**
 Intl. Assn. of Professional Bureaucrats **[22595]**
 Intl. Banana Club **[22596]**
 Intl. Banana Club **[IO]**
 Intl. Laughter Soc. **[10188]**
 Intl. Order of the Armadillo **[22597]**
 Intl. Save the Pun Found. **[IO]**
 Intl. Shrine Clown Assn. **[21952]**
 Intl. Soc. for Humor Stud. **[10210]**
 Intl. Soc. for Humor Stud. **[IO]**
 Jokewriters Guild **[IO]**
 Jokewriters Guild **[10211]**
 Joygerms Unlimited **[10190]**
 Laughter Therapy **[16622]**
 Man Will Never Fly Memorial Soc. Internationale **[22598]**
 Man Will Never Fly Memorial Soc. Internationale **[IO]**
 Marx Brotherhood **[24832]**
 Natl. Org. Taunting Safety and Fairness Everywhere **[22599]**
 Peter Sellers Appreciation Soc. **[24767]**
 Sarcastics Anonymous **[22600]**
 Secret Soc. of Happy People **[10212]**
 Soc. for the Preservation and Enhancement of the Recognition of Millard Fillmore, Last of the Whigs **[22601]**
 Stephen Leacock Assn. **[IO]**
 Universal Perkehner Soc. **[22602]**
 World Clown Assn. **[21953]**
Humor; Amer. Assn. for Therapeutic **[★16605]**
Humor Assn. **[★10208]**
Humor; Assn. for Applied and Therapeutic **[16605]**
Humor Correspondence Club **[★10211]**
Humor Correspondence Club **[★IO]**
Humor Helps! **[10208]**, 14224 SE 88th Ave., Summerfield, FL 34491, (352)307-7993
Humor and Irony Membership; Western **[★10210]**
Humor and Irony Membership; World **[★10210]**
Humor and Irony Movement; World **[★10210]**
HUMOR Proj. **[10209]**, 480 Broadway, Ste. 210, Saratoga Springs, NY 12866-2288, (518)587-8770
Humor Stamp Club **[22827]**
Hump Pilot Assn; China-Burma-India **[21391]**
Humper Dears - Defunct.
Humperdinck, Engelbert
 Engelbert's "Goils" **[24883]**
 Englebert's Golden Eagles **[24884]**
 Engel's Angels in Humperdinck Heaven Fan Club **[24885]**
 FR-ENGE Intl. **[24889]**
Humperdinck "Goils" **[24883]**
Humperdinck Heaven Fan Club; Engel's Angels in **[24885]**
The Huna Fellowship **[★12349]**
The Huna Fellowship **[★IO]**
Huna Forschunggesellschaft **[★IO]**
Huna Intl. **[★IO]**
Huna Intl. **[★12340]**

HUNA Res. **[12349]**, 1760 Anna St., Cape Girardeau, MO 63701-4504, (573)334-3478
HUNA Research **[IO]**, Cape Girardeau, MO, United States
Huna Res. Assn. **[IO]**, Zurich, Switzerland
Hundred Million Club - Address unknown since 1995.
Hundredth Monkey - Address unknown since 2003.
Hungarian
 Amer. Hungarian Educators' Assn. **[8533]**
 Amer. Hungarian Educators' Assn. **[IO]**
 Amer. Hungarian Fed. **[19104]**
 Amer. Hungarian Folklore Centrum **[10213]**
 Amer. Hungarian Found. **[10214]**
 Amer. Hungarian Lib. and Historical Soc. **[10215]**
 Amer. Liszt Soc. **[9807]**
 First Hungarian Literary Soc. **[19105]**
 Hungarian Amer. Coalition **[12451]**
 Hungarian/American Friendship Soc. **[19106]**
 Hungarian Human Rights Found. **[18571]**
 Hungarian Pumi Club of Am. **[22284]**
 Hungarian Reformed Fed. of Am. **[19107]**
 Hungarian Scouts Assn. **[12999]**
 Hungarian-U.S. Bus. Coun. **[724]**
 Intl. Assn. of Hungarian Stud. **[IO]**
 Kuvasz Club of Am. **[22302]**
 Natl. Fed. of American Hungarians **[19108]**
 Natl. Tour Assn. **[3930]**
 Soc. for Hungarian Philately **[22873]**
Hungarian Acad. of Sciences **[IO]**, Budapest, Hungary
Hungarian ACM Chap. **[IO]**, Szeged, Hungary
Hungarian Advt. Assn. **[IO]**, Budapest, Hungary
Hungarian Aeronautical Assn. **[IO]**, Budaors, Hungary
Hungarian Agricultural Journalists Assn. **[IO]**, Budapest, Hungary
Hungarian Alcological Soc. **[IO]**, God, Hungary
Hungarian Alliance of Reprographic Rights **[IO]**, Budapest, Hungary
Hungarian Amer. Coalition **[IO]**, Washington, DC, United States
Hungarian Amer. Coalition **[12451]**, 1120 Connecticut Ave. NW, Ste. 280, Washington, DC 20036, (202)296-9505
Hungarian/American Friendship Soc. **[19106]**, c/o Douglas P. Holmes, Dir., 17327 W Carmen Dr., Surprise, AZ 85388, (916)690-4293
Hungarian-Americans; Natl. Federation of **[★19108]**
Hungarian Anatomical Soc. **[IO]**, Budapest, Hungary
Hungarian Assn. of Competition Law **[IO]**, Budapest, Hungary
Hungarian Assn. of Customs Affairs **[IO]**, Budapest, Hungary
Hungarian Assn. of Foundries **[★IO]**
Hungarian Assn. for Geo-Information **[IO]**, Budapest, Hungary
Hungarian Assn. of IT Companies **[IO]**, Budapest, Hungary
Hungarian Assn. of Landscape Architects **[IO]**, Budapest, Hungary
Hungarian Assn. of Packaging and Materials Handling **[IO]**, Budapest, Hungary
Hungarian Assn. of Pedodontics and Orthodontics **[IO]**, Budapest, Hungary
Hungarian Assn. of Rheumatologists **[IO]**, Budapest, Hungary
Hungarian Badminton Assn. **[IO]**, Budapest, Hungary
Hungarian Banking Assn. **[IO]**, Budapest, Hungary
Hungarian Biophysical Soc. **[IO]**, Budapest, Hungary
Hungarian Bur. for the Protection of Authors' Rights **[IO]**, Budapest, Hungary
Hungarian Catholic League of America - Address unknown since 2004.
Hungarian Catholic Priests' Assn. in Am. **[19637]**, St. Stephen's Church, 223 3rd St., Passaic, NJ 07055, (973)779-0332
Hungarian Catholic Soc; Amer. **[★19144]**
Hungarian Central Comm. for Books and Education - Defunct.
Hungarian Chap. of the ILAE **[IO]**, Budapest, Hungary

Hungarian Chem. Indus. **[★IO]**
Hungarian Chem. Indus. Assn. **[IO]**, Budapest, Hungary
Hungarian Chem. Soc. **[IO]**, Budapest, Hungary
Hungarian Comm. - Address unknown since 1995.
Hungarian Comm. of Socialist Labor Party - Defunct.
Hungarian Cong. - Address unknown since 2002.
Hungarian Cost Engg. Club **[IO]**, Budapest, Hungary
Hungarian Cultural Found. - Address unknown since 2004.
Hungarian Dancesport Assn. **[IO]**, Budapest, Hungary
Hungarian Data Center - Defunct.
Hungarian Dermatological Soc. **[IO]**, Budapest, Hungary
Hungarian Economic Assn. **[IO]**, Budapest, Hungary
Hungarian Fed. of Forestry and Wood Indus. **[IO]**, Budapest, Hungary
Hungarian Floorball Fed. **[IO]**, Budapest, Hungary
Hungarian Folklore Centrum; Amer. **[10213]**
Hungarian Franchise Assn. **[IO]**, Budapest, Hungary
Hungarian Freedom Fighters Federation U.S.A. **[IO]**, Berkeley Springs, WV, United States
Hungarian Freedom Fighters Fed. U.S.A. **[17791]**, PO Box 867, Berkeley Springs, WV 25411, (304)258-4051
Hungarian Geological Soc. **[IO]**, Budapest, Hungary
Hungarian Gerontological Assn. **[IO]**, Budapest, Hungary
Hungarian Horse Assn. **[★4891]**
Hungarian Horse Assn. of Am. **[4891]**, c/o George Cooksley, Treas., HC 71 Box 108, Anselmo, NE 68813, (308)749-2411
Hungarian Hospice Assn. **[IO]**, Budapest, Hungary
Hungarian Human Rights Found. **[IO]**, New York, NY, United States
Hungarian Human Rights Found. **[18571]**, PO Box J, Gracie Sta., New York, NY 10028, (212)289-5488
Hungarian Hydrological Soc. **[IO]**, Budapest, Hungary
Hungarian Kuvasz
 Kuvasz Club of Am. **[22302]**
Hungarian Lancia Delta Fan Club **[IO]**, Szigetszentmiklos, Hungary
Hungarian Literary Soc. **[★19105]**
Hungarian Marketing Assn. **[IO]**, Budapest, Hungary
Hungarian Memorial Found. - Defunct.
Hungarian Mining and Metallurgical Soc. **[IO]**, Budapest, Hungary
Hungarian Multiple Sclerosis Soc. **[IO]**, Szekesfehervar, Hungary
Hungarian Natl. Baseball and Softball Fed. **[IO]**, Budapest, Hungary
Hungarian Natl. Skating Fed. **[IO]**, Budapest, Hungary
Hungarian Natl. Tourist Off. **[IO]**, Budapest, Hungary
Hungarian Olympic Comm. **[IO]**, Budapest, Hungary
Hungarian Operational Res. Soc. **[IO]**, Budapest, Hungary
Hungarian Osteoporosis Patients Assn. **[IO]**, Budapest, Hungary
Hungarian Pain Soc. **[IO]**, Budapest, Hungary
Hungarian Paralympic Comm. **[IO]**, Budapest, Hungary
Hungarian Philately; Soc. for **[22873]**
Hungarian Physiological Soc. **[IO]**, Budapest, Hungary
Hungarian Psychological Assn. **[IO]**, Budapest, Hungary
Hungarian Publishers and Booksellers Assn. **[IO]**, Budapest, Hungary
Hungarian Pumi Club of Am. **[22284]**, c/o Diane Bushwick-Klauber, Sec., PO Box 94, Chappaqua, NY 10514, (914)261-2965
Hungarian Real Estate Assn. **[IO]**, Budapest, Hungary
Hungarian Reformed Fed. of Am. **[19107]**, 2001 Massachusetts Ave. NW, Washington, DC 20036-1011, (202)328-2630
Hungarian Schoolsport Fed. **[IO]**, Budapest, Hungary
Hungarian Sci. Soc. for Building **[IO]**, Budapest, Hungary
Hungarian Sci. Soc. of Energy Economics **[IO]**, Budapest, Hungary

Reference to "IO" in place of a book number signifies that the association may be found in the 45th edition of International Organizations.

Hungarian Scouts Assn. **[12999]**, 2850 State Rte. 23 N, Newfoundland, NJ 07435-1443, (973)208-0450
Hungarian Soc. for Chemotherapy **[IO]**, Budapest, Hungary
Hungarian Soc. of Hypertension **[IO]**, Budapest, Hungary
Hungarian Soc. for Microscopy **[IO]**, Veszprem, Hungary
Hungarian Soc. for Osteoporosis and Osteoarthrology **[IO]**, Budapest, Hungary
Hungarian Soc. of Psychosomatic Obstetrics and Gynaecology **[IO]**, Debrecen, Hungary
Hungarian Soc. of Sports Medicine **[IO]**, Budapest, Hungary
Hungarian Soc. of Surveying, Mapping and Remote Sensing **[IO]**, Budapest, Hungary
Hungarian Soc. of Textile Tech. and Sci. **[IO]**, Budapest, Hungary
Hungarian Stud. Found.; Amer. **[★10214]**
Hungarian Taekwondo Fed. **[IO]**, Budapest, Hungary
Hungarian Tenants Assn. **[IO]**, Budapest, Hungary
Hungarian-U.S. Bus. Coun. **[IO]**, Washington, DC, United States
Hungarian-U.S. Bus. Coun. **[724]**, c/o Chamber of Commerce of the U.S., 1615 H St. NW, Washington, DC 20062-2000, (202)463-5460
Hungarian Venture Capital and Private Equity Assn. **[IO]**, Budapest, Hungary
Hungarian Water Ski and Wakeboard Fed. **[IO]**, Budapest, Hungary
Hungarian World Fed. of the Defense of a Nation - Defunct.
Hungarian Yachting Assn. **[IO]**, Budapest, Hungary
Hungary
   Hungarian Amer. Coalition **[12451]**
   Hungarian Freedom Fighters Fed. U.S.A. **[17791]**
   Hungarian Freedom Fighters Federation U.S.A. **[IO]**
   Hungarian Pumi Club of Am. **[22284]**
   Hungarian Scouts Assn. **[12999]**
   Kuvasz Club of Am. **[22302]**
   Soc. for Hungarian Philately **[22873]**
Hunger
   Action Against Hunger - France **[IO]**
   Alliance to End Hunger **[12387]**
   America's Children Hunger Network **[11558]**
   America's Second Harvest **[12388]**
   Angelcare **[11672]**
   Bread for the World **[17792]**
   Bread for the World **[IO]**
   Canadian Assn. of Food Banks **[IO]**
   Canadian Feed The Children **[IO]**
   Canadian Food for the Hungry Intl. **[IO]**
   Catholic Charities USA **[13158]**
   Center for Community Action of B'Nai B'rith Intl. **[11766]**
   CHF - Partners in Rural Development **[IO]**
   Children's Network Intl. **[11579]**
   Chol Chol Found. for Human Development **[IO]**
   Comm. on World Food Security **[IO]**
   Educational Concerns for Hunger Org. **[IO]**
   Educational Concerns for Hunger Org. **[12389]**
   End Hunger Network **[17793]**
   Euronaid **[IO]**
   Feed the Children **[12854]**
   Feeding Hungry Children Intl. **[12390]**
   Feeding Hungry Children Intl. **[IO]**
   Food Aid Comm. **[IO]**
   Food for the Hungry **[12391]**
   Food for the Hungry - UK **[IO]**
   Food Providers of Am. **[12392]**
   Food Res. and Action Center **[12393]**
   FoodFirst Info. and Action Network **[IO]**
   Freedom from Hunger **[12394]**
   The Hunger Proj. **[17794]**
   The Hunger Proj. **[IO]**
   IFDC - An Intl. Center for Soil Fertility and Agricultural Development **[4665]**
   Inst. for Food and Development Policy **[17795]**
   Inst. for Food and Development Policy **[IO]**
   Intl. Food Policy Res. Inst. **[IO]**
   Intl. Food Policy Res. Inst. **[17796]**
   Japan Intl. Food for the Hungry **[IO]**
   Just Act: Youth Action for Global Justice **[12435]**
   Korea Food for the Hungry Intl. **[IO]**

Malawi Proj. **[11266]**
MAZON **[12395]**
MAZON **[IO]**
Meals on Wheels Assn. of Am. **[12284]**
Meals4Israel **[12459]**
Millennium Promise **[11485]**
Natl. Student Campaign Against Hunger and Homelessness **[12396]**
Need **[12875]**
New Forests Proj. **[12436]**
OXFAM Am. **[12438]**
Partners for Development/Cambodia **[IO]**
People Helping People **[12385]**
Permanent End Intl. **[IO]**
Presbyterian Hunger Prog. **[12397]**
RESULTS **[17797]**
RESULTS **[IO]**
Self Help Intl. **[12442]**
Senior Gleaners **[12398]**
Share Our Strength **[12399]**
Soc. of St. Andrew **[20088]**
Tilapia Intl. Found. **[IO]**
Touching Hearts **[11267]**
Trees for Life **[12400]**
Trees for Life **[IO]**
United Nations Sys. Standing Comm. on Nutrition **[IO]**
U.S. Natl. Comm. for World Food Day **[IO]**
U.S. Natl. Comm. for World Food Day **[12401]**
U.S.A. Harvest **[12402]**
World Food Programme - Afghanistan **[IO]**
World Food Programme - Algeria **[IO]**
World Food Programme - Angola **[IO]**
World Food Programme - Armenia **[IO]**
World Food Programme - Azerbaijan **[IO]**
World Food Programme - Bangladesh **[IO]**
World Food Programme - Benin **[IO]**
World Food Programme - Bhutan **[IO]**
World Food Programme - Bolivia **[IO]**
World Food Programme - Burkina Faso **[IO]**
World Food Programme - Burundi **[IO]**
World Food Programme - Cambodia **[IO]**
World Food Programme - Cameroon **[IO]**
World Food Programme - Cape Verde **[IO]**
World Food Programme - Central African Republic **[IO]**
World Food Programme - Chad **[IO]**
World Food Programme - China **[IO]**
World Food Programme - Colombia **[IO]**
World Food Programme - Congo **[IO]**
World Food Programme - Cote d'Ivoire **[IO]**
World Food Programme - Cuba **[IO]**
World Food Programme - Djibouti **[IO]**
World Food Programme - Dominican Republic **[IO]**
World Food Programme - Ecuador **[IO]**
World Food Programme - Egypt **[IO]**
World Food Programme - El Salvador **[IO]**
World Food Programme - Eritrea **[IO]**
World Food Programme - Ethiopia **[IO]**
World Food Programme - Gambia **[IO]**
World Food Programme - Georgia **[IO]**
World Food Programme - Ghana **[IO]**
World Food Programme - Guatemala **[IO]**
World Food Programme - Guinea **[IO]**
World Food Programme - Guinea Bissau **[IO]**
World Food Programme - Haiti **[IO]**
World Food Programme - Honduras **[IO]**
World Food Programme - India **[IO]**
World Food Programme - Indonesia **[IO]**
World Food Programme - Iran **[IO]**
World Food Programme - Italy **[IO]**
World Food Programme - Jordan **[IO]**
World Food Programme - Kenya **[IO]**
World Food Programme - Korea (DPR) **[IO]**
World Food Programme - Laos **[IO]**
World Food Programme - Lesotho **[IO]**
World Food Programme - Liberia **[IO]**
World Food Programme - Madagascar **[IO]**
World Food Programme - Malawi **[IO]**
World Food Programme - Mali **[IO]**
World Food Programme - Mauritania **[IO]**
World Food Programme - Mozambique **[IO]**
World Food Programme - Myanmar **[IO]**
World Food Programme - Nepal **[IO]**

World Food Programme - Nicaragua **[IO]**
World Food Programme - Niger **[IO]**
World Food Programme - Occupied Palestinian Territories **[IO]**
World Food Programme - Pakistan **[IO]**
World Food Programme - Peru **[IO]**
World Food Programme - Russia **[IO]**
World Food Programme - Rwanda **[IO]**
World Food Programme - Sao Tome and Principe **[IO]**
World Food Programme - Senegal **[IO]**
World Food Programme - Sierra Leone **[IO]**
World Food Programme - Sri Lanka **[IO]**
World Food Programme - Sudan **[IO]**
World Food Programme - Swaziland **[IO]**
World Food Programme - Syria **[IO]**
World Food Programme - Tajikistan **[IO]**
World Food Programme - Tanzania **[IO]**
World Food Programme - Thailand **[IO]**
World Food Programme - Uganda **[IO]**
World Food Programme - United Arab Emirates **[IO]**
World Food Programme - Yemen **[IO]**
World Food Programme - Zambia **[IO]**
World Food Programme - Zimbabwe **[IO]**
World Hunger Educ. Ser. **[IO]**
World Hunger Educ. Ser. **[17798]**
World Hunger Year **[17799]**
World Hunger Year **[IO]**
Hunger Action Coalition - Defunct.
Hunger Found; Freedom from **[★12394]**
Hunger Found; Meals for Millions/Freedom from **[★12394]**
Hunger; Natl. Student Campaign Against **[★12396]**
Hunger/Presbyterian Church in the U.S; Task Force on World **[★12397]**
Hunger Prog. Comm. of the United Presbyterian Church of the U.S.A. in 1981 **[★12397]**
The Hunger Proj. **[17794]**, 5 Union Sq. W, New York, NY 10003, (212)251-9100
The Hunger Proj. **[IO]**, New York, NY, United States
Hunger Relief and Development - Address unknown since 2004.
Hungry; Food for the **[12391]**
Hunt Assn; Natl. Steeplechase and **[★23509]**
Hunt Assn; One-Arm Dove **[23358]**
Hunt Saboteurs Assn. **[IO]**, London, United Kingdom
Hunter and Angler Issues Program **[★4413]**
Hunter Archaeological Soc. **[IO]**, Sheffield, United Kingdom
Hunter Assn. USA; Clan **[20832]**
Hunter Club of America - Defunct.
Hunter Educ. Assn. **[★23545]**
Hunter Educ. Assn. **[★IO]**
Hunter Educ. Found; Natl. Bow **[23053]**
Hunter Educ. Program; International Bow **[★23053]**
Hunter Jumper Assn; Natl. **[23530]**
Hunter/Jumper Coun; Natl. **[23531]**
Hunter Olive Assn. **[IO]**, Narrabeen, Australia
Hunter Safety Coordinators; North Amer. Assn. of **[★23545]**
Hunterian Society **[IO]**, London, United Kingdom
Hunters of Am; Christian Bow **[23051]**
Hunters Helping Hunters **[22604]**, PO Box 836796, Richardson, TX 75083-6796, (877)317-3367
Hunter's Shooting Assn. **[23543]**, N8881 Hwy. D, Belleville, WI 53508
Hunter's Soc; Professional Bow **[23057]**
Hunting
   Amateur Field Trial Clubs of Am. **[22184]**
   Amer. Chesapeake Club **[22195]**
   Amer. Coon Hunters Assn. **[23541]**
   Amer. Crossbow Fed. **[23542]**
   Amer. Kennel Club **[22201]**
   Amer. Pointer Club **[22206]**
   Amer. Single Shot Rifle Assn. **[23714]**
   Animal Rights Coalition **[11356]**
   Archery Shooters Assn. **[23050]**
   Assn. Of Hunt Saboteurs - Ireland **[IO]**
   Assn. of Ohio Longrifle Collectors **[22425]**
   Australian Bowhunters Assn. **[IO]**
   Basset Hound Club of Am. **[22226]**
   Bluetick Breeders of Am. **[22233]**
   Bowhunting Preservation Alliance **[22603]**
   British Assn. for Shooting and Conservation **[IO]**

A star before a book entry number signifies that the name is not listed separately, but is mentioned within the entry.

Browning Collectors Assn. [22426]
Citizens to End Animal Suffering and Exploitation [11375]
Coalition to Protect Animals in Parks and Refuges [11379]
Comm. to Abolish Sport Hunting [11380]
Dream Catchers, USA [11943]
European Fed. Against Hunting [IO]
Fed. of Associations for Hunting and Conservation of the E.U. [IO]
Friends of Animals [11397]
Fur Free Alliance [4153]
German Gun Collectors' Assn. [22029]
Humane Soc. of the U.S. [11412]
Hunt Saboteurs Assn. [IO]
Hunters Helping Hunters [22604]
Hunter's Shooting Assn. [23543]
Hunting Assn. of Ireland [IO]
Hunting Retriever Club [22285]
Intl. Bowhunting Org. [23544]
International Bowhunting Organization [IO]
Intl. Fed. of Sound Hunters [IO]
Intl. Handgun Metallic Silhouette Assn. [23719]
Intl. Hunter Educ. Assn. [23545]
International Hunter Education Association [IO]
Intl. Hunting Land Assn. [IO]
Intl. Hunting Land Assn. [22605]
Irish Water Spaniel Club of Am. [22294]
Masters of Foxhounds Assn. of Am. [23546]
Midwest Decoy Collectors Assn. [22071]
Natl. Amateur Retriever Club [22309]
Natl. Archery Assn. of the U.S. [23052]
Natl. Assn. of Regional Game Councils [IO]
Natl. Beagle Club of Am. [22314]
Natl. Bird Dog Challenge Assn. [22315]
Natl. Bowhunter Educ. Found. [23053]
The Natl. Crossbowmen of the U.S.A. [23054]
Natl. Field Archery Assn. [23055]
Natl. Hunters Assn. [23547]
Natl. Muzzle Loading Rifle Assn. [23722]
North Amer. Bowhunting Coalition [22606]
North Amer. Hunting Club [23548]
North Amer. Pt-to-Pt Assn. [23511]
North Amer. Squirrel Assn. [22773]
North Amer. Trap Collector Assn. [22095]
North-South Skirmish Assn. [23727]
Physically Challenged Bowhunters of Am. [23549]
Pope and Young Club [23056]
Professional Bowhunter's Soc. [23057]
Professional Hunters' Assn. of South Africa [IO]
Rabbits Unlimited Inc. [4161]
Safari Club Intl. [5377]
Salisbury Hunt Club [IO]
Theodore Roosevelt Conservation Partnership [4458]
Treeing Walker Breeders and Fanciers Assn. [22368]
Tufts Center for Animals and Public Policy [11466]
United Sportsmans Assn. of North Am. [23058]
U.S. Revolver Assn. [23731]
U.S. Sportsmen's Alliance [23550]
Vizsla Club of Am. [22378]
Weatherby Collectors Assn. [22432]
Western Gamebird Alliance [4466]
Wirehaired Vizsla Club of Am. [22384]
World Atlatl Assn. [22611]
Hunting Assn. of Ireland [IO], Kilmallock, Ireland
Hunting; Comm. to Abolish Sport [11380]
Hunting Dogs
Amateur Field Trial Clubs of Am. [22184]
Amer. Chesapeake Club [22195]
Amer. Kennel Club [22201]
Amer. Pointer Club [22206]
Basset Hound Club of Am. [22226]
Bluetick Breeders of Am. [22233]
Epagneul Breton USA [22264]
French Brittany Gun Dog Assn. [22270]
Hunting Retriever Club [22285]
Irish Water Spaniel Club of Am. [22294]
Natl. Amateur Retriever Club [22309]
Natl. Beagle Club of Am. [22314]
Natl. Bird Dog Challenge Assn. [22315]
Natl. Retriever Club [23386]
North Amer. Teckel Club [22329]

Treeing Walker Breeders and Fanciers Assn. [22368]
Vizsla Club of Am. [22378]
Wirehaired Vizsla Club of Am. [22384]
Hunting Retriever Club [22285], c/o Jim Reichman, Pres., PO Box 210, Alexandria, LA 71309, (318)446-0075
Huntington Assn. of Russia [IO], Moscow, Russia
Huntington Assn. of Slovenia [IO], Ljubljana, Slovenia
Huntington Disease Care and Cure Soc. of Pakistan [IO], Peshawar, Pakistan
Huntington Disease Found. of Am. [★15329]
Huntington Disease Soc. of Argentina [IO], Buenos Aires, Argentina
Huntington Disease Soc. of Colombia [IO], Juan de Acosta, Colombia
Huntington Espoir [IO], Cuvry, France
Huntington Foreningen I Sverige [IO], Stockholm, Sweden
Huntington Liga [IO], Bierbeek, Belgium
Huntington Self Support Gp. Malta [IO], Kappara, Malta
Huntington Soc. of Canada [IO], Kitchener, ON, Canada
Huntington's Assn. of South Africa [IO], Cape Town, Republic of South Africa
Huntington's Disease
Hereditary Disease Found. [15328]
Huntington's Disease Soc. of Am. [15329]
Huntington's Disease Assn. [IO], London, United Kingdom
Huntington's Disease Assn. - Canterbury, New Zealand [IO], Christchurch, New Zealand
Huntington's Disease Assn. of Ireland [IO], Dublin, Ireland
Huntington's Disease Assn; Natl. [★15329]
Huntington's Disease Soc. of Am. [15329], 505 8th Ave., Ste. 902, New York, NY 10018, (212)242-1968
Huntington's Org. [IO], Gurgaon, India
Huntington's United Gp. South Africa [IO], Johannesburg, Republic of South Africa
Hunts Racing Assn; United [★23509]
Hunza Res. Soc. - Defunct.
Hupmobile Club - Address unknown since 1995.
Huququalinsan.org [12374], 955 Massachusetts Ave., No. 242, Cambridge, MA 02139, (617)588-0224
Hurlingham Polo Assn. [IO], Faringdon, United Kingdom
Hurst/Olds Club of Am. [21661], 3626 Meadowview Ct., Decatur, IL 62526
Hurston Soc; Zora Neale [9729]
Husband-Coached Childbirth; Amer. Acad. of [15579]
Husky; Adopt A [11340]
Husky Club of Am; Siberian [22359]
Hutmen's Assn. - Address unknown since 1995.
Hutterian Brethren [★20481]
Hutterian Soc. of Bros. [★20481]
Huxley Inst. for Biosocial Res. - Defunct.
Hyacinth Control Soc. [★6630]
Hyborean Legion - Defunct.
Hybrid Intl. Assn; Bison [★4123]
Hybrid Microelectronics; Intl. Soc. for [★6930]
Hybridizers Assn; Gesneriad [22514]
Hybridizers Assn; Rose [22539]
Hyderabad Race Club [IO], Hyderabad, India
Hydrangea Soc; Amer. [22494]
Hydraulic Inst. [2024], 9 Sylvan Way, Parsippany, NJ 07054, (973)267-9700
Hydraulic Tool Mfrs. Assn. [2025], PO Box 5416, Glendale Heights, IL 60139-5416, (630)893-7755
Hydraulics Training Assn; Indus. [★7084]
Hydrauliikka-ja Pneumatiikkayhdistys r.y. [★IO]
Hydrocephalus Assn. [15330], 870 Market St., Ste. 705, San Francisco, CA 94102, (415)732-7040
Hydrocephalus Assn. of Canada; Spina Bifida and [IO]
Hydrocephalus; Assn. for Spina Bifida and [IO]
Hydrocephalus Found; Natl. [14280]
Hydrocephalus; Irish Assn. for Spina Bifida and [IO]
Hydrocephalus Res. Found. - Defunct.
Hydrocephalus Res. Found; Guardians of [15326]
Hydrocephalus and Spina Bifida; Soc. for Res. into [IO]

Hydrofoil Assn; U.S. [23978]
Hydrogen Assn; Amer. [6940]
Hydrogen Assn; Canadian [IO]
Hydrogen Assn; Natl. [7619]
Hydrogen Org. for Progress, Education and Cooperation - Defunct.
Hydrographic Bur; Intl. [IO]
Hydrographic Soc. [★IO]
The Hydrographic Soc. of Am. [7718], PO Box 732, Rockville, MD 20848-0732, (301)460-4768
Hydrological Sciences; Intl. Assn. of [IO]
Hydrology
Amer. Meteorological Soc. [7325]
Hungarian Hydrological Soc. [IO]
The Hydrographic Soc. of Am. [7718]
Hydrology; Amer. Inst. of [7823]
Hydrology and Climatology; Intl. Soc. of Medical [IO]
Hydrology; Universities Coun. on [★7844]
Hydrolyzed Protein Coun; Intl. [1529]
Hydronic Radiant Heating Assn. [★1884]
Hydronics Inst. [★1884]
Hydronics Inst. Division of GAMA [1884], PO Box 218, Berkeley Heights, NJ 07922-0218, (908)464-8200
Hydroponic Merchants Assn. [1988], 10210 Leatherleaf Ct., Manassas, VA 20111-4245, (703)392-5890
Hydroponic Soc. of Am. [4174], c/o Bill Graham, VP, 569 E Evelyn Ave., Mountain View, CA 94041, (650)968-4070
Hydroponics
Hydroponic Merchants Assn. [1988]
Hydropower Assn; European Small [IO]
Hydropower Assn; Natl. [6964]
Hydrotherapy; Intl. Assn. for Colon [14567]
Hygiene; Acad. of Indus. [★15627]
Hygiene; Amer. Bd. of Indus. [15623]
Hygiene; Amer. Soc. of Tropical Medicine and [16693]
Hygiene Assn; Amer. Indus. [15627]
Hygiene Assn; Amer. Social [★16410]
Hygiene; Hong Kong Inst. of Occupational and Environmental [IO]
Hygiene; Intl. Comm. for Mental [★15237]
Hygiene; Natl. Comm. for Mental [★15211]
Hygiene Soc; Amer. Natural [★15279]
Hygiene Soc; Amer. Physiological and Natural [★15279]
Hygiene Veterinarians; Amer. Assn. of Food [16745]
Hygienic Community Network - Address unknown since 2006.
Hygienists; Amer. Conf. of Governmental Indus. [15625]
Hygienists' Assn; Amer. Dental [14132]
Hygienists' Assn; Natl. Dental [14177]
Hygienists; Natl. Conf. of Governmental Indus. [★15625]
Hymn Soc. of Am. [★20432]
Hymn Soc. of Great Britain and Ireland [IO], Lancaster, United Kingdom
Hymn Soc. in the U.S. and Canada [20432], Boston Univ. School of Theology, 745 Commonwealth Ave., Boston, MA 02215-1401, (617)353-6493
Hynek Center for UFO Stud; J. Allen [7479]
Hypatia Cluster - Defunct.
Hyperactivity
Feingold Assn. of the U.S. [15557]
Hyperactivity Disorder; Children and Adults With Attention Deficit/ [15314]
Hyperbaric Medical Soc; Undersea and [16697]
Hyperbaric Medicine
Baromedical Nurses Assn. [15471]
Undersea and Hyperbaric Medical Soc. [16697]
Hyperlexia Assn; Amer. [13940]
Hyperoxaluria Found; Oxalosis and [15296]
Hypertension
Algerian Soc. of Hypertension [IO]
Amer. Soc. of Hypertension [IO]
Amer. Soc. of Hypertension [14905]
Argentine Soc. of Hypertension [IO]
Arterial Hypertension Soc. of Mexico [IO]
Austrian Soc. of Hypertension [IO]
Belgian Hypertension Comm. [IO]
Brazilian Soc. of Hypertension [IO]
British Hypertension Soc. [IO]
Bulgarian Hypertension League [IO]

Reference to "IO" in place of a book number signifies that the association may be found in the 45th edition of International Organizations.

Canadian Coalition for High Blood Pressure Prevention and Control [IO]
Canadian Hypertension Soc. [IO]
Chilean Soc. of Hypertension [IO]
Chinese Hypertension League [IO]
Costa Rican Hypertension League [IO]
Croatian Soc. of Hypertension [IO]
Cuban Natl. Comm. for the Stud. of Hypertension [IO]
Czech Soc. of Hypertension [IO]
Danish Hypertension Soc. [IO]
Egyptian Hypertension Soc. [IO]
Estonian Soc. of Hypertension [IO]
Finnish Hypertension Soc. [IO]
French Comm. Against Hypertension [IO]
German Soc. of Hypertension [IO]
Hellenic Soc. of Hypertension [IO]
HELLP Syndrome Soc. [IO]
HELLP Syndrome Soc. [14906]
Hong Kong Coll. of Cardiology [IO]
Hungarian Soc. of Hypertension [IO]
Intl. Pediatric Hypertension Assn. [IO]
Intl. Pediatric Hypertension Assn. [14907]
Intl. Soc. of Hypertension [14908]
Intl. Soc. of Hypertension [IO]
Intl. Soc. on Hypertension in Blacks [IO]
Intl. Soc. on Hypertension in Blacks [14909]
Intl. Soc. for the Stud. of Hypertension in Pregnancy [IO]
Israel Hypertension Soc. [IO]
Italian League Against Hypertension [IO]
Kenya Hypertension League [IO]
Korean Soc. of Hypertension [IO]
Lebanese Hypertension League [IO]
Lithuanian Hypertension League [IO]
Natl. Hypertension Assn. [14910]
Natl. League for the Control of Cardiovascular Disease [IO]
Netherlands Soc. of Hypertension [IO]
Nigerian Hypertension Soc. [IO]
North Amer. Soc. for the Stud. of Hypertension in Pregnancy [16342]
Nurses' Hypertension Assn. [IO]
Pakistan Hypertension League [IO]
Pan-African Soc. of Cardiology [IO]
Paraguayan Soc. of Hypertension [IO]
Peruvian Soc. of Arterial Hypertension [IO]
Philippine Soc. of Hypertension [IO]
Polish Soc. of Hypertension [IO]
Portuguese League Against Hypertension [IO]
Pulmonary Hypertension Assn. [14911]
Pulmonary Hypertension Assn. - United Kingdom [IO]
Russian Soc. of Hypertension [IO]
Slovak League Against Hypertension [IO]
Slovene Hypertension Soc. [IO]
Southern African Hypertension Soc. [IO]
Spanish Soc. and League of Hypertension [IO]
Swedish Hypertension Soc. [IO]
Swiss Soc. of Hypertension [IO]
Thai Hypertension League [IO]
Turkish Assn. for Hypertension Control [IO]
Uruguayan Hypertension Comm. [IO]
Uruguayan League Against Arterial Hypertension [IO]
World Hypertension League [IO]
World Hypertension League [14912]
Zimbabwe Hypertension Soc. [IO]
Hypertension Assn; Pulmonary [14911]
Hypertension Coun. [★14562]
Hypertension; Japanese Soc. of [IO]
Hypertension; United Patients Assn. for Pulmonary [★14911]
Hyperthermia Assn. of the U.S; Malignant [14464]
Hyperthermia Soc; North Amer. [★16639]
Hyperthermic Oncology; European Soc. for [IO]
Hypertrophic Cardiomyopathy Association [IO], Hibernia, NJ, United States
Hypertrophic Cardiomyopathy Assn. [14782], PO Box 306, Hibernia, NJ 07842, (973)983-7429
Hyphenate Lobby [★17165]
Hypnosis
Acad. of Scientific Hypnotherapy [14913]
Amer. Acad. of Medical Hypnoanalysts [14914]
Amer. Assn. of Professional Hypnotherapists [14915]

Amer. Bd. of Hypnotherapy [14916]
Amer. Bd. of Psychological Hypnosis [14917]
Amer. Coun. of Hypnotist Examiners [14918]
Amer. Guild of Hypnotherapists [14919]
Amer. Hypnosis Assn. [14920]
Amer. Soc. of Clinical Hypnosis [14921]
Amer. Soc. of Clinical Hypnosis - Educ. and Res. Found. [14922]
Assn. of Qualified Curative Hypnotherapists [IO]
Australian Soc. of Clinical Hypnotherapists [IO]
Australian Soc. of Hypnosis [IO]
British Soc. of Experimental and Clinical Hypnosis [IO]
British Soc. of Hypnotherapists [IO]
British Soc. of Medical and Dental Hypnosis [IO]
European Coll. of Hypnotherapy [IO]
Hypnotherapy Assn. [IO]
Intl. Assn. of Counselors and Therapists [IO]
Intl. Assn. of Counselors and Therapists [14923]
Intl. Assn. for Regression Res. and Therapies [16617]
Intl. Medical and Dental Hypnotherapy Assn. [14924]
Intl. Medical and Dental Hypnotherapy Assn. [IO]
Intl. Soc. of Hypnosis [IO]
Intl. Soc. for Medical and Psychological Hypnosis [IO]
Milton H. Erickson Found. [16221]
Natl. Bd. for Certified Clinical Hypnotherapists [14925]
Natl. Guild of Hypnotists [14926]
Soc. for Clinical and Experimental Hypnosis [14927]
Soc. of Psychological Hypnosis [16178]
Hypnosis; Amer. Bd. of Examiners in Psychological [★14917]
Hypnosis; Amer. Bd. of Professional Psychology in [★14917]
Hypnosis Educational Coun. Intl. [★14926]
Hypnosis Found; Seminars on [★14922]
Hypnosis; International Soc. of [★14927]
Hypnosis and Psychotherapy; Natl. Coll. of [IO]
Hypnotherapists; Assn. of Qualified Curative [IO]
Hypnotherapy Assn. [IO], Lancashire, United Kingdom
Hypnotherapy; European Coll. of [IO]
Hypnotists Examining Coun. [★14918]
Hypoglycemia
HELP - Inst. for Body Chemistry [14928]
Hypoglycemia Assn. - Defunct.
Hypoparathyroidism Assn. [14356], PO Box 2258, Idaho Falls, ID 83403, (208)524-3857
Hypoparathyroidism Assn. [IO], Idaho Falls, ID, United States
Hypopigmentation; Natl. Org. for Albinism and [15255]
Hyresgasternas Riksforbund [★IO]
Hysterectomy Educational Resources and Services Foundation [IO], Bala Cynwyd, PA, United States
Hysterectomy Educational Resources and Services Found. [15601], 422 Bryn Mawr Ave., Bala Cynwyd, PA 19004, (610)667-7757

I

I Am Your Child Found. [★12682]
I-ANON - Address unknown since 2004.
I CAN [IO], London, United Kingdom
I-CAR [★415]
The I Hate Barney Secret Soc. - Address unknown since 1999.
I Have a Dream Found. [13487], 330 7th Ave., 20th Fl., New York, NY 10001-5010, (212)293-5480
I Have Lived Before Club - Defunct.
I KARE - Individuals Against Killing Animals for Recreational Enjoyment [★5332]
I KARE - Individuals Against Killing Animals for Recreational Enjoyment [★IO]
I Love Lucy Fan Club - Defunct.
I Seek a Transsexual Female and Intros - Defunct.
IAB Partners [1464], 462 E 800 N, Orem, UT 84097, (801)805-1361
IACP Law Enforcement Info. Mgt. Sect. [5819], c/o Intl. Assn. of Chiefs of Police, 515 N Washington St., Alexandria, VA 22314-2357, (703)836-6767

IADT, The Intl. Assn. for Document Technologies [★3679]
IADT, The Intl. Assn. for Document Technologies - Defunct.
IAESTE Polska [★IO]
IAHI, The Owners' Assn. [IO], Atlanta, GA, United States
IAHI, The Owners' Assn. [1946], 3 Ravinia Dr., Ste. 100, Atlanta, GA 30346, (770)604-5555
IANA [★3872]
IARF - Australian and New Zealand Unitarian Assn. [IO], Norwood, Australia
IARF - Europe and the Middle East [IO], Budapest, Hungary
IARF - Philippines [IO], Dumaguete City, Philippines
IARF - South Asia [IO], Bangalore, India
IATROS - Defunct.
IBEC Res. Inst. [★4103]
Iberamerican Fed. of the World Coun. for Gifted and Talented Children [IO], Valladolid, Spain
Iberian Sport Horse and Warmblood Registry [4892], c/o Dolores Dougherty, Pres., PO Box 998, Ridgefield, WA 98642, (360)887-3259
Ibero-American Bur. of Educ. [★IO]
Ibero-American Fed. of Acoustics [IO], Madrid, Spain
Ibero-American Fed. of Exchanges [IO], Buenos Aires, Argentina
Ibero-American Inst. of Aeronautic and Space Law and Commercial Aviation [IO], Madrid, Spain
Ibero-American Univ. Assn. for Postgraduate Universities [IO], Salamanca, Spain
Ibero-Latin Amer. Coll. of Dermatology [IO], Buenos Aires, Argentina
Ibero-Latin Amer. Fed. of Plastic Surgery [IO], Santiago, Chile
Iberoamerican Assn. of Educational TV [IO], Madrid, Spain
Iberoamerican Cultural Exchange Program - Defunct.
IBM
Common-A Users Gp. [6791]
IBM Employees Credit Unions; League of [★1111]
IBM PC
Capital PC User Gp. [6788]
Ibsen Soc. of Am. [9660], c/o Prof. Arne Lunde, Dept. of German, Scandinavian, and Dutch, Univ. of Minnesota, 205 Folwell Hall, Minneapolis, MN 55455
Ibsen Soc. of Am. [IO], Minneapolis, MN, United States
ICA - Australia [IO], Highgate Hill, Australia
ICA Bunka Jigyo Kyokai - Japan [★IO]
ICA Gender Equality Comm. [IO], Geneva, Switzerland
ICA Gp. [1249], 1 Harvard St., Ste. 200, Brookline, MA 02445, (617)232-8765
ICA Women's Comm. [★IO]
ICAR - Interstate Cinderellans and Revenuers: Educational Club - Defunct.
ICC - Austria [IO], Vienna, Austria
ICC Belgique-Belgie [★IO]
ICC Commercial Crime Services [IO], Barking, United Kingdom
ICC Counterfeiting Intelligence Bur. [IO], London, United Kingdom
ICC - Finland [IO], Helsinki, Finland
ICC Intl. Maritime Bur. [IO], Barking, United Kingdom
ICC - Polska [IO], Bydgoszcz, Poland
ICC - Russia [IO], Moscow, Russia
Ice Assn; Intl. Packaged [1891]
Ice Assn; Natl. [★1891]
Ice Carving Assn; Natl. [9458]
Ice Cream
Assn. of Ice Cream and Related Products Manufacturers [IO]
Danish Ice Cream Indus. [IO]
Ice Screamers [22041]
Natl. Confed. of Ice Cream Producers [IO]
Ice Cream Alliance [IO], Derby, United Kingdom
Ice Cream Assn; Quality Chekd [★1139]
Ice Cream Connoisseurs Club - Defunct.
Ice Cream Machinery and Supplies Assn; Dairy and [★1133]
Ice Cream Manufacturers; Natl. Assn. of Retail [★1137]

A star before a book entry number signifies that the name is not listed separately, but is mentioned within the entry.

Ice Cream Retailers Assn; Natl. **[1137]**
Ice Cream Retailers Assn; Natl. **[★1137]**
Ice Cream Vendors; Intl. Assn. of **[3970]**
Ice Cream and Yogurt Retailers Assn; Natl. **[★1137]**
Ice Hockey Assn; Intercollegiate **[★23484]**
Ice Hockey Fed; Intl. **[IO]**
Ice Hockey UK **[IO]**, Romford, United Kingdom
Ice Indus; Natl. Assn. of the **[★1891]**
Ice Mgt. Assn; Snow and **[6325]**
Ice Screamers **[22041]**, c/o Judy Snyder, PO Box 465, Warrington, PA 18976, (215)343-2676
Ice Skating Assn. of India **[IO]**, New Delhi, India
Ice Skating Assn. of the United Kingdom; Natl. **[IO]**
Ice Skating Australia **[IO]**, North Strathfield, Australia
Ice Skating Institute **[IO]**, Dallas, TX, United States
Ice Skating Inst. **[3600]**, 17120 N Dallas Pkwy., Ste. 140, Dallas, TX 75248-1187, (972)735-8800
Ice Skating Inst. of Am. **[★3600]**
Ice Skating Inst. of Am. **[★IO]**
Ice Speed Skating New Zealand **[IO]**, Christchurch, New Zealand
Iceberg Athletic Club - Defunct.
Iceland Assn. of Women Entrepreneurs FKA **[IO]**, Reykjavik, Iceland
Iceland Chamber of Commerce **[IO]**, Reykjavik, Iceland
Iceland Music Info. Centre **[IO]**, Reykjavik, Iceland
Iceland Squash Comm. **[IO]**, Reykjavik, Iceland
Iceland Veterans - Defunct.
Icelandic Amateur Theatre Assn. **[IO]**, Reykjavik, Iceland
Icelandic Amer. Chamber of Commerce **[IO]**, New York, NY, United States
Icelandic Amer. Chamber of Commerce **[24282]**, 800 3rd Ave., 36th Fl., New York, NY 10022-7604, (212)593-2700
The Icelandic Aquaculture Assn. **[IO]**, Reykjavik, Iceland
Icelandic Assn. of the Deaf **[IO]**, Reykjavik, Iceland
Icelandic Athletic Fed. **[IO]**, Reykjavik, Iceland
Icelandic Auto. Assn. **[IO]**, Reykjavik, Iceland
Icelandic Bible Soc. **[IO]**, Reykjavik, Iceland
Icelandic Cardiac Soc. **[IO]**, Reykjavik, Iceland
Icelandic Center for Res. **[IO]**, Reykjavik, Iceland
Icelandic Church Aid **[IO]**, Reykjavik, Iceland
Icelandic Comm. for UNICEF **[IO]**, Reykjavik, Iceland
Icelandic Dance Sport Fed. **[IO]**, Reykjavik, Iceland
Icelandic Geotechnical Soc. **[IO]**, Reykjavik, Iceland
Icelandic Heart Assn. **[IO]**, Reykjavik, Iceland
Icelandic Horse Assn. of America - Address unknown since 2006.
Icelandic Horse Cong; U.S. **[4962]**
Icelandic Horse Trekkers **[4893]**
Icelandic League against Rheumatism - Gigtarfelag Islands **[IO]**, Reykjavik, Iceland
Icelandic Lib. and Info. Sci. Assn. **[IO]**, Reykjavik, Iceland
Icelandic Literary Soc. **[IO]**, Reykjavik, Iceland
Icelandic Medical Assn. **[IO]**, Kopavogur, Iceland
Icelandic Mountainbike Club **[IO]**, Reykjavik, Iceland
Icelandic Natl. Gp. of IFPI **[IO]**, Reykjavik, Iceland
Icelandic Nurses' Assn. **[IO]**, Reykjavik, Iceland
Icelandic Orthodontic Soc. **[IO]**, Reykjavik, Iceland
Icelandic Physical Soc. **[IO]**, Reykjavik, Iceland
Icelandic Pony Club and Registry - Defunct.
Icelandic Pony Trekkers **[★4893]**
Icelandic Pre-School Teachers Union **[IO]**, Reykjavik, Iceland
Icelandic Publishers' Assn. **[IO]**, Reykjavik, Iceland
Icelandic Radio Amateurs **[IO]**, Reykjavik, Iceland
Icelandic Red Cross **[IO]**, Reykjavik, Iceland
Icelandic Sailing Assn. **[IO]**, Reykjavik, Iceland
Icelandic Sheepdog Assn. of Am. **[22286]**, 7 S Kansas Ct., Newton, KS 67114
Icelandic Skating Assn. **[IO]**, Reykjavik, Iceland
Icelandic Ski Assn. **[IO]**, Reykjavik, Iceland
Icelandic Soc. for Info. Processing **[IO]**, Reykjavik, Iceland
Icelandic Taekwondo Fed. **[IO]**, Reykjavik, Iceland
Icelandic Teachers' Union **[IO]**, Reykjavik, Iceland
Icelandic Tennis Assn. **[IO]**, Reykjavik, Iceland
Icelandic Weightlifting Fed. **[IO]**, Reykjavik, Iceland
ICES Users Group - Defunct.
ICHCA Intl. Limited **[IO]**, Romford, United Kingdom

Ichthyologists and Herpetologists; Amer. Soc. of **[7158]**
Ichthyology
    Amer. Fisheries Soc. **[7169]**
    Amer. Fisheries Soc. **[IO]**
    Amer. Inst. of Fishery Res. Biologists **[7170]**
    Amer. Soc. of Ichthyologists and Herpetologists **[7158]**
    Aquatic Res. Inst. **[7171]**
    Australian Soc. for Fish Biology **[IO]**
    Bonefish and Tarpon Unlimited **[4987]**
    Environmental and Contamination Res. Center **[7172]**
    European Ichthyological Soc. **[IO]**
    Fed. of Amer. Aquarium Societies **[7173]**
    Intl. Assn. of Astacology **[7174]**
    Intl. Assn. of Astacology **[IO]**
    Natl. Shellfisheries Assn. **[7255]**
    Native Fish Soc. **[5347]**
    North Amer. Native Fishes Assn. **[7175]**
    North Amer. Native Fishes Assn. **[IO]**
    Pacific Ocean Res. Found. **[7176]**
    Soc. for the Protection of Old Fishes **[7177]**
    Society for the Protection of Old Fishes **[IO]**
Ichthyosis Found; Natl. **[★14201]**
Ichthyosis and Related Skin Types; Found. for **[14201]**
Ichud Habonim Dror Labor Zionist Youth **[★20138]**
Ichud Habonim Labor Zionist Youth **[★20138]**
ICIA - Defunct.
ICLARM: The World Fish Center **[★IO]**
ICOM Energy Assn. **[IO]**, Lemington Spa, United Kingdom
ICOMOS Canada **[IO]**, Ottawa, ON, Canada
ICOMOS Documentation Centre **[★IO]**
ICOMOS Documentation Centre **[★10074]**
Ida P. Rolf Found. for Structural Integration **[★13652]**
Idaho Forest Indus. Coun. **[★1608]**
Idaho Potato Commn. **[4735]**, 661 S Rivershore Ln., Eagle, ID 83616-5396, (208)334-2350
Idaho Potato and Onion Commn. **[★4735]**
Idara Aaghosh **[★IO]**
IDB Family Assn. **[19436]**, One Democracy Plz., 6701 Democracy Blvd., Ste. 103, Bethesda, MD 20817, (301)493-6576
IDB Forum **[7736]**, 43588 Wild Ginger Terr., Lansdowne, VA 20176-8439, (571)333-1394
IDC - Address unknown since 2006.
IDEA Hea. and Fitness Assn. **[15965]**, 10455 Pacific Center Ct., San Diego, CA 92121-3773, (858)535-8979
IDEA: Intl. Dance Exercise Assn. **[★15965]**
IDEA: The Assn. for Fitness Professionals **[★15965]**
Idea, The Hea. & Fitness Source **[★15965]**
IDEA, The Hea. and Fitness Source **[★15965]**
IDEA: The Intl. Debate Educ. Assn. **[18677]**, 400 W 59th St., New York, NY 10019, (212)548-0185
Idealism; Inst. for Practical **[★8665]**
Idealist and Action Without Borders **[★17640]**
Idealist and Action Without Borders **[★IO]**
Idealist Intl. - Defunct.
Idealist.org; Action Without Borders/ **[17640]**
IDEAlliance - Intl. Digital Enterprise Alliance **[1773]**, 1421 Prince St., Ste. 230, Alexandria, VA 22314, (703)837-1070
IDEAlliance - Intl. Digital Enterprise Alliance **[IO]**, Alexandria, VA, United States
Ideas Soc; Sharing **[★10905]**
IDEEA Inc. **[★1343]**
IDEEA Inc. **[★IO]**
Ident-A-Pet **[★11463]**
Identification Assn; Personalization and **[★2837]**
Identification Center; Bromeliad **[★22505]**
Identification Center; Bromeliad **[★IO]**
Identification Mfrs; Natl. Assn. of Graphic and Prdt. **[2720]**
Identity Formation; Soc. for Res. on **[8960]**
Identity; Oper. **[11258]**
Identity Theft Rsrc. Center **[18007]**, PO Box 26833, San Diego, CA 92196, (858)693-7935
IDMA **[★IO]**
IDOC/North America - Defunct.
Idol of My Heart Elvis Presley Fan Club - Address unknown since 1995.

IDRA - Intl. Disaster Recovery Assn. **[★7774]**
IDRA - Intl. Disaster Recovery Assn. **[★IO]**
IEC Sys. for Conformity Testing and Certification of Elecl. Equip. **[IO]**, Geneva, Switzerland
IEC Sys. for Conformity Testing to Standards for Safety of Elecl. Equip. **[★IO]**
IEEE Aerospace and Electronics Systems Soc. **[6912]**, c/o IEEE Admission and Advancement Dept., 445 Hoes Ln., Piscataway, NJ 08854-4141, (732)981-0060
IEEE Antennas and Propagation Soc. **[6913]**, c/o Mike Shields, Sec.-Treas., MIT Lincoln Lab., 244 Wood St., Lexington, MA 02421, (781)981-4919
IEEE Broadcast Tech. Soc. **[7768]**, c/o Kathy Colabaugh, Admin., 445 Hoes Ln., PO Box 1331, Piscataway, NJ 08854, (732)562-3906
IEEE Circuits and Systems Soc. **[6914]**, c/o IEEE CASS Executive Off., 445 Hoes Ln., Piscataway, NJ 08854, (732)465-5821
IEEE Communications Soc. **[7769]**, 3 Park Ave., 17th Fl., New York, NY 10016, (212)705-8900
IEEE Components, Hybrids, and Mfg. Tech. Soc. **[★6915]**
IEEE Components, Packaging, and Mfg. Tech. Soc. **[6915]**, 445 Hoes Ln., Piscataway, NJ 08854, (732)562-5529
IEEE Cmpt. Soc. **[6727]**, 1730 Massachusetts Ave. NW, Washington, DC 20036-1992, (202)371-0101
IEEE Consumer Electronics Soc. **[6916]**, c/o Charlotte Kobert, Sec., 4115 Clendenning Rd., Gibsonia, PA 15044
IEEE Control Systems Soc. **[6514]**, 445 Hoes Ln., PO Box 1331, Piscataway, NJ 08855-1331, (732)981-0060
IEEE Dielectrics and Elecl. Insulation Soc. **[6902]**, c/o Hulya Kirkici, VP for Admin., Auburn Univ., Elecl. and Cmpt. Engg., 200 Broun Hall, Auburn, AL 36849-5201, (334)844-5201
IEEE Educ. Soc. **[8262]**, c/o Joseph L.A. Hughes, Pres., Georgia Inst. of Tech., 777 Atlantic Dr. NW, Atlanta, GA 30332, (404)894-2975
IEEE Elecl. Insulation Soc. **[★6902]**
IEEE Electromagnetic Compatibility Soc. **[6917]**, c/o Bruce Archambeault, Awards Chm., PO Box 12195, Research Triangle Park, NC 27709, (919)486-0120
IEEE Electron Devices Soc. **[6918]**, c/o IEEE Operations Center, 445 Hoes Ln., Piscataway, NJ 08854, (732)562-3926
IEEE Engg. Mgt. Soc. **[7014]**, c/o IEEE Admission and Advancement, 445 Hoes Ln., PO Box 6804, Piscataway, NJ 08855-6804, (732)981-0025
IEEE Engg. in Medicine and Biology Soc. **[6608]**, 445 Hoes Ln., Piscataway, NJ 08855-1331, (732)981-3433
IEEE Engg. in Medicine and Biology Soc. **[IO]**, Piscataway, NJ, United States
IEEE Geoscience and Remote Sensing Soc. **[7144]**, c/o IEEE Admission and Advancement Dept., PO Box 6804, Piscataway, NJ 08854-6804, (206)685-7537
IEEE Indus. Electronics Soc. **[6919]**, c/o Dr. John Y. Hung, Treas., Elecl. Engg. Dept., Auburn Univ., Auburn, AL 36849-5201, (334)844-1813
IEEE Industrial Electronics Society **[IO]**, Auburn, AL, United States
IEEE Indus. Applications Soc. **[7183]**, 799 N Beverly Glen, Los Angeles, CA 90077, (310)446-8280
IEEE Info. Theory Gp. **[7770]**, c/o IEEE Corporate Off., 3 Park Ave., 17th Fl., New York, NY 10016-5997, (212)419-7900
IEEE Info. Theory Soc. **[★7770]**
IEEE Instrumentation and Measurement Soc. **[7219]**, c/o Ruth A. Dyer, PhD, VP of Membership, Kansas State Univ., 106 Anderson Hall, Manhattan, KS 66506, (785)532-6224
IEEE Lasers and Electro-Optics Soc. **[6920]**, 445 Hoes Ln., Piscataway, NJ 08854-1331, (732)562-3891
IEEE Lasers and Electro-Optics Society **[IO]**, Piscataway, NJ, United States
IEEE Magnetics Soc. **[6921]**, c/o IEEE Membership Development, 445 Hoes Ln., PO Box 459, Piscataway, NJ 08855-0459, (908)981-0060
IEEE Microwave Theory and Techniques Soc. **[7337]**, c/o IEEE Corporate Off., 3 Park Ave., 17th Fl., New York, NY 10016-5997, (212)705-7900

Reference to "IO" in place of a book number signifies that the association may be found in the 45th edition of International Organizations.

IEEE Neural Networks Coun. [★7009]
IEEE Nuclear and Plasma Sciences Soc. [7386], 445 Hoes Ln., PO Box 6801, Piscataway, NJ 08855, (212)419-7900
IEEE Oceanic Engg. Soc. [7397], c/o Kenneth Ferer, 114 S Fork Ct., Hertford, NC 27944, (252)426-1226
IEEE Power Electronics Coun. [★6922]
IEEE Power Electronics Soc. [6922], c/o Robert Myers, Exec. Dir., 799 N Beverly Glen, Los Angeles, CA 90077, (310)592-5431
IEEE Power Engg. Soc. [6903], c/o IEEE Operations Center, 445 Hoes Ln., Piscataway, NJ 08854-1331, (732)562-3883
IEEE Professional Commun. Soc. [6923], PO Box 6804, Piscataway, NJ 08854-6804, (732)981-0060
IEEE Reliability Soc. [6924], c/o IEEE Corporate Off. , 3 Park Ave., 17th Fl., New York, NY 10016-5997, (212)419-7900
IEEE Robotics and Automation Soc. [7582], c/o Ms. Rosalyn Graham Snyder, Admin., 3603 Octavia St., Raleigh, NC 27606, (919)851-3603
IEEE Signal Processing Soc. [6365], 445 Hoes Ln., Piscataway, NJ 08854-4141, (732)562-3888
IEEE Soc. Social Implications of Tech. [7737], c/o IEEE Corporate Off., 445 Hoes Ln., Piscataway, NJ 08855-0459, (732)981-0060
IEEE Solid-State Circuits Coun. [★6904]
IEEE Solid-State Circuits Soc. [6904], c/o Katherine Olstein, Admin., 445 Hoes Ln., Piscataway, NJ 08855-1331, (732)981-3400
IEEE Sonics and Ultrasonics Soc. [★6366]
IEEE Systems, Man, and Cybernetics Soc. [6728], c/o IEEE Admission and Advancement Dept., 3 Park Ave., 17th Fl., New York, NY 10016-5997, (212)419-7900
IEEE Ultrasonics, Ferroelectrics, and Frequency Control Soc. [6366], c/o IEEE Operations Center, 445 Hoes Ln., Piscataway, NJ 08854-4141, (732)981-0060
IEEE Vehicular Tech. Soc. [6925], c/o IEEE Admission and Advancement, PO Box 6804, Piscataway, NJ 08855-6804, (732)981-0225
IES, Inst. for the Intl. Educ. of Students [8405], 33 N LaSalle St., 15th Fl., Chicago, IL 60602-2602, (312)944-1750
IES, Inst. for the Intl. Educ. of Students [IO], Chicago, IL, United States
IETF [★IO]
IETF [★15331]
IFA Aquaculture [IO], Bluebell, Ireland
IFA Assn. [★IO]
Ifa Fish Farming Sect. [★IO]
IFCA Intl. [IO], Grandville, MI, United States
IFCA Intl. [19849], PO Box 810, Grandville, MI 49468-0810, (616)531-1840
IFDA Educational Found. [★2264]
IFDA Educational Found. [★IO]
IFDC - An Intl. Center for Soil Fertility and Agricultural Development [IO], Muscle Shoals, AL, United States
IFDC - An Intl. Center for Soil Fertility and Agricultural Development [4665], PO Box 2040, Muscle Shoals, AL 35662, (256)381-6600
IFO Institut fur Wirtschaftsforschung [★IO]
IFO Inst. for Economic Res. [IO], Munich, Germany
IFPA Film and Video Communicators [★IO]
IFPA Film and Video Communicators [★1384]
IFRA [IO], Darmstadt, Germany
IFS Nepal Children Welfare Prog. [IO], Kathmandu, Nepal
Iglesia De Malabo [★IO]
Iglesias Fan Club; Amer. Friends of Julio [24833]
Iglesias, Julio
    Amer. Friends of Julio Iglesias Fan Club [24833]
    Friends of Julio Intl. [24894]
    Julio - Am. Fan Club [24834]
    Official Julio Iglesias Intl. Fan Club [24835]
Ignation Soc. - Defunct.
Igorot Global Org. [10225], PO Box 4471, West Covina, CA 91791, (626)919-1094
Igorot Global Org. [IO], West Covina, CA, United States
IHM Volunteer Prog. of the Sisters, Servants of the Immaculate Heart of Mary [20346], IHM Center, 2300 Adams Ave., Scranton, PA 18509, (570)346-5413

IHM Volunteer Services of the Sisters, Servants of the Immaculate Heart of Mary; We Care - [★20346]
IHRA Motor-cycle Assn. - Defunct.
IHRA World Championship Series [★23077]
IIE/Europe [IO], Budapest, Hungary
IIEC-Asia [IO], Bangkok, Thailand
IIEC; CERF/ [★6699]
IISRP [★3432]
IISRP [★IO]
Ijaw Natl. Alliance of the Americas [12639], PO Box 24435, Brooklyn, NY 11202-4435
Ikatan Ahli Ilmu Faal Indonesia [★IO]
Ikatan Penerbit Indonesia [★IO]
Ikatan Sarjana Wanita Indonesia [IO], Jakarta, Indonesia
Ikatan Sekretaris Indonesia [IO], Jakarta, Indonesia
Ikebana Intl. [IO], Tokyo, Japan
Ikenobo Ikebana Soc. of Japan - Address unknown since 1995.
Iklimlendirme Sogutma Klima Imalatcilari Dernegi [★IO]
Il Circolo Italiano [★24614]
ILA, AFL-CIO; Intl. Org. of Masters, Mates and Pilots, [24128]
ILEIA: Centre for Info. on Low External Input and Sustainable Agriculture [IO], Amersfoort, Netherlands
Ileitis and Colitis; Found. for [★14414]
Ileitis and Colitis; Natl. Found. for [★14414]
Ileitis and Colitis; Reach Out for Youth with [16548]
Ileostomy and Internal Pouch Support Gp. [IO], Ballyclare, United Kingdom
Ill for Animal Res; Incurably [13697]
Ill Kids; Natl. Org. for Chronically [★11638]
Illinois Archaeology; Found. for [★6442]
Illinois Central Railroad Historical Soc. [10120], PO Box 288, Paxton, IL 60957
Illness and Loss (Division of Found. of Thanatology); Amer. Inst. of Life Threatening [11908]
Illness; Natl. Found. for Depressive [15225]
Illuminating and Allied Glassware Mfrs. Assn. - Defunct.
Illuminating Companies; Assn. of Edison [3952]
Illuminating Engg. Res. Inst. [★7251]
Illuminating Engg. Soc. [★IO]
Illuminating Engg. Soc. of North Am. [7250], 120 Wall St., 17th Fl., New York, NY 10005-4001, (212)248-5000
Illumination Comm. of Great Britain; Natl. [IO]
Illumination; U.S. Natl. Comm. of the Intl. Commn. on [7252]
Illusion Theater [12030], 528 Hennepin Ave., Ste. 704, Minneapolis, MN 55403, (612)339-4944
Illusion Theater and School [★12030]
Illustrators; Amer. Soc. of Architectural [289]
Illustrators; Assn. of [IO]
Illustrators; Assn. of Medical [13707]
Illustrators; Guild of Natural Sci. [7153]
Illustrators; Soc. of [9527]
Illustrators; Soc. of Children's Book Writers and [11194]
Image Consultants; Assn. of [★957]
Image Consultants; Assn. of Fashion and [★957]
Image Consultants Intl; Assn. of [957]
Image Indus. Coun. International/Institute for Image Mgt. [964], PO Box 190007, San Francisco, CA 94119, (415)863-2573
Image Industry Council International/Institute for Image Management [IO], San Francisco, CA, United States
Image Mgt; Assn. for Info. and [★2095]
Image; Natl. [19102]
IMAGE Soc. [6729], PO Box 6221, Chandler, AZ 85246-6221
Imagers; Independent Photo [2998]
Imaginary Basketball Fed. - Address unknown since 2001.
Imagine Canada [IO], Toronto, ON, Canada
Imagine Canada [IO], Toronto, ON, Canada
Imagine World Hea. [IO], Ponte Vedra Beach, FL, United States
Imagine World Hea. [14566], 105 E Dolphin Blvd., Ponte Vedra Beach, FL 32082-1714, (904)285-0240

Imaging; Acad. of Molecular [15150]
Imaging Assn; Automated [7581]
Imaging Assn; Digital Printing and [1764]
Imaging Assn; Optical [2735]
Imaging Assn; Pacific Printing and [1783]
Imaging; Coun. on Diagnostic [16288]
Imaging and Geospatial Info. Soc; ASPRS - The [7495]
Imaging Mfrs. Assn; Photographic and [★3002]
Imaging Media
    Canadian Imaging Trade Assn. [IO]
    DICOM Standards Comm. [7178]
    Intl. Soc. for Magnetic Resonance in Medicine - German Chap. [IO]
    Law Enforcement Thermographers' Assn. [5982]
    Pacific Printing and Imaging Assn. [1783]
    UK Indus. Vision Assn. [IO]
    WHTour [IO]
Imaging; North Amer. Soc. for Cardiac [13920]
Imaging Sci. and Tech; Soc. for [7497]
Imaging Soc; Computerized Medical [16287]
Imaging Supplies Coalition [5845], 1435 E Venice Ave., No. 104, MBN 249, Venice, FL 34292, (941)961-7897
Imaging Supplies Coalition [IO], Avalon, NJ, United States
Imaging Technologies Assn. - Address unknown since 2008.
IMAGO - European Fed. of Cinematographers [IO], Tallinn, Estonia
IMCR Dispute Resolution Center [★5455]
IMDR [★5000]
IMDR [★IO]
Immaculata Movement; Militia of the [19660]
Immaculate Heart of Mary; IHM Volunteer Prog. of the Sisters, Servants of the [20346]
Immaculate Heart of Mary; Reparation Soc. of the [19709]
Immaculate Heart of Mary; We Care - IHM Volunteer Services of the Sisters, Servants of the [★20346]
Immaculate Mary Fan Club - Defunct.
Immigrant Aid Soc; Hebrew Sheltering and [★12471]
Immigrant Genealogical Soc. [21121], PO Box 7369, Burbank, CA 91510-7369, (818)848-3122
Immigrant Genealogical Soc. [IO], Burbank, CA, United States
Immigrant Lib. [★IO]
Immigrant Lib. [★21121]
Immigrant and Visible Minority Women Against Abuse [★IO]
Immigrant Women Services Ottawa [IO], Ottawa, ON, Canada
Immigrants; Rav Tov Comm. to Aid New [★12817]
Immigrants' Rights; Natl. Center for [★17807]
Immigration
    Afghan Community in Am. [12801]
    Afghan Women Counselling and Integration Community Support Org. [IO]
    Amer. Civic Assn. [12403]
    Amer. Coun. on Intl. Personnel [1252]
    Amer. Fund for Czechoslovak Relief [12802]
    Amer. Immigration Control Found. [17800]
    Amer. Immigration Law Found. [5806]
    Amer. Immigration Lawyers Assn. [5807]
    Americans for Better Immigration [17801]
    Americans for Immigration Control [17802]
    Assn. for New Canadians [IO]
    The Blue Card [12468]
    Calgary Immigrant Women's Assn. [IO]
    Canadian Assn. of Professional Immigration Consultants [IO]
    Canadian Ukrainian Immigrant Aid Soc. [IO]
    Catholic Legal Immigration Network [20089]
    Center for Commun. Programs [12755]
    Center for Equal Opportunity [10216]
    Center for Immigration Stud. [17803]
    Centre for Medical, Legal and Cultural Assistance for Foreigners in Austria [IO]
    Chinese-American Arts Coun. [9608]
    CitizensLobby.com [18435]
    Comm. for Humanitarian Assistance to Iranian Refugees [12808]
    Conf. on Jewish Material Claims Against Germany [12470]
    Ellis Island Medal of Honor Soc. [19044]

A star before a book entry number signifies that the name is not listed separately, but is mentioned within the entry.

Emerald Isle Immigration Center [17804]
Emerald Isle Immigration Center [IO]
Estonian Relief Comm. [12853]
Fed. for Amer. Immigration Reform [17805]
Federation for American Immigration Reform [IO]
Immigration Advisory Ser. [IO]
Immigration Equality [12237]
Immigration and Refugee Services of Am. [12404]
Immigration and Refugee Services of Am. [IO]
Indo-Canadian Women's Assn. [IO]
Intl. Rescue Comm. - USA [12812]
Israeli Assn. for Immigrant Children [IO]
Joint Coun. for the Welfare of Immigrants [IO]
Legal Immigrant Assn. [5808]
Liberty's Promise [5809]
Lutheran Immigration and Refugee Ser. [12815]
Natl. Center for Urban Ethnic Affairs [11753]
Natl. Coalition of Anti-Deportation Campaigns [IO]
Natl. Ethnic Coalition of Organizations [19046]
Natl. Immigration Forum [17806]
Natl. Immigration Forum [IO]
National Immigration Law Center [IO]
Natl. Immigration Law Center [17807]
Natl. Immigration Proj. of the Natl. Lawyers Guild
  [5810]
Natl. Network to End Violence Against Immigrant
  Women [13433]
Natl. Network for Immigrant and Refugee Rights
  [17808]
Negative Population Growth [12756]
New York Assn. for New Americans [12479]
Nordic Immigration Comm. [IO]
Political Ecology Group [17502]
Population Action Intl. [12758]
Population Commun. [12759]
Population Connection [12761]
Population Coun. [12762]
Population-Environment Balance [12763]
Population Inst. [12764]
Population Rsrc. Center [12765]
ProjectUSA [17809]
Racial Justice 911 [18493]
Rav Tov Intl. Jewish Rescue Org. [12817]
Refugee Coun. USA [18500]
Refugees Intl. [12818]
Res. Found. for Jewish Immigration [10469]
Southeast Asia Rsrc. Action Center [12820]
Spanish Refugee Aid [12821]
Tibetan Aid Proj. [12822]
United to Secure Am. [18596]
U.S. Border Control [17810]
U.S. Catholic Conference/Migration and Refugee
  Services [12823]
Upwardly Global [3186]
Immigration Advisory Ser. [IO], London, United
  Kingdom
Immigration and Citizenship Conf; Amer. [★17806]
Immigration Equality [12237], 40 Exchange Pl., 17th
  Fl., New York, NY 10005, (212)714-2904
Immigration and Ethnic History Soc. [10121], c/o
  Betty A. Bergland, Sec., Univ. of Wisconsin, Dept.
  of History, River Falls, WI 54022, (715)425-3164
Immigration and Ethnic History Soc. [IO], River
  Falls, WI, United States
Immigration and History Soc. [★IO]
Immigration and History Soc. [★10121]
Immigration and Nationality Lawyers; Assn. of
  [★5807]
Immigration Reform Movement; Irish [★17804]
Immigration Refugee Citizenship Forum; Natl.
  [★17806]
Immigration and Refugee Ser; Lutheran [12815]
Immigration and Refugee Services of Am. [12404],
  c/o U.S. Comm. for Refugees and Immigrants,
  1717 Massachusetts Ave. NW, 2nd Fl.,
  Washington, DC 20036, (202)347-3507
Immigration and Refugee Services of Am. [IO],
  Washington, DC, United States
Immigration; Res. Found. for Jewish [10469]
Immigration Rights Task Force; Lesbian and Gay
  [★12237]
Immigration Union; Canada Employment and [IO]
Immortalist Soc. [6845], 24355 Sorrentino Ct., Clin-
  ton Township, MI 48035, (586)791-5961
Immortality; Intl. Inst. for the Stud. of Death and
  [★13315]

Immune Deficiency
  Amer. Found. for AIDS Res. [13557]
  Ataxia Telangiectasia Children's Proj. [14253]
  CFIDS Assn. of Am. [14256]
  Fed. of Clinical Immunology Societies [14935]
  Gay Men's Hea. Crisis [13564]
  Haitian Coalition on AIDS [13567]
  Natl. Jewish Medical and Res. Center [16361]
  Norwegian Immune Deficiency Found. [IO]
  Primary Immunodeficiency Assn. [IO]
  Vasculitis Found. [16552]
Immune Deficiency Found. [14936], 40 W
  Chesapeake Ave., Ste. 308, Towson, MD 21204,
  (410)321-6647
Immunization Action Coalition [14937], 1573 Selby
  Ave., Ste. 234, St. Paul, MN 55104, (651)647-9009
Immunization; Natl. Coalition for Adult [14583]
Immunogenetics; Amer. Soc. for Histocompatibility
  and [14931]
Immunologists; Amer. Assn. of Veterinary [16752]
Immunology
  Amer. Acad. of Allergy, Asthma and Immunology
    [13592]
  Amer. Acad. of Otolaryngic Allergy and Found.
    [13593]
  Amer. Assn. of Certified Allergists [13594]
  Amer. Assn. of Immunologists [14929]
  Amer. Autoimmune Related Diseases Assn.
    [14930]
  Amer. Bd. of Allergy and Immunology [13595]
  Amer. Coll. of Allergy, Asthma and Immunology
    [13596]
  Amer. Soc. for Histocompatibility and Immunoge-
    netics [14931]
  Assn. of Medical Lab. Immunologists [14932]
  Asthma and Allergy Found. of Am. [13598]
  Australasian Soc. of Clinical Immunology and Al-
    lergy [IO]
  British Soc. for Immunology [IO]
  Canadian Soc. of Allergy and Clinical Immunology
    [IO]
  Canadian Soc. for Immunology [IO]
  Chronic Syndrome Support Assn. [14259]
  Clinical Immunology Soc. [14933]
  European Fed. of Immunological Societies [IO]
  European Soc. for Immunodeficiencies [IO]
  European Soc. of Reproductive and Development
    Immunology [IO]
  Evans Syndrome Research and Support Group
    [IO]
  Evans Syndrome Res. and Support Gp. [14934]
  Every Child By Two [13959]
  Fed. of Clinical Immunology Societies [14935]
  Fed. of Immunological Societies of Asia-Oceania
    [IO]
  Immune Deficiency Found. [14936]
  Immunization Action Coalition [14937]
  Immunology of Diabetes Soc. [14225]
  Intl. Complement Soc. [14938]
  Intl. Complement Soc. [IO]
  Intl. Correspondence Soc. of Allergists and Clini-
    cal Immunologists [13601]
  Intl. Endotoxin and Innate Immunity Soc. [7803]
  Intl. Patient Assn. for Primary Immunodeficiencies
    [IO]
  Intl. Soc. of Exercise and Immunology [IO]
  Intl. Union of Immunological Societies [IO]
  Jeffrey Modell Found. [14939]
  Joint Coun. of Allergy, Asthma and Immunology
    [13602]
  Natl. Assn. on HIV Over Fifty [14952]
  Natl. Immunotherapy Cancer Res. Found. [14940]
  Natl. Jewish Medical and Res. Center [16361]
  Natl. Network for Immunization Info. [14941]
  Natl. Partnership for Immunization [14942]
  Natl. Vaccine Info. Center [13972]
  Nightingale Res. Found. [IO]
  Norwegian Soc. for Immunology [IO]
  Scandinavian Soc. for Immunology [IO]
  Society for Mucosal Immunology [IO]
  Soc. for Mucosal Immunology [14943]
  Task Force for Child Survival and Development
    [12542]
  Think Twice Global Vaccine Inst. [14944]
  Transverse Myelitis Assn. [15368]

  Vasculitis Found. [16552]
  World Allergy Org. [13605]
Immunology and Allergy; Amer. Assn. for Clinical
  [★13596]
Immunology; Amer. Acad. of Allergy, Asthma and
  [13592]
Immunology; Amer. Bd. of Allergy and [13595]
Immunology; Amer. Coll. of Allergy and [★13596]
Immunology; Amer. Coll. of Allergy, Asthma and
  [13596]
Immunology of Diabetes Soc. [14225], c/o Matthias
  Von Herrath, Treas., La Jolla Inst. of Allergy & Im-
  munology, 9420 Athena Cir., La Jolla, CA 92037,
  (858)205-0646
Immunology; European Soc. of Paediatric Allergy
  and Clinical [IO]
Immunology; Intl. Assn. of Allergology and Clinical
  [★13605]
Immunology; Joint Coun. of Allergy, Asthma and
  [13602]
Immunology and Respiratory Medicine; Natl. Jewish
  Center for [★16361]
Impac - Address unknown since 1999.
Impact on Hunger - Address unknown since 1988.
Impaired Drivers; Citizens Against Drug [13230]
Impaired Enterprisers; Independent Visually [16855]
Impaired; Natl. Accreditation Coun. for Agencies
  Serving the Blind and Visually [16870]
Impaired; Natl. Assn. for Parents of the Visually
  [★16873]
Impaired Physician Prog. [13246], c/o Talbott
  Recovery Campus, 5448 Yorketowne Dr., Atlanta,
  GA 30349, (770)994-0185
Impairment; Coun. of Families with Visual [16844]
Impairments; Div. on Visual [9145]
Impairments; Natl. Assn. for Parents of Children With
  Visual [16873]
Impala Assn; Natl. [21733]
IMPALA (Intl. Motion Picture and Lecturers Assn.);
  Travelogues by [★1386]
Impartial Justice; Citizens for [17957]
Imperial Byzantine Soc. - Address unknown since
  1995.
Imperial Club; Online [21750]
Imperial Coun. of the Ancient Arabic Order of the
  Nobles of the Mystic Shrine for North Am. [19238],
  c/o Intl. Shriners HQ, 2900 Rocky Point Dr.,
  Tampa, FL 33607-1460, (813)281-0300
Imperial Court - Daughters of Isis - Address
  unknown since 1995.
Imperial German Military Collector's Assn. - Defunct.
Imperial Glass Collectors Soc. [★22565]
Imperial Glass Collectors Soc; Natl. [22565]
Imperial Inst. [★IO]
Imperial Klingon Embassy/Star Trek - Address
  unknown since 2004.
Imperial Order of the Dragon - Defunct.
Imperial Owners Club, Intl. - Defunct.
Imperial Soc. of Teachers of Dancing [★IO]
Imperial Soc. of Teachers of Dancing [IO], London,
  United Kingdom
Imperial Valley Dune Buggy Assn. - Address
  unknown since 1995.
Imperial War Graves Commn. [★IO]
Imperialist; Vietnam Veterans Against the War Anti-
  [18785]
Implant Dentistry; Amer. Acad. of [14101]
Implant Dentures; Amer. Acad. of [★14101]
Implant Prosthodontics; Amer. Acad. of [14102]
Implant Soc; Amer. Intra-Ocular [★15665]
Implantologists; Intl. Coll. of Oral [★14165]
Implants and Transplants; Acad. for [14087]
Implements
  Amer. Collectors of Infant Feeders [21959]
  Amer. Edge Collectors Assn. [22612]
  Amer. Spoon Collectors [21966]
  Case Collectors Club [22613]
  Cast Iron Seat Collectors Assn. [22607]
  Intermuseum Conservation Assn. [10505]
  Mid-West Tool Collectors Assn. [22608]
  Natl. Reamer Collectors Assn. [22609]
  Potomac Antique Tools and Indus. Assn. [22610]
  World Atlatl Assn. [22611]
  World Atlatl Assn. [IO]
Import Comm. of the Amer. Paper Industry - Defunct.

Reference to "IO" in place of a book number signifies that the association may be found in the 45th edition of International Organizations.

Import Shippers Assn; Amer. [3557]
Imported Auto. Dealers Assn; Amer. [★404]
Imported Car Gp. [★343]
Imported Car Gp. [★IO]
Imported Hardwood Plywood Assn. [★IO]
Imported Hardwood Plywood Assn. [★1609]
Imported Hardwood Plywood Assn. of Am. [★1609]
Imported Hardwood Plywood Assn. of Am. [★IO]
Imported Hardwood Products Assn. [★IO]
Imported Hardwood Products Assn. [★1609]
Imported Tyre Mfrs'. Assn. [IO], London, United
Kingdom
Importers of Am; Auto. [★343]
Importers; Amer. Assn. of Exporters and [2297]
Importers Assn. of Am; Cheese [1131]
Importers Assn. of Am; Diamond Mfrs. and [2362]
Importers Assn. of Am; Woodworking Machinery
[★2081]
Importers Assn; Amer. [★2297]
Importers Assn; Amer. Flower [★1489]
Importers Assn; Asian Amer. [226]
Importers Assn; Oriental Rug [2272]
Importers Assn. of the U.S; Amer. [2298]
Importers and Breeders of Belgian Draft Horses;
Amer. Assn. of [★4865]
Importers Coun. of Am; Meat [2660]
Importers' Coun; Meat [★2660]
Importers and Exporters Assn. of Taipei [IO], Taipei,
Taiwan
Importers; Natl. Assn. of Alcoholic Beverage [★206]
Importers; Natl. Assn. of Beverage [206]
Importers; Natl. Coun. of Amer. [★2297]
Importers of Textiles and Apparel; U.S. Assn. of
[3807]
Importing
North Amer. Importers Assn. [2311]
Sporting Goods Shippers Assn. [3590]
Imports; Coalition for Fair Lumber [1641]
Impotence
Intl. Soc. for Sexual Medicine [IO]
Sexual Dysfunction Assn. [IO]
Soc. for the Stud. of Male Reproduction [16344]
Impotence Assn. [★IO]
Impotence Inst. of America - Address unknown since
2004.
Imprisoned Persons; People Organized to Stop
Rape of [★11894]
Improved Benevolent Protective Order of Elks of the
World [19036], PO Box 159, Winton, NC 27986,
(252)358-7661
Improved Benevolent Protective Order of Elks of the
World [IO], Winton, NC, United States
Improved Learning Environments; Center for
[★9085]
Improvement Assn; Young Women's Mutual
[★20209]
Improvement Coun; Natl. Home [★643]
Impuls - Vorming, Training en Procesbeheer [IO],
Aarschot, Belgium
Impulse Intl. Auto Club - Defunct.
IMS Forum [7771], 211 Summit Pl., No. 292, Silver-
thorne, CO 80498, (970)262-6100
IMS Forum [IO], Fremont, CA, United States
IMTEC - Intl. Learning Cooperative [★IO]
IMZ Intl. Music Media Centre [IO], Vienna, Austria
IMZ Internationales Musik Medienzentrum [★IO]
IMZ - Vienna [★IO]
Imzadi Intl. - Address unknown since 2000.
In Appreciation of the Hollies - Defunct.
In Coun. on Hotel, Restaurant and Institutional Educ.
[★8525]
In Coun. on Hotel, Restaurant and Institutional Educ.
[★IO]
In Defense of Animals [11413], 3010 Kerner Blvd.,
San Rafael, CA 94901, (415)388-9641
In Kind Canada [IO], Mississauga, ON, Canada
In Our Own Way - Address unknown since 2004.
In-Plant Mgt. Assn. [★1776]
In-Plant Mgt. Assn. [★IO]
In-Vitro Diagnostics Assn; British [IO]
INADES Formation Intl. - Kenya [IO], Machakos,
Kenya
Inbred Livestock Registry Assn. - Address unknown
since 1999.
Inca-Fiej Res. Assn. [★IO]

Incandescent Lamp Mfrs. Assn. - Defunct.
Incarcerated Mothers; Aid to [11851]
Incarnate Word Missionaries - Congregation of the
Sisters of Charity of the Incarnate Word; CCVI
[19607]
Incentive Fed. [2629], 5008 Castlerock Way, Naples,
FL 34112-7926, (239)775-7527
Incentive Mfrs. and Representatives Alliance [2536],
1601 N Bond St., Ste. 303, Naperville, IL 60563,
(630)369-7786
Incentive Mfrs. and Representatives Assn. [★2536]
Incentive Travel Executives; Soc. of [★3935]
Incest Anonymous; Survivors of [13085]
Incest Concerned Effort; Victims of [★13086]
Incest Natl. Network; Rape, Abuse and [12791]
Incest Survivors Anonymous [13076]
Incest Survivors Anonymous [IO], Long Beach, CA,
United States
Incest Survivors Resource Network, Intl. - Address
unknown since 2006.
Incineration; Coalition for Responsible Waste [3990]
Incinerator Inst. of America - Defunct.
INCITE! Women of Color Against Violence [18788],
PO Box 226, Redmond, WA 98073, (484)932-3166
INCITS - InterNational Comm. for Info. Tech.
Standards [7738], c/o Info. Tech. Indus. Coun.,
1250 Eye St. NW, Ste. 200, Washington, DC
20005-5977, (202)737-8888
Inclusion Intl. [IO], London, United Kingdom
Inclusion Ireland [IO], Dublin, Ireland
INCODA - Defunct.
Income Housing Coalition; Ad Hoc Low [★12330]
Incontinence
Continence Restored, Inc. [16707]
Intl. Continence Soc. [IO]
Pull-thru Network [14427]
Simon Found. for Continence [16711]
Incontinent People; Help for [★16709]
Incontinentia Pigmenti Found; Natl. [14470]
Incontinentia Pigmenti Found; Natl. [★14455]
Incontinentia Pigmenti Intl. Found. [14455], c/o Sus-
anne Bross Emmerich, Founder/Exec. Dir., 30 E
72nd St., New York, NY 10021, (212)452-1231
Incontinentia Pigmenti Intl. Found. [IO], New York,
NY, United States
Inconvenienced Sportsmen's Assn; Natl. [★23343]
Incorporated Assn. of Architects and Surveyors
[★IO]
Incorporated Assn. of Asst. Masters in Secondary
Schools [★IO]
Incorporated Assn. of Organists [IO], Birmingham,
United Kingdom
Incorporated Assn. of Preparatory Schools [IO],
Leamington Spa, United Kingdom
Incorporated Phonographic Soc. [IO], Harrow, United
Kingdom
Incorporated Soc. of British Advertisers [IO], London,
United Kingdom
Incorporated Soc. of Irish/American Lawyers [5939],
c/o Stacey Harb, 15140 Farmington Rd., Livonia,
MI 48154
Incorporated Soc. of Musicians [IO], London, United
Kingdom
Incorporated Soc. of Organ Builders - England [IO],
Hebden Bridge, United Kingdom
Incubation Assn; Natl. Bus. [746]
Incurably Ill for Animal Res. [13697], 2510
Champion Way, Lansing, MI 48910, (517)887-1141
INDA, Assn. of the Nonwoven Fabrics Indus. [3785],
PO Box 1288, Cary, NC 27512-1288, (919)233-
1210
Indenlandsk Somandsmission [★IO]
INDENT, Dutch Dental Assn. [IO], Zoetermeer,
Netherlands
Independence; Community Found. for [★17219]
Independence for the Disabled and Elderly; P.R.I.
D.E. Found. - Promote Real [11982]
Independence Dogs - Defunct.
Independence; Extensions for [11945]
Independence Inst. [17120], 13952 Denver W Pkwy.,
Ste. 400, Golden, CO 80401, (303)279-6536
Independence; New Avenues to [12578]
Independence Plan for Neighborhood Councils
[17219], 201 W Maple, Independence, MO 64050,
(816)833-4225

Independence Seaport Museum [21266], Penn's
Landing, 211 S Columbus Blvd., Walnut St.,
Philadelphia, PA 19106, (215)413-8655
Independence Think Tank [★17219]
Independence for Women; Justice, Economic Dignity
and [18812]
Independent Action - Address unknown since 1999.
Independent Aeronautical Dealers Assn. - Defunct.
Independent Air Carriers Assn. - Defunct.
Independent Airforwarder and Cargo Agents Coun. -
Defunct.
Independent Airlines Assn. - Address unknown since
1995.
Independent Aluminum Residential Fabricators Assn.
- Defunct.
Independent Americans [17294], 704 W 1100 S,
Payson, UT 84651, (801)465-3228
Independent Armored Car Operators Assn. [3568],
7101 N Mesa St., No. 518, El Paso, TX 79912-
3613, (661)726-9864
Independent Artists; Natl. Assn. of [9513]
Independent Assn. of German Dentists [IO], Bonn,
Germany
Independent Assn. of Publishers' Employees
[24174], 5 Schalks Crossing Rd., Ste. 220, Plains-
boro, NJ 08536, (609)275-6020
Independent Assn. of Questioned Document
Examiners [5762], c/o Julie C. Edison, PO Box
1231, McLean, VA 22101-1231, (703)437-9801
Independent Assn. of Stocking Mfrs. - Defunct.
Independent Auto. Dealers Assn; Natl. [423]
Independent Automotive Damage Appraisers Assn.
[281], PO Box 12291, Columbus, GA 31917-2291,
(800)369-4232
Independent Automotive Ser. Assn. [★410]
Independent Bakers Assn. [452], PO Box 3731,
Washington, DC 20007, (202)333-8190
Independent Bakery Employees Union - Address
unknown since 2003.
Independent Bank Equip. and Systems Assn; Natl.
[★476]
Independent Bankers Assn. of Am. [★480]
Independent Bankers; Western [500]
Independent Bar Assn. - Defunct.
Independent Battery Mfrs. Assn. - Defunct.
Independent Bd. for Presbyterian Foreign Missions
[20467], PO Box 1346, Blue Bell, PA 19422-0435,
(610)279-0952
Independent Bus. Alliance [★3602]
Independent Bus; Natl. Fed. of [3622]
Independent Catholic Churches Intl. [20497], 1035
Indiana St., Vallejo, CA 94590, (707)853-0440
Independent Catholic Churches Intl. [IO], Vallejo,
CA, United States
Independent Charities of Am. [1688], 1100 Larkspur
Landing Cir., Ste. 340, Larkspur, CA 94939,
(415)924-1108
Independent Cinema Artists and Producers -
Defunct.
Independent Citizens Res. Found. for the Study of
Degenerative Diseases [14263]
Independent Cold Extruders Inst. - Defunct.
Independent Coll. Funds of Am. [★8537]
Independent Coll. and Univ. Presidents; Amer. Assn.
of [★8534]
Independent Colleges and Schools; Accrediting
Coun. for [7874]
Independent Colleges and Universities; Fed. of State
Associations of [★8539]
Independent Colleges and Universities; Natl. Coun.
of [★8539]
Independent Colleges and Universities; Natl. Inst. of
[★8539]
Independent Commercial Producers; Assn. of [90]
Independent Community Bankers of Am. [480], 1615
L St. NW, Ste. 900, Washington, DC 20036,
(202)659-8111
Independent Community Consultants - Defunct.
Independent Cmpt. Consultants Assn. [902], 11131
S Towne Sq., Ste. F, St. Louis, MO 63123,
(314)892-1675
Independent Conservative Party - Defunct.
Independent Contractors of Australia [IO], Oakleigh,
Australia
Independent Cosmetic Manufacturers and Distribu-
tors [1847], 1220 W Northwest Hwy., Palatine, IL
60067, (847)991-4499

A star before a book entry number signifies that the name is not listed separately, but is mentioned within the entry.

Independent Curators Incorporated [★9444]

Independent Curators Incorporated [★IO]

Independent Curators Intl. [IO], New York, NY, United States

Independent Curators Intl. [9444], 799 Broadway, Ste. 205, New York, NY 10003, (212)254-8200

Independent Data Communications Mfrs. Assn. - Defunct.

Independent Dealer Comm. Dedicated to Action - Address unknown since 1994.

Independent Dentist's Assn; Amer. [14136]

Independent Distributors Assn. - Defunct.

Independent Documentary; Center for [9934]

Independent Educ. Union of Australia [IO], South Melbourne, Australia

Independent Educational Consultants Assn. [7871], 3251 Old Lee Hwy., Ste. 510, Fairfax, VA 22030-1504, (703)591-4850

Independent Educational Counselors Assn. [★7871]

Independent Educational Services [1263]

Independent Elecl. Contractors [1018], 4401 Ford Ave., Ste. 1100, Alexandria, VA 22302-1432, (703)549-7351

Independent Electrical Mfrs. Assn. - Defunct.

Independent Electronic Music Center - Defunct.

Independent Fabric Retailers Assn. - Defunct.

Independent Feature Proj. [1381], c/o Michelle Byrd, Exec. Dir., 104 W 29th St., 12th Fl., New York, NY 10001-5310, (212)465-8200

Independent Fed. of Chinese Students and Scholars [17062], 733 15th St. NW, Ste. 700, Washington, DC 20005, (202)347-0017

Independent Fed. of Chinese Students and Scholars [IO], Washington, DC, United States

Independent Fed. of Flight Attendants - Address unknown since 2000.

Independent Film Producers Export Corp. - Defunct.

Independent Film and TV Alliance [1382], 10850 Wilshire Blvd., 9th Fl., Los Angeles, CA 90024-4321, (310)446-1000

Independent Film and Television Alliance [IO], Los Angeles, CA, United States

Independent Film and Video Alliance [★IO]

Independent Financial Brokers of Canada [IO], Mississauga, ON, Canada

Independent Fluorspar Producers Assn. - Defunct.

Independent Foodservice Companies; ComSource [★1566]

Independent Footwear Retailers' Assn. [IO], Surrey, United Kingdom

Independent Forest Products Assn. - Address unknown since 2006.

Independent Free Papers of Am. [3226], 107 Hemlock Dr., Rio Grande, NJ 08242, (609)408-8000

Independent Fuel Oil Marketers of America - Defunct.

Independent Fundamental Churches of Am. [★19849]

Independent Fundamental Churches of Am. [★IO]

Independent Gasoline Marketers of Am; Soc. of [2947]

Independent Gasoline Marketers Coun. - Defunct.

Independent Glass Assn. [1730], 385 Garrisonville Rd., Ste. 116, Stafford, VA 22554, (540)720-7484

Independent Health Insurance Inst. - Address unknown since 1989.

Independent Hermetic Rebuilders Assn. [★1887]

Independent Hermetic Rebuilders Assn. [★IO]

Independent Hospital Workers Union - Address unknown since 1999.

The Independent Inst. [18452], 100 Swan Way, Oakland, CA 94621-1428, (510)632-1366

Independent Insurance Adjusters; Natl. Assn. of [2209]

Independent Insurance Agents of Am. [★2169]

Independent Insurance Agents and Brokers of Am. [2169], 127 S Peyton St., Alexandria, VA 22314, (703)683-4422

Independent Insurance Auditors and Engineers; Natl. Assn. of [2210]

Independent Insurers; Natl. Assn. of [★2232]

Independent Insurers Safety Association; National Assn. of [★12964]

Independent Investor Protective League [2334], PO Box 5031, Fort Lauderdale, FL 33310, (954)749-1551

Independent Jewelers Org. [2366], 25 Seir Hill Rd., Norwalk, CT 06850, (203)846-4215

Independent Label Assn. - Address unknown since 1988.

Independent Labs; Amer. Coun. of [★7236]

Independent Labs. Inst. [2391], c/o Amer. Coun. of Independent Labs., 1629 K St. NW, Ste. 400, Washington, DC 20006-1633, (202)887-5872

Independent Lab. Distributors Assn. [3483], PO Box 1464, Fairplay, CO 80440, (719)836-9091

Independent Life Brokerage Agencies; Natl. Assn. of [2211]

Independent Liquid Terminals Assn. [3977], 1444 I St. NW, No. 400, Washington, DC 20005, (202)842-9200

Independent Literary Agents Assn. [★171]

Independent Living - Defunct.

Independent Living; Natl. Coun. on [11968]

Independent Living; Res. and Training Center on [11984]

Independent Lubricant Mfrs. Assn. [2927], 400 N Columbus St., Ste. 201, Alexandria, VA 22314-2264, (703)684-5574

Independent Lubricant Mfrs. Assn. [IO], Alexandria, VA, United States

Independent Mailing Equip. Dealers; Assn. of [★2448]

Independent Manufacturers'/Representatives; Assn. of [2534]

Independent Mfrs. Representatives Forum - Defunct.

Independent Media Arts Alliance [IO], Montreal, QC, Canada

Independent Media Arts Preservation [10454], c/o Electronic Arts Intermix, 535 W 22nd St., 5th Fl., New York, NY 10011, (212)560-7259

Independent Medical Distributors Assn. [1862], 5204 Fairmount Ave., Downers Grove, IL 60515, (866)463-2937

Independent Medical Examiners; Amer. Bd. of [8877]

Independent Meeting Planners Assn. of Canada [IO], Newmarket, ON, Canada

Independent Midwives Assn. [IO], Abingdon, United Kingdom

Independent Motion Picture Producers Assn. - Defunct.

Independent Motorcycle Retailers of America - Defunct.

Independent Music Assn. - Address unknown since 2004.

Independent Music Companies Assn. [IO], Brussels, Belgium

Independent Music New Zealand [IO], Auckland, New Zealand

Independent Music Publishers; Assn. of [2800]

Independent Music Retailers Assn. [2806], 912 Carlton Rd., Tarpon Springs, FL 34689, (727)938-0571

Independent Natural Gas Assn. of Am. [★1680]

Independent News Distributors; Amer. Assn. of [3078]

Independent Off. Products and Furniture Dealers Assn. [1698], 301 N Fairfax St., Alexandria, VA 22314, (703)549-9040

Independent Oil Compounders Assn. [★2927]

Independent Oil Compounders Assn. [★IO]

Independent Online Booksellers Assn. [530], c/o Sandra L. Morris, Membership Sec., Nan's Book Shop, 350 N Main St., Glen Ellyn, IL 60137-5065

Independent Optical Wholesalers; Assn. of [★1864]

Independent Order of B'nai B'rith [★20125]

Independent Order of B'nai B'rith [★IO]

Independent Order of Brith Sholom [★19178]

Independent Order of Foresters [IO], Toronto, ON, Canada

Independent Order Free Sons of Israel [★19182]

Independent Order Ladies of Vikings - Address unknown since 1995.

Independent Order of Odd Fellows [19295], 422 Trade St., Winston-Salem, NC 27101, (336)725-5955

Independent Order of Odd Fellows; Junior Lodge, [19297]

Independent Order of St. Luke - Defunct.

Independent Order of Svithiod [19344], 5518 W Lawrence Ave., Chicago, IL 60630, (773)736-1191

Independent Order of Vikings [19127], PO Box 5147, Springfield, IL 62705-5147, (877)241-6006

Independent Organic Inspectors Assn. [5067], PO Box 6, Broadus, MT 59317-0006, (406)436-2031

Independent Party; Comm. for a Unified [18321]

Independent Pet and Animal Trans. Assn. Intl. [2958], 745 Winding Trail, Holly Lake Ranch, TX 75765-7148, (903)769-2267

Independent Petroleum Assn. of Am. [2928], 1201 15th St. NW, Ste. 300, Washington, DC 20005, (202)857-4722

Independent Photo Imagers [2998], 2510 Anthem Village Pkwy., Ste. 110, Henderson, NV 89052, (702)617-1141

Independent Pilots Assn. [24000], 3607 Fern Valley Rd., Louisville, KY 40219

Independent Postal System of America - Address unknown since 1995.

Independent Poster Exchanges of America - Address unknown since 1995.

Independent Practice; Amer. Psychological Assn. Division of [16126]

Independent Press Assn. [3116], 65 Battery, 2nd Fl., San Francisco, CA 94111, (415)445-0230

Independent Press Assn. [IO], Chisinau, Moldova

Independent Print Indus. Assn. [IO], Shepshed, United Kingdom

Independent and Private School Data Educ; Soc. of [★8132]

Independent Producers; Natl. Assn. of Latino [1390]

Independent Producers and Royalty Owners Assn; Texas [2949]

Independent Professional Earth Scientists; Soc. of [7135]

Independent Professional Painting Contractors Assn. of Am. [1019]

Independent Professional Painting Contractors Assn. of Am. [IO], Huntington, NY, United States

Independent Professional Representatives Org. [330], 34157 W 9 Mile Rd., Farmington Hills, MI 48335, (248)474-0522

Independent Professional Seedsmen Assn. [187], 2320 S 48th St., Ste. 102, Lincoln, NE 68506-5810, (402)483-2571

Independent Professional Typists Network - Defunct.

Independent Progressive Politics Network [18619], PO Box 1041, Bloomfield, NJ 07003, (973)338-5398

Independent Property Managers' Assn. [IO], Christchurch, New Zealand

Independent Psychiatric Assn. of Russia [IO], Moscow, Russia

Independent Public Broadcasting; Citizens for [17025]

Independent Public Finance Advisors; Natl. Assn. of [1467]

Independent Publishers Guild [IO], Royston, United Kingdom

Independent Publishers League - Defunct.

Independent Publishers; Natl. Assn. of [3238]

Independent Publishing; Small Press Center for [3252]

Independent Res. Libraries Assn. [10359], c/o Dr. Charles F. Bryan, Jr., Pres., PO Box 7311, Richmond, VA 23221-0311, (804)342-9656

Independent Res. Service - Defunct.

Independent Retail Tobacconists Assn. of America - Defunct.

Independent Road Service Assn. - Defunct.

Independent Scholars of Asia [9957], c/o Dr. Ruth-Inge Heinze, Natl. Dir., 2321 Russell, No. 3C, Berkeley, CA 94705-1959, (510)849-3791

Independent Scholars of Asia [IO], Berkeley, CA, United States

Independent Scholars; Natl. Coalition of [8491]

Independent Scholarship Natl. Program - Defunct.

Independent Schools

Amer. Assn. of Presidents of Independent Colleges and Universities [8534]

Coun. of Independent Colleges [8535]

Coun. for Spiritual and Ethical Educ. [8536]

European Coun. of Natl. Associations of Independent Schools [IO]

Found. for Independent Higher Educ. [8537]

Independent Schools Assn. of the Central States [8538]

Independent Schools Assn. of Southern Africa [IO]

Reference to "IO" in place of a book number signifies that the association may be found in the 45th edition of International Organizations.

Independent Schools Coun. of Australia [IO]
Natl. Assn. of Independent Colleges and Universities [8539]
Natl. Assn. of Independent Schools [8540]
Quebec Assn. of Independent Schools [IO]
Independent Schools Assn. of the Central States [8538], 1165 N Clark St., Ste. 311, Chicago, IL 60610, (312)255-1244
Independent Schools Assn. of Southern Africa [IO], Houghton, Republic of South Africa
Independent Schools Coun. [IO], London, United Kingdom
Independent Schools Coun. of Australia [IO], Deakin West, Australia
Independent Schools Coun. Info. Ser. [IO], London, United Kingdom
Independent Schools Educ. Bd. [★8540]
Independent Schools; Natl. Coun. of [★8540]
Independent Schools Talent Search Prog. [★8321]
Independent Sealing Distributors [4022], 105 Eastern Ave., Ste. 104, Annapolis, MD 21403, (410)263-1014
Independent Search Consultants [11246], PO Box 10192, Costa Mesa, CA 92627
Independent Search Consultants [IO], Costa Mesa, CA, United States
Independent Sector [12725], 1200 18th St. NW, Ste. 200, Washington, DC 20036, (202)467-6100
Independent Security and Police Union - Address unknown since 2002.
Independent Shoemen of America - Defunct.
Independent Show Organizers; Soc. of [1348]
Independent Signcrafters of America - Address unknown since 1990.
Independent Snowmobile Medical Res. - Defunct.
Independent Social Ideas; Found. for the Stud. of [18010]
Independent Soc. of the Blind [IO], Singapore, Singapore
Independent Space Res. Group - Address unknown since 1990.
Independent Study; ERIS Roundtable for [10792]
Independent Telephone Assn. of Am. [★3965]
Independent Telephone Assn; Natl. [★3965]
Independent Telephone Assn; U.S. [★3965]
Independent Telephony; Museum of [★22985]
Independent TV Assn. [IO], London, United Kingdom
Independent TV News Assn. - Defunct.
Independent Terminal Operators Assn. [2929], 1150 Connecticut NW, 9th Fl., Washington, DC 20036, (202)828-4100
Independent Textile Rental Assn. [3786], PO Box 190, Hogansville, GA 30230, (800)477-7843
Independent Textile Rental Assn. [IO], Hogansville, GA, United States
Independent Theatre Coun. [IO], London, United Kingdom
Independent Thinking; Resources for [10827]
Independent Travel Agencies of America Assn. - Defunct.
Independent Truck Owner/Operator Assn. - Address unknown since 2002.
Independent Truckers and Drivers Assn. [3870], 1109 Plover Dr., Baltimore, MD 21227, (410)242-0507
Independent Truckers League - Address unknown since 1995.
Independent Turf and Ornamental Distributors Assn. [2394], 174 Crestview Dr., Bellefonte, PA 16823-8516, (814)326-5995
Independent Union Coun; Natl. [★24210]
Independent Union of Petroleum Workers [★24163]
Independent Union of Plant Protection Employees [★24188]
Independent Unions; Cong. of [24205]
Independent Unions; Natl. Fed. of [24210]
Independent United Order of Mechanics - Western Hemisphere [19265]
Independent U.S. Tanker Owners Comm. - Defunct.
Independent Univ., Washington-Paris-Moscow [★8597]
Independent Univ., Washington-Paris-Moscow [★IO]
Independent Video and Filmmakers; Assn. of [9931]
Independent Video Programmers Assn. - Defunct.
Independent Visually Impaired Enterprisers [16855], c/o Ardis Bazyn, Pres., 500 S 3rd St., Apt. H, Burbank, CA 91502, (818)238-9321

Independent Waste Paper Processors Assn. [IO], Daventry, United Kingdom
Independent Wire Producers Assn. [★1999]
Independent Women's Forum [18311], 1726 M St. NW, 10th Fl., Washington, DC 20036-4527, (202)419-1820
Independent Workers Assn. - Defunct.
Independent Workers Union [IO], Cork, Ireland
Independent Zinc Alloyers Assn. - Address unknown since 2001.
Indevestors [★17219]
Indexers; Amer. Soc. of [10322]
Indexing and Abstracting Soc. of Canada [IO], Toronto, ON, Canada
Indexing Services; Natl. Fed. of Abstracting and [★7205]
Indexing Services; Natl. Fed. of Sci. Abstracting and [★7205]

India
Amer. Hindu Assn. [20077]
Amer. Inst. of Indian Stud. [8541]
Amer. Telugu Assn. [9848]
Assn. of Indian Entomologists in North Am. [7057]
Assn. of Kannada Kootas of Am. [19111]
Bhojpuri Assn. of North Am. [10299]
Bibles For The World [20305]
Bihar Assn. of North Am. [10220]
Brahman Samaj of North Am. [9998]
Congregation Bina [10277]
Cultural Assn. of Bengal [9737]
East-West Cultural Center [9619]
Engg. Export Promotion Coun. of India [2304]
Friends of Christ in India [20090]
Help the Helpless [12405]
Hindustan Bible Inst. [19927]
India Amer. Cultural Assn. [10217]
India Development Ser. [18572]
India Literacy Proj. [8790]
India Partners [17811]
India Stud. Circle for Philately [22828]
Indian Dental Assn., U.S.A. [14157]
Indian Muslim Relief Comm. of ISNA [12860]
Indicorps [12406]
Indify [13488]
Indo-American Arts Coun. [9570]
Intl. Alumni Assn. of Shri Mahavir Jain Vidyalaya [19346]
Intl. Soc. of India Chemists and Chem. Engineers [6685]
Jagannath Org. for Global Awareness [20527]
Kashmiri Amer. Coun. [12753]
Leuva Patidar Samaj of USA [10221]
Malayalee Engineers Assn. in North Am. [7026]
Milan Cultural Assn. [10222]
Natl. Ayurvedic Medical Assn. [13642]
North Amer. Dhrupad Assn. [10677]
North Amer. Sankethi Assn. [9802]
Patidar Cultural Assn. of USA [10218]
PlanetRead [8796]
Punjabi-American Cultural Assn. [10223]
Ramakrishna - Vivekananda Center [20610]
Seva Found. [12443]
Solidarity and Action Against the HIV Infection in India [16969]
Tibetan Aid Proj. [12822]
U.S. Indian Amer. Chamber of Commerce [24331]
U.S. Indian Amer. Chamber of Commerce [IO]
USA Sanatan Sports and Cultural Assn. [23787]
Uttaranchal Assn. of North Am. [10219]
World Assn. for Vedic Stud. [9854]
India Alert - Address unknown since 1994.
India-America Chamber of Commerce - Address unknown since 2003.
India-America Soc. - Address unknown since 1995.
India America Trade Coun. - Address unknown since 1995.
India Amer. Cultural Assn. [10217], 1281 Cooper Lake Rd. SE, Smyrna, GA 30082, (770)436-3719
India Amer. Cultural Assn. [IO], Smyrna, GA, United States
India Chemists and Chem. Engineers Club [★IO]
India Chemists and Chem. Engineers Club [★6685]
India Development Ser. [18572], PO Box 980, Chicago, IL 60690, (630)495-4200
India Development Ser. [IO], Chicago, IL, United States

India Hump Pilot Assn; China-Burma- [21391]
India Literacy Proj. [8790], PO Box 361143, Milpitas, CA 95035-9998
India Literacy Proj. [IO], Milpitas, CA, United States
The India Mission [★IO]
The India Mission [★20315]
India-Net - Address unknown since 1999.
India Partners [17811], PO Box 5470, Eugene, OR 97405-0470, (541)683-0696
India Pepper and Spice Trade Assn. [IO], Kochi, India
India; Ramakrishna Order of [★20610]
India Semiconductor Assn. [IO], Bangalore, India
India Stud. Circle for Philately [IO], Washington, DC, United States
India Stud. Circle for Philately [22828], PO Box 7326, Washington, DC 20044, (202)564-6876
India; Tea Bd. of [515]
India Trade Promotion Org. [IO], New Delhi, India
India-U.S. Found. - Address unknown since 2000.

Indian
All-American Indian Motorcycle Club [22663]
Amer. Indian Liberation Crusade [12622]
Amer. Indian Lib. Assn. [10319]
Amer. Indian Youth Running Strong [12623]
Amer. Inst. of Indian Stud. [8541]
Amer. Telugu Assn. [9848]
Americans for Indian Opportunity [12624]
Asian Amer. Arts Centre [9553]
Asian Indian Chamber of Commerce [24228]
Assoc. Comm. of Friends on Indian Affairs [20039]
Assn. of Indian Entomologists in North Am. [7057]
Assn. of Indian Muslims of Am. [19109]
Assn. of Indians in Am. [19110]
Assn. of Kannada Kootas of Am. [19111]
Bear Butte Intl. Alliance [19446]
Bhojpuri Assn. of North Am. [10299]
Bihar Assn. of North Am. [10220]
Bihar Assn. of North Am. [IO]
Black and Indian Mission Off. [19587]
Brahman Samaj of North Am. [9998]
Bur. of Catholic Indian Missions [19591]
Friends of India Soc. Intl. [19112]
Friends of India Soc. Intl. [IO]
Gathering of Nations [10742]
Global Org. of People of Indian Origin [19113]
India Amer. Cultural Assn. [IO]
India Stud. Circle for Philately [22828]
Indian Dental Assn., U.S.A. [14157]
Indian Heritage Coun. [10744]
Indian Motor-Cycle Club of America [22682]
Indian Muslim Relief Comm. of ISNA [12860]
Indian Youth of Am. [12626]
Indicorps [12406]
Indify [13488]
Indo-American Arts Coun. [9570]
Inst. for the Stud. of Amer. Cultures [10746]
Intl. Alumni Assn. of Shri Mahavir Jain Vidyalaya [19346]
Jagannath Org. for Global Awareness [20527]
Leuva Patidar Samaj of USA [10221]
Malayalee Engineers Assn. in North Am. [7026]
Milan Cultural Assn. [10222]
Natl. Amer. Indian Court Judges Assn. [5905]
Natl. Assn. of Canadians of Origins in India [IO]
Natl. Center for Amer. Indian and Alaska Native Mental Hea. Res. [15220]
Natl. Centre for the Performing Arts [IO]
Natl. Coun. of Urban Indian Hea. [15277]
Natl. Fed. of Indian Amer. Associations [19114]
Natl. Indian Hea. Bd. [12629]
Natl. Indian Wars Assn. [9371]
Native Amer. Indian Info. and Trade Center [24358]
Native Tourism Alliance [24381]
Network of Indian Professionals [19115]
North Am. Native Amer. (Indian) Info. and Trade Center [10752]
North Amer. Dhrupad Assn. [10677]
North Amer. Sikh Medical and Dental Assn. [16416]
Old Sleepy Eye Collectors' Club of Am. [21934]
Order of the Indian Wars [10479]
Pan Amer. Indian Assn. [10753]

A star before a book entry number signifies that the name is not listed separately, but is mentioned within the entry.

Patidar Cultural Assn. of USA [10218]
Punjabi-American Cultural Assn. [10223]
Seva Found. [12443]
Sikh Amer. Legal Defense and Educ. Fund [18600]
Sikh Coun. on Religion and Educ. [20558]
Tekakwitha Conf. Natl. Center [19727]
United Indian Missions, Intl. [20405]
United South and Eastern Tribes [12632]
U.S. Indian Amer. Chamber of Commerce [24331]
USA Sanatan Sports and Cultural Assn. [23787]
Uttaranchal Assn. of North Am. [10219]
World Assn. for Vedic Stud. [9854]
Indian Acad. of Neurology - Clinical Neurophysiology [IO], New Delhi, India
Indian Acad. of Sciences [IO], Bangalore, India
Indian Adult Educ. Assn. [IO], New Delhi, India
Indian Affairs; Amer. Assn. on [★18092]
Indian Affairs; Assoc. Comm. of Friends on [20039]
Indian Affairs; Assn. on Amer. [18092]
Indian Affairs; Natl. Assn. of [★18092]
Indian AIDS Hotline; Natl. [★16968]
Indian and Alaska Native Mental Hea. Res; Natl. Center for Amer. [15220]
Indian Amer. Forum for Political Educ. [18352], c/o Sakhuja Ravi, Pres., 259 Amherst Ave., Colonia, NJ 07067, (781)861-6797
Indian Archaeological Inst; Amer. [★6447]
Indian Arts Coun; Amer. [10730]
Indian Arts and Crafts Assn. [10743], 4010 Carlisle NE, Ste. C, Albuquerque, NM 87107, (505)265-9149
Indian Arts; Inst. of Amer. [10745]
Indian Assn. of Amusement Parks and Indus. [IO], Bombay, India
Indian Assn. of Cardiovascular Thoracic Anaesthesiologists [IO], Chennai, India
Indian Assn. for the Cultivation of Sci. [IO], Calcutta, India
Indian Assn. of Gastrointestinal Endosurgeons [IO], Bangalore, India
Indian Assn. of Ghana [IO], Accra, Ghana
Indian Assn; Pan Amer. [10753]
Indian Assn. of Physiotherapists [IO], Bombay, India
Indian Assn. of Secretaries and Administrative Professionals [IO], Bombay, India
Indian Assn. of Social Sci. Institutions [IO], New Delhi, India
Indian Assn. of Sports Medicine [IO], New Delhi, India
Indian Assn. of Surgical Oncology [IO], New Delhi, India
Indian Banks' Assn. [IO], Bombay, India
Indian Biophysical Soc. [IO], Bombay, India
Indian Bus. Assn; Natl. [751]
Indian Bus. Leaders; Amer. [2830]
Indian Cancer Soc. [IO], Bombay, India
Indian Cattlemen's Assn; Natl. Amer. [4273]
Indian Ceramic Soc. [IO], Calcutta, India
Indian Ceremonial Assn; Inter-Tribal [10747]
Indian Chamber of Commerce; Asian [24228]
Indian Chamber of Commerce - Calcutta [IO], Calcutta, India
Indian Chamber of Commerce Hong Kong [IO], Hong Kong, People's Republic of China
Indian Chamber of Commerce of North Am; North Amer. [★24358]
Indian Chap. of Intl. Hepato Pancreato Biliary Assn. [IO], Bombay, India
Indian Chem. Coun. [IO], Bombay, India
Indian Chem. Mfrs. Assn. [★IO]
Indian Chem. Soc. [IO], Calcutta, India
Indian Child Welfare Assn; Natl. [19277]
Indian Children's Fund Australia [IO], Sydney, Australia
Indian Cotton Mills' Fed. [★IO]
Indian Coun. on Aging; Natl. [11311]
Indian Coun. of Agricultural Res. [IO], New Delhi, India
Indian Coun. of Architects and Engineers; Amer. [6462]
Indian Coun. for Cultural Relations [IO], New Delhi, India
Indian Coun. of Medical Res. [IO], New Delhi, India
Indian Coun. of Social Sci. Res. [IO], New Delhi, India

Indian Court Judges Assn; Natl. Amer. [5905]
Indian Cultural Center - Defunct.
Indian Culture Res. Center; Amer. [10731]
Indian Dairy Assn. [IO], New Delhi, India
Indian Dancers; Thunderbird Amer. [10754]
Indian Defense Assn; Amer. [★18092]
Indian Defense League of Am. [19273], c/o Joseph Rickard, Sr., Pres., PO Box 305, Niagara Falls, NY 14302
Indian Dental Assn. [IO], Bombay, India
Indian Dental Assn., U.S.A. [14157], 146-02 89th Ave., Jamaica, NY 11435, (718)639-0192
Indian Development Assn; United [★12628]
Indian Development; Seventh Generation Fund for [18099]
Indian Diamond and Colorstone Assn. [2367], 56 W 45th St., No. 705, New York, NY 10036, (212)921-4488
Indian Drug Mfrs'. Assn. [IO], Bombay, India
Indian Economic Assn. [IO], Calcutta, India
Indian Educ. Assn; Natl. [8941]
Indian Educ; Coun. for [8937]
Indian Educ; Montana Coun. for [★8937]
Indian Educators Fed. [8938], 2309 Renard Pl. SE, Ste. 202, Albuquerque, NM 87106, (505)243-4088
Indian Elecl. and Electronics Mfrs. Assn. [IO], Bombay, India
Indian Enterprise Development; Natl. Center for Amer. [12628]
Indian Epilepsy Soc. [IO], Gurgaon, India
Indian Ethnohistoric Conf; Amer. [★9918]
Indian Fed. of Tenants Coun. [IO], Calcutta, India
Indian Fish and Wildlife Commn; Great Lakes [5323]
Indian Footwear Components Mfrs. Assn. [IO], Noida, India
Indian Gaming Assn; Natl. [5771]
Indian Geotechnical Soc. [IO], New Delhi, India
Indian Graduate Center; Amer. [8426]
Indian Hea. Bd; Natl. [12629]
Indian Heritage Coun. [10744]
Indian Heritage Found; Amer. [10732]
Indian Higher Educ. Consortium; Amer. [8935]
Indian, Hispanic, and Asian Women in Action; Black, [13420]
Indian Historical Soc. [★10740]
Indian Homoeopathic Medical Assn. [IO], Ernakulam, India
Indian Horse Registry; Amer. [4827]
Indian Housing Coun; Natl. Amer. [5791]
Indian Info. Center; South Amer. [★17818]
Indian Info. Center; South and Central Amer. [★17818]
Indian Info. Center; South and Meso-American [★17818]
Indian Info. and Trade Center; Native Amer. [24358]
Indian Info. and Trade Center; North Am. Native Amer. [10752]
Indian Inst; Amer. [10733]
Indian Inst. of Architects [IO], Bombay, India
Indian Inst. of Materials Mgt. [IO], Bombay, India
Indian Inst. of Metals [IO], Calcutta, India
Indian Inst. of Packaging [IO], Bombay, India
Indian Jaycees [IO], Tiruvannamalai, India
Indian Justice Center; Natl. [19278]
Indian Jute Mills Assn. [IO], Calcutta, India
Indian Law Inst. [IO], New Delhi, India
Indian Law; Inst. for the Development of [18095]
Indian Law Rsrc. Center [18094], 602 N Ewing St., Helena, MT 59601, (406)449-2006
Indian Law Students Assn; Amer. [★8772]
Indian Liberation Crusade; Amer. [12622]
Indian Lib. Assn; Amer. [10319]
Indian Lore Assn; Amer. [★10751]
Indian Managers; Management Inst.: Training for [★12628]
Indian Medical Assn. [IO], New Delhi, India
Indian Medical Assn. - Bangalore Br. [IO], Bangalore, India
Indian Medical Assn. - Chandigarh [IO], Chandigarh, India
Indian Medical Assn. - Udupi-Karavali Br. [IO], Udupi, India
Indian Memorial Assn; Creek [10740]
Indian Merchants' Chamber [IO], Bombay, India
Indian Military Historical Soc. [IO], Huntingdon, United Kingdom

Indian Ministries; North Am. [★20376]
Indian Mission; North Am. [★20376]
Indian Mission Off; Black and [19587]
Indian Mission; South Amer. [★20397]
Indian Missions; Bur. of Catholic [19591]
Indian Motion Picture Producers' Assn. [IO], Bombay, India
Indian Motor-Cycle Club of America [22682]
Indian Motorcycle Club; All-American [22663]
Indian Movement; Amer. [18090]
Indian Music Indus. [IO], Bombay, India
Indian Muslim Relief Comm. of ISNA [IO], Palo Alto, CA, United States
Indian Muslim Relief Comm. of ISNA [12860], 1000 San Antonio Rd., Palo Alto, CA 94303, (650)856-0440
Indian Muslims; Assn. of [★19109]
Indian Natl. Sci. Acad. [IO], New Delhi, India
Indian Natl. Shipowners' Assn. [IO], Bombay, India
Indian Natl. Trade Union Cong. [IO], New Delhi, India
Indian Navy Found. [IO], New Delhi, India
Indian Newspaper Soc. [IO], New Delhi, India
Indian and Northern Affairs Canada [IO], Ottawa, ON, Canada
Indian Ocean Commn. [IO], Quatre Bornes, Mauritius
Indian Oil Seeds and Produce Exporters' Assn. [IO], Bombay, India
Indian Olympic Assn. [IO], New Delhi, India
Indian Opportunity; Americans for [12624]
Indian People's Assn. in North America - Address unknown since 1995.
Indian Pepper and Spice Trade Assn. [IO], Kochi, India
Indian Peptide Soc. [IO], New Delhi, India
Indian Pest Control Assn. [IO], New Delhi, India
Indian Pharmaceutical Assn. [IO], Bombay, India
Indian Pharmacological Soc. [IO], Ahmedabad, India
Indian Philosophy Assn; Amer. [19268]
Indian Physicians; Assn. of Amer. [15989]
Indian Physics Assn. [IO], Bombay, India
Indian Phytopathological Soc. [IO], New Delhi, India
Indian Plumbing Assn. [IO], New Delhi, India
Indian Political Action Coun. - Address unknown since 2004.
Indian Polyurethane Assn. [IO], Chennai, India
Indian Pueblo Coun; All [18089]
Indian Pueblo Cultural Center [★18089]
Indian Red Cross Soc. [IO], New Delhi, India
Indian Refractory Makers Assn. [IO], Calcutta, India
Indian Res. and Development; Amer. [8464]
Indian Rheumatology Assn. [IO], Hyderabad, India
Indian Rights Assn. - Address unknown since 1999.
Indian Ritual Object Repatriation Found; Amer. [18091]
Indian Rubber Mfrs. Res. Assn. [IO], Thane, India
Indian Scholarships; Amer. [★8426]
Indian School; Sante Fe [★10745]
Indian Sci. Cong. Assn. [IO], Calcutta, India
Indian Sci. and Engg. Soc; Amer. [6987]
Indian Silk Export Promotion Coun. [IO], Bombay, India
Indian Soc. of Advertisers [IO], Bombay, India
Indian Soc. of Agricultural Economics [IO], Bombay, India
Indian Soc. for Antimicrobial Chemotherapy [IO], New Delhi, India
Indian Soc. for Assisted Reproduction [IO], Bombay, India
Indian Soc. of Cinematographers [IO], Thiruvananthapuram, India
Indian Soc. of Clinical Neurophysiology [★IO]
Indian Soc. of Critical Care Medicine [IO], Bombay, India
Indian Soc. of Geomatics [IO], Ahmedabad, India
Indian Soc. of Landscape Architects [IO], Ahmedabad, India
Indian Soc. for Mathematical Modelling and Cmpt. Simulation [IO], Kanpur, India
Indian Soc. for Medical Statistics [IO], Jhansi, India
Indian Soc. of Nephrology [IO], Lucknow, India
Indian Soc. of Neuroradiology [IO], Dispur, India
Indian Soc. for Parenteral and Enteral Nutrition [IO], Chennai, India

Reference to "IO" in place of a book number signifies that the association may be found in the 45th edition of International Organizations.

Indian Soc. of Psychosomatic Obstetrics and Gynae-cology [IO], Calcutta, India
Indian Soc. of Soil Sci. [IO], New Delhi, India
Indian Soc. for Trenchless Tech. [IO], New Delhi, India
Indian Soc. of Vascular and Interventional Radiology [IO], New Delhi, India
Indian Space Res. Org. [IO], Bangalore, India
Indian Spina Bifida Assn. [IO], Jaipur, India
Indian Stainless Steel Development Assn. [IO], New Delhi, India
Indian Steam Railway Soc. [IO], New Delhi, India
Indian Stud; Inst. for Amer. [6447]
Indian Sugar Mills Assn. [IO], New Delhi, India
Indian Tea Assn. [IO], Calcutta, India
Indian Textile Accessories and Machinery Mfrs'. Assn. [IO], Bombay, India
Indian Trade and Info. Center; North Amer. [★10750]
Indian Trade Promotion Org. [IO], New Delhi, India
Indian Tribal Youth; United Natl. [10756]
Indian Unit for Pattern Recognition and Artificial Intelligence [IO], Calcutta, India
Indian Venture Capital Assn. [IO], New Delhi, India
Indian Volunteers for Community Ser. [IO], Middle-sex, United Kingdom
Indian Wars; Order of the [10479]
Indian Wars of the U.S; Order of [★10482]
Indian Wind Energy Assn. [IO], New Delhi, India
Indian Women's Assn. [IO], Singapore, Singapore
Indian Youth of Am. [12626]
Indian Youth Coun; Natl. [10749]
Indian Youth Running Strong; Amer. [12623]
Indiana Found. for Hand Surgical Res. [★14526]
Indiana Limestone Inst. of Am. [3694], 400 Stone City Bank Bldg., Bedford, IN 47421, (812)275-4426
Indiana Limestone; Natl. Assn. for [★3694]
Indiana Pioneers; Soc. of [21256]
Indiana State Univ. Alumni Assn. [18899], c/o Indiana State Univ., 200 N 7th St., Terre Haute, IN 47809-9989, (812)237-3707
Indians of All Tribes Found; United [18100]
Indians in Am; Assn. of Asian [★19110]
Indians; Continental Confed. of Adopted [10737]
Indians; Coun. for Native Amer. [10738]
Indians for Democracy - Defunct.
Indians Into Communications Assn. - Defunct.
Indians Into Medicine [8865], UNDSMHS, Rm. 2101, 501 N Columbia Rd., Stop 9037, Grand Forks, ND 58202-9037, (701)777-3037
Indians; Natl. Cong. of Amer. [18096]
India's Natl. Acad. of Letters [IO], New Delhi, India
Indicorps [12406], 3418 Hwy. 6 S, Ste. B, No. 309, Houston, TX 77082, (617)500-2677
Indify [13488], 3418 Hwy. 6 S, Ste. B, No. 309, Houston, TX 77082
Indigenous Affairs and Human Rights Proj. [★17993]
Indigenous Affairs and Human Rights Proj. [★IO]
Indigenous Communications Assn. - Defunct.
Indigenous Environmental Network [4624], PO Box 485, Bemidji, MN 56619, (218)751-4967
Indigenous Ministries; North Am. [20376]
Indigenous Peoples
  Aboriginal Rights Coalition [IO]
  Assn. of Iroquois and Allied Indians [IO]
  Assn. of Kannada Kootas of Am. [19111]
  Assn. for the Stud. of Persianate Societies [8668]
  Assn. for the Stud. of the Worldwide African Di-aspora [7929]
  Australian Indigenous Doctors' Assn. [IO]
  Australian Inst. of Aboriginal and Torres Strait Islander Stud. [IO]
  Calmeadow Charitable Found. [IO]
  Canadian Native Friendship Centre [IO]
  Center for World Indigenous Stud. [IO]
  Center for World Indigenous Stud. [17812]
  Circolo Amerindiano [IO]
  Cong. of Aboriginal Peoples [IO]
  Cultural Conservancy [10741]
  Cultural Survival [10171]
  Egbe Omo Yoruba: Natl. Assn. of Yoruba Descendants in North America [19289]
  First Peoples Worldwide [10224]
  First Peoples Worldwide [IO]
  For Mother Earth [17813]

  Fourth World Documentation Proj. [17814]
  Fourth World Documentation Proj. [IO]
  Hmong Natl. Development [17815]
  Igorot Global Org. [10225]
  Igorot Global Org. [IO]
  Ijaw Natl. Alliance of the Americas [12639]
  Indian Defense League of Am. [19273]
  Indigenous Peoples Coun. on Biocolonialism [12407]
  Inst. for the Advancement of Hawaiian Affairs [10883]
  Intl. Alliance of Indigenous and Tribal Peoples of Tropical Forests [IO]
  Intl. Comm. for the Indians of the Americas [IO]
  Intl. Indian Treaty Coun. [IO]
  Intl. Indian Treaty Coun. [17816]
  Intl. Work Gp. for Indigenous Affairs [IO]
  Just Transition Alliance [24105]
  Lakota Student Alliance [19275]
  Milan Cultural Assn. [10222]
  Natl. Aboriginal Islander Skills Development Assn. [IO]
  Natl. Haitian Soc. [IO]
  Natl. Haitian Soc. [17817]
  Natl. Tribal Child Support Assn. [11713]
  Native Amer. Leadership Alliance [20455]
  Native Women's Assn. of Canada [IO]
  Netherlands Centre for Indigenous Peoples [IO]
  Pacific Peoples' Partnership [IO]
  PARTIZANS [IO]
  Pauktuutit Inuit Women's Assn. [IO]
  Racial Justice 911 [18493]
  Russian Assn. of Indigenous Peoples of the North, Siberia and Far East [IO]
  Saq' Be': Organization for Mayan and Indigenous Spiritual Bodies [IO]
  Saq' Be': Org. for Mayan and Indigenous Spiritual Bodies [10226]
  SisterSong Women of Color Reproductive Hea. Collective [18826]
  Slavic Heritage Coalition [10969]
  South and Meso-American Indian Rights Center [17818]
  South and Meso-American Indian Rights Center [IO]
  SurfAid Intl. [11791]
  SURVIVAL [IO]
  Survival Deutschland [IO]
  Survival Intl. - Espana [IO]
  Survival Intl. - France [IO]
  Survival Intl. - Italia [IO]
  Ugbajo Itsekiri USA [19260]
  Wordcraft Circle of Native Writers and Storytellers [9859]
Indigenous Peoples Coun. on Biocolonialism [12407], PO Box 72, Nixon, NV 89424, (775)574-0248
Indigenous People's Network - Address unknown since 1995.
Indigenous Women's Network - Address unknown since 1999.
Indigent; Natl. Off. for the Rights of the [★17130]
Individual and Community Development; Center for [★12365]
Individual Freedom Fed. - Address unknown since 2006.
Individual Investors; Amer. Assn. of [8422]
Individual Investors; National Assn. of [★2342]
Individual Liberty; Soc. for [★18015]
Individual Rights and Responsibilities; Sect. of [17153]
Individualists; Intercollegiate Soc. of [★17271]
Individuals for a Rational Soc. - Defunct.
Indo-American Arts Coun. [9570], 118 E 25th St., Third Fl., New York, NY 10010, (212)529-2347
Indo-American Arts Coun. [IO], New York, NY, United States
Indo-American Chamber of Commerce [IO], Bom-bay, India
Indo Amer. Garment Assn. [★226]
Indo-Amer. Soc. of Interventional Cardiology [13908], 185 Shore Dr. S, Miami, FL 33131, (305)285-4171
Indo-Amer. Soc. of Interventional Cardiology [IO], Miami, FL, United States

Indo-Burma Pioneer Mission [★IO]
Indo-Burma Pioneer Mission [★20305]
Indo-Canadian Women's Assn. [IO], Edmonton, AB, Canada
Indo-French Chamber of Commerce and Indus. [IO], Bombay, India
Indo-German Chamber of Commerce [IO], Bombay, India
Indo-Pacific Prehistory Assn. [IO], Canberra, Australia
Indochina
  Amer. Fund for Czechoslovak Relief [12802]
  Indochina Center [10122]
Indochina; Assn. of Chinese from [★18502]
Indochina Center [10122], c/o Center for Southeast Asia Stud., Univ. of California, Berkeley, 2223 Ful-ton St., Rm. 617, MC2318, Berkeley, CA 94720-2318, (510)642-3609
Indochina Curriculum Group - Defunct.
IndoChina Inst. [★10122]
Indochina Refugee Action Center [★12820]
Indochina Rsrc. Action Center [★12820]
Indochina Solidarity Comm. - Defunct.
Indonesia
  Amer. Indonesian Chamber of Commerce [24332]
  Asian Amer. Arts Centre [9553]
  Indonesian Stud. Comm. [9620]
  Soc. for Indonesian-Americans [19116]
  Subud U.S.A. [20589]
  Sumatran Orangutan Soc. USA [5384]
  United States-Indonesia Soc. [775]
  Volunteers in Asia [13407]
Indonesia Amateur Baseball and Softball Fed. [IO], Jakarta, Indonesia
Indonesia-Amer. Soc. of the U.S. - Defunct.
Indonesia Archery Assn. [IO], Jakarta, Indonesia
Indonesia Human Rights Campaign [IO], Thornton Heath, United Kingdom
Indonesia Sailing Fed. [IO], Jakarta, Indonesia
Indonesia Skateboarding Assn. [IO], Bandung, Indonesia
Indonesian Amateur Dancesport Assn. [IO], Jakarta, Indonesia
Indonesian Assn. of Advt. Agencies [IO], Jakarta, Indonesia
Indonesian Assn. of Investment Managers [IO], Jakarta, Indonesia
Indonesian Assn. for Sports Hea. [IO], Jakarta, Indonesia
Indonesian Book Publishers' Assn. [IO], Jakarta, Indonesia
Indonesian Bus. Professional Assns. of the U.S. - Address unknown since 2003.
Indonesian Chamber of Commerce and Indus. [IO], Jakarta, Indonesia
Indonesian Consumers Org. [IO], Jakarta, Indonesia
Indonesian Furniture Indus. and Handicraft Assn. [IO], Jakarta, Indonesia
Indonesian Gas Assn. [IO], Jakarta, Indonesia
Indonesian Heart Assn. [IO], Jakarta, Indonesia
Indonesian Internet Ser. Provider Assn. [IO], Jakarta, Indonesia
Indonesian Osteoporosis Soc. [IO], Jakarta, Indonesia
Indonesian Physiological Soc. [IO], Surabaya, Indonesia
Indonesian Physiotherapists Assn. [IO], Jakarta, Indonesia
Indonesian Planned Parenthood Assn. [IO], Jakarta, Indonesia
Indonesian Pulp and Paper Assn. [IO], Jakarta, Indonesia
Indonesian Soc. Against Epilepsy [IO], Bandung, Indonesia
Indonesian Soc. for Chemotherapy [IO], Jakarta, Indonesia
Indonesian Soc. for Clinical Neurophysiology [IO], Jakarta, Indonesia
Indonesian Soc. of Dermatology and Venereology [IO], Jakarta, Indonesia
Indonesian Soc. of Digestive Endoscopy [IO], Jakarta, Indonesia
Indonesian Soc. for Geotechnical Engg. [IO], Jakarta, Indonesia
Indonesian Soc. of Landscape Architects [IO], Jakarta, Indonesia

A star before a book entry number signifies that the name is not listed separately, but is mentioned within the entry.

Indonesian Students Assn. in the U.S. - Address unknown since 1995.

Indonesian Stud. Comm. [9620], c/o Dr. Karl Heider, Off. of Provost, Univ. of South Carolina, Columbia, SC 29208, (803)777-2808

Indonesian Taekwondo Assn. [IO], Jakarta, Indonesia

Indonesian Telecommunications Soc. [IO], Jakarta, Indonesia

Indonesian Tennis Assn. [IO], Jakarta, Indonesia

Indoor Air Quality Assn. [5093], 12339 Carroll Ave., Rockville, MD 20852, (301)231-8388

Indoor Air Quality Coun; Amer. [5082]

Indoor Citrus and Rare Fruit Soc. - Defunct.

Indoor Gardening Soc. of Am. [22519], c/o Jacqueline Hodes, 763 Ave. A, New York, NY 10009, (212)242-6785

Indoor Light Gardening Soc. of Am. [★22519]

Indoor Soccer Coaches Assn. [23288]

Indoor Sports Club [11951], 16 Liberty St., Larkspur, CA 94939, (415)924-3549

Indoor Tennis Assn. [★3021]

Indoor Tennis Assn. [★IO]

Indoor Tennis Assn; Natl. [★3021]

Indore Mgt. Assn. [IO], Indore, India

Indus Women Leaders [18003], 236 W Portal Ave., No. 473, San Francisco, CA 94127

Industria; Camara Venezolano Americana de Comercio e [★24305]

Industria Nacional de Autopartes [★IO]

Indus. Accident Prevention Assn. [IO], Mississauga, ON, Canada

Indus. and Applied Mathematics; Soc. for [7294]

Indus. Archeology; Soc. for [6458]

Indus. Areas Found. [17220], 220 W Kinzie St., 5th Fl., Chicago, IL 60610, (312)245-9211

Indus. Arts Assn; Amer. [★9231]

Indus. Arts Supervisors; Amer. Coun. of [★9232]

Indus. Arts Teacher Educ; Amer. Coun. on [★8543]

Industrial Assn. of House Dress, Robe and Uniform Mfrs. - Defunct.

Industrial Assn. of Juvenile Apparel Mfrs. - Defunct.

Indus. Assn. of Macau [IO], Macau, Macao

Industrial Assn. of Production Engineers - Address unknown since 1995.

Indus. Audio-Visual Assn. [★329]

Indus. Bag and Cover Assn. [★2875]

Indus. Bankers Assn; Amer. [★2422]

Indus. Biotechnology Assn. [★520]

Indus. Caterers' Assn; Mobile [★1938]

Indus., Chem. and Energy Workers Intl. Union; Paper, Allied- [24211]

Industrial Chemical Res. Assn. [810]

Indus. Chiropractic Consultants; Acad. of Forensic and [830]

Indus. Cleaning Machine Mfrs'. Assn. [IO], Solihull, United Kingdom

Indus. Commun. Coun. [★876]

Indus. Communications Assn. [★3748]

Indus. Communications Assn. [★IO]

Industrial Compressor Distributors Assn. - Address unknown since 2003.

Indus. Cmpt. Mfrs. Gp; PCI [6818]

Indus. Conf. Bd; Natl. [★6877]

Indus. Cooperative Assn. [★1249]

Industrial Coun. of Cloak, Suit and Skirt Mfrs. [★253]

Indus. Coun; Natl. [★2555]

Indus. Coun; Southern States [★17639]

Indus. Coun; U.S. [★17639]

Indus. Coun; U.S. Bus. and [★17639]

Indus. Crops; Assn. for the Advancement of [4110]

Industrial Design

Assn. of Chartered Indus. Designers of Ontario [IO]

Assn. of Women Indus. Designers [IO]

Assn. of Women Indus. Designers [7179]

Danish Designers [IO]

Design Coun. [IO]

Design Mgt. Inst. [1807]

Finnish Assn. of Designers Ornamo [IO]

Indus. Designers Soc. of Am. [7180]

Indus. Perforators Assn. [2709]

Intl. Coun. of Societies of Indus. Design [IO]

Japan Indus. Design Promotion Org. [IO]

Japan Indus. Designers' Assn. [IO]

Org. of Black Designers [9907]

Union of Designers in Belgium [IO]

Indus. Design Educ. Assn. [★7180]

Indus. Designers Inst. [★7180]

Indus. Designers Soc. of Am. [7180], 45195 Bus. Ct., Ste. 250, Dulles, VA 20166-6717, (703)707-6000

Industrial Development

1394 High Performance Serial Bus Trade Assn. [3720]

All India Assn. of Indus. [IO]

Amer. Indus. Extension Alliance [2546]

Assn. of Defense Communities [5811]

Assn. of Lebanese Industrialists [IO]

Bus. and Indus. Advisory Comm. to the OECD [IO]

China Natl. Light Indus. Coun. [IO]

Confed. of Indus. of the Czech Republic [IO]

Confed. of Italian Indus. [IO]

Employer Assn. Gp. [2555]

European Indus. Assn. [IO]

European Logistics Assn. [IO]

Fabless Semiconductor Assn. [1215]

Fed. of Icelandic Indus. [IO]

Glass Mfg. Indus. Coun. [1729]

Gulf Org. for Indus. Consulting [IO]

Intl. Aviation Ground Support Assn. [436]

Intl. Economic Development Coun. [5812]

Intl. Economic Development Coun. [IO]

Intervention and Coiled Tubing Assn. [7512]

Irish Productivity Centre [IO]

Japan Productivity Center for Socio-Economic Development [IO]

Mfg. Enterprise Solutions Assn. Intl. [7722]

Mfg. Skill Standards Coun. [7696]

Mexican Assn. of Indus. Parks [IO]

Turkish Amer. Scientists and Scholars Assn. [7636]

Indus. Development Bd. of Ceylon [IO], Moratuwa, Sri Lanka

Indus. Development Bond Issuers; Coun. of [★17458]

Indus. Development; Maritime Inst. for Res. and [6060]

Indus. Diamond Assn. [2026], PO Box 29460, Columbus, OH 43229, (614)797-2265

Indus. Diamond Assn. of Am. [★2026]

Indus. Diamond Assn. of Japan [IO], Tokyo, Japan

Indus. Distribution Assn. [★2027]

Indus. Ecology; Intl. Soc. for [4580]

Industrial Education

Assn. for Skilled and Tech. Sciences [8542]

Coun. on Tech. Teacher Educ. [8543]

Coun. on Tech. Teacher Educ. [IO]

European Consortium of Innovative Universities [IO]

Iota Lambda Sigma [24724]

Natl. Assn. of Indus. and Tech. Teacher Educators [8544]

Natl. Assn. of Indus. Tech. [8545]

SkillsUSA [8546]

Tech. Student Assn. [8547]

Indus. Electronics Soc; IEEE [6919]

Industrial Engineering

Alpha Pi Mu [24458]

APICS - The Assn. for Operations Mgt. [7181]

APICS - The Association for Operations Management [IO]

Completion Engg. Assn. [7182]

European Students of Indus. Engg. and Mgt. [IO]

IEEE Indus. Applications Soc. [7183]

Inst. of Indus. Engineers [IO]

Intl. Soc. of Coating Sci. and Tech. [6705]

Intervention and Coiled Tubing Assn. [7512]

Miles Value Found. [7184]

Natl. Inst. of Mgt. Counsellors [2508]

SAVE Intl. [7185]

SAVE Intl. [IO]

SOLE - The Intl. Soc. of Logistics [IO]

SOLE - The Intl. Soc. of Logistics [7186]

Indus. Engineers; Amer. Inst. of [★7016]

Indus. Engineers; Inst. of [7016]

Indus. Engineers; Soc. of [★2515]

Industrial Equipment

Abrasive Engg. Soc. [1989]

Abrasive Engineering Society [IO]

Amer. Apparel Machinery Trade Assn. [1990]

Amer. Bearing Mfrs. Assn. [1991]

Amer. Boiler Mfrs. Assn. [1992]

Amer. Chain Assn. [1993]

Amer. Gear Mfrs. Assn. [1994]

Amer. Gear Mfrs. Assn. [IO]

Amer. Machine Tool Distributors' Assn. [1995]

Amer. Mold Builders Assn. [1996]

Amer. Textile Machinery Assn. [1997]

Amer. Wire Cloth Inst. [1998]

Amer. Wire Producers Assn. [1999]

Antique Caterpillar Machinery Owners Club [22619]

Antique Small Engine Collectors Club [22409]

Associacao de Industriais Metalurgicos, Metalomecanicos e Afins de Portugal [IO]

Assoc. Equip. Distributors [2000]

Assoc. Wire Rope Fabricators [2001]

Assn. of British Mining Equip. Companies [IO]

Assn. of Equip. Mgt. Professionals [2442]

Assn. of European Gas Meter Mfrs. [IO]

Assn. of Ingersoll-Rand Distributors [2002]

Assn. of Loading and Elevating Equip. Mfrs. [IO]

Assn. of Mfrs. of Power Generating Systems [IO]

Assn. of Progressive Rental Organizations [3379]

Assn. of Suppliers to the Paper Indus. [2003]

Automated Material Handling Systems Assn. [IO]

Automated Storage/Retrieval Systems [2004]

Automatic Guided Vehicle Systems Sect. of the Material Handling Inst. [2005]

AVEM Intl. [2006]

AVEM Intl. [IO]

Ball and Roller Bearing Mfrs. Assn. [IO]

Bearing Specialists Assn. [2007]

Boiler and Radiator Manufacturers Assn. [IO]

Brazilian Assn. of Infrastructure and Basic Indus. [IO]

British Abrasives Fed. [IO]

British Fluid Power Distributors Assn. [IO]

British Gear Assn. [IO]

British Hardmetal and Engineers' Cutting Tool Assn. [IO]

British Indus. Furnace Constructors Assn. [IO]

British Pump Mfrs'. Assn. [IO]

British Textile Machinery Assn. [IO]

British Turned-Parts Mfrs. Assn. [IO]

British Valve and Actuator Assn. [IO]

Cast Bronze Inst. [2008]

Casting Indus. Suppliers Assn. [2009]

China Bearing Indus. Assn. [IO]

China Chamber of Commerce for Import and Export of Machinery and Electronic Products [IO]

China Feather and Down Indus. Assn. [IO]

China Food and Packaging Machinery Indus. Assn. [IO]

China Sewing Machinery Assn. [IO]

China Welding Assn. [IO]

Cleaning and Hygiene Suppliers' Assn. [IO]

Comm. for European Constr. Equip. [IO]

Compressed Air and Gas Inst. [2010]

Constr. Equip. Assn. [IO]

Contractors Pump Bur. [2011]

Converting Equip. Mfrs. Assn. [2012]

Conveyor Equip. Mfrs. Assn. [2013]

Conveyor Sect. of the Material Handling Inst. [2014]

Coordinating Res. Coun. [2921]

Coun. of Indus. Boiler Owners [2015]

Crane Mfrs. Assn. of Am. [2016]

Energy Traffic Assn. [2923]

Equip. Appraisers Assn. of North Am. [279]

Equip. Ser. Assn. [3549]

European Assn. of Machine Tool Merchants [IO]

European Assn. of Pump Mfrs. [IO]

European Comm. of Mfrs. of Compressors, Vacuum Pumps, and Pneumatic Tools [IO]

European Comm. for the Valve Indus. [IO]

European Confed. of Iron and Steel Indus. [IO]

European Demolition Assn. [IO]

European Fed. of Materials Handling and Storage Equip. [IO]

European Indus. Fasteners Inst. [IO]

European Lift Components Assn. [IO]

Reference to "IO" in place of a book number signifies that the association may be found in the 45th edition of International Organizations.

European Oil Hydraulic and Pneumatic Comm. [IO]
European Power Tool Assn. [IO]
European Rental Assn. [IO]
European Resin Mfrs'. Assn. [IO]
Fabricators and Mfrs. Assn., Intl. [IO]
Fabricators and Mfrs. Assn., Intl. [2017]
Fed. of European Producers of Abrasives [IO]
Fed. of the Italian Associations of Mech. and Engg. Indus. [IO]
Finnish Hydraulics and Pneumatics Assn. [IO]
Floor Installation Assn. of North Am. [623]
Fluid Controls Inst. [2018]
Fluid Power Distributors Assn. [2019]
Fluid Sealing Assn. [2020]
Forecourt Equip. Fed. [IO]
Foundry Equip. and Supplies Assn. [IO]
Gases and Welding Distributors Assn. [2021]
Gasket Fabricators Assn. [2022]
Gauge and Tool Makers' Assn. [IO]
German Machine Tool Builders' Assn. [IO]
Heat Exchange Inst. [1881]
Hoist Mfrs. Inst. [2023]
Hydraulic Inst. [2024]
Hydraulic Tool Mfrs. Assn. [2025]
ICOM Energy Assn. [IO]
Indus. Cleaning Machine Mfrs'. Assn. [IO]
Indus. Diamond Assn. [2026]
Indus. Diamond Assn. of Japan [IO]
Indus. Supply Assn. [2027]
Indus. Truck Assn. [387]
Institut fuer Naehtechnik [IO]
Inst. of Caster Manufacturers [2028]
Intl. Assn. of Diecutting and Diemaking [2029]
Intl. Assn. of Diecutting and Diemaking [IO]
Intl. Aviation Ground Support Assn. [436]
Intl. Certified Floorcovering Installers Assn. [1025]
Intl. Coun. for Machinery Lubrication [7253]
Intl. Glove Assn. [2030]
Intl. Glove Assn. [IO]
Intl. Powered Access Fed. [IO]
Intl. Safety Equip. Assn. [3445]
Intl. Special Tooling and Machining Assn. [2031]
Intl. Special Tooling and Machining Assn. [IO]
Intervention and Coiled Tubing Assn. [7512]
Investment Casting Inst. [2032]
Investment Casting Inst. [IO]
Iron Casting Res. Inst. [2033]
Italian Assn. of Fasteners Mfrs. [IO]
Italian Assn. of Precision Moulds, Dies and Tooling Manufacturers [IO]
Japan Automotive Ser. Equip. Assn. [IO]
Japan Machine Tool Importers' Assn. [IO]
Japan Sewing Machinery Mfrs. Assn. [IO]
Japan Soc. of Indus. Machinery Mfrs. [IO]
Kibbutz Indus. Assn. [IO]
Korea Machine Tool Mfrs'. Assn. [IO]
Lift and Escalator Indus. Assn. [IO]
Lift Mfrs. Prdt. Sect. - Material Handling Indus. of Am. [2034]
Lifting Equip. Engineers Assn. [IO]
Loading Dock Equip. Mfrs. [2035]
Machine Knife Assn. [2036]
Machinery Dealers Natl. Assn. [2037]
Machinery Dealers Natl. Assn. [IO]
Mfrs. of Aerial Devices and Digger-Derricks Coun. [2038]
Mfrs. Alliance/MAPI [2039]
Mfrs. Standardization Soc. of the Valve and Fittings Indus. [2040]
Manufacturers Standardization Society of the Valve and Fittings Industry [IO]
Mfrs. of Telescoping and Articulated Cranes Coun. [2041]
Mfg. Technologies Assn. [IO]
Material Handling Accessory Mfrs., Production Sect. of the Material Handling Indus. [2042]
Material Handling Equip. Distributors Assn. [2043]
Material Handling Indus. of Am. [2044]
Mech. Equip. Mfrs. Representatives Assn. [2540]
Mech. Power Transmission Assn. [2045]
Metal Treating Inst. [2717]
Metalforming Machinery Makers' Assn. [IO]
Millwright Gp. [24102]
Monorail Mfrs. Assn. [2046]

Natl. Assn. of Hose and Accessories Distribution [2047]
Natl. Assn. of Vertical Trans. Professionals [2048]
Natl. Drilling Assn. [1044]
Natl. Elevator Indus., Inc. [2049]
Natl. Fluid Power Assn. [2050]
Natl. Fluid Power Assn. [IO]
Natl. Indus. Belting Assn. [2051]
Natl. New England Lead Burning Assn. [2052]
Natl. Pavement Contractors Assn. [651]
Non-Ferrous Founders' Soc. [2053]
North Amer. Die Casting Assn. [2054]
North Amer. Power Sweeping Assn. [2473]
North Amer. Punch Mfrs. Assn. [2055]
Offshore Marine Ser. Assn. [2590]
Paper, Allied-Indus., Chem. and Energy Workers Intl. Union [IO]
Paper Machine Clothing Coun. [2056]
Pattern, Model, and Mould Mfrs. Assn. [IO]
Petroleum Equip. Inst. [2941]
Petroleum Equip. Suppliers Assn. [2942]
Picon [IO]
Powder Actuated Tool Mfrs'. Inst. [2057]
Power Crane and Shovel Assn. [2058]
Power-Motion Tech. Representatives Assn. [2059]
Power Transmission Distributors Assn. [2060]
Power Transmission Distributors Association [IO]
Pressure Gauge and Dial Thermometer Assn. [IO]
Pressure Vessel Mfrs. Assn. [2061]
Pressure Washer Mfrs. Assn. [2062]
Process Equip. Mfrs. Assn. [2063]
Pump Distributors Assn. [IO]
Rack Manufacturers Institute [IO]
Rack Mfrs. Inst. [2064]
Resistance Welding Mfg. Alliance [2065]
Sci. and Indus. Valve Mfrs. Assn. [IO]
Scottish Plant Owners Assn. [IO]
Secondary Materials and Recycled Textiles [IO]
Secondary Materials and Recycled Textiles [2066]
Sewn Products Equip. and Suppliers of the Americas [2067]
Soc. of Laundry Engineers and Allied Trades [IO]
Soc. of Professional Rope Access Technicians [2068]
Solids Handling and Processing Assn. [IO]
Spanish Textile Machinery Mfrs. Assn. [IO]
Specialist Access Engg. and Maintenance Assn. [IO]
Specialty Tools and Fasteners Distributors Assn. [2069]
Steel Founders' Soc. of Am. [2070]
Steel Founders' Soc. of Am. [IO]
Steel Tube Inst. of North Am. [997]
Storage Equip. Mfrs. Assn. [2071]
Surface Mount Tech. Assn. [2072]
Swedish Assn. of Suppliers of Effluent and Water Treatment Equip. [IO]
Swedish Machine Tool and Cutting Tool Mfrs. Assn. [IO]
Swedish Special Tooling Assn. [IO]
Swissmem - Swiss Mech. and Elecl. Engg. Indus. [IO]
Taiwan Assn. of Machinery Indus. [IO]
Tool and Gauge Manufacturers Assn. of India [IO]
Tooling, Mfg. and Technologies Assn. [2073]
The Transformer Assn. [1836]
Tubular Exchanger Mfrs. Assn. [1902]
Unified Abrasives Mfrs'. Assn. - Grain Div. [2074]
Unified Abrasives Mfrs'. Assn. - Superabrasives Div. [2075]
United Kingdom Weighing Fed. [IO]
U.S. Bus. and Indus. Coun. Educational Found. [18638]
U.S. Cutting Tool Inst. [2076]
U.S. Microscopic Welding Assn. [7849]
Valve Mfrs. Assn. of Am. [1838]
Valves and Fittings Sweden [IO]
Verband Deutscher Maschinen- und Anlagenbau [IO]
Water Jetting Assn. [IO]
Water and Wastewater Equip. Mfrs. Assn. [2077]
Web Sling and Tie Down Assn. [2078]
The Welding Inst. [IO]
Welding Mfrs. Assn. [IO]
Wire and Cable Indus. Suppliers Assn. [1231]

Wire Industry Suppliers Assn. [2079]
Wood Machinery Mfrs. of Am. [2080]
Woodworking Machinery Indus. Assn. [2081]
Woodworking Machinery Suppliers Assn. [IO]
Woven Wire Products Assn. [2082]
Indus. Fabrics Assn. Intl. [3787], 1801 County Rd. B W, Roseville, MN 55113-4061, (651)225-2508
Indus. Fabrics Assn. Intl. [IO], Roseville, MN, United States
Indus. Fabrics Inst; U.S. [3808]
Indus. Fasteners Inst. [1823], 6363 Oak Tree Blvd., Independence, OH 44131, (216)241-1482
Indus. Fiber Soc. [★7078]
Industrial Finishing Equipment Mfrs. Assn. - Defunct.
Indus. Forestry Assn. [★1613]
Indus. Forum; Atomic [★6969]
Indus. Found. of Am. [1264], 402 E San Antonio Ave., Boerne, TX 78006, (830)249-7899
Indus. Furnace Mfrs. Assn. [★1885]
Indus. Gas Cleaning Inst. [★3071]
Industrial Health Coun; Amer. [15626]
Indus. Heating Equip. Assn. [1885], PO Box 54172, Cincinnati, OH 45254, (513)231-5613
Indus. Hemp Coun; North Amer. [7079]
Indus. Heritage Assn. of Ireland [IO], Dublin, Ireland
Indus. Hydraulics Training Assn. [★7084]
Indus. Hygiene; Amer. Bd. of [15623]
Indus. Hygiene Assn; Amer. [15627]
Indus. Hygienists; Amer. Conf. of Governmental [15625]
Indus. Hygienists; Natl. Conf. of Governmental [★15625]
Indus. Instructors; Natl. Assn. of Trade and [9233]
Indus. Insurers' Conf. [★2194]
Indus. Insurers' Conf; Southern [★2194]
Industrial Jacks Product Sect. of the Material Handling Inst. - Defunct.
Indus. Launderers; Inst. of [★2408]
Industrial Lift and Loading Ramp Inst. - Defunct.
Industrial Lighting Distributors of America - Address unknown since 1995.
Indus. Mgt; Amer. Assn. of [2480]
Indus. Mgt. Soc. [★7016]
Indus. Mfrs. Representatives Assn; Agricultural and [2533]
Industrial Marketing Associates - Defunct.
Industrial Mathematics Soc. - Defunct.
Indus. Medal Containers, Sect. of the Material Handling Inst. [★983]
Indus. Metal Containers and Wire Decking, a Prdt. Sect. of the Material Handling Indus. [983], 8720 Red Oak Blvd., Ste. 201, Charlotte, NC 28217, (704)676-1190
Indus. Metallizers, Coaters and Laminators; Assn. of [851]
Indus. Methods Soc. [★2515]
Indus. Microbiology; Soc. for [6599]
Indus. Minerals Assn. - North Am. [2742], 2011 Pennsylvania Ave. NW, Ste. 301, Washington, DC 20006, (202)457-0200
Indus. Minerals Assn. - North Am. [IO], Washington, DC, United States
Indus. Naval Air Stations; Natl. Coun. of [6088]
Indus. Network [★2867]
Indus. Noise Control Assn; Community [★7383]
Indus. Nurses; Amer. Assn. of [★15439]
Indus. and Off. Parks; Natl. Assn. of [★3320]
Indus. and Off. Properties; Natl. Assn. of [3320]
Indus. and Off. Realtors; Soc. of [3343]
Industrial Oil Consumers Group - Address unknown since 1994.
Indus. and Organizational Psychology; Soc. for [16173]
Indus. Organizations; Cong. of [★24096]
Indus. Packaging Assn; Reusable [994]
Indus. Parks; Natl. Assn. of [★3320]
Indus. Perforators Assn. [2709], 5157 Deerhurst Crescent Cir., Boca Raton, FL 33486, (561)447-7511
Industrial Photographers of New Jersey - Defunct.
Industrial Policy Coun. - Defunct.
Indus. Property Mgt. Assn; Natl. [★3190]
Industrial Publicity Assn. - Address unknown since 1995.
Indus. Radio Ser. Assn; Special [★3742]

A star before a book entry number signifies that the name is not listed separately, but is mentioned within the entry.

Indus. Radium and X-Ray Soc; Amer. [★7787]
Indus. Realtors; Soc. of [★3343]
Industrial Relations Assn; Natl. Trucking [★2906]
Industrial Relations Assn; North Amer. Trucking [2906]
Indus. Relations Conf; Airline [136]
Industrial Relations Coun. - Address unknown since 2002.
Industrial Relations Coun. for the Plumbing and Pipe Fitting Industry - Address unknown since 2001.
Industrial Relations Counselors - Address unknown since 1995.
Indus. Relations; Inst. of Labor and [24114]
Indus. Relations Res. Assn. [★24115]
Indus. Res. Inst. [7568], 2200 Clarendon Blvd., Ste. 1102, Arlington, VA 22201, (703)647-2580
Indus. Resources; Natl. Assn. for the Exchange of [8336]
Indus. Safety Equip. Assn. [★3445]
Indus. Safety Equip. Assn. [★IO]
Indus. Sand Assn; Natl. [2743]
Indus. Sanitation Mgt. Assn. [★2463]
Industrial Security
    ASIS Intl. [2083]
    ASIS Intl. [IO]
    Assn. of Certified Fraud Examiners [IO]
    Assn. of Certified Fraud Examiners [2084]
    Assn. of Certified Fraud Examiners, Belgium Chap. 127 [IO]
    Assn. of Certified Fraud Examiners, Hong Kong Chap. [IO]
    Assn. of Certified Fraud Examiners, South African Chap. [IO]
    Assn. of Certified Fraud Examiners, United Kingdom Chap. [IO]
    Assn. of Certified Fraud Specialists [2085]
    Australian Information Security Assn. [IO]
    Business Espionage Controls and Countermeasures Association [IO]
    Bus. Espionage Controls and Countermeasures Assn. [2086]
    Canadian Soc. for Indus. Security [IO]
    Communications Fraud Control Association [IO]
    Communications Fraud Control Assn. [2087]
    Cmpt. Security Inst. [2088]
    Energy Security Coun. [2089]
    Help the Helpless [12405]
    Info. Systems Security Assn. [2090]
    Information Systems Security Association [IO]
    Info. Systems Security Assn. Brussels-European Chap. [IO]
    Info. Systems Security Assn. - Netherlands Chap. [IO]
    Natl. Assn. of Indus. Security Companies [IO]
    Natl. Center for Computer Crime Data [2091]
    NCMS — Soc. of Indus. Security Professionals &lsqb2092]
    U.S. Contract Security Assn. [3543]
Indus. Security; Amer. Soc. for [★2083]
Indus. Ser. Assn; Natl. [★1180]
Industrial Silencer Mfrs. Assn. - Defunct.
Indus. Soc. [IO], Santiago, Chile
Indus. Soc. [★IO]
Industrial Specialty Chemical Assn. - Defunct.
Indus. Stapling Mfrs. Inst. [★1825]
Indus. Stapling Mfrs. Inst. [★IO]
Indus. Stapling and Nailing Tech. Assn. [★IO]
Indus. Stapling and Nailing Tech. Assn. [★1825]
Indus. Supply Assn. [2027], 100 N 20th St., 4th Fl., Philadelphia, PA 19103, (215)320-3862
Indus. Supply and Machinery Mfrs. Assn. [★2027]
Indus. Supply Mfrs. Assn. [★2027]
Indus. Teacher Educators; Natl. Assn. of [★8544]
Indus. Teacher Trainers; Natl. Assn. of [★8544]
Indus. Telecommunications Assn. [★3742]
Indus. TV Assn; Natl. [★1388]
Indus. TV Soc. [★1388]
Indus. TV Soc. [★IO]
Indus. Traffic League; Natl. [★3879]
Indus. Trans. League; Natl. [3879]
Indus. Truck Assn. [387], 1750 K St. NW, Ste. 460, Washington, DC 20006, (202)296-9880
Indus. Truck Assn; Elec. [★387]
Industrial Union Dept. (of AFL-CIO) - Defunct.
Indus. Union of Marine and Ship Building Workers of Am. [24125], 122 Main St., Ste. 4A, Topsham, ME 04086, (207)721-8996

Indus. Unit Heater Assn. [★1876]
Indus. Unit Heater Assn. [★IO]
Industrial Vegetation Mgt. Assn. - Defunct.
Industrial Water Conditioning Inst. - Address unknown since 2001.
Indus. Wire Cloth Inst. [★1998]
Industrial Workers
    AFL-CIO [24096]
    Amer. Assn. of Indus. Mgt. [2480]
    Amer. Bd. of Indus. Hygiene [15623]
    Amer. Conf. of Governmental Indus. Hygienists [15625]
    Amer. Industrial Health Coun. [15626]
    Amer. Indus. Hygiene Assn. [15627]
    Australian Mfg. Workers' Union [IO]
    Community: The Union for Life [IO]
    Confed. of Icelandic Employers [IO]
    Economiesuisse, The Swiss Bus. Fed. [IO]
    Fed. of German Indus. [IO]
    Fed. of Greek Indus. [IO]
    Fed. of Luxembourg Industrialists [IO]
    Finnish Confed. of Salaried Employees [IO]
    Gen. Ser. Employees Union Local 73 [24097]
    Gen. Union of Workers [IO]
    Indus. Workers of the World [IO]
    Indus. Workers of the World [24098]
    Indus. Workers of the World Starbucks Workers Union [24206]
    Inst. of the Ironworking Indus. [24133]
    Intl. Union of Elevator Constructors [24099]
    Intl. Union of Elevator Constructors [IO]
    Intl. Union of Indus. and Independent Workers [24208]
    Intl. Union of Petroleum and Indus. Workers [24163]
    Intl. Union of Tool, Die and Mold Makers [24100]
    Machinists Non-Partisan Political League [24101]
    Malta Fed. of Indus. [IO]
    Metal Trades Dept., AFL-CIO [24135]
    Millwright Gp. [24102]
    Natl. Inst. for Metalworking Skills [7321]
    Natl. Org. of Indus. Trade Unions [24103]
    Oilfields Workers' Trade Union [IO]
    Social Accountability Intl. [18828]
    Soc. for Occupational and Environmental Hea. [15633]
    United Paperworkers Intl. Union [24104]
    United Paperworkers Intl. Union [IO]
Indus. Workers; Intl. Union of Petroleum and [24163]
Indus. Workers of the World [24098], PO Box 23085, Cincinnati, OH 45223, (513)591-1905
Indus. Workers of the World [IO], Cincinnati, OH, United States
Indus. Workers of the World Starbucks Workers Union [24206], 347 Maujer St., Apt. C, Brooklyn, NY 11206, (917)577-1110
Industrial Yarns Mfrs; Intl. Soc. of [★3790]
Industrialists' Assn. of Panama [IO], Panama City, Panama
Industrialization Centers of Am; Opportunities [12096]
Industrialization Centers Intl; Opportunities [13181]
Industrialized Housing Mfrs. Assn. - Address unknown since 1994.
Industrias Venezolanas de Buena Voluntad [★IO]
Industrie Mondiale de l'Automedication Responsable [★IO]
Industriegewerkschaft Bergbau, Chemie, and Energie [★IO]
Indus; Adventist-Laymen's Services and [20553]
Indus. Assn. of Am; Aerospace [130]
Indus. Assn. of Canada; Aerospace [★154]
Indus. Assn. of Canada; Aerospace [★IO]
Indus. Assn; Early Amer. [9481]
Indus. for the Blind; Natl. [16878]
Indus. of Chicago; Textile Merchants and Assoc. [★221]
Indus; Materials Tech. Inst. of the Chem. Process [★812]
Indus. of St. Louis; Textile Merchants and Assoc. [★221]
Industrieverband Heimtierbedarf [★IO]
Industrieverband Korperpflege-und Waschmittel e.V. [★IO]
Industrievereinigung Chemiefaser [★IO]

Indus. Advisory Comm. to the OECD; U.S.A. - Bus. and [17466]
Indus; American-Arab Assn. for Commerce and [★24357]
Indus. Applications Soc; IEEE [7183]
Indus. Assn; Intl. Fence [★938]
Indus. Assn; Korea-America Commerce and [★24350]
Indus. Assn; MDS [★3764]
Indus. Assn; Returns [2981]
Industry Assn; United Dairy [1140]
Indus. Assn; Woodworking Machinery [2081]
Indus. Associations; Coun. of Defense and Space [147]
Indus. Bar Code Alliance [★338]
Indus. Bd. of the Elecl. Indus; Joint [1030]
Industry Center for Trade Negotiations - Defunct.
Industry Coalition for Fire Safety - Defunct.
Industry Coalition on Technology Transfer [1217]
Indus. Comm; ERISA [1238]
Industry Conf. on Auto Collision Repair; Inter- [415]
Indus. Coun. Educational Found; U.S. Bus. and [18638]
Indus. Coun. for Electronic Equip. Recycling [IO], London, United Kingdom
Indus. Coun. for Packaging and the Env. [IO], Reading, United Kingdom
Indus. Coun. for Tangible Assets [3713], PO Box 1365, Severna Park, MD 21146-8365, (410)626-7005
Indus. Coun; U.S. Bus. and [17639]
Industry-Education Cooperation; Natl. Assn. for [8048]
Indus. Educ. Found; Exhibit [★1349]
Indus. Film Producers Assn. [★1384]
Indus. Film Producers Assn. [★IO]
Indus. Mfrs. Representatives; Assn. of [★2534]
Industry Planning Coun. - Defunct.
Industry Political Action Comm; Business- [18284]
Indus. Prog; Projects With [★11271]
Industry Res. Advisory Coun; All- [★2183]
Indus. Res; Center for Exhibition [1335]
Indus; School Facilities Coun. of Architecture, Educ. and [★7892]
Indus. for a Sound Env; Responsible [2912]
Indus. Tech. Facilitator [IO], Aberdeen, United Kingdom
Indus. of the U.S. and Canada; Assn. of Govt. Officials in [★5917]
Indy 500 Collectors Club; Natl. [21734]
Ineqartut Peqatigiiffiisa Kattuffiat [★IO]
Infact [★IO]
Infact [★18149]
Infant Death Rsrc. Center; Natl. SIDS/ [16526]
Infant Death and Stillbirth Support Gp; Miscarriage [16540]
Infant Death Syndrome Alliance; Sudden [★16525]
Infant Death Syndrome CH; Natl. Sudden [★16526]
Infant Death Syndrome Found; Natl. Sudden [★16525]
Infant Death Syndrome Inst; Amer. Sudden [16523]
Infant Feeders; Amer. Collectors of [21959]
Infant Feeding Action Coalition - Canada [IO], Toronto, ON, Canada
Infant Formula Coun. [★2387]
Infant and Juvenile Mfrs. Assn. [240]
Infant Loss Center; Pregnancy and [★12668]
Infant Loss Support; SHARE-Pregnancy and [12690]
Infant - Maternal Nutrition Educ. [★IO]
Infant Mental Hea; Intl. Assn. for [★16098]
Infant Mortality Programs; Assn. of SIDS and [16524]
Infant and Nursery Products Assn. of Australia [IO], Boronia, Australia
Infant Programs; Natl. Center for Clinical [★13944]
Infant Psychiatry; World Assn. for Allied Disciplines and [★16098]
Infant Services; Natl. Inst. of [★2389]
Infant Survival; Amer. Guild for [16522]
Infantile Paralysis; Natl. Found. for [★13756]
Infantry Assn; 325th Glider [21374]
Infantry Assn; 509th Parachute [21380]
Infantry Assn; U.S. [★6071]
Infantry Battalion Assn; 526th Armored [21382]
Infantry Div. (2id), Korean War Veterans Alliance; 2nd [21167]

Reference to "IO" in place of a book number signifies that the association may be found in the 45th edition of International Organizations.

Infantry Div. Assn; 24th [20686]
Infantry Div. Assn; 25th [20687]
Infantry Div. Assn; 29th [20679]
Infantry Div. Assn; 33rd [20680]
Infantry Div. Assn; 43rd [★20689]
Infantry Div. Assn; 63rd [20690]
Infantry Div. Assn; 70th [21366]
Infantry Div. Assn; 94th [21369]
Infantry Div. Assn; 95th [20691]
Infantry Div. Assn; 96th [20692]
Infantry Div. Assn; 99th [21370]
Infantry Div. Assn; 100th [20693]
Infantry Div. Assn; 106th [21371]
Infantry Div. Korean War Veterans; Assn. of 40th [21168]
Infantry Div; Natl. Assn. of the Sixth [20704]
Infantry Div. Natl. Timberwolf Assn; 104th [20695]
Infantry Div; Soc. of the 3rd [21186]
Infantry Div; Soc. of the First [20706]
Infantry Div. Veterans Assn; 32nd [20688]
Infantry Div. Veterans Assn; 43rd [20689]
Infantry (Ivy) Div. Assn; Natl. 4th [20703]
Infantry Regiment Assn; 504th Parachute [21378]
Infantry Regiment Assn; 508th Parachute [21379]
Infants
Amer. Center for Law and Justice [12901]
Amer. Collectors of Infant Feeders [21959]
Amer. Found. for Maternal and Child Health [15586]
Amer. Sudden Infant Death Syndrome Inst. [16523]
Assn. for Birth Psychology [16137]
Assn. of Breastfeeding Mothers [IO]
Assn. for Pre- and Perinatal Psychology and Hea. [13979]
Assn. for Retinopathy of Prematurity and Related Diseases [15673]
Assn. of SIDS and Infant Mortality Programs [16524]
Australian Breastfeeding Assn. [IO]
Baby Milk Action [IO]
Birth Defect Res. for Children [13752]
Childbirth and Postpartum Professional Assn. [13980]
Children with AIDS Proj. of Am. [11238]
Coun. of Women's and Infants' Specialty Hospitals [14880]
Danny Found. [12959]
Diaper Ser. Accreditation Coun. [2386]
Fairview Pregnancy and Newborn Loss Information [12668]
Fed. of Pediatric Organizations [15887]
First Candle/SIDS Alliance [16525]
FORMULA Inc. [12408]
Found. for the Stud. of Infant Deaths [IO]
Geneva Infant Feeding Assn. [IO]
Global Neuro Rescue [15324]
Human Lactation Center [12409]
Human Lactation Center [IO]
Infant Feeding Action Coalition - Canada [IO]
Infant and Nursery Products Assn. of Australia [IO]
Inst. for Consumer Protection [IO]
Intl. Assn. of Infant Massage [15029]
Intl. Baby Food Action Network - Africa [IO]
Intl. Baby Food Action Network - Asia [IO]
Intl. Baby Food Action Network - Brazil [IO]
Intl. Baby Food Action Network - Latin Am. [IO]
Intl. Baby Food Action Network - South Am. [IO]
Intl. Formula Coun. [2387]
Intl. Lactation Consultant Assn. [12410]
Intl. Lactation Consultant Assn. [IO]
Intl. Soc. on Infant Stud. [13963]
Juvenile Products Mfrs. Assn. [2388]
La Leche League Intl. [12411]
La Leche League Intl. [IO]
La Leche League of New Zealand [IO]
March of Dimes Birth Defects Found. [13756]
Natl. Abandoned Infants Assistance Rsrc. Center [12412]
Natl. Assn. of Diaper Services [2389]
Natl. Assn. of Pro-Life Nurses [18378]
Natl. Healthy Mothers, Healthy Babies Coalition [15612]
Natl. Healthy Start Assn. [15613]

Natl. Infant Torticollis Assn. [14945]
Natl. SIDS/Infant Death Rsrc. Center [16526]
Newborn Rights Soc. [12413]
Newborn Rights Soc. [IO]
Non-Circumcision Educational Found. [11735]
Non-Circumcision Info. Center [11736]
Nursing Mothers Counsel [12414]
Parents of Infants and Children with Kernicterus [15358]
Peaceful Beginnings [11669]
Postpartum Support Intl. [12689]
Soc. for Pediatric Radiology [16301]
Soc. for Pediatric Res. [15899]
U.S. Coalition for Life [12929]
Wellstart Intl. [14666]
Women Exploited by Abortion [12932]
World Assn. for Infant Mental Hea. [16098]
Zero to Three: Natl. Center for Infants, Toddlers and Families [13944]
Infants', Children's and Girls' Sportswear and Coat Assn. - Defunct.
Infants' and Children's Novelties Assn. - Address unknown since 1995.
Infants', Children's and Teens' Wear Buyers Assn. - Address unknown since 1995.
Infants' and Children's Wear Salesmen's Guild - Address unknown since 1991.
Infants Ser; Retarded [★12566]
Infants, Toddlers and Families; Natl. Center for [★13944]
Infants, Toddlers and Families; Zero to Three: Natl. Center for [13944]
INFARMA - Employers' Union of Innovative Pharmaceutical Companies [IO], Warsaw, Poland
Infection Control Assn. Australian Capital Territory [IO], Garran, Australia
Infection Control Assn. New South Wales [IO], Burwood, Australia
Infection Control Assn. (Singapore) [IO], Singapore, Singapore
Infection Control Assn. of South Australia [IO], North Adelaide, Australia
Infection Control Assn. of Western Australia [IO], Claremont, Australia
Infection Control and Epidemiology; Assn. for Professionals in [14947]
Infection Control and Epidemiology; Certification Bd. of [14702]
Infection Control Nurses' Assn. [IO], Bathgate, United Kingdom
Infection Control Practitioners Assn. of Queensland [IO], Buranda, Australia
Infectionists Sci. Soc. of Republic Belarus [IO], Vitebsk, Belarus
Infectious Disease Soc. of the Netherlands [IO], Utrecht, Netherlands
Infectious Diseases
Aid for AIDS [13547]
AIDS Empowerment and Treatment Intl. [13550]
AIDS Treatment Activists Coalition [11324]
Alliance for Microbicide Development [13555]
Amer. Sepsis Alliance [14946]
Argentine Soc. of Infectious Diseases [IO]
Assn. for Professionals in Infection Control and Epidemiology [14947]
Australian Infection Control Assn. [IO]
Certification Bd. of Infection Control and Epidemiology [14702]
Chilean Soc. of Infectious Diseases [IO]
Comm. to Reduce Infection Deaths [14877]
Czech Soc. for Infectious Disease [IO]
Deutsche Gesellschaft fur Infektiologie [IO]
Deutsche Gesellschaft fur Padiatrische Infektiologie [IO]
Deutsche Vereinigung zur Bekampfung der Viruskrankheiten [IO]
European Res. Org. of Genital Infection and Neoplasia [IO]
European Soc. of Clinical Microbiology and Infectious Diseases [IO]
Frontline Hepatitis Awareness [14806]
Global Bus. Coalition on HIV/AIDS [11329]
Global Strategies for HIV Prevention [13566]
Grassroot Soccer [11330]
Hellenic Soc. for Infectious Diseases [IO]

Hepatitis C Assn. [14807]
Hepatitis C Caring Ambassadors Prog. [14808]
Hepatitis Rsrc. Network [14810]
Herpes Viruses Assn. [IO]
Hong Kong Soc. for Infectious Diseases [IO]
Infection Control Assn. Australian Capital Territory [IO]
Infection Control Assn. New South Wales [IO]
Infection Control Assn. (Singapore) [IO]
Infection Control Assn. of South Australia [IO]
Infection Control Assn. of Western Australia [IO]
Infection Control Practitioners Assn. of Queensland [IO]
Infectionists Sci. Soc. of Republic Belarus [IO]
Infectious Disease Soc. of the Netherlands [IO]
Infectious Diseases Soc. of Am. [14948]
Infectious Diseases Soc. of Am. Emerging Infections Network [14949]
Intl. Fed. of Infection Control [IO]
Intl. Leptospirosis Soc. [IO]
Intl. Leptospirosis Soc. [14950]
Intl. Lyme and Assoc. Diseases Soc. [14267]
Intl. Partnership for Microbicides [13572]
Intl. Soc. for Infectious Diseases [14951]
Intl. Soc. for Infectious Diseases [IO]
Intl. Soc. for Pharmacoepidemiology [15939]
Intl. Treatment Preparedness Coalition [13573]
Israeli Soc. for Infectious Diseases [IO]
Japanese Assn. for Infectious Diseases [IO]
Lebanese Soc. for Infectious Diseases [IO]
Lyme Disease Assn. [14271]
Natl. Assn. of Hepatitis Task Forces [14812]
Natl. Assn. on HIV Over Fifty [14952]
Natl. Found. for Infectious Diseases [14953]
Natl. Hepatitis C Advocacy Coun. [14813]
Natl. Viral Hepatitis Roundtable [14815]
Parents of Kids with Infectious Diseases [14954]
Pediatric Infectious Diseases Soc. [14955]
Pediatric Infectious Diseases Soc. [IO]
Philippine Soc. for Microbiology and Infectious Diseases [IO]
Portuguese Soc. of Infectious Diseases [IO]
Romanian Soc. for the Stud. of Chemotherapeutics [IO]
Slovak Medical Soc. of Infectiology [IO]
Soc. of Infectious Diseases (Singapore) [IO]
Solidarity and Action Against the HIV Infection in India [16969]
Swiss Soc. for Infectious Diseases [IO]
Taipei Soc. of Infectious Diseases [IO]
Tasmanian Infection Control Assn. [IO]
Transatlantic Partners Against AIDS [13586]
Victorian Infection Control Professionals Assn. [IO]
Women Alive Coalition [13588]
Infectious Diseases; Canadian Assn. for Clinical Microbiology and [IO]
Infectious Diseases Pharmacists; Soc. of [15952]
Infectious Diseases Soc. of Am. [14948], 1300 Wilson Blvd., Ste. 300, Arlington, VA 22209, (703)299-0200
Infectious Diseases Soc. of Am. Emerging Infections Network [14949], c/o Susan Beekmann, RN, Prog. Coor., Univ. of Iowa, Carver Coll. of Medicine, SW 34 GH, 200 Hawkins Dr., Iowa City, IA 52242, (319)384-8622
Infertility Associates - Address unknown since 1990.
Infertility Assn; Resolve, The Natl. [14394]
Infertility Awareness Assn. of Canada [IO], Montreal, QC, Canada
Infertility Info. Dissemination; Intl. Coun. on [14392]
Infertility; Intl. Soc. of Infectious Diseases and Human [★16347]
Infertility Network Exchange; Natl. [12678]
Infertility Network UK [IO], Bexhill-on-Sea, United Kingdom
Infinite Dreams [IO], Ebikon, Switzerland
Infiniti Car Owners Club; Nissan [21742]
Infinium UserNet [★3728]
Inflammation Res. Assn. [14264], c/o William M. Selig, PhD, Pres., CombinatoRx, Inc., 245 First St., Cambridge, MA 02142, (617)301-7225
Inflammatory Skin Disease Inst. [14265], PO Box 1074, Newport News, VA 23601, (757)223-0795
Inflatable Advt. Dealers Assn. [101], 136 S Keowee St., Dayton, OH 45402, (937)222-1024

A star before a book entry number signifies that the name is not listed separately, but is mentioned within the entry.

Inflation Study Group - Defunct.
Inflight Food Ser. Assn. [★1583]
Inflight Food Ser. Assn. [★IO]
INFO Nepal [IO], Kathmandu, Nepal
InfoComm Intl. [IO], Fairfax, VA, United States
InfoComm Intl. [331], 11242 Waples Mill Rd., Ste.
200, Fairfax, VA 22030-6079, (703)273-7200
Infomercial Marketing Assn; Natl. [★2626]
INFORM [18644], 5 Hanover Sq., New York, NY
10004-2638, (212)361-2400
Inform; Proj. [13583]
Informal Logic and Critical Thinking; Assn. for
[10785]
Informatics
African Soc. for Bioinformatics and Computational
Biology [IO]
Assn. of Medical Directors of Info. Systems
[14957]
Assn. for Pathology Informatics [15864]
Bioinformatics Italian Soc. [IO]
Brazilian Assn. for Bioinformatics and
Computational Biology [IO]
Fed. of Hellenic Info. Tech. and Communications
Enterprises [IO]
Info. Resources Mgt. Assn. [2101]
Intl. Assn. of Info. Tech. Asset Managers [2093]
Intl. Assn. of Info. Tech. Asset Managers [IO]
International Society for Computational Biology
[IO]
Intl. Soc. for Computational Biology [2094]
Israeli Soc. for Bioinformatics and Computational
Biology [IO]
Japanese Soc. for Bioinformatics [IO]
Natl. Alliance of Primary Care Informatics [14956]
Informatics Assn; Amer. Medical [14079]
Informatics Assn; Amer. Nursing [15453]
Informatikai Vallalkozasok Szovetsege [★IO]
Information Access Inst. - Address unknown since
2006.
Info. for Action [IO], Perth, Australia
Info. Brokers; Intl. Assn. of Independent [★2097]
Info. Bur; Guatemala News and [17680]
Info. Bur; Medical [★14961]
Info. Bur; Natl. Charities [★17309]
Info. Center; Albanian Catholic [★18506]
Info. Center for Amer. Music; U.S. [★10541]
Info. Center for the Blind; Radio [★16831]
Info. Center for Children and Youth with Disabilities;
Natl. [★11971]
Information Center on Children's Cultures - Defunct.
Info. Center Comm; Fed. Lib. and [10356]
Info. Center for individuals with Disabilities; Moss
Regional Rsrc. and [★13345]
Info. Center; Freedom of [18413]
Information Center on the Mature Woman - Defunct.
Information Center; Natl. Employee Union [24076]
Info. Center; Natl. Hea. [14588]
Info. Center; Natural Hazards Res. and Applications
[7355]
Info. Center; North Amer. Indian Trade and
[★10750]
Info. Center Prog; Fed. [★5817]
Info. Center; Southwest Res. and [17345]
Info. Centre for Low External Input Agriculture [★IO]
Info. Centre for Regional Planning and Building
Constr. of the Fraunhofer Soc. [★IO]
Info. Centre on Southern Africa [IO], Bonn, Germany
Info. CH; Freedom of [18414]
Info. CH; Natl. Digestive Diseases Educ. and
[★14422]
Info. CH; Natl. Hea. [★14588]
Info. CH; Natl. Kidney and Urologic Diseases
[16710]
Info. CH; Natl. Pesticide [★13327]
Info. Comm; Elec. Consumers [★17321]
Info. and Communications Tech. Coun. [IO], Ottawa,
ON, Canada
Info. and Communications Tech. Ireland [IO], Dublin,
Ireland
Info. Coun. of Am; Sex [★16400]
Information Coun. of the Americas [18415]
Info. Coun; Intl. Food [1525]
Info. Directors of Am; Coll. Sports [23814]
Info. Display; Soc. for [6745]
Info. and Dissemination Centers; Assn. of [★7189]

Info. Div., Taipei Economic and Cultural Off. in New
York [★9792]
Info; Essential [17175]
The Information Exchange - Defunct.
Info. Exchange; Ethnic and Multicultural [★10354]
Info. Exchange; Homelessness [★12296]
Info. Exchange Round Table; Ethnic Materials and
[★10354]
Info. Exchange Roundtable; Ethnic and Multicultural
[10354]
Information Exchange; Travelers' [★1936]
Info. Film Producers of Am. [★1384]
Info. Film Producers of Am. [★IO]
Info. and Image Mgt; Assn. for [★2095]
Info. Indus. Assn; Software and [5858]
Information Industry Liaison Comm. - Defunct.
Info. Indus. South Africa [IO], Midrand, Republic of
South Africa
Information Management
African Info. Soc. Initiative [IO]
AIIM - The Enterprise Content Mgt. Assn. [2095]
Alliance of Info. and Referral Systems [7187]
Alliance of Information and Referral Systems [IO]
Amer. Assn. of Webmasters [896]
Amer. Booksellers Found. for Free Expression
[17641]
Amer. Coll. of Healthcare Info. Administrators
[14611]
Amer. Coun. for Tech. [5813]
Amer. Hea. Info. Mgt. Assn. [15097]
Amer. Lib. Assn. - Off. for Res. and Statistics
[10934]
Amer. Lib. Assn. - Public Info. Off. [10897]
Amer. Medical Informatics Assn. [14079]
Amer. Soc. of Access Professionals [5814]
Amer. Soc. for Info. Sci. and Tech. [7188]
Arab Knowledge and Mgt. Soc. [IO]
Argentine Assn. of Medical Informatics [IO]
ARMA Intl. - Canadian Region [IO]
ARMA Intl. - The Assn. of Info. Mgt. Professionals
[IO]
ARMA Intl. - The Assn. of Info. Mgt. Professionals
[2096]
Assn. for the Development of Religious Info.
Systems [20091]
Assn. for Fed. Info. Resources Mgt. [5815]
Assn. of Independent Info. Professionals [2097]
Assn. of Independent Info. Professionals [IO]
Assn. of Info. and Dissemination Centers [IO]
Assn. of Info. and Dissemination Centers [7189]
Assn. for Info. Mgt. [IO]
Assn. of Info. Specialists [IO]
Assn. for Medical and Bio-Informatics, Singapore
[IO]
Assn. of Medical Directors of Info. Systems
[14957]
Assn. for Pathology Informatics [15864]
Assn. of Public Data Users [7190]
Assn. of Records Managers and Administrators
[IO]
Assn. for Terminology and Knowledge Transfer
[IO]
Belgian Assn. for Documentation [IO]
Belgian Medical Informatics Assn. [IO]
Black Info. Tech. Forum [IO]
Brazilian Inst. for Info. in Sci. and Tech. [IO]
Brazilian Soc. of Hea. Informatics [IO]
British Columbia Tech. Indus. Assn. [IO]
Bulgarian Assn. of Info. Technologies [IO]
Canadian Assn. for Info. Sci. [IO]
Canadian Comm. on MARC [IO]
Canadian IT Law Assn. [IO]
China Medical Informatics Assn. [IO]
CIMTECH [IO]
clickITnigeria [IO]
COACH: Canada's Hea. Informatics Assn. [IO]
Coalition for Networked Info. [7191]
Coll. of Healthcare Info. Mgt. Executives [2098]
Comm. on Data for Sci. and Tech. [IO]
Commonwealth Network of Info. Tech. for
Development [IO]
Coun. of Professional Associations on Fed.
Statistics [5816]
Coun. of Regional Info. Tech. Associations [7192]
Coun. of Regional Info. Tech. Associations [IO]

Croatian Soc. for Medical Informatics [IO]
Data Mgt. Assn. Intl. [IO]
Data Mgt. Assn. Intl. [7193]
Demos [IO]
DSL Forum [2099]
Electronic Document Systems Found. [2100]
Electronic Govt. Directorate [IO]
Electronic Privacy Info. Center [7194]
ENCOMPASS [6792]
ESPRIT [IO]
Estonian Assn. of Info. Tech. and Telecommunica-
tions [IO]
European Assn. of Info. Services [IO]
European Assn. for the Transfer of Technologies,
Innovation, and Indus. Info. [IO]
European Centre for Parliamentary Res. and
Documentation [IO]
European Commn. on Preservation and Access
[IO]
European Fed. for Medical Informatics [IO]
European Info. Assn. [IO]
Fed. Consumer Info. Center Prog. [5817]
Females in Info. Tech. and Telecommunications
[IO]
Finnish Social and Hea. Informatics Assn. [IO]
Freedom of Info. Center [18413]
Freedom of Info. CH [18414]
German Soc. for Info. Sci. and Practice [IO]
Govt. Mgt. Info. Sciences [5818]
Greek Hea. Informatics Assn. [IO]
Hea. Informatics New Zealand [IO]
Healthcare Informatics Soc. of Ireland [IO]
Healthcare Info. and Mgt. Systems Soc. [14885]
Higher Educ. Info. Tech. Alliance [8489]
IACP Law Enforcement Info. Mgt. Sect. [5819]
Indexing and Abstracting Soc. of Canada [IO]
Info. Rsrc. Mgt. Assn. of Canada [IO]
Information Resources Management Association
[IO]
Info. Resources Mgt. Assn. [2101]
Info. Systems Audit and Control Assn. and Found.
[65]
Info. Systems Mgt. Benchmarking Consortium
[725]
Info. Tech. Assn. of Am. [6768]
Info. Tech. Assn. of Canada [IO]
Info. Tech. Assn. of Jordan [IO]
Info. Tech. Assn. of New Zealand [IO]
Info. Tech. Assn., South Africa [IO]
Info. Tech. Indus. Coun. [904]
Info. Tech. Mgt. Assn. Singapore [IO]
Info. Tech. Professionals Assn. of Am. [7195]
Info. Tech. Solution Provider Alliance [2102]
Inst. of Certified Records Managers [2103]
Inst. for Cmpt. Capacity Mgt. [7196]
Inst. for Educational Services [8265]
Inst. of Electronics, Info. and Commun. Engineers
[IO]
Inst. for the Future [7105]
Inst. for the Mgt. of Info. Systems [IO]
Intl. Assn. for Documentation Technologies [729]
Intl. Assn. for Info. and Data Quality [7197]
Intl. Assn. of Info. Tech. Asset Managers [2093]
Intl. Assn. for the Mgt. of Tech. [7740]
Intl. Assn. of Messaging Professionals [6711]
Intl. Assn. of Privacy Professionals [6711]
Intl. Assn. of Privacy Professionals [2104]
Intl. Coun. for Sci. and Tech. Info. [IO]
Intl. Coun. for Tech. Commun. [IO]
Intl. DB2 Users Gp. [6856]
Intl. Info. Systems Security Certification
Consortium [6758]
Intl. Mgt. Development Assn. [735]
Intl. Medical Informatics Assn. [IO]
Intl. Records Mgt. Trust [IO]
Intl. Security, Trust and Privacy Alliance [3535]
Intl. Soc. for Ethics and Info. Tech. [IO]
Intl. Soc. for Ethics and Info. Tech. [7198]
Intl. Soc. of Info. Fusion [7199]
Intl. Soc. of Info. Fusion [IO]
Intl. Soc. for Knowledge Org. [IO]
Internet Content Rating Assn. [12060]
Iranian Medical Informatics Assn. [IO]
Israeli Assn. for Medical Informatics [IO]
Italy Medical Informatics Soc. [IO]

Reference to "IO" in place of a book number signifies that the association may be found in the 45th edition of International Organizations.

Ithaka [7200]
Japan Assn. for Medical Informatics [IO]
Japan Info. Tech. Services Indus. Assn. [IO]
Japanese Assn. of Healthcare Info. Systems
  Indus. [IO]
Knowbility [11958]
Korea Info. Tech. Network [6736]
Korean Soc. of Medical Informatics [IO]
Latin Amer. Info. Agency [IO]
Latinos in Info. Sciences and Tech. Assn. [7201]
Latvian Info. Tech. and Telecommunications Assn.
  [IO]
Macedonian Assn. of Info. Tech. [IO]
Mgt. Info. Systems Gp. [2105]
Media Rsrc. Ser. [7202]
Medical Pharmaceutical Info. Assn. [IO]
Medical Records Inst. [15098]
Natl. Alliance of Primary Care Informatics [14956]
Natl. Assn. of Govt. Archives and Records
  Administrators [5820]
Natl. Assn. for Info. Destruction [2106]
Natl. Assn. for Info. Destruction [IO]
Natl. Assn. for Justice Info. Systems [5648]
Natl. Assn. for Public Hea. Info. Tech. [7203]
Natl. Assn. of Regional Media Centers [7204]
Natl. Assn. of State Chief Info. Officers [5821]
Natl. Environmental Satellite, Data, and Info. Ser.
  [4590]
Natl. Fed. of Abstracting and Info. Services [IO]
Natl. Fed. of Abstracting and Info. Services [7205]
Natl. Freedom of Info. Coalition [5822]
Natl. Info. Standards Org. [7206]
Natl. MIS User Gp. [7207]
Natl. Public Records Res. Assn. [2107]
Natl. Quality Forum [14658]
NiUG Intl. [7208]
Nordic Info. Center for Media and Commun. Res.
  [IO]
Nordic Info. Center for Media and Commun. Res.
  - Denmark [IO]
Norwegian Soc. for Medical Informatics [IO]
ODF Alliance [7209]
Open DeviceNet Vendor Assn. [892]
The Open Gp. [2108]
Panel on World Data Centers [7210]
Panel on World Data Centers [IO]
Philippine Medical Informatics Soc. [IO]
PRISM International - Professional Records and
  Information Services Management [IO]
PRISM Intl. - Professional Records and Info.
  Services Mgt. [2109]
Privacy Rights CH [3176]
Professional Cmpt. Assn. of Lebanon [IO]
Programmers Guild [7757]
Property Records Indus. Assn. [3187]
Records Mgt. Assn. of Australasia [IO]
Records Mgt. Soc. [IO]
Regis Sys. Users' Gp. [6801]
Romanian Soc. of Medical Informatics [IO]
SCSI Trade Assn. [2110]
SEARCH - The Natl. Consortium for Justice Info.
  and Statistics [11892]
Slovene Medical Informatics Assn. [IO]
Society of Competitive Intelligence Professionals
  [IO]
Soc. of Competitive Intelligence Professionals
  [7211]
Soc. of Info. Tech. Mgt. [IO]
Soc. for Medical Informatics of Bosnia and Herze-
  govina [IO]
Soc. of Public Info. Networks [IO]
South African Assn. of Competitive Intelligence
  Professionals [IO]
South African Hea. Informatics Assn. [IO]
Spanish Soc. of Hea. Informatics [IO]
Special Interest Gp. on Info. Retrieval [7212]
Special Interest Gp. on Mgt. Info. Systems [6824]
Supply-Chain Coun. [IO]
Supply-Chain Coun. [2111]
Supply-Chain Coun. - Brazil Chap. [IO]
Supply-Chain Coun. - Europe Chap. [IO]
Supply-Chain Coun. - Greater China Chap. [IO]
Supply-Chain Coun. - South East Asia Chap. [IO]
Supply-Chain Coun. - Southern African Chap. [IO]
Swiss Assn. for Documentation [IO]

Swiss Soc. for Medical Informatics [IO]
Technology Resource Consortium [7213]
Tech. Without Borders [7763]
Turkish Medical Informatics Assn. [IO]
Unicorn Users Gp. Intl. [7214]
U.S. Internet Ser. Provider Assn. [911]
U.S. Prdt. Data Assn. [2112]
Urban and Regional Info. Systems Assn. [7215]
Uruguayan Soc. of Hea. Informatics [IO]
Usability Professionals' Assn. [IO]
Usability Professionals' Assn. [2113]
Women in ICT [IO]
World Org. of Webmasters [IO]
World Org. of Webmasters [2114]
Zangle Natl. Users' Gp. [7216]
Info. Mgt. Inst; Jimi Hendrix [24921]
Info. Mgt. Open Systems Alliance; Machinery [2560]
Information Mgt. and Processing Assn. - Defunct.
Info. Media and Equip; Assn. for [328]
Info. Network on Educ. in European [IO], Brussels,
  Belgium
Info. Network; SATELLIFE Global Hea. [14663]
Info. Officers Assn; Natl. [6231]
Info. Officers; Natl. Assn. of County [5620]
Information Processing
Amer. Medical Informatics Assn. [14079]
Application Ser. Provider Indus. Consortium
  [3722]
Assn. for Educ. in Healthcare Info. Tech. [15132]
Assn. for Electronic Hea. Care Transactions
  [14618]
Assn. of Medical Directors of Info. Systems
  [14957]
Assn. for Pathology Informatics [15864]
Bangladesh Assn. of Software and Info. Services
  [IO]
Canadian Healthcare Info. Tech. Trade Assn. [IO]
Coun. of Regional Info. Tech. Associations [7192]
European Assn. for Microprocessing and
  Microprogramming [IO]
Higher Educ. Info. Tech. Alliance [8489]
Hong Kong Info. Tech. Fed. [IO]
Info. Resources Mgt. Assn. [2101]
Info. Tech. Assn. of Am. [6768]
Info. Tech. Solution Provider Alliance [2102]
Inst. for Educational Services [8265]
Intl. Assn. for Info. and Data Quality [7197]
Intl. Assn. of Info. Tech. Asset Managers [2093]
Intl. Assn. of Messaging Professionals [6711]
Intl. Audiotex Regulators Network [IO]
Intl. DB2 Users Gp. [6856]
Intl. Soc. for Ethics and Info. Tech. [7198]
Irish Internet Assn. [IO]
Ithaka [7200]
Japan Electronic Data Interchange Coun. [IO]
Korea Info. Tech. Network [6736]
Latinos in Info. Sciences and Tech. Assn. [7201]
Metro Ethernet Forum [7748]
Natl. Alliance of Primary Care Informatics [14956]
Natl. Assn. for Justice Info. Systems [5648]
Natl. Assn. for Public Hea. Info. Tech. [7203]
Natl. Assn. of State Chief Info. Officers [5821]
Natl. Centre for Trade Info. [IO]
Natl. Environmental Satellite, Data, and Info. Ser.
  [4590]
Natl. MIS User Gp. [7207]
NiUG Intl. [7208]
ODF Alliance [7209]
Open Data Acquisition Assn. [891]
Open DeviceNet Vendor Assn. [892]
Polish Info. Processing Soc. [IO]
Property Records Indus. Assn. [3187]
SCSI Trade Assn. [2110]
SkyTruth [4637]
Soc. for Conservation GIS [6831]
Unicorn Users Gp. Intl. [7214]
Union of Info. Tech. Enterprises [IO]
U.S. Prdt. Data Assn. [2112]
Zangle Natl. Users' Gp. [7216]
Info. Processing Assn; Finnish [IO]
Info. Processing Org; Biological [★6783]
Info. Processing Soc. of Japan [IO], Tokyo, Japan
Info. Processing Soc; North Amer. Fuzzy [6741]
Info. Processing; Special Interest Gp. for Biomedical
  [★6783]

Information Processing Supplies Coun. - Defunct.
Info. Prog; The Road [3892]
Information Project for Africa - Address unknown
  since 2008.
Info. Proj; Parent Training and [★12569]
Info. and Records Mgt. Assn; Nuclear [7389]
Info. Rsrc. Mgt. Assn. of Canada [IO], Toronto, ON,
  Canada
Info. and Rsrc. Ser; Nuclear [18132]
Info. Resources Mgt. Assn. [2101], 701 E Chocolate
  Ave., Ste. 200, Hershey, PA 17033, (717)533-8879
Information Resources Management Association
  [IO], Hershey, PA, United States
Info. Resources for Nursing; Interagency Coun. on
  [10360]
Info. Retrieval Center; UFO [7486]
Info. for School and Coll. Governors [IO], London,
  United Kingdom
Info. Sci. and Automation Div. [★10368]
Info. Sci. Educ; Assn. for Lib. and [8782]
Info. Ser; Environmental Data and [★4590]
Info. Ser; European Community [★17507]
Info. Ser; The Hospitality and [17896]
Info. Services on Latin Am. [17990], PO Box 6103,
  Albany, CA 94706, (510)996-2318
Info. Services; Organized Adoption Search [11259]
Info. Soc; Geoscience [7142]
Info. Specialists; Substance Abuse Librarians and
  [10390]
Info. Standards; Org. for the Advancement of
  Structured [7756]
Info. Storage Indus. Consortium [903], 3655 Ruffin
  Rd., Ste. 335, San Diego, CA 92123-1833,
  (858)279-7230
Info. Systems; Assn. for [6722]
Info. Systems Audit and Control Assn. and Found.
  [65], 3701 Algonquin Rd., Ste. 1010, Rolling
  Meadows, IL 60008, (847)253-1545
Info. Systems Audit and Control Assn. and Found.
  [IO], Rolling Meadows, IL, United States
Info. Systems Audit and Control Assn. and Found.
  Singapore [IO], Singapore, Singapore
Info. Systems; Comm. on [★5821]
Information Systems Consultants Assn. - Address
  unknown since 2006.
Info. Systems Integrators Assn; Control and [3704]
Info. Systems Mgt; Amer. Assn. of Public Welfare
  [★13152]
Info. Systems Mgt; Amer. Public Human Services
  Assn. - [13152]
Info. Systems Mgt. Benchmarking Consortium [725],
  4606 FM 1960 W, Ste. 250, Houston, TX 77069-
  9949, (281)440-5044
Info. Systems; Natl. Assn. for State [★5821]
Info. Systems Security Assn. [2090], 9220 SW Bar-
  bur Blvd., No. 119-333, Portland, OR 97219,
  (206)388-4584
Information Systems Security Association [IO],
  Portland, OR, United States
Info. Systems Security Assn. Brussels-European
  Chap. [IO], Brussels, Belgium
Info. Systems Security Assn. - Netherlands Chap.
  [IO], Badhoevedorp, Netherlands
Info. Systems; Soc. for Mgt. [★2516]
Info. Technologies Credit Union Assn. [1110], PO
  Box 160, Del Mar, CA 92014-0160, (858)792-3883
Information Technology Acquisition and Marketing
  Assn. - Defunct.
Info. Tech. Assn. of Am. [6768], 1401 Wilson Blvd.,
  Ste. 1100, Arlington, VA 22209, (703)522-5055
Info. Tech. Assn. of Canada [IO], Mississauga, ON,
  Canada
Info. Tech; Assn. for Educ. in Healthcare [15132]
Info. and Tech. Assn; Geospatial [900]
Info. Tech. Assn; Hospitality [6717]
Info. Tech. Assn. of Jordan [IO], Amman, Jordan
Info. Tech. Assn; Lib. and [10368]
Info. Tech. Assn. of New Zealand [IO], Wellington,
  New Zealand
Info. Tech. Assn., South Africa [IO], Randburg,
  Republic of South Africa
Info. Tech; Charles Babbage Inst. for the History of
  [10100]
Info. Tech. Commn. [★IO]
Info. Tech. Contract and Recruitment Assn. [IO],
  Melbourne, Australia

A star before a book entry number signifies that the name is not listed separately, but is mentioned within the entry.

Info. Tech. Indus. Coun. [904], 1250 Eye St. NW, Ste. 200, Washington, DC 20005, (202)737-8888

Info. Tech. Mgt. Assn. Singapore [IO], Singapore, Singapore

Info. Tech; Natl. Alliance for Hea. [15142]

Info. Tech. Professionals Assn. of Am. [7195], PO Box 7912, Wilmington, DE 19803

Information Technology Resellers Assn. - Defunct.

Information Technology Society [IO], Frankfurt am Main, Germany

Info. Tech. Solution Provider Alliance [2102], PO Box 10641, Portland, OR 97296, (503)231-3086

Info. Tech. Standards; INCITS - InterNational Comm. for [7738]

Info. Tech. and Teacher Educ; Soc. for [9243]

Information Technology Training Assn. - Address unknown since 2005.

Info. and Telecommunications Technologies Gp. of Electronic Indus. Assn. [★3759]

Info. Theory Gp; IEEE [7770]

Info. Theory Soc; IEEE [★7770]

Info. and Training; Eiseman Center for Color [6707]

Informationsstelle Sudliches Afrika [★IO]

Informed Amers. Monitor Assn. - Defunct.

Informed Consent [★11732]

Informed Consent [★IO]

Informed Family Life [★15602]

Informed Homebirth [★15602]

Informed Homebirth/Informed Birth and Parenting [15602]

Informed Medical Decision Making; Found. for [15137]

Infoshare Intl. [16965], 584 Castro St., Ste. 671, San Francisco, CA 94114, (415)437-1873

Infoshare Intl. [IO], San Francisco, CA, United States

Infrared Data Assn. [IO], Walnut Creek, CA, United States

Infrared Data Assn. [6855], PO Box 3883, Walnut Creek, CA 94598, (925)943-6546

Infrastructure Assn; PCIA - The Wireless [3752]

Infusion Nurses Soc. [16614], 315 Norwood Park S, Norwood, MA 02062, (781)440-9408

Infusion Therapy Assn; Outpatient Intravenous [16631]

Infusion Therapy; Natl. Alliance for [14839]

Ingalls Wilder Memorial Soc; Laura [9679]

Ingenieros Cubanos; Asociacion de [7002]

Ingenieurs Canada [★IO]

Ingenieurs Sans Frontieres (Canada) [★IO]

Ingeniorforeningen i Danmark [★IO]

Ingenjorsforbundet [★IO]

Ingersoll-Rand Distributors; Assn. of [2002]

Ingestive Behavior; Soc. for the Stud. of [13742]

Inglewood Region Olive Co-operative [IO], Warwick, Australia

Ingot Industry; Brass and Bronze [2701]

Ingot Institute; Brass and Bronze [★2701]

Ingot Manufacturers; Association of Brass and Bronze [★2701]

Ingot Manufacturers; Brass and Bronze [★2701]

Ingredient Marketing Specialists; Natl. [★1554]

Ingredient Marketing Specialists; Network of [1554]

Ingredient Marketing Specialists; Northamerican [★1554]

Ingredient Rev; Cosmetic [1844]

Ingredient Systems; Natl. Assn. of Flavors and Food- [1539]

Inhalant Prevention Coalition; Natl. [16514]

Inhalation Therapists; Amer. Assn. of [★16599]

Inhalation Therapists; Amer. Registry of [★16626]

Inhalation Therapy; Amer. Assn. for [★16599]

Inhalation Therapy Assn. [★16599]

Inhalation Therapy; Bd. of Schools of [★16610]

Inhlangano Yezokusakaza Eningizimu Afrika [★IO]

Inholders Assn; Natl. [★6187]

Inholders Assn; Natl. Parks [★6187]

Initiative America - Address unknown since 1999.

Initiative America Found. - Defunct.

Initiative Comm. for Natl. Economic Planning - Address unknown since 1995.

Initiative Resource Center - Defunct.

Initiativen der Veranderung [★IO]

Initiatives of Change [IO], Washington, DC, United States

Initiatives of Change [17734], 1156 15th St. NW, Ste. 910, Washington, DC 20005-1704, (202)872-9077

Initiatives of Change - Switzerland [IO], Lucerne, Switzerland

Initiatives Support Corp; Local [17224]

Initiators - Defunct.

Injection Molding Assn; Metal [2713]

Injuries; Natl. Alliance for the Primary Prevention of Sharps [16381]

Injuries and Physical Fitness; Amer. Chiropractic Assn. Coun. on Sports [13989]

Injury Assn; Amer. Spinal [16461]

Injury Assn; Natl. Spinal Cord [16468]

Injury Control Center [★16690]

Injury Control Res. Center [★16690]

Injury Control Res. Center; Harvard [16690]

Injury Found; Natl. Spinal Cord [★16468]

Injury Nurses; Amer. Assn. of Spinal Cord [15441]

Injury Prevention Directors Assn; State and Territorial [18581]

Injury Prevention; Found. for Aquatic [12963]

Injury Prevention Res. Center; Univ. of Iowa [7588]

Injury Psychologists and Social Workers; Amer. Assn. of Spinal Cord [16459]

Injury Safety Found; Aquatic [★12963]

Ink Makers; Natl. Assn. of Printing [★1803]

Ink Mfrs; Natl. Assn. of Printing [1803]

Ink Res. Institute; National Printing [★1803]

Inkjet Cartridge Recycling Assn. - Defunct.

Inkwell Collectors; Soc. of [22114]

Inland Bird Banding Assn. [7420], c/o James Ingold, Pres., Dept. of Biology Sci., Louisiana State Univ., Shreveport, LA 71115, (318)797-5236

Inland Commercial Fisheries Assn. - Address unknown since 2001.

Inland Forest Rsrc. Coun. [★1608]

Inland Intl. Trade Assn. - Defunct.

Inland Lake Yachting Assn. [23175], PO Box 311, Fontana, WI 53125, (262)275-6921

Inland Marine Underwriters Assn. [2170], 14 Wall St., 8th Fl., New York, NY 10005, (212)233-0550

Inland Press Assn. [3227], 701 Lee St., Ste. 925, Des Plaines, IL 60016, (847)795-0380

Inland Rivers Ports and Terminals [2604], 316 Bd. of Trade Pl., New Orleans, LA 70130, (504)585-0715

Inland Seas Educ. Assn. [2577], 100 Dame St., Suttons Bay, MI 49682, (231)271-3077

Inland Waterways Amenity Advisory Coun. [IO], London, United Kingdom

Inland Waterways Assn. of England [IO], Rickmansworth, United Kingdom

Inland Waterways Assn. of Ireland [IO], Dublin, Ireland

Inland Waterways Common Carriers Assn. - Defunct.

Inlandboatman's Union of the Pacific [2605], 1711 W Nickerson St., Ste. D, Seattle, WA 98119, (206)284-6001

Inliners Intl. [21662], c/o Jean Weigt, Membership Chair, 14 E Main St., Winters, CA 95694, (530)795-0224

Inliners Intl. [IO], Winters, CA, United States

INMED Partnerships for Children [IO], Sterling, VA, United States

INMED Partnerships for Children [14981], 45449 Severn Way, Ste. 161, Sterling, VA 20166, (703)444-4477

Inn Club; Intl. B and B Fly- [21451]

Inn Sign Soc. [IO], Wolverhampton, United Kingdom

Inner Circle - Address unknown since 1999.

Inner Circle of Advocates [6043], c/o Dennis Donnelly, Pres., 1 Main St., Chatham, NJ 07928, (973)635-5400

Inner Light Found. [7569], PO Box 750265, Petaluma, CA 94975, (707)765-2200

Inner Peace Movement [10173], PO Box 681757, San Antonio, TX 78268, (877)475-7792

Inner Wheel New Zealand [IO], Wellington, New Zealand

Innerspring Manufacturers; Amer. [1969]

Innerspring Manufacturers; Assn. of [★1969]

Innes Clan Soc. [20950], c/o Ms. Carole A. Innes, Membership Chair, 129 Ravenna Dr., Long Beach, CA 90803

Innes Clan Society [IO], Long Beach, CA, United States

Innholders' Company [IO], London, United Kingdom

Innkeepers Soc. of America - Defunct.

Innocence in Danger - USA [11601], 22 River Terr., PH-G, New York, NY 10282, (866)552-7840

Innocence in Danger - USA [IO], New York, NY, United States

Innocence Proj. [5643], 100 5th Ave., 3rd Fl., New York, NY 10011, (212)364-5340

Innovation

Assn. for Strategic Planning [3042]

Athena Alliance [17468]

Chaordic Commons [7409]

Engg. and Sci. Network on Thinking [7217]

Innovation Network [2115]

Intl. Assn. for Prdt. Development [3177]

Intl. Soc. for Law and Tech. [5945]

Intl. Soc. for Presence Res. [7572]

Natl. Collegiate Inventors and Innovators Alliance [7218]

One Economy [7755]

ResearchChannel [7575]

Innovation in the Community Coll; League for [8120]

Innovation Mgt. Assn. of Canada [IO], Ottawa, ON, Canada

Innovation; Mfrs. Alliance for Productivity and [★2039]

Innovation in Medicine; Found. for [15166]

Innovation Network [2115], c/o Joyce Wycoff, Co-Founder, 8200 Kroll Way, No. 72, Bakersfield, CA 93311, (870)656-4141

Innovation Norway - U.S. [24283], 655 3rd Ave., Rm. 1810, New York, NY 10017-9111, (212)885-9700

Innovation Norway - U.S. [IO], New York, NY, United States

Innovations in Civic Participation [IO], Washington, DC, United States

Innovations in Civic Participation [17075], 1776 Massachusetts Ave. NW, Ste. 201, Washington, DC 20036, (202)775-0290

Innovations et Reseaux pour le Developpement [★IO]

Innovative Schools; Network of [★8295]

Innovators and Entrepreneurs Assn. [IO], Singapore, Singapore

Innovators Intl. - Defunct.

Inns; Amer. Historic [1909]

Inns; Amer. Travel [1929]

Inns of North Am; Select Registry, Distinguished [1965]

Inorganic Feed Phosphates/CEFIC Sector Gp. [IO], Brussels, Belgium

Inpatient Physicians; Natl. Assn. of [★14897]

Input/Output Systems Assn. - Defunct.

INROADS [8749], 10 S Broadway, Ste. 300, St. Louis, MO 63102, (314)241-7488

INSA, The Intl. Ser. Assn. for Hea. [★14978]

INSA, The Intl. Ser. Assn. for Hea. [★IO]

Insane; Assn. of Medical Superintendents of Amer. Institutions for [★16076]

Insect Ecologists; Assn. of Applied [★5073]

Insect Screening Weavers Assn. - Defunct.

Insecticide and Disinfectant Manufacturers; Natl. Assn. [★806]

Insecticide and Fungicide Assn; Agricultural [★807]

Insecticides

Amer. Assn. of Pesticide Safety Educators [4627]

The Pesticide Stewardship Alliance [7068]

Insecticides and Fungicide Manufacturers Assn; Agricultural [★807]

Insects

Acarological Soc. of Am. [7056]

Amer. Apitherapy Soc. [13614]

Amer. Lyme Disease Found. [14249]

Amer. Mosquito Control Assn. [5072]

Assn. of Applied IPM Ecologists [5073]

Assn. of Indian Entomologists in North Am. [7057]

Coun. of Entomology Dept. Administrators [7060]

Eastern Apicultural Soc. of North Am. [4165]

Entomological Soc. of Am. [7062]

Intl. Dragonfly Fund [IO]

Intl. Lyme and Assoc. Diseases Soc. [14267]

Lyme Disease Assn. [14271]

Lyme Disease Found. [14272]

Reference to "IO" in place of a book number signifies that the association may be found in the 45th edition of International Organizations.

Mosquito Control Assn. of Australia **[IO]**
Natl. Gypsy Moth Mgt. Bd. **[5078]**
North Amer. Forensic Entomology Assn. **[7064]**
Selected Independent Funeral Homes **[2791]**
Soc. for Insect Stud. **[IO]**
Young Entomologists' Soc. **[7066]**
INSEE Info Ser. **[IO]**, Paris, France
INSEE Observatoire Economique de Paris **[★IO]**
Insignia Collectors; Amer. Soc. of Military **[22627]**
Insititut Bank-Bank Malaysia **[★IO]**
Inslee Family Assn. - Defunct.
Insol Intl. **[IO]**, London, United Kingdom
Insolvency
    Insolvency Practitioners Assn. of Australia **[IO]**
Insolvency Aid Soc. **[IO]**, Brighton, United Kingdom
Insolvency Practitioners Assn. **[IO]**, London, United Kingdom
Insolvency Practitioners Assn. of Australia **[IO]**, Sydney, Australia
Insolvency and Restructuring Advisors; Assn. of **[15]**
Inspection Agencies-Americas Comm; Intl. Fed. of **[2120]**
Inspection of Bd. of Underwriters of New York; Bur. of **[★3576]**
Inspection Bur; Southern Pine **[1623]**
Inspection Bur; West Coast Lumber **[1628]**
Inspection Engineers; Natl. Acad. of Building **[640]**
Inspection Foundation/Association of Home Inspectors; Housing **[★2119]**
Inspection Found; Housing **[2119]**
Inspection Ser; Redwood **[1618]**
Inspection and Weighing Agencies; Amer. Assn. of Grain **[1747]**
Inspectors
    Amer. Inst. of Inspectors **[2116]**
    Amer. Soc. of Home Inspectors **[592]**
    Assn. of Constr. Inspectors **[2117]**
    Assn. of Fruit and Vegetable Inspection and Standardization Agencies **[1674]**
    Assn. of Inspectors Gen. **[5777]**
    Canadian Assn. of Home and Property Inspectors **[IO]**
    Canadian Inst. of Professional Home Inspectors **[IO]**
    Environmental Assessment Assn. **[4559]**
    Examination Bd. of Professional Home Inspectors **[2118]**
    Found. of Real Estate Appraisers **[280]**
    Healthcare Laundry Accreditation Coun. **[2403]**
    Housing Inspection Found. **[2119]**
    Intl. Assn. of Bedding and Furniture Law Officials **[5823]**
    Intl. Fed. of Inspection Agencies-Americas Comm. **[2120]**
    Natl. Assn. of Certified Home Inspectors **[2121]**
    National Association of Certified Home Inspectors **[IO]**
    Natl. Assn. of Home Inspectors **[2122]**
    Natl. Assn. of Mold Professionals **[1330]**
    Natl. Assn. for Professional Inspectors and Testers **[IO]**
    Natl. Assn. of Property Inspectors **[2123]**
    Natl. Bd. of Boiler and Pressure Vessel Inspectors **[5824]**
    Natl. Org. of Remediators and Mold Inspectors **[1331]**
Inspectors of Am; Apiary **[4164]**
Inspectors; Amer. Inst. of **[2116]**
Inspectors; Amer. Soc. of Home **[592]**
Inspectors' Inst. of Am; Mine **[6117]**
Inspectors; Intl. Assn. of Dairy and Milk **[★5739]**
Inspectors; Intl. Assn. of Factory **[★5917]**
Inspectors; Natl. Bd. of Boiler and Pressure Vessel **[5824]**
Inspectors of Plumbing and Sanitary Engg; Amer. Soc. of **[★7590]**
Inspiration Ministries **[11952]**, PO Box 948, Corner State Rd. 67 and County F, Walworth, WI 53184, (262)275-6131
Inspiration through the Written Word - Defunct.
Installation Assn; Custom Electronic Design **[3548]**
Installation Assn. of North Am; Floor **[623]**
Installation Contractors Assn; Floor Covering **[1016]**
Installation Developers; Natl. Assn. of **[★5811]**
Installers Assn; Intl. Certified Floorcovering **[1025]**

Instant Potato Products Assn. - Defunct.
Institiuid Ceimice Na hEireann **[★IO]**
Institue Goree **[★IO]**
Institusi Jurutera, Malaysia **[★IO]**
Institut de recherche en politiques publiques **[★IO]**
Institut international du developpement durable **[★IO]**
Institut canadien du droit des ressources **[★IO]**
L'Institut canadien de recherches avancees **[★IO]**
L'Institut canadien pour la resolution des conflits **[★IO]**
Institut canadien de la construction en acier **[★IO]**
Institut Aeronautique et Spatial du Canada **[★IO]**
Institut Africain de Developpement Economique et de Planification **[★IO]**
Institut Africain Intl. **[★IO]**
Institut fur Afrika-Kunde **[★IO]**
Institut Americain Universitaire **[★IO]**
Institut Americain Universitaire **[★8643]**
Institut agree de la logistique et des transports Amerique du Nord **[★IO]**
Institut de Biologie Physico-Chimique **[IO]**, Paris, France
L'Institut de chimie du Canada **[★IO]**
L'Institut Canadien **[★IO]**
Institut Canadien des Actuaires **[★IO]**
Institut Canadien d Admin. de la Justice **[★IO]**
Institut Canadien des Affaires Internationales **[★IO]**
Institut Canadien du Beton Prefabrique et Precontraint **[★IO]**
Institut Canadien des Comptables Agrees **[★IO]**
Institut Canadien des Condominiums **[★IO]**
Institut Canadien de Conservation **[★IO]**
Institut Canadien d'Etudes Strategiques **[★IO]**
Institut Canadien d'Etudes Ukrainiennes **[★IO]**
Institut Canadien des Economistes en Constr. **[★IO]**
Institut Canadien des Engrais **[★IO]**
Institut Canadien des Experts en Evaluation d'Enterprises **[★IO]**
Institut Canadien du Film **[★IO]**
Institut Canadien de Gestion **[★IO]**
Institut Canadien de l'immeuble **[★IO]**
Institut Canadien des Ingenieurs **[★IO]**
Institut Canadien des Inspecteurs en Sante Publique **[★IO]**
Institut Canadien de l'Energie **[★IO]**
Institut Canadien du Marketing **[★IO]**
Institut Canadien de Planification Finaniere **[★IO]**
L'Institut Canadien de Plomberie et de Chauffage **[★IO]**
Institut Canadien des Professionels de la Logistique **[★IO]**
Institut Canadien de la Recherche sur la Condition Physique et le Mode de Vie **[★IO]**
Institut Canadien de Recherches sur les Femmes **[★IO]**
Institut Canadien de Recherches sur le Judaisme **[★IO]**
Institut Canadien de Relations avec les Investisseurs **[★IO]**
Institut Canadien de la Retraite et des Avantages Sociaux **[★IO]**
Institut Canadien de la Sante Infantile **[★IO]**
L'Institut Canadien de Sci. et Technologie Alimentaires **[★IO]**
Institut Canadien du Sucre **[★IO]**
Institut Canadien du Tapis **[★IO]**
Institut Canadien des Technologies Scenographiques **[★IO]**
Institut Canadien des Textiles **[★IO]**
Institut Canadien du Trafic et du Transport **[★IO]**
Institut Canadien des Urbanistes **[★IO]**
Institut Canadien des Valeurs Mobilieres **[★IO]**
Institut Canadiens des Conseillers en Voyages **[★IO]**
Institut C.D. Howe **[★IO]**
Institu du Chrysotile **[★IO]**
L'Institut d'administration publique du Canada **[★IO]**
Institut Des Fonds D'Investissement Du Canada **[★IO]**
Institut d'Estudis Catalans **[★IO]**
Institut d'Europe pour la Prevention du Crime et la Lutte Contre la Delinquance Affile a l'Organisation des Nations Unies **[★IO]**
Institut d'Histoire de l'Amerique Francaise **[★IO]**

Institut canadien d'information sur la sante **[★IO]**
Institut de Droit Intl. **[★IO]**
Institut des Etudes Ethiopiennes **[★IO]**
Institut fur Europaische Politik **[★IO]**
Institut Europeen d'Administration Publique **[★IO]**
Institut Europeen d'Education et de Polikique Sociale **[★IO]**
Institut Europeen d'Education et de Politique Sociale **[★IO]**
Institut Europeen des Itineraires Culturels **[★IO]**
Institut Europeen de Recherches et d'Etudes Superieures en Mgt. **[★IO]**
Institut Feuerverzinken **[★IO]**
Institut Forestier du Canada **[★IO]**
Institut de la Fourrure du Canada **[★IO]**
Institut Francais d'Histoire Sociale **[★IO]**
Institut Francais du Petrole **[★IO]**
Institut Francais de Pondichery **[★IO]**
Institut Francais des Relations Internationales **[★IO]**
Institut de France Academie des Sciences **[★IO]**
Institut Intl. du Canada pour le Grain **[★IO]**
Institut Intl. des Communications **[★IO]**
Institut Intl. d'Agriculture Tropicale **[★IO]**
Institut Intl. d'Aluminium **[★IO]**
Institut Intl. d'Anthropologie **[★IO]**
Institut Intl. d'Etudes Sociales **[★IO]**
Institut Intl. d'Etudes Strategiques **[★IO]**
Institut Intl. de Droit Humanitaire **[★IO]**
Institut Intl. de Droit Spatial **[★IO]**
Institut Intl. des Droits de l'Homme **[★IO]**
Institut Intl. de Finances Publiques **[★IO]**
Institut Intl. du Froid **[★IO]**
Institut Intl. pour l'Analyse des Systemes Appliques **[★IO]**
Institut Intl. de l'Ocean **[★IO]**
Institut Intl. de l'Ombudsman **[★IO]**
Institut Intl. pour l'Unification du Droit Prive **[★IO]**
Institut Intl. du Manganese **[★IO]**
Institut Intl. de Planification de l'Education **[★IO]**
Institut Intl. de la Potasse **[★IO]**
Institut Intl. de Recherches Betteravieres **[★IO]**
Institut Intl. des Sciences Administratives **[★IO]**
Institut Intl. des Sciences Humaines Integrales **[★IO]**
Institut Intl. de la Soudure **[★IO]**
Institut Intl. de Statistique **[★IO]**
Institut Internationale du Theatre **[★IO]**
L'institut canadien du droit et de la politique en l'environnement **[★IO]**
L'Institut de l'euro **[★IO]**
Institut de l'Horticulture **[★IO]**
Institut de l'UNESCO pour l'apprentissage tout au long de la vie **[★IO]**
Institut za Medunarodne Odnose **[★IO]**
Institut canadien des mines, Metallurgie et Petrole **[★IO]**
Institut du Monde Arabe **[★IO]**
Institut fuer Naehtechnik **[IO]**, Aachen, Germany
L'Institut Natl. Canadien pour les Aveugles **[★IO]**
Institut Natl. du Cancer du Canada **[★IO]**
Institut Natl. de Recherche en Informatique et en Automatique **[★IO]**
Institut des Nations Unies pour la Formation et la Recherche **[★IO]**
L'Institut Nord-Sud **[★IO]**
Institut Orientaliste **[★IO]**
Institut Pan-Africain pour le Developpement - Afrique de l'Ouest-Sahel **[★IO]**
Institut Pierre Richet **[IO]**, Bouake, Cote d'Ivoire
Institut de Radioprotection du Canada **[★IO]**
Institut de Recherche des Nations Unies pour le Developpement Social **[★IO]**
Institut de Recherches et d'Etudes sur le Monde Arabe et Musulman **[★IO]**
Institut de Recherches et d'Etudes Publicitaires **[★IO]**
Institut des Reviseurs d'Entreprises - Luxembourg **[IO]**, Luxembourg, Luxembourg
Institut Royal d'Architecture du Canada **[★IO]**
Institut Royal des Relations Internationale **[★IO]**
Institut Ruder Boskovic **[★IO]**
Institut des Sciences de l'Environnement **[★IO]**
Institut fur Seeverkehrswirtschaft und Logistik **[★IO]**
Institut fur Sportwissenschaft **[★IO]**
Institut Suisse de Recherche Experimentale sur le Cancer **[★IO]**

A star before a book entry number signifies that the name is not listed separately, but is mentioned within the entry.

Institut pour une Synthese Planetaire [★IO]
Institut Tal-Gurnalisti Maltin [★IO]
Institut Tropical Suisse [★IO]
Institut du Verre [★IO]
Institut der Wirtschaftspruefer in Deutschland e.V. [★IO]
Inst. for 21st Century Stud. [★17647]
Inst. of Accounting Staff [★IO]
Inst. of Accounting Technicians in Ireland [IO], Dublin, Ireland
Inst. of Acoustics [IO], St. Albans, United Kingdom
Inst. of Actuaries of Australia [IO], Sydney, Australia
Inst. of Actuaries of Australia and New Zealand [★IO]
Inst. of Actuaries - United Kingdom [IO], London, United Kingdom
Inst. of Administrative Mgt. [IO], London, United Kingdom
Inst. for Adoption Info. [11247], PO Box 4405, Bennington, VT 05201, (802)442-2845
Inst. for Advanced Judaic Stud. [IO], Toronto, ON, Canada
Inst. of Advanced Motorists [IO], London, United Kingdom
Inst. for Advanced Pastoral Stud. [★19924]
Inst. for Advanced Philosophic Res. [10795], PO Box 805, Moultonborough, NH 03254, (603)253-3311
Inst. for Advanced Res. in Asian Sci. and Medicine [★14986]
Inst. for Advanced Res. in Asian Sci. and Medicine [★IO]
Inst. for Advanced Strategic and Political Stud. [IO], Jerusalem, Israel
Inst. for Advanced Studies in the Theatre Arts - Address unknown since 2000.
Inst. for Advanced Stud. of World Religions [9275]
Inst. for Advanced Stud. of World Religions [IO], Carmel, NY, United States
Inst. for the Advanced Stud. of Black Family Life and Culture [9359], 1012 Linden St., Oakland, CA 94607, (510)836-3705
Inst. for Advanced Stud. in Rational Psychotherapy [★16197]
Inst. for the Advancement of Criminal Justice [★13262]
Inst. for the Advancement of Hawaiian Affairs [10883], 86-649 Puuhulu Rd., Waianae, HI 96792-2723, (808)696-5157
Inst. for the Advancement of Health - Defunct.
Inst. for the Advancement of Human Behavior [13735], 4370 Alpine Rd., Ste. 209, Portola Valley, CA 94028, (650)851-8411
Inst. for the Advancement of Journalism [IO], Houghton, Republic of South Africa
Inst. for Advancement of Medical Communication - Defunct.
Inst. for the Advancement of Notary Public Education - Address unknown since 1985.
Inst. for the Advancement of Philosophy for Children [10796], c/o Montclair State Univ., Univ. Hall 2151, Montclair, NJ 07043, (973)655-7049
Institute for the Advancement of Philosophy for Children [IO], Montclair, NJ, United States
Inst. of Advt. Practitioners in Ireland [IO], Dublin, Ireland
Inst. of Advt. Stud. and Res. [IO], Paris, France
Inst. for Aerobics Res. [★IO]
Inst. for Aerobics Res. [★15962]
Inst. of Aeronautical Engineers [★IO]
Inst. of the Aerospace Sciences [★6369]
Inst. of African Affairs [IO], Hamburg, Germany.
Inst. of African Affairs - Address unknown since 2001.
Inst. of African Stud. [IO], Accra, Ghana
Inst. Against Prejudice and Violence; Natl. [★17146]
Inst. Against Violence - Address unknown since 2000.
Inst. of Agricultural Mgt. [IO], Reading, United Kingdom
Inst. of Agricultural Secretaries and Administrators [IO], Kenilworth, United Kingdom
Inst. for Agriculture and Trade Policy [16955], 2105 1st Ave. S, Minneapolis, MN 55404, (612)870-0453
Inst. for Alternative Energy Sources - Defunct.
Inst. for Alternative Futures [7104], 100 N Pitt St., Alexandria, VA 22314-3134, (703)684-5880

Institute for Alternative Futures [IO], Alexandria, VA, United States
Inst. of Amateur Cinematographers, Amer. Chap. - Defunct.
Inst. for Amer. Church Growth [★20536]
Inst. for Amer. Democracy - Address unknown since 1995.
Inst. on Amer. Freedoms - Defunct.
Inst. of Amer. Indian Arts [10745], 83 Avan. Nu Po Rd., Santa Fe, NM 87508, (505)424-2300
Inst. for Amer. Indian Stud. [6447], 38 Curtis Rd., PO Box 1260, Washington, CT 06793-0260, (860)868-0518
Inst. of Amer. Inventors - Defunct.
Inst. of Amer. Meat Packers [★2658]
Inst. of the Amer. Musical [10610], 121 N Detroit St., Los Angeles, CA 90036-2915, (323)934-1221
Inst. of Amer. Relations - Defunct.
Inst. for Amer. Strategy [★16986]
Inst. for Amer. Universities [8643], 1830 Sherman Ave., Ste. 402, Evanston, IL 60201, (847)864-6876
Inst. for Amer. Universities [IO], Evanston, IL, United States
Inst. for Amer. Values [12158], 1841 Broadway, Ste. 211, New York, NY 10023, (212)246-3942
Inst. for Amer. Values Investing - Address unknown since 2004.
Inst. of America's Future [18353], c/o Campaign for America's Future, 1025 Connecticut Ave. NW, Ste. 205, Washington, DC 20036, (202)955-5665
Inst. of Andean Res. [9386]
Inst. of Andean Stud. [9387], PO Box 9307, Berkeley, CA 94709, (510)222-6284
Inst. of Andean Stud. [IO], Berkeley, CA, United States
Inst. of Animal Hea. [IO], Newbury, United Kingdom
Inst. of Animal Physiology [★IO]
Inst. of Animal Physiology and Genetics Res. [★IO]
Inst. of Animal Tech. [IO], Oxford, United Kingdom
Institute for Animals and Soc; Animal Rights Network/ [11359]
Inst. of Apostolic Oblates [19638], 205 S Pine Dr., Fullerton, CA 92833, (714)956-1020
Inst. of Appliance Manufacturers [★265]
Inst. for Applied Epistemics - Address unknown since 1994.
Inst. of Applied Natural Science - Address unknown since 1989.
Inst. for Appropriate Tech; Southern [★17001]
Inst. of Archaeo-Metallurgical Stud. [IO], London, United Kingdom
Inst. of Arctic Medicine [★IO]
Inst. of Art Stud. [IO], Sofia, Bulgaria
Inst. for Art and Urban Resources [★9595]
Inst. of Asian Res. [IO], Vancouver, BC, Canada
Inst. of Asian Stud. [★IO]
Inst. of Asian Stud. [★7985]
Inst. of Assn. Mgt. [IO], London, United Kingdom
Inst. of Assn. Mgt. Companies [★IO]
Inst. of Assn. Mgt. Companies [★314]
Inst. of Athletic Motivation [★23665]
Inst. of Australian Geographers [IO], Hobart, Australia
Inst. of Automotive Engineer Assessors [IO], Lichfield, United Kingdom
Inst. of Automotive Mech. Engineers [IO], Auburn, Australia
Institute for Axiomatic Knowledge and Education [IO], Annapolis, MD, United States
Inst. for Axiomatic Knowledge and Educ. [7606], 208-G Victor Pkwy., Annapolis, MD 21403, (410)974-9012
Inst. for Axiomatic Knowledge and Systematic Core Educ. [★7606]
Inst. for Axiomatic Knowledge and Systematic Core Educ. [★IO]
Inst. of Balkan Stud. [IO], Sofia, Bulgaria
Inst. of Bankers in Ireland [IO], Dublin, Ireland
Inst. of Bankers Malaysia [IO], Kuala Lumpur, Malaysia
Inst. of Bankers in South Africa [IO], Marshalltown, Republic of South Africa
Inst. of Bankers of Zimbabwe [IO], Harare, Zimbabwe
Inst. in Basic Life Principles [13489], Box 1, Oak Brook, IL 60522-3001, (630)323-9800

Inst. in Basic Youth Conflicts [★13489]
Inst. for Behavioral Healthcare [★13735]
Inst. for Better Packaging [★2877]
Inst. for Biblical Res. [19519], c/o Michael W. Holmes, Sec., Bethel Coll., 3900 Bethel Dr., St. Paul, MN 55112
Inst. for Bioenergetic Anal. [★IO]
Inst. of Biology [IO], London, United Kingdom
Inst. of Biomedical Sci. [IO], London, United Kingdom
Inst. of Black Elected Officials - Defunct.
Inst. of Black Studies - Defunct.
Inst. of the Black World - Defunct.
Inst. of Boiler and Radiator Mfrs. [★1884]
Inst. for Briquetting and Agglomeration - Defunct.
Inst. for British Carriage and Auto. Mfrs. [★IO]
Inst. of British Foundrymen [IO], West Midlands, United Kingdom
Inst. of British Foundrymen [★IO]
Inst. of Broadcasting Financial Mgt. [★553]
Inst. of Bus. Admin. [★IO]
Inst. of Bus. Admin. and Mgt. [IO], Petaling Jaya, Malaysia
Inst. of Bus. Advisers [IO], Chesterfield, United Kingdom
Inst. of Bus. Appraisers [282], PO Box 17410, Plantation, FL 33318, (954)584-1144
Inst. of Bus. Counsellors [★IO]
Inst. of Bus. Designers, Coun. for Fed. Interior Designers [★IO]
Inst. of Bus. Designers, Coun. for Fed. Interior Designers [★2265]
Inst. for Bus. and Home Safety [2171], 4775 E Fowler Ave., Tampa, FL 33617, (813)286-3400
Inst. Canadien du Credit [★IO]
Inst. for Cancer Prevention - Defunct.
Inst. of Career Guidance [IO], Stourbridge, United Kingdom
Institute of Caribbean Studies [IO], Washington, DC, United States
Inst. of Caribbean Stud. [12430], 7306 Georgia Ave. NW, Washington, DC 20012, (202)829-1887
Inst. of Carpenters [IO], Nottingham, United Kingdom
Inst. of Cartography [★IO]
Inst. of Cast Metals Engineers [★IO]
Inst. of Cast Metals Engineers [IO], West Bromwich, United Kingdom
Inst. of Caster Manufacturers [2028]
Inst. of Catalan Stud. [IO], Barcelona, Spain
Inst. for Central European Res. - Address unknown since 2005.
Inst. for Certification of Computing Professionals [8131], 2350 E Devon Ave., Ste. 115, Des Plaines, IL 60018-4610, (847)299-4227
Inst. for the Certification of Engg. Technicians [★7033]
Inst. for Certification of Tax Professionals - Address unknown since 2001.
Inst. of Certified Bus. Counselors [726], 18615 Willamette Dr., West Linn, OR 97068, (877)ICB-CORG
Inst. of Certified Financial Planners [★1420]
Inst. of Certified Financial Planners [★IO]
Inst. for Certified Investment Mgt. Consultants [★IO]
Inst. for Certified Investment Mgt. Consultants [★2336]
Inst. for Certified Investment Mgt. Consultants - Defunct.
Inst. of Certified Professional Managers [2497], James Madison Univ., MSC 5504, Harrisonburg, VA 22807, (540)568-3247
Inst. of Certified Professional Managers [IO], Harrisonburg, VA, United States
Inst. of Certified Records Managers [2103], 5818 Molloy Rd., Syracuse, NY 13211, (315)234-1904
Inst. of Certified Travel Agents [3918], 148 Linden St., Ste. 305, Wellesley, MA 02482, (781)237-0280
Inst. of Charity Fundraising Managers [★IO]
Inst. of Chartered Accountants in Australia [IO], Sydney, Australia
Inst. of Chartered Accountants of Bermuda [IO], Hamilton, Bermuda
Inst. of Chartered Accountants in England and Wales [IO], London, United Kingdom

Reference to "IO" in place of a book number signifies that the association may be found in the 45th edition of International Organizations.

Inst. of Chartered Accountants of Guyana [IO], Georgetown, Guyana

Inst. of Chartered Accountants of India [IO], New Delhi, India

Inst. of Chartered Accountants in Ireland [IO], Belfast, United Kingdom

Inst. of Chartered Accountants of New Zealand [IO], Wellington, New Zealand

Inst. of Chartered Accountants of Nigeria [IO], Lagos, Nigeria

Inst. of Chartered Accountants of Scotland [IO], Edinburgh, United Kingdom

Inst. of Chartered Accountants of Zimbabwe [IO], Harare, Zimbabwe

Inst. of Chartered Financial Analysts [★IO]

Inst. of Chartered Financial Analysts [★2331]

Inst. of Chartered Financial Analysts of India [IO], Hyderabad, India

Inst. of Chartered Foresters [IO], Edinburgh, United Kingdom

Inst. of Chartered Secretaries and Administrators - Canada [IO], Toronto, ON, Canada

Inst. of Chartered Secretaries and Administrators in Hong Kong [★IO]

Inst. of Chartered Secretaries and Administrators - United Kingdom [IO], London, United Kingdom

Inst. of Chartered Secretaries and Administrators - Zimbabwe [IO], Harare, Zimbabwe

Inst. of Chartered Shipbrokers - England [IO], London, United Kingdom

Inst. for Chem. Educ. [8062], Univ. of Wisconsin, Dept. of Chemistry, 1101 Univ. Ave., Madison, WI 53706-1396, (608)262-3033

Inst. of Chemistry of Ireland [IO], Dublin, Ireland

Inst. for Childhood Resources [8068], 268 Bush St., Ste. 2811, San Francisco, CA 94104, (415)864-1169

Inst. for Children and Poverty [11602], 50 Cooper Sq., New York, NY 10003, (212)674-2137

Inst. of Chinese Culture [9791], 10550 Westoffice Dr., Houston, TX 77042, (281)980-5172

Inst. of Chiropodists [★IO]

Inst. of Chiropodists and Podiatrists [IO], Southport, United Kingdom

Inst. on the Church in Urban-Industrial Soc. - Defunct.

Inst. of Civil Defence and Disaster Stud. [IO], Camberley, United Kingdom

Inst. of Civil War Studies - Address unknown since 2001.

Inst. of Clean Air Companies [3071], 1730 M St. NW, Ste. 206, Washington, DC 20036, (202)457-0911

Inst. of Clerks of Works of Great Britain [IO], Peterborough, United Kingdom

Inst. of Clinical Res. [IO], Marlow, United Kingdom

Inst. of Collective Bargaining and Group Relations - Address unknown since 2002.

Inst. for Coll. and Univ. Administrators [★8745]

Inst. for Commercial Forestry Res. [IO], Scottsville, Republic of South Africa

Inst. of Commercial Mgt. [IO], Christchurch, United Kingdom

Inst. of Commonwealth Stud. [IO], London, United Kingdom

Inst. of Communications and Advt. [IO], Toronto, ON, Canada

Inst. for Community Design Analysis - Address unknown since 2001.

Inst. for Community Economics [17221], 57 School St., Springfield, MA 01105-1331, (413)746-8660

Inst. of Community Studies - Defunct.

Inst. for Complementary Medicine [IO], London, United Kingdom

Inst. of Complementary Sciences - Defunct.

Inst. for Composite Materials - Defunct.

Inst. for Comprehensive Planning - Defunct.

Inst. for Cmpt. Capacity Mgt. [7196], c/o Joanne Decker, Chief Financial Off., 9148 Bonita Beach Rd., Ste. 210, Bonita Springs, FL 34135-4265, (239)261-8945

Inst. for Computers in Jewish Life [8562], 8170 N McCormick Blvd., Ste. 111, Skokie, IL 60076, (312)533-4240

Inst. of Concrete Tech. [IO], Camberley, United Kingdom

Inst. for Conservation Leadership [4573], 6930 Carroll Ave., Ste. 420, Takoma Park, MD 20912, (301)270-2900

Inst. for Constitutional Res. - Defunct.

Inst. of Consumer Affairs [IO], London, United Kingdom

Inst. for Consumer Financial Educ. [8424], PO Box 34070, San Diego, CA 92163-4070, (619)239-1401

Inst. for Consumer Protection [IO], Port Louis, Mauritius

Inst. of Contemporary Arts [IO], London, United Kingdom

Inst. for Contemporary Stud. [18453], 3100 Harrison St., Oakland, CA 94611-5526, (510)238-5010

Inst. for Continuing Studies in Design, Mgt. and Communication - Defunct.

Inst. for Control Therapy, Reality Therapy, and Quality Mgt. [★16233]

Inst. for the Cooperative Stud. of Intl. Sea-food Markets [★1484]

Inst. for the Cooperative Stud. of Intl. Sea-food Markets [★IO]

Inst. of Corrosion [IO], Leighton Buzzard, United Kingdom

Inst. of Cost Anal. [★1448]

Inst. of Cost and Mgt. Accountants [★IO]

Inst. of Cost and Mgt. Accountants [★IO]

Inst. for Counter-Terrorism [IO], Herzlia, Israel

Inst. for Court Mgt. of the Natl. Center for State Courts - Address unknown since 1999.

Inst. for Creation Res. [20538], 10946 Woodside Ave., Santee, CA 92071, (619)448-0900

Inst. of Credit Mgt. [IO], South Luffenham, United Kingdom

Inst. of Cultural Affairs [12350], 4750 N Sheridan Rd., Chicago, IL 60640, (773)769-6363

Inst. of Cultural Affairs - Australia [IO], Cleveland, Australia

Inst. of Cultural Affairs Brazil [IO], Rio de Janeiro, Brazil

Inst. of Cultural Affairs Chile [IO], Santiago, Chile

Inst. of Cultural Affairs Cote D'Ivoire [IO], Abidjan, Cote d'Ivoire

Inst. of Cultural Affairs Egypt [IO], Cairo, Egypt

Inst. of Cultural Affairs Ghana [IO], Accra, Ghana

Inst. of Cultural Affairs Guatemala [IO], Guatemala City, Guatemala

Inst. of Cultural Affairs India [IO], Pune, India

Inst. of Cultural Affairs Intl. - Belgium [IO], Brussels, Belgium

Inst. of Cultural Affairs - Japan [IO], Tokyo, Japan

Inst. of Cultural Affairs Kenya [IO], Nairobi, Kenya

Inst. of Cultural Affairs Malaysia [IO], Kuala Lumpur, Malaysia

Inst. of Cultural Affairs - Middle East and North Africa [IO], Cairo, Egypt

Inst. of Cultural Affairs - Mumbai [IO], Bombay, India

Inst. of Cultural Affairs Nepal [IO], Kathmandu, Nepal

Inst. of Cultural Affairs - Netherlands [IO], Amsterdam, Netherlands

Inst. of Cultural Affairs Nigeria [IO], Lagos, Nigeria

Inst. of Cultural Affairs Peru [IO], Lima, Peru

Inst. of Cultural Affairs - Pune [IO], Pune, India

Inst. of Cultural Affairs Taiwan [IO], Taipei, Taiwan

Inst. of Cultural Affairs Tanzania [IO], Moshi, United Republic of Tanzania

Inst. of Cultural Affairs Uganda [IO], Kyambogo, Uganda

Inst. of Cultural Affairs - United Kingdom [IO], Manchester, United Kingdom

Inst. of Cultural Affairs Zambia [IO], Lusaka, Zambia

Inst. of Cultural Affairs - Zimbabwe [IO], Harare, Zimbabwe

Inst. for Cultural Studies - Address unknown since 2006.

Inst. of Current World Affairs [18837], 4545 42nd St. NW, Ste. 311, Washington, DC 20016, (202)364-4068

Inst. of Current World Affairs [IO], Hanover, NH, United States

Inst. of Data Processing [★IO]

Inst. of Data Processing Mgt. [★IO]

Inst. of Decontamination Sciences [IO], Chesterfield, United Kingdom

Inst. for Defense Analyses [6256], 4850 Mark Center Dr., Alexandria, VA 22311-1882, (703)845-2000

Inst. for Defense and Disarmament Stud. [17430], 675 Massachusetts Ave., Cambridge, MA 02139, (617)354-4337

Inst. for Defense Policy [★IO]

Inst. for Delphinid Res. [★7261]

Inst. for Democracy in Eastern Europe [17446], 1718 M St. NW, No. 147, Washington, DC 20036, (202)466-7105

Inst. for Democracy in Eastern Europe [IO], Washington, DC, United States

Inst. for Democratic Educ. [★17091]

Inst. for Democratic Socialism - Address unknown since 1999.

Inst. of Designers in Ireland [IO], Dublin, Ireland

Inst. d'Etudes de Securite [★IO]

Inst. for Developing Countries [★IO]

Inst. of Developing Economies, Japan External Trade Org. [IO], Chiba, Japan

Inst. for Development Anthropology - Defunct.

Inst. for Development of Educational Activities [8263]

Inst. for the Development of Emotional and Life Skills [★15201]

Inst. for the Development of Emotional and Life Skills/National Inst. of Relationship Enhancement [15201], 4400 East-West Hwy., Ste. 28, Bethesda, MD 20814-4501, (301)986-1479

Inst. for the Development of the Harmonious Human Being [12351], PO Box 370, Nevada City, CA 95959, (530)272-0180

Inst. for the Development of Indian Law [18095]

Inst. for Development and Intl. Relations [★IO]

Inst. for Development Policy and Mgt. [IO], Manchester, United Kingdom

Inst. for Development Res. [★IO]

Inst. for Development Res. [★7918]

Inst. of Development Stud. [IO], Brighton, United Kingdom

Inst. for Development Training [★IO]

Inst. for Development Training [★14978]

Inst. for Diagnostic Radiology [★IO]

Inst. of Directors - England [IO], London, United Kingdom

Inst. of Directors in Ireland [IO], Dublin, Ireland

Inst. of Directors - Zimbabwe [IO], Harare, Zimbabwe

Inst. of Distribution - Defunct.

Inst. for Diversity in Hea. Mgt. [14704], 1 N Franklin, 30th Fl., Chicago, IL 60606, (312)422-2630

Inst. of Diving [23961]

Inst. of Domestic Heating and Environmental Engineers [IO], Southampton, United Kingdom

Inst. for a Drug-Free Workplace [13247], 8614 Westwood Center Dr., Ste. 950, Vienna, VA 22182, (202)842-7400

Inst. of Early Amer. History and Culture [★10140]

Institute for Early Learning Through the Arts [★9602]

Inst. for Earth Educ. [8389], Cedar Cove, PO Box 115, Greenville, WV 24945, (304)832-6404

Inst. for Earth Educ. [IO], Greenville, WV, United States

Inst. for East West Stud. [★IO]

Inst. for East West Stud. [★17823]

Inst. of Eastern Culture [IO], Tokyo, Japan

Inst. for Ecological Policies - Defunct.

Inst. of Ecology and Environmental Mgt. [IO], Winchester, United Kingdom

Inst. for Econometric Res. - Address unknown since 2003.

Inst. of Economic Affairs [IO], London, United Kingdom

Inst. for Economic Anal. [6880], 262 Harvard St., No. 12, Cambridge, MA 02139, (617)864-9933

Institute for Economic Development of Cuba [★17367]

Institute for Economic Development of Cuba [★IO]

Inst. of Economics, Inst. for Govt. Res. [★18424]

Inst. of Ecotechnics [IO], London, United Kingdom

Inst. for Ecumenical Res. [IO], Strasbourg, France

Inst. for Educ. in Peace and Justice [★18209]

Inst. for Education for Working Class Women - Defunct.

Inst. for Educational Development - Defunct.

Inst. for Educational Innovation [★8253]

A star before a book entry number signifies that the name is not listed separately, but is mentioned within the entry.

Inst. for Educational Innovation [★IO]

Inst. for Educational Leadership [8264], 4455 Connecticut Ave. NW, Ste. 310, Washington, DC 20008, (202)822-8405

Inst. of Educational Res. - Defunct.

Inst. for Educational Services [8265], 108 Johnston St., Savannah, GA 31405-5605, (912)355-2259

Inst. of Elecl. and Electronics Engineers [6926], 445 Hoes Ln., Piscataway, NJ 08854, (732)981-0060

Inst. of Elecl. and Electronics Engineers - Nigerian Sect. [IO], Port Harcourt, Nigeria

Inst. of Elecl. and Electronics Engineers - USA [7015], 1828 L St. NW, Ste. 1202, Washington, DC 20036-5104, (202)785-0017

Inst. of Elecl. Engineers of Japan [IO], Tokyo, Japan

Inst. of Electronics, Info. and Commun. Engineers [IO], Tokyo, Japan

Institute of Employment Consultants [★IO]

Inst. of Employment Rights [IO], Liverpool, United Kingdom

Inst. for Energy and Environmental Res. [6955], 6935 Laurel Ave., Ste. 201, Takoma Park, MD 20912, (301)270-5500

Inst. of Entertainment and Arts Mgt. [IO], Horsham, United Kingdom

Inst. for Env. and Development Stud. [IO], Dhaka, Bangladesh

Inst. of Environmental Engineers [★IO]

Inst. of Environmental Engineers [★7570]

Inst. of Environmental Sciences [★7570]

Inst. of Environmental Sciences [★IO]

Institute of Environmental Sciences and Technology [IO], Rolling Meadows, IL, United States

Inst. of Environmental Sciences and Tech. [7570], 5005 Newport Dr., Ste. 506, Rolling Meadows, IL 60008-3841, (847)255-1561

Inst. for Epidemiologic Studies of Violence - Defunct.

Institute for Esperanto in Commerce and Industry [★9914]

Inst. for Estuarine and Coastal Stud. [IO], Hull, United Kingdom

Institute of Ethics [★19931]

Inst. of Ethiopian Stud. [IO], Addis Ababa, Ethiopia

Inst. of European and Asian Stud. [★IO]

Inst. of European and Asian Stud. [★7985]

Inst. for European Environmental Policy [IO], London, United Kingdom

Inst. of European Politics [IO], Berlin, Germany

Inst. for European Stud. [★IO]

Inst. of European Stud. [★IO]

Inst. of European Stud. [★8405]

Inst. of European Stud. [★7985]

Inst. of Explosives Engineers [IO], Swindon, United Kingdom

Inst. of Export [IO], Peterborough, United Kingdom

Inst. for Expressive Anal. [16217], 50 W 97th St., No. 1H, New York, NY 10025, (212)988-1809

Inst. of Family History and Genealogy - Address unknown since 1999.

Inst. for Family Res. and Education - Defunct.

Inst. of Farm Brokers [★3342]

Inst. for Female Alternative Medicine [16345], 6815 Noble Ave., Ste. 410, Van Nuys, CA 91405, (818)997-5000

Inst. of Field Archaeologists [IO], Reading, United Kingdom

Inst. of Finance Professionals New Zealand [IO], Wellington, New Zealand

Inst. of Financial Accountants [IO], Sevenoaks, United Kingdom

Inst. for Financial Crime Prevention [★IO]

Inst. for Financial Crime Prevention [★2084]

Inst. of Financial Planning [IO], Bristol, United Kingdom

Inst. of Financial Services - England [IO], London, United Kingdom

Inst. of Fireplace Equipment Mfrs. - Address unknown since 1995.

Inst. for First Amendment Studies - Defunct.

Inst. of Fiscal and Political Education - Defunct.

Inst. for Fiscal Stud. [IO], London, United Kingdom

Inst. of Fisheries Mgt. [IO], Nottingham, United Kingdom

Inst. for Fluitronics Education - Defunct.

Inst. de la Fondation D'Acupuncture du Canada [★IO]

Inst. for Food and Development Policy [IO], Oakland, CA, United States

Inst. for Food and Development Policy [17795], 398 60th St., Oakland, CA 94618, (510)654-4400

Inst. of Food Sci. and Tech. - UK [IO], London, United Kingdom

Inst. of Food Technologists [7094], 525 W Van Buren, Ste. 1000, Chicago, IL 60607, (312)782-8424

Inst. of Foreign Bankers [★481]

Inst. of Foreign Bankers [★IO]

Inst. for Foreign Policy Anal. [17612], Central Plz. Bldg., 10th Fl., 675 Massachusetts Ave., Cambridge, MA 02139-3309, (617)492-2116

Inst. for Forest Improvement [★IO]

Inst. of Foresters [★IO]

Inst. of Forestry, Policy and Info. [★IO]

Inst. for Friendship Through Learning - Address unknown since 2003.

Inst. of Fundraising [IO], London, United Kingdom

Inst. for the Future [IO], Palo Alto, CA, United States

Inst. for the Future [7105], 124 Univ. Ave., 2nd Fl., Palo Alto, CA 94301, (650)854-6322

Inst. of Gas Tech. [★1678]

Inst. of Gen. Semantics [10962], 2260 Coll. Ave., Fort Worth, TX 76110, (817)922-9950

Institute of General Semantics [IO], Fort Worth, TX, United States

Inst. of Geologists of Ireland [IO], Belfield, Ireland

Inst. of Gerontology [IO], London, United Kingdom

Inst. for Global Communications [IO], San Francisco, CA, United States

Inst. for Global Communications [7772], PO Box 29047, San Francisco, CA 94129-0047

Inst. on Global Drug Policy [13248], c/o Drug Free Am. Found., Inc., 2600 9th St. N, Ste. 200, St. Petersburg, FL 33704-2744, (727)828-0211

Inst. on Global Drug Policy [IO], St. Petersburg, FL, United States

Inst. of Global Env. and Soc. [IO], Beltsville, MD, United States

Inst. of Global Env. and Soc. [4574], 4041 Powder Mill Rd., Ste. 302, Beltsville, MD 20705-3106, (301)595-7000

Inst. for Global Ethics [7070], PO Box 563, Camden, ME 04843, (207)236-6658

Inst. for Global Ethics [IO], Camden, ME, United States

Inst. for Graphic Communication - Defunct.

Inst. for Gravitational Strain Pathology - Address unknown since 2003.

Inst. of the Great Plains [9994], PO Box 68, Lawton, OK 73502, (580)581-3460

Inst. of Grocery Distribution [IO], Watford, United Kingdom

Inst. of Groundsmanship [IO], Milton Keynes, United Kingdom

Inst. of Gp. Anal. [IO], London, United Kingdom

Inst. of Hazardous Materials Mgt. [4805], 11900 Parklawn Dr., Ste. 450, Rockville, MD 20852-2624, (301)984-8969

Inst. for Hea. Policy Solutions [14689], 1444 Eye St. NW, Ste. 900, Washington, DC 20005, (202)789-1491

Inst. for Hea. and Productivity Mgt. [2498], 4435 Waterfront Dr., Ste. 101, Glen Allen, VA 23060, (804)527-1905

Inst. for Hea. and Productivity Mgt. [IO], Glen Allen, VA, United States

Inst. of Hea. Promotion and Educ. [IO], Manchester, United Kingdom

Inst. of Hea. Services Mgt. [★IO]

Inst. of Healthcare Engg. and Estate Mgt. [IO], Portsmouth, United Kingdom

Inst. of Healthcare Improvement [14637], 20 Univ. Rd., 7th Fl., Cambridge, MA 02138, (617)301-4800

Inst. of Healthcare Mgt. - United Kingdom [IO], London, United Kingdom

Inst. of HeartMath [10174], 14700 W Park Ave., Boulder Creek, CA 95006, (831)338-8500

Inst. for Hemp - Address unknown since 2001.

Inst. of Heraldic and Genealogical Stud. [IO], Canterbury, United Kingdom

Inst. of High Fidelity [★1212]

Institute of Higher Tibetan Studies [★11055]

Inst. of Highway Incorporated Engineers [IO], London, United Kingdom

Inst. for Historical Rev. [17711], PO Box 2739, Newport Beach, CA 92659, (949)631-1490

Inst. of Home Office Underwriters - Defunct.

Inst. of Horticulture [IO], London, United Kingdom

Inst. for Hospital Clinical Nursing Education - Address unknown since 1999.

Inst. on Hosp. and Community Psychiatry [★16085]

Inst. of Hosp. Engg. [★IO]

Inst. for Human-Animal Relationship - Address unknown since 1995.

Inst. for the Human Env. [4575]

Inst. of Human Origins [7072], Arizona State Univ., PO Box 874101, Tempe, AZ 85287-4101, (480)727-6580

Inst. for Human Progress - Defunct.

Inst. for Human Rights - Defunct.

Inst. for Humane Stud. [12375], George Mason Univ., 3301 N Fairfax Dr., Ste. 440, Arlington, VA 22201-4432, (703)993-4880

Inst. for Humanist Stud. [8528], 48 Howard St., Albany, NY 12207-1608, (518)432-7820

Institute for Image Mgt; Image Indus. Coun. International/ [964]

Inst. of Incorporated Public Accountants [IO], Naas, Ireland

Inst. for Independent Education - Defunct.

Inst. of Indian Foundrymen [IO], Calcutta, India

Inst. for Individual and World Peace [IO], Santa Monica, CA, United States

Inst. for Individual and World Peace [12352], 2101 Wilshire Blvd., Ste. 119, Santa Monica, CA 90403-5745, (310)315-3451

Inst. of Indus. Economics of China [★IO]

Inst. of Indus. Engineers [IO], Dublin, Ireland

Inst. of Indus. Engineers [7016], 3577 Parkway Ln., Ste. 200, Norcross, GA 30092, (770)449-0460

Inst. of Indus. Engineers (Hong Kong) [IO], Hong Kong, People's Republic of China

Inst. of Indus. Launderers [★2408]

Inst. of Inspection, Cleaning and Restoration Certification [2259], 2715 E Mill Plain Blvd., Vancouver, WA 98661, (360)693-5675

Inst. of Insurance Brokers [IO], Higham Ferrers, United Kingdom

Inst. for Integral Development [13249], PO Box 2172, Colorado Springs, CO 80901, (719)634-7943

Inst. for the Integration of Latin Am. and the Caribbean [IO], Buenos Aires, Argentina

Inst. for Interconnecting and Packaging Electronic Circuits [★1221]

Inst. for Intercultural Stud. [10234], 67A E 77th St., New York, NY 10021-1813, (212)737-1011

Inst. on Interdenominational Stud. [★19931]

Inst. for Interindustry Data - Defunct.

Inst. of Intermodal Repairers - Address unknown since 2003.

Inst. of Internal Auditors [33], 247 Maitland Ave., Altamonte Springs, FL 32701-4201, (407)937-1100

Inst. of Internal Auditors [IO], Altamonte Springs, FL, United States

Inst. of Internal Auditors - Australia [IO], Sydney, Australia

Inst. of Internal Auditors - Hong Kong [IO], Hong Kong, People's Republic of China

Inst. of Internal Auditors - UK and Ireland [IO], London, United Kingdom

Inst. of Intl. Bankers [IO], New York, NY, United States

Inst. of Intl. Bankers [481], 299 Park Ave., 17th Fl., New York, NY 10171, (212)421-1611

Inst. of Intl. Container Lessors [984], 555 Pleasantville Rd., Ste. 140 S, Briarcliff Manor, NY 10510, (914)747-9100

Inst. of Intl. Container Lessors [IO], Briarcliff Manor, NY, United States

Inst. for Intl. Cooperation and Development [IO], Williamstown, MA, United States

Inst. for Intl. Cooperation and Development [12431], PO Box 520, Williamstown, MA 01267, (413)441-5126

Inst. for Intl. Economic Co-operation [IO], Milan, Italy

Inst. for Intl. Economic Cooperation and Development [IO], Rome, Italy

Inst. for Intl. Economics [IO], Seoul, Republic of Korea

Reference to "IO" in place of a book number signifies that the association may be found in the 45th edition of International Organizations.

Inst. of Intl. Educ. [IO], New York, NY, United States

Inst. of Intl. Educ. [8616], 809 United Nations Plz., New York, NY 10017-3580, (212)883-8200

Inst. of Intl. Educ; Arts Intl. Prog. of the [★9551]

Inst. of Intl. Educ. - China [IO], Hong Kong, People's Republic of China

Inst. of Intl. Educ. - Egypt [IO], Cairo, Egypt

Inst. of Intl. Educ. - India [IO], New Delhi, India

Inst. of Intl. Educ. - Latin Am. [IO], Mexico City, Mexico

Inst. of Intl. Educ. - Russia [IO], Moscow, Russia

Inst. of Intl. Educ. - Southeast Asia [IO], Bangkok, Thailand

Inst. for the Intl. Educ. of Students [IO], Chicago, IL, United States

Inst. for the Intl. Educ. of Students [7985], 33 N La-Salle St., 15th Fl., Chicago, IL 60602-2602, (312)944-1750

Inst. of Intl. Educ. - Ukraine [IO], Kiev, Ukraine

Inst. for Intl. Entrepreneurship [727]

Inst. of Intl. Finance [482], 1333 H St. NW, Ste. 800E, Washington, DC 20005-4770, (202)857-3600

Inst. of Intl. Finance [IO], Washington, DC, United States

Inst. for Intl. and Foreign Trade Law [★IO]

Inst. for Intl. and Foreign Trade Law [★5867]

Inst. for Intl. Govt. [★17620]

Inst. for Intl. Govt. [★IO]

Inst. for Intl. Health and Development - Address unknown since 1999.

Inst. for Intl. Human Resources [★2907]

Inst. for Intl. Human Resources [★IO]

Inst. of Intl. Labor Res. - Defunct.

Inst. of Intl. Law [IO], Geneva, Switzerland

Inst. of Intl. Licensing Practitioners [IO], Oxford, United Kingdom

Inst. for Intl. Mediation and Conflict Resolution [IO], Washington, DC, United States

Inst. for Intl. Mediation and Conflict Resolution [5454], 1424 K St. NW, Ste. 650, Washington, DC 20005, (202)347-2042

Inst. for Intl. Order [★17620]

Inst. for Intl. Order [★IO]

Inst. for Intl. Peace Stud; Joan B. Kroc [18216]

Inst. for Intl. Policy [★17748]

Inst. for Intl. Policy [★IO]

Inst. for Intl. Political Stud. [IO], Milan, Italy

Inst. for Intl. Relations [IO], Zagreb, Croatia

Inst. for Intl. Relations - Czech Republic [★IO]

Inst. of Intl. Relations Prague [IO], Prague, Czech Republic

Inst. of Intl. Trade and Development - Address unknown since 1991.

Inst. of Intl. Trade of Ireland [IO], Dublin, Ireland

Inst. for Intl. Youth Affairs - Address unknown since 1995.

Inst. of Inventors [IO], London, United Kingdom

Inst. of Investment Mgt. and Res. [★IO]

Inst. of the Ironworking Indus. [24133], 1750 New York Ave. NW, Washington, DC 20006, (202)783-3998

Inst. of Islamic and Arabic Sciences in Am. [8670], 8500 Hilltop Rd., Fairfax, VA 22031, (703)641-4986

Inst. for Jewish-Christian Relations - Defunct.

Inst. for Jewish Medical Ethics [20143], c/o Lisa Kampner Hebrew Acad., 645 14th Ave., San Francisco, CA 94118, (415)752-7333

Inst. for Jewish Policy Planning and Res. - Defunct.

Inst. for Jewish Policy Res. [IO], London, United Kingdom

Institute for Jewish Studies [★20167]

Inst. of Judicial Admin. [5902], c/o Prof. Oscar G. Chase, Exec. Co-Dir., New York Univ. School of Law, Vanderbilt Hall, 40 Washington Square Park, Rm. 413, New York, NY 10012, (212)998-6217

Inst. for Justice [5940], 901 N Glebe Rd., Ste. 900, Arlington, VA 22203, (703)682-9320

Inst. of Labor and Indus. Relations [24114], Univ. of Michigan, Victor Vaughan Bldg., 1111 E Catherine St., Ann Arbor, MI 48109-2054, (734)763-3116

Inst. for Labor and Mental Health [15202]

Inst. for Lab. Animal Res. [13698], 500 Fifth St. NW, Washington, DC 20001, (202)334-2590

Inst. of Lab. Animal Resources [★13698]

Inst. of Landscape Architects of South Africa [IO], Groenkloof, Republic of South Africa

Inst. of Landscape Architects of Southern Africa [★IO]

Inst. of Language and Literature [IO], Kuala Lumpur, Malaysia

Inst. for Latin Amer. Integration [★IO]

Inst. of Leadership and Mgt. [IO], Lichfield, United Kingdom

Inst. for Learning Technologies [8355], c/o John B. Black, Dir., Columbia Univ., 2960 Broadway, New York, NY 10027-6902, (212)678-4007

Inst. of Legal Cashiers [★IO]

Inst. of Legal Cashiers and Administrators [IO], Kent, United Kingdom

Inst. of Legal Executives [IO], Kempston, United Kingdom

Inst. of Legal Executives (Victoria) [IO], Burwood, Australia

Institute for Legislative Action [★22913]

Inst. of Leisure and Amenity Mgt. [IO], Reading, United Kingdom

Inst. for Liberty and Community - Defunct.

Inst. for Liberty and Justice [★17108]

Inst. of Licensed Trade Stock Auditors [IO], Halifax, United Kingdom

Inst. of Lithuanian Stud. [IO], Chicago, IL, United States

Inst. of Lithuanian Stud. [10435], 5600 S Claremont Ave., Chicago, IL 60636-1039, (773)434-4545

Inst. for Local Self-Reliance [11747], 927 15th St. NW, 4th Fl., Washington, DC 20005, (202)898-1610

Inst. of Logistics and Transport [★IO]

Inst. of London Underwriters [★IO]

Inst. of Maintenance and Building Mgt. [IO], Farnham, United Kingdom

Inst. of Makers of Explosives [1351], 1120 19th St. NW, Ste. 310, Washington, DC 20036-3605, (202)429-9280

Inst. of Maltese Journalists [IO], Valletta, Malta

Inst. of Mgt. [IO], London, United Kingdom

Inst. of Mgt. Accountants [34], 10 Paragon Dr., Montvale, NJ 07645, (201)573-9000

Inst. of Mgt. Consultancy [IO], London, United Kingdom

Inst. of Mgt. Consultants [IO], Surrey Hills, Australia

Inst. of Mgt. Consultants in Ireland [IO], Dublin, Ireland

Inst. of Mgt. Consultants USA [2499], 2025 M St. NW, Ste. 800, Washington, DC 20036-3309, (202)367-1134

Inst. for the Mgt. of Info. Systems [IO], Orpington, United Kingdom

The Inst. of Mgt. Sciences [★IO]

The Inst. of Mgt. Sciences [★2500]

Inst. of Mgt. Services [IO], Lichfield, United Kingdom

Inst. for Mfg. [IO], Cambridge, United Kingdom

Inst. of Marine Engg., Sci. and Tech. [IO], London, United Kingdom

Inst. for Marine Information - Defunct.

Inst. of Marketing Mgt. Graduate School of Marketing [IO], Johannesburg, Republic of South Africa

Inst. of Marriage and for Family Relations - Address unknown since 2002.

Inst. of Masonry Res. - Defunct.

Inst. of Masters of Wine [IO], London, United Kingdom

Inst. of Materials Engg. Australasia [IO], Parkville, Australia

Inst. of Materials, Minerals, and Mining [IO], London, United Kingdom

Inst. of Materials, Minerals and Mining and Inst. of Packaging - United Kingdom [★IO]

Inst. of Mathematical Statistics [7706], PO Box 22718, Beachwood, OH 44122, (216)295-2340

Inst. of Mathematics and its Applications [IO], Essex, United Kingdom

Inst. of Measurement and Control [IO], London, United Kingdom

Inst. of Measurement and Control of New Zealand [IO], Auckland, New Zealand

Inst. for Media Analysis - Address unknown since 1999.

Inst. for Mediation and Conflict Resolution [5455], 384 E 149th St., Ste. 330, Bronx, NY 10455, (718)585-1190

Inst. for Medical Quality [16263], 221 Main St., Ste. 210, San Francisco, CA 94105, (415)882-5151

Inst. for Medical Record Economics [★15098]

Inst. of Medicine [7607], 500 5th St. NW, Washington, DC 20001, (202)334-2352

Inst. of Medicine; Comm. on Human Rights of the U.S. Natl. Acad. of Sciences, Natl. Acad. of Engg., and [★17753]

Inst. for Mediterranean Affairs - Address unknown since 1999.

Inst. for Mediterranean Art and Archaeology - Defunct.

Inst. for Mental Hea. Initiatives [15203], 2175 K St. NW, Ste. No. 700, Washington, DC 20037, (202)467-2285

Inst. of Mental Physics [★20503]

Inst. of Metal Finishing [IO], Birmingham, United Kingdom

Inst. of Metal Repair - Address unknown since 2003.

Inst. of Microwavable Food and Packaging - Address unknown since 2006.

Inst. of Mine Surveyors of South Africa [IO], Marshalltown, Republic of South Africa

Inst. for Minority Business Education - Defunct.

Inst. of Modern Procedures - Defunct.

Inst. for Molecular Mfg. [7263], 555 Bryant St., Ste. 354, Palo Alto, CA 94301, (650)917-1120

Inst. for Monetary Freedom - Address unknown since 1994.

Inst. on Money and Inflation - Defunct.

Inst. of the Motor Indus. [IO], Hertford, United Kingdom

Inst. of Municipal Engg. [★IO]

Inst. for Muscle Disease - Defunct.

Inst. of Musical Instrument Tech. [IO], Croydon, United Kingdom

Inst. of Natl. Affairs [IO], Port Moresby, Papua New Guinea

Inst. of Nautical Archaeology [IO], College Station, TX, United States

Inst. of Nautical Archaeology [6448], PO Drawer HG, College Station, TX 77841-5137, (979)845-6694

Inst. of Navigation [7369], 3975 Univ. Dr., Ste. 390, Fairfax, VA 22030, (703)383-9688

Inst. of Near Eastern and African Stud. [8266], PO Box 425125, Cambridge, MA 02142, (617)864-6327

Inst. of Near Eastern and African Stud. [IO], Cambridge, MA, United States

Inst. for Neighborhood Reinvestment and Minority Business Res. - Defunct.

Inst. for New Enterprise Development - Address unknown since 1991.

Inst. for a New Middle East Policy - Defunct.

Inst. of Newspaper Controllers and Finance Officers [★1428]

Inst. of Newspaper Controllers and Finance Officers [★IO]

Inst. of Noetic Sciences; IONS - [10976]

Inst. of Noise Control Engg. [7382], 210 Marston Hall, Ames, IA 50011-2153, (515)294-6142

Inst. of the Northamerican West - Defunct.

Inst. of Nuclear Materials Mgt. [7387], 60 Revere Dr., Ste. 500, Northbrook, IL 60062, (847)480-9573

Inst. of Nuclear Power Operations [7392], c/o U.S. Department of Energy, 1000 Independence Ave. SW, Washington, DC 20585, (202)586-5575

Inst. for Numerical Computation and Anal. [IO], Dublin, Ireland

Inst. of Nutrition of Central Am. and Panama [IO], Guatemala City, Guatemala

Inst. for Objectivist Stud. [★10821]

Inst. of Occupational and Environmental Hea. [★IO]

Inst. of Occupational Medicine [IO], Edinburgh, United Kingdom

Inst. of Operations Mgt. [IO], Coventry, United Kingdom

Inst. for Operations Res. and the Mgt. Sciences [IO], Hanover, MD, United States

Inst. for Operations Res. and the Mgt. Sciences [2500], 7240 Parkway Dr., Ste. 310, Hanover, MD 21076-1310, (443)757-3500

Inst. of Ophthalmology [IO], London, United Kingdom

Inst. of Outdoor Drama [11018], UNC-Chapel Hill, 1700 Martin Luther King Jr. Blvd., CB No. 3240, Chapel Hill, NC 27599-3240, (919)962-1328

A star before a book entry number signifies that the name is not listed separately, but is mentioned within the entry.

Inst. for Outdoor Learning [IO], Penrith, United Kingdom

Inst. of Packaging Professionals [7426], 1601 Bond St., Ste. 101, Naperville, IL 60563, (630)544-5050

Inst. of Packaging - South Africa [IO], Pinegowrie, Republic of South Africa

Inst. for Palestine Stud. [IO], Washington, DC, United States

Inst. for Palestine Stud. [9397], 3501 M St. NW, Washington, DC 20007, (202)342-3990

Inst. of Paper [IO], Chertsey, United Kingdom

Inst. of Paper Chemistry [★IO]

Inst. of Paper Chemistry [★7435]

Inst. of Paper Conservation [IO], Upton-upon-Severn, United Kingdom

Institute of Paper Science and Technology [IO], Atlanta, GA, United States

Inst. of Paper Sci. and Tech. [7435], 500 10th St. NW, Atlanta, GA 30332-0620, (404)894-5700

Inst. for Parapsychology; Rhine Res. Center - [7452]

Inst. of Pastoral Care [★19915]

Inst. of Patentees and Inventors [IO], London, United Kingdom

Inst. of Payroll and Pensions Mgt. [IO], Solihull, United Kingdom

Inst. for Peace and Intl. Security - Address unknown since 2004.

Inst. for Peace and Justice [18209], 475 E Lockwood Ave., St. Louis, MO 63119, (314)918-2630

Inst. of People Mgt. (South Africa) [IO], Johannesburg, Republic of South Africa

Inst. for People's Educ. and Action [8267], 73 Willow St., Florence, MA 01062, (413)585-8755

Inst. for Personal Computing - Address unknown since 1995.

Inst. of Personal Image Consultants - Defunct.

Inst. of Personnel Mgt. [★IO]

Inst. of Personnel Mgt. of Zimbabwe [IO], Harare, Zimbabwe

Institute of Petroleum [★IO]

Inst. of Pharmacy Mgt. Intl. [IO], Glasgow, United Kingdom

Inst. for Philosophy and Public Policy [18454], Maryland School of Public Affairs, 3111 Van Munching, College Park, MD 20742, (301)405-4753

Inst. of Photographic Tech. [IO], Melbourne, Australia

Inst. of Physics [IO], London, United Kingdom

Inst. of Physics [★IO]

Inst. of Physics [7501], c/o Inst. of Physics Publishing, The Public Ledger Bldg., 150 S Independence Mall W, Ste. 929, Philadelphia, PA 19106, (215)627-0880

Inst. of Physics and Engg. in Medicine [IO], York, United Kingdom

Inst. of Physics, Singapore [IO], Singapore, Singapore

Inst. for Planetary Synthesis - Switzerland [IO], Geneva, Switzerland

Inst. of Plumbing - Australia [IO], Marmion, Australia

Inst. of Plumbing and Heating Engg. [IO], Hornchurch, United Kingdom

Inst. on Pluralism and Group Identity - Address unknown since 1999.

Inst. of Policy Anal. and Res. [IO], Nairobi, Kenya

Inst. for Policy and Legal Stud. [IO], Tirana, Albania

Inst. for Policy Stud. [IO], Washington, DC, United States

Inst. for Policy Stud. [18455], 1112 16th St. NW, Ste. 600, Washington, DC 20036, (202)234-9382

Inst. of Political Campaign Consultants - Address unknown since 2003.

Inst. for Polyacrylate Absorbents [811], c/o Synthetic Organic Chem. Mfrs. Assn., 1850 M St. NW, Ste. 700, Washington, DC 20036-5810, (202)721-4100

Institute for Polyacrylate Absorbents [IO], Washington, DC, United States

Institute for Polynesian Studies [★IO]

Institute for Polynesian Studies [★10885]

Inst. for Practical Idealism [★8665]

Inst. for Practical Idealism [★IO]

Inst. of Practitioners in Advt. [IO], London, United Kingdom

Inst. for Prevention and Control of Violence and Extremism [★17146]

Inst. of Printed Circuits [★1221]

Inst. of Professional Engg. Technologists [IO], Randburg, Republic of South Africa

Inst. for Professional Enrichment [★7901]

Inst. for Professional Environmental Practice [4576], 333 Fisher Hall, 600 Forbes Ave., Pittsburgh, PA 15282, (412)396-1703

Inst. for Professional Environmental Practice [IO], Pittsburgh, PA, United States

Inst. of Professional Soil Scientists [IO], Aberdeen, United Kingdom

Inst. for Professionals in Taxation [6294], 600 Northpark Town Center, 1200 Abernathy Rd. NE, Ste. L-2, Atlanta, GA 30328, (404)240-2300

Inst. of Property Taxation [★6294]

Inst. for Prospective Technological Stud. [IO], Seville, Spain

Inst. for the Protection of Lesbian and Gay Youth [★12234]

Inst. on Psychiatric Services/American Psychiatric Assn. [16085], 1000 Wilson Blvd., Ste. 1825, Arlington, VA 22209-3901, (703)907-7300

Inst. of Psychiatry [IO], London, United Kingdom

Inst. for Psychiatry and Foreign Affairs - Defunct.

Inst. for Psychohistory [10123], 140 Riverside Dr., New York, NY 10024-2605, (212)799-2294

Inst. of Psychosexual Medicine [IO], London, United Kingdom

Inst. for Public Accuracy [18456], 65 9th St., Ste. 3, San Francisco, CA 94103, (415)552-5378

Inst. of Public Admin. [IO], Dublin, Ireland

Inst. of Public Admin. Australia [IO], Brisbane, Australia

Inst. of Public Admin. of Canada [IO], Toronto, ON, Canada

Inst. of Public Admin. - USA [IO], New York, NY, United States

Inst. of Public Admin. - USA [6192]

Inst. of Public Affairs [IO], Melbourne, Australia

Inst. of Public Auditors in Germany [IO], Dusseldorf, Germany

Inst. of Public Loss Assessors [IO], Chesham, United Kingdom

Inst. of Public Media Arts - Address unknown since 2004.

Inst. for Public Relations [9031], PO Box 118400, Gainesville, FL 32611-8400, (352)392-0280

Inst. of Public Relations [★IO]

Inst. for Public Relations Res. and Educ. [★9031]

Inst. for Public Representation; Citizens Commun. Center of the [★17171]

Inst. for Public Representation; Citizens Communications Center Proj. of the [17171]

Inst. of Public Understanding - Defunct.

Inst. of Public Utilities [3958], Michigan State Univ., W157 Owen Graduate Hall, East Lansing, MI 48825-1109, (517)355-1876

Inst. of Public Works Engg. Australia [IO], Sydney, Australia

Inst. for Puerto Rican Arts and Culture - Address unknown since 2001.

Inst. of Purchasing and Supply of Hong Kong [IO], Hong Kong, People's Republic of China

Inst. of Qualified Private Secretaries [★IO]

Inst. of Qualified Professional Secretaries [IO], Windsor, United Kingdom

Inst. of Quality Assurance [★IO]

Inst. of Quantity Surveyors [★IO]

Inst. of Quarrying - Australia [IO], North Ryde, Australia

Inst. of Quarrying - England [IO], Nottingham, United Kingdom

Inst. of Quarrying - Hong Kong Br. [IO], Hong Kong, People's Republic of China

Inst. of Quarrying - Southern Africa [IO], Gallo Manor, Republic of South Africa

Inst. of Race Relations [IO], London, United Kingdom

Inst. of Radio Engineers [★6926]

Inst. for Rational-Emotive Therapy [★16197]

Inst. for Rational Living [★16197]

Inst. of Real Estate Mgt. [3312], 430 N Michigan Ave., Chicago, IL 60611-3900, (312)329-6000

Inst. for Reality Therapy [★16233]

Inst. for Reduction of Crime [★9085]

Inst. of Refrigeration [IO], Carshalton, United Kingdom

Inst. for Regional and Intl. Stud. [IO], Boulder, CO, United States

Inst. for Regional and Intl. Stud. [17047], 5735 Arapahoe Ave., No. A-5, Boulder, CO 80303

Inst. on Religion in an Age of Sci. [20550], c/o David A. Klotz, Membership Chm., 82 Goose Ln., Coventry, CT 06238

Inst. on Religion and Democracy [17393], 1023 15th St. NW, Ste. 601, Washington, DC 20005-2601, (202)682-4131

Inst. on Religious Life [19639], PO Box 7500, Libertyville, IL 60048-7500, (847)573-8975

Inst. for Religious and Social Stud. [★19931]

Inst. for Reproductive Hea. [★16345]

Inst. on Res. and Development on Asbestos [★IO]

Inst. for Res. and Education on Human Rights - Defunct.

Inst. for Res. in Hypnosis and Psychotherapy - Address unknown since 2008.

Institute for Res. in Modern History of Poland [★10878]

Institute for Res. in Modern History of Poland [★IO]

Inst. for Res. in Psychotherapy [★16227]

Inst. for Res. on Public Policy [IO], Montreal, QC, Canada

Inst. for Res. of Rheumatic Diseases - Defunct.

Institute for Res. in Social Sci. [★11066]

Institute for Res. in Social Sci. [★IO]

Inst. for Res. and Stud. of the Arab and Muslim World [IO], Aix-en-Provence, France

Inst. for Research on Women's Health - Address unknown since 2003.

Inst. for Rsrc. Mgt. [★4373]

Inst. for Rsrc. and Security Stud. [18457], 27 Ellsworth Ave., Cambridge, MA 02139, (617)491-5177

Inst. for Responsible Housing Preservation [5790], 401 9th St. NW, Ste. 900, Washington, DC 20004, (202)585-8739

Inst. for Responsive Educ. [8408], Cambridge Colorado School of Educ., 80 Prospect St., 3rd Fl., Cambridge, MA 02138, (617)873-0610

Inst. for Retired Professionals [12898], New School Univ., 66 W 12th St., Rm. 502, New York, NY 10011, (212)229-5682

Inst. for Retirement Stud. [★8153]

Inst. of Revenues, Rating and Valuation [IO], London, United Kingdom

Inst. of Risk Mgt. [IO], London, United Kingdom

Inst. of Risk Mgt. [★2244]

Inst. of Road Safety Officers [IO], Gillingham, United Kingdom

Inst. of Road Transport Engineers [★IO]

Inst. of Roofing [IO], London, United Kingdom

Inst. of Roofing and Waterproofing Consultants - Defunct.

Inst. for Safe Medication Practices [14638], 1800 Byberry Rd., Ste. 810, Huntingdon Valley, PA 19006, (215)947-7797

Inst. of Saint Francis de Sales; Secular [19716]

Inst. of Sales and Marketing Mgt. [IO], Luton, United Kingdom

Inst. of Salesian Studies - Address unknown since 1995.

Inst. of Sanitation Mgt. [★2463]

Inst. for Sci. and Intl. Security [18583], 236 Massachusetts Ave. NE, Ste. 500, Washington, DC 20002, (202)547-3633

Inst. for Sci. and Intl. Security [IO], Washington, DC, United States

Inst. of Sci. Tech. [IO], Sheffield, United Kingdom

Inst. for Sci. Info. - Europe, Middle East, and Africa [★IO]

Inst. of Sci. and Tech. Communicators [IO], Peterborough, United Kingdom

Inst. of Scrap Iron and Steel [★IO]

Inst. of Scrap Iron and Steel [★3995]

Inst. of Scrap Recycling Indus. [3995], 1615 L St. NW, Ste. 600, Washington, DC 20036-5610, (202)662-8500

Institute of Scrap Recycling Industries [IO], Washington, DC, United States

Institute for Secular Humanistic Judaism [★IO]

Reference to "IO" in place of a book number signifies that the association may be found in the 45th edition of International Organizations.

Institute for Secular Humanistic Judaism [★20086]

Inst. for Security and Cooperation in Outer Space - Address unknown since 1999.

Inst. for Security Stud. [IO], Pretoria, Republic of South Africa

Inst. of Sheet Metal Engg. [IO], Stafford, United Kingdom

Inst. of Shipping Economics and Logistics [IO], Bremen, Germany

Inst. of Shortening and Edible Oils [2851], 1750 New York Ave. NW, Ste. 120, Washington, DC 20006-5301, (202)783-7960

Inst. of Shortening Mfrs. [★2851]

Inst. of Signage Res. [★1189]

Inst. of Signage Res. [★IO]

Inst. of Singles Dynamics [20281], c/o Don Davidson, Dir./Founder, PO Box 27222, Overland Park, KS 66225-7222, (816)763-9401

Inst. of Small Enterprise and Development [IO], Kochi, India

Inst. for Social Dance Studies - Defunct.

Inst. of Social Ethics - Defunct.

Inst. for Social Inventions [IO], London, United Kingdom

Inst. for Social Justice [11796]

Inst. for Social Res. [7650], Univ. of Michigan, PO Box 1248, Ann Arbor, MI 48106-1248, (734)764-8354

Inst. of Social Services Alternatives - Defunct.

Inst. of Social Stud. Trust [IO], New Delhi, India

Inst. of Soc., Ethics, and the Life Sciences [★12125]

Inst. for SocioEconomic Stud. [18458], 10 New King St., White Plains, NY 10604-1204, (914)686-7112

Inst. for Soil, Climate and Water [IO], Pretoria, Republic of South Africa

Inst. of South African Architects [★IO]

Inst. for Southern Stud. [9377], PO Box 531, Durham, NC 27707, (919)419-8311

Inst. for Soviet Amer. Relations [★17899]

Inst. for Soviet Amer. Relations [★IO]

Inst. for Space and Security Stud. [18155], 5115 S A1A Hwy., Melbourne, FL 32951, (407)952-0601

Inst. of Speculative Philosophy [IO], Ottawa, ON, Canada

Inst. for Spiritual and Environmental Awareness [20572], PO Box 310, Bangor, ME 04402-0310

Inst. of Sport and Recreation Mgt. [IO], Loughborough, United Kingdom

Institute of Sports Sponsorship [★IO]

Inst. of Spring Tech. [IO], Sheffield, United Kingdom

Inst. of Statehood and Democracy [IO], Kiev, Ukraine

Inst. of Sterile Services Mgt. [★IO]

Institute of Store Planners [IO], Tarrytown, NY, United States

Inst. of Store Planners [3408], 25 N Broadway, Tarrytown, NY 10591-3221, (914)332-0040

Inst. of Strategic Studies on Terrorism - Address unknown since 2002.

Inst. for Stud. in Amer. Music [8911], Brooklyn Coll. of CUNY, 2900 Bedford Ave., Brooklyn, NY 11210-2889, (718)951-5655

Inst. for the Stud. of Amer. Cultures [10746], PO Box 2707, Columbus, GA 31902

Inst. for the Study of Animal Problems - Defunct.

Inst. for the Study of Antisocial Behavior in Youth [IO], Oakville, ON, Canada

Inst. for the Study of Anxiety in Learning - Defunct.

Inst. for the Stud. of Athletic Motivation [★23665]

Inst. for the Stud. of Athletic Motivation and Inst. of Athletic Motivation [★23665]

Inst. for the Study of Conscious Evolution - Defunct.

Inst. for the Study of Developing Nations - Address unknown since 1995.

Inst. for the Stud. of Drug Dependence [★IO]

Inst. for the Study of Drug Misuse - Defunct.

Inst. for the Stud. of Genocide [17764], John Jay Coll. of Criminal Justice, City Univ. of New York, 899 10th Ave., Rm. 325, New York, NY 10019

Inst. for the Stud. of Genocide [IO], New York, NY, United States

Inst. for the Study of Health and Soc. - Address unknown since 1995.

Inst. for the Stud. of Human Ideas on Ultimate Reality and Meaning [IO], Pickering, ON, Canada

Inst. for the Study of Human Issues - Address unknown since 1995.

Inst. for the Stud. of Human Knowledge [10175], PO Box 176, Los Altos, CA 94023, (650)948-9428

Inst. for the Stud. of Human Resources [★12251]

Inst. for the Stud. of Labor and Economic Crisis [★18448]

Inst. for the Stud. of Labor and Economic Crisis [★IO]

Inst. for the Stud. of Man [6418], 1133 13th St. NW, Ste. C-2, Washington, DC 20005, (202)371-2700

Inst. for the Study of Matrimonial Laws - Defunct.

Inst. for the Study of Natural Systems - Defunct.

Inst. for the Study of Nonviolence - Defunct.

Inst. for Study of Regulation - Defunct.

Inst. for the Study of Sexual Assault - Defunct.

Inst. for the Study of Sport and Soc. - Defunct.

Inst. for the Stud. of Traditional Amer. Indian Arts - Defunct.

Inst. for the Stud. and Treatment of Pain (iSTOP) [IO], Vancouver, BC, Canada

Inst. for the Study of Universal History Through Arts and Artifacts - Defunct.

Inst. for the Study of the USSR - Defunct.

Inst. for Supervision and Mgt. [★IO]

Inst. of Supervisory Mgt. [★IO]

Inst. for Supply Mgt. [3263], PO Box 22160, Tempe, AZ 85285-2160, (480)752-6276

Inst. of Surplus Dealers - Defunct.

Inst. for Sustainable Communities [11780], 535 Stone Cutters Way, Montpelier, VT 05602, (802)229-2900

Inst. for Sustainable Communities [IO], Montpelier, VT, United States

Inst. for Sustainable Desert Occupancy [4510]

Inst. of Systems, Control and Info. Engineers [IO], Kyoto, Japan

Inst. of Tax Consultants [6295], 7500 212th SW, Ste. 205, Edmonds, WA 98026-7617, (425)774-3521

Inst. on Taxation and Economic Policy [17470], Washington Off., 1616 P St. NW, Ste. 200, Washington, DC 20036, (202)299-1066

Inst. of Tech. and Polytechnics of New Zealand [IO], Wellington, New Zealand

Inst. of Temporary Services [★1254]

Inst. of Terrestrial Ecology [★IO]

Inst. of Textiles and Clothing [IO], Hong Kong, People's Republic of China

Inst. for Theological Encounter With Sci. and Tech. [12353], c/o Sister Marianne Postiglione, Dir. of Communications, 3601 Lindell Blvd., St. Louis, MO 63108, (314)633-4626

Inst. for Theological and Philosophical Studies - Address unknown since 1995.

Inst. of Thread Machiners - Defunct.

Inst. of Totally Useless Skills [22593], c/o Rick Davis, PO Box 181, Temple, NH 03084, (603)654-5875

Inst. of Trade Mark Attorneys [IO], Croydon, United Kingdom

Inst. of Trading Standards Admin. [★IO]

Institute for Traditional Medicine and Preventive Health Care [IO], Portland, OR, United States

Inst. for Traditional Medicine and Preventive Hea. Care [13635], 2017 SE Hawthorne Blvd., Portland, OR 97214, (503)233-4907

Inst. of Traffic Engineers [★7812]

Inst. of Traffic Engineers [★IO]

Inst. of Training and Development [★IO]

Inst. of Training Professionals [IO], Hong Kong, People's Republic of China

Inst. of Transactional Anal. [IO], Cambridge, United Kingdom

Inst. for the Transfer of Tech. to Educ. [8563], c/o Natl. School Boards Assn., 1680 Duke St., Alexandria, VA 22314, (703)838-6722

Inst. of Translation and Interpreting [IO], Milton Keynes, United Kingdom

Inst. of Transport Admin. [IO], Westoning, United Kingdom

Inst. of Transport Economics [IO], Oslo, Norway

Inst. for Trans. and Development Policy [IO], New York, NY, United States

Inst. for Trans. and Development Policy [17840], 127 W 26th St., Ste. 1002, New York, NY 10001, (212)629-8001

Inst. of Trans. Engineers [7812], 1099 14th St. NW, Ste. 300 W, Washington, DC 20005-3438, (202)289-0222

Institute of Transportation Engineers [IO], Washington, DC, United States

Inst. of Transportation and Regional Planning - Address unknown since 1995.

Inst. of Travel and Tourism [IO], Ware, United Kingdom

Inst. for Tribal Environmental Professionals [19274], PO Box 15004, Flagstaff, AZ 86011, (928)523-9555

Inst. of Trichologists [IO], London, United Kingdom

Inst. of Turkish Stud. [11061], Intercultural Center, Georgetown Univ., Box 571033, Washington, DC 20057-1033, (202)687-0295

Inst. for Twenty-First Century Studies - Defunct.

Inst. for UFO Contactee Studies - Defunct.

Inst. for Univ. Cooperation [IO], Rome, Italy

Inst. for Urban Design [6475], PO Box 835, New York, NY 10014, (212)741-2041

Inst. of Urban Life - Defunct.

Inst. of Vehicle Engineers [IO], Birmingham, United Kingdom

Inst. of Vehicle Recovery [IO], West Drayton, United Kingdom

Inst. for Victims of Terrorism [★13362]

Inst. for Victims of Trauma [13362], 6801 Market Square Dr., McLean, VA 22101, (703)847-8456

Inst. of Vitreous Enamellers [IO], Cannock, United Kingdom

Inst. of Welfare [IO], Birmingham, United Kingdom

Inst. of Welfare Officers [★IO]

Inst. for Wildlife Res. - Defunct.

Inst. on Women and Tech. [★12754]

Inst. on Women and Tech. [★IO]

Inst. of Women Today [17538], 7315 S Yale Ave., Chicago, IL 60621, (773)651-8372

Inst. for Women in Trades, Tech. and Sci. [4042], 1150 Ballena Blvd., Ste. 102, Alameda, CA 94501-3696, (510)749-0200

Inst. for Women's Policy Res. [17539], 1707 L St. NW, Ste. 750, Washington, DC 20036, (202)785-5100

Inst. for Women's Stud. in the Arab World [IO], Beirut, Lebanon

Inst. of Wood Sci. [IO], London, United Kingdom

Inst. of World Affairs [IO], Washington, DC, United States

Inst. of World Affairs [★IO]

Inst. of World Affairs [8663], 1321 Pennsylvania Ave. SE, Washington, DC 20003, (571)214-5293

Inst. of World Affairs [★8663]

Institute of World Affairs; Amer. Universities Field Staff - [★8663]

Inst. for World Economics of the Hungarian Acad. of Sciences [IO], Budapest, Hungary

Inst. for World Order [★IO]

Inst. for World Order [★17620]

Inst. for World Understanding of Peoples, Cultures, and Languages - Address unknown since 2003.

Institutes for the Achievement of Human Potential [11700], 8801 Stenton Ave., Wyndmoor, PA 19038, (215)233-2050

Insts. for Behavior Resources - Defunct.

Institutes for Org. Mgt. [★24301]

Instituti Per Studimet Publike Dhe Ligjore [★IO]

Institution of Agricultural Engineers [IO], Bedford, United Kingdom

Institution of Analysts and Programmers [IO], London, United Kingdom

Institution of British Telecommunications Engineers [★IO]

Institution of Certificated Mech. and Elecl. Engineers, South Africa [IO], Yeoville, Republic of South Africa

Institution of Chem. Engineers [IO], Rugby, United Kingdom

Institution of Civil Engg. Surveyors [IO], Sale, United Kingdom

Institution of Civil Engineers [IO], London, United Kingdom

Institution of Civil Engineers [★IO]

Institution of Diagnostic Engineers [IO], Leicester, United Kingdom

Institution of Diesel and Gas Turbine Engineers [IO], Bedford, United Kingdom

A star before a book entry number signifies that the name is not listed separately, but is mentioned within the entry.

Institution of Economic Development [IO], High Wy-
combe, United Kingdom
Institution of Elecl. Engineers [★IO]
Institution of Elecl. Engineers - England [IO],
London, United Kingdom
Institution of Electronic and Radio Engineers [★IO]
Institution of Electronics and Elecl. Incorporated
Engineers [★IO]
Institution of Electronics and Telecommunication
Engineers [IO], New Delhi, India
Institution of Engg. Designers [IO], Westbury, United
Kingdom
Institution of Engineers Australia/Engineers Australia
[IO], Barton, Australia
Institution of Engineers - India [IO], Calcutta, India
Institution of Engineers of - Ireland [★IO]
Institution of Engineers - Malaysia [IO], Petaling
Jaya, Malaysia
Institution of Engineers, Pakistan [IO], Karachi,
Pakistan
Institution of Engineers, Sri Lanka [IO], Colombo, Sri
Lanka
Institution of Engineers and Technicians [★IO]
Institution of Environmental Hea. Offices [★IO]
Institution of Environmental Sciences [IO], London,
United Kingdom
Institution of Fire Engineers - England [IO], Moreton-
in-Marsh, United Kingdom
Institution of Fire Engineers in South Africa [IO],
Houghton, Republic of South Africa
Institution of Gas Engineers and Managers [IO],
Loughborough, United Kingdom
Institution of Geologists [★IO]
Institution of Heating and Ventilating Engineers
[★IO]
Institution of Highways and Trans. [IO], London,
United Kingdom
Institution of Incorporated Engineers [IO], London,
United Kingdom
Institution of Lighting Engineers [IO], Rugby, United
Kingdom
Institution of Mfg. Engineers [★IO]
Institution of Mech. Engineers [IO], London, United
Kingdom
Institution of Mech. Incorporated Engineers [★IO]
Institution of Mining and Metallurgy [★IO]
Institution of Municipal Engg. of Southern Africa [IO],
Ferndale, Republic of South Africa
Institution of Nuclear Engineers [IO], London, United
Kingdom
Institution of Occupational Safety and Hea. [IO],
Wigston, United Kingdom
Institution of Plant Engineers [★IO]
Institution of Professional Engineers New Zealand
[IO], Wellington, New Zealand
Institution of Railway Signal Engineers [IO], London,
United Kingdom
Institution for School and Coll. Governors [★IO]
Institution of Structural Engineers [IO], London,
United Kingdom
Institution of Structural Engineers - United Kingdom
[★IO]
Institution of Surveyors, Australia [IO], Deakin,
Australia
Institution of Water Officers [IO], Gateshead, United
Kingdom
Institutional Cooperation; Comm. on [8104]
Institutional Development and Economic Affairs
Service - Defunct.
Institutional Educ; In Coun. on Hotel, Restaurant and
[★8525]
Institutional Financing Organizations; Natl. Assn. of
Church and [2426]
Institutional Food Distributors Assn; Natl. [★1566]
Institutional Food Editorial Coun. [★3119]
Institutional Food Editorial Coun. [★IO]
Institutional Food Mfrs. of Am. [★IO]
Institutional Food Mfrs. of Am. [★1526]
Institutional Food Mfrs. Assn. [★1526]
Institutional Food Mfrs. Assn. [★IO]
Institutional Food-Service Mfrs. Assn. [★IO]
Institutional Food-Service Mfrs. Assn. [★1526]
Institutional Furniture Manufacturer's Assn; Bus. and
[1692]
Institutional and Industrial Food Brokers Assn. -
Defunct.

Institutional and Intl. Initiatives; Center for [★8745]
Institutional Investors; Coun. of [3512]
Institutional Linen Mgt; Natl. Assn. of [★2401]
Institutional Locksmiths' Assn. [1164], PO Box
24772, Philadelphia, PA 19111
Institutional and Municipal Parking Cong. [★2899]
Institutional and Municipal Parking Cong. [★IO]
Institutional Res; Assn. for [8997]
Institutional Res. Coun. - Defunct.
Institutional and Ser. Textile Distributors Assn.
[3788], 1609 Connecticut Ave. NW, Ste. 200,
Washington, DC 20009, (202)986-0105
Institutional Teacher Placement Assn; Natl. [★8994]
Institutions and Alternatives; Natl. Center on [11878]
Institutions; Assn. of Free Methodist Educational
[8447]
Institutions; Commn. on Benevolent [★13165]
Instituto Africano di Diritto Internazionale [★IO]
Instituto Argentino del Envase [★IO]
Instituto de Assuntos Culturais - Brasil [★IO]
Instituto de Asuntos Culturales [★IO]
Instituto Boliviano de Comercio Exterior [★IO]
Instituto Brasileiro de Bibliografia e Documentacao
[★IO]
Instituto Brasileiro de Economia [★IO]
Instituto Brasileiro de Informacao em Ciencia e Tec-
nologia [★IO]
Instituto Centroamericano de la Salud [★IO]
Instituto Colombiano de Productores de Cemento
[★IO]
Instituto per la Cooperazione Economica Internazio-
nale e i Problemi dello Sviluppo [★IO]
Instituto de Desarrollo y Medio Ambiente [★IO]
Instituto EcoBrasil [★IO]
Instituto Ecuatoriano de Investigaciones y Capacita-
cion de la Mujer [IO], Quito, Ecuador
Instituto de las Espanas [★10004]
Instituto Forestal Latinoamericano [★IO]
Instituto Geografico Militar - Chile [★IO]
Instituto Historico y Geografico Brasileiro [★IO]
Instituto Humanista para la Cooperacion con los
Paises en Desarrollo [★IO]
Instituto Iberoamericano de Derecho Aeronautico y
del Espacio y de la Aviacion Comercial [★IO]
Instituto para la Integracion de Am. Latina y el Car-
ibe [★IO]
Instituto Interamericano de Cooperacion para la Agri-
cultura [★IO]
Instituto Interamericano de Cooperacion para la Agri-
cultura - Guyana [★IO]
Instituto Interamericano de Cooperacion para la Agri-
cultura - Paraguay [★IO]
Instituto Interamericano de Cooperacion para la Agri-
cultura - St. Lucia [★IO]
Instituto Interamericano de Cooperacion para la Agri-
cultura - Dominican Republic [★IO]
Instituto Interamericano de Cooperacion para la
Agriculture - Grenada [★IO]
Instituto Interamericano - Defunct.
Instituto Interamericano de Derechos Humanos
[★IO]
Instituto Interamericano de Derechos Humanos -
Programa Mujer y Derechos Humanos [IO], San
Jose, Costa Rica
Instituto Interamericano de Estadistica [★IO]
Instituto Interamericano del Nino [★IO]
Instituto Latino-Americano de Estudos Avancados
[★IO]
Instituto Latinoamericano de Derecho Tributario
[★IO]
Instituto Latinoamericano del Fierro y el Acero [★IO]
Instituto Latinoamericano de Investigaciones So-
ciales [★IO]
Instituto di Medicina Pa Deporte di Aruba [IO], San
Nicolas, Aruba
Instituto de la Mujer [★IO]
Instituto Nacional de Estadistica [IO], Madrid, Spain
Instituto Nacional Hispano de Liturgia [19640], PO
Box 18, Washington, DC 20064, (202)319-6450
Instituto Nacional de Liturgia Para Hispanos
[★19640]
Instituto Nacional de Metrologia, Normalizacao e
Qualidade Indus. [★IO]
Instituto Nacional de las Mujeres [IO], San Jose,
Costa Rica

Instituto Nacional de Vitivinicultura [★IO]
Instituto de Nutricion de Centro Am. y Panama
[★IO]
Instituto Panamericano de Geografia e Historia
[★IO]
Instituto Panamericano de Ingenieria Naval [★IO]
Instituto Papelero Espanol [★IO]
Instituto Peruano de Educacion en Derechos Hu-
manos y la Paz [★IO]
Instituto Peruano de Paternidad Responsible [IO],
Lima, Peru
Instituto Portugues da Voz [★IO]
Instituto Textil de Chile [★IO]
Instituto Venezolano de Genealogia [★IO]
Instituto da Vinha e do Vinho [★IO]
Instituto do Vinho do Porto [★IO]
Instituto Zooprofilattico Sperimentale dell'Abruzzo e
del Molise 'G.Caporale' [★IO]
Instituut vir Gediplomeerde Werktuigkundige en Ele-
ktegniese Ingenieurs, Suid-Afrika [★IO]
Instituut van Landskapargitekte van Suid Afrika
[★IO]
Instruction; Assn. for Direct [8232]
Instruction Consortium; Cmpt. Assisted Language
[8553]
Instruction Consortium; Cmpt. Assisted Language,
Learning and [★8553]
Instruction; Natl. Soc. for Performance and [★9252]
Instruction; Natl. Soc. for Programmed [★9252]
Instructional Language Programs; Natl. Assn. of
Self- [8736]
Instructional Materials; Amer. Assn. for Vocational
[9298]
Instructional Materials Prog; PALTEX - Expanded
Textbook and [9261]
Instructional Materials Reference Center [★16829]
Instructional Media
 ACUTA: The Assn. for Communications Tech.
 Professionals in Higher Educ. [8548]
 Agency for Instructional Tech. [8549]
 Assn. of Amer. Univ. Presses [8550]
 Assn. for Educational Communications and Tech.
 [8551]
 British Universities Film and Video Coun. [IO]
 British Universities Film and Video Coun. and
 Soc. for Screen-Based Learning [IO]
 Center for Teaching About China [8552]
 Cmpt. Assisted Language Instruction Consortium
 [8553]
 Computer Assisted Language Instruction
 Consortium [IO]
 Concord Video and Film Coun. [IO]
 Consortium of Coll. and Univ. Media Centers
 [8554]
 Consortium for School Networking [8555]
 Educ., Training and Res. Associates [8556]
 Educ. Turnkey Inst. [8557]
 EDUCAUSE [8558]
 EPIE Inst. [8559]
 French Amer. Cultural Exchange [8560]
 GalaxyGoo [8065]
 Hea. Sciences Consortium [8561]
 Inst. for Computers in Jewish Life [8562]
 Inst. for Learning Technologies [8355]
 Inst. for the Transfer of Tech. to Educ. [8563]
 Instructional Systems Assn. [8564]
 Instructional Tech. Coun. [8565]
 Instructional Technology Council [IO]
 Intl. Univ. Consortium [IO]
 Intl. Univ. Consortium [8566]
 Intl. Visual Literacy Assn. [8271]
 Manpower Educ. Inst. [8567]
 Natl. Assn. of State Educational Media Profes-
 sionals [8568]
 Natl. Info. Center for Educational Media [8569]
 North Amer. Coun. for Online Learning [7949]
 Playing 2 Win [8570]
 Soc. for Applied Learning Tech. [8571]
 Soc. for Info. Tech. and Teacher Educ. [9243]
 Univ. and Coll. Designers Assn. [8572]
 University and College Designers Association [IO]
 Vocational Instructional Materials Sect. [8573]
Instructional Systems Assn. [8564], 12427 Hedges
Run Dr., No. 120, Lake Ridge, VA 22192,
(703)730-2838

Reference to "IO" in place of a book number signifies that the association may be found in the 45th edition of International Organizations.

Instructional Technology
  State Educational Tech. Directors Assn. [9244]
Instructional Tech. Coun. [8565], 1 Dupont Cir. NW, Ste. 360, Washington, DC 20036-1143, (202)293-3110
Instructional Technology Council [IO], Washington, DC, United States
Instructional Telecommunications Consortium [★IO]
Instructional Telecommunications Consortium [★8565]
Instructional Telecommunications Coun. [★8565]
Instructional Telecommunications Coun. [★IO]
Instructors of Am. Educational Foundation; Professional Ski [★23755]
Instructors of Am; Professional Ski [23755]
Instructors Assn; Amateur Ski [23748]
Instructors Assn; Natl. Photography [8973]
Instructors; Assn. of Women Martial Arts [23585]
Instructors of the Deaf; Coun. of Amer. [14750]
Instructors; Natl. Assn. of Coll. Wind and Percussion [8919]
Instructors; Natl. Assn. of Dog Obedience [22312]
Instructors; Natl. Assn. of Flight [161]
Instructors; Natl. Assn. of Rehabilitation [16324]
Instructors; Natl. Assn. of Trade and Indus. [9233]
Instructors; Natl. Assn. of Underwater [23963]
Instructors Training Assn; NDEITA - Natl. Dance Exercise [★23037]
Instrument Contracting and Engg. Assn. [1020], c/o Nick Theisen Exec. Dir., 4312 Rochard Ln., Fort Mill, SC 29707-5851, (704)905-0319
Instrument Engineers; Amer. Soc. of [★7220]
Instrument Guild of Am; Fretted [10597]
Instrument Makers
  British Violin Making Assn. [IO]
  Guild of Amer. Luthiers [2804]
  Intl. Horn Soc. [10620]
Instrument Mfrs; Natl. Assn. of Band [★2810]
Instrument Manufacturers' Software Assn; Hearing [14758]
Instrument Repair Technicians; Natl. Assn. of Professional Band [2818]
Instrument Soc. of Am. [★7220]
Instrument Soc. of Am. [★IO]
Instrument Soc; Amer. Musical [10544]
Instrument Technicians Labor-Mgt. Cooperation Fund [1021]
Instrumental Directors Assn; Christian [★20427]
Instrumentalists and Directors Assn; Christian [20427]
Instrumentation
  IEEE Instrumentation and Measurement Soc. [7219]
  Inst. of Measurement and Control of New Zealand [IO]
  Instrumentation Testing Assn. [IO]
  Instrumentation Testing Assn. [2124]
  ISA - Instrumentation, Systems, and Automation Soc. [7220]
  ISA - Instrumentation, Systems, and Automation Society [IO]
  Japan Analytical Instruments Manufacturers Assn. [IO]
  Mexican Soc. of Instrumentation [IO]
Instrumentation; Assn. for the Advancement of Medical [6606]
Instrumentation Engineers; Soc. of Photo-Optical [★7408]
Instrumentation Engineers; Soc. of Photographic [★7408]
Instrumentation, Systems, and Automation Soc; ISA - [7220]
Instrumentation Testing Assn. [2124], 631 N Stephanie St., No. 279, Henderson, NV 89014, (702)568-1445
Instrumentation Testing Assn. [IO], Henderson, NV, United States
Instruments Association; Opto-Precision [★3488]
Instruments; Fellowship of Makers and Researchers of Historical [IO]
Insulated Cable Engineers Assn. [7017], PO Box 1568, Carrollton, GA 30112, (770)830-0369
Insulated Panel Assn; Structural [675]
Insulated Power Cable Engineers Assn. [★7017]
Insulated Render and Cladding Assn. [IO], Haslemere, United Kingdom

Insulated Steel Door Inst. [628]
Insulating Concrete Form Assn. [925], 1730 Dewes St., Ste. No. 2, Glenview, IL 60025, (847)657-9730
Insulating Glass Certification Coun. [1731], PO Box 9, Henderson Harbor, NY 13651, (315)646-2234
Insulating Glass Mfrs. Alliance [IO], Ottawa, ON, Canada
Insulating Glass Mfrs. Assn. of Canada [★IO]
Insulating Siding Assn. - Defunct.
Insulating Siding Core Bd. Assn. - Defunct.
Insulation Assn; Natl. [1048]
Insulation Contractors Assn. of Am. [1022], 1321 Duke St., Ste. 303, Alexandria, VA 22314, (703)739-0356
Insulation Contractors Assn; Natl. [★1048]
Insulation Contractors; Natl. Assn. of Cold Storage [★1886]
Insulation Distributor Contractors Natl. Assn. [★1048]
Insulation Fabricators Assn. - Defunct.
Insulation Manufacturers Assn; Cellulose [610]
Insulation Manufacturers Assn; Exterior [★618]
Insulation Manufacturers Assn; Mineral [★659]
Insulation Manufacturers Assn; North Amer. [659]
Insulation Mfrs. Assn; Polyisocyanurate [661]
Insulation Soc; IEEE Dielectrics and Elecl. [6902]
Insulation Soc; IEEE Elecl. [★6902]
Insulator Assn; Natl. [22408]
Insulator-Line Jewels - Defunct.
Insulators and Asbestos Workers; Intl. Assn. of Heat and Frost [24093]
Insulin-Free World Found. [14226]
Insulin-Free World Found. [IO], St. Louis, MO, United States
Insulin for Life Australia [IO], Ballarat, Australia
Insurance
  ACORD [IO]
  ACORD [2125]
  Actuarial Assn. [IO]
  Actuarial Soc. of Hong Kong [IO]
  Actuarial Soc. of South Africa [IO]
  ADVOCIS [IO]
  African Insurance Org. [IO]
  African Reinsurance Corp. [IO]
  Alliance of Claims Assistance Professionals [2126]
  Alliance of Transylvanian Saxons [19117]
  Amer. Acad. of Actuaries [2127]
  Amer. Agents Assn. [2128]
  Amer. Assn. of Crop Insurers [2129]
  Amer. Assn. of Dental Consultants [2130]
  Amer. Assn. of Insurance Mgt. Consultants [953]
  Amer. Assn. of Insurance Services [2131]
  Amer. Assn. for Long-Term Care Insurance [2132]
  Amer. Assn. of Managing Gen. Agents [2133]
  Amer. Assn. of State Compensation Insurance Funds [2134]
  Amer. Assn. of State Compensation Insurance Funds [2134]
  Amer. Auto. Assn. [403]
  Amer. Coun. of Life Insurers [2135]
  Amer. Equestrian Alliance [1923]
  Amer. Foreign Ser. Protective Assn. [19118]
  Amer. Fraternal Union [19119]
  Amer. Horseman Alliance [1924]
  Amer. Hull Insurance Syndicate [2136]
  Amer. Inst. for CPCU [2137]
  Amer. Inst. of Marine Underwriters [2138]
  Amer. Insurance Assn. [2139]
  Amer. Insurance Marketing and Sales Soc. [2140]
  Amer. Risk and Insurance Assn. [8574]
  Amer. Tort Reform Assn. [5926]
  Americas Assn. of Cooperative/Mutual Insurance Societies [2141]
  America's Hea. Insurance Plans [14682]
  APIW [2142]
  Applied Systems Client Network [2143]
  Argentine Assn. of Insurance Companies [IO]
  Artisans Order of Mutual Protection [19120]
  Asia-Pacific Risk and Insurance Assn. [IO]
  Asian Reinsurance Corp. [IO]
  Asociacion de Administradores de Riesgos de la Republica Argentina [IO]
  Asociacion Espanola de Gerencia de Riesgos y Seguros [IO]

  Asociacion Latinoamericana de Administradores de Riesgos y Seguros [IO]
  Associacao Brasileira de Gerencia de Riscos [IO]
  Assn. for Advanced Life Underwriting [2144]
  Assn. of Average Adjusters [IO]
  Assn. of Average Adjusters of the U.S. [2145]
  Assn. of British Insurers [IO]
  Assn. of Consulting Actuaries [IO]
  Assn. of Czech Insurance Brokers [IO]
  Assn. of Defense Trial Attorneys [5825]
  Assn. of European Cooperative and Mutual Insurers [IO]
  Assn. of Finance and Insurance Professionals [2146]
  Assn. of Financial Guaranty Insurers [2147]
  Assn. of Hea. Insurance Advisors [14958]
  Assn. of Home Off. Underwriters [2148]
  Association of Home Office Underwriters [IO]
  Assn. of Insurance Companies - Greece [IO]
  Assn. of Insurance and Reinsurance Companies of Turkey [IO]
  Assn. of Insurance and Risk Managers [IO]
  Assn. Internationale de la Mutualite [IO]
  Assn. of Life Insurance Counsel [5826]
  Assn. of Lloyd's Members [IO]
  Assn. of Malaysian Loss Adjusters [IO]
  Assn. of Online Insurance Agents [2149]
  Assn. of Policy Market Makers [IO]
  Assn. of Risk Mgt. - Japan [IO]
  Assn. of Trinidad and Tobago Insurance Companies [IO]
  Associazione Nazionale di Risk Managers e Responsabili Assicurazioni Aziendali [IO]
  Australian Insurance Law Assn. [IO]
  Austrian Fed. of Independent Loss Adjusters [IO]
  Aviation Insurance Assn. [2150]
  Bank Insurance and Securities Assn. [2151]
  Belgian Risk Mgt. Assn. [IO]
  Beroepsvereniging van de Experten B.O.A.R. [IO]
  Blue Cross and Blue Shield Assn. [14959]
  Bolivian Assn. of Insurance Companies [IO]
  British Hea. Care Assn. [IO]
  British Insurance Broker's Assn. [IO]
  British Insurance Law Assn. [IO]
  Bundesverband Deutscher Versicherungskaufleute e.V. [IO]
  Burkina Insurance Union [IO]
  Canadian Assn. of Insurance Women [IO]
  Canadian Assn. of Mutual Insurance Companies [IO]
  Canadian Bar Insurance Assn. [IO]
  Canadian Bd. of Marine Underwriters [IO]
  Canadian Coalition Against Insurance Fraud [IO]
  Canadian Independent Adjusters' Assn. [IO]
  Canadian Inst. of Actuaries [IO]
  Canadian Insurance Claims Managers' Assn. [IO]
  Canadian Life and Hea. Insurance Assn. [IO]
  Canadian Life Insurance Medical Officers Assn. [IO]
  Captive Insurance Companies Assn. [2152]
  Casualty Actuarial Soc. [2153]
  Chamber of Commerce of the Apparel Indus. [24269]
  Chartered Inst. of Loss Adjusters [IO]
  Chartered Insurance Inst. [IO]
  Citizens' Coun. on Hea. Care [17696]
  Claims Support Professional Assn. [2154]
  Coalition Against Insurance Fraud [2155]
  Coalition for Auto-Insurance Reform [17316]
  Comm. of Annuity Insurers [2156]
  Compagnie des Experts Agrees [IO]
  Conf. of Consulting Actuaries [2157]
  Consumer Credit Industry Association [2158]
  Consumer Hea. Educ. Coun. [14685]
  Coun. of Insurance Agents and Brokers [2159]
  Coun. of Insurance Agents and Brokers [IO]
  Cover the Uninsured [14960]
  CPCU Soc. [2160]
  Crop Insurance Res. Bur. [2161]
  Czech Insurance Assn. [IO]
  Danish Insurance Assn. [IO]
  Degree of Honor Protective Assn. [19121]
  Direct Marketing Insurance and Financial Services Coun. [2162]
  Eastern Claims Conf. [2163]

A star before a book entry number signifies that the name is not listed separately, but is mentioned within the entry.

Ebix Users Assn. [340]
Environmental Risk Resources Assn. [4563]
Equitable Reserve Assn. [19122]
Estonian Insurance Assn. [IO]
European Actuarial Consultative Gp. [IO]
European Fed. of Insurance Intermediaries [IO]
European Fed. of Loss Adjusting Experts [IO]
European Insurance Coun. [IO]
European Insurance Fed. [IO]
Export Credit Insurance Org. [IO]
Faculty of Actuaries [IO]
Fed. of African Natl. Insurance Companies [IO]
Fed. of Asian, Pacific and African Risk Mgt. Organisations [IO]
Fed. of Defense and Corporate Counsel [5827]
Fed. of Finnish Insurance Companies [IO]
Fed. Life Insurance of Am. [19123]
Fire Mark Circle of the Americas [22420]
Flight Safety Found. [148]
Floodplain Mgt. Assn. [5038]
Foreign Credit Insurance Assn. [2164]
Fraternal Field Managers' Assn. [2165]
French Fed. of Insurance Companies [IO]
GAMA Intl. [IO]
GAMA Intl. [2166]
Gamma Iota Sigma [24520]
Gamma Iota Sigma [IO]
Gen. Insurance Assn. of Japan [IO]
Gen. Insurance Assn. of Singapore [IO]
Gleaner Life Insurance Soc. [19124]
Global Assn. of Risk Professionals [1423]
Global Mobile Entertainers Assn. [1302]
Grand Lodge Order of the Sons of Hermann in Texas [19125]
Gp. Underwriters Assn. of Am. [2167]
Highway Loss Data Inst. [2168]
Hong Kong Fed. of Insurers [IO]
Honorable Order of the Blue Goose, Intl. [IO]
Honorable Order of the Blue Goose, Intl. [19126]
IAB Partners [1464]
Independent Financial Brokers of Canada [IO]
Independent Insurance Agents and Brokers of Am. [2169]
Independent Order of Foresters [IO]
Independent Order of Vikings [19127]
Inland Marine Underwriters Assn. [2170]
Inst. of Actuaries of Australia [IO]
Inst. of Actuaries - United Kingdom [IO]
Inst. for Bus. and Home Safety [2171]
Inst. for Hea. Policy Solutions [14689]
Inst. of Insurance Brokers [IO]
Inst. of Public Loss Assessors [IO]
Inst. of Risk Mgt. [IO]
Insurance Accounting and Systems Association [IO]
Insurance Accounting and Systems Assn. [2172]
Insurance Assn. of the Caribbean [IO]
Insurance Assn. of Cyprus [IO]
Insurance Brokers and Agents of the West [2173]
Insurance Brokers' Assn. [IO]
Insurance Brokers Assn. of Canada [IO]
Insurance Bur. of Canada [IO]
Insurance Consumer Affairs Exchange [2174]
Insurance Coun. of Australia [IO]
Insurance Coun. of New Zealand [IO]
Insurance Data Mgt. Assn. [2175]
Insurance Educ. Found. [8575]
Insurance Employees' Union [IO]
Insurance Info. Inst. [2176]
Insurance Inst. of Am. [2177]
Insurance Inst. of Hong Kong [IO]
Insurance Inst. of India [IO]
Insurance Inst. of Ireland [IO]
Insurance Inst. of London [IO]
Insurance Loss Control Assn. [2178]
Insurance Managers Assn. of Cayman [IO]
Insurance Marketing Communications Assn. [2179]
Insurance Marketplace Standards Assn. [2180]
Insurance Premium Finance Assn. [2181]
Insurance Regulatory Examiners Soc. [2182]
Insurance Res. Coun. [2183]
Insurance Soc. of New York [2184]
Insurers' Company [IO]
Interamerican Fed. of Insurance Companies [IO]

Intermediaries and Reinsurance Underwriters Assn. [2185]
Intl. Actuarial Assn. [IO]
Intl. Assn. of Black Actuaries [IO]
Intl. Assn. of Black Actuaries [2186]
Intl. Assn. of Engg. Insurers [IO]
Intl. Assn. of Hail Insurers [IO]
Intl. Assn. of Insurance Fraud Agencies [IO]
Intl. Assn. of Insurance Fraud Agencies [5828]
Intl. Assn. for Insurance Law in the U.S. [5829]
Intl. Assn. for Insurance Law in the U.S. [IO]
International Association of Insurance Receivers [IO]
Intl. Assn. of Insurance Receivers [2187]
Intl. Assn. of Mutual Insurance Companies [IO]
International Association of Special Investigation Units [IO]
Intl. Assn. of Special Investigation Units [2188]
Intl. Assn. for the Stud. of Insurance Economics [IO]
Intl. Claim Assn. [IO]
Intl. Claim Assn. [2189]
Intl. Cooperative and Mutual Insurance Fed. [IO]
Intl. Credit Insurance and Surety Assn. [IO]
Intl. Insurance Soc. [IO]
Intl. Insurance Soc. [2190]
Intl. Risk Mgt. Soc. of Japan [IO]
Intl. Underwriting Assn. of London [IO]
Intl. Union of Aviation Insurers [IO]
Intl. Union of Credit and Investment Insurers/ The Berne Union [IO]
Intl. Union of Marine Insurance [IO]
Intersure - Singer Nelson Charlmers [2191]
Investment and Financial Services Assn. [IO]
Investment Savings and Insurance Assn. [IO]
Irish Brokers Assn. [IO]
Irish Insurance Fed. [IO]
Italian Inst. of Actuaries [IO]
Italian Natl. Assn. of Insurance Adjusters [IO]
Jordan Insurance Fed. [IO]
Knights of the Golden Eagle [19128]
Korea Life Insurance Assn. [IO]
Korea Non-Life Insurance Assn. [IO]
Liability Insurance Res. Bur. [2192]
Life Insurance Assn. of Japan [IO]
Life Insurance Assn. - Singapore [IO]
Life Insurance Settlement Assn. [2193]
Life Insurers Coun. [2194]
Life Underwriter Training Coun. [8576]
Life Underwriters Assn. of Hong Kong [IO]
LIMRA Europe [IO]
LIMRA Intl. [IO]
LIMRA Intl. [2195]
LOMA [2196]
LOMA [IO]
Loss Adjusters Assn. of Japan [IO]
Loss Executives Assn. [2197]
Loyal Christian Benefit Assn. [19129]
Luso-American Fraternal Fed. [19130]
Luso-American Life Insurance Soc. [19131]
Malaysian Assn. of Risk and Insurance Mgt. [IO]
Mass Marketing Insurance Inst. [2198]
Member Insurance Assn. [1827]
MIB Gp. [14961]
Million Dollar Round Table [2199]
Mortgage Insurance Companies of Am. [2200]
Mutual Atomic Energy Liability Underwriters [2201]
Natl. African-American Insurance Assn. [2202]
Natl. Alliance for Insurance Educ. and Res. [2203]
Natl. Assn. of Alternative Benefits Consultants [1867]
Natl. Assn. of Bar-Related Title Insurers [2204]
Natl. Assn. of Catastrophe Adjusters [2205]
Natl. Assn. of Dental Plans [14962]
Natl. Assn. of Disability Examiners [14034]
Natl. Assn. of Fire Investigators [2206]
Natl. Assn. of Fraternal Insurance Counsellors [2207]
Natl. Assn. of Hea. Underwriters [2208]
Natl. Assn. of Independent Insurance Adjusters [2209]
Natl. Assn. of Independent Insurance Auditors and Engineers [2210]
Natl. Assn. of Independent Life Brokerage Agencies [2211]

Natl. Assn. of Insurance Commissioners [5830]
Natl. Assn. of Insurance and Financial Advisors [2212]
Natl. Assn. of Insurance Women Intl. [2213]
Natl. Assn. of Mutual Insurance Companies [2214]
Natl. Assn. of Professional Insurance Agents [2215]
Natl. Assn. of Professional Surplus Lines Offices [2216]
Natl. Assn. of Public Insurance Adjusters [2217]
Natl. Assn. of State Comprehensive Hea. Insurance Plans [14691]
Natl. Assn. of State Farm Agents [2218]
Natl. Assn. of Surety Bond Producers [2219]
Natl. Assn. of Unemployment Insurance Appellate Boards [5831]
Natl. Assn. for Variable Annuities [2220]
Natl. Chamber of Insurance Businesses [IO]
Natl. Coalition on Hea. Care [17698]
Natl. Conf. of Insurance Legislators [5832]
Natl. Coun. on Compensation Insurance [2221]
Natl. Coun., Daughters of America [19132]
Natl. Coun. of Self-Insurers [2222]
Natl. Crop Insurance Services [2223]
Natl. Fraternal Cong. of Am. [19133]
Natl. Fraternal Soc. of the Deaf [19134]
Natl. Hea. Care Anti-Fraud Assn. [14963]
Natl. InStar Users Gp. [7221]
Natl. Insurance Crime Bur. [2224]
Natl. Org. of Life and Hea. Insurance Guaranty Associations [1852]
Natl. Risk Retention Assn. [2225]
Natl. Soc. of Insurance Premium Auditors [2226]
Natl. Soc. of Professional Insurance Investigators [2227]
Natl. Truck and Heavy Equip. Claims Coun. [2228]
Order of United Commercial Travelers of Am. [19135]
Organized Flying Adjusters [2229]
Physician Insurers Assn. of Am. [14964]
Police and Firemen's Insurance Assn. [19136]
Professional Insurance Marketing Assn. [2230]
Professional Liability Underwriting Soc. [2231]
Professional Liability Underwriting Soc. [IO]
Professional Union of Insurance Companies [IO]
Property Casualty Insurers Assn. of Am. [2232]
Property Loss Res. Bur. [2233]
Public Agency Risk Managers Assn. [5833]
Public Risk Mgt. Assn. [5834]
Reinsurance Assn. of Am. [2234]
Reinsurance Brokers' Assn. (Singapore) [IO]
Risk and Insurance Mgt. Assn. of Singapore [IO]
Risk and Insurance Mgt. Soc. [2235]
Risk Mgt. Institution of Australasia [IO]
Risk Mgt. Soc. of Finland [IO]
Risk Mgt. Soc. of Taiwan, R.O.C. [IO]
Risk Managers and Consultants Assn. of Japan [IO]
Royal Neighbors of Am. [19137]
Securities and Insurance Licensing Assn. [2236]
Self-Insurance Inst. of Am. [2237]
Shipowners Claims Bur. [2238]
Singapore Reinsurers' Assn. [IO]
Societe Culinaire Philanthropique [19138]
Soc. of Actuaries [2239]
Soc. of Certified Insurance Counselors [8577]
Soc. of Financial Ser. Professionals [2240]
Society of Financial Service Professionals [IO]
Soc. of Insurance Res. [2241]
Soc. of Insurance Trainers and Educators [8578]
Soc. of Registered Professional Adjusters [2242]
Soc. of Registered Professional Adjusters [IO]
Soc. for Risk Anal. [2243]
Soc. of Risk Mgt. Consultants [2244]
South African Insurance Assn. [IO]
SPJST [19139]
Supreme Coun. of the Royal Arcanum [19140]
Surety and Fidelity Assn. of Am. [2245]
Swedish Assn. of Marine Underwriters [IO]
Swedish Insurance Soc. [IO]
Swiss Assn. of Insurance and Risk Managers [IO]
Teachers Insurance and Annuity Assn. [8579]
Thai Life Assurance Assn. [IO]

Reference to "IO" in place of a book number signifies that the association may be found in the 45th edition of International Organizations.

Travel Trust Assn. [IO]
Travelers Protective Assn. of Am. [19141]
United Agribusiness League [4084]
U.S. Letter Carriers Mutual Benefit Assn. [19142]
Univ. Risk Mgt. and Insurance Assn. [8580]
Vasa Order of Am. [19143]
Vasa Order of Am. [IO]
Venezuelan Chamber of Insurance Companies [IO]
Volunteers in Hea. Care [14665]
Water Quality Insurance Syndicate [2246]
Weather Risk Mgt. Assn. [4015]
William Penn Assn. [19144]
Woman's Life Insurance Soc. [19145]
Women in Insurance and Financial Services [2247]
Women in Insurance and Financial Services [IO]
Workers Compensation Insurance Organizations [2248]
Workmen's Benefit Fund of the U.S.A. [19146]
Workmen's Circle [19147]
Workplace Benefits Assn. [1247]
Worldwide Assurance for Employees of Public Agencies [5776]
WSA Fraternal Life [19148]
Insurance Accounting and Statistical Assn. [★2172]
Insurance Accounting and Statistical Assn. [★IO]
Insurance Accounting and Systems Association [IO], Durham, NC, United States
Insurance Accounting and Systems Assn. [2172], PO Box 51340, Durham, NC 27717, (919)489-0991
Insurance Actuarial Assn; Crop-Hail [★2223]
Insurance Advt. Conf. [★2179]
Insurance Agency Mgt. Assn; Life [★2195]
Insurance Agents of Am; Independent [★2169]
Insurance Agents; Assn. of Intl. [★2191]
Insurance Agents; Natl. Assn. of [★2169]
Insurance Agents; Natl. Assn. of Mutual [★2215]
Insurance; Amer. Assn. of Univ. Teachers of [★8574]
Insurance Assn; Amer. [★2139]
Insurance Assn. of the Caribbean [IO], St. Michael, Barbados
Insurance Assn. of Cyprus [IO], Nicosia, Cyprus
Insurance Assn; Member [1827]
Insurance Assn; Natl. Crop [★2223]
Insurance Attorneys; Assn. of [★5825]
Insurance Brokers and Agents of the West [2173], 7041 Koll Center Pkwy., Ste. 290, Pleasanton, CA 94566-3128, (800)772-8998
Insurance Brokers' Assn. [IO], Bangkok, Thailand
Insurance Brokers Assn. of Canada [IO], Toronto, ON, Canada
Insurance Bur. of Canada [IO], Toronto, ON, Canada
Insurance Buyers Assn; Natl. [★2235]
Insurance; Catholic Family Life [18993]
Insurance Commissioners; Natl. Convention of [★5830]
Insurance Communicators of Am; Professional [884]
Insurance Companies; Natl. Assn. of Mutual [2214]
Insurance Company; Amer. Fraternal [★19146]
Insurance Company Educ. Directors Soc. [★8578]
Insurance Consultants Soc. [★2244]
Insurance Consumer Affairs Exchange [2174], PO Box 746, Lake Zurich, IL 60047, (847)991-8454
Insurance and Corporate Counsel; Fed. of [★5827]
Insurance Coun. of Australia [IO], Sydney, Australia
Insurance Coun. of Canada 1998-2000 [★IO]
Insurance Coun; Direct Marketing [★2162]
Insurance Coun. of New Zealand [IO], Wellington, New Zealand
Insurance Counsel; Fed. of [★5827]
Insurance Counsel; Intl. Assn. of [★5499]
Insurance Counsellors Assn; Fraternal [★2207]
Insurance Crime Prevention Inst. [★2224]
Insurance Data Mgt. Assn. [2175], c/o Richard Penberthy, Exec. Dir., 545 Washington Blvd., 22-16, Jersey City, NJ 07310-1686, (201)469-3069
Insurance Economics Soc. of America - Defunct.
Insurance Educ. Found. [8575], 3601 Vincennes Rd., Indianapolis, IN 46268, (317)876-6046
Insurance Employees' Union [IO], Helsinki, Finland
Insurance Engineers; Assn. of Mutual [★2178]
Insurance Engineers; Assn. of Mutual Fire [★2178]
Insurance Fund; United Furniture Workers [24065]

Insurance Guaranty Associations; Natl. Org. of Life and Hea. [1852]
Insurance Highway Safety Association; American [★12964]
Insurance Info. Inst. [2176], 110 William St., New York, NY 10038, (212)346-5500
Insurance Inst. of Am. [2177], 720 Providence Rd., Ste. 100, Malvern, PA 19355, (610)644-2100
Insurance Inst. for Highway Safety [12964], 1005 N Glebe Rd., Ste. 800, Arlington, VA 22201, (703)247-1500
Insurance Inst. of Hong Kong [IO], Hong Kong, People's Republic of China
Insurance Inst. of India [IO], Bombay, India
Insurance Inst. of Ireland [IO], Dublin, Ireland
Insurance Inst. of London [IO], London, United Kingdom
Insurance Inst. for Property Loss Reduction [★2171]
Insurance Law, U.S. Chap; Intl. Assn. for [★5829]
Insurance Loss Control Assn. [2178], 118 Treetops Dr., Lancaster, PA 17601-1790, (440)946-8397
Insurance Mgt; Amer. Soc. of [★2235]
Insurance Mgt. Consultants; Amer. Assn. of [953]
Insurance Managers Assn. of Cayman [IO], Grand Cayman, Cayman Islands
Insurance Managers Assn; Univ. [★8580]
Insurance Managers Assn; Univ. Risk and [★8580]
Insurance Marketing Communications Assn. [2179], 4916 Point Fosdick Dr. NW, No. 180, Gig Harbor, WA 98335, (206)219-9811
Insurance Marketing and Res. Assn; Life [★2195]
Insurance Marketplace Standards Assn. [2180], 4550 Montgomery Ave., Ste. 700N, Bethesda, MD 20814, (240)744-3030
Insurance; Natl. Acad. of Social [18647]
Insurance; Natl. Comm. on Property [★2171]
Insurance; Natl. Coun. on Workmen's Compensation [★2221]
Insurance Plans; America's Hea. [14682]
Insurance Premium Finance Assn. [2181], 2890 Niagara Falls Blvd., PO Box 726, Amherst, NY 14226, (716)695-8757
Insurance Rating Bur; Trans. [★2131]
Insurance Regulatory Examiners Soc. [2182], 12710 S Pflumm Rd., Ste. 200, Olathe, KS 66062, (913)768-4700
Insurance Res. Coun. [2183], PO Box 3025, Malvern, PA 19355-0725, (610)644-2212
Insurance Sales Res. Bur; Life [★2195]
Insurance Security Assn. - Defunct.
Insurance Seminars; Intl. [★2190]
Insurance Services; Alternative Hea. [★13609]
Insurance Soc; Catholic Knights [★18994]
Insurance Soc. of New York [2184], c/o School of Risk Mgt., 101 Murray St., New York, NY 10007-2165, (212)341-9346
Insurance Soc; Sloga Fraternal Life [★19022]
Insurance Soc; United Natl. Life [★19131]
Insurance Soc; Woodmen of the World/Omaha Woodmen Life [19441]
Insurance Testing Inst. - Defunct.
Insurance Union; Catholic Life [18996]
Insurance Women; Assn. of Professional [★2142]
Insurance Women; Natl. Assn. of [★2213]
Insurance Workers Intl. Union [★24061]
Insured Locksmiths and Safemen of America - Defunct.
Insurers; Alliance of Amer. [★2232]
Insurers; Amer. Assn. of Crop [2129]
Insurers; Amer. Coun. of Life [2135]
Insurers; Amer. Nuclear [3948]
Insurers; Assn. of Financial Guaranty [2147]
Insurers; Comm. of Annuity [2156]
Insurers' Company [IO], London, United Kingdom
Insurers' Conf; Indus. [★2194]
Insurers' Conf; Southern Indus. [★2194]
Insurers Coun; Life [2194]
Insurers; Natl. Assn. of Bar-Related Title [2204]
Insurers; Natl. Assn. of Independent [★2232]
Insurers; Natl. Assn. of Property and Casualty Re [★2234]
Insurers; Natl. Conf. of Bar-Related Title [★2204]
Insurers Safety Association; National Assn. of Independent [★12964]
INTACT Educational Found. [★11732]

INTACT Educational Found. [★IO]
INTACT of Pennsylvania [★IO]
INTACT of Pennsylvania [★12413]
Integral Development; Inst. for [13249]
Integrated Bus. Communications Alliance [338], 81 Cottage St., Doylestown, PA 18901, (215)489-1722
Integrated Healthcare Delivery Systems; Amer. Assn. of [15048]
Integrated Library System Users Soc. - Defunct.
Integrated Mfg. Tech. Initiative [7264], PO Box 5296, Oak Ridge, TN 37830, (865)862-5667
Integrated Waste Services Assn. [5270], 1331 H St. NW, Ste. 801, Washington, DC 20005, (202)467-6240
Integration
  Fund for an OPEN Soc. [17819]
  Natl. Assn. for Neighborhood Schools [17820]
Integration Fellowship; Cultural [9618]
Integrative and Comparative Biology; Soc. for [7867]
Integrative Medicine; Amer. Assn. of [15152]
Integrative Medicine; Veterinary Inst. of [16815]
Integrative Stud; Assn. for [10227]
Integrators; NASBA - The Assn. of Sys. Builders and [3706]
Integrity [20058], 620 Park Ave., No. 311, Rochester, NY 14607-2943, (800)462-9498
Integrity; Center for Public [17667]
Integrity Intl. [★11817]
Intel Alumni Assn; Defense [18892]
Intel - Former and Current Employees of Intel; FACE [1262]
Intellect [IO], London, United Kingdom
Intellectual Disability Rights Ser. [IO], Redfern, Australia
Intellectual Freedom; Off. for [6047]
Intellectual History; Intl. Soc. for [10126]
Intellectual Life; Assn. for Religion and [19916]
Intellectual Property
  Access Copyright, The Canadian Copyright Licensing Agency [IO]
  African Intellectual Property Org. [IO]
  African Regional Indus. Property Org. [IO]
  AIPPI Gp. of Lithuania [IO]
  Alliance Against IP and Theft [IO]
  Amer. Intellectual Property Law Assn. [5835]
  Amer. Soc. of Composers, Authors and Publishers [5836]
  Americans for the Enforcement of Intellectual Property Rights [5837]
  Anti Copying In Design [IO]
  Anti-Counterfeiting Gp. [IO]
  Arab Soc. for Intellectual Property [IO]
  Asociacion Uruguaya para la Tutela Organizada de los derechos Reprograficos [IO]
  Associacao Brasileira de Direitos Reprograficos [IO]
  Assn. of European Trade Mark Owners [IO]
  Assn. of Photographers [IO]
  Assn. of Univ. Tech. Managers [5838]
  Associazione Italiana per i Diritti di Riproduzione delle Opere dell'ingegno [IO]
  ASSUCOPIE [IO]
  Australasian Mech. Copyright Owners Soc. [IO]
  Australian Copyright Coun. [IO]
  Bildkonst Upphovsratt i Sverige [IO]
  Bonus Presskopia [IO]
  Brand Names Educ. Found. [5839]
  British Brands Gp. [IO]
  British Copyright Coun. [IO]
  Bur. Togolais du Droit d'Auteur [IO]
  Bus. Software Alliance [5840]
  Camara Uruguaya del Libro [IO]
  Canadian Alliance Against Software Theft [IO]
  Canadian Copyright Inst. [IO]
  Canadian Musical Reproduction Rights Agency [IO]
  Center for Social and Legal Res. [IO]
  Center for Social and Legal Res. [5841]
  Centro Administracion de Derechos Reprograficos Asociacion Civil [IO]
  Cerebrals Soc. [IO]
  Chartered Inst. of Patent Agents [IO]
  Chilean Assn. of Publishers, Distributors and Booksellers [IO]
  Copy-Dan [IO]

A star before a book entry number signifies that the name is not listed separately, but is mentioned within the entry.

COPYGHANA **[IO]**
Copyright Agency Limited **[IO]**
Copyright Clearance Center **[5842]**
Copyright Info. and Anti-piracy Centre **[IO]**
Copyright Licensing and Admin. Soc. of Singapore
   [IO]
Copyright Licensing Agency **[IO]**
Copyright Licensing Limited **[IO]**
Copyright Soc. of the U.S.A. **[5843]**
Design and Artists Copyright Soc. **[IO]**
Deutscher Journalisten-Verband e.V. **[IO]**
Dramatic, Artistic and Literary Rights Org. **[IO]**
Ethiopian Free-Press Journalists Assn. **[IO]**
European Brands Assn. **[IO]**
European Fed. of Agents of Indus. in Indus.
   Property **[IO]**
European Grouping of Societies of Authors and
   Composers **[IO]**
European Patent Off. **[IO]**
Fed. Against Software Theft **[IO]**
Fed. Luxembourgeoise des Editeurs de Livres
   [IO]
Fjolis **[IO]**
Future of Music Coalition **[10598]**
GESTAUTOR **[IO]**
Greek Collecting Soc. for Literary Works **[IO]**
Home Recording Rights Coalition **[5844]**
Hong Kong Reprographic Rights Licensing Soc.
   [IO]
Hungarian Alliance of Reprographic Rights **[IO]**
Hungarian Bur. for the Protection of Authors'
   Rights **[IO]**
ICC Counterfeiting Intelligence Bur. **[IO]**
Imaging Supplies Coalition **[IO]**
Imaging Supplies Coalition **[5845]**
Inst. for Axiomatic Knowledge and Educ. **[7606]**
Inst. of Intl. Licensing Practitioners **[IO]**
Inst. of Trade Mark Attorneys **[IO]**
Intellectual Property Owners Assn. **[5846]**
Inter-American Assn. of Indus. Property **[IO]**
Intergovernmental Comm. of the Universal
   Copyright Convention **[IO]**
Intl. Assn. for the Advancement of Teaching and
   Res. in Intellectual Property **[IO]**
Intl. Assn. for the Protection of Intellectual
   Property **[IO]**
Intl. Confed. of Societies of Authors and Compos-
   ers **[IO]**
Intl. Intellectual Property Alliance **[IO]**
Intl. Intellectual Property Alliance **[5847]**
Intl. Intellectual Property Assn. **[5848]**
Intl. Intellectual Property Assn. **[IO]**
Intl. ISBN Agency **[IO]**
Intl. Licensing Indus. Merchandisers' Assn. **[IO]**
Intl. Licensing Indus. Merchandisers' Assn. **[5849]**
Intl. Trademark Assn. **[5850]**
Intl. Trademark Assn. **[IO]**
Inventors Workshop Intl. Educ. Foundation/
   Entrepreneurs Workshop **[IO]**
Inventors Workshop Intl. Educ. Foundation/
   Entrepreneurs Workshop **[5851]**
IP Justice **[5852]**
Irish Copyright Licensing Agency **[IO]**
Irish Music Rights Org. **[IO]**
Irish Visual Artists' Rights Org. **[IO]**
ISSN Intl. Centre **[IO]**
Japan Academic Assn. for Copyright Clearance
   [IO]
KOPIKEN **[IO]**
KOPINOR **[IO]**
KOPIOSTO **[IO]**
KOPIPOL **[IO]**
Licensing Executives Soc. **[5853]**
Licensing Executives Soc. Andean Community
   [IO]
Licensing Executives Soc. Arab Countries **[IO]**
Licensing Executives Soc. Argentina **[IO]**
Licensing Executives Soc. of Australia and New
   Zealand **[IO]**
Licensing Executives Soc. Austria **[IO]**
Licensing Executives Soc. Benelux **[IO]**
Licensing Executives Soc. Brazil **[IO]**
Licensing Executives Soc. - Britain and Ireland
   [IO]
Licensing Executives Soc. China **[IO]**

Licensing Executives Soc. Croatia **[IO]**
Licensing Executives Soc. France **[IO]**
Licensing Executives Soc. Germany **[IO]**
Licensing Executives Soc. Hungary **[IO]**
Licensing Executives Soc. India **[IO]**
Licensing Executives Soc. Israel **[IO]**
Licensing Executives Soc. Italy **[IO]**
Licensing Executives Soc. Japan **[IO]**
Licensing Executives Soc. Korea **[IO]**
Licensing Executives Soc. Malaysia **[IO]**
Licensing Executives Soc. Mexico **[IO]**
Licensing Executives Soc. Philippines **[IO]**
Licensing Executives Soc. Poland **[IO]**
Licensing Executives Soc. Russia **[IO]**
Licensing Executives Soc. Scandinavia **[IO]**
Licensing Executives Soc. Singapore **[IO]**
Licensing Executives Soc. South Africa **[IO]**
Licensing Executives Soc. Switzerland **[IO]**
LITA, Soc. of Authors **[IO]**
Literary and Artistic Assn. Canada **[IO]**
Los Angeles Copyright Soc. **[5854]**
Luxembourg Org. for Reproduction Rights **[IO]**
MARQUES - Assn. of European Trademark Own-
   ers **[IO]**
Mechanical-Copyright Protection Soc. **[IO]**
Natl. Assn. of Artists and Crafters **[301]**
Natl. Assn. of Patent Practitioners **[6167]**
Natl. Coun. of Intellectual Property Law Assns.
   [5855]
Patent Off. Professional Assn. **[5856]**
Patent and Trademark Off. Soc. **[5857]**
Performing Right Soc. **[IO]**
Phonographic Performances New Zealand **[IO]**
ProLitteris **[IO]**
REPROBEL **[IO]**
Reproduction Rights Soc. of Nigeria **[IO]**
Romanian Visual Arts Copyright Collecting Soc.
   [IO]
Russian Authors' Soc. **[IO]**
Russian Rightholders' Soc. for Collective Mgt. of
   Reprographic Reproduction Rights **[IO]**
Screenrights **[IO]**
Sociedad de Gestion de Derechos Literarios **[IO]**
Societate de Gestiune Colectiva a Dreptunior de
   Autor **[IO]**
Societe quebecoise de gestion collective des
   droits de reproduction **[IO]**
Societe des Editeurs et Auteurs de Musique **[IO]**
Societes des Auters dans les Arts Graphiques et
   Plastiques **[IO]**
Software and Info. Indus. Assn. **[5858]**
Songwriters Guild of Am. **[5859]**
Spanish Reproduction Rights Centre **[IO]**
Theatrical, Literary and Audiovisual Agency **[IO]**
Trade Marks Patents and Designs Fed. **[IO]**
Trademark Soc. **[5860]**
Trinidad and Tobago Reproduction Rights Org.
   [IO]
Visual Artists and Galleries Assn. **[5861]**
VPP: Assn. of Intellectual Property Rights **[IO]**
World Intellectual Property Org. **[IO]**
ZimCopy **[IO]**
Intellectual Property Owners **[★5846]**
Intellectual Property Owners Assn. **[5846]**, 1255
   23rd St. NW, Ste. 200, Washington, DC 20037,
   (202)466-2396
Intelligence
   Amer. Mensa **[9981]**
   Assn. of Former Intelligence Officers **[5878]**
   Consortium for the Stud. of Intelligence **[17821]**
   Hollingworth Center for Highly Gifted Children
      [9982]
   Intl. Assn. for Intelligence Educ. **[8581]**
   Intl. Assn. of Law Enforcement Intelligence
      Analysts **[5882]**
   Intl. High IQ Soc. **[19149]**
   International High IQ Society **[IO]**
   Intl. Soc. for Philosophical Enquiry **[9983]**
   INTERTEL **[9984]**
   Lewis M. Terman Soc. **[9985]**
   Marine Corps CounterIntelligence Assn. **[19224]**
   Marine Corps Intelligence Assn. **[19225]**
   Mega Soc. **[9986]**
   Military Intelligence Corps Assn. **[5862]**
   Nathan Hale Inst. **[17822]**

   Natl. Counter Intelligence Corps Assn. **[21164]**
   Prometheus Soc. **[9987]**
Intelligence; Amer. Assn. for Artificial **[6483]**
Intelligence Assn; Natl. Military **[5889]**
Intelligence and Criminal Justice Acad. - Defunct.
Intelligence Industries Assn. - Address unknown
   since 1995.
Intelligence; International Legion of **[★9984]**
Intelligence Professionals; Naval **[6096]**
Intelligence Professionals; Soc. of Competitive
   [7211]
Intelligence Professionals; Soc. of Competitor
   [★7211]
Intelligence Proj. **[17121]**, 400 Washington Ave.,
   Montgomery, AL 36104, (334)956-8200
Intelligence; Special Interest Gp. on Artificial **[6487]**
Intelligent Building Gp. **[IO]**, London, United
   Kingdom
Intelligent Buildings Inst. - Defunct.
Intelligent Network Forum - Address unknown since
   2006.
Intelligent Transport Systems - Arab **[IO]**, London,
   United Kingdom
Intelligent Transport Systems - Australia **[IO]**, Port
   Melbourne, Australia
Intelligent Transport Systems - Japan **[IO]**, Tokyo,
   Japan
Intelligent Transport Systems - Singapore **[IO]**, Sin-
   gapore, Singapore
Intelligent Transport Systems - South Africa **[IO]**,
   Gauteng, Republic of South Africa
Intelligent Transport Systems for the United Kingdom
   [IO], London, United Kingdom
Intelligent Trans. Soc. of Am. **[3871]**, 1100 17th St.
   NW, Ste. 1200, Washington, DC 20036, (202)484-
   4847
Intenieria Sanitaria; Asociacion Interamericana de
   [★7589]
Intensive Care
   Acute Long Term Hosp. Assn. **[14852]**
   Natl. Assn. of Neonatal Nurses **[15495]**
   Soc. for Neonatology and Paediatric Intensive
      Care **[IO]**
Intensive Care Medicine; German Soc. of Anaesthe-
   siology and **[IO]**
Intensive Care Soc. **[IO]**, London, United Kingdom
Intensive Caring Unlimited - Address unknown since
   2001.
Intentional Community; Fellowship for **[17216]**
Inter-African Coffee Org. **[IO]**, Abidjan, Cote d'Ivoire
Inter-America Travel Agents Soc. **[★3920]**
Inter-Amer. Assn. for Democracy and Freedom - Ad-
   dress unknown since 1999.
Inter-American Assn. of Indus. Property **[IO]**, Asun-
   cion, Paraguay
Inter-American Assn. of Sanitary Engg. **[★IO]**
Inter-American Assn. of Sanitary Engg. **[★7589]**
Inter-American Assn. of Sanitary Engg. and Env.
   [★7589]
Inter-American Assn. of Sanitary Engg. and Env.
   [★IO]
Inter-American Assn. of Sanitary Engg. and
   Environmental Sciences **[★IO]**
Inter-American Assn. of Sanitary Engg. and
   Environmental Sciences **[★7589]**
Inter-American Assn. of Sanitary Engineers **[★7589]**
Inter-American Assn. of Sanitary Engineers **[★IO]**
Inter-American Assn. of Sanitary and Environmental
   Engg. **[★IO]**
Inter-American Assn. of Sanitary and Environmental
   Engg. **[★7589]**
Inter-American Bar Assn. **[5941]**, 1211 Connecticut
   Ave. NW, Ste. 202, Washington, DC 20036,
   (202)466-5944
Inter-American Bar Assn. **[IO]**, Washington, DC,
   United States
Inter-Amer. Bar Found. - Address unknown since
   2006.
Inter-Amer. Bibliographical and Library Assn. -
   Defunct.
Inter-American Children's Inst. **[IO]**, Montevideo,
   Uruguay
Inter-Amer. Coll. Assn. - Address unknown since
   2001.
Inter-American Commercial Arbitration Commn.
   [5456], c/o Amer. Arbitration Assn., 140 W 51st St.,
   New York, NY 10020-1201, (212)484-4000

Reference to "IO" in place of a book number signifies that the association may be found in the 45th edition of International Organizations.

Inter-American Commn. on Human Rights [17765], 1889 F St. NW, Washington, DC 20006, (202)458-6002

Inter-American Commn. on Human Rights [IO], Washington, DC, United States

Inter-American Commn. of Women [IO], Washington, DC, United States

Inter-Amer. Commn. of Women [17540], c/o Org. of Amer. States, 17th St. and Constitution Ave. NW, Washington, DC 20006, (202)458-3000

Inter-Amer. Comm. on Peaceful Settlement - Defunct.

Inter-Amer. Comm. of Shipowners - Address unknown since 1995.

Inter Amer. Commun. and Action; Ecumenical Prog. for [★17987]

Inter-American Conductive Educ. Assn. [9146], PO Box 3169, Toms River, NJ 08756-3169, (732)797-2566

Inter-American Conductive Educ. Assn. [IO], Toms River, NJ, United States

Inter-American Confed. for Catholic Educ. [IO], Bogota, Colombia

Inter-American Conf. of Ministers of Labor [IO], Washington, DC, United States

Inter-American Conf. of Ministers of Labor [17394], c/o Org. of Amer. States, 1889 F St. NW, 6th Fl., Washington, DC 20006-4401, (202)458-3000

Inter-American Conf. of Social Security [IO], Mexico City, Mexico

Inter-Amer. Coun. for Education, Science and Culture - Defunct.

Inter-Amer. Cultural Assn. - Address unknown since 1995.

Inter-American Defense Bd. [17378], 2600 NW 16th St., Washington, DC 20441, (202)939-6041

Inter-American Defense Bd. [IO], Washington, DC, United States

Inter-American Development Bank [IO], Washington, DC, United States

Inter-American Development Bank [17460], 1300 New York Ave. NW, Washington, DC 20577, (202)623-1000

Inter-American Development Bank's Wives Assn. [★19436]

Inter-Amer. Economic and Social Coun. - Address unknown since 1999.

Inter-Amer. Education Assn. - Address unknown since 1995.

Inter-American Elecl. Commun. Commn. [★3744]

Inter-Amer. Elecl. Commun. Commn. [★IO]

Inter-Amer. Fed. of Textile, Garment and Leather Workers - Address unknown since 1995.

Inter-American Fed. of Touring and Auto. Clubs [IO], Buenos Aires, Argentina

Inter-American Found. [IO], Arlington, VA, United States

Inter-American Found. [18573], 901 N Stuart St., 10th Fl., Balston, Arlington, VA 22203-1821, (703)306-4301

Inter-Amer. Found. for the Arts - Defunct.

Inter-Amer. Freight Conf. - Address unknown since 1999.

Inter-Amer. Hospital Assn. - Defunct.

Inter-Amer. Hotel Assn. - Address unknown since 1995.

Inter-American Inst. for Cooperation on Agriculture - Costa Rica [IO], San Jose, Costa Rica

Inter-American Inst. for Cooperation on Agriculture - Dominican Republic [IO], Santo Domingo, Dominican Republic

Inter-American Inst. for Cooperation on Agriculture - Grenada [IO], St. George's, Grenada

Inter-American Inst. for Cooperation on Agriculture - Guyana [IO], Georgetown, Guyana

Inter-American Inst. for Cooperation on Agriculture - Paraguay [IO], Asuncion, Paraguay

Inter-American Inst. for Cooperation on Agriculture - St. Lucia [IO], Castries, St. Lucia

Inter-American Inst. for Global Change Res. [IO], Sao Jose dos Campos, Brazil

Inter-American Inst. of Human Rights [IO], San Jose, Costa Rica

Inter-Amer. Inst. of Intl. Legal Studies - Address unknown since 1995.

Inter-Amer. Investment Development Center - Defunct.

Inter-Amer. Legal Services Assn. - Defunct.

Inter-Amer. Music Coun. - Address unknown since 2002.

Inter-American Nuclear Energy Commn. - Address unknown since 1999.

Inter-American Org. for Higher Educ. [IO], Quebec, QC, Canada

Inter-American Parliamentary Gp. on Population and Development [IO], New York, NY, United States

Inter-American Parliamentary Gp. on Population and Development [12432], 420 Lexington Ave., Rm. 303, New York, NY 10170-0002, (646)240-4055

Inter Amer. Press Assn. [17181], 1801 SW 3rd Ave., Jules Dubois Bldg., Miami, FL 33129, (305)634-2465

Inter Amer. Press Assn. [IO], Miami, FL, United States

Inter-American Res. and Documentation Centre on Vocational Training [IO], Montevideo, Uruguay

Inter-Amer. Safety Coun. [12965]

Inter-American School Ser. [★8647]

Inter-American School Ser. [★IO]

Inter-American Soc. of Cardiology [IO], Mexico City, Mexico

Inter-American Statistical Inst. [IO], Panama City, Panama

Inter-American Telecommunication Commn. [IO], Washington, DC, United States

Inter-American Telecommunication Commn. [3744], 1889 F St. NW, Washington, DC 20006, (202)458-3004

Inter-American Telecommunication Conf. [★3744]

Inter-American Telecommunication Conf. [★IO]

Inter-Amer. Translators Assn. - Defunct.

Inter-Amer. Travel Agents Soc. - Address unknown since 2002.

Inter-American Travel Cong. [3919], c/o Org. of Amer. States, 1889 F St. NW, Washington, DC 20006, (202)458-3221

Inter-American Travel Cong. [IO], Washington, DC, United States

Inter-American Tropical Tuna Commn. [IO], La Jolla, CA, United States

Inter-American Tropical Tuna Commn. [5730], 8604 La Jolla Shores Dr., La Jolla, CA 92037-1508, (858)546-7100

Inter-Amer. Univ. Coun. for Economic and Social Development - Address unknown since 1999.

Inter-Association Task Force on Alcohol Issues [★13250]

Inter-Association Task Force on Alcohol and Other Substance Abuse Issues [13250], c/o Dr. Herbert Songer, VP for Student Affairs, Fort Hays State Univ., 600 Park St., Hays, KS 67601-4099, (785)628-4277

Inter-Association Task Force on Campus Alcohol and Other Substance Abuse Issues [★13250]

Inter-Celtic Soc. - Address unknown since 1995.

Inter-Church Ministries [★19516]

Inter-Church Ministries - Defunct.

Inter Circle - Address unknown since 2008.

Inter-collegiate Men's Chorus, A Natl. Assn. of Male Choruses [★10611]

Inter-collegiate Men's Chorus, A Natl. Assn. of Male Choruses [★IO]

Inter-Collegiate Sailing Assn. of North Am. [23176], c/o Capt. Eric Wallischeck, U.S.A. Merchant Marine Acad., 300 Steamboat Rd., Kings Point, NY 11024-1699, (516)773-5232

Inter-Collegiate Yacht Racing Assn. [★23176]

Inter-Collegiate Yacht Racing Assn. of North Am. [★23176]

Inter-cultural Relations; Coun. on [★10234]

Inter-Faith Community Services [12775], 3370 S Irving St., Englewood, CO 80110-1816, (303)789-0501

Inter-Faith Compassionists - Address unknown since 1995.

Inter-Faith Task Force [★12775]

Inter-Faith Task Force for Community Services [★12775]

Inter-Financial Assn. - Address unknown since 1990.

Inter-fraternity Conf; Professional [★24488]

Inter-Galactic Spacecraft UFO Intercontinental Res. and Analytic Network - Defunct.

Inter-Governmental Philatelic Corp. [22829], 460 W 34th St., 10th Fl., New York, NY 10001, (212)629-7979

Inter-Hemispheric Educ. Rsrc. Center [★16976]

Inter-Hemispheric Educ. Rsrc. Center [★IO]

Inter-Industry Conf. on Auto Collision Repair [415], 5125 Trillium Blvd., Hoffman Estates, IL 60192-3600, (800)422-7872

Inter-Industry Emission Control Program - Defunct.

Inter-Industry Farm Elec. Utilization Coun. [★6963]

Inter-Lake Yachting Assn. [23177], c/o Daniel Van Heeckeren, Advisory Comm. Chm., 600 Battles Rd., Gates Mills, OH 44040, (440)423-3244

Inter-National Assn. of Bus., Indus. and Rehabilitation [17417], PO Box 15242, Washington, DC 20003, (202)543-6353

Inter-Natl. Assn. for Widowed People - Address unknown since 1995.

Inter-Pacific Bar Assn. [IO], Tokyo, Japan

Inter Pares [IO], Ottawa, ON, Canada

Inter-Parliamentary Conf. for Intl. Arbitration [★IO]

Inter-Parliamentary Consultative Coun. of Benelux [IO], Brussels, Belgium

Inter-Parliamentary Union [IO], Geneva, Switzerland

Inter Press Ser. Intl. Assn. [IO], Rome, Italy

Inter-Religious Task Force on Central America - Defunct.

Inter-Society Color Coun. [6708], 11491 Sunset Hills Rd., Reston, VA 20190, (703)318-0263

Inter-Society Color Coun. [IO], Reston, VA, United States

Inter-Soc. Corrosion Comm. - Defunct.

Inter-Society Cytology Coun. [★14075]

Inter-Society for the Electronic Arts [IO], Amsterdam, Netherlands

Inter-Tribal Indian Ceremonial Assn. [10747]

Inter-Union Commn. on Frequency Allocations for Radio Astronomy and Space Sci. [★IO]

Inter-Union Commn. on Solar Terrestrial Physics [★IO]

Inter-Union Commn. on Solar Terrestrial Physics [★7508]

Inter-Univ. Comm. for Debate on Foreign Policy - Defunct.

Inter-Univ. Comm. for Res. on Consumer Behavior - Address unknown since 1995.

Inter-University Comm. on the Superior Student [★8290]

Inter-University Consortium for Political and Social Res. [7525], Univ. of Michigan Inst. for Social Res., PO Box 1248, Ann Arbor, MI 48106-1248, (734)647-5000

Inter-University Coun. for East Africa [IO], Kampala, Uganda

Inter-University Prog. for Latino Res. [19045], Univ. of Notre Dame, Inst. for Latino Stud., 230 McKenna Hall, PO Box 764, Notre Dame, IN 46556-5685, (574)631-3481

Inter-University Seminar on Armed Forces and Soc. [6077], Political Sci. Dept., Loyola Univ. Chicago, 6525 N Sheridan Rd., Chicago, IL 60626, (773)508-2930

Inter Varsity Christian Fellowship [20347], PO Box 7895, Madison, WI 53707-7895, (608)274-9001

Inter Varsity Missions Fellowship [★20347]

Interact Ministries [20348], 31000 SE Kelso Rd., Boring, OR 97009, (503)668-5571

Interact Ministries [IO], Boring, OR, United States

Interact Worldwide [IO], London, United Kingdom

Interaction/American Coun. for Voluntary Intl. Action [IO], Washington, DC, United States

Interaction/American Coun. for Voluntary Intl. Action [12433], 1400 16th St. NW, Ste. 210, Washington, DC 20036, (202)667-8227

InterAction Coun. of Former Heads of Govt. - Address unknown since 1999.

Interaction Design Assn. [6863], PO Box 2833, Westport, CT 06880

Interaction Design Assn. [IO], Westport, CT, United States

Interaction; Soc. for the Stud. of Symbolic [7669]

Interactive Advt. Bur. [102], 116 E 27th St., 7th Fl., New York, NY 10016, (212)380-4700

A star before a book entry number signifies that the name is not listed separately, but is mentioned within the entry.

Interactive Advt. Bur. **[IO]**, New York, NY, United States

Interactive Advt. Bur. - Europe **[IO]**, Brussels, Belgium

Interactive Audio Special Interest Gp. **[2807]**, c/o MIDI Mfrs. Assn., PO Box 3173, La Habra, CA 90632-3173, (714)736-9774

Interactive Digital Software Assn. **[★6766]**

Interactive Entertainment Assn. of Australia **[IO]**, Eveleigh, Australia

Interactive Gaming Coun. **[IO]**, Vancouver, BC, Canada

Interactive Marketing; Assn. for **[3734]**

Interactive Media; Assn. for **[★3734]**

Interactive Multimedia; Assn. for Applied **[2666]**

Interactive Multimedia Assn. - Defunct.

Interactive Services; Natl. Assn. for **[★737]**

Interactive TV Assn. **[★3734]**

Interactive Travel Services Assn. **[3946]**, 1156 15th St. NW, Ste. 900, Washington, DC 20005, (202)955-0089

Interactive Videodisc Consortium - Defunct.

Interagency Coalition on AIDS and Development **[IO]**, Ottawa, ON, Canada

Interagency Comm. on Intl. Athletics - Defunct.

Interagency Coun. on Info. Resources for Nursing **[10360]**, c/o Richard J. Barry, Pres., Amer. Nurses Assn. Lib., 8515 Georgia Ave., Ste. 400, Silver Spring, MD 20910-3492, (301)628-5143

Interagency Group for Interactive Training Technologies - Address unknown since 1999.

Interamerican Accounting Assn. **[35]**, 275 Fountainebleau Blvd., Ste. 245, Miami, FL 33172, (305)225-1991

Interamerican Accounting Assn. **[IO]**, Miami, FL, United States

Interamerican Accounting Conf. **[★IO]**

Interamerican Accounting Conf. **[★35]**

Interamerican Assn. for Environmental Defense **[4630]**, c/o Earthjustice, 426 17th St., 6th Fl., Oakland, CA 94612, (510)550-6753

Interamerican Assn. for Environmental Defense **[IO]**, Oakland, CA, United States

Interamerican Assn. of Pediatric Otolaryngology - Address unknown since 2004.

Interamerican Coll. of Physicians and Surgeons **[16000]**, 233 Broadway, Ste. 771, New York, NY 10279, (212)777-3642

Interamerican Coll. of Physicians and Surgeons **[IO]**, New York, NY, United States

Interamerican Confed. of Cattlemen - Address unknown since 1999.

Interamerican Fed. of Insurance Companies **[IO]**, Bogota, Colombia

Interamerican Heart Cardiology Found. **[★13909]**

InterAmerican Heart Found. **[13909]**, 7272 Greenville Ave., Dallas, TX 75231-4596, (214)706-1301

Interamerican Medical and Health Assn. - Address unknown since 2006.

InterAmerican Soc. for Tropical Horticulture **[4979]**, c/o Dr. Richard Campbell, Exec. Sec.-Treas., Fairchild Tropical Garden, 11935 SW Old Cutler Rd., Miami, FL 33156, (305)667-1651

InterAmerican Travel Agents Soc. **[3920]**, c/o Jackie Alton, CTC, Bd. Member, CWT/Almeda Travel, 450 Meyerland Plz., Houston, TX 77096, (713)592-8000

Interamericana de Contabilidad; Asociacion **[★35]**

Interamericana de Engenharia Sanitaria; Asociacao **[★7589]**

Interamericana de Intenieria Sanitaria; Asociacion **[★7589]**

Interamericano de Seguridad; Consejo **[★12965]**

Interbank Marketing Assn. - Defunct.

Interbank Merchants Assn. - Address unknown since 1994.

Intercambio de Casas **[★22580]**

Intercampus Comm. for Handicapped Students - Defunct.

Intercare - Address unknown since 2003.

Intercessors for Am. **[19803]**, PO Box 915, Purcellville, VA 20134, (540)751-0980

Interchange - Address unknown since 2005.

Interchange Resource Center - Address unknown since 1989.

Interchangeable Virtual Instruments **[★6814]**

The Interchurch Center **[19896]**, 475 Riverside Dr., New York, NY 10115-0002, (212)870-2200

Interchurch Medical Assistance **[20242]**, 500 Main St., Old Main Bldg., PO Box 429, New Windsor, MD 21776, (410)635-8720

Interchurch Medical Assistance **[IO]**, New Windsor, MD, United States

Interchurch Org. for Development Cooperation **[IO]**, Utrecht, Netherlands

Intercoastal Steamship Freight Assn. - Defunct.

Intercoiffure Am. **[1080]**, c/o Joy Warner, Membership Chair, 154 Rte. 206, Chester, NJ 07930, (908)879-6211

InterCol London **[IO]**, London, United Kingdom

Intercollegiate Assn. of Amateur Athletes of Am. **[23820]**, c/o Eastern Coll. Athletic Conf., PO Box 3, Centerville, MA 02632, (508)771-5060

Intercollegiate Assn. for the Study of the Alcohol Problem - Defunct.

Intercollegiate Athletic Assn; Central **[23811]**

Intercollegiate Athletics; Natl. Assn. of **[23835]**

Intercollegiate Basketball Assn; Metropolitan **[23131]**

Intercollegiate Basketball; Natl. Assn. of **[★23835]**

Intercollegiate Broadcasting Sys. **[8004]**, 367 Windsor Hwy., New Windsor, NY 12553-7900, (845)565-0003

Intercollegiate Dramatic Assn. - Defunct.

Intercollegiate Fencing Assn. **[23401]**, c/o Eastern Coll. Athletic Conf., 1311 Craigville Beach Rd., Centerville, MA 02632, (508)771-5060

Intercollegiate Flying Assn; Natl. **[21466]**

Intercollegiate Gymnastic League; Eastern **[23475]**

Intercollegiate Horse Show Assn. **[23526]**, c/o Naomi Blumenthal, Treas., 8125 Verbeck Dr., Manlius, NY 13104

Intercollegiate Ice Hockey Assn. **[★23484]**

Intercollegiate Knights **[24507]**, PO Box 7264, Provo, UT 84602-7264, (801)489-0458

Intercollegiate Lacrosse Assn; U.S. **[23571]**

Intercollegiate Men's Choruses, An Intl. Assn. of Male Choruses **[10611]**, c/o Gerald Polich, Exec. Sec., Dept. of Music, McCain Auditorium, Kansas State Univ., Manhattan, KS 66506-4706, (913)532-5740

Intercollegiate Men's Choruses, An Intl. Assn. of Male Choruses **[IO]**, Manhattan, KS, United States

Intercollegiate Musical Coun., A Natl. Assn. of Male Choruses **[★IO]**

Intercollegiate Musical Coun., A Natl. Assn. of Male Choruses **[★10611]**

Intercollegiate Opera Group - Defunct.

Intercollegiate Outing Club Assn. **[23941]**, c/o Michelle Moon, Exec. Sec., 2711 Blanchard, Mt. Holyoke Coll., South Hadley, MA 01075, (518)833-6816

Intercollegiate Rodeo Assn; Natl. **[23691]**

Intercollegiate Rowing Assn. **[23700]**, c/o ECAC Rowing Off., 1311 Craigville Beach Rd., Centerville, MA 02632-4129, (508)771-5060

Intercollegiate Soccer Assn. of America - Address unknown since 2001.

Intercollegiate Soccer Officials Assn; Natl. **[23778]**

Intercollegiate Soc. of Individualists **[★17271]**

Intercollegiate Stud. Inst. **[17271]**, PO Box 4431, Wilmington, DE 19807-0431, (302)652-4600

Intercollegiate Taiwanese Amer. Students Assn. **[19401]**, PO Box 961856, Boston, MA 02196

Intercollegiate Tennis Assn. **[23902]**, 174 Tamarack Cir., Skillman, NJ 08558-2021, (609)497-6920

Intercollegiate Tennis Coaches Assn. **[★23902]**

Intercomm Users' Group - Address unknown since 2002.

Interconnecting and Packaging Electronic Circuits; Inst. for **[★1221]**

Intercontainer-Interfrigo **[IO]**, Basel, Switzerland

Intercontinental Church Soc. **[IO]**, Warwick, United Kingdom

Intercontinental Fed. of Behavioral Optometry **[IO]**, Santa Ana, CA, United States

Intercontinental Fed. of Behavioral Optometry **[15719]**, c/o Robert Williams, Exec. Dir., 1921 E Carnegie Ave., Ste. 3L, Santa Ana, CA 92705, (949)250-8070

Intercontinental Press Publishing Assn. - Defunct.

Intercristo **[19804]**, 19303 Fremont Ave. N, MS No. 20, Seattle, WA 98133

Intercultural
African Amer. Museum **[9352]**
Amer. Nyckelharpa Assn. **[10546]**
American-Paraguayan Cultural Center **[IO]**
Anglo Chilean Soc. **[IO]**
Assn. for Africanist Anthropology **[6408]**
Assn. for Cultural Exchange, ACE Stud. Tours **[IO]**
Assn. for Formation and Activities Intercultural for Youth **[IO]**
Assn. for Intl. Youth-work - Christian Women's Working Group **[IO]**
Assn. of Latina and Latino Anthropologists **[6410]**
Australia-Britain Soc. **[IO]**
Australian Assn. of Hong Kong **[IO]**
Austrian Cultural Forum **[9625]**
Belarusian Canadian Alliance **[IO]**
Belgian Amer. Educational Found. **[9736]**
Bihar Assn. of North Am. **[10220]**
Bridges to Community **[13389]**
British Coun. Canada **[IO]**
British Inst. of Persian Stud. **[IO]**
Butimar Productions **[9849]**
Caribbean Amer. Intercultural Org. **[9774]**
Champa Cultural Preservation Assn. of USA **[11082]**
Cultural Integration Fellowship **[9618]**
Cultural Union Brazil U.S. **[IO]**
Delta Sigma Chi Sorority **[24706]**
Delta Xi Phi Multicultural Sorority **[24685]**
European Assn. for Middle Eastern Stud. **[IO]**
European Soc. of Culture **[IO]**
F. Scott Fitzgerald Soc. **[9649]**
First Peoples Worldwide **[10224]**
Friends of Nepal Assn. **[IO]**
German-Armenian Soc. **[IO]**
German China Assn. **[IO]**
German-Chinese Friendship Assn. **[IO]**
Hellenic Amer. Natl. Coun. **[9995]**
Hmong Natl. Development **[17815]**
Ijaw Natl. Alliance of the Americas **[12639]**
Indian Volunteers for Community Ser. **[IO]**
Indo-American Arts Coun. **[9570]**
Interracial Family Alliance of Houston **[12160]**
Interracial-Intercultural Pride **[12162]**
Kobe YMCA Cross Cultural Center **[IO]**
Leuva Patidar Samaj of USA **[10221]**
Mediterranean Stud. Assn. **[10466]**
Milan Cultural Assn. **[10222]**
My Travel Bug **[9279]**
Nepali Amer. Friendship Assn. **[19288]**
New Zealand Ireland Assn. **[IO]**
North Amer. Assn. for Belarusian Stud. **[9735]**
North Amer. Assn. for the Stud. of Welsh Culture and History **[11083]**
North Amer. Taiwan Stud. Assn. **[9205]**
Patidar Cultural Assn. of USA **[10218]**
Pogranicze Found. **[IO]**
Publishers Assn. for Cultural Exchange, Japan **[IO]**
Saq' Be': Org. for Mayan and Indigenous Spiritual Bodies **[10226]**
Slavic and East European Folklore Assn. **[9962]**
Slavic Heritage Coalition **[10969]**
Soc. for Anglo-Chinese Understanding **[IO]**
Soc. for the Anthropology of North Am. **[6425]**
Soc. for the History of the Germans in Maryland **[9980]**
South Asian Women's Centre **[IO]**
Student Org. of North Am. **[9194]**
Turkish Amer. Alliance for Fairness **[19410]**
USA Sanatan Sports and Cultural Assn. **[23787]**
Uttaranchal Assn. of North Am. **[10219]**
Wimbum Cultural and Development Assn. in the U.S.A. **[9344]**
Women Welcome Women World Wide **[IO]**
World Assn. of Cultural Psychiatry **[16097]**
World Cultural Coun. **[IO]**
Intercultural Cancer Coun. **[IO]**, Houston, TX, United States
Intercultural Cancer Coun. **[13830]**, 6655 Travis, Ste. 322, Houston, TX 77030-1312, (713)798-4617
Intercultural Development Res. Assn. **[7998]**, 5835 Callaghan Rd., Ste. 350, San Antonio, TX 78228-1190, (210)444-1710

Reference to "IO" in place of a book number signifies that the association may be found in the 45th edition of International Organizations.

Intercultural Development Res. Assn. **[IO]**, San Antonio, TX, United States
Intercultural Educ; Amer. Coun. on Intl. **[8651]**
Intercultural Educ., Training and Res; Intl. Soc. for **[★8667]**
Intercultural Educ., Training and Res; Soc. for **[★8667]**
Intercultural Pride; Interracial- **[12162]**
Intercultural Student Exchange; Amer. **[8596]**

Intercultural Studies
Assn. for Africanist Anthropology **[6408]**
Assn. of Latina and Latino Anthropologists **[6410]**
Assn. for Low Countries Stud. in Great Britain and Ireland **[IO]**
Assn. for the Stud. of Persianate Societies **[8668]**
Cultural Integration Fellowship **[9618]**
Intl. Assn. for the Stud. of Sexuality, Culture and Soc. **[9124]**
Interracial-Intercultural Pride **[12162]**
Mediterranean Stud. Assn. **[10466]**
Natl. Assn. for Multicultural Educ. **[8582]**
National Association for Multicultural Education **[IO]**
Salzburg Seminar **[10229]**
Saq' Be': Org. for Mayan and Indigenous Spiritual Bodies **[10226]**
Soc. for the Anthropology of North Am. **[6425]**
Soc. for German-American Stud. **[9979]**
Soc. for Urban, Natl. and Transnational/Global Anthropology **[6435]**
Intercultural Stud; Inst. for **[10234]**
Interdenominational Foreign Mission Assn. of North Am. **[★20349]**
Interdenominational Foreign Missions Assn. **[20349]**, PO Box 398, Wheaton, IL 60189-0398, (630)682-9270
Interdisciplinary Biblical Res. Inst. **[19928]**, PO Box 423, 200 N Main St., Hatfield, PA 19440-0423, (215)368-5000

Interdisciplinary Education
Amer. Acad. of Arts and Sciences **[9605]**
Amer. Soc. for Eighteenth-Century Stud. **[10089]**
Assn. for Integrative Stud. **[10227]**
Global Stud. Assn. North Am. **[8583]**
Interdisciplinary Environmental Assn. **[4988]**
Interdisciplinary Environmental Assn. **[IO]**
Intl. Assn. for Dialogue Anal. **[7244]**
Leonardo, The Intl. Soc. for the Arts, Sciences and Tech. **[9610]**
Soc. for Cross-Cultural Res. **[10230]**
Soc. for Textual Scholarship **[10432]**
Interdisciplinary Environmental Assn. **[4988]**, c/o Dr. Michael A. Reiter, Chm., Delaware State Univ., Dept. of Agriculture and Natural Resources, 1200 N DuPont Hwy., Dover, DE 19901, (302)857-6412
Interdisciplinary Environmental Assn. **[IO]**, Dover, DE, United States

Interdisciplinary Studies
Africa-Europe Gp. for Interdisciplinary Stud. **[IO]**
Amer. Acad. of Arts and Sciences **[9605]**
Amer. Culture Assn. **[10886]**
Amer. Soc. for Eighteenth-Century Stud. **[10089]**
Assn. for Integrative Stud. **[10227]**
Assn. for the Stud. of Free Institutions **[8481]**
Coun. of Christian Scholarly Societies **[8085]**
Educational Center for Applied Ekistics **[10228]**
Global Stud. Assn. North Am. **[8583]**
Global Stud. Assn. North Am. **[IO]**
Inst. for Psychohistory **[10123]**
Inst. for the Stud. of Human Ideas on Ultimate Reality and Meaning **[IO]**
Inst. for the Stud. of Human Knowledge **[10175]**
Intl. Assn. for Dialogue Anal. **[7244]**
Intl. Assn. for the Stud. of Sexuality, Culture and Soc. **[9124]**
Intl. Maledicta Soc. **[10404]**
Intl. Psychohistorical Assn. **[10125]**
Intl. Soc. for Gesture Stud. **[6712]**
Intl. Soc. for Language Stud. **[10302]**
Intl. Stud. Assn. **[10235]**
Leonardo, The Intl. Soc. for the Arts, Sciences and Tech. **[9610]**
Mediterranean Stud. Assn. **[10466]**
Modernist Stud. Assn. **[8780]**
Natl. Coun. on Family Relations **[12164]**

Salzburg Seminar **[10229]**
Soc. for Cross-Cultural Res. **[10230]**
Soc. of Educators and Scholars **[10231]**
Soc. of Educators and Scholars **[IO]**
Soc. for Res. in Child Development **[11546]**
Soc. for Textual Scholarship **[10432]**
Interested Veterans of the Central City **[★21308]**
InterEuropean Comission en Eglise et Ecole **[★IO]**
InterEuropean Commn. on Church and School **[IO]**, Oslo, Norway
INTEREX **[6795]**
InterExchange **[8617]**, 161 6th Ave., New York, NY 10013, (212)924-0446
InterExchange **[IO]**, New York, NY, United States
Interface Consortium; Biometric Application Programming **[6572]**

Interfaith
Amer. Freedom Alliance **[18507]**
Covenant of Unitarian Universalist Pagans **[20459]**
FaithWorks Intl. **[11777]**
Interfaith Alliance **[20498]**
Interfaith Thrift Stores Assn. **[IO]**
Interfaith Worker Justice **[20092]**
Sacred Dance Soc. **[19878]**
Sikh Coun. on Religion and Educ. **[20558]**
Interfaith Alliance **[20498]**, 1212 New York Ave., Washington, DC 20005, (202)238-3300
Interfaith Center on Corporate Responsibility **[17353]**, 475 Riverside Dr., Rm. 1842, New York, NY 10115, (212)870-2295
Interfaith Center to Reverse the Arms Race - Address unknown since 1999.
Interfaith Church of Metaphysics **[20573]**, 163 Moon Valley Rd., Windyville, MO 65783, (417)345-8411
Interfaith Coalition on Aging; Natl. **[11314]**
Interfaith Coalition on Energy - Defunct.
Interfaith Commn. on Marriage and Family - Defunct.
Interfaith Comm. on Released Time Religious Education - Address unknown since 1995.
Interfaith Comm. on Social Responsibility in Investments **[★17353]**
Interfaith Coun. for Human Rights - Address unknown since 2003.
Interfaith Coun. for the Protection of Animals and Nature **[4409]**, 3691 Tuxedo Rd. NW, Atlanta, GA 30305, (404)814-1371
Interfaith Encounter Assn. **[IO]**, Jerusalem, Israel
Interfaith Hospitality Network; Natl. **[★12290]**
Interfaith Hunger Appeal - Address unknown since 2003.
Interfaith Impact Found. - Address unknown since 2003.
Interfaith Movement - Defunct.
Interfaith Office on Accompaniment - Address unknown since 1999.
Interfaith Services; Org. for Attempters and Survivors of Suicide in **[13290]**
Interfaith Thrift Stores Assn. **[IO]**, Calgary, AB, Canada
Interfaith Worker Justice **[20092]**, 1020 W Bryn Mawr Ave., 4th Fl., Chicago, IL 60660, (773)728-8400
Interfaith Working Group **[12887]**, PO Box 11706, Philadelphia, PA 19101, (215)235-3050
Interferon and Cytokine Res; Intl. Soc. for **[16351]**
Interferon Found. - Defunct.
Interferry **[IO]**, Victoria, BC, Canada
Interflora - Address unknown since 2001.
Interfraternity Conf; Natl. **[★24487]**
Interfraternity Found; Natl. **[★24486]**
Interfraternity Res. and Advisory Coun. - Defunct.
InterFuture **[8664]**, c/o David L. Robbins, Pres., PO Box 282, State House Sta., Boston, MA 02133, (617)573-8267
InterFuture **[IO]**, Boston, MA, United States
Intergalactic Ranch House **[★24951]**
Intergalactic Sysop Alliance - Address unknown since 1995.
Intergovernmental Authority on Development **[IO]**, Djibouti, Djibouti
Intergovernmental Comm. of the Universal Copyright Convention **[IO]**, Paris, France
Intergovernmental Comm. on Urban and Regional Res. **[IO]**, Toronto, ON, Canada

Intergovernmental Copyright Comm. **[★IO]**
Intergovernmental Gp. on Meat and Dairy Products **[IO]**, Rome, Italy
Intergovernmental Hea. Policy Proj. **[★17689]**
Intergovernmental Maritime Consultative Org. **[★IO]**
Intergovernmental Oceanographic Commn. **[IO]**, Paris, France
Intergovernmental Org. for Intl. Carriage by Rail **[IO]**, Bern, Switzerland
Intergovernmental Panel on Climate Change **[IO]**, Geneva, Switzerland
Intergovernmental Relations Officials; Natl. Assn. of **[★5622]**
Intergovernmental Steering Comm. on World Food Day - Address unknown since 1999.
Interhelp **[18620]**, PO Box 61, Delmar, NY 12054, (518)475-1929
Interhelp **[IO]**, Delmar, NY, United States
Interhemispheric Rsrc. Center **[★IO]**
Interhemispheric Rsrc. Center **[★16976]**
Interhostel **[8618]**, Univ. of New Hampshire, 6 Garrison Ave., Durham, NH 03824, (603)862-1147
Interights, the Intl. Centre for the Legal Protection of Human Rights **[IO]**, London, United Kingdom
Interim Comm. for Coordination of Investigations of the Lower Mekong Basin **[★IO]**
Interim Mgt. Assn. **[IO]**, London, United Kingdom
Interior Decorators and Designers Assn. and Intl. Interior Design Assn. United Kingdom **[★IO]**

Interior Design
Access Flooring Assn. **[IO]**
Allied Bd. of Trade **[2249]**
Amer. Floorcovering Alliance **[2250]**
Amer. Soc. of Interior Designers **[2251]**
Assn. for Contract Textiles **[3775]**
Assn. of European Candle Mfrs. **[IO]**
Assn. of German Home Textiles Indus. **[IO]**
Assn. of Interior Specialists **[IO]**
Assn. of Univ. Interior Designers **[2252]**
British Contract Furnishing Assn. **[IO]**
British Interior Design Assn. **[IO]**
Bund Osterreichischer Innenarchitekten **[IO]**
Canadian Carpet Inst. **[IO]**
Carpet Cushion Coun. **[2253]**
Carpet and Rug Inst. **[2254]**
Central Carpet Indus. Assn. **[IO]**
Certified Interior Decorators Intl. **[IO]**
Certified Interior Decorators Intl. **[2255]**
Contract Flooring Assn. **[IO]**
Contractors Co-Op Coun. **[2256]**
Coun. for Interior Design Accreditation **[8584]**
Coun. for Qualification of Residential Interior Designers **[2257]**
European Acad. of Design **[IO]**
Floor Installation Assn. of North Am. **[623]**
Found. for Design Integrity **[1152]**
German Carpet Res. Inst. **[IO]**
German Interior Architects Assn. **[IO]**
Home Fashion Products Assn. **[2258]**
Hong Kong Interior Design Assn. **[IO]**
Independent Off. Products and Furniture Dealers Assn. **[1698]**
Inst. of Inspection, Cleaning and Restoration Certification **[2259]**
Interior Design Educators Coun. **[8585]**
Interior Design Soc. **[2260]**
Intl. Assn. of Home Staging Professionals **[2261]**
Intl. Assn. of Home Staging Professionals **[IO]**
Intl. Assn. of Lighting Designers **[IO]**
Intl. Assn. of Lighting Designers **[2262]**
Intl. Certified Floorcovering Installers Assn. **[1025]**
Intl. Confed. of Mfrs. of Furnishing Fabrics **[IO]**
Intl. Design Center Berlin **[IO]**
Intl. Design Guild **[IO]**
Intl. Design Guild **[2263]**
Intl. Fed. of Interior Architects/Designers **[IO]**
Intl. Feng Shui Guild **[9906]**
Intl. Furnishings and Design Assn. **[2264]**
Intl. Furnishings and Design Assn. **[IO]**
Intl. Interior Design Assn. **[IO]**
Intl. Interior Design Assn. **[2265]**
Intl. Wallcovering Mfrs. Assn. **[IO]**
Jute Carpet Backing Coun. and Burlap and Jute Assn. **[2266]**
Kitchen Cabinet Mfrs. Assn. **[2267]**

A star before a book entry number signifies that the name is not listed separately, but is mentioned within the entry.

Lighting Union [IO]
Natl. Assn. of Shopfitters [IO]
Natl. Candle Assn. [2268]
Natl. Coun. for Interior Design Qualification [2269]
Natl. Coun. for Interior Design Qualification [IO]
Natl. Floor Covering Assn. [IO]
Natl. Guild of Professional Paperhangers [2270]
Natl. Kitchen and Bath Assn. [2271]
North Amer. Laminate Flooring Assn. [660]
Norwegian Org. of Interior Architects and
    Furniture Designers [IO]
Org. of Black Designers [9907]
Oriental Rug Importers Assn. [2272]
Oriental Rug Retailers of Am. [2273]
Paint and Decorating Retailers Assn. [2274]
Paint and Decorating Retailers Assn. [IO]
Painting and Decorating Assn. of Great Britain
    [IO]
Painting and Decorating Contractors of Am. .
    [1057]
Residential Space Planners Intl. [2275]
Residential Space Planners Intl. [IO]
Scottish Decorators Fed. [IO]
Set Decorators Soc. of Am. [2276]
Soc. of Certified Kitchen Designers [2277]
Soc. for Marketing Professional Services [2649]
Wallcoverings Assn. [2278]
Wax Chandlers' Company [IO]
Window Covering Mfrs. Assn. [2279]
Window Coverings Assn. of Am. [2280]
Interior Design Educ. Foundation [★8585]
Interior Design Educators Coun. [8585], 7150 Win-
    ton Dr., Ste. 300, Indianapolis, IN 46268, (317)328-
    4437
Interior Design Soc. [2260], 3910 Tinsley Dr., Ste.
    101, High Point, NC 27265, (800)888-9590
Interior Designer; Intl. Soc. of [★2265]
Interior Designers; Inst. of Bus. Designers, Coun. for
    Fed. [★2265]
Interior Designers; Natl. Soc. of [★2251]
Interior Insulating Window Inst. - Defunct.
Interior Plantscape Div. - Address unknown since
    1994.
Interior Systems Constr. Assn; Ceilings and [1008]
Interkerkelijke Organisatie voor Ontwikkelingssamen-
    werking [★IO]
Interlac [22042], c/o Kevin McConnell, 6 Stoney
    Bridge Rd., Rockaway, NJ 07866
Interlake Sailing Class Assn. [23178], c/o Ron Gall,
    Sec.-Treas., 2022 Glencove Dr., Toledo, OH
    43609-1945, (419)356-7296
Interlingua Inst. - Defunct.
Interlink Rural Info. Ser. [IO], Nairobi, Kenya
Interlochen Center for the Arts [IO], Interlochen, MI,
    United States
Interlochen Center for the Arts [9571], PO Box 199,
    Interlochen, MI 49643-0199, (231)276-7472
Interlocking Concrete Pavement Inst. [926], 1444 I
    St. NW, Ste. 700, Washington, DC 20005-2210,
    (202)712-9036
Interlocking Concrete Pavement Institute [IO],
    Washington, DC, United States
Interlocking Paving Mfrs. Assn. - Defunct.
Intermarket Agency Network [103], 5307 S 92nd St.,
    Hales Corners, WI 53130, (414)425-8800
Intermarket Agency Network [IO], Hales Corners,
    WI, United States
Intermarket Assn. of Advt. Agencies [★IO]
Intermarket Assn. of Advt. Agencies [★103]
Intermed Intl. [14982], 125-28 Queens Blvd., Ste.
    538, Kew Gardens, NY 11415, (212)327-4940
Intermed Intl. [IO], New York, NY, United States
Intermedia [★IO]
Intermedia [★12376]
Intermediaries and Reinsurance Underwriters Assn.
    [2185], 971 Rte. 202 N, Branchburg, NJ 08876,
    (908)203-0211
Intermediate Technology - Address unknown since
    2003.
Intermediate Tech. Development Gp. - Bangladesh
    [★IO]
Intermediate Tech. Development Gp. - England
    [★IO]
Intermediate Tech. Development Gp. of North Am.
    [16997]

Intermediate Tech. Development Gp. - Peru [IO],
    Lima, Peru
Intermediate Tech. Development Gp. - United
    Kingdom [★IO]
Intermission [★IO]
Intermission [★11985]
Intermodal Assn. of North Am. [3872], 11785 Belts-
    ville Dr., Ste. 1100, Calverton, MD 20705-4049,
    (301)982-3400
Intermodal Inst; Containerization and [978]
Intermodal Marketing Assn. - Defunct.
Intermodal Tank Container Assn. - Defunct.
Intermountain Forest Assn. [1608], 3731 N Ramsey
    Rd., Ste. 110, Coeur d'Alene, ID 83815, (208)667-
    4641
Intermountain Forest Indus. Assn. [★1608]
Intermountain Forestry Services [★1608]
Intermountain Veterinary Medical Assn. [★16817]
Intermuseum Conservation Assn. [10505], 2915
    Detroit Ave., Cleveland, OH 44113, (216)658-8700
Intern Matching Prog; Natl. [★8872]
Intern Programs; Center for Environmental [★8388]
Intern and Resident Matching Prog; Natl. [★8872]
Internacia Esperanto-Asocio de Bibliotekistoj -
    Defunct.
Internacia Esperanto Instituto [★IO]
Internacia Katolika Unio Esperantista [★9915]
Internacia Libro-Klubo Esperanta [IO], Arhus,
    Denmark
Internacia Ligo de Esperantistaj Instruistoj [★IO]
Internacional Socialista [★IO]
Internal Admin. Textbook Prog. [★9261]
Internal Audit Gp; Healthcare [★15061]
Internal Auditors; Assn. of Credit Union [1104]
Internal Auditors; Assn. of Healthcare [15061]
Internal Combustion Engine Inst. [★1291]
Internal Mgt. Consultants; Assn. of [2484]
Internal Medicine
    Alliance for Academic Internal Medicine [8586]
    Amer. Bd. of Internal Medicine [14965]
    Amer. Coll. of Physicians-American Soc. of
        Internal Medicine [14966]
    Amer. Coll. of Veterinary Internal Medicine
        [16767]
    Assn. of Prog. Directors in Internal Medicine
        [14967]
    Assn. of Specialty Professors [8587]
    Assn. of Specialty Professors [IO]
    Clerkship Directors in Internal Medicine [IO]
    Clerkship Directors in Internal Medicine [14968]
    European Fed. of Internal Medicine [IO]
    Intl. Assn. of Colon Therapy [16061]
    Intestinal Disease Found. [14421]
    Italian Soc. of Internal Medicine [IO]
    Japanese Soc. of Internal Medicine [IO]
    Natl. MedPeds Residents' Assn. [14969]
    Soc. of Gen. Internal Medicine [14970]
Internal Medicine; Amer. Coll. of Veterinary [16767]
Internal Medicine Overseas [★15778]
Internal Medicine Overseas [★IO]
Internal Medicine; Soc. of Gen. [14970]
Internal Medicine; Soc. for Res. and Educ. in
    Primary Care [★14970]
Internal Revenue Code; Natl. Org. for the Repeal of
    the Fed. Reserve Act and the [★17666]
Internal Revenue Employees; Natl. Assn. of
    [★24080]
Internal Revenue; Natl. Assn. of Employees of Col-
    lectors of [★24080]
Internal Secretions; Assn. for Stud. of [★14355]
Internasjonal Kvinneliga for Fred og Frihet [★IO]
Internatinaal Juridisch Instituut [★IO]
Internationaal Archief Vromnenbeweging [★IO]
Internationaal Instituut voor Sociale Geschiedenis
    [★IO]
Intl. 50 Foot Yacht Club Assn. - Address unknown
    since 1999.
Intl. 5.5 Class Assn. [IO], The Hague, Netherlands
Intl. 99/4 Users Group - Defunct.
Intl. 190SL Gp. [21663], c/o Shirley Freese,
    Membership Mgr., 258 E Paul Revere Dr., Chester-
    ton, IN 46304-9370, (219)926-3216
Intl. 190SL Lone Gp., Inc. [★21663]
Intl. 210 Assn. [23179], c/o Greg Sullivan, Pres., 59
    Water St., Hingham, MA 02043, (781)749-4141

Intl. 505 Yacht Racing Assn., Amer. Sect. [23180],
    c/o G. Macy Nelson, 401 Washington Ave., Ste.
    803, Towson, MD 21204, (757)897-2127
Intl. Acad. of Aquatic Art [23884], c/o Nadine Pi-
    etrantoni, VP, Membership, 803 E Washington
    Blvd., Lombard, IL 60148
International Academy of Aquatic Art [IO], Lombard,
    IL, United States
Intl. Acad. of Architecture - Bulgaria [IO], Sofia,
    Bulgaria
Intl. Acad. of Astronautics [IO], Paris, France
Intl. Acad. of Aviation and Space Medicine [IO],
    Brossard, QC, Canada
Intl. Acad. for Axiomatic Knowledge, Sci. and Educ.
    [★IO]
Intl. Acad. for Axiomatic Knowledge, Sci. and Educ.
    [★7606]
Intl. Acad. of Behavioral Medicine, Counseling and
    Psychotherapy - Address unknown since 2006.
Intl. Acad. of Biological Medicine - Defunct.
Intl. Acad. of Broadcasting [IO], Dublin, Ireland
Intl. Acad. of Ceramics [IO], Geneva, Switzerland
Intl. Acad. of Child Brain Development [IO], Wynd-
    moor, PA, United States
Intl. Acad. for Child Brain Development [15389], c/o
    Institutes for the Achievement of Human Potential,
    8801 Stenton Ave., Wyndmoor, PA 19038,
    (215)233-2050
Intl. Acad. of Comparative Law [IO], Paris, France
Intl. Acad. of Compounding Pharmacists [15935],
    PO Box 1365, Sugar Land, TX 77487, (281)933-
    8400
Intl. Acad. of Cosmetic Dermatology [14202], c/o
    Larry Millikan, MD, Sec.-Treas., Dept. of Dermatol-
    ogy and Cutaneous Biology, Jefferson Medical
    Coll., 233 S 10th St., Ste. 450, Philadelphia, PA
    19107, (215)503-5786
Intl. Acad. of Cosmetic Dermatology [IO],
    Philadelphia, PA, United States
Intl. Acad. of Cosmetic Surgery [IO], Tokyo, Japan
Intl. Acad. of Cytology [IO], Freiburg, Germany
Intl. Acad. of Gnathology-American Sect. [14158],
    3868 Riviera Dr., Ste. 3B, San Diego, CA 92109-
    6351, (858)273-9263
Intl. Acad. of Health Care Professionals [14705]
Intl. Acad. of Law and Mental Hea. [IO], Montreal,
    QC, Canada
Intl. Acad. of Legal Medicine [IO], Zurich,
    Switzerland
Intl. Acad. of Legal and Social Medicine [★IO]
Intl. Acad. of Linguistic Law [IO], Montreal, QC,
    Canada
Intl. Acad. of Mgt. [IO], Barcelona, Spain
Intl. Acad. of Mgt. - U.S. Br. - Defunct.
Intl. Acad. of Matrimonial Lawyers [IO], Harrogate,
    United Kingdom
Intl. Acad. of Myodontics [IO], Doylestown, PA,
    United States
Intl. Acad. of Myodontics [14159], c/o Dr. Harry N.
    Cooperman, DDS, Pres., 777 Ferry Rd., P-6,
    Doylestown, PA 18901, (215)345-1149
Intl. Acad. of Nutrition and Preventative Medicine
    [★15560]
Intl. Acad. of Nutrition and Preventative Medicine
    [★IO]
Intl. Acad. of Nutritional Consultants [★15540]
Intl. Acad. of Olympic Chiropractic Officers [14006],
    c/o Dr. Stephen J. Press, DC, Chm., 546 Broad
    Ave., Englewood, NJ 07631, (201)569-1444
Intl. Acad. of Olympic Chiropractic Officers [IO],
    Englewood, NJ, United States
Intl. Acad. of Opticianry [★15707]
Intl. Acad. of Optimum Dentistry - Defunct.
Intl. Acad. of Oral Dynamics [★14090]
Intl. Acad. of Oral Medicine and Toxicology [14160],
    8297 Champions Gate Blvd., No. 193, Champions
    Gate, FL 33896, (863)420-6373
Intl. Acad. of Oral Medicine and Toxicology [IO],
    Champions Gate, FL, United States
Intl. Acad. of Orthodontics [★IO]
Intl. Acad. of Orthodontics [★14162]
Intl. Acad. of Osteopathy [IO], Alkmaar, Netherlands
Intl. Acad. of Pathology [IO], Washington, DC,
    United States
Intl. Acad. of Pathology [15868], c/o Dr. Florabel G.
    Mullick, Pres.-Elect, WRAMC, Bldg. 54, Rm.
    N1610, 14th St. and Alaska Ave. NW, Washington,
    DC 20306-6000

Reference to "IO" in place of a book number signifies that the association may be found in the 45th edition of International Organizations.

Intl. Acad. of Periodontology **[IO]**, Bern, Switzerland
Intl. Acad. of Podiatric Medicine - Defunct.
Intl. Acad. of Preventive Medicine **[★15560]**
Intl. Acad. of Preventive Medicine **[★IO]**
Intl. Acad. of Proctology - Defunct.
Intl. Acad. for Quality **[7553]**, c/o ASQ Global Development, 600 N Plankinton Ave., PO Box 3005, Milwaukee, WI 53201, (414)272-8575
Intl. Acad. for Quality **[IO]**, Milwaukee, WI, United States
Intl. Acad. at Santa Barbara - Defunct.
Intl. Acad. of Sciences **[IO]**, Paderborn, Germany
Intl. Acad. for Sports Dentistry **[IO]**, Farmersville, IL, United States
Intl. Acad. for Sports Dentistry **[16481]**, c/o Shelly Lott, Exec. Sec., 118 Faye St., Farmersville, IL 62533, (217)227-3431
Intl. Acad. of Sports Vision - Address unknown since 2005.
Intl. Acad. of TV Arts and Sciences **[560]**, 888 7th St., 5th Fl., New York, NY 10019, (212)489-6969
Intl. Acad. of TV Arts and Sciences **[IO]**, New York, NY, United States
Intl. Acad. of Toxicological Risk Assessment **[★IO]**
Intl. Acad. of Toxicological Risk Assessment **[★4593]**
Intl. Acad. of Trial Lawyers **[5497]**, 5841 Cedar Lake Rd., Ste. 204, Minneapolis, MN 55416-5657, (952)546-2364
Intl. Acad. of Trial Lawyers **[IO]**, Minneapolis, MN, United States
Intl. Acad. of Twirling Teachers - Defunct.
Intl. Accidental War Info. Sharing Proj. **[★18229]**
Intl. Accidental War Info. Sharing Proj. **[★IO]**
Intl. Accounting Standards Bd. **[IO]**, London, United Kingdom
Intl. Accrediting Commn. for Real Estate and Appraisal Educ. and Training **[IO]**, Alexandria, MN, United States
Intl. Accrediting Commn. for Real Estate and Appraisal Educ. and Training **[3313]**, c/o Robert G. Johnson, Exec. Dir., 1224 N Nokomis NE, Alexandria, MN 56308-5072, (320)763-7626
Intl. Acetylene Assn. **[★1721]**
Intl. Action Against Hunger - Cambodia **[★IO]**
Intl. Action Center **[IO]**, New York, NY, United States
Intl. Action Center **[18076]**, 5C Solidarity Center, 55 W 17th St., New York, NY 10011, (212)633-6646
Intl. Action Network on Small Arms **[IO]**, London, United Kingdom
Intl. Actuarial Assn. **[IO]**, Ottawa, ON, Canada
Intl. Acupuncture Assn. of Physical Therapists **[IO]**, Timaru, New Zealand
International Adhesions Society **[IO]**, Dallas, TX, United States
Intl. Adhesions Soc. **[15840]**, c/o Dr. David Wiseman, PhD, Founder, Synechion, Inc., 6757 Arapaho Rd., Ste. 711, No. 238, Dallas, TX 75248, (972)931-5596
Intl. Adoption Assn. - Ireland **[IO]**, Dublin, Ireland
Intl. Advanced Microlithography Soc. - Defunct.
Intl. Advt. Assn. **[104]**, 521 5th Ave., Ste. 1807, New York, NY 10175, (212)557-1133
Intl. Advt. Assn. **[IO]**, New York, NY, United States
Intl. Advt. Festival **[IO]**, London, United Kingdom
Intl. Advisory Coun. for Homosexual Men and Women in Alcoholics Anonymous **[★13283]**
Intl. Aerobatic Club **[23040]**, EAA Aviation Center, PO Box 3086, Oshkosh, WI 54903-3086, (920)426-4800

International Affairs
 Alliance for Peacebuilding **[17248]**
 Amer. Assn. for the Intl. Commn. of Jurists **[17742]**
 Amer. Comm. for Rescue and Resettlement of Iraqi Jews **[17943]**
 Amer. Ireland Fund **[17929]**
 American-Kuwaiti Alliance **[2299]**
 Bridging Nations **[17861]**
 Bus. Assn. Italy Am. **[2300]**
 Bus. Coun. for Intl. Understanding **[17862]**
 Carnegie Coun. for Ethics in Intl. Affairs **[20093]**
 Carnegie Coun. for Ethics in Intl. Affairs **[IO]**
 Carnegie Endowment for Intl. Peace **[17863]**
 Center for Russian and East European Jewry **[17946]**

Coalition of 9/11 Families **[13307]**
Commn. of the Churches on Intl. Affairs **[20094]**
Commission of the Churches on International Affairs **[IO]**
Commn. on Intl. Programs **[17832]**
Comm. for Economic Development **[17455]**
Coun. on Foreign Relations **[17608]**
Croatian Amer. Assn. **[17868]**
EastWest Inst. **[17823]**
Families of September 11 **[18729]**
Foreign Policy Assn. **[17610]**
Found. for Rational Economics and Educ. **[17293]**
Global Interdependence Center **[18835]**
Global Stud. Assn. North Am. **[8583]**
Henry L. Stimson Center **[17824]**
Henry M. Jackson Found. **[17480]**
High Frontier Org. **[18686]**
Hispanic Coun. on Intl. Relations **[17869]**
Intl. Assn. of Space Entrepreneurs **[3634]**
Intl. Center **[17613]**
Intl. Forum on Globalization **[17825]**
Intl. Forum on Globalization **[IO]**
Intl. Peace Operations Assn. **[18213]**
Irish Amer. Unity Conf. **[17932]**
Minority Peace Corps Assn. **[18261]**
Natl. Comm. on Amer. Foreign Policy **[17615]**
Natl. Memorial Inst. for the Prevention of Terrorism **[18734]**
Peace Action **[18166]**
Planning Assistance **[17846]**
Secretary's Open Forum **[17617]**
Sierra Visions **[12444]**
Swiss-American Bus. Coun. **[2314]**
Transnational Diplomatic Network **[17874]**
Trilateral Commn. **[17875]**
Turkish Coalition of Am. **[18754]**
US-Azerbaijan Coun. **[17876]**
U.S.A. - Bus. and Indus. Advisory Comm. to the OECD **[17466]**
Voices of September 11th **[18737]**
William J. Clinton Found. **[17855]**
Win Without War **[18124]**
World Soc. of Mixed Jurisdiction Jurists **[5957]**
Intl. Affairs CH; Women and **[★17578]**
Intl. Affairs CH; Women and **[★IO]**
Intl. Affairs; Commn. on **[★17832]**
Intl. Affairs; Coun. on Religion and **[★20093]**
Intl. Affairs; Natl. Republican Inst. for **[★17396]**
Intl. Affiliation of Sales and Advertising Clubs - Defunct.
Intl. African Inst. **[IO]**, London, United Kingdom
Intl. Afro-American Museum **[★IO]**
Intl. Afro-American Museum **[★9358]**
Intl. Afro-American Museum Comm. **[★9358]**
Intl. Afro-American Museum Comm. **[★IO]**
Intl. Agency for the Prevention of Blindness **[IO]**, Hyderabad, India
Intl. Agency for Res. on Cancer **[IO]**, Lyon, France
Intl. Agnetha Benny Bjorn Frida Fan Club **[IO]**, Roosendaal, Netherlands
Intl. Agricultural Aviation Centre - Defunct.
Intl. Agricultural Aviation Found. - Address unknown since 2004.
Intl. Agricultural Centre **[IO]**, Wageningen, Netherlands
Intl. Agricultural Club - Address unknown since 2003.
Intl. Agricultural Exchange Assn. - United Kingdom **[IO]**, Kenilworth, United Kingdom
Intl. Agriculture Development Ser. **[★IO]**
Intl. Agriculture Development Ser. **[★16959]**
Intl. Aid **[12861]**, 17011 W Hickory, Spring Lake, MI 49456-9712, (616)846-7490
Intl. Aid **[IO]**, Spring Lake, MI, United States
Intl. Aid and Adoption; Amerasians for **[★11642]**
Intl. Aid Services **[IO]**, Vallingby, Sweden
Intl. Aid Serving Kids **[IO]**, Orem, UT, United States
Intl. Aid Serving Kids **[11603]**, c/o Illens Dort, Pres., 1135 N 650 E, Orem, UT 84097
Intl. Aid Sweden **[★IO]**
Intl. AIDS Prospective Epidemiology Network - Defunct.
Intl. AIDS Soc. - USA **[13570]**, 425 California St., Ste. 1450, San Francisco, CA 94104-2120, (415)544-9400
Intl. AIDS Soc. - USA **[IO]**, San Francisco, CA, United States

Intl. AIDS Vaccine Initiative **[IO]**, New York, NY, United States
Intl. AIDS Vaccine Initiative **[13571]**, New York Off., 110 William St., Fl. 27, New York, NY 10038-3901, (212)847-1111
Intl. Aikido Assn. **[23048]**, PO Box 4528, Dallas, TX 75208, (214)943-7530
Intl. Aikido Assn. **[IO]**, Dallas, TX, United States
International Air Cadet Exchange **[★5538]**
The Intl. Air Cargo Assn. **[3873]**, PO Box 661510, Miami, FL 33266-1510, (786)265-7011
The International Air Cargo Association **[IO]**, Miami, FL, United States
Intl. Air Carrier Assn. **[IO]**, Brussels, Belgium
Intl. Air Rail Org. **[IO]**, London, United Kingdom
Intl. Air Transport Assn. - Argentina **[IO]**, Buenos Aires, Argentina
Intl. Air Transport Assn. - Australia **[IO]**, Sydney, Australia
Intl. Air Transport Assn. - Austria **[IO]**, Vienna, Austria
Intl. Air Transport Assn. - Bolivia **[IO]**, La Paz, Bolivia
Intl. Air Transport Assn. - Brazil **[IO]**, Sao Paulo, Brazil
Intl. Air Transport Assn. - Canada **[IO]**, Montreal, QC, Canada
Intl. Air Transport Assn. - Chile **[IO]**, Santiago, Chile
Intl. Air Transport Assn. - Colombia **[IO]**, Bogota, Colombia
Intl. Air Transport Assn. - Costa Rica **[IO]**, San Jose, Costa Rica
Intl. Air Transport Assn. - Ecuador **[IO]**, Quito, Ecuador
Intl. Air Transport Assn. - Egypt **[IO]**, Cairo, Egypt
Intl. Air Transport Assn. - El Salvador **[IO]**, San Salvador, El Salvador
Intl. Air Transport Assn. - India **[IO]**, Bombay, India
Intl. Air Transport Assn. - Indonesia **[IO]**, Jakarta, Indonesia
Intl. Air Transport Assn. - Israel **[IO]**, Tel Aviv, Israel
Intl. Air Transport Assn. - Japan **[IO]**, Tokyo, Japan
Intl. Air Transport Assn. - Jordan **[IO]**, Amman, Jordan
Intl. Air Transport Assn. - Kenya **[IO]**, Nairobi, Kenya
Intl. Air Transport Assn. - Korea **[IO]**, Seoul, Republic of Korea
Intl. Air Transport Assn. - Malaysia **[IO]**, Kuala Lumpur, Malaysia
Intl. Air Transport Assn. - Mexico **[IO]**, Mexico City, Mexico
Intl. Air Transport Assn. - New Zealand **[IO]**, Auckland, New Zealand
Intl. Air Transport Assn. - Panama **[IO]**, Panama City, Panama
Intl. Air Transport Assn. - Philippines **[IO]**, Makati City, Philippines
Intl. Air Transport Assn. - Poland **[IO]**, Warsaw, Poland
Intl. Air Transport Assn. - Portugal **[IO]**, Lisbon, Portugal
Intl. Air Transport Assn. - Romania **[IO]**, Bucharest, Romania
Intl. Air Transport Assn. - Russia **[IO]**, Moscow, Russia
Intl. Air Transport Assn. - Saudi Arabia **[IO]**, Jeddah, Saudi Arabia
Intl. Air Transport Assn. - Singapore **[IO]**, Singapore, Singapore
Intl. Air Transport Assn. - Slovenia **[IO]**, Ljubljana, Slovenia
Intl. Air Transport Assn. - South Africa **[IO]**, Sandton, Republic of South Africa
Intl. Air Transport Assn. - Spain **[IO]**, Madrid, Spain
Intl. Air Transport Assn. - Sweden **[IO]**, Solna, Sweden
Intl. Air Transport Assn. - Switzerland **[IO]**, Geneva, Switzerland
Intl. Air Transport Assn. - Taiwan **[IO]**, Taipei, Taiwan
Intl. Air Transport Assn. - Thailand **[IO]**, Bangkok, Thailand
Intl. Air Transport Assn. - Trinidad and Tobago **[IO]**, Port of Spain, Trinidad and Tobago
Intl. Air Transport Assn. - Turkey **[IO]**, Istanbul, Turkey
Intl. Air Transport Assn. - Uruguay **[IO]**, Montevideo, Uruguay

A star before a book entry number signifies that the name is not listed separately, but is mentioned within the entry.

Intl. Air Transport Assn. - Venezuela **[IO]**, Caracas, Venezuela

Intl. Airforwarders and Agents Assn. - Address unknown since 1990.

Intl. Airline Navigators Coun. - Defunct.

Intl. Airline Passengers Assn. **[23015]**, PO Box 700188, Dallas, TX 75370-0188, (972)404-9980

Intl. Airline Passengers Assn. **[IO]**, Dallas, TX, United States

Intl. Airline Passengers Assn. - London **[IO]**, Croydon, United Kingdom

Intl. Airline Passengers' Assn. - United Kingdom **[IO]**, London, United Kingdom

Intl. Al Jolson Soc. **[IO]**, Orlando, FL, United States

Intl. Al Jolson Soc. **[24911]**, c/o Mr. Tom Nestor, Treas., 1709 Billingshurst Ct., Orlando, FL 32825

Intl. Alban Berg Soc. - Address unknown since 2002.

Intl. Allergy Assn. - Defunct.

Intl. Alliance of ALS/MND Associations **[IO]**, Northampton, United Kingdom

The Intl. Alliance, An Assn. of Executive and Professional Women **[★IO]**

The Intl. Alliance, An Assn. of Executive and Professional Women **[★728]**

Intl. Alliance for Animal Therapy and Healing **[13703]**, c/o Maryann Adams, PO Box 1255, Winters, CA 95694, (530)795-5040

International Alliance for Animal Therapy and Healing **[IO]**, Winters, CA, United States

Intl. Alliance of Avaya Users **[3745]**, c/o Renee Seay, CEO, Bldg. 960, 2nd Fl., 1 Franklin Pkwy., San Mateo, CA 94403, (781)251-7857

Intl. Alliance of Bill Posters, Billers and Distributors of U.S. and Canada - Defunct.

Intl. Alliance for Child and Adolescent Mental Hea. and Schools **[15204]**, Educ. Development Center, Inc., Hea. and Human Development Programs, 55 Chapel St., Newton, MA 02458-1060

Intl. Alliance of Equestrian Journalists **[IO]**, Aurora, ON, Canada

Intl. Alliance of Grant Writers and Nonprofit Consultants - Address unknown since 2006.

Intl. Alliance of Healthcare Educators **[8475]**, 11211 Prosperity Farms Rd., Ste. D-325, Palm Beach Gardens, FL 33410, (561)622-4334

Intl. Alliance of Holistic Lawyers **[5498]**, PO Box 371, Milton, DE 19968

Intl. Alliance of Indigenous and Tribal Peoples of Tropical Forests **[IO]**, Chiang Mai, Thailand

International Alliance for Interoperability **[IO]**, Washington, DC, United States

Intl. Alliance for Interoperability **[7018]**, 1090 Vermont Ave. NW, Ste. 700, Washington, DC 20005-4905, (202)289-7800

Intl. Alliance of Law Firms **[IO]**, London, United Kingdom

Intl. Alliance of Messianic Congregations and Synagogues **[IO]**, Sarasota, FL, United States

Intl. Alliance of Messianic Congregations and Synagogues **[20254]**, PO Box 20006, Sarasota, FL 34276-3006, (941)923-0193

Intl. Alliance of New Catholic Churches - Address unknown since 2004.

Intl. Alliance of Nutrimedical Assns. - Address unknown since 1999.

Intl. Alliance of Patients' Organizations **[IO]**, London, United Kingdom

Intl. Alliance in Ser. and Educ. **[11748]**, 101 California St., Ste. 2450, San Francisco, CA 94111, (415)982-1296

Intl. Alliance for Sustainable Agriculture **[★4641]**

Intl. Alliance of Theatrical Stage Employees, Motion Picture Technicians, Artists and Allied Crafts of the U.S. and Canada **[★24156]**

Intl. Alliance of Theatrical Stage Employees, Motion Picture Technicians, Artists and Allied Crafts of the U.S. and Canada **[★IO]**

Intl. Alliance of Theatrical Stage Employees, Motion Picture Technicians, Artists and Allied Crafts of the U.S., U.S. Territories and Canada **[★IO]**

Intl. Alliance of Theatrical Stage Employees, Motion Picture Technicians, Artists and Allied Crafts of the U.S., U.S. Territories and Canada **[★24156]**

Intl. Alliance of Theatrical Stage Employees, Moving Picture Technicians, Artists and Allied Crafts of the U.S., Its Territories and Canada **[24156]**, 1430 Broadway, 20th Fl., New York, NY 10018, (212)730-1770

Intl. Alliance of Theatrical Stage Employees, Moving Picture Technicians, Artists and Allied Crafts of the U.S., Its Territories and Canada **[IO]**, New York, NY, United States

Intl. Alliance of Women **[IO]**, Ansfelden, Austria

Intl. Alliance of Women **[IO]**, Vienna, Austria

The Intl. Alliance for Women **[IO]**, McLean, VA, United States

The Intl. Alliance for Women **[728]**, 8405 Greensboro Dr., Ste. 800, McLean, VA 22102-5120, (703)506-3284

Intl. Alliance for Women in Music **[10612]**, Univ. of Maryland/Baltimore County, Dept. of Music, FA 509, 1000 Hilltop Cir., Baltimore, MD 21250, (623)556-2276

Intl. Alliance for Women in Music **[IO]**, Winter Park, FL, United States

Intl. Alliance for Youth Sports **[23994]**, 2050 Vista Pkwy., West Palm Beach, FL 33411, (561)684-1141

Intl. Allied Printing Trades Assn. **[24084]**, 501 3rd St. NW, Ste. 950, Washington, DC 20001, (202)434-1248

Intl. Aloe Sci. Coun. **[1863]**, 415 E Airport Fwy., Ste. 150, Irving, TX 75062-6350, (972)258-8772

Intl. Aloe Sci. Coun. **[IO]**, Irving, TX, United States

Intl. Aluminium Inst. **[IO]**, London, United Kingdom

Intl. Alumni Assn. of Shri Mahavir Jain Vidyalaya **[IO]**, Garner, NC, United States

Intl. Alumni Assn. of Shri Mahavir Jain Vidyalaya **[19346]**, 1119 Flanders St., Garner, NC 27529, (919)772-8473

Intl. Amateur Athletic Fed. **[★IO]**

Intl. Amateur Basketball Fed. **[★IO]**

Intl. Amateur Boat Building Soc. - Defunct.

Intl. Amateur Boxing Assn. - Address unknown since 1990.

Intl. Amateur-Professional Photoelectric Photometry **[6505]**, 4229 Franklin Rd., Nashville, TN 37204, (615)383-4630

International Amateur-Professional Photoelectric Photometry **[IO]**, Brentwood, TN, United States

Intl. Amateur Radio Union **[IO]**, Newington, CT, United States

Intl. Amateur Radio Union **[21501]**, PO Box 310905, Newington, CT 06131-0905, (860)594-0200

Intl. Amateur Snowshoe Racing Fed. - Address unknown since 2007.

Intl. Amateur Swimming Fed. **[IO]**, Lausanne, Switzerland

Intl. Amateur Theatre Assn. **[IO]**, Tallinn, Estonia

Intl. Amateur Wrestling Fed. **[★IO]**

Intl. Amer. Albino Assn. **[★4855]**

Intl. and Amer. Assn. of Clinical Nutritionists **[IO]**, Addison, TX, United States

Intl. and Amer. Associations of Clinical Nutritionists **[15560]**, 15280 Addison Rd., Ste. 130, Addison, TX 75001, (972)407-9089

Intl. Amer. Saddlebred Pleasure Horse Assn. **[★4842]**

Intl. Ammunition Assn. - Defunct.

Intl. Amphicar Owners Club **[21664]**, 202 E Nebraska Ave., Berthoud, CO 80513

Intl. Anchoritic Soc. **[10460]**, c/o Susannah Mary Chewning, Founder, Union County Coll., Dept. of English, 1033 Springfield Ave., Cranford, NJ 07016, (908)709-7182

Intl. Andalusian and Lusitano Horse Assn. **[4894]**, 101 Carnoustie N, Box 200, Birmingham, AL 35242, (205)995-8900

International Andalusian and Lusitano Horse Association **[IO]**, Birmingham, AL, United States

Intl. Anesthesia Res. Soc. **[IO]**, Cleveland, OH, United States

Intl. Anesthesia Res. Soc. **[13684]**, 2 Summit Park Dr., Ste. 140, Cleveland, OH 44131-2571, (216)642-1124

Intl. Animal Rescue - UK **[IO]**, Uckfield, United Kingdom

Intl. Animal Rights Alliance - Defunct.

Intl. Animated Film Assn. **[IO]**, Zagreb, Croatia

Intl. Animated Film Assn. - Canada **[IO]**, Ville St.-Laurent, QC, Canada

Intl. Animated Film Soc., ASIFA - Hollywood **[1383]**, 2114 Burbank Blvd., Burbank, CA 91506, (818)842-8330

Intl. Animated Film Soc. - Hollywood **[★1383]**

Intl. A.N.S.W.E.R. Coalition - Act Now to Stop War and End Racism **[18210]**, 1247 E St. SE, Washington, DC 20003, (202)544-3389

Intl. A.N.S.W.E.R. Coalition - Act Now to Stop War and End Racism **[IO]**, Washington, DC, United States

Intl. Antarctic Glaciological Project - Defunct.

Intl. Anti-Euthanasia Task Force **[★12133]**

Intl. Anticounterfeiting Coalition **[17333]**, 1730 M St. NW, Ste. 1020, Washington, DC 20036, (202)223-6667

International Anticounterfeiting Coalition **[IO]**, Washington, DC, United States

Intl. Apparel Fed. **[IO]**, Zeist, Netherlands

Intl. Apple Assn. **[★IO]**

Intl. Apple Assn. **[★4768]**

Intl. Apple Inst. **[★4768]**

Intl. Apple Inst. **[★IO]**

Intl. Appropriate Technology Assn. - Defunct.

Intl. Aquaculture Found. - Defunct.

Intl. Aquarium Soc. - Address unknown since 2002.

Intl. Arabian Horse Assn. **[4895]**

International Arabian Horse Association **[IO]**, Aurora, CO, United States

Intl. Arabian Horse Registry of North America - Address unknown since 2001.

Intl. Archery Fed. **[IO]**, Lausanne, Switzerland

Intl. Architects Designers Planners for Social Responsibility **[IO]**, Stockholm, Sweden

Intl. Arctic Sci. Comm. **[IO]**, Stockholm, Sweden

Intl. Arid Lands Consortium **[IO]**, Tucson, AZ, United States

Intl. Arid Lands Consortium **[4577]**, c/o Dr. Jim P.M. Chamie, Managing Dir., 1955 E 6th St., Tucson, AZ 85719-5224, (520)621-3024

Intl. Aroid Soc. **[22520]**, c/o Dan Levin, Pres., 255 King Ave., Piedmont, CA 94610, (510)547-5052

Intl. Aroid Soc. **[IO]**, Piedmont, CA, United States

Intl. Aromatherapy and Herb Assn. **[IO]**, Phoenix, AZ, United States

Intl. Aromatherapy and Herb Assn. **[13636]**, c/o Jeffrey Schiller, Pres., 3541 W Acapulco Ln., Phoenix, AZ 85053, (602)938-4439

Intl. Arthroscopy Assn. **[★15771]**

Intl. Arthroscopy Assn. **[★IO]**

Intl. Arthur Schnitzler Res. Assn. - Address unknown since 2002.

Intl. Arthurian Soc., North Amer. Br. **[10422]**, c/o Logan E. Whalen, Sec.-Treas., Univ. of Oklahoma, Dept. of Modern Languages, Literatures, and Linguistics, 780 Van Vleet Oval, Rm. 206, Norman, OK 73019-2032, (405)325-6181

Intl. Arthurian Soc., North Amer. Br. **[IO]**, Norman, OK, United States

Intl. Article Numbering Assn. - EAN **[★IO]**

Intl. Artificial Intelligence in Educ. Soc. **[IO]**, Falmer, United Kingdom

Intl. Artist Managers' Assn. **[IO]**, London, United Kingdom

Intl. Artists Network **[9506]**

Intl. Arts and Artists **[9572]**, 9 Hillyer Ct. NW, 2nd Fl., Washington, DC 20008, (202)338-0680

Intl. Arts and Artists **[IO]**, Washington, DC, United States

Intl. Arts Medicine Assn. **[IO]**, Bryn Mawr, PA, United States

Intl. Arts Medicine Assn. **[7972]**, 714 Old Lancaster Rd., Bryn Mawr, PA 19010, (610)525-3784

Intl. Asclepiad Soc. **[IO]**, Burgess Hill, United Kingdom

International Assembly for Collegiate Business Education **[IO]**, Olathe, KS, United States

Intl. Assembly for Collegiate Bus. Educ. **[8024]**, PO Box 3960, Olathe, KS 66063, (913)631-3009

Intl. Assembly of Grocery Mfrs. Associations **[★1521]**

Intl. Assembly of Grocery Mfrs. Associations **[★IO]**

Intl. Assembly of Leathercraftsmen - Defunct.

Intl. Assn. of Accident and Hea. Underwriters **[★2208]**

Intl. Assn. of Accident Reconstruction Specialists **[2410]**, PO Box 534, Grand Ledge, MI 48837-0534, (517)622-3135

International Association of Accident Reconstruction Specialists **[IO]**, Grand Ledge, MI, United States

---

Reference to "IO" in place of a book number signifies that the association may be found in the 45th edition of International Organizations.

International Association of Addictions and Offender Counselors **[IO]**, Baltimore, MD, United States

Intl. Assn. of Addictions and Offender Counselors **[11824]**, PO Box 791006, Baltimore, MD 21279-1006, (800)347-6647

Intl. Assn. of Administrative Professionals **[66]**, 10502 NW Ambassador Dr., PO Box 20404, Kansas City, MO 64195-0404, (816)891-6600

Intl. Assn. of Administrative Professionals **[IO]**, Kansas City, MO, United States

Intl. Assn. for Adolescent Hea. **[IO]**, Christchurch, New Zealand

Intl. Assn. for the Advancement of Earth and Environmental Sciences **[4511]**

Intl. Assn. for the Advancement of Ethnology and Eugenics **[★4512]**

Intl. Assn. for the Advancement of Ethnology and Eugenics **[★IO]**

Intl. Assn. for the Advancement of High Pressure Science and Technology - Address unknown since 1995.

Intl. Assn. for the Advancement of Teaching and Res. in Intellectual Property **[IO]**, Montreal, QC, Canada

Intl. Assn. of African and Amer. Black Business People - Address unknown since 1999.

Intl. Assn. of African-American Music **[10613]**, PO Box 382, Gladwyne, PA 19035, (610)664-8292

Intl. Assn. of African-American Music **[IO]**, Gladwyne, PA, United States

Intl. Assn. Against Painful Experiments on Animals **[IO]**, Hayling Island, United Kingdom

Intl. Assn. of Agricultural Economists **[IO]**, Oak Brook, IL, United States

Intl. Assn. of Agricultural Economists **[6881]**, c/o Dr. Walter J. Armbruster, Sec.-Treas., 1301 W 22nd St., Ste. 615, Oak Brook, IL 60523-2197, (630)571-9393

Intl. Assn. of Agricultural Info. Specialists **[IO]**, Wallingford, United Kingdom

Intl. Assn. of Agricultural Librarians and Documentalists **[★IO]**

Intl. Assn. of Agricultural Medicine and Rural Hea. **[IO]**, Budapest, Hungary

Intl. Assn. of Agricultural Museums **[IO]**, Roznov pod Radhostem, Czech Republic

Intl. Assn. of Agricultural Students **[★IO]**

Intl. Assn. of Air Travel Couriers **[IO]**, Ames, IA, United States

Intl. Assn. of Air Travel Couriers **[153]**, PO Box 1832, Ames, IA 50010, (515)292-2458

Intl. Assn. of Air Travel Couriers - UK **[IO]**, Chepstow, United Kingdom

Intl. Assn. of Airborne Veterans **[21303]**

Intl. Assn. of Airline Internal Auditors **[IO]**, Dubai, United Arab Emirates

Intl. Assn. of Airline Nurses - Address unknown since 2002.

Intl. Assn. of Airport Duty Free Stores **[3409]**, 2025 M St. NW, Ste. 800, Washington, DC 20036-3309, (202)367-1184

Intl. Assn. of Airport Duty Free Stores **[IO]**, Washington, DC, United States

Intl. Assn. of Airport and Seaport Police **[IO]**, Coquitlam, BC, Canada

Intl. Assn. of Allergology **[★IO]**

Intl. Assn. of Allergology **[★13605]**

Intl. Assn. of Allergology and Clinical Immunology **[★13605]**

Intl. Assn. of Allergology and Clinical Immunology **[★IO]**

Intl. Assn. of ALS/MND Associations **[★IO]**

Intl. Assn. of Amateur Baseball **[★IO]**

Intl. Assn. of Amateur Boat Builders - Address unknown since 1987.

Intl. Assn. for Ambulatory Surgery **[IO]**, London, United Kingdom

Intl. Assn. of Amusement Parks **[★IO]**

Intl. Assn. of Amusement Parks **[★1303]**

Intl. Assn. of Amusement Parks & Attractions **[★1296]**

Intl. Assn. of Amusement Parks and Attractions **[1303]**, 1448 Duke St., Alexandria, VA 22314, (703)836-4800

Intl. Assn. of Amusement Parks & Attractions **[★IO]**

Intl. Assn. of Amusement Parks and Attractions **[IO]**, Alexandria, VA, United States

Intl. Assn. for Analytical Psychology **[IO]**, Zurich, Switzerland

Intl. Assn. of Animal Behavior Consultants **[7864]**, 505 Timber Ln., Jefferson Hills, PA 15025

Intl. Assn. of Animal Massage and Bodywork **[15028]**, 3347 McGregor Ln., Toledo, OH 43623, (419)727-6917

Intl. Assn. of Animal Massage and Bodywork **[IO]**, Toledo, OH, United States

International Association of Antarctica Tour Operators **[IO]**, Basalt, CO, United States

Intl. Assn. of Antarctica Tour Operators **[3921]**, c/o Denise Landau, Exec. Dir., PO Box 2178, Basalt, CO 81621, (970)704-1047

Intl. Assn. of Applied Linguistics **[IO]**, Erfurt, Germany

Intl. Assn. of Applied Psychology **[IO]**, Madrid, Spain

Intl. Assn. of Approved Basketball Officials **[IO]**, Germantown, MD, United States

Intl. Assn. of Approved Basketball Officials **[23130]**, PO Box 1300, Germantown, MD 20875-1300, (301)540-5180

Intl. Assn. for Aquatic Animal Medicine **[16792]**, c/o Judy St. Leger, DVM, Membership Chair, 500 Sea World Dr., San Diego, CA 92109-7904, (619)225-4259

Intl. Assn. for Aquatic Animal Medicine **[IO]**, San Diego, CA, United States

Intl. Assn. of Aquatic and Marine Sci. Libraries and Info. Centers **[IO]**, Newport, OR, United States

Intl. Assn. of Aquatic and Marine Sci. Libraries and Info. Centers **[10361]**, c/o Janet Webster, Librarian, Hatfield Marine Sci. Center, Oregon State Univ., 2030 S Marine Sci. Dr., Newport, OR 97365

Intl. Assn. of Architectural Photographers **[2999]**, 2901 136th St. NW, Gig Harbor, WA 98332-9111, (877)845-4783

Intl. Assn. of Architectural Photographers **[IO]**, Gig Harbor, WA, United States

Intl. Assn. of Arson Investigators **[IO]**, Crofton, MD, United States

Intl. Assn. of Arson Investigators **[5716]**, 2151 Priest Bridge Dr., Ste. 25, Crofton, MD 21114, (410)451-FIRE

Intl. Assn. for Art, Creativity and Therapy **[IO]**, Basel, Switzerland

Intl. Assn. of Art Critics - Canada Sect. **[IO]**, Toronto, ON, Canada

Intl. Assn. of Art Critics - France **[IO]**, Paris, France

Intl. Assn. of Art Critics - Germany **[IO]**, Cologne, Germany

Intl. Assn. of Art Critics - Hong Kong **[IO]**, Hong Kong, People's Republic of China

Intl. Assn. of Art Critics - Ireland **[IO]**, Dublin, Ireland

Intl. Assn. of Art Critics - Taiwan **[IO]**, Changhua City, Taiwan

Intl. Assn. of Art Critics - U.S. Sect. **[9573]**, 333 E 55th St., No. 3B, New York, NY 10022, (212)838-2475

Intl. Assn. for Artificial Intelligence and Law **[6730]**, c/o Carole D. Hafner, Sec.-Treas., Coll. of Cmpt. and Info. Sci., Northeastern Univ., 202 WVH, Boston, MA 02115, (617)373-5116

Intl. Assn. of Arts and Cultural Mgt. **[IO]**, Montreal, QC, Canada

Intl. Assn. of Asian Crime Investigators **[IO]**, Marina, CA, United States

Intl. Assn. of Asian Crime Investigators **[5636]**, PO Box 1327, Marina, CA 93933, (831)901-4595

Intl. Assn. of Asian Stud. **[7986]**, PO Box 6670, Scarborough, ME 04070-6670, (207)839-8004

Intl. Assn. of Asian Stud. **[IO]**, Scarborough, ME, United States

Intl. Assn. of Assembly Managers **[IO]**, Coppell, TX, United States

Intl. Assn. of Assembly Managers **[2671]**, 635 Fritz Dr., Ste. 100, Coppell, TX 75019-4442, (972)906-7441

Intl. Assn. of Assessing Officers **[6296]**, 314 W 10th St., Kansas City, MO 64105-1616, (816)701-8100

Intl. Assn. of Assessing Officers **[IO]**, Kansas City, MO, United States

Intl. Assn. of Assistance Dog Partners **[14241]**, c/o Editor/Information and Advocacy Center, 38691 Filly Dr., Sterling Heights, MI 48310, (586)826-3938

International Assn. of Assn. Mgt. Companies **[★314]**

International Assn. of Assn. Mgt. Companies **[★IO]**

Intl. Assn. of Astacology **[IO]**, Auburn University, AL, United States

Intl. Assn. of Astacology **[7174]**, c/o Bill Daniels, Sec., Auburn Univ., Dept. of Fisheries and Allied Aquaculture, Rm. 123, Swingle Hall, Auburn University, AL 36849-5419, (334)844-9123

Intl. Assn. of Asthmology **[IO]**, Telese Terme, Italy

Intl. Assn. of Athletics Federations **[IO]**, Monaco, Monaco

International Association of Attorneys and Executives in Corporate Real Estate **[IO]**, Frankfort, IL, United States

Intl. Assn. of Attorneys and Executives in Corporate Real Estate **[3314]**, c/o Lisa V. Carreras, Exec. VP/Dir., 20106 S Sycamore Dr., Frankfort, IL 60423, (815)464-6019

Intl. Assn. of Audio Info. Services **[16856]**, c/o Linda Ornt, Sec., Triangle Radio Reading Ser., 211 E Six Forks Rd., No. 103, Raleigh, NC 27609, (919)832-5138

Intl. Assn. of Audio Info. Services **[IO]**, Durham, NC, United States

Intl. Assn. of Audio Visual Communicators **[IO]**, Ocotillo, CA, United States

Intl. Assn. of Audio Visual Communicators **[1384]**, 57 W Palo Verde Ave., PO Box 250, Ocotillo, CA 92259-0250, (760)358-7000

Intl. Assn. for Audio-Visual Media in Historical Res. and Education - Address unknown since 1995.

Intl. Assn. of Auditorium Managers **[★2671]**

Intl. Assn. of Auditorium Managers **[★IO]**

Intl. Assn. Auto Theft Investigators **[IO]**, Clinton, NY, United States

Intl. Assn. Auto Theft Investigators **[5971]**, c/o John V. Abounader, Exec. Dir., PO Box 223, Clinton, NY 13323-0223, (315)853-1913

Intl. Assn. of Automotive Modelers - Defunct.

Intl. Assn. of Avian Trainers and Educators **[21847]**, 350 St. Andrews Fairway, Memphis, TN 38111, (901)685-9122

Intl. Assn. of Avian Trainers and Educators **[IO]**, Memphis, TN, United States

Intl. Assn. of Baptist Colleges and Universities **[9276]**, 8120 Sawyer Brown Rd., Ste. 108, Nashville, TN 37221-1410, (615)673-1896

Intl. Assn. for Bear Res. and Mgt. **[5325]**, c/o Joseph Clark, Sec., Southern Appalachian Field Lab., Univ. of Tennessee, 274 Ellington Hall, Knoxville, TN 37996, (865)974-4790

Intl. Assn. for Bear Res. and Mgt. **[★5325]**

International Association for Bear Research and Management **[IO]**, Knoxville, TN, United States

Intl. Assn. for Bear Res. and Mgt. **[★IO]**

Intl. Assn. of Bedding and Furniture Law Officials **[5823]**, c/o Joan C. Jordan, Pres., Dept. of Consumer Protection, 165 Capitol Ave., Hartford, CT 06106, (860)713-6123

Intl. Assn. of Biblical Counselors **[19867]**, 11500 Sheridan Blvd., Westminster, CO 80020, (303)469-4222

Intl. Assn. of Biblical Counselors **[IO]**, Westminster, CO, United States

Intl. Assn. of Bioethics **[IO]**, Quezon City, Philippines

Intl. Assn. for Biological Oceanography **[IO]**, Warkworth, New Zealand

Intl. Assn. of Biological Standardization **[★IO]**

Intl. Assn. of Biological Technicians **[IO]**, Neuilly-sur-Marne, France

Intl. Assn. for Biologicals **[IO]**, Acacias-Geneva, Switzerland

Intl. Assn. of Biomedical Lab. Sci. **[★IO]**

Intl. Assn. for Biometrics **[IO]**, Northampton, United Kingdom

Intl. Assn. of Black Actuaries **[IO]**, Chicago, IL, United States

Intl. Assn. of Black Actuaries **[2186]**, c/o Mosher and Associates, 19 S LaSalle St., Ste. 1400, Chicago, IL 60603, (919)317-4105

Intl. Assn. of Black Business Educators - Defunct.

Intl. Assn. of Black Professional Fire Fighters **[5717]**, 1020 N Taylor Ave., St. Louis, MO 63113, (786)229-6914

Intl. Assn. of Black Professional Fire Fighters **[IO]**, St. Louis, MO, United States

A star before a book entry number signifies that the name is not listed separately, but is mentioned within the entry.

International Association of Bloodstain Pattern Analysts [IO], Tucson, AZ, United States

Intl. Assn. of Bloodstain Pattern Analysts [5637], 12139 E Makohoh Trail, Tucson, AZ 85749-8179, (520)760-6620

Intl. Assn. of Blue Print and Allied Indus. [★1801]

Intl. Assn. of Blue Print and Allied Indus. [★IO]

Intl. Assn. of Boards of Examiners in Optometry [★IO]

Intl. Assn. of Boards of Examiners in Optometry [★15716]

Intl. Assn. of Bomb Technicians and Investigators [7077], PO Box 160, Goldvein, VA 22720-0160, (540)752-4533

Intl. Assn. of Bomb Technicians and Investigators [IO], Goldvein, VA, United States

Intl. Assn. of Book-Keepers [IO], Sevenoaks, United Kingdom

Intl. Assn. of Book Publishing Consultants - Address unknown since 2004.

Intl. Assn. of Book Trade Consultants - Defunct.

Intl. Assn. of Botanical and Mycological Societies [IO], Vienna, Austria

Intl. Assn. for Bridge Maintenance and Safety [IO], Bethlehem, PA, United States

Intl. Assn. for Bridge Maintenance and Safety [538], c/o Prof. Dan M. Frangopol, Pres., ATLSS Ctr., Lehigh Univ., 117 ATLSS Dr., Imbt Labs, Bethlehem, PA 18015-4729, (610)758-6103

Intl. Assn. for Bridge and Structural Engg. [IO], Zurich, Switzerland

Intl. Assn. of Bridge, Structural, Ornamental and Reinforcing Iron Workers [24134], 1750 New York Ave. NW, Ste. 400, Washington, DC 20006, (202)383-4800

Intl. Assn. of Broadcast Meteorology [IO], Wexford, Ireland

Intl. Assn. of Broadcast Monitors [IO], Meriden, NH, United States

Intl. Assn. of Broadcast Monitors [561], c/o Clara McNamara, Exec. Dir./Librarian, PO Box 422, Meriden, NH 03770, (603)469-3054

Intl. Assn. of Broadcasting Mfrs. [IO], Reading, United Kingdom

Intl. Assn. of Buddhist Stud. [IO], Lausanne, Switzerland

Intl. Assn. of Building Companions [IO], Vienna, Austria

Intl. Assn. of Building Services Contractors [IO], Munich, Germany

Intl. Assn. of Bus. - Address unknown since 2004.

Intl. Assn. of Bus. Communicators [879], 1 Hallidie Plz., Ste. 600, San Francisco, CA 94102-2818, (415)544-4700

Intl. Assn. of Bus. Communicators [IO], Calgary, AB, Canada

Intl. Assn. of Bus. Communicators [IO], San Francisco, CA, United States

Intl. Assn. of Bus. Communicators - BC Chap. [IO], Vancouver, BC, Canada

Intl. Assn. of Bus. Communicators Calgary [IO], Calgary, AB, Canada

Intl. Assn. of Bus. Communicators - Hong Kong [IO], Hong Kong, People's Republic of China

Intl. Assn. of Bus. Communicators Malaysia Chap. [IO], Petaling Jaya, Malaysia

Intl. Assn. of Bus. Communicators Manitoba [IO], Winnipeg, MB, Canada

Intl. Assn. of Bus. Communicators Newfoundland and Labrador [IO], St. John's, NL, Canada

Intl. Assn. of Bus. Communicators Ottawa [IO], Ottawa, ON, Canada

Intl. Assn. of Bus. Communicators Philippines [IO], Makati City, Philippines

Intl. Assn. of Bus. Communicators Polar Chap. [IO], Yellowknife, NT, Canada

Intl. Assn. of Bus. Communicators Regina [IO], Regina, SK, Canada

Intl. Assn. of Bus. Communicators Saskatoon [IO], Saskatoon, SK, Canada

Intl. Assn. of Bus. Forecasting - Address unknown since 2006.

Intl. Assn. for Bus. Organizations [3610], 3 Woodthorn Ct., Ste. 12, Owings Mills, MD 21117, (410)581-1373

Intl. Assn. for Bus. Organizations [IO], Owings Mills, MD, United States

Intl. Assn. for Bus. and Soc. [IO], Washington, DC, United States

Intl. Assn. for Bus. and Soc. [8025], c/o Jenn Griffin, Exec. Dir., 2201 G St. NW, Funger 615, George Washington Univ. School of Bus., Washington, DC 20052, (202)994-2536

Intl. Assn. of Business Strategy Consultants - Defunct.

Intl. Assn. of Businesses [★1464]

Intl. Assn. of Butterfly Exhibitions [1341], PO Box 240757, St. Paul, MN 55124, (952)212-4757

Intl. Assn. of Butterfly Exhibitions [IO], St. Paul, MN, United States

Intl. Assn. of Calculator Collectors - Defunct.

Intl. Assn. of Campus Law Enforcement Administrators [9084], 342 N Main St., Ste. 301, West Hartford, CT 06117-2507, (860)586-7517

Intl. Assn. of Campus Law Enforcement Administrators [IO], West Hartford, CT, United States

Intl. Assn. of Cancer Registries [IO], Lyon, France

Intl. Assn. of Cancer Victims and Friends [★IO]

Intl. Assn. of Cancer Victims and Friends [★13831]

Intl. Assn. of Cancer Victors and Friends [13831], 7740 W Manchester Ave., Ste. 203, Playa del Rey, CA 90293, (310)822-5032

Intl. Assn. of Cancer Victors and Friends [IO], Santa Clarita, CA, United States

Intl. Assn. of Canine Professionals [IO], Montverde, FL, United States

Intl. Assn. of Canine Professionals [1161], PO Box 560156, Montverde, FL 34756-0156, (407)469-2008

Intl. Assn. of Career Consulting Firms - Defunct.

Intl. Assn. of Career Mgt. Professionals [★782]

Intl. Assn. of Career Mgt. Professionals [★IO]

Intl. Assn. for Cereal Sci. and Tech. [IO], Vienna, Austria

Intl. Assn. of Chain Stores [★IO]

Intl. Assn. of Chain Stores [★3404]

Intl. Assn. of Character Cities [11781], 520 W Main St., Oklahoma City, OK 73102, (405)815-0001

Intl. Assn. of Character Cities [IO], Oklahoma City, OK, United States

Intl. Assn. of Charities [IO], Louvain-la-Neuve, Belgium

Intl. Assn. of Chiefs of Police [IO], Alexandria, VA, United States

Intl. Assn. of Chiefs of Police [5972], 515 N Washington St., Alexandria, VA 22314-2344, (703)836-6767

Intl. Assn. for Child and Adolescent Psychiatry and Allied Professions [IO], Stockholm, Sweden

Intl. Assn. for Child and Adolescent Psychiatry and Allied Professions Germany [IO], Stockholm, Sweden

Intl. Assn. for Child Psychiatry and Allied Professions [★IO]

Intl. Assn. of Children's Intl. Simmer Villages [★IO]

Intl. Assn. for the Child's Right to Play - Address unknown since 1999.

Intl. Assn. of Chinese Linguistics [7243], c/o Audrey Li, Treas., East Asian Languages and Cultures, THH 356M, Univ. of Southern California, Los Angeles, CA 90089-0357

Intl. Assn. of Chinese Linguistics [IO], Los Angeles, CA, United States

Intl. Assn. of Christian Chaplains [19748], 5804 Babcock Rd., San Antonio, TX 78240-2134, (210)696-7313

Intl. Assn. for Chronic Fatigue Syndrome [14266], 27 N Wacker Dr., Ste. 416, Chicago, IL 60606, (847)258-7248

Intl. Assn. of Cities and Ports [IO], Le Havre, France

Intl. Assn. for Citizenship Social and Economics Educ. [IO], Stoke-On-Trent, United Kingdom

Intl. Assn. of Civil Aviation Chaplains [IO], Johannesburg, Republic of South Africa

Intl. Assn. of Civil Defense Public Information Officers - Defunct.

Intl. Assn. of Civil Engg. Students [IO], Wuppertal, Germany

Intl. Assn. of Clan MacInnes [20951], c/o Randy McInnis, Chm., Scholarship Comm., 1413 Autumn Ridge Ln., Fort Mill, SC 29708

Intl. Assn. for Classical Archaeology [IO], Rome, Italy

Intl. Assn. of Classification Societies [IO], London, United Kingdom

Intl. Assn. for Clear Thinking - Address unknown since 2001.

Intl. Assn. of Clerks, Recorders, Election Officials and Treasurers [5775], 2400 Augusta Dr., Ste. 250, Houston, TX 77057, (630)407-5600

Intl. Assn. of Clerks, Recorders, Election Officials and Treasurers [IO], Houston, TX, United States

Intl. Assn. of Clinical BioChemists [★IO]

Intl. Assn. of Clinical Laser Acupuncturists - Address unknown since 1999.

Intl. Assn. of Clothing Designers [★241]

Intl. Assn. of Clothing Designers [★IO]

Intl. Assn. of Clothing Designers and Executives [IO], Oklahoma City, OK, United States

Intl. Assn. of Clothing Designers and Executives [241], 835 NW 36th Terr., Oklahoma City, OK 73118, (405)602-8037

Intl. Assn. of Club Executives - Defunct.

Intl. Assn. on Coffee Sci. [IO], Lausanne, Switzerland

Intl. Assn. for Cognitive Psychotherapy [IO], New York, NY, United States

Intl. Assn. for Cognitive Psychotherapy [16218], c/o Lata K. McGinn, PhD, Sec.-Treas./Membership Coor., Amer. Inst. for Cognitive Therapy, 136 E 57th St., Ste. 1101, New York, NY 10022, (718)430-3965

Intl. Assn. for Cold Storage Constr. [1886], 1500 King St., Ste. 201, Alexandria, VA 22314, (703)373-4300

Intl. Assn. for Cold Storage Constr. [IO], Alexandria, VA, United States

Intl. Assn. of Cold Storage Contractors [★IO]

Intl. Assn. of Cold Storage Contractors [★1886]

Intl. Assn. of Coll. and Univ. Security Directors [★9084]

Intl. Assn. of Coll. and Univ. Security Directors [★IO]

Intl. Assn. of Colloid and Interface Scientists [IO], Wageningen, Netherlands

International Association for Colon Hydrotherapy [IO], San Antonio, TX, United States

Intl. Assn. for Colon Hydrotherapy [14567], PO Box 461285, San Antonio, TX 78246-1285, (210)366-2888

Intl. Assn. of Colon Therapy [16061], c/o A.R. Hoenninger, III, Exec. Dir., PO Box 461285, San Antonio, TX 78246-1285, (210)366-2888

Intl. Assn. of Colon Therapy [IO], San Antonio, TX, United States

International Association of Color Manufacturers [IO], Washington, DC, United States

Intl. Assn. of Color Mfrs. [869], 1620 I St. NW, Ste. 925, Washington, DC 20006, (202)293-5800

Intl. Assn. to Combat Terrorism - Defunct.

Intl. Assn. of Commercial Collectors [1147], 4040 W 70th St., Minneapolis, MN 55435, (952)925-0760

Intl. Assn. of Commercial Collectors [IO], Minneapolis, MN, United States

Intl. Assn. of Community TeleService Centres [IO], Nice, France

Intl. Assn. for Comparative Res. on Leukemia and Related Diseases [IO], Boston, MA, United States

Intl. Assn. for Comparative Res. on Leukemia and Related Diseases [15647], c/o The de Burlo Gp., 50 Fed. St., Boston, MA 02110

International Assn. of Computational Mechanics [★7300]

Intl. Assn. for Computational Mechanics [IO], Barcelona, Spain

Intl. Assn. of Computer Crime Investigators - Defunct.

Intl. Assn. for Cmpt. Info. Systems [8132], c/o Dr. G. Daryl Nord, Managing Dir., Oklahoma State Univ., 220 College of Business, Stillwater, OK 74078, (405)744-8632

Intl. Assn. for Cmpt. Info. Systems [IO], Stillwater, OK, United States

Intl. Assn. of Cmpt. Investigative Specialists [IO], Fairmont, WV, United States

Intl. Assn. of Cmpt. Investigative Specialists [8133], PO Box 1728, Fairmont, WV 26555, (888)884-2247

Reference to "IO" in place of a book number signifies that the association may be found in the 45th edition of International Organizations.

Intl. Assn. of Computer Programmers - Defunct.

Intl. Assn. for Cmpt. Systems Security **[905]**, 6 Swathmore Ln., Dix Hills, NY 11746, (631)499-1616

Intl. Assn. for Cmpt. Systems Security **[IO]**, Dix Hills, NY, United States

Intl. Assn. of Computer Users Groups - Address unknown since 2001.

Intl. Assn. for Computing in Educ. **[★8134]**

Intl. Assn. for Computing in Educ. **[★IO]**

Intl. Assn. of Concrete Repair Specialists **[★IO]**

Intl. Assn. of Concrete Repair Specialists **[★927]**

Intl. Assn. of Conf. Center Administrators **[1947]**, 5976 20th St., Ste. 80, Vero Beach, FL 32966, (772)562-4017

Intl. Assn. of Conf. Center Administrators **[IO]**, Melbourne, FL, United States

Intl. Assn. of Conf. Centers **[IO]**, St. Louis, MO, United States

Intl. Assn. of Conf. Centers **[2672]**, 243 N Lindbergh Blvd., St. Louis, MO 63141, (314)993-8575

Intl. Assn. of Conf. Interpreters **[IO]**, Geneva, Switzerland

Intl. Assn. of Conf. Translators **[IO]**, Geneva, Switzerland

Intl. Assn. for Conservation of Natural Rsrcs. and Energy - Address unknown since 1999.

Intl. Assn. for Consumer Law **[IO]**, Brussels, Belgium

Intl. Assn. of Contact Lens Educators **[IO]**, Sydney, Australia

Intl. Assn. for Continuing Educ. and Training **[IO]**, McLean, VA, United States

Intl. Assn. for Continuing Educ. and Training **[8150]**, 8405 Greensboro Dr., Ste. 800, McLean, VA 22102, (703)506-3275

Intl. Assn. for Contract and Commercial Mgt. **[772]**, 90 Grove St., Ridgefield, CT 06877, (203)431-8741

International Association for Contract and Commercial Management **[IO]**, Ridgefield, CT, United States

Intl. Assn. of Convention and Visitor Bureaus **[★IO]**

Intl. Assn. of Convention and Visitor Bureaus **[★2678]**

Intl. Assn. of Cooking Professionals **[★1582]**

Intl. Assn. of Cooking Professionals **[★IO]**

Intl. Assn. of Cooking Schools **[★IO]**

Intl. Assn. of Cooking Schools **[★1582]**

Intl. Assn. of Coroners and Medical Examiners **[15093]**, c/o Mr. John Fudenberg, 1st VP/Sec., 1704 Pinto Ln., Las Vegas, NV 89106, (702)455-3210

Intl. Assn. of Coroners and Medical Examiners **[IO]**, Las Vegas, NV, United States

International Association of Corporate and Professional Recruitment **[IO]**, Beverly Hills, CA, United States

Intl. Assn. of Corporate and Professional Recruitment **[1265]**, 327 N Palm Dr., Ste. 201, Beverly Hills, CA 90210, (310)550-0304

Intl. Assn. of Corporate and Professional Resources **[★1265]**

Intl. Assn. of Corporate and Professional Resources **[★IO]**

Intl. Assn. of Corporate Real Estate Executives **[★IO]**

Intl. Assn. of Corporate Real Estate Executives **[★3305]**

Intl. Assn. of Correctional Officers **[11870]**

Intl. Assn. of Correctional Training Personnel **[11871]**, PO Box 6604, Jefferson City, MO 65102, (573)896-4560

International Association of Correctional Training Personnel **[IO]**, Jefferson City, MO, United States

Intl. Assn. of Counseling Services **[IO]**, Alexandria, VA, United States

Intl. Assn. of Counseling Services **[8169]**, 101 S Whiting St., Ste. 211, Alexandria, VA 22304, (703)823-9840

Intl. Assn. of Counselors and Therapists **[14923]**, RR No. 2, Box 2468, Laceyville, PA 18623, (570)869-1021

Intl. Assn. of Counselors and Therapists **[IO]**, Laceyville, PA, United States

International Association for Counterterrorism and Security Professionals **[IO]**, Arlington, VA, United States

Intl. Assn. for Counterterrorism and Security Professionals **[18731]**, PO Box 10265, Arlington, VA 22210, (703)243-0993

Intl. Assn. for Creative Dance **[9883]**, c/o Douglas R. Victor, 103 Princeton Ave., Providence, RI 02907, (401)521-0546

Intl. Assn. for Creative Dance **[IO]**, Providence, RI, United States

Intl. Assn. of Credit Cards **[★IO]**

Intl. Assn. of Credit Cards **[★5881]**

Intl. Assn. of Crime Analysts **[5658]**, 9218 Metcalf Ave., No. 364, Overland Park, KS 66212, (800)609-3419

Intl. Assn. of Crime Analysts **[IO]**, Overland Park, KS, United States

Intl. Assn. of Crime Writers **[IO]**, Havana, Cuba

Intl. Assn. of Crime Writers, North Amer. Br. **[IO]**, New York, NY, United States

Intl. Assn. of Crime Writers, North Amer. Br. **[11175]**, PO Box 8674, New York, NY 10116-8674

Intl. Assn. for Criminal Identification **[★5763]**

Intl. Assn. for Criminal Identification **[★IO]**

Intl. Assn. for Critical Realism **[IO]**, Lancaster, United Kingdom

Intl. Assn. for Cross-Cultural Psychology **[IO]**, Bremen, Germany

Intl. Assn. of Cross-Reference Dir. Publishers **[3228]**, c/o Bresser Co., 684 W Baltimore St., Detroit, MI 48202-2902, (313)874-0570

Intl. Assn. for Cryptologic Res. **[6849]**, c/o IACR Gen. Secretary, Univ. of California, Santa Rosa Administrative Center, Santa Barbara, CA 93106-6120

Intl. Assn. for Cryptologic Res. **[IO]**, Santa Barbara, CA, United States

Intl. Assn. of Culinary Professionals **[IO]**, Louisville, KY, United States

Intl. Assn. of Culinary Professionals **[1582]**, 304 W Liberty St., Ste. 201, Louisville, KY 40202, (502)581-9786

Intl. Assn. of Culinary Professionals Found. **[★8174]**

Intl. Assn. of Culinary Professionals Found. **[★IO]**

Intl. Assn. for Cultural Freedom - Defunct.

Intl. Assn. for Cybernetics **[IO]**, Namur, Belgium

Intl. Assn. of Cylindrical Hydraulic Engineers - Address unknown since 1995.

Intl. Assn. of Dairy and Milk Inspectors **[★5739]**

Intl. Assn. of Dairy and Milk Inspectors **[★IO]**

Intl. Assn. for Dance Medicine and Sci. **[15170]**, 1214 Univ. of Oregon, Dept. of Dance, Eugene, OR 97403-1214, (541)465-1763

Intl. Assn. for the Defense of Artists - U.S.A. - Defunct.

Intl. Assn. of Defense Counsel **[5499]**, 1 N Franklin St., Ste. 1205, Chicago, IL 60606, (312)368-1494

Intl. Assn. of Defense Counsel **[IO]**, Chicago, IL, United States

Intl. Assn. of Democratic Lawyers **[IO]**, Brussels, Belgium

Intl. Assn. for Dental Res. **[IO]**, Alexandria, VA, United States

Intl. Assn. of Dental Res. **[14161]**, 1619 Duke St., Alexandria, VA 22314-3406, (703)548-0066

Intl. Assn. of Dental Students **[IO]**, Ferney-Voltaire, France

Intl. Assn. of Dental Traumatology **[IO]**, Reykjavik, Iceland

Intl. Assn. of Dentistry for the Handicapped **[★IO]**

Intl. Assn. of Dentistry for the Handicapped **[★14242]**

Intl. Assn. of Dento-Maxillo-Facial Radiology - Defunct.

Intl. Assn. of Dept. Stores **[IO]**, Paris, France

Intl. Assn. for the Development of Agri- Bus. **[★IO]**

Intl. Assn. for the Development and Mgt. of Existing and New Towns **[★IO]**

Intl. Assn. for Dialogue Anal. **[IO]**, Chicago, IL, United States

Intl. Assn. for Dialogue Anal. **[7244]**, c/o Lawrence N. Berlin, PhD, Sec., Northeastern Illinois Univ., 5500 N St. Louis Ave., Chicago, IL 60625, (773)442-5493

Intl. Assn. of Diecutting and Diemaking **[2029]**, 651 W Terra Cotta Ave., Ste. 132, Crystal Lake, IL 60014, (815)455-7519

Intl. Assn. of Diecutting and Diemaking **[IO]**, Crystal Lake, IL, United States

International Association of Dinnerware Matchers **[IO]**, Hawthorne, NJ, United States

Intl. Assn. of Dinnerware Matchers **[1971]**, c/o Richard Goldberg, 67 Beverly Rd., Hawthorne, NJ 07506

Intl. Assn. of Directors of Law Enforcement Standards and Training **[5973]**, c/o Patrick J. Judge, Exec. Dir., 2521 Country Club Way, Albion, MI 49224, (517)857-3828

Intl. Assn. of Directory Publishers - Address unknown since 2001.

Intl. Assn. for Disability and Oral Hea. **[14242]**, c/o Dr. Daniel E. Jolly, Ohio State Univ. Coll. of Dentistry, 305 W 12th Ave., PO Box 182357, Columbus, OH 43218-2357, (614)292-1232

Intl. Assn. for Disability and Oral Hea. **[IO]**, Columbus, OH, United States

Intl. Assn. for Disability and Oral Hea. - Sweden **[IO]**, Wentworthville, Australia

Intl. Assn. of Dive Rescue Specialists **[IO]**, Fort Collins, CO, United States

Intl. Assn. of Dive Rescue Specialists **[23574]**, 201 N Link Ln., Fort Collins, CO 80524, (970)482-1562

Intl. Assn. for Documentalists and Information Officers - Defunct.

Intl. Assn. for Documentation Technologies **[729]**

Intl. Assn. of Dollbaby Parents - Defunct.

Intl. Assn. of Dredging Companies **[IO]**, The Hague, Netherlands

Intl. Assn. of Drilling Contractors **[IO]**, Houston, TX, United States

Intl. Assn. of Drilling Contractors **[2930]**, PO Box 4287, Houston, TX 77210-4287, (713)292-1945

Intl. Assn. of Dry Cargo Shipowners **[IO]**, London, United Kingdom

International Association of Duncan Certified Ceramic Teachers **[IO]**, Toledo, OH, United States

Intl. Assn. of Duncan Certified Ceramic Teachers **[21928]**, c/o Larry Knight, Pres., 1463 Sabra Rd., Toledo, OH 43612, (419)476-7489

Intl. Assn. of Dutch Stud. **[IO]**, Woubrugge, Netherlands

Intl. Assn. for Earthquake Engg. **[IO]**, Tokyo, Japan

Intl. Assn. of Eating Disorders Professionals **[IO]**, Pekin, IL, United States

Intl. Assn. of Eating Disorders Professionals **[14300]**, PO Box 1295, Pekin, IL 61555-1295, (309)346-3341

Intl. Assn. for Ecology **[IO]**, Seoul, Republic of Korea

Intl. Assn. for the Educ. of Deafblind People **[★IO]**

Intl. Assn. for Educ. to a Life Without Drugs - Norway **[IO]**, Arendal, Norway

Intl. Assn. for Educational Assessment **[IO]**, Bridgetown, Barbados

Intl. Assn. of Educational Peace Officers - Address unknown since 2001.

Intl. Assn. for Educational and Vocational Guidance **[IO]**, Croydon, United Kingdom

Intl. Assn. of Educators for World Peace - Canada **[IO]**, Toronto, ON, Canada

Intl. Assn. of Educators for World Peace - USA **[IO]**, Huntsville, AL, United States

Intl. Assn. of Educators for World Peace - USA **[18211]**, PO Box 3282, Mastin Lake Sta., Huntsville, AL 35810-0282, (256)534-5501

Intl. Assn. of Egyptologists **[IO]**, Munich, Germany

Intl. Assn. of Elecl. Inspectors **[IO]**, Richardson, TX, United States

Intl. Assn. of Elecl. Inspectors **[1186]**, PO Box 830848, Richardson, TX 75083-0848, (972)235-1455

Intl. Assn. of Elecl. Inspectors - Japan Chap. **[IO]**, Tokyo, Japan

Intl. Assn. of Elecl. Inspectors - Korea Chap. **[IO]**, Seoul, Republic of Korea

Intl. Assn. of Elecl. Inspectors - Mexico Chap. **[IO]**, Coyoacan, Mexico

Intl. Assn. of Elecl. Inspectors - Saudi Arabia Chap. **[IO]**, Ras Tanura, Saudi Arabia

Intl. Assn. of Elecl. Leagues **[★IO]**

Intl. Assn. of Elecl. Leagues **[★1188]**

Intl. Assn. of Electronic Keyboard Mfrs. **[2808]**, c/o Korg USA, 316 S Ser. Rd., Melville, NY 11747, (631)390-6500

A star before a book entry number signifies that the name is not listed separately, but is mentioned within the entry.

Intl. Assn. of Electronic Keyboard Mfrs. **[IO]**, Melville, NY, United States

Intl. Assn. of Electronics Recyclers **[IO]**, Albany, NY, United States

Intl. Assn. of Electronics Recyclers **[1218]**, PO Box 16222, Albany, NY 12212-6222, (888)989-4237

Intl. Assn. Emergency Managers **[5563]**, c/o Elizabeth B. Armstrong, CAE, Exec. Dir, 201 Park Washington Ct., Falls Church, VA 22046-4527, (703)538-1795

Intl. Assn. Emergency Managers **[IO]**, Falls Church, VA, United States

Intl. Assn. of Empirical Aesthetics **[IO]**, Oldenburg, Germany

Intl. Assn. of Employment Web Sites **[IO]**, Stamford, CT, United States

Intl. Assn. of Employment Web Sites **[1266]**, 2052 Shippan Ave., Stamford, CT 06902, (203)964-1888

Intl. Assn. of EMTs and Paramedics **[24051]**, 159 Burgin Pkwy., Quincy, MA 02169, (617)376-0220

Intl. Assn. of EMTs and Paramedics **[IO]**, Quincy, MA, United States

Intl. Assn. of Endocrine Surgeons **[IO]**, Halle, Germany

Intl. Assn. for Energy Economics **[IO]**, Cleveland, OH, United States

Intl. Assn. for Energy Economics **[6956]**, 28790 Chagrin Blvd., Ste. 350, Cleveland, OH 44122-4630, (216)464-5365

Intl. Assn. for Energy Economics - Austria **[IO]**, Vienna, Austria

Intl. Assn. for Energy Economics - Canada **[IO]**, Edmonton, AB, Canada

Intl. Assn. for Energy Economics - Czech Republic **[IO]**, Prague, Czech Republic

Intl. Assn. for Energy Economics - Denmark **[IO]**, Frederiksberg, Denmark

Intl. Assn. for Energy Economics - Finland **[IO]**, Espoo, Finland

Intl. Assn. for Energy Economics - France **[IO]**, Nogent-sur-Marne, France

Intl. Assn. for Energy Economics - Germany **[IO]**, Berlin, Germany

Intl. Assn. for Energy Economics - Japan **[IO]**, Tokyo, Japan

Intl. Assn. for Energy Economics - Korea **[IO]**, Seoul, Republic of Korea

Intl. Assn. for Energy Economics - Latvia **[IO]**, Riga, Latvia

Intl. Assn. for Energy Economics - Lithuania **[IO]**, Kaunas, Lithuania

Intl. Assn. for Energy Economics - Mexico **[IO]**, Mexico City, Mexico

Intl. Assn. for Energy Economics - Oceania **[IO]**, Sydney, Australia

Intl. Assn. for Energy Economics - Poland **[IO]**, Katowice, Poland

Intl. Assn. for Energy Economics - Spain **[IO]**, Vigo, Spain

Intl. Assn. for Energy Economics - Sweden **[IO]**, Stockholm, Sweden

Intl. Assn. for Energy Economics - Switzerland **[IO]**, Zurich, Switzerland

Intl. Assn. for Energy Economics - Taiwan **[IO]**, Taipei, Taiwan

Intl. Assn. for Energy Economics - Turkey **[IO]**, Istanbul, Turkey

Intl. Assn. of Energy Economists **[★IO]**

Intl. Assn. of Energy Economists **[★6956]**

Intl. Assn. of Engg. Geology and the Env. **[IO]**, Subiaco, Australia

Intl. Assn. of Engg. Insurers **[IO]**, Macclesfield, United Kingdom

Intl. Assn. for Enterostomal Therapy **[★IO]**

Intl. Assn. for Enterostomal Therapy **[★15533]**

Intl. Assn. of Entertainment Lawyers - France **[IO]**, London, United Kingdom

Intl. Assn. of Entertainment Lawyers - United Kingdom **[IO]**, London, United Kingdom

Intl. Assn. of Environmental Analytical Chemistry **[IO]**, Allschwil, Switzerland

International Association of Environmental Mutagen Societies **[IO]**, Cambridge, MA, United States

Intl. Assn. of Environmental Mutagen Societies **[6578]**, c/o Leona Samson, VP, Massachusetts Inst. of Tech., CEHS/Bio Engg., Rm. 56-235, 77 Massachusetts Ave., Cambridge, MA 02139, (617)258-7813

Intl. Assn. of Environmental Testing Laboratories - Address unknown since 2004.

Intl. Assn. of Equine Professionals **[1925]**

Intl. Assn. of Ethicists - Address unknown since 2001.

Intl. Assn. for the Evaluation of Educational Achievement **[IO]**, Amsterdam, Netherlands

Intl. Assn. for the Exchange of Students for Tech. Experience **[IO]**, Banbridge, United Kingdom

Intl. Assn. for the Exchange of Students for Tech. Experience - Argentina **[IO]**, Buenos Aires, Argentina

Intl. Assn. for the Exchange of Students for Tech. Experience - Armenia **[IO]**, Yerevan, Armenia

Intl. Assn. for the Exchange of Students for Tech. Experience - Australia **[IO]**, Hawthorn, Australia

Intl. Assn. for the Exchange of Students for Tech. Experience - Austria **[IO]**, Vienna, Austria

Intl. Assn. for the Exchange of Students for Tech. Experience - Belarus **[IO]**, Minsk, Belarus

Intl. Assn. for the Exchange of Students for Tech. Experience - Belgium **[IO]**, Gent, Belgium

Intl. Assn. for the Exchange of Students for Tech. Experience - Bosnia and Herzegovina **[IO]**, Banja Luka, Bosnia-Hercegovina

Intl. Assn. for the Exchange of Students for Tech. Experience - Botswana **[IO]**, Gaborone, Botswana

Intl. Assn. for the Exchange of Students for Tech. Experience - Brazil **[IO]**, Sao Paulo, Brazil

Intl. Assn. for the Exchange of Students for Tech. Experience - Bulgaria **[IO]**, Plovdiv, Bulgaria

Intl. Assn. for the Exchange of Students for Tech. Experience - Canada **[IO]**, Kingston, ON, Canada

Intl. Assn. for the Exchange of Students for Tech. Experience - China **[IO]**, Shanghai, People's Republic of China

Intl. Assn. for the Exchange of Students for Tech. Experience - Columbia **[IO]**, Ibague, Colombia

Intl. Assn. for the Exchange of Students for Tech. Experience - Croatia **[IO]**, Zagreb, Croatia

Intl. Assn. for the Exchange of Students for Tech. Experience - Cyprus **[IO]**, Nicosia, Cyprus

Intl. Assn. for the Exchange of Students for Tech. Experience - Czech Republic **[IO]**, Prague, Czech Republic

Intl. Assn. for the Exchange of Students for Tech. Experience - Denmark **[IO]**, Lyngby, Denmark

Intl. Assn. for the Exchange of Students for Tech. Experience - Ecuador **[IO]**, Quito, Ecuador

Intl. Assn. for the Exchange of Students for Tech. Experience - Egypt **[IO]**, Giza, Egypt

Intl. Assn. for the Exchange of Students for Tech. Experience - Estonia **[IO]**, Tallinn, Estonia

Intl. Assn. for the Exchange of Students for Tech. Experience - Finland **[IO]**, Helsinki, Finland

Intl. Assn. for the Exchange of Students for Tech. Experience - France **[IO]**, Villeurbanne, France

Intl. Assn. for the Exchange of Students for Tech. Experience - Gambia **[IO]**, Banjul, Gambia

Intl. Assn. for the Exchange of Students for Tech. Experience - Georgia **[IO]**, Tbilisi, Georgia

Intl. Assn. for the Exchange of Students for Tech. Experience - Germany **[IO]**, Bonn, Germany

Intl. Assn. for the Exchange of Students for Tech. Experience - Ghana **[IO]**, Kumasi, Ghana

Intl. Assn. for the Exchange of Students for Tech. Experience - Greece **[IO]**, Athens, Greece

Intl. Assn. for the Exchange of Students for Tech. Experience - Hong Kong **[IO]**, Hong Kong, People's Republic of China

Intl. Assn. for the Exchange of Students for Tech. Experience - Hungary **[IO]**, Budapest, Hungary

Intl. Assn. for the Exchange of Students for Tech. Experience - Iceland **[IO]**, Reykjavik, Iceland

Intl. Assn. for the Exchange of Students for Tech. Experience - India **[IO]**, Coimbatore, India

Intl. Assn. for the Exchange of Students for Tech. Experience - Iran **[IO]**, Tehran, Iran

Intl. Assn. for the Exchange of Students for Tech. Experience - Iraq **[IO]**, Sulaimany, Iraq

Intl. Assn. for the Exchange of Students for Tech. Experience - Israel **[IO]**, Haifa, Israel

Intl. Assn. for the Exchange of Students for Tech. Experience - Italy **[IO]**, Milan, Italy

Intl. Assn. for the Exchange of Students for Tech. Experience - Japan **[IO]**, Osaka, Japan

Intl. Assn. for the Exchange of Students for Tech. Experience - Jordan **[IO]**, Amman, Jordan

Intl. Assn. for the Exchange of Students for Tech. Experience - Kazakhstan **[IO]**, Almaty, Kazakhstan

Intl. Assn. for the Exchange of Students for Tech. Experience - Kenya **[IO]**, Nairobi, Kenya

Intl. Assn. for the Exchange of Students for Tech. Experience - Kyrgyzstan **[IO]**, Bishkek, Kirgizstan

Intl. Assn. for the Exchange of Students for Tech. Experience - Latvia **[IO]**, Riga, Latvia

Intl. Assn. for the Exchange of Students for Tech. Experience - Lebanon **[IO]**, Beirut, Lebanon

Intl. Assn. for the Exchange of Students for Tech. Experience - Liechtenstein **[IO]**, Vaduz, Liechtenstein

Intl. Assn. for the Exchange of Students for Tech. Experience - Lithuania **[IO]**, Kaunas, Lithuania

Intl. Assn. for the Exchange of Students for Tech. Experience - Luxembourg **[IO]**, Kirchberg, Luxembourg

Intl. Assn. for the Exchange of Students for Tech. Experience - Macao **[IO]**, Macau, Macao

Intl. Assn. for the Exchange of Students for Tech. Experience - Macedonia **[IO]**, Skopje, Macedonia

Intl. Assn. for the Exchange of Students for Tech. Experience - Malta **[IO]**, Msida, Malta

Intl. Assn. for the Exchange of Students for Tech. Experience - Mexico **[IO]**, Mexico City, Mexico

Intl. Assn. for the Exchange of Students for Tech. Experience - Mongolia **[IO]**, Ulan Bator, Mongolia

Intl. Assn. for the Exchange of Students for Tech. Experience - Nigeria **[IO]**, Lagos, Nigeria

Intl. Assn. for the Exchange of Students for Tech. Experience - Norway **[IO]**, Trondheim, Norway

Intl. Assn. for the Exchange of Students for Tech. Experience - Oman **[IO]**, Muscat, Oman

Intl. Assn. for the Exchange of Students for Tech. Experience - Pakistan **[IO]**, Karachi, Pakistan

Intl. Assn. for the Exchange of Students for Tech. Experience - Panama **[IO]**, Panama City, Panama

Intl. Assn. for the Exchange of Students for Tech. Experience - Peru **[IO]**, Lima, Peru

Intl. Assn. for the Exchange of Students for Tech. Experience - Poland **[IO]**, Warsaw, Poland

Intl. Assn. for the Exchange of Students for Tech. Experience - Portugal **[IO]**, Lisbon, Portugal

Intl. Assn. for the Exchange of Students for Tech. Experience - Romania **[IO]**, Bucharest, Romania

Intl. Assn. for the Exchange of Students for Tech. Experience - Russia **[IO]**, Moscow, Russia

Intl. Assn. for the Exchange of Students for Tech. Experience - Sierra Leone **[IO]**, Freetown, Sierra Leone

Intl. Assn. for the Exchange of Students for Tech. Experience - Slovakia **[IO]**, Bratislava, Slovakia

Intl. Assn. for the Exchange of Students for Tech. Experience - Slovenia **[IO]**, Ljubljana, Slovenia

Intl. Assn. for the Exchange of Students for Tech. Experience - South Africa **[IO]**, Pretoria, Republic of South Africa

Intl. Assn. for the Exchange of Students for Tech. Experience - Spain **[IO]**, Valencia, Spain

Intl. Assn. for the Exchange of Students for Tech. Experience - Sri Lanka **[IO]**, Moratuwa, Sri Lanka

Intl. Assn. for the Exchange of Students for Tech. Experience - Sweden **[IO]**, Stockholm, Sweden

Intl. Assn. for the Exchange of Students for Tech. Experience - Switzerland **[IO]**, Zurich, Switzerland

Intl. Assn. for the Exchange of Students for Tech. Experience - Syria **[IO]**, Aleppo, Syrian Arab Republic

Intl. Assn. for the Exchange of Students for Tech. Experience - Tajikistan **[IO]**, Dushanbe, Tajikistan

Intl. Assn. for the Exchange of Students for Tech. Experience - Thailand **[IO]**, Bangkok, Thailand

Intl. Assn. for the Exchange of Students for Tech. Experience - Tunisia **[IO]**, Tunis, Tunisia

Intl. Assn. for the Exchange of Students for Tech. Experience - Turkey **[IO]**, Istanbul, Turkey

Intl. Assn. for the Exchange of Students for Tech. Experience - Ukraine **[IO]**, Kiev, Ukraine

Intl. Assn. for the Exchange of Students for Tech. Experience - United Arab Emirates **[IO]**, Sharjah, United Arab Emirates

Intl. Assn. for the Exchange of Students for Tech. Experience - United Kingdom **[IO]**, London, United Kingdom

Reference to "IO" in place of a book number signifies that the association may be found in the 45th edition of International Organizations.

Intl. Assn. for the Exchange of Students for Tech. Experience (U.S.) [★IO]

Intl. Assn. for the Exchange of Students for Tech. Experience (U.S.) [★8601]

Intl. Assn. for the Exchange of Students for Tech. Experience - Uruguay [IO], Montevideo, Uruguay

Intl. Assn. for the Exchange of Students for Tech. Experience - Uzbekistan [IO], Tashkent, Uzbekistan

Intl. Assn. for the Exchange of Students for Tech. Experience [IO], Columbia, MD, United States

Intl. Assn. for the Exchange of Students for Tech. Experience [9181], 10400 Little Patuxent Pkwy., Ste. 250, Columbia, MD 21044-3519, (410)997-3069

Intl. Assn. for Exhibition Mgt. [★2682]

Intl. Assn. for Exhibition Mgt. [IO], Dallas, TX, United States

Intl. Assn. of Exhibitions and Events [2682], PO Box 802425, Dallas, TX 75380, (972)458-8002

Intl. Assn. for Exposition Mgt. [★2682]

Intl. Assn. for Exposition Mgt. [★IO]

Intl. Assn. of Facilitators [IO], St. Paul, MN, United States

Intl. Assn. of Facilitators [3183], 14985 Glazier Ave., Ste. 550, St. Paul, MN 55124, (952)891-3541

Intl. Assn. of Factory Inspectors [★5917]

Intl. Assn. of Fairs and Expositions [2683], PO Box 985, Springfield, MO 65801, (417)862-5771

Intl. Assn. of Fairs and Expositions [IO], Springfield, MO, United States

Intl. Assn. of Family Entertainment Centers [★IO]

Intl. Assn. of Family Entertainment Centers [★1305]

Intl. Assn. for the Fantastic in the Arts [10945], c/o Stacie L. Hanes, Membership/Registration Coor., PO Box 3701, Youngstown, OH 44513

Intl. Assn. for Feminist Economics - Europe [IO], Amsterdam, Netherlands

Intl. Assn. for Feminist Economics - USA [IO], Middlebury, VT, United States

Intl. Assn. for Feminist Economics - USA [6882], 4800 McCullough, Middlebury Coll., Middlebury, VT 05753

Intl. Assn. of Filipino Patriots - Defunct.

Intl. Assn. of Film and TV Schools [IO], Brussels, Belgium

Intl. Assn. of Financial Crimes [★IO]

Intl. Assn. of Financial Crimes [★5881]

Intl. Assn. of Financial Crimes Investigators [5881], 1020 Suncast Ln., Ste. 102, El Dorado Hills, CA 95762, (916)939-5000

Intl. Assn. of Financial Crimes Investigators [IO], El Dorado Hills, CA, United States

Intl. Assn. of Financial Engineers [1424], 560 Lexington Ave., 9th Fl., New York, NY 10022, (212)317-7479

Intl. Assn. of Financial Executives Institutes [IO], Vienna, Austria

Intl. Assn. for Financial Planning [★IO]

Intl. Assn. for Financial Planning [★1420]

Intl. Assn. of Fire Chiefs [5718], 4025 Fair Ridge Dr., Ste. 300, Fairfax, VA 22033-2868, (703)273-0911

Intl. Assn. of Fire Chiefs [IO], Fairfax, VA, United States

Intl. Assn. of Fire Chiefs Found. - Address unknown since 2002.

Intl. Assn. of Fire Fighters [24057], 1750 New York Ave. NW, Washington, DC 20006, (202)737-8484

Intl. Assn. for Fire Safety Sci. [7080], c/o Soc. of Fire Protection Engineers, 7315 Wisconsin Ave., Ste. 620E, Bethesda, MD 20814, (301)718-2910

Intl. Assn. for Fire Safety Sci. [IO], Bethesda, MD, United States

Intl. Assn. of Fish and Wildlife Agencies [★IO]

Intl. Assn. of Fish and Wildlife Agencies [★4360]

Intl. Assn. of Flight Paramedics [14334], 4835 Riveredge Cove, Snellville, GA 30039, (770)979-6372

Intl. Assn. of Flower Seed Breeders and Distributors [★IO]

International Association of Fly Fishing Veterinarians [IO], Tucson, AZ, United States

Intl. Assn. of Fly Fishing Veterinarians [22451], c/o Walter E. Weirich, PhD, Sec.-Treas., 7957 W Juniper Shadows Way, Tucson, AZ 85743, (715)325-2628

Intl. Assn. of Food Indus. Suppliers [★1133]

Intl. Assn. of Food Indus. Suppliers [★IO]

Intl. Assn. of Food Indus. Suppliers and Food Processing Machinery Assn. [★IO]

Intl. Assn. of Food Indus. Suppliers and Food Processing Machinery Assn. [★1133]

Intl. Assn. for Food Protection [5739], 6200 Aurora Ave., Ste. 200W, Des Moines, IA 50322-2864, (515)276-3344

Intl. Assn. for Food Protection [IO], Des Moines, IA, United States

Intl. Assn. of Forensic Nurses [IO], Arnold, MD, United States

Intl. Assn. of Forensic Nurses [15483], 1517 Ritchie Hwy., Ste. 208, Arnold, MD 21012, (410)626-7805

Intl. Assn. for Forensic Psychotherapy [IO], London, United Kingdom

The Intl. Assn. of Forensic Toxicologists [IO], Gent, Belgium

Intl. Assn. of Former Soviet Political Prisoners and Victims of the Communist Regime [IO], Brooklyn, NY, United States

Intl. Assn. of Former Soviet Political Prisoners and Victims of the Communist Regime [17766], 1310 Ave. R, Ste. 6-F, Brooklyn, NY 11229, (718)339-4563

Intl. Assn. of Found. Drilling [★1000]

Intl. Assn. of Found. Drilling [★IO]

Intl. Assn. of Found. Drilling; ADSC: The [1000]

Intl. Assn. of French Language Archives [IO], Ste.-Foy, QC, Canada

Intl. Assn. of French Language Demographers [IO], Paris, France

Intl. Assn. of French Language Sociologists [IO], Toulouse, France

Intl. Assn. of French-Speaking Directors of Educational Institutions [IO], Montreal, QC, Canada

Intl. Assn. for Game Educ. and Res. [IO], Pasadena, CA, United States

Intl. Assn. for Game Educ. and Res. [8823], 530 S Lake Ave., Ste. 171, Pasadena, CA 91101

Intl. Assn. of Game, Fish, and Conservation Commissioners [★4360]

Intl. Assn. of Game, Fish, and Conservation Commissioners [★IO]

Intl. Assn. of Gay/Lesbian Country Western Dance Clubs [IO], Nashville, TN, United States

Intl. Assn. of Gay/Lesbian Country Western Dance Clubs [9884], PMB 107, 5543 Edmondson Pike, Nashville, TN 37211

Intl. Assn. of Gay and Lesbian Martial Artists [23588], PO Box 590601, San Francisco, CA 94159-0601

Intl. Assn. of Gay and Lesbian Martial Artists [IO], San Francisco, CA, United States

Intl. Assn. of Gay Square Dance Clubs [IO], Denver, CO, United States

Intl. Assn. of Gay Square Dance Clubs [9885], PO Box 9176, Denver, CO 80209-0176, (303)722-5276

Intl. Assn. on the Genesis of Ore Deposits [IO], Oslo, Norway

Intl. Assn. of Genocide Scholars [IO], Tuscaloosa, AL, United States

Intl. Assn. of Genocide Scholars [17661], c/o Dr. Steven Leonard Jacobs, Sec.-Treas., Univ. of Alabama, Dept. of Religious Stud., 212 Manly Hall, Box 870264, Tuscaloosa, AL 35487-0264, (205)348-0473

Intl. Assn. of Geochemistry [IO], Pinawa, MB, Canada

Intl. Assn. of Geodesy [IO], Copenhagen, Denmark

Intl. Assn. of Geomagnetism and Aeronomy [IO], Canberra, Australia

Intl. Assn. of Geomorphologists [IO], Oxford, United Kingdom

Intl. Assn. of Geophysical Contractors [IO], Houston, TX, United States

Intl. Assn. of Geophysical Contractors [2931], 2550 N Loop W, Ste. 104, Houston, TX 77092, (713)957-8080

Intl. Assn. of Geosynthetic Installers [1023], PO Box 18012, St. Paul, MN 55118, (651)554-1895

Intl. Assn. of Geosynthetic Installers [IO], St. Paul, MN, United States

Intl. Assn. for Gerda Alexander Eutony [★IO]

Intl. Assn. of Gerontology European Region [IO], Madrid, Spain

Intl. Assn. of Gerontology and Geriatrics [IO], Rio de Janeiro, Brazil

Intl. Assn. of Golf Administrators [IO], North Hollywood, CA, United States

Intl. Assn. of Golf Administrators [1737], 3740 Cahuenga Blvd., North Hollywood, CA 91604, (818)980-3630

Intl. Assn. of Golf Tour Operators [IO], London, United Kingdom

Intl. Assn. of Governmental Labor Officials [★5917]

Intl. Assn. of Graphic Communications - Address unknown since 1995.

Intl. Assn. of Great Lakes Ports - Address unknown since 1994.

Intl. Assn. for Great Lakes Res. [7239], 2205 Commonwealth Blvd., Ann Arbor, MI 48105, (734)665-5303

Intl. Assn. for Great Lakes Res. [IO], Ann Arbor, MI, United States

Intl. Assn. for Greek Philosophy [IO], Alimos, Greece

Intl. Assn. of Gp. Psychotherapy [IO], Singapore, Singapore

Intl. Assn. of Gyro Clubs [★IO]

Intl. Assn. of Gyro Clubs [★13043]

Intl. Assn. of Hail Insurers [IO], Zurich, Switzerland

Intl. Assn. of Hand Papermakers and Paper Artists [IO], Mainburg, Germany

Intl. Assn. for Handicapped Divers [IO], Middenmeer, Netherlands

Intl. Assn. of Haunted Attractions [IO], Niles, MI, United States

Intl. Assn. of Haunted Attractions [1304], 1508 Rolling Hills Dr., Niles, MI 49120

Intl. Assn. of Hea. Underwriters [★2208]

Intl. Assn. of Healthcare Central Ser. Materiel Mgt. [14886], 213 W Inst. Pl., Ste. 307, Chicago, IL 60610, (312)440-0078

Intl. Assn. of Healthcare Central Ser. Materiel Mgt. [IO], Chicago, IL, United States

Intl. Assn. of Healthcare Practitioners [IO], Palm Beach Gardens, FL, United States

Intl. Assn. of Healthcare Practitioners [14639], 11211 Prosperity Farms Rd., Ste. D-325, Palm Beach Gardens, FL 33410, (561)622-4334

Intl. Assn. for Healthcare Security and Safety [14887], PO Box 5038, Glendale Heights, IL 60139, (630)529-3913

Intl. Assn. for Healthcare Security and Safety [IO], Glendale Heights, IL, United States

Intl. Assn. of Heat and Frost Insulators and Asbestos Workers [24093], 9602 Martin Luther King Jr. Hwy., Lanham, MD 20706, (301)731-9101

The Intl. Assn. of Hewlett-Packard Computing Professionals [★6795]

Intl. Assn. of Hispanic Meeting Professionals [2684], 1120 NASA Rd. 1, Ste. 405, Houston, TX 77058, (281)333-1552

Intl. Assn. of Hispanic Meeting Professionals [IO], Houston, TX, United States

Intl. Assn. of Hispanists [IO], Rennes, France

Intl. Assn. of Historical Societies for the Stud. of Jewish History [★IO]

Intl. Assn. for the History of Glass [IO], Corning, NY, United States

Intl. Assn. for the History of Glass [10124], c/o Jane Shadel Spillman, Gen. Sec., Corning Museum of Glass, 1 Museum Way, Corning, NY 14830, (607)974-8357

Intl. Assn. for the History of Physical Educ. and Sport [★IO]

Intl. Assn. for the History of Religions [IO], Odense, Denmark

Intl. Assn. of Holiday Inns [★IO]

Intl. Assn. of Holiday Inns [★1946]

Intl. Assn. of Holistic Health Practitioners - Address unknown since 1999.

Intl. Assn. of Holistic Medicine - Address unknown since 2003.

Intl. Assn. of Home Improvement Councils - Defunct.

Intl. Assn. of Home Safety and Security Professionals [3527]

International Association of Home Safety and Security Professionals [IO], Erie, PA, United States

A star before a book entry number signifies that the name is not listed separately, but is mentioned within the entry.

Intl. Assn. of Home Staging Professionals **[IO]**, Concord, CA, United States

Intl. Assn. of Home Staging Professionals **[2261]**, 4807 Clayton Rd., Ste. 200, Concord, CA 94521, (925)686-2413

Intl. Assn. of Homes and Services for the Ageing **[11289]**, 2519 Connecticut Ave. NW, Washington, DC 20008, (202)508-9468

Intl. Assn. of Homes and Services for the Ageing **[IO]**, Washington, DC, United States

Intl. Assn. of Horticultural Producers **[IO]**, Zoetermeer, Netherlands

Intl. Assn. for Hospice and Palliative Care **[IO]**, Houston, TX, United States

Intl. Assn. for Hospice and Palliative Care **[14838]**, 5535 Memorial Dr., Ste. F, PMB 509, Houston, TX 77007, (936)321-9846

Intl. Assn. of Hosp. Central Ser. Mgt. **[★14886]**

Intl. Assn. of Hosp. Central Ser. Mgt. **[★IO]**

Intl. Assn. for Hosp. Security **[★IO]**

Intl. Assn. for Hosp. Security **[★14887]**

Intl. Assn. of Hospitality Accountants **[★32]**

Intl. Assn. of Hospitality Accountants **[★IO]**

Intl. Assn. for Housing Sci. **[IO]**, Coral Gables, FL, United States

Intl. Assn. for Housing Sci. **[12316]**, PO Box 340254, Coral Gables, FL 33134, (305)446-9462

Intl. Assn. of Human-Animal Interaction Organizations **[16615]**, c/o Delta Soc., 875 124th Ave. NE, Ste. 101, Bellevue, WA 98005-2531, (425)226-7357

Intl. Assn. of Human-Animal Interaction Organizations **[IO]**, Bellevue, WA, United States

Intl. Assn. of Human Biologists **[IO]**, Zagreb, Croatia

International Association for Human Caring **[IO]**, Harrisburg, PA, United States

Intl. Assn. for Human Caring **[14640]**, c/o Christine Filipovich, Admin., 2090 Linglestown Rd., Ste. 107, Harrisburg, PA 17110, (717)703-0033

Intl. Assn. for Human Rsrc. Info. Mgt. **[67]**, PO Box 1086, Burlington, MA 01803-6086, (800)804-3983

Intl. Assn. for Human Rsrc. Info. Mgt. **[IO]**, Burlington, MA, United States

Intl. Assn. for Human Rights of the Kurds **[IO]**, Bonn, Germany

Intl. Assn. of Hungarian Stud. **[IO]**, Budapest, Hungary

Intl. Assn. of Hydraulic Engg. and Res. **[IO]**, Madrid, Spain

Intl. Assn. for Hydraulic Res. **[★IO]**

Intl. Assn. for Hydrogen Energy **[IO]**, Miami, FL, United States

Intl. Assn. for Hydrogen Energy **[6957]**, 5783 SW 40 St., No. 303, Miami, FL 33155, (305)284-4666

Intl. Assn. of Hydrogeologists **[7830]**, c/o Todd Halihan, Sec.-Treas., 105 NRC, School of Geology, Oklahoma State Univ., Stillwater, OK 74078, (405)372-8611

Intl. Assn. of Hydrogeologists **[IO]**, Stillwater, OK, United States

Intl. Assn. of Hydrogeologists - Argentina **[IO]**, Santa Fe, Argentina

Intl. Assn. of Hydrogeologists - Australia **[IO]**, Perth, Australia

Intl. Assn. of Hydrogeologists - Australian Capital Territory **[IO]**, Kingston, Australia

Intl. Assn. of Hydrogeologists - Belgium **[IO]**, Brussels, Belgium

Intl. Assn. of Hydrogeologists - Bulgaria **[IO]**, Sofia, Bulgaria

Intl. Assn. of Hydrogeologists - Canadian Natl. Chap. **[IO]**, Milton, ON, Canada

Intl. Assn. of Hydrogeologists - Chile **[IO]**, Santiago, Chile

Intl. Assn. of Hydrogeologists - China **[IO]**, Beijing, People's Republic of China

Intl. Assn. of Hydrogeologists - Columbia **[IO]**, Bogota, Colombia

Intl. Assn. of Hydrogeologists - Croatia **[IO]**, Zagreb, Croatia

Intl. Assn. of Hydrogeologists - Czech Republic **[IO]**, Prague, Czech Republic

Intl. Assn. of Hydrogeologists - Egypt **[IO]**, Cairo, Egypt

Intl. Assn. of Hydrogeologists - France **[IO]**, Orleans, France

Intl. Assn. of Hydrogeologists - Georgia **[IO]**, Tbilisi, Georgia

Intl. Assn. of Hydrogeologists - Germany **[IO]**, Hannover, Germany

Intl. Assn. of Hydrogeologists - Hungary **[IO]**, Budapest, Hungary

Intl. Assn. of Hydrogeologists - Irish Gp. **[IO]**, Dublin, Ireland

Intl. Assn. of Hydrogeologists - Italy **[IO]**, Cagliari, Italy

Intl. Assn. of Hydrogeologists - Japan **[IO]**, Chiba, Japan

Intl. Assn. of Hydrogeologists - Mexico **[IO]**, Coyoacan, Mexico

Intl. Assn. of Hydrogeologists - Morocco **[IO]**, Agadir, Morocco

Intl. Assn. of Hydrogeologists - Netherlands **[IO]**, Utrecht, Netherlands

Intl. Assn. of Hydrogeologists - Northern Territory **[IO]**, Winnellie, Australia

Intl. Assn. of Hydrogeologists - Norway **[IO]**, Trondheim, Norway

Intl. Assn. of Hydrogeologists - Peru **[IO]**, Lima, Peru

Intl. Assn. of Hydrogeologists - Poland **[IO]**, Warsaw, Poland

Intl. Assn. of Hydrogeologists - Queensland **[IO]**, Brisbane, Australia

Intl. Assn. of Hydrogeologists - Republic of Korea **[IO]**, Taejeon, Republic of Korea

Intl. Assn. of Hydrogeologists - Romania **[IO]**, Bucharest, Romania

Intl. Assn. of Hydrogeologists - Russia **[IO]**, Moscow, Russia

Intl. Assn. of Hydrogeologists - Slovakia **[IO]**, Bratislava, Slovakia

Intl. Assn. of Hydrogeologists - Slovenia **[IO]**, Ljubljana, Slovenia

Intl. Assn. of Hydrogeologists - Spain **[IO]**, Barcelona, Spain

Intl. Assn. of Hydrogeologists - United Kingdom **[IO]**, Shrewsbury, United Kingdom

Intl. Assn. of Hydrogeologists - Western Australia **[IO]**, East Perth, Australia

Intl. Assn. of Hydrological Sciences **[IO]**, Fontainebleau, France

Intl. Assn. for Hydromagnetic Phenomena and Applications **[IO]**, Ilmenau, Germany

Intl. Assn. of Hygienic Physicians **[IO]**, Youngstown, OH, United States

Intl. Assn. of Hygienic Physicians **[15278]**, 4620 Euclid Blvd., Youngstown, OH 44512, (330)788-0526

Intl. Assn. of Ice Cream Vendors **[3970]**, 100 N 20th St., 4th Fl., Philadelphia, PA 19103-1443, (215)564-3484

International Association of Ice Cream Vendors **[IO]**, Philadelphia, PA, United States

Intl. Assn. for Identification **[IO]**, Mendota Heights, MN, United States

Intl. Assn. for Identification **[5763]**, 2535 Pilot Knob Rd., Ste. 117, Mendota Heights, MN 55120-1120, (651)681-8566

Intl. Assn. for Identification - Great Britain **[IO]**, Sidcup, United Kingdom

Intl. Assn. for Identification - New Zealand **[IO]**, Wellington, New Zealand

Intl. Assn. for Identification - Russia **[IO]**, Moscow, Russia

Intl. Assn. for Identification - Switzerland **[IO]**, Lausanne, Switzerland

Intl. Assn. for Impact Assessment **[IO]**, Fargo, ND, United States

Intl. Assn. for Impact Assessment **[7739]**, 1330 23rd St. S, Ste. C, Fargo, ND 58103, (701)297-7908

Intl. Assn. of Independent Colleges and Universities - Address unknown since 1986.

Intl. Assn. of Independent Info. Brokers **[★2097]**

Intl. Assn. of Independent Info. Brokers **[★IO]**

Intl. Assn. of Independent Producers - Address unknown since 1995.

Intl. Assn. of Independent Scholars - Address unknown since 2001.

Intl. Assn. of Independent Tanker Owners **[IO]**, Oslo, Norway

Intl. Assn. of Individual Psychology **[IO]**, Reggio Emilia, Italy

Intl. Assn. of Indus. Accident Boards and Commissions **[IO]**, Madison, WI, United States

Intl. Assn. of Indus. Accident Boards and Commissions **[5678]**, 5610 Medical Cir., Ste. 24, Madison, WI 53719-1295, (608)663-6355

Intl. Assn. of Infant Massage **[15029]**, PO Box 6370, Ventura, CA 93006, (805)644-8524

Intl. Assn. of Infant Massage **[IO]**, Ventura, CA, United States

Intl. Assn. of Infant Massage Instructors **[★IO]**

Intl. Assn. of Infant Massage Instructors **[★15029]**

Intl. Assn. for Infant Mental Hea. **[★16098]**

Intl. Assn. for Infant Mental Hea. **[★IO]**

Intl. Assn. for Info. and Data Quality **[7197]**, 19239 N Dale Mabry Hwy., No. 137, Lutz, FL 33548, (813)343-2163

Intl. Assn. of Info. Tech. Asset Managers **[2093]**, 1915A Gingerich St. NW, Hartville, OH 44632, (330)877-1437

Intl. Assn. of Info. Tech. Asset Managers **[IO]**, Hartville, OH, United States

Intl. Assn. of Insurance Counsel **[★IO]**

Intl. Assn. of Insurance Counsel **[★5499]**

Intl. Assn. of Insurance Fraud Agencies **[5828]**, PO Box 10018, Kansas City, MO 64171, (816)756-5285

Intl. Assn. of Insurance Fraud Agencies **[IO]**, Kansas City, MO, United States

Intl. Assn. for Insurance Law in the U.S. **[IO]**, Mount Vernon, NY, United States

Intl. Assn. for Insurance Law in the U.S. **[5829]**, PO Box 9001, Mount Vernon, NY 10552, (914)966-3180

Intl. Assn. for Insurance Law, U.S. Chap. **[★5829]**

Intl. Assn. for Insurance Law, U.S. Chap. **[★IO]**

International Association of Insurance Receivers **[IO]**, Altamonte Springs, FL, United States

Intl. Assn. of Insurance Receivers **[2187]**, c/o Paula Keyes, CPCU, Exec. Dir., 174 Grace Blvd., Altamonte Springs, FL 32714, (407)682-4513

Intl. Assn. of Integrative Coaches **[11740]**, c/o Deborah Dowe, Treas., PO Box 2635, Kennebunkport, ME 04046

Intl. Assn. of Integrative Coaches **[IO]**, Kennebunkport, ME, United States

Intl. Assn. for Intelligence Educ. **[8581]**, c/o Heather Tate, PO Box 10508, Erie, PA 16514, (814)824-2131

Intl. Assn. of Interaction Design **[IO]**, Paris, France

Intl. Assn. of Intermodal Equipment Surveyors - Defunct.

Intl. Assn. of Investigative Locksmiths **[3528]**, 1507 Whitmarsh Cir., Severn, MD 21144

Intl. Assn. of Investigative Locksmiths **[IO]**, Severn, MD, United States

Intl. Assn. of Iranian Art and Archaeology - Address unknown since 1995.

Intl. Assn. of Jai Alai Players - Address unknown since 2001.

Intl. Assn. of Jazz Appreciation **[22713]**

Intl. Assn. for Jazz Educ. **[8912]**, Box 724, Manhattan, KS 66505, (785)776-8744

Intl. Assn. for Jazz Educ. **[IO]**, Manhattan, KS, United States

Intl. Assn. of Jazz Educators **[★IO]**

Intl. Assn. of Jazz Educators **[★8912]**

Intl. Assn. of Jazz Record Collectors **[22714]**, c/o Perry Huntoon, Registrar, 1047 Mattande Ln., Naperville, IL 60540

Intl. Assn. of Jazz Record Collectors **[IO]**, Louisville, KY, United States

Intl. Assn. of Jesuit Bus. Schools **[IO]**, Detroit, MI, United States

Intl. Assn. of Jesuit Bus. Schools **[8026]**, c/o Dr. Gregory W. Ulferts, Exec. Dir./Corporate Sec., 4001 W McNichols Rd., Detroit, MI 48221, (313)993-1219

Intl. Assn. of Jewish Genealogical Societies **[21122]**, c/o Anne Feder Lee, Pres., 7207 Kuahono St., Honolulu, HI 96825, (808)395-0115

Intl. Assn. of Jewish Genealogical Societies **[IO]**, Honolulu, HI, United States

Intl. Assn. of Jewish Lawyers and Jurists **[IO]**, Tel Aviv, Israel

Intl. Assn. of Jewish Vocational Services **[IO]**, Philadelphia, PA, United States

Reference to "IO" in place of a book number signifies that the association may be found in the 45th edition of International Organizations.

Intl. Assn. of Jewish Vocational Services **[9305]**, 1845 Walnut St., Ste. 640, Philadelphia, PA 19103, (215)854-0233

Intl. Assn. of Jim Beam Bottle and Specialties Clubs **[21889]**, 2965 Waubesa Ave., Madison, WI 53711-5964, (608)663-9661

Intl. Assn. of Jim Beam Bottle and Specialties Clubs **[IO]**, Madison, WI, United States

Intl. Assn. of Judges **[IO]**, Rome, Italy

Intl. Assn. for Jungian Stud. **[IO]**, London, United Kingdom

Intl. Assn. of Justice Volunteerism - Address unknown since 2007.

Intl. Assn. of Juvenile Court Judges **[★IO]**

Intl. Assn. of Knowledge Engineers **[IO]**, Gaithersburg, MD, United States

Intl. Assn. of Knowledge Engineers **[6485]**, 973 Russell Ave., Ste. D, Gaithersburg, MD 20879, (301)948-5390

Intl. Assn. of Labour History Institutions **[IO]**, Paris, France

Intl. Assn. of Labour Inspection **[IO]**, Strassen, Luxembourg

Intl. Assn. of Language Centres **[IO]**, Canterbury, United Kingdom

Intl. Assn. for Language Learning Tech. **[IO]**, Victoria, BC, Canada

Intl. Assn. of Laryngectomees **[IO]**, Jacksonville, NC, United States

Intl. Assn. of Laryngectomees **[11953]**, c/o Gary L. Miner, Sr., Pres., 1203 Wolf Swamp Rd., Jacksonville, NC 28546, (910)340-4519

Intl. Assn. of Law Enforcement Firearms Instructors **[5974]**, 25 Country Club Rd., Ste. 707, Gilford, NH 03249-6977, (603)524-8787

Intl. Assn. of Law Enforcement Firearms Instructors **[IO]**, Gilford, NH, United States

Intl. Assn. of Law Enforcement Intelligence Analysts **[IO]**, Richmond, VA, United States

Intl. Assn. of Law Enforcement Intelligence Analysts **[5882]**, PO Box 13857, Richmond, VA 23225, (520)547-8760

Intl. Assn. of Law Enforcement Planners **[5644]**, PO Box 11437, Torrance, CA 90510-1437, (310)225-5148

Intl. Assn. of Law Enforcement Planners **[IO]**, Torrance, CA, United States

Intl. Assn. of Law, Ethics and Sci. **[IO]**, Paris, France

Intl. Assn. of Law Firms - Defunct.

Intl. Assn. of Law Schools **[8767]**, 1201 Connecticut Ave. NW, Ste. 800, Washington, DC 20036-2717, (202)296-8851

Intl. Assn. of Law Schools **[IO]**, Washington, DC, United States

Intl. Assn. of Lawyers **[IO]**, Paris, France

Intl. Assn. of Lawyers Against Nuclear Arms **[IO]**, Marburg, Germany

Intl. Assn. for Learning Alternatives **[7945]**, 449 Desnoyer Ave., St. Paul, MN 55104-4946, (651)644-2805

Intl. Assn. for Learning Labs. **[★IO]**

Intl. Assn. for the Leisure and Entertainment Indus. **[IO]**, Hershey, PA, United States

Intl. Assn. for the Leisure and Entertainment Indus. **[1305]**, 10 Briarcrest Sq., Hershey, PA 17033, (717)533-0534

Intl. Assn. of Lemon Law Administrators **[5536]**, c/o Ms. Carol Roberts, Exec. Dir., 89 Annabessacook Dr., Winthrop, ME 04364, (207)377-8752

Intl. Assn. of Lesbian and Gay Judges **[5903]**, c/o Hon. D. Zeke Zeidler, Treas., 137 N Larchmont Blvd., No. 206, Los Angeles, CA 90004

Intl. Assn. of Lesbian and Gay Judges **[IO]**, Los Angeles, CA, United States

Intl. Assn. of Lesbian/Gay Pride Coordinators **[★IO]**

Intl. Assn. of Lesbian/Gay Pride Coordinators **[★12240]**

Intl. Assn. for Lichenology **[IO]**, Birmensdorf, Switzerland

Intl. Assn. of Lighting Designers **[IO]**, Chicago, IL, United States

Intl. Assn. of Lighting Designers **[2262]**, Merchandise Mart, Ste. 9-104, 200 World Trade Ctr., Chicago, IL 60654, (312)527-3677

Intl. Assn. of Lighting Mgt. Companies **[2432]**, East Grand Office Park, 100 E Grand Ave., Ste. 330, Des Moines, IA 50309-1835, (515)243-2360

Intl. Assn. of Lighting Mgt. Companies **[IO]**, Des Moines, IA, United States

Intl. Assn. of Lions Clubs **[★IO]**

Intl. Assn. of Lions Clubs **[★13050]**

Intl. Assn. of Literary Critics **[IO]**, Paris, France

Intl. Assn. of Logopedics and Phoniatrics **[IO]**, Ulrum, Netherlands

Intl. Assn. of Machinists **[IO]**, Upper Marlboro, MD, United States

Intl. Assn. of Machinists **[24011]**, 9000 Machinists Pl., Upper Marlboro, MD 20772-2687, (301)967-4500

Intl. Assn. of Machinists **[★24012]**

Intl. Assn. of Machinists and Aerospace Workers **[24012]**, 9000 Machinists Pl., Upper Marlboro, MD 20772-2687, (301)967-4500

Intl. Assn. of Machinists and Aerospace Workers, Woodworkers District Lodge W1 **[24026]**, 25 Cornell Ave., Gladstone, OR 97027, (503)656-1475

International Assn. of Mgt; Assn. of Management/ **[6528]**

Intl. Assn. for the Mgt. of Tech. **[7740]**, PO Box 248294, Coral Gables, FL 33124-8294, (305)284-2344

Intl. Assn. of Marine Aids to Navigation and Lighthouse Authorities **[IO]**, St.-Germain-en-Laye, France

Intl. Assn. of Marine Aids to Navigation and Lighthouse Authorities **[★IO]**

Intl. Assn. for Marine Electronics Companies **[IO]**, London, United Kingdom

Intl. Assn. of Marine Investigators **[IO]**, Medford, OR, United States

Intl. Assn. of Marine Investigators **[2578]**, 711 Medford Ctr., No. 419, Medford, OR 97504, (541)776-8601

Intl. Assn. of Marine Sciences Libraries and Info. Centers **[★10361]**

Intl. Assn. of Marine Sciences Libraries and Info. Centers **[★IO]**

Intl. Assn. of Maritime Institutions **[IO]**, South Shields, United Kingdom

Intl. Assn. for Marriage and Family Counselors **[IO]**, Corpus Christi, TX, United States

Intl. Assn. for Marriage and Family Counselors **[11825]**, c/o Dr. Robert Smith, Exec. Dir., Texas A&M Univ. - Corpus Christi, Coll. of Educ., 6300 Ocean Dr., Corpus Christi, TX 78412, (361)825-2307

Intl. Assn. for Mass Commun. Res. **[★IO]**

Intl. Assn. for Maternal and Neonatal Hea. **[IO]**, Basel, Switzerland

Intl. Assn. for Mathematical Geology **[IO]**, Kingston, ON, Canada

Intl. Assn. of Mathematical Physics **[IO]**, Prague, Czech Republic

Intl. Assn. of Mathematical Sciences **[IO]**, Osaka, Japan

Intl. Assn. for Mathematics and Computers in Simulation **[IO]**, New Brunswick, NJ, United States

Intl. Assn. for Mathematics and Computers in Simulation **[6731]**, c/o Robert Vichnevetsky, Honorary Pres., Rutgers Univ. - Bush Campus, Dept. of Cmpt. Sci., Hill Center, Brett Rd., New Brunswick, NJ 08903, (732)445-2081

Intl. Assn. of Mayors Responsible for Capital Cities or Metropolises Partially or Entirely French-Speaking **[IO]**, Paris, France

Intl. Assn. on Mechanization of Field Experiments **[IO]**, St. Petersburg, Russia

Intl. Assn. for Media and Commun. Res. **[IO]**, London, United Kingdom

Intl. Assn. for Media and Communications Res. **[IO]**, London, United Kingdom

Intl. Assn. for Media and History **[IO]**, Amsterdam, Netherlands

Intl. Assn. of Media Tie-in Writers **[IO]**, Calabasas, CA, United States

Intl. Assn. of Media Tie-in Writers **[11176]**, PO Box 8212, Calabasas, CA 91372

Intl. Assn. for Medical Assistance to Travellers **[13343]**, 1623 Military Rd., No. 279, Niagara Falls, NY 14304-1745, (716)754-4883

Intl. Assn. for Medical Assistance to Travellers **[IO]**, Niagara Falls, NY, United States

Intl. Assn. for Medical Assistance to Travellers - Canada **[IO]**, Guelph, ON, Canada

Intl. Assn. for Medical Assistance to Travellers - New Zealand **[IO]**, Christchurch, New Zealand

Intl. Assn. for Medical Assistance to Travellers - Switzerland **[IO]**, Geneva, Switzerland

Intl. Assn. of Medical Equip. Remarketers **[★IO]**

Intl. Assn. of Medical Equip. Remarketers **[★15139]**

Intl. Assn. of Medical Equip. Remarketers and Servicers **[15139]**, 183 Lucy Ln., Wylie, TX 75098-7244, (201)833-2021

Intl. Assn. of Medical Equip. Remarketers and Servicers **[IO]**, Wylie, TX, United States

International Association of Medical Intuitives **[IO]**, Spokane, WA, United States

Intl. Assn. of Medical Intuitives **[15040]**, c/o Charles Lightwalker, Treas., PO Box 30752, Spokane, WA 99223-3021

Intl. Assn. of Medical Lab. Technologists **[★IO]**

Intl. Assn. of Medical Museums **[★IO]**

Intl. Assn. of Medical Museums **[★15868]**

Intl. Assn. of Medical Sci. Educators **[15090]**, 1 Crested Butte, Huntington, WV 25705, (304)733-1270

International Association of Medical Science Educators **[IO]**, Huntington, WV, United States

International Association for Medicinal Compliance **[IO]**, Washington, DC, United States

Intl. Assn. for Medicinal Compliance **[15041]**, 1441 Rhode Island Ave. NW, No. 601, Washington, DC 20005

Intl. Assn. of Medicine and Biology of Env. **[IO]**, Paris, France

Intl. Assn. for Mediterranean Forests **[IO]**, Marseille, France

Intl. Assn. of Meiobenthologists **[IO]**, Gent, Belgium

Intl. Assn. Merger and Acquisition Consultants **[★IO]**

Intl. Assn. Merger and Acquisition Consultants **[★730]**

Intl. Assn. of Merger and Acquisition Professionals **[730]**, 525 SW 5th St., Des Moines, IA 50309, (515)282-8192

Intl. Assn. of Merger and Acquisition Professionals **[IO]**, Des Moines, IA, United States

Intl. Assn. of Messaging Professionals **[IO]**, Manhattan Beach, CA, United States

Intl. Assn. of Messaging Professionals **[6711]**, 1501 Harkness St., Manhattan Beach, CA 90266, (816)414-4972

Intl. Assn. of Meteorology and Atmospheric Physics **[★IO]**

Intl. Assn. of Meteorology and Atmospheric Sciences **[IO]**, Toronto, ON, Canada

Intl. Assn. Microscopy - Defunct.

Intl. Assn. of Microsoft Certified Partners **[6769]**, 346 Brigham St., Marlborough, MA 01752

Intl. Assn. of Microsoft Certified Partners **[IO]**, Markham, ON, Canada

International Association of Military Flight Surgeon-Pilots **[IO]**, Portsmouth, VA, United States

Intl. Assn. of Military Flight Surgeon-Pilots **[13541]**, c/o Dave Hiland, VP, Navy Environmental Hea. Ctr., 620 John Paul Jones Cir., Ste. 1100, Portsmouth, VA 23708-2103

Intl. Assn. of Milk Control Agencies **[5740]**, c/o Charles Huff, Sec.-Treas., New York Dept. of Agriculture and Markets, 10 B Airline Dr., Albany, NY 12235, (518)457-5731

Intl. Assn. of Milk Control Agencies **[IO]**, Albany, NY, United States

Intl. Assn. of Milk, Food and Environmental Sanitarians **[★IO]**

Intl. Assn. of Milk, Food and Environmental Sanitarians **[★5739]**

Intl. Assn. of Milk and Food Sanitarians **[★5739]**

Intl. Assn. of Milk and Food Sanitarians **[★IO]**

Intl. Assn. of Milk Sanitarians **[★IO]**

Intl. Assn. of Milk Sanitarians **[★5739]**

Intl. Assn. of Ministers Wives and Ministers Widows **[19897]**, 26 Fowler St., New Haven, CT 06515, (203)397-3400

Intl. Assn. of Ministers Wives and Ministers Widows **[IO]**, New Haven, CT, United States

Intl. Assn. for Mission Stud. **[IO]**, Nijmegen, Netherlands

A star before a book entry number signifies that the name is not listed separately, but is mentioned within the entry.

Intl. Assn. of Model and Talent Scouts - Defunct.

Intl. Assn. for Modular Exhibitry **[1342]**

Intl. Assn. of Music Info. Centres **[IO]**, Brussels, Belgium

Intl. Assn. of Music Libraries, Archives and Documentation Centers (Australia Br.) **[IO]**, South Brisbane, Australia

Intl. Assn. of Music Libraries, Archives and Documentation Centers, U.S. Br. **[10362]**, c/o Mary Wallace Davidson, Pres., Indiana Univ., 620 S Park Ave., Bloomington, IN 47401, (812)334-1410

Intl. Assn. of Music Libraries Archives and Documentation Centres **[IO]**, Wellington, New Zealand

Intl. Assn. of Music Libraries, Archives and Documentation Centres - New Zealand Br. **[IO]**, Auckland, New Zealand

Intl. Assn. of Music Libraries, Archives and Documentation Centres - United Kingdom and Ireland **[IO]**, Manchester, United Kingdom

Intl. Assn. of Music Libraries, U.S. Br. **[★10362]**

Intl. Assn. of Mutual Insurance Companies **[IO]**, Brussels, Belgium

Intl. Assn. of Nanotechnology **[IO]**, Sacramento, CA, United States

Intl. Assn. of Nanotechnology **[7741]**, 1290 Parkmoor Ave., San Jose, CA 95126, (408)277-3071

Intl. Assn. of Native Amer. Stud. **[8939]**, c/o NAAAS and Affiliates, PO Box 6670, Scarborough, ME 04070-6670, (207)839-8004

Intl. Assn. for Natural Gas Vehicles **[IO]**, Auckland, New Zealand

Intl. Assn. of Natural Rsrc. Pilots **[4187]**, c/o Fred Kruger, Treas., 27102 County Rd. A, Spooner, WI 54801, (715)635-7788

Intl. Assn. for Near-Death Stud. **[7476]**, PO Box 502, East Windsor Hill, CT 06028-0502, (860)882-1211

Intl. Assn. for Near-Death Stud. **[IO]**, East Windsor Hill, CT, United States

Intl. Assn. for Neo-Latin Stud. **[IO]**, Copenhagen, Denmark

Intl. Assn. of Neuro-Linguistic Programming **[★IO]**

Intl. Assn. for Neuro-Linguistic Programming **[★IO]**

Intl. Assn. of Neuro-Linguistic Programming **[★IO]**

Intl. Assn. for Neuro-Linguistic Programming **[★16219]**

Intl. Assn. of Neuro-Linguistic Programming **[★16219]**

Intl. Assn. for Neuro-Linguistic Programming **[★16219]**

Intl. Assn. of Nitrox and Tech. Divers **[23379]**, 1545 NE 104th St., Miami Shores, FL 33138-2665, (305)754-1027

Intl. Assn. of Nitrox and Tech. Divers **[IO]**, Miami Shores, FL, United States

Intl. Assn. of Non-Vessel Operating Common Carriers - Address unknown since 2007.

Intl. Assn. of NVOCCs - Address unknown since 2001.

Intl. Assn. of Obituarists **[4062]**, c/o Carolyn Milford Gilbert, Founder, 8409 Pickwick Ln., No. 312, Dallas, TX 75225, (214)502-7801

Intl. Assn. of Obituarists **[IO]**, Dallas, TX, United States

Intl. Assn. for Obsidian Stud. **[IO]**, Seattle, WA, United States

Intl. Assn. for Obsidian Stud. **[6449]**, c/o S. Colby Phillips, Sec.-Treas., Univ. of Washington, Dept. of Anthropology, Box 353100, Seattle, WA 98195-3100

Intl. Assn. of Occitan Stud. **[IO]**, Montpellier, France

Intl. Assn. of Ocular Surgeons **[15684]**

Intl. Assn. of Official Human Rights Agencies **[5802]**, 444 N Capitol St. NW, Ste. 536, Washington, DC 20001, (202)624-5410

Intl. Assn. of Official Human Rights Agencies **[IO]**, Washington, DC, United States

Intl. Assn. for Official Statistics **[IO]**, Voorburg, Netherlands

Intl. Assn. of Open Systems Professionals **[★IO]**

Intl. Assn. of Open Systems Professionals **[★6805]**

Intl. Assn. of Operative Millers **[2737]**, 5001 Coll. Blvd., Ste. 104, Leawood, KS 66211, (913)338-3377

Intl. Assn. of Operative Millers **[IO]**, Leawood, KS, United States

Intl. Assn. of Optometric Executives **[IO]**, West Des Moines, IA, United States

Intl. Assn. of Optometric Executives **[15720]**

Intl. Assn. of Oral and Maxillofacial Surgeons **[15736]**, 17 W 220 22nd St., Ste. 420, Oakbrook Terrace, IL 60181, (630)833-0945

Intl. Assn. of Oral and Maxillofacial Surgeons **[IO]**, Oakbrook Terrace, IL, United States

Intl. Assn. of Oral Pathologists **[IO]**, Heidelberg, Australia

Intl. Assn. for Organ Donation **[16671]**, PO Box 545, Dearborn, MI 48121, (313)745-2379

Intl. Assn. of Orofacial Myology **[15869]**, 2000 NE 42nd Ave., Portland, OR 97213-1305, (503)280-0614

Intl. Assn. for Orthodontics **[14162]**, 750 N Lincoln Memorial Dr., Ste. 422, Milwaukee, WI 53202, (414)272-2757

Intl. Assn. for Orthodontics **[IO]**, Milwaukee, WI, United States

Intl. Assn. of Outsourcing Professionals **[IO]**, Lagrangeville, NY, United States

Intl. Assn. of Outsourcing Professionals **[2871]**, c/o Christina L. Powers, Exec. Dir., 2600 South Rd., Ste. 44-240, Poughkeepsie, NY 12601, (845)452-0600

Intl. Assn. for Oxygen Therapy **[16616]**, PO Box 502, Nordman, ID 83848, (208)443-4319

Intl. Assn. for Oxygen Therapy **[IO]**, Nordman, ID, United States

Intl. Assn. of Paediatric Dentistry **[IO]**, Ferney-Voltaire, France

Intl. Assn. of Panoramic Photographers **[IO]**, New York, NY, United States

Intl. Assn. of Panoramic Photographers **[3000]**, PO Box 3371, New York, NY 10008

Intl. Assn. of Paper Historians **[IO]**, Eupen, Belgium

Intl. Assn. of Papyrologists **[IO]**, Brussels, Belgium

Intl. Assn. of Paratuberculosis **[16793]**, 2015 Linden Dr., Madison, WI 53706-1102, (608)262-8457

Intl. Assn. of Parents of the Deaf **[★14742]**

Intl. Assn. of Parents and Professionals for Safe Alternatives in Childbirth **[15603]**, Rte. 4, Box 646, Marble Hill, MO 63764, (573)238-2010

Intl. Assn. of Parents and Professionals for Safe Alternatives in Childbirth **[IO]**, Marble Hill, MO, United States

Intl. Assn. for Past and Present History of the Art of Printing; Gutenberg Soc.: **[IO]**

International Association of Pastel Societies **[IO]**, Falls Church, VA, United States

Intl. Assn. of Pastel Societies **[9445]**, PO Box 2057, Falls Church, VA 22042, (703)241-2826

Intl. Assn. of Pastoral Psychologists **[16151]**, 981 S Third St., Louisville, KY 40203

Intl. Assn. of Pastoral Psychologists **[IO]**, Louisville, KY, United States

Intl. Assn. for Patristic Stud. **[IO]**, Virginia, Australia

Intl. Assn. for Pattern Recognition **[IO]**, Hamamatsu, Japan

Intl. Assn. of Pediatric Lab. Medicine **[IO]**, McLean, VA, United States

Intl. Assn. of Pediatric Lab. Medicine **[15888]**, 6728 Old McLean Village Dr., McLean, VA 22101

Intl. Assn. of Pedodontics - Defunct.

Intl. Assn. for Penal Law **[IO]**, Pau, France

Intl. Assn. for Penal Law - Austria **[IO]**, Pau, France

Intl. Assn. of Penal Law - Switzerland **[IO]**, Zurich, Switzerland

Intl. Assn. of People Who Dine Over the Kitchen Sink **[IO]**, Sacramento, CA, United States

Intl. Assn. of People Who Dine Over the Kitchen Sink **[22594]**, PO Box 221413, Sacramento, CA 95822

Intl. Assn. of Personnel in Employment Security **[★5679]**

Intl. Assn. of Personnel in Employment Security **[★IO]**

Intl. Assn. for Personnel Women **[★2905]**

Intl. Assn. of Pet Cemeteries **[★2959]**

Intl. Assn. of Pet Cemeteries **[★IO]**

Intl. Assn. of Pet Cemeteries and Crematories **[IO]**, Ellenburg Depot, NY, United States

Intl. Assn. of Pet Cemeteries and Crematories **[2959]**, PO Box 163, 5055 Rte. 11, Ellenburg Depot, NY 12935-0163, (518)594-3000

Intl. Assn. of Philatelic Experts **[IO]**, Innsbruck, Austria

Intl. Assn. for Philosophy of Law and Social Philosophy, Amer. Sect. - Defunct.

Intl. Assn. for Philosophy and Literature **[10797]**, c/o Prof. Hugh J. Silverman, Exec. Dir., Stony Brook Univ., Philosophy Dept., Stony Brook, NY 11794-3750, (631)331-4598

Intl. Assn. for Philosophy and Literature **[★10806]**

Intl. Assn. of Philosophy and Literature **[★10840]**

Intl. Assn. for Philosophy and Literature **[IO]**, Stony Brook, NY, United States

Intl. Assn. for Philosophy and Literature **[★IO]**

Intl. Assn. of Philosophy and Literature **[★IO]**

Intl. Assn. of Photoplatemakers **[★IO]**

Intl. Assn. of Photoplatemakers **[★7154]**

Intl. Assn. of Physical Activity **[★11281]**

Intl. Assn. of Physical Educ. and Sport for Girls and Women **[8980]**

Intl. Assn. of Physical Educ. and Sport for Girls and Women **[IO]**, Newark, DE, United States

Intl. Assn. of Physical Oceanography **[★IO]**

Intl. Assn. of Physical Oceanography **[★7398]**

Intl. Assn. for the Physical Sciences of the Oceans **[7398]**, c/o Dr. Fred E. Camfield, Sec. Gen., PO Box 820440, Vicksburg, MS 39182-0440, (601)636-1363

Intl. Assn. for the Physical Sciences of the Oceans **[IO]**, Vicksburg, MS, United States

Intl. Assn. of Physicians in AIDS Care **[IO]**, Chicago, IL, United States

Intl. Assn. of Physicians in AIDS Care **[16001]**, 33 N LaSalle St., Ste. 1700, Chicago, IL 60602-2601, (312)795-4930

Intl. Assn. of Physicians in Audiology **[IO]**, Copenhagen, Denmark

International Association of Physicians and Health Care Professionals **[IO]**, Tallahassee, FL, United States

Intl. Assn. of Physicians and Hea. Care Professionals **[16002]**, PO Box 13089, Tallahassee, FL 32317, (850)878-3134

Intl. Assn. of Physics Students **[IO]**, Oslo, Norway

Intl. Assn. of Piano Builders and Technicians **[IO]**, Kansas City, KS, United States

Intl. Assn. of Piano Builders and Technicians **[2809]**, c/o Piano Technicians Guild, 4444 Forest Ave., Kansas City, KS 66106, (913)432-9975

Intl. Assn. of Pipe Smokers Clubs **[22897]**, c/o Paul T. Spaniola, Chm., 647 S Saginaw St., Flint, MI 48502, (810)235-0581

Intl. Assn. of Pipe Smokers Clubs **[IO]**, Flint, MI, United States

International Association for the Plant Protection Sciences **[IO]**, Blacksburg, VA, United States

Intl. Assn. for the Plant Protection Sciences **[6397]**, c/o Dr. E.A. "Short" Heinrichs, Sec. Gen., 2270 Litton Reaves Hall, Virginia Tech, Blacksburg, VA 24061-0334, (540)231-3516

Intl. Assn. for Plant Taxonomy **[IO]**, Vienna, Austria

Intl. Assn. of Plastics Distributors **[IO]**, Leawood, KS, United States

Intl. Assn. of Plastics Distributors **[3051]**, 4707 Coll. Blvd., Ste. 105, Leawood, KS 66211, (913)345-1005

Intl. Assn. of Plumbing and Mech. Officials **[5549]**, 5001 E Philadelphia St., Ontario, CA 91761, (909)472-4100

Intl. Assn. of Plumbing and Mech. Officials **[IO]**, Ontario, CA, United States

Intl. Assn. of Police Professors **[★11850]**

Intl. Assn. of Political Consultants **[IO]**, Krefeld, Germany

Intl. Assn. for Pollution Control - Defunct.

Intl. Assn. of Ports and Harbors **[IO]**, Tokyo, Japan

Intl. Assn. of Practising Accountants **[IO]**, Farnham, United Kingdom

Intl. Assn. for Presentation Professionals - Defunct.

Intl. Assn. of Printing House Craftsmen **[1774]**, 7042 Brooklyn Blvd., Minneapolis, MN 55429-1370, (763)560-1620

Intl. Assn. of Printing House Craftsmen **[IO]**, Minneapolis, MN, United States

Intl. Assn. of Privacy Professionals **[IO]**, York, ME, United States

Reference to "IO" in place of a book number signifies that the association may be found in the 45th edition of International Organizations.

Intl. Assn. of Privacy Professionals **[2104]**, 266 York St., York, ME 03909, (207)351-1500

Intl. Assn. Private Investigators **[★2325]**

Intl. Assn. for Prdt. Development **[3177]**, PO Box 998, New Canaan, CT 06840, (203)254-3677

Intl. Assn. for Prdt. Development **[IO]**, New Canaan, CT, United States

International Association for Professional Art Advisors **[IO]**, Brooklyn, NY, United States

Intl. Assn. for Professional Art Advisors **[24002]**, c/o Kimberly Maier, Exec. Dir., 433 Third St., Ste. 3, Brooklyn, NY 11215, (718)788-1425

Intl. Assn. of Professional Bureaucrats **[22595]**, c/o Dr. Jim H. Boren, Pres./Founder, 2400 Jolinda Ln., Whitesboro, TX 76273, (903)564-9290

International Association of Professional Bureaucrats **[IO]**, Whitesboro, TX, United States

Intl. Assn. of Professional and Bus. Women in Bulgaria **[IO]**, Sofia, Bulgaria

Intl. Assn. of Professional Cong. Organizers **[IO]**, London, United Kingdom

Intl. Assn. of Professional Event Photographers **[★IO]**

Intl. Assn. of Professional Event Photographers **[★3015]**

Intl. Assn. of Professional Natural Hygienists **[★15278]**

Intl. Assn. of Professional Natural Hygienists **[★IO]**

Intl. Assn. of Professional Numismatists **[IO]**, Brussels, Belgium

International Association of Professional Protection Specialists **[IO]**, Santa Clara, CA, United States

Intl. Assn. of Professional Protection Specialists **[13009]**

Intl. Assn. of Professional Security Consultants **[3529]**, 525 SW 5th St., Ste. A, Des Moines, IA 50309-4501, (515)282-8192

Intl. Assn. of Professional Security Consultants **[IO]**, Des Moines, IA, United States

Intl. Assn. for the Promotion of Cooperation with Scientists from the New Independent States of the Former Soviet Union **[IO]**, Brussels, Belgium

Intl. Assn. for the Properties of Steam **[★IO]**

Intl. Assn. for the Properties of Steam **[★6268]**

Intl. Assn. for the Properties of Water and Steam **[6268]**, c/o Dr. R. Barry Dooley, Exec. Sec., EPRI, 1300 W W.T. Harris Blvd., Charlotte, NC 28262

Intl. Assn. for the Properties of Water and Steam **[IO]**, Charlotte, NC, United States

International Association for Property and Evidence **[IO]**, Burbank, CA, United States

Intl. Assn. for Property and Evidence **[5975]**, 903 N San Fernando Blvd., Ste. 4, Burbank, CA 91504-4327, (818)846-2926

Intl. Assn. of Prosecutors **[IO]**, The Hague, Netherlands

Intl. Assn. for the Protection of Intellectual Property **[IO]**, Zurich, Switzerland

International Association of Protocol Consultants **[IO]**, McLean, VA, United States

Intl. Assn. of Protocol Consultants **[965]**, PO Box 6150, McLean, VA 22106-6150, (703)555-1212

Intl. Assn. of Psychosocial Rehabilitation Services **[★16336]**

Intl. Assn. of Psychosocial Rehabilitation Services **[★IO]**

Intl. Assn. of Public Employment Services **[★IO]**

Intl. Assn. of Public Employment Services **[★5679]**

Intl. Assn. for Public Participation Practitioners **[6236]**, 11166 Huron St., Ste. 27, Denver, CO 80234-3339, (303)451-5945

Intl. Assn. for Public Participation Practitioners **[IO]**, Denver, CO, United States

Intl. Assn. of Public Transport **[IO]**, Brussels, Belgium

Intl. Assn. of Public Works Officials **[★6233]**

Intl. Assn. of Pupil Personnel Workers **[★8326]**

Intl. Assn. of Pupil Personnel Workers **[★IO]**

Intl. Assn. of Quality Circles **[★7555]**

Intl. Assn. of Quality Technicians in the Automotive Industry **[358]**, c/o Rachel Vandongen, 9705 Sterling, Allen Park, MI 48101

Intl. Assn. of Quality Technicians in the Automotive Industry **[IO]**, Allen Park, MI, United States

Intl. Assn. for Radio, Telecommunications and Electromagnetics **[7773]**, 167 Village St., Medway, MA 02053, (508)533-8333

Intl. Assn. of Radio Women **[★IO]**

Intl. Assn. of Radiopharmacology **[IO]**, Edmonton, AB, Canada

Intl. Assn. of Railway Employees - Address unknown since 1995.

Intl. Assn. of Railway Operating Officers - Address unknown since 1999.

Intl. Assn. of Railway Operations Res. **[IO]**, Delft, Netherlands

Intl. Assn. of Rattan Mfrs. and Importers - Defunct.

Intl. Assn. of Rebekah Assemblies, IOOF **[19296]**, 422 Trade St., Winston-Salem, NC 27101, (336)725-6037

Intl. Assn. of Rebekah Assemblies, IOOF **[IO]**, Winston-Salem, NC, United States

Intl. Assn. of Reentry **[17355]**, PO Box 14125, Columbus, OH 43214-0125

Intl. Assn. of Refrigerated Warehouses **[3978]**, 1500 King St., Ste. 201, Alexandria, VA 22314, (703)373-4300

Intl. Assn. of Refrigerated Warehouses **[IO]**, Alexandria, VA, United States

Intl. Assn. for Regional and Urban Statistics **[★IO]**

Intl. Assn. of Registered Financial Consultants **[IO]**, Middletown, OH, United States

Intl. Assn. of Registered Financial Consultants **[1425]**, PO Box 42506, 2507 N Verity Pkwy., Middletown, OH 45042-0506, (513)424-6395

Intl. Assn. for Regression Res. and Therapies **[16617]**, PO Box 20151, Riverside, CA 92516, (951)784-1570

Intl. Assn. of Rehabilitation Facilities **[★16312]**

Intl. Assn. of Rehabilitation Professionals **[16322]**, 1926 Waukegan Rd., Ste. 1, Glenview, IL 60025, (847)657-6964

Intl. Assn. of Reiki Professionals **[13637]**, PO Box 6182, Nashua, NH 03063-6182, (603)881-8838

Intl. Assn. of Reiki Professionals **[IO]**, Nashua, NH, United States

Intl. Assn. for Relational Psychoanalysis and Psychotherapy **[IO]**, New York, NY, United States

Intl. Assn. for Relational Psychoanalysis and Psychotherapy **[16108]**, 22 Cortlandt St., 20th Fl., New York, NY 10007, (212)669-6123

Intl. Assn. for Relationship Res. **[7571]**, c/o Rebecca Adams, Ed., PO Box 26170, Greensboro, NC 27402-6170, (336)334-3578

Intl. Assn. for Relationship Res. **[IO]**, Greensboro, NC, United States

Intl. Assn. for Religion and Parapsychology **[IO]**, Tokyo, Japan

Intl. Assn. for Religious Freedom **[IO]**, Oxford, United Kingdom

Intl. Assn. for Religious Freedom - Japan **[IO]**, Suzuka, Japan

Intl. Assn. of Religious Sci. Churches **[★IO]**

Intl. Assn. of Religious Sci. Churches **[★20525]**

Intl. Assn. for Res. on Epstein Barr Virus **[IO]**, Guangzhou, People's Republic of China

Intl. Assn. for Res. in Income and Wealth **[IO]**, New York, NY, United States

Intl. Assn. for Res. in Income and Wealth **[18407]**, c/o Periodicals Service Company, 11 Main St., Germantown, NY 12526, (212)924-4386

Intl. Assn. for Res. in Vietnamese Music **[10614]**, 2005 Willow Ridge Cir., Kent, OH 44240, (330)673-3763

Intl. Assn. for Res. in Vietnamese Music **[IO]**, Kent, OH, United States

Intl. Assn. of Reservation Executives **[IO]**, Centennial, CO, United States

Intl. Assn. of Reservation Executives **[3828]**, 7400 E Arapahoe Rd., Ste. 211, Centennial, CO 80112, (303)694-4728

Intl. Assn. of Residential and Community Alternative **[★11872]**

Intl. Assn. of Residential and Community Alternative **[★IO]**

Intl. Assn. for Retail Excellence in Awards - Defunct.

Intl. Assn. for the Retractable Awning Industry **[629]**, c/o Lily Harrison, 16677 Racho Rd., Taylor, MI 48180, (734)383-4082

Intl. Assn. for the Retractable Awning Industry **[IO]**, Taylor, MI, United States

Intl. Assn. for the Rhine Ships Register **[IO]**, Rotterdam, Netherlands

Intl. Assn. of Rolling Stock Builders **[★IO]**

Intl. Assn. of Rotary Clubs **[★IO]**

Intl. Assn. of Rotary Clubs **[★13060]**

Intl. Assn. of Round Dance Teachers **[9886]**, 176 S Cole Rd., Boise, ID 83709-0932, (208)377-1232

Intl. Assn. of Round Dance Teachers **[★9886]**

Intl. Assn. of Round Dance Teachers **[★IO]**

Intl. Assn. of Round Dance Teachers **[IO]**, Boise, ID, United States

International Association of R.S. Prussia Collectors **[IO]**, Lost Nation, IA, United States

Intl. Assn. of R.S. Prussia Collectors **[22043]**, PO Box 583, Mukwonago, WI 53149

Intl. Assn. of Sales Professionals - Address unknown since 2003.

Intl. Assn. of Sand Castle Builders **[22971]**

Intl. Assn. of Sanskrit Stud. **[IO]**, Edinburgh, United Kingdom

Intl. Assn. of Satellite Users **[★3746]**

Intl. Assn. of Satellite Users and Suppliers **[3746]**

Intl. Assn. of School Security Directors **[★9087]**

Intl. Assn. of Schools and Institutes of Admin. **[IO]**, Brussels, Belgium

Intl. Assn. of Schools of Social Work **[IO]**, Addis Ababa, Ethiopia

Intl. Assn. of Sci. Parks **[IO]**, Malaga, Spain

Intl. Assn. of Sci. and Tech. for Development **[IO]**, Calgary, AB, Canada

Intl. Assn. for Sci., Tech. and Soc. **[7608]**, c/o Franz Foltz, Treas., Rochester Inst. of Tech., One Lomb Memorial Dr., Rochester, NY 14623-5603

Intl. Assn. of Sci. Experts in Tourism **[IO]**, St. Gallen, Switzerland

Intl. Assn. of Sci. Hydrology **[★IO]**

Intl. Assn. for the Sci. Stud. of Intellectual Disabilities **[IO]**, Cardiff, United Kingdom

Intl. Assn. for the Sci. Stud. of Intellectual Disabilities - Ireland **[IO]**, Cardiff, United Kingdom

Intl. Assn. for the Sci. Stud. of Mental Deficiency **[★IO]**

Intl. Assn. of Sci., Tech. and Medical Publishers **[IO]**, The Hague, Netherlands

Intl. Assn. of Security Service - Address unknown since 2002.

Intl. Assn. of Sedimentologists **[IO]**, Gent, Belgium

Intl. Assn. of Seismology and Physics of the Earth's Interior **[IO]**, Boulder, CO, United States

Intl. Assn. of Seismology and Physics of the Earth's Interior **[7639]**, c/o Prof. Thorne Lay, Univ. of California - Santa Cruz, Earth Sci. Dept., Santa Cruz, CA 95064, (831)459-3164

Intl. Assn. for Seminar Mgt. - Address unknown since 1994.

Intl. Assn. for Semiotic Stud. **[IO]**, Vienna, Austria

Intl. Assn. Service Companies **[★907]**

Intl. Assn. of Ser. Evaluators **[3269]**, c/o Evelyn Arnette, 815 Pavilion Ct., McDonough, GA 30253, (770)288-2717

Intl. Assn. of Severe Weather Specialists - Defunct.

Intl. Assn. for Shell and Spatial Structures **[IO]**, Madrid, Spain

Intl. Assn. for Shopping Center Security - Address unknown since 2001.

Intl. Assn. of Sickle Cell Nurses And Physician Assistants **[14706]**, c/o Jane Hennessy, RNCNP, MPH, Treas., Hematology/Oncology Clinic, 2525 Chicago Ave. S, Ste. 4150, Minneapolis, MN 55404, (612)813-6998

Intl. Assn. of Sickle Cell Nurses And Physician Assistants **[IO]**, Minneapolis, MN, United States

Intl. Assn. of Siderographers - Defunct.

Intl. Assn. of Silver Art Collectors **[22044]**

Intl. Assn. of Silver Art Collectors **[IO]**, Seattle, WA, United States

Intl. Assn. of Silver Bar Collectors **[★IO]**

Intl. Assn. of Silver Bar Collectors **[★22044]**

Intl. Assn. of Skateboard Companies **[23679]**, 22431 Antonio Pkwy., Ste. B160-412, Rancho Santa Margarita, CA 92688, (949)455-1112

Intl. Assn. of Skateboard Companies **[IO]**, Rancho Santa Margarita, CA, United States

Intl. Assn. of the Skubinna Family **[IO]**, Washington, DC, United States

Intl. Assn. of the Skubinna Family **[20952]**, 16 3rd St. NE, Washington, DC 20002-7312, (202)546-0126

A star before a book entry number signifies that the name is not listed separately, but is mentioned within the entry.

International Assn. of the Soap and Detergent Indus. [★IO]

Intl. Assn. for Soaps, Detergents and Maintenance Products [IO], Brussels, Belgium

Intl. Assn. for Social Psychiatry [★IO]

Intl. Assn. for Social Psychiatry [★16099]

Intl. Assn. for Soc. and Natural Resources [5039], c/o Richard S. Krannich, Exec. Dir., Inst. for Social Sci. Res. on Natural Resources, Utah State Univ., 0730 Old Main Hill, Logan, UT 84322-0730, (435)797-1241

Intl. Assn. for Soc. and Natural Resources [IO], Logan, UT, United States

Intl. Assn. of Software Architects [IO], Austin, TX, United States

Intl. Assn. of Software Architects [6770], PO Box 204253, Austin, TX 78720, (866)399-4272

Intl. Assn. of Sound Archives [★IO]

Intl. Assn. of Sound and Audiovisual Archives [IO], Stockholm, Sweden

Intl. Assn. of Space Entrepreneurs [IO], Leesburg, VA, United States

Intl. Assn. of Space Entrepreneurs [3634], 206 Stoneledge Pl, NE, Leesburg, VA 20176, (703)386-9737

Intl. Assn. of Space Philatelists - Address unknown since 1994.

Intl. Assn. of Speakers Bureaus [10900], 7150 Winton Dr., Ste. 300, Indianapolis, IN 46268, (317)328-7790

Intl. Assn. of Speakers Bureaus [IO], Indianapolis, IN, United States

International Association of Special Investigation Units [IO], Baltimore, MD, United States

Intl. Assn. of Special Investigation Units [2188], c/o The Mgt. Alliance, 8015 Corporate Dr., Ste. A, Baltimore, MD 21236, (410)931-3332

Intl. Assn. for Spiritual Consciousness [20574], 401 W Intl. Airport Rd., No. 17, Anchorage, AK 99518-1168, (907)344-5533

Intl. Assn. for Spiritual Consciousness [IO], Anchorage, AK, United States

Intl. Assn. of Sport Kinetics [IO], Warsaw, Poland

Intl. Assn. of Sports Fans - Address unknown since 2003.

Intl. Assn. for Sports Info. [IO], Barcelona, Spain

Intl. Assn. for Sports and Leisure Facilities [IO], Cologne, Germany

Intl. Assn. of Sports Marketing Executives - Defunct.

Intl. Assn. of Sports Museums and Halls of Fame [★23827]

Intl. Assn. of Sports Physicians - Defunct.

Intl. Assn. of Sports Surface Sciences [IO], Eschenz, Switzerland

Intl. Assn. of State Lotteries [★IO]

Intl. Assn. of State Trading Organizations of Developing Countries [★IO]

Intl. Assn. for Statistical Computing [IO], Voorburg, Netherlands

Intl. Assn. for Statistical Educ. [IO], Voorburg, Netherlands

Intl. Assn. of Structural Integrators [IO], Missoula, MT, United States

Intl. Assn. of Structural Integrators [13638], PO Box 8664, Missoula, MT 59807, (406)543-4856

Intl. Assn. for Structural Mechanics in Reactor Tech. [7742], c/o Bonnie Diaz, Center for Nuclear Power Plants Structures, Equip and Piping, Campus Box 7908, North Carolina State Univ., Raleigh, NC 27695-7908, (919)515-7736

Intl. Assn. for Structural Mechanics in Reactor Tech. [IO], Raleigh, NC, United States

Intl. Assn. of Structural Movers [IO], Lexington, SC, United States

Intl. Assn. of Structural Movers [3569], PO Box 2637, Lexington, SC 29071-2637, (803)951-9304

Intl. Assn. of Students in Agriculture and Related Sciences [IO], Heverlee, Belgium

Intl. Assn. of Students in Agriculture and Related Sciences - Algarve [IO], Faro, Portugal

Intl. Assn. of Students in Agriculture and Related Sciences - Ancona [IO], Ancona, Italy

Intl. Assn. of Students in Agriculture and Related Sciences - Austria [IO], Vienna, Austria

Intl. Assn. of Students in Agriculture and Related Sciences - Bandung [IO], Bandung, Indonesia

Intl. Assn. of Students in Agriculture and Related Sciences - Belarus [IO], Minsk, Belarus

Intl. Assn. of Students in Agriculture and Related Sciences - Berlin [IO], Berlin, Germany

Intl. Assn. of Students in Agriculture and Related Sciences - Bogor [IO], Bogor, Indonesia

Intl. Assn. of Students in Agriculture and Related Sciences - Bologna [IO], Bologna, Italy

Intl. Assn. of Students in Agriculture and Related Sciences - Bonn [IO], Bonn, Germany

Intl. Assn. of Students in Agriculture and Related Sciences - Brawijaya Univ. [IO], Malang, Indonesia

Intl. Assn. of Students in Agriculture and Related Sciences - Bulgaria [IO], Stara Zagora, Bulgaria

Intl. Assn. of Students in Agriculture and Related Sciences - Cape Coast [IO], Cape Coast, Ghana

Intl. Assn. of Students in Agriculture and Related Sciences - Coimbra [IO], Coimbra, Portugal

Intl. Assn. of Students in Agriculture and Related Sciences - Cordoba [IO], Cordoba, Spain

Intl. Assn. of Students in Agriculture and Related Sciences - Croatia [IO], Zagreb, Croatia

Intl. Assn. of Students in Agriculture and Related Sciences - Czech Republic [IO], Prague, Czech Republic

Intl. Assn. of Students in Agriculture and Related Sciences - Denmark [IO], Frederiksberg, Denmark

Intl. Assn. of Students in Agriculture and Related Sciences - Finland [IO], Helsinki, Finland

Intl. Assn. of Students in Agriculture and Related Sciences - France [IO], Nancy, France

Intl. Assn. of Students in Agriculture and Related Sciences - Gent [IO], Gent, Belgium

Intl. Assn. of Students in Agriculture and Related Sciences - Georgia [IO], Tbilisi, Georgia

Intl. Assn. of Students in Agriculture and Related Sciences - Greece [IO], Athens, Greece

Intl. Assn. of Students in Agriculture and Related Sciences - Hungary [IO], Mosonmagyarovar, Hungary

Intl. Assn. of Students in Agriculture and Related Sciences - Ibadan [IO], Ibadan, Nigeria

Intl. Assn. of Students in Agriculture and Related Sciences - Indonesia [IO], Malang, Indonesia

Intl. Assn. of Students in Agriculture and Related Sciences - Italy [IO], Sassari, Italy

Intl. Assn. of Students in Agriculture and Related Sciences - Kendari [IO], Kendari, Indonesia

Intl. Assn. of Students in Agriculture and Related Sciences - Kenya [IO], Nairobi, Kenya

Intl. Assn. of Students in Agriculture and Related Sciences - Lautech [IO], Ogbomosho, Nigeria

Intl. Assn. of Students in Agriculture and Related Sciences - Lisbon [IO], Lisbon, Portugal

Intl. Assn. of Students in Agriculture and Related Sciences - Ljubljana [IO], Ljubljana, Slovenia

Intl. Assn. of Students in Agriculture and Related Sciences - Macedonia [IO], Skopje, Macedonia

Intl. Assn. of Students in Agriculture and Related Sciences - Madrid [IO], Madrid, Spain

Intl. Assn. of Students in Agriculture and Related Sciences - Maribor [IO], Maribor, Slovenia

Intl. Assn. of Students in Agriculture and Related Sciences - Milan [IO], Milan, Italy

Intl. Assn. of Students in Agriculture and Related Sciences - Monterrey [IO], Monterrey, Mexico

Intl. Assn. of Students in Agriculture and Related Sciences - Nepal [IO], Kathmandu, Nepal

Intl. Assn. of Students in Agriculture and Related Sciences - Netherlands [IO], Wageningen, Netherlands

Intl. Assn. of Students in Agriculture and Related Sciences - Niger [IO], Niamey, Niger

Intl. Assn. of Students in Agriculture and Related Sciences - Norway [IO], Aas, Norway

Intl. Assn. of Students in Agriculture and Related Sciences - Osijek [IO], Osijek, Croatia

Intl. Assn. of Students in Agriculture and Related Sciences - Piacenza [IO], Piacenza, Italy

Intl. Assn. of Students in Agriculture and Related Sciences - Poland [IO], Warsaw, Poland

Intl. Assn. of Students in Agriculture and Related Sciences - Ponte de Lima [IO], Ponte de Lima, Portugal

Intl. Assn. of Students in Agriculture and Related Sciences - Porto [IO], Vila do Conde, Portugal

Intl. Assn. of Students in Agriculture and Related Sciences - Portugal [IO], Lisbon, Portugal

Intl. Assn. of Students in Agriculture and Related Sciences - Queretaro [IO], Santiago de Queretaro, Mexico

Intl. Assn. of Students in Agriculture and Related Sciences - Russia [IO], Moscow, Russia

Intl. Assn. of Students in Agriculture and Related Sciences - St. Petersburg [IO], St. Petersburg, Russia

Intl. Assn. of Students in Agriculture and Related Sciences - Santarem [IO], Santarem, Portugal

Intl. Assn. of Students in Agriculture and Related Sciences - Sassari [IO], Sassari, Italy

Intl. Assn. of Students in Agriculture and Related Sciences - Switzerland [IO], Zurich, Switzerland

Intl. Assn. of Students in Agriculture and Related Sciences - Thailand [IO], Khon Kaen, Thailand

Intl. Assn. of Students in Agriculture and Related Sciences - Thessaloniki [IO], Thessaloniki, Greece

Intl. Assn. of Students in Agriculture and Related Sciences - Togo [IO], Palime, Togo

Intl. Assn. of Students in Agriculture and Related Sciences - Turin [IO], Turin, Italy

Intl. Assn. of Students in Agriculture and Related Sciences - Uganda [IO], Kampala, Uganda

Intl. Assn. of Students in Agriculture and Related Sciences - Ukraine [IO], Kiev, Ukraine

Intl. Assn. of Students in Agriculture and Related Sciences - Ultuna [IO], Uppsala, Sweden

Intl. Assn. of Students in Agriculture and Related Sciences - Uzbekistan [IO], Tashkent, Uzbekistan

Intl. Assn. of Students in Agriculture and Related Sciences - Vila Real [IO], Vila Real, Portugal

Intl. Assn. of Students in Agriculture and Related Sciences - Viterbo [IO], Viterbo, Italy

Intl. Assn. of Students in Agriculture and Related Sciences - Zambia [IO], Lusaka, Zambia

Intl. Assn. of Students in Agriculture and Related Sciences - Zimbabwe [IO], Harare, Zimbabwe

Intl. Assn. of Students in Economics and Bus. Management—United States [IO]

Intl. Assn. of Students in Economics and Bus. Management—United States [8012]

Intl. Assn. of Students in Economics and Mgt. - Hong Kong Natl. Comm. [IO], Hong Kong, People's Republic of China

Intl. Assn. of Students in Economics and Mgt. Netherlands [★IO]

Intl. Assn. for Stud. of Men [IO], Oslo, Norway

Intl. Assn. for the Stud. of Ancient Mosaics [IO], Paris, France

Intl. Assn. for the Stud. of Clays [IO], Brisbane, Australia

Intl. Assn. for the Stud. of Common Property [IO], Gary, IN, United States

Intl. Assn. for the Stud. of Common Property [4410], PO Box 2355, Gary, IN 46409, (219)980-1433

Intl. Assn. for the Stud. of Dreams [16426], 1672 Univ. Ave., Berkeley, CA 94703, (209)724-0889

Intl. Assn. for the Stud. of Forced Migration [IO], Oxford, United Kingdom

Intl. Assn. for the Stud. of Fossil Cnidaria and Porifera [IO], Cologne, Germany

Intl. Assn. for the Stud. of Insurance Economics [IO], Geneva, Switzerland

Intl. Assn. for the Stud. of Irish Literatures [IO], Moorhead, MN, United States

Intl. Assn. for the Stud. of Irish Literatures [8800], c/o Dr. Dawn Duncan, PhD, Exec. Sec., Concordia Coll., Dept. of English, 901 8th St. S, Moorhead, MN 56562, (218)299-3961

Intl. Assn. for the Stud. of the Liver [IO], Munich, Germany

Intl. Assn. for the Stud. of Lung Cancer [13832], c/o Pia Hirsch, PO Box 6511, Aurora, CO 80045-0511, (303)724-3155

Intl. Assn. for the Stud. of Maritime Mission [IO], York, United Kingdom

Intl. Assn. for the Stud. of Obesity [IO], London, United Kingdom

Intl. Assn. for the Stud. of Organized Crime [IO], Bloomington, IN, United States

Intl. Assn. for the Stud. of Organized Crime [11837], c/o Dina Siegel, Pres., Indiana Univ., Dept. of Criminal Justice, 302 Sycamore Hall, Bloomington, IN 47405, (812)855-0889

Reference to "IO" in place of a book number signifies that the association may be found in the 45th edition of International Organizations.

Intl. Assn. for the Stud. of Pain [15841], 111 Queen Anne Ave. N, Ste. 501, Seattle, WA 98109-4955, (206)547-6409

Intl. Assn. for the Stud. of Pain [IO], Seattle, WA, United States

Intl. Assn. for the Stud. of Popular Music [IO], Liverpool, United Kingdom

Intl. Assn. for the Stud. of Sexuality, Culture and Soc. [IO], San Francisco, CA, United States

Intl. Assn. for the Stud. of Sexuality, Culture and Soc. [9124], c/o Niels Teunis, Sec.-Treas., 2017 Mission St., No. 300, San Francisco, CA 94110, (415)437-1473

Intl. Assn. of Sublimation Printers - Defunct.

Intl. Assn. of Sufism [20101], 14 Commercial Blvd., Ste. 101, Novato, CA 94949, (415)382-7834

Intl. Assn. for Suicide Prevention [IO], Gondrin, France

Intl. Assn. of Supreme Administrative Jurisdictions [IO], Paris, France

Intl. Assn. for Surgical Metabolism and Nutrition [IO], Pratteln, Switzerland

Intl. Assn. of Survey Statisticians [IO], Libourne, France

Intl. Assn. of System Operators - Address unknown since 1999.

Intl. Assn. for Tartan Stud. [19354], PO Box 138, Skippack, PA 19474, (610)584-4220

Intl. Assn. for Tartan Stud. [IO], Skippack, PA, United States

Intl. Assn. of Teachers of Czech [IO], Austin, TX, United States

Intl. Assn. of Teachers of Czech [9861], c/o Prof. Hana Pichova, Exec. Off., Univ. of Texas, PO Box 7217, Austin, TX 78713

Intl. Assn. of Teachers of English as a Foreign Language [IO], Kent, United Kingdom

Intl. Assn. of Teachers of Italian [IO], Brussels, Belgium

Intl. Assn. of Teachers of Russian Language and Literature [IO], Moscow, Russia

Intl. Assn. of Technological Univ. Libraries [IO], Dublin, Ireland

Intl. Assn. of Telecomputer Networks - Address unknown since 1999.

Intl. Assn. for Textile Care Labelling [IO], Clichy, France

Intl. Assn. Textile Dyers [★IO]

Intl. Assn. of Textile Dyers and Printers [★IO]

Intl. Assn. of Theatre for Children and Young People [IO], Johanneshov, Sweden

Intl. Assn. of Theatre Critics [IO], Isleworth, United Kingdom

Intl. Assn. of Theoretical and Applied Limnology [IO], Chapel Hill, NC, United States

Intl. Assn. of Theoretical and Applied Limnology [7240], c/o Dr. William M. Lewis, Jr., Acting Gen. Sec.-Treas., Univ. of North Carolina at Chapel Hill, School of Public Hea., Dept. of Environmental Sciences and Engg., 124 Rosenau Hall, CB No. 7431, Chapel Hill, NC 27599-7431, (336)376-9362

Intl. Assn. of Therapeutic Drug Monitoring and Clinical Toxicology [IO], Kingston, ON, Canada

Intl. Assn. for Time Use Res. [IO], Halifax, NS, Canada

Intl. Assn. of Tool Craftsmen - Address unknown since 2003.

Intl. Assn. of Torch Clubs [10894], 749 Boush St., Norfolk, VA 23510-1517, (757)622-3927

Intl. Assn. of Tour Managers [IO], London, United Kingdom

Intl. Assn. of Tour Managers - Central Europe [IO], Lucerne, Switzerland

Intl. Assn. of Tour Managers - France [IO], London, United Kingdom

Intl. Assn. of Tour Managers - Israel [IO], Tel Aviv, Israel

Intl. Assn. of Tour Managers - Italy [IO], Rome, Italy

Intl. Assn. of Tour Managers - North Amer. Region [IO], Kerhonkson, NY, United States

Intl. Assn. of Tour Managers - North Amer. Region [3922], 24 Blevins Rd., Kerhonkson, NY 12446-1302, (212)208-6800

Intl. Assn. of Tour Managers - Pacific [IO], Sydney, Australia

Intl. Assn. of Tour Managers - Spain [IO], London, United Kingdom

Intl. Assn. of Tour Managers - Taiwan [IO], Taipei, Taiwan

Intl. Assn. of Touring Theatre Presentors - Defunct.

Intl. Assn. of Trade Exchanges [★3841]

Intl. Assn. of Trade Exchanges [★IO]

Intl. Assn. of Trading Organizations for a Developing World [IO], Ljubljana, Slovenia

Intl. Assn. of Traffic and Safety Sciences [IO], Tokyo, Japan

International Association of Transpersonal Therapists and Physicians [IO], Virginia Beach, VA, United States

Intl. Assn. of Transpersonal Therapists and Physicians [15205], 485 S Independence Blvd., Ste. 111, Virginia Beach, VA 23452, (757)216-8096

Intl. Assn. of Trauma Counseling [★11821]

Intl. Assn. of Trauma Counseling [★IO]

Intl. Assn. of Travel Exhibitors - Defunct.

Intl. Assn. of Travel Journalists - Defunct.

Intl. Assn. of Triathlon Clubs - Address unknown since 2001.

Intl. Assn. of Trichologists [IO], Sydney, Australia

Intl. Assn. for Truancy and Dropout Prevention [IO], Houston, TX, United States

Intl. Assn. for Truancy and Dropout Prevention [8326], c/o Henrietta Pryor, Sec., 812 W 28th St., Houston, TX 77008, (713)293-9711

Intl. Assn. of Undercover Officers [5976], 142 Banks Dr., Brunswick, GA 31523, (800)876-5943

International Association of Undercover Officers [IO], Brunswick, GA, United States

Intl. Assn. for a Union of Democracies - Defunct.

Intl. Assn. of Universities [IO], Paris, France

Intl. Assn. of Univ. Professors of English [IO], Mex, Switzerland

Intl. Assn. of Univ. Res. Parks [★9054]

Intl. Assn. for Urban Climate [IO], Singapore, Singapore

International Association of Used Equipment Dealers [IO], Wilmington, DE, United States

Intl. Assn. of Used Equip. Dealers [3052], 214 Edgewood Dr., Ste. 100, Wilmington, DE 19809, (302)765-3571

Intl. Assn. for Vegetation Sci. [IO], Wageningen, Netherlands

Intl. Assn. for Vehicle Sys. Dynamics [IO], Prague, Czech Republic

Intl. Assn. of Voice Identification [★IO]

Intl. Assn. of Voice Identification [★5763]

Intl. Assn. for Voice Movement Therapy [13711], 912 Hunters Ln., Oreland, PA 19075, (267)625-5451

Intl. Assn. for Voice Movement Therapy [IO], Oreland, PA, United States

Intl. Assn. of Volcanology and Chemistry of the Earth's Interior [IO], Campbell, Australia

Intl. Assn. for Volunteer Effort [IO], Washington, DC, United States

Intl. Assn. for Volunteer Effort [13396], c/o Civil Soc. Consulting Gp., LLC, 805 15th St. NW, Ste. 100, Washington, DC 20005, (202)628-4360

Intl. Assn. for Volunteer Effort - Belarus [IO], Minsk, Belarus

Intl. Assn. for Volunteer Effort - Bolivia [IO], Santa Cruz, Bolivia

Intl. Assn. for Volunteer Effort - Botswana [IO], Gaborone, Botswana

Intl. Assn. for Volunteer Effort - Brazil [IO], Rio de Janeiro, Brazil

Intl. Assn. for Volunteer Effort - Chile [IO], Santiago, Chile

Intl. Assn. for Volunteer Effort - Colombia [IO], Bogota, Colombia

Intl. Assn. for Volunteer Effort - Cyprus [IO], Nicosia, Cyprus

Intl. Assn. for Volunteer Effort - Czech Republic [IO], Prague, Czech Republic

Intl. Assn. for Volunteer Effort - Ecuador [IO], Quito, Ecuador

Intl. Assn. for Volunteer Effort - France [IO], Paris, France

Intl. Assn. for Volunteer Effort - Greece [IO], Athens, Greece

Intl. Assn. for Volunteer Effort - Hong Kong [IO], Hong Kong, People's Republic of China

Intl. Assn. for Volunteer Effort - India [IO], New Delhi, India

Intl. Assn. for Volunteer Effort - Korea [IO], Seoul, Republic of Korea

Intl. Assn. for Volunteer Effort - Liberia [IO], Monrovia, Liberia

Intl. Assn. for Volunteer Effort - Nepal [IO], Lalitpur, Nepal

Intl. Assn. for Volunteer Effort - Nigeria [IO], Umuahia, Nigeria

Intl. Assn. for Volunteer Effort - Russia [IO], Moscow, Russia

Intl. Assn. for Volunteer Effort - Sierra Leone [IO], Freetown, Sierra Leone

Intl. Assn. for Volunteer Effort - Slovenia [IO], Ljubljana, Slovenia

Intl. Assn. for Volunteer Effort - Switzerland [IO], Geneva, Switzerland

Intl. Assn. for Volunteer Effort - Uruguay [IO], Montevideo, Uruguay

Intl. Assn. for Volunteer Effort - Venezuela [IO], Caracas, Venezuela

Intl. Assn. of Wagner Societies [IO], Freiburg, Germany

Intl. Assn. on Water Pollution Res. and Control [★IO]

Intl. Assn. of Water Polo Referees [IO], Genoa, Italy

Intl. Assn. on Water Quality [★IO]

Intl. Assn. of Waterworks in the Rhine Basin Area [IO], Cologne, Germany

International Association of Webmasters and Designers [IO], Wellington, FL, United States

Intl. Assn. of Webmasters and Designers [888], 11924 Forest Hill Blvd., Executive Ste. 22-276, Wellington, FL 33414, (561)248-5507

Intl. Assn. of Wholesale Markets within IULA [★IO]

Intl. Assn. of Wholesalers - Defunct.

Intl. Assn. of Wildland Fire [4686], PO Box 261, Hot Springs, SD 57747-0261, (605)890-2348

Intl. Assn. of Wildland Fire [IO], Hot Springs, SD, United States

Intl. Assn. of Wiping Cloth Mfrs. [★IO]

Intl. Assn. of Wiping Cloth Mfrs. [★2066]

Intl. Assn. of Women Chefs and Restaurateurs [★794]

Intl. Assn. for Women of Color Day [17541], 3325 Northrop Ave., Sacramento, CA 95864, (916)483-9804

Intl. Assn. for Women of Color Day [IO], Sacramento, CA, United States

Intl. Assn. of Women Ministers [IO], Stroudsburg, PA, United States

Intl. Assn. of Women Ministers [20619], c/o Rev. Carol S. Brown, Treas., 579 Main St., Stroudsburg, PA 18360, (570)421-7751

Intl. Assn. of Women in Radio and TV [IO], New Delhi, India

Intl. Assn. of Wood Anatomists [IO], Leiden, Netherlands

Intl. Assn. of Wool Textile Labs. [IO], Bradford, United Kingdom

Intl. Assn. of Word and Image Stud. [IO], Ann Arbor, MI, United States

Intl. Assn. of Word and Image Stud. [9060], c/o Dr. Michele Hannoosh, Sec., Univ. of Michigan, Dept. of Romance Languages and Literature, Modern Languages Bldg., Ann Arbor, MI 48109, (734)764-5344

Intl. Assn. of Word Processing Specialists - Defunct.

Intl. Assn. of Workforce Professionals [5679], 1801 Louisville Rd., Frankfort, KY 40601, (502)223-4459

Intl. Assn. of Workforce Professionals [IO], Frankfort, KY, United States

Intl. Assn. of Young Lawyers [IO], Brussels, Belgium

Intl. Assn. of Youth and Family Judges and Magistrates [IO], The Hague, Netherlands

Intl. Assn. of Youth Magistrates [★IO]

Intl. Astronautical Fed. [IO], Paris, France

Intl. Astronomical Union [IO], Paris, France

Intl. Atherosclerosis Soc. [IO], Houston, TX, United States

Intl. Atherosclerosis Soc. [13910]

Intl. Athletic Found. [IO], Monaco, Monaco

Intl. Atlantic Economic Soc. [IO], St. Louis, MO, United States

A star before a book entry number signifies that the name is not listed separately, but is mentioned within the entry.

Intl. Atlantic Economic Soc. [6883], 4949 W Pine Blvd., 2nd Fl., St. Louis, MO 63108-1431, (314)454-0100

International Atlantic Salmon Found. [★IO]

Intl. Atomic Energy Agency [IO], Vienna, Austria

Intl. Audiotex Regulators Network [IO], Dusseldorf, Germany

Intl. Audiovisual Soc. - Defunct.

Intl. Autistic Res. Org. [IO], Croydon, United Kingdom

Intl. Auto Sound Challenge Assn. [1219], 2129 S Ridgewood Ave., South Daytona, FL 32119, (386)322-1551

Intl. Autograph Collectors Club and Dealers Alliance [22045], PO Box 848486, Hollywood, FL 33084

Intl. Auto. Fed. [IO], Paris, France

Intl. Automotive Hall of Shame - Address unknown since 2000.

Intl. Automotive Remarketers Alliance [359], PO Box 431, Mount Arlington, NJ 07856, (973)398-2774

Intl. Aviation Ground Support Assn. [436], 201 Park Washington Ct., Falls Church, VA 22046-4527, (703)533-0251

Intl. Aviation Ground Support Assn. [IO], Falls Church, VA, United States

Intl. Aviation Theft Bur. [★433]

Intl. Aviation Womens Assn. [437], PO Box 1088, Edgewater, MD 21037, (410)571-1990

International Aviation Womens Association [IO], Edgewater, MD, United States

Intl. Aviculturists Soc. [IO], Memphis, TN, United States

Intl. Aviculturists Soc. [4199], PO Box 341852, Memphis, TN 38184

Intl. B-24 Liberator Club [21394], 1672 Main St., Ste. E-124, Ramona, CA 92065-5257, (760)788-3624

Intl. B-24 Liberator Club [IO], Ramona, CA, United States

Intl. B and B Fly-Inn Club [21451]

Intl. Baby Food Action Network - Africa [IO], Mbabane, Swaziland

Intl. Baby Food Action Network - Asia [IO], Pitampura, India

Intl. Baby Food Action Network - Brazil [IO], Paraguacu Paulista, Brazil

Intl. Baby Food Action Network - Latin Am. [IO], San Jose, Costa Rica

Intl. Baby Food Action Network - South Am. [IO], Buenos Aires, Argentina

Intl. Baccalaureate Org. [IO], Geneva, Switzerland

Intl. Bach Soc. - Defunct.

Intl. Backgammon Assn. [22466]

Intl. Backpackers Assn. [★23934]

Intl. Badminton Fed. [★IO]

Intl. Balance Disorder Assn. - Defunct.

Intl. Ballet Competition for the U.S. - Defunct.

Intl. Balloon Assn. - Address unknown since 1999.

Intl. Baltic Sea Fishery Commn. [IO], Warsaw, Poland

International Banana Association [IO], Washington, DC, United States

Intl. Banana Assn. [4736], 1901 Pennsylvania Ave. NW, Ste. 1100, Washington, DC 20006, (540)314-3214

Intl. Banana Club [22596], 16367 Main St., Hesperia, CA 92345-3547, (760)244-5488

Intl. Banana Club [IO], Hesperia, CA, United States

Intl. Band and Orchestral Products Assn. [IO], New York, NY, United States

Intl. Band and Orchestral Products Assn. [2810], PO Box 757, New York, NY 10033, (212)795-3630

Intl. Bank Note Soc. [22739], c/o Marcus Turner, Pres., PO Box 191, Danville, IN 46122

Intl. Bank Note Soc. [IO], Danville, IN, United States

Intl. Bank for Reconstruction and Development [IO], Washington, DC, United States

Intl. Bank for Reconstruction and Development [17841], 1818 H St. NW, Washington, DC 20433, (202)473-1000

Intl. Bankers Forum [IO], Frankfurt am Main, Germany

Intl. Banknotes Soc. - England [IO], London, United Kingdom

Intl. Bar Assn. [IO], London, United Kingdom

Intl. Barbed Wire Collectors Assn. - Address unknown since 1995.

Intl. Barbeque Cookers Assn. [22570], PO Box 300556, Arlington, TX 76007-0556, (817)469-1579

Intl. Barbie Doll Collectors Club - Defunct.

Intl. Barrel Racing Assn. [23500], PO Box 425, Valley City, OH 44280, (330)483-9608

International Barrel Racing Association [IO], Valley City, OH, United States

Intl. Baseball Fed. [IO], Lausanne, Switzerland

Intl. Basketball Assn. - Defunct.

Intl. Basketball Fed. [IO], Geneva, Switzerland

Intl. Baton Twirling Assn. of America and Abroad - Defunct.

Intl. Battleship Galactica Soc. - Defunct.

Intl. BBSing and Electronic Communications Corp. [3747], PO Box 21766, Denver, CO 80221-0766, (303)426-1847

Intl. Bear Assn. [★5325]

Intl. Bear Assn. [★IO]

Intl. Bee Res. Assn. [IO], Cardiff, United Kingdom

Intl. Beefalo Breeders Registry [★IO]

Intl. Beefalo Breeders Registry [★4123]

Intl. Beer Tasting Soc. - Defunct.

Intl. Behavioral Neuroscience Soc. [15408], c/o Marianne Van Wagner, Exec. Coor., 8181 Tezel Rd., No. 10269, San Antonio, TX 78250, (830)796-9393

Intl. Behavioral Neuroscience Soc. [IO], San Antonio, TX, United States

Intl. Behavioural and Neural Genetics Soc. [IO], Seoul, Republic of Korea

Intl. Benchrest Shooters [IO], Springville, PA, United States

Intl. Benchrest Shooters [23717], c/o Joan Borden, Recording Sec., RR1, Box 250 BB, Springville, PA 18844, (570)965-2505

Intl. Benevolent Soc. - Address unknown since 2007.

The Intl. Bengal Breeders' Assn. [4205], 2336 Pleasant Grove, Westmoreland, TN 37186, (615)644-2992

The International Bengal Breeders' Association [IO], Westmoreland, TN, United States

The International Bengal Cat Society [IO], Long Beach, CA, United States

The Intl. Bengal Cat Soc. [4206], PO Box 50198, Long Beach, CA 90815

Intl. Benjamin Franklin Soc. - Defunct.

Intl. Bentham Soc. [★IO]

Intl. Berkeley Soc. [10798], Dept. of Philosophy, Texas A and M Univ., College Station, TX 77843, (979)845-5660

Intl. Betta Cong. [22441], c/o Steve Van Camp, Membership Chm./Sec., 923 Wadsworth St., Syracuse, NY 13208, (315)454-4792

Intl. Betta Cong. [IO], Syracuse, NY, United States

International Beverage Dispensing Equipment Association [IO], Baltimore, MD, United States

Intl. Beverage Dispensing Equip. Assn. [507], 3837 Naylors Ln., Baltimore, MD 21208, (410)602-0616

Intl. Beverage Packaging Assn. [508], c/o Brian Bishop, Pres., Anheuser-Busch, Inc., Fort Collins, CO 80524

Intl. Bi-Rak-It Assn. [23676]

Intl. Biathlon Union [IO], Salzburg, Austria

Intl. Bible Mission - Defunct.

Intl. Bible Soc. [19520], PO Box 35700, Colorado Springs, CO 80935-3570, (719)488-9200

Intl. Bible Soc. [IO], Colorado Springs, CO, United States

Intl. Bible Students Assn. [IO], Brooklyn, NY, United States

Intl. Bible Students Assn. [19521], 25 Columbia Heights, Brooklyn, NY 11201-2483, (718)560-5000

Intl. Bicycle Fund [13338], 4887 Columbia Dr. S, Seattle, WA 98108-1919, (206)767-0848

Intl. Bicycle Fund [IO], Seattle, WA, United States

Intl. Bicycle Touring Soc. - Address unknown since 1999.

Intl. Biliary Assn. [★14802]

Intl. Biliary Assn. [★IO]

Intl. Bio-Environmental Found. - Address unknown since 2004.

Intl. Bioacoustics Coun. [IO], London, United Kingdom

Intl. Biodeterioration and Biodegradation Soc. [IO], Northwich, United Kingdom

Intl. Biogeography Soc. [7122], c/o Glen M. MacDonald, PhD, 2133 Basswood Ct., Westlake Village, CA 91361

Intl. BioIron Soc. [15269], 1111 N Plaza Dr., Ste. 550, Schaumburg, IL 60173, (847)517-7225

Intl. BioIron Soc. [IO], Schaumburg, IL, United States

Intl. Biomass Inst. - Defunct.

Intl. Biometric Assn. - Address unknown since 1995.

Intl. Biometric Indus. Assn. [7743], 1666 K St. NW, Washington, DC 20006, (202)293-8133

Intl. Biometric Soc. [7707], 1444 I St. NW, Ste. 700, Washington, DC 20005, (202)712-9049

Intl. Biometric Soc. [IO], Washington, DC, United States

Intl. Biometric Soc., Eastern North Amer. Region [7708], 12100 Sunset Hills Rd., Ste. 130, Reston, VA 20190, (703)437-4377

Intl. Biometric Soc., Western North Amer. Region [7709], c/o Cancer Res. and Biostatistics, 1730 Minor Ave., Ste. 1900, Seattle, WA 98101-1468

Intl. Biometric Soc., Western North Amer. Region [IO], Seattle, WA, United States

Intl. Biopharmaceutical Assn. [IO], Austin, TX, United States

Intl. Biopharmaceutical Assn. [15936], PMB 143, 11521 N FM 620, No. 250, Austin, TX 78726, (914)206-4640

Intl. Biotechnology Scientific Assn. - Address unknown since 2001.

Intl. Bird Beer Label Assn. [21491], PO Box 2551, Homer, AK 99603

Intl. Bird Beer Label Assn. [IO], Homer, AK, United States

Intl. Bird Dog Assn. [21452], c/o Suzanne Cobb, Membership Dir., 1845 Port Stanhope Pl., Newport Beach, CA 92660

Intl. Bird Rescue Res. Center [5326], 4369 Cordelia Rd., Fairfield, CA 94534, (707)207-0380

Intl. Bird Rescue Res. Center [IO], Fairfield, CA, United States

Intl. Bird Strike Comm. [IO], The Hague, Netherlands

Intl. Black Peoples' Found. - Defunct.

Intl. Black Toy Mfrs. Assn. - Address unknown since 1994.

Intl. Black Women for Wages for Housework [18811], PO Box 86681, Los Angeles, CA 90086-0681, (323)292-7405

Intl. Black Women's Cong. [17542], 645 Church St., Ste. 200, Norfolk, VA 23510, (800)280-0122

International Black Women's Congress [IO], Norfolk, VA, United States

Intl. Black Writers [★IO]

Intl. Black Writers [★11177]

Intl. Black Writers and Artists [11177], PO Box 43576, Los Angeles, CA 90043, (213)964-3721

Intl. Black Writers and Artists [IO], Los Angeles, CA, United States

Intl. Black Writers Conf. [★IO]

Intl. Black Writers Conf. [★11177]

Intl. Blade Collectors - Defunct.

Intl. Blind Sports Assn. [★IO]

Intl. Blind Sports Fed. [IO], Madrid, Spain

Intl. Blind Sports Fed. Europe [IO], Olival Basto, Portugal

Intl. Blind Sports Fed. Oceania [IO], Auckland, New Zealand

Intl. Blue Crescent Relief and Development Found. [IO], Istanbul, Turkey

Intl. Blue Jay Class Assn. [IO], Mantoloking, NJ, United States

Intl. Blue Jay Class Assn. [23181], c/o William K. Dunbar, III, Pres., 12 Sandpiper Point Rd., Old Lyme, CT 06371, (732)295-0238

Intl. Bluegrass Music Assn. [10615], 2 Music Cir. S, Ste. 100, Nashville, TN 37203, (615)256-3222

International Bluegrass Music Association [IO], Nashville, TN, United States

Intl. Blues Soc. [21865]

Intl. Bd. on Books for Young People [IO], Basel, Switzerland

Intl. Board on Books for Young People - Dutch Section [IO], Amsterdam, Netherlands

International Bd. of Electrologist Certification [★14308]

Intl. Bd. of Environmental Medicine [14365], 65 Wehrle Dr., Cheektowaga, NY 14225, (716)837-1320

Reference to "IO" in place of a book number signifies that the association may be found in the 45th edition of International Organizations.

Encyclopedia of Associations, 46th Edition

3645

Intl. Bd. of Environmental Medicine **[IO]**, Cheektowaga, NY, United States

Intl. Bd. of Jewish Missions **[IO]**, Hixson, TN, United States

Intl. Bd. of Jewish Missions **[20014]**, PO Box 1386, Hixson, TN 37343, (423)876-8150

Intl. Bd. of Lactation Consultant Examiners **[13775]**, 7245 Arlington Blvd., Ste. 200, Falls Church, VA 22042-3217, (703)560-7330

Intl. Bd. of Lactation Consultant Examiners **[IO]**, Falls Church, VA, United States

Intl. Bd. for Regression Therapy **[IO]**, Lafayette, CA, United States

Intl. Bd. for Regression Therapy **[16618]**, 3702 Mt. Diablo Blvd., Lafayette, CA 94549, (925)283-3941

Intl. Bd. of Standards and Practices for Certified Financial Planners **[★1459]**

Intl. Bobath Alumni Assn. **[★15399]**

Intl. Bocce Assn. - Address unknown since 2008.

Intl. Boer Goat Assn. **[4783]**, PO Box 1045, Whitewright, TX 75491, (903)364-5735

Intl. Boer Goat Assn. **[IO]**, Whitewright, TX, United States

Intl. Boethius Soc. **[10799]**, c/o Noel Harold Kaylor, Jr., Exec. Dir., Dept. of English, Univ. of Northern Iowa, Cedar Falls, IA 50614-0502

Intl. Bond and Share Soc. **[22046]**, PO Box 430, Hackensack, NJ 07602-0430, (201)489-2440

Intl. Bond and Share Soc. **[IO]**, Hackensack, NJ, United States

Intl. Bone Marrow Transplant Registry **[★IO]**

Intl. Bone Marrow Transplant Registry **[★13771]**

Intl. Bonefishing Soc. **[22452]**, 205A Plaza Dr., Greenville, NC 27858, (252)353-4440

International Bonefishing Society **[IO]**, Greenville, NC, United States

Intl. Book Bank **[IO]**, Baltimore, MD, United States

Intl. Book Bank **[8619]**, PO Box 1662, Baltimore, MD 21203, (410)362-0334

Intl. Book Proj. **[8620]**, Van Meter Bldg., 1440 Delaware Ave., Lexington, KY 40505, (859)254-6771

Intl. Book Proj. **[IO]**, Lexington, KY, United States

Intl. Booksellers Fed. **[IO]**, Brussels, Belgium

Intl. Border Fancy Canary Club - Address unknown since 1999.

Intl. Borzoi Coun. **[22287]**, c/o Shen Smith, Intl. Conf. Coor., PO Box 175, Elk Rapids, MI 49629, (231)264-6665

Intl. Borzoi Coun. **[IO]**, Elk Rapids, MI, United States

Intl. Bossons Collectors Soc. **[22047]**, 8316 Woodlake Pl., Tampa, FL 33615-1728, (813)885-2038

Intl. Bottled Water Assn. **[509]**, 1700 Diagonal Rd., Ste. 650, Alexandria, VA 22314, (703)683-5213

Intl. Bottled Water Assn. **[IO]**, Alexandria, VA, United States

Intl. Boundaries Res. Unit **[IO]**, Durham, United Kingdom

International Bowhunter Educ. Program **[★23053]**

Intl. Bowhunting Org. **[23544]**, PO Box 398, Vermilion, OH 44089, (440)967-2137

International Bowhunting Organization **[IO]**, Vermilion, OH, United States

Intl. Bowling Fed. **[IO]**, Pasig City, Philippines

Intl. Bowling Pro Shop and Instructors Assn. **[531]**, 615 Six Flags Dr., Arlington, TX 76011-6305, (817)649-0079

Intl. Boxing Fed. **[23260]**, 516 Main St., 2nd Fl., East Orange, NJ 07018, (973)414-0300

Intl. Boxing Fed. **[IO]**, East Orange, NJ, United States

Intl. Boxing Hall of Fame Museum **[23261]**, 1 Hall of Fame Dr., Canastota, NY 13032, (315)697-7095

Intl. Boxing Writers Assn. - Address unknown since 2001.

Intl. Boys' Schools Coalition **[8268]**, c/o Christopher Wadsworth, Assoc. Exec. Dir., PO Box 117, Dennis, MA 02638-0117, (508)385-4563

Intl. Boys' Schools Coalition **[IO]**, Dennis, MA, United States

Intl. Braford Assn. **[★4295]**

Intl. Brain Res. Org. **[IO]**, Paris, France

Intl. Brain Tumour Alliance **[IO]**, Tadworth, United Kingdom

Intl. Brancusi Soc. - Address unknown since 1994.

Intl. Brangus Breeders Assn. **[4265]**, PO Box 696020, San Antonio, TX 78269-6020, (210)696-4343

Intl. Brecht Soc. **[9661]**, c/o Paula Hanssen, Sec.-Treas., Webster Univ., 470 E Lockwood, St. Louis, MO 63119, (314)968-6900

Intl. Brecht Soc. **[IO]**, St. Louis, MO, United States

Intl. Brick Collectors' Assn. **[22048]**, c/o Ken D. Jones, Treas., 100 Manor Dr., Columbia, MO 65203-1728

Intl. Bridge Press Assn. **[IO]**, Sliema, Malta

Intl. Bridge Press Assn. - Address unknown since 1999.

Intl. Bridge, Tunnel and Turnpike Assn. **[6318]**, 1146 19th St. NW, Ste. 800, Washington, DC 20036-3725, (202)659-4620

Intl. Bridge, Tunnel and Turnpike Assn. **[IO]**, Washington, DC, United States

Intl. Broadcasting Union **[★IO]**

Intl. Bronchoesophagological Soc. **[IO]**, Scottsdale, AZ, United States

Intl. Bronchoesophagological Soc. **[13779]**, Mayo Clinic Arizona, 13400 E Shea Blvd., Scottsdale, AZ 85259, (480)301-8000

Intl. Broom and Whisk Makers' Union of America - Defunct.

Intl. Brotherhood of Bikers' Teardrops - Address unknown since 2005.

Intl. Brotherhood of Boilermakers **[★24001]**

Intl. Brotherhood of Boilermakers, Iron Ship Builders, Blacksmiths, Forgers and Helpers **[24021]**, 753 State Ave., Ste. 570, Kansas City, KS 66101, (913)371-2640

Intl. Brotherhood of Boilermakers; Stove, Furnace, Energy, and Allied Appliance Workers Division of the **[24001]**

Intl. Brotherhood of DuPont Workers **[24034]**, PO Box 10, Waynesboro, VA 22980

Intl. Brotherhood of Elecl. Workers **[24048]**, 900 Seventh St. NW, Washington, DC 20001, (202)833-7000

Intl. Brotherhood of Live Steamers - Defunct.

Intl. Brotherhood of Locomotive Engineers **[★24176]**

Intl. Brotherhood of Locomotive Engineers **[★IO]**

International Brotherhood of Magicians **[IO]**, St. Louis, MO, United States

Intl. Brotherhood of Magicians **[22620]**, 11155-C S Towne Sq., St. Louis, MO 63123-7813, (314)845-9200

Intl. Brotherhood of Motorcycle Campers **[23624]**, PO Box 375, Helper, UT 84526, (435)650-3290

Intl. Brotherhood of Motorcycle Campers **[IO]**, Helper, UT, United States

Intl. Brotherhood of Painters and Allied Trades **[★IO]**

Intl. Brotherhood of Painters and Allied Trades **[★12082]**

Intl. Brotherhood of Police Officers **[24120]**, 159 Burgin Pkwy., Quincy, MA 02169, (617)376-0220

Intl. Brotherhood of Pottery and Allied Workers **[★24066]**

Intl. Brotherhood of Silica Structure Engineers **[★22971]**

Intl. Brotherhood of Stationary Firemen **[★24058]**

Intl. Brotherhood of Teamsters **[★24083]**

Intl. Brotherhood of Teamsters **[24198]**, 25 Louisiana Ave. NW, Washington, DC 20001, (202)624-6800

Intl. Brotherhood of Teamsters, Chauffeurs, Stablemen and Helpers of Am. **[★24198]**

Intl. Brotherhood of Teamsters; Graphic Communications Conf. of the **[24083]**

Intl. Buckskin Horse Assn. **[4896]**, PO Box 268, Shelby, IN 46377, (219)552-1013

International Buckskin Horse Association **[IO]**, Shelby, IN, United States

Intl. Buckskin Horse Registry **[★IO]**

Intl. Buckskin Horse Registry **[★4896]**

Intl. Buddhist Meditation Center - Defunct.

Intl. Buddy Rich Fan Club - Address unknown since 2001.

Intl. Budget Proj. of the Center on Budget and Policy Priorities **[16915]**, 820 1st St. NE, Ste. 510, Washington, DC 20002, (202)408-1080

Intl. Budget Proj. of the Center on Budget and Policy Priorities **[IO]**, Washington, DC, United States

International Builders Exchange Executives **[IO]**, San Antonio, TX, United States

Intl. Builders Exchange Executives **[1024]**, 4047 Naco Perrin, Ste. 201A, San Antonio, TX 78232, (210)653-3900

Intl. Building Performance Simulation Assn. **[6652]**, c/o Jeff Haberl, Energy Sys. Lab., Dept. of Architecture, Texas A&M Univ., College Station, TX 77843-3581, (979)845-1015

International Building Performance Simulation Association **[IO]**, College Station, TX, United States

Intl. Bulb Soc. **[IO]**, Sanger, CA, United States

Intl. Bulb Soc. **[6637]**, PO Box 336, Sanger, CA 93657-0336, (305)254-3635

Intl. Bundle Br. Block Assn. **[13911]**

Intl. Bundle Br. Block Assn. **[IO]**, Los Angeles, CA, United States

Intl. Bunker Indus. Assn. **[IO]**, Southampton, United Kingdom

Intl. Bur. Against Alcoholism **[★IO]**

Intl. Bur. of Educ. **[IO]**, Geneva, Switzerland

Intl. Bur. for Epilepsy **[IO]**, Dublin, Ireland

Intl. Bur. of Fiscal Documentation **[IO]**, Amsterdam, Netherlands

Intl. Bur. for Precast Concrete **[IO]**, Brussels, Belgium

Intl. Bur. of Social Tourism **[IO]**, Brussels, Belgium

Intl. Bur. for the Standardisation of Man-Made Fibres **[IO]**, Brussels, Belgium

Intl. Bur. of Weights and Measures **[IO]**, Sevres, France

Intl. Bus Collectors Club **[21895]**

Intl. Bus. Aviation Coun. **[IO]**, Montreal, QC, Canada

Intl. Bus. Brokers Assn. **[IO]**, Chicago, IL, United States

Intl. Bus. Brokers Assn. **[3315]**, 401 N Michigan Ave., Ste. 2200, Chicago, IL 60611-4267, (703)453-2226

Intl. Bus. Coun. **[★2284]**

Intl. Bus. Coun. **[★IO]**

Intl. Bus. Coun. Midamerica **[★IO]**

Intl. Bus. Coun. Midamerica **[★2284]**

Intl. Business Forms Industries **[★729]**

Intl. Bus. Law Consortium **[IO]**, Salzburg, Austria

Intl. Business Writers - Defunct.

Intl. Buster Keaton Soc; Damfinos: The **[24797]**

Intl. Butterfly Breeders Assn. **[4203]**, c/o Renee Cooke, Exec. Dir., 7917 Breeezy Point Rd., Melrose, FL 32666, (352)258-0324

International Butterfly Breeders Association **[IO]**, Springfield, NE, United States

Intl. C Class Catamaran Assn. of America - Defunct.

Intl. Cable Protection Comm. **[IO]**, Totton and Eling, United Kingdom

Intl. Cablemakers' Fed. **[IO]**, Vienna, Austria

Intl. Cadmium Assn. **[IO]**, Brussels, Belgium

Intl. Cadmium Assn. - Belgium **[IO]**, Brussels, Belgium

Intl. Call Center Benchmarking Consortium **[IO]**, Houston, TX, United States

Intl. Call Center Benchmarking Consortium **[731]**, c/o The Benchmarking Network, 4606 FM 1960 W, Ste. 250, Houston, TX 77069-9949, (281)440-5044

Intl. Camaro Club **[21665]**, 2001 Pittston Ave., Dept. HOL, Scranton, PA 18505, (570)585-4082

Intl. Camaro Club **[IO]**, Scranton, PA, United States

Intl. Camellia Soc. **[IO]**, Waiuku, New Zealand

Intl. Campaign for Abortion Rights **[★IO]**

Intl. Campaign to Ban Landmines **[IO]**, Washington, DC, United States

Intl. Campaign to Ban Landmines **[17431]**, c/o US Campaign to Ban Landmines, Friends Comm. on Natl. Legislation, 245 2nd St. NE, Washington, DC 20002, (202)547-6000

Intl. Campaign to Free Geronimo ji jaga Pratt - Defunct.

Intl. Campaign for Tibet **[18738]**, 1825 Jefferson Pl. NW, Washington, DC 20036, (202)785-1515

Intl. Campaign for Tibet **[IO]**, Washington, DC, United States

Intl. Cancer League - Defunct.

Intl. Canoe Fed. **[IO]**, Lausanne, Switzerland

International Canopy Network **[IO]**, Olympia, WA, United States

Intl. Canopy Network **[6579]**, 2103 Harrison Ave. NW, PMB 612, Olympia, WA 98502-2607, (360)866-6788

A star before a book entry number signifies that the name is not listed separately, but is mentioned within the entry.

Intl. Capital Market Assn. [IO], Zurich, Switzerland

Intl. Capital Market Assn., Zurich [IO], Zurich, Switzerland

Intl. Car Wash Inst. - Defunct.

Intl. Card Mfrs. Assn. [3053], PO Box 727, Princeton Junction, NJ 08550, (609)799-4900

Intl. Card Manufacturers Assn. [IO], Princeton Junction, NJ, United States

Intl. Cardiology Fed. [★IO]

Intl. Cardiology Found. [★13909]

Intl. Cargo Gear Bur. [6050], 321 W 44th St., New York, NY 10036, (212)757-2011

Intl. Cargo Gear Bur. [IO], New York, NY, United States

Intl. Cargo Handling Coordination Assn. [★IO]

Intl. Cargo Security Coun. [3530], 1400 Eye St. NW, Ste. 1050, Washington, DC 20005, (202)962-0190

Intl. Carnival Glass Assn. [22559], c/o Brian Pitman, Pres., 10750 NW 13th St., Topeka, KS 66615, (785)478-9004

Intl. Carnival Glass Assn. [IO], Topeka, KS, United States

International Carnivorous Plant Society [IO], Pinole, CA, United States

Intl. Carnivorous Plant Soc. [22521], 1564-A Fitzgerald Dr., Pinole, CA 94564-2229

Intl. Cartographic Assn. [IO], Utrecht, Netherlands

Intl. Cartographic Assn. - The Intl. Soc. for Cartography and Geographical [★IO]

Intl. Cartridge Recycling Assn. [3996]

Intl. Carwash Assn. [416], 401 N Michigan Ave., Ste. 2200, Chicago, IL 60611-4267, (312)321-5199

Intl. Carwash Assn. [★416]

Intl. Carwash Assn. [IO], Chicago, IL, United States

Intl. Carwash Assn. [★IO]

Intl. Cast Polymer Assn. [IO], Arlington, VA, United States

Intl. Cast Polymer Assn. [630], 1010 N Glebe Rd., Ste. 450, Arlington, VA 22201, (703)525-0320

Intl. Castor Oil Assn. [2852], 521 Pomona Rd., Cinnaminson, NJ 08077-4225, (856)786-2893

Intl. Castor Oil Assn. [IO], Cinnaminson, NJ, United States

The Intl. Cat Assn. [IO], Harlingen, TX, United States

The Intl. Cat Assn. [21910], PO Box 2684, Harlingen, TX 78551, (956)428-8046

Intl. Catacomb Soc. [10039], 50 Cross St., Winchester, MA 01890, (781)729-1150

International Catacomb Society [IO], Winchester, MA, United States

Intl. Catalina 27/270 Assn. [23182], c/o Phil Agur, Sec.-Treas., 2963 Mt. View Ct., Cameron Park, CA 95682, (530)677-6229

Intl. Catalina 27 Assn. [★23182]

Intl. Catalina 400 Assn. [21875], c/o Lloyd Clauss, Commodore, 15742 Intrepid Ln., Huntington Beach, CA 92649, (562)592-4085

Intl. Caterers Assn. - Defunct.

Intl. Catholic Child Bur. [IO], Paris, France

Intl. Catholic Child Bur. - Switzerland [IO], Geneva, Switzerland

Intl. Catholic Deaf Assn. - U.S. Sect. [19641], 7202 Buchanan St., Landover Hills, MD 20784-2236, (301)429-0697

Intl. Catholic Esperanto Assn. [9915]

Intl. Catholic Esperanto Union [★9915]

Intl. Catholic Film Off. [★IO]

Intl. Catholic Film Org. [★IO]

Intl. Catholic Migration Commn. - Switzerland [IO], Geneva, Switzerland

Intl. Catholic Org. for Cinema and Audiovisual [★IO]

Intl. Catholic Rural Assn. [IO], Vatican City, Vatican City

Intl. Catholic Stewardship Coun. [IO], Washington, DC, United States

Intl. Catholic Stewardship Coun. [19642], 1275 K St. NW, Ste. 880, Washington, DC 20005-4077, (202)289-1093

Intl. Catholic Union of the Press [IO], Geneva, Switzerland

Intl. CBX Owners Assn. [IO], Fort Lee, NJ, United States

Intl. CBX Owners Assn. [22683], c/o Bill Herting, PO Box 2826, Bluffton, SC 29909, (717)697-5559

Intl. Cell Death Soc. [6854], c/o Zahra Zakeri, PhD, Pres., Queens Coll. of CUNY, 65-30 Kissena Blvd., Flushing, NY 11367, (718)997-3417

Intl. Cell Death Soc. [IO], Flushing, NY, United States

Intl. Cell Res. Org. [IO], Paris, France

Intl. Cemetery and Funeral Assn. [IO], Sterling, VA, United States

Intl. Cemetery and Funeral Assn. [2781], 107 Carpenter Dr., Ste. 100, Sterling, VA 20164, (703)391-8400

Intl. Cemetery Supply Assn. [★2782]

Intl. Cemetery Supply Assn. [★IO]

Intl. Center [IO], Washington, DC, United States

Intl. Center [17613], 731 8th St. SE, Washington, DC 20003, (202)547-3800

Intl. Center for African Social and Economic Documentation - Defunct.

Intl. Center for Agricultural Res. in the Dry Areas [IO], Aleppo, Syrian Arab Republic

International Center for Alcohol Policies [IO], Washington, DC, United States

Intl. Center for Alcohol Policies [203], 1519 New Hampshire Ave. NW, Washington, DC 20036, (202)986-1159

Intl. Center for Attitudinal Healing [15206], 33 Buchanan Dr., Sausalito, CA 94965, (415)331-6161

Intl. Center for Canadian-Amer. Trade - Address unknown since 2006.

Intl. Center for Comparative Criminology [IO], Montreal, QC, Canada

Intl. Center for Coordination of Portuguese Studies - Defunct.

Intl. Center for Development Policy [★17613]

Intl. Center for Development Policy [★IO]

Intl. Center for Dynamics of Development - Address unknown since 1995.

Intl. Center for Earth Tides [IO], Brussels, Belgium

Intl. Center for Economic Policy Stud. [★18408]

Intl. Center for Fabry Disease [16537], Mt. Sinai School of Medicine, Dept. of Genetics and Genomic Sciences, 5th Ave. at 100th St., Box 1498, New York, NY 10029, (866)322-7963

International Center for Fabry Disease [IO], New York, NY, United States

Intl. Center for the Health Sciences [IO], Charlottesville, VA, United States

Intl. Center for the Health Sciences [8476]

Intl. Center for Holocaust Stud. [★17715]

Intl. Center for Jefferson Stud. [★9003]

Intl. Center for Jefferson Stud; Robert H. Smith [9003]

Intl. Center for Job's Daughters [★19239]

Intl. Center for Job's Daughters [★IO]

Intl. Center for Journalists [IO], Washington, DC, United States

Intl. Center for Journalists [3117], 1616 H St. NW, 3rd Fl., Washington, DC 20006, (202)737-3700

Intl. Center for Law in Development [5942]

Intl. Center for Law in Development [IO], New York, NY, United States

Intl. Center of Medical and Psychological Hypnosis [★IO]

Intl. Center for Medicine and Law - Defunct.

Intl. Center of Medieval Art [10461], The Cloisters, Ft. Tryon Park, New York, NY 10040, (212)928-1146

Intl. Center of Medieval Art [IO], New York, NY, United States

Intl. Center for Monetary and Banking Stud. [IO], Geneva, Switzerland

Intl. Center in New York [IO], New York, NY, United States

Intl. Center in New York [17897], 50 W 23rd St., 7th Fl., New York, NY 10010-5205, (212)255-9555

Intl. Center for Not-for-Profit Law [5943], 1126 16th St. NW, Ste. 400, Washington, DC 20036, (202)452-8600

Intl. Center for Not-for-Profit Law [IO], Washington, DC, United States

Intl. Center of Photography [IO], New York, NY, United States

Intl. Center of Photography [8972], 1114 Ave. of the Americas, 43rd St., New York, NY 10036, (212)857-0001

Intl. Center for Positive Psychotherapy, Transcultural Family Therapy and Psychosomatic Medicine [IO], Wiesbaden, Germany

Intl. Center for Positive and Transcultural Psychotherapy [★IO]

Intl. Center for Promotion of Enterprises [IO], Ljubljana, Slovenia

Intl. Center for Public Enterprises in Developing Countries [★IO]

International Center for Reiki Training [IO], Southfield, MI, United States

Intl. Center for Reiki Training [22969], 21421 Hilltop St., Unit 28, Southfield, MI 48034, (248)948-8112

Intl. Center of Religion and Culture - Address unknown since 1995.

Intl. Center for Res. on Women [17543], 1717 Massachusetts Ave. NW, Ste. 302, Washington, DC 20036, (202)797-0007

Intl. Center for Res. on Women [IO], Washington, DC, United States

Intl. Center for Social Gerontology [★11280]

Intl. Center for the Solution of Environmental Problems [4578], 5120 Woodway, Ste. 8009, Houston, TX 77056-1788, (713)527-8711

Intl. Center for the Solution of Environmental Problems [IO], Alpine, TX, United States

Intl. Center for Spirit at Work [20575], 36 Sylvan Hills Rd., East Haven, CT 06513, (203)467-9084

Intl. Center for the Stud. of Bird Migration, Latrun [IO], Tel Aviv, Israel

International Center for the Study of Psychiatry and Psychology [IO], Township of Washington, NJ, United States

Intl. Center for the Stud. of Psychiatry and Psychology [16086], c/o Dominick Riccio, PhD, Exec. Dir., 1036 Park Ave., Ste. 1B, New York, NY 10028, (212)861-7400

Intl. Center for Transitional Justice [17767], 5 Hanover Sq., 24th Fl., New York, NY 10004, (917)637-3800

Intl. Center for Transitional Justice [IO], New York, NY, United States

Intl. Center for the Typographic Arts - Address unknown since 1995.

International Center for Youth Studies [★13474]

Intl. Centre for Advanced Mediterranean Agronomic Stud. [IO], Paris, France

Intl. Centre for Agricultural Educ. [IO], Bern, Switzerland

Intl. Centre for Child Stud. [IO], Bristol, United Kingdom

Intl. Centre for Conservation Educ. [IO], Cheltenham, United Kingdom

Intl. Centre for Criminal Law Reform and Criminal Justice Policy [IO], Vancouver, BC, Canada

Intl. Centre for Ethnic Stud. [IO], Colombo, Sri Lanka

Intl. Centre of Films for Children and Young People [IO], Montreal, QC, Canada

Intl. Centre for Genetic Engg. and Biotechnology [IO], Trieste, Italy

Intl. Centre for Information on Palestinian and Lebanese Prisoners, Deportees and Missing Persons - Defunct.

Intl. Centre of Insect Physiology and Ecology [IO], Nairobi, Kenya

Intl. Centre for Integrated Mountain Development [IO], Kathmandu, Nepal

Intl. Centre for Island Tech. [IO], Stromness, United Kingdom

Intl. Centre for Local Credit [IO], The Hague, Netherlands

Intl. Centre for Mathematical Sciences [IO], Edinburgh, United Kingdom

Intl. Centre for Mech. Sciences [IO], Udine, Italy

Intl. Centre for Pure and Applied Mathematics [IO], Nice, France

Intl. Centre for Res. in Agroforestry [★IO]

Intl. Centre for Res. on Anarchism [IO], Lausanne, Switzerland

Intl. Centre of Res. and Info. on Public and Cooperative Economy [IO], Liege, Belgium

Intl. Centre for Res. and Stud. on Tourism [IO], Aix-en-Provence, France

Intl. Centre for Settlement of Investment Disputes [IO], Washington, DC, United States

Reference to "IO" in place of a book number signifies that the association may be found in the 45th edition of International Organizations.

Intl. Centre for Settlement of Investment Disputes [5457], 1818 H St. NW, Washington, DC 20433, (202)458-1534

Intl. Centre for Sports History and Culture [IO], Leicester, United Kingdom

Intl. Centre for Stud. in Religious Educ. - Lumen Vitae [★IO]

Intl. Centre for the Stud. of the Preservation and Restoration of Cultural Property [IO], Rome, Italy

Intl. Centre for Theoretical Physics [★IO]

Intl. Centre for Training and Exchanges in the Geosciences [IO], Orleans, France

Intl. Centre for Tropical Agriculture [IO], Cali, Colombia

Intl. Ceramic Assn. [IO], Prior Lake, MN, United States

Intl. Ceramic Assn. [787], c/o Helen Daum, Treas., 17098 Pheasant Meadow Ln. SW, Prior Lake, MN 55372, (952)447-6421

Intl. Certified Floorcovering Installers Assn. [1025], 2400 E Truman Rd., Kansas City, MO 64127, (816)231-4646

International Certified Floorcovering Installers Association [IO], Kansas City, MO, United States

Intl. Cesarean Awareness Network [IO], Redondo Beach, CA, United States

Intl. Cesarean Awareness Network [15604], 1304 Kingsdale Ave., Redondo Beach, CA 90278, (310)542-6400

Intl. Cessna 120/140 Assn. [21453], PO Box 830092, Richardson, TX 75083-0092, (405)391-6773

Intl. Cessna 120/140 Assn. [IO], Richardson, TX, United States

The Intl. Cessna 170 Assn. [IO], Cody, WY, United States

The Intl. Cessna 170 Assn. [21454], 22 Vista View Ln., Cody, WY 82414-9606, (307)587-6397

Intl. Chain Salon Assn. [1081], 207 E Ohio St., No. 361, Chicago, IL 60611, (866)444-ICSA

Intl. Chain Salon Assn. [IO], Chicago, IL, United States

Intl. Chain Saw Wood Sculptors Assn. [9446]

Intl. Chamber of Commerce - Austria [IO], Vienna, Austria

Intl. Chamber of Commerce - Belgium [IO], Brussels, Belgium

Intl. Chamber of Commerce - Czech Republic [IO], Prague, Czech Republic

Intl. Chamber of Commerce - Deutschland [IO], Berlin, Germany

Intl. Chamber of Commerce - Finland [IO], Helsinki, Finland

Intl. Chamber of Commerce - France [IO], Paris, France

Intl. Chamber of Commerce - Georgia [IO], Tbilisi, Georgia

Intl. Chamber of Commerce - Hellas [IO], Athens, Greece

Intl. Chamber of Commerce - Hrvatska [IO], Zagreb, Croatia

Intl. Chamber of Commerce - Hungary [IO], Budapest, Hungary

Intl. Chamber of Commerce - Italia [IO], Rome, Italy

Intl. Chamber of Commerce - Lithuania [IO], Vilnius, Lithuania

Intl. Chamber of Commerce - Luxembourg [IO], Luxembourg, Luxembourg

Intl. Chamber of Commerce - Netherlands [IO], The Hague, Netherlands

Intl. Chamber of Commerce - UK [IO], London, United Kingdom

Intl. Chamber of Commerce; U.S. Associates of the [★766]

Intl. Chamber of Commerce; U.S. Coun. of the [★766]

Intl. Chamber of Commerce - USA [24284], c/o US Coun. for Intl. Bus., 1212 Ave. of the Americas, New York, NY 10036-1689, (212)354-4480

Intl. Chamber of Commerce - USA [IO], New York, NY, United States

Intl. Chamber of Shipping [IO], London, United Kingdom

Intl. Chaplain's Ministry - Address unknown since 2002.

Intl. Charollaise Assn. [★4228]

Intl. Charollaise Assn. [★IO]

Intl. Cheerleading Found. - Defunct.

Intl. Cheese Coun. of Canada [IO], Toronto, ON, Canada

Intl. Cheese and Deli Assn. [★IO]

Intl. Cheese and Deli Assn. [★1522]

Intl. Cheese and Deli Seminar [★1522]

Intl. Cheese and Deli Seminar [★IO]

Intl. Chem. Workers Union [★24061]

Intl. Chessology Club - Address unknown since 1985.

Intl. Child Amputee Network [11954], PO Box 514, Abilene, TX 79604-0514, (325)675-6434

International Child Amputee Network [IO], Abilene, TX, United States

Intl. Child Care - Canada [IO], Mississauga, ON, Canada

Intl. Child Care U.S.A. [IO], Columbus, OH, United States

Intl. Child Care U.S.A. [11701], 3620 N High St., Ste. 110, Columbus, OH 43214-0485, (614)447-9952

Intl. Child Hea. Found. [★13950]

Intl. Child Hea. Found. [★13950]

Intl. Child Hea. Found. [★IO]

Intl. Child Hea. Found. [★IO]

Intl. Child Neurology Assn. [IO], Uppsala, Sweden

Intl. Child Rsrc. Inst. [IO], Berkeley, CA, United States

Intl. Child Rsrc. Inst. [11604], 1581 Leroy Ave., Berkeley, CA 94708, (510)644-1000

Intl. Childbirth Educ. Assn. [15605], PO Box 20048, Minneapolis, MN 55420, (952)854-8660

Intl. Childbirth Educ. Assn. [IO], Minneapolis, MN, United States

Intl. Children's Anophthalmia Network [IO], Philadelphia, PA, United States

Intl. Children's Anophthalmia Network [16857], c/o Center for Developmental Medicine and Genetics, 5501 Old York Rd., Genetics, Levy 2 W, Philadelphia, PA 19141, (800)580-4226

Intl. Children's Services; Joint Coun. on [11250]

Intl. Chili Soc. [22571], PO Box 1027, San Juan Capistrano, CA 92693, (949)496-2651

Intl. Chili Soc. [IO], San Juan Capistrano, CA, United States

Intl. Chinese Boxing Assn. [IO], Plano, TX, United States

Intl. Chinese Boxing Assn. [23262], 6205 Coit Rd., Ste. 336-194, Plano, TX 75024

Intl. Chinese Hand Tissue Soc. - Address unknown since 2002.

Intl. Chinese Snuff Bottle Soc. [21890], 2601 N Charles St., Baltimore, MD 21218, (410)467-9400

Intl. Chinese Snuff Bottle Soc. [IO], Baltimore, MD, United States

Intl. Chiropractic Pediatric Assn. [IO], Media, PA, United States

Intl. Chiropractic Pediatric Assn. [14007], 327 N Middletown Rd., Media, PA 19063, (610)565-2360

Intl. Chiropractors Assn. [14008], 1110 N Glebe Rd., Ste. 650, Arlington, VA 22201, (703)528-5000

Intl. Chiropractors Assn. [IO], Arlington, VA, United States

Intl. Chiropractors Res. Found. [★14003]

Intl. Choral Network [IO], Marktoberdorf, Germany

Intl. Christian Accrediting Assn. [IO], Tulsa, OK, United States

International Christian Accrediting Association [★8089]

Intl. Christian Accrediting Assn. [7876], 2448 E 81st St., Tulsa, OK 74137, (918)493-8880

Intl. Christian Alert Network - Defunct.

Intl. Christian Broadcasters - Defunct.

Intl. Christian Classic Motorcyclists - Address unknown since 1999.

Intl. Christian Concern [19805], 2020 Pennsylvania Ave. NW, No. 941, Washington, DC 20006-1846, (301)989-1708

Intl. Christian Concern [IO], Washington, DC, United States

Intl. Christian Cycling Club USA [IO], Aurora, CO, United States

Intl. Christian Cycling Club USA [23309], PO Box 441757, Aurora, CO 80044-1757

Intl. Christian Dance Fellowship [IO], Lane Cove, Australia

Intl. Christian Education Assn. - Defunct.

Intl. Christian Esperanto Assn. [★19812]

Intl. Christian Esperanto Assn. [★IO]

Intl. Christian Leadership - Address unknown since 2001.

Intl. Christian Leprosy Mission [15009]

Intl. Christian Leprosy Mission [IO], Forest Grove, OR, United States

Intl. Christian Media Commn. [IO], Kingsburg, CA, United States

Intl. Christian Media Commn. [19538], 1601 Windsor Dr., Kingsburg, CA 93631

Intl. Christian Org. [★19804]

Intl. Christian Ser. for Peace [IO], Neuwied, Germany

Intl. Christian Stud. Assn. [IO], Pasadena, CA, United States

Intl. Christian Stud. Assn. [19806], c/o Dr. Oskar Gruenwald, Pres., 1065 Pine Bluff Dr., Pasadena, CA 91107, (626)351-0419

Intl. Christian Technologists Assn. [20282], 1271 Kelly Johnson Blvd., Ste. 240, Colorado Springs, CO 80920, (719)785-0120

Intl. Christian Technologists Assn. [IO], Colorado Springs, CO, United States

Intl. Christian Union of Bus. Executives [IO], Brussels, Belgium

International Christian University [★IO]

International Christian University [★19929]

Intl. Christian Women's Fellowship [★20620]

Intl. Christian Women's Fellowship [★IO]

Intl. Christian Youth - Defunct.

Intl. Chromium Development Assn. [IO], Paris, France

Intl. Church of Metaphysics [★20573]

Intl. Churchill Societies - Defunct.

Intl. Churchill Soc. - Canada [IO], Markham, ON, Canada

Intl. Churchill Soc. - U.S. [★11109]

Intl. Cigar Band Soc. - Defunct.

Intl. Cinema Tech. Assn. [3811], 770 Broadway, 5th Fl., New York, NY 10003-9522, (646)654-7680

Intl. Cinema Tech. Assn. [IO], New York, NY, United States

Intl. Circle for the Promotion of Creation [IO], Bafoussam, Cameroon

Intl. Circulation Managers Assn. [★3244]

International Circus Exchange [★9796]

Intl. City/County Mgt. Assn. [6123], 777 N Capitol St. NE, Ste. 500, Washington, DC 20002-4201, (202)289-4262

Intl. City/County Mgt. Assn. [IO], Washington, DC, United States

Intl. City Mgt. Assn. [★IO]

Intl. City Mgt. Assn. [★6123]

Intl. City Mgt. Assn; Tech. Applications Prog., [★6197]

Intl. City Managers' Assn. [★6123]

Intl. City Managers' Assn. [★IO]

Intl. Civil Aviation Org. [IO], Montreal, QC, Canada

Intl. Civil Aviation Org. Asia Pacific Off. [IO], Bangkok, Thailand

Intl. Civil Aviation Org. Eastern and Southern African Off. [IO], Nairobi, Kenya

Intl. Civil Defence Org. [IO], Geneva, Switzerland

Intl. Civil Servants - New York; Assn. of Former [5566]

Intl. Civil Ser. Commn. [24143], 2 United Nations Plz., 10th Fl., New York, NY 10017, (212)963-5465

Intl. Civil Ser. Commn. [IO], New York, NY, United States

Intl. Claim Assn. [IO], Washington, DC, United States

Intl. Claim Assn. [2189], 1155 15th St. NW, Ste. 500, Washington, DC 20005, (202)452-0143

Intl. Clarinet Assn. [10616], PO Box 1310, Lyons, CO 80540, (801)867-4335

Intl. Clarinet Assn. [IO], Lyons, CO, United States

Intl. Clarinet Soc. [★IO]

Intl. Clarinet Soc. [★10616]

Intl. Clarinet Society/Clarinetwork Intl. [★10616]

Intl. Clarinet Society/Clarinetwork Intl. [★IO]

Intl. Classified Media Assn. [IO], Amsterdam, Netherlands

A star before a book entry number signifies that the name is not listed separately, but is mentioned within the entry.

Intl. Cleaning Companies Assn. **[IO]**, Moscow, Russia

Intl. Clearinghouse on the Military and the Environment - Address unknown since 2006.

Intl. Clematis Soc. **[IO]**, Waltham Cross, United Kingdom

Intl. Clergy Coun. - Defunct.

Intl. Cliff Richard Movement **[IO]**, Amsterdam, Netherlands

Intl. Climatology Assn. **[IO]**, Rennes, France

Intl. Clinical Epidemiology Network **[14375]**, 1420 Walnut St., Ste. 411, Philadelphia, PA 19102-4003, (215)222-7700

Intl. Clinical Phonetics and Linguistics Assn. **[10403]**, c/o Nicole Mueller, Univ. of Louisiana at Lafayette, Dept. of Communicative Disorders, PO Box 43107, Lafayette, LA 70504-3170, (337)482-1077

Intl. Clinical Phonetics and Linguistics Assn. **[IO]**, Lafayette, LA, United States

International Clinicians Program **[★IO]**

International Clinicians Program **[★14163]**

Intl. Club of Magic **[★22622]**

Intl. Club of Magic **[★IO]**

Intl. Co-operative Alliance - Switzerland **[IO]**, Geneva, Switzerland

Intl. Co-operative Women's Guild **[★IO]**

Intl. Coach Fed. **[IO]**, Lexington, KY, United States

Intl. Coach Fed. **[836]**, 2365 Harrodsburg Rd., Ste. A325, Lexington, KY 40504, (859)219-3580

Intl. Coach Fed. - Australasian Region **[IO]**, Kariong, Australia

Intl. Coalition for Addiction Stud. Educ. **[9197]**, PO Box 224, Vermillion, SD 57069-0224, (480)517-8522

Intl. Coalition Against Violent Entertainment - Address unknown since 2005.

Intl. Coalition for Children and the Env. **[4636]**, 161 Water St., Norwich, CT 06360, (860)885-1000

Intl. Coalition for Children and the Env. **[IO]**, Norwich, CT, United States

International Coalition for Genital Integrity **[IO]**, West Lafayette, IN, United States

Intl. Coalition for Genital Integrity **[11731]**, 1970 North River Rd., West Lafayette, IN 47906, (765)497-0150

Intl. Coalition of Lib. Consortia **[8784]**, c/o Tom Sanville, 2455 N Star Rd., Ste. 300, Columbus, OH 43221, (614)728-3600

Intl. Coalition of Lib. Consortia **[IO]**, Columbus, OH, United States

Intl. Coalition for Religious Freedom **[IO]**, Falls Church, VA, United States

Intl. Coalition for Religious Freedom **[18511]**, 7777 Leesburg Pike, Ste. 404 N, Falls Church, VA 22043, (703)790-1500

Intl. Coalition for Sustainable Production and Consumption **[17222]**, c/o Integrative Strategies Forum, 11426 Rockville Pike, No. 306, Rockville, MD 20852, (301)770-6375

Intl. Coalition for Sustainable Production and Consumption **[IO]**, Rockville, MD, United States

Intl. Cocoa Org. **[IO]**, London, United Kingdom

Intl. Code Coun. **[IO]**, Washington, DC, United States

Intl. Code Coun. **[5550]**, 500 New Jersey Ave. NW, 6th Fl., Washington, DC 20001-2070, (562)699-0541

Intl. Coenzyme Q10 Assn. **[IO]**, Ancona, Italy

Intl. Coffee Org. **[IO]**, London, United Kingdom

Intl. Cogeneration Soc. - Address unknown since 1988.

Intl. Coil Winding Assn. **[★1183]**

Intl. Coleman Collectors Club **[22049]**, c/o Charleen Becker, Treas., 1822 E Fernwood, Wichita, KS 67216

Intl. Collector's Club of Hatpins and Hatpin Holders **[22050]**

Intl. Collectors Guild **[22051]**

Intl. Collectors Guild **[IO]**, Artesia, CA, United States

Intl. Coll. of Angiology **[IO]**, Nesconset, NY, United States

Intl. Coll. of Angiology **[16724]**, 5 Daremy Ct., Nesconset, NY 11767-1547, (631)366-1429

Intl. Coll. of Applied Kinesiology - U.S.A. **[14827]**, 6405 Metcalf Ave., Ste. 503, Shawnee Mission, KS 66202-3929, (913)384-5336

International College of Applied Kinesiology - U.S.A. **[IO]**, Shawnee Mission, KS, United States

Intl. Coll. of Applied Nutrition **[★IO]**

Intl. Coll. of Applied Nutrition **[★15560]**

Intl. Coll. of Cranio-Mandibular Orthopedics **[15770]**, 619 N 35th St., Ste. 307, Seattle, WA 98103, (206)633-4355

International College of Cranio-Mandibular Orthopedics **[IO]**, Seattle, WA, United States

Intl. Coll. of Dentists **[IO]**, Rockville, MD, United States

Intl. Coll. of Dentists **[14163]**, 51 Monroe St., Ste. 1400, Rockville, MD 20850-2408, (301)251-8861

Intl. Coll. for Hea. Cooperation in Developing Countries - Italy **[IO]**, Padua, Italy

Intl. Coll. of Nuclear Medicine Physicians **[IO]**, Mexico City, Mexico

Intl. Coll. of Oral Implantologists **[★IO]**

Intl. Coll. of Oral Implantologists **[★14165]**

Intl. Coll. of Prosthodontists **[14164]**, PO Box 99119, San Diego, CA 92169-1119, (858)270-1814

Intl. Coll. of Prosthodontists **[IO]**, San Diego, CA, United States

Intl. Coll. of Real Estate Consulting Professionals - Address unknown since 2001.

Intl. Coll. of Surgeons **[16583]**, 1516 N Lake Shore Dr., Chicago, IL 60610, (312)642-3555

Intl. Coll. of Surgeons **[IO]**, Chicago, IL, United States

Intl. Colleges and Universities; Assn. of **[★8641]**

Intl. Collegiate Licensing Assn. **[2630]**, c/o NACDA, PO Box 16428, Cleveland, OH 44116, (440)892-4000

Intl. Collegiate Sports Found. - Address unknown since 1999.

Intl. Color Computer Club - Defunct.

Intl. Color Consortium **[870]**, 1899 Preston White Dr., Reston, VA 20191, (703)264-7200

Intl. Color Vision Soc. **[IO]**, Manchester, United Kingdom

International Colored Appaloosa Association **[IO]**, Shipshewana, IN, United States

Intl. Colored Appaloosa Assn. **[4897]**, PO Box 99, Shipshewana, IN 46565, (574)825-3331

Intl. Colored Gemstone Assn. **[3695]**, 19 W 21st St., Ste. 705, New York, NY 10010-6805, (212)620-0900

International Colored Gemstone Association **[IO]**, New York, NY, United States

Intl. Colour Assn. **[IO]**, Granada, Spain

Intl. Columbian Quincentenary Alliance - Address unknown since 2007.

Intl. Coma Recovery Inst. - Address unknown since 1991.

Intl. Comic Arts Assn. **[9447]**, 533 Johnson Ave., Morris, IL 60450, (815)942-1819

Intl. Comic Arts Assn. **[IO]**, Morris, IL, United States

Intl. Comic Book Org. - Defunct.

Intl. Commercial Exchange - Defunct.

Intl. Commn. of Agricultural Engg. **[IO]**, Tsukuba, Japan

Intl. Commn. for Agricultural and Food Indus. **[IO]**, Paris, France

Intl. Commn. for Alpine Rescue **[IO]**, Marthalen, Switzerland

Intl. Commn. on Atmospheric Chemistry and Global Pollution **[IO]**, Greenbelt, MD, United States

Intl. Commn. on Atmospheric Chemistry and Global Pollution **[5094]**, c/o Dr. Anne M. Thompson, Pres., NASA/Goddard Flight Ctr., Code 916, Bldg. 33, Rm. E417, Greenbelt, MD 20771, (301)614-5731

Intl. Commn. on Biological Effects of Noise **[IO]**, Sydney, Australia

Intl. Commn. of Catholic Prison Chaplaincies **[★IO]**

Intl. Commn. of Catholic Prison Pastoral Care **[IO]**, Zeist, Netherlands

Intl. Commn. on Civil Status **[IO]**, Strasbourg, France

Intl. Commn. for the Conservation of Atlantic Tunas **[IO]**, Madrid, Spain

Intl. Commn. on Gen. Relativity and Gravitation **[IO]**, London, United Kingdom

Intl. Commn. on Glass **[IO]**, Sheffield, United Kingdom

Intl. Commn. for Historical Demography **[IO]**, Paris, France

Intl. Commn. on the History of the Geological Sciences **[IO]**, Paris, France

Intl. Commn. on the History of Mathematics **[IO]**, Arhus, Denmark

Intl. Commn. for the History of Representative and Parliamentary Institutions **[IO]**, Ottawa, ON, Canada

Intl. Commn. for the History of Representative and Parliamentary Institutions, Amer. Sect. - Defunct.

Intl. Commission for the History of Salt - Address unknown since 2007.

Intl. Commn. for the History of Towns **[IO]**, Kiel, Germany

Intl. Commn. for Human Ecology and Ethnology **[★IO]**

Intl. Commn. for Human Ecology and Ethnology **[★4512]**

Intl. Commn. on Illumination **[IO]**, Vienna, Austria

Intl. Commn. on Illumination; U.S. Natl. Comm. of the **[7252]**

Intl. Commn. on Irrigation and Drainage - England **[IO]**, London, United Kingdom

Intl. Commn. on Irrigation and Drainage - India **[IO]**, New Delhi, India

Intl. Commn. of Jurists - Canadian Sect. **[IO]**, Ottawa, ON, Canada

Intl. Commn. of Jurists - Switzerland **[IO]**, Geneva, Switzerland

Intl. Commn. on Large Dams **[IO]**, Paris, France

Intl. Commn. on Mathematical Instruction **[IO]**, Quebec, QC, Canada

Intl. Commn. on Microbiological Specifications for Foods **[IO]**, Lyngby, Denmark

Intl. Commn. on Missing Persons **[IO]**, Sarajevo, Bosnia-Hercegovina

Intl. Commn. on Natl. Parks **[★IO]**

Intl. Commn. on Natl. Parks and Protected Areas **[★IO]**

Intl. Commn. for the Northwest Atlantic Fisheries **[★IO]**

Intl. Commn. on Occupational Hea. **[IO]**, Rome, Italy

Intl. Commn. for Optics **[IO]**, Madrid, Spain

Intl. Commn. on Physics Educ. **[IO]**, New Delhi, India

Intl. Commn. for the Prevention of Alcoholism **[★IO]**

Intl. Commn. for the Prevention of Alcoholism **[★13251]**

Intl. Commn. for the Prevention of Alcoholism and Drug Dependency **[13251]**, 12501 Old Columbia Pike, Silver Spring, MD 20904, (301)680-6719

Intl. Commn. for the Prevention of Alcoholism and Drug Dependency **[IO]**, Silver Spring, MD, United States

Intl. Commn. for Protection Against Environmental Mutagens and Carcinogens - Defunct.

Intl. Commn. for the Protection of the Alps **[★IO]**

Intl. Commn. for the Protection of the Rhine **[IO]**, Koblenz, Germany

Intl. Commn. on Radiation Units and Measurements **[IO]**, Bethesda, MD, United States

Intl. Commn. on Radiation Units and Measurements **[5161]**, 7910 Woodmont Ave., Ste. 400, Bethesda, MD 20814-3076, (301)657-2652

Intl. Commn. on Radiological Units **[★5161]**

Intl. Commn. on Radiological Units **[★IO]**

Intl. Commn. on Radiological Units and Measurements **[★IO]**

Intl. Commn. on Radiological Units and Measurements **[★5161]**

Intl. Commn. of Sugar Tech. **[IO]**, Berlin, Germany

Intl. Commn. for Uniform Methods of Sugar Anal. **[IO]**, Peterborough, United Kingdom

Intl. Commn. on Zoological Nomenclature **[IO]**, London, United Kingdom

Intl. Comm. Against Mental Illness **[IO]**, New York, NY, United States

Intl. Comm. Against Mental Illness **[15207]**, PO Box 1921, Grand Central Sta., New York, NY 10163-1921, (212)263-6214

Intl. Comm. Against Racism - Defunct.

Intl. Comm. Agricultural Librarians **[★IO]**

Intl. Comm. for Animal Performance Recording **[★IO]**

Intl. Comm. for Animal Recording **[IO]**, Rome, Italy

Intl. Comm. for the Anthropology of Food and Food Habits - Defunct.

Reference to "IO" in place of a book number signifies that the association may be found in the 45th edition of International Organizations.

Intl. Comm. of Applied Res. on Population - Defunct.

Intl. Comm. for Breaking the Language Barrier - Defunct.

Intl. Comm. for the Children of Chechnya [11605], PO Box 381305, Cambridge, MA 02238

Intl. Comm. for the Children of Chechnya [IO], Cambridge, MA, United States

Intl. Comm. for Coal and Organic Petrology [IO], Keiraville, Australia

Intl. Comm. for Coal Petrology [★IO]

Intl. Comm. of Conscience on Vietnam - Defunct.

Intl. Comm. on Consumers Unions - Address unknown since 1999.

Intl. Comm. for the Defense of Salman Rushdie and His Publishers - Defunct.

Intl. Comm. for Documentation of the Intl. Coun. of Museums [IO], Berlin, Germany

Intl. Comm. on Economic and Applied Microbiology - Defunct.

Intl. Comm. on English in the Liturgy - Defunct.

Intl. Comm. of Food Sci. and Tech. [★IO]

Intl. Comm. for Foundry Tech. Associations [★IO]

Intl. Comm. of Hard of Hearing Young People [★IO]

Intl. Comm. for Historical Metrology [IO], Lille, France

Intl. Comm. of Historical Sciences [IO], Montreal, QC, Canada

Intl. Comm. for the History of the Second World War [IO], Paris, France

Intl. Comm. for the History of Tech. [IO], Bochum, Germany

Intl. Comm. for the Indians of the Americas [IO], Zurich, Switzerland

InterNational Comm. for Info. Tech. Standards; IN-CITS - [7738]

Intl. Comm. for Life, Disability and Hea. Insurance Medicine [IO], Vienna, Austria

Intl. Comm. for Mental Hygiene [★IO]

Intl. Comm. for Mental Hygiene [★15237]

Intl. Comm. on Microbial Biology - Defunct.

Intl. Comm. of Military Medicine [IO], Brussels, Belgium

Intl. Comm. of Military Medicine and Pharmacy [★IO]

Intl. Comm. on Modern Literary History [★IO]

Intl. Comm. of the Paper and Bd. Converting Indus. (Common Market Gp.) [★IO]

Intl. Comm. on Physical Fitness Res. [★IO]

Intl. Comm. of Plastics in Agriculture [IO], Paris, France

Intl. Comm. to Preserve Catacombs in Italy [★IO]

Intl. Comm. to Preserve Catacombs in Italy [★10039]

Intl. Comm. of Public Relations Consultancies Associations [★IO]

Intl. Comm. for Radiological Units [★IO]

Intl. Comm. for Radiological Units [★5161]

Intl. Comm. for Recording the Productivity of Milk Animals [★IO]

Intl. Comm. of the Red Cross - Armenia [IO], Yerevan, Armenia

Intl. Comm. of the Red Cross - Azerbaijan [IO], Baku, Azerbaijan

Intl. Comm. of the Red Cross - Switzerland [IO], Geneva, Switzerland

Intl. Comm. for the Release of Anatoly Scharansky - Defunct.

Intl. Comm. for the Rescue of KAL 007 Survivors [18541], 408 Parkwood Pl., Niceville, FL 32578, (617)780-5088

Intl. Comm. of Sarcoidosis [★IO]

Intl. Comm. on Seafarer's Welfare [IO], Watford, United Kingdom

Intl. Comm. for Social Sci. Info. and Documentation [IO], Buenos Aires, Argentina

Intl. Comm. of Sport and Physical Educ. [★IO]

Intl. Comm. of Sports for the Deaf/DEAFLYMPICS [IO], Frederick, MD, United States

Intl. Comm. of Sports for the Deaf/DEAFLYMPICS [23345], 528 Trail Ave., Frederick, MD 21701

Intl. Comm. of Tensio-Active Derivatives - Address unknown since 1995.

Intl. Comm. on Ultra-High Intensity Lasers [7245], c/o Christopher P.J. Barty, Co-Chm., PO Box 808, Livermore, CA 94551, (925)423-8486

Intl. Comm. on Ultra-High Intensity Lasers [IO], Livermore, CA, United States

Intl. Comm. on Veterinary Anatomical Nomenclature - Address unknown since 2002.

Intl. Comm. for World Day of Prayer [★20629]

Intl. Comm. for World Day of Prayer [★IO]

Intl. Common Law Exchange Soc. - Address unknown since 1988.

Intl. Communal Stud. Assn. [IO], Ramat Efal, Israel

Intl. Commun. Assn. [IO], Washington, DC, United States

Intl. Commun. Assn. [3748], 1500 21st St. NW, Washington, DC 20036, (202)955-1444

Intl. Communications Agency Network [105], PO Box 490, Rollinsville, CO 80474-0490, (303)258-9511

Intl. Communications Agency Network [IO], Rollinsville, CO, United States

Intl. Communications Consultancy Org. [IO], Hilversum, Netherlands

Intl. Communications Indus. Assn. [★IO]

Intl. Communications Indus. Assn. [★331]

Intl. Community Corrections Assn. [11872], 1730 Rhode Island Ave. NW, Ste. 403, Washington, DC 20006, (202)828-5605

Intl. Community Corrections Assn. [IO], Washington, DC, United States

Intl. Community for the Relief of Starvation and Suffering - Defunct.

Intl. Comparative Literature Assn. [10423], Brigham Young Univ., HRCB, Provo, UT 84602-4538, (801)422-5598

Intl. Comparative Literature Assn. [IO], Provo, UT, United States

Intl. Comparative Literature Assn. - Italy [IO], Venice, Italy

Intl. Complement Soc. [IO], Philadelphia, PA, United States

Intl. Complement Soc. [14938], c/o John D. Lambris, Pres., Univ. of Pennsylvania, Dept. of Pathology and Lab. Medicine, 401 Stellar Chance, Philadelphia, PA 19104, (215)746-5765

Intl. Compost Tea Coun. [5244], 14150 NE 20th St., Ste. 293, Bellevue, WA 98007, (425)614-4282

Intl. Compressor Remanufacturers Assn. [1887], PO Box 33092, Kansas City, MO 64114, (816)333-7205

Intl. Compressor Remanufacturers Assn. [IO], Kansas City, MO, United States

Intl. Cmpt. Chess Assn. [★IO]

International Cmpt. Educ. Project [★IO]

International Cmpt. Educ. Project [★18763]

Intl. Cmpt. Games Assn. [IO], London, United Kingdom

Intl. Cmpt. Music Assn. [IO], San Francisco, CA, United States

Intl. Cmpt. Music Assn. [2811], 1819 Polk St., Ste. 330, San Francisco, CA 94109

Intl. Computer Products Remanufacturing Assn. [★3996]

Intl. Computer Users Groups Assn. - Defunct.

Intl. Computing Centre [IO], Geneva, Switzerland

Intl. Concerns for Children - Defunct.

Intl. Concert Alliance [10617], 47 W 85th St., Ste. 2B, New York, NY 10024

Intl. Concrete Repair Inst. [927], 3166 S River Rd., Ste. 132, Des Plaines, IL 60018, (847)827-0830

Intl. Concrete Repair Inst. [IO], Des Plaines, IL, United States

Intl. Confectionery Assn. [IO], Brussels, Belgium

Intl. Confed. of Accordionists [IO], Ikaalinen, Finland

Intl. Confed. of Agricultural Credit [IO], Zurich, Switzerland

Intl. Confed. of Architectural Museums [IO], Rotterdam, Netherlands

Intl. Confed. of Art Dealers [IO], Brussels, Belgium

Intl. Confed. of Art Dealers - Austria [IO], Vienna, Austria

Intl. Confed. of Book Actors - Defunct.

Intl. Confed. for Electroacoustic Music [IO], Bourges, France

Intl. Confed. of European Sugar-Beet Growers [IO], Paris, France

Intl. Confed. of Free Trade Unions [IO], Brussels, Belgium

Intl. Confed. of Free Trade Unions - African Regional Org. [IO], Nairobi, Kenya

Intl. Confed. of Mfrs. of Carpets and Furnishing Fabrics [★IO]

Intl. Confed. of Mfrs. of Furnishing Fabrics [IO], Wuppertal, Germany

Intl. Confed. of Meat and Meat Processing Indus. [IO], Brussels, Belgium

Intl. Confed. of Midwives [IO], The Hague, Netherlands

Intl. Confed. of Paper and Bd. Converters in Europe [IO], Brussels, Belgium

Intl. Confed. for Plastic, Reconstructive and Aesthetic Surgery [IO], Albany, NY, United States

Intl. Confed. for Plastic, Reconstructive and Aesthetic Surgery [14047], 45 Lyme Rd., Ste. 304, Hanover, NH 03755, (603)643-2325

Intl. Confed. for Plastic Reconstructive and Aesthetic Surgery Asia-Pacific Sect. [IO], Chennai, India

Intl. Confed. of Popular Banks [IO], Brussels, Belgium

Intl. Confed. of Popular Credit [★IO]

Intl. Confed. for Printing and Allied Indus. [IO], Brussels, Belgium

Intl. Confed. of Societies of Authors and Composers [IO], Neuilly-sur-Seine, France

Intl. Confed. for Thermal Anal. [★IO]

Intl. Confed. for Thermal Anal. and Calorimetry [IO], Sao Carlos, Brazil

Intl. Conf. of Administrators of Residential Centers for Youth - Defunct.

Intl. Conf. of Agricultural Economists [★6881]

Intl. Conf. of Agricultural Economists [★IO]

Intl. Conf. of Building Officials [IO], Whittier, CA, United States

Intl. Conf. of Building Officials [5551], c/o Intl. Code Coun., Los Angeles District Off., 5360 Workman Mill Rd., Whittier, CA 90601, (888)422-7233

Intl. Conf. on the Fantastic in the Arts; Lord Ruthven Assembly [10426]

Intl. Conf. of Funeral Ser. Examining Boards of the U.S. [6120], 1885 Shelby Ln., Fayetteville, AR 72704, (479)442-7076

Intl. Conf. Group - Address unknown since 1990.

Intl. Conf. of Historians of the Labour Movement [IO]

Intl. Conf. Industry Assn. - Defunct.

Intl. Conf. of Labour Historians [★IO]

Intl. Conf. of Labour and Social History [IO], Vienna, Austria

Intl. Conf. on Mechanics in Medicine and Biology - Address unknown since 2006.

Intl. Conf. on the Medical Aspects of Telemedicine [★IO]

Intl. Conf. of Police Assns. - Defunct.

Intl. Conf. of Police Chaplains [19749], PO Box 5590, Destin, FL 32540-5590, (850)654-9736

International Conference of Police Chaplains [IO], Destin, FL, United States

Intl. Conf. of Symphony and Opera Musicians [IO], New York, NY, United States

Intl. Conf. of Symphony and Opera Musicians [10618], c/o Leonard Leibowitz, 120 W 86th St., Ste. 9B, New York, NY 10024, (917)863-2897

Intl. Conf. of Weekly Newspaper Editors [★3125]

Intl. Conf. of Weekly Newspaper Editors [★IO]

Intl. Cong. and Convention Assn. [IO], Amsterdam, Netherlands

Intl. Cong. of Dealers Assns. - Address unknown since 1988.

Intl. Cong. on High-Speed Photography and Photonics - Address unknown since 1999.

International Cong. for the History of Discoveries [★10158]

International Cong. for the History of Discoveries [★IO]

Intl. Cong. of Maritime Museums [IO], Mystic, CT, United States

Intl. Cong. of Maritime Museums [10506], c/o Stuart Parnes, Sec. Gen., PO Box 326, Mystic, CT 06355, (860)767-8269

International Cong. on Medieval Studies [★10459]

International Cong. on Medieval Studies [★IO]

Intl. Cong. of Oral Implantologists [IO], Upper Montclair, NJ, United States

Intl. Cong. of Oral Implantologists [14165], 248 Lorraine Ave., Ste. 3, Upper Montclair, NJ 07043, (973)783-6300

A star before a book entry number signifies that the name is not listed separately, but is mentioned within the entry.

Intl. Cong. on Smoking and Health - Defunct.
Intl. Cong. on Women in Music - Defunct.
Intl. Congresses of Labour Law [★IO]
Intl. Connoisseurs of Green and Red Chile [22572],
  c/o NMSU Alumni Assn., PO Box 30001, MSC
  3AS, Las Cruces, NM 88003-8001, (505)646-3616
Intl. Consortium for Emergency Contraception
  [12183], c/o Family Care Intl., 588 Broadway, Ste.
  503, New York, NY 10012, (212)941-5300
International Consortium for Emergency Contracep-
  tion [IO], New York, NY, United States
Intl. Consortium on Governmental Financial Mgt.
  [IO], Washington, DC, United States
Intl. Consortium on Governmental Financial Mgt.
  [1426], 444 N Capitol St., Ste. 234, Washington,
  DC 20001, (202)624-8461
Intl. Consultants and Contractors Assn. of Iran [IO],
  Tehran, Iran
Intl. Consultative Res. Gp. on Rapeseed [IO], Paris,
  France
International Consumer Product Health and Safety
  Organization [IO], Germantown, MD, United States
Intl. Consumer Prdt. Hea. and Safety Org. [3178],
  PO Box 1785, Germantown, MD 20875-1785,
  (301)528-0310
Intl. Contact Dermatitis Res. Gp. [IO], Brussels,
  Belgium
Intl. Contemporary Music Exchange - Defunct.
Intl. Continence Soc. [IO], Bristol, United Kingdom
Intl. Contraception, Abortion and Sterilization
  Campaign [★IO]
International Conure Association [IO], Las Vegas,
  NV, United States
Intl. Conure Assn. [21848], c/o Brent Andrus, Treas.,
  PO Box 70123, Las Vegas, NV 89170
Intl. Convention of Bible Students - Address
  unknown since 2002.
Intl. Convention of Faith, Churches and Ministers
  [★19807]
Intl. Convention of Faith, Churches and Ministers
  [★IO]
Intl. Convention of Faith Ministries [IO], Arlington,
  TX, United States
Intl. Convention of Faith Ministries [19807], 5500
  Woodland Park Blvd., Arlington, TX 76013,
  (817)451-9620

International Cooperation

Africa-American Friendship Soc. [18862]
Amer. Bahraini Friendship Soc. [19150]
Amer. Red Cross Overseas Assn. [12831]
Amer. Soc. for Kurds [13154]
Assembly of European Regions [IO]
Assn. of Caribbean States [IO]
Assn. for Sciences and Politics [IO]
Assn. of Space Explorers - U.S.A. [6371]
Assn. of Thai Professionals in Am. and Canada
  [19406]
Austrian North-South Inst. for Development
  Cooperation [IO]
Caribbean-Central Amer. Action [12421]
Chinese Amer. Assn. of Engg. [7008]
Chinese Amer. Forum [9786]
Christian Friends of Israel - USA [19777]
Common Market for Eastern and Southern Africa
  [IO]
Commonwealth Secretariat [IO]
Coun. of Europe [IO]
East-West Center [17882]
EastWest Inst. [IO]
Estonian Inst. [IO]
European Acad. Otzenhausen [IO]
European Assn. of Teachers [IO]
European Centre for Development Policy Mgt.
  [IO]
Golden Rule Found. [10186]
Hungarian Amer. Coalition [12451]
Indian Ocean Commn. [IO]
Interamerican Assn. for Environmental Defense
  [4630]
Intl. Assn. for Counterterrorism and Security
  Professionals [18731]
Intl. Assn. of Protocol Consultants [965]
Intl. Assn. of Space Entrepreneurs [3634]
Intl. Counter-Terrorism Officers Assn. [18732]
Intl. Fed. of Europe Houses [IO]

Intl. Paneuropean Union [IO]
Kanazawa Goodwill Guide Network [IO]
Laotian Amer. Natl. Alliance [19192]
Laotian Amer. Soc. [19193]
Macedonian Amer. Friendship Assn. [19220]
MS Nepal: Danish Assn. for Intl. Cooperation [IO]
Network of European Foundations for Innovative
  Cooperation [IO]
New Zealand Inst. of Intl. Affairs [IO]
Nordic Coun. [IO]
Nordic Coun. of Ministers [IO]
Org. of Eastern Caribbean States [IO]
Org. of the Black Sea Economic Cooperation [IO]
Sistema de la Integracion CentroAmericana [IO]
Soc. for Indonesian-Americans [19116]
South Centre [IO]
Trust for Mutual Understanding [IO]
Trust for Mutual Understanding [10232]
Turkish Coalition of Am. [18754]
United Nations [18769]
USA for the United Nations High Commissioner
  for Refugees [12824]
Win Without War [18124]
World Youth Alliance [18860]
Intl. Cooperation Coun. [★17916]
Intl. Cooperation Coun. [★IO]
Intl. Cooperation for Development and Solidarity
  [IO], Brussels, Belgium
Intl. Cooperation for Development and Solidarity -
  Vietnam [IO], Hanoi, Vietnam
Intl. Cooperative Development Assn. [★IO]
Intl. Cooperative Development Assn. [★4481]
Intl. Cooperative Housing Development Assn. -
  Defunct.
Intl. Cooperative and Mutual Insurance Fed. [IO],
  Altrincham, United Kingdom
Intl. Cooperative Petroleum Assn. - Address
  unknown since 1994.
Intl. Coordinating Comm. on Solid State Sensors
  and Actuators Res. [6927], c/o Mr. John Huggins,
  Exec. Dir., Berkeley Sensor and Actuator Center,
  Univ. of California, 483 Cory Hall, No. 1774,
  Berkeley, CA 94720-1774, (510)643-5663
Intl. Coordinating Comm. on Solid State Sensors
  and Actuators Res. [IO], Berkeley, CA, United
  States
Intl. Coordinating Comm. on Solid State Transducers
  Res. [★IO]
Intl. Coordinating Comm. on Solid State Transducers
  Res. [★6927]
Intl. Coordinating Coun. of Aerospace Indus. As-
  sociations [154], 1000 Wilson Blvd., Ste. 1700,
  Arlington, VA 22209-3901, (703)358-1000
Intl. Coordinating Coun. of Aerospace Indus. As-
  sociations [IO], Arlington, VA, United States
Intl. Coordination Coun. of Educational Institutions
  Alumni [IO], Moscow, Russia
Intl. Copper Assn. [IO], New York, NY, United States
Intl. Copper Assn. [★IO]
Intl. Copper Assn. [7315], 260 Madison Ave., 16th
  Fl., New York, NY 10016-2401, (212)251-7240
Intl. Copper Res. Assn. [★7315]
Intl. Copper Res. Assn. [★IO]
Intl. Cops for Christ [19808], PO Box 444, Liverpool,
  PA 17045, (717)329-0470
Intl. Copyright Information Center - Defunct.
Intl. Coral Reef Action Network [IO], Cambridge,
  United Kingdom
Intl. Cornish Bantam Breeders' Assn. - Address
  unknown since 2000.
Intl. Coronelli Soc. for the Stud. of Globes [IO], Vi-
  enna, Austria
Intl. Corrections and Prisons Assn. [IO], Ottawa, ON,
  Canada
Intl. Correspondence of Corkscrew Addicts [IO],
  Camp Hill, PA, United States
Intl. Correspondence of Corkscrew Addicts [22052],
  c/o Dr. Bert Giulian, 649 Johns Dr., Camp Hill, PA
  17011, (717)737-5828
Intl. Correspondence Inst. [★19802]
Intl. Correspondence Inst. [★IO]
Intl. Correspondence Soc. of Allergists [★IO]
Intl. Correspondence Soc. of Allergists [★13601]
Intl. Correspondence Soc. of Allergists and Clinical
  Immunologists [13601], 6806 W 83rd St., Overland
  Park, KS 66204, (913)469-4043

Intl. Correspondence Soc. of Allergists and Clinical
  Immunologists [IO], Overland Park, KS, United
  States
Intl. Correspondence Soc. of Obstetricians and
  Gynecologists - Address unknown since 2004.
Intl. Corrosion Coun. [IO], Erlangen, Germany
Intl. Corrugated Case Assn. [IO], Elk Grove Village,
  IL, United States
Intl. Corrugated Case Assn. [985], 25 NW Point
  Blvd., Ste. 510, Elk Grove Village, IL 60007,
  (847)364-9600
Intl. Corrugated Packaging Found. [12726], 113 S
  West St., Alexandria, VA 22314, (703)549-8580
Intl. Corrugated Packaging Found. [IO], Alexandria,
  VA, United States
Intl. Cost Engg. Coun. [IO], Deakin West, Australia
Intl. Cotton Advisory Comm. [IO], Washington, DC,
  United States
Intl. Cotton Advisory Comm. [4306], 1629 K St. NW,
  Ste. 702, Washington, DC 20006-1636, (202)463-
  6660
Intl. Coun. of Academies of Engg. and Technological
  Sciences [9104], 3601 N Peary St., Arlington, VA
  22207, (703)527-5782
Intl. Coun. of Academies of Engg. and Technological
  Sciences [IO], Arlington, VA, United States
Intl. Coun. of Accrediting Assn. [★IO]
Intl. Coun. for Adult Educ. [IO], Montevideo, Uruguay
Intl. Coun. of the Aeronautical Sciences [IO], Stock-
  holm, Sweden
Intl. Coun. Against Bullfighting [★IO]
Intl. Coun. of Air Shows [IO], Leesburg, VA, United
  States
Intl. Coun. of Air Shows [21455], 751 Miller Dr. SE,
  Ste. F4, Leesburg, VA 20175, (703)779-8510
Intl. Coun. of Aircraft Owner and Pilot Associations
  [155], 421 Aviation Way, Frederick, MD 21701,
  (301)695-2220
Intl. Coun. of Aircraft Owner and Pilot Associations
  [IO], Frederick, MD, United States
Intl. Coun. on Alcohol and Addictions [IO], Lau-
  sanne, Switzerland
Intl. Coun. on Alcohol, Drugs and Traffic Safety [IO],
  Lafayette, CA, United States
Intl. Coun. on Alcohol, Drugs and Traffic Safety
  [16504], c/o Barry M. Sweedler, 3798 Mosswood
  Dr., Lafayette, CA 94549, (925)962-1810
Intl. Coun. for Applied Mineralogy [IO], Hannover,
  Germany
Intl. Coun. for Archaeozoology [IO], Sheffield, United
  Kingdom
Intl. Coun. on Archives [IO], Paris, France
Intl. Coun. of Associations for Sci. Educ. [IO], Tartu,
  Estonia
Intl. Coun. of Associations of Theological Libraries
  [★IO]
Intl. Coun. of Ballroom Dancing [★IO]
Intl. Coun. for Bird Preservation [★5290]
Intl. Coun. Bird Protection [★IO]
Intl. Coun. of Bottled Water Associations [IO],
  Richmond Hill, ON, Canada
Intl. Coun. for Brainstorming and Expertise on Issues
  of Pure and Applied Linguistics - Address unknown
  since 2004.
Intl. Coun. for Building Res., Stud. and Documenta-
  tion [★IO]
Intl. Coun. for Canadian Stud. [IO], Ottawa, ON,
  Canada
Intl. Coun. for Central and East European Stud. [IO],
  Toronto, ON, Canada
Intl. Coun. of Christian Churches [IO], Tulsa, OK,
  United States
Intl. Coun. of Christian Churches [20015], 10977 E
  23rd St., Tulsa, OK 74129, (918)234-0462
Intl. Coun. of Christians and Jews [IO], Heppenheim,
  Germany
Intl. Coun. of Community Churches [IO], Frankfort,
  IL, United States
Intl. Coun. of Community Churches [★IO]
Intl. Coun. of Community Churches [19850], 21116
  Washington Pkwy., Frankfort, IL 60423, (815)464-
  5690
Intl. Coun. of Community Churches [★19850]
Intl. Coun. for Computer Communication - Defunct.
Intl. Coun. for Computers in Educ. [★8134]

Reference to "IO" in place of a book number signifies that the association may be found in the 45th edition of International Organizations.

Intl. Coun. for Computers in Educ. [★IO]
Intl. Coun. for the Control of Iodine Deficiency Disorders - Australia [IO], Westmead, Australia
Intl. Coun. for Correspondence Educ. [★IO]
Intl. Coun. of Cruise Lines [3923], 2111 Wilson Blvd., 8th Fl., Arlington, VA 22201, (703)522-8463
Intl. Coun. on Disability - Defunct.
Intl. Coun. on Dispute Resolution - Defunct.
Intl. Coun. on Educ. for Teaching [9216], c/o Natl. Louis Univ., 1000 Capitol Dr., Wheeling, IL 60090-7201, (847)465-0191
Intl. Coun. on Educ. for Teaching [IO], Wheeling, IL, United States
Intl. Coun. for Educational Development - Address unknown since 1995.
Intl. Coun. of Employers of Bricklayers and Allied Craftsworkers [★1029]
Intl. Coun. of Employers of Bricklayers and Allied Craftsworkers [★IO]
Intl. Coun. for Engg. and Tech. [IO], Paris, France
Intl. Coun. of Environmental Law [IO], Bonn, Germany
Intl. Coun. for Evangelical Theological Educ. [IO], Veenendaal, Netherlands
Intl. Coun. for the Exploration of the Sea [IO], Copenhagen, Denmark
Intl. Coun. of Fan Clubs - Defunct.
Intl. Coun. of Fine Arts Deans [7973], c/o Liz Cole, Exec. Dir., 8725 SR 70 E, Ste. 127, Bradenton, FL 34211, (941)753-0080
Intl. Coun. of Fine Arts Deans [IO], Bradenton, FL, United States
Intl. Coun. of the French Language [IO], Paris, France
Intl. Coun. on the Future of the Univ. - Defunct.
Intl. Coun. of Goodwill Industries - Defunct.
Intl. Coun. of Graphic Design Associations [IO], Montreal, QC, Canada
Intl. Coun. of Grocery Mfrs. Associations [IO], Washington, DC, United States
Intl. Coun. of Grocery Mfrs. Associations [1521], 1350 I St. NW, Ste. 300, Washington, DC 20005, (202)337-9400
Intl. Coun. for Hea., Physical Educ., Recreation, Sport, and Dance [8981], 1900 Assn. Dr., Reston, VA 20191-1598, (703)476-3486
Intl. Coun. for Hea., Physical Educ., Recreation, Sport, and Dance [IO], Reston, VA, United States
Intl. Coun. of Hides, Skins and Leather Traders Associations [IO], Paris, France
Intl. Coun. on Hotel, Restaurant, and Institutional Educ. [IO], Richmond, VA, United States
Intl. Coun. on Hotel, Restaurant, and Institutional Educ. [8525], 2810 N Parham Rd., Ste. 230, Richmond, VA 23294, (804)346-4800
Intl. Coun. on Human Ecology [★4512]
Intl. Coun. on Human Ecology [★IO]
Intl. Coun. for Human Ecology and Ethnology [IO], New York, NY, United States
Intl. Coun. for Human Ecology and Ethnology [4512], PO Box 7024, New York, NY 10128-0010, (212)410-6560
Intl. Coun. for the Improvement of Reading and Instruction [★9043]
Intl. Coun. for the Improvement of Reading and Instruction [★IO]
Intl. Coun. of Indus. Editors [★IO]
Intl. Coun. of Indus. Editors [★879]
Intl. Coun. on Infertility Info. Dissemination [14392], PO Box 6836, Arlington, VA 22206, (703)379-9178
International Council on Infertility Information Dissemination [IO], Arlington, VA, United States
Intl. Coun. of Iranian Christians [IO], Colorado Springs, CO, United States
Intl. Coun. of Iranian Christians [19809], PO Box 25607, Colorado Springs, CO 80936, (719)596-0010
Intl. Coun. of Jewish Women [IO], Zur Hadassah, Israel
Intl. Coun. of Kinetography Laban [IO], Columbus, OH, United States
Intl. Coun. of Kinetography Laban [9887], c/o Valerie Mockabee, Treas., 2801 Northwest Blvd., Columbus, OH 43221, (614)469-9984
Intl. Coun. on Large Elec. Systems [IO], Paris, France

Intl. Coun. for Lathing and Plastering [★IO]
Intl. Coun. for Lathing and Plastering [★1026]
Intl. Coun. of Library Assn. Executives - Address unknown since 2001.
Intl. Coun. for Local Environmental Initiatives [IO], Toronto, ON, Canada
Intl. Coun. for Machinery Lubrication [IO], Tulsa, OK, United States
Intl. Coun. for Machinery Lubrication [7253], 3015 E Skelly Dr., Ste. 443F, Tulsa, OK 74105, (918)742-2950
Intl. Coun. of Marine Indus. Associations [IO], Egham, United Kingdom
Intl. Coun. on Metals and the Env. [★IO]
Intl. Coun. on Mining and Metals [IO], London, United Kingdom
Intl. Coun. on Monuments and Sites [IO], Paris, France
Intl. Coun. on Monuments and Sites - Canada [★IO]
Intl. Coun. on Monuments and Sites - France [IO], Paris, France
Intl. Coun. of the Museum of Modern Art [IO], New York, NY, United States
Intl. Coun. of the Museum of Modern Art [9448], 11 W 53rd St., New York, NY 10019, (212)708-9400
Intl. Coun. of Museums [IO], Paris, France
Intl. Coun. - Natl. Acad. of TV Arts and Sciences [★IO]
Intl. Coun. - Natl. Acad. of TV Arts and Sciences [★560]
Intl. Coun. of Nurses [IO], Geneva, Switzerland
Intl. Coun. for Open and Distance Educ. [IO], Oslo, Norway
Intl. Coun. of Organizations for Folklore Festivals and Folk Art [IO], Confolens, France
Intl. Coun. of Perfusion Societies - Defunct.
Intl. Coun. for Philosophy and Humanistic Stud. [IO], Paris, France
Intl. Coun. for Physical Activity and Fitness Res. [IO], Padua, Italy
Intl. Coun. for Physical Fitness Res. [★IO]
Intl. Coun. of Psychologists - Defunct.
Intl. Coun. of Reflexologists [IO], Paris, ON, Canada
Intl. Coun. for Res. and Innovation in Building and Constr. [IO], Rotterdam, Netherlands
Intl. Coun. for Rhodesia - Defunct.
Intl. Coun. for Sci. [IO], Paris, France
Intl. Coun. for Sci. and Tech. Info. [IO], Paris, France
Intl. Coun. for Sci. Unions [★IO]
Intl. Coun. of Sci. Unions Abstracting Bd. [★IO]
Intl. Coun. of Seamen's Agencies [★IO]
Intl. Coun. of Seamen's Agencies [★13007]
Intl. Coun. of Sex Education and Parenthood - Address unknown since 1995.
Intl. Coun. of Shopping Centers [3410], 1221 Ave. of the Americas, 41st Fl., New York, NY 10020-1099, (646)728-3800
Intl. Coun. of Shopping Centers [IO], New York, NY, United States
Intl. Coun. for Small Bus. [IO], Washington, DC, United States
Intl. Coun. for Small Bus. [3611], The George Washington Univ., Scholarship of Bus., Dept. of Mgt., 2201 G St. NW, Funger 315, Washington, DC 20052, (202)994-0704
Intl. Coun. of Social Democratic Women [★IO]
Intl. Coun. on Social Welfare - Canada [IO], Utrecht, Netherlands
Intl. Coun. of Societies of Indus. Design [IO], Montreal, QC, Canada
Intl. Coun. of Societies of Pathology - Address unknown since 2001.
Intl. Coun. for Soviet and East European Stud. [★IO]
Intl. Coun. of Sport Sci. and Physical Educ. [IO], Berlin, Germany
Intl. Coun. on Systems Engg. [IO], Seattle, WA, United States
Intl. Coun. on Systems Engg. [7019], 2150 N 107th St., Ste. 205, Seattle, WA 98133-9009, (206)361-6607
Intl. Coun. on Systems Engg. - South Africa [IO], Highveld Park, Republic of South Africa
Intl. Coun. of Tanners [IO], Northampton, United Kingdom

Intl. Coun. for Tech. Commun. [IO], Kuesnacht, Switzerland
Intl. Coun. of Toy Indus. [IO], New York, NY, United States
Intl. Coun. of Toy Indus. [3831], 1115 Broadway, 4th Fl., New York, NY 10010, (212)675-1141
Intl. Coun. for Traditional Music - Address unknown since 2001.
Intl. Coun. of Voluntary Agencies [IO], Geneva, Switzerland
Intl. Coun. of Women [IO], Paris, France
Intl. Coun. for Women in the Arts - Address unknown since 2002.
Intl. Councils on Higher Education - Defunct.
Intl. Counseling Center [★11829]
Intl. Counter-Terrorism Officers Assn. [18732], Empire State Bldg., 350 5th Ave., Ste. 3304 - No. 16P, New York, NY 10118, (212)564-5048
International Counter-Terrorism Officers Association [IO], New York, NY, United States
Intl. Courtly Literature Soc. [IO], Madison, WI, United States
Intl. Courtly Literature Soc. [10424], c/o Maureen Boulton, North American Branch Pres., Univ. of Notre Dame, 343 O'Shaughnessy Hall, Notre Dame, IN 46556
Intl. Crane Found. [5327], PO Box 447, E-11376 Shady Lane Rd., Baraboo, WI 53913-0447, (608)356-9462
International Crane Foundation [IO], Baraboo, WI, United States
Intl. Craniofacial Foundations [★14057]
Intl. Craniopathic Soc. [★14013]
Intl. Craniopathic Soc. [★IO]
Intl. Creative Writers League - Address unknown since 1995.
Intl. Credit Assn. - Defunct.
Intl. Credit Insurance Assn. [★IO]
Intl. Credit Insurance and Surety Assn. [IO], Amsterdam, Netherlands
Intl. Cremation Fed. [IO], The Hague, Netherlands
Intl. Criminal Court Alliance [5654], 11835 W Olympic Blvd., Ste. 1090, Los Angeles, CA 90064, (310)473-0777
Intl. Criminal Investigators Assn. - Defunct.
Intl. Criminal Justice Assn. - Address unknown since 1995.
Intl. Criminal Law Commn. - Address unknown since 2003.
Intl. Criminal Law Network [IO], The Hague, Netherlands
Intl. Criminal Police Org. - Interpol [IO], Lyon, France
Intl. Crisis Gp., Washington Off. [IO], Washington, DC, United States
Intl. Crisis Gp., Washington Off. [17246], 1629 K St. NW, Ste. 450, Washington, DC 20006, (202)785-1601
Intl. Critical Incident Stress Found. [16491], 3290 Pine Orchard Ln., Ste. 106, Ellicott City, MD 21042, (410)750-9600
International Critical Incident Stress Foundation [IO], Ellicott City, MD, United States
Intl. Crocodilian Soc. - Defunct.
Intl. Crop Improvement Assn. [★5436]
Intl. Crops Res. Inst. for the Semi-Arid Tropics - Bulawayo [IO], Bulawayo, Zimbabwe
Intl. Crosby Circle [24804], 5608 N 34th St., Arlington, VA 22207, (703)241-5608
Intl. Cruise Passengers Assn. - Defunct.
Intl. Cryogenic Engineering Committee [IO], Dresden, Germany
Intl. Cryogenic Materials Conf. [6846], c/o Centennial Conferences, 901 Front St., Ste. 130, Louisville, CO 80027, (303)499-2299
Intl. Cuemakers Assn. [519], c/o Chris Hightower, Intl. Dir., 444 Flint Hill Rd., Aragon, GA 30104, (770)684-7004
Intl. Cuemakers Assn. [IO], Aragon, GA, United States
Intl. Cultic Stud. Assn. [17368], PO Box 2265, Bonita Springs, FL 34133, (239)514-3081
Intl. Cultural Centers for Youth - Address unknown since 2001.
Intl. Cultural Exchange - Address unknown since 2000.

A star before a book entry number signifies that the name is not listed separately, but is mentioned within the entry.

Intl. Cultural Soc. of Korea [★IO]
Intl. Cultural Youth Exchange - Bolivia [IO], La Paz, Bolivia
Intl. Cultural Youth Exchange - Colombia [IO], Bogota, Colombia
Intl. Cultural Youth Exchange - Denmark [IO], Arhus, Denmark
Intl. Cultural Youth Exchange in Europe [IO], Arhus, Denmark
Intl. Cultural Youth Exchange - Ghana [IO], Accra, Ghana
Intl. Cultural Youth Exchange - Japan [IO], Tokyo, Japan
Intl. Cultural Youth Exchange - Kenya [IO], Nairobi, Kenya
Intl. Cultural Youth Exchange - New Zealand [IO], Tauranga, New Zealand
Intl. Cultural Youth Exchange - Nigeria [IO], Lagos, Nigeria
Intl. Cultural Youth Exchange - South Korea [IO], Seoul, Republic of Korea
Intl. Cultural Youth Exchange - Switzerland [IO], Bern, Switzerland
Intl. Cultural Youth Exchange - Taiwan [IO], Tainan, Taiwan
Intl. Cultural Youth Exchange - United Kingdom [IO], London, United Kingdom
Intl. Curling Fed. [★IO]
Intl. Curling Fed. - Ladies Comm. - Defunct.
Intl. Curly Horse Org. [4898], c/o Tina Estridge, Off. Mgr., 2690 Carpenter Rd., Jamestown, OH 45335, (515)204-6211
International Curly Horse Organization [IO], Jamestown, OH, United States
Intl. Customer Ser. Assn. [3551], 401 N Michigan Ave., Chicago, IL 60611, (312)321-6800
Intl. Customs Tariffs Bur. [IO], Brussels, Belgium
Intl. Cut Flower Growers Assn. [IO], Haslett, MI, United States
Intl. Cut Flower Growers Assn. [4980], PO Box 99, Haslett, MI 48840, (517)655-3726
Intl. Cut Stone Quarrymen's Assn. [★3692]
Intl. Cycling Union [IO], Aigle, Switzerland
Intl. Cystic Fibrosis-Mucoviscidosis Assn. [IO], Valencia, Spain
International Cytokine Society [IO], Augusta, GA, United States
Intl. Cytokine Soc. [6580], c/o Dr. Sherwood M. Reichard, Exec. Mgr., 119 Davis Rd., Ste. 5A, Augusta, GA 30907-0219, (706)228-4655
Intl. Dairy-Deli-Bakery Assn. [1522], PO Box 5528, Madison, WI 53705-0528, (608)310-5000
Intl. Dairy-Deli-Bakery Assn. [★1522]
International Dairy-Deli-Bakery Association [IO], Madison, WI, United States
Intl. Dairy-Deli-Bakery Assn. [★IO]
Intl. Dairy Fed. [IO], Brussels, Belgium
Intl. Dairy Fed. - Canadian Natl. Comm. [IO], Ottawa, ON, Canada
Intl. Dairy Foods Assn. [IO], Washington, DC, United States
Intl. Dairy Foods Assn. [1134], 1250 H St. NW, Ste. 900, Washington, DC 20005, (202)737-4332
Intl. Dalkon Shield Victims Educ. Assn. [16898], PO Box 84151, Seattle, WA 98124, (206)329-1371
International Dalkon Shield Victims Education Association [IO], Seattle, WA, United States
Intl. Dams Newsl. [★IO]
Intl. Dams Newsl. [★7833]
Intl. Dance Alliance - Address unknown since 2003.
Intl. Dance Coun. [IO], Paris, France
Intl. Dance Sport Fed. [IO], Duisburg, Germany
Intl. Dance Teachers' Assn. [IO], Brighton, United Kingdom
Intl. Dark-Sky Assn. [IO], Tucson, AZ, United States
Intl. Dark-Sky Assn. [6506], 3225 N 1st Ave., Tucson, AZ 85719-2103, (520)293-3198
Intl. Data Base Mgt. Assn. - Defunct.
Intl. Data Warehousing Assn. - Address unknown since 2004.
Intl. Database Assn. - Defunct.
Intl. DB2 Users Gp. [6856], 401 N Michigan Ave., Chicago, IL 60611-4267, (312)321-6881
Intl. Debate Educ. Assn; IDEA: The [18677]
Intl. Defenders of Animals [11414], PO Box 5634, Weybosset Hill Sta., Providence, RI 02903-0634, (401)738-3710

Intl. Defenders of Animals [IO], Providence, RI, United States
Intl. Defense and Aid Fund for Southern Africa, U.S. Comm. - Defunct.
Intl. Defense Equip. Exhibitors Assn. [1343], 6233 Nelway Dr., McLean, VA 22101, (703)760-0762
International Defense Equipment Exhibitors Association [IO], McLean, VA, United States
International Defensive Pistol Association [IO], Berryville, AR, United States
Intl. Defensive Pistol Assn. [23718], 2232 CR 719, Berryville, AR 72616, (870)545-3886
Intl. Deli-Bakery Assn. - Defunct.
Intl. Democrat Union [IO], Oslo, Norway
Intl. Dendrology Soc. [IO], Kington, United Kingdom
Intl. Dental Hea. Found. [IO], Reston, VA, United States
Intl. Dental Hea. Found. [14166]
Intl. Desalination Assn. [7831], PO Box 387, Topsfield, MA 01983, (978)887-0410
Intl. Desalination Assn. [IO], Topsfield, MA, United States
Intl. Desalination and Environmental Assn. [★IO]
Intl. Desalination and Environmental Assn. [★7831]
Intl. Desert Lynx Cat Assn. [4207], PO Box 511, Selma, OR 97538
International Desert Lynx Cat Association [IO], Selma, OR, United States
Intl. Desert Racing Assn. - Address unknown since 1995.
Intl. Design Center Berlin [IO], Berlin, Germany
Intl. Design Conf. in Aspen [9905]
Intl. Design Guild [2263], 670 Commercial St., Manchester, NH 03101, (800)205-4345
Intl. Design Guild [IO], Manchester, NH, United States

International Development

ABANTU for Development - Regional Off. for West Africa [IO]
ActionAid Intl. USA [11758]
Adventist Development and Relief Agency Intl. [12826]
Africa 2000Plus Network - Zimbabwe [IO]
Africa Leadership Forum [IO]
AFRICALINK [16922]
African Capacity Building Found. [IO]
African, Caribbean and Pacific Gp. of States [IO]
African Development Found. [IO]
African Development Fund [IO]
African Development Inst. [16923]
African Found. for Development [IO]
African Medical and Res. Found. [14971]
African Training and Res. Centre in Admin. for Development [IO]
Aga Khan Found. Canada [IO]
Aga Khan Found. - India [IO]
Aga Khan Found. - Kyrgyz Republic [IO]
AGIR Ici [IO]
Agri-Energy Roundtable [IO]
Agri-Energy Roundtable [17826]
Aid to Artisans [12415]
Aid for Intl. Medicine [14972]
Aide et Action - France [IO]
Alliance for Communities in Action [12416]
Alliance for Intl. Reforestation [4344]
Alliance of Small Island States [17827]
Alliance of Small Island States [IO]
Alliance for Southern African Progress [IO]
Alliance for Southern African Progress [12417]
Alternatives, Action and Commun. Network for Intl. Development [IO]
Amer. Coll. of Intl. Physicians [14973]
Amer. Comm. for KEEP [12418]
Amer. Friends Ser. Comm. [13148]
Amer. Red Cross Overseas Assn. [12831]
Angelcare [11672]
Ashoka: Innovators for the Public [12419]
Ashoka: Innovators for the Public [IO]
Asian Inst. for Development Commun. [IO]
Aspen Inst. Berlin [IO]
Associacao Brasileira Para o Desenvolvimento de Liderancas [IO]
Assn. for the Advancement of Policy, Res. and Development in the Third World [17828]
Assn. for India's Development [12420]

Assn. for India's Development [IO]
Assn. of PVO Financial Managers [1458]
Assn. of Thai Professionals in Am. and Canada [19406]
Assn. on Third World Affairs [17829]
Assn. on Third World Affairs [IO]
Assn. of Third World Stud. [IO]
Assn. of Third World Stud. [17830]
Assn. for Women's Rights in Development [IO]
Associazione Bertoni per la Cooperazione e lo Sviluppo nel Terzo Mondo [IO]
Associazione di Cooperazione Cristiana Internazionale [IO]
Associazione per gli Interventi di Cooperazione allo Sviluppo [IO]
Associazione Studi Am. Latina [IO]
Australian Agency for Intl. Development [IO]
Australian Coun. for Intl. Development [IO]
Austrian Found. for Development Res. [IO]
Banana Link [IO]
Bangladesh Inst. of Development Stud. [IO]
Baptist World Aid Australia [IO]
Bellanet [IO]
Berne Declaration [IO]
BIO Ventures for Global Hea. [14975]
Bd. of Intl. Ministries [19483]
Bridges to Community [13389]
Bridging Nations [17861]
British Overseas NGOs for Development [IO]
Brother's Brother Found. [12837]
Canadian Assn. for the Stud. of Intl. Development [IO]
Canadian Coun. for Intl. Co-operation [IO]
Canadian Crossroads Intl. [IO]
Canadian Org. for Development Through Educ. [IO]
Caribbean Assn. of Indus. and Commerce [IO]
Caribbean-Central Amer. Action [IO]
Caribbean-Central Amer. Action [12421]
Catholic Medical Mission Bd. [12515]
Catholic Network of Volunteer Ser. [19602]
Centre for Development and Population Activities [12422]
Centro Informazione ed Educazione allo Sviluppo [IO]
China Connection [IO]
China Connection [12423]
China Medical Bd. of New York [14976]
Christian Children's Fund [11688]
Christian Found. for Children and Aging [13159]
Christian Reformed World Relief Comm. [12424]
Christian Reformed World Relief Comm. [IO]
Christians for Peace in El Salvador [20322]
Church World Ser. - Vietnam [IO]
Citizens Development Corps [IO]
Citizens Development Corps [17831]
Claretian Volunteers and Lay Missionaries [19612]
Club of Budapest [IO]
Coady Intl. Inst. [IO]
Comhlamh [IO]
Comitato di Coordinamento dell Organizzazioni per il Servizio Volontario [IO]
Commn. on Intl. Programs [IO]
Commn. on Intl. Programs [17832]
Comm. for the Economic Growth of Israel [24337]
Comm. for the Promotion and Advancement of Cooperatives [IO]
Commonwealth Found. [IO]
Commonwealth Fund for Tech. Co-Operation [IO]
Concern Am. [12845]
Concord [IO]
Consultative Group to Assist the Poor [IO]
Consultative Gp. to Assist the Poor [17833]
Consultative Gp. on Intl. Agricultural Res. [12425]
Consultative Gp. on Intl. Agricultural Res. [IO]
Cooperation for the Development of Emerging Countries [IO]
Coun. for Intl. Development [IO]
Counterpart Intl. [IO]
Counterpart Intl. [12426]
Counterpart - U.S. Off. [17834]
Counterpart - U.S. Off. [IO]
CUSO - Canada [IO]
Dag Hammarskjold Found. [IO]

Reference to "IO" in place of a book number signifies that the association may be found in the 45th edition of International Organizations.

Danish Inst. for Intl. Stud. [IO]
Delegation Catholique pour la Cooperation [IO]
Dept. for Intl. Development [IO]
Development Gp. [IO]
Development Gp. for Alternative Policies [IO]
Development Gp. for Alternative Policies [17835]
Development Innovations and Networks - Switzerland [IO]
Development Network of Indigenous Voluntary Associations [IO]
Development Rsrc. Centre [IO]
DOCARE Intl., N.F.P. [12518]
East Meets West Found. [17836]
East Meets West Found. [IO]
Educational Concerns for Hunger Org. [12389]
Egyptians Relief Assn. [11774]
Emergency Relief Response Fund [20562]
ENDA Caribe [IO]
European Assn. of Development Agencies [IO]
European Movement - Ireland [IO]
FARMS Intl. [IO]
FARMS Intl. [12427]
Fed. of Australia-Japan Societies [IO]
Fellowship Intl. Mission [20338]
FEMCONSULT [IO]
Financial Services Volunteer Corps [IO]
Financial Services Volunteer Corps [17837]
Floresta U.S.A. [17838]
Floresta U.S.A. [IO]
Flying Doctors of Am. [12523]
Food and Agriculture Org. of the United Nations - Regional Off. for Europe [IO]
Food and Agriculture Org. of the United Nations - Regional Off. for Latin Am. and the Caribbean [IO]
Food and Agriculture Org. of the United Nations - Trinidad and Tobago [IO]
Food for the Hungry [12391]
Food for the Poor [12772]
Forum on Debt and Development [IO]
Found. for Development Cooperation [IO]
Found. for the Peoples of the South Pacific - Kiribati [IO]
Found. for the Support of Intl. Medical Training [14977]
Fourth World Documentation Proj. [17814]
Freedom from Hunger [12394]
Futures for Children [11695]
GALA: Globalization and Localization Assn. [1168]
Global Envision [12194]
Global Healing [12450]
Global Hea. Coun. [14979]
Global Outreach Mission [12525]
Global Policy Forum [17839]
Global Ser. Corps [13392]
Global Teams [19961]
Global Youth Connect [18851]
God's Child Proj. [11597]
Grassroots Intl. [12428]
Grassroots Intl. [IO]
Gruppo Autonomo di Volontariato Civile in Italia [IO]
Healing the Children [11697]
Hea. Volunteers Overseas [12526]
Heifer Proj. Intl. [12429]
Heifer Proj. Intl. [IO]
Helvetas - Swiss Assn. for Intl. Cooperation [IO]
Hesperian Found. [14980]
Hispanic Coun. on Intl. Relations [17869]
Humanist Inst. for Development Co-operation [IO]
Humanistic Inst. for Cooperation with Developing Countries [IO]
Humanity Intl. [12859]
Indian Muslim Relief Comm. of ISNA [12860]
Inst. of Caribbean Stud. [12430]
Institute of Caribbean Studies [IO]
Inst. for Development Policy and Mgt. [IO]
Inst. for Intl. Cooperation and Development [IO]
Inst. for Intl. Cooperation and Development [12431]
Inst. for Intl. Economic Cooperation and Development [IO]
Inst. for Trans. and Development Policy [IO]
Inst. for Trans. and Development Policy [17840]
Inst. for Univ. Cooperation [IO]

Inter-American Parliamentary Gp. on Population and Development [IO]
Inter-American Parliamentary Gp. on Population and Development [12432]
Interaction/American Coun. for Voluntary Intl. Action [12433]
Interaction/American Coun. for Voluntary Intl. Action [IO]
Interchurch Org. for Development Cooperation [IO]
Intergovernmental Authority on Development [IO]
Intermed Intl. [14982]
Intl. Bank for Reconstruction and Development [17841]
Intl. Bank for Reconstruction and Development [IO]
Intl. Center for Promotion of Enterprises [IO]
Intl. Center for Res. on Women [17543]
Intl. Coalition for Sustainable Production and Consumption [17222]
Intl. Cooperation for Development and Solidarity [IO]
Intl. Development Assn. [IO]
Intl. Development Assn. [17842]
Intl. Development Center of Japan [IO]
Intl. Development Educ. Rsrc. Assn. [IO]
The Intl. Found. [IO]
The Intl. Found. [12434]
Intl. Inst. for Env. and Development [IO]
Intl. Inst. of Rural Reconstruction, U.S. Chap. [12938]
Intl. Inst. for Sustainable Development [IO]
Intl. Medical Corps [12862]
Intl. NGO Training and Res. Centre [IO]
Intl. Peace Operations Assn. [18213]
Intl. Relief And Development [11782]
Intl. Relief Friendship Found. [13171]
Intl. Solidarity Found. [IO]
Intl. Task Force for the Rural Poor [IO]
InterServe U.S.A. [20351]
Japan External Trade Org. [24342]
Japanese NGO Center for Intl. Cooperation [IO]
Jewish Natl. Fund [20150]
Jubilee Res. [IO]
Just Act: Youth Action for Global Justice [IO]
Just Act: Youth Action for Global Justice [12435]
Kids 4 Afghan Kids [11610]
Lalmba Assn. [12866]
Latin Amer. Assn. of Development Organizations [IO]
Lay Mission-Helpers Assn. [19648]
LEAD - Afrique Francophone [IO]
LEAD - Benin [IO]
LEAD - Canada [IO]
LEAD - China [IO]
LEAD - CIS [IO]
LEAD - Indonesia [IO]
LEAD Intl. - United Kingdom [IO]
LEAD - Mexico [IO]
LEAD - Nigeria [IO]
LEAD - Pakistan [IO]
LEAD - Southern Africa [IO]
LEAD - Togo [IO]
Los Ninos [12589]
Lutheran World Relief [20230]
Malawi Proj. [11266]
Marjorie Mayrock Center for CIS and East European Res. [IO]
MATCH Intl. Centre [IO]
MediSend Intl. [12530]
Mennonite Central Comm. [20247]
Mennonite Economic Development Associates [20249]
Mennonite Economic Development Associates [IO]
Mirrer Yeshiva Central Inst. [12477]
Mission Doctors Assn. [12532]
Natl. Student Campaign Against Hunger and Homelessness [12396]
Need [12875]
NetAid [11486]
Netherlands Development Org. [IO]
Netherlands Org. for Intl. Development Cooperation [IO]
New Forests Proj. [12436]

New Wineskins Missionary Network [20375]
NGO Coordination for Development [IO]
Nordic Proj. Fund [IO]
North-South Inst. [IO]
Occupational Knowledge Intl. [5099]
One Earth One Justice [12437]
One Village [IO]
One World Action [IO]
OPEC Fund for Intl. Development [IO]
Oper. Smile [12534]
Our Little Bros. and Sisters [20380]
Outstretched Hands [IO]
Overseas Development Inst. [IO]
OXFAM Am. [IO]
OXFAM Am. [12438]
Oxfam Australia [IO]
OXFAM - Canada [IO]
OXFAM - GB in Vietnam [IO]
Oxfam - Germany [IO]
OXFAM - Hong Kong [IO]
OXFAM - Ireland [IO]
Oxfam - New Zealand [IO]
OXFAM - Solidarity [IO]
OXFAM - U.K. [IO]
Pacific Basin Development Coun. [17843]
PACT [12439]
Panos Inst. [12440]
Panos Inst. [IO]
Panos Inst. - London [IO]
Partners for Democratic Change [17844]
Partners for Peace [18230]
Pax World Ser. [17845]
Pax World Ser. [IO]
People-to-People Hea. Found. [14984]
Planning Assistance [17846]
Planning Assistance [IO]
Plenty Intl. [12878]
Pontifical Mission for Palestine [12816]
Presbyterian Hunger Prog. [12397]
Prince of Wales Intl. Bus. Leaders Forum [IO]
Probe Intl. [IO]
Progressio [IO]
Proj. South: Inst. for the Elimination of Poverty and Genocide [17872]
PROTOS [IO]
Red Sea Team Intl. [20385]
Restoration Proj. Intl. [12441]
Restoration Proj. Intl. [IO]
Sabre Found. [IO]
Sabre Found. [17847]
Sahel and West Africa Club [IO]
Salesian Missioners [20391]
Save the Children [11720]
Scottish Catholic Intl. Aid Fund [IO]
Secretariat of the Pacific Community [IO]
Self Help Intl. [IO]
Self Help Intl. [12442]
Seva Found. [12443]
Seva Found. [IO]
Sierra Visions [IO]
Sierra Visions [12444]
Single Global Currency Assn. [17021]
Social Relief Intl. [12445]
Social Relief Intl. [IO]
Soc. of African Missions [19719]
Soc. for the Development of Austrian Economics [6894]
Soc. for Intl. Development - Italy [IO]
Soc. for Intl. Development - USA [IO]
Soc. for Intl. Development - USA [17848]
Soc. of Missionaries of Africa [19721]
Soc. for Res. and Initiatives for Sustainable Technologies and Institution [IO]
Solidaridad Internacional [IO]
SOS Sahel Intl. - UK [IO]
South Asian Assn. for Regional Cooperation [IO]
Southern African Non-Governmental Org. Network [IO]
Swiss Alliance of Development Organisations [IO]
Task Force for Child Survival and Development [12542]
TechnoServe [17849]
TechnoServe [IO]
Teen Missions Intl. [20402]
Terre des Hommes [IO]

A star before a book entry number signifies that the name is not listed separately, but is mentioned within the entry.

Third World Conf. Found. [IO]
Third World Conf. Found. [17850]
Third World Forum - African Off. [IO]
Third World Forum - Middle East Off. [IO]
Third World Network - Malaysia [IO]
Transnational Diplomatic Network [17874]
Trickle Up Prog. [12446]
UNA Intl. Ser. [IO]
UNESCO Co-Action Programme [IO]
UNESCO-IHE Inst. for Water Educ. [IO]
UNIDO Center for Regional Cooperation in Turkey [IO]
United Methodist Comm. on Relief [20267]
United Nations Conf. on Trade and Development [IO]
United Nations Development Prog. - Mali [IO]
United Nations Development Prog. - Mauritania [IO]
United Nations Development Prog. - Mauritius and Seychelles [IO]
United Nations Development Prog. - Nigeria [IO]
United Nations Development Prog. - Rwanda [IO]
United Nations Development Prog. - Togo [IO]
United Nations Development Programme [IO]
United Nations Development Programme [17851]
United Nations Development Programme - Cameroon [IO]
United Nations Development Programme - Cote d'Ivoire [IO]
United Nations Development Programme - Djibouti [IO]
United Nations Development Programme - Ethiopia [IO]
United Nations Development Programme - Gambia [IO]
United Nations Development Programme - Ghana [IO]
United Nations Development Programme - Malawi [IO]
United Nations Development Programme - Mozambique [IO]
United Nations Development Programme - Namibia [IO]
United Nations Development Programme - Regional Bur. for Asia and the Pacific [IO]
United Nations Development Programme - Regional Bur. for Asia and the Pacific [17852]
United Nations Development Programme - South Africa [IO]
United Nations Development Programme - Tanzania [IO]
United Nations Development Programme - Uganda [IO]
United Nations Indus. Development Org. [IO]
United Nations Indus. Development Org. - Algeria [IO]
United Nations Indus. Development Org. - Bolivia [IO]
United Nations Indus. Development Org. - Cameroon [IO]
United Nations Indus. Development Org. - China [IO]
United Nations Indus. Development Org. - Colombia [IO]
United Nations Indus. Development Org. - Cote d'Ivoire [IO]
United Nations Indus. Development Org. - Egypt [IO]
United Nations Indus. Development Org. - Eritrea [IO]
United Nations Indus. Development Org. - Ethiopia [IO]
United Nations Indus. Development Org. - Ghana [IO]
United Nations Indus. Development Org. - Guinea [IO]
United Nations Indus. Development Org. - India [IO]
United Nations Indus. Development Org. - Indonesia [IO]
United Nations Indus. Development Org. - Iran [IO]
United Nations Indus. Development Org. - Kenya [IO]
United Nations Indus. Development Org. - Lebanon [IO]

United Nations Indus. Development Org. - Madagascar [IO]
United Nations Indus. Development Org. - Mexico [IO]
United Nations Indus. Development Org. - Morocco [IO]
United Nations Indus. Development Org. - Mozambique [IO]
United Nations Indus. Development Org. - Nigeria [IO]
United Nations Indus. Development Org. - Pakistan [IO]
United Nations Indus. Development Org. - Philippines [IO]
United Nations Indus. Development Org. - Senegal [IO]
United Nations Indus. Development Org. - Sudan [IO]
United Nations Indus. Development Org. - Thailand [IO]
United Nations Indus. Development Org. - Tunisia [IO]
United Nations Indus. Development Org. - Uruguay [IO]
United Nations Indus. Development Org. - Vietnam [IO]
United Nations Indus. Development Org. - Zimbabwe [IO]
United Nations Info. Centre - Nigeria [IO]
United Nations Res. Inst. for Social Development [IO]
United Nations Volunteers [IO]
U.S. African Development Found. [17853]
U.S. Peace Corps - Zambia [IO]
Univ. of Bremen, Res. Gp. on African Development Perspectives [IO]
U.S.A. for Africa [12882]
Vienna Inst. for Development and Cooperation [IO]
Visions in Action [IO]
Visions in Action [12447]
Volunteer Missionary Movement - U.S. Off. [19736]
Volunteer Ser. Overseas - United Kingdom [IO]
Volunteers in Tech. Assistance [12448]
Water for People [17854]
William J. Clinton Found. [17855]
Wings of Hope [12883]
World Bank Gp. [17856]
World Bank Gp. [IO]
World Development Fed. [IO]
World Development Fed. [12449]
World Development Movement [IO]
World Fed. of Public Hea. Associations [16258]
World House [IO]
World Mercy Fund [12886]
World Neighbors - Southeast Asia [IO]
World Relief [19985]
World Resources Inst. [4477]
Worldwatch Inst. [18844]
Youth Soc. for Peace and Development of the Balkans [IO]
Intl. Development Assn. [IO], Washington, DC, United States
Intl. Development Assn. [17842], The World Bank, 1818 H St. NW, Washington, DC 20433, (202)473-1000
Intl. Development Assn. of the Furniture Indus. of Japan [IO], Tokyo, Japan
Intl. Development Center of Japan [IO], Tokyo, Japan
Intl. Development Educ. Rsrc. Assn. [IO], Vancouver, BC, Canada
Intl. Development Enterprises - India [IO], New Delhi, India
Intl. Development Found. - Address unknown since 2005.
Intl. Development Law Org. [IO], Rome, Italy
Intl. Development and Relief Found. [IO], Toronto, ON, Canada
Intl. Development Res. Centre - Canada [IO], Ottawa, ON, Canada
Intl. Development Res. Coun. [★IO]
Intl. Development Res. Coun. [★3305]
Intl. Development Services - Address unknown since 1995.

Intl. Development; Volunteers for [★18239]
Intl. Diabetes Fed. [IO], Brussels, Belgium
Intl. Diabetic Athletes Assn. [★14222]
Intl. Diana Ross Fan Club - Defunct.
Intl. Diastema Club - Defunct.
Intl. Die Sinkers Conf. [★24012]
Intl. Digital Imaging Assn. - Defunct.
Intl. Disaster Recovery Assn. [7774], c/o BWT Associates, PO No. 4515, Shrewsbury, MA 01545, (508)845-6000
Intl. Disc Dog Handlers' Assn. [23373], 1690 Julius Bridge Rd., Ball Ground, GA 30107, (770)735-6200
Intl. Disciples Women's Ministries [20620], PO Box 1986, Indianapolis, IN 46206, (317)713-2679
Intl. Disciples Women's Ministries [IO], Indianapolis, IN, United States
Intl. Discotheque Assn. - Defunct.
Intl. Discus Assn. - Address unknown since 2001.
Intl. Disk Drive Equip. and Materials Assn. [6732], 470 Lakeside Dr., Ste. A, Sunnyvale, CA 94085-4720, (408)991-9430
Intl. Disk Drive Equip. and Materials Assn. [IO], Sunnyvale, CA, United States
Intl. District Energy Assn. [IO], Westborough, MA, United States
Intl. District Energy Assn. [1888], 125 Turnpike Rd., Ste. 4, Westborough, MA 01581-2841, (508)366-9339
Intl. District Heating Assn. [★1888]
Intl. District Heating Assn. [★IO]
Intl. District Heating and Cooling Assn. [★IO]
Intl. District Heating and Cooling Assn. [★1888]
Intl. Diving Schools Assn. - Address unknown since 1988.
Intl. DJ Guild [2812], c/o Rembrandt, Turner and Griswold, 395 Lockwood Dr., Shirley, NY 11967, (631)772-2020
Intl. D.N. Ice Yacht Racing Assn. [23183], c/o John Harper, Commodore, 1369 Hawthorne Rd., Grosse Pointe Woods, MI 48236-1443, (313)882-3420
Intl. D.N. Ice Yacht Racing Assn. [IO], Lambertville, MI, United States
Intl. Doctors in Alcoholics Anonymous [IO], Lexington, KY, United States
Intl. Doctors in Alcoholics Anonymous [13252], c/o Gordon L. Hyde, MD, Exec. Dir., 3311 Brookhill Cir., Lexington, KY 40502, (859)277-9379
Intl. Doctors Soc. [10895], PO Box 21088, Detroit, MI 48221, (313)368-8701
Intl. Doctors Soc. [IO], Detroit, MI, United States
Intl. Documentary Assn. [IO], Los Angeles, CA, United States
Intl. Documentary Assn. [1385], 1201 W 5th St., Ste. M320, Los Angeles, CA 90017, (213)534-3600
Intl. Documentary Found. [★1385]
Intl. Documentary Found. [★IO]
Intl. Documents Service - Defunct.
Intl. Dodge Ball Fed. [23821], 3451A Washington Ave., Gulfport, MS 39507, (228)860-9000
International Dodge Ball Federation [IO], Gulfport, MS, United States
Intl. Doll Assn. - Defunct.
Intl. Doll Makers Assn. [22397], c/o Judy Kroeger, Pres., 2512 White Pole Rd., Casey, IA 50048, (641)524-5139
Intl. Doll Makers Assn. [★22397]
Intl. Doll Makers Assn. [IO], Duncanville, TX, United States
Intl. Doll Makers Assn. [★IO]
Intl. Doll Makers Assn. - Internationals [★IO]
Intl. Doll Makers Assn. - Internationals [★22397]
Intl. Door Assn. [631], PO Box 246, West Milton, OH 45383-0246, (937)698-8042
Intl. Door Assn. [IO], West Milton, OH, United States
Intl. Dostoevsky Soc. [IO], Geneva, Switzerland
Intl. Double Reed Soc. [IO], Finksburg, MD, United States
Intl. Double Reed Soc. [10619], c/o Norma R. Hooks, Exec. Sec.-Treas., 2423 Lawndale Rd., Finksburg, MD 21048-1401, (410)871-0658
Intl. DOVE Assn. [IO], Olds, AB, Canada
Intl. Dove Soc. - Defunct.
Intl. Downtown Assn. [732], 1250 H St. NW, 10th Fl., Washington, DC 20005, (202)393-6801
Intl. Downtown Assn. [IO], Washington, DC, United States

Reference to "IO" in place of a book number signifies that the association may be found in the 45th edition of International Organizations.

Intl. Downtown Executives Assn. [★IO]
Intl. Downtown Executives Assn. [★732]
Intl. Dragon Boat Assn. - Defunct.
Intl. Dragon Class Assn. - Address unknown since 2001.
Intl. Dragonfly Fund [IO], Zerf, Germany
Intl. Drapery Assn. [★2256]
Intl. Drilling Fed. [★1044]
Intl. Drilling Fed. [★IO]
Intl. Drip Irrigation Assn. [★IO]
Intl. Drip Irrigation Assn. [★182]
Intl. Drug Strategy Inst. [★13248]
Intl. Drug Strategy Inst. [★IO]
Intl. Drycleaners Cong. [IO], Oxford, OH, United States
Intl. Drycleaners Cong. [2404], c/o Carolyn Portwood, Exec. Sec., PO Box 261, West College Corner, IN 47003, (403)685-4755
Intl. Dull Folks Unlimited - Defunct.
Intl. Dull Men's Club - Defunct.
Intl. Dwarf Fruit Tree Assn. [★5257]
International Dwarf Fruit Tree Association [IO], Wenatchee, WA, United States
Intl. Dyslexia Assn. [IO], Baltimore, MD, United States
Intl. Dyslexia Assn. [14295], 40 York Rd., 4th Fl., Baltimore, MD 21204-5202, (410)296-0232
Intl. E-22 Class Assn. [★23184]
Intl. E-22 Class Assn. [★IO]
Intl. Ecology Inst. [IO], Oldendorf, Germany
Intl. Ecology Soc. - Defunct.
Intl. Economic Assn. [IO], Paris, France
Intl. Economic Conversion Campaign - Defunct.
Intl. Economic Development Coun. [5812], 734 15th St. NW, Ste. 900, Washington, DC 20005, (202)223-7800
Intl. Economic Development Coun. [IO], Washington, DC, United States
Intl. Economic History Assn. [IO], Tuebingen, Germany
Intl. Economic Policy Assn. - Address unknown since 1990.
Intl. Economics and Finance Soc. [6884], c/o Prof. Eric W. Bond, Pres., Vanderbilt Univ., Dept. of Economics, VU Sta. B, No. 351819, 2301 Vanderbilt Pl., Nashville, TN 37235-1819, (615)322-3237
Intl. Economics and Philosophy Soc. [IO], Kensington, Australia
The Intl. Ecotourism Soc. [IO], Washington, DC, United States
The Intl. Ecotourism Soc. [3829], 1333 H St. NW, Ste. 300, East Tower, Washington, DC 20005, (202)347-9203
Intl. Edsel Club [21666], 6990 NW 6th Dr., Ankeny, IA 50023-9512
Intl. Edsel Club [IO], Lindenhurst, IL, United States
Intl. Education Assn. - Defunct.
Intl. Educ; Leadership Network for [★8659]
Intl. Educ; Leadership Network for [★IO]
Intl. Educ. Res. Found. [IO], Culver City, CA, United States
Intl. Educ. Res. Found. [8644], PO Box 3665, Culver City, CA 90231-3665, (310)258-9451
Intl. Educ. and Rsrc. Network [8269], 475 Riverside Dr., Ste. 450, New York, NY 10115, (212)870-2693
Intl. Educ. and Rsrc. Network [IO], New York, NY, United States
Intl. Educ. and Rsrc. Network - Armenia [IO], Yerevan, Armenia
Intl. Educ. and Rsrc. Network - Canada [IO], Cochrane, AB, Canada
Intl. Educ. and Rsrc. Network - Egypt [IO], Cairo, Egypt
Intl. Educ. and Rsrc. Network of Nepal [IO], Kathmandu, Nepal
Intl. Educ. and Rsrc. Network of Sierra Leone [IO], Freetown, Sierra Leone
Intl. Educ. and Rsrc. Network - Trinidad and Tobago [IO], Port of Spain, Trinidad and Tobago
Intl. Educational and Cultural Exchange; Fulbright Assn. of Alumni of [★8613]
Intl. Educational Exchange; Liaison Gp. for [★8591]
Intl. Educator's Inst. [8645], PO Box 513, Cummaquid, MA 02637, (508)790-1990
Intl. Educator's Inst. [IO], Cummaquid, MA, United States

Intl. EECP Therapists Assn. [IO], Vero Beach, FL, United States
Intl. EECP Therapists Assn. [16619], PO Box 650005, Vero Beach, FL 32965-0005, (772)794-0861
Intl. Egg Commn. [IO], London, United Kingdom
Intl. Elecl. Testing Assn. [IO], Portage, MI, United States
Intl. Elecl. Testing Assn. [1187], 2700 W Centre Ave., Ste. A, Portage, MI 49024, (269)488-6382
Intl. Electrology Educators - Address unknown since 2006.
Intl. Electronic Article Surveillance Mfg. Assn. - Address unknown since 2003.
Intl. Electronic Facsimile Users Assn. - Defunct.
Intl. Electronics Mfg. Initiative [7265], 2214 Rock Hill Rd., Ste. 110, Herndon, VA 20170-4214, (703)834-0330
Intl. Electronics Packaging Soc. - Address unknown since 2003.
Intl. Electrophoresis Soc. [★6900]
Intl. Electrotechnical Commn. [IO], Geneva, Switzerland
Intl. Elvis Presley Fan Club (Hong Kong) [IO], Hong Kong, People's Republic of China
Intl. Embryo Transfer Soc. [IO], Savoy, IL, United States
Intl. Embryo Transfer Soc. [16794], 1111 N Dunlap Ave., Savoy, IL 61874, (217)356-3182
Intl. Enamellers Inst. [IO], Milan, Italy
Intl. Endotoxin and Innate Immunity Soc. [IO], Stevensville, MT, United States
Intl. Endotoxin and Innate Immunity Soc. [7803], c/o Nancy Pollman, 3777 Eastside Hwy., Stevensville, MT 59870
Intl. Energy Agency [IO], Paris, France
Intl. Energy Credit Assn. [IO], St. John, IN, United States
Intl. Energy Credit Assn. [1427], 8325 Lantern View Ln., St. John, IN 46373, (219)365-7313
Intl. Energy Found. [IO], Okotoks, AB, Canada
Intl. Engg. Consortium [IO], Chicago, IL, United States
Intl. Engg. Consortium [6928], 300 W Adams St., Ste. 1210, Chicago, IL 60606-5114, (312)559-4600
Intl. English Shepherd Registry - Address unknown since 2001.
Intl. Enneagram Assn. [15904], 4100 Executive Park Dr., Ste. 16, Cincinnati, OH 45241, (513)232-5054
Intl. Enneagram Assn. [IO], Cincinnati, OH, United States
Intl. Enterprise Singapore [IO], Singapore, Singapore
Intl. Entertainment Buyers Assn. [1306], PO Box 128376, Nashville, TN 37212, (615)251-9000
Intl. Epidemiological Assn. [IO], Alexandria, Egypt
Intl. Equestrian Drill Team Alliance [23527]
Intl. Equestrian Fed. [★IO]
Intl. Ergonomics Assn. [IO], Ivanhoe East, Australia
Intl. Erosion Control Assn. [IO], Steamboat Springs, CO, United States
Intl. Erosion Control Assn. [4411], 3001 S Lincoln Ave., Ste. A, Steamboat Springs, CO 80487, (970)879-3010
Intl. Erosion Control Assn. - Iberoamerican [IO], Buenos Aires, Argentina
Intl. Erosion Control Assn. - Malaysia [IO], Kuala Lumpur, Malaysia
Intl. Erosion Control Assn. - South Africa [IO], Gauteng, Republic of South Africa
Intl. Esperanto Inst. [IO], The Hague, Netherlands
International Essential Tremor Foundation [IO], Lenexa, KS, United States
Intl. Essential Tremor Found. [15331], PO Box 14005, Lenexa, KS 66285-4005, (913)341-3880
Intl. Etchells Class Assn. [23184], 2812 Canon St., San Diego, CA 92106, (619)222-0252
Intl. Etchells Class Assn. [IO], Jamestown, RI, United States
Intl. European Constr. Fed. [★IO]
International Exchange
Academic Travel Abroad [8588]
AFS Intercultural Programs [8589]
AFS Intercultural Programs [IO]
AFS Interculture Canada [IO]
AHA Intl. [IO]

AHA Intl. [8590]
Alliance for Intl. Educational and Cultural Exchange [8591]
Alliance for Intl. Educational and Cultural Exchange [IO]
Amer. Coun. for Intl. Stud. [IO]
Amer. Coun. for Intl. Stud. [8592]
Amer. Forum for Global Educ. [8593]
Amer. Home Life Intl. [8594]
Amer. Home Life Intl. [IO]
Amer. Inst. for Foreign Stud. Found. [8595]
Amer. Intercultural Student Exchange [8596]
Amer. Univ. in Moscow [8597]
Amer. Univ. in Moscow [IO]
Asian Amer. Curriculum Proj. [IO]
Asian Amer. Curriculum Proj. [8598]
ASPECT Found. [8599]
ASSE Intl. Student Exchange Programs [8600]
ASSE Intl. Student Exchange Programs [IO]
Assn. for the Advancement of Dutch-American Stud. [9908]
Assn. for Intl. Practical Training [8601]
Assn. for Intl. Practical Training [IO]
Assn. for World Travel Exchange [IO]
Assn. for World Travel Exchange [8602]
Au Pair in Am. [8603]
Belgian Amer. Educational Found. [9736]
Brazilian Stud. Assn. [8604]
Brazilian Stud. Assn. [IO]
British Amer. Educational Found. [8605]
British Universities North Am. Club [8606]
Bus. Assn. Italy Am. [2300]
Canada World Youth [IO]
Canadian Bur. for Intl. Educ. [IO]
Canadian Host Family Assn. [IO]
Center for Citizen Initiatives [IO]
Center for Global Educ. [IO]
China Educ. Assn. for Intl. Exchange [IO]
Chinese Amer. Assn. of Engg. [7008]
Chinese Amer. Forum [9786]
CISV Intl. [IO]
Commonwealth Youth Exchange Coun. [IO]
Community Colleges for Intl. Development [IO]
Community Colleges for Intl. Development [8607]
Coun. on Intl. Educational Exchange - USA [8608]
Coun. on Intl. Educational Exchange - USA [IO]
Coun. for Intl. Exchange of Scholars/Institute of Intl. Educ. [IO]
Coun. for Intl. Exchange of Scholars/Institute of Intl. Educ. [8609]
Coun. on Standards for Intl. Educational Travel [8610]
Coun. on Standards for Intl. Educational Travel [IO]
Crosscurrents Intl. Inst. [IO]
Delphi International Program of World Learning [IO]
Denmark-America Found. [IO]
East-West Center [IO]
EF Found. for Foreign Stud. [IO]
EF Found. for Foreign Stud. [8611]
Erasmus Student Network [IO]
Euro-Children [IO]
European Assn. for Intl. Educ. [IO]
Fed. of Intl. Youth Travel Organisations [IO]
Found. for Intl. Cooperation [IO]
Found. for Intl. Cooperation [8612]
French-American Found. [IO]
Friends of Malawi [9851]
Friends of Togo [IO]
Friendship Ambassadors Found. [IO]
Friendship Force Intl. [IO]
Fulbright Assn. [IO]
Fulbright Assn. [8613]
Fulbright Assn. of Uzbekistan [IO]
German Academic Exchange Ser. [IO]
German Academic Exchange Ser. [8614]
German Marshall Fund of the U.S. [IO]
Global Educ. Associates [IO]
Global Nomads Intl. [IO]
Global Outreach [IO]
Global Outreach [8615]
Global Volunteers [IO]
Golden Rule Found. [10186]
Inst. of Intl. Educ. [8616]

A star before a book entry number signifies that the name is not listed separately, but is mentioned within the entry.

Inst. of Intl. Educ. [IO]
Inst. of Intl. Educ. - China [IO]
Inst. of Intl. Educ. - Egypt [IO]
Inst. of Intl. Educ. - India [IO]
Inst. of Intl. Educ. - Latin Am. [IO]
Inst. of Intl. Educ. - Russia [IO]
Inst. of Intl. Educ. - Southeast Asia [IO]
Inst. of Intl. Educ. - Ukraine [IO]
Inst. of World Affairs [IO]
InterExchange [IO]
InterExchange [8617]
InterFuture [8664]
InterFuture [IO]
Interhostel [8618]
Intl. Assn. for the Exchange of Students for Tech. Experience [IO]
Intl. Assn. for the Exchange of Students for Tech. Experience - Argentina [IO]
Intl. Assn. for the Exchange of Students for Tech. Experience - Armenia [IO]
Intl. Assn. for the Exchange of Students for Tech. Experience - Australia [IO]
Intl. Assn. for the Exchange of Students for Tech. Experience - Austria [IO]
Intl. Assn. for the Exchange of Students for Tech. Experience - Belarus [IO]
Intl. Assn. for the Exchange of Students for Tech. Experience - Belgium [IO]
Intl. Assn. for the Exchange of Students for Tech. Experience - Bosnia and Herzegovina [IO]
Intl. Assn. for the Exchange of Students for Tech. Experience - Botswana [IO]
Intl. Assn. for the Exchange of Students for Tech. Experience - Brazil [IO]
Intl. Assn. for the Exchange of Students for Tech. Experience - Bulgaria [IO]
Intl. Assn. for the Exchange of Students for Tech. Experience - Canada [IO]
Intl. Assn. for the Exchange of Students for Tech. Experience - China [IO]
Intl. Assn. for the Exchange of Students for Tech. Experience - Columbia [IO]
Intl. Assn. for the Exchange of Students for Tech. Experience - Croatia [IO]
Intl. Assn. for the Exchange of Students for Tech. Experience - Cyprus [IO]
Intl. Assn. for the Exchange of Students for Tech. Experience - Czech Republic [IO]
Intl. Assn. for the Exchange of Students for Tech. Experience - Denmark [IO]
Intl. Assn. for the Exchange of Students for Tech. Experience - Ecuador [IO]
Intl. Assn. for the Exchange of Students for Tech. Experience - Egypt [IO]
Intl. Assn. for the Exchange of Students for Tech. Experience - Estonia [IO]
Intl. Assn. for the Exchange of Students for Tech. Experience - Finland [IO]
Intl. Assn. for the Exchange of Students for Tech. Experience - France [IO]
Intl. Assn. for the Exchange of Students for Tech. Experience - Gambia [IO]
Intl. Assn. for the Exchange of Students for Tech. Experience - Georgia [IO]
Intl. Assn. for the Exchange of Students for Tech. Experience - Germany [IO]
Intl. Assn. for the Exchange of Students for Tech. Experience - Ghana [IO]
Intl. Assn. for the Exchange of Students for Tech. Experience - Greece [IO]
Intl. Assn. for the Exchange of Students for Tech. Experience - Hong Kong [IO]
Intl. Assn. for the Exchange of Students for Tech. Experience - Hungary [IO]
Intl. Assn. for the Exchange of Students for Tech. Experience - Iceland [IO]
Intl. Assn. for the Exchange of Students for Tech. Experience - India [IO]
Intl. Assn. for the Exchange of Students for Tech. Experience - Iran [IO]
Intl. Assn. for the Exchange of Students for Tech. Experience - Iraq [IO]
Intl. Assn. for the Exchange of Students for Tech. Experience - Israel [IO]
Intl. Assn. for the Exchange of Students for Tech. Experience - Italy [IO]

Intl. Assn. for the Exchange of Students for Tech. Experience - Japan [IO]
Intl. Assn. for the Exchange of Students for Tech. Experience - Jordan [IO]
Intl. Assn. for the Exchange of Students for Tech. Experience - Kazakhstan [IO]
Intl. Assn. for the Exchange of Students for Tech. Experience - Kenya [IO]
Intl. Assn. for the Exchange of Students for Tech. Experience - Kyrgyzstan [IO]
Intl. Assn. for the Exchange of Students for Tech. Experience - Latvia [IO]
Intl. Assn. for the Exchange of Students for Tech. Experience - Lebanon [IO]
Intl. Assn. for the Exchange of Students for Tech. Experience - Liechtenstein [IO]
Intl. Assn. for the Exchange of Students for Tech. Experience - Lithuania [IO]
Intl. Assn. for the Exchange of Students for Tech. Experience - Luxembourg [IO]
Intl. Assn. for the Exchange of Students for Tech. Experience - Macao [IO]
Intl. Assn. for the Exchange of Students for Tech. Experience - Macedonia [IO]
Intl. Assn. for the Exchange of Students for Tech. Experience - Malta [IO]
Intl. Assn. for the Exchange of Students for Tech. Experience - Mexico [IO]
Intl. Assn. for the Exchange of Students for Tech. Experience - Mongolia [IO]
Intl. Assn. for the Exchange of Students for Tech. Experience - Nigeria [IO]
Intl. Assn. for the Exchange of Students for Tech. Experience - Norway [IO]
Intl. Assn. for the Exchange of Students for Tech. Experience - Oman [IO]
Intl. Assn. for the Exchange of Students for Tech. Experience - Pakistan [IO]
Intl. Assn. for the Exchange of Students for Tech. Experience - Panama [IO]
Intl. Assn. for the Exchange of Students for Tech. Experience - Peru [IO]
Intl. Assn. for the Exchange of Students for Tech. Experience - Poland [IO]
Intl. Assn. for the Exchange of Students for Tech. Experience - Portugal [IO]
Intl. Assn. for the Exchange of Students for Tech. Experience - Romania [IO]
Intl. Assn. for the Exchange of Students for Tech. Experience - Russia [IO]
Intl. Assn. for the Exchange of Students for Tech. Experience - Sierra Leone [IO]
Intl. Assn. for the Exchange of Students for Tech. Experience - Slovakia [IO]
Intl. Assn. for the Exchange of Students for Tech. Experience - Slovenia [IO]
Intl. Assn. for the Exchange of Students for Tech. Experience - South Africa [IO]
Intl. Assn. for the Exchange of Students for Tech. Experience - Spain [IO]
Intl. Assn. for the Exchange of Students for Tech. Experience - Sri Lanka [IO]
Intl. Assn. for the Exchange of Students for Tech. Experience - Sweden [IO]
Intl. Assn. for the Exchange of Students for Tech. Experience - Switzerland [IO]
Intl. Assn. for the Exchange of Students for Tech. Experience - Syria [IO]
Intl. Assn. for the Exchange of Students for Tech. Experience - Tajikistan [IO]
Intl. Assn. for the Exchange of Students for Tech. Experience - Thailand [IO]
Intl. Assn. for the Exchange of Students for Tech. Experience - Tunisia [IO]
Intl. Assn. for the Exchange of Students for Tech. Experience - Turkey [IO]
Intl. Assn. for the Exchange of Students for Tech. Experience - Ukraine [IO]
Intl. Assn. for the Exchange of Students for Tech. Experience - United Arab Emirates [IO]
Intl. Assn. for the Exchange of Students for Tech. Experience - United Kingdom [IO]
Intl. Assn. for the Exchange of Students for Tech. Experience - Uruguay [IO]
Intl. Assn. for the Exchange of Students for Tech. Experience - Uzbekistan [IO]

Intl. Book Bank [IO]
Intl. Book Bank [8619]
Intl. Book Proj. [8620]
Intl. Book Proj. [IO]
Intl. Center in New York [IO]
Intl. Cultural Youth Exchange - Bolivia [IO]
Intl. Cultural Youth Exchange - Colombia [IO]
Intl. Cultural Youth Exchange - Denmark [IO]
Intl. Cultural Youth Exchange in Europe [IO]
Intl. Cultural Youth Exchange - Ghana [IO]
Intl. Cultural Youth Exchange - Japan [IO]
Intl. Cultural Youth Exchange - Kenya [IO]
Intl. Cultural Youth Exchange - New Zealand [IO]
Intl. Cultural Youth Exchange - Nigeria [IO]
Intl. Cultural Youth Exchange - South Korea [IO]
Intl. Cultural Youth Exchange - Switzerland [IO]
Intl. Cultural Youth Exchange - Taiwan [IO]
Intl. Cultural Youth Exchange - United Kingdom [IO]
Intl. Exchange Center [IO]
Intl. Executive Ser. Corps [733]
Intl. Healthy Cities Found. [13349]
Intl. Mgt. Development Assn. [735]
Intl. Meeting in Community Ser. [IO]
Intl. Multiracial Shared Cultural Org. [IO]
Intl. Pen Friends [22138]
Intl. Res. and Exchanges Bd. [8621]
Intl. Res. and Exchanges Bd. [IO]
ISAR: Resources for Environmental Activists [IO]
Japan-America Student Conf. [8622]
Japan Center for Intl. Exchange - USA [IO]
Japan Info. Access Proj. [10265]
Legacy Intl. [IO]
Lisle Intercultural [IO]
Lisle Intercultural [8623]
Meridian Intl. Center [IO]
Metro Intl. Prog. Services of New York [8624]
Mexican Arts and Tech. Network [9611]
Minato Intl. Assn. [IO]
Mobility Intl. USA [11961]
NACEL Open Door [8625]
Natl. Coun. for Intl. Visitors [IO]
Natl. Registration Center for Stud. Abroad [IO]
Natl. Registration Center for Stud. Abroad [8626]
Our Developing World [IO]
Palestine Center [8627]
People to People Ambassador Prog. [IO]
People to People Intl. [IO]
Perhaps Kids Meeting Kids Can Make a Difference [IO]
Prog. of Academic Exchange [IO]
Prog. of Academic Exchange [8628]
Proj. Harmony [8629]
The Russian-American Center/Track Two Institute for Citizen Diplomacy [IO]
Scandinavian Seminar [IO]
Scandinavian Seminar [8630]
Sister Cities Intl. [IO]
Soc. for Intercultural Educ., Training and Res. U.S.A. [IO]
Stelios M. Stelson Found. [8631]
Student Letter Exchange [22144]
U.S.-China Educ. Found. [8632]
U.S.-China Educ. Found. [IO]
U.S. Comm. for Sci. Cooperation With Vietnam [IO]
U.S. Comm. for Sci. Cooperation With Vietnam [8633]
U.S. Servas [IO]
Unity-and-Diversity World Coun. [IO]
Volunteers for Peace [IO]
Wisconsin Coordinating Coun. on Nicaragua [IO]
World Bamboo Org. [5041]
World Heritage [8634]
World Heritage [IO]
World Learning [IO]
World Learning [8635]
World Neighbors [IO]
World Peace Found. [IO]
World Pen Pals [IO]
World Pen Pals [8636]
Worldwide Friendship Intl. [22147]
Yale-China Assn. [8637]
YMCA Intl. Camp Counselor Prog. [8638]
YMCA Intl. Camp Counselor Prog. [IO]

Reference to "IO" in place of a book number signifies that the association may be found in the 45th edition of International Organizations.

Youth Challenge International-Canada **[IO]**
Youth For Understanding USA **[IO]**
Youth For Understanding USA **[8639]**
Intl. Exchange Assn. **[★8591]**
Intl. Exchange Assn. **[★IO]**
Intl. Exchange Center **[IO]**, Riga, Latvia
Intl. Exchangors Assn. - Defunct.
Intl. Executive Housekeepers Assn. **[2464]**, 1001
  Eastwind Dr., Ste. 301, Westerville, OH 43081-
  3361, (614)895-7166
Intl. Executive Housekeepers Assn. **[IO]**, Westerville,
  OH, United States
Intl. Executive Ser. Corps **[IO]**, Washington, DC,
  United States
Intl. Executive Ser. Corps **[733]**, 1900 M St. NW,
  Ste. 500, Washington, DC 20036, (202)589-2600
Intl. Exer-Safety Assn. **[★15963]**
Intl. Exhibition Logistics Associates **[IO]**, Grand-
  Saconnex, Switzerland
Intl. Exhibitions Bur. **[IO]**, Paris, France
Intl. Exhibitions Found. **[★IO]**
Intl. Exhibitions Found. **[★9426]**
Intl. Exhibitors Assn. **[★1349]**
Intl. Experiential Marketing Assn. **[2631]**, 380
  Alabama St., No. 10, San Francisco, CA 94110,
  (415)355-1586
Intl. Experiential Marketing Assn. **[IO]**, San
  Francisco, CA, United States
Intl. Experimental Aerospace Soc. **[IO]**, Apple Valley,
  MN, United States
Intl. Experimental Aerospace Soc. **[6375]**, 14870
  Granada Ave., No. 316, Apple Valley, MN 55124,
  (952)432-3918
Intl. Expressive Arts Therapy Assn. **[13712]**, PO Box
  320399, San Francisco, CA 94132-0399, (415)522-
  8959
Intl. Expressive Arts Therapy Assn. **[IO]**, San
  Francisco, CA, United States
Intl. Eye Found. **[IO]**, Kensington, MD, United States
Intl. Eye Found. **[15685]**, 10801 Connecticut Ave.,
  Kensington, MD 20895-2134, (240)290-0263
Intl. Fabricare Inst. **[2405]**, 14700 Sweitzer Ln.,
  Laurel, MD 20707, (301)622-1900
Intl. Fabricare Inst. **[IO]**, Laurel, MD, United States
Intl. Fac. Mgt. Assn. **[IO]**, Houston, TX, United
  States
Intl. Fac. Mgt. Assn. **[3188]**, 1 E Greenway Plz., Ste.
  1100, Houston, TX 77046-0104, (713)623-4362
Intl. Fac. Mgt. Assn. - Toronto Chap. **[IO]**, Toronto,
  ON, Canada
Intl. Facsimile Consultative Coun. - Address
  unknown since 2004.
Intl. Fainting Goat Assn. **[4784]**, c/o Lottie Long,
  Registrar, 2455 Deanburg Rd., Pinson, TN 38366,
  (402)782-2089
International Fainting Goat Association **[IO]**, Terril,
  IA, United States
International Family Recreation Association **[IO]**,
  Gonzalez, FL, United States
Intl. Family Recreation Assn. **[12798]**, PO Box 520,
  Gonzalez, FL 32560-0520, (850)937-8354
Intl. Fan Club Assn. - Defunct.
Intl. Fan Club; David Birney **[24737]**
Intl. Fan Club Org. **[24912]**, PO Box 40328,
  Nashville, TN 37204-0328, (615)371-9596
Intl. Fan Club Org. **[IO]**, Nashville, TN, United States
Intl. Fancy Guppy Assn. **[IO]**, Snellville, GA, United
  States
Intl. Fancy Guppy Assn. **[22442]**, c/o Mr. Alan Op-
  dyke, Pres., PO Box 1183, Snellville, GA 30078-
  1183, (770)979-3878
Intl. Fantasy Gaming Soc. **[22467]**, PO Box 3577,
  Boulder, CO 80307, (303)443-1012
Intl. Fantasy Gaming Soc. **[IO]**, Boulder, CO, United
  States
Intl. Farm Mgt. Assn. **[IO]**, Cambridge, United
  Kingdom
Intl. Farmers Assn. for Education - Defunct.
Intl. Fatigue Syndromes Share and Prayer and Pen
  Pal Chain - Address unknown since 2001.
Intl. Fed. of ACAT (Action by Christians for the Aboli-
  tion of Torture) **[IO]**, Paris, France
Intl. Fed. of Accountants **[IO]**, New York, NY, United
  States
Intl. Fed. of Accountants **[36]**, 545 5th Ave., 14th Fl.,
  New York, NY 10017, (212)286-9344

Intl. Fed. of Actors **[IO]**, London, United Kingdom
Intl. Fed. of Advt. Agencies **[★IO]**
Intl. Fed. of Advt. Agencies **[★105]**
Intl. Fed. of Aestheticians **[IO]**, Brussels, Belgium
Intl. Fed. on Ageing **[IO]**, Montreal, QC, Canada
Intl. Fed. of Agricultural Journalists **[IO]**, Vantaa,
  Finland
Intl. Fed. of Agricultural Producers **[IO]**, Paris,
  France
Intl. Fed. of Air Line Pilots Associations **[IO]**, Chert-
  sey, United Kingdom
Intl. Fed. of Air Traffic Controllers' Associations **[IO]**,
  Montreal, QC, Canada
Intl. Fed. of Air Traffic Safety Electronics Assn. **[IO]**,
  London, United Kingdom
Intl. Fed. of Airworthiness **[IO]**, East Grinstead,
  United Kingdom
Intl. Fed. of Airworthiness Tech. and Engg. **[★IO]**
Intl. Fed. of Amer. Football **[IO]**, La Courneuve,
  France
Intl. Fed. of Amer. Homing Pigeon Fanciers **[IO]**,
  Hicksville, NY, United States
Intl. Fed. of Amer. Homing Pigeon Fanciers **[22895]**,
  c/o Val Matteucci, Sec.-Treas., PO Box 374, Hicks-
  ville, NY 11802, (516)794-3612
Intl. Fed. of Anatomists - Address unknown since
  2002.
Intl. Fed. of Anti-Leprosy Associations **[IO]**, London,
  United Kingdom
Intl. Fed. for the Application of Standards **[★IO]**
Intl. Fed. of Aquarium Societies - Defunct.
Intl. Fed. of Aromatherapists (Australian Br.) **[IO]**,
  Burwood, Australia
Intl. Fed. of Arts Councils and Culture Agencies **[IO]**,
  Strawberry Hills, Australia
Intl. Fed. of Asian and Pacific Associations of
  Optometrists **[★IO]**
Intl. Fed. of Asian and Pacific Associations of
  Optometrists **[★15715]**
Intl. Fed. of Asian and Western Pacific Contractors'
  Associations **[IO]**, Pasig City, Philippines
Intl. Fed. of Assoc. Wrestling Styles **[IO]**, Vevey,
  Switzerland
Intl. Fed. of Assn. Football **[IO]**, Zurich, Switzerland
Intl. Fed. of Associations of Pharmaceutical Physi-
  cians **[IO]**, Mijdrecht, Netherlands
Intl. Fed. of Audit Bureaux of Circulations **[IO]**, Petal-
  ing Jaya, Malaysia
Intl. Fed. of Automatic Control - Canada **[IO]**, Out-
  remont, QC, Canada
Intl. Fed. of Automatic Control - Natl. Member Org.
  of Hungary **[IO]**, Budapest, Hungary
Intl. Fed. of Auto. Experts **[IO]**, Rixensart-Genval,
  Belgium
Intl. Fed. of Automotive Aftermarket Distributors **[IO]**,
  Brussels, Belgium
Intl. Fed. of Automotive Engg. Societies **[IO]**,
  London, United Kingdom
Intl. Fed. of Ball Badminton - Address unknown
  since 1999.
Intl. Fed. of Basque Pelota **[IO]**, Pamplona, Spain
Intl. Fed. of Beekeepers' Associations **[IO]**, Rome,
  Italy
Intl. Fed. of Bike Messenger Associations **[IO]**, San
  Francisco, CA, United States
Intl. Fed. of Bike Messenger Associations **[517]**, PO
  Box 191443, San Francisco, CA 94119-1443
Intl. Fed. of Biomedical Lab. Sci. **[IO]**, Hamilton, ON,
  Canada
Intl. Fed. of Biomedical Sci. **[★IO]**
Intl. Fed. of Black Prides **[12238]**, PO Box 1301,
  Washington, DC 20013
Intl. Fed. of the Blind **[★IO]**
Intl. Fed. of Blood Donor Organizations **[IO]**, Fred-
  eriksberg, Denmark
Intl. Fed. of the Blue Cross **[IO]**, Bern, Switzerland
Intl. Fed. of Boat Show Organisers **[IO]**, Woking,
  United Kingdom
Intl. Fed. of Bodybuilders and Fitness **[IO]**, Montreal,
  QC, Canada
Intl. Fed. of Bowlers **[★IO]**
Intl. Fed. of Building and Wood Workers **[IO]**, Ca-
  rouge, Switzerland
Intl. Fed. of Bus. and Professional Women **[★IO]**
Intl. Fed. of Camping and Caravanning **[IO]**, Brus-
  sels, Belgium

Intl. Fed. of Catholic Alumnae - Address unknown
  since 1995.
Intl. Fed. of Catholic Medical Associations **[IO]**, Vati-
  can City, Vatican City
Intl. Fed. of Catholic Parochial Youth Communities
  [IO], Antwerp, Belgium
Intl. Fed. of Catholic Universities **[IO]**, Paris, France
International Federation of Cell Biology **[IO]**,
  Huntington, WV, United States
Intl. Fed. of Cell Biology **[6581]**, c/o Dr. W. Elaine
  Hardman, Treas., Marshall Univ. School of
  Medicine, 1542 Spring Valley Dr., Huntington, WV
  25704-9388, (304)696-7339
Intl. Fed. for Cervical Pathology and Colposcopy
  [IO], Buenos Aires, Argentina
Intl. Fed. of Chem., Energy, Mine and Gen. Workers'
  Unions **[IO]**, Brussels, Belgium
Intl. Fed. of Children's Choirs - Address unknown
  since 2003.
Intl. Fed. for Choral Music **[IO]**, Louvigny, France
Intl. Fed. of Christian Agricultural Workers' Unions
  [★IO]
Intl. Fed. of City Sport and Multi-Purpose Halls
  [★IO]
Intl. Fed. of Clinical Chemistry **[★IO]**
Intl. Fed. of Clinical Chemistry and Lab. Medicine
  [IO], Milan, Italy
Intl. Fed. of Clinical Neurophysiology **[IO]**, Vancou-
  ver, BC, Canada
Intl. Fed. of Competitive Eating **[IO]**, New York, NY,
  United States
Intl. Fed. of Competitive Eating **[23822]**, 151 W 25th
  St., 4th Fl., New York, NY 10001, (212)627-5766
Intl. Fed. of Consular Corps and Associations **[IO]**,
  Brussels, Belgium
Intl. Fed. of Consulting Engineers **[IO]**, Geneva,
  Switzerland
Intl. Fed. of Cosmopolitan Clubs **[★IO]**
Intl. Fed. of Cosmopolitan Clubs **[★13039]**
Intl. Fed. of Customs Brokers Associations **[IO]**, Ot-
  tawa, ON, Canada
Intl. Fed. of Dalit Orgs. - Defunct.
Intl. Fed. of Denturists **[IO]**, Winnipeg, MB, Canada
Intl. Fed. of Disabled Workers and Civilian
  Handicapped **[★IO]**
Intl. Fed. of Elvis Presley Fan Clubs - Defunct.
Intl. Fed. of Employees in Public Ser. **[IO]**, Brussels,
  Belgium
Intl. Fed. for Equestrian Sports **[IO]**, Lausanne,
  Switzerland
Intl. Fed. of Essential Oils and Aroma Trades **[IO]**,
  London, United Kingdom
Intl. Fed. of Esthetic Dentistry **[IO]**, Boston, MA,
  United States
Intl. Fed. of Esthetic Dentistry **[IO]**, Taubate, Brazil
Intl. Fed. of Esthetic Dentistry **[14167]**, c/o Dan
  Nathanson, VP, Boston Univ., 100 E Newton St.,
  Boston, MA 02118, (617)638-5590
Intl. Fed. of Europe Houses **[IO]**, Saarbrucken,
  Germany
Intl. Fed. of Exhibition and Event Services **[IO]**,
  Brussels, Belgium
Intl. Fed. of Fabric Printers **[★IO]**
Intl. Fed. of Family Associations of Missing Persons
  from Armed Conflicts **[IO]**, Rockford, IL, United
  States
Intl. Fed. of Family Associations of Missing Persons
  from Armed Conflicts **[12609]**, PO Box 6888,
  Rockford, IL 61125
Intl. Fed. for Family Life Promotion - Address
  unknown since 1994.
Intl. Fed. of Festival Organizations **[1307]**, 4230
  Stansbury Ave., Ste. 105, Sherman Oaks, CA
  91423, (818)789-7596
Intl. Fed. of Festival Organizations **[IO]**, Sherman
  Oaks, CA, United States
Intl. Fed. of Film Archives **[IO]**, Brussels, Belgium
Intl. Fed. of Film Producers Associations **[IO]**, Paris,
  France
Intl. Fed. of Foot and Ankle Societies **[IO]**, Rose-
  mont, IL, United States
Intl. Fed. of Foot and Ankle Societies **[16045]**, 6300
  N River Rd., Ste. 510, Rosemont, IL 60018,
  (847)698-4654
Intl. Fed. of Football History and Statistics **[IO]**,
  Bonn, Germany

A star before a book entry number signifies that the name is not listed separately, but is mentioned within the entry.

Intl. Fed. of Free Teachers' Union [★IO]

Intl. Fed. of Freight Forwarders Associations [IO], Glattbrugg, Switzerland

Intl. Fed. of Fruit Juice Producers [IO], Paris, France

Intl. Fed. for Gerda Alexander Eutony [IO], St. Thibault, France

Intl. Fed. of Gynecology and Obstetrics [IO], London, United Kingdom

Intl. Fed. of the Hard of Hearing [★IO]

Intl. Fed. of Hard of Hearing People [IO], Stockholm, Sweden

Intl. Fed. of Hard of Hearing Young People [IO], St. Petersburg, Russia

Intl. Fed. of Hardware and Housewares Associations [IO], Birmingham, United Kingdom

Intl. Fed. of Hea. Funds [★IO]

Intl. Fed. of Hea. Plans [IO], London, United Kingdom

Intl. Fed. for Heat Treatment and Surface Engg. [IO], London, United Kingdom

Intl. Fed. of High Rise Structures [IO], Bangalore, India

Intl. Fed. for Home Economics - USA [IO], Silver Spring, MD, United States

Intl. Fed. for Home Economics - USA [8512], 122 Point Ln., Ridgeway, SC 29130

Intl. Fed. of Horseracing Authorities [IO], Boulogne, France

Intl. Fed. for Housing and Planning [IO], The Hague, Netherlands

Intl. Fed. of Human Genetics Societies [IO], Bethesda, MD, United States

Intl. Fed. of Human Genetics Societies [14500], c/o Off. of the Secretariat, 9650 Rockville Pike, Bethesda, MD 20814-3998, (301)634-7300

Intl. Fed. for Human Rights Leagues [IO], Paris, France

Intl. Fed. of Hydrographic Societies [IO], Plymouth, United Kingdom

Intl. Fed. of Indus. Energy Consumers [IO], Geneva, Switzerland

Intl. Fed. of Infection Control [IO], Uppsala, Sweden

Intl. Fed. for Info. Processing [IO], Laxenburg, Austria

Intl. Fed. of Inspection Agencies-Americas Comm. [2120], 3942 N Upland St., Arlington, VA 22207, (703)533-9539

Intl. Fed. of Interior Architects/Designers [IO], Singapore, Singapore

Intl. Fed. of Intl. Furniture Removers [IO], Brussels, Belgium

Intl. Fed. of Inventors' Associations [IO], Budapest, Hungary

Intl. Fed. of Iranian Refugees [IO], Eindhoven, Netherlands

Intl. Fed. of Ironmongers and Iron Merchants Assn. [★IO]

Intl. Fed. of Jeunesses Musicales [★IO]

Intl. Fed. of Journalists [IO], Brussels, Belgium

Intl. Fed. of Kennel Clubs [IO], Thuin, Belgium

Intl. Fed. of Landscape Architects [IO], Christchurch, New Zealand

Intl. Fed. of Latin Amer. Stud. Centers [IO], Mexico City, Mexico

Intl. Fed. of Leather Guilds [2413], c/o Ernie Wayman, Exec. Dir., 3117 Babette Dr., Southport, IN 46227, (317)787-2586

Intl. Fed. of Liberal and Radical Youth [IO], Brussels, Belgium

Intl. Fed. of Lib. Associations and Institutions [IO], The Hague, Netherlands

Intl. Fed. of Lib. Associations and Institutions - Metropolitan Libraries Sect. [IO], The Hague, Netherlands

Intl. Fed. of the Little Bros. of the Poor [IO], Paris, France

Intl. Fed. for Manual/Musculoskeletal Medicine [IO], Warsage, Belgium

Intl. Fed. of Mfrs. and Converters of Pressure-Sensitive and Heatseals on Paper and Other Base Materials [★IO]

Intl. Fed. of Mfrs. of Gummed Paper [IO], Hoofddorp, Netherlands

Intl. Fed. of Marfan Syndrome Organizations [IO], Port Washington, NY, United States

Intl. Fed. of Marfan Syndrome Organizations [14456], c/o Natl. Marfan Found., 22 Manhassett Ave., Port Washington, NY 11050

Intl. Fed. of Maritime Philately - Address unknown since 1999.

Intl. Fed. of Martial Arts and Oriental Medicine [15021], 622 W Colorado St., Glendale, CA 91204, (323)512-2538

Intl. Fed. of Martial Arts and Oriental Medicine [IO], Glendale, CA, United States

Intl. Fed. for Medical and Biological Engg. [IO], Zagreb, Croatia

Intl. Fed. of Medical Students' Associations [IO], Ferney-Voltaire, France

Intl. Fed. of Messianic Jews [IO], Tampa, FL, United States

Intl. Fed. of Messianic Jews [20255], PO Box 271708, Tampa, FL 33688, (813)920-0864

Intl. Fed. for Modern Languages and Literatures [IO], London, United Kingdom

Intl. Fed. of the Movements of Modern School [IO], Belfort, France

Intl. Fed. of Multiple Sclerosis Societies [★IO]

Intl. Fed. of Municipal Engineers [IO], Rome, Italy

Intl. Fed. of Musicians [IO], Paris, France

Intl. Fed. for Narcotic Education - Address unknown since 1995.

Intl. Fed. of Nematology Societies [IO], Richmond, BC, Canada

Intl. Fed. of Netball Associations [IO], Manchester, United Kingdom

Intl. Fed. of Newspaper Publishers [★IO]

Intl. Fed. of Nonlinear Analysts [IO], Melbourne, FL, United States

Intl. Fed. of Nonlinear Analysts [7609], c/o Dr. V. Lakshmikantham, Ed.-in-Chief, Florida Inst. of Tech., 150 W Univ. Blvd., Melbourne, FL 32901, (321)674-7412

Intl. Fed. of Ophthalmological Societies [15686], c/o Bruce E. Spivey, MD, Pres., 945 Green St., San Francisco, CA 94133, (415)409-8410

Intl. Fed. of Ophthalmological Societies [IO], San Francisco, CA, United States

Intl. Fed. of Organic Agriculture Movements [IO], Bonn, Germany

Intl. Fed. of Oto-Rhino-Laryngological Societies [IO], Leiden, Netherlands

Intl. Fed. of Park and Recreation Admin. [IO], Reading, United Kingdom

Intl. Fed. of Pedestrians - Address unknown since 2002.

Intl. Fed. of Pediatric and Adolescent Gynecology [IO], Helsinki, Finland

Intl. Fed. of the Periodical Press [IO], London, United Kingdom

Intl. Fed. of Persons with Physical Disabilities [IO], Bonn, Germany

Intl. Fed. of Petanque and Provencal Games [IO], Marseille, France

Intl. Fed. of Petroleum and Chemical Workers - Defunct.

Intl. Fed. of Pharmaceutical Mfrs. and Associations [IO], Geneva, Switzerland

International Federation of Pharmaceutical Wholesalers [IO], Manassas, VA, United States

Intl. Fed. of Pharmaceutical Wholesalers [2976], 10569 Crestwood Dr., Manassas, VA 20109, (703)331-3714

Intl. Fed. of Philosophical Societies [10800], c/o William L. McBride, Sec. Gen., Purdue Univ., Dept. of Philosophy, 100 N Univ. St., West Lafayette, IN 47907-2098, (765)494-4285

Intl. Fed. of Philosophical Societies [IO], West Lafayette, IN, United States

Intl. Fed. of the Phonographic Indus. - Belgium [IO], Brussels, Belgium

Intl. Fed. of the Phonographic Indus. - Chile [IO], Santiago, Chile

Intl. Fed. of the Phonographic Indus. - Czech Republic [IO], Prague, Czech Republic

Intl. Fed. of the Phonographic Indus. - Denmark [IO], Copenhagen, Denmark

Intl. Fed. of the Phonographic Indus. - England [IO], London, United Kingdom

Intl. Fed. of the Phonographic Indus. - Finland [IO], Helsinki, Finland

Intl. Fed. of the Phonographic Indus. - Finland [★IO]

Intl. Fed. of the Phonographic Indus. - Germany [IO], Berlin, Germany

Intl. Fed. of the Phonographic Indus. - Hong Kong [IO], Hong Kong, People's Republic of China

Intl. Fed. of the Phonographic Indus. - Israel [IO], Ramat Gan, Israel

Intl. Fed. of the Phonographic Indus. - Jamaica [IO], Kingston, Jamaica

Intl. Fed. of the Phonographic Indus. - Nigeria [IO], Lagos, Nigeria

Intl. Fed. of the Phonographic Indus. - Russia and CIS [IO], Moscow, Russia

Intl. Fed. of the Phonographic Indus. - Slovak Republic [IO], Bratislava, Slovakia

Intl. Fed. of the Phonographic Indus. - Sweden [IO], Stockholm, Sweden

Intl. Fed. of the Phonographic Indus. - Switzerland [IO], Zurich, Switzerland

Intl. Fed. of the Phonographic Indus. - Taiwan [IO], Taipei, Taiwan

Intl. Fed. of Photographic Art [IO], Paris, France

Intl. Fed. for Physical Educ. [IO], Foz do Iguacu, Brazil

Intl. Fed. for Postcard Dealers [IO], Manassas, VA, United States

Intl. Fed. of Postcard Dealers [22906], PO Box 1765, Manassas, VA 20108-1765

Intl. Fed. of Press Cutting Agencies [IO], Zurich, Switzerland

Intl. Fed. of Professional Aromatherapists [IO], Hinckley, United Kingdom

Intl. Fed. of Professional and Tech. Engineers [24052], 8630 Fenton St., Ste. 400, Silver Spring, MD 20910-3803, (301)565-9016

Intl. Fed. for the Protection of the Rights of Ethnic, Religious, Linguistic and Other Minorities [17768]

International Federation for the Protection of the Rights of Ethnic, Religious, Linguistic and Other Minorities [IO], Long Island City, NY, United States

Intl. Fed. of Psoriasis Associations [IO], Portland, OR, United States

Intl. Fed. of Psoriasis Associations [14203], c/o Gail Zimmerman, Pres./CEO, 6600 SW 92nd, Ste. 300, Portland, OR 97223-7195, (503)244-7404

Intl. Fed. for Psychoanalytic Educ. [9028], c/o Stuart Spence, Interim Admin., 8234 McGroarty St., Sunland, CA 91040, (818)352-3882

Intl. Fed. for Psychoanalytic Educ. [IO], Sunland, CA, United States

Intl. Fed. of Psychoanalytic Societies [IO], Mexico City, Mexico

Intl. Fed. of Purchasing and Materials Mgt. [★IO]

Intl. Fed. of Purchasing and Supply Mgt. [IO], Aarau, Austria

Intl. Fed. of Rabbis [IO], Chevy Chase, MD, United States

Intl. Fed. of Rabbis [20144], 5600 Wisconsin Ave., No. 1107, Chevy Chase, MD 20815, (919)833-8430

Intl. Fed. of Ragtime - Defunct.

Intl. Fed. of Record Libraries - Defunct.

Intl. Fed. of Red Cross and Red Crescent Societies [IO], Geneva, Switzerland

Intl. Fed. of Red Cross and Red Crescent Societies - Vietnam [IO], Hanoi, Vietnam

Intl. Fed. of Registered Equine Massage Therapists [IO], St. Thomas, ON, Canada

Intl. Fed. of Reproduction Rights Org. [IO], Brussels, Belgium

Intl. Fed. for Res. in Women's History [IO], Sofia, Bulgaria

Intl. Fed. of Robotics [IO], Paris, France

Intl. Fed. of Rock Art Organizations [IO], Caulfield South, Australia

Intl. Fed. of Roofing Contractors [★IO]

Intl. Fed. for the Roofing Trade [IO], Cologne, Germany

Intl. Fed. of Rowing Associations [IO], Lausanne, Switzerland

Intl. Fed. of Rural Adult Catholic Movements [IO], Assesse, Belgium

Intl. Fed. of Sanitarians Orgs. - Defunct.

Intl. Fed. of Scientific Editors' Assns. - Address unknown since 1994.

Reference to "IO" in place of a book number signifies that the association may be found in the 45th edition of International Organizations.

Intl. Fed. of Secular Humanistic Jews [20086], 28611 W 12 Mile Rd., Farmington Hills, MI 48334, (248)476-9532

International Federation of Secular Humanistic Jews [IO], Farmington Hills, MI, United States

Intl. Fed. for Secular Humanistic Judaism [★IO]

Intl. Fed. for Secular Humanistic Judaism [★20086]

Intl. Fed. of Settlements and Neighbourhood Centres [IO], Toronto, ON, Canada

Intl. Fed. of Settlements and Neighbourhood Centres - Defunct.

Intl. Fed. of Shipmasters' Associations [IO], London, United Kingdom

International Federation of Sleddog Sports [IO], Grand Marais, MN, United States

Intl. Fed. of Sleddog Sports [23393], c/o Tim White, VP of Development, 881 County Rd. 14, Grand Marais, MN 55604, (218)387-2712

Intl. Fed. of Social Workers [IO], Bern, Switzerland

Intl. Fed. of the Societies of Classical Stud. [IO], Neuchatel, Switzerland

Intl. Fed. of Societies of Cosmetic Chemists [IO], Luton, United Kingdom

Intl. Fed. of Societies of Electron Microscopy [★IO]

Intl. Fed. of Societies of Electron Microscopy [★7333]

Intl. Fed. of Societies for Hand Therapy [IO], Gauteng, Republic of South Africa

Intl. Fed. of Societies for Histochemistry and Cytochemistry [IO], Seattle, WA, United States

Intl. Fed. of Societies for Histochemistry and Cytochemistry [14077], c/o Denis G. Baskin, PhD, Pres., PO Box 357420, Seattle, WA 98195-9420, (206)616-5894

Intl. Fed. of Societies for Microscopy [7333], c/o Prof. C. Barry Carter, Gen. Sec., Dept. of Chem. Engg. & Materials Sci., 151 Amundson Hall, 421 Washington Ave. SE, Minneapolis, MN 55455, (612)625-8805

Intl. Fed. of Societies for Microscopy [IO], Minneapolis, MN, United States

Intl. Fed. of Societies for Surgery of the Hand [IO], Durham, NC, United States

Intl. Fed. of Societies for Surgery of the Hand [14527], c/o Dr. James R. Urbaniak, MD, Sec. Gen., PO Box 2912, Duke Univ. Medical Center, Durham, NC 27710, (919)684-5388

Intl. Fed. of Sound Hunters [IO], Bern, Switzerland

Intl. Fed. for Spina Bifida and Hydrocephalus [IO], Brussels, Belgium

Intl. Fed. of Spine Assns. - Defunct.

Intl. Fed. of Sports Chiropractic [IO], Lausanne, Switzerland

Intl. Fed. of Sports Medicine [IO], Nicosia, Cyprus

Intl. Fed. of Stamp Dealers' Associations [IO], Arhus, Denmark

Intl. Fed. of Standards Users [IO], Geneva, Switzerland

Intl. Fed. for the Surgery of Obesity [IO], Munich, Germany

Intl. Fed. of Surgical Colleges [IO], Bogis-Bossey, Switzerland

Intl. Fed. of Surveyors [IO], Copenhagen, Denmark

Intl. Fed. for Systems Res. [IO], Linz, Austria

Intl. Fed. of Teachers of Dalcroze Eurhythmics [IO], Bienne, Switzerland

Intl. Fed. of Teachers of French [IO], Sevres, France

Intl. Fed. for the Teaching of English [IO], Winnipeg, MB, Canada

Intl. Fed. of the Temperance Blue Cross Societies [★IO]

Intl. Fed. of Teratology Societies [IO], London, United Kingdom

Intl. Fed. Terre des Hommes [IO], Geneva, Switzerland

Intl. Fed. of Thanatologists Assn. [IO], Amsterdam, Netherlands

Intl. Fed. for Theatre Res. [IO], Lancaster, United Kingdom

Intl. Fed. of Trade Unions of Transport Workers [IO], Brussels, Belgium

Intl. Fed. of Training Centers for the Promotion of Progressive Educ. [IO], Paris, France

Intl. Fed. of Training and Development Organizations [IO], New Delhi, India

Intl. Fed. of Translators [IO], Montreal, QC, Canada

Intl. Fed. for Tropical Medicine [IO], Lima, Peru

Intl. Fed. of Univ. Women - Switzerland [IO], Geneva, Switzerland

Intl. Fed. of Vexillological Associations [IO], Houston, TX, United States

Intl. Fed. of Vexillological Associations [11075], c/o Mr. Charles A. Spain, Jr., Sec. Gen., 504 Branard St., Houston, TX 77006-5018, (713)529-2545

Intl. Fed. of Voluntary Hea. Ser. Funds [★IO]

Intl. Fed. of Wargaming - Defunct.

Intl. Fed. of Wholesalers, Importers and Exporters in Auto. Fittings [★IO]

Intl. Fed. of Wines and Spirits [IO], Paris, France

Intl. Fed. of Women Lawyers - Address unknown since 2003.

Intl. Fed. of Women's Hockey Associations [★IO]

Intl. Fed. of Women's Travel Organizations [IO], Torremolinos, Spain

Intl. Fed. of Workers' Educ. Associations [IO], Manchester, United Kingdom

Intl. Feed Indus. Fed. [IO], Cheltenham, United Kingdom

Intl. Fellowship of Christians and Jews [IO], Chicago, IL, United States

Intl. Fellowship of Christians and Jews [20533], 30 N La Salle St., Ste. 2600, Chicago, IL 60602-3356, (312)641-7200

Intl. Fellowship of Evangelical Students [IO], Oxford, United Kingdom

Intl. Fellowship of Fishing Rotarians [IO], Citra, FL, United States

Intl. Fellowship of Fishing Rotarians [22453], c/o Greg Foster, Admin./Membership Chair, 7600 NE 137 Pl., Citra, FL 32113, (352)236-4504

Intl. Fellowship of Reconciliation - Austria [IO], Vienna, Austria

Intl. Fellowship of Reconciliation - Bangladesh [IO], Dhaka, Bangladesh

Intl. Fellowship of Reconciliation - Belgium [IO], Brussels, Belgium

Intl. Fellowship of Reconciliation - England [IO], Oxford, United Kingdom

Intl. Fellowship of Reconciliation - France [IO], Paris, France

Intl. Fellowship of Reconciliation - Germany [IO], Minden, Germany

Intl. Fellowship of Reconciliation - India [IO], Trivandrum, India

Intl. Fellowship of Reconciliation - Italy [IO], Turin, Italy

Intl. Fellowship of Reconciliation - Japan [IO], Tokyo, Japan

Intl. Fellowship of Reconciliation - Madagascar [IO], Antananarivo, Madagascar

Intl. Fellowship of Reconciliation - Netherlands [IO], Alkmaar, Netherlands

Intl. Fellowship of Reconciliation - Norway [IO], Oslo, Norway

Intl. Fellowship of Reconciliation - Sweden [IO], Sundbyberg, Sweden

Intl. Fellowship of Reconciliation - Uganda [IO], Kampala, Uganda

Intl. Fellowship of Reconciliation - Wales [IO], Caernarfon, United Kingdom

Intl. Fellowship of Reconciliation - Zimbabwe [IO], Harare, Zimbabwe

Intl. Fellowship Soc. [★1474]

Intl. Female Boxers Assn. [23263], 50B Peninsula Center Dr., No. 120, Rolling Hills Estates, CA 90274, (310)428-1402

Intl. Female Boxers Assn. [IO], Rolling Hills Estates, CA, United States

Intl. Feminist Approaches to Bioethics [★IO]

Intl. Feminist Approaches to Bioethics [★12126]

Intl. Fence Indus. Assn. [★938]

Intl. Fence Indus. Assn. [★IO]

Intl. Feng Shui Guild [IO], Portland, OR, United States

Intl. Feng Shui Guild [9906], 6663 SW Beaverton Hillsdale Hwy., Ste. 333, Portland, OR 97225-1403, (888)881-IFSG

Intl. Ferret Assn. - Address unknown since 1994.

Intl. Fertiliser Soc. - England [IO], York, United Kingdom

Intl. Fertility Assn., U.S. Div. - Defunct.

Intl. Fertility Res. Prog. [★12181]

Intl. Fertility Res. Prog. [★IO]

Intl. Fertilizer Development Center - USA [★IO]

Intl. Fertilizer Development Center - USA [★4665]

Intl. Fertilizer Indus. Assn. [IO], Paris, France

Intl. Festivals Assn. [★IO]

Intl. Festivals Assn. [★1308]

Intl. Festivals and Events Assn. [1308], 2603 Eastover Terr., Boise, ID 83706, (208)433-0950

Intl. Festivals and Events Assn. [IO], Boise, ID, United States

Intl. Fibre Drum Inst. - Address unknown since 2006.

Intl. Fibrodysplasia Ossificans Progressiva Assn. [14457], PO Box 196217, Winter Springs, FL 32719-6217, (407)365-4194

Intl. Fiction Rev. [IO], Fredericton, NB, Canada

Intl. FidoNet Assn. - Defunct.

Intl. Fight'n Rooster Cutlery Club [22614], PO Box 936, Lebanon, TN 37088, (615)444-8070

Intl. Fight'n Rooster Cutlery Club [IO], Lebanon, TN, United States

Intl. Figure Skating Writers Assn. - Defunct.

Intl. Film Importers and Distributers of America - Defunct.

Intl. Film Seminars [9940], 6 E 39th St., 12th Fl., New York, NY 10016, (212)448-0457

Intl. Film Seminars [IO], New York, NY, United States

Intl. Finance Corp. [IO], Washington, DC, United States

Intl. Finance Corp. [17461], 2121 Pennsylvania Ave. NW, Washington, DC 20433, (202)473-1000

Intl. Financial Printers Assn. - Defunct.

Intl. Financial Services Assn. [483], 9 Sylvan Way, Ste. 130, Parsippany, NJ 07054-3817, (973)656-1900

Intl. Financial Soc. for Investment and Development in Africa [★IO]

International Fine Print Dealers Association [IO], New York, NY, United States

Intl. Fine Print Dealers Assn. [309], 250 W 26th St., Ste. 405, New York, NY 10001, (212)674-6095

Intl. Finn Assn. [IO], Pezilla-la-Riviere, France

Intl. Finn Assn. - Antigua [IO], English Harbour, Antigua-Barbuda

Intl. Finn Assn. - Argentina [IO], Buenos Aires, Argentina

Intl. Finn Assn. - Australia [IO], Patterson Lakes, Australia

Intl. Finn Assn. - Austria [IO], Salzburg, Austria

Intl. Finn Assn. - Belarus [IO], Minsk, Belarus

Intl. Finn Assn. - Belgium [IO], Antwerp, Belgium

Intl. Finn Assn. - Bermuda [IO], Pembroke, Bermuda

Intl. Finn Assn. - Brazil [IO], Sao Paulo, Brazil

Intl. Finn Assn. - Canada [IO], Milton, ON, Canada

Intl. Finn Assn. - Costa Rica [IO], San Jose, Costa Rica

Intl. Finn Assn. - Croatia [IO], Split, Croatia

Intl. Finn Assn. - Czech Republic [IO], Prague, Czech Republic

Intl. Finn Assn. - Denmark [IO], Valby, Denmark

Intl. Finn Assn. - Estonia [IO], Parnu, Estonia

Intl. Finn Assn. - Finland [IO], Espoo, Finland

Intl. Finn Assn. - France [IO], Meyzieu, France

Intl. Finn Assn. - Germany [IO], Neumunster, Germany

Intl. Finn Assn. - Greece [IO], Moschato, Greece

Intl. Finn Assn. - Hong Kong [IO], Hong Kong, People's Republic of China

Intl. Finn Assn. - Hungary [IO], Budapest, Hungary

Intl. Finn Assn. - Iceland [IO], Hafnarfjorour, Iceland

Intl. Finn Assn. - India [IO], Hyderabad, India

Intl. Finn Assn. - Japan [IO], Tokyo, Japan

Intl. Finn Assn. - Lithuania [IO], Kaunas, Lithuania

Intl. Finn Assn. - Mexico [IO], Guadalajara, Mexico

Intl. Finn Assn. - Monaco [IO], Monaco, Monaco

Intl. Finn Assn. - Netherlands [IO], Amsterdam, Netherlands

Intl. Finn Assn. - New Zealand [IO], Auckland, New Zealand

Intl. Finn Assn. - Philippines [IO], Quezon City, Philippines

Intl. Finn Assn. - Poland [IO], Olsztyn, Poland

Intl. Finn Assn. - Portugal [IO], Lisbon, Portugal

A star before a book entry number signifies that the name is not listed separately, but is mentioned within the entry.

Intl. Finn Assn. - Romania [IO], Constanta, Romania
Intl. Finn Assn. - Russia [IO], Moscow, Russia
Intl. Finn Assn. - Slovakia [IO], Bratislava, Slovakia
Intl. Finn Assn. - Slovenia [IO], Koper, Slovenia
Intl. Finn Assn. - South Africa [IO], Cape Town, Republic of South Africa
Intl. Finn Assn. - Spain [IO], Cartagena, Spain
Intl. Finn Assn. - Switzerland [IO], Bern, Switzerland
Intl. Finn Assn. - Thailand [IO], Bangkok, Thailand
Intl. Finn Assn. - Turkey [IO], Istanbul, Turkey
Intl. Finn Assn. - Ukraine [IO], Yuzhny, Ukraine
Intl. Finn Assn. - Zimbabwe [IO], Harare, Zimbabwe
Intl. Fire Buff Associates [IO], Mequon, WI, United States
Intl. Fire Buff Associates [22421], c/o Mr. William M. Mokros, Exec. VP, 11017 N Redwood Tree Ct., Mequon, WI 53092
Intl. Fire Chiefs' Assn. of Asia [IO], Tokyo, Japan
Intl. Fire Marshals Assn. [IO], Quincy, MA, United States
Intl. Fire Marshals Assn. [5719], c/o Steven Sawyer, Exec. Sec., 1 Batterymarch Park, Quincy, MA 02169-7471
Intl. Fire Photographers Assn. [3001], c/o David Sassaman, Membership Coor., 146 W Caracas Ave., Hershey, PA 17033-1510, (717)533-4133
Intl. Fire Photographers Assn. [IO], Hershey, PA, United States
Intl. Fire Ser. Training Assn. [IO], Stillwater, OK, United States
Intl. Fire Ser. Training Assn. [9230], Oklahoma State Univ., 930 N Willis, Stillwater, OK 74078-8045, (405)744-5723
Intl. FireStop Coun. [7081], 17209 Bradgate Ave., Cleveland, OH 44111, (877)241-3769
Intl. FireStop Coun. [IO], Cleveland, OH, United States
Intl. Fiscal Assn. [IO], Rotterdam, Netherlands
Intl. Fiscal Assn. - Belgium [IO], Brussels, Belgium
Intl. Fiscal Assn. - Brazil [IO], Rio de Janeiro, Brazil
Intl. Fiscal Assn. - Canada Br. [IO], Kingston, ON, Canada
Intl. Fiscal Assn. - China [IO], Shanghai, People's Republic of China
Intl. Fiscal Assn. - Colombia [IO], Bogota, Colombia
Intl. Fiscal Assn. - Cyprus [IO], Limassol, Cyprus
Intl. Fiscal Assn. - Czech Republic [IO], Prague, Czech Republic
Intl. Fiscal Assn. - Egypt [IO], Cairo, Egypt
Intl. Fiscal Assn. - Estonia [IO], Tartu, Estonia
Intl. Fiscal Assn. - Finland [IO], Helsinki, Finland
Intl. Fiscal Assn. - France [IO], Paris, France
Intl. Fiscal Assn. - Germany [IO], Frankfurt am Main, Germany
Intl. Fiscal Assn. - Greece [IO], Athens, Greece
Intl. Fiscal Assn. - Hong Kong [IO], Hong Kong, People's Republic of China
Intl. Fiscal Assn. - Hungary [IO], Budapest, Hungary
Intl. Fiscal Assn. - Indonesia [IO], Jakarta, Indonesia
Intl. Fiscal Assn. - Ireland [IO], Dublin, Ireland
Intl. Fiscal Assn. - Israel [IO], Tel Aviv, Israel
Intl. Fiscal Assn. - Italy [IO], Rome, Italy
Intl. Fiscal Assn. - Japan [IO], Tokyo, Japan
Intl. Fiscal Assn. - Luxembourg [IO], Luxembourg, Luxembourg
Intl. Fiscal Assn. - Malaysia [IO], Kuala Lumpur, Malaysia
Intl. Fiscal Assn. - Malta [IO], Sliema, Malta
Intl. Fiscal Assn. - Mauritius [IO], Port Louis, Mauritius
Intl. Fiscal Assn. - Poland [IO], Warsaw, Poland
Intl. Fiscal Assn. - Russia [IO], Moscow, Russia
Intl. Fiscal Assn. - Singapore [IO], Singapore, Singapore
Intl. Fiscal Assn. - Spain [IO], Salamanca, Spain
Intl. Fiscal Assn. - Sri Lanka [IO], Colombo, Sri Lanka
Intl. Fiscal Assn. - Uruguay [IO], Montevideo, Uruguay
Intl. Fiscal Intl. - Australia [IO], Sydney, Australia
Intl. Fish Meal and Fish Oil Org. [IO], St. Albans, United Kingdom
Intl. Fish Meal and Oil Mfr. Assn. [★IO]
Intl. Flat Earth Res. Soc. [7145]
Intl. Flattie Yacht Racing Assn. [★23172]

Intl. Flight Catering Assn. [★IO]
International Flight Service Association [IO], Atlanta, GA, United States
International Flight Service Association [1583], 1100 Johnson Ferry Rd., Ste. 300, Atlanta, GA 30342, (404)252-3663
Intl. Floor Covering Representatives Assn. - Address unknown since 2004.
Intl. Floorball Fed. [IO], Helsinki, Finland
Intl. Flow Aids Assn. - Defunct.
Intl. Fluid Power Soc. [7084], PO Box 1420, Cherry Hill, NJ 08034-0054, (856)489-8983
Intl. Fly Fishing Assn. [IO], Perth, United Kingdom
Intl. Flying Bankers Assn. - Defunct.
Intl. Flying Dutchman Class Assn. of the U.S. [23185], c/o John Sayles, Sec.-Treas., 291 Cromwell Ln., West Chester, PA 19380, (610)429-9765
Intl. Flying Dutchman Class Assn. of the U.S. [IO], West Chester, PA, United States
Intl. Flying Farmers [IO], Wichita, KS, United States
Intl. Flying Farmers [4646], PO Box 9124, Wichita, KS 67277-0124, (316)943-4234
Intl. Flying Nun Fan Club - Address unknown since 2006.
Intl. Flying Nurses Assn. - Address unknown since 1995.
Intl. Folk Dance Found. [★9592]
Intl. Food Additives Coun. [1523], 5775 Peachtree-Dunwoody Rd., Ste. 500G, Atlanta, GA 30342, (404)252-3663
Intl. Food Additives Coun. [IO], Atlanta, GA, United States
Intl. Food and Agribusiness Mgt. Assn. [IO], College Station, TX, United States
Intl. Food and Agribusiness Mgt. Assn. [1524], 333 Blocker Bldg., 2124 TAMU, College Station, TX 77843-2124, (979)845-2118
Intl. Food Info. Coun. [1525], 1100 Connecticut Ave. NW, Ste. 430, Washington, DC 20036, (202)296-6540
Intl. Food Info. Ser. (IFIS Publishing) [IO], Reading, United Kingdom
Intl. Food Policy Res. Inst. [IO], Washington, DC, United States
Intl. Food Policy Res. Inst. [17796], 2033 K St. NW, 4th Fl., Washington, DC 20006-1002, (202)862-5600
Intl. Food Res. and Educational Center - Defunct.
Intl. Food Safety Coun. [17605], c/o Natl. Restaurant Assn. Educational Found., 175 W Jackson Blvd., Ste. 1500, Chicago, IL 60604, (312)715-1010
Intl. Food Safety Coun. [IO], Chicago, IL, United States
Intl. Food Ser. Executives Assn. [IO], Louisville, KY, United States
Intl. Food Ser. Executives Assn. [1584], 2609 Surfwood Dr., Las Vegas, NV 89128, (702)430-9217
Intl. Food, Wine and Travel Writers Assn. [3118], 1142 S Diamond Bar Blvd., No. 177, Diamond Bar, CA 91765-2203, (909)860-6914
Intl. Food, Wine and Travel Writers Assn. [IO], Diamond Bar, CA, United States
International Foodservice Distributors Association [IO], Falls Church, VA, United States
Intl. Foodservice Distributors Assn. [1585], 201 Park Washington Ct., Falls Church, VA 22046-4521, (703)532-9400
Intl. Foodservice Editorial Coun. [3119], PO Box 491, Hyde Park, NY 12538-0491, (845)229-6973
Intl. Foodservice Editorial Coun. [IO], Hyde Park, NY, United States
Intl. Foodservice Mfrs. Assn. [IO], Chicago, IL, United States
Intl. Foodservice Mfrs. Assn. [1526], 2 Prudential Plz., 180 N Stetson Ave., Ste. 4400, Chicago, IL 60601, (312)540-4400
Intl. Footprint Assn. [5977], PO Box 1652, Walnut, CA 91788-1652, (877)432-3668
Intl. Footwear Assn. - Address unknown since 1991.
Intl. FOP Assn. [★14457]
Intl. Ford Retractable Club - Address unknown since 2004.
Intl. Formalwear Assn. [242], 401 N Michigan Ave., Chicago, IL 60611-4267, (312)321-5139
International Formalwear Association [IO], Chicago, IL, United States

Intl. Formula Coun. [2387], 5775 Peachtree-Dunwoody Rd., Bldg. G, Ste. 500, Atlanta, GA 30342-1558, (404)252-3663
Intl. Fortean Org. [7477], PO Box 50088, Baltimore, MD 21210
Intl. Fortean Org. [IO], Baltimore, MD, United States
Intl. Forum - Address unknown since 1985.
Intl. Forum of Alan's - Defunct.
Intl. Forum on Globalization [17825], 1009 Gen. Kennedy Ave., No. 2, San Francisco, CA 94129, (415)561-7650
Intl. Forum on Globalization [IO], San Francisco, CA, United States
Intl. Forwarders Assn. of Australia [★IO]
The Intl. Found. [IO], Brookfield, WI, United States
The Intl. Found. [12434], PO Box 69, Brookfield, WI 53008-0069, (888)334-3327
Intl. Found. for Agricultural Development - Defunct.
Intl. Found. for Airline Passengers - Address unknown since 1994.
Intl. Found. for Art Res. [9449], 500 5th Ave., Ste. 935, New York, NY 10110, (212)391-6234
Intl. Found. for Art Res. [IO], New York, NY, United States
International Foundation of Bio-Magnetics [IO], Tucson, AZ, United States
Intl. Found. of Bio-Magnetics [16654], 5634 E Pima St., Tucson, AZ 85712, (520)751-7751
Intl. Found; China [★12434]
Intl. Found. for the Conservation of Game [★IO]
Intl. Found. for the Conservation of Wildlife [IO], Paris, France
Intl. Found. for Dermatology [IO], Belfast, United Kingdom
Intl. Found. of Doll Makers [22398]
Intl. Found. for Election Systems [17487], 1101 15th St. NW, 3rd Fl., Washington, DC 20005, (202)350-6700
Intl. Found. for Electoral Systems [★17487]
Intl. Found. of Employee Benefit Plans [1240], PO Box 69, Brookfield, WI 53008-0069, (262)786-6700
Intl. Found. of Employee Benefit Plans [IO], Brookfield, WI, United States
Intl. Found. for Ethical Res. [IO], Chicago, IL, United States
Intl. Found. for Ethical Res. [11415], 53 W Jackson Blvd., Ste. 1552, Chicago, IL 60604, (312)427-6025
Intl. Found. for Functional Gastrointestinal Disorders [14419], PO Box 170864, Milwaukee, WI 53217, (414)964-1799
International Foundation for Functional Gastrointestinal Disorders [IO], Milwaukee, WI, United States
Intl. Found. for Gender Educ. [13091], PO Box 540229, Waltham, MA 02454, (781)899-2212
Intl. Found. of the High-Altitude Res. Stations Jungfraujoch and Gornergrat [IO], Bern, Switzerland
Intl. Found. for Homeopathy [14849]
Intl. Found. for Independence - Address unknown since 1995.
Intl. Found. for Music Res. [★10653]
Intl. Found. of Oriental Medicine - Address unknown since 2004.
Intl. Found. for the Promotion of Homeopathy [★14849]
Intl. Found. for Protection Officers [3531], PO Box 771329, Naples, FL 34107-1329, (239)430-0534
Intl. Found. for Protection Officers [IO], Naples, FL, United States
Intl. Found. for Stutterers [16447], 304 Hampshire Dr., Plainsboro, NJ 08536, (609)275-3806
Intl. Found. for Telemetering [7786], 5959 Topanga Canyon Blvd., Ste. 150, Woodland Hills, CA 91367
Intl. Found. for Telemetering [IO], Woodland Hills, CA, United States
Intl. Found. for Terror Act Victims [IO], Southampton, PA, United States
Intl. Found. for Terror Act Victims [12942], PO Box 444, Southampton, PA 18966, (321)213-0198
Intl. Found. for Theatrical Res. - Address unknown since 1999.
Intl. Fox-Tango Club - Defunct.
Intl. Fragrance Assn. [IO], Brussels, Belgium
Intl. Franchise Assn. [IO], Washington, DC, United States

Intl. Franchise Assn. **[1668]**, 1501 K St. NW, Ste. 350, Washington, DC 20005, (202)628-8000

Intl. Frankenstein Soc. **[24822]**, 29 Washington Sq. W, Penthouse N, New York, NY 10011

Intl. Frankenstein Soc. **[IO]**, New York, NY, United States

Intl. Fraternity of Lambda Alpha **[★24445]**

Intl. Freedom of Expression Exchange CH **[IO]**, Toronto, ON, Canada

Intl. Freedom Found. **[17272]**, 200 G St. NE, Ste. 300, Washington, DC 20002-4328, (202)546-5788

Intl. Freedom to Publish Comm. **[17041]**, c/o Assn. of Amer. Publishers, 71 5th Ave., 2nd Fl., New York, NY 10003, (212)255-0200

Intl. Freedom to Publish Comm. **[IO]**, New York, NY, United States

Intl. Freeze-Dry Floral Assn. **[IO]**, Des Moines, IA, United States

Intl. Freeze-Dry Floral Assn. **[1492]**, c/o Connie Johnson, Pres., 320 Scandia Ave., Des Moines, IA 50315, (515)953-2211

Intl. French Brittany Club of Am. **[22288]**, PO Box 104, Pettibone, ND 58475-0104

Intl. French Brittany Club of Am. **[IO]**, Pettibone, ND, United States

Intl. French-Speaking Cultural Assn. of the ONU - USA - Address unknown since 2007.

Intl. Friendly Circle of the Blind - Address unknown since 2004.

Intl. Friends of the London Lib. **[10363]**, c/o John W. Spurdle, Sec., 515 Madison Ave., Ste. 3702, New York, NY 10022, (212)644-4858

Intl. Friends of the London Lib. **[IO]**, New York, NY, United States

Intl. Friends of Nature **[IO]**, Vienna, Austria

Intl. Friendship Found. **[★8631]**

Intl. Friendship League - Defunct.

Intl. Frisbee Disc Assn. - Defunct.

International Frog Collectors Club; Beyond the Pond. **[21977]**

Intl. Frozen Food Assn. **[1527]**, 2000 Corporate Ridge, Ste. 1000, McLean, VA 22102, (703)821-0770

Intl. Frozen Food Assn. **[IO]**, McLean, VA, United States

Intl. Fruit Tree Assn. **[5257]**, c/o Susan M. Pheasant, PhD, Exec. Dir., PO Box 5006, Wenatchee, WA 98807-5006, (509)884-5651

Intl. Function Point Users Gp. **[734]**, 191 Clarksville Rd., Princeton Junction, NJ 08550, (609)799-4900

Intl. Functional Elecl. Stimulation Soc. **[15390]**, c/o Paul Meadows, MS, Pres., 1854 Los Encinos Ave., Glendale, CA 91208-2240, (661)362-1755

Intl. Functional Elecl. Stimulation Soc. **[IO]**, Glendale, CA, United States

Intl. Fund for Agricultural Development - Italy **[IO]**, Rome, Italy

Intl. Fund for Animal Welfare **[IO]**, Yarmouth Port, MA, United States

Intl. Fund for Animal Welfare **[11416]**, 411 Main St., PO Box 193, Yarmouth Port, MA 02675-0193, (508)744-2000

Intl. Fund for Concerned Photography **[★8972]**

Intl. Fund for Concerned Photography **[★IO]**

Intl. Fund for Horses **[★IO]**

Intl. Fund for Horses **[★4159]**

Intl. Fund-Raising Assn. - Address unknown since 2000.

Intl. Fur Trade Fed. **[IO]**, Weybridge, United Kingdom

Intl. Furnishings and Design Assn. **[IO]**, Princeton Junction, NJ, United States

Intl. Furnishings and Design Assn. **[2264]**, 150 S Warner Rd., Ste. 156, King of Prussia, PA 19406, (610)535-6422

Intl. Furniture and Accessory Assn. - Address unknown since 1987.

Intl. Furniture Rental Assn. **[1699]**, 5229 Coll. Hill Rd., Woodstock, VT 05091

Intl. Furniture Rental Assn. **[IO]**, Woodstock, VT, United States

Intl. Furniture Suppliers Assn. **[IO]**, High Point, NC, United States

Intl. Furniture Suppliers Assn. **[1700]**, 3910 Tinsley Dr., Ste. 101, High Point, NC 27265, (336)801-6130

Intl. Furniture and Trans. Logistics Coun. **[3570]**, PO Box 889, Gardner, MA 01440-0889, (978)632-1913

Intl. Furniture and Trans. Logistics Coun. **[IO]**, Gardner, MA, United States

Intl. G. G. Drayton Assn. - Defunct.

Intl. Galapagos Tour Operators Assn. **[24383]**, PO Box 1043, Winchester, MA 01890

Intl. Galapagos Tour Operators Assn. **[IO]**, Winchester, MA, United States

Intl. Galdos Assn. - Defunct.

Intl. Game Developers Assn. **[6733]**, 19 Mantua Rd., Mount Royal, NJ 08061, (856)423-2990

Intl. Game Developers Assn. **[IO]**, San Francisco, CA, United States

Intl. Game Fish Assn. **[IO]**, Dania Beach, FL, United States

Intl. Game Fish Assn. **[23417]**, IGFA Fishing Hall of Fame and Museum, 300 Gulf Stream Way, Dania Beach, FL 33004, (954)927-2628

Intl. Gamers Assn. - Address unknown since 2002.

Intl. Garden Club **[10040]**, Bartow-Pell Mansion Museum, 895 Shore Rd., Pelham Bay Park, Bronx, NY 10464, (718)885-1461

Intl. Garden Club **[IO]**, Bronx, NY, United States

Intl. Garden Horticultural Indus. Assn. **[★IO]**

Intl. Garden Horticultural Indus. Assn. **[★4975]**

Intl. Gas Turbine Inst. **[★7001]**

Intl. Gas Turbine Inst. **[★IO]**

Intl. Gas Union **[IO]**, Hoersholm, Denmark

Intl. Gay Assn. **[★IO]**

Intl. Gay Bowling Org. **[23251]**, c/o Greg Edenfield, Pres., PO Box 30722, Charlotte, NC 28230-0722

Intl. Gay Figure Skating Union **[23736]**, PO Box 945, New York, NY 10116

International Gay Figure Skating Union **[IO]**, New York, NY, United States

Intl. Gay Information Center - Defunct.

Intl. Gay and Lesbian Aquatics **[23885]**, c/o Bernie LaFianza, Treas., 7423 Hollywood Blvd., Los Angeles, CA 90046-2819

Intl. Gay and Lesbian Aquatics **[IO]**, Los Angeles, CA, United States

Intl. Gay and Lesbian Football Assn. **[IO]**, Seattle, WA, United States

Intl. Gay and Lesbian Football Assn. **[23777]**, c/o Brendan Patrick, Treas., 723 ML King Jr. Way, Seattle, WA 98122

Intl. Gay and Lesbian Franchise Assn. - Address unknown since 2000.

Intl. Gay and Lesbian Human Rights Commn. **[12239]**, 80 Maiden Ln., Ste. 1505, New York, NY 10038, (212)268-8040

Intl. Gay and Lesbian Human Rights Commn. **[IO]**, New York, NY, United States

Intl. Gay and Lesbian Travel Assn. **[3924]**, 4331 N Fed. Hwy., No. 304, Fort Lauderdale, FL 33308, (954)776-2626

Intl. Gay Rodeo Assn. **[23685]**, PO Box 460504, Aurora, CO 80046-0504

Intl. Gay Rodeo Assn. **[IO]**, Aurora, CO, United States

Intl. Gender and Trade Network - Central Asia **[IO]**, Tashkent, Uzbekistan

Intl. Gender and Trade Network - Europe **[IO]**, Brussels, Belgium

Intl. Genealogy Consumer Org. - Address unknown since 1999.

Intl. Genealogy and Heraldry Fellowship of Rotarians - Address unknown since 2003.

Intl. General - Address unknown since 1989.

Intl. Gen. Produce Assn. **[IO]**, London, United Kingdom

Intl. Generic Horse Assn. **[4899]**, PO Box 6778, Eastview, San Pedro, CA 90734-6778

Intl. Genetic Epidemiology Soc. **[14376]**, c/o Michael A. Province, Sec.-Treas., Washington Univ. School of Medicine, Div. of Biostatistics, Box 8067, 660 S Euclid Ave., St. Louis, MO 63108, (314)362-3616

Intl. Genetic Epidemiology Soc. **[IO]**, St. Louis, MO, United States

Intl. Genetic Resources Programme **[★IO]**

Intl. Genetic Resources Programme **[★4108]**

Intl. Genetics Fed. **[IO]**, Parkville, Australia

Intl. Geographical Union - Commn. on Geographical Educ. **[IO]**, Helsinki, Finland

Intl. Geosphere-Biosphere Programme **[IO]**, Stockholm, Sweden

International Geosynthetics Society **[IO]**, Easley, SC, United States

Intl. Geosynthetics Soc. **[6700]**, PO Box 347, Easley, SC 29641, (864)855-0504

Intl. Geosynthetics Soc. - Brazilian Chap. **[IO]**, Sao Paulo, Brazil

Intl. Geosynthetics Soc. - Chinese Chap. **[IO]**, Shanghai, People's Republic of China

Intl. Geosynthetics Soc. - Indian Chap. **[IO]**, New Delhi, India

Intl. Geosynthetics Soc. - Turkish Chap. **[IO]**, Istanbul, Turkey

Intl. Geothermal Assn. **[IO]**, Reykjavik, Iceland

Intl. Geranium Soc. - Address unknown since 2001.

Intl. Glaciological Soc. **[IO]**, Cambridge, United Kingdom

Intl. Glaucoma Assn. **[IO]**, Kent, United Kingdom

Intl. Gloster Breeders Assn. **[21849]**, c/o Candace Pezzuti, Sec.-Treas., 3844 Lindell Rd., Las Vegas, NV 89103, (702)876-8949

Intl. Glove Assn. **[2030]**, PO Box 146, Brookville, PA 15825, (814)328-5208

Intl. Glove Assn. **[IO]**, Brookville, PA, United States

International Glutamate Technical Committee **[IO]**, Atlanta, GA, United States

Intl. Glutamate Tech. Comm. **[1528]**, 1100 Johnson Ferry Rd., Atlanta, GA 30342, (404)252-3663

Intl. Goat Assn. **[4785]**, c/o Christian DeVries, Operations Dir., 1 World Ave., Little Rock, AR 72202, (501)454-1641

Intl. Goat Assn. **[IO]**, Little Rock, AR, United States

Intl. Goebel Collectors Club **[★22040]**

Intl. Gold and Silver Plate Soc. **[18977]**, c/o Intl. Foodservice Manufacturers Assn., 2 Prudential Plz., 180 N Stetson, Ste. 4400, Chicago, IL 60601, (312)540-4400

Intl. Gold Star Pig Registry - Address unknown since 2001.

Intl. Golf Associates **[23452]**, 1040 Genter St., No. 103, La Jolla, CA 92037-5550, (858)546-4737

Intl. Golf Associates **[IO]**, San Diego, CA, United States

Intl. Golf Assn. **[★IO]**

Intl. Golf Assn. **[★23452]**

Intl. Golf Fed. **[23453]**, PO Box 708, Far Hills, NJ 07931-0708, (908)234-2300

Intl. Golf Fed. **[IO]**, Far Hills, NJ, United States

Intl. Golf Sponsors Assn. **[★23461]**

Intl. Good Template Youth Fed. **[★IO]**

Intl. Gottfried Wilhelm Leibniz Soc. **[IO]**, Hannover, Germany

Intl. Govt; Inst. for **[★17620]**

Intl. Graduate Achievement - Defunct.

International Grail Movement **[★19630]**

Intl. Grains Coun. **[IO]**, London, United Kingdom

International Graphic Arts Education Association **[IO]**, Reston, VA, United States

Intl. Graphic Arts Educ. Assn. **[8470]**, 1899 Preston White Dr., Reston, VA 20191-4367, (703)758-0595

Intl. Graphic Arts Soc. - Address unknown since 1995.

Intl. Graphics - Address unknown since 2003.

Intl. Graphoanalysis Soc. **[11210]**, 842 5th Ave., New Kensington, PA 15068, (724)472-9701

Intl. Graphoanalysis Soc. **[IO]**, New Kensington, PA, United States

Intl. Graphological Soc. **[11211]**

Intl. Graphology Assn. **[IO]**, Bath, United Kingdom

Intl. Graphonomics Soc. **[IO]**, Montreal, QC, Canada

Intl. Gravity Bur. **[IO]**, Toulouse, France

International Gravity Sports Association **[IO]**, Glendora, CA, United States

Intl. Gravity Sports Assn. **[23823]**, 638 N Crestview Dr., Glendora, CA 91741, (951)532-6378

Intl. Green Alliance - Address unknown since 1985.

Intl. Green Party - Address unknown since 2007.

Intl. Grooving and Grinding Assn. **[928]**, 12573 Rte. 9W, West Coxsackie, NY 12192, (518)731-7450

Intl. Grooving and Grinding Assn. **[IO]**, West Coxsackie, NY, United States

International Ground Source Heat Pump Association **[IO]**, Stillwater, OK, United States

Intl. Ground Source Heat Pump Assn. **[1889]**, 374 Cordell S, Stillwater, OK 74078-8018, (405)744-5175

A star before a book entry number signifies that the name is not listed separately, but is mentioned within the entry.

Intl. Gp. of Accounting Firms [37], 3235 Satellite Blvd., Bldg. 400, Ste. 300, Duluth, GA 30096, (678)417-7730

Intl. Gp. of Accounting Firms [IO], Duluth, GA, United States

Intl. Gp. of Agencies and Bureaus [★IO]

Intl. Gp. of Agencies and Bureaus [★10900]

Intl. Group for Co-Operation and Res. on Documentation - Defunct.

Intl. Guards Union of Am. [24185], Rte. 8, Box 32-14, Amarillo, TX 79118-9427, (806)622-2424

Intl. Guiding Eyes [★16851]

Intl. Guild of Artists [IO], Ilkley, United Kingdom

Intl. Guild of Candle Artisans [IO], Fremont, NE, United States

Intl. Guild of Candle Artisans [9831], 1640 Garfield St., Fremont, NE 68025

Intl. Guild of Craft Journalists, Authors and Photographers - Defunct.

Intl. Guild of Glass Artists [299], c/o Katherine Bell, Membership Dir., 4735 Waverly Ln., Jacksonville, FL 32210

Intl. Guild of Glass Artists [IO], Jacksonville, FL, United States

Intl. Guild of Hair Removal Specialists [IO], Columbus, OH, United States

Intl. Guild of Hair Removal Specialists [14309], 1918 Bethel Rd., Columbus, OH 43220, (614)457-0448

Intl. Guild of Hypnotists - Address unknown since 1994.

Intl. Guild of Knot Tyers [IO], Chester, United Kingdom

Intl. Guild of Lamp Researchers [22618], Lamplighters Farm, 10111 Lincoln Way W, St. Thomas, PA 17252-9513

Intl. Guild of Lay Ministers and Acolytes [★19963]

Intl. Guild of Lay Ministers and Acolytes [★IO]

International Guild of Miniature Artisans [IO], Freedom, CA, United States

Intl. Guild of Miniature Artisans [22159], PO Box 629, Freedom, CA 95019-0629, (831)724-7974

Intl. Guild of Musicians in Dance [10774], c/o Larry Attaway, Sec.-Treas., 5144 Boulevard Pl., Indianapolis, IN 46208

Intl. Guild of Musicians in Dance [IO], Indianapolis, IN, United States

Intl. Guild of Nobles [19056], PO Box 7264, Univ. Sta., Provo, UT 84602-7264, (801)489-0458

Intl. Guild of Prestidigitators - Defunct.

Intl. Guild of Professional Butlers [24040], 134 W 82nd St., Ste. 3b, New York, NY 10024, (646)290-6527

Intl. Guild of Professional Butlers [IO], New York, NY, United States

Intl. Guild of Professional Consultants [IO], Winter Springs, FL, United States

Intl. Guild of Professional Consultants [966], 5703 Red Bug Lake Rd., Ste. 403, Winter Springs, FL 32708, (407)687-7853

Intl. Guild of Professional Electrologists [★14309]

Intl. Guild of Professional Electrologists [★IO]

Intl. Guild of Realism [9574], 4400 N Scottsdale Rd., No. 9539, Scottsdale, AZ 85251

Intl. Guild of Symphony, Opera and Ballet Musicians [24157], c/o Matthew Kocmieroski, Treas., 12724 19th Ave. NE, Seattle, WA 98125, (206)524-7050

Intl. Guild of Vatican Philatelists - Defunct.

Intl. Gustav Mahler Soc. [IO], Vienna, Austria

Intl. Gymnastic Fed. [IO], Moutier, Switzerland

Intl. H Boat Class Assn. - Defunct.

Intl. Hahnemannian Assn. - Defunct.

Intl. Hajji Baba Soc. [9450], c/o Virginia Day, Treas., 6500 Pinecrest Ct., Annandale, VA 22003, (703)354-4880

Intl. Hajji Baba Soc. [IO], Annandale, VA, United States

Intl. Halfway House Assn. [★IO]

Intl. Halfway House Assn. [★11872]

Intl. Halley Watch - Defunct.

Intl. Hand Protection Assn. [★2030]

Intl. Hand Protection Assn. [★IO]

Intl. Handball Fed. [IO], Basel, Switzerland

Intl. Handgun Metallic Silhouette Assn. [IO], Sandy, UT, United States

Intl. Handgun Metallic Silhouette Assn. [23719], PO Box 901120, Sandy, UT 84090-1120, (801)733-2423

Intl. Handicappers' Net [21502], 300 Luman Rd., No. 40, Phoenix, OR 97535, (541)535-6797

Intl. Harbour Masters' Assn. [IO], Fareham, United Kingdom

International Hard Anodizing Association [IO], Moorestown, NJ, United States

Intl. Hard Anodizing Assn. [2710], PO Box 579, Moorestown, NJ 08057-0579, (856)234-0330

Intl. Hardware Distributors Assn. - Defunct.

Intl. Hardwood Products Assn. [★1609]

Intl. Hardwood Products Assn. [★IO]

Intl. Harm Reduction Assn. [IO], North Melbourne, Australia

Intl. Harvester Collectors [IO], Cygnet, OH, United States

Intl. Harvester Collectors [23003], c/o Bill Swope, Pres., 9980 Five Point Rd., Perrysburg, OH 43551, (419)874-2759

Intl. Hazard Control Manager Certification Bd. [★3440]

Intl. Headache Soc. [IO], London, United Kingdom

International Health

Adopt a Dr. [12750]

Adventist Development and Relief Agency Intl. [12826]

African Medical and Res. Found. [14971]

African Medical and Res. Found. [IO]

Aid for Intl. Medicine [IO]

Aid for Intl. Medicine [14972]

Amer. Coll. of Intl. Physicians [14973]

Amer. Coll. of Intl. Physicians [IO]

Amer. Medical Resources Found. [IO]

Amer. Medical Resources Found. [14974]

Amer. Physicians Fellowship for Medicine in Israel [12456]

Amer. Red Cross Overseas Assn. [12831]

Amer. Soc. of Tropical Medicine and Hygiene [16693]

Amer. Women's Hospitals Ser. Comm. of AMWA [14870]

Ashoka: Innovators for the Public [12419]

Assn. for Intl. Medical Study [12834]

BIO Ventures for Global Hea. [14975]

BIO Ventures for Global Hea. [IO]

Brother's Brother Found. [12837]

Canadian Soc. of Internal Medicine [IO]

Catholic Medical Mission Bd. [12515]

Children's Wish Found. Intl. [11687]

China Medical Bd. of New York [14976]

Christian Children's Fund [11688]

Christian Connections for Intl. Hea. [14551]

Christian Found. for Children and Aging [13159]

Commn. on Graduates of Foreign Nursing Schools [15473]

Concern Am. [12845]

DOCARE Intl., N.F.P. [12518]

Egyptians Relief Assn. [11774]

Flying Doctors of Am. [12523]

Food for the Poor [12772]

Found. for the Support of Intl. Medical Training [14977]

Found. for the Support of Intl. Medical Training [IO]

Futures for Children [11695]

Global Healing [12450]

Global Healing [IO]

Global Hea. Action [IO]

Global Hea. Action [14978]

Global Hea. Coun. [14979]

Global Hea. Coun. [IO]

Global Outreach Mission [12525]

God's Child Proj. [11597]

Healing the Children [11697]

Hea. Volunteers Overseas [12526]

Hesperian Found. [14980]

Hesperian Found. [IO]

Humanity Intl. [12859]

Indian Muslim Relief Comm. of ISNA [12860]

INMED Partnerships for Children [14981]

INMED Partnerships for Children [IO]

Intermed Intl. [IO]

Intermed Intl. [14982]

Intl. Acad. of Health Care Professionals [14705]

Intl. Fed. of Ophthalmological Societies [15686]

Intl. Medical Corps [12862]

Intl. Relief Friendship Found. [13171]

Intl. Vitamin A Consultative Gp. [15564]

Interplast [14049]

Just Act: Youth Action for Global Justice [12435]

Lalmba Assn. [12866]

Lay Mission-Helpers Assn. [19648]

Los Ninos [12589]

Medical Missions Response [20246]

Mission Doctors Assn. [12532]

Missions Intl. [20037]

Natl. Latina Health Org. [14983]

Natl. Latina Health Org. [IO]

Natl. Student Campaign Against Hunger and Homelessness [12396]

Need [12875]

Oper. Smile [12534]

Orthopaedics Overseas [15778]

Pan Amer. Hea. and Educ. Found. [12536]

Pan Amer. Hea. Org. [14592]

People-to-People Hea. Found. [14984]

People-to-People Hea. Found. [IO]

Proj. Concern Intl. [IO]

Proj. Concern Intl. [14985]

Save the Children [11720]

Tang Center for Herbal Medicine Res. [14986]

Tang Center for Herbal Medicine Research [IO]

Task Force for Child Survival and Development [12542]

Intl. Hea. Consultants [★14575]

Intl. Health Coun. - Address unknown since 1994.

Intl. Hea. Evaluation Assn. [14568], 846 S Hotel St., Ste. 301, Honolulu, HI 96813-2583, (808)524-4411

Intl. Hea. Evaluation Assn. [IO], Honolulu, HI, United States

Intl. Hea. Exchange [IO], London, United Kingdom

Intl. Health Industries Assn. - Defunct.

Intl. Hea. Org., India [IO], Patna, India

Intl. Health Policy and Mgt. Inst. - Address unknown since 2001.

Intl. Hea., Racquet and Sportsclub Assn. [3021], 263 Summer St., Boston, MA 02210, (617)951-0055

Intl. Hea., Racquet and Sportsclub Assn. [IO], Boston, MA, United States

Intl. Hea. and Safety Assn. for Radio and TV [IO], Brussels, Belgium

Intl. Health Soc. - Defunct.

Intl. Hea. and Temperance Assn. [13304], 12501 Old Columbia Pike, Silver Spring, MD 20904, (301)680-6702

Intl. Hea. and Temperance Assn. [IO], Silver Spring, MD, United States

Intl. Healthcare Safety Professional Certification Bd. [IO], Rockville, MD, United States

Intl. Healthcare Safety Professional Certification Bd. [16379]

Intl. Healthy Cities Found. [13349], 555 12th St., 10th Fl., Oakland, CA 94607, (510)642-1715

International Healthy Cities Foundation [IO], Oakland, CA, United States

Intl. Hearing Dog, Inc. [IO], Henderson, CO, United States

Intl. Hearing Dog, Inc. [14762], 5901 E 89th Ave., Henderson, CO 80640, (303)287-3277

Intl. Hearing Soc. [14763], 16880 Middlebelt Rd., Ste. 4, Livonia, MI 48154-3374, (734)522-7200

Intl. Hearing Soc. [IO], Livonia, MI, United States

Intl. Heart Hea. Soc. [IO], Burnaby, BC, Canada

International Heart and Lung Transplantation Registry [★IO]

International Heart and Lung Transplantation Registry [★16674]

Intl. Hearts Air Supply Fan Club - Defunct.

Intl. Hebrew Christian Alliance [★20016]

Intl. Hebrew Christian Alliance [★IO]

Intl. Hedgehog Assn. [IO], Divide, CO, United States

Intl. Hedgehog Assn. [11417], PO Box 1060, Divide, CO 80814

Intl. Hedgehog Club [★11417]

Intl. Hedgehog Club [★IO]

Intl. Hedgehog Fanciers Soc. [★IO]

Intl. Hedgehog Fanciers Soc. [★11417]

Intl. Heinrich Schutz Soc. [IO], Kassel, Germany

Intl. Helicopter Found. [★IO]

Intl. Helicopter Found. [★151]

Intl. Helsinki Fed. for Human Rights [IO], Vienna, Austria

Reference to "IO" in place of a book number signifies that the association may be found in the 45th edition of International Organizations.

Intl. Hepato-Biliary Pancreatic Assn. [★IO]
Intl. Hepato-Biliary Pancreatic Assn. [★14802]
Intl. Hepato-Pancreato-Biliary Assn. [★14802]
Intl. Hepato-Pancreato-Biliary Assn. [★IO]
Intl. Herb Assn. [IO], Jacksonville, FL, United States
Intl. Herb Assn. [1907], PO Box 5667, Jacksonville, FL 32247-5667, (904)399-3241
Intl. Herb Growers and Marketers Assn. [★1907]
Intl. Herb Growers and Marketers Assn. [★IO]
Intl. High Five Soc. - Defunct.
Intl. High IQ Soc. [19149], PO Box 3882, New York, NY 10163
International High IQ Society [IO], New York, NY, United States
Intl. Hobie Class Assn. [IO], Portage, MI, United States
Intl. Hobie Class Assn. [23186], c/o David Brookes, Exec. Dir., 2812 E Shore Dr., Portage, MI 49002, (269)327-4565
Intl. Hockey Fed. [IO], Lausanne, Switzerland
Intl. Hockey League - Address unknown since 2004.
Intl. Hologram Mfrs. Assn. [IO], Shepperton, United Kingdom
International Home Exchange [★22580]
Intl. Home Furnishings Market Authority [1701], PO Box 5243, High Point, NC 27262, (336)869-1000
Intl. Home Furnishings Marketing Assn. [★1701]
Intl. Home Furnishings Representatives Assn. [1702], PO Box 670, High Point, NC 27261, (336)889-3920
Intl. Home Furnishings Representatives Assn. [IO], High Point, NC, United States
Intl. Home and Private Poker Players' Assn. - Defunct.
Intl. Homeopathic Medical League [IO], Berlin, Germany
International Homicide Investigators Association [IO], Fredericksburg, VA, United States
Intl. Homicide Investigators Assn. [5883], 10711 Spotsylvania Ave., Fredericksburg, VA 22408, (877)843-4442
Intl. Horn Soc. [10620], PO Box 630158, Lanai City, HI 96763-0158, (808)565-7273
Intl. Horn Soc. [IO], Lanai City, HI, United States
Intl. Hosp. Fed. [IO], Ferney-Voltaire, France
Intl. Hot Rod Assn. [23077], 9 1/2 E Main St., Norwalk, OH 44857, (419)663-6666
Intl. Hotel Assn. [★IO]
Intl. Hotel and Restaurant Assn. [IO], Paris, France
Intl. House Assn. - Defunct.
Intl. House - World Trade Center [★2295]
Intl. House - World Trade Center [★IO]
Intl. Housewares Assn. [IO], Rosemont, IL, United States
Intl. Housewares Assn. [1972], 6400 Shafer Ct., Ste. 650, Rosemont, IL 60018, (847)292-4200
Intl. Housewares Representatives Assn. [1973], 175 N Harbor Dr., Ste. 3807, Chicago, IL 60601, (312)240-0774
Intl. Housewares Representatives Assn. [IO], Chicago, IL, United States
Intl. Hug Center - Defunct.
Intl. Human Assistance Programs - Address unknown since 1990.
Intl. Human Powered Vehicle Assn. [★7811]
Intl. Human Powered Vehicle Assn. [★IO]
Intl. Human Resources, Business and Legal Res. Assn. - Address unknown since 1994.
Intl. Human Rights Assn. of Amer. Minorities [IO], Nanaimo, BC, Canada
Intl. Human Rights Law Gp. [★IO]
Intl. Human Rights Law Gp. [★17758]
Intl. Human Rights; Lawyers Comm. for [★17759]
Intl. Humanist and Ethical Union [IO], London, United Kingdom
Intl. Humic Substances Soc. [IO], Ames, IA, United States
Intl. Humic Substances Soc. [7610], c/o Dr. Dan Olk, Natl. Coor., Natl. Soil Tilth Lab., 2110 Univ. Blvd., Ames, IA 50011-3120, (515)294-8412
Intl. Hunter Educ. Assn. [23545], 2727 W 92nd Ave., Ste. 103, Federal Heights, CO 80260, (303)430-7233
International Hunter Education Association [IO], Federal Heights, CO, United States

Intl. Hunting Land Assn. [IO], Johnstown, PA, United States
Intl. Hunting Land Assn. [22605], 476 Dorothy Ave., Johnstown, PA 15906-1455, (814)536-1898
Intl. Huntington Assn. [IO], Harfsen, Netherlands
Intl. Huntington Assn. - Chile [IO], Santiago, Chile
Intl. Huntington Assn. - Ecuador [IO], Quito, Ecuador
Intl. Huntington Assn. - Egypt [IO], Giza, Egypt
Intl. Huntington Assn. - Hungary [IO], Szeged, Hungary
Intl. Huntington Assn. - Iceland [IO], Reykjavik, Iceland
Intl. Huntington Assn. - Korea [IO], Seoul, Republic of Korea
Intl. Huntington Assn. - Lebanon [IO], Beirut, Lebanon
Intl. Huntington Assn. - Lithuania [IO], Kaunas, Lithuania
Intl. Huntington Assn. - Moldova [IO], Kishinev, Moldova
Intl. Huntington Assn. - Oman [IO], Muscat, Oman
Intl. Huntington Assn. - Paraguay [IO], Asuncion, Paraguay
Intl. Huntington Assn. - Peru [IO], Lima, Peru
Intl. Huntington Assn. - Philippines [IO], Quezon City, Philippines
Intl. Huntington Assn. - Taiwan [IO], Taipei, Taiwan
Intl. Huntington Assn. - Thailand [IO], Chiang Mai, Thailand
Intl. Huntington Assn. - Tunisia [IO], Tunis, Tunisia
Intl. Huntington Assn. - Uruguay [IO], Montevideo, Uruguay
Intl. Huntington Assn. - Zimbabwe [IO], Bulawayo, Zimbabwe
Intl. Huntington Org. - Iran [IO], Tehran, Iran
Intl. Husserl and Phenomenological Res. Soc. [IO], Hanover, NH, United States
Intl. Husserl and Phenomenological Res. Soc. [10801], c/o World Phenomenology Inst., 1 Ivy Pointe Way, Hanover, NH 03755, (802)295-3487
Intl. Hydrofoil Soc. [21876], PO Box 51, Cabin John, MD 20818
Intl. Hydrofoil Soc. [IO], Cabin John, MD, United States
Intl. Hydrographic Bur. [IO], Monte Carlo, Monaco
Intl. Hydrographic Org. [★IO]
International Hydrolyzed Protein Council [IO], Washington, DC, United States
Intl. Hydrolyzed Protein Coun. [1529], 555 13th St. NW, Washington, DC 20004-1109, (202)637-5926
Intl. Hyperhidrosis Soc. [14357], 520 Walnut St., Ste. 1160, Philadelphia, PA 19106, (215)351-9050
Intl. Hyperhidrosis Soc. [IO], Philadelphia, PA, United States
Intl. Hypnological Assn. [★14926]
Intl. Hypnological Assn. - Defunct.
Intl. Ice Hockey Fed. [IO], Zurich, Switzerland
Intl. Illawarra Assn. - Defunct.
Intl. Imagery Assn. [10183], c/o Leslie J. Dagnall, Dir. of Training, 18 Edgeclif Terr., Yonkers, NY 10705, (914)476-0781
Intl. Imagery Assn. [IO], Yonkers, NY, United States
Intl. Imaging Indus. Assn. [IO], White Plains, NY, United States
Intl. Imaging Indus. Assn. [3002], 701 Westchester Ave., Ste. 317W, White Plains, NY 10604-3018, (914)285-4933
Intl. Independence Inst. [★17221]
Intl. Indian Treaty Coun. [17816], 2390 Mission St., Ste. 301, San Francisco, CA 94110, (415)641-4482
Intl. Indian Treaty Coun. [IO], San Francisco, CA, United States
Intl. Industrial Marketing Club - Defunct.
Intl. Indus. Photographers Assn. [IO], Rotterdam, Netherlands
Intl. Indus. Relations Assn. [IO], Geneva, Switzerland
Intl. Indus. TV Assn. [★IO]
Intl. Indus. TV Assn. [★1388]
Intl. Indus. Assn. for Standardizing Info. and Commun. Systems [IO], Geneva, Switzerland
Intl. Inflatable Products and Games Assn. [861], 10 E Athens Ave., Ste. 208, Ardmore, PA 19003, (610)645-6940
Intl. Inflight Food Ser. Assn. [★1583]

Intl. Inflight Food Ser. Assn. [★1583]
Intl. Inflight Food Ser. Assn. [★IO]
Intl. Informatiecentrum en Archief voor de Vrouwenbeweging [★IO]
Intl. Info. Centre and Archives for the Women's Movement [IO], Amsterdam, Netherlands
Intl. Info. Centre for Terminology [IO], Vienna, Austria
Intl. Information Management Congress - Address unknown since 2003.
Intl. Info. Systems Security Certification Consortium [6758], 2494 Bayshore Blvd., Ste. 201, Dunedin, FL 34698, (727)738-8657
International Information Systems Security Certification Consortium [IO], Dunedin, FL, United States
Intl. Initiatives of the Amer. Coun. on Educ. [IO], Washington, DC, United States
Intl. Initiatives of the Amer. Coun. on Educ. [8659], 1 Dupont Cir. NW, Washington, DC 20036-1193, (202)939-9300
Intl. Inline Skating Assn. [IO], Cleveland Heights, OH, United States
Intl. Inline Skating Assn. - Defunct.
Intl. Input-Output Assn. [IO], Vienna, Austria
Intl. Inst. of Administrative Sciences [IO], Brussels, Belgium
Intl. Inst. of African Languages and Cultures [★IO]
Intl. Inst. on Ageing [IO], Valletta, Malta
Intl. Inst. of Amer. Ideals - Address unknown since 1995.
Intl. Inst. of Ammonia Refrigeration [1890], 1110 N Glebe Rd., Ste. 250, Arlington, VA 22201, (703)312-4200
Intl. Inst. of Ammonia Refrigeration [IO], Arlington, VA, United States
Intl. Inst. of Anthropology [IO], Paris, France
Intl. Inst. for Applied Systems Anal. [IO], Laxenburg, Austria
Intl. Inst. for Arab-Amer. Relations - Defunct.
Intl. Inst. for Baubiologie and Ecology [4513], PO Box 387, Clearwater, FL 33757, (727)461-4371
Intl. Inst. for Beet Res. [IO], Gottingen, Germany
Intl. Inst. for Bioenergetic Anal. [IO], Zurich, Switzerland
Intl. Inst. for Biological and Botanical Res. - Defunct.
Intl. Inst. of Biological Control [★IO]
Intl. Inst. of Biophysics [IO], Neuss, Germany
Intl. Inst. of Carpet and Upholstery Certification [★2259]
Intl. Inst. of Catechetics and Pastoral Stud. [IO], Brussels, Belgium
Intl. Inst. of Central Asia Biodiversity [IO], Tashkent, Uzbekistan
Intl. Inst. for Children's Juvenile and Popular Literature [★IO]
Intl. Inst. for Children's Literature and Reading Res. [IO], Vienna, Austria
Intl. Inst. of Children's Nature and Their Rights - Address unknown since 1989.
Intl. Inst. of Communications [IO], London, United Kingdom
Intl. Inst. of Comparative Linguistic Law [★IO]
Intl. Inst. of Concern for Public Hea. [IO], Toronto, ON, Canada
Intl. Inst. of Conf. Mgt. [★IO]
Intl. Inst. of Conf. Mgt. [★2676]
Intl. Inst. for Conflict Prevention and Resolution; CPR [11488]
Intl. Inst. of Connector and Interconnection Tech. [6929], PO Box 399, Waretown, NJ 08758, (609)242-2445
Intl. Inst. of Connector and Interconnection Tech. [IO], Waretown, NJ, United States
Intl. Inst. for Conservation of Historic and Artistic Works [IO], London, United Kingdom
Intl. Inst. for Conservation of Historic and Artistic Works—American Gp. [IO]
Intl. Inst. for Conservation of Historic and Artistic Works—American Gp. [10011]
Intl. Inst. of Convention Mgt. [★2676]
Intl. Inst. of Convention Mgt. [★IO]
Intl. Inst. for Educational Planning [IO], Paris, France
Intl. Inst. of Embryology [★IO]
International Institute for Energy Conservation [IO], Vienna, VA, United States

A star before a book entry number signifies that the name is not listed separately, but is mentioned within the entry.

Intl. Inst. for Energy Conservation [6958], 10005 Leamoore Ln., No. 100, Vienna, VA 22181, (703)281-7263

Intl. Inst. for Energy Conservation - Asia Off. [★IO]

Intl. Inst. for Env. and Development [IO], London, United Kingdom

Intl. Inst. for Environmental Affairs [★IO]

Intl. Inst. for Ethnic Gp. Rights and Regionalism [IO], Munich, Germany

Intl. Inst. for Field-Being [8968], Fairfield Univ., Dept. of Philosophy, 332 Donnarumma Hall, Fairfield, CT 06824-5195, (203)254-4000

Intl. Inst. of Fisheries Economics and Trade [1484], Dept. of Agricultural and Rsrc. Economics, Oregon State Univ., Corvallis, OR 97331-3601, (541)737-1439

Intl. Inst. of Fisheries Economics and Trade [IO], Corvallis, OR, United States

Intl. Inst. of Foods and Family Living - Defunct.

Intl. Inst. of Forecasters [7106], c/o Ms. Pamela Stroud, Bus. Mgr., 53 Tesla Ave., Medford, MA 02155, (781)234-4077

Intl. Inst. of Forecasters [IO], Medford, MA, United States

Intl. Inst. for Frame Stud. [9991]

Intl. Inst. for Geo-Information Sci. and Earth Observation [IO], Enschede, Netherlands

International Inst. for Hearing Instruments Stud. [★IO]

International Inst. for Hearing Instruments Stud. [★14763]

Intl. Inst. of Human Rights [IO], Strasbourg, France

Intl. Inst. of Humanitarian Law [IO], Sanremo, Italy

Intl. Inst. of Iberoamerican Literature [IO], Pittsburgh, PA, United States

Intl. Inst. of Iberoamerican Literature [10425], Univ. of Pittsburgh, 1312 Cathedral of Learning, Pittsburgh, PA 15260, (412)624-3359

Intl. Inst. for Infrastructural, Hydraulic and Environmental Engg. [★IO]

Intl. Inst. of Integral Human Sciences [IO], Montreal, QC, Canada

Intl. Inst. of Investment and Merchant Banking - Defunct.

Intl. Inst. of Islamic Thought [10247], 500 Grove St., Herndon, VA 20170, (703)471-1133

Intl. Inst. of Islamic Thought [IO], Herndon, VA, United States

Intl. Inst. of Islamic Thought and Civilization [IO], Kuala Lumpur, Malaysia

Intl. Inst. for Labour Stud. [IO], Geneva, Switzerland

Intl. Inst. for Land Reclamation and Improvement [IO], Wageningen, Netherlands

International Institute for Lath and Plaster [IO], Lafayette, CA, United States

Intl. Inst. for Lath and Plaster [1026], PO Box 1663, Lafayette, CA 94549, (925)283-5160

Intl. Inst. for Ligurian Stud. [IO], Bordighera, Italy

Intl. Inst. for Mgt. Development [IO], Lausanne, Switzerland

Intl. Inst. for the Mgt. of Technology - Defunct.

Intl. Inst. of Municipal Clerks [6124], 8331 Utica Ave., Ste. 200, Rancho Cucamonga, CA 91730, (909)944-4162

Intl. Inst. of Municipal Clerks [IO], Rancho Cucamonga, CA, United States

Intl. Inst. for Music, Dance, and Theatre in the Audio-Visual Media [★IO]

Intl. Inst. of Peace Stud. and Global Philosophy [IO], Llanerfyl, United Kingdom

Intl. Inst. of Philosophy - U.S. Center - Defunct.

Intl. Inst. of Photographic Arts [3003], 1690 Frontage Rd., Chula Vista, CA 91911, (619)628-1466

Intl. Inst. of Photographic Arts [IO], Chula Vista, CA, United States

Intl. Inst. for Promotion and Prestige [IO], Geneva, Switzerland

Intl. Inst. of Public Finance [IO], Munich, Germany

International Institute of Reflexology [IO], St. Petersburg, FL, United States

Intl. Inst. of Reflexology [IO], Sheffield, United Kingdom

Intl. Inst. of Reflexology [16620], PO Box 12642, St. Petersburg, FL 33733-2642, (727)343-4811

Intl. Inst. of Refrigeration [IO], Paris, France

Intl. Inst. of Rehabilitation - Defunct.

Intl. Inst. for Resource Economics - Defunct.

Intl. Inst. of Risk and Safety Mgt. [IO], London, United Kingdom

Intl. Inst. for Robotics - Defunct.

Intl. Inst. of Rural Reconstruction, U.S. Chap. [12938], 333 E 38th St., 6th Fl., New York, NY 10016-2772, (212)880-9147

Intl. Inst. of Rural Reconstruction, U.S. Chap. [IO], New York, NY, United States

Intl. Inst. for Safety in Transportation - Address unknown since 1995.

Intl. Inst. for the Sci. of Sintering [IO], Belgrade, Serbia

Intl. Inst. of Security [IO], Paignton, United Kingdom

Intl. Inst. of Seismology and Earthquake Engg. [IO], Tsukuba, Japan

Intl. Inst. of Site Planning [IO], Washington, DC, United States

Intl. Inst. of Site Planning [5465], 715 G St. SE, Washington, DC 20003, (202)546-2322

Intl. Inst. of Social History [IO], Amsterdam, Netherlands

Intl. Inst. of Sociology [IO], Stanford, CA, United States

Intl. Inst. of Sociology [7663], c/o Prof. Karen S. Cook, Gen. Sec.-Treas., Stanford Univ., Dept. of Sociology, Stanford, CA 94305

Intl. Inst. of Space Law [IO], Paris, France

Intl. Inst. of Space Law; Assn. of U.S. Members of the [6372]

Intl. Inst. for Strategic Stud. [IO], London, United Kingdom

Intl. Inst. for Strategic Stud. - US [IO], Washington, DC, United States

Intl. Inst. for Strategic Stud. - US [18396], 1850 K St. NW, Ste. 300, Washington, DC 20006, (202)659-1490

Intl. Inst. for the String Bass [★10625]

Intl. Inst. for the String Bass [★IO]

Intl. Inst. for the Stud. of Death [IO], Aventura, FL, United States

Intl. Inst. for the Stud. of Death [13315], 1000 Island Blvd., No. 512, Aventura, FL 33160, (305)936-1408

Intl. Inst. for the Stud. of Death and Immortality [★13315]

Intl. Inst. for the Stud. of Death and Immortality [★IO]

Intl. Inst. for Sustainable Development [IO], Winnipeg, MB, Canada

Intl. Inst. of Synthetic Rubber Producers [IO], Houston, TX, United States

Intl. Inst. of Synthetic Rubber Producers [3432], 2077 S Gessner Rd., Ste. 133, Houston, TX 77063, (713)783-7511

Intl. Inst. of Tropical Agriculture [IO], Ibadan, Nigeria

Intl. Inst. of Tropical Agriculture - United Kingdom [IO], Croydon, United Kingdom

Intl. Inst. for the Unification of Private Law [IO], Rome, Italy

Intl. Inst. for the Visually Impaired [★16834]

Intl. Inst. of Welding [IO], Roissy, France

Intl. Inst. of Welding; Amer. Coun. of the [7846]

Intl. Inst. for Women's Political Leadership - Defunct.

Intl. -Inst. of World Affairs; Universities Field Staff [★8663]

Intl. Institution for Production Engg. Res. [IO], Paris, France

Intl. Institutional Services - Address unknown since 2001.

Intl. Insurance Coun. - Defunct.

Intl. Insurance Seminars [★2190]

Intl. Insurance Seminars [★IO]

Intl. Insurance Soc. [IO], New York, NY, United States

Intl. Insurance Soc. [2190], 101 Murray St., New York, NY 10007-2165, (212)815-9291

Intl. Intellectual Property Alliance [5847], c/o Eric H. Smith, Pres./Co-Founder, 800 Connecticut Ave. NW, Ste. 500, Washington, DC 20006, (202)833-4198

Intl. Intellectual Property Alliance [IO], Washington, DC, United States

Intl. Intellectual Property Assn. [IO], Washington, DC, United States

Intl. Intellectual Property Assn. [5848], 1255 23rd St. NW, Ste. 200, Washington, DC 20037, (202)466-2396

Intl. Intelligence Network [3532], PO Box 350, Gladwyne, PA 19035, (610)520-9222

Intl. Intelligence Network [IO], Gladwyne, PA, United States

Intl. Intelligent Buildings Assn. - Defunct.

Intl. Interior Design Assn. [2265], 222 Merchandise Mart Plz., Ste. 1540, Chicago, IL 60654, (312)467-1950

Intl. Interior Design Assn. [IO], Chicago, IL, United States

Intl. Internet Leather Crafters' Guild [IO], Cary, MS, United States

Intl. Internet Leather Crafters' Guild [2414], c/o Pat Hay, Treas., PO Box 98, Cary, MS 39054

Intl. Internet Marketing Assn. [IO], Vancouver, BC, Canada

Intl. Intradiscal Therapy Soc. [IO], Belgium, WI, United States

Intl. Intradiscal Therapy Soc. [16464], 810 North St., Belgium, WI 53004-9531, (262)285-4487

Intl. Inventor's Assn. - Defunct.

Intl. Iridology Practitioners Assn. [15687], PO Box 72601, Newnan, GA 30271, (888)682-2208

International Iridology Practitioners Association [IO], Pinehurst, TX, United States

Intl. Iridology Res. Assn. [★IO]

Intl. Iridology Res. Assn. [★15687]

Intl. Iron and Steel Inst. [IO], Brussels, Belgium

Intl. Irrigation Mgt. Inst. [★IO]

Intl. ISBN Agency [IO], London, United Kingdom

Intl. Islamic Charitable Org. - Defunct.

Intl. Islamic Fed. of Student Orgs. [10248]

Intl. Islamic News Agency [IO], Jeddah, Saudi Arabia

Intl. Isotope Soc. [IO], Litchfield, CT, United States

Intl. Isotope Soc. [6548], c/o Dr. Brad D. Maxwell, Pres., PO Box 4000, Princeton, NJ 08543, (609)252-5015

Intl. Ivory Soc. [9832], c/o Robert Weisblut, Founder, 11109 Nicholas Dr., Wheaton, MD 20902

Intl. Ivory Soc. [IO], Wheaton, MD, United States

Intl. J/22 Class Assn. [IO], Lakewood, OH, United States

Intl. J/22 Class Assn. [23187], c/o Christopher E. Howell, Exec. Sec., 12900 Lake Ave., No. 2001, Lakewood, OH 44107, (440)796-3100

Intl. Jack Benny Fan Club [24798], PO Box 11288, Piedmont, CA 94611

Intl. Jack Benny Fan Club [IO], Piedmont, CA, United States

Intl. Japanese Philatelic Specialists Stud. Club [★IO]

Intl. Japanese Philatelic Specialists Stud. Club [★22830]

Intl. Jazz Fed. [★10632]

Intl. Jazz Fed. [★IO]

Intl. Jelly and Preserve Assn. [IO], Atlanta, GA, United States

Intl. Jelly and Preserve Assn. [1530], 5775 Peachtree-Dunwoody Rd., Ste. 500-G, Atlanta, GA 30342, (404)252-3663

Intl. Jet Ski Boating Assn. [★23976]

Intl. Jet Ski Boating Assn. [★IO]

Intl. Jet Sports Boating Assn. and Amer. Watercraft Assn. [IO], Half Moon Bay, CA, United States

Intl. Jet Sports Boating Assn. and Amer. Watercraft Assn. [23976], 330 Purissima St., Ste. C, Half Moon Bay, CA 94019, (714)751-8695

Intl. Jewelry Design Guild [2368], c/o Stacy Blackshaw, Exec. Dir., 19 Mantua Rd., Mount Royal, NJ 08061, (856)423-7222

Intl. Jewelry Design Guild [IO], Mount Royal, NJ, United States

Intl. Jewelry Workers Union [★IO]

Intl. Jewelry Workers Union [★24189]

Intl. Jewish Comm. on Interreligious Consultations - Address unknown since 1999.

Intl. Jewish Media Assn. - Address unknown since 2000.

Intl. Jewish Vegetarian Soc. [IO], London, United Kingdom

Intl. Jigsaw Puzzle Soc. - Defunct.

Intl. John Steinbeck Soc. - Defunct.

Intl. Joint Commn. [5040], 1250 23rd St. NW, Ste. 100, Washington, DC 20440, (202)736-9024

Reference to "IO" in place of a book number signifies that the association may be found in the 45th edition of International Organizations.

Intl. Joint Commn. [IO], Washington, DC, United States

Intl. Joint Painting, Decorating and Drywall Apprenticeship and Manpower Training Fund [★IO]

Intl. Joint Painting, Decorating and Drywall Apprenticeship and Manpower Training Fund [★12082]

Intl. Joseph A. Schumpeter Soc. [IO], Augsburg, Germany

Intl. Joseph Disease Found. - Defunct.

Intl. Judo Fed. [IO], Seoul, Republic of Korea

Intl. Jugglers' Assn. [IO], Austin, TX, United States

Intl. Jugglers' Assn. [23557], PO Box 7307, Austin, TX 78713-7307, (415)596-3307

Intl. Jumper Futurity [23528], PO Box 1445, Georgetown, KY 40324, (502)535-6787

Intl. Junior Brangus Breeders Assn. [4266], 5750 Epsilon Dr., San Antonio, TX 78249, (210)696-4343

International Junior Brangus Breeders Association [IO], San Antonio, TX, United States

International Junior Charolais Association [★IO]

International Junior Charolais Association [★4228]

Intl. Juridical Inst. [★IO]

Intl. Justice and Human Rights, Natl. Coun. of Churches of Christ USA [IO], New York, NY, United States

Intl. Justice and Human Rights, Natl. Coun. of Churches of Christ USA [12376], c/o NCC Communications Dept., 475 Riverside Dr., Ste. 880, New York, NY 10115, (212)870-2227

Intl. Justice Mission [5803], PO Box 58147, Washington, DC 20037-8147, (703)465-5495

Intl. Justice Mission [IO], Washington, DC, United States

Intl. Justice Network - Defunct.

Intl. Justice and Peace; Office of [★19613]

Intl. Justice and Peace; Office of [★IO]

Intl. Juvenile Officers' Assn. - Address unknown since 2005.

Intl. Kart Fed. [23568], 1609 S Grove Ave., Ste. 105, Ontario, CA 91761, (909)923-4999

Intl. Kart Fed. [IO], Ontario, CA, United States

Intl. KCI [★IO]

Intl. KCI [★13046]

Intl. Kennel Club of Chicago [22289], 6222 W North Ave., Chicago, IL 60639, (773)237-5100

Intl. Kennel Soc. [22290]

Intl. Kennel Soc. [IO], Blooming Prairie, MN, United States

Intl. Kindergarten Union [★IO]

Intl. Kindergarten Union [★8064]

Intl. King Midget Car Club [21667], c/o Paula Jasper, Sec., 2425 Ervin Ln., Stockport, OH 43787, (740)559-3983

Intl. Kirlian Res. Assn. - Defunct.

Intl. Kitchen Exhaust Cleaning Assn. [1475], 12339 Carroll Ave., Rockville, MD 20852, (301)230-0099

Intl. Kitefliers Assn. - Defunct.

Intl. Klaus Tennstedt Soc. - Defunct.

Intl. Kodak Historical Soc. [10850], PO Box 21, Flourtown, PA 19031

International Kodak Historical Society [IO], Flourtown, PA, United States

Intl. Kodaly Soc. [IO], Budapest, Hungary

Intl. Kolping Soc. [IO], Cologne, Germany

Intl. Korfball Fed. [IO], Zeist, Netherlands

Intl. Labelling Centre - Defunct.

Intl. Labor Communications Assn., AFL-CIO/CLC [3229], 815 16th St. NW, Washington, DC 20006, (202)637-5068

Intl. Labor History Assn. [5916], 706 Bruce Ct., Madison, WI 53705, (608)231-1886

Intl. Labor History Assn. [IO], Madison, WI, United States

Intl. Labor Off. [★IO]

Intl. Labor Off. [★24207]

Intl. Labor Org. - U.S. [24207]

Intl. Labor Org. - U.S. [IO], Washington, DC, United States

Intl. Labor Press of Am. [★3229]

Intl. Labor Press Assn. [★3229]

Intl. Labor Rights Educ. and Res. Fund [★17973]

Intl. Labor Rights Educ. and Res. Fund [★IO]

Intl. Labor Rights Fund [IO], Washington, DC, United States

Intl. Labor Rights Fund [17973], 2001 South St. NW, No. 420, Washington, DC 20009, (202)347-4100

Intl. Labor and Working Class History Study Group - Defunct.

Intl. Labour Film Inst. - Defunct.

Intl. Labour Off. - Switzerland [IO], Geneva, Switzerland

Intl. Labour Org. [IO], Geneva, Switzerland

Intl. Labour Org. Ankara [IO], Ankara, Turkey

Intl. Labour Org. Beijing Off. [IO], Beijing, People's Republic of China

Intl. Labour Org. Cairo Off. [IO], Cairo, Egypt

Intl. Labour Org. Caribbean Off. [IO], Port of Spain, Trinidad and Tobago

Intl. Labour Org. Jakarta Off. [IO], Jakarta, Indonesia

Intl. Labour Org. Off. for the European Union and the Benelux countries [IO], Brussels, Belgium

Intl. Labour Org. Off. in Germany: ILO-Berlin [IO], Berlin, Germany

Intl. Labour Org. Off. for Italy and San Marino [IO], Rome, Italy

Intl. Labour Org. Off. for the United Kingdom and Republic of Ireland [IO], London, United Kingdom

Intl. Labour Org. Regional Off. for Africa [IO], Abidjan, Cote d'Ivoire

Intl. Labour Org. Regional Off. for the Arab States [IO], Beirut, Lebanon

Intl. Labour Org. Regional Off. for Asia and the Pacific [IO], Bangkok, Thailand

Intl. Labour Org. Subregional Off. - Budapest Off. [IO], Budapest, Hungary

Intl. Labour Org. Subregional Off. for East Asia [IO], Bangkok, Thailand

Intl. Labour Org. Subregional Off. for Eastern Europe and Central Asia [IO], Moscow, Russia

Intl. Labour Org. Subregional Off. for South Asia [IO], New Delhi, India

Intl. Labour Org. Subregional Off. for South-East Asia and the Pacific [IO], Makati City, Philippines

Intl. Labour Org. Subregional Off. for Southern Africa [IO], Harare, Zimbabwe

Intl. Labour Org. Suva Off. [IO], Suva, Fiji

Intl. Lacrosse Fed. [IO], Gilgo Beach, NY, United States

Intl. Lacrosse Fed. [23570], 4117 Gilgo E, Gilgo Beach, NY 11702, (631)630-4433

Intl. Lactation Consultant Assn. [12410], 1500 Sunday Dr., Ste. 102, Raleigh, NC 27607, (919)861-5577

Intl. Lactation Consultant Assn. [IO], Raleigh, NC, United States

Intl. Lama Registry [IO], Kalispell, MT, United States

Intl. Lama Registry [21519], PO Box 8, Kalispell, MT 59903, (406)755-3438

Intl. Landslide Res. Gp. [7146], c/o Earl E. Brabb, Emeritus Pres./Ed., 4377 Newland Heights Dr., Rocklin, CA 95765

Intl. Landslide Res. Gp. [IO], Rocklin, CA, United States

Intl. Laser Acupuncture Soc. - Address unknown since 1999.

Intl. Laser Display Assn. [1309], 7062 Edgeworth Dr., Orlando, FL 32819, (407)797-7654

Intl. Laser Display Assn. [IO], Orlando, FL, United States

Intl. Laser Tag Assn. [1716], 5351 E Thompson Rd., Ste. 236, Indianapolis, IN 46237, (317)786-9755

Intl. Latino Gang Investigator's Assn. [5884], 4057 Hwy. 9, PMB 108, Howell, NJ 07731-3307

International Latino Gang Investigator's Association [IO], Howell, NJ, United States

Intl. Laughter Soc. [IO], Los Gatos, CA, United States

Intl. Laughter Soc. [10188], 16000 Glen Una Dr., Los Gatos, CA 95030, (408)354-3456

International Law

African Inst. of Private Intl. Law [IO]

Amer. Bar Assn. Sect. of Intl. Law [IO]

Amer. Bar Assn. Sect. of Intl. Law [5863]

Amer. Foreign Law Assn. [5864]

Amer. Soc. of Comparative Law [5865]

Amer. Soc. of Intl. Law [5866]

Amer. Soc. of Intl. Law [IO]

Assn. of Attenders and Alumni of The Hague Acad. of Intl. Law [IO]

Australian and New Zealand Soc. of Intl. Law [IO]

British Inst. of Intl. and Comparative Law [IO]

Canadian Coun. on Intl. Law [IO]

Centre for Stud. and Res. in Intl. Law and Intl. Relations [IO]

Chinese Law Soc. of Am. [5933]

Coalition for an Intl. Criminal Court [17361]

Friends of Sabeel - North Am. [18205]

Hague Conf. on Private Intl. Law [IO]

Inst. of Intl. Law [IO]

Intl. Criminal Court Alliance [5654]

Intl. Law Assn. [IO]

Intl. Law Assn., Japan Br. [IO]

Intl. Law Assn., Swiss Br. [IO]

Intl. Law Inst. [IO]

Intl. Law Inst. [5867]

Intl. Law Students Assn. [5868]

Intl. Law Students Assn. [IO]

Intl. Legal Defense Counsel [IO]

Intl. Legal Defense Counsel [5869]

Intl. Legal Inst. [IO]

A Jewish Voice for Peace [19184]

Law of the Sea Inst. [6054]

Singapore Inst. of Intl. Affairs [IO]

Win Without War [18124]

World Assn. of Judges [5870]

World Assn. of Judges [IO]

World Assn. of Law Professors [IO]

World Assn. of Law Professors [5871]

World Assn. of Law Students and Young Jurists [5872]

World Assn. of Law Students and Young Jurists [IO]

World Assn. of Lawyers [IO]

World Assn. of Lawyers [5873]

World Bus. Associates [5874]

World Bus. Associates [IO]

World Jurist Assn. [IO]

World Jurist Assn. [5875]

World Soc. of Mixed Jurisdiction Jurists [5957]

Intl. Law Assn. [IO], London, United Kingdom

Intl. Law Assn., German Br. [IO], Saarbrucken, Germany

Intl. Law Assn., Indian Br. [IO], New Delhi, India

Intl. Law Assn., Japan Br. [IO], Tokyo, Japan

Intl. Law Assn., Korean Br. [IO], Seoul, Republic of Korea

Intl. Law Assn., Norwegian Br. [IO], Oslo, Norway

Intl. Law Assn., South African Br. [IO], Durban, Republic of South Africa

Intl. Law Assn., Swedish Br. [IO], Stockholm, Sweden

Intl. Law Assn., Swiss Br. [IO], Zurich, Switzerland

Intl. Law Enforcement Educators and Trainers Assn. [IO], Twin Lakes, WI, United States

Intl. Law Enforcement Educators and Trainers Assn. [5978], PO Box 1003, Twin Lakes, WI 53181-1003, (262)279-7879

Intl. Law Enforcement Officers Assn. - Address unknown since 1990.

Intl. Law Enforcement Stress Assn. - Address unknown since 2002.

Intl. Law Inst. [5867], The Foundry Bldg., 1055 Thomas Jefferson St. NW, Washington, DC 20007, (202)247-6006

Intl. Law Inst. [IO], Washington, DC, United States

Intl. Law Students Assn. [IO], Chicago, IL, United States

Intl. Law Students Assn. [5868], 25 E Jackson Blvd., Ste. 518, Chicago, IL 60604, (312)362-5025

Intl. Lawrence Durrell Soc. [9662], c/o Paul H. Lorenz, Sec.-Treas., 3201 S Beech St., No. 40, Pine Bluff, AR 71603, (870)575-8618

International Lawrence Durrell Society [IO], Pine Bluff, AR, United States

Intl. Lawyers in Alcoholics Anonymous [13253], c/o Eli Gauna, Sec., 14123 Victory Blvd., Van Nuys, CA 91401

Intl. Lead Zinc Res. Org. [7316], 2525 Meridian Pkwy., Ste. 100, Durham, NC 27713, (919)361-4647

Intl. Lead Zinc Res. Org. [IO], Durham, NC, United States

Intl. Lead and Zinc Study Group [IO], Lisbon, Portugal

A star before a book entry number signifies that the name is not listed separately, but is mentioned within the entry.

Intl. Leadership Center - Defunct.

Intl. League Against Epilepsy [IO], Brussels, Belgium

Intl. League Against Epilepsy of United Kingdom [IO], London, United Kingdom

Intl. League Against Rheumatism [★IO]

Intl. League of Antiquarian Booksellers [IO], Merchantville, NJ, United States

Intl. League of Antiquarian Booksellers [3411], c/o Tom Congalton, 35 W Maple Ave., Merchantville, NJ 08109-5141, (856)665-2284

Intl. League of Associations for Rheumatology [IO], Brisbane, Australia

Intl. League for Bolivarian Action - Address unknown since 1995.

Intl. League of Competition Law [IO], Lausanne, Switzerland

Intl. League of Competition Law, Austria [IO], Vienna, Austria

Intl. League for Competition Law, Brazil [IO], Rio de Janeiro, Brazil

Intl. League for Competition Law, Czech Republic [IO], Prague, Czech Republic

Intl. League for Competition Law, Japan [IO], Tokyo, Japan

Intl. League for Competition Law, Nordic Countries [IO], Stockholm, Sweden

Intl. League of Conservation Photographers [IO], Great Falls, VA, United States

Intl. League of Conservation Photographers [5080], 432 Walker Rd., Great Falls, VA 22066, (703)304-1440

Intl. League of Elecl. Associations [1188], 12165 W Center Rd., Ste. 59, Omaha, NE 68144, (402)330-7227

Intl. League of Elecl. Associations [IO], Omaha, NE, United States

Intl. League of Esperantist Teachers [IO], The Hague, Netherlands

Intl. League for Human Rights [IO], New York, NY, United States

Intl. League for Human Rights [17769], 352 7th Ave., Ste. 1234, New York, NY 10001, (212)661-0480

Intl. League of New York - Defunct.

Intl. League of Non-Religious and Atheists [IO], Hagen, Germany

Intl. League of Professional Baseball Clubs [23110], 55 S High St., Ste. 202, Dublin, OH 43017, (614)791-9300

Intl. League for the Protection of Horses [IO], Snetterton, United Kingdom

Intl. League for the Repatriation of Russian Jews - Defunct.

Intl. League for the Rights of Man [★17769]

Intl. League for the Rights of Man [★IO]

Intl. League of Societies for the Mentally Handicapped [★IO]

Intl. League of Societies for Persons with Mental Handicap [★IO]

Intl. League of Women Composers - Address unknown since 2001.

Intl. Leather Goods, Plastic and Novelty Workers' Union - Address unknown since 2005.

Intl. Legal Aid Assn. - Defunct.

Intl. Legal Center [★5942]

Intl. Legal Center [★IO]

Intl. Legal Defense Counsel [IO], New York, NY, United States

Intl. Legal Defense Counsel [5869], 405 Lexington Ave., 26th Fl., New York, NY 10174, (212)907-6442

Intl. Legal Inst. [IO], The Hague, Netherlands

International Legion of Intelligence [★9984]

Intl. Leprosy Assn. [IO], New Delhi, India

Intl. Leptospirosis Soc. [IO], La Jolla, CA, United States

Intl. Leptospirosis Soc. [14950], c/o Prof. Joseph Vinetz, Sec., Univ. of California San Diego School of Medicine, Div. of Infectious Diseases, 9500 Gilman Dr., La Jolla, CA 92093-0741, (858)822-4469

Intl. Lesbian and Gay Assn. [IO], Brussels, Belgium

Intl. Lesbian and Gay Assn. - Intl. Assn. of Lesbians/Gay Women and Gay Men [★IO]

Intl. Lexical Functional Grammar Assn. [IO], Palo Alto, CA, United States

Intl. Lexical Functional Grammar Assn. [8732], c/o Tracy Holloway King, Palo Alto Res. Ctr., 3333 Coyote Hill Rd., Palo Alto, CA 94304, (650)812-4808

Intl. Liaison of Lay Volunteers in Mission (U.S. Catholic Network of Lay Mission Programs) [★19602]

Intl. Liaison U.S. Catholic Coordinating Center for Lay Missioners [★19602]

Intl. Liaison, U.S. Catholic Coordinating Center for Lay Volunteer Ministries [★19602]

Intl. Liaison for Volunteer Ser. [★19602]

Intl. Library Information Center - Defunct.

Intl. Licensing Indus. Merchandisers' Assn. [5849], 350 5th Ave., Ste. 1408, New York, NY 10118, (212)244-1944

Intl. Licensing Indus. Merchandisers' Assn. [IO], New York, NY, United States

Intl. Life Saving Fed. [IO], Leuven, Belgium

Intl. Life Sciences Inst., European Br. [IO], Brussels, Belgium

Intl. Life Sciences Inst. - North Am. [IO], Washington, DC, United States

Intl. Life Sciences Inst. - North Am. [15561], 1 Thomas Cir. NW, 9th Fl., Washington, DC 20005, (202)659-0074

Intl. Life Sciences Inst; North Amer. Br. of [★15561]

Intl. Life Sciences Inst. - Nutrition Found. [★15561]

Intl. Life Sciences Inst. - Nutrition Found. [★IO]

International Life Services [IO], Kennewick, WA, United States

Intl. Life Services [12916], c/o Life Org, 941 S Johnson St., Kennewick, WA 99336, (509)735-8518

Intl. Life Services Found. - Defunct.

Intl. Lifeboat Fed. [★IO]

Intl. Lifeline - Address unknown since 2004.

Intl. Lifesaving Museum and Water Safety Center - Defunct.

Intl. Light Tackle Tournament Assn. - Address unknown since 2002.

Intl. Lighter Collectors; On the Lighter Side, [22100]

Intl. Lightning Class Assn. [23188], c/o Jan Davis, Exec. Sec., 7625 S Yampa St., Centennial, CO 80016, (303)325-5886

Intl. Lightning Class Assn. [IO], Centennial, CO, United States

Intl. Lignin Inst. [IO], Lausanne, Switzerland

International Lilac Society [IO], Cohoes, NY, United States

Intl. Lilac Soc. [22522], c/o William F. Tschumi, 3 Paradise Ct., Cohoes, NY 12047-1422, (440)946-4400

Intl. Linear Algebra Soc. [7290], c/o Jeffrey L. Stuart, Sec.-Treas., Pacific Lutheran Univ., Dept. of Mathematics, Tacoma, WA 98447

Intl. Linear Algebra Soc. [IO], Tacoma, WA, United States

Intl. Linen Promotion Commn. - Defunct.

Intl. Liquid Crystal Soc. [6853], c/o Joseph E. Maclennan, Dept. of Physics, Univ. of Colorado, 390 UCB, Boulder, CO 80309-0390, (303)492-7543

Intl. Liquid Crystal Soc. [IO], Boulder, CO, United States

Intl. Listening Assn. [IO], River Falls, WI, United States

Intl. Listening Assn. [8270], PO Box 744, River Falls, WI 54022, (715)425-3377

Intl. Livedo Reticularis Network - Address unknown since 2002.

Intl. Liver Transplantation Soc. [16672], 15000 Commerce Pkwy., Ste. C, Mount Laurel, NJ 08054, (856)439-0500

Intl. Liver Transplantation Soc. [IO], Mount Laurel, NJ, United States

Intl. Livestock Brand Conf. [★4998]

Intl. Livestock Brand and Theft Conf. [★4998]

Intl. Livestock Identification Assn. [4998], c/o Rick Wahlert, Sec.-Treas., 4701 Marion St., Ste. 201, Denver, CO 80216, (303)294-0895

Intl. Livestock Identification and Theft Investigators Assn. [★4998]

Intl. Livestock Investigators Assn. [4999], c/o Rick Wahlert, Sec.-Treas., Capitol Sta., PO Box 202001, Helena, MT 59620-2001, (406)444-2043

Intl. Livestock Investigators Assn. [IO], Helena, MT, United States

Intl. Livestock Res. Inst. - Kenya [IO], Nairobi, Kenya

Intl. Llama Assn. - Defunct.

Intl. Log Rolling Assn. [23824], 711 Glenna Dr., Hudson, WI 54016

Intl. Log Rolling Assn. [IO], Hudson, WI, United States

International Longshore and Warehouse Union [IO], San Francisco, CA, United States

Intl. Longshore and Warehouse Union [24126], 1188 Franklin St., 4th Fl., San Francisco, CA 94109, (415)775-0533

Intl. Longshoremen's Assn. [24127], 17 Battery Pl., Ste. 930, New York, NY 10004, (212)425-1200

Intl. Longshoremen's and Warehousemen's Union [★24126]

Intl. Longshoremen's and Warehousemen's Union [★IO]

Intl. Loran Assn. [IO], Santa Barbara, CA, United States

Intl. Loran Assn. [7370], 741 Cathedral Pointe Ln., Santa Barbara, CA 93111, (805)967-8649

Intl. Luge Fed. [IO], Berchtesgaden, Germany

Intl. Luggage Repair Assn. [IO], Mayfield Heights, OH, United States

Intl. Luggage Repair Assn. [2440], 5102 Mayfield Rd., Mayfield Heights, OH 44124, (440)442-5910

Intl. Lunar Soc. - Address unknown since 1995.

Intl. Lutheran Deaf Assn. [20217], c/o John Krause, Treas., 9905 Madison St. NE, Blaine, MN 55434

Intl. Lutheran Deaf Assn. [IO], Blaine, MN, United States

Intl. Lutheran Laymen's League [IO], St. Louis, MO, United States

Intl. Lutheran Laymen's League [20218], 660 Mason Ridge Center, St. Louis, MO 63141, (800)876-9880

Intl. Lutheran Women's Missionary League [★20229]

Intl. Lyceum Assn. [★10901]

Intl. Lyceum Club Deutschland [★IO]

Intl. Lyme and Assoc. Diseases Soc. [IO], Bethesda, MD, United States

Intl. Lyme and Assoc. Diseases Soc. [14267], PO Box 341461, Bethesda, MD 20827-1461, (301)263-1080

Intl. Machine Quilters Assn. [22160], PO Box 419, Higginsville, MO 64037, (660)584-8171

Intl. Machine Quilters Assn. [IO], Higginsville, MO, United States

Intl. Machinery Insurers Assn. [★IO]

Intl. Magic Dealers Assn. - Address unknown since 2001.

Intl. Magnesium Assn. [2711], 1000 N Rand Rd., Ste. 214, Wauconda, IL 60084, (847)526-2010

Intl. Magnesium Assn. [IO], Wauconda, IL, United States

Intl. Magnetics Assn. [IO], Chicago, IL, United States

Intl. Magnetics Assn. [1824], 8 S Michigan Ave., Ste. 1000, Chicago, IL 60603, (312)456-5590

Intl. Mail Art Network - Defunct.

Intl. Mail Dealers Assn. - Address unknown since 1988.

Intl. Mailers Union [★24086]

Intl. Maillard Reaction Soc. [6683], Wolstein Bldg., 2103 Cornell Rd., Rm. 5127, Cleveland, OH 44106, (216)368-2930

Intl. Maine-Anjou Assn. [★4234]

Intl. Maintenance Inst. [2465], PO Box 751896, Houston, TX 77275-1896, (281)481-0869

Intl. Maintenance Inst. [IO], Houston, TX, United States

Intl. Maize and Wheat Improvement Center [IO], Mexico City, Mexico

Intl. Maledicta Soc. [IO], Santa Rosa, CA, United States

Intl. Maledicta Soc. [10404], PO Box 14123, Santa Rosa, CA 95402-6123, (707)795-8178

Intl. Mgt. Assn. of Japan [IO], Tokyo, Japan

Intl. Mgt. Coun. of the YMCA [★2509]

Intl. Mgt. Coun. of the YMCA - Defunct.

Intl. Mgt. Development Assn. [735], PO Box 216, Hummelstown, PA 17036, (717)566-3054

Intl. Mgt. Development Assn. [IO], Hummelstown, PA, United States

Reference to "IO" in place of a book number signifies that the association may be found in the 45th edition of International Organizations.

Intl. Managers Forum [★IO]
Intl. Manganese Inst. [IO], Paris, France
Intl. Manuel Ponce Soc. [IO], Dallas, TX, United States
Intl. Manuel Ponce Soc. [10621], PO Box 59152, Dallas, TX 75229, (972)293-5360
Intl. Mfrs. Representatives Assn. [360], PO Box 702678, Tulsa, OK 74170
Intl. Map Collectors' Soc. [IO], London, United Kingdom
Intl. Map Dealers Assn. [★IO]
Intl. Map Dealers Assn. [★6655]
Intl. Map Trade Assn. [6655], PMB 281, 2629 Manhattan Ave., Hermosa Beach, CA 90254-2411, (310)376-7731
Intl. Map Trade Assn. [IO], Hermosa Beach, CA, United States
Intl. Maple Syrup Inst. [IO], Ferrisburg, VT, United States
Intl. Maple Syrup Inst. [1531], c/o Larry Myott, Exec. Sec., 5014 Rte. 7, Ferrisburg, VT 05456, (802)877-2250
Intl. Marble Collectors Assn. - Defunct.
Intl. Marchigiana Soc; Amer. [4229]
Intl. Marina Inst. [★2602]
Intl. Marina Inst. [★IO]
International Marine Animal Trainers Association [IO], Chicago, IL, United States
Intl. Marine Animal Trainers Assn. [6401], 1200 S Lake Shore Dr., Chicago, IL 60605, (312)692-3193
Intl. Marine Contractors Assn. [IO], London, United Kingdom
Intl. Marine Minerals Soc. [IO], Honolulu, HI, United States
Intl. Marine Minerals Soc. [5009], Univ. of Hawaii, 1000 Pope Rd., MSB 303, Honolulu, HI 96822, (808)956-6036
Intl. Marinelife Alliance - Philippines [IO], Quezon City, Philippines
Intl. Maritime Comm. [IO], Antwerp, Belgium
Intl. Maritime Hea. Assn. [IO], Antwerp, Belgium
Intl. Maritime Indus. Forum [IO], London, United Kingdom
Intl. Maritime Org. [IO], London, United Kingdom
Intl. Maritime Pilots' Assn. [IO], London, United Kingdom
Intl. Maritime Rescue Fed. [IO], Poole, United Kingdom
Intl. Maritime Satellite Org. [IO], London, United Kingdom
Intl. Mark Twain Soc. - Defunct.
Intl. Marketing Audit Assn. - Defunct.
Intl. Marketing Inst. - Defunct.
Intl. Marking and Identification Assn. [3683], 655 Rockland Rd., Ste. 5, Lake Bluff, IL 60044, (847)283-9810
Intl. Marking and Identification Assn. [IO], Lake Bluff, IL, United States
Intl. Martial Arts Fed. [IO], Tokyo, Japan
Intl. Martial Arts League [IO], Fort Wayne, IN, United States
Intl. Martial Arts League [23589], c/o John Pendergrass, Pres., 12820 N Shore Dr., Fort Wayne, IN 46818, (219)625-2389
Intl. Martial Arts Pen Pal Assn. - Defunct.
Intl. Masonry Inst. [1027], The James Brice House, 42 East St., Annapolis, MD 21401, (410)280-1305
Intl. Masonry Inst. [IO], Annapolis, MD, United States
Intl. Mass Transit Assn. - Address unknown since 1994.
Intl. Massage Assn. [15030], PO Box 421, Warrenton, VA 20188-0421, (540)351-0800
Intl. Massage Assn. [IO], Warrenton, VA, United States
Intl. Match Safe Assn. [IO], Malaga, NJ, United States
Intl. Match Safe Assn. [22053], PO Box 791, Malaga, NJ 08328, (856)694-4167
Intl. Material Mgt. Soc. [★7282]
Intl. Material Mgt. Soc. [★IO]
Intl. Mathematical Union [IO], La Jolla, CA, United States
Intl. Matrix Gp. [★IO]
Intl. Matrix Gp. [★7290]

Intl. MC Class Sailboat Racing Assn. [★23199]
Intl. Measurement Confed. [IO], Budapest, Hungary
Intl. Meat Secretariat [IO], Paris, France
Intl. Medalist Assn. [IO], Baltimore, MD, United States
Intl. Medalist Assn. [23825], 1 E Chase St., Ste. 11, Baltimore, MD 21202, (240)464-7444
Intl. Media Buyers Assn. - Defunct.
Intl. Medical Assn. for Radio and TV [★IO]
Intl. Medical Cooperation Comm. [IO], Copenhagen, Denmark
Intl. Medical Corps [IO], Santa Monica, CA, United States
Intl. Medical Corps [12862], 1919 Santa Monica Blvd., Ste. 400, Santa Monica, CA 90404, (310)826-7800
Intl. Medical and Dental Hypnotherapy Assn. [14924], Box 2468, Laceyville, PA 18623, (570)869-1021
Intl. Medical and Dental Hypnotherapy Assn. [IO], Laceyville, PA, United States
Intl. Medical Equip. Collaborative [IO], North Andover, MA, United States
Intl. Medical Equip. Collaborative [14569], 1600 Osgood St., 30-1 Y-8, North Andover, MA 01845, (978)557-5510
Intl. Medical Exchange - Defunct.
Intl. Medical Informatics Assn. [IO], Edmonton, AB, Canada
Intl. Medical Relief Fund/Salvadoran Medical Relief Fund - Defunct.
Intl. Medical and Res. Found. [★14971]
Intl. Medical and Res. Found. [★IO]
Intl. Medical Services for Hea. [★IO]
Intl. Medical Services for Hea. [★14981]
Intl. Medical Soc. for Bio-Physical Info. - Therapy Assn. [IO], Freiburg, Germany
Intl. Medical Soc. of Paraplegia [★IO]
Intl. Medical Spa Assn. [IO], Union City, NJ, United States
Intl. Medical Spa Assn. [1870], 310 17th St., Union City, NJ 07087, (201)865-2065
Intl. Medical Volunteers Assn. [15075], PO Box 205, Woodville, MA 01784, (508)435-7377
Intl. Medical Volunteers Assn. [IO], Woodville, MA, United States
Intl. Meeting in Community Ser. [IO], Stuttgart, Germany
Intl. Memorialization Supply Assn. [IO], Export, PA, United States
Intl. Memorialization Supply Assn. [2782], PO Box 663, Export, PA 15632, (800)864-4174
Intl. Meniere Fed. [IO], Vilvoorde, Belgium
Intl. Menopause Soc. [IO], Lancaster, United Kingdom
Intl. Mental Game Coaching Assn. [23289], 1523 Alma Terr., San Jose, CA 95125, (408)294-2776
Intl. Mentoring Network Org. [11520], 766 E 560 N, No. 206, Provo, UT 84606, (801)361-9942
Intl. Mentoring Network Org. [IO], Provo, UT, United States
Intl. Mercury Owners Assn. [21668], 6445 W Grand Ave., Chicago, IL 60707-3410, (773)622-6445
Intl. Messianic Jewish Alliance [20016], 72-877 Dinah Shore Dr., Ste. 103-141, Rancho Mirage, CA 92270, (760)668-3011
Intl. Messianic Jewish Alliance [IO], Rancho Mirage, CA, United States
Intl. Messianic Outreach - Address unknown since 1999.
Intl. Metal Decorators Assn. [1775], 9616 Deereco Rd., Timonium, MD 21093, (410)252-5205
Intl. Metallographic Soc. - Address unknown since 1993.
Intl. Metalworkers' Fed. [IO], Geneva, Switzerland
Intl. Metaphysical Assn. - Defunct.
Intl. Meteor Org. [IO], Hove, Belgium
International Meteorite Collectors Association [IO], Lehigh Acres, FL, United States
Intl. Meteorite Collectors Assn. [22981], c/o Mr. Norbert Classen, Pres., 115 Maple Ave. N, Lehigh Acres, FL 33936-6482
Intl. Meteorological Org. [★IO]
Intl. Methodist Historical Soc. [★IO]
Intl. Methodist Historical Soc. [★20273]

Intl. Methodist Historical Union [★20273]
Intl. Methodist Historical Union [★IO]
Intl. Microelectric and Packing Soc. [★IO]
Intl. Microelectric and Packing Soc. [★6930]
Intl. Microelectronic and Packaging Soc. [6930], 611 2nd St. NE, Washington, DC 20002-4909, (202)548-4001
Intl. Microelectronic and Packaging Soc. [IO], Washington, DC, United States
Intl. Microwave Power Inst. [IO], Mechanicsville, VA, United States
Intl. Microwave Power Inst. [7338], 7076 Drinkard Way, Mechanicsville, VA 23111, (804)559-6667
Intl. Midas Dealers Assn. [417], 14 W 3rd St., Ste. 200, Kansas City, MO 64152, (972)489-0602
Intl. Midas Dealers Assn. [IO], Kansas City, MO, United States
Intl. Middle East Associates - Address unknown since 1999.
Intl. MIDI Assn. - Address unknown since 2001.
Intl. Military Archives - Address unknown since 2001.
Intl. Military Community Executives Assn. [834], 1530 Dunwoody Village Pkwy., Ste. 203, Atlanta, GA 30338, (770)396-2101
Intl. Military Community Executives Assn. [IO], Atlanta, GA, United States
Intl. Military Recreation Assn. - Defunct.
Intl. Military Sports Coun. [IO], Brussels, Belgium
Intl. Milk Dealers Assn. [★IO]
Intl. Milk Dealers Assn. [★1135]
Intl. Milk Producers Assn. [4487], c/o NMPF, 2101 Wilson Blvd., Ste. 400, Arlington, VA 22201, (703)243-6111
Intl. Milk Producers Assn. [IO], Arlington, VA, United States
Intl. Mimes and Pantomimists - Defunct.
Intl. Mine Water Assn. [IO], Munich, Germany
Intl. Mineralogical Assn. [IO], Nancy, France
International Miniature Aircraft Association [IO], Redding, CA, United States
Intl. Miniature Aircraft Assn. [22938], c/o Jim Giffin, Pres./AMA Liaison, PO Box 494688, Redding, CA 96049, (916)760-8291
Intl. Miniature Cattle Breeders Soc. and Registry [4267], 25204 156th Ave. SE, Covington, WA 98042, (253)631-1911
Intl. Miniature Donkey Registry [5000], 1338 Hughes Shop Rd., Westminster, MD 21158, (410)875-0118
Intl. Miniature Donkey Registry [IO], Westminster, MD, United States
Intl. Miniature Horse Registry [★4830]
Intl. Miniature Zebu Assn. [4268], c/o Maureen Neidhardt, Registrar, PO Box 66, Crawford, NE 69339, (308)665-3919
Intl. Minilab Assn. - Defunct.
Intl. Ministerial Fed. - Defunct.
Intl. Ministries to Israel - Address unknown since 2000.
Intl. Mission Bd. [20350], PO Box 6767, Richmond, VA 23230-0767, (800)999-3113
Intl. Mission Bd. [IO], Richmond, VA, United States
Intl. Mission Radio Assn. - Address unknown since 2005.
Intl. Missions [★20315]
Intl. Missions [★IO]
Intl. Mistral Class Org. [23710], c/o Laura Lewandowski, 125 Eighth Ave., Indialantic, FL 32903, (321)953-5858
Intl. Mobile Air Conditioning Assn. - Defunct.
Intl. Mobile Hea. Assn. [14724], PO Box 7611, Huntington, WV 25777-7611, (228)238-9676
Intl. Mobile Hea. Assn. [IO], Huntington, WV, United States
Intl. Mobile Satellite Org. [IO], London, United Kingdom
International Mobjack Association [IO], Glen Allen, VA, United States
Intl. Mobjack Assn. [23189], 4803 Croft Ct., Glen Allen, VA 23060, (804)346-8761
Intl. Model Power Boat Assn. [22645], PO Box 1951, Huntsville, AL 35807-0951, (256)684-2986
Intl. Model Power Boat Assn. [IO], Huntsville, AL, United States
Intl. Modena Club [22896], c/o B. Tim Taylor, Sec.-Treas., 10032 Goodrich Rd., Bloomington, MN 55437-2413

A star before a book entry number signifies that the name is not listed separately, but is mentioned within the entry.

Intl. Modern Arnis Fed. Philippines **[IO]**, Mandaluyong City, Philippines

Intl. Molded Pulp Environmental Packaging Assn. **[IO]**, Mequon, WI, United States

Intl. Molded Pulp Environmental Packaging Assn. **[2888]**, 1425 W Mequon Rd., Ste. A, Mequon, WI 53092, (262)241-0522

Intl. Molders' and Allied Workers' Union **[★24066]**

The Intl. Molinological Soc. **[IO]**, Vaihingen, Germany

Intl. Molybdenum Assn. **[IO]**, Brussels, Belgium

Intl. Molyneux Family Assn. **[20953]**, PO Box 10306, Bainbridge Island, WA 98110, (206)842-0565

Intl. MOMS Club - Defunct.

Intl. Monetary Fund **[17462]**, 700 19th St. NW, Washington, DC 20431, (202)623-7000

Intl. Monetary Fund **[IO]**, Washington, DC, United States

Intl. Montessori Accreditation Coun. **[IO]**, Silver Spring, MD, United States

Intl. Montessori Accreditation Coun. **[8893]**, c/o Lee Havis, 9525 Georgia Ave., No. 200, Silver Spring, MD 20910, (301)589-1127

Intl. Montessori Assn. **[IO]**, Amsterdam, Netherlands

Intl. Montessori Soc. **[IO]**, Silver Spring, MD, United States

Intl. Montessori Soc. **[8894]**, 9525 Georgia Ave., No. 200, Silver Spring, MD 20910, (301)589-1127

Intl. Morab Breeders' Assn. **[4900]**, 24 Bauneg Rd., Sanford, ME 04073, (866)667-2246

International Morab Breeders' Association **[IO]**, Decatur, IL, United States

Intl. Morab Registry **[4901]**, c/o Intl. Morab Breeders Assn., 24 Bauneg Beg Rd., Sanford, ME 04073, (866)667-2246

Intl. Mothers' Peace Day Comm. **[18212]**, PO Box 102, West Liberty, WV 26074, (304)336-7159

Intl. Mothers' Peace Day Comm. **[IO]**, West Liberty, WV, United States

Intl. Motion Picture and Lecturers Assn. **[IO]**, San Leandro, CA, United States

Intl. Motion Picture and Lecturers Assn. **[1386]**

Intl. Motor Contest Assn. **[23078]**, PO Box 921, Vinton, IA 52349, (319)472-2201

Intl. Motor Press Assn. **[3120]**, 4 Park St., Harrington Park, NJ 07640, (201)750-3533

Intl. Motor Press Assn. **[IO]**, Harrington Park, NJ, United States

Intl. Motor Sports Assn. **[23079]**, 1394 Broadway Ave., Braselton, GA 30517, (706)658-2120

Intl. Motor Vehicle Inspection Comm. **[IO]**, Brussels, Belgium

Intl. Motorcycling Fed. **[IO]**, Mies, Switzerland

International Mountain Bicycling Association **[IO]**, Boulder, CO, United States

Intl. Mountain Bicycling Assn. **[23310]**, PO Box 7578, Boulder, CO 80306, (303)545-9011

Intl. Mountain Soc. - Defunct.

Intl. Movement Against All Forms of Discrimination and Racism **[IO]**, Tokyo, Japan

Intl. Movement of Catholic Agricultural and Rural Youth **[IO]**, Brussels, Belgium

Intl. Movement of Catholic Students - African Secretariat **[IO]**, Nairobi, Kenya

Intl. Movement of Catholic Students - Pax Romana **[IO]**, Paris, France

Intl. Movement Towards Educational Change **[IO]**, Oslo, Norway

Intl. MS Support Found. - Defunct.

Intl. Multimedia Telecommunications Consortium **[7775]**, 2400 Camino Ramon, Ste. 375, San Ramon, CA 94583, (925)275-6600

International Multimedia Telecommunications Consortium **[IO]**, San Ramon, CA, United States

Intl. Multiracial Shared Cultural Org. **[IO]**, New York, NY, United States

Intl. Multiracial Shared Cultural Org. **[17898]**, PO Box 3865, New York, NY 10163, (212)532-5449

Intl. Municipal Lawyers Assn. **[5500]**, 1110 Vermont Ave. NW, Ste. 200, Washington, DC 20005, (202)466-5424

Intl. Municipal Lawyers Assn. **[IO]**, Washington, DC, United States

Intl. Municipal Parking Cong. **[★IO]**

Intl. Municipal Parking Cong. **[★2899]**

Intl. Municipal Signal Assn. **[6251]**, PO Box 539, Newark, NY 14513-0539, (315)331-2182

Intl. Municipal Signal Assn. **[IO]**, Newark, NY, United States

Intl. Musculoskeletal Laser Soc. **[IO]**, Oldham, United Kingdom

Intl. Museum Photographers Assn. - Address unknown since 2001.

Intl. Museum Theatre Alliance **[10507]**, c/o Putnam Museum, 1717 W 12th St., Davenport, IA 52804

International Museum Theatre Alliance **[IO]**, Davenport, IA, United States

Intl. Music Center **[★IO]**

Intl. Music Coun. **[IO]**, Paris, France

Intl. Music League - Defunct.

Intl. Music Products Assn; NAMM, the **[2817]**

Intl. Music Study Group **[★IO]**

Intl. Musicological Soc. **[IO]**, Basel, Switzerland

Intl. Muslim Students Union - Address unknown since 1999.

Intl. Mustang Bullitt Owners Club **[21669]**, PO Box 376, Springboro, OH 45066

Intl. Mustang Club **[★5330]**

Intl. Mustang Club **[★IO]**

Intl. Mustard Assn. - Defunct.

Intl. Mycological Assn. **[7351]**, c/o Mycological Soc. of Am., PO Box 7065, Lawrence, KS 66044, (800)627-0629

Intl. Mycological Assn. **[IO]**, Lawrence, KS, United States

Intl. Mycological Inst. **[★IO]**

Intl. Mycophagist Assn. - Address unknown since 1995.

Intl. Myeloma Found. **[13833]**, 12650 Riverside Dr., Ste. 206, North Hollywood, CA 91607-3421, (818)487-7455

Intl. Myeloma Found. **[IO]**, North Hollywood, CA, United States

Intl. Myomassethics Fed. - Address unknown since 2002.

Intl. MYOPAIN Soc. **[15842]**, c/o Barbara Runnels, MEd, Admin. Off., PO Box 690402, San Antonio, TX 78269, (210)567-4661

Intl. Myopia Prevention Assn. - Defunct.

Intl. Mystery Shopping Alliance **[3412]**, c/o Arcadio Roselli, 210 Crossways Park Dr., Woodbury, NY 11797, (516)576-1188

Intl. NACRA Class Racing Assn. **[★23192]**

Intl. Nanny Assn. **[11527]**, 3801 Kirby Dr., Ste. 540, Houston, TX 77098, (713)526-2670

Intl. Nanny Assn. **[IO]**, Houston, TX, United States

Intl. Nanocasting Assn. **[562]**, 1010 N Central Ave., Glendale, CA 91202, (320)210-1857

Intl. Naples Sabot Assn. **[23190]**, c/o Aimee Graham, Sec.-Treas., PO Box 6808, San Diego, CA 92166, (949)645-1245

Intl. Narcotic Enforcement Officers Assn. **[5741]**, 112 State St., Ste. 1200, Albany, NY 12207-2023, (518)463-6232

Intl. Narcotic Enforcement Officers Assn. **[IO]**, Albany, NY, United States

Intl. Narcotics Control Bd. **[IO]**, Vienna, Austria

Intl. Narcotics Interdiction Assn. **[IO]**, Conroe, TX, United States

Intl. Narcotics Interdiction Assn. **[5742]**, 2523 Sand Shore Dr., Conroe, TX 77304, (936)447-6759

Intl. Native Amer. Flute Assn. **[10622]**, 3351 Mintonville Point Dr., Suffolk, VA 23435, (757)538-0468

International Native American Flute Association **[IO]**, Suffolk, VA, United States

Intl. Natural Bodybuilding and Fitness Fed. **[IO]**, Pocono Lake, PA, United States

Intl. Natural Bodybuilding and Fitness Fed. **[23243]**, PO Box 4, Pocono Lake, PA 18347

Intl. Natural Sausage Casing Assn. **[2659]**, c/o North Amer. Natural Casing Assn., 494 Eight Ave., Ste. 805, New York, NY 10001, (206)682-6845

Intl. Natural Sausage Casing Assn. **[IO]**, Seattle, WA, United States

Intl. Naturist Fed. **[IO]**, Antwerp, Belgium

Intl. Naturist Org. for Esperanto **[IO]**, San Francisco, CA, United States

Intl. Naturist Org. for Esperanto **[9916]**, c/o Leif Heilberg, Pres., Viking Photography, Inc., PO Box 22159, San Francisco, CA 94122

Intl. Naval Res. Org. **[10476]**, 5905 Reinwood Dr., Toledo, OH 43613-5605, (419)472-1331

Intl. Naval Res. Org. **[IO]**, Toledo, OH, United States

Intl. Navigation Assn. - Belgium **[IO]**, Brussels, Belgium

Intl. Navigation Assn. - USA **[IO]**, Charlotte Hall, MD, United States

Intl. Navigation Assn. - USA - Defunct.

Intl. .NET Assn. **[6771]**, PO Box 6713, Bellevue, WA 98008-0713, (401)885-4943

Intl. Netherland Group - Address unknown since 2004.

Intl. Netsuke Collectors Soc. - Defunct.

Intl. Network of Alternative Financial Institution **[IO]**, Nairobi, Kenya

Intl. Network for the Availability of Sci. Publications **[IO]**, Oxford, United Kingdom

Intl. Network of Boutique Law Firms **[5501]**, c/o Gallion and Spielvogel, 1225 Franklin Ave., Ste. 325, Garden City, NY 11530, (516)512-8899

Intl. Network for Cancer Treatment and Res. **[IO]**, Brussels, Belgium

Intl. Network of Children of Jewish Holocaust Survivors **[IO]**, North Miami Beach, FL, United States

Intl. Network of Children of Jewish Holocaust Survivors **[17720]**, c/o Rositta Kenigsberg, Exec. VP, 13899 Biscayne Blvd., Ste. 404, North Miami Beach, FL 33181, (305)919-5690

Intl. Network of Children's Ministry **[19758]**, 1025 S Perry St., No. 101C, Castle Rock, CO 80104, (800)324-4543

Intl. Network of Children's Ministry **[IO]**, Castle Rock, CO, United States

Intl. Network for Contemporary Iraqi Artists **[IO]**, London, United Kingdom

Intl. Network of Engineers and Scientists Against Proliferation **[IO]**, Darmstadt, Germany

Intl. Network of Engineers and Scientists for Global Responsibility **[IO]**, Berlin, Germany

Intl. Network on Family Poultry Development **[IO]**, Rome, Italy

Intl. Network on Feminist Approaches to Bioethics **[IO]**, Hastings on Hudson, NY, United States

Intl. Network on Feminist Approaches to Bioethics **[12126]**, c/o Anne Donchin, Treas., 5 Riverpoint Rd., Hastings-on-Hudson, NY 10706, (914)674-0122

Intl. Network for the History of Public Hea. **[IO]**, Linkoping, Sweden

Intl. Network of Liberal Women **[IO]**, London, United Kingdom

Intl. Network on Participatory Irrigation Mgt. **[IO]**, Washington, DC, United States

Intl. Network on Participatory Irrigation Mgt. **[7233]**, 333 1/2 Pennsylvania Ave. SE, 3rd Fl., Washington, DC 20003, (202)546-7005

Intl. Network of Performing and Visual Arts Schools **[★7974]**

Intl. Network of Performing and Visual Arts Schools **[★IO]**

Intl. Network on Personal Meaning **[IO]**, Langley, BC, Canada

Intl. Network for the Prevention of Elder Abuse **[IO]**, Buenos Aires, Argentina

Intl. Network of Prison Ministries **[IO]**, Dallas, TX, United States

Intl. Network of Prison Ministries **[20283]**, Box 227475, Dallas, TX 75222

Intl. Network for Religion and Animals - Defunct.

Intl. Network of Schools for the Advancement of Arts Educ. **[7974]**, 173 Ridge View Dr., Berkeley Springs, WV 25411, (304)258-1799

Intl. Network of Schools for the Advancement of Arts Educ. **[IO]**, Berkeley Springs, WV, United States

Intl. Network for Social Network Anal. **[IO]**, Alhambra, CA, United States

Intl. Network for Social Network Anal. **[7651]**, c/o Tom Valente, Univ. of Southern California, Dept. of Preventive Medicine, 1000 Fremont Ave., Unit No. 8, Bldg. A, Rm. 5133, Alhambra, CA 91803, (626)457-6678

Intl. Network of Somewhere in Time Enthusiasts **[24825]**, c/o Jo Addie, Pres., 8110 S Verdev Dr., Oak Creek, WI 53154, (708)579-3749

Reference to "IO" in place of a book number signifies that the association may be found in the 45th edition of International Organizations.

Intl. Network of Somewhere in Time Enthusiasts [IO], Oak Creek, WI, United States

Intl. Network for Sustainable Energy [IO], Hjortshoj, Denmark

Intl. Network for Terminology [IO], Vienna, Austria

Intl. Network for Urban Development [IO], The Hague, Netherlands

Intl. Network of Utility Professionals; Women's [1200]

Intl. Network of Women Against Tobacco [18744], c/o Pressing Issues, PO Box 224, Metuchen, NJ 08840, (732)549-9054

Intl. Network for Women in Enterprise and Trade - Address unknown since 2003.

Intl. Network of Women in Tech. [★7764]

Intl. Network of Women in Tech. [★IO]

Intl. Neural Network Soc. [IO], Madison, WI, United States

Intl. Neural Network Soc. [15391], 2810 Crossroads Dr., Ste. 3800, Madison, WI 53718, (608)443-2461

Intl. Neuro-Linguistic Programming Assn. [16219], 42 Spruce Ridge, Rte. 9P, Saratoga Springs, NY 12866, (518)587-3478

Intl. Neuro-Linguistic Programming Assn. [IO], Saratoga Springs, NY, United States

Intl. Neuroendocrine Fed. [IO], Edinburgh, United Kingdom

International Neuromodulation Society [IO], San Francisco, CA, United States

Intl. Neuromodulation Soc. [15392], 2000 Van Ness Ave., Ste. 402, San Francisco, CA 94109, (415)567-1219

Intl. Neuropsychiatric Assn. [IO], Randwick, Australia

Intl. Neuropsychological Soc: [IO], Columbus, OH, United States

Intl. Neuropsychological Soc. [15393], 700 Ackerman Rd., Ste. 625, Columbus, OH 43202, (614)263-4200

Intl. New Thought Alliance [10802], 5003 E Broadway Rd., Mesa, AZ 85206, (480)830-2461

Intl. New Towns Assn. [★IO]

Intl. News Ser. [★IO]

Intl. News Ser. [★3169]

Intl. Newspaper Advt. and Marketing Executives [★3244]

Intl. Newspaper Collector's Club - Defunct.

Intl. Newspaper Financial Executives [1428], 21525 Ridgetop Cir., Ste. 200, Sterling, VA 20166, (703)421-4060

Intl. Newspaper Financial Executives [IO], Sterling, VA, United States

Intl. Newspaper Gp. [3121], c/o Marty Donner, Sec.-Treas., 64 Spyglass Dr., Jackson, NJ 08527

Intl. Newspaper Marketing Assn. [3230], 10300 N Central Expy., Ste. 467, Dallas, TX 75231-8654, (214)373-9111

Intl. Newspaper Marketing Assn. [IO], Dallas, TX, United States

Intl. Newspaper Promotion Assn. [★IO]

Intl. Newspaper Promotion Assn. [★3230]

Intl. Newsreel and News Film Assn. [IO], Brussels, Belgium

Intl. NGO Forum on Indonesian Development - European Liaison Off. [IO], Brussels, Belgium

Intl. NGO Forum on Indonesian Development - Indonesia [IO], Jakarta, Indonesia

Intl. NGO Training and Res. Centre [IO], Oxford, United Kingdom

Intl. Nick Tate Club [IO], Birmingham, United Kingdom

Intl. Nippon Collectors Club [IO], Thurmont, MD, United States

Intl. Nippon Collectors Club [21929], c/o Dick Bittner, 8 Geoley Ct., Thurmont, MD 21788

Intl. Non-Violence and Vegetarian Soc. - Defunct.

Intl. Nonviolent Initiatives [18115]

Intl. Nonwovens and Disposables Assn. [★3785]

Intl. Nortel Networks Meridian Users Gp. [★7776]

Intl. Nortel Networks Users Assn. [7776], 401 N Michigan Ave., Ste. 2200, Chicago, IL 60611, (312)673-6102

Intl. North Amer. Highway Assn. - Defunct.

Intl. Norton Owners' Assn. [22684], c/o Tari Norum, 276 Butterworth Ln., Langhorne, PA 19047, (215)741-0110

Intl. Norton Owners' Assn. [IO], Stockbridge, MI, United States

Intl. Nubian Breeders Assn. [IO], Pine Bush, NY, United States

Intl. Nubian Breeders Assn. [4135], c/o Caroline Lawson, Sec.-Treas., 5124 FM 1940, Franklin, TX 77856, (845)744-6089

Intl. Nuclear and Energy Assn. - Defunct.

Intl. Nuclear Law Assn. [IO], Brussels, Belgium

Intl. Numismatic Commn. [IO], Paris, France

Intl. Numismatic Soc. Authentication Bur. - Address unknown since 2004.

Intl. Nurses Anonymous [16505], c/o Kathy Kavanaugh, RN, Sec.-Treas., 14542 Greenpoint Ln., Huntersville, NC 28078, (704)992-0678

International Nurses Anonymous [IO], Huntersville, NC, United States

Intl. Nurses Soc. on Addictions [IO], Denver, CO, United States

Intl. Nurses Soc. on Addictions [15484], PO Box 163635, Columbus, OH 43216, (614)221-9989

Intl. Nursing Assn. for Clinical Simulation and Learning [15485], c/o Dr. Christine Hooper, VP of Finance, San Jose State Univ. - School of Nursing, One Washington Sq., San Jose, CA 95192-0057

International Nursing Association for Clinical Simulation and Learning [IO], San Jose, CA, United States

Intl. Nursing Coalition for Mass Casualty Educ. [IO], Nashville, TN, United States

Intl. Nursing Coalition for Mass Casualty Educ. [8946], c/o Colleen Conway-Welch, PhD, Dir., Vanderbilt Univ. School of Nursing, 461 21st Ave. S, 111 Godchaux Hall, Nashville, TN 37240, (615)343-8876

Intl. Nursing Services Assn. [★14978]

Intl. Nursing Services Assn. [★IO]

Intl. Nutrition Res. Found. - Defunct.

Intl. Oak Soc. [5258], c/o Richard Jensen, Membership Chm., Dept. of Biology, St. Mary's Coll., Notre Dame, IN 46556, (574)284-4674

International Oak Society [IO], Notre Dame, IN, United States

Intl. Occultation Timing Assn. [IO], Stillwater, OK, United States

Intl. Occultation Timing Assn. [6507], c/o Chad Ellington, Sec.-Treas., PO Box 6356, Kent, WA 98064-6356

Intl. Ocean Inst. [IO], Gzira, Malta

Intl. Ocean Pollution Symposium - Defunct.

Intl. Oceanographic Found. [7399]

Intl. Oceanographic Found. [IO], Miami, FL, United States

Intl. Ocular Inflammation Soc. [IO], Alicante, Spain

Intl. Oculoplastic Soc. - Address unknown since 2004.

Intl. Off. of Cocoa and Chocolate [★IO]

Intl. Off. of Cocoa, Chocolate, and Sugar Confectionery [★IO]

Intl. Off. for Water [IO], Paris, France

Intl. Oil Pollution Compensation Funds [IO], London, United Kingdom

Intl. Oil Scouts Assn. [IO], Houston, TX, United States

Intl. Oil Scouts Assn. [2932], PO Box 940310, Houston, TX 77094-7310, (512)472-7173

Intl. Okinawa Kobudo Assn. [23590], 1666 San Diego St., Fairfield, CA 94533, (707)428-7266

Intl. Old Lacers, Inc. [22161], c/o Laurie J. Hughes, Membership Chair, 1151 Shenandoah Dr., Sunnyvale, CA 94087-2221

Intl. Old Lacers, Inc. [IO], Sunnyvale, CA, United States

Intl. Oleander Soc. [IO], Galveston, TX, United States

Intl. Oleander Soc. [22523], PO Box 3431, Galveston, TX 77552-0431, (409)762-9334

Intl. Olive Oil Coun. [IO], Madrid, Spain

Intl. Olympic Comm. [IO], Lausanne, Switzerland

Intl. Ombudsman Assn. [736], 203 Towne Centre Dr., Hillsborough, NJ 08844-4693, (908)359-0246

Intl. Ombudsman Inst. [IO], Edmonton, AB, Canada

Intl. Omega Assn. [★IO]

Intl. Oncology Stud. Gp. - Address unknown since 2008.

Intl. Open Finance Assn. [17584], 10201 Hammocks Blvd., No. 153, Miami, FL 33196, (305)773-7663

Intl. Open Finance Assn. [IO], Miami, FL, United States

Intl. Opticians Assn. [IO], Canterbury, United Kingdom

Intl. Oracle Users Gp. [IO], Chicago, IL, United States

Intl. Oracle Users Gp. [6796], 401 N Michigan Ave., 22nd Fl., Chicago, IL 60611-4267, (312)245-1579

Intl. Oracle Users Gp. - Americas [★6796]

Intl. Oracle Users Gp. - Americas [★IO]

Intl. Orchid Soc. - Defunct.

Intl. Order of Alhambra [19001], 4200 Leeds Ave., Baltimore, MD 21229, (410)242-0660

Intl. Order of the Alhambra [★19001]

Intl. Order of the Alhambra [★IO]

International Order of Alhambra [IO], Baltimore, MD, United States

Intl. Order of the Armadillo [22597]

Intl. Order of E.A.R.S. [10979], PO Box 17141, Louisville, KY 40217, (502)245-0643

Intl. Order of E.A.R.S. [IO], Louisville, KY, United States

International Order of the Golden Rule [IO], St. Louis, MO, United States

Intl. Order of the Golden Rule [2783], PO Box 28689, St. Louis, MO 63146-1189, (314)209-7142

Intl. Order of Handicapped Radio Amateurs [★21502]

Intl. Order of Hoo-Hoo [★19103]

Intl. Order; Inst. for [★17620]

Intl. Order of Job's Daughters, Supreme Guardian Coun. [19239], c/o Susan M. Goolsby, Exec. Mgr., 233 W 6th St., Papillion, NE 68046-2210, (402)592-7987

International Order of Job's Daughters, Supreme Guardian Council [IO], Papillion, NE, United States

Intl. Order of the King's Daughters and Sons [IO], Chautauqua, NY, United States

Intl. Order of the King's Daughters and Sons [19810], PO Box 1017, Chautauqua, NY 14722-1017, (716)357-4951

Intl. Order of Runeberg [9952], 6094 Myrtle Ave., Eureka, CA 95503, (707)445-2364

Intl. Order of Runeberg [IO], Eureka, CA, United States

Intl. Order of Saint Luke the Physician [IO], San Antonio, TX, United States

Intl. Order of Saint Luke the Physician [20499], PO Box 780909, San Antonio, TX 78278-0909, (210)698-7141

Intl. Order of St. Vincent [19963], 126 Coming St., Charleston, SC 29403, (843)722-7345

Intl. Order of St. Vincent [IO], Charleston, SC, United States

Intl. Organ Festival at St. Albans [IO], St. Albans, United Kingdom

Intl. Org. of Aluminum Aerosol Can Mfrs. [IO], Dusseldorf, Germany

Intl. Org. for Biological Control of Noxious Animals and Plants [IO], Wageningen, Netherlands

Intl. Org. for Biotechnology and Bioengineering [IO], Kenmore, Australia

Intl. Org. of Consumers Unions [★IO]

Intl. Org. for the Elimination of All Forms of Racial Discrimination [IO], Geneva, Switzerland

Intl. Org. of Motor Vehicle Mfrs. [IO], Paris, France

Intl. Org. for the Ornamental Plants Indus. [IO], Noordwijk, Netherlands

Intl. Org. for the Transition of Professional Dancers [IO], Lausanne, Switzerland

Intl. Org. of Vine and Wine [IO], Paris, France

International Organization for Adolescents [IO], Brooklyn, NY, United States

Intl. Org. for Adolescents [11606], PO Box 25792, Brooklyn, NY 11202-2218, (718)222-5802

Intl. Org. for Biological Control of Noxious Animals and Plants [IO], Palermo, Italy

Intl. Org. of Black Security Executives [3533], PO Box 92, Fairfield, CA 94533, (888)884-6273

Intl. Org. for Chem. Sciences in Development [6684], PO Box 8156, Falls Church, VA 22041, (703)845-9078

Intl. Org. for Chem. Sciences in Development [IO], Falls Church, VA, United States

---

A star before a book entry number signifies that the name is not listed separately, but is mentioned within the entry.

Intl. Org. of Citrus Virologists [IO], Riverside, CA, United States

Intl. Org. of Citrus Virologists [6638], c/o Chester N. Roistacher, Sec., Dept. of Plant Pathology, Univ. of California, Riverside, CA 92521, (951)787-1012

Intl. Org. of Consumers Unions [★IO]

Intl. Org. of Consumers Unions - USA - Defunct.

Intl. Org. for the Defense of Human Rights in Iraq - Address unknown since 1994.

Intl. Org. for the Elimination of All Forms of Racial Discrimination [IO], Geneva, Switzerland

International Org. of Employers [★IO]

International Org. of Employers [★766]

Intl. Org. of the Flavor Indus. [IO], Geneva, Switzerland

Intl. Org. for Forensic Odonto-Stomatology [IO], Oslo, Norway

International Organization of Glutaric Acidemia [IO], Blairsville, PA, United States

Intl. Org. of Glutaric Acidemia [15332], RD No. 4, Box 299-A, Blairsville, PA 15717, (724)459-0179

Intl. Org. of Legal Metrology [IO], Paris, France

Intl. Org. of Masters, Mates and Pilots, ILA, AFL-CIO [24128], 700 Maritime Blvd., Ste. B, Linthicum Heights, MD 21090-1941, (410)850-8700

Intl. Org. for Medical Physics [16018], c/o Saiyid M. Shah, PhD, Corporate Liaison Off., Evansville Cancer Center, 706 N Burkhardt Rd., Evansville, IN 47715-2740, (812)474-1110

Intl. Org. for Medical Physics [IO], Evansville, IN, United States

Intl. Org. for Migration - Abidjan, Cote d'Ivoire [IO], Abidjan, Cote d'Ivoire

Intl. Org. for Migration - Abuja, Nigeria [IO], Abuja, Nigeria

Intl. Org. for Migration - Accra, Ghana [IO], Accra, Ghana

Intl. Org. for Migration - Addis Ababa, Ethiopia [IO], Addis Ababa, Ethiopia

Intl. Org. for Migration - Amman, Jordan [IO], Amman, Jordan

Intl. Org. for Migration - Armenia [IO], Yerevan, Armenia

Intl. Org. for Migration - Ashgabat, Turkmenistan [IO], Ashgabat, Turkmenistan

Intl. Org. for Migration - Athens, Greece [IO], Athens, Greece

Intl. Org. for Migration - Austria [IO], Vienna, Austria

Intl. Org. for Migration - Azerbaijan [IO], Baku, Azerbaijan

Intl. Org. for Migration - Bamako, Mali [IO], Bamako, Mali

Intl. Org. for Migration - Belgium [IO], Brussels, Belgium

Intl. Org. for Migration - Bosnia and Herzegovina [IO], Sarajevo, Bosnia-Hercegovina

Intl. Org. for Migration - Bratislava, Slovakia [IO], Bratislava, Slovakia

Intl. Org. for Migration - Bucharest, Romania [IO], Bucharest, Romania

Intl. Org. for Migration - Budapest, Hungary [IO], Budapest, Hungary

Intl. Org. for Migration - Cambodia [IO], Phnom Penh, Cambodia

Intl. Org. for Migration - Canberra, Australia [IO], Canberra, Australia

Intl. Org. for Migration - China [IO], Hong Kong, People's Republic of China

Intl. Org. for Migration - Colombia [IO], Bogota, Colombia

Intl. Org. for Migration - Colombo, Sri Lanka [IO], Colombo, Sri Lanka

Intl. Org. for Migration - Conakry, Guinea [IO], Conakry, Guinea

Intl. Org. for Migration - Costa Rica [IO], San Pedro, Costa Rica

Intl. Org. for Migration - Dar es Salaam, Tanzania [IO], Dar es Salaam, United Republic of Tanzania

Intl. Org. for Migration - Dhaka, Bangladesh [IO], Dhaka, Bangladesh

Intl. Org. for Migration - Dublin, Ireland [IO], Dublin, Ireland

Intl. Org. for Migration - Dushanbe [IO], Dushanbe, Tajikistan

Intl. Org. for Migration - Freetown, Sierra Leone [IO], Freetown, Sierra Leone

Intl. Org. for Migration - Germany [IO], Berlin, Germany

Intl. Org. for Migration - Guatemala [IO], Guatemala City, Guatemala

Intl. Org. for Migration - Harare, Zimbabwe [IO], Harare, Zimbabwe

Intl. Org. for Migration - Islamabad, Pakistan [IO], Islamabad, Pakistan

Intl. Org. for Migration - Istanbul, Turkey [IO], Ankara, Turkey

Intl. Org. for Migration - Jakarta, Indonesia [IO], Jakarta, Indonesia

Intl. Org. for Migration - Kabul, Afghanistan [IO], Kabul, Afghanistan

Intl. Org. for Migration - Kampala, Uganda [IO], Kampala, Uganda

Intl. Org. for Migration - Kazakhstan [IO], Almaty, Kazakhstan

Intl. Org. for Migration - Khartoum, Sudan [IO], Khartoum, Sudan

Intl. Org. for Migration - Kiev, Ukraine [IO], Kiev, Ukraine

Intl. Org. for Migration - Kingston, Jamaica [IO], Kingston, Jamaica

Intl. Org. for Migration - Kinshasa, Democratic Republic of the Congo [IO], Kinshasa, Democratic Republic of the Congo

Intl. Org. for Migration - Kyrgyz Republic [IO], Bishkek, Kirgizstan

Intl. Org. for Migration - La Paz, Bolivia [IO], La Paz, Bolivia

Intl. Org. for Migration - Lima, Peru [IO], Lima, Peru

Intl. Org. for Migration - Lisbon, Portugal [IO], Lisbon, Portugal

Intl. Org. for Migration - Ljubljana [IO], Ljubljana, Slovenia

Intl. Org. for Migration - Luanda, Angola [IO], Luanda, Angola

Intl. Org. for Migration - Lusaka, Zambia [IO], Lusaka, Zambia

Intl. Org. for Migration - Madrid, Spain [IO], Madrid, Spain

Intl. Org. for Migration - Managua, Nicaragua [IO], Managua, Nicaragua

Intl. Org. for Migration - Mexico [IO], Mexico City, Mexico

Intl. Org. for Migration - Minsk, Belarus [IO], Minsk, Belarus

Intl. Org. for Migration - Moldova [IO], Chisinau, Moldova

Intl. Org. for Migration - Moscow, Russia [IO], Moscow, Russia

Intl. Org. for Migration - Nairobi, Kenya [IO], Nairobi, Kenya

Intl. Org. for Migration - Netherlands [IO], The Hague, Netherlands

Intl. Org. for Migration - Norway [IO], Oslo, Norway

Intl. Org. for Migration - Ottawa, Canada [IO], Ottawa, ON, Canada

Intl. Org. for Migration - Paris, France [IO], Paris, France

Intl. Org. for Migration - Philippines [IO], Makati City, Philippines

Intl. Org. for Migration - Port au Prince, Haiti [IO], Port-au-Prince, Haiti

Intl. Org. for Migration - Prague, Czech Republic [IO], Prague, Czech Republic

Intl. Org. for Migration - Quito, Ecuador [IO], Quito, Ecuador

Intl. Org. for Migration - Regional Off. for the Baltic and Nordic States [IO], Helsinki, Finland

Intl. Org. for Migration - Riga, Latvia [IO], Riga, Latvia

Intl. Org. for Migration - Riyadh, Saudi Arabia [IO], Riyadh, Saudi Arabia

Intl. Org. for Migration - Rome, Italy [IO], Rome, Italy

Intl. Org. for Migration - San Salvador, El Salvador [IO], San Salvador, El Salvador

Intl. Org. for Migration - Santiago, Chile [IO], Santiago, Chile

Intl. Org. for Migration - Santo Domingo, Dominican Republic [IO], Santo Domingo, Dominican Republic

Intl. Org. for Migration - Seoul, Republic of Korea [IO], Seoul, Republic of Korea

Intl. Org. for Migration - Skopje [IO], Skopje, Macedonia

Intl. Org. for Migration - Sofia, Bulgaria [IO], Sofia, Bulgaria

Intl. Org. for Migration - Southern Africa [IO], Arcadia, Republic of South Africa

Intl. Org. for Migration - Switzerland [IO], Geneva, Switzerland

Intl. Org. for Migration - Tallinn, Estonia [IO], Tallinn, Estonia

Intl. Org. for Migration - Tbilisi, Georgia [IO], Tbilisi, Georgia

Intl. Org. for Migration - Tegucigalpa, Honduras [IO], Tegucigalpa, Honduras

Intl. Org. for Migration - Tehran, Iran [IO], Tehran, Iran

Intl. Org. for Migration - Thailand [IO], Bangkok, Thailand

Intl. Org. for Migration - Tirana, Albania [IO], Tirana, Albania

Intl. Org. for Migration - Tokyo, Japan [IO], Tokyo, Japan

Intl. Org. for Migration - Tunis, Tunisia [IO], Tunis, Tunisia

Intl. Org. for Migration - United Kingdom [IO], London, United Kingdom

Intl. Org. for Migration - Vietnam [IO], Hanoi, Vietnam

Intl. Org. for Migration - Vilnius, Lithuania [IO], Vilnius, Lithuania

Intl. Org. for Migration - Warsaw, Poland [IO], Warsaw, Poland

Intl. Org. for Migration - Zagreb, Croatia [IO], Zagreb, Croatia

Intl. Org. of Multiple Sclerosis Nurses [IO], Teaneck, NJ, United States

Intl. Org. of Multiple Sclerosis Nurses [15486], PO Box 450, Teaneck, NJ 07666, (201)837-0727

Intl. Org. for Mycoplasmology [6582], c/o Jacqueline Fletcher, Treas., Oklahoma State Univ., 127 Noble Res. Ctr., Stillwater, OK 74078, (405)744-9948

Intl. Org. for Mycoplasmology [IO], Stillwater, OK, United States

Intl. Org. of Nerds - Defunct.

Intl. Org. of Overhead Catenary Engineers [IO], Wellingborough, United Kingdom

Intl. Org. of Plant Biosystematists [IO], St. Louis, MO, United States

Intl. Org. of Plant Biosystematists [6639], c/o Peter C. Hoch, PhD, Treas., Missouri Botanical Garden, PO Box 299, St. Louis, MO 63166-0299, (314)577-5175

Intl. Org. of Psychophysiology [IO], Montreal, QC, Canada

Intl. Org. of Scenographers, Theatre Architects, and Technicians [IO], Taipei, Taiwan

Intl. Org. for Sci. and Tech. Educ. [IO], Kiel, Germany

Intl. Org. of Securities Commissions [IO], Madrid, Spain

Intl. Org. for Septuagint and Cognate Stud. [IO], Winona Lake, IN, United States

Intl. Org. for Septuagint and Cognate Stud. [19522], c/o Eisenbrauns, PO Box 275, Winona Lake, IN 46590-0275, (574)269-2011

Intl. Org. on Shape Memory and Superelastic Technologies [7317], c/o Sarina Pastoric, Admin., Affl. Societies, Customer Ser. Dept., 9639 Kinsman Rd., Novelty, OH 44073, (440)338-5151

Intl. Org. on Shape Memory and Superelastic Technologies [IO], Novelty, OH, United States

Intl. Org. of Space Communications [IO], Moscow, Russia

Intl. Org. for Standardization [IO], Geneva, Switzerland

Intl. Org. for Statistical Stud. on Diseases of the Esophagus [★IO]

Intl. Org. for the Stud. of Gp. Tensions [IO], New York, NY, United States

Intl. Org. for the Stud. of Gp. Tensions [10189], c/o Dr. Herbert Krauss, PhD, Co-Pres., Pace Univ., 1 Pace Plz., New York, NY 10038, (212)346-1506

Intl. Org. for the Study of Human Development - Defunct.

Intl. Org. for Succulent Plant Stud. [IO], Zurich, Switzerland

Reference to "IO" in place of a book number signifies that the association may be found in the 45th edition of International Organizations.

Encyclopedia of Associations, 46th Edition

3671

Intl. Org. of Sugar Cane Technologists [★IO]

Intl. Org. of Supreme Audit Institutions [IO], Vienna, Austria

Intl. Org. for Transportation by Rope - North Amer. Continental Sect. - Address unknown since 1994.

Intl. Org. of Women Executives - Defunct.

Intl. Org. of Women Pilots [★163]

Intl. Org. of Women Pilots [★IO]

Intl. Org. of Women in Telecommunications - Defunct.

Intl. Org. of Wooden Money Collectors - Address unknown since 1999.

Intl. Org. for World Peace, Disarmament, Development and Human Rights - Address unknown since 2001.

Intl. Orienteering Fed. [IO], Helsinki, Finland

Intl. Orphans, Inc. [★11680]

Intl. Orthodox Christian Charities [19811], 110 West Rd., Ste. 360, Baltimore, MD 21204, (410)243-9820

Intl. Orthodox Christian Charities [IO], Baltimore, MD, United States

Intl. Orthokeratology Soc. - Address unknown since 2002.

Intl. Orthoptic Assn. [IO], London, United Kingdom

The International Osprey Foundation [IO], Sanibel, FL, United States

The Intl. Osprey Found. [5328], PO Box 250, Sanibel, FL 33957-0250

Intl. Osteopathic Assn., North Amer. Div. - Defunct.

Intl. Ostomy Assn. [IO], Toronto, ON, Canada

Intl. Otter Survival Fund [IO], Broadford, United Kingdom

Intl. Oxygen Mfrs. Assn. [IO], Washington, DC, United States

Intl. Oxygen Mfrs. Assn. [1723], 1255 23rd St. NW, Ste. 200, Washington, DC 20037, (202)521-9300

Intl. Ozone Assn. [7109], PO Box 28873, Scottsdale, AZ 85255, (480)529-3787

Intl. Ozone Assn. [IO], Scottsdale, AZ, United States

Intl. Ozone Assn. - EA3G [IO], Poitiers, France

Intl. Ozone Inst. [★IO]

Intl. Ozone Inst. [★7109]

Intl. Pacific Halibut Commn. [5731], PO Box 95009, Seattle, WA 98145-2009, (206)634-1838

Intl. Pacific Halibut Commn. [IO], Seattle, WA, United States

Intl. Pacific Salmon Fisheries Commn. [★IO]

Intl. Packaged Ice Assn. [1891], PO Box 1199, Tampa, FL 33601-1199, (813)258-1690

Intl. Packet Communications Consortium [★7771]

Intl. Packet Communications Consortium [★IO]

Intl. Paddle Assn. [★23678]

Intl. Paddle Rackets Assn. [★23678]

Intl. Pain Found. - Defunct.

Intl. Paintball Players Assn. - Address unknown since 2001.

Intl. Palm Soc. [6640], PO Box 1897, Lawrence, KS 66044-8897, (785)843-1274

Intl. Palm Soc. [IO], Lawrence, KS, United States

International Palmtherapy Association [IO], Van Nuys, CA, United States

Intl. Palmtherapy Assn. [16621], PO Box 7453, Van Nuys, CA 91409-7453, (661)944-4909

Intl. Paneuropean Union [IO], Munich, Germany

Intl. Paperweight Soc. [22776], 761 Chestnut St., Santa Cruz, CA 95060, (800)538-0766

Intl. Paralegal Mgt. Assn. [5944], PO Box 659, Avondale Estates, GA 30002-0659, (404)292-4762

Intl. Paralegal Mgt. Assn. [IO], Avondale Estates, GA, United States

Intl. Paralympic Comm. [IO], Bonn, Germany

Intl. Parents' Org. [★14776]

International Parking CH Foundation [★2899]

International Parking CH Foundation [★IO]

Intl. Parking Inst. [IO], Fredericksburg, VA, United States

Intl. Parking Inst. [2899], 701 Kenmore Ave., Ste. 200, Fredericksburg, VA 22401, (540)371-7535

Intl. Parliamentary Group for Human Rights in the Soviet Union - Defunct.

Intl. Parrotlet Soc. [21850], PO Box 2428, Santa Cruz, CA 95063-2428, (831)688-5560

International Parrotlet Society [IO], Santa Cruz, CA, United States

Intl. Partners in Prayer - Address unknown since 2003.

Intl. Partnership for Microbicides [13572], 1010 Wayne Ave., Ste. 1450, Silver Spring, MD 20910, (301)608-2221

Intl. Partnership for Microbicides [IO], Silver Spring, MD, United States

Intl. Passenger Ship Assn. [★IO]

Intl. Passenger Ship Assn. [★3915]

Intl. Patent Inst. [★IO]

Intl. Patent and Trademark Assn. [★IO].

Intl. Patent and Trademark Assn. [★5848]

Intl. Patient Assn. for Primary Immunodeficiencies [IO], Cornwall, United Kingdom

Intl. Patient Education Coun. - Address unknown since 1999.

Intl. PBX/Telecommunicators - Address unknown since 1995.

Intl. Peace Acad. [17735], 777 UN Plz., 4th Fl., New York, NY 10017-3521, (212)687-4300

Intl. Peace Acad. [IO], New York, NY, United States

Intl. Peace Bur. [IO], Geneva, Switzerland

Intl. Peace Center - Defunct.

Intl. Peace Clubs; Pat's Peace Kids [★18196]

Intl. Peace Clubs; Pat's Peace Kids [★IO]

Intl. Peace Lantern Exchange Project - Defunct.

Intl. Peace Operations Assn. [18213], 1900 L St. NW, Ste. 320, Washington, DC 20036, (202)464-0721

Intl. Peace Operations Assn. [IO], Washington, DC, United States

International Peace Scholarship Fund [★IO]

International Peace Scholarship Fund [★9325]

Intl. Peace Walk - Address unknown since 2003.

Intl. Peasant Union - Address unknown since 1995.

Intl. Peat Soc. [IO], Jyvaskyla, Finland

Intl. Peat Soc; U.S. Natl. Comm. of the [7459]

Intl. Pectin Producers Assn. [IO], Neuenbuerg, Germany

Intl. Pediatric Endosurgery Gp. [IO], Los Angeles, CA, United States

Intl. Pediatric Endosurgery Gp. [15889], 11300 W Olympic Blvd., No. 600, Los Angeles, CA 90064, (310)437-0553

Intl. Pediatric Hypertension Assn. [14907], c/o Kathy Franco, Coor., Univ. of Texas Houston Hea. Sci. Center, Dept. of Pediatrics/Div. of Nephrology and Hypertension, 6431 Fannin St., MSB 3.124, Houston, TX 77030, (713)500-5113

Intl. Pediatric Hypertension Assn. [IO], Houston, TX, United States

Intl. Pediatric Nephrology Assn. [IO], Los Angeles, CA, United States

Intl. Pediatric Nephrology Assn. [15292], c/o Isidro B. Salusky, MD, Sec. Gen., Gen. Clinical Res. Center, 10833 Le Conte Ave., 27-066 CHS, Los Angeles, CA 90095-1697, (310)206-9295

Intl. Pediatric Transplant Assn. [16673], 15000 Commerce Pkwy., Ste. C, Mount Laurel, NJ 08054, (856)439-0500

Intl. Pediatric Transplant Assn. [IO], Mount Laurel, NJ, United States

Intl. Pedigree Assignment and Bloodline Res. Assn. [IO], Lombard, IL, United States

Intl. Pedigree Assignment and Bloodline Res. Assn. [4902], c/o Chris Wallbruch, Pres./Treas., 321 N Martha St., Lombard, IL 60148

Intl. Pelvic Pain Soc. [15843], c/o C. Paul Perry, MD, Bd. Chm., C. Paul Perry Pelvic Pain Center, 2006 Brookwood Medical Center Drive, Ste. 402, Women's Medical Plz., Birmingham, AL 35209, (205)877-2950

International Pelvic Pain Society [IO], Birmingham, AL, United States

Intl. Pemphigus Found. [14268], 1540 River Park Dr., Ste. 208, Sacramento, CA 95815, (916)922-1298

Intl. P.E.N. - England [IO], London, United Kingdom

Intl. Pen Friend Ser. [IO], Ivrea, Italy

Intl. Pen Friends [IO], Honolulu, HI, United States

Intl. Pen Friends [22138], c/o Lorrin Lee, Rep., 500 Univ. Ave., No. 2415, Honolulu, HI 96826, (808)949-5000

Intl. Pen Friends - Australia [IO], Suffolk Park, Australia

Intl. P.E.N. - Guatemalan Writers Abroad - Address unknown since 2001.

Intl. Pen Pal Support Group Network for Chronic Dizziness and Balance Disorders - Defunct.

Intl. P.E.N. - Scottish Centre [IO], Edinburgh, United Kingdom

Intl. PEN - U.S.A West [★11186]

Intl. P.E.N. Women Writers' Comm. [IO], Gardenvale, Australia

Intl. PEN Writers Assn. [IO], London, United Kingdom

Intl. P.E.N. - Yiddish - Address unknown since 1999.

Intl. Penguin Class Dinghy Assn. [23191], c/o Charles Krafft, 8300 Waverly Rd., Owings, MD 20736

Intl. Penguin Class Dinghy Assn. [IO], Owings, MD, United States

Intl. Penpal Club [IO], Bombay, India

Intl. Pentecostal Press Assn. [IO], Oklahoma City, OK, United States

Intl. Pentecostal Press Assn. [3122], c/o Homer Rhea, PO Box 12609, Oklahoma City, OK 73157, (405)787-7110

Intl. People's Democratic Uhuru Movement [17395], 1245 18th Ave. S, St. Petersburg, FL 33705, (727)502-0575

International People's Democratic Uhuru Movement [IO], St. Petersburg, FL, United States

Intl. People's Sports - U.S.A. [★23803]

Intl. Pepper Community [IO], Jakarta, Indonesia

Intl. Percy Grainger Soc. [IO], White Plains, NY, United States

Intl. Percy Grainger Soc. [9810], c/o Lucinda Hess, 7 Cromwell Pl., White Plains, NY 10601, (914)582-1237

Intl. Perfume Bottle Assn. [22054], c/o Susan Arthur, Membership Sec., PO Box 425, Pennington, NJ 08534

Intl. Perfume Bottle Assn. [IO], Paradise, CA, United States

Intl. Perfume and Scent Bottle Collectors Assn. [★IO]

Intl. Perfume and Scent Bottle Collectors Assn. [★22054]

Intl. Perimetric Soc. [15688], c/o Dr. Richard P. Mills, MD, Glaucoma Consultants Northwest, 1221 Madison St., Ste. 1124, Seattle, WA 98104, (206)682-3447

Intl. Perimetric Soc. [IO], Seattle, WA, United States

Intl. Periodical Distributors Assn. - Address unknown since 1991.

Intl. Peritoneal Dialysis Org. [★IO]

Intl. Permafrost Assn. - Argentina [IO], Mendoza, Argentina

Intl. Permafrost Assn. - Austria [IO], Graz, Austria

Intl. Permafrost Assn. - Belgium [IO], Gent, Belgium

Intl. Permafrost Assn. - Canada [IO], Calgary, AB, Canada

Intl. Permafrost Assn. - China [IO], Lanzhou, People's Republic of China

Intl. Permafrost Assn. - Finland [IO], Helsinki, Finland

Intl. Permafrost Assn. - France [IO], Orsay, France

Intl. Permafrost Assn. - Germany [IO], Giessen, Germany

Intl. Permafrost Assn. - Iceland [IO], Reykjavik, Iceland

Intl. Permafrost Assn. - Japan [IO], Sapporo, Japan

Intl. Permafrost Assn. - Kazakhstan [IO], Almaty, Kazakhstan

Intl. Permafrost Assn. - Mongolia [IO], Ulan Bator, Mongolia

Intl. Permafrost Assn. - Netherlands [IO], Amsterdam, Netherlands

Intl. Permafrost Assn. - Norway [IO], Longyearbyen, Norway

Intl. Permafrost Assn. - Poland [IO], Lublin, Poland

Intl. Permafrost Assn. - Russia [IO], Tyumen, Russia

Intl. Permafrost Assn. - South Africa [IO], Pretoria, Republic of South Africa

Intl. Permafrost Assn. - Spain [IO], Madrid, Spain

Intl. Permafrost Assn. - Sweden [IO], Lund, Sweden

Intl. Permafrost Assn. - Switzerland [IO], Basel, Switzerland

Intl. Permafrost Assn. - United Kingdom [IO], Brighton, United Kingdom

A star before a book entry number signifies that the name is not listed separately, but is mentioned within the entry.

Intl. Personhood of Illiterate Programmers - Address unknown since 1995.

Intl. Personnel Mgt. Assn. [★1267]

Intl. Personnel Mgt. Assn. [★IO]

Intl. Personnel Mgt. Assn. - Canada [IO], Edmonton, AB, Canada

Intl. Peruvian Paso Horse Assn. [★IO]

Intl. Peruvian Paso Horse Assn. [★4934]

Intl. Pesticide Applicators Assn. [★2909]

Intl. Petroleum Credit Assn. [★1427]

Intl. Petroleum Credit Assn. [★IO]

Intl. Petroleum Indus. Environmental Conservation Assn. [IO], London, United Kingdom

Intl. Petula Clark Soc. [IO], Ramsgate, United Kingdom

Intl. Pharmaceutical Excipients Coun. [★IO]

Intl. Pharmaceutical Excipients Coun. [★2977]

Intl. Pharmaceutical Excipients Coun. of the Americas [2977], 1655 N Ft. Myer Dr., Ste. 700, Arlington, VA 22209, (703)875-2127

Intl. Pharmaceutical Excipients Coun. of the Americas [IO], Arlington, VA, United States

Intl. Pharmaceutical Fed. [IO], The Hague, Netherlands

Intl. Pharmaceutical Students' Fed. [IO], The Hague, Netherlands

Intl. Phenomenological Soc. [IO], Providence, RI, United States

Intl. Phenomenological Soc. [10803], c/o Brown Univ., 54 Coll. St., Box 1947, Providence, RI 02912, (401)863-3215

Intl. Philatelic Fed. [IO], Zurich, Switzerland

Intl. Philatelic Press Club - Defunct.

Intl. Philosophers for the Prevention of Nuclear Omnicide [18156], c/o Ms. Shireen Parsons, Treas., 306 Miller St., Christiansburg, VA 24073, (519)458-8137

Intl. Philosophers for the Prevention of Nuclear Omnicide [IO], Christiansburg, VA, United States

Intl. Phonetic Assn. [IO], Thessaloniki, Greece

Intl. Photo Optical Show Assn. - Defunct.

Intl. Photodynamic Assn. [IO], Tokyo, Japan

International Photographic Historical Organization [IO], San Francisco, CA, United States

Intl. Photographic Historical Org. [10851], PO Box 16074, San Francisco, CA 94116, (415)681-4356

Intl. Photonics Commercialization Alliance [2862], c/o David A. Gottfried, Operations Mgr., The Javelin Gp. Inc., 5450 Campus Dr., Canandaigua, NY 14424, (585)919-3081

Intl. Photonics Commercialization Alliance [IO], Canandaigua, NY, United States

Intl. Phototherapy Assn. [IO], Vancouver, BC, Canada

Intl. Phototherapy Inst. - Defunct.

Intl. Physical Fitness Assn. [3665], 415 W Court St., Flint, MI 48503, (810)239-2166

International Physical Fitness Association [IO], Flint, MI, United States

Intl. Physicians Commn. [★IO]

Intl. Physicians Commn. [★17444]

Intl. Physicians for the Prevention of Nuclear War [18157], 727 Massachusetts Ave., Cambridge, MA 02139, (617)868-5050

Intl. Physicians for the Prevention of Nuclear War [IO], Cambridge, MA, United States

Intl. Pianists' Guild - Defunct.

Intl. Piano Guild [10623]

Intl. Piano Guild [IO], Austin, TX, United States

Intl. Piano Teachers Assn. - Defunct.

Intl. Pietenpol Assn. [21456], PO Box 127, Blakesburg, IA 52536, (641)938-2773

Intl. Pietenpol Assn. [IO], Blakesburg, IA, United States

Intl. Pin Collectors Club - Defunct.

Intl. Pinball Assn. - Address unknown since 1995.

Intl. Pipe Line and Offshore Contractors Assn. [IO], Vernier, Switzerland

Intl. Planetarium Soc. [IO], Greenville, NC, United States

Intl. Planetarium Soc. [6508], c/o Shawn Laatsch, Membership Chm./Treas., Imiloa Astronomy Center of Hawaii, 600 Imiloa Pl., Hilo, HI 96720, (808)969-9735

Intl. Planned Parenthood Fed. - Africa Regional Off. [IO], Nairobi, Kenya

Intl. Planned Parenthood Fed. - East and South East Asia and Oceania Regional Off. [IO], Kuala Lumpur, Malaysia

Intl. Planned Parenthood Fed. European Network [IO], Brussels, Belgium

Intl. Planned Parenthood Fed. - United Kingdom [IO], London, United Kingdom

Intl. Planned Parenthood Fed., Western Hemisphere Region [IO], New York, NY, United States

Intl. Planned Parenthood Fed., Western Hemisphere Region [12184], 120 Wall St., 9th Fl., New York, NY 10005, (212)248-6400

Intl. Planning History Soc. [IO], Birmingham, United Kingdom

Intl. Plant Biotech Network - Defunct.

Intl. Plant Genetic Resources Inst. [IO], Rome, Italy

International Plant Propagators Society [IO], State College, PA, United States

Intl. Plant Propagators Soc. [4981], 615 Williams Grove Rd., Mechanicsburg, PA 17055-7512, (717)691-8898

Intl. Plant Propagators Soc., Eastern Region - Address unknown since 1989.

Intl. Plantation Walking Horse Assn. - Address unknown since 2004.

Intl. Plasma Fractionation Assn. [IO], Amsterdam, Netherlands

Intl. Plastic Modelers Society/United States Br. [22646], PO Box 2475, North Canton, OH 44720-0475, (330)374-3682

Intl. Plate Printers, Die Stampers, and Engravers' Union of North Am. [24085]

Intl. Platform Assn. [10901]

Intl. Plato Soc. [IO], Dublin, Ireland

Intl. Play Equip. Manufacturers Assn. [IO], Harrisburg, PA, United States

Intl. Play Equip. Manufacturers Assn. [3060], 4305 N 6th St., Ste. A, Harrisburg, PA 17110, (717)238-1744

Intl. Playground Contractors Assn. [1028], PO Box 2364, Salt Lake City, UT 84110-2364, (888)908-9519

Intl. Playground Contractors Assn. [IO], Salt Lake City, UT, United States

International Poetry Forum [IO], Pittsburgh, PA, United States

Intl. Poetry Forum [10862], c/o Grace Lib., 3333 5th Ave., Pittsburgh, PA 15213, (412)621-9893

Intl. Police Assn. [IO], Nottingham, United Kingdom

Intl. Police Dogs - Defunct.

Intl. Police and Fire Athletic Assn. - Defunct.

Intl. Police and Fire Chaplain's Assn. [19750], 9393 Pardee Rd., Taylor, MI 48180, (800)994-7322

Intl. Police Mountain Bike Assn. [6172], 583 Frederick Rd., Ste. 5B, Baltimore, MD 21228, (410)744-2400

Intl. Police Work Dog Assn. [5979], PO Box 7455, Greenwood, IN 46143

Intl. Police Work Dog Assn. [IO], Greenwood, IN, United States

Intl. Policy Inst. for Counter-Terrorism [★IO]

Intl. Polio Network [★IO]

Intl. Polio Network [★11981]

Intl. Polka Assn. [10624], 4608 S Archer Ave., Chicago, IL 60632-2932, (800)TO-POLKA

Intl. Polka Assn. [IO], Chicago, IL, United States

Intl. Pompe Assn. [IO], Baarn, Netherlands

Intl. Popcorn Assn. [★1589]

Intl. Population and Family Assn. - Address unknown since 1999.

Intl. Population Inst. - Defunct.

Intl. Population Res. - Defunct.

Intl. Porcelain Art Teachers - Defunct.

Intl. Possibilities Unlimited [18642], 8403 Colesville Rd., Metro Plaza II, Silver Spring, MD 20910, (301)562-0883

Intl. Possibilities Unlimited [IO], Silver Spring, MD, United States

Intl. Post Polio Support Org. [IO], Central Point, OR, United States

Intl. Post Polio Support Org. [16048], 6901 Old Stage Rd., No. 3, Central Point, OR 97502, (541)664-4348

Intl. Postal Collectors League - Address unknown since 1995.

Intl. Postal Stationery Soc. [★22885]

Intl. Postcard Collectors Assn. - Defunct.

Intl. Pot and Kettle Clubs - Defunct.

Intl. Potash Inst. [IO], Horgen, Switzerland

Intl. Potato Center [IO], Lima, Peru

Intl. Powered Access Fed. [IO], Milnthorpe, United Kingdom

Intl. Practical Shooting Confed. Australia [IO], Victoria Park, Australia

Intl. Prader-Willi Syndrome Org. [IO], Costozza, Italy

Intl. Pragmatics Assn. [IO], Antwerp, Belgium

Intl. Prayer Fellowship [IO], Lake Junaluska, NC, United States

Intl. Prayer Fellowship [19898], c/o SEJ Ministry, PO Box 237, Lake Junaluska, NC 28745, (828)454-6710

Intl. Precancel Club [★22861]

Intl. Precious Metals Inst. [7318], 5101 N 12th Ave., Ste. C, Pensacola, FL 32504, (850)476-1156

Intl. Precious Metals Inst. [IO], Pensacola, FL, United States

Intl. Premature Ovarian Failure Assn. [15606], PO Box 23643, Alexandria, VA 22304, (703)913-4787

Intl. Prepaid Communications Assn. [3767]

Intl. Prepress Assn. [★7154]

Intl. Prepress Assn. [★IO]

Intl. Press Assn. - Defunct.

Intl. Press Inst. [IO], Vienna, Austria

Intl. Press Inst., Amer. Comm. [3123], c/o IPI Global Journalist, Missouri Scholarship of Journalism, 132A Neff Annex, Columbia, MO 65211, (573)884-1599

Intl. Press Telecommunications Coun. [IO], Windsor, United Kingdom

Intl. Preview Soc. - Defunct.

Intl. Primary Aluminum Inst. [★IO]

Intl. Primary Market Assn. and Intl. Securities Market Assn. - London [★IO]

Intl. Primate Protection League [IO], Summerville, SC, United States

Intl. Primate Protection League [11418], PO Box 766, Summerville, SC 29484-0766, (843)871-2280

Intl. Primatological Soc. [6419], c/o Richard Wrangham, Pres., Harvard Univ., Peabody Museum, 11 Divinity Ave., Cambridge, MA 02138, (617)495-5948

International Primatological Society [IO], Cambridge, MA, United States

Intl. Primitive Money Soc. - Defunct.

Intl. Prindle Class Racing Assn. [23192], c/o Performance Catamarans Inc., 1800 E Borchard Ave., Santa Ana, CA 92705, (714)835-6416

Intl. Print Triennial Soc. - Krakow [IO], Krakow, Poland

Intl. Printers Supply Salesmen's Guild - Address unknown since 2002.

Intl. Printing and Graphics Communications Union [★24083]

Intl. Prison Ministry [11873], PO Box 2868, Costa Mesa, CA 92628-2868, (800)527-1212

Intl. Prison Ministry [IO], Costa Mesa, CA, United States

Intl. Prisoners Aid Assn. - Defunct.

Intl. Private Energy Assn. - Address unknown since 1999.

Intl. Private Practitioners Assn. [IO], Worcester, United Kingdom

Intl. Probate Research Assn. - Address unknown since 1999.

Intl. Produce Fed. - Defunct.

Intl. Prdt. Safety Mgt. Certification Bd. [★3441]

Intl. Production Planning and Scheduling Assn. [8809], PO Box 5031, Incline Village, NV 89450, (775)833-3922

International Production Planning and Scheduling Association [IO], Incline Village, NV, United States

Intl. Professional Groomers [2960], 120 Turner Ave., Elk Grove Village, IL 60007, (847)758-1938

Intl. Professional Rodeo Assn. [23686], PO Box 83377, Oklahoma City, OK 73148, (405)235-6540

Intl. Professional Security Assn. - England [IO], London, United Kingdom

Intl. Professional Ski Racers Assn. - Address unknown since 1995.

Intl. Professional Surrogates Assn. [16403], 3428 Motor Ave., Los Angeles, CA 90034, (310)836-1662

Reference to "IO" in place of a book number signifies that the association may be found in the 45th edition of International Organizations.

Intl. Professional Surrogates Assn. **[IO]**, Los Angeles, CA, United States
Intl. Professional Vinyl Repair Assn. - Address unknown since 1994.
Intl. Program for Human Resource Development - Defunct.
Intl. Prog. Off. **[★17832]**
Intl. Prog. Off. **[★IO]**
Intl. Programme on Chem. Safety **[IO]**, Geneva, Switzerland
Intl. Programs and Stud. Off. **[★IO]**
Intl. Programs and Stud. Off. **[★17832]**
Intl. Progress Org. **[IO]**, Vienna, Austria
Intl. Proj. Mgt. Assn. **[IO]**, Nijkerk, Netherlands
Intl. Project for Soft Energy Paths - Defunct.
Intl. Proteolysis Soc. **[6549]**, Wayne State Univ. School of Medicine, Scott Hall, Rm. 6304, 540 E Canfield, Detroit, MI 48201, (313)577-0514
Intl. Proteolysis Soc. **[IO]**, Detroit, MI, United States
Intl. Psycho-Oncology Soc. **[IO]**, Charlottesville, VA, United States
Intl. Psycho-Oncology Soc. **[13834]**, c/o Custom Mgt. Gp., 2365 Hunters Way, Charlottesville, VA 22911, (434)293-5350
Intl. Psychoanalytical Assn. **[IO]**, London, United Kingdom
Intl. Psychogeriatric Assn. **[IO]**, Northfield, IL, United States
Intl. Psychogeriatric Assn. **[14512]**, 550 Frontage Rd., Ste. 3759, Northfield, IL 60093, (847)501-3310
Intl. Psychohistorical Assn. **[10125]**, PO Box 314, New York, NY 10024
Intl. Psychohistorical Assn. **[IO]**, New York, NY, United States
Intl. Public Debate Assn. **[IO]**, Monticello, AR, United States
Intl. Public Debate Assn. **[9041]**, c/o Scott Kuttenkuler, Exec. Sec., Box 3460, Monticello, AR 71656
Intl. Public Hea. Watch **[IO]**, Meadowbrook, Australia
Intl. Public Mgt. Assn. for Human Resources **[IO]**, Alexandria, VA, United States
Intl. Public Mgt. Assn. for Human Resources **[1267]**, 1617 Duke St., Alexandria, VA 22314, (703)549-7100
Intl. Public Relations Assn. **[IO]**, Surrey, United Kingdom
Intl. Public Works Fed. - Defunct.
The Intl. Publication Planning Assn. **[3231]**, 1840 41st Ave., Stes. 102-132, Capitola, CA 95010, (704)889-1288
The Intl. Publication Planning Assn. **[IO]**, Capitola, CA, United States
Intl. Publishers Assn. **[IO]**, Geneva, Switzerland
Intl. Publishing Mgt. Assn. **[IO]**, Kearney, MO, United States
Intl. Publishing Mgt. Assn. **[1776]**, 710 Regency Dr., Ste. 6, Kearney, MO 64060, (816)902-4762
Intl. Pugwash **[★17247]**
Intl. Pugwash **[★IO]**
International Pugwash Conferences on Sci. and World Affairs **[★18842]**
Intl. Pulse Trade and Indus. Confed. **[IO]**, Paris, France
Intl. Pumpkin Assn. - Address unknown since 2003.
Intl. Quail Found. - Defunct.
Intl. Quantitative Linguistics Assn. **[IO]**, Toronto, ON, Canada
Intl. Quantum Structure Assn. **[IO]**, Brussels, Belgium
International Quarab Horse Association **[IO]**, Hopkins, MI, United States
Intl. Quarab Horse Assn. **[4903]**, PO Box 263, Hopkins, MI 49328-0263, (269)672-9175
Intl. Quarter Horse Registry **[★4922]**
Intl. Quarter Pony Assn. **[4904]**, PO Box 125, Sheridan, CA 95681, (916)645-9313
Intl. Quick Printing Found. - Defunct.
Intl. Quilt Assn. **[22162]**, 7660 Woodway, Ste. 550, Houston, TX 77063, (713)781-6864
International Quilt Association **[IO]**, Houston, TX, United States
Intl. R/C Helicopter Assn. **[22647]**, 5161 E Memorial Dr., Muncie, IN 47302-9050, (765)287-1256
Intl. Rabbinic Comm. for the Safety of Israel - Address unknown since 1988.

Intl. Rack Assn. - Defunct.
Intl. Racquet Sports Assn. **[★3021]**
Intl. Racquet Sports Assn. **[★IO]**
Intl. Racquetball Assn. **[★23678]**
Intl. Racquetball Fed. **[23677]**, 1631 Mesa Ave., Colorado Springs, CO 80906, (719)477-6934
Intl. Racquetball Fed. **[IO]**, Colorado Springs, CO, United States
Intl. Radiation Protection Assn. **[IO]**, Fontenay-aux-Roses, France
Intl. Radiator Standards Assn. **[★IO]**
Intl. Radiator Standards Assn. **[★19897]**
Intl. Radio Club of Am. **[21503]**, PO Box 60241, Lafayette, LA 70596
Intl. Radio and TV Soc. **[★563]**
Intl. Radio and TV Soc. Found. **[563]**, 420 Lexington Ave., Ste. 1601, New York, NY 10170, (212)867-6650
Intl. RadioSurgery Assn. **[16269]**, 3005 Hoffman St., Harrisburg, PA 17110, (717)260-9808
Intl. RadioSurgery Assn. **[IO]**, Harrisburg, PA, United States
Intl. Ragdoll Cat Assn. - Address unknown since 1999.
Intl. Raiffeisen Union **[IO]**, Bonn, Germany
Intl. Rail Transport Comm. **[IO]**, Bern, Switzerland
Intl. Railroad and Transportation Postcard Collectors Club **[22055]**
Intl. Railway Gen. Foremen's Associations **[★3283]**
Intl. Rainwater Catchment Systems Assn. **[7832]**, c/o Trisha Macomber, UH-CTAHR-NREM, 875 Komohana St., Hilo, HI 96720
International Rainwater Catchment Systems Association **[IO]**, Hilo, HI, United States
Intl. Randonneurs - Defunct.
Intl. Ranger Fed. **[IO]**, Mount Beauty, Australia
Intl. Rare Breed Dog Club **[★IO]**
Intl. Rare Breed Dog Club **[★22290]**
Intl. Ray Price Fan Club **[★24963]**
Intl. Rayon and Synthetic Fibres Comm. **[IO]**, Brussels, Belgium
Intl. Reading Assn. **[IO]**, Newark, DE, United States
Intl. Reading Assn. **[9043]**, PO Box 8139, Newark, DE 19714-8139, (302)731-1600
Intl. Real Estate Fed; FIABCI-U.S.A. - U.S. Chap., **[3310]**
Intl. Real Estate Fed. - France **[IO]**, Paris, France
Intl. Real Estate Inst. **[IO]**, Alexandria, MN, United States
Intl. Real Estate Inst. **[3316]**, 1224 N Nokomis NE, Alexandria, MN 56308-5072, (320)763-4648
Intl. Rebecca West Soc. **[11178]**, c/o Helen Macleod, Sec.-Treas., 129 Columbia Heights, No. 42, Brooklyn, NY 11202
Intl. Reception Operators - Defunct.
Intl. Reciprocal Trade Assn. **[3841]**, 140 Metro Park Dr., Rochester, NY 14623-2641, (585)424-2940
Intl. Reciprocal Trade Assn. **[IO]**, Rochester, NY, United States
Intl. Recording Media Assn. **[IO]**, Princeton, NJ, United States
Intl. Recording Media Assn. **[1370]**, 182 Nassau St., Ste. 204, Princeton, NJ 08542, (609)279-1700
Intl. Records Mgt. Trust **[IO]**, London, United Kingdom
Intl. Recreational Go-Kart Assn. **[IO]**, Fort Worth, TX, United States
Intl. Recreational Go-Kart Assn. **[1310]**, 1113 Belle Pl., Fort Worth, TX 76107, (817)738-3344
Intl. Red Locust Control Org. for Central and Southern Africa **[IO]**, Ndola, Zambia
Intl. Red Locust Control Ser. **[★IO]**
Intl. Reference Centre for Community Water Supply and Sanitation **[★IO]**
Intl. Reference Org. in Forensic Medicine and Sciences - Address unknown since 1999.
Intl. Reform Fed. - Address unknown since 2005.
Intl. Refractive Surgery Club **[15689]**, c/o Marcie B. Stein, 4000 Legato Rd., No. 850, Fairfax, VA 22033, (703)591-2220
Intl. Refractive Surgery Club **[IO]**, Fairfax, VA, United States
Intl. Regional Magazine Assn. **[2443]**, c/o Herman Kelly, Exec. Dir., 1320 E Univ. Ave., Georgetown, TX 78626, (512)819-9500

Intl. Regional Org. of Plant Protection and Animal Hea. **[IO]**, San Salvador, El Salvador
International Register of Rural Sociologists **[★IO]**
International Register of Rural Sociologists **[★7664]**
Intl. Registry of Early Corvettes - Address unknown since 1987.
Intl. Registry of Org. Development Professionals **[2865]**, c/o The Org. Development Inst., 11234 Walnut Ridge Rd., Chesterland, OH 44026, (440)729-7419
Intl. Registry of Org. Development Professionals **[IO]**, Chesterland, OH, United States
Intl. Registry for Religious-Wo/men-Artists - Defunct.
Intl. Rehabilitation Coun. for Torture Victims **[IO]**, Copenhagen, Denmark
International Relations
ACP-EU Joint Parliamentary Assembly **[IO]**
Advocates Intl. **[17998]**
Africa Action **[16918]**
Africa-America Inst. **[16919]**
Africa-American Friendship Soc. **[18862]**
Africa Faith and Justice Network **[16920]**
Africa News Ser. **[16921]**
Africare **[16924]**
Alliance for Peacebuilding **[17248]**
America-Georgia Bus. Coun. **[2296]**
Amer. and African Bus. Women's Alliance **[691]**
Amer. Bahraini Friendship Soc. **[19150]**
Amer. Ditchley Found. **[17857]**
Amer. Iranian Coun. **[17926]**
American-Kuwaiti Alliance **[2299]**
Amer. Peace Soc. **[17858]**
Amer. Psychological Assn. - Div. of Intl. Psychology **[16127]**
Amer. Red Cross Overseas Assn. **[12831]**
American-Russian Chamber of Commerce and Indus. **[24261]**
Amer. Sovereignty Task Force **[17859]**
Amer. Task Force on Palestine **[17860]**
Armenian Amer. Chamber of Commerce **[24263]**
ASEAN Regional Forum **[IO]**
Assn. for the Advancement of Dutch-American Stud. **[9908]**
Assn. of Concerned African Scholars **[16926]**
Assn. of European Border Regions **[IO]**
Australia Bhutan Friendship Assn. **[IO]**
Australian Amer. Assn. **[IO]**
Australian Inst. of Intl. Affairs **[IO]**
Australian and New Zealand Stud. Assn. of North Amer. **[8484]**
Austrian Cultural Forum **[9625]**
Bhutan Soc. of the United Kingdom **[IO]**
Bilateral US-Arab Chamber of Commerce **[24226]**
Botswana-Sweden Friendship Assn. **[IO]**
Bridging Nations **[IO]**
Bridging Nations **[17861]**
British-Yemeni Soc. **[IO]**
Bus. Coun. for Intl. Understanding **[IO]**
Bus. Coun. for Intl. Understanding **[17862]**
Cameroon-USA Chamber of Commerce **[24249]**
Canadian/American Border Trade Alliance **[3838]**
Canadian Inst. of Intl. Affairs **[IO]**
Caribbean-Central Amer. Action **[12421]**
Carnegie Endowment for Intl. Peace **[17863]**
Carnegie Endowment for Intl. Peace **[IO]**
Center for New Natl. Security **[17864]**
Center for War/Peace Stud. **[17865]**
Centre for Applied Stud. in Intl. Negotiations **[IO]**
Chile-U.S. Chamber of Commerce **[24270]**
Christian Friends of Israel - USA **[19777]**
Citizens Network for Foreign Affairs **[17866]**
Coalition for Amer. Leadership Abroad **[17867]**
Coalition for Amer. Leadership Abroad **[IO]**
Comm. on US/Latin Amer. Relations **[19194]**
Conflict Resolution Prog. **[18111]**
Consumers for World Trade **[17325]**
Coun. for Asia-Europe Cooperation **[IO]**
Coun. on Foreign Relations **[17608]**
Croatian Amer. Assn. **[17868]**
Croatian-American Chamber of Commerce **[24314]**
Czech-North Amer. Chamber of Commerce **[24274]**
Danish Foreign Policy Soc. **[IO]**
Delegation of the European Commn. to Guyana, Suriname, Trinidad and Tobago, Aruba and the Netherlands Antilles **[IO]**

A star before a book entry number signifies that the name is not listed separately, but is mentioned within the entry.

Delegation of the European Commn. - Jamaica, Belize, The Bahamas, Turks and Caicos Islands and the Cayman Islands [IO]
Diplomatic and Consular Officers, Retired [5745]
Ditchley Found. [IO]
East-West Center [17882]
Egyptian Student Assn. in North Am. [9179]
Eisenhower Fellowships [17884]
European Commn. - Barbados and Eastern Caribbean Delegation [IO]
European Commn. - Congo Delegation [IO]
European Commn. - Kenya Delegation [IO]
European Commn. - Mozambique Delegation [IO]
European Commn. - Pacific Delegation [IO]
European Commn. - Suriname Off. [IO]
European Commn. - Tanzania Delegation [IO]
European Commn. - Togo Delegation [IO]
European Commn. - Trinidad and Tobago Delegation [IO]
Fed. of Philippine Amer. Chambers of Commerce [24277]
Foreign Policy Assn. [17610]
French Inst. of Intl. Relations [IO]
Friends of Malawi [9851]
Friends of Sabeel - North Am. [18205]
Friendship Ambassadors Found. [17888]
Friendship Force Intl. [17889]
Georgia-USA Chamber of Commerce [24278]
German Coun. on Foreign Relations [IO]
German Inst. for Intl. and Security Affairs [IO]
Ghana-USA Chamber of Commerce [24279]
Global Interdependence Center [18835]
Global Majority [17249]
Global Options [18448]
Golden Rule Found. [10186]
Greek Amer. Chamber of Commerce [24280]
Hispanic Coun. on Intl. Relations [17869]
Hispanic Coun. on Intl. Relations [IO]
The Hospitality and Info. Ser. [17896]
Hungarian Amer. Coalition [12451]
Hungarian Amer. Coalition [IO]
Inst. for Intercultural Stud. [10234]
Inst. of Intl. Relations Prague [IO]
Intl. Center [17613]
Intl. Center in New York [17897]
Intl. Peace Operations Assn. [18213]
Intl. Pen Friends [22138]
Iraqi Amer. Chamber of Commerce and Indus. [24285]
Israel/Palestine Center for Res. and Info. [IO]
Jamaica USA Chamber of Commerce [24287]
Japan-America Soc. of Washington, D.C. [10263]
Japan Info. Access Proj. [10265]
Japan Inst. of Intl. Affairs [IO]
A Jewish Voice for Peace [19184]
Joan B. Kroc Inst. for Intl. Peace Stud. [18216]
Laotian Amer. Natl. Alliance [19192]
Laotian Amer. Soc. [19193]
Macedonian Amer. Friendship Assn. [19220]
Meridian Intl. Center [17901]
Nanoose Conversion Campaign [IO]
Natl. Comm. on Amer. Foreign Policy [17615]
Natl. Comm. on United States-China Relations [17064]
Natl. Coun. for Intl. Visitors [17903]
Natl. Democratic Inst. for Intl. Affairs [17870]
Natl. Democratic Inst. for Intl. Affairs [IO]
Natl. Fed. of Croatian Americans [17362]
Netherlands Soc. for Intl. Affairs [IO]
Network 20/20 [18004]
No Peace Without Justice [18227]
North American-Bulgarian Chamber of Commerce [24291]
Norwegian Inst. of Intl. Affairs [IO]
Open Soc. Inst. [IO]
Open Soc. Inst. [17871]
Oper. Crossroads Africa [16932]
Org. of Chinese Americans [17065]
Pakistan Chamber of Commerce USA [24364]
Pakistan Inst. of Intl. Affairs [IO]
Partners for Peace [18230]
People to People Intl. [17909]
Play for Peace [12699]
Polish Amer. Chamber of Commerce [24293]
Polish-American-Jewish Alliance for Youth Action [13510]

Proj. South: Inst. for the Elimination of Poverty and Genocide [17872]
Proj. South: Inst. for the Elimination of Poverty and Genocide [IO]
Royal Inst. of Intl. Relations [IO]
The Russian-American Center/Track Two Inst. for Citizen Diplomacy [17912]
Russian-American Chamber of Commerce [24294]
Russian-American Chamber of Commerce in the USA [24371]
Salvadoran Amer. Leadership and Educational Fund [17484]
Scholars for Peace in the Middle East [18070]
Secretary's Open Forum [17617]
Serbian-American Chamber of Commerce [24373]
Sierra Visions [12444]
Sister Cities Intl. [17913]
Soc. for Historians of Amer. Foreign Relations [10156]
Soc. for Indonesian-Americans [19116]
South African Inst. of Intl. Affairs [IO]
South African USA Chamber of Commerce [24295]
Sovereignty Intl. [17873]
Sovereignty Intl. [IO]
StandWithUs [17941]
Student Letter Exchange [22144]
Swedish Inst. of Intl. Affairs [IO]
TransAfrica Forum [16934]
Transnational Diplomatic Network [17874]
Transnational Diplomatic Network [IO]
Trilateral Commn. [IO]
Trilateral Commn. [17875]
Trinidad and Tobago/USA Chamber of Commerce [24298]
Trust for Mutual Understanding [10232]
Turkish-American Chamber of Commerce and Indus. [24384]
Turkish Coalition of Am. [18754]
U.S. of America-China Chamber of Commerce [24310]
U.S.-Bahrain Bus. Coun. [2315]
U.S. Canada Peace Anniversary Assn. [19299]
U.S.-China Peoples Friendship Assn. [17066]
U.S.-Cuba Trade Assn. [2316]
United States-Indonesia Soc. [775]
U.S.-Japan Bus. Coun. [24347]
U.S.-Kazakhstan Bus. Assn. [2317]
Uniterra Found. [17915]
Unity Coalition for Israel [8672]
US-Azerbaijan Coun. [17876]
US-Ireland Alliance [776]
Voices of September 11th [18737]
Voices in the Wilderness [18253]
Wales North Am. Bus. Chamber [24306]
Washington Inst. of Foreign Affairs [17877]
Washington Inst. of Foreign Affairs [IO]
Washington Off. on Africa [16935]
Weatherhead Center for Intl. Affairs [17878]
Weatherhead Center for Intl. Affairs [IO]
William J. Clinton Found. [17855]
Win Without War [18124]
Workshop 3 [IO]
World Neighbors [17921]
World Policy Inst. [17620]
World Soc. of Mixed Jurisdiction Jurists [5957]
Worldwide Friendship Intl. [22147]
Young Koreans United [12485]
Intl. Relations Center [16976], PO Box 2178, Silver City, NM 88062, (505)388-0208
Intl. Relations Center [IO], Silver City, NM, United States
Intl. Relief And Development [IO], Arlington, VA, United States
Intl. Relief And Development [11782], 1621 N Kent St., 4th Fl., Arlington, VA 22209, (703)248-0161
Intl. Relief Assn. [★12812]
Intl. Relief Assn. [★IO]
Intl. Relief Friendship Found. [IO], Barrytown, NY, United States
Intl. Relief Friendship Found. [13171], 30 Seminary Dr., No. 228, Barrytown, NY 12507, (917)319-6802
Intl. Relief Teams [12863], 4560 Alvarado Canyon Rd., Ste. 2G, San Diego, CA 92120, (619)284-7979

Intl. Relief Teams [IO], San Diego, CA, United States
Intl. Religious Fine Art Program - Address unknown since 1989.
Intl. Religious Liberty Assn. [18512], c/o Carol Rasmussen, Admin. Asst., 12501 Old Columbia Pike, Silver Spring, MD 20904-6600, (301)680-6686
Intl. Religious Liberty Assn. [IO], Silver Spring, MD, United States
Intl. Religious Studies Unit - Defunct.
Intl. Relocation Center - Address unknown since 2006.
Intl. Reprographic Assn. [1801], 401 N Michigan Ave., Chicago, IL 60611, (312)245-1026
Intl. Reprographic Assn. [IO], Chicago, IL, United States
Intl. Reprographic Blueprint Assn. [★IO]
Intl. Reprographic Blueprint Assn. [★1801]
Intl. Reptile Soc. - Defunct.
Intl. Republican Inst. - USA [17396], 1225 Eye St. NW, Ste. 700, Washington, DC 20005, (202)408-9450
Intl. Republican Inst. - USA [IO], Washington, DC, United States
Intl. Rescue Comm. - USA [IO], New York, NY, United States
Intl. Rescue Comm. - USA [12812], 122 E 42nd St., New York, NY 10168-1289, (212)551-3000
Intl. Rescue and Emergency Care Assn. [14316], PO Box 431000, Minneapolis, MN 55443, (301)741-0455
Intl. Rescue and Emergency Care Assn. [IO], Minneapolis, MN, United States
Intl. Rescue and First Aid Assn. [★IO]
Intl. Rescue and First Aid Assn. [★14316]
Intl. Res. Coun. [★IO]
Intl. Res. Coun. of Neuromuscular Disorders - Address unknown since 2008.
Intl. Res. and Exchanges Bd. [8621], 2121 K St. NW, Ste. 700, Washington, DC 20037, (202)628-8188
Intl. Res. and Exchanges Bd. [IO], Washington, DC, United States
Intl. Res. Gp. on Coloru Vision Deficiencies [★IO]
Intl. Res. Gp. on Time Budgets and Social Activities [★IO]
Intl. Res. Gp. on Wood Preservation [IO], Stockholm, Sweden
Intl. Res. Inst. for Media, Commun. and Cultural Development [IO], Vienna, Austria
Intl. Res. Soc. for Children's Literature [IO], Newcastle upon Tyne, United Kingdom
Intl. Res. Training Center on Erosion and Sedimentation [IO], Beijing, People's Republic of China
Intl. Resources Gp. [IO], Washington, DC, United States
Intl. Resources Gp. [5564], 1211 Connecticut Ave. NW, Ste. 700, Washington, DC 20036, (202)289-0100
Intl. REST Investigators Soc. [16220]
Intl. Restoration Artists Assn. - Address unknown since 2002.
Intl. Rett Syndrome Assn. [15333], 9121 Piscataway Rd., No. 2B, Clinton, MD 20735, (301)856-3334
Intl. Rett Syndrome Assn. [IO], Clinton, MD, United States
Intl. Rett's Syndrome Assn. [★IO]
Intl. Rett's Syndrome Assn. [★15333]
Intl. Rhythm and Blues Assn. - Address unknown since 1997.
Intl. Rice Commn. [IO], Rome, Italy
Intl. Rice Res. Inst. [IO], Manila, Philippines
Intl. Right of Way Assn. [IO], Torrance, CA, United States
Intl. Right of Way Assn. [6246], 19750 S Vermont Ave., Ste. 220, Torrance, CA 90502-1144, (310)538-0233
Intl. Risk Mgt. Soc. of Japan [IO], Tokyo, Japan
Intl. Rivers Network [IO], Berkeley, CA, United States
Intl. Rivers Network [7833], 1847 Berkeley Way, Berkeley, CA 94703, (510)848-1155
Intl. Road Fed. [3874], 500 Montgomery St., 5th Fl., Alexandria, VA 22314-1565, (703)535-1001

Reference to "IO" in place of a book number signifies that the association may be found in the 45th edition of International Organizations.

Intl. Road Fed. **[IO]**, Alexandria, VA, United States

Intl. Road Safety Org. **[IO]**, Lisbon, Portugal

Intl. Road Transport Union **[IO]**, Geneva, Switzerland

Intl. Rock 'n' Roll Music Assn. - Address unknown since 2001.

Intl. Rodeo Assn. **[★23686]**

Intl. Romani Writers' Assn. **[IO]**, Helsinki, Finland

Intl. Rope Skipping Org. **[★23698]**

Intl. Rorschach Soc. **[IO]**, Enencourt-Leage, France

Intl. Rose O'Neill Club **[★IO]**

Intl. Rose O'Neill Club **[★22399]**

Intl. Rose O'Neill Club Found. **[22399]**, c/o Arlene Asher, Treas., 103 W Locust, Aurora, MO 65605-1416

Intl. Rose O'Neill Club Found. **[IO]**, Branson, MO, United States

Intl. Royal Enterprises - Address unknown since 1987.

Intl. Rubber Conf. Org. **[IO]**, Frankfurt am Main, Germany

Intl. Rubber Study Group **[IO]**, Wembley, United Kingdom

Intl. Rural Development Off. **[★IO]**

Intl. Rural Development Off. **[★17832]**

Intl. Rural Sociology Assn. **[7664]**, c/o David O. Hansen, RSS, Sec.-Treas., Ohio State Univ., Intl. Prog. for Agriculture, 2120 Fyfe Rd., Columbus, OH 43085, (614)292-7252

Intl. Rural Sociology Assn. **[IO]**, Columbus, OH, United States

Intl. Safe Transit Assn. **[IO]**, East Lansing, MI, United States

Intl. Safe Transit Assn. **[3571]**, 1400 Abbott Rd., Ste. 160, East Lansing, MI 48823-1900, (517)333-3437

International Safe Transit Assn; National/ **[★3571]**

Intl. Safety Equip. Assn. **[3445]**, 1901 N Moore St., Arlington, VA 22209-1762, (703)525-1695

Intl. Safety Equip. Assn. **[IO]**, Arlington, VA, United States

Intl. Safety Inst. - Defunct.

Intl. Sailing Fed. **[IO]**, Southampton, United Kingdom

Intl. Sailing Schools Assn. **[IO]**, Douarnenez, France

Intl. Salon of Cartoons - Address unknown since 1989.

Intl. Salvage Union **[IO]**, London, United Kingdom

Intl. Salzedo Soc. **[IO]**, Dornach, Switzerland

Intl. Sand Collectors Soc. **[IO]**, North Haven, CT, United States

Intl. Sand Collectors Soc. **[22056]**, PO Box 117, North Haven, CT 06473-0117, (203)239-5488

Intl. Sanitary Supply Assn. **[2466]**, 7373 N Lincoln Ave., Lincolnwood, IL 60712-1799, (847)982-0800

Intl. Sanitary Supply Assn. **[IO]**, Lincolnwood, IL, United States

The International Savannah Breeders' Association **[IO]**, Lancaster, PA, United States

The Intl. Savannah Breeders' Assn. **[4208]**, 571 Millcross Rd., Lancaster, PA 17601

Intl. Savant Soc. - Address unknown since 1994.

Intl. Save the Pun Found. **[IO]**, Toronto, ON, Canada

Intl. Saw and Knife Assn. **[IO]**, Fresno, CA, United States

Intl. Saw and Knife Assn. **[2390]**, c/o Mr. Kirk M. Wethey, Membership Chm., Ideal Saw Works, 351 O St., Fresno, CA 93721, (559)237-0809

Intl. Scale Soaring Assn. **[22648]**, c/o Rick Briggs, Treas./Webmaster, 3015 Volk Ave., Long Beach, CA 90808, (562)421-4864

Intl. Scale Soaring Assn. **[IO]**, Long Beach, CA, United States

Intl. Schizophrenia Found. **[IO]**, Toronto, ON, Canada

Intl. School Art Program - Defunct.

Intl. School Psychology Assn. **[IO]**, Amsterdam, Netherlands

International Schools

Assn. for the Advancement of Intl. Educ. **[IO]**

Assn. for the Advancement of Intl. Educ. **[8640]**

Assn. of Amer. Intl. Colleges and Universities **[8641]**

Assn. of Amer. Intl. Colleges and Universities **[IO]**

Assn. of Amer. Schools in South Am. **[8642]**

Assn. of Intl. Schools in Africa **[IO]**

East Asia Regional Coun. of Overseas Schools **[IO]**

European Coun. of Intl. Schools **[IO]**

Inst. for Amer. Universities **[IO]**

Inst. for Amer. Universities **[8643]**

Intl. Educ. Res. Found. **[8644]**

Intl. Educ. Res. Found. **[IO]**

Intl. Educator's Inst. **[IO]**

Intl. Educator's Inst. **[8645]**

Intl. Schools Assn. **[8646]**

Intl. Schools Assn. **[IO]**

Intl. Schools Assn. of Thailand **[IO]**

Intl. Schools Services **[IO]**

Intl. Schools Services **[8647]**

Intl. Univ. Found. **[8648]**

Intl. Univ. Found. **[IO]**

United Bd. for Christian Higher Educ. in Asia **[IO]**

United Bd. for Christian Higher Educ. in Asia **[8649]**

Intl. Schools Assn. **[8646]**, 10333 Diego Dr. S, Boca Raton, FL 33428, (561)883-3854

Intl. Schools Assn. **[IO]**, Boca Raton, FL, United States

Intl. Schools Assn. of Thailand **[IO]**, Nonthaburi, Thailand

Intl. Schools Found. **[★IO]**

Intl. Schools Found. **[★8647]**

International Schools Internship Program **[★8645]**

International Schools Internship Program **[★IO]**

Intl. Schools Services **[IO]**, Princeton, NJ, United States

Intl. Schools Services **[8647]**, PO Box 5910, 15 Roszel Rd., Princeton, NJ 08543, (609)452-0990

Intl. Science Found. - Address unknown since 2000.

Intl. Sci. Writers Assn. **[3124]**, c/o James C. Cornell, Pres., 6666 N Mesa View Terr., Tucson, AZ 85718, (520)529-6835

Intl. Sci. Writers Assn. **[IO]**, Tucson, AZ, United States

Intl. Sci. Assn. for World Economy and World Economics **[IO]**, Berlin, Germany

Intl. Scientific Collectors Assn. - Address unknown since 2004.

Intl. Scleroderma Fed. **[★16389]**

Intl. Scleroderma Network **[16387]**, 7455 France Ave. S, No. 266, Edina, MN 55435, (952)831-3091

Intl. Scleroderma Network **[IO]**, Edina, MN, United States

Intl. Scouting Collectors Assn. **[IO]**, Pleasanton, CA, United States

Intl. Scouting Collectors Assn. **[22057]**, c/o Craig Leighty, Pres., 1035 Golden Sands Way, Leland, NC 28451

Intl. Screen Advertising Producers' Assn. - Defunct.

Intl. Sculpture Center **[10958]**, 14 Fairgrounds Rd., Ste. B, Hamilton, NJ 08619-3447, (609)689-1051

Intl. Seahorse and Marine Invertebrate Soc. - Address unknown since 2001.

Intl. SeaKeepers Soc. **[5010]**, 4101 Ravenswood Rd., Ste. 128, Fort Lauderdale, FL 33312, (954)766-7100

Intl. SeaKeepers Soc. **[IO]**, Fort Lauderdale, FL, United States

Intl. Seal, Label and Cigar Band Soc. - Defunct.

Intl. Seapost Cover Club **[★22841]**

Intl. Seapost Cover Club **[★IO]**

Intl. Seaweed Assn. **[IO]**, Sao Paulo, Brazil

Intl. Secret Ser. Assn. **[★IO]**

Intl. Secretariat for Volunteer Service - Defunct.

Intl. Sect. of the Natl. Coun. on Family Relations **[12159]**, 3989 Central Ave. NE, Ste. 550, Minneapolis, MN 55421, (763)781-9331

Intl. Sect. of the Natl. Coun. on Family Relations **[IO]**, Minneapolis, MN, United States

Intl. Securities Market Assn. and Intl. Primary Market Assn. **[★IO]**

Intl. Security Coun. - Address unknown since 1999.

Intl. Security and Detective Alliance **[2323]**

Intl. Security Mgt. Assn. **[3534]**, PO Box 623, Buffalo, IA 52728, (800)368-1894

Intl. Security Mgt. Assn. **[IO]**, Buffalo, IA, United States

Intl. Security Officer's Police and Guard Union - Address unknown since 2001.

Intl. and Security Stud. at Maryland; Center for **[★18598]**

Intl. and Security Stud. at Maryland; Center for **[★IO]**

Intl. Security, Trust and Privacy Alliance **[3535]**, 3525 Del Mar Heights Rd., Ste. 327, San Diego, CA 92130-2122, (703)478-7600

Intl. Seebeck Study Soc. - Defunct.

Intl. Seed Fed. **[IO]**, Nyon, Switzerland

Intl. Seed Testing Assn. **[IO]**, Bassersdorf, Switzerland

Intl. Seismological Centre **[IO]**, Newbury, United Kingdom

Intl. Seminars on Training for Nonviolent Action **[★18115]**

Intl. Senior Citizens Assn. - Address unknown since 2003.

Intl. Senior Lawyers Proj. **[5502]**, c/o Ms. Jean C. Berman, Esq., Exec. Dir., 31 W 52nd St., 3rd Fl., New York, NY 10019, (212)880-5836

Intl. Senior Lawyers Proj. **[IO]**, New York, NY, United States

Intl. Senior Softball Assn. **[IO]**, Manassas, VA, United States

Intl. Senior Softball Assn. **[23790]**, 9401 East St., Manassas, VA 20110, (703)368-1188

Intl. Seppala Assn. **[22291]**, c/o Jack R. Murray, Sec.-Treas., Tullibardine Farm LLP, 808 Starks Rd., New Sharon, ME 04955

Intl. Serials Data Sys. **[★IO]**

Intl. Ser. for the Acquisition of Agri-biotech Applications **[IO]**, Ithaca, NY, United States

Intl. Ser. for the Acquisition of Agri-biotech Applications **[6398]**, c/o Ms. Patricia Meenen, Financial Mgr., Cornell Univ., 417 Bradfield Hall, Ithaca, NY 14853, (607)255-1724

Intl. Ser. for Human Rights - Switzerland **[IO]**, Geneva, Switzerland

International Service Organization - COSA **[IO]**, Minneapolis, MN, United States

Intl. Ser. Org. - COSA **[13072]**, PO Box 14537, Minneapolis, MN 55414, (763)537-6904

Intl. Service Robot Assn. - Defunct.

Intl. Seven-Star Mantis Style Lee Kam Wing Martial Art Assn. - USA **[23591]**, c/o Raul Ortiz, Ortiz Chinese Boxing Acad., 148-B Middle Neck Rd., Great Neck, NY 11021, (516)972-1670

Intl. Sewing Machine Assn. **[★3784]**

Intl. Sex Worker Found. for Art, Culture and Educ. **[13092]**, 8801 Cedros Ave., No. 7, Panorama City, CA 91402, (818)892-2029

Intl. SGML/XML Users' Gp. **[IO]**, Swindon, United Kingdom

Intl. Shade Tree Conf. **[★IO]**

Intl. Shade Tree Conf. **[★5259]**

Intl. Shadow Project - Defunct.

Intl. Shaolin Kenpo Assn. **[23592]**, 69 Washington St., Daly City, CA 94014, (650)755-8996

Intl. Shaolin Kenpo Assn. **[IO]**, Daly City, CA, United States

Intl. Sharps Injury Prevention Soc. **[IO]**, South Jordan, UT, United States

Intl. Sharps Injury Prevention Soc. **[16380]**, 10046 Prestwick Cir., South Jordan, UT 84095, (801)280-8797

Intl. Sheep Dog Soc. **[IO]**, Bedford, United Kingdom

Intl. Ship Elec. Ser. Assn. **[★IO]**

Intl. Ship Elecl. and Engg. Ser. Assn. **[IO]**, Ware, United Kingdom

Intl. Ship Managers Assn. **[IO]**, Monaco, Monaco

Intl. Ship Masters' Assn. **[IO]**, Toledo, OH, United States

Intl. Ship Masters' Assn. **[2579]**, c/o ISMA-Toledo Lodge No. 9, PO Box 167820, Oregon, OH 43616, (440)933-4376

Intl. Ship Suppliers Assn. **[IO]**, London, United Kingdom

Intl. Shipmasters Assn. of the Great Lakes **[★IO]**

Intl. Shipmasters Assn. of the Great Lakes **[★2579]**

Intl. Shipping Conf. **[★IO]**

Intl. Shipping Fed. **[IO]**, London, United Kingdom

Intl. Ships-In-Bottles Assn. **[★22658]**

Intl. Shooting Coaches Assn. - Address unknown since 2003.

Intl. Shooting Sport Fed. **[IO]**, Munich, Germany

Intl. Show Caves Assn. **[IO]**, Ancona, Italy

Intl. Shrine Clown Assn. **[IO]**, Marine, IL, United States

Intl. Shrine Clown Assn. **[21952]**, PO Box 102, Marine, IL 62061-0102, (618)887-4544

A star before a book entry number signifies that the name is not listed separately, but is mentioned within the entry.

Intl. Shuffleboard Assn. **[23735]**, c/o Joe Messier, Pres./Treas., 390 Santa Fe Trail, North Fort Myers, FL 33917, (239)543-1235

Intl. Shuffleboard Assn. **[IO]**, North Fort Myers, FL, United States

Intl. Siberian Husky Club - Address unknown since 1995.

Intl. Side Saddle Org. **[23529]**, PO Box 161, Stevensville, MD 21666-0161, (410)643-1497

International Side-Saddle Org. and World Sidesaddle Fed., Inc. **[★23529]**

Intl. Sign Assn. **[1189]**, 707 N St. Asaph St., Alexandria, VA 22314, (703)836-4012

Intl. Sign Assn. **[IO]**, Alexandria, VA, United States

International Sikh Org; Coun. of Khalistan/ **[20557]**

Intl. Silk Assn. - U.S.A. **[3789]**, c/o Seritex, One Madison St., East Rutherford, NJ 07073, (973)472-4200

Intl. Silo Assn. **[181]**, E106 Church Rd., Luxemburg, WI 54217, (920)655-3301

Intl. Silo Assn. **[IO]**, Luxemburg, WI, United States

Intl. Simulation and Gaming Assn. **[IO]**, Washington, DC, United States

Intl. Simulation and Gaming Assn. **[8454]**, c/o John F. Lobuts, George Washington Univ., School of Bus. and Public Mgt., Monroe Hall, Washington, DC 20052, (202)994-6918

Intl. Sinatra Soc. **[24913]**

Intl. Single Comb Black Minorca Club - Address unknown since 2003.

Intl. Sivananda Yoga Vedanta Center **[IO]**, Val Morin, QC, Canada

International Size Acceptance Association **[IO]**, Austin, TX, United States

Intl. Size Acceptance Assn. **[12645]**, PO Box 82126, Austin, TX 78758, (206)600-3089

Intl. Skateboard Assn. - Defunct.

Intl. Skating Union **[IO]**, Lausanne, Switzerland

Intl. Skeeter Assn. - Address unknown since 1995.

Intl. Skeletal Soc. **[16289]**, c/o Lynne S. Steinbach, Univ. of California San Francisco, Dept. of Radiology, San Francisco, CA 94143-0628

Intl. Skeletal Soc. **[IO]**, San Francisco, CA, United States

Intl. Ski Dancing Assn. **[23751]**, c/o Cheryl Malfetti, Co-Founder/Co-Exec. Dir., 30 Tumalum Cir., Westerly, RI 02891, (401)596-8009

Intl. Ski Fed. **[IO]**, Oberhof, Switzerland

Intl. Skiing History Assn. **[IO]**, South Burlington, VT, United States

Intl. Skiing History Assn. **[10965]**, 530 Cheese Factory Rd., South Burlington, VT 05403, (802)863-2511

Intl. Skin Care Nursing Gp. **[IO]**, Southampton, United Kingdom

Intl. Sled Dog Racing Assn. **[IO]**, Merrifield, MN, United States

Intl. Sled Dog Racing Assn. **[23394]**, c/o Dave Steele, Exec. Dir., 22702 Rebel Rd., Merrifield, MN 56465, (218)765-4297

Intl. Sleep Products Assn. **[1974]**, 501 Wythe St., Alexandria, VA 22314-1917, (703)683-8371

Intl. Sleep Products Assn. **[IO]**, Alexandria, VA, United States

Intl. Slurry Seal Assn. **[★IO]**

Intl. Slurry Seal Assn. **[★632]**

Intl. Slurry Surfacing Assn. **[632]**, 3 Church Cir., PMB 250, Annapolis, MD 21401, (410)267-0023

Intl. Slurry Surfacing Assn. **[IO]**, Annapolis, MD, United States

Intl. Small Bus. Consortium **[IO]**, Norman, OK, United States

Intl. Small Bus. Consortium **[3612]**, 3309 Windjammer St., Norman, OK 73072

Intl. Snow Leopard Trust **[5329]**, 4649 Sunnyside Ave. N, Ste. 325, Seattle, WA 98103, (206)632-2421

Intl. Snow Leopard Trust **[IO]**, Seattle, WA, United States

Intl. Snowmobile Mfrs. Assn. **[IO]**, Haslett, MI, United States

Intl. Snowmobile Mfrs. Assn. **[3368]**, 1640 Haslett Rd., Ste. 170, Haslett, MI 48840, (517)339-7788

Intl. Snowshoe Coun. - Defunct.

Intl. Snowshoe Fed. - Defunct.

Intl. Soap Box Derby **[23770]**, PO Box 7225, Akron, OH 44306, (330)733-8723

Intl. Soccer League - Defunct.

Intl. Social Affiliation of Women Airline Pilots **[★157]**

Intl. Social Affiliation of Women Airline Pilots **[★IO]**

Intl. Social Insurance Conf. **[★IO]**

Intl. Social Sci. Coun. **[IO]**, Paris, France

Intl. Social Security Assn. **[IO]**, Geneva, Switzerland

Intl. Social Ser., Amer. Br. **[★IO]**

Intl. Social Ser., Amer. Br. **[★12595]**

Intl. Social Ser. - Australian Br. **[IO]**, Melbourne, Australia

Intl. Social Ser. Canada **[IO]**, Ottawa, ON, Canada

Intl. Social Ser. - Gen. Secretariat **[IO]**, Geneva, Switzerland

Intl. Social Ser. - Hong Kong **[IO]**, Hong Kong, People's Republic of China

Intl. Social Ser. - Japan **[IO]**, Tokyo, Japan

Intl. Social Ser., U.S.A. Br. **[12595]**, 207 E Redwood St., Ste. 300, Baltimore, MD 21202, (443)451-1200

Intl. Social Ser., U.S.A. Br. **[IO]**, Baltimore, MD, United States

Intl. Socialist Org. **[IO]**, Chicago, IL, United States

Intl. Socialist Org. **[18654]**, PO Box 16085, Chicago, IL 60616-0085, (773)583-5069

Intl. Socialist Org. Australia **[IO]**, Sydney, Australia

Intl. Soc. for the Abolition of Data Processing Machines - Address unknown since 1995.

Intl. Soc. of Acoustic Remote Sensing of the Atmosphere and Oceans **[IO]**, Cambridge, United Kingdom

Intl. Soc. of Active Youth **[IO]**, Delmas, Haiti

Intl. Soc. for Adaptive Behavior **[IO]**, Honolulu, HI, United States

Intl. Soc. for Adaptive Behavior **[6533]**, c/o Prof. Herb Roitblat, VP, Dept. of Psychology, Univ. of Hawaii at Manoa, 2430 Campus Rd., Honolulu, HI 96822, (808)956-6727

Intl. Soc. for Adolescent Psychiatry and Psychology **[16087]**, c/o Rosalie J. Landy, Admin. Dir. for USA-Asia-SA, 223 Sunset Blvd., Bronx, NY 10473, (718)892-4868

Intl. Soc. for Adolescent Psychiatry and Psychology **[IO]**, Bronx, NY, United States

Intl. Soc. for Adult Congenital Cardiac Disease **[IO]**, Raleigh, NC, United States

Intl. Soc. for Adult Congenital Cardiac Disease **[13912]**, 1500 Sunday Dr., Ste. 102, Raleigh, NC 27607, (919)861-5578

Intl. Soc. for the Advancement of Humanistic Studies in Gynecology - Address unknown since 1999.

Intl. Soc. of Aeronauts **[★23097]**

Intl. Soc. for Aerosols in Medicine **[IO]**, Gemunden, Germany

Intl. Soc. of African Scientists **[IO]**, Wilmington, DE, United States

Intl. Soc. of African Scientists **[7611]**, PO Box 9209, Wilmington, DE 19809

Intl. Soc. of Agile Mfg. **[2558]**, c/o Suren Dwivedi, PhD, IJAMS Chief Ed., 2851 Johnston St., PMB No. 325, Lafayette, LA 70503, (337)989-7262

Intl. Soc. of Agile Mfg. **[IO]**, Lafayette, LA, United States

Intl. Soc. for Aging and Physical Activity **[IO]**, Urbana, IL, United States

Intl. Soc. for Aging and Physical Activity **[13545]**, c/o Wojtek Chodzko-Zajko, PhD, Pres., Dept. of Kinesiology, Univ. of Illinois at Urbana-Champaign, Louise Freer Hall, 906 S Goodwin Ave., Urbana, IL 61801, (217)244-0823

Intl. Soc. of Air Safety Investigators **[12966]**, 107 E Holly Ave., Ste. 11, Sterling, VA 20164, (703)430-9668

Intl. Soc. of Air Safety Investigators **[IO]**, Sterling, VA, United States

Intl. Soc. for Alstrom Syndrome Families **[★IO]**

Intl. Soc. for Alstrom Syndrome Families **[★14440]**

Intl. Soc. for Alternative and Augmentative Commun. - Finland **[IO]**, Helsinki, Finland

International Society for Anaesthetic Pharmacology **[IO]**, Cleveland, OH, United States

Intl. Soc. for Anaesthetic Pharmacology **[13685]**, 2 Summit Park Dr., No. 140, Cleveland, OH 44131-2571, (216)447-7862

Intl. Soc. for Analytical Cytology **[6583]**, 9650 Rockville Pike, Bethesda, MD 20814-3998, (301)634-7435

Intl. Soc. for Analytical Cytology **[IO]**, Bethesda, MD, United States

Intl. Soc. of Andrology **[IO]**, Rotterdam, Netherlands

Intl. Soc. of Anglo-Saxonists **[IO]**, Tallahassee, FL, United States

Intl. Soc. of Anglo-Saxonists **[8379]**, c/o David F. Johnson, PhD, Exec. Dir., Florida State Univ., 432 Diffenbaugh, Tallahassee, FL 32306

Intl. Soc. for Animal Genetics **[IO]**, Jouy-en-Josas, France

Intl. Soc. for Animal License Collectors **[IO]**, Clinton, KY, United States

Intl. Soc. of Animal License Collectors **[22058]**, 928 SR 2206, Clinton, KY 42031, (270)653-6060

Intl. Soc. for Animal Rights **[11419]**, 965 Griffin Pond Rd., Clarks Summit, PA 18411-9214, (570)586-2200

Intl. Soc. for Animal Rights **[IO]**, Clarks Summit, PA, United States

Intl. Soc. for Anthrozoology **[IO]**, London, United Kingdom

Intl. Soc. of Antique Scale Collectors **[IO]**, Los Angeles, CA, United States

Intl. Soc. of Antique Scale Collectors **[22059]**, 3616 Noakes St., Los Angeles, CA 90023, (323)263-6878

International Soc. for Apple Parer Enthusiasts - Address unknown since 2001.

Intl. Soc. for Applied Ethology **[IO]**, Helsinki, Finland

Intl. Soc. of Applied Intelligence **[IO]**, San Marcos, TX, United States

Intl. Soc. of Applied Intelligence **[6486]**, Texas State Univ., San Marcos, Dept. of Cmpt. Sci., 601 Univ. Dr., San Marcos, TX 78666-4616, (512)245-3409

Intl. Soc. of Appraisers **[283]**, 1131 SW 7th St., Ste. 105, Renton, WA 98055, (206)241-0359

Intl. Soc. of Appraisers **[IO]**, Renton, WA, United States

Intl. Soc. of Arachnology **[IO]**, Berlin, Germany

Intl. Soc. of Arboriculture **[IO]**, Champaign, IL, United States

Intl. Soc. of Arboriculture **[5259]**, PO Box 3129, Champaign, IL 61826-3129, (217)355-9411

Intl. Soc. of Arboriculture - United Kingdom and Ireland **[IO]**, Wednesbury, United Kingdom

Intl. Soc. of Arthroscopy, Knee Surgery and Orthopaedic Sports Medicine **[IO]**, San Ramon, CA, United States

Intl. Soc. of Arthroscopy, Knee Surgery and Orthopaedic Sports Medicine **[15771]**, 2678 Bishop Dr., Ste. 250, San Ramon, CA 94583-2338, (925)807-1197

Intl. Soc. of Artificial Life **[6584]**, Reed Coll., 3203 SE Woodstock Blvd., Portland, OR 97202-8199, (503)788-6697

International Society of Artificial Life **[IO]**, Portland, OR, United States

Intl. Soc. of Artists - Defunct.

Intl. Soc. for the Arts, Sciences and Tech; Leonardo, The **[9610]**

Intl. Soc. for Astrological Res. **[6494]**, PO Box 38613, Los Angeles, CA 90038, (805)525-0461

Intl. Soc. for Astrological Res. **[IO]**, Los Angeles, CA, United States

Intl. Soc. for Augmentative and Alternative Commun. **[IO]**, Toronto, ON, Canada

Intl. Soc. for Autistic Children - Defunct.

Intl. Soc. of Aviation Writers - Defunct.

Intl. Soc. of Barristers **[6331]**, 802 Legal Res. Bldg., Univ. of Michigan Law School, Ann Arbor, MI 48109-1215, (734)763-0165

Intl. Soc. of Barristers **[IO]**, Ann Arbor, MI, United States

Intl. Soc. of Bassists **[IO]**, Dallas, TX, United States

Intl. Soc. of Bassists **[10625]**, 14070 Proton Rd., Ste. 100, Dallas, TX 75244, (972)233-9107

Intl. Soc. for Bayesian Anal. **[7291]**, c/o Prof. Bruno Sanso, Treas., Dept. of Applied Mathematics and Statistics, School of Engg., Univ. of California, 1156 High St., MS: SOE2, Santa Cruz, CA 95064, (831)459-1484

Intl. Soc. for Bayesian Anal. **[IO]**, Santa Cruz, CA, United States

Intl. Soc. of Behavioral Medicine **[IO]**, Ulm, Germany

Intl. Soc. for Behavioral Nutrition and Physical Activity **[13745]**, c/o Marti Kubik, PhD, Univ. of Minnesota, 308 Harvard St. SE, Minneapolis, MN 55455, (612)625-0606

Reference to "IO" in place of a book number signifies that the association may be found in the 45th edition of International Organizations.

Intl. Soc. of Beverage Technologists [6543], 3340 Pilot Knob Rd., St. Paul, MN 55121, (651)454-7250

Intl. Soc. of Beverage Technologists [IO], St. Paul, MN, United States

Intl. Soc. of Bible Collectors [IO], Minneapolis, MN, United States

Intl. Soc. of Bible Collectors [19523], c/o Carl V. Johnson, Pres., PO Box 26654, Minneapolis, MN 55426

Intl. Soc. for Bioengineering and the Skin [★IO]

Intl. Soc. of Bioethics [IO], Asturias, Spain

Intl. Soc. for Biological and Environmental Repositories [IO], Bethesda, MD, United States

Intl. Soc. for Biological and Environmental Repositories [6585], 9650 Rockville Pike, Bethesda, MD 20814-3993, (301)634-7949

Intl. Soc. of Biological Therapy of Cancer [13835], 555 E Wells St., Ste. 1100, Milwaukee, WI 53202-3823, (414)271-2456

International Society for Biological Therapy of Cancer [IO], Milwaukee, WI, United States

Intl. Soc. for Bioluminescence and Chemiluminescence [IO], Madison, WI, United States

Intl. Soc. for Bioluminescence and Chemiluminescence [7612], c/o Erika Hawkins, Treas./Membership Sec., 2800 Woods Hollow Rd., Madison, WI 53711, (608)274-4330

Intl. Soc. of Biomechanics [IO], Wollongong, Australia

Intl. Soc. for Biomedical Res. on Alcoholism [IO], Denver, CO, United States

Intl. Soc. for Biomedical Res. on Alcoholism [16506], PO Box 202332, Denver, CO 80220-8332, (303)355-6420

Intl. Soc. for Biophysics and Imaging of the Skin [IO], Hamburg, Germany

Intl. Soc. for Biosafety Res. [IO], Riverside, CA, United States

Intl. Soc. for Biosafety Res. [6586], c/o Alan McHughen, PhD, Treas., Batchelor Hall 3110, Univ. of California, Riverside, CA 92521-0124

Intl. Soc. of Blood Purification [14791], c/o Prof. Thomas A. Golper, MD, Sec., S-3303 MCN, Vanderbilt Univ. Medical Ctr., 1161 21st Ave. S, Nashville, TN 37232-2372, (615)343-2220

Intl. Soc. of Blood Purification [IO], Nashville, TN, United States

Intl. Soc. of Blood Transfusion [IO], Amsterdam, Netherlands

Intl. Soc. for British Genealogy and Family History [IO], Westminster, CO, United States

Intl. Soc. for British Genealogy and Family History [21123], PO Box 350459, Westminster, CO 80035-0459, (303)422-9371

Intl. Soc. for Burn Injuries [13783], c/o Elisabeth Greenfield McManus, RN, Admin., 2172 US Hwy. 181 S, Floresville, TX 78114-5015

Intl. Soc. for Burn Injuries [IO], Boston, MA, United States

Intl. Soc. of Bus. Astrologers [IO], Bronshoj, Denmark

Intl. Soc. for Bus. Educ. [IO], Athens, GA, United States

Intl. Soc. for Bus. Educ. [8027], c/o John Lightle, Gen. Sec., PO Box 2083, Marion, IN 46952, (765)654-7753

Intl. Soc. of Cardiology [★IO]

Intl. Soc. for Cardiovascular Res. [★IO]

Intl. Soc. for Cardiovascular Surgery - Address unknown since 2006.

Intl. Soc. for Cell Biology [★6581]

Intl. Soc. for Cell Biology [★IO]

Intl. Soc. of Certified Electronics Technicians [IO], Fort Worth, TX, United States

Intl. Soc. of Certified Electronics Technicians [1220], 3608 Pershing Ave., Fort Worth, TX 76107-4527, (817)921-9101

Intl. Soc. of Certified Employee Benefit Specialists [1241], PO Box 209, Brookfield, WI 53008-0209, (262)786-8771

Intl. Soc. of Certified Employee Benefit Specialists [IO], Brookfield, WI, United States

Intl. Soc. of Chem. Ecology [IO], Fargo, ND, United States

Intl. Soc. of Chem. Ecology [6550], c/o Dr. Stephen Foster, Sec., Dept. of Entomology, North Dakota State Univ., Fargo, ND 58105, (701)231-6444

Intl. Soc. of Chemotherapy [IO], Aberdeen, United Kingdom

Intl. Soc. for Chronobiology [IO], Galveston, TX, United States

Intl. Soc. for Chronobiology [6587], Univ. of Texas, Medical Br., Dept. of Neuroscience and Cell Biology, Galveston, TX 77555-1069, (409)772-1294

Intl. Soc. of Citriculture [4737], c/o Dr. Carol Lovatt, Sec.-Treas., Univ. of California, Dept. of Botany and Plant Sciences, Riverside, CA 92521-0124, (909)787-4663

International Society of Citriculture [IO], Riverside, CA, United States

Intl. Soc. of City and Regional Planners [IO], The Hague, Netherlands

Intl. Soc. of Cleaning Technicians [★2477]

Intl. Soc. for Clinical Biostatistics [IO], Birkerod, Denmark

Intl. Soc. for Clinical Densitometry [IO], West Hartford, CT, United States

Intl. Soc. for Clinical Densitometry [15788], 342 N Main St., West Hartford, CT 06117-2507, (860)586-7563

Intl. Soc. for Clinical Electrophysiology of Vision [IO], Glasgow, United Kingdom

Intl. Soc. for Clinical Haemorheology [IO], Beijing, People's Republic of China

Intl. Soc. of Clinical Pathology [★IO]

Intl. Soc. of Coating Sci. and Tech. [IO], Hockessin, DE, United States

Intl. Soc. of Coating Sci. and Tech. [6705], 146 Dewberry Dr., Hockessin, DE 19707, (530)752-8780

Intl. Soc. for Commodity Sci. and Tech. [IO], Vienna, Austria

Intl. Soc. of Commun. Specialists [IO], Marietta, GA, United States

Intl. Soc. of Commun. Specialists [332], 201 Blue Sky Dr., Marietta, GA 30068-3511, (770)973-0662

Intl. Soc. for Community Development - Defunct.

Intl. Soc. of Comparative Adult Educ. [IO], Bamberg, Germany

Intl. Soc. for Comparative Psychology [IO], Detroit, MI, United States

Intl. Soc. for Comparative Psychology [16152], c/o Dr. Ty Partridge, Treas., Dept. of Psychology, Wayne State Univ., 71 W Waren, Detroit, MI 48202, (313)577-2813

Intl. Soc. for the Comparative Stud. of Civilizations [7652], c/o Dr. Lee Daniel Snyder, Pres., New Coll. of Florida, Dept. of History, Sarasota, FL 34243, (941)359-4482

Intl. Soc. for the Comparative Stud. of Civilizations [IO], Sarasota, FL, United States

Intl. Soc. for Complementary Medicine Res. [IO], Ann Arbor, MI, United States

Intl. Soc. for Complementary Medicine Res. [13639], 715 E Huron St., Ste. 2E, Ann Arbor, MI 48104-1555, (734)998-9553

Intl. Soc. for a Complete Earth [12354], PO Box 1952, Kapaa, HI 96746, (808)245-3820

Intl. Soc. for a Complete Earth [IO], Kapaa, HI, United States

International Society for Computational Biology [IO], La Jolla, CA, United States

Intl. Soc. for Computational Biology [2094], c/o San Diego Supercomputer Ctr., UC San Diego, 9500 Gilman Dr., MC 0505, La Jolla, CA 92093-0505, (858)822-0852

Intl. Soc. for Cmpt. Assisted Orthopaedic Surgery [15772], Inst. for Cmpt. Assisted Orthopaedic Surgery, The Western Pennsylvania Hosp., Mellon Pavillon, Ste. 242, 4815 Liberty Ave., Pittsburgh, PA 15224, (412)578-2267

Intl. Soc. for Cmpt. Assisted Orthopaedic Surgery [IO], Pittsburgh, PA, United States

International Society for Computerized Electrocardiology [IO], Solomons, MD, United States

Intl. Soc. for Computerized Electrocardiology [13913], 11495 Emmanuel Way, No. 518, Solomons, MD 20688-3031, (301)855-1004

Intl. Soc. for Contemporary Music - Netherlands [IO], Amsterdam, Netherlands

Intl. Soc. for Contemporary Music - Uruguayan Sect. [IO], Montevideo, Uruguay

Intl. Soc. for Contemporary Music - USA [IO], New York, NY, United States

Intl. Soc. for Contemporary Music - USA [10626], c/o David Mcmullin, 332 Jamaicaway, No. 208, Boston, MA 02130, (617)901-1677

Intl. Soc. of Copier Artists [9507], 759 Pres. St., No. 2H, Brooklyn, NY 11215, (718)638-3264

Intl. Soc. of Copier Artists [IO], Brooklyn, NY, United States

Intl. Soc. of Corvette Owners - Defunct.

Intl. Soc. of Cosmetic and Laser Surgeons [14048], 737 N Michigan Ave., Ste. 2100, Chicago, IL 60611-5405, (312)981-6799

Intl. Soc. of Cosmetic and Laser Surgeons [IO], Tallahassee, FL, United States

Intl. Soc. for Cow Protection [IO], Moundsville, WV, United States

Intl. Soc. for Cow Protection [4155], RD 1, Box 322A, Moundsville, WV 26041, (304)843-1658

Intl. Soc. of Crime Prevention Practitioners [11838], c/o Richard Cannady, Exec. Dir., PO Box 476, Simpsonville, SC 29681, (864)884-8466

Intl. Soc. of Crime Prevention Practitioners [IO], Simpsonville, SC, United States

Intl. Soc. of Criminology [IO], Paris, France

Intl. Soc. for Crippled Children [★IO]

Intl. Soc. for Crippled Children [★16333]

Intl. Soc. of Cryosurgery [IO], Trieste, Italy

Intl. Soc. of Cryptozoology [IO], Tucson, AZ, United States

Intl. Soc. of Cryptozoology [7865]

Intl. Soc. for Cultural and Activity Res. [IO], Copenhagen, Denmark

Intl. Soc. for Cutaneous Lymphomas [IO], Florence, Italy

Intl. Soc. of Cybernetic Medicine - Defunct.

Intl. Soc. Daughters of Utah Pioneers [21252], 300 N Main St., Salt Lake City, UT 84103-1699, (801)532-6479

Intl. Soc. Daughters of Utah Pioneers [IO], Salt Lake City, UT, United States

Intl. Soc. for Dermatologic Surgery [IO], New York, NY, United States

Intl. Soc. for Dermatologic Surgery [14204], c/o Perry Robins, MD, Founder/Pres., 530 1st Ave., New York, NY 10016, (212)686-4663

Intl. Soc. of Dermatology [14205], 138 Palm Coast Pkwy. NE, No. 333, Palm Coast, FL 32137, (386)437-4405

Intl. Soc. of Dermatology [IO], Palm Coast, FL, United States

Intl. Soc. of Dermatology: Tropical, Geographic, and Ecologic [★IO]

Intl. Soc. of Dermatology: Tropical, Geographic, and Ecologic [★14205]

Intl. Soc. of Developmental Biologists [IO], Kobe, Japan

Intl. Soc. for Developmental Neuroscience [IO], Vancouver, BC, Canada

Intl. Soc. for Developmental Psychobiology [IO], San Antonio, TX, United States

Intl. Soc. for Developmental Psychobiology [16153], 8181 Tezel Rd., No. 10269, San Antonio, TX 78250, (866)377-4416

Intl. Soc. for Dialectology and Geolinguistics [IO], Umea, Sweden

Intl. Soc. for Dialogical Sci. [7544], c/o Prof. Vincent W. Hevern, Le Moyne Coll., Psychology Dept., 1419 Salt Springs Rd., Syracuse, NY 13214

Intl. Soc. of Difference Equations [7292], c/o Saber Elaydi, Pres., Trinity Univ., Dept. of Mathematics, Marrs-McLean Sci. Bldg., Rm. 115-D, One Trinity Pl., San Antonio, TX 78212-7200, (210)999-8246

Intl. Soc. of Difference Equations [IO], San Antonio, TX, United States

Intl. Soc. of Differentiation [IO], St. Paul, MN, United States

Intl. Soc. of Differentiation [6588], PO Box 10854, St. Paul, MN 55110, (651)659-9493

Intl. Soc. for Digestive Surgery [14420], Univ. of Washington Medical Center, Box 356410, BB487, Seattle, WA 98195-6410, (206)543-3106

Intl. Soc. for Digestive Surgery [IO], Seattle, WA, United States

A star before a book entry number signifies that the name is not listed separately, but is mentioned within the entry.

Intl. Soc. for Disease Surveillance [IO], Boston, MA, United States

Intl. Soc. for Disease Surveillance [14269], 136 Harrison Ave., Boston, MA 02111

Intl. Soc. of Doctors for the Env. [IO], Basel, Switzerland

Intl. Soc. of Doctors for the Env. - Germany [IO], Bremen, Germany

Intl. Soc. of Dramatists - Address unknown since 2003.

Intl. Soc. of Dynamic Games [IO], Espoo, Finland

Intl. Soc. for Ecological Economics [IO], West Allis, WI, United States

Intl. Soc. for Ecological Economics [1173], c/o Marsha Kopan, PO Box 44194, West Allis, WI 53214, (414)453-0030

Intl. Soc. for Ecological Modelling [4514], PMB 255, 550 M Ritchie Hwy., Severna Park, MD 21146

Intl. Soc. for Ecological Modelling [IO], Severna Park, MD, United States

Intl. Soc. for Ecological Psychology [IO], Hartford, CT, United States

Intl. Soc. for Ecological Psychology [7545], c/o William M. Mace, Dept. of Psychology, 300 Summit St., Hartford, CT 06106-3100, (860)297-2343

Intl. Soc. for Ecology and Culture [IO], Darlington, United Kingdom

Intl. Soc. for Educ. Through Art [IO], DeKalb, IL, United States

Intl. Soc. for Educ. Through Art - Netherlands [IO], Arnhem, Netherlands

Intl. Soc. for Educational Planning [IO], Youngstown, NY, United States

Intl. Soc. for Educational Planning [★IO]

Intl. Soc. for Educational Planning [★8999]

Intl. Soc. for Educational Planning [8999], c/o Dr. Walter S. Polka, Superintendent, Lewiston-Porter Central School, 4061 Creek Rd., Youngstown, NY 14174, (716)878-5028

Intl. Soc. for Educative Communities [IO], Frankfurt am Main, Germany

Intl. Soc. for Eighteenth-Century Stud. [IO], Oxford, United Kingdom

Intl. Soc. of Electrocardiology [IO], Glasgow, United Kingdom

Intl. Soc. of Electrochemistry [IO], Lausanne, Switzerland

Intl. Soc. of Electrophysiology and Kinesiology [IO], Aachen, Germany

Intl. Soc. of Emergency Medical Services - Address unknown since 1999.

Intl. Soc. of Endangered Cats [4209], 3070 Riverside Dr., Ste. 160, Columbus, OH 43221, (614)487-8760

International Society for Endangered Cats [IO], Columbus, OH, United States

Intl. Soc. for Endangered Cats [IO], Calgary, AB, Canada

Intl. Soc. for Endocrinology [IO], Birmingham, United Kingdom

Intl. Soc. of Endovascular Specialists [IO], Phoenix, AZ, United States

Intl. Soc. of Endovascular Specialists [16725], 1928 E Highland Ave., Ste. F104-605, Phoenix, AZ 85016, (602)650-1334

Intl. Soc. for Engg. Educ. [IO], Manno, Switzerland

Intl. Soc. of Environmental Botanists [IO], Lucknow, India

Intl. Soc. for Environmental Ethics [IO], Fairfield, CT, United States

Intl. Soc. for Environmental Ethics [4579], c/o Dr. Lisa Newton, Treas., Fairfield Univ., Prog. in Environmental Stud., Fairfield, CT 06824, (203)254-4128

Intl. Soc. of Environmental Forensics [7098], 150 Fearing St., Ste. 21, Amherst, MA 01002, (413)549-5170

Intl. Soc. of Environmental Forensics [IO], Amherst, MA, United States

Intl. Soc. for Environmental Protection [IO], Vienna, Austria

Intl. Soc. for Environmental Toxicology and Cancer - Defunct.

Intl. Soc. for Equity in Hea. [IO], Toronto, ON, Canada

Intl. Soc. for Ethics and Info. Tech. [IO], Charlottesville, VA, United States

Intl. Soc. for Ethics and Info. Tech. [7198], c/o Philosophy Documentation Center, PO Box 7147, Charlottesville, VA 22906-7147, (414)229-3973

Intl. Soc. of Exercise and Immunology [IO], Copenhagen, Denmark

Intl. Soc. for Existential Psychology and Psychotherapy [IO], Langley, BC, Canada

Intl. Soc. for Experimental Cytology [★IO]

Intl. Soc. for Experimental Cytology [★6581]

Intl. Soc. for Experimental Hematology [14792], 2025 M St. NW, Ste. 800, Washington, DC 20036-3309, (202)367-1183

International Society for Experimental Hematology [IO], Washington, DC, United States

Intl. Soc. of Explosives Engineers [IO], Cleveland, OH, United States

Intl. Soc. of Explosives Engineers [7020], 30325 Bainbridge Rd., Cleveland, OH 44139-2295, (440)349-4400

Intl. Soc. of Explosives Specialists - Address unknown since 1995.

Intl. Soc. of Facilities Executives [2467], c/o INSITE, 200 Corporate Pl., Ste. 6B, Peabody, MA 01960-3840, (978)536-0100

Intl. Soc. for Fat Res. [7405], c/o Amer. Oil Chemists' Soc., PO Box 3489, Champaign, IL 61826-3489, (217)359-2344

International Society for Fat Research [IO], Champaign, IL, United States

Intl. Soc. and Fed. of Cardiology [★IO]

Intl. Soc. of Financiers [IO], Naples, NC, United States

Intl. Soc. of Financiers [1429]

Intl. Soc. of Fine Art Photographers [10852]

Intl. Soc. of Fine Art Photographers [IO], Miami, FL, United States

Intl. Soc. of Fine Arts Appraisers - Address unknown since 2001.

Intl. Soc. for Fire Ser. Instructors [5720], 2425 Hwy. 49 E, Pleasant View, TN 37146, (800)435-0005

Intl. Soc. for Fire Ser. Instructors [IO], Pleasant View, TN, United States

Intl. Soc. of First Responders [IO], Cincinnati, OH, United States

Intl. Soc. of First Responders [14317], 128 E 6th St., Cincinnati, OH 45202, (513)333-7800

Intl. Soc. for Fluoride Res. [IO], Dunedin, New Zealand

Intl. Soc. of Flying Engineers - Defunct.

Intl. Soc. of Folk Harpers and Craftsmen [10627], 1614 Pittman Dr., Missoula, MT 59803, (406)542-1976

Intl. Soc. of Folk Harpers and Craftsmen [IO], Missoula, MT, United States

Intl. Soc. of Folk Narrative Res. [IO], Tartu, Estonia

Intl. Soc. For Apheresis [IO], Otsu, Japan

Intl. Soc. for Forensic Genetics [IO], Santiago de Compostela, Spain

Intl. Soc. of Forensic Odonto-Stomatology [★IO]

Intl. Soc. of the Friends of Georges Cziffra - Amer. Branch - Address unknown since 2002.

Intl. Soc. of Friendship and Good Will [9917], c/o D. Gary Grady, Pres., 3119 Lassiter St., Durham, NC 27707-3888

Intl. Soc. of Friendship and Good Will [IO], Durham, NC, United States

Intl. Soc. of Gastroenterological Carcinogenesis [IO], Hiroshima, Japan

Intl. Soc. for Gen. Relativity and Gravitation [IO], London, United Kingdom

Intl. Soc. for Gen. Systems Res. [★IO]

Intl. Soc. of Geographical and Epidemiological Ophthalmology [IO], Vancouver, BC, Canada

Intl. Soc. for Geothermal Engineering - Defunct.

Intl. Soc. for Gesture Stud. [6712], Dept. of Commun. Stud., The Univ. of Texas at Austin, 1 Univ. Sta., Austin, TX 78712-0115

Intl. Soc. for Gesture Stud. [IO], Austin, TX, United States

Intl. Soc. of Glass Beadmakers [IO], Cleveland, OH, United States

Intl. Soc. of Glass Beadmakers [311], 1120 Chester Ave., No. 470, Cleveland, OH 44114, (888)742-0242

Intl. Soc. of Gourmet and Specialty Retailers - Defunct.

Intl. Soc. of Guatemala Collectors - Address unknown since 1995.

Intl. Soc. of Gynaecologic Endoscopy [IO], Morphett Vale, Australia

Intl. Soc. of Haematology - European and African Div. [IO], Ankara, Turkey

Intl. Soc. of Hair Restoration Surgery [14521], 13 S 2nd St., Geneva, IL 60134, (630)262-5399

Intl. Soc. of Healthcare Executives - Address unknown since 1995.

Intl. Soc. for Heart and Lung Transplantation [16674], 14673 Midway Rd., Ste. 200, Addison, TX 75001, (972)490-9495

Intl. Soc. for Heart and Lung Transplantation [IO], Addison, TX, United States

Intl. Soc. for Heart Res. [IO], London, United Kingdom

Intl. Soc. for Heart Transplantation [★IO]

Intl. Soc. for Heart Transplantation [★16674]

Intl. Soc. of Heterocyclic Chemistry [IO], Auckland, New Zealand

Intl. Soc. for Hildegard Von Bingen Stud. [IO], Cambridge, MA, United States

Intl. Soc. for Hildegard Von Bingen Stud. [11124], c/o Prof. Pozzi Escot, Pres., 24 Avon Hill, Cambridge, MA 02140, (617)868-0215

Intl. Soc. for History Didactics [IO], Nuremberg, Germany

Intl. Soc. for the History of Ideas - Defunct.

Intl. Soc. for the History of Medicine [IO], St.-Germain-en-Laye, France

Intl. Soc. for the History of the Neurosciences [IO], Puyallup, WA, United States

Intl. Soc. for the History of the Neurosciences [7376], c/o Laurie Swan, Sec., 15518 87th Ave. E, Puyallup, WA 98375, (253)209-7837

Intl. Soc. for the History of Pharmacy [IO], Eschborn, Germany

Intl. Soc. for the History of Philosophy of Sci; HOPOS - The [9103]

Intl. Soc. for the History, Philosophy, and Social Stud. of Biology [8507], c/o Dr. Roberta Millstein, Sec., UC Davis, Dept. of Philosophy, One Shields Ave., Davis, CA 95616

Intl. Soc. for the History, Philosophy, and Social Stud. of Biology [IO], Vashon, WA, United States

Intl. Soc. for the History of Physical Educ. and Sport [IO], Ambleside, United Kingdom

Intl. Soc. for the History of Rhetoric [IO], Berkeley, CA, United States

Intl. Soc. for the History of Rhetoric [10936], c/o Dr. Stephen McKenna, Sec. Gen., The Catholic Univ. of Am., Dept. of Media Stud., Washington, DC 20064, (202)319-5488

Intl. Soc. for HIV/AIDS Education and Prevention - Defunct.

Intl. Soc. for Home Educ. [★IO]

Intl. Soc. for Horticultural Sci. [IO], Leuven, Belgium

Intl. Soc. of Hospitality Consultants [IO], Naples, FL, United States

Intl. Soc. of Hospitality Consultants [967], c/o Lori E. Raleigh, Exec. Dir., 411 6th St. S, No. 204, Naples, FL 34102, (239)436-3915

Intl. Soc. of Hospitality Purchasers [1948], c/o Mr. Larry Carver, Pres., 4177 NE Expy., Atlanta, GA 30340, (770)446-2677

Intl. Soc. of Hospitality Purchasers [IO], Calabasas, CA, United States

Intl. Soc. of Hotel Assn. Executives - Address unknown since 2003.

Intl. Soc. for Human and Animal Mycology [IO], Helsinki, Finland

Intl. Soc. for Human Ethology [IO], Charleston, SC, United States

Intl. Soc. for Human Ethology [6534], c/o Dori LeCroy, Treas., 175 King St., Charleston, SC 29401, (843)534-0526

Intl. Soc. for Human Rights - Germany [IO], Frankfurt am Main, Germany

Intl. Soc. for Human Rights/U.S.A. Sect. - Defunct.

Intl. Soc. for Humor Stud. [10210], c/o Martin D. Lampert, PhD, Exec. Sec.-Treas., Holy Names Univ., Psychology Dept., 3500 Mountain Blvd., Oakland, CA 94619-1627, (510)436-1532

Reference to "IO" in place of a book number signifies that the association may be found in the 45th edition of International Organizations.

Intl. Soc. for Humor Stud. **[IO]**, Oakland, CA, United States

Intl. Soc. for Hybrid Microelectronics **[★IO]**

Intl. Soc. for Hybrid Microelectronics **[★6930]**

Intl. Soc. of Hypertension **[14908]**, 2045 Manchester St. NE, Atlanta, GA 30324

Intl. Soc. of Hypertension **[IO]**, Atlanta, GA, United States

Intl. Soc. on Hypertension in Blacks **[IO]**, Atlanta, GA, United States

Intl. Soc. on Hypertension in Blacks **[14909]**, 157 Summit View Dr., McDonough, GA 30253, (404)880-0343

International Soc. of Hypnosis **[★14927]**

Intl. Soc. of Hypnosis **[IO]**, Tiel, Netherlands

Intl. Soc. for Imaging in the Eye **[IO]**, Thorofare, NJ, United States

Intl. Soc. for Imaging in the Eye **[15690]**, 6900 Grove Rd., Bldg. 100, Thorofare, NJ 08086-0308, (856)994-9400

Intl. Soc. of India Chemists and Chem. Engineers **[6685]**, c/o Dr. Dayal T. Meshri, Pres., Advanced Res. Chemicals, 1110 W Keystone Ave., Catoosa, OK 74015, (918)266-6789

Intl. Soc. of India Chemists and Chem. Engineers **[IO]**, Catoosa, OK, United States

Intl. Soc. for Individual Liberty **[IO]**, Benicia, CA, United States

Intl. Soc. for Individual Liberty **[18015]**, 836-B Southampton Rd., No. 299, Benicia, CA 94510, (707)746-8796

Intl. Soc. of Indoor Air Quality and Climate **[IO]**, Espoo, Finland

International Society for Industrial Ecology **[IO]**, New Haven, CT, United States

Intl. Soc. for Indus. Ecology **[4580]**, c/o Yale School of Forestry and Environmental Stud., Yale Univ., 205 Prospect St., New Haven, CT 06511-2189, (203)436-4835

Intl. Soc. of Industrial Fabric Mfrs. **[3790]**

Intl. Soc. of Industrial Yarns Mfrs. **[★3790]**

Intl. Soc. on Infant Stud. **[13963]**, c/o Lawrence Erlbaum Associates, Inc., 10 Indus. Ave., Mahwah, NJ 07430

Intl. Soc. on Infant Stud. **[IO]**, Mahwah, NJ, United States

Intl. Soc. for Infectious Diseases **[IO]**, Brookline, MA, United States

Intl. Soc. for Infectious Diseases **[14951]**, 1330 Beacon St., Ste. 228, Brookline, MA 02446, (617)277-0551

Intl. Soc. of Infectious Diseases and Human Infertility **[★16347]**

Intl. Soc. of Infectious Diseases and Human Infertility **[★IO]**

Intl. Soc. of Info. Fusion **[IO]**, Fairborn, OH, United States

Intl. Soc. of Info. Fusion **[7199]**, c/o Dr. Erik Blasch, Pres., 2393 Fieldstone Cir., Fairborn, OH 45324, (937)255-2632

Intl. Soc. of Integral Psychoanalysis **[IO]**, Sao Paulo, Brazil

International Society for Intellectual History **[IO]**, Princeton, NJ, United States

Intl. Soc. for Intellectual History **[10126]**, c/o Mr. Steven Lestition, PhD, Membership Sec., B41 Holder Hall, Mathey Coll., Princeton, NJ 08544, (609)258-3317

Intl. Soc. for the Interaction of Mechanics and Mathematics **[IO]**, Padua, Italy

Intl. Soc. for Intercultural Educ., Training and Res. **[★IO]**

Intl. Soc. for Intercultural Educ., Training and Res. **[★8667]**

Intl. Soc. for Interferon and Cytokine Res. **[16351]**, c/o Fed. of Amer. Societies for Experimental Biology, 9650 Rockville Pike, Bethesda, MD 20814-3998, (301)634-7250

International Society for Interferon and Cytokine Research **[IO]**, Bethesda, MD, United States

Intl. Soc. of Interior Designer **[★IO]**

Intl. Soc. of Interior Designer **[★2265]**

Intl. Soc. of Internal Medicine **[IO]**, Langenthal, Switzerland

Intl. Soc. of Introduction Services - Defunct.

Intl. Soc. for Iranian Stud. **[10238]**, c/o Hamid Akbari, Exec. Dir., Northeastern Illinois Univ., 5500 N St. Louis Ave., Chicago, IL 60625, (773)442-6126

Intl. Soc. of Iraqi Scientists **[7613]**, PO Box 4445, Dearborn, MI 48126, (248)538-9121

Intl. Soc. of Iraqi Scientists **[IO]**, Dearborn, MI, United States

Intl. Soc. for Japanese Philately **[IO]**, Haddonfield, NJ, United States

Intl. Soc. for Japanese Philately **[22830]**, PO Box 1283, Haddonfield, NJ 08033

Intl. Soc. of the Knee **[★15771]**

Intl. Soc. of the Knee **[★IO]**

Intl. Soc. for Knowledge Org. **[IO]**, Granada, Spain

Intl. Soc. for Krishna Consciousness **[IO]**, Alachua, FL, United States

Intl. Soc. for Krishna Consciousness **[20203]**, c/o New Raman Reti ISKCON of Alachua, PO Box 819, Alachua, FL 32616, (386)462-2017

Intl. Soc. for Labor Law and Social Security U.S. Natl. Br. - Defunct.

Intl. Soc. for Labor and Social Security Law **[IO]**, Geneva, Switzerland

Intl. Soc. for Language Stud. **[IO]**, Storrs Mansfield, CT, United States

Intl. Soc. for Language Stud. **[10302]**, c/o OSBORN, Fordham Univ., Graduate School of Educ., 113 W 60th St., Rm. 1102, New York, NY 10023

Intl. Soc. for Law and Tech. **[5945]**, 1811 W Katella Ave., No. 101, Anaheim, CA 92804, (714)778-3230

Intl. Soc. for Law and Tech. **[IO]**, Anaheim, CA, United States

Intl. Soc. for Liturgical Stud. and Renewal **[★IO]**

Intl. Soc. for Liturgical Stud. and Renewal **[★19911]**

Intl. Soc. of Livestock Husbandry **[IO]**, Liestal, Switzerland

Intl. Soc. of Lymphology **[IO]**, Tucson, AZ, United States

Intl. Soc. of Lymphology **[15016]**, c/o M.H. Witte, MD, Sec. Gen., Univ. of Arizona, Coll. of Medicine, Dept. of Surgery, PO Box 245200, Tucson, AZ 85724-5200, (520)626-6118

Intl. Soc. of Lyophilization - Freeze Drying **[6616]**, 112A Bala Ave., Bala Cynwyd, PA 19004, (610)660-9665

Intl. Soc. for Magnetic Resonance in Medicine **[16290]**, 2030 Addison St., 7th Fl., Berkeley, CA 94704, (510)841-1899

Intl. Soc. for Magnetic Resonance in Medicine **[IO]**, Berkeley, CA, United States

Intl. Soc. of Magnetic Resonance in Medicine - British Chap. **[IO]**, Sutton, United Kingdom

Intl. Soc. for Magnetic Resonance in Medicine - German Chap. **[IO]**, Frankfurt, Germany

Intl. Soc. for Mangrove Ecosystems **[IO]**, Okinawa, Japan

International Society for Mannosidosis and Related Diseases **[IO]**, Dexter, MI, United States

Intl. Soc. for Mannosidosis and Related Diseases **[14458]**, c/o Terri Klein, Exec. Dir., PO Box 328, Dexter, MI 48130, (734)449-8222

Intl. Soc. for Medical Education - U.S. **[15091]**

Intl. Soc. of Medical Hydrology **[★IO]**

Intl. Soc. of Medical Hydrology and Climatology **[IO]**, Sarow, Germany

Intl. Soc. for Medical and Psychological Hypnosis **[IO]**, Milan, Italy

Intl. Soc. for Medical and Psychological Hypnosis, U.S.A. Office - Address unknown since 2006.

Intl. Soc. for Medical Publication Professionals **[16259]**, PO Box 2523, Briarcliff Manor, NY 10510, (914)945-0507

Intl. Soc. for Medical Publication Professionals **[IO]**, Briarcliff Manor, NY, United States

Intl. Soc. of Meeting Planners **[IO]**, Alexandria, MN, United States

Intl. Soc. of Meeting Planners **[2685]**, 1224 N Nokomis NE, Alexandria, MN 56308-5072, (320)763-4919

Intl. Soc. for Mental Hea. Online **[15208]**, c/o Patricia Kennington, PhD, Sec.-Treas., 388 Chester St. SE, Marietta, GA 30060-2086, (888)875-3570

Intl. Soc. for Mental Hea. Online **[IO]**, Marietta, GA, United States

Intl. Soc. on Metabolic Eye Disease **[IO]**, New York, NY, United States

Intl. Soc. on Metabolic Eye Disease **[15691]**, 1125 Park Ave., New York, NY 10128, (212)427-1246

Intl. Soc. for Microbial Ecology **[4515]**, c/o David A. Stahl, Univ. of Washington, Dept. of Civil and Env. Engg., 302 More Hall, Seattle, WA 98195-2700, (206)685-3464

Intl. Soc. for Microbial Ecology **[IO]**, East Lansing, MI, United States

Intl. Soc. for Military Law and Law of War **[IO]**, Brussels, Belgium

Intl. Soc. of Mine Safety Professionals **[IO]**, Jasper, GA, United States

Intl. Soc. of Mine Safety Professionals **[15270]**, PO Box 772, Jasper, GA 30143, (706)253-3675

Intl. Soc. for Minimally Invasive Cardiac Surgery **[★13914]**

Intl. Soc. for Minimally Invasive Cardiac Surgery **[★IO]**

International Society for Minimally Invasive Cardiothoracic Surgery **[IO]**, Beverly, MA, United States

Intl. Soc. for Minimally Invasive Cardiothoracic Surgery **[13914]**, 900 Cummings Ctr., Ste. 221-U, Beverly, MA 01915, (978)927-8330

Intl. Soc. for Molecular Plant Microbe Interactions **[6641]**, 3340 Pilot Knob Rd., St. Paul, MN 55121, (651)454-7250

International Society for Molecular Plant Microbe Interactions **[IO]**, St. Paul, MN, United States

Intl. Soc. of Motor Control **[IO]**, Newark, DE, United States

Intl. Soc. of Motor Control **[7377]**, c/o Slobodan Jaric, Sec., Univ. of Delaware, Human Performance Lab, Rm. 146, 547 S Coll. Ave., Newark, DE 19716

Intl. Soc. for Mountain Medicine **[15171]**, PO Box 31142, Colorado Springs, CO 80931

Intl. Soc. for Mountain Medicine **[IO]**, Colorado Springs, CO, United States

Intl. Soc. for Mushroom Sci. **[IO]**, Pretoria, Republic of South Africa

Intl. Soc. for Music Educ. - Australia **[IO]**, Nedlands, Australia

Intl. Soc. for Music and Educ. - Germany **[IO]**, Bramsche, Germany

Intl. Soc. for Music in Medicine **[IO]**, Ludenscheid, Germany

Intl. Soc. for Nanoscale Sci., Computation and Engg. **[IO]**, Tampa, FL, United States

Intl. Soc. for Nanoscale Sci., Computation and Engg. **[7614]**, c/o Natasha Jonoska, Treas., Dept. of Mathematics, Univ. of South Florida, 4202 E Fowler Ave., PHY 114, Tampa, FL 33620-5700

Intl. Soc. for Neoplatonic Stud. **[10804]**, c/o Michael Wagner, Sec.-Treas., Univ. of San Diego, 5998 Alcala Park, San Diego, CA 92110-2492, (619)260-4600

Intl. Soc. for Neoplatonic Stud. **[IO]**, San Diego, CA, United States

Intl. Soc. of Nephrology **[IO]**, Brussels, Belgium

Intl. Soc. of Neuro-Semantics **[IO]**, Clifton, CO, United States

Intl. Soc. of Neuro-Semantics **[16396]**, c/o L. Michael Hall, PhD, Co-Founder, PO Box 8, Clifton, CO 81520, (970)523-7877

Intl. Soc. for Neurochemistry **[IO]**, Montreal, QC, Canada

Intl. Soc. for Neurofeedback and Res. **[15394]**, 1925 Francisco Blvd. E, No. 12, San Rafael, CA 94901, (415)485-1344

Intl. Soc. for Neuroimmunomodulation **[15395]**, c/o Jeannine A. Majde-Cottrell, PhD, Exec. Dir./Treas., PO Box 41269, Arlington, VA 22204-8269

Intl. Soc. for Neuroimmunomodulation **[IO]**, Arlington, VA, United States

Intl. Soc. for Neuronal Regulation **[IO]**, Greeley, CO, United States

Intl. Soc. for Neuronal Regulation **[★15394]**

Intl. Soc. of Neuropathology **[IO]**, Bristol, United Kingdom

Intl. Soc. for NeuroVirology **[IO]**, Philadelphia, PA, United States

Intl. Soc. for NeuroVirology **[15396]**, Temple Univ., Bio-Life Sciences Bldg., 1900 N 12th St., Rm. 203-N, Philadelphia, PA 19122, (215)204-0680

Intl. Soc. for New Atlantis - Address unknown since 1986.

A star before a book entry number signifies that the name is not listed separately, but is mentioned within the entry.

Intl. Soc. for New Institutional Economics **[6885]**, Washington Univ., Dept. of Economics, Campus Box 1208, One Brookings Dr., St. Louis, MO 63130-4899

Intl. Soc. for New Institutional Economics **[IO]**, St. Louis, MO, United States

Intl. Soc. of Nurses in Cancer Care **[IO]**, Macclesfield, United Kingdom

International Society of Nurses in Genetics **[IO]**, Pittsburgh, PA, United States

Intl. Soc. of Nurses in Genetics **[14501]**, 461 Cochran Rd., Box 246, Pittsburgh, PA 15228, (412)344-1414

Intl. Soc. of Offshore and Polar Engineers **[7021]**, PO Box 189, Cupertino, CA 95015-0189, (650)254-1871

Intl. Soc. of Offshore and Polar Engineers **[IO]**, Cupertino, CA, United States

Intl. Soc. of Olympic Historians **[IO]**, Fochteloo, Netherlands

Intl. Soc. for Oncodevelopmental Biology and Medicine **[IO]**, Munich, Germany

Intl. Soc. of Oncology Pharmacy Practitioners **[15937]**, c/o Terri Davidson, 305 W Country Dr., Duluth, GA 30097-5906, (678)584-9661

Intl. Soc. for Optical Engineering - Defunct.

Intl. Soc. on Optics within Life Sciences **[IO]**, Munster, Germany

Intl. Soc. for Oral Laser Applications **[IO]**, Vienna, Austria

Intl. Soc. for Oral Literature in Africa **[IO]**, London, United Kingdom

Intl. Soc. for Organ History and Preservation **[10628]**

Intl. Soc. of Organbuilders **[IO]**, Lidingo, Sweden

Intl. Soc. of Oriental Medicine **[IO]**, Seoul, Republic of Korea

Intl. Soc. for Orthomolecular Medicine **[IO]**, Toronto, ON, Canada

Intl. Soc. of Orthopaedic Surgery and Traumatology **[IO]**, Brussels, Belgium

Intl. Soc. of Paediatric Oncology **[IO]**, Eindhoven, Netherlands

International Society for Panetics **[IO]**, College Park, MD, United States

Intl. Soc. for Panetics **[18621]**, PO Box 142, College Park, MD 20741

Intl. Soc. of Parametric Analysts **[6734]**, 527 Maple Ave. E, Ste. 301, Vienna, VA 22180, (703)938-5090

Intl. Soc. of Parametric Analysts **[IO]**, Vienna, VA, United States

International Society for Paranormal Research **[IO]**, Marina del Rey, CA, United States

Intl. Soc. for Paranormal Res. **[2897]**, 4712 Admiralty Way, No. 541, Marina del Rey, CA 90292, (323)644-8866

Intl. Soc. for Pathophysiology **[IO]**, Budapest, Hungary

Intl. Soc. for Pediatric and Adolescent Diabetes **[IO]**, Berlin, Germany

Intl. Soc. for Pediatric Neurosurgery **[IO]**, Graz, Austria

Intl. Soc. for Performance Improvement **[IO]**, Silver Spring, MD, United States

Intl. Soc. for Performance Improvement **[9252]**, 1400 Spring St., Ste. 260, Silver Spring, MD 20910, (301)587-8570

Intl. Soc. for Performance Improvement - Arabia **[IO]**, Dubai, United Arab Emirates

Intl. Soc. for Performance Improvement - Argentina **[IO]**, Buenos Aires, Argentina

Intl. Soc. for Performance Improvement - Cameroon **[IO]**, Bamenda, Cameroon

Intl. Soc. for Performance Improvement - Europe **[IO]**, Walldorf, Germany

Intl. Soc. for Performance Improvement - India **[IO]**, Chennai, India

Intl. Soc. for Performance Improvement - Israel **[IO]**, Haifa, Israel

Intl. Soc. for Performance Improvement - Italy **[IO]**, Rome, Italy

Intl. Soc. for Performance Improvement - Japan **[IO]**, Tokyo, Japan

Intl. Soc. for Performance Improvement - Kurachi, Pakistan **[IO]**, Karachi, Pakistan

Intl. Soc. for Performance Improvement - Melbourne **[IO]**, St. Kilda, Australia

Intl. Soc. for Performance Improvement - Mexico **[IO]**, Ciudad Obregon, Mexico

Intl. Soc. for Performance Improvement - Montreal **[IO]**, Montreal, QC, Canada

Intl. Soc. for Performance Improvement - Nigeria **[IO]**, Lagos, Nigeria

Intl. Soc. for Performance Improvement - South Africa **[IO]**, Johannesburg, Republic of South Africa

Intl. Soc. for Performance Improvement - Sydney **[IO]**, Sydney, Australia

Intl. Soc. for Performance Improvement - United Kingdom **[IO]**, Horsham, United Kingdom

Intl. Soc. for Performance Improvement - Vancouver **[IO]**, North Vancouver, BC, Canada

Intl. Soc. for the Performing Arts **[IO]**, Rye, NY, United States

Intl. Soc. for the Performing Arts **[9575]**, 17 Purdy Ave., PO Box 909, Rye, NY 10580, (914)921-1550

Intl. Soc. of Performing Arts Administrators **[★9575]**

Intl. Soc. of Performing Arts Administrators **[★IO]**

Intl. Soc. for the Performing Arts Found. **[IO]**, Rye, NY, United States

Intl. Soc. for the Performing Arts Found. **[9576]**, PO Box 909, Rye, NY 10580, (914)921-1550

Intl. Soc. for Peritoneal Dialysis **[IO]**, Hong Kong, People's Republic of China

Intl. Soc. for Pharmaceutical Engg. **[IO]**, Tampa, FL, United States

Intl. Soc. for Pharmaceutical Engg. **[7468]**, 3109 W Dr. Martin Luther King Jr. Blvd., Ste. 250, Tampa, FL 33607, (813)960-2105

Intl. Soc. of Pharmaceutical Engineers **[★7468]**

Intl. Soc. of Pharmaceutical Engineers **[★IO]**

International Society for Pharmacoeconomics and Outcomes Research **[IO]**, Lawrenceville, NJ, United States

Intl. Soc. for Pharmacoeconomics and Outcomes Res. **[15938]**, 3100 Princeton Pike, Bldg. 3, Ste. E, Lawrenceville, NJ 08648, (609)219-0773

Intl. Soc. for Pharmacoepidemiology **[15939]**, 5272 River Rd., Ste. 630, Bethesda, MD 20816, (301)718-6500

Intl. Soc. for Phenomenological Stud. **[10805]**, c/o Prof. William Blattner, Dir., Georgetown Univ., Dept. of Philosophy, 240 New North Bldg., Washington, DC 20057-1133, (202)687-4528

Intl. Soc. for Phenomenological Stud. **[IO]**, Washington, DC, United States

Intl. Soc. of Phenomenology, Aesthetics, and the Fine Arts **[IO]**, Hanover, NH, United States

Intl. Soc. of Phenomenology, Aesthetics, and the Fine Arts **[9577]**, c/o The World Phenomenology Inst., 1 Ivy Pointe Way, Hanover, NH 03755, (802)295-3487

Intl. Soc. for Phenomenology and the Human Sciences **[★10807]**

Intl. Soc. for Phenomenology and the Human Sciences **[★IO]**

Intl. Soc. for Phenomenology and Literature **[IO]**, Hanover, NH, United States

Intl. Soc. for Phenomenology and Literature **[10806]**, c/o World Phenomenology Inst., 1 Ivy Pointe Way, Hanover, NH 03755, (802)295-3487

Intl. Soc. for Phenomenology and the Sciences of Life **[10807]**, c/o World Phenomenology Inst., 1 Ivy Pointe Way, Hanover, NH 03755, (802)295-3487

Intl. Soc. for Phenomenology and the Sciences of Life **[IO]**, Hanover, NH, United States

Intl. Soc. for Philosophical Enquiry **[IO]**, Wall Township, NJ, United States

Intl. Soc. for Philosophical Enquiry **[9983]**, c/o John A. Kosinski, PhD, Acting Admissions Off., 1200 Remsen Mill Rd., Wall Township, NJ 07753-7206, (732)280-8799

Intl. Soc. for the Philosophy of Chemistry **[IO]**, Bradford, United Kingdom

Intl. Soc. of Phonetic Sciences **[IO]**, Budapest, Hungary

Intl. Soc. for Photogrammetry and Remote Sensing **[IO]**, Istanbul, Turkey

Intl. Soc. of Photosynthesis Res. **[IO]**, Turku, Finland

Intl. Soc. for Phylogenetic Nomenclature **[IO]**, New Haven, CT, United States

Intl. Soc. for Phylogenetic Nomenclature **[7116]**, c/o Nico Cellinese, Treas., Florida Museum of Natural History, Univ. of Florida, PO Box 117800, Gainesville, FL 32611-7800, (352)392-1721

Intl. Soc. of Physical and Rehabilitation Medicine **[IO]**, Assenede, Belgium

Intl. Soc. of Planetarium Educators **[★IO]**

Intl. Soc. of Planetarium Educators **[★6508]**

Intl. Soc. for Plant Molecular Biology **[6589]**, Univ. of Georgia, Biochemistry and Molecular Biology Dept., Athens, GA 30602, (706)542-3000

Intl. Soc. for Plant Molecular Biology **[IO]**, Athens, GA, United States

Intl. Soc. of Plant Morphologists **[IO]**, New Delhi, India

Intl. Soc. for Plant Pathology **[IO]**, Christchurch, New Zealand

International Society for Plastination **[IO]**, Knoxville, TN, United States

Intl. Soc. for Plastination **[15870]**, c/o Robert W. Henry, PhD, Treas., Univ. of Tennessee, Dept. of Animal Sciences, Rm. A-130, 2407 River Dr., Knoxville, TN 37996-4500, (423)974-5822

Intl. Soc. of Podiatric Laser Surgery - Defunct.

Intl. Soc. of Political Psychology **[16154]**, ISPP Central Off., Moynihan Inst. of Global Affairs, 346 Eggers Hall, Syracuse Univ., Syracuse, NY 13244, (315)443-4470

Intl. Soc. of Political Psychology **[IO]**, Syracuse, NY, United States

Intl. Soc. for Portuguese Philately - Address unknown since 2003.

Intl. Soc. of Postmasters **[IO]**, Busselton, Australia

Intl. Soc. of Prenatal and Perinatal Psychology and Medicine **[IO]**, Heidelberg, Germany

Intl. Soc. for Presence Res. **[7572]**, c/o Matthew Lombard, Pres., Temple Univ., Dept. of Broadcasting, Telecommunications, and Mass Media, Annenberg Hall (011-00), Philadelphia, PA 19122, (215)204-7182

Intl. Soc. for Preservation of the Tropical Rainforest **[5162]**, c/o Roxanne Kremer, Exec. Dir./Founder, 3302 N Burton Ave., Rosemead, CA 91770, (626)572-0233

Intl. Soc. for Preservation of the Tropical Rainforest **[IO]**, Rosemead, CA, United States

Intl. Soc. for Prevention of Child Abuse and Neglect **[IO]**, West Chicago, IL, United States

Intl. Soc. for Prevention of Child Abuse and Neglect **[11607]**, c/o Secretariat Off., 245 W Roosevelt Rd., Bldg. 6, Ste. 39, West Chicago, IL 60185, (630)876-6913

Intl. Soc. for Preventive Oncology **[15648]**, c/o Herbert E. Nieburgs, Sec. Gen./Ed., Univ. of Massachusetts Medical School, Cancer Detection and Prevention, 365 Plantation St., Ste. 175, Worcester, MA 01605-2398, (508)856-1822

Intl. Soc. for Preventive Oncology **[IO]**, Worcester, MA, United States

Intl. Soc. of Primerus Law Firms **[IO]**, Grand Rapids, MI, United States

Intl. Soc. of Primerus Law Firms **[5503]**, 171 Monroe Ave. NW, Ste. 750, Grand Rapids, MI 49503, (616)454-9939

Intl. Soc. for Productivity Enhancement **[7022]**, c/o Dr. Biren Prasad, Managing Dir./Managing Ed., CERA Inst., PO Box 3882, Tustin, CA 92781-3882, (714)505-0662

International Society for Productivity Enhancement **[IO]**, Tustin, CA, United States

Intl. Soc. of Professional Ambulance Services - Defunct.

International Soc. of Professional Aromatherapists **[★IO]**

Intl. Soc. for Professional Hypnosis - Defunct.

Intl. Soc. for Prosthetics and Orthotics **[IO]**, Copenhagen, Denmark

Intl. Soc. for Prosthetics and Orthotics - United Kingdom **[IO]**, Glasgow, United Kingdom

Intl. Soc. for Prosthetics and Orthotics - U.S. Natl. Member Soc. - Address unknown since 1995.

Intl. Soc. for the Protection of Animals **[★IO]**

Intl. Soc. for the Protection of Mustangs and Burros **[IO]**, Lantry, SD, United States

Intl. Soc. for the Protection of Mustangs and Burros **[5330]**, PO Box 55, Lantry, SD 57636-0055, (605)964-6866

Reference to "IO" in place of a book number signifies that the association may be found in the 45th edition of International Organizations.

Intl. Soc. of Protistologists **[7866]**, Dept. of Biological Sciences, Univ. of Alabama, Box 870344, Tuscaloosa, AL 35487, (205)348-1830

Intl. Soc. of Protozoologists **[IO]**, Salzburg, Austria

Intl. Soc. of Psychiatric Consultation Liaison Nurses - Defunct.

Intl. Soc. of Psychiatric Genetics **[14502]**, 650 1st Ave., 5th Fl., Rm. 543, New York, NY 10016, (212)263-3420

Intl. Soc. of Psychiatric Genetics **[IO]**, New York, NY, United States

Intl. Soc. of Psychiatric-Mental Hea. Nurses **[IO]**, Madison, WI, United States

Intl. Soc. of Psychiatric-Mental Hea. Nurses **[15487]**, 2810 Crossroads Dr., Ste. 3800, Madison, WI 53718, (608)443-2463

Intl. Soc. for the Psychological Treatments of the Schizophrenias and Other Psychoses - USA **[15209]**, PO Box 491, Narberth, PA 19072, (610)308-4744

Intl. Soc. of Psychoneuroendocrinology **[15108]**, c/o Alan F. Schatzberg, MD, Sec. Gen., Dept. of Psychiatry and Behavioral Sciences, Stanford Univ. School of Medicine, 401 Quarry Rd., Stanford, CA 94305-5717, (650)723-6811

International Society of Psychoneuroendocrinology **[IO]**, Stanford, CA, United States

Intl. Soc. for the Psychopathology of Expression and Art Therapy **[IO]**, Pau, France

Intl. Soc. for Psychophysics **[IO]**, Marseille, France

Intl. Soc. of Psychosomatic Obstetrics and Gynaecology **[IO]**, Linkoping, Sweden

Intl. Soc. for Quality in Healthcare **[IO]**, East Melbourne, Australia

International Society for Quality-of-Life Studies **[IO]**, Blacksburg, VA, United States

Intl. Soc. for Quality-of-Life Stud. **[7997]**, 1800 Kraft Dr., Ste. 111, Blacksburg, VA 24060-6370, (540)231-5110

Intl. Soc. of Radiographers and Radiological Technicians **[★IO]**

Intl. Soc. of Radiographers and Radiological Technologists **[IO]**, Cardiff, United Kingdom

Intl. Soc. of Radiolabeled Blood Elements **[IO]**, New Hyde Park, NY, United States

Intl. Soc. of Radiolabeled Blood Elements **[13763]**, c/o Prof. Christopher J. Palestro, Pres., Chief Division of Nuclear Medicine, Long Island Jewish Medical Center, 270-05 76th Ave., New Hyde Park, NY 11040

Intl. Soc. of Radiology **[16291]**, 7910 Woodmont Ave., Ste. 800, Bethesda, MD 20814, (301)657-2652

Intl. Soc. of Radiology **[IO]**, Bethesda, MD, United States

Intl. Soc. for Range Mgt. **[★5166]**

Intl. Soc. for Reef Stud. **[4581]**, c/o Richard Aronson, Pres., Dauphin Island Sea Lab, 101 Bienville Blvd., Dauphin Island, AL 36528

Intl. Soc. for Reef Stud. **[IO]**, Newcastle upon Tyne, United Kingdom

International Society for Reef Studies **[IO]**, Dauphin Island, AL, United States

International Society of Regulatory Toxicology and Pharmacology **[IO]**, Columbia, MD, United States

Intl. Soc. of Regulatory Toxicology and Pharmacology **[14570]**, 6546 Belleview Dr., Columbia, MD 21046-1054, (410)992-9083

Intl. Soc. for Rehabilitation of the Disabled **[★16333]**

Intl. Soc. for Rehabilitation of the Disabled **[★IO]**

Intl. Soc. of Reply Coupon Collectors - Defunct.

Intl. Soc. of Reproductive Medicine - Address unknown since 2005.

Intl. Soc. for Res. on Aggression **[6535]**, c/o L. Rowell Huesmann, Ed., 426 Thompson St., Ann Arbor, MI 48106-1248

International Society for Research on Aggression **[IO]**, Augusta, GA, United States

International Society for Research in Human Milk and Lactation **[IO]**, Madison, WI, United States

Intl. Soc. for Res. in Human Milk and Lactation **[13776]**, c/o Dr. Frank R. Greer, MD, Sec.-Treas., Meriter Hosp., Perinatal Center, 202 S Park St., Madison, WI 53715, (608)262-6561

Intl. Soc. for Res. on Impulsivity **[16088]**, c/o Christina Oyervides, Managing Sec., Univ. of Texas at Houston, 1300 Moursund Ave., Ste. 206, Houston, TX 77030, (713)500-2550

Intl. Soc. for Res. on Impulsivity **[IO]**, Houston, TX, United States

Intl. Soc. for Res. in Stereoencephalotomy **[★IO]**

Intl. Soc. for Res. in Stereoencephalotomy **[★15418]**

Intl. Soc. for Res. in Stereoencephalotomy, Amer. Br. **[★15412]**

Intl. Soc. for Res. in Stereoencephalotomy, Amer. Br. **[★IO]**

Intl. Soc. of Restaurant Assn. Executives **[IO]**, Baltimore, MD, United States

Intl. Soc. of Restaurant Assn. Executives **[3394]**, 5024-R Campbell Blvd., Baltimore, MD 21236, (410)931-8100

Intl. Soc. for Retirement and Life Planning - Defunct.

Intl. Soc. for Rock Mechanics **[IO]**, Lisbon, Portugal

Intl. Soc. for the Scholarship of Teaching and Learning **[IO]**, Alexandria, VA, United States

Intl. Soc. for the Scholarship of Teaching and Learning **[9073]**, c/o Barbara Cambridge, Pres., Natl. Coun. of Teachers of English, 1410 King St., Alexandria, VA 22314, (202)316-6828

Intl. Soc. of Scientist-Artists **[★9610]**

Intl. Soc. of Scientist-Artists **[★IO]**

Intl. Soc. for Scientometrics and Informetrics **[IO]**, Leuven, Belgium

Intl. Soc. for Self and Identity **[IO]**, Ann Arbor, MI, United States

Intl. Soc. for Self and Identity **[7546]**, c/o Jennifer Crocker, Pres., Univ. of Michigan, Dept. of Psychology, 530 Church St., Ann Arbor, MI 48109-1043

Intl. Soc. for Sexual and Impotence Res. **[★IO]**

Intl. Soc. for Sexual Medicine **[IO]**, Maarn, Netherlands

Intl. Soc. of Six Sigma Professionals **[IO]**, Scottsdale, AZ, United States

Intl. Soc. of Six Sigma Professionals **[7534]**, 10446 N 74th St., Ste. 140, Scottsdale, AZ 85258, (480)368-7083

Intl. Soc. for Ski Traumatology and Medicine of Winter Sports **[IO]**, Avoriaz, France

Intl. Soc. for Skin Imaging **[IO]**, Freudenberg, Germany

Intl. Soc. for Social Defence **[IO]**, Milan, Italy

Intl. Soc. for Social Law **[★IO]**

Intl. Soc. for the Sociology of Religion **[IO]**, Leuven, Belgium

Intl. Soc. for Soil Mechanics and Geotechnical Engg. **[IO]**, London, United Kingdom

Intl. Soc. of Soil Mechanics and Geotechnical Engg. **[IO]**, Reston, VA, United States

Intl. Soc. of Soil Mechanics and Geotechnical Engg. **[7147]**, c/o Geo-Institute of the ASCE, 1801 Alexander Bell Dr., Reston, VA 20191-4400, (703)295-6350

Intl. Soc. of Soil Sci. **[★IO]**

Intl. Soc. of Speakers, Authors and Consultants - Defunct.

Intl. Soc. of Spelaeological Art **[IO]**, Kidderminster, United Kingdom

Intl. Soc. of Sports Nutrition **[IO]**, Woodland Park, CO, United States

Intl. Soc. of Sports Nutrition **[15562]**, c/o Maelu Fleck, Exec. Dir., 600 Pembrook Dr., Woodland Park, CO 80863, (866)472-4650

Intl. Soc. of Sports Psychology **[16155]**, c/o Judy Van Raalte, VP, Psychology Dept., 263 Alden St., Springfield, MA 01109, (413)748-3388

Intl. Soc. of Sports Psychology **[IO]**, Springfield, MA, United States

Intl. Soc. of Statistical Sci. **[IO]**, Santa Rosa, CA, United States

Intl. Soc. of Statistical Sci. **[7710]**, 536 Oasis Dr., Santa Rosa, CA 95407, (707)575-3529

Intl. Soc. of Statistical Sci. in Economics **[★7710]**

Intl. Soc. of Statistical Sci. in Economics **[★IO]**

International Society for Stem Cell Research **[IO]**, Northbrook, IL, United States

Intl. Soc. for Stem Cell Res. **[14503]**, 60 Revere Dr., Ste. 500, Northbrook, IL 60062, (847)509-1944

Intl. Soc. for Stereology **[IO]**, Fontainebleau, France

Intl. Soc. of Stress Analysts **[IO]**, Kissimmee, FL, United States

Intl. Soc. of Stress Analysts **[5764]**

Intl. Soc. for the Stud. of Behavioural Development **[IO]**, Jena, Germany

Intl. Soc. for the Study of Dendrobatid Frogs - Defunct.

Intl. Soc. for the Stud. of Dissociation **[★15210]**

Intl. Soc. for the Stud. of Dissociation **[★IO]**

Intl. Soc. for the Study of Expressionism - Defunct.

Intl. Soc. for the Stud. of Ghosts and Apparitions **[7445]**, Penthouse N, 29 Washington Sq. W, New York, NY 10011-9180, (212)533-5018

Intl. Soc. for the Stud. of Ghosts and Apparitions **[IO]**, New York, NY, United States

Intl. Soc. for the Stud. of the Human-Companion Animal Bond **[★IO]**

Intl. Soc. for the Stud. of the Human-Companion Animal Bond **[★16615]**

Intl. Soc. for the Stud. of Human Ideas on Ultimate Reality and Meaning **[IO]**, Pickering, ON, Canada

Intl. Soc. for the Stud. of Hypertension in Pregnancy **[IO]**, Rotterdam, Netherlands

Intl. Soc. for the Stud. of the Lumbar Spine **[IO]**, Toronto, ON, Canada

Intl. Soc. for the Stud. of Medieval Philosophy **[IO]**, Freiburg, Germany

Intl. Soc. for the Stud. of Multiple Personalities and Dissociation **[★IO]**

Intl. Soc. for the Stud. of Multiple Personalities and Dissociation **[★15210]**

Intl. Soc. for the Stud. of the Origin of Life **[IO]**, Valencia, Spain

Intl. Soc. for the Stud. of Pilgrimage Art **[IO]**, Carrollton, GA, United States

Intl. Soc. for the Stud. of Pilgrimage Art **[9451]**, c/o Rita Tekippe, Exec. Ed., Univ. of West Georgia, Art Dept., 324 Humanities Hall, Carrollton, GA 30118, (770)836-4532

Intl. Soc. for the Stud. of Subtle Energies and Energy Medicine **[14035]**, c/o Denise Lewis Premschak, CEO, 11005 Ralston Rd., Ste. 100D, Arvada, CO 80004, (303)425-4625

Intl. Soc. for the Stud. of Subtle Energies and Energy Medicine **[IO]**, Arvada, CO, United States

Intl. Soc. for the Study of Symbols - Defunct.

Intl. Soc. for the Stud. of Tension in Performance **[IO]**, London, United Kingdom

Intl. Soc. for the Stud. of Time **[IO]**, Narberth, PA, United States

Intl. Soc. for the Stud. of Time **[11056]**, 442 Brookhurst Ave., Narberth, PA 19072

Intl. Soc. for the Stud. of Trauma and Dissociation **[15210]**, 8201 Greensboro Dr., Ste. 300, McLean, VA 22102, (703)610-9087

Intl. Soc. for the Stud. of Trauma and Dissociation **[IO]**, McLean, VA, United States

Intl. Soc. for the Stud. of Women's Sexual Hea. **[IO]**, Schaumburg, IL, United States

Intl. Soc. for the Stud. of Women's Sexual Hea. **[16404]**, Two Woodfield Lake, 1100 E Woodfield Rd., Ste. 520, Schaumburg, IL 60173, (847)517-7225

Intl. Soc. of Sugar Cane Technologists **[IO]**, Quatre Bornes, Mauritius

Intl. Soc. of Surgery **[IO]**, Pratteln, Switzerland

Intl. Soc. for Systematic and Comparative Musicology **[IO]**, Hamburg, Germany

Intl. Soc. for the Systems Sciences **[IO]**, York, United Kingdom

Intl. Soc. for Teacher Educ. **[IO]**, Vordingborg, Denmark

Intl. Soc. for Tech. in Educ. **[IO]**, Eugene, OR, United States

Intl. Soc. for Tech. in Educ. **[8134]**, 175 W Broadway, Ste. 300, Eugene, OR 97401-3003, (541)302-3777

Intl. Soc. for Telemedicine **[IO]**, Regensburg, Germany

Intl. Soc. for Terrain-Vehicle Systems **[IO]**, Arlington, VA, United States

Intl. Soc. for Terrain-Vehicle Systems **[6518]**, c/o George L. Blaisdell, Gen. Sec., Natl. Sci. Found., 4201 Wilson Blvd., Arlington, VA 22230, (703)292-7447

Intl. Soc. for Theoretical Chem. Physics **[IO]**, Uppsala, Sweden

Intl. Soc. for Third-Sector Res. **[IO]**, Baltimore, MD, United States

Intl. Soc. for Third-Sector Res. **[12654]**, 559 Wyman Park Bldg., 3400 N Charles St., Baltimore, MD 21218-2688, (410)516-4678

A star before a book entry number signifies that the name is not listed separately, but is mentioned within the entry.

Intl. Soc. on Thrombosis and Haemostasis **[14793]**, 610 Jones Ferry Rd., Ste. 205, Carrboro, NC 27510, (919)929-3807

Intl. Soc. on Thrombosis and Haemostasis **[★14793]**

Intl. Soc. on Thrombosis and Haemostasis **[IO]**, Chapel Hill, NC, United States

Intl. Soc. on Thrombosis and Haemostasis **[★IO]**

Intl. Soc. on Toxinology **[IO]**, Frankfurt, Germany

Intl. Soc. for Training and Culture - Address unknown since 1995.

Intl. Soc. of Transport Aircraft Trading **[156]**, 401 N Michigan Ave., Chicago, IL 60611, (312)321-5169

Intl. Soc. of Transport Aircraft Trading **[IO]**, Chicago, IL, United States

International Society for Traumatic Stress Studies **[IO]**, Northbrook, IL, United States

Intl. Soc. for Traumatic Stress Stud. **[16489]**, 60 Revere Dr., Ste. 500, Northbrook, IL 60062, (847)480-9028

Intl. Soc. of Travel Medicine **[15172]**, PO Box 871089, Stone Mountain, GA 30087-0028, (770)736-7060

Intl. Soc. of Travel Medicine **[IO]**, Stone Mountain, GA, United States

Intl. Soc. of Travel and Tourism Educators **[IO]**, St. Clair Shores, MI, United States

Intl. Soc. of Travel and Tourism Educators **[3925]**, 23220 Edgewater, St. Clair Shores, MI 48082-2037, (586)294-0208

Intl. Soc. for Trenchless Tech. **[IO]**, Moreton-in-Marsh, United Kingdom

Intl. Soc. of Tropical Dermatology **[★IO]**

Intl. Soc. of Tropical Dermatology **[★14205]**

Intl. Soc. of Tropical Foresters **[4687]**, 5400 Grosvenor Ln., Bethesda, MD 20814, (301)897-8720

Intl. Soc. of Tropical Foresters **[IO]**, Bethesda, MD, United States

Intl. Soc. for Tropical Root Crops **[IO]**, Chatham, United Kingdom

Intl. Soc. for Twin Stud. **[IO]**, Brisbane, Australia

Intl. Soc. of Typographic Designers **[IO]**, Taunton, United Kingdom

Intl. Soc. on Ultrasonic Diagnostics in Ophthalmology **[IO]**, Naples, Italy

Intl. Soc. of Ultrasound in Obstetrics and Gynecology **[IO]**, London, United Kingdom

Intl. Soc. for Utilitarian Stud. **[IO]**, London, United Kingdom

Intl. Soc. for Vascular Surgery **[IO]**, Smithtown, NY, United States

Intl. Soc. for Vascular Surgery **[16584]**, 11 Scott Dr., Smithtown, NY 11787, (631)979-3780

Intl. Soc. for Vehicle Preservation **[21670]**, PO Box 50046, Tucson, AZ 85703-1046, (520)622-2201

Intl. Soc. for Vehicle Preservation **[IO]**, Tucson, AZ, United States

Intl. Soc. of Veterinary Dermatopathology **[IO]**, Venice, CA, United States

Intl. Soc. of Veterinary Dermatopathology **[16795]**, c/o Emily J. Walder, VMD, Treas., 626 Venice Blvd., Venice, CA 90291

Intl. Soc. of Wang Users - Defunct.

Intl. Soc. of Weekly Newspaper Editors **[3125]**, c/o Dr. Chad Stebbins, Exec. Dir., Inst. of Intl. Stud., Missouri Southern State Univ., 3950 E Newman Rd., Joplin, MO 64801-1512, (417)625-9736

Intl. Soc. of Weekly Newspaper Editors **[IO]**, Joplin, MO, United States

Intl. Soc. of Weighing and Measurement **[IO]**, Rockville, MD, United States

Intl. Soc. of Weighing and Measurement **[4016]**, 15245 Shady Grove Rd., Ste. 130, Rockville, MD 20850, (301)258-1115

Intl. Soc. for the Welfare of Cripples **[★16333]**

Intl. Soc. for the Welfare of Cripples **[★IO]**

Intl. Soc. of Wine Tasters - Defunct.

Intl. Soc. of Women Airline Pilots **[157]**, 2250 E Tropicana Ave., Ste. 19-395, Las Vegas, NV 89119-6573, (772)228-6719

Intl. Soc. of Women Airline Pilots **[IO]**, Las Vegas, NV, United States

Intl. Soc. for Work Options - Defunct.

Intl. Soc. of Worldwide Stamp Collectors **[22831]**, c/o Dr. Terry Myers, Exec. Dir., 9463 Benbrook Blvd., No. 14, Benbrook, TX 76126

Intl. Soc. of Worldwide Stamp Collectors **[IO]**, Benbrook, TX, United States

Intl. Sociological Assn. **[IO]**, Madrid, Spain

Intl. Softball Fed. **[IO]**, Plant City, FL, United States

Intl. Softball Fed. **[23791]**, 1900 S Park Rd., Plant City, FL 33563-8113, (813)864-0100

Intl. Softbill Soc. - Defunct.

Intl. Software A.G. Users' Group - Address unknown since 2003.

Intl. Soil Reference and Info. Centre **[IO]**, Wageningen, Netherlands

Intl. Solar Energy Soc. **[IO]**, Freiburg, Germany

Intl. Solid Surface Fabricators Assn. **[IO]**, Henderson, NV, United States

Intl. Solid Surface Fabricators Assn. **[2559]**, 975 Amer. Pacific Dr., Ste. 102, Henderson, NV 89014-7823, (702)567-8150

Intl. Solid Waste and Public Cleansing Assn. **[★IO]**

Intl. Solid Wastes Assn. **[IO]**, Copenhagen, Denmark

Intl. Solidarity Found. **[IO]**, Helsinki, Finland

Intl. Songwriters Assn. **[IO]**, Limerick, Ireland

Intl. Songwriters' Assn. - Ireland **[IO]**, Limerick, Ireland

Intl. Songwriters Guild **[2828]**, c/o Russ Robinson, Pres., 5108 Louvre Ave., Orlando, FL 32812-1028, (407)851-5328

Intl. Sonoran Desert Alliance **[4582]**, PO Box 687, Ajo, AZ 85321, (520)387-6823

International Sonoran Desert Alliance **[IO]**, Ajo, AZ, United States

International Soundex Reunion Registry **[IO]**, Carson City, NV, United States

Intl. Soundex Reunion Registry **[11248]**, PO Box 371179, Las Vegas, NV 89137, (775)882-7755

Intl. Sourdough Reunion - Address unknown since 1995.

Intl. Spa Assn. **[3355]**, 2365 Harrodsburg Rd., Ste. A325, Lexington, KY 40504, (859)226-4326

Intl. Spa Assn. **[IO]**, Lexington, KY, United States

Intl. Spa and Fitness Assn. - Address unknown since 2000.

Intl. Spa and Tub Coun. - Defunct.

Intl. Space: 1999 Alliance - Defunct.

Intl. Space Exploration and Colonization Company **[6376]**, PO Box 60885, Fairbanks, AK 99706-0885, (907)488-1001

Intl. Space Exploration and Colonization Company **[IO]**, Fairbanks, AK, United States

Intl. Space Sci. Inst. **[IO]**, Bern, Switzerland

International Special Events Society **[IO]**, Chicago, IL, United States

Intl. Special Events Soc. **[1311]**, 401 N Michigan Ave., Chicago, IL 60611-4267, (312)321-6853

Intl. Special Tooling Assn. **[★2031]**

Intl. Special Tooling Assn. **[★IO]**

Intl. Special Tooling and Machining Assn. **[IO]**, Covina, CA, United States

Intl. Special Tooling and Machining Assn. **[2031]**, c/o Mr. Egon Jaeggin, VP, 2200 Foster Ave., Wheeling, IL 60090, (847)394-3610

Intl. Specialty Car Assn. - Address unknown since 1999.

Intl. Speech Commun. Assn. **[IO]**, Baixas, France

Intl. Spenser Soc. **[9663]**, c/o Prof. Craig Berry, Sec.-Treas., 1518 W Thorndale, No. 2W, Chicago, IL 60660

Intl. Sphynx Breeders and Fanciers' Assn. - Defunct.

Intl. Sphynx Soc. **[21911]**, c/o Patricia Hawk, Sec.-Treas., 320 E Beresford Ave., DeLand, FL 32724

Intl. Sphynx Soc. **[IO]**, Deland, FL, United States

Intl. Spin Fishing Assn. **[★IO]**

Intl. Spin Fishing Assn. **[★23417]**

Intl. Spinal Cord Soc. **[IO]**, Aylesbury, United Kingdom

Intl. Spinal Development and Res. Found. **[IO]**, Las Vegas, NV, United States

Intl. Spinal Development and Res. Found. **[16465]**, 600 S Rancho Dr., Ste. 101, Las Vegas, NV 89108

Intl. Spinal Injection Soc. **[★16466]**

Intl. Spinal Res. Trust **[IO]**, Guildford, United Kingdom

Intl. Spine Intervention Soc. **[16466]**, c/o Jordon Moncrief, Chief Operating Off., 5 Ash Ave., Kentfield, CA 94904-1504, (415)457-4747

Intl. Sport Horses of Color **[4905]**, PO Box 1710, Cottage Grove, OR 97424, (541)836-3000

Intl. Sport Press Assn. **[IO]**, Budapest, Hungary

Intl. Sport Show Producers Assn. **[1344]**, c/o Dianne Seymour, Exec. Sec., PO Box 480084, Denver, CO 80248-0084, (303)892-6800

Intl. Sporthorse Registry **[4906]**, 517 DeKalb Ave., Sycamore, IL 60178, (815)899-7803

Intl. Sports Engg. Assn. **[IO]**, Sheffield, United Kingdom

Intl. Sports Exchange **[IO]**, Plainfield, IN, United States

Intl. Sports Exchange **[23826]**, 5982 Mia Ct., Plainfield, IN 46168, (317)839-9257

Intl. Sports Fed. for Persons with Intellectual Disability **[IO]**, Birmingham, United Kingdom

Intl. Sports Heritage Assn. **[23827]**, PO Box 2384, Florence, OR 97439, (904)955-0126

Intl. Sports Massage Fed. **[16482]**

Intl. Spotted Horse Registry Assn. **[4907]**, PO Box 412, Anderson, MO 64831-0412, (417)475-6273

International Spotted Horse Registry Association **[IO]**, Anderson, MO, United States

Intl. Spotted Pony Club - Defunct.

Intl. Sprout Growers Assn. **[4090]**, 2150 N 107th St., Ste. 205, Seattle, WA 98133-9009, (206)367-8704

Intl. Sprout Growers Assn. **[IO]**, Seattle, WA, United States

Intl. Squash Players Assn. **[★IO]**

Intl. St Rabismological Assn. - Address unknown since 2002.

Intl. Stained Glass Assn. - Defunct.

Intl. Stamp and Coin Collectors Soc. **[22832]**, c/o Israel I. Bick, Pres., PO Box 854, Van Nuys, CA 91408, (818)997-6496

Intl. Stamp and Coin Collectors Soc. **[IO]**, Van Nuys, CA, United States

Intl. Stamp Mfrs. Assn. **[★IO]**

Intl. Stamp Mfrs. Assn. **[★3683]**

International Standards

African Economic Community **[IO]**

African Forum and Network on Debt and Development **[IO]**

Albanian-American Trade and Development Assn. **[IO]**

Albanian-American Trade and Development Assn. **[24333]**

ASEAN Free Trade Area **[IO]**

Canadian Fed. of Trading House Associations **[IO]**

Canadian Norwegian Bus. Assn. **[IO]**

Coun. for Intl. Tax Educ. **[IO]**

Coun. for Intl. Tax Educ. **[2281]**

FCIB-NACM Corp. **[2282]**

FCIB-NACM Corp. **[IO]**

Fed. of Intl. Trade Associations **[IO]**

Fed. of Intl. Trade Associations **[2283]**

Freshfel Europe **[IO]**

Inst. of Intl. Trade of Ireland **[IO]**

Intl. Trade Club of Chicago **[IO]**

Intl. Trade Club of Chicago **[2284]**

Intl. Trade Coun. **[2285]**

Iranian Trade Assn. **[2286]**

Iranian Trade Assn. **[IO]**

Moroccan Amer. Bus. Coun. **[IO]**

Moroccan Amer. Bus. Coun. **[2287]**

Natl. Coun. on Intl. Trade Development **[2288]**

Natl. Coun. on Intl. Trade Development **[IO]**

Natl. Foreign Trade Coun. **[IO]**

Natl. Foreign Trade Coun. **[2289]**

New Zealand Pacific Bus. Coun. **[IO]**

Org. of Women in Intl. Trade **[2290]**

Soc. of Intl. Bus. Fellows **[2291]**

Soc. of Intl. Bus. Fellows **[IO]**

U.S. Bus. Coun. for Southeastern Europe **[2292]**

U.S.-Russia Bus. Coun. **[2293]**

U.S.-Russia Bus. Coun. **[IO]**

US-Taiwan Bus. Coun. **[IO]**

US-Taiwan Bus. Coun. **[2294]**

World Trade Center of New Orleans **[2295]**

World Trade Center of New Orleans **[IO]**

World Trade Center Tripoli **[IO]**

Intl. Standing Comm. of the Intl. Cong. on Animal Reproduction **[IO]**, Sydney, Australia

Intl. Standing Comm. of the Intl. Cong. on Animal Reproduction and Artificial Insemination **[★IO]**

Intl. Standing Comm. of the Intl. Cong. of Physiology and Pathology of Animal Reproduction **[★IO]**

Reference to "IO" in place of a book number signifies that the association may be found in the 45th edition of International Organizations.

Intl. Standing Conf. on Philanthropy - North America - Defunct.

Intl. Staple, Nail and Tool Assn. **[1825]**, 512 W Burlington Ave., Ste. 203, La Grange, IL 60525-2245, (708)482-8138

Intl. Staple, Nail and Tool Assn. **[IO]**, La Grange, IL, United States

International Star Class Yacht Racing Association **[IO]**, Glenview, IL, United States

Intl. Star Class Yacht Racing Assn. **[23193]**, 1545 Waukegan Rd., Ste. 8, Glenview, IL 60025-2185, (847)729-0630

Intl. Star Riders Assn. **[22685]**, PO Box 532, Linden, VA 22642

Intl. Stationary Steam Engine Soc. **[22977]**, c/o Rick Rowlands, Membership Sec., 2261 Hubbard Rd., Youngstown, OH 44505, (330)728-2799

Intl. Stationary Steam Engine Soc. **[IO]**, Youngstown, OH, United States

Intl. Statistical Inst. **[IO]**, Voorburg, Netherlands

Intl. Steamboat Soc. - Address unknown since 2000.

Intl. Steel Guitar Convention **[10629]**, 9535 Midland Blvd., St. Louis, MO 63114-3314, (314)427-7794

Intl. Steel Guitar Convention **[IO]**, St. Louis, MO, United States

Intl. Steel Trade Assn. **[IO]**, London, United Kingdom

Intl. Step by Step Assn. **[IO]**, Amsterdam, Netherlands

Intl. Stewards and Caterers Assn. **[★IO]**

Intl. Stewards and Caterers Assn. **[★1584]**

Intl. Stillbirth Alliance **[13982]**, 1314 Bedford Ave., Ste. 210, Baltimore, MD 21208

Intl. Stiltwalkers Assn. - Address unknown since 1995.

Intl. Stoke Mandeville Games Fed. **[★IO]**

Intl. Stop Continental Drift Soc. - Defunct.

Intl. Strategic Stud. Assn. **[17379]**, PO Box 20407, Alexandria, VA 22320, (703)548-1070

Intl. Strategic Stud. Assn. **[IO]**, Alexandria, VA, United States

Intl. Street and Evangelism Ministries Assn. - Defunct.

Intl. Stress Mgt. Assn. **[IO]**, South Petherton, United Kingdom

Intl. Stress Mgt. Assn. - India **[IO]**, Hyderabad, India

Intl. String Figure Assn. **[IO]**, Pasadena, CA, United States

Intl. String Figure Assn. **[9833]**, PO Box 5134, Pasadena, CA 91117, (626)398-1057

Intl. Stroke Soc. **[IO]**, Osaka, Japan

Intl. Student Helpers Program - Defunct.

Intl. Student Pugwash **[★18842]**

Intl. Student Visitors Ser. **[★8617]**

Intl. Student Visitors Ser. **[★IO]**

Intl. Student Week Ilmenau **[IO]**, Ilmenau, Germany

Intl. Student/Young Pugwash - Netherlands **[IO]**, Delft, Netherlands

Intl. Student/Young Pugwash - Norway **[IO]**, Oslo, Norway

Intl. Students, Inc. **[IO]**, Colorado Springs, CO, United States

Intl. Students, Inc. **[20017]**, PO Box C, Colorado Springs, CO 80901, (719)576-2700

Intl. Students Soc. - Defunct.

International Studies

Amer. Assn. for Ukrainian Stud. **[8650]**

Amer. Assn. for Ukrainian Stud. **[IO]**

American Council on International Intercultural Education **[IO]**

Amer. Coun. on Intl. Intercultural Educ. **[8651]**

Amer. Inst. for Foreign Stud. **[8652]**

Asia Soc. **[9616]**

Assn. for Borderlands Stud. **[8653]**

Assn. for Borderlands Stud. **[IO]**

Assn. of Professional Schools of Intl. Affairs **[IO]**

Assn. of Professional Schools of Intl. Affairs **[8654]**

Assn. for the Stud. of Persianate Societies **[8668]**

Australian and New Zealand Stud. Assn. of North Amer. **[8484]**

Central Eurasian Stud. Soc. **[10233]**

Central Eurasian Stud. Soc. **[IO]**

Comparative and Intl. Educ. Soc. **[IO]**

Comparative and Intl. Educ. Soc. **[8655]**

Cordell Hull Found. for Intl. Educ. **[8656]**

Cordell Hull Found. for Intl. Educ. **[IO]**

East-West Center **[17882]**

Global Alliance for Transnational Educ. **[8657]**

Global Alliance for Transnational Educ. **[IO]**

Global Learning **[8658]**

Inst. for Intercultural Stud. **[10234]**

Intl. Initiatives of the Amer. Coun. on Educ. **[8659]**

Intl. Initiatives of the Amer. Coun. on Educ. **[IO]**

Intl. Stud. Assn. **[IO]**

Intl. Stud. Assn. **[10235]**

Island Resources Found. **[10236]**

Maryknoll Mission Center of New England **[8660]**

Natl. Coun. for Languages and Intl. Stud. **[10306]**

Natl. Model United Nations **[8661]**

Intl. Stud. Assn. **[10235]**, Univ. of Arizona, 324 Social Sciences Bldg., Tucson, AZ 85721, (520)621-7715

Intl. Stud. Assn. **[IO]**, Tucson, AZ, United States

Intl. Stud; Coun. for Languages and Other **[★10306]**

Intl. Stud; Natl. Coun. on Foreign Language and **[★8593]**

Intl. Stud. Assn. for Teachers and Teaching **[IO]**, Reading, United Kingdom

Intl. Study Group for the Detection and Prevention of Cancer - Defunct.

Intl. Study Group for Waterworks in the Rhine Catchment Area **[★IO]**

Intl. Stuttering Assn. **[IO]**, Tucson, AZ, United States

Intl. Stuttering Assn. **[16498]**, c/o Judith Eckardt, Sec., 65208 E Desert Sands Ct., Tucson, AZ 85739, (520)825-9875

Intl. Substance Abuse and Addiction Coalition **[IO]**, Reading, United Kingdom

Intl. Sufi Movement **[IO]**, The Hague, Netherlands

Intl. Sugar Confectionary Mfrs. Assn. **[★IO]**

Intl. Sugar Glider Assn. **[11483]**, 824 130th Ave. NE, Bellevue, WA 98005-2612

Intl. Sugar Org. **[IO]**, London, United Kingdom

Intl. Sugar Res. Found. **[★IO]**

Intl. Sumo Fed. **[IO]**, Tokyo, Japan

Intl. Sunfish Class Assn. **[★IO]**

Intl. Sunfish Class Assn. **[IO]**, Waterford, MI, United States

Intl. Sunfish Class Assn. **[23194]**, PO Box 300128, Waterford, MI 48330-0128, (248)673-2750

Intl. Sunfish Class Assn. **[★23194]**

Intl. Sunflower Assn. **[IO]**, Paris, France

Intl. Sungja-Do Assn. **[23593]**, c/o George I. Petrotta, Dir./Founder, 1366 St. Andrews Blvd., Florence, SC 29505, (843)669-1444

Intl. Sunshine Soc. - Defunct.

Intl. Superphosphate and Compound Mfrs. Assn. **[★IO]**

Intl. Superphosphate Mfrs. Assn. **[★IO]**

International Supreme Coun. Order of DeMolay **[★IO]**

International Supreme Coun. Order of DeMolay **[★19375]**

Intl. Supreme Coun. of World Masons - Address unknown since 1986.

Intl. Surfing Assn. **[23879]**, 5580 La Jolla Blvd., PMB 145, La Jolla, CA 92037, (760)931-0111

Intl. Surfing Assn. **[IO]**, La Jolla, CA, United States

Intl. Surfing League - Address unknown since 2006.

Intl. Survey Lib. Assn. **[10364]**, c/o Roper Center for Public Opinion Res., Univ. of Connecticut, Homer Babbidge Lib., 369 Fairfield Way, Unit 2164, Storrs Mansfield, CT 06269-2164, (860)486-4440

Intl. Survey Lib. Assn. **[IO]**, Storrs Mansfield, CT, United States

Intl. Swaps and Derivatives Assn. **[2335]**, 360 Madison Ave., 16th Fl., New York, NY 10017, (212)901-6000

Intl. Sweeteners Assn. **[IO]**, Brussels, Belgium

Intl. Swift Assn. **[★21481]**

Intl. Swimming Hall of Fame **[23886]**, 1 Hall of Fame Dr., Fort Lauderdale, FL 33316, (954)462-6536

Intl. Swimming Hall of Fame **[IO]**, Fort Lauderdale, FL, United States

Intl. Swizzle Stick Collectors Assn. **[IO]**, Bellingham, WA, United States

Intl. Swizzle Stick Collectors Assn. **[22060]**, c/o Ray P. Hoare, Co-Chm., PO Box 1117, Bellingham, WA 98227-1117, (604)936-7636

Intl. Sybil Jason Fan Club **[24746]**, c/o Gary L. Heckman, Pres., 745 S 31st St., Lincoln, NE 68510, (402)477-7875

Intl. Symbiosis Soc. **[18622]**, c/o Prof. Douglas Zook, Pres./Acting Treas., Boston Univ., 2 Sherborn St., Boston, MA 02215

Intl. Symbiosis Soc. **[IO]**, Boston, MA, United States

Intl. Symposium on Nitrogen Fixation - Defunct.

Intl. Symposium on Radiopharmaceutical Dosimetry - Defunct.

Intl. Sysop Guild - Address unknown since 2001.

Intl. Systems Dealers Assn. **[★2847]**

Intl. Systems Security Engg. Assn. **[7023]**, c/o Dana McCulloch, Relations Coor., 13873 Park Center Rd., Ste. 200, Herndon, VA 20171, (703)478-7615

Intl. Systems Security Engg. Assn. **[IO]**, Herndon, VA, United States

Intl. Table Tennis Fed. **[IO]**, Lausanne, Switzerland

Intl. Table Tennis League - Address unknown since 1999.

Intl. Tandem Users' Gp. **[6797]**, 401 N Michigan Ave., Ste. 2200, Chicago, IL 60611-4267, (312)321-6851

Intl. Tandem Users' Gp. **[IO]**, Chicago, IL, United States

Intl. Tank Container Org. **[IO]**, Overijse, Belgium

Intl. Tanker Owners Pollution Fed. **[IO]**, London, United Kingdom

Intl. Tap Assn. **[9888]**, PO Box 356, Boulder, CO 80306, (303)443-7989

Intl. Tape Assn. **[★1370]**

Intl. Tape Assn. **[★IO]**

Intl. Tape/Disc Assn. **[★IO]**

Intl. Tape/Disc Assn. **[★1370]**

Intl. Tarot Soc. - Defunct.

Intl. Task Force on Euthanasia and Assisted Suicide **[12133]**, PO Box 760, Steubenville, OH 43952, (740)282-3810

Intl. Task Force on Prevention of Nuclear Terrorism - Defunct.

Intl. Task Force for the Rural Poor **[IO]**, Moradabad, India

Intl. Tax Inst. - Address unknown since 1999.

Intl. Tax Planning Assn. **[IO]**, Jersey, United Kingdom

Intl. Taxicab Assn. **[★IO]**

Intl. Taxicab Assn. **[★3894]**

Intl. Taxicab and Livery Assn. **[★3894]**

Intl. Taxicab and Livery Assn. **[★IO]**

Intl. Tea Comm. **[IO]**, London, United Kingdom

International Tea Masters Association - Address unknown since 2002.

Intl. Tech. Assistance; Volunteers for **[★12448]**

Intl. Tech. Caramel Assn. **[1532]**, c/o McKenna Long & Aldridge LLP, 1900 K St. NW, Ste. 100, Washington, DC 20006, (202)496-7111

Intl. Tech. Caramel Assn. **[IO]**, Washington, DC, United States

Intl. Tech. Tropical Timber Assn. **[IO]**, Paris, France

Intl. Technology Coun. - Defunct.

Intl. Tech. Educ. Assn. **[9231]**, 1914 Assn. Dr., Ste. 201, Reston, VA 20191-1539, (703)860-2100

Intl. Tech. Educ. Assn. **[IO]**, Reston, VA, United States

Intl. Tech. Educ. Assn. - Coun. for Supervisors **[IO]**, Salt Lake City, UT, United States

Intl. Tech. Educ. Assn. - Coun. for Supervisors **[9232]**, c/o Melvin L. Robinson, Commun. Chm., PO Box 144200, Salt Lake City, UT 84114-4200, (801)538-7598

Intl. Tech. Inst. **[7744]**, PO Box 23166, San Diego, CA 92193-3166, (858)279-0483

Intl. Tech. Inst. **[IO]**, San Diego, CA, United States

Intl. Tech. Law Assn. **[5582]**, 401 Edgewater Pl., Ste. 600, Wakefield, MA 01880, (781)876-8877

Intl. Tele-Education - Defunct.

Intl. Telecard Assn. **[★3767]**

Intl. Telecommunication Union **[IO]**, Geneva, Switzerland

Intl. (Telecommunications) Disaster Recovery Assn. **[IO]**, Shrewsbury, MA, United States

Intl. Telecommunications Satellite Org. **[IO]**, Washington, DC, United States

Intl. Telecommunications Satellite Org. **[7777]**, 3400 Intl. Dr. NW, Washington, DC 20008-3006, (202)243-5096

Intl. Telecommunications Soc. **[3749]**, c/o Leland W. Schmidt, Treas./Finance Comm. Chm., 33 Alpine Dr., Gilford, NH 03249, (603)293-4094

A star before a book entry number signifies that the name is not listed separately, but is mentioned within the entry.

Intl. Telecommunications Soc. **[IO]**, Gilford, NH, United States

Intl. Telecommunications Users Gp. **[IO]**, Driebergen, Netherlands

Intl. Teleconferencing Assn. - Address unknown since 2003.

Intl. Telegraph Consultative Comm. **[★IO]**

Intl. Telegraph and Telephone Consultative Comm. **[★IO]**

Intl. Telephone Credit Union Assn. **[★1110]**

Intl. Televent - Address unknown since 2008.

Intl. TV Assn. **[★1388]**

Intl. TV Assn. **[★IO]**

Intl. TV Assn. Deutschland **[IO]**, Frankfurt, Germany

Intl. TV Assn. - Japan **[IO]**, Tokyo, Japan

Intl. TV Assn. - New Zealand **[IO]**, Auckland, New Zealand

Intl. Telework Assn. and Coun. **[IO]**, Scottsdale, AZ, United States

Intl. Telework Assn. and Coun. **[3750]**, 14040 N Northsight Blvd., Scottsdale, AZ 85260, (480)348-7285

Intl. Temperance Assn. **[★13304]**

Intl. Temperance Assn. **[★IO]**

Intl. Tennis Fed. **[IO]**, London, United Kingdom

Intl. Tennis Hall of Fame **[IO]**, Newport, RI, United States

Intl. Tennis Hall of Fame **[23903]**, 194 Bellevue Ave., Newport, RI 02840, (401)849-3990

Intl. Tesla Soc. - Address unknown since 2004.

Intl. Test and Evaluation Assn. **[7791]**, 4400 Fair Lakes Ct., Ste. 104, Fairfax, VA 22033-3801, (703)631-6220

Intl. Test and Evaluation Assn. **[IO]**, Fairfax, VA, United States

International Texas Longhorn Association **[IO]**, Fort Worth, TX, United States

Intl. Texas Longhorn Assn. **[4269]**, PO Box 2610, Glen Rose, TX 76043, (254)898-0157

Intl. Textile and Apparel Assn. **[3791]**, 6060 Sunrise Vista Dr., Ste. 1300, Citrus Heights, CA 95610, (916)723-1628

Intl. Textile and Apparel Assn. **[IO]**, Citrus Heights, CA, United States

Intl. Textile, Garment and Leather Workers' Fed. **[IO]**, Brussels, Belgium

Intl. Textile Mfrs. Fed. **[IO]**, Zurich, Switzerland

Intl. Thai Therapists Assn. **[IO]**, Grass Valley, CA, United States

Intl. Thai Therapists Assn. **[15031]**, PO Box 367, Talbotton, GA 31827, (706)358-8646

Intl. Theatre Equip. Assn. **[★3811]**

Intl. Theatre Equip. Assn. **[★IO]**

Intl. Theatre Inst. - France **[IO]**, Paris, France

Intl. Theatre Inst. - Switzerland **[IO]**, Basel, Switzerland

Intl. Theatre Inst. of the U.S. - Defunct.

Intl. Theodore Dreiser Soc. **[9664]**, c/o Donna Packer-Kinlaw, Sec.-Treas., Univ. of Maryland, Dept. of English, 3101 Susquehanna Hall, College Park, MD 20742

Intl. Theodore Dreiser Soc. **[IO]**, College Park, MD, United States

Intl. Thermal Storage Advisory Coun. - Defunct.

Intl. Thermionic Soc. - Defunct.

Intl. Thermoelectric Soc. **[IO]**, Nagoya, Japan

Intl. Thermographers Assn. **[2889]**

Intl. Thespian Soc. **[★9264]**

Intl. Third World Legal Stud. Assn. - Defunct.

Intl. Thomas Merton Soc. **[9665]**, Bellarmine Univ., Thomas Merton Center, 2001 Newburg Rd., Louisville, KY 40205-0671, (502)452-8177

Intl. Thomas Merton Soc. **[IO]**, Louisville, KY, United States

Intl. Thriller Writers **[IO]**, Eureka, CA, United States

Intl. Thriller Writers **[11179]**, PO Box 311, Eureka, CA 95502

Intl. Thunderbird Assn. **[★23195]**

Intl. Thunderbird Class Assn. **[23195]**, PO Box 1033, Mercer Island, WA 98040-1033

Intl. Thunderbird Club **[21671]**, c/o Kitty Mummert, Treas., 20 Northview Dr., Hanover, PA 17331-4521, (717)632-2818

Intl. Thunderbird Club **[IO]**, Hanover, PA, United States

Intl. Ticketing Assn. **[IO]**, New York, NY, United States

Intl. Ticketing Assn. **[1312]**, 330 W 38th St., No. 605, New York, NY 10018, (212)629-4036

Intl. Time Bur. - Time Sect. **[★IO]**

International Time Capsule Society **[IO]**, Atlanta, GA, United States

Intl. Time Capsule Soc. **[10041]**, c/o Oglethorpe Univ., 4484 Peachtree Rd. NE, Atlanta, GA 30319, (404)261-1441

Intl. Tin Res. Coun. **[★IO]**

Intl. Tire Assn. **[IO]**, Hebron, CT, United States

Intl. Tire Assn. **[3813]**

Intl. Tire and Rubber Assn. **[★3814]**

Intl. Tit Soc. - Defunct.

Intl. Titanium Assn. **[2712]**, 2655 W Midway Blvd., Ste. 300, Broomfield, CO 80020-7187, (303)404-2221

Intl. Titanium Assn. **[IO]**, Broomfield, CO, United States

Intl. Tobacco Growers Assn. **[IO]**, Castelo Branco, Portugal

Intl. Touring Alliance **[IO]**, Geneva, Switzerland

Intl. Toy Buff's Assn. - Defunct.

Intl. Toy Libraries Assn. **[IO]**, Gauteng, Republic of South Africa

International Trachoma Initiative **[IO]**, New York, NY, United States

Intl. Trachoma Initiative **[16858]**, 441 Lexington Ave., Ste. 1101, New York, NY 10017-3910, (212)490-6460

Intl. Tracing Ser. **[IO]**, Bad Arolsen, Germany

Intl. Track and Field Coaches Assn. **[IO]**, Kalamazoo, MI, United States

Intl. Track and Field Coaches Assn. **[23919]**, 1705 Evanston St., Kalamazoo, MI 49008, (269)349-1008

International Trade

Alliance for Responsible Trade **[3836]**

America-Georgia Bus. Coun. **[2296]**

Amer. Assn. of Exporters and Importers **[2297]**

Amer. Importers Assn. of the U.S. **[2298]**

Amer. Intl. Chamber of Commerce **[24247]**

American-Kuwaiti Alliance **[2299]**

American-Russian Chamber of Commerce and Indus. **[24261]**

Armenian Amer. Chamber of Commerce **[24263]**

Asia Pacific - USA Chamber of Commerce **[24264]**

Assn. for Intl. Bus. **[701]**

Assn. of Trade and Forfaiting in the Americas **[1404]**

Australian New Zealand - Amer. Chambers of Commerce **[24248]**

Automotive Trade Policy Coun. **[350]**

Bilateral US-Arab Chamber of Commerce **[24226]**

Bus. Assn. Italy Am. **[2300]**

Cameroon-USA Chamber of Commerce **[24249]**

Canada-United States Bus. Assn. **[2301]**

Chile-U.S. Chamber of Commerce **[24270]**

Chinese Amer. Assn. of Engg. **[7008]**

Commercial Mortgage Securities Assn. **[3304]**

Croatian-American Chamber of Commerce **[24314]**

Czech-North Amer. Chamber of Commerce **[24274]**

Czech and Slovak-U.S. Bus. Coun. **[2302]**

Emergency Comm. for Amer. Trade **[2303]**

Engg. Export Promotion Coun. of India **[2304]**

Fashion Exports New York **[233]**

Fed. of Philippine Amer. Chambers of Commerce **[24277]**

Georgia-USA Chamber of Commerce **[24278]**

Ghana-USA Chamber of Commerce **[24279]**

Global Offset and Countertrade Assn. **[2305]**

Greek Amer. Chamber of Commerce **[24280]**

Inst. for Intl. Entrepreneurship **[727]**

Inter-American Commercial Arbitration Commn. **[5456]**

Intl. Economics and Finance Soc. **[6884]**

Intl. Wood Products Assn. **[1609]**

Iraqi Amer. Chamber of Commerce and Indus. **[24285]**

Jamaica USA Chamber of Commerce **[24287]**

Joint Indus. Gp. **[2306]**

Mfrs. for Fair Trade **[2538]**

Natl. Assn. of Export Companies **[2307]**

Natl. Assn. of Foreign-Trade Zones **[2308]**

Natl. Customs Brokers and Forwarders Assn. of Am. **[2309]**

North America-Mongolia Bus. Coun. **[2310]**

North America-Mongolia Bus. Coun. **[IO]**

North American-Bulgarian Chamber of Commerce **[24291]**

North Amer. Importers Assn. **[2311]**

North Amer. Importers Assn. **[IO]**

North America's SuperCorridor Coalition **[3887]**

Overseas Sales and Marketing Assn. of Am. **[2312]**

Pakistan Chamber of Commerce USA **[24364]**

Polish Amer. Chamber of Commerce **[24293]**

Representative of German Indus. and Trade **[762]**

Russian-American Chamber of Commerce **[24294]**

Russian-American Chamber of Commerce in the USA **[24371]**

Serbian-American Chamber of Commerce **[24373]**

Singapore Amer. Bus. Assn. **[763]**

Small Bus. Exporters Assn. of the U.S. **[2313]**

South African USA Chamber of Commerce **[24295]**

Southern U.S. Trade Assn. **[4083]**

Swiss-American Bus. Coun. **[2314]**

Trinidad and Tobago/USA Chamber of Commerce **[24298]**

Turkish-American Chamber of Commerce and Indus. **[24384]**

U.S. of America-China Chamber of Commerce **[24310]**

U.S.-Bahrain Bus. Coun. **[2315]**

U.S.-Cuba Trade Assn. **[2316]**

U.S. Indian Amer. Chamber of Commerce **[24331]**

United States-Indonesia Soc. **[775]**

U.S.-Kazakhstan Bus. Assn. **[2317]**

United States-New Zealand Coun. **[2318]**

US-China Bus. Coun. **[2319]**

US-Ireland Alliance **[776]**

Wales North Am. Bus. Chamber **[24306]**

Intl. Trade Action Coun. - Address unknown since 1999.

Intl. Trade Assn. - Defunct.

Intl. Trade Center **[★IO]**

Intl. Trade Centre **[IO]**, Geneva, Switzerland

Intl. Trade Club of Chicago **[IO]**, Chicago, IL, United States

Intl. Trade Club of Chicago **[★IO]**

Intl. Trade Club of Chicago **[2284]**, 134 N LaSalle St., Ste. 1300, Chicago, IL 60602, (312)368-9197

Intl. Trade Club of Chicago **[★2284]**

Intl. Trade Commn. Trial Lawyers Assn. **[★6332]**

Intl. Trade Coun. **[2285]**

Intl. Trade Exhibitions in France **[1345]**, 1611 N Kent St., Ste. 903, Arlington, VA 22209, (703)522-5000

Intl. Trade Exhibitions in France **[IO]**, Arlington, VA, United States

Intl. Trade Mart **[★IO]**

Intl. Trade Mart **[★2295]**

International Trade Specialist Training Prog. **[★5592]**

Intl. Trademark Assn. **[5850]**, 655 3rd Ave., 10th Fl., New York, NY 10017-5617, (212)642-1700

Intl. Trademark Assn. **[IO]**, New York, NY, United States

Intl. Traders Assn. - Address unknown since 2006.

Intl. Traders Club - Address unknown since 1995.

Intl. Traders Club - Real Estate - Defunct.

Intl. Traditional Country Music Fan Club **[24914]**, PO Box 161, Watauga, TN 37694, (423)542-5543

Intl. Traditional Karate Fed. **[23562]**, 1930 Wilshire Blvd., Ste. 1007, Los Angeles, CA 90057-3603, (213)483-8261

Intl. Traditional Karate Fed. **[IO]**, Los Angeles, CA, United States

International Training and Simulation Alliance **[IO]**, Arlington, VA, United States

Intl. Training and Simulation Alliance **[6735]**, 2111 Wilson Blvd., Ste. 400, Arlington, VA 22201-3061, (703)247-9471

Intl. Transactional Anal. Assn. **[16089]**, 2186 Rheem Dr., No. B-1, Pleasanton, CA 94588, (925)600-8110

Reference to "IO" in place of a book number signifies that the association may be found in the 45th edition of International Organizations.

Intl. Transactional Anal. Assn. [IO], Pleasanton, CA, United States

Intl. Transfer Printing Inst. - Address unknown since 1994.

Intl. Transplant Coordinators Soc. [IO], Linden, Belgium

Intl. Transplant Nurses Soc. [IO], Pittsburgh, PA, United States

Intl. Transplant Nurses Soc. [15488], PO Box 351, 1739 E Carson St., Pittsburgh, PA 15203-0351, (412)343-4867

Intl. Transport Workers' Fed. [IO], London, United Kingdom

International Transportation Management Association [IO], Houston, TX, United States

Intl. Trans. Mgt. Assn. [6319], PO Box 924146, Houston, TX 77292-4146, (713)747-4909

Intl. Trauma Anesthesia and Critical Care Soc. [13686], PO Box 4826, Baltimore, MD 21211

International Trauma Anesthesia and Critical Care Society [IO], Baltimore, MD, United States

Intl. Travel-Adventure Film Guild - Defunct.

Intl. Travel Catering Assn. [IO], Godalming, United Kingdom

Intl. Travel and Trailer Club - Defunct.

Intl. Travel Writers and Editors Assn. [3926], 1224 N Nolcomis NE, Alexandria, MN 56308, (320)763-7626

Intl. Travel Writers and Editors Assn. [IO], Alexandria, MN, United States

Intl. Travelers Health Inst. - Address unknown since 1995.

Intl. Treatment Preparedness Coalition [13573], c/o Collaborative Fund for HIV Treatment Preparedness, Tides Found., 40 Exchange Pl., Ste. 1111, New York, NY 10005, (212)509-1049

Intl. Treatment Preparedness Coalition [IO], New York, NY, United States

Intl. Tree Crops Inst. U.S.A. - Address unknown since 2002.

Intl. Tree Found. [IO], Crawley Down, United Kingdom

Intl. Tree Nut Coun. [IO], Reus, Spain

Intl. Tremor Found. [★IO]

Intl. Tremor Found. [★15331]

Intl. Triathlon Union [IO], North Vancouver, BC, Canada

Intl. Trombone Assn. [IO], Coventry, United Kingdom

Intl. Tropical Fern Soc. - Defunct.

Intl. Trotting and Pacing Assn. [23501], 60 Gulf Rd., Gouverneur, NY 13642, (315)287-2294

Intl. Trotting and Pacing Assn. [IO], Gouverneur, NY, United States

Intl. Truck Parts Assn. [IO], Bethesda, MD, United States

Intl. Truck Parts Assn. [388], 7127 Braeburn Pl., Bethesda, MD 20817, (202)544-3090

Intl. Trumpet Guild [10630], c/o Dixie Burress, Treas., PO Box 2688, Davenport, IA 52809-2688

Intl. Trumpet Guild [IO], Westfield, MA, United States

International Truss Plate Assn. [★IO]

Intl. Tsunami Info. Center [IO], Honolulu, HI, United States

Intl. Tsunami Info. Center [7640], 737 Bishop St., Ste. 2200, Honolulu, HI 96813, (808)532-6423

Intl. Tuba-Euphonium Assn. [10631], c/o Kathy Aylsworth Brantigan, Treas., 2253 Downing St., Denver, CO 80205, (303)832-4676

Intl. Tuba-Euphonium Assn. [IO], Denver, CO, United States

Intl. Tube Assn. [IO], Leamington Spa, United Kingdom

Intl. Tug-of-War Assn. - Address unknown since 1988.

Intl. Tungsten Indus. Assn. [IO], Brussels, Belgium

Intl. Tunnelling Assn. [IO], Lausanne, Switzerland

Intl. Turf Producers Found. [IO], East Dundee, IL, United States

Intl. Turf Producers Found. [4793], c/o Turfgrass Producers Intl., 2 E Main St., East Dundee, IL 60118, (847)649-5555

Intl. Turquoise Assn. - Defunct.

Intl. Turtle and Tortoise Soc. - Defunct.

Intl. Twins Assn. - Defunct.

Intl. Typographical Union [★24086]

Intl. Tyre, Rubber, and Plastics Fed. [IO], Warrington, United Kingdom

Intl. UFO Museum and Res. Center at Roswell, New Mexico [IO], Roswell, NM, United States

Intl. UFO Museum and Res. Center at Roswell, New Mexico [7478], 114 N Main St., Roswell, NM 88203, (800)822-3545

International Understanding

Abwenzi African Stud. [18863]

Africa-American Friendship Soc. [18862]

Alliance of Amer. and Russian Women [13418]

Alliance for Communities in Action [12416]

Alliance for Peacebuilding [17248]

Amer. Bahraini Friendship Soc. [19150]

Amer. Iranian Coun. [17926]

Amer. Portuguese Soc. [10889]

Amer. Red Cross Overseas Assn. [12831]

Asia Soc. [9616]

Assn. for the Advancement of Dutch-American Stud. [9908]

Assn. of Nepalis in the Americas [19286]

Belgian Amer. Educational Found. [9736]

Center for Citizen Initiatives [17879]

Center for Global Educ. [8662]

Chinese Amer. Forum [9786]

Christian Friends of Israel - USA [19777]

Croatian Amer. Assn. [17868]

Crosscurrents Intl. Inst. [17880]

Delphi Intl. Prog. of World Learning [17881]

East-West Center [17882]

Educators for Social Responsibility [17883]

Eisenhower Fellowships [17884]

English in Action [17885]

French-American Found. [17886]

French Inst. Alliance Francaise [9968]

Friends of Sabeel - North Am. [18205]

Friends of Togo [17887]

Friendship Ambassadors Found. [17888]

Friendship Force Intl. [17889]

German Marshall Fund of the U.S. [17890]

Global Educ. Associates [17891]

Global Nomads Intl. [17892]

Global Volunteers [17893]

Golden Rule Found. [10186]

Ground Zero Pairing Proj. [17894]

Hospitality Comm. for United Nations Delegations [17895]

The Hospitality and Info. Ser. [17896]

Inst. of World Affairs [8663]

InterFuture [8664]

Intl. Center in New York [17897]

Intl. Multiracial Shared Cultural Org. [17898]

Intl. Peace Operations Assn. [18213]

ISAR: Resources for Environmental Activists [17899]

Japan Center for Intl. Exchange - USA [17900]

Japan Info. Access Proj. [10265]

Kiwanis Intl. [13047]

The Korea Soc. [24350]

Laotian Amer. Natl. Alliance [19192]

Laotian Amer. Soc. [19193]

Legacy Intl. [8665]

Macedonian Amer. Friendship Assn. [19220]

Makassed Found. of Am. [12730]

Meridian Intl. Center [17901]

Meridian Intl. Center Programming Div. [17902]

Moorhead Kennedy Gp. [8666]

Natl. Assn. for Multicultural Educ. [8582]

Natl. Comm. for Labor Israel [12460]

Natl. Comm. on United States-China Relations [17064]

Natl. Coun. for Intl. Visitors [17903]

Nepalese Americas Coun. [19287]

Never Again Campaign [18162]

Org. of Chinese Americans [17065]

Org. for Intl. Cooperation [17904]

Org. for Intl. Professional Exchanges [17905]

Our Developing World [17906]

Pacific Arts Assn. [9463]

Pan-Pacific and Southeast Asia Women's Assn. of the U.S.A. [17907]

People to People Ambassador Prog. [17908]

People to People Intl. [17909]

Perhaps Kids Meeting Kids Can Make a Difference [17910]

Polish-American-Jewish Alliance for Youth Action [13510]

Proj. Handclasp [17911]

Punjabi-American Cultural Assn. [10223]

The Russian-American Center/Track Two Inst. for Citizen Diplomacy [17912]

Salvadoran Amer. Leadership and Educational Fund [17484]

Scholars for Peace in the Middle East [18070]

Sister Cities Intl. [17913]

Soc. for Indonesian-Americans [19116]

Soc. for Intercultural Educ., Training and Res. U.S.A. [8667]

Sovereignty Intl. [17873]

StandWithUs [17941]

Student Letter Exchange [22144]

Symphony for United Nations [9601]

Transnational Diplomatic Network [17874]

Turkish Coalition of Am. [18754]

United Religions Initiative [20518]

U.S.-China Peoples Friendship Assn. [17066]

U.S.-Japan Culture Center [10268]

U.S. Servas [17914]

Uniterra Found. [17915]

Unity-and-Diversity World Coun. [17916]

Unity Coalition for Israel [8672]

US-Azerbaijan Coun. [17876]

USA for the United Nations High Commissioner for Refugees [12824]

Venceremos Brigade [17917]

Veterans for Am. [17918]

Volunteers for Peace [17919]

Wisconsin Coordinating Coun. on Nicaragua [17920]

World Congress of Poets [10873]

World Neighbors [17921]

World Peace Found. [17922]

World Press Inst. [17202]

Intl. Underwater Spearfishing Assn. [23418], 31169 Nassau Ct., Temecula, CA 92591

International Underwater Spearfishing Association [IO], Temecula, CA, United States

Intl. Underwater Spearfishing Soc. - Address unknown since 1995.

Intl. Underwriting Assn. of London [IO], London, United Kingdom

Intl. Unicycling Fed. [23311], PO Box 790, North Bend, WA 98045-0790

Intl. Union of Advertisers Assn. [★IO]

Intl. Union Against Alcoholism [★IO]

Intl. Union Against Cancer [IO], Geneva, Switzerland

Intl. Union Against Sexually Transmitted Infections, Regional Off. for North Am. [IO], Baltimore, MD, United States

Intl. Union Against Sexually Transmitted Infections, Regional Off. for North Am. [16414], c/o Prof. King K. Holmes, Pres.-Elect, Harbor Medical Center, Box 359931, 325 9th Ave., Seattle, WA 98104, (206)731-4239

Intl. Union Against Sexually Transmitted Infections - United Kingdom [IO], Southampton, United Kingdom

Intl. Union Against Tuberculosis [★IO]

Intl. Union Against Tuberculosis and Lung Disease [IO], Paris, France

Intl. Union Against the Venereal Diseases and the Treponematoses, Regional Off. for North Am. [★IO]

Intl. Union Against the Venereal Diseases and the Treponematoses, Regional Off. for North Am. [★16414]

Intl. Union of Air Pollution Prevention Associations [★IO]

Intl. Union of Air Pollution Prevention and Environmental Protection Associations [IO], Brighton, United Kingdom

Intl. Union of Allied Novelty and Prdt.ion Workers [24196]

Intl. Union of Angiology [IO], Rome, Italy

Intl. Union of Anthropological and Ethnological Sciences [IO], Leiden, Netherlands

Intl. Union of Architects [IO], Paris, France

Intl. Union of Aviation Insurers [IO], London, United Kingdom

Intl. Union of Biochemistry [★IO]

A star before a book entry number signifies that the name is not listed separately, but is mentioned within the entry.

3686   Encyclopedia of Associations, 46th Edition

Intl. Union of Biochemistry and Molecular Biology **[IO]**, Strasbourg, France

Intl. Union of Biological Sciences **[IO]**, Paris, France

Intl. Union of Bricklayers and Allied Craftsmen **[★24027]**

Intl. Union of Bricklayers and Allied Craftsworkers **[1029]**, 620 F St. NW, Washington, DC 20004, (202)783-3788

International Union of Bricklayers and Allied Craftsworkers **[IO]**, Washington, DC, United States

Intl. Union of Bricklayers and Allied Craftworkers **[24027]**, 620 F St. NW, Washington, DC 20004, (202)783-3788

Intl. Union of Building Centres **[IO]**, Helsinki, Finland

Intl. Union of Building Societies and Savings Associations **[★IO]**

Intl. Union for Conservation of Nature and Natural Resources **[★IO]**

Intl. Union for Conservation of Nature and Natural Resources - Botswana **[IO]**, Gaborone, Botswana

Intl. Union for the Conservation of Nature and Natural Resources U.S. **[IO]**, Washington, DC, United States

Intl. Union for the Conservation of Nature and Natural Resources U.S. **[4412]**, 1630 Connecticut Ave. NW, 3rd Fl., Washington, DC 20009, (202)387-4826

Intl. Union for the Conservation of Nature and Natural Resources - Vietnam **[IO]**, Hanoi, Vietnam

Intl. Union for Conservation of Nature and Natural Resources - Zambia **[IO]**, Lusaka, Zambia

Intl. Union for the Conservation of Nature's Primate Specialist Group - Defunct.

Intl. Union of Credit and Investment Insurers/ The Berne Union **[IO]**, London, United Kingdom

Intl. Union of Criminal Law **[★IO]**

Intl. Union of Crystallography **[IO]**, Chester, United Kingdom

Intl. Union of District 50, Allied and Tech. Workers of the U.S. and Canada **[★24137]**

Intl. Union of Doll and Toy Workers of the U.S. and Canada **[★24196]**

Intl. Union of Dolls, Toys, Playthings, Novelties and Allied Prdts. of the U.S. and Canada **[★24196]**

Intl. Union of Elecl., Radio and Machine Workers **[★24049]**

Intl. Union of Elecl. Workers **[★IO]**

Intl. Union for Electricity Applications **[IO]**, Puteaux, France

Intl. Union for Electroheat **[★IO]**

Intl. Union of Electronic, Elecl., Salaried, Machine, and Furniture Workers **[24049]**, 501 Third St. NW, Washington, DC 20001, (202)513-6300

Intl. Union of Electronic, Elecl., Tech., Salaried, Machine, and Furniture Workers **[★24049]**

Intl. Union of Elevator Constructors **[24099]**, 7154 Columbia Gateway Dr., Columbia, MD 21046, (410)953-6150

Intl. Union of Elevator Constructors **[IO]**, Columbia, MD, United States

Intl. Union of Exhibitions and Fairs **[★IO]**

Intl. Union of Food, Agricultural, Hotel, Restaurant, Catering, Tobacco, and Allied Workers' Associations **[IO]**, Petit-Lancy, Switzerland

Intl. Union of Food and Allied Workers' Associations **[★IO]**

Intl. Union of Food Sci. and Tech. **[IO]**, Oakville, ON, Canada

Intl. Union of Forest Res. Organizations **[IO]**, Vienna, Austria

Intl. Union of Francophone Press **[IO]**, Paris, France

Intl. Union of Geodesy and Geophysics **[IO]**, Boulder, CO, United States

Intl. Union of Geological Sciences **[IO]**, Ottawa, ON, Canada

Intl. Union of Gospel Missions **[★IO]**

Intl. Union of Gospel Missions **[★13155]**

Intl. Union of Guards and Watchmen **[★24186]**

Intl. Union of Guides and Scouts of Europe **[IO]**, Chateau Landon, France

Intl. Union for Hea. Promotion and Educ. **[IO]**, St.-Denis, France

Intl. Union of Heat Distributors **[★IO]**

Intl. Union of the History and Philosophy of Sci. **[IO]**, Athens, Greece

Intl. Union of the History of Sciences **[★IO]**

Intl. Union for Housing Finance **[IO]**, London, United Kingdom

Intl. Union of Housing Finance Institutions **[★IO]**

Intl. Union of Immunological Societies **[IO]**, Zurich, Switzerland

Intl. Union of Indus. and Independent Workers **[IO]**, Paramount, CA, United States

Intl. Union of Indus. and Independent Workers **[24208]**, 8131 E Rosecrans Ave., Ste. 203, Paramount, CA 90723, (682)438-3382

Intl. Union for Inland Navigation **[★IO]**

Intl. Union of Journeymen Horseshoers of the U.S. and Canada - Address unknown since 2004.

Intl. Union of Judges **[★IO]**

Intl. Union of Labs. and Experts in Constr. Materials, Systems and Structures **[IO]**, Bagneux, France

Intl. Union for Land Value Taxation and Free Trade **[IO]**, London, United Kingdom

Intl. Union of Liberal Democratic and Radical Youth **[★IO]**

Intl. Union of Life Insurance Agents - Address unknown since 1994.

Intl. Union for the Logic, Methodology and Philosophy of Sci. **[★IO]**

Intl. Union of Marine Insurance **[IO]**, Zurich, Switzerland

Intl. Union of Microbiological Societies **[IO]**, Utrecht, Netherlands

Intl. Union of Mine, Mill and Smelter Workers **[★24137]**

Intl. Union of Non-Professional Cinema **[IO]**, Dronten, Netherlands

Intl. Union of Nutritional Sciences **[IO]**, Los Angeles, CA, United States

Intl. Union of Nutritional Sciences **[15563]**, c/o Dr. Osman M. Galal, Sec. Gen., UCLA School of Public Hea., Dept. of Community Hea. Sciences, PO Box 951772, Los Angeles, CA 90095-1772, (310)206-9639

Intl. Union of Official Travel Organizations **[★IO]**

Intl. Union of Operating Engineers **[24028]**, 1125 17th St. NW, Washington, DC 20036, (202)429-9100

Intl. Union of Painters and Allied Trades **[24146]**, 1750 New York Ave. NW, Washington, DC 20006, (202)637-0700

Intl. Union of Painters and Allied Trades/Joint Apprenticeship and Training Fund **[12082]**, 1750 New York Ave. NW, Washington, DC 20006, (202)637-0700

Intl. Union of Painters and Allied Trades/Joint Apprenticeship and Training Fund **[IO]**, Washington, DC, United States

Intl. Union of Petroleum and Indus. Workers **[24163]**

Intl. Union of Petroleum Workers **[★24163]**

Intl. Union for Physical and Engg. Sciences in Medicine **[IO]**, Stockholm, Sweden

Intl. Union of Physiological Sciences **[IO]**, Nara, Japan

Intl. Union of Police Associations **[24121]**, 1549 Ringling Blvd., Ste. 600, Sarasota, FL 34236, (941)487-2560

Intl. Union of Police Syndicates **[★IO]**

Intl. Union for Prehistoric and Protohistoric Sciences **[IO]**, Gent, Belgium

Intl. Union of Private Wagons **[IO]**, Brussels, Belgium

Intl. Union of Professional Drivers **[IO]**, Ruggell, Liechtenstein

Intl. Union for the Protection of New Varieties of Plants **[IO]**, Geneva, Switzerland

Intl. Union of Psychological Sci. **[IO]**, Ottawa, ON, Canada

Intl. Union of Public Transport **[★IO]**

Intl. Union for Pure and Applied Biophysics **[IO]**, Garching, Germany

Intl. Union of Pure and Applied Chemistry **[IO]**, Research Triangle Park, NC, United States

Intl. Union of Pure and Applied Chemistry **[6686]**, c/o Dr. John W. Jost, Exec. Dir., PO Box 13757, Research Triangle Park, NC 27709-3757, (919)485-8700

Intl. Union of Pure and Applied Physics **[IO]**, Victoria, BC, Canada

Intl. Union of Pure and Applied Physics - USA **[IO]**, College Park, MD, United States

Intl. Union of Pure and Applied Physics - USA **[7502]**, c/o Jackie Beamon-Kiene, Amer. Physical Soc., One Physics Ellipse, College Park, MD 20740-3844, (301)209-3269

Intl. Union for Quaternary Res. **[IO]**, Dublin, Ireland

Intl. Union of Radio Sci. **[IO]**, Gent, Belgium

Intl. Union of Radio Sci; U.S. Natl. Comm. of the **[7785]**

Intl. Union of Radioecology **[IO]**, St. Paul, France

Intl. Union of Railways **[IO]**, Paris, France

Intl. Union for the Sci. Stud. of Population **[IO]**, Paris, France

Intl. Union of Security Officers **[24186]**, 2201 Broadway St., Ste. 101, Oakland, CA 94612, (800)772-3326

Intl. Union, Security, Police and Fire Professionals of Am. **[24187]**, 25510 Kelly Rd., Roseville, MI 48066, (586)772-7250

International Union, Security, Police and Fire Professionals of America **[IO]**, Roseville, MI, United States

Intl. Union of Sex Workers **[IO]**, London, United Kingdom

Intl. Union of Shoe Indus. Technicians **[IO]**, Elda, Spain

Intl. Union of Societies of Foresters - Defunct.

Intl. Union of Soil Sciences **[IO]**, Reading, United Kingdom

Intl. Union of Speleology **[IO]**, Prague, Czech Republic

Intl. Union of Students **[IO]**, Prague, Czech Republic

Intl. Union for the Stud. of Social Insects **[IO]**, Charlotte, NC, United States

Intl. Union for the Stud. of Social Insects **[7063]**, c/o Stan Schneider, Sec.-Treas., Univ. of North Carolina, Dept. of Biology, 9201 Univ. City Blvd., Charlotte, NC 28223, (704)687-4053

Intl. Union of Tech. Associations and Organizations **[IO]**, Paris, France

Intl. Union of Tenants **[IO]**, Stockholm, Sweden

Intl. Union of Testing and Res. Labs. for Materials and Structures **[★IO]**

Intl. Union of Theoretical and Applied Mechanics **[IO]**, Eindhoven, Netherlands

Intl. Union of Tool, Die and Mold Makers **[24100]**, 71 E Cherry St., Rahway, NJ 07065, (732)388-3323

Intl. Union, UAW - Community Action Prog. **[18298]**, 8000 E Jefferson Ave., Solidarity House, Detroit, MI 48214, (313)926-5000

Intl. Union, United Auto., Aerospace and Agricultural Implement Workers of Am. **[24004]**, 8000 E Jefferson Ave., Solidarity House, Detroit, MI 48214, (313)926-5000

Intl. Union, United Auto., Aircraft, and Agricultural Implement Workers of Am. **[★24004]**

Intl. Union of United Brewery, Flour, Cereal, Soft Drink and Distillery Workers of Am. (AFL-CIO) **[★24020]**

Intl. Union United Mine Workers of Am. **[★24139]**

Intl. Union United Plant Guard Workers of Am. **[★24187]**

Intl. Union United Plant Guard Workers of Am. **[★IO]**

Intl. Union, United Welders **[★24028]**

Intl. Union for Vacuum Sci., Technique and Applications **[IO]**, Chester, United Kingdom

Intl. Union of Wine, Spirits, Brandy and Liqueur Industrialists and Wholesalers **[★IO]**

Intl. Union of Workers in Public Services **[★IO]**

Intl. Universities' Sports Bd. - Defunct.

Intl. Univ. Consortium **[8566]**, Univ. of Maryland Univ. Coll., 3501 Univ. Blvd. E, Adelphi, MD 20783, (301)985-7826

Intl. Univ. Consortium **[IO]**, Adelphi, MD, United States

Intl. Univ. Consortium for Telecommunications in Learning **[★IO]**

Intl. Univ. Consortium for Telecommunications in Learning **[★8566]**

Intl. Univ. Found. **[8648]**, 1301 S Noland Rd., Independence, MO 64055, (816)461-3633

Intl. Univ. Found. **[IO]**, Independence, MO, United States

Intl. Univ. Sports Fed. **[IO]**, Brussels, Belgium

Reference to "IO" in place of a book number signifies that the association may be found in the 45th edition of International Organizations.

Intl. Utilities Revenue Protection Assn. [IO], Wauchula, FL, United States

Intl. Utilities Revenue Protection Assn. [6338], c/o Jeff Cornelius, Chm., PO Box 1310, Wauchula, FL 33873, (800)282-3824

Intl. VAR Assn. - Defunct.

Intl. Vaulting Club [23968], c/o Suzanne E. Detol, VP, 34142 SW Johnson School Rd., Cornelius, OR 97113, (503)357-9651

Intl. Vaulting Club [IO], Cornelius, OR, United States

Intl. Vegetarian Union [IO], Altrincham, United Kingdom

International Ventilator Users Network [★IO]

International Ventilator Users Network [★11981]

Intl. Venture Capital Inst. - Defunct.

Intl. Veteran Boxers Assn. [23264]

Intl. Veterinary Acupuncture Soc. [16796], PO Box 271395, Fort Collins, CO 80527-1395, (970)266-0666

Intl. Veterinary Acupuncture Soc. [IO], Fort Collins, CO, United States

Intl. Veterinary Assistance [IO], Mosinee, WI, United States

Intl. Veterinary Assistance [11420], c/o Dr. Angela L. Witt, DVM, Sec., 1972 Woodcrest Cir., Mosinee, WI 54455

Intl. Veterinary Students' Assn. [IO], Frederiksberg, Denmark

Intl. Veterinary Ultrasound Soc. [IO], Madison, WI, United States

Intl. Veterinary Ultrasound Soc. [16797], PO Box 46391, Madison, WI 53744, (608)827-7239

Intl. Video Fed. [IO], Brussels, Belgium

Intl. Vine and Wine Off. [★IO]

International Vintage Poster Dealers Association [IO], New York, NY, United States

Intl. Vintage Poster Dealers Assn. [106], PO Box 501, New York, NY 10113-0501

Intl. Virginia Woolf Soc. [9666], c/o Bonnie Kime Scott, Pres., Dept. of Women's Stud., San Diego State Univ., 5500 Campanile Dr., San Diego, CA 92182-8138, (619)594-6460

Intl. Virginia Woolf Soc. [IO], San Diego, CA, United States

Intl. Virtual Assistants Assn. [68], 561 Keystone Ave., Ste. 309, Reno, NV 89503, (888)259-2487

International Visitors
Global Nomads Intl. [17892]

Intl. Visitors Information Service - Defunct.

Intl. Visitors; Natl. Coun. for Community Services to [★17903]

International Visitors Program [★17902]

Intl. Visual Commun. Assn. [IO], London, United Kingdom

Intl. Visual Literacy Assn. [IO], Broken Arrow, OK, United States

Intl. Visual Literacy Assn. [8271], c/o Dr. Constance L. Cassity, Exec. Treas., Northeastern State Univ., 3100 E New Orleans St., Broken Arrow, OK 74014

Intl. Vitamin A Consultative Gp. [15564], c/o ILSI Human Nutrition Inst., One Thomas Cir. NW, Washington, DC 20005-5802, (202)659-9024

Intl. Vitamin A Consultative Gp. [IO], Washington, DC, United States

Intl. Vladimir Nabokov Soc. [IO], Lawrence, KS, United States

Intl. Vladimir Nabokov Soc. [9667], c/o Prof. Stephen Jan Parker, Sec.-Treas./Ed., Dept. of Slavic Languages and Literatures, Univ. of Kansas - Wescoe Hall, 1445 Jayhawk Blvd., Rm. 2134, Lawrence, KS 66045-7590, (785)864-3313

Intl. Vocational Educ. and Training Assn. [9306], c/o Barbara Herrmann, Exec. Sec./Treas., 186 Wedgewood Dr., Mahtomedi, MN 55115, (651)770-6719

International Vocational Education and Training Association [IO], Mahtomedi, MN, United States

Intl. Volleyball Assn. - Defunct.

Intl. Volleyball Fed. - Switzerland [IO], Lausanne, Switzerland

Intl. Voluntary Action and Voluntary Assn. Res. Org. - Defunct.

Intl. Voluntary Ser. [★13404]

Intl. Voluntary Ser. [IO], Edinburgh, United Kingdom

Intl. Voluntary Ser. [★IO]

Intl. Voluntary Ser. Assn. [★IO]

Intl. Voluntary Ser. - Scotland [★IO]

Intl. Voluntary Services - Address unknown since 2006.

Intl. Volunteer Org. for Women, Educ. and Development [IO], Rome, Italy

Intl. Volunteer Prog. [IO], Oakland, CA, United States

Intl. Volunteer Prog. [13397], 678 13th St., Ste. 100, Oakland, CA 94612, (510)433-0414

Intl. Volunteer Programs Assn. [13398], c/o Found. of Sustainable Development, 870 Market St., Ste. 321, San Francisco, CA 94102, (201)221-4105

Intl. Volunteer Programs Assn. [IO], San Francisco, CA, United States

Intl. Volunteers for Development [IO], Rome, Italy

Intl. Voyage Alliance - Address unknown since 1995.

Intl. Wages for Housework Campaign [13428], c/o Crossroads Women's Centre, PO Box 86681, Los Angeles, CA 90086-0681, (323)292-7405

Intl. Wages for Housework Campaign [IO], Los Angeles, CA, United States

Intl. Wallcovering Mfrs. Assn. [IO], Brussels, Belgium

Intl. Wallpaper Mfrs. Assn. [★IO]

Intl. War Veterans' Alliance - Address unknown since 1995.

Intl. Warehouse Logistics Assn. [3979], 2800 S River Rd., Ste. 260, Des Plaines, IL 60018-6003, (847)813-4699

Intl. Warehouse Logistics Assn. [IO], Des Plaines, IL, United States

International Warlander Society and Registry [IO], Palm Bay, FL, United States

Intl. Warlander Soc. and Registry [4908], PO Box 110545, Palm Bay, FL 32911-0545, (321)953-1410

Intl. Watch Collectors Soc. [22988], 244 Madison Ave., No. 258, New York, NY 10016

Intl. Watch Fob Assn. [22989], 601 Patriot Pl., Holmen, WI 54636, (608)385-7237

Intl. Watch Fob Assn. [IO], Holmen, WI, United States

Intl. Water Assn. [IO], London, United Kingdom

Intl. Water History Assn. [IO], Bergen, Norway

Intl. Water Lily Soc. [★IO]

Intl. Water Lily Soc. [★22524]

Intl. Water Mgt. Inst. [IO], Colombo, Sri Lanka

Intl. Water Resources Assn. [IO], Carbondale, IL, United States

Intl. Water Resources Assn. [7834], c/o Southern Illinois Univ., 4535 Faner Hall, Carbondale, IL 62901-4516, (618)453-6021

Intl. Water Ski Fed. [IO], Unteraegeri, Switzerland

Intl. Water Ski Racing Assn. - Address unknown since 2003.

Intl. Waterlily and Water Gardening Soc. [22524], c/o Paula Biles, Exec. Dir., 6828 26th St. W, Bradenton, FL 34207, (941)756-0880

International Waterlily and Water Gardening Society [IO], Bradenton, FL, United States

Intl. Waterproofing Assn. [★IO]

International Webcasting Association [IO], Chantilly, VA, United States

Intl. Webcasting Assn. [2667], 4206 F Tech. Ct., Chantilly, VA 20151

Intl. Webmasters Assn. [6812], 119 E Union St., Ste. F, Pasadena, CA 91103, (626)449-3709

Intl. Webmasters Assn. [IO], Pasadena, CA, United States

Intl. Weed Sci. Soc. [IO], Davis, CA, United States

Intl. Weed Sci. Soc. [4102], c/o Dr. Albert Fischer, Sec.-Treas., Univ. of California-Davis, Plant Sciences Dept., Mail Stop No. 4, 1 Shields Ave., Davis, CA 95616, (530)752-7386

Intl. Weight Pull Assn. [23384], c/o Rodney Martin, Membership Chm., 3407 17th Ave., Evans, CO 80620, (970)339-9264

International Weight Pull Association [IO], Evans, CO, United States

Intl. Weightlifting Fed. [IO], Budapest, Hungary

Intl. Well Control Forum [IO], Montrose, United Kingdom

Intl. Western Music Assn. [★10723]

Intl. Whaling Commn. [IO], Cambridge, United Kingdom

Intl. Wheat Coun. [★IO]

Intl. Wheat Gluten Assn. [IO], Overland Park, KS, United States

Intl. Wheat Gluten Assn. [1533], 9300 Metcalf Ave., Ste. 300, Overland Park, KS 66212, (913)381-8180

Intl. Wheelchair and Amputee Sports Fed. [IO], Aylesbury, United Kingdom

Intl. Wheelchair Aviators [IO], Big Bear City, CA, United States

Intl. Wheelchair Aviators [21457], PO Box 4140, Big Bear Lake, CA 92315-4140, (951)529-2644

Intl. Wheelchair Road Racers Club [23346], c/o Joseph M. Dowling, Pres., 30 Myano Ln., PO Box 3, Stamford, CT 06902, (203)967-2231

Intl. Wheelchair Road Racers Club [IO], Stamford, CT, United States

Intl. Wholesale Furniture Assn. [★IO]

Intl. Wholesale Furniture Assn. [★1700]

Intl. Wild Rice Assn. [★4307]

Intl. Wild Rice Assn. [★IO]

Intl. Wild Rice Exchange [IO], Woodland, CA, United States

Intl. Wild Rice Exchange [4307], PO Box 1247, Woodland, CA 95776-1247, (530)669-0150

Intl. Wild Waterfowl Assn. [5331], c/o John Nuccitelli, Treas., 438 Quaker Meeting House Rd., Honeoye Falls, NY 14472, (585)624-4608

Intl. Wild Waterfowl Assn. [IO], Honeoye Falls, NY, United States

Intl. Wildlife Carving Assn. [IO], Centralia, WA, United States

Intl. Wildlife Carving Assn. [22163], c/o Byrn Watson, Pres., 194 Summerside Dr., Centralia, WA 98531, (360)736-1082

Intl. Wildlife Coalition - USA [5332], 70 E Falmouth Hwy., East Falmouth, MA 02536, (508)457-1898

Intl. Wildlife Coalition - USA [IO], East Falmouth, MA, United States

Intl. Wildlife Rehabilitation Coun. [IO], San Jose, CA, United States

Intl. Wildlife Rehabilitation Coun. [5333], PO Box 8187, San Jose, CA 95155, (408)271-2685

Intl. Willie Nelson Fan Club [24915], PO Box 7104, Lancaster, PA 17604-7104

International Willie Nelson Fan Club [IO], Lancaster, PA, United States

Intl. Willow Collectors [IO], Des Moines, IA, United States

Intl. Willow Collectors [22061], c/o Edie Cronk, Membership Chm., 2408 46th St., Des Moines, IA 50310

Intl. Window Cleaning Assn. [2468], 14 W 3rd St., Ste. 200, Kansas City, MO 64105, (816)471-4922

Intl. Window Cleaning Assn. [IO], Kansas City, MO, United States

International Window Film Association [IO], Martinsville, VA, United States

Intl. Window Film Assn. [633], PO Box 3871, Martinsville, VA 24115-3871, (276)666-4932

Intl. Wine and Food Soc. - London [IO], London, United Kingdom

Intl. Wine Soc. - Address unknown since 1995.

Intl. Wire and Machinery Assn. [IO], Leamington Spa, United Kingdom

Intl. Wireless Telecommunications Assn. - Address unknown since 2008.

Intl. Wizard of Oz Club [9668], PO Box 2657, Alameda, CA 94501

Intl. Wizard of Oz Club [IO], Alameda, CA, United States

Intl. Women Fly Fishers [IO], Pleasant Hill, CA, United States

Intl. Women Fly Fishers [22443], 141 Wiggins Ct., Pleasant Hill, CA 94523, (925)934-2461

Intl. Women's Anthropology Conf. [6420], Anthropology Dept., 25 Waverly Pl., New York Univ., New York, NY 10003, (212)998-8550

Intl. Women's Anthropology Conf. [IO], New York, NY, United States

Intl. Women's Club of Bari [IO], Bari, Italy

Intl. Women's Coffee Alliance [11783], c/o Charlene Farmer, Chief Financial Off., Green Mountain Coffee Roasters, 33 Coffee Ln., Waterbury, VT 05676, (800)545-2326

Intl. Women's Cricket Coun. [IO], Christchurch, New Zealand

Intl. Women's Film Project - Address unknown since 1995.

A star before a book entry number signifies that the name is not listed separately, but is mentioned within the entry.

Intl. Women's Fishing Assn. **[23419]**, PO Box 21066, Fort Lauderdale, FL 33335-1066

Intl. Women's Fishing Assn. **[IO]**, Fort Lauderdale, FL, United States

Intl. Women's Forum **[IO]**, Washington, DC, United States

Intl. Women's Forum **[13429]**, 2120 L St. NW, Ste. 460, Washington, DC 20037, (202)387-1010

Intl. Women's Hea. Coalition **[16899]**, 333 7th Ave., 6th Fl., New York, NY 10001, (212)979-8500

Intl. Women's Hea. Coalition **[IO]**, New York, NY, United States

International Women's Media Foundation **[IO]**, Washington, DC, United States

Intl. Women's Media Found. **[4043]**, 1625 K St. NW, Ste. 1275, Washington, DC 20006, (202)496-1992

Intl. Women's Media Project - Defunct.

Intl. Women's Network **[★IO]**

Intl. Women's Rights Action Watch **[IO]**, Minneapolis, MN, United States

Intl. Women's Rights Action Watch **[17770]**, c/o Human Rights Center, Univ. of Minnesota, 229-19th Ave. S, Minneapolis, MN 55455, (612)625-4985

Intl. Women's Tribune Centre/Women, Ink **[17544]**, 777 United Nations Plz., New York, NY 10017, (212)687-8633

Intl. Women's Tribune Centre/Women, Ink **[IO]**, New York, NY, United States

Intl. Women's Writing Guild **[IO]**, New York, NY, United States

Intl. Women's Writing Guild **[11180]**, PO Box 810, Gracie Sta., New York, NY 10028-0082, (212)737-7536

Intl. Women's Year/Tribune Proj. **[★17544]**

Intl. Women's Year/Tribune Proj. **[★IO]**

Intl. Wood Collectors Soc. **[IO]**, Greencastle, IN, United States

Intl. Wood Collectors Soc. **[23031]**, c/o William Cockrell, Sec.-Treas., 2300 W Rangeline Rd., Greencastle, IN 46135-7875, (765)653-6483

Intl. Wood Products Assn. **[1609]**, 4214 King St. W, Alexandria, VA 22302, (703)820-6696

Intl. Wood Products Assn. **[IO]**, Alexandria, VA, United States

Intl. Wooden Bow Tie Club **[243]**, 24B Rosemary Ln., Middlefield, CT 06455, (860)349-9328

Intl. Woodworkers of Am. **[★24026]**

Intl. Woodworkers of Am., U.S. AFL-CIO **[★24026]**

Intl. Wool Textile Org. **[IO]**, Brussels, Belgium

Intl. Work Gp. for Indigenous Affairs **[IO]**, Copenhagen, Denmark

International Work Platform Assn. **[★IO]**

Intl. Workcamp Org. **[IO]**, Seoul, Republic of Korea

Intl. Workcamps Morocco **[IO]**, Safi, Morocco

International Workers' Compensation College **[★IO]**

International Workers' Compensation College **[★5678]**

Intl. World Calendar Assn. - Defunct.

Intl. World Games Assn. **[IO]**, Hoensbroek, Netherlands

Intl. World Wide Web Conf. Comm. **[IO]**, Hong Kong, People's Republic of China

Intl. Wrought Copper Coun. **[★IO]**

Intl. Wrought Copper Coun. **[IO]**, London, United Kingdom

Intl. WWOOF Assn. **[IO]**, Maur, Switzerland

Intl. X-Ray Unit Comm. **[★IO]**

Intl. X-Ray Unit Comm. **[★5161]**

Intl. Yacht Racing Union **[★IO]**

Intl. Yak Assn. **[IO]**, Hillside, CO, United States

Intl. Yak Assn. **[5001]**, c/o Cynthia Huber, Sec.-Treas./Registrar, PO Box 27, Hillside, CO 81232, (719)942-4181

Intl. Yan Xin Qigong Assn. **[13640]**, PO Box 1332, Church Sta., New York, NY 10008-1332

Intl. Yan Xin Qigong Assn. **[IO]**, New York, NY, United States

International Yang Style Tai Chi Chuan Association **[IO]**, Redmond, WA, United States.

Intl. Yang Style Tai Chi Chuan Assn. **[23594]**, 4076-148th Ave. NE, Redmond, WA 98052, (425)869-1185

Intl. Yoga Soc. **[★20637]**

Intl. Yoga Teachers' Assn. **[IO]**, Thornleigh, Australia

Intl. Young Catholic Students **[IO]**, Paris, France

Intl. Young Christian Workers - Belgium **[IO]**, Brussels, Belgium

Intl. Young Democrat Union **[IO]**, London, United Kingdom

Intl. Youth Assn. **[IO]**, Tallinn, Estonia

Intl. Youth Found. **[IO]**, Baltimore, MD, United States

Intl. Youth Found. **[13490]**, 32 South St., Ste. 500, Baltimore, MD 21202, (410)951-1500

Intl. Youth Hostel Fed. **[IO]**, Welwyn Garden City, United Kingdom

Intl. Youth Lib. **[IO]**, Munich, Germany

Intl. Youth Year Commn. - Defunct.

Intl. Zebu Breeders Assn. - Address unknown since 1995.

Intl. Zen Assn. **[IO]**, Paris, France

Intl. Zinc Assn. - Belgium **[IO]**, Brussels, Belgium

Intl. Zinc Assn. - Europe **[IO]**, Brussels, Belgium

Intl. Zuma Class Assn. - Address unknown since 1991.

Internationale AlpenschutzKommission **[IO]**, Schaan, Liechtenstein

Internationale Arbeitsgemeinschaft der Papier historiker **[★IO]**

Internationale Arbeitsgemeinschaft der Wasserwerke im Rheineinzugsgebiet **[★IO]**

Internationale Arzte-Gesellschaft fur Biophysikalische Informations - Therapie e.V. **[★IO]**

Internationale Begegnung in Gemeinschaftsdiensten **[★IO]**

Internationale Buchhaendler-Vereinigung **[★IO]**

Internationale des Coiffures de Dames **[★1080]**

Internationale Coronelli-Gesellschaft fuer Globenkunde **[★IO]**

Internationale Democrate Chretienne **[★IO]**

Internationale Foderation des Dachdeckerhandwerks **[★IO]**

Internationale Foderation Vexillologischer Gesellschaften **[★IO]**

Internationale Foderation Vexillologischer Gesellschaften **[★11075]**

Internationale Frauenliga fur Frieden und Freiheit **[★IO]**

Internationale Gesellchhaft der Stadt and Regionaplaner **[★IO]**

Internationale Gesellschaft fur die Geschichte der Pharmazie **[★IO]**

Internationale Gesellschaft fur Geschichtsdidaktik **[★IO]**

Internationale Gesellschaft fur Ingenieurpadagogik **[★IO]**

Internationale Gesellschaft fur Menschenrechte **[★IO]**

Internationale Gesellschaft fur Musik in der Medizin **[★IO]**

Internationale Gesellschaft fur Musikwissenschaft **[★IO]**

Internationale Gesellschaft fur Nutztierhaltung **[★IO]**

Internationale Gesellschaft fur Warenkunde und Technologie **[★IO]**

Internationale Gesselschaft Fur Kunst, Gestaltung Und Therapie **[★IO]**

Internationale Gustav Mahler Gesellschaft **[★IO]**

Internationale Hegel-Gesellschaft **[IO]**, Berlin, Germany

Internationale Hegel-Vereinigung **[IO]**, Heidelberg, Germany

Internationale Heinrich Schutz-Gesellschaft **[★IO]**

Internationale Jugendbibliothek **[★IO]**

Internationale Kolpingwerk **[★IO]**

Internationale Kommission fur Alpines Rettungswesen **[★IO]**

Internationale Kommission fur Geschichte der Geologischen Wissenschaften **[★IO]**

Internationale Kommission zum Schutz des Rheins **[★IO]**

Internationale de l'Education **[★IO]**

Internationale Liberale **[★IO]**

Internationale Messtechnische Konfoderation **[★IO]**

Internationale Org. fur Sukkulentenforschung **[★IO]**

Internationale Orientierungslauf Foderation **[★IO]**

Internationale Paneuropa Union **[★IO]**

Internationale des Resistants a la Guerre **[★IO]**

Internationale Sektion der IVSS fur die Verhutung von Arbeitsunfallen und Berufskrankheiten durch Elektrizitat-Gas-Fernwarme-Wasser **[★IO]**

Internationale des Services Publics **[★IO]**

Internationale Socialiste des Femmes **[★IO]**

Internationale Studiengemeinschaft fur Pranatale und Perinatale Psychologie und Medizin **[★IO]**

Internationale Tagung der Historikerinnen und Historiker der Arbeiter-und anderer sozialer Bewegungen **[★IO]**

Internationale Terminologienetz **[★IO]**

Internationale Union der Lebensmittel-, Landwirschafts-, Hotel-, Restaurant-, Cafe und Genussmittelarbeiter-Gewerkschaften **[★IO]**

Internationale Vereinigung fur Bruckenbau und Hochbau **[★IO]**

Internationale Vereinigung fur Okologie **[★IO]**

Internationale Vereinigung der Schall-und Audiovisuellen Archv. **[★IO]**

Internationale Vereinigung fur Schul-und Berufsberatung **[★IO]**

Internationale Vereinigung Sport- und Freizeiteinrichtungen **[★IO]**

Internationale Vereinigung van Telecommunicatiegebruikers **[★IO]**

Internationale Vereinigung fur Vegetationskunde **[★IO]**

Internationale Vereniging voor Neerlandistiek **[★IO]**

Internationale Verkehrssicherheit LA Prevention Routiere Internationale **[★IO]**

Internationale Versohnungsbund **[★IO]**

Internationale Vredesbrigades Belgie **[★IO]**

Internationalen Raiffeisen Union **[★IO]**

Internationalen Rat der Christen und Juden **[★IO]**

Internationalen Wissenschaftlichen Vereinigung Weltwirtschaft und Weltpolitik, e.V. **[★IO]**

Internationaler Arbeitskreis fur Musik **[★IO]**

Internationaler Arbeitskreis Systematische und Vergleichende Musikwissenschaft **[★IO]**

Internationaler Bauorden **[★IO]**

Internationaler Bund der Konfessionslosen und Atheisten **[★IO]**

Internationaler Christlicher Friedensdienst **[★IO]**

Internationaler Draht- und Maschinenverband **[★IO]**

Internationaler Kunstkritikerverband **[★IO]**

Internationaler Suchdienst **[★IO]**

Internationaler Verband des Erwerbsgartenbaues **[★IO]**

Internationaler Verein fuer Menschenrechte der Kurden **[★IO]**

Internationaler Versohnungsbund - Osterreichischer Zweig **[★IO]**

Internationales Design Zentrum Berlin **[★IO]**

Internationales Forschungsinstitut fur Medien, Kommunikation und Kulturelle Entwicklung **[★IO]**

Internationales Institut fur Jugendliteratur und Leseforschung **[★IO]**

Internationales Institut fur Nationalitatenrecht und Regionalismus **[★IO]**

Internationales Katholisches Missionswerk **[★IO]**

Internationales Komitee Fur Die Indianer Amerikas **[★IO]**

Internationales Komitte fur die Indigenen Amerikas **[★IO]**

Internationales Theater-Institut, Zentrum Schweiz **[★IO]**

Internationalle Gesellschaft fur Erzieherische Hilfen **[★IO]**

Internationella Forsurningssekretariatet **[★IO]**

Internationella Kvinnoforbundet for Fred och Frihet **[★IO]**

Internet

Advanced Media Workflow Assn. **[3721]**

Amer. Assn. of Webmasters **[896]**

Anti-Child Pornography Org. **[12766]**

Assn. Global View **[8017]**

Assn. of Sites Advocating Child Protection **[11560]**

Consumer Web Watch **[17322]**

CyberAngels **[12452]**

eMarketing Assn. **[1166]**

Enough Is Enough **[17923]**

EPIC - Electronically Published Internet Connection **[22914]**

Hi-Ethics - Hea. Internet Ethics **[14676]**

HomePlug Powerline Alliance **[1216]**

HumanHorizons.Net **[IO]**

Independent Online Booksellers Assn. **[530]**

Indonesian Internet Ser. Provider Assn. **[IO]**

Reference to "IO" in place of a book number signifies that the association may be found in the 45th edition of International Organizations.

Interactive Travel Services Assn. [3946]
Intl. Assn. of Employment Web Sites [1266]
Intl. Assn. of Messaging Professionals [6711]
Intl. Assn. of Webmasters and Designers [888]
Intl. Educ. and Rsrc. Network [8269]
Intl. Info. Systems Security Certification
  Consortium [6758]
Intl. Nanocasting Assn. [562]
Intl. .NET Assn. [6771]
Intl. Webcasting Assn. [2667]
Internet Assn. Japan [IO]
Internet and Mobile Assn. of India [IO]
Internet Professional Publishers Assn. [1777]
Internet Ser. Providers Assn. of Bangladesh [IO]
Internet Ser. Providers Assn. of India [IO]
Internet Soc. of China [IO]
Internet Soc. Nederland [IO]
Internet Soc. of New Zealand [IO]
Internet Telephony Services Providers' Assn. [IO]
Israel Internet Assn. [IO]
Metro Ethernet Forum [7748]
North Amer. Coun. for Online Learning [7949]
One Economy [7755]
Other Minds [10684]
PANGEA - Comunicacio per a la Cooperacio [IO]
People for Internet Responsibility [12453]
Privacy Rights CH [3176]
Reporters Network [3160]
Rhizome [9596]
SATELLIFE Global Hea. Info. Network [14663]
SavetheInternet.com Coalition [17924]
Search Engine Marketing Professional Org.
  [2648]
SeniorNet [13302]
Sloan Consortium [8304]
Teaching, Learning and Tech. Gp. [6898]
TeleTruth: The Alliance for Customers' Telecom-
  munications Rights [17346]
Thailand Chap. of the Internet Soc. [IO]
Ukrainian Internet Assn. [IO]
Virtual Private Network Consortium [IO]
Virtual Private Network Consortium [2320]
VON Coalition [2321]
Web Analytics Assn. [7222]
WECAI Network [1167]
Wi-Fi Alliance [6829]
World Internet Numismatic Soc. [22768]
Internet Advt. Bur. [IO], London, United Kingdom
Internet Alliance [IO], Washington, DC, United
  States
Internet Alliance [737], c/o Emily T. Hackett, Exec.
  Dir., 1111 19th St. NW, Ste. 1100, Washington, DC
  20035-5782, (202)861-2476
Internet Assn; Asia and Pacific [IO]
Internet Assn; Irish [IO]
Internet Assn. Japan [IO], Tokyo, Japan
Internet Bus. Alliance [3730], PO Box 11518,
  Seattle, WA 98110-5518
Internet Business Assn. Intl. - Defunct.
Internet Censorship; Families Against [17039]
Internet Connection; EPIC - Electronically Published
  [22914]
Internet Content Rating Assn. [12060], c/o Family
  Online Safety Inst., 666 11th St. NW, Ste. 1100,
  Washington, DC 20001, (202)331-8651
Internet Content Rating Assn. [IO], Washington, DC,
  United States
Internet Corp. for Assigned Names and Numbers
  [6813], 4676 Admiralty Way, Ste. 330, Marina del
  Rey, CA 90292, (310)823-9358
Internet Ethics; Hi-Ethics - Hea. [14676]
Internet Exchange Assn; Commercial [★911]
Internet Fraud Watch; Natl. Fraud Info. Center/
  [17339]
Internet Indus. Assn. [IO], Manuka, Australia
Internet Indus. Assn; U.S. [893]
Internet Infidels [7490], PO Box 142, Colorado
  Springs, CO 80901-0142
Internet: Intl. Human Rights Documentation Network
  [★IO]
Internet Local Advt. and Commerce Assn. [★IO]
Internet Local Advt. and Commerce Assn. [★737]
Internet Local Advertising and Commerce Assn. -
  Defunct.
Internet Marketing and Advt. Assn. [★98]

Internet and Mobile Assn. of India [IO], Bombay,
  India
Internet Professional Assn. [IO], Hong Kong,
  People's Republic of China
Internet Professional Publishers Assn. [1777], c/o
  Digital Minute, PO Box 670446, Coral Springs, FL
  33067, (954)426-3507
Internet Professionals Assn. - Address unknown
  since 2001.
Internet Professionals; Soc. of [IO]
Internet Providers; Canadian Assn. of [IO]
Internet Ser. Providers Assn. [IO], Parklands,
  Republic of South Africa
Internet Ser. Providers Assn. of Bangladesh [IO],
  Dhaka, Bangladesh
Internet Ser. Providers Assn. of India [IO], New
  Delhi, India
Internet Services Providers Assn; European [IO]
Internet Soc. [IO], Reston, VA, United States
Internet Soc. [906], 1775 Wiehle Ave., Ste. 102, Re-
  ston, VA 20190-5109, (703)326-9880
Internet Soc. of Australia [IO], Sydney, Australia
Internet Soc. of China [IO], Beijing, People's
  Republic of China
Internet Soc. Nederland [IO], The Hague,
  Netherlands
Internet Soc. of New Zealand [IO], Wellington, New
  Zealand
Internet Soc. - Republic of South Africa [IO], Cape
  Town, Republic of South Africa
Internet Software Consortium [★6772]
Internet Systems Consortium [6772], 950 Charter
  St., Redwood City, CA 94063, (650)423-1300
Internet and Telecom Assn. of Hong Kong [★IO]
Internet Telephony Services Providers' Assn. [IO],
  London, United Kingdom
Internetworking Forum; Optical [3726]
Internews Network [18027], PO Box 4448, Arcata,
  CA 95518-4448, (707)826-2030
Internews Network [IO], Arcata, CA, United States
InterNICHE [IO], Leicester, United Kingdom
Internists; Amer. Coll. of Osteopathic [15794]
Interns; Canadian Assn. of Pharmacy Students and
  [IO]
Interns; Natl. Assn. of Residents and [15175]
Interns for Peace [17736], c/o Middle East Peace
  Dialogue Network, 200 Country Club Pkwy., Mount
  Laurel, NJ 08054, (856)235-3111
Interns for Peace [IO], Mount Laurel, NJ, United
  States
Interns and Residents; Comm. of [24089]
Interns and Residents in New York City; Comm. of
  [★24089]
Internship Assn; Cooperative Educ. and [8157]
Internship Centers; Assn. of Psychology [★8854]
Internship Centers; Assn. of Psychology Postdoc-
  toral and [8854]
Internship Prog; Academic Admin. [★7881]
Internship Program; Natl. Consumer Affairs [17337]
Internships; Natl. InterAssociation Comm. on
  [★8872]
Interoperability Assn; LonMark [★3705]
Interoperability; Intl. Alliance for [7018]
INTERPAVE [IO], Leicester, United Kingdom
Interplast [IO], Mountain View, CA, United States
Interplast [14049], 857 Maude Ave., Mountain View,
  CA 94043, (650)962-0123
INTERPRED - World Trade Center Sofia [IO], Sofia,
  Bulgaria
Interpretation Mgt. Institute [★7363]
Interpretation; Natl. Assn. for [7363]
Interpreters Assn; Western [★7363]
Interpreters for the Deaf; Registry of [14778]
Interpreters Guild; Translators and [3855]
Interpreters; Natl. Alliance of Black [3854]
Interpreters and Translators Assn; Court [★5628]
Interpreters and Translators for the Deaf; Natl.
  Registry of Professional [★14778]
Interpreters and Translators; Natl. Assn. of Judiciary
  [5628]
Interpretive Naturalists; Assn. of [★7363]
InterPride [12240], c/o Southern Maine Pride, PO
  Box 9715, Portland, ME 04104-5015, (207)773-
  4188
InterPride [IO], Portland, ME, United States

Interprofessional Fostering of Ophthalmic Care for
  Underserved Sectors [16859], 19728 Saums Rd.,
  PMB No. 136, Houston, TX 77084, (281)398-7525
Interprofessional Res. Comm. on Pupil Personnel
  Services - Defunct.
Interracial
  Amegroid Soc. of Am. [9366]
  Interracial Family Alliance of Houston [12160]
  Interracial Family Circle [12161]
  Interracial-Intercultural Pride [12162]
  John La Farge Inst. [19645]
  Natl. Catholic Conf. for Interracial Justice [17133]
Interracial Cooperation; Commn. on [★17156]
Interracial Coun. for Business Opportunity - Address
  unknown since 2000.
Interracial Family Alliance [★12160]
Interracial Family Alliance of Houston [12160]
Interracial Family Circle [12161], 4923 E Chalk Point
  Rd., West River, MD 20778
Interracial-Intercultural Pride [12162], PO Box 11811,
  Berkeley, CA 94712-2811, (510)644-1000
Interracial Justice; Natl. Catholic Conf. for [17133]
Interregional Assn. for Clinical Microbiology and
  Antimicrobial Chemotherapy [IO], Smolensk, Rus-
  sia
Interreligious Affairs; Bishops' Comm. for Ecumenical
  and [19584]
Interreligious Comm. of General Secretaries - Ad-
  dress unknown since 2002.
Interreligious Emergency Campaign for Economic
  Justice - Defunct.
Interreligious Found. for Community Org. [11797],
  418 W 145th St., New York, NY 10031, (212)926-
  5757
Interreligious Inst; Graymoor Ecumenical and
  [19895]
Interreligious and Intl. Fed. for World Peace
  [★18251]
Interreligious and Intl. Fed. for World Peace [IO],
  Tarrytown, NY, United States
Interrogator Translator Teams Assn; Marine Corps
  [19226]
Interscholastic Athletic Administrators Assn; Natl.
  [8989]
Interscholastic Music Assn; Natl. Fed. [★8928]
Interscholastic Officials Assn; Natl. Fed. [★23874]
Interscholastic Spirit Assn; Natl. Fed. [★23295]
Interscholastic Spirit Association; National Fed.
  [★23841]
Interscholastic Swimming Coaches Assn. of Am;
  Natl. [23887]
Interscience Res. Inst. [★13649]
InterServe U.S.A. [20351], PO Box 418, Upper
  Darby, PA 19082-0418, (800)809-4440
InterServe U.S.A. [IO], Upper Darby, PA, United
  States
Interservice Sports Comm. [★6069]
Interservice Sports Coun. [★6069]
Intersex Soc. of North Am. [13093], 979 Golf Course
  Dr., No. 282, Rohnert Park, CA 94928
Intersex Soc. of North Am. [IO], Rohnert Park, CA,
  United States
Intersocietal Commn. for the Accreditation of
  Vascular Labs. [★16726]
Intersocietal Commn. for the Accreditation of
  Vascular Labs. [16726], 8830 Stanford Blvd., Ste.
  306, Columbia, MD 21045-5442, (410)872-0100
Intersociety Commn. for Heart Disease Resources
  [★13890]
Intersociety Comm. on Methods for Air Sampling and
  Analysis - Address unknown since 2007.
Intersociety Comm. on Pathology Info. [★15871]
Intersociety Coun. for Pathology Info. [15871], 9650
  Rockville Pike, Bethesda, MD 20814-3993,
  (301)634-7200
Intersociety Professional Nutrition Educ. Consortium
  [15565], c/o Univ. of Alabama at Birmingham, 439
  Susan Mott Webb Nutrition Sciences Bldg., 1675
  Univ. Blvd., Birmingham, AL 35294-3360,
  (205)996-2513
Interspecies [7223], 301 Hidden Meadow, Friday
  Harbor, WA 98250
Interspecies [IO], Friday Harbor, WA, United States
Interspecies Commun. [★IO]
Interspecies Commun. [★7223]

A star before a book entry number signifies that the name is not listed separately, but is mentioned within the entry.

Interspecies Communication
Gorilla Found. [7533]
Interspecies [7223]
Interspecies [IO]
Interstate Carriers Conf. [★3899]
Interstate Clearing House on Mental Health - Defunct.
Interstate Club [21458], c/o Brent Taylor, PO Box 127, Blakesburg, IA 52536, (641)938-2773
Interstate Commerce Commn; Assn. of Practitioners Before the [★6316]
Interstate Commerce Commn. Practitioners; Assn. of [★6316]
Interstate Compact for Education [★8252]
Interstate Compact on the Placement of Children; Assn. of Administrators of the [11559]
Interstate Conf. of Employment Security Agencies [★5680]
Interstate Conf. of Unemployment Compensation Agencies [★5680]
Interstate Conf. on Water Policy [★6138]
Interstate Cong. for Equal Rights and Responsibili- ties - Defunct.
Interstate Cotton Seed Crushers' Assn. [★2854]
Interstate Coun. of State Boards of Cosmetology [★5616]
Interstate Coun. of State Boards of Cosmetology; Natl. - [5616]
Interstate Coun. on Water Policy [6138], 51 Monroe St., Ste. PE-08A, Rockville, MD 20850, (301)984-1908
Interstate Dental Assn. [★14175]
Interstate Migrant Educ. Coun. [12588], 1 Mas- sachusetts Ave., Ste. 700, Washington, DC 20001, (202)336-7078
Interstate Migrant Educ. Task Force [★12588]
Interstate Milk Shipments; Natl. Conf. on [4493]
Interstate Mining Compact Commn. [6116], 445-A Carlisle Dr., Herndon, VA 20170, (703)709-8654
Interstate Natural Gas Assn: of Am. [1680], 10 G St. NE, Ste. 700, Washington, DC 20002, (202)216-5900
Interstate Oil Compact Commn. [★5684]
Interstate Oil and Gas Compact Commn. [5684], PO Box 53127, Oklahoma City, OK 73152-3127, (405)525-3556
Interstate Postgraduate Medical Assn. of North Am. [14386], PO Box 5474, Madison, WI 53705, (608)231-9045
Interstate Producers Livestock Assn. [★5030]
Interstate Professional Applicators Assn. [2909], PO Box 13262, Salem, OR 97309, (503)363-7205
Interstate Renewable Energy Coun. [6959], PO Box 1156, Latham, NY 12110-1156, (518)458-6059
Interstate Rodeo Assn. [★23686]
Interstate Solar Coordination Coun. - Address unknown since 2003.
Interstate Towing Assn. - Defunct.
Interstate Trolley Club of New York [★10915]
Interstate Truckload Carriers Conf. [★3899]
Interstate Water Pollution Control Administrators; Assn. of State and [5688]
Interstitial Cystitis Assn. [16708], 110 N Washington St., Ste. 340, Rockville, MD 20850, (301)610-5300
Intersure [★2191]
Intersure - Singer Nelson Charlmers [2191], PO Box 16, Teaneck, NJ 07666, (201)837-1100
INTERTECT [★5564]
INTERTECT [★IO]
INTERTEL [9984], PO Box 1083, Tulsa, OK 74101, (918)583-2928
Intertribal Bison Cooperative [5036], 2497 W Chicago St., Rapid City, SD 57702, (605)394-9730
Intertribal Native Amer. Assn; Black Indians and [19269]
Interuniversity Consortium for Political Res. [★7525]
Interval Intl. [22581], PO Box 431920, Miami, FL 33243-1920, (305)666-1884
Interval Intl. [IO], Miami, FL, United States
InterVarsity Link [IO], Madison, WI, United States
InterVarsity Link [9182], PO Box 7895, Madison, WI 53707-7895, (608)274-9001
Intervega - Movement for Compassionate Living (the Vegan Way) [IO], Swansea, United Kingdom
Intervenor Org. of Ontario [IO], Toronto, ON, Canada

Intervention and Coiled Tubing Assn. [7512], PO Box 1082, Montgomery, TX 77356, (936)520-1549
Interventional Nephrology; Amer. Soc. of Diagnostic and [15287]
Interventional Radiology; Soc. of [16300]
Interventional Radiology; Soc. of Cardiovascular and [★16300]
Interventional and Therapeutic Neuroradiology; Amer. Soc. of [16280]
Interventionists; Amer. Assn. for Home-Based Early [17056]
Interventions; Soc. for Cardiac Angiography and [13924]
Interweave Continental (Unitarian Universalists for Lesbian, Gay, Bisexual and Transgender Concerns) [20059], 45 State St., No. 380, Montpelier, VT 05602
Intestinal Disease Found. [14421]
Intestinal and Endoscopic Surgeons; Soc. of Amer. Gastro [14428]
Intimate Apparel Associates - Defunct.
Intimate Apparel Mfrs. Assn. - Defunct.
Intimate Apparel Square Club [12201], 326 Field Rd., Clinton Corners, NY 12514, (845)758-5752
Intinet [★13101]
Intinet Rsrc. Center [★13101]
InTouch Networks [16860], c/o Jewish Guild for the Blind, 15 W 65th St., New York, NY 10023, (212)769-6270
Intoxicated Drivers - U.S.A; Remove [★12987]
Intramural Assn; Natl. [★23842]
Intramural-Recreational Sports Assn; Natl. [23842]
Intraocular Lens Mfrs. Assn. - Defunct.
Intravenous Infusion Therapy Assn; Outpatient [16631]
Intravenous Nurses Soc. [★16614]
Intrepid Assn. of Former Crew Members; USS [21225]
Intuitives; Intl. Assn. of Medical [15040]
Inuit Art Found. [IO], Ottawa, ON, Canada
Invasive Cardiovascular Professionals; Soc. of [13928]
Invasive Specialists; Amer. Coll. of Cardiovascular [★13885]
Invasive Species Specialist Gp. [IO], Auckland, New Zealand
Invent Am.! [7227], PO Box 26065, Alexandria, VA 22313, (703)942-7121
Invention Marketing Inst. [★7228]
Inventors
Affiliated Inventors Found. [7224]
Amer. Assn. of Inventors [7225]
Amer. Assn. of Inventors [IO]
Amer. Soc. of Inventors [7226]
Assn. of Hungarian Inventors [IO]
Belgian Chamber of Inventors [IO]
Canadian Innovation Centre [IO]
China Assn. of Inventions [IO]
Czech Union of Inventors and Rationalizers [IO]
Danish Inventors Assn. [IO]
Edison Birthplace Assn. [11110]
Hong Kong Invention Assn. [IO]
Innovators and Entrepreneurs Assn. [IO]
Inst. of Inventors [IO]
Inst. of Patentees and Inventors [IO]
Inst. for Social Inventions [IO]
Intl. Fed. of Inventors' Associations [IO]
Invent Am.! [7227]
Inventors Assistance League [7228]
Inventors Clubs of Am. [7229]
Inventors Workshop Intl. Educ. Foundation/ Entrepreneurs Workshop [5851]
Japan Inst. of Invention and Innovation [IO]
John Ericsson Soc. [11130]
Natl. Collegiate Inventors and Innovators Alliance [7218]
Natl. Cong. of Inventors Organizations [7230]
Natl. Inventors Found. [7231]
Norwegian Inventors' Assn. [IO]
Singapore Inventors' Development Assn. [IO]
Spanish Inventors Club [IO]
Swedish Inventors Assn. [IO]
Swiss Assn. of Inventors and Researchers [IO]
Tesla Memorial Soc. [11151]
Union of Inventors of Bulgaria [IO]

United Inventors Assn. of the U.S.A. [7232]
Inventors Assistance League [7228], 1053 Colorado Blvd., Los Angeles, CA 90041, (818)246-6546
Inventors Assn. of America - Address unknown since 1995.
Inventors Clubs of Am. [7229], 524 Curtis Rd., East Lansing, MI 48823, (517)332-3561
Inventor's Guild - Address unknown since 2001.
Inventors Hall of Fame Found; Natl. [★5855]
Inventor's League - Defunct.
Inventors Workshop Intl. [★5851]
Inventors Workshop Intl. [★IO]
Inventors Workshop Intl. Educ. Foundation/ Entrepreneurs Workshop [IO], Santa Barbara, CA, United States
Inventors Workshop Intl. Educ. Foundation/ Entrepreneurs Workshop [5851], PO Box 285, Santa Barbara, CA 93102-0285, (805)969-9250
Inventory Control Soc; Amer. Production and [★7181]
Inventory Services; North Amer. Assn. of [755]
Inventrepreneurs' Forum - Defunct.
Inverell and District Olive Growers Assn. [IO], Inver- ell, Australia
Invest to Compete Alliance [738], 1010 Pennsylvania Ave. SE, Washington, DC 20003, (202)546-4995
Invest-in-America Found. - Defunct.
Invest in Kids; Fight Crime: [17057]
InvesteringsForeningsRadet [★IO]
Investigate Assassinations; Comm. to [★18787]
Investigation
Amer. Guild of Court Videographers [6019]
Amer. Rescue Dog Assn. [12889]
Assn. of British Investigators [IO]
Assn. of Christian Investigators [5876]
Assn. for Explosive Detection K-9s, Intl. [5964]
Assn. of Former Agents of the U.S. Secret Ser. [5877]
Assn. of Former Intelligence Officers [5878]
Assn. of Former Intelligence Officers [IO]
Assn. of Inspectors Gen. [5777]
Coun. of Intl. Investigators [2322]
Coun. of Intl. Investigators [IO]
Doe Network [12608]
Fed. Criminal Investigators Assn. [5653]
Fed. Law Enforcement Officers Assn. [5879]
Food Safety Consortium [5031]
High Tech. Crime Investigation Assn. Intl. [5880]
High Tech. Crime Investigation Assn. Intl. [IO]
Intl. Assn. of Asian Crime Investigators [5636]
Intl. Assn. of Bloodstain Pattern Analysts [5637]
Intl. Assn. of Cmpt. Investigative Specialists [8133]
Intl. Assn. of Financial Crimes Investigators [5881]
Intl. Assn. of Financial Crimes Investigators [IO]
Intl. Assn. for Intelligence Educ. [8581]
Intl. Assn. of Investigative Locksmiths [3528]
Intl. Assn. of Law Enforcement Intelligence Analysts [5882]
Intl. Assn. of Law Enforcement Intelligence Analysts [IO]
Intl. Assn. of Marine Investigators [2578]
Intl. Assn. for Property and Evidence [5975]
Intl. Assn. of Ser. Evaluators [3269]
Intl. Homicide Investigators Assn. [5883]
International Homicide Investigators Association [IO]
Intl. Intelligence Network [3532]
Intl. Latino Gang Investigator's Assn. [5884]
International Latino Gang Investigator's Associa- tion [IO]
Intl. Security and Detective Alliance [2323]
Intl. Soc. of Environmental Forensics [7098]
ION [2324]
London Club [11900]
Military Intelligence Corps Assn. [5862]
Natl. Assn. for Civilian Oversight of Law Enforce- ment [5985]
Natl. Assn. of Drug Diversion Investigators [5986]
Natl. Assn. of Investigative Specialists [2325]
Natl. Assn. of Legal Investigators [5885]
Natl. Assn. of Legal Search Consultants [2326]
Natl. Assn. of Professional Accident Reconstruc- tionists [6252]
Natl. Assn. of Property Recovery Investigators [5886]

Reference to "IO" in place of a book number signifies that the association may be found in the 45th edition of International Organizations.

National Association of Property Recovery Investigators **[IO]**
Natl. Assn. of Traffic Accident Reconstructionists and Investigators **[5887]**
Natl. Constr. Investigators Assn. **[5606]**
Natl. Defender Investigator Assn. **[5888]**
Natl. District Attorneys Assn. **[5668]**
Natl. Military Intelligence Assn. **[5889]**
Natl. Narcotic Detector Dog Assn. **[5997]**
Natl. Native Amer. Law Enforcement Assn. **[5998]**
Naval Intelligence Professionals **[6096]**
Soc. of Professional Investigators **[5890]**
World Assn. of Detectives **[IO]**
World Assn. of Professional Investigators **[IO]**
World Investigators Network **[IO]**
World Investigators Network **[2327]**
Investigation Agents Assn; Fed. Bur. of **[5968]**
Investigation Assn; High Tech. Crime **[★5880]**
Investigation of Claims of the Paranormal; Comm. for the Sci. **[7444]**
Investigation Comm. on Aerial Phenomena; Natl. **[★7479]**
Investigation League; Vivisection **[11474]**
Investigation and Security Services; Natl. Coun. of **[3539]**
Investigation; Soc. of Former Special Agents of the Fed. Bur. of **[19202]**
Investigation; Soc. for Gynecologic **[15618]**
Investigations Comm. on Unidentified Flying Objects; Natl. **[7482]**
Investigative Commission; Clinton **[★18309]**
Investigative Journalism; Fund for **[17178]**
Investigative Journalism Project **[★17669]**
Investigative Open Network **[★2324]**
Investigative Pathology; Amer. Soc. for **[15860]**
Investigative Reporters and Editors **[3126]**, Missouri School of Journalism, 138 Neff Annex, Columbia, MO 65211, (573)882-2042
Investigative Reporters and Editors **[IO]**, Columbia, MO, United States
Investigative Reporting; Center for **[17168]**
Investigator Assn; Natl. Defender **[5888]**
Investigators; Amer. Assn. of Paranormal **[2896]**
Investigators Anywhere Rsrc. Line **[★2324]**
Investigators Assn; Fed. **[★5653]**
Investigators; Assn. of Fed. **[★5653]**
Investigators Assn; Fed. Criminal **[5653]**
Investigators Assn; Fed. Criminal **[★5653]**
Investigators Assn; Intl. Livestock Identification and Theft **[★4998]**
Investigators Assn; Natl. Constr. **[5606]**
Investigators Associations; Natl. Alliance of Gang **[5638]**
Investigators; Intl. Assn. Private **[★2325]**
Investigators; Natl. Assn. of Drug Diversion **[5986]**
Investigators; Natl. Assn. of Fire **[2206]**
Investigators; Natl. Assn. of Legal **[5885]**
Investigators; Natl. Assn. of Traffic Accident Reconstructionists and **[5887]**
Investigators; Soc. of Air Safety **[★12966]**
Investigators; Soc. of Professional **[5890]**
Investment Adviser Assn. **[3514]**, 1050 17th St. NW, Ste. 725, Washington, DC 20036-5503, (202)293-4222
Investment Advisory Publishers; Natl. Assn. of the **[★3258]**
Investment; Assn. for Intl. **[★18473]**
Investment Assn. of New York; Young Women's **[★1421]**
Investment Bankers Assn. of Am. **[★3523]**
Investment Bankers Conf. **[★3517]**
Investment Casting Inst. **[2032]**, 136 Summit Ave., Montvale, NJ 07645-1745, (201)573-9770
Investment Casting Inst. **[IO]**, Montvale, NJ, United States
Investment Clubs; Natl. Assn. of **[★2342]**
Investment Companies; Amer. Assn. of Minority Enterprise Small Bus. **[★2764]**
Investment Companies; Natl. Assn. of **[★3515]**
Investment Companies; Natl. Assn. of **[2764]**
Investment Companies; Natl. Assn. of Small Bus. **[3618]**
Investment Company Inst. **[3515]**, 1401 H St. NW, 12th Fl., Washington, DC 20005, (202)326-5800
Investment Counsel Assn. of Am. **[★3514]**

Investment Dealers Assn. of Canada **[IO]**, Toronto, ON, Canada
Investment Educ. Inst. **[8425]**, PO Box 220, Royal Oak, MI 48068, (248)583-6242
Investment and Financial Services Assn. **[IO]**, Sydney, Australia
Investment Forum; Social **[18646]**
Investment Funds Inst. of Canada **[IO]**, Toronto, ON, Canada
Investment Mgt. Assn. **[IO]**, London, United Kingdom
Investment Mgt. Assn. of Singapore **[IO]**, Singapore, Singapore
Investment Management Consultants Association **[IO]**, Greenwood Village, CO, United States
Investment Mgt. Consultants Assn. **[2336]**, 5619 DTC Pkwy., Ste. 500, Greenwood Village, CO 80111, (303)770-3377
Investment Mgt. Consultants; Inst. for Certified **[★2336]**
Investment Mgt. and Res; Assn. for **[★2331]**
Investment Managers; Natl. Assn. of Real Estate **[3326]**
Investment Off; British Trade and **[★24241]**
Investment; Org. for Fair Treatment of Intl. **[★18473]**
Investment Partnership Prog. **[★2337]**
Investment Prog. Assn. **[2337]**, 1140 Connecticut Ave. NW, Ste. 1040, Washington, DC 20036, (202)775-9750
Investment Recovery Assn. **[3702]**, 638 W 39th St., Kansas City, MO 64111, (816)561-5323
Investment Savings and Insurance Assn. **[IO]**, Wellington, New Zealand
Investment; Sponsors of Open Housing **[★17819]**
Investment Trusts Assn. **[IO]**, Tokyo, Japan
Investment Trusts; Natl. Assn. of Real Estate **[3327]**
Investments
Alliance in Support of Independent Res. **[3390]**
Alternative Investment Mgt. Assn. **[IO]**
Alternative Investment Mgt. Assn. - Australia **[IO]**
Alternative Investment Mgt. Assn. - Japan **[IO]**
America-Georgia Bus. Coun. **[2296]**
Amer. and African Bus. Women's Alliance **[691]**
Amer. Entrepreneurs for Economic Growth **[695]**
Amer. Intl. Chamber of Commerce **[24247]**
American-Russian Chamber of Commerce and Indus. **[24261]**
Amer.-Southern Africa Chamber of Trade and Indus. **[24375]**
Armenian Amer. Chamber of Commerce **[24263]**
Asia Pacific - USA Chamber of Commerce **[24264]**
Asset Managers Forum **[1401]**
Assn. of Asset Mgt. Companies **[IO]**
Assn. of Chinese Finance Professionals **[1402]**
Assn. of Foreign Investors in Real Estate **[2328]**
Assn. of Foreign Investors in Real Estate **[IO]**
Assn. of Independent Financial Advisers **[IO]**
Assn. of Investment Companies **[IO]**
Assn. of Investment Mgt. Sales Executives **[2329]**
Assn. of Mutual Funds in India **[IO]**
Assn. of Private Client Investment Managers and Stockbrokers **[IO]**
Australian Shareholders' Assn. **[IO]**
Australian Trade Commn. **[24229]**
Automotive Trade Policy Coun. **[350]**
Bd. of Investment of Sri Lanka **[IO]**
Brazil-U.S. Bus. Coun. **[24266]**
Brazilian-American Chamber of Commerce **[24239]**
Brazilian Govt. Trade Bur. of the Consulate Gen. of Brazil in New York **[24240]**
British Trade Off. at Consulate-General **[24241]**
BritishAmerican Bus. Inc. of New York and London **[24267]**
Cameroon-USA Chamber of Commerce **[24249]**
Canadian/American Border Trade Alliance **[3838]**
Canadian Assn. of Income Funds **[IO]**
Canadian Investor Relations Inst. **[IO]**
Canadian ShareOwners Assn. **[IO]**
Center for Venture Res. **[2330]**
CFA Inst. **[2331]**
CFA Inst. **[IO]**
CFA Soc. of the Netherlands **[IO]**
Chartered Alternative Investment Analyst Assn. **[2332]**

Chinese Amer. Assn. of Commerce **[24308]**
Chinese Chamber of Commerce of Hawaii **[24309]**
Commercial Off. of Spain **[24376]**
Comm. for the Economic Growth of Israel **[24337]**
Community Development Venture Capital Alliance **[11771]**
Corporate Coun. on Africa **[169]**
Czech-North Amer. Chamber of Commerce **[24274]**
Dominican Assn. of Foreign Investment Enterprises **[IO]**
Emerging Markets Private Equity Assn. **[1415]**
Estonian Amer. Chamber of Commerce and Indus. **[24318]**
Ethical Investment Assn. **[IO]**
European Assn. for Investors in Non-listed Real Estate Vehicles **[IO]**
European Assn. for Share Promotion **[IO]**
European Funds and Asset Mgt. Assn. **[IO]**
European Mutual Guarantee Assn. **[IO]**
European Private Equity and Venture Capital Assn. **[IO]**
Fed. of Danish Investment Associations **[IO]**
Fed. of Philippine Amer. Chambers of Commerce **[24277]**
Financial Markets Assn. **[1419]**
Foreign Investors Assn. of Albania **[IO]**
Found. for Investment and Development of Exports **[IO]**
Gender Action **[18825]**
Georgia-USA Chamber of Commerce **[24278]**
Ghana-USA Chamber of Commerce **[24279]**
Greek Amer. Chamber of Commerce **[24280]**
Gp. of Thirty **[1172]**
Guild of Investment and Financial Analysts **[IO]**
Hedge Fund Assn. **[IO]**
Hedge Fund Assn. **[2333]**
IAB Partners **[1464]**
Independent Investor Protective League **[2334]**
Intl. Assn. of Financial Engineers **[1424]**
Intl. Assn. of Space Entrepreneurs **[3634]**
Intl. Centre for Settlement of Investment Disputes **[5457]**
Intl. Swaps and Derivatives Assn. **[2335]**
Investment Adviser Assn. **[3514]**
Investment Company Inst. **[3515]**
Investment Dealers Assn. of Canada **[IO]**
Investment Funds Inst. of Canada **[IO]**
Investment Mgt. Assn. **[IO]**
Investment Mgt. Assn. of Singapore **[IO]**
Investment Management Consultants Association **[IO]**
Investment Mgt. Consultants Assn. **[2336]**
Investment Prog. Assn. **[2337]**
Investment Recovery Assn. **[3702]**
Investor Relations Soc. **[IO]**
Investorside Res. Assn. **[2338]**
Iraqi Amer. Chamber of Commerce and Indus. **[24285]**
Irish Assn. of Investment Managers **[IO]**
Irish Funds Indus. Assn. **[IO]**
Jamaica USA Chamber of Commerce **[24287]**
Japan External Trade Org. **[24342]**
Korean Amer. Soc. of Entrepreneurs **[773]**
Latin Amer. Venture Capital Assn. **[1431]**
Liechtenstein Investment Fund Assn. **[IO]**
Loan Syndications and Trading Assn. **[484]**
London Intl. Financial Futures and Options Exchange **[IO]**
Managed Funds Assn. **[24334]**
MicroComputer Investors Assn. **[2339]**
Natl. Assn. of Christian Financial Consultants **[1465]**
Natl. Assn. of Equity Source Banks **[488]**
Natl. Assn. of Govt. Defined Contribution Administrators **[2340]**
Natl. Assn. of Investment Professionals **[2341]**
Natl. Assn. of Investors Corp. **[2342]**
Natl. Assn. of Legal Investigators **[5885]**
Natl. Assn. of Publicly Traded Partnerships **[2343]**
Natl. Assn. of State Treasurers **[6208]**
Natl. Coun. of Asian Amer. Bus. Associations **[774]**
Natl. Coun. of Real Estate Investment Fiduciaries **[2344]**

A star before a book entry number signifies that the name is not listed separately, but is mentioned within the entry.

Natl. Investment Company Ser. Assn. [2345]
Natl. Investor Relations Inst. [2346]
Natl. Real Estate Investors Assn. [2347]
Natl. United States-Arab Chamber of Commerce [24290]
Natl. Venture Capital Assn. [2348]
North America-Mongolia Bus. Coun. [2310]
North American-Bulgarian Chamber of Commerce [24291]
North American-Chilean Chamber of Commerce [24307]
Norwegian Venture Capital and Private Equity Assn. [IO]
NZX [IO]
Pakistan Chamber of Commerce USA [24364]
Pakistani Amer. Bus. Executives Assn. [758]
Polish Amer. Chamber of Commerce [24293]
Private Equity CFO Assn. [1445]
Pro Vita Advisors [20479]
Professional Assn. for Investment Communications Resources [2349]
Public Investors Arbitration Bar Assn. [5891]
Resourceful Women [2350]
Romanian-U.S. Bus. Coun. [24370]
Russian-American Chamber of Commerce [24294]
Savers and Investors League [18699]
Securities Investors Assn. - Singapore [IO]
Serbian-American Chamber of Commerce [24373]
Shareholders Res. Alliance [3391]
Small Investor Protection Assn. [IO]
Social Investment Org. [IO]
South African USA Chamber of Commerce [24295]
Springboard Enterprises [4046]
Stable Value Investment Assn. [2351]
Swedish-American Chambers of Commerce, USA [24297]
Swedish Trade Coun. [3847]
Trinidad and Tobago/USA Chamber of Commerce [24298]
Turkish-American Chamber of Commerce and Indus. [24384]
UK Soc. of Investment Professionals [IO]
U.S. of America-China Chamber of Commerce [24310]
U.S.-Bahrain Bus. Coun. [2315]
U.S.-Kazakhstan Bus. Assn. [2317]
Venezuelan Amer. Assn. of the U.S. [24386]
Wales North Am. Bus. Chamber [24306]
World Fed. of Investors Corp. [IO]
Investments; Interfaith Comm. on Social Responsibility in [★17353]
Investments in Southern Africa; Church Proj. on U.S. [★17353]
Investor Advice; Forum for [1463]
Investor Relations Soc. [IO], London, United Kingdom
Investors; Amer. Assn. of Individual [8422]
Investors Arbitration Bar Assn; Public [5891]
Investors; Coun. of Institutional [3512]
Investors League - Address unknown since 1995.
Investors; National Assn. of Individual [★2342]
Investors in U.S. Real Estate; Assn. of Foreign [★2328]
Investorside Res. Assn. [2338], 1050 Connecticut Ave. NW, Ste. 1000, Washington, DC 20036, (202)223-2769
Invisible Empire Knights of the Ku Klux Klan - Address unknown since 1999.
Involvement and Participation Assn. [IO], London, United Kingdom
IOCALUM [23942], c/o Roland Vinyard, Exec. Sec., 597 State Hwy. 162, Sprakers, NY 12166-4008, (518)673-3212
Iolani Place Irregulars - Defunct.
IOMEC Users Assn. - Defunct.
IOMI [★23501]
IOMI [★IO]
ION [2324], 4548 Jones Rd., Oak Harbor, WA 98277, (360)279-8343
Ionosphere Center; National Astronomy and [★7622]
IONS - Inst. of Noetic Sciences [10976], 101 San Antonio Rd., Petaluma, CA 94952, (707)775-3500
IoP: The Packaging Soc. [IO], Grantham, United Kingdom

Iota Alpha Pi - Defunct.
Iota Beta Sigma [24410], 367 Windsor Hwy., New Windsor, NY 12553-7900, (845)565-0003
Iota Lambda Sigma [24724], c/o Anna Skinner, Exec. Sec.-Treas., 607 Pkwy. W, Oregon, OH 43616, (419)693-6860
Iota Nu Delta Fraternity [24631], PO Box 312152, Jamaica, NY 11431
Iota Phi Lambda [24421], 1462 W 113th Pl., Chicago, IL 60643, (773)445-1315
Iota Sigma Pi [24429], c/o Kathryn Louie, Natl. VP, Univ. of Arizona, Arizona Research Labs, Gould Simpson Bldg., Rm. 615A, 1040 E 4th St., Tucson, AZ 85721, (520)626-8812
Iota Tau Sigma - Address unknown since 2002.
Iota Tau Tau - Address unknown since 2004.
Iowa Alumni Assn; Univ. of [18933]
Iowa Mountaineers - Defunct.
Iowa; Veteran's Assn. of the USS [21233]
Iowa Wesleyan Coll. Alumni Assn. [18900], 601 N Main St., Mount Pleasant, IA 52641, (319)385-8021
IP Justice [5852], 1192 Haight St., San Francisco, CA 94117, (415)553-6261
The IPA Assn. of Am. [3022], 17120 Jami Lynn Ln., Village of Loch Lloyd, MO 64012, (816)322-7906
IPA The Assn. of Graphic Solutions Providers [7154], 7200 France Ave. S, Ste. 223, Edina, MN 55435, (952)896-1908
IPA The Association of Graphic Solutions Providers [IO], Edina, MN, United States
IPC - Assn. Connecting Electronics Indus. [1221], 3000 Lakeside Dr., 309 S, Bannockburn, IL 60015, (847)615-7100
IPM Ecologists; Assn. of Applied [5073]
IPREX [3193], 2861 Kingsland Ct., Atlanta, GA 30339, (770)433-9084
IPS - Inter Press Ser. Intl. Assn. [IO], Rome, Italy
IQ Soc; Intl. High [19149]
IQNet Assn. - Intl. Certification Network [IO], Bern, Switzerland
Ira F. Brilliant Center for Beethoven Studies [★9803]
Iracambi Rainforest Conservation and Res. Center [IO], Rosario da Limeira, Brazil
Irakiska Riksforbundet i Sverige [★IO]
Iran
  Amer. Inst. of Iranian Stud. [10237]
  Amer. Iranian Coun. [17926]
  Assn. for the Stud. of Persianate Societies [8668]
  British Inst. of Persian Stud. - United Kingdom [IO]
  Coalition for Democracy in Iran [17389]
  Comm. for Humanitarian Assistance to Iranian Refugees [12808]
  Intl. Coun. of Iranian Christians [19809]
  Intl. Soc. for Iranian Stud. [10238]
  Iran Freedom Found. [17925]
  Iran Freedom Found. [IO]
  Iranian Amer. Bar Assn. [5504]
  Iranian B'nei Torah Movement [20145]
  Iranian Muslim Assn. of North Am. [20438]
  Mission for Est. of Human Rights in Iran [17777]
  Natl. Coun. of Resistance of Iran [IO]
  Natl. Iranian Amer. Coun. [19151]
Iran Amer. Chamber of Commerce - Defunct.
Iran-Amer. Comm. for Protection of Iranian Integrity - Defunct.
Iran Found. - Defunct.
Iran Freedom Found. [17925], PO Box 422, Bethesda, MD 20817, (301)215-6677
Iran Freedom Found. [IO], Bethesda, MD, United States
Iran Interior Mission [★IO]
Iran Interior Mission [★20315]
Iran School Sport Fed. [IO], Tehran, Iran
Iran Small Indus. and Indus. Parks Org. [IO], Tehran, Iran
Iran Squash Fed. [IO], Tehran, Iran
Iran Taekwondo Union [IO], Tehran, Iran
Iranian
  Amer. Inst. of Iranian Stud. [IO]
  Amer. Inst. of Iranian Stud. [10237]
  Amer. Iranian Coun. [17926]
  Amer. Iranian Coun. [IO]
  Assn. for the Stud. of Persianate Societies [8668]

Children of Persia [11576]
Coalition for Democracy in Iran [17389]
Comm. for Humanitarian Assistance to Iranian Refugees [12808]
Intl. Coun. of Iranian Christians [19809]
Intl. Soc. for Iranian Stud. [10238]
Iran Freedom Found. [17925]
Iranian Amer. Bar Assn. [5504]
Iranian Amer. Medical Assn. [15173]
Iranian Amer. Tech. Coun. [2352]
Iranian Chemists' Assn. of the Amer. Chem. Soc. [6687]
Iranian Muslim Assn. of North Am. [20438]
Iranian Refugees' Alliance [12813]
Mission for Est. of Human Rights in Iran [17777]
Natl. Iranian Amer. Coun. [19151]
Network of Iranian Amer. Soc. [13507]
Iranian Amer. Bar Assn. [5504], 1025 Connecticut Ave. NW, Ste. 1012, Washington, DC 20036
Iranian Amer. Medical Assn. [15173]
Iranian Amer. Medical Assn. [IO], Haledon, NJ, United States
Iranian Amer. Tech. Coun. [2352], PO Box 123, Sterling, VA 20167-0123, (800)788-7824
Iranian Assn. for Energy Economics [IO], Tehran, Iran
Iranian Assn. of Environmental Hea. [IO], Tehran, Iran
Iranian B'nei Torah Movement [20145]
Iranian Chemists' Assn. of the Amer. Chem. Soc. [6687], c/o Dr. Ali R. Banijamali, Dir. of Membership, 35 Meadowbrook Ln., Woodbury, CT 06798, (203)573-3220
Iranian Cultural and Social Stud; Soc. For [★10238]
Iranian Democratic Comm. - Defunct.
Iranian Geotechnical Subcomm. [IO], Tehran, Iran
Iranian Heart Assn. [IO], Tehran, Iran
Iranian Homeopathic Assn. [IO], Tehran, Iran
Iranian Human Rights Working Group - Address unknown since 2006.
Iranian Medical Informatics Assn. [IO], Tehran, Iran
Iranian Medical Laser Assn. [IO], Tehran, Iran
Iranian Muslim Assn. of North Am. [IO], Los Angeles, CA, United States
Iranian Muslim Assn. of North Am. [20438], 3376 Motor Ave., Los Angeles, CA 90034, (310)202-8181
Iranian Pain Soc. [IO], Tehran, Iran
Iranian Physiotherapy Assn. [IO], Tehran, Iran
Iranian Red Crescent [IO], Tehran, Iran
Iranian Refugees' Alliance [IO], New York, NY, United States
Iranian Refugees' Alliance [12813], Cooper Sta., PO Box 316, New York, NY 10276-0316, (212)260-7460
Iranian Soc. of Consulting Engineers [IO], Tehran, Iran
Iranian Soc. of Environmentalists [IO], Tehran, Iran
Iranian Soc. of Fertility and Sterility [IO], Tehran, Iran
Iranian Soc. of Physiology and Pharmacology [IO], Tehran, Iran
Iranian Students Counseling Center - Defunct.
Iranian Stud; Intl. Soc. for [10238]
Iranian Stud; Soc. for [★10238]
Iranian Trade Assn. [2286], PO Box 927743, San Diego, CA 92192, (619)368-6790
Iranian Trade Assn. [IO], San Diego, CA, United States
Iran's Assn. of Flour Producers [IO], Tehran, Iran
Iraq
  Amer. Comm. for Rescue and Resettlement of Iraqi Jews [17943]
  Amer. Soc. for Kurds [13154]
  Coalition to Salute America's Heroes [21294]
  Educ. for Peace in Iraq Center [17927]
  Fed. of Iraqi Associations in Sweden [IO]
  Historians Against the War [18795]
  Iraq Action Coalition [17928]
  Iraq Action Coalition [IO]
  Iraq War Veterans Org. [21304]
  Iraqi Amer. Chamber of Commerce and Indus. [24285]
  Iraqi Assn. [IO]
  Iraqi Medical Sciences Assn. [IO]
  Iraqi Medical Sciences Assn. [14987]

Reference to "IO" in place of a book number signifies that the association may be found in the 45th edition of International Organizations.

Middle East Children's Alliance [**17774**]
Mothers Against War [**18221**]
Oper. Truth [**21317**]
Voices in the Wilderness [**18253**]
Win Without War [**18124**]
Iraq Action Coalition [**17928**], 7309 Haymarket Ln., Raleigh, NC 27615
Iraq Action Coalition [**IO**], Raleigh, NC, United States
Iraq and Afghanistan Veterans of Am. [**21335**], 770 Broadway, 2nd Fl., New York, NY 10003, (212)982-9699
Iraq Occupation Focus [**IO**], London, United Kingdom
Iraq Soc. Against Epilepsy [**IO**], Baghdad, Iraq
Iraq Veterans Against the War [**21356**], PO Box 8296, Philadelphia, PA 19101, (215)241-7123
Iraq War Veterans Org. [**21304**], PO Box 571, Yucaipa, CA 92399, (909)494-6218
Iraq War Veterans Org. [**IO**], Yucaipa, CA, United States
Iraqi Amateur Athletic Fed. [**IO**], Baghdad, Iraq
Iraqi Amateur Radio Soc. [**IO**], Baghdad, Iraq
Iraqi Amer. Chamber of Commerce and Indus. [**24285**], 15265 Maturin Dr., No. 184, San Diego, CA 92127, (858)613-9215
Iraqi Assn. [**IO**], London, United Kingdom
Iraqi Badminton Fed. [**IO**], Baghdad, Iraq
Iraqi Fertility Soc. [**IO**], Baghdad, Iraq
Iraqi Jews; Amer. Comm. for Rescue and Resettlement of [**17943**]
Iraqi Medical Sciences Assn. [**14987**], 3912 Maple Hill E, West Bloomfield, MI 48323, (248)738-5995
Iraqi Medical Sciences Assn. [**IO**], West Bloomfield, MI, United States
Iraqi Natl. Paralympic Comm. [**IO**], Baghdad, Iraq
Iraqi Reproductive Hea. and Family Planning Assn. [**IO**], Baghdad, Iraq
Iraqi Taekwondo Fed. [**IO**], Baghdad, Iraq
Iraqi Tennis Fed. [**IO**], Baghdad, Iraq
Iraqi Widows Org. [**IO**], Ad-Diwaniyah, Iraq
IRC Intl. Water and Sanitation Centre [**IO**], Delft, Netherlands
IRCDA/SDA [**★910**]
IRE Mgt. Engg. Gp. [**★7014**]
Ireland
Amer. Conf. for Irish Stud. [**10239**]
Amer. Ireland Fund [**17929**]
Amer. Ireland Fund [**IO**]
Amer. Irish Historical Soc. [**10240**]
Children's Friendship Proj. for Northern Ireland [**13478**]
Christian Ireland Ministries [**17930**]
Christian Ireland Ministries [**IO**]
Doors of Hope [**IO**]
Doors of Hope [**17931**]
Eire Philatelic Assn. [**22817**]
Irish Amer. Cultural Inst. [**10241**]
Irish Amer. Unity Conf. [**17932**]
Irish Amer. Unity Conf. [**IO**]
Irish Arts Center - An Claidheamh Soluis [**10243**]
Irish Natl. Caucus [**17933**]
Irish Natl. Caucus [**IO**]
Irish Northern Aid Comm. [**17934**]
Irish Special Interest Gp. of Mensa [**10244**]
Northern Ireland Human Rights Commn. [**IO**]
Proj. Children [**11717**]
Tourism Ireland [**24335**]
Ulster-Scots Soc. of Am. [**21154**]
US-Ireland Alliance [**776**]
Ireland Chamber of Commerce U.S.A. [**24286**], 556 Central Ave., New Providence, NJ 07974, (908)286-1300
Ireland Chamber of Commerce U.S.A. [**IO**], New Providence, NJ, United States
Ireland; Children's Friendship Proj. for Northern [**13478**]
Ireland China Assn. [**IO**], Dublin, Ireland
Ireland Japan Assn. [**IO**], Dublin, Ireland
Irelands Architectural Heritage Soc. [**★IO**]
IRG Ltd. [**★IO**]
IRG Ltd. [**★5564**]
IRI Res. Inst. [**4103**], PO Box 1276, 169 Greenwich Ave., Stamford, CT 06904-1276, (203)327-5985
Iridology Practitioners Assn; Intl. [**15687**]
Iridology Res. Assn; Intl. [**★15687**]

Iris Feminist Collective; Iris Films/ [**11086**]
Iris Films [**★11086**]
Iris Films/Iris Feminist Collective [**11086**], 2600 Tenth St., Ste. 413, Berkeley, CA 94710, (510)845-5414
Iris Gp. of North Am; Species [**22545**]
Iris Soc. of Am; Dwarf [**22509**]
Iris Soc; Amer. [**22495**]
Iris Soc; British [**IO**]
Iris Soc; Median [**22525**]
Iris; Soc. for Pacific Coast Native [**22543**]
Iris Soc; Reblooming [**22538**]
Iris Soc; Spuria [**22546**]
Irises; Soc. for Japanese [**22541**]
Irises; Soc. for Louisiana [**22542**]
Irises; Soc. for Siberian [**22544**]
Irish
Amer. Conf. for Irish Stud. [**10239**]
Amer. Conf. for Irish Stud. [**IO**]
Amer. Irish Historical Soc. [**10240**]
Ancient Order of Hibernians in Am. [**19152**]
Eire Philatelic Assn. [**22817**]
Emerald Soc. of the Fed. Law Enforcement Agencies [**19199**]
European Fed. of Associations and Centres of Irish Stud. [**IO**]
Incorporated Soc. of Irish/American Lawyers [**5939**]
Intl. Rebecca West Soc. [**11178**]
Irish Amer. Cultural Inst. [**10241**]
Irish Amer. Partnership [**10242**]
Irish Amer. Partnership [**IO**]
The Irish Ancestral Res. Assn. [**19069**]
Irish Arts Center - An Claidheamh Soluis [**10243**]
Irish Graduates Assn. of Singapore [**IO**]
Irish Heritage [**IO**]
Irish Inst. [**19153**]
Irish Quaternary Assn. [**IO**]
Irish Special Interest Gp. of Mensa [**10244**]
Irish Terrier Club of Am. [**22293**]
Irish Texts Soc. [**IO**]
Irish Water Spaniel Club of Am. [**22294**]
James Joyce Soc. [**9671**]
James Joyce Soc. of Southern Colorado [**9672**]
Knights of Equity [**19154**]
Royal Soc. of Antiquaries of Ireland [**IO**]
Soc. of the Friendly Sons of St. Patrick in the City of New York [**19155**]
Tourism Ireland [**24335**]
Ulster-Scots Soc. of Am. [**21154**]
US-Ireland Alliance [**776**]
Irish Aikido Fed. [**IO**], Dublin, Ireland
Irish Airmail Soc. [**IO**], Rochford, United Kingdom
Irish Amateur Rowing Union [**IO**], Dublin, Ireland
Irish Amateur Swimming Assn. [**★IO**]
Irish Amateur Weightlifting Assn. [**IO**], Dublin, Ireland
Irish Amer. Cultural Inst. [**10241**], 1 Lackawanna Pl., Morristown, NJ 07960, (973)605-1991
Irish Amer. Defense Fund - Defunct.
Irish-American Labor Coalition - Address unknown since 2003.
Irish/American Lawyers; Incorporated Soc. of [**5939**]
Irish Amer. Partnership [**10242**], 33 Broad St., Boston, MA 02109, (617)723-2707
Irish Amer. Partnership [**IO**], Boston, MA, United States
Irish Amer. Sports Found. - Address unknown since 1999.
Irish Amer. Unity Conf. [**17932**], PO Box 78, Selma, IN 47383, (800)947-4282
Irish Amer. Unity Conf. [**IO**], Washington, DC, United States
The Irish Ancestral Res. Assn. [**IO**], Auburndale, MA, United States
The Irish Ancestral Res. Assn. [**19069**], Dept. W, 2120 Commonwealth Ave., Auburndale, MA 02466
Irish Angus Cattle Soc. [**IO**], Carrick-On-Shannon, Ireland
Irish Anti-Vivisection Soc. [**IO**], Greystones, Ireland
Irish Antique Dealers Assn. [**IO**], Dublin, Ireland
Irish Arts Center - An Claidheamh Soluis [**10243**], 553 W 51st St., New York, NY 10019, (212)757-3318
Irish Assn. for Amer. Stud. [**IO**], Dublin, Ireland
Irish Assn. for Counselling and Psychotherapy [**IO**], Dun Laoghaire, Ireland

Irish Assn. of Creative Arts Therapists [**IO**], Dublin, Ireland
Irish Assn. of Dermatologists [**IO**], Dublin, Ireland
Irish Assn. for Economic Geology [**IO**], Dublin, Ireland
Irish Assn. of Investment Managers [**IO**], Dublin, Ireland
Irish Assn. for Nurses in Oncology [**IO**], Dublin, Ireland
Irish Assn. of Pastoral Care in Educ. [**IO**], Dublin, Ireland
Irish Assn. of Pension Funds [**IO**], Dublin, Ireland
Irish Assn. for Quaternery Stud. [**★IO**]
Irish Assn. of Social Workers [**IO**], Dublin, Ireland
Irish Assn. of the Sovereign Military Order of Malta [**IO**], Dublin, Ireland
Irish Assn. for Spina Bifida and Hydrocephalus [**IO**], Dublin, Ireland
Irish Assn. of Suicidology [**IO**], Castlebar, Ireland
Irish Assn. of Teachers in Special Educ. [**IO**], Dublin, Ireland
Irish Astronomical Assn. [**IO**], Antrim, Ireland
Irish Astronomical Soc. [**★IO**]
Irish Auctioneers' and Valuers' Inst. [**IO**], Dublin, Ireland
Irish Australian Chamber of Commerce [**IO**], Melbourne, Australia
Irish Bankers Fed. [**IO**], Dublin, Ireland
Irish Biblical Assn. [**IO**], Dublin, Ireland
Irish Bioenergy Assn. [**IO**], Waterford, Ireland
Irish Blacks Assn. [**4270**], 25377 Weld County Rd. 17, Johnstown, CO 80534, (970)587-2252
Irish Blue Cross [**IO**], Dublin, Ireland
Irish Book Publishers' Assn. [**IO**], Dublin, Ireland
Irish Brokers Assn. [**IO**], Dublin, Ireland
Irish Bus. and Employers' Confed. [**IO**], Dublin, Ireland
Irish Campaign for Nuclear Disarmament [**IO**], Dublin, Ireland
Irish Cancer Soc. [**IO**], Dublin, Ireland
Irish Canoe Union [**IO**], Dublin, Ireland
Irish Cardiac Soc. [**IO**], Dublin, Ireland
Irish Cattle and Sheep Farmers Assn. [**IO**], Portlaoise, Ireland
Irish Cattle Traders' and Stockowners Assn. [**★IO**]
Irish Centre for European Law [**IO**], Dublin, Ireland
Irish Chamber of Shipping [**IO**], Dublin, Ireland
Irish Christmas Tree Growers [**IO**], Dublin, Ireland
Irish Commercial Horticultural Assn. [**★IO**]
Irish Cmpt. Soc. [**IO**], Dublin, Ireland
Irish Cong. of Trade Unions [**IO**], Dublin, Ireland
Irish Copyright Licensing Agency [**IO**], Dublin, Ireland
Irish Cosmetics, Detergent and Allied Products Assn. [**IO**], Dublin, Ireland
Irish Coun. for Civil Liberties [**IO**], Dublin, Ireland
Irish Creamery Milk Suppliers' Assn. [**IO**], Limerick, Ireland
Irish Cricket Union [**IO**], Dublin, Ireland
Irish Cultural Society - Defunct.
Irish Curling Assn. [**IO**], Blessington, Ireland
Irish Dairy Bd. [**IO**], Dublin, Ireland
Irish Deaf Soc. [**IO**], Dublin, Ireland
Irish Dental Assn. [**IO**], Dublin, Ireland
Irish Diabetes Assn. [**IO**], Dublin, Ireland
Irish Dinghy Racing Assn. [**★IO**]
Irish Direct Marketing Assn. [**IO**], Dublin, Ireland
Irish Distributive and Administrative Trade Union [**★IO**]
Irish Doctors Environmental Assn. [**IO**], Dublin, Ireland
Irish Draught Horse Soc. [**IO**], Collinstown, Ireland
Irish Draught Horse Society of North America [**IO**], Pleasant Mount, PA, United States
Irish Draught Horse Soc. of North Am. [**4909**], c/o Rachel Cox, Info. Off., HC65 Box 45, Pleasant Mount, PA 18453-9605, (866)434-7621
Irish Economic Assn. [**IO**], Dublin, Ireland
Irish Economic Assn. [**IO**], Belfield, Ireland
Irish Emigrant Soc. - Defunct.
Irish Engg. Enterprises Fed. [**IO**], Dublin, Ireland
Irish Epilepsy League [**IO**], Dublin, Ireland
Irish Ergonomics Soc. [**IO**], Limerick, Ireland
Irish Exporters Assn. [**IO**], Dublin, Ireland
Irish Family History Forum [**9974**], PO Box 67, Plainview, NY 11803-0067

A star before a book entry number signifies that the name is not listed separately, but is mentioned within the entry.

Irish Family History Soc. [★21125]
Irish Family History Soc. [IO], Naas, Ireland
Irish Family Jour. [★IO]
Irish Family Jour. [★21124]
Irish Family Names Soc. - Defunct.
Irish Family Planning Assn. [IO], Dublin, Ireland
Irish Farmers' Assn. [IO], Bluebell, Ireland
Irish Fed. of Univ. Teachers [IO], Dublin, Ireland
Irish Fed. of Univ. Women [IO], Newtownabbey,
   United Kingdom
Irish Feis Inst. [★19153]
Irish Fish Producers Org. [IO], Dublin, Ireland
Irish Flying Disc Assn. [IO], Clonskea, Ireland
Irish Foster Care Assn. [IO], Dublin, Ireland
Irish Fragile X Soc. [IO], Dublin, Ireland
Irish Franchise Assn. [IO], Dublin, Ireland
Irish Funds Indus. Assn. [IO], Dublin, Ireland
Irish Genealogical Found. [IO], Kansas City, MO,
   United States
Irish Genealogical Found. [21124], PO Box 7575,
   Kansas City, MO 64116
Irish Genealogical Res. Soc. [IO], Rainham, United
   Kingdom
Irish Genealogical Soc. Intl. [21125], 5768 Olson
   Memorial Hwy., Golden Valley, MN 55422
Irish Georgian Soc. [IO], Dublin, Ireland
Irish Gerontological Soc. [IO], Dublin, Ireland
Irish Girl Guides [IO], Dublin, Ireland
Irish Graduates Assn. of Singapore [IO], Singapore,
   Singapore
Irish Grain and Feed Assn. [IO], Portlaoise, Ireland
Irish Grassland Assn. [IO], Borris-in-Ossory, Ireland
Irish Greyhound Bd. [IO], Limerick, Ireland
Irish Guide Dogs for the Blind [IO], Cork, Ireland
Irish Haemophilia Soc. [IO], Dublin, Ireland
Irish Handball Coun. [IO], Dublin, Ireland
Irish Hard of Hearing Assn. [IO], Dublin, Ireland
Irish Hardware and Building Materials Assn. [IO],
   Dublin, Ireland
Irish Heritage [IO], London, United Kingdom
Irish Heritage Found. - Address unknown since
   2006.
Irish Holstein Friesian Assn. [IO], Clonakilty, Ireland
Irish Home Builders Assn. [IO], Dublin, Ireland
Irish Hosp. Consultants Assn. [IO], Dublin, Ireland
Irish Hospitality Inst. [IO], Dublin, Ireland
Irish Hotel and Catering Inst. [★IO]
Irish Hotels Fed. [IO], Dublin, Ireland
Irish Immigration Reform Movement [★IO]
Irish Immigration Reform Movement [★17804]
Irish Inst. [19153]
Irish Inst. of Credit Mgt. [IO], Dublin, Ireland
Irish Inst. of Purchasing and Materials Mgt. [IO],
   Dublin, Ireland
Irish Inst. of Training and Development [IO], Naas,
   Ireland
Irish Insurance Fed. [IO], Dublin, Ireland
Irish Intl. Freight Assn. [IO], Dublin, Ireland
Irish Internet Assn. [IO], Dublin, Ireland
Irish Jet Sport Assn. [IO], Newtownards, United
   Kingdom
Irish Kidney Assn. [IO], Dublin, Ireland
Irish Ladies Golf Union [IO], Dublin, Ireland
Irish Landscape Inst. [IO], Dublin, Ireland
Irish Linen Guild [IO], Hillsborough, United Kingdom
Irish Linen Guild - Defunct.
Irish LP Gas Assn. [IO], Drogheda, Ireland
Irish Mgt. Inst. Intl. [IO], Dublin, Ireland
Irish Marine Fed. [IO], Dublin, Ireland
Irish Mathematical Soc. [IO], Maynooth, Ireland
Irish Medical Devices Assn. [IO], Dublin, Ireland
Irish Medical Org. [IO], Dublin, Ireland
Irish Meteorological Soc. [IO], Dublin, Ireland
Irish Mining and Quarrying Soc. [IO], Dublin, Ireland
Irish Missionary Union [IO], Dublin, Ireland
Irish Moiled Cattle Soc. [IO], Claverdon, United
   Kingdom
Irish Motor Neurone Disease Assn. [IO], Dublin,
   Ireland
Irish Music Rights Org. [IO], Dublin, Ireland
Irish Natl. Assn. of Tenants [IO], Dublin, Ireland
Irish Natl. Caucus [IO], Washington, DC, United
   States
Irish Natl. Caucus [17933], PO Box 15128,
   Washington, DC 20003-0849, (202)544-0568

Irish Natl. Teachers' Org. [IO], Dublin, Ireland
Irish Northern Aid Comm. [17934], 252 W 38th St.,
   Ste. 1404, New York, NY 10018, (212)736-1916
Irish Nutrition and Dietetic Inst. [IO], Dun Laoghaire,
   Ireland
Irish Offshore Operators' Assn. [IO], Dublin, Ireland
Irish Organic Farmers and Growers Assn. [IO], New-
   townforbes, Ireland
Irish Org. for Geographic Info. [IO], Naas, Ireland
Irish Orienteering Assn. [IO], Dublin, Ireland
Irish Pain Soc. [IO], Dublin, Ireland
Irish Pattern Recognition and Classification Soc.
   [IO], Belfast, United Kingdom
Irish Payment Services Org. [IO], Dun Laoghaire,
   Ireland
Irish Peatland Conservation Coun. [IO], Rathangan,
   Ireland
Irish Pharmaceutical and Chem. Manufacturers' Fed.
   [★IO]
Irish Pharmaceutical Healthcare Assn. [IO], Dublin,
   Ireland
Irish Playwrights and Screenwriters Guild [IO], Dub-
   lin, Ireland
Irish Productivity Centre [IO], Dublin, Ireland
Irish Quaternary Assn. [IO], Blessington, Ireland
Irish Radio Transmitters Soc. [IO], Dublin, Ireland
Irish Railway Record Soc. [IO], Dublin, Ireland
Irish Raynaud's and Scleroderma Soc. [IO], Dublin,
   Ireland
Irish Recorded Music Assn. [IO], Dun Laoghaire,
   Ireland
Irish Refugee Coun. [IO], Dublin, Ireland
Irish Res. Scientists' Assn. [IO], Sandyford, Ireland
Irish Road Haulage Assn. [IO], Dublin, Ireland
Irish Rounders Coun. [★IO]
Irish Rugby Football Union [IO], Dublin, Ireland
Irish Rugby Union Players Assn. [IO], Dublin, Ireland
Irish Sailing Assn. [IO], Dun Laoghaire, Ireland
Irish Salmon Growers' Assn. [IO], Dublin, Ireland
Irish Schoolsport Fed. [IO], Dublin, Ireland
Irish Security Indus. Assn. [IO], Dublin, Ireland
Irish Setter Club of Am. [22292], c/o Mr. Robert A.
   Robinson, Pres., 1826 Palmcroft Way NE,
   Phoenix, AZ 85007-1740, (602)253-6260
Irish Small and Medium Enterprises Assn. [IO], Dub-
   lin, Ireland
Irish Soc. for Archives [IO], Dublin, Ireland
Irish Soc. for Autism [IO], Dublin, Ireland
Irish Soc. of Chartered Physiotherapists [IO], Dublin,
   Ireland
Irish Soc. of Homeopaths [IO], Galway, Ireland
Irish Soc. of Human Genetics [IO], Dublin, Ireland
Irish Soc. of Occupational Medicine [IO], Dublin,
   Ireland
Irish Soc; Pennsylvania Scotch- [★21151]
Irish Soc. of Periodontology [IO], Dublin, Ireland
Irish Soc. for the Prevention of Cruelty to Animals
   [IO], Longford, Ireland
Irish Soc. for Quality and Safety in Healthcare [IO],
   Dublin, Ireland
Irish Soc. for Rheumatology [IO], Dublin, Ireland
Irish Soc. of Surveying, Photogrammetry and
   Remote Sensing [IO], Dublin, Ireland
Irish Soc. of the U.S.A; Scotch- [21151]
Irish South and West Fish Producers Org. [IO],
   Castletownbere, Ireland
Irish Special Interest Gp. of Mensa [10244], c/o Shir-
   ley Starke, Coor., Box 230, Rte. 2, Valley City, ND
   58072, (701)845-2382
Irish Sports Coun. [IO], Dublin, Ireland
Irish Squash [IO], Dublin, Ireland
Irish Squash Assn. [★IO]
Irish Squash Rackets Assn. [★IO]
Irish Stammering Assn. [IO], Dublin, Ireland
Irish Stud; Amer. Comm. for [★10239]
Irish Sudden Infant Death Assn. [IO], Dublin, Ireland
Irish Taekwondo Union [IO], Dublin, Ireland
Irish Taxation Inst. [IO], Dublin, Ireland
Irish Terrier Club of Am. [22293], c/o Gale Cum-
   mings, Corresponding Sec., 37 Clapp St., Norton,
   MA 02766-2709, (508)285-9655
Irish Texts Soc. [IO], London, United Kingdom
Irish Timber Growers' Assn. [IO], Dublin, Ireland
Irish Tour Operators Assn. [IO], Bray, Ireland
Irish Tourist Bd. [★24335]

Irish Tourist Indus. Confed. [IO], Monkstown, Ireland
Irish Transport and Gen. Workers Union [★IO]
Irish Travel Agents Assn. [IO], Dublin, Ireland
Irish United Nations Veterans Assn. [IO], Dublin,
   Ireland
Irish Visual Artists' Rights Org. [IO], Dublin, Ireland
Irish Vocational Educ. Assn. [IO], Dublin, Ireland
Irish Water Spaniel Club of Am. [22294], c/o Kim
   Kezer, 86 High St., Amesbury, MA 01913
Irish Waterski Fed. [IO], Cork, Ireland
Irish Wheelchair Assn. [IO], Dublin, Ireland
Irish Wind Energy Assn. [IO], Carrick-On-Shannon,
   Ireland
Irish Wolfhound
   Irish Wolfhound Club of Am. [22295]
Irish Wolfhound Club of Am. [22295], c/o Judy Si-
   mon, Sec., 7155 Co. Rd. 26, Maple Plain, MN
   55359, (763)479-1638
Irish Women's Squash Rackets Assn. [★IO]
Irish Woodturners' Guild [IO], Dublin, Ireland
Irish Youth Found. [IO], Dublin, Ireland
Irish Youth Hostel Assn. [IO], Dublin, Ireland
IRM Services - Defunct.
Iron Architecture; Friends of Cast [10025]
Iron Butterfly Information Network - Address
   unknown since 1999.
Iron Casting Res. Inst. [2033], 2802 Fisher Rd.,
   Columbus, OH 43204, (614)275-4201
Iron Cookware Assn; Griswold and Cast [22588]
Iron Curtain; Jesus to the [★20410]
Iron Maiden Fan Club [IO], Sudbury, United
   Kingdom
Iron Mfrs. Assn; Natl. Ornamental [★2722]
Iron Ore Assn; Lake Superior [★2696]
Iron Ore Assn; Western [★2696]
Iron Overload Diseases Assn. [15249], PO Box
   15857, West Palm Beach, FL 33416-5857,
   (561)586-8246
Iron Overload Diseases Association [IO], West Palm
   Beach, FL, United States
Iron Pipe Inst; Cast [★3029]
Iron Pipe Publicity Bur; Cast [★3029]
Iron Pipe Res. Assn; Cast [★3029]
Iron Pipe Res. Assn; Ductile [3029]
Iron Res. Inst; Gray [★2033]
Iron Seat Collectors Assn; Cast [22607]
Iron Ship Builders, Blacksmiths, Forgers and Help-
   ers; Intl. Brotherhood of Boilermakers, [24021]
Iron Soc; Ductile [7313]
Iron Soil Pipe Inst; Cast [3027]
Iron and Steel Assn; Amer. [★2697]
Iron and Steel Division of the Metallurgical Soc. of
   AIME [★7312]
Iron and Steel Engineers; Assn. of [★7312]
Iron and Steel Inst; Amer. [2697]
Iron and Steel; Inst. of Scrap [★3995]
Iron and Steel Institution of Japan [IO], Tokyo, Japan
Iron and Steel Soc. [★7312]
Iron and Steel Trades Confed. and Natl. Union of
   Knitwear, Footwear and Apparel Trades [★IO]
Iron and Steel Trades Confed. and Natl. Union of
   Knitwear, Footwear and Apparel Trades [★IO]
Iron Workers; Intl. Assn. of Bridge, Structural,
   Ornamental and Reinforcing [24134]
Ironmongers' Company [IO], London, United
   Kingdom
Ironstone China Assn; White [21940]
Ironworking Indus; Inst. of the [24133]
Iroquois Stud. Assn. [10748], 28 Zevan Rd.,
   Johnson City, NY 13790, (607)729-0016
Irregular Route; Common Carrier Conf. - [★3899]
Irrigation
   Amer. Soc. of Irrigation Consultants [7826]
   Intl. Network on Participatory Irrigation Mgt.
      [7233]
   Intl. Network on Participatory Irrigation Mgt. [IO]
   Irrigation Assn. [182]
   U.S. Comm. on Irrigation and Drainage [7842]
   Western Snow Conf. [7845]
Irrigation Assn. [182], 6540 Arlington Blvd., Falls
   Church, VA 22042-6638, (703)536-7080
Irrigation Assn. [IO], Falls Church, VA, United States
Irrigation Assn. of Australia [IO], Sydney, Australia
Irrigation Assn; Intl. Drip [★182]
Irrigation Assn; U.K. [IO]

Reference to "IO" in place of a book number signifies that the association may be found in the 45th edition of International Organizations.

Irrigation Consultants; Amer. Soc. of [7826]
Irrigation, Drainage and Flood Control; U.S. Comm. on [★7842]
Irrigation and Drainage - India; Intl. Commn. on [IO]
Irrigation and Drainage; U.S. Comm. on [7842]
Irrigation and Drainage; U.S. Natl. Comm., Intl. Commn. on [★7842]
Irritable Bowel Info. and Support Assn. [IO], Sippy Downs, Australia
IRSA, The Assn. of Quality Clubs [★IO]
IRSA, The Assn. of Quality Clubs [★3021]
Irvine Group - Address unknown since 2003.
Irving; Amer. Friends of Henry [24727]
Irwin Allen Fan Club - Defunct.
Irwin Assn; Clan [20833]
I.S. Financial Mgt. Assn. [★1430]
ISA - Instrumentation, Systems, and Automation Soc. [7220], c/o Mr. Pat Gouhin, Exec. Dir., 67 Alexander Dr., PO Box 12277, Research Triangle Park, NC 27709, (919)549-8411
ISA - Instrumentation, Systems, and Automation Society [IO], Research Triangle Park, NC, United States
Isaac Garrison Family Assn. [20954], 5567 Ecton Rd., Winchester, KY 40391, (859)842-3028
Isabel Hampton Robb Memorial Fund [★15516]
Isabel; Portuguese Soc. Queen St. [19322]
ISAR: CH on Grassroots in Eurasia [★17899]
ISAR: CH on Grassroots in Eurasia [★IO]
ISAR: Initiative for Social Action and Renewal in Eurasia [★IO]
ISAR: Initiative for Social Action and Renewal in Eurasia [★17899]
ISAR: Resources for Environmental Activists [17899], PO Box 70029, Washington, DC 20024-0029, (202)966-0880
ISAR: Resources for Environmental Activists [IO], Washington, DC, United States
ISBE Employers of Am. [★3608]
ISCO Careerscope [IO], Camberley, United Kingdom
ISDA - Assn. of Storage and Retrieval Professionals [2847], 4060 Pike Ln., Concord, CA 94520, (925)687-3100
ISDA - The Off. Systems Cooperative [★2847]
Isis Internacional [IO], Santiago, Chile
Isis International-Manila [IO], Quezon City, Philippines
ISIS - Women's Intl. Cross-Cultural Exchange [IO], Kampala, Uganda
Islam
  Amer. Soc. for Muslim Advancement [10245]
  Arab World and Islamic Resources and School Services [9393]
  Assn. of Islamic Charitable Projects [20096]
  Comm. for Crescent Observation Intl. [10246]
  Coun. on American-Islamic Relations [19156]
  Coun. on Islamic Educ. [8669]
  Coun. of Masajid of U.S. [20097]
  Fed. of Islamic Associations in the U.S. and Canada [20098]
  Fiqh Coun. of North America [20099]
  Free Muslims Coalition [18084]
  Gamma Gamma Chi Sorority [24711]
  Intl. Inst. of Islamic Thought [10247]
  Iranian Muslim Assn. of North Am. [20438]
  Islamic Amer. Relief Agency [12864]
  Islamic Center of New York [20104]
  Islamic Correctional Reunion Assn. [20105]
  Islamic Food and Nutrition Coun. of Am. [2353]
  Islamic Info. Center of Am. [20106]
  Islamic Medical Assn. of North Am. [16003]
  Islamic Relief USA [12865]
  Islamic Soc. of North Am. [10249]
  Life for Relief and Development [12867]
  Middle East Inst. [18062]
  Muslim Amer. Soc. [20440]
  Muslim Public Affairs Coun. [18085]
  Natl. Assn. of Muslim Lawyers [5511]
  Natl. Young Adult Assn. [13504]
  North Amer. Islamic Trust [10250]
  Thought and Educ. Club [7957]
  Universal Muslim Assn. of Am. [20442]
Islam and Christian/Muslim Relations; Duncan Black Macdonald Center for the Stud. of [★20100]
Islamic
  Ahl-ul-Bait World Assembly [IO]

Ahmadiyya Muslim Community [IO]
Al-Rashid Islamic Inst. [IO]
Amer. Druze Soc. [20095]
Amer. Soc. for Muslim Advancement [10245]
Arab World and Islamic Resources and School Services [9393]
Assn. of Indian Muslims of Am. [19109]
Assn. of Islamic Charitable Projects [20096]
Canadian Coun. of Muslim Women [IO]
Comm. for Crescent Observation Intl. [IO]
Comm. for Crescent Observation Intl. [10246]
Coun. on American-Islamic Relations [19156]
Coun. on Islamic Educ. [8669]
Coun. of Masajid of U.S. [20097]
Egyptian Student Assn. in North Am. [9179]
Fed. of Islamic Associations in the U.S. and Canada [20098]
Fed. of Islamic Associations in the U.S. and Canada [IO]
Fiqh Coun. of North America [20099]
Free Muslims Coalition [18084]
Gamma Gamma Chi Sorority [24711]
Hartford Seminary [20100]
Hartford Seminary [IO]
Human Assistance and Development Intl. [20437]
Inst. of Islamic and Arabic Sciences in Am. [8670]
Intl. Assn. of Sufism [20101]
Intl. Inst. of Islamic Thought [10247]
Intl. Inst. of Islamic Thought [IO]
Intl. Inst. of Islamic Thought and Civilization [IO]
Intl. Islamic Fed. of Student Orgs. [10248]
Iranian Muslim Assn. of North Am. [20438]
Islamic Amer. Relief Agency [12864]
Islamic Assembly of North Am. [20102]
Islamic Assembly of North Am. [IO]
Islamic Center of Am. [20103]
Islamic Center of New York [20104]
Islamic Circle of North Am. [20439]
Islamic Correctional Reunion Assn. [20105]
Islamic Food and Nutrition Coun. of Am. [2353]
Islamic Food and Nutrition Coun. of Am. [IO]
Islamic Info. Center of Am. [20106]
Islamic Medical Assn. of North Am. [16003]
Islamic Mission of America [20107]
Islamic Relief USA [12865]
Islamic Res. Found. Intl. [8671]
Islamic Res. Found. Intl. [IO]
Islamic Soc. of North Am. [10249]
Islamic States Broadcasting Org. [IO]
Islamic Text Soc. [IO]
Lahore Ahmadiyya Movement for the Propagation of Islam, Canada [IO]
Lahore Ahmadiyya Movement for the Propagation of Islam - Pakistan [IO]
Muslim Amer. Soc. [20440]
Muslim Women's Natl. Network of Australia [IO]
Muslim World League [IO]
Muslim Youth Movement of South Africa [IO]
Natl. Assn. of Muslim Lawyers [5511]
Natl. Young Adult Assn. [13504]
North Amer. Islamic Trust [10250]
Res. Centre for Islamic History, Art and Culture [IO]
Stud. of Islam Sect. [20108]
Universal Muslim Assn. of Am. [20442]
World Fed. of Islamic Missions [IO]
Islamic Acad. of Sciences [IO], Amman, Jordan
Islamic Affairs; Amer. Inst. for [★18062]
Islamic Amer. Relief Agency [12864]
Islamic Amer. Relief Agency [IO], Columbia, MO, United States
Islamic and Arabic Sciences in Am; Inst. of [8670]
Islamic Assembly of North Am. [20102], 3588 Plymouth Rd., PMB 270, Ann Arbor, MI 48105, (734)528-0006
Islamic Assembly of North Am. [IO], Ann Arbor, MI, United States
Islamic Center of Am. [20103], 19500 Ford Rd., Dearborn, MI 48128, (313)593-0000
Islamic Center of New York [20104]
Islamic Centre for Development of Trade [IO], Casablanca, Morocco
Islamic Chamber of Commerce and Indus. [IO], Karachi, Pakistan
Islamic Chamber of Commerce, Indus. and Commodity Exchange [★IO]

Islamic Circle of North Am. [20439], 166-26 89th Ave., Jamaica, NY 11432, (718)658-1199
Islamic Correctional Reunion Assn. [20105], PO Box 774, Tinley Park, IL 60477, (708)429-0093
Islamic Development Bank [IO], Jeddah, Saudi Arabia
Islamic Educational, Sci., and Cultural Org. [IO], Rabat, Morocco
Islamic Food and Nutrition Coun. of Am. [IO], Chicago, IL, United States
Islamic Food and Nutrition Coun. of Am. [2353], 5901 N Cicero Ave., Ste. 309, Chicago, IL 60646, (773)283-3708
Islamic Info. Center of Am. [20106], PO Box 4052, Des Plaines, IL 60016, (847)541-8141
Islamic Law
  Islamic Food and Nutrition Coun. of Am. [2353]
  Thought and Educ. Club [7957]
Islamic Medical Assn. [★16003]
Islamic Medical Assn. of North Am. [16003], 101 W 22nd St., Ste. 106, Lombard, IL 60148, (630)932-0000
Islamic Mission of America [20107]
Islamic Org. for Medical Sciences [IO], Sulaibekhat, Kuwait
Islamic Party of Malaysia [IO], Selangor, Malaysia
Islamic Relief USA [IO], Buena Park, CA, United States
Islamic Relief USA [12865], PO Box 5640, Buena Park, CA 90622, (714)676-1300
Islamic Res. Found. for Advancement of Knowledge [★8671]
Islamic Res. Found. for Advancement of Knowledge [★IO]
Islamic Res. Found. Intl. [IO], Louisville, KY, United States
Islamic Res. Found. Intl. [8671], 7102 W Shefford Ln., Louisville, KY 40242-6462, (502)287-6262
Islamic Resources and School Services; Arab World and [9393]
Islamic Soc. of North Am. [10249], PO Box 38, Plainfield, IN 46168, (317)839-8157
Islamic Soc. of North America Fiqh Comm. [★20099]
Islamic States Broadcasting Org. [IO], Jeddah, Saudi Arabia
Islamic Sufism; School of [★20576]
Islamic Text Soc. [IO], Cambridge, United Kingdom
Islamic Univ. of Tech. [IO], Gazipur, Bangladesh
Island Missionary Soc. - Address unknown since 1995.
Island Proj; Sister [11788]
Island Resources Found. [10236], 1718 P St. NW, Ste. T-4, Washington, DC 20036, (202)265-9712
Islander Mental Hea. Assn; Natl. Asian Amer. Pacific [15215]
Islanders Booster Club; New York [25009]
Islanders' Cultural Assn; Pacific [10767]
Islands Res. Found. - Defunct.
Islandsdeild Amnesty Intl. [★IO]
Isle of Man Chamber of Commerce [IO], Douglas, United Kingdom
Isle of Wight Chamber of Commerce [IO], Newport, United Kingdom
Islensk Tonverkamistod [★IO]
Islenskir Radioamatorar [★IO]
ISNA [★IO]
ISNA [★13093]
Iso and Bizzarrini Owners Club [21672], 2025 Drake Dr., Oakland, CA 94611
Iso and Bizzarrini Owners Club [IO], Oakland, CA, United States
Isotta Fraschini Owner's Assn. - Defunct.
Israel
  Agudath Israel of Am. [20110]
  All4Israel [IO]
  All4Israel [12454]
  America-Israel Chamber of Commerce and Indus. [24336]
  America-Israel Cultural Found. [10251]
  America-Israel Friendship League [10252]
  Amer. Bd. of Rabbis - Vaad Harabonim of Am. [20111]
  American Committee for Shaare Zedek Hospital in Jerusalem [IO]

A star before a book entry number signifies that the name is not listed separately, but is mentioned within the entry.

Amer. Comm. for Shaare Zedek Hosp. in Jerusalem [12455]
Amer. Comm. for Shenkar Coll. [8674]
Amer. Comm. for the Weizmann Inst. of Sci. [7597]
Amer. Friends of Beth Hatefutsoth [10253]
Amer. Friends of the Israel Museum [10491]
American-Israel Environmental Coun. [10254]
American-Israel Numismatic Assn. [22723]
Amer. Israeli Lighthouse [16827]
Amer. Jewish League for Israel [20116]
Amer. Physicians Fellowship for Medicine in Israel [IO]
Amer. Physicians Fellowship for Medicine in Israel [12456]
Amer. Red Magen David for Israel - Amer. Friends of Magen David Adom [12832]
Amer. Soc. for the Protection of Nature in Israel [4353]
Amer. Soc. for Technion-Israel Inst. of Tech. [8677]
Amer. Veterans of Israel [21165]
Americans for Peace Now [17935]
Americans for Peace Now [IO]
Americans United for Israel [19157]
Anti-Defamation League [17091]
Artists for Israel Intl. [9428]
Associates for Biblical Res. [19507]
Assn. of Israel's Decorative Arts [9556]
Bnos Agudath Israel [20127]
Boys Town Jerusalem Found. of Am. [13473]
Canada-Israel Comm. [IO]
Canadian Zionist Fed. [IO]
Central Rabbinical Cong. of the U.S.A. and Canada [20130]
Christ for the Nations [20314]
Christian Friends of Israel - USA [19777]
Christians' Israel Public Action Campaign [IO]
Christians' Israel Public Action Campaign [17936]
Comm. for the Economic Growth of Israel [24337]
Concern for Helping Animals in Israel [11383]
Emunah of Am. [12457]
Emunah Women of Am. [20136]
Friends of Israel Disabled Veterans [21166]
Friends of Sabeel - North Am. [18205]
Hashomer Hatzair Zionist Youth Movement [20140]
Hebrew Christian Fellowship [20012]
Inst. for Palestine Stud. [9397]
Israel Aliyah Center [20146]
Israel Humanitarian Foundation [IO]
Israel Humanitarian Found. [12458]
Jewish Coun. for Public Affairs [12474]
Jewish Inst. for Natl. Security Affairs [17380]
Jewish Natl. Fund [20150]
Jewish Peace Lobby [17614]
A Jewish Voice for Peace [19184]
Jewish War Veterans of the U.S.A. - Natl. Ladies Auxiliary [21196]
Jews Against the Occupation [17952]
Kibbutz Prog. Center [17937]
Kolel Chibas Jerusalem [20156]
Kolel Shomre Hachomos/Reb Meir Baal Haness [17938]
LATET - Israeli Humanitarian Aid Org. [IO]
Maccabi USA/Sports for Israel [23828]
Meals4Israel [IO]
Meals4Israel [12459]
Natl. Christian Leadership Conf. for Israel [IO]
Natl. Christian Leadership Conf. for Israel [17939]
Natl. Comm. for Labor Israel [12460]
National Committee for Labor Israel [IO]
Natl. Museum of Amer. Jewish Military History [21312]
New Israel Fund [17940]
PEF Israel Endowment Funds [12461]
PEF Israel Endowment Funds [IO]
Pups for Peace [12700]
Rebuilding Alliance [12336]
Religious Zionist Youth Movement - Bnei Akiva of the U.S. and Canada [20178]
Sabra Automobile Connection [21779]
Scholars for Peace in the Middle East [18070]
Soc. of Israel Philatelists [22874]
StandWithUs [17941]

United Charity Institutions of Jerusalem [12462]
United Charity Institutions of Jerusalem [IO]
United Synagogue of Conservative Judaism [20188]
United Tiberias Institutions Relief Soc. [12463]
Unity Coalition for Israel [8672]
USS Liberty Veterans Assn. [21227]
Volunteers for Israel [17942]
Volunteers for Israel [IO]
World Confed. of United Zionists [20195]
World Coun. of Conservative/Masorti Synagogues [20196]
Zionist Org. of Am. [20201]
Israel Acad. of Sciences and Humanities [IO], Jerusalem, Israel
Israel Aliyah Center [20146], 633 3rd Ave., 21st Fl., New York, NY 10017-6706, (212)339-6063
Israel or Am; Agudath [20110]
Israel-American Chamber of Commerce and Indus. [IO], Tel Aviv, Israel
Israel; Amer. Jewish League for [20116]
Israel; Americans for a Safe [18052]
Israel Antiquities Authority [IO], Jerusalem, Israel
Israel Assn. of Baseball [IO], Tel Aviv, Israel
Israel Assn. for Computational Methods in Mechanics [IO], Haifa, Israel
Israel Assn. for Cmpt. Vision and Pattern Recognition [IO], Haifa, Israel
Israel Assn. of Electronics Indus. [★IO]
Israel Assn. of Electronics and Info. Indus. [IO], Tel Aviv, Israel
Israel Assn. for Ethiopian Jews [IO], Jerusalem, Israel
Israel Assn. for the Habilitation of the Mentally Handicapped [★IO]
Israel Assn. of Illustrators [IO], Tel Aviv, Israel
Israel Assn. for Info. Systems [IO], Raanana, Israel
Israel Assn. of Univ. Women [IO], Jerusalem, Israel
Israel Badminton Assn. [IO], Tel Aviv, Israel
Israel Barlow Family Assn. - Address unknown since 2006.
Israel Biochemical Soc. [★IO]
Israel; Bnos Agudath [20127]
Israel Cancer Assn. [IO], Givatayim, Israel
Israel Chamber of Commerce and Indus; American- [★24336]
Israel Chap. of the ILAE [IO], Tel Aviv, Israel
Israel Chem. Soc. [IO], Ramat Gan, Israel
Israel; Christians Concerned for [★17939]
Israel; Coun. for a Beautiful [★10254]
Israel Coun. for Israeli-Palestinian Peace; America- [18047]
Israel Coun. of Rabbis; Young [20197]
Israel Cricket Assn. [IO], Tel Aviv, Israel
Israel Dance Sport Assn. [IO], Ashdod, Israel
Israel Democracy Institute [IO], Jerusalem, Israel
Israel Disabled War Veterans (Beit Halochem); Friends of [★21166]
Israel Emergency Alliance [★17941]
Israel Export and Intl. Cooperation Inst. [IO], Tel Aviv, Israel
Israel Family Planning Assn. [IO], Tel Aviv, Israel
Israel Flying Disc Assn. [IO], Hertzelia, Israel
Israel; Free Sons of [19182]
Israel Genealogical Soc. [IO], Jerusalem, Israel
Israel Geological Soc. [IO], Jerusalem, Israel
Israel Gospel Ministry; Friends of [20010]
Israel Heart Soc. [IO], Ramat Gan, Israel
Israel Histadrut Campaign [★IO]
Israel Histadrut Campaign [★12460]
Israel Histadrut Found. [★12458]
Israel Histadrut Found. [★IO]
Israel Hotel Assn. [IO], Tel Aviv, Israel
Israel Hotel Managers Assn. [IO], Tel Aviv, Israel
Israel Humanitarian Foundation [IO], New York, NY, United States
Israel Humanitarian Found. [12458], 276 5th Ave., Ste. 404, New York, NY 10001, (212)683-5676
Israel Hypertension Soc. [IO], Tel Aviv, Israel
Israel Ice Skating Fed. [IO], Metula, Israel
Israel; Independent Order Free Sons of [★19182]
Israel Institutions; Amer. Fund for [★10251]
Israel Internet Assn. [IO], Ramat Gan, Israel
Israel Jewelry Mfrs. Assn. [IO], Kfar-Saba, Israel
Israel; Maccabi USA/Sports for [23828]

Israel; Machne [12476]
Israel Mathematical Union [IO], Beersheba, Israel
Israel Medical Assn; Amer. Physicians Fellowship for the [★12456]
Israel Medical Org. [IO], Ramat Gan, Israel
Israel Missionary and Relief SOC; Friends of [★20010]
Israel Mobile Assn. [IO], Tel Aviv, Israel
Israel Museum; Amer. Friends of the [10491]
Israel Music Found. - Address unknown since 1995.
Israel Music Inst. [IO], Tel Aviv, Israel
Israel Musicological Soc. [IO], Jerusalem, Israel
Israel Natl. Commn. for UNESCO [IO], Jerusalem, Israel
Israel; Natl. Coun. of Young [20167]
Israel Numismatic Assn; American- [22723]
Israel Oriental Soc. [IO], Jerusalem, Israel
Israel Orienteering Assn. [★IO]
Israel Pain Assn. [IO], Haifa, Israel
Israel/Palestine Center for Res. and Info. [IO], Jerusalem, Israel
Israel-Palestine Philatelic Soc. of Am. [★22874]
Israel Philatelists; Soc. of [22874]
Israel Physical Soc. [IO], Haifa, Israel
Israel; Pirchei Agudath [8699]
Israel Plate Block Soc. [22833]
Israel Psoriasis Assn. [IO], Holon, Israel
Israel Public Affairs Comm; Amer. [18050]
Israel; Remnant Of [20030]
Israel; Search for Justice and Equality in Palestine/ [18071]
Israel Shippers' Coun. [IO], Haifa, Israel
Israel Soc; America- [★10251]
Israel Soc. of Anesthesiologists [IO], Tel Hashomer, Israel
Israel Soc. for Biochemistry and Molecular Biology [IO], Ramat Efal, Israel
Israel Soc. of Dermatology and Venereology [IO], Tel Aviv, Israel
The Israel Soc. for Developmental Biology [IO], Rehovot, Israel
Israel Soc. for Microbiology [IO], Tel Aviv, Israel
Israel Soc. for Microscopy [IO], Haifa, Israel
Israel Soc. for Neuroscience [IO], Rishon LeZion, Israel
Israel Soc. for Physiology and Pharmacology [IO], Ramat Gan, Israel
Israel Soc. for Quality [IO], Azor, Israel
Israel Soc. of Sports Medicine [IO], Jerusalem, Israel
Israel Sport Orienteering Assn. [IO], Hod Hasharon, Israel
Israel Sports Assn. for the Disabled [IO], Caesarea, Israel
Israel Squash Rackets Assn. [IO], Raanana, Israel
Israel Taekwondo Fed. [IO], Jerusalem, Israel
Israel Tennis Assn. [IO], Tel Aviv, Israel
Israel Tourist and Travel Agents' Assn. [IO], Tel Aviv, Israel
Israel Translators Assn. [IO], Tel Aviv, Israel
Israel; United Sons of [20187]
Israel; U.S. Comm. Sports for [★23828]
Israel; U.S. Comm. for Sports in [★23828]
Israel Vacuum Soc. [IO], Haifa, Israel
Israel Venture Assn. [IO], Savyon, Israel
Israel Veterinary Medical Assn. [IO], Raanana, Israel
Israel; Wingate Inst. for Physical Educ. in [★23828]
Israel; Women's League for [20194]
Israel Women's Network [IO], Ramat Gan, Israel
Israel Yachting Assn. [IO], Tel Aviv, Israel
Israel; Young Men's Division-Zeirei Agudath [20199]
Israel Youth Hostels Assn. [IO], Jerusalem, Israel
Israel; Zeirei Agudath [20200]
Israeli
Agudath Israel of Am. [20110]
All4Israel [12454]
America-Israel Cultural Found. [10251]
America-Israel Cultural Found. [IO]
America-Israel Friendship League [10252]
Amer. Associates, Ben-Gurion Univ. of the Negev [8673]
Amer. Comm. for Shaare Zedek Hosp. in Jerusalem [12455]
Amer. Comm. for Shenkar Coll. [8674]
Amer. Friends of the Alliance Israelite Universelle [8675]

Reference to "IO" in place of a book number signifies that the association may be found in the 45th edition of International Organizations.

Amer. Friends of Beth Hatefutsoth [10253]
Amer. Friends of the Israel Museum [10491]
Amer. Friends of The Hebrew Univ. [8676]
American-Israel Environmental Coun. [10254]
American-Israel Environmental Coun. [IO]
American-Israel Numismatic Assn. [22723]
Amer. Israeli Lighthouse [16827]
Amer. Jewish League for Israel [20116]
Amer. Physicians Fellowship for Medicine in Israel [12456]
Amer. Red Magen David for Israel - Amer. Friends of Magen David Adom [12832]
Amer. Soc. for Technion-Israel Inst. of Tech. [8677]
Amer. Soc. for Technion-Israel Inst. of Tech. [IO]
Artists for Israel Intl. [9428]
Associates for Biblical Res. [19507]
Assn. of Israel's Decorative Arts [9556]
Boys Town Jerusalem Found. of Am. [13473]
Christian Friends of Israel - USA [19777]
Comm. for the Economic Growth of Israel [24337]
Concern for Helping Animals in Israel [11383]
Friends of Bezalel Acad. of Arts [10255]
Friends of Sabeel - North Am. [18205]
Inst. for Palestine Stud. [9397]
Israeli Students' Org. in the U.S.A. and Canada [19158]
Jewish War Veterans of the U.S.A. - Natl. Ladies Auxiliary [21196]
Maccabi USA/Sports for Israel [23828]
Meals4Israel [12459]
Natl. Comm. for Labor Israel [12460]
Natl. Museum of Amer. Jewish Military History [21312]
Ohr Torah Institutions of Israel [8678]
Partners for Peace [18230]
PEF Israel Endowment Funds [12461]
Pups for Peace [12700]
Rebuilding Alliance [12336]
Russian Amer. Jews for Israel [18576]
Sabra Automobile Connection [21779]
Scholars for Peace in the Middle East [18070]
Soc. of Israel Philatelists [22874]
StandWithUs [17941]
Tel Aviv Univ.: Amer. Coun. [8679]
Unity Coalition for Israel [8672]
Unity Coalition for Israel [IO]
Israeli Assn. for Aerosol Res. [IO], Jerusalem, Israel
Israeli Assn. of Automatic Control [IO], Haifa, Israel
Israeli Assn. of Creative and Expressive Therapies [IO], Jerusalem, Israel
Israeli Assn. of Creative-Expressive Therapy [★IO]
Israeli Assn. of Gastroenterology and Hepatology [IO], Beersheba, Israel
Israeli Assn. of Grid Technologies [IO], Hertzelia, Israel
Israeli Assn. for Immigrant Children [IO], Rehovot, Israel
Israeli Assn. of Landscape Architects [IO], Tel Aviv, Israel
Israeli Assn. for Medical Informatics [IO], Tel Aviv, Israel
Israeli Assn. of Physiotherapists [IO], Tel Aviv, Israel
Israeli Assn. for Psychoanalytic Psychotherapy [IO], Tel Aviv, Israel
Israeli Assn. of Software Houses [IO], Tel Aviv, Israel
Israeli Athletic Assn. [IO], Tel Aviv, Israel
Israeli Boy and Girl Scout Federation [★13004]
Israeli Coun. for Israeli-Palestinian Peace [IO], Holon, Israel
Israeli Dance Inst. [9889], JCRC, 12th Fl., 711 Third Ave., New York, NY 10017, (212)983-4806
Israeli Draughts Fed. [IO], Rehovot, Israel
Israeli Export Assn. [★IO]
Israeli Feldenkrais Qualified Practitioners Assn. [IO], Tel Aviv, Israel
Israeli Intelligent Transport Systems Assn. [IO], Herzlia, Israel
Israeli Metrological Soc. [IO], Jerusalem, Israel
Israeli Org. of Occupational Therapy [IO], Tel Aviv, Israel
Israeli Soc. for Bioinformatics and Computational Biology [IO], Haifa, Israel
Israeli Soc. of Botany [★IO]
Israeli Soc. of Gene Therapy [IO], Jerusalem, Israel

Israeli Soc. for Infectious Diseases [IO], Petah Tikva, Israel
Israeli Soc. of Photogrammetry and Remote Sensing [IO], Tel Aviv, Israel
Israeli Soc. of Plant Sciences [IO], Ramat Gan, Israel
Israeli Soc. of Psychosomatic Obstetrics and Gynaecology [IO], Tel Aviv, Israel
Israeli Soc. for Res. and Treatment of Obesity [IO], Beersheba, Israel
Israeli Students' Org. in the U.S.A. and Canada [19158], c/o Intl. Student Org., 250 W 49th St., Ste. 806, New York, NY 10019, (212)262-8922
Israeli Support Gp. for HD Families [IO], Gedera, Israel
Israelite Universelle; Alliance [★IO]
Israelite Universelle; Alliance [★8675]
Israelite Universelle; Alliance [★17947]
Israelite Universelle; Canadian Friends of the Alliance [★17947]
Israelite Universelle; Canadian Friends of the Alliance [★IO]
Israelites en France; Assn. pour le Retablissement des Institutions et Oeuvres [20121]
ISSA Sect. on the Prevention of Occupational Risks Due to Electricity-Gas-Long-Distance Heating-Water [IO], Cologne, Germany
ISSHII Assn. [★479]
ISSN Intl. Centre [IO], Paris, France
The Issue Exchange [★2501]
Issue Mgt. Coun. [2501], 207 Loudoun St. SE, Leesburg, VA 20175-3115, (703)777-8450
ISSUE, the Natl. Fertility Assn. and CHILD [★IO]
Issues Forums Inst; Natl. [18467]
Issues Forums; Natl. [★18467]
Issues Mgt. Assn. - Address unknown since 2002.
Issues Rsrc. Center; Global [18151]
Istanbul Chamber of Commerce [IO], Istanbul, Turkey
Istanbul Found. for Culture and Arts [IO], Istanbul, Turkey
Istanbul Ticaret Odasi [★IO]
ISTD Dance Examinations Bd. [IO], London, United Kingdom
Istituto Cooperazione Economica Internazionale [★IO]
Istituto per la Cooperazione Universitaria [★IO]
Istituto Internazionale di Studi Liguri [★IO]
Istituto Internazionale Suore di Santa Marcellina [IO], Milan, Italy
Istituto Italiano Alimenti Surgelati [★IO]
Istituto Italiano degli Attuari [★IO]
Istituto Italiano di Cultura [10257], 686 Park Ave., New York, NY 10021-5009, (212)879-4242
Istituto Italiano Imballaggio [★IO]
Istituto Italiano della Saldatura [★IO]
Istituto Italo-Latino Americano [★IO]
Istituto Nazionale per la Diffusione della Codifica dei Prodotti [★IO]
Istituto Paolo VI: Centro Internazionale di Studi e Documentazione [★IO]
Istituto Paolo VI: Intl. Centre for Stud. and Documentation [IO], Brescia, Italy
Istituto Siciliano di Bioetica [★IO]
Istituto per gli Studi di Politica Internazionale [★IO]
IT-Brancheforeningen [★IO]
I.T. Financial Mgt. Assn. [1430], PO Box 30188, Santa Barbara, CA 93130, (805)687-7390
IT Indus. Assn. [IO], Copenhagen, Denmark
ITA - Intl. Assn. of Magnetic and Optical Media Manufacturers and Related Indus. [★IO]
ITA - Intl. Assn. of Magnetic and Optical Media Manufacturers and Related Indus. [★1370]
Italia Camera di Commercio Internazionale [★IO]
Italia Camera Di Commercio Internazionale [★IO]
Italian
  Abarth Register, U.S.A. [21562]
  Amer. Assn. of Teachers of Italian [8680]
  Amer. Assn. of Teachers of Italian [IO]
  Amer. Boccaccio Assn. [9629]
  Amer. Comm. on Italian Migration [19159]
  Amer. Inst. for Verdi Stud. [10539]
  Amer. Italian Historical Assn. [10256]
  Amer. Italian Historical Assn. [IO]
  Assn. of Student and Professional Italian-Americans [19160]

Bus. Assn. Italy Am. [2300]
Canadian Soc. for Italian Stud. [IO]
Commn. for Social Justice [17108]
Dante Soc. of Am. [9644]
Gruppo Esponenti Italiani [19161]
Guild of Italian Amer. Actors [24155]
Istituto Italiano di Cultura [10257]
Italian-American Chamber of Commerce [24338]
Italian Amer. Cultural Soc. [19162]
Italian Car Registry [21673]
Italian Catholic Fed. Central Coun. [19163]
Italian Charities of Am. [19164]
Italian Cultural Soc. of Hong Kong [IO]
Italian Culture Coun. [IO]
Italian Culture Coun. [10258]
Italian Folk Art Fed. of Am. [10259]
Italian Genealogical Gp. [21126]
Italian Genealogical Soc. of Am. [10260]
Italian Historical Soc. of Am. [10261]
Italian Historical Soc. of Am. [IO]
Italian Sons and Daughters of Am. [19165]
Italian Trade Commn. [634]
Italic Inst. of Am. [10262]
Maserati Info. Exchange [21696]
Natl. Italian Amer. Found. [19166]
Natl. Italian Amer. Found. [IO]
Natl. Org. of Italian-American Women [19167]
Order Sons of Italy in Am. [19168]
Pirandello Soc. of Am. [9701]
Soc. for Italian Historical Stud. [8681]
Unico Natl. [19169]
Italian ACM SIGCHI [IO], Udine, Italy
Italian Actors Union [★24155]
Italian-American Chamber of Commerce [24338], 500 N Michigan Ave., Ste. 506, Chicago, IL 60611, (312)553-9137
Italian-Amer. Civil Rights League - Address unknown since 1995.
Italian Amer. Cultural Soc. [19162], 43843 Romeo Plank Rd., Clinton Township, MI 48038, (586)226-1582
Italian Amer. Forum - Defunct.
Italian Amer. Found. [★19166]
Italian Amer. Found. [★IO]
Italian Amer. Foundation; Affiliates of the Natl. [★IO]
Italian Amer. Foundation; Affiliates of the Natl. [★19166]
Italian Amer. Librarians Caucus - Defunct.
Italian Amer. Stamp Club - Address unknown since 2001.
Italian Amer. War Veterans of the U.S. - Defunct.
Italian Assn. for Advanced Documentation [IO], Rome, Italy
Italian Assn. of Cost Mgt. [IO], Milan, Italy
Italian Assn. of Energy Economists [IO], Rome, Italy
Italian Assn. of Fasteners Mfrs. [IO], Milan, Italy
Italian Assn. for the Fight against Parkinson's Disease, Extrapyramidal Disorders and Dementia [IO], Rome, Italy
Italian Assn. of Friends of Raoul Follereau [IO], Bologna, Italy
Italian Assn. for Hydrogen and Fuel Cells [IO], Milan, Italy
Italian Assn. of Indus. Producers, Exporters and Importers of Wine, Spirits, Syrups and Vinegars [IO], Rome, Italy
Italian Assn. for Inflammatory Bowel Diseases [IO], Milan, Italy
Italian Assn. for Info. Systems [IO], Rome, Italy
Italian Assn. for Japanese Stud. [IO], Venice, Italy
Italian Assn. of Leather and Leather Substitute Mfrs. [IO], Milan, Italy
Italian Assn. of Mfg. and Trading Companies in Fluid Power Equip. and Components [IO], Milan, Italy
Italian Assn. of Medical Physics [IO], Gazzada, Italy
Italian Assn. for Metallurgy [IO], Milan, Italy
Italian Assn. of Milk and Cheese Producers [IO], Milan, Italy
Italian Assn. of Osteoporosis Patients [IO], Florence, Italy
Italian Assn. for Pattern Recognition [IO], Pavia, Italy
Italian Assn. of Pediatric Hematology and Oncology [IO], Bologna, Italy
Italian Assn. of Precision Moulds, Dies and Tooling Manufacturers [IO], Milan, Italy

A star before a book entry number signifies that the name is not listed separately, but is mentioned within the entry.

Italian Assn. of Sporting Goods Mfrs. **[IO]**, Treviso, Italy
Italian Atlantic Comm. **[IO]**, Rome, Italy
Italian Automotive Ser. Equip. Mfrs. Assn. **[IO]**, Bologna, Italy
Italian Banking Assn. **[IO]**, Rome, Italy
Italian Booksellers' Assn. **[IO]**, Rome, Italy
Italian Car Registry **[21673]**
Italian Catholic Fed. Central Coun. **[19163]**, 675 Hegenberger Rd., Ste. 230, Oakland, CA 94621, (510)633-9058
Italian Cement Assn. **[IO]**, Rome, Italy
Italian Center of Solidarity **[IO]**, Rome, Italy
Italian Chamber of Commerce and Indus. in Australia - SA **[IO]**, Adelaide, Australia
Italian Chamber of Commerce and Indus. in Queensland **[IO]**, Milton, Australia
Italian Chamber of Commerce and Indus. for the UK **[IO]**, London, United Kingdom
Italian Charities of Am. **[19164]**
Italian Charity and Welfare Center **[★19164]**
Italian Chem. Soc. **[IO]**, Rome, Italy
Italian Civic League; Natl. **[★19169]**
Italian Confed. of Retailers, Commerce, Tourism and Ser. **[IO]**, Rome, Italy
Italian Cooperatives Assn. **[IO]**, Rome, Italy
Italian Cricket Fed. **[IO]**, Turin, Italy
Italian Cultural and Community Center **[★19162]**
Italian Cultural Exchange in the U.S. - Address unknown since 2002.
Italian Cultural Inst. **[★10257]**
Italian Cultural Soc. of Hong Kong **[IO]**, Hong Kong, People's Republic of China
Italian Culture Coun. **[IO]**, Union, NJ, United States
Italian Culture Coun. **[10258]**, c/o Patricia A. McDorman, Exec.Dir., 35 W Sumner Ave., Apt. 105, Union, NJ 07083-9414, (908)206-1288
Italian Dance Sport Fed. **[IO]**, Rome, Italy
Italian Dental Indus. Assn. **[IO]**, Milan, Italy
Italian Elecl. and Electronics Assn. **[IO]**, Milan, Italy
Italian Fed. of the Chem. Indus. **[IO]**, Milan, Italy
Italian Fed. of Goldsmiths, Jewelry and Silver Retailers and Wholesalers **[IO]**, Rome, Italy
Italian Fed. of the Mineral and Soft Drinks Indus. **[IO]**, Rome, Italy
Italian Fed. of Tour Operators and Travel Agencies **[IO]**, Rome, Italy
Italian Fed. of Univ. Women **[IO]**, Cava Manara, Italy
Italian Fed. of Urban Cyclists and Bicycle Tourism **[IO]**, Mestre, Italy
Italian Fed. of the Wool, Cork, Furniture and Furnishing Indus. **[IO]**, Milan, Italy
Italian Fed. of the YMCA **[IO]**, Rome, Italy
Italian Florists Natl. Assn. **[IO]**, Rome, Italy
Italian Folk Art Fed. of Am. **[10259]**, PO Box 1192, Rockford, IL 61105, (800)601-6888
Italian Food Indus. Fed. **[IO]**, Rome, Italy
Italian Food Retailers' Fed. **[IO]**, Rome, Italy
Italian Franchising Assn. **[IO]**, Milan, Italy
Italian Frozen Food Inst. **[IO]**, Rome, Italy
Italian Garage Equip. Mfrs. Assn. **[IO]**, Bologna, Italy
Italian Genealogical Gp. **[21126]**, PO Box 626, Bethpage, NY 11714-0626
Italian Genealogical Soc. of Am. **[10260]**, PO Box 3572, Peabody, MA 01961-3572
Italian Geological Soc. **[IO]**, Rome, Italy
Italian Greyhound Club of Am. **[22296]**, c/o Lynette Coyner, VP, 10061 S Deer Creek Rd., Littleton, CO 80127-9514, (303)697-7527
Italian Historical Soc. of Am. **[10261]**, 410 Park Ave., Ste. 1530, New York, NY 10022, (718)852-2929
Italian Historical Soc. of Am. **[IO]**, New York, NY, United States
Italian Historical Soc; Amer. **[★10261]**
Italian Independent Record Producers' Assn. **[IO]**, Milan, Italy
Italian Indus. Assn. for Aerospace Systems and Defence **[IO]**, Rome, Italy
Italian Inst. of Actuaries **[IO]**, Rome, Italy
Italian Inst. of Packaging **[IO]**, Milan, Italy
Italian Inst. of Welding **[IO]**, Genoa, Italy
Italian-Latin Amer. Inst. **[IO]**, Rome, Italy
Italian Lay Center for Missions **[★IO]**
Italian League Against Epilepsy **[IO]**, Bologna, Italy
Italian League Against Hypertension **[IO]**, Ancona, Italy

Italian Lib. Assn. **[IO]**, Rome, Italy
Italian Mathematical Union **[IO]**, Bologna, Italy
Italian Meteorological Soc. **[IO]**, Bussoleno, Italy
Italian Moebius Syndrome Assn. **[IO]**, Muggio, Italy
Italian Natl. Assn. of Insurance Adjusters **[IO]**, Rome, Italy
Italian Natl. Res. Coun. **[IO]**, Rome, Italy
Italian Neuroscience Soc. **[IO]**, Turin, Italy
Italian Newspaper Publishers' Assn. **[IO]**, Rome, Italy
Italian Oddities; Registry of **[★21673]**
Italian Paralympic Comm. **[IO]**, Rome, Italy
Italian Pasta Makers' Union **[IO]**, Rome, Italy
Italian PEN Club **[IO]**, Milan, Italy
Italian Pharmacists' Fed. **[IO]**, Rome, Italy
Italian Pharmacological Soc. **[IO]**, Milan, Italy
Italian Photographic Assn. **[IO]**, Rome, Italy
Italian Physical Soc. **[IO]**, Bologna, Italy
Italian Private Equity and Venture Capital Assn. **[IO]**, Milan, Italy
Italian Publishers Assn. **[IO]**, Milan, Italy
Italian Radio Relay Ser. **[★IO]**
Italian Remote Sensing Assn. **[IO]**, Rome, Italy
Italian Rice Millers Assn. **[IO]**, Pavia, Italy
Italian Sailing Fed. **[IO]**, Genoa, Italy
Italian Soc. of Agriculture Genetics **[IO]**, Portici, Italy
Italian Soc. of Anatomy **[IO]**, Rome, Italy
Italian Soc. of Authors, Composers and Publishers - Address unknown since 1995.
Italian Soc. of Biophysics **[IO]**, Naples, Italy
Italian Soc. of Chemotherapy **[IO]**, Florence, Italy
Italian Soc. of Dermatology **[IO]**, Brescia, Italy
Italian Soc. of Digestive Endoscopy **[IO]**, Naples, Italy
Italian Soc. of Ecology **[IO]**, Parma, Italy
Italian Soc. for Endoscopic Surgery and New Technologies **[IO]**, Rome, Italy
Italian Soc. for Environmental Geology **[IO]**, Rome, Italy
Italian Soc. of Fertility, Sterility and Reproductive Medicine **[IO]**, Cattolica, Italy
Italian Soc. of Gerontology and Geriatrics **[IO]**, Florence, Italy
Italian Soc. for Hosp. Pharmacy **[IO]**, Milan, Italy
Italian Soc. of Internal Medicine **[IO]**, Rome, Italy
Italian Soc. for Intl. Org. **[IO]**, Rome, Italy
Italian Soc. for Microscopical Sciences **[IO]**, Modena, Italy
Italian Soc. for Plant Pathology **[IO]**, Bari, Italy
Italian Soc. of Psychosomatic Obstetrics and Gynaecology **[IO]**, Turin, Italy
Italian Soc. of Radiology **[IO]**, Milan, Italy
Italian Soc. of Reumatologia **[IO]**, Milan, Italy
Italian Soc. of Surgical and Oncological Dermatology **[IO]**, Rome, Italy
Italian Soc. of Therapeutic Psychosynthesis **[IO]**, Florence, Italy
Italian Soc. of Toxicology **[IO]**, Milan, Italy
Italian Sons and Daughters of Am. **[19165]**, 419 Wood St., Pittsburgh, PA 15222, (412)261-3550
Italian Sports Medicine Fed. **[IO]**, Rome, Italy
Italian Squash Fed. **[IO]**, Riccione, Italy
Italian Stainless Steel Development Assn. **[IO]**, Milan, Italy
Italian Textile Assn. **[IO]**, Milan, Italy
Italian Tile Center **[★634]**
Italian Tobacconists' Fed. **[IO]**, Rome, Italy
Italian Trade Commn. **[634]**, 33 E 67th St., New York, NY 10021-5949, (212)980-1500
Italian Unihockey and Floorball Assn. **[IO]**, Rodano, Italy
Italian Union of the Blind **[IO]**, Rome, Italy
Italian Vacuum Assn. **[IO]**, Milan, Italy
Italian Vending Machines' Assn. **[IO]**, Milan, Italy
Italian Venture Capital Assn. **[★IO]**
Italian Welfare League - Address unknown since 2001.
Italian Wine and Food Inst. **[1534]**, PO Box 789, New York, NY 10150-0789, (212)867-4111
Italiano di Cultura; Istituto **[10257]**
Italic Inst. of Am. **[10262]**, PO Box 818, Floral Park, NY 11001, (516)488-7400
Italic Stud. Inst. **[★10262]**
Italo Amer. Natl. Union **[★19165]**
Italo Svevo Intl. Assn. - Defunct.

Italy
  Abarth Register, U.S.A. **[21562]**
  Alpine Tourist Commn. **[24223]**
  Amer. Friends of the Vatican Lib. **[10318]**
  Amer. Italian Historical Assn. **[10256]**
  Aurora Ministries **[20276]**
  Boys' Towns of Italy **[13474]**
  Bus. Assn. Italy Am. **[2300]**
  Istituto Italiano di Cultura **[10257]**
  Italian Car Registry **[21673]**
  Italian Culture Coun. **[10258]**
  Italian Folk Art Fed. of Am. **[10259]**
  Italian Historical Soc. of Am. **[10261]**
  Italic Inst. of Am. **[10262]**
  Italy-America Chamber of Commerce **[24339]**
  Maserati Info. Exchange **[21696]**
  Soc. for Italian Historical Stud. **[8681]**
Italy-America Chamber of Commerce **[24339]**, 730 5th Ave., Ste. 600, New York, NY 10019, (212)459-0044
Italy; Amer. Relief for **[★13474]**
Italy; Boys' Towns of **[13474]**
Italy; Intl. Comm. to Preserve Catacombs in **[★10039]**
Italy Medical Informatics Soc. **[IO]**, Rome, Italy
Itasca Travelers; Winnebago- **[22968]**
ITC Trial Lawyers Assn. **[6332]**, PO Box 6186, Benjamin Franklin Sta., Washington, DC 20004, (202)429-3770
ITC/USA/2003 **[★7786]**
ITC/USA/2003 **[★IO]**
ITEM Coalition **[14690]**, 1875 Eye St. NW, 12th Fl., Washington, DC 20006, (202)349-4260
Ithaca; EcoVillage at **[4557]**
Ithaca Railroad Assn. - Defunct.
Ithaka **[7200]**, 151 E 61st St., New York, NY 10021, (212)500-2600
ITS The Assn. of Imaging Technology and Sound - Defunct.
Ittleson Found. **[13122]**, 15 E 67th St., New York, NY 10021, (212)794-2008
IUCN: Centre for Mediterranean Cooperation of the World Conservation Union **[IO]**, Campanillas, Spain
IUCN - Environmental Law Programme Germany **[IO]**, Bonn, Germany
IUCN - Russia **[IO]**, Moscow, Russia
IUCN - The World Conservation Union **[IO]**, Gland, Switzerland
IUCN: The World Conservation Union Regional Off. for Southern Africa **[IO]**, Harare, Zimbabwe
IUCN World Conservation Union - Bangladesh **[IO]**, Dhaka, Bangladesh
IUCN: World Conservation Union - Botswana **[IO]**, Gaborone, Botswana
IUCN: World Conservation Union - Cambodia **[IO]**, Phnom Penh, Cambodia
IUCN: World Conservation Union - China **[IO]**, Beijing, People's Republic of China
IUCN: World Conservation Union - Congo **[IO]**, Pointe-Noire, Republic of the Congo
IUCN: World Conservation Union - Ethiopia **[IO]**, Addis Ababa, Ethiopia
IUCN: World Conservation Union - Guinea - Bissau **[IO]**, Bissau, Guinea-Bissau
IUCN: World Conservation Union - Kenya **[IO]**, Nairobi, Kenya
IUCN: World Conservation Union - Lao People's Democratic Republic **[IO]**, Vientiane, Lao People's Democratic Republic
IUCN: World Conservation Union - Mali **[IO]**, Bamako, Mali
IUCN: World Conservation Union - Mauritania **[IO]**, Nouakchott, Mauritania
IUCN: World Conservation Union - Mozambique **[IO]**, Maputo, Mozambique
IUCN: World Conservation Union - Nepal **[IO]**, Kathmandu, Nepal
IUCN: World Conservation Union - Niger **[IO]**, Niamey, Niger
IUCN: World Conservation Union - Oficina Regional para Am. del Sur **[IO]**, Quito, Ecuador
IUCN: World Conservation Union - Pakistan **[IO]**, Karachi, Pakistan
IUCN: World Conservation Union Programme Off. for Central Europe **[IO]**, Warsaw, Poland

Reference to "IO" in place of a book number signifies that the association may be found in the 45th edition of International Organizations.

IUCN: World Conservation Union - Protected Area Mgt. and Wildlife Conservation Proj. Wildlife Dept. [IO], Accra, Ghana

IUCN - World Conservation Union Regional Off. for Europe [IO], Brussels, Belgium

IUCN: World Conservation Union - Senegal [IO], Dakar, Senegal

IUCN: World Conservation Union - Sri Lanka [IO], Colombo, Sri Lanka

IUCN: World Conservation Union - Tanzania [IO], Dar es Salaam, United Republic of Tanzania

IUCN: World Conservation Union - Thailand [IO], Bangkok, Thailand

IUCN: World Conservation Union - Uganda [IO], Kampala, Uganda

IUCN: World Conservation Union - Vietnam [IO], Hanoi, Vietnam

IUD Claims Info. Source [6216], PO Box 84151, Seattle, WA 98124, (206)329-1371

Iuliu Maniu Amer. Romanian Relief Found. [19332]

IVAS [★16796]

IVAS [★IO]

I've Known Rivers - Defunct.

Ives Soc; Charles [10574]

IVH Parents - Defunct.

IVI Found. [6814], PO Box 1016, Niwot, CO 80544-1016, (303)652-2585

Ivory Family Assn. - Defunct.

Ivy Div. Assn; Natl. 4th Infantry [20703]

Ivy Gp. Presidents; Coun. of [23817]

Ivy League [★23817]

Ixquic, The Woman in Guatemala - Address unknown since 1988.

Iyengar Yoga Natl. Assn. of the U.S; B.K.S. [23992]

Izaak Walton League of Am. [4413], 707 Conservation Ln., Gaithersburg, MD 20878, (301)548-0150

Izaak Walton League of Am. Endowment [4414], c/o Charles L. Eldridge, Pres., 523 14th St., Des Moines, IA 50309, (515)244-0932

J

J/24 Class Assn. [★23227]

J/24 Class Assn. [★IO]

J/24 Class Assn; U.S. [23227]

J/29 Assn. - Address unknown since 1999.

J. Allen Hynek Center for UFO Stud. [7479], 2457 W Peterson Ave., Ste. 6, Chicago, IL 60659, (773)271-3611

J. L. Inst; Better World Builders [★12142]

J-Road Open Club [IO], Kadoma, Japan

J2CP Online Services - Address unknown since 2001.

Jaan Tonisson Inst. [IO], Tallinn, Estonia

Jaan Tonissoni Instituut [★IO]

Jack Inst. - Defunct.

Jack and Jennet Registry of Am; Standard [★4130]

Jack and Jill of Am. [11702], 1930 17th St. NW, Washington, DC 20009, (202)667-7010

Jack and Jill of Am. Found. [11703], 1930 17th St. NW, Washington, DC 20009, (202)232-5290

Jack Knight Air Mail Soc. [22834], PO Box 1239, Elgin, IL 60121-1239

Jack Knight Air Mail Soc. [IO], Elgin, IL, United States

Jack London Foundation [★9669]

Jack London Res. Center [9669], PO Box 337, Glen Ellen, CA 95442, (707)996-2888

Jack M. Blount Found. for the Eradication of Rheumatoid Disease; Roger Wyburn-Mason and [16375]

Jack Point Preservation Soc. [9811], PO Box 179, New Ellenton, SC 29809, (803)652-3492

Jack Russell Terrier Assn. of Am. [★22337]

Jack Russell Terrier Club of Am. [22297], PO Box 4527, Lutherville, MD 21094-4527, (410)561-3655

Jack Scalia Fan Club - Address unknown since 1994.

Jack Stock Registry; Amer. Mammoth [★4130]

Jackie Chan Charitable Found. [IO], Hong Kong, People's Republic of China

Jackie Chan Fan Club, Australia [★IO]

Jackie Chan and Friends [IO], Gladesville, Australia

Jackie Chan Intl. Fan Club, Japan [IO], Tokyo, Japan

Jackie Chan UK Fan Club [IO], Bath, United Kingdom

Jackie Robinson Found. [13491], One Hudson Sq., 75 Varick St., 2nd Fl., New York, NY 10013-1947, (212)290-8600

Jackson, Andrew
 Ladies' Hermitage Assn. [11133]

Jackson Fan Club; Alan [24839]

Jackson Found; Henry M. [17480]

Jackson Orthopaedic Soc; Ruth [15781]

Jackson State Univ. Natl. Alumni Assn. [18901], PO Box 17144, Jackson, MS 39217, (601)979-2282

Jackstock Registry; Amer. Mammoth [4130]

Jacky Ward Fan Club - Defunct.

Jaclyn Smith's Official Fan Club - Address unknown since 1999.

Jacob Blaustein Inst. for the Advancement of Human Rights [17771], c/o Amer. Jewish Comm., PO Box 705, New York, NY 10150, (212)751-4000

Jacob Blaustein Inst. for Desert Research [★8673]

Jacob Hochstetler Family Assn. [20955], 1102 S 13th St., Goshen, IN 46526, (574)533-7819

Jacob Horning Family Org. - Address unknown since 2002.

Jacob More Soc. - Address unknown since 2001.

Jacob Schools; Federated Coun. of Beth [8691]

Jacob Sheep Breeders Assn. [5203], c/o Lane Harris, Membership Sec., PO Box 10427, Bozeman, MT 59719, (406)580-6832

Jacob Sheep Soc. [IO], Warwick, United Kingdom

Jacob Wetterling Found. [11608], 2314 Univ. Ave. W, Ste. 14, St. Paul, MN 55114-1863, (651)714-4673

Jacobs Inst. of Women's Hea. [14641], 2021 K St. NW, Ste. 800, Washington, DC 20006, (202)530-2376

Jacques Timothe Boucher Sieur de Montbrun Heritage Soc. [20741], c/o Peggy Binkley, Treas., 4009 Ivy Dr., Nashville, TN 37216

Jae Fan Club; Jana [24916]

Jaeger/Loretan/Steiner/Ross Soc; Pellien/ [21022]

Jafari Intl. Travel Club; Jayco [★22955]

Jaffa Inst; Jaffa, Israel

Jagannath Org. for Global Awareness [IO], Dayton, MD, United States

Jagannath Org. for Global Awareness [20527], c/o Dr. Naresh C. Das, Chm., 4525 Rutherford Way, Dayton, MD 21036, (410)531-7445

Jaguar Assn; Classic [21616]

Jaguar Clubs of North Am. [21674], c/o Nelson Rath, Admin. Mgr./Treas., 234 Buckland Trace, Louisville, KY 40245, (502)244-1672

Jaguar Clubs of North Am. [IO], Louisville, KY, United States

Jail Assn; Amer. [11856]

Jail Assn; Natl. [★11856]

Jail Managers Assn; Natl. [★11856]

Jail and Prison Ministry; Good News [★11869]

Jail Workers; Christian [★19745]

Jama'at Ahmadiyyah [★IO]

Jamaica
 Assn. of Racing Commissioners Intl. [6240]
 Jamaica Tourist Bd. [24340]
 Jamaica USA Chamber of Commerce [24287]

Jamaica Agricultural Soc. [IO], Kingston, Jamaica

Jamaica Amateur Athletic Assn. [IO], Kingston, Jamaica

Jamaica Assn. of Evangelicals [★IO]

Jamaica Assn. of Secretaries and Administrative Professionals [IO], Kingston, Jamaica

Jamaica Assn. of Villas and Apartments [IO], Ocho Rios, Jamaica

Jamaica Badminton Assn. [IO], Kingston, Jamaica

Jamaica Bankers' Assn. [IO], Kingston, Jamaica

Jamaica Baseball Assn. [IO], Kingston, Jamaica

Jamaica (BWI) Study Group - Defunct.

Jamaica Cancer Soc. [IO], Kingston, Jamaica

Jamaica Exporters Assn. [IO], Kingston, Jamaica

Jamaica Family Planning Assn. [★IO]

Jamaica Hotel and Tourist Assn. [IO], Kingston, Jamaica

Jamaica Mfrs'. Assn. [IO], Kingston, Jamaica

Jamaica Olympic Assn. [IO], Kingston, Jamaica

Jamaica Physiotherapy Assn. [IO], Kingston, Jamaica

Jamaica Red Cross [IO], Kingston, Jamaica

Jamaica Squash Assn. [IO], Kingston, Jamaica

Jamaica Taekwondo Fed. [IO], Kingston, Jamaica

Jamaica Teachers' Assn. [IO], Kingston, Jamaica

Jamaica Tourist Bd. [24340], 5201 Blue Lagoon Dr., Ste. 670, Miami, FL 33126, (305)665-0557

Jamaica Union of Teachers [★IO]

Jamaica USA Chamber of Commerce [24287], 4770 Biscayne Blvd., Ste. 1050, Miami, FL 33137, (305)573-3235

Jamaica Yachting Assn. [IO], Kingston, Jamaica

Jamaican Airline Pilots' Assn. [IO], Kingston, Jamaica

Jamaican Assn. for the Deaf [IO], Kingston, Jamaica

Jamaican Chap. of ILAE [IO], Kingston, Jamaica

Jamaicans For Justice [IO], Kingston, Jamaica

James A. Michener Soc. [9670], c/o A. Richard Boera, Treas., PO Box 1126, Lyndonville, VT 05851, (505)296-9047

James Allen Fan Club - Address unknown since 1989.

James Beard Found. [11125], 167 W 12th St., New York, NY 10011, (212)675-4984

James Bond 007 Fan Club - Defunct.

James Bond Intl. Fan Club [IO], York, United Kingdom

James Branch Cabell Soc. - Defunct.

James Buchanan Found. [★11126]

James Buchanan Found. for the Preservation of Wheatland [11126], 1120 Marietta Ave., Lancaster, PA 17603, (717)392-8721

James Darren Fan Club - Defunct.

James Dean Memory Club - Address unknown since 1995.

James Dickey Soc. [10875], c/o Prof. William B. Thesing, Dir./Ed., Univ. of South Carolina, Dept. of English, 1620 Coll. St., Columbia, SC 29208

James Doohan Intl. Fan Club - Defunct.

James Ewing Soc. [★15655]

James Family Assn. - Address unknown since 1991.

James; Fellowship of Saint [19800]

James Happy Family Org. [20956]

James Intl. Fan Club; Joni [24818]

James Joyce Soc. [9671], c/o A. Nicholas Fargnoli, Pres., 26 Varick Ct., Rockville Centre, NY 11570

James Joyce Soc. of Southern Colorado [9672], PO Box 62482, Colorado Springs, CO 80962, (719)594-9164

James K. Polk Memorial Assn. [11127], c/o Polk Home, PO Box 741, Columbia, TN 38402, (931)388-2354

James Leonard Williams Family Org. [20957]

James Madison Found. [★18444]

James Monroe Freedom Scholarship Program [★11128]

James Monroe Law Off. Museum and Memorial Lib. [★11128]

James Monroe Memorial Found. [11128], 1009 Bainbridge St., Richmond, VA 23224, (804)231-1827

James O'Gwynn Fan Club - Defunct.

James "Rebel" O'Leary Fan Club - Address unknown since 2004.

James "Rebel" O'Leary and Jammie Ann Tape Club - Defunct.

James Redman Miller Family Org. [20958]

James Renwick Alliance [9452], 4405 East-West Hwy., Ste. 510, Bethesda, MD 20814, (301)907-3888

James Robison Evangelistic Assn. [★20021]

James Robison Life Intl. [★20021]

James Weldon Johnson Family and Children's Counseling Center [★12785]

James Willard Schultz Soc. - Defunct.

James William McIlhaney Family Assn. - Address unknown since 2003.

Jamestown Found. [17447], 1111 16th St. NW, Ste. No. 320, Washington, DC 20036, (202)483-8888

Jamestown Found. [IO], Washington, DC, United States

Jamestowne Soc. [20742], PO Box 17426, Richmond, VA 23226, (804)673-6006

Jami'at Al Islam - Defunct.

Jammie Ann Fan Club - Address unknown since 2004.

Jan Berry and the Alohas Fan Club - Address unknown since 1989.

A star before a book entry number signifies that the name is not listed separately, but is mentioned within the entry.

Jan and Dean Fan Club; Surfun: The Official **[24977]**
Jan Howard Friends Club - Address unknown since 1995.
Jana Jae Fan Club **[24916]**, PO Box 35726, Tulsa, OK 74153, (918)786-8896
Jane Addams Peace Assn. **[18214]**, 777 United Nations Plz., 6th Fl., New York, NY 10017, (212)682-8830
Jane Addams Peace Assn. **[IO]**, New York, NY, United States
Jane Austen Soc. - England **[★IO]**
Jane Austen Soc. of North Am. **[IO]**, Milwaukee, WI, United States
Jane Austen Soc. of North Am. **[9673]**, c/o Bobbie Gay, Membership Sec., 7230 N San Blas Dr., Tucson, AZ 85704, (800)836-3911
Jane Austen Soc. of the United Kingdom **[IO]**, Havant, United Kingdom
Jane Badler Soc. - Address unknown since 1995.
Jane Goodall Inst. for Wildlife Res., Educ., and Conservation **[5334]**, 4245 N Fairfax Dr., Ste. 600, Arlington, VA 22203, (703)682-9220
Jane Powell Fan Club **[24747]**, 847 S Carpenter Ave., Oak Park, IL 60304, (708)386-2587
Jane Seymour Fan Club - Defunct.
Janet Jackson's Official Fan Club - Address unknown since 2002.
JANGO - Defunct.
Janie's Friends - Address unknown since 1999.
Janis Ian Fan Club - Address unknown since 1994.
Jans and Everardus Bogardus Descendants Assn; Anneke **[20782]**
January 2nd Coalition for the Defense of Haitian Refugees - Address unknown since 1995.
January 12th 1888 Blizzard Club - Defunct.
Japan
All Japan Ju-Jitsu Intl. Fed. **[23577]**
Amer. Bonsai Soc. **[22483]**
Amer. Comm. for KEEP **[12418]**
Assoc. Koi Clubs of Am. **[22437]**
Bonsai Clubs Intl. **[22504]**
High School Evangelism Fellowship **[20013]**
Inter-American Tropical Tuna Commn. **[5730]**
Intl. Nippon Collectors Club **[21929]**
Intl. Soc. for Japanese Philately **[22830]**
Japan Aikido Assn. U.S.A. **[23595]**
Japan-America Soc. of Washington, D.C. **[10263]**
Japan-America Student Conf. **[8622]**
Japan Auto. Mfrs. Assn., Washington Off. **[389]**
Japan Convention Bur. **[24341]**
Japan External Trade Org. **[24342]**
Japan Found. **[10264]**
Japan Info. Access Proj. **[10265]**
Japan Intl. Center for the Rights of the Child **[IO]**
Japan Intl. Christian Univ. Found. **[19929]**
Japan Light Machinery Info. Center of Central New York **[24343]**
Japan Natl. Tourist Org. **[24344]**
Japan Soc. **[10266]**
Japanese Akita Club of Am. **[22298]**
Japanese Amer. Veterans Assn. **[21305]**
Japanese Chamber of Commerce and Industry of Hawaii **[24345]**
Japanese Chamber of Commerce and Indus. of New York **[24346]**
Japanese Chin Club of Am. **[22299]**
Jin Shin Do Found. for Bodymind Acupressure **[15746]**
Never Again Campaign **[18162]**
Nichiren Buddhist Assn. of Am. **[19555]**
North Amer. Coordinating Coun. on Japanese Lib. Resources **[8781]**
Northern Far East Returned Missionaries Assn. **[20504]**
Occupied Japan Club **[22098]**
Origami USA **[22771]**
Shudokan Martial Arts Assn. **[23603]**
Soc. for Japanese Irises **[22541]**
Soc. for the Stud. of Japanese Religions **[20529]**
Tanka Soc. of Am. **[10871]**
U.S. Aikido Fed. **[23049]**
U.S.-Japan Bus. Coun. **[24347]**
U.S.-Japan Culture Center **[10268]**
Urasenke Tea Ceremony Soc. **[10269]**
Japan Academic Assn. for Copyright Clearance **[IO]**, Tokyo, Japan

Japan Advertisers Assn. **[IO]**, Tokyo, Japan
Japan Advt. Agencies Assn. **[IO]**, Tokyo, Japan
Japan Aeronautic Assn. **[IO]**, Tokyo, Japan
Japan Aikido Assn. U.S.A. **[23595]**, 5752 S Kingston Way, Englewood, CO 80111, (303)740-7424
Japan Aluminium Fed. **[IO]**, Tokyo, Japan
Japan Amateur Radio League **[IO]**, Tokyo, Japan
Japan-America Inst. - Defunct.
Japan-America Societies; Natl. Assn. of **[19171]**
Japan-America Societies of the U.S; Assoc. **[★19171]**
Japan-America Soc. of Washington, D.C. **[10263]**, 1819 L St. NW, 1B Level, Washington, DC 20036, (202)833-2210
Japan-America Soc. of Washington, D.C. **[IO]**, Washington, DC, United States
Japan-America Student Conf. **[8622]**, 1819 L St. NW, Ste. LL2, Washington, DC 20036, (202)289-4231
Japan; Amer. Comm. for the Brotherhood of Saint Andrew in **[★12418]**
Japan Amyotrophic Lateral Sclerosis Assn. **[IO]**, Tokyo, Japan
Japan Analytical Instruments Manufacturers Assn. **[IO]**, Tokyo, Japan
Japan Ankylosing Spondylitis Club **[IO]**, Tokyo, Japan
Japan Art Academy **[IO]**, Tokyo, Japan
Japan Art Assn. **[IO]**, Tokyo, Japan
Japan Art History Forum **[9480]**, c/o Ms. Sarah Thompson, Treas., Art of Asia, Oceania and Africa, Museum of Fine Arts, Boston, 465 Huntington Ave., Boston, MA 02115, (617)369-3223
Japan Asian Assn. and Asian Friendship Soc. **[IO]**, Osaka, Japan
Japan Assn. of Adult Orthodontics **[IO]**, Tokyo, Japan
Japan Assn. for African Stud. **[IO]**, Kyoto, Japan
Japan Assn. of Athletics Federations **[IO]**, Tokyo, Japan
Japan Assn. of Automatic Control Engineers **[★IO]**
Japan Assn. of Coll. English Teachers **[IO]**, Tokyo, Japan
Japan Assn. of Corporate Executives **[IO]**, Tokyo, Japan
Japan Assn. of Graphic Arts Tech. **[IO]**, Tokyo, Japan
Japan Assn. for Intl. Chem. Info. **[IO]**, Tokyo, Japan
Japan Assn. for Intl. Collaboration of Agriculture and Forestry **[IO]**, Tokyo, Japan
Japan Assn. for Intl. Horse Racing **[IO]**, Tokyo, Japan
Japan Assn. for Language Teaching **[IO]**, Tokyo, Japan
Japan Assn. of Legal Philosophy **[IO]**, Chiba, Japan
Japan Assn. of Manufacturers and Distributors of Educational Materials **[★IO]**
Japan Assn. for Medical Informatics **[IO]**, Tokyo, Japan
Japan Assn. of New Bus. Incubation Org. **[IO]**, Tokyo, Japan
Japan Assn. for Philosophy of Sci. **[IO]**, Tokyo, Japan
Japan Assn. for Quaternary Res. **[IO]**, Tokyo, Japan
Japan Assn. for Trade with Russia and Central-Eastern Europe **[IO]**, Tokyo, Japan
Japan Assn. of Translators **[IO]**, Tokyo, Japan
Japan Assn. of Travel Agents **[IO]**, Tokyo, Japan
Japan Atherosclerosis Soc. **[IO]**, Tokyo, Japan
Japan Audio Soc. **[IO]**, Tokyo, Japan
Japan Audio Visual Educ. Assn. **[IO]**, Tokyo, Japan
Japan Auto Parts Indus. Assn. **[IO]**, Tokyo, Japan
Japan Auto. Fed. **[IO]**, Tokyo, Japan
Japan Auto. Importers' Assn. **[IO]**, Tokyo, Japan
Japan Auto. Mfrs. Assn. **[IO]**, Tokyo, Japan
Japan Auto. Mfrs. Assn., Washington Off. **[389]**, 1050 17th St. NW, Ste. 410, Washington, DC 20036, (202)296-8537
Japan Auto. Tyre Mfrs. Assn. **[IO]**, Tokyo, Japan
Japan Automotive Products' Assn. **[IO]**, Tokyo, Japan
Japan Automotive Ser. Equip. Assn. **[IO]**, Tokyo, Japan
Japan Bamboo Soc. **[IO]**, Kyoto, Japan
Japan Bearing Indus. Assn. **[IO]**, Tokyo, Japan

Japan Binoculars Assn. - Defunct.
Japan Biscuit Assn. **[IO]**, Tokyo, Japan
Japan Boating Indus. Assn. **[IO]**, Tokyo, Japan
Japan Book Publishers Assn. **[IO]**, Tokyo, Japan
Japan Bus. Aviation Assn. **[IO]**, Tokyo, Japan
Japan Bus. Fed. **[IO]**, Tokyo, Japan
Japan Bus. Machine and Info. Sys. Indus. Assn. **[IO]**, Tokyo, Japan
Japan Cartographers Assn. **[IO]**, Tokyo, Japan
Japan Center for Intl. Exchange **[IO]**, Tokyo, Japan
Japan Center for Intl. Exchange - USA **[IO]**, New York, NY, United States
Japan Center for Intl. Exchange - USA **[17900]**, 274 Madison Ave., Ste. 1102, New York, NY 10016, (212)679-4130
Japan Chap. of Intl. Geosynthetics Soc. **[IO]**, Saitama, Japan
Japan Chem. Fibers Assn. **[IO]**, Tokyo, Japan
Japan Chem. Indus. Assn. **[IO]**, Tokyo, Japan
Japan Clock and Watch Assn. **[IO]**, Tokyo, Japan
Japan Club; Occupied **[22098]**
Japan Coal Assn. **[★IO]**
Japan Coal Energy Center **[IO]**, Tokyo, Japan
Japan Commercial Arbitration Assn. **[IO]**, Tokyo, Japan
Japan Confed. of Railway Workers' Unions **[IO]**, Tokyo, Japan
Japan Constr. Mechanization Assn. **[IO]**, Tokyo, Japan
Japan Convention Bur. **[24341]**, 1 Rockefeller Plz., Ste. 1250, New York, NY 10020, (212)757-5640
Japan Copper Development Assn. **[IO]**, Tokyo, Japan
Japan Cotton Traders Assn. **[IO]**, Osaka, Japan
Japan Coun. Against A and H Bombs **[IO]**, Tokyo, Japan
Japan Craft Beer Assn. **[IO]**, Nishinomiya, Japan
Japan Cricket Assn. **[IO]**, Tokyo, Japan
Japan Customs Brokers Assn. **[IO]**, Tokyo, Japan
Japan Dam Found. **[IO]**, Tokyo, Japan
Japan Dancesport Fed. **[IO]**, Tokyo, Japan
Japan Die and Mold Indus. Assn. **[IO]**, Tokyo, Japan
Japan Direct Marketing Assn. **[IO]**, Tokyo, Japan
Japan Donor Family Club **[IO]**, Tokyo, Japan
Japan Economic Inst. of America - Defunct.
Japan Economic Policy Assn. **[IO]**, Kobe, Japan
Japan Elec. Lamp Mfrs. Assn. **[IO]**, Tokyo, Japan
Japan Elec. Measuring Instruments Mfrs'. Assn. **[IO]**, Tokyo, Japan
Japan Elecl. Mfrs. Assn. **[IO]**, Tokyo, Japan
Japan Electronic Data Interchange Coun. **[IO]**, Tokyo, Japan
Japan Electronic Products Importers Assn. **[IO]**, Tokyo, Japan
Japan Electronics and Info. Tech. Indus. Assn. **[IO]**, Tokyo, Japan
Japan Electronics Show Assn. **[IO]**, Tokyo, Japan
Japan Embedded Systems Tech. Assn. **[IO]**, Tokyo, Japan
Japan Environmental Mgt. Assn. for Indus. **[IO]**, Tokyo, Japan
Japan Epilepsy Soc. **[IO]**, Tokyo, Japan
Japan Evangelical Lutheran Church **[IO]**, Tokyo, Japan
Japan Explosives Soc. **[IO]**, Tokyo, Japan
Japan External Trade Org. **[IO]**, Tokyo, Japan
Japan External Trade Org. **[24342]**, 1221 Ave. of the Americas, McGraw Hill Bldg., 42nd Fl., New York, NY 10020, (212)997-0400
Japan Farm Machinery Manufacturers Assn. **[IO]**, Tokyo, Japan
Japan Fashion Color Assn. **[IO]**, Tokyo, Japan
Japan Fed. of Bar Associations **[IO]**, Tokyo, Japan
Japan Fed. of Commercial Workers Unions **[★IO]**
Japan Fed. of Composers **[IO]**, Tokyo, Japan
Japan Fed. of Economic Organizations **[★IO]**
Japan Fed. of Ser. and Distributive Workers Unions **[IO]**, Tokyo, Japan
Japan Fed. of Telecommunications, Electronic Info. and Allied Workers **[IO]**, Tokyo, Japan
Japan Film Center **[★IO]**
Japan Film Center **[★10266]**
Japan Fisheries Assn. **[IO]**, Tokyo, Japan
Japan Flax, Ramie and Jute Spinners' Assn. **[★IO]**
Japan Floorball Assn. **[IO]**, Saitama, Japan

Reference to "IO" in place of a book number signifies that the association may be found in the 45th edition of International Organizations.

Japan Fluid Power Assn. [IO], Tokyo, Japan
Japan Flying Disc Assn. [IO], Tokyo, Japan
Japan Foreign Trade Coun. [IO], Tokyo, Japan
Japan Forest Tech. Assn. [IO], Tokyo, Japan
Japan Found. [10264], New York Off., 152 W 57th St., 17th Fl., New York, NY 10019, (212)489-0299
Japan Fur Assn. [IO], Tokyo, Japan
Japan Gas Assn. [IO], Tokyo, Japan
Japan Gastroenterological Endoscopy Soc. [IO], Tokyo, Japan
Japan Gear Manufacturers Assn. [IO], Tokyo, Japan
Japan Geriatrics Soc. [IO], Tokyo, Japan
Japan Gerontological Soc. [IO], Tokyo, Japan
Japan Golf Goods Assn. [IO], Tokyo, Japan
Japan Heterocerists' Soc. [IO], Tokyo, Japan
Japan Hour Broadcasting - Address unknown since 2001.
Japan Image and Info. Mgt. Assn. [IO], Tokyo, Japan
Japan Indus. Design Promotion Org. [IO], Tokyo, Japan
Japan Indus. Designers' Assn. [IO], Tokyo, Japan
Japan Indus. Mgt. Assn. [IO], Tokyo, Japan
Japan Indus. Safety and Hea. Assn. [IO], Tokyo, Japan
Japan Indus. Assn. of Radiation Apparatus [★IO]
Japan Indus. Assn. of Radiological Systems [IO], Tokyo, Japan
Japan Info. Access Proj. [IO], Washington, DC, United States
Japan Info. Access Proj. [10265], 2000 P St. NW, Ste. 620, Washington, DC 20036-6920, (202)822-6040
Japan Info. Tech. Services Indus. Assn. [IO], Tokyo, Japan
Japan Inst. - Defunct.
Japan Inst. of Intl. Affairs [IO], Tokyo, Japan
Japan Inst. of Invention and Innovation [IO], Tokyo, Japan
Japan Inst. of Metals [IO], Sendai, Japan
Japan Inst. of Navigation [IO], Tokyo, Japan
Japan Intl. Center for the Rights of the Child [IO], Osaka, Japan
Japan Intl. Christian Univ. Found. [IO], New York, NY, United States
Japan Intl. Christian Univ. Found. [19929], 475 Riverside Dr., Ste. 439, New York, NY 10115-0439, (212)870-3386
Japan Intl. Food and Aquaculture Soc. [IO], Tokyo, Japan
Japan Intl. Food for the Hungry [IO], Osaka, Japan
Japan Intl. League of Artists [IO], Tokyo, Japan
Japan Intl. Volunteer Center [IO], Tokyo, Japan
Japan Iron and Steel Fed. [IO], Tokyo, Japan
Japan Karate-Do Org. [IO], San Diego, CA, United States
Japan Karate-Do Org. [23563], 3545 Midway Dr., Ste. C, San Diego, CA 92110-4922, (619)223-7405
Japan Legal History Assn. [IO], Yokohama, Japan
Japan Lib. Assn. [IO], Tokyo, Japan
Japan Light Machinery Info. Center of Central New York [24343]
Japan Lime Assn. [IO], Tokyo, Japan
Japan Linen, Ramie and Jute Spinners' Assn. [IO], Tokyo, Japan
Japan Machine Tool Builders' Assn. [IO], Tokyo, Japan
Japan Machine Tool Importers' Assn. [IO], Tokyo, Japan
Japan Machinery Center for Trade and Investment [IO], Tokyo, Japan
Japan Machinery Exporters' Assn. [★IO]
Japan Machinery Fed. [IO], Tokyo, Japan
Japan Magazine Advt. Assn. [IO], Tokyo, Japan
Japan Maillard Reaction Soc. [IO], Nishinomiya, Japan
Japan Mgt. Assn. [IO], Tokyo, Japan
Japan Marketing Assn. [IO], Tokyo, Japan
Japan Marketing Res. Assn. [IO], Tokyo, Japan
Japan Medical Assn. [IO], Tokyo, Japan
Japan Mini Vehicles Assn. [IO], Tokyo, Japan
Japan Natl. Assembly of Disabled People's Intl. [IO], Tokyo, Japan
Japan Natl. Tourist Assn. [★24344]
Japan Natl. Tourist Org. [24344], 1 Rockefeller Plz., Ste. 1250, New York, NY 10020, (212)757-5640

Japan Natl. Tourist Org. [IO], Tokyo, Japan
Japan Neuroendocrine Soc. [IO], Kyoto, Japan
Japan Neuroscience Soc. [IO], Tokyo, Japan
Japan Neurosurgical Soc. [IO], Tokyo, Japan
Japan Newspaper Publishers and Editors Assn. [IO], Tokyo, Japan
Japan-North Amer. Commn. on Cooperative Mission - Address unknown since 2003.
Japan Oil Chemists' Soc. [IO], Tokyo, Japan
Japan Optical Measuring Instrument Mfrs'. Assn. [IO], Tokyo, Japan
Japan Organ Transplant Network [IO], Tokyo, Japan
Japan Overseas Christian Medical Cooperative Ser. [IO], Tokyo, Japan
Japan Overseas Enterprises' Assn. [IO], Tokyo, Japan
Japan Overseas Rolling Stock Assn. [IO], Tokyo, Japan
Japan Paint Mfrs. Assn. [IO], Tokyo, Japan
Japan Palestine Medical Assn. [IO], Tokyo, Japan
Japan Paper Exporters' Assn. [IO], Tokyo, Japan
Japan Paper Importers' Assn. [IO], Tokyo, Japan
Japan Pearl Exporters' Assn. [IO], Kobe, Japan
Japan Pediatric Soc. [IO], Tokyo, Japan
Japan Petroleum Development Assn. [IO], Tokyo, Japan
Japan Pharmaceutical Mfrs'. Assn. [IO], Tokyo, Japan
Japan Philatelic Soc. [IO], Tokyo, Japan
Japan Powder Metallurgy Assn. [IO], Tokyo, Japan
Japan Printing Machinery Mfrs'. Assn. [IO], Tokyo, Japan
Japan Productivity Center for Socio-Economic Development [IO], Tokyo, Japan
Japan Proj. [★IO]
Japan Proj. [★10265]
Japan Public Hea. Assn. [IO], Tokyo, Japan
Japan Racing Assn. [IO], Tokyo, Japan
Japan Radiation Res. Soc. [IO], Nara, Japan
Japan Radiological Soc. [IO], Tokyo, Japan
Japan Railway Engineers Assn. [IO], Tokyo, Japan
Japan Railway Trade Unions Confed. [IO], Tokyo, Japan
Japan Recording Media Indus'. Assn. [IO], Tokyo, Japan
Japan Refrigeration and Airconditioning Indus. Assn. [IO], Tokyo, Japan
Japan Restaurant Assn. [IO], Tokyo, Japan
Japan Road Contractors Assn. [IO], Tokyo, Japan
Japan Robot Assn. [IO], Tokyo, Japan
Japan Rose Soc. [IO], Tokyo, Japan
Japan Rubber Mfrs'. Assn. [IO], Tokyo, Japan
Japan Sailing Fed. [IO], Tokyo, Japan
Japan Scholarship Found. - Address unknown since 1995.
Japan Sci. and Tech. Corp. [IO], Saitama, Japan
Japan Scientists' Assn. [IO], Tokyo, Japan
Japan Secretaries Assn. [IO], Tokyo, Japan
Japan Securities Dealers' Assn. [IO], Tokyo, Japan
Japan Seed Trade Assn. [IO], Tokyo, Japan
Japan Sewing Machinery Mfrs. Assn. [IO], Tokyo, Japan
Japan Sheep Casing Importers' Assn. [IO], Tokyo, Japan
Japan Ship Exporters' Assn. [IO], Tokyo, Japan
Japan Silk Assn. [IO], Tokyo, Japan
Japan Silk and Rayon Weavers' Assn. [IO], Tokyo, Japan
Japan Skating Fed. [IO], Tokyo, Japan
Japan Smoking Articles Corporate Assn. [IO], Tokyo, Japan
Japan Soap and Detergent Assn. [IO], Tokyo, Japan
Japan Soc. [IO], New York, NY, United States
Japan Soc. [10266], 333 E 47th St., New York, NY 10017, (212)832-1155
Japan Soc. for Analytical Chemistry [IO], Tokyo, Japan
Japan Soc. of Applied Physics [IO], Tokyo, Japan
Japan Soc. for Bioscience, Biotechnology and Agrochemistry [IO], Tokyo, Japan
Japan Soc. of Blood Transfusion [IO], Tokyo, Japan
Japan Soc. of Bus. Admin. [IO], Tokyo, Japan
Japan Soc. of Civil Engineers [IO], Tokyo, Japan
Japan Soc. of Clinical Oncology [IO], Kyoto, Japan
Japan Soc. of Cost and Proj. Engineers [IO], Kanagawa, Japan

Japan Soc. of Indus. Machinery Mfrs. [IO], Tokyo, Japan
Japan Soc. of Lib. and Info. Sci. [IO], Tsukuba, Japan
Japan Soc. of Materials Sci. [IO], Kyoto, Japan
Japan Soc. of Mech. Engineers [IO], Tokyo, Japan
Japan Soc. of Medical Entomology and Zoology [IO], Tokyo, Japan
Japan Soc. of Microgravity Application [IO], Tokyo, Japan
Japan Soc. of Nuclear and Radiochemical Sciences [IO], Ibaraki, Japan
Japan Soc. of Obstetrics and Gynecology [IO], Tokyo, Japan
Japan Soc. of Photogrammetry and Remote Sensing [IO], Tokyo, Japan
Japan Soc. of Political Economy [IO], Tokyo, Japan
Japan Soc. for the Promotion of Machine Indus. [IO], Tokyo, Japan
Japan Soc. for the Promotion of Sci. [IO], Tokyo, Japan
Japan Soc. of Radiological Tech. [IO], Kyoto, Japan
Japan Soc. of Refrigerating and Air Conditioning Engineers [IO], Tokyo, Japan
Japan Soc. for Reproductive Medicine [IO], Tokyo, Japan
Japan Soc. of Risk Mgt. for Preventive Medicine [IO], Tokyo, Japan
Japan Soc. for Southeast Asian History [IO], Kyoto, Japan
Japan Soft Drinks Assn. [IO], Tokyo, Japan
Japan Special Libraries Assn. [IO], Tokyo, Japan
Japan Spinners' Assn. [IO], Osaka, Japan
Japan Squash Assn. [IO], Tokyo, Japan
Japan Statistical Soc. [IO], Tokyo, Japan
Japan Surgical Soc. [IO], Tokyo, Japan
Japan for Sustainability [IO], Kanagawa, Japan
Japan Sys. House Assn. [★IO]
Japan Table Tennis Assn. [IO], Tokyo, Japan
Japan Telescope Mfrs. Assn. [IO], Tokyo, Japan
Japan Telework Assn. [IO], Tokyo, Japan
Japan Textile Finishers' Assn. [IO], Tokyo, Japan
Japan Textile Machinery Assn. [IO], Tokyo, Japan
Japan Touch Assn. [IO], Tokyo, Japan
Japan Toy Assn. [IO], Tokyo, Japan
Japan Trucking Assn. [IO], Tokyo, Japan
Japan-U.S. Bus. Alliance - Defunct.
Japan UNIX Soc. [IO], Tokyo, Japan
Japan Valve Mfrs'. Assn. [IO], Tokyo, Japan
Japan Vending Machine Mfrs. Assn. [IO], Tokyo, Japan
Japan Video Assn. [★IO]
Japan Video Software Assn. [IO], Tokyo, Japan
Japan Watch Importers' Assn. [IO], Tokyo, Japan
Japan Weather Assn. [IO], Tokyo, Japan
Japan Whaling Assn. [IO], Tokyo, Japan
Japan Wines and Spirits Importers' Assn. [IO], Tokyo, Japan
Japan Wood Res. Soc. [IO], Tokyo, Japan
Japan Youth Hostels [IO], Tokyo, Japan
Japanese
Aikido Assn. of Am. [23046]
Aikido Assn. of North Am. [23047]
All Japan Ju-Jitsu Intl. Fed. [23577]
Amer. Bonsai Soc. [22483]
Amer. Wagyu Assn. [4250]
Asian Amer. Arts Centre [9553]
Asian Amer. Curriculum Proj. [8598]
Assoc. Koi Clubs of Am. [22437]
Assn. of Teachers of Japanese [8682]
Austrian-Japan Soc. for Sci. and Art [IO]
Bonsai Clubs Intl. [22504]
British Assn. for Japanese Stud. [IO]
European Assn. for Japanese Stud. [IO]
Haiku Soc. of Am. [10861]
Honolulu Japanese Chamber of Commerce [24348]
Inst. of Eastern Culture [IO]
Intl. Aikido Assn. [23048]
Intl. Nippon Collectors Club [21929]
Intl. Soc. for Japanese Philately [22830]
Italian Assn. for Japanese Stud. [IO]
Japan Aikido Assn. U.S.A. [23595]
Japan-America Soc. of Washington, D.C. [10263]
Japan-America Soc. of Washington, D.C. [IO]

A star before a book entry number signifies that the name is not listed separately, but is mentioned within the entry.

Japan Art History Forum [9480]
Japan Convention Bur. [24341]
Japan External Trade Org. [24342]
Japan Found. [10264]
Japan Info. Access Proj. [10265]
Japan Info. Access Proj. [IO]
Japan Intl. Christian Univ. Found. [19929]
Japan Natl. Tourist Org. [24344]
Japan Soc. [10266]
Japan Soc. [IO]
Japanese Akita Club of Am. [22298]
Japanese Amer. Citizens League [19170]
Japanese Amer. Veterans Assn. [21305]
Japanese Chamber of Commerce and Industry of
  Hawaii [24345]
Japanese Chin Club of Am. [22299]
Japanese Natl. Honor Soc. [24521]
Jin Shin Do Found. for Bodymind Acupressure
  [15746]
Natl. Assn. of Japan-America Societies [19171]
Natl. Coun. of Japanese Language Teachers
  [9226]
Natl. Japanese Amer. Historical Soc. [10267]
Netherlands Assn. for Japanese Stud. [IO]
Nichiren Buddhist Assn. of Am. [19555]
Nippon Club [19172]
North Amer. Coordinating Coun. on Japanese Lib.
  Resources [8781]
Occupied Japan Club [22098]
Origami USA [22771]
Shudokan Martial Arts Assn. [23603]
Soc. for Japanese Arts [IO]
Soc. for Japanese Irises [22541]
Soc. for the Stud. of Japanese Religions [20529]
Tanka Soc. of Am. [10871]
U.S. Aikido Fed. [23049]
U.S.-Japan Culture Center [10268]
U.S.-Japan Culture Center [IO]
Urasenke Tea Ceremony Soc. [10269]
Yuki Teikei Haiku Soc. [10874]
Japanese Aerospace Companies; Society of [★154]
Japanese Aerospace Companies; Society of [★IO]
Japanese Agricultural Journalists Assn. [IO], Tokyo,
  Japan
Japanese Akita Club of Am. [22298], c/o Pat Szy-
  manski, Pres., 11313 White Oak Way, Conroe, TX
  77304, (936)441-3205
Japanese Amer. Citizens League [19170], 1765 Sut-
  ter St., San Francisco, CA 94115, (415)921-5225
Japanese-Amer. Cultural Trade Assn. - Address
  unknown since 2006.
Japanese Amer. Curriculum Proj. [★8598]
Japanese Amer. Curriculum Proj. [★IO]
Japanese Amer. Soc. for Legal Studies - Defunct.
Japanese Amer. Soc. for Philately - Defunct.
Japanese Amer. Veterans Assn. [21305], c/o Gerald
  Yamada, Esq., 1666 K St. NW, Ste. 500,
  Washington, DC 20006, (703)503-3431
Japanese Animation Fans Western Australia [IO],
  Perth, Australia
Japanese Animation Network - Address unknown
  since 2005.
Japanese Animation Soc. [IO], Leicester, United
  Kingdom
Japanese Animation; Soc. for the Promotion of
  [9473]
Japanese Assn. for Acute Medicine [IO], Osaka,
  Japan
Japanese Assn. for Amer. Stud. [IO], Tokyo, Japan
Japanese Assn. for Behavior Anal. [IO], Kyoto,
  Japan
Japanese Assn. of Chiropractors [IO], Tokyo, Japan
Japanese Assn. for Death Educ. and Grief Counsel-
  ling [★IO]
Japanese Assn. for Death Stud. and Bereavement
  Support [IO], Tokyo, Japan
Japanese Assn. on Disability and Difficulty [IO],
  Tokyo, Japan
Japanese Assn. of Healthcare Info. Systems Indus.
  [IO], Tokyo, Japan
Japanese Assn. for Infectious Diseases [IO], Tokyo,
  Japan
Japanese Assn. for Legal Philosophy [★IO]
Japanese Assn. of Mathematical Sciences [★IO]
Japanese Assn. of Mineralogists, Petrologists and
  Economic Geologists [IO], Sendai, Japan

Japanese Assn. of Occupational Therapists [IO],
  Tokyo, Japan
Japanese Assn. for Petroleum Tech. [IO], Tokyo,
  Japan
Japanese Assn. of Real Estate Appraisal [IO],
  Tokyo, Japan
Japanese Assn. of Refrigeration [★IO]
Japanese Assn. of Rural Medicine [IO], Tokyo,
  Japan
Japanese Assn. for Semiotic Stud. [IO], Tokyo,
  Japan
Japanese Assn. of Speech-Language-Hearing
  Therapists [IO], Tokyo, Japan
Japanese Assn. of Univ. Women [IO], Tokyo, Japan
Japanese Assn. for Women in Sport [IO], Tokyo,
  Japan
Japanese Bankers Assn. [IO], Tokyo, Japan
Japanese Biochemical Soc. [IO], Tokyo, Japan
Japanese Chamber of Commerce and Industry of
  Hawaii [24345]
Japanese Chamber of Commerce and Indus. of New
  York [24346], 145 W 57th St., New York, NY
  10019, (212)246-8001
Japanese Chamber of Commerce of New York
  [★24346]

Japanese Chin
  Japanese Chin Club of Am. [22299]
Japanese Chin Club of Am. [22299], c/o Trish Swa-
  gerty, Treas., PO Box 90056, Houston, TX 77290
Japanese Circulation Soc. [IO], Kyoto, Japan
Japanese Communist Party [IO], Tokyo, Japan
Japanese Confed. of Port and Transport Workers'
  Unions [IO], Tokyo, Japan
Japanese Consumers' Co-operative Union [IO],
  Tokyo, Japan
Japanese Dermatological Assn. [IO], Tokyo, Japan
Japanese Elec. Wire and Cable Makers Assn. [IO],
  Tokyo, Japan
Japanese Elecl., Electronic and Info. Union [IO],
  Tokyo, Japan
Japanese Fed. of Pulp and Paper Workers' Unions
  [IO], Tokyo, Japan
Japanese Geotechnical Soc. [IO], Tokyo, Japan
Japanese Huntington's Disease Network [IO], Na-
  gano, Japan
Japanese Inst. of Certified Public Accountants [IO],
  Tokyo, Japan
Japanese Irises; Soc. for [22541]
Japanese Marine Equip. Assn. [IO], Tokyo, Japan
Japanese Midwives' Assn. [IO], Tokyo, Japan
Japanese Natl. Honor Soc. [24521], c/o Karla Ves-
  covi, Dir., Lockport Township High School, 1333 E
  7th St., Lockport, IL 60441
Japanese NGO Center for Intl. Cooperation [IO],
  Tokyo, Japan
Japanese Nursing Assn. [IO], Tokyo, Japan
Japanese Olympic Comm. [IO], Tokyo, Japan
Japanese Ophthalmological Soc. [IO], Tokyo, Japan
Japanese Organic Inspectors Assn. [IO], Tokyo,
  Japan
Japanese Org. for Intl. Cooperation in Family Plan-
  ning [IO], Tokyo, Japan
Japanese Orthodontic Soc. [IO], Tokyo, Japan
Japanese Orthopaedic Assn. [IO], Tokyo, Japan
Japanese Peptide Soc. [IO], Minoh, Japan
Japanese Pharmacological Soc. [IO], Tokyo, Japan
Japanese Philatelic Specialists Stud. Club; Intl.
  [★22830]
Japanese Physical Therapy Assn. [IO], Tokyo, Japan
Japanese Psychological Assn. [IO], Tokyo, Japan
Japanese Red Cross Soc. [IO], Tokyo, Japan
Japanese Rubber Workers' Union Confed. [IO],
  Tokyo, Japan
Japanese Shipowners' Assn. [IO], Tokyo, Japan
Japanese Shipowners Assn. - United Kingdom [IO],
  London, United Kingdom
Japanese Soc. of Adlerian Psychology [IO], Osaka,
  Japan
Japanese Soc. of Agricultural Informatics [IO],
  Ibaraki, Japan
Japanese Soc. of Agricultural Machinery [IO],
  Saitama, Japan
Japanese Soc. of Allergology [IO], Tokyo, Japan
Japanese Soc. of Anesthesiologists [IO], Tokyo,
  Japan

Japanese Soc. of Animal Sci. [IO], Tokyo, Japan
Japanese Soc. of Applied Entomology and Zoology
  [IO], Tokyo, Japan
Japanese Soc. of Applied Glycoscience [IO], Tokyo,
  Japan
Japanese Soc. for Bioinformatics [IO], Tokyo, Japan
Japanese Soc. of Breeding [IO], Kyoto, Japan
Japanese Soc. of Certified Pension Actuaries [IO],
  Tokyo, Japan
Japanese Soc. for Chemotherapy [IO], Tokyo, Japan
Japanese Soc. of Cinematographers [IO], Tokyo,
  Japan
Japanese Soc. of Clinical Neurophysiology [IO],
  Tokyo, Japan
Japanese Soc. of Computational Statistics [IO],
  Tokyo, Japan
Japanese Soc. for Dental Hea. [IO], Tokyo, Japan
Japanese Soc. of Developmental Biologists [IO],
  Kobe, Japan
Japanese Soc. for Dialysis Therapy [IO], Tokyo,
  Japan
Japanese Soc. of Electron Microscopy [★IO]
Japanese Soc. of Fertility and Sterility [★IO]
Japanese Soc. of Fisheries Sci. [IO], Tokyo, Japan
Japanese Soc. of Hematology [IO], Kyoto, Japan
Japanese Soc. for the History of Economic Thought
  [IO], Yokohama, Japan
Japanese Soc. of Hypertension [IO], Tokyo, Japan
Japanese Soc. of Internal Medicine [IO], Tokyo,
  Japan
Japanese Soc. of Legal Medicine [IO], Tokyo, Japan
Japanese Soc. of Limnology [IO], Osaka, Japan
Japanese Soc. of Medical Imaging Tech. [IO], Tokyo,
  Japan
Japanese Soc. of Microscopy [IO], Tokyo, Japan
Japanese Soc. of Nephrology [IO], Tokyo, Japan
Japanese Soc. of Neurology [IO], Tokyo, Japan
Japanese Soc. of Nuclear Medicine [IO], Tokyo,
  Japan
Japanese Soc. of Pathology [IO], Tokyo, Japan
Japanese Soc. of Pharmacognosy [IO], Tokyo,
  Japan
Japanese Soc. of Plant Physiologists [IO], Kyoto,
  Japan
Japanese Soc. for Plant Systematics [IO], Fuku-
  shima, Japan
Japanese Soc. of Psychiatry and Neurology [IO],
  Tokyo, Japan
Japanese Soc. of Snow and Ice [IO], Tokyo, Japan
Japanese Soc. of Social Psychology [IO], Tokyo,
  Japan
Japanese Soc. of Soil Sci. and Plant Nutrition [IO],
  Tokyo, Japan
Japanese Soc. for the Stud. of Educ. [IO], Tokyo,
  Japan
Japanese Soc. for Theatre Res. [IO], Osaka, Japan
Japanese Soc. for Tissue Engg. [IO], Kobe, Japan
Japanese Soc. of Tribologists [IO], Tokyo, Japan
Japanese Soc. of Tropical Medicine [IO], Nagasaki,
  Japan
Japanese Soc. of Veterinary Sci. [IO], Tokyo, Japan
Japanese Sociological Soc. [IO], Tokyo, Japan
Japanese Spaniel Club of Am. [★22299]
Japanese Standards Assn. [IO], Tokyo, Japan
Japanese Sword Soc. of the U.S. [IO], Albuquerque,
  NM, United States
Japanese Sword Soc. of the U.S. [21537], PO Box
  513, Albuquerque, NM 87103-0513
Japanese Tenants Assn. [IO], Tokyo, Japan
Japanese Urological Assn. [IO], Tokyo, Japan
JAPOS Study Group - Defunct.
Jar Assn; Amer. Cookie [22577]
Jar Collectors; Soc. of Tobacco [21936]
JARC [12570], 30301 Northwestern Hwy., Ste. 100,
  Farmington Hills, MI 48334, (248)538-6611
Jardine Clan Soc. [IO], Lindsay, ON, Canada
Jared Martin Fan Club - Defunct.
Jargon Press [★9958]
Jargon Soc. [9958], PO Box 15458, Winston-Salem,
  NC 27113
Jarrett Fan Club; Dale [25003]
Jason Fan Club; Intl. Sybil [24746]
Jathika Pusthakala Ha Pralekhana Seva Mandalaya
  [★IO]
Javelin Class Assn. - Address unknown since 2004.

Reference to "IO" in place of a book number signifies that the association may be found in the 45th edition of International Organizations.

JAW-Jidoshasoren [★IO]

Jaw Joints and Allied Musculo-Skeletal Disorders Found. [15773], c/o The Forsyth Inst., 140 Fenway, Boston, MA 02115-3782, (617)266-2550

Jaw Stud. Club; Northern Virginia Functional [★14115]

Jay Black and the Americans Fan Club - Defunct.

Jay Robinson Fan Club - Defunct.

Jaycees Intl. [★13044]

Jaycees Intl. [★IO]

Jaycees; U.S. [★24390]

Jayco Jafari Intl. Travel Club [★22955]

Jayco Travel Club [22955], PO Box 192, Osceola, IN 46561-0192, (800)262-5178

Jazz

Amer. Bop Assn. [9863]

Amer. Fed. of Jazz Societies [10270]

Amer. Pianists Assn. [22709]

Assn. for the Advancement of Creative Musicians [10558]

Collectors Record Club [22712]

The Duke Ellington Soc. [10590]

Helen Forrest Fan Club [24910]

Intl. Assn. of Jazz Appreciation [22713]

Intl. Assn. for Jazz Educ. [8912]

Intl. Assn. of Jazz Record Collectors [22714]

Jazz Journalists Assn. [3127]

Jazz World Soc. [10632]

Jazzmobile [10633]

Natl. Assn. of Rhythm and Blues Dee Jay's [10659]

Natl. Fastdance Assn. [9894]

Natl. Found. for Advancement in the Arts [9587]

New Orleans Jazz Club [10671]

Rhythm and Blues Rock and Roll Soc., Inc. [10692]

Jazz Appreciation; Intl. Assn. of [22713]

Jazz Arts Soc. - Address unknown since 1995.

Jazz Club; New Orleans [10671]

Jazz Composers Orchestra Assn. - Address unknown since 2002.

Jazz Educators; Intl. Assn. of [★8912]

Jazz Fed; European [★10632]

Jazz Fed; Intl. [★10632]

Jazz Interactions - Defunct.

Jazz Journalists Assn. [3127], c/o Arnold Jay Smith, 436 State St., Brooklyn, NY 11217

Jazz Journalists Assn. [IO], Brooklyn, NY, United States

Jazz for Life Project - Defunct.

Jazz-Lift - Defunct.

Jazz Nation [22715]

Jazz Soc; Duke Ellington [★10590]

Jazz World Soc. [10632], PO Box 35, New York, NY 10018

Jazz World Soc. [IO], New York, NY, United States

Jazzmobile [10633], 154 W 127th St., New York, NY 10027, (212)866-4900

JBI Intl. - Jewish Braille Inst. of Am. [16861], 110 E 30th St., New York, NY 10016, (212)889-2525

JBI Intl. - Jewish Braille Inst. of Am. [IO], New York, NY, United States

JCC Assn. [★12473]

JCI Auckland [IO], Auckland, New Zealand

JCI Belgium [IO], Brussels, Belgium

JCI Cameroon [IO], Douala, Cameroon

JCI Dublin [IO], Dublin, Ireland

Jean-Baptiste; Union Saint- [19065]

Jean Piaget Soc. [★16156]

Jean Piaget Soc.: Soc. for the Stud. of Knowledge and Development [16156], c/o Nancy Budwig, Pres., Clark Univ., Dept. of Psychology, 950 Main St., Worcester, MA 01610-1477, (508)793-7250

Jean S. Harris Defense Fund Comm. - Address unknown since 1999.

Jeanette MacDonald Intl. Fan Club [24748], 1617 SW Indian Trail, Topeka, KS 66604-1951, (785)271-7468

Jeanette MacDonald Intl. Fan Club [IO], Topeka, KS, United States

Jeanne Pruett Fan Club - Address unknown since 1995.

Jeannie Seely's Circle of Friends [24917], c/o Ann Allen, 1128 Mayors Dr., Sevierville, TN 37862

Jeanswear Communications - Address unknown since 2006.

JEDEC [1222], 2500 Wilson Blvd., Ste. 220, Arlington, VA 22201-3834, (703)907-7515

Jedi Knights of Orange County [25021], 12291 Meade St., Garden Grove, CA 92841, (760)244-9593

Jedi Knights/Science Fiction [★25021]

Jednota Ceskych Matematiku a Fyziku [★IO]

Jeepster Assn; Midstates [21705]

Jeepster Club; Amer. [21572]

Jeepster Club; Willys Overland [21818]

Jeff Carson Intl. Fan Club [24918], PO Box 1332, Franklin, TN 37065, (615)321-5080

Jeffers Assn; Robinson [11190]

Jefferson Davis Assn. [11129], Rice Univ., MS 43, PO Box 1892, Houston, TX 77251-1892, (713)348-4990

Jefferson Educational Found. [17273]

Jefferson Equal Tax Soc; Thomas [18720]

Jefferson Found. [17295], 809 Quail St., Bldg. No. 1, Lakewood, CO 80215, (303)982-2210

Jefferson Legacy Found. [9002], PO Box 76, Ripton, VT 05766-0076, (802)388-7676

Jefferson Stud; Intl. Center for [★9003]

Jefferson Stud; Robert H. Smith Intl. Center for [9003]

Jefferson's Poplar Forest; Thomas [10069]

Jeffrey Modell Found. [14939], 747 3rd Ave., New York, NY 10017, (212)819-0200

Jehovah's Witnesses

Jehovah's Witnesses for Animal Rights [11421]

Watchtower Bible and Tract Soc. of New York [20109]

Jehovah's Witnesses for Animal Rights [11421], 1090 Sunnyvale Saratoga Rd., No. 19, Sunnyvale, CA 94087-2513, (408)737-0935

Jehovah's Witnesses Gay Support Group - Defunct.

Jenkins Christian Writers Guild; Jerry B. [20630]

Jennet Registry of Am; Standard Jack and [★4130]

Jennifer Bassey Fan Club - Address unknown since 1990.

Jennifer Burnett Fan Club - Address unknown since 1989.

Jennifer Trust for Spinal Muscular Atrophy [IO], Stratford-Upon-Avon, United Kingdom

Jensen Healey Preservation Soc. [21675], c/o Greg Fletcher, 4 Estrade Ln., Foothill Ranch, CA 92610

Jensen Interceptor Owners Club - Address unknown since 2005.

Jeofizik Muhendisleri Odasi [★IO]

Jeremiah Greene Family Org. - Address unknown since 2004.

Jernkontoret [★IO]

Jerome K. Jerome Soc. [IO], Walsall, United Kingdom

Jerry B. Jenkins Christian Writers Guild [20630], 5525 N Union Blvd., Ste. 200, Colorado Springs, CO 80918, (719)495-5177

Jerry Campbell and Five Star Band Fan Club - Address unknown since 1990.

Jerry Jeff Walker Fan Club [24919], c/o Tried and True Music, PO Box 39, Austin, TX 78767, (512)477-0036

Jerry Reed Fan Club - Defunct.

Jersey

Societe Jersiaise [IO]

Jersey; Assoc. Humane Societies of New [★11366]

Jersey Cattle Assn; Amer. [4230]

Jersey Cattle Club; Amer. [★4230]

Jersey Cattle Registry; Amer. Miniature [4238]

Jersey Chamber of Commerce and Indus. [IO], Jersey, United Kingdom

Jersey; National All- [★4230]

Jersey Touch Assn. [IO], Jersey, United Kingdom

Jersey Wildlife Preservation Trust [★IO]

Jerusalem; Amer. Friends of Boys Town [★13473]

Jerusalem Found. of Am; Boys Town [13473]

Jerusalem Institutions for the Blind [★16863]

Jerusalem Institutions for the Blind [★IO]

Jerusalem Intl. YMCA [IO], Jerusalem, Israel

Jerusalem; Kolel Chibas [20156]

Jerusalem Media and Communications Centre [IO], East Jerusalem, Israel

Jerusalem; Soc. of the Devotees of [★20156]

Jerusalem; United Charity Institutions of [12462]

Jesse Couch Fan Club - Address unknown since 1989.

Jesse Stuart Found. [9674], 1645 Winchester Ave., PO Box 669, Ashland, KY 41105, (606)326-1667

Jessie Ball duPont Fund [12727], One Independent Dr., Ste. 1400, Jacksonville, FL 32202-0511, (904)353-0890

Jessie Smith Noyes Found. [4583], 6 E 39th St., 12th Fl., New York, NY 10016-0112, (212)684-6577

Jesuit Assn. of Student Personnel Administrators [7896], c/o JASPA Newsl. Ed., 2500 California Plz., Omaha, NE 68178, (402)280-2717

Jesuit Center for Social Studies - Defunct.

Jesuit Centre for Social Faith and Justice [IO], Toronto, ON, Canada

Jesuit Colleges and Universities; Assn. of [8052]

Jesuit Conf. [19643], 1616 P St. NW, Ste. 300, Washington, DC 20036-1408, (202)462-0400

Jesuit Educational Assn. [★8055]

Jesuit Educational Assn. [★8052]

Jesuit Missionary Assn; Amer. [★19643]

Jesuit Missions [★19643]

Jesuit Off. of Social Ministry [★13172]

Jesuit Off. of Social Ministry [★IO]

Jesuit Philosophical Assn. [9778], c/o Rev. Joseph Koterski, SJ, Sec., Fordham Univ., Dept. of Philosophy, Bronx, NY 10458, (718)817-3291

Jesuit Philosophical Assn. of the U.S. and Canada [★9778]

Jesuit Refugee Ser. Italy [IO], Rome, Italy

Jesuit Refugee Service/U.S.A. [IO], Washington, DC, United States

Jesuit Refugee Service/U.S.A. [12814], 1616 P St. NW, Ste. 300, Washington, DC 20036-1405, (202)462-0400

Jesuit Res. Coun. of Am. [★8052]

Jesuit Secondary Educ. Assn. [8055], 1616 P St. NW, Ste. 400, Washington, DC 20036-1418, (202)667-3888

Jesuit Seismological Assn. - Defunct.

Jesuit Social and Intl. Ministries [13172], 1616 P St. NW, Ste. 300, Washington, DC 20036-1420, (202)462-0400

Jesuit Social and Intl. Ministries [IO], Washington, DC, United States

Jesuit Student Personnel Administrators; Conf. on [★7896]

Jesuit Volunteer Corps: Northwest [19644], PO Box 3928, Portland, OR 97208-3928, (503)335-8202

Jesuits

Alpha Sigma Nu [24500]

Assn. of Jesuit Colleges and Universities [8052]

Canadian Jesuits Intl. [IO]

Intl. Assn. of Jesuit Bus. Schools [8026]

Jesuit Assn. of Student Personnel Administrators [7896]

Jesuit Conf. [19643]

Jesuit Philosophical Assn. [9778]

Jesuit Refugee Service/U.S.A. [12814]

Jesuit Secondary Educ. Assn. [8055]

John La Farge Inst. [19645]

Jesuits in Communication in the U.S. - Defunct.

Jesus Christ of Latter-day Saints; Genealogical Soc. of the Church of [★21115]

Jesus to the Communist World [★20410]

Jesus; Ex-Masons for [19795]

Jesus to the Iron Curtain [★20410]

Jesus; Saints Alive in [20032]

Jet 14 Class Assn. [23196], c/o Dave Michos, Pres., 27180 Edgecliff Dr., Euclid, OH 44132, (216)496-2135

Jet Pioneers Assn. of the U.S.A. - Address unknown since 2001.

Jet Registry; Muntz [21721]

Jet Ski Boating Assn; Intl. [★23976]

Jet Sports Boating Assn. of Serbia and Montenegro [IO], Belgrade, Serbia

Jet Sports Racing Assn. of Great Britain [IO], Penistone, United Kingdom

Jet Tech. Assn; Water [7086]

Jetsons Fan Club; New [25037]

Jett Set Family Assn. - Address unknown since 2001.

Jeune Chambre Economique Francaise [IO], Paris, France

Jeune Chambre Economique de Madagascar [IO], Antananarivo, Madagascar

A star before a book entry number signifies that the name is not listed separately, but is mentioned within the entry.

Jeune Chambre Economique du Mali [★IO]
Jeune Chambre Economique de Maurice [★IO]
Jeune Chambre Economique Suisse [★IO]
Jeune Chambre Internationale - Togo [IO], Lome, Togo
Jeunesse Canada Monde [★IO]
Jeunesse des Chantiers Marocains [★IO]
Jeunesse Etudiante Catholique Internationale [★IO]
Jeunesse Ouvriere Chretienne Internationale [★IO]
Jeunesses Musicales Deutschland [★IO]
Jeunesses Musicales Intl. [IO], Brussels, Belgium
Jeunesses Musicales de Suisse [IO], Geneva, Switzerland
Jewel Heart [19552], 207 E Washington St., Ann Arbor, MI 48104, (734)994-3387
Jeweler's Advisory Gp. [2369], PO Box 17241, Richmond, VA 23226, (804)673-9046
Jewelers of Am. [2370], 52 Vanderbilt Ave., 19th Fl., New York, NY 10017-3827, (646)658-0246
Jewelers of Am; Retail [★2370]
Jewelers Assn; Rocky Mountain [2382]
Jewelers Bd. of Trade [2371], PO Box 6928, Providence, RI 02940, (401)467-0055
Jewelers' Book Club - Defunct.
Jewelers Memorandum Bur. - Address unknown since 1995.
Jewelers Org; Independent [2366]
Jewelers Protective Assn; Amer. [★2374]
Jewelers' Security Alliance [2372], 6 E 45th St., New York, NY 10017, (800)537-0067
Jewelers Security Alliance of the U.S. [★2372]
Jewelers Shipping Assn. [2373], 125 Carlsbad St., Cranston, RI 02920, (401)943-6020
Jewelers and Suppliers of Am; Mfg. [2378]
Jewelers Vigilance Comm. [2374], 25 W 45th St., Ste. 1406, New York, NY 10036, (212)997-2002
Jewellers Assn. of Australia [IO], Crows Nest, Australia
Jewellers Vigilance Canada [IO], Toronto, ON, Canada
Jewellers and Watchmakers of New Zealand [IO], Christchurch, New Zealand
Jewellery and Allied Indus. Training Coun. [IO], Birmingham, United Kingdom
Jewellery Distributors' Assn. of the United Kingdom [IO], Birmingham, United Kingdom
Jewelry
  Accredited Gemologists Assn. [2354]
  Amer. Diamond Industry Assn. [2355]
  Amer. Gem Soc. [2356]
  Amer. Gem Trade Assn. [2357]
  Amer. Soc. of Jewelry Historians [10271]
  Amer. Soc. of Jewelry Historians [IO]
  Amer. Watch Assn. [2358]
  Amer. Watchmakers-Clockmakers Inst. [2359]
  Antique Comb Collectors Club Intl. [21970]
  Antwerp Diamond High Coun. [IO]
  Assn. of Spanish Costume Jewelry Mfrs. and Exporters [IO]
  Bead Soc. of Los Angeles [21975]
  Beyond the Pond.International Frog Collectors Club [21977]
  British Horological Fed. [IO]
  British Jewellers' Assn. [IO]
  British Jewellery, Giftware and Finishing Fed. [IO]
  Canadian Gemmological Assn. [IO]
  Canadian Inst. of Gemmology [IO]
  Canadian Jewellers Assn. [IO]
  Coun. of Fashion Designers of Am. [230]
  Diamond Coun. of Am. [2360]
  Diamond Dealers Club [2361]
  Diamond Mfrs. and Importers Assn. of Am. [2362]
  Diamond Trade and Precious Stone Assn. of America [2363]
  Diamond Trade and Precious Stone Assn. of America [IO]
  Dutch Jewelry, Watch and Clock Makers' Br. [IO]
  Fed. Assn. of the Gem, Stone and Diamond Indus. [IO]
  Fed. of Hong Kong Watch Trades and Indus. [IO]
  Fed. of the Swiss Watch Indus. [IO]
  Gem and Jewelry Export Promotion Coun. [IO]
  Gem and Lapidary Dealers Assn. [2364]
  Gemmological Assn. of Australia [IO]
  Gemological Inst. of Am. [2365]

Gemological Inst. of Am. Alumni Assn. [19173]
Gemological Inst. of Am.: Alumni Assn. [IO]
Gems, Minerals and Jewelry Stud. Unit [22821]
Goldsmiths' Company [IO]
Guild of Philippine Jewellers [IO]
Hong Kong Gemstone Mfrs'. Assn. [IO]
Hong Kong Jade and Stone Manufacturers Assn. [IO]
Hong Kong Jewelers' and Goldsmiths' Assn. [IO]
Hong Kong Jewellery and Jade Mfrs. Assn. [IO]
Hong Kong Jewelry Mfrs. Assn. [IO]
Hong Kong Watch Mfrs. Assn. Ltd. [IO]
Independent Jewelers Org. [2366]
Indian Diamond and Colorstone Assn. [2367]
Intl. Colored Gemstone Assn. [3695]
Intl. Jewelry Design Guild [2368]
Intl. Jewelry Design Guild [IO]
Israel Jewelry Mfrs. Assn. [IO]
Italian Fed. of Goldsmiths, Jewelry and Silver Retailers and Wholesalers [IO]
Japan Clock and Watch Assn. [IO]
Japan Pearl Exporters' Assn. [IO]
Jeweler's Advisory Gp. [2369]
Jewelers of Am. [2370]
Jewelers Bd. of Trade [2371]
Jewelers' Security Alliance [2372]
Jewelers Shipping Assn. [2373]
Jewelers Vigilance Comm. [2374]
Jewellers Assn. of Australia [IO]
Jewellers Vigilance Canada [IO]
Jewellers and Watchmakers of New Zealand [IO]
Jewellery and Allied Indus. Training Coun. [IO]
Jewellery Distributors' Assn. of the United Kingdom [IO]
Jewelry Indus. Distributors Assn. [2375]
Jewelry Info. Center [2376]
Leading Jewelers of the World [2377]
Leading Jewelers of the World [IO]
Mfg. Jewelers and Suppliers of Am. [2378]
Metal Findings Mfrs. Assn. [2379]
Natl. Assn. of Goldsmiths [IO]
Natl. Assn. of Jewelry Appraisers [2380]
Natl. Fed. of Goldsmiths [IO]
Platinum Guild Intl. USA [IO]
Platinum Guild Intl. USA [2381]
Rocky Mountain Jewelers Assn. [2382]
Silver Users Assn. [2728]
Singapore Jewellers Assn. [IO]
Soc. of Bead Researchers - Canada [IO]
Soc. of North Amer. Goldsmiths [9841]
Spanish Jewelry, Silverware and Watches Assn. [IO]
Taiwan Jewelry Indus. Assn. [IO]
Thai Gem and Jewelry Traders' Assn. [IO]
Twenty-Four Karat Club of the City of New York [2383]
U.S. Faceters Guild [1121]
Women's Jewelry Assn. [2384]
Jewelry Club; Vintage Fashion and Costume [22128]
Jewelry Distributors Assn; Watch Material and [★2375]
Jewelry Indus. Coun. [★2376]
Jewelry Indus. Distributors Assn. [2375], 701 Enterprise Dr., Harrison, OH 45030, (513)367-2357
Jewelry Industry Tax Comm. - Defunct.
Jewelry Info. Center [2376], 52 Vanderbilt Ave., 19th Fl., New York, NY 10017, (646)658-0240
Jewelry Mfrs. Assn. - Address unknown since 2003.
Jewelry Mfrs. Guild - Address unknown since 2004.
Jewelry Stud. Unit; Gems, Minerals and [22821]
Jewelry Workers Union; Intl. [★24189]
Jewett Owners Club [21676]
Jewish
  Agudath Israel of Am. [20110]
  Ameinu [19174]
  Amer. Bd. of Rabbis - Vaad Harabonim of Am. [20111]
  Amer. Comm. for Rescue and Resettlement of Iraqi Jews [17943]
  American Committee for Rescue and Resettlement of Iraqi Jews [IO]
  Amer. Conf. of Cantors [20112]
  Amer. Coun. for Judaism [20113]
  Amer. Fed. of Jews From Central Europe [17944]
  American Federation of Jews From Central Europe [IO]

Amer. Forum for Jewish-Christian Cooperation [19887]
Amer. Friends of the Alliance Israelite Universelle [8675]
Amer. Friends of Beth Hatefutsoth [10253]
Amer. Friends of The Hebrew Univ. [8676]
Amer. Gathering of Jewish Holocaust Survivors [17712]
Amer. Guild of Judaic Art [9414]
American-Israel Numismatic Assn. [22723]
Amer. Jewish Comm. [20114]
Amer. Jewish Cong. [20115]
Amer. Jewish Historical Soc. [10272]
Amer. Jewish Joint Distribution Comm. [12464]
Amer. Jewish Joint Distribution Comm. [IO]
Amer. Jewish League for Israel [20116]
Amer. Jewish Philanthropic Fund [12803]
Amer. Jewish Press Assn. [3081]
Amer. Jewish Soc. for Ser. [12465]
Amer. Jewish World Ser. [12829]
Amer. Sephardi Fed. [20117]
Amer. Soc. for Jewish Heritage in Poland [10273]
Amer. Soc. for Jewish Heritage in Poland [IO]
Amer. Soc. for Jewish Music [10550]
Amer. Zionist Movement [20118]
Americans for Peace Now [17935]
AMF Intl. [19988]
AMIT [20119]
Anglo-Jewish Assn. [IO]
Anne Frank Center U.S.A. [17713]
Anti-Defamation League [17091]
Artists for Israel Intl. [9428]
ARZA - Canada [IO]
Assn. of Advanced Rabbinical and Talmudic Schools [8683]
Assn. for Canadian Jewish Stud. [IO]
Assn. of Hebrew Catholics [19575]
Assn. of Humanistic Rabbis [20120]
Assn. of Jewish Aging Services [11277]
Assn. of Jewish Center Professionals [12466]
Assn. of Jewish Chaplains of the Armed Forces [19743]
Assn. of Jewish Family and Children's Agencies [12467]
Assn. of Jewish Libraries [10332]
Assn. of Jewish Religious Professionals from the Commonwealth of Independent States and Eastern Europe [IO]
Assn. of Jewish Sponsored Camps [23275]
Assn. for Jewish Stud. [8684]
Assn. for Jewish Stud. [IO]
Assn. of Orthodox Jewish Scientists [7601]
Assn. of Orthodox Jewish Teachers [9210]
Assn. for Religion and Intellectual Life [19916]
Assn. pour le Retablissement des Institutions et Oeuvres Israelites en France [20121]
Assn. for the Social Sci. Stud. of Jewry [8685]
Assn. for the Social Sci. Stud. of Jewry [IO]
Assn. of Yugoslav Jews in the U.S.A. [19175]
Athra Kadisha: The Soc. for the Preservation of Jewish Holy Sites [10274]
AUFBAU Trust [19176]
AUFBAU Trust [IO]
Australasian Union of Jewish Students [IO]
AZRA/World Union for Progressive Judaism North America [IO]
AZRA/World Union for Progressive Judaism North Am. [20122]
Beth Din of Am. [20123]
The Blue Card [12468]
B'nai B'rith [20124]
B'nai B'rith [IO]
B'nai Brith Canada [IO]
B'nai B'rith Intl. [IO]
B'nai B'rith Intl. [20125]
B'nai B'rith International's Center for Jewish Identity [8686]
B'nai B'rith International's Center for Jewish Identity [IO]
B'nai B'rith Senior Citizens Housing Comm. [12469]
B'nai B'rith Youth Org. [20126]
Bnai Zion Found. [19177]
Bnos Agudath Israel [20127]
Brandeis - Bardin Inst. [8687]

Reference to "IO" in place of a book number signifies that the association may be found in the 45th edition of International Organizations.

Brith Sholom [19178]
British-Israel-World Fed. (Canada) [IO]
Campus Ministry Women [19918]
Canadian Coun. for Reform Judaism [IO]
Canadian Found. for Masorti Judaism [IO]
Canadian Friends of Givat Haviva [IO]
Canadian Inst. for Jewish Res. [IO]
Canadian Jewish Cong. [IO]
Cantors Assembly [IO]
Cantors Assembly [20128]
Center for Christian/Jewish Understanding of
    Sacred Heart Univ. [19888]
Center for Jewish Community Stud. [17945]
Center for Jewish History [19179]
Center for Russian and East European Jewry
    [17946]
Center for Russian and East European Jewry [IO]
Central Agency for Jewish Educ. [19180]
Central Conf. of Amer. Rabbis [20129]
Central Conference of American Rabbis [IO]
Central Org. for Jewish Educ. [8688]
Central Rabbinical Cong. of the U.S.A. and
    Canada [20130]
Central Yiddish Culture Org. [10275]
Chabad Lubavitch [20131]
Chicago Action for Jews in the Former Soviet
    Union [17444]
Chosen People Ministries [19998]
Christian Friends of Israel - USA [19777]
Church and Synagogue Lib. Assn. [10348]
CLAL: Natl. Jewish Center for Learning and
    Leadership [20132]
Coalition for the Advancement of Jewish Educ.
    [8689]
Commn. on Outreach and Synagogue Community
    [20133]
Commn. for Women's Equality [17522]
Comm. for the Implementation of the Standard-
    ized Yiddish Orthography [10276]
Concern for Helping Animals in Israel [11383]
Conf. of European Rabbis [IO]
Conf. on Jewish Material Claims Against Germany
    [12470]
Conf. of Presidents of Major Amer. Jewish
    Organizations [20134]
Congregation Bina [10277]
Congregation Shema Yisrael [20135]
Cong. for Jewish Culture [10278]
Cong. of Secular Jewish Organizations [10279]
Consultative Coun. of Jewish Organizations
    [17947]
Consultative Coun. of Jewish Organizations [IO]
Coun. of Amer. Jewish Museums [10500]
Coun. of Archives and Res. Libraries in Jewish
    Stud. [10351]
Coun. for Jewish Educ. [8690]
Coun. for Jewish Educ. [IO]
Coun. of Jewish Orgs. in Civil Service [5567]
Coun. of Jewish Women of New Zealand [IO]
Dysautonomia Found. [15317]
Eleanor Leff Jewish Women's Rsrc. Center
    [10280]
Emunah of Am. [12457]
Emunah Women of Am. [20136]
Emunah Women of Am. [IO]
Emunah Women of Canada [IO]
European Assn. for Jewish Stud. [IO]
European Union of Jewish Students [IO]
Federated Coun. of Beth Jacob Schools [8691]
Fed. of Jewish Men's Clubs [20137]
Found. for the Advancement of Sephardic Stud.
    and Culture [19181]
Free Sons of Israel [19182]
Friends of Israel Disabled Veterans [21166]
Friends of Israel Gospel Ministry [20010]
GesherCity [19183]
Gp. Proj. for Holocaust Survivors and Their
    Children [17716]
Habonim Dror North Am. [20138]
Hadassah, The Women's Zionist Org. of Am.
    [20139]
Hadassah, The Women's Zionist Org. of Am. [IO]
Hadassah WIZO Org. of Canada [IO]
Hashomer Hatzair Zionist Youth Movement
    [20140]

Hebrew Christian Fellowship [20012]
Hebrew Free Burial Assn. [20141]
Hebrew Immigrant Aid Soc. [12471]
Hebrew Immigrant Aid Soc. [IO]
Hillel: The Found. for Jewish Campus Life [20142]
Hineni [10281]
Hineni [IO]
Historical Soc. of Jews from Egypt [10282]
Humanitarian Assn. of Jewish Women [IO]
Inst. for Advanced Judaic Stud. [IO]
Inst. for Computers in Jewish Life [8562]
Inst. for Jewish Medical Ethics [20143]
Inst. for Jewish Policy Res. [IO]
Intl. Assn. of Jewish Vocational Services [9305]
Intl. Bd. of Jewish Missions [20014]
Intl. Catacomb Soc. [10039]
Intl. Coun. of Jewish Women [IO]
Intl. Fed. of Messianic Jews [20255]
Intl. Fed. of Rabbis [20144]
Intl. Fed. of Rabbis [IO]
Intl. Fed. of Secular Humanistic Jews [20086]
Intl. Fellowship of Christians and Jews [20533]
Intl. Network of Children of Jewish Holocaust
    Survivors [17720]
Intl. Org. for Septuagint and Cognate Stud.
    [19522]
Interns for Peace [17736]
Iranian B'nei Torah Movement [20145]
Israel Aliyah Center [20146]
JARC [12570]
JBI Intl. - Jewish Braille Inst. of Am. [16861]
Jesuit Social and Intl. Ministries [13172]
Jewish Assn. for Services for the Aged [11290]
Jewish Bd. of Family and Children's Services/
    Youth Counseling League Div. [13492]
Jewish Book Coun. [9751]
Jewish Chautauqua Soc. [20147]
Jewish Children's Adoption Network [11249]
Jewish Communal Ser. Assn. of North Am.
    [12472]
Jewish Communal Service Association of North
    America [IO]
Jewish Community Centers Assn. of North Am.
    [12473]
Jewish Community of Estonia [IO]
Jewish Coun. for Public Affairs [12474]
Jewish Defense Org. [17948]
Jewish Defense Org. Youth Movement [17949]
Jewish Educ. Ser. of North Am. [8692]
Jewish Educators Assembly [8693]
Jewish Educators Assembly [IO]
Jewish Free Loan Assn. [20148]
Jewish Funeral Directors of Am. [2784]
Jewish Guild for the Blind [16862]
Jewish Historical Soc. of England [IO]
Jewish Inst. for Natl. Security Affairs [17380]
Jewish Labor Comm. [17950]
Jewish Lawyer Guild [20149]
Jewish Natl. Fund [20150]
Jewish Philanthropic Fund of 1933 [12475]
Jewish Publication Soc. [10283]
Jewish Reconstructionist Fed. [20151]
Jewish Restitution Successor Org. [20152]
Jewish Socialists Gp. [IO]
Jewish Storytelling Coalition [10980]
Jewish Student Press Ser. [8694]
Jewish Telegraphic Agency [17951]
Jewish Telegraphic Agency [IO]
Jewish Vegetarian Soc. - North Am. [11068]
Jewish Vegetarians of North Am. [11069]
A Jewish Voice for Peace [19184]
Jewish War Veterans of the U.S.A. - Natl. Ladies
    Auxiliary [21196]
Jewish Women Intl. [20153]
Jewish Women Intl. [IO]
Jewish Women Intl. of Canada [IO]
Jewish Women's Coalition [13430]
Jews Against the Occupation [17952]
Jews for Animal Rights [11422]
Jews for Judaism [20500]
Jews for Morality [20154]
Joint Action in Community Ser. [11803]
JWB Jewish Chaplains Coun. [19751]
Kadima [20155]
Kolel Chibas Jerusalem [20156]

League of Jewish Women [IO]
League for Yiddish, Inc. [20157]
Lederer Messianic Ministries [20019]
Leo Baeck Inst. [10284]
Leo Baeck Inst. [IO]
Louis Finkelstein Inst. for Religious and Social
    Stud. at the Louis Stein Center [19931]
Lubavitch Youth Org. [20158]
Maccabi USA/Sports for Israel [23828]
Machne Israel [12476]
Marcus Center of the Amer. Jewish Archives
    [10285]
Masada/Maccabi Israel Summer Programs
    [20159]
MAZON [12395]
Memorial Found. for Jewish Culture [10286]
Memorial Found. for Jewish Culture [IO]
Men of Reform Judaism [20160]
MERCAZ USA [20161]
MERCAZ USA [IO]
A Messianic Jewish Perspective [20259]
Mirrer Yeshiva Central Inst. [12477]
Mirrer Yeshiva Central Inst. [IO]
Mutual Israelite Assn. - Argentina [IO]
Na'amat U.S.A. [20162]
Nathan Cummings Found. [13125]
Natl. Assn. of Professors of Hebrew [8695]
Natl. Assn. of Temple Administrators [20163]
Natl. Assn. of Temple Educators [20164]
National Association of Temple Educators [IO]
Natl. Center for Jewish Healing [10287]
Natl. Comm. for the Furtherance of Jewish Educ.
    [8696]
Natl. Comm. for Labor Israel [12460]
Natl. Conf. for Community and Justice [19904]
Natl. Conf. of Shomrim Societies [12478]
Natl. Conf. of Synagogue Youth [20165]
Natl. Conf. of Yeshiva Principals [9017]
Natl. Coun. of Jewish Women [20166]
Natl. Coun. of Jewish Women in Australia [IO]
Natl. Coun. of Young Israel [20167]
Natl. Havurah Comm. [20168]
Natl. Inst. for Jewish Hospice [14857]
Natl. Jewish Coalition for Literacy [8795]
Natl. Jewish Comm. on Scouting [13003]
Natl. Jewish Girl Scout Comm. [13004]
Natl. Jewish Medical and Res. Center [16361]
Natl. Museum of Amer. Jewish Military History
    [21312]
Natl. Ramah Commn. [8697]
Natl. Ramah Commn. [IO]
Natl. Religious Partnership for the Env. [19941]
Natl. Yiddish Book Center [10288]
New York Assn. for New Americans [12479]
North Amer. Assn. of Jewish High Schools [8698]
North Amer. Assn. of Jewish High Schools [IO]
North Amer. Assn. of Synagogue Executives
    [20517]
North Amer. Conf. on Ethiopian Jewry [17953]
North Amer. Conf. on Ethiopian Jewry [IO]
North Amer. Fed. of Temple Youth [19185]
North Amer. Levinas Soc. [10817]
Ohr Torah Institutions of Israel [8678]
OK Kosher Certification [20169]
ORT Am. [12480]
ORT Am. [IO]
ORT Canada [IO]
Orthodox Union - Union of Orthodox Jewish
    Congregations of Am. [20170]
Ozar Hatorah [20171]
Pirchei Agudath Israel [8699]
Polish-American-Jewish Alliance for Youth Action
    [13510]
Pomegranate Guild of Judaic Needlework [9837]
Proj. Genesis [8700]
Rabbinical Alliance of Am. [20172]
Rabbinical Assembly [20173]
Rabbinical Assembly [IO]
Rabbinical Coun. of Am. [20174]
Rav Tov Intl. Jewish Rescue Org. [12817]
Reconstructionist Rabbinical Assn. [20175]
Reform Jewish Appeal [20176]
Reform Judaism [20177]
Religious Action Center of Reform Judaism
    [17954]

A star before a book entry number signifies that the name is not listed separately, but is mentioned within the entry.

Religious Action Center of Reform Judaism [IO]
Religious Zionist Youth Movement - Bnei Akiva of the U.S. and Canada [20178]
Remnant Of Israel [20030]
Root and Br. Assn. [IO]
Russian Amer. Jews for Israel [18576]
Scholars for Peace in the Middle East [18070]
Secretariat for Catholic-Jewish Relations [19910]
Sephardic Jewish Brotherhood of Am. [20179]
Sharsheret [13872]
Shomrim Soc. [12481]
Simon Wiesenthal Center [17724]
Soc. for the Advancement of Judaism [20180]
Soc. for the History of Czechoslovak Jews [10289]
Soc. for Humanistic Judaism [20181]
Soc. for Humanistic Judaism [IO]
Soc. of Jewish Sci. [20202]
Soc. of Saint Stephen [20523]
Solomon Schechter Day School Assn. [8701]
StandWithUs [17941]
Struggle to Save Ethiopian Jewry [20182]
Struggle to Save Ethiopian Jewry [IO]
Swiss Comm. for the Jews in the Former Soviet Union [IO]
Tel Aviv Univ.: Amer. Coun. [8679]
Temple Inst. [IO]
Thanks to Scandinavia [8436]
Touro Synagogue Found. [10070]
Toward Tradition [20508]
Tzivos Hashem [10290]
UJA Fed. - Jewish Info. Ser. of Greater Toronto [IO]
Union of Orthodox Rabbis of the U.S. and Canada [20183]
Union for Reform Judaism [20184]
Union of Sephardic Congregations [20185]
Union for Traditional Judaism [20186]
United Charity Institutions of Jerusalem [12462]
United Hebrew Trades - New York Division of the Jewish Labor Comm. [24214]
United Israel World Union [20424]
United Jewish Appeal - Fed. of Jewish Philanthropies of New York [12482]
United Jewish Communities [12483]
United Sons of Israel [20187]
U.S. Holocaust Memorial Coun. [17725]
United Synagogue of Conservative Judaism [20188]
United Synagogue of Conservative Judaism [IO]
United Synagogue of Conservative Judaism Commn. on Jewish Educ. [8702]
United Synagogue Youth [20189]
Unity Coalition for Israel [8672]
Universal Torah Registry [20190]
Volunteers for Israel [17942]
Warsaw Ghetto Resistance Org. [20191]
Women of Reform Judaism, The Fed. of Temple Sisterhoods [20192]
Women's Intl. Zionist Org. - Israel [IO]
Women's Intl. Zionist Org. - Netherlands [IO]
Women's League for Conservative Judaism [20193]
Women's League for Israel [20194]
World Confed. of Jewish Community Centers [IO]
World Confed. of United Zionists [IO]
World Confed. of United Zionists [20195]
World Cong. of Gay, Lesbian, Bisexual, and Transgender Jews [20069]
World Coun. of Conservative/Masorti Synagogues [20196]
World Coun. of Conservative/Masorti Synagogues [IO]
World Fed. of Bergen-Belsen Associations [17726]
World Jewish Cong., Amer. Sect. [17955]
World Jewish Cong., Amer. Sect. [IO]
World Jewish Genealogy Org. [21158]
World Jewish Relief [IO]
World ORT [IO]
World Union of Jewish Students [IO]
Yiddish Theatrical Alliance [11053]
Yiddisher Kultur Farband [10291]
YIVO Inst. for Jewish Res. [10292]
YIVO Inst. for Jewish Res. [IO]

Young Israel Coun. of Rabbis [20197]
Young Judaea [20198]
Young Men's Division-Zeirei Agudath Israel [20199]
Yugntruf - Youth for Yiddish [10293]
Yugntruf - Youth for Yiddish [IO]
Zalman Shazar Center for Jewish History [IO]
Zarrow Families Found. [13197]
Zeirei Agudath Israel [20200]
Zionist Fed. of Great Britain and Northern Ireland [IO]
Zionist Org. of Am. [20201]
Jewish Acad. of Arts and Sciences - Address unknown since 1995.
Jewish Aging Services; Assn. of [11277]
Jewish Alcoholics, Chemically Dependent Persons and Significant Others [13254], 120 W 57th St., New York, NY 10019, (212)397-4197
Jewish Alcoholics, Chemically Dependent Persons and Significant Others [IO], New York, NY, United States
Jewish Alliance of Am; Messianic [20257]
Jewish Alliance; Young Messianic [★20257]
Jewish Anti-Abortion League [18555]
Jewish Appeal of Greater New York; United [★12482]
Jewish Archives; Amer. [★10285]
Jewish Assn; Anglo- [★17947]
Jewish Assn; Anglo- [★IO]
Jewish Assn. of Residential Care [★12570]
Jewish Assn. for Retarded Citizens [★12570]
Jewish Assn. for Services for the Aged [11290], 132 W 31st St., 15th Fl., New York, NY 10001, (212)273-5272
Jewish Blind; New York Guild for the [★16862]
Jewish Bd. of Deputies; South African [★20124]
Jewish Bd. of Deputies; South African [★IO]
Jewish Bd. of Family and Children's Services/Youth Counseling League Div. [13492], 120 W 57th St., New York, NY 10019, (212)582-9100
Jewish Book Coun. [9751], 520 8th Ave., 4th Fl., New York, NY 10018, (212)201-2920
Jewish Book Coun. of the Jewish Community Center Assn. of North Am. [★9751]
Jewish Book Coun; JWB [★9751]
Jewish Braille Inst. of Am. [★16861]
Jewish Braille Inst. of Am. [★IO]
Jewish Camp Info. Services [★23275]
Jewish Center for Immunology and Respiratory Medicine; Natl. [★16361]
Jewish Center Workers; Assn. of [★12466]
Jewish Center Workers; Natl. Assn. of [★12466]
Jewish Chaplaincy; Commn. on [★19751]
Jewish Chaplains of the Armed Forces; Assn. of [19743]
Jewish Chaplains Coun; JWB [19751]
Jewish Charities in Brooklyn; Fed. of [★12482]
Jewish Chautauqua Soc. [20147], 633 3rd Ave., New York, NY 10017, (212)650-4100
Jewish Children's Adoption Network [11249], PO Box 147016, Denver, CO 80214-7016, (303)573-8113
Jewish Coalition; Republican [18530]
Jewish Comm. for Israeli-Palestinian Peace - Address unknown since 2003.
Jewish Comm. on the Middle East [18060], PO Box 18367, Washington, DC 20036, (202)362-5266
Jewish Comm. on the Middle East [IO], Washington, DC, United States
Jewish Comm. on Scouting; Natl. [13003]
Jewish Communal Ser. Assn. of North Am. [12472], 520 Eighth Ave., 4th Fl., New York, NY 10018, (212)532-0167
Jewish Communal Service Association of North America [IO], New York, NY, United States
Jewish Community Centers Assn. of North Am. [12473], 520 8th Ave., New York, NY 10018, (212)532-4949
Jewish Community of Estonia [IO], Tallinn, Estonia
Jewish Community Services of Long Island [★12075]
Jewish Conf. on Soviet Jewry; Amer. [★17448]
Jewish Coun. for Public Affairs [12474], 116 E 27th St., New York, NY 10016-7322, (212)684-6950
Jewish Cultural Clubs and Societies - Address unknown since 1999.

Jewish Cultural Soc. [★IO]
Jewish Defense Org. [17948], PO Box 159, FDR Sta., New York, NY 10150, (212)252-3383
Jewish Defense Org. Youth Movement [17949], PO Box 159, FDR Sta., New York, NY 10150, (212)252-3383
Jewish Educ; Amer. Assn. for [★8692]
Jewish Educ; B'nai B'rith Intl. Commn. on Adult [★8686]
Jewish Educ; Coalition for Alternatives in [★8689]
Jewish Educ; Natl. Coun. for [★8690]
Jewish Educ. Ser. of North Am. [8692], 111 8th Ave., 11th Fl., New York, NY 10011, (212)284-6950
Jewish Educ; United Synagogue Commn. on [★8702]
Jewish Educators Assembly [8693], PO Box 413, Cedarhurst, NY 11516, (516)569-2537
Jewish Educators Assembly [IO], Cedarhurst, NY, United States
Jewish Film; Natl. Center for [9943]
The Jewish Found. for Christian Rescue [★17721]
The Jewish Found. for Christian Rescue [★IO]
Jewish Found. for the Righteous [IO], New York, NY, United States
Jewish Found. for the Righteous [17721], 305 7th Ave., 19th Fl., New York, NY 10001-6008, (212)727-9955
Jewish Free Loan Assn. [20148], 6505 Wilshire Blvd., Ste. 715, Los Angeles, CA 90048, (323)761-8830
Jewish Friends Soc. - Address unknown since 1995.
Jewish Fund for Justice [12776], New York Off., 330 7th Ave., Ste. 1902, New York, NY 10001, (212)213-2113
Jewish Funeral Directors of Am. [2784], 150 Lynnway, Ste. 506, Seaport Landing, Lynn, MA 01902, (781)477-9300
Jewish Genealogical Societies; Assn. of [★21122]
Jewish Genealogical Soc. [21127], PO Box 286398, New York, NY 10128-0004, (212)294-8326
Jewish Girl Scout Comm; Natl. [13004]
Jewish Girl Scout Comm. of the Synagogue Coun. of Amer; Natl. [★13004]
Jewish Guild for the Blind [16862], 15 W 65th St., New York, NY 10023, (212)769-6200
Jewish Healing Center [★10287]
Jewish Historical Soc. of England [IO], London, United Kingdom
Jewish Holocaust Survivors; Amer. Gathering of [17712]
Jewish Homes for the Aged; Natl. Assn. of [★11277]
Jewish Homes and Housing for the Aging; North Amer. Assn. of [★11277]
Jewish Hospice; Natl. Inst. for [14857]
Jewish Hospital/National Asthma Center; Natl. [★16361]
Jewish Hosp. and Res. Center; Natl. [★16361]
Jewish Immigration; Res. Found. for [10469]
Jewish Information Bur. - Defunct.
Jewish Information Soc. of America - Address unknown since 1995.
Jewish Inst. for Natl. Security Affairs [17380], 1779 Massachusetts Ave. NW, Ste. 515, Washington, DC 20036, (202)667-3900
Jewish Inst. for Natl. Security Affairs [IO], Washington, DC, United States
Jewish Joint Distribution Comm; Migration Dept. of the Amer. [★12471]
Jewish Labor Bund - Address unknown since 2007.
Jewish Labor Comm. [17950], 25 E 21st St., New York, NY 10010, (212)477-0707
Jewish Labor Comm; United Hebrew Trades Division of the [★24214]
Jewish Labor Comm; United Hebrew Trades - New York Division of the [24214]
Jewish Lawyer Guild [20149], c/o Bruce N. Lederman, Pres., Cozen O'Connor, 909 3rd Ave., New York, NY 10022, (212)453-3819
Jewish Librarians Assn. [★10332]
Jewish Librarians Assn. [★IO]
Jewish Librarians Task Force - Address unknown since 1994.
Jewish Lib. Assn. [★10332]
Jewish Lib. Assn. [★IO]
Jewish Life; Inst. for Computers in [8562]

Reference to "IO" in place of a book number signifies that the association may be found in the 45th edition of International Organizations.

Jewish Liturgical Music Soc. of America - Address unknown since 1995.
Jewish Loan Fund [★20148]
Jewish Media Service - Defunct.
Jewish Medical and Res. Center; Natl. [16361]
Jewish Men's Clubs; Natl. Fed. of [★20137]
Jewish Military History; Natl. Museum of Amer. [21312]
Jewish Ministers and Cantors' Assn. of America - Address unknown since 2002.
Jewish Museum Soc. - Defunct.
Jewish Museums; Coun. of Amer. [10500]
Jewish Music Alliance - Address unknown since 2006.
Jewish Music Coun. of the Jewish Community Center Assn. of North America - Defunct.
Jewish Music Educators Assn. - Defunct.
Jewish Natl. Fund [20150], 42 E 69th St., New York, NY 10021, (212)879-9300
Jewish Natl. Fund; Found. for the [★20150]
Jewish Nazi Victims Org. of America - Address unknown since 1995.
Jewish Newspapers; Amer. Assn. of English [★3081]
Jewish Occupational Coun. [★9305]
Jewish Occupational Coun. [★IO]
Jewish Orgs. in Civil Service; Coun. of [5567]
Jewish Organizations; Coordinating Bd. of [★20124]
Jewish Peace Fellowship [18215], Box 271, Nyack, NY 10960-0271, (845)358-4601
Jewish Peace Lobby [17614], 817 Silver Spring Ave., Ste. 301, Silver Spring, MD 20910, (301)589-8764
Jewish Peace Lobby [IO], Silver Spring, MD, United States
Jewish Perspective; A Messianic [20259]
Jewish Pharmaceutical Soc. of America - Defunct.
Jewish Philanthropic Fund of 1933 [12475]
Jewish Philanthropic Fund; Amer. [12803]
Jewish Philanthropic Societies of New York; Fed. for the Support of [★12482]
Jewish Philanthropies of Greater New York; Fed. of [★12482]
Jewish Physicians' Comm.; Amer. [★8676]
Jewish Press Assn; Amer. [3081]
Jewish Publication Soc. [10283], 2100 Arch St., 2nd Fl., Philadelphia, PA 19103-4599, (215)832-0608
Jewish Publication Soc. of Am. [★10283]
Jewish Publication Soc; Amer. [★10283]
Jewish Reconstructionist Fed. [20151], 101 Greenwood Ave., Jenkintown, PA 19046, (215)885-5601
Jewish Reconstructionist Found. [★20151]
Jewish Relations; Secretariat for Catholic- [19910]
Jewish Relations; Subcommn. for Catholic- [★19910]
Jewish Relief Comm; Amer. [★12464]
Jewish Residential Care; Parents Assn. for [★12570]
Jewish Restitution Successor Org. [20152], 15 E 26th St., Rm. 906, New York, NY 10010, (212)696-4944
Jewish Retarded; Assn. for [★12570]
The Jewish Right - Address unknown since 1999.
Jewish Science
　Soc. of Jewish Sci. [20202]
Jewish Scientists; Assn. of Orthodox [7601]
Jewish Socialist Verband of America - Defunct.
Jewish Socialists Gp. [IO], London, United Kingdom
Jewish Soc. of America - Defunct.
Jewish Soc. for the Blind - Address unknown since 1995.
Jewish Sponsored Camps; Assn. of [23275]
Jewish Statistical Bur. - Address unknown since 1995.
Jewish Storytelling Coalition [10980], 63 Gould Rd., Waban, MA 02468, (617)244-2884
Jewish Student Editorial Projects [★8694]
Jewish Student Press Ser. [8694], 114 W 26th St., Ste. 1004, New York, NY 10001, (212)675-1168
Jewish Students; World Union of [IO]
Jewish Stud; Coun. of Archives and Res. Libraries in [10351]
Jewish Studies; Institute for [★20167]
Jewish Teachers Assn. - Morim - Address unknown since 2001.

Jewish Teachers; Assn. of Orthodox [9210]
Jewish Telegraphic Agency [17951], 330 7th Ave., 17th Fl., New York, NY 10001, (212)643-1890
Jewish Telegraphic Agency [IO], New York, NY, United States
Jewish Theatre Assn. - Defunct.
Jewish Theatrical Guild of America - Defunct.
Jewish Trust Corp. [★IO]
Jewish Understanding; Center for Christian/ [★19888]
Jewish Understanding of Sacred Heart Univ; Center for Christian/ [19888]
Jewish Vacation Assn. [★23275]
Jewish Vegetarian Soc. - Am. [★11068]
Jewish Vegetarian Soc; Amer. [★11068]
Jewish Vegetarian Soc. - North Am. [11068], PO Box 5722, Baltimore, MD 21282-5722
Jewish Vegetarians [★11069]
Jewish Vegetarians of North Am. [11069], 6938 Reliance Rd., Federalsburg, MD 21632-2722, (410)754-5550
Jewish Visual Artists Assn. - Defunct.
Jewish Vocational Services; Natl. Assn. of [★9305]
A Jewish Voice for Peace [19184], 1611 Telegraph Ave., Ste. 806, Oakland, CA 94612, (510)465-1777
Jewish War Dead; Natl. Shrine to the [★21312]
Jewish War Sufferers; Joint Distribution Comm. for Relief of [★12464]
Jewish War Veterans of Canada [IO], Downsview, ON, Canada
Jewish War Veterans of the U.S.A. [21306], 1811 R St. NW, Washington, DC 20009, (202)265-6280
Jewish War Veterans of the U.S.A. - Natl. Ladies Auxiliary [21196], 1811 R St. NW, Washington, DC 20009-1603, (202)265-6280
Jewish War Veterans, U.S.A. Natl. Memorial [★21312]
Jewish Welfare Bd; Natl. [★12473]
Jewish Women Intl. [20153], 2000 M St. NW, Ste. 720, Washington, DC 20036, (202)857-1300
Jewish Women Intl. [IO], Washington, DC, United States
Jewish Women Intl. of Canada [IO], Toronto, ON, Canada
Jewish Women's Coalition [13430]
Jewish Women's Rsrc. Center [★10280]
Jewish Women's Soc. of Azerbaijan [★IO]
Jewish Workers in Palestine; Natl. Labor Comm. for the [★12460]
Jewish Youth Educ. in the Middle East and North Africa; Soc. for [★20171]
Jewry; Amer. Jewish Conf. on Soviet [★17448]
Jewry; Assn. of the Sociological Stud. of [★8685]
Jewry; Natl. Conf. on Soviet [★17448]
Jewry; Student Struggle for Soviet [17451]
Jews Against the Occupation [17952], PO Box 494, Prince St. Sta., New York, NY 10012, (212)539-6683
Jews; Amer. Bd. of Missions to the [★19998]
Jews; Amer. Fed. of Polish [19302]
Jews, Amer. Sect; World Fed. of Polish [★19302]
Jews for Animal Rights [11422], 255 Humphrey St., Marblehead, MA 01945, (781)631-7601
Jews; Board of Deputies of British [★20124]
Jews; Board of Deputies of British [★IO]
Jew's Harp Guild [10634], 69954 Hidden Valley Ln., Cove, OR 97824
Jews; Intl. Fed. of Secular Humanistic [20086]
Jews for Jesus [20256], 60 Haight St., San Francisco, CA 94102-5802, (415)864-2600
Jews for Jesus [IO], San Francisco, CA, United States
Jews for Jews - Defunct.
Jews for Judaism [20500], c/o Rabbi Bentzion Kravitz, Dir., PO Box 351235, Los Angeles, CA 90035-1235, (310)556-3344
Jews for Judaism [IO], Los Angeles, CA, United States
Jews for Morality [20154], Gravesend Sta., PO Box 262, Brooklyn, NY 11223
Jews; Natl. Conf. of Christians and [★19904]
Jews for the Preservation of Firearms Ownership [17122], PO Box 270143, Hartford, WI 53027, (262)673-9745
Jews in Russia, Ukraine, the Baltic States and Eurasia; NCSJ: Advocates on Behalf of [17448]

Jews; Union of Councils for Soviet [★17452]
Jews in the U.S; Fed. of Polish [★19302]
JFK Assassination Information Center - Address unknown since 1999.
JIAP [★10265]
JIAP [★IO]
JILA [7503], c/o Univ. of Colorado, Box 440 UCB, Boulder, CO 80309-0440, (303)492-7789
Jim Beam Bottle and Specialties Clubs; Natl. Assn. of [★21889]
Jim Hubbard Fan Club [24920], c/o Kim Davis, Pres., 5361 Opportunity Dr., Crestview, FL 32539
Jim and Jesse Fan Club - Defunct.
Jim Marlboro Intl. Fan Club - Address unknown since 2004.
Jim Smith Soc. [19377], c/o East Berlin Jim, 256 Lake Meade Dr., East Berlin, PA 17316, (985)384-0790
Jim Smith Soc. [IO], East Berlin, PA, United States
Jimi Hendrix Info. Mgt. Inst. [24921], 3369 Morgan St., West Lafayette, IN 47906, (765)464-3175
Jimmie Dale Fan Club - Address unknown since 1989.
Jimmy C. Newman Fan CLub - Address unknown since 1999.
Jimmy Connors Fan Club - Defunct.
Jimmy Kish "The Flying Cowboy" Fan Club [24922], PO Box 140316, Nashville, TN 37214, (615)889-6675
Jimmy Murphy Fan Club - Address unknown since 1995.
Jimmy Wakely Fan Club - Defunct.
Jim's Neighbors - Address unknown since 1995.
Jin Shin Do Found. for Bodymind Acupressure [15746], PO Box 416, Idyllwild, CA 92549, (951)659-5707
Jin Shin Do Foundation for Bodymind Acupressure [IO], Idyllwild, CA, United States
Jiu Jitsu Black Belt Fed. of the U.S. of America - Address unknown since 2002.
J.N. "Ding" Darling Found. - Defunct.
Joan B. Kroc Inst. for Intl. Peace Stud. [18216], PO Box 639, Notre Dame, IN 46556-0639, (574)631-6970
Joan B. Kroc Institute for International Peace Studies [IO], Notre Dame, IN, United States
Joan Jett Fan Club - Address unknown since 1989.
Joan Lunden Fan Club - Defunct.
Joanie Dale Fan Club - Address unknown since 1989.
Joaquim Nabuco Found. [IO], Recife, Brazil
Job Accommodation Network [11955], PO Box 6080, Morgantown, WV 26506-6080, (304)293-7186
Job Corps Alumni Assn; Natl. [12093]
A Job is a Right Campaign [12083], PO Box 06053, Milwaukee, WI 53206, (414)374-1034
Job Shops Assn; Mass Finishing [1473]
Jobbers Assn; Appliance Parts [★263]
Jobbers Assn; Elecl. Supply [★1190]
Jobbers Assn; Northern Sash and Door [★600]
Jobbers Assn; Southern Sash and Door [★600]
Jobbers Coun; Natl. [★2943]
JOBCAP [★6063]
Jobs for America's Graduates [12084], 1729 King St., Ste. 100, Alexandria, VA 22314, (703)684-9479
Job's Daughters [★19239]
Job's Daughters [★IO]
Job's Daughters Intl. [★IO]
Job's Daughters Intl. [★19239]
Job's Daughters, Supreme Guardian Coun; Intl. Order of [19239]
Jobs in Energy - Defunct.
Jobs for the Future [12085], 88 Broad St., Boston, MA 02110, (617)728-4446
Jobs for Older Women Action Project - Defunct.
Jobs, Peace, and Freedom in the Americas; Coalition for [★18463]
Jobs for Progress Natl; SER - [12100]
Jobs for Progress; SER - [★12100]
Jobs for Survival Program [★12780]
Jobs for Veterans Natl. Comm. - Defunct.
Jobs With Justice [18827], 1325 Massachusetts Ave. NW, Ste. 200, Washington, DC 20005, (202)393-1044
The Jockey Club [23502], 821 Corporate Dr., Lexington, KY 40503, (859)224-2700

A star before a book entry number signifies that the name is not listed separately, but is mentioned within the entry.

Jockey Club [IO], London, United Kingdom
Jockey Club; Arabian [23494]
Jockey Club Argentina [IO], Buenos Aires, Argentina
Jockey Club of Canada [IO], Etobicoke, ON, Canada
Jockey Club Ceske Republiky [★IO]
Jockey Club Czech Republic [IO], Prague, Czech Republic
Jockey Club Res. Found. [★4886]
Jockey Club Res. Found; Grayson- [4886]
Jockey Club Royal de Belgique [IO], Brussels, Belgium
Jockey Club of Turkey [IO], Istanbul, Turkey
Jockey Clube de Macau [★IO]
Jockey's Community Fund and Guild [★23503]
Jockeys' Guild [23503], PO Box 150, Monrovia, CA 91017-0150, (626)305-5605
Joe Diffie Fan Club [24923], PO Box 479, Velma, OK 73491-0479, (580)444-2315
Joe Gallison Fan Club - Address unknown since 2001.
Joe Stampley Fan Club - Defunct.
Joe Waters Fan Club - Defunct.
Joey Lawrence Fan Club - Defunct.
Joggers Assn; Amer. Medical [★23650]
Jogging Assn; Natl. [★23651]
Johan Andreas Scheible Family Assn. - Address unknown since 2002.
Johann Frederick Mouser Family Org. [20959]
Johann Strauss Soc. of Great Britain [IO], Caterham, United Kingdom
Johannes Schwalm Historical Assn. [21128], PO Box 127, Scotland, PA 17254-0127
Johannesburg Metropolitan Chamber of Commerce and Indus. [IO], Johannesburg, Republic of South Africa
John A. Andrew Clinical Soc. - Defunct.
John A. Hartford Found. [11291], 55 E 59th St., 16th Fl., New York, NY 10022-1178, (212)832-7788
John Agar Fan Club - Defunct.
John AIDS Found; Elton [16963]
John Anderson Fan Club - Defunct.
John Augustus Found. - Address unknown since 1999.
John Berry's Fan Club [24924], c/o Clear Sky Records, Inc., 1720 Epps Bridge Rd., Ste. 108, Athens, GA 30606, (615)297-7002
John Birch Soc. [17274], PO Box 8040, Appleton, WI 54912, (920)749-3780
John Bosher Family Org. [20960]
John Brown Anti-Klan Comm. - Defunct.
John Burroughs Assn. [7362], c/o Lisa Breslof, Sec., 15 W 77th St., New York, NY 10024-5192, (212)769-5169
John Burroughs Memorial Assn. [★7362]
John Carver Family Org. [20961], c/o Jay G. Burrup, Genealogist, 6602 W King Valley Rd., West Valley City, UT 84128-4217, (801)250-9017
John Clare Soc. [IO], Ely, United Kingdom
John Clough Genealogical Soc. [20962], c/o John R. Clough, Treas., PO Box 242, Harwich, MA 02645
John Conlee Fan Club - Address unknown since 2003.
John Denver Early Warning Network - Address unknown since 1999.
John Denver Heart to Heart Fan Club [★24909]
John Denver; Hearts in Harmony - World Family of [24909]
John Dewey Soc. [8272], c/o Dr. Robert C. Morris, Sec.-Treas., Educational Leadership, Univ. of West Georgia, Carrollton, GA 30118, (678)839-6132
John the Divine; Fellowship of St. [19882]
John and Elizabeth Curtis/Curtiss Soc. [★20876]
John Ericsson Soc. [11130], c/o Mr. Leif Brisfjord, Pres., 5 E 48th St., New York, NY 10017, (973)464-2038
John F. Kennedy Center Dakar [IO], Dakar, Senegal
John F. Kennedy First Day Cover Stud. Unit [22835]
John F. Kennedy Lib. Found. [10365], Columbia Point, Boston, MA 02125, (617)514-1600
John F. Kennedy Philatelic Soc. - Address unknown since 2008.
John F. Kennedy Res. Found. for Mental Health - Defunct.
John Fricke Fan Club - Defunct.
John Gabriel Fan Club - Defunct.

John Gary Intl. Fan Club [24925], 7 Briarwood Cir., Richardson, TX 75080
John Gary International Fan Club [IO], Richardson, TX, United States
John Gary Memorial Fan Club [★IO]
John Gary Memorial Fan Club [★24925]
John Gray Intl. Fan Club [★24925]
John Gray Intl. Fan Club [★IO]
John Hall and Mary Bates Family Org. - Defunct.
John Hampden Soc. [IO], High Wycombe, United Kingdom
John Henry Cardinal Newman Honorary Soc. - Defunct.
John Howard Assn. [11874], 300 W Adams St., Ste. 423, Chicago, IL 60606, (312)782-1901
John Innes Mfrs. Assn. [IO], Harrogate, United Kingdom
John La Farge Inst. [19645], 106 W 56th St., New York, NY 10019-3803, (212)581-4640
John Libby Family Assn. [20963], c/o Patricia Libbey Davis, Sec., 195 Deacon Haynes Rd., Concord, MA 01742-4711, (978)369-6250
John M. Olin Found. [12047]
John Marshall Found. [10042], c/o Lynn Brackenridge, Exec. Dir., 209 W Franklin St., Richmond, VA 23220, (804)775-0861
John McLaren Soc. - Defunct.
John Mellencamp Official Intl. Fan Club [24926]
John Mellencamp Official Intl. Fan Club [IO], Bloomington, IN, United States
John Milton Soc. for the Blind in Canada [IO], Toronto, ON, Canada
John Milton Soc. for the Blind - USA - Defunct.
John More Assn. [20964], c/o Judith Erikson, Treas., 188 Bay Shore Dr., Plymouth, MA 02360
John Morgan Evans of Merthyr Tydil [20965]
John Muir Inst. for Environmental Studies - Defunct.
John Pelham Historical Assn. [11131], c/o Bill Gilmore, Treas., 210 Old Gabblettville Rd., West Point, GA 31833
John R. Schneider No. 1 Fan Club - Address unknown since 1994.
John Reich Collectors Soc. [22740], PO Box 135, Harrison, OH 45030-0135
John Roger Found. [★12352]
John Roger Found. [★IO]
John S. and James L. Knight Found. [12484], Wachovia Financial Ctr., Ste. 3300, 200 S Biscayne Blvd., Miami, FL 33131-2349, (305)908-2600
John T. Conner Center for East/West Reconciliation - Defunct.
John Templeton Found. [20501], 300 Conshohocken State Rd., Ste. 500, West Conshohocken, PA 19428, (610)941-2828
John Thomas Martin Family Org. [20966]
John Tracy Clinic [14764], 806 W Adams Blvd., Los Angeles, CA 90007, (213)748-5481
John Updike Soc. - Defunct.
John Von Neumann Cmpt. Soc. - Hungary [IO], Budapest, Hungary
John and Walter Cusick Family Assn. - Defunct.
John Wilson Gill Fan Club - Address unknown since 1999.
Johnnie Ray Intl. Fan Club [24927], 220 S 8th St., 4th Fl., Eunice, LA 70535
Johnny Alfalfa Sprout - Defunct.
Johnny Benson Fan Club [24784], PO Box 150619, Grand Rapids, MI 49515-0619
Johnny Bernard Fan Club - Address unknown since 1989.
Johnny Cash and June Carter Cash Intl. Fan Club - Defunct.
Johnny Gatewood Fan Club - Defunct.
Johnny and Jack Fan Club - Address unknown since 1989.
Johnny Len Fan Club [24928], PO Box 1714, Manitowoc, WI 54221-1714, (920)682-4414
Johnny Mathis Aficionados - Defunct.
Johnny Mathis East Coast Fan Club [24929]
Johnny Mathis Intl. Fan Club - Address unknown since 1989.
Johnny Mathis Soc. - Defunct.
Johnny Rodriguez Fan Club - Address unknown since 1995.

Johnny Wright-Bobby Wright Intl. Fan Club; Kitty Wells- [24936]
Johns and Call Girls United Against Repression [13094]
Johns Hopkins Center for Alternatives to Animal Testing [11423], 111 Market Pl., Ste. 840, Baltimore, MD 21202-6709, (410)223-1692
Johnson Family Assn; A.D. [20771]
Johnson Family and Children's Counseling Center; James Weldon [★12785]
Johnson Found; Magic [13175]
Johnson Soc. - Lichfield [IO], Lichfield, United Kingdom
Johnson Soc. of London [IO], London, United Kingdom
The Johnsonians - Address unknown since 1999.
The Johnsons Fan Club - Address unknown since 2001.
Johnston(e) in Am; Clan [20834]
Johnston(e) Clan in Am. [★20834]
Johnston(e) Clan in Am. [★IO]
Joho-Shori Gakkai [★IO]
Join Hands Day [17203], 1315 W 22nd St., Ste. 400, Oak Brook, IL 60523, (630)522-6322
Join Hands - Defunct.
Join Together [18689], 715 Albany St., 580-3rd Fl., Boston, MA 02118, (617)437-1500
Joiners of Am; United Brotherhood of Carpenters and [24032]
Joiners' and Ceilers' Company [IO], Woking, United Kingdom
Joint Action in Community Ser. [11803], 5225 Wisconsin Ave. NW, Ste. 404, Washington, DC 20015, (202)537-0996
Joint Assn. of Classical Teachers [IO], London, United Kingdom
Joint Assn. of Head Masters and Head Mistresses [★IO]
Joint Baltic Amer. Comm. [★IO]
Joint Baltic Amer. Comm. [★17020]
Joint Baltic Amer. Natl. Comm. [17020], 400 Hurley Ave., Rockville, MD 20850-3121, (301)340-1954
Joint Baltic Amer. Natl. Comm. [IO], Rockville, MD, United States
Joint Blood Coun. - Defunct.
Joint Center for Political and Economic Stud. [7526], 1090 Vermont Ave. NW, Ste. 1100, Washington, DC 20005-4928, (202)789-3500
Joint Center for Political Stud. [★7526]
Joint Church Aid - U.S.A. - Defunct.
Joint Commn. on Accreditation of Healthcare Organizations [14888], One Renaissance Blvd., Oakbrook Terrace, IL 60181, (630)792-5000
Joint Commn. on Accreditation of Hospitals [★14888]
Joint Commn. on Allied Hea. Personnel in Ophthalmology [15692], 2025 Woodlane Dr., St. Paul, MN 55125-2998, (651)731-2944
Joint Commn. on Church Music [19973]
Joint Commn. on Competitive Safeguards and the Medical Aspects of Sports [★16483]
Joint Commn. on Correctional Manpower and Training - Defunct.
Joint Commn. on Dance and Theatre Accreditation - Defunct.
Joint Commn. of Orgs. Concerned About Status of Women in the Catholic Church - Defunct.
Joint Commn. on Sports Medicine and Sci. [16483], c/o Eve Becker-Doyle, CAE, Exec. Advisor, 2952 Stemmons Fwy., Ste. 200, Dallas, TX 75247, (214)637-6282
Joint Comm. on Careers in Nursing [★15510]
Joint Comm. on Clinical Investigation Involving Children - Defunct.
Joint Comm. on Contemporary China - Address unknown since 1995.
Joint Comm. on Continuing Legal Educ. - of ALI-ABA [★8758]
Joint Comm. on Grassland Farming [★5165]
Joint Comm. on Health Problems in Education on NEA-AMA - Defunct.
Joint Comm. on Intersociety Coordination - Defunct.
Joint Comm. on Lib. Ser. to Labor Groups; AFL-CIO/ALA [10314]
Joint Comm. on Mortuary Educ. [★8896]

Reference to "IO" in place of a book number signifies that the association may be found in the 45th edition of International Organizations.

Joint Comm. of Orgs. Concerned With the Status of Women in the Church - Defunct.

Joint Comm. of Schools of Journalism [★8703]

Joint Comm. of the States [5445], c/o Natl. Alcohol Beverage Control Assn., 4401 Ford Ave., Ste. 700, Alexandria, VA 22302-1473, (703)578-4200

Joint Comm. of the States to Stud. Alcohol Beverage Laws [★5445]

Joint Comm. on Tall Buildings [★6474]

Joint Comm. on Tall Buildings [★IO]

Joint Coun. of Allergy, Asthma and Immunology [13602], 50 N Brockway, Ste. 3-3, Palatine, IL 60067, (847)934-1918

Joint Coun. in Economic Educ. [★8217]

Joint Coun. on Educational Telecommunications - Defunct.

Joint Coun. of Fire Service Orgs. - Defunct.

Joint Coun. to Improve Health Care of the Aged - Defunct.

Joint Coun. on Intl. Children's Services [11250], 117 S St. Asaph St., Alexandria, VA 22314, (703)535-8045

Joint Council on International Children's Services [IO], Alexandria, VA, United States

Joint Coun. for the Physically and Mentally Disabled - Hong Kong [IO], Hong Kong, People's Republic of China

Joint Coun. for Repatriation - Address unknown since 1995.

Joint Coun. of Socio Economics of Allergy [★13602]

Joint Coun. for the Welfare of Immigrants [IO], London, United Kingdom

Joint Cultural Appeal - Defunct.

Joint Custody Assn. [12011], c/o James A. Cook, Pres., 10606 Wilkins Ave., Los Angeles, CA 90024, (310)475-5352

Joint Defense Appeal - Defunct.

Joint Distribution Comm. [★12464]

Joint Distribution Comm. [★IO]

Joint Distribution Comm. for Relief of Jewish War Sufferers [★IO]

Joint Distribution Comm. for Relief of Jewish War Sufferers [★12464]

Joint Educational Development - Defunct.

Joint Electron Device Engg. Coun. [★1222]

Joint FAO-WHO Codex Alimentarius Commn. [IO], Rome, Italy

Joint Found. Support - Address unknown since 1995.

Joint Govt. Liaison Comm. - Defunct.

Joint Industrial Coun. - Defunct.

Joint Indus. Bd. of the Elecl. Indus. [1030], 158-11 Harry Van Arsdale Jr. Ave., Flushing, NY 11365, (718)591-2000

Joint Indus. Gp. [2306], 1620 I St. NW, Ste. 615, Washington, DC 20006, (202)466-5490

Joint Info. Systems Comm. [IO], Bristol, United Kingdom

Joint Inst. for Nuclear Res. [IO], Dubna, Russia

Joint Labor Mgt. Comm. of the Retail Food Indus. [24059], 711 Jorie Blvd., Oak Brook, IL 60523, (301)942-5400

Joint Mfrs. Assn; Expansion [3030]

Joint Maritime Cong. [★6057]

Joint Media Comm. on News Coverage Problems - Address unknown since 1995.

Joint Natl. Comm. for Languages [10303], 4646 40th St. NW, Ste. 310, Washington, DC 20016, (202)966-8477

Joint Nature Conservation Comm. [IO], Peterborough, United Kingdom

Joint Org. of Nordic Women's Rights Associations [★IO]

Joint Radio Comm. [★IO]

Joint Radio Comm. for the Fuel and Power Indus. [★IO]

Joint Radio Comm. for the Nationalised Fuel and Power Indus. [★IO]

Joint Radio Co. [IO], London, United Kingdom

Joint Rev. Commn. for the Opthalmic Medical Personnel [★8834]

Joint Rev. Comm. on Educ. in Diagnostic Medical Sonography [8837], 2025 Woodlane Dr., St. Paul, MN 55125-2998, (651)731-1582

Joint Rev. Comm. on Educ. in Radiologic Tech. [8838], 20 N Wacker Dr., Ste. 2850, Chicago, IL 60606-3182, (312)704-5300

Joint Rev. Comm. on Educ. for the Surgical Technologist [★15123]

Joint Rev. Comm. on Educational Programs for the EMT-Paramedic [★8833]

Joint Rev. Comm. on Educational Programs for Physician's Assistants [★15972]

Joint Rev. Comm. for the Opthalmic Medical Asst. [★8834]

Joint Rev. Comm. for Opthalmic Medical Personnel [★8834]

Joint Rev. Comm. for Respiratory Therapy Educ. [★16610]

Joint Rev. on Educational Programs for Physician Assistants [★15972]

Joint Schools Comm. for Academic Excellence Now - Address unknown since 1995.

Joint Strategy and Action Comm. - Defunct.

Joint Surgeons; Assn. of Bone and [15763]

Joint Telecommunications Advisory Bd. - Defunct.

Joint Univ. Coun. [IO], Nottingham, United Kingdom

Joint Users Group - Defunct.

Joint Users of Siemens Technologies U.S. [880], 401 N Michigan Ave., Chicago, IL 60611, (312)321-6804

Joint Venture - Defunct.

Joint Venture: Silicon Valley Network [7745], 84 W Santa Clara St., Ste. 440, San Jose, CA 95113-1820, (408)271-7213

Joints and Allied Musculo-Skeletal Disorders Found; Jaw [15773]

Joints; Res. Coun. on Riveted and Bolted Structural [★7712]

Joist Inst; Steel [673]

Jojoba Growers Assn. - Defunct.

Joker; 52 Plus [21955]

Jokewriters Guild [10211]

Jokewriters Guild [IO], Brooklyn, NY, United States

Jon Beryl Fan Club Intl. - Defunct.

Jon-Erik Hexum Fan Club [24749], c/o Alan J. Carell, Sec., 3003 NE Knott St., Portland, OR 97212-3536

Jones Employees Assn; Dow [★24174]

Jones Evangelistic Assn; Larry [★12854]

Jones Family Assn. - Address unknown since 2002.

Jones Railroad Unit - ATA; Casey [22800]

Jones Railroad Unit; Casey [★22800]

Jones "Tom Terrific" Fan Club; Tom 24986

Jongerenwerkgroep voor Sterrenkunde [★IO]

Joni and Friends [11956], PO Box 3333, Agoura Hills, CA 91376-3333, (818)707-5664

Joni James Intl. Fan Club [24818], PO Box 7207, Westchester, IL 60154-7207

Joplin Commemorative Comm; Scott [★10694]

Joplin Found. of Sedalia; Scott [★10694]

Joplin Ragtime Festival Comm; Scott [★10694]

Joplin Ragtime Festival; Scott [★10694]

Jorbrugsakademikernes Forbund [★IO]

Jordan

Jordan Info. Bur. [24349]

Jordan Amateur Athletic Fed. [IO], Amman, Jordan

Jordan Badminton Fed. [IO], Amman, Jordan

Jordan Chap. of Epilepsy [IO], Amman, Jordan

Jordan Exporters and Producers Assn. of Fruit and Vegetables [IO], Amman, Jordan

Jordan Hotel Assn. [IO], Amman, Jordan

Jordan Info. Bur. [24349], 3504 Intl. Dr. NW, Washington, DC 20008, (202)265-1606

Jordan Insurance Fed. [IO], Amman, Jordan

Jordan Is Palestine Comm. - Address unknown since 2003.

Jordan Register [21677], 2099 Pheasant Dr., Yuba City, CA 95993, (530)673-7382

Jordan Squash Assn. [IO], Amman, Jordan

Jordan Tennis Fed. [IO], Amman, Jordan

Jordanian Assn. for Family Planning and Protection [IO], Amman, Jordan

Jordanian Astronomical Soc. [IO], Amman, Jordan

Jordanian Chem. Soc. [IO], Amman, Jordan

Jordanian Natl. Comm. for Women [IO], Amman, Jordan

Jordanian Occupational Therapy Assn. [★IO]

Jordanian Osteoporosis Prevention Soc. [IO], Amman, Jordan

Jordanian Physiotherapy Soc. [IO], Amman, Jordan

Jordanian Soc. for Fertility and Genetics [IO], Amman, Jordan

Jordanian Soc. of Gastroenterology [IO], Amman, Jordan

Jordanian Soc. for Occupational Therapy [IO], Amman, Jordan

Joring Assn; North Amer. Ski [23845]

Jose Carreras Club Vienna [IO], Vienna, Austria

Jose Carreras Intl. Leukaemia Found. [IO], Barcelona, Spain

Jose Carreras Intl. Leukemia Found; Friends of the [13825]

Joseph Campbell Found. [9206], PO Box 36, San Anselmo, CA 94979-0036, (800)330-6984

Joseph Conrad Soc. of Am. [9675], c/o Prof. Mary Morzinski, Ed., Dept. of English, Univ. of Wisconsin-La Crosse, 1725 State St., La Crosse, WI 54601

Joseph Cox and Mary Rue Family Assn. [20967]

Joseph Drown Found. [12051], 1999 Ave. of the Stars, Ste. 2330, Los Angeles, CA 90067, (310)277-4488

Joseph and Edna Josephson Inst. of Ethics [17505], 9841 Airport Blvd., Ste. 300, Los Angeles, CA 90045-5415, (310)846-4800

Joseph Goodbrake Montgomery Family Org. [20968], 5750 Carr Factory Rd., Benton, WI 53803, (608)759-2755

Joseph P. Kennedy, Jr. Found. [12571], 1133 19th St. NW, 12th Fl., Washington, DC 20036-3604, (202)393-1250

Joseph P. and Rose F. Kennedy Inst. of Ethics [17506], Box 571212, Georgetown Univ., Healy Hall, 4th Fl., Washington, DC 20057-1212, (202)687-8099

Joseph Soc. [★IO]

Josephine Porter Inst. for Applied Bio-Dynamics [4104], PO Box 133, Woolwine, VA 24185, (276)930-2463

Josephson Inst. of Ethics; Joseph and Edna [17505]

Joshua Gibbons Family Assn. - Address unknown since 2002.

Joshua Slocum Soc. Intl. [23197], c/o Ted Jones, Commodore, 15 Codfish Hill Rd. Extension, Bethel, CT 06801, (203)790-6616

Josiah Macy, Jr. Found. [14571], 44 E 64th St., New York, NY 10021, (212)486-2424

Joslin Clinic [★14227]

Joslin Diabetes Center [14227], One Joslin Pl., Boston, MA 02215, (617)732-2400

Joslin Diabetes Found. [★14227]

Joubert Syndrome Found. [★14459]

Joubert Syndrome Found. and Related Cerebellar Disorders [14459], 6931 S Carlinda Ave., Columbia, MD 21046, (410)997-8084

Joubert Syndrome Parents in Touch Network [★14459]

Journalism

Accrediting Coun. on Educ. in Journalism and Mass Communications [8703]

Action Coalition for Media Educ. [18026]

Africa News Ser. [16921]

Alliance of Area Bus. Publications [3199]

Amer. Amateur Press Assn. [22910]

Amer. Assn. of Dental Editors [3077]

Amer. Auto Racing Writers and Broadcasters Assn. [23069]

Amer. Jewish Press Assn. [3081]

Amer. News Women's Club [3083]

Amer. Philatelic Soc. Writers Unit [22786]

Amer. Press Inst. [8704]

Amer. Soc. of Newspaper Editors [3086]

Arab-American Press Guild [3087]

Assoc. Collegiate Press [8705]

Assoc. Press [3089]

Assoc. Press Managing Editors [3090]

Assn. of Capitol Reporters and Editors [6181]

Assn. for Commun. Admin. [9154]

Assn. of Directors of Journalism Programs in Canadian Universities [IO]

Assn. for Educ. in Journalism and Mass Commun. [8706]

Assn. of Food Journalists [3094]

Assn. of Hea. Care Journalists [3095]

Assn. of Schools of Journalism and Mass Commun. [7893]

Assn. for Women in Communications [874]

A star before a book entry number signifies that the name is not listed separately, but is mentioned within the entry.

Assn. of Young Journalists [3098]
Auto. Journalists Assn. of Canada [IO]
Canadian Univ. Press [IO]
Carol Burnett Fund for Responsible Journalism [8707]
Catholic News Ser. [3103]
Center for Campus Organizing [18195]
Coll. Media Advisers [8708]
Collegiate Network [8709]
Community Coll. Journalism Assn. [8710]
Dog Writers' Assn. of Am. [3110]
Dow Jones Newspaper Fund [8711]
European Journalism Training Assn. [IO]
Football Writers Assn. of Am. [23430]
Found. for Amer. Communications [17177]
Garden Writers Assn. [22512]
Golf Writers Assn. of Am. [23450]
Gridiron Club of Washington, DC [3114]
Inst. for the Advancement of Journalism [IO]
Inst. for Public Accuracy [18456]
Intl. Center for Journalists [3117]
Intl. Food Info. Coun. [1525]
Intl. Food, Wine and Travel Writers Assn. [3118]
Intl. Labor Communications Assn., AFL-CIO/CLC [3229]
Intl. Soc. of Weekly Newspaper Editors [3125]
Internews Network [18027]
Investigative Reporters and Editors [3126]
Journalism Assn. of Community Colleges [8712]
Journalism Educ. Assn. [8713]
Kappa Tau Alpha [24522]
The Media Inst. [17184]
Military Reporters and Editors [6182]
Natl. Agricultural Communicators of Tomorrow [8714]
Natl. Amateur Press Assn. [22911]
Natl. Assn. of Black Journalists [3129]
Natl. Assn. of Hispanic Journalists [3130]
Natl. Assn. of Real Estate Editors [3132]
Natl. Assn. of Shortwave Broadcasters [541]
Natl. Conf. of Editorial Writers [3136]
Natl. Journalism Center [17634]
Natl. Newspaper Assn. [3140]
Natl. Newspaper Assn. Found. [8715]
Natl. Press Club [3141]
Natl. Press Found. [3142]
Natl. Press Photographers Assn. [3005]
Natl. Sportscasters and Sportswriters Assn. [3144]
Natl. Writers Union [24219]
Newspaper Collectors Soc. of Am. [22092]
Newswomen's Club of New York [3150]
Nieman Found. [8716]
North Amer. St. Newspaper Assn. [18102]
People's News Agency [3155]
Professional Hockey Writers' Assn. [3156]
Proj. Censored [17043]
Quill and Scroll Soc. [24523]
Reporters Network [3160]
Scripps Howard Foundation [8717]
Sigma Delta Chi Found. [24524]
Soc. of Environmental Journalists [8718]
Soc. for News Design [3163]
Student Press Law Center [17194]
Thomas Nast Soc. [9477]
Thomson Found. [IO]
Travel Journalists Guild [3167]
United Amateur Press Assn. of Am. [22912]
United Nations Correspondents Assn. [3168]
United Press Intl. [3169]
U.S. Basketball Writers Assn. [23137]
UNITY: Journalists of Color [3172]
Univ. Photographers Assn. of Am. [8977]
Washington Journalism Center [8719]
White House Correspondents' Assn. [3173]
White House News Photographers Assn. [3018]
William Allen White Found. [9723]
World Media Assn. [18035]
Journalism; Amer. Assn. of Schools and Dept. of [★7893]
Journalism; Amer. Assn. of Teachers of [★8706]
Journalism; Amer. Coun. on Educ. for [★8703]
Journalism; Assn. of Accredited School and Departments of [★7893]
Journalism Assn. of Community Colleges [8712], PO Box 18846, Oakland, CA 94619, (408)864-8588

Journalism Assn; Junior Coll. [★8710]
Journalism Assn. of Junior Colleges [★8712]
Journalism Directors; Natl. Assn. of [★8713]
Journalism Educ. Assn. [8713], Kansas State Univ., 103 Kedzie Hall, Manhattan, KS 66506-1505, (785)532-5532
Journalism; Fund for Investigative [17178]
Journalism Historians Assn; Amer. [8501]
Journalism; Joint Comm. of Schools of [★8703]
Journalism and Mass Commun; Assn. of Schools of [7893]
Journalism; Natl. Assn. of High School Teachers of [★8713]
Journalism; Natl. Assn. of Supervisors and Teachers of High School [★8713]
Journalism Project; Investigative [★17669]
Journalism School Administrators; Amer. Soc. of [★7893]
Journalists
   Amer. Auto Racing Writers and Broadcasters Assn. [23069]
   Amer. Chesterton Soc. [9630]
   Amer. Philatelic Soc. Writers Unit [22786]
   Assn. of Capitol Reporters and Editors [6181]
   Assn. of Hungarian Journalists [IO]
   Assn. of Music Writers and Photographers [10562]
   Assn. of Yiddish Writers and Journalists in Israel [IO]
   Brazilian Press Assn. [IO]
   British Assn. of Journalists [IO]
   European Fed. of Journalists [IO]
   European Journalism Centre [IO]
   Food Editors Club Deutschland [IO]
   Football Writers Assn. of Am. [23430]
   Foreign Correspondents' Club of Japan [IO]
   Foreign Press Assn. - Israel [IO]
   Foreign Press Center Japan [IO]
   Foreign Press in Japan [IO]
   Garden Writers Assn. [22512]
   Golf Writers Assn. of Am. [23450]
   Intl. Alliance of Equestrian Journalists [IO]
   Intl. Assn. of Obituarists [4062]
   Internews Network [18027]
   Jazz Journalists Assn. [3127]
   John S. and James L. Knight Found. [12484]
   Journalists, Authors and Poets on Stamps Stud. Unit [10778]
   Journalists' Union of Moldova [IO]
   Kuwait Journalists Assn. [IO]
   Medical Journalists' Assn. [IO]
   Military Reporters and Editors [6182]
   Natl. Writers Union [24219]
   Newspaper Collectors Soc. of Am. [22092]
   Outer Critics Circle [11037]
   Polish Journalists' Assn. [IO]
   Public Radio News Directors Incorporated [579]
   Reporters Network [3160]
   Sindh Journalists' Network for Children [IO]
   Soc. for Editors and Proofreaders [IO]
   Student Press Law Center [17194]
   Syndicate of Journalists of the Czech Republic [IO]
   Union of Journalists in Finland [IO]
   U.S. Basketball Writers Assn. [23137]
   UNITY: Journalists of Color [3172]
   William Allen White Found. [9723]
   World Media Assn. [18035]
   Zambia Union of Journalists [IO]
Journalists of Am; Chess [3104]
Journalists Assn; Asian Amer. [3088]
Journalists; Assn. of Food [3094]
Journalists Assn; Native Amer. [3147]
Journalists; Assn. of U.S. Chess [★3104]
Journalists; Assn. for Women [3096]
Journalists and Authors; Amer. Soc. of [11158]
Journalists, Authors and Poets on Stamps Stud. Unit [10778], 800 E River Dr., Unit B, De Pere, WI 54115-4159, (920)339-9117
Journalists, Authors and Poets on Stamps Study Unit [IO], Green Bay, WI, United States
Journalists Guild; Travel [3167]
Journalists; Natl. Acad. of TV [3128]
Journalists; Natl. Assn. of Black [3129]
Journalists; Natl. Assn. of Hispanic [3130]

Journalists; Soc. of Environmental [8718]
Journalists; Soc. of Professional [3164]
Journalists' Union of Moldova [IO], Chisinau, Moldova
Journeymen and Apprentices of the Plumbing and Pipe Fitting Indus. of the U.S. and Canada; United Assn. of [★24164]
Journeymen and Apprentices of the Plumbing, Pipe Fitting, Sprinkler Fitting Indus. of the U.S. and Canada; United Assn. of [24164]
Journeymen Stone Cutters Assn. of North America - Defunct.
Jousting
   Natl. Jousting Assn. [23551]
Jove Cambra de Barcelona [★IO]
Jove Cambra De Girona [★IO]
Jove Cambra De Terrassa [★IO]
Jove Cambra D'empresaris de Barcelona [★IO]
Jove Cambra Internacional Igualada [★IO]
Jove Cambra de Lleida [★IO]
Jove Cambra de Manresa [★IO]
Jove Cambra de Reus [★IO]
Jove Cambra de Sabadell [★IO]
Jove Cambra de Tarragona [★IO]
Joves Cambres de Catalunya [IO], Barcelona, Spain
Jowett Car Club [IO], Coventry, United Kingdom
Joy Found. - Address unknown since 1999.
Joyce, James
   James Joyce Soc. [9671]
Joyce Soc; James [9671]
Joyce Soc. of Southern Colorado; James [9672]
Joygerms Unlimited [10190], PO Box 555, Syracuse, NY 13206, (315)472-2779
Joygerms Unlimited [IO], Syracuse, NY, United States
Joyner Family Assn. - Address unknown since 2007.
Jozef Pilsudski Inst. of Am. for Res. in the Modern History of Poland [10878], 180 2nd Ave., New York, NY 10003-5778, (212)505-9077
Jozef Pilsudski Institute of America for Research in the Modern History of Poland [IO], New York, NY, United States
Jubilation - Paul Anka Admiration Soc. - Defunct.
Jubilee 2000 [★IO]
Jubilee Action - UK [IO], Guildford, United Kingdom
Jubilee Res. [IO], London, United Kingdom
Jubilee USA Network [IO], Washington, DC, United States
Jubilee USA Network [17585], 212 E Capitol St. NE, Washington, DC 20003, (202)783-3566
Judaea; Young [★20198]
Judaic Needlework; Pomegranate Guild of [9837]
Judaica Captioned Film Center - Address unknown since 2006.
Judaica Historical Philatelic Soc. - Address unknown since 2003.
Judaism; Combined Campaign for Amer. Reform [★20176]
Judaism; Commn. on Social Action of Reform [★20177]
Judaism; Intl. Fed. for Secular Humanistic [★20086]
Judas Priest Fan Club - Address unknown since 1989.
Jude League; St. [19713]
Judean Soc. - Defunct.
Judge Advocates Assn. [6078], c/o Col. Amy Griese, USAFR, 8109 Overlake Ct., Fairfax Station, VA 22039, (703)474-7691
Judge Assn; Greater North Amer. Color-Bred [★21845]
Judge Convertible Registry; 1971 GTO and [21559]
Judge David L. Bazelon Center for Mental Hea. Law [17123], 1101 15th St. NW, Ste. 1212, Washington, DC 20005, (202)467-5730
The Judge GTO Intl. [21678], 114 Prince George Dr., Hampton, VA 23669, (757)838-2059
Judgement and Decision Making; Soc. for [8041]
Judges; Assn. of Administrative Law [5894]
Judges Assn; Amer. [5892]
Judges Assn. Educ. Fund; Senior Conformation [★22193]
Judges Assn; Greater North Amer. Aviculturist and Cage Bird [★21845]
Judges Assn; Natl. [5913]
Judges Assn; Natl. Amer. Indian Court [5905]

Reference to "IO" in place of a book number signifies that the association may be found in the 45th edition of International Organizations.

Judges Assn; Natl. Gymnastics [23478]
Judges Assn; North Amer. [★5892]
Judges Assn; Senior Conformation [22358]
Judges Conf; Fed. Administrative Law [5899]
Judges, Dept. of Hea. and Human Services; Assn.
of Administrative Law [★5894]
Judges Educ. and Res. Foundation; National
[★5913]
Judges; Found. for Women [★5907]
Judges; Natl. Assn. of Municipal [★5892]
Judges; Natl. Assn. of Women [5907]
Judges; Natl. Coll. of State Trial [★5914]
Judges; Natl. Conf. of Bankruptcy [5909]
Judges; Natl. Conf. of Fed. Trial [5910]
Judges; Natl. Conf. of Special Court [★5911]
Judges; Natl. Conf. of Specialized Court [5911]
Judges; Natl. Coun. of Juvenile Court [★5912]
Judges; Natl. Coun. of Juvenile and Family Court
[5912]
Judicature Soc; Amer. [5893]
Judicial Conduct Organizations; Center for [★5893]
Judicial Coun. of the Natl. Bar Assn. - Address
unknown since 1995.
Judicial Ethics; Americans for the Enforcement of
[12124]
Judicial Reform
Center for Judicial Accountability [17956]
Citizens for Impartial Justice [17957]
Citizens for Law and Order [17958]
Criminal Justice Policy Found. [17959]
Fully Informed Jury Assn. [17960]
HALT - An Org. of Americans for Legal Reform
[17961]
Lawyers for Civil Justice [17962]
Natl. Comm. for Judicial Reform [17963]
Natl. Judicial Educ. Prog. [17964]
Judicial Res. Found. - Defunct.
Judicial Selection Proj. [★6219]
Judiciary
Amer. Judges Assn. [5892]
Amer. Judicature Soc. [5893]
Americans for the Enforcement of Judicial Ethics
[12124]
Assn. of Administrative Law Judges [5894]
Assn. of Reporters of Judicial Decisions [5895]
Canadian Assn. of Provincial Court Judges [IO]
Canadian Inst. for the Admin. of Justice [IO]
Commonwealth Magistrates and Judges' Assn.
[IO]
Conf. of Chief Justices [5896]
Coun. for Court Excellence [5897]
Enforcement Services Assn. [IO]
Equal Justice Works [5898]
Fair Elections Legal Network [5491]
Fed. Administrative Law Judges Conf. [5899]
Federalist Soc. for Law and Public Policy Stud.
[5900]
Fund for Modern Courts [5901]
Inst. of Judicial Admin. [5902]
Intl. Assn. of Judges [IO]
Intl. Assn. of Lesbian and Gay Judges [IO]
Intl. Assn. of Lesbian and Gay Judges [5903]
Intl. Assn. of Supreme Administrative Jurisdictions
[IO]
Intl. Assn. of Youth and Family Judges and
Magistrates [IO]
John Marshall Found. [10042]
Justices' Clerks' Soc. [IO]
Magistrates' Assn. of England and Wales [IO]
A Matter of Justice Coalition [6012]
Natl. Alliance for Family Court Justice [5904]
National Alliance for Family Court Justice [IO]
Natl. Amer. Indian Court Judges Assn. [5905]
Natl. Assn. of Hearing Officials [5906]
Natl. Assn. of State Sentencing Commissions
[5650]
Natl. Assn. of Women Judges [5907]
Natl. Center for State Courts [5908]
Natl. Conf. of Appellate Court Clerks [5629]
Natl. Conf. of Bankruptcy Judges [5909]
Natl. Conf. of Fed. Trial Judges [5910]
Natl. Conf. of Specialized Court Judges [5911]
Natl. Coun. of Juvenile and Family Court Judges
[5912]
Natl. Judges Assn. [5913]

Natl. Judicial Coll. [5914]
People Before Lawyers [5528]
Judiciary Interpreters and Translators; Natl. Assn. of
[5628]
Judiciary; Natl. Coll. of the State [★5914]
Judkins Family Assn. [20969], c/o Kathi Judkins
Abendroth, 1538 NW 60th St., Seattle, WA 98107-
2328
Judo
Amer. Judo Assn. [23552]
Amer. Judo and Jujitsu Fed. [23553]
Judo Scotland [IO]
U.S. Judo [23554]
U.S. Judo Assn. [23555]
U.S. Judo Fed. [23556]
Welsh Judo Assn. [IO]
World Martial Arts Assn. [23616]
Judo Assn; Amateur [★23556]
Judo Assn; Armed Forces [★23555]
Judo Assn; Strategic Air Command [★23555]
Judo Assn; U.S. [23555]
Judo Assn; U.S. Air Force [★23555]
Judo Black Belt Fed. of the U.S.A. [★23556]
Judo Fed; Intl. [IO]
Judo Hall of Fame; National [★23555]
Judo Scotland [IO], Newbridge, United Kingdom
Judson Scott Is Number 1 Official Fan Club -
Defunct.
Judson Welliver Soc. [10127], c/o Gordon Stewart,
Sec., Insurance Info. Inst., 110 William St., New
York, NY 10038, (212)346-5501
Judson Welliver Society [IO], New York, NY, United
States
Judy Fields Fan Club - Address unknown since
1991.
Judy Garland Memorial Club - Defunct.
Juggling
Clowns of Am., Intl. [21951]
European Juggling Assn. [IO]
Intl. Jugglers' Assn. [IO]
Intl. Jugglers' Assn. [23557]
World Juggling Fed. [23558]
Jugoslavia Study Group [22836], 1514 N 3rd Ave.,
Wausau, WI 54401-1903, (715)675-2833
Jugoslovensko udruzenje za plasticnu, rekonstruk-
tivnu i estetsku hirurgiju [★IO]
Juice Assn; Natl. Orange [★510]
Juice Newton Fan Club - Defunct.
Juice Processors; Natl. Assn. of Citrus [★510]
Juice Products Assn. [510], 1156 15th St. NW, Ste.
900, Washington, DC 20005, (202)785-3232
Juice Products Assn. and Processed Apples Inst;
Natl. [★510]
Jujitsu Fed; Amer. Judo and [23553]
Julia Morgan Assn. - Defunct.
Julia Roberts Fan Club - Address unknown since
2002.
Julio - Am. Fan Club [24834], c/o Barbara Rush, 400
Dutch Neck Rd., No. H-8, East Windsor, NJ 08512
Julio; Friends of [★24894]
Julio Iglesias Fan Club; Amer. Friends of [24833]
Julio Iglesias Fan Club - Defunct.
Julio Iglesias Intl. Fan Club; Official [24835]
Julio Intl; Friends of [24894]
Julius A. Thomas Fellowship Program [★8047]
Julius E. Farr Family Org. - Defunct.
Jumel Mansion; Morris- [11137]
Jump Rope Fed; U.S. Amateur [23698]
Jumper Assn; Natl. Hunter [23530]
Jumper Coun; Natl. Hunter/ [23531]
Jumper Futurity; Intl. [23529]
Jumpers-Riggers Assn; Natl. Parachute [★23648]
Jumping Assn; Michigan Barrel [★23743]
Jumping Assn; U.S. Barrel [23743]
JUMV - Jugoslovensko drustvo za motore i vozila
[★IO]
June 4th Found. [★IO]
June 4th Found. [★17062]
June 4th Found. [17063], 733 15th St. NW, Ste.
700, Washington, DC 20005, (202)347-0017
June Carter Cash Fan Club - Address unknown
since 1989.
June Wilkinson Fan Club [24750], c/o Scott Hughes,
Pres., 7901 Iroquois Ct., Woodridge, IL 60517-
3332, (630)985-4714

Juneteenth Observance Found; Natl. [16945]
Jung Found. for Analytical Psychology; C.G. [16147]
Junge Liberalen Bonn [IO], Bonn, Germany
Junge Wirtschaft Osterreich [★IO]
Jungle Cock; Brotherhood of the [23412]
Junior Achievement [8028], 1 Educ. Way, Colorado
Springs, CO 80906, (719)540-8000
Junior Achievement [IO], Colorado Springs, CO,
United States
Junior Achievement of Canada [IO], Toronto, ON,
Canada
Junior Achievement China [IO], Beijing, People's
Republic of China
Junior Achievement Ireland [IO], Monkstown, Ireland
Junior Achievement Russia [IO], Moscow, Russia
Junior Activities Dept. of the Amer. Angus Assn.
[★4275]
Junior Ambassadors - Defunct.
Junior Amer. Citizens [11335], 1776 D St. NW,
Washington, DC 20006-5303, (202)628-1776
Junior Amer. Coin Klub - Address unknown since
1990.
Junior Amer. Horse Protection Assn. - Defunct.
Junior Angus Assn; Natl. [4275]
Junior Art Club [IO], Accra, Ghana
Junior Assn; North Amer. Limousin [4280]
Junior Astronomical Soc. [★IO]
Junior Auxiliaries; Natl. Assn. of [13052]
Junior Beta Club [★24592]
Junior Bluejackets of America - Address unknown
since 1995.
Junior Bowhunter Program - Address unknown since
2001.
Junior Brahman Assn; Amer. [4231]
Junior Brangus Breeders Assn; Intl. [4266]
Junior Catholic Daughters of the Americas - Defunct.
Junior Chamber Austria [IO], Vienna, Austria
Junior Chamber Barcelona [IO], Barcelona, Spain
Junior Chamber Belarus [IO], Minsk, Belarus
Junior Chamber of Commerce; U.S. [24390]
Junior Chamber Cyprus [IO], Lefkosia, Cyprus
Junior Chamber Empresaris de Barcelona [IO], Bar-
celona, Spain
Junior Chamber Germany [IO], Berlin, Germany
Junior Chamber Girona [IO], Girona, Spain
Junior Chamber Igualada [IO], Igualada, Spain
Junior Chamber Intl. [IO], Chesterfield, MO, United
States
Junior Chamber Intl. [13044], 15645 Olive Blvd.,
Chesterfield, MO 63017, (636)449-3100
Junior Chamber Intl. Australia [IO], Montmorency,
Australia
Junior Chamber Intl. - Bangladesh [IO], Dhaka,
Bangladesh
Junior Chamber Intl. - Benin [IO], Cotonou, Benin
Junior Chamber Intl., Bolivia [IO], Cochabamba,
Bolivia
Junior Chamber Intl. - Botswana [IO], Gaborone,
Botswana
Junior Chamber Intl. Brasil [IO], Curitiba, Brazil
Junior Chamber Intl. - Burkina [IO], Ouagadougou,
Burkina Faso
Junior Chamber Intl. Canada [IO], Toronto, ON,
Canada
Junior Chamber Intl. Colombia [IO], Bogota,
Colombia
Junior Chamber Intl. Denmark [IO], Holstebro,
Denmark
Junior Chamber Intl. of Dominican Republic [IO],
Santo Domingo, Dominican Republic
Junior Chamber Intl., Ecuador [IO], Manabi, Ecuador
Junior Chamber Intl. Estonia [IO], Tallinn, Estonia
Junior Chamber Intl. Finland [IO], Pori, Finland
Junior Chamber Intl. - Gabon [IO], Libreville, Gabon
Junior Chamber Intl. - Greece [IO], Piraeus, Greece
Junior Chamber Intl. Hong Kong [IO], Hong Kong,
People's Republic of China
Junior Chamber Intl. Hungary [IO], Budapest,
Hungary
Junior Chamber Intl., Indonesia [IO], Jakarta,
Indonesia
Junior Chamber Intl. Ireland [IO], Dublin, Ireland
Junior Chamber Intl. Island [IO], Reykjavik, Iceland
Junior Chamber Intl. Japan [IO], Tokyo, Japan
Junior Chamber Intl. - Jordan [IO], Amman, Jordan

A star before a book entry number signifies that the name is not listed separately, but is mentioned within the entry.

Junior Chamber Intl. Korea [IO], Seoul, Republic of Korea
Junior Chamber Intl. Latvia [IO], Riga, Latvia
Junior Chamber Intl. Limerick [IO], Limerick, Ireland
Junior Chamber Intl. Lithuania [IO], Kaunas, Lithuania
Junior Chamber Intl. Lleida [IO], Lleida, Spain
Junior Chamber Intl. Malaysia [IO], Kuala Lumpur, Malaysia
Junior Chamber Intl. - Mali [IO], Bamako, Mali
Junior Chamber Intl. - Mauritius [IO], Port Louis, Mauritius
Junior Chamber Intl., Mexico [IO], Mexico City, Mexico
Junior Chamber Intl. New Zealand [IO], Wellington, New Zealand
Junior Chamber Intl. - Nigeria [IO], Lagos, Nigeria
Junior Chamber Intl. Pakistan [IO], Karachi, Pakistan
Junior Chamber Intl., Peru [IO], Lima, Peru
Junior Chamber Intl. Philippines [IO], Quezon City, Philippines
Junior Chamber Intl. South Africa [IO], Pretoria, Republic of South Africa
Junior Chamber Intl. Sweden [IO], Stockholm, Sweden
Junior Chamber Intl. The Netherlands [IO], Alkmaar, Netherlands
Junior Chamber Intl. Tunisie [IO], Tunis, Tunisia
Junior Chamber Intl. Turkey [IO], Istanbul, Turkey
Junior Chamber Intl. Ukraine [IO], Kiev, Ukraine
Junior Chamber Intl. United Kingdom [IO], Grantham, United Kingdom
Junior Chamber Intl. of Venezuela [IO], Valencia, Venezuela
Junior Chamber Intl. Waterford [IO], Waterford, Ireland
Junior Chamber Italiana [IO], Busto Arsizio, Italy
Junior Chamber Manresa [IO], Manresa, Spain
Junior Chamber Namibia [IO], Windhoek, Namibia
Junior Chamber Nepal [IO], Kathmandu, Nepal
Junior Chamber Poland [IO], Katowice, Poland
Junior Chamber Reus [IO], Reus, Spain
Junior Chamber Romania [IO], Bucharest, Romania
Junior Chamber Sabadell [IO], Sabadell, Spain
Junior Chamber Serbia [IO], Novi Sad, Serbia
Junior Chamber Singapore [IO], Singapore, Singapore
Junior Chamber Switzerland [IO], Glarus, Switzerland
Junior Chamber Tarragona [IO], Tarragona, Spain
Junior Chamber Terrassa [IO], Terrassa, Spain
Junior Chamber Thailand [IO], Bangkok, Thailand
Junior Chamber Zimbabwe [IO], Harare, Zimbabwe
Junior Chaplain's Corps [★19855]
Junior Chianina Assn; Amer. [4232]
Junior Classical League [★8095]
Junior Coll. Athletic Assn; Natl. [23843]
Junior Coll. Journalism Assn. [★8710]
Junior Coll. Mathematics Club; Natl. High School and [★24538]
Junior Daughters of Peter Claver [19002], PO Box 8278, Montgomery, AL 36110-0278, (504)821-4225
Junior Engg. Tech. Soc. [8368], 1420 King St., Ste. 405, Alexandria, VA 22314-2794, (703)548-5387
Junior Engg. Training for Schools [★8368]
Junior Golf Assn; Amer. [23444]
Junior Golf Assn; Natl. Pan-American [23459]
Junior Good Will Ambassadors for a Better World [★12142]
Junior Hadassah [★20198]
Junior Hereford Assn; Amer. [★4276]
Junior Hereford Assn; Natl. [4276]
Junior Hollywood Radio and TV Soc. [564], PO Box 16173, Beverly Hills, CA 90209
Junior Honor Soc; Natl. [24513]
Junior Horticultural Assn; Natl. [22530]
Junior Intl. Club - Address unknown since 2001.
Junior Knights of Peter Claver [19003], PO Box 8278, Montgomery, AL 36110-0278, (334)265-3214
Junior League Football; Pop Warner [★23436]
Junior Lodge, Independent Order of Odd Fellows [19297], c/o Sovereign Grand Lodge Off., 422 Trade St., Winston-Salem, NC 27101, (336)725-5955
Junior Naval Reserve of Am. [★20718]

Junior Optimist Clubs [★13045]
Junior Optimist Clubs [★IO]
Junior Optimist Octagon International [IO], St. Louis, MO, United States
Junior Optimist Octagon Intl. [13045], 4494 Lindell Blvd., St. Louis, MO 63108, (314)371-6000
Junior Order, Knights of Pythias [19187], c/o Supreme Lodge Knights of Pythias, 59 Coddington St., Ste. 202, Quincy, MA 02169-4510, (617)472-8800
Junior Paint Horse Assn; Amer. [4828]
Junior Panel Outdoor Advt. Assn. [★99]
Junior Philatelic Soc. of Am. [★22837]
Junior Philatelists of Am. [22837]
Junior Santa Gertrudis Assn; Natl. [4277]
Junior Shag Assn. [9890], c/o Keith Dallas, Pres., 437 Palmer Ct., Eden, NC 27288, (336)635-1353
Junior Shorthorn Assn; Amer. [4233]
Junior Simmental Assn; Amer. [★4248]
Junior Slovak Catholic Sokol [★19365]
Junior State of Am. [8750], 400 S El Camino Real, Ste. 300, San Mateo, CA 94402, (650)347-1600
Junior Statesmen of Am. [★8750]
Junior Statesmen Found. [8751], 400 S El Camino Real, Ste. 300, San Mateo, CA 94402, (650)347-1600
Junior Tennis Found. - Address unknown since 2002.
Junior Town Meeting League - Defunct.
Junior Wireless Club, Limited [★22928]
Junior Writers Unit, Amer. Philatelic Soc. [★22837]
Junkins Family Assn. [20970], c/o Kathy Junkins, 9 Springside Ct., Yardley, PA 19067, (215)428-9491
Junta Civico-Militar Cubana [17366]
Junta Internacional de Fiscalizacion de Estupefacientes [★IO]
Juridisk Radgivning for Kvinner [★IO]
Jurisprudence; Soc. of Medical [15006]
Jurisprudence and State Medicine; Soc. of Medical [★15006]
Jury Assn; Fully Informed [17960]
Jussi Bjorling Soc. - USA [9508], c/o Laura Homonnay-Demilio, 2354 Buena Vista Ave., Pittsburgh, PA 15218
Just Act: Youth Action for Global Justice [12435]
Just Act: Youth Action for Global Justice [IO], San Francisco, CA, United States
Just David - Intl. David Cassidy Fan Club - Address unknown since 2002.
Just One Break [11957], 570 Seventh Ave., New York, NY 10018, (212)785-7300
Just for Openers [22062], PO Box 64, Chapel Hill, NC 27514
Just Plain Folks Songwriting/Musician Networking Org. [2829], 5327 Kit Dr., Indianapolis, IN 46237
Just Think [18852], 39 Mesa St., Ste. 106, San Francisco, CA 94129, (415)561-2900
Just Transition Alliance [24105], 2434 Southport Way, Ste. D, National City, CA 91950, (619)474-4001
Just Transition Alliance [IO], National City, CA, United States
Just World Partners [IO], Edinburgh, United Kingdom
JustAct: Youth Action for Global Justice [18853]
Justice; Ad Hoc Comm. to Bring Nazi War Criminals to [★17719]
Justice for All; And [18639]
Justice; Alliance for [6219]
Justice; Amer. Center for Law and [12901]
Justice; Amer. Citizens for [17083]
Justice of the Amer. Citizens for Justice; Asian Amer. Center for [17094]
Justice; Arkansas Inst. for Social [★11796]
Justice; Center for Community [★5451]
Justice; Center for Correctional [★5451]
Justice; Center For Hea., Env. and [5266]
Justice; Center for Public [18431]
Justice; Center for Stud. in Criminal [11859]
Justice for Children Intl. [★11620]
Justice for Children Intl. [IO], New Haven, CT, United States
Justice; Citizens for Impartial [17957]
Justice; Citizens for Tax [18706]
Justice CH; Juvenile [6363]

Justice; Coalition for Juvenile [5915]
Justice Coalition; A Matter of [6012]
Justice Coalition; Natl. Black [18643]
Justice; Commn. for Social [17108]
Justice Concerns; Maryknoll Center for [★8660]
Justice, Economic Dignity and Independence for Women [18812]
Justice Educ. Fund; Assn. for Public [★18431]
Justice and Equality in Palestine/Israel; Search for [18071]
Justice and Equality in Palestine; Search for [★18071]
Justice Fellowship [11875], 44180 Riverside Pkwy., Landsowne, VA 20176, (703)478-0100
Justice Found. [★17298]
Justice Found. of Am; Natl. [17298]
Justice Found; U.S. [6228]
Justice Fund; Farmworker [12587]
Justice; Holocaust Survivors and Friends in Pursuit of [17719]
Justice Info. and Statistics; SEARCH - The Natl. Consortium for [11892]
Justice; Inst. for [5940]
Justice; Inst. for the Advancement of Criminal [★13262]
Justice Inst; Amer. [11835]
Justice Inst; Economic [6221]
Justice; Inst. for Liberty and [★17108]
Justice; Inst. for Peace and [18209]
Justice; Inst. for Social [11796]
Justice Intl; Center for Law and [6017]
Justice; Jewish Fund for [12776]
Justice; Lawyers for Civil [17962]
Justice Legal Defense and Educ. Fund; Partnership for Civil [17142]
Justice Lobby; NETWORK, A Natl. Catholic Social [18624]
Justice in the Maquiladoras; Coalition for [18610]
Justice and the Media; Leadership Coun. for Mental Hea., [★12031]
Justice; Natl. Assn. of Blacks in Criminal [11877]
Justice; Natl. Catholic Conf. for Interracial [17133]
Justice; Natl. Center for Juvenile [11879]
Justice; Natl. Conf. for Community and [19904]
Justice; Natl. Interfaith Comm. for Worker [★20092]
Justice Network; Africa Faith and [16920]
Justice Now - Address unknown since 2001.
Justice at NYU School of Law; Brennan Center for [6176]
Justice and Peace Commn. of the Hong Kong Catholic Diocese [IO], Hong Kong, People's Republic of China
Justice and Peace; Office of Intl. [★IO]
Justice and Peace; Office of Intl. [★19613]
Justice Res. Assn. [5655], PO Drawer 23557, Hilton Head Island, SC 29925, (843)689-6298
Justice Res. and Statistics Assn. [11876], 777 N Capitol St. NE, Ste. 801, Washington, DC 20002, (202)842-9330
Justice Sciences; Acad. of Criminal [11850]
Justice Sect; Amer. Bar Assn. Criminal [5922]
Justice Statistics Assn; Criminal [★11876]
Justice Stud. Assn. [13109], Mohawk Valley Community Coll., Social Science/Criminal Justice Dept., Utica, NY 13501, (315)792-5653
Justice Stud. Assn; Peace and [18233]
Justice System Training Assn. - Defunct.
Justice; Trial Lawyers for Public [★6227]
Justice; United Church of Christ Ministers for Racial and Social [★20608]
Justice; Vera Inst. of [11895]
Justice for Veteran Victims of the Veterans Administration - Defunct.
Justice Without Borders [6025], PO Box 2400, Madison, WI 53701-2400
Justice Without Borders [IO], Madison, WI, United States
Justice and Witness Ministries; United Church of Christ [20608]
Justice; Women Judges' Fund for [★5907]
Justice Working Group; Eco- [18613]
Justices' Clerks' Soc. [IO], Liverpool, United Kingdom
Justices; Conf. of Chief [5896]
Justin Tubb Fan Club - Address unknown since 2006.

Reference to "IO" in place of a book number signifies that the association may be found in the 45th edition of International Organizations.

JustLife - Defunct.
Jute Assn; Burlap and [3778]
Jute Assn; Jute Carpet Backing Coun. and Burlap and [2266]
Jute Carpet Backing Coun. [★2266]
Jute Carpet Backing Coun. and Burlap and Jute Assn. [2266], c/o Dayton Natl. Sales Off. and Plant, 322 Davis Ave., Dayton, OH 45403, (937)258-8000
Jute Manufacturers Development Coun. [IO], Calcutta, India
Juvenile
    Amer. Juvenile Arthritis Org. [16368]
    Amer. Specialty Toy Retailing Assn. [2385]
    Amer. Youth Work Center [13469]
    Australian Toy Assn. [IO]
    Boys Hope Girls Hope [13472]
    British Toy and Hobby Assn. [IO]
    Canadian Toy Assn. [IO]
    Canadian Toy Testing Coun. [IO]
    Children Now [11575]
    Diaper Ser. Accreditation Coun. [2386]
    Empower Prog. [8945]
    Equitoy [IO]
    Fresh Lifelines for Youth [13484]
    Hong Kong Toys Coun. [IO]
    Intl. Formula Coun. [2387]
    Intl. Org. for Adolescents [11606]
    Intl. Toy Libraries Assn. [IO]
    Japan Toy Assn. [IO]
    Jobs for America's Graduates [12084]
    Juvenile Diabetes Res. Found. Intl. [14228]
    Juvenile Products Mfrs. Assn. [2388]
    Natl. Assn. of Diaper Services [2389]
    Natl. Assn. of Police Athletic Leagues [13496]
    Natl. Child Support Enforcement Assn. [5701]
    Natl. Coun. of Juvenile and Family Court Judges [5912]
    Natl. Court Appointed Special Advocate Assn. [11636]
    Natl. Juvenile Court Services Assn. [5702]
    Natl. Youth Court Center [18854]
    Robert F. Kennedy Memorial [13513]
    St. Law [6035]
    Toy Indus. Assn. [3832]
    Toy Retailers Assn. [IO]
    United League Toy Representatives Associations [3833]
    Voices for America's Children [11662]
    What Kids Can Do [18859]
    Women in Toys [3834]
Juvenile Arthritis Org; Amer. [16368]
Juvenile Court Judges; Natl. Coun. of [★5912]
Juvenile Court Services Assn; Natl. [5702]
Juvenile and Criminal Justice; Center on [5640]
Juvenile Delinquency
    Amer. Youth Work Center [13469]
    Boys Hope Girls Hope [13472]
    Center on Juvenile and Criminal Justice [5640]
    Children Now [11575]
    Coalition for Juvenile Justice [5915]
    Fresh Lifelines for Youth [13484]
    Jobs for America's Graduates [12084]
    Natl. Assn. of Police Athletic Leagues [13496]
    Natl. Assn. of Public Child Welfare Administrators [11629]
    Natl. Commn. on Correctional Hea. Care [14729]
    Robert F. Kennedy Memorial [13513]
    Voices for America's Children [11662]
Juvenile Detention Assn; Natl. [11882]
Juvenile Diabetes Found. [★14228]
Juvenile Diabetes Found. [★IO]
Juvenile Diabetes Found. of Australia [★IO]
Juvenile Diabetes Res. Found. [IO], St. Leonards, Australia
Juvenile Diabetes Res. Found. - Hellas [IO], Athens, Greece
Juvenile Diabetes Res. Found. Intl. [IO], New York, NY, United States
Juvenile Diabetes Res. Found. Intl. [14228], 120 Wall St., 19th Fl., New York, NY 10005-4001, (212)785-9500
Juvenile and Family Court Judges; Natl. Coun. of [5912]
Juvenile Justice CH [6363], c/o Stephanie Bush-Baskette, Prog. Dir., School of Criminology and Criminal Justice, Florida State Univ., Bellamy Bldg., Rm. 155C, Tallahassee, FL 32306-2170, (850)644-4299

Juvenile Justice; Natl. Center for [11879]
Juvenile Mfrs. Assn; Infant and [240]
Juvenile Products Mfrs. Assn. [2388], 15000 Commerce Pkwy., Ste. C, Mount Laurel, NJ 08054, (856)638-0420
Juvenile Scleroderma Network [16388], 1204 W 13th St., San Pedro, CA 90731, (310)519-9511
Juventude Social-Democratica [IO], Lisbon, Portugal
JWB [★12473]
JWB Jewish Book Coun. [★9751]
JWB Jewish Chaplains Coun. [19751], c/o Jewish Community Center Assn., 520 Eighth Ave., New York, NY 10018, (212)532-4949

K

K-9 Assn; Police [★6008]
K-9 Assn; U.S. [★6008]
K Phi P - Defunct.
K-T Support Gp. [★13755]
K-W and Area Right to Life Assn. [IO], Kitchener, ON, Canada
KA-BAR Knife Collectors Club - Defunct.
KaBOOM! [12751], 4455 Connecticut Ave. NW, Ste. B100, Washington, DC 20008, (202)659-0215
Kach Intl. - Address unknown since 1999.
Kadets of America - Address unknown since 1995.
Kadima [20155], 155 5th Ave., New York, NY 10010-6802, (212)533-7800
Kafka Soc. of Am. and Jour. [9676], c/o Dr. Marie Luise Caputo-Mayr, Dir., 160 E 65th St., 2C, New York, NY 10021, (212)744-0821
Kafka Soc. of Am. and Jour. [IO], New York, NY, United States
Kagaku Gijutsu Shinko Jigyodan [★IO]
Kagaku Kisoron Gakkai [★IO]
Kahayag Found. [IO], Davao City, Philippines
Kahlil Gibran Centennial Found. [★11132]
Kahlil Gibran Memorial Found. [11132], The Carriage House, 1 St. Matthews Ct. NW, Washington, DC 20036, (202)331-7738
Kai Martial Arts Assn; Zen-do [★23619]
Kaigai Consulting Kigyo Kyokai [★IO]
Kaiser-Darrin Owners Roster [21679], 734 Antram Rd., Somerset, PA 15501-8856, (814)445-6135
Kaiser Family Found. [14642], 2400 Sand Hill Rd., Menlo Park, CA 94025, (650)854-9400
Kaiser Family Found. [IO], Menlo Park, CA, United States
Kaiser-Frazer Owners Club Intl. [IO], Kimberly, WI, United States
Kaiser-Frazer Owners Club Intl. [21680], PO Box 182, Kimberly, WI 54136
Kaiser-Frazer Owners Clubs of Am. [★21680]
Kaiser-Frazer Owners Clubs of Am. [★IO]
Kajagoogoo Fan Club - Defunct.
KAL Project [★17669]
Kalabaw-No-Kai [IO], Yokohama, Japan
Kalatalouden Keskusliitto [★IO]
Kalatalouden Keskusliitto [★IO]
Kaleidoscope Theatre Productions Soc. [IO], Victoria, BC, Canada
Kaleidoscopes
    Brewster Kaleidoscope Soc. [21980]
Kamer van Koophandel Amsterdam [★IO]
Kamer van Koophandel en Fabrieken [★IO]
Kamer van Koophandel The Haag [★IO]
KampGround Owners Assn. [3356], 3416 Primm Ln., Birmingham, AL 35216, (205)824-0022
Kampuchea
    Assn. of Cambodian Survivors of America [12806]
Kampuchean
    Cambodian Buddhist Soc. [9769]
Kamut Assn. of North Am. [4308], 333 Kamut Ln., Big Sandy, MT 59520, (406)378-3105
Kanada Esperanto-Asocio [★IO]
Kanata Cross Country Ski Club [IO], Kanata, ON, Canada
Kanazawa Goodwill Guide Network [IO], Kanazawa, Japan
Kangaroo Protection Found. - Address unknown since 1994.
Kansainvalinen Romanikirjailijaliitto [★IO]
Kansainvalinen Solidaarisuussaatio [★IO]
Kansallinen Kokoomus [★IO]

Kansas City Barbeque Society [IO], Kansas City, MO, United States
Kansas City Barbeque Soc. [22573], 11514 Hickman Mills Dr., Kansas City, MO 64134, (816)765-5891
Kansas City Bd. of Trade [4327], 4800 Main St., Ste. 303, Kansas City, MO 64112, (816)753-7500
Kansas City, Missouri; Bd. of Trade [★4327]
Kansas Wheat Improvement Assn. Hard Winter Wheat Quality Coun. [★4322]
Kant Soc; North Amer. [10816]
Kappa Alpha [★24634]
Kappa Alpha Order [24632], PO Box 1865, Lexington, VA 24450, (540)463-1865
Kappa Alpha Psi Fraternity [24633], 2322-24 N Broad St., Philadelphia, PA 19132, (215)228-7184
Kappa Alpha Psi Fraternity [IO], Philadelphia, PA, United States
Kappa Alpha Soc. [24634], 3109 N Triphammer Rd., Lansing, NY 14882, (877)895-1825
Kappa Alpha Theta [24688], 8740 Founders Rd., Indianapolis, IN 46268, (317)876-1870
Kappa Beta Pi - Address unknown since 1995.
Kappa Delta [24689], 3205 Players Ln., Memphis, TN 38125-8897, (901)748-1897
Kappa Delta Epsilon [24452], c/o Mrs. Patricia Clark, Natl. Treas., 619 34th Ave. E, Tuscaloosa, AL 35404
Kappa Delta Epsilon Sorority [★24452]
Kappa Delta Phi - Address unknown since 2002.
Kappa Delta Pi [24453], 3707 Woodview Trace, Indianapolis, IN 46268-1158, (317)871-4900
Kappa Delta Rho [24635], 331 S Main St., Greensburg, PA 15601-3111, (724)838-7100
Kappa Delta Rho Found. [★24635]
Kappa Epsilon - Defunct.
Kappa Eta Kappa [24460], 718 E Pearson St., Milwaukee, WI 53202, (414)273-9843
Kappa Gamma Pi [24508], 10215 Chardon Rd., Chardon, OH 44024-9700, (440)286-3764
Kappa Gamma Pi Natl. Off. [★24508]
Kappa Kappa Gamma [24690], PO Box 38, Columbus, OH 43216-0038, (614)228-6515
Kappa Kappa Iota [★24454]
Kappa Kappa Iota; Natl. [24454]
Kappa Kappa Psi [24551], PO Box 849, Stillwater, OK 74076-0849, (800)543-6505
Kappa Mu Epsilon [24537], c/o Dr. Don Tosh, Pres., Evangel Univ., Dept. of Sci. and Tech., Springfield, MO 65802, (417)865-2811
Kappa Omicron Nu [24496], 4990 Northwind Dr., Ste. 140, East Lansing, MI 48823-5031, (517)351-8335
Kappa Omicron Phi [★24496]
Kappa Phi Gamma Sorority [24712], 3439 Woodbrook Ln., Sugar Land, TX 77478
Kappa Phi Kappa - Address unknown since 2004.
Kappa Pi Intl. Honorary Art Fraternity [24404], c/o Ron Koehler, Pres., 400 S Bolivar Ave., Cleveland, MS 38732, (662)846-6271
Kappa Pi Intl. Honorary Art Fraternity [IO], Cleveland, MS, United States
Kappa Pi Sigma - Defunct.
Kappa Psi [24568], c/o Kappa Psi Central Off., SWOSU College of Pharmacy, 100 Campus Dr., Weatherford, OK 73096, (580)774-7171
Kappa Psi Kappa - Address unknown since 2003.
Kappa Psi Kappa Fraternity [24480], 108 Forrister St., Columbia, SC 29223
Kappa Sigma [24636], PO Box 5066, Charlottesville, VA 22905-5066, (434)295-3193
Kappa Sigma Alpha Epsilon [★24463]
Kappa Sigma Kappa [★24669]
Kappa Tau Alpha [24522], c/o Dr. Keith P. Sanders, Exec. Dir., Univ. of Missouri, Scholarship of Journalism, Columbia, MO 65211-1200, (573)882-7685
Karachi ACM Chap. [IO], Karachi, Pakistan
Karakul Fur Sheep Registry [★5186]
Karakul Fur Sheep Registry; Amer. [★5186]
Karakul Registry; Empire [★5186]
Karakul Sheep Registry; Amer. [5186]
Karaoke Intl. Sing-Along Assn. - Defunct.
Karat Club of the City of New York; Twenty-Four [2383]
Karate
    Amer. Amateur Karate Fed. [23559]

A star before a book entry number signifies that the name is not listed separately, but is mentioned within the entry.

Amer. Kempo-Karate Assn. [23579]
Amer. Kenpo Karate Intl. [23560]
Amer. Shorin Kempo Karate Assn. [23581]
Bulgarian Natl. Fed. of Karate-Do [IO]
Choy Lee Fut Martial Arts Fed. of Am. [23586]
Feminist Karate Union [23561]
Hong Kong Amateur Karatedo Assn. [IO]
Intl. Traditional Karate Fed. [IO]
Intl. Traditional Karate Fed. [23562]
Japan Karate-Do Org. [23563]
Japan Karate-Do Org. [IO]
Pan-American Union of Karatedo Organizations
    [IO]
Pan-American Union of Karatedo Organizations
    [23564]
Shudokan Martial Arts Assn. [23603]
U.S. Isshinryu Karate Assn. [23565]
U.S. Martial Arts Assn. [23607]
U.S.A. Karate Fed. [23566]
World Martial Arts Assn. [23616]
World Traditional Karate Org. [23567]
World Traditional Karate Org. [IO]
Zen-do Kai Martial Arts [23619]
Karate Assn; Amer. Shorin Kempo [23581]
Karate Fed; All Am. [★23559]
Karate Intl; Kenpo [★23560]
Karate Union/Alternatives to Fear; Feminist
    [★23561]
Karate Union; Feminist [★23561]
Karen Brooks Fan Club - Address unknown since
    2001.
Karen Carpenter Fan Club - Defunct.
Karen; Friends of [11694]
Karen Horney Clinic [16109], 329 E 62nd St., New
    York, NY 10021, (212)838-4333
Karen Horney Psychoanalytic Clinic [★16109]
Karen Horney Psychoanalytic Inst. and Center;
    Assn. for Advancement of Psychoanalysis of the
    [16105]
Karen Taylor-Good Intl. Fan Club - Defunct.
Karg-Elert Archv. [IO], Twickenham, United Kingdom
Karisoke Res. Center [★IO]
Karisoke Res. Center [★5310]
Karl Jaspers Soc. of North Am. [10808], c/o Andrew
    Gluck, Sec.-Treas., 3145 Rte. 44/55, Gardiner, NY
    12525
Karl Kuebel Found. for Child and Family [IO], Ben-
    sheim, Germany
Karl Kuebel Stiftung fuer Kind und Familie [★IO]
Karmann Ghia Club of North Am. [IO], Oakland, CA,
    United States
Karmann Ghia Club of North Am. [21681], 4200
    Park Blvd., No. 151, Oakland, CA 94602,
    (510)567-9957
Karmann-Ghia Registry - Address unknown since
    1999.
Karnkraftskommunernas Samarbetsorgan [★IO]
Kart Marketing Assn. of America - Defunct.
Kart Racing
    Intl. Kart Fed. [23568]
    Intl. Kart Fed. [IO]
    Young Racers of Am. [23674]
Kartografiska Sallskapet [★IO]
Karuna Trust [IO], London, United Kingdom
Kas Hastaliklari Dernegi [★IO]
Kashmiri Amer. Coun. [IO], Washington, DC, United
    States
Kashmiri Amer. Coun. [12753], 1111 16th St. NW,
    Ste. 400, Washington, DC 20036, (202)628-6789
Kassian Benevolent Soc. in America - Address
    unknown since 2003.
Kastorians "Omonoia"; Soc. of 19092
Kasturba Inst. of Rural Stud. [IO], Delhi, India
Katalysis Found. [★IO]
Katalysis Found. [★17048]
Katalysis North/South Development Partnership
    [★17048]
Katalysis North/South Development Partnership
    [★IO]
Katalysis Partnership [IO], Stockton, CA, United
    States
Katalysis Partnership [17048], c/o Christina Jen-
    nings, Exec. Dir., Katalysis Bootstrap Fund, 3601
    Pacific Ave., Stockton, CA 95211, (209)644-6245
Kate Greenaway Soc. [22063], c/o Deltiologists of
    Am., PO Box 8, Norwood, PA 19074

Kate Greenaway Soc. - Address unknown since
    1999.
Kate Jackson Fan Club - Address unknown since
    2003.
Kate Smith Commemorative Soc. [24930], PO Box
    3575, Cranston, RI 02910, (401)461-7457
Kate Smith Commemorative Society [IO], Cranston,
    RI, United States
Kate Smith; Friends of [★24930]
Kate Smith/God Bless Am. Found. [★24930]
Kate Smith/God Bless Am. Found. [★IO]
Kateri Tekakwitha League; Blessed [19588]
Kathmandu Environmental Educ. Proj. [IO], Kath-
    mandu, Nepal
Kathmandu Environmental Educ. Proj. - Nepal [IO],
    Kathmandu, Nepal
Katholiek Vormingswerk van Landelijke Vrouwen
    [IO], Leuven, Belgium
Katholiken Fursorgeverein fur Madchen, Frauen und
    Kinder [★IO]
Katholische Bibelfoederation [★IO]
Katholischer Deutscher Frauenbund [★IO]
Katholischer Gesellenverein [★IO]
Kathy Lynn Sacra Intl. Fan Club - Defunct.
Kathy Mattea Fan Club [24931], PO Box 1776,
    Orem, UT 84059-1776, (801)229-7048
Katipunang Manggagawang Filipino [★IO]
Katolicky Delnik [★18998]
Katolika Unio Esperantista; Internacia [★9915]
Kauffman Center for Entrepreneurial Leadership
    [739], 4801 Rockhill Rd., Kansas City, MO 64110-
    2046, (816)932-1000
Kaufman Found; Ewing Marion [18846]
Kaunihera mo te Whakapakari Ao Whanul [★IO]
Kaup Assn. - Defunct.
Kaupan Keskusliitto [★IO]
Kavak Ve Hizli Gelisen Orman Agaclari Arastirma
    Enstitusu [★IO]
Kayak; USA Canoe/ [23280]
Kazak fiziologtardyn uiymy [★IO]
Kazak Agrarian Expertise [IO], Astana, Kazakhstan
Kazakh Physiology Soc. [IO], Almaty, Kazakhstan
Kazakhistanian Assn. of Sports Medicine [IO], Al-
    maty, Kazakhstan
Kazakhstan Assn. of Bus. Incubators and Innovation
    Centers [IO], Almaty, Kazakhstan
Kazakhstan Assn. Inst. of Non-Proliferation [IO], Al-
    maty, Kazakhstan
Kazakhstan Badminton Fed. [IO], Almaty, Kazakh-
    stan
Kazakhstan Geotechnical Soc. [IO], Astana, Kazakh-
    stan
Kazakhstan Natl. League Against Epilepsy [IO], Al-
    maty, Kazakhstan
Kazakhstan Sailing Fed. [IO], Almaty, Kazakhstan
Kazakhstan Stomatological Assn. [IO], Almaty, Kaza-
    khstan
Kazakhstan Tennis Fed. [IO], Almaty, Kazakhstan
Kazan; Friends of Lainie [24743]
KCZT Tape Club - Defunct.
KDK [★22961]
KDWB Variety Family Center [13964], Div. of Gen.
    Pediatrics, McNamara Alumni Ctr., Univ. of Min-
    nesota Gateway, 200 Oak St. SE, Ste. 160, Min-
    neapolis, MN 55455-2002, (612)626-3087
Keanu Reeves Fan Club - Address unknown since
    2001.
Keaton Soc; Damfinos: The Intl. Buster [24797]
Keats-Shelley Assn. of Am. [9677], 476 5th Ave.,
    New York Public Lib., Rm. 226, New York, NY
    10018, (212)764-0655
Keck Found; W.M. [15115]
Keeler Soc; Harry Stephen [9656]
Keep Am. Beautiful [4584], 1010 Washington Blvd.,
    Stamford, CT 06901, (203)323-8987
Keep America Independent - Defunct.
KEEP; Amer. Comm. for [12418]
Keep Fit Assn. [IO], London, United Kingdom
Keepers of the Treasures-Cultural Coun. of Amer.
    Indians, Alaska Natives and Native Hawaiians -
    Address unknown since 2006.
Keepers of the Waters [5273], 1415 SE Tacoma St.,
    Portland, OR 97202
Keeping Track [5335], PO Box 444, Huntington, VT
    05462, (802)434-7000

Keeshond Club of Am. [22300], c/o Carolyn Schal-
    decker, Corresponding Sec., 1571 Twin Valley Dr.
    NE, Solon, IA 52333
Kehot Publications Society [★20131]
Keidanren Nature Conservation Fund [IO], Tokyo,
    Japan
Keisoku Jidouseigyo Gakkai [★IO]
Keith Bulluck Fan Club [24830], PO Box 1827,
    Brentwood, TN 37024-1827
Keith Intl. Fan Club; Toby [24985]
Keith Keating Soc. for the Arts - Defunct.
Keith Sewell Fan Club - Defunct.
Keith Soc; Clan [20835]
Keizai Doyukai [★IO]
Keizai Riron Gakkai [★IO]
Keller Natl. Center for Deaf-Blind Youths and Adults;
    Helen [14760]
Kelley; Fans of Leonard Nimoy and DeForest
    [24739]
Kelley's Kobras [★20658]
Kelli Warren Fan Club - Defunct.
Kellogg Found; W.K. [18400]
Kelly Lang Fan Club [24932], 242 W Main St., PMB
    311, Hendersonville, TN 37075
Kelly Soc; Pogo Fan Club and Walt [24794]
Kelsey Kindred of Am. [20971], c/o Mrs. Suzanne
    Kelsey Hall, Membership Sec., 244 Mountain Rd.,
    North Granby, CT 06060, (860)653-8233
Kemian Keskuslitto [★IO]
Kemianteollisuus [★IO]
Kemisk Forening [★IO]
Kemisk-Tekniska Leverantoerfoerbundet [★IO]
Kempe Children's Center [11609], c/o Donald C.
    Bross, PhD, Dir. of Educ. and Legal Counsel, 1825
    Marion St., Denver, CO 80218, (303)864-5300
Kempe Natl. Center for the Prevention and Treat-
    ment of Child Abuse and Neglect [★11609]
Kempo Karate Assn; Amer. Shorin [23581]
Kemps of Am; Kustom [21683]
Kenevan of Ireland Assn. - Defunct.
Kennarasamband Islands [★IO]
Kennedy Center Alliance for Arts Educ. Network
    [7975], John F. Kennedy Center for the Performing
    Arts, 2700 F St. NW, Washington, DC 20566,
    (202)416-8817
Kennedy Center; Friends of the [9568]
Kennedy First Day Cover Stud. Unit; John F. [22835]
Kennedy Gp; Moorhead [8666]
Kennedy Inst. of Ethics; Joseph P. and Rose F.
    [17506]
Kennedy, John F.
    John F. Kennedy Center Dakar [IO]
    John F. Kennedy First Day Cover Stud. Unit
    [22835]
Kennedy, Jr. Found; Joseph P. [12571]
Kennedy Lib. Found; John F. [10365]
Kennedy Memorial; Robert F. [13513]
Kennedy's Disease Assn. [15334], PO Box 1105,
    Coarsegold, CA 93614-1105, (559)658-5950
Kennel Assn. of Am; Ladies [22303]
Kennel Club [IO], London, United Kingdom
Kennel Club; Amer. [22201]
Kennel Club Boliviano [IO], La Paz, Bolivia
Kennel Club of Chicago; Intl. [22289]
Kennel Club; United [22370]
Kennel Club; Westminster [22382]
Kennels Assn; Amer. Boarding [2954]
Kenneth Branagh Fan Assn. - Defunct.
Kenny Antcliff Fan Club - Defunct.
Kenny Chesney Fan Club [24933], PO Box 1873,
    Charlottesville, VA 22903
Kenny Dale Fan Club - Address unknown since
    1989.
Kenny Found; Sister [★16335]
Kenny Inst; Sister [★16335]
Kenny Rehabilitation Inst; Sister [16335]
Kenny Roberts and Bettyanne Fan Club - Defunct.
Kenpo Karate Intl. [★23560]
Kent State Univ. Alumni Assn. [18902], Williamson
    Alumni Center, PO Box 5190, Kent, OH 44242-
    0001, (330)672-5368
Kent Waldrep Intl. Spinal Cord Res. Found.
    [★16463]
Kent Waldrep Natl. Paralysis Found. [16467]
Kentucky Callers Assn. - Address unknown since
    2001.

Reference to "IO" in place of a book number signifies that the association may be found in the 45th edition of International Organizations.

Kenya AIDS Intervention/Prevention Proj. Gp. [IO], Kakamega, Kenya

Kenya Air Sports Assn. [IO], Nairobi, Kenya

Kenya Assn. of Hotelkeepers and Caterers [IO], Nairobi, Kenya

Kenya Assn. of Mfrs. [IO], Nairobi, Kenya

Kenya Assn. of Producers and Videograms [IO], Nairobi, Kenya

Kenya Assn. of Tour Operators [IO], Nairobi, Kenya

Kenya Badminton Assn. [IO], Nairobi, Kenya

Kenya Bankers Assn. [IO], Nairobi, Kenya

Kenya Bur. of Standards [IO], Nairobi, Kenya

Kenya Cricket Assn. [IO], Nairobi, Kenya

Kenya Diabetes Assn. [IO], Nairobi, Kenya

Kenya Disabled Development Soc. [IO], Nairobi, Kenya

Kenya Female Advisory Org. [IO], Kisumu, Kenya

Kenya Hypertension League [IO], Nairobi, Kenya

Kenya Inst. of Mgt. [IO], Nairobi, Kenya

Kenya Junior Chamber [IO], Nairobi, Kenya

Kenya Lawn Tennis Assn. [IO], Nairobi, Kenya

Kenya Medical Assn. [IO], Nairobi, Kenya

Kenya Natl. Acad. of Sciences [IO], Nairobi, Kenya

Kenya Occupational Therapists Assn. [IO], Nairobi, Kenya

Kenya Programmes of Disabled Persons [IO], Nairobi, Kenya

Kenya Scouts Assn. [IO], Nairobi, Kenya

Kenya Soc. for Epilepsy [IO], Nairobi, Kenya

Kenya Soc. of Physiotherapists [IO], Nairobi, Kenya

Kenya Squash Rackets Assn. [IO], Nairobi, Kenya

Kenya Taekwondo Assn. [IO], Nairobi, Kenya

Kenya Wildlife Soc. [★IO]

Kenya Yachting Assn. [IO], Nairobi, Kenya

Kenya Youth Hostels Assn. [IO], Nairobi, Kenya

Kenyan Geotechnical Soc. [IO], Nairobi, Kenya

Kenyan Physiological Soc. [IO], Nairobi, Kenya

Kenyan Publishers Assn. [IO], Nairobi, Kenya

Kenyan Sect. of the Intl. Commn. of Jurists [IO], Nairobi, Kenya

Keramos [24461], c/o Dr. Robert W. Schwartz, Pres., Univ. of Missouri - Rolla, 110 ERL, Rolla, MO 65409-0330, (573)341-7887

Kerato-Refractive Soc. - Address unknown since 2005.

Keratoconjunctivitis Sicca

Sjogren's Syndrome Found. [16376]

Keren Kayemeth Leisrael [★20150]

Keren Or [16863], 350 7th Ave., Ste. 701, New York, NY 10001, (212)279-4070

Keren Or [IO], New York, NY, United States

Keren-Or Center for Multi-Handicapped Blind Children [★IO]

Keren-Or Center for Multi-Handicapped Blind Children [★16863]

Keresztyen Ifjusagi Egyesulet [★IO]

Kerntechnischer Ausschuss [★IO]

Kerosene Heater Assn; Natl. [1896]

Kerouac!; Lowell Celebrates [9683]

Kerr Family Assn. of North Am. [20972], c/o Mr. Joe F. Kerr, Jr., 7980 Ridgewood Rd., Goodlettsville, TN 37072-9461

Kerr Family Assn. of North Am. [IO], Goodlettsville, TN, United States

Kerry Blue Terrier Club; U.S. [22374]

Kerry Bog Pony Soc; Amer. [4829]

Kerry and Dexter Club; Amer. [★4221]

Kershaw Fan Club; Sammy [24973]

Kershner Family Assn. [20973], 101 Potters Way, Lexington, SC 29073

Kesatuan Guru-Guru Melayu Singapura [★IO]

Kesrawan Soc; United [19206]

Keston USA - Address unknown since 1995.

Kettering Family Found. [12728], 2833 S Colorado Blvd., Denver, CO 80222

Kettering Found; Charles F. [★8263]

Keuda Cat Assn; Amer. [4204]

Keuka Coll. Alumni Assn. [18903], Off. of Alumni and Family Relations, Keuka Park, NY 14478, (315)279-5238

Kevin Collins Found. for Missing Children - Address unknown since 2001.

Kevin Gray Fan Club - Defunct.

Kevin Sorbo's Official Fan Club [24820], PO Box 1418, Aliquippa, PA 15001

Kex Natl. Assn. - Address unknown since 1995.

Key Chain Collectors Club [★22011]

Key Chain and Mini License Plate Collectors Club; License Plate [★22011]

Key Chain Tag and Mini License Plate Collectors Club [★22011]

Key Club Intl. [13046], 3636 Woodview Trace, Indianapolis, IN 46268-3196, (317)875-8755

Key Club Intl. [IO], Indianapolis, IN, United States

Key Collectors Intl. - Defunct.

Keyboard Mfrs; Natl. Assn. of Electronic [★2808]

Keychain Tag and Chauffeur's Badge Collectors Newsl; Disabled Veterans [22011]

Keyette Intl. - Address unknown since 2008.

Keystone Bituminous Coal Assn. [★847]

The Keystone Center [7746], 1628 St. John Rd., Keystone, CO 80435, (970)513-5800

Keystone Center for Continuing Educ. [★7746]

Khalistan/International Sikh Org; Coun. of [20557]

Khmer Amateur Athletic Assn. [IO], Phnom Penh, Cambodia

Khmer Weightlifting Fed. [IO], Phnom Penh, Cambodia

Khorassan; Dramatic Order Knights of [19186]

Khoury Assn. of Baseball Leagues; George [23109]

Ki-Wives Intl. - Address unknown since 2001.

Kibbutz Indus. Assn. [IO], Tel Aviv, Israel

Kibbutz Movement; Garin Yarden - Young [★17937]

Kibbutz Prog. Center [17937], 114 W 26th St., Ste. 1004, New York, NY 10001, (212)462-2764

Kibris Turk Universiteli Kadinlar Dernegi [★IO]

Kid; AASK - Adopt a Special [11226]

Kid; Adopt a Special [★11226]

Kid-To-Kid; Oper. [19757]

Kidney

Amer. Assn. of Kidney Patients [15283]

Amer. Kidney Fund [15284]

Amer. Nephrology Nurses' Assn. [15286]

Amer. Soc. of Diagnostic and Interventional Nephrology [15287]

Amer. Soc. of Nephrology [15288]

Cystinosis Found. [15246]

Cystinosis Res. Network [15247]

DaVita Patient Citizens [15291]

Intl. Pediatric Nephrology Assn. [15292]

Kidney Transplant/Dialysis Assn. [16675]

Natl. Kidney Found. [15294]

Natl. Renal Administrators Assn. [15072]

North Amer. Soc. for Dialysis and Transplantation [15295]

Renal Pathology Soc. [15872]

Renal Physicians Assn. [15298]

Renal Support Network [15299]

Sunshine Found. [11726]

Kidney Assn; Irish [IO]

Kidney Cancer Assn. [13836], 1234 Sherman Ave., Ste. 203, Evanston, IL 60202-1375, (847)332-1051

Kidney Cancer UK [IO], Uttoxeter, United Kingdom

Kidney Disease Found; Natl. [★15294]

Kidney Found; Natl. [15294]

Kidney Fund; Amer. [15284]

Kidney Patients; Amer. Assn. of [15283]

Kidney Transplant/Dialysis Assn. [16675], PO Box 51362 GMF, Boston, MA 02205-1362, (781)641-4000

Kidney and Urologic Diseases Info. CH; Natl. [16710]

Kidpower Teenpower Fullpower Intl. [12967], PO Box 1212, Santa Cruz, CA 95061, (831)426-4407

Kidpower Teenpower Fullpower Intl. [IO], Santa Cruz, CA, United States

Kids 4 Afghan Kids [IO], Northville, MI, United States

Kids 4 Afghan Kids [11610], c/o Khris Nedam, Exec. Dir., Amerman Elementary School, 847 North Ctr., Northville, MI 48167, (248)344-8405

Kids Against Junk Food - Defunct.

Kids: America's Challenge; Drug Free [18687]

Kids; Athletes and Entertainers for [★13560]

Kids; Athletics and Entertainers for [13560]

Kids Campaign; Natl. Safe [★11651]

Kids for a Clean Env. [4585], PO Box 158254, Nashville, TN 37215, (615)331-7381

Kid's Clubs Network [★IO]

Kids Coalition; City [★13479]

KIDS COUNT [11611], c/o The Annie E. Casey Found., 701 St. Paul St., Baltimore, MD 21202, (410)547-6600

Kids to the Cup [23504], 2905 Circle Crest Ct., Prospect, KY 40059, (626)695-3433

Kids and Families; Covering [12271]

Kids First Parent Assn. of Canada [IO], Calgary, AB, Canada

Kids Fund [11704], 416 Benninghaus Rd., Baltimore, MD 21212, (410)532-9330

Kids and Guns; Common Sense about [8443]

Kids at Hope [11705], 2501 W Dunlap Ave., Phoenix, AZ 85021, (602)674-0026

Kids In Danger [11612], 116 W Illinois, Ste. 5E, Chicago, IL 60610-4532, (312)595-0649

Kids In a Drug-Free Soc. - Address unknown since 2006.

Kids Internationally Distributed Superstation - Address unknown since 2001.

Kids Konnected [11706], 27071 Cabot Rd., Ste. 102, Laguna Hills, CA 92653, (949)582-5443

Kids Korps USA [13399], 265 Santa Helena, Ste. 130, Solana Beach, CA 92075, (858)259-3602

Kids Kottage Found. [IO], Edmonton, AB, Canada

Kids Meeting Kids [★IO]

Kids Meeting Kids [★17910]

Kids; Mothers and Fathers Aligned Saving [17059]

Kids Need Both Parents [17509], c/o James P. Whinston, PO Box 6481, Portland, OR 97228-6481, (503)727-3686

Kids Program; Toughlove for [★12694]

Kids Program; Toughlove for [★IO]

Kids for Saving Earth [8390], PO Box 421118, Minneapolis, MN 55442, (763)559-1234

Kids; Trips for [8396]

Kids Universe, Inc. [8320], c/o Janeczka Eberhart, CFO, PO Box 465552, Lawrenceville, GA 30042, (678)407-1331

Kids With A Cause [11613], 400 Corporate Pointe, Ste. 300, Culver City, CA 90230, (310)590-4505

Kids With Food Allergies [13603], 73 Old Dublin Pike, Ste. 10, No. 163, Doylestown, PA 18901, (215)230-5394

Kids With Heart Natl. Assn. for Children's Heart Disorders [13915], PO Box 12504, Green Bay, WI 54307-2504, (800)538-5390

Kids Without Borders [11614], PO Box 24, Bellevue, WA 98009-0024, (206)484-4830

Kids Without Borders [IO], Bellevue, WA, United States

Kids the World Found; Give [★11696]

Kids the World Trust; Give [★11696]

Kidsave Intl. [11251], 11835 W Olympic Blvd., Ste. 295, Los Angeles, CA 90064, (310)479-5437

Kidsave Intl. [IO], Los Angeles, CA, United States

KIDSCOPE [11518], 2045 Peachtree Rd., Ste. 150, Atlanta, GA 30309, (404)892-1437

KidsPeace [11615], c/o Kids Peace Hosp., 5300 Kids Peace Dr., Orefield, PA 18069, (800)8KID-123

Kidwell Family Assn. - Defunct.

Kiger Mesteno Assn. [4910], 11124 NE Halsey, Ste. 591, Portland, OR 97220

Kiko Goat Assn; Amer. [4780]

Kill Devil Hills Memorial Assn. [★21447]

Killarney Chamber of Commerce [IO], Killarney, Ireland

Killifish Assn; Amer. [22434]

Killing Animals for Recreational Enjoyment; I KARE - Individuals Against [★5332]

Kiln Drying Assn; New England [1610]

Kiln Recycling Coalition; Cement [4337]

Kilner Family Org. - Defunct.

Kilts Family Assn. [20974], c/o Herman W. Witthoft, Sr., 141 Hudson Ave., Chatham, NY 12037, (518)392-4544

Kilvert Soc. [IO], Abergavenny, United Kingdom

Kimberly McCullough Fan Club - Address unknown since 1990.

Kin Canada [IO], Cambridge, ON, Canada

Kincaid Clan U.S.A. - Address unknown since 1995.

Kindel Family Org; William [21087]

Kinder Goat Breeders Assn. [4786], PO Box 1575, Snohomish, WA 98291-1575, (360)668-4559

Kinder- und Jugendfilmzentrum in Deutschland [★IO]

Kindergarten Assn. of North Am; Waldorf [★9008]

Kindergarten Program; Get Set Pre- [★11539]

Kindergarten Union; Intl. [★8064]

A star before a book entry number signifies that the name is not listed separately, but is mentioned within the entry.

Kindernothilfe e.V. [IO], Duisburg, Germany
Kindernothilfe Osterreich [★IO]
Kindness in Suffering [IO], Frederick, MD, United States
Kindness in Suffering [11616]
Kinesiology and Physical Educ; Amer. Acad. of [8978]
Kinesiology - U.S.A; Intl. Coll. of Applied [14827]
Kinesiotherapy Assn; Amer. [16311]
Kinetic Art Org. [9453], 301 Clematis St., No. 3000, West Palm Beach, FL 33401, (561)655-2745
Kinetics Soc; Cell [★6573]
King Baudouin Found. [IO], Brussels, Belgium
King Charles the Martyr; Soc. of [19455]
King; Daughters of the [★19969]
King, Jr. Center for Nonviolent Social Change; Martin Luther [18116]
King Midget and Eshelman Registry - Defunct.
King; Order of the Daughters of the [19969]
King of Our Hearts Elvis Presley Fan Club - Defunct.
Kings Booster Club; Los Angeles [25007]
King's Garden [★13166]
Kingston Hard of Hearing Club [IO], Kingston, ON, Canada
Kingston Korner [24934], 705 S Washington St., Naperville, IL 60540-3535, (630)305-0770
Kingston Trio
   Kingston Korner [24934]
Kinkade Collectors' Soc; Thomas [21545]
Kinship Alliance - Intl. - Address unknown since 2000.
Kinship Intl; SDA [★20066]
Kinship Intl; Seventh Day Adventist [20066]
Kinsmen and Kinette Clubs of Canada [★IO]
Kipling Soc. [IO], London, United Kingdom
Kippe Brannon Fan Club - Defunct.
Kirche in Not Ostpriesterhilfe [★IO]
Kiribati Athletics Assn. [IO], Tarawa, Kiribati
Kiribati Natl. Olympic Comm. [IO], Tarawa, Kiribati
Kiribati Tennis Assn. [IO], Tarawa, Kiribati
Kiribati and Tungaru Assn. [IO], Chesham, United Kingdom
Kiribati Weightlifting Fed. [IO], Tarawa, Kiribati
Kirjakauppaliitto [★IO]
Kirkon Ulkomaanapu [★IO]
Kish "The Flying Cowboy" Fan Club; Jimmy 24922
KISS - Flaming Youth - Defunct.
KISS Konnection Fan Club - Address unknown since 2003.
KISS Rocks Fan Club [24935], c/o Jon Rubin, Pres./ Founder, 2 Tudor City Pl., New York, NY 10017
KISS Rocks Fan Club [IO], New York, NY, United States
Kissel Kar Klub [IO], Hartford, WI, United States
Kissel Kar Klub [21682], c/o Wisconsin Automotive Museum, 147 N Rural St., Hartford, WI 53027, (262)673-7999
Kit Collector's Clearinghouse - Defunct.
Kit Collectors Intl. [22649], PO Box 38, Stanton, CA 90680, (714)826-5218
Kit Collectors Intl. [IO], Stanton, CA, United States
Kitchen and Bath Assn; Natl. [2271]
Kitchen, Bathroom, Bedroom Specialists Assn. [IO], Worcester, United Kingdom
Kitchen Cabinet Assn; Natl. [★2267]
Kitchen Cabinet Mfrs. Assn. [2267], 1899 Preston White Dr., Reston, VA 20191-5435, (703)264-1690
Kitchen Cabinets; Natl. Inst. of Wood [★2267]
Kitchen Dealers; Amer. Inst. of [★2271]
Kitchen Designers; Soc. of Certified [2277]
Kitchen Exhaust Cleaning Assn; Intl. [1475]
Kitchen Gardeners Intl. [9966], 3 Powderhorn Dr., Scarborough, ME 04074, (207)883-5341
Kitchen Gardeners Intl. [IO], Scarborough, ME, United States
Kitchen Klutzs of America - Defunct.
Kitchen Specialists Assn. [★IO]
Kite Flying
   Amer. Kitefliers Assn. [23569]
   Australian Kite Assn. [IO]
   Kite Trade Assn. Intl. [3643]
Kite Trade Assn. Intl. [3643], PO Box 443, Otis, OR 97368, (541)994-9647
Kite Trade Association International [IO], Otis, OR, United States

Kitts-Nevis Tourist Off; Saint [★24254]
Kitts Tourism Authority; Saint [24254]
Kitty Fan Club; Princess [24778]
Kitty Wells Appreciation Soc. [★24936]
Kitty Wells-Johnny Wright-Bobby Wright Intl. Fan Club [24936], PO Box 1189, Madison, TN 37116, (615)865-1900
Kitty Wells/Johnny Wright Fan Club [★24936]
Kituo cha Elimuya Demokrasia kwa Wanawake [★IO]
Kiviteollisuusliitto ry [★IO]
Kiwanis Club of Te Awamutu [IO], Te Awamutu, New Zealand
Kiwanis Intl. [IO], Indianapolis, IN, United States
Kiwanis Intl. [13047], 3636 Woodview Trace, Indianapolis, IN 46268-3196, (317)875-8755
Kiwifruit Commn; California [4717]
Kiwifruit Growers of California - Defunct.
Kjaerulf Family Assn. [20975], c/o Cap Kjaerulf, 358 S Bentley Ave., Los Angeles, CA 90049-3219, (310)472-9206
Kjottbransjens Landsforbund [★IO]
Klaas Found; Polly [12604]
Klan Network; Natl. Anti- [★17098]
Klanwatch [★17121]
Klassieke Vereniging van Suid-Afrika [★IO]
Kleptonian; Neo-American Church, The Original [20456]
Klinefelter Syndrome and Associates [16538], 11 Keats Ct., Coto de Caza, CA 92679, (949)858-9428
Klinefelter Syndrome Info. and Support; Amer. Assn. for [14538]
Klingenstein Fund; Esther A. and Joseph [15106]
Klingenstein Third Generation Found. [13965], 787 Seventh Ave., 6th Fl., New York, NY 10019-6016, (212)492-6179
Klingon Empire - Address unknown since 1999.
Klingon Strike Force [25015]
Klippel-Trenaunay Support Gp. [13755], 5404 Dundee Rd., Edina, MN 55436, (952)925-2596
Klondike Visitors Assn. [IO], Dawson City, YT, Canada
Klub Hateufah Leisrael [★IO]
Klub Inteligencji Katolickiej [★IO]
Knattspyrnusamband Islands [★IO]
Knee; Intl. Soc. of the [★15771]
Knee Surgeons; Amer. Assn. of Hip and [16559]
KNH Austria [IO], Vienna, Austria
Knife Assn; Machine [2036]
Knife Assn; Metal Cutting [★2036]
Knife Collectors Club [22615], 2900 S 26th St., US 540 Exit 81, Rogers, AR 72758-8571, (479)631-0130
Knife and Fork Club Intl. [19378]
Knife Mfrs. Assn; Machine [★2036]
Knifemakers' Guild [9834], c/o Gil Hibben, Pres., 2914 Winters Ln., La Grange, KY 40031, (502)222-1937
Knight Automobiles; Natl. Registry of Willys - [★21819]
Knight Bros. Found. [★12484]
Knight Club - Address unknown since 1989.
Knight Found; John S. and James L. [12484]
Knight Registry; Willys-Overland- [21819]
Knights of the Altar Intl. - Address unknown since 2006.
Knights of America; Catholic [18995]
Knights Boxing Team - Intl. [23265], 12086 Flat Shoals Rd., Covington, GA 30016-4708, (770)787-3131
Knights; Catholic [18994]
Knights of Columbus [19004], 1 Columbus Plz., New Haven, CT 06510, (203)752-4000
Knights of Columbus [IO], New Haven, CT, United States
Knights of Dunamis [★13002]
Knights of Equity [19154], 1135 8th Ave., Freedom, PA 15042, (412)204-8450
Knights of the Golden Eagle [19128], c/o Tim Chubb, 412 Brookside Dr., Perkasie, PA 18944, (215)345-0929
Knights of the Holy Sepulchre of Jerusalem; Religious and Military Order of [19008]
Knights of the Hook [★24507]

Knights of the Immaculata Movement [★19660]
Knights Insurance Soc; Catholic [★18994]
Knights; Intercollegiate [24507]
Knights of Khorassan; Dramatic Order [19186]
Knights of the Ku Klux Klan [18799], PO Box 2222, Harrison, AR 72601, (870)427-3414
Knights and Ladies of Sta. Peter Claver [★19005]
Knights of Life Motorcycle Club [12968], PO Box 96, Wharton, NJ 07885
Knights of Lithuania - Address unknown since 1999.
Knights of Malta; Ancient and Illustrious Order [19325]
Knights of the Mystic Light; Aladdin [22617]
Knights of Peter Claver [19005], 1825 Orleans Ave., New Orleans, LA 70116, (504)821-4225
Knights of Peter Claver; Junior [19003]
Knights of Pythias
   Dramatic Order Knights of Khorassan [19186]
   Junior Order, Knights of Pythias [19187]
   Supreme Lodge Knights of Pythias [19188]
   Supreme Temple Order Pythian Sisters [19189]
Knights of Pythias; Junior Order, [19187]
Knights of the Round Table; Loyal [★13061]
Knights of Saint Andrew [★20073]
Knights of Saint George; Catholic [★19144]
Knights of Saint John Intl. [19006], 89 S Pine Ave., Albany, NY 12208-2214, (518)453-5675
Knights of Saint John Intl. [IO], Albany, NY, United States
Knights of St. John of Jerusalem, Palestine, Rhodes [★19325]
Knights of Saint John; Supreme Ladies Auxiliary [19009]
Knights of Scorpius, Honorary Leadership Soc; Natl. Assn. of the [24511]
Knights of the Square Table - Defunct.
Knights Templar Educational Foundation [★19240]
Knights Templar Eye Foundation [★19240]
Knights Templar, Grand Encampment, U.S.A. [19240], 5909 West Loop S, Ste. 495, Bellaire, TX 77401-2402, (713)349-8700
Knights of the Vine; Brotherhood of the [5411]
Knights of the White Cross [★19293]
Knights of the White Cross [★IO]
Knitgoods Dyers and Processors Assn. - Defunct.
Knitted Outerwear Assn; New England [★20816]
Knitted Outerwear Manufacturers Assn; New England [★20816]
Knitted Textile Assn. [★3795]
The Knitting Guild of Am. [★22164]
The Knitting Guild Assn. [22164], 1100-H Brandywine Blvd., Zanesville, OH 43701-7303, (740)452-4541
Knitting Indus'. Fed. [IO], Leicester, United Kingdom
Knitting Machine Mfrs. Assn. - Defunct.
Knitting Technologists; Amer. Soc. of [7795]
Knitwear Designers Guild; Professional [★228]
Knitwear Div.-Amer. Apparel Mfrs. Assn. - Address unknown since 2004.
Knitwear Employers Assn. - Defunct.
Knitwear Mill Representatives Assn. - Defunct.
Knitwear and Sportswear Assn; Natl. [251]
Knives
   Amer. Edge Collectors Assn. [22612]
   Case Collectors Club [22613]
   Intl. Fight'n Rooster Cutlery Club [22614]
   Intl. Fight'n Rooster Cutlery Club [IO]
   Intl. Saw and Knife Assn. [IO]
   Intl. Saw and Knife Assn. [2390]
   Knife Collectors Club [22615]
   Knifemakers' Guild [9834]
   Natl. Knife Collectors Assn. [22616]
   Professional Knifemakers Assn. [9839]
Knoles/Noles Family Assn; Knowles/ [21129]
Knollwood [★21192]
Knollwood; Army Distaff Foundation/ [21192]
Knothole Assn; Christopher Morley [9643]
Know, Inc. [17545], 807 Penn Ave., Wilkinsburg, PA 15221, (412)241-4844
Knowbility [11958], 3925 W Braker Ln., 3rd Fl., Austin, TX 78759, (512)305-0310
Knowledge Alliance [9061], 850 Connecticut Ave. NW, Ste. 220, Washington, DC 20006, (202)518-0847
Knowledge of the Church; Soc. for Promoting and Encouraging Arts and [19972]

Reference to "IO" in place of a book number signifies that the association may be found in the 45th edition of International Organizations.

Knowledge and Development; Jean Piaget Soc.: Soc. for the Stud. of [16156]

Knowledge Intl; Occupational [5099]

Knowledge for Iraqi Woman Soc. [IO], Baghdad, Iraq

Knowledge; Org. for the Advancement of [4313]

Knowledge Rescue; Amer. [★12287]

Knowles/Knoles/Noles Family Assn. [21129], c/o Robert B. Noles, Historian, 133 Acadian Ln., Mandeville, LA 70471, (985)845-4688

Koala Found; Friends of the Australian [5319]

Kobe YMCA Cross Cultural Center [IO], Kobe, Japan

Kodak Historical Soc; Intl. [10850]

Kodaly Educators; Org. of Amer. [8929]

Kodaly, Zoltan

Org. of Amer. Kodaly Educators [8929]

Kodbranchens Faellesraad [★IO]

Koepel van Christelijke Werknemersorganisaties [IO], Brussels, Belgium

Koi Clubs of Am; Assoc. [22437]

Koinonia Caritas [IO], Nicosia, Cyprus

Koinonia Found. [19899], 6037 Franconia Rd., Alexandria, VA 22310, (703)971-1991

Kokoomuksen Nuorten Liitto [★IO]

Koko.org [★7533]

Kokuren Josei Kaihatsu Kikin Nihon Kokunai Iinkai [★IO]

Kokusai Jishin Kogaku-kai [★IO]

Kokusai Kanko Shinko-kai [★IO]

Kokusai Koryu Kikin [★10264]

Kokusai Kotsu Anzen Gakkai [★IO]

Kokusai Kowan Kyokai [★IO]

Kokusai Kyoryoku BGO Center [★IO]

Kokusai Yoshoku Sangyo Kai [★IO]

Kolan Olive Growers Assn. [IO], Bucca, Australia

Kolel Chibas Jerusalem [20156], 4802-A 12th Ave., Brooklyn, NY 11219, (718)633-7112

Kolel Shomre Hachomos [★17938]

Kolel Shomre Hachomos/Reb Meir Baal Haness [17938]

Kollel America - Address unknown since 1995.

Kolping Soc. of Am; Catholic [19599]

Komei [★IO]

Komen Breast Cancer Found; Susan G. [13878]

Komen Found; Susan G. [★13878]

Kommission der Kirchen fur Migranten in Europa [★IO]

Kommission fur Musikforschung der Osterreichischen Akademie der Wissenschaften [★IO]

Kommission Reinhaltung der Luft im VDI und DIN - Normenausschuss [★IO]

Kommunalberatung - Unternehmensberatung fur Wirtschaft und Verwaltung [★IO]

Komondor Club of Am. [22301], c/o Ann Quigley, Pres., 159 Beville Rd., Chehalis, WA 98532, (360)245-3464

Komondorok

Komondor Club of Am. [22301]

Komoradanoych poradcu CR [★IO]

Kona Coffee Coun. - Defunct.

Kongelig Dansk Aeroklub [★IO]

Kongelige Danske Geografiske Selskab [★IO]

Kongelige Danske Landhusholdningsselskab [★IO]

Kongelige Danske Videnskabernes Selskab [★IO]

Koninklijk Belgisch Genootschap voor Numismatiek [★IO]

Koninklijk Belgisch Yachting Verbond [★IO]

Koninklijk Genootschap Voor Landbouwwetenschap [★IO]

Koninklijk Instituut van Ingenieurs [★IO]

Koninklijk Instituut voor den Tropen [★IO]

Koninklijk Nederlands Aardrijkskundig Genootschap [★IO]

Koninklijk Nederlands Geologisch Mijnbouwkundig Genootschap [★IO]

Koninklijk Nederlands Korfbalverbond [★IO]

Koninklijke Academie voor Nederlandse Taal-en Letterkunde [★IO]

Koninklijke Belgische Baseball en Softball Federatie [IO], Liege, Belgium

Koninklijke Belgische Vereniging der Elektrotechnici [★IO]

Koninklijke Hollandsche Maatschappij der Wetenschappen [★IO]

Koninklijke Landbouwkundige Vereniging [★IO]

Koninklijke Maatschappij tot Bevordering der Bouwkunst - Bond van Nederlandse Architekten [★IO]

Koninklijke Nederlandsche Maatschappij tot bevordering der Geneeskunst [★IO]

Koninklijke Nederlandse Akademie van Wetenschappen [★IO]

Koninklijke Nederlandse Atletiek Unie [IO], Arnhem, Netherlands

Koninklijke Nederlandse Cricket Bond [★IO]

Koninklijke Nederlandse Lawn Tennis Bond [IO], Amersfoort, Netherlands

Koninklijke Nederlandse Toonkunstenaars Vereniging [★IO]

Koninklijke Nederlandse Vereniging voor de Koffiehandel [IO], Amsterdam, Netherlands

Koninklijke Nederlandse Vereniging Voor Luchtvaart [IO], The Hague, Netherlands

Koninklijke Vereniging voor Nederlandse Muziekgeschiedenis [★IO]

Koninklijke Vereniging van Nederlandse Reders [★IO]

Koninklijke Vereniging van Nederlandse Wijnhandelaren [★IO]

Koninklijke Vlaamse Academie voor Taal-en Letterkunde [★IO]

Konoinklijke Nederlandse Chemische Vereniging [★IO]

Konrad Adenauer Found. - Germany [IO], St. Augustin, Germany

Konrad Adenauer Found. - South Africa [IO], Johannesburg, Republic of South Africa

Konrad Adenauer Found. - Zimbabwe [IO], Harare, Zimbabwe

Konrad-Adenauer Stiftung [★IO]

Konrad Adenauer Stiftung [★IO]

Konservativ Ungdom [★IO]

Konservative Folkeparti [★IO]

Kopenhagen Fur [IO], Glostrup, Denmark

KOPIKEN [IO], Nairobi, Kenya

KOPINOR [IO], Oslo, Norway

KOPIOSTO [IO], Helsinki, Finland

KOPIPOL [IO], Kielce, Poland

Korea

Amer. Fighter Aces Assn. [20647]

Amer. Legion Auxiliary [21189]

China Stamp Soc. [22803]

EAA Warbirds of Am. [21443]

Korea Economic Inst. [17965]

Korea Info. Tech. Network [6736]

Korea Postcard Collectors Gp. [22907]

The Korea Soc. [24350]

Korea Stamp Soc. [22838]

Korea Trade Promotion Center [24351]

Korean-American Medical Assn. [15174]

Korean Amer. Peace Inst. [17966]

Korean American Peace Institute [IO]

Korean Amer. Soc. of Entrepreneurs [773]

Korean War Proj. [6344]

Northern Far East Returned Missionaries Assn. [20504]

Traditional Tae Kwon Do Chung Do Assn. [23604]

Young Koreans United [12485]

Korea ACM SIGCHI [IO], Daejeon, Republic of Korea

Korea Agro-Fisheries Trade Corp. [IO], Seoul, Republic of Korea

Korea-America Commerce and Indus. Assn. [★24350]

Korea Auto Indus. Cooperative Assn. [IO], Seoul, Republic of Korea

Korea Auto. Manufacturers' Assn. [IO], Seoul, Republic of Korea

Korea Badminton Assn. [IO], Seoul, Republic of Korea

Korea; Campaign for the Peace and Reunification of [★17966]

Korea Certified Investment Analysts Assn. [IO], Seoul, Republic of Korea

Korea Chamber of Commerce and Indus. [IO], Seoul, Republic of Korea

Korea Chem. Fibers Assn. [IO], Seoul, Republic of Korea

Korea Church Coalition for Peace, Justice and Reunification [★IO]

Korea Church Coalition for Peace, Justice and Reunification [★17966]

Korea Cricket Assn. [IO], Seoul, Republic of Korea

Korea Dairy Indus. Assn. [IO], Seoul, Republic of Korea

Korea Die and Mold Indus. Cooperative [IO], Seoul, Republic of Korea

Korea Economic Coun; U.S.- [★24350]

Korea Economic Inst. [17965], 1201 F St. NW, Ste. 910, Washington, DC 20004, (202)464-1982

Korea Economic Inst. of Am. [★17965]

Korea Elecl. Contractors' Assn. [IO], Seoul, Republic of Korea

Korea Elecl. Mfrs'. Co-operative [IO], Seoul, Republic of Korea

Korea Electronic Indus. Cooperative [IO], Seoul, Republic of Korea

Korea Employers Fed. [IO], Seoul, Republic of Korea

Korea Fed. of Advt. Associations [IO], Seoul, Republic of Korea

Korea Fed. of Banks [IO], Seoul, Republic of Korea

Korea Fed. of Furniture Indus. Cooperatives [IO], Seoul, Republic of Korea

Korea Fed. of Small and Medium Bus. [IO], Seoul, Republic of Korea

Korea Fed. of Textile Indus. [IO], Seoul, Republic of Korea

Korea Floorball Fed. [IO], Seoul, Republic of Korea

Korea Food for the Hungry Intl. [IO], Seoul, Republic of Korea

Korea Found. [IO], Seoul, Republic of Korea

Korea Indus. Safety Assn. [IO], Seoul, Republic of Korea

Korea Info. Sci. Soc. [IO], Seoul, Republic of Korea

Korea Info. Tech. Network [IO], San Jose, CA, United States

Korea Info. Tech. Network [6736], 3003 N First St., San Jose, CA 95134, (408)432-5006

Korea Intl. Freight Forwarders Assn. [IO], Seoul, Republic of Korea

Korea Iron and Steel Assn. [IO], Seoul, Republic of Korea

Korea Life Insurance Assn. [IO], Seoul, Republic of Korea

Korea Machine Tool Mfrs'. Assn. [IO], Seoul, Republic of Korea

Korea Musical Instrument Indus. Assn. [IO], Seoul, Republic of Korea

Korea Non-Life Insurance Assn. [IO], Seoul, Republic of Korea

Korea; North Amer. Coalition for Human Rights in [★17966]

Korea Orienteering Fed. [IO], Seoul, Republic of Korea

Korea Paper Manufacturers' Assn. [IO], Seoul, Republic of Korea

Korea PC Gp. [★22907]

Korea Petrochemical Indus. Assn. [IO], Seoul, Republic of Korea

Korea Pharmaceutical Manufacturers Assn. [IO], Seoul, Republic of Korea

Korea Polio Found. [IO], Seoul, Republic of Korea

Korea Postcard Collectors Gp. [22907], c/o Deltiologists of Am., PO Box 8, Norwood, PA 19074

Korea Racing Assn. [IO], Gwacheon, Republic of Korea

Korea Shipbuilders' Assn. [IO], Seoul, Republic of Korea

Korea Skating Union [IO], Seoul, Republic of Korea

The Korea Soc. [24350], 950 3rd Ave., 8th Fl., New York, NY 10022, (212)759-7525

Korea Soc; U.S.- [★24350]

Korea Sports Assn. for the Disabled [IO], Seoul, Republic of Korea

Korea Squash Fed. [IO], Seoul, Republic of Korea

Korea Stamp Soc. [IO], Oak Ridge, TN, United States

Korea Stamp Soc. [22838], c/o John E. Talmage, Jr., Sec.-Treas., PO Box 6889, Oak Ridge, TN 37831

Korea Stationery Indus. Cooperative [IO], Seoul, Republic of Korea

Korea Taekwondo Assn. [IO], Seoul, Republic of Korea

Korea Tennis Assn. [IO], Seoul, Republic of Korea

A star before a book entry number signifies that the name is not listed separately, but is mentioned within the entry.

Korea Textile Trade Assn. **[IO]**, Seoul, Republic of Korea
Korea Trade Promotion Center **[24351]**, 460 Park Ave., Ste. 402, New York, NY 10022, (212)826-0900
Korea Trade Promotion Corp. **[IO]**, Seoul, Republic of Korea
Korea Veterans Assn. of Canada **[IO]**, Caledonia, ON, Canada
Korea Water Ski Assn. **[IO]**, Seoul, Republic of Korea
Korea Welfare Found. **[IO]**, Seoul, Republic of Korea
Korean
    Asian Amer. Curriculum Proj. **[8598]**
    Assn. for Korean Music Res. **[10561]**
    Coalition for Healthy Korean Americans **[14988]**
    Intercollegiate Taiwanese Amer. Students Assn. **[19401]**
    Intl. Comm. for the Rescue of KAL 007 Survivors **[18541]**
    Korea Found. **[IO]**
    Korea Postcard Collectors Gp. **[22907]**
    The Korea Soc. **[24350]**
    Korea Stamp Soc. **[22838]**
    Korea Trade Promotion Center **[24351]**
    Korean Amer. Coalition **[19190]**
    Korean-American Medical Assn. **[15174]**
    Korean Amer. Professional Tennis Assn. **[23904]**
    Korean-American Scientists and Engineers Assn. **[7024]**
    Korean Amer. Soc. of Entrepreneurs **[773]**
    Natl. Assn. of Korean Americans **[17131]**
    Oh Ji Ho Intl. Fan Club **[24781]**
    U.S. Hapki Hae **[23606]**
    World Kouk Sun Do Soc. **[10294]**
    World Kouk Sun Do Soc. **[IO]**
    Young Koreans United **[IO]**
    Young Koreans United **[12485]**
Korean Acad. of Psychotherapists **[IO]**, Seoul, Republic of Korea
Korean Acad. of Psychotherapists **[★IO]**
Korean Acad. of Psychotherapy Res. **[★IO]**
Korean Advertisers Assn. **[IO]**, Seoul, Republic of Korea
Korean Affairs Inst. - Address unknown since 1995.
Korean Amateur Radio League **[IO]**, Seoul, Republic of Korea
Korean Amer. Coalition **[19190]**, 3727 W 6th St., Ste. 515, Los Angeles, CA 90020, (213)365-5999
Korean Amer. Cultural Found. - Address unknown since 1995.
Korean-American Medical Assn. **[15174]**, 40 Bennett Rd., Englewood, NJ 07631-3306, (201)541-1345
Korean-American Medical Assn. of Am. **[★15174]**
Korean Amer. Peace Inst. **[17966]**, 60 Cedar St., Ridgefield Park, NJ 07660, (973)200-0071
Korean American Peace Institute **[IO]**, Ridgefield Park, NJ, United States
Korean Amer. Professional Tennis Assn. **[23904]**, 1515 N Glenoaks Blvd., Burbank, CA 91504
Korean-American Scientists and Engineers Assn. **[7024]**, 1952 Gallows Rd., Ste. 300, Vienna, VA 22182, (703)748-1221
Korean Amer. Soc. of Entrepreneurs **[773]**, 2882 Sand Hill Rd., Ste. 100, Menlo Park, CA 94025
Korean Americans; Natl. Assn. of **[17131]**
Korean Americans Reaching for Excellence - Address unknown since 2004.
Korean Assn. of Orthodontics **[IO]**, Seoul, Republic of Korea
Korean Assn. of Univ. Women **[IO]**, Seoul, Republic of Korea
Korean Athletics Fed. **[IO]**, Seoul, Republic of Korea
Korean Baseball Assn. **[IO]**, Seoul, Republic of Korea
Korean Bible Soc. **[IO]**, Seoul, Republic of Korea
Korean Chamber of Commerce in Hong Kong **[IO]**, Hong Kong, People's Republic of China
Korean Chem. Soc. **[IO]**, Seoul, Republic of Korea
Korean Commun. Workers Union **[★IO]**
Korean Conflict Res. Found. - Defunct.
Korean Cultural and Freedom Found. - Defunct.
Korean Culture and Arts Found. **[IO]**, Seoul, Republic of Korea
Korean Customs Brokers Assn. **[IO]**, Seoul, Republic of Korea

Korean Dermatological Assn. **[IO]**, Seoul, Republic of Korea
Korean Economic Assn. **[IO]**, Seoul, Republic of Korea
Korean EMDR Assn. **[IO]**, Seoul, Republic of Korea
Korean Energy Forum **[IO]**, Seoul, Republic of Korea
Korean Epilepsy Soc. **[IO]**, Seoul, Republic of Korea
Korean Fed. of DanceSport **[IO]**, Seoul, Republic of Korea
Korean Footwear Exporters Assn. **[★IO]**
Korean Footwear Indus. Assn. **[IO]**, Seoul, Republic of Korea
Korean Foster Care Assn. **[IO]**, Seoul, Republic of Korea
Korean Geotechnical Soc. **[IO]**, Seoul, Republic of Korea
Korean Inst. for Human Rights - Address unknown since 1999.
Korean Inst. of Intl. Stud. **[IO]**, Seoul, Republic of Korea
Korean Inst. of Landscape Architecture **[IO]**, Seoul, Republic of Korea
Korean Inst. for Women and Politics **[IO]**, Seoul, Republic of Korea
Korean Medical Assn. **[IO]**, Seoul, Republic of Korea
Korean Natl. Assn. - Address unknown since 2002.
Korean Natl. Commn. for UNESCO **[IO]**, Seoul, Republic of Korea
Korean Nuclear Soc. **[IO]**, Daejeon, Republic of Korea
Korean Olympic Comm. **[IO]**, Seoul, Republic of Korea
Korean Operations Res. and Mgt. Sci. Soc. **[IO]**, Seoul, Republic of Korea
Korean Pain Res. Soc. **[IO]**, Seoul, Republic of Korea
Korean Patriotic Women's Assn. in America - Defunct.
Korean Physical Therapy Assn. **[IO]**, Seoul, Republic of Korea
Korean Physiological Soc. **[IO]**, Seoul, Republic of Korea
Korean Postal Workers Union **[IO]**, Seoul, Republic of Korea
Korean Psychotherapy Case Study Group **[★IO]**
Korean Radiological Soc. **[IO]**, Seoul, Republic of Korea
Korean Red Cross **[IO]**, Seoul, Republic of Korea
Korean Sailing Fed. **[IO]**, Seoul, Republic of Korea
Korean Scientists and Engineers Assn. in Am. **[★7024]**
Korean Soc. of Anesthesiologists **[IO]**, Seoul, Republic of Korea
Korean Soc. for the Cerebral Palsied **[IO]**, Seoul, Republic of Korea
Korean Soc. of Chemotherapy **[IO]**, Seoul, Republic of Korea
Korean Soc. of Circulation **[IO]**, Seoul, Republic of Korea
Korean Soc. of Electron Microscopy **[IO]**, Seoul, Republic of Korea
Korean Soc. of Fertility and Sterility **[IO]**, Seoul, Republic of Korea
Korean Soc. of Gastrointestinal Endoscopy **[IO]**, Seoul, Republic of Korea
Korean Soc. of Geodesy, Photogrammetry and Cartography **[IO]**, Seoul, Republic of Korea
Korean Soc. of Hypertension **[IO]**, Seoul, Republic of Korea
Korean Soc. of Medical Informatics **[IO]**, Seoul, Republic of Korea
Korean Soc. of Pharmacology **[IO]**, Seoul, Republic of Korea
Korean Soc. of Remote Sensing **[IO]**, Seoul, Republic of Korea
Korean Soc. of Soil Sci. and Fertilizer **[IO]**, Suwon, Republic of Korea
Korean Soc. of Woman Composers **[IO]**, Seoul, Republic of Korea
Korean Standards Assn. **[IO]**, Seoul, Republic of Korea
Korean Veterans Intl. - Address unknown since 1995.
Korean War
    2nd Infantry Div. (2id), Korean War Veterans Alliance **[21167]**

2nd Infantry Division (2id), Korean War Veterans Alliance **[IO]**
77th Artillery Assn. **[21342]**
Amer. Fighter Aces Assn. **[20647]**
Amer. Legion Auxiliary **[21189]**
Assn. of 40th Infantry Div. Korean War Veterans **[21168]**
Chosin Few **[21169]**
Chosin Few **[IO]**
EAA Warbirds of Am. **[21443]**
Korean War Proj. **[6344]**
Korean War Veterans Assn. **[21170]**
Korean War Veterans Assn. **[IO]**
Mosquito Assn. **[20663]**
Natl. Alliance of Families for the Return of America's Missing Servicemen **[21263]**
Korean War Proj. **[6344]**, PO Box 180190, Dallas, TX 75218-0190, (214)320-0342
Korean War Veterans Assn. **[21170]**, 163 Deerbrook Trail, Pineville, LA 71360, (318)641-8033
Korean War Veterans Assn. **[IO]**, Pineville, LA, United States
Korean War Veterans Memorial - Defunct.
Korean Women Entrepreneurs Assn. **[IO]**, Seoul, Republic of Korea
Korean Women Workers Associations United **[IO]**, Seoul, Republic of Korea
Korean Women's Inst. **[IO]**, Seoul, Republic of Korea
Korean YMCA **[IO]**, Seoul, Republic of Korea
Korfball
    British Korfball Assn. **[IO]**
    Intl. Korfball Fed. **[IO]**
    Royal Dutch Korfball Assn. **[IO]**
Korps USA; Kids **[13399]**
Kosciuszko Found. **[10879]**, 15 E 65th St., New York, NY 10021-6595, (212)734-2130
Kosciuszko Found. **[IO]**, New York, NY, United States
Kosher Certification; OK **[20169]**
Kosher Certification; OK Labs - **[★20169]**
Kosher Certification Service **[★20170]**
Kosher Wine Inst. - Defunct.
Kosovo
    Direct Aid Intl. **[12849]**
Kossuth Found. - Defunct.
Kost och Naring- en branchforening inom Ledarna **[★IO]**
Kosuto Kougaku Ken'Kyusho **[★IO]**
Kott och Chark Foretagen **[★IO]**
Kotzebue Area Hea. Corp. **[★12627]**
Kotzebue Area Hea. Corp. **[★12627]**
Kowloon Chamber of Commerce **[IO]**, Hong Kong, People's Republic of China
Krajowa Izba Gospodarcza **[★IO]**
Krasner Found; Pollock- **[17004]**
KRC Development Coun. - Defunct.
Kreis Katholischer Frauen im Heliand-Bund **[IO]**, Frankfurt, Germany
Kresge Found. **[IO]**, Troy, MI, United States
Kresge Found. **[13123]**, 3215 W Big Beaver Rd., Troy, MI 48084, (248)643-9630
Kress Found; Samuel H. **[13132]**
Kring voor Toegeporte Fysioch Geografie **[★IO]**
Kris Kristofferson Intl. Fan Club - Defunct.
Krishna Consciousness
    Intl. Soc. for Krishna Consciousness **[20203]**
    Intl. Soc. for Krishna Consciousness **[IO]**
Krishnamurti Found. of Am. **[12355]**, PO Box 1560, Ojai, CA 93024, (805)646-2726
Kristana Esperantista Ligo Internacia **[19812]**, 3578 S Taylor Ave., Milwaukee, WI 53207-3439, (414)482-8903
Kristana Esperantista Ligo Internacia **[IO]**, Milwaukee, WI, United States
Kristana Esperantista Ligo Usona - Defunct.
Kristelige Foreninger av Unge Vinner **[★IO]**
Kristelijke Beweging van Gepensioneerden **[IO]**, Brussels, Belgium
Kristelijke Werknemersbeweging **[IO]**, Brussels, Belgium
Kristna Fredsrorelsen **[★IO]**
Kroc Inst. for Intl. Peace Stud; Joan B. **[18216]**
Kroeber Anthropological Soc. **[6421]**, c/o Univ. of California, Berkeley, Dept. of Anthropology, 232 Kroeber Hall, Berkeley, CA 94720-3710, (510)642-3391

Reference to "IO" in place of a book number signifies that the association may be found in the 45th edition of International Organizations.

Krousar Thmey [IO], Paris, France
Krystonia Collector's Club [22064], 125 W Ellsworth, Ann Arbor, MI 48108, (734)332-8773
KS and Associates [★16538]
Ku Klux Klan
    Anti-Repression Rsrc. Team [17093]
    Center for Democratic Renewal [17098]
    Intelligence Proj. [17121]
Ku Klux Klan; Knights of the [18799]
Kuban; All Cossack Assn. New [★19019]
Kuban Educ. and Welfare Assn; New [19019]
Kuban Historical Museum; New [★19019]
Kuebel Stiftung fur Hilfe zur Selbdthilfe [★IO]
Kuki-Chowa Eisei Kogakkai [★IO]
Kultana Orchids [IO], Bangkok, Thailand
Kultur Farband; Yiddisher [10291]
Kultura Centro Esperantista [★IO]
Kumitat Olimpiku Malta [★IO]
Kumiteollisuus ry [★IO]
Kump Family Assn. [20976], 7783 S 4950 W, West Jordan, UT 84084-5516
Kump Family Org. [★20976]
Kumpulan Kebudayaan Malaysia [★IO]
Kundalini Res. Inst. [★20631]
Kundalini Res. Network [14828], c/o Lawrence Edwards, PhD, VP, PO Box 215, Bedford Hills, NY 10507, (914)234-4800
Kungfu Fed; U.S.A. Wushu- [23605]
Kungl. Vetenskapsakademien [★IO]
Kungliga Fysiografiska Sallskapet [★IO]
Kungliga Vitterhets Historie och Antikvitets Akademien [★IO]
Kunzang Palyul Choling [19553], 18400 River Rd., Poolesville, MD 20837, (301)349-0440
Kuratorium fur die Tagungen der Nobelpreistrager [★IO]
Kurdish
    Amer. Kurdish Info. Network [IO]
    Amer. Kurdish Info. Network [17967]
    Amer. Soc. for Kurds [13154]
    Kurdish Heritage Found. of Am. [19191]
    Kurdish Heritage Found. of Am. [IO]
Kurdish Heritage Found. of Am. [IO], Brooklyn, NY, United States
Kurdish Heritage Found. of Am. [19191], 345 Park Pl., Brooklyn, NY 11238, (718)783-7930
Kurdish Human Rights Proj. [IO], London, United Kingdom
Kurk Sanayicileri ve Is Adamlari Dernegi [★IO]
Kurt-Godel-Gesellschaft [★IO]
Kurt Goedel Soc. [IO], Vienna, Austria
Kurt Weill Foundation for Music [IO], New York, NY, United States
Kurt Weill Found. for Music [10635], 7 E 20th St., New York, NY 10003-1106, (212)505-5240
Kurtis-Kraft Register - Defunct.
Kushner Breast Cancer Advisory Center; Rose [13870]
Kustom Kemps of Am. [21683], 26 Main St., Cassville, MO 65625-9400, (417)847-2940
Kustoms of Am. [22921], c/o Jeff Wortman, Pres., 4427 Ginger Dr., Gastonia, NC 28056, (704)865-4433
Kuvasz Assn; Amer. [12015]
Kuvasz Club of Am. [22302], c/o Richard Rosenthal, Treas., 6050 Peachtree Pkwy., Ste. 240-216, Norcross, GA 30092
Kuwait Amateur Radio Soc. [IO], Safat, Kuwait
Kuwait Assn. of Athletic Fed. [IO], Safat, Kuwait
Kuwait Badminton Fed. [IO], Hawalli, Kuwait
Kuwait Boxing and Weightlifting Assn. [IO], Hawalli, Kuwait
Kuwait Chamber of Commerce and Indus. [IO], Safat, Kuwait
Kuwait Dental Assn. [IO], Hawalli, Kuwait
Kuwait Jet Ski Fed. [IO], Safat, Kuwait
Kuwait Journalists Assn. [IO], Safat, Kuwait
Kuwait Judo and Taekwondo Fed. [IO], Safat, Kuwait
Kuwait Medical Assn. [IO], Safat, Kuwait
Kuwait Natl. Commn. for Educ., Sci. and Culture [IO], Safat, Kuwait
Kuwait Olympic Comm. [IO], Safat, Kuwait
Kuwait Soc. of Dermatologists [IO], Khaldeyah, Kuwait

Kuwait Soc. for the Handicapped [IO], Hawalli, Kuwait
Kuwait Sports Medicine Assn. [IO], Safat, Kuwait
Kuwait Squash Fed. [IO], Hawalli, Kuwait
Kuwait Tennis Fed. [IO], Hawalli, Kuwait
Kuwaiti Soc. for Traumatic Stress Stud. [IO], Safat, Kuwait
Kvindernes Internationale Liga for Fred og Frihed [★IO]
KVINFO - Danish Centre for Info. on Women and Gender [IO], Copenhagen, Denmark
Kvinnliga Akademikers Forening [★IO]
KXE6S Verein Chess Soc. - Address unknown since 1985.
Kyongsang Bankers Club [★IO]
Kyosiga Community Christians Assn. for Development [IO], Kampala, Uganda
Kypriaki Aerathlitiki Omospondia [★IO]
Kypriakos Syndesmos Biomichanion Endysis [★IO]
Kyrghyz Natl. Badminton Fed. [IO], Bishkek, Kirgizstan
Kyrgyz League Against Epilepsy [IO], Bishkek, Kirgizstan
Kyrgyzstan Medical Assn. [IO], Bishkek, Kirgizstan
Kyrgyzstan Taekwondo Assn. [IO], Bishkek, Kirgizstan
Kyrgyzstan Tennis Fed. [IO], Bishkek, Kirgizstan
Kythe [IO], Quezon City, Philippines
KZ Owners' Assn. - Defunct.

L

L. E. Support Club - Defunct.
L. Mike Assn. [13124]
L. Q. C. Lamar Soc. - Defunct.
L Walkers; Natl. Org. of [23971]
L5 Soc. [★6378]
La federation humaniste europeenne [★IO]
La Asociacion Pro-Bienestar de la Familia Colombia [IO], Bogota, Colombia
La Buena Fe Assn. - Address unknown since 2002.
La Camara De Comercio Americana En Espana [★IO]
La Camara De Comercio Americana En Espana [★IO]
La societe des comptables professionnels du Canada [★IO]
La Chambre Canadienne Allemande de l'Industrie et du Commerce [★IO]
La Chambre de Commerce Canada - Grande Bretagne [★IO]
La Cle d'la Baie en Huronie [★IO]
La Communaute Baha'ie du Canada [★IO]
La Conseil Canadien des Ministres de l'Environnement [★IO]
La Corp. Canadienne des Retraites Interesses [★IO]
La Croix Rouge Monegasque [★IO]
La Farge Inst; John [19645]
La Federacion Dominicana de Badminton [IO], Santo Domingo, Dominican Republic
La Fed. Canadienne de Bridge [★IO]
La Fed. Canado-Arabe [★IO]
La Fed. des associations europeennes d'ecrivains [★IO]
La Fed. des Societes Canadiennes d'Assistance aux Animaux [★IO]
La Fed. de Tir du Canada [★IO]
La Fleur Fraternity - Address unknown since 1995.
La Fondation des ecrivains canadiens [★IO]
La Fondation Canadienne MedicAlert [★IO]
La Fondation Canadienne de Recherche en Publicite [★IO]
La Guilde Canadienne des Realisateurs [★IO]
La Leche League [IO], Charlemagne, QC, Canada
La Leche League Intl. [IO], Schaumburg, IL, United States
La Leche League Intl. [12411], PO Box 4079, Schaumburg, IL 60168-4079, (847)519-7730
La Leche League of New Zealand [IO], Wellington, New Zealand
La Otra Bolsa de Valores [IO], Mexico City, Mexico
La Plate-forme Europeenne des Personnes Agees [★IO]
La Prevention Routiere Internationale [★IO]
La Raza Legal Alliance Joint Guatemala Delegation - Defunct.

La Raza Natl. Bar Assn. [★5496]
La Raza; Natl. Coun. of [12278]
La Raza Natl. Lawyers Assn. [★5496]
La Raza; Southwest Coun. of [★12278]
La Raza Unida Party [18326], 11663 Herrick Ave., PO Box 13, San Fernando, CA 91340, (619)420-3826
La Sertoma Intl. [13048], 21710 S Race, Spring Hill, KS 66083, (913)686-3000
La Sertoma Intl. [IO], Spring Hill, KS, United States
La Societe canadienne des etudes mesopotamiennes [★IO]
La Societe des sculpteurs du Canada [★IO]
La Societe Canadienne D' Histoire de L'Eglise Catholique [★IO]
La Societe Canadienne d'Addison [★IO]
La Societe Canadienne De La Douleur [★IO]
La Societe Canadienne d'Etudes Ethniques [★IO]
La Societe Canadienne des Eleveurs de Moutons [★IO]
La Societe Canadienne de l'Ouie [★IO]
La Societe Canadienne de Neurophysiologie Clinique [★IO]
La Societe Canadienne de Physiologie [★IO]
La Societe Canadienne de Sante Internationale [★IO]
La Societe Canadienne de Sciences de la Nutrition [★IO]
La Societe Canadienne de Texels [★IO]
La Societe d'histoire nationale du Canada [★IO]
La Societe de Genetique du Canada [★IO]
La Societe Guernesiaise [IO], Guernsey, United Kingdom
La Societe canadienne des eleveurs de bovins Highland [★IO]
La Societe John Milton Pour Les Aveugles du Canada [★IO]
La Societe pour l'etude de l'architecture au Canada [★IO]
La Societe Opimian [★IO]
La Societe de Philosophie Exacte [★IO]
La Societe de Philosophie Exacte [★10833]
La Societe de Protection des Infirmies et infirmiers du Canada [★IO]
La Societe Royale de Philatelie du Canada [★IO]
Laakarin Sosiaalinen Vastuu [★IO]
Lab Personnel; Natl. Certification Agency for Medical [★15145]
Laban/Bartenieff Inst. of Movement Stud. [9891], 520 8th Ave., Rm. 304, New York, NY 10018, (212)643-8888
Laban Guild [IO], Knutsford, United Kingdom
Laban Inst. of Movement Stud. [★9891]
Label Collectors Club; Aeronautica and Air [21422]
Label Collectors; Tri-County Citrus [★21995]
Label Mfrs. Assn. - Defunct.
Label Mfrs. Inst; Tag and [3687]
Label Printing Indus. of Am. [3684], 200 Deer Run Rd., Sewickley, PA 15143-2600, (412)741-6860
Label and Ser. Trades Dept., AFL-CIO; Union [24213]
Label Soc; Citrus [21995]
Label Soc; Pacific Antique [★21995]
Labels
    Citrus Label Soc. [21995]
    Intl. Bird Beer Label Assn. [21491]
    Packaging and Label Gravure Assn. Global [1784]
Labonte Fan Club; Bobby [24999]
Labor
    A. Philip Randolph Inst. [18604]
    Actors' Equity Assn. [24148]
    AFL-CIO [24096]
    AFL-CIO Community Action Field Mobilization Dept. [11801]
    AFL-CIO Working for Am. Inst. [12065]
    AFT Healthcare [24087]
    Air Line Pilots Assn., Intl. [24005]
    Aircraft Mechanics Fraternal Assn. [24006]
    Alliance for Sustainable Jobs and the Env. [24053]
    Alliance for Worker Freedom [24217]
    Amalgamated Transit Union [24197]
    Amer. Assn. of Classified School Employees [24041]
    Amer. Fed. of Govt. Employees [24068]

A star before a book entry number signifies that the name is not listed separately, but is mentioned within the entry.

Amer. Fed. of Musicians of the U.S. and Canada [24149]

Amer. Fed. of Security Officers [24184]

Amer. Fed. of State, County and Municipal Employees [24069]

Amer. Fed. of Teachers [24042]

Amer. Fed. of TV and Radio Artists [24022]

Amer. Foreign Ser. Assn. [24070]

Amer. Guild of Musical Artists [24150]

Amer. Guild of Variety Artists [24151]

Amer. Independent Cockpit Alliance [24008]

Amer. Inst. for Full Employment [12068]

Amer. Labor Education Center [8720]

Amer. Musicians Union [24152]

Amer. Postal Workers Union [24166]

Amer. Radio Assn. [24023]

Amer. Rights at Work [17968]

Amer. Train Dispatchers Dept. of the BLE [24175]

Andolan - Organizing South Asian Workers [24138]

Assoc. Actors and Artistes of Am. [24153]

Associates of the Amer. Foreign Ser. Worldwide [24071]

Assn. for Behavioral Hea. and Wellness [24088]

Assn. of Civilian Technicians [24072]

Assn. of Farmworker Opportunity Programs [12585]

Assn. of Flight Attendants - CWA [24009]

Assn. of Labor Relations Agencies [24112]

Assn. for Measurement and Evaluation of Commun. [IO]

Assn. of Minor League Umpires [23104]

Assn. of Theatrical Press Agents and Managers [24154]

Assn. for Union Democracy [24113]

Assn. of Volleyball Professionals [24191]

Assn. of Western Pulp and Paper Workers [24064]

Bakery, Confectionery, Tobacco Workers and Grain Millers Intl. Union [24017]

Brewery and Soft Drink Workers Conf. - U.S.A. and Canada [24020]

Brotherhood of Locomotive Engineers and Trainmen, A Division of the Rail Conf. of the Intl. Brotherhood of Teamsters [24176]

Brotherhood of Maintenance of Way Employees [24177]

Brotherhood of Railroad Signalmen [24178]

Brotherhood Railway Carmen Division/Transportation Communications Union [24179]

Brotherhood of Shoe and Allied Craftsmen [24063]

Brotherhood of Utility Workers of New England [24215]

Building and Constr. Trades Dept. - AFL-CIO [24025]

California Public Employee Relations Prog. [17969]

Cement, Lime, Gypsum, and Allied Workers Div. [24038]

Center for Labor and Community Res. [17970]

Center for Labor Res. and Educ. [8721]

Change to Win [24201]

Child Labor Coalition [11567]

Christian Labor Assn. of the U.S.A. [24035]

Civil Ser. Employees Assn. [24073]

Coalition of Black Trade Unionists [24202]

Coalition of Labor Union Women [24203]

Coalition of Labor Union Women Center for Educ. and Res. [24204]

Comm. of Interns and Residents [24089]

Community Food Security Coalition [12192]

Concerned Educators Against Forced Unionism - A Special Proj. of the Natl. Right to Work Legal Defense Found. [17971]

Confed. of Labour "Podkrepa" [IO]

Cong. of Independent Unions [24205]

Constr. Labour Relations Assn. of Manitoba [IO]

Coun. of Engineers and Scientists Organizations [7817]

Coun. of the United Textile Workers of Am. [24194]

Dept. for Professional Employees, AFL-CIO [24173]

Directors Guild of Am. [24055]

Distribution Contractors Assn. [24162]

Eugene V. Debs Found. [10295]

European Assn. of Labour Economists [IO]

European Assn. of Natl. Productivity Centres [IO]

Farm Labor Organizing Comm. [23997]

Farm Labor Res. Proj. [23998]

Farm Worker Hea. Services [12586]

Fed. Educ. Assn. [24043]

Fed. of Westinghouse Independent Salaried Unions [24047]

Freelancers Union [24218]

French Democratic Union of Labour [IO]

Gen. Ser. Employees Union Local 73 [24097]

Glass Molders, Pottery, Plastics, and Allied Workers Intl. Union [24066]

Global Workers Justice Alliance [18074]

Graphic Arts Employers of Am. [24082]

Graphic Communications Conf. of the Intl. Brotherhood of Teamsters [24083]

Guild of Italian Amer. Actors [24155]

Hard Hatted Women [4040]

HR Policy Assn. [17972]

Indus. Union of Marine and Ship Building Workers of Am. [24125]

Indus. Workers of the World [24098]

Indus. Workers of the World Starbucks Workers Union [24206]

Inst. of the Ironworking Indus. [24133]

Inst. of Labor and Indus. Relations [24114]

Intl. Alliance of Theatrical Stage Employees, Moving Picture Technicians, Artists and Allied Crafts of the U.S., Its Territories and Canada [24156]

Intl. Allied Printing Trades Assn. [24084]

Intl. Assn. of Bridge, Structural, Ornamental and Reinforcing Iron Workers [24134]

Intl. Assn. of EMTs and Paramedics [24051]

Intl. Assn. of Fire Fighters [24057]

Intl. Assn. of Labour Inspection [IO]

Intl. Assn. of Machinists [24011]

Intl. Assn. of Machinists and Aerospace Workers [24012]

Intl. Assn. of Machinists and Aerospace Workers, Woodworkers District Lodge W1 [24010]

Intl. Brotherhood of Boilermakers, Iron Ship Builders, Blacksmiths, Forgers and Helpers [24021]

Intl. Brotherhood of DuPont Workers [24034]

Intl. Brotherhood of Elecl. Workers [24048]

Intl. Brotherhood of Police Officers [24120]

Intl. Civil Ser. Commn. [24143]

Intl. Fed. of Professional and Tech. Engineers [24052]

Intl. Guards Union of Am. [24185]

Intl. Guild of Symphony, Opera and Ballet Musicians [24157]

Intl. Inst. for Labour Stud. [IO]

Intl. Labor History Assn. [IO]

Intl. Labor History Assn. [5916]

Intl. Labor Rights Fund [17973]

Intl. Labor Rights Fund [IO]

Intl. Longshore and Warehouse Union [24126]

Intl. Longshoremen's Assn. [24127]

Intl. Org. of Masters, Mates and Pilots, ILA, AFL-CIO [24128]

Intl. Plate Printers, Die Stampers, and Engravers' Union of North Am. [24085]

Intl. Soc. for Labor and Social Security Law [IO]

Intl. Union of Allied Novelty and Prdt.ion Workers [24196]

Intl. Union of Bricklayers and Allied Craftworkers [24027]

Intl. Union of Electronic, Elecl., Salaried, Machine, and Furniture Workers [24049]

Intl. Union of Elevator Constructors [24099]

Intl. Union of Indus. and Independent Workers [24208]

Intl. Union of Operating Engineers [24028]

Intl. Union of Painters and Allied Trades/Joint Apprenticeship and Training Fund [12082]

Intl. Union of Petroleum and Indus. Workers [24163]

Intl. Union of Police Associations [24121]

Intl. Union of Security Officers [24186]

Intl. Union, Security, Police and Fire Professionals of Am. [24187]

Intl. Union of Tool, Die and Mold Makers [24100]

Intl. Union, United Auto., Aerospace and Agricultural Implement Workers of Am. [24004]

Joint Labor Mgt. Comm. of the Retail Food Indus. [24059]

Just Transition Alliance [24105]

Just Transition Alliance [IO]

Labor Coun. for Latin Amer. Advancement [24094]

Labor and Employment Relations Assn. [24115]

Labor Heritage Found. [9578]

Labor Proj. for Working Families [24117]

Labor Res. Assn. [24118]

Labor and Working Class History Assn. [8723]

Laborers' Intl. Union of North Am. [24029]

Lithuanian Labour Fed. [IO]

Machinists Non-Partisan Political League [24101]

Major League Baseball Players Assn. [24018]

Manpower Educ. Inst. [8567]

Maritime Trades Dept., AFL-CIO [24129]

Metal Trades Dept., AFL-CIO [24135]

Migrant Hea. Promotion [12590]

Millwright Gp. [24102]

Natl. Air Traffic Controllers Assn. [24013]

Natl. Alliance for Fair Contracting [24030]

Natl. Alliance for Migrant and Seasonal Farmworker Vocational Rehabilitation [12591]

Natl. Alliance of Postal and Fed. Employees [24167]

Natl. Alliance for Worker and Employer Rights [24110]

Natl. Assn. of Air Traffic Specialists [24014]

Natl. Assn. Broadcast Employees and Technicians - Communications Workers of Am. [24024]

Natl. Assn. of Govt. Employees [24075]

Natl. Assn. of Governmental Labor Officials [5917]

Natl. Assn. of Letter Carriers of the U.S.A. [24168]

Natl. Assn. of Postal Supervisors [24169]

Natl. Assn. of State Directors of Migrant Educ. [12592]

Natl. Assn. of Unemployment Insurance Appellate Boards [5831]

Natl. Basketball Players Assn. [24192]

Natl. Center for the Stud. of Collective Bargaining in Higher Educ. and the Professions [24036]

Natl. Comm. on the Educ. of Migrant Children (of the Natl. Child Labor Comm.) [12593]

Natl. Comm. for Labor Israel [12460]

Natl. Conf. of Firemen and Oilers [24058]

Natl. Conservation District Employees Assn. [24209]

Natl. Coun. on Teacher Retirement [24044]

Natl. Day Laborer Organizing Network [24111]

Natl. Educ. Assn. [24045]

Natl. Employment Law Proj. [12092]

Natl. Farm Worker Ministry [12594]

Natl. Fed. of Fed. Employees [24077]

Natl. Fed. of Independent Unions [24210]

Natl. Inst. for Work and Learning [17974]

Natl. Labor Alliance of Hea. Care Coalitions [24091]

Natl. League of Postmasters of the U.S. [24170]

Natl. Mobilization Against Sweatshops [17975]

Natl. Org. of Indus. Trade Unions [24103]

Natl. Org. of Legal Services Workers, UAW Local 2320 [24079]

Natl. Postal Mail Handlers Union [24171]

Natl. Public Employer Labor Relations Assn. [5918]

Natl. Rural Letter Carriers' Assn. [24172]

Natl. Treasury Employees Union [24080]

Natl. Union of Law Enforcement Associations [24124]

Natl. Writers Union [24219]

New York Coun. of Motion Picture and TV Unions [24056]

The Newspaper Guild [24140]

NLRB Professional Assn. [24081]

North Amer. Assn. of Educational Negotiators [24046]

OAS Staff Assn. [24144]

Off. and Professional Employees Intl. Union [23995]

Operative Plasterers and Cement Masons Intl. Assn. of U.S. and Canada [24031]

Pacific Coast Marine Firemen, Oilers, Watertenders and Wipers Assn. [24130]

Reference to "IO" in place of a book number signifies that the association may be found in the 45th edition of International Organizations.

Plant Protection Assn. [24188]
Printing, Publishing and Media Workers Sector of the CWA [24086]
Professional Airways Systems Specialists [24015]
Public Ser. Res. Coun. [17976]
Rescue Amer. Jobs [17984]
Res. Associates of Am. [24060]
Residential Constr. Workers' Assn. [948]
Retail, Wholesale and Dept. Store Union [24182]
Sailors' Union of the Pacific [24131]
Samuel Gompers Stamp Club [22867]
Screen Actors Guild [24158]
Seafarers' Intl. Union of North Am. [24132]
SEIU, District 925, AFL-CIO [23996]
Ser. Employees Intl. Union [24189]
Ser. Workers United [24190]
Sheet Metal Workers' Intl. Assn. [24136]
Soc. of Fed. Labor and Employee Relations Professionals [5919]
Soc. of Stage Directors and Choreographers [24159]
Stove, Furnace, Energy, and Allied Appliance Workers Division of the Intl. Brotherhood of Boilermakers [24001]
Student/Farmworker Alliance [24054]
SweatFree Communities [24106]
Sweatshop Watch [17977]
Teamsters for a Democratic Union [24199]
Textile Converters Assn. [24195]
Transport Workers Union of Am. [24200]
Trans. Communications Intl. Union [24180]
Union of Amer. Physicians and Dentists [24092]
Union Label and Ser. Trades Dept., AFL-CIO [24213]
UNITE HERE [24095]
United Assn. of Journeymen and Apprentices of the Plumbing, Pipe Fitting, Sprinkler Fitting Indus. of the U.S. and Canada [24164]
United Assn. for Labor Educ. [8722]
United Brotherhood of Carpenters and Joiners of Am. [24032]
United Food and Commercial Workers Intl. Union [24061]
United Furniture Workers Insurance Fund [24065]
United Hebrew Trades - New York Division of the Jewish Labor Comm. [24214]
United Mine Workers of Am. [24139]
United Nations Staff Union [24145]
United Scenic Artists [24160]
U.S./Labor Educ. in the Americas Proj. [17978]
U.S./Labor Educ. in the Americas Proj. [IO]
United Steel Workers of Am., Rubber/Plastics Indus. Conf. [24183]
United Steelworkers of Am. [24137]
United Trans. Union [24181]
United Union of Roofers, Waterproofers and Allied Workers [24033]
USWA Flint/Glass Workers Conf. [24067]
Utility Workers Union of Am., AFL-CIO [24216]
Verite [12063]
W. E. Upjohn Inst. for Employment Res. [12104]
Wal-Mart Alliance for Reform Now [24107]
Wal-Mart Workers of Am. [24108]
Wal-Mart Workers Assn. [24109]
Welfare to Work Partnership [13146]
Women's Bur. of the U.S. Department of Labor [6361]
Women's Natl. Basketball Players Assn. [23140]
Workers' Defense League [17159]
Writers Guild of Am., East [24220]
Writers Guild of Am., West [24221]
Youth for Intl. Socialism [18663]
Labor; Amer. Fed. of [★24096]
Labor Assistants and Childbirth Educators; Assn. of [13977]
Labor; Assn. of Chiefs and Officials of Bureaus of [★5917]
Labor Assn. of the U.S.A; Christian [24035]
The Labor Center [★8721]
Labor Coalition; Child [★17338]
Labor Comm; Jewish [17950]
Labor Comm. for the Jewish Workers in Palestine; Natl. [★12460]
Labor Comm; Natl. Child [13500]
Labor Comm; Natl. Comm. on the Educ. of Migrant Children of the Natl. Child [12593]

Labor Comm. for Safe Energy and Full Employment - Defunct.
Labor Comm. in Support of Worker and Human Rights in Central Am; Natl. [★17049]
Labor Comm. for Worker and Human Rights; Natl. [17049]
Labor Communications Assn., AFL-CIO/CLC; Intl. [3229]
Labor Conf; Natl. Railway [3288]
Labor Cooperative Educational and Publishing Soc. - Defunct.
Labor Coun. for Latin Amer. Advancement [24094], 815 16th St. NW, 4th Fl., Washington, DC 20006, (202)508-6919
Labor and Economic Crisis; Inst. for the Stud. of [★18448]
Labor Education Advancement Program - Defunct.
Labor Educ. Assn; Univ. [★8722]
Labor Educ. Proj; U.S./Guatemala [★17978]
Labor Educ. and Res. Proj. [★24116]
Labor and Employment Relations Assn. [24115], Univ. of Illinois, 121 LIR Bldg., 504 E Armory Ave., Champaign, IL 61820, (217)333-0072
Labor Groups; AFL-CIO/ALA Joint Comm. on Lib. Ser. to [10314]
Labor Heritage Found. [9578], 815 16th St. NW, Washington, DC 20006, (202)637-3963
Labor Historians - Defunct.
Labor-Industry Coalition for Intl. Trade - Address unknown since 2002.
Labor Inst. of Public Affairs - Defunct.
Labor Israel; Natl. Comm. for [12460]

Labor Management

Actors' Equity Assn. [24148]
AFL-CIO [24096]
AFT Healthcare [24087]
Air Line Pilots Assn., Intl. [24005]
Aircraft Mechanics Fraternal Assn. [24006]
Amalgamated Transit Union [24197]
Amer. Assn. of Classified School Employees [24041]
Amer. Fed. of Govt. Employees [24068]
Amer. Fed. of Musicians of the U.S. and Canada [24149]
Amer. Fed. of Security Officers [24184]
Amer. Fed. of State, County and Municipal Employees [24069]
Amer. Fed. of Teachers [24042]
Amer. Fed. of TV and Radio Artists [24022]
Amer. Foreign Ser. Assn. [24070]
Amer. Guild of Musical Artists [24150]
Amer. Guild of Variety Artists [24151]
Amer. Independent Cockpit Alliance [24008]
Amer. Musicians Union [24152]
Amer. Postal Workers Union [24166]
Amer. Radio Assn. [24023]
Amer. Train Dispatchers Dept. of the BLE [24175]
Assoc. Actors and Artistes of Am. [24153]
Associates of the Amer. Foreign Ser. Worldwide [24071]
Assn. for Behavioral Hea. and Wellness [24088]
Assn. of Civilian Technicians [24072]
Assn. of Flight Attendants - CWA [24009]
Assn. of Labor Relations Agencies [24112]
Assn. of Labour Providers [IO]
Assn. of Minor League Umpires [23104]
Assn. of Theatrical Press Agents and Managers [24154]
Assn. for Union Democracy [24113]
Assn. of Volleyball Professionals [24191]
Assn. of Western Pulp and Paper Workers [24064]
Bakery, Confectionery, Tobacco Workers and Grain Millers Intl. Union [24017]
Brewery and Soft Drink Workers Conf. - U.S.A. and Canada [24020]
Brotherhood of Locomotive Engineers and Trainmen, A Division of the Rail Conf. of the Intl. Brotherhood of Teamsters [24176]
Brotherhood of Maintenance of Way Employees [24177]
Brotherhood of Railroad Signalmen [24178]
Brotherhood Railway Carmen Division/Transportation Communications Union [24179]
Brotherhood of Shoe and Allied Craftsmen [24063]

Brotherhood of Utility Workers of New England [24215]
Building and Constr. Trades Dept. - AFL-CIO [24025]
Canadian Indus. Relations Assn. [IO]
Canadian Labour and Bus. Centre [IO]
Caribbean Employers' Confed. [IO]
Cement, Lime, Gypsum, and Allied Workers Div. [24038]
Change to Win [24201]
Christian Labor Assn. of the U.S.A. [24035]
Civil Ser. Employees Assn. [24073]
Coalition of Black Trade Unionists [24202]
Coalition of Labor Union Women [24203]
Coalition of Labor Union Women Center for Educ. and Res. [24204]
Comm. of Interns and Residents [24089]
Confed. of German Employers' Associations [IO]
Confed. of Swiss Employers [IO]
Cong. of Independent Unions [24205]
Coun. of Indian Employers [IO]
Coun. of the United Textile Workers of Am. [24194]
Dept. for Professional Employees, AFL-CIO [24173]
Directors Guild of Am. [24055]
Distribution Contractors Assn. [24162]
Employers' Consultative Assn. of Malawi [IO]
Employers' Consultative Assn. of Trinidad and Tobago [IO]
Employers' Fed. of Hong Kong [IO]
Farm Labor Organizing Comm. [23997]
Fed. Educ. Assn. [24043]
Fed. of Westinghouse Independent Salaried Unions [24047]
Fiji Employers' Fed. [IO]
Gen. Ser. Employees Union Local 73 [24097]
Ghana Employers Assn. [IO]
Glass Molders, Pottery, Plastics, and Allied Workers Intl. Union [24066]
Graphic Arts Employers of Am. [24082]
Graphic Communications Conf. of the Intl. Brotherhood of Teamsters [24083]
Guild of Italian Amer. Actors [24155]
Indus. Union of Marine and Ship Building Workers of Am. [24125]
Indus. Workers of the World [24098]
Indus. Workers of the World Starbucks Workers Union [24206]
Inst. of the Ironworking Indus. [24133]
Inst. of Labor and Indus. Relations [24114]
Intl. Alliance of Theatrical Stage Employees, Moving Picture Technicians, Artists and Allied Crafts of the U.S., Its Territories and Canada [24156]
Intl. Allied Printing Trades Assn. [24084]
Intl. Assn. of Bridge, Structural, Ornamental and Reinforcing Iron Workers [24134]
Intl. Assn. of EMTs and Paramedics [24051]
Intl. Assn. of Fire Fighters [24057]
Intl. Assn. of Machinists [24011]
Intl. Assn. of Machinists and Aerospace Workers [24012]
Intl. Assn. of Machinists and Aerospace Workers, Woodworkers District Lodge W1 [24026]
Intl. Brotherhood of Boilermakers, Iron Ship Builders, Blacksmiths, Forgers and Helpers [24021]
Intl. Brotherhood of DuPont Workers [24034]
Intl. Brotherhood of Elecl. Workers [24048]
Intl. Brotherhood of Police Officers [24120]
Intl. Civil Ser. Commn. [24143]
Intl. Fed. of Professional and Tech. Engineers [24052]
Intl. Guards Union of Am. [24185]
Intl. Guild of Symphony, Opera and Ballet Musicians [24157]
Intl. Longshore and Warehouse Union [24126]
Intl. Longshoremen's Assn. [24127]
Intl. Org. of Masters, Mates and Pilots, ILA, AFL-CIO [24128]
Intl. Plate Printers, Die Stampers, and Engravers' Union of North Am. [24085]
Intl. Union of Allied Novelty and Prdt.ion Workers [24196]
Intl. Union of Bricklayers and Allied Craftworkers [24027]

A star before a book entry number signifies that the name is not listed separately, but is mentioned within the entry.

Intl. Union of Electronic, Elecl., Salaried, Machine, and Furniture Workers [24049]
Intl. Union of Elevator Constructors [24099]
Intl. Union of Indus. and Independent Workers [24208]
Intl. Union of Operating Engineers [24028]
Intl. Union of Painters and Allied Trades/Joint Apprenticeship and Training Fund [12082]
Intl. Union of Petroleum and Indus. Workers [24163]
Intl. Union of Police Associations [24121]
Intl. Union of Security Officers [24186]
Intl. Union, Security, Police and Fire Professionals of Am. [24187]
Intl. Union of Tool, Die and Mold Makers [24100]
Intl. Union, United Auto., Aerospace and Agricultural Implement Workers of Am. [24004]
Joint Labor Mgt. Comm. of the Retail Food Indus. [24059]
Just Transition Alliance [24105]
Korea Employers Fed. [IO]
Labor Coun. for Latin Amer. Advancement [24094]
Labor and Employment Relations Assn. [24115]
Labor Proj. for Working Families [24117]
Labor Res. Assn. [24118]
Laborers' Intl. Union of North Am. [24029]
Machinists Non-Partisan Political League [24101]
Major League Baseball Players Assn. [24018]
Malaysian Employers' Fed. [IO]
Maritime Trades Dept., AFL-CIO [24129]
Metal Trades Dept., AFL-CIO [24135]
Millwright Gp. [24102]
Natl. Air Traffic Controllers Assn. [24013]
Natl. Alliance for Fair Contracting [24030]
Natl. Alliance for Migrant and Seasonal Farmworker Vocational Rehabilitation [12591]
Natl. Alliance of Postal and Fed. Employees [24167]
Natl. Alliance for Worker and Employer Rights [24110]
Natl. Assn. of Air Traffic Specialists [24014]
Natl. Assn. Broadcast Employees and Technicians - Communications Workers of Am. [24024]
Natl. Assn. of Govt. Employees [24075]
Natl. Assn. of Governmental Labor Officials [5917]
Natl. Assn. of Letter Carriers of the U.S.A. [24168]
Natl. Assn. of Postal Supervisors [24169]
Natl. Basketball Players Assn. [24192]
Natl. Center for the Stud. of Collective Bargaining in Higher Educ. and the Professions [24036]
Natl. Conf. of Firemen and Oilers [24058]
Natl. Conservation District Employees Assn. [24209]
Natl. Coun. on Teacher Retirement [24044]
Natl. Educ. Assn. [24045]
Natl. Fed. of Fed. Employees [24077]
Natl. Fed. of Independent Unions [24210]
Natl. Labor-Management Assn. [24119]
Natl. League of Postmasters of the U.S. [24170]
Natl. Org. of Indus. Trade Unions [24103]
Natl. Org. of Legal Services Workers, UAW Local 2320 [24079]
Natl. Postal Mail Handlers Union [24171]
Natl. Public Employer Labor Relations Assn. [5918]
Natl. Rural Letter Carriers' Assn. [24172]
Natl. Treasury Employees Union [24080]
Natl. Writers Union [24219]
New York Coun. of Motion Picture and TV Unions [24056]
The Newspaper Guild [24140]
NLRB Professional Assn. [24081]
North Amer. Assn. of Educational Negotiators [24046]
OAS Staff Assn. [24144]
Off. and Professional Employees Intl. Union [23995]
Operative Plasterers and Cement Masons Intl. Assn. of U.S. and Canada [24031]
Pacific Coast Marine Firemen, Oilers, Watertenders and Wipers Assn. [24130]
Plant Protection Assn. [24188]
Printing, Publishing and Media Workers Sector of the CWA [24086]

Professional Airways Systems Specialists [24015]
Professional Pilots Fed. [24016]
Rescue Amer. Jobs [17984]
Res. Associates of Am. [24060]
Retail, Wholesale and Dept. Store Union [24182]
Sailors' Union of the Pacific [24131]
Samuel Gompers Stamp Club [22867]
Screen Actors Guild [24158]
Seafarers' Intl. Union of North Am. [24132]
SEIU, District 925, AFL-CIO [23996]
Ser. Employees Intl. Union [24189]
Ser. Workers United [24190]
Sheet Metal Workers' Intl. Assn. [24136]
Soc. of Fed. Labor and Employee Relations Professionals [5919]
Soc. of Stage Directors and Choreographers [24159]
Stove, Furnace, Energy, and Allied Appliance Workers Division of the Intl. Brotherhood of Boilermakers [24001]
SweatFree Communities [24106]
Teamsters for a Democratic Union [24199]
Textile Converters Assn. [24195]
Transport Workers Union of Am. [24200]
Trans. Communications Intl. Union [24180]
Union of Amer. Physicians and Dentists [24092]
Union Label and Ser. Trades Dept., AFL-CIO [24213]
UNITE HERE [24095]
United Assn. of Journeymen and Apprentices of the Plumbing, Pipe Fitting, Sprinkler Fitting Indus. of the U.S. and Canada [24164]
United Brotherhood of Carpenters and Joiners of Am. [24032]
United Food and Commercial Workers Intl. Union [24061]
United Furniture Workers Insurance Fund [24065]
United Hebrew Trades - New York Division of the Jewish Labor Comm. [24214]
United Mine Workers of Am. [24139]
United Nations Staff Union [24145]
United Scenic Artists [24160]
United Steel Workers of Am., Rubber/Plastics Indus. Conf. [24183]
United Steelworkers of Am. [24137]
United Trans. Union [24181]
United Union of Roofers, Waterproofers and Allied Workers [24033]
USWA Flint/Glass Workers Conf. [24067]
Utility Workers Union of Am., AFL-CIO [24216]
Verite [12063]
Wal-Mart Alliance for Reform Now [24107]
Wal-Mart Workers of Am. [24108]
Wal-Mart Workers Assn. [24109]
Writers Guild of Am., East [24220]
Writers Guild of Am., West [24221]
Labor Mgt. Comm. of the Retail Food Indus; Joint [24059]
Labor-Mgt. Cooperation Fund; Instrument Technicians [1021]
Labor Mgt. Maritime Comm., Inc. - Address unknown since 2008.
Labor-Mgt. Relations Service of the U.S. Conf. of Mayors - Defunct.
Labor and Mental Health; Inst. for [15202]
Labor Notes [24116], 7435 Michigan Ave., Detroit, MI 48210, (313)842-6262
Labor Officials; Assn. of Governmental [★5917]
Labor Officials; Intl. Assn. of Governmental [★5917]
Labor Organizing Comm; Farm [23997]
Labor Palestine; Natl. Comm. for [★12460]
Labor Party of Am; Socialist [18334]
Labor Party; Progressive [18331]
Labor Party; Socialist [★18335]
Labor Party; Socialistic [★18334]
Labor Policy Assn. [★17972]
Labor Press of Am; Intl. [★3229]
Labor Press Assn; Intl. [★3229]
Labor Proj. for Working Families [24117], 2521 Channing Way, No. 5555, Berkeley, CA 94720, (510)643-7088
Labor Reform
Alliance for Sustainable Jobs and the Env. [24053]
Amer. Rights at Work [17968]

Americans Against Union Control of Govt. [17979]
Center on Natl. Labor Policy [17980]
CorpWatch [17756]
Eugene V. Debs Found. [10295]
Indus. Workers of the World Starbucks Workers Union [24206]
Just Transition Alliance [24105]
Labor Heritage Found. [9578]
Natl. Alliance for Worker and Employer Rights [24110]
Natl. Assn. of Orchestra Leaders [17981]
Natl. Day Laborer Organizing Network [24111]
Natl. Farm Worker Ministry [12594]
Natl. Labor Alliance of Hea. Care Coalitions [24091]
Natl. Mobilization Against Sweatshops [17975]
Natl. Right to Work Comm. [17982]
Natl. Right to Work Legal Defense and Educ. Found. [17983]
POWER: People Organized to Win Employment Rights [17494]
Rescue Amer. Jobs [17984]
Student/Farmworker Alliance [24054]
SweatFree Communities [24106]
Wal-Mart Alliance for Reform Now [24107]
Wal-Mart Workers of Am. [24108]
Wal-Mart Workers Assn. [24109]
Women's Natl. Basketball Players Assn. [23140]
Labor Relations Professionals; Soc. of Fed. [★5919]
Labor Res. Assn. [24118], 330 W 42nd St., 13th Fl., New York, NY 10036, (212)714-1677
Labor Res. Fund; Natl. Coun. on Agricultural Life and [12322]
Labor Res; Midwest Center for [★17970]
Labor Res. Proj; Farm [23998]
Labor Rights Educ. and Res. Fund; Intl. [★17973]
Labor Studies
Actors' Equity Assn. [24148]
AFL-CIO [24096]
AFT Healthcare [24087]
Air Line Pilots Assn., Intl. [24005]
Aircraft Mechanics Fraternal Assn. [24006]
Amalgamated Transit Union [24197]
Amer. Assn. of Classified School Employees [24041]
Amer. Fed. of Govt. Employees [24068]
Amer. Fed. of Musicians of the U.S. and Canada [24149]
Amer. Fed. of Security Officers [24184]
Amer. Fed. of State, County and Municipal Employees [24069]
Amer. Fed. of Teachers [24042]
Amer. Fed. of TV and Radio Artists [24022]
Amer. Foreign Ser. Assn. [24070]
Amer. Guild of Musical Artists [24150]
Amer. Guild of Variety Artists [24151]
Amer. Musicians Union [24152]
Amer. Postal Workers Union [24166]
Amer. Radio Assn. [24023]
Amer. Train Dispatchers Dept. of the BLE [24175]
Assoc. Actors and Artistes of Am. [24153]
Associates of the Amer. Foreign Ser. Worldwide [24071]
Assn. for Behavioral Hea. and Wellness [24088]
Assn. of Civilian Technicians [24072]
Assn. of Flight Attendants - CWA [24009]
Assn. of Labor Relations Agencies [24112]
Assn. of Labor Relations Agencies [IO]
Assn. of Theatrical Press Agents and Managers [24154]
Assn. for Union Democracy [24113]
Assn. of Volleyball Professionals [24191]
Assn. of Western Pulp and Paper Workers [24064]
Bakery, Confectionery, Tobacco Workers and Grain Millers Intl. Union [24017]
Brewery and Soft Drink Workers Conf. - U.S.A. and Canada [24020]
Brotherhood of Locomotive Engineers and Trainmen, A Division of the Rail Conf. of the Intl. Brotherhood of Teamsters [24176]
Brotherhood of Maintenance of Way Employees [24177]
Brotherhood of Railroad Signalmen [24178]
Brotherhood Railway Carmen Division/Transportation Communications Union [24179]

Reference to "IO" in place of a book number signifies that the association may be found in the 45th edition of International Organizations.

Brotherhood of Shoe and Allied Craftsmen [24063]
Brotherhood of Utility Workers of New England [24215]
Building and Constr. Trades Dept. - AFL-CIO [24025]
Cement, Lime, Gypsum, and Allied Workers Div. [24038]
Christian Labor Assn. of the U.S.A. [24035]
Civil Ser. Employees Assn. [24073]
Coalition of Black Trade Unionists [24202]
Coalition of Labor Union Women [24203]
Coalition of Labor Union Women Center for Educ. and Res. [24204]
Comm. of Interns and Residents [24089]
Cong. of Independent Unions [24205]
Coun. of the United Textile Workers of Am. [24194]
Dept. for Professional Employees, AFL-CIO [24173]
Directors Guild of Am. [24055]
Distribution Contractors Assn. [24162]
Farm Labor Organizing Comm. [23997]
Fed. Educ. Assn. [24043]
Fed. of Westinghouse Independent Salaried Unions [24047]
Gen. Ser. Employees Union Local 73 [24097]
Glass Molders, Pottery, Plastics, and Allied Workers Intl. Union [24066]
Graphic Arts Employers of Am. [24082]
Graphic Communications Conf. of the Intl. Brotherhood of Teamsters [24083]
Guild of Italian Amer. Actors [24155]
Indus. Union of Marine and Ship Building Workers of Am. [24125]
Indus. Workers of the World [24098]
Indus. Workers of the World Starbucks Workers Union [24206]
Inst. of the Ironworking Indus. [24133]
Inst. of Labor and Indus. Relations [24114]
Intl. Alliance of Theatrical Stage Employees, Moving Picture Technicians, Artists and Allied Crafts of the U.S., Its Territories and Canada [24156]
Intl. Allied Printing Trades Assn. [24084]
Intl. Assn. of Bridge, Structural, Ornamental and Reinforcing Iron Workers [24134]
Intl. Assn. of Fire Fighters [24057]
Intl. Assn. of Machinists [24011]
Intl. Assn. of Machinists and Aerospace Workers [24012]
Intl. Assn. of Machinists and Aerospace Workers, Woodworkers District Lodge W1 [24026]
Intl. Brotherhood of Boilermakers, Iron Ship Builders, Blacksmiths, Forgers and Helpers [24021]
Intl. Brotherhood of DuPont Workers [24034]
Intl. Brotherhood of Elecl. Workers [24048]
Intl. Brotherhood of Police Officers [24120]
Intl. Civil Ser. Commn. [24143]
Intl. Fed. of Professional and Tech. Engineers [24052]
Intl. Guards Union of Am. [24185]
Intl. Guild of Symphony, Opera and Ballet Musicians [24157]
Intl. Indus. Relations Assn. [IO]
Intl. Longshore and Warehouse Union [24126]
Intl. Longshoremen's Assn. [24127]
Intl. Org. of Masters, Mates and Pilots, ILA, AFL-CIO [24128]
Intl. Plate Printers, Die Stampers, and Engravers' Union of North Am. [24085]
Intl. Union of Allied Novelty and Prdt.ion Workers [24196]
Intl. Union of Bricklayers and Allied Craftworkers [24027]
Intl. Union of Electronic, Elecl., Salaried, Machine, and Furniture Workers [24049]
Intl. Union of Elevator Constructors [24099]
Intl. Union of Operating Engineers [24028]
Intl. Union of Petroleum and Indus. Workers [24163]
Intl. Union of Police Associations [24121]
Intl. Union of Security Officers [24186]
Intl. Union, Security, Police and Fire Professionals of Am. [24187]
Intl. Union of Tool, Die and Mold Makers [24100]

Intl. Union, United Auto., Aerospace and Agricultural Implement Workers of Am. [24004]
Joint Labor Mgt. Comm. of the Retail Food Indus. [24059]
Labor Coun. for Latin Amer. Advancement [24094]
Labor and Employment Relations Assn. [24115]
Labor Notes [24116]
Labor Proj. for Working Families [24117]
Labor Res. Assn. [24118]
Labor and Working Class History Assn. [8723]
Laborers' Intl. Union of North Am. [24029]
Machinists Non-Partisan Political League [24101]
Major League Baseball Players Assn. [24018]
Maritime Trades Dept., AFL-CIO [24129]
Metal Trades Dept., AFL-CIO [24135]
Millwright Gp. [24102]
Natl. Air Traffic Controllers Assn. [24013]
Natl. Alliance of Postal and Fed. Employees [24167]
Natl. Assn. of Air Traffic Specialists [24014]
Natl. Assn. Broadcast Employees and Technicians - Communications Workers of Am. [24024]
Natl. Assn. of Govt. Employees [24075]
Natl. Assn. of Letter Carriers of the U.S.A. [24168]
Natl. Assn. of Postal Supervisors [24169]
Natl. Basketball Players Assn. [24192]
Natl. Center for the Stud. of Collective Bargaining in Higher Educ. and the Professions [24036]
Natl. Conf. of Firemen and Oilers [24058]
Natl. Coun. on Teacher Retirement [24044]
Natl. Educ. Assn. [24045]
Natl. Fed. of Fed. Employees [24077]
Natl. Fed. of Independent Unions [24210]
Natl. Labor-Management Assn. [24119]
Natl. League of Postmasters of the U.S. [24170]
Natl. Org. of Indus. Trade Unions [24103]
Natl. Org. of Legal Services Workers, UAW Local 2320 [24079]
Natl. Postal Mail Handlers Union [24171]
Natl. Rural Letter Carriers' Assn. [24172]
Natl. Treasury Employees Union [24080]
Natl. Writers Union [24219]
New York Coun. of Motion Picture and TV Unions [24056]
The Newspaper Guild [24140]
NLRB Professional Assn. [24081]
North Amer. Assn. of Educational Negotiators [24046]
OAS Staff Assn. [24144]
Off. and Professional Employees Intl. Union [23995]
Operative Plasterers and Cement Masons Intl. Assn. of U.S. and Canada [24031]
Pacific Coast Marine Firemen, Oilers, Watertenders and Wipers Assn. [24130]
Plant Protection Assn. [24188]
Printing, Publishing and Media Workers Sector of the CWA [24086]
Professional Airways Systems Specialists [24015]
Res. Associates of Am. [24060]
Retail, Wholesale and Dept. Store Union [24182]
Sailors' Union of the Pacific [24131]
Samuel Gompers Stamp Club [22867]
Screen Actors Guild [24158]
Seafarers' Intl. Union of North Am. [24132]
SEIU, District 925, AFL-CIO [23996]
Ser. Employees Intl. Union [24189]
Sheet Metal Workers' Intl. Assn. [24136]
Soc. of Stage Directors and Choreographers [24159]
Stove, Furnace, Energy, and Allied Appliance Workers Division of the Intl. Brotherhood of Boilermakers [24001]
SweatFree Communities [24106]
Teamsters for a Democratic Union [24199]
Textile Converters Assn. [24195]
Transport Workers Union of Am. [24200]
Trans. Communications Intl. Union [24180]
Union of Amer. Physicians and Dentists [24092]
Union Label and Ser. Trades Dept., AFL-CIO [24213]
UNITE HERE [24095]
United Assn. of Journeymen and Apprentices of the Plumbing, Pipe Fitting, Sprinkler Fitting Indus. of the U.S. and Canada [24164]

United Brotherhood of Carpenters and Joiners of Am. [24032]
United Food and Commercial Workers Intl. Union [24061]
United Furniture Workers Insurance Fund [24065]
United Hebrew Trades - New York Division of the Jewish Labor Comm. [24214]
United Mine Workers of Am. [24139]
United Nations Staff Union [24145]
United Scenic Artists [24160]
United Steel Workers of Am., Rubber/Plastics Indus. Conf. [24183]
United Steelworkers of Am. [24137]
United Trans. Union [24181]
United Union of Roofers, Waterproofers and Allied Workers [24033]
USWA Flint/Glass Workers Conf. [24067]
Utility Workers Union of Am., AFL-CIO [24216]
Wal-Mart Workers of Am. [24108]
Writers Guild of Am., East [24220]
Writers Guild of Am., West [24221]
Labor and Supply Company; Planters' [★5228]
Labor Union Cong. of Quebec [IO], Montreal, QC, Canada
Labor Union Women Center for Educ. and Res; Coalition of [24204]
Labor Union Women; Coalition of [24203]
Labor Unions
Actors' Equity Assn. [24148]
AFL-CIO [24096]
AFL-CIO/ALA Joint Comm. on Lib. Ser. to Labor Groups [10314]
AFL-CIO Community Action Field Mobilization Dept. [11801]
AFL-CIO Working for Am. Inst. [12065]
Africa Action [16918]
AFT Healthcare [24087]
Air Line Pilots Assn., Intl. [24005]
Aircraft Mechanics Fraternal Assn. [24006]
Amalgamated Transit Union [24197]
Amer. Assn. of Classified School Employees [24041]
Amer. Fed. of Govt. Employees [24068]
Amer. Fed. of Musicians of the U.S. and Canada [24149]
Amer. Fed. of Security Officers [24184]
Amer. Fed. of State, County and Municipal Employees [24069]
Amer. Fed. of Teachers [24042]
Amer. Fed. of TV and Radio Artists [24022]
Amer. Foreign Ser. Assn. [24070]
Amer. Guild of Musical Artists [24150]
Amer. Guild of Variety Artists [24151]
Amer. Independent Cockpit Alliance [24008]
Amer. Musicians Union [24152]
Amer. Postal Workers Union [24166]
Amer. Radio Assn. [24023]
Amer. Train Dispatchers Dept. of the BLE [24175]
Amer. Union of Pizza Delivery Drivers [24062]
Assoc. Actors and Artistes of Am. [24153]
Associates of the Amer. Foreign Ser. Worldwide [24071]
Assn. for Behavioral Hea. and Wellness [24088]
Assn. of Civilian Technicians [24072]
Assn. of Flight Attendants - CWA [24009]
Assn. of Independent Commercial Producers [90]
Assn. of Labor Relations Agencies [24112]
Assn. of Minor League Umpires [23104]
Assn. of Theatrical Press Agents and Managers [24154]
Assn. for Union Democracy [24113]
Assn. of Volleyball Professionals [24191]
Assn. of Western Pulp and Paper Workers [24064]
Bakery, Confectionery, Tobacco Workers and Grain Millers Intl. Union [24017]
Brewery and Soft Drink Workers Conf. - U.S.A. and Canada [24020]
Brotherhood of Locomotive Engineers and Trainmen, A Division of the Rail Conf. of the Intl. Brotherhood of Teamsters [24176]
Brotherhood of Maintenance of Way Employees [24177]
Brotherhood of Railroad Signalmen [24178]
Brotherhood Railway Carmen Division/Transportation Communications Union [24179]

A star before a book entry number signifies that the name is not listed separately, but is mentioned within the entry.

Brotherhood of Shoe and Allied Craftsmen [24063]
Brotherhood of Utility Workers of New England [24215]
Building and Constr. Trades Dept. - AFL-CIO [24025]
Cement, Lime, Gypsum, and Allied Workers Div. [24038]
Change to Win [24201]
Christian Labor Assn. of the U.S.A. [24035]
Civil Ser. Employees Assn. [24073]
Coalition of Black Trade Unionists [24202]
Coalition of Labor Union Women [24203]
Coalition of Labor Union Women Center for Educ. and Res. [24204]
Comm. of Interns and Residents [24089]
Concerned Educators Against Forced Unionism - A Special Proj. of the Natl. Right to Work Legal Defense Found. [17971]
Cong. of Independent Unions [24205]
Coun. of the United Textile Workers of Am. [24194]
Dept. for Professional Employees, AFL-CIO [24173]
Directors Guild of Am. [24055]
Distribution Contractors Assn. [24162]
Farm Labor Organizing Comm. [23997]
Fed. Educ. Assn. [24043]
Fed. of Westinghouse Independent Salaried Unions [24047]
Flight Attendants and Related Services Assn. [IO]
Freelancers Union [24218]
Gen. Ser. Employees Union Local 73 [24097]
Glass Molders, Pottery, Plastics, and Allied Workers Intl. Union [24066]
Graphic Arts Employers of Am. [24082]
Graphic Communications Conf. of the Intl. Brotherhood of Teamsters [24083]
Guild of Italian Amer. Actors [24155]
Indus. Union of Marine and Ship Building Workers of Am. [24125]
Indus. Workers of the World [24098]
Indus. Workers of the World Starbucks Workers Union [24206]
Inst. of the Ironworking Indus. [24133]
Inst. of Labor and Indus. Relations [24114]
Intl. Alliance of Theatrical Stage Employees, Moving Picture Technicians, Artists and Allied Crafts of the U.S., Its Territories and Canada [24156]
Intl. Allied Printing Trades Assn. [24084]
Intl. Assn. of Bridge, Structural, Ornamental and Reinforcing Iron Workers [24134]
Intl. Assn. of EMTs and Paramedics [24051]
Intl. Assn. of Fire Fighters [24057]
Intl. Assn. of Heat and Frost Insulators and Asbestos Workers [24093]
Intl. Assn. of Machinists [24011]
Intl. Assn. of Machinists and Aerospace Workers [24012]
Intl. Assn. of Machinists and Aerospace Workers, Woodworkers District Lodge W1 [24026]
Intl. Brotherhood of Boilermakers, Iron Ship Builders, Blacksmiths, Forgers and Helpers [24021]
Intl. Brotherhood of DuPont Workers [24034]
Intl. Brotherhood of Elecl. Workers [24048]
Intl. Brotherhood of Police Officers [24120]
Intl. Brotherhood of Teamsters [24198]
Intl. Civil Ser. Commn. [24143]
Intl. Fed. of Professional and Tech. Engineers [24052]
Intl. Guards Union of Am. [24185]
Intl. Guild of Symphony, Opera and Ballet Musicians [24157]
Intl. Labor Communications Assn., AFL-CIO/CLC [3229]
Intl. Longshore and Warehouse Union [24126]
Intl. Longshoremen's Assn. [24127]
Intl. Org. of Masters, Mates and Pilots, ILA, AFL-CIO [24128]
Intl. Plate Printers, Die Stampers, and Engravers' Union of North Am. [24085]
Intl. Union of Allied Novelty and Prdt.ion Workers [24196]
Intl. Union of Bricklayers and Allied Craftworkers [24027]

Intl. Union of Electronic, Elecl., Salaried, Machine, and Furniture Workers [24049]
Intl. Union of Elevator Constructors [24099]
Intl. Union of Indus. and Independent Workers [24208]
Intl. Union of Operating Engineers [24028]
Intl. Union of Painters and Allied Trades [24146]
Intl. Union of Petroleum and Indus. Workers [24163]
Intl. Union of Police Associations [24121]
Intl. Union of Security Officers [24186]
Intl. Union, Security, Police and Fire Professionals of Am. [24187]
Intl. Union of Tool, Die and Mold Makers [24100]
Intl. Union, United Auto., Aerospace and Agricultural Implement Workers of Am. [24004]
Joint Labor Mgt. Comm. of the Retail Food Indus. [24059]
Labor Coun. for Latin Amer. Advancement [24094]
Labor and Employment Relations Assn. [24115]
Labor Heritage Found. [9578]
Labor Proj. for Working Families [24117]
Labor Res. Assn. [24118]
Laborers' Intl. Union of North Am. [24029]
Machinists Non-Partisan Political League [24101]
Major League Baseball Players Assn. [24018]
Malta Workers' Union [IO]
Maritime Trades Dept., AFL-CIO [24129]
Metal Trades Dept., AFL-CIO [24135]
Millwright Gp. [24102]
Natl. Air Traffic Controllers Assn. [24013]
Natl. Alliance of Postal and Fed. Employees [24167]
Natl. Alliance for Worker and Employer Rights [24110]
Natl. Assn. of Air Traffic Specialists [24014]
Natl. Assn. Broadcast Employees and Technicians - Communications Workers of Am. [24024]
Natl. Assn. of Govt. Employees [24075]
Natl. Assn. of Letter Carriers of the U.S.A. [24168]
Natl. Assn. of Postal Supervisors [24169]
Natl. Basketball Players Assn. [24192]
Natl. Center for the Stud. of Collective Bargaining in Higher Educ. and the Professions [24036]
Natl. Comm. for Labor Israel [12460]
Natl. Conf. of Firemen and Oilers [24058]
Natl. Conservation District Employees Assn. [24209]
Natl. Coun. on Teacher Retirement [24044]
Natl. Day Laborer Organizing Network [24111]
Natl. Educ. Assn. [24045]
Natl. Farm Worker Ministry [12594]
Natl. Fed. of Fed. Employees [24077]
Natl. Fed. of Independent Unions [24210]
Natl. League of Postmasters of the U.S. [24170]
Natl. Org. of Indus. Trade Unions [24103]
Natl. Org. of Legal Services Workers, UAW Local 2320 [24079]
Natl. Postal Mail Handlers Union [24171]
Natl. Rural Letter Carriers' Assn. [24172]
Natl. Treasury Employees Union [24080]
Natl. Union of Law Enforcement Associations [24124]
Natl. Writers Union [24219]
New Ways to Work [12094]
New York Coun. of Motion Picture and TV Unions [24056]
The Newspaper Guild [24140]
NLRB Professional Assn. [24081]
North Amer. Assn. of Educational Negotiators [24046]
OAS Staff Assn. [24144]
Odborovy svaz Unios [IO]
Off. and Professional Employees Intl. Union [23995]
Operative Plasterers and Cement Masons Intl. Assn. of U.S. and Canada [24031]
Pacific Coast Marine Firemen, Oilers, Watertenders and Wipers Assn. [24130]
Plant Protection Assn. [24188]
Printing, Publishing and Media Workers Sector of the CWA [24086]
Professional Airways Systems Specialists [24015]
Rescue Amer. Jobs [17984]

Res. Associates of Am. [24060]
Retail, Wholesale and Dept. Store Union [24182]
Sailors' Union of the Pacific [24131]
Samuel Gompers Stamp Club [22867]
Screen Actors Guild [24158]
Seafarers' Intl. Union of North Am. [24132]
SEIU, District 925, AFL-CIO [23996]
Ser. Employees Intl. Union [24189]
Ser. Workers United [24190]
Sheet Metal Workers' Intl. Assn. [24136]
Soc. of Stage Directors and Choreographers [24159]
Stove, Furnace, Energy, and Allied Appliance Workers Division of the Intl. Brotherhood of Boilermakers [24001]
Student/Farmworker Alliance [24054]
SweatFree Communities [24106]
Teamsters for a Democratic Union [24199]
Textile Converters Assn. [24195]
Transport Workers Union of Am. [24200]
Trans. Communications Intl. Union [24180]
Union of Amer. Physicians and Dentists [24092]
Union Label and Ser. Trades Dept., AFL-CIO [24213]
UNITE HERE [24095]
United Assn. of Journeymen and Apprentices of the Plumbing, Pipe Fitting, Sprinkler Fitting Indus. of the U.S. and Canada [24164]
United Brotherhood of Carpenters and Joiners of Am. [24032]
United Food and Commercial Workers Intl. Union [24061]
United Furniture Workers Insurance Fund [24065]
United Hebrew Trades - New York Division of the Jewish Labor Comm. [24214]
United Mine Workers of Am. [24139]
United Nations Staff Union [24145]
United Scenic Artists [24160]
U.S. Maritime Alliance [2594]
United Steel Workers of Am., Rubber/Plastics Indus. Conf. [24183]
United Steelworkers of Am. [24137]
United Trans. Union [24181]
United Union of Roofers, Waterproofers and Allied Workers [24033]
USWA Flint/Glass Workers Conf. [24067]
Utility Workers Union of Am., AFL-CIO [24216]
Women's Natl. Basketball Players Assn. [23140]
Writers Guild of Am., East [24220]
Writers Guild of Am., West [24221]
Labor; Women's Bur. of the U.S. Department of [6361]
Labor and Working Class History Assn. [8723], c/o Max Krochmal, Exec. Sec., Stanford Indus., Duke Univ., Box 90239, Durham, NC 27708-0239, (919)613-7399
Labor Zionist Alliance [★19174]
Labor Zionist Order; Farbard [★19174]
Labor Zionist Org. of Am; Pioneer Women/Na'amat, the Women's [★20162]
Labor Zionist Org. of Am; Pioneer Women, The Women's [★20162]
Labor Zionist Org. of Am; Poale Zion - United [★19174]
Labor Zionist Youth; Habonim Dror [★20138]
Labor Zionist Youth; Ichud Habonim [★20138]
Labor Zionist Youth; Ichud Habonim Dror [★20138]
Laboratoires des assureurs de Canada [★IO]
Labs; Amer. Coun. of Commercial [★7236]
Labs; Amer. Coun. of Independent [★7236]
Labs; Assn. of Cinema [★1367]
Labs; Assn. of Cinema and Video [1367]
Labs. Assn; Optical [1864]
Labs; Cable TV [780]
Laboratories; Construction Tech. [★933]
Labs; Natl. Assn. of Dental [14170]
Labs; Underwriters [3459]
Laboratory
Accreditation Rev. Comm. on Educ. in Surgical Tech. [15123]
Amer. Assn. of Bioanalysts [14989]
Amer. Assn. of Bioanalysts Bd. of Registry [15126]
Amer. Assn. for Clinical Chemistry [13936]
Amer. Assn. for Lab. Accreditation [7234]

Reference to "IO" in place of a book number signifies that the association may be found in the 45th edition of International Organizations.

Amer. Assn. for Lab. Animal Sci. [13693]
Amer. Assn. of Physician Offices and Labs.
   [14990]
Amer. Assn. of Veterinary Lab. Diagnosticians
   [16753]
Amer. Bd. of Bioanalysis [7235]
Amer. Clinical Lab. Assn. [14991]
Amer. Coun. of Independent Labs. [7236]
Amer. Fed. for Medical Res. [14019]
Amer. Inst. of Biological Sciences [6560]
Amer. Soc. for Clinical Investigation [14020]
Amer. Soc. for Clinical Lab. Sci. [14992]
Analytical Lab. Managers Assn. [7237]
Asia Pacific Lab. Accreditation Cooperation [IO]
Assn. for Assessment and Accreditation of Lab.
   Animal Care Intl. [13695]
Assn. of Biomolecular Rsrc. Facilities [7238]
Assn. of Clinical Scientists [14022]
Assn. of Kenya Medical Lab. Sci. Officers [IO]
Assn. for Lab. Automation [6515]
Canadian Assn. for Environmental Analytical Labs.
   [IO]
Canadian Coun. of Independent Labs. [IO]
Central Soc. for Clinical Res. [14023]
Clinical Lab. Mgt. Assn. [14993]
Clinical and Lab. Standards Inst. [14994]
Clinical and Lab. Standards Inst. [14995]
Clinical Ligand Assay Soc. [14995]
European Comm. for External Quality Assessment
   Programmes in Lab. Medicine [IO]
European Fed. of Natl. Associations of Measure-
   ment, Testing and Analytical Labs. [IO]
Forbes Norris MDA/ALS Res. Center [15323]
Found. for Biomedical Res. [13696]
Histochemical Soc. [13938]
Hong Kong Assn. of Certification Labs. [IO]
Independent Labs. Inst. [2391]
Independent Lab. Distributors Assn. [3483]
Inst. for Chem. Educ. [8062]
Inst. for Lab. Animal Res. [13698]
Intl. Assn. of Pediatric Lab. Medicine [15888]
Intl. Soc. for Biological and Environmental
   Repositories [6585]
Lab. Animal Mgt. Assn. [13699]
Natl. Accrediting Agency for Clinical Lab. Sciences
   [15141]
Natl. Assn. for Biomedical Res. [13700]
Natl. Assn. of Dental Labs. [14170]
Natl. Assn. of Marine Labs. [7274]
Natl. Bd. for Certification in Dental Lab. Tech.
   [14172]
Natl. Credentialing Agency for Lab. Personnel
   [15145]
Natl. Registry of Certified Chemists [13939]
Natl. Soc. for Histotechnology [15146]
North Amer. Specialized Coagulation Lab. Assn.
   [14996]
Scottish Soc. for Contamination Control [IO]
Soc. for Applied Immunohistochemistry [15873]
Soc. for Clinical Trials [14028]
World Assn. of Veterinary Lab. Diagnosticians
   [16819]
Laboratory Animal Breeders Assn. - Defunct.
Lab. Animal Care; Amer. Assn. for Accreditation of
   [★13695]
Lab. Animal Mgt. Assn. [13699], 7500 Flying Cloud
   Dr., Ste. 900, Eden Prairie, MN 55344, (952)253-
   6235
Lab. Animal Managers Assn. [★13699]
Lab. Animal Medicine; Amer. Bd. of [★16762]
Lab. Animal Medicine; Amer. Coll. of [16762]
Lab. Animal Res; Inst. for [13698]
Lab. Animal Resources; Inst. of [★13698]
Lab. Animal Sci; Amer. Assn. for [13693]
Lab. Animal Sci. Assn. [IO], Tamworth, United
   Kingdom
Lab. Diagnosticians; Amer. Assn. of Veterinary
   [16753]
Lab. Directors; Amer. Soc. of Crime [5754]
Lab. Distributors Assn; Independent [3483]
Lab. Immunologists; Assn. of Medical [14932]
Lab. Managers Assn; Univ. [★7237]
Lab. of Ornithology; Cornell [7416]
Lab. of Ornithology; Cornell Univ. [★7416]
Lab. Personnel; Natl. Credentialing Agency for
   [15145]

Lab. Products Assn. [3484], 225 Reinekers Ln., Ste.
   625, Alexandria, VA 22314, (703)836-1360
Laboratory Products Association [★3488]
Lab. Schools; Accrediting Bur. of Medical [★15124]
Lab. Sciences; Natl. Accrediting Agency for Clinical
   [15141]
Lab. Standards; Natl. Comm. for Clinical [★14994]
Lab. Technicians; Amer. Soc. of Clinical [★14992]
Lab. Tech; Natl. Bd. for Certification in Dental
   [14172]
Laborers' Intl. Union of North Am. [24029], 905 16th
   St. NW, Washington, DC 20006, (202)737-8320
Laborers' Intl. Union of North Am. [IO], Washington,
   DC, United States
Laborers' Political League [18354], 905 16th St. NW,
   Washington, DC 20006, (202)737-8320
Labor's League for Political Educ. [★18303]
Labour Party - Britain [IO], London, United Kingdom
Labour Party - Ireland [IO], Dublin, Ireland
Labour Party - Netherlands [IO], Amsterdam,
   Netherlands
Labour Women's Coun. [IO], Wellington, New
   Zealand
Labour Women's Network [IO], Malmesbury, United
   Kingdom
Labrador Retriever Club [★22319]
Lace and Embroidery Mfrs. Assn; Schiffli [3797]
Lace Guild [IO], Stourbridge, United Kingdom
Lace Importers Assn. - Defunct.
Lace Paper Inst; Linen and [★1157]
Lacers; Natl. Old [★22161]
Lackey Family Assn. - Defunct.
Laconia Sled Dog Club [★23395]
Lacquer Assn; Natl. Paint, Varnish and [★2884]
Lacrosse
   Atlantic Coast Conf. [23806]
   Big East Conf. [23807]
   Big Ten Conf. [23808]
   Canadian Lacrosse Assn. [IO]
   Coun. of Ivy Gp. Presidents [23817]
   Eastern Collegiate Hockey Assn. [23485]
   English Lacrosse Assn. [IO]
   Hong Kong Lacrosse Assn. [IO]
   Intl. Lacrosse Fed. [IO]
   Intl. Lacrosse Fed. [23570]
   Natl. Assn. of Intercollegiate Athletics [23835]
   Natl. Christian Coll. Athletic Assn. [23837]
   Natl. Collegiate Athletic Assn. [23838]
   Natl. Junior Coll. Athletic Assn. [23843]
   Pacific 10 Conf. [23847]
   Southeastern Conf. [23851]
   Southern Conf. [23852]
   U.S. Collegiate Athletic Assn. [23859]
   U.S. Collegiate Sports Coun. [23860]
   U.S. Intercollegiate Lacrosse Assn. [23571]
   U.S. Lacrosse [23572]
   U.S. Lacrosse Assn., Women's Div. [23573]
Lacrosse Assn; U.S. Intercollegiate [23571]
The Lacrosse Found. [★23572]
Lacrosse Players Assn; Professional [24193]
Lactation; Intl. Soc. for Res. in Human Milk and
   [13776]
Lacy J. Dalton Fan Club - Address unknown since
   2001.
Ladder Inst; Amer. [1816]
Ladies Against Women - Address unknown since
   2003.
Ladies Apparel Contractors Assn. [244]
Ladies Assn; First Catholic Slovak [19361]
Ladies' Assn; Mount Vernon [11138]
Ladies' Assn. of the Union; Mount Vernon [★11138]
Ladies Auxiliary; Jewish War Veterans of the U.S.A.
   - Natl. [21196]
Ladies Auxiliary Knights of Saint John; Supreme
   [19009]
Ladies Auxiliary, Military Order of the Purple Heart,
   U.S.A. [20713], 5413-B Backlick Rd., Springfield,
   VA 22151-3960, (703)642-5360
Ladies Auxiliary; Polish Legion of Amer. Veterans,
   U.S.A., [21260]
Ladies Auxiliary to the Veterans of Foreign Wars of
   the U.S. [21307], 406 W 34th St., 10th Fl., Kansas
   City, MO 64111, (816)561-8655
Ladies Auxiliary to Veterans of World War I of the
   U.S.A; Natl. [21359]

Ladies Catholic Benevolent Assn. [★19129]
Ladies Charity Societies; United Hasroun Men's and
   St. Laba [19732]
Ladies of Charity of the U.S.A. [13173], PO Box
   31697, St. Louis, MO 63131
Ladies Garment Assn; Merchants [★253]
Ladies of the Golden Eagle [★19128]
Ladies' Golf Union [IO], St. Andrews, United
   Kingdom
Ladies of the Grand Army of the Republic [20727],
   c/o Judy Rock, Sec., 36091 Hathaway, No. D, New
   Baltimore, MI 48047, (330)279-4393
Ladies' Hermitage Assn. [11133], 4580 Rachel's Ln.,
   Hermitage, TN 37076, (615)889-2941
Ladies Kennel Assn. of Am. [22303], c/o Ms. Tracey
   E. Monahan, Chair, 190 Merrits Rd., Farmingdale,
   NY 11735, (516)777-1512
Ladies Oriental Shrine of North Am. [19241], 1111 E
   54th St., Ste. 111, Indianapolis, IN 46220
Ladies Philoptochos Soc; Greek Orthodox [20071]
Ladies Professional Golf Assn. [23454], 100 Intl.
   Golf Dr., Daytona Beach, FL 32124-1092,
   (386)274-6200
Ladies of Sta. Peter Claver; Knights and [★19005]
Ladies' Tea and Rhetoric Soc. - Address unknown
   since 2005.
Lady Bird Johnson Wildflower Center [6642], 4801
   La Crosse Ave., Austin, TX 78739, (512)232-0100
Ladyslipper [11087], PO Box 3124, Durham, NC
   27715, (919)383-8773
Laekemedelsindustrifoereningen [★IO]
Lafayette; Amer. Friends of [11102]
Lafayette Fellowship Found. - Defunct.
Lafayette; Order of [21418]
Lagonda Club, U.S. Sect. - Address unknown since
   2002.
LaHaye Family History Assn. - Address unknown
   since 2006.
Lahore Ahmadiyya Movement for the Propagation of
   Islam, Canada [IO], Toronto, ON, Canada
Lahore Ahmadiyya Movement for the Propagation of
   Islam - Pakistan [IO], Lahore, Pakistan
Laine Soc. of Am; Frankie [24890]
Laity
   Men for Missions Intl. [20357]
   Natl. Assn. for Lay Ministry [20204]
   Natl. Bible Assn. [20205]
   Natl. Center for the Laity [20206]
   Natl. Labor Comm. for Worker and Human Rights
      [17049]
Laity of the Episcopal Church; Concerned Clergy
   and [19950]
Laity and Family Life; Secretariat on [★12167]
Laity, Women, and Youth; Secretariat for Family,
   [12167]
Lakare for Miljon [★IO]
Lakasberlok es Lakok Egyesulete [★IO]
Lake Carriers' Assn. [2606], 614 W Superior Ave.,
   Cleveland, OH 44113-1383, (216)621-1107
Lake Erie Cleanup Comm. - Defunct.
Lake Erie Steam Assn. - Defunct.
Lake Freight Assn. - Defunct.
Lake Superior Iron Ore Assn. [★2696]
Lake Superior Iron Ore Assn. [★IO]
Lake Tahoe; League to Save [4417]
Lake Yachting Assn; Inter- [23177]
Lakeland Terrier Club; U.S. [22375]
Lakemedelsindustriforeningen [★IO]
Lakes
   Amer. Soc. of Limnology and Oceanography
      [7393]
   Intl. Assn. for Great Lakes Res. [7239]
   Intl. Assn. for Great Lakes Res. [IO]
   Intl. Assn. of Theoretical and Applied Limnology
      [IO]
   Intl. Assn. of Theoretical and Applied Limnology
      [7240]
   Japanese Soc. of Limnology [IO]
   League to Save Lake Tahoe [4417]
   New Zealand Freshwater Sciences Soc. [IO]
   North Amer. Lake Mgt. Soc. [7241]
Lakes Commn; Great [6137]
Lakes Dove Assn; Great [★21839]
Lakes Historical Soc; Great [10438]
Lakes Indian Fish and Wildlife Commn; Great [5323]

A star before a book entry number signifies that the name is not listed separately, but is mentioned within the entry.

Lakes Maritime Inst; Great **[10439]**

Lakes Region Sled Dog Club **[23395]**, PO Box 382, Laconia, NH 03247, (603)524-4314

Lakes United; Great **[4405]**

Lakota Student Alliance **[19275]**, PO Box 225, Kyle, SD 57752, (605)441-9453

Lalmba Assn. **[12866]**, 7685 Quartz St., Arvada, CO 80007, (303)420-1810

Lalmba Assn. **[IO]**, Arvada, CO, United States

LAM Found. **[14270]**, 4015 Executive Park Dr., Ste. 320, Cincinnati, OH 45241, (513)777-6889

Lama Found. **[10176]**, PO Box 240, San Cristobal, NM 87564, (505)586-1269

Lamaze Birth Without Pain Educ. Assn. **[15607]**, 20134 Snowden, Detroit, MI 48235, (313)341-3816

Lamaze Intl. **[15608]**, 2025 M St. NW, Ste. 800, Washington, DC 20036-3309, (202)367-1128

Lamaze Intl. **[IO]**, Washington, DC, United States

Lamaze Method

 Lamaze Intl. **[15608]**

Lamb Comm. - Defunct.

Lamb Coun; Amer. **[5187]**

Lamb Feeders Assn; Natl. **[5206]**

Lambda Alpha **[24402]**, Ball State Univ., Dept. of Anthropology, Muncie, IN 47306-0435, (765)285-1575

Lambda Alpha Epsilon **[★11855]**

Lambda Alpha Epsilon; Amer. Criminal Justice Assn. **[11855]**

Lambda Alpha Intl. **[24445]**, c/o Terry Stevenson, Exec. Dir., 214 N Hale St., Wheaton, IL 60187, (630)510-4584

Lambda Alpha; Intl. Fraternity of **[★24445]**

Lambda Amateur Radio Club **[21504]**, PO Box 21669, Cleveland, OH 44121-0669

Lambda Chi Alpha **[24637]**, 8741 Founders Rd., Indianapolis, IN 46268-1389, (317)803-7329

Lambda Delta Lambda **[24586]**, Wayne State Coll., Carhart Sci. Bldg., 1111 Main St., Wayne, NE 68787, (402)375-7000

Lambda Iota Tau **[24533]**, Ball State Univ., Dept. of English, 2000 W Univ. Ave., Muncie, IN 47306-0460, (765)285-8456

Lambda Kappa Sigma **[24569]**, W179 S6769 Muskego Dr., Muskego, WI 53150, (800)557-1913

Lambda Legal Defense and Educ. Fund **[12241]**, 120 Wall St., Ste. 1500, New York, NY 10005-3904, (212)809-8585

Lambda Omicron Gamma Medical Soc. - Defunct.

Lambda Pi Alumni Assn. **[24481]**, PO Box 1133, Chico, CA 95927, (530)332-9347

Lambda Psi Delta Sorority **[24713]**, PO Box 260128, Hartford, CT 06126

Lambda Theta Phi **[24482]**, 565 Main Ave., 2nd Fl., Passaic, NJ 07055

Lamborghini Club Am. **[21684]**, PO Box 649, Orinda, CA 94563, (925)253-9399

Lamborghini Club; Nuova **[★21684]**

The Lambs **[11019]**, 3 W 51st St., New York, NY 10019, (212)586-0306

Laminate Coun. of America - Defunct.

Laminated Fiberglass Insulation Producers Assn. - Defunct.

Laminated Foil Mfrs. Assn. - Defunct.

Laminating Materials Assn. **[★1643]**

Laminating Materials Assn. **[★IO]**

Laminators; Assn. of Indus. Metallizers, Coaters and **[851]**

Laminators Safety Glass Assn. **[★1728]**

Lamp Club; Fairy **[22019]**

Lamp of Hope Proj. **[17031]**, PO Box 305, League City, TX 77574-0305

Lamp and Shade Inst. of America - Defunct.

Lamps

 Aladdin Knights of the Mystic Light **[22617]**

 Assn. of Stained Glass Lamp Artists **[2392]**

 Intl. Guild of Lamp Researchers **[22618]**

 Magic Lantern Soc. of the U.S. and Canada **[21531]**

Lancashire Welsh Pony and Cob Assn. **[IO]**, Manchester, United Kingdom

Lancaster District Chamber of Commerce, Trade and Indus. **[IO]**, Lancaster, United Kingdom

Lancaster Mennonite Historical Society **[IO]**, Lancaster, PA, United States

Lancaster Mennonite Historical Soc. **[21130]**, 2215 Millstream Rd., Lancaster, PA 17602-1499, (717)393-9745

Lancaster (Pennsylvania) Railway and Locomotive Historical Soc. **[★10915]**

Lancia Club; Amer. **[21573]**

Lancia Club Belgio **[IO]**, Dilbeek, Belgium

Lancia Club Deutschland **[IO]**, Stuttgart, Germany

Lancia Club Finland **[IO]**, Pori, Finland

Lancia Club France **[IO]**, Paris, France

Lancia Club Japan **[IO]**, Tokyo, Japan

Lancia Club Nederland **[IO]**, Zandvoort, Netherlands

Lancia Club Suisse **[IO]**, Feuerthalen, Switzerland

Lancia Club Vincenzo **[IO]**, Neuenburg am Rhein, Germany

Lancia Motor Club **[IO]**, Southport, United Kingdom

Lancia Motor Club New South Wales **[IO]**, Northbridge, Australia

Lancisti Norvegesi **[IO]**, Oslo, Norway

Land Advisory Service **[★4380]**

Land Assistance Fund; Fed. of Southern Cooperatives **[12937]**

Land Brokers; Natl. Inst. of Farm and **[★3342]**

Land Conservation Rsrc; Equestrian **[5130]**

Land Control

 Alliance for Am. **[11807]**

 Amer. Land Rights Assn. **[6187]**

 Amer. Lands Access Assn. **[22937]**

 Big Thicket Natural Heritage Trust **[4368]**

 Black Farmers and Agriculturists Assn. **[4111]**

 Land Loss Fund **[12486]**

 League of Private Property Voters **[17985]**

 Lincoln Inst. of Land Policy **[5920]**

 Natl. Brownfield Assn. **[3191]**

 People Food and Land Found. **[4656]**

 Sustainable Obtainable Solutions **[5129]**

Land Development Assn; Amer. **[★3298]**

Land Educational Associates Found. - Defunct.

Land Found; People Food and **[4656]**

Land Found; Urban **[★18777]**

Land; Friends of the **[★4413]**

Land Fund; Emergency **[★12937]**

Land-Grant Colleges; Natl. Assn. of State Universities and **[8110]**

Land-Grant Colleges; Off. for the Advancement of Public Black Colleges of the Natl. Assn. of State Universities and **[8112]**

Land-Grant Colleges; Off. for Advancement of Public Negro Colleges - of the Natl. Assn. of State Universities and **[★8112]**

Land-Grant Colleges and State Universities; Assn. of **[★8110]**

Land Improvement Contractors of Am. **[4415]**, 3080 Ogden Ave., Ste. No. 300, Lisle, IL 60532, (630)548-1984

The Land Inst. **[4647]**, 2440 E Water Well Rd., Salina, KS 67401-9051, (785)823-5376

Land Inst; Farm and **[★3342]**

Land Inst; Realtors **[3342]**

Land Inst; Urban **[5597]**

Land; James Buchanan Found. for the Preservation of Wheat **[11126]**

Land Loss Fund **[12486]**, PO Box 61, Tillery, NC 27887

Land Mgt; Bureau of **[★4468]**

Land Mgt; Bureau of **[★IO]**

Land Mgt. Natl. Wild Horse and Burro Prog; Bur. of **[4868]**

Land Mobile Communications Coun. **[3751]**, 8484 Westpark Dr., Ste. 630, McLean, VA 22102-5117, (703)528-5115

Land for People; Natl. **[★4656]**

Land Reclamationists; Natl. Assn. of State **[6118]**

Land Rights **[★6187]**

Land Rights Assn; Amer. **[6187]**

Land Rover Owner Austria **[IO]**, Willendorf, Austria

Land Rover Owners Assn., U.S.A. - Defunct.

Land Title Assn; Amer. **[3297]**

Land Trust; Acres **[4339]**

Land Trust Alliance **[4416]**, 1660 L St. NW, Ste. 1100, Washington, DC 20036, (202)638-4725

Land Trust Center; Natl. Community **[★17221]**

Land Trust Exchange **[★4416]**

Land; Trust for Public **[4461]**

Landau-Bain Fan Assn. **[★24730]**

Landau-Bain Fan Assn. **[★IO]**

Landau/Bain Fan Assn. - Defunct.

Landau Network - Centry Volta **[IO]**, Como, Italy

LandboUngdom **[★IO]**

Landers Fund; Barb **[★8399]**

Landing Craft Infantry Natl. Assn. **[★21328]**

Landmarks Assn; Literary **[★10358]**

Landmen; Amer. Assn. of Professional **[2913]**

Landmen's Assn; Natl. Oil Scouts and **[★2932]**

Landmine Survivors Network **[11959]**, 2100 M St. NW, Ste. 302, Washington, DC 20037, (202)464-0007

Landmines; Physicians Against **[17434]**

Landowners Assn; Forest **[4683]**

Landrace Assn; Amer. **[5232]**

Lands Access Assn; Amer. **[22937]**

Lands Alliance; Amer. **[4533]**

Lands Coun; Public **[5127]**

Lands Found; Public **[5128]**

Lands Stud; Assn. for Arid **[4498]**

Landscape Architects; Amer. Soc. of **[6466]**

Landscape Architects Found; Amer. Soc. of **[★6476]**

Landscape Architectural Registration Boards; Coun. of **[6473]**

Landscape Architecture Found. **[6476]**, 818 18th St. NW, Ste. 810, Washington, DC 20006, (202)331-7070

Landscape Artists Intl. **[9509]**, c/o Karl Eric Leitzel, Founder/Dir., Karl Eric Leitzel Studio, 155 Murray School Ln., Spring Mills, PA 16875, (814)422-8461

Landscape Artists Intl. **[IO]**, Spring Mills, PA, United States

Landscape Assn; Amer. Nursery and **[5042]**

Landscape Assn. Executives of North Am; Nursery and **[5047]**

Landscape Conf; Professional Turf and **[★2397]**

Landscape Designers; Assn. of Professional **[2393]**

Landscape Ecology; Polish Assn. for **[IO]**

Landscape Indus. Assn. Singapore **[IO]**, Singapore, Singapore

Landscape Inst. **[IO]**, London, United Kingdom

Landscape Nursery Coun. **[5045]**, 1611 Creekview Dr., Florence, KY 41042, (859)525-1809

Landscape Nurserymen's Assn; Natl. **[★2396]**

Landscape Res. Gp. **[IO]**, Sheffield, United Kingdom

Landscaping

 Alberta Assn. of Landscape Architects **[IO]**

 Amer. Conifer Soc. **[5253]**

 Amer. Nursery and Landscape Assn. **[5042]**

 Amer. Soc. of Landscape Architects **[6466]**

 Arizona Cactus and Succulent Res. **[6631]**

 Asociacion Peruana de Arquitetura del Paisaje **[IO]**

 Associacao Brasileira de Arquitetos Paisagistas **[IO]**

 Associacion Costarricense de Arquitectos Paisajistas **[IO]**

 Assn. Belge des Architectes de Jardins et des Architectes Paysagistes **[IO]**

 Assn. of Danish Landscape Architects **[IO]**

 Association of Professional Landscape Designers **[IO]**

 Assn. of Professional Landscape Designers **[2393]**

 Assn. of Professional Landscapers **[IO]**

 Associazione Italiana di Architettura del Paesaggio **[IO]**

 Australian Inst. of Landscape Architects **[IO]**

 Bermuda Assn. of Landscape Architects **[IO]**

 British Assn. of Golf Course Constructors **[IO]**

 British Assn. of Landscape Indus. **[IO]**

 British and Intl. Golf Greenkeepers Assn. **[IO]**

 Canadian Soc. of Landscape Architects **[IO]**

 Centro Argentino de Arquitectos Paisajistas **[IO]**

 Chinese Taiwan Landscape Architects Soc. **[IO]**

 Colombian Assn. of Landscape Architects **[IO]**

 Coun. of Educators in Landscape Architecture **[8724]**

 Coun. of Landscape Architectural Registration Boards **[6473]**

 Ecological Landscaping Assn. **[4989]**

 Ecological Landscaping Assn. **[IO]**

 European Found. for Landscape Architecture **[IO]**

 European Inst. of Golf Course Architects **[IO]**

 European Landscape Contractors Assn. **[IO]**

Reference to "IO" in place of a book number signifies that the association may be found in the 45th edition of International Organizations.

Encyclopedia of Associations, 46th Edition

3727

Fed. of German Landscape Architects [IO]
Fed. of Icelandic Landscape Architects [IO]
Finnish Assn. of Landscape Architects [IO]
French Assn. of Landscape Contractors [IO]
Garden Design Soc. of New Zealand [IO]
German Coun. for Land Stewardship [IO]
Hong Kong Inst. of Landscape Architects [IO]
Hungarian Assn. of Landscape Architects [IO]
Independent Turf and Ornamental Distributors
    Assn. [2394]
Indian Soc. of Landscape Architects [IO]
Indonesian Soc. of Landscape Architects [IO]
Inst. of Groundsmanship [IO]
Inst. of Landscape Architects of South Africa [IO]
Intl. Erosion Control Assn. [4411]
Intl. Fed. of Landscape Architects [IO]
Irish Landscape Inst. [IO]
Israeli Assn. of Landscape Architects [IO]
Korean Inst. of Landscape Architecture [IO]
Landscape Architecture Found. [6476]
Landscape Indus. Assn. Singapore [IO]
Landscape Inst. [IO]
Landscape Nursery Coun. [5045]
Landscape Res. Gp. [IO]
Latvian Soc. of Landscape Architects [IO]
Lawn and Garden Marketing and Distribution
    Assn. [2395]
Lithuanian Assn. of Landscape Architects [IO]
Natl. Assn. for Areas of Outstanding Natural
    Beauty [IO]
Natl. Hedgelaying Soc. [IO]
Natl. Landscape Assn. [2396]
Natl. Pavement Contractors Assn. [651]
Natl. Roadside Vegetation Mgt. Assn. [4802]
Netherlands Assn. for Landscape Architecture [IO]
New York State Turf and Landscape Assn. [2397]
New Zealand Inst. of Landscape Architects [IO]
Northeastern Weed Sci. Soc. [4990]
Norwegian Assn. of Landscape Architects [IO]
Osterreichische Gesellschaft fur Landschaftspla-
    nung und Landschaftsarchitektur [IO]
Outdoor Power Equip. Inst. [1294]
Panhellenic Assn. of Landscape Architects [IO]
Philippines Assn. of Landscape Architects [IO]
Professional Grounds Mgt. Soc. [4803]
Professional Landcare Network [2398]
Professional Plant Users Gp. [IO]
Proj. EverGreen [4991]
Singapore Inst. of Landscape Architects [IO]
Slovak Assn. of Landscape Architects [IO]
Slovenian Assn. of Landscape Architects [IO]
Sociedad de Arquitectos Paisajistas, Ecologia y
    Medio Ambiente [IO]
Soc. of Garden Designers [IO]
Sports Turf Managers Association [IO]
Sports Turf Managers Assn. [2399]
Thai Assn. of Landscape Architects [IO]
Turf and Ornamental Communicators Assn.
    [2400]
Venezuelan Soc. of Landscape Architects [IO]
Walter Burley Griffin Soc. of Am. [9398]
Landsforeningen for Marfan Syndrom [★IO]
Landslaget Fysisk Fostring I Skolen [IO], Tonsberg,
    Norway
Landsorganisationen i Danmark [★IO]
Landsradet for Sveriges Ungdomsorganisationer
    [★IO]
Landssamband KFUM [★IO]
Lane Brody and Eleni Global Fan Club; Official
    [24953]
Lane Operators Assn; Archery [★3657]
Langbrugsraadet [★IO]
Lange Parents Gp; Cornelia de [★13754]
Langshan Club; Amer. [5105]
Langston Hughes Soc. [9678], c/o Inst. for African
    Amer. Stud., 312 Holmes/Hunter Academic Bldg.,
    Univ. of Georgia, Athens, GA 30602, (706)542-
    5197
Language
    Academic Language Therapy Assn. [12488]
    Acad. of Aphasia [13704]
    Acad. of Rehabilitative Audiology [14734]
    ADARA: Professionals Networking for Excellence
        in Ser. Delivery with Individuals who are Deaf
        or Hard of Hearing [14735]

African Assn. for Lexicography [IO]
African Language Assn. of Southern Africa [IO]
African Language Teachers Assn. [9207]
Alexander Graham Bell Assn. for the Deaf and
    Hard of Hearing [14736]
Alliance of Rhetoric Societies [10935]
Alpha Mu Gamma Natl. [24525]
Amer. Assn. of Phonetic Sciences [10842]
Amer. Assn. of Teachers of Arabic [7958]
Amer. Assn. of Teachers of Slavic and East
    European Languages [9125]
Amer. Assn. of Teachers of Spanish and
    Portuguese [8725]
Amer. Assn. of Teachers of Spanish and
    Portuguese [IO]
Amer. Assn. of Teachers of Turkic Languages
    [9282]
Amer. Classical League [8726]
Amer. Coun. on the Teaching of Foreign
    Languages [8727]
Amer. Cryptogram Assn. [22178]
Amer. Dialect Soc. [10398]
Amer. Hearing Res. Found. [14740]
Amer. Literary Translators Assn. [11058]
Amer. Philological Assn. [10296]
Amer. Portuguese Stud. Assn. [9004]
Amer. Soc. for Deaf Children [14742]
Amer. Soc. of Geolinguistics [10399]
Amer. Speech Language Hearing Assn. [16442]
Assn. for the Advancement of Documentation Sci-
    ences and Techniques [IO]
Assn. of Departments of Foreign Languages
    [8728]
Assn. for the History of Language [IO]
Assn. for Language Learning [IO]
Assn. of Language Testers in Europe [IO]
Assn. of Language Travel Organisations [IO]
Assn. of Literary Scholars and Critics [10413]
Assn. for Machine Translation in the Americas
    [7807]
Assn. of Univ. Professors of French and Heads of
    Departments of French in Universities in the UK
    and Ireland [IO]
Assn. of Visual Language Interpreters of New
    Brunswick [IO]
Assyrian Academic Soc. [IO]
Assyrian Academic Soc. [10297]
AUI Peace Language Intl. [10298]
Australasian Universities Language and Literature
    Assn. [IO]
Better Hearing Inst. [14745]
Bhojpuri Assn. of North Am. [10299]
Bhojpuri Assn. of North Am. [IO]
Canada Language Coun. [IO]
Canadian Assn. for Translation Stud. [IO]
Canadian Parents for French [IO]
Cantonese Language Assn. [7242]
Center for Applied Linguistics [10401]
Chinese Language Assn. of Secondary-
    Elementary Schools [8075]
CILT - The Natl. Centre for Languages [IO]
Clarity [6011]
Coll. Language Assn. [8729]
Cmpt. Assisted Language Instruction Consortium
    [8553]
Conf. of Educational Administrators of Schools
    and Programs for the Deaf [14749]
Coun. of Amer. Instructors of the Deaf [14750]
Coun. on Educ. of the Deaf [14751]
Coun. of Teachers of Southeast Asian Languages
    [7990]
Cultural Assn. of Bengal [9737]
Deafness Res. Found. [14753]
Dogs for the Deaf [14754]
Endangered Language Fund [10300]
English First [9911]
English UK [IO]
ERIC CH on Languages and Linguistics [8730]
Esperanto League for North Am. [9914]
Eurocentres Bus. Inst. [IO]
European Assn. for Cmpt. Assisted Language
    Learning [IO]
European Assn. of Linguists and Language
    Teachers [IO]
European Assn. for Terminology [IO]

European Bur. for Lesser-Used Languages [IO]
European Centre for Modern Language of the
    Coun. of Europe [IO]
European Language Coun. [IO]
European Language Resources Assn. [IO]
Finno-Ugrian Soc. [IO]
Found. for European Language and Educational
    Centres [IO]
Found. for European Language and Educational
    Centres U.S.A. [IO]
Found. for European Language and Educational
    Centres U.S.A. [8731]
German Language Soc. [IO]
Glosa Educ. Org. [IO]
Gp. of Universities for the Advancement of
    Vietnamese Abroad [9296]
Hanen Centre [IO]
Hankes Found. [10301]
HEAR Center [14756]
Hearing Loss Assn. of Am. [14759]
Helen Keller Natl. Center for Deaf-Blind Youths
    and Adults [14760]
House Ear Inst. [16446]
Inst. of Gen. Semantics [10962]
Inst. of Language and Literature [IO]
Intl. Assn. of Chinese Linguistics [IO]
Intl. Assn. of Chinese Linguistics [7243]
Intl. Assn. for Dialogue Anal. [7244]
Intl. Assn. for Dialogue Anal. [IO]
Intl. Assn. of Language Centres [IO]
Intl. Assn. for Language Learning Tech. [IO]
Intl. Assn. of Teachers of English as a Foreign
    Language [IO]
Intl. Assn. of Teachers of Italian [IO]
Intl. Assn. of Univ. Professors of English [IO]
Intl. Catholic Esperanto Assn. [9915]
Intl. Dyslexia Assn. [14295]
Intl. Fed. for Modern Languages and Literatures
    [IO]
Intl. Fed. of Teachers of French [IO]
Intl. Hearing Dog, Inc. [14762]
Intl. Hearing Soc. [14763]
Intl. Lexical Functional Grammar Assn. [8732]
Intl. Lexical Functional Grammar Assn. [IO]
Intl. Maledicta Soc. [10404]
Intl. Soc. for Dialectology and Geolinguistics [IO]
Intl. Soc. for Dialogical Sci. [7544]
Intl. Soc. of Friendship and Good Will [9917]
Intl. Soc. for Gesture Stud. [6712]
Intl. Soc. for Language Stud. [10302]
Intl. Soc. for Language Stud. [IO]
Irish Special Interest Gp. of Mensa [10244]
Italic Inst. of Am. [10262]
Japan Assn. for Language Teaching [IO]
Japanese Natl. Honor Soc. [24521]
Joint Natl. Comm. for Languages [10303]
Language Materials Proj. [8733]
Language Origins Soc. [IO]
League for Yiddish, Inc. [20157]
Less Commonly Taught Languages Proj. [8734]
Linguistic Assn. of Canada and the U.S. [10405]
Linguistic Data Consortium [2437]
Linguistic Soc. of Am. [10406]
Logical Language Gp. [10304]
Marine Corps Interrogator Translator Teams Assn.
    [19226]
Media Access Gp. [12487]
Mediterranean Editors and Translators [IO]
Mend Our Tongues Soc. [10407]
Model Secondary School for the Deaf [14766]
Modern Language Assn. of Am. [8735]
Modern Language Assn. of Am. [IO]
Natl. Alliance to Save Native Languages [10305]
Natl. Assn. for Bilingual Educ. [7999]
Natl. Assn. of the Deaf [14767]
Natl. Assn. of Language Advisers [IO]
Natl. Assn. of Self-Instructional Language
    Programs [8736]
Natl. Assn. for the Teaching of English [IO]
Natl. Assn. for Teaching English and other Com-
    munity Languages to Adults [IO]
Natl. Captioning Inst. [14769]
Natl. Chinese Honor Soc. [24432]
Natl. Comm. for Latin and Greek [9800]
Natl. Coun. on Interpreting in Hea. Care [1851]

A star before a book entry number signifies that the name is not listed separately, but is mentioned within the entry.

Natl. Coun. of Japanese Language Teachers [9226]
Natl. Coun. for Languages and Intl. Stud. [10306]
Natl. Coun. for Languages and Intl. Stud. [IO]
Natl. Coun. of Less Commonly Taught Languages [IO]
Natl. Coun. of Less Commonly Taught Languages [8737]
Natl. Coun. of State Supervisors of Foreign Languages [8738]
Natl. Fed. of Modern Language Teachers Associations [8739]
Natl. Foreign Language Center [8740]
Natl. Registration Center for Stud. Abroad [8626]
Natl. Ser. Dog Center [14774]
Natl. Student Speech Language Hearing Assn. [16453]
Noah Webster House [10053]
North Amer. Assn. for Celtic Language Teachers [8741]
North Amer. Chap. of the Assn. for Computational Linguistics [10408]
North Amer. Sankethi Assn. [9802]
Northeast Conf. on the Teaching of Foreign Languages [8742]
Oral Hearing-Impaired Sect. [14775]
Parents' Sect. of the Alexander Graham Bell Assn. for the Deaf and Hard of Hearing [14776]
Phi Sigma Iota [24526]
PlanetRead [8796]
ProEnglish [9912]
Punjabi-American Cultural Assn. [10223]
Registry of Interpreters for the Deaf [14778]
Rhetoric Soc. of Am. [10937]
SEAMEO Regional Language Centre [IO]
Selective Mutism Found. [15233]
Slovenian Res. Center of Am. [10972]
Soc. for Endangered Languages [IO]
Soc. of Modern Grammar [IO]
Soc. for Name Stud. in Britain and Ireland [IO]
Soc. for New Language Stud. [10307]
Soc. for the Stud. of Indigenous Languages of the Americas [10308]
Soc. for the Stud. of Indigenous Languages of the Americas [IO]
Swedish Translators in North Am. [11059]
Telecommunications for the Deaf and Hard of Hearing, Inc. [14780]
Ulster-Scots Language Soc. [IO]
United Kingdom Literacy Assn. [IO]
U.S. Br. of the Intl. Comm. for the Defense of the Breton Language [9758]
Vietnamese Nom Preservation Found. [10433]
Language Acad; Amer. [★8785]
Language Acquisition and Language Instruction Educational Programs; Natl. CH for English [8287]
Language Arts; Canadian Coun. of Teachers of English [IO]

Language Assimilation
U.S.English [18307]
Language and Cultural Preservation Comm; Comanche [10736]
Language Hearing Assn; Amer. Speech [16442]
Language Hearing Assn; Natl. Student Speech [16453]
Language and Hearing; Natl. Black Assn. for Speech- [16448]
Language Instruction Consortium; Cmpt. Assisted [8553]
Language and Intl. Stud; Natl. Coun. on Foreign [★8593]
Language and Literature; Soc. for the Preservation of English [8381]
Language Materials Proj. [8733], 1337 Rolfe Hall, Box 951487, Los Angeles, CA 90095-1487, (310)267-4720
Language Origins Soc. [IO], Nijmegen, Netherlands
Language; Pan Amer. Coun. for the Preservation of the Hellenic Orthodox Church and the Hellenic [20074]
Language Stud; Amer. Coun. of Teachers of Russian/American Coun. for Collaboration and [★8226]
Language Teachers Assn; Chinese [8076]
Language Teachers Assn; South Asian [7991]

Language Therapy Assn; Academic [12488]
Languages; Amer. Assn. of Teachers of Slavic and East European [9125]
Languages; Amer. Assn. of Teachers of Turkic [9282]
Languages; Coun. of Teachers of Southeast Asian [7990]
Languages and Other Intl. Stud; Coun. for [★10306]
Languages; Special Interest Gp. on Programming [7541]
Languages; Teachers of English to Speakers of Other [8382]
Lansforeningen mod Huntingtons Chorea [★IO]
Lansforeningen for Huntington's Sykdom [IO], Trondheim, Norway
Lantbrukarnas Riksfoerbund [★IO]
Lantern Soc. of the U.S. and Canada; Magic [21531]
Lao Amateur Athletic Assn. [IO], Vientiane, Lao People's Democratic Republic
Lao Badminton Fed. [IO], Vientiane, Lao People's Democratic Republic
Lao Disabled People's Assn. [IO], Vientiane; Lao People's Democratic Republic
Lao Medical Assn. [IO], Vientiane, Lao People's Democratic Republic
Lao Natl. Chamber of Commerce and Indus. [IO], Vientiane, Lao People's Democratic Republic
Lao Taekwondo Fed. [IO], Vientiane, Lao People's Democratic Republic
Lao Tennis Fed. [IO], Vientiane, Lao People's Democratic Republic
Laogai Res. Found. [IO], Washington, DC, United States
Laogai Res. Found. [17772], 1420 K St., 3rd Fl., Washington, DC 20005, (202)833-8770

Laotian
Laotian Amer. Natl. Alliance [19192]
Laotian Amer. Soc. [19193]
Volunteers in Asia [13407]
Laotian Amer. Natl. Alliance [19192], c/o Newcomer Community Ser. Center, 1628 16th St. NW, Washington, DC 20009, (202)370-7841
Laotian Amer. Soc. [19193], PO Box 48432, Atlanta, GA 30362
Laotian Cultural and Res. Center - Address unknown since 2002.
Laparoendoscopic Surgeons; Soc. of [16589]
Laparoscopists; Amer. Assn. of Gynecologic [15581]
Laparoscopists; Amer. Assn. of Gynecological [★15581]
LaPerm Soc. of Am. [21912], c/o Diane Dunn, Treas., PO Box 417, Hygiene, CO 80533-0417, (303)651-0919
Lapidary Dealers Assn; Gem and [2364]
Laptops for the Wounded [11741], 1526 19th St., Cody, WY 82414, (307)587-9371
Lararforbundet [★IO]
Lararnas Riksforbund [★IO]
Large Families of America - Defunct.
Large Format Cinema Assn. [1387], c/o Jeannie Moore, Exec. Dir., 28241 Crown Valley Pkwy., PMB 401, Laguna Niguel, CA 92677, (949)831-1142
Largely Positive [18177], c/o Carol A. Johnson, MA, Founder/Pres., PO Box 170223, Milwaukee, WI 53217-8021, (414)299-9295
Largesse, the Network for Size Esteem [12646]
Largesse, the Network for Size Esteem [IO], New Haven, CT, United States
Larry Gatlin and the Gatlin Brothers Intl. Fan Club - Address unknown since 1999.
Larry Jones Evangelistic Assn. [★12854]
Larry Jones Evangelistic Assn. [★IO]
Larry Jones Intl. Ministries [★IO]
Larry Jones Intl. Ministries [★12854]
Larry Winters Fan Club - Defunct.
Laryngectomy Clubs; Natl. Assn. of [IO]
Laryngological Assn; Amer. [15820]
Laryngological, Rhinological and Otological Soc; Amer. [15821]
Laryngology and Head/Neck Nurses; Soc. of Otorhino [15526]
Laryssa Lauret Fan Club - Defunct.
Las Hermanas-U.S.A. - Address unknown since 2000.

LaSalle Club; Cadillac- [21602]
Lasallian Volunteers [20352], Hecker Ctr., Ste. 300, 3025 Fourth St. NE, Washington, DC 20017, (202)529-0041
Laser Assn. of Am. [★7246]
Laser Dentistry; Acad. of [14088]
Laser and Electro-Optics Mfrs. Assn. [7246], 123 Kent Rd., Pacifica, CA 94044, (650)738-1492
Laser Indus. Assn. [★7247]
Laser Inst. of Am. [7247], 13501 Ingenuity Dr., Ste. 128, Orlando, FL 32826, (407)380-1553
Laser Medicine
Amer. Soc. for Laser Medicine and Surgery [14997]
Assn. of Indus. Laser Users [IO]
British Medical Laser Assn. [IO]
European Soc. for Laser Aesthetic Surgery [IO]
Hong Kong Surgical Laser Assn. [IO]
Intl. Musculoskeletal Laser Soc. [IO]
Intl. Photodynamic Assn. [IO]
Intl. Soc. of Cosmetic and Laser Surgeons [14048]
Iranian Medical Laser Assn. [IO]
Laser Tag Assn; Intl. [1716]
Lasers
Amer. Soc. for Laser Medicine and Surgery [14997]
Intl. Comm. on Ultra-High Intensity Lasers [7245]
Intl. Comm. on Ultra-High Intensity Lasers [IO]
Intl. Soc. of Cosmetic and Laser Surgeons [14048]
Laser and Electro-Optics Mfrs. Assn. [7246]
Laser Inst. of Am. [7247]
Lasers and Electro-Optics Soc; IEEE [6920]
Lasers in Publishing Users Group - Address unknown since 2002.
Lasher Family Assn. [20977], PO Box 1194, Kingston, NY 12402, (845)339-5279
LASPAU: Academic and Professional Programs for the Americas [8108], 25 Mt. Auburn St., Cambridge, MA 02138-6095, (617)495-5255
LASPAU: Academic and Professional Programs for the Americas [IO], Cambridge, MA, United States
Lassen Legacy Proj; Leo [24789]
Last Acts Partnership - Defunct.
Last Chance for Animals [11424], 8033 Sunset Blvd., No. 835, Los Angeles, CA 90046, (310)271-6096
Last Chance Corral [11425], 5350 Pomeroy Rd., Athens, OH 45701, (740)594-4336
Last Chance Forever [5336], PO Box 460993, San Antonio, TX 78246-0993, (210)499-4080
Last Harvest [★12917]
Last Harvest Ministries [12917], PO Box 462192, Garland, TX 75046-2192, (214)703-0505
Last Mfrs. Assn. - Defunct.
Lastensuojelun Keskusliitto [★IO]
Late-Deafened Adults; Assn. of [14743]
Late Great Chevrolet Assn. [21685], 5140 S Washington Ave., Titusville, FL 32780, (800)285-7461
Late Model Racing Assn; Northern [23084]
Late Model Smoothie Div. [★21683]
Late-Onset Tay-Sachs Found. [14460]
LATER - Defunct.
Lateral Sclerosis Assn; Amyotrophic [15306]
Lateral Sclerosis Soc. of Am; Amyotrophic [★15306]
LATET - Israeli Humanitarian Aid Org. [IO], Tel Aviv, Israel
Latex Allergy Assn; Amer. [13597]
Latex Coun; SB [820]
Latex Foam Rubber Coun. - Defunct.
Lath and Plaster; Assoc. Institutes for [★1026]
Lath and Plaster; Intl. Inst. for [1026]
Latham Found. [11426], Latham Plaza Bldg., 1826 Clement Ave., Alameda, CA 94501, (510)521-0920
Lathers' Intl. Union; Wood, Wire and Metal [★24032]
Lathing and Plastering; Intl. Coun. for [★1026]
Latin
Alpha Psi Lambda Natl. [24615]
Amer. Soc. of Greek and Latin Epigraphy [11207]
Assn. of Amer. Chambers of Commerce in Latin Am. [24352]
Coun. of the Americas [24353]
Eta Sigma Phi, Natl. Classics Honorary Soc. [24433]

Reference to "IO" in place of a book number signifies that the association may be found in the 45th edition of International Organizations.

Encyclopedia of Associations, 46th Edition

3729

Hemispheric Cong. of Latin Chambers of Commerce [24281]
Hispanic Org. of Latin Actors [10001]
Labor Coun. for Latin Amer. Advancement [24094]
Latin Amer. Paper Money Soc. [22741]
Latin Chamber of Commerce of U.S.A. [24354]
Natl. Comm. for Latin and Greek [9800]
Natl. Junior Classical League [8095]
Puerto Rican Traveling Theatre Company [11040]
Latin Actors; Hispanic Org. of [10001]

Latin America
ACCION Intl. [17205]
Alliance for Communities in Action [12416]
Alpha Psi Lambda Natl. [24615]
Amer. Youth Understanding Diabetes Abroad [14219]
Assn. of Amer. Chambers of Commerce in Latin Am. [24352]
Assn. of Teachers of Latin Amer. Stud. [10309]
Comm. on US/Latin Amer. Relations [19194]
Community Action on Latin Am. [17986]
Community Action on Latin Am. [IO]
Conf. on Latin Amer. History [10310]
Coun. of the Americas [24353]
Delta Tau Lambda Sorority [24707]
Ecumenical Prog. on Central Am. and the Caribbean [17987]
Ecumenical Prog. on Central Am. and the Caribbean [IO]
Fellowship of Reconciliation Task Force on Latin Am. and Caribbean [IO]
Fellowship of Reconciliation Task Force on Latin Am. and Caribbean [17988]
Food for the Poor [12772]
Hemispheric Cong. of Latin Chambers of Commerce [24281]
Hermandad [17046]
Hispanic Coun. for Reform and Educational Options [8260]
Human Rights Documentation Exchange [17989]
Human Rights Documentation Exchange [IO]
Info. Services on Latin Am. [17990]
Inter-American Development Bank [17460]
Labor Coun. for Latin Amer. Advancement [24094]
Latin Am. Data Base [17991]
Latin Am. Data Base [IO]
Latin Am. Mission [20353]
Latin Am. Parents Assn. [11252]
Latin Am. Working Group [17992]
Latin Am. Working Group [IO]
Latin Amer. Aeronautical Assn. [438]
Latin Amer. Art Song Alliance [10636]
Latin Amer. Paper Money Soc. [22741]
Latin Chamber of Commerce of U.S.A. [24354]
Letelier-Moffitt Memorial Fund for Human Rights [17993]
Letelier-Moffitt Memorial Fund for Human Rights [IO]
Liga Intl. [12528]
Natl. Assn. of Latino Arts and Culture [9584]
Natl. Latino Officers Assn. [5921]
Panamerican Cultural Circle [10312]
Puerto Rican Traveling Theatre Company [11040]
Reach-Out Intl. [17994]
Reach-Out Intl. [IO]
Soc. for Latin Amer. Anthropology [6431]
South Amer. Missionary Soc. - USA [20398]
Washington Off. on Latin Am. [17995]
Washington Off. on Latin Am. [IO]
Women's Alliance for Theology, Ethics and Ritual [20626]
Latin Am. Bur. [IO], London, United Kingdom
Latin Am; Coun. for [★24353]
Latin Am. Data Base [17991], 1 Univ. of New Mexico, MSC 02 1690, Albuquerque, NM 87131-1016, (505)277-6839
Latin Am. Data Base [IO], Albuquerque, NM, United States
Latin Am. Gender and Trade Network [IO], Montevideo, Uruguay
Latin Am; Info. Services on [17990]
Latin Am. Mission [20353], PO Box 527900, Miami, FL 33152-7900, (305)884-8400
Latin Am. Mission [IO], Miami, FL, United States
Latin Am; North Amer. Cong. on [16977]

Latin Am. Parents Assn. [11252], PO Box 339-340, Brooklyn, NY 11234, (718)236-8689
Latin Am. Working Group [17992], 424 C St. NE, Washington, DC 20002, (202)546-7010
Latin Am. Working Group [IO], Washington, DC, United States
Latin Am. Working Group Educ. Fund [★IO]
Latin Am. Working Group Educ. Fund [★17992]

Latin American
ACCION Intl. [17205]
African Asian Latina Lesbians United [17649]
Alliance for Communities in Action [12416]
Alpha Psi Lambda Natl. [24615]
Alpha Rho Lambda Sorority [24703]
Amer. Portuguese Stud. Assn. [9004]
Assn. of Amer. Chambers of Commerce in Latin Am. [24352]
Assn. of Latina and Latino Anthropologists [6410]
Assn. of Teachers of Latin Amer. Stud. [10309]
Assn. of Teachers of Latin Amer. Stud. [IO]
Before Columbus Found. [10416]
Centre for Development and Population Activities [12422]
Comm. on US/Latin Amer. Relations [19194]
Conf. on Latin Amer. History [10310]
Coun. of the Americas [24353]
Coun. of Latin-American Students of Architecture [292]
Delta Tau Lambda Sorority [24707]
DIVAS of Lambda Fe Uson Sorority [24709]
Fed. Hispanic Law Enforcement Officers Assn. [5969]
Feministas Unidas [10000]
Gamma Alpha Omega Sorority [24599]
Hemispheric Cong. of Latin Chambers of Commerce [24281]
Hispanas Organized for Political Equality [17703]
Hispanic Coun. for Reform and Educational Options [8260]
Hispanic Marketing and Commun. Assn. [2628]
Inter-University Prog. for Latino Res. [19045]
Intl. Assn. of Hispanic Meeting Professionals [2684]
Labor Coun. for Latin Amer. Advancement [24094]
Latin Am. Bur. [IO]
Latin Am. Mission [20353]
Latin Am. Parents Assn. [11252]
Latin Amer. Aeronautical Assn. [438]
Latin Amer. Art Song Alliance [10636]
Latin Amer. Paper Money Soc. [22741]
Latin Amer. Stud. Assn. [10311]
Latin Amer. Stud. Assn. [IO]
Latin Amer. Venture Capital Assn. [1431]
Latin Chamber of Commerce of U.S.A. [24354]
Latino Amer. Mgt. Assn. [24288]
Latino Issues Forum [19098]
Latino Org. for Liver Awareness [14811]
Latinos in Info. Sciences and Tech. Assn. [7201]
Lawyers for One Am. [6028]
Leadership Enterprise for a Diverse Am. [9183]
Mexican Amer. Cultural Center [20286]
Mexican Amer. Grocers Assn. [1536]
Minority Student Achievement Network [8401]
Natl. Assn. for Direct Care Workers of Color [14709]
Natl. Assn. of Hispanic and Latino Stud. [9920]
Natl. Assn. of Latina Leaders [2411]
Natl. Assn. of Latino Arts and Culture [9584]
Natl. Assn. of Latino Independent Producers [1390]
Natl. Community for Latino Leadership [19203]
Natl. Hispanic Bus. Assn. [8039]
Natl. Hispanic Employee Assn. [12279]
Natl. Latina Hea. Network [14589]
Natl. Latina/Latino Law Student Assn. [17996]
Natl. Latino Alliance for the Elimination of Domestic Violence [12037]
Natl. Latino Behavioral Hea. Assn. [15227]
Natl. Latino Coun. on Alcohol and Tobacco Prevention [12269]
Natl. Latino Officers Assn. [5921]
Natl. Latino Peace Officers Assn. [19195]
Natl. Org. for Mexican Amer. Rights [17709]
Natl. Soc. for Hispanic Professionals [1908]
New Am. Alliance [1169]

Pan Amer. Hea. and Educ. Found. [12536]
Panamerican Cultural Circle [10312]
Panamerican Cultural Circle [IO]
Puerto Rican Traveling Theatre Company [11040]
RARE [5373]
Salvadoran Amer. Leadership and Educational Fund [17484]
Seminar on the Acquisition of Latin Amer. Lib. Materials [10386]
Sigma Lambda Alpha Sorority [24714]
Soc. for Latin Amer. Stud. [10313]
South Amer. Missionary Soc. - USA [20398]
Tinker Found. [10313]
Tinker Found. [IO]
Tomas Rivera Policy Inst. [19196]
William C. Velasquez Inst. [19197]
Women's Alliance for Theology, Ethics and Ritual [20626]
Latin Amer. Acad. of Sciences [IO], Caracas, Venezuela
Latin Amer. Advancement; Labor Coun. for [24094]
Latin Amer. Aeronautical Assn. [438], 5100 S Collins, Arlington Airport, Arlington, TX 76018, (817)284-0431
Latin Amer. Aeronautical Assn. [IO], Arlington, TX, United States
Latin Amer. Anthropology; Ad Hoc Gp. on [★6431]
Latin Amer. Anthropology Gp. [★6431]
Latin Amer. Anthropology Gp. [★IO]
Latin Amer. Art Song Alliance [10636], 18204 NE 23rd St., Vancouver, WA 98684
Latin Amer. Assn. of Communications Researchers [IO], La Paz, Bolivia
Latin Amer. Assn. of Development Financing Institutions [IO], Lima, Peru
Latin Amer. Assn. of Development Organizations [IO], San Jose, Costa Rica
Latin Amer. Assn. of Natl. Academies of Medicine - Defunct.
Latin Amer. Banking Fed. [IO], Bogota, Colombia
Latin Amer. Blind Union - Uruguay [IO], Havana, Cuba
Latin Amer. Book Programs - Defunct.
Latin Amer. Botanical Assn. [IO], Bogota, Colombia
Latin Amer. Brewers Assn. [IO], Caracas, Venezuela
Latin Amer. and Caribbean Comm. for the Defense of Women's Rights [IO], Lima, Peru
Latin Amer. and Caribbean Demographic Centre [IO], Santiago, Chile
Latin Amer. and Caribbean Economic Assn. [IO], Bogota, Colombia
Latin Amer. and Caribbean Economic Sys. [IO], Caracas, Venezuela
Latin Amer.-Caribbean Labor Inst. - Address unknown since 2001.
Latin Amer. and Caribbean Solidarity Assn. [★18104]
Latin Amer. and Caribbean Solidarity Assn. [★IO]
Latin Amer. and Caribbean Women's Hea. Network [IO], Santiago, Chile
Latin Amer. Center of Physics [IO], Rio de Janeiro, Brazil
Latin Amer. Center of Social Ecology [IO], Montevideo, Uruguay
Latin Amer. Centre for Development Admin. [IO], Caracas, Venezuela
Latin Amer. Citizens; League of United [19099]
Latin Amer. Coun. of Churches [IO], Quito, Ecuador
Latin Amer. Diabetes Assn. [IO], San Luis Potosi, Mexico
Latin Amer. Economic Sys. [★IO]
Latin Amer. Educational Found. [8496], 561 Santa Fe Dr., Denver, CO 80204, (303)446-0541
Latin Amer. Energy Org. [IO], Quito, Ecuador
Latin Amer. Evangelistic Campaign [★IO]
Latin Amer. Evangelistic Campaign [★20353]
Latin Amer. Fed. of Associations for Relatives of the Detained-Disappeared [IO], Caracas, Venezuela
Latin Amer. Fed. of the Pharmaceutical Indus. [IO], Buenos Aires, Argentina
Latin Amer. Forestry Inst. [IO], Merida, Venezuela
Latin Amer. Human Rights Assn. - Address unknown since 1985.
Latin Amer. Indian Literatures Assn. - Address unknown since 1995.

A star before a book entry number signifies that the name is not listed separately, but is mentioned within the entry.

Latin Amer. Info. Agency [IO], Quito, Ecuador
Latin Amer. Inst. for Advanced Stud. [IO], Porto Alegre, Brazil
Latin Amer. Inst. for Social Res. [IO], Quito, Ecuador
Latin Amer. Iron and Steel Inst. [IO], Santiago, Chile
Latin Amer. Mfrs. Assn. [★24288]
Latin Amer. Notaphilic Soc. [★22741]
Latin Amer. Paper Money Soc. [22741], 3304 Milford Mill Rd., Baltimore, MD 21244
Latin Amer. Petrochemical Assn. [IO], Buenos Aires, Argentina
Latin Amer. Phytopathology Assn. [IO], Lima, Peru
Latin Amer. Railway Assn. [IO], Buenos Aires, Argentina
Latin Amer. Refugee Support Comm. - Defunct.
Latin Amer. Resource Center and Clearinghouse - Defunct.
Latin Amer. Scholarship Prog. of Amer. Universities [★8108]
Latin Amer. Scholarship Prog. of Amer. Universities [★IO]
Latin Amer. Secretariat for Academic Services - Defunct.
Latin Amer. Soc. for Interventional Cardiology [IO], Buenos Aires, Argentina
Latin Amer. Soc. of Nephrology and Hypertension [IO], Maracaibo, Venezuela
Latin-American Students of Architecture; Coun. of [292]
Latin Amer. Stud. Assn. [10311], Univ. of Pittsburgh, 416 Bellefield Hall, Pittsburgh, PA 15260, (412)648-7929
Latin Amer. Stud. Assn. [IO], Pittsburgh, PA, United States
Latin Amer. Tax Law Inst. [IO], Montevideo, Uruguay
Latin Amer. Thoracic Soc. [IO], Buenos Aires, Argentina
Latin Amer. Thyroid Soc. [IO], Sao Paulo, Brazil
Latin Amer. Venture Capital Assn. [1431], 28 E Jackson Blvd., Ste. 1700, Chicago, IL 60604, (503)239-7449
Latin Bus. Assn. [740], 120 S San Pedro St., Ste. 530, Los Angeles, CA 90012, (213)628-8510
Latin Chamber of Commerce [★24354]
Latin Chamber of Commerce of U.S.A. [24354], 1417 W Flagler St., 3rd Fl., Miami, FL 33135, (305)642-3870
Latin and Greek; Natl. Comm. for [9800]
Latin and Greek; Natl. Coordinating Off. for [★9800]
Latin Liturgy Assn. [19646], c/o Mr. James F. Pauer, Pres., PO Box 16517, Rocky River, OH 44116
Latin Mass Soc. [IO], London, United Kingdom
Latina/o Lesbian, Gay, Bisexual, and Transgender Org; Natl. [9972]
Latina Org; MANA, A Natl. [17548]
Latinas and Latinos for Social Change [18104], PO Box 1279, Cambridge, MA 02238, (617)290-5614
Latinas and Latinos for Social Change [IO], Cambridge, MA, United States
Latino Alumni Assn; Stanford Chicano/ [18925]
Latino Amer. Mgt. Assn. [24288], 419 New Jersey Ave. SE, Washington, DC 20003, (202)546-3803
Latino Appointed Democratic Officials; Natl. Assn. of [★17706]
Latino Elected and Appointed Officials; Natl. Assn. of [17706]
Latino Fraternal Organizations; Natl. Assn. of [19059]
Latino Gang Investigator's Assn; Intl. [5884]
Latino Gerontological Center [11292], 75 Maiden Ln., Ste. 208, New York, NY 10038, (212)402-5474
Latino Gerontological Center [IO], New York, NY, United States
Latino Issues Forum [19098], 160 Pine St., Ste. 700, San Francisco, CA 94111, (415)284-7220
Latino Org. for Liver Awareness [14811], PO Box 842, Throggs Neck Sta., Bronx, NY 10465, (718)892-8697
Latino Professionals in Finance and Accounting; Assn. of [16]
Latino Res; Inter-University Prog. for [19045]
Latino Stud; Natl. Assn. of Hispanic and [9920]
Latinos in Info. Sciences and Tech. Assn. [7201], 500 W 37th St., 4th Fl., New York, NY 10018, (347)632-4542

Latter Day Saints
Affirmation/Gay and Lesbian Mormons [20046]
Assn. of Mormon Counselors and Psychotherapists [16212]
Dialogue Found. [20207]
Family and Church History Dept. of the Church of Jesus Christ of Latter-Day Saints [21115]
Mormon History Assn. [20208]
Northern Far East Returned Missionaries Assn. [20504]
Recovery from Mormonism [12888]
Young Women of the Church of Jesus Christ of Latter-Day Saints [20209]
Latter-day Saints; Genealogical Soc. of the Church of Jesus Christ of [★21115]
Latvia
Assn. for the Advancement of Baltic Stud. [9730]
World Fed. of Free Latvians [17997]
World Fed. of Free Latvians [IO]
Latvia Sports Medicine Assn. [IO], Riga, Latvia
Latvia Tenants Soc. of Liepaja [IO], Liepaja, Latvia
Latvian
Amer. Latvian Assn. [19198]
Latvian Choir Assn. of the U.S. [10637]
Latvian Acad. of Sciences [IO], Riga, Latvia
Latvian Assn. of Consulting Engineers [IO], Riga, Latvia
Latvian Assn. of Foresters in the U.S. - Defunct.
Latvian Assn. of Gastrointestinal Endoscopy [IO], Riga, Latvia
Latvian Assn. of Language Teachers [IO], Riga, Latvia
Latvian Assn. of Occupational Therapists [IO], Jurmala, Latvia
Latvian Assn. of Rheumatologists [IO], Riga, Latvia
Latvian Assn. for the Stud. of Pain [IO], Riga, Latvia
Latvian Assn. of Univ. Women [IO], Salaspils, Latvia
Latvian Athletic Fed. [IO], Riga, Latvia
Latvian Authorized Auto. Dealers' Assn. [IO], Riga, Latvia
Latvian Badminton Fed. [IO], Riga, Latvia
Latvian Bible Soc. [IO], Riga, Latvia
Latvian Biochemical Soc. [IO], Riga, Latvia
Latvian Canadian Cultural Centre [IO], Toronto, ON, Canada
Latvian Chamber of Commerce and Indus. [IO], Riga, Latvia
Latvian Choir Assn. of the U.S. [10637]
Latvian Dancesport Fed. [IO], Riga, Latvia
Latvian Floorball Union [IO], Riga, Latvia
Latvian Flying Disc Fed. [IO], Ogre, Latvia
Latvian Football Fed. [IO], Riga, Latvia
Latvian Fund for Nature [IO], Riga, Latvia
Latvian Info. Tech. and Telecommunications Assn. [IO], Riga, Latvia
Latvian League Against Epilepsy [IO], Riga, Latvia
Latvian Memorial Comm. - Defunct.
Latvian Multiple Sclerosis Assn. [IO], Riga, Latvia
Latvian Natl. Found. [IO], Stockholm, Sweden
Latvian Ornithological Soc. [IO], Riga, Latvia
Latvian Paralympic Comm. [IO], Riga, Latvia
Latvian Physical Soc. [IO], Riga, Latvia
Latvian Physicians Assn. [IO], Riga, Latvia
Latvian Physiological Soc. [IO], Riga, Latvia
Latvian Physiotherapists Assn. [IO], Riga, Latvia
Latvian Press Publishers Assn. [IO], Riga, Latvia
Latvian Publishers' Assn. [IO], Riga, Latvia
Latvian Rheumatic Assn. [IO], Riga, Latvia
Latvian Schoolsport Fed. [IO], Riga, Latvia
Latvian Skating Assn. [IO], Riga, Latvia
Latvian Social Democratic Workers' Party [IO], Riga, Latvia
Latvian Soc. of Cardiology [IO], Riga, Latvia
Latvian Soc. for Electron Microscopy [IO], Riga, Latvia
Latvian Soc. of Geodesy and Photogrammetry [IO], Riga, Latvia
Latvian Soc. of Landscape Architects [IO], Riga, Latvia
Latvian Soc. of Osteoporosis [IO], Riga, Latvia
Latvian Soc. of Pharmacology [IO], Riga, Latvia
Latvian Squash Fed. [IO], Riga, Latvia
Latvian Students Union [★IO]
Latvian Taekwondo Fed. [IO], Riga, Latvia
Latvian Tennis Union [IO], Jurmala, Latvia

Latvian Traders' Assn. [IO], Riga, Latvia
Latvian Venture Capital and Private Equity Assn. [IO], Riga, Latvia
Latvia's Assn. for Family Planning and Sexual Hea. Assn. [IO], Riga, Latvia
Latviesu Nacionalais Fonds [★IO]
Latvijas Aeroklubs [IO], Riga, Latvia
Latvijas Bibeles biedriba [★IO]
Latvijas Dabas Fonds [★IO]
Latvijas Farmakologijas Biedriba [★IO]
Latvijas Fizikas Biedriba [★IO]
Latvijas Florbola Savieniba [★IO]
Latvijas Frisbija Federacija [★IO]
Latvijas Futbola Federacija [★IO]
Latvijas Gimenes Planosanas un Seksualas Veselibas Asociacija [★IO]
Latvijas Gramatizdeveju Asociacija [★IO]
Latvijas Informacijas un Komunikacijas Tehnologijas Asociacija [★IO]
Latvijas Inzenierkonsultantu Asociacija [★IO]
Latvijas Komercbanku Asociacija [★IO]
Latvijas Multiplas Sklerozes Asociacijas [★IO]
Latvijas Ornitologijas Biedriba [★IO]
Latvijas Pilnvaroto Autotirgotaju Asociacija [★IO]
Latvijas Riska Kapitala Asociacija [★IO]
Latvijas Sapju Izpetes Biedriba [★IO]
Latvijas Slidosanas Asociacija [★IO]
Latvijas Socialdemokratiska Stradnieku Partija [★IO]
Latvijas Sports Deju Federacija [★IO]
Latvijas Studentu apvieniba [★IO]
Latvijas Tirdzniecibas Un Rupniecibas Kamera [★IO]
Latvijas Tirgotaju Asociacija [★IO]
Latvijas Valodu Skolotaju Asociacija [★IO]
Laubach Literacy of Canada [IO], Ottawa, ON, Canada
Laubach Literacy Intl. [★IO]
Laubach Literacy Intl. [★8797]
Laucks Found. - Address unknown since 2008.
Laugh Lovers [★22600]
Laughlin China Collectors Assn; Homer [22036]
Laughter Therapy [16622], PO Box 827, Monterey, CA 93942
Launderers; Inst. of Indus. [★2408]
Laundering; Amer. Inst. of [★2405]
Laundry
Association for Linen Management [2401]
Coin Laundry Assn. [2402]
Drycleaning Inst. of Australia [IO]
Healthcare Laundry Accreditation Coun. [2403]
Independent Textile Rental Assn. [3786]
Intl. Drycleaners Cong. [2404]
Intl. Drycleaners Cong. [IO]
Intl. Fabricare Inst. [IO]
Intl. Fabricare Inst. [2405]
Multi-Housing Laundry Assn. [2406]
Natl. Assn. of the Launderette Indus. [IO]
Ontario Fabricare Assn. [IO]
Textile Care Allied Trades Assn. [2407]
Textile Rental Services Assn. of Am. [3386]
Uniform and Textile Ser. Assn. [2408]
Laundry Allied Trades Assn; Natl. [★2407]
Laundry and Cleaners Allied Trades Assn. [★2407]
Laundry and Cleaning Coun; Natl. Automatic [★2402]
Laundry and Dry Cleaners Machinery Mfrs. Assn. [★2407]
Laundry Equip. Operators; Natl. Assn. of Coin [★2406]
Laundry and Linen College; American [★2401]
Laundry Managers; Natl. Assn. of Institutional [★2401]
Laundry Manufacturers Assn; Amer. Home [★264]
Laura Branigan Fan Club - Address unknown since 1995.
Laura Hendler Fan Club [24751]
Laura Ingalls Wilder Memorial Soc. [9679], PO Box 426, De Smet, SD 57231, (800)880-3383
Laura Lee McBride Fan Club - Address unknown since 1989.
Lauralee Bell Fan Club - Address unknown since 2001.
Laurel and Hardy
Sons of the Desert [24828]
Lauren Robbins Intl. Fan Club - Address unknown since 2001.

Reference to "IO" in place of a book number signifies that the association may be found in the 45th edition of International Organizations.

Laurence-Moon-Bardet-Biedl Syndrome Network [14461], c/o Mary Morris, 15205 W Port Royale Lane Ave., Surprise, AZ 85379-7011
Laurence-Moon-Biedl Syndrome Network [★14461]
Lauritz Melchior Heldentenor Found. - Address unknown since 2007.
Lavender Families Resource Network - Address unknown since 2000.
Laverda Owner's Club - Defunct.
Law
  Acad. of Criminal Justice Sciences [11850]
  Advocates Intl. [17998]
  Advocates Intl. [IO]
  Alliance Against the Uniformed Services Former Spouses Protection Act (USFSPA) Law [6112]
  Alliance of Guardian Angels [11834]
  Alliance for Justice [6219]
  Alston Wilkes Veterans Home [11852]
  Amer. Acad. of Psychiatry and the Law [5780]
  Amer. Alliance of Paralegals, Inc. [6149]
  Amer. Assn. for Correctional and Forensic Psychology [11853]
  Amer. Assn. of Law Libraries [10316]
  Amer. Assn. of Motor Vehicle Administrators [5535]
  Amer. Assn. of Nurse Attorneys [15000]
  Amer. Bar Assn. [5475]
  Amer. Bar Assn. Center on Children and the Law [11555]
  Amer. Bar Assn. Center for Professional Responsibility [5476]
  Amer. Bar Assn. Criminal Justice Sect. [5922]
  Amer. Bar Assn. Sect. of Dispute Resolution [5449]
  Amer. Bar Found. [5923]
  Amer. Catholic Lawyers Assn. [5558]
  Amer. Coll. of Legal Medicine [15001]
  Amer. Coll. of Tax Counsel [5924]
  Amer. Constitution Soc. for Law and Policy [5603]
  Amer. Correctional Assn. [11854]
  Amer. Court and Commercial Newspapers [3202]
  Amer. Criminal Justice Assn. (Lambda Alpha Epsilon) [11855]
  Amer. Fed. of Police and Concerned Citizens [5962]
  Amer. Foreign Law Assn. [5864]
  Amer. Immigration Lawyers Assn. [5807]
  Amer. Indian Law Alliance [16973]
  Amer. Intellectual Property Law Assn. [5835]
  Amer. Jail Assn. [11856]
  Amer. Judges Assn. [5892]
  Amer. Judicature Soc. [5893]
  Amer. Law Inst. [5925]
  Amer. Lawyers Auxiliary [5480]
  Amer. Mock Trial Assn. [9281]
  Amer. Pro Se Assn. [6021]
  Amer. Prosecutors Res. Inst. [5481]
  Amer. Psychology-Law Soc. [16133]
  Amer. Soc. of Access Professionals [5814]
  Amer. Soc. of Comparative Law [5865]
  Amer. Soc. of Criminology [11899]
  Amer. Soc. of Intl. Law [5866]
  Amer. Soc. of Law, Medicine and Ethics [15002]
  Amer. Soc. for Legal History [10090]
  Amer. Soc. for Pharmacy Law [15003]
  Amer. Soc. of Separated and Divorced Men [12005]
  Amer. Tort Reform Assn. [5926]
  Amer. Veterinary Medical Law Assn. [5927]
  Americans for Effective Law Enforcement [5652]
  Animal Legal Defense Fund [11351]
  Asia Pacific Forum on Women, Law and Development [IO]
  Asian-African Legal Consultative Org. [IO]
  Asian Amer. Legal Defense and Educ. Fund [17095]
  Asian Law Caucus [5928]
  Assn. of Administrative Law Judges [5894]
  Assn. of Amer. Pesticide Control Officials [6170]
  Assn. of Danish Lawyers and Economists [IO]
  Assn. of Defense Trial Attorneys [5825]
  Assn. of Family and Conciliation Courts [5699]
  Assn. for Honest Attorneys [5486]
  Assn. of Inspectors Gen. [5777]
  Assn. of Legal Administrators [5929]

  Association of Legal Administrators [IO]
  Assn. on Programs for Female Offenders [11857]
  Assn. of Real Estate License Law Officials [6243]
  Assn. of Reporters of Judicial Decisions [5895]
  Assn. of State Correctional Administrators [11858]
  Assn. of Trans. Law Professionals [6316]
  Atlantic Legal Found. [5930]
  Australian Corporate Lawyers Assn. [IO]
  Australian Inst. of Administrative Law [IO]
  Australian Women Lawyers [IO]
  Azerbaijan Young Lawyers' Union [IO]
  Bermuda Bar Assn. [IO]
  British - German Jurists Assn. [IO]
  Canadian Law and Economics Assn. [IO]
  Canadian Law and Soc. Assn. [IO]
  Canon Law Soc. of Am. [19592]
  Center for Amer. and Intl. Law [5931]
  Center for Amer. and Intl. Law [IO]
  Center for Democracy [5932]
  Center for Philosophy, Law, Citizenship [18271]
  Center for Stud. in Criminal Justice [11859]
  Center for Stud. of Responsive Law [17315]
  Charity Law Assn. [IO]
  China Law Soc. [IO]
  Chinese Law Soc. of Am. [5933]
  Citizens Communications Center Proj. of the Inst. for Public Representation [17171]
  Citizens Equal Rights Alliance [5800]
  Clarity [6011]
  Clinical Legal Educ. Assn. [8763]
  Coalition for an Intl. Criminal Court [17361]
  Coalition for Intl. Justice [5934]
  Coalition for Intl. Justice [IO]
  Commercial Law League of Am. [5576]
  Commn. on Accreditation for Law Enforcement Agencies [5967]
  Commn. on Law and Aging [5935]
  Commn. on Women in the Profession [5936]
  Comm. for Legal Aid to Poor [IO]
  Commonwealth Lawyers' Assn. [IO]
  Conf. of Chief Justices [5896]
  Conf. on Consumer Finance Law [5608]
  Correctional Educ. Assn. [11862]
  Coun. of the Bars and Law Societies of Europe [IO]
  Coun. for Court Excellence [5897]
  Coun. on Governmental Ethics Laws [6270]
  CPR Intl. Inst. for Conflict Prevention and Resolution [11488]
  Croatian Amer. Bar Assn. [5489]
  Czech Bar Assn. [IO]
  Defense Res. Inst. [6042]
  Delta Theta Phi [24527]
  Deutscher Juristinnenbund [IO]
  District Courts Assn. [IO]
  Drug Policy Alliance [17112]
  Economic Justice Inst. [6221]
  Educ. Law Assn. [5676]
  Emerald Soc. of the Fed. Law Enforcement Agencies [19199]
  Energy and Mineral Law Found. [6136]
  Environmental Defense [4562]
  Equal Justice Works [5898]
  European Assn. of Psychology and Law [IO]
  European Coun. for Rural Law [IO]
  European Food Law Assn. [IO]
  European Law Students' Assn. [IO]
  European Network on Law and Soc. [IO]
  Fair Elections Legal Network [5491]
  Fed. Administrative Law Judges Conf. [5899]
  Fed. Circuit Bar Assn. [5493]
  Fed. Communications Bar Assn. [5580]
  Fed. Hispanic Law Enforcement Officers Assn. [5969]
  Fellowship of Christian Peace Officers - U.S.A. [19798]
  Fiji Law Soc. [IO]
  Food and Drug Law Inst. [5738]
  Fortune Soc. [11867]
  Found. of the Fed. Bar Assn. [5937]
  Friends Outside [11868]
  Fund for Modern Courts [5901]
  German-American Lawyers Assn. [IO]
  German Bar Assn. [IO]
  German - Brazilian Lawyers Assn. [IO]

  German Fed. Bar [IO]
  German - Japanese Jurists Assn. [IO]
  Global Advt. Lawyers Alliance [IO]
  Global Advt. Lawyers Alliance [5938]
  Global Alliance for Justice Educ. [8766]
  Global Rights [17758]
  Global Village Inst. [6235]
  Guild of Catholic Lawyers [19631]
  Hea. Law Sect. - Amer. Bar Assn. [5783]
  Hellenic Found. for European and Foreign Policy [IO]
  Hispanic Natl. Bar Assn. [5496]
  Hong Kong Bar Assn. [IO]
  Human Rights Advocates [5801]
  Human Rights First [17759]
  Identity Theft Rsrc. Center [18007]
  Incorporated Soc. of Irish/American Lawyers [5939]
  Indian Law Inst. [IO]
  Indian Law Rsrc. Center [18094]
  Inst. for the Development of Indian Law [18095]
  Inst. of Employment Rights [IO]
  Inst. for Justice [5940]
  Inst. of Legal Executives (Victoria) [IO]
  Inter-American Bar Assn. [IO]
  Inter-American Bar Assn. [5941]
  Inter-Pacific Bar Assn. [IO]
  Intl. Acad. of Comparative Law [IO]
  Intl. Acad. of Law and Mental Hea. [IO]
  Intl. Alliance of Holistic Lawyers [5498]
  Intl. Assn. of Cmpt. Investigative Specialists [8133]
  Intl. Assn. of Correctional Officers [11870]
  Intl. Assn. of Correctional Training Personnel [11871]
  Intl. Assn. of Defense Counsel [5499]
  Intl. Assn. of Directors of Law Enforcement Standards and Training [5973]
  Intl. Assn. of Entertainment Lawyers - United Kingdom [IO]
  Intl. Assn. of Financial Crimes Investigators [5881]
  Intl. Assn. for Insurance Law in the U.S. [5829]
  Intl. Assn. of Jewish Lawyers and Jurists [IO]
  Intl. Assn. of Law Enforcement Firearms Instructors [5974]
  Intl. Assn. of Law, Ethics and Sci. [IO]
  Intl. Assn. of Law Schools [8767]
  Intl. Assn. of Lemon Law Administrators [5536]
  Intl. Assn. of Official Human Rights Agencies [5802]
  Intl. Assn. for Penal Law [IO]
  Intl. Assn. for Property and Evidence [5975]
  Intl. Assn. for the Stud. of Organized Crime [11837]
  Intl. Assn. of Undercover Officers [5976]
  Intl. Bar Assn. [IO]
  Intl. Brotherhood of Police Officers [24120]
  Intl. Center for Law in Development [5942]
  Intl. Center for Law in Development [IO]
  Intl. Center for Not-for-Profit Law [IO]
  Intl. Center for Not-for-Profit Law [5943]
  Intl. Centre for Criminal Law Reform and Criminal Justice Policy [IO]
  Intl. Community Corrections Assn. [11872]
  Intl. Conf. of Police Chaplains [19749]
  Intl. Criminal Court Alliance [5654]
  Intl. Development Law Org. [IO]
  Intl. Intelligence Network [3532]
  Intl. Law Assn., German Br. [IO]
  Intl. Law Assn., Indian Br. [IO]
  Intl. Law Assn., Korean Br. [IO]
  Intl. Law Assn., Norwegian Br. [IO]
  Intl. Law Assn., South African Br. [IO]
  Intl. Law Assn., Swedish Br. [IO]
  Intl. Law Students Assn. [5868]
  Intl. Legal Defense Counsel [5869]
  Intl. Municipal Lawyers Assn. [5500]
  Intl. Narcotics Interdiction Assn. [5742]
  Intl. Network of Boutique Law Firms [5501]
  Intl. Paralegal Mgt. Assn. [5944]
  Intl. Paralegal Mgt. Assn. [IO]
  Intl. Police Work Dog Assn. [5979]
  Intl. Senior Lawyers Proj. [5502]
  Intl. Soc. for Law and Tech. [5945]
  Intl. Soc. for Law and Tech. [IO]

A star before a book entry number signifies that the name is not listed separately, but is mentioned within the entry.

Intl. Soc. of Primerus Law Firms [5503]
Intl. Union of Police Associations [24121]
Intl. Utilities Revenue Protection Assn. [6338]
IP Justice [5852]
Iranian Amer. Bar Assn. [5504]
Irish Centre for European Law [IO]
IUD Claims Info. Source [6216]
Japan Fed. of Bar Associations [IO]
John Howard Assn. [11874]
Joint Comm. of the States [5445]
Judge David L. Bazelon Center for Mental Hea.
    Law [17123]
Justice Res. and Statistics Assn. [11876]
Law Assn. for Asia and the Pacific [IO]
Law Coun. of Australia [IO]
Law Enforcement Against Prohibition [17999]
Law Enforcement and Emergency Services Video
    Assn. [6350]
Law and Soc. Assn. [5946]
Law and Soc. Assn. [IO]
Law Soc. of England and Wales [IO]
Law Soc. of Hong Kong [IO]
Law Soc. of Ireland [IO]
Law Soc. of Northern Ireland [IO]
Law Soc. of Singapore [IO]
Law Soc. of South Africa [IO]
Law and Soc. Trust [IO]
Law Students for Choice [18517]
Lawyers Alliance for World Security [18158]
Lawyers Assoc. Worldwide [5505]
Lawyers Without Borders [18008]
Legal Immigrant Assn. [5808]
Lithuanian-American Bar Assn. [5507]
London Club [11900]
Los Angeles Copyright Soc. [5854]
Malaysian Bar Coun. [IO]
Maritime Law Assn. of the U.S. [6055]
Media Access Proj. [17182]
Minority Corporate Counsel Assn. [5615]
Mongolian Women Lawyers Assn. [IO]
Murder Victims' Families for Reconciliation
    [17032]
NALS [6013]
NARAL Pro-Choice Am. [18518]
Natl. Action for Former Military Wives [12012]
Natl. African Amer. Drug Policy Coalition [17440]
Natl. Alliance Against Racist and Political Repres-
    sion [17128]
Natl. Alliance for Family Court Justice [5904]
Natl. Alliance for Model State Drug Laws [5671]
Natl. Amer. Indian Court Judges Assn. [5905]
Natl. Asian Pacific Amer. Bar Assn. [5947]
Natl. Assn. of Bar Executives [5948]
Natl. Assn. for Civilian Oversight of Law Enforce-
    ment [5985]
Natl. Assn. of Counsel for Children [11711]
Natl. Assn. of Crime Commissions [11840]
Natl. Assn. of Criminal Defense Lawyers [5656]
Natl. Assn. of Fed. Defenders [5646]
Natl. Assn. for Justice Info. Systems [5648]
National Association of Legal Fee Analysis [2409]
Natl. Assn. of Legal Investigators [5885]
Natl. Assn. of Muslim Lawyers [5511]
Natl. Assn. of Patent Practitioners [6167]
Natl. Assn. of Professional Process Servers
    [6184]
Natl. Assn. of State Boating Law Administrators
    [5545]
Natl. Assn. of State Sentencing Commissions
    [5650]
Natl. Assn. of Town Watch [11841]
Natl. Assn. of Unclaimed Property Administrators
    [6186]
Natl. Assn. of Women and the Law [IO]
Natl. Assn. of Women Law Enforcement Execu-
    tives [5989]
Natl. Assn. of Women Lawyers [5514]
Natl. Bar Assn. [5515]
Natl. Center on Institutions and Alternatives
    [11878]
Natl. Center for Juvenile Justice [11879]
Natl. Center for Law and Economic Justice [6232]
Natl. Center for State Courts [5908]
Natl. Center for Youth Law [5700]
Natl. Chamber Litigation Center [6223]

Natl. Child Support Enforcement Assn. [5701]
Natl. Client Protection Org. [5949]
National Client Protection Organization [IO]
Natl. Comm. to Reopen the Rosenberg Case
    [17135]
Natl. Comm. on Uniform Traffic Laws and
    Ordinances [6309]
Natl. Conf. of Bankruptcy Judges [5909]
Natl. Conf. of Bar Examiners [5950]
Natl. Conf. of Bar Foundations [5951]
Natl. Conf. of Bar Foundations [IO]
Natl. Conf. of Bar Presidents [5516]
Natl. Conf. of Black Lawyers [5517]
Natl. Conf. of Commissioners on Uniform State
    Laws [6282]
Natl. Conf. of Fed. Trial Judges [5910]
Natl. Conf. of Specialized Court Judges [5911]
Natl. Conf. of State Trans. Specialists [6323]
Natl. Cong. of Amer. Indians [18096]
Natl. Correctional Indus. Assn. [11880]
Natl. Coun. on Crime and Delinquency [11843]
Natl. Coun. of Juvenile and Family Court Judges
    [5912]
Natl. Crime Prevention Coun. [11844]
Natl. Crime Prevention Inst. [11845]
Natl. Crime Victim Bar Assn. [6349]
Natl. Criminal Justice Assn. [11881]
Natl. Defender Investigator Assn. [5888]
Natl. Employment Law Proj. [12092]
Natl. Employment Lawyers Assn. [5520]
Natl. Endangered Species Act Reform Coalition
    [17504]
Natl. Housing Law Proj. [5796]
Natl. Immigration Proj. of the Natl. Lawyers Guild
    [5810]
Natl. - Interstate Coun. of State Boards of
    Cosmetology [5616]
Natl. Italian Amer. Bar Assn. [5952]
Natl. Judges Assn. [5913]
Natl. Judicial Coll. [5914]
Natl. Juvenile Detention Assn. [11882]
Natl. Latino Officers Assn. [5921]
Natl. Lawyers Assn. [5521]
Natl. Lawyers Guild [5522]
Natl. Legal Found. [6225]
Natl. Liquor Law Enforcement Assn. [5996]
Natl. Major Gang Task Force [5651]
Natl. Narcotic Detector Dog Assn. [5997]
Natl. Org. of Bar Counsel [5953]
Natl. Org. of Legal Services Workers, UAW Local
    2320 [24079]
Natl. Prison Proj. of the ACLU [11883]
Natl. Senior Citizens Law Center [11316]
Natl. South Asian Bar Assn. [6018]
Natl. Union of Law Enforcement Associations
    [24124]
Natl. Women Law Students Assn. [9322]
Native Amer. Rights Fund [18098]
Network of Trial Law Firms [5525]
New Zealand Law Soc. [IO]
Nigerian Lawyers Assn. [5526]
Nine Lives Associates [3540]
NLRB Professional Assn. [24081]
No Peace Without Justice [18227]
North Amer. Assn. of Wardens and
    Superintendents [11884]
North Amer. South Asian Bar Assn. [5527]
North Amer. South Asian Law Student Assn.
    [8773]
Order of the Coif [24516]
Osborne Assn. [11885]
Pacific Legal Found. [6226]
Park Law Enforcement Assn. [6162]
Phi Alpha Delta [24528]
Phi Delta Phi Intl. Legal Fraternity [24530]
Prison Fellowship Intl. [11887]
Prison Fellowship Ministries [11888]
Prison Ministry of Yokefellow's Intl. [11889]
Prisoners' Rights Union [11890]
Privacy Rights CH [3176]
Public Justice [6227]
Public Responsibility in Medicine and Res.
    [18585]
Renaissance Lawyer Soc. [5529]
Safer Soc. Found. [11891]

Scribes - The Amer. Soc. of Legal Writers [5584]
Selden Soc. [IO]
Serbian Bar Assn. of Am. [5531]
Soc. for Animal Protective Legislation [11459]
Soc. of Constr. Law [IO]
Soc. for Court Stud. [IO]
Soc. for Evolutionary Anal. in Law [6539]
Soc. for Healthcare Consumer Advocacy of the
    Amer. Hosp. Assn. [15005]
Soc. of Medical Jurisprudence [15006]
Soc. of Professional Investigators [5890]
Southeastern Legal Found. [5954]
Southern Center for Human Rights [17036]
Sport and Recreation Law Assn. [23870]
St. Law [6035]
Swedish-American Bar Assn. [5532]
Swiss Bar Assn. [IO]
Taiwanese Amer. Lawyers Assn. [5533]
Tau Epsilon Rho Law Soc. [24529]
TechLaw Gp. [5955]
Tokyo Bar Assn. [IO]
Traffic Court Prog. of the Amer. Bar Assn. [6310]
Tribal Court CH [5956]
U.S. Law Firm Gp. [5534]
Volunteer Lawyers for the Arts [6036]
Volunteers in Prevention, Probation, Prisons
    [11896]
Washington Legal Found. [6229]
We Care Prog. [11897]
WeTip [11849]
WITNESS [17789]
Women in Fed. Law Enforcement [6010]
Women in Law and Development in Africa [IO]
Women's Prison Assn. [11898]
WomensLaw.org [18823]
World Assn. of Judges [5870]
World Assn. of Law Professors [5871]
World Assn. of Law Students and Young Jurists
    [5872]
World Assn. of Lawyers [5873]
World Bus. Associates [5874]
World Jurist Assn. [5875]
World Soc. of Mixed Jurisdiction Jurists [5957]
World Soc. of Mixed Jurisdiction Jurists [IO]
Youth Law Center [13522]
Law Administrators; Natl. Assn. of State Boating
    [5545]
Law; Amer. Acad. of Psychiatry and the [5780]
Law; Amer. Assn. for the Comparative Stud. of
    [★5865]
Law; Amer. Bar Assn. Center on Children and the
    [11555]
Law; Amer. Bar Assn. - Commn. on Mental and
    Physical Disability [5781]
Law; Amer. Soc. of Comparative [5865]
Law; Amer. Soc. for Pharmacy [15003]
Law Assn; Amer. Agricultural [5431]
Law Assn; Amer. Bus. [★8757]
Law Assn; Amer. Foreign [5864]
Law Assn; Amer. Intellectual Property [5835]
Law Assn; Amer. Patent [★5835]
Law Assn. for Asia and the Pacific [IO], Brisbane,
    Australia
Law Assn; Christian [19780]
Law Assn; Cmpt. [★5582]
Law Assn; Educ. [5676]
Law; Assn. of U.S. Members of the Intl. Inst. of
    Space [6372]
Law Assn. of the U.S; Maritime [6055]
Law Assn. of Washington; Patent [★5835]
Law Assns; Natl. Coun. of Intellectual Property
    [5855]
Law Assns; Natl. Coun. of Patent [★5855]
Law Attorneys; Natl. Acad. of Elder [6029]
Law Attorneys; Natl. Assn. of Securities and Com-
    mercial [★5579]
Law Center; Child Care [11525]
Law Center for Children and Families; Natl. [5703]
Law Center for Constitutional Rights [★17097]
Law Center on Homelessness and Poverty; Natl.
    [12297]
Law Center; Natl. Consumer [5611]
Law Center; Natl. Economic Development and
    [17464]
Law Center; Natl. Immigration [17807]

Reference to "IO" in place of a book number signifies that the association may be found in the 45th edition of International Organizations.

Law Center; Natl. Senior Citizens [11316]
Law Center; Natl. Women's [17565]
Law; Center on Social Welfare Policy and [★6232]
Law Center; Southern Poverty [17155]
Law Center; Student Press [17194]
Law; Center for Stud. of Responsive [17315]
Law Center; World Peace Through [★5875]
Law, Citizenship; Center for Philosophy, [18271]
Law; Committee on Soviet and East European [★5475]
Law; Conf. on Consumer Finance [5608]
Law; Conf. on Personal Finance [★5608]
Law Coun. of Australia [IO], Canberra, Australia
Law; Coun. for Public Interest [★6219]
Law and Educ; Center for [5675]
Law Educ. Fund; Peace Through [18236]

Law Enforcement
African Amer. Criminal Justice Soc. [17359]
Airborne Law Enforcement Assn. [5958]
Alliance of Guardian Angels [11834]
Amer. Acad. of Matrimonial Lawyers [5698]
Amer. Assn. of Code Enforcement [5959]
Amer. Assn. of State Troopers [5960]
Amer. Deputy Sheriffs' Assn. [5961]
Amer. Fed. of Police and Concerned Citizens [5962]
Amer. Judges Assn. [5892]
Amer. Judicature Soc. [5893]
Amer. Soc. of Criminology [11899]
Amer. Soc. of Law Enforcement Training [5963]
Assn. of Chief Police Officers of England, Wales and Northern Ireland [IO]
Assn. of Chief Police Officers in Scotland [IO]
Assn. of Christian Investigators [5876]
Assn. for Explosive Detection K-9s, Intl. [5964]
Assn. for Explosive Detection K-9s, Intl. [IO]
Assn. of Food and Drug Officials [5736]
Assn. of Former Agents of the U.S. Secret Ser. [5877]
Australian Fed. Police Assn. [IO]
Aviation Crime Prevention Inst. [433]
Black Cops Against Police Brutality [5965]
Blacks in Law Enforcement [5966]
Blue Knights Intl. Law Enforcement Motorcycle Club [22669]
Campaign to End the Death Penalty [17028]
Canadian Assn. of Chiefs of Police [IO]
Canadian Assn. of Police Boards [IO]
Canadian Assn. of Police Educators [IO]
Canadian Police Assn. [IO]
Commn. on Accreditation for Law Enforcement Agencies [5967]
Concerns of Police Survivors [12752]
Conf. of Chief Justices [5896]
Coun. for Court Excellence [5897]
Doe Network [12608]
Emerald Soc. of the Fed. Law Enforcement Agencies [19199]
Emerald Society of the Federal Law Enforcement Agencies [IO]
Equal Justice Works [5898]
European Confed. of Police [IO]
European Network of Policewomen [IO]
Evidence Photographers Intl. Coun. [5759]
Fed. Administrative Law Judges Conf. [5899]
Fed. Bur. of Investigation Agents Assn. [5968]
Fed. Hispanic Law Enforcement Officers Assn. [5969]
Fed. Hispanic Law Enforcement Officers Assn. [IO]
Fellowship of Christian Peace Officers - U.S.A. [19798]
Fraternal Order of Police, Grand Lodge [19200]
Gay Officers' Action League [12231]
Hispanic Amer. Police Command Officers Assn. [5970]
IACP Law Enforcement Info. Mgt. Sect. [5819]
Intl. Assn. of Accident Reconstruction Specialists [2410]
International Association of Accident Reconstruction Specialists [IO]
Intl. Assn. of Airport and Seaport Police [IO]
Intl. Assn. of Arson Investigators [5716]
Intl. Assn. Auto Theft Investigators [5971]
Intl. Assn. Auto Theft Investigators [IO]

Intl. Assn. of Chiefs of Police [IO]
Intl. Assn. of Chiefs of Police [5972]
Intl. Assn. of Cmpt. Investigative Specialists [8133]
Intl. Assn. of Directors of Law Enforcement Standards and Training [5973]
Intl. Assn. of Financial Crimes Investigators [5881]
Intl. Assn. of Investigative Locksmiths [3528]
Intl. Assn. of Law Enforcement Firearms Instructors [5974]
Intl. Assn. of Law Enforcement Firearms Instructors [IO]
International Association for Property and Evidence [IO]
Intl. Assn. for Property and Evidence [5975]
Intl. Assn. for the Stud. of Organized Crime [11837]
Intl. Assn. of Undercover Officers [5976]
International Association of Undercover Officers [IO]
Intl. Brotherhood of Police Officers [24120]
Intl. Conf. of Police Chaplains [19749]
Intl. Criminal Police Org. - Interpol [IO]
Intl. Footprint Assn. [5977]
Intl. Found. for Protection Officers [3531]
Intl. Homicide Investigators Assn. [5883]
Intl. Law Enforcement Educators and Trainers Assn. [5978]
Intl. Law Enforcement Educators and Trainers Assn. [IO]
Intl. Narcotic Enforcement Officers Assn. [5741]
Intl. Narcotics Interdiction Assn. [5742]
Intl. Police Assn. [IO]
Intl. Police and Fire Chaplain's Assn. [19750]
Intl. Police Work Dog Assn. [5979]
Intl. Police Work Dog Assn. [IO]
Intl. Soc. of Crime Prevention Practitioners [11838]
Intl. Union of Police Associations [24121]
Law Enforcement Against Prohibition [17999]
Law Enforcement Against Prohibition [IO]
Law Enforcement Alliance of Am. [5980]
Law Enforcement Assn. of Asian Pacifics [19201]
Law Enforcement and Emergency Services Video Assn. [6350]
Law Enforcement Memorial Assn. [5981]
Law Enforcement Thermographers' Assn. [5982]
Law Enforcement Thermographers' Association [IO]
London Club [11900]
Natl. Alliance of Gang Investigators Associations [5638]
Natl. Amer. Indian Court Judges Assn. [5905]
Natl. Asian Peace Officers' Assn. [5983]
Natl. Assn. of Asian Amer. Law Enforcement Commanders [5984]
Natl. Assn. Citizens on Patrol [12970]
Natl. Assn. for Civilian Oversight of Law Enforcement [5985]
Natl. Assn. of Crime Commissions [11840]
Natl. Assn. of Drug Diversion Investigators [5986]
Natl. Assn. of Field Training Officers [5987]
Natl. Assn. of Police Athletic Leagues [13496]
Natl. Assn. of Police Organizations [5988]
Natl. Assn. of Special Police and Security Officers [24122]
Natl. Assn. of Town Watch [11841]
Natl. Assn. of Women Law Enforcement Executives [5989]
Natl. Black Police Assn. [5990]
Natl. Black Police Assn. - UK [IO]
Natl. Border Patrol Coun. [24123]
Natl. Center for Women and Policing [5991]
Natl. Child Safety Coun. [12972]
Natl. Conf. of State Liquor Administrators [5447]
Natl. Constables Assn. [5992]
Natl. Cops for Life [18558]
Natl. Coun. on Crime and Delinquency [11843]
Natl. Coun. of Juvenile and Family Court Judges [5912]
Natl. Crime Prevention Coun. [11844]
Natl. Crime Prevention Inst. [11845]
Natl. Defender Investigator Assn. [5888]
Natl. Drug Enforcement Officers Assn. [5993]
Natl. Fed. of Officers for Life [18559]

Natl. Latino Officers Assn. [5921]
Natl. Latino Peace Officers Assn. [19195]
Natl. Law Enforcement Coun. [5994]
Natl. Law Enforcement Officers Memorial Fund [5995]
Natl. Liquor Law Enforcement Assn. [5996]
Natl. Major Gang Task Force [5651]
Natl. Narcotic Detector Dog Assn. [5997]
Natl. Native Amer. Law Enforcement Assn. [5998]
Natl. Org. of Black Law Enforcement Executives [5999]
Natl. Police Bloodhound Assn. [6000]
Natl. Police Officers Assn. of Am. [6001]
Natl. Sheriffs' Assn. [6002]
Natl. Tactical Officers Assn. [6175]
Natl. Union of Law Enforcement Associations [24124]
New Zealand Police Assn. [IO]
Nine Lives Associates [3540]
North Amer. Police Work Dog Assn. [6003]
North Amer. Wildlife Enforcement Officers Assn. [5357]
Park Law Enforcement Assn. [6162]
People of Faith Against the Death Penalty [17034]
Police Assn. for Coll. Educ. [6004]
Police Executive Res. Forum [6005]
Police Fed. of England and Wales [IO]
Police Found. [6006]
Police Marksman Assn. [6007]
Police Superintendents' Assn. of England and Wales [IO]
Scottish Police Fed. [IO]
Soc. of Former Special Agents of the Fed. Bur. of Investigation [19202]
Soc. of Professional Investigators [5890]
Southern Center for Human Rights [17036]
U.S. Police Canine Assn. [6008]
U.S. Secret Ser. Uniformed Div. Retirement Assn. [6009]
WeTip [11849]
Women in Fed. Law Enforcement [6010]
World Assn. of Judges [5870]
Law Enforcement Against Prohibition [17999], 121 Mystic Ave., Medford, MA 02155, (781)393-6985
Law Enforcement Against Prohibition [IO], Medford, MA, United States
Law Enforcement Alliance of Am. [5980], 7700 Leesburg Pike, Ste. 421, Falls Church, VA 22043, (703)847-2677
Law Enforcement Assn. of Asian Pacifics [19201], PO Box 11336, Glendale, CA 91226
Law Enforcement; Blacks in [★5966]
Law Enforcement Communication Network - Address unknown since 1999.
Law Enforcement and Emergency Services Video Assn. [6350], PO Box 547, Midlothian, TX 76065, (972)291-5888
Law Enforcement Info. Mgt. Sect. [★5819]
Law Enforcement Info. Mgt. Sect; IACP [5819]
Law Enforcement Memorial Assn. [5981], PO Box 72835, Roselle, IL 60172-0835, (312)623-1391
Law Enforcement Officer - Defunct.
Law Enforcement Officers Assn; Amer. [★5962]
Law Enforcement Officers Assn; Fed. [5879]
Law Enforcement Officers; Natl. Assn. of School Safety and [9087]
Law Enforcement Steering Comm. - Address unknown since 1999.
Law Enforcement Study Unit - Defunct.
Law Enforcement Thermographers' Assn. [5982], PO Box 6485, Edmond, OK 73083-6485, (405)330-6988
Law Enforcement Thermographers' Association [IO], Edmond, OK, United States
Law Firm Gp; State Capital [★324]
Law Firm Gp; State Capital Global [324]
Law Firm Marketing Administrators; Natl. Assn. of [★2632]
Law Firm Marketing Assn; Natl. [★2632]
Law Firm Recruiters Assn. - Defunct.
Law Firm Services Assn. [38], 10831 Old Mill Rd., Ste. 400, Omaha, NE 68154, (402)778-7922
Law Found; Energy and Mineral [6136]
Law Found; Rocky Mountain Mineral [6141]
Law Fraternity; Tau Epsilon Rho [★24529]

A star before a book entry number signifies that the name is not listed separately, but is mentioned within the entry.

Law in Higher Educ; Coun. on [8317]
Law Inst; Banking [5543]
Law; Inst. for the Development of Indian [18095]
Law Inst; Food [★5738]
Law Inst; Food and Drug [5738]
Law; Inst. for Intl. and Foreign Trade [★5867]
Law Inst; Natl. St. [★6035]
Law Inst; Practising [8774]
Law; Judge David L. Bazelon Center for Mental Hea. [17123]
Law Judges; Assn. of Administrative [5894]
Law Judges Conf; Fed. Administrative [5899]
Law Judges, Dept. of Hea. and Human Services; Assn. of Administrative [★5894]
Law and Justice; Amer. Center for [12901]
Law; Lawyers' Comm. for Civil Rights Under [6027]
Law League of Am; Commercial [5576]
Law and Liberty Project - Defunct.
Law Libraries; Amer. Assn. of [10316]
Law, Logistics and Policy; Assn. for Trans. [★6316]
Law and Medicine; Amer. Soc. of [★15002]
Law, Medicine and Ethics; Amer. Soc. of [15002]
Law and Medicine; Massachusetts Soc. of [★15002]
Law; Natl. Assn. for Public Interest [★5898]
Law; Natl. Center for Youth [5700]
Law; Natl. Inst. for Citizen Educ. in the [★6035]
Law Off. Museum and Memorial Lib; James Monroe [★11128]
Law Officials; Intl. Assn. of Bedding and Furniture [5823]
Law Opposition Forum; Seatbelt [12990]
Law and Order; Citizens for [17958]
Law; Pierce Butler, Jr. Found. for Educ. in World [★18834]
Law Placement; Natl. Assn. for [8770]
Law and Policy; Center for Oceans [7394]
Law and Policy; Center for Reproductive [★18516]
Law and Politics; Center for the Stud. of [★5693]
Law and Poverty; Western Center on [6037]
Law Prog; Natl. Hea. [5784]
Law Proj; Mental Hea. [★17123]
Law Proj; Natl. Employment [12092]
Law Proj; Natl. Housing [5796]
Law Proj; Women's [17579]
Law and Public Policy; Natl. Inst. for Sci., [4105]
Law and Public Policy; Newport Inst. for Ethics, [18470]
Law and Public Policy Stud; Federalist Soc. for [5900]
Law and Religious Freedom; Center for [18510]
Law Res. Found; Family [★12138]
Law Rsrc. Center; Indian [18094]
Law School Admission Coun. [8768], PO Box 40, Newtown, PA 18940, (215)968-1001
Law School Admission Coun. [IO], Newtown, PA, United States
Law School Computer Group - Defunct.
Law Schools; Assn. of Amer. [8760]
Law Schools; Sect. on Gay and Lesbian Legal Is-sues, Assn. of Amer. [★8761]
Law of the Sea Inst. [6054], c/o Inst. of Legal Res., 381 Boalt Hall, Univ. of California, Berkeley, Berkeley, CA 94720-7200, (510)642-5125
Law; Sect. of Criminal [★5922]
Law Services [★8768]
Law Services [★IO]
Law and Social Policy; Center for [6220]
Law and Social Policy; Women's Rights Proj. of the Center for [★17565]
Law Societies; Assn. of Student Intl. [★5868]
Law Societies; Natl. Assn. of Environmental [5697]
Law Soc. [IO], London, United Kingdom
Law Soc; Amer. Psychology- [16133]
Law and Soc. Assn. [5946], 217 Draper Hall, Univ. of Massachusetts, 40 Campus Center Way, Am-herst, MA 01003-9244, (413)545-4617
Law and Soc. Assn. [IO], Amherst, MA, United States
Law Soc. of England [IO], London, United Kingdom
Law Soc. of England and Wales [IO], London, United Kingdom
Law Soc; Harvard Environmental [5695]
Law Soc. of Hong Kong [IO], Hong Kong, People's Republic of China
Law Soc. of Ireland [IO], Dublin, Ireland

Law Soc; Natural [10813]
Law Soc. of Northern Ireland [IO], Belfast, United Kingdom
Law Soc. of Scotland [IO], Edinburgh, United Kingdom
Law Soc. of Singapore [IO], Singapore, Singapore
Law Soc. of South Africa [IO], Pretoria, Republic of South Africa
Law and Soc. Trust [IO], Colombo, Sri Lanka
Law; St. [6035]
Law Student Assn; Amer. [★8769]
Law Student Div. [8769], c/o Amer. Bar Assn., 321 N Clark St., Chicago, IL 60610, (312)988-5623
Law Students Assn; Amer. Indian [★8772]
Law Students Assn; Black Amer. [★8771]
Law Students Assn; Natl. Black [8771]
Law Students Assn; Natl. Native Amer. [8772]
Law Students Assn; Native Amer. [★8772]
Law Students for Choice [18517], 111 Pine St., Ste. 1500, San Francisco, CA 94111, (650)281-3661
Law Students Civil Rights Res. Coun. - Address unknown since 1991.
Law Task Force; Military [6083]
Law, U.S. Chap; Intl. Assn. for Insurance [★5829]
Lawman History; Natl. Assn. for Outlaw and [9380]
Lawn Bowls Assn. of Alberta [IO], Edmonton, AB, Canada
Lawn Bowls Assn; Amer. [★23256]
Lawn Bowls Assn; Amer. Women's [★23256]
Lawn Bowls Assn; U.S. [23256]
Lawn and Garden Dealers Assn. [1720], 5616 S 122nd East Ave., Ste. N, Tulsa, OK 74146, (800)752-5296
Lawn and Garden Distributors Assn. [★2395]
Lawn and Garden Distributors Assn; Natl. [★2395]
Lawn and Garden Mfrs. Assn. - Defunct.
Lawn and Garden Marketing and Distribution Assn. [2395], 2105 Laurel Bush Rd., Ste. 200, Bel Air, MD 21015, (443)640-1080
Lawn Inst. [4794], 2 E Main St., East Dundee, IL 60118, (847)649-5555
Lawn Inst. [IO], East Dundee, IL, United States
Lawn Mower Inst. [★1294]
Lawn Mower Racing Assn; U.S. [23673]
Lawn Tennis Assn. [IO], London, United Kingdom
Lawn Tennis Assn. of Malawi [IO], Blantyre, Malawi
Lawn Tennis Assn. of Thailand [IO], Nonthaburi, Thailand
Lawn Tennis Assn; U.S. [★23915]
Lawn and Turf Institute/American Sod Producers Assn; Better [★4794]
Lawrence Durrell Soc; Intl. [9662]
Lawrence Technological Univ. Alumni Assn. [18904], 21000 W 10 Mile Rd., Southfield, MI 48075-1058, (248)204-2308
Laws; Citizens Coalition for Rational Traffic [★13340]
Laws; Comm. to Support the Antitrust [17626]
Laws; Coun. on Governmental Ethics [6270]
Laws; Joint Comm. of the States to Stud. Alcohol Beverage [★5445]
Laws; Natl. Conf. of Commissioners on Uniform State [6282]
Laws and Ordinances; Natl. Comm. on Uniform Traf-fic [6309]
Laws; Victims of Child Abuse [★13365]
Lawton Collector's Guild [22400], c/o The Lawton Doll Co., 1651 Lander Ave., Ste. 125, Turlock, CA 95380-6236, (209)632-3655
Lawyer Guild; Jewish [20149]
Lawyer Marketing Assn; Trial [★2651]
Lawyer-Pilots Assn. [★5539]
Lawyer-Pilots Bar Assn. [5539], PO Box 1510, Edgewater, MD 21037, (410)571-1750
Lawyers in Alcoholics Anonymous; Intl. [13253]
Lawyers Alliance for Nuclear Arms Control [★18158]
Lawyers Alliance for Nuclear Arms Control [★IO]
Lawyers Alliance for World Security [IO], Washington, DC, United States
Lawyers Alliance for World Security [18158], c/o Center for Defense Info., 1779 Massachusetts Ave. NW, Ste. 615, Washington, DC 20036-2109, (202)745-2450
Lawyers of Am; Assn. of Trial [★6328]
Lawyers; Amer. Acad. of Appellate [5472]

Lawyers; Amer. Acad. of Matrimonial [5698]
Lawyers; Amer. Coll. of Real Estate [5479]
Lawyers; Amer. Coll. of Trial [6330]
Lawyers for the Arts; Volunteer [6036]
Lawyers Assoc. Worldwide [5505], 15424 Holdridge Dr. E, Wayzata, MN 55391, (952)404-1546
Lawyers Assn; Amer. Blind [★5474]
Lawyers Assn; Amer. Hea. [5782]
Lawyers Assn; Amer. Immigration [5807]
Lawyers Assn; Amer. Trial [★6328]
Lawyers Assn; Black Entertainment [★5687]
Lawyers Assn; Black Entertainment and Sports [5687]
Lawyers Assn; First Amendment [5605]
Lawyers; Assn. of Immigration and Nationality [★5807]
Lawyers Assn; Intl. Trade Commn. Trial [★6332]
Lawyers Assn; ITC Trial [6332]
Lawyers Assn; La Raza Natl. [★5496]
Lawyers Assn; Motor Carrier [★6326]
Lawyers; Association of Muslim Amer. [★20097]
Lawyers Assn; Natl. Employment [5520]
Lawyers; Assn. of Professional Responsibility [5487]
Lawyers Assn; Scandinavian Amer. [5530]
Lawyers Assn; Sports [6266]
Lawyers Assn; Trans. [6326]
Lawyers Auxiliary; Amer. [5480]
Lawyers' Campaign to Free Nelson Mandela - Defunct.
Lawyers for Children Am. [6026], c/o Swidler Berlin Shereff Friedman LLP, 3000 K St. NW, Ste. 125, Washington, DC 20007, (202)339-8943
Lawyers Christian Fellowship, U.S.A. - Address unknown since 2001.
Lawyers for Civil Justice [17962], 1140 Connecticut Ave. NW, Ste. 503, Washington, DC 20036, (202)429-0045
Lawyers Comm. on Amer. Policy Towards Vietnam - Defunct.
Lawyers Comm. on Central America - Defunct.
Lawyers' Comm. for Civil Rights Under Law [6027], 1401 New York Ave. NW, Ste. 400, Washington, DC 20005, (202)662-8600
Lawyers Comm. for Human Rights [★17759]
Lawyers Comm. for Human Rights [★IO]
Lawyers Comm. for Intl. Human Rights [★IO]
Lawyers Comm. for Intl. Human Rights [★17759]
Lawyers' Comm. on Nuclear Policy [18159], 675 Third Ave., Ste. 315, New York, NY 10017, (212)818-1861
Lawyers Constitutional Defense Comm. - Defunct.
Lawyers in Criminal Cases; Natl. Assn. of Defense [★5656]
Lawyers; Decalogue Soc. of [5490]
Lawyers Div; Amer. Bar Assn. Young [5477]
Lawyers Found; Roscoe Pound-American Trial [★6335]
Lawyers; Guild of Catholic [19631]
Lawyers Guild; Natl. [5522]
Lawyers Guild; Natl. Immigration Proj. of the Natl. [5810]
Lawyers; Incorporated Soc. of Irish/American [5939]
Lawyers for an Independent Judiciary - Defunct.
Lawyers Marketing; Trial [2651]
Lawyers; Natl. Assn. of Bond [6255]
Lawyers; Natl. Assn. of Criminal Defense [5656]
Lawyers; Natl. Assn. of Women [5514]
Lawyers; National Conference of Black [★5519]
Lawyers; Natl. Counsel of Black [5519]
Lawyers for One Am. [6028], 4136 Redwood Hwy., Ste. 9, San Rafael, CA 94903, (415)479-3636
Lawyers and Physicians; Global [14558]
Lawyers Protecting People From Malicious and Unjustified Lawsuits - Defunct.
Lawyers for Public Justice; Trial [★6227]
Lawyers' Second Amendment Soc. - Address unknown since 2003.
Lawyers Training Institutes [★8765]
Lawyers Wines; Natl. [★5480]
Lawyers Without Borders [18008], 750 Main St., Hartford, CT 06103, (860)541-2288
Lawyers Without Borders [IO], Hartford, CT, United States
Lay Associates of the Sisters, Servants of the Im-maculate Heart of Mary [★20346]

Reference to "IO" in place of a book number signifies that the association may be found in the 45th edition of International Organizations.

Lay Carmelite Order of the Blessed Virgin Mary of Mount Carmel **[19647]**, 8501 Bailey Rd., Darien, IL 60561-8417, (630)969-5050

Lay Carmelites **[★19647]**

Lay Commn. on Catholic Social Teaching and the U.S. Economy - Defunct.

Lay Comm; Presbyterian **[20472]**

Lay Ministers and Acolytes; Intl. Guild of **[★19963]**

Lay Ministry Coordinators; Natl. Assn. of **[★20204]**

Lay Mission-Helpers Assn. **[19648]**, 3435 Wilshire Blvd., Ste. 1035, Los Angeles, CA 90010-1911, (213)368-1870

Lay Mission-Helpers Assn. **[IO]**, Los Angeles, CA, United States

Lay Missioners; Intl. Liaison U.S. Catholic Coordinating Center for **[★19602]**

The Layman Tithing Company **[★20595]**

Layman Tithing Company; The **[★20595]**

Layman Tithing Found. **[★20595]**

Laymen's Commn. of the Amer. Coun. of Christian Churches - Address unknown since 2003.

Laymen's Home Missionary Movement **[20018]**, 1156 St. Matthews Rd., Chester Springs, PA 19425-2700, (610)827-7665

Laymen's Home Missionary Movement **[IO]**, Chester Springs, PA, United States

Laymen's League; Lutheran **[★20218]**

Laymen's Movement for a Christian World **[★20588]**

Laymen's Natl. Bible Assn. **[★20205]**

Laymen's Natl. Bible Comm. **[★20205]**

Laymen's Services and Indus; Adventist- **[20553]**

L.C. Smith Collectors Assn. **[22429]**, c/o Frank Finch, Exec. Dir./Corresponding Sec., 1322 Bay Ave., Mantoloking, NJ 08738

LCI Natl. Assn; U.S.S. **[21328]**

LDS Bus. Coll. Alumni Assn. **[18905]**, 411 E South Temple, Salt Lake City, UT 84111, (801)524-8172

Le Centre Parlementaire **[★IO]**

Le Centre de Recherches pour le Developpement Intl. **[★IO]**

Le Club BMW du Canada **[★IO]**

Le Coll. canadien des enseignantes et des enseignants **[★IO]**

Le Coll. Royal Canadien des Organistes **[★IO]**

Le Coll. Royal des Medecins et Chirurgiens du Canada **[★IO]**

Le Comite international pour la documentation du Conseil international des musees **[★IO]**

Le Conseil canadiene des distributeurs de vehicules hors route **[★IO]**

Le Conseil Africain pour l'Enseignement de la Commun. **[★IO]**

Le Conseil des Arts du Canada **[★IO]**

Le Conseil Atlantique du Canada **[★IO]**

Le Conseil Canadien pour le Commerce Autochtone **[★IO]**

Le Conseil Canadien de la Readaptation et du Travail **[★IO]**

Le Conseil canadien de l'agrement des programmes de pharmacie **[★IO]**'

Le Conseil canadien pour l'avancement de l'education **[★IO]**

Le Front Des Artistes Canadiens **[★IO]**

Le Groupe Canadien de Recherche en Geomorphologie **[★IO]**

Le Havre World Trade Center **[IO]**, Le Havre, France

Le Paradis Des Orchidees **[IO]**, Laval, QC, Canada

Le Reseau Canadien pour la Sante des Femmes **[★IO]**

Le Syndicat canadien de la fonction publique **[★IO]**

LE TRIPTYQUE **[IO]**, Paris, France

Lea-Francis Owners' Club **[IO]**, Abingdon, United Kingdom

Lead
Alliance for Healthy Homes **[13320]**
Natl. Comm. to Reopen the Rosenberg Case **[17135]**

LEAD - Afrique Francophone **[IO]**, Dakar, Senegal

Lead Belly Soc. - Address unknown since 2007.

LEAD - Benin **[IO]**, Porto Novo, Benin

Lead Burning Assn; Natl. **[★2052]**

Lead Burning Assn; Natl. New England **[2052]**

LEAD - Canada **[IO]**, Chelsea, QC, Canada

LEAD - China **[IO]**, Beijing, People's Republic of China

LEAD - CIS **[IO]**, Moscow, Russia

Lead Contractors Assn. **[IO]**, East Grinstead, United Kingdom

Lead Development Assn. Intl. **[IO]**, London, United Kingdom

LEAD - Indonesia **[IO]**, Jakarta, Indonesia

Lead Industries Assn. - Defunct.

LEAD Intl.: Leadership for Env. and Development **[IO]**, London, United Kingdom

LEAD Intl. - United Kingdom **[IO]**, London, United Kingdom

LEAD - Mexico **[IO]**, Mexico City, Mexico

LEAD - Nigeria **[IO]**, Lagos, Nigeria

LEAD - Pakistan **[IO]**, Islamabad, Pakistan

Lead Poisoning; Alliance to End Childhood **[★13320]**

Lead Poisoning; Coalition to End Childhood **[4543]**

Lead Sheet Assn. **[IO]**, Tunbridge Wells, United Kingdom

Lead Smelters and Refiners Assn. **[IO]**, London, United Kingdom

LEAD - Southern Africa **[IO]**, Lusaka, Zambia

LEAD - Togo **[IO]**, Lome, Togo

Lead-Zinc Producers **[★2723]**

Lead-Zinc Producers Comm. **[★2723]**

Lead-Zinc Producers Comm; Emergency **[★2723]**

The Leader **[★2780]**

Leader Dog League for the Blind **[★16864]**

Leader Dog League for the Blind **[★IO]**

Leader Dogs for the Blind **[IO]**, Rochester, MI, United States

Leader Dogs for the Blind **[16864]**, 1039 S Rochester Rd., Rochester, MI 48307, (248)651-9011

Leaders of Am; Family, Career and Community **[8417]**

Leaders of Am. - Phi Beta Lambda; Future Bus. **[24420]**

Leaders; Natl. Assn. of Business **[3614]**

Leaders Online/Women Organizing For Change; Women **[18818]**

Leadership
Amer. Coun. of Young Political Leaders **[18000]**
Amer. Coun. of Young Political Leaders **[IO]**
Amer. Humanics **[8743]**
Amer. Leadership Forum **[18001]**
Amer. Student Govt. Assn. **[9175]**
Amer. Youth Found. **[20638]**
Asian Americans/Pacific Islanders in Philanthropy **[12710]**
Assn. of Leadership Educators **[8744]**
Assn. of Univ. Leaders for a Sustainable Future **[8483]**
Black Leadership Forum **[18867]**
Bridging Nations **[17861]**
Center for Excellence in Assn. Leadership **[316]**
Center for Intl. Initiatives **[8745]**
Center for Visionary Leadership **[18002]**
The Christophers **[19611]**
Community Leadership Assn. **[11795]**
Educational Leadership Inst. **[8746]**
Empower Prog. **[8945]**
Euro-American Women's Coun. **[17530]**
The Fund for Amer. Stud. **[IO]**
The Fund for Amer. Stud. **[8747]**
Global Action Proj. **[18849]**
Hugh O'Brian Youth Leadership **[8748]**
Independence Plan for Neighborhood Councils **[17219]**
Indicorps **[12406]**
Indify **[13488]**
Indus Women Leaders **[18003]**
INROADS **[8749]**
Junior Chamber Intl. **[13044]**
Junior State of Am. **[8750]**
Junior Statesmen Found. **[8751]**
Kauffman Center for Entrepreneurial Leadership **[739]**
Leadership Am. **[8752]**
Leadership Enterprise for a Diverse Am. **[9183]**
Leadership Inst. **[8753]**
Mid-American Greek Coun. Assn. **[24483]**
Natl. Assn. of the Knights of Scorpius, Honorary Leadership Soc. **[24511]**
Natl. Assn. of Latina Leaders **[2411]**
Natl. Assn. for Tech Prep Leadership **[9239]**
Natl. Community for Latino Leadership **[19203]**
Natl. Employment Counseling Assn. **[12091]**
Natl. Hispana Leadership Inst. **[17707]**
Natl. Hispanic Employee Assn. **[12279]**
Natl. Inst. for Leadership Development **[2412]**
Natl. Organizations for Youth Safety **[13502]**
Natl. Partnership for Community Leadership **[11805]**
Natl. Soc. of Leadership and Success **[9189]**
Natl. Young Adult Assn. **[13504]**
Natl. Youth Leadership Coun. **[8754]**
Native Amer. Leadership Alliance **[20455]**
Network 20/20 **[18004]**
New Leaders for New Schools **[8755]**
Portuguese Amer. Leadership Coun. of the U.S. **[19320]**
Presidential Classroom **[8756]**
Presidential Prayer Team **[20210]**
Proj. South: Inst. for the Elimination of Poverty and Genocide **[17872]**
Public Hea. Leadership Soc. **[16252]**
Public Leadership Educ. Network **[9326]**
Rising Leaders **[18005]**
Salvadoran Amer. Leadership and Educational Fund **[17484]**
Seeking Common Ground **[13514]**
Sigma Alpha Lambda **[24519]**
Soc. for Executive Leadership in Academic Medicine Intl. **[15179]**
South Asian Amer. Leaders of Tomorrow **[18667]**
Student African Amer. Brotherhood **[19444]**
SustainUS **[13517]**
Toastmasters Intl. **[10904]**
Women Leaders Online **[18817]**
Women of the World **[13448]**
Youth Advocate Prog. Intl. **[11668]**

Leadership Agenda; Natl. Hispanic **[17708]**

Leadership Am. **[8752]**, PO Box 191009, Dallas, TX 75219, (214)397-0900

Leadership; Center for Creative **[2488]**

Leadership Center; DeMolay Ser. and **[★19375]**

Leadership Center; DeMolay Ser. and **[★IO]**

Leadership Center; Entrepreneurial **[17627]**

Leadership; CLAL: Natl. Jewish Center for Learning and **[20132]**

Leadership Conf; Amer. Clergy **[19858]**

Leadership Conf. on Civil Rights **[17124]**, 1629 K St. NW, 10th Fl., Washington, DC 20006, (202)466-3311

Leadership Conf. Educ. Fund **[8094]**, 1629 K St. NW, No. 1010, Washington, DC 20006, (202)466-3311

Leadership Conf. of Women Religious **[19649]**, 8808 Cameron St., Silver Spring, MD 20910-4113, (301)588-4955

Leadership Conf. of Women Religious of the U.S.A. **[★19649]**

Leadership Coun. of Aging Organizations **[11293]**, c/o Scott Frey, 10 G St. NE, Ste. 600, Washington, DC 20002, (202)216-8380

Leadership Coun; Arab Amer. **[17003]**

Leadership Coun. on Child Abuse and Interpersonal Violence **[12031]**, 191 Presidential Blvd., Ste. C-132, Bala Cynwyd, PA 19004, (610)664-5007

Leadership Coun; Democratic **[17403]**

Leadership Coun; Executive **[2762]**

Leadership Coun. for Mental Hea., Justice and the Media **[★12031]**

Leadership Coun; Trade Union **[17158]**

Leadership Coun. of the U.S; Portuguese Amer. **[19320]**

Leadership Couns. of America - Defunct.

Leadership Development and Academic Admin; Center for **[★8745]**

Leadership Development Network **[17223]**, PO Box 70, Silver Point, TN 38582, (931)858-6399

Leadership Educ. for Asian Pacifics **[9621]**, 327 E 2nd St., Ste. 226, Los Angeles, CA 90012, (213)485-1422

Leadership in Educ; Assn. for Gender Equity **[8399]**

Leadership Education and Development U.S.A. - Address unknown since 1999.

Leadership Educ. Network; Public **[9326]**

Leadership Enterprise for a Diverse Am. **[9183]**, 39 Hamilton Terr., New York, NY 10031, (212)234-1384

A star before a book entry number signifies that the name is not listed separately, but is mentioned within the entry.

Leadership Forum; Amer. [18001]
Leadership Found; African Wildlife [★5289]
Leadership in Hea. Care; Soc. for Social Work [13209]
Leadership Initiative on Cancer; Natl. Black [13847]
Leadership Inst. [8753], 1101 N Highland St., Arlington, VA 22201, (703)247-2000
Leadership; Inst. for Educational [8264]
Leadership Inst; Natl. Hispana [17707]
Leadership to Keep Children Alcohol Free [11334], c/o The CDM Gp., Inc., 7500 Old Georgetown Rd., Ste. 900, Bethesda, MD 20814, (301)654-6740
Leadership Ministries Commn; Natl. Coun. of Churches, Educ. and [19935]
Leadership; Natl. Assn. for Community [★11795]
Leadership; Natl. Assn. for Rehabilitation [16325]
Leadership; Natl. Conf. on Student [9188]
Leadership Network for Intl. Educ. [★8659]
Leadership Network for Intl. Educ. [★IO]
Leadership Network, Natl. Student Educ. Fund; Women's [★9195]
Leadership Network; Student [9193]
Leadership Organizations; Natl. Assn. of Community [★11795]
Leadership Prog; Educational [8779]
Leadership Project - Defunct.
Leadership; Project Volunteer Info., Tech. Assistance, and [★13580]
Leadership Soc; Natl. Assn. of the Knights of Scorpius, Honorary [24511]
Leadership Training
   Amer. Student Govt. Assn. [9175]
   Amer. Youth Found. [20638]
   Center for Visionary Leadership [18002]
   The Christophers [19611]
   Community Leadership Assn. [11795]
   Global Action Proj. [18849]
   Jackie Robinson Found. [13491]
   Junior Chamber Intl. [13044]
   Kauffman Center for Entrepreneurial Leadership [739]
   Leadership Enterprise for a Diverse Am. [9183]
   Mid-American Greek Coun. Assn. [24483]
   Natl. Community for Latino Leadership [19203]
   Natl. Employment Counseling Assn. [12091]
   Natl. Soc. of Leadership and Success [9189]
   Natl. Young Adult Assn. [13504]
   Network 20/20 [18004]
   New Leaders for New Schools [8755]
   Paraclete [20381]
   Rising Leaders [18005]
   State Educational Tech. Directors Assn. [9244]
   Toastmasters Intl. [10904]
   Women's Learning Partnership for Rights, Development, and Peace [13452]
   World Youth Alliance [18860]
   Youth Advocate Prog. Intl. [11668]
Leadership and World Soc. - Defunct.
Leadership Youth Found; Conservative [★8753]
Leading Edge Alliance [39], 621 Cedar St., St. Charles, IL 60174, (630)513-9814
Leading Jewelers of the World [2377], 500 7th Ave., 12th Fl., New York, NY 10018, (212)768-2744
Leading Jewelers of the World [IO], New York, NY, United States
Leading Spas of Canada [IO], Sooke, BC, Canada
Leaf Tobacco Dealers and Exporters; Assn. of Dark [3817]
Leaf Tobacco Exporters Assn. - Defunct.
Leafy Greens Coun. [4738], c/o Ray L. Clark, Exec. Dir., 33 Pheasant Ln., St. Paul, MN 55127, (651)484-3321
League for the Advancement of States' Equal Rights - Address unknown since 1995.
League of Advertising Agencies - Address unknown since 2007.
League Against Cruel Sports [IO], London, United Kingdom
League Against Epilepsy of Republic Macedonia [IO], Skopje, Macedonia
League Against Nuclear Dangers - Defunct.
League of Amer. Bicyclists [23312], 1612 K St. NW, Ste. 800, Washington, DC 20006-2850, (202)822-1333
League of Amer. Theatres and Producers [11020], 226 W 47th St., New York, NY 10036, (212)764-1122

League of Amer. Wheelmen [★23312]
League of Amer. Wheelmen/Bicycle U.S.A. [★23312]
League of Amers. of Ukrainian Descent - Address unknown since 1990.
League of Canadian Poets [IO], Toronto, ON, Canada
League of Composers - Intl. Soc. for Contemporary Music, U.S. Sect. [★IO]
League of Composers - Intl. Soc. for Contemporary Music, U.S. Sect. [★10626]
League of Conservation Voters [18312], 1920 L St. NW, Ste. 800, Washington, DC 20036, (202)785-8683
League of Distilled Spirits Rectifiers - Defunct.
League for Ecological Democracy - Defunct.
League of Elderly Gentlemen in Reduced Circumstances - Defunct.
League for Equitable General Aviation Legislation - Address unknown since 1995.
League of European Res. Universities [IO], Leuven, Belgium
League of Evangelical-Catholic Reunion - Defunct.
League for the Exchange of Commonwealth Teachers [IO], London, United Kingdom
League of Federal Recreation Assns. - Defunct.
League of Finnish-American Societies [IO], Helsinki, Finland
League Football; Pop Warner Junior [★23436]
League of Free Nations Assn. [★17610]
League of Free Nations Assn. [★IO]
League of Friendship - Defunct.
League for the Hard of Hearing [14765], 50 Broadway, 6th Fl., New York, NY 10004, (917)305-7700
League of Historic Amer. Theatres [11021], 334 N Charles St., 2nd Fl., Baltimore, MD 21201, (410)659-9533
League of Homeowners' Associations - Habitat [IO], Bucharest, Romania
League for Human Rights and Freedoms [★IO]
League of IBM Employees Credit Unions [★1111]
League of Independent Ferret Enthusiasts - Address unknown since 1999.
League for Industrial Democracy - Address unknown since 2004.
League for Innovation in the Community Coll. [8120], 4505 E Chandler Blvd., Ste. 250, Phoenix, AZ 85048, (480)705-8200
League for Intl. Food Education - Defunct.
League/ISCM [★10626]
League/ISCM [★IO]
League of Jewish Women [IO], London, United Kingdom
League of Lefthanders - Defunct.
League for Liberty - Defunct.
League for Mutual Aid - Defunct.
League for Natl. Defense - Address unknown since 2007.
League for Natl. Labor in Israel - Address unknown since 1995.
League of New York Theatres [★11020]
League of New York Theatres and Producers [★11020]
League of Night Adoration in the Home [★19695]
League of Off-Broadway Theatres and Producers - Address unknown since 2002.
League of Pace Amendment Advocates - Address unknown since 1995.
League of Prayer for Unity - Defunct.
League of Private Property Owners [★6187]
League of Private Property Voters [17985], PO Box 423, Battle Ground, WA 98604, (360)687-2471
League of Professional Sys. Administrators [6815], 15000 Commerce Pkwy., Ste. C, Mount Laurel, NJ 08054, (856)439-0500
League of Professional Sys. Administrators [IO], Mount Laurel, NJ, United States
League of Professional Theatre Training Programs - Defunct.
League for Programming Freedom [7536], PO Box 9171, 1 Kendall Sq., No. 143, Cambridge, MA 02139, (617)243-4091
League for Religious Labor in Eretz Israel - Address unknown since 1995.

League of Religious Settlements - Address unknown since 1995.
League of Resident Theatres [11022], c/o Adam Knight, Mgt. Assoc., 1501 Broadway, Ste. 2401, New York, NY 10036, (212)944-1501
League of Revolutionaries for a New Am. [18299], PO Box 477113, Chicago, IL 60647, (773)486-0028
League for the Revolutionary Party [18655], PO Box 1936, Murray Hill Sta., New York, NY 10156, (212)330-9017
League for the Rights of Man; Intl. [★17769]
League of Rural Voters Educ. Proj. [★16955]
League for Safeguarding the Fixity of the Sabbath Against Possible Encroachment by Calendar Reform - Address unknown since 1995.
League of St. Dymphna [19650], Natl. Shrine of St. Dymphna, 3000 Erie St. S, PO Box 4, Massillon, OH 44648-0004, (330)833-8478
League of Saint Gerard - Defunct.
League to Save Lake Tahoe [4417], 955 Emerald Bay Rd., South Lake Tahoe, CA 96150, (530)541-5388
League of Shut-In Sodalists - Address unknown since 1995.
League of the South [17125], PO Box 760, Killen, AL 35645, (256)757-6789
League of Tarcisians [19651], c/o Natl. Enthronement Center, PO Box 111, Fairhaven, MA 02719-0111, (508)999-2680
League of Tarcisians of the Sacred Heart [★19651]
League of Ukrainian Catholics of Am. [19411], c/o Dr. Michael Labuda, Membership Dir., 14 Prince St., Plains, PA 18705-1211
League of Ukranian Canadian Women [IO], Toronto, ON, Canada
League of United Latin Amer. Citizens [19099], 2000 L St. NW, Ste. 610, Washington, DC 20036, (202)833-6130
League to Uphold Congregational Principles - Defunct.
League of Winant Volunteers [★13409]
League of Winant Volunteers [★IO]
League of Women Voters Educ. Fund [18459], 1730 M St. NW, Ste. 1000, Washington, DC 20036-4508, (202)429-1965
League of Women Voters of the U.S. [18355], 1730 M St. NW, Ste. 1000, Washington, DC 20036-4508, (202)429-1965
League of World War I Aviation Historians [21459], 16820 25th Ave. N, Plymouth, MN 55447
League of World War I Aviation Historians [IO], Plymouth, MN, United States
League for Yiddish, Inc. [20157], 45 E 33rd St., No. 203, New York, NY 10016, (212)889-0380
League of Young Voters [18356], 45 Main St., Ste. 628, Brooklyn, NY 11201, (718)305-4245
League of Zarvona - Defunct.
Leak Detection Technology Assn. - Defunct.
Lean Line - Address unknown since 2003.
Leann Hunley Fan Club - Defunct.
LEANON - Lupus Erythematosus Anonymous - Defunct.
Leap South Africa [IO], Cardiff, United Kingdom (LEAPA); Legion Amateur Publishing Alliance [★22042]
Leapfrog Gp. [14643], c/o Acad. Hea., 1801 K St. NW, Ste. 701-L, Washington, DC 20006, (202)292-6713
Learned Societies; Amer. Coun. of [10197]
Learning About Aging; Natl. Acad. for Teaching and [11297]
Learning and Activism; Amer. Muslims Intent on [10728]
Learning; Assn. for Bus. Simulation and Experiential [8015]
Learning Assn; Coll. Reading and [9042]
Learning Assn; Equine Assisted Growth and [16216]
Learning Assn; Family [8419]
Learning Assn; U.S. Distance [8523]
Learning Assn; Western Coll. Reading and [★9042]
Learning; Center for Adaptive [★7104]
Learning; Coun. for Adult and Experiential [8412]
Learning; Delphi Intl. Prog. of World [17881]
Learning and Development Kenya [IO], Nakuru, Kenya

Reference to "IO" in place of a book number signifies that the association may be found in the 45th edition of International Organizations.

Learning Disabilities Assn. of Alberta [IO], Edmonton, AB, Canada

Learning Disabilities Assn. of Alberta - Calgary Chap. [IO], Calgary, AB, Canada

Learning Disabilities Assn. of Alberta - Edmonton Chap. [IO], Edmonton, AB, Canada

Learning Disabilities Assn. of Alberta - Red Deer Chap. [IO], Red Deer, AB, Canada

Learning Disabilities Assn. of Am. [12492], 4156 Lib. Rd., Pittsburgh, PA 15234-1349, (412)341-1515

Learning Disabilities Assn. of Canada [IO], Ottawa, ON, Canada

Learning Disabilities; Assn. for Children with [★12492]

Learning Disabilities; Assn. for Children and Adults with [★12492]

Learning Disabilities Assn. of Halton [IO], Burlington, ON, Canada

Learning Disabilities Assn. of Kingston [IO], Kingston, ON, Canada

Learning Disabilities Assn. of Kitchener - Waterloo [IO], Kitchener, ON, Canada

Learning Disabilities Assn. of Lambton County [IO], Sarnia, ON, Canada

Learning Disabilities Assn. - London Region [IO], London, ON, Canada

Learning Disabilities Assn. of Manitoba [IO], Winnipeg, MB, Canada

Learning Disabilities Assn. - Mississauga Chap. [IO], Mississauga, ON, Canada

Learning Disabilities Assn. of New Brunswick [IO], Fredericton, NB, Canada

Learning Disabilities Assn. of Newfoundland and Labrador [IO], St. John's, NL, Canada

Learning Disabilities Assn. - North Peel Chap. [IO], Brampton, ON, Canada

Learning Disabilities Assn. of Nova Scotia [IO], Dartmouth, NS, Canada

Learning Disabilities Assn. of the NWT [IO], Yellowknife, NT, Canada

Learning Disabilities Assn. of Ontario [IO], Toronto, ON, Canada

Learning Disabilities Assn. of Ontario - Durham Region [IO], Pickering, ON, Canada

Learning Disabilities Assn. of Ontario - Niagara Chap. [IO], St. Catharines, ON, Canada

Learning Disabilities Assn. of Ontario - Thunder Bay Chap. [IO], Thunder Bay, ON, Canada

Learning Disabilities Assn. of Ottawa - Carleton [IO], Ottawa, ON, Canada

Learning Disabilities Assn. of PEI [IO], Charlottetown, PE, Canada

Learning Disabilities Assn. of Peterborough [IO], Peterborough, ON, Canada

Learning Disabilities Assn. of Quebec [IO], Montreal, QC, Canada

Learning Disabilities Assn. of Quebec - Laval Sect. [IO], Laval, QC, Canada

Learning Disabilities Assn. of Saskatchewan [IO], Saskatoon, SK, Canada

Learning Disabilities Assn. of Saskatchewan - Prince Albert Br. [IO], Prince Albert, SK, Canada

Learning Disabilities Assn. of Saskatchewan - Regina Br. [IO], Regina, SK, Canada

Learning Disabilities Assn. of Sault Ste. Marie [IO], Sault Ste. Marie, ON, Canada

Learning Disabilities Assn. of Simcoe County [IO], Barrie, ON, Canada

Learning Disabilities Assn. - South Vancouver Island Chap. [IO], Victoria, BC, Canada

Learning Disabilities Assn. of Sudbury [IO], Sudbury, ON, Canada

Learning Disabilities Assn. of Toronto District [IO], Toronto, ON, Canada

Learning Disabilities Assn. of Vancouver [IO], Vancouver, BC, Canada

Learning Disabilities Assn. of Wellington County [IO], Guelph, ON, Canada

Learning Disabilities Assn. of York Region [IO], Richmond Hill, ON, Canada

Learning Disabilities Assn. of Yukon Territory [IO], Whitehorse, YT, Canada

Learning Disabilities; Div. for Children with [★12490]

Learning Disabilities; Found. for Children with [★12494]

Learning Disabilities Special Interest Group - Address unknown since 2003.

Learning Disabled

Academic Language Therapy Assn. [12488]

Acad. of Learning and Developmental Disorders [12489]

Ackerman Inst. for the Family [12134]

Assn. for Children with Down Syndrome [12562]

Attention Deficit Info. Network [15308]

Autism Network Intl. [13719]

Autism Services Center [13722]

Autism Soc. of Am. [13723]

Autism Speaks [13724]

AVKO Dyslexia Res. Found. [9138]

Children and Adults With Attention Deficit/ Hyperactivity Disorder [15314]

Coun. for Learning Disabilities [12490]

Education-A-Must [12056]

First Signs [13942]

Foster Grandparent Prog. [11693]

Friends of LADDERS [12491]

Global Autism Proj. [13725]

Intl. Dyslexia Assn. [14295]

Learning Disabilities Assn. of Am. [12492]

Natl. Alliance for Autism Res. [13726]

Natl. Assn. for the Educ. of African Amer. Children with Learning Disabilities [12493]

Natl. Assn. of Therapeutic Schools and Programs [13738]

Natl. Attention Deficit Disorder Assn. [15343]

Natl. Autism Assn. [13727]

Natl. Center for Learning Disabilities [12494]

Natl. Fed. of Arch Clubs [IO]

Natl. Networker [12495]

Neurofibromatosis [14471]

Nonverbal Learning Disorders Assn. [14998]

Nonverbal Learning Disorders Assn. [IO]

RESCARE [IO]

Schwab Learning - A Prog. of the Charles Schwab Found. [12496]

Social Workers in the Field of Learning Disability [IO]

South African Assn. for Learning and Educational Difficulties [IO]

STRIDE: Sports and Therapeutic Recreation Instruction/Developmental Educ. [8205]

Williams Syndrome Assn. [14490]

Young Adult Institute/National Inst. for People with Disabilities [12584]

Learning Disabled Adults; Natl. Network of [★12495]

Learning Environments; Center for Improved [★9085]

The Learning Exchange - Defunct.

Learning First Alliance [8273], 4455 Connecticut Ave., Ste. 310, Washington, DC 20008, (202)296-5220

Learning How [★11978]

Learning Inst; OMNI [8299]

Learning and Instruction Consortium; Cmpt. Assisted Language, [★8553]

Learning; Intl. Nursing Assn. for Clinical Simulation and [15485]

Learning and Leadership; CLAL: Natl. Jewish Center for [20132]

Learning Light Found. [10177], 1212 E Lincoln Ave., Anaheim, CA 92805-4249, (714)533-2311

Learning; Natl. Inst. for Work and [17974]

Learning is Necessary to Care [★12562]

Learning Needs; Natl. Assn. for Adults with Special [8204]

Learning Resources Inst. - Defunct.

Learning Resources Network [8151], PO Box 9, River Falls, WI 54022, (715)426-9777

Learning; Soc. for Organizational [2868]

Learning and Teaching Scotland [IO], Glasgow, United Kingdom

Learning Technologies; Inst. for [8355]

Learning and Tech. Gp; Teaching, [6898]

Learning Tech; Soc. for Applied [8571]

LearnWell Resources [13142], PO Box 944, Camino, CA 95709, (530)644-2123

Lease; Amtra [3378]

Leased Housing Assn; Natl. [12329]

Leased Housing Assn; Sect. 23 [★12329]

Leasing

Natl. Retail Tenants Assn. [3383]

Leasing Assn. of Am; Equip. [★3381]

Leasing Assn; Amer. Automotive [3375]

Leasing Assn; Automotive Fleet and [406]

Leasing Assn; California Vehicle [★3385]

Leasing Assn; Equip. [★3381]

Leasing Assn; Natl. Staff [★1273]

Leasing Assn; Natl. Vehicle [3385]

Leasing Assn; Truck Renting and [3387]

Leasing Assn; Western Vehicle [★3385]

Leasing Brokers; Natl. Assn. of Equip. [3382]

Leasing Coun. of Am; Driver [★3867]

Leasing and Finance; Assn. for Governmental [6202]

Leasing Sys; Natl. Truck [3384]

Leather

All India Skin and Hide Tanners' and Merchants' Assn. [IO]

Amer. Leather Chemists Assn. [6667]

Assn. of the German Leather Indus. [IO]

Assn. of Leather Exporters [IO]

Australian Plaiters and Whipmakers Assn. [IO]

BLC Leather Tech. Centre [IO]

British Travelgoods and Accessories Assn. [IO]

Confed. of Natl. Associations of Tanners and Dressers of the European Community [IO]

Fed. Assn. of Leather Goods, Toys and Fitness Equip. [IO]

Intl. Coun. of Hides, Skins and Leather Traders Associations [IO]

Intl. Coun. of Tanners [IO]

Intl. Fed. of Leather Guilds [2413]

Intl. Internet Leather Crafters' Guild [2414]

Intl. Internet Leather Crafters' Guild [IO]

Italian Assn. of Leather and Leather Substitute Mfrs. [IO]

Leather Apparel Assn. [2415]

Leather Garment Mfrs'. Assn. [IO]

Leather Indus. of Am. [2416]

Leather Indus. Assn. [IO]

Leathercraft Guild [2417]

Natl. Leather Coun. [IO]

Natl. Luggage Dealers Assn. [2418]

Natl. Union of the Leather Indus. [IO]

New Zealand Leather and Shoe Res. Assn. [IO]

Portuguese Leather Indus. Assn. [IO]

Saddle, Harness and Allied Trades Assn. [2419]

Skinners' Company [IO]

Soc. of Leather Technologists and Chemists [IO]

Sponge and Chamois Inst. [2420]

Tanners' Coun. of Japan [IO]

Travel Goods Assn. [2441]

U.S. Hide, Skin and Leather Assn. [2421]

Leather Apparel Assn. [2415], 19 W 21st St., Ste. 403, New York, NY 10010, (212)727-1210

Leather Assn. - Intl; Natl. [13098]

Leather Assn; Natl. [★13098]

Leather Assn; Natl. Indus. [★2051]

Leather Belting Assn; Amer. [★2051]

Leather Chemists Assn; Amer. [6667]

Leather Garment Mfrs'. Assn. [IO], Istanbul, Turkey

Leather Guilds; Fed. of [★2413]

Leather Guilds; Intl. Fed. of [2413]

Leather Indus. of Am. [2416], 3050 K St. NW, Ste. 400, Washington, DC 20007, (202)342-8497

Leather Indus. Assn. [IO], Vienna, Austria

Leather Mfrs. Assn; Patent and Enamelled [★2416]

Leather Merchants; Amer. Assn. of Hide, Skin and [★2421]

Leather Processing Assn; Textiles, Clothing and [IO]

Leather and Shoe Finders Assn; Natl. [★1600]

Leather Workers Intl. Union [★23995]

Leathercraft Guild [2417], c/o Robert Ambriz, 1434 S Pine Ave., Ontario, CA 91762, (909)983-9544

Leatherhead Food Intl. [IO], Leatherhead, United Kingdom

Leathermasters Intl. - Address unknown since 2006.

Leatherneck Assn. [★6079]

Leavers Lace Mfrs. of America - Defunct.

Lebanese

Amer. Lebanese Engg. Soc. [6989]

Amer. Task Force for Lebanon [19204]

Beirut Veterans of Am. [21287]

Kahlil Gibran Memorial Found. [11132]

Lebanese Amer. Professional Soc. [19205]

United Hasroun Men's and St. Laba Ladies Charity Societies [19732]

A star before a book entry number signifies that the name is not listed separately, but is mentioned within the entry.

United Kesrawan Soc. [19206]
United North Lebanon Soc. [18954]
U.S. Comm. for a Free Lebanon [18006]
Lebanese Aikido Fed. [IO], Beirut, Lebanon
Lebanese Amer. Organizations; Coun. of [9396]
Lebanese Amer. Professional Soc. [19205], 4000
Gypsy Ln., Unit 732, Philadelphia, PA 19129,
(215)848-6825
Lebanese-Amer. Soc. of Greater New York -
Defunct.
Lebanese Assn. of Public Accountants [IO], Beirut,
Lebanon
Lebanese Coun. of Disabled People [IO], Beirut,
Lebanon
Lebanese Coun. to Resist Violence Against Women
[IO], Beirut, Lebanon
Lebanese Dermatological Soc. [IO], Beirut, Lebanon
Lebanese Engg. Soc; Amer. [6989]
Lebanese Hypertension League [IO], Beirut,
Lebanon
Lebanese Info. Center [IO], Alexandria, VA, United
States
Lebanese Info. Center [18061], 4900 Leesburg Pike,
Ste. 203, Alexandria, VA 22302, (703)578-4214
Lebanese League Against Epilepsy [IO], Beirut,
Lebanon
Lebanese Medical Association [★15154]
Lebanese Medical Assn; Amer. [15154]
Lebanese Olympic Comm. [IO], Beirut, Lebanon
Lebanese Orthodontic Soc. [IO], Beirut, Lebanon
Lebanese Osteoporosis Prevention Soc. [IO], Beirut,
Lebanon
Lebanese Ostomy Assn. [IO], Keserwan, Lebanon
Lebanese Paralympics Comm. [IO], Beirut, Lebanon
Lebanese Red Cross [IO], Beirut, Lebanon
Lebanese Soc. of Gastroenterology [IO], Beirut,
Lebanon
Lebanese Soc. for Infectious Diseases [IO], Beirut,
Lebanon
Lebanese Soc. for the Stud. of Pain [IO], Beirut,
Lebanon
Lebanese Squash Fed. [IO], Beirut, Lebanon
Lebanon Family Planning Assn. [IO], Beirut,
Lebanon
Lebanon of North Am; Tall Cedars of [19255]
Lebanon Soc; United North [18954]
Lectura; Asociacion Internacional de [★9043]
Lecturers Assn; Travelogues by IMPALA Intl. Motion
Picture and [★1386]
Lederer Found. [★20019]
Lederer Messianic Ministries [20019], c/o Messianic
Jewish Communications, 6120 Day Long Ln.,
Clarksville, MD 21029, (410)531-6644
Ledernes Hovedeorganisation [IO], Copenhagen,
Denmark
LeDoux Intl. Fan Club; Chris [24861]
Lee Fan Club; Cecilia [★24856]
Lee Fan Club/Michele Lee Online; Michele [24761]
Lee Intl. Fan Club; Cecilia [24856]
Lee Moore Fan Club - Defunct.
Lee Music Found; Tom [IO]
Lee Roy Parnell Fan Network - Address unknown
since 2006.
Leeds Chamber of Commerce [IO], Leeds, United
Kingdom
Leeds Philosophical and Literary Soc. [IO], Leeds,
United Kingdom
The Leek Growers Assn. [IO], Louth, United
Kingdom
Lee's Familee [24937], PO Box 287, Ironton, OH
45638
Leff Jewish Women's Rsrc. Center; Eleanor [10280]
Left Green Network - Address unknown since 1995.
Left-Handed Golfers; Natl. Assn. of [23458]
Left-Handers
Natl. Assn. of Left-Handed Golfers [23458]
Left-Handers Against the World - Defunct.
Lefthanders Intl. [19379]
A Leg To Stand On [12659], 267 Fifth Ave., Ste.
301, New York, NY 10016, (212)683-8805
Lega Italiana contro l'Epilessia [★IO]
Lega Italiana per la Lotta contro la Malattia di Par-
kinson, le Sindromi Extrapiramidali e le Demenze
[★IO]
Lega Italiana Osteoporosi [IO], Milan, Italy

LEGACY - Defunct.
Legacy Found; Amer. [18743]
Legacy Intl. [8665], 1020 Legacy Dr., Bedford, VA
24523, (540)297-5982
Legacy Intl. [IO], Bedford, VA, United States
Legal
Acad. of Criminal Justice Sciences [11850]
African Amer. Criminal Justice Soc. [17359]
Alston Wilkes Veterans Home [11852]
Amer. Alliance of Paralegals, Inc. [6149]
Amer. Assn. for Correctional and Forensic
Psychology [11853]
Amer. Assn. of Law Libraries [10316]
Amer. Assn. of Legal Nurse Consultants [14999]
Amer. Assn. of Nurse Attorneys [15000]
Amer. Bar Assn. Center on Children and the Law
[11555]
Amer. Catholic Lawyers Assn. [5558]
Amer. Coll. of Legal Medicine [15001]
Amer. Conservative Union [17261]
Amer. Correctional Assn. [11854]
Amer. Criminal Justice Assn. (Lambda Alpha
Epsilon) [11855]
Amer. Guild of Court Videographers [6019]
Amer. Jail Assn. [11856]
Amer. Pro Se Assn. [6021]
Amer. Psychology-Law Soc. [16133]
Amer. Soc. of Law, Medicine and Ethics [15002]
Amer. Soc. for Legal History [10090]
Amer. Soc. for Pharmacy Law [15003]
Amer. Veterinary Medical Law Assn. [5927]
Animal Legal Defense Fund [11351]
Asian Amer. Legal Defense and Educ. Fund
[17095]
Assn. of Certified Anti-Money Laundering Special-
ists [463]
Assn. for Continuing Legal Educ. [8762]
Assn. of Forensic DNA Analysts and Administra-
tors [5756]
Assn. of Forensic Quality Assurance Managers
[5758]
Assn. for Honest Attorneys [5486]
Assn. of Inspectors Gen. [5777]
Assn. for Political and Legal Anthropology [6411]
Assn. on Programs for Female Offenders [11857]
Assn. of State Correctional Administrators [11858]
Center for Philosophy, Law, Citizenship [18271]
Center for Stud. in Criminal Justice [11859]
Center for Stud. of Responsive Law [17315]
Children's Healthcare Is a Legal Duty [15004]
Chinese Law Soc. of Am. [5933]
Citizens Equal Rights Alliance [5800]
Clarity [6011]
Clinical Legal Educ. Assn. [8763]
Correctional Educ. Assn. [11862]
Croatian Amer. Bar Assn. [5489]
Custom Legal Plans, LLC [6022]
Equal Justice Soc. [6258]
Fair Elections Legal Network [5491]
Fed. Circuit Bar Assn. [5493]
Forensic Expert Witness Assn. [5760]
Fortune Soc. [11867]
Free Enterprise Legal Defense Fund [17630]
Friends Outside [11868]
Global Alliance for Justice Educ. [8766]
Global Rights [17758]
HALT - An Org. of Americans for Legal Reform
[17961]
Harvard Environmental Law Soc. [5695]
Human Rights First [17759]
Indian Law Rsrc. Center [18094]
Inst. for the Development of Indian Law [18095]
Intl. Alliance of Holistic Lawyers [5498]
Intl. Assn. of Cmpt. Investigative Specialists
[8133]
Intl. Assn. of Correctional Officers [11870]
Intl. Assn. of Correctional Training Personnel
[11871]
Intl. Assn. of Law Schools [8767]
Intl. Assn. of Lemon Law Administrators [5536]
Intl. Community Corrections Assn. [11872]
Intl. Legal Defense Counsel [5869]
Intl. Network of Boutique Law Firms [5501]
Intl. Senior Lawyers Proj. [5502]
Intl. Soc. for Law and Tech. [5945]

Intl. Soc. of Primerus Law Firms [5503]
Intl. Utilities Revenue Protection Assn. [6338]
Iranian Amer. Bar Assn. [5504]
John Howard Assn. [11874]
Judge David L. Bazelon Center for Mental Hea.
Law [17123]
Justice Res. and Statistics Assn. [11876]
Law Enforcement and Emergency Services Video
Assn. [6350]
Lawyers Assoc. Worldwide [5505]
Lawyers' Comm. for Civil Rights Under Law
[6027]
Lawyers for One Am. [6028]
Legal Counsel for the Elderly [12497]
Legal Immigrant Assn. [5808]
Legal Sers. for the Elderly [12499]
Lithuanian-American Bar Assn. [5507]
A Matter of Justice Coalition [6012]
Media Access Proj. [17182]
Mexican Amer. Legal Defense and Educational
Fund [17705]
Minority Corporate Counsel Assn. [5615]
NALS [6013]
Natl. Alliance for Family Court Justice [5904]
Natl. Alliance of Senior Citizens [11299]
Natl. Assn. of Area Agencies on Aging [11301]
Natl. Assn. of Coll. and Univ. Attorneys [5677]
Natl. Assn. of Consumer Bankruptcy Attorneys
[5510]
Natl. Assn. of Counsel for Children [11711]
Natl. Assn. of Litigation Support Managers [6014]
Natl. Assn. of Muslim Lawyers [5511]
Natl. Assn. of State Units on Aging [11305]
Natl. Center on Institutions and Alternatives
[11878]
Natl. Center for Juvenile Justice [11879]
Natl. Client Protection Org. [5949]
Natl. Coalition of Concerned Legal Professionals
[12501]
Natl. Cong. of Amer. Indians [18096]
Natl. Correctional Indus. Assn. [11880]
Natl. Criminal Justice Assn. [11881]
Natl. Economic Development and Law Center
[17464]
Natl. Justice Found. of Am. [17298]
Natl. Juvenile Detention Assn. [11882]
Natl. Lawyers Assn. [5521]
Natl. Legal Center for the Public Interest [6224]
Natl. Legal Sanctuary for Community Advance-
ment [6015]
Natl. Legal Video Assn. [6016]
Natl. Org. of Legal Services Workers, UAW Local
2320 [24079]
Natl. Prison Proj. of the ACLU [11883]
Natl. Senior Citizens Law Center [11316]
Natl. South Asian Bar Assn. [6018]
Native Amer. Rights Fund [18098]
Network of Trial Law Firms [5525]
Nigerian Lawyers Assn. [5526]
NLRB Professional Assn. [24081]
North Amer. Assn. of Wardens and
Superintendents [11884]
North Amer. South Asian Bar Assn. [5527]
North Amer. South Asian Law Student Assn.
[8773]
Osborne Assn. [11885]
People Before Lawyers [5528]
Phi Delta Phi Intl. Legal Fraternity [24530]
Prison Fellowship Intl. [11887]
Prison Fellowship Ministries [11888]
Prison Ministry of Yokefellow's Intl. [11889]
Prisoners' Rights Union [11890]
Professional Mediation Assn. [5462]
Puerto Rican Legal Defense and Educ. Fund
[17149]
Renaissance Lawyer Soc. [5529]
Safer Soc. Found. [11891]
Sikh Amer. Legal Defense and Educ. Fund
[18600]
Soc. for Healthcare Consumer Advocacy of the
Amer. Hosp. Assn. [15005]
Soc. of Medical Jurisprudence [15006]
Sport and Recreation Law Assn. [23870]
Swedish-American Bar Assn. [5532]
Taiwanese Amer. Lawyers Assn. [5533]

Reference to "IO" in place of a book number signifies that the association may be found in the 45th edition of International Organizations.

United Black Republican Coalition [18538]
U.S. Law Firm Gp. [5534]
Victims' Assistance Legal Org. [5639]
Volunteers in Prevention, Probation, Prisons [11896]
We Care Prog. [11897]
Women's Prison Assn. [11898]
World Soc. of Mixed Jurisdiction Jurists [5957]
Legal Action Prog; Migrant [12500]
Legal Action for Women [16912], PO Box 11061, Pensacola, FL 32524, (334)962-3554
Legal Administrators; Assn. of [5929]
Legal Advice for Women [IO], Oslo, Norway
Legal Advocacy Fund; AAUW [5573]
Legal Advocates for Women - Address unknown since 1995.

Legal Aid
Amer. Pro Se Assn. [6021]
Assn. for Honest Attorneys [5486]
Assn. of Legal Administrators [5929]
Center for Law and Justice Intl. [6017]
Farmers' Legal Action Gp. [6023]
Homeowners Against Deficient Dwellings [12314]
Intl. Legal Defense Counsel [5869]
Intl. Senior Lawyers Proj. [5502]
Intl. Tech. Law Assn. [5582]
Iranian Refugees' Alliance [12813]
Joint Action in Community Ser. [11803]
Justice Without Borders [6025]
Lawyers' Comm. for Civil Rights Under Law [6027]
Lawyers for One Am. [6028]
Legal Counsel for the Elderly [12497]
Legal Environmental Assistance Found. [4586]
Legal Sers. for the Elderly [12499]
Natl. Assn. of Litigation Support Managers [6014]
Natl. Center for Lesbian Rights [12246]
Natl. Coalition of Concerned Legal Professionals [12501]
Natl. Coun. for Support of Disability Issues [13212]
Natl. Crime Victim Bar Assn. [6349]
Natl. Domestic Violence Hotline [12036]
Natl. Org. of Fed. Employees Against Abuse and Retaliation [24078]
Natl. Org. of Veterans' Advocates [6348]
Natl. Senior Citizens Law Center [11316]
Rutherford Inst. [18513]
Sikh Amer. Legal Defense and Educ. Fund [18600]
Victims' Assistance Legal Org. [5639]
WITNESS [17789]
Legal Aid Warranty Fund - Address unknown since 1995.
Legal Asst. Mgt. Assn. [★5944]
Legal Asst. Mgt. Assn. [★IO]
Legal Assistants; Natl. Assn. of [6150]
Legal Assn; Natl. Para [6152]
Legal Center; Intl. [★5942]
Legal Center for the Public Interest; Natl. [6224]
Legal Comm; NOW [★17546]
Legal Consortium; Natl. Asian Pacific Amer. [★5470]
Legal Counsel for the Elderly [12497], 601 E St. NW, Bldg. A, 4th Fl., Washington, DC 20049, (202)434-2120
Legal Defense Assn; Home School [8339]
Legal Defense and Educ. Found; Natl. Right to Work [17983]
Legal Defense and Educ. Fund; Asian Amer. [17095]
Legal Defense and Educ. Fund; Lambda [12241]
Legal Defense and Educ. Fund; Minority Bus. Enterprise [2763]
Legal Defense and Educ. Fund; NOW [★17546]
Legal Defense and Educ. Fund; Partnership for Civil Justice [17142]
Legal Defense and Educ. Fund; Puerto Rican [17149]
Legal Defense and Educational Fund; Mexican Amer. [17705]
Legal Defense and Educational Fund; Natl. Assn. for the Advancement of Colored People [17130]
Legal Defense Found; Natl. Right to Work [★17983]
Legal Defense Fund; Animal [11351]
Legal Defense Fund; Civil Rights [★17097]
Legal Defense Fund; Free Enterprise [17630]

Legal Defense Fund; Sierra Club [★5690]
Legal Defense Fund; Women's [★17561]
Legal Defense Network; Servicemembers [6113]
Legal Eagles [★5539]
Legal Education
Acad. of Criminal Justice Sciences [11850]
Acad. of Legal Stud. in Bus. [8757]
Academy of Legal Studies in Business [IO]
ALI-ABA Comm. on Continuing Professional Educ. [8758]
Amer. Alliance of Paralegals, Inc. [6149]
Amer. Assn. for Paralegal Educ. [8759]
Amer. Mock Trial Assn. [9281]
Amer. Soc. for Legal History [10090]
Assn. of Amer. Law Schools [8760]
Assn. of Amer. Law Schools Sect. on Sexual Orientation and Gender Identity Issues [8761]
Assn. for Continuing Legal Educ. [8762]
Assn. for Honest Attorneys [5486]
Assn. of Law Teachers [IO]
British and Irish Law, Educ. and Tech. Assn. [IO]
Canadian Assn. for the Practical Stud. of Law in Educ. [IO]
Chinese Law Soc. of Am. [5933]
Clinical Legal Educ. Assn. [8763]
Coun. on Legal Educ. Opportunity [8764]
Earl Warren Legal Training Prog. [8765]
European Law Faculties Assn. [IO]
Fed. Bar Assn. [5492]
Fed. Circuit Bar Assn. [5493]
Fed. Communications Bar Assn. [5580]
Global Alliance for Justice Educ. [8766]
Global Alliance for Justice Educ. [IO]
Identity Theft Rsrc. Center [18007]
Intl. Assn. of Law Schools [8767]
Intl. Assn. of Law Schools [IO]
Law School Admission Coun. [IO]
Law School Admission Coun. [8768]
Law Student Div. [8769]
Law Students for Choice [18517]
Natl. Assn. for Law Placement [8770]
Natl. Assn. of Legal Assistants [6150]
Natl. Black Law Students Assn. [8771]
Natl. Criminal Defense Coll. [5657]
Natl. Inst. for Trial Advocacy [6334]
Natl. Native Amer. Law Students Assn. [8772]
Natl. South Asian Bar Assn. [6018]
Natl. Women Law Students Assn. [9322]
Network of Trial Law Firms [5525]
North Amer. South Asian Law Student Assn. [8773]
North Amer. South Asian Law Student Assn. [IO]
Phi Delta Phi Intl. Legal Fraternity [IO]
Phi Delta Phi Intl. Legal Fraternity [24530]
Pound Civil Justice Inst. [6335]
Practising Law Inst. [8774]
Renaissance Lawyer Soc. [5529]
Soc. of Legal Scholars in the United Kingdom and Ireland [IO]
Legal Educ. Administrators; Assn. of Continuing [★8762]
Legal Educ. - of ALI-ABA; Joint Comm. on Continuing [★8758]
Legal Environmental Assistance Found. [4586], 1114 Thomasville Rd., Ste. E, Tallahassee, FL 32303-6290, (850)681-2591
Legal Found; Amer. [★6229]
Legal Found; Atlantic [5930]
Legal Found; Criminal Justice [5642]
Legal Found; Natl. [6225]
Legal Found; Pacific [6226]
Legal Found; Southwestern [★5931]
Legal Found; Washington [6229]
Legal Fund; Get Oil Out Educ. and [★5092]
Legal Fund; Omega First Amendment [17140]
Legal History; Amer. Soc. for [10090]
Legal Immigrant Assn. [5808], PO Box 2082, Santa Clara, CA 95055
Legal Immigration Network; Catholic [20089]
Legal Industry Advisory Coun. - Address unknown since 1994.
Legal Inst; Phi Delta Phi [★24530]
Legal Inst; Phi Delta Phi [★IO]
Legal Instruction; Center for Computer-Assisted [6789]

Legal Investigators; Natl. Assn. of [5885]
Legal Marketing Assn. [2632], 1926 Waukegan Rd., Ste. 1, Glenview, IL 60025, (847)657-6717
Legal Marketing Assn. [IO], Glenview, IL, United States
Legal Momentum [★17546]
Legal Momentum: Advancing Women's Rights [17546], 395 Hudson St., New York, NY 10014, (212)925-6635
Legal Nurse Consultants; Amer. Assn. of [14999]
Legal and Policy Center; Natl. [17671]
Legal Problems of Educ; Natl. Org. on [★5676]
Legal Reform; HALT - Americans for [★17961]
Legal Reform; HALT - An Org. of Americans for [17961]
Legal Res. Services and Databases; Mental and Physical Disability [★5781]
Legal Rsrc. Center for Child Advocacy and Protection; Natl. [★11555]
Legal Rsrc. Center; Mental Disability [★5781]
Legal Resources Centre [IO], Johannesburg, Republic of South Africa
Legal Resources Found. - Zambia [IO], Lusaka, Zambia
Legal Resources Found. - Zimbabwe [IO], Harare, Zimbabwe
Legal Rights and Natural Resources Center - Kasama sa Kalikasan [IO], Quezon City, Philippines
Legal Search Consultants; Natl. Assn. of [2326]
Legal Secretaries, Inc. [★71]
Legal Secretaries, Inc. [★IO]
Legal Secretaries Intl. [IO], Houston, TX, United States
Legal Secretaries Intl. [69], 2302 Fannin St., Ste. 500, Houston, TX 77002-9136, (713)659-7617
Legal Services
Acad. of Criminal Justice Sciences [11850]
Access to Justice Network [IO]
Advice UK [IO]
Alston Wilkes Veterans Home [11852]
Amer. Alliance of Paralegals, Inc. [6149]
Amer. Assn. for Correctional and Forensic Psychology [11853]
Amer. Catholic Lawyers Assn. [5558]
Amer. Correctional Assn. [11854]
Amer. Criminal Justice Assn. (Lambda Alpha Epsilon) [11855]
Amer. Guild of Court Videographers [6019]
Amer. Jail Assn. [11856]
Amer. Prepaid Legal Services Inst. [6020]
Amer. Pro Se Assn. [6021]
Animal Legal Defense Fund [11351]
Assn. of Child Abuse Lawyers [IO]
Assn. of Forensic Quality Assurance Managers [5758]
Assn. for Honest Attorneys [5486]
Assn. of Lawyers for Children [IO]
Assn. of Life Insurance Counsel [5826]
Assn. of Personal Injury Lawyers [IO]
Assn. on Programs for Female Offenders [11857]
Assn. of State Correctional Administrators [11858]
Center for Medicare Advocacy [14684]
Center for Stud. in Criminal Justice [11859]
Child Care Law Center [11525]
Clarity [6011]
Correctional Educ. Assn. [11862]
Croatian Amer. Bar Assn. [5489]
Custom Legal Plans, LLC [6022]
Custom Legal Plans, LLC [IO]
Fair Elections Legal Network [5491]
Farmers' Legal Action Gp. [6023]
Fed. Law Enforcement Officers Assn. [5879]
Forensic Expert Witness Assn. [5760]
Fortune Soc. [11867]
Friends Outside [11868]
Guam Bar Assn. [6024]
Identity Theft Rsrc. Center [18007]
Intl. Alliance of Holistic Lawyers [5498]
Intl. Assn. of Correctional Officers [11870]
Intl. Assn. of Correctional Training Personnel [11871]
Intl. Bus. Law Consortium [IO]
Intl. Community Corrections Assn. [11872]
Intl. Network of Boutique Law Firms [5501]

A star before a book entry number signifies that the name is not listed separately, but is mentioned within the entry.

Intl. Soc. of Primerus Law Firms [5503]
Intl. Utilities Revenue Protection Assn. [6338]
Iranian Amer. Bar Assn. [5504]
Japan Legal History Assn. [IO]
John Howard Assn. [11874]
Judge David L. Bazelon Center for Mental Hea. Law [17123]
Justice Res. and Statistics Assn. [11876]
Justice Without Borders [6025]
Justice Without Borders [IO]
Law Enforcement and Emergency Services Video Assn. [6350]
Lawyers Assoc. Worldwide [5505]
Lawyers for Children Am. [6026]
Lawyers' Comm. for Civil Rights Under Law [6027]
Lawyers for One Am. [6028]
Lawyers Without Borders [18008]
Lawyers Without Borders [IO]
Legal Advice for Women [IO]
Legal Counsel for the Elderly [12497]
Legal Environmental Assistance Found. [4586]
Legal Immigrant Assn. [5808]
Legal Resources Centre [IO]
Legal Resources Found. - Zambia [IO]
Legal Resources Found. - Zimbabwe [IO]
Legal Services for Children [12498]
Legal Sers. for the Elderly [12499]
Lithuanian-American Bar Assn. [5507]
Media Access Proj. [17182]
Migrant Legal Action Prog. [12500]
Natl. Acad. of Elder Law Attorneys [6029]
Natl. Alliance of Senior Citizens [11299]
Natl. Assn. for the Advancement of Colored People Legal Defense and Educational Fund [17130]
Natl. Assn. of Area Agencies on Aging [11301]
Natl. Assn. of Counsel for Children [11711]
Natl. Assn. of Muslim Lawyers [5511]
Natl. Bd. of Trial Advocacy [6333]
Natl. Center on Institutions and Alternatives [11878]
Natl. Center for Juvenile Justice [11879]
Natl. Center for Lesbian Rights [12246]
Natl. Center on Poverty Law [6030]
Natl. Coalition of Concerned Legal Professionals [12501]
Natl. Correctional Indus. Assn. [11880]
Natl. Crime Victim Bar Assn. [6349]
Natl. Criminal Justice Assn. [11881]
Natl. Employment Law Proj. [12092]
Natl. Juvenile Detention Assn. [11882]
Natl. Law Center on Homelessness and Poverty [12297]
Natl. Lawyers Assn. [5521]
Natl. Legal Aid and Defender Assn. [6031]
Natl. Legal Center for the Medically Dependent and Disabled [6032]
Natl. Legal Sanctuary for Community Advancement [6015]
Natl. Legal Video Assn. [6016]
Natl. Org. of Veterans' Advocates [6348]
Natl. Prison Proj. of the ACLU [11883]
Natl. Senior Citizens Law Center [11316]
Natl. Structured Settlements Trade Assn. [6033]
Natl. Veterans Legal Services Prog. [21314]
Network of Trial Law Firms [5525]
Nigerian Lawyers Assn. [5526]
North Amer. Assn. of Wardens and Superintendents [11884]
North Amer. South Asian Bar Assn. [5527]
Osborne Assn. [11885]
People Before Lawyers [5528]
Pretrial Justice Indus. [6034]
Prison Fellowship Intl. [11887]
Prison Fellowship Ministries [11888]
Prison Ministry of Yokefellow's Intl. [11889]
Prisoners' Rights Union [11890]
Puerto Rican Legal Defense and Educ. Fund [17149]
Renaissance Lawyer Soc. [5529]
Safer Soc. Found. [11891]
Sikh Amer. Legal Defense and Educ. Fund [18600]
Soc. for Advanced Legal Stud. [IO]

Socio-Legal Stud. Assn. [IO]
St. Law [6035]
Swedish-American Bar Assn. [5532]
Taiwanese Amer. Lawyers Assn. [5533]
United Kingdom Assn. for European Law [IO]
U.S. Law Firm Gp. [5534]
Victims' Assistance Legal Org. [5639]
Volunteer Lawyers for the Arts [6036]
Volunteers in Prevention, Probation, Prisons [11896]
We Care Prog. [11897]
Western Center on Law and Poverty [6037]
Women's Prison Assn. [11898]
World Soc. of Mixed Jurisdiction Jurists [5957]
Zambia Civic Educ. Assn. [IO]
Legal Services for Children [12498], 1254 Market St., 3rd Fl., San Francisco, CA 94102, (415)863-3762
Legal Sers. for the Elderly [12499]
Legal Sers. for the Elderly Poor [★12499]
Legal Services; Natl. CH for [★6030]
Legal Services; Natl. Consumer Center for [★6022]
Legal Services for Prisoners With Children - Address unknown since 1989.
Legal Services Prog; Natl. Veterans [21314]
Legal Services; Rsrc. Center for Consumers of [★6022]
Legal Services Staff Assn. [★24079]
Legal Services Workers; Natl. Org. of [★24079]
Legal Services Workers, UAW Local 2320; Natl. Org. of [24079]
Legal Soc; Christian [19781]
Legal Soc; Medico- [★15006]
Legal Software Suppliers Assn. [IO], Grantham, United Kingdom
Legal Subjects; Amer. Soc. of Writers on [★5584]
Legal Support of Alternative Schools; Natl. Assn. for [7946]
Legal Support Ser; Refugee [★17989]
Legal Support Ser; Refugee [★IO]
Legal Tech. Insider [IO], Harleston, United Kingdom
Legal Tyranny; HALT - Help Abolish [★17961]
Legambiente [IO], Rome, Italy
Legambiente Campania [IO], Naples, Italy
Legambiente Ecopolis, Turin [IO], Turin, Italy
Legatus [19652], 2640 Golden Gate Pkwy., Ste. 118, Naples, FL 34105, (239)435-3852
Legemiddel Industri Foreningen [★IO]
Legemiddelindustriforeningen [★IO]
Legend Club-Marilyn Monroe - Address unknown since 2004.
Legends; Pro [★23433]
Legion Amateur Publishing Alliance (LEAPA) [★22042]
Legion of Christ the King - Defunct.
Legion Fan Club [★22042]
Legion of Guardsmen Auxiliaries - Defunct.
Legion of Guardsmen - Defunct.
Legion of Honor; Amer. Soc. of the French [19061]
Legion Royale Canadienne [★IO]
Legion of Valor of the U.S.A. [20714], c/o Philip J. Conran, AFC, Natl. Adj., 4706 Calle Reina, Santa Barbara, CA 93110-2018, (805)692-2244
Legion of Young Polish Women [19304]
Legionarios del Trabajo in America [19057]
Legis 50/The Center for Legislative Improvement - Defunct.
Legislation; Activists for Protective Animal [11338]
Legislation; Friends Comm. on Natl. [20041]
Legislation; Natl. Comm. Against Repressive [17134]
Legislation; Soc. for Animal Protective [11459]
Legislative Action; Institute for [★22913]
Legislative Action Now; Psychologists For [★16136]
Legislative Alliance of Creative Arts Therapies - Defunct.
Legislative Coun. [★5027]
Legislative Coun; Alcohol Beverage [5444]
Legislative Coun. for Photogrammetry [★7496]
Legislative Coun; Small Bus. [3627]
Legislative Exchange Coun; Amer. [18422]
Legislative Fund of Am; Wildlife [★23550]
Legislative Leaders; Natl. Conf. of State [★6283]
Legislative Reform
Amer. Coun. on Alcohol Problems [13220]
Amer. Coun. for Tech. [5813]

Amer. Entrepreneurs for Economic Growth [695]
Amer. Hea. Lawyers Assn. [5782]
Amer. Rights at Work [17968]
Equal Justice Soc. [6258]
Fed. Managers Assn. [5708]
HALT - An Org. of Americans for Legal Reform [17961]
Inst. for Policy and Legal Stud. [IO]
Intl. Senior Lawyers Proj. [5502]
Law Enforcement Against Prohibition [17999]
Leadership Conf. on Civil Rights [17124]
Natl. Adult Day Services Assn. [11298]
Natl. Assn. of Area Agencies on Aging [11301]
Natl. Assn. of State Units on Aging [11305]
Natl. Coalition on Rural Aging [11307]
Natl. Endangered Species Act Reform Coalition [17504]
Natl. Meals on Wheels Found. [11315]
Natl. Order of Women Legislators [6038]
Public Responsibility in Medicine and Res. [18585]
ReclaimDemocracy.org [17398]
Soc. for Animal Protective Legislation [11459]
Legislators Assn; Amer. [★6273]
Legislators; Natl. Black Caucus of State [6281]
Legislators; Natl. Found. for Women [6359]
Legislators; Natl. Order of Women [6038]
Legislators; Natl. Soc. of State [★6283]
Legislatures; Natl. Conf. of State [6283]
Legitimerade Sjukgymnasters Riksforbund [★IO]
Legs Syndrome Found; Restless [16549]
Lehman Educ. Fund; Herbert [★17130]
Leibniz Soc. of North Am. [10809], c/o Glenn A. Hartz, Ed., Philosophy Dept., Ohio State Univ., 1680 Univ. Dr., Mansfield, OH 44906, (419)755-4354
Leicester Assn; Amer. Border [5177]
Leicestershire Chamber of Commerce and Indus. [IO], Leicester, United Kingdom
Leieboerforeningen [★IO]
Leieboerforeningen Bergen [★IO]
Leif Ericson Soc. Intl. [★11134]
Leif Ericson Viking Ship [11134], PO Box 393, Swarthmore, PA 19081-0393, (410)275-8516
Leigh McCloskey Fan Club - Address unknown since 2001.
Leighton; Anglican Order of Archbishop Robert [19453]
Leinster Soc. of Chartered Accountants [IO], Dublin, Ireland
Leisure and Outdoor Furniture Assn. [IO], Chichester, United Kingdom
Leisure Stud. Assn. [IO], Eastbourne, United Kingdom
Lejernes Landsorganisation [★IO]
Lelio Basso Intl. Found. for the Rights and Liberation of Peoples [IO], Rome, Italy
LeMans Am. [22686], c/o Donald Boyd, Pres., 8075 Tipsico Trail, Holly, MI 48442
Lembaga Getah Malaysia [★IO]
Lembaga Koko Malaysia [★IO]
Lembaga Lada Malaysia [★IO]
Lembaga Perindustrian Nanas Malaysia [★IO]
Lemberg Center for the Study of Violence - Defunct.
Lemko Assn. of U.S. and Canada [19338], c/o Alexander Herenchak, Pres., PO Box 156, Allentown, NJ 08501, (609)758-1115
Lemko Housing Org. [15537]
Lemon Administrative Comm. - Defunct.
Len Fan Club; Johnny [24928]
Lenders; Natl. Assn. of Govt. Guaranteed [6039]
Lending
Alliance Credit Counseling [11833]
Amer. Financial Services Assn. [2422]
Canadian Assn. of Accredited Mortgage Professionals [IO]
Commercial Finance Association [IO]
Commercial Finance Assn. [2423]
Consumer Mortgage Coalition [2424]
Intl. Centre for Local Credit [IO]
Intl. Confed. of Popular Banks [IO]
Mortgage and Finance Assn. of Australia [IO]
Natl. Aircraft Finance Assn. [2425]
Natl. Assn. of Church and Institutional Financing Organizations [2426]

Reference to "IO" in place of a book number signifies that the association may be found in the 45th edition of International Organizations.

Natl. Assn. of Development Companies [2427]
Natl. Assn. of Govt. Guaranteed Lenders [6039]
Natl. Assn. of Mortgage Planners [490]
Natl. Automotive Finance Assn. [421]
Natl. Found. for Credit Counseling [2428]
Natl. Pawnbrokers Assn. [2429]
Natl. Reverse Mortgage Lenders Assn. [2430]
New Zealand Mortgage Brokers Assn. [IO]
Structured Employment Economic Development Corp. [12045]
Lending and Credit Risk; Robert Morris Associates/ Association of [★498]
Lennon Sisters Fan Club - Address unknown since 2008.
Lenny Kravitz's Official Fan Club - Address unknown since 2002.
Lens Soc. of Am; Contact [1857]
Lenten Desert Experience [★18161]
Lentz Peace Res. Assn. [18217], c/o Univ. of Missouri-St. Louis, One Univ. Blvd., St. Louis, MO 63121-4400, (314)516-5000
Lenya Res. Center; Weill/ [★10635]
Lenya Res. Center; Weill/ [★IO]
Leo Baeck Inst. [IO], New York, NY, United States
Leo Baeck Inst. [10284], 15 W 16th St., New York, NY 10011, (212)744-6400
Leo Clubs [★13050]
Leo Clubs [★IO]
Leo Lassen Legacy Proj. [24789]
Leon Jordan Fan Club - Address unknown since 1989.
Leonard Cheshire Intl. [IO], London, United Kingdom
Leonard Nimoy Club - Defunct.
Leonard Nimoy and DeForest Kelley; Fans of [24739]
Leonard Peltier Defense Comm. [17381], 3800 N Mesa St., Ste. A2, El Paso, TX 79902, (915)533-6655
Leonard Peltier Defense Committee [IO], El Paso, TX, United States
Leonard Wood Memorial - Amer. Leprosy Found. [IO], Rockville, MD, United States
Leonard Wood Memorial - Amer. Leprosy Found. [15010], 11600 Nebel St., Rockville, MD 20852, (301)984-1336
Leonard Wood Memorial for the Eradication of Leprosy [★15010]
Leonard Wood Memorial for the Eradication of Leprosy [★IO]
Leonardo, The International Society for the Arts, Sciences and Technology [IO], San Francisco, CA, United States
Leonardo, The Intl. Soc. for the Arts, Sciences and Tech. [9610], 211 Sutter St., Ste. 501, San Francisco, CA 94108, (415)391-1110
Leonardo da Vinci Soc. - Defunct.
Leonine Commn. [★19714]
Leopold Stokowski Club [9812], 3900 SE 33 Ave., Ocala, FL 34480
Leopold Stokowski Soc. [IO], Deal, United Kingdom
Leopold Stokowski Soc. of Am. [★9812]
Lepidoptera; Assn. for Tropical [7058]
Lepidoptera Res. Found. - Defunct.
Lepidopterological Soc. of Finland [IO], Helsinki, Finland

Lepidopterology
Butterfly Lovers Intl. [7248]
Intl. Butterfly Breeders Assn. [4203]
North Amer. Butterfly Assn. [7249]
LEPRA - England [IO], Colchester, United Kingdom
Lepra Soc. [IO], Secunderabad, India

Leprosy
All Africa Leprosy, Tuberculosis and Rehabilitation Training Centre [IO]
Amer. Leprosy Missions [IO]
Amer. Leprosy Missions [15007]
British Leprosy Relief Assn. [IO]
Damien-Dutton Soc. for Leprosy Aid [15008]
Damien Found. - Belgium [IO]
Intl. Christian Leprosy Mission [IO]
Intl. Christian Leprosy Mission [15009]
Intl. Fed. of Anti-Leprosy Associations [IO]
Intl. Leprosy Assn. [IO]
Italian Assn. of Friends of Raoul Follereau [IO]
Leonard Wood Memorial - Amer. Leprosy Found. [IO]

Leonard Wood Memorial - Amer. Leprosy Found. [15010]
LEPRA - England [IO]
Lepra Soc. [IO]
Leprosy Relief Assn. [IO]
Leprosy Assn; Intl. [IO]
Leprosy Found; Amer. [★15010]
Leprosy; Leonard Wood Memorial for the Eradication of [★15010]
Leprosy Mission; Philippine [★15010]
Leprosy Mission; Philippine [★IO]
Leprosy Relief Assn. [IO], Colchester, United Kingdom
Leroy Van Dyke Intl. Fan Club - Address unknown since 1999.
Les amis canadiens de la birmanie [★IO]
Les Amis d'Escoffier Society of New York [IO], Millburn, NJ, United States
Les Amis d'Escoffier Soc. of New York [1535], 787 Ridgewood Rd., Millburn, NJ 07041, (212)414-5820
Les Amis du Louvre [★IO]
Les Amis de Panhard and Deutsch Bonnet [21686], 7992 Oak Creek Dr., Reno, NV 89511-1065, (775)853-8452
Les Amis du Plein Air [★IO]
Les Amis de la Rose Luxembourg [IO], Luxembourg, Luxembourg
Les Amis de la Terre - France [★IO]
Les Amis du Togo [★IO]
Les Amis du Vin - Address unknown since 1999.
Les Anciens Combattants Juifs du Canada [★IO]
Les Anciens Combattants de l'Armee, de la Marine et des Forces Aeriennes Au Canada [★IO]
Les Choeurs de l'Union Europeenne [★IO]
Les Clefs d'Or U.S.A. [1949], 68 Laurie Ave., Boston, MA 02132, (617)469-5397
Les Dames d'Escoffier Intl. [1123], PO Box 4961, Louisville, KY 40204, (502)456-1851
Les Dietetistes du Canada [★IO]
Les Femmes d'Entreprises Mondiales [★IO]
Les Grands Freres Grandes Soeurs du Canada [★IO]
Les Humains Associes [★IO]
Les Meres contre L'alcool au volant [★IO]
LES Osterreich [★IO]
Les Unions d'Agents et Organizateurs de Voyages en Europe [★IO]
Lesbian Adolescent Social Services; Gay and [18847]
Lesbian Advocates and Defenders; Gay and [17118]
Lesbian Alliance Against Defamation; Gay [17652]
Lesbian Alliance Against Defamation New York; Gay and [★17652]
Lesbian Alliance; Columbia Gay and [★12224]
Lesbian Alumni/ae Assn; Northeastern Gay and [★18913]
Lesbian Alumni/ae Associations; Network of Gay and [18913]
Lesbian Assn. of Choruses; Gay and [10599]
Lesbian, and Bisexual Caucus of the Amer. Psychiatric Assn; Gay, [★12217]
Lesbian Bisexual Gay Coalition [★12224]
Lesbian, Bisexual, Gay and Transgendered United Employees at AT&T [12242], c/o Mr. Charles Eader, Pres., One AT&T Way, Rm. 4B214J, Bedminster, NJ 07921-2694, (703)691-5734
Lesbian, and Bisexual Issues in Counseling; Assn. for Gay, [12216]
Lesbian, and Bisexual Members of the Amer. Psychiatric Assn; Caucus of Gay, [★12217]
Lesbian, Bisexual, and Transgender Natl. Hotline; Gay, [12230]
Lesbian, Bisexual, and Transgendered Disabled Veterans of Am; Gay, [20765]
Lesbian, Bisexual and Transgendered Round Table; Amer. Lib. Association/Gay, [12214]
Lesbian, and Bisexual Veterans of Am; Gay, [★12215]
Lesbian Coalition Intl; Gay and [★12227]
Lesbian Couples; Partners Task Force for Gay and [17654]
Lesbian Disabled Veterans of Am. [★20765]
Lesbian Feminist Liberation - Address unknown since 1999.

Lesbian-Feminist Study Clearinghouse - Defunct.
Lesbian and Gay Academic Union - Defunct.
Lesbian/Gay Addiction Professionals; Natl. Assn. of [13263]
Lesbian/Gay Alcoholism Professionals; Natl. Assn. of [★13263]
Lesbian and Gay Anthropologists; Soc. of [6432]
Lesbian and Gay Assoc. Engineers and Scientists [★7620]
Lesbian and Gay Band Assn. [10638], PO Box 14874, San Francisco, CA 94114-0874
Lesbian and Gay Bands of Am. [★10638]
Lesbian, Gay and Bisexual Concerns; Affirmation: United Methodists for [20047]
Lesbian, Gay and Bisexual Issues; Natl. Assn. of Social Workers Natl. Comm. on [12245]
Lesbian, Gay and Bisexual Issues; Soc. for the Psychological Stud. of [16180]
Lesbian, Gay and Bisexual People in Medicine [★12243]
Lesbian, Gay and Bisexual Returned Peace Corps Volunteers [★18260]
Lesbian, Gay, Bisexual and Transgender Concerns; Interweave Continental Unitarian Universalists for [20059]
Lesbian, Gay, Bisexual and Transgender Concerns; More Light Presbyterians for [20063]
Lesbian, Gay, Bisexual and Transgender Concerns; United Church of Christ Coalition for [20067]
Lesbian, Gay, Bisexual and Transgender Interest; Brethren/Mennonite Coun. for [20050]
Lesbian, Gay, Bisexual, and Transgender Org; Natl. Latina/o [9972]
Lesbian, Gay, Bisexual, and Transgender People in Medicine [12243], c/o Amer. Medical Student Assn., 1902 Assn. Dr., Reston, VA 20191, (703)620-6600
Lesbian, Gay, Bisexual and Transgender US Peace Corps Alumni [18260], PO Box 14332, San Francisco, CA 94114-4332, (800)424-8580
Lesbian and Gay Caucus of Public Health Workers - Address unknown since 2001.
Lesbian and Gay Christian Movement [IO], London, United Kingdom
Lesbian and Gay Christians [★IO]
Lesbian/Gay Concerns; Affirmation: United Methodists for [★20047]
Lesbian and Gay Concerns; Brethren/Mennonite Coun. for [★20050]
Lesbian and Gay Concerns; Presbyterians for [★20063]
Lesbian and Gay Concerns; Unitarian Universalists for [★20059]
Lesbian/Gay Concerns; United Church Coalition for [★20067]
Lesbian and Gay Immigration Rights Task Force [★12237]
Lesbian and Gay Issues; Natl. Assn. of Social Workers Comm. on [★12245]
Lesbian and Gay Issues; Natl. Assn. of Social Workers- Natl. Comm. on [★12245]
Lesbian and Gay Issues; Soc. for the Psychological Stud. of [★16180]
Lesbian/Gay Issues; Task Force on [★9132]
Lesbian and Gay Journalists Assn; Natl. [3138]
Lesbian and Gay Law Assn; Natl. [5523]
Lesbian and Gay Lawyers Assn; Natl. [★5523]
Lesbian and Gay People in Medicine [★12243]
Lesbian/Gay Pride Coordinators; Intl. Assn. of [★12240]
Lesbian/Gay Rights Monitoring Group - Address unknown since 1989.
Lesbian and Gay Stud; Center for [12222]
Lesbian and Gay Youth; Inst. for the Protection of [★12234]
Lesbian Hea. Fund [14432], c/o Gay and Lesbian Medical Assn., 459 Fulton St., Ste. 107, San Francisco, CA 94102, (415)255-4547
Lesbian Health Fund [IO], San Francisco, CA, United States
Lesbian Hea; Mautner Proj. for [14433]
Lesbian Herstory Archives [★11088]
Lesbian Herstory Archives [★IO]
Lesbian Herstory Educational Found. [IO], New York, NY, United States

A star before a book entry number signifies that the name is not listed separately, but is mentioned within the entry.

Lesbian Herstory Educational Found. [11088], PO Box 1258, New York, NY 10116, (718)768-3953
Lesbian Issues in Social work Educ; Commn. on Gay/ [★9132]
Lesbian Legal Issues, Assn. of Amer. Law Schools; Sect. on Gay and [★8761]
Lesbian Media Coalition; Gay and [★9944]
Lesbian Medical Assn; Gay and [14431]
Lesbian Mormons; Affirmation/Gay and [20046]
Lesbian Psychiatrists; Assn. of Gay and [12217]
Lesbian Rsrc. Center [12244], 227 S Orcas St., Seattle, WA 98108, (206)322-3953
Lesbian Rights; Natl. Center for [12246]
Lesbian Rights Proj. [★12246]
Lesbian Scientists and Tech. Professionals; Natl. Org. of Gay and [7620]
Lesbian Sports Fed; European Gay and [IO]
Lesbian Task Force; Natl. Gay and [12249]
Lesbian Travel Assn; Intl. Gay and [3924]
Lesbian Travel Desk; Natl. Gay/ [24322]
Lesbian Visual Artists [★9454]
Lesbian Visual Artists [★IO]
Lesbians with Cancer; Mautner Proj. for [★14433]
Lesbians; Conf. for Catholic [20051]
Lesbians in Foreign Affairs Agencies USA; Gays and [24074]
Lesbians in Foreign Affairs; Gays and [★24074]
Lesbians and Gays Everywhere; Children of [★12223]
Lesbians and Gays; Parents, Families, and Friends of [12253]
Lesbians and Gays; Parents and Friends of [★12253]
Lesbians Organizing for Change; Old [11317]
Lesbians Organizing; Old [★11317]
Lesbians; Pro-Life Alliance of Gay and [12927]
Lesbians United Non-Nuclear Action - Defunct.
Lesbians in the Visual Arts [9454]
Lesbians in the Visual Arts [IO], San Francisco, CA, United States
Leschetizky Assn. [10639], c/o Ms. Young Drago, Treas./Registrar/Corresponding Sec., 37-21 90th St., Apt. 2R, Jackson Heights, NY 11372, (718)205-8271
Lesley Gore Fan Club [24938], PO Box 1548, Ocean Pines, MD 21811, (410)208-6369
Leslie Charleson Fan Club [24752], c/o Gen. Hosp. - ABC, Inc., 4151 Prospect Ave., Los Angeles, CA 90027
Leslie-Lohman Gay Art Found. [9455], 26 Wooster St., New York, NY 10013, (212)431-2609
Leslie Soc; Clan [★20836]
Leslie Soc. Intl; Clan [20836]
Lesotho Amateur Athletics Assn. [IO], Maseru, Lesotho
Lesotho Badminton Assn. [IO], Maseru, Lesotho
Lesotho Baseball and Softball Assn. [IO], Maseru, Lesotho
Lesotho Lawn Tennis Assn. [IO], Maseru, Lesotho
Lesotho Lib. Assn. [IO], Maseru, Lesotho
Lesotho Natl. Coun. of Women [IO], Maseru, Lesotho
Lesotho Squash Fed. [IO], Maseru, Lesotho
Lesotho Taekwondo Assn. [IO], Maseru, Lesotho
Lesotho Weightlifting Fed. [IO], Maseru, Lesotho
Less Commonly Taught Languages Proj. [8734], c/o Center for Advanced Res. on Language Acquisition, 619 Heller Hall, 271 19th Ave. S, Minneapolis, MN 55455, (612)626-8600
Lessing Soc. [9680], Germanic Languages Dept., Univ. of Cincinnati, 733 Old Chem, Cincinnati, OH 45221-0372, (513)556-2752
Lessing Soc; Amer. [★9680]
Lessors; Natl. Coun. of Coal [845]
Let Nicaragua Live - Defunct.
Letelier-Moffitt Memorial Fund for Human Rights [17993], c/o Inst. for Policy Stud., 1112 16th St. NW, Ste. 600, Washington, DC 20036, (202)234-9382
Letelier-Moffitt Memorial Fund for Human Rights [IO], Washington, DC, United States
Let's Face It USA [IO], Ann Arbor, MI, United States
Let's Face It USA [14064], Univ. of Michigan, School of Dentistry, Dentistry Lib., 1011 North Univ., Ann Arbor, MI 48109-1078

Letter Carriers' Assn; Natl. Rural [24172]
Letter Carriers Mutual Benefit Assn; U.S. [19142]
Letter Carriers; Natl. Assn. of [★24168]
Letter Carriers of the U.S.A; Natl. Assn. of [24168]
Letter Enjoyers Assn. - Address unknown since 1999.
Letter Exchange - Defunct.
Letter Exchange; Student [22144]
Letters Abroad - Defunct.
Letters Comm; News and [18656]
Letters; Natl. Soc. of Arts and [10201]
Letzebuerger Chreschtleche Gewerkschafts-Bond [★IO]
Leukaemia CARE [IO], Worcester, United Kingdom
Leukemia
  Children's Blood Found. [14786]
  Children's Leukemia Res. Assn. [13813]
  Chronic Lymphocytic Leukaemia Support Assn. [IO]
  City of Hope Natl. Medical Center [15102]
  Friends of the Jose Carreras Intl. Leukemia Found. [13825]
  Intl. Assn. for Comparative Res. on Leukemia and Related Diseases [15647]
  Jose Carreras Intl. Leukemia Found. [IO]
  Leukaemia CARE [IO]
  Leukemia and Lymphoma Soc. [13837]
  Sunshine Found. [11726]
Leukemia Assn; Natl. [★13813]
Leukemia Found; Friends of the Jose Carreras Intl. [13825]
Leukemia and Lymphoma Soc. [13837], 1311 Mamaroneck Ave., White Plains, NY 10605, (914)949-5213
Leukemia Res. Assn; Children's [13813]
Leukemia Soc. of Am. [★13837]
Leukemia Stricken Amer. Children; Aiding [★13946]
Leukocyte Biology; Soc. for [16365]
Leukodystrophy Found; United [15372]
Leuva Patidar Samaj of USA [10221], c/o Gunvant Prema, Knights Inn, 1111B Bell Rd., Antioch, TN 37013, (615)731-3205
Levitt Found. [13493], c/o The Philanthropic Gp., 630 Fifth Ave., 20th Fl., New York, NY 10111, (212)501-7785
Levnedsmiddelselskabet [★IO]
Lew DeWitt Fan Club - Defunct.
Lewa Wildlife Conservancy (USA) [5337], c/o Paula Morris, Admin., PO Box 7943, Woodbridge, VA 22195, (703)680-3182
Lewis Carroll Soc. [IO], London, United Kingdom
Lewis Carroll Soc. of North Am. [9681], c/o Clare Imholtz, Sec., 11935 Beltsville Dr., Beltsville, MD 20705
Lewis and Clark Soc. of America - Address unknown since 1995.
Lewis and Clark Trail Heritage Found. [10128], 4201 Giant Springs Rd., Great Falls, MT 59405, (406)454-1234
Lewis D. and John J. Gilbert, Corporate Democracy - Defunct.
Lewis J. Smith Assn. [8274], PO Box 30093, Raleigh, NC 27622, (919)755-3952
Lewis M. Terman Soc. [9985], PO Box 539, New York, NY 10101-0539
Lewis Soc; New York C.S. [9696]
Lewy Body Dementia Assn. [15335], PO Box 451429, Atlanta, GA 31145-9429, (404)935-6444
Lewy Body Dementia Assn. [IO], Atlanta, GA, United States
Lex Mundi [IO], Houston, TX, United States
Lex Mundi [5506], 2100 W Loop S, Ste. 1000, Houston, TX 77027, (713)626-9393
Lexicography; African Assn. for [IO]
Lexicography; European Assn. for [IO]
Lexicography; Soc. for the Stud. of Dictionaries and [★9747]
Lexington Gp. in Trans. History [10913], c/o Don L. Hofsommer, Treas./Ed., Dept. of History, St. Cloud State Univ., St. Cloud, MN 56301, (320)308-4906
Leyte CV32 Assn; USS [21226]
Lhasa Apso Club; Amer. [22202]
Liability
  Amer. Bd. of Professional Disability Consultants [6040]

Amer. Bd. of Professional Liability Attorneys [6041]
  Defense Res. Inst. [6042]
  Inner Circle of Advocates [6043]
  Natl. Assn. of Forensic Economics [6044]
  The Prdt. Liability Alliance [3452]
Liability and Access; Hea. Coalition on [14635]
Liability Alliance; Hea. Care [★14635]
Liability Alliance; The Prdt. [3452]
Liability Common Defense; Prdt. [★3453]
Liability Insurance Res. Bur. [2192], 3025 Highland Pkwy., Ste. 800, Downers Grove, IL 60515-1291, (630)724-2250
Liability Prevention and Defense; Prdt. [3453]
Liability Underwriters; Amer. Inst. for Property and [★2137]
Liability Underwriters; Mutual Atomic Energy [2201]
Liaison Comm. on Continuing Medical Educ. [★15151]
Liaison Comm. of Cooperating Oil and Gas Associations [2933], c/o Texas Independent Producers and Royalty Owners Assn., 919 Cong. Ave., Ste. 1000, Austin, TX 78701, (512)477-4452
Liaison Comm. on Graduate Medical Educ. [★7872]
Liaison Comm. on Medical Educ. [8839], c/o Amer. Medical Assn., 515 N State St., Chicago, IL 60610, (312)464-4933
Liaison Coun. on Certification for the Surgical Technologist [★13534]
Liaison Endorsement Comm. [★14343]
Liaison Gp. of the European Mech., Elecl., Electronic, and Metalworking Indus. [IO], Brussels, Belgium
Liaison Gp. for Intl. Educational Exchange [★IO]
Liaison Gp. for Intl. Educational Exchange [★8591]
Liaison Off. of the European Ceramic Indus. [IO], Brussels, Belgium
Liaison Officers; Natl. Assn. of State Outdoor Recreation [6157]
Liars Club; Burlington [22592]
Liatris Intl. - Address unknown since 2003.
Libby Family Assn; John [20963]
Libel
  Media Law Rsrc. Center [6045]
Libel Defense Rsrc. Center [★6045]
Liberace Club of Las Vegas - Address unknown since 1999.
Liberal Arts
  Amer. Acad. for Liberal Educ. [8775]
  Assn. for Core Texts and Courses [8776]
  Assn. for Core Texts and Courses [IO]
  Assn. for Gen. and Liberal Stud. [8777]
  Assn. of Graduate Liberal Stud. Programs [8778]
  Educational Leadership Prog. [8779]
  Educational Leadership Program [IO]
  Higher Educ. Consortium for Urban Affairs [9286]
  Modernist Stud. Assn. [8780]
  Phi Beta Kappa [24406]
  Phi Sigma Pi Natl. Honor Fraternity [24531]
Liberal Democractic Party of Switzerland [★IO]
Liberal Democrat Youth and Students - UK [IO], London, United Kingdom
Liberal Democratic Party of Japan [IO], Tokyo, Japan
Liberal Educ. for Adoptive Families [11253], 1295 Omaha Ave. N, Stillwater, MN 55082, (651)436-2215
Liberal Intl. [IO], London, United Kingdom
Liberal League; Natl. [★19838]
Liberal Party of Australia [IO], Kingston, Australia
Liberal Party of Canada [IO], Ottawa, ON, Canada
Liberal Party of Norway [IO], Oslo, Norway
Liberal Religious Educ. Directors Assn. [★20599]
Liberal Religious Educators Assn. [20599], PO Box 691254, San Antonio, TX 78269, (210)641-7247
Liberal Religious Peace Fellowship - Address unknown since 1995.
Liberal Religious Youth - Defunct.
Liberal Studies
  Assn. for Core Texts and Courses [8776]
  Modernist Stud. Assn. [8780]
Liberal Stud; Assn. for Gen. and [8777]
Liberal Unionists [★IO]
Liberalism
  Americans for Democratic Action [18009]

Reference to "IO" in place of a book number signifies that the association may be found in the 45th edition of International Organizations.

Found. for the Stud. of Independent Social Ideas [18010]
Helen Suzman Found. [IO]
Trusteeship Inst. [18011]
Liberate Life; Collegians Activated to [12911]
Liberation Action Gp; Animal [11352]
Liberation Found; Male [18037]
Liberation Movement of the German Reich - Address unknown since 1999.
Liberation News Service - Defunct.
Liberation Support Movement Information Center - Defunct.
Liberator Atlanta - Address unknown since 1994.
Liberator Club [★21394]
Liberator Club [★IO]
Liberia
   Liberian Shipowners' Coun. [2607]
Liberia Baseball and Softball Assn. [IO], Monrovia, Liberia
Liberia Chamber of Commerce [IO], Monrovia, Liberia
Liberia Res. and Information Project - Address unknown since 2001.
Liberia Taekwondo Fed. [IO], Monrovia, Liberia
Liberia Tennis Assn. [IO], Monrovia, Liberia
Liberia Track and Field Fed. [IO], Monrovia, Liberia
Liberian Philatelic Soc. - Defunct.
Liberian Shipowners' Coun. [2607], 99 Park Ave., Ste. 1700, New York, NY 10016, (212)973-3896
Liberian Shipowners' Coun. [IO], New York, NY, United States
Libertarian Alliance [IO], London, United Kingdom
Libertarian Campaign Fund - Defunct.
Libertarian Coun. of Churches - Defunct.
Libertarian Defense Caucus - Defunct.
Libertarian Feminists; Assn. of [18013]
Libertarian Futurist Soc. [18016], 650 Castro St., Ste. 120-433, Mountain View, CA 94041
Libertarian Information Service - Address unknown since 1999.
Libertarian Intl. [★18015]
Libertarian Intl. [★IO]
Libertarian Lawyers Alliance - Defunct.
Libertarian League - Defunct.
Libertarian Nation Found. [6046], 335 Mulberry St., Raleigh, NC 27604
Libertarian Natl. Comm. [18327], 2600 Virginia Ave. NW, Ste. 200, Washington, DC 20037, (202)333-0008
Libertarian Party [★18327]
Libertarian Party Abolitionist Caucus - Defunct.
Libertarian Republican Alliance - Defunct.
Libertarian Republican Organizing Comm. - Defunct.
Libertarian SIG [10810], c/o Amer. Mensa, 1229 Corporate Dr. W, Arlington, TX 76006-6103, (817)607-0060
Libertarianism
   Advocates for Self-Government [18012]
   Assn. of Libertarian Feminists [18013]
   Center for Libertarian Stud. [18014]
   Inst. for Justice [5940]
   Intl. Soc. for Individual Liberty [18015]
   Intl. Soc. for Individual Liberty [IO]
   Libertarian Alliance [IO]
   Libertarian Futurist Soc. [18016]
   Libertarian Nation Found. [6046]
   Libertarians for Life [18017]
   Natl. Org. Taunting Safety and Fairness Everywhere [22599]
   Republican Liberty Caucus [18531]
   The Voluntaryists [18018]
   World Libertarian Order [18019]
Libertarians for Animal Rights - Address unknown since 1994.
Libertarians for Gay and Lesbian Concerns - Address unknown since 2001.
Libertarians for Life [18017], 13424 Hathaway Dr., Silver Spring, MD 20906, (301)460-4141
Libertel de la Capitale Nationale [★IO]
Liberty [IO], London, United Kingdom
Liberty Alliance - Defunct.
Liberty Amendment Comm. of the U.S.A. [17296], PO Box 188785, Sacramento, CA 95818, (916)443-7769
Liberty; Amer. Sons of [17087]

Liberty; Americans for Religious [17090]
Liberty Assn; Natl. Religious [★18512]
Liberty; Becket Fund for Religious [18509]
Liberty Bell Matchcover Club - Address unknown since 1999.
Liberty Caucus; Republican [18531]
Liberty Comm; Radio [★17191]
Liberty Fed. - Address unknown since 2001.
Liberty Found. [★17298]
Liberty Godparent Home [12918], PO Box 4199, Lynchburg, VA 24502, (434)845-3466
Liberty Godparent Ministry [★12918]
Liberty and Justice; Inst. for [★17108]
Liberty Lobby - Defunct.
Liberty Movement Assn; ALMA Soc. - Adoptees' [11232]
Liberty Museum and Educ. Center [★17723]
Liberty Museum and Educ. Center [★IO]
Liberty Natl. Coun. for Civil Liberties [★IO]
Liberty; National Endowment for [★17293]
Liberty; Radio Free Europe/Radio [17191]
Liberty Seated Collectors Club [22742], c/o Leonard Augsburger, Sec.-Treas., PO Box 261, Wellington, OH 44090
Liberty Services [17666], 225 N Stockwell Rd., Evansville, IN 47715-2456, (812)473-5250
Liberty; Soc. for Individual [★18015]
Liberty Veterans Assn; USS [21227]
Liberty for Women; Life and [11222]
Liberty's Promise [5809], 1010 Pendleton St., Alexandria, VA 22314-1837, (703)549-9950
LibertyTree [17275], 100 Swan Way, Oakland, CA 94621-1428, (800)927-8733
LibertyTree Network [★17275]
Librarians Assn; Chinese [★10347]
Librarians Assn; Jewish [★10332]
Librarians Assn. of Malaysia [IO], Kuala Lumpur, Malaysia
Librarians Assn; Mid-West Chinese Amer. [★10347]
Librarians; Assn. of Visual Sci. [★10341]
Librarians; East Coast Marine Sci. [★10361]
Librarians' Fellowship; Christian [★10330]
Librarians Guild; Progressive [★10381]
Librarians in the History of the Hea. Sciences; Assn. of [★10326]
Librarians of Institutes and Schools of Educ. [IO], Worcester, United Kingdom
Librarians; Natl. Freedom Fund for [★17040]
Librarians of North Am; Assn. of Record [★15097]
Librarians for Nuclear Arms Control - Defunct.
Librarians; REFORMA: Natl. Assn. of Spanish-Speaking [★10384]
Librarians United to Fight Costly, Silly, Unnecessary Serial Title Changes - Defunct.
Libraries
   AFL-CIO/ALA Joint Comm. on Lib. Ser. to Labor Groups [10314]
   African-American Lib. and Info. Sci. Assn. [IO]
   Agricultural Libraries Network [IO]
   Alternatives in Publication Task Force [10315]
   Amer. Antiquarian Soc. [10008]
   Amer. Assn. of Law Libraries [10316]
   Amer. Assn. of School Librarians [10317]
   Amer. Assn. of Teachers of Slavic and East European Languages [9125]
   Amer. Friends of the Vatican Lib. [10318]
   Amer. Indian Lib. Assn. [10319]
   Amer. Lib. Assn. [10320]
   Amer. Lib. Association/Gay, Lesbian, Bisexual and Transgendered Round Table [12214]
   Amer. Lib. Assn. - Off. for Res. and Statistics [10934]
   Amer. Lib. Assn. - Public Info. Off. [10897]
   Amer. Merchant Marine Lib. Assn. [10321]
   Amer. Soc. of Indexers [10322]
   Amer. Theological Lib. Assn. [10323]
   Americans for Libraries Coun. [10324]
   AMIGOS Lib. Services [10325]
   Archivists and Librarians in the History of the Hea. Sciences [10326]
   Armenian Lib. Assn. [IO]
   Art Libraries Soc. of North Am. [IO]
   Asia/Pacific Amer. Librarians Assn. [IO]
   Asia/Pacific Amer. Librarians Assn. [10327]
   Assn. of Architecture School Librarians [10328]

Assn. of Austrian Librarians [IO]
Assn. of Book Gp. Readers and Leaders [9738]
Assn. of British Theological and Philosophical Libraries [IO]
Assn. of Canadian Map Libraries and Archives [IO]
Assn. of Caribbean Univ., Res. and Institutional Libraries [IO]
Assn. of Caribbean Univ., Res. and Institutional Libraries [10329]
Assn. of Christian Librarians [10330]
Association of Christian Librarians [IO]
Assn. of Coll. and Res. Libraries [10331]
Assn. of the Dutch Univ. Libraries and the Royal Lib. [IO]
Assn. of German Librarians [IO]
Assn. of Graduate Librarians of Argentina [IO]
Assn. for Hea. Info. and Libraries in Africa [IO]
Assn. of Hungarian Librarians [IO]
Assn. of Independent Libraries [IO]
Assn. of Jewish Libraries [IO]
Assn. of Jewish Libraries [10332]
Assn. pour l'Avancement des Sciences et des Techniques de la Documentation [IO]
Assn. for Lib. Collections and Tech. Services [10333]
Assn. of Lib. and Info. Professionals of the Czech Republic [IO]
Assn. of Lib. and Info. Professionals - Germany [IO]
Assn. for Lib. Ser. to Children [10334]
Assn. for Lib. Trustees and Advocates [10335]
Assn. for Population/Family Planning Libraries and Info. Centers-International [10336]
Assn. for Population/Family Planning Libraries and Info. Centers-International [IO]
Assn. des Professionnels de l'information et de la Documentation [IO]
Association for Recorded Sound Collections [IO]
Assn. for Recorded Sound Collections [10337]
Assn. of Res. Libraries [10338]
Assn. of Seventh-Day Adventist Librarians [10339]
Assn. of Specialized and Cooperative Lib. Agencies [10340]
Assn. of United Kingdom Media Librarians [IO]
Assn. of Vision Sci. Librarians [10341]
Associazione Italiana Biblioteche [IO]
Athenaeum of Philadelphia [10342]
Australian Lib. and Info. Assn. [IO]
Azerbaijan Lib. Development Assn. [IO]
Belarusian Lib. Assn. [IO]
Beta Phi Mu [24532]
Black Caucus of the Amer. Lib. Assn. [10343]
Bliss Classification Assn. [IO]
Britain and Ireland Assn. of Aquatic Sciences Libraries and Info. Centres [IO]
British Assn. of Picture Libraries and Agencies [IO]
British and Irish Assn. of Law Librarians [IO]
Calibre Audio Lib. [IO]
Canadian Assn. of Children's Librarians [IO]
Canadian Assn. of Coll. and Univ. Libraries [IO]
Canadian Assn. of Law Libraries [IO]
Canadian Assn. of Music Libraries, Archives, and Documentation Centres [IO]
Canadian Assn. of Public Libraries [IO]
Canadian Assn. of Res. Libraries [IO]
Canadian Assn. for School Libraries [IO]
Canadian Assn. of Special Libraries and Info. Services [IO]
Canadian Comm. on Cataloguing [IO]
Canadian Hea. Libraries Assn. [IO]
Canadian Lib. Assn. [IO]
Canadian Lib. Trustees Assn. [IO]
Catholic Lib. Assn. [10344]
Center for Res. Libraries [10345]
Chartered Inst. of Lib. and Info. Professionals [IO]
Chartered Inst. of Lib. and Info. Professionals in Scotland [IO]
Chief Officers of State Lib. Agencies [10346]
Chinese Amer. Librarians Assn. [10347]
Christian Librarians Network - Australia and New Zealand [IO]
Church and Synagogue Lib. Assn. [10348]

A star before a book entry number signifies that the name is not listed separately, but is mentioned within the entry.

Comm. on Res. Materials on Southeast Asia [10349]
Comm. on Res. Materials on Southeast Asia [IO]
Conf. of European Natl. Librarians [IO]
Cong. of Southeast Asian Librarians [IO]
Consortium of European Res. Libraries [IO]
Continuing Lib. Educ. Network and Exchange Round Table [10350]
Coun. of Archives and Res. Libraries in Jewish Stud. [10351]
Coun. on Botanical and Horticultural Libraries [10352]
Council on Botanical and Horticultural Libraries [IO]
Coun. for Culture [IO]
Coun. on Lib. and Info. Resources [10353]
Estonian Librarians' Assn. [IO]
Ethnic and Multicultural Info. Exchange Round-table [10354]
European Assn. for Hea. Info. and Libraries [IO]
European Theological Libraries [IO]
Evangelical Church Lib. Assn. [10355]
Fed. Lib. and Info. Center Comm. [10356]
Fed. of Organizations in the Field of Libraries, Info. and Documentation [IO]
Finnish Lib. Assn. [IO]
FOCAL Intl. [IO]
Freedom to Read Found. [17040]
Friends of Libraries for Blind and Physically Handicapped Individuals in North America [10357]
Friends of Libraries U.S.A. [10358]
Friends of the Natl. Libraries [IO]
Fundza [IO]
Green Lib. - Sweden [IO]
Harry S. Truman Lib. Inst. for Natl. and Intl. Affairs [11120]
Higher Educ. Info. Tech. Alliance [8489]
Hong Kong Lib. Assn. [IO]
Icelandic Lib. and Info. Sci. Assn. [IO]
Independent Res. Libraries Assn. [10359]
Interagency Coun. on Info. Resources for Nursing [10360]
Intl. Assn. of Agricultural Info. Specialists [IO]
Intl. Assn. of Aquatic and Marine Sci. Libraries and Info. Centers [IO]
Intl. Assn. of Aquatic and Marine Sci. Libraries and Info. Centers [10361]
Intl. Assn. of Music Libraries, Archives and Documentation Centers, U.S. Br. [10362]
Intl. Assn. of Music Libraries, Archives and Documentation Centres - New Zealand Br. [IO]
Intl. Assn. of Music Libraries, Archives and Documentation Centres - United Kingdom and Ireland [IO]
Intl. Assn. of Technological Univ. Libraries [IO]
Intl. Coun. for Hea., Physical Educ., Recreation, Sport, and Dance [8981]
Intl. Fed. of Lib. Associations and Institutions [IO]
Intl. Fed. of Lib. Associations and Institutions - Metropolitan Libraries Sect. [IO]
Intl. Friends of the London Lib. [IO]
Intl. Friends of the London Lib. [10363]
Intl. Reading Assn. [9043]
Intl. Survey Lib. Assn. [10364]
Intl. Survey Lib. Assn. [IO]
Italian Assn. for Advanced Documentation [IO]
Italian Lib. Assn. [IO]
Japan Soc. of Lib. and Info. Sci. [IO]
Japan Special Libraries Assn. [IO]
John F. Kennedy Lib. Found. [10365]
Lesotho Lib. Assn. [IO]
Librarians Assn. of Malaysia [IO]
Librarians of Institutes and Schools of Educ. [IO]
Lib. Admin. and Mgt. Assn. [10366]
Lib. Assn. of Austria [IO]
Lib. Assn. of Ireland [IO]
Lib. Assn. of Singapore [IO]
Lib. Binding Inst. [1778]
Lib. Cat Soc. [10367]
Lib. and Info. Assn. of New Zealand Aotearoa [IO]
Lib. and Info. Assn. of South Africa [IO]
Lib. and Info. Res. Gp. [IO]
Lib. and Info. Tech. Assn. [10368]
Lib. Public Relations Coun. [10369]

Lib. Users of Am. [10370]
Lithuanian Librarians' Assn. [IO]
Major Orchestra Librarians' Assn. [10371]
Malta Lib. and Info. Assn. [IO]
Maritime Info. Assn. [IO]
Medical Lib. Assn. [10372]
Middle East Librarians Assn. [10373]
Middle East Librarians Assn. [IO]
Music Lib. Assn. [10374]
Natl. Church Lib. Assn. [10375]
Natl. Lib. and Documentation Services Bd. [IO]
Natl. Lib. of Uganda [IO]
Natl. Serials Data Prog. [10376]
Natural Resources Info. Coun. [10377]
Natural Resources Info. Coun. [IO]
NBLC Dutch Assn. of Public Libraries [IO]
Netherlands Assn. for Lib., Info. and Knowledge Professionals [IO]
Network of Govt. Lib. and Info. Specialists [IO]
Nordic Fed. of Res. Libraries Associations [IO]
North Amer. Coordinating Coun. on Japanese Lib. Resources [IO]
North Amer. Coordinating Coun. on Japanese Lib. Resources [8781]
North Amer. Serials Interest Gp. [10378]
North Amer. Sport Lib. Network [IO]
Norwegian Assn. of Special Libraries [IO]
Off. for Intellectual Freedom [6047]
Online Audiovisual Catalogers [10379]
Org. of Amer. Kodaly Educators [8929]
Patent and Trademark Depository Lib. Prog. [6168]
Philomathean Soc. of the Univ. of Pennsylvania [10429]
Polar Libraries Colloquy [10380]
Polar Libraries Colloquy [IO]
Polish Librarians Assn. [IO]
Private Libraries Assn. [IO]
Prdt. Liability Prevention and Defense [3453]
Progressive Librarians Guild [10381]
Public Lib. Assn. [10382]
Reading Is Fundamental [9047]
Reference and User Services Assn. of Amer. Lib. Assn. [10383]
REFORMA: Natl. Assn. to Promote Lib. Services to the Spanish-Speaking [10384]
Res. Libraries Gp. [10385]
Russian Lib. Assn. [IO]
Saskatchewan Lib. Assn. [IO]
Schomburg Center for Res. in Black Culture [9363]
School Lib. Assn. [IO]
Seminar on the Acquisition of Latin Amer. Lib. Materials [IO]
Seminar on the Acquisition of Latin Amer. Lib. Materials [10386]
Social Responsibilities Round Table of the American Library Association [10387]
Soc. of Coll., Natl. and Univ. Libraries [IO]
Soc. of Indexers [IO]
Society of School Librarians International [IO]
Soc. of School Librarians Intl. [10388]
Special Libraries Assn. [10389]
Special Libraries Assn. [IO]
Sri Lanka Lib. Assn. [IO]
Standing Conf. on Lib. Materials on Africa [IO]
Stelios M. Stelson Found. [8631]
Substance Abuse Librarians and Info. Specialists [10390]
Substance Abuse Librarians and Information Specialists [IO]
Tanzania Lib. Assn. [IO]
Theatre Lib. Assn. [10391]
Union of Associations of Slovene Librarians [IO]
Union of Librarians and Info. Services Officers [IO]
U.S. Book Exchange [10392]
Univ. and Res. Librarians Assn. [IO]
Urban Libraries Coun. [10393]
Values and Visions [8155]
Western Assn. of Map Libraries [10394]
Women's Natl. Book Assn. [3174]
Young Adult Lib. Services Assn. [10395]
Zambia Lib. Assn. [IO]
Libraries; Amer. Book Center for War Devastated [★10392]

Libraries; Assn. of Coll. and Reference [★10331]
Libraries Assn; Marine Sci. [★10361]
Libraries for Children and Young People of the Amer. Lib. Assn; Sect. of the Division of [★10317]
Libraries Colloquy; Northern [★10380]
Libraries Division of the Amer. Lib. Assn; School [★10317]
Libraries Div; Public [★10382]
Libraries for the Future [★10324]
Libraries and Info. Centers; Intl. Assn. of Marine Sci-ences [★10361]
Lib. Admin. Division of ALA [★10366]
Lib. Admin. and Mgt. Assn. [10366], c/o Amer. Lib. Assn., 50 E Huron St., Chicago, IL 60611-2729, (312)280-5032
Lib. Agencies; Assn. of State [★10340]
Lib; Amer. Choral Found. [★10588]
Lib; Amer. Philatelic Res. [22784]
Lib. and Archives; Southern Baptist Historical [19499]
Lib. Assn. of Austria [IO], Vienna, Austria
Lib. Assn; Children's [★10334]
Lib. Association/Gay, Lesbian, Bisexual and Trans-gendered Round Table; Amer. [12214]
Lib. Assn; Herbert Hoover Presidential [11122]
Lib. Assn. of Ireland [IO], Dublin, Ireland
Lib. Assn; Jewish [★10332]
Lib. Assn; Napa Valley Wine [23027]
Lib. Assn; Philatelic [★22784]
Lib. Assn. of Singapore [IO], Singapore, Singapore
Lib. Assn. of Slovenia [★IO]
Lib. Assn; U.S.A. Toy [11548]
Lib. Binding Inst. [1778], 4300 S U.S. Hwy. One, No. 203-296, Jupiter, FL 33477, (561)745-6821
Lib. Binding Inst. [IO], Jupiter, FL, United States
Lib. Cat Soc. [10367], PO Box 274, Moorhead, MN 56560, (218)236-7205
Lib. Center; Found. [★12653]
Library Center; Midwest Inter [★10345]
Lib. of Choral Music; Drinker [10588]
Library Club of America - Defunct.
Library-Coll. Associates - Defunct.
Lib. Comm; Fed. [★10356]
Library Education Div. - Defunct.
Lib. Educ. Network and Exchange; Continuing [★10350]
Library Found. for Voluntary Orgs. - Defunct.
Lib. of the High Seas; Public [★10321]
Lib. and Historical Soc; Amer. Hungarian [10215]
Lib. and Info. Assn. of New Zealand Aotearoa [IO], Wellington, New Zealand
Lib. and Info. Assn. of South Africa [IO], Pretoria, Republic of South Africa
Lib. and Info. Res. Gp. [IO], Sheffield, United Kingdom
Lib. and Info. Tech. Assn. [10368], c/o Amer. Lib. Assn., 50 E Huron St., Chicago, IL 60611-2795, (312)280-4268
Lib. Materials - of ALA; Bd. of Acquisitions of [★10333]
Lib. Media Supervisors Assn; State School [★8568]
Lib. Organizations; Assn. of Cooperative [★10340]
Lib. of Presidential Papers [★17069]
Lib. Program; New Believer [★20368]
Lib. Public Relations Coun. [10369], 2576 Broadway, No. 532, New York, NY 10025
Lib. Resources on South Asia; Comm. on Amer. [★10349]
Lib. Resources on Southeast Asia; Comm. on Amer. [★10349]
Library Science
Assn. of Danish Res. Libraries [IO]
Assn. Internationale des Ecoles des Sciences de l'Information [IO]
Assn. for Lib. and Info. Sci. Educ. [8782]
Beta Phi Mu [24532]
Beta Phi Mu [IO]
British Assn. for Info. and Lib. Educ. Res. [IO]
Continuing Lib. Educ. Network and Exchange Round Table [10350]
Coun. on Library-Media Technicians [8783]
Croatian Lib. Assn. [IO]
Danish Lib. Assn. [IO]
Danish Music Lib. Assn. [IO]
Danish School Librarian Assn. [IO]

Reference to "IO" in place of a book number signifies that the association may be found in the 45th edition of International Organizations.

European Bur. of Lib., Info. and Documentation Associations [IO]
Intl. Coalition of Lib. Consortia [IO]
Intl. Coalition of Lib. Consortia [8784]
Japan Lib. Assn. [IO]
Mita Society for Library and Information Science [IO]
North Amer. Serials Interest Gp. [10378]
Norwegian Lib. Assn. [IO]
Swedish Lib. Assn. [IO]
Lib. Services; Hea. and Rehabilitative [★10340]
Lib. Services to the Spanish-Speaking; REFORMA: Natl. Assn. of [★10384]
Lib. Soc; Percy Grainger [★9810]
Lib. Technical-Assistants; Coun. on [★8783]
Lib. Tech; Coun. on [★8783]
Library Technology Program - Defunct.
Lib. Trustee Assn; Amer. [★10335]
Lib. Trustees; Amer. Assn. of [★10335]
Lib. Trustees Coun; Urban [★10393]
Lib. Users of Am. [10370], c/o Amer. Coun. of the Blind, 1155 15th St. NW, Ste. 1004, Washington, DC 20005, (202)467-5081
Libya Amateur Athletic Fed. [IO], Tripoli, Libyan Arab Jamahiriya
Libyan
  Soc. for Libyan Stud. [IO]
Libyan Arab Tennis and Squash Fed. [IO], Tripoli, Libyan Arab Jamahiriya
Libyan Fed. of Sports for Disabled [IO], Tripoli, Libyan Arab Jamahiriya
Libyan Sailing Fed. [IO], Tripoli, Libyan Arab Jamahiriya
Libyan Taekwondo Fed. [IO], Tripoli, Libyan Arab Jamahiriya
Lice
  Natl. Pediculosis Assn. [16247]
License Plate Collectors Assn; Auto. [21587]
License Plate Collectors Club; Key Chain Tag and Mini [★22011]
License Plate Collectors Club; License Plate Key Chain and Mini [★22011]
License Plate Key Chain and Mini License Plate Collectors Club [★22011]
Licensed Agencies for Relief in Asia - Defunct.
Licensed Beverage Assn; Natl. [★193]
Licensed Beverage Indus. [★199]
Licensed Beverage Information Coun. - Defunct.
Licensed Merchandisers' Assn. [★5849]
Licensed Merchandisers' Assn; Intl. [★5849]
Licensed Practical Nurses Assn; Amer. [15450]
Licensed Practical Nurses; Natl. Assn. of [★8869]
Licensed Practical Nurses; Natl. Fed. of [15509]
Licensed Taxi Drivers Assn. [IO], London, United Kingdom
Licensed Vintners' Assn. [IO], Dublin, Ireland
Licensee Assn; Avis [3380]
Licensees; Amer. Beverage [193]
Licensing
  Accreditation Coun. on Optometric Educ. [15710]
  Amer. Acad. of Optometry [15711]
  Amer. Bd. of Opticianry [15704]
  Amer. Optometric Assn. [15712]
  Amer. Optometric Found. [15713]
  Amer. Optometric Student Assn. [15714]
  Assn. of Commercial Stock Image Licensors [1378]
  Assn. of Real Estate License Law Officials [6243]
  Assn. of Regulatory Boards of Optometry [15716]
  Assn. of Schools and Colleges of Optometry [15717]
  Assn. of Univ. Tech. Managers [5838]
  Auto. License Plate Collectors Assn. [21587]
  Coll. of Optometrists in Vision Development [15718]
  Coun. on Licensure, Enforcement and Regulation [6271]
  Disabled Veterans Keychain Tag and Chaffeur's Badge Collectors Newsl. [22011]
  Fed. for Accessible Nursing Educ. and Licensure [15478]
  Intl. Assn. of Optometric Executives [15720]
  Intl. Conf. of Funeral Ser. Examining Boards of the U.S. [6120]
  Intl. Intellectual Property Assn. [5848]

Intl. Licensing Indus. Merchandisers' Assn. [5849]
Intl. Soc. of Animal License Collectors [22058]
Natl. Acad. of Opticianry [15707]
Natl. Assn. for Alternative Certification [8360]
Natl. Assn. of Optometrists and Opticians [15721]
Natl. Assn. for Regulatory Admin. [15011]
Natl. Assn. of State Contractors Licensing Agencies [1040]
Natl. Bd. of Examiners in Optometry [15722]
Natl. Coun. of State Boards of Nursing [15508]
Natl. Optometric Assn. [15725]
Natl. Org. of Alternative Programs [16382]
Natl. Org. for Competency Assurance [14591]
Opticians Assn. of Am. [15709]
Optometric Extension Prog. Found. [15727]
Optometric Historical Soc. [15728]
Pediatric Nursing Certification Bd. [15522]
Securities and Insurance Licensing Assn. [2236]
Women in Toys [3834]
Licensing Administrators; Assn. of Collegiate [★2630]
Licensing Assn; Intl. Collegiate [2630]
Licensing Boards; Fed. of Chiropractic [14000]
Licensing Executives Soc. [5853], 1800 Diagonal Rd., Ste. 280, Alexandria, VA 22314, (703)836-3106
Licensing Executives Soc. Andean Community [IO], Quito, Ecuador
Licensing Executives Soc. Arab Countries [IO], Amman, Jordan
Licensing Executives Soc. Argentina [IO], Buenos Aires, Argentina
Licensing Executives Soc. of Australia and New Zealand [IO], Pakenham Upper, Australia
Licensing Executives Soc. Austria [IO], Vienna, Austria
Licensing Executives Soc. Benelux [IO], Wijk bij Durstede, Netherlands
Licensing Executives Soc. Brazil [IO], Rio de Janeiro, Brazil
Licensing Executives Soc. - Britain and Ireland [IO], Glasgow, United Kingdom
Licensing Executives Soc. China [IO], Beijing, People's Republic of China
Licensing Executives Soc. Croatia [IO], Zagreb, Croatia
Licensing Executives Soc. France [IO], Lille, France
Licensing Executives Soc. Germany [IO], Hamburg, Germany
Licensing Executives Soc. Hungary [IO], Budapest, Hungary
Licensing Executives Soc. India [IO], New Delhi, India
Licensing Executives Soc. Israel [IO], Tel Aviv, Israel
Licensing Executives Soc. Italy [IO], Milan, Italy
Licensing Executives Soc. Japan [IO], Tokyo, Japan
Licensing Executives Soc. Korea [IO], Seoul, Republic of Korea
Licensing Executives Soc. Malaysia [IO], Kuala Lumpur, Malaysia
Licensing Executives Soc. Mexico [IO], Mexico City, Mexico
Licensing Executives Soc. Philippines [IO], Makati City, Philippines
Licensing Executives Soc. Poland [IO], Warsaw, Poland
Licensing Executives Soc. Russia [IO], Moscow, Russia
Licensing Executives Soc. Scandinavia [IO], Arhus, Denmark
Licensing Executives Soc. Singapore [IO], Singapore, Singapore
Licensing Executives Soc. South Africa [IO], Killarney, Republic of South Africa
Licensing Executives Soc. Switzerland [IO], Zurich, Switzerland
Licensing Indus. Assn. [★IO]
Licensing Indus. Assn. [★5849]
Licensure and Certification Directors; Assn. of Hea. Fac. [★6210]
Licensure, Enforcement and Regulation; Coun. on [6271]
Licensure, Enforcement, and Regulation; Natl. CH on [★6271]
Licensure; Fed. for Accessible Nursing Educ. and [15478]

Licentiate Ministers and Certified Mediums Soc. [20450], c/o Rev. Janet Tisdale, NST, Sec., 9106 W Willow Haven Ct., Sun City, AZ 85351, (805)965-4474
Lichenological Soc; Amer. Bryological and [6621]
LICU [1111], 1 Credit Union Plz., 24 McKinley Ave., Endicott, NY 13760, (607)754-7900
; LICU [1111]
Lido 14 Intl. Class Assn. [23198], PO Box 1252, Newport Beach, CA 92663, (714)437-1370
Liechtenstein Bankers Assn. [IO], Vaduz, Liechtenstein
Liechtenstein Floorball Assn. [IO], Schaan, Liechtenstein
Liechtenstein Investment Fund Assn. [IO], Vaduz, Liechtenstein
Liechtenstein Squash Rackets Assn. [IO], Vaduz, Liechtenstein
Liechtenstein Unihockey Verband [★IO]
Liechtensteiner Tanzsportverband [IO], Schaan, Liechtenstein
Liechtensteiner Tennisverband [IO], Triesen, Liechtenstein
Liechtensteinischer Anlagefondsverband [★IO]
Liechtensteinischer Bankenverband [★IO]
Liechtensteinischer Hangegleiter Verband [IO], Triesenberg, Liechtenstein
Liederkranz Found. [10640], 6 E 87th St., New York, NY 10128, (212)534-0880
Lietuviu Tautininku Sajunga [★IO]
Lietuvos tautinis olimpinis komitetas [★IO]
Lietuvos bibliotekininku draugija [★IO]
Lietuvos Aeroklubas [★IO]
Lietuvos Aprangos ir Tekstiles Imoniu Asociacija [★IO]
Lietuvos Banku Asociacija [★IO]
Lietuvos Beisbolo Asociacija [★IO]
Lietuvos Biblijos Draugija [★IO]
Lietuvos Buriuotoju Sajunga [★IO]
Lietuvos Darbo Federacija [★IO]
Lietuvos Energetikos Institutas [★IO]
Lietuvos Fiziku Draugija [★IO]
Lietuvos Gydytoju Sajunga [★IO]
Lietuvos Kompiuterininku Sajunga [★IO]
Lietuvos Kompozitoriu Sajunga [★IO]
Lietuvos Laivu Statytoju ir Remontininku Asociacija [★IO]
Lietuvos Lengvosios Atletikos Federacija [★IO]
Lietuvos Mesiniu Galviju Augintoju ir Gerintoju Asociacija [★IO]
Lietuvos Mokslu Akademija [★IO]
Lietuvos Mokytoju Profesine Sajunga [★IO]
Lietuvos Nekilnojamojo Turto Pletros Asociacija [★IO]
Lietuvos Orientavimosi Sporto Federacija [★IO]
Lietuvos Pakuotoju Asociacija [★IO]
Lietuvos Pramoninku Konfederacija [★IO]
Lietuvos prekybos, pramones ir amatu rumu asociacija [★IO]
Lietuvos Projektavimo Imoniu Asociacija [★IO]
Lietuvos Radijo Megeju Draugija [★IO]
Lietuvos Sirdies Asociacija [★IO]
Lietuvos Sportiniu Sokiu Federacija [★IO]
Lietuvos Taekwondo Federija [★IO]
Lietuvos Teniso Sajunga [★IO]
Lietuvos Universitetu Moteru Asociacija [IO], Kaunas, Lithuania
Lietuvos Vejo Energetiku Asociacija [★IO]
Lietuvos Zaliuju Judejimas [★IO]
Lietuvos Zemes Ukio Inzinieriu Asociacija [★IO]
Lietvus Respublikos Odontologu Rumai [★IO]
Lieutenant Governors Assn; Natl. [6285]
Lieutenant Governors; Natl. Conf. of [★6285]
LIFE [20060], PO Box 353, New York, NY 10185, (212)768-2366
LIFE [IO], Leamington Spa, United Kingdom
Life Acad. [IO], Guildford, United Kingdom
Life Action League; Pro- [18565]
Life Action Ministries [★20020]
Life Action Revival Ministries [20020], PO Box 31, Buchanan, MI 49107-0031, (269)697-8600
Life After Assault League [13363], 1336 W Lindbergh St., Appleton, WI 54914, (920)739-4489
Life After Divorce Is Eventually Sane - Address unknown since 1994.

A star before a book entry number signifies that the name is not listed separately, but is mentioned within the entry.

Life After Exoneration Prog. **[17360]**, PO Box 10208, Berkeley, CA 94709, (510)292-6010
Life Agency Officers; Assn. of **[★2195]**
Life Alliance of Gays and Lesbians; Pro- **[12927]**
Life Amendment; Natl. Comm. for a Human **[18557]**
Life Amendment Political Action Comm. - Defunct.
Life of Am; Democrats for **[18549]**
Life of Am; Feminists for **[18552]**
Life; Amer. Collegians for **[★12928]**
Life; Americans United for **[12904]**
Life Assn; Amer. Mutual **[19368]**
Life Assn; Western Fraternal **[19030]**
Life Assurance Soc; Catholic Family Protective **[★18993]**
Life Assurance Soc; North Amer. Union **[★19010]**
Life Assurance of Trinidad and Tobago **[★IO]**
Life; Baptists for **[12907]**
Life; Black Americans for **[12909]**
Life Brokerage Agencies; Natl. Assn. of Independent **[2211]**
Life; Care for **[★11981]**
Life; Catholics United for **[12910]**
Life Center; Natl. **[12922]**
Life Coalition Intl. **[12919]**, PO Box 360221, Melbourne, FL 32936-0221, (321)726-0444
Life Coalition Intl. **[IO]**, Melbourne, FL, United States
Life; Collegians Activated to Liberate **[12911]**
Life Comm; Natl. Right to **[12923]**
Life Decisions Intl. **[12920]**, PO Box 75161, Washington, DC 20013-0161, (540)631-0380
Life Decisions Intl. **[IO]**, Washington, DC, United States
Life; Dentists for **[18550]**
Life Educ. and Res. Trust; Amer. **[★12902]**
Life and Env; Center for Respect of **[4620]**
Life; Eternal **[18551]**
Life Extension Found; Alcor **[14072]**
Life Extension Soc. **[14074]**, 990 N Powhatan St., Arlington, VA 22205, (202)483-1760
Life Found; Holistic **[★12345]**
Life Found; Human **[12914]**
Life Fund; March for **[18556]**
Life and Hea. Insurance Guaranty Associations; Natl. Org. of **[1852]**
Life History Stud. Center **[★11261]**
Life and Human Sciences; Assn. for Commun. Excellence in Agriculture, Natural Resources, and **[4098]**
Life Insurance Adjustment Bur. - Defunct.
Life Insurance Agency Mgt. Assn. **[★2195]**
Life Insurance Agency Mgt. Assn. **[★IO]**
Life Insurance of Am; Fed. **[19123]**
Life Insurance Assn. of Japan **[IO]**, Tokyo, Japan
Life Insurance Assn; Korea **[IO]**
Life Insurance Assn. - Singapore **[IO]**, Singapore, Singapore
Life Insurance Cashiers' and Office Managers Assn. of the U.S. and Canada - Address unknown since 1995.
Life Insurance; Catholic Family **[18993]**
Life Insurance Comm. for Social Responsibility - Address unknown since 2006.
Life Insurance Counsel; Assn. of **[5826]**
Life Insurance Marketing and Res. Assn. **[★2195]**
Life Insurance Marketing and Res. Assn. **[★IO]**
Life Insurance Marketing and Res. Assn. **[★IO]**
Life Insurance Medical Res. Fund - Defunct.
Life Insurance Sales Res. Bur. **[★2195]**
Life Insurance Sales Res. Bur. **[★IO]**
Life Insurance Settlement Assn. **[2193]**, 1011 E Colonial Dr., Ste. 500, Orlando, FL 32803, (407)894-3797
Life Insurance Soc. of America - Defunct.
Life Insurance Soc; Gleaner **[19124]**
Life Insurance Soc; Luso-American **[19131]**
Life Insurance Soc; United Natl. **[★19131]**
Life Insurance Soc; Woman's **[19145]**
Life Insurance Soc; Woodmen of the World/Omaha Woodmen **[19441]**
Life Insurance Union; Catholic **[18996]**
Life Insurers; Amer. Coun. of **[2135]**
Life Insurers Coun. **[2194]**, 2300 Windy Ridge Pkwy., Ste. 600, Atlanta, GA 30339-8443, (770)951-1770
Life Intl; Champions for **[19996]**

Life Issues in Formal Education - Defunct.
Life League; Amer. **[12902]**
Life; Libertarians for **[18017]**
Life and Liberty for Women **[11222]**, PO Box 271778, Fort Collins, CO 80527-1778, (970)416-6872
Life; Lutherans For **[12921]**
Life Ministries; Alliance for **[19760]**
Life; Natl. Fed. of Officers for **[18559]**
Life; Natl. Teens for **[12924]**
Life Obstetricians and Gynecologists; Amer. Assn. of Pro **[18545]**
Life Off. Assn. of New Zealand **[★IO]**
Life Off. Mgt. Assn. **[★IO]**
Life Off. Mgt. Assn. **[★2196]**
Life Outreach Intl. **[20021]**, PO Box 982000, Fort Worth, TX 76182-8000, (817)267-4211
Life Pediatricians; Amer. Assn. of Pro- **[18546]**
Life; People for **[12925]**
Life; Pharmacists for **[★18563]**
Life; Prayers for **[19907]**
Life; Presbyterians Pro- **[12926]**
Life; Priests for **[18564]**
Life Raft Gp. **[13838]**, 40 Galesi Dr., Wayne, NJ 07470, (973)837-9092
Life for Relief and Development **[12867]**, 17300 W 10 Mile Rd., Southfield, MI 48075, (248)424-7493
Life for Relief and Development **[IO]**, Southfield, MI, United States
Life, Reproduction and Rhythm; Natl. Commn. on Human **[16008]**
Life; Republican Natl. Coalition for **[18566]**
Life Res. Inst. **[14572]**, 4279 Armand Dr., Concord, CA 94521
Life Resources Inst. **[14829]**, 116 High St., Ashland, OR 97520, (541)482-1289
Life Saving Assn. of Am; Natl. Surf **[★12894]**
Life Sci. Systems Association; Analytical **[★3488]**
Life Sciences; Assn. for Politics and the **[7522]**
Life Sciences; Coalition for Educ. in the **[9098]**
Life Sciences Inst; North Amer. Br. of Intl. **[★15561]**
Life Sciences Inst. - Nutrition Found; Intl. **[★15561]**
Life Sciences; Inst. of Soc., Ethics, and the **[★12125]**
Life Sciences; Soc. for Chaos Theory in Psychology and **[7547]**
Life Seed Found; Abundant **[4338]**
Life Services for the Handicapped **[★11941]**
Life Services; Intl. **[12916]**
Life Sharing Found. - Address unknown since 2004.
Life; Sisters of **[20480]**
Life Skills/National Inst. of Relationship Enhancement; Inst. for the Development of Emotional and **[15201]**
Life Threatening Illness and Loss (Division of Found. of Thanatology); Amer. Inst. of **[11908]**
Life Understanding Found. **[20484]**
Life Underwriter Training Coun. **[8576]**, 7625 Wisconsin Ave., Bethesda, MD 20814, (610)526-1000
Life Underwriters Assn; Home Off. **[★2148]**
Life Underwriters Assn. of Hong Kong **[IO]**, Hong Kong, People's Republic of China
Life Underwriters Conf. of the Natl. Assn. of Life Underwriters; Women **[★2247]**
Life Underwriting; Academy **[★2148]**
Life Underwriting; Academy **[★IO]**
Life Underwriting; Assn. for Advanced **[2144]**
Life; U.S. Coalition for **[12929]**
LifeBanc **[14290]**, 20600 Chagrin Blvd., Ste. 350, Cleveland, OH 44122, (216)752-5433
Lifeboat Found. **[18668]**, 1638 Esmeralda Ave., Minden, NV 89423, (775)972-0180
Lifeforce Found. **[IO]**, Vancouver, BC, Canada
Lifegain Inst. **[14573]**, 151 Dunder Rd., Burlington, VT 05401, (802)862-8855
Lifeline Found. - Defunct.
Lifelong Establishment of Paternity; Org. for the **[11714]**
Lifelong Fitness Alliance **[23920]**, 658 Bair Island Rd., Ste. 200, Redwood City, CA 94063, (650)361-8282
Lifesaver; Oper. **[12983]**
Lifesaving
  Alcor Life Extension Found. **[14072]**

Amer. Cryonics Soc. **[14073]**
Australian Resuscitation Coun. **[IO]**
Carnegie Hero Fund Commn. **[13036]**
Cryonics Inst. **[1120]**
Intl. Assn. of Dive Rescue Specialists **[23574]**
Intl. Assn. of Dive Rescue Specialists **[IO]**
Intl. Life Saving Fed. **[IO]**
Oper. Lifesaver **[12983]**
Royal Life Saving Soc. **[IO]**
Royal Life Saving Soc. Australia **[IO]**
Surf Life Saving Assn. of Great Britain **[IO]**
Surf Life Saving Australia **[IO]**
Swiss Lifesaving Assn. **[IO]**
Lifesaving Assn; U.S. **[12894]**
Lifesaving Emergency Response Team; Amer. **[★12894]**
Lifespan Resources **[11294]**, PO Box 995, New Albany, IN 47151-0995, (812)948-8330
Lifespire **[12572]**, Empire State Bldg., 350 5th Ave., Ste. 301, New York, NY 10118, (212)741-0100
Lifestyles Org. **[13095]**, 2641 W La Palma Ave., Ste. F, Anaheim, CA 92801, (714)821-9953
Lifetime Sports Found. - Defunct.
LifeWind Intl. **[20284]**, PO Box 576645, Modesto, CA 95357-6645, (209)524-0600
LifeWorks Inst. **[12551]**, 33 Creekside Dr., Wimberley, TX 78676, (512)423-5638
Lift and Escalator Indus. Assn. **[IO]**, London, United Kingdom
Lift Mfrs. Prdt. Sect. - Material Handling Indus. of Am. **[2034]**, 8720 Red Oak Blvd., Ste. 201, Charlotte, NC 28217-3996, (704)676-1190
Lifters Sect. of the Material Handling Inst; Below/Hook **[★2042]**
Lifters; World Assn. of Benchers and Dead **[23986]**
Lifting Equip. Engineers Assn. **[IO]**, Huntingdon, United Kingdom
Liga Argentina Contra la Epilepsia **[★IO]**
Liga Asociatiilor de Proprietari - Habitat **[★IO]**
Liga Brasileira de Epilepsia **[★IO]**
Liga Colombiana Contra la Epilepsia **[★IO]**
Liga Colombiana de Lucha contra la Osteoporosis **[IO]**, Bogota, Colombia
Liga Espanola Contra La Epilepsia **[★IO]**
Liga Internacional de Mujeres pro Paz y Libertad - Costa Rica **[★IO]**
Liga Intl. **[IO]**, Rialto, CA, United States
Liga Intl. **[12528]**, 1464 N Fitzgerald Hangar 2, Rialto, CA 92376, (909)875-6300
Liga Medicorum Homeopathica Internationalis **[★IO]**
Liga Portuguesa Contra as Doencas Reumaticas **[IO]**, Lisbon, Portugal
Liga Portuguesa Contra a Epilepsia **[★IO]**
Liga Portuguesa contra a Hipertensao **[★IO]**
Liga Reumatologica Espanola **[IO]**, Madrid, Spain
Liga Uruguaya Contra La Epilepsia **[★IO]**
Ligand Assay Soc; Clinical **[14995]**
Ligeia Assn. pour le Renouvellement de la Culture Artistique Europeenne **[IO]**, Paris, France
Light Aircraft Mfrs. Assn. - Address unknown since 2002.
Light; Art Inst. of **[9425]**
Light of Cambodian Children **[11617]**, 181 Market St., Lowell, MA 01852
Light Commercial Vehicle Assn. - Defunct.
Light of Divine Truth Found. - Address unknown since 1995.
Light Gardening Soc. of Am; Indoor **[★22519]**
Light Intl; Gospel **[★20342]**
Light Living Library **[23272]**
Light Machinery Info. Center of Central New York; Japan **[24343]**
Light Music Soc. **[IO]**, Clitheroe, United Kingdom
Light to the Nations **[IO]**, Jerusalem, Israel
Light Rail Transit Assn. **[IO]**, Walsall, United Kingdom
Light Truck Accessory Alliance **[390]**, c/o Specialty Equip. Market Assn., PO Box 4910, Diamond Bar, CA 91765, (909)396-0289
Light on Yoga Italia **[IO]**, Florence, Italy
Light of Yoga Soc. **[★11216]**
Lighter Assn. **[1826]**, 1700 Pennsylvania Ave. NW, Ste. 400, Washington, DC 20036, (202)349-4190
Lighter Collectors' Intl. Soc. - Defunct.
Lighter Collectors; On the Lighter Side, Intl. **[22100]**

Reference to "IO" in place of a book number signifies that the association may be found in the 45th edition of International Organizations.

Lighter-Than-Air Soc. [21460], 526 S Main St., Ste. 232, Akron, OH 44311, (330)535-5827
Lighter-Than-Air Soc. [IO], Akron, OH, United States
LightHawk [4418], PO Box 653, Lander, WY 82520, (307)332-3242
Lighthouse Intl. [16865], 111 E 59th St., New York, NY 10022-1202, (212)821-9200
Lighthouse Intl. [IO], New York, NY, United States
Lighthouse Intl. - Japan [IO], Saitama, Japan
Lighthouse Keepers Assn. [★10030]
Lighthouse Keepers Assn; Great Lakes [10030]
Lighthouse Soc; U.S. [10073]
Lighthouse Study Unit - Defunct.
Lighting
   Aladdin Knights of the Mystic Light [22617]
   Amer. Lighting Assn. [2431]
   Art Inst. of Light [9425]
   Assn. of Lighting and Mercury Recyclers [5168]
   Australasian Lighting Indus. Assn. [IO]
   China Assn. of the Lighting Indus. [IO]
   Fairy Lamp Club [22019]
   Golden Glow of Christmas Past [22975]
   Illuminating Engg. Soc. of North Am. [7250]
   Institution of Lighting Engineers [IO]
   Intl. Assn. of Lighting Designers [2262]
   Intl. Assn. of Lighting Mgt. Companies [2432]
   Intl. Assn. of Lighting Mgt. Companies [IO]
   Intl. Coleman Collectors Club [22049]
   Intl. Commn. on Illumination [IO]
   Intl. Dark-Sky Assn. [6506]
   Intl. Guild of Lamp Researchers [22618]
   Intl. Soc. for Bioluminescence and Chemiluminescence [7612]
   Lighting Controls Assn. [2433]
   Lighting Res. Off. [7251]
   Magic Lantern Soc. of the U.S. and Canada [21531]
   Natl. Assn. of Independent Lighting Distributors [2434]
   Natl. Candle Assn. [2268]
   Natl. Coun. on Qualifications for the Lighting Professions [2435]
   Natl. Illumination Comm. of Great Britain [IO]
   Natl. Lighting Bur. [IO]
   Natl. Lighting Bur. [2436]
   Professional Lighting and Sound Assn. [IO]
   Rushlight Club [10396]
   Set Decorators Soc. of Am. [2276]
   Suppliers Assn. for Professional Audio, Video and Lighting Equip. in Sweden [IO]
   U.S. Natl. Comm. of the Intl. Commn. on Illumination [7252]
Lighting Assn. [IO], Telford, United Kingdom
Lighting Assn; Amer. Home [★2431]
Lighting Controls Assn. [2433], c/o NEMA, 1300 N 17th St., Ste. 1847, Rosslyn, VA 22209, (703)841-3226
Lighting-Electrical Materials Distributors Assn. - Address unknown since 2002.
Lighting Indus. Fed. [IO], London, United Kingdom
Lighting Res. Inst. [★7251]
Lighting Res. Off. [7251], c/o Philip F. Keebler, Proj. Mgr., Elec. Power Res. Inst., 942 Corridor Park Blvd., Knoxville, TN 37932, (865)218-8015
Lighting Union [IO], Paris, France
Lightmongers' Company [IO], London, United Kingdom
Lightning Protection Assn; United [3461]
Lightning Protection Inst. [3446], PO Box 99, Maryville, MO 64468, (804)314-8955
Lightning Rod Mfrs. Assn. - Defunct.
Lightning Strike and Elec. Shock Survivors Intl. [14304], PO Box 1156, Jacksonville, NC 28541-1156, (910)346-4708
Lightning Strike and Elec. Shock Survivors Intl. [IO], Jacksonville, NC, United States
Lightning Strike and Elec. Shock Victims [★IO]
Lightning Strike and Elec. Shock Victims [★14304]
Lightweight Aggregate Producers Assn. - Address unknown since 1989.
Lignin Inst. [1650], 5775 Peachtree-Dunwoody Rd., Bldg. G, Ste. 500, Atlanta, GA 30342, (404)252-3663
Lignin Inst. [IO], Atlanta, GA, United States
Ligue des Associations Sportives Estudiantes Luxembourgeoises [IO], Strassen, Luxembourg

Ligue pour le bien-etre de l'enfance du Canada [★IO]
Ligue des Cadets de l'Air du Canada [★IO]
Ligue des Cadets de l'Armee du Canada [★IO]
Ligue Canadienne des Compositeurs [★IO]
Ligue Cardiologique Belge [★IO]
Ligue Europeene de Cooperation Economique [★IO]
Ligue Europeenne Contre le Rhumatisme [★IO]
Ligue Francaise contre la Sclerose En Plaques [IO], Paris, France
Ligue Huntington Francophone Belge [IO], Liege, Belgium
Ligue Internationale du Droit de la Concurrence [★IO]
Ligue Internationale de Femmes pour la Paix et la Liberte [★IO]
Ligue Internationale de Femmes pour la Paix et la Liberte [★IO]
Ligue La Leche [★IO]
Ligue pour la Lecture de la Bible - Brazzaville [IO], Brazzaville, Republic of the Congo
Ligue pour la Lecture de la Bible - Burkina Faso [IO], Ouagadougou, Burkina Faso
Ligue pour la Lecture de la Bible Cameroun [★IO]
Ligue pour la Lecture de la Bible - Central African Republic [IO], Bangui, Central African Republic
Ligue pour la Lecture de la Bible - Cote d'Ivoire [IO], Abidjan, Cote d'Ivoire
Ligue pour la Lecture de la Bible - Guinea [IO], Conakry, Guinea
Ligue pour la Lecture de la Bible - Madagascar [IO], Antananarivo, Madagascar
Ligue pour la Lecture de la Bible Togo [★IO]
Ligue canadienne contre l'epilepsie [★IO]
Ligue Monarchiste du Canada [★IO]
Ligue Nationale Belge de la Sclerose en Plaques [IO], Brussels, Belgium
Ligue des Pays du Commonwealth [★IO]
Ligue Trotskyste du Canada [★IO]
Likud-Herut U.S.A. - Address unknown since 1995.
Lilac Rabbit Club of Am; Natl. [5153]
Lilac Soc; Intl. [22522]
Lillard Family Assn. [20978]
Lilliputian Bottle Club - Defunct.
Lily Soc; Intl. Water [★22524]
Lily Soc; North Amer. [22534]
Lily and Water Gardening Soc; Intl. Water [22524]
Lima Bean Advisory Bd. - Defunct.
Lima Chamber of Commerce [IO], Lima, Peru
Limb Mfrs. of Am; Assn. of [★1855]
Limb Mfrs. Assn; Orthopedic Appliance and [★1855]
Limbless Assn. [IO], London, United Kingdom
Lime Assn; Natl. [816]
Lime, Gypsum, and Allied Workers Div; Cement, [24038]
Limerick Chamber of Commerce [IO], Limerick, Ireland
Limestone Assn; Pulverized [★3699]
Limestone Inst. of Am; Indiana [3694]
Limestone Inst; Natl. [★3699]
Limestone; Natl. Assn. for Indiana [★3694]
Limitation Comm; Natl. Tax- [18713]
Limited Edition Dealers; Natl. Assn. of [862]
Limnology and Oceanography; Amer. Soc. of [7393]
Limnology Soc. of Am. [★7393]
Limnology Soc. of Am. [★IO]
Limousin Found; North Amer. [4279]
Limousin Junior Assn; North Amer. [4280]
Limousine Assn; Natl. [3880]
Limousine Indus. Mfrs. Org. [391], 3603 Fredericksbury Rd., San Antonio, TX 78201, (210)732-5466
Limousine and Paratransit Assn; Taxicab, [3894]
LIMRA Europe [IO], Watford, United Kingdom
LIMRA Intl. [IO], Windsor, CT, United States
LIMRA Intl. [2195], 300 Day Hill Rd., Windsor, CT 06095, (860)688-3358
Linceorum Academia [★IO]
Lincoln
   Abraham Lincoln Assn. [11100]
   Abraham Lincoln Natl. Cemetery Support Comm. [21160]
   Ford's Theatre Soc. [11015]
   Friends of the Abraham Lincoln Museum [11113]
   Lincoln and Continental Owners Club [21687]
   Lincoln Owners' Club [21688]

   Road Race Lincoln Register [21773]
   Soc. of Lincoln Cent Collectors [22756]
   Surratt Soc. [10067]
Lincoln Assn; Abraham [11100]
Lincoln Brigade; Veterans of the Abraham [21269]
Lincoln Cent Collectors; Soc. of [22756]
Lincoln Centennial Assn. [★11100]
Lincoln Civil War Coun; Natl. [★11113]
Lincoln Continental Owners Club [★21687]
Lincoln and Continental Owners Club [21687], PO Box 1715, Maple Grove, MN 55311-6715, (763)420-7829
Lincoln Cosmopolitan Owners Registry - Defunct.
Lincoln Educational Found. - Defunct.
Lincoln Heritage Trail Found. [23943]
Lincoln Highway Assn. [10043], PO Box 308, Franklin Grove, IL 61031, (815)456-3030
Lincoln Inst. of Land Policy [5920], 113 Brattle St., Cambridge, MA 02138, (617)661-3016
Lincoln Inst. for Res. and Educ. [16940], PO Box 254, Great Falls, VA 22066, (703)759-4278
Lincoln, Mercury Minority Dealers Assn; Ford, [★413]
Lincoln Museum; Friends of the Abraham [11113]
Lincoln Natl. Cemetery Support Comm; Abraham [21160]
Lincoln Owners' Club [21688], c/o Reuben Taylor, Membership Chm., 699 Revere Rd., Glen Ellyn, IL 60137, (630)469-1447
Lincoln Register; Road Race [21773]
Lincoln Registry; Fifty-Six Fifty-Seven [★21773]
Lincoln Republican Coun. - Defunct.
Lincoln Sheep Breeders' Assn; Natl. [5207]
Lincoln Soc. of Philately - Defunct.
Lincoln Univ. Alumni Assn. [18906], Lincoln Univ., Memorial Hall, 818 Chestnut St., Jefferson City, MO 65102-0029, (573)681-5572
Lincoln Zephyr Owner's Club [21689], c/o Shirley Hopkins, Membership Dir., PO Box 733, Loleta, CA 95551-0733, (707)768-1938
Lincoln Zephyr Owner's Club [IO], Loleta, CA, United States
Lincolnshire Chamber of Commerce and Indus. [IO], Lincoln, United Kingdom
Linda Davis Fan Club [24939], c/o Linda Davis, Inc., PO Box 767, Hermitage, TN 37076
Linda Gray's Official Fan Club [24753], PO Box 5064, Sherman Oaks, CA 91403
Lindbergh Found; Charles A. and Anne Morrow [4539]
Lindbergh Fund; Charles A. [★4539]
Lindbergh Kidnapping Network - Address unknown since 2002.
Lindbergh Memorial Fund [★4539]
Lindenwald; Friends of [10027]
Lindesmith Center [★17112]
Lindesmith Center - Defunct.
Lindsay Assn; Vachel [9718]
Lindsay Wagner's Official Fan Club [24754], PO Box 5002, Sherman Oaks, CA 91403
Line Dance Assn. of Australia [IO], Baulkham Hills, Australia
Line Dance Soc. Singapore [IO], Singapore, Singapore
Linen College; American Laundry and [★2401]
Linen and Lace Paper Inst. [★1157]
Linen Mgt; Natl. Assn. of Institutional [★2401]
Linen Supply Assn. of Am. [★3386]
Linen Trade Assn. - Defunct.
Liner Operators/Trans-Pacific Amer. Flag Berth Operators; Trans-Atlantic Amer. Flag [3592]
Lineweaver Found; Danny [★12959]
Lingerie Indus. Coun. [★221]
Linguistic Assn. of Canada and the U.S. [10405], c/o Lilly Lee Chen, Sec.-Treas., Rice Univ., Center for the Stud. of Languages, MS 36, Houston, TX 77251-1892, (713)348-2820
Linguistic Assn. of Canada and the U.S. [IO], Houston, TX, United States
Linguistic Assn. of Finland [IO], Helsinki, Finland
Linguistic Data Consortium [IO], Philadelphia, PA, United States
Linguistic Data Consortium [2437], 3600 Market St., Ste. 810, Philadelphia, PA 19104-2653, (215)898-0464

A star before a book entry number signifies that the name is not listed separately, but is mentioned within the entry.

Linguistic Institute [★10406]
Linguistic Institute [★IO]
Linguistic and Other Minorities; Intl. Fed. for the Protection of the Rights of Ethnic, Religious, [17768]
Linguistic Programming; Intl. Assn. for Neuro- [★16219]
Linguistic Programming; Intl. Assn. of Neuro- [★16219]
Linguistic Programming; Intl. Assn. of Neuro- [★16219]
Linguistic Programming; North Amer. Assn. of Neuro- [★16219]
Linguistic Soc. of Am. [10406], 1325 18th St. NW, Ste. 211, Washington, DC 20036-6501, (202)835-1714
Linguistic Soc. of Am. [IO], Washington, DC, United States
Linguistic Soc. of Europe [IO], Vienna, Austria
Linguistic Soc. of Hong Kong [IO], Hong Kong, People's Republic of China
Linguistic Soc. of New Zealand [IO], Christchurch, New Zealand
Linguistic Soc. of Southern Africa [IO], Bloemfontein, Republic of South Africa
Linguistics
Amer. Assn. for Applied Linguistics [10397]
Amer. Assn. of Language Specialists [3852]
Amer. Cryptogram Assn. [22178]
Amer. Dialect Soc. [10398]
Amer. Hyperlexia Assn. [13940]
Amer. Name Soc. [10764]
Amer. Soc. of Geolinguistics [10399]
Amer. Soc. of Geolinguistics [IO]
Amer. Translators Assn. [3853]
Anthropology Film Center [6407]
Applied Linguistics Assn. of New Zealand [IO]
Assn. for Computational Linguistics [IO]
Assn. for Computational Linguistics [10400]
Assn. for Linguistic Typology [IO]
Australian Linguistic Soc. [IO]
British Assn. of Academic Phoneticians [IO]
British Assn. for Applied Linguistics [IO]
Canadian Linguistic Assn. [IO]
Center for Applied Linguistics [10401]
Chartered Inst. of Linguists [IO]
Coun. of Teachers of Southeast Asian Languages [7990]
Elvish Linguistic Fellowship [10402]
Elvish Linguistic Fellowship [IO]
Epigraphic Soc. [6445]
ERIC CH on Languages and Linguistics [8730]
Generative Linguistics in the Old World [IO]
German Soc. for Linguistics [IO]
Gp. of Universities for the Advancement of Vietnamese Abroad [9296]
Hong Kong Assn. for Applied Linguistics [IO]
Intl. Assn. of Applied Linguistics [IO]
Intl. Clinical Phonetics and Linguistics Assn. [IO]
Intl. Clinical Phonetics and Linguistics Assn. [10403]
Intl. Inst. of Iberoamerican Literature [10425]
Intl. Maledicta Soc. [10404]
Intl. Maledicta Soc. [IO]
Intl. Quantitative Linguistics Assn. [IO]
Intl. Soc. for Humor Stud. [10210]
Intl. Soc. for Language Stud. [10302]
Intl. Soc. of Phonetic Sciences [IO]
Linguistic Assn. of Canada and the U.S. [IO]
Linguistic Assn. of Canada and the U.S. [10405]
Linguistic Assn. of Finland [IO]
Linguistic Data Consortium [IO]
Linguistic Data Consortium [2437]
Linguistic Soc. of Am. [10406]
Linguistic Soc. of Am. [IO]
Linguistic Soc. of Europe [IO]
Linguistic Soc. of Hong Kong [IO]
Linguistic Soc. of New Zealand [IO]
Linguistic Soc. of Southern Africa [IO]
Linguistics Assn. of Great Britain [IO]
Logical Language Gp. [10304]
Mend Our Tongues Soc. [10407]
Natl. Alliance to Save Native Languages [10305]
North Amer. Chap. of the Assn. for Computational Linguistics [10408]

North Amer. Chap. of the Assn. for Computational Linguistics [IO]
Philological Soc. [IO]
Poetics and Linguistics Assn. [IO]
Soc. for Caribbean Linguistics [IO]
Soc. for Linguistic Anthropology [6433]
Soc. of Neuro-Linguistic Programming [15012]
Society of Neuro-Linguistic Programming [IO]
Union Mundial pro Interlingua [IO]
Wycliffe Bible Translators [19531]
Linguistics Assn. of Great Britain [IO], London, United Kingdom
Linguistics; Assn. for Machine Translation and Computational [★10400]
Linguistics; ERIC CH on Languages and [8730]
Link Fence Manufacturers Inst; Chain [1362]
Link Found. [7765], c/o Binghamton Univ. Found., PO Box 6005, Binghamton, NY 13902-6005
Links [13049], 1200 Massachusetts Ave. NW, Washington, DC 20005-4501, (202)842-8686
The Linkup - Survivors of Clergy Abuse [11522], PO Box 429, Pewee Valley, KY 40056-0429, (502)241-5544
Linnean Soc. of London [IO], London, United Kingdom
Linograph Soc. - Defunct.
Linseed Assn. of New York - Defunct.
Linseed Castor Seed Assn. of New York [★2852]
Linseed Castor Seed Assn. of New York [★IO]
Linus Pauling Inst. of Science and Medicine - Defunct.
Linux Consortium; Embedded [6726]
Lion Found; Mountain [5341]
Lion Preservation Found; Mountain [★5341]
Lionel Collectors Club of Am. [22633], c/o Richard H. Johnson, Pres., 8750 E Kemper Rd., Cincinnati, OH 45249-2506, (513)469-7774
Lionel Kids Club - Defunct.
Lionel Railroader Club [22634], 50625 Richard W Blvd., Chesterfield, MI 48051, (586)949-4100
Lions; Amer. Coun. of the Blind [16825]
Lions Blind Sports Found. - Address unknown since 1995.
Lions Clubs Intl. [13050], 300 W 22nd St., Oak Brook, IL 60523-8842, (630)571-5466
Lions Clubs Intl. [IO], Oak Brook, IL, United States
Lions Clubs; Intl. Assn. of [★13050]
Lions Intl. [★13050]
Lions Intl. [★IO]
Lions Philatelic Unit - Address unknown since 1999.
Lions-Quest [8199], PO Box 304, Annapolis Junction, MD 20701-0304, (630)571-5466
Lions-Quest Programs [★8199]
Lipid Nurse Task Force [★15523]
Lipizzan Assn. of Am. [★4911]
Lipizzan Assn. of Amer. [★4911]
Lipizzan Assn. of North Am. [4911], PO Box 1133, Anderson, IN 46015-1133
Lipizzan Club; Royal Intl. [★4911]
Lipizzan Registry; U.S. [4963]
Lipizzan Soc. of North Am. [★4911]
Lipo-Suction Surgery; Amer. Soc. of [16572]
Lippitt Morgan Breeders Assn. [4912], c/o Brenda Vincent, 6395W US Hwy. 2, Manistique, MI 49854, (906)341-6372
Liquefied Petroleum Gas Assn. [★1681]
Liquid Food Carton Mfrs. Assn. [★IO]
Liquid Terminals Assn; Independent [3977]
Liquified Petroleum Gas Indus. Tech. Assn. [★IO]
Liquor Administrators; Natl. Conf. of State [★5445]
Liquor Administrators; Natl. Conf. of State [5447]
Liquor, Hospitality and Miscellaneous Workers' Union [IO], Haymarket, Australia
Liquor Merchants Assn. of Australia [IO], Chatswood, Australia
Liquor Package Stores Assn; Natl. Retail [★193]
Liquor Stores Assn; Natl. [★193]
Lisa Madonia Memorial Fund - Address unknown since 2000.
Lisa Prog; Paul and [13082]
Lisbon Acad. of Sciences [IO], Lisbon, Portugal
Lisle Fellowship [★IO]
Lisle Fellowship [★8623]
Lisle Inc. [★8623]
Lisle Inc. [★IO]

Lisle Intercultural [IO], Leander, TX, United States
Lisle Intercultural [8623], 900 County Rd. 269, Leander, TX 78641, (800)477-1538
Lissencephaly Network [15336], c/o Dianna Fitzgerald, Pres., 10408 Bitterroot Ct., Fort Wayne, IN 46804, (260)432-4310
Lissencephaly Network [IO], Fort Wayne, IN, United States
Lissner Found; Gerda [10765]
Listen - Address unknown since 2007.
Listen to the Band - Address unknown since 1995.
Listeners Club; Amer. Shortwave [21495]
Listening and Mediation; Child Abuse [11565]
Listening Program - Defunct.
Listin Diario [IO], Santo Domingo, Dominican Republic
Liszt Soc; Amer. [9807]
LITA, Soc. of Authors [IO], Bratislava, Slovakia
Litchfield Inst. - Defunct.
Literacy
ABLE: Assn. for Better Living and Educ. Intl. [11756]
Action Coalition for Media Educ. [18026]
Alliance for a Media Literate Am. [8830]
Amer. Literacy Coun. [8785]
Assn. for Non-Traditional Students in Higher Educ. [7916]
Australian Literacy Educators' Assn. [IO]
Barbara Bush Found. for Family Literacy [8786]
Book Aid Intl. [IO]
Books for the Barrios [12049]
Books For Africa [9744]
Bunyad Literacy Community Coun. [IO]
Center for Applied Linguistics [10401]
Children's Literacy Initiative [8787]
Christian Literacy Associates [8788]
Christian Literacy Associates [IO]
Coll. Reading and Learning Assn. [9042]
Educational Paperback Assn. [3221]
Family Literacy Alliance [18020]
First Book [8789]
India Literacy Proj. [8790]
India Literacy Proj. [IO]
Intl. Reading Assn. [9043]
Laubach Literacy of Canada [IO]
Literacy and Evangelism International [IO]
Literacy and Evangelism Intl. [8791]
Literacy USA [8792]
Natl. Center for Family Literacy [8793]
Natl. Coalition for Literacy [8794]
Natl. Jewish Coalition for Literacy [8795]
Natl. Reading Conf. [9044]
Phonics Inst. [9046]
PlanetRead [8796]
PlanetRead [IO]
Proj. READ Literacy Network [IO]
ProLiteracy Worldwide [IO]
ProLiteracy Worldwide [8797]
Reading Is Fundamental [9047]
Reading Recovery Coun. of North Am. [9048]
Rolling Readers [12502]
Room to Read [12053]
Seedlings Braille Books for Children [9297]
Simplified Spelling Soc. [IO]
World Literacy of Canada [IO]
Literacy Campaign; Hebrew [★20137]
Literacy; Coalition for [★8794]
Literacy and Community Ser. of local clubs [★13033]
Literacy and Community Ser. of local clubs [★IO]
Literacy; Conf. on Visual [★8271]
Literacy Education; National Center for ESL [★10401]
Literacy and Evangelism Intl. [8791], 1800 S Jackson Ave., Tulsa, OK 74107, (918)585-3826
Literacy and Evangelism International [IO], Tulsa, OK, United States
Literacy, Inc; World [★7918]
Literacy Intl. [★8791]
Literacy Intl. [★IO]
Literacy Intl; Laubach [★8797]
Literacy Proj; Natl. Cued Speech Association/Deaf Children's [16452]
Literacy USA [8792], 3131 W Alabama, Ste. 110, Houston, TX 77098, (713)961-3922

Reference to "IO" in place of a book number signifies that the association may be found in the 45th edition of International Organizations.

Literacy Volunteers [★8797]
Literacy Volunteers [★IO]
Literacy Volunteers of Am. [★IO]
Literacy Volunteers of Am. [★8797]
Literary
  Assn. of Book Gp. Readers and Leaders [9738]
  Assn. of Literary Scholars and Critics [10413]
  Benjamin Franklin Literary and Medical Soc.
    [14549]
  Center for the Book [10417]
  G. Unger Vetlesen Found. [12719]
  Literary Source [3232]
  Mountains and Plains Booksellers Assn. [741]
  Parallax Soc. [10947]
  Philomathean Soc. of the Univ. of Pennsylvania
    [10429]
  Vietnamese Nom Preservation Found. [10433]
Literary Agents Assn; Independent [★171]
Literary and Artistic Assn. Canada [IO], Montreal,
  QC, Canada
Literary/Arts Center; Beyond Baroque [9559]
Literary Club; Ship's [★10321]
Literary Guild; Numismatic [22749]
Literary Landmarks Assn. [★10358]
Literary Magazines and Presses; Coun. of [10893]
Literary Managers and Dramaturgs of the Americas
  [11023], PO Box 728, New York, NY 10014,
  (212)561-0315
Literary and Medical Soc; Benjamin Franklin [14549]
Literary Press Gp. of Canada [IO], Toronto, ON,
  Canada
Literary Scholars and Critics; Assn. of [10413]
Literary Societies; Assn. of Amer. Collegiate [10412]
Literary Soc; Confederate Memorial [10105]
Literary Soc; First Hungarian [19105]
Literary Soc. Found. - Address unknown since 1995.
Literary Soc; Hungarian [★19105]
Literary Source [3232]
Literary Translators Assn; Amer. [11058]
Literary Translators' Assn. of Canada [IO], Montreal,
  QC, Canada
Literature
  Academi - Yr Academi Gymreig [IO]
  Academie des Inscriptions et Belles-Lettres [IO]
  African Amer. Literature and Culture Soc. [8798]
  African Language Teachers Assn. [9207]
  Alice in Wonderland Collectors Network [21957]
  Alliance of Literary Societies [IO]
  Amer. Acad. of Arts and Letters [10196]
  Amer. Assn. of Teachers of Arabic [7958]
  Amer. Assn. of Teachers of Spanish and
    Portuguese [8725]
  Amer. Christian Fiction Writers [11156]
  Amer. Comparative Literature Assn. [10409]
  Amer. Friends of the Hakluyt Soc. [10410]
  Amer. Literary Translators Assn. [11058]
  Amer. Literature Assn. [10411]
  Amer. Soc. for Aesthetics [9545]
  Amer. Soc. of Greek and Latin Epigraphy [11207]
  Arthur Miller Soc. [11159]
  Assn. of Amer. Collegiate Literary Societies
    [10412]
  Assn. of Book Gp. Readers and Leaders [9738]
  Assn. for Commonwealth Literature and Language
    Stud. [IO]
  Assn. of Departments of English [8374]
  Assn. of Literary Scholars and Critics [10413]
  Assn. for Scottish Literary Stud. [IO]
  Assn. for the Stud. of Amer. Indian Literatures
    [10734]
  Assn. for the Stud. of Literature and Env. [10414]
  Assn. for Textual Scholarship in Art History [9432]
  Assn. of Writers and Writing Programs [11160]
  August Derleth Soc. [9634]
  Augustan Reprint Soc. [10415]
  Barbara Pym Soc. [9635]
  Before Columbus Found. [10416]
  British Comparative Literature Assn. [IO]
  Butimar Productions [9849]
  Canadian Comparative Literature Assn. [IO]
  Carson McCullers Soc. [11164]
  Cassie Edwards Intl. Fan Club [24782]
  Catharine Maria Sedgwick Soc. [11165]
  Center for the Book [10417]
  Children's Literature Assn. [10418]

Coll. English Assn. [8375]
Conf. for Chinese Oral and Performing Literature
  [9790]
Conf. on Christianity and Literature [8799]
Conf. on Coll. Composition and Commun. [8376]
Conf. on English Educ. [8377]
Cormac McCarthy Soc. [11168]
Coun. for Indian Educ. [8937]
Coun. on Natl. Literatures [10419]
Count Dracula Soc. [10420]
Danish Literature Centre [IO]
D.H. Lawrence Soc. of North Am. [9645]
Dickens Soc. [9646]
Don DeLillo Soc. [11169]
Edgar Allan Poe Soc. of Baltimore [9647]
Elizabethan Club of Yale Univ. [10421]
English Centre of Intl. PEN [IO]
European Assn. for Commonwealth Literature and
  Language Stud. [IO]
European Fairytale Assn. [IO]
Evelyn Scott Soc. [11170]
Feministas Unidas [10000]
Finnish Literature Info. Centre [IO]
Found. for Australian Literary Stud. [IO]
Found. for the Stud. of Women's Literature [IO]
Friends of Amer. Writers [11171]
Georgia Writers Assn. and Young Georgia Writers
  [11172]
German Acad. of Language and Poetry [IO]
Great Books Found. [9748]
Hakluyt Soc. - Australia [IO]
Hakluyt Soc. - England [IO]
Harriet Beecher Stowe Soc. [11173]
Hemingway Found. and Soc. [9658]
Icelandic Literary Soc. [IO]
India's Natl. Acad. of Letters [IO]
Intl. Arthurian Soc., North Amer. Br. [IO]
Intl. Arthurian Soc., North Amer. Br. [10422]
Intl. Assn. of Crime Writers, North Amer. Br.
  [11175]
Intl. Assn. for the Fantastic in the Arts [10945]
Intl. Assn. of Literary Critics [IO]
Intl. Assn. of Media Tie-in Writers [11176]
Intl. Assn. for Philosophy and Literature [10797]
Intl. Assn. for the Stud. of Irish Literatures [8800]
Intl. Assn. for the Stud. of Irish Literatures [IO]
Intl. Comparative Literature Assn. [IO]
Intl. Comparative Literature Assn. [10423]
Intl. Comparative Literature Assn. - Italy [IO]
Intl. Courtly Literature Soc. [IO]
Intl. Courtly Literature Soc. [10424]
Intl. Fiction Rev. [IO]
Intl. Frankenstein Soc. [24822]
Intl. Inst. of Iberoamerican Literature [10425]
Intl. Inst. of Iberoamerican Literature [IO]
Intl. Soc. for Oral Literature in Africa [IO]
Intl. Soc. for Phenomenology and Literature
  [10806]
Intl. Spenser Soc. [9663]
Intl. Theodore Dreiser Soc. [9664]
Intl. Thriller Writers [11179]
Intl. Virginia Woolf Soc. [9666]
Intl. Vladimir Nabokov Soc. [9667]
Intl. Wizard of Oz Club [9668]
Irish Special Interest Gp. of Mensa [10244]
Jack London Res. Center [9669]
James A. Michener Soc. [9670]
James Dickey Soc. [10875]
James Joyce Soc. [9671]
James Joyce Soc. of Southern Colorado [9672]
Jargon Soc. [9958]
Kafka Soc. of Am. and Jour. [9676]
Keats-Shelley Assn. of Am. [9677]
Lambda Iota Tau [24533]
Lessing Soc. [9680]
Literary Source [3232]
Longfellow Soc. [10863]
Lord Ruthven Assembly Intl. Conf. on the
  Fantastic in the Arts [10426]
Lowell Celebrates Kerouac! [9683]
Malone Soc. [IO]
Margery Allingham Soc. [IO]
Marlowe Lives! Assn. [9689]
Mordechai Bernstein Literary Prizes Assn. [IO]
Mythopoeic Soc. [IO]

Mythopoeic Soc. [10427]
Nathaniel Hawthorne Soc. [9694]
Natl. Assn. for Literature Development [IO]
Natl. Assn. for Visually Handicapped [16874]
Natl. Coun. of Teachers of English [8380]
Natl. Steinbeck Center [9695]
Natl. Story League [10982]
Native Writers' Circle of the Americas [19283]
Nietzsche Soc. [10814]
North Amer. Conf. on British Stud. [9760]
North Amer. Jules Verne Soc. [11184]
North Amer. Nietzsche Soc. [10818]
North Amer. Victorian Stud. Assn. [11079]
Norwegian Literature Abroad [IO]
Norwegian PEN [IO]
Parallax Soc. [10947]
PEN Amer. Center [11185]
Philip Roth Soc. [11187]
Philippine Amer. Writers and Artists [11188]
Philolexian Soc. [10428]
Philomathean Soc. of the Univ. of Pennsylvania
  [10429]
Poe Found. [9703]
Poe Stud. Assn. [9704]
Poets and Writers [10870]
Powys Soc. of North Am. [9705]
Ralph Waldo Emerson Memorial Assn. [9706]
Reading Is Fundamental [9047]
Renaissance Artists and Writers Assn. [10202]
Richard Wright Circle [9707]
Royal Soc. of Literature [IO]
Saint Karl Borromaus Assn. for the Dissemination
  of Good Literature [IO]
Sci. Fiction and Fantasy Writers of Am. [11193]
Shakespeare Oxford Soc. [9709]
Shakespeare Soc. [9710]
Shakespeare Soc. of Southern Africa [IO]
Shakespeare Theatre Assn. of Am. [11042]
Societe Royale des Sciences de Liege [IO]
Soc. for the History of Authorship, Reading and
  Publishing [9754]
Soc. of Netherlands Literature [IO]
Soc. for New Language Stud. [10307]
Soc. for the Preservation of English Language
  and Literature [8381]
Soc. for the Promotion of African, Asian, and Latin
  Amer. Literature [IO]
Soc. of Spanish and Spanish-American Stud.
  [10974]
Soc. for the Stud. of Amer. Women Writers
  [11195]
Soc. for the Stud. of Midwestern Literature
  [10430]
Soc. for the Stud. of Southern Literature [10431]
Soc. for Textual Scholarship [10432]
Space Coast Writers' Guild [11196]
Spellbinders [10984]
Susan Glaspell Soc. [11197]
Swedenborg Found. [9711]
Swedish Translators in North Am. [11059]
Tanka Soc. of Am. [10871]
The Thomas Hardy Assn. [9712]
Thomas Wolfe Soc. [9713]
Thornton Wilder Soc. [11200]
Twentieth Century Spanish Assn. of Am. [10975]
U.S. Bd. on Books for Young People [9756]
Unity Corps [19017]
Vietnamese Nom Preservation Found. [10433]
Vietnamese Nom Preservation Found. [IO]
Walt Whitman Birthplace Assn. [9721]
Western Literature Assn. [10434]
William Dean Howells Soc. [9724]
The Wodehouse Soc. [9726]
Women Writing the West [4071]
Women's Classical Caucus [9801]
Women's World Org. for Rights, Literature and
  Development [18822]
Wordcraft Circle of Native Writers and Storytellers
  [9859]
World Literature Ministries [19832]
Literature Assn; Philatelic [★22784]
Literature; Conf. for Chinese Oral and Performing
  [9790]
Literature Found; Church [★19964]
Literature; Intl. Assn. for Philosophy and [★10806]

A star before a book entry number signifies that the name is not listed separately, but is mentioned within the entry.

Literature; Intl. Assn. of Philosophy and [★10840]
Literature Intl; Bible [★19512]
Literature Ministries; Christian Reformed Church World [★19832]
Literature Ministries; CRC World [★19832]
Literature Ministries; Moody [★20368]
Literature Mission; Moody [★20368]
Literature Org; Electronic [1202]
Literature and Reading Res; Intl. Inst. for Children's [IO]
Literature; Soc. of Biblical [19530]
Literature; Soc. for the Preservation of English Language and [8381]
Literature for Women and Children; Comm. on Christian [★12376]
Literatures; Assn. for the Stud. of Amer. Indian [10734]
Lithium Inst. - Defunct.
Litho Clubs; Natl. Assn. of [1779]
Lithographers; Natl. Assn. of Printers and [★1780]
Lithographers and Printers Natl. Assn. [★1788]
Lithographers and Woodcutters; Soc. of Amer. Etchers, Gravers, [★9992]
Lithographic Engravers and Plate Makers Assn. - Address unknown since 1995.
Lithographic Indus; Tech. Assn. of the [★7155]
Lithographic Tech. Found. [★1769]
Lithography Workshop; Tamarind [★8471]
Lithophane Collectors Club - Address unknown since 1999.
Lithotripsy Soc; Amer. [15285]
Lithuania
   Assn. for the Advancement of Baltic Stud. [9730]
   Inst. of Lithuanian Stud. [10435]
   Lithuanian-American Bar Assn. [5507]
   Lithuanian Catholic Religious Aid [19653]
   Lithuanian Natl. Found. [18021]
   Lithuanian Natl. Found. [IO]
   Lithuanian Numismatic Assn. [22743]
Lithuanian
   Amer. Lithuanian Musicians Alliance [10540]
   Amer. Lithuanian Press and Radio Assn. - Viltis [19207]
   Amer. Lithuanian Press and Radio Assn. - Viltis [IO]
   Inst. of Lithuanian Stud. [IO]
   Inst. of Lithuanian Stud. [10435]
   Lithuanian Alliance of Am. [19208]
   Lithuanian-American Bar Assn. [5507]
   Lithuanian-American Community [19209]
   Lithuanian Amer. Coun. [19210]
   Lithuanian Amer. Roman Catholic Women's Alliance [19211]
   Lithuanian Catholic Alliance [19212]
   Lithuanian Catholic Press Soc. [19213]
   Lithuanian Catholic Religious Aid [19653]
   Lithuanian Numismatic Assn. [22743]
   Lithuanian Roman Catholic Fed. of America [19214]
   Lituanus Found. [10436]
   Natl. Lithuanian Soc. of Am. [19215]
   North Amer. Levinas Soc. [10817]
   United Lithuanian Relief Fund of Am. [19216]
Lithuanian Acad. of Sciences [IO], Vilnius, Lithuania
Lithuanian Alliance of Am. [19208], 307 W 30th St., New York, NY 10001, (212)563-2210
Lithuanian Amateur Radio Soc. [IO], Vilnius, Lithuania
Lithuanian-American Bar Assn. [5507], c/o Patricia A. Streeter, Pres., 221 N Main St., Ste. 300, Ann Arbor, MI 48104, (734)222-0088
Lithuanian-Amer. Catholic Services - Defunct.
Lithuanian-American Community [19209], 2715 E Allegheny Ave., Philadelphia, PA 19134, (800)625-1170
Lithuanian-American Community of the U.S. [★19209]
Lithuanian Amer. Coun. [19210], 6500 S Pulaski Rd., Ste. 200, Chicago, IL 60629, (773)735-6677
Lithuanian Amer. Information Center - Defunct.
Lithuanian Amer. Natl. Alliance - Address unknown since 1995.
Lithuanian Amer. Roman Catholic Women's Alliance [19211]
Lithuanian Apparel and Textile Indus. Assn. [IO], Vilnius, Lithuania

Lithuanian Arthritis Assn. [IO], Vilnius, Lithuania
Lithuanian Assn. of Beef Cattle Breeders and Improvers [IO], Kaunas, Lithuania
Lithuanian Assn. of Consulting Companies [IO], Vilnius, Lithuania
Lithuanian Assn. of Landscape Architects [IO], Vilnius, Lithuania
Lithuanian Athletic Fed. [IO], Vilnius, Lithuania
Lithuanian Badminton Fed. [IO], Kaunas, Lithuania
Lithuanian Baseball Assn. [IO], Vilnius, Lithuania
Lithuanian Boy Scouts - Address unknown since 2007.
Lithuanian Catholic Acad. of Sciences - Address unknown since 2007.
Lithuanian Catholic Alliance [19212], c/o Ladies Pennsylvania Slovak Catholic Union, 71 S Washington St., Wilkes-Barre, PA 18701, (570)823-3513
Lithuanian Catholic Alliance of Am. [★19212]
Lithuanian Catholic Fed. Ateitis/USA Section - Address unknown since 2008.
Lithuanian Catholic Press Soc. [19213], 4545 W 63rd St., Chicago, IL 60629, (773)585-9500
Lithuanian Catholic Religious Aid [19653], 64-25 Perry Ave., Maspeth, NY 11378-2411, (718)326-5202
Lithuanian Catholic Students' Assn. "Ateitis" - Defunct.
Lithuanian Catholic Women [★19211]
Lithuanian Catholic Youth Assn. Ateitis - Address unknown since 2003.
Lithuanian Chamber of Commerce of America - Address unknown since 1999.
Lithuanian Composers' Union [IO], Vilnius, Lithuania
Lithuanian Cmpt. Soc. [IO], Vilnius, Lithuania
Lithuanian Confed. of Industrialists [IO], Vilnius, Lithuania
Lithuanian Cultural Soc. - Defunct.
Lithuanian Dancesport Fed. [IO], Vilnius, Lithuania
Lithuanian Draughts Fed. [IO], Vilnius, Lithuania
Lithuanian Flying Disc Fed. [IO], Vilnius, Lithuania
Lithuanian Gas Assn. [IO], Vilnius, Lithuania
Lithuanian Geotechnical Soc. [IO], Vilnius, Lithuania
Lithuanian Green Movement [IO], Kaunas, Lithuania
Lithuanian Heart Assn. [IO], Vilnius, Lithuania
Lithuanian Hypertension League [IO], Kaunas, Lithuania
Lithuanian Information Center - Defunct.
Lithuanian Kinezitherapy Assn. [IO], Kaunas, Lithuania
Lithuanian Labour Fed. [IO], Vilnius, Lithuania
Lithuanian Librarians' Assn. [IO], Vilnius, Lithuania
Lithuanian Mfrs. Confed. [★IO]
Lithuanian Medical Assn. [IO], Vilnius, Lithuania
Lithuanian Musicians Alliance; Amer. [10540]
Lithuanian Natl. Found. [18021], 307 W 30th St., New York, NY 10001-2703, (212)868-5860
Lithuanian Natl. Found. [IO], New York, NY, United States
Lithuanian Natl. League of America - Address unknown since 1995.
Lithuanian Natl. Union [IO], Vilnius, Lithuania
Lithuanian Numismatic Assn. [IO], Baltimore, MD, United States
Lithuanian Numismatic Assn. [22743], PO Box 22696, Baltimore, MD 21203, (410)233-9279
Lithuanian Organist Musicians Alliance; Amer. [★10540]
Lithuanian Orienteering Fed. [IO], Vilnius, Lithuania
Lithuanian Packaging Assn. [IO], Kaunas, Lithuania
Lithuanian Paralympic Comm. [IO], Vilnius, Lithuania
Lithuanian Philatelic Soc. of New York - Defunct.
Lithuanian Physical Soc. [IO], Vilnius, Lithuania
Lithuanian Physiological Soc. [IO], Kaunas, Lithuania
Lithuanian Printers' Assn. [IO], Vilnius, Lithuania
Lithuanian Psychological Assn. [IO], Vilnius, Lithuania
Lithuanian Real Estate Development Assn. [IO], Vilnius, Lithuania
Lithuanian Regeneration Assn. - Address unknown since 2002.
Lithuanian Republic Chamber of Odontologists [IO], Vilnius, Lithuania
Lithuanian Rheumatologists Assn. [IO], Vilnius, Lithuania

Lithuanian Roads Assn. [IO], Vilnius, Lithuania
Lithuanian Roman Catholic Fed. of America [19214]
Lithuanian Roman Catholic Organist Alliance; Amer. [★10540]
Lithuanian Roman Catholic Priests' League of America - Address unknown since 2001.
Lithuanian Skating Fed. [IO], Kaunas, Lithuania
Lithuanian Soc. of Agricultural Engineers [IO], Kaunas, Lithuania
Lithuanian Soc. of Cardiology [IO], Vilnius, Lithuania
Lithuanian Soc. of Gastrointestinal Endoscopy [IO], Kaunas, Lithuania
Lithuanian Soc. of Palliative Care [IO], Kaunas, Lithuania
Lithuanian Speed Skating Assn. [IO], Vilnius, Lithuania
Lithuanian Sports Medicine Assn. [IO], Vilnius, Lithuania
Lithuanian Squash Fed. [IO], Vilnius, Lithuania
Lithuanian Stuttering Problem Club [IO], Vilnius, Lithuania
Lithuanian Taekwondo Fed. [IO], Vilnius, Lithuania
Lithuanian Teachers' Union [IO], Vilnius, Lithuania
Lithuanian Tennis Assn. [IO], Vilnius, Lithuania
Lithuanian-U.S. Bus. Coun. [IO], Washington, DC, United States
Lithuanian-U.S. Bus. Coun. [24289], c/o Chamber of Commerce of the U.S., 1615 H St. NW, Washington, DC 20062, (202)463-5460
Lithuanian Veterans Assn. Ramove - Address unknown since 1995.
Lithuanian Weightlifting Fed. [IO], Vilnius, Lithuania
Lithuanian Wind Energy Assn. [IO], Klaipeda, Lithuania
Lithuanian World Community [IO], Lemont, IL, United States
Lithuanian World Community [18979], c/o Lithuanian World Center, 14911 W 127th St., Lemont, IL 60439, (630)257-8787
Lithuanian World Youth Assn. Communications Center - Defunct.
Lithuanian Yachting Union [IO], Vilnius, Lithuania
Litigation Center; Natl. Chamber [6223]
Litigation CH; Firearms [★17592]
Litigation Gp; Asbestos [13321]
Litigation Gp; Public Citizen [17342]
Little Apostoles of Charity [IO], Ponte Lambro, Italy
Little Big Horn Associates [★11135]
Little Bigger League [★23106]
Little Bighorn History Alliance [11135], PO Box 1752, Niceville, FL 32588, (850)897-4505
Little Book Collector's Club of Am; Big [★21978]
Little Book Collector's Club; Big [21978]
Little Britches Rodeo [★23692]
Little Britches Rodeo Assn; Natl. [23692]
Little Bros. - Friends of the Elderly [11295], 28 E Jackson Blvd., Ste. 405, Chicago, IL 60604-2357, (312)786-1032
Little Bros. of the Poor [★11295]
Little City Found. [12573], 1760 W Algonquin Rd., Palatine, IL 60067, (847)358-5510
Little Coll. Athletic Assn; Natl. [★23859]
Little Company of Mary Generalate [IO], London, United Kingdom
Little Elegance Memories of Yesterday [22065]
Little Flower Mission Clubs - Defunct.
Little Flower Mission League [19654]
Little Flower; Soc. of the [19720]
Little Flower Soc. [★19720]
Little Hearts [13966], PO Box 171, Cromwell, CT 06416
Little League Baseball [★23111]
Little League Baseball [★IO]
Little League Baseball and Softball [IO], Williamsport, PA, United States
Little League Baseball and Softball [23111], PO Box 3485, Williamsport, PA 17701-0485, (570)326-1921
Little League Found. [23112], 539 US Rte. 15 Hwy., PO Box 3485, Williamsport, PA 17701-0485, (570)326-1921
Little Mouse Club [22413], c/o Mike Chiodo, PO Box 1802, New York, NY 10009, (212)529-9843
Little Mouse Club [IO], New Cumberland, PA, United States
Little Nash Rambler Club - Defunct.

Reference to "IO" in place of a book number signifies that the association may be found in the 45th edition of International Organizations.

Little People of Am. [13105], 5289 NE Elam Young Pkwy., Ste. F-100, Hillsboro, OR 97124, (503)846-1562
Little Rock Cotton Exchange - Defunct.
Little Sisters of the Assumption - France [IO], Paris, France
Little Sisters of Jesus [IO], Rome, Italy
Little Theatre Guild of Great Britain [IO], Carlisle, United Kingdom
Little Way Circle - Address unknown since 1994.
Littlefield CH and Info. Exchange [★20979]
Littlefield Family Newsl. [20979], PO Box 912, Ogunquit, ME 03907-0912
Littoral Soc. - Northeast Region; Amer. [7269]
Lituanus Found. [10436], 47 W Polk St., Ste. 100-300, Chicago, IL 60605, (312)341-9396
Liturgia; Instituto Nacional Hispano de [19640]
Liturgia Para Hispanos; Instituto Nacional de [★19640]
Liturgical Apostolate; Bishops' Comm. on the [★19585]
Liturgical Arts Soc. - Address unknown since 1995.
Liturgical Commissions; Fed. of Diocesan [19623]
Liturgical Conf. [19900], PO Box 31, Evanston, IL 60204
Liturgical Conf. [IO], Evanston, IL, United States
Liturgical Conf; Benedictine [★19900]
Liturgical Stud. and Renewal; Intl. Soc. for [★19911]
Liturgies of Initiation [★19698]
Liturgies of Initiation [★19698]
Liturgy; ADOREMUS - Soc. for the Renewal of the Sacred [19561]
Liturgy Assn; Latin [19646]
Liturgy; Bishops' Comm. on the [19585]
Liturgy and Mission; Assoc. Parishes for [19945]
Liturgy; Soc. for the Renewal of the Sacred [★19561]
Litzenberg Assn; Litzenberger- [20980]
Litzenberger-Litzenberg Assn. [20980], c/o Homer L. Litzenberg, III, Pres., 3233 Simberlan Dr., San Jose, CA 95148-3128, (408)270-7227
Livable Communities; Partners for [5594]
Live Aid Found. - Address unknown since 1990.
Live Food Singles Club - World Wide - Defunct.
Live-Free, Inc. [★9203]
Live-Free, Inc. [★IO]
Live-Free Intl. [★IO]
Live-Free Intl. [★9203]
Live-Free, USA [9203], PO Box 375, Dolton, IL 60419-9998
Live-Free, USA [IO], Dolton, IL, United States
Live Oak Soc. [4688], 3609 Purdue Dr., Metairie, LA 70003, (504)887-1800
Live Performance Australia [IO], Melbourne, Australia
Live Stock Marketing Assn; Natl. [★5024]
Live Stock Record Associations; Natl. Soc. of [★4141]
Lively Families; Natl. Assn. of [21007]
Liver Awareness; Latino Org. for [14811]
Liver Diseases; Amer. Assn. for the Stud. of [14801]
Liver Found; Amer. [14803]
Liver; Intl. Assn. for the Stud. of the [IO]
Liver Transplant Network; Biliary Atresia and [16529]
Liveries and Outfitters; Natl. Associations of Canoe [★3650]
Livermore Action Group - Defunct.
Liverpool Chamber of Commerce and Indus. [IO], Liverpool, United Kingdom
Livery Assn; Intl. Taxicab and [★3894]
Livestock
    Alpaca Breeders of the Rockies [4992]
    Amer. Assn. of Bovine Practitioners [16741]
    Amer. Assn. of Swine Veterinarians [16750]
    Amer. Dorper Sheep Breeders' Soc. [5183]
    Amer. Embryo Transfer Assn. [4149]
    Amer. Emu Assn. [4993]
    Amer. Grassfed Assn. [2438]
    Amer. Guinea Hog Assn. [5231]
    Amer. Kiko Goat Assn. [4780]
    Amer. Livestock Breeds Conservancy [4994]
    Amer. Miniature Cheviot Sheep Breeders Assn. [5188]
    Amer. Miniature Llama Assn. [21513]
    Amer. Pastured Poultry Producers Assn. [5106]

    Amer. Royal Assn. [4995]
    Amer. Soc. of Animal Sci. [4150]
    Amer. Water Buffalo Assn. [4996]
    American Water Buffalo Association [IO]
    ARCA: Amer. Romeldale/CVM Assn. [5197]
    Australian Cattle Dog Club of Am. [22221]
    Barbados Blackbelly Sheep Assn. Intl. [5198]
    Bluefaced Leicester Union of North Am. [5200]
    British Angora Goat Soc. [IO]
    British Goat Soc. [IO]
    British Llama and Alpaca Assn. [IO]
    British Mule Soc. [IO]
    British Pig Assn. [IO]
    British Rabbit Coun. [IO]
    Canadian Bison Assn. [IO]
    Canadian Goat Soc. [IO]
    Canadian Livestock Records Corp. [IO]
    Canadian Llama and Alpaca Assn. [IO]
    Canadian Pork Coun. [IO]
    Colored Angora Goat Breeders Assn. [4782]
    Cow Observers Worldwide [22002]
    Cowboys for Christ [19792]
    Food Animal Concerns Trust [4997]
    Food Safety Consortium [5031]
    Heifer Proj. Intl. [12429]
    Intl. Assn. for Paratuberculosis [16793]
    Intl. Fainting Goat Assn. [4784]
    Intl. Goat Assn. [4785]
    Intl. Livestock Identification Assn. [4998]
    Intl. Livestock Investigators Assn. [4999]
    Intl. Livestock Investigators Assn. [IO]
    Intl. Livestock Res. Inst. - Kenya [IO]
    Intl. Miniature Donkey Registry [IO]
    Intl. Miniature Donkey Registry [5000]
    Intl. Soc. for Cow Protection [4155]
    Intl. Soc. of Livestock Husbandry [IO]
    Intl. Yak Assn. [IO]
    Intl. Yak Assn. [5001]
    Livestock Marketing Assn. [5021]
    Miniature Hereford Breeders Assn. [4272]
    Miniature and Novelty Sheep Breeders Assn. and Registry [5204]
    Natl. Assn. of Animal Breeders [5002]
    Natl. Cattlemen's Beef Assn. [5023]
    Natl. Inst. for Animal Agriculture [5003]
    Natl. Junior Swine Assn. [5237]
    Natl. Livestock Producers Assn. [5024]
    Natl. Miniature Donkey Assn. [5004]
    Natl. Pedigreed Livestock Coun. [4141]
    Natl. Sheep Assn. [IO]
    New Zealand Deer Farmers Assn. [IO]
    Nigerian Dwarf Goat Assn. [4788]
    NMC [16802]
    North Amer. Babydoll Southdown Sheep Assn. and Registry [5211]
    North Amer. Rhea Assn. [5005]
    North Amer. Wensleydale Sheep Assn. [5214]
    Painted Desert Sheep Soc. [5215]
    Producers Livestock Marketing Assn. [5029]
    Public Lands Coun. [5127]
    Ranchers-Cattlemen Action Legal Fund, United Stockgrowers of Am. [4290]
    Rare Breeds Canada [IO]
    Serama Coun. of North Am. [4201]
    Soays of Am. [5218]
    Umbrella Assn. of German Pig Production [IO]
    U.S. Animal Hea. Assn. [16811]
    U.S. Boer Goat Assn. [4789]
Livestock Assn; Interstate Producers [★5030]
Livestock Auctioneers' Assn. [IO], Carlisle, United Kingdom
Livestock Brand Conf; Intl. [★4998]
Livestock Brand Conf; Natl. [★4998]
Livestock Brand and Theft Conf; Intl. [★4998]
Livestock Conservation, Inc. [★5003]
Livestock Conservation Inst. [★5003]
Livestock Coun; Natl. Pedigreed [4141]
Livestock Dealers Assn; Natl. [★5021]
Livestock Equipment Coun. - Defunct.
Livestock Hea. Officials; Natl. Assembly of Chief [★16811]
Livestock Identification and Theft Investigators Assn; Intl. [★4998]
Livestock Industry Inst. - Address unknown since 2003.

Livestock Loss Prevention Bd; Natl. [★5003]
Livestock Marketing Assn. [5021], 10510 NW Ambassador Dr., Kansas City, MO 64153, (816)891-0502
Livestock Marketing Assn; Competitive [★5021]
Livestock Marketing Assn; Producers [5029]
Livestock Producers Assn; Natl. [5024]
Livestock Publications Coun. [3233], 910 Currie St., Fort Worth, TX 76107, (817)336-1130
Livestock Res. and Training Center; Winrock Intl. [★16959]
Livestock Sanitary Assn; U.S. [★16811]
Livestock Sanitary Comm; Natl. [★5003]
Living Arts Found. - Address unknown since 1995.
The Living Bank [★14291]
The Living Bank [★IO]
The Living Bank Intl. [IO], Houston, TX, United States
The Living Bank Intl. [14291], PO Box 6725, Houston, TX 77265-6725, (713)528-2971
Living Bibles Intl. [★19520]
Living Bibles Intl. [★IO]
Living Church Found. [19964], PO Box 514036, Milwaukee, WI 53203-3436, (414)276-5420
Living Colour Fan Club - Address unknown since 1991.
Living/Dying Proj. [13316], PO Box 357, Fairfax, CA 94978-0357, (415)456-3915
Living Fed. of Am; Assisted [12306]
Living in Freedom Eternally [★20060]
Living History, Farm and Agricultural Museums; Assn. for [10497]
The Living Room [★16231]
Living Stream Prayer Circle - Address unknown since 2003.
Living Streets [IO], London, United Kingdom
Living Tree Centre - Address unknown since 1995.
Living Water Ministry; Spring of [20556]
Living With Cancer - Defunct.
Liza Minnelli Fan Club - Address unknown since 2004.
Lizzie High Soc. [22401], 220 N Main St., Sellersville, PA 18960, (215)453-8200
Lladro Soc. [21930], c/o Lladro Museum, 43 W 57th St., New York, NY 10019, (212)838-9352
Llama and Alpaca Assn; Rocky Mountain [4148]
Llama Assn; Amer. Miniature [21513]
Llama Assn. of North Am. [4136], 1800 S Obenchain Rd., Eagle Point, OR 97524, (541)830-5262
Llama RescueNet [11427], c/o Jim Krowka, Pres., PO Box 215, Bow, WA 98232-0215, (541)937-2507
Llama Show Assn; Alpaca [21514]
LLGAF [★9455]
Lloyd
    Borgward Owners' Club [21594]
Lloyd Shaw Found. [8187], c/o Bob Fuller, Pres., 293 Stone Rd., Paris, KY 40361, (813)662-2341
Lloyd Wood Fan Club - Defunct.
LMBS Network [16539], c/o Found. Fighting Blindness, 11435 Cronhill Dr., Owings Mills, MD 21117-2220, (410)568-0150
LMBS Network [★14461]
LO/TCO Bistandsnamnd [★IO]
Lo/Tco Coun. of Intl. Trade Union [★IO]
LO/TCO Secretariat of Intl. Trade Union Development [IO], Stockholm, Sweden
Loading Dock Equip. Mfrs. [2035], 8720 Red Oak Blvd., Ste. 201, Charlotte, NC 28217, (704)676-1190
Loan Administrators; Assn. of Small [★5610]
Loan Administrators; Natl. Assn. of Student [8432]
Loan Assn; Jewish Free [20148]
Loan Controllers; Soc. of Savings and [★1418]
Loan Fund; Jewish [★20148]
Loan; Hebrew Free [★20148]
Loan Leagues; Amer. Savings and [★459]
Loan Programs; Natl. Coun. of Higher Educ. [8351]
Loan Supervisors; Natl. Assn. of Small [★5610]
Loan Supervisors; Natl. Assn. of State Savings and [★458]
Loan Syndications and Trading Assn. [484], 366 Madison Ave., 15th Fl., New York, NY 10017, (212)880-3000
Loan Syndications and Trading Assn. [IO], New York, NY, United States

A star before a book entry number signifies that the name is not listed separately, but is mentioned within the entry.

Lobby Europeen des Femmes [★IO]
Lobby; Natl. Student [★9195]
Lobby; NETWORK, A Natl. Catholic Social Justice [18624]
Lobbyists; Amer. League of [18343]
Lobbyists and Lawyers for Campaign Finance Reform - Address unknown since 1999.
Lobster Assn; Atlantic Offshore Fish and [★5728]
Lobstermen's Assn; Atlantic Offshore [5728]
Lobstermen's Assn; Maine [3492]
Local 747 Union, New Jersey [★24100]
Local Alliance Networking Project [★9116]
Local Authorities Confronting Disasters and Emergencies [IO], Tel Aviv, Israel
Local Authorities Coordinators of Regulatory Services [IO], London, United Kingdom
Local Authorities Res. and Intelligence Assn. [IO], Middlesborough, United Kingdom
Local Authority Caterers Assn. [IO], Woking, United Kingdom
Local Authority Recycling Advisory Comm. [IO], Knighton, United Kingdom
Local Authority Road Safety Officers' Assn. [IO], Lincoln, United Kingdom
Local Bankers Assn. of Korea [★IO]
Local Boards of Hea; Natl. Assn. of [16244]
Local Elected Officials; Natl. Black Caucus of [6127]
Local Elected Officials Project of the Center for Innovative Diplomacy - Defunct.
Local Environmental Hea. Administrators; Conf. of [★16246]
Local Environmental Hea. Administrators; Natl. Conf. of [16246]
Local Govt; Acad. for State and [18417]
Local Govt. Center [★6131]
Local Govt. Environmental Professionals; Natl. Assn. of [6125]
Local Govt; Natl. Assn. of Volunteer Programs in [6352]
Local History; Amer. Assn. for State and [10084]
Local Housing Finance Agencies; Assn. of [★5794]
Local Housing Finance Agencies; Natl. Assn. of [5794]
Local Independent Charities of Am. [12729], Natl. HQ, 1100 Larkspur Landing Cir., Ste. 340, Larkspur, CA 94939, (800)876-0413
Local Initiatives Support Corp. [17224], 501 7th Ave., New York, NY 10018, (212)455-9800
Local Officials' Admin. Network [★23873]
Local Officials; Hispanic Elected [6122]
Local Policies; Conf. on Alternative State and [★18429]
Local Post Collectors Club - Address unknown since 2007.
Local Post Collectors Soc. - Defunct.
Local Public Human Ser. Administrators; Natl. Coun. of [13178]
Local Public Policies; Conf. on Alternative State and [★18429]
Local Public Welfare Administrators; Natl. Coun. of [★13178]
Local Self-Reliance; Inst. for [11747]
Localization Indus. Standards Assn. [IO], Romainmotier, Switzerland
Location Managers Guild of Am. [2522], 8033 Sunset Blvd., Ste. 1017, West Hollywood, CA 90046, (310)967-2007
Loch Ness Investigation Bur. - Defunct.
Lock Collectors Assn; Amer. [21962]
Lock Museum of Am. [9835], 230 Main St., Rte. 6, PO Box 104, Terryville, CT 06786-0104, (860)589-6359
Lockdown; Comm. to End the Marion [11861]
Locke Surname Org. [20981], 7650 Fairview Rd., Tillamook, OR 97141-9714, (503)842-6036
Locknut Mfrs. Assn; Aircraft [1814]
Locks of Love [17055], 2925 10th Ave. N, Ste. 102, Lake Worth, FL 33461, (561)963-1677
Locksmith Security Assn. - Address unknown since 2003.
Locksmith Suppliers Assn; Natl. [★1834]
Locksmiths of Am; Assoc. [1818]
Locksmiths' Assn; Institutional [1164]
Locksmiths Assn; Master [IO]
Loco & Carr Inst [★IO]

Locomotive and Carriage Institution [IO], Derby, United Kingdom
Locomotive Engineers; Grand Intl. Brotherhood of [★24176]
Locomotive Engineers; Intl. Brotherhood of [★24176]
Locomotive Firemen and Enginemen; Brotherhood of [★24181]
Locomotive Historical Soc; Lancaster (Pennsylvania) Railway and [★10915]
Locomotive Historical Soc; Railway and [10921]
Locomotive Maintenance Officers' Assn. [3283], c/o Ron Pondel, Sec.-Treas., 701 Maple Ln., Bensenville, IL 60106, (630)860-5511
Lodging Assn; Amer. Hotel and [1927]
Lodging Inst; Foodservice and [★1957]
Lodgings
  Broker Mgt. Coun. [1937]
Lodi District Vintners Assn. - Address unknown since 1994.
Lodzer Young Men's Benevolent Soc. - Address unknown since 1989.
Log Analysts; Soc. of Petrophysicists and Well [7466]
Log Analysts; Soc. of Professional Well [★7466]
Log Cabin Fed. [★18523]
Log Cabin Republicans [18523], 1901 Pennsylvania Ave. NW, Ste. 902, Washington, DC 20006, (202)347-5306
Log Home Builders Assn. of North Am. [1031], 14241 NE Woodinville-Duvall Rd., Ste. 345, Woodinville, WA 98072-8564, (360)794-4469
Log Homes Coun. [★2525]
Log Homes Coun. [2525], c/o Natl. Assn. of Home Builders, 1201 15th St. NW, Washington, DC 20005, (202)266-8577
Log Homes Coun; Amer. [★2525]
Log House Assn. of North Am. [★1031]
Log House Builder's Assn. of North Am. [★1031]
Logan Community Resources [11960], 2505 E Jefferson Blvd., South Bend, IN 46615, (574)289-4831
Loggers Assn; Northeastern [1612]
Logging Conf; Redwood Region [4694]
Logic; Assn. for Symbolic [7287]
Logic and Critical Thinking; Assn. for Informal [10785]
Logical Language Gp. [10304], 2904 Beau Ln., Fairfax, VA 22031, (703)385-0273
Logistics; Amer. Soc. of Trans. and [3861]
Logistics Assn; Amer. [6064]
Logistics Engineers; Natl. Inst. of Packaging, Handling and [7427]
Logistics Mgt; Coun. of [★4018]
Logistics Mgt. Inst. [5607], 2000 Corporate Ridge, McLean, VA 22102-7805, (703)917-9800
Logistics NZ [★IO]
Logistics Officer Association [IO], Arlington, VA, United States
Logistics Officer Assn. [2736], PO Box 2264, Arlington, VA 22202, (703)693-8395
Logistics and Policy; Assn. for Trans. Law, [★6316]
Logistics and Transport New Zealand [IO], Auckland, New Zealand
Logo Forum on Compuserve - Defunct.
LOGOI [19930], 14540 SW 136 St., Ste. 200, Miami, FL 33186, (305)232-5880
LOGOI [IO], Miami, FL, United States
Logsplitter Mfrs. Assn. - Defunct.
Lohman Gay Art Found; Leslie- [9455]
Lois Intl. [★19380]
Lois Intl. [★IO]
Lois Link Intl. - USA [IO], Orange, CA, United States
Lois Link Intl. - USA [19380], c/o Lois Widly, Chair, 11155 Meads Ave., Orange, CA 92869
Lok Chi Assn. [IO], Hong Kong, People's Republic of China
Lollard Soc. [20524], c/o Dr. Jill C. Havens, Membership Dir., Texas Christian Univ., Dept. of English, Box 297270, Fort Worth, TX 76129
LOMA [2196], 2300 Windy Ridge Pkwy., Ste. 600, Atlanta, GA 30339-8443, (770)951-1770
LOMA [IO], Atlanta, GA, United States
London & Provincial Antique Dealers Assn. [★IO]
London Animal Action [IO], London, United Kingdom

London Assn. of Eyesight Training [★IO]
London Assn. of Primal Psychotherapists [IO], London, United Kingdom
London Chamber of Commerce and Indus. [IO], London, United Kingdom
London Club [11900]
London Foundation; Jack [★9669]
London Intl. Financial Futures and Options Exchange [IO], London, United Kingdom
London Intl. Insurance and Reinsurance Market Assn. [★IO]
London Investment Banking Assn. [IO], London, United Kingdom
London Mathematical Soc. [IO], London, United Kingdom
London and Middlesex Archaeological Soc. [IO], London, United Kingdom
London Natl. Soc. for Women's Suffrage [★IO]
London Natural History Soc. [IO], London, United Kingdom
London Record Soc. [IO], London, United Kingdom
London Region Campaign for Nuclear Disarmament [IO], London, United Kingdom
London Regional Passengers Comm. [★IO]
London Res. Center; Jack [9669]
London Soc. [IO], London, United Kingdom
London Soc. of Obtaining Political Rights for Women [★IO]
London Subterranean Survey Assn. [IO], London, United Kingdom
London Swing Dance Soc. [IO], Middlesex, United Kingdom
London Topographical Soc. [IO], Richmond, United Kingdom
London Transport Users Comm. [IO], London, United Kingdom
London Underground Railway Soc. [IO], Worcester Park, United Kingdom
London Vintage Taxi Assn. [IO], Uxbridge, United Kingdom
London Vintage Taxi Assn. - Amer. Sect. [21690], PO Box 445, Windham, NH 03087-0445, (603)893-8919
London Women and Manual Trades [★IO]
Londonderry Chamber of Commerce [IO], Londonderry, United Kingdom
Lone Gp., Inc; Intl. 190SL [★21663]
Lone Indian Fellowship - Address unknown since 1999.
Lone Ranger Fan Club [25032], PO Box 9561, Amarillo, TX 79105, (806)373-3969
Lonergan Philosophical Soc. [18272], c/o Dr. Elizabeth A. Murray, Founder/Pres., Dept. of Philosophy, Loyola Marymount Univ., 1 LMU Dr., Ste. 3600, Los Angeles, CA 90045-2659
Lonergan Philosophical Soc. [IO], Los Angeles, CA, United States
Loners of Am. [22956]
Loners on Wheels [22957], PO Box 1060 - WB, Cape Girardeau, MO 63702, (505)546-4058
Lonestar Fatherhood Initiative [★18038]
Long Distance Love [★22136]
Long Distance Running Directors Assn. - Defunct.
Long Distance Telephone Companies; Assn. of [★3955]
Long Distance Walkers Assn. [IO], Manchester, United Kingdom
Long Island Soc. of Anesthetists [★13674]
Long Island Univ. - Southampton Coll. Alumni Assn. [18907], 720 Northern Blvd., Brookville, NY 11548-1300, (516)299-4052
Long Staple Yarn Assn. [★3774]
Long Term Care Administrators; Natl. Assn. of Boards of Examiners of [15538]
Long Term Care Campaign - Address unknown since 2005.
Long Term Care; Natl. Assn. of Directors of Nursing Admin. in [15493]
Long Term Care; Natl. Assn. for the Support of [14651]
Long-Term Care; Natl. Inst. on Community-Based [11312]
Long Term Care and Rehabilitation; Sect. for [14894]
Long-term Conditions Alliance [IO], London, United Kingdom

Reference to "IO" in place of a book number signifies that the association may be found in the 45th edition of International Organizations.

Long-term Medical Conditions Alliance [★IO]
Longfellow Club [★10863]
Longfellow Poetry Soc. [★10863]
Longfellow Soc. [10863], c/o Dawn L. Stewart, Pres., 106 Richard Rd., Holliston, MA 01746
Longfellow Soc. of Sudbury at the Wayside Inn [★10863]
Longhorn Assn; Intl. Texas [4269]
Longhorn Breeders Assn. of Am; Texas [4294]
Longhorn Cattle Soc. [IO], Devon, United Kingdom
Longrifle Collectors; Assn. of Ohio [22425]
Longshore and Warehouse Union; Intl. [24126]
Longshoremen's Assn; Intl. [24127]
Longshoremen's and Warehousemen's Union; Intl. [★24126]
Longwave Club of Am. [21505], 45 Wildflower Rd., Levittown, PA 19057, (215)945-0543
LonMark Intl. [3705], 550 Meridian Ave., San Jose, CA 95126, (408)938-5266
LonMark Interoperability Assn. [★3705]
Looking Up - Address unknown since 1994.
Loon Fund; North Amer. [5355]
Loops for Lupus - Defunct.
Lop Rabbit Club of Am. [5148], c/o Jeanne Welch, Sec.-Treas., PO Box 236, Hornbrook, CA 96044, (530)475-3371
LORAN
    Intl. Loran Assn. [7370]
    MacLellan Clan in Am. [20988]
Lord Byron
    Byron Soc. of Am. [9641]
Lord Ruthven Assembly [★10426]
Lord Ruthven Assembly Intl. Conf. on the Fantastic in the Arts [10426]
Lord's Day Alliance of the U.S. [20544], PO Box 941745, Atlanta, GA 31145-0745, (404)693-5530
Lord's Day Observance Soc. [IO], Leominster, United Kingdom
Lords of the Maryland Manors; Natl. Soc. of Descendants of [20747]
Loretan/Steiner/Ross Soc; Pellien/Jaeger/ [21022]
Loretta Ellis Fan Club - Defunct.
Loretta Lynn Fan Club - Defunct.
l'Organisation hydrographique internationale [★IO]
Lorin Elias Bassett Family Org. [20982], c/o Irvin Gene Bassett, Pres., 1055 E Hillcrest Dr., Springville, UT 84663, (801)489-6298
Lorrie Morgan Intl. Fan Club [24940], PO Box 121739, Nashville, TN 37212, (615)332-8947
Los Algarrobos - Asociacion Civil para el Desarrollo Sustentable [★IO]
Los Algarrobos - Assn. for Sustainable Development [IO], Cordoba, Argentina
Los Amigos [★24612]
Los Angeles Advt. Agencies Assn. [107], 4223 Glencoe Ave., Ste. C-100, Marina del Rey, CA 90292, (310)823-7320
Los Angeles Copyright Soc. [5854], c/o Greg P. Goeckner, Treas., 15503 Ventura Blvd., Encino, CA 91436
Los Angeles Found. of Otology [★16446]
Los Angeles Grain Exchange - Address unknown since 2004.
Los Angeles Intl. Fern Soc. - Address unknown since 2002.
Los Angeles Kings Booster Club [25007], Staples Center, 1111 S Figueroa St., Ste. 3100, Los Angeles, CA 90015, (310)712-5435
Los Californianos [20719], PO Box 600522, San Diego, CA 92160-0522, (858)538-3027
Los Ninos [12589], 287 G St., Chula Vista, CA 91910, (619)426-9110
Los P.A.D.R.E.S. - Address unknown since 1995.
Loss Adjusters Assn. of Japan [IO], Tokyo, Japan
Loss Data Inst; Highway [2168]
Loss Executives Assn. [2197], PO Box 37, Tenafly, NJ 07670, (201)569-3346
Loss and Healing; William Wendt Center for [13317]
Loss in Multiple Birth; Center for [12665]
Loss Prevention Coun. [★IO]
Loss Prog; AARP Grief and [13414]
Loss Support; SHARE-Pregnancy and Infant [12690]
Lost Chord Clubs [★11953]
Lost Chord Clubs [★IO]
Lost Music Network - Defunct.

Lost Planes - Defunct.
Lost Seska - Defunct.
Lost in Space Fannish Alliance [25033], c/o Flint Mitchell, PO Box 510442, St. Louis, MO 63151-0442, (314)416-4071
Lotteries
    European Lotteries [IO]
    Global Lottery Collectors Soc. [22030]
    Lotteries Coun. [IO]
    North Amer. Assn. of State and Provincial Lotteries [IO]
    North Amer. Assn. of State and Provincial Lotteries [6048]
    World Lottery Assn. - Canada [IO]
Lotteries Coun. [IO], London, United Kingdom
Lotteries; Natl. Assn. of State [★6048]
Lottery Collectors Soc. [★22030]
Lottery Collectors Soc; Global [22030]
Lotus [★21691]
Lotus
    Club Elite North Am. [21618]
Lotus Cortina of America Register - Defunct.
Lotus Lantern Intl. Buddhist Center [IO], Seoul, Republic of Korea
Lotus, Ltd. [21691], PO Box L, College Park, MD 20741, (301)982-4054
Lotus Outreach [13143], PO Box 1184, Cathedral City, CA 92235, (888)831-9990
Lotus West - Address unknown since 1995.
Lou Christie Intl. Fan Club [24941], c/o Harry Young, Pres., PO Box 260172, St. Louis, MO 63126
Lou Rawls Natl. Appreciation Soc. - Defunct.
Loudspeaker Mfrs. Assn; Amer. [★1206]
Louis Braille Found. for Blind Musicians - Defunct.
Louis Finkelstein Inst. for Religious and Social Stud. at the Louis Stein Center [19931], c/o Jewish Theological Seminary, 3080 Broadway, New York, NY 10027, (212)678-8000
Louis and Harold Price Found. [13174], 1371 Hecla Dr., Ste. B-1, Louisville, CO 80027-2318, (303)665-9201
Louisa May Alcott Memorial Assn. [9682], c/o Orchard House, 399 Lexington Rd., PO Box 343, Concord, MA 01742-0343, (978)369-4118
Louise Brooks Soc. [24755], 1518 Church St., San Francisco, CA 94131-2018
Louise Brooks Soc. [IO], San Francisco, CA, United States
Louise Mandrell Fan Club - Address unknown since 1999.
Louisiana Alumni Assn; Centenary Coll. of [18886]
Louisiana Catahoulas; Natl. Assn. of [22313]
Louisiana Iris Soc; Mary Swords Debaillon [★22542]
Louisiana Irises; Soc. for [22542]
Louisiana Pecan Growers' Assn. - Address unknown since 1995.
Louisiana Sugar Exchange - Defunct.
Louisiana Sugar Planters Assn., Amer. Cane Growers Assn. and [★5225]
Louisville Alumni Assn; Univ. of [18934]
Louvre Museum; Friends of the [IO]
Love - 5 - Defunct.
Love in Action [19868], 4780 Yale Rd., Memphis, TN 38128, (901)751-2468
Love Addicts Anonymous; Sex and [13074]
"Love is All" for Enge - Address unknown since 2002.
Love Assn; North Amer. Man/Boy [13099]
Love Bird Soc; African [21832]
Love Campaign; Natl. Black on Black [11842]
Love is Feeding Everyone - Address unknown since 2003.
Love Found; Simply [10191]
Love Humanity [IO], Bombay, India
Love Humanity - India [★IO]
Love Humanity Intl. [IO], Bombay, India
Love Humanity - USA [IO], Tustin, CA, United States
Love Humanity - USA [11618], 17702 Irvine Blvd., Ste. 202, Tustin, CA 92780, (714)749-3613
Love on a Leash - The Found. for Pet Provided Therapy [16623], PO Box 4115, Oceanside, CA 92052-4115, (760)740-2326
Love; Long Distance [★22136]
Love-N-Addiction - Address unknown since 2007.
Love Notes [★10191]

Love Our Children USA [11619], 220 E 57th St., 9th Fl., Ste. G, New York, NY 10022-2820, (212)629-2099
Love Proj. [★12364]
Love; Soc. for the Philosophy of Sex and [10836]
Love Token Soc. [22744], c/o Sid Gale, Sec., PO Box 970, Mandeville, LA 70470, (985)626-3867
"Love Yourself" Stop the Violence [17250], PO Box 101054, Brooklyn, NY 11210
Love146 [11620], PO Box 8266, New Haven, CT 06530, (203)772-4420
Loved Ones and Drivers Support [13347], PO Box 544, Plover, WI 54467-0544
LOVEfords [21692], c/o John Rotella, Pres./Founder, 2484 W Genesee Tpke., Camillus, NY 13031-9610, (315)672-5548
LOVEfords [IO], Camillus, NY, United States
Lovers of the Stinking Rose - Address unknown since 2001.
Loving More [13096], PO Box 4358, Boulder, CO 80306-4358, (303)543-7540
LOVW [★22580]
Low Impact Living Initiative [IO], Winslow, United Kingdom
Low Income Housing Coalition; Ad Hoc [★12330]
Low Income Housing Coalition; Natl. [12330]
Low Income Housing Info. Ser. [★12330]
Low-Mintage Coin Club - Defunct.
Low Power Radio Assn. [IO], Zaventem, Belgium
Low Temperature Calorimetry Conf. [★7796]
Low Vision; Coun. of Citizens With [★11934]
Low Vision Intl; Coun. of Citizens With [11934]
Lowe Syndrome Assn. [14462], 18919 Voss Rd., Dallas, TX 75287, (612)869-5693
Lowell Celebrates Kerouac! [9683], c/o Lawrence Carradini, Pres., PO Box 1111, Lowell, MA 01853-1111, (877)KER-OUAC
Loyal Assn. - Address unknown since 1995.
Loyal Christian Benefit Assn. [19129], PO Box 13005, 700 Peach St., Erie, PA 16514-1305, (814)453-4331
Loyal Escorts of the Green Garter [21173], c/o Jeanne Cantrell, Treas., 11 Brown St., Irving, TX 75061
Loyal Knights of the Round Table [★13061]
Loyal Knights of the Round Table [★IO]
Loyal League of the Yiddish Sons of Erin - Address unknown since 1995.
Loyal Legion of the Medal of Honor - Address unknown since 1995.
Loyal Legion of the U.S; Military Order of the [20728]
Loyal Orange Institution of U.S.A. - Address unknown since 1995.
Loyal Orange Ladies Institution - Address unknown since 1995.
Loyal Order of the Boar - Address unknown since 1987.
Loyal Order of Catfish Lovers - Address unknown since 1999.
Loyal Order of Pessimists; Benevolent and [22591]
Loyal Temperance Legion [★13306]
Loyalists and Patriots of the Amer. Revolution; Hereditary Order of Descendants of the [20673]
Loyola Extension Services [IO], Trivandrum, India
LP Gas Assn. [IO], Ringwood, United Kingdom
LP-Gas Coun; Natl. [★1681]
LPG Australia [IO], Strawberry Hills, Australia
LPG Australia [IO], Strawberry Hills, Australia
LPTV Assn; Natl. Translator [★576]
LS ESSI, Inc. [★14304]
LS ESSI, Inc. [★IO]
LSM Natl. Assn. [★21228]
LTD Shippers Assn. [3842], 1230 Pottstown Pike, Ste. 6, Glenmoore, PA 19343, (610)458-3636
LTD Shippers Assn. [IO], Glenmoore, PA, United States
LTL Carriers Assn; Distribution and [3564]
LTN - Defunct.
Lubavitch; Chabad [20131]
Lubavitch Movement [★20131]
Lubavitch Women's Org. - Address unknown since 2008.
Lubavitch Youth Org. [20158], 770 Eastern Pkwy., Brooklyn, NY 11213, (718)953-1000

A star before a book entry number signifies that the name is not listed separately, but is mentioned within the entry.

Lubes; Natl. Assn. of Independent [★408]
Lubricants
  Intl. Coun. for Machinery Lubrication [7253]
  Intl. Coun. for Machinery Lubrication [IO]
  Japanese Soc. of Tribologists [IO]
  Metal Powder Producers Assn. [2715]
  Soc. of Tribologists and Lubrication Engineers [7047]
Lubricating Grease Inst; Natl. [2937]
Lubrication Engineers; Amer. Soc. of [★7047]
Lucas Educational Found; George [8258]
Luce Found; Henry [12050]
Lucio Fan Club [24942], c/o Sue Fetcho, Pres., 315 Cypress Glen Dr., Mount Juliet, TN 37122-3083
Lucis Trust [17737], 120 Wall St., 24th Fl., New York, NY 10005, (212)292-0707
Lucis Trust [IO], New York, NY, United States
Lucky Mee Family Assn. [20983]
Lucy Stone League [17547], 133 Walton St., No. 126, Syracuse, NY 13202, (315)443-2173
Lucy Stone League [IO], Newcastle, ME, United States
Ludwick Family Found. [17646], PO Box 1796, Glendora, CA 91740, (626)852-0092
Ludwig Boltzman Gesellschaft - Osterreichische Vereinigung zur Forderung der Wissenschaftlichen Forschung [★IO]
Ludwig Boltzmann Assn. - Austrian Soc. for the Promotion of Sci. Res. [IO], Vienna, Austria
Luge
  Bobsleigh Canada Skeleton [IO]
  Intl. Luge Fed. [IO]
  Norwegian Luge, Bobsleigh and Skeleton Fed. [IO]
  U.S. Luge Assn. [23575]
Luggage
  Amer. Luggage Dealers Cooperative [2439]
  Intl. Luggage Repair Assn. [2440]
  Intl. Luggage Repair Assn. [IO]
  Natl. Luggage Dealers Assn. [2418]
  Travel Goods Assn. [2441]
Luggage Dealers Assn; Natl. [2418]
Luggage and Leather Goods Mfrs. of America - Address unknown since 2005.
Luggage and Leather Goods Salesmen's Assn. of America - Address unknown since 2005.
Luis Palau Assn. [20022], PO Box 50, Portland, OR 97207, (503)614-1500
Luis Palau Assn. [IO], Portland, OR, United States
Luis Palau Evangelistic Assn. [★IO]
Luis Palau Evangelistic Assn. [★20022]
Luis Palau Evangelistic Team [★20022]
Luis Palau Evangelistic Team [★IO]
LULAC Found. - Defunct.
LULAC Natl. Educational Ser. Centers [8275], 2000 L St. NW, Ste. 610, Washington, DC 20036, (202)835-9646
LULAC Natl. Scholarship Fund Program [★8275]
Lulu; Friends of [22134]
Lum and Abner Soc; Natl. [22925]
Lumber Assn; North Amer. Wholesale [1611]
Lumber Assn; Northeastern Retail [1655]
Lumber Assn; Northwestern [1614]
Lumber and Building Material Dealers Assn; Natl. [1653]
Lumber and Building Materials Assn. of Ontario [IO], Mississauga, ON, Canada
Lumber Dealers Assn; Natl. Retail [★1653]
Lumber Dealers Res. Coun. - Defunct.
Lumber Distributing Yard Assn; Natl. Wholesale [★1647]
Lumber Exporters Assn; Natl. [★1603]
Lumber Exporters Assn; Pacific [1616]
Lumber Imports; Coalition for Fair [1641]
Lumber Inspection Bur; West Coast [1628]
Lumber Mfrs. Assn; Northeastern [1654]
Lumber Mfrs. Assn; Southeastern [1620]
Lumber Mfrs. Assn; Southern Hardwood [★1648]
Lumber Manufacturers; Southern Pine [★1623]
Lumber Standard Comm; Amer. [1634]
Lumber Standards; Central Comm. on [★1634]
Lumberjack Assn; Amer. [23800]
Lumberman's Assn; Northeastern Retail [★1655]
Lumbermen's Assn; Northwestern [★1614]
Lumbermen's Assn; West Coast [★1631]

Lumbermen's Assn; Western Retail [★1629]
Lumen Vitae - Centre Intl. d'Etudes de la Formation Religieuse [★IO]
Luminescent Stamp Club - Defunct.
Lunar and Planetary Observers; Assn. of [21550]
Lunar Res; Trans [6391]
Lunar Soc; Amer. [6499]
Lundberg School of Seamanship; Seafarers/Harry [★24132]
Lunds Botaniska Forening [★IO]
Lundy Collectors Club - Address unknown since 2001.
Lung Assn; Amer. [16354]
Lung Assn; Black [13323]
Lung Assn. Staff; Cong. of [16357]
Lung Assn; White [13332]
Lung Assn. of Zurich [IO], Zurich, Switzerland
Lung Cancer
  Alliance for Lung Cancer Advocacy, Support and Educ. [13788]
  Amer. Lung Assn. [16354]
  Cong. of Lung Assn. Staff [16357]
  Cystic Fibrosis Found. [16358]
  Global Lung Cancer Coalition [IO]
  Lung Cancer Alliance [13839]
  Natl. Jewish Medical and Res. Center [16361]
  Natl. Lung Cancer Partnership [13854]
Lung Cancer Advocacy, Support and Educ; Alliance for [13788]
Lung Cancer Alliance [13839]
Lung Transplantation Registry; International Heart and [★16674]
Lung Transplantation Registry; International Heart and [★IO]
Lungenliga Zurich [★IO]
Luontaistuotealan Tukkukauppiaiden Liitto ry [★IO]
Luovan Saveltaiteen Edistamissaatio [★IO]
Lupus Assn. of NSW [IO], North Ryde, Australia
Lupus Assn. Singapore [IO], Singapore, Singapore
Lupus Erythematosus
  Alliance for Lupus Res. [IO]
  Alliance for Lupus Res. [15013]
  European Lupus Erythematosus Fed. [IO]
  Lupus Assn. of NSW [IO]
  Lupus Assn. Singapore [IO]
  Lupus Found. of Am. [15014]
  Lupus Info. Network [15015]
Lupus Found. of Am. [15014], 2000 L St. NW, Ste. 710, Washington, DC 20036, (202)349-1155
Lupus Info. Network [15015], 230 Ranch Dr., Bridgeport, CT 06606-1747, (203)372-5795
Lupus Network [★15015]
Lure Collectors Club; Natl. Fishing [22082]
Luscombe Assn. [★21461]
Luscombe Assn; Continental [21439]
Luscombe Endowment [21461], 2487 S Gilbert Rd., Ste. 106, PMB 113, Gilbert, AZ 85296, (480)650-0883
Lusitano Breed Soc. of Great Britain [IO], Machynlleth, United Kingdom
Lusitano Horse Assn; Intl. Andalusian and [4894]
Luso-American Educ. Found. [10890], PO Box 2967, Dublin, CA 94568, (925)828-3883
Luso-American Fraternal Fed. [19130], PO Box 2968, Dublin, CA 94568, (925)828-4884
Luso-American Fraternal Fed. Scholarship Comm. [★10890]
Luso-American Life Insurance Soc. [19131], PO Box 2968, Dublin, CA 94568, (925)828-4884
Lute Soc. [IO], Guildford, United Kingdom
Lute Soc. of Am. [10641], c/o Garald Farnham, Treas., 255 W 98th St., No. 5C, New York, NY 10025-7282, (925)686-5800
Luther Family Assn. [20984], 2027 Spyglass Ct., Lakeland, FL 33810-6737, (863)815-2505
Luther League - Defunct.
Luther Vandross Intl. Fan Club - Address unknown since 2006.
Lutheran
  African Amer. Lutheran Assn. [20211]
  Amer. Lutheran Publicity Bur. [20212]
  Assn. of Lutheran Secondary Schools [8801]
  Australian Lutheran World Ser. [IO]
  Concordia Deaconess Conf. [20213]
  Concordia Gospel Outreach [20214]

  Concordia Gospel Outreach [IO]
  Concordia Historical Inst. [20215]
  Disability Ministries [20216]
  Evangelical Lutheran Educ. Assn. [8802]
  Global Hea. Ministries [14630]
  Hea. Ministries [20241]
  Intl. Lutheran Deaf Assn. [20217]
  Intl. Lutheran Deaf Assn. [IO]
  Intl. Lutheran Laymen's League [IO]
  Intl. Lutheran Laymen's League [20218]
  Japan Evangelical Lutheran Church [IO]
  Lutheran Bible Translators [19524]
  Lutheran Braille Workers [16867]
  Lutheran Deaconess Assn. [20219]
  Lutheran Deaconess Conf. [20220]
  Lutheran Educ. Assn. [8803]
  Lutheran Education Association [IO]
  Lutheran Educational Conf. of North Am. [8804]
  Lutheran Fraternities of Am. [19217]
  Lutheran Girl Pioneers [20221]
  Lutheran Historical Conf. [20222]
  Lutheran Human Relations Assn. [20223]
  Lutheran Immigration and Refugee Ser. [12815]
  Lutheran Laymen's League of Canada [IO]
  Lutheran Men in Mission [20224]
  Lutheran Mission Societies [20225]
  Lutheran Services in Am. [20226]
  Lutheran Student Movement - U.S.A. [20227]
  Lutheran Volunteer Corps [20228]
  Lutheran Women's Missionary League [20229]
  Lutheran World Fed. [IO]
  Lutheran World Relief [IO]
  Lutheran World Relief [20230]
  Lutherans Concerned/North Am. [20061]
  Natl. Church Lib. Assn. [10375]
  Natl. Lutheran Outdoors Ministry Assn. [20231]
  Phi Beta Chi [24691]
  Seafarers and Intl. House [20232]
  Thrivent Financial for Lutherans [19218]
  Trinity Medical Center [14900]
  United Lutheran Soc. [19219]
  Wheat Ridge Ministries [20233]
  World Mission Prayer League [20234]
  World Mission Prayer League [IO]
  Youth Ministry [20235]
Lutheran Acad. for Scholarship - Defunct.
Lutheran Benevolent Assn. - Defunct.
Lutheran Bible Translators [19524], PO Box 2050, Aurora, IL 60507-2050, (630)897-0660
Lutheran Bible Translators of Canada [IO], Kitchener, ON, Canada
Lutheran Bible Translators; Messengers of Christ- [★19524]
Lutheran Braille Evangelism Assn. [16866], 1740 Eugene St., White Bear Lake, MN 55110-3312, (651)426-0469
Lutheran Braille Evangelism Association [IO], White Bear Lake, MN, United States
Lutheran Braille Workers [IO], Yucaipa, CA, United States
Lutheran Braille Workers [16867], PO Box 5000, Yucaipa, CA 92399, (909)795-8977
Lutheran Brotherhood Found. [★19218]
Lutheran Campus Ministry Assn. - Defunct.
Lutheran Church in Am. [★20224]
Lutheran Church; Amer. [★20224]
Lutheran Church; Assn. of Evangelical [★20224]
Lutheran Church; Brotherhood of the Amer. [★20224]
Lutheran Church and Indian People - Defunct.
Lutheran Church Lib. Assn. [★10375]
Lutheran Church Men; Amer. [★20224]
Lutheran Coalition on Latin America - Address unknown since 2001.
Lutheran Collegiate Assn. - Defunct.
Lutheran Conf. on Social Concerns - Defunct.
Lutheran Coun. in the U.S.A. [★19915]
Lutheran Coun. in the U.S.A. - Defunct.
Lutheran Deaconess Assn. [20219], 1304 LaPorte Ave., Valparaiso, IN 46383, (219)464-6925
Lutheran Deaconess Conf. [20220], 1304 LaPorte Ave., Valparaiso, IN 46383, (219)464-6925
Lutheran Educ. Assn. [8803], 7400 Augusta St., River Forest, IL 60305, (708)209-3343
Lutheran Education Association [IO], River Forest, IL, United States

Reference to "IO" in place of a book number signifies that the association may be found in the 45th edition of International Organizations.

Lutheran Educ. Assn; Amer. [★8802]

Lutheran Educ. Conf; Natl. [★8804]

Lutheran Educational Conf. of North Am. [8804], First Financial Center, 110 S Phillips Ave., Ste. 306, Sioux Falls, SD 57104, (605)782-4003

Lutheran Found. for Religious Drama - Address unknown since 1995.

Lutheran Fraternities of Am. [19217], PO Box 182033, Shelby Township, MI 48318-2033, (586)677-5020

Lutheran Fraternity; Beta Sigma Psi Natl. [24619]

Lutheran Gen. Hea. Sys. [★14821]

Lutheran Girl Pioneers [20221], 1611 Caledonia St., La Crosse, WI 54603, (608)781-5232

Lutheran Good Samaritan Soc; Evangelical [13168]

Lutheran Historical Conf. [20222], c/o Marvin A. Huggins, Membership Sec., 5732 White Pine Dr., St. Louis, MO 63129-2936, (314)505-7921

Lutheran Homes and Services; Bethesda [12565]

Lutheran Hospitals and Homes Soc. - Address unknown since 1999.

Lutheran Human Relations Assn. [20223], 1821 N 16th St., Milwaukee, WI 53205, (414)536-0585

Lutheran Human Relations Assn. of Am. [★20223]

Lutheran Immigration and Refugee Ser. [12815], 700 Light St., Baltimore, MD 21230, (410)230-2700

Lutheran Immigration and Refugee Service [IO], Baltimore, MD, United States

Lutheran Immigration Ser. [★IO]

Lutheran Immigration Ser. [★12815]

Lutheran Laymen's League [★20218]

Lutheran Laymen's League [★IO]

Lutheran Laymen's League of Canada [IO], Kitchener, ON, Canada

Lutheran Medical Mission Assn. - Defunct.

Lutheran Men; Assn. of [★20224]

Lutheran Men in Mission [20224], Evangelical Lutheran Church in Am., 8765 W Higgins Rd., Chicago, IL 60631, (773)380-2700

Lutheran Mission; Salem Hebrew [★20019]

Lutheran Mission Societies [20225]

Lutheran Outdoors Ministry Assn. [★20231]

Lutheran Peace Fellowship [18218], 1710 11th Ave., Seattle, WA 98122-2420, (206)720-0313

Lutheran Sanatorium Assn; Evangelical [★20233]

Lutheran Seaman's Center [★20232]

Lutheran Secondary Schools; Assn. of [8801]

Lutheran Services in Am. [20226], c/o Jill Schumann, Pres./CEO, 700 Light St., Baltimore, MD 21230-3850, (410)230-2702

Lutheran Soc. for Worship, Music and the Arts [★19900]

Lutheran Soc. for Worship, Music and the Arts [★IO]

Lutheran Student Assn. of Am. [★20227]

Lutheran Student Movement - U.S.A. [20227], 8765 W Higgins Rd., Chicago, IL 60631-4194, (773)380-2852

Lutheran Volunteer Corps [20228], 1226 Vermont Ave. NW, Washington, DC 20005, (202)387-3222

Lutheran Women's Missionary League [20229], PO Box 411993, St. Louis, MO 63141-1993, (800)252-5965

Lutheran Women's Missionary League [★20229]

Lutheran Women's Missionary League; Intl. [★20229]

Lutheran World Fed. [IO], Geneva, Switzerland

Lutheran World Fed. - Switzerland [★IO]

Lutheran World Fed., U.S.A. Natl. Comm. - Defunct.

Lutheran World Relief [20230], 700 Light St., Baltimore, MD 21230, (410)230-2700

Lutheran World Relief [IO], Baltimore, MD, United States

Lutheran World Ser. - India [IO], Calcutta, India

Lutheran Young People's Societies of America; Federated Norwegian [★20225]

Lutheran Youth Fellowship [★20235]

Lutherans Concerned for Gay People [★20061]

Lutherans Concerned/North Am. [20061], PO Box 4707, St. Paul, MN 55104-0707, (651)665-0861

Lutherans For Life [12921], 1120 S G Ave., Nevada, IA 50201-2774, (515)382-2077

Lutherans for Life - Australia [IO], Adelaide, Australia

Luthiers; Guild of Amer. [2804]

Luvers of David Jones United - Address unknown since 1999.

Luxembourg Amateur Dance Fed. [IO], Hautcharage, Luxembourg

Luxembourg Badminton Fed. [IO], Luxembourg, Luxembourg

Luxembourg Bankers' Assn. [IO], Luxembourg, Luxembourg

Luxembourg Baseball Fed. [IO], Dudelange, Luxembourg

Luxembourg Brotherhood of America - Address unknown since 1995.

Luxembourg Chamber of Notaries [IO], Luxembourg, Luxembourg

Luxembourg Confed. of Christian Trade Unions [IO], Luxembourg, Luxembourg

Luxembourg Cricket Fed. [IO], Luxembourg, Luxembourg

Luxembourg Dietetic Assn. [IO], Walferdange, Luxembourg

Luxembourg Fed. of Hospitals [IO], Luxembourg, Luxembourg

Luxembourg Fed. of Hotels, Restaurants and Coffee Shops [IO], Luxembourg, Luxembourg

Luxembourg Naturalist Soc. [IO], Luxembourg, Luxembourg

Luxembourg-Nicaragua Solidarity Assn. [IO], Luxembourg, Luxembourg

Luxembourg Org. for Reproduction Rights [IO], Luxembourg, Luxembourg

Luxembourg Philatelic Study Club - Defunct.

Luxembourg Socialist Workers' Party [IO], Luxembourg, Luxembourg

Luxembourg Soc. of Gastroenterology and Digestive Endoscopy [IO], Luxembourg, Luxembourg

Luxembourg Water Ski Fed. [IO], Luxembourg, Luxembourg

Luxembourg Youth Hostels Assn. [IO], Luxembourg, Luxembourg

Luxury Hotels Assn; Small [★1966]

Luxury Hotels Intl; Assoc. [1931]

Luxury Hotels; Small [★1966]

Luxury Hotels of the World; Small [1966]

Luxury Suite Directors; Assn. of [3676]

Luz Social Services [13255], 2797 N Introspect Dr., Tucson, AZ 85745, (520)882-6216

Lybarger Memorial Assn. [20985], PO Box 611, Delaware, OH 43015-0611, (419)774-9830

Lyceum Assn; Amer. [★10901]

Lyceum Assn; Intl. [★10901]

Lychee Growers Assn; Florida [4732]

Lydia - A Women's Cooperative Interchange - Defunct.

Lyman A. Brewer III, Intl. Surgical Soc. - Defunct.

Lyman Boat Owners Assn. [21877], PO Box 40052, Cleveland, OH 44140, (440)954-4005

Lyme Borreliosis Found. [★14272]

Lyme Disease Assn. [14271], PO Box 1438, Jackson, NJ 08527, (888)366-6611

Lyme Disease Found. [14272], PO Box 332, Tolland, CT 06084-0332, (860)870-0070

Lyme Disease Found; Amer. [14249]

Lymphatic Res. Found. [15017], 100 Forest Dr., Greenvale, NY 11548, (516)625-9675

Lymphedema Network; Natl. [15018]

Lymphology

Australasian Lymphology Assn. [IO]

Intl. Soc. for Cutaneous Lymphomas [IO]

Intl. Soc. of Lymphology [IO]

Intl. Soc. of Lymphology [15016]

Lymphatic Res. Found. [15017]

Lymphovenous Canada [IO]

Natl. Lymphedema Network [15018]

North Amer. Vodder Assn. of Lymphatic Therapy [15019]

North Amer. Vodder Assn. of Lymphatic Therapy [IO]

Soc. for Hematopathology [15874]

Lymphoma Assn. [IO], Aylesbury, United Kingdom

Lymphoma Found; Cure For [★13840]

Lymphoma Res. Found. [13840], 8800 Venice Blvd., Ste. 207, Los Angeles, CA 90034, (310)204-7040

Lymphoma. Res. Found. of Am. [★13840]

Lymphoma Soc; Leukemia and [13837]

Lymphovenous Canada [IO], Toronto, ON, Canada

Lynn Anderson Fan Club - Address unknown since 1989.

Lynx Cat Assn; Intl. Desert [4207]

Lyon Commerce Intl. [IO], Lyon, France

Lyre Assn. of North Am. [22716], c/o Samantha Embrey, Treas., PO Box 7745, Charlottesville, VA 22906-7745, (434)295-9571

Lyre Assn. of North America-Esther Centers [★22716]

Lysosomal Diseases New Zealand [IO], Lower Hutt, New Zealand

M

M-20 Sailing Assn. - Address unknown since 1999.

M. T. Bottle Collectors Assn. [22066], PO Box 1581, DeLand, FL 32721, (386)734-3651

M Technology Assn. -, Address unknown since 2002.

Maa- ja Metsataloustuottajain Keskusliitto [★IO]

Maan ystavat ry [★IO]

Ma'an Development Center [IO], Jerusalem, Israel

MAAP Services for Autism and Asperger Syndrome [15337], c/o Susan J. Moreno, Pres./Founder/Ed., PO Box 524, Crown Point, IN 46308, (219)662-1311

Maaseutukeskusten Liitto [★IO]

MAB Community Services [16868], 200 Ivy St., Brookline, MA 02446, (617)738-5110

Macadamia Soc; California [5053]

Macao Chamber of Commerce [IO], Macau, Macao

Macaroni Manufacturers Assn; Natl. [★1550]

MacArthur Memorial Found; Rizal- [12541]

Macau Amateur Weightlifting Fed. [IO], Macau, Macao

Macau DanceSport Fed. [IO], Macau, Macao

Macau Importers and Exporters Assn. [IO], Macau, Macao

Macau Jockey Club [IO], Taipa, Macao

Macau Junior Chamber China [IO], Macau, Macao

Macau Sports Medicine Assn. [IO], Macau, Macao

Macbride Museum Soc. [IO], Whitehorse, YT, Canada

The Maccabees - Address unknown since 2003.

Maccabi USA/Sports for Israel [23828], 1926 Arch St., No. 4R, Philadelphia, PA 19103, (215)561-6900

MacCartney Clan Soc. [20986]

Macclesfield Chamber of Commerce and Enterprise [IO], Macclesfield, United Kingdom

MacDowell Artists Assn. - Address unknown since 2003.

MacDuff Soc. of Am; Clan [20837]

Macedonia Taekwondo Fed. [IO], Skopje, Macedonia

Macedonian

Macedonian Amer. Friendship Assn. [19220]

Macedonian Arts Coun. [10437]

Macedonian Arts Coun. [IO]

Macedonian Orthodox Youth Assn. of North Am. [19883]

Macedonian Outreach [20236]

Macedonian Outreach [IO]

Macedonian Patriotic Org. of U.S. and Canada [IO]

Macedonian Patriotic Org. of U.S. and Canada [19221]

Macedonian Amer. Friendship Assn. [19220], 57 Jefferson Ave., Columbus, OH 43215, (614)668-9656

Macedonian Arts Coun. [10437], PO Box 23905, New York, NY 10023, (212)799-0009

Macedonian Arts Coun. [IO], New York, NY, United States

Macedonian Assn. Against Rheumatism [IO], Skopje, Macedonia

Macedonian Assn. of Info. Tech. [IO], Skopje, Macedonia

Macedonian Dance Assn. [IO], Skopje, Macedonia

Macedonian Dermatovenerologic Soc. [IO], Skopje, Macedonia

Macedonian Geotechnical Soc. [IO], Skopje, Macedonia

Macedonian Medical Assn. [IO], Skopje, Macedonia

Macedonian Olympic Comm. [IO], Skopje, Macedonia

Macedonian Orthodox Youth Assn. of North Am. [IO], Syracuse, NY, United States

Macedonian Orthodox Youth Assn. of North Am. [19883], 5083 Onondaga Rd., Syracuse, NY 13215, (315)487-1265

A star before a book entry number signifies that the name is not listed separately, but is mentioned within the entry.

Macedonian Outreach [20236], PO Box 398, Danville, CA 94526-0398, (925)820-4107
Macedonian Outreach [IO], Danville, CA, United States
Macedonian Patriotic Org. of U.S. and Canada [IO], Fort Wayne, IN, United States
Macedonian Patriotic Org. of U.S. and Canada [19221], 124 W Wayne St., Fort Wayne, IN 46802, (260)422-5900
Macedonian Political Organizations; Union of [★19221]
Macedonian School Sport Fed. [IO], Skopje, Macedonia
Macedonian Tennis Fed. [IO], Skopje, Macedonia
MacFaddien Family Soc. [20987], c/o Norman J. McFaddien, Sr., 5297 Black River Rd., Gn D1, Sardinia, SC 29143, (803)473-2643
Machine Accountants Assn; Natl. [★8128]
Machine Affiliates Trading Corp. - Defunct.
Machine Assn; Amer. Amusement [1296]
Machine Cancel Soc. [22839], c/o William Barlow, III, Pres., 3097 Frobisher Ave., Dublin, OH 43017-1652
Machine Chain Mfrs. Assn. - Address unknown since 1995.
Machine Dealers Assn; Natl. Off. [★2844]
Machine Dealers Assn; Natl. Typewriter and Off. [★2844]
Machine, and Furniture Workers; Intl. Union of Electronic, Elecl., Salaried, [24049]
Machine, and Furniture Workers; Intl. Union of Electronic, Elecl., Tech., Salaried, [★24049]
Machine Inst; Cold Formed Parts and [1820]
Machine Inst; Tubular Rivet and [★1820]
Machine Knife Assn. [2036], 30200 Detroit Rd., Cleveland, OH 44145-1967, (440)899-0010
Machine Knife Mfrs. Assn. [★2036]
Machine Printers and Engravers Assn. of the U.S. - Address unknown since 2002.
Machine Records Conf; Coll. and Univ. [★7894]
Machine Tool Distributors' Assn; Amer. [1995]
Machine Tool Importers Assn. of Japan [★IO]
Machine Tool Technologies Assn. [★IO]
Machine Translation and Computational Linguistics; Assn. for [★10400]
Machine Vision Assn. of the Soc. of Mfg. Engineers [7583], PO Box 930, Dearborn, MI 48121-0930, (313)271-1500
Machine Vision Assn. of the Soc. of Mfg. Engineers [IO], Dearborn, MI, United States
Machine Workers of Am; United Elecl., Radio and [24050]
Machine Workers; Intl. Union of Elecl., Radio and [★24049]
Machined Products Assn; Precision [1832]
Machinery
    Agricultural and Forestry Machinery Assn. [IO]
    Antique Caterpillar Machinery Owners Club [22619]
    Antique Small Engine Collectors Club [22409]
    Assn. of Equip. Mgt. Professionals [2442]
    Association of Equipment Management Professionals [IO]
    Canadian Assn. of Equip. Distributors [IO]
    Early Typewriter Collectors Assn. [22015]
    Equip. Appraisers Assn. of North Am. [279]
    Intl. Assn. of Machinists and Aerospace Workers [24012]
    Intl. Assn. of Machinists and Aerospace Workers, Woodworkers District Lodge W1 [24026]
    Intl. Coun. for Machinery Lubrication [7253]
    Intl. Union of Electronic, Elecl., Salaried, Machine, and Furniture Workers [24049]
    Japan Light Machinery Info. Center of Central New York [24343]
    Japan Machinery Fed. [IO]
    Japan Soc. for the Promotion of Machine Indus. [IO]
    Japan Textile Machinery Assn. [IO]
    Machinery Dealers Natl. Assn. [2037]
    Machinists Non-Partisan Political League [24101]
    Mfrs. Alliance/MAPI [2039]
    Marine Machinery Assn. [2608]
    Mech. and Metal Trades Confed. [IO]
    Motor Trades Assn. of Australia [IO]

Natl. Threshers Assn. [9484]
Packaging Machinery Mfrs. Inst. [2876]
Power Crane and Shovel Assn. [2058]
Rough and Tumble Engineers' Historical Assn. [22979]
Tooling Indus. Forum of Australia [IO]
Turbine Inlet Cooling Assn. [7055]
United Elecl., Radio and Machine Workers of Am. [24050]
Wire and Cable Indus. Suppliers Assn. [1231]
Wire Industry Suppliers Assn. [2079]
Wood Machinery Mfrs. of Am. [2080]
Woodworking Machinery Indus. Assn. [2081]
Machinery and Allied Products Inst. [★2039]
Machinery Assn; Amer. Paper [★2003]
Machinery Assn; Amer. Textile [1997]
Machinery; Assn. for Computing [6783]
Machinery Assn; Fabricating [★2017]
Machinery Assn; Intl. Assn. of Food Indus. Suppliers and Food Processing [★1133]
Machinery Assn; Pulp and Paper [★2003]
Machinery Builders Assn; Wire [★2079]
Machinery Dealers Natl. Assn. [2037], 315 S Patrick St., Alexandria, VA 22314-3501, (703)836-9300
Machinery Dealers Natl. Assn. [IO], Alexandria, VA, United States
Machinery and Equip. Appraisers; Assn. of [277]
Machinery Importers Assn. of Am; Woodworking [★2081]
Machinery Indus. Assn; Woodworking [2081]
Machinery Info. Center of Central New York; Japan Light [24343]
Machinery Info. Mgt. Open Systems Alliance [2560], 2704 8th St., Tuscaloosa, AL 35401, (949)625-8616
Machinery Mfrs. of Am; Wood [2080]
Machinery Mfrs. Assn; Amer. Supply and [★2027]
Machinery Mfrs. Assn; Indus. Supply and [★2027]
Machinery Mfrs. Assn; Laundry and Dry Cleaners [★2407]
Machinery Mfrs. Assn; Pulp and Paper [★2003]
Machinery Mfrs. Inst; Meat [★2661]
Machinery Mfrs. Inst; Packaging [2876]
Machinery Mfrs; Natl. Assn. of Textile [★1997]
Machinery and Supplies Assn; Dairy and Ice Cream [★1133]
Machinery Trade Assn; Amer. Apparel [1990]
Machinery Trade Assn; Farm Tractor and [IO]
Machining Assn; Natl. Tool, Die and Precision [★2031]
Machining Inst; Photo-Chemical [2725]
Machining and Material Removal Community [7025], PO Box 930, Dearborn, MI 48121, (313)271-1500
Machining and Material Removal Community of the Soc. of Mfg. Engineers [7747], c/o Soc. Of Mfg. Engineers, PO Box 930, Dearborn, MI 48121-0930, (313)425-3000
Machining Tech. Assn. of SME [★7025]
Machinists and Aerospace Workers; Intl. Assn. of [24012]
Machinists and Aerospace Workers, Woodworkers District Lodge W1; Intl. Assn. of [24026]
Machinists; Intl. Assn. of [★24012]
Machinists Non-Partisan Political League [24101], 9000 Machinists Pl., Upper Marlboro, MD 20772-2687, (301)967-4500
Machinists Vise Assn. [★1822]
Machne Israel [12476], 770 Eastern Pkwy., Brooklyn, NY 11213, (718)774-4000
MacInnes Soc; Clan [★20951]
Macintosh User Gp; Christian [6790]
Macintosh Users Gp; Arizona [6782]
MacIntyre Assn; Clan [20838]
MacIntyre Soc; Clan [20839]
Mack Vickery Fan Club - Address unknown since 2003.
MacKay Soc; Clan [20840]
Mackenzie Inst. [IO], Toronto, ON, Canada
MacKenzie Soc. in the Americas; Clan [20841]
Mackintosh of North Am; Clan [20842]
MacLellan Clan in Am. [20988], c/o Ms. Nancy Sears, Treas., PO Box 397, Simpsonville, KY 40067-0397, (502)722-5067
Maclellan Found. [20502], 820 Broad St., Ste. 300, Chattanooga, TN 37402, (423)755-1366

Maclellan Found. [IO], Chattanooga, TN, United States
MacLennan Assn., U.S.A; Clan [20843]
Macneil Assn. of Am; Clan [20844]
Macpherson Assn; Clan [20845]
Macra Na Feirme [IO], Dublin, Ireland
MacRae Soc. of North Am; Clan [20846]
Macro Soc. [10184], PO Box 26880, Tempe, AZ 85285-6880
Macrocosm USA [3234], PO Box 185, Cambria, CA 93428, (805)927-2515
MacThomas North Am. [20989], 210 Belford Ave., Huntington, WV 25701
MacThomas Soc; Clan [★20989]
Macular Degeneration Found. [16869], PO Box 531313, Henderson, NV 89053, (888)633-3937
Macular Disease Soc. [IO], Andover, United Kingdom
Macular Diseases; Assn. for [15669]
Macy, Jr. Found; Josiah [14571]
MAD DADS (Men Against Destruction - Defending Against Drugs and Social Disorder) [12043], 555 Stockton St., Jacksonville, FL 32204, (904)388-8171
Mad World Campaign - Defunct.
Madagascar Aviation Assn. [IO], Antsirabe, Madagascar
Made Up Textiles Assn. [★IO]
Made in the U.S.A. Found. - Address unknown since 2003.
Madge Sinclair Fan Club - Defunct.
Madison Center for Educational Affairs - Address unknown since 2003.
Madison Found; James [★18444]
Madison Proj. [6245], PO Box 66128, Washington, DC 20035-6128, (202)747-1245
The Madison Proj. [8824], c/o James Madison Univ., Graduate School of Educ., 800 S Main St., PO Box 8298, Harrisonburg, VA 22801
Madness Network News - Address unknown since 1990.
Mado Robin Soc. - Defunct.
Madonna House Apostolate [IO], Combermere, ON, Canada
Madonna Intl. Fan Club - Defunct.
MADRE [12529], 121 W 27th St., Rm. 301, New York, NY 10001, (212)627-0444
Madrid Chamber of Commerce and Indus. [IO], Madrid, Spain
Maffucci Self-Help Gp; Ollier's/ [★15749]
Magazine Advertising Sales Club - Defunct.
Magazine Assn. of America; Comics [3219]
Magazine Assn; City and Regional [3218]
Magazine Editors; Amer. Soc. of [3085]
Magazine Editors; Soc. of Bus. [★3084]
Magazine and Paperback Marketing Inst. - Address unknown since 1999.
Magazine Photographers; Amer. Soc. of [★2992]
Magazine Photographers; Soc. of [★2992]
Magazine Printers Sect. - Defunct.
Magazine Promotion Group - Defunct.
Magazine Publishers of Am. [3235], 810 7th Ave., 24th Fl., New York, NY 10019, (212)872-3700
Magazine Publishers Assn. [★3235]
Magazine Publishers' Assn. - Brazil [IO], Sao Paulo, Brazil
Magazine Publishers' Assn. of New Zealand [IO], Auckland, New Zealand
Magazine Publishers of Australia [IO], Sydney, Australia
Magazine Publishers; Natl. Assn. of [★3235]
Magazine Writers; Soc. of [★11158]
Magazines
    Alberta Magazine Publishers Assn. [IO]
    Alternative Press Center [10892]
    Amer. Amateur Press Assn. [22910]
    Amer. Bus. Media [3201]
    Amer. Horse Publications [3203]
    Amer. Soc. of Magazine Editors [3085]
    Argentine Magazine Publishers' Assn. [IO]
    Assoc. Church Press [3205]
    Assn. of Food Journalists [3094]
    Audit Bur. of Circulations - India [IO]
    Benjamin Franklin Literary and Medical Soc. [14549]

Reference to "IO" in place of a book number signifies that the association may be found in the 45th edition of International Organizations.

Encyclopedia of Associations, 46th Edition   3757

Boating Writers Intl. [3100]
British Soc. of Magazine Editors [IO]
Catholic Press Assn. [3215]
The Christian Sci. Publishing Soc. [3216]
City and Regional Magazine Assn. [3218]
Comics Magazine Assn. of America [3219]
Coun. of Literary Magazines and Presses [10893]
Dog Writers' Assn. of Am. [3110]
Football Writers Assn. of Am. [23430]
Golf Writers Assn. of Am. [23450]
Hollywood Foreign Press Assn. [3115]
Intl. Artists Network [9506]
Intl. Press Inst., Amer. Comm. [3123]
Intl. Regional Magazine Assn. [2443]
Livestock Publications Coun. [3233]
Magazine Publishers of Am. [3235]
Magazine Publishers' Assn. - Brazil [IO]
Magazine Publishers' Assn. of New Zealand [IO]
Media Credit Assn. [1432]
Natl. Amateur Press Assn. [22911]
Natl. Assn. of Black Journalists [3129]
Natl. Geographic Soc. [7123]
Natl. News Bur. [3139]
Natl. Press Club [3141]
Natl. Scholastic Press Assn. [9013]
Natl. Trade Press Assn. [IO]
Newswomen's Club of New York [3150]
Outdoor Writers Assn. of Am. [3153]
Periodical and Book Assn. of Am. [3247]
Publishers Info. Bur. [128]
Reader's Digest Assn. [3250]
Religion News Ser. [3158]
Religion Newswriters Assn. [3159]
Swedish Magazine Publishers' Assn. [IO]
United Amateur Press Assn. of Am. [22912]
United Press Intl. [3169]
White House Correspondents' Assn. [3173]
Magazines Assoc; Agricultural Coll. [★8714]
Magazines Associated; Engineering Coll. [3222]
Magazines Canada [IO], Toronto, ON, Canada
Magazines for Friendship - Address unknown since 1995.
Magazines and Presses; Coun. of Literary [10893]
Magdalene; Soc. of Saint Mary [19724]
Maghrib Stud. in Tunis; Center for [★7927]
Maghrib Stud. in Tunis; Center for [★IO]
Magic
  Australian Soc. of Magicians [IO]
  British Magical Soc. [IO]
  Clowns of Am., Intl. [21951]
  Fellowship of Christian Magicians [19797]
  Intl. Brotherhood of Magicians [22620]
  International Brotherhood of Magicians [IO]
  Intl. Shrine Clown Assn. [21952]
  Magic Circle [IO]
  Magic Collectors' Assn. [22621]
  Magic Lantern Soc. of the U.S. and Canada [21531]
  Magic Youth Intl. [22622]
  Magic Youth Intl. [IO]
  Magicians' Assn. of Macao [IO]
  Magicians Without Borders [12503]
  Proj. Magic [16634]
  Soc. of Amer. Magicians [22623]
  World Clown Assn. [21953]
Magic of Bewitched Fan Club [25034], c/o Gina Hill-Meyers, Pres., PO Box 26734, Fresno, CA 93729, (559)433-1727
Magic Bus, India [IO], Bombay, India
Magic Circle [IO], London, United Kingdom
Magic Collectors' Assn. [22621]
Magic of Engelbert Fan Club - Address unknown since 2002.
MAGIC Found. [13967], 6645 W North Ave., Oak Park, IL 60302, (708)383-0808
MAGIC Found. for Children's Growth [★13967]
Magic; Intl. Club of [★22622]
Magic Johnson Found. [13175], 9100 Wilshire Blvd., Ste. 700 E, Beverly Hills, CA 90212, (310)246-4400
Magic Lantern Soc. of the U.S. and Canada [21531], c/o Richard Moore, Sec.-Treas., 259 Fitch Hill Rd., Guilford, CT 06437-1028, (360)830-5209
Magic; Proj. [16634]
Magic Youth Intl. [22622], 11155C S Towne Sq., St. Louis, MO 63123-7823, (314)845-9200

Magic Youth Intl. [IO], St. Louis, MO, United States
The Magical Child - Belgian Michael Jackson Fan Club [IO], Overpelt, Belgium
Magical Youths Intl. [★IO]
Magical Youths Intl. [★22622]
Magicians
  Clowns of Am., Intl. [21951]
  Fellowship of Christian Magicians [19797]
  Intl. Brotherhood of Magicians [22620]
  Intl. Shrine Clown Assn. [21952]
  Magic Collectors' Assn. [22621]
  Magic Youth Intl. [22622]
  Magicians Without Borders [12503]
  Magicians Without Borders [IO]
  Proj. Magic [16634]
  Soc. of Amer. Magicians [22623]
  World Clown Assn. [21953]
Magicians' Assn. of Macao [IO], Macau, Macao
Magicians; Australian Soc. of [IO]
Magicians; Fellowship of Christian [19797]
Magicians; Intl. Brotherhood of [22620]
Magicians Without Borders [12503], 100 Geary Rd., Lincoln, VT 05443, (802)453-5425
Magicians Without Borders [IO], Lincoln, VT, United States
Magistrates' Assn. of England and Wales [IO], London, United Kingdom
Magna Charta Earls and Barons [★IO]
Magna Charta Earls and Barons [★10096]
Magnesium Assn. [★2711]
Magnesium Assn. [★IO]
Magnet Distributors and Fabricators Assn. - Address unknown since 2007.
Magnet Producers Assn; Permanent [★1824]
Magnetic Compatibility Soc; IEEE Electro [6917]
Magnetic Materials Producers Assn. [★1824]
Magnetic Materials Producers Assn. [IO]
Magnetic and Optical Media Manufacturers and Related Indus; ITA - Intl. Assn. of [★1370]
Magnetic Reading Indus. Assn. [★1212]
Magnetic Resonance; European Chinese Soc. for Clinical [IO]
Magnetic Resonance Managers Soc. [16292], 615 Valley View Dr., Ste. 102, Moline, IL 61265, (309)762-7227
Magnetic Resonance; Soc. for [★16290]
Magnetic Resonance Soc; Clinical [14024]
Magnetic Resonance; Soc. of Computed Body To-mography and [16297]
Magnetic Resonance Technologists; Sect. for [16594]
Magnetics Soc; Bioelectro [6555]
Magnetics Soc; IEEE [6921]
Magnetics Special Interest Gp; Bioelectro [6556]
Magnificent 13 [★11834]
Magnificent 13 [★IO]
The Magnolia Soc. [★6643]
Magnolia Soc; Amer. [★6643]
Magnolia Soc. Intl. [6643], c/o Elizabeth Edward, Sec., 3000 Henneberry Rd., Jamesville, NY 13078, (315)677-7813
Magnum Memorabilia [25035], c/o David Romas, Dir., 438 Leroy St., Ferndale, MI 48220
Magnum Memorabilia [IO], Ferndale, MI, United States
Magnus Hirschfeld Center for Human Rights [IO], Bloomfield, NJ, United States
Magnus Hirschfeld Center for Human Rights [17773], c/o Crosswicks House, PO Box 1974, Bloomfield, NJ 07003-1974, (862)823-1767
Magny Families Assn. [20990], 5 Fieldstone Ct., Newburgh, NY 12550
Magyar Algologiai Tarsasag [★IO]
Magyar Bankzovetzeg [★IO]
Magyar Biofizikai Tarsasag [★IO]
Magyar Communion of Friends - Address unknown since 2001.
Magyar Dermatologiai Tarsulat [★IO]
Magyar Ensz Tarsasag [★IO]
Magyar Fallabda (Squash) Szovetseg [IO], Budapest, Hungary
Magyar Feltalalok Egyesuletenek [★IO]
Magyar Floorball Szovetseg [★IO]
Magyar Franchise Szovetseg [★IO]
Magyar Geofizikusok Egyesulete [★IO]

Magyar Gepjarmuipari Szovetseg [★IO]
Magyar Gerontologiai Tarsasag [★IO]
Magyar Hanglemezkiadok Szovetsege [★IO]
Magyar Hidrologiai Tarsasag [★IO]
Magyar Ingatlanszovetseg [★IO]
Magyar Kockazati es Magantoke Egyesulet [★IO]
Magyar Konyvtarosok Egyesulete [★IO]
Magyar Kozgazdasagi Tarsasag [★IO]
Magyar Marketing Szovetseg [★IO]
Magyar Mezogazdasag [★IO]
Magyar Onteszeti Szovetseg [★IO]
Magyar Orszagos Baseball es Softball Szovetseg [★IO]
Magyar Orvostudomanyi Tarsasagok es Egyesuletek Szovetsege [★IO]
Magyar Paralimpiai Bizottsg [★IO]
Magyar Pszichologiai Tarsasag [★IO]
Magyar Reklamszovetseg [★IO]
Magyar Reprografiai Szovetseg [★IO]
Magyar Repulo Szovetseg [★IO]
Magyar Szakszervezetek Orszagos Szovettsege [★IO]
Magyar Szallodaszovetseg [★IO]
Magyar Taekwon-Do Szovetseg [★IO]
Magyar Tanacsado Mernokok es Epiteszek Szovetsege [★IO]
Magyar Tenisz Szovetseg [IO], Budapest, Hungary
Magyar Termeszetvedok Szovetsege [★IO]
Magyar Termeszetvedok Szovetsege [★IO]
Magyar Tollaslabda Szovetseg [★IO]
Magyar Tudomanyos Akademia Vilaggazdasagi Ku-tatointezet [★IO]
Magyar Ujsagirok Orszagos Szovetsege [★IO]
Magyar Vamugyi Szovetseg [★IO]
Magyar Vas- Es Acelipari Egyesules [★IO]
Magyar Vegyipari Szovetseg [★IO]
Magyar Versenyjogi Egyesulet [★IO]
Magyarhoni Foldtani Tarsulat [★IO]
Magyarorszag Nemzetkozi Csereprogram Alapitvany [★IO]
Magyarorszagi Fajdalom Tarsasag [★IO]
Magyarorszagi Kiallitas-es Vasarszervezok Szovetsege [★IO]
Mah Jongg League; Natl. [22468]
Mahayana Tradition; Found. for the Preservation of the [19550]
Mahogany Assn. - Defunct.
Mai Wah Soc. [9622], PO Box 404, Butte, MT 59703, (406)723-3231
Mai Wah Soc. [IO], Butte, MT, United States
Maids of Athena [19089], 1909 Q St. NW, Ste. 500, Washington, DC 20009, (202)232-6300
Maids of Athens [★19089]
Mail
  Air Mail Pioneers [21425]
  Airforwarders Assn. [2444]
  Alaska Collectors' Club [22779]
  All Ser. Postal Chess Club [21941]
  Alliance of Nonprofit Mailers [2445]
  Amer. Air Mail Soc. [22780]
  Amer. First Day Cover Soc. [22781]
  Amer. Helvetia Philatelic Soc. [22782]
  Amer. Philatelic Cong. [22783]
  Amer. Philatelic Res. Lib. [22784]
  Amer. Philatelic Soc. [22785]
  Amer. Philatelic Soc. Writers Unit [22786]
  Amer. Plate Number Single Soc. [22787]
  Amer. Racing Pigeon Union [22894]
  Amer. Revenue Assn. [22788]
  Amer. Soc. of Polar Philatelists [22789]
  Amer. Topical Soc. [22790]
  Amer. Topical Assn., Americana Unit [22791]
  Amer. Topical Assn., Biology Unit [22792]
  Armed Forces Stamp Exchange Club [22793]
  Assoc. Collectors of El Salvador [22794]
  Assoc. Mail and Parcel Centers [2446]
  Assn. of Alternate Postal Systems [2447]
  Assn. of Mailing, Shipping, and Off. Automation Specialists [2448]
  Assn. for Postal Commerce [2449]
  Astronomy Stud. Unit [22795]
  Bicycle Stamps Club [22796]
  Brazil Philatelic Assn. [22797]
  Carriers and Locals Soc. [22904]
  CartoPhilatelic Soc. [22799]

A star before a book entry number signifies that the name is not listed separately, but is mentioned within the entry.

Casey Jones Railroad Unit - ATA [22800]
Cats on Stamps Stud. Unit [22801]
Chemistry and Physics on Stamps Stud. Unit [22802]
China Stamp Soc. [22803]
Christmas Philatelic Club [22804]
Christopher Columbus Philatelic Soc. [22805]
Citizens' Stamp Advisory Comm. [22806]
Civil Censorship Study Group [22807]
Collectors Club [22808]
Collectors of Religion on Stamps [22809]
Confederate Stamp Alliance [22811]
Cover Collectors Circuit Club [22812]
Croatian Philatelic Soc. [22813]
Dogs on Stamps Stud. Unit [22815]
Earth's Physical Features Stud. Unit [22816]
Eire Philatelic Assn. [22817]
Errors, Freaks and Oddities Collector's Club [22818]
Fine Arts Philatelists [22819]
France and Colonies Philatelic Soc. [22820]
Gems, Minerals and Jewelry Stud. Unit [22821]
German Colonies Collectors Gp. [22822]
Germany Philatelic Soc. [22823]
Graphics Philately Assn. [22824]
Haiti Philatelic Soc. [22825]
Hellenic Philatelic Soc. of Am. [22826]
Humor Stamp Club [22827]
India Stud. Circle for Philately [22828]
Inter-Governmental Philatelic Corp. [22829]
Intl. Fed. of Amer. Homing Pigeon Fanciers [22895]
Intl. Pen Friends [22138]
Intl. Soc. for Japanese Philately [22830]
Intl. Soc. of Worldwide Stamp Collectors [22831]
Intl. Stamp and Coin Collectors Soc. [22832]
Irish Airmail Soc. [IO]
Jack Knight Air Mail Soc. [22834]
Junior Philatelists of Am. [22837]
Korea Stamp Soc. [22838]
Machine Cancel Soc. [22839]
Mail for Me Club [11621]
Mail Systems Mgt. Assn. [2450]
Mailers Coun. [2451]
Mailer's Postmark Permit Club [22840]
Maritime Postmark Soc. [22841]
Mathematical Stud. Unit [22842]
Medical Subjects Unit [22843]
Meter Stamp Soc. [22844]
Metropolitan Air Post Soc. [22845]
Mexico Elmhurst Philatelic Soc. Intl. [22846]
Military Postal History Soc. [22847]
Mobile Post Off. Soc. [22848]
Natl. Assn. of Presort Mailers [2452]
Natl. Mail Order Assn. [2643]
Natl. Postal Arts Assn. [22139]
Natl. Star Route Mail Contractors Assn. [2453]
Nepal and Tibet Philatelic Stud. Circle [22852]
Parcel Shippers Assn. [2454]
Perfins Club [22854]
Periodical Publications Assn. [2455]
Philatelic Found. [22855]
Philatelic Friends Exchange Circuit [22856]
Polonus Philatelic Soc. [22857]
Post Mark Collectors Club [22858]
Postal Commemorative Soc. [22859]
Postal History Soc. [22860]
Precancel Stamp Soc. [22861]
Red Tag News Publications Assn. [2456]
Rossica Soc. of Russian Philately [22862]
Rotary on Stamps Fellowship [22863]
Russian Zone Handoverprint Stud. and Res. Gp. [22864]
Ryukyu Philatelic Specialist Soc. [22865]
St. Helena, Ascension, and Tristan da Cunha Philatelic Soc. [22866]
Samuel Gompers Stamp Club [22867]
Scandinavian Collectors Club [22868]
Scouts on Stamps Soc. Intl. [22869]
Ships on Stamps Unit [22870]
Soc. of Australasian Specialists/Oceania [22871]
Soc. for Hungarian Philately [22873]
Soc. of Israel Philatelists [22874]
Soc. for Thai Philately [22875]
Space Topic Stud. Unit [22876]

Sports Philatelists Intl. [22877]
Stamps on Stamps Collectors Club [22878]
Stamps for the Wounded [22879]
State Revenue Soc. [22880]
Student Letter Exchange [22144]
Ukrainian Philatelic and Numismatic Soc. [22883]
United Nations Philatelists, Inc. [22884]
United Postal Stationery Soc. [22885]
U.S. Cancellation Club [22886]
U.S. Stamp Soc. [22888]
Universal Ship Cancellation Soc. [22889]
Unmarried-Catholics Correspondence Club [22145]
Western Cover Soc. [22890]
Worldwide Friendship Intl. [22147]
Young Stamp Collectors of Am. [22891]
Zeppelin Collectors Club [22892]
Mail Advt. Assn; Direct [★2625]
Mail Advt. Ser. Assn. Intl. [★108]
Mail Assn; Third Class [★2449]
Mail Educational Found; Direct [★8816]
Mail Found; Bus. [★2625]
Mail Fundraisers Assn; Direct [★1685]
Mail Handlers Union; Natl. Postal [24171]
Mail Handlers, Watchmen, Messengers, and Gp. Leaders; Natl. Post Off. [★24171]
Mail Handlers, Watchmen and Messengers; Natl. Assn. of Post Off. and Postal Trans. Ser. [★24171]
Mail/Marketing Assn; Direct [★2625]
Mail/Marketing Educational Found; Direct [★8816]
Mail for Me Club [11621], PO Box 225, Mentone, CA 92359, (909)794-9676
Mail Order
  Amer. Mailorder Assn. [2457]
  Call For Action [11802]
Mail Order Assn. of America - Address unknown since 2004.
Mail Order Assn; Natl. [2643]
Mail Order Traders' Assn. [IO], London, United Kingdom
Mail Pioneers; Air [21425]
Mail Publications; Assn. of Second Class [★2455]
Mail Publications; Second Class [★2455]
Mail Publishers; Assn. of Second Class [★2455]
Mail Ser. Veterans Assn; Navy [21216]
Mail Soc; Amer. Air [22780]
Mail Systems Mgt. Assn. [2450], PO Box 1145, North Riverside, IL 60546-1145, (708)853-0471
Mail for Tots - Address unknown since 1994.
Mail Users; Assoc. Third Class [★2449]
Mail Users' Assn. [IO], Emsworth, United Kingdom
The Mailbox Club [IO], Valdosta, GA, United States
The Mailbox Club [19525], 404 Eager Rd., Valdosta, GA 31602, (229)244-6812
Mailbox Club Books [★19525]
Mailbox Club Books [★IO]
Mailers Coun. [2451], c/o Robert E. McLean, Exec. Dir., 2001 Jefferson Davis Hwy., Ste. 1004, Arlington, VA 22202-3617, (703)418-0390
Mailers Fed; Nonprofit [★317]
Mailer's Postmark Permit Club [22840], c/o Charlie Myers, PO Box 3, Portland, TN 37148-0003
Mailer's Postmark Permit Club [IO], Portland, TN, United States
Mailers Union; Intl. [★24086]
Mailing Equip. Dealers; Assn. of Independent [★2448]
Mailing and Fulfillment Ser. Assn. [108], 1421 Prince St., Ste. 410, Alexandria, VA 22314-2806, (703)836-9200
Mailing List Brokers Professional Assn. - Defunct.
Mailing List User and Supplier Assn. - Defunct.
Mailman Family Found; A.L. [11671]
Mailorder Assn. of Nurserymen - Defunct.
Mailorder Gardening Assn. [3413], 5836 Rockburn Woods Way, Elkridge, MD 21075, (410)540-9830
Maimed Soldiers League; U.S. [★21320]
Main St. Center; Natl. [17237]
Main St. Coalition for Postal Fairness [18375], c/o The Aker Partners, Inc., 2000 K St. NW, Ste. 801, Washington, DC 20006, (202)789-2424
Main St. Proj. [★17237]
Maine-Anjou Assn; Amer. [4234]
Maine-Anjou Soc. [★4234]
Maine Folklife Center [9959], 5773 S Stevens Hall, Rm. 112B, Orono, ME 04469-5773, (207)581-1891

Maine Lobster Fishermen's Assn. - Address unknown since 1995.
Maine Lobstermen's Assn. [3492], 21C Western Ave., Box 1, Kennebunk, ME 04043, (207)967-4555
Maine Sardine Coun. - Defunct.
Maine Sardine Packers Assn. - Defunct.
Maine Wholesale Lobster Dealers Assn. - Defunct.
Mainland Miniature Horse Club [IO], Belfast, New Zealand
Mainostajien Liitto [★IO]
Mainstream - Address unknown since 2005.
Mainstream Media Proj. [18494], 854 9th St., Ste. B, Arcata, CA 95521, (707)826-9111
Mainstream Media Proj. [IO], Arcata, CA, United States
Maintenance
  Amer. Homeowners Assn. [2458]
  Amer. Soc. for Healthcare Engg. of the Amer. Hosp. Assn. [14865]
  Assn. des Aides Familiales du Quebec [IO]
  Assn. of Healthcare Professionals [IO]
  Aviation Maintenance Found. Intl. [143]
  British Cleaning Coun. [IO]
  British Inst. of Cleaning Sci. [IO]
  British Inst. of Facilities Mgt. [IO]
  Building Maintenance Contractors Assn. of Canada [IO]
  Building Ser. Contractors Assn. Intl. [IO]
  Building Ser. Contractors Assn. Intl. [2459]
  Canadian Assn. Environmental Mgt. [IO]
  Canadian Sanitation Supply Assn. [IO]
  Chimney Safety Inst. of Am. [2460]
  Cleaning Equip. Trade Assn. [2461]
  Cleaning Equipment Trade Association [IO]
  Cleaning Mgt. Inst. [2462]
  Cleaning and Support Services Assn. [IO]
  Domestic Appliance Ser. Assn. [IO]
  Environmental Mgt. Assn. [2463]
  European Fed. of Cleaning Indus. [IO]
  Global Environmental Mgt. Initiative [4628]
  Healthcare Laundry Accreditation Coun. [2403]
  Home Laundering Consultative Coun. [IO]
  Intl. Assn. for Bridge Maintenance and Safety [538]
  Intl. Cleaning Companies Assn. [IO]
  Intl. Executive Housekeepers Assn. [IO]
  Intl. Executive Housekeepers Assn. [2464]
  Intl. Fac. Mgt. Assn. - Toronto Chap. [IO]
  Intl. Maintenance Inst. [IO]
  Intl. Maintenance Inst. [2465]
  Intl. Sanitary Supply Assn. [2466]
  Intl. Sanitary Supply Assn. [IO]
  Intl. Soc. of Facilities Executives [2467]
  Intl. Window Cleaning Assn. [2468]
  Intl. Window Cleaning Assn. [IO]
  Locomotive Maintenance Officers' Assn. [3283]
  Logistics Officer Assn. [2736]
  Master Window Cleaners of Am. [2469]
  Natl. Air Duct Cleaners Assn. [2470]
  Natl. Assn. of Chimney Sweeps [IO]
  Natl. Chimney Sweep Guild [2471]
  Natl. Railroad Constr. and Maintenance Assn. [3287]
  Natl. Uniform Certification of Building Operators [2472]
  North Amer. Power Sweeping Assn. [2473]
  Power Washers of North Am. [2474]
  Power Washers of North Am. [IO]
  Professional Aviation Maintenance Assn. [165]
  Railway Engineering-Maintenance Suppliers Assn. [3289]
  Restoration Indus. Assn. [2475]
  Sanitary Supply Wholesaling Assn. [2476]
  Soc. of Cleaning and Restoration Technicians [2477]
  Soc. of Hosp. Linen Ser. and Laundry Managers [IO]
  Soc. for Maintenance and Reliability Professionals [2478]
  World Coun. for Venue Mgt. [1350]
  World Fed. of Building Ser. Contractors [2479]
  World Fed. of Building Ser. Contractors [IO]
Maintenance Assn; Natl. Railroad Constr. and [3287]
Maintenance Assn; Professional Aviation [165]

Reference to "IO" in place of a book number signifies that the association may be found in the 45th edition of International Organizations.

Maintenance Assn; Railroad Constr. and [★3287]
Maintenance Conf; Avionics [144]
The Maintenance Coun. of the Amer. Trucking Associations [★3895]
Maintenance Coun; Equip. [★2442]
Maintenance Officers' Assn; Locomotive [3283]
Maintenance Suppliers Assn; Railway Engineering- [3289]
Maintenance of Way Employees; Brotherhood of [24177]
Maison de Commerce l'autre facon d'Exporter [★IO]
Maitland Soc. of North Am; Clan [20847]
Maize Assn. of Australia [IO], Darlington Point, Australia
Majestic Circle, Military Order of Lady Bugs of U.S.A. - Address unknown since 1995.
Majlis Belia Malaysia [★IO]
Majlis Kanser Nasional [★IO]
Majlis Olimpik Malaysia [★IO]
Majolica Intl. Soc. [IO], New York, NY, United States
Majolica Intl. Soc. [21931], PMB 103, New York, NY 10021
Major Appliance Consumer Action Program - Address unknown since 2000.
Major Aspects of Growth in Children Found. [★13967]
Major Contractors' Gp. [IO], London, United Kingdom
Major Energy Users Coun. [IO], London, United Kingdom
Major Indoor Soccer League - Defunct.
Major Indoor Soccer League Players Assn. - Address unknown since 2003.
Major League Baseball [23113], 75 9th Ave., 5th Fl., New York, NY 10011
Major League Baseball Players Alumni Assn. [23114], 1631 Mesa Ave., Ste. B, Colorado Springs, CO 80906-2956
Major League Baseball Players Assn. [24018], 12 E 49th St., 24th Fl., New York, NY 10017-8207, (212)826-0808
Major League Umpires Assn. - Defunct.
Major Orchestra Librarians' Assn. [10371], c/o Patrick McGinn, Admin., Milwaukee Symphony Orchestra, 700 N Water St., Ste. 700, Milwaukee, WI 53202
Major Superiors of Men; Conf. of [19615]
Major Wingfield Club [★23905]
Major Wingfield Historical Soc. [23905], c/o Stanley Malless, Pres., 5401 Greenwillow Rd., Indianapolis, IN 46226, (317)547-1336
Majorette Associations; Global Alliance of Natl. Baton Twirling and [23141]
Majorette Associations; World Fed. of Baton Twirling and [★23141]
Majority Cong. Comm. - Defunct.
Majority Rule Assn. - Address unknown since 1995.
Makassed Found. of Am. [12730], 3231 P St. NW, 2nd Fl., Washington, DC 20007, (202)783-7979
Makassed Found. of Am. [IO], Washington, DC, United States
Makassed Philanthropic Islamic Assn. [IO], Beirut, Lebanon
Makatab Tarighat Oveyssi Shahmaghsoudi [20576], PO Box 5827, Washington, DC 20016, (202)342-0022
Make-A-Wish Found. of Am. [11707], 3550 N Central Ave., Ste. 300, Phoenix, AZ 85012-2127, (602)279-9474
Make a Child Smile [11708], 11110 W Oakland Park Blvd., No. 292, Sunrise, FL 33351
Make Early Diagnosis to Prevent Early Death [14463], Univ. of Utah, School of Medicine, 420 Chipeta Way, Rm. 1160, Salt Lake City, UT 84108, (801)581-8720
Make Early Diagnosis to Prevent Early Death [IO], Salt Lake City, UT, United States
Make Today Count [13841], 1235 E Cherokee St., Springfield, MO 65804-2203, (417)820-2588
Makeni Ecumenical [★IO]
Makeni Ecumenical Centre [IO], Lusaka, Zambia
Makers of Explosives; Inst. of [1351]
Makina Muehendisleri Odasi [★IO]
Making Music [IO], London, United Kingdom
Malacological Soc. of Japan [IO], Tokyo, Japan

Malacological Soc. of London [IO], York, United Kingdom
Malacological Soc. of the Philippines [IO], Quezon City, Philippines
Malacology
  Amer. Malacological Soc. [7254]
  Malacological Soc. of Japan [IO]
  Malacological Soc. of the Philippines [IO]
  Natl. Shellfisheries Assn. [IO]
  Natl. Shellfisheries Assn. [7255]
  Soc. for Experimental and Descriptive Malacology [7256]
  Western Soc. of Malacologists [7257]
Malagasy Bible Soc. [IO], Antananarivo, Madagascar
Malagasy Fed. of Taekwondo [IO], Antananarivo, Madagascar
Malamute Assistance League; Alaskan [11342]
Malamute Club of Am; Alaskan [22182]
Malamute Protection League; Alaskan [★11342]
Malaria Philatelists Intl. - Address unknown since 1999.
Malaria Soc; Natl. [★16693]
Malawi Assn. of Christian Support [IO], Enfield, United Kingdom
Malawi Junior Chamber [IO], Lilongwe, Malawi
Malawi Proj. [IO], Indianapolis, IN, United States
Malawi Proj. [11266], 3314 Van Tassel Dr., Indianapolis, IN 46240
Malawi Red Cross Soc. [IO], Lilongwe, Malawi
Malay Chamber of Commerce Malaysia [IO], Kuala Lumpur, Malaysia
Malay for Natl. Consciousness Movement [IO], Penang, Malaysia
Malayalee Engineers Assn. in North Am. [7026], 6807 Fieldstone Dr., Burr Ridge, IL 60527, (630)851-1690
Malayan Pharmaceutical Assn. [★IO]
Malaysia
  Australian Malaysian Singaporean Assn. [IO]
  Malaysia/Singapore/Brunei Stud. Gp. of the Southeast Asia Coun. Assn. for Asian Stud. [7987]
  Malaysia Tourism Promotion Bd. [24355]
  Malaysian Assn. in France [IO]
  Malaysian Assn. of the Netherlands [IO]
Malaysia Amateur Athletic Union [IO], Kuala Lumpur, Malaysia
Malaysia Automotive Tyre Mfrs. Indus. Gp. [IO], Kuala Lumpur, Malaysia
Malaysia Budget Hotel Assn. [IO], Kuala Lumpur, Malaysia
Malaysia Mold and Die Assn. [IO], Kuala Lumpur, Malaysia
Malaysia Occupational Therapists Assn. [IO], Kuala Lumpur, Malaysia
Malaysia Retailers' Assn. [IO], Selangor, Malaysia
Malaysia/Singapore/Brunei Stud. Gp. of the Southeast Asia Coun. Assn. for Asian Stud. [IO], Salem, OR, United States
Malaysia/Singapore/Brunei Stud. Gp. of the Southeast Asia Coun. Assn. for Asian Stud. [7987], c/o Greg Felker, Chm., Dept. of Politics, Willamette Univ., 900 State St., Salem, OR 97301, (503)370-6261
Malaysia South-South Assn. [IO], Kuala Lumpur, Malaysia
Malaysia Taekwondo Assn. [IO], Kuala Lumpur, Malaysia
Malaysia Tourism Promotion Bd. [IO], Kuala Lumpur, Malaysia
Malaysia Tourism Promotion Bd. [24355], 818 W 7th St., Ste. 970, Los Angeles, CA 90017-3431, (213)689-9702
Malaysia Tourist Info. Center [★24355]
Malaysian Advertisers Assn. [IO], Petaling Jaya, Malaysia
Malaysian AIDS Coun. [IO], Kuala Lumpur, Malaysia
Malaysian Airlines Pilots' Assn. [IO], Selangor, Malaysia
Malaysian Amateur Radio Transmitter's Soc. [IO], Kuala Lumpur, Malaysia
Malaysian Assoc. Indian Chambers of Commerce and Indus. [IO], Kuala Lumpur, Malaysia
Malaysian Assn. for the Blind [IO], Kuala Lumpur, Malaysia

Malaysian Assn. of Clinical Biochemists [IO], Kuala Lumpur, Malaysia
Malaysian Assn. in France [IO], Paris, France
Malaysian Assn. of Hotels [IO], Kuala Lumpur, Malaysia
Malaysian Assn. of the Netherlands [IO], Rotterdam, Netherlands
Malaysian Assn. of Professional Secretaries and Administrators [IO], Kuala Lumpur, Malaysia
Malaysian Assn. of Risk and Insurance Mgt. [IO], Kuala Lumpur, Malaysia
Malaysian Assn. of Speech Language and Hearing [IO], Selangor, Malaysia
Malaysian Assn. of Tour and Travel Agents [IO], Kuala Lumpur, Malaysia
Malaysian Automotive Components and Parts Mfrs. Assn. [IO], Kuala Lumpur, Malaysia
Malaysian Bar Coun. [IO], Kuala Lumpur, Malaysia
Malaysian Br. of the Royal Asiatic Soc. [IO], Kuala Lumpur, Malaysia
Malaysian Chamber of Mines [IO], Kuala Lumpur, Malaysia
Malaysian Chinese Assn. [IO], Kuala Lumpur, Malaysia
Malaysian Cocoa Bd. [IO], Kota Kinabalu, Malaysia
Malaysian Cocoa Mfrs'. Gp. [IO], Kuala Lumpur, Malaysia
Malaysian Cosmetics and Toiletries Indus. Gp. [IO], Kuala Lumpur, Malaysia
Malaysian Cricket Assn. [IO], Puchong, Malaysia
Malaysian Cultural Gp. [IO], Kuala Lumpur, Malaysia
Malaysian Danish Assn. [IO], Frederiksberg, Denmark
Malaysian Dental Assn. [IO], Kuala Lumpur, Malaysia
Malaysian Dietitians Assn. [IO], Kuala Lumpur, Malaysia
Malaysian Economic Assn. [IO], Kuala Lumpur, Malaysia
Malaysian Elecl. Appliances Indus. Gp. [IO], Kuala Lumpur, Malaysia
Malaysian Employers' Fed. [IO], Petaling Jaya, Malaysia
Malaysian Floorball Assn. [IO], Petaling Jaya, Malaysia
Malaysian Food Mfg. Gp. [IO], Kuala Lumpur, Malaysia
Malaysian Franchise Assn. [IO], Kuala Lumpur, Malaysia
Malaysian Furniture Indus. Coun. [IO], Kuala Lumpur, Malaysia
Malaysian Gas Assn. [IO], Kuala Lumpur, Malaysia
Malaysian Golf Assn. [IO], Kuala Lumpur, Malaysia
Malaysian Inst. of Architects [IO], Kuala Lumpur, Malaysia
Malaysian Inst. of Certified Public Accountants [IO], Kuala Lumpur, Malaysia
Malaysian Inst. of Chartered Secretaries and Administrators [IO], Kuala Lumpur, Malaysia
Malaysian Intl. Chamber of Commerce and Indus. [IO], Kuala Lumpur, Malaysia
Malaysian Iron and Steel Indus. Fed. [IO], Shah Alam, Malaysia
Malaysian Medical Assn. [IO], Kuala Lumpur, Malaysia
Malaysian Medical Relief Soc. [★IO]
Malaysian Menopause Soc. [IO], Kuala Lumpur, Malaysia
Malaysian Natl. Cmpt. Confed. [IO], Petaling Jaya, Malaysia
Malaysian Nature Soc. [IO], Kuala Lumpur, Malaysia
Malaysian Nuclear Soc. [IO], Selangor, Malaysia
Malaysian Org. of Pharmaceutical Indus. [IO], Selangor, Malaysia
Malaysian Osteoporosis Soc. [IO], Selangor, Malaysia
Malaysian Palm Oil Assn. [IO], Kuala Lumpur, Malaysia
Malaysian Panel-Products Manufacturers' Assn. [IO], Kuala Lumpur, Malaysia
Malaysian Pepper Bd. [IO], Sarawak, Malaysia
Malaysian Physiotherapy Assn. [IO], Kuala Lumpur, Malaysia
Malaysian Pineapple Indus. Bd. [IO], Johor Bahru, Malaysia

A star before a book entry number signifies that the name is not listed separately, but is mentioned within the entry.

Malaysian Plastic Manufacturers Assn. **[IO]**, Petaling Jaya, Malaysia

Malaysian Plastics Manufacturers Assn. **[IO]**, Petaling Jaya, Malaysia

Malaysian Printers' Assn. **[IO]**, Kuala Lumpur, Malaysia

Malaysian Red Crescent Soc. **[IO]**, Kuala Lumpur, Malaysia

Malaysian Rubber Bd. **[IO]**, Kuala Lumpur, Malaysia

Malaysian Rubber Bur. - Address unknown since 2004.

Malaysian Rubber Glove Manufacturers' Assn. **[IO]**, Petaling Jaya, Malaysia

Malaysian Rubber Producers' Res. Assn. **[★IO]**

Malaysian Rubber Products Manufacturers Assn. **[IO]**, Petaling Jaya, Malaysia

Malaysian Rubber Res. and Development Bd. **[★IO]**

Malaysian Sci. Assn. **[IO]**, Petaling Jaya, Malaysia

Malaysian Senior Scientists' Assn. **[IO]**, Petaling Jaya, Malaysia

Malaysian Soc. of Allergy and Immunology **[IO]**, Kuala Lumpur, Malaysia

Malaysian Soc. of Anaesthesiologists **[IO]**, Kuala Lumpur, Malaysia

Malaysian Soc. of Gastroenterology and Hepatology **[IO]**, Kuala Lumpur, Malaysia

Malaysian Soc. of Infectious Diseases and Chemotherapy **[IO]**, Kuala Lumpur, Malaysia

Malaysian Soc. of Nephrology **[IO]**, Kuala Lumpur, Malaysia

Malaysian Soc. of Pharmacology and Physiology **[IO]**, Kelantan, Malaysia

Malaysian Soc. for Quality in Hea. **[IO]**, Selangor, Malaysia

Malaysian Soc. of Radiographers **[IO]**, Kuala Lumpur, Malaysia

Malaysian Soc. of Transplantation **[IO]**, Kuala Lumpur, Malaysia

Malaysian Textile Mfrs'. Assn. **[IO]**, Kuala Lumpur, Malaysia

Malaysian Timber Coun. **[IO]**, Kuala Lumpur, Malaysia

Malaysian Timber Indus. Bd. **[IO]**, Kuala Lumpur, Malaysia

Malaysian Tin Bur. - Defunct.

Malaysian Venture Capital Assn. **[IO]**, Kuala Lumpur, Malaysia

Malaysian Wood Indus. Assn. **[IO]**, Kuala Lumpur, Malaysia

Malaysian Youth Coun. **[IO]**, Kuala Lumpur, Malaysia

Malcolm Wain Fan Club **[24756]**

Male Choruses; Intercollegiate Musical Coun., A Natl. Assn. of **[★10611]**

Male Liberation Found. **[18037]**, 701 NE 67th St., Miami, FL 33138, (305)756-6249

Male Nurse Assn; Natl. **[★15431]**

Male Reproduction and Urology; Soc. for **[16343]**

Male Sexual Victimization; Natl. Org. on **[★13077]**

Male Survivor: The Natl. Org. Against Male Sexual Victimization **[13077]**, PMB 103, 5505 Connecticut Ave. NW, Washington, DC 20015-2601, (800)738-4181

Male Violence; Emerge: Counseling and Educ. to Stop **[★12026]**

Males; Natl. Org. to Halt the Abuse and Routine Mutilation of **[11733]**

Mali Fed. of Sport for the Disabled **[IO]**, Bamako, Mali

Malian Found. **[IO]**, Sydney, Australia

Malignant Hyperthermia Assn. of the U.S. **[14464]**, 11 E State St., PO Box 1069, Sherburne, NY 13460, (607)674-7901

Malik Sigma Psi - Address unknown since 1994.

Malleable Chain Mfrs. Inst. **[★1993]**

Malone Soc. **[IO]**, London, United Kingdom

Malpractice
P.U.L.S.E. **[14662]**

Malpractice Assn. - Address unknown since 1995.

Malt Anal. Standardization Comm. **[★6670]**

Malt Anal. Standardization Comm. **[★IO]**

Malt Distillers Assn. of Scotland **[IO]**, Elgin, United Kingdom

Malta Amateur Athletic Assn. **[IO]**, Marsa, Malta

Malta Amateur Radio League **[IO]**, Valletta, Malta

Malta Amateur Weightlifting Assn. **[IO]**, San Gwann, Malta

Malta; Ancient and Illustrious Order Knights of **[19325]**

Malta Article Numbering Coun. **[★IO]**

Malta Assn. of Occupational Therapists **[IO]**, Guardamangia, Malta

Malta Assn. of Physiotherapists **[IO]**, Msida, Malta

Malta Assn. of Women in Bus. **[IO]**, Msida, Malta

Malta Bible Soc. **[IO]**, Floriana, Malta

Malta Chamber of Commerce and Enterprise **[IO]**, Valletta, Malta

Malta Cricket Assn. **[IO]**, Marsa, Malta

Malta Dancesport Assn. **[IO]**, Attard, Malta

Malta Ecological Found. **[IO]**, Valletta, Malta

Malta Employers' Assn. **[IO]**, Valletta, Malta

Malta Fed. of Indus. **[IO]**, Floriana, Malta

Malta Feline Guardians Club **[IO]**, Zejtun, Malta

Malta Football Assn. **[IO]**, Valletta, Malta

Malta Handball Assn. **[IO]**, Gzira, Malta

Malta Hotels and Restaurants Assn. **[IO]**, Sliema, Malta

Malta Labour Party **[IO]**, Hamrun, Malta

Malta Lib. Assn. **[★IO]**

Malta Lib. and Info. Assn. **[IO]**, Msida, Malta

Malta Olympic Comm. **[IO]**, Gzira, Malta

The Malta Press Club **[★IO]**

Malta Red Cross **[IO]**, Valletta, Malta

Malta Tennis Fed. **[IO]**, Sliema, Malta

Malta Tourism Authority **[IO]**, Valletta, Malta

Malta Union of Teachers **[IO]**, Valletta, Malta

Malta Veterinary Assn. **[IO]**, B'Kara, Malta

Malta Workers' Union **[IO]**, Floriana, Malta

Maltase Deficiency Assn; Acid **[13535]**

Maltese
Amer. Maltese Assn. **[22203]**
Maltese-Amer. Benevolent Soc. **[19222]**

Maltese-Amer. Benevolent Soc. **[19222]**

Maltese Assn; Amer. **[22203]**

Maltese Assn. of Dermatology and Venereology **[IO]**, San Gwann, Malta

Maltese Assn. of Gerontology and Geriatrics **[IO]**, Msida, Malta

Maltese Diabetes Assn. **[IO]**, Valletta, Malta

Maltese Ecological Soc. **[★IO]**

Maltese Falcon Soc. - Defunct.

Maltese Union Club - Address unknown since 1995.

Malteurs de France **[★IO]**

Malting Barley Assn; Amer. **[4303]**

Malting Barley Improvement Assn. **[★4303]**

Maltsters' Assn. of Great Britain **[IO]**, Newark, United Kingdom

Mamas and the Papas Fan Club - Address unknown since 2001.

Mamie Doud Eisenhower Birthplace Found. **[10044]**, 709 Caroll St., Boone, IA 50036, (515)432-1907

Mamie Van Doren Fan Club **[24757]**, c/o Bob Bethia, Pres., 1067 Lake View Terr., Azusa, CA 91702

Mammal Center; Friends of the Sea Lion Marine **[★5361]**

Mammal Center; Pacific Marine **[5361]**

Mammal Conservation Fund; Marine **[★4435]**

Mammal Soc. **[IO]**, London, United Kingdom

Mammal Soc; Pacific Northwest Bird and **[★7364]**

Mammal Stranding Center; Marine **[5338]**

Mammalogy
Alliance of Marine Mammal Parks and Aquariums **[5006]**
Amer. Cetacean Soc. **[7258]**
Amer. Soc. of Mammalogists **[7259]**
Center for Whale Res. **[7260]**
Dolphin Res. Center **[7261]**
Polar Bears Intl. **[5367]**
Sirenian Intl. **[5016]**
Soc. for Marine Mammalogy **[5017]**
Soc. for Northwestern Vertebrate Biology **[7364]**
Water Planet USA **[5018]**
World Whale Police **[IO]**

Mammoth Jack Stock Registry; Amer. **[★4130]**

Mammoth Jackstock Registry; Amer. **[4130]**

Mamselle Sorority **[★13102]**

Man and the Biosphere Programme **[IO]**, Paris, France

Man/Boy Love Assn; North Amer. **[13099]**

MAN for ERA - Defunct.

Man; Found. for Res. on the Nature of **[★7452]**

Man; Intl. League for the Rights of **[★17769]**

Man from U.N.C.L.E.
Man from U.N.C.L.E. Fan Club **[25036]**
U.N.C.L.E. HQ **[25044]**

Man from U.N.C.L.E. Fan Club **[25036]**, c/o Sue Cole, Pres., PO Box 1733, Oshkosh, WI 54903

Man Watchers **[★22580]**

Man Watchers Intl. - Address unknown since 2006.

Man Will Never Fly Memorial Soc. Internationale **[22598]**, 103 Caribbean Ave., Virginia Beach, VA 23451-4716

Man Will Never Fly Memorial Soc. Internationale **[IO]**, Virginia Beach, VA, United States

MANA, A Natl. Latina Org. **[17548]**, 1725 K St. NW, Ste. 201, Washington, DC 20006, (202)833-0060

Managed Care Dentists; Assn. of **[14145]**

Managed Care Nurses; Amer. Assn. of **[15435]**

Managed Care Nursing; Amer. Bd. of **[15442]**

Managed Care Pharmacy; Acad. of **[15905]**

Managed Care Physicians; Natl. Assn. of **[16005]**

Managed Care Providers; Acad. of **[14677]**

Managed Funds Assn. **[24334]**, 2025 M St. NW, Ste. 800, Washington, DC 20036-3309, (202)367-1140

Managed Futures Trade Assn. - Address unknown since 1994.

Managed Hea. Care Assn; Employers' **[★14682]**

Managed Healthcare Organizations; Assn. of **[★14680]**

Management
Acad. of Mgt. **[8805]**
Alliance for Nonprofit Mgt. **[313]**
Alliance in Support of Independent Res. **[3390]**
Amer. Assn. of Airport Executives **[138]**
Amer. Assn. of Indus. Mgt. **[2480]**
Amer. Assn. of Ser. Coordinators **[1985]**
Amer. Case Mgt. Assn. **[15051]**
Amer. Coll. of Healthcare Executives **[14862]**
Amer. Mgt. Assn. **[2481]**
Amer. Mgt. Assn. **[IO]**
Amer. Soc. for Engg. Mgt. **[6994]**
Amer. Soc. for Healthcare Engg. of the Amer. Hosp. Assn. **[14865]**
Amer. Soc. for Healthcare Risk Mgt. **[14869]**
APQC **[2482]**
Asia Acad. of Mgt. **[IO]**
Asian Assn. of Mgt. Organisations **[IO]**
Asian Inst. of Mgt. **[IO]**
Assn. of British Certification Bodies **[IO]**
Assn. of Bus. Executives **[IO]**
Assn. of Call Center Managers **[2520]**
Assn. of Certified Adizes Practitioners Intl. **[2483]**
Association of Certified Adizes Practitioners International **[IO]**
Assn. for Corporate Growth - Toronto Chap. **[IO]**
Assn. for Healthcare Rsrc. and Materials Mgt. **[14872]**
Assn. of Internal Mgt. Consultants **[2484]**
Association of Internal Management Consultants **[IO]**
Assn. of Mgt. Consulting Firms **[2485]**
Assn. of MBA's **[IO]**
Association of Productivity Specialists **[IO]**
Assn. of Productivity Specialists **[2486]**
Assn. for Proj. Mgt. **[IO]**
Assn. for Proj. Mgt. Hong Kong **[IO]**
Assn. of Proposal Mgt. Professionals **[2487]**
Assn. of PVO Financial Managers **[1458]**
Assn. for Strategic Alliance Professionals **[2521]**
Australian Inst. of Mgt. **[IO]**
Australian Inst. of Proj. Mgt. **[IO]**
Automotive Training Managers Coun. **[351]**
Bd. of Certified Prdt. Safety Mgt. **[3441]**
Brazilian Assn. for Proj. Mgt. **[IO]**
Canadian Inst. of Certified Administrative Managers **[IO]**
Canadian Inst. of Mgt. **[IO]**
Canadian. Mgt. Centre **[IO]**
Canadian Payroll Assn. **[IO]**
Center for Creative Leadership **[IO]**
Center for Creative Leadership **[2488]**
Center for Mgt. Effectiveness **[2489]**
Center for Mgt. Tech. **[2490]**
Central Asian Found. for Mgt. Development **[IO]**
Central and East European Mgt. Development Assn. **[IO]**

Reference to "IO" in place of a book number signifies that the association may be found in the 45th edition of International Organizations.

Coll. of Performance Mgt. [IO]
Coll. of Performance Mgt. [2491]
Congressional Mgt. Found. [5599]
The Consortium [8806]
Constr. Mgt. Assn. of Am. [2492]
Cost Mgt. Gp. [2493]
Coun. of Commun. Mgt. [876]
Coun. for Hospitality Mgt. Educ. [IO]
Croatian Managers' and Entrepreneurs Assn. [IO]
Delhi Mgt. Assn. [IO]
DFK International/USA [28]
Eastern and Southern Africa Mgt. Inst. [IO]
Employers Coun. on Flexible Compensation [1237]
Employers Gp. [2494]
European Assn. for Personnel Mgt. [IO]
European Fac. Mgt. Network [IO]
European Fed. of Mgt. Consultancies Associations [IO]
European Found. for Mgt. Development [IO]
European Inst. for Advanced Stud. in Mgt. [IO]
European Operations Mgt. Assn. [IO]
European Women's Mgt. Development Asia/Pacific [IO]
European Women's Mgt. Development Austria [IO]
European Women's Mgt. Development Belgium [IO]
European Women's Mgt. Development Italy [IO]
European Women's Mgt. Development Network [IO]
European Women's Mgt. Development Sweden [IO]
European Women's Mgt. Development Switzerland [IO]
Expediting Mgt. Assn. [IO]
Fed. of European Risk Mgt. Associations [IO]
Found. for Educational Futures [318]
Global Assn. of Risk Professionals [1423]
Global Environmental Mgt. Initiative [4628]
Governance Inst. [2495]
Graduate Mgt. Admission Coun. [8807]
Graduate Mgt. Admission Coun. [IO]
Graduate Mgt. Assn. of Australia [IO]
GS1 Hong Kong [IO]
Hea. Res. and Educational Trust [14884]
Healthcare Info. and Mgt. Systems Soc. [14885]
Hong Kong Mgt. Assn. [IO]
Hong Kong Productivity Coun. [IO]
Hospitality Asset Managers Assn. [1942]
Human Rsrc. Planning Soc. [2496]
Incentive Mfrs. and Representatives Alliance [2536]
Inst. of Administrative Mgt. [IO]
Inst. of Certified Professional Managers [IO]
Inst. of Certified Professional Managers [2497]
Inst. of Commercial Mgt. [IO]
Inst. of Directors - England [IO]
Inst. of Directors - Zimbabwe [IO]
Inst. for Hea. and Productivity Mgt. [IO]
Inst. for Hea. and Productivity Mgt. [2498]
Inst. of Leadership and Mgt. [IO]
Inst. of Mgt. [IO]
Inst. of Mgt. Consultancy [IO]
Inst. of Mgt. Consultants [IO]
Inst. of Mgt. Consultants USA [2499]
Inst. of Mgt. Services [IO]
Inst. for Operations Res. and the Mgt. Sciences [IO]
Inst. for Operations Res. and the Mgt. Sciences [2500]
Inst. of Personnel Mgt. of Zimbabwe [IO]
Inst. for Supply Mgt. [3263]
Interim Mgt. Assn. [IO]
Intl. Acad. of Mgt. [IO]
Intl. Assn. of Healthcare Central Ser. Materiel Mgt. [14886]
Intl. Assn. of Jesuit Bus. Schools [8026]
Intl. Assn. for the Mgt. of Tech. [7740]
Intl. Assn. for Prdt. Development [3177]
Intl. City/County Mgt. Assn. [6123]
Intl. Fac. Mgt. Assn. [3188]
Intl. Proj. Mgt. Assn. [IO]
Intl. Soc. of Agile Mfg. [2558]
Intl. Soc. of Facilities Executives [2467]

IQNet Assn. - Intl. Certification Network [IO]
Irish Inst. of Purchasing and Materials Mgt. [IO]
Irish Mgt. Inst. Intl. [IO]
Issue Mgt. Coun. [2501]
Japan Mgt. Assn. [IO]
Kenya Inst. of Mgt. [IO]
Leading Edge Alliance [39]
Ledernes Hovedeorganisation [IO]
Logistics Mgt. Inst. [5607]
Mgt. Consultancies Assn. [IO]
Mgt. Educ. Alliance [8029]
Mananga Centre for Regional Integration and Mgt. Development [IO]
Marketing and Advt. Global Network [109]
Moore Stephens North Am. [41]
MRA-The Mgt. Assn. [2502]
NAED Educ. and Res. Found. [2503]
Natl. Assn. of Church Facilities Managers [20514]
Natl. Assn. of Corporate Directors [2504]
Natl. Assn. of Healthcare Access Mgt. [14890]
Natl. Assn. of Ser. Managers [3552]
Natl. Assn. of State Treasurers [6208]
Natl. Biosolids Partnership [5096]
Natl. Black MBA Assn. [8035]
Natl. Bd. of the Fac. Mgt. Assn. of Australia [IO]
Natl. Bur. of Certified Consultants [2505]
Natl. Conf. of Executives of the Arc [2506]
Natl. Food Ser. Mgt. Inst. [1590]
Natl. Grants Mgt. Assn. [2507]
Natl. Inst. for Hea. Care Mgt. Res. and Educational Found. [14655]
Natl. Inst. of Mgt. Counsellors [2508]
Natl. Mgt. Assn. [2509]
Natl. Productivity Coun. [IO]
Native Financial Educ. Coalition [8442]
New Zealand Inst. of Mgt. [IO]
North Amer. Performing Arts Managers and Agents [175]
Oper. Enterprise [8808]
Org. Design Forum [2510]
Organization Design Forum [IO]
Prdt. Development and Mgt. Assn. [2511]
Production Managers Assn. [IO]
Production and Operations Management Society [IO]
Production and Operations Mgt. Soc. [2512]
Professional Services Mgt. Assn. [2513]
Proj. Mgt. Inst. [2514]
Proj. Mgt. Inst. [IO]
Public Agency Risk Managers Assn. [5833]
Public Employees Roundtable [5572]
Public Risk Mgt. Assn. [5834]
SCORE [3625]
Sigma Iota Epsilon [24534]
Soc. for Advancement of Mgt. [2515]
Soc. for Human Rsrc. Mgt. [2908]
Soc. for Info. Mgt. [2516]
Soc. of Trust and Estate Practitioners USA [1332]
Southern Africa Inst. for Mgt. Services [IO]
Special Interest Gp. on Mgt. Info. Systems [6824]
Statistical Process Controls [7554]
Strategic Planning Soc. [IO]
Swiss Mgt. Assn. [IO]
Tech. Mgt. Educ. Assn. [9245]
Transworld Advt. Agency Network [124]
Turnaround Mgt. Assn. [2517]
U.S. Maritime Alliance [2594]
Women Executives in Public Relations [3197]
Women in Mgt. [2518]
World Confed. of Productivity Sci. [IO]
Mgt; Acad. of Pharmacy Practice and [★15918]
Mgt. Accountants; Inst. of [34]
Mgt. Admission Search Service; Graduate [★8807]
Mgt. Admission Search Service; Graduate [★IO]
Mgt; Amer. Acad. of Podiatric [★16024]
Mgt; Amer. Assn. of Public Welfare Info. Systems [★13152]
Mgt; Amer. Pharmaceutical Assn. - Acad. of Pharmacy Practice and [★15918]
Mgt; Amer. Pharmacists Assn. - Acad. of Pharmacy Practice and [15918]
Mgt; Amer. Soc. for Engg. [6994]
Mgt; Amer. Soc. for Healthcare Risk [14869]
Mgt. Assistance Gp. [12655], 1555 Connecticut Ave. NW, 3rd Fl., Washington, DC 20036-1103, (202)659-1963

Mgt. Assistance Proj. of the Center for Community Change; Planning and [★12655]
Mgt; Assn. of [★6528]
Mgt. Assn; Agricultural Personnel [4638]
Mgt. Assn; AIIM - The Enterprise Content [2095]
Mgt. Assn. of Am; Govt. Contract [★1744]
Mgt. Assn; Amer. Hea. Info. [15097]
Mgt. Assn; Audiovisual [★329]
Mgt. Assn; Broadcast Cable Financial [553]
Mgt. Assn; Broadcast Financial [★553]
Mgt. Assn; Christian [20511]
Mgt. Assn; Clinical Lab. [14993]
Mgt. Assn; Communications Media [329]
Mgt. Assn; Constr. Financial [1012]
Mgt; Assn. for Convention Operations [2674]
Mgt. Assn; Dealer [717]
Mgt. Assn; Dental Gp. [15065]
Mgt. Assn; Distribution Bus. [4019]
Mgt. Assn; Environmental [2463]
Mgt; Assn. for Fed. Info. Resources [5815]
Mgt. Assn; Fulfillment [3224]
Mgt. Assn; Healthcare Financial [15066]
Mgt; Assn. for Healthcare Rsrc. and Materials [14872]
Mgt. Assn; In-Plant [★1776]
Mgt. Assn; Indus. Sanitation [★2463]
Mgt. Assn; Info. Resources [2101]
Mgt. Assn; Intl. City [★6123]
Mgt. Assn; Intl. Trans. [6319]
Mgt. Assn; Lab. Animal [13699]
Mgt. Assn; Latino Amer. [24288]
Mgt. Assn; Legal Asst. [★5944]
Mgt. Assn; Lib. Admin. and [10366]
Mgt. Assn; Life Insurance Agency [★2195]
Mgt. Assn; Life Off. [★2196]
Mgt. Assn; Mail Systems [2450]
Mgt. Assn; Medical Gp. [15067]
Mgt. Assn; MRA-The [2502]
Mgt. Assn; Natl. Account [★2650]
Mgt. Assn; Natl. Assistance [★2507]
Mgt. Assn; Natl. Contract [1744]
Mgt. Assn; Natl. Corporate Cash [★1403]
Mgt. Assn; Natl. Credit Union [1117]
Mgt. Assn; Natl. Fac. [★3188]
Mgt. Assn; Natl. Indus. Property [★3190]
Management Assn; Natl. Labor- [24119]
Mgt. Assn; Natl. Property [3190]
Mgt. Assn; North Amer. Hazardous Materials [4806]
Mgt. Assn; Paper Indus. [2893]
Mgt. Assn. for Private Photogrammetric Surveyors [7496], 1760 Reston Pkwy., Ste. 515, Reston, VA 20190, (703)787-6996
Mgt. Assn; Professional Convention [2689]
Mgt. Assn; Professional Services Bus. [★2513]
Mgt. Assn; Property [3336]
Mgt. Assn; Public Broadcasting [578]
Mgt; Assn. for Public Policy Anal. and [18423]
Mgt. Assn; Public Risk [5834]
Mgt. Assn; Radiology Bus. [15074]
Mgt. Assn; Strategic Account [2650]
Mgt. Assn; Tech. Applications Prog., Intl. City [★6197]
Mgt. Assn; Telecommunications Risk [3761]
Mgt. Assn; Treasury [★1403]
Mgt. Benchmarking Consortium; Info. Systems [725]
Mgt; Bd. of Certified Hazard Control [3440]
Mgt; Bd. of Certified Prdt. Safety [3441]
Mgt; Bureau of Land [★4468]
Mgt; Bureau of Land [★IO]
Mgt. Caucus; Groundwater [7829]
Mgt; Center for Rsrc. [4373]
Mgt. Centre Europe [IO], Brussels, Belgium
Mgt. Comm. of the Retail Food Indus; Joint Labor [24059]
Mgt. Company for Amer. Poultry U.S.A. [★5108]
Mgt. Company for Amer. Poultry U.S.A. [★IO]
Mgt. Consultancies Assn. [IO], London, United Kingdom
Mgt. Consultants; Amer. Assn. of Insurance [953]
Mgt. Consultants Assn; Investment [2336]
Mgt. Consultants; Inst. for Certified Investment [★2336]
Mgt. Consultants; Natl. Bur. of Professional [★2505]
Mgt. Consultants; Soc. of Risk [2244]
Mgt. and Controls Soc; Energy [★6942]

A star before a book entry number signifies that the name is not listed separately, but is mentioned within the entry.

Mgt. Cooperation Fund; Instrument Technicians Labor- [1021]
Mgt. Coun. of the Amer. Trucking Assns. - Defunct.
Mgt. Coun; Broker [1937]
Mgt; Coun. of Commun. [876]
Mgt; Coun. of Logistics [★4018]
Mgt. Coun; Paper and Plastic Representatives [2645]
Mgt. of Data; Special Interest Gp. on [6750]
Mgt. Development; Natl. Comm. for Small Bus. [★3611]
Mgt. Educ; AACSB-The Intl. Assn. for [★8010]
Mgt. Educ. Alliance [8029], c/o Francis J. Aguilar, Exec. Dir., 300 Cumnock Hall, Boston, MA 02163, (617)495-6494
Mgt. Educ. Assn; Natl. Farm and Ranch Bus. [4639]
Mgt. Education and Res. Found; Operations [7167]
Mgt. Employer Coalition; Disability [1259]
Mgt. Engg; Center for Hosp. [★14885]
Mgt. Engg. Gp; IRE [★7014]
Mgt. Executives; Coll. of Healthcare Info. [2098]
Mgt; Forum on Res. [★6530]
Mgt. Found; ACEC Res. and [6980]
Mgt. Gp; Bus. Process Mgt. Initiative and Object [★706]
Mgt; Hospitality Inst. of Tech. and [1943]
Mgt. Info. in Financial Services; Assn. for [464]
Mgt. Info. Sciences; Govt. [5818]
Mgt. Info. Systems Gp. [2105], 10 Lab. Dr., Research Triangle Park, NC 27709-3966, (919)406-8829
Management Institute [★1780]
Mgt. Institute; Christian [★20511]
Mgt. Inst; Cleaning [2462]
Mgt; Inst. for Control Therapy, Reality Therapy, and Quality [★16233]
Mgt. Inst; Design [1807]
Mgt. Inst; Multiple Assn. [★314]
Mgt. Inst; Natl. Food Ser. [1590]
Mgt. Inst; North Amer. Trans. [8212]
Mgt; Inst. of Nuclear Materials [7387]
Mgt. Inst; Professional Arts [9594]
Mgt; Inst. of Real Estate [3312]
Mgt. Inst; Reliability Engg. and [★7038]
Mgt. Institute/Reliability Testing Inst; Reliability Engg. and [7038]
Mgt; Inst. of Risk [★2244]
Mgt. Inst; Service [★3552]
Mgt; Inst. for Supply [3263]
Management Inst.: Training for Indian Managers [★12628]
Mgt. Intl; Box Off. [★1312]
Mgt; Moderation [16507]
Mgt; Natl. Assn. of Credit [1436]
Mgt; Natl. Assn. for Environmental [★4588]
Mgt; Natl. Assn. of Healthcare Access [14890]
Mgt; Natl. Assn. of Purchasing [★3263]
Mgt; Natl. Assn. of Purchasing [★2718]
Mgt; Natl. Center for Housing [12321]
Mgt. Open Systems Alliance; Machinery Info. [2560]
Mgt. in Podiatry; Amer. Acad. of Practice [★16024]
Mgt. Policy Reform and Sustainable Forestry Prog; Timber [★4354]
Mgt. Professionals; Assn. of Equip. [2442]
Mgt. Professionals; Total Energy [★6942]
Mgt. Res; Amer. Found. for [★2481]
Mgt. and Res; Assn. for Investment [★2331]
Mgt. Sales Executives; Assn. of Investment [2329]
Mgt. Sci. Soc. of Ireland [IO], Dublin, Ireland
Mgt. Sect; IACP Law Enforcement Info. [5819]
Mgt. Soc. of Am; Case [15063]
Mgt. Soc. for Foodservice [1594]
Mgt. Soc. for Healthcare Professionals [IO], Hong Kong, People's Republic of China
Mgt; Soc. for Human Rsrc. [2908]
Mgt. Soc; Mineral Economics and [6139]
Mgt. Soc; Natl. Classification [★2092]
Mgt. Soc; Natl. Safety [12980]
Mgt. Soc; Risk and Insurance [2235]
Mgt; Special Interest Group for Business Data Processing and [76]
Mgt. Systems Gp; NAQP [★6798]
Mgt. Systems; Natl. Center for Higher Educ. [7905]
Mgt. Systems Soc; Healthcare Info. and [14885]
Mgt. Systems Soc; Hosp. [★14885]

Mgt. and Tech. Assistance Centers; Natl. Assn. of [★9309]
Managerial and Professional Staff Assn. [★IO]
Managers
All India Mgt. Assn. [IO]
Alliance in Support of Independent Res. [3390]
Amer. Soc. for the Advancement of Proj. Mgt. [2519]
American Society for the Advancement of Project Management [IO]
Asset Managers Forum [1401]
Assn. of Call Center Managers [2520]
Assn. of Forensic Quality Assurance Managers [5758]
Assn. for Global Bus. [8016]
Assn. of PVO Financial Managers [1458]
Assn. for Strategic Alliance Professionals [2521]
Assn. for Strategic Alliance Professionals [IO]
Assn. of Univ. Tech. Managers [5838]
Assn. of Users of Res. Agencies [IO]
Constr. Indus. Round Table [940]
Elephant Managers Assn. [4158]
European Confed. of Executives and Managerial Staff [IO]
European Mgt. Assistants [IO]
Global Assn. of Risk Professionals [1423]
Governance Inst. [2495]
Guatemalan Managers' Assn. [IO]
Hellenic Assn. of Professional Cong. Organisers [IO]
Hospitality Asset Managers Assn. [1942]
Indian Inst. of Materials Mgt. [IO]
Indore Mgt. Assn. [IO]
Inst. of Directors in Ireland [IO]
Inst. of Maintenance and Building Mgt. [IO]
Inst. of People Mgt. (South Africa) [IO]
Intl. Assn. for Contract and Commercial Mgt. [772]
Intl. Assn. of Info. Tech. Asset Managers [2093]
Intl. Food and Agribusiness Mgt. Assn. [1524]
Intl. Mgt. Assn. of Japan [IO]
Japan Indus. Mgt. Assn. [IO]
Location Managers Guild of Am. [2522]
Mgt. Centre Europe [IO]
Music Managers Forum [IO]
Natl. Assn. of Senior Move Managers [2523]
Natl. Assn. of Women Law Enforcement Executives [5989]
Natl. Conf. of Personal Managers [174]
Natl. Hospitality Mgt. Club [IO]
Natl. Workforce Assn. [1739]
North Amer. Weed Mgt. Assn. [4106]
Southern Classified Advt. Managers Assn. [119]
Talent Managers Assn. [1325]
Value Engg. Soc. Intl. [7052]
World Coun. for Venue Mgt. [1350]
Managers; Acad. of Certified Hazardous Materials [4804]
Managers and Agent; Natl. Assn. Performing Arts [★175]
Managers and Agents; North Amer. Performing Arts [175]
Managers; Amer. Coll. of Clinic [★15054]
Managers; Amer. Guild of Patient Account [★15047]
Managers Assn. of Am; Club [833]
Managers Assn; Athletic Equip. [23805]
Managers Assn; Coll. Athletic Bus. [★23813]
Managers Assn; Dietary [15555]
Managers Assn; Fed. [5708]
Managers' Assn; Fraternal Field [2165]
Managers' Assn; Gen. Agents and [★2166]
Managers Assn; Intl. Circulation [★3244]
Managers' Assn; Intl. City [★6123]
Managers Assn; Natl. Catalog [3134]
Managers Assn; Naval Civilian [6094]
Managers Assn; Northwest Farm [4640]
Managers Assn; Professional [5712]
Managers Assn; Radiologists Bus. [★15074]
Managers Assn; Religious Convention [★2690]
Managers; Assn. of Sales Admin. [3464]
Managers Assn; Sports Turf [2399]
Managers Assn; Stadium [23869]
Managers Assn; Subscription Fulfillment [★3224]
Managers Assn; Teleprofessional [★2619]
Managers; Assn. of Theatrical Press Agents and [24154]

Managers Assn; Univ. Insurance [★8580]
Managers Assn; Univ. Lab. [★7237]
Managers Assn; Univ. Risk and Insurance [★8580]
Managers; Assn. of Vacation Home Rental [★3344]
Managers Assn; Vacation Rental [3344]
Managers Assn; Veterinary Hosp. [16814]
Managers; Automotive Trade Assn. [★349]
Managers Club of Chicago; Export [★2284]
Managers Conf. of NALU; Gen. Agents and [★2166]
Managers Coun. of Am; Equip. [943]
Managers Coun; Automotive Training [351]
Managers Coun; Real Estate Brokerage [★3306]
Managers and Dramaturgs of the Americas; Literary [11023]
Managers, East; Conf. of Personal [★174]
Managers Guild; Artists [★172]
Managers Guild; Banquet [★1951]
Managers; Inst. of Certified Records [2103]
Managers Inst. Intl; Building Owners and [9027]
Managers; Management Inst.: Training for Indian [★12628]
Managers; Natl. Assn. of Employment [★2481]
Managers; Natl. Assn. of Exposition [★2682]
Managers; Natl. Assn. of Produce Market [5022]
Managers; Natl. Assn. of Sales [★2481]
Managers; Natl. Assn. of Ser. [3552]
Managers; Natl. Conf. of Personal [174]
Managers; Natl. Network for Social Work [13207]
Managers; Newspaper Assn. [3149]
Managers and Planners; Org. of Facility [★7167]
Managers and Rural Appraisers; Amer. Soc. of Farm [274]
Managers Soc; CUES [★1106]
Managers Soc; Financial [1418]
Managers, West; Conf. of Personal [★174]
Managing Editors; Assoc. Press [3090]
Managing Gen. Agents; Amer. Assn. of [2133]
Manakin in the Colony of Virginia; Huguenot Soc. of the Founders of [21162]
Mananga Centre for Regional Integration and Mgt. Development [IO], Mbabane, Swaziland
Mananga Mgt. Centre [★IO]
Manatee; Adopt-a- [★5378]
Manatee Club; Save the [5378]
Manchester Chamber of Commerce and Indus. [IO], Manchester, United Kingdom
Manchester Geological Assn. [IO], Cheadle, United Kingdom
Manchester Terrier Club; Amer. [22204]
Mancuso Fan Network; Nick [24762]
Mandala Holistic Health - Defunct.
Mandala Soc. [12356], PO Box 1233, Del Mar, CA 92014, (858)481-7751
Mandate Trade Union [IO], Dublin, Ireland
Mandibular Orthopedics; Intl. Coll. of Cranio- [15770]
M&M's Collectors Club [22067], c/o Dennis Hudson, Treas., RD 7, Box 7711, Stroudsburg, PA 18360
Mandolinists and Guitarists; Amer. Guild of Banjoists, [★10536]
Manee, Maney, Manney, Manny, Many [★20990]
Manganese Centre [★IO]
Manganese Inst; Intl. [IO]
Manhattan Bowery Corp. [★13277]
Manhattan Chess Club - Defunct.
Manhattan Inst. for Policy Res. [18408], 52 Vanderbilt Ave., New York, NY 10017, (212)599-7000
Manhattan Publishing Group - Address unknown since 1994.
Manhattan Ryegrass Growers Assn. [4795]
Mani Tese [★IO]
Manic-Depressive Assn. - Defunct.
Manic Depressive Assn; Natl. Depressive and [★15196]
Manic Depressive and Depressive Assn. [★15196]
Manichaean Soc. - Defunct.
Maniilaq Assn. [12627], PO Box 256, Kotzebue, AK 99752, (907)442-7660
Manilow's Michigan Medley - Defunct.
Manipulative Therapeutic and Clinical Res. Assn; Osteopathic [★15790]
Manitoba 4-H [IO], Brandon, MB, Canada
Manitoba Amateur Boxing Assn. [IO], Winnipeg, MB, Canada
Manitoba Brain Injury Assn. [IO], Winnipeg, MB, Canada

Reference to "IO" in place of a book number signifies that the association may be found in the 45th edition of International Organizations.

Manitoba Cricket Assn. [IO], Winnipeg, MB, Canada

Manitoba Epilepsy Assn. [IO], Winnipeg, MB, Canada

Manitoba Psychological Soc. [IO], Winnipeg, MB, Canada

Manitoba Wheelchair Sports Assn. [IO], Winnipeg, MB, Canada

ManKind Proj. [13021], PO Box 230, Malone, NY 12953-0230, (800)870-4611

Mankind Res. Found. - Address unknown since 2004.

Mann League of the U.S.A; Horace [9036]

Manna House [12293], PO Box 675, Concordia, KS 66901, (785)243-4428

Mannerheim League for Child Welfare [IO], Helsinki, Finland

Mannerheimin Lastensuojeluliitto [★IO]

Mannlicher Collectors Assn. - Address unknown since 2001.

Mannosidosis and Related Diseases; Intl. Soc. for [14458]

Manorial Soc. of Great Britain [IO], London, United Kingdom

Manors; Natl. Soc. of Descendants of Lords of the Maryland [20747]

Manpower Analysis and Planning Soc. - Address unknown since 1999.

Manpower Commn; Sci. [★7604]

Manpower Demonstration Res. Corp. [12777], 16 E 34th St., 19th Fl., New York, NY 10016-4326, (212)532-3200

Manpower Demonstration Res. Corp. [IO], New York, NY, United States

Manpower and Development Inst. - Defunct.

Manpower Educ. Inst. [8567], 715 Ladd Rd., Bronx, NY 10471-1203, (718)548-4200

Manpower Franchise Owners; Assn. of [1257]

Manpower Inst; The [★17974]

The Manpower Inst. [★17974]

Manpower Inst; Natl. [★17974]

Manpower Soc. [★IO]

Mantel Contractors Assn. of Am; Tile and [★1066]

Manufactured Buildings Assn. - Defunct.

Manufactured Home Owners; Natl. Found. of [12323]

Manufactured Housing

Building Systems Councils of NAHB [2524]
Canadian Manufactured Housing Inst. [IO]
Homeowners Against Deficient Dwellings [12314]
Log Homes Coun. [2525]
Manufactured Housing Assn. for Regulatory Reform [2526]
Manufactured Housing Inst. [2527]
Metal Building Contractors and Erectors Assn. [2528]
Modular Building Systems Coun. [2529]
Natl. Dome Coun. [2530]
Panelized Building Systems Coun. [2531]
Teton Club Intl. [22632]
Western Manufactured Housing Communities Assn. [2532]

Manufactured Housing Assn. for Regulatory Reform [2526], c/o Manufactured Housing Inst., 2101 Wilson Blvd., Ste. 610, Arlington, VA 22201, (703)558-0400

Manufactured Housing Fed; Natl. [★2527]

Manufactured Housing Inst. [2527], 2101 Wilson Blvd., Ste. 610, Arlington, VA 22201-3062, (703)558-0400

Manufactured Housing Inst; Southeastern [★2527]

Manufactured Housing Res. Alliance [1976], 2109 Broadway, Ste. 200, New York, NY 10023, (212)496-0900

Manufactured Housing Task Force - Defunct.

Manufactured Imports Promotion Org. [IO], Tokyo, Japan

Manufactured Imports Promotion Org. - Defunct.

Mfr. Assn; Game [1301]

Mfr. Assn; Small Motor [★1198]

Mfrs. of Aerial Devices and Digger-Derricks Coun. [2038], 6737 W Washington St., Ste. 2400, Milwaukee, WI 53214-5647, (414)272-0943

Mfrs'. Agents' Assn. of Great Britain and Ireland [IO], Harpenden, United Kingdom

Mfrs. Agents for Food Ser. Indus. [★1575]

Mfrs'. Agents for the Foodservice Indus. [1575], 2814 Spring Rd., Ste. 211, Atlanta, GA 30339, (770)433-9844

Mfrs'. Agents Natl. Assn. [2537], 1 Spectrum Pointe, Ste. 150, Lake Forest, CA 92630-2283, (949)859-4040

Mfrs. Aircraft Assn. - Defunct.

Mfrs. Alliance/MAPI [2039], 1600 Wilson Blvd., Ste. 1100, Arlington, VA 22209-2594, (703)841-9000

Mfrs. Alliance for Productivity and Innovation [★2039]

Mfrs. of Am; Bur. of Envelope [★3681]

Mfrs. of Am; Dental [★1859]

Manufacturers of Am; Pharmaceutical Res. and [2980]

Mfrs. of Am; Toy [★3832]

Mfrs. of Am; Wood Machinery [2080]

Mfrs; Amer. Assn. of Automatic Door [1163]

Manufacturers. Amer. Innerspring [1969]

Mfrs; Amer. Inst. of Bolt, Nut and Rivet [★1823]

Mfrs; Associated Corset and Brassiere [227]

Mfrs; Assoc. Glass and Pottery [3709]

Manufacturers Assn; Accessibility Equip. [1156]

Mfrs. Assn; Agricultural Insecticides and Fungicide [★807]

Mfrs. Assn; Aircraft Locknut [1814]

Manufacturers Assn; Aluminum Foil Container [971]

Manufacturers Assn; Aluminum Window [★588]

Manufacturers Assn. of Am; Casket [★2775]

Mfrs. Assn. of Am; Crane [2016]

Mfrs. Assn. of Am; Envelope [★3681]

Mfrs. Assn. of Am; Hack and Band Saw [★1830]

Mfrs. Assn. of Am; Valve [1838]

Manufacturers Assn; Amer. Apparel [★221]

Manufacturers Assn; Amer. Apparel and Footwear [★221]

Manufacturers Assn; Amer. Architectural [588]

Manufacturers Assn; Amer. Award [★441]

Mfrs. Assn; Amer. Bearing [1991]

Mfrs. Assn; Amer. Boiler [1992]

Mfrs. Assn; Amer. Brush [1968]

Manufacturers; Assn. of Amer. Ceramic Component [785]

Mfrs. Assn; Amer. Cloak and Suit [223]

Mfrs. Assn; Amer. Composites [589]

Mfrs. Assn; Amer. Cotton [★3772]

Manufacturers Assn; Amer. Drug [★2980]

Manufacturers Assn; Amer. Edged Products [3708]

Mfrs. Assn; Amer. Envelope [★3681]

Manufacturers Assn; Amer. Feed [★1357]

Mfrs. Assn; Amer. Fiber [3769]

Mfrs. Assn; Amer. Furniture [★1690]

Mfrs. Assn; Amer. Hardware [1815]

Manufacturers Assn; Amer. Home Laundry [★264]

Mfrs. Assn; Amer. Loudspeaker [★1206]

Mfrs. Assn; Amer. Metal Detector [1817]

Mfrs. Assn; Amer. Paint [★2884]

Mfrs. Assn; Amer. Pet Products [2956]

Mfrs. Assn; Amer. Precision Optics [3480]

Mfrs. Assn; Amer. Sprocket Chain [★1993]

Mfrs. Assn; Amer. Supply and Machinery [★2027]

Manufacturers Assn; Amer. Walnut [1635]

Mfrs. Assn; Amer. Window Covering [★2279]

Mfrs. Assn; Anti-Friction Bearing [★1991]

Mfrs. Assn; Apparel [225]

Manufacturers Assn; Archery [★3638]

Manufacturers Assn; Asphalt Emulsion [594]

Manufacturers Assn; Asphalt Roofing [597]

Manufacturers Assn; Athletic Goods [★3652]

Manufacturers Assn; Aviation Distributors and [141]

Manufacturers Assn; Biscuit and Cracker [450]

Mfrs. Assn; Boat [★2587]

Mfrs. Assn; Braided Trimming [★3780]

Manufacturers Assn; Brake Lining [★385]

Manufacturers Assn; Brick [★604]

Mfrs. Assn; Bridge Grid Flooring [605]

Mfrs. Assn; Builders Hardware [1819]

Manufacturer's Assn; Bus. and Institutional Furniture [1692]

Manufacturers Assn; Carbonated Beverage Container [★974]

Manufacturers Assn; Cellulose Insulation [610]

Mfrs. Assn; Ceramic [786]

Manufacturers Assn; Chem. Specialties [★806]

Manufacturers Assn; Closure [975]

Manufacturers Assn; Color Pigments [868]

Mfrs. Assn; Concrete Anchor [921]

Manufacturers Assn; Constr. Indus. [★177]

Manufacturers Assn; Consumer Products Division of the Natl. Elecl. [★264]

Mfrs. Assn; Converting Equip. [2012]

Mfrs. Assn; Conveyor Equip. [2013]

Mfrs. Assn; Cookware [1970]

Mfrs. Assn; Diamond [★2362]

Manufacturers Assn; Diving Equip. [★3642]

Manufacturers Assn; Dry Color [★868]

Mfrs. Assn; Elastic Braid [★3780]

Manufacturers; Assn. of Electronic [★1212]

Manufacturers Assn; Engine [1291]

Manufacturers Assn; Engine Generator Set [★1182]

Mfrs. Assn; Engraved Stationery [3680]

Mfrs. Assn; Envelope [3681]

Mfrs. Assn; Expansion Joint [3030]

Manufacturers Assn; Exterior Insulation [★618]

Mfrs. Assn; Fabricating [★2017]

Manufacturers Assn; Farm Equip. [179]

Mfrs'. Assn; Fire Equip. [3443]

Mfrs. Assn; Flexible Polyurethane Foam [★3057]

Mfrs. Assn; Food Equipment [1573]

Mfrs. Assn. Found; Pharmaceutical [★2980]

Manufacturers Assn; Gas Appliance [265]

Mfrs. Assn; Gasoline Pump [2926]

Manufacturers Assn; Gen. Aviation [149]

Mfrs. Assn; Guitar and Accessory [★2805]

Mfrs. Assn; Hardwood [1648]

Mfrs. Assn; Hardwood Dimension [★1656]

Mfrs. Assn; Hea. Indus. [★14669]

Mfrs. Assn; Heavy Duty [2557]

Manufacturers; Assn. of Home Appliance [264]

Mfrs. Assn; Hydraulic Tool [2025]

Mfrs. Assn; Infant and Juvenile [240]

Manufacturers; Assn. of Innerspring [★1969]

Mfrs. Assn. of Israel [IO], Tel Aviv, Israel

Mfrs. Assn; Juvenile Products [2388]

Mfrs. Assn; Kitchen Cabinet [2267]

Mfrs. Assn; Latin Amer. [★24288]

Mfrs. Assn; Laundry and Dry Cleaners Machinery [★2407]

Manufacturers Assn; Maple Flooring [635]

Mfrs. Assn; Marine Engine [★2587]

Manufacturers Assn; Mayonnaise and Salad Dressing [★1502]

Mfrs. Assn; Medical Device [3486]

Mfrs; Assn. of Medical Diagnostics [3482]

Mfrs. Assn; Medical-Surgical [★14669]

Manufacturers Assn; Metal Building [637]

Mfrs. Assn; Metal Cookware [★1970]

Mfrs. Assn; Metal Findings [2379]

Manufacturers Assn; Metal Framing [639]

Mfrs; Assn. of Microbiological Diagnostic [★3482]

Mfrs. Assn; MIDI [2813]

Manufacturers Assn; Midwest Feed [★1357]

Manufacturers Assn; Mineral Insulation [★659]

Mfrs. Assn; Monorail [2046]

Mfrs. Assn; Natl. Beauty and Barber [★1086]

Mfrs. Assn; Natl. Dress [★225]

Manufacturers Assn; Natl. Elecl. [1191]

Manufacturers Assn; Natl. Greenhouse [184]

Mfrs. Assn; Natl. Housewares [★1972]

Manufacturers Assn; Natl. Marine [2587]

Manufacturers Assn; Natl. Oak Flooring [★656]

Mfrs. Assn; Natl. Reloading [1481]

Mfrs. Assn; Natl. Seasoning [1552]

Manufacturers Assn; Natl. Tile Roofing [★681]

Mfrs. Assn; Natl. Wooden Pallet [★989]

Manufacturers Assn; New England Knitted Outerwear [★20816]

Manufacturers Assn; New England Rainwear [★221]

Manufacturers Assn; NOFMA: The Wood Flooring [656]

Manufacturers Assn; North Amer. Insulation [659]

Mfrs. Assn; North Amer. Punch [2055]

Mfrs. Assn; Northeastern Lumber [1654]

Mfrs. Assn; Outboard Motor [2587]

Manufacturers Assn; Pacific Coast Garment [★221]

Mfrs'. Assn; Pacific Coast Paper Box [990]

Manufacturers' Assn; Paper Shipping Sack [991]

Manufacturers Assn; Peanut Butter [★1556]

Manufacturers Assn; Peanut Butter Sandwich and Cookie [★1556]

A star before a book entry number signifies that the name is not listed separately, but is mentioned within the entry.

Mfrs. Assn; Pipe Fittings [★3025]
Mfrs. Assn; Plastic and Metal Products [3056]
Mfrs. Assn; Plumbing and Drainage [★3065]
Mfrs. Assn; Political Products [3069]
Mfrs. Assn; Polyisocyanurate Insulation [661]
Mfrs. Assn; Polyurethane [3058]
Manufacturers Assn; Power Fan [★1876]
Manufacturers Assn; Precision Potentiometer [★1230]
Mfrs. Assn; Pressure Vessel [2061]
Mfrs. Assn; Private Label [2646]
Mfrs. Assn; Process Equip. [2063]
Mfrs. Assn; Producers and [★5225]
Manufacturers Assn; Production Engine Re [1295]
Mfrs. Assn. of Products From Corn; Amer. [★1508]
Mfrs. Assn; Pulp and Paper Machinery [★2003]
Mfrs. Assn; Railway Car [★3278]
Manufacturers Assn; Refrigeration Equip. [★1873]
Mfrs. Assn. of Robes, Leisurewear, Shirts and Rainwear - Defunct.
Manufacturers Assn; Roof Coatings [855]
Mfrs. Assn; Rubber [3434]
Mfrs. Assn; Scale [4017]
Mfrs. Assn; Schiffli Lace and Embroidery [3797]
Mfrs. Assn; Screen [1833]
Mfrs. Assn; Southeastern Lumber [1620]
Mfrs. Assn; Southern Cypress [1621]
Mfrs. Assn; Southern Furniture [★1690]
Manufacturers Assn; Southern Garment [★221]
Mfrs. Assn; Southern Hardwood Lumber [★1648]
Mfrs. Assn; Southern Plywood [★1649]
Mfrs. Assn; Speciality Automotive [★396]
Manufacturers Assn; Specialty Equip. [★397]
Manufacturers Assn; Speed Equip. [★397]
Manufacturers Assn; Sporting Goods [★3652]
Mfrs. Assn; Steel [2732]
Manufacturers Assn; Storage Equip. [2071]
Manufacturers Assn; Stucco [676]
Mfrs. Assn; Summer and Casual Furniture [1706]
Mfrs. Assn; Sump and Sewage Pump [678]
Manufacturers Assn; Synthetic Organic Chem. [827]
Mfrs; Assn. of Synthetic Yarn [★3774]
Mfrs. Assn; Tank Conf. of the Truck Trailer [998]
Manufacturers Assn; Tennis [★3653]
Mfrs. Assn; Timber Products [★1626]
Mfrs. Assn; Trailer [★2583]
Mfrs. Assn; Trailer Coach [★2527]
Manufacturers Assn; Trophy Dealers and [★441]
Mfrs. Assn; Truck Trailer [401]
Mfrs. Assn; Tubular Exchanger [1902]
Mfrs. Assn; Tufted Textile [★2254]
Mfrs'. Assn; Unified Abrasives [2567]
Manufacturers Assn. of the U.S; Flavor and Extract [1509]
Mfrs. Assn; U.S. Sugar [★1567]
Mfrs. Assn. of the U.S.A; Chocolate [1506]
Mfrs. Assn. of the U.S.A; Clothing [229]
Manufacturers Assn; Vacuum Cleaner [★264]
Mfrs. Assn., Washington Off; Japan Auto. [389]
Mfrs. Assn; Water and Wastewater Equip. [2077]
Manufacturers Assn; West Coast Electronics [★1203]
Manufacturers Assn; Western Apparel and Equip. [★259]
Manufacturers Assn; Western Electronics [★1203]
Manufacturers Assn; Western and English [★259]
Mfrs. Assn; Window Covering [2279]
Manufacturer's Assn; Wiring Harness [1199]
Mfrs. Assn; Wood Products [1657]
Mfrs. Assn; Wood Tank [3366]
Mfrs. Assn; Work Glove [★2030]
Mfrs. Assn; Woven Elastic [★3780]
Mfrs. Assn; Woven Fabric Belting [★3792]
Mfrs. Assn; Writing Instrument [3688]
Mfrs; Associations Coun. of the Natl. Assn. of [★2562]
Mfrs; Basic Acrylic Monomer [800]
Manufacturers; Brass and Bronze Ingot [★2701]
Mfrs. Bur; Embroidery [★3797]
Mfrs. Bur; Truck Mixer [400]
Mfrs'. Clubs Assn; RV [22961]
Manufacturers Coun; Automotive Filter [★384]
Manufacturers Coun; Brake [381]
Manufacturers Coun; Brake Sys. Parts [★381]
Mfrs. Coun. on Color and Appearance - Defunct.

Mfrs. Coun; Equip. [178]
Mfrs. Coun. of Mfg. Associations; Natl. Assn. of [2562]
Mfrs. Coun. of NAHB; Dome Comm. of the Home [★2530]
Mfrs. Coun. of the Natl. Textile Assn; Elastic Fabric [3780]
Manufacturers Coun; Rubber and Plastic Adhesive and Sealant [★56]
Manufacturers Coun; Tune-Up [402]
Manufacturers Coun; Valve Re [★1839]
Mfrs. Coun; Wool [3809]
Manufacturers and Dealers Assn; Archery [★3638]
Mfrs. and Distributors Assn; Photoimaging [3007]
Manufacturers and Distributors; Independent Cosmetic [1847]
Manufacturers and Distributors; Natl. Assn. of Uniform [248]
Mfrs. Div; Ambulance [369]
Mfrs. Div; Commercial Refrigerator [1878]
Mfrs. Div., Natl. Assn. of Amusement Parks [★1298]
Manufacturers Div., Natl. Assn. of Amusement Parks [★IO]
Manufacturers EDP Coun; Automotive [★70]
Mfrs. of Educational and Commercial Stationery European Assn. [IO], Paris, France
Manufacturers of Elecl. and Supplies; Assoc. [★1191]
Mfrs. of Emission Controls Assn. [3072], 1730 M St. NW, Ste. 206, Washington, DC 20036, (202)296-4797
Manufacturers Exchange; Uniform [★248]
Mfrs. for Fair Trade [2538], PO Box 310, Cranesville, PA 16410, (814)756-5765
Mfrs. Gp; Popular Priced Dress [★225]
Mfrs. of Illumination Products - Defunct.
Mfrs. and Importers Assn. of Am; Diamond [2362]
Manufacturers, Inc; Appalachian Hardwood [1638]
Mfrs; Industrial Coun. of Cloak, Suit and Skirt [★253]
Mfrs. Inst; Amer. Textile [3772]
Manufacturers; Inst. of Appliance [★265]
Manufacturers' Inst; Book [1761]
Manufacturers Inst; Can [974]
Manufacturers Inst; Chain Link Fence [1362]
Mfrs. Inst; Elastic Fabric [★3780]
Manufacturers Inst; Equip. [★177]
Manufacturers Inst; Glass Container [★982]
Mfrs. Inst; Hardwood [★1648]
Mfrs. Inst; Hoist [2023]
Mfrs. Inst; Packaging Machinery [2876]
Mfrs. Inst; Plumbing [3066]
Mfrs'. Inst; Powder Actuated Tool [2057]
Mfrs. Inst; Rack [2064]
Mfrs. Inst; Sporting Arms and Ammunitions [1482]
Mfrs. Inst; Spring [1835]
Mfrs. Inst; Tag and Label [3687]
Manufacturers Inst; Tune-up [★402]
Mfrs; Intl. Assn. of Color [869]
Mfrs. Intl; Assn. of Vacuum Equip. [★2006]
Mfrs; Intl. Assn. of Wiping Cloth [★2066]
Mfrs; Loading Dock Equip. [2035]
Mfrs. Medical Device Assn; Smaller [★3486]
Manufacturers Members of the Natl. Warm Air Heating and Air Conditioning Assn. [★1873]
Manufacturers and Merchants Org; Archery [★3638]
Manufacturers; Natl. Assn. of [★565]
Mfrs; Natl. Assn. of [2561]
Mfrs; Natl. Assn. of Architectural Metal [2719]
Mfrs; Natl. Assn. of Band Instrument [★2810]
Mfrs; Natl. Assn. of Bedding [★1974]
Mfrs; Natl. Assn. of Blouse [245]
Mfrs; Natl. Assn. of Chewing Gum [1538]
Mfrs; Natl. Assn. of Cotton Cloth Glove [★2030]
Mfrs; Natl. Assn. of Dome Home [★2530]
Mfrs; Natl. Assn. of Electronic Keyboard [★2808]
Mfrs; Natl. Assn. of Engine and Boat [★2587]
Manufacturers; Natl. Assn. of Fan [★1876]
Mfrs; Natl. Assn. of Furniture [★1690]
Manufacturers; Natl. Assn. Insecticide and Disinfectant [★806]
Mfrs; Natl. Assn. of Margarine [2853]
Mfrs; Natl. Assn. of Meat and Food Seasoning [★1552]
Mfrs; Natl. Assn. of Meat Seasoning [★1552]

Mfrs; Natl. Assn. of Metal Name Plate [★2720]
Mfrs; Natl. Assn. of Musical Merchandise [★2805]
Mfrs; Natl. Assn. of Popcorn [★1589]
Mfrs; Natl. Assn. of Printing Ink [1803]
Manufacturers; Natl. Assn. of Relay [★1197]
Manufacturers; Natl. Assn. of Retail Ice Cream [★1137]
Mfrs; Natl. Assn. of Scale [★4017]
Manufacturers; Natl. Assn. of Silo [★181]
Mfrs; Natl. Assn. of Steam and Fluid Specialty [★2018]
Manufacturers; Natl. Assn. of Store Fixture [644]
Mfrs; Natl. Assn. of Textile Machinery [★1997]
Mfrs; Natl. Assn. of Trailer [393]
Mfrs; Natl. Assn. of Wool [★3772]
Mfrs; Natl. Clay Pipe [★3034]
Mfrs; Natl. Clay Pot [183]
Mfrs; North Amer. Assn. of Food Equip. [1576]
Manufacturers and Nut Salters Assn; Peanut Butter [★1556]
Mfrs. Operating Comm. of ETAD; U.S. Dye [★5089]
Manufacturers Org; Archery [★3638]
Mfrs. Prdt. Sect. of the Material Handling Inst; Overhead Components [★2042]
Mfrs. Promotion Fund; Schiffli Embroidery [3796]
Manufacturers Radio Frequency Advisory Comm. [565], 899-A Harrison Dr. SE, Leesburg, VA 20175, (703)669-0320
Manufacturers and Related Indus; ITA - Intl. Assn. of Magnetic and Optical Media [★1370]
Manufacturers Representatives
Agricultural and Indus. Mfrs. Representatives Assn. [2533]
Alliance of Auto. Mfrs. [368]
Assn. of Independent Manufacturers'/Representatives [2534]
Assn. of Visual Merchandise Representatives [2535]
Chem. Producers and Distributors Assn. [803]
Incentive Mfrs. and Representatives Alliance [2536]
Mfrs'. Agents Natl. Assn. [2537]
Mfrs. for Fair Trade [2538]
Mfrs. Representatives Educational Res. Found. [2539]
Mech. Equip. Mfrs. Representatives Assn. [2540]
NAGMR [2541]
Natl. Mobility Equip. Dealers Assn. [2542]
Natl. Mobility Equip. Dealers Assn. [IO]
North Amer. Industrial Representatives Assn. [2543]
United Assn. Mfrs. Representatives [2544]
United League Toy Representatives Associations [3833]
Manufacturers Representatives of Am. [1158], PO Box 150229, Arlington, TX 76015, (682)518-6008
Mfrs. and Representatives Assn; Incentive [★2536]
Mfrs. Representatives Assn; Mech. Equip. [2540]
Manufacturers Representatives Assn; Natl. Elecl. [1192]
Mfrs. Representatives Educational Res. Found. [2539], 8329 Cole St., Arvada, CO 80005, (303)463-1801
Manufacturers Representatives; Natl. Assn. of Diversified [★2541]
Manufacturers Representatives; Natl. Assn. of Drug [★2541]
Manufacturers; Southern Pine Lumber [★1623]
Mfrs. Standardization Soc. of the Valve and Fittings Indus. [2040], 127 Park St. NE, Vienna, VA 22180-4602, (703)281-6613
Manufacturers Standardization Society of the Valve and Fittings Industry [IO], Vienna, VA, United States
Mfrs. Standards Assn; Mortar [★636]
Mfrs. of Telescoping and Articulated Cranes Coun. [2041], c/o Assn. of Equip. Mfrs., 6737 W Washington St., Ste. 2400, Milwaukee, WI 53214-5647, (414)298-4132
Mfrs; Timber Products [1626]
Manufacturers of Toilet Articles; Assoc. [★1845]
Mfrs. Trade Assn; Amer. Metal Etching [★2720]
Manufacturiers et Exportateurs du Canada [★IO]
Manufacturing
Agile Mfg. Benchmarking Consortium [2545]

Reference to "IO" in place of a book number signifies that the association may be found in the 45th edition of International Organizations.

Aircraft Fleet Recycling Assn. [12800]
Alkylphenols and Ethoxylates Res. Coun. [796]
All India Manufacturer's Org. [IO]
Amer. Assn. of Indus. Mgt. [2480]
Amer. Indus. Extension Alliance [2546]
Amer. Mfg. Trade Action Coalition [2547]
APICS Region 8 [IO]
APQC [2482]
Assn. of Amer. Ceramic Component Manufacturers [785]
Assn. for Automatic Identification and Mobility North Am. [336]
Assn. for Electronics Mfg. of the Soc. of Mfg. Engineers [6907]
Assn. of European Wheel Mfrs. [IO]
Assn. for Mfg. Excellence [IO]
Assn. for Mfg. Excellence [2548]
Assn. for Mfg. Tech. [7262]
Assn. of Mauritian Mfrs. [IO]
Assn. of Needle-Free Injection Mfrs. [2549]
Aviation Suppliers Assn. [2550]
Barbados Mfrs'. Assn. [IO]
British Ladder Mfrs. Assn. [IO]
Bulgarian Indus. Assn. [IO]
CAMUS Intl. [IO]
CAMUS Intl. [2551]
Canadian Assn. of Defence and Security Indus. [IO]
Canadian Boiler Soc. [IO]
Canadian Mfrs. and Exporters [IO]
Canadian Tooling and Machining Assn. [IO]
Chinese Mfrs. Assn. of Hong Kong [IO]
Clean Production Action [4631]
Coalition for Justice in the Maquiladoras [18610]
CompactFlash Assn. [6723]
Composite Lumber Mfrs. Assn. [1642]
Composites Assn. of New Zealand [IO]
Composites Mfg. Assn. of the Soc. of Mfg. Engineers [IO]
Composites Mfg. Assn. of the Soc. of Mfg. Engineers [2552]
Concrete Tile Manufacturers Assn. [924]
Confed. of Danish Indus. [IO]
Confed. of Indian Indus. [IO]
Consortium for Advanced Mfg. Intl. [IO]
Consortium for Advanced Mfg. Intl. [2553]
Consortium for Energy Efficiency [1286]
Corrugated Packaging Coun. [2874]
Door and Access Systems Mfrs. Assn. Intl. [2554]
Door and Access Systems Manufacturers Assn. Intl. [IO]
The Elecl. and Electronics Assn. of Malaysia [IO]
Elecl. Generating Systems Assn. [1182]
Electro-Federation Canada [IO]
Employer Assn. Gp. [2555]
Entertainment Services and Tech. Assn. [2556]
Entertainment Services and Technology Association [IO]
European Assn. of Fibre Drum Mfrs. [IO]
European Assn. of Flexible Polyurethane Foam Blocks Mfrs. [IO]
European Comm. of Associations of Manufacturers of Gears and Transmission Parts [IO]
European Liaison Comm. of Machine Tool Importers [IO]
Fed. of British Engineers' Tool Manufacturers [IO]
Fed. of Hong Kong Indus. [IO]
Fed. of Malaysian Mfrs. [IO]
Fed. of Norwegian Indus. [IO]
Flag Mfrs. Assn. of Am. [1487]
Floor Installation Assn. of North Am. [623]
Gasket Cutters Assn. [IO]
Gen. Union of Romanian Manufacturers [IO]
German Machinery and Plant Mfrs. Assn. - Japan Liaison Off. [IO]
Glass Mfg. Indus. Coun. [1729]
Guyana Manufacturers' Assn. [IO]
Handcrafted Soap Makers Guild [1155]
Healthcare Mfrs. Marketing Coun. [14673]
Heavy Duty Mfrs. Assn. [2557]
Heavy Duty Representatives Assn. [386]
HomePlug Powerline Alliance [1216]
Indus. Assn. of Macau [IO]
Indus. Minerals Assn. - North Am. [2742]
Inst. for Mfg. [IO]

Inst. for Molecular Mfg. [7263]
Inst. of Shortening and Edible Oils [2851]
Instituto Nacional de Estadistica [IO]
Integrated Mfg. Tech. Initiative [7264]
Intl. Assn. of Dinnerware Matchers [1971]
Intl. Aviation Ground Support Assn. [436]
Intl. Coun. of Toy Indus. [3831]
Intl. Cuemakers Assn. [519]
Intl. Electronics Mfg. Initiative [7265]
Intl. Play Equip. Manufacturers Assn. [3060]
Intl. Production Planning and Scheduling Assn. [8809]
International Production Planning and Scheduling Association [IO]
Intl. Soc. of Agile Mfg. [IO]
Intl. Soc. of Agile Mfg. [2558]
Intl. Soc. of Transport Aircraft Trading [156]
Intl. Solid Surface Fabricators Assn. [2559]
Intl. Solid Surface Fabricators Assn. [IO]
Inventors Clubs of Am. [7229]
Japan Gear Manufacturers Assn. [IO]
Japan Machine Tool Builders' Assn. [IO]
Kenya Assn. of Mfrs. [IO]
Lithuanian Apparel and Textile Indus. Assn. [IO]
Lithuanian Confed. of Industrialists [IO]
Machinery Info. Mgt. Open Systems Alliance [2560]
Machining and Material Removal Community of the Soc. of Mfg. Engineers [7747]
Manufactured Housing Inst. [2527]
Mfrs. Alliance/MAPI [2039]
Mfrs. Assn. of Israel [IO]
Mfrs. for Fair Trade [2538]
Mfrs. Representatives Educational Res. Found. [2539]
Mfg. Enterprise Solutions Assn. Intl. [7722]
Mfg. Skill Standards Coun. [7696]
Materials Marketing Associates [2636]
Measurement, Control, and Automation Assn. [3485]
MultiMediaCard Assn. [7305]
Natl. Assn. of Mfrs. [2561]
Natl. Assn. of Mfrs. Coun. of Mfg. Associations [2562]
Natl. Assn. of Tobacco Outlets [3820]
Natl. Chamber of Mfrs. [IO]
Natl. Coun. for Advanced Mfg. [2563]
Natl. Indus. Assn. [IO]
Natl. Marine Mfrs. Assn. [2587]
Natl. Retail Hobby Stores Assn. [753]
Natl. Storm Shelter Assn. [2831]
Natl. Utility Locating Contractors Assn. [1055]
Netherlands Defence Mfrs. Assn. [IO]
North Amer. Insulation Manufacturers Assn. [659]
North Amer. Laminate Flooring Assn. [660]
North Amer. Mfg. Res. Institution of the Soc. of Mfg. Engineers [7266]
Packaging and Label Gravure Assn. Global [1784]
Percussion Marketing Coun. [1165]
PET Resin Assn. [3054]
Pressure Sensitive Manufacturers Assn. [IO]
Production Engg. Res. Assn. [IO]
Pump Indus. Australia [IO]
Rapid Technologies and Additive Mfg. Community [7267]
Refractory Ceramic Fibers Coalition [788]
The Remanufacturing Inst. [2564]
The Remanufacturing Inst. [IO]
Retailers of Art Glass and Supplies [1734]
Samoa Assn. of Mfrs. and Exporters [IO]
Schiffli Embroidery Mfrs. Promotion Fund [3796]
SD Card Assn. [6743]
SEAMS Assn. [2565]
Singapore Mfrs. Fed. [IO]
Soc. of Mfg. Engineers [7268]
Southern Pine Coun. [4057]
Swedish Crystal Mfrs. Assn. [IO]
Thermoset Resin Formulators Assn. [857]
Tooling and Mfg. Assn. [2566]
Trinidad and Tobago Mfrs. Assn. [IO]
Truck Mfrs. Assn. [366]
Unified Abrasives Mfrs'. Assn. [2567]
United Assn. Mfrs. Representatives [2544]
United Kingdom Indus. Vision Assn. [IO]
United Kingdom Spring Mfrs. Assn. [IO]

United League Toy Representatives Associations [3833]
U.S. Indus. Fabrics Inst. [3808]
Verite [12063]
Vibration Isolation and Seismic Control Mfrs. Assn. [7643]
Virtual Private Network Consortium [2320]
Women in Toys [3834]
Worldwide Responsible Apparel Production [261]
Mfg; Assn. of Refrigerant and Desuperheating [1877]
Mfg. Credit Assn; Natl. Radiator [★1422]
Mfg. Credit Assn; Natl. Radiator Core [★1422]
Mfg. Engineers; Amer. Soc. of Tool and [★7268]
Mfg. Engineers Educ. Found; Soc. of [8373]
Mfg. Engineers; Machining and Material Removal Community of the Soc. of [7747]
Mfg. Enterprise Solutions Assn. Intl. [7722], 107 S Southgate Dr., Chandler, AZ 85226, (480)893-6883
Manufacturing Enterprise Solutions Association International [IO], Chandler, AZ, United States
Mfg. Integration Tech Gp. of the Soc. of Mfg. Engineers [IO], Dearborn, MI, United States
Mfg. Integration Tech Gp. of the Soc. of Mfg. Engineers [6737], PO Box 930, One SME Dr., Dearborn, MI 48121, (313)271-1500
Mfg. Jewelers and Silversmiths of Am. [★2378]
Mfg. Jewelers and Suppliers of Am. [2378], 45 Royal Little Dr., Providence, RI 02904, (401)274-3840
Mfg. and Packaging Assn; Contract [★2873]
Mfg. Perfumers Assn. of the U.S. [★1845]
Mfg. Services Assn; CPA [26]
Mfg. Skill Standards Coun. [7696], 5020 Overlook Rd. NW, Washington, DC 20036, (202)237-2300
Mfg. Technologies Assn. [IO], London, United Kingdom
Mfg. Tech. Soc; IEEE Components, Packaging, and [6915]
Manuscript Soc. [22068], 1960 E Fairmont Dr., Tempe, AZ 85282-2844
Manushi for Sustainable Development [IO], Kathmandu, Nepal
Manx
North Amer. Manx Assn. [IO]
North Amer. Manx Assn. [19223]
Maoism
Maoist Internationalist Movement [6049]
Maoist Intl. Movement [★6049]
Maoist Intl. Movement [★IO]
Maoist Internationalist Movement [6049], c/o MIM Distributors, PO Box 29670, Los Angeles, CA 90029-0670
Map Collectors of Am; Road [★22111]
Map Collectors Assn; Road [22111]
Map Collectors Circle - Defunct.
Map Dealers Assn; Intl. [★6655]
MAP Intl. [20243], 2200 Glynco Pkwy., Brunswick, GA 31525-6800, (912)265-6010
MAP Intl. [IO], Brunswick, GA, United States
MAP Intl. - Eastern Africa Off. [IO], Nairobi, Kenya
Map Intl. - Latin Am. Off. [IO], Quito, Ecuador
Map Libraries; Western Assn. of [10394]
Map Online Users Group - Defunct.
Map Soc; Chicago [21528]
Mapendo Intl. [12868], 689 Massachusetts Ave., 2nd Fl., Cambridge, MA 02139, (617)864-7800
Mapendo Intl. [IO], Somerville, MA, United States
MAPI; Mfrs. Alliance/ [2039]
Maple Flooring Manufacturers Assn. [635], 60 Revere Dr., Ste. 500, Northbrook, IL 60062, (847)480-9138
Maple Flooring Manufacturers Association [IO], Northbrook, IL, United States
Maple Indus. Coun; Vermont [1569]
Maple Leaf Club [10642], 15522 Ricky Ct., Grass Valley, CA 95949
Maple Syrup Urine Disease; Families with [★15250]
Maple Syrup Urine Family Support Gp. [15250], 82 Ravine Rd., Powell, OH 43065, (740)548-4475
Mapping; Amer. Cong. on Surveying and [7717]
Mapping; Cartography Division of the Amer. Cong. on Surveying and [★6654]
Mapping; Control Surveys Division of the Amer. Cong. on Surveying and [★7716]
Mapping; Org. for Human Brain [7379]
Mapping Sciences Inst., Australia [IO], Brisbane, Australia

A star before a book entry number signifies that the name is not listed separately, but is mentioned within the entry.

MAPS Air Museum - Military Aviation Preservation Soc. [9342], 2260 Intl. Pkwy., North Canton, OH 44720, (330)896-6332

Maquiladoras; Coalition for Justice in the [18610]

MAR-Bulgarian Youth Alliance for Development [IO], Sofia, Bulgaria

Maranatha Gospel Bottle Crusade [★19993]

Maranatha Volunteers Intl. [20023], 1600 Sacramento Inn Way, Ste. 116, Sacramento, CA 95815, (916)920-1900

Maranatha Volunteers Intl. [IO], Sacramento, CA, United States

Marangopoulos Found. for Human Rights [IO], Athens, Greece

Maraschino Cherry and Glace Fruit Processors - Defunct.

Marathon Cycling Assn; Ultra [23318]

Marathon Skating Intl. [23737], PO Box 89, Norwich, VT 05055, (802)649-3939

Marauder Club - Defunct.

Marauder Historical Soc; B-26 [21389]

Marauders Assn; Merrill's [21395]

Marble Club of America; Natl. [22084]

Marble Collectors' Soc. of Am. [22624], c/o Stanley A. Block, Chm., PO Box 222, Trumbull, CT 06611, (203)261-3223

Marble Collectors Unlimited - Address unknown since 2007.

Marble Contractors and Affiliates; Assn. of Tile, Terrazzo, [★1053]

Marble Dealers; Natl. Assn. of [★3696]

Marble Inst. of Am. [3696], 28901 Clemens Rd., Ste. 100, Cleveland, OH 44145, (440)250-9222

Marble Inst. of Am. [IO], Cleveland, OH, United States

Marble Inst; Cultured [★630]

Marble Mfrs; Natl. Assn. of Cultured [★630]

Marble, Terrazzo, Finishers, Shopworkers, and Granite Cutters Intl. Union; Tile, [★24032]

Marbles
   Assn. of Game and Puzzle Collectors [22460]
   Marble Collectors' Soc. of Am. [22624]
   Natl. Marble Club of America [22084]

Marce Soc. [IO], London, United Kingdom

Marcel Soc; Gabriel [10794]

March of Dimes Birth Defects Found. [13756], 1275 Mamaroneck Ave., White Plains, NY 10605, (914)997-4488

March of Dimes; Natl. Found. - [★13756]

March of Dimes Natl. Registry for MPS/ML Disorders - Defunct.

March of Faces; ALS [13666]

March for Life [★18556]

March for Life Fund [18556], PO Box 90300, Washington, DC 20090, (202)543-3377

Marchigiana Soc; Amer. Intl. [4229]

Marchigiana Soc; Amer. Intl. [★4271]

Marching Bands of Am. [★10564]

Marching New Zealand [IO], Nelson, New Zealand

Marco Polo Club - Defunct.

Marcus Center of the Amer. Jewish Archives [10285], 3101 Clifton Ave., Cincinnati, OH 45220, (513)221-1875

Maremma Sheepdog Club of Am. [22304], c/o Mary C. Jarvis, Sec.-Treas., 2862 S Peterson Rd., Poplar, WI 54864, (715)364-2646

Marfan Argentina [IO], Buenos Aires, Argentina

Marfan Assn. UK [IO], Fleet, United Kingdom

Marfan Brasil [IO], Sao Luis, Brazil

Marfan Found; Natl. [16652]

Marfan Hilfe (Deutschland) e.V. [IO], Eutin, Germany

Marga Inst., Sri Lanka Centre for Development Stud. [IO], Colombo, Sri Lanka

Margaret River Olive Indus. Assn. [IO], Margaret River, Australia

Margaret Sanger Res. Bur. - Defunct.

Margarine Mfrs; Natl. Assn. of [2853]

Margarine and Shortening Mfrs. Assn. [★IO]

Margarine and Spreads Assn. [IO], London, United Kingdom

Margery Allingham Soc. [IO], King's Lynn, United Kingdom

Marguerite Rawalt Rsrc. Center [★11084]

MARHO: The Radical Historians' Org. [10129], c/o Amer. Historical Assn., 400 A St. SE, Washington, DC 20003-3889, (202)544-2422

Maria Comm; Pro [19704]

Maria Mitchell Assn. [6509], 4 Vestal St., Nantucket, MA 02554, (508)228-9198

Mariah Carey French Fan Club [IO], Paris, France

Mariah Carey Official Intl. Fan Club [IO], Branford, CT, United States

Mariah Carey Official Intl. Fan Club [24943]

Marian Helpers; Assn. of [19576]

Marian Philatelic Study Group - Defunct.

Marianist Writers' Guild - Defunct.

Mariannhill Mission Soc. [19655], 23715 Ann Arbor Trail, Dearborn Heights, MI 48127, (313)561-7140

Mariannhill Missionaries; U.S. Province of Congregation of [★19655]

Mariannhill Missionaries; U.S. Region of Congregation of [★19655]

Mariculture Soc; World [★4185]

Marie Curie Cancer Care [IO], London, United Kingdom

Marie Stopes Intl. - United Kingdom [IO], London, United Kingdom

Marie Stopes Intl. - Vietnam [IO], Hanoi, Vietnam

Marigold Soc. of Am. - Defunct.

Marijuana
   Addiction Res. and Treatment Corp. [13213]
   Amer. Alliance for Medical Cannabis [15020]
   Amer. Coun. for Drug Educ. [13222]
   Amer. Outreach Assn. [13223]
   Do It Now Found. [13235]
   Drug Peace Campaign [18022]
   Friends and Families of Cannabis Consumers [18023]
   Hea. Connection [13245]
   Inst. on Global Drug Policy [13248]
   Marijuana Policy Proj. [18024]
   Narcotic Educational Found. of Am. [13256]
   Narcotics Anonymous [13257]
   Natl. Assn. on Drug Abuse Problems [13262]
   Natl. Families in Action [13269]
   Natl. Family Partnership [13270]
   Natl. Narcotic Detector Dog Assn. [5997]
   Natl. Org. for the Reform of Marijuana Laws [17137]
   November Coalition [18690]
   Phoenix House [13273]
   Pills Anonymous [13275]
   PRIDE Youth Programs [13276]
   Women for Sobriety [13284]
   Women's Drug Res. Project [13285]

Marijuana Anonymous World Services [13022], PO Box 2912, Van Nuys, CA 91404, (800)766-6779

Marijuana Laws; Natl. Org. for the Reform of [17137]

Marijuana and Other Psychoactive Drugs; Amer. Coun. on [★13222]

Marijuana Policy Proj. [18024], PO Box 77492, Washington, DC 20013, (202)462-5747

Marilyn Monroe Intl. Fan Club - Address unknown since 2004.

Marin Self-Publishers Assn. [★3212]

Marin Small-Publishers Assn. [★3212]

Marina Assn. of America - Defunct.

Marina Operators Assn. of Am. - Defunct.

MARINALG Intl., World Assn. of Seaweed Processors [IO], Brussels, Belgium

Marine
   Aircraft Carrier Indus. Base Coalition [1148]
   Alberg 37 Intl. Owners Assn. [21866]
   All Japan Seamen's Union [IO]
   Alliance of Marine Mammal Parks and Aquariums [IO]
   Alliance of Marine Mammal Parks and Aquariums [5006]
   Alliance of Maritime Regional Interests in Europe [IO]
   Amer. Boat Builders and Repairers Assn. [2568]
   Amer. Boat and Yacht Coun. [2569]
   Amer. Bur. of Shipping [2600]
   Amer. Hull Insurance Syndicate [2136]
   Amer. Inst. of Marine Underwriters [2138]
   Amer. Littoral Soc. - Northeast Region [7269]
   Amer. Marinelife Dealers Assn. [5007]
   Amer. Maritime Cong. [6057]
   Amer. Maritime Safety, Inc. [2570]
   Amer. Pilots' Assn. [2571]
   Amer. Soc. of Marine Artists [9494]

   Amer. Soc. of Naval Engineers [7270]
   Amer. Waterways Operators [2601]
   Aquaculture Intl. [4169]
   Aquatic Animal Life Support Operators [7279]
   Armed Forces Sports [6069]
   ASEAN Ports Assn. [IO]
   Assn. of Average Adjusters of the U.S. [2145]
   Assn. of Brokers and Yacht Agents [IO]
   Assn. of Canadian Port Authorities [IO]
   Assn. of Certified Marine Surveyors [2572]
   Assn. for the History of the Northern Seas [IO]
   Assn. of Marina Indus. [2602]
   Assn. of Marine Technicians [2573]
   Assn. for Professional Observers [4667]
   Assn. of Ship Brokers and Agents - U.S.A. [2603]
   Atlantic States Marine Fisheries Commn. [5729]
   Australian Coral Reef Soc. [IO]
   Australian Inst. of Marine Sci. [IO]
   Australian Marine Sciences Assn. [IO]
   Baltic Marine Biologists [IO]
   Blue Dolphin Alliance [5008]
   Bonsai and Orchid Assn. [4975]
   Breeder's Registry [22438]
   British and Intl. Sailors Soc. [IO]
   British Marine Life Stud. Soc. [IO]
   Canadian Centre for Marine Communications [IO]
   Canadian Marine Mfrs. Assn. [IO]
   Canadian Marine Officers' Union [IO]
   Canadian Marine Pilots' Assn. [IO]
   Canadian Merchant Ser. Guild [IO]
   Canadian Nautical Res. Soc. [IO]
   Captain Cook Soc. [IO]
   Caribbean Conservation Corp. and Sea Turtle Survival League [5305]
   Central Commn. for the Navigation on the Rhine [IO]
   Challenger Soc. for Marine Sci. [IO]
   Clean Beaches Coun. [4540]
   The Coastal Soc. [7395]
   Coastal States Org. [7396]
   Commercial Boat Operators Assn. [IO]
   Comm. for Private Offshore Rescue and Towing [2574]
   Coun. of Amer. Master Mariners [2575]
   Cruise Lines Intl. Assn. [3915]
   Diving Historical Soc. Norway [IO]
   Dredging Contractors of Am. [2576]
   EarthEcho Intl. [4391]
   Environmental and Contamination Res. Center [7172]
   Estuarine Res. Fed. [7271]
   European Fed. of Marine Sci. and Tech. Societies [IO]
   European Marine Equip. Coun. [IO]
   European Sea Ports Org. [IO]
   European Soc. for Oceanists [IO]
   Franck Goddio Soc. [IO]
   German Soc. for Marine Res. [IO]
   Great Lakes Historical Soc. [10438]
   Great Lakes Maritime Inst. [10439]
   Historic Naval Ships Assn. [10440]
   Historic Naval Ships Association [IO]
   Historical Diving Soc. [IO]
   Historical Diving Soc. Canada [IO]
   Historical Diving Soc. Germany [IO]
   Historical Diving Soc. Italia [IO]
   Historical Diving Soc. Mexico [IO]
   Historical Diving Soc. South Africa [IO]
   Historical Diving Soc. USA [23576]
   Indus. Union of Marine and Ship Building Workers of Am. [24125]
   Inland Marine Underwriters Assn. [2170]
   Inland Rivers Ports and Terminals [2604]
   Inland Seas Educ. Assn. [2577]
   Inland Waterways Assn. of England [IO]
   Inland Waterways Assn. of Ireland [IO]
   Inst. of Estuarine and Coastal Stud. [IO]
   Intl. Assn. for Aquatic Animal Medicine [16792]
   Intl. Assn. of Aquatic and Marine Sci. Libraries and Info. Centers [10361]
   Intl. Assn. of Marine Investigators [2578]
   Intl. Assn. of Marine Investigators [IO]
   Intl. Bunker Indus. Assn. [IO]
   Intl. Cargo Gear Bur. [IO]
   Intl. Cargo Gear Bur. [6050]

Reference to "IO" in place of a book number signifies that the association may be found in the 45th edition of International Organizations.

Intl. Catalina 400 Assn. [21875]
Intl. Centre for Island Tech. [IO]
Intl. Coun. for the Exploration of the Sea [IO]
International Longshore and Warehouse Union [IO]
Intl. Longshore and Warehouse Union [24126]
Intl. Longshoremen's Assn. [24127]
Intl. Marine Minerals Soc. [5009]
Intl. Marine Minerals Soc. [IO]
Intl. Military Community Executives Assn. [834]
Intl. Org. of Masters, Mates and Pilots, ILA, AFL-CIO [24128]
Intl. SeaKeepers Soc. [5010]
Intl. SeaKeepers Soc. [IO]
Intl. Seaweed Assn. [IO]
Intl. Ship Masters' Assn. [IO]
Intl. Ship Masters' Assn. [2579]
Intl. Soc. for Reef Stud. [IO]
Intl. Stationary Steam Engine Soc. [22977]
John Ericsson Soc. [11130]
Lake Carriers' Assn. [2606]
Liberian Shipowners' Coun. [2607]
LTD Shippers Assn. [3842]
Lyman Boat Owners Assn. [21877]
Marine Aquarium Coun. [4175]
Marine Bd. [7272]
Marine Corps Assn. [6079]
Marine Corps Engineer Assn. [6142]
Marine Corps Recruiters Assn. [5799]
Marine Embassy Guard Assn. [21177]
Marine Fish Conservation Network [4419]
Marine Machinery Assn. [2608]
Marine Mammal Stranding Center [5338]
Marine Retailers Assn. of Am. [2580]
Marine Soc. [IO]
Marine Soc. of the City of New York [2581]
Marine Tech. Soc. [7273]
Maritime Assn. of the Port of New York/New Jersey [3572]
Maritime Trades Dept., AFL-CIO [24129]
Maritime Union of Australia [IO]
Maritime Union of New Zealand [IO]
Monaco Sci. Center [IO]
Montford Point Marine Assn. [6084]
Mystic Seaport [10441]
Natl. Aquarium Soc. [10442]
Natl. Assn. of Charterboat Operators [2582]
Natl. Assn. of Marine Labs. [7274]
Natl. Assn. of Marine Products and Services [2583]
Natl. Assn. of Marine Services [2584]
Natl. Assn. of Marine Surveyors [7275]
Natl. Assn. of Waterfront Employers [2609]
Natl. Cargo Bur. [3576]
Natl. Coalition for Marine Conservation [4423]
Natl. Counter Intelligence Corps Assn. [21164]
Natl. Fed. of Fishermen's Organisations [IO]
Natl. Marine Charter Assn. [2610]
Natl. Marine Distributors Assn. [2585]
Natl. Marine Educators Assn. [8810]
Natl. Marine Electronics Assn. [2586]
Natl. Marine Mfrs. Assn. [2587]
Natl. Marine Representatives Assn. [2588]
Natl. Naval Officers Assn. [6093]
Natl. Pearson Yacht Owners Assn. [21878]
Natl. Waterways Conf. [3581]
Nautical Inst. [IO]
Naval Enlisted Reserve Assn. [6095]
New York Shipping Assn. [3583]
Nippon Kaiji Kyokai [IO]
North Amer. Soc. for Oceanic History [IO]
North Amer. Soc. for Oceanic History [10443]
Northwest Marine Trade Assn. [2589]
Ocean Conservancy [4435]
Ocean Res. and Conservation Assn. [4436]
Oceanic Navigation Res. Soc. [10444]
Oceanic Soc. Expeditions [23016]
Offshore Marine Ser. Assn. [2590]
Oper. We Do Care [11499]
Pacific Coast Marine Firemen, Oilers, Watertenders and Wipers Assn. [24130]
Pacific Marine Mammal Center [5361]
Pacific Maritime Assn. [3585]
Pacific Seabird Gp. [5362]
Pacific Whale Found. [5363]

PACON Intl. [5011]
PACON Intl. [IO]
Passenger Vessel Assn. [2591]
Penobscot Marine Museum [10445]
Professional Boatman's Assn. [IO]
Propeller Club of the U.S. [3586]
Recreational Fishing Alliance [17603]
Reef Check [5012]
Reef Check [IO]
Reef Check Europe [IO]
Reef Relief [IO]
Reef Relief [5013]
ReefGuardian Intl. [5014]
ReefGuardian Intl. [IO]
Reserve Officers Assn. of the U.S. [6103]
Royal Natl. Lifeboat Institution - Ireland [IO]
Russian Assn. of Marine and River Bunker Suppliers [IO]
Sailors for the Sea [4447]
Sailors' Union of the Pacific [24131]
SATS/EAF Assn. [21179]
Save the Manatee Club [5378]
Save Our Seas [4449]
Scottish Assn. for Marine Sci. [IO]
Sea Educ. Assn. [8811]
Sea Grant Assn. [7276]
Sea Kayak Operators Assn. of New Zealand [IO]
Sea Stud. Found. [IO]
Seafarers' Intl. Union of North Am. [24132]
Seafloor Geosciences Div. [7404]
Seafood Choices Alliance [3503]
SeaWeb [5015]
Shark Res. Inst. [5019]
Shipbuilders Coun. of Am. [2592]
Shipowners Claims Bur. [2238]
Sirenian Intl. [5016]
Sirenian Intl. [IO]
Soc. for Marine Mammalogy [IO]
Soc. for Marine Mammalogy [5017]
Soc. of Marine Port Engineers [3588]
Soc. for Nautical Res. [IO]
Soc. of Small Craft Designers [2593]
South St. Seaport Museum [10446]
Steamship Assn. of Louisiana [3591]
Submarine Indus. Base Coun. [1149]
Titanic Historical Soc. [10447]
Titanic Historical Society [IO]
Titanic Intl. Soc. [IO]
Titanic Intl. Soc. [10448]
Trans. Inst. [3593]
Tugboat Enthusiasts Soc. of the Americas [21886]
U.S. Aquaculture Soc. [4183]
U.S. Life-Saving Ser. Heritage Assn. [10072]
U.S. Marine Safety Assn. [6051]
U.S. Maritime Alliance [2594]
U.S. Surveyors Assn. [7721]
USMC Vietnam Tankers Assn. [21337]
USS Constellation Museum [10449]
USS St. Louis CL-49 Assn. [10450]
Vietnam Era Seabees [21339]
Water Planet USA [5018]
Water Planet USA [IO]
Water Quality Insurance Syndicate [2246]
West African Discussion Agreement [3597]
West Gulf Maritime Assn. [2595]
Western Dredging Assn. [2596]
Whaling Museum Soc. [10451]
Women's Aquatic Network [7277]
World Org. of Dredging Associations [2597]
World Org. of Dredging Associations [IO]
World Ship Trust - United Kingdom [IO]
World Whale Police [5285]
Yacht Brokers Assn. of Am. [2598]
Marine Accessories and Services Assn. [★2583]
Marine Affairs; Women's Network in Aquatic and [★7277]
Marine Animal Trainers Assn; Intl. [6401]
Marine Aquarium Coun. [4175], 923 Nu'uanu Ave., Honolulu, HI 96817, (808)550-8217
Marine Aquarium Coun. [IO], Honolulu, HI, United States
Marine Aquarium Coun. - Indonesia [IO], Bali, Indonesia
Marine Aquarium Societies of North Am. [4176], c/o Bob Lemcke, Treas., 937 Roper Rd., Canton, GA 30115, (770)565-9841

Marine Artists; Amer. Soc. of [9494]
Marine Assn; Montford Point [6084]
Marine Assn; Women's [★21173]
Marine Aviation Force Veterans Assn; First [★6080]
Marine Bankers Assn; Natl. [495]
Marine Beirut Relief Fund - Defunct.
Marine Biological Assn. of the United Kingdom [IO], Plymouth, United Kingdom
Marine Biology
  Alliance of Marine Mammal Parks and Aquariums [5006]
  Amer. Cetacean Soc. [7258]
  Amer. Elasmobranch Soc. [7278]
  Amer. Marinelife Dealers Assn. [5007]
  Aquaculture Intl. [4169]
  Aquatic Animal Life Support Operators [7279]
  Blue Dolphin Alliance [5008]
  CEDAM Intl. [4371]
  Coastal Conservation Assn. [4376]
  Freshwater Mollusk Conservation Soc. [5034]
  Intl. Assn. for Aquatic Animal Medicine [16792]
  Intl. Soc. for Reef Stud. [4581]
  Marine Biological Assn. of the United Kingdom [IO]
  New Zealand Marine Sciences Soc. [IO]
  Ocean Conservancy [4435]
  Ocean Futures Soc. [5280]
  Ocean Res. and Conservation Assn. [4436]
  Ocean Soc. [7401]
  Pacific Marine Mammal Center [5361]
  Pacific Shellfish Inst. [4182]
  PACON Intl. [5011]
  Reef Check [5012]
  Sailors for the Sea [4447]
  Save the Manatee Club [5378]
  Save Our Seas [4449]
  SeaWeb [5015]
  Shark Res. Inst. [5019]
  Sirenian Intl. [5016]
  Soc. for Marine Mammalogy [5017]
  U.S. Aquaculture Soc. [4183]
  Water Planet USA [5018]
  World Whale Police [5285]
Marine Bd. [7272], c/o Keck Center of the Natl. Academies, 500 5th St. NW, Washington, DC 20001, (202)334-3119
Marine Conf; Mutual [★2131]
Marine Connection [IO], London, United Kingdom
Marine Conservation; Center for [★4435]
Marine Conservation; Natl. Coalition for [4423]
Marine Conservation Soc. [IO], Ross-On-Wye, United Kingdom
Marine Constr. Companies; Amer. Assn. for Small Dredging and [★2576]
Marine Cooks and Stewards Union [★24132]
Marine Corps
  1st Marine Div. Assn. [21171]
  AdoptaPlatoon [11489]
  All Navy Women's Natl. Alliance [6144]
  Any Soldier [11490]
  Beirut Veterans of Am. [21287]
  Books For Soldiers [11491]
  Devil Pups [21172]
  Judge Advocates Assn. [6078]
  Loyal Escorts of the Green Garter [21173]
  Marine Corps Aviation Reconnaissance Assn. [6052]
  Marine Corps CounterIntelligence Assn. [19224]
  Marine Corps Cryptologic Assn. [21174]
  Marine Corps Engineer Assn. [6142]
  Marine Corps Heritage Found. [10477]
  Marine Corps Intelligence Assn. [19225]
  Marine Corps Interrogator Translator Teams Assn. [19226]
  Marine Corps League Auxiliary [21175]
  Marine Corps Mustang Assn. [21176]
  Marine Corps Recruiters Assn. [5799]
  Marine Corps Reserve Assn. [6082]
  Marine Embassy Guard Assn. [21177]
  Marine Toys for Tots Found. [11709]
  Military Officers Assn. of Am. [21235]
  Military Order of the Devil Dog Fleas [21178]
  Navy Club of the U.S.A. Auxiliary [6100]
  Navy League of the U.S. [6101]
  Navy Seabee Veterans of Am. [21217]

A star before a book entry number signifies that the name is not listed separately, but is mentioned within the entry.

Navy Wifeline Assn. [21199]
Oper. AC [11492]
Oper. Homelink [11494]
Oper. Sandbox [11495]
Oper. ShoeBox [11496]
Oper. Soldier Support [11497]
Oper.: Take a Soldier to the Movies [11498]
Oper. We Do Care [11499]
Salute Our Services [11500]
SATS/EAF Assn. [21179]
Second Marine Div. Assn. [21180]
Sixth Marine Div. Assn. [21406]
Support Our Soldiers Am. [11502]
Tin Can Sailors - The Natl. Assn. of Destroyer
  Veterans [21220]
Tragedy Assistance Prog. for Survivors [11503]
U.S. Marine Corps Combat Correspondents Assn.
  [3171]
U.S. Marine Corps Drill Instructors Assn. [6109]
U.S. Marine Corps Scout/Sniper Assn. [21181]
U.S. Naval Cryptologic Veterans Assn. [21327]
U.S. Naval Inst. [6110]
USMC Motor Transport Assn. [2599]
USMC Vietnam Tankers Assn. [21337]
USS Wainwright Veterans Assn. [21329]
Vietnam Era Seabees [21339]
Women Marines Assn. [21182]
Marine Corps Assn. [6079], 715 Broadway St.,
  Quantico, VA 22134, (703)640-6161
Marine Corps Aviation Assn. [6080], 715 Broadway
  St., PO Box 296, Quantico, VA 22134, (703)630-
  1903
Marine Corps Aviation Reconnaissance Assn. [6052]
Marine Corps Combat Correspondents Assn; U.S.
  [3171]
Marine Corps CounterIntelligence Assn. [19224], PO
  Box 1298, Seminole, OK 74818-1298
Marine Corps Cryptologic Assn. [21174], 4486
  Sandalwood St., Napa, CA 94558-1766, (877)856-
  9562
Marine Corps Drill Instructors Assn; U.S. [6109]
Marine Corps Engineer Assn. [6142], PO Box 566,
  Jacksonville, NC 28541, (910)265-2701
Marine Corps Fathers Assn. of New York - Defunct.
Marine Corps Heritage Found. [10477], 307 5th
  Ave., Quantico, VA 22134, (703)640-7965
Marine Corps Historical Found. [★10477]
Marine Corps Intelligence Assn. [19225], PO Box
  1028, Quantico, VA 22134-1028
Marine Corps Interrogator Translator Teams Assn.
  [19226], 3224 N 109th Ave., Avondale, AZ 85392-
  4043
Marine Corps League [6081], c/o Mr. Michael A.
  Blum, Exec. Dir., PO Box 3070, Merrifield, VA
  22116-3070, (703)207-9588
Marine Corps League Auxiliary [21175], 8626 Lee
  Hwy., Ste. 207, Fairfax, VA 22031, (703)207-0626
Marine Corps Mustang Assn. [21176], Bunker 127,
  Mountain City, GA 30562, (866)937-6262
Marine Corps Recruiters Assn. [5799], c/o Sgt.
  James Simmons, Sec.-Treas., 1705 N Main St.,
  Nevada, MO 64772
Marine Corps Relief Soc; Navy- [18960]
Marine Corps Reserve Assn. [6082], 2020 Gen.
  Booth Blvd., Ste. 200, Virginia Beach, VA 23454,
  (757)301-2032
Marine Corps Reserve Officers' Assn. [★6082]
Marine Corps Toys for Tots Found. [★11709]
Marine Debris Info. Office [★4435]
Marine Debris Info. Office [★IO]
Marine Div. Assn; Sixth [21406]
Marine Div. Assn. WWII; 4th [21361]
Marine Educ. Assn; Natl. [★8810]
Marine Educators Assn; Natl. [8810]
Marine Embassy Guard Assn. [21177], c/o Tony Lo-
  pez, Sec., 70 Stringari Ln., Belfry, MT 59008,
  (406)664-3130
Marine Engine Mfrs. Assn. [★2587]
Marine Engineers' Beneficial Assn. [7308], 444 N
  Capitol St., Ste. 800, Washington, DC 20001,
  (202)638-5355
Marine Engineers Beneficial Association/National
  Maritime Union and Professional Airways Systems
  Specialists; District 1 of [★24015]
Marine Engineers; Soc. of Naval Architects and
  [7368]

Marine and Fire Insurance Assn. of Japan [★IO]
Marine Firemen, Oilers and Watertenders of the
  Pacific [★24130]
Marine Firemen's Union [★24130]
Marine Firemen's Union; Pacific Coast [★24130]
Marine Fish Conservation Network [4419], 600
  Pennsylvania Ave. SE, Ste. 210, Washington, DC
  20003, (202)543-5509
Marine Fisheries Commn; Atlantic States [5729]
Marine Fisheries Commn; Pacific States [5733]
Marine Industries
  All Japan Dockworkers' Union [IO]
  Amer. Bur. of Shipping [2600]
  Amer. Marinelife Dealers Assn. [5007]
  Amer. Waterways Operators [2601]
  Assn. of Australian Ports and Marine Authorities
    [IO]
  Assn. of British Sailmakers [IO]
  Assn. of Lithuania Shipbuilders and Shiprepairers
    [IO]
  Assn. of Marina Indus. [IO]
  Assn. of Marina Indus. [2602]
  Assn. of Ship Brokers and Agents - U.S.A. [2603]
  Assn. of Singapore Marine Indus. [IO]
  Australian Shipbuilders Assn. [IO]
  Australian Shipowners Assn. [IO]
  Baltic Exchange [IO]
  Baltic and Intl. Maritime Coun. [IO]
  Baltic Ports Org. [IO]
  British Marine Fed. [IO]
  British Marine Fed. - Scotland [IO]
  British Naval Equip. Assn. [IO]
  British Ports Assn. [IO]
  Canadian Shipowners Assn. [IO]
  Central Dredging Assn. [IO]
  Chamber of Shipping [IO]
  Chart and Nautical Instrument Trade Assn. [IO]
  Cruise Lines Intl. Assn. [3915]
  Danish Maritime [IO]
  Danish Shipowner's Assn. [IO]
  European Community Shipowners' Assn. [IO]
  European Fed. of Inland Ports [IO]
  European Maritime Pilots' Assn. [IO]
  European Shippers' Coun. [IO]
  Fed. of ASEAN Shipowners' Associations [IO]
  Fed. of Natl. Associations of Shipbrokers and
    Agents [IO]
  Filipino Shipowners Assn. [IO]
  Finnish Port Assn. [IO]
  Finnish Shipowners' Assn. [IO]
  French Natl. Shipowners Assn. [IO]
  German Shipbuilding and Ocean Indus. Assn. [IO]
  German Shipowners' Assn. [IO]
  German Shipsupplier Assn. [IO]
  Hong Kong Shipowners Assn. [IO]
  Honourable Company of Master Mariners [IO]
  Indian Natl. Shipowners' Assn. [IO]
  Inland Rivers Ports and Terminals [2604]
  Inlandboatman's Union of the Pacific [2605]
  Inst. of Chartered Shipbrokers - England [IO]
  Inst. of Shipping Economics and Logistics [IO]
  Interferry [IO]
  Intl. Assn. of Dredging Companies [IO]
  Intl. Assn. of Dry Cargo Shipowners [IO]
  Intl. Assn. for Marine Electronics Companies [IO]
  Intl. Assn. of Maritime Institutions [IO]
  Intl. Assn. of Ports and Harbors [IO]
  Intl. Assn. for the Rhine Ships Register [IO]
  Intl. Chamber of Shipping [IO]
  Intl. Coun. of Marine Indus. Associations [IO]
  Intl. Fed. of Shipmasters' Associations [IO]
  Intl. Harbour Masters' Assn. [IO]
  Intl. Marine Contractors Assn. [IO]
  Intl. Maritime Indus. Forum [IO]
  Intl. Maritime Pilots' Assn. [IO]
  Intl. Ship Elecl. and Engg. Ser. Assn. [IO]
  Intl. Ship Suppliers Assn. [IO]
  Intl. Shipping Fed. [IO]
  Irish Chamber of Shipping [IO]
  Irish Marine Fed. [IO]
  Japan Boating Indus. Assn. [IO]
  Japan Ship Exporters' Assn. [IO]
  Japanese Marine Equip. Assn. [IO]
  Japanese Shipowners' Assn. [IO]
  Korea Shipbuilders' Assn. [IO]

Lake Carriers' Assn. [2606]
Liberian Shipowners' Coun. [2607]
Liberian Shipowners' Coun. [IO]
Marine Machinery Assn. [2608]
Maritime Assn. of the Port of New York/New
  Jersey [3572]
Natl. Assn. of Waterfront Employers [2609]
Natl. Marine Charter Assn. [2610]
Natl. Waterways Conf. [3581]
Netherlands' Shipbuilding Indus. Assn. [IO]
New York Shipping Assn. [3583]
Norwegian Shipowners' Assn. [IO]
Pacific Maritime Assn. [3585]
Pacific Shellfish Inst. [4182]
Professional Yachtsmen's Assn. [IO]
Propeller Club of the U.S. [3586]
Royal Assn. of Netherlands' Shipowners [IO]
Royal Belgian Shipowners' Assn. [IO]
Sailing Barge Assn. [IO]
Salvage Assn. [IO]
Shipbuilders' Assn. of Japan [IO]
Shipbuilders and Shiprepairers Assn. [IO]
Shipbuilding Assn. of Canada [IO]
Soc. of Boat and Yacht Designers [1154]
Soc. of Intl. Gas Tanker and Terminal Operators
  [IO]
Soc. of Marine Port Engineers [3588]
Soc. of Maritime Indus. [IO]
Steamship Assn. of Louisiana [3591]
Swedish Shipbrokers' Assn. [IO]
Swedish Shipowners' Assn. [IO]
Trans. Inst. [3593]
United Kingdom Major Ports Gp. [IO]
United Kingdom Maritime Pilots' Assn. [IO]
West African Discussion Agreement [3597]
Women's Intl. Shipping and Trading Assn. Hellas
  [IO]
Worshipful Company of Shipwrights [IO]
Yacht Brokers, Designers and Surveyors Assn.
  [IO]
Yacht Harbour Assn. [IO]
Marine Indus; Northwest [★2589]
Marine Inst; Amer. Merchant [★6059]
Marine Insurance Syndicate; Amer. [★2136]
Marine Librarians Assn. [★IO]
Marine Lib. Assn; Amer. Merchant [10321]
Marine Machinery Assn. [2608], 8665 Sudley Rd.,
  Ste. 270, Manassas, VA 20110-4588, (703)791-
  4800
Marine Mammal Center; Friends of the Sea Lion
  [★5361]
Marine Mammal Center; Pacific [5361]
Marine Mammal Conservation Fund [★4435]
Marine Mammal Conservation Fund [★IO]
Marine Mammal Events Program - Address unknown
  since 1995.
Marine Mammal Stranding Center [5338], PO Box
  773, 3625 Brigantine Blvd., Brigantine, NJ 08203,
  (609)266-0538
Marine Mfrs. Safety Equipment Assn. - Defunct.
Marine Medical Mission [★20376]
Marine Port Engineers; Soc. of [3588]
Marine Retailers Assn. of Am. [2580], PO Box 1127,
  Oak Park, IL 60304, (708)763-9210
Marine Sci. Librarians; East Coast [★10361]
Marine Sci. Libraries Assn. [★10361]
Marine Sci. Libraries Assn. [★IO]
Marine Sciences Libraries and Info. Centers; Intl.
  Assn. of [★10361]
Marine Ser. Assn; Gulf Offshore [★2590]
Marine Ser; Radio Tech. Commn. for [★3753]
Marine Soc. [IO], London, United Kingdom
Marine Soc. of the City of New York [2581], 17 Bat-
  tery Pl., Ste. 714, New York, NY 10004, (212)425-
  0448
Marine Staff Officers - Address unknown since 2001.
Marine Stewardship Coun. [5171], 2110 N Pacific
  St., Ste. 102, Seattle, WA 98103, (206)691-0188
Marine Stewardship Coun. [IO], London, United
  Kingdom
Marine Suppliers; Natl. Assoc. [★2584]
Marine Surveyors; Soc. of Accredited [7720]
Marine Tech. Soc. [7273], 5565 Sterrett Pl., Ste.
  108, Columbia, MD 21044, (410)884-5330
Marine Towing and Transportation Employers Assn. -
  Defunct.

Reference to "IO" in place of a book number signifies that the association may be found in the 45th edition of International Organizations.

Marine Toys for Tots Found. [11709], PO Box 1947, Quantico, VA 22134, (703)640-9433
Marine Underwriters; Amer. Inst. of [2138]
Marine Underwriters Assn; Inland [2170]
Marine Underwriters of San Francisco; Bd. of [★3576]
Marine Veterans; Amer. Merchant [21387]
Marine Veterans of World War II; U.S. Merchant [21408]
Mariner Class Assn; U.S. [23228]
Mario Santo Domingo Found. [IO], Barranquilla, Colombia
Mariological Soc. of Am. [19656], Marian Lib., Univ. of Dayton, Dayton, OH 45469-1390, (937)229-4294
Marion Kaufman Found; Ewing [18846]
Marion Lockdown; Comm. to End the [11861]
Marionnette; UNIMA-U.S.A., Amer. Center of the Union Internationale de la [22916]
Mariposa Folk Found. [IO], Orillia, ON, Canada
Mariposa In The Schools [IO], Toronto, ON, Canada
Marist Bros. of the Schools [IO], Rome, Italy
Marist Missionary Sisters; Missionary Sisters of the Soc. of Mary - [20365]
Marist Volunteer Program - Defunct.
Marists; Third Order of Mary/ [19728]
Maritain Assn; Amer. [10782]
Marital and Date Rape; Natl. CH on [12790]
Maritime
   Alberg 37 Intl. Owners Assn. [21866]
   Amer. Maritime Assn. [6056]
   Amer. Maritime Cong. [6057]
   Amer. Maritime Officers Ser. [6058]
   Amer. Power Boat Assn. [23152]
   Amer. Sail Training Assn. [23153]
   Amer. Sailing Assn. [23154]
   Amer. Shark Assn. [23156]
   Amer. Soc. of Marine Artists [9494]
   Antique and Classic Boat Soc. [21868]
   Apostleship of the Sea in the U.S.A. [19570]
   Blind Sailing Intl. [23151]
   Boat Owners Assn. of the U.S. [23160]
   Boston Shipping Assn. [3561]
   Bullseye Assn. [23161]
   Catboat Assn. [23163]
   Center for Seafarers' Rights [6053]
   Center for Wooden Boats [21869]
   Chamber of Shipping of Am. [6059]
   Classic Yacht Assn. [21871]
   Coun. of Amer. Maritime Museums [10501]
   Coun. of Sailing Associations [23165]
   Day Sailer Assn. [23167]
   El Toro Intl. Yacht Racing Assn. [23168]
   FJ U.S. [23169]
   The Floating Hosp. [14882]
   Flying Scot Sailing Assn. [23170]
   Force 5 Class Assn. [23171]
   Gar Wood Soc. [21873]
   Geary 18 Intl. Yacht Racing Assn. [23172]
   Grays Harbor Historical Seaport Authority [8812]
   Great Lakes Lighthouse Keepers Assn. [10030]
   Great Lakes Maritime Inst. [10439]
   Harbour Lights Collectors Soc. [22034]
   Highlander Class Intl. Assn. [23174]
   Historic Naval Ships Assn. [10440]
   Horn and Whistle Enthusiasts Gp. [22037]
   Inst. of Nautical Archaeology [6448]
   Inst. of Navigation [7369]
   Inter-Collegiate Sailing Assn. of North Am. [23176]
   Inter-Lake Yachting Assn. [23177]
   Intl. Assn. for the Stud. of Maritime Mission [IO]
   Intl. Blue Jay Class Assn. [23181]
   Intl. Cargo Gear Bur. [6050]
   Intl. Catalina 400 Assn. [21875]
   Intl. D.N. Ice Yacht Racing Assn. [23183]
   Intl. Etchells Class Assn. [23184]
   Intl. Flying Dutchman Class Assn. of the U.S. [23185]
   Intl. Hobie Class Assn. [23186]
   Intl. Jet Sports Boating Assn. and Amer. Watercraft Assn. [23976]
   Intl. Lightning Class Assn. [23188]
   Intl. Naval Res. Org. [10476]
   Intl. Penguin Class Dinghy Assn. [23191]

Intl. Prindle Class Racing Assn. [23192]
Intl. Sunfish Class Assn. [23194]
Jet 14 Class Assn. [23196]
Lido 14 Intl. Class Assn. [23198]
Lyman Boat Owners Assn. [21877]
Marine Bd. [7272]
Maritime Inst. for Res. and Indus. Development [6060]
Maritime Postmark Soc. [22841]
Maritime Trades Dept., AFL-CIO [24129]
MC Sailing Assn. [23199]
Mystic Seaport [10441]
Natl. Assn. of Marine Labs. [7274]
Natl. Assn. of Maritime Educators [8813]
Natl. Boating Fed. [23201]
Natl. Butterfly Assn. [23202]
Natl. Class E Scow Assn. [23204]
Natl. Offshore Dept. [23205]
Natl. One Design Racing Assn. [23206]
Natl. Pearson Yacht Owners Assn. [21878]
Nautical Res. Guild [21880]
Naval Historical Found. [10478]
North Amer. Formula 18 Assn. [23208]
North Amer. Maritime Ministry Assn. [13007]
North Amer. Model Boat Assn. [22654]
North Amer. Steam Boat Assn. [21881]
North Amer. Tornado Assn. [23209]
One-Design Class Coun. [23211]
Pacific Coast Marine Firemen, Oilers, Watertenders and Wipers Assn. [24130]
Penobscot Marine Museum [10445]
Prindle Class Assn. [23212]
Rhodes 19 Class Assn. [23213]
Rhodes Bantam Class Assn. [23214]
Sailors for the Sea [4447]
Sailors' Union of the Pacific [24131]
Santana 20 Class Assn. [23216]
Seafarers' Intl. Union of North Am. [24132]
Seven Seas Cruising Assn. [23217]
Ships-in-Bottles Assn. of Am. [22658]
Ships on Stamps Unit [22870]
Snipe Class Intl. Racing Assn. [23219]
South St. Seaport Museum [10446]
Swan Owners Assn. of Am. [23221]
Titanic Intl. Soc. [10448]
Traditional Small Craft Assn. [21885]
Tugboat Enthusiasts Soc. of the Americas [21886]
United Seamen's Ser. [13008]
U.S. A-Class Catamaran Assn. [23225]
U.S. Albacore Assn. [23226]
U.S. J/24 Class Assn. [23227]
U.S. Lighthouse Soc. [10073]
U.S. Mariner Class Assn. [23228]
U.S. Power Squadrons [23231]
U.S. Sailing Assn. [23232]
U.S. Sailing Found. [23233]
U.S. Wayfarer Assn. [23235]
U.S. Windsurfing Assn. [23236]
Universal Ship Cancellation Soc. [22889]
U.S.A. Finn Assn. [23238]
USS Wainwright Veterans Assn. [21329]
Windmill Class Assn. [23239]
Women's Intl. Shipping and Trading Assn. [3598]
World Ocean and Cruise Liner Soc. [23020]
Yachting Club of Am. [23240]
Maritime Arbitrators; Soc. of [5463]
Maritime Assn; Amer. [6056]
Maritime Assn; Brownsville [★2595]
Maritime Assn; Galveston [★2595]
Maritime Assn; Houston [★2595]
Maritime Assn; Pacific [3585]
Maritime Assn. of the Port of New York [★3572]
Maritime Assn. of the Port of New York/New Jersey [3572], 17 Battery Pl., Ste. 913, New York, NY 10004, (212)425-5704
Maritime Assn; West Gulf [2595]
Maritime Cong; Amer. [6057]
Maritime Cong; Joint [★6057]
Maritime Educators; Natl. Assn. of Independent [★8813]
Maritime Fiddlers Assn. [IO], Riverview, NB, Canada
Maritime Info. Assn. [IO], Cambridge, United Kingdom
Maritime Inst; Great Lakes [10439]
Maritime Inst. for Res. and Indus. Development [6060]

Maritime Inst. of Tech. and Graduate Stud. [★24128]
Maritime Law
   British Maritime Law Assn. [IO]
   Canadian Maritime Law Assn. [IO]
   Center for Seafarers' Rights [6053]
   Chamber of Shipping of Am. [6059]
   Intl. Maritime Comm. [IO]
   Intl. Maritime Org. [IO]
   Law of the Sea Inst. [6054]
   Maritime Law Assn. of the U.S. [6055]
   Northern Shipowners' Defence Club [IO]
   Permanent Commn. for the South Pacific [IO]
   Scandinavian Inst. of Maritime Law [IO]
Maritime Law Assn. of the U.S. [6055], 80 Pine St., New York, NY 10005-1759, (212)425-1900
Maritime Museum Assn; Natl. [★10513]
Maritime Museums; Coun. of Amer. [10501]
Maritime Natl. Park Assn; San Francisco [10513]
Maritime Officers Ser; Amer. [6058]
Maritime Postmark Soc. [22841], c/o Tom Hirschinger, Pres., PO Box 497, Wadsworth, OH 44282
Maritime Postmark Society [IO], Wadsworth, OH, United States
Maritime Res; Andrew Furuseth Found. for [★3593]
Maritime Res. Dept. - Defunct.
Maritime Service Comm. - Address unknown since 2004.
Maritime Trades Dept., AFL-CIO [24129], 815 16th St. NW, Washington, DC 20006, (202)628-6300
Maritime Training Assn. - Address unknown since 1999.
Maritime Transit Assn. [★IO]
Maritime Trans. Res. Bd. [★7272]
Maritime Union of Australia [IO], Sydney, Australia
Maritime Union of New Zealand [IO], Wellington, New Zealand
Maritime Union and Professional Airways Systems Specialists; District 1 of Marine Engineers Beneficial Association/National [★24015]
Marjorie Mayrock Center for CIS and East European Res. [IO], Jerusalem, Israel
Mark Examiners; Assn. of Firearm and Tool [7083]
Mark Lindsay Intl. Fan Club - Defunct.
Mark Slade Fan Club [24758], 38 Joppa Rd., Worcester, MA 01603
Mark Twain Assn. of New York [★9685]
Mark Twain Boyhood Home Associates [9684], 120 N Main St., Hannibal, MO 63401, (573)221-9010
Mark Twain Circle of New York [9685], c/o Salwen Bus. Communications, 156 5th Ave., Ste. 517, New York, NY 10010-7002, (212)242-5546
Mark Twain Home Found. [9686], 120 N Main St., Hannibal, MO 63401, (573)221-9010
Mark Twain House and Museum [9687], 351 Farmington Ave., Hartford, CT 06105-4401, (860)247-0998
Mark Twain Memorial [★9687]
Mark Twain Res. Found. [9688], c/o Mark Twain Birthplace, 37352 Shrine Rd., Florida, MO 65283, (573)565-3449
Mark Twain Soc. - Defunct.
Market Assn; Communications [★3738]
Market Assn; Specialty Equip. [397]
Market Authority; Intl. Home Furnishings [1701]
Market Comm; Container [977]
Market Decision Making; Comm. on Non- [★7527]
Market Developers; Natl. Alliance of [2641]
Market Developers; Natl. Assn. of [★2641]
Market Development Advisory Comm. [IO], Kent Town, Australia
Market Development of the Amer. Hosp. Assn; Soc. for Healthcare Strategy and [14896]
Market Res. Assn. of Australia [★IO]
Market Res. Coun; Automotive [347]
Market Res. Soc. of New Zealand [IO], Auckland, New Zealand
Market Res. Soc. of the United Kingdom [IO], London, United Kingdom
Market; Southern Furniture [★1701]
Marketers of Am; Soc. of Independent Gasoline [2947]
Marketers Assn. of Am; Petroleum [2943]
Marketers Assn; Amer. Wholesale [1500]
Marketers Assn; Gulf Oil Wholesale [★2920]
Marketers Assn; Intl. Herb Growers and [★1907]

A star before a book entry number signifies that the name is not listed separately, but is mentioned within the entry.

Marketers Assn; Natl. Advisory Gp., Convenience Stores/Petroleum [★3420]
Marketers Assn; Natl. Energy [1288]
Marketing
ABA Marketing Network [2611]
Acad. of Marketing Sci. [8814]
Advt. Club of New York [77]
Advt. Women of New York [81]
Agricultural Products Marketing Bd. [IO]
AIM - European Brands Assn. [IO]
Alliance for Healthcare Strategy and Marketing [2612]
Alliance of Intl. Market Res. Institutes [IO]
Amer. Agri-Women [16948]
Amer. Collegiate Retailing Assn. [8815]
Amer. Mailorder Assn. [2457]
Amer. Marketing Assn. [2613]
Amer. Teleservices Assn. [2614]
Argentine Bank Marketing Assn. [IO]
Argentine Marketing Assn. [IO]
Asia Pacific Marketing Fed. [IO]
Asia-Pacific Professional Services Marketing Assn. [IO]
Assn. for Accounting Marketing [2615]
Assn. for Convention Marketing Executives [1933]
Assn. of Dir. Marketing [2616]
Assn. of Govt. Marketing Assistance Specialists [1740]
Assn. of Needle-Free Injection Mfrs. [2549]
Assn. for Postal Commerce [2449]
Assn. of Qualitative Res. [IO]
Assn. for Rehabilitation Marketing [2617]
Assn. of Travel Marketing Executives [3912]
Assn. of Visual Merchandise Representatives [2535]
Australian Direct Marketing Assn. [IO]
Australian Market and Social Res. Soc. [IO]
Belgian Direct Marketing Assn. [IO]
BP Amoco Marketers Assn. [2920]
Branding Assn. of Malaysia [IO]
Brazilian Assn. of Sales and Marketing Directors [IO]
Brazilian Direct Selling Assn. [IO]
British Promotional Merchandise Assn. [IO]
British Web Design and Marketing Assn. [IO]
Calendar Marketing Assn. [2618]
Canadian Inst. of Marketing [IO]
Canadian Produce Marketing Assn. [IO]
Catalog and Multichannel Marketing Coun. [1763]
CCNG Intl. [2619]
Chartered Inst. of Marketing [IO]
Circulation Coun. of DMA [2620]
Color Marketing Gp. [867]
Confed. of Commercial Associations of Brazil [IO]
Corporate Event Marketing Assn. [2621]
Coun. of Intl. Restaurant Real Estate Brokers [3392]
Coun. for Marketing and Opinion Res. [2622]
CPExchange [7280]
CUES Financial Suppliers Forum [2623]
Danish Marketing Forum [IO]
Diagnostic Marketing Assn. [2624]
Diamond Walnut Growers [5055]
Direct Marketing Assn. [2625]
Direct Marketing Assn. [IO]
Direct Marketing Assn. India [IO]
Direct Marketing Assn. - United Kingdom [IO]
Direct Marketing Educational Found. [8816]
Direct Selling Assn. - Hungary [IO]
Direct Selling Assn. - South Africa [IO]
Distributive Educ. Clubs of Am. [8817]
Dominicans on Wall St. [1413]
eBusiness Assn. [98]
Electronic Retailing Assn. [2626]
Electronic Retailing Assn. [IO]
eMarketing Assn. [1166]
ESOMAR: World Assn. of Opinion and Marketing Res. Professionals [IO]
European Distance Selling Trade Assn. [IO]
European Fed. of Associations of Market Res. Organisations [IO]
Fed. of European Direct and Interactive Marketing [IO]
Finnish Direct Marketing Assn. [IO]
Finnish Marketing Assn. [IO]

Fitness Indus. Suppliers Assn. - North Am. [3020]
Foodservice Sales and Marketing Assn. [1581]
German Agricultural Marketing Bd. - CMA [5020]
German Direct Marketing Assn. [IO]
Ghana Cocoa Marketing Bd. [IO]
Graphic Arts Sales Found. [1768]
Hea. Indus. Representatives Assn. [2627]
Healthcare Mfrs. Marketing Coun. [14673]
Hispanic Marketing and Commun. Assn. [2628]
Hispanic Marketing and Commun. Assn. [IO]
Hospitality Sales and Marketing Assn. Intl. [1944]
Hungarian Marketing Assn. [IO]
Incentive Fed. [2629]
Inst. of Marketing Mgt. Graduate School of Marketing [IO]
Inst. of Sales and Marketing Mgt. [IO]
Insurance Marketing Communications Assn. [2179]
Insurance Marketplace Standards Assn. [2180]
Intl. Assn. of Butterfly Exhibitions [1341]
Intl. Assn. for Prdt. Development [3177]
Intl. Automotive Remarketers Alliance [359]
Intl. Collegiate Licensing Assn. [2630]
Intl. Design Guild [2263]
Intl. Experiential Marketing Assn. [2631]
Intl. Experiential Marketing Assn. [IO]
Intl. Internet Marketing Assn. [IO]
Intl. Newspaper Marketing Assn. [3230]
Intl. Play Equip. Manufacturers Assn. [3060]
Intl. Ticketing Assn. [1312]
Irish Direct Marketing Assn. [IO]
Japan Direct Marketing Assn. [IO]
Japan Marketing Assn. [IO]
Japan Marketing Res. Assn. [IO]
Lawn and Garden Marketing and Distribution Assn. [2395]
Legal Marketing Assn. [2632]
Legal Marketing Assn. [IO]
Livestock Marketing Assn. [5021]
Market Res. Soc. of New Zealand [IO]
Market Res. Soc. of the United Kingdom [IO]
Marketing and Advt. Global Network [109]
Marketing Agencies Assn. Worldwide [3468]
Marketing Assn. of Pakistan [IO]
Marketing Assn. of Thailand [IO]
Marketing Educ. Assn. [8818]
Marketing Executive Networking Gp. [2633]
Marketing Res. Assn. [2634]
Marketing Sci. Inst. [2635]
Marketing Soc. of Ireland [IO]
Marketing Soc. of Kenya [IO]
Marketing Soc. - United Kingdom [IO]
Materials Marketing Associates [2636]
Medical Marketing Assn. [2637]
Mexican Assn. of Marketing and Public Opinion Res. Agencies [IO]
Mexican Market Res. and Opinion Polls Assn. [IO]
Mobile Marketing Assn. [110]
Mu Kappa Tau [24535]
Multi-Level Marketing Intl. Assn. [2638]
Multi-Level Marketing Intl. Assn. [IO]
Mystery Shopping Providers Assn. [2639]
Mystery Shopping Providers Assn. - Europe [IO]
Natl. Agri-Marketing Assn. [2640]
Natl. Alliance of Market Developers [2641]
Natl. Assn. of African Americans for Positive Imagery [16941]
Natl. Assn. of Collegiate Marketing Administrators [23834]
Natl. Assn. of Display Indus. [2642]
Natl. Assn. of Farmers' Market Nutrition Programs [4648]
Natl. Assn. of Major Mail Users [IO]
Natl. Assn. of Produce Market Managers [5022]
Natl. Cattlemen's Beef Assn. [5023]
Natl. Energy Marketers Assn. [1288]
Natl. Fraud Info. Center/Internet Fraud Watch [17339]
Natl. Healthcare Collectors Assn. [1869]
Natl. Livestock Producers Assn. [5024]
Natl. Mail Order Assn. [2643]
Natl. Marine Charter Assn. [2610]
Natl. Org. for Diversity in Sales and Marketing [2644]
Natl. Retail Hobby Stores Assn. [753]

Natl. Watermelon Assn. [4747]
Natural Products Marketing Coun. [IO]
Network of Ingredient Marketing Specialists [1554]
New Zealand Direct Marketing Assn. [IO]
North Amer. Agricultural Marketing Officials [5025]
North Amer. Bramble Growers Res. Found. [1675]
North Amer. Farmers' Direct Marketing Assn. [5026]
Organic Trade Assn. [5027]
Overseas Sales and Marketing Assn. of Am. [2312]
Pacific Asia Travel Assn. [3933]
Paper and Plastic Representatives Mgt. Coun. [2645]
Percussion Marketing Coun. [1165]
Petroleum Marketers Assn. of Am. [2943]
Photo Marketing Assn. Intl. [IO]
Pi Sigma Epsilon [24536]
PMA - Independent Book Publishers Assn. [3248]
Point-of-Purchase Advt. Intl. [115]
Polaris Intl. North Amer. Network [51]
Private Label Mfrs. Assn. [2646]
Produce Marketing Assn. [5028]
Produce Marketing Assn. [IO]
Producers Livestock Marketing Assn. [5029]
Professional Soc. for Sales and Marketing Training [3472]
Proj. EverGreen [4991]
Promotion Marketing Assn. [2647]
Promotional Products Assn. Intl. [116]
Radio Advt. Bur. [117]
Ranchers-Cattlemen Action Legal Fund, United Stockgrowers of Am. [4290]
Religion Communicators Coun. [20483]
Retail Advt. and Marketing Assn. [118]
Russian Marketing Assn. [IO]
Sales and Marketing Executives Intl. [3473]
Search Engine Marketing Professional Org. [2648]
Shop and Display Equip. Assn. [IO]
Soc. for Consumer Psychology [17344]
Soc. for Healthcare Strategy and Market Development of the Amer. Hosp. Assn. [14896]
Soc. for Marketing Professional Services [2649]
Southern African Marketing Res. Assn. [IO]
Specialty Wine Retailers Assn. [4031]
Sport Marketing Assn. [3672]
Strategic Account Mgt. Assn. [2650]
Strategic Account Management Association [IO]
Swedish Direct Marketing Assn. [IO]
TV Bur. of Advt. [121]
Traffic Audit Bur. for Media Measurement [123]
Transworld Advt. Agency Network [124]
Trial Lawyers Marketing [2651]
Turkish Assn. of Marketing and Public Opinion Researchers [IO]
Ukrainian Marketing Assn. [IO]
United Producers [5030]
U.S. Potato Bd. [4770]
Walnut Marketing Bd. [5066]
Women in Direct Marketing Intl. [2652]
Women in Direct Marketing Intl. [IO]
Word of Mouth Marketing Assn. [2653]
World Assn. of Res. Professionals [IO]
Marketing Administrators; Natl. Assn. of Collegiate [23834]
Marketing Administrators; Natl. Assn. of Law Firm [★2632]
Marketing Administrators; Professional Independent Mass [★2230]
Marketing and Advt. Assn; Internet [★98]
Marketing and Advt. Global Network [109], 1017 Perry Hwy., Ste. 5, Pittsburgh, PA 15237, (412)366-6850
Marketing and Advt. Global Network [IO], Pittsburgh, PA, United States
Marketing Agencies; Assn. of Direct [★2625]
Marketing Agencies Assn. Worldwide [3468], 460 Summer St., 4th Fl., Stamford, CT 06901, (203)978-1590
Marketing Agencies Assn. Worldwide [IO], Stamford, CT, United States
Marketing Agencies Worldwide; Assn. of Promotion [★3468]

Reference to "IO" in place of a book number signifies that the association may be found in the 45th edition of International Organizations.

Marketing Agents for Food Ser. Indus. [★1575]
Marketing of the Amer. Hosp. Assn; Soc. for Health-care Planning and [★14896]
Marketing Assistance Specialists; Assn. of Govt. [1740]
Marketing Associates; Chain Drug [★2972]
Marketing Associates; Natl. Foodservice [★3467]
Marketing Assn. of Am; Overseas Sales and [2312]
Marketing Assn; Bank [★2611]
Marketing Assn; Bank Public Relations and [★2611]
Marketing Assn; Bus. [94]
Marketing Assn; Commercial Development and [6677]
Marketing Assn; Communications [3738]
Marketing Assn; Competitive Livestock [★5021]
Marketing Assn; Direct Mail/ [★2625]
Marketing Assn; Elecl. Generating Systems [★1182]
Marketing Assn; Flat Glass [★1728]
Marketing Assn; Guitar and Accessories [2805]
Marketing Assn; Guitar and Accessories Music [★2805]
Marketing; Assn. for Interactive [3734]
Marketing Assn; Intl. Home Furnishings [★1701]
Marketing Assn; Intl; Photo [★3009]
Marketing Assn., Intl; Retail Advt. and [★118]
Marketing Assn; Natl. Account [★2650]
Marketing Assn; Natl. Agricultural Advt. and [★2640]
Marketing Assn; Natl. Infomercial [★2626]
Marketing Assn; Natl. Law Firm [★2632]
Marketing Assn; Natl. Live Stock [★5024]
Marketing Assn; Natl. Sugar Ingredient [1553]
Marketing Assn; Natural [★13609]
Marketing Assn. of Pakistan [IO], Karachi, Pakistan
Marketing Assn; Produce Packaging and [★5028]
Marketing Assn; Professional Insurance [2230]
Marketing Assn; Publishers [★3248]
Marketing Assn; Retail Advt. and [118]
Marketing Assn. of the South; Furniture Factories [★1701]
Marketing Assn. of Thailand [IO], Bangkok, Thailand
Marketing Assn; Trial Lawyer [★2651]
Marketing Commun; Center for [★87]
Marketing Communications Assn; Insurance [2179]
Marketing Communications Coun; AEM [★82]
Marketing Communications Coun; CIMA [★82]
Marketing and Communications Coun; Healthcare [100]
Marketing Communications Executives Intl. - Ad-dress unknown since 1995.
Marketing Companies; Assn. of Sales and [★1518]
Marketing Cmpt. Assn; Direct [★2625]
Marketing Coun; AEM [82]
Marketing Council; National Sales and [★1035]
Marketing; CTAM - Cable and Telecommunications Assn. for [558]
Marketing and Development Associate Coun. on Economic Priorities - Address unknown since 2006.
Marketing and Distribution Assn; Lawn and Garden [2395]
Marketing and Distributive Educ. Assn. [★8818]
Marketing Educ. Assn. [8818], PO Box 27473, Tempe, AZ 85285-7473, (602)750-6735
Marketing Educational Found; Direct Mail/ [★8816]
Marketing and Electronic Commerce; Alliance Against Fraud in Tele [17302]
Marketing Executive Networking Gp. [2633], 15 Bond St., East Norwalk, CT 06855
Marketing Executives; Assn. of Travel [3912]
Marketing Executives; Broadcast Promotion and [★577]
Marketing Executives; Intl. Newspaper Advt. and [★3244]
Marketing Fundraisers Assn; Direct [1685]
Marketing Inst; Auction [★326]
Marketing Inst; Cherry [4723]
Marketing Inst; Food [3406]
Marketing Inst; Invention [★7228]
Marketing Insurance Coun; Direct [★2162]
Marketing Insurance and Financial Services Coun; Direct [2162]
Marketing Insurance Inst; Mass [2198]
Marketing Mgt. Coun. [★3306]
Marketing Mgt. Coun. [★IO]
Marketing Network; Herb Growing and [1906]

Marketing Officials; Natl. Agricultural [★5025]
Marketing Officials; Natl. Assn. of [★5025]
Marketing and Public Relations; Amer. Soc. for Healthcare [★14896]
Marketing and Public Relations; Amer. Soc. for Hosp. [★14896]
Marketing and Public Relations; Natl. Coun. for [9032]
Marketing Res. Assn. [2634], 110 Natl. Dr., 2nd Fl., Glastonbury, CT 06033-1212, (860)682-1000
Marketing and Res. Assn; Life Insurance [★2195]
Marketing Res. Trade Assn. [★2634]
Marketing Sci. Inst. [2635], 1000 Massachusetts Ave., Cambridge, MA 02138-5396, (617)491-2060
Marketing Services; Assn. of Retail [3463]
Marketing Services; Natl. Assn. for Retail [3418]
Marketing Services; TSIA—The Assn. of Retail [3463]
Marketing Soc; Amer. [★2613]
Marketing Soc. of Ireland [IO], Bray, Ireland
Marketing Soc. of Kenya [IO], Nairobi, Kenya
Marketing Soc. - United Kingdom [IO], Teddington, United Kingdom
Marketing Specialists; Natl. Ingredient [★1554]
Marketing Specialists; Network of Ingredient [1554]
Marketing Teachers; Natl. Assn. of [★2613]
Marketing Training; Professional Soc. for Sales and [3472]
Marketing; Women in Advt. and [★874]
Markets Assn; Financial [1419]
Markets; Inst. for the Cooperative Stud. of Intl. Sea-food [★1484]
Markham Prayer Card Apostolate - Defunct.
Marking Device Assn. [★3683]
Marking Device Assn. [★IO]
Marking Device Assn. Intl. [★IO]
Marking Device Assn. Intl. [★3683]
Markkinointiviestinnan Toismistojen Liitto [★IO]
Markle Found. [6713], 10 Rockefeller Plz., 16th Fl., New York, NY 10020-1903, (212)713-7600
Marklin Digital Special Interest Gp. [22635], PO Box 510559, New Berlin, WI 53151-0559, (262)784-8854
Marksman Assn; Police [6007]
Marky Cattle Assn. [4271], PO Box 198, Walton, KS 67151-0198, (620)837-3303
Marley Family Assn. [20991], c/o Michael D. Frost, PhD, Archivist, 8910 W 62nd Terr., Merriam, KS 66202, (913)362-4600
Marlin Auto Club [21693], 7580 Old Dayton Rd., Dayton, OH 45427, (408)269-7788
Marlin Owners' Club - Address unknown since 2004.
Marlowe Lives! Assn. [9689], 402 S Illinois Ave., Carbondale, IL 62901-2813, (618)549-3495
Marlowe Soc. [IO], Teddington, United Kingdom
Marlowe Soc. of Am. [9690], c/o Prof. Bruce E. Brandt, Pres., South Dakota State Univ., Dept. of English, Box 504, Brookings, SD 57007-1397, (605)688-4058
Marmon Club [21694], c/o Marge Iaccino, Sec., No. 4 Country Rte. 22, Hudson, NY 12534-9521, (518)828-5581
Marmon Club [IO], Hudson, NY, United States
Marquandia Soc. - Address unknown since 2001.
MARQUES - Assn. of European Trademark Owners [IO], Leicester, United Kingdom
Marquetry Soc. of America - Defunct.
Marquette League for Catholic Indian Missions - Defunct.
Marquette Univ. Alumni Assn. [18908], c/o Marquette Univ., PO Box 1881, Milwaukee, WI 53201-1881, (414)288-7441
Marquis Giuseppe Scicluna Intl. Univ. Found. - Ad-dress unknown since 2000.

Marriage

Albert Ellis Inst. [16197]
Alliance for Children and Families [12136]
Alliance for Marriage [12504]
Alternatives to Marriage Proj. [18025]
Alternatives to Marriage Proj. [IO]
Amer. Assn. for Marriage and Family Therapy [16200]
Amer. Assn. of Wedding Planners [2654]
Amer. Family Communiversity [12138]
Amer. Professional Wedding Photographers Assn. [2991]

Amer. Soc. of Separated and Divorced Men [12005]
Assn. for Couples in Marriage Enrichment [12505]
Bonus Families [12143]
Bridal Assn. of Am. [534]
Catholics United for Life [12910]
Christian Family Life [12146]
Commn. on Accreditation for Marriage and Family Therapy Educ. [8819]
Commn. on Outreach and Synagogue Community [20133]
CORPUS - Natl. Assn. for an Inclusive Priesthood [19619]
Inst. in Basic Life Principles [13489]
Intl. Acad. of Matrimonial Lawyers [IO]
Intl. Assn. for Marriage and Family Counselors [11825]
Loved Ones and Drivers Support [13347]
Marriage Equality USA [12506]
Natl. Action for Former Military Wives [12012]
Natl. Black Bridal Assn. [535]
Natl. Commn. on Human Life, Reproduction and Rhythm [16008]
Natl. Coun. on Family Relations [12164]
Natl. Marriage Encounter [12507]
Natl. Right to Life Comm. [12923]
Northern Ireland Mixed Marriage Assn. [IO]
Rabbinic Center for Res. and Counseling [16229]
Secretariat for Family, Laity, Women, and Youth [12167]
Stepfamily Found. [12168]
Straight Spouse Network [12508]
United Fathers of Am. [12014]
Wives of Older Men [12509]
Worldwide Marriage Encounter [12510]
Worldwide Marriage Encounter [IO]
Marriage Care [IO], London, United Kingdom
Marriage Counselling Scotland [IO]
Marriage Counselors; Amer. Assn. of [★16200]
Marriage Encounter; Natl. [12507]
Marriage Equality USA [12506], 4096 Piedmont Ave., Ste. 257, Oakland, CA 94611, (510)496-2700
Marriage and Family Counselors; Amer. Assn. of [★16200]
Marriage and Family Therapy; Amer. Assn. for [16200]
Married Priesthood; CORPUS - Natl. Assn. for a [★19619]
Marrow Donor Prog; Natl. [14292]
Marrow Donor Registry; Amer. Bone [13768]
Marrow Donor Registry; Natl. Bone [★14292]
Marrow Found; Bone [13769]
Marrow Transplant Link; Natl. Bone [16676]
Marrow Transplantation; Amer. Soc. for Blood and [16665]
Mars Investigation Group - Defunct.
Mars Soc. [7683], 11111 W 8th Ave., Unit A, Lakewood, CO 80215, (303)984-9653
Mars Soc. [IO], Edinburgh, United Kingdom
Marshall Found; George C. [11118]
Marshall Found; John [10042]
Marshall Islands Athletics [IO], Majuro, Marshall Islands
Marshall Islands Tennis Fed. [IO], Majuro, Marshall Islands
Marshall Islands Weightlifting Fed. [IO], Majuro, Mar-shall Islands
Marshall Scholarship Fund; Thurgood [7932]
Martha Movement - Defunct.
Martha Org. [IO], Helsinki, Finland
Martha and the Vandellas Fan Club; Supremes, Mar-vellettes, and [★24975]

Martial Arts

Aikido Assn. of Am. [23046]
Aikido Assn. of North Am. [23047]
Aikido Yoshokai Assn. of North Am. [7943]
Albanian Taekwondo Fed. [IO]
Algerian Taekwondo Fed. [IO]
All Japan Ju-Jitsu Intl. Fed. [IO]
All Japan Ju-Jitsu Intl. Fed. [23577]
All Japan Taekwondo Fed. [IO]
Amer. Amateur Karate Fed. [23559]
Amer. Chen Style Tai Chi Assn. [23578]
Amer. Judo Assn. [23552]
Amer. Judo and Jujitsu Fed. [23553]

A star before a book entry number signifies that the name is not listed separately, but is mentioned within the entry.

Amer. Kempo-Karate Assn. [23579]
Amer. Kenpo Karate Intl. [23560]
Amer. Sambo Assn. [23580]
Amer. Self-Protection Assn. [23712]
Amer. Shorin Kempo Karate Assn. [23581]
American Shorin Kempo Karate Association [IO]
Amer. Tai Chi Assn. [16593]
Amer. Teachers Assn. of the Martial Arts [23582]
Amer. Wu Shu Soc. [23583]
Amer. Wu Shu Soc. [IO]
Amer. Yangjia Michuan Taijiquan Assn. [23584]
Angolan Taekwondo Fed. [IO]
Aruba Taekwondo Assn. [IO]
Asociacion Panamena de Taekwondo [IO]
Associacao desportiva Taekwondo de Mocambique [IO]
Assn. Costarricense de Taekwondo [IO]
Assn. Haitienne de Taekwondo [IO]
Assn. for Renaissance Martial Arts [IO]
Assn. for Renaissance Martial Arts [8820]
Assn. of Women Martial Arts Instructors [23585]
Austrian Taekwondo Fed. [IO]
Azerbaijan Taekwondo Fed. [IO]
Bahamas Taekwondo Fed. [IO]
Bangladesh Taekwondo Fed. [IO]
Barbados Taekwondo Assn. [IO]
Belarusian Republican Taekwondo Fed. [IO]
Belgian Natl. Taekwondo Union [IO]
Belize Taekwondo Fed. [IO]
Bermuda Taekwondo Assn. [IO]
Bhutan Taekwondo Fed. [IO]
British Aikido Assn. [IO]
British Judo Assn. [IO]
British Kendo Assn. [IO]
British Taekwondo Control Bd. [IO]
Bulgarian Taekwondo Fed. [IO]
Canadian Chinese Kuo Shu Fed. [IO]
Canadian Ging Wu Kung Fu Martial Art Assn. [IO]
Canadian Kendo Fed. [IO]
Chinese-American Arts Coun. [9608]
Chinese Taekwondo Assn. [IO]
Choy Lee Fut Martial Arts Fed. of Am. [23586]
Combat Martial Art Practitioners Assn. [23587]
Confederacao Brasileira de Taekwondo [IO]
Confederacion Paraguaya de Taekwondo [IO]
Croatian Taekwondo Fed. [IO]
Cyprus Amateur Judo, Taekwondo Fed. [IO]
Czech Taekwondo Fed. WTF [IO]
Danish Taekwondo Fed. [IO]
Deutsche Taekwondo Union [IO]
Dominica Taekwondo Fed. [IO]
Egyptian Taekwondo Fed. [IO]
Estonian Taekwondo Fed. [IO]
Ethiopian World Taekwondo Fed. [IO]
European Judo Union [IO]
European Taekwondo Union [IO]
Federacao Portuguesa de Taekwondo [IO]
Federacion Boliviana de Taekwondo [IO]
Federacion Chilena de Taekwondo [IO]
Federacion Colombiana de Taekwondo [IO]
Federacion Cuban de Taekwondo [IO]
Federacion Deportiva Peruana de Taekwondo [IO]
Federacion Dominicana de Taekwondo [IO]
Federacion Ecuatoriana de Taekwondo [IO]
Federacion Equatiguineana de Taekwondo [IO]
Federacion Espanola de Taekwondo [IO]
Federacion Nacional Taekwondo de Guatemala [IO]
Federacion Nacional de Taekwondo de Honduras [IO]
Federacion Nicaraguense de Taekwondo [IO]
Federacion Salvadorena de Taekwondo [IO]
Federacion Uruguaya de Taekwondo [IO]
Fed. Andorrana de Taekwondo [IO]
Fed. Beninoise de Taekwondo [IO]
Fed. Burkinabe de Taekwondo [IO]
Fed. Camerounaise de Taekwondo [IO]
Fed. Centrafricaine Taekwondo [IO]
Fed. Congolaise de Taekwondo [IO]
Fed. Francaise de Taekwondo et Disciplines Associees [IO]
Fed. Gabonaise de Taekwondo [IO]
Fed. Guineenne de Taekwondo [IO]
Fed. Ivoirienne de Taekwondo [IO]
Fed. Malienne de Taekwondo [IO]

Fed. Nigerienne de Taekwondo [IO]
Fed. Royale Marocaine de Taekwondo [IO]
Fed. Senegalaise de Taekwondo [IO]
Fed. of Taekwondo of the Republic of Moldova [IO]
Fed. Tchadienne de Taekwondo [IO]
Fed. Togolaise de Taekwondo [IO]
Federazione Italiana Taekwondo [IO]
Fiji Taekwondo Assn. [IO]
Finnish Taekwondo Fed. [IO]
Georgian Taekwondo Fed. [IO]
Ghana Taekwondo Assn. [IO]
Hong Kong Taekwondo Assn. [IO]
Hungarian Taekwondo Fed. [IO]
Icelandic Taekwondo Fed. [IO]
Indonesian Taekwondo Assn. [IO]
Intl. Aikido Assn. [23048]
Intl. Assn. of Gay and Lesbian Martial Artists [23588]
Intl. Assn. of Gay and Lesbian Martial Artists [IO]
Intl. Chinese Boxing Assn. [23262]
Intl. Fed. of Martial Arts and Oriental Medicine [15021]
Intl. Fed. of Martial Arts and Oriental Medicine [IO]
Intl. Judo Fed. [IO]
Intl. Martial Arts Fed. [IO]
Intl. Martial Arts League [IO]
Intl. Martial Arts League [23589]
Intl. Modern Arnis Fed. Philippines [IO]
Intl. Okinawa Kobudo Assn. [23590]
Intl. Seven-Star Mantis Style Lee Kam Wing Martial Art Assn. - USA [23591]
Intl. Shaolin Kenpo Assn. [23592]
Intl. Shaolin Kenpo Assn. [IO]
Intl. Sungja-Do Assn. [23593]
Intl. Traditional Karate Fed. [23562]
Intl. Yang Style Tai Chi Chuan Assn. [23594]
International Yang Style Tai Chi Chuan Association [IO]
Iran Taekwondo Union [IO]
Iraqi Taekwondo Fed. [IO]
Irish Taekwondo Union [IO]
Israel Taekwondo Fed. [IO]
Jamaica Taekwondo Fed. [IO]
Japan Aikido Assn. U.S.A. [23595]
Kenya Taekwondo Assn. [IO]
Korea Taekwondo Assn. [IO]
Kuwait Judo and Taekwondo Fed. [IO]
Kyrgyzstan Taekwondo Assn. [IO]
Lao Taekwondo Fed. [IO]
Latvian Taekwondo Fed. [IO]
Lesotho Taekwondo Assn. [IO]
Liberia Taekwondo Fed. [IO]
Libyan Taekwondo Fed. [IO]
Lithuanian Taekwondo Fed. [IO]
Macedonia Taekwondo Fed. [IO]
Malagasy Fed. of Taekwondo [IO]
Malaysia Taekwondo Assn. [IO]
Martial Arts Development Commn. [IO]
Martial Arts Indus. Assn. [IO]
Martial Arts Indus. Assn. [IO]
Martial Arts Indus. Assn. [2655]
Martial Arts Intl. Fed. [23596]
Martial Arts Intl. Fed. [IO]
Martial Arts USA [23597]
Mauritius Taekwondo Assn. [IO]
Mongolian Taekwondo Fed. [IO]
Myanmar Taekwondo Fed. [IO]
Natl. Assn. of Karate and Martial Arts Schools [IO]
Natl. Assn. of Professional Martial Artists [23598]
Natl. Coun. for Taekwondo Masters Certification [23599]
Natl. Women's Martial Arts Fed. [23600]
Nepal Taekwondo Assn. [IO]
New Zealand Taekwondo Coun. [IO]
Nigeria Taekwondo Fed. [IO]
North Am. Wu(Hao) Taiji Fed. [IO]
North Am. Wu(Hao) Taiji Fed. [23601]
North Amer. Tang Shou Tao Assn. [13645]
Norwegian Martial Arts Fed. [IO]
Osterreichischer Judo Verband [IO]
Pakistan Taekwondo Fed. [IO]
Pan Amer. Taekwondo Union [IO]
Pan Amer. Taekwondo Union [23602]

Pan-American Union of Karatedo Organizations [23564]
Philippine Ling Ming Martial Arts Assn. [IO]
Philippine Taekwondo Assn. [IO]
Police Martial Arts Assn. [IO]
Polish Taekwondo Fed. [IO]
Qatar Taekwondo and Karate Fed. [IO]
Republic of Trinidad and Tobago Taekwondo Assn. [IO]
Romanian Taekwondo Fed. [IO]
Russian Taekwondo Union [IO]
St. Kitts and Nevis Taekwondo Fed. [IO]
Samoa Taekwondo Assn. [IO]
Saudi Arabian Judo and Taekwondo Fed. [IO]
Scottish Ju Jitsu Assn. [IO]
Shudokan Martial Arts Assn. [23603]
Singapore Taekwondo Fed. [IO]
Slovenian Taekwondo Assn. [IO]
Solomon Islands Taekwondo Union [IO]
South African Taekwondo Fed. [IO]
Sudanese Taekwondo Fed. [IO]
Suriname Taekwondo Associatie [IO]
Syrian Arab Taekwondo Fed. [IO]
Taekwondo Assn. of Thailand [IO]
Taekwondo Australia [IO]
Taekwondo Bond Nederland [IO]
Taekwondo Fed. of Armenia [IO]
Taekwondo Fed. of Bosnia and Herzegovina [IO]
Taekwondo Fed. of India [IO]
Taekwondo Fed. of Islamic Republic of Iran [IO]
Taekwondo Fed. of the Republic of Kazakhstan [IO]
Taekwondo Fed. of the Republic of Tajikistan [IO]
Taekwondo Fed. of Turkey [IO]
Taekwondo Papua New Guinea [IO]
Tai Chi Assn. of Australia [IO]
Takemusu Aiki Assn. of Australia [IO]
Taoist Tai Chi Soc. of Australia [IO]
Traditional Tae Kwon Do Chung Do Assn. [23604]
Ukrainian Taekwondo Fed. [IO]
Union of Taekwondo Tanzania [IO]
United Kingdom Jujitsu Assn. Intl. [IO]
United Kingdom Tang Soo (Soo Bahk) Do Fed. [IO]
U.S. Aikido Fed. [23049]
U.S.A. Wushu-Kungfu Fed. [23605]
U.S. Hapki Hae [23606]
U.S. Isshinryu Karate Assn. [23565]
U.S. Judo [23554]
U.S. Judo Assn. [23555]
U.S. Martial Arts Assn. [23607]
U.S. Martial Arts Assn. [IO]
U.S. Muay Thai Assn. [23608]
U.S. Sport Jujitsu Assn. [23609]
U.S. Taekwondo Union [23610]
U.S. Yudo Assn. [23611]
Universal Martial Arts Brotherhood [23612]
Universal Martial Arts Brotherhood [IO]
US Cheng Ming Martial Arts Assn. [23613]
U.S.A. Karate Fed. [23566]
Uzbekistan Taekwondo Assn. [IO]
Vanuatu Taekwondo Assn. [IO]
Vietnam Taekwondo Assn. [IO]
World Head of Family Sokeship Coun. [23614]
World Jeet Kune Do Fed. [23615]
World Karate Fed. [IO]
World Martial Arts Assn. [IO]
World Martial Arts Assn. [23616]
World Modern Arnis Alliance [23617]
World Taekwondo Fed. [IO]
World Traditional Karate Org. [23567]
World Ving Tsun Athletic Assn. [23618]
WTF Taekwondo Assn. of Canada [IO]
Yemen Taekwondo Fed. [IO]
Zen-do Kai Martial Arts [23619]
Zimbabwe Taekwondo Assn. [IO]
Martial Arts Assn; Zen-do Kai [★23619]
Martial Arts Development Commn. [IO], Wembley, United Kingdom
Martial Arts Indus. Assn. [IO], Oklahoma City, OK, United States
Martial Arts Indus. Assn. [IO], Kenthurst, Australia
Martial Arts Indus. Assn. [2655], 1000 Century Blvd., Oklahoma City, OK 73110, (866)626-7481
Martial Arts Intl. Fed. [23596], 1850 Columbia Pike, Ste. No. 613, Arlington, VA 22204, (703)920-1590

Reference to "IO" in place of a book number signifies that the association may be found in the 45th edition of International Organizations.

Martial Arts Intl. Fed. [IO], Arlington, VA, United States
Martial Arts USA [23597], 1619 Fairway Dr. SW, Jacksonville, AL 36265, (256)782-5078
Martime Assn. of Greater Boston [★3561]
Martin Colony Registry Program; Purple [★5369]
Martin Conservation Assn; Purple [5369]
Martin De Porres Guild; St. [20389]
Martin Family Org; John Thomas [20966]
Martin Fan Center; Dean [24816]
Martin Landau Aficionados - Defunct.
Martin Luther King, Jr. Center for Nonviolent Social Change [18116], 449 Auburn Ave. NE, Atlanta, GA 30312, (404)526-8900
Martin Luther King, Jr. Center for Social Change [★18116]
Martin Luther King, Jr. Fellowship Program - Defunct.
Martin Steinberg Center for Jewish Artists - Amer. Jewish Cong. - Defunct.
Martin Van Buren Fan Club [11136], c/o Gary L. Holloway, Pres., 778 14th St., San Francisco, CA 94114, (415)626-0676
Martina McBride Fan Club [24944], PO Box 291627, Nashville, TN 37229-1627
Marttaliitto [★IO]
Marty Stuart Fan Club [24945]
Martyrs; Voice of the [20410]
Marusho/Lilac Owners Club - Defunct.
Marvellettes, and Martha and the Vandellas Fan Club; Supremes, [★24975]
Marx Brotherhood [24832], 335 Fieldstone Dr., New Hope, PA 18938-1012
Marx Bros. Stud. Unit [★24832]
Marxism
    News and Letters Comm. [18656]
    Soc. for the Philosophical Stud. of Marxism [10452]
    Youth for Intl. Socialism [18663]
Marxist-Leninist Party of the U.S.A. - Defunct.
Mary Alumni Assn; Univ. of [18935]
Mary; Ambassadors of [19565]
Mary Ellen Kinney Family Org. - Address unknown since 2006.
Mary; IHM Volunteer Prog. of the Sisters, Servants of the Immaculate Heart of [20346]
Mary Jo Cattlett Fan Club [24759]
Mary Magdalene; Soc. of Saint [19724]
Mary - Marist Missionary Sisters; Missionary Sisters of the Soc. of [20365]
Mary/Marists; Third Order of [19728]
Mary Moran Official Fan Club - Address unknown since 2004.
Mary Morstan's Companions - Defunct.
Mary; Reparation Soc. of the Immaculate Heart of [19709]
Mary Rue Family Assn; Joseph Cox and [20967]
Mary Stuart Soc. of America - Address unknown since 1990.
Mary Swords Debaillon Louisiana Iris Soc. [★22542]
Mary Wilson Fan Club [★24954]
Mary Wilson Message Bd. and Fan Club; Official [24954]
Marycrest Intl. Univ. Alumni Assn. - Defunct.
Maryheart Crusaders [19657], 22 Button St., Meriden, CT 06450, (203)238-9735
MaryKnoll Associate Lay Missioners [★20354]
MaryKnoll Associate Lay Missioners [★IO]
Maryknoll Call and Response Prog. [★20309]
Maryknoll Center for Justice Concerns [★8660]
Maryknoll Fathers and Bros. [19658], PO Box 304, Maryknoll, NY 10545-0304, (914)941-7590
Maryknoll Fathers and Bros. [IO], Maryknoll, NY, United States
Maryknoll Mission Assn. of the Faithful [IO], Maryknoll, NY, United States
Maryknoll Mission Assn. of the Faithful [20354], Bethany Bldg., PO Box 307, Maryknoll, NY 10545-0307, (914)762-6364
Maryknoll Mission Center of New England [8660]
Maryknoll Mission Family [★19658]
Maryknoll Mission Family [★IO]
Maryknoll Priests, Bros., and Priest and Brother Associates [★IO]

Maryknoll Priests, Bros., and Priest and Brother Associates [★19658]
Maryknoll Sisters of Saint Dominic [20355], PO Box 311, Maryknoll, NY 10545-0311, (914)941-7575
Maryland Assn. of Railway and Maintenance - Address unknown.
Maryland Independent Truckers and Drivers Assn. [★3870]
Maryland Manors; Natl. Soc. of Descendants of Lords of the [20747]
Maryland Soc. on Alcoholism [★13221]
Maryland; Soc. for the History of the Germans in [9980]
Maryland Suicide Found. [★13287]
Maryland Truk Stop Found. [★8948]
Masada the Holocaust Survivors Org. [17722]
Masada the Holocaust Survivors Org. [IO], Brooklyn, NY, United States
Masada/Maccabi Israel Summer Programs [20159], 520 8th Ave., New York, NY 10018, (212)532-4949
Masajid of U.S; Coun. of [20097]
Masaryk Inst. - Address unknown since 1995.
Mascular Degeneration; Assn. for [★15669]
The Maserati Club [21695], 325 Walden Ave., Harriman, TN 37748, (865)882-9230
The Maserati Club [IO], Harriman, TN, United States
Maserati Club of Am. [★IO]
Maserati Club of Am. [★21695]
Maserati Info. Exchange [21696], 1620 Indus. Dr. SW, Ste. F, Auburn, WA 98001-6555, (253)833-2598
Maserati Owners Club of North Am. [★21695]
Maserati Owners Club of North Am. [★IO]
Maserati Owners Club of North Am. - Defunct.
Mason Contractors Assn. of Am. [1032], 33 S Roselle Rd., Schaumburg, IL 60193, (847)301-0001
Mason Dixon Intl. Fan Club - Address unknown since 1999.
Masonic Homes Executives' Assn. of North America - Address unknown since 2005.
Masonic Jurisdiction; Supreme Coun. 33rd Degree, Ancient and Accepted Scottish Rite of Freemasonry - Southern [★19251]
Masonic Jurisdiction; Supreme Coun., Ancient Accepted Scottish Rite of Free-Masonry Northern [19252]
Masonic Relief Assn. of U.S.A. and Canada [★19229]
Masonic Ser. Assn. of North Am. [19242], 8120 Fenton St., Ste. 203, Silver Spring, MD 20910-4785, (301)588-4010
Masonic Services Assn. of the U.S. [★19242]
Masonic Study Unit - Defunct.
Masonry
    British Masonry Soc. [IO]
    Building and Constr. Trades Dept. - AFL-CIO [24025]
    Intl. Brick Collectors' Assn. [22048]
    Intl. Union of Bricklayers and Allied Craftsworkers [1029]
    The Masonry Soc. [6837]
    Operative Plasterers and Cement Masons Intl. Assn. of U.S. and Canada [24031]
Masonry Assn; Natl. Concrete [929]
Masonry Heater Assn. of North Am. [1892], c/o Richard Smith, Admin., 2180 S Flying Q Ln., Tucson, AZ 85713, (520)883-0191
Masonry Indus. Comm. [★1027]
Masonry Indus. Comm. [★IO]
Masonry Res. Found. [★IO]
Masonry Res. Found. [★1027]
The Masonry Soc. [6837], 3970 Broadway, Ste. 201-D, Boulder, CO 80304-1135, (303)939-9700
The Masonry Soc. [IO], Boulder, CO, United States
Masonry - Southern Jurisdiction; Supreme Coun. 33rd Degree, Ancient and Accepted Scottish Rite of Free [19251]
Masons
    Ancient Egyptian Arabic Order Nobles of the Mystic Shrine [19227]
    Ancient Egyptian Order of Sciots [19228]
    Assn. of Masonic Boards of Relief of the U.S. and Canada [19229]
    Conf. of Prince Hall Grand Masters [19230]

    Daughters of Mokanna [19231]
    Daughters of the Nile, Supreme Temple [19232]
    Ex-Masons for Jesus [19795]
    Fed. of Masons of the World [19233]
    Gen. Grand Chap., Order of the Eastern Star [19234]
    General Grand Chapter, Order of the Eastern Star [IO]
    Gen. Grand Chap. of Royal Arch Masons Intl. [IO]
    Gen. Grand Chap. of Royal Arch Masons Intl. [19235]
    Heroes of '76 [19236]
    High Twelve Intl. [19237]
    High Twelve Intl. [IO]
    Imperial Coun. of the Ancient Arabic Order of the Nobles of the Mystic Shrine for North Am. [19238]
    Intl. Brick Collectors' Assn. [22048]
    Intl. Order of Job's Daughters, Supreme Guardian Coun. [19239]
    International Order of Job's Daughters, Supreme Guardian Council [IO]
    Knights Templar, Grand Encampment, U.S.A. [19240]
    Ladies Oriental Shrine of North Am. [19241]
    Masonic Ser. Assn. of North Am. [19242]
    The Masonry Soc. [6837]
    Modern Free and Accepted Masons of the World [19243]
    Modern Free and Accepted Masons of the World [IO]
    Natl. Federated Craft [19244]
    Natl. League of Masonic Clubs [19245]
    Natl. Sojourners [19246]
    Philalethes Soc. [19247]
    Red Cross of Constantine - United Grand Imperial Coun. [19248]
    Royal Order of Scotland [19249]
    Supreme Assembly, Intl. Order of Rainbow for Girls [19250]
    Supreme Assembly, Intl. Order of Rainbow for Girls [IO]
    Supreme Coun. 33rd Degree, Ancient and Accepted Scottish Rite of Freemasonry - Southern Jurisdiction [19251]
    Supreme Coun., Ancient Accepted Scottish Rite of Free-Masonry (Northern Masonic Jurisdiction) [19252]
    Supreme Coun., Mystic Order of Veiled Prophets of the Enchanted Realm [19253]
    Supreme Coun. Order of the Amaranth [19254]
    Tall Cedars of Lebanon of North Am. [19255]
    Universal Masonic Brotherhood [19256]
Masons' Company [IO], London, United Kingdom
Masons and Plasterers Intl. of Amer; Bricklayers, [★24027]
The Masquers [11024], 105 Park Pl., Point Richmond, CA 94801-3922, (510)232-3888
Mass Commun; Assn. for Educ. in Journalism and [8706]
Mass Commun; Assn. of Schools of Journalism and [7893]
Mass Communications; Accrediting Coun. on Educ. in Journalism and [8703]
Mass Finishing Job Shops Assn. [1473], 808 13th St., East Moline, IL 61244-1628, (309)755-1101
Mass Marketing Administrators; Professional Independent [★2230]
Mass Marketing Insurance Inst. [2198], 14 W 3rd St., Ste. 200, Kansas City, MO 64105, (816)221-7575
Mass Media; Task Force on Using [★8565]
Mass Merchandising Distributors' Assn. - Defunct.
Mass Merchandising Res. Found. [★3427]
Mass Retailing Inst. [★3427]
Mass Spectrometry; Amer. Soc. for [7688]
Massachusetts; Ancient and Honorable Artillery Company of [21191]
Massachusetts Assn. for the Blind; Vision Community Services - A Division of the [★16868]
Massachusetts Assn. for the Blind and Vision Found. [★16868]
Massachusetts Catholic Order of Foresters [★18991]
Massachusetts; Colonial Soc. of [10104]

A star before a book entry number signifies that the name is not listed separately, but is mentioned within the entry.

Massachusetts Coun. for the Humanities - Defunct.
Massachusetts Physicians Against the Death Penalty - Defunct.
Massachusetts Soc. of Examining Physicians [★15002]
Massachusetts Soc. of Law and Medicine [★15002]
Massage
  Amer. Massage Therapy Assn. [15022]
  Amer. Medical Massage Assn. [15023]
  Amer. Org. for Bodywork Therapies of Asia [15024]
  Amer. Reiki Master Assn. [13622]
  Assoc. Bodywork and Massage Professionals [15025]
  Australian Assn. of Massage Therapists [IO]
  Canadian Massage Therapist Alliance [IO]
  Day-Break Geriatric Massage Inst. [15026]
  Hospital-Based Massage Network [15027]
  Intl. Assn. of Animal Massage and Bodywork [15028]
  Intl. Assn. of Animal Massage and Bodywork [IO]
  Intl. Assn. of Infant Massage [IO]
  Intl. Assn. of Infant Massage [15029]
  Intl. Inst. of Reflexology [16620]
  Intl. Massage Assn. [15030]
  Intl. Massage Assn. [IO]
  Intl. Medical Spa Assn. [1870]
  Intl. Sports Massage Fed. [16482]
  Intl. Thai Therapists Assn. [15031]
  Intl. Thai Therapists Assn. [IO]
  Massage Therapy Assn. [IO]
  Medical Spa Soc. [1871]
  Natl. Certification Bd. for Therapeutic Massage and Bodywork [15032]
  Reflexology Assn. of Am. [13650]
  Shiatsu Therapy Assn. of Australia [IO]
  Spa Bus. Assn. [IO]
  Thai Spa Assn. [IO]
  U.S. Medical Massage Assn. [15033]
  U.S. Sports Massage Fed. [16485]
Massage Fed; Intl. Sports [16482]
Massage Fed; U.S. Sports [16485]
Massage Therapists and Allied Hea. Practitioners Intl; Assoc. Professional [★15025]
Massage Therapists and Bodyworkers; Assoc. Professional [★15025]
Massage Therapists; Intl. Fed. of Registered Equine [IO]
Massage Therapists; Natl. Assn. of Nurse [15496]
Massage Therapy Assn. [IO], Kenilworth, Republic of South Africa
Massenet Soc. - Defunct.
Master Animal - Address unknown since 1995.
Master Appraisers; Natl. Assn. of [3321]
Master Barbers and Beauticians of America; Associated [★1079]
Master Barbers and Beauticians of America; Hair Intl./Associated [1079]
Master Boilermakers' Assn. [★3283]
Master Brewers Assn. of Am. [★6544]
Master Brewers Assn. of Am. [★IO]
Master Brewers Assn. of the Americas [IO], St. Paul, MN, United States
Master Brewers Assn. of the Americas [6544], 3340 Pilot Knob Rd., St. Paul, MN 55121-2097, (651)454-7250
Master Builders Assn. - Australian Capital Territory [IO], Canberra, Australia
Master Builders Assn. - Malaysia [IO], Kuala Lumpur, Malaysia
Master Builders Assn. - New South Wales [IO], Forest Lodge, Australia
Master Builders Assn. - South Australia [IO], Adelaide, Australia
Master Builders Assn. - Tasmania [IO], Hobart, Australia
Master Builders Assn. - Victoria [IO], East Melbourne, Australia
Master Builders Assn. - Western Australia [IO], West Perth, Australia
Master Builders Australia [IO], Yarralumla, Australia
Master Builders South Africa [IO], Halfway House, Republic of South Africa
Master of Business Administration Executives; Assn. of [702]

Master Carvers Assn. [IO], London, United Kingdom
Master Drawings Assn. [9456], 225 Madison Ave., New York, NY 10016, (212)590-0369
Master Dyers Assn. - Address unknown since 1995.
Master Furriers Guild of America - Address unknown since 1990.
Master Gemology Soc. - Defunct.
Master Heart Found. - Defunct.
Master Hosts - Defunct.
Master Inst. of United Arts - Defunct.
Master Locksmiths Assn. [IO], Daventry, United Kingdom
Master Mariners; Coun. of Amer. [2575]
Master Painters Assn. of Finland [IO], Helsinki, Finland
Master Painters Australia - Western Australian Assn. [IO], Maylands, Australia
Master Photo Dealers' and Finishers' Assn. [★IO]
Master Photo Dealers' and Finishers' Assn. [★3009]
Master Photo Finishers and Dealers Assn. [★3009]
Master Photo Finishers and Dealers Assn. [★IO]
Master Photographers Assn. [IO], Darlington, United Kingdom
Master Plumbers and Mech. Services Assn. of Australia [IO], West Melbourne, Australia
Master Printers of Am. [★1765]
Master Textile Printers Assn. - Defunct.
Master Weavers Inst. - Defunct.
Master Window Cleaners of Am. [2469], PO Box 495, Cumberland, MD 21501
Master Workmen of Navy Yards and Naval Stations; Natl. Assn. of [★6085]
Masterkey Assn. - Address unknown since 1995.
Mastermind Alliance - Address unknown since 2008.
Masters of Foxhounds Assn. of Am. [23546], PO Box 363, Millwood, VA 22646, (540)955-5680
Masters of Foxhounds Club of America and England - Defunct.
Masters, Mates and Pilots, ILA, AFL-CIO; Intl. Org. of [24128]
Master's Men of the Free Will Baptist Church [★19490]
Master's Men of the Natl. Assn. of Free Will Baptists [19490], PO Box 5002, Antioch, TN 37011-5002, (615)760-6142
Masters Swimming Comm. of the AAU [★23891]
Masters Track and Field Comm. - Address unknown since 2001.
Mastic Asphalt Coun. [IO], Hastings, United Kingdom
Mastic Asphalt Coun. and Employer's Fed. [★IO]
Mastiff and Bullmastiff Club in France [IO], Bordeaux, France
Mastiff Club of Am. [22305], c/o Jodi LaBombard, Membership Sec., 30 Blue Heron Dr., Rochester, NY 14624, (585)594-5354
Mastiff Club of Am; Pyrenean [22349]
The Mastocytosis Soc. [14273], c/o Regina Rentz, Treas., PO Box 511, Plainville, CT 06062, (413)862-4556
Masyarakat Telematika Indonesia [★IO]
Matagiri Sri Aurobindo Center [★20636]
Match Inst. - Defunct.
MATCH Intl. Centre [IO], Nepean, ON, Canada
Matchbox Collectors Club - Defunct.
Matchbox U.S.A. [22069], 62 Saw Mill Rd., Durham, CT 06422, (860)349-1655
Matchcover
  Amer. Matchcover Collecting Club [21963]
  Denver Strikers Matchcover Club [22625]
  Intl. Match Safe Assn. [22053]
  Rathkamp Matchcover Soc. [22626]
Matchcover Collecting Club; Amer. [21963]
Matchcover Collecting Club; Amer. [★21963]
Matchcover Soc; Rathkamp [22626]
Matching Prog; Ophthalmology [★15675]
Material Aerospatial; Association Europeenne des Constructeurs de [★154]
Material Aerospatial; Association Europeenne des Constructeurs de [★IO]
Material Aid Comm. of Central America - Defunct.
Material Handling Accessory Mfrs., Production Sect. of the Material Handling Indus. [2042], 8720 Red Oak Blvd., Ste. 201, Charlotte, NC 28217-3992, (704)676-1190

Material Handling Consultants; Assn. of Professional [961]
Material Handling Equip. Distributors Assn. [2043], 201 U.S. Hwy. 45, Vernon Hills, IL 60061-2398, (847)680-3500
Material Handling Indus. [★2044]
Material Handling Indus. of Am. [2044], 8720 Red Oak Blvd., Ste. 201, Charlotte, NC 28217-3992, (704)676-1190
Material Handling Indus. of Am; Lift Mfrs. Prdt. Sect. - [2034]
Material Handling Inst. [★2044]
Material Handling Inst; Automatic Guided Vehicle Systems Sect. of the [2005]
Material Handling Inst; Below/Hook Lifters Sect. of the [★2042]
Material Handling Inst; Conveyor Sect. of the [2014]
Material Handling Inst; Overhead Components Mfrs. Prdt. Sect. of the [★2042]
Material Handling Soc; Amer. [★7282]
Material Mgt. Soc; Intl. [★7282]
Material and Process Engineers; Soc. of Aerospace [★7285]
Material and Process Engineers; Soc. of Aircraft [★7285]
Material Removal Community of the Soc. of Mfg. Engineers; Machining and [7747]
Materials
  Amer. Soc. for Testing and Materials [7789]
  ASM Intl. [7311]
  Assn. of Professional Material Handling Consultants [961]
  Automatic Guided Vehicle Systems Sect. of the Material Handling Inst. [2005]
  British Materials Handling Fed. [IO]
  Building Materials Reuse Assn. [608]
  Chinese Material Res. Soc. [IO]
  Clinical Res. Associates [14148]
  Conveyor Sect. of the Material Handling Inst. [2014]
  Deutsche Gesellschaft fur Materialkunde [IO]
  Deutscher Verband fur Materialforschung und -prufung [IO]
  European Materials Res. Soc. [IO]
  European Pultrusion Tech. Assn. [IO]
  European Soc. for Biomaterials [IO]
  Fed. of European Materials Societies [IO]
  Fed. of Materials Societies [7281]
  Inst. of Caster Manufacturers [2028]
  Inst. of Nuclear Materials Mgt. [7387]
  Inst. of Operations Mgt. [IO]
  Intl. Org. on Shape Memory and Superelastic Technologies [7317]
  Japan Soc. of Materials Sci. [IO]
  Material Handling Accessory Mfrs., Production Sect. of the Material Handling Indus. [2042]
  Material Handling Equip. Distributors Assn. [2043]
  Material Handling Indus. of Am. [2044]
  Materials Handling and Mgt. Soc. [7282]
  Materials Handling and Mgt. Soc. [IO]
  Materials Properties Coun. [7319]
  Materials Res. Soc. [7283]
  Materials Tech. Inst. [812]
  Natl. Inst. for Materials Sci. [IO]
  Natl. Materials Advisory Bd. [7284]
  PET Resin Assn. [3054]
  Soc. for the Advancement of Material and Process Engg. [7285]
  Steel Framing Alliance [2731]
  Steel Truss and Component Assn. [2733]
  Storage and Handling Equip. Distributors' Assn. [IO]
  Telemark Technological Res. and Development Centre, Dept. of Powder Sci. and Tech. [IO]
  United Kingdom Warehousing Assn. [IO]
Materials Advisory Bd. [★7284]
Materials Assn; Suppliers of Advanced Composite [★589]
Materials Australia [★IO]
Materials Engg. Institute [★IO]
Materials Engg. Institute [★7311]
Materials Handling Engineers Assn. [IO], Stockton on Tees, United Kingdom
Materials Handling and Mgt. Soc. [IO], Charlotte, NC, United States

---

Reference to "IO" in place of a book number signifies that the association may be found in the 45th edition of International Organizations.

Materials Handling and Mgt. Soc. **[7282]**, 8720 Red Oak Blvd., Ste. 201, Charlotte, NC 28217, (704)676-1190

Materials Info. Exchange Task Force (SRRT); Ethnic **[★10354]**

Materials Inst; Semiconductor Equip. and **[★1228]**

Materials Intl; Semiconductor Equip. and **[★1228]**

Materials Mgt; Amer. Soc. for Hosp. Purchasing and **[★14872]**

Materials Managers; Acad. of Certified Hazardous **[4804]**

Materials Managers; Natl. Assn. of Sci. **[3487]**

Materials Marketing Associates **[2636]**, 136 S Keowee St., Dayton, OH 45402, (937)222-1024

Materials and Methods Standards Assn. **[636]**, 4000 Pinemont, Houston, TX 77292

Materials Properties Coun. **[7319]**, PO Box 1942, New York, NY 10156, (216)658-3847

Materials Properties Data Network; National **[★7319]**

Materials Res. Soc. **[7283]**, 506 Keystone Dr., Warrendale, PA 15086-7573, (724)779-3003

Materials Soc; Minerals, Metals, and **[7320]**

Materials Tech. Inst. **[812]**, 1215 Fern Ridge Pkwy., Ste. 206, St. Louis, MO 63141-4408, (314)576-7712

Materials Tech. Inst. of the Chem. Process Indus. **[★812]**

Maternal and Child Health; Amer. Found. for **[15586]**

Maternal and Child Hea; Natl. Center for Educ. in **[13969]**

Maternal and Child Hea. Programs; Assn. of **[13947]**

Maternal Life Intl. **[16341]**, 326 S Jackson St., Butte, MT 59701, (406)782-1719

Maternal Life Intl. **[IO]**, Butte, MT, United States

Maternity Center Assn. **[★15595]**

Maternity Coalition **[IO]**, Blackburn, Australia

Maternity Services; Coalition for Improving **[15596]**

Mates Of Mel Gibson - Defunct.

Mates and Pilots, ILA, AFL-CIO; Intl. Org. of Masters, **[24128]**

Math/Science Network **[8825]**, Mills Coll., 5000 MacArthur Blvd., Oakland, CA 94613, (510)430-2222

Mathematical Assn. **[IO]**, Leicester, United Kingdom

Mathematical Assn. of Am. **[7293]**, 1529 18th St. NW, Washington, DC 20036-1358, (202)387-5200

Mathematical Biology; Soc. for **[6600]**

Mathematical Org. of Japan **[★IO]**

Mathematical Sciences; Assn. of Christians in the **[19766]**

Mathematical Soc. of Japan **[IO]**, Tokyo, Japan

Mathematical Soc; New York **[★7286]**

Mathematical Stud. Unit **[22842]**, c/o Estelle A. Buccino, Sec.-Treas., 5615 Glenwood Rd., Bethesda, MD 20817-6727

Mathematical Union of Argentina **[IO]**, Buenos Aires, Argentina

Mathematicians; Assn. of Women **[★7288]**

Mathematics

Adhesion Soc. **[6661]**

Advocates for Women in Sci., Engg., and Mathematics **[7593]**

Alliance for Sci. and Tech. Res. in Am. **[7595]**

Amer. Mathematical Assn. of Two-Year Colleges **[8821]**

Amer. Mathematical Soc. **[7286]**

Amer. Philosophical Soc. **[7598]**

Amer. Statistical Assn. **[7702]**

Assn. of Christians in the Mathematical Sciences **[19766]**

Assn. for Mathematics Applied to Economic and Social Sciences **[IO]**

Assn. of State Supervisors of Mathematics **[8822]**

Assn. for Symbolic Logic **[7287]**

Association for Symbolic Logic **[IO]**

Assn. of Teachers of Mathematics **[IO]**

Assn. for Women in Mathematics **[7288]**

Australasian Soc. for Gen. Relativity and Gravitation **[IO]**

Australian Mathematical Soc. **[IO]**

Belgian Mathematical Soc. **[IO]**

Beta Kappa Chi **[24585]**

Canadian Mathematical Soc. **[IO]**

Caucus for Women in Statistics **[7703]**

Chinese Mathematical Soc. **[IO]**

Comm. of Presidents of Statistical Societies **[7704]**

Conf. Bd. of the Mathematical Sciences **[7289]**

Danish Mathematical Soc. **[IO]**

Domino Players Assn. of Am. **[22465]**

Dozenal Soc. of Am. **[7695]**

Econometric Soc. **[7705]**

Edinburgh Mathematical Soc. **[IO]**

Euler Soc. **[10453]**

European Consortium for Mathematics in Indus. **[IO]**

European Mathematical Soc. **[IO]**

European Res. Consortium for Informatics and Mathematics **[IO]**

European Women in Mathematics **[IO]**

Fiber Soc. **[7078]**

Fibonacci Assn. **[IO]**

For Inspiration and Recognition of Sci. and Tech. **[8319]**

German Mathematical Assn. **[IO]**

German Natl. Mathematical Soc. **[IO]**

Glasgow Mathematical Assn. **[IO]**

Hands On Sci. Outreach **[8067]**

Hong Kong Mathematical Soc. **[IO]**

HOPOS - The Intl. Soc. for the History of Philosophy of Sci. **[9103]**

Inst. of Mathematical Statistics **[7706]**

Inst. of Mathematics and its Applications **[IO]**

Intl. Assn. for Cryptologic Res. **[6849]**

Intl. Assn. for Game Educ. and Res. **[8823]**

Intl. Assn. for Game Educ. and Res. **[IO]**

Intl. Assn. of Mathematical Sciences **[IO]**

Intl. Biometric Soc. **[7707]**

Intl. Biometric Soc., Eastern North Amer. Region **[7708]**

Intl. Biometric Soc., Western North Amer. Region **[7709]**

Intl. Centre for Mathematical Sciences **[IO]**

Intl. Centre for Pure and Applied Mathematics **[IO]**

Intl. Commn. on the History of Mathematics **[IO]**

Intl. Commn. on Mathematical Instruction **[IO]**

Intl. Fed. of Nonlinear Analysts **[7609]**

Intl. Linear Algebra Soc. **[7290]**

Intl. Linear Algebra Soc. **[IO]**

Intl. Mathematical Union **[IO]**

Intl. Soc. for Bayesian Anal. **[IO]**

Intl. Soc. for Bayesian Anal. **[7291]**

Intl. Soc. for Computational Biology **[2094]**

Intl. Soc. of Difference Equations **[7292]**

Intl. Soc. of Difference Equations **[IO]**

Intl. Soc. for the Interaction of Mechanics and Mathematics **[IO]**

Intl. Soc. of Statistical Sci. **[7710]**

Irish Mathematical Soc. **[IO]**

Israel Mathematical Union **[IO]**

Italian Mathematical Union **[IO]**

Junior Engg. Tech. Soc. **[8368]**

Kappa Mu Epsilon **[24537]**

Kurt Goedel Soc. **[IO]**

London Mathematical Soc. **[IO]**

The Madison Proj. **[8824]**

Math/Science Network **[8825]**

Mathematical Assn. **[IO]**

Mathematical Assn. of Am. **[7293]**

Mathematical Soc. of Japan **[IO]**

Mathematical Stud. Unit **[22842]**

Mathematical Union of Argentina **[IO]**

Mu Alpha Theta **[24538]**

Natl. Alliance of State Sci. and Mathematics Coalitions **[9106]**

Natl. Assn. of Mathematics Advisers **[IO]**

Natl. Assn. of PreCollege Directors **[8371]**

Natl. Coun. of Supervisors of Mathematics **[8826]**

Natl. Coun. of Teachers of Mathematics **[8827]**

New York Cipher Soc. **[6850]**

New Zealand Mathematical Soc. **[IO]**

North Amer. Computational Social and Org. Sciences **[6740]**

Oughtred Soc. **[22101]**

Pi Mu Epsilon **[24539]**

Real Sociedad Matematica Espanola **[IO]**

School Sci. and Mathematics Assn. **[9115]**

Sigma Zeta **[24589]**

Singapore Mathematical Soc. **[IO]**

Sociedad Colombiana de Matematicas **[IO]**

Sociedad de Matematica de Chile **[IO]**

Sociedad Matematica Mexicana **[IO]**

Soc. for Exact Philosophy **[10833]**

Soc. for Indus. and Applied Mathematics **[7294]**

Soc. of Kabalarians of Canada **[IO]**

Soc. for Natural Philosophy **[7295]**

South African Mathematical Soc. **[IO]**

Special Interest Gp. for Symbolic and Algebraic Manipulation **[7296]**

Swedish Mathematical Soc. **[IO]**

Women and Mathematics Educ. **[8828]**

World Sci. and Engg. Acad. and Soc. **[7054]**

Mathematics Assn; School Sci. and **[9115]**

Mathematics; British Soc. for the History of **[IO]**

Mathematics Club; Natl. High School and Junior Coll. **[★24538]**

Mathematics Educ. of Girls and Women; Assn. for the Promotion of the **[★8828]**

Mathematics Educators; Commonwealth Assn. of Sci., Tech. and **[IO]**

Mathematics Teachers; Central Assn. of Sci. and **[★9115]**

Matheson Soc; Clan **[20848]**

Mathis East Coast Fan Club; Johnny **[24929]**

Mathis Soc. - Defunct.

Matkailun Edistamiskeskus **[★IO]**

Matrimonial Lawyers; Amer. Acad. of **[5698]**

Matrix Biology Soc. of Australia and New Zealand **[IO]**, North Adelaide, Australia

Matrix Found. **[18813]**, 3337 Duke St., Alexandria, VA 22314

Mattachine Soc. of New York - Defunct.

Mattea Fan Club; Kathy **[24931]**

A Matter of Justice Coalition **[6012]**, PO Box 1209, Dahlgren, VA 22448-1209, (540)663-0486

Matthay Assn; Amer. **[8901]**

Matthew McCune Family Assn. **[★20996]**

Mature Market Inst. - Defunct.

Mature Market Rsrc. Center **[11296]**

Mature Outlook - Defunct.

Maturity; Action for Independent **[★12895]**

Maulik Chahida Karmashuchi **[IO]**, Dhaka, Bangladesh

Mauneluk Assn. **[★12627]**

Mauritius Amateur Radio Soc. **[IO]**, Quatre Bornes, Mauritius

Mauritius Assn. of Quantity Surveyors **[IO]**, Quatre Bornes, Mauritius

Mauritius Badminton Assn. **[IO]**, Rose Hill, Mauritius

Mauritius Chamber of Commerce and Indus. **[IO]**, Port Louis, Mauritius

Mauritius Employers' Fed. **[IO]**, Port Louis, Mauritius

Mauritius Export Processing Zone Assn. **[IO]**, Port Louis, Mauritius

Mauritius Squash Rackets Assn. **[IO]**, Riambel, Mauritius

Mauritius Taekwondo Assn. **[IO]**, Port Louis, Mauritius

Mauritius Tennis Fed. **[IO]**, Phoenix, Mauritius

Mauritius Turf Club **[IO]**, Port Louis, Mauritius

Mauritius Union of Journalists **[IO]**, Flic en Flac, Mauritius

Mauritius Yachting Assn. **[IO]**, Port Louis, Mauritius

Mautner Proj. for Lesbian Hea. **[14433]**, 1707 L St. NW, Ste. 230, Washington, DC 20036, (202)332-5536

Mautner Proj. for Lesbians with Cancer **[★14433]**

Maverick/Comet Club Intl. **[21697]**, 421 E State St., Albany, IN 47320, (765)789-6036

Max-Eyth-Gesselschaft Agrartechnik im VDI **[★IO]**

Max-Eyth Soc. for Agricultural Engg. of the VDI **[IO]**, Dusseldorf, Germany

Maxey Flats Radioactive Protective Assn. - Address unknown since 1995.

Maxfield Family Org. **[20992]**, 250 S 100th E, Hyrum, UT 84319, (435)245-6984

Maxillo-Faciale; Assn. Internationale de Chirurgie Buccale et **[★15736]**

Maxillofacial Pathology; Amer. Acad. of Oral and **[15852]**

Maxillofacial Pathology; Amer. Bd. of Oral and **[15855]**

Maxillofacial Prosthetics; Amer. Acad. of **[14103]**

Maxillofacial Radiology; Amer. Acad. of Oral and **[14104]**

Maxillofacial Surgeons; Amer. Assn. of Oral and **[15732]**

A star before a book entry number signifies that the name is not listed separately, but is mentioned within the entry.

Maxillofacial Surgeons; Amer. Coll. of Oral and [15734]
Maxillofacial Surgeons; Amer. Soc. of [15735]
Maxillofacial Surgeons; British Assn. of Oral and [IO]
Maxillofacial Surgery; Amer. Bd. of Oral and [15733]
Maximilian Numismatic and Historical Soc. - Defunct.
Maximum Card Study Unit - Address unknown since 1999.
Maximum Ser. TV; Assn. for [549]
Maxwell Soc. of the USA; Clan [20849]
Maxwell's Official Fan Club - Address unknown since 2003.
May 2nd Movement - Defunct.
May 19 Coalition - Address unknown since 1997.
May I Speak Freely Media [18028], 20 Greenleaf Ave., Medford, MA 02155, (781)393-0906
Mayan and Indigenous Spiritual Bodies; Saq' Be': Org. for [10226]
Maybee Soc. [20993], 10809 16th Ave. SE, No. 218, Everett, WA 98208
Mayflower Descendants; Gen. Soc. of [21247]
Mayflower Soc. [★21247]
Mayflower Soc. [★IO]
Mayflower Warehousemen's Assn. - Defunct.
Maynard Bernstein Resource Center on Cults - Defunct.
Maynard Listener Library - Defunct.
Mayo Smith Soc. - Address unknown since 1999.
Mayonnaise and Salad Dressing Inst. [★1502]
Mayonnaise and Salad Dressing Manufacturers Assn. [★1502]
Mayors; Natl. Conf. of Black [6129]
Mayors; Southern Conf. of Black [★6129]
Mayors; U.S. Conf. of [6132]
Mazda Club [21698], PO Box 11238, Chicago, IL 60611, (773)769-6262
Mazda RX-7 Club - Defunct.
Mazdaznan Assn. - Address unknown since 2001.
MAZON [12395], 1990 S Bundy Dr., Ste. 260, Los Angeles, CA 90025, (310)442-0020
MAZON [IO], Los Angeles, CA, United States
Mazur Surname Org. [20994]
MBA Assn; Natl. Black [8035]
MBA Executives; Assn. of [★702]
MBAs; Natl. Soc. of Hispanic [754]
MBD-foreningen [★IO]
Mbong Found., Intl. [IO], Mexico City, Mexico
MC Class Sailboat Racing Assn; Intl. [★23199]
MC Sailing Assn. [23199], c/o Ronald G. Stryker, Exec. Sec., PO Box 250, Lewis Center, OH 43035-0250, (740)549-4700
MCAD Family Support Gp. [★15248]
MCAD Family Support Gp. [★IO]
McAdams Historical Soc. [20995], 14018 Davana Terr., Sherman Oaks, CA 91423, (818)789-1086
McAlpin(e) Family Assn. - Defunct.
MCAP Group - Address unknown since 2006.
McArdle Fan Club; Andrea [24728]
McArdles's Disease
  Muscular Dystrophy Assn. [15339]
McAuley Institute [12317]
McBride Fan Club; Martina [24944]
McCarver Sisters Fan Club - Address unknown since 1989.
McCleave Family Org; George [20912]
McCoon Family Assn. [★20996]
McCoy Pottery Collectors' Soc. [21932], PO Box 5286, Delanco, NJ 08075
McCullough/McCulloch Clan Soc. - Defunct.
McCune Family Assn. [20996]
McCurdy Family Assn. [20997]
McDonald's Collectors Club [22070], 1153 S Lee St., PMB 200, Des Plaines, IL 60016, (216)941-7127
McDonald's Hispanic Operators Assn. [3395], c/o Ronald McDonald House Charities, One Kroc Dr., Oak Brook, IL 60523, (630)623-7048
McDonald's Operators Assn. - Defunct.
McDonald's Operators Assn; Natl. Black [1955]
McDonnell Douglas Computer Systems Company Vendors' Assn. - Defunct.
McEwan Family Assn. [★20996]
McGahen/McGhen/McGahn/McGahan Family Assn. - Address unknown since 2005.
McGoohan, Patrick
  Once Upon A Time (The Prisoner Fan Club) [25040]

Six of One Club: The Prisoner Appreciation Soc. [25043]
McGrath Family Assn. - Defunct.
McGregor Family Assn. [20998]
MCIA [★IO]
McKeown Family Assn. [★20996]
McLaren Assn. of North America; Clan [20850]
McLaughlin Buick Club of Canada [IO], Alliston, ON, Canada
McLibel Support Campaign - UK [IO], London, United Kingdom
McLibel Support Campaign - U.S.A. - Defunct.
MDA/ALS Res. Center; Forbes Norris [15323]
MDS Indus. Assn. [★3764]
MDS Indus. Assn. [★IO]
Meader Family Assn. [20999], 158 Ashdown Rd., Ballston Lake, NY 12019, (518)399-5013
Meal and Oil Assn; Natl. Fish [2855]
Meal Providers; Natl. Assn. of Home Delivered and Congregate [★12284]
Meals for Millions Found. [★12394]
Meals for Millions/Freedom from Hunger Found. [★12394]
Meals-on-Wheels America - Defunct.
Meals on Wheels Assn. of Am. [12284], 203 S Union St., Alexandria, VA 22314-3355, (703)548-5558
Meals4Israel [12459], 11301 W Olympic Blvd., No. 580, Los Angeles, CA 90064, (877)647-7235
Meals4Israel [IO], Los Angeles, CA, United States
Meaning; Found. for Ethics and [7069]
Measure; Americans for Customary Weight and [18679]
Measurement Assn; Customer Satisfaction [716]
Measurement Bur; Out-of-Home [★123]
Measurement Control; Amer. Soc. for [★7220]
Measurement, Control, and Automation Assn. [3485], PO Box 3698, Williamsburg, VA 23187-3698, (757)258-3100
Measurement in Educ; Natl. Coun. on [9256]
Measurement and Evaluation in Counseling and Development; Assn. for [★9247]
Measurement and Evaluation in Guidance; Assn. for [★9247]
Measurement and Evaluation; Special Interest Gp. on [6751]
Measurement Gp; Cmpt. [6724]
Measurement Soc; IEEE Instrumentation and [7219]
Measurement Techniques Assn; Antenna [6905]
Measurement; Traffic Audit Bur. for Media [123]
Measurements Assn. for Standards and Res; Methods Time [★7165]
Measurements; Intl. Commn. on Radiological Units and [★5161]
Measurements; Natl. Coun. on Radiation Protection and [6242]
Measurements Used in Educ; Natl. Coun. on [★9256]
Measures; Natl. Conf. on Weights and [6269]
Measuring Tool Mfrs. Assn; Amer. [7694]
Meat
  Amer. Assn. of Meat Processors [2656]
  Amer. Meat Goat Assn. [2657]
  Amer. Meat Inst. [2658]
  Animal Agriculture Alliance [1501]
  AUS-MEAT [IO]
  Australian Meat Indus. Coun. [IO]
  Beef Info. Centre [IO]
  British Contract Mfrs. and Packers Assn. [IO]
  Butchers' Company [IO]
  Canada Beef Export Fed. [IO]
  Canada Pork Intl. [IO]
  Canadian Meat Coun. [IO]
  Central Assn. of German Pork Producers [IO]
  Central Org. for the Meat Indus. [IO]
  Danish Butchers' Assn. [IO]
  Danish Slaughterhouses [IO]
  Deutscher Fleischer-Verband [IO]
  Dutch Fed. of Traders in Livestock [IO]
  Estonian Meat Assn. [IO]
  European Livestock and Meat Trading Union [IO]
  Fats and Proteins Res. Found. [2850]
  Fed. Butchers' Assn. [IO]
  Federatie van het Belgisch Vlees [IO]
  Food Safety Consortium [5031]
  German Meat Assn. [IO]

  Independent Workers Union [IO]
  Intergovernmental Gp. on Meat and Dairy Products [IO]
  Intl. Confed. of Meat and Meat Processing Indus. [IO]
  Intl. Meat Secretariat [IO]
  Intl. Natural Sausage Casing Assn. [IO]
  Intl. Natural Sausage Casing Assn. [2659]
  Intl. Yak Assn. [5001]
  Irish Cattle and Sheep Farmers Assn. [IO]
  Livestock Auctioneers' Assn. [IO]
  Meat Bd. [IO]
  Meat Bd. of Namibia [IO]
  Meat Importers Coun. of Am. [2660]
  Meat Indus'. Assn. [IO]
  Meat Indus. Suppliers Assn. [2661]
  Meat and Livestock Australia [IO]
  Meat Processing Indus'. Assn. of Spain [IO]
  Meat and Wool New Zealand [IO]
  Natl. Assn. of Catering Butchers [IO]
  Natl. Assn. of Wholesale Butchers and Meat Merchants [IO]
  Natl. Fed. of Meat and Food Traders [IO]
  Natl. Meat Assn. [2662]
  Natl. Renderers Assn. [2858]
  New Zealand Pork Indus. Bd. [IO]
  North Amer. Meat Processors Assn. [IO]
  North Amer. Meat Processors Assn. [2663]
  Northern Ireland Meat Exporters Assn. [IO]
  Norwegian Independent Meat Assn. [IO]
  Piedmontese Assn. of the U.S. [4287]
  Polish Assn. of Meat Producers, Exporters and Importers [IO]
  Quality Meat Scotland [IO]
  Ranchers-Cattlemen Action Legal Fund, United Stockgrowers of Am. [4290]
  Rural Assn. of Paraguay [IO]
  Scottish Assn. of Meat Wholesalers [IO]
  Scottish Fed. of Meat Traders Assn. [IO]
  Shelf-Stable Food Processors Assn. [2664]
  Spanish Assn. of the Meat Indus. [IO]
  Swedish Meat Indus. Assn. [IO]
  U.S. Boer Goat Assn. [4789]
  U.S. Meat Export Fed. [2665]
  U.S. Meat Export Fed. [IO]
  Weston A. Price Found. [15572]
Meat Assn; Natl. [★2658]
Meat Assn; Pacific Coast [★2662]
Meat Bd. [IO], Zoetermeer, Netherlands
Meat Bd. of Namibia [IO], Windhoek, Namibia
Meat Conf; Reciprocal [★7088]
Meat Cutters and Bucher Workmen of North Am; Amalgamated [★24061]
Meat and Food Seasoning Mfrs; Natl. Assn. of [★1552]
Meat Importers' Coun. [★2660]
Meat Importers Coun. of Am. [2660], 1901 N Ft. Myer Dr., Arlington, VA 22209, (703)522-1910
Meat Indus'. Assn. [IO], Rozzano, Italy
Meat Indus. Suppliers Assn. [2661], 201 Park Washington Ct., Falls Church, VA 22046-4527, (703)533-0251
Meat Indus. Supply and Equip. Assn. [★2661]
Meat and Livestock Australia [IO], North Sydney, Australia
Meat Loaf UK Fanclub [IO], Cheadle, United Kingdom
Meat Machinery Mfrs. Inst. [★2661]
Meat New Zealand [★IO]
Meat Packers Assn; Amer. [★2658]
Meat Packers Assn; Western States [★2662]
Meat Packers; Inst. of Amer. [★2658]
Meat and Poultry Export Assn. - Address unknown since 1995.
Meat Processing Indus'. Assn. of Spain [IO], Madrid, Spain
Meat Purveyors; Natl. Assn. of [★2663]
Meat Purveyors; Natl. Assn. of Hotel and Restaurant [★2663]
Meat Sci. Assn; Amer. [7088]
Meat Seasoning Mfrs; Natl. Assn. of [★1552]
Meat and Wool New Zealand [IO], Wellington, New Zealand
Mech. Bank Collectors of Am. [21826], PO Box 13323, Pittsburgh, PA 15242

Reference to "IO" in place of a book number signifies that the association may be found in the 45th edition of International Organizations.

Mech. Bank Collectors of Rhode Island [★21826]
Mech. Contractors Assn. of Am. [1033], 1385 Pic-
card Dr., Rockville, MD 20850-4329, (301)869-
5800
Mech. Contractors Assn. of Canada [IO], Ottawa,
ON, Canada
Mech. Contractors Coun; Natl. [1049]
Mechanical-Copyright Protection Soc. [IO], London,
United Kingdom
Mechanical Engineering
  Aircraft Mechanics Fraternal Assn. [24006]
  Amer. Soc. of Mech. Engineers [7298]
  Amer. Soc. of Mech. Engineers Auxiliary [7299]
  Cessna Pilots Assn. [21436]
  Chamber of Mech. Engineers [IO]
  Chinese Mech. Engg. Soc. [IO]
  Fed. of Mech. Engg. of the Slovak Republic [IO]
  Inst. of Automotive Mech. Engineers [IO]
  Japan Soc. of Mech. Engineers [IO]
  Materials Properties Coun. [7319]
  Pi Tau Sigma [24465]
  Tire Soc. [7798]
  U.S. Natl. Comm. on Theoretical and Applied
    Mechanics [7301]
  Vibration Inst. [7302]
Mech. Engineers; Woman's Auxiliary to the Amer.
Soc. of [★7299]
Mech. Equip. Mfrs. Representatives Assn. [2540],
c/o Engg. Center, 11 W Mt. Vernon Pl., Baltimore,
MD 21201, (410)793-0202
Mechanical Jack Mfrs. Assn. - Defunct.
Mech. and Metal Trades Confed. [IO], Paisley,
United Kingdom
Mech. Packing Assn. [★2020]
Mech. Power Transmission Assn. [2045], 6724 Lone
Oak Blvd., Naples, FL 34109, (239)514-3441
Mech. Power Transmission Equip. Distributors Assn.
[★2060]
Mech. Power Transmission Equip. Distributors Assn.
[★IO]
Mech. Specialty Contracting Indus; Coun. of
[★1006]
Mech. Storage Systems; Controlled [★2004]
Mech. Trade Coun; Natl. [★1049]
Mechanics
  Aircraft Mechanics Fraternal Assn. [24006]
  Amer. Acad. of Mechanics [7297]
  Amer. Soc. of Mech. Engineers [7298]
  Amer. Soc. of Mech. Engineers Auxiliary [7299]
  Assn. of Chairmen of Departments of Mechanics
    [8829]
  Cessna Pilots Assn. [21436]
  Championship Assn. of Mechanics [23075]
  Chinese Soc. of Theoretical and Applied Mechan-
    ics [IO]
  Czech Soc. for Mechanics [IO]
  European Mechanics Soc. [IO]
  Intl. Assn. for Computational Mechanics [IO]
  Intl. Assn. for Vehicle Sys. Dynamics [IO]
  Intl. Centre for Mech. Sciences [IO]
  Intl. Institution for Production Engg. Res. [IO]
  Intl. Union of Theoretical and Applied Mechanics
    [IO]
  Israel Assn. for Computational Methods in
    Mechanics [IO]
  Nordic Assn. for Computational Mechanics [IO]
  U.S. Assn. for Computational Mechanics [7300]
  U.S. Natl. Comm. on Theoretical and Applied
    Mechanics [7301]
  Vibration Inst. [7302]
Mechanics; Championship Assn. of [23075]
Mechanics Educational Soc. of America - Defunct.
Mechanics and Foreman of Naval Shore Establish-
ments; Natl. Assn. of Master [★6085]
Mechanics Fraternal Assn; Aircraft [24006]
Mechanics Institute [★9229]
Mechanics; International Assn. of Computational
[★7300]
Mechanics; Soc. for Experimental [7713]
Mechanics and Tradesmen of the City of New York;
Gen. Soc. of [9229]
Mechanics and Tradesmen; Gen. Soc. of [★9229]
Med Help Intl. [15042], 6300 N Wickham Rd., Ste.
130, PMB No. 188, Melbourne, FL 32940,
(321)259-7505

Med Help Intl. [IO], Melbourne, FL, United States
Med; Tel- [14601]
MEDACT [IO], London, United Kingdom
Medailles Militares of New York, U.S.A. - Defunct.
Medal; Central Assn. of the Miraculous [19609]
Medal Collectors of Am. [22745], c/o John W. Ad-
ams, Pres., 99 High St., 11th Fl., Boston, MA
02110
Medal of Honor Historical Soc. - Defunct.
Medal of Honor Legion [★20714]
Medal of Honor Soc; Congressional [20710]
Medal of Honor Soc; Ellis Island [19044]
Medal Soc; Token and [22763]
Medals Soc. of Am; Orders and [22631]
MEDASSET: Mediterranean Assn. to Save the Sea
Turtles - Greece [IO], Athens, Greece
MEDASSET: Mediterranean Assn. to Save the Sea
Turtles - United Kingdom [IO], London, United
Kingdom
Medau Movement [IO], Horsham, United Kingdom
Medecins en Faveur de l'Environnement [★IO]
Medecins du Monde UK [IO], London, United
Kingdom
Medecins Sans Frontieres [★IO]
Medecins Sans Frontieres [★IO]
Medecins Sans Frontieres [★IO]
Medecins Sans Frontieres [★12850]
Medecins Sans Frontieres - Australia [★IO]
Medecins Sans Frontieres - Hong Kong [IO], Hong
Kong, People's Republic of China
Medecins Sans Frontieres - UAE [IO], Abu Dhabi,
United Arab Emirates
Medecins Sans Frontieres - UK [IO], London, United
Kingdom
Medem Jewish Socialist Group - Defunct.
Media
  About-Face [13415]
  Acad. of Motion Picture Arts and Sciences [1374]
  Acad. of TV Arts and Sciences [542]
  Action Coalition for Media Educ. [18026]
  Advanced Media Workflow Assn. [3721]
  Africa-America Inst. [16919]
  Africa News Ser. [16921]
  AIIM - The Enterprise Content Mgt. Assn. [2095]
  Alliance of Area Bus. Publications [3199]
  Alliance for Community Media [17161]
  Alliance for a Media Literate Am. [8830]
  Amateur Movie Makers Assn. [22418]
  American-Arab Anti-Discrimination Comm. [17082]
  Amer. Assn. of Electronic Reporters and
    Transcribers [3180]
  Amer. Assn. of Independent News Distributors
    [3078]
  Amer. Bus. Media [3201]
  Amer. Cable Assn. [779]
  Amer. Commun. Assn. [6710]
  Amer. Coun. on Consumer Interests [17305]
  Amer. Court and Commercial Newspapers [3202]
  Amer. Family Assn. [17162]
  Amer. Guild of Court Videographers [6019]
  Amer. Horse Publications [3203]
  Amer. Jewish Press Assn. [3081]
  Amer. Lib. Assn. - Public Info. Off. [10897]
  Amer. News Women's Club [3083]
  Amer. Psychological Assn. - Media Psychology
    Div. [16131]
  Amer. Soc. of Bus. Publication Editors [3084]
  Amer. Soc. of Magazine Editors [3085]
  Amer. Soc. of Media Photographers [2992]
  Amer. Soc. of Newspaper Editors [3086]
  America's Angel [12140]
  Artists for Israel Intl. [9428]
  The Asia Found. [17005]
  Asian Amer. Journalists Assn. [3088]
  Asian CineVision [9930]
  Assoc. Church Press [3205]
  Assoc. Press [3089]
  Assoc. Press Managing Editors [3090]
  Assn. of Amer. Editorial Cartoonists [3092]
  Assn. for Applied Interactive Multimedia [2666]
  Assn. of Capitol Reporters and Editors [6181]
  Assn. of Commercial Stock Image Licensors
    [1378]
  Assn. of Food Journalists [3094]
  Assn. for Info. Media and Equip. [328]

  Assn. for Interactive Marketing [3734]
  Assn. for Media Literacy [IO]
  Assn. for Women in Sports Media [3097]
  Assn. of Young Journalists [3098]
  Baseball Writers Assn. of Am. [3099]
  Black Awareness in TV [17164]
  Blue-ray Disc Assn. [1207]
  Boating Writers Intl. [3100]
  Bowling Writers Assn. of Am. [3101]
  Cable Positive [11327]
  Cable and Telecommunications Human
    Resources Assn. [1980]
  Canadian Assn. of Media Educ. Organizations
    [IO]
  Catholic Press Assn. [3215]
  Caucus for TV Producers, Writers, and Directors
    [17165]
  Challenge Intl. [17415]
  Christian Media Assn. [20237]
  The Christian Sci. Publishing Soc. [3216]
  Citizens Communications Center Proj. of the Inst.
    for Public Representation [17171]
  City and Regional Magazine Assn. [3218]
  Coll. Media Advisers [8708]
  Comics Magazine Assn. of America [3219]
  Constr. Writers Assn. [3106]
  Coun. on Foreign Relations [17608]
  Coun. of Sci. Editors [3108]
  CrossRef [3220]
  Digital Cinema Soc. [1380]
  Digital Media Assn. of Alberta [IO]
  Digital Media Device Assn. [7303]
  Dog Writers' Assn. of Am. [3110]
  DVD Assn. [7304]
  EMS/Science Commun. Network [5032]
  European Multimedia Forum [IO]
  Fed. Without TV [18725]
  Foreign Press Assn. [3113]
  Found. for Amer. Communications [17177]
  Fulfillment Mgt. Assn. [3224]
  Game Audio Network Guild [1715]
  Global Action Proj. [18849]
  Global Alliance of Performers [10773]
  Gridiron Club of Washington, DC [3114]
  Hispanic Marketing and Commun. Assn. [2628]
  Hollywood Foreign Press Assn. [3115]
  Independent Free Papers of Am. [3226]
  Independent Media Arts Preservation [10454]
  Inst. for Public Accuracy [18456]
  Interaction Design Assn. [6863]
  Intl. Assn. of Audio Visual Communicators [1384]
  Intl. Assn. of Bus. Communicators [879]
  Intl. Assn. of Media Tie-in Writers [11176]
  Intl. Assn. of Obituarists [4062]
  Intl. Food, Wine and Travel Writers Assn. [3118]
  Intl. Motor Press Assn. [3120]
  Intl. Nanocasting Assn. [562]
  Intl. Newspaper Gp. [3121]
  Intl. Newspaper Marketing Assn. [3230]
  Intl. Pentecostal Press Assn. [3122]
  Intl. Press Inst., Amer. Comm. [3123]
  Intl. Soc. of Commun. Specialists [332]
  Intl. Soc. of Weekly Newspaper Editors [3125]
  Intl. Webcasting Assn. [2667]
  International Webcasting Association [IO]
  Internews Network [IO]
  Internews Network [18027]
  Investigative Reporters and Editors [3126]
  Jazz Journalists Assn. [3127]
  Just Think [18852]
  Law Enforcement and Emergency Services Video
    Assn. [6350]
  Livestock Publications Coun. [3233]
  Magazine Publishers of Am. [3235]
  Mainstream Media Proj. [18494]
  Markle Found. [6713]
  May I Speak Freely Media [18028]
  Media Access Gp. [12487]
  Media Access Proj. [17182]
  Media Action Network for Asian Americans
    [18029]
  Media Communications Assn. Intl. [1388]
  Media Credit Assn. [1432]
  Media Ecology Assn. [8831]
  Media Guilds Intl. [2668]

A star before a book entry number signifies that the name is not listed separately, but is mentioned within the entry.

Media Human Resources Assn. [2903]
The Media Inst. [17184]
Media in Ministry Assn. [20285]
Media Res. Center [12511]
MediaChannel.org [18030]
Mediascope [18031]
Military Reporters and Editors [6182]
Mobile Voter [18032]
MultiMediaCard Assn. [7305]
MultiMediaCard Assn. [IO]
Natl. Acad. of Sports [23831]
Natl. Agri-Marketing Assn. [2640]
Natl. Alliance for Media Arts and Culture [9580]
Natl. Assn. of Black Female Executives in Music
    and Entertainment [12117]
Natl. Assn. of Black Journalists [3129]
Natl. Assn. of Hispanic Journalists [3130]
Natl. Assn. of Latino Independent Producers
    [1390]
Natl. Assn. of Media Brokers [3322]
Natl. Assn. of Media and Tech. Centers [2669]
Natl. Assn. of Public Affairs Networks [17026]
Natl. Assn. of Regional Media Centers [7204]
Natl. Assn. of State Educational Media Profes-
    sionals [8568]
Natl. Assn. of Video Distributors [1391]
Natl. Club Indus. Assn. of Am. [1320]
Natl. Coalition Against Censorship [17042]
Natl. Conf. of Editorial Writers [3136]
Natl. Fed. of Hispanic Owned Newspapers [3240]
Natl. Fed. of Press Women [3137]
Natl. Geographic Soc. [7123]
Natl. Info. Officers Assn. [6231]
Natl. News Bur. [3139]
Natl. Newspaper Assn. [3140]
Natl. Newspaper Publishers Assn. [3241]
Natl. Press Club [3141]
Natl. Press Found. [3142]
Natl. Sportscasters and Sportswriters Assn.
    [3144]
Natl. Telemedia Coun. [9766]
Natl. Trade Circulation Found., Inc. [3242]
New Dimensions Radio [17738]
New Media Development Assn. [IO]
Newspaper Assn. of Am. [3244]
Newspaper Assn. Managers [3149]
The Newspaper Guild [24140]
Newswomen's Club of New York [3150]
North Amer. St. Newspaper Assn. [18102]
Org. of Asia Pacific News Agencies [IO]
Org. of News Ombudsmen [3152]
Other Minds [10684]
Overseas Press Club of Am. [3154]
Pacific Islanders in Communications [10455]
People's News Agency [3155]
PlanetRead [8796]
Printing, Publishing and Media Workers Sector of
    the CWA [24086]
Pro Players Assn. [13402]
Professional Hockey Writers' Assn. [3156]
Public Educ. Center [18398]
Public Media Center [17190]
Public Media Found. [18033]
Publishers Info. Bur. [128]
Radio Free Europe/Radio Liberty [17191]
Reader's Digest Assn. [3250]
Red Tag News Publications Assn. [2456]
Religion News Ser. [3158]
Religion Newswriters Assn. [3159]
ResearchChannel [7575]
Rhizome [9596]
SD Card Assn. [6743]
Set Decorators Soc. of Am. [2276]
Soc. for the Eradication of TV [17193]
Soc. of Motion Picture and TV Engineers [7044]
South African Freelancer's Assn. [IO]
Special Interest Gp. on Data Communications of
    the Assn. for Computing Machinery [6804]
Special Interest Gp. on Multimedia [6826]
Specialized Info. Publishers Assn. [3258]
Stop the Violence, Face The Music [13376]
Teachers Resisting Unhealthy Children's
    Entertainment [11657]
Telecommunications Res. and Action Center
    [17195]

Traffic Audit Bur. for Media Measurement [123]
Traffic Directors Guild of Am. [584]
Transworld Advt. Agency Network [124]
Travel Journalists Guild [3167]
Union for Democratic Communications [17196]
United Nations Correspondents Assn. [3168]
United Press Intl. [3169]
U.S. Marine Corps Combat Correspondents Assn.
    [3171]
U.S. Tour Operators Assn. [3943]
UNITY: Journalists of Color [3172]
We Interrupt This Message [18034]
White House Correspondents' Assn. [3173]
Women Leaders Online [18817]
World Bowling Writers [3175]
World Media Assn. [18035]
World Media Assn. [IO]
Young Media Australia [IO]
Media Access Gp. [12487], 125 Western Ave.,
    Boston, MA 02134, (617)300-3600
Media Access Proj. [17182], 1625 K St. NW, Ste.
    1000, Washington, DC 20006, (202)232-4300
Media; Accuracy in [17160]
Media Action Coalition - Defunct.
Media Action Network for Asian Americans [18029],
    PO Box 11105, Burbank, CA 91510, (213)486-
    4433
Media Action Res. Center - Defunct.
Media-Advertising Partnership for a Drug-Free Am.
    [★13272]
Media Advisers; Coll. [8708]
Media Alliance [17183], 1904 Franklin St., Ste. 500,
    Oakland, CA 94612, (510)832-9000
Media; Alliance for Community [17161]
Media; Amer. Bus. [3201]
Media Analysis Project - Defunct.
Media Arts Preservation; Independent [10454]
Media Associates Intl. [19981], 351 S Main Pl., Ste.
    230, Carol Stream, IL 60188-2455, (630)260-9063
Media Associates Intl. [IO], Carol Stream, IL, United
    States
Media Associates Res. Coalition - Address unknown
    since 2002.
Media; Assn. for Interactive [★3734]
Media Assn; Yellow Pages Integrated [★3261]
Media-Based Continuing Educ. for Engineers; Assn.
    for [8367]
Media Brokers; Natl. Assn. of [3322]
Media Center; Public [17190]
Media Centers; Consortium of Coll. and Univ. [8554]
Media Centers; Natl. Assn. of Regional [7204]
Media Coalition [★17126]
Media Coalition [17126], 275 Seventh Ave., Ste.
    1504, New York, NY 10003, (212)587-4025
Media Coalition/Americans for Constitutional
    Freedom [★17126]
Media Coalition; Gay and Lesbian [★9944]
Media Coalition; Natl. Hispanic [17187]
Media Commentary Coun. - Defunct.
Media Communications Assn. - Denmark [IO],
    Copenhagen, Denmark
Media Communications Assn. Intl. [IO], Madison, WI,
    United States
Media Communications Assn. Intl. [1388], c/o Susan
    M. Rees, Exec. Dir., 2810 Crossroads Dr., Ste.
    3800, Madison, WI 53718, (608)443-2464
Media Coun; Natl. Tele [9766]
Media Credit Assn. [1432]
Media Credit Executives Assn; Advt. [1397]
Media Ecology Assn. [8831], c/o Stephanie Bennett,
    PhD, Dir. of Commun., Palm Beach Atlantic
    University, Gregory Hall 457, West Palm Beach,
    FL 33401, (561)803-2617
Media and Educational Technology Unit of the Amer.
    Assn. for Adult and Continuing Education -
    Defunct.
Media, Entertainment and Arts Alliance [IO],
    Strawberry Hills, Australia
Media and Entertainment; Fellowship of Christians in
    the Arts, [★20024]
Media and Equip; Assn. for Info. [328]
Media Executives; Natl. Assn. of Minority [882]
Media Fellowship Intl. [20024], PO Box 82685, Ken-
    more, WA 98028, (425)488-3965
Media Fellowship Intl. [IO], Kenmore, WA, United
    States

Media Forum - Address unknown since 1991.
Media Found; Intl. Women's [4043]
Media Fund for Human Rights - Address unknown
    since 1995.
Media Guilds Intl. [2668], 10020 Benjamin Nicholas
    Pl., No. 103, Las Vegas, NV 89144, (702)255-1179
Media Human Resources Assn. [2903], c/o Soc. for
    Human Rsrc. Mgt., 1800 Duke St., Alexandria, VA
    22314, (703)548-3440
Media Human Resources Assn. [IO], Alexandria, VA,
    United States
The Media Inst. [17184], 2300 Clarendon Blvd., Ste.
    503, Arlington, VA 22201, (703)243-5700
Media Inst. of Southern Africa - Namibia [IO], Wind-
    hoek, Namibia
Media Inst. of Southern Africa - South Africa [IO],
    Johannesburg, Republic of South Africa
Media Inst. of Southern Africa - Swaziland [IO],
    Mbabane, Swaziland
Media Inst. of Southern Africa - Tanzania [IO], Dar
    es Salaam, United Republic of Tanzania
Media Inst. of Southern Africa - Zambia [IO],
    Lusaka, Zambia
Media Law Rsrc. Center [6045], North Tower, 20th
    Fl., 520 Eight Ave., New York, NY 10018,
    (212)337-0200
Media; Leadership Coun. for Mental Hea., Justice
    and the [★12031]
Media Mgt. Assn; Communications [329]
Media Manufacturers and Related Indus; ITA - Intl.
    Assn. of Magnetic and Optical [★1370]
Media Measurement; Traffic Audit Bur. for [123]
Media in Ministry Assn. [20285], c/o Gene Blanken-
    ship, 2549 Newbolt Dr., Orlando, FL 32817,
    (407)678-0159
Media; Morality in [18373]
Media Network - Defunct.
Media; Natl. Info. Center for Educational [8569]
Media Photographers; Amer. Soc. of [2992]
Media Producers; Assn. of [★331]
Media Professionals; Natl. Assn. of State
    Educational [8568]
Media Proj; Advocates for Youth's [12174]
Media and Public Affairs; Center for [17169]
Media Rating Coun. [566], 370 Lexington Ave., Ste.
    902, New York, NY 10017, (212)972-0300
Media Res. Center [12511], 325 S Patrick St.,
    Alexandria, VA 22314-3580, (703)683-9733
Media Res. Directors Assn. - Address unknown
    since 2001.
Media Rsrc. Ser. [7202], PO Box 13975, Research
    Triangle Park, NC 27709, (919)547-5259
Media; Special Interest Gp. on Multi [6826]
Media Supervisors Assn; State School Lib. [★8568]
Media; Task Force on Using Mass [★8565]
Media Technicians; Coun. on Library- [8783]
Media Watch [17185], PO Box 618, Santa Cruz, CA
    95061-0618, (831)423-6355
Media Watch [IO], Santa Cruz, CA, United States
Media; Willow Mixed [17199]
Media Workers Sector of the CWA; Printing, Publish-
    ing and [24086]
MediaChannel.org [18030], 575 8th Ave., New York,
    NY 10018, (212)246-0202
MEDIACULT Intl. Inst. for Audio-Visual Commun.
    and Cultural Development [★IO]
Median Iris Soc. [22525], c/o Ann Henson, Sec.,
    6401 Cedar Rd., Iuka, IL 62849-2815, (618)822-
    6584
Mediascope [18031]
Mediation Assn; Professional [5462]
Mediation Canada; Family [IO]
Mediation; Center for Medical Ethics and [5452]
Mediation; Child Abuse Listening and [11565]
Mediation and Conflict Resolution; Inst. for [5455]
Mediation Educ; Natl. Center for [5461]
Mediation League; Bible [★19512]
Mediation; Natl. Assn. for Community [5460]
Mediation, and Peacemaking; Training Inst. for
    Conflict Resolution, [★8139]
Mediators; Acad. of Family [★5450]
Mediators Inst. Ireland [IO], Dublin, Ireland
Mediators Without Borders [5458], 1807 Jancey St.,
    Pittsburgh, PA 15206-1065, (412)441-1151
Mediawatch - UK [IO], Ashford, United Kingdom

Reference to "IO" in place of a book number signifies that the association may be found in the 45th edition of International Organizations.

Medicaid Directors; Natl. Assn. of State [14692]
Medicaid/SCHIP Dental Assn. [14168], 212 Huerta
    Pl., Davis, CA 95616, (916)464-3794
Medical
    A-T Medical Res. Found. [14436]
    Academic Orthopaedic Soc. [15750]
    Acad. of Ambulatory Foot and Ankle Surgery
        [16023]
    Acad. of Dental Materials [14084]
    Acad. of Dentistry Intl. [14085]
    Acad. of Gen. Dentistry [14086]
    Acad. for Implants and Transplants [14087]
    Acad. of Managed Care Providers [14677]
    Acad. on Mental Retardation [15238]
    Acad. of Operative Dentistry [14089]
    Acad. of Oral Dynamics [14090]
    Acad. of Pharmaceutical Res. and Sci. [15906]
    Acad. of Scientific Hypnotherapy [14913]
    AcademyHealth [14535]
    Accelerated Cure Proj. for Multiple Sclerosis
        [15301]
    Accreditation Assn. for Ambulatory Hea. Care
        [13661]
    Accreditation Commn. for Acupuncture and
        Oriental Medicine [15739]
    Accreditation Coun. on Optometric Educ. [15710]
    Accreditation Coun. for Pharmacy Educ. [15907]
    Accreditation Rev. Commn. on Educ. for the
        Physician Asst. [15972]
    Accreditation Rev. Comm. on Educ. in Surgical
        Tech. [15123]
    Acoustic Neuroma Assn. [15816]
    Action on Smoking and Hea. [16431]
    Acupuncturists Without Borders [13536]
    Acute Long Term Hosp. Assn. [14852]
    Adolescent Scoliosis Soc. of North Am. [16392]
    Adult Congenital Heart Assn. [13884]
    Advocate Hea. Care [14821]
    Advocates for the Amer. Osteopathic Assn.
        [15789]
    Aerospace Medical Assn. [13538]
    Aesculapian Club [15982]
    African Medical and Res. Found. [14971]
    AFT Healthcare [24087]
    Aicardi Syndrome Newsl. [14437]
    Aid for AIDS [13547]
    Aid for Intl. Medicine [14972]
    AIDS Clinical Trials Gp. [13549]
    AIDS, Medicine and Miracles [13551]
    Air Charity Network [14312]
    Air and Surface Transport Nurses Assn. [15427]
    Airlines Medical Directors Assn. [13539]
    Albinism World Alliance [15242]
    Alcor Life Extension Found. [14072]
    Allergy and Asthma Network Mothers of Asthmat-
        ics [16352]
    Alliance for Academic Internal Medicine [8586]
    Alliance for Advancing Nonprofit Hea. Care
        [14606]
    Alliance of Cardiovascular Professionals [13885]
    Alliance for Childhood Cancer [13787]
    Alliance for Lupus Res. [15013]
    Alliance for Microbicide Development [13555]
    Alliance of Minority Medical Associations [14607]
    Alliance for the Prudent Use of Antibiotics [15908]
    Alpha Epsilon Delta [24541]
    Alpha Omega Alpha Honor Medical Soc. [24542]
    Alpha Tau Delta [24559]
    Alpha Zeta Omega [24567]
    ALSAC/Saint Jude Children's Res. Hosp. [13946]
    Alumni Assn. of the Universidad del Valle [18872]
    Ambulatory Pediatric Assn. [15879]
    Amer. Acad. of Allergy, Asthma and Immunology
        [13592]
    Amer. Acad. of Alternative Medicine [13612]
    Amer. Acad. of Ambulatory Care Nursing [15428]
    Amer. Acad. for Cerebral Palsy and
        Developmental Medicine [13934]
    Amer. Acad. of Clinical Psychiatrists [16064]
    Amer. Acad. of Clinical Toxicology [16657]
    Amer. Acad. of Cosmetic Surgery [14037]
    Amer. Acad. of Craniofacial Pain [15751]
    Amer. Acad. of Dental Gp. Practice [14094]
    Amer. Acad. of Dental Practice Admin. [14095]
    Amer. Acad. of Dermatology [14189]

Amer. Acad. of Disability Evaluating Physicians
    [14033]
Amer. Acad. of Environmental Medicine [14360]
Amer. Acad. of Esthetic Dentistry [14096]
Amer. Acad. of Facial Plastic and Reconstructive
    Surgery [14038]
Amer. Acad. of Family Physicians [14383]
Amer. Acad. of Fixed Prosthodontics [14097]
Amer. Acad. of Gnathologic Orthopedics [14098]
Amer. Acad. of the History of Dentistry [14100]
Amer. Acad. of HIV Medicine [13556]
Amer. Acad. of Implant Dentistry [14101]
Amer. Acad. of Medical Administrators [15045]
Amer. Acad. of Medical Administrators Res. and
    Educational Found. [15046]
Amer. Acad. of Medical Hypnoanalysts [14914]
Amer. Acad. of Neurological and Orthopaedic
    Surgeons [15409]
Amer. Acad. of Neurology [15376]
Amer. Acad. of Nurse Practitioners [15429]
Amer. Acad. of Nursing [15430]
Amer. Acad. of Ophthalmology [15656]
Amer. Acad. of Optometry [15711]
Amer. Acad. of Oral and Maxillofacial Pathology
    [15852]
Amer. Acad. of Oral and Maxillofacial Radiology
    [14104]
Amer. Acad. of Oral Medicine [14105]
Amer. Acad. of Orofacial Pain [14106]
Amer. Acad. of Orthodontics for the Gen.
    Practitioner [14107]
Amer. Acad. of Orthopaedic Surgeons [15752]
Amer. Acad. of Orthotists and Prosthetists [15782]
Amer. Acad. of Osteopathy [15790]
Amer. Acad. of Otolaryngic Allergy and Found.
    [13593]
Amer. Acad. of Otolaryngology - Head and Neck
    Surgery [15817]
Amer. Acad. of Pediatric Dentistry [14108]
Amer. Acad. of Pediatrics [15880]
Amer. Acad. of Periodontology [14109]
Amer. Acad. of Physical Medicine and Rehabilita-
    tion [16307]
Amer. Acad. of Physician Assistants [15973]
Amer. Acad. of Restorative Dentistry [14110]
Amer. Acad. of Sleep Medicine [16418]
Amer. Acad. of Somnology [16419]
Amer. Acad. of Tropical Medicine [16692]
Amer. Acad. of Veterinary and Comparative
    Toxicology [16736]
Amer. Acad. of Veterinary Pharmacology and
    Therapeutics [16738]
Amer. Acupuncture Assn. [15741]
Amer. Aging Assn. [14507]
Amer. Alliance for Medical Cannabis [15020]
Amer. Ambulance Assn. [14313]
Amer. Animal Hosp. Assn. [16739]
Amer. Assembly for Men in Nursing [15431]
Amer. Assn. for Accreditation of Ambulatory
    Surgery Facilities [16557]
Amer. Assn. of Ambulatory Surgery Centers
    [16558]
Amer. Assn. of Avian Pathologists [16740]
Amer. Assn. of Bioanalysts Bd. of Registry
    [15126]
Amer. Assn. of Birth Centers [15580]
Amer. Assn. of Blood Banks [13761]
Amer. Assn. for Bovine Practitioners [16741]
Amer. Assn. for Cancer Educ. [13789]
Amer. Assn. of Cardiovascular and Pulmonary
    Rehabilitation [13886]
Amer. Assn. of Certified Allergists [13594]
Amer. Assn. of Chairs of Departments of
    Psychiatry [16065]
Amer. Assn. for Clinical Chemistry [13936]
Amer. Assn. of Clinical Endocrinologists [14350]
Amer. Assn. of Colleges of Osteopathic Medicine
    [15791]
Amer. Assn. of Colleges of Pharmacy [15909]
Amer. Assn. of Colleges of Podiatric Medicine
    [16025]
Amer. Assn. of Critical-Care Nurses [15433]
Amer. Assn. of Dental Examiners [14112]
Amer. Assn. for Dental Res. [14113]
Amer. Assn. of Diabetes Educators [14217]

Amer. Assn. of Endodontists [14114]
Amer. Assn. of Equine Veterinary Technicians
    [16743]
Amer. Assn. of Eye and Ear Hospitals [14859]
Amer. Assn. for Functional Orthodontics [14115]
Amer. Assn. of Genito-Urinary Surgeons [16699]
Amer. Assn. of Gynecologic Laparoscopists
    [15581]
Amer. Assn. for Hand Surgery [14522]
Amer. Assn. on Hea. and Disability [14235]
Amer. Assn. for Hea. Educ. [16234]
Amer. Assn. of Heart Failure Nurses [15434]
Amer. Assn. for Homecare [14670]
Amer. Assn. of Hosp. Dentists [14116]
Amer. Assn. of Hosp. Podiatrists [16026]
Amer. Assn. of Human-Animal Bond Veterinarians
    [13702]
Amer. Assn. of Immunologists [14929]
Amer. Assn. of Integrated Healthcare Delivery
    Systems [15048]
Amer. Assn. on Intellectual and Developmental
    Disabilities [15239]
Amer. Assn. of Kidney Patients [15283]
Amer. Assn. of Legal Nurse Consultants [14999]
Amer. Assn. of Managed Care Nurses [15435]
Amer. Assn. of Medical Assistants [15081]
Amer. Assn. of Medical Audit Specialists [15049]
Amer. Assn. for Medical Chronobiology and Chro-
    notherapeutics [13751]
Amer. Assn. of Medical Milk Commissions [16384]
Amer. Assn. of Medical Soc. Executives [15153]
Amer. Assn. of Mental Hea. Professionals in Cor-
    rections [15186]
Amer. Assn. of Neurological Surgeons [15410]
Amer. Assn. of Neuromuscular and Electrodiag-
    nostic Medicine [15303]
Amer. Assn. of Neuropathologists [15853]
Amer. Assn. of Neuroscience Nurses [15436]
Amer. Assn. of Nurse Anesthetists [15437]
Amer. Assn. of Nurse Attorneys [15000]
Amer. Assn. of Nurse Life Care Planners [15438]
Amer. Assn. of Nutritional Consultants [15540]
Amer. Assn. of Occupational Hea. Nurses [15439]
Amer. Assn. of Off. Nurses [15440]
Amer. Assn. for Ophthalmic Standardized Echog-
    raphy [15659]
Amer. Assn. of Oral and Maxillofacial Surgeons
    [15732]
Amer. Assn. of Oriental Medicine [15742]
Amer. Assn. of Orthodontists [14117]
Amer. Assn. of Orthopedic Medicine [15753]
Amer. Assn. of Pathologists' Assistants [15854]
Amer. Assn. for Pediatric Ophthalmology and
    Strabismus [15660]
Amer. Assn. of Physician Offices and Labs.
    [14990]
Amer. Assn. of Physician Specialists [15792]
Amer. Assn. of Plastic Surgeons [14040]
Amer. Assn. of Poison Control Centers [16658]
Amer. Assn. of Preferred Provider Organizations
    [14680]
Amer. Assn. of Professional Hypnotherapists
    [14915]
Amer. Assn. of Psychiatric Administrators [14861]
Amer. Assn. of Public Hea. Dentistry [14118]
Amer. Assn. of Public Hea. Veterinarians [16747]
Amer. Assn. for Respiratory Care [16599]
Amer. Assn. of Retired Veterinarians [16748]
Amer. Assn. of Small Ruminant Practitioners
    [16749]
Amer. Assn. of Spinal Cord Injury Nurses [15441]
Amer. Assn. of Spinal Cord Injury Psychologists
    and Social Workers [16459]
Amer. Assn. for the Stud. of Liver Diseases
    [14801]
Amer. Assn. for the Surgery of Trauma [16687]
Amer. Assn. of Swine Veterinarians [16750]
Amer. Assn. for Thoracic Surgery [16640]
Amer. Assn. of Tissue Banks [16663]
Amer. Assn. of Veterinary Lab. Diagnosticians
    [16753]
Amer. Assn. of Veterinary Parasitologists [16754]
Amer. Assn. of Veterinary State Boards [16755]
Amer. Assn. of Wildlife Veterinarians [16756]
Amer. Assn. of Women Dentists [14119]

A star before a book entry number signifies that the name is not listed separately, but is mentioned within the entry.

Amer. Assn. of Zoo Veterinarians [16757]
Amer. Athletic Trainers Assn. and Certification Bd. [23953]
Amer. Autonomic Soc. [15406]
Amer. Behcet's Disease Assn. [13746]
Amer. Bd. of Abdominal Surgery [16561]
Amer. Bd. of Anesthesiology [13671]
Amer. Bd. of Cardiovascular Perfusion [13887]
American Bd. of Clinical Metal Toxicology [16659]
Amer. Bd. of Colon and Rectal Surgery [16059]
Amer. Bd. of Dental Public Hea. [14120]
Amer. Bd. of Dermatology [14190]
Amer. Bd. of Emergency Medicine [14325]
Amer. Bd. of Endodontics [14121]
Amer. Bd. of Family Dentistry [14122]
Amer. Bd. of Genetic Counseling [14492]
Amer. Bd. of Indus. Hygiene [15623]
Amer. Bd. of Internal Medicine [14965]
Amer. Bd. of Medical Psychotherapists and Psy-chodiagnosticians [16202]
Amer. Bd. of Medical Specialties [15117]
Amer. Bd. of Neurological Surgery [15411]
Amer. Bd. of Nuclear Medicine [15419]
Amer. Bd. of Nutrition [15541]
Amer. Bd. of Obstetrics and Gynecology [15582]
Amer. Bd. for Occupational Hea. Nurses [15445]
Amer. Bd. of Ophthalmology [15661]
Amer. Bd. of Opticianry [15704]
Amer. Bd. of Oral and Maxillofacial Pathology [15855]
Amer. Bd. of Oral and Maxillofacial Surgery [15733]
Amer. Bd. of Orthodontics [14124]
Amer. Bd. of Orthopaedic Surgery [15755]
Amer. Bd. of Otolaryngology [15818]
Amer. Bd. of Pathology [15856]
Amer. Bd. of Pediatrics [15881]
Amer. Bd. of Periodontology [14125]
Amer. Bd. of Physical Medicine and Rehabilitation [16309]
Amer. Bd. of Plastic Surgery [14041]
Amer. Bd. of Podiatric Orthopedics and Primary Podiatric Medicine [16030]
Amer. Bd. of Podiatric Surgery [16031]
Amer. Bd. of Preventive Medicine [16050]
Amer. Bd. of Prosthodontics [14126]
Amer. Bd. of Psychological Hypnosis [14917]
Amer. Bd. of Quality Assurance and Utilization Rev. Physicians [16260]
Amer. Bd. of Radiology [16272]
Amer. Bd. of Surgery [16563]
Amer. Bd. of Thoracic Surgery [16641]
Amer. Bd. of Urology [16700]
Amer. Bd. of Veterinary Specialties [16759]
Amer. Bd. of Veterinary Toxicology [16760]
Amer. Broncho-Esophagological Assn. [13778]
Amer. Burn Assn. [13781]
Amer. Case Mgt. Assn. [15051]
Amer. Celiac Society/Dietary Support Coalition [15543]
Amer. Central European Dental Inst. [14127]
Amer. Chiropractic Assn. [13988]
Amer. Chiropractic Registry of Radiologic Technologists [16273]
Amer. Chronic Pain Assn. [15834]
Amer. Cleft Palate-Craniofacial Assn. [14055]
Amer. Clinical and Climatological Assn. [14018]
Amer. Clinical Lab. Assn. [14991]
Amer. Clinical Neurophysiology Soc. [14306]
Amer. Coll. for Advancement in Medicine [16051]
Amer. Coll. of Allergy, Asthma and Immunology [13596]
Amer. Coll. of Angiology [16719]
Amer. Coll. of Apothecaries [15912]
Amer. Coll. of Cardiology [13888]
Amer. Coll. of Cardiovascular Administrators [15052]
Amer. Coll. of Chest Physicians [13889]
Amer. Coll. of Clinical Pharmacology [15913]
Amer. Coll. of Clinical Pharmacy [15914]
Amer. Coll. of Dentists [14128]
Amer. Coll. of Domiciliary Midwives [15583]
Amer. Coll. of Emergency Physicians [14326]
Amer. Coll. of Epidemiology [14373]
Amer. Coll. of Foot and Ankle Orthopedics and Medicine [16032]

Amer. Coll. of Foot and Ankle Pediatrics [16033]
Amer. Coll. of Foot and Ankle Surgeons [16034]
Amer. Coll. of Gastroenterology [14405]
Amer. Coll. Hea. Assn. [14714]
Amer. Coll. of Hea. Care Administrators [15535]
Amer. Coll. of Hea. Plan Mgt. [15053]
Amer. Coll. of Healthcare Executives [14862]
Amer. Coll. of Intl. Physicians [14973]
Amer. Coll. of Legal Medicine [15001]
Amer. Coll. of Medical Genetics [14494]
Amer. Coll. of Medical Practice Executives [15054]
Amer. Coll. of Medical Quality [16261]
Amer. Coll. of Medical Toxicology [16660]
Amer. Coll. of Mohs Micrographic Surgery and Cutaneous Oncology [15636]
Amer. Coll. of Neuropsychopharmacology [15915]
Amer. Coll. of Nuclear Medicine [15421]
Amer. Coll. of Nuclear Physicians [15422]
Amer. Coll. of Nurse-Midwives [15447]
Amer. Coll. of Nutrition [15544]
Amer. Coll. of Obstetricians and Gynecologists [15584]
Amer. Coll. of Occupational and Environmental Medicine [15624]
Amer. Coll. of Oral and Maxillofacial Surgeons [15734]
Amer. Coll. of Orgonomy [15738]
Amer. Coll. of Osteopathic Emergency Physicians [14327]
Amer. Coll. of Osteopathic Family Physicians [15793]
Amer. Coll. of Osteopathic Internists [15794]
Amer. Coll. of Osteopathic Obstetricians and Gynecologists [15585]
Amer. Coll. of Osteopathic Pediatricians [15795]
Amer. Coll. of Osteopathic Surgeons [15797]
Amer. Coll. of Physician Executives [15056]
Amer. Coll. of Physicians-American Soc. of Internal Medicine [14966]
Amer. Coll. of Preventive Medicine [16052]
Amer. Coll. of Prosthodontists [14129]
Amer. Coll. of Radiation Oncology [16267]
Amer. Coll. of Radiology [16274]
Amer. Coll. of Rheumatology [16367]
Amer. Coll. of Surgeons [16565]
Amer. Coll. of Theriogenologists [16763]
Amer. Coll. of Veterinary Anesthesiologists [16764]
Amer. Coll. of Veterinary Dermatology [16765]
Amer. Coll. of Veterinary Internal Medicine [16767]
Amer. Coll. of Veterinary Ophthalmologists [16768]
Amer. Coll. of Veterinary Pathologists [16769]
Amer. Coll. of Veterinary Radiology [16770]
Amer. Coll. of Veterinary Surgeons [16771]
Amer. Conf. of Governmental Indus. Hygienists [15625]
Amer. Cong. of Rehabilitation Medicine [16310]
Amer. Correctional Hea. Services Assn. [14715]
Amer. Coun. of Applied Clinical Nutrition [15545]
Amer. Coun. of Hypnotist Examiners [14918]
Amer. Coun. on Sci. and Hea. [14539]
Amer. Cryonics Soc. [14073]
Amer. Dental Assistants Assn. [14130]
Amer. Dental Assn. [14131]
Amer. Dental Hygienists' Assn. [14132]
Amer. Dental Soc. of Anesthesiology [14133]
Amer. Diabetes Assn. [14218]
Amer. Dietetic Assn. [15546]
Amer. Electrology Assn. [14308]
Amer. Endodontic Soc. [14134]
Amer. Epilepsy Soc. [14379]
Amer. Equilibration Soc. [14135]
Amer. Fed. for Aging Res. [14508]
Amer. Fed. for Medical Res. [14019]
Amer. Found. for Aging Res. [14509]
Amer. Found. for AIDS Res. [13557]
Amer. Found. for Maternal and Child Health [15586]
Amer. Found. for Pharmaceutical Educ. [15916]
Amer. Found. for the Prevention of Venereal Disease [16409]
Amer. Fracture Assn. [15756]

Amer. Gastroenterological Assn. [14406]
Amer. Geriatrics Soc. [14510]
Amer. Guild of Hypnotherapists [14919]
Amer. Gynecological and Obstetrical Soc. [15587]
Amer. Hair Loss Assn. [14519]
Amer. Head and Neck Soc. [15819]
Amer. Headache Soc. [14531]
Amer. Hea. Assistance Found. [15100]
Amer. Hea. Care Assn. [14540]
Amer. Hea. Decisions [14541]
Amer. Hea. Info. Mgt. Assn. [15097]
Amer. Hea. Planning Assn. [14542]
Amer. Healthcare Radiology Administrators [16275]
Amer. Heartworm Soc. [16772]
Amer. Herbalists Guild [14817]
Amer. Holistic Nurses' Assn. [14825]
Amer. Holistic Veterinary Medical Assn. [16773]
Amer. Horticultural Therapy Assn. [16601]
Amer. Industrial Health Coun. [15626]
Amer. Indus. Hygiene Assn. [15627]
Amer. Inst. of the History of Pharmacy [15917]
Amer. Inst. of Homeopathy [14845]
Amer. Inst. of Medical Ethics [12122]
Amer. Inst. of Oral Biology [14137]
Amer. Inst. for Preventive Medicine [16053]
Amer. Inst. of Stress [16487]
American Institute for Teen AIDS Prevention [13558]
Amer. Inst. of Ultrasound in Medicine [16436]
Amer. Integrative Medical Assn. [15034]
Amer. Juvenile Arthritis Org. [16368]
Amer. Kidney Fund [15284]
Amer. Kinesiotherapy Assn. [16311]
Amer. Laryngological, Rhinological and Otological Soc. [15821]
Amer. Latex Allergy Assn. [13597]
Amer. Licensed Practical Nurses Assn. [15450]
Amer. Liver Found. [14803]
Amer. Lung Assn. [16354]
Amer. Lyme Disease Found. [14249]
Amer. Manual Medicine Assn. [13618]
Amer. Massage Therapy Assn. [15022]
Amer. Medical Assn. [15155]
Amer. Medical Assn. Alliance [15156]
Amer. Medical Athletic Assn. [23650]
Amer. Medical Directors Assn. [15536]
Amer. Medical Gp. Assn. [14717]
Amer. Medical Informatics Assn. [14079]
Amer. Medical Rehabilitation Providers Assn. [16312]
Amer. Medical Technologists [15127]
Amer. Medical Tennis Assn. [23898]
Amer. Medical Women's Assn. [14696]
Amer. Medical Writers Assn. [3082]
Amer. Mental Hea. Alliance [15188]
Amer. Mental Hea. Counselors Assn. [15189]
Amer. Naprapathic Assn. [15276]
Amer. Nephrology Nurses' Assn. [15286]
Amer. Neuroendocrine Soc. [15035]
Amer. Nurses Assn. [15451]
Amer. Nurses Found. [15452]
Amer. Occupational Therapy Assn. [16602]
Amer. Ophthalmological Soc. [15662]
Amer. Optometric Assn. [15712]
Amer. Optometric Found. [15713]
Amer. Optometric Student Assn. [15714]
Amer. Organ Transplant Assn. [16664]
Amer. Org. for Bodywork Therapies of Asia [15024]
Amer. Org. of Nurse Executives [15454]
Amer. Orthodontic Soc. [14138]
Amer. Orthopaedic Assn. [15757]
Amer. Orthopaedic Foot and Ankle Soc. [15758]
Amer. Orthoptic Coun. [15663]
Amer. Osler Soc. [15157]
Amer. Osteopathic Acad. of Orthopedics [15759]
Amer. Osteopathic Assn. [15798]
Amer. Osteopathic Bd. of Emergency Medicine [14328]
Amer. Osteopathic Bd. of Family Physicians [15799]
Amer. Osteopathic Bd. of Pediatrics [15800]
Amer. Osteopathic Coll. of Anesthesiologists [13672]

Reference to "IO" in place of a book number signifies that the association may be found in the 45th edition of International Organizations.

Amer. Osteopathic Coll. of Dermatology [14194]

Amer. Osteopathic Coll. of Occupational and Preventive Medicine [15802]

Amer. Osteopathic Coll. of Physical Medicine and Rehabilitation [15805]

Amer. Osteopathic Coll. of Radiology [16276]

Amer. Osteopathic Colleges of Ophthalmology and Otolaryngology-Head and Neck Surgery [15664]

Amer. Osteopathic Found. [15806]

Amer. Otological Soc. [15822]

Amer. Pain Soc. [15836]

Amer. Paraplegia Soc. [16460]

Amer. Parkinson Disease Assn. [15304]

Amer. Partnership for Eosinophilic Disorders [14408]

Amer. Pathology Found. [15857]

Amer. Pediatric Soc. [15882]

Amer. Pharmacists Assn. - Acad. of Pharmacy Practice and Mgt. [15918]

Amer. Pharmacists Assn. Acad. of Student Pharmacists [15919]

Amer. Physical Therapy Assn. [16603]

Amer. Physicians Fellowship for Medicine in Israel [12456]

Amer. Podiatric Circulatory Soc. [16036]

Amer. Podiatric Medical Assn. [16037]

Amer. Podiatric Medical Students' Assn. [16038]

Amer. Podiatric Medical Writers Assn. [16039]

Amer. Porphyria Found. [15243]

Amer. Pre-Veterinary Medical Assn. [16774]

Amer. Prostate Soc. [16701]

Amer. Prosthodontic Soc. [14139]

Amer. Psychosocial Oncology Soc. [15638]

Amer. Public Hea. Assn. [16236]

Amer. Radiological Nurses Assn. [15457]

Amer. Radium Soc. [15639]

Amer. Registry of Diagnostic Medical Sonography [16437]

Amer. Registry of Medical Assistants [15082]

Amer. Registry of Pathology [15858]

Amer. Registry of Radiologic Technologists [15128]

Amer. Rehabilitation Counseling Assn. [16313]

Amer. Rehabilitation Economics Assn. [16314]

Amer. Rhinologic Soc. [15823]

Amer. Roentgen Ray Soc. [16277]

Amer. Running Assn. [23651]

Amer. School Hea. Assn. [14718]

Amer. Sepsis Alliance [14946]

Amer. Social Hea. Assn. [16410]

Amer. Soc. of Abdominal Surgeons [16568]

Amer. Soc. for the Advancement of Pharmacotherapy [16134]

Amer. Soc. for Aesthetic Plastic Surgery [14042]

Amer. Soc. of Anesthesiologists [13674]

Amer. Soc. for Apheresis [13706]

Amer. Soc. of Bariatric Physicians [15575]

Amer. Soc. for Bone and Mineral Res. [15787]

Amer. Soc. of Breast Disease [13772]

Amer. Soc. of Breast Surgeons [16570]

Amer. Soc. of Cataract and Refractive Surgery [15665]

Amer. Soc. of Childbirth Educators [15589]

Amer. Soc. of Clinical Hypnosis [14921]

Amer. Soc. of Clinical Hypnosis - Educ. and Res. Found. [14922]

Amer. Soc. for Clinical Investigation [14020]

Amer. Soc. for Clinical Lab. Sci. [14992]

Amer. Soc. for Clinical Nutrition [15547]

Amer. Soc. for Clinical Oncology [15640]

Amer. Soc. for Clinical Pathology [15859]

Amer. Soc. for Clinical Pharmacology and Therapeutics [15920]

Amer. Soc. of Colon and Rectal Surgeons [16060]

Amer. Soc. for Colposcopy and Cervical Pathology [15590]

Amer. Soc. of Consultant Pharmacists [15922]

Amer. Soc. of Contemporary Medicine, Surgery, and Ophthalmology [15666]

Amer. Soc. of Cytopathology [14075]

Amer. Soc. of Cytotechnology [14076]

Amer. Soc. for Dental Aesthetics [14140]

Amer. Soc. for Dermatologic Surgery [14196]

Amer. Soc. of Echocardiography [13891]

Amer. Soc. of Electroneurodiagnostic Technologists [14307]

Amer. Soc. of Extra-Corporeal Tech. [15129]

Amer. Soc. of Forensic Odontology [14142]

Amer. Soc. for Gastrointestinal Endoscopy [14409]

Amer. Soc. of Hand Therapists [14524]

Amer. Soc. of Hea. Sys. Pharmacists [15923]

Amer. Soc. for Healthcare Central Ser. Professionals [14864]

Amer. Soc. for Healthcare Engg. of the Amer. Hosp. Assn. [14865]

Amer. Soc. for Healthcare Environmental Services of the Amer. Hosp. Assn. [14866]

Amer. Soc. for Healthcare Food Ser. Administrators [14867]

Amer. Soc. for Healthcare Risk Mgt. [14869]

Amer. Soc. of Hematology [14783]

Amer. Soc. for Histocompatibility and Immunogenetics [14931]

Amer. Soc. of Interventional Pain Physicians [15837]

Amer. Soc. of Interventional and Therapeutic Neuroradiology [16280]

Amer. Soc. for Investigative Pathology [15860]

Amer. Soc. for Laser Medicine and Surgery [14997]

Amer. Soc. of Law, Medicine and Ethics [15002]

Amer. Soc. of Lipo-Suction Surgery [16572]

Amer. Soc. of Master Dental Technologists [14143]

Amer. Soc. of Maxillofacial Surgeons [15735]

Amer. Soc. for Mohs Histotechnology [15130]

Amer. Soc. for Mohs Surgery [15641]

Amer. Soc. of Nephrology [15288]

Amer. Soc. for Neural Transplantation and Repair [15380]

Amer. Soc. of Neuroimaging [16281]

Amer. Soc. of Neurophysiological Monitoring [15381]

Amer. Soc. of Neuroradiology [16282]

Amer. Soc. for Nutrition [15548]

Amer. Soc. of Ophthalmic Registered Nurses [15458]

Amer. Soc. for Ophthalmic Ultrasonography [15667]

Amer. Soc. of Pain Educators [15838]

Amer. Soc. for Parenteral and Enteral Nutrition [15549]

Amer. Soc. of Pharmacognosy [15924]

Amer. Soc. for Pharmacology and Experimental Therapeutics [15925]

Amer. Soc. for Pharmacy Law [15003]

Amer. Soc. of Plastic Surgeons and Plastic Surgery Educ. Found. [14045]

Amer. Soc. of Plastic Surgical Nurses [15461]

Amer. Soc. of Podiatric Medical Assistants [16040]

Amer. Soc. of Radiologic Technologists [15131]

Amer. Soc. for Reconstructive Microsurgery [16573]

Amer. Soc. of Regional Anesthesia and Pain Medicine [13676]

Amer. Soc. for Reproductive Medicine [14389]

Amer. Soc. for Stereotactic and Functional Neurosurgery [15412]

Amer. Soc. for the Stud. of Orthodontics [14144]

Amer. Soc. for Surgery of the Hand [14525]

Amer. Soc. for Therapeutic Radiology and Oncology [16285]

Amer. Soc. of Transplant Surgeons [16667]

Amer. Soc. of Tropical Medicine and Hygiene [16693]

Amer. Soc. of Veterinary Ophthalmology [16775]

Amer. Spinal Injury Assn. [16461]

Amer. Sudden Infant Death Syndrome Inst. [16523]

Amer. Surgical Assn. [16575]

Amer. Surgical Hosp. Assn. [15036]

Amer. Syringomyelia Alliance Proj. [15305]

Amer. Thoracic Soc. [16642]

Amer. Trauma Soc. [16689]

Amer. Urological Assn. [16704]

Amer. Urological Assn. Found. [16705]

Amer. Veterinary Dental Soc. [16778]

Amer. Veterinary Medical Assn. [16779]

Amer. Veterinary Medical Law Assn. [5927]

Amer. Veterinary Soc. of Animal Behavior [16780]

Americans for Medical Progress Educational Found. [13694]

America's Blood Centers [13762]

Amyloidosis Support Groups [14250]

Amyloidosis Support Network [14251]

Amyotrophic Lateral Sclerosis Assn. [15306]

Androgen Insensitivity Syndrome Support Gp. - USA [14441]

Anesthesia Awareness Campaign [13677]

Angioma Alliance [15307]

Archaeus Proj. [13625]

Archivists and Librarians in the History of the Hea. Sciences [10326]

Armed Forces Inst. of Pathology [15261]

Army Distaff Foundation/Knollwood [21192]

Army Nurse Corps Assn. [15262]

Arthritis Found. [16369]

Arthroscopy Assn. of North Am. [15762]

The Arts We Need [13710]

Ashoka: Innovators for the Public [12419]

ASHP Found. [15926]

Asian Amer./Pacific Islander Nurses Assn. [15463]

Assembly of Episcopal Healthcare Chaplains [19944]

Assn. of Academic Hea. Centers [14546]

Assn. of Academic Physiatrists [16316]

Assn. for Academic Surgery [16576]

Assn. of Accredited Naturopathic Medical Colleges [8943]

Assn. of Air Medical Services [14314]

Assn. for Ambulatory Behavioral Healthcare [16080]

Assn. of Amer. Cancer Institutes [13794]

Assn. of Amer. Physicians and Surgeons [15990]

Assn. for Applied Psychophysiology and Biofeedback [13749]

Assn. for Applied and Therapeutic Humor [16605]

Assn. for Assistive Tech. Act Programs [14237]

Assn. for Behavioral Hea. and Wellness [24088]

Assn. of Behavioral Healthcare Mgt. [15191]

Assn. of Biomedical Communications Directors [14030]

Assn. for the Bladder Exstrophy Community [14252]

Assn. of Bone and Joint Surgeons [15763]

Assn. of Camp Nurses [15464]

Assn. for Childbirth at Home, Intl. [15591]

Assn. of Children's Prosthetic-Orthotic Clinics [15784]

Assn. of Chinese Amer. Physicians [15991]

Assn. of Chiropractic Colleges [13993]

Assn. of Clinical Scientists [14022]

Assn. for Community Affiliated Plans [14617]

Assn. of Community Cancer Centers [13797]

Assn. for Community Hea. Improvement [16238]

Assn. for the Educ. of Children with Medical Needs [8072]

Assn. for Eradication of Heart Attack [13894]

Assn. of Family Practice Administrators [15060]

Assn. of Family Practice Physician Assistants [14698]

Assn. for Healthcare Documentation Integrity [15084]

Assn. for Healthcare Philanthropy [14871]

Assn. for Healthcare Rsrc. and Materials Mgt. [14872]

Assn. for Hosp. Medical Educ. [14873]

Assn. for Integrative Hea. Care Practitioners [15037]

Assn. of Intl. Hea. Researchers [14548]

Assn. for Intl. Medical Study [12834]

Assn. for Macular Diseases [15669]

Assn. of Maternal and Child Hea. Programs [13947]

Assn. of Medical Device Reprocessors [15038]

Assn. of Medical Directors of Info. Systems [14957]

Assn. for Medical Humanities [IO]

Assn. of Medical Illustrators [13707]

Assn. of Medical Lab. Immunologists [14932]

Assn. of Medical School Pediatric Dept. Chairs [15884]

A star before a book entry number signifies that the name is not listed separately, but is mentioned within the entry.

Assn. of Medicine and Psychiatry [16081]
Assn. of Military Osteopathic Physicians and Surgeons [15807]
Assn. of Military Surgeons of the U.S. [15263]
Assn. of Minority Hea. Professions Schools [8850]
Assn. of Needle-Free Injection Mfrs. [2549]
Assn. of Nurses in AIDS Care [13559]
Assn. of Nurses Endorsing Transplantation [15670]
Assn. for Ocular Pharmacology and Therapeutics [15671]
Assn. of Organ Procurement Organizations [14287]
Assn. of Osteopathic State Executive Directors [15809]
Assn. of Otolaryngology Administrators [15062]
Assn. of Pakistani Physicians of North Am. [15993]
Assn. of Pathology Chairs [15863]
Assn. for Pathology Informatics [15864]
Assn. of Pediatric Hematology/Oncology Nurses [15467]
Assn. of Pediatric Oncology Social Workers [15885]
Assn. of Pediatric Therapists [16606]
Assn. of PeriOperative Registered Nurses [15468]
Assn. of Physician Assistants in Cardiovascular Surgery [13895]
Assn. for Prevention Teaching and Res. [16054]
Assn. for Professionals in Infection Control and Epidemiology [14947]
Assn. of Professors of Cardiology [13896]
Assn. of Professors of Gynecology and Obstetrics [15592]
Assn. of Professors of Human and Medical Genetics [14497]
Assn. of Prog. Directors in Internal Medicine [14967]
Assn. of Prog. Directors in Vascular Surgery [16578]
Assn. of Regulatory Boards of Optometry [15716]
Assn. of Rehabilitation Nurses [15469]
Assn. for Res. of Childhood Cancer [13798]
Assn. for Res. in Vision and Ophthalmology [15672]
Assn. of Rheumatology Hea. Professionals [16370]
Assn. of Schools and Colleges of Optometry [15717]
Assn. of Schools of Public Hea. [16240]
Assn. of Shelter Veterinarians [16784]
Assn. of SIDS and Infant Mortality Programs [16524]
Assn. of State and Territorial Dental Directors [14146]
Assn. of Surgical Technologists [15133]
Assn. of Tech. Personnel in Ophthalmology [15674]
Assn. for Therapeutic Eurythmy in North Am. [16608]
Assn. of Univ. Anesthesiologists [13680]
Assn. of Univ. Professors of Ophthalmology [15675]
Assn. of Univ. Radiologists [16286]
Assn. of Veterans Affairs Ophthalmologists [15676]
Assn. of Veterinary Hematology and Transfusion Medicine [16785]
Assn. of Vision Educators [15677]
Assn. for Women Veterinarians [16786]
Assn. of Women's Hea., Obstetric and Neonatal Nurses [15470]
Assyrian Medical Soc. [13715]
Asthma and Allergy Found. of Am. [13598]
Australian Soc. of Teachers of the Alexander Technique [IO]
Auxiliary to the Natl. Medical Assn. [15161]
Avenues, Natl. Support Gp. for Arthrogryposis Multiplex Congenita [15309]
Bangladesh Medical Assn. of North Am. [15162]
Bay Area Physicians for Human Rights [12218]
Behavior Genetics Assn. [14498]
Benign Essential Blepharospasm Res. Found. [15311]
Benjamin Franklin Literary and Medical Soc. [14549]

Better Sleep Coun. [16424]
Better Vision Inst. [15678]
BIO Ventures for Global Hea. [14975]
BioCommunications Assn. [14031]
Bladder Cancer Advocacy Network [13799]
Blue Cross and Blue Shield Assn. [14959]
Brain Injury Assn. of Am. [14528]
Brave Kids [13949]
Brother's Brother Found. [12837]
Bur. of Professional Educ. of the Amer. Osteopathic Assn. [15810]
Burns United Support Groups [13782]
C/SEC [15593]
Cajal Club [15385]
Cancer Care [13803]
Cancer Control Soc. [13804]
Cancer Fed. [13805]
Cancer Info. Ser. [13807]
Cancer Prevention Coalition [13808]
Cancer Quality Alliance [13809]
Candlelighters Childhood Cancer Found. [13810]
Cardiovascular Credentialing Intl. [13898]
Care4Dystonia [15312]
Catholic Hea. Assn. of the U.S. [14874]
Catholic Medical Assn. [15996]
Catholic Medical Mission Bd. [12515]
CCHS Family Network [14255]
CDC Natl. Prevention Info. Network [13563]
Center for Humane Options in Childbirth Experiences [15594]
Center for Medical Consumers [14550]
Center for Organ Recovery and Educ. [16670]
Center for Professional Well-Being [14700]
Center for Res. in Ambulatory Hea. Care Admin. [15064]
Center for Sports and Osteopathic Medicine [16055]
Center for the Stud. of Multiple Birth [15272]
Central Soc. for Clinical Res. [14023]
Certification Bd. for Music Therapists [16213]
Certification Bd. for Urologic Nurses and Associates [16706]
CFIDS Assn. of Am. [14256]
Charles Ray III Diabetes Assn. [14220]
Chem. Injury Info. Network [16656]
Chemotherapy Found. [15644]
Chi Eta Phi Sorority [24560]
Child Life Coun. [13951]
Child Neurology Soc. [15386]
Childbirth Connection [15595]
Childhood Arthritis and Rheumatology Res. Alliance [16371]
Children's Blood Found. [14786]
Children's Cause for Cancer Advocacy [13812]
Children's Craniofacial Assn. [14057]
Children's Eye Found. [15679]
Children's Hemiplegia and Stroke Assn. [16493]
Children's Hospice Intl. [14853]
Children's Leukemia Res. Assn. [13813]
Children's Liver Assn. for Support Services [14804]
Children's PKU Network [15245]
Children's Tumor Found. [15315]
China Medical Bd. of New York [14976]
Chinese Amer. Medical Soc. [15163]
Christian Chiropractors Assn. [19773]
Christian Dental Soc. [14147]
Christian Medical and Dental Associations [IO]
Christian Medical and Dental Associations [20238]
Christian Medical Found. Intl. [20239]
Christian Medical Found. Intl. [IO]
Christopher and Dana Reeve Found. [16463]
Chromosome 9P Network [14443]
Chromosome 18 Registry and Res. Soc. [14444]
Chronic Syndrome Support Assn. [14259]
Citizens Alliance for VD Awareness [16411]
City of Hope Natl. Medical Center [15102]
CityMatch [13957]
Civil Aviation Medical Assn. [13540]
Cleft Lip and Palate Assn. of Ireland [IO]
Clinical Lab. Mgt. Assn. [14993]
Clinical and Lab. Standards Inst. [14994]
Clinical Ligand Assay Soc. [14995]
Coalition of Cancer Cooperative Groups [13814]
Coalition for Healthcare Commun. [14622]

Coalition for Hemophilia B [14787]
Coffin-Lowry Syndrome Found. [14447]
Cognitive Neuroscience Soc. [15407]
COLA [15039]
Coll. of Amer. Pathologists [15866]
Coll. of Optometrists in Vision Development [15718]
Coll. of Osteopathic Healthcare Executives [14876]
Collegium Internationale Neuro-Psychopharmacologicum [15929]
Coma Recovery Assn. [14029]
Commn. on Graduates of Foreign Nursing Schools [15473]
Comm. on Accreditation for Respiratory Care [16610]
Comm. for Freedom of Choice in Medicine [13628]
Comm. of Interns and Residents [24089]
Comm. for the Promotion of Medical Res. [15104]
Comm. to Reduce Infection Deaths [14877]
Community Systems Found. [15552]
Comparative Nutrition Soc. [15553]
Competency and Credentialing Inst. [14878]
Computerized Medical Imaging Soc. [16287]
Conf. of Res. Workers in Animal Diseases [16790]
Congenital Cardiac Anesthesia Soc. [13682]
Congenital Heart Defects Awareness [13900]
Congenital Heart Info. Network [13901]
Cong. of Lung Assn. Staff [16357]
Conservative Orthopedics Intl. Assn. [15767]
Consultant Dietitians in Hea. Care Facilities [15554]
Contact Lens Assn. of Ophthalmologists [15680]
Continuing Care Accreditation Commn. [16318]
Corporate Angel Network [13817]
Coun. for Affordable Quality Healthcare [14625]
Coun. on Arteriosclerosis, Thrombosis and Vascular Biology of the Amer. Heart Assn. [13902]
Coun. on Certification of Nurse Anesthetists [15475]
Coun. on Chiropractic Educ. [13998]
Coun. on Chiropractic Orthopedics [15768]
Coun. of Colleges of Acupuncture and Oriental Medicine [15743]
Coun. on Diagnostic Imaging [16288]
Coun. on Educ. for Public Hea. [16242]
Coun. on Hea. Info. and Educ. [14553]
Coun. of Medical Specialty Societies [15120]
Coun. of Pediatric Subspecialties [15886]
Coun. on Podiatric Medical Educ. [16042]
Coun. on Resident Educ. in Obstetrics and Gynecology [15597]
Coun. of State Administrators of Vocational Rehabilitation [16320]
Coun. of State and Territorial Epidemiologists [14374]
Coun. of Teaching Hospitals [14879]
Coun. of Women's and Infants' Specialty Hospitals [14880]
Cranial Acad. [15811]
Crigler-Najjar Assn. [14805]
Crohn's and Colitis Found. of Am. [14414]
CTSNet: Cardiothoracic Surgery Network [16643]
Cure Res. Found. [13818]
CyberKnife Soc. [16581]
Cyclic Vomiting Syndrome Assn. [14415]
Cystic Fibrosis Found. [16358]
Cystic Fibrosis Worldwide [16359]
Cystinosis Found. [15246]
Cystinosis Res. Network [15247]
Damon Runyon Cancer Res. Found. [13819]
Dana Alliance for Brain Initiatives [15387]
Dannemiller Memorial Educational Found. [13683]
Delta Dental Plans Assn. [14687]
Delta Omega [24582]
Dental Assisting Natl. Bd. [14151]
Dental Hea. Intl. [14152]
Depression and Bipolar Support Alliance [15196]
Dermatology Found. [14199]
Dermatology Nurses' Assn. [15476]
DES Action, U.S.A. [13821]
Diabetes Res. Assn. of Am. [14223]

Reference to "IO" in place of a book number signifies that the association may be found in the 45th edition of International Organizations.

Diabetes Res. Inst. Found. [14224]
Diagnostic Marketing Assn. [2624]
Dietary Managers Assn. [15555]
Digestive Disease Natl. Coalition [14416]
Direct Care Alliance [1868]
DOCARE Intl., N.F.P. [12518]
Docs for Tots [13958]
Drs. for Artists [12520]
Doctors Ought to Care [14554]
Drug Info. Assn. [15931]
Dysautonomia Found. [15317]
Dystonia Medical Res. Found. [15319]
Dystrophic Epidermolysis Bullosa Res. Assn. of Am. [14200]
Ear Found. [15825]
ECRI [15136]
Educational Commn. for Foreign Medical Graduates [15997]
Ehlers Danlos Natl. Found. [16651]
EMDR Intl. Assn. [16215]
Emergency Medicine Found. [14331]
Emergency Medicine Residents' Assn. [14332]
Emergency Nurses Assn. [14333]
Endocrine Soc. [14355]
Endometriosis Assn. [15599]
Environmental Res. Found. [13599]
Epilepsy Found. [14380]
Esophageal Cancer Awareness Assn. [13822]
Ethiopian Pharmacists Assn. in North Am. [15932]
European Diagnostic Mfrs. Assn. [IO]
European Fed. of Organizations for Medical Physics [IO]
European Medical Writers Assn. [IO]
Everyday Ayurveda [13606]
Extensions for Independence [11945]
Eye Bank Assn. of Am. [14288]
Eye-Bank for Sight Restoration [14289]
Fabry Support and Info. Gp. [14262]
FACES: The Natl. Craniofacial Assn. [14061]
Facioscapulohumeral (FSH) Soc. [15320]
Family and Hea. Sect. of the Natl. Coun. on Family Relations [14385]
Fanconi Anemia Res. Fund [14450]
Fed. Physicians Assn. [15998]
Federated Ambulatory Surgery Assn. [16582]
Fed. for Accessible Nursing Educ. and Licensure [15478]
Fed. of Amer. Hospitals [14881]
Fed. of Associations of Regulatory Boards [14555]
Fed. of Chinese Amer. and Chinese Canadian Medical Societies [13985]
Fed. of Clinical Immunology Societies [14935]
Fed. of Pediatric Organizations [15887]
Fed. of Podiatric Medical Boards [16043]
Fed. of State Medical Boards of the U.S. [15165]
Fed. of State Physician Hea. Programs [15999]
Fed. of Straight Chiropractors and Organizations [14001]
Fellowship of Associates of Medical Evangelism [20240]
Fertility Res. Found. [14391]
Fibromuscular Dysplasia Soc. of Am. [15322]
Filipino Amer. Medical Inc. [14722]
First Candle/SIDS Alliance [16525]
Floating Harbor Syndrome Support Gp. of North Am. [14451]
Flower Essence Soc. [14818]
Flying Chiropractors Assn. [14002]
Flying Dentists Assn. [14153]
Flying Physicians Assn. [13731]
Focus [15681]
FOD Family Support Gp. [15248]
Food and Nutrition Bd. [15558]
Forbes Norris MDA/ALS Res. Center [15323]
Foreign Pharmacy Graduate Examination Comm. [15933]
Found. for Advancement in Cancer Therapy [13824]
Found. for the Advancement of Chiropractic Tenets and Sci. [14003]
Found. for Chiropractic Educ. and Res. [14004]
Found. for Hea. [14556]
Found. for Ichthyosis and Related Skin Types [14201]

Found. for Informed Medical Decision Making [15137]
Found. for Innovation in Medicine [15166]
Found. for the Support of Intl. Medical Training [14977]
Friedreich's Ataxia Res. Alliance [14403]
Friends of the Jose Carreras Intl. Leukemia Found. [13825]
Frontier Nursing Ser. [15479]
Frontline Hepatitis Awareness [14806]
Gay and Lesbian Medical Assn. [14431]
Gay Men's Hea. Crisis [13564]
German Phytomedical Soc. [IO]
Gerontological Soc. of Am. [14511]
Gift of Life Intl. [12524]
Glaucoma Res. Found. [15683]
Global Alliance for Medical Educ. [8862]
Global Alliance of Mental Illness Advocacy Networks [15200]
Global Assn. for Interpersonal Neurobiology Stud. [7375]
Global Bus. Coalition on HIV/AIDS [11329]
Global Healing [12450]
Global Hea. Coun. [14979]
Global Neuro Rescue [15324]
Global Outreach Mission [12525]
Global and Regional Asperger Syndrome Partnership [15325]
Gluten Intolerance Gp. [15559]
Guardians of Hydrocephalus Res. Found. [15326]
Haitian Coalition on AIDS [13567]
Harvey Soc. [15168]
Hastings Center [12125]
Hea. Acad. [14883]
Hea. Educ. Found. [16243]
Hea. Educ. Rsrc. Org. [13568]
Hea. for Humanity [14563]
Hea. Indus. Distributors Assn. [1860]
Hea. Info. Rsrc. Center [14564]
Hea. Ministries [20241]
Hea. Res. and Educational Trust [14884]
Hea. Sci. Communications Assn. [14032]
Hea. Volunteers Overseas [12526]
Healthcare Financial Mgt. Assn. [15066]
Healthcare Info. and Mgt. Systems Soc. [14885]
Heart Disease Res. Found. [13905]
Heart Failure Soc. of Am. [13906]
Heart Rhythm Soc. [13907]
HELLP Syndrome Soc. [14906]
HELP - Inst. for Body Chemistry [14928]
Hemochromatosis Found. [14799]
Hemochromatosis Info. Soc. [14800]
Hemophilia Fed. of Am. [14789]
Hepatitis C Assn. [14807]
Hepatitis C Caring Ambassadors Prog. [14808]
Hepatitis Rsrc. Network [14810]
Hereditary Colon Cancer Assn. [13829]
Herpes Rsrc. Center - Amer. Social Hea. Assn. [16412]
Hesperian Found. [14980]
HHT Found. Intl. [14454]
Hip Soc. [15769]
Histochemical Soc. [13938]
Holistic Dental Assn. [14156]
Homeopathic Nurses Assn. [14846]
Hospice Educ. Inst. [14854]
Hospice and Palliative Nurses Assn. [15482]
Hospitalized Veterans Writing Proj. [16321]
Human Ecology Action League [14364]
Human Growth Found. [16020]
Huntington's Disease Soc. of Am. [15329]
Hydrocephalus Assn. [15330]
Hypoparathyroidism Assn. [14356]
Hysterectomy Educational Resources and Services Found. [15601]
Immune Deficiency Found. [14936]
Immunology of Diabetes Soc. [14225]
Incurably Ill for Animal Res. [13697]
Independent Citizens Res. Found. for the Study of Degenerative Diseases [14263]
Independent Medical Distributors Assn. [1862]
Infectious Diseases Soc. of Am. [14948]
Informed Homebirth/Informed Birth and Parenting [15602]
Infusion Nurses Soc. [16614]

Inst. for the Development of Emotional and Life Skills/National Inst. of Relationship Enhancement [15201]
Inst. for Labor and Mental Health [15202]
Interamerican Coll. of Physicians and Surgeons [16000]
InterAmerican Heart Found. [13909]
Interchurch Medical Assistance [IO]
Interchurch Medical Assistance [20242]
Intermed Intl. [14982]
Intl. Acad. for Child Brain Development [15389]
Intl. Acad. of Health Care Professionals [14705]
Intl. Acad. of Myodontics [14159]
Intl. and Amer. Associations of Clinical Nutritionists [15560]
Intl. Anesthesia Res. Soc. [13684]
Intl. Assn. for Aquatic Animal Medicine [16792]
Intl. Assn. of Cancer Victors and Friends [13831]
Intl. Assn. for Cognitive Psychotherapy [16218]
Intl. Assn. for Colon Hydrotherapy [14567]
Intl. Assn. for Comparative Res. on Leukemia and Related Diseases [15647]
Intl. Assn. of Coroners and Medical Examiners [15093]
Intl. Assn. for Dental Res. [14161]
Intl. Assn. of Flight Paramedics [14334]
Intl. Assn. of Healthcare Central Ser. Materiel Mgt. [14886]
Intl. Assn. for Healthcare Security and Safety [14887]
Intl. Assn. of Human-Animal Interaction Organizations [16615]
Intl. Assn. of Hygienic Physicians [15278]
Intl. Assn. for Medical Assistance to Travellers [13343]
Intl. Assn. of Medical Equip. Remarketers and Servicers [15139]
International Association of Medical Intuitives [IO]
Intl. Assn. of Medical Intuitives [15040]
Intl. Assn. for Medicinal Compliance [15041]
International Association for Medicinal Compliance [IO]
Intl. Assn. of Ocular Surgeons [15684]
Intl. Assn. of Optometric Executives [15720]
Intl. Assn. of Oral and Maxillofacial Surgeons [15736]
Intl. Assn. for Organ Donation [16671]
Intl. Assn. of Orofacial Myology [15869]
Intl. Assn. for Orthodontics [14162]
Intl. Assn. for Oxygen Therapy [16616]
Intl. Assn. for Paratuberculosis [16793]
Intl. Assn. of Pediatric Lab. Medicine [15888]
Intl. Assn. of Rehabilitation Professionals [16322]
Intl. Assn. of Reiki Professionals [13637]
Intl. Assn. for Relational Psychoanalysis and Psychotherapy [16108]
Intl. Assn. of Sickle Cell Nurses And Physician Assistants [14706]
Intl. Assn. of Structural Integrators [13638]
Intl. Assn. for the Stud. of Pain [15841]
Intl. Atherosclerosis Soc. [13910]
Intl. Behavioral Neuroscience Soc. [15408]
Intl. Biopharmaceutical Assn. [15936]
Intl. Bd. of Environmental Medicine [14365]
Intl. Bronchoesophagological Soc. [13779]
Intl. Bundle Br. Block Assn. [13911]
Intl. Center for Attitudinal Healing [15206]
Intl. Cesarean Awareness Network [15604]
Intl. Childbirth Educ. Assn. [15605]
Intl. Chiropractors Assn. [14008]
Intl. Coll. of Dentists [14163]
Intl. Coll. of Surgeons [16583]
Intl. Comm. Against Mental Illness [15207]
Intl. Cong. of Oral Implantologists [14165]
Intl. Correspondence Soc. of Allergists and Clinical Immunologists [13601]
Intl. Cytokine Soc. [6580]
Intl. Dalkon Shield Victims Educ. Assn. [16898]
Intl. Embryo Transfer Soc. [16794]
Intl. Eye Found. [15685]
Intl. Fed. of Catholic Medical Associations [IO]
Intl. Fed. of Esthetic Dentistry [14167]
Intl. Fed. of Foot and Ankle Societies [16045]
Intl. Fed. of Marfan Syndrome Organizations [14456]

A star before a book entry number signifies that the name is not listed separately, but is mentioned within the entry.

Intl. Fed. of Martial Arts and Oriental Medicine [15021]
Intl. Fed. of Psoriasis Associations [14203]
Intl. Found. for Homeopathy [14849]
Intl. Functional Elecl. Stimulation Soc. [15390]
Intl. Genetic Epidemiology Soc. [14376]
Intl. Guild of Hair Removal Specialists [14309]
Intl. Hea. Evaluation Assn. [14568]
Intl. Healthcare Safety Professional Certification Bd. [16379]
Intl. Hyperhidrosis Soc. [14357]
Intl. Leptospirosis Soc. [14950]
Intl. Life Sciences Inst. - North Am. [15561]
Intl. Liver Transplantation Soc. [16672]
Intl. Lyme and Assoc. Diseases Soc. [14267]
Intl. Medical Corps [12862]
Intl. Medical and Dental Hypnotherapy Assn. [14924]
Intl. Medical Equip. Collaborative [14569]
Intl. Medical Spa Assn. [1870]
Intl. Medical Volunteers Assn. [15075]
Intl. Mobile Hea. Assn. [14724]
Intl. Org. of Glutaric Acidemia [15332]
Intl. Org. of Multiple Sclerosis Nurses [15486]
Intl. Pediatric Hypertension Assn. [14907]
Intl. Pediatric Nephrology Assn. [15292]
Intl. Pediatric Transplant Assn. [16673]
Intl. Premature Ovarian Failure Assn. [15606]
Intl. Psycho-Oncology Soc. [13834]
The Intl. Publication Planning Assn. [3231]
Intl. RadioSurgery Assn. [16269]
Intl. Refractive Surgery Club [15689]
Intl. Scleroderma Network [16387]
Intl. Sharps Injury Prevention Soc. [16380]
Intl. Skeletal Soc. [16289]
Intl. Soc. of Arthroscopy, Knee Surgery and Orthopaedic Sports Medicine [15771]
Intl. Soc. for Clinical Densitometry [15788]
Intl. Soc. for Complementary Medicine Res. [13639]
Intl. Soc. for Cmpt. Assisted Orthopaedic Surgery [15772]
Intl. Soc. of Cosmetic and Laser Surgeons [14048]
Intl. Soc. for Dermatologic Surgery [14204]
Intl. Soc. of Dermatology [14205]
Intl. Soc. of First Responders [14317]
Intl. Soc. for Heart and Lung Transplantation [16674]
Intl. Soc. for the History of the Neurosciences [7376]
Intl. Soc. for Imaging in the Eye [15690]
Intl. Soc. for Infectious Diseases [14951]
Intl. Soc. of Lymphology [15016]
Intl. Soc. for Medical Publication Professionals [16259]
Intl. Soc. on Metabolic Eye Disease [15691]
Intl. Soc. of Motor Control [7377]
Intl. Soc. of Neuro-Semantics [16396]
Intl. Soc. of Oncology Pharmacy Practitioners [15937]
Intl. Soc. for Pharmacoepidemiology [15939]
Intl. Soc. for Plastination [15870]
Intl. Soc. of Psychiatric Genetics [14502]
Intl. Soc. for the Psychological Treatments of the Schizophrenias and Other Psychoses - USA [15209]
Intl. Soc. for Res. on Impulsivity [16088]
Intl. Soc. of Sports Nutrition [15562]
Intl. Soc. for the Stud. of Women's Sexual Hea. [16404]
Intl. Soc. on Thrombosis and Haemostasis [14793]
Intl. Soc. for Traumatic Stress Stud. [16489]
Intl. Soc. of Travel Medicine [15172]
Intl. Soc. for Vascular Surgery [16584]
Intl. Soc. of Veterinary Dermatopathology [16795]
Intl. Stuttering Assn. [16498]
Intl. Trachoma Initiative [16858]
Intl. Union Against Sexually Transmitted Infections, Regional Off. for North Am. [16414]
Intl. Veterinary Acupuncture Soc. [16796]
Intl. Veterinary Ultrasound Soc. [16797]
Intl. Vitamin A Consultative Gp. [15564]
Intersociety Coun. for Pathology Info. [15871]

Interstate Postgraduate Medical Assn. of North Am. [14386]
Interstitial Cystitis Assn. [16708]
Iraqi Medical Sciences Assn. [14987]
Islamic Medical Assn. of North Am. [16003]
ITEM Coalition [14690]
Jaw Joints and Allied Musculo-Skeletal Disorders Found. [15773]
Jin Shin Do Found. for Bodymind Acupressure [15746]
Joint Commn. on Accreditation of Healthcare Organizations [14888]
Joint Commn. on Allied Hea. Personnel in Ophthalmology [15692]
Joint Coun. of Allergy, Asthma and Immunology [13602]
Juvenile Diabetes Res. Found. Intl. [14228]
Kennedy's Disease Assn. [15334]
Kids With Heart Natl. Assn. for Children's Heart Disorders [13915]
Korean Medical Assn. [IO]
Lamaze Birth Without Pain Educ. Assn. [15607]
Lambda Kappa Sigma [24569]
Lesbian, Gay, Bisexual, and Transgender People in Medicine [12243]
Leukemia and Lymphoma Soc. [13837]
Lewy Body Dementia Assn. [15335]
LifeBanc [14290]
Lifegain Inst. [14573]
The Living Bank Intl. [14291]
LMBS Network [16539]
Lung Cancer Alliance [13839]
Lupus Found. of Am. [15014]
Lupus Info. Network [15015]
Lyme Disease Assn. [14271]
Lyme Disease Found. [14272]
Make Today Count [13841]
Malignant Hyperthermia Assn. of the U.S. [14464]
MAP Intl. [IO]
MAP Intl. [20243]
Marijuana Policy Proj. [18024]
Med Help Intl. [IO]
Med Help Intl. [15042]
Medicaid/SCHIP Dental Assn. [14168]
Medical Assurance Soc. [IO]
Medical Defence Assn. of Victoria [IO]
Medical Defence Malaysia [IO]
Medical Defence Union [IO]
Medical Device Mfrs. Assn. [3486]
Medical Equip. and Tech. Assn. [7306]
Medical Gp. Mgt. Assn. [15067]
Medical Image Perception Soc. [15140]
Medical Letter [15940]
Medical Lib. Assn. [10372]
Medical Marketing Assn. [2637]
Medical Missions Response [20246]
Medical Missions Response [IO]
Medical Outcomes Trust [14644]
Medical Records Inst. [15098]
Medical Res. Modernization Comm. [15109]
Medical Software Indus. Assn. [IO]
Medical Spa Soc. [1871]
Medical Subjects Unit [22843]
MedicAlert Found. Intl. [14318]
Medicine for Peace [12789]
MediSend Intl. [12530]
MedShare Intl. [12531]
Mended Hearts, Inc. [13916]
Meniere's Network [15826]
Mental Hea. Am. [15211]
Mental Res. Inst. [13737]
Michael E. DeBakey Intl. Surgical Soc. [13917]
Midwifery Educ. Accreditation Coun. [8063]
Midwives Alliance of North Am. [15610]
Mitochondrial Medicine Soc. [14078]
Mothers' Voices [13574]
Multiple Sclerosis Found. [15338]
Musculoskeletal Ultrasound Soc. [16696]
Myasthenia Gravis Found. of Am. [15340]
Nail Patella Syndrome Worldwide [14467]
NANDA Intl. [15489]
Natl. Acad. of Neuropsychology [16158]
Natl. Acad. of Opticianry [15707]
Natl. Accrediting Agency for Clinical Lab. Sciences [15141]

Natl. Adrenal Diseases Found. [14358]
Natl. AIDS Fund [13576]
Natl. Alliance of Advocates for Buprenorphine Treatment [16511]
Natl. Alliance for Infusion Therapy [14839]
Natl. Alliance of Medical Researchers and Teaching Physicians [15143]
Natl. Alliance on Mental Illness [15214]
Natl. Alliance for the Primary Prevention of Sharps Injuries [16381]
Natl. Alliance of State Pharmacy Associations [15943]
Natl. Alopecia Areata Found. [16386]
Natl. Amer. Arab Nurses Assn. [15490]
Natl. Anemia Action Coun. [14794]
Natl. Assn. for the Advancement of Orthotics and Prosthetics [15786]
Natl. Assn. of Boards of Examiners of Long Term Care Administrators [15538]
Natl. Assn. of Boards of Pharmacy [15944]
Natl. Assn. for Children's Behavioral Hea. [16090]
Natl. Assn. of Community Hea. Centers [14574]
Natl. Assn. for Continence [16709]
Natl. Assn. of County Hea. Fac. Administrators [15069]
Natl. Assn. of Dental Assistants [14169]
Natl. Assn. of Dental Labs. [14170]
Natl. Assn. for Direct Care Workers of Color [14709]
Natl. Assn. of Disability Evaluating Professionals [14575]
Natl. Assn. of Disability Examiners [14034]
Natl. Assn. of Emergency Medical Technicians [14335]
Natl. Assn. of Fed. Veterinarians [16799]
Natl. Assn. of First Responders [14320]
Natl. Assn. of Free Clinics [14727]
Natl. Assn. of Geriatric Educ. Centers [14513]
Natl. Assn. of Hea. Care Assistants [14514]
Natl. Assn. of Hea. Educ. Centers [14675]
Natl. Assn. of Hea. Unit Coordinators [14578]
Natl. Assn. for Healthcare Quality [16264]
Natl. Assn. for Healthcare Recruitment [15070]
Natl. Assn. of Hepatitis Task Forces [14812]
Natl. Assn. of Hispanic Nurses [15494]
Natl. Assn. for Home Care and Hospice [14840]
Natl. Assn. of Hosp. Hospitality Houses [14891]
Natl. Assn. of Locum Tenens Org. [16004]
Natl. Assn. of Medical Examiners [15094]
Natl. Assn. Medical Staff Services [15071]
Natl. Assn. of Myofascial Trigger Point Therapists [16624]
Natl. Assn. of Nurse Practitioners in Women's Hea. [15497]
Natl. Assn. of Optometrists and Opticians [15721]
Natl. Assn. of Orthopaedic Nurses [15498]
Natl. Assn. of People With AIDS [13578]
Natl. Assn. of Physician Nurses [15500]
Natl. Assn. for Proton Therapy [15649]
Natl. Assn. for Pseudoxanthoma Elasticum [14207]
Natl. Assn. of Public Hospitals and Hea. Systems [14892]
Natl. Assn. of Rehabilitation Instructors [16324]
Natl. Assn. of Rehabilitation Providers and Agencies [16326]
Natl. Assn. of Residents and Interns [15175]
Natl. Assn. for Rural Mental Hea. [15217]
Natl. Assn. of School Nurses [15501]
Natl. Assn. of State EMS Officials [14337]
Natl. Assn. of State Mental Hea. Prog. Directors [15219]
Natl. Assn. of Subacute and Post-Acute Care [14728]
Natl. Assn. of VA Physicians and Dentists [16007]
Natl. Assn. of Vietnamese Nurses [15504]
Natl. Assn. of Vision Professionals [15693]
Natl. Ataxia Found. [15342]
Natl. Athletic Trainers' Assn. [23954]
Natl. Black Nurses Assn. [15505]
Natl. Bd. for Certification in Dental Lab. Tech. [14172]
Natl. Bd. for Certification in Dental Tech. [14173]
Natl. Bd. for Certification in Occupational Therapy [16625]

Reference to "IO" in place of a book number signifies that the association may be found in the 45th edition of International Organizations.

Natl. Bd. for Certification of Orthopaedic Technologists [15774]
Natl. Bd. of Examiners in Optometry [15722]
Natl. Bd. of Medical Examiners [15095]
Natl. Bd. of Osteopathic Medical Examiners [15812]
Natl. Bd. of Podiatric Medical Examiners [16046]
Natl. Bd. for Respiratory Care [16626]
Natl. Burn Victim Found. [13784]
Natl. Catholic Pharmacists Guild of the U.S. [15945]
Natl. Center for Educ. in Maternal and Child Hea. [13969]
Natl. Center for Farmworker Hea. [14581]
Natl. Center for Hea. Educ. [14582]
Natl. Certification Commn. for Acupuncture and Oriental Medicine [15747]
Natl. Chronic Pain Soc. [15845]
Natl. Coalition for Cancer Survivorship [13852]
Natl. Coalition of Creative Arts Therapies Associations [16224]
Natl. Coalition of Ethnic Minority Nurse Associations [15507]
Natl. Coalition for Res. in Neurological Disorders [15346]
Natl. Commn. on Certification of Physician Assistants [15975]
Natl. Commn. on Correctional Hea. Care [14729]
Natl. Comm. for Quality Assurance [16265]
Natl. Conf. of Local Environmental Hea. Administrators [16246]
Natl. Contact Lens Examiners [15723]
Natl. Coordinating Coun. for Medication Error Reporting and Prevention [14653]
Natl. Coun. on Interpreting in Hea. Care [1851]
Natl. Coun. on Minority Educ. in Transplantation [16677]
Natl. Coun. on Patient Info. and Educ. [15946]
Natl. Coun. on Rehabilitation Educ. [16329]
Natl. Coun. of State Boards of Nursing [15508]
Natl. Coun. for Therapeutic Recreation Certification [16627]
Natl. Coun. on Women's Hea. [16904]
Natl. Credentialing Agency for Lab. Personnel [15145]
Natl. Dental Assistants Assn. [14174]
Natl. Dental Assn. [14175]
Natl. Dental Hygienists' Assn. [14177]
Natl. Denturist Assn. [14178]
Natl. Digestive Diseases Info. CH [14422]
Natl. Educ. Alliance for Borderline Personality Disorder [15224]
Natl. Environmental Hea. Assn. [14367]
Natl. Eosinophilia-Myalgia Syndrome Network [16662]
Natl. Eye Res. Found. [15724]
Natl. Fed. of Licensed Practical Nurses [15509]
Natl. Found. for Brain Res. [15397]
Natl. Found. of Dentistry for the Handicapped [14179]
Natl. Found. for Depressive Illness [15225]
Natl. Found. for Ectodermal Dysplasias [14468]
Natl. Found. for Facial Reconstruction [14065]
Natl. Found. for Infectious Diseases [14953]
Natl. Found. for Transplants [16678]
Natl. Fragile X Found. [14469]
Natl. Free Clinic Found. of Am. [14585]
Natl. Gaucher Found. [15252]
Natl. Guideline CH [14654]
Natl. Headache Found. [14533]
Natl. Hea. Assn. [15279]
Natl. Hea. Coun. [14586]
Natl. Hea. Fed. [14587]
Natl. Hea. Info. Center [14588]
Natl. Heartburn Alliance [14423]
Natl. Hemophilia Found. [14795]
Natl. Hepatitis C Advocacy Coun. [14813]
Natl. Home Infusion Assn. [15043]
Natl. Hospice and Palliative Care Org. [14856]
Natl. Infant Torticollis Assn. [14945]
Natl. Inst. of Electromedical Info. [14311]
Natl. Inst. for Jewish Hospice [14857]
Natl. Jewish Medical and Res. Center [16361]
Natl. Kidney Found. [15294]
Natl. League for Nursing [15510]

Natl. Lung Cancer Partnership [13854]
Natl. Lymphedema Network [15018]
Natl. Marfan Found. [16652]
Natl. Medical Assn. [15176]
Natl. Meningitis Assn. [14281]
Natl. Minority AIDS Coun. [13580]
Natl. Multiple Sclerosis Soc. [15349]
Natl. Optometric Assn. [15725]
Natl. Org. for Albinism and Hypopigmentation [15255]
Natl. Org. for Associate Degree Nursing [15512]
Natl. Org. for Competency Assurance [14591]
Natl. Osteoporosis Found. [15775]
Natl. Pain Educ. Coun. [15846]
Natl. Parkinson Found. [15351]
Natl. Perinatal Assn. [15900]
Natl. Pharmaceutical Assn. [15947]
Natl. Phlebotomy Assn. [14796]
Natl. Physicians Alliance [16009]
Natl. Podiatric Medical Assn. [16047]
Natl. Postdoctoral Assn. [9064]
Natl. Prison Hospice Assn. [14858]
Natl. Prostate Cancer Coalition [13856]
Natl. Registry of Emergency Medical Technicians [14342]
Natl. Rehabilitation Assn. [16330]
Natl. Rehabilitation Info. Center [16332]
Natl. Reye's Syndrome Found. [16366]
Natl. Rural Hea. Assn. [16248]
Natl. Scoliosis Found. [16393]
Natl. SIDS/Infant Death Rsrc. Center [16526]
Natl. Soc. of Genetic Counselors [14506]
Natl. Soc. for Histotechnology [15146]
Natl. Spasmodic Dysphonia Assn. [15352]
Natl. Spasmodic Torticollis Assn. [15353]
Natl. Spinal Cord Injury Assn. [16468]
Natl. Strength and Conditioning Assn. [23957]
Natl. Stroke Assn. [16494]
Natl. Tay-Sachs and Allied Diseases Assn. [15354]
Natl. Therapeutic Recreation Soc. [16628]
Natl. Tuberculosis Controllers Assn. [14283]
Natl. Vaccine Info. Center [13972]
Natl. Viral Hepatitis Roundtable [14815]
Natl. Women's Hea. Network [16906]
NBIA Disorders Assn. [15355]
Neuro-Optometric Rehabilitation Assn., Intl. [15300]
Neuroblastoma Children's Cancer Soc. [13858]
Neurocritical Care Soc. [14070]
Neurofibromatosis [14471]
Neurosurgeons to Preserve Hea. Care Access [15414]
NIDCD - Natl. Temporal Bone, Hearing and Balance Pathology Rsrc. Registry [15121]
NMC [16802]
North Amer. Assn. for Ambulatory Urgent Care [13663]
North Amer. Assn. of Medical Educ. and Commun. Companies [8874]
North Amer. Clinical Dermatologic Soc. [14212]
North Amer. Menopause Soc. [15614]
North Amer. Sikh Medical and Dental Assn. [16416]
North Amer. Soc. for Dialysis and Transplantation [15295]
North Amer. Soc. of Obstetric Medicine [15615]
North Amer. Soc. for Pediatric Gastroenterology, Hepatology and Nutrition [14424]
North Amer. Tang Shou Tao Assn. [13645]
North Amer. Transplant Coordinators Org. [16681]
North Amer. Vascular Biology Org. [16728]
North Amer. Vodder Assn. of Lymphatic Therapy [15019]
Norwegian Medical Assn. [IO]
NSF Intl. [16249]
Nuclear Medicine Tech. Certification Bd. [15423]
Nurses Educational Funds [15516]
Nurses' House [15518]
Nurses Org. of Veterans Affairs [15519]
Nutrition for Optimal Hea. Assn. [15567]
Obesity Action Coalition [15577]
Ohashi Inst. [15748]
Oncology Nursing Soc. [15521]
Oper. Smile [12534]

Oper. U.S.A. [12535]
Ophthalmic Photographers' Soc. [15696]
Opticians Assn. of Am. [15709]
Optometric Extension Prog. Found. [15727]
Optometric Historical Soc. [15728]
ORBIS Intl. [15697]
Organic Acidemia Assn. [14472]
Org. for Autism Res. [13728]
Orthodontic Education and Res. Found. [14183]
Orthopaedic Res. Soc. [15776]
Orthopaedic Sect., Amer. Physical Therapy Assn. [16630]
Osteogenesis Imperfecta Found. [15779]
Osteopathic Intl. Alliance [15813]
Outpatient Ophthalmic Surgery Soc. [15698]
Pacific Dermatologic Assn. [14213]
Paget Found. for Paget's Disease of Bone and Related Disorders [15256]
Pain Mgt. and Sclerotherapy [15814]
Pan-American Allergy Soc. [13604]
Pan-American Assn. of Ophthalmology [15699]
Pan Amer. Hea. and Educ. Found. [12536]
Pan Amer. Hea. Org. [14592]
Pancreatic Cancer Action Network [15851]
Paratuberculosis Awareness and Res. Assn. [14425]
Parents Against Childhood Epilepsy [14382]
Parents of Infants and Children with Kernicterus [15358]
Parents of Kids with Infectious Diseases [14954]
Parkinson Alliance [15359]
Parkinson's Disease Found. [15360]
Partners in Hea. [12270]
Partnership for Quality Medical Donations [12537]
Patient Advocate Found. [14660]
PBCers Org. [14816]
Pediatric Infectious Diseases Soc. [14955]
Pediatric Keratoplasty Assn. [15700]
Pediatric Nursing Certification Bd. [15522]
Pediatric Orthopedic Soc. of North Am. [15780]
People-Animals-Love [16632]
People, Animals, Nature [13319]
People-to-People Hea. Found. [14984]
Performing Arts Medicine Assn. [16164]
Perfusion Prog. Directors' Coun. [13921]
Peripheral Arterial Disease Coalition [13922]
Peruvian Heart Assn. [13923]
Pharmacy Technician Educators Coun. [8963]
Phi Alpha Sigma [24543]
Phi Chi Medical Fraternity [24544]
Phi Delta Chi [24570]
Phi Delta Epsilon Medical Fraternity [24540]
Philippine Nurses Assn. of Am. [2840]
Physician Asst. Educ. Assn. [15976]
Physicians for Peace [15078]
Pierre Fauchard Acad. [14184]
Pierre Robin Network [14473]
Pituitary Network Assn. [16022]
Plastic Surgery Educational Found. [14051]
Plastic Surgery Res. Coun. [14052]
Platelet Disorder Support Assn. [13730]
Polio Soc. [15362]
Prader-Willi Found. [14474]
Prader-Willi Syndrome Assn. (U.S.A.) [14475]
Premier Advocacy [14597]
Price-Pottenger Nutrition Found. [15568]
Private Practice Section/American Physical Therapy Assn. [16633]
Professional Women in Healthcare [4045]
Progressive Osseous Heteroplasia Assn. [14477]
Proj. Inform [13583]
Proj. Magic [16634]
PSRC of Am. [16266]
Public Citizen Hea. Res. Gp. [16250]
Public Hosp. Pharmacy Coalition [15949]
Pull-thru Network [14427]
Purine Res. Soc. [15258]
QiGong Res. Soc. [13647]
R.A. Bloch Cancer Found. [13867]
Radiation Therapy Oncology Gp. [15653]
Radiological Soc. of North Am. [16293]
Radiology Bus. Mgt. Assn. [15074]
Radiology Mammography Intl. [13774]
Ray Helfer Soc. [13976]
Regulatory Affairs Professionals Soc. [14599]

A star before a book entry number signifies that the name is not listed separately, but is mentioned within the entry.

Rehabilitation Intl. [16333]
Rehabilitation Tech. Assn. [16334]
Reiki Alliance [13651]
Renal Pathology Soc. [15872]
Renal Physicians Assn. [15298]
Resolve, The Natl. Infertility Assn. [14394]
Retinoblastoma Intl. [13869]
Riders for Hea. [15271]
Roger Wyburn-Mason and Jack M. Blount Found.
    for the Eradication of Rheumatoid Disease
    [16375]
Rolf Inst. of Structural Integration [13652]
Rose Kushner Breast Cancer Advisory Center
    [13870]
Royal Soc. of Medicine Found. [15178]
Safety Pharmacology Soc. [15950]
Salvadoran Amer. Medical Soc. [15092]
San Francisco AIDS Found. [13584]
Schizophrenia Intl. Res. Soc. [15232]
School Nurse Achievement Prog. [15525]
Scleroderma Found. [16389]
Scleroderma Res. Found. [16390]
Scleroderma Support Gp. [16391]
Scoliosis Assn., Inc. [16394]
Scoliosis Res. Soc. [16395]
Sect. for Long Term Care and Rehabilitation
    [14894]
Sect. for Metropolitan Hospitals [14895]
Serbian Amer. Medical and Dental Soc. [14185]
Serendipity Assn. [14832]
Seventh-Day Adventist Dietetic Assn. [15569]
Sexual Medicine Soc. of North Am. [16405]
Shriners Hospitals for Children [13973]
Shy Drager Syndrome/Multiple Sys. Atrophy Sup-
    port Gp. [15364]
Sickle Cell Disease Assn. of Am. [14797]
Simon Found. for Continence [16711]
Sino-American Pharmaceutical Professionals
    Assn. [15951]
Sister Kenny Rehabilitation Inst. [16335]
Skin Cancer Found. [13874]
Sleep Res. Soc. [16429]
Smokenders [16435]
Soc. for Academic Continuing Medical Educ.
    [8875]
Soc. for Academic Emergency Medicine [14344]
Soc. for Acupuncture Res. [13537]
Soc. for the Advancement of Blood Mgt. [14798]
Soc. for the Advancement of Women's Imaging
    [16294]
Soc. of Air Force Physicians [15264]
Soc. of Amer. Gastrointestinal and Endoscopic
    Surgeons [14428]
Soc. for Applied Immunohistochemistry [15873]
Soc. for Assisted Reproductive Tech. [16346]
Soc. of Cardiovascular Anesthesiologists [13689]
Soc. for Clinical and Experimental Hypnosis
    [14927]
Soc. for Clinical and Medical Hair Removal
    [14310]
Soc. of Clinical Res. Associates [14027]
Soc. for Clinical Trials [14028]
Soc. of Correctional Physicians [16011]
Soc. of Critical Care Medicine [14071]
Soc. of Diagnostic Medical Sonography [16438]
Soc. for Ear, Nose, and Throat Advances in
    Children [15827]
Soc. for Epidemiologic Res. [14377]
Soc. of Eye Surgeons [15703]
Soc. of Gastroenterology Nurses and Associates
    [14429]
Soc. of Govt. Ser. Urologists [16714]
Soc. for Gynecologic Investigation [15618]
Soc. of Gynecologic Oncologists [15654]
Soc. for Healthcare Consumer Advocacy of the
    Amer. Hosp. Assn. [15005]
Soc. for Healthcare Strategy and Market Develop-
    ment of the Amer. Hosp. Assn. [14896]
Soc. for Hematopathology [15874]
Soc. of Interventional Pain Mgt. Surgery Centers
    [16588]
Soc. of Interventional Radiology [16300]
Soc. of Invasive Cardiovascular Professionals
    [13928]
Soc. for Investigative Dermatology [14214]

Soc. for Leukocyte Biology [16365]
Soc. for Male Reproduction and Urology [16343]
Soc. of Medical Consultants to the Armed Forces
    [15265]
Soc. of Medical Jurisprudence [15006]
Soc. for Melanoma Res. [13875]
Soc. for Menstrual Cycle Res. [15619]
Soc. of Military Orthopaedic Surgeons [15266]
Soc. of Military Otolaryngologists - Head and
    Neck Surgeons [15267]
Soc. for Molecular Imaging [15181]
Soc. of Nuclear Medicine [15424]
Soc. of Nuclear Medicine Technologist Sect.
    [15425]
Soc. for Obstetric Anesthesia and Perinatology
    [15903]
Soc. for Occupational and Environmental Hea.
    [15633]
Soc. of Otorhinolaryngology and Head/Neck
    Nurses [15526]
Soc. for Pediatric Dermatology [14215]
Soc. of Pediatric Nurses [15527]
Soc. for Pediatric Radiology [16301]
Soc. for Pediatric Res. [15899]
Soc. for Pediatric Urology [16715]
Soc. of Primary Care Policy Fellows [14664]
Soc. for Public Hea. Educ. [16254]
Soc. for Radiation Oncology Administrators
    [16302]
Soc. of Reproductive Surgeons [16349]
Soc. for Simulation in Healthcare [15148]
Soc. for the Stud. of Male Reproduction [16344]
Soc. for the Stud. of Reproduction [16350]
Soc. of Surgical Oncology [15655]
Soc. of Teachers of Family Medicine [14387]
Soc. for Tech. in Anesthesia [13692]
Soc. for Theriogenology [16806]
Soc. of Thoracic Radiology [16305]
Soc. of Thoracic Surgeons [16644]
Soc. of Toxicologic Pathology [15876]
Soc. of Univ. Otolaryngologists - Head and Neck
    Surgeons [15828]
Soc. of Univ. Surgeons [16591]
Soc. of Univ. Urologists [16716]
Soc. for Vascular Surgery [16730]
Soc. for Vascular Ultrasound [16731]
Soc. for Veterinary Medical Ethics [16808]
Soc. for Whole Body Autoradiography [15149]
Spina Bifida Assn. of Am. [16458]
Spinal Cord Soc. [16469]
Spirit of Women Hosp. Network [14898]
Spondylitis Assn. of Am. [16377]
State EMS Training Coordinators Coun. of
    NASEMSO [14345]
Stratis Hea. [14600]
Stroke Awareness for Everyone [16495]
Stroke Clubs, Intl. [16496]
Sturge-Weber Found. [15365]
Sudden Cardiac Arrest Assn. [13933]
Sun Safety Alliance [13876]
Support Org. for Trisomy 18, 13, and Related
    Disorders [14485]
Support for People with Oral and Head and Neck
    Cancer [13877]
Surgical Dressing Manufacturers Assn. [IO]
Surgical Instrument Manufacturers Assn. of
    Pakistan [IO]
Swiss Soc. of Radiobiology and Medical Physics
    [IO]
Sword Swallowers Assn. Intl. [10776]
Syndrome X Assn. [15259]
Take Charge! Cure Parkinson's [15366]
Taking Control of Your Diabetes [14231]
Tear Film and Ocular Surface Soc. [15729]
TECH, Tech. Exchange for Christian Healthcare
    [20244]
Tel-Med [14601]
Thai Physicians Assn. of Am. [16012]
Therapy Dogs.Intl. [16638]
Theta Psi [24566]
Thoracic Surgery Residents Assn. [16645]
Tissue Engg. Soc. Intl. [6610]
Tourette Syndrome Assn. [15367]
Transatlantic Partners Against AIDS [13586]
Transplant Recipients Intl. Org. [16682]

Transplant Speakers Intl. [16683]
Treatment Action Gp. [13587]
Tremor Action Network [15369]
Trinity Medical Center [14900]
Trust for America's Hea. [16255]
Tuberous Sclerosis Alliance [15371]
Turner Syndrome Soc. of the U.S. [14486]
Ukrainian Medical Assn. of North Am. [15182]
Undersea and Hyperbaric Medical Soc. [16697]
Union of Amer. Physicians and Dentists [24092]
United Brachial Plexus Network [15403]
United Cerebral Palsy Associations [13935]
United Methodist Assn. of Hea. and Welfare
    Ministries [14602]
United Network for Organ Sharing [16684]
U.S. Adult Cystic Fibrosis Assn. [16364]
U.S. Hereditary Angioedema Assn. [14487]
U.S. Medical Massage Assn. [15033]
U.S. Pharmacopeia [15953]
Urgent Care Assn. of Am. [13665]
Urgenta Found. [IO]
Us TOO Intl. [13879]
USAF Medical Ser. Corps Assn. [13590]
Venous Soc. of Am. [16732]
Veterinary Botanical Medicine Assn. [16812]
Veterinary Orthopedic Soc. [16816]
VHA [14901]
Vision World Wide [16890]
Visiting Nurse Associations of Am. [15532]
Vitamin Angel Alliance [15571]
Vocational Evaluation and Career Assessment
    Professionals [16337]
Volunteer Trustees of Not-for-Profit Hospitals
    [14902]
Wellness Associates [16058]
Western Surgical Assn. [16592]
Western Veterinary Conf. [16817]
Wilderness Medical Soc. [15184]
Williams Syndrome Assn. [14490]
Women in Neurotrauma Res. [15404]
WomenHeart: Natl. Coalition for Women with
    Heart Disease [13929]
Women's Auxiliary of the ICA [14016]
World Allergy Org. [13605]
World Assn. of Medical Editors [14303]
World Assn. for Psychosocial Rehabilitation - U.S.
    Br. [16338]
World Assn. of Sleep Medicine [16430]
World Assn. of Veterinary Lab. Diagnosticians
    [16819]
World Coun. for Cardiovascular and Pulmonary
    Rehabilitation [13930]
World.Fed. for Mental Hea. [15237]
World Fed. of Neurology Res. Gp. on Motor
    Neuron Diseases [15373]
World Fed. of Neuroradiological Societies [16306]
World Homecare and Hospice Org. [14844]
World Medical Mission [IO]
World Medical Mission [20245]
World Soc. for Stereotactic and Functional Neuro-
    surgery [15418]
World Spine Soc. [15405]
World Sports Medicine Assn. of Registered
    Therapists [16486]
Wound, Ostomy and Continence Nurses Soc.; An
    Assn. of E.T. Nurses [15533]
Zero to Three: Natl. Center for Infants, Toddlers
    and Families [13944]

Medical Accreditation
Accreditation Commn. for Acupuncture and
    Oriental Medicine [15739]
Amer. Assn. of Managed Care Nurses [15435]
Amer. Assn. of Medical Assistants [15081]
Amer. Bd. for Certification in Orthotics, Prosthetics
    and Pedorthics [15783]
Amer. Bd. of Internal Medicine [14965]
Amer. Bd. for Occupational Hea. Nurses [15445]
Amer. Coll. of Cardiovascular Administrators
    [15052]
Amer. Coll. of Hea. Plan Mgt. [15053]
Amer. Coll. of Veterinary Anesthesiologists
    [16764]
Amer. Integrative Medical Assn. [15034]
Coll. of Diplomates of the Amer. Bd. of
    Orthodontics [14149]

Reference to "IO" in place of a book number signifies that the association may be found in the 45th edition of International Organizations.

Commn. on Accreditation of Allied Hea. Educ. Programs [8832]
Commn. on Collegiate Nursing Educ. [8859]
Comm. on Accreditation for Educational Programs for the EMS Professions [8833]
Comm. on Accreditation for Opthalmic Medical Personnel [8834]
Competency and Credentialing Inst. [14878]
Coun. on Accreditation of Nurse Anesthesia Educational Programs [8835]
Coun. on Medical Educ. of the Amer. Medical Assn. [8836]
Fed. for Accessible Nursing Educ. and Licensure [15578]
Fed. of Associations of Regulatory Boards [14555]
Intl. Nursing Coalition for Mass Casualty Educ. [8946]
Joint Commn. on Accreditation of Healthcare Organizations [14888]
Joint Rev. Comm. on Educ. in Diagnostic Medical Sonography [8837]
Joint Rev. Comm. on Educ. in Radiologic Tech. [8838]
Liaison Comm. on Medical Educ. [8839]
Natl. Assn. of Hea. Unit Coordinators [14578]
Natl. Bd. for Certification of Orthopaedic Technologists [15774]
Natl. Bd. of Medical Examiners [15095]
Natl. Coun. of State Boards of Nursing [15508]
Natl. Fitness Therapy Assn. [15968]
Natl. Org. for Competency Assurance [14591]
Nuclear Medicine Tech. Certification Bd. [15423]
Pediatric Nursing Certification Bd. [15522]
Soc. for Assisted Reproductive Tech. [16346]
Soc. of Reproductive Surgeons [16349]
World Sports Medicine Assn. of Registered Therapists [16486]
Medical Acupuncture; Amer. Acad. of [15740]
Medical Administration
Acad. for Intl. Hea. Stud. [15044]
Acad. for Intl. Hea. Stud. [IO]
Alliance for Academic Internal Medicine [8586]
Amer. Acad. of Ambulatory Care Nursing [15428]
Amer. Acad. of Medical Administrators [15045]
Amer. Acad. of Medical Administrators Res. and Educational Found. [15046]
Amer. Assn. of Healthcare Administrative Mgt. [15047]
Amer. Assn. of Integrated Healthcare Delivery Systems [15048]
Amer. Assn. of Medical Audit Specialists [15049]
Amer. Assn. of Medical Billers [15050]
Amer. Assn. of Medical Soc. Executives [15153]
Amer. Assn. of Physician Offices and Labs. [14990]
Amer. Assn. of Psychiatric Administrators [14861]
Amer. Bd. of Internal Medicine [14965]
Amer. Case Mgt. Assn. [15051]
Amer. Coll. of Cardiovascular Administrators [15052]
Amer. Coll. of Hea. Care Administrators [15535]
Amer. Coll. of Hea. Plan Mgt. [15053]
Amer. Coll. of Healthcare Executives [14862]
Amer. Coll. of Medical Practice Executives [15054]
Amer. Coll. of Mental Hea. Admin. [15187]
Amer. Coll. of Oncology Administrators [15055]
Amer. Coll. of Physician Executives [15056]
Amer. Healthcare Radiology Administrators [16275]
Amer. Medical Assn. [15155]
Amer. Medical Billing Assn. [15057]
Amer. Medical Directors Assn. [15536]
Amer. Org. of Nurse Executives [15454]
Amer. Soc. for Healthcare Environmental Services of the Amer. Hosp. Assn. [14866]
Amer. Soc. for Healthcare Risk Mgt. [14869]
Amer. Soc. of Law, Medicine and Ethics [15002]
Amer. Soc. of Ophthalmic Administrators [15058]
Assn. of Behavioral Healthcare Mgt. [15191]
Assn. of Biomedical Communications Directors [14030]
Assn. for Electronic Hea. Care Transactions [14618]

Assn. of Family Medicine Residency Directors [15059]
Assn. of Family Practice Administrators [15060]
Assn. of Healthcare Internal Auditors [15061]
Assn. for Healthcare Rsrc. and Materials Mgt. [14872]
Assn. of Medical Directors of Info. Systems [14957]
Assn. of Otolaryngology Administrators [15062]
Assn. of Professors of Cardiology [13896]
Assn. of Prog. Directors in Internal Medicine [14967]
Assn. of Prog. Directors in Vascular Surgery [16537]
Australian Medical Coun. [IO]
Canadian Inst. of Hea. Care and Bus. [IO]
Case Management Society of America [IO]
Case Mgt. Soc. of Am. [15063]
Case Mgt. Soc. of Australia [IO]
Center for Res. in Ambulatory Hea. Care Admin. [15064]
Coll. of Osteopathic Healthcare Executives [14876]
Coun. for Affordable Quality Healthcare [14625]
Coun. of Women's and Infants' Specialty Hospitals [14880]
Dental Gp. Mgt. Assn. [15065]
Fed. of Associations of Regulatory Boards [14555]
Hea. Res. and Educational Trust [14884]
Healthcare Financial Mgt. Assn. [15066]
Healthcare Info. and Mgt. Systems Soc. [14885]
Intl. Assn. of Healthcare Central Ser. Materiel Mgt. [14886]
Intl. Assn. for Healthcare Security and Safety [14887]
Intl. Assn. for Medicinal Compliance [15041]
Medical Dental Hosp. Bus. Associates [40]
Medical Gp. Mgt. Assn. [15067]
NAMDRC [15068]
Natl. Assn. of Boards of Examiners of Long Term Care Administrators [15538]
Natl. Assn. of County Hea. Fac. Administrators [15069]
Natl. Assn. of Directors of Nursing Admin. in Long Term Care [15493]
Natl. Assn. of Hea. Unit Coordinators [14578]
Natl. Assn. for Healthcare Recruitment [15070]
Natl. Assn. of Locum Tenens Org. [16004]
Natl. Assn. Medical Staff Services [15071]
Natl. Assn. of Urban Hospitals [14893]
Natl. Coun. of State Boards of Nursing [15508]
Natl. Org. for Competency Assurance [14591]
Natl. Renal Administrators Assn. [15072]
Perfusion Prog. Directors' Coun. [13921]
Professional Assn. of Hea. Care Off. Mgt. [15073]
Radiology Bus. Mgt. Assn. [15074]
Soc. of Medical Banking Excellence [1449]
USAF Medical Ser. Corps Assn. [13590]
Volunteer Trustees of Not-for-Profit Hospitals [14902]
Medical Aid
Acute Long Term Hosp. Assn. [14852]
African Medical and Res. Found. [14971]
Aid for Intl. Medicine [14972]
Air Charity Network [14312]
All4Israel [12454]
Amer. Ambulance Assn. [14313]
Amer. Belarussian Relief Org. [12828]
Amer. Bd. of Emergency Medicine [14325]
Amer. Bd. of Urgent Care Medicine [13662]
Amer. Coll. of Emergency Physicians [14326]
Amer. Coll. of Intl. Physicians [14973]
Amer. Coll. of Osteopathic Emergency Physicians [14327]
Amer. Osteopathic Bd. of Emergency Medicine [14328]
Amer. Physicians Fellowship for Medicine in Israel [12456]
Amer. Veterans Medical Airlift Ser. [6342]
Angel Flight West [12512]
Ashoka: Innovators for the Public [12419]
Assist Intl. [12513]
Assist Intl. [IO]
Assn. of Air Medical Services [14314]

Assn. of Assistive Tech. Act Programs [14237]
Assn. for Community Affiliated Plans [14617]
Assn. for Intl. Medical Study [12834]
Batey Relief Alliance [12835]
Blessings Intl. [IO]
Blessings Intl. [12514]
Blue Cross and Blue Shield Assn. [14959]
Brother's Brother Found. [12837]
Catholic Medical Mission Bd. [12515]
Catholic Medical Mission Bd. [IO]
Center for Medicare Advocacy [14684]
Center for Res. in Ambulatory Hea. Care Admin. [15064]
Children's HeartLink [13899]
Children's Wish Found. Intl. [11687]
China Medical Bd. of New York [14976]
Chinese Amer. Medical Soc. [15163]
CHOSEN [12516]
Christian Found. for Children and Aging [13159]
Christian Orthopaedic Partners [15765]
Christian Pilots Assn. [20321]
Community Voices [11745]
Direct Relief Intl. [12517]
Direct Relief Intl. [IO]
DOCARE Intl., N.F.P. [IO]
DOCARE Intl., N.F.P. [12518]
Docs for Tots [13958]
Dr. to Dr. [12519]
Dr. to Dr. [IO]
Drs. for Artists [12520]
Doctors for Developing Countries [IO]
Doctors Without Borders - France [IO]
Doctors to the World [IO]
Doctors to the World [IO]
Doctors to the World [12522]
Doctors of the World [12521]
Doctors Worldwide [12851]
EMDR - Humanitarian Assistance Programs [12767]
Emergency Medicine Found. [14331]
Emergency Medicine Residents' Assn. [14332]
Emergency Nurses Assn. [14333]
Filipino Amer. Medical Inc. [14722]
Flying Doctors of Am. [12523]
Flying Doctors of Am. [IO]
Found. for the Support of Intl. Medical Training [14977]
Fred Hollows Found. - Australia [IO]
Fred Hollows Found. - Vietnam [IO]
Gift of Life Intl. [IO]
Gift of Life Intl. [12524]
Global Healing [12450]
Global Hea. Coun. [14979]
Global Hea. Ministries [14630]
Global Neuro Rescue [15324]
Global Outreach Mission [12525]
Global Outreach Mission [IO]
God's Child Proj. [11597]
Hea. for Humanity [14563]
Hea. Volunteers Overseas [IO]
Hea. Volunteers Overseas [12526]
Hesperian Found. [14980]
HOPE Worldwide - Malaysia [IO]
Humanitarian Medical Relief [12527]
Humanity Intl. [12859]
Humanity United in Giving Internationally [11699]
Hunters Helping Hunters [22604]
Indian Medical Assn. [IO]
Indian Medical Assn. - Bangalore Br. [IO]
Indian Medical Assn. - Chandigarh [IO]
Indian Medical Assn. - Udupi-Karavali Br. [IO]
INMED Partnerships for Children [14981]
Interchurch Medical Assistance [20242]
Intermed Intl. [14982]
Intl. Assn. for Medical Assistance to Travellers [13343]
Intl. Hea. Exchange [IO]
Intl. Medical Corps [12862]
Intl. Medical Equip. Collaborative [14569]
Intl. Medical Volunteers Assn. [IO]
Intl. Medical Volunteers Assn. [15075]
Intl. Relief Teams [12863]
Intl. Soc. of First Responders [14317]
Iranian Amer. Medical Assn. [15173]
Israel Humanitarian Found. [12458]

A star before a book entry number signifies that the name is not listed separately, but is mentioned within the entry.

ITEM Coalition [14690]
Joint Action in Community Ser. [11803]
Lalmba Assn. [12866]
Lay Mission-Helpers Assn. [19648]
Liga Intl. [12528]
Liga Intl. [IO]
MADRE [12529]
Malawi Proj. [11266]
MAP Intl. [20243]
Medecins du Monde UK [IO]
Medical Missions Response [20246]
Medicine for Peace [12789]
MediSend Intl. [12530]
MediSend Intl. [IO]
Meds and Food for Kids [11622]
MedShare Intl. [IO]
MedShare Intl. [12531]
Mercy Ships Intl. Operations Center [15076]
Mercy Ships Intl. Operations Center [IO]
Mission Doctors Assn. [IO]
Mission Doctors Assn. [12532]
Mission to Haiti [12267]
Missions Intl. [20037]
Natl. Assn. of First Responders [14320]
Natl. Assn. of State EMS Officials [14337]
Natl. Christ Child Soc. [19679]
Natl. Comm. for Quality Assurance [16265]
Natl. Registry of Emergency Medical Technicians
   [14342]
Natl. Transplant Soc. [16680]
Natl. Voluntary Organizations Active in Disaster
   [12874]
New Eyes for the Needy [12533]
North Amer. Assn. for Ambulatory Urgent Care
   [13663]
Oper. Rainbow [15077]
Oper. Smile [12534]
Oper. Smile [IO]
Oper. U.S.A. [12535]
Pan Amer. Hea. and Educ. Found. [12536]
Pan Amer. Hea. and Educ. Found. [IO]
Pan Amer. Hea. Org. [14592]
Partners in Hea. [12270]
Partnership for Quality Medical Donations [IO]
Partnership for Quality Medical Donations [12537]
People-to-People Hea. Found. [14984]
Physicians for Peace [15078]
Physicians for Peace [IO]
Proj.: Hearts and Minds [12538]
Rapha Intl. [12539]
Recovered Medical Equip. for the Developing
   World [15079]
Recovered Medical Equip. for the Developing
   World [IO]
Red Sea Team Intl. [20385]
Refugee Relief Intl. [IO]
Refugee Relief Intl. [12540]
Rizal-MacArthur Memorial Found. [12541]
Soc. for Academic Emergency Medicine [14344]
State EMS Training Coordinators Coun. of
   NASEMSO [14345]
SurfAid Intl. [11791]
Task Force for Child Survival and Development
   [12542]
United Amputee Services Assn. [15080]
United Seniors Assn. [11322]
Uplift Internationale [15737]
Vietnam Veteran Wives [21332]
Vitamin Angel Alliance [15571]
VOSH Intl. [12543]
VOSH Intl. [IO]
World Medical Mission [20245]
World Medical Relief [IO]
World Medical Relief [12544]
World Rehabilitation Fund [11997]
Medical Aid for El Salvador - Defunct.
Medical Aid for Indochina - Address unknown since
   1995.
Medical Aid; Restoring Hope through Educational
   and [★12881]
Medical Airlift Ser; Amer. Veterans [6342]
Medical Alumni Assn; Univ. of Colorado [18931]
Medical Ambassadors Intl. [★20284]
Medical Ambassadors Intl. [IO], Modesto, CA, United
   States

Medical Anthropology; Soc. for [6434]
Medical Aspects of Sports; Joint Commn. on
   Competitive Safeguards and the [★16483]
Medical Assistance Programs [★20243]
Medical Assistance Programs [★IO]
Medical Assistants
   Accreditation Rev. Comm. on Educ. in Surgical
      Tech. [15123]
   Amer. Assn. of Bioanalysts Bd. of Registry
      [15126]
   Amer. Assn. of Medical Assistants [15081]
   Amer. Medical Technologists [15127]
   Amer. Registry of Medical Assistants [15082]
   Amer. Registry of Radiologic Technologists
      [15128]
   Amer. Soc. of Anesthesia Technologists and
      Technicians [15083]
   Amer. Soc. for Clinical Lab. Sci. [14992]
   Amer. Soc. of Extra-Corporeal Tech. [15129]
   Amer. Soc. of Podiatric Medical Assistants
      [16040]
   Amer. Soc. of Radiologic Technologists [15131]
   Amer. Soc. for Reconstructive Microsurgery
      [16573]
   Assn. for Healthcare Documentation Integrity
      [15084]
   Coun. on Podiatric Medical Educ. [16042]
   FireFlag/EMS [5773]
   Intl. Assn. of Sickle Cell Nurses And Physician
      Assistants [14706]
   Medicine for Peace [12789]
   Natl. Accrediting Agency for Clinical Lab. Sciences
      [15141]
   Natl. Credentialing Agency for Lab. Personnel
      [15145]
   Natl. Dental Assistants Assn. [14174]
   Natl. Soc. for Histotechnology [15146]
   Partners in Hea. [12270]
   Russian Amer. Medical Assn. [16378]
   SurfAid Intl. [11791]
Medical Assistants; Amer. Soc. of Podiatric [16040]
Medical Associates; Provident [★8871]
Medical Assn. Abroad; Haitian [★15159]
Medical Assn; Aero [★13538]
Medical Assn. Alliance; Amer. [15156]
Medical Assn; Amer. [15155]
Medical Assn; Amer. Holistic [14824]
Medical Assn; Amer. Holistic Veterinary [16773]
Medical Assn; Amer. Lebanese [15154]
Medical Assn; Amer. Occupational [★15624]
Medical Assn; Amer. Osteopathic Occupational
   [★15802]
Medical Assn; Amer. Physicians Fellowship for the
   Israel [★12456]
Medical Assn; Amer. Podiatric [16037]
Medical Assn; Amer. Preventive [★16049]
Medical Assn; Amer. Veterinary [16779]
Medical Assn; Amer. Veterinary Holistic [★16773]
Medical Assn; Arab Amer. [★14707]
Medical Assn. Auxiliary; Amer. [★15156]
Medical Assn. Auxiliary to the Natl. [15161]
Medical Assn. of the Bahamas [IO], Nassau,
   Bahamas
Medical Assn. in Brunei [IO], Bandar Seri Begawan,
   Brunei Darussalam
Medical Assn; Catholic [15996]
Medical Assn. Educ. and Res. Found; Amer.
   [★8843]
Medical Assn. Found; American Veterinary [★16779]
Medical Assn; Gay and Lesbian [14431]
Medical Assn; Intermountain Veterinary [★16817]
Medical Assn; Islamic [★16003]
Medical Assn. of Jamaica [IO], Kingston, Jamaica
Medical Assn; Korean-American [15174]
Medical Assn. of Malta [IO], Gzira, Malta
Medical Assn; Natl. [15176]
Medical Assn; Natl. Arab Amer. [14707]
Medical Assn; Natl. Ayurvedic [13642]
Medical Assn; Natl. Hispanic [14820]
Medical Assn; Natl. Podiatric [16047]
Medical Assn. of North Am; Bangladesh [15162]
Medical Assn. of North Am; Interstate Postgraduate
   [14386]
Medical Assn. of North Am; Islamic [16003]
Medical Assn. of North Am; Ukrainian [15182]

Medical Assn. for Prevention of War - Australia [IO],
   Carlton, Australia
Medical Assn. of South Africa [★IO]
Medical Assn. of South East Asian Nations [IO], Sin-
   gapore, Singapore
Medical Assn; Student Amer. [★8844]
Medical Assn; Student Osteopathic [15815]
Medical Assn. of Turkey [IO], Ankara, Turkey
Medical Assn; U.S. Veterinary [★16779]
Medical Assn; Women's Auxiliary to the Amer.
   [★15156]
Medical Assn; Women's Auxiliary to the Natl.
   [★15161]
Medical Assn; Women's Veterinary [★16786]
Medical Assurance Soc. [IO], Wellington, New
   Zealand
Medical Athletic Assn; Amer. [23650]
Medical Audio Visual Inst. - Defunct.
Medical Banking Excellence; Soc. of [1449]
Medical Banking Proj. [1433], 320 Main St., Ste.
   230, Franklin, TN 37064, (615)794-2009
Medical Benevolence Found. [14725], PO Box
   770636, Houston, TX 77215-0636, (800)547-7627
Medical and Biological Engg; Amer. Inst. for [7112]
Medical Bd. of New York; China [14976]
Medical Boards; Amer. Confed. of Reciprocating,
   Examining and Licensing [★15165]
Medical Boards; Fed. of Podiatric [16043]
Medical Boards; Fed. of Podiatry [★16043]
Medical Boards of the U.S; Fed. of State [15165]
Medical Book Publishers; Assn. of Amer. [★3204]
Medical Care; Symposium on Cmpt. Applications in
   [★14079]
Medical Center; Animal [11353]
Medical Center; City of Hope Natl. [15102]
Medical Chess Club of America - Defunct.
Medical Clinics; Amer. Assn. of [★14717]
Medical Colleges; Assn. of Amer. Veterinary [9293]
Medical Comm. for Civil Rights - Defunct.
Medical Comm. for Human Rights - Defunct.
Medical Communications Directors; Assn. of Bio
   [14030]
Medical Computing Soc; Bio [★6783]
Medical Consultants to the Armed Forces; Soc. of
   [15265]
Medical Consultants in World War II; Soc. of U.S.
   [★15265]
Medical Consumers; Center for [14550]
Medical Consumers and Hea. Care Info; Center for
   [★14550]
Medical Corps; World [★12862]
Medical Correctional Assn. - Defunct.
Medical Correctional Soc. of the Amer. Correctional
   Assn. [★15186]
Medical Coun. of India [IO], New Delhi, India
Medical Cybernetics Found. - Address unknown
   since 2002.
Medical Decision Making; Soc. for [15180]
Medical Defence Assn. of Victoria [IO], Carlton,
   Australia
Medical Defence Malaysia [IO], Kuala Lumpur,
   Malaysia
Medical Defence Union [IO], London, United
   Kingdom
Medical and Dental Assn; Natl. [19305]
Medical-Dental Comm. on Evaluation of Fluoridation
   - Defunct.
Medical-Dental-Hospital Burs. of America - Address
   unknown since 1999.
Medical Dental Hosp. Bus. Associates [40], 350
   Poplar Ave., Elmhurst, IL 60126, (630)941-8100
Medical and Dental Soc; Christian [★20238]
Medical and Dental Soc; Global Hea. Outreach of
   the Christian [★20238]
Medical Dermatology Soc. [14206], 820 W Superior
   Ave., Ste. 700, Cleveland, OH 44113-1807,
   (216)579-9300
Medical Device Assn; Smaller Mfrs. [★3486]
Medical Device Mfrs. Assn. [3486], 1350 I St. NW,
   Ste. 540, Washington, DC 20005, (202)354-7171
Medical Diagnostics Mfrs; Assn. of [3482]
Medical Direction of Respiratory Care; Natl. Assn. for
   [★15068]
Medical Directors; Amer. Acad. of [★15056]
Medical Directors Assn; Airlines [13539]

Reference to "IO" in place of a book number signifies that the association may be found in the 45th edition of International Organizations.

Medical Directors Assn; Amer. [15536]
Medical Distributors Assn; Independent [1862]
Medical Editors' Assn; Mississippi Valley [★3082]
Medical Education
Acad. of Pharmaceutical Physicians and
Investigators [8840]
Accreditation Coun. for Continuing Medical Educ.
[15151]
Alliance for Academic Internal Medicine [8586]
Alliance for Continuing Medical Educ. [8841]
Alliance of Independent Academic Medical
Centers [15085]
Amer. Acad. of Medical Mgt. [15086]
Amer. Assn. of Colleges of Nursing [8842]
Amer. Assn. of Colleges of Osteopathic Medicine
[15791]
Amer. Bd. of Urgent Care Medicine [13662]
Amer. Medical Assn. Found. [8843]
Amer. Medical Student Assn. [8844]
Amer. Soc. for Bioethics and Humanities [8845]
Anesthesia History Assn. [13678]
Assn. of Accredited Naturopathic Medical Col-
leges [8943]
Assn. of Amer. Indian Physicians [15989]
Assn. of Amer. Medical Colleges [8846]
Assn. of Amer. Medical Colleges-Women in
Medicine Prog. [8847]
Assn. of Black Nursing Faculty [8848]
Assn. for Continuing Dental Educ. [8195]
Assn. of Faculties of Medicine of Canada [IO]
Assn. for Hosp. Medical Educ. [14873]
Assn. for Medical Educ. in the Eastern Mediter-
ranean Region [IO]
Assn. for Medical Educ. in Europe [IO]
Assn. for Medical Educ. and Res. in Substance
Abuse [8849]
Assn. for Medical Educ. in the Western Pacific
Region [IO]
Assn. of Medical Schools in Europe [IO]
Assn. of Minority Hea. Professions Schools [8850]
Assn. of Native Amer. Medical Students [15087]
Assn. of Optometric Educators [8851]
Assn. of Pediatric Prog. Directors [8852]
Assn. of Professors of Gynecology and Obstetrics
[15592]
Assn. of Professors of Medicine [8853]
Assn. of Prog. Directors in Internal Medicine
[14967]
Assn. of Prog. Directors in Radiology [15088]
Assn. of Psychology Postdoctoral and Internship
Centers [8854]
Assn. of Schools of Allied Hea. Professions
[8855]
Assn. of Schools of Public Hea. in the European
Region [IO]
Assn. of Specialty Professors [8587]
Assn. for the Stud. of Medical Educ. [IO]
Assn. for Surgical Educ. [IO]
Assn. for Surgical Educ. [8856]
Assn. of Univ. Programs in Hea. Admin. [8857]
Bangladesh Medical Stud. and Res. Inst. [IO]
Bates Assn. for Vision Educ. [IO]
Boston Intl. Found. for Medical Education/
Exchange [IO]
Boston Intl. Found. for Medical Education/
Exchange [15089]
Canadian Assn. of Schools of Nursing [IO]
Canadian Chiropractic Examining Bd. [IO]
Canadian Coun. for Accreditation of Pharmacy
Programs [IO]
Canadian Coun. on Continuing Educ. in
Pharmacy [IO]
Canadian Post-MD Educ. Registry [IO]
Clerkship Directors in Internal Medicine [14968]
Coalition of Natl. Hea. Educ. Organizations [8858]
Commn. on Collegiate Nursing Educ. [8859]
Comprehensive Hea. Educ. Found. [8860]
Coun. on Medical Student Educ. in Pediatrics
[8861]
Coun. of Teaching Hospitals [14879]
Ethiopian Pharmacists Assn. in North Am. [15932]
Fed. for Accessible Nursing Educ. and Licensure
[15478]
Global Alliance for Medical Educ. [8862]
Global Alliance for Medical Educ. [IO]

Hea. Occupations Students of Am. [8863]
Hispanic-Serving Hea. Professions Schools
[8864]
Hong Kong Sex Educ. Assn. [IO]
Indians Into Medicine [8865]
Inst. of Hea. Promotion and Educ. [IO]
International Association of Medical Science
Educators [IO]
Intl. Assn. of Medical Sci. Educators [15090]
Intl. Childbirth Educ. Assn. [15605]
Intl. Nursing Coalition for Mass Casualty Educ.
[8946]
Intl. Soc. for Medical Education - U.S. [15091]
Joint Rev. Comm. on Educ. in Diagnostic Medical
Sonography [8837]
Med Help Intl. [15042]
Medical Educ. for South African Blacks [IO]
MediSend Intl. [12530]
Natl. Assn. of Advisors for the Hea. Professions
[8866]
Natl. Assn. of EMS Educators [8867]
National Association of EMS Educators [IO]
Natl. Assn. of Geriatric Educ. Centers [14513]
Natl. Assn. of Hea. Educ. Centers [14675]
Natl. Assn. of Medical Minority Educators [8868]
Natl. Assn. for Practical Nurse Educ. and Ser.
[8869]
Natl. Assn. of Supervisors and Administrators of
Hea. Occupations Educ. [8870]
Natl. Center for Hea. Educ. [14582]
Natl. Educ. Alliance for Borderline Personality
Disorder [15224]
Natl. Medical Fellowships [8871]
Natl. Resident Matching Prog. [8872]
Natl. Student Nurses' Assn. [8873]
Network for Continuing Medical Educ. [15177]
Nordic Inst. for Advanced Training in Occupational
Hea. [IO]
North Amer. Assn. of Medical Educ. and Commun.
Companies [8874]
Nurses Educational Funds [15516]
Orthopaedic Res. and Educ. Found. [8949]
People-to-People Hea. Found. [14984]
Perfusion Prog. Directors' Coun. [13921]
Phi Delta Epsilon Medical Fraternity [24540]
Phi Delta Epsilon Medical Fraternity [IO]
Physicians for Peace [15078]
Royal Australian Coll. of Gen. Practitioners [IO]
Royal Coll. of Surgeons of Edinburgh [IO]
Salvadoran Amer. Medical Soc. [15092]
Scottish Coun. for Postgraduate Medical and
Dental Educ. [IO]
SEAMEO Regional Centre for Medical Microbiol-
ogy, Parasitology and Entomology [IO]
SEAMEO Regional Centre for Public Hea. [IO]
Sex Info. and Educ. Coun. of Canada [IO]
Society for Academic Continuing Medical Educa-
tion [IO]
Soc. for Academic Continuing Medical Educ.
[8875]
Soc. of Gen. Internal Medicine [14970]
Student Natl. Medical Assn. [8876]
Student Osteopathic Medical Assn. [15815]
Tropical Hea. and Educ. Trust [IO]
Upledger Inst. [13657]
World Fed. for Medical Educ. [IO]
Medical Educ; Accreditation Coun. for Continuing
[15151]
Medical Educ; Accreditation Coun. for Graduate
[7872]
Medical Educ; Assn. for the Behavioral Sciences and
[6527]
Medical Educ; Assn. for Hosp. [14873]
Medical Educ; Coun. on Podiatric [16042]
Medical Educ. Found; Amer. [★8843]
Medical Educ. Fund for Podiatric [16044]
Medical Educ; Liaison Comm. on Continuing
[★15151]
Medical Educ; Liaison Comm. on Graduate [★7872]
Medical Educ; Network for Continuing [15177]
Medical Educ. and Res. Foundation [★14549]
Medical Educ. for South African Blacks [IO],
Washington, DC, United States
Medical Educ. for South African Blacks - Defunct.
Medical, Educational, Social Service Assn. - Address
unknown since 1990.

Medical Educators; Assn. of Osteopathic Directors
and [15808]
Medical Electrologists; Soc. of Clinical and [★14310]
Medical Electronics Soc. - Defunct.
Medical Equestrian Assn; Amer. [★16474]
Medical Equestrian Association/Safe Riders Found;
Amer. [16474]
Medical Equip. Companies; Natl. Affiliation of
Durable [★14670]
Medical Equip. Services; Natl. Assn. for [★14670]
Medical Equip. Suppliers; Assn. of Independent
[★14670]
Medical Equip. Suppliers; Natl. Assn. of [★14670]
Medical Equip. and Tech. Assn. [7306], 220 S Bus.
Park Dr., Ste. A-1, Oostburg, WI 53070, (804)693-
3916
Medical Ethics; Amer. Inst. of [12122]
Medical Ethics; Inst. for Jewish [20143]
Medical Ethics and Mediation; Center for [5452]
Medical Examiners
Amer. Bd. of Independent Medical Examiners
[8877]
American Board of Independent Medical Examin-
ers [IO]
Amer. Bd. of Surgery [16563]
Fed. of Podiatric Medical Boards [16043]
Fed. of State Medical Boards of the U.S. [15165]
Intl. Assn. of Coroners and Medical Examiners
[15093]
Intl. Assn. of Coroners and Medical Examiners
[IO]
Natl. Assn. of Medical Examiners [15094]
Natl. Bd. of Medical Examiners [15095]
Medical Examiners Assn; Airline [★13540]
Medical Examiners; Natl. Bd. of Osteopathic [15812]
Medical Examiners; Natl. Bd. of Podiatric [16046]
Medical Examining Boards; Amer. Confed. of State
[★15165]
Medical Exchange; Boston Intl. Found. for [★15089]
Medical Exhibitors Assn. [★1340]
Medical Fitness Assn. [15966], PO Box 73103,
Richmond, VA 23235-8026, (804)897-5701
Medical Fly Fishing Assn; Amer. [4349]
Medical Found. [IO], Sydney, Australia
Medical Found; AIDS [★13557]
Medical Found. for AIDS and Sexual Hea. [IO],
London, United Kingdom
Medical Fraternity; Phi Chi [24544]
Medical Friends of Wine; Soc. of [23028]
Medical Genetics; Amer. Bd. of [14493]
Medical Genetics; Amer. Coll. of [14494]
Medical Graduates; Educational Coun. for Foreign
[★15997]
Medical Graduates; Natl. Assn. of Foreign [★14973]
Medical Gp. Administrators; Amer. Coll. of [★15054]
Medical Gp. Assn; Amer. [14717]
Medical Gp. Mgt. Assn. [15067], 104 Inverness Terr.
E, Englewood, CO 80112-5306, (303)799-1111
Medical Gp. Missions of the Christian Medical and
Dental Soc. [★20238]
Medical Gp. Missions of the Christian Medical and
Dental Soc. [★IO]
Medical Hair Removal; Soc. for Clinical and [14310]
Medical Hypnoanalysts; Amer. Acad. of [14914]
Medical Identification
Action Against Medical Accidents [IO]
Amer. Veterans Medical Airlift Ser. [6342]
Asociacion Medica Argentina [IO]
Canadian MedicAlert Found. [IO]
Coeliac Soc. of Ireland [IO]
European Medical Students' Assn. [IO]
Fund for Podiatric Medical Educ. [16044]
Japan Medical Assn. [IO]
Kenya Medical Assn. [IO]
MAAP Services for Autism and Asperger
Syndrome [15337]
Medical Assn. of Malta [IO]
MedicAlert Found. Intl. [14318]
Natl. Medical and Dental Assn. [19305]
Surfer's Medical Assn. [15096]
Medical Illustration
Assn. of Medical Illustrators [13707]
Medical Illustrators; Assn. of [13707]
Medical Image Perception Soc. [15140], c/o Jannick
Rolland, PhD, CREOL, Univ. Central Florida, 4000
Central Florida Blvd., Orlando, FL 32816-2700,
(407)823-6870

A star before a book entry number signifies that the name is not listed separately, but is mentioned within the entry.

Medical Imaging Soc; Computerized [16287]
Medical Indus. Assn. of Australia [IO], St. Leonards, Australia
Medical Informatics; Amer. Coll. of [★14079]
Medical Informatics Assn; Amer. [14079]
Medical Info. Bur. [★14961]
Medical Info; Natl. Inst. of Electro [14311]
Medical Info. Processing; Special Interest Gp. for Bio [★6783]
Medical Inst; Howard Hughes [15107]
Medical Institute; Tibetan [★11055]
Medical Instrumentation; Assn. for the Advancement of [6606]
Medical Interfraternity Conf. - Defunct.
Medical Joggers Assn; Amer. [★23650]
Medical Journalists' Assn. [IO], Heathfield, United Kingdom
Medical Jurisprudence; Soc. of [15006]
Medical Jurisprudence and State Medicine; Soc. of [★15006]
Medical Lab Personnel; Natl. Certification Agency for [★15145]
Medical Lab. Schools; Accrediting Bur. of [★15124]
Medical Letter [15940], 1000 Main St., New Rochelle, NY 10801, (914)235-0500
Medical Liability Commn. - Defunct.
Medical Liberation Front - Address unknown since 1995.
Medical Lib. Assn. [10372], 65 E Wacker Pl., Ste. 1900, Chicago, IL 60601-7246, (312)419-9094
Medical Mgt. Assn; Biotech [14683]
Medical Marketing Assn. [2637], 1525 Valley Center Pkwy., Ste. 150, Bethlehem, PA 18017, (610)868-8530
Medical Marketing Assn; Bio [★2624]
Medical Milk Commissions; Amer. Assn. of [16384]
Medical Ministries; Children's [13955]
Medical Mission; Marine [★20376]
Medical Mission Sisters [20356], 8400 Pine Rd., Philadelphia, PA 19111, (215)742-6100
Medical Mission Sisters [IO], Philadelphia, PA, United States
Medical Missions Response [IO], Oklahoma City, OK, United States
Medical Missions Response [20246], PO Box 57011, Oklahoma City, OK 73157-7011, (866)667-8996
Medical Museum; Army [★15261]
Medical Museums; Intl. Assn. of [★15868]
Medical Mycological Soc. of the Americas [15275], c/o Dr. James Harris, 2501 Timberline Dr., Austin, TX 78746, (512)458-7566
Medical Network for Missing Children - Address unknown since 2007.
Medical Nurses Assn; Baro [15471]
Medical Officers of Amer. Institutions of Idiotic and Feebleminded Children; Assn. of [★15239]
Medical Officers of Schools Assn. [IO], Sevenoaks, United Kingdom
Medical Outcomes Trust [14644], 275 Wyman St., Ste. 120, Waltham, MA 02451, (781)890-4884
Medical Outreach for Armenians - Address unknown since 2002.
Medical Passport Found. - Defunct.
Medical Peer Rev. Assn; Amer. [★16262]
Medical Pharmaceutical Info. Assn. [IO], Almaty, Kazakhstan
Medical Physician Assn; Air [15983]
Medical Physics; Amer. Coll. of [16016]
Medical Political Action Comm; Amer. [18279]
Medical Practice Mgt; Amer. Coll. of [★15086]
Medical Preventics; Amer. Acad. of [★16051]
Medical Professionals with Hearing Losses; Assn. of [14744]
Medical Progress Educational Found; Americans for [13694]
Medical Protection Soc. [IO], London, United Kingdom
Medical Psychotherapists and Psychodiagnosticians; Amer. Bd. of [16202]
Medical Publications; Assn. of [3209]
Medical Publishers' Assn; Amer. [3204]
Medical Quality; Amer. Coll. of [16261]
Medical Quality; Inst. for [16263]
Medical Record Economics; Inst. for [★15098]
Medical Record Librarians; Amer. Assn. of [★15097]

Medical Records
Amer. Assn. of Medical Audit Specialists [15049]
Amer. Assn. of Medical Billers [15050]
Amer. Hea. Info. Mgt. Assn. [15097]
Amer. Nursing Informatics Assn. [15453]
Canadian Hea. Info. Mgt. Assn. [IO]
Canadian Inst. for Hea. Info. [IO]
Dutch Assn. for Medical Records Admin. [IO]
Hong Kong Soc. of Medical Informatics [IO]
Medical Records Inst. [15098]
Medical Transcription Indus. Assn. [2670]
Privacy Rights CH [3176]
Medical Records Assn; Amer. [★15097]
Medical Records Inst. [15098], 425 Boylston St., Boston, MA 02116-3315, (617)964-3923
Medical Reform
Chromosome Deletion Outreach [14445]
Gilda Radner Familial Ovarian Cancer Registry [13826]
Incontinentia Pigmenti Intl. Found. [14455]
Make Early Diagnosis to Prevent Early Death [14463]
Natl. Coordinating Coun. for Medication Error Reporting and Prevention [14653]
Nature of Wellness [13701]
Medical Rehabilitation Center for Torture Victims [IO], Athens, Greece
Medical Rehabilitation Providers Assn; Amer. [16312]
Medical Relief Broadcasts - Defunct.
Medical Rescue Ser; Parachute [★12540]
Medical Research
A-T Medical Res. Found. [14436]
Acad. of Behavioral Medicine Res. [13732]
Acad. on Mental Retardation [15238]
Acad. of Pharmaceutical Res. and Sci. [15906]
Acad. of Surgical Res. [15099]
AcademyHealth [14535]
Accelerated Cure Proj. for Multiple Sclerosis [15301]
Accreditation Coun. for Pharmacy Educ. [15907]
Alliance for Human Res. Protection [17741]
Alliance for Lupus Res. [15013]
Alliance for the Prudent Use of Antibiotics [15908]
Amer. Acad. of Medical Administrators Res. and Educational Found. [15046]
Amer. Acad. of Neurological and Orthopaedic Surgeons [15409]
Amer. Acad. of Neurology [15376]
Amer. Acad. of Sleep Medicine [16418]
Amer. Acad. of Somnology [16419]
Amer. Animal Hosp. Assn. [16739]
Amer. Assn. for Clinical Chemistry [13936]
Amer. Assn. of Colleges of Pharmacy [15909]
Amer. Assn. for Dental Res. [14113]
Amer. Assn. of Immunologists [14929]
Amer. Assn. on Intellectual and Developmental Disabilities [15239]
Amer. Assn. for Medical Chronobiology and Chronotherapeutics [13751]
Amer. Assn. of Neurological Surgeons [15410]
Amer. Assn. of Neuropathologists [15853]
Amer. Assn. for the Stud. of Liver Diseases [14801]
Amer. Bd. of Neurological Surgery [15411]
Amer. Bd. of Preventive Medicine [16050]
Amer. Bd. of Urgent Care Medicine [13662]
Amer. Clinical and Climatological Assn. [14018]
Amer. Clinical Lab. Assn. [14991]
Amer. Coll. for Advancement in Medicine [16051]
Amer. Coll. of Angiology [16719]
Amer. Coll. of Apothecaries [15912]
Amer. Coll. of Clinical Pharmacology [15913]
Amer. Coll. of Clinical Pharmacy [15914]
Amer. Coll. of Medical Genetics [14494]
Amer. Coll. of Neuropsychopharmacology [15915]
Amer. Coll. of Preventive Medicine [16052]
Amer. Coll. of Rheumatology [16367]
Amer. Fed. for Medical Res. [14019]
Amer. Found. for Pharmaceutical Educ. [15916]
Amer. Headache Soc. [14531]
Amer. Hea. Assistance Found. [15100]
Amer. Horticultural Therapy Assn. [16601]
Amer. Inst. of the History of Pharmacy [15917]
Amer. Inst. of Stress [16487]

Amer. Liver Found. [14803]
Amer. Pain Soc. [15836]
Amer. Parkinson Disease Assn. [15304]
Amer. Pharmacists Assn. - Acad. of Pharmacy Practice and Mgt. [15918]
Amer. Pharmacists Assn. Acad. of Student Pharmacists [15919]
Amer. Podiatric Medical Writers Assn. [16039]
Amer. Registry of Pathology [15858]
Amer. Soc. for Clinical Investigation [14020]
Amer. Soc. for Clinical Nutrition [15547]
Amer. Soc. for Clinical Pharmacology and Therapeutics [15920]
Amer. Soc. of Consultant Pharmacists [15922]
Amer. Soc. of Cytopathology [14075]
Amer. Soc. for Cytotechnology [14076]
Amer. Soc. of Electroneurodiagnostic Technologists [14307]
Amer. Soc. of Hea. Sys. Pharmacists [15923]
Amer. Soc. for Histocompatibility and Immunogenetics [14931]
Amer. Soc. of Interventional and Therapeutic Neuroradiology [16280]
Amer. Soc. of Neuroradiology [16282]
Amer. Soc. for Nutrition [15548]
Amer. Soc. of Pharmacognosy [15924]
Amer. Soc. for Pharmacology and Experimental Therapeutics [15925]
Amer. Soc. for Stereotactic and Functional Neurosurgery [15412]
Amer. Spinal Injury Assn. [16461]
Amer. Urological Assn. Found. [16705]
Americans for Medical Progress Educational Found. [13694]
Amyotrophic Lateral Sclerosis Assn. [15306]
Applied Res. Ethics Natl. Assn. [15101]
Arthritis Found. [16369]
ASHP Found. [15926]
Asian Soc. for Pigment Cell Res. [IO]
Assoc. Professional Sleep Societies [16422]
Assn. of Amer. Cancer Institutes [13794]
Assn. of Clinical Scientists [14022]
Assn. of Freestanding Radiation Oncology Centers [16268]
Assn. of Intl. Hea. Researchers [14548]
Assn. of Medical Lab. Immunologists [14932]
Assn. of Medical Res. Charities [IO]
Assn. for Ocular Pharmacology and Therapeutics [15671]
Assn. of Polysomnographic Technologists [16423]
Assn. of Prevention Teaching and Res. [16054]
Assn. for Res. in Vision and Ophthalmology [15672]
Assn. of Rheumatology Hea. Professionals [16370]
Assn. of Veterans Affairs Ophthalmologists [15676]
Australian Soc. for Medical Res. [IO]
Autism Speaks [13724]
Avenues, Natl. Support Gp. for Arthrogryposis Multiplex Congenita [15309]
Benign Essential Blepharospasm Res. Found. [15311]
Benjamin Franklin Literary and Medical Soc. [14549]
Better Sleep Coun. [16424]
Bladder Cancer Advocacy Network [13799]
Cajal Club [15385]
Cancer Info. Ser. [13807]
Carrie Estelle Doheny Found. [13156]
Center for Sports and Osteopathic Medicine [16055]
Center for the Stud. of Multiple Birth [15272]
Central Soc. for Clinical Res. [14023]
Centre for Arctic Medicine [IO]
Cervical Spine Res. Soc. [16462]
Chem. Injury Info. Network [16656]
Child Neurology Soc. [15386]
Childhood Arthritis and Rheumatology Res. Alliance [16371]
Children's Cause for Cancer Advocacy [13812]
Children's Tumor Found. [15315]
Christopher and Dana Reeve Found. [16463]
City of Hope Natl. Medical Center [15102]
Clinical Lab. Mgt. Assn. [14993]

Reference to "IO" in place of a book number signifies that the association may be found in the 45th edition of International Organizations.

Clinical and Lab. Standards Inst. [14994]
Clinical Ligand Assay Soc. [14995]
Coalition for the Advancement of Medical Res. [15103]
Coalition of Cancer Cooperative Groups [13814]
Coalition for Hemophilia B [14787]
Cognitive Neuroscience Soc. [15407]
Collegium Internationale Neuro-Psychopharmacologicum [15929]
Comm. for the Promotion of Medical Res. [15104]
Consortium for Conservation Medicine [15164]
Cornea Res. Found. of Am. [15105]
Crohn's and Colitis Found. of Am. [14414]
Cure Res. Found. [13818]
Cystinosis Res. Network [15247]
Damon Runyon Cancer Res. Found. [13819]
Dana Alliance for Brain Initiatives [15387]
Diabetes Action Res. and Educ. Found. [14221]
Diabetes Res. Assn. of Am. [14223]
Diabetes Res. Inst. Found. [14224]
Donald W. Reynolds Found. [13903]
Drug Info. Assn. [15931]
Dysautonomia Found. [15317]
Dystonia Medical Res. Found. [15319]
ECRI [15136]
Endocrine Soc. [14355]
Environmental Res. Found. [13599]
Epilepsy Therapy Development Proj. [14381]
Esther A. and Joseph Klingenstein Fund [15106]
European Fed. for the Sci. and Tech. of Lipids [IO]
European Sci. Found. [IO]
Facioscapulohumeral (FSH) Soc. [15320]
Fanconi Anemia Res. Fund [14450]
Fertile Hope [14390]
Foreign Pharmacy Graduate Examination Comm. [15933]
Found. for the Advancement of Chiropractic Tenets and Sci. [14003]
Found. for Chiropractic Educ. and Res. [14004]
Found. for Innovation in Medicine [15166]
French Found. for Medical Res. [IO]
Friedreich's Ataxia Res. Alliance [14403]
Gait and Clinical Movement Anal. Soc. [14557]
Genetics Policy Inst. [14499]
German Medical Assn. [IO]
The Glaucoma Found. [15682]
Global Assn. for Interpersonal Neurobiology Stud. [7375]
Global Bus. Coalition on HIV/AIDS [11329]
Global Perioperative Res. Org. [14026]
Guardians of Hydrocephalus Res. Found. [15326]
Hea. Res. Coun. of New Zealand [IO]
Heart Disease Res. Found. [13905]
Heart Rhythm Soc. [13907]
Hemophilia Fed. of Am. [14789]
Histochemical Soc. [13938]
Howard Hughes Medical Inst. [15107]
Howard Hughes Medical Institute [IO]
Human Growth Found. [16020]
Huntington's Disease Soc. of Am. [15329]
Indian Coun. of Medical Res. [IO]
Indo-Amer. Soc. of Interventional Cardiology [13908]
Intl. Assn. of Cancer Victors and Friends [13831]
Intl. Assn. of Human-Animal Interaction Organizations [16615]
Intl. Assn. for Paratuberculosis [16793]
Intl. Assn. for the Stud. of Pain [15841]
Intl. Atherosclerosis Soc. [13910]
Intl. Behavioral Neuroscience Soc. [15408]
Intl. Biopharmaceutical Assn. [15936]
Intl. Bundle Br. Block Assn. [13911]
Intl. Cell Death Soc. [6854]
Intl. Complement Soc. [14938]
Intl. Cystic Fibrosis-Mucoviscidosis Assn. [IO]
Intl. Fed. of Marfan Syndrome Organizations [14456]
Intl. Genetic Epidemiology Soc. [14376]
Intl. Hea. Evaluation Assn. [14568]
Intl. Hyperhidrosis Soc. [14357]
Intl. Leptospirosis Soc. [14950]
Intl. Soc. for Biological Therapy of Cancer [13835]
Intl. Soc. for Complementary Medicine Res. [13639]

Intl. Soc. for the History of the Neurosciences [7376]
Intl. Soc. for Interferon and Cytokine Res. [16351]
Intl. Soc. of Lymphology [15016]
Intl. Soc. on Metabolic Eye Disease [15691]
Intl. Soc. of Motor Control [7377]
Intl. Soc. for Plastination [15870]
Intl. Soc. of Psychiatric Genetics [14502]
Intl. Soc. of Psychoneuroendocrinology [15108]
International Society of Psychoneuroendocrinology [IO]
Intl. Soc. for Res. on Impulsivity [16088]
Intl. Soc. for Stem Cell Res. [14503]
Intl. Soc. on Thrombosis and Haemostasis [14793]
Intl. Stuttering Assn. [16498]
Interstate Postgraduate Medical Assn. of North Am. [14386]
John A. Hartford Found. [11291]
Joseph Drown Found. [12051]
Joseph P. Kennedy, Jr. Found. [12571]
Kennedy's Disease Assn. [15334]
Lupus Found. of Am. [15014]
Lyme Disease Assn. [14271]
Medical Image Perception Soc. [15140]
Medical Letter [15940]
Medical Res. Modernization Comm. [15109]
Medical Res. Soc. [IO]
Mended Hearts, Inc. [13916]
Mental Res. Inst. [13737]
Mitochondrial Medicine Soc. [14078]
Multiple Sclerosis Found. [15338]
Myasthenia Gravis Found. of Am. [15340]
NARSAD: Mental Hea. Res. Assn. [15213]
Natl. Alliance for Autism Res. [13726]
Natl. Alliance for Eye and Vision Res. [16872]
Natl. Alliance of Medical Researchers and Teaching Physicians [15143]
Natl. Alliance of State Pharmacy Associations [15943]
Natl. Alopecia Areata Found. [16386]
Natl. Assn. of Boards of Pharmacy [15944]
Natl. Assn. for Res. and Therapy of Homosexuality [14434]
Natl. Ataxia Found. [15342]
Natl. Catholic Pharmacists Guild of the U.S. [15945]
Natl. Center for Voice and Speech [16451]
Natl. Coalition for Res. in Neurological Disorders [15346]
Natl. Comm. for Medical Res. Ethics [IO]
Natl. Coun. on Patient Info. and Educ. [15946]
Natl. Educ. Alliance for Borderline Personality Disorder [15224]
Natl. Eye Res. Found. [15724]
Natl. Found. for Brain Res. [15397]
Natl. Headache Found. [14533]
Natl. Hea. and Medical Res. Coun. [IO]
Natl. Hemophilia Found. [14795]
Natl. Hepatitis C Advocacy Coun. [14813]
Natl. Multiple Sclerosis Soc. [15349]
Natl. Parkinson Found. [15351]
Natl. Pharmaceutical Assn. [15947]
Natl. Spasmodic Torticollis Assn. [15353]
Natl. Spinal Cord Injury Assn. [16468]
Natl. Stroke Assn. [16494]
Natl. Tay-Sachs and Allied Diseases Assn. [15354]
Nature of Wellness [13701]
NCI Alliance for Nanotechnology in Cancer [15110]
Netherlands Org. for Hea. Res. and Development [IO]
Neurofibromatosis [14471]
North Amer. Vodder Assn. of Lymphatic Therapy [15019]
Org. for Autism Res. [13728]
Org. for Human Brain Mapping [7379]
Orthopaedic Res. and Educ. Found. [8949]
Osteogenesis Imperfecta Found. [15779]
PanAmerican Soc. for Pigment Cell Res. [15111]
Paratuberculosis Awareness and Res. Assn. [14425]
Parents Against Childhood Epilepsy [14382]
Parkinson Alliance [15359]

Parkinson's Action Network [14285]
Parkinson's Disease Found. [15360]
PBCers Org. [14816]
Peruvian Heart Assn. [13923]
Plastic Surgery Res. Coun. [14052]
Proj. Magic [16634]
Purine Res. Soc. [15258]
QiGong Res. Soc. [13647]
Res.! Am. [15112]
Res. Soc. on Alcoholism [16517]
Retinoblastoma Intl. [13869]
RGK Found. [15113]
Schizophrenia Intl. Res. Soc. [15232]
Scleroderma Found. [16389]
Scleroderma Res. Found. [16390]
Sickle Cell Disease Assn. of Am. [14797]
Sino-American Pharmaceutical Professionals Assn. [15951]
Sleep Res. Soc. [16429]
Soc. for Acupuncture Res. [13537]
Soc. for Applied Immunohistochemistry [15873]
Soc. of Clinical Res. Associates [14027]
Soc. for Clinical Trials [14028]
Soc. of Govt. Ser. Urologists [16714]
Soc. for Melanoma Res. [13875]
Soc. for Molecular Imaging [15181]
Soc. for Simulation in Healthcare [15148]
Soc. of Teachers of Family Medicine [14387]
Soc. for Whole Body Autoradiography [15149]
South African Medical Res. Coun. [IO]
Spina Bifida Assn. of Am. [16458]
Spinal Cord Soc. [16469]
Student Soc. for Stem Cell Res. [15114]
Student Society for Stem Cell Research [IO]
Take Charge! Cure Parkinson's [15366]
Tear Film and Ocular Surface Soc. [15729]
Tenovus Scotland [IO]
Thyroid Soc. for Educ. and Res. [16650]
Tourette Syndrome Assn. [15367]
Treatment and Res. Advancements Assn. for Personality Disorder [15235]
Tremor Action Network [15369]
Tuberous Sclerosis Alliance [15371]
United Mitochondrial Disease Found. [16363]
U.S. Pharmacopeia [15953]
William H. Donner Found. [13880]
Williams Syndrome Assn. [14490]
W.M. Keck Found. [15115]
Women in Neurotrauma Res. [15404]
World Assn. of Sleep Medicine [16430]
World Fed. of Neurology Res. Gp. on Motor Neuron Diseases [15373]
World Fed. of Neuroradiological Societies [16306]
World Soc. for Stereotactic and Functional Neurosurgery [15418]
Young Onset Parkinson's Assn. [15374]
Zarrow Families Found. [13197]
Medical Res; Amer. Fed. for [14019]
Medical and Res. Center; Natl. Jewish [16361]
Medical Res; Comm. for the Promotion of [15104]
Medical Res. Coun. of New Zealand [★IO]
Medical Res; Fisher Inst. for [17628]
Medical Res. Found; A-T [14436]
Medical and Res. Found; African [★14971]
Medical Res. Found; Amer. [★8843]
Medical Res. Found; for Bio [13696]
Medical Res. Found; Dystonia [15319]
Medical and Res. Found; Intl. [★14971]
Medical Res. Found; Santa Barbara [★15568]
Medical Res. Funding; Ad Hoc Gp. for [17686]
Medical Res. Modernization Comm. [15109], 3200 Morley Rd., Shaker Heights, OH 44122, (216)283-6702
Medical Res; Natl. Assn. for Bio [13700]
Medical Res; Natl. Soc. for [★13700]
Medical Res. Soc. [IO], Cambridge, United Kingdom
Medical Rev; Amer. Coll. of Podiatric [16035]
Medical School Departments of Pathology; Amer. Assn. of Chairmen of [★15863]
Medical School Pediatric Dept. Chairs; Assn. of [15884]
Medical Self-Help Program - Defunct.
Medical Seminars Intl. - Address unknown since 1994.
Medical Ser. Assn. of Am; Ambulance and [★14313]

A star before a book entry number signifies that the name is not listed separately, but is mentioned within the entry.

Medical Services; Amer. Soc. of Hospital-Based Emergency Air [★14314]
Medical Services Assn; Natl. Ambulance and [★14313]
Medical Social Workers; Amer. Assn. of [★13206]
Medical Soc. on Alcoholism; New York City [★16501]
Medical Soc. on Alcoholism and Other Drug Dependencies; Amer. [★16501]
Medical Soc; Amer. Chinese [★15163]
Medical Soc; Amer. Ukrainian [★15182]
Medical Soc; Benjamin Franklin Literary and [14549]
Medical Soc; Chinese Amer. [15163]
Medical Soc; Christian [★20238]
Medical Soc. Executives; Amer. Assn. of [15153]
Medical Soc. Executives Assn. [★15153]
Medical Soc; People's [17694]
Medical Soc. for Sports Medicine; Amer. [16475]
Medical Soc; Undersea and Hyperbaric [16697]
Medical Soc. of the U.S. and Mexico - Address unknown since 2000.
Medical Soc; Wilderness [15184]
Medical Software Indus. Assn. [IO], Kenmore, Australia
Medical Sonography; Amer. Registry of Diagnostic [16437]
Medical Spa Soc. [1871], 60 E 56th St., 2nd Fl., New York, NY 10022, (866)633-4772

Medical Specialties
Amer. Acad. of Allergy, Asthma and Immunology [13592]
Amer. Acad. of Somnology [16419]
Amer. Assn. of Dispensing Ophthalmologists [15658]
Amer. Assn. of Medical Dosimetrists [15116]
Amer. Assn. of Medical Rev. Officers [14695]
Amer. Assn. for Ophthalmic Standardized Echography [15659]
Amer. Assn. of Physician Specialists [15792]
Amer. Bd. of Abdominal Surgery [16561]
Amer. Bd. of Anesthesiology [13671]
Amer. Bd. of Medical Specialties [15117]
Amer. Bd. of Nuclear Medicine [15419]
Amer. Bd. of Quality Assurance and Utilization Rev. Physicians [16260]
Amer. Bd. of Radiology [16272]
Amer. Bd. of Surgery [16563]
Amer. Coll. of Angiology [16719]
Amer. Coll. of Medical Quality [16261]
Amer. Coll. of Nuclear Medicine [15421]
Amer. Coll. of Nuclear Physicians [15422]
Amer. Coll. of Radiology [16274]
Amer. Healthcare Radiology Administrators [16275]
Amer. Laryngological, Rhinological and Otological Soc. [15821]
Amer. Neuroendocrine Soc. [15035]
Amer. Osteopathic Coll. of Anesthesiologists [13672]
Amer. Osteopathic Coll. of Occupational and Preventive Medicine [15802]
Amer. Osteopathic Coll. of Radiology [16276]
Amer. Osteopathic Colleges of Ophthalmology and Otolaryngology-Head and Neck Surgery [15664]
Amer. Radium Soc. [15639]
Amer. Roentgen Ray Soc. [16277]
Amer. Soc. of Abdominal Surgeons [16568]
Amer. Soc. of Anesthesiologists [13674]
Amer. Soc. of Bariatric Physicians [15575]
Amer. Soc. of Hematology [14783]
Amer. Soc. of Interventional Pain Physicians [15837]
Amer. Soc. of Neuroimaging [16281]
Amer. Soc. of Ocularists [15118]
Amer. Soc. of Regional Anesthesia and Pain Medicine [13676]
Amer. Soc. for Therapeutic Radiology and Oncology [16285]
Assn. of Medical Device Reprocessors [15038]
Assn. for Ocular Pharmacology and Therapeutics [15671]
Assn. of Prog. Directors in Vascular Surgery [16578]
Assn. of Specialty Professors [8587]

Assn. for Surgical Educ. [8856]
Assn. of Univ. Anesthesiologists [13680]
Assn. of Univ. Radiologists [16286]
Certification Bd. for Sterile Processing and Distribution [15119]
Children's Blood Found. [14786]
Computerized Medical Imaging Soc. [16287]
Congenital Cardiac Anesthesia Soc. [13682]
Coun. on Diagnostic Imaging [16288]
Coun. of Medical Specialty Societies [15120]
Coun. of Pediatric Subspecialties [15886]
Coun. of Women's and Infants' Specialty Hospitals [14880]
CyberKnife Soc. [16581]
Dannemiller Memorial Educational Found. [13683]
Hip Soc. [15769]
Indo-Amer. Soc. of Interventional Cardiology [13908]
Intl. Anesthesia Res. Soc. [13684]
Intl. Assn. of Sickle Cell Nurses And Physician Assistants [14706]
Intl. Fed. of Foot and Ankle Societies [16045]
Intl. Refractive Surgery Club [15689]
Intl. Skeletal Soc. [16289]
Intl. Soc. for Anaesthetic Pharmacology [13685]
Intl. Soc. of Cosmetic and Laser Surgeons [14048]
Intl. Soc. for Vascular Surgery [16584]
Mitochondrial Medicine Soc. [14078]
Musculoskeletal Ultrasound Soc. [16696]
Natl. Assn. for Healthcare Quality [16264]
NIDCD - Natl. Temporal Bone, Hearing and Balance Pathology Rsrc. Registry [15121]
Nuclear Medicine Tech. Certification Bd. [15423]
Periodic Paralysis Assn. [15122]
Radiological Soc. of North Am. [16293]
Renal Pathology Soc. [15872]
Russian Amer. Medical Assn. [16378]
Soc. for the Advancement of Women's Imaging [16294]
Soc. for Applied Immunohistochemistry [15873]
Soc. of Cardiovascular Anesthesiologists [13689]
Soc. of Interventional Radiology [16300]
Soc. of Nuclear Medicine [15424]
Soc. of Nuclear Medicine Technologist Sect. [15425]
Soc. for Radiation Oncology Administrators [16302]
Soc. for Tech. in Anesthesia [13692]
Soc. for Vascular Surgery [16730]
Soc. for Vascular Ultrasound [16731]
Medical and Sports Music Inst. of America - Defunct.
Medical Students' Assn; Amer. Podiatric [16038]
Medical Study; Assn. for Intl. [12834]
Medical Subjects Unit [22843]
Medical Subjects Unit [IO], Bridgewater, NJ, United States
Medical Superintendents of Amer. Institutions for Insane; Assn. of [★16076]
Medical Superintendents of Mental Hospitals; Assn. of [★14861]
Medical Support Comm. for Nigeria/Biafra Relief - Defunct.
Medical-Surgical Mfrs. Assn. [★14669]
Medical Surgical Nurses; Acad. of [15426]
Medical and Surgical Relief Comm. - Defunct.
Medical Systems and Informatics; Amer. Assn. for [★14079]
Medical Teams Intl. [12869], PO Box 10, Portland, OR 97207-0010, (503)624-1000
Medical Technicians - Ambulance; Registry of Emergency [★14342]
Medical Technicians; Natl. Assn. of Emergency [14335]
Medical Technicians; Natl. Registry of Emergency [14342]
Medical Technologists; Amer. Soc. of [★14992]
Medical Technology
Accreditation Rev. Comm. on Educ. in Surgical Tech. [15123]
Accrediting Bur. of Hea. Educ. Schools [15124]
Advanced Medical Tech. Assn. [14669]
Alcor Life Extension Found. [14072]
Alliance of Cardiovascular Professionals [13885]
Amer. Acad. of Anti-Aging Medicine [15125]

Amer. Assn. of Bioanalysts Bd. of Registry [15126]
Amer. Assn. for Ophthalmic Standardized Echography [15659]
Amer. Cryonics Soc. [14073]
Amer. Electrology Assn. [14308]
Amer. Inst. of Ultrasound in Medicine [16436]
Amer. Lithotripsy Soc. [15285]
Amer. Medical Technologists [15127]
Amer. Registry of Diagnostic Medical Sonography [16437]
Amer. Registry of Radiologic Technologists [15128]
Amer. Soc. of Emergency Radiology [16278]
Amer. Soc. of Extra-Corporeal Tech. [15129]
Amer. Soc. for Mohs Histotechnology [15130]
Amer. Soc. for Neural Transplantation and Repair [15380]
Amer. Soc. of Radiologic Technologists [15131]
Assn. of Assistive Tech. Act Programs [14237]
Assn. for Educ. in Healthcare Info. Tech. [15132]
Assn. for Electronic Hea. Care Transactions [14618]
Assn. for Politics and the Life Sciences [7522]
Assn. of Surgical Technologists [15133]
Australian Inst. of Radiography [IO]
BioCommunications Assn. [14031]
Bd. of Registered Polysomnographic Technologists [15134]
British In-Vitro Diagnostics Assn. [IO]
British Inst. of Dental and Surgical Technologists [IO]
Canadian Assn. of Cardio-Pulmonary Technologists [IO]
Canadian Assn. of Electroneurophysiology Technologists [IO]
Canadian Assn. of Medical Radiation Technologists [IO]
Canadian Soc. for Medical Lab. Sci. [IO]
Computerized Medical Imaging Soc. [16287]
Cryonics Inst. [1120]
CuresNow [15135]
ECRI [15136]
ECRI [IO]
Eucomed [IO]
European Assn. for Professions in Biomedical Sci. [IO]
European Chinese Soc. for Clinical Magnetic Resonance [IO]
European Soc. of Gene and Cell Therapy [IO]
European Soc. for Magnetic Resonance in Medicine and Biology [IO]
Extensions for Independence [11945]
Found. for Informed Medical Decision Making [15137]
Hea. Level Seven [14636]
Hea. Tech. Center [15138]
Inst. of Decontamination Sciences [IO]
Intl. Assn. of Medical Equip. Remarketers and Servicers [IO]
Intl. Assn. of Medical Equip. Remarketers and Servicers [15139]
Intl. Biopharmaceutical Assn. [15936]
Intl. Fed. of Biomedical Lab. Sci. [IO]
Intl. Functional Elecl. Stimulation Soc. [15390]
Intl. Guild of Hair Removal Specialists [14309]
The Intl. Publication Planning Assn. [3231]
Intl. RadioSurgery Assn. [16269]
Intl. Sharps Injury Prevention Soc. [16380]
Intl. Soc. for Clinical Densitometry [15788]
Intl. Soc. For Apheresis [IO]
Intl. Soc. of Magnetic Resonance in Medicine - British Chap. [IO]
Intl. Soc. of Radiographers and Radiological Technologists [IO]
Intl. Soc. for Skin Imaging [IO]
Intl. Veterinary Ultrasound Soc. [16797]
ITEM Coalition [14690]
Japanese Soc. of Medical Imaging Tech. [IO]
Korean Radiological Soc. [IO]
Malaysian Soc. of Radiographers [IO]
Medical Equip. and Tech. Assn. [7306]
Medical Image Perception Soc. [15140]
Medical Outcomes Trust [14644]
Musculoskeletal Ultrasound Soc. [16696]

Reference to "IO" in place of a book number signifies that the association may be found in the 45th edition of International Organizations.

Natl. Accrediting Agency for Clinical Lab. Sciences [15141]
Natl. Alliance for Hea. Info. Tech. [15142]
Natl. Alliance of Medical Researchers and Teaching Physicians [15143]
Natl. Alliance of Primary Care Informatics [14956]
Natl. Alliance for the Primary Prevention of Sharps Injuries [16381]
Natl. Assn. of Orthopaedic Technologists [15144]
Natl. Bd. for Certification in Dental Tech. [14173]
Natl. Credentialing Agency for Lab. Personnel [15145]
Natl. Inst. of Electromedical Info. [14311]
Natl. Soc. for Histotechnology [15146]
NCI Alliance for Nanotechnology in Cancer [15110]
Neuro-Optometric Rehabilitation Assn., Intl. [15300]
New Zealand Inst. of Medical Radiation Tech. [IO]
Radiology Bus. Mgt. Assn. [15074]
Regulatory Affairs Professionals Soc. [14599]
Rehabilitation Tech. Assn. [16334]
Soc. for the Advancement of Women's Imaging [16294]
Soc. for Assisted Reproductive Tech. [16346]
Soc. of Breast Imaging [16295]
Soc. for Cardiological Sci. and Tech. [IO]
Soc. for Cardiovascular Magnetic Resonance [IO]
Soc. for Cardiovascular Magnetic Resonance [15147]
Soc. for Clinical and Medical Hair Removal [14310]
Soc. of Diagnostic Medical Sonography [16438]
Soc. of Medical Lab. Technologists of South Africa [IO]
Soc. of Radiographers of South Africa [IO]
Soc. for Simulation in Healthcare [IO]
Soc. for Simulation in Healthcare [15148]
Soc. for Tech. in Anesthesia [13692]
Soc. of Uroradiology [16717]
Soc. for Vascular Surgery [16730]
Soc. for Vascular Ultrasound [16731]
Soc. for Whole Body Autoradiography [15149]
Stratis Hea. [14600]
Tissue Engg. Soc. Intl. [6610]
Medical Tech; Amer. Soc. for [★14992]
Medical Tech. Assn; Advanced [14669]
Medical Tech; Bd. of Schools of [★15141]
Medical Tennis Assn; Amer. [23898]
Medical Toxicology; Amer. Bd. of [★16660]
Medical Toxicology; Amer. Coll. of [16660]
Medical Transcription Indus. Alliance [★2670]
Medical Transcription Indus. Assn. [2670], 4230 Kiernan Ave., Ste. 130, Modesto, CA 95356, (209)527-9620
Medical Transport Systems; Comm. on Accreditation of [14347]
Medical Wings Intl. [14645], PO Box 610542, Dallas, TX 75261, (817)467-5020
Medical Wings Intl. [IO], Dallas, TX, United States
Medical Women's Assn; Amer. [14696]
Medical Women's Fed. [IO], London, United Kingdom
Medical Women's Intl. Assn. [IO], Dortmund, Germany
Medical Work; Coun. for Christian [★20241]
Medical Writers Assn; Amer. [3082]
Medical Writers Assn; Amer. Podiatric [16039]
MedicAlert Found. Intl. [14318], 2323 Colorado Ave., Turlock, CA 95382, (209)668-3333
MedicAlert Found. Intl. [IO], Turlock, CA, United States
Medically Dependent and Disabled; Natl. Legal Center for the [6032]
Medicare Advocacy; Center for [14684]
Medicare Beneficiaries Defense Fund [★17690]
Medicare; Natl. Comm. to Preserve Social Security and [18649]
Medicare Rights Center [17690], 520 8th Ave., North Wing, 3rd Fl., New York, NY 10018, (212)869-3850
Medication Compliance Inst. [15941], PO Box 437, Lakeside, CA 92040, (619)443-0531
Medication Compliance Inst. [IO], Lakeside, CA, United States
Medication Practices; Inst. for Safe [14638]

Medicine
Academic Orthopaedic Soc. [15750]
Acad. of Medicine, Singapore [IO]
Acad. on Mental Retardation [15238]
Acad. of Molecular Imaging [15150]
Acad. of Pharmaceutical Res. and Sci. [15906]
Acad. of Psychosomatic Medicine [16195]
Acad. of Scientific Hypnotherapy [14913]
AcademyHealth [14535]
Accademia di Medicina di Torino [IO]
Accreditation Commn. for Acupuncture and Oriental Medicine [15739]
Accreditation Coun. for Continuing Medical Educ. [15151]
Accreditation Coun. on Optometric Educ. [15710]
Accreditation Coun. for Pharmacy Educ. [15907]
Acute Long Term Hosp. Assn. [14852]
Adolescent Scoliosis Soc. of North Am. [16392]
Advanced Medical Tech. Assn. [14669]
Advocates for the Amer. Osteopathic Assn. [15789]
Aerospace Medical Assn. [13538]
African Medical and Res. Found. [14971]
Aid for Intl. Medicine [14972]
AIDS, Medicine and Miracles [13551]
Air and Surface Transport Nurses Assn. [15427]
Albert Ellis Inst. [16197]
Alcor Life Extension Found. [14072]
Alliance for Lupus Res. [15013]
Alliance for Microbicide Development [13555]
Alliance for the Prudent Use of Antibiotics [15908]
Alpha Epsilon Delta [24541]
Alpha Omega Alpha Honor Medical Soc. [24542]
Alpha Tau Delta [24559]
Amer. Acad. of Alternative Medicine [13612]
Amer. Acad. of Ambulatory Care Nursing [15428]
Amer. Acad. of Clinical Psychiatrists [16064]
Amer. Acad. of Environmental Medicine [14360]
Amer. Acad. of Family Physicians [14383]
Amer. Acad. of HIV Medicine [13556]
Amer. Acad. of Medical Administrators [15045]
Amer. Acad. of Medical Administrators Res. and Educational Found. [15046]
Amer. Acad. of Neurological and Orthopaedic Surgeons [15409]
Amer. Acad. of Neurology [15376]
Amer. Acad. of Nursing [15430]
Amer. Acad. of Ophthalmology [15656]
Amer. Acad. of Optometry [15711]
Amer. Acad. of Orthopaedic Surgeons [15752]
Amer. Acad. of Osteopathy [15790]
Amer. Acad. of Psychotherapists [16198]
Amer. Acad. of Tropical Medicine [16692]
Amer. Alliance for Medical Cannabis [15020]
Amer. Alternative Medical Assn. [13613]
Amer. Ambulance Assn. [14313]
Amer. Animal Hosp. Assn. [16739]
Amer. Apitherapy Soc. [13614]
Amer. Art Therapy Assn. [16199]
Amer. Assembly for Men in Nursing [15431]
Amer. Assn. of Birth Centers [15580]
Amer. Assn. of Chairs of Departments of Psychiatry [16065]
Amer. Assn. of Clinical Directors [15986]
Amer. Assn. of Colleges of Osteopathic Medicine [15791]
Amer. Assn. of Colleges of Pharmacy [15909]
Amer. Assn. of Food Hygiene Veterinarians [16745]
Amer. Assn. of Gynecologic Laparoscopists [15581]
Amer. Assn. for Hand Surgery [14522]
Amer. Assn. for the History of Medicine [10082]
Amer. Assn. of Housecall Veterinarians [16746]
Amer. Assn. of Immunologists [14929]
Amer. Assn. of Integrative Medicine [15152]
Amer. Assn. on Intellectual and Developmental Disabilities [15239]
Amer. Assn. of Kidney Patients [15283]
Amer. Assn. for Marriage and Family Therapy [16200]
Amer. Assn. of Medical Assistants [15081]
Amer. Assn. of Medical Milk Commissions [16384]
Amer. Assn. of Medical Rev. Officers [14695]
Amer. Assn. of Medical Soc. Executives [15153]

Amer. Assn. of Neurological Surgeons [15410]
Amer. Assn. of Neuromuscular and Electrodiagnostic Medicine [15303]
Amer. Assn. of Neuropathologists [15853]
Amer. Assn. of Neuroscience Nurses [15436]
Amer. Assn. of Nurse Anesthetists [15437]
Amer. Assn. of Nurse Attorneys [15000]
Amer. Assn. of Nutritional Consultants [15540]
Amer. Assn. of Occupational Hea. Nurses [15439]
Amer. Assn. of Oriental Medicine [15742]
Amer. Assn. of Orthopedic Medicine [15753]
Amer. Assn. for Pediatric Ophthalmology and Strabismus [15660]
Amer. Assn. of Physician Specialists [15792]
Amer. Assn. of Professional Hypnotherapists [14915]
Amer. Assn. of Psychiatric Administrators [14861]
Amer. Assn. of Retired Veterinarians [16748]
Amer. Assn. of Spinal Cord Injury Nurses [15441]
Amer. Assn. for the Stud. of Liver Diseases [14801]
Amer. Assn. of Women Emergency Physicians [14324]
Amer. Autonomic Soc. [15406]
Amer. Bd. of Genetic Counseling [14492]
Amer. Bd. of Indus. Hygiene [15623]
Amer. Bd. of Internal Medicine [14965]
Amer. Bd. of Medical Genetics [14493]
Amer. Bd. of Medical Specialties [15117]
Amer. Bd. of Neurological Surgery [15411]
Amer. Bd. of Nuclear Medicine [15419]
Amer. Bd. of Nutrition [15541]
Amer. Bd. of Obstetrics and Gynecology [15582]
Amer. Bd. of Ophthalmology [15661]
Amer. Bd. of Opticianry [15704]
Amer. Bd. of Orthopaedic Surgery [15755]
Amer. Bd. of Preventive Medicine [16050]
Amer. Bd. of Psychological Hypnosis [14917]
Amer. Celiac Society/Dietary Support Coalition [15543]
Amer. Clinical Lab. Assn. [14991]
Amer. Coll. for Advancement in Medicine [16051]
Amer. Coll. of Apothecaries [15912]
Amer. Coll. of Cardiology [13888]
Amer. Coll. of Clinical Pharmacology [15913]
Amer. Coll. of Clinical Pharmacy [15914]
Amer. Coll. of Gastroenterology [14405]
Amer. Coll. of Hea. Care Administrators [15535]
Amer. Coll. of Healthcare Executives [14862]
Amer. Coll. of Intl. Physicians [14973]
Amer. Coll. of Legal Medicine [15001]
Amer. Coll. of Neuropsychopharmacology [15915]
Amer. Coll. of Nuclear Medicine [15421]
Amer. Coll. of Nuclear Physicians [15422]
Amer. Coll. of Nurse-Midwives [15447]
Amer. Coll. of Nutrition [15544]
Amer. Coll. of Obstetricians and Gynecologists [15584]
Amer. Coll. of Occupational and Environmental Medicine [15624]
Amer. Coll. of Oral and Maxillofacial Surgeons [15734]
Amer. Coll. of Osteopathic Family Physicians [15793]
Amer. Coll. of Osteopathic Internists [15794]
Amer. Coll. of Osteopathic Obstetricians and Gynecologists [15585]
Amer. Coll. of Osteopathic Pediatricians [15795]
Amer. Coll. of Osteopathic Surgeons [15797]
Amer. Coll. of Physician Executives [15056]
Amer. Coll. of Physicians-American Soc. of Internal Medicine [14966]
Amer. Coll. of Preventive Medicine [16052]
Amer. Conf. of Governmental Indus. Hygienists [15625]
Amer. Coun. of Applied Clinical Nutrition [15545]
Amer. Coun. on Sci. and Hea. [14539]
Amer. Cryonics Soc. [14073]
Amer. Dance Therapy Assn. [16203]
Amer. Dietetic Assn. [15546]
Amer. Epilepsy Soc. [14379]
Amer. Fed. for Medical Res. [14019]
Amer. Found. for Maternal and Child Health [15586]
Amer. Found. for Pharmaceutical Educ. [15916]

A star before a book entry number signifies that the name is not listed separately, but is mentioned within the entry.

Amer. Fracture Assn. [15756]
Amer. Gastroenterological Assn. [14406]
Amer. Gp. Psychotherapy Assn. [16204]
Amer. Guild of Hypnotherapists [14919]
Amer. Gynecological and Obstetrical Soc. [15587]
Amer. Head and Neck Soc. [15819]
Amer. Headache Soc. [14531]
Amer. Hea. Care Assn. [14540]
Amer. Hea. Planning Assn. [14542]
Amer. Herbalists Guild [14817]
Amer. Holistic Nurses' Assn. [14825]
Amer. Industrial Health Coun. [15626]
Amer. Indus. Hygiene Assn. [15627]
Amer. Inst. of the History of Pharmacy [15917]
Amer. Inst. of Homeopathy [14845]
Amer. Inst. of Medical Ethics [12122]
Amer. Inst. for Preventive Medicine [16053]
Amer. Inst. of Ultrasound in Medicine [16436]
Amer. Kidney Fund [15284]
Amer. Laryngological, Rhinological and Otological Soc. [15821]
Amer. Lebanese Medical Assn. [15154]
Amer. Liver Found. [14803]
Amer. Manual Medicine Assn. [13618]
Amer. Massage Therapy Assn. [15022]
Amer. Medical Assn. [15155]
Amer. Medical Assn. Alliance [15156]
Amer. Medical Directors Assn. [15536]
Amer. Mental Hea. Alliance [15188]
Amer. Mental Hea. Counselors Assn. [15189]
Amer. Music Therapy Assn. [16205]
Amer. Naprapathic Assn. [15276]
Amer. Nephrology Nurses' Assn. [15286]
Amer. Neuroendocrine Soc. [15035]
Amer. Nurses Assn. [15451]
Amer. Nurses Found. [15452]
Amer. Ophthalmological Soc. [15662]
Amer. Optometric Assn. [15712]
Amer. Optometric Found. [15713]
Amer. Optometric Student Assn. [15714]
Amer. Org. of Nurse Executives [15454]
Amer. Orthopaedic Assn. [15757]
Amer. Orthopaedic Foot and Ankle Soc. [15758]
Amer. Orthoptic Coun. [15663]
Amer. Osler Soc. [15157]
Amer. Osteopathic Acad. of Orthopedics [15759]
Amer. Osteopathic Assn. [15798]
Amer. Osteopathic Bd. of Family Physicians [15799]
Amer. Osteopathic Bd. of Pediatrics [15800]
Amer. Osteopathic Coll. of Physical Medicine and Rehabilitation [15805]
Amer. Osteopathic Colleges of Ophthalmology and Otolaryngology-Head and Neck Surgery [15664]
Amer. Osteopathic Found. [15806]
Amer. Parkinson Disease Assn. [15304]
Amer. Pharmacists Assn. - Acad. of Pharmacy Practice and Mgt. [15918]
Amer. Pharmacists Assn. Acad. of Student Pharmacists [15919]
Amer. Physicians Fellowship for Medicine in Israel [12456]
Amer. Professional Wound Care Assn. [16688]
Amer. Psychosomatic Soc. [16196]
Amer. Psychotherapy Assn. [16207]
Amer. Registry of Diagnostic Medical Sonography [16437]
Amer. Soc. for the Advancement of Pharmacotherapy [16134]
Amer. Soc. of Cataract and Refractive Surgery [15665]
Amer. Soc. of Childbirth Educators [15589]
Amer. Soc. of Clinical Hypnosis [14921]
Amer. Soc. of Clinical Hypnosis - Educ. and Res. Found. [14922]
Amer. Soc. for Clinical Investigation [14020]
Amer. Soc. for Clinical Nutrition [15547]
Amer. Soc. for Clinical Pharmacology and Therapeutics [15920]
Amer. Soc. for Colposcopy and Cervical Pathology [15590]
Amer. Soc. of Consultant Pharmacists [15922]
Amer. Soc. of Contemporary Medicine, Surgery, and Ophthalmology [15666]

Amer. Soc. of Echocardiography [13891]
Amer. Soc. for Gastrointestinal Endoscopy [14409]
Amer. Soc. for Genomic Medicine [14496]
Amer. Soc. of Hand Therapists [14524]
Amer. Soc. of Hea. Sys. Pharmacists [15923]
Amer. Soc. for Healthcare Central Ser. Professionals [14864]
Amer. Soc. for Healthcare Engg. of the Amer. Hosp. Assn. [14865]
Amer. Soc. for Healthcare Risk Mgt. [14869]
Amer. Soc. for Histocompatibility and Immunogenetics [14931]
Amer. Soc. of Interventional Pain Physicians [15837]
Amer. Soc. for Laser Medicine and Surgery [14997]
Amer. Soc. of Law, Medicine and Ethics [15002]
Amer. Soc. of Maxillofacial Surgeons [15735]
Amer. Soc. of Nephrology [15288]
Amer. Soc. of Neuroradiology [16282]
Amer. Soc. for Nutrition [15548]
Amer. Soc. of Ophthalmic Registered Nurses [15458]
Amer. Soc. for Ophthalmic Ultrasonography [15667]
Amer. Soc. for Parenteral and Enteral Nutrition [15549]
Amer. Soc. of Pharmacognosy [15924]
Amer. Soc. for Pharmacology and Experimental Therapeutics [15925]
Amer. Soc. for Pharmacy Law [15003]
Amer. Soc. of Plastic Surgical Nurses [15461]
Amer. Soc. for Reproductive Medicine [14389]
Amer. Soc. for Stereotactic and Functional Neurosurgery [15412]
Amer. Soc. for Surgery of the Hand [14525]
Amer. Soc. of Tropical Medicine and Hygiene [16693]
Amer. Tai Chi Assn. [16593]
Amer. Uveitis Soc. [15668]
Americans for Free Choice in Medicine [15158]
Amyotrophic Lateral Sclerosis Assn. [15306]
Anesthesia Patient Safety Found. [13679]
Armenian Medical Assn. [IO]
Army Nurse Corps Assn. [15262]
Arthroscopy Assn. of North Am. [15762]
ASHP Found. [15926]
Asian Amer./Pacific Islander Nurses Assn. [15463]
Asian Pacific Assn. for the Stud. of the Liver [IO]
Asociacion Medica Nacional de la Republica de Panama [IO]
Asociacion Mexicana de Facultades y Escuelas de Medicina [IO]
Associacao Medica Braseleira [IO]
Assn. of Academic Hea. Centers [14546]
Assn. of Accredited Naturopathic Medical Colleges [8943]
Assn. for the Advancement of Psychotherapy [16210]
Assn. of Behavioral Healthcare Mgt. [15191]
Assn. for the Behavioral Sciences and Medical Educ. [6527]
Assn. Belge des Syndicats Medicaux [IO]
Assn. of Black Nursing Faculty [8848]
Assn. of Bone and Joint Surgeons [15763]
Assn. for Childbirth at Home, Intl. [15591]
Assn. of Chinese Amer. Physicians [15991]
Assn. of Clinical Scientists [14022]
Assn. of Haitian Physicians Abroad [15159]
Assn. for Healthcare Documentation Integrity [15084]
Assn. for Healthcare Philanthropy [14871]
Assn. for Healthcare Rsrc. and Materials Mgt. [14872]
Assn. for Hosp. Medical Educ. [14873]
Assn. of Hungarian Medical Societies [IO]
Assn. for Intl. Medical Study [12834]
Assn. for Macular Diseases [15669]
Assn. des Medecins et Medecins Dentistes du Grand-Duche de Luxembourg [IO]
Assn. of Medical Directors of Info. Systems [14957]
Assn. of Medical Doctors of Kazakhstan [IO]
Assn. of Medical Illustrators [13707]

Assn. Medicale Francaise [IO]
Assn. Medicale Haitienne [IO]
Assn. of Medicine and Psychiatry [16081]
Assn. of Natural Medicine Pharmacists [15282]
Assn. of Nurses Endorsing Transplantation [15670]
Assn. of Osteopathic State Executive Directors [15809]
Assn. of Otolaryngology Administrators [15062]
Assn. for Palliative Medicine of Great Britain and Ireland [IO]
Assn. of Pediatric Hematology/Oncology Nurses [15447]
Assn. of PeriOperative Registered Nurses [15468]
Assn. for Prevention Teaching and Res. [16054]
Assn. for Professionals in Infection Control and Epidemiology [14947]
Assn. of Professors of Gynecology and Obstetrics [15592]
Assn. of Prog. Directors in Internal Medicine [14967]
Assn. of Regulatory Boards of Optometry [15716]
Assn. of Rehabilitation Nurses [15469]
Assn. for Res. in Vision and Ophthalmology [15672]
Assn. of Schools and Colleges of Optometry [15717]
Assn. of the Sci. Medical Societies of Germany [IO]
Assn. of Shelter Veterinarians [16784]
Assn. of Specialty Professors [8587]
Assn. of Systematic Kinesiology [IO]
Assn. of Tech. Personnel in Ophthalmology [15674]
Assn. of Telehealth Ser. Providers [15160]
Assn. of Ukrainian Doctors [IO]
Assn. of Univ. Professors of Ophthalmology [15675]
Assn. of Veterans Affairs Anesthesiologists [13681]
Assn. of Veterinary Hematology and Transfusion Medicine [16785]
Assn. of Women's Hea., Obstetric and Neonatal Nurses [15470]
Australian Medical Assn. [IO]
Australian Military Medicine Assn. [IO]
Australian Traditional-Medicine Soc. [IO]
Austrian Medical Chamber [IO]
Auxiliary to the Natl. Medical Assn. [15161]
Avenues, Natl. Support Gp. for Arthrogryposis Multiplex Congenita [15309]
Azerbaijan Medical Assn. [IO]
Bangladesh Medical Assn. of North Am. [15162]
Barbados Assn. of Medical Practitioners [IO]
Bay Area Physicians for Human Rights [12218]
Behavior Genetics Assn. [14498]
Benign Essential Blepharospasm Res. Found. [15311]
Benjamin Franklin Literary and Medical Soc. [14549]
Berufsverband der Pharmaberater [IO]
Better Vision Inst. [15678]
Biological Stain Commn. [6571]
Brain Injury Assn. of Am. [14528]
Brazilian Assn. of Homeopathic Medicine [IO]
Brazilian Soc. of Aesthetic Medicine [IO]
British Assn. of Medical Managers [IO]
British Assn. for Performing Arts Medicine [IO]
British Assn. for Sexual Hea. and HIV [IO]
British Fertility Soc. [IO]
British Medical Assn. [IO]
British Soc. for Oral Medicine [IO]
Brother's Brother Found. [12837]
Bulgarian Medical Assn. [IO]
Bur. of Professional Educ. of the Amer. Osteopathic Assn. [15810]
Byelorussian Assn. of the Physicians [IO]
C/SEC [15593]
Cajal Club [15385]
Cambodia Medical Assn. [IO]
Canadian Medical Assn. [IO]
Canadian Medical Protective Assn. [IO]
Canadian Thoracic Soc. [IO]
Cardiovascular Credentialing Intl. [13898]
Care4Dystonia [15312]

Reference to "IO" in place of a book number signifies that the association may be found in the 45th edition of International Organizations.

Catholic Hea. Assn. of the U.S. [14874]
Cell Stress Soc. Intl. [16488]
Center for Humane Options in Childbirth Experiences [15594]
Center for Medical Consumers [14550]
Center for Professional Well-Being [14700]
Center for Sports and Osteopathic Medicine [16055]
Center for the Stud. of Multiple Birth [15272]
Central Soc. for Clinical Res. [14023]
Charles Ray III Diabetes Assn. [14220]
Chi Eta Phi Sorority [24560]
Child Neurology Soc. [15386]
Childbirth Connection [15595]
Children's Eye Found. [15679]
Children's Hospice Intl. [14853]
Children's Tumor Found. [15315]
China Acad. of Traditional Chinese Medicine [IO]
Chinese Amer. Medical Soc. [15163]
Chinese Assn. of Integrated Traditional and Western Medicine [IO]
Chinese Medical Assn. [IO]
Citizens Against Drug Impaired Drivers [13230]
Clinical Lab. Mgt. Assn. [14993]
Clinical and Lab. Standards Inst. [14994]
Clinical Ligand Assay Soc. [14995]
Coll. of Optometrists in Vision Development [15718]
Coll. of Osteopathic Healthcare Executives [14876]
Colleges of Medicine of South Africa [IO]
Collegium Internationale Neuro-Psychopharmacologicum [15929]
Comm. for Freedom of Choice in Medicine [13628]
Community Guidance Ser. [16214]
Community Systems Found. [15552]
Complementary Alternative Medical Assn. [13629]
Confederacion Medica Republica Argentina [IO]
Confed. of African Medical Associations and Societies [IO]
Conservative Orthopedics Intl. Assn. [15767]
Consortium for Conservation Medicine [15164]
Consortium for Conservation Medicine [IO]
Contact Lens Assn. of Ophthalmologists [15680]
Coun. on Arteriosclerosis, Thrombosis and Vascular Biology of the Amer. Heart Assn. [13902]
Coun. on Chiropractic Orthopedics [15768]
Coun. of Colleges of Acupuncture and Oriental Medicine [15743]
Coun. on Hea. Info. and Educ. [14553]
Coun. for Intl. Organizations of Medical Sciences [IO]
Coun. of Medical Specialty Societies [15120]
Coun. of Pediatric Subspecialties [15886]
Coun. on Resident Educ. in Obstetrics and Gynecology [15597]
Coun. for Responsible Telemedicine [16596]
Coun. of State and Territorial Epidemiologists [14374]
Coun. of Teaching Hospitals [14879]
Cranial Acad. [15811]
Croatian Medical Assn. [IO]
Crohn's and Colitis Found. of Am. [14414]
Cryonics Inst. [1120]
Cure Res. Found. [13818]
CyberKnife Soc. [16581]
Czech Medical Assn. of J.E. Purkyne [IO]
Danish Medical Soc. [IO]
Dermatology Nurses' Assn. [15476]
Dietary Managers Assn. [15555]
Digestive Disease Natl. Coalition [14416]
Doctors Ought to Care [14554]
Doctors Worldwide [12851]
Drug Info. Assn. [15931]
Dysautonomia Found. [15317]
Dystonia Medical Res. Found. [15319]
Educational Commn. for Foreign Medical Graduates [15997]
Egyptian Medical Assn. [IO]
Endometriosis Assn. [15599]
Epilepsy Found. [14380]
Ethiopian Medical Assn. [IO]
Ethiopian Pharmacists Assn. in North Am. [15932]

European Assn. of Centres of Medical Ethics [IO]
European Assn. for the History of Medicine and Hea. [IO]
European Hernia Soc. [IO]
European Medical Assn. [IO]
European Sci. Cooperative on Phytotherapy [IO]
European Union of Medical Specialists [IO]
Federacion Medica Colombiana [IO]
Federacion Medica Venezolana [IO]
Fed. for Accessible Nursing Educ. and Licensure [15478]
Fed. of Amer. Hospitals [14881]
Fed. of Associations of Regulatory Boards [14555]
Fed. of Chinese Amer. and Chinese Canadian Medical Societies [13985]
Fed. of Medical Societies of Hong Kong [IO]
Federation of State Medical Boards of the United States [IO]
Fed. of State Medical Boards of the U.S. [15165]
Fertility Res. Found. [14391]
Fiji Medical Assn. [IO]
Finnish Medical Assn. [IO]
Flower Essence Soc. [14818]
Focus [15681]
Food and Nutrition Bd. [15558]
Forbes Norris MDA/ALS Res. Center [15323]
Foreign Pharmacy Graduate Examination Comm. [15933]
Found. for Innovation in Medicine [15166]
Found. for the Support of Intl. Medical Training [14977]
Friends of the Natl. Lib. of Medicine [15167]
Frontier Nursing Ser. [15479]
Gay and Lesbian Medical Assn. [14431]
Gen. Medical Coun. [IO]
Georgian Medical Assn. [IO]
German Soc. for Physical Medicine and Rehabilitation [IO]
Ghana Medical Assn. [IO]
Glaucoma Res. Found. [15683]
Global Alliance for Medical Educ. [8862]
Global Healing [12450]
Global Hea. Coun. [14979]
Global Perioperative Res. Org. [14026]
Global and Regional Asperger Syndrome Partnership [15325]
Gluten Intolerance Gp. [15559]
Harvey Soc. [15168]
Hea. Acad. [14883]
Hea. Global Access Proj. [11331]
Hea. Res. and Educational Trust [14884]
Healthcare Billing and Mgt. Assn. [15169]
Healthcare Info. and Mgt. Systems Soc. [14885]
Heart Disease Res. Found. [13905]
Heart Rhythm Soc. [13907]
Hemochromatosis Found. [14799]
Herbalists Without Borders [13634]
Hesperian Found. [14980]
Hong Kong Medical Assn. [IO]
Hong Kong Telemedicine Assn. [IO]
Human Ecology Action League [14364]
Huntington's Disease Soc. of Am. [15329]
Icelandic Medical Assn. [IO]
Independent Citizens Res. Found. for the Study of Degenerative Diseases [14263]
Informed Homebirth/Informed Birth and Parenting [15602]
Inst. for the Development of Emotional and Life Skills/National Inst. of Relationship Enhancement [15201]
Inst. for Expressive Anal. [16217]
Inst. for Labor and Mental Health [15202]
Inst. of Medicine [7607]
Inst. for Traditional Medicine and Preventive Hea. Care [13635]
InterAmerican Heart Found. [13909]
Intermed Intl. [14982]
Intl. and Amer. Associations of Clinical Nutritionists [15560]
Intl. Arts Medicine Assn. [7972]
Intl. Assn. for Cognitive Psychotherapy [16218]
Intl. Assn. for Colon Hydrotherapy [14567]
Intl. Assn. of Coroners and Medical Examiners [15093]

Intl. Assn. for Dance Medicine and Sci. [15170]
Intl. Assn. of Environmental Mutagen Societies [6578]
Intl. Assn. of Healthcare Central Ser. Materiel Mgt. [14886]
Intl. Assn. for Healthcare Security and Safety [14887]
Intl. Assn. for Medicinal Compliance [15041]
Intl. Assn. of Ocular Surgeons [15684]
Intl. Assn. of Optometric Executives [15720]
Intl. Assn. for Oxygen Therapy [16616]
Intl. Assn. of Pediatric Lab. Medicine [15888]
Intl. Assn. of Reiki Professionals [13637]
Intl. Assn. of Structural Integrators [13638]
Intl. Biopharmaceutical Assn. [15936]
Intl. Bd. of Environmental Medicine [14365]
Intl. Bundle Br. Block Assn. [13911]
Intl. Center for Attitudinal Healing [15206]
Intl. Cesarean Awareness Network [15604]
Intl. Childbirth Educ. Assn. [15605]
Intl. Coll. of Angiology [16724]
Intl. Comm. Against Mental Illness [15207]
Intl. Comm. for Life, Disability and Hea. Insurance Medicine [IO]
Intl. Complement Soc. [14938]
Intl. Eye Found. [15685]
Intl. Fed. of Marfan Syndrome Organizations [14456]
Intl. Fed. of Martial Arts and Oriental Medicine [15021]
Intl. Found. for Homeopathy [14849]
Intl. Functional Elecl. Stimulation Soc. [15390]
Intl. Hea. Evaluation Assn. [14568]
Intl. Leptospirosis Soc. [14950]
Intl. Life Sciences Inst. - North Am. [15561]
Intl. Maillard Reaction Soc. [6683]
Intl. Medical and Dental Hypnotherapy Assn. [14924]
The Intl. Publication Planning Assn. [3231]
Intl. REST Investigators Soc. [16220]
Intl. Sharps Injury Prevention Soc. [16380]
Intl. Soc. for Anaesthetic Pharmacology [13685]
Intl. Soc. of Andrology [IO]
Intl. Soc. of Arthroscopy, Knee Surgery and Orthopaedic Sports Medicine [15771]
Intl. Soc. for Complementary Medicine Res. [13639]
Intl. Soc. for the History of Medicine [IO]
Intl. Soc. for Imaging in the Eye [15690]
Intl. Soc. of Internal Medicine [IO]
Intl. Soc. on Metabolic Eye Disease [15691]
Intl. Soc. of Mountain Medicine [15171]
Intl. Soc. for Mountain Medicine [IO]
Intl. Soc. for Oncodevelopmental Biology and Medicine [IO]
Intl. Soc. of Oncology Pharmacy Practitioners [15937]
Intl. Soc. of Oriental Medicine [IO]
Intl. Soc. for Orthomolecular Medicine [IO]
Intl. Soc. for Pharmacoepidemiology [15939]
Intl. Soc. for Res. on Impulsivity [16088]
Intl. Soc. for the Stud. of the Lumbar Spine [IO]
Intl. Soc. for Telemedicine [IO]
Intl. Soc. of Travel Medicine [IO]
Intl. Soc. of Travel Medicine [15172]
Intl. Soc. for Vascular Surgery [16584]
Intl. Vitamin A Consultative Gp. [15564]
Interstate Postgraduate Medical Assn. of North Am. [14386]
Iranian Amer. Medical Assn. [15173]
Iranian Amer. Medical Assn. [IO]
Iraqi Medical Sciences Assn. [14987]
Irish Medical Org. [IO]
Israel Medical Org. [IO]
Japanese Assn. for Acute Medicine [IO]
Joint Commn. on Accreditation of Healthcare Organizations [14888]
Joint Commn. on Allied Hea. Personnel in Ophthalmology [15692]
Joseph P. and Rose F. Kennedy Inst. of Ethics [17506]
Kappa Psi [24568]
Korean-American Medical Assn. [15174]
Kuwait Medical Assn. [IO]
Kyrgyzstan Medical Assn. [IO]

A star before a book entry number signifies that the name is not listed separately, but is mentioned within the entry.

Lamaze Birth Without Pain Educ. Assn. [15607]
Lao Medical Assn. [IO]
Latvian Physicians Assn. [IO]
Life Extension Soc. [14074]
Lithuanian Medical Assn. [IO]
Lupus Found. of Am. [15014]
Macedonian Medical Assn. [IO]
Malaysian Medical Assn. [IO]
Malignant Hyperthermia Assn. of the U.S. [14464]
Mgt. Soc. for Healthcare Professionals [IO]
Med Help Intl. [15042]
Medical Assn. of the Bahamas [IO]
Medical Assn. in Brunei [IO]
Medical Assn. of Jamaica [IO]
Medical Assn. of South East Asian Nations [IO]
Medical Assn. of Turkey [IO]
Medical Coun. of India [IO]
Medical Found. [IO]
Medical Image Perception Soc. [15140]
Medical Letter [15940]
Medical Protection Soc. [IO]
Medical Subjects Unit [22843]
MedicAlert Found. Intl. [14318]
Medication Compliance Inst. [15941]
Mended Hearts, Inc. [13916]
Mental Hea. Am. [15211]
Michael E. DeBakey Intl. Surgical Soc. [13917]
Midwives Alliance of North Am. [15610]
Milton H. Erickson Found. [16221]
Mitochondrial Medicine Soc. [14078]
Musculoskeletal Ultrasound Soc. [16696]
Myanmar Medical Assn. [IO]
Myasthenia Gravis Found. of Am. [15340]
Natl. Acad. of Medicine [IO]
Natl. Acad. of Opticianry [15707]
Natl. Alliance on Mental Illness [15214]
Natl. Alliance for the Primary Prevention of Sharps
  Injuries [16381]
Natl. Alliance of State Pharmacy Associations
  [15943]
Natl. Amer. Arab Nurses Assn. [15490]
Natl. Assn. of Boards of Pharmacy [15944]
Natl. Assn. of Community Hea. Centers [14574]
Natl. Assn. of County Hea. Fac. Administrators
  [15069]
Natl. Assn. of Disability Examiners [14034]
Natl. Assn. for Drama Therapy [16222]
Natl. Assn. of Hea. Unit Coordinators [14578]
Natl. Assn. for Healthcare Recruitment [15070]
Natl. Assn. of Hispanic Nurses [15494]
Natl. Assn. for Home Care and Hospice [14840]
Natl. Assn. of Medical Examiners [15094]
Natl. Assn. of Optometrists and Opticians [15721]
Natl. Assn. of Orthopaedic Nurses [15498]
Natl. Assn. of Physician Nurses [15500]
Natl. Assn. for Poetry Therapy [16223]
Natl. Assn. of Public Hospitals and Hea. Systems
  [14892]
Natl. Assn. of Residents and Interns [15175]
Natl. Assn. for Rural Mental Hea. [15217]
Natl. Assn. of School Nurses [15501]
Natl. Assn. of State Mental Hea. Prog. Directors
  [15219]
Natl. Assn. of Vietnamese Nurses [15504]
Natl. Assn. of Vision Professionals [15693]
Natl. Ataxia Found. [15342]
Natl. Black Nurses Assn. [15505]
Natl. Bd. of Examiners in Optometry [15722]
Natl. Bd. of Medical Examiners [15095]
Natl. Bd. of Osteopathic Medical Examiners
  [15812]
Natl. Catholic Pharmacists Guild of the U.S.
  [15945]
Natl. Certification Commn. for Acupuncture and
  Oriental Medicine [15747]
Natl. Coalition of Ethnic Minority Nurse Associa-
  tions [15507]
Natl. Coalition for Res. in Neurological Disorders
  [15346]
Natl. Comm. for Quality Assurance [16265]
Natl. Contact Lens Examiners [15723]
Natl. Coordinating Coun. for Medication Error
  Reporting and Prevention [14653]
Natl. Coun. on Patient Info. and Educ. [15946]
Natl. Coun. of State Boards of Nursing [15508]

Natl. Digestive Diseases Info. CH [14422]
Natl. Environmental Hea. Assn. [14367]
Natl. Eye Res. Found. [15724]
Natl. Fed. of Licensed Practical Nurses [15509]
Natl. Found. for Ectodermal Dysplasias [14468]
Natl. Found. for Infectious Diseases [14953]
Natl. Gaucher Found. [15252]
Natl. Headache Found. [14533]
Natl. Hea. Assn. [15279]
Natl. Hea. Coun. [14586]
Natl. Hea. Fed. [14587]
Natl. Hea. Info. Center [14588]
Natl. Hospice and Palliative Care Org. [14856]
Natl. Inst. of Electromedical Info. [14311]
Natl. Kidney Found. [15294]
Natl. League for Nursing [15510]
Natl. Medical Assn. [15176]
Natl. Multiple Sclerosis Soc. [15349]
Natl. Optometric Assn. [15725]
Natl. Org. for Competency Assurance [14591]
Natl. Parkinson Found. [15351]
Natl. Perinatal Assn. [15900]
Natl. Pharmaceutical Assn. [15947]
Natl. Physicians Alliance [16009]
Natl. Postdoctoral Assn. [9064]
Natl. Scoliosis Found. [16393]
Natl. Soc. of Genetic Counselors [14506]
Natl. Spasmodic Torticollis Assn. [15353]
Natl. Tay-Sachs and Allied Diseases Assn.
  [15354]
Nepal Medical Assn. [IO]
Network for Continuing Medical Educ. [15177]
New Zealand Medical Assn. [IO]
Nigerian Medical Assn. [IO]
Nordic Telemedicine Assn. [IO]
North Amer. Assn. of Medical Educ. and Commun.
  Companies [8874]
North Amer. Assn. for the Stud. of Obesity
  [15576]
North Amer. Soc. of Obstetric Medicine [15615]
North Amer. Soc. for Pediatric Gastroenterology,
  Hepatology and Nutrition [14424]
North Amer. Soc. for Pediatric Medicine [15891]
North Amer. Vascular Biology Org. [16728]
Nuclear Medicine Tech. Certification Bd. [15423]
Nurses Educational Funds [15516]
Nurses' House [15518]
Nurses Org. of Veterans Affairs [15519]
Nutrition for Optimal Hea. Assn. [15567]
Ohashi Inst. [15748]
Oncology Nursing Soc. [15521]
Ophthalmic Photographers' Soc. [15696]
Opticians Assn. of Am. [15709]
Optometric Extension Prog. Found. [15727]
ORBIS Intl. [15697]
Ordem dos Medicos [IO]
Org. for Autism Res. [13728]
Orthopaedic Res. Soc. [15776]
Osteopathic Intl. Alliance [15813]
Outpatient Ophthalmic Surgery Soc. [15698]
Pain Mgt. and Sclerotherapy [15814]
Pan-American Assn. of Ophthalmology [15699]
Pan Amer. Hea. and Educ. Found. [12536]
Parkinson's Disease Found. [15360]
Partnership for Quality Medical Donations [12537]
Patient Advocate Found. [14660]
Pediatric Nursing Certification Bd. [15522]
Performing Arts Medicine Assn. [16164]
Pharmacy Technician Educators Coun. [8963]
Phi Alpha Sigma [24543]
Phi Chi Medical Fraternity [24544]
Phi Rho Sigma Medical Soc. [24545]
Philippine Medical Assn. [IO]
Philippine Nurses Assn. of Am. [2840]
Physicians Assn. of Uzbekistan [IO]
Physicians for Social Responsibility [18169]
Polish Medical Assn. [IO]
Postgraduate Center for Mental Hea. [16227]
Price-Pottenger Nutrition Found. [15568]
Psychotherapy Network [16228]
Public Hosp. Pharmacy Coalition [15949]
Rabbinic Center for Res. and Counseling [16229]
Recovery, Inc. [16230]
Regulatory Affairs Professionals Soc. [14599]

Reiki Alliance [13651]
Renal Physicians Assn. [15298]
Resolve, The Natl. Infertility Assn. [14394]
Riders for Hea. [15271]
Romanian Medical Assn. [IO]
Royal Acad. of Medicine of Belgium [IO]
Royal Acad. of Medicine in Ireland [IO]
Royal Dutch Medical Assn. [IO]
Royal Medical Soc. [IO]
Royal Soc. of Medicine [IO]
Royal Soc. of Medicine Found. [15178]
Russian Amer. Medical Assn. [16378]
Russian Medical Soc. [IO]
Russian Soc. of Aesthetic Medicine [IO]
Safety Pharmacology Soc. [15950]
Scoliosis Assn., Inc. [16394]
Scoliosis Res. Soc. [16395]
Scottish Soc. of the History of Medicine [IO]
Sect. for Long Term Care and Rehabilitation
  [14894]
Sect. for Metropolitan Hospitals [14895]
Sexual Medicine Soc. of North Am. [16405]
Singapore Medical Assn. [IO]
Sino-American Pharmaceutical Professionals
  Assn. [15951]
Slovak Medical Assn. [IO]
Slovenian Medical Assn. [IO]
Social/Vocational Rehabilitation Clinic [16231]
Societa Italiana di Medicina Generale [IO]
Soc. for Academic Continuing Medical Educ.
  [8875]
Soc. for Acupuncture Res. [13537]
Soc. of Air Force Physicians [15264]
Soc. of Amer. Gastrointestinal and Endoscopic
  Surgeons [14428]
Soc. for Clinical and Experimental Hypnosis
  [14927]
Soc. of Clinical Res. Associates [14027]
Soc. for Clinical Trials [14028]
Soc. of Correctional Physicians [16011]
Soc. of Critical Care Medicine [14071]
Soc. for Cryobiology [6847]
Soc. of Diagnostic Medical Sonography [16438]
Soc. for Epidemiologic Res. [14377]
Soc. for Executive Leadership in Academic
  Medicine Intl. [15179]
Soc. for Executive Leadership in Academic
  Medicine Intl. [IO]
Soc. for Experimental Biology and Medicine
  [6597]
Soc. for Eye Surgeons [15703]
Soc. for Fetal Urology [16713]
Soc. for Free Radical Biology and Medicine
  [6613]
Soc. of Gastroenterology Nurses and Associates
  [14429]
Soc. for Gynecologic Investigation [15618]
Soc. for Healthcare Consumer Advocacy of the
  Amer. Hosp. Assn. [15005]
Soc. for Healthcare Strategy and Market Develop-
  ment of the Amer. Hosp. Assn. [14896]
Soc. of Interventional Pain Mgt. Surgery Centers
  [16588]
Soc. of Medical Consultants to the Armed Forces
  [15265]
Soc. for Medical Decision Making [15180]
Soc. of Medical Jurisprudence [15006]
Soc. for Menstrual Cycle Res. [15619]
Soc. of Military Orthopaedic Surgeons [15266]
Soc. for Molecular Imaging [15181]
Soc. for Molecular Imaging [IO]
Soc. of Nuclear Medicine [15424]
Soc. of Nuclear Medicine Technologist Sect.
  [15425]
Soc. for Obstetric Anesthesia and Perinatology
  [15903]
Soc. for Occupational and Environmental Hea.
  [15633]
Soc. of Otorhinolaryngology and Head/Neck
  Nurses [15526]
Soc. for Social Medicine [IO]
Soc. of Teachers of Family Medicine [14387]
Soc. for Tropical Veterinary Medicine [16807]
Soc. for Vascular Surgery [16730]
Soc. for Vascular Ultrasound [16731]

Reference to "IO" in place of a book number signifies that the association may be found in the 45th edition of International Organizations.

South African Assn. of Physicists in Medicine and Biology [IO]
South African Medical Assn. [IO]
South African Soc. of Teachers of the Alexander Technique [IO]
South African Soc. of Travel Medicine [IO]
Spanish Confed. of Medical and Tech. Advisers Associations [IO]
Stroke Awareness for Everyone [16495]
Student Natl. Medical Assn. [8876]
Support Org. for Trisomy 18, 13, and Related Disorders [14485]
Swedish Soc. of Medicine [IO]
Swiss Medical Assn. [IO]
Taiwan Medical Assn. [IO]
Tel-Med [14601]
Theta Psi [24566]
Tissue Engg. Soc. Intl. [6610]
Tourette Syndrome Assn. [15367]
Treatment and Res. Advancements Assn. for Personality Disorder [15235]
Tremor Action Network [15369]
Trinity Medical Center [14900]
Trust for America's Hea. [16255]
Tuberous Sclerosis Alliance [15371]
Uganda Medical Assn. [IO]
Ukrainian Medical Assn. of North Am. [15182]
Undersea and Hyperbaric Medical Soc. [16697]
Union Medica Nacional [IO]
United Methodist Assn. of Hea. and Welfare Ministries [14602]
United Plant Savers [13655]
U.S. Pharmacopeia [15953]
U.S. Psychiatric Rehabilitation Assn. [16336]
U.S. Sports Chiropractic Fed. [23282]
U.S. Trager Assn. [13656]
Univ. of Colorado Hea. Sciences Center Alumni Assn. [24494]
Vietnam Gen. Assn. of Medicine and Pharmacy [IO]
Vietnam Medical Assn. [IO]
Vietnamese Medical Assn. of the U.S.A. [IO]
Vietnamese Medical Assn. of the U.S.A. [15183]
Visiting Nurse Associations of Am. [15532]
Volunteer Trustees of Not-for-Profit Hospitals [14902]
Wellness Associates [16058]
Wilderness Medical Soc. [15184]
William Glasser Inst. [16233]
Women in Sci. and Engg. [7635]
World Fed. of Catholic Medical Associations [IO]
World Fed. for Mental Hea. [15237]
World Fed. of Neurology Res. Gp. on Motor Neuron Diseases [15373]
World Fed. for Ultrasound in Medicine and Biology [IO]
World Homecare and Hospice Org. [14844]
World Medical Assn. [IO]
World Self-Medication Indus. [IO]
World Soc. for Stereotactic and Functional Neurosurgery [15418]
World Spine Soc. [15405]
Wound, Ostomy and Continence Nurses Soc.: An Assn. of E.T. Nurses [15533]
Zimbabwe Medical Assn. [IO]
Medicine; Acad. of Psychosomatic [16195]
Medicine Alliance; Acupuncture and Oriental [13607]
Medicine; Amer. Acad. of Acupuncture and Oriental [13611]
Medicine; Amer. Acad. of Anti-Aging [15125]
Medicine; Amer. Acad. for Cerebral Palsy and Developmental [13934]
Medicine; Amer. Acad. of Emergency [14323]
Medicine; Amer. Acad. of Occupational [★15624]
Medicine; Amer. Acad. of Oral [14105]
Medicine; Amer. Acad. of Pain [15832]
Medicine; Amer. Acad. of Podiatric Sports [16471]
Medicine; Amer. Acad. of Tropical [16692]
Medicine; Amer. Assn. for Automotive [★12951]
Medicine; Amer. Assn. of Colleges of Osteopathic [15791]
Medicine; Amer. Assn. of Colleges of Podiatric [16025]
Medicine; Amer. Assn. for the History of [10082]
Medicine; Amer. Assn. of Neuromuscular and Electrodiagnostic [15303]

Medicine; Amer. Assn. of Oriental [15742]
Medicine; Amer. Assn. of Orthopedic [15753]
Medicine; Amer. Assn. of Physicists in [16014]
Medicine; Amer. Bd. of Emergency [14325]
Medicine; Amer. Bd. of Internal [14965]
Medicine; Amer. Bd. of Lab. Animal [★16762]
Medicine; Amer. Bd. of Nuclear [15419]
Medicine; American Bd. of Oral [★8197]
Medicine; Amer. Bd. of Pain [15833]
Medicine; Amer. Bd. of Podiatric Orthopedics and Primary [★16030]
Medicine; Amer. Bd. of Podiatric Orthopedics and Primary Podiatric [16030]
Medicine; Amer. Bd. of Preventive [16050]
Medicine; Amer. Bd. of Sleep [16420]
Medicine; Amer. Coll. of Foot and Ankle Orthopedics and [16032]
Medicine; Amer. Coll. of Lab. Animal [16762]
Medicine; Amer. Coll. of Legal [15001]
Medicine; Amer. Coll. of Nuclear [15421]
Medicine; Amer. Coll. of Occupational [★15624]
Medicine; Amer. Coll. of Occupational and Environmental [15624]
Medicine; Amer. Coll. of Physicians-American Soc. of Internal [14966]
Medicine; Amer. Coll. of Preventive [16052]
Medicine; Amer. Coll. of Sports [16473]
Medicine; Amer. Coll. of Veterinary Internal [16767]
Medicine; Amer. Cong. of Physical [★16310]
Medicine; Amer. Cong. of Rehabilitation [16310]
Medicine; Amer. Inst. of Ultrasound in [16436]
Medicine; Amer. Medical Soc. for Sports [16475]
Medicine; Amer. Orthopaedic Soc. for Sports [16476]
Medicine; Amer. Osteopathic Acad. of Public Hea. and Preventive [★15802]
Medicine; Amer. Osteopathic Acad. of Sports [16477]
Medicine; Amer. Osteopathic Bd. of Emergency [14328]
Medicine; American Osteopathic Bd. of Rehabilitation [★15805]
Medicine; Amer. Osteopathic Coll. of Occupational and Preventive [15802]
Medicine; Amer. Osteopathic Coll. of Preventive [★15802]
Medicine; Amer. Osteopathic Coll. of Rehabilitation [★15805]
Medicine; Amer. Soc. of Addiction [16501]
Medicine; Amer. Soc. of Law and [★15002]
Medicine; Amer. Soc. of Tropical [★16693]
Medicine; Assn. for the Advancement of Automotive [12951]
Medicine Assn; Amer. Canine Sports [16761]
Medicine Assn; Complementary [13630]
Medicine; Assn. of Deans of Amer. Colleges of Veterinary [★9293]
Medicine Assn; Natl. Emergency [14340]
Medicine; Assn. of Professors of [8853]
Medicine; Assn. of Prog. Directors in Internal [14967]
Medicine; Assn. for Psychoanalytic [16107]
Medicine; Assn. for Psychoanalytic and Psychosomatic [★16107]
Medicine; Assn. of Teachers of Preventive [★16054]
Medicine and Biology; Soc. for Vascular [16729]
Medicine Cabinet Mfrs. Assn. - Defunct.
Medicine Cabinet Mfrs. Coun. - Defunct.
Medicine; Center for Sports and Osteopathic [16055]
Medicine; Comm. for Freedom of Choice in [13628]
Medicine; Comm. on Human Rights of the U.S. Natl. Acad. of Sciences, Natl. Acad. of Engg., and Inst. of [★17753]
Medicine; Conf. of Professors of Preventive [★16054]
Medicine; Coun. of Colleges of Acupuncture and Oriental [15743]
Medicine; CTR for Dance [★16055]
Medicine and Ethics; Amer. Soc. of Law, [15002]
Medicine; Gay People in [★12243]
Medicine and Hygiene; Amer. Soc. of Tropical [16693]
Medicine; Indians Into [8865]
Medicine; Inst. of [7607]
Medicine; Intl. Acad. of Nutrition and Preventative [★15560]

Medicine; Intl. Acad. of Preventive [★15560]
Medicine; Lesbian, Gay and Bisexual People in [★12243]
Medicine; Lesbian, Gay, Bisexual, and Transgender People in [12243]
Medicine; Lesbian and Gay People in [★12243]
Medicine; Massachusetts Soc. of Law and [★15002]
Medicine; Natl. Assn. for Ambulatory Care [★13663]
Medicine; Natl. Center for Complementary and Alternative [13643]
Medicine; Natl. Inst. for the Clinical Application of Behavioral [13739]
Medicine; New Frontiers of [★12834]
Medicine; North Amer. Assn. of Urgent Care [★13663]
Medicine for Peace [12789], 2732 Unicorn Ln. NW, Washington, DC 20015, (202)362-9121
Medicine for Peace [IO], Washington, DC, United States
Medicine; Physicians' Assn. for Anthroposophical [13646]
Medicine; Physicians Comm. for Responsible [14595]
Medicine Prog; Assn. of Amer. Medical Colleges-Women in [8847]
Medicine, Psychology and Religion; Orthodox Christian Assn. of [16163]
Medicine and Public Hea; Amer. Bd. of Preventive [★16050]
Medicine in the Public Interest - Defunct.
Medicine and Rehabilitation; Amer. Acad. of Physical [16307]
Medicine and Rehabilitation; Amer. Bd. of Physical [16309]
Medicine and Rehabilitation; Amer. Cong. of Physical [★16310]
Medicine and Rehabilitation; Amer. Osteopathic Acad. of Physical [★15805]
Medicine and Rehabilitation; Amer. Osteopathic Coll. of Physical [★15805]
Medicine and Rehabilitation; Amer. Soc. of Physical [★16307]
Medicine Res; Acad. of Behavioral [13732]
Medicine and Res; Public Responsibility in [18585]
Medicine; Residency Rev. Comm. for Emergency [14343]
Medicine Residents' Assn; Emergency [14332]
Medicine and Sci; Found. for Advances in [14025]
Medicine and Sci; Joint Commn. on Sports [16483]
Medicine; Soc. for Academic Emergency [14344]
Medicine; Soc. for Adolescent [13974]
Medicine; Soc. of Behavioral [13740]
Medicine; Soc. for Experimental Biology and [6597]
Medicine; Soc. of Gen. Internal [14970]
Medicine; Soc. of Medical Jurisprudence and State [★15006]
Medicine; Soc. of Nuclear [15424]
Medicine; Soc. for Res. and Educ. in Primary Care Internal [★14970]
Medicine; Soc. of Teachers of Emergency [★14344]
Medicine and Surgery; Amer. Coll. of Gen. Practitioners in Osteopathic [★15793]
Medicine and Surgery; Amer. Soc. for Laser [14997]
Medicine; Technologist Sect. of the Soc. of Nuclear [★15425]
Medicine Technologist Sect; Soc. of Nuclear [15425]
Medicine Tech. Certification Bd; Nuclear [15423]
Medicine; Univ. Assn. for Emergency [★14344]
Medicines Australia [IO], Deakin, Australia
Medico-Legal Soc. [★15006]
Medico Psychological Assn; Amer. [★16076]
Medicus Mundi Intl. [IO], Brussels, Belgium
Mediebedriftenes Landsforening [★IO]
Medienplanung fur Entwicklungslander, Mittel und Osteuropa [★IO]

Medieval
Assn. for Renaissance Martial Arts [8820]
Australian and New Zealand Assn. for Medieval and Early Modern Stud. [IO]
Australian and New Zealand Assn. for Medieval and Renaissance Stud. [IO]
Center for Medieval and Renaissance Stud. [10456]
Center for Medieval and Renaissance Stud. [10457]

A star before a book entry number signifies that the name is not listed separately, but is mentioned within the entry.

Centers and Regional Associations [10458]
Charles Homer Haskins Soc. [10459]
Charles Homer Haskins Society [IO]
De Re Militari: The Soc. for Medieval Military History [10474]
Early English Text Soc. [IO]
Hagiography Soc. [20526]
Intl. Anchoritic Soc. [10460]
Intl. Boethius Soc. [10799]
Intl. Center of Medieval Art [10461]
Intl. Center of Medieval Art [IO]
Intl. Soc. for the Stud. of Medieval Philosophy [IO]
Intl. Soc. for the Stud. of Pilgrimage Art [9451]
Lollard Soc. [20524]
Medieval Acad. of Am. [10462]
North Amer. Soc. of Ancient and Medieval Wargamers [22471]
Renaissance English Text Soc. [10932]
Soc. for Creative Anachronism [10463]
Soc. for Creative Anachronism, New Zealand [IO]
Soc. for Medieval and Renaissance Philosophy [10464]
Soc. for the Stud. of Medieval Languages and Literature [IO]
Medieval Acad. of Am. [10462], 104 Mt. Auburn St., 5th Fl., Cambridge, MA 02138, (617)491-1622
Medieval Acad. Reprints for Teaching [★10458]
Medieval and Early Renaissance Stud; Center for [★10456]
Medieval Languages and Literature; Soc. for the Stud. of [IO]
Medieval and Renaissance Philosophy; Soc. for [10464]
Medieval and Renaissance Stud; Assn. of Centers of [★10458]
Medieval and Renaissance Stud; Center for [10456]
Medieval and Renaissance Stud; Center for [10457]
Medieval Spain; Amer. Acad. of Res. Historians of [10081]
Medieval Studies; International Cong. on [★10459]
Medieval Studies; International Cong. on [★IO].
Mediocrity
Soc. for the Preservation and Enhancement of the Recognition of Millard Fillmore, Last of the Whigs [22601]
MediSend Intl. [12530], 9244 Markville Dr., Dallas, TX 75243, (214)575-5006
MediSend Intl. [IO], Dallas, TX, United States
Medisinsk teknisk forening [★IO]
Meditation
Amer. Buddhist Assn. [19540]
Amer. Buddhist Movement [19541]
Amer. Buddhist Stud. Center [19542]
Amer. Yangjia Michuan Taijiquan Assn. [23584]
Amer. Yoga Assn. [11216]
Ananda Marga [20633]
Ananda Yoga Teachers Assn. [11217]
Assn. of Himalayan Yoga Meditation Societies [11218]
Bear Butte Intl. Alliance [19446]
Buddhist Churches of Am. Fed. of Buddhist Women's Associations [19543]
Burma-America Buddhist Assn. [19546]
Cambridge Buddhist Assn. [19547]
Center for Confucian Sci. [19879]
Consciousness Res. and Training Project [12343]
Dharma Realm Buddhist Assn. [19548]
First Zen Inst. of Am. [19549]
Found. of Human Understanding [10465]
Friends of Falun Gong [17061]
Hanuman Found. [12347]
Himalayan Intl. Inst. of Yoga Sci. and Philosophy of the U.S.A. [12348]
Hong Kong Found. for the Sci. of Creative Intelligence [IO]
Kunzang Palyul Choling [19553]
Lama Found. [10176]
Mentalphysics [20503]
Nichiren Buddhist Assn. of Am. [19555]
North Amer. Yoga Fed. [11219]
Patience T'ai Chi Assn. [23897]
Patient Advocate Found. [14660]
SOL [13030]
Somatics Soc. [12363]
Supreme Master Ching Hai Meditation Assn. [19557]

Tayu Center [20581]
Theosophical Book Assn. for the Blind [20592]
U.S. Trager Assn. [13656]
Wainwright House [20588]
Well-Springs Found. [10179]
Western Young Buddhist League [19558]
Yoga Alliance [11220]
Yoga Res. Found. [20637]
Zen Stud. Soc. [19559]
Meditation Assn; Supreme Master Ching Hai [19557]
Mediterranean
Mediterranean Stud. Assn. [10466]
Mediterranean Editors and Translators [IO], Barcelona, Spain
Mediterranean Soc. of Chemotherapy [IO], Athens, Greece
Mediterranean Stud. Assn. [10466], PO Box 212, East Sandwich, MA 02537
Mediums Soc; Licentiate Ministers and Certified [20450]
MedPed [★14463]
MedPed [★IO]
MedPeds Residents' Assn; Natl. [14969]
Meds and Food for Kids [11622], c/o Patricia B. Wolff, MD, Founder/Exec. Dir., 4488 Forest Park Ave., Ste. 230, St. Louis, MO 63108, (314)726-0168
Meds and Food for Kids [IO], St. Louis, MO, United States
MedSearch [★21262]
MedShare Intl. [12531], 3240 Clifton Springs Rd., Decatur, GA 30034, (770)323-5858
MedShare Intl. [IO], Decatur, GA, United States
Medtner Soc., U.S.A. - Address unknown since 1994.
Medugorje Center - Defunct.
MEDUSA - Landelijk Bur. Ontwikkeling Beleid & Hulpverlening Seksueel Gweld [★IO]
Meduxnekeag River Assn. [IO], Woodstock, NB, Canada
Medzinarodna federacia fonografickeho priemyslu Narodna skupina slovenskej republiky [★IO]
Mee Family Assn; Lucky [20983]
Meet A Mum Assn. [IO], Norton Radstock, United Kingdom
Meet Americans - Defunct.
Meet the Composer [10643], 75 9th Ave., Fl. 3R, Ste. C, New York, NY 10011-7006, (212)645-6949
Meeting and Events Australia [IO], North Sydney, Australia
Meeting of Friends; Five Years [★20044]
Meeting Places
European Assn. of Event Centers [IO]
Green Meeting Indus. Coun. [2681]
Intl. Assn. of Assembly Managers [2671]
Intl. Assn. of Assembly Managers [IO]
Intl. Assn. of Conf. Centers [IO]
Intl. Assn: of Conf. Centers [2672]
Natl. Convention Assn. [2688]
Netherlands Bd. of Tourism and Conventions [IO]
Venue Mgt. Assn. - Asia Pacific [IO]
World Coun. for Venue Mgt. [1350]
Meeting Planners
Amer. Assn. of Cmpt. Rental Professionals [895]
Assn. of Collegiate Conf. and Events Directors-International [2673]
Assn. of Collegiate Conf. and Events Directors-International [IO]
Association for Convention Operations Management [IO]
Assn. for Convention Operations Mgt. [2674]
Assn. of Intl. Meeting Planners [2675]
Connected Intl. Meeting Professionals Assn. [2676]
Connected Intl. Meeting Professionals Assn. [IO]
Coun. of Protocol Executives [2677]
Destination Marketing Assn. Intl. [2678]
Destination Marketing Assn. Intl. [IO]
Exposition Ser. Contractors Assn. [2679]
Found. for Intl. Meetings [2680]
Found. for Intl. Meetings [IO]
German Convention Bur. [IO]
Golf Tournament Assn. of Am. [23449]
Green Meeting Indus. Coun. [2681]
Independent Meeting Planners Assn. of Canada [IO]

Intl. Assn. for Exhibition Mgt. [IO]
Intl. Assn. of Exhibitions and Events [2682]
Intl. Assn. of Fairs and Expositions [2683]
Intl. Assn. of Fairs and Expositions [IO]
Intl. Assn. of Hispanic Meeting Professionals [IO]
Intl. Assn. of Hispanic Meeting Professionals [2684]
Intl. Assn. of Professional Cong. Organizers [IO]
Intl. Assn. of Protocol Consultants [965]
Intl. Cong. and Convention Assn. [IO]
Intl. Exhibitions Bur. [IO]
Intl. Soc. of Meeting Planners [IO]
Intl. Soc. of Meeting Planners [2685]
Meeting and Events Australia [IO]
Meeting Professionals Intl. [IO]
Meeting Professionals Intl. [2686]
Meetings and Events Australia - Australian Capital Territory Br. [IO]
Meetings and Events Australia - New South Wales Br. [IO]
Meetings and Events Australia - Northern Territory Br. [IO]
Meetings and Events Australia - Queensland Br. [IO]
Meetings and Events Australia - Tasmania Br. [IO]
Meetings and Events Australia - Victoria Br. [IO]
Meetings and Events Australia - Western Australia Br. [IO]
Natl. Assn. of Golf Tournament Directors [23457]
Natl. Coalition of Black Meeting Planners [2687]
Natl. Convention Assn. [2688]
Professional Convention Mgt. Assn. [2689]
Religious Conf. Mgt. Assn. [2690]
Religious Conf. Mgt. Assn. [IO]
Soc. of Govt. Meeting Professionals [2691]
Thailand Incentive and Convention Assn. [IO]
Meeting Planners Coalition; Natl. Black [★2687]
Meeting Planners Intl. [★2686]
Meeting Planners Intl. [★IO]
Meeting Professionals; Assn. of [1934]
Meeting Professionals Intl. [2686], 3030 Lyndon B. Johnson Fwy., Ste. 1700, Dallas, TX 75234-2759, (972)702-3000
Meeting Professionals Intl. [IO], Dallas, TX, United States
Meetings and Events Australia - Australian Capital Territory Br. [IO], Sydney, Australia
Meetings and Events Australia - New South Wales Br. [IO], Annandale, Australia
Meetings and Events Australia - Northern Territory Br. [IO], Cleveland, Australia
Meetings and Events Australia - Queensland Br. [IO], Cleveland, Australia
Meetings and Events Australia - Tasmania Br. [IO], Sydney, Australia
Meetings and Events Australia - Victoria Br. [IO], Melbourne, Australia
Meetings and Events Australia - Western Australia Br. [IO], Sydney, Australia
Meetings Indus. Assn. of Australia - Australian Capital Territory Br. [★IO]
Meetings Indus. Assn. of Australia - New South Wales Br. [★IO]
Meetings Indus. Assn. of Australia - Northern Territory Br. [★IO]
Meetings Indus. Assn. of Australia - Queensland Br. [★IO]
Meetings Indus. Assn. of Australia - Tasmania Br. [★IO]
Meetings Indus. Assn. of Australia - Victoria Br. [★IO]
Meetings Indus. Assn. of Australia - Western Australia Br. [★IO]
Meetings Industry Microcomputer Users Group - Defunct.
Meetings Inst. Assn. of Australia [★IO]
Mega Soc. [9986], 13155 Wimberly Sq., No. 284, San Diego, CA 92128
Megadeth's Official Fan Club - Address unknown since 2003.
Meginfelag Ahugaleikara Feroya [★IO]
Meiklejohn Civil Liberties Inst. [5804], PO Box 673, Berkeley, CA 94701-0673, (510)848-0599
Mejeriforeningen [★IO]
Mekong River Commn. [IO], Vientiane, Lao People's Democratic Republic

Reference to "IO" in place of a book number signifies that the association may be found in the 45th edition of International Organizations.

Mel Anderson Fan Club - Defunct.
The Mel Gablers [★9259]
The Mel Gibson Fan Club - Address unknown since 2006.
Mel Tillis Fan Club [24946], c/o Mel Tellis Enterprise, PO Box 305, Silver Springs, FL 34489
Mel Tillis Fan Club [IO], Silver Springs, FL, United States
Melamine Coun. - Defunct.
Melamine Tableware Assn. - Defunct.
Melanoma Res. Found. [13842], 24 Old Georgetown Rd., Princeton, NJ 08540, (800)MRF-1290
Melbourne ACM SIGGRAPH [IO], Parkville, Australia
Melbourne Anime Soc. (Australia) [IO], Melbourne, Australia
Melbourne Argonauts Queer Rowing Club [IO], Richmond, Australia
Melbourne Nordic Ski Club [IO], Camberwell, Australia
Melbourne Trail Horse Riders Club [IO], Healesville, Australia
Melissa Etheridge Official Fan Club - Address unknown since 2002.
Mellemfolkeligt Samvirke [★IO]
Mellon Found; Andrew W. [10777]
Melodious Accord [10644], c/o Alice Parker, Artistic Dir./Founder, 96 Middle Rd., Hawley, MA 01339, (413)339-8508
Melon Res. Bd; California [4718]
Melpomene Inst. [16900], 550 Rice St., Ste. 104, St. Paul, MN 55103, (651)789-0140
Melpomene Inst. for Women's Hea. Res. [★16900]
Melungeon Heritage Assn. [18950], PO Box 4042, Wise, VA 24293
Melvil Dui Marching and Chowder Assn. - Defunct.
Melville Soc. [9691], c/o Christopher Sten, Sec., Dept. of English, George Washington Univ., Washington, DC 20052
MEMA Info. Services Coun. [70], 10 Lab. Dr., PO Box 13966, Research Triangle Park, NC 27709-3966, (919)406-8830
Member Insurance Assn. [1827]
Members Prime Club - Defunct.
Membership Development; Natl. Assn. for [319]
Membership Sect. for Health Care Systems - Address unknown since 1999.

Membrane Science
Coalition for the Advancement of Medical Res. [15103]
European Membrane Soc. [IO]
North Amer. Membrane Soc. [7307]
Membrane Soc. of Japan [IO], Tokyo, Japan
Membrane Tech. Assn; Amer. [7824]
Memoir Writers Assn. - Address unknown since 2008.
Memorandum Club - Defunct.
Memorial Assn; 381st Bomb Gp. [20655]
Memorial Assn; Confederate [9368]
Memorial Assn; Creek Indian [10740]
Memorial Found; Crazy Horse [10739]
Memorial Found. of the Germanna Colonies in Virginia [10045], PO Box 279, Locust Grove, VA 22508-0279, (540)423-1700
Memorial Found. for Jewish Culture [10286], c/o Dr. Jerry Hochbaum, Exec. VP, 50 Broadway, 34th Fl., New York, NY 10004-1690, (212)425-6606
Memorial Found. for Jewish Culture [IO], New York, NY, United States
Memorial Found; Professor Chen Wen-Chen [18694]
Memorial Found; U.S. Navy [21221]
Memorial Found; Vietnam Women's [21353]
Memorial Found; Weston A. Price [★15568]
Memorial Found; Women in Military Ser. for Am. [6360]
Memorial Industry Promotion Fund - Defunct.
Memorial Inst. for the Prevention of Terrorism; Natl. [18734]
Memorial; Jewish War Veterans, U.S.A. Natl. [★21312]
Memorial Proj; Vietnam Women's [★21353]
Memorial Societies of Am; Funeral and [★2780]
Memorial Societies; Continental Assn. of Funeral and [★2780]
Memorial Soc; Elvis Presley [24809]
Memorial Soc; Laura Ingalls Wilder [9679]

Memories of Elvis Fan Club [IO], Auckland, New Zealand
Memories of Yesterday Collectors Soc. [★22065]
Memory Syndrome Found; False [16150]
Memphis Cotton Exchange [4328], c/o Cotton Museum, 65 Union Ave., Memphis, TN 38103, (901)531-7826

Men
100 Black Men of Am. [18865]
Amer. Men's Stud. Assn. [12341]
Career Gear [12705]
Father Matters [18180]
Hard Hat Brotherhood [19257]
Intl. Assn. for Stud. of Men [IO]
Iota Nu Delta Fraternity [24631]
Kappa Psi Kappa Fraternity [24480]
Men's Educational Support Assn. [IO]
Men's Rights Agency of Australia [IO]
Natl. Coalition of Men's Ministries [19816]
Natl. Compadres Network [12545]
Native Amer. Fatherhood and Families Assn. [12681]
Phi Sigma Nu Native Amer. Fraternity [24647]
Pi Delta Psi Fraternity [24649]
Promise Keepers [19834]
Psi Sigma Phi Multicultural Fraternity [24594]
Reel Recovery [11519]
Sigma Phi Beta Fraternity [24659]
Single and Custodial Fathers Network [12691]
Soc. for the Psychological Stud. of Men and Masculinity [16181]
Soc. for the Stud. of Male Reproduction [16344]
Student African Amer. Brotherhood [19444]
Men Against Breast Cancer [13843], PO Box 150, Adamstown, MD 21710-0150, (866)547-6222
Men Against Destruction - Defending Against Drugs and Social Disorder; MAD DADS [12043]
Men Against Rape - Defunct.
Men Against Sexism; Natl. Org. for [17779]
Men; Aid to Divorced and Separated [★18039]
Men of Am; Bald-Headed [19373]
Men; Amer. Soc. of Separated and Divorced [12005]
Men of the Church Coun. [★20473]
Men; Conf. of Major Superiors of [19615]
Men to End Spouse Abuse - Address unknown since 1989.
Men Exploring New Directions; Abusive [★12020]
Men/Fathers Hotline [★18038]
Men and Fathers Rsrc. Center [18038], c/o LoneStar Fatherhood Initiative, 807 Brazos St., Ste. 315, Austin, TX 78701-2508, (512)472-3237
Men of the Free Will Baptist Church; Master's [★19490]
Men of Goodwill [★17739]
Men of Goodwill [★IO]
Men Intl., U.S. Area; Y's [13464]
Men for Missions Intl. [20357], PO Box A, Greenwood, IN 46142-6599, (317)881-6752
Men for Missions Intl. [IO], Greenwood, IN, United States
Men; Natl. Assn. of Deans and Advisers of [★7904]
Men of the Natl. Assn. of Free Will Baptists; Master's [19490]
Men; Natl. Coll. Physical Educ. Assn. for [★8985]
Men; Natl. Org. of Restoring [11734]
Men in Nursing; Amer. Assembly for [15431]
Men Our Masters/Women Our Wonders - Address unknown since 1995.
Men; Presbyterian [20473]
Men of Reform Judaism [20160], 633 3rd Ave., New York, NY 10017, (212)650-4100
Men of the Sacred Heart [19659]
Men Societies; Amer. Fed. of Reformed Young [★19831]
Men Stopping Violence [12643], 533 W Howard Ave., Ste. C, Decatur, GA 30030, (404)270-9894
Men of the Trees [★IO]
Men of the Trees (WA) [IO], Guildford, Australia
Men; Wives of Older [12509]
Men and Women in Alcoholics Anonymous; Intl. Advisory Coun. for Homosexual [★13283]
MENC: The Natl. Assn. for Music Educ. [8913], 1806 Robert Fulton Dr., Reston, VA 20191, (703)860-4000
Mencken Soc. [9692], PO Box 16218, Baltimore, MD 21210

MEND - Mothers Embracing Nuclear Disarmament - Defunct.
Mend Our Tongues Soc. [10407]
Mended Hearts Club [★13916]
Mended Hearts, Inc. [13916], 7272 Greenville Ave., Dallas, TX 75231-4596, (214)360-6149
Mendoza Hall of Fame - Defunct.
Meniere's Network [15826], c/o The Ear Found., PO Box 330867, Nashville, TN 37203, (615)627-2724
Meningitis Assn; Natl. [14281]
Meningitis and Schistosomiasis; Res. Center Against [IO]

Mennonite
Anabaptist Sociology and Anthropology Assn. [7559]
Brethren/Mennonite Coun. for Lesbian, Gay, Bisexual and Transgender Interest [20050]
Canadian Conf. of Mennonite Brethren Churches [IO]
Mennonite Central Comm. [IO]
Mennonite Central Comm. [20247]
Mennonite Church USA Historical Comm. [20248]
Mennonite Economic Development Associates [20249]
Mennonite Educ. Agency [20250]
Mennonite Voluntary Ser. [20251]
Mennonite Women USA [20252]
Rosedale Mennonite Missions [20253]
Rosedale Mennonite Missions [IO]
Mennonite Assn. of Retired Persons [12899], 771 Rte. 113, Souderton, PA 18964, (215)721-7730
Mennonite Bd. of Educ. [★20250]
Mennonite Bd. of Missions and Charities; Conservative [★20253]
Mennonite Central Comm. [20247], 21 S 12th St., PO Box 500, Akron, PA 17501-0500, (717)859-1151
Mennonite Central Comm. [IO], Akron, PA, United States
Mennonite Central Comm. Overseas Peace Off. [IO], Akron, PA, United States
Mennonite Central Comm. Overseas Peace Off. [18219], 21 S 12th St., PO Box 500, Akron, PA 17501-0500, (717)859-1151
Mennonite Church; Historical Comm. of the [★20248]
Mennonite Church USA Historical Comm. [20248], 1700 S Main St., Goshen, IN 46526, (574)535-7477
Mennonite Church; Women's Missionary and Ser. Commn. of the [★20252]
Mennonite Coun. for Lesbian, Gay, Bisexual and Transgender Interest; Brethren/ [20050]
Mennonite Coun. for Lesbian and Gay Concerns; Brethren/ [★20050]
Mennonite Disaster Ser. [12870], 1018 Main St., Akron, PA 17501, (717)859-2210
Mennonite Disaster Service [IO], Akron, PA, United States
Mennonite Economic Development Associates [IO], Waterloo, ON, Canada
Mennonite Economic Development Associates [20249], 1821 Oregon Pike, Ste. 201, Lancaster, PA 17601-6466, (717)560-6546
Mennonite Educ. Agency [20250], 63846 County Rd. 35, Ste. 1, Goshen, IN 46528-9621, (574)642-3164
Mennonite Health Assn. - Defunct.
Mennonite Historical Soc; Lancaster [21130]
Mennonite Indus. and Bus. Assn. [★20249]
Mennonite Voluntary Ser. [20251], PO Box 347, Newton, KS 67114-0347, (316)283-5100
Mennonite Women USA [20252], 722 Main St., PO Box 347, Newton, KS 67114-0347, (316)283-5100
Menopause Found; Amer. [16894]
Menopause Soc; Australasian [IO]
Menopause Soc; Intl. [IO]
Menopause Soc; North Amer. [15614]
Menorah Assn. - Defunct.
Men's Apparel Club of New York City - Address unknown since 1994.
Men's Apparel Indus; Young Men's Assn. of the [★262]
Men's Apparel Indus; Young Menswear Assn. of [★262]
Men's and Boys' Wear Inter-Industry Coun. - Defunct.

A star before a book entry number signifies that the name is not listed separately, but is mentioned within the entry.

Men's Chorus, A Natl. Assn. of Male Choruses; Inter-
collegiate [★10611]
Men's Christian Associations of North Am; Assn. of
Secretaries, Young [★13460]
Men's Christian Associations in the U.S; Assn. of
Professional Directors, Young [★13460]
Men's Clothing Mfrs. Assn. [IO], Montreal, QC,
Canada
Men's Clubs; Fed. of Jewish [20137]
Men's Clubs; Natl. Fed. of Jewish [★20137]
Men's Counseling Ser. on Domestic Violence;
Emerge: A [★12026]
Men's Curling Assn; U.S. [★23302]
Men's Defense Assn. [18039], 17854 Lyons, Forest
Lake, MN 55025, (651)464-7887
Men's Educational Support Assn. [IO], Calgary, AB,
Canada
Men's Equality Now Intl. [IO], Forest Lake, MN,
United States
Men's Equality Now Intl. [★IO]
Men's Equality Now Intl. [18040], 17854 Lyons St.,
Forest Lake, MN 55025, (651)464-7663
Men's Equality Now Intl. [★18040]
Men's Garden Clubs of Am. [★22513]
Men's Garden Clubs of Am; The Gardeners of
America/ [4778]
Men's Hat Linings and Trimmings Assn. - Defunct.
Men's Hea. Crisis; Gay [13564]
Men's Hebrew and Kindred Associations; Coun. of
Young [★12473]
Men's Institutes of the U.S; Conf. of Major Religious
Superiors of [★19615]
Men's Intl. Peace Exchange [18220], 612 Kenney
Ln., Brookhaven, PA 19015, (610)872-8178
Men's Intl. Peace Exchange [IO], Brookhaven, PA,
United States
Men's Intl. Professional Tennis Coun. - Defunct.
Men's League of New York; Advt. [★77]
Men's Liberation - Defunct.
Men's Neckwear Mfrs. Assn. of New York - Defunct.
Men's Neckwear Mfrs. Inst. of America - Defunct.
Men's Rsrc. Center [12357], 12 SE 14th Ave.,
Portland, OR 97214, (503)235-3433
Men's Resources Hot Line [★18043]
Men's Rights [18041]
Men's Rights
  Amer. Union of Men [18036]
  Fathers for Equal Rights [12010]
  Male Liberation Found. [18037]
  Men and Fathers Rsrc. Center [18038]
  Men's Defense Assn. [18039]
  Men's Equality Now Intl. [18040]
  Men's Equality Now Intl. [IO]
  Men's Rights [18041]
  Natl. Center for Men [18042]
  Natl. Coalition of Free Men [18043]
  Natl. Men's Rsrc. Center [18044]
  Natl. Org. for Men [18045]
  Single and Custodial Fathers Network [12691]
Men's Rights Agency of Australia [IO], Waterford,
Australia
Men's Rights Assn. [★18039]
Men's and St. Laba Ladies Charity Societies; United
Hasroun [19732]
Men's Sportswear Buyers; Natl. Assn. of [247]
Men's Stud. Assn; Amer. [12341]
Men's Tie Found. [★252]
Mensa; Amer. [9981]
Mensa, the High IQ Soc. [★9981]
Mensa Intl. [IO], Wolverhampton, United Kingdom
Mensa; Irish Special Interest Gp. of [10244]
Mensa South Africa [IO], Pinegowrie, Republic of
South Africa
Menstrual Cycle Res; Soc. for [15619]
Menstruation and Women's Hea; Museum of [15611]
Menswear
  Career Gear [12705]
  Clothing Mfrs. Assn. of the U.S.A. [229]
  Intl. Wooden Bow Tie Club [243]
  Neckwear Assn. of America [252]
  Young Menswear Assn. [262]
Menswear Assn. of Men's Apparel Indus; Young
[★262]
Menswear Assn; Young [262]
Mental After Care Assn. [★IO]

Mental Deficiency; Amer. Assn. on [★15239]
Mental Development; Assn. for Children with
Retarded [★12572]
Mental Disability Legal Rsrc. Center [★5781]
Mental Disability Rights Intl. [12574], 1156 15th St.
NW, Ste. 1001, Washington, DC 20005, (202)296-
0800
Mental Disability Rights Intl. [IO], Washington, DC,
United States
Mental Disease; Assn. for Res. in Nervous and
[16082]
Mental Health
  ABIL - Agoraphobics Building Independent Lives
  [12546]
  Acad. of Psychosomatic Medicine [16195]
  Acad. of Scientific Hypnotherapy [14913]
  Addiction Res. and Treatment Corp. [13213]
  Advocate Hea. Care [14821]
  African Regional Coun. for Mental Hea. [IO]
  Agoraphobics in Motion [12742]
  Albert Ellis Inst. [16197]
  Alfred Adler Inst. [16117]
  Alliance for Eating Disorders Awareness [14297]
  Amer. Acad. of Child and Adolescent Psychiatry
  [16063]
  Amer. Acad. of Clinical Psychiatrists [16064]
  Amer. Acad. of Psychoanalysis and Dynamic
  Psychiatry [16101]
  Amer. Acad. of Psychotherapists [16198]
  Amer. Acad. of Sleep Medicine [16418]
  Amer. Art Therapy Assn. [16199]
  Amer. Assn. of Anger Mgt. Providers [15185]
  Amer. Assn. of Applied and Preventive Psychol-
  ogy [16119]
  Amer. Assn. of Behavioral Therapists [13744]
  Amer. Assn. of Chairs of Departments of
  Psychiatry [16065]
  Amer. Assn. of Children's Residential Centers
  [13467]
  Amer. Assn. of Community Psychiatrists [16066]
  Amer. Assn. of Directors of Psychiatric Residency
  Training [16067]
  Amer. Assn. for Geriatric Psychiatry [16068]
  Amer. Assn. for Hea. Educ. [16234]
  Amer. Assn. for Marriage and Family Therapy
  [16200]
  Amer. Assn. of Mental Hea. Professionals in Cor-
  rections [15186]
  Amer. Assn. of Professional Hypnotherapists
  [14915]
  Amer. Assn. of Psychiatric Administrators [14861]
  Amer. Assn. of Psychiatric Technicians [16069]
  Amer. Assn. for Tech. in Psychiatry [16070]
  Amer. Bd. of Examiners of Psychodrama, Sociom-
  etry, and Gp. Psychotherapy [16201]
  Amer. Bd. of Medical Psychotherapists and Psy-
  chodiagnosticians [16202]
  Amer. Bd. of Professional Psychology [16121]
  Amer. Bd. of Psychiatry and Neurology [16071]
  Amer. Bd. of Psychological Hypnosis [14917]
  Amer. Coll. of Mental Hea. Admin. [15187]
  Amer. Correctional Hea. Services Assn. [14715]
  Amer. Coun. for Drug Educ. [13222]
  Amer. Counseling Assn. [11815]
  Amer. Dance Therapy Assn. [16203]
  Amer. Gp. Psychotherapy Assn. [16204]
  Amer. Guild of Hypnotherapists [14919]
  Amer. Inst. of Stress [16487]
  Amer. Mental Hea. Alliance [15188]
  Amer. Mental Hea. Counselors Assn. [15189]
  Amer. Music Therapy Assn. [16205]
  Amer. Orthopsychiatric Assn. [16075]
  Amer. Psychiatric Assn. [16076]
  Amer. Psychiatric Assn. Alliance [16077]
  Amer. Psychoanalytic Assn. [16102]
  Amer. Psychological Assn. [16122]
  Amer. Psychological Assn. - Addictions Div.
  [16123]
  American Psychological Association Division 31 -
  State, Provincial, and Territorial Psychological
  Association Affairs [16124]
  Amer. Psychological Assn. - Division of Family
  Psychology [16125]
  Amer. Psychological Assn. Division of
  Independent Practice [16126]

  Amer. Psychological Assn. - Div. of Intl. Psychol-
  ogy [16127]
  Amer. Psychological Assn. - Div. of Trauma
  Psychology [16128]
  Amer. Psychological Assn. of Graduate Students
  [16129]
  Amer. Psychological Assn. - Hea. Psychology Div.
  [16130]
  Amer. Psychological Assn. - Media Psychology
  Div. [16131]
  Amer. Psychological Assn. - Psychology of
  Religion (Division 36) [16132]
  Amer. Psychology-Law Soc. [16133]
  Amer. Psychopathological Assn. [16190]
  Amer. Psychosomatic Soc. [16196]
  Amer. Psychotherapy Assn. [16207]
  Amer. Public Hea. Assn. [16236]
  Amer. School Hea. Assn. [14718]
  Amer. Soc. for Adolescent Psychiatry [16078]
  Amer. Soc. for the Advancement of Pharmaco-
  therapy [16134]
  Amer. Soc. of Clinical Hypnosis [14921]
  Amer. Soc. of Clinical Hypnosis - Educ. and Res.
  Found. [14922]
  Amer. Soc. of Psychoanalytic Physicians [16104]
  AMHS [11817]
  Anxiety Disorders Assn. of Am. [12743]
  Anxiety Disorders Special Interest Gp. [12744]
  Anxiety and Phobia Treatment Center [12745]
  Armenian Amer. Soc. for Stud. on Stress and
  Genocide [15190]
  Arts in Therapy Network [13709]
  The Arts We Need [13710]
  Assn. for Advanced Training in the Behavioral Sci-
  ences [8878]
  Assn. for Advancement of Psychoanalysis (of the
  Karen Horney Psychoanalytic Inst. and Center)
  [16105]
  Assn. for the Advancement of Psychology [16136]
  Assn. for the Advancement of Psychotherapy
  [16210]
  Assn. for Behavioral and Cognitive Therapies
  [13733]
  Assn. for Behavioral Hea. and Wellness [24088]
  Assn. of Behavioral Healthcare Mgt. [15191]
  Assn. for Birth Psychology [16137]
  Assn. of Black Psychologists [16138]
  Assn. for Child Psychoanalysis [16106]
  Assn. for Convulsive Therapy [15192]
  Association for Convulsive Therapy [IO]
  Assn. for Happiness Advancement [18046]
  Assn. for Humanistic Psychology [16140]
  Assn. for Infant Mental Hea., United Kingdom [IO]
  Assn. of Medicine and Psychiatry [16081]
  Assn. for Multicultural Counseling and Develop-
  ment [11819]
  Assn. for Psychoanalytic Medicine [16107]
  Assn. for Psychoanalytic Self Psychology [16141]
  Assn. for Psychological Type Intl. [16143]
  Assn. for Res. in Personality [7543]
  Assn. of Schools of Public Hea. [16240]
  Assn. for Specialists in Gp. Work [11820]
  Assn. of State and Provincial Psychology Boards
  [16144]
  Assn. for Women in Psychology [16145]
  Australian False Memory Assn. [IO]
  Australian Infant, Child, Adolescent and Family
  Mental Hea. Assn. [IO]
  Autism Speaks [13724]
  Better Sleep Coun. [16424]
  Black Mental Hea. Alliance [15193]
  British Columbia Schizophrenia Soc. [IO]
  British False Memory Soc. [IO]
  British Psychodrama Assn. [IO]
  Canadian Mental Hea. Assn. [IO]
  Canadian Mental Hea. Assn. - Alberta Div. [IO]
  Canadian Mental Hea. Assn., Barrie - Simcoe Br.
  [IO]
  Canadian Mental Hea. Assn., Bas-du-Fleuve Br.
  [IO]
  Canadian Mental Hea. Assn. - Battlefords Br. [IO]
  Canadian Mental Hea. Assn. - BC Div. [IO]
  Canadian Mental Hea. Assn. - Brant County Br.
  [IO]
  Canadian Mental Hea. Assn. - Calgary Region
  [IO]

Reference to "IO" in place of a book number signifies that the association may be found in the 45th edition of International Organizations.

Canadian Mental Hea. Assn. - Central Region [IO]
Canadian Mental Hea. Assn., Chatham - Kent Br. [IO]
Canadian Mental Hea. Assn., Chaudiere - Appa-laches Br. [IO]
Canadian Mental Hea. Assn. - Cochrane Timiska-ming Br. [IO]
Canadian Mental Hea. Assn. - Courtenay Br. [IO]
Canadian Mental Hea. Assn. - Cowichan Valley Br. [IO]
Canadian Mental Hea. Assn. - Dartmouth Br. [IO]
Canadian Mental Hea. Assn. - Durham Br. [IO]
Canadian Mental Hea. Assn. - East Central Region [IO]
Canadian Mental Hea. Assn. - Edmonton Region [IO]
Canadian Mental Hea. Assn. - Elgin County Br. [IO]
Canadian Mental Hea. Assn. - Estevan Br. [IO]
Canadian Mental Hea. Assn. - Fredericton/Oro-mocto Region [IO]
Canadian Mental Hea. Assn., Grey - Bruce Br. [IO]
Canadian Mental Hea. Assn. - Hamilton Br. [IO]
Canadian Mental Hea. Assn. - Hastings and Prince Edward Br. [IO]
Canadian Mental Hea. Assn., Haut-Richelieu Br. [IO]
Canadian Mental Hea. Assn. - Huron - Perth Br. [IO]
Canadian Mental Hea. Assn. - Interlake Region [IO]
Canadian Mental Hea. Assn. - Kamloops Br. [IO]
Canadian Mental Hea. Assn. - Kelowna Br. [IO]
Canadian Mental Hea. Assn. - Kingston Br. [IO]
Canadian Mental Hea. Assn. for the Kootenays [IO]
Canadian Mental Hea. Assn. - Lac St. Jean Br. [IO]
Canadian Mental Hea. Assn. - Lambton County Br. [IO]
Canadian Mental Hea. Assn., Leeds - Grenville Br. [IO]
Canadian Mental Hea. Assn., London - Middlesex Br. [IO]
Canadian Mental Hea. Assn. - Manitoba Div. [IO]
Canadian Mental Hea. Assn. - Melfort Br. [IO]
Canadian Mental Hea. Assn. - Mid-Island Br. [IO]
Canadian Mental Hea. Assn. - Moncton Region [IO]
Canadian Mental Hea. Assn. - Montreal Br. [IO]
Canadian Mental Hea. Assn. - Moose Jaw Br. [IO]
Canadian Mental Hea. Assn. - New Brunswick Div. [IO]
Canadian Mental Hea. Assn. - Newfoundland and Labrador Div. [IO]
Canadian Mental Hea. Assn. - Niagara Br. [IO]
Canadian Mental Hea. Assn. - Nipissing Regional Br. [IO]
Canadian Mental Hea. Assn. - North and South Okanagan Br. [IO]
Canadian Mental Hea. Assn. - North West Region [IO]
Canadian Mental Hea. Assn. - North and West Vancouver Br. [IO]
Canadian Mental Hea. Assn. - Northwest Ter-ritories Div. [IO]
Canadian Mental Hea. Assn. - Nova Scotia Div. [IO]
Canadian Mental Hea. Assn. - Ontario Div. [IO]
Canadian Mental Hea. Assn. - Ottawa Br. [IO]
Canadian Mental Hea. Assn. - Oxford County Br. [IO]
Canadian Mental Hea. Assn. - Peel Br. [IO]
Canadian Mental Hea. Assn. - Peterborough Br. [IO]
Canadian Mental Hea. Assn. - Pincher Creek Br. [IO]
Canadian Mental Hea. Assn. - Port Alberni Br. [IO]
Canadian Mental Hea. Assn. - Prince Albert Br. [IO]
Canadian Mental Hea. Assn. - Prince County Br. [IO]
Canadian Mental Hea. Assn. - Prince Edward Island Div. [IO]

Canadian Mental Hea. Assn. - Prince George Br. [IO]
Canadian Mental Hea. Assn. - Quebec Div. [IO]
Canadian Mental Hea. Assn. - Regina Br. [IO]
Canadian Mental Hea. Assn. - Region I Moncton [IO]
Canadian Mental Hea. Assn. - Region III Br. [IO]
Canadian Mental Hea. Assn. - Region IV Ed-mundston [IO]
Canadian Mental Hea. Assn. - Region V Camp-bellton [IO]
Canadian Mental Hea. Assn. - Region VII Mirami-chi [IO]
Canadian Mental Hea. Assn. - Richmond Br. [IO]
Canadian Mental Hea. Assn., Rive-Sud de Mont-real Br. [IO]
Canadian Mental Hea. Assn., S. D. and G. Pres-cott - Russel Br. [IO]
Canadian Mental Hea. Assn. - Saint John Br. [IO]
Canadian Mental Hea. Assn. - Saskatchewan Div. [IO]
Canadian Mental Hea. Assn. - Saskatoon Br. [IO]
Canadian Mental Hea. Assn. - Sault Ste. Marie Br. [IO]
Canadian Mental Hea. Assn. - Simon Fraser Br. [IO]
Canadian Mental Hea. Assn. - South East Region [IO]
Canadian Mental Hea. Assn. - South Okanagan Similkameen Br. [IO]
Canadian Mental Hea. Assn. - South Region [IO]
Canadian Mental Hea. Assn. - Swift Current Br. [IO]
Canadian Mental Hea. Assn. - Thompson Region [IO]
Canadian Mental Hea. Assn. - Thunder Bay Br. [IO]
Canadian Mental Hea. Assn. - Toronto Br. [IO]
Canadian Mental Hea. Assn. - Vancouver/Burnaby Br. [IO]
Canadian Mental Hea. Assn. - Vernon District Br. [IO]
Canadian Mental Hea. Assn. - Waterloo Regional Br. [IO]
Canadian Mental Hea. Assn., Wellington - Dufferin Br. [IO]
Canadian Mental Hea. Assn. - Westman Region [IO]
Canadian Mental Hea. Assn. - Weyburn Br. [IO]
Canadian Mental Hea. Assn., Windsor - Essex County Br. [IO]
Canadian Mental Hea. Assn. - Winnipeg Region [IO]
Canadian Mental Hea. Assn. - Yorkton Br. [IO]
Canadian Mental Hea. Assn. - Yukon Div. [IO]
Center for Applications of Psychological Type [16146]
Center for Attitudinal Healing [IO]
Center for Psychological and Spiritual Hea. [15194]
Center for the Stud. of Aging of Albany [11281]
CFC Intl. [14435]
C.G. Jung Found. for Analytical Psychology [16147]
Chicano Family Center [17701]
Childbirth and Postpartum Professional Assn. [13980]
Christian Assn. for Psychological Stud. [16148]
Clowns Without Borders [IO]
Clowns Without Borders - USA [11768]
Cognitive Neuroscience Soc. [15407]
Comm. for Truth in Psychiatry [15195]
Community Guidance Ser. [16214]
CONTACT USA [19865]
Corporate and Found. Relations [12075]
Coun. on Accreditation [13164]
Coun. on Educ. for Public Hea. [16242]
Coun. for the Natl. Register of Hea. Ser. Providers in Psychology [16149]
Deaf-REACH [14752]
Depression Alliance [IO]
Depression and Bipolar Support Alliance [15196]
Depression and Related Affective Disorders Assn. [15197]
Depressives Anonymous: Recovery From Depres-sion [12547]

Devereux Natl. [13734]
Disaster Psychiatry Outreach [16083]
Double Trouble in Recovery [12548]
Dual Disorders Anonymous [13237]
EMDR - Humanitarian Assistance Programs [12767]
EMDR Intl. Assn. [16215]
Emotions Anonymous Intl. Ser. Center [12549]
Emotions Anonymous Intl. Ser. Center [IO]
European Fed. of Associations of Families of People with Mental Illness
Families for Depression Awareness [15198]
Feathered Pipe Found. [12345]
Fed. of Families for Children's Mental Hea. [12550]
Feldenkrais Guild of North Am. [10182]
Finnish Assn. for Mental Hea. [IO]
First Person Plural [IO]
First Steps to Freedom [IO]
Freedom From Fear [15199]
Gift From Within [12768]
Global Alliance of Mental Illness Advocacy Networks [15200]
Global Alliance of Mental Illness Advocacy Networks [IO]
Global Autism Proj. [13725]
Global and Regional Asperger Syndrome Partner-ship [15325]
Gp. for the Advancement of Psychiatry [16084]
Gp. Proj. for Holocaust Survivors and Their Children [17716]
Hea. Connection [13245]
Hea. Educ. Found. [16243]
Hea. Promotion Inst. [11288]
Inst. for the Advanced Stud. of Black Family Life and Culture [9359]
Inst. for the Development of Emotional and Life Skills/National Inst. of Relationship Enhance-ment [15201]
Inst. for Expressive Anal. [16217]
Inst. for Integral Development [13249]
Inst. for Labor and Mental Health [15202]
Inst. for Mental Hea. Initiatives [15203]
Inst. on Psychiatric Services/American Psychiatric Assn. [16085]
Intl. Alliance for Child and Adolescent Mental Hea. and Schools [15204]
Intl. Assn. for Cognitive Psychotherapy [16218]
Intl. Assn. of Pastoral Psychologists [16151]
Intl. Assn. for Relational Psychoanalysis and Psychotherapy [16108]
Intl. Assn. for the Sci. Stud. of Intellectual Dis-abilities - Ireland [IO]
Intl. Assn. for the Stud. of Dreams [16426]
Intl. Assn. of Transpersonal Therapists and Physi-cians [15205]
International Association of Transpersonal Therapists and Physicians [IO]
Intl. Center for Attitudinal Healing [15206]
Intl. Comm. Against Mental Illness [15207]
Intl. Comm. Against Mental Illness [IO]
Intl. Critical Incident Stress Found. [16491]
Intl. Expressive Arts Therapy Assn. [13712]
Intl. Fed. for Psychoanalytic Educ. [9028]
Intl. Mental Game Coaching Assn. [23289]
Intl. REST Investigators Soc. [16220]
Intl. Schizophrenia Found. [IO]
Intl. Soc. for Adolescent Psychiatry and Psychol-ogy [16087]
Intl. Soc. for Developmental Psychobiology [16153]
Intl. Soc. for Mental Hea. Online [15208]
Intl. Soc. for Mental Hea. Online [IO]
Intl. Soc. of Psychiatric Genetics [14502]
Intl. Soc. for the Psychological Treatments of the Schizophrenias and Other Psychoses - USA [15209]
Intl. Soc. for Res. on Impulsivity [16088]
Intl. Soc. for Self and Identity [7546]
Intl. Soc. for the Stud. of Trauma and Dissociation [15210]
Intl. Soc. for the Stud. of Trauma and Dissociation [IO]
Intl. Transactional Anal. Assn. [16089]
Ittleson Found. [13122]

A star before a book entry number signifies that the name is not listed separately, but is mentioned within the entry.

Jean Piaget Soc.: Soc. for the Stud. of Knowledge and Development [16156]
Jewish Bd. of Family and Children's Services/ Youth Counseling League Div. [13492]
Joseph P. Kennedy, Jr. Found. [12571]
Judge David L. Bazelon Center for Mental Hea. Law [17123]
Karen Horney Clinic [16109]
LifeWorks Inst. [12551]
Macro Soc. [10184]
ManKind Proj. [13021]
Marce Soc. [IO]
Marijuana Policy Proj. [18024]
Mental Hea. Am. [15211]
Mental Hea. Assn. NSW [IO]
Mental Hea. Assn. Queensland [IO]
Mental Hea. Coalition of South Australia [IO]
Mental Hea. Corporations of Am. [13736]
Mental Hea. Coun. of Australia [IO]
Mental Hea. Found. [IO]
Mental Hea. Ireland [IO]
Mental Health Workers Without Borders [IO]
Mental Hea. Workers Without Borders [15212]
Milton H. Erickson Found. [16221]
Mind - Natl. Assn. for Mental Hea. [IO]
NADD - An Assn. for Persons with Developmental Disabilities and Mental Hea. Needs [12552]
NAMM Found. Res. Div. [10653]
Narcotic Educational Found. of Am. [13256]
NARSAD: Mental Hea. Res. Assn. [15213]
Natl. Alliance of Advocates for Buprenorphine Treatment.[16511]
Natl. Alliance on Mental Illness [15214]
Natl. Asian Amer. Pacific Islander Mental Hea. Assn. [15215]
Natl. Assn. for the Advancement of Psychoanalysis [16110]
Natl. Assn. for Children's Behavioral Hea. [16090]
Natl. Assn. for Drama Therapy [16222]
Natl. Assn. on Drug Abuse Problems [13262]
Natl. Assn. for Human Development [11303]
Natl. Assn. of Mental Hea. Planning and Advisory Councils [15216]
Natl. Assn. for Poetry Therapy [16223]
Natl. Assn. for Psychiatric Hea. Systems [16091]
Natl. Assn. of Qualified Mental Retardation Professionals [15241]
Natl. Assn. for Regulatory Admin. [15011]
Natl. Assn. for Res. and Therapy of Homosexuality [14434]
Natl. Assn. for Rural Mental Hea. [15217]
Natl. Assn. of School Psychologists [16160]
Natl. Assn. for Self Esteem [15218]
Natl. Assn. of State Mental Hea. Prog. Directors [15219]
Natl. Assn. of Therapeutic Schools and Programs [13738]
Natl. Autism Assn. [13727]
Natl. Benevolent Assn. of the Christian Church [13177]
Natl. Center for Amer. Indian and Alaska Native Mental Hea. Res. [15220]
Natl. Coalition of Mental Hea. Professionals and Consumers [15221]
Natl. Coalition of Psychiatrists Against Motorcoach Therapy [15222]
Natl. Coun. for Community Behavioral Healthcare [15223]
Natl. Eating Disorders Assn. [14302]
Natl. Educ. Alliance for Borderline Personality Disorder [15224]
Natl. Families in Action [13269]
Natl. Family Partnership [13270]
Natl. Found. for Depressive Illness [15225]
Natl. Fragile X Found. [14469]
Natl. Inst. of Mental Hea. [15226]
Natl. Latino Behavioral Hea. Assn. [15227]
Natl. Mental Hea. Consumers' Self-Help CH [12553]
Natl. Org. for People of Color Against Suicide [13289]
Natl. Psychological Assn. for Psychoanalysis [16111]
Natl. Rehabilitation Counseling Assn. [16331]
Natl. Remotivation Therapy Org. [16226]

Natl. Rsrc. Center on Homelessness and Mental Illness [12298]
Natl. Stigma CH [15228]
Network Against Coercive Psychiatry [12554]
North Amer. Soc. of Adlerian Psychology [16162]
North Amer. Soc. for Childhood Onset Schizophrenia [15229]
Northamerican Assn. of Masters in Psychology [9030]
Northern Ireland Assn. for Mental Hea. [IO]
Obsessive-Compulsive Anonymous [12555]
Obsessive-Compulsive Found. [15230]
Org. for Attempters and Survivors of Suicide in Interfaith Services [13290]
Pan Amer. Hea. Org. [14592]
Phoenix House [13273]
Postgraduate Center for Mental Hea. [16227]
PRIDE Youth Programs [13276]
Psi Beta [24579]
Psychiatric Rehabilitation Services [15231]
Psychohistory Forum [16113]
Psychology Soc. [16165]
Psychometric Soc. [16166]
Psychonomic Soc. [16167]
Psychotherapy Network [16228]
Rabbinic Center for Res. and Counseling [16229]
The Radiance Technique Intl. Assn. [13648]
Radical Caucus in Psychiatry [16092]
Radix Inst. [13649]
Reclamation Inc. [12556]
Recovery, Inc. [16230]
Rethink [IO]
Richmond Fellowship Intl. [IO]
S.A.F.E. Alternatives [12557]
Sandtray Network [16114]
SANE Australia [IO]
Schizophrenia Assn. of Great Britain [IO]
Schizophrenia Intl. Res. Soc. [15232]
Schizophrenia Ireland [IO]
Schizophrenia Soc. of Canada [IO]
Schizophrenics Anonymous [12558]
Scottish Assn. for Mental Hea. [IO]
Selective Mutism Found. [15233]
Serendipity Assn. [14832]
Sex and Love Addicts Anonymous [13074]
Sidran Inst. for Traumatic Stress Educ. [12559]
Sigmund Freud Archives [16115]
Sleep Res. Soc. [16429]
Social, Emotional and Behavioural Difficulties Assn. [IO]
Social Psychiatry Res. Inst. [16094]
Social/Vocational Rehabilitation Clinic [16231]
Soc. of Biological Psychiatry [16095]
Soc. of Clinical Child and Adolescent Psychology [16171]
Soc. for Clinical and Experimental Hypnosis [14927]
Soc. of Consulting Psychology [16172]
Soc. for the Exploration of Psychotherapy Integration [16232]
Soc. of Jewish Sci. [20202]
Soc. of Multivariate Experimental Psychology [16174]
Soc. for Pediatric Psychology [16175]
Soc. for Personality Assessment [16176]
Soc. of Professors of Child and Adolescent Psychiatry [16096]
Soc. of Psychological Hypnosis [16178]
Soc. for the Psychological Stud. of Lesbian, Gay and Bisexual Issues [16180]
Soc. for the Psychological Stud. of Men and Masculinity [16181]
Soc. for Psychophysiological Res. [16183]
Soc. for Sex Therapy and Res. [16408]
Soc. for the Stud. of Ingestive Behavior [13742]
Soc. for the Stud. of Peace, Conflict, and Violence: Peace Psychology Div. of the Amer. Psychological Assn. [16185]
Soul Friends [16637]
Southeast Inst. for Gp. and Family Therapy [18629]
Stop it Now! [11653]
Suicide and Mental Hea. Assn. Intl. [15234]
Suicide and Mental Hea. Assn. Intl. [IO]
Suicide Prevention Action Network USA [13292]

Tatry Housing Org. [12300]
Tech. Assistance Collaborative [13145]
Together [IO]
Top End Assn. for Mental Hea. [IO]
TOPS Club (Take Off Pounds Sensibly) [12649]
Treatment and Res. Advancements Assn. for Personality Disorder [15235]
Trichotillomania Learning Center [15236]
UK Soc. for the Stud. of Dissociation [IO]
U.S.A. Transactional Anal. Assn. [13743]
U.S. Psychiatric Rehabilitation Assn. [16336]
Weight Watchers Intl. [14603]
Wellness Associates [16058]
Western Australian Assn. for Mental Hea. [IO]
William Glasser Inst. [16233]
Women's Drug Res. Project [13285]
World Assn. of Cultural Psychiatry [16097]
World Assn. for Infant Mental Hea. [16098]
World Assn. for Psychosocial Rehabilitation - U.S. Br. [16338]
World Assn. for Social Psychiatry [16099]
World Fed. for Mental Hea. [15237]
World Fed. for Mental Hea. [IO]
Mental Hea. Am. [15211], 2000 N Beauregard St., 6th Fl., Alexandria, VA 22311, (703)684-7722
Mental Hea. Am. [★15211]
Mental Hea. Assn. NSW [IO], East Sydney, Australia
Mental Hea. Assn. Queensland [IO], Brisbane, Australia
Mental Hea. Bus. Administrators; Amer. Soc. of [★15191]
Mental Hea. Coalition of South Australia [IO], Adelaide, Australia
Mental Hea. Corporations of Am. [13736], 1876-A Eider Ct., Tallahassee, FL 32308, (850)942-4900
Mental Hea. Coun. of Australia [IO], Canberra, Australia
Mental Hea. Counselors; Acad. of Clinical [★11828]
Mental Health Film Bd. - Address unknown since 1994.
Mental Hea. Film Coun. [★IO]
Mental Hea. Found. [IO], London, United Kingdom
Mental Hea. Found; Natl. [★15211]
Mental Hea; Intl. Assn. for Infant [★16098]
Mental Hea. Ireland [IO], Dun Laoghaire, Ireland
Mental Hea. Law; Judge David L. Bazelon Center for [17123]
Mental Hea. Law Proj. [★17123]
Mental Health Materials Center - Defunct.
Mental Hea. Media [IO], London, United Kingdom
Mental Hea. Media Coun. [★IO]
Mental Hea; Natl. Assn. for [★15211]
Mental Hea. Organizations; Coalition of Spanish Speaking [★13176]
Mental Health Policy Resource Center - Defunct.
Mental Hea; Postgraduate Center for [16227]
Mental Hea. and Psychiatric Services; Special Constituency Sect. for [★16093]
Mental Hea. Specialties; Assn. of [★11817]
Mental Health Workers for Peace - Defunct.
Mental Hea. Workers Without Borders [15212], c/o Martin Gittelman, 100 W 94th St., New York, NY 10025
Mental Health Workers Without Borders [IO], New York, NY, United States
Mental Healthcare Coun; Natl. Community [★15223]
Mental Hospitals; Assn. of Medical Superintendents of [★14861]
Mental Hygiene; Intl. Comm. for [★15237]
Mental Hygiene; Natl. Comm. for [★15211]
Mental Illness Found. - Defunct.
Mental Illness; Natl. Rsrc. Center on Homelessness and [12298]
Mental Patient Civil Liberties Project - Defunct.
Mental Patients; Recovery, Inc., The Assn. of Nervous and Former [★16230]
Mental and Physical Disability Law; Amer. Bar Assn. - Commn. on [5781]
Mental and Physical Disability Legal Res. Services and Databases [★5781]
Mental Physics; Inst. of [★20503]
Mental Rehabilitation; Assn. for Physical and [★16311]
Mental Res. Inst. [13737], 555 Middlefield Rd., Palo Alto, CA 94301, (650)321-3055

Reference to "IO" in place of a book number signifies that the association may be found in the 45th edition of International Organizations.

Mental Retardation; Amer. Acad. on [★15238]
Mental Retardation Assn. of America - Defunct.
Mental Retardation; Natl. Apostolate with People with [★20026]
Mentally Disabled
Acad. on Mental Retardation [15238]
Action for Autism [IO]
Activ Found. [IO]
Aicardi Syndrome Newsl. [14437]
Amer. Assn. on Intellectual and Developmental Disabilities [15239]
Amer. Assn. of Mental Hea. Professionals in Corrections [15186]
Amer. Bd. of Disability Analysts [16308]
Amer. Correctional Hea. Services Assn. [14715]
Amer. Network of Community Options and Resources [12560]
Amer. Occupational Therapy Assn. [16602]
Amer. Physical Therapy Assn. [16603]
Amer. Psychiatric Assn. [16076]
Amer. Psychiatric Assn. Alliance [16077]
Arc of the U.S. [12561]
Assn. for the Advancement of Blind and Retarded [16832]
Assn. for Children with Down Syndrome [12562]
Assn. for the Help of Retarded Children [15240]
Assn. for Real Change [IO]
Assn. of Univ. Centers on Disabilities [12563]
Autism Soc. in Norway [IO]
Autism Speaks [13724]
Best Buddies Intl. [12564]
Best Buddies Intl. [IO]
Bethesda Lutheran Homes and Services [12565]
Canadian Assn. for Community Living [IO]
Center for Family Support [12566]
Children and Adults With Attention Deficit/ Hyperactivity Disorder [15314]
Christian Coun. on Persons with Disabilities [11931]
Christos Stelios Ioannou Found. [IO]
Chromosome 9P Network [14443]
Coffin-Lowry Syndrome Found. [14447]
Confederacion Espanola de Organizaciones en favor de las Personas con Discapacidad Intelectual [IO]
Coun. on Quality and Leadership [IO]
Coun. on Quality and Leadership [12567]
Devereux Natl. [13734]
Differently Abled Proud People Exercising Rights [12568]
Elwyn [12383]
ENABLE Scotland [IO]
Fed. for Children with Special Needs [12569]
First Signs [13942]
Friends of LADDERS [12491]
Fundacion de Asistencia Sicopedagogica para Ninos, Adolescentes y Adultos con Retardo Mental [IO]
Global Autism Proj. [13725]
Gospel Assn. for the Blind [16848]
Hong Chi Assn. [IO]
Hong Kong Down Syndrome Assn. [IO]
Inclusion Intl. [IO]
Inclusion Ireland [IO]
Institutes for the Achievement of Human Potential [11700]
Intl. Assn. for the Sci. Stud. of Intellectual Disabilities [IO]
Intl. Rett Syndrome Assn. [15333]
Irish Fragile X Soc. [IO]
JARC [12570]
Joseph P. Kennedy, Jr. Found. [12571]
Joubert Syndrome Found. and Related Cerebellar Disorders [14459]
Lifespire [12572]
Little City Found. [12573]
Lok Chi Assn. [IO]
Mental Disability Rights Intl. [IO]
Mental Disability Rights Intl. [12574]
Mentally Retarded Welfare Soc. [IO]
Natl. Asian Amer. Pacific Islander Mental Hea. Assn. [15215]
Natl. Assn. of Councils on Developmental Disabilities [12575]
Natl. Assn. for the Habilitation of the Mentally Handicapped in Israel [IO]

Natl. Assn. of Mental Hea. Planning and Advisory Councils [15216]
Natl. Assn. for Persons with Intellectual Disabilities of Germany [IO]
Natl. Assn. of Qualified Mental Retardation Professionals [15241]
Natl. Assn. for Regulatory Admin. [15011]
Natl. Assn. of State Directors of Developmental Disabilities Services [12576]
Natl. Attention Deficit Disorder Assn. [15343]
Natl. Autism Assn. [13727]
Natl. Autistic Soc. [IO]
Natl. Benevolent Assn. of the Christian Church [13177]
Natl. Coun. on Intellectual Disability [IO]
Natl. Down Syndrome Cong. [12577]
Natl. Fragile X Found. [14469]
Natl. Guardianship Assn. [1813]
Natl. Networker [12495]
Natl. Special Needs Network Found. [14232]
New Avenues to Independence [12578]
New Zealand Down Syndrome Assn. [IO]
Parents of Down Syndrome [12579]
People First Intl. [12580]
People First Intl. [IO]
Pilot Parents of Southern Arizona [12581]
Proj. Magic [16634]
Rehabilitation Intl. [16333]
Res. and Training Center on Independent Living [11984]
Royal Mencap Soc. [IO]
Sidran Inst. for Traumatic Stress Educ. [12559]
Sister Kenny Rehabilitation Inst. [16335]
Special Olympics [23362]
Support Org. for Trisomy 18, 13, and Related Disorders [14485]
Symbral Found. [12582]
Vocational Evaluation and Career Assessment Professionals [16337]
Voice of the Retarded [12583]
Young Adult Institute/National Inst. for People with Disabilities [12584]
Mentally Disabled; Commn. on the [★5781]
Mentally Ill Children; Natl. Org. for [★15211]
Mentally Retarded; Accreditation Coun. for Facilities for the [★12567]
Mentally Retarded Children; Natl. Assn. of Parents and Friends of [★12561]
Mentally Retarded; Natl. Apostolate for the [★20026]
Mentally Retarded; Natl. Assn. of Coordinators of State Programs for the [★12576]
Mentally Retarded; Natl. Assn. of Private Residential Facilities for the [★12560]
Mentally Retarded and Other Developmentally Disabled Persons; Accreditation Coun. for Services for [★12567]
Mentally Retarded Persons; Natl. Apostolate with [★20026]
Mentally Retarded Welfare Soc. [IO], Guntur, India
Mentalphysics [20503], PO Box 1000, Joshua Tree, CA 92252, (760)365-8371
Mentor Prog. [★19167]
Mentoring Centers; Natl. Org. of Tutoring and [★9283]
Menzies Soc., North Amer. Br; Clan [20851]
Mercantile Exchange; New York [4333]
MERCAZ USA [20161], 155 5th Ave., New York, NY 10010, (212)533-7800
MERCAZ USA [IO], New York, NY, United States
Mercedes-Benz Club of Am. [21699], 1907 Lelaray St., Colorado Springs, CO 80909-2872, (719)633-6427
Mercedes-Benz M-100 Owner's Gp. [21700], 910 Suellen Dr., Reading, PA 19605, (610)921-0462
Mercenary Assn. - Address unknown since 1997.
Mercer Associates - Address unknown since 1999.
Mercers' Company [IO], London, United Kingdom
Merchandise Chains; Assn. of Gen. [★3427]
Merchandise Distributors Coun; Gen. [4021]
Merchandise Mfrs; Natl. Assn. of Musical [★2805]
Merchandise Mart Apparel Assn. - Defunct.
Merchandise Representatives; Assn. of Visual [2535]
Merchandise Wholesalers; Natl. Assn. of Musical [★2814]
Merchandisers; Assn. of Golf [3639]

Merchandisers; Natl. Assn. of Record [★3349]
Merchandisers; Natl. Assn. of Recording [3349]
Merchandisers; Natl. Assn. of Visual [1153]
Merchandising Assn; Natl. Automatic [3971]
Merchandising and Distributing Assn; Photographic [★3007]
Merchandising Res. Found; Mass [★3427]
Merchandising Services; Natl. Assn. for Retail [★3418]
Merchant Bakers of Am; Retail [★454]
Merchant Marine
Amer. Maritime Assn. [6056]
Amer. Maritime Cong. [6057]
Amer. Maritime Officers Ser. [6058]
Chamber of Shipping of Am. [6059]
Marine Engineers' Beneficial Assn. [7308]
Maritime Inst. for Res. and Indus. Development [6060]
New Zealand Merchant Ser. Guild [IO]
North Amer. Maritime Ministry Assn. [13007]
Propeller Club of the U.S. [3586]
United Seamen's Ser. [13008]
Merchant Marine Inst; Amer. [★6059]
Merchant Marine Lib. Assn; Amer. [10321]
Merchant Marine Officers Guild - Defunct.
Merchant Marine Veterans; Amer. [21387]
Merchant Marine Veterans of World War II; U.S. [21408]
Merchant Member Group of Bicycle Inst. of America - Defunct.
Merchant Seamen and Privateers; Brotherhood of [★21408]
Merchant Tailors and Designers Assn. of Am. [★231]
Merchant Taylors' Company [IO], London, United Kingdom
Merchant Token Collectors Assn. - Defunct.
Merchants and Assoc. Indus. of Chicago; Textile [★221]
Merchants and Assoc. Indus. of St. Louis; Textile [★221]
Merchants' Assn. of Am; Cocoa [1507]
Merchants Assn; Hydroponic [1988]
Merchants Assn; Natl. Retail [★3423]
Merchants Assn; Tobacco [3824]
Merchants' Chamber of Agricultural Products [IO], Montevideo, Uruguay
Merchants' Exchange of St. Louis - Defunct.
Merchants Ladies Garment Assn. [★253]
Merchants and Mfrs. Assn. [★2494]
Merchants; Natl. Assn. of Blind [525]
Merchants Org; Archery Manufacturers and [★3638]
Merck Family Fund [4587], 303 Adams St., Milton, MA 02186, (617)696-3580
Mercury
Assn. of Lighting and Mercury Recyclers [5168]
Consumers for Dental Choice [11912]
Cyclone Montego Torino Registry [21626]
Intl. Mercury Owners Assn. [21668]
Mercury Policy Proj. [18745]
Mid-Century Mercury Car Club [21704]
Mercury Car Club; Mid-Century [21704]
Mercury Club - Defunct.
Mercury Enthusiast Restorer Custom Performance Auto Club - Address unknown since 2001.
Mercury Minority Dealers Assn; Ford, Lincoln, [★413]
Mercury Owners Assn; Intl. [21668]
Mercury Policy Proj. [18745], c/o Michael Bender, Exec. Dir./Co-Founder, 1420 North St., Montpelier, VT 05602, (802)223-9000
Mercury Recyclers; Assn. of Lighting and [5168]
Mercy Colleges; Assn. of [8053]
Mercy Corps [12778], Dept. W, PO Box 2669, Portland, OR 97208-2669, (800)256-1900
Mercy Corps [★17845]
Mercy Corps [★IO]
Mercy Corps [IO], Portland, OR, United States
Mercy For Animals [11336], PO Box 363, Columbus, OH 43216, (866)MFA-OHIO
Mercy; Hands of [12291]
Mercy Intl. Hea. Services [★14731]
MERCY Malaysia [IO], Selangor, Malaysia
Mercy Medical Airlift - Defunct.
Mercy Ships Intl. Operations Center [15076], PO Box 2020, Garden Valley, TX 75771-2020, (903)939-7000

A star before a book entry number signifies that the name is not listed separately, but is mentioned within the entry.

Mercy Ships Intl. Operations Center [IO], Garden Valley, TX, United States

Mercy Universal [IO], Greenford, United Kingdom

Mercy-USA for Aid and Development [IO], Plymouth, MI, United States

Mercy-USA for Aid and Development [12871], 44450 Pinetree Dr., Ste. 201, Plymouth, MI 48170-3869, (734)454-0011

Merger and Acquisition Advisors; Alliance of [54]

Merger and Acquisition Consultants; Intl. Assn. [★730]

Meridian House Found. [★17901]

Meridian House Found. [★IO]

Meridian House Intl. [★IO]

Meridian House Intl. [★17901]

Meridian Intl. Center [17901], 1630 Crescent Pl. NW, Washington, DC 20009, (202)667-6800

Meridian Intl. Center [IO], Washington, DC, United States

Meridian Intl. Center Programming Div. [17902], 1630 Crescent Pl. NW, Washington, DC 20009, (202)667-6800

Merier-Gourley-Roark Family Org. [21000], Gourley Hill, 80 Ivy & N Bowen's Mill Rd., Broxton, GA 31519, (912)384-1033

Merino Record Assn; Amer. Delaine and [5182]

Merino Sheep Assn; Black Top and Natl. Delaine [5199]

Merion Bluegrass Assn. - Defunct.

Merit Contractors Assn. [IO], Edmonton, AB, Canada

Merkos L'inyonei Chinuch [★8688]

Merle Haggard Fan Club - Address unknown since 1989.

Merle Thorpe, Jr. Found. [★18058]

Merle Thorpe, Jr. Found. [★IO]

Merleau-Ponty Circle [10811], c/o Prof. Galen A. Johnson, Gen. Sec., Univ. of Rhode Island, Dept. of Philosophy, Lippitt Hall, No. 206, Kingston, RI 02881

Merrell's Fan Club - Address unknown since 1989.

Merrill's Marauders Assn. [21395], c/o Philip Piazza, Pres., 13033 Azalea Dr., Seneca, SC 29678-4508

Merseyside Campaign for Nuclear Disarmament [IO], Liverpool, United Kingdom

Merthyr Tydil; John Morgan Evans of [20965]

Mertonvrienden of Belgium and the Netherlands [IO], Dave, Belgium

Merwin Assn; Miles [21001]

MESHWORK - Address unknown since 1999.

Mesoamerican Archeology Study Unit - Defunct.

Mesothelioma Applied Res. Found. [14274], 3944 State St., Ste. 340, Santa Barbara, CA 93105, (805)563-8400

Message! Products [18645], PO Box 700, Edgewood, MD 21040-0700, (800)243-2565

Messenger Courier Assn. of Am. [★3573]

Messenger Courier Assn. of the Americas [3573], 1156 15th St. NW, Ste. 900, Washington, DC 20005, (202)785-3298

Messengers of Christ-Lutheran Bible Translators [★19524]

Messengers, and Gp. Leaders; Natl. Post Off. Mail Handlers, Watchmen, [★24171]

Messengers; Natl. Assn. of Post Off. and Postal Trans. Ser. Mail Handlers, Watchmen and [★24171]

Messerschmitt Owners Club, U.S. Div. - Defunct.

Messianic Fellowship; Amer. [★19988]

Messianic Jewish Alliance of Am. [20257], PO Box 274, Springfield, PA 19064, (610)338-0451

Messianic Jewish Alliance; Young [★20257]

Messianic Jewish Movement Intl. [20258], PO Box 1212, Chandler, AZ 85244-1212, (480)786-6564

Messianic Jewish Movement Intl. [IO], Chandler, AZ, United States

A Messianic Jewish Perspective [20259], 60 Haight St., San Francisco, CA 94102, (415)864-2600

Messianic Judaism

Congregation Shema Yisrael [20135]

Intl. Alliance of Messianic Congregations and Synagogues [20254]

Intl. Alliance of Messianic Congregations and Synagogues [IO]

Intl. Fed. of Messianic Jews [IO]

Intl. Fed. of Messianic Jews [20255]

Jews for Jesus [20256]

Jews for Jesus [IO]

Messianic Jewish Alliance of Am. [20257]

Messianic Jewish Movement Intl. [20258]

Messianic Jewish Movement Intl. [IO]

A Messianic Jewish Perspective [20259]

Messianic Ministries; Lederer [20019]

Messies Anonymous [13023], 5025 SW 114th Ave., Miami, FL 33165, (786)243-2793

Messinian Benevolent Assn. "Aristomenis" - Address unknown since 1995.

MEST Org. - Address unknown since 2007.

Mesteno Assn; Kiger [4910]

Metaalunie, Nederlandse Organisatie van Ondernemers in het Midden- en Kleinbedrijf in de Metaal [★IO]

Metaalunie, Netherlands Org. for Small- and Medium-Sized Enterprises in the Metal Indus. [IO], Nieuwegein, Netherlands

Metabolic Dietary Disorder Assn. [IO], Montrose, Australia

Metabolic Disorders

Albinism World Alliance [IO]

Albinism World Alliance [15242]

Alteraciones de Crecimiento/Desarrollo y Enfermedades Lisosomales [IO]

Amer. Bd. of Nutrition [15541]

Amer. Porphyria Found. [15243]

Assn. for Glycogen Storage Disease [15244]

British Porphyria Assn. [IO]

Children Living with Inherited Metabolic Diseases [IO]

Children's PKU Network [15245]

City of Hope Natl. Medical Center [15102]

Crigler-Najjar Assn. [14805]

Cystinosis Found. [15246]

Cystinosis Res. Network [15247]

European Soc. for the Stud. of Purine and Pyrimidine Metabolism in Man [IO]

Fatty Oxidation Disorders (FOD) Family Support Gp. [16532]

FOD Family Support Gp. [15248]

FOD Family Support Group [IO]

German MPS Soc. [IO]

Hemochromatosis Found. [14799]

Intl. Soc. on Metabolic Eye Disease [15691]

Iron Overload Diseases Assn. [15249]

Iron Overload Diseases Association [IO]

Lysosomal Diseases New Zealand [IO]

Maple Syrup Urine Family Support Gp. [15250]

Metabolic Dietary Disorder Assn. [IO]

MPS Australia [IO]

MPS Austria [IO]

MPS Brazil [IO]

Natl. Center for the Study of Wilson's Disease [15251]

Natl. Gaucher Found. [15252]

Natl. MPS Soc. [15253]

Natl. Niemann Pick Disease Found. [15254]

Natl. Org. for Albinism and Hypopigmentation [15255]

Organic Acidemia Assn. [14472]

Oxalosis and Hyperoxaluria Found. [15296]

Paget Found. for Paget's Disease of Bone and Related Disorders [15256]

Parents of Galactosemic Children [15257]

Purine Res. Soc. [15258]

Soc. of Children with Mucopolysaccharidosis and Diseases Related [IO]

Soc. for Mucopolysaccharide Diseases (The MPS Soc.) [IO]

Soc. for the Stud. of Inborn Errors of Metabolism [IO]

Syndrome X Assn. [15259]

Taking Control of Your Diabetes [14231]

Wilson's Disease Assn. Intl. [15260]

Metabolism; Assn. of Prog. Directors in Endocrinology and [★14351]

Metabolism; Assn. of Prog. Directors in Endocrinology, Diabetes and [14351]

Metabolism; Soc. for the Stud. of Inborn Errors of [IO]

Metal

All India Stainless Steel Indus. Assn. [IO]

Aluminium Extruders Assn. [IO]

Aluminium Fed. [IO]

Aluminium Powder and Paste Assn. [IO]

Aluminium Primary Producers Assn. [IO]

Aluminium Rolled Products Mfrs. Assn. [IO]

Aluminium Stockholders Assn. [IO]

Aluminum Assn. [2692]

Aluminum Extruders Coun. [2693]

Amer. Copper Coun. [2694]

Amer. Inst. for Intl. Steel [2695]

Amer. Inst. for Intl. Steel [IO]

Amer. Inst. of Mining, Metallurgical, and Petroleum Engineers [7346]

Amer. Inst. of Steel Constr. [6834]

Amer. Iron Ore Assn. [2696]

Amer. Iron Ore Assn. [IO]

Amer. Iron and Steel Inst. [2697]

Amer. Metal Detector Mfrs. Assn. [1817]

Amer. Soc. for Nondestructive Testing [7787]

Amer. Tin Trade Assn. [2698]

Amer. Wire Producers Assn. [1999]

Amer. Zinc Assn. [2699]

APMI Intl. [7310]

ASM Intl. [7311]

Assn. of the Austrian Machinery and Metalware Indus. [IO]

Assn. of the German Hotdip Galvanizing Indus. [IO]

Assn. of Hungarian Foundries [IO]

Assn. of Hungarian Steel Indus. [IO]

Assn. for Iron and Steel Tech. [7312]

Assn. of Steel Distributors [2700]

Assn. of Steel and Metal Forming Indus. [IO]

Australian Stainless Steel Development Assn. [IO]

Australian Steel Inst. [IO]

Brass and Bronze Ingot Industry [2701]

British Artist Blacksmiths Assn. [IO]

British Hallmarking Coun. [IO]

British Hardmetal Assn. [IO]

British Metals Recycling Assn. [IO]

British Stainless Steel Assn. [IO]

Canadian Assn. of Metal Finishers [IO]

Canadian Assn. of Moldmakers [IO]

Canadian Copper and Brass Development Assn. [IO]

Canadian Die Casters Assn. [IO]

Canadian Foundry Assn. [IO]

Canadian Steel Producers Assn. [IO]

Cast Iron Soil Pipe Inst. [3027]

Cast Metals Fed. [IO]

Cemented Carbide Producers Assn. [2702]

Chinese Soc. for Metals [IO]

Cobalt Development Inst. [IO]

Cold Finished Steel Bar Inst. [2703]

Community [IO]

Confed. of British Metalforming [IO]

Container Market Comm. [977]

Copper and Brass Fabricators Coun. [2704]

Copper and Brass Servicenter Assn. [2705]

Copper Development Assn. [2750]

Copper Development Assn. [IO]

Copper Development Assn. - United Kingdom [IO]

Coun. for Aluminium in Building [IO]

Coun. of European Employers of the Metal, Engg. and Technology-Based Indus. [IO]

Custom Roll Forming Inst. [2706]

Ductile Iron Pipe Res. Assn. [3029]

Ductile Iron Soc. [7313]

European Aluminium Assn. [IO]

European Assn. of Metals [IO]

European Convention for Constructional Steelwork [IO]

European Copper Inst. [IO]

European Ferrous Recovery and Recycling Fed. [IO]

European Metal Trade and Recycling Fed. [IO]

European Metal Union [IO]

European Metallizers Assn. [IO]

European Metalworkers' Fed. [IO]

European Perforators Assn. [IO]

European Stabiliser Producers Assn. [IO]

Fed. Des Minerais, Mineraux Industriels Et Metaux Non Ferreux [IO]

Firearms Engravers Guild of Am. [9830]

Foil Stamping and Embossing Assn. [2707]

Forging Indus. Assn. [2708]

Reference to "IO" in place of a book number signifies that the association may be found in the 45th edition of International Organizations.

Galvanizers Assn. [IO]
German Metal Dealers Assn. [IO]
German Steel Constr. Assn. [IO]
Gold Prospectors Assn. of Am. [22913]
Guild of Architectural Ironmongers [IO]
Hammered Aluminum Collectors Assn. [22033]
Hong Kong Metal Finishing Soc. [IO]
Indus. Perforators Assn. [2709]
Indus. Coun. for Tangible Assets [3713]
Inst. of Indian Foundrymen [IO]
Inst. of the Ironworking Indus. [24133]
Inst. of Materials Engg. Australasia [IO]
Inst. of Metal Finishing [IO]
Intl. Aluminium Inst. [IO]
Intl. Assn. of Bridge, Structural, Ornamental and
    Reinforcing Iron Workers [24134]
Intl. Assn. of Used Equip. Dealers [3052]
Intl. Cadmium Assn. [IO]
Intl. Cadmium Assn. - Belgium [IO]
Intl. Copper Assn. [7315]
Intl. Hard Anodizing Assn. [2710]
International Hard Anodizing Association [IO]
Intl. Iron and Steel Inst. [IO]
Intl. Lead Zinc Res. Org. [7316]
Intl. Lead and Zinc Study Group [IO]
Intl. Magnesium Assn. [IO]
Intl. Magnesium Assn. [2711]
Intl. Manganese Inst. [IO]
Intl. Metalworkers' Fed. [IO]
Intl. Org. on Shape Memory and Superelastic
    Technologies [7317]
Intl. Precious Metals Inst. [7318]
Intl. Steel Trade Assn. [IO]
Intl. Titanium Assn. [IO]
Intl. Titanium Assn. [2712]
Intl. Tungsten Indus. Assn. [IO]
Intl. Wrought Copper Coun. [IO]
Intl. Zinc Assn. - Belgium [IO]
Intl. Zinc Assn. - Europe [IO]
Intervention and Coiled Tubing Assn. [7512]
Iron Casting Res. Inst. [2033]
Iron and Steel Institution of Japan [IO]
Ironmongers' Company [IO]
Japan Aluminium Fed. [IO]
Japan Copper Development Assn. [IO]
Japan Inst. of Metals [IO]
Korea Iron and Steel Assn. [IO]
Latin Amer. Iron and Steel Inst. [IO]
Lead Development Assn. Intl. [IO]
Lead Sheet Assn. [IO]
Lead Smelters and Refiners Assn. [IO]
Malaysian Iron and Steel Indus. Fed. [IO]
Mass Finishing Job Shops Assn. [1473]
Metaalunie, Netherlands Org. for Small- and
    Medium-Sized Enterprises in the Metal Indus.
    [IO]
Metal Boat Soc. [526]
Metal Injection Molding Assn. [2713]
Metal Powder Indus. Fed. [2714]
Metal Powder Producers Assn. [2715]
Metal Roofing Alliance [2716]
Metal Trades Dept., AFL-CIO [24135]
Metal Treating Inst. [2717]
Metal Treating Inst. [IO]
Metals Ser. Center Inst. [2718]
Minerals, Metals, and Materials Soc. [7320]
Mining and Metallurgical Soc. of Am. [7347]
Minor Metals Trade Assn. [IO]
Natl. Assn. of Architectural Metal Mfrs. [2719]
Natl. Assn. of Graphic and Prdt. Identification
    Mfrs. [2720]
Natl. Assn. of Hose and Accessories Distribution
    [2047]
Natl. Assn. of Steel Pipe Distributors [3032]
Natl. Assn. of Stockholders and Traders in Iron
    and Steel, Non-Ferrous Metals, Ferros and
    Non-Ferros Scrap [IO]
Natl. Assn. for Surface Finishing [1474]
Natl. Corrugated Steel Pipe Assn. [3035]
Natl. Inst. of Steel Detailing [2721]
National Institute of Steel Detailing [IO]
Natl. Metal Trades Fed. [IO]
Natl. New England Lead Burning Assn. [2052]
Natl. Ornamental and Miscellaneous Metals Assn.
    [2722]

Natl. Steel Bridge Alliance [539]
Natl. Union of Metalworkers of South Africa [IO]
Nickel Inst. - North Am. [IO]
Nickel Inst. - UK [IO]
Non-Ferrous Founders' Soc. [2053]
Non-Ferrous Metals Producers Comm. [2723]
Nonferrous Metals Soc. of China [IO]
Nordic IN [IO]
North Amer. Die Casting Assn. [2054]
North Amer. Steel Alliance [2724]
Org. of European Aluminium Refiners and Remelt-
    ers [IO]
Pewter Collectors Club of Am. [22107]
Pewterers' Company [IO]
Photo-Chemical Machining Institute [IO]
Photo-Chemical Machining Inst. [2725]
Plastic and Metal Products Mfrs. Assn. [3056]
Platinum Guild Intl. USA [2381]
Precious Metal Clay Guild [8172]
Precision Metalforming Assn. [2726]
Scandinavian Copper Development Assn. [IO]
Sheet Metal Occupational Hea. Inst. Trust [12991]
Sheet Metal Workers' Intl. Assn. [24136]
Silver Inst. [2727]
Silver Users Assn. [2728]
Soc. for Mining, Metallurgy, and Exploration
    [7349]
South East Asia Iron and Steel Inst. [IO]
Specialty Steel Indus. of North Am. [2729]
SSPC: The Soc. for Protective Coatings [2885]
Steel Alliance [2730]
Steel Founders' Soc. of Am. [2070]
Steel Framing Alliance [2731]
Steel Framing Alliance [IO]
Steel Lintel Manufacturers Assn. [IO]
Steel Mfrs. Assn. [2732]
Steel Recycling Inst. [4004]
Steel Truss and Component Assn. [2733]
Surface Engg. Assn. [IO]
Swedish Steel Producers' Assn. [IO]
Swiss Aluminium Assn. [IO]
Tantalum-Niobium Intl. Stud. Center [IO]
Tech. Indus. of Finland [IO]
Tin Tech. [IO]
UK Steel [IO]
UK Steel Assn. [IO]
United Steel Workers of Am., Rubber/Plastics
    Indus. Conf. [24183]
United Steelworkers of Am. [24137]
United Steelworkers of Am. - Canadian Br. [IO]
Vanadium Producers and Reclaimers Assn.
    [2734]
Venezuelan Assn. of Mining and Metallurgical
    Indus. [IO]
Wire Assn. Intl. [7323]
Wirtschaftsverband Grosshandel Metallhalbzeug
    [IO]
World Foundrymen Org. - United Kingdom [IO]
World Nuclear Assn. [IO]
Worshipful Company of Farriers [IO]
Worshipful Company of Pewterers [IO]
Worshipful Company of Tin Plate Workers [IO]
Metal and Air Conditioning Contractors' Natl. Assn;
    Sheet [1900]
Metal Belt Inst. - Defunct.
Metal Boat Soc. [526], PO Box 61856, Vancouver,
    WA 98666, (360)695-4100
Metal Boat Soc. [IO], Vancouver, WA, United States
Metal Building Component Mfrs. Assn. - Defunct.
Metal Building Contractors and Erectors Assn.
    [2528], PO Box 499, Shawnee Mission, KS 66201,
    (913)432-3800
Metal Building Dealers Assn. [★2528]
Metal Building Manufacturers Assn. [637], 1300
    Sumner Ave., Cleveland, OH 44115-2851,
    (216)241-7333
Metal Buildings Inst. [8006], c/o Ray Barbieri, Pres.-
    Elect, 588 Winsted Rd., Torrington, CT 06790,
    (860)496-7503
Metal Constr. Assn. [638], 4700 W Lake Ave., Glen-
    view, IL 60025-1485, (847)375-4718
Metal Containers and Wire Decking, a Prdt. Sect. of
    the Material Handling Indus; Indus. [983]
Metal Contractors Natl. Assn; Sheet [★1900]
Metal Cookware Mfrs. Assn. [★1970]

Metal Cutting Knife Assn. [★2036]
Metal Cutting Tool Inst. [★2076]
Metal Decorators Assn; Natl. [★1775]
Metal Detector and Archaeological Clubs; Fed. of
    [22578]
Metal Detector Mfrs. Assn; Amer. [1817]
Metal Etching and Fabricating Assn. [★2720]
Metal Etching Mfrs. Trade Assn; Amer. [★2720]
Metal Fabricating Inst. - Defunct.
Metal Findings Mfrs. Assn. [2379]
Metal Finishers and Amer. Electroplaters and
    Surface Finishers Soc; Metal Finishing Suppliers'
    Assn., Natl. Assn. of [★1474]
Metal Finishing Assn. [★IO]
Metal Finishing Suppliers' Assn., Natl. Assn. of Metal
    Finishers and Amer. Electroplaters and Surface
    Finishers Soc. [★1474]
Metal Framing Manufacturers Assn. [639], 401 N
    Michigan Ave., Chicago, IL 60611-4267, (312)644-
    6610
Metal Grating Inst. - Defunct.
Metal Industry Promotion Plan; Sheet [1065]
Metal Injection Molding Assn. [2713], c/o Metal
    Powder Indus. Fed., 105 Coll. Rd. E, Princeton, NJ
    08540-6692, (609)452-7700
Metal Injection Molding Association [★2714]
Metal Inst; Pressed [★2726]
Metal Ladder Mfrs. Assn. - Defunct.
Metal Lathers' Intl. Union; Wood, Wire and [★24032]
Metal Mfrs. Assn; Natl. Ornamental [★2722]
Metal Mfrs; Natl. Assn. of Ornamental [★2719]
Metal Mouldings Mfrs. Assn. - Defunct.
Metal Name Plate Mfrs; Natl. Assn. of [★2720]
Metal Occupational Hea. Inst; Sheet [★12991]
Metal Occupational Hea. Inst. Trust; Sheet [12991]
Metal Packaging Mfrs. Assn. [IO], Reading, United
    Kingdom
Metal Pipe Assn; Corrugated [★3035]
Metal Pipe Assn; Natl. Corrugated [★3035]
Metal Polishers, Buffers, Platers and Allied Workers
    Intl. Union [★24021]
Metal Powder Assn. [★2714]
Metal Powder Indus. Fed. [2714], 105 Coll. Rd. E,
    Princeton, NJ 08540-6692, (609)452-7700
Metal Powder Producers Assn. [2715], c/o Metal
    Powder Indus. Fed., 105 Coll. Rd. E, Princeton, NJ
    08540-6692, (609)452-7700
Metal Powder Producers Association [★2714]
Metal Products Mfrs. Assn; Plastic and [3056]
Metal Properties Coun. [★7319]
Metal Roofing Alliance [2716], E 4142 Hwy. 302,
    Belfair, WA 98528, (360)275-6164
Metal Stamping Assn; Amer. [★2726]
Metal Trades Assn; Natl. [★2480]
Metal Trades Dept., AFL-CIO [24135], 815 16th St.
    NW, Washington, DC 20006, (202)508-3705
Metal Treating Inst. [2717], 1550 Roberts Dr.,
    Jacksonville Beach, FL 32250-3222, (904)249-
    0448
Metal Treating Inst. [IO], Jacksonville Beach, FL,
    United States
Metal Tube Assn; Collapsible [★2881]
Metal Tube Packaging Coun. of North Am. [★2881]
Metal Ventilator Inst. - Address unknown since 1995.
Metalforming Machinery Makers' Assn. [IO], Ban-
    bury, United Kingdom
Metallic Yarns Inst. - Defunct.
Metallizers Assn; Vacuum [★851]
Metallizers, Coaters and Laminators; Assn. of Indus.
    [851]
Metallurgic and Metal Mech. Indus'. Assn. [IO], San-
    tiago, Chile
Metallurgical Engineers; Amer. Inst. of Mining and
    [★7346]
Metallurgical and Petroleum Engineers; Mining Br.,
    Amer. Inst. of Mining, [★7349]
The Metallurgical Soc. [★7320]
Metallurgical Soc. of AIME; Iron and Steel Division of
    the [★7312]
Metallurgical Soc. of Am; Mining and [7347]
Metallurgistes Unis d'Amerique [★IO]
Metallurgy
    Aluminium Assn. of India [IO]
    Aluminum Assn. [2692]
    Aluminum Extruders Coun. [2693]

A star before a book entry number signifies that the name is not listed separately, but is mentioned within the entry.

Amer. Bur. of Metal Statistics [7309]
Amer. Copper Coun. [2694]
Amer. Inst. for Intl. Steel [2695]
Amer. Inst. of Mining, Metallurgical, and
    Petroleum Engineers [7346]
Amer. Iron Ore Assn. [2696]
Amer. Iron and Steel Inst. [2697]
Amer. Metal Detector Mfrs. Assn. [1817]
Amer. Soc. for Nondestructive Testing [7787]
Amer. Wire Producers Assn. [1999]
APMI Intl. [7310]
APMI Intl. [IO]
Argentine Chamber of the Aluminum, Metals and
    Related Indus. [IO]
Argentine Metallurgical Indus'. Assn. [IO]
ASM Intl. [IO]
ASM Intl. [7311]
Assn. for Iron and Steel Tech. [7312]
Assn. of Steel Distributors [2700]
Associazione Italiana di Metallurgia [IO]
Australian Die Casting Assn. [IO]
Brass and Bronze Ingot Industry [2701]
Brazilian Metallurgy and Materials Assn. [IO]
Castings Tech. Intl. [IO]
Centro Nacional para el Desarrollo del Acero in-
    oxidable [IO]
Cold Finished Steel Bar Inst. [2703]
Container Market Comm. [977]
Copper and Brass Fabricators Coun. [2704]
Copper and Brass Servicenter Assn. [2705]
Copper Development Assn. [2750]
Custom Roll Forming Inst. [2706]
Ductile Iron Soc. [7313]
Electrochemical Soc. [6680]
European Investment Casters' Fed. [IO]
European Powder Metallurgy Assn. [IO]
European Slag Assn. [IO]
Forging Indus. Assn. [2708]
Forging Indus. Educational and Res. Found.
    [7314]
French Soc. for Metallurgy and Materials [IO]
Historical Metallurgy Soc. [IO]
Indian Inst. of Metals [IO]
Indian Stainless Steel Development Assn. [IO]
Indus. Perforators Assn. [2709]
Inst. of Archaeo-Metallurgical Stud. [IO]
Inst. of Corrosion [IO]
Inst. of Sheet Metal Engg. [IO]
Intl. Chromium Development Assn. [IO]
Intl. Copper Assn. [IO]
Intl. Copper Assn. [7315]
Intl. Inst. for the Sci. of Sintering [IO]
Intl. Lead Zinc Res. Org. [IO]
Intl. Lead Zinc Res. Org. [7316]
Intl. Magnesium Assn. [2711]
Intl. Molybdenum Assn. [IO]
Intl. Org. on Shape Memory and Superelastic
    Technologies [IO]
Intl. Org. on Shape Memory and Superelastic
    Technologies [7317]
Intl. Precious Metals Inst. [7318]
Intl. Precious Metals Inst. [IO]
Intl. Titanium Assn. [2712]
Iron Casting Res. Inst. [2033]
Italian Assn. for Metallurgy [IO]
Italian Stainless Steel Development Assn. [IO]
Japan Die and Mold Indus. Assn. [IO]
Japan Iron and Steel Fed. [IO]
Japan Powder Metallurgy Assn. [IO]
Korea Die and Mold Indus. Cooperative [IO]
Malaysia Mold and Die Assn. [IO]
Materials Properties Coun. [7319]
Metal Powder Indus. Fed. [2714]
Metal Treating Inst. [2717]
Metallurgic and Metal Mech. Indus'. Assn. [IO]
Metallurgy Union C.F.E.-C.G.C. [IO]
Metals Ser. Center Inst. [2718]
Minerals, Metals, and Materials Soc. [7320]
Mining and Metallurgical Soc. of Am. [7347]
Natl. Assn. of Architectural Metal Mfrs. [2719]
Natl. Assn. for Surface Finishing [1474]
Natl. Inst. for Metalworking Skills [7321]
Natl. Inst. of Steel Detailing [2721]
Natl. New England Lead Burning Assn. [2052]
Natl. Ornamental and Miscellaneous Metals Assn.
    [2722]

New Zealand Stainless Steel Development Assn.
    [IO]
Non-Ferrous Founders' Soc. [2053]
Non-Ferrous Metals Producers Comm. [2723]
North Amer. Steel Alliance [2724]
Photo-Chemical Machining Inst. [2725]
Precision Metalforming Assn. [2726]
Silver Inst. [2727]
Silver Users Assn. [2728]
Singapore Metal and Machinery Assn. [IO]
Small and Mid-Size Metallurgic Indus. Assn. [IO]
Soc. of Carbide and Tool Engineers [7322]
Soc. of Mineral Analysts [7345]
Soc. for Mining, Metallurgy, and Exploration
    [7349]
Spanish Stainless Steel Development Assn. [IO]
Steel Founders' Soc. of Am. [2070]
Steel Framing Alliance [2731]
Steel Mfrs. Assn. [2732]
Steel Recycling Inst. [4004]
Steel Truss and Component Assn. [2733]
Taiwan Mold and Die Indus. Assn. [IO]
Turkish Foundrymen's Assn. [IO]
Turkish Iron and Steel Producers Assn. [IO]
United Engg. Found. [7051]
Vanadium Producers and Reclaimers Assn.
    [2734]
Wire Assn. Intl. [7323]
Wire Assn. Intl. [IO]
World Bur. of Metal Statistics [IO]
World Foundrymen Org. [IO]
Metallurgy, and Exploration; Soc. for Mining, [7349]
Metallurgy Inst; Amer. Powder [★7310]
Metallurgy Union C.F.E.-C.G.C. [IO], Paris, France

Metals
    Aluminum Assn. [2692]
    Aluminum Extruders Coun. [2693]
    Amer. Copper Coun. [2694]
    Amer. Galvanizers Assn. [850]
    Amer. Inst. for Intl. Steel [2695]
    Amer. Inst. of Mining, Metallurgical, and
        Petroleum Engineers [7346]
    Amer. Iron Ore Assn. [2696]
    Amer. Iron and Steel Inst. [2697]
    Amer. Metal Detector Mfrs. Assn. [1817]
    Amer. Soc. for Nondestructive Testing [7787]
    Amer. Wire Producers Assn. [1999]
    APMI Intl. [7310]
    ASM Intl. [7311]
    Assn. of Indus. Metallizers, Coaters and Lamina-
        tors [851]
    Assn. for Iron and Steel Tech. [7312]
    Assn. of Steel Distributors [2700]
    Brass and Bronze Ingot Industry [2701]
    Cold Finished Steel Bar Inst. [2703]
    Container Market Comm. [977]
    Copper and Brass Fabricators Coun. [2704]
    Copper and Brass Servicenter Assn. [2705]
    Copper Development Assn. [2750]
    Custom Roll Forming Inst. [2706]
    Ductile Iron Soc. [7313]
    Electrochemical Soc. [6680]
    Fabricators and Mfrs. Assn., Intl. [2017]
    Forging Indus. Assn. [2708]
    Indus. Perforators Assn. [2709]
    Intl. Copper Assn. [7315]
    Intl. Lead Zinc Res. Org. [7316]
    Intl. Magnesium Assn. [2711]
    Intl. Org. on Shape Memory and Superelastic
        Technologies [7317]
    Intl. Precious Metals Inst. [7318]
    Intl. Titanium Assn. [2712]
    Iron Casting Res. Inst. [2033]
    Metal Building Contractors and Erectors Assn.
        [2528]
    Metal Injection Molding Assn. [2713]
    Metal Powder Indus. Fed. [2714]
    Metal Treating Inst. [2717]
    Metals Ser. Center Inst. [2718]
    Minerals, Metals, and Materials Soc. [7320]
    Mining and Metallurgical Soc. of Am. [7347]
    Natl. Assn. of Architectural Metal Mfrs. [2719]
    Natl. Assn. for Surface Finishing [1474]
    Natl. Inst. for Metalworking Skills [7321]
    Natl. Inst. of Steel Detailing [2721]

    Natl. New England Lead Burning Assn. [2052]
    Natl. Ornamental and Miscellaneous Metals Assn.
        [2722]
    Natl. Slag Assn. [652]
    Natl. Steel Bridge Alliance [539]
    Non-Ferrous Founders' Soc. [2053]
    Non-Ferrous Metals Producers Comm. [2723]
    North Amer. Steel Alliance [2724]
    Photo-Chemical Machining Inst. [2725]
    Precision Metalforming Assn. [2726]
    Sheet Metal Industry Promotion Plan [1065]
    Silver Inst. [2727]
    Silver Users Assn. [2728]
    Soc. for Mining, Metallurgy, and Exploration
        [7349]
    Steel Founders' Soc. of Am. [2070]
    Steel Framing Alliance [2731]
    Steel Mfrs. Assn. [2732]
    Steel Recycling Inst. [4004]
    Steel Truss and Component Assn. [2733]
    Truss Plate Inst. [683]
    Vanadium Producers and Reclaimers Assn.
        [2734]
    Welders Without Borders [7850]
    Wire Assn. Intl. [7323]
    Wire Reinforcement Inst. [687]
Metals; Amer. Soc. for [★7311]
Metals Assn; Amer. Cast [★9227]
Metals Inst; Cast [★9227]
Metals, and Materials Soc; Minerals, [7320]
Metals Res. and Development Found. - Defunct.
Metals Ser. Center Inst. [2718], 4201 Euclid Ave.,
    Rolling Meadows, IL 60008-2025, (847)485-3000
Metalworking Skills; Natl. Inst. for [7321]
Metamorphic Assn. [IO], London, United Kingdom
Metanoia Ministries [19869], PO Box 448,
    Washington, NH 03280, (603)495-0035
Metaphysical Energy
    Amer. Ghost Soc. [7438]
    Internet Infidels [7490]
Metaphysical Soc. of Am. [10812], c/o Dept. of
    Philosophy, Univ. of Alabama—Huntsville,
    Huntsville, AL 35899, (205)895-6555
Metaphysicians; Soc. of [IO]
Metaphysics
    Amer. Ghost Soc. [7438]
    Astara [20443]
    Found. for Philosophy of Creativity [10793]
    Interfaith Church of Metaphysics [20573]
    Intl. New Thought Alliance [10802]
    Metaphysical Soc. of Am. [10812]
    Soc. of Pragmatic Mysticism [20448]
    Soc. for the Stud. of Process Philosophies
        [10838]
Metapsychic Investigations and Sci. Res. Soc. [IO],
    Istanbul, Turkey
MetaScience Found. [7446], c/o MetaScience An-
    nual, Box 32, Kingston, RI 02881
Meteor Soc; Amer. [6500]
Meteorite Collectors Assn; Intl. [22981]
Meteorites; Soc. for Res. on [★7148]
Meteoritical Soc. [7148], c/o Jeffrey N. Grossman,
    Sec., US Geological Survey, 954 Natl. Ctr., Re-
    ston, VA 20192, (703)648-6184
Meteoritical Soc. [IO], Cologne, Germany
Meteorological Soc. of Japan [IO], Tokyo, Japan
Meteorological Soc. of New Zealand [IO], Welling-
    ton, New Zealand
Meteorological Soc. of the Republic of China [IO],
    Taipei, Taiwan
Meteorology
    African Centre of Meteorological Applications for
        Development [IO]
    Amer. Assn. of State Climatologists [7324]
    Amer. Meteor Soc. [6500]
    Amer. Meteorological Soc. [7325]
    Asia Pacific Network for Global Change Res. [IO]
    Assn. of British Climatologists [IO]
    Australian Severe Weather Assn. [IO]
    Canadian Inst. for Climate Stud. [IO]
    Canadian Meteorological and Oceanographic Soc.
        [IO]
    Caribbean Inst. for Meteorology and Hydrology
        [IO]
    Caribbean Meteorological Org. [IO]

Reference to "IO" in place of a book number signifies that the association may be found in the 45th edition of International Organizations.

Chinese Acad. of Meteorological Sciences [IO]
Commercial Weather Services Assn. [7326]
Czech Bioclimatological Soc. [IO]
Czech Meteorological Soc. [IO]
European Centre for Medium-Range Weather Forecasts [IO]
European Meteorological Soc. [IO]
European Org. for the Exploitation of Meteorological Satellites [IO]
German Meteorological Soc. [IO]
Inst. of Global Env. and Soc. [4574]
Intl. Assn. of Broadcast Meteorology [IO]
Intl. Assn. of Meteorology and Atmospheric Sciences [IO]
Intl. Assn. for Urban Climate [IO]
Intl. Climatology Assn. [IO]
Intl. Glaciological Soc. [IO]
Intl. Meteor Org. [IO]
Intl. Soc. of Medical Hydrology and Climatology [IO]
Irish Meteorological Soc. [IO]
Italian Meteorological Soc. [IO]
Japan Weather Assn. [IO]
Meteoritical Soc. [IO]
Meteoritical Soc. [7148]
Meteorological Soc. of Japan [IO]
Meteorological Soc. of New Zealand [IO]
Meteorological Soc. of the Republic of China [IO]
Natl. Assn. of Storm Chasers and Spotters [13413]
Natl. Assn. for the Stud. of Snow and Avalanches [IO]
Natl. Soaring Found. [23042]
Natl. Weather Assn. [7327]
North Amer. Meteor Network [7328]
North Amer. Meteor Network [IO]
Royal Meteorological Soc. [IO]
Soaring Soc. of Am. [23043]
Stonehenge Study Group [6459]
Tech. Commn. for Oceanography and Marine Meteorology [IO]
Tornado and Storm Res. Org. [IO]
Univ. Corp. for Atmospheric Res. [7329]
Weather Modification Assn. [7330]
World Meteorological Org. [IO]
Meteorology Study Unit - Defunct.
Meter Reading Assn; Automatic [3953]
Meter-Slogan Associates [★22844]
Meter Stamp Soc. [22844], c/o Douglas Kelsey, Sec., PO Box 16178, Tucson, AZ 85732-6178
Metering and Utility Allocation Assn; Natl. Sub [3961]
Methacrylate Producers Assn. [813], 17260 Vannes Ct., Hamilton, VA 20158, (540)751-2093
Methadone Advocates; Natl. Alliance of [14293]
Methanol Inst. [7110], 4100 N Fairfax Dr., Ste. 740, Arlington, VA 22203, (703)248-3636
Methanol Inst; Amer. [★7110]

Methodist
Affirmation: United Methodists for Lesbian, Gay and Bisexual Concerns [20047]
Bible Holiness Movement [IO]
Black Methodists for Church Renewal [20260]
Center for the Evangelical United Brethren Heritage [19976]
Fellowship of United Methodists in Music and Worship Arts [20261]
Forum for Scriptural Christianity [20262]
Gen. Bd. of Church and Soc. of the United Methodist Church [20263]
Gen. Commn. on Archives and History of the United Methodist Church [10467]
Gen. Commn. on the Status and Role of Women [17535]
Historical Soc. of the United Methodist Church [10113]
The Interchurch Center [19896]
Methodist Church of New Zealand [IO]
Methodist Fed. for Social Action [20264]
Methodist Women in Ireland [IO]
Mission Soc. for United Methodists [20265]
Natl. Assn. of Schools, Colleges and Universities of the United Methodist Church [8879]
Natl. Fed. of Asian-Amer. United Methodists [20266]
Reconciling Ministries Network [20065]

United Methodist Assn. of Hea. and Welfare Ministries [14602]
United Methodist Comm. on Relief [20267]
United Methodist Comm. on Relief [IO]
United Methodist Youth Org. [20268]
Women's Division of the Gen. Bd. of Global Ministries of the United Methodist Church [20269]
Women's Missionary Coun. of the Christian Methodist Episcopal Church [20270]
Women's Network of the Methodist Church [IO]
World Fed. of Methodist and Uniting Church Women - USA [IO]
World Fed. of Methodist and Uniting Church - Women - USA [20271]
World Methodist Coun. [20272]
World Methodist Coun. [IO]
World Methodist Historical Soc. [IO]
World Methodist Historical Soc. [20273]
Methodist Assn. of Hea. and Welfare Ministries; United [14602]
Methodist Church; Bd. of Hospitals and Homes of The [★14602]
Methodist Church; Christian Educators Fellowship of the United [19923]
Methodist Church; Division of Hea. and Welfare Ministries of The United [★14602]
Methodist Church; Historical Soc. of the United [10113]
Methodist Church; Natl. Assn. of Hea. and Welfare Ministries of The United [★14602]
Methodist Church of New Zealand [IO], Christchurch, New Zealand
Methodist Comm. for Overseas Relief [★IO]
Methodist Comm. for Overseas Relief [★20267]
Methodist Comm. on Overseas Relief; United [★20267]
Methodist Coun. on Youth Ministry [★20268]
Methodist Coun. on Youth Ministry; United [★20268]
Methodist Educational Institutions; Assn. of Free [8447]
Methodist Fed. for Social Action [20264], 212 E Capitol St. NE, Washington, DC 20003, (202)546-8806
Methodist Fed. for Social Ser. [★20264]
Methodist Historical Societies; Assn. of [★10467]
Methodist Historical Soc; Intl. [★20273]
Methodist Historical Union [★20273]
Methodist Historical Union [★IO]
Methodist Historical Union; Intl. [★20273]
Methodist Musicians; Fellowship of United [★20261]
Methodist Musicians; Natl. Fellowship of [★20261]
Methodist Peace Fellowship - Defunct.
Methodist Student Movement - Defunct.
Methodist Women in Ireland [IO], Bangor, United Kingdom
Methodists for Church Renewal - Address unknown since 1995.
Methodists for Lesbian, Gay and Bisexual Concerns; Affirmation: United [20047]
Methodists for Lesbian/Gay Concerns; Affirmation: United [★20047]
Methodists for Life - Defunct.
Methodists in Worship, and Other Arts; Fellowship of United [★20261]
Methods of Moderation - Address unknown since 1994.
Methods Standards Assn; Materials and [636]
Methods Time Measurements Assn. for Standards and Res. [★7165]
Methyl Chloride Indus. Assn. [814], 555 11th St. NW, Ste. 1000, Washington, DC 20004-1327, (202)637-2200
Methyl Tertiary Butyl Ether Task Force - Address unknown since 2000.
Metopera [★10645]
Metric
Americans for Customary Weight and Measure [18679]
U.S. Metric Assn. [7701]
Metric Assn. [★7701]
Metric Assn; U.S. [7701]
Metric Coun; Amer. Natl. [18678]
Metric Opposition Forum [18682]
Metro Ethernet Forum [7748], 19900 MacArthur Blvd., Ste. 810, Irvine, CA 92612, (949)250-7188

Metro Ethernet Forum [IO], Irvine, CA, United States
Metro Intl. Prog. Services of New York [8624], 285 W Broadway, Ste. 450, New York, NY 10013, (212)431-1195
Metrology; Intl. Comm. for Historical [IO]
Metrology; Intl. Org. of Legal [IO]
Metrology Soc. of Australia [IO], Lindfield, Australia
Metrology Soc. of Thailand [IO], Bangkok, Thailand
Metropolitan Air Post Society [IO], Sterling, NY, United States
Metropolitan Air Post Soc. [22845], c/o Fred Dietz, Pres., 14834 Hadcock Dr., Sterling, NY 13156-4196
Metropolitan Airmail Cover Club [★22845]
Metropolitan Airmail Cover Club [★IO]
Metropolitan Area Apparel Assn. - Address unknown since 2003.
Metropolitan Assn. of Urban Designers and Environmental Planners - Defunct.
Metropolitan Coll. Mental Health Assn. - Defunct.
Metropolitan Collegiate Athletic Conf. - Address unknown since 1999.
Metropolitan Community Church [★20062]
Metropolitan Community Churches [20062], PO Box 1374, Abilene, TX 79604, (310)360-8640
Metropolitan Community Churches; Universal Fellowship of [★20062]
Metropolitan Districts; Natl. Assn. of Teacher Educ. Institutions of [★9208]
Metropolitan Hospitals; Sect. for [14895]
Metropolitan Intercollegiate Basketball Assn. [23131], 60 E 42nd St., Ste. 660, New York, NY 10165-0659, (212)425-6510
Metropolitan Microchemical Soc. [★6668]
Metropolitan Mutual Housing Assn. - Defunct.
Metropolitan Opera Assn. [10645], Lincoln Center, New York, NY 10023, (212)799-3100
Metropolitan Opera Guild [10646], 70 Lincoln Center Plz., New York, NY 10023, (212)769-7000
Metropolitan Owners' Club [IO], Pulborough, United Kingdom
Metropolitan Owners Club of North Am. [21701], c/o Betty Jacobson, Treas., 2308 Co. Hwy. V, Sun Prairie, WI 53590
Metropolitan Pharmaceutical Secretaries Assn. - Address unknown since 1994.
Metropolitan Planning Organizations; Assn. of [17207]
Metropolitan Sewerage Agencies; Assn. of [★6237]
Metropolitan Travel Agents - Defunct.
Metropolitan Tree Improvement Alliance [5260], c/o Dr. Bert Cregg, Sec.-Treas., Michigan State Univ., Dept. of Horticulture, East Lansing, MI 48824-1325
Metropolitan Veterans Ser. [★21308]
Metropolitan Water Agencies; Assn. of [6135]
Metropolitan YMCA Singapore [IO], Singapore, Singapore
Metz Owners Club Library - Defunct.
MEU, FCU, MOA [★IO]
Mexican Acad. of Dermatology [IO], Mexico City, Mexico
Mexican Acad. of Sciences [IO], Tlalpan, Mexico
Mexican Advt. Agencies' Assn. [IO], Mexico City, Mexico
Mexican Airmail Collectors Club - Defunct.
Mexican Amer. Cultural Center [20286], PO Box 28185, 3115 W Ashby Pl., San Antonio, TX 78228-5104, (210)732-2156
Mexican-American Engg. Soc. [★7043]
Mexican Amer. Engineers and Scientists; Soc. of [7043]
Mexican Amer. Grocers Assn. [1536], 405 N San Fernando Rd., Los Angeles, CA 90031, (323)227-1565
Mexican Amer. Legal Defense and Educational Fund [17705], 634 S Spring St., Los Angeles, CA 90014, (213)629-2512
Mexican American Legal Defense and Educational Fund [IO], Los Angeles, CA, United States
Mexican Amer. Music Assn. [10647], 103 Broadway Ave., Dodson, TX 79230, (806)493-4938
Mexican-American Opportunity Found. [12276], 401 N Garfield Ave., Montebello, CA 90640, (323)890-9600
Mexican Amer. Rights; Natl. Org. for [17709]

A star before a book entry number signifies that the name is not listed separately, but is mentioned within the entry.

Mexican Amer. Unity Coun. [12277], 2300 W Commerce St., Ste. 200, San Antonio, TX 78207, (210)978-0500
Mexican Amer. Women's Natl. Assn. [★17548]
Mexican Americans; Assn. for the Advancement of [11763]
Mexican Article Numbering Assn. [IO], Mexico City, Mexico
Mexican Arts and Tech. Network [9611]
Mexican Assn. of Car Dealers [IO], Mexico City, Mexico
Mexican Assn. for Cmpt. Vision, Neurocomputing and Robotics [IO], Guadalajara, Mexico
Mexican Assn. of Fair, Exhibition, and Convention Professionals [IO], Mexico City, Mexico
Mexican Assn. of Farm Equip. Distributors [IO], Mexico City, Mexico
Mexican Assn. of Gifts, Decorative Goods and Folk Art Producers [IO], Mexico City, Mexico
Mexican Assn. of Indus. Parks [IO], Mexico City, Mexico
Mexican Assn. of Marketing and Public Opinion Res. Agencies [IO], Mexico City, Mexico
Mexican Assn. of Restaurants [IO], Mexico City, Mexico
Mexican Automotive Assn. [IO], Mexico City, Mexico
Mexican Border Veterans - Address unknown since 1974.
Mexican Chamber of Commerce of the U.S. - Address unknown since 1999.
Mexican Chamber of the Constr. Indus. [IO], Mexico City, Mexico
Mexican Coffee Inst. - Address unknown since 1990.
Mexican Commn. for the Defense and Promotion of Human Rights [IO], Mexico City, Mexico
Mexican Epigraphic Soc. [10130]
Mexican Food and Beverage Bd. - Address unknown since 1994.
Mexican Found. for Family Planning [IO], Mexico City, Mexico
Mexican Govt. Tourism Off. [★24356]
Mexican Industrialists' Assn. [IO], Mexico City, Mexico
Mexican League Against Epilepsy [IO], Mexico City, Mexico
Mexican Market Res. and Opinion Polls Assn. [IO], Mexico City, Mexico
Mexican Olympic Comm. [IO], Lomas de Sotelo, Mexico
Mexican Org. for the History of Sci. and Tech. [IO], Mexico City, Mexico
Mexican Pharmaceutical Assn. [IO], Mexico City, Mexico
Mexican Professional Assn. of Conf. Interpreters [IO], Cuauhtemoc, Mexico
Mexican Pulp and Paper Indus'. Assn. [IO], Mexico City, Mexico
Mexican Soc. of Dermatologic Surgery and Oncology [IO], Mexico City, Mexico
Mexican Soc. of Dermatology [IO], Mexico City, Mexico
Mexican Soc. of Economic, Financial and Cost Engg. [IO], Mexico City, Mexico
Mexican Soc. of Instrumentation [IO], Mexico City, Mexico
Mexican Soc. on Mechatronics [IO], Queretaro, Mexico
Mexican Soc. of Psychology [IO], Mexico City, Mexico
Mexican War
    Descendants of Mexican War Veterans [21183]
Mexican War Veterans; Descendants of [21183]
Mexico
    Amerind Found. [6406]
    Assn. for Mexican Cave Stud. [7691]
    Assn. of Racing Commissioners Intl. [6240]
    Coalition for Justice in the Maquiladoras [18610]
    Congressional Border Caucus [5598]
    DOCARE Intl., N.F.P. [12518]
    Los Ninos [12589]
    Mexican Amer. Legal Defense and Educational Fund [17705]
    Mexican Amer. Music Assn. [10647]
    Mexican Epigraphic Soc. [10130]
    Mexico Elmhurst Philatelic Soc. Intl. [22846]

Mexico Tourism Bd. [24356]
Missionary Gospel Fellowship [20363]
    Seva Found. [12443]
    Soc. of Mexican Amer. Engineers and Scientists [7043]
    U.S. Mexican Numismatic Assn. [22765]
Mexico ACM SIGCHI [IO], Cholula, Mexico
Mexico Apparel Chamber [IO], Mexico City, Mexico
Mexico Border Hea. Assn; United States- [★16256]
Mexico City ACM SIGGRAPH [IO], Mexico City, Mexico
Mexico Elmhurst Philatelic Soc. Intl. [IO], New York, NY, United States
Mexico Elmhurst Philatelic Soc. Intl. [22846], c/o Geoffrey Goodridge, Circuit Book Mgr., PO Box 1217, New York, NY 10113
Mexico/Monterrey Chap. of the Assn. of Energy Engineers [IO], Monterrey, Mexico
Mexico Pilgrims Found. - Address unknown since 1995.
Mexico Tourism Bd. [24356], 400 Madison Ave., Ste. 11C, New York, NY 10017, (212)308-2110
Mexico-U.S. Inst. - Address unknown since 1999.
Mexico-U.S.A. CrossBorder Hea. Insurance Initiative [★15044]
Mexico-U.S.A. CrossBorder Hea. Insurance Initiative [★IO]
Meyers Aircraft Owners Assn. - Address unknown since 1989.
Mezogazdasagi Szovetkezok es Termelok Orszagos Szovetsege [★IO]
Mezzanine Mfrs; Assn. of [★2071]
MFM Publishing [★12880]
MG Car Club [IO], Abingdon, United Kingdom
MG Drivers Club of North Am. [21702], 18 George's Pl., Clinton, NJ 08809-1334, (908)713-6251
MG Octagon Car Club [IO], Rugeley, United Kingdom
M.G. "T" Register Limited; New England 21740
MG Vintage Racers [22922], 55 Belden Rd., Burlington, CT 06013
M.G.A. Twin-Cam Register - Address unknown since 1995.
MGB Assn; Amer. [21574]
MGC Register; Amer. [21575]
MHE Coalition [14465], 6783 York Rd., Apt. No. 104, Parma Heights, OH 44130-4569, (440)842-8817
M.I. Hummel Club [21933], Goebel Plz., PO Box 11, Pennington, NJ 08534-0011, (800)666-2582
MIB Gp. [14961], 160 Univ. Ave., Westwood, MA 02090-2307, (781)329-4500
Mica Industry Assn. - Defunct.
Micah [★11422]
Michael Biehn Fan Club; Official [24764]
Michael Bolton Platinum Club [24947], c/o Fan Asylum, PO Box 7149, San Francisco, CA 94120
Michael Crawford Intl. Fan Assn. [24760], 2272 Colorado Blvd., PMB No. 1367, Los Angeles, CA 90041
Michael E. DeBakey Intl. Cardiovascular Soc. [★13917]
Michael E. DeBakey Intl. Cardiovascular Soc. [★IO]
Michael E. DeBakey International Surgical Society [IO], Houston, TX, United States
Michael E. DeBakey Intl. Surgical Soc. [13917], c/o Kenneth L. Mattox, MD, Sec.-Treas., 1 Baylor Plz., Houston, TX 77030, (713)798-4557
Michael Fund/International Found. for Genetic Res. [14466], 4371 Northern Pike, Monroeville, PA 15146-2837, (412)374-0111
Michael Fund/International Found. for Genetic Res. [IO], Monroeville, PA, United States
Michael Harding Intl. Fan Club - Address unknown since 1995.
Michael Hurst Fan Club - Defunct.
Michael J. Stark Fan Club - Defunct.
Michael Jackson Fan Club [24948], PO Box 181275, Corpus Christi, TX 78480
Michael Jackson Fan Club 3 Generations [IO], Neuchatel, Switzerland
Michael Moriarty Official Fan Club - Address unknown since 2001.
Michael Oakeshott Assn. [7491], c/o Timothy Fuller, Political Sciences Dept., Colorado Coll., 14 E Cache La Poudre St., Colorado Springs, CO 80903

Michael O'Leary Fan Club - Defunct.
Michael York Fan Club; Official Intl. [24763]
Michele Lee Fan Club [★24761]
Michele Lee Fan Club/Michele Lee Online [24761], c/o Peter Roth, Pres., 4000 Warner Blvd., Burbank, CA 91522
Michelle Lynn Intl. Fan Club - Address unknown since 1995.
Michener Soc; James A. [9670]
Michigan; Alumni Assn. of the Univ. of [18873]
Michigan Apple Comm. [4739], 13105 Schavey Rd., Ste. 2, DeWitt, MI 48820, (517)669-8353
Michigan Assn. of Cherry Producers [4740], c/o Cherry Marketing Inst., PO Box 30285, Lansing, MI 48909-7785, (517)669-4264
Michigan Barrel Jumping Assn. [★23743]
Michigan Bigfoot Info. Center [★7480]
Michigan Bigfoot Info. Center [★IO]
Michigan/Canadian Bigfoot Info. Center [IO], Caro, MI, United States
Michigan/Canadian Bigfoot Info. Center [7480], 152 W Sherman, Caro, MI 48723, (989)673-2715
Michigan Tooling Assn. [★2073]
Mickey Gilley Fan Club - Defunct.
Mickey Mantle Found. - Defunct.
"Micky the D" Show/Metal Micky Fan Club - Address unknown since 1995.
Micro Cmpt. Educ. Application Network [★8557]
Micro Development Corps - Address unknown since 2007.
Micro Enterprise Alliance [IO], Braamfontein, Republic of South Africa
Micro Indus. Development Assistance and Services [IO], Dhaka, Bangladesh
Micro Indus. Development Assistance Soc. [★IO]
Microalgae Intl. Union - Address unknown since 2001.
Microbe Interactions; Intl. Soc. for Molecular Plant [6641]
Microbeam Anal. Soc. [7334], c/o Mr. Louis Ross, Membership Chm., Univ. of Missouri, Veterinary Sciences Bldg., Electron Microscopy Core Fac., W136 Veterinary Medicine Bldg., Columbia, MO 65211, (573)882-4777
Microbiological Diagnostic Mfrs; Assn. of [★3482]
Microbiological Media Mfrs; Assn. for [★3482]
Microbiologists; Canadian Soc. of [IO]
Microbiology
    Amer. Acad. of Microbiology [6559]
    Amer. Soc. for Microbiology [6565]
    Amer. Type Culture Coll. [6567]
    AOAC Intl. [6671]
    Assn. of Medical Microbiologists [IO]
    Assn. of Medical Microbiology and Infectious Disease Canada [IO]
    Australian Soc. for Antimicrobials [IO]
    Biochemical, Biophysical and Microbiological Soc. of Finland [IO]
    Comm. on the Status of Women in Microbiology [6574]
    European Soc. of Clinical Microbiology and Infectious Diseases - Switzerland [IO]
    Hellenic Soc. for Microbiology [IO]
    Israel Soc. for Microbiology [IO]
    Matrix Biology Soc. of Australia and New Zealand [IO]
    Natl. Meningitis Assn. [14281]
    New Zealand Microbiological Soc. [IO]
    Puerto Rico Soc. of Microbiologists [7331]
    Scottish Microbiology Assn. [IO]
    Soc. for Anaerobic Microbiology [IO]
    Soc. for Indus. Microbiology [6599]
    Soil Sci. Soc. of Am. [7674]
    U.S. Fed. for Culture Collections [6603]
    Waksman Found. for Microbiology [6605]
Microbiology; Amer. Acad. of [6559]
Microbiology; Amer. Soc. for [6565]
Microbiology; Australian Soc. for [IO]
Microbiology; Comm. on the Status of Women in [6574]
MicroBiology; Found. for [★6605]
Microbiology and Infectious Diseases; Canadian Assn. for Clinical [IO]
Microbiology and Infectious Diseases; European Soc. of Clinical [IO]

Reference to "IO" in place of a book number signifies that the association may be found in the 45th edition of International Organizations.

Microbiology; Soc. for Applied [IO]
Microbiology; Soc. for Gen. [IO]
Microbiology; Soc. for Indus. [6599]
Microbiology; Waksman Found. for [6605]
Microcar and Minicar Club [21703], PO Box 43137, Upper Montclair, NJ 07043-0137
Microchemical Soc; Amer. [6668]
Microchemical Soc; Metropolitan [★6668]
Microchemical Soc; New York-New Jersey Sect. of the [★6668]
Microcirculatory Soc. [16727], c/o Dr. Cynthia Meininger, Pres., Dept. of Systems Biology and Translational Medicine, Coll. of Medicine, Texas A&M Hea. Sci. Center, College Station, TX 77843-1114, (254)742-7037
Microcomputer Indus. Assn; ABCD: The [★898]
MicroComputer Investors Assn. [2339], 264 Anderson Dr., Fredericksburg, VA 22405, (703)371-5474
Microcomputer Software Assn. - of ADAPSO [★6768]
Microdealers; Assn. of Independent [★2827]
Microelectronic Indus. Design Assn. - Ireland [IO], Cork, Ireland
Microelectronics; Intl. Soc. for Hybrid [★6930]
Microfilm Assn; Natl. [★2095]
Microfilm and Info. Processing Assn. [★IO]
Microfilm Res. Centers Project - Defunct.
Micrographic Surgery and Cutaneous Oncology; Amer. Coll. of Mohs [15636]
Micrographics Assn; Natl. [★2095]
Microlight Assn. of South Africa [IO], Germiston, Republic of South Africa
Micronesia Coalition - Defunct.
Micronesia Inst. - Defunct.
Microneurography Soc. - Defunct.
Microorganisms; World Data Center for Collections of [★IO]
Microscopical Soc. of Canada [IO], Halifax, NS, Canada
Microscopical Soc. of Ireland [IO], Belfast, United Kingdom
Microscopical Soc. of London [★IO]
Microscopists Div; Amer. Assn. of Feed [★4662]
Microscopy
    Amer. Microscopical Soc. [7332]
    Armenian Electron Microscopy Soc. [IO]
    Australian Microscopy and Microanalysis Soc. [IO]
    Austrian Soc. for Electron Microscopy [IO]
    Belgian Soc. for Microscopy [IO]
    Brazilian Soc. for Microscopy and Microanalysis [IO]
    Bulgarian Soc. for Electron Microscopy [IO]
    Columbian Soc. for Electron Microscopy [IO]
    Croatian Microscopy Soc. [IO]
    Czechoslovak Microscopy Soc. [IO]
    Dutch Soc. for Microscopy [IO]
    Ecuadorian Electron Microscopy Soc. [IO]
    Electron Microscope Soc. of India [IO]
    Electron Microscopy Sect. of Moldova Republic [IO]
    European Microscopy Soc. [IO]
    Hungarian Soc. for Microscopy [IO]
    Intl. Fed. of Societies for Microscopy [IO]
    Intl. Fed. of Societies for Microscopy [7333]
    Intl. Soc. for Stereology [IO]
    Israel Soc. for Microscopy [IO]
    Italian Soc. for Microscopical Sciences [IO]
    Japanese Soc. of Microscopy [IO]
    Korean Soc. of Electron Microscopy [IO]
    Latvian Soc. for Electron Microscopy [IO]
    Microbeam Anal. Soc. [7334]
    Microscopical Soc. of Canada [IO]
    Microscopical Soc. of Ireland [IO]
    Microscopy New Zealand [IO]
    Microscopy Soc. of Am. [7335]
    Microscopy Soc. (Singapore) [IO]
    Microscopy Soc. of Southern Africa [IO]
    New York Microscopical Soc. [7336]
    Nordic Microscopy Soc. [IO]
    Optical Imaging Assn. [2735]
    Polish Commn. for Electron Microscopy [IO]
    Quekett Microscopical Club [IO]
    Romanian Soc. for Electron Microscopy [IO]
    Royal Microscopical Soc. [IO]

    Russian Soc. for Electron Microscopy [IO]
    Russian Soc. of Scanning Probe Microscopy and Nanotechnology [IO]
    Slovene Soc. for Microscopy [IO]
    Societe Francaise des Microscopies [IO]
    Spanish Microscopy Soc. [IO]
    Swiss Soc. for Optics and Microscopy [IO]
    Turkish Soc. for Electron Microscopy [IO]
    U.S. Microscopic Welding Assn. [7849]
Microscopy New Zealand [IO], Auckland, New Zealand
Microscopy Soc. of Am. [7335], 230 E Ohio St., Ste. 400, Chicago, IL 60611, (312)644-1527
Microscopy Soc. of Am; Electron [★7335]
Microscopy Soc. (Singapore) [IO], Singapore, Singapore
Microscopy Soc. of Southern Africa [IO], Pretoria, Republic of South Africa
Microsoft Certified Partners; Intl. Assn. of [6769]
Microsoft Healthcare Users Gp. [14726], 230 E Ohio St., Ste. 500, Chicago, IL 60611, (312)664-4467
Microsurgery; Amer. Soc. for Reconstructive [16573]
Microtonal Music; Amer. Festival of [10533]
Microwave Assn. [★IO]
Microwave Communications Assn. [★IO]
Microwave Communications Assn. [★3764]
Microwave Technologies Assn. [IO], Iver, United Kingdom
Microwaves
    IEEE Microwave Theory and Techniques Soc. [7337]
    Intl. Microwave Power Inst. [7338]
    Intl. Microwave Power Inst. [IO]
MICRU Intl. - Address unknown since 1995.
Mid-Am Antique Appraisers Assn. - Address unknown since 2008.
Mid-America; Black Archives of [9400]
Mid-America Buddhist Assn. [19554], 299 Heger Ln., Augusta, MO 63332-1445, (636)482-4037
Mid-America Coun. on Intl. Banking [★483]
Mid-America Periodical Distributors Assn. - Address unknown since 1995.
Mid-America State Universities Assn. - Defunct.
Mid-American Greek Coun. Assn. [24483], 3308 Snowbrush Ct., Fort Collins, CO 80521, (970)372-1174
Mid-American Res. Lib. [★18586]
Mid-Atlantic Equity Consortium [8276], 5272 River Rd., Ste. 340, Bethesda, MD 20816, (301)657-7741
Mid Atlantic Fiber Assn. [310], PO Box 5053, Delanco, NJ 08075
Mid-Atlantic Radical Historians Org. [★10129]
Mid-Atlantic States Assn. of Avian Veterinarians [16798], 610 N Main St., Memorial Bldg., Ste. 291, Blacksburg, VA 24060-3311, (540)951-2559
Mid-Century Mercury Car Club [21704], c/o Rusty Bethley, 1816 E Elmwood Dr., Lindenhurst, IL 60046, (847)356-2555
Mid-Continent Oil and Gas Assn. [★2950]
Mid-Continent Railway Historical Soc. [22934], PO Box 358, North Freedom, WI 53951, (608)522-4261
Mid Continent Wildcatters Assn. - Defunct.
Mid-Missions; Baptist [19480]
Mid North Coast Olive Assn. [IO], Willawarrin, Australia
Mid-Peninsula Conversion Proj. [★17423]
Mid Somerset Campaign for Nuclear Disarmament [IO], Shepton Mallet, United Kingdom
Mid-U.S. Honey Producers Marketing Assn. [4166], 3499 75th St. SW, Waverly, MN 55390, (763)658-4645
Mid-West Chinese Amer. Librarians Assn. [★10347]
Mid-West Tool Collectors Assn. [22608], PO Box 355, Humboldt, IA 50548-0355
Mid-West Truckers Assn. [3875], 2727 N Dirksen Pkwy., Springfield, IL 62702, (217)525-0310
Midamerica Commodity Exchange - Defunct.
Middle Atlantic Conf. - Defunct.
Middle Atlantic Fisheries Assn. [3493]
Middle Atlantic Planetarium Soc. [9105], c/o John Meader, PO Box 302, Fairfield, ME 04937, (207)453-7668
Middle Atlantic Water Polo Conf. [★23972]

Middle East
Afro-Asian People's Solidarity Org. [IO]
All4Israel [12454]
America-Israel Coun. for Israeli-Palestinian Peace [18047]
America-MidEast Educational and Training Services [18048]
America-MidEast Educational and Training Services [IO]
Amer. Educational Trust [18049]
Amer. Israel Public Affairs Comm. [18050]
Amer. Mideast Bus. Associates [24357]
Amer. Near East Refugee Aid [12804]
Americans for Middle East Understanding [18051]
Americans for Middle East Understanding [IO]
Americans for a Safe Israel [IO]
Americans for a Safe Israel [18052]
Arab Palestine Assn. [IO]
Assn. for the Stud. of Persianate Societies [8668]
Bethlehem Assn. [18053]
Bilateral US-Arab Chamber of Commerce [24226]
Canadian Lebanon Soc. of Halifax [IO]
Catholic Near East Welfare Assn. [IO]
Catholic Near East Welfare Assn. [18054]
Centre for Development and Population Activities [12422]
Comm. for Accuracy in Middle East Reporting in Am. [18055]
Comm. for Accuracy in Middle East Reporting in Am. [IO]
Coun. for the Natl. Interest [18056]
Democracy and Workers Rights Center [IO]
Facts and Logic About the Middle East [18057]
Found. for Middle East Peace [18058]
Foundation for Middle East Peace [IO]
Givat Haviva Educational Foundation [IO]
Givat Haviva Educational Found. [18059]
Inst. for Palestine Stud. [9397]
Intl. Soc. of Iraqi Scientists [7613]
Jewish Comm. on the Middle East [18060]
Jewish Comm. on the Middle East [IO]
Lebanese Info. Center [IO]
Lebanese Info. Center [18061]
Meals4Israel [12459]
Middle East Children's Alliance [17774]
Middle East Genetics Assn. [7117]
Middle East Info. Network [19258]
Middle East Info. Network [IO]
Middle East Inst. [IO]
Middle East Inst. [18062]
Middle East Librarians Assn. [10373]
Middle East Policy Coun. [18063]
Middle East Policy Coun. [IO]
Middle East Res. and Info. Proj. [IO]
Middle East Res. and Info. Proj. [18064]
Middle East Stud. Assn. of North Am. [18065]
Middle East Stud. Assn. of North Am. [IO]
Natl. Comm. for Labor Israel [12460]
Natl. Coun. on U.S.-Arab Relations [18066]
Natl. Coun. on U.S.-Arab Relations [IO]
Natl. PAC [18067]
Near East Found. [18068]
Near East Found. [IO]
Nordic Soc. for Middle Eastern Stud. [IO]
Palestine Liberation Org. [18069]
Partners for Peace [18230]
Pontifical Mission for Palestine [12816]
Scholars for Peace in the Middle East [18070]
Scholars for Peace in the Middle East [IO]
Search for Justice and Equality in Palestine/Israel [IO]
Search for Justice and Equality in Palestine/Israel [18071]
Soc. for Asian Music [10699]
StandWithUs [17941]
Syrian Stud. Assn. [8880]
U.S. Comm. for a Free Lebanon [18006]
Unity Coalition for Israel [8672]
USS Liberty Veterans Assn. [21227]
Writers and Artists for Peace in the Middle East [18072]
Youth Inst. for Peace in the Middle East [18073]
Middle East; Amer. Friends of the [★18048]
Middle East Assn. [IO], London, United Kingdom
Middle East Assn. for the Stud. of Pain [IO], Cairo, Egypt

A star before a book entry number signifies that the name is not listed separately, but is mentioned within the entry.

Middle East Children's Alliance [IO], Berkeley, CA, United States

Middle East Children's Alliance [17774], 901 Parker St., Berkeley, CA 94710, (510)548-0542

Middle East Coun. of Shopping Centres [IO], Dubai, United Arab Emirates

Middle East Development and Science Inst. - Address unknown since 2004.

Middle East Genetics Assn. [7117], c/o Mohammad Rafi, PhD, Pres., Dept. of Neurology, Jefferson Medical Coll., 1020 Locust St., JAH394, Philadelphia, PA 19107, (215)503-5715

Middle East Genetics Assn. [IO], Washington, DC, United States

Middle East Info. Network [IO], Boston, MA, United States

Middle East Info. Network [19258], 197 Fairmount Ave., Unit 2, Boston, MA 02136

Middle East Inst. [18062], 1761 N St. NW, Washington, DC 20036-2882, (202)785-1141

Middle East Inst. [IO], Washington, DC, United States

Middle East Librarians Assn. [IO], Philadelphia, PA, United States

Middle East Librarians Assn. [10373], c/o Mr. William J. Kopycki, Sec.-Treas., Univ. of Pennsylvania Lib., 3420 Walnut St., Philadelphia, PA 19104-6206, (215)898-2196

Middle East Nonviolence and Democracy [IO], Jerusalem, Israel

Middle East Peace Action Coalition - Defunct.

Middle East Peace Project - Defunct.

Middle East Policy Coun. [18063], 1730 M St. NW, Ste. 512, Washington, DC 20036, (202)296-6767

Middle East Policy Coun. [IO], Washington, DC, United States

Middle East Project [★IO]

Middle East Project [★18122]

Middle East Res. and Info. Proj. [18064], 1500 Massachusetts Ave. NW, Ste. 119, Washington, DC 20005, (202)223-3677

Middle East Res. and Info. Proj. [IO], Washington, DC, United States

Middle East Resource Center - Defunct.

Middle East Stud. Assn. of North Am. [18065], 1219 N Santa Rita Ave., Univ. of Arizona, Tucson, AZ 85721, (520)621-5850

Middle East Stud. Assn. of North Am. [IO], Tucson, AZ, United States

Middle East Watch - Address unknown since 2001.

Middle East; Writers and Artists for Peace in the [18072]

Middle East; Youth Comm. for Peace and Democracy in the [★18073]

Middle East; Youth Inst. for Peace in the [18073]

Middle Eastern Dance Assn. of New Zealand [IO], Timaru, New Zealand

Middle School Assn; Midwest [★8881]

Middle Schools

Natl. Middle Level Sci. Teachers' Assn. [9112]

Natl. Middle School Assn. [8881]

Middle States Assn. of Colleges and Schools [8277], 3624 Market St., Philadelphia, PA 19104, (215)662-5600

Middle States Assn. of Colleges and Secondary Schools [★8277]

Middle States Regatta Assn. [23701], 5035 Pulaski Ave., Philadelphia, PA 19144, (215)951-9549

Midget Ocean Racing Club [23200], c/o Rene Valliant, 711 Warren Dr., Annapolis, MD 21403, (410)263-6632

MIDI Mfrs. Assn. [2813], PO Box 3173, La Habra, CA 90632-3173

Midland Authors; Soc. of [4070]

Midmarch Arts Press [★9510]

Midmarch Associates [9510], 300 Riverside Dr., New York, NY 10025-5239, (212)666-6990

Midori Found. [★7976]

Midori and Friends [7976], 352 7th Ave., New York, NY 10001, (212)767-1300

Midsouth Indemnity Assn. and Asian Amer. Hotel Owners Assn. [★1930]

Midsouth Indemnity Assn. and Asian Amer. Hotel Owners Assn. [★IO]

Midstates Jeepster Assn. [21705], c/o Barb Conrad, Sec.-Treas., 7721 Howick Rd., Celina, OH 45822

Midtown Churches Community Assn. [★12293]

Midtown Intl. Center [★17897]

Midtown Intl. Center [★IO]

Midtown Outreach Program [★13277]

Midweek - North America - Address unknown since 1999.

Midwest Acad. [11751], 28 E Jackson St., No. 605, Chicago, IL 60604, (312)427-2304

Midwest Archives Conf. [9401], c/o Gregory Brooks, Admin./Membership Coor., 4300 S U.S. Hwy. 1, No. 203-293, Jupiter, FL 33477

Midwest Assn. of Fish and Wildlife Agencies [5339], c/o Ollie Torgerson, Coor., Wisconsin Dept. of Natural Resources, 107 Sutliff Ave., Rhinelander, WI 54501, (715)365-8924

Midwest Benthological Soc. [★4516]

Midwest Benthological Soc. [★IO]

Midwest Center for Environmental Sci. and Public Policy [5095], 1845 N Farewell Ave., Ste. 100, Milwaukee, WI 53202, (414)271-7280

Midwest Center for Labor Res. [★17970]

Midwest Collegiate Ski Assn. [★23760]

Midwest Comm. for Military Counseling - Address unknown since 1999.

Midwest Compensation Assn. [★1283]

Midwest Compensation Assn. [★IO]

Midwest Curling Assn. - Defunct.

Midwest Decoy Collectors Assn. [22071], 6 E Scott St., No. 3, Chicago, IL 60610-2321, (312)337-7957

Midwest Energy Education Consortium - Defunct.

Midwest Energy Efficiency Program [★4413]

Midwest Equip. Dealers Assn. [4092], 5330 Wall St., Ste. 100, Madison, WI 53718, (608)240-4700

Midwest Feed Manufacturers Assn. [★1357]

Midwest Fish and Game Commissioners; Assn. of [★5339]

Midwest Fish and Wildlife Commissioners; Assn. of [★5339]

Midwest Free Community Papers [3236], PO Box 1350, Iowa City, IA 52244-1350, (319)341-4352

Midwest Inst; Northeast- [18471]

Midwest Interlibrary Center [★10345]

Midwest Job Galvanizers Assn. - Defunct.

Midwest Middle School Assn. [★8881]

Midwest Migrant Hea. Info. Off. [★12590]

Midwest Old Settlers and Threshers Assn. [9483], 405 E Threshers Rd., Mount Pleasant, IA 52641, (319)385-8937

Midwest Olive Assn. [IO], Dongara, Australia

Midwest Open Land Assn. - Defunct.

Midwest Org. Development Network [★2866]

Midwest Org. Development Network [★IO]

Midwest Parentcraft Center [15609]

Midwest Railway Historical Soc. - Address unknown since 2001.

Midwest Resources Assn. - Defunct.

Midwest Rugby Football Union [★23706]

Midwest Sci. Center [★7172]

Midwest Senate Coalition; Northeast- [18472]

Midwest Ski Representatives Assn. [★3666]

Midwest Stock Exchange [★3510]

Midwest Sunbeam Registry [21706], 20700 Huntington Way, Prior Lake, MN 55372-9725, (952)440-6300

Midwest Treaty Network [19276], 21 S Barstow St., Ste. 206, Eau Claire, WI 54701, (715)833-1777

Midwest UFO Network [★7481]

Midwest United Drag Racers Assn. [★23070]

Midwest Winter Ski Representative Assn. [★3666]

Midwest Winter Sports Representatives Assn. [3666], PO Box 76, Hazelhurst, WI 54531, (715)358-6262

Midwest Women's Legal Group - Address unknown since 1995.

Midwestern Advt. Agency Network [★109]

Midwestern Advt. Agency Network [★IO]

Midwestern Assn. for Behavior Anal. [★6526]

Midwestern Celiac Sprue Assn. [★14413]

Midwestern Fast-Draw Assn. [★23733]

Midwestern Gilbert and Sullivan Soc. [9813], c/o Sarah Cole, Sec., 613 W State St., North Aurora, IL 60542-1538, (630)896-8860

Midwestern Literature; Soc. for the Stud. of [10430]

Midwestern Psychological Assn. [16157], c/o Dr. Mary Kite, Sec.-Treas., Dept. of Psychology Sci., Ball State Univ., Muncie, IN 47306, (765)285-1690

Midwifery; Amer. Coll. of Nurse- [★15447]

Midwifery; Citizens for [13981]

Midwifery Educ. Accreditation Coun. [8063], 20 E Cherry Ave., Flagstaff, AZ 86001-4607, (928)214-0997

Midwifery and Family Nursing; Frontier School of [★15479]

Midwives Alliance of North Am. [15610], 375 Rockbridge Rd., Ste. 172-313, Lilburn, GA 30047, (888)923-6262

Midwives; Amer. Assn. of Nurse- [★15447]

Midwives; Amer. Coll. of Domiciliary [15583]

Midwives; Amer. Coll. of Nurse- [15447]

Midwives Assn; Independent [IO]

Midwives Info. and Rsrc. Ser. [IO], Bristol, United Kingdom

Midwives; Intl. Confed. of [IO]

Midwives; North Amer. Registry of [13983]

MIE Corp. [★21696]

Mietervereinigung Osterreichs [IO], Vienna, Austria

Migraine Action Assn. [IO], Great Oakley, United Kingdom

Migraine Assn. of Ireland [IO], Dublin, Ireland

Migraine Awareness Gp.: A Natl. Understanding for "Migraineurs" [14532], 100 N Union St., Ste. B, Alexandria, VA 22314, (703)349-1929

Migraine Found; Natl. [★14533]

Migrant Children's Fund [★12593]

Migrant Dropout Reconnection Program - Defunct.

Migrant Educ. Task Force; Interstate [★12588]

Migrant Hea. Info. Off; Midwest [★12590]

Migrant Hea. Proj; East Coast [★12587]

Migrant Hea. Promotion [12590], 224 W Michigan Ave., Saline, MI 48176, (734)944-0244

Migrant Legal Action Prog. [12500], 1001 Connecticut Ave. NW, Ste. 915, Washington, DC 20036, (202)775-7780

Migrant Ministry [★12594]

Migrant Referral Proj; Natl. [★14581]

Migrant Workers

Andolan - Organizing South Asian Workers [24138]

Assn. of Farmworker Opportunity Programs [12585]

Farm Labor Organizing Comm. [23997]

Farm Worker Hea. Services [12586]

Farmworker Justice Fund [12587]

Global Workers Justice Alliance [18074]

Global Workers Justice Alliance [IO]

Interstate Migrant Educ. Coun. [12588]

Legal Immigrant Assn. [5808]

Los Ninos [12589]

Migrant Hea. Promotion [12590]

Migrant Legal Action Prog. [12500]

Natl. Alliance for Migrant and Seasonal Farmworker Vocational Rehabilitation [12591]

Natl. Assn. of State Directors of Migrant Educ. [12592]

Natl. Center for Farmworker Hea. [14581]

Natl. Child Labor Comm. [13500]

Natl. Comm. on the Educ. of Migrant Children (of the Natl. Child Labor Comm.) [12593]

Natl. Farm Worker Ministry [12594]

United Farm Workers of Am. [23999]

Migrant Workers; Bishops' Comm. for [★12282]

Migrant Workers Coun; Natl. [★12590]

Migration

Andolan - Organizing South Asian Workers [24138]

Asia-Pacific Migration Res. Network [IO]

Assn. of European Migration Institutions [IO]

Center for Migration Stud. of New York [IO]

Center for Migration Stud. of New York [10468]

Churches' Commn. for Migrants in Europe [IO]

Comm. on Migration, Refugees, and Population [IO]

Corona Worldwide [IO]

Ecumenical Migration Centre [IO]

Found. Info-Turk [IO]

Hebrew Immigrant Aid Soc. [12471]

Immigration and Ethnic History Soc. [10121]

Intl. Assn. for the Stud. of Forced Migration [IO]

Intl. Catholic Migration Commn. - Switzerland [IO]

Intl. Org. for Migration - Abidjan, Cote d'Ivoire [IO]

Intl. Org. for Migration - Abuja, Nigeria [IO]

Reference to "IO" in place of a book number signifies that the association may be found in the 45th edition of International Organizations.

Intl. Org. for Migration - Accra, Ghana [IO]
Intl. Org. for Migration - Addis Ababa, Ethiopia [IO]
Intl. Org. for Migration - Amman, Jordan [IO]
Intl. Org. for Migration - Armenia [IO]
Intl. Org. for Migration - Ashgabat, Turkmenistan [IO]
Intl. Org. for Migration - Athens, Greece [IO]
Intl. Org. for Migration - Austria [IO]
Intl. Org. for Migration - Azerbaijan [IO]
Intl. Org. for Migration - Bamako, Mali [IO]
Intl. Org. for Migration - Belgium [IO]
Intl. Org. for Migration - Bosnia and Herzegovina [IO]
Intl. Org. for Migration - Bratislava, Slovakia [IO]
Intl. Org. for Migration - Bucharest, Romania [IO]
Intl. Org. for Migration - Budapest, Hungary [IO]
Intl. Org. for Migration - Cambodia [IO]
Intl. Org. for Migration - Canberra, Australia [IO]
Intl. Org. for Migration - China [IO]
Intl. Org. for Migration - Colombia [IO]
Intl. Org. for Migration - Colombo, Sri Lanka [IO]
Intl. Org. for Migration - Conakry, Guinea [IO]
Intl. Org. for Migration - Costa Rica [IO]
Intl. Org. for Migration - Dar es Salaam, Tanzania [IO]
Intl. Org. for Migration - Dhaka, Bangladesh [IO]
Intl. Org. for Migration - Dublin, Ireland [IO]
Intl. Org. for Migration - Dushanbe [IO]
Intl. Org. for Migration - Freetown, Sierra Leone [IO]
Intl. Org. for Migration - Germany [IO]
Intl. Org. for Migration - Guatemala [IO]
Intl. Org. for Migration - Harare, Zimbabwe [IO]
Intl. Org. for Migration - Islamabad, Pakistan [IO]
Intl. Org. for Migration - Istanbul, Turkey [IO]
Intl. Org. for Migration - Jakarta, Indonesia [IO]
Intl. Org. for Migration - Kabul, Afghanistan [IO]
Intl. Org. for Migration - Kampala, Uganda [IO]
Intl. Org. for Migration - Kazakhstan [IO]
Intl. Org. for Migration - Khartoum, Sudan [IO]
Intl. Org. for Migration - Kiev, Ukraine [IO]
Intl. Org. for Migration - Kingston, Jamaica [IO]
Intl. Org. for Migration - Kinshasa, Democratic Republic of the Congo [IO]
Intl. Org. for Migration - Kyrgyz Republic [IO]
Intl. Org. for Migration - La Paz, Bolivia [IO]
Intl. Org. for Migration - Lima, Peru [IO]
Intl. Org. for Migration - Lisbon, Portugal [IO]
Intl. Org. for Migration - Ljubljana [IO]
Intl. Org. for Migration - Luanda, Angola [IO]
Intl. Org. for Migration - Lusaka, Zambia [IO]
Intl. Org. for Migration - Madrid, Spain [IO]
Intl. Org. for Migration - Managua, Nicaragua [IO]
Intl. Org. for Migration - Mexico [IO]
Intl. Org. for Migration - Minsk, Belarus [IO]
Intl. Org. for Migration - Moldova [IO]
Intl. Org. for Migration - Moscow, Russia [IO]
Intl. Org. for Migration - Nairobi, Kenya [IO]
Intl. Org. for Migration - Netherlands [IO]
Intl. Org. for Migration - Norway [IO]
Intl. Org. for Migration - Ottawa, Canada [IO]
Intl. Org. for Migration - Paris, France [IO]
Intl. Org. for Migration - Philippines [IO]
Intl. Org. for Migration - Port au Prince, Haiti [IO]
Intl. Org. for Migration - Prague, Czech Republic [IO]
Intl. Org. for Migration - Quito, Ecuador [IO]
Intl. Org. for Migration - Regional Off. for the Baltic and Nordic States [IO]
Intl. Org. for Migration - Riga, Latvia [IO]
Intl. Org. for Migration - Riyadh, Saudi Arabia [IO]
Intl. Org. for Migration - Rome, Italy [IO]
Intl. Org. for Migration - San Salvador, El Salvador [IO]
Intl. Org. for Migration - Santiago, Chile [IO]
Intl. Org. for Migration - Santo Domingo, Dominican Republic [IO]
Intl. Org. for Migration - Seoul, Republic of Korea [IO]
Intl. Org. for Migration - Skopje [IO]
Intl. Org. for Migration - Sofia, Bulgaria [IO]
Intl. Org. for Migration - Southern Africa [IO]
Intl. Org. for Migration - Switzerland [IO]
Intl. Org. for Migration - Tallinn, Estonia [IO]

Intl. Org. for Migration - Tbilisi, Georgia [IO]
Intl. Org. for Migration - Tegucigalpa, Honduras [IO]
Intl. Org. for Migration - Tehran, Iran [IO]
Intl. Org. for Migration - Thailand [IO]
Intl. Org. for Migration - Tirana, Albania [IO]
Intl. Org. for Migration - Tokyo, Japan [IO]
Intl. Org. for Migration - Tunis, Tunisia [IO]
Intl. Org. for Migration - United Kingdom [IO]
Intl. Org. for Migration - Vietnam [IO]
Intl. Org. for Migration - Vilnius, Lithuania [IO]
Intl. Org. for Migration - Warsaw, Poland [IO]
Intl. Org. for Migration - Zagreb, Croatia [IO]
Intl. Social Ser. - Australian Br. [IO]
Intl. Social Ser., U.S.A. Br. [IO]
Intl. Social Ser., U.S.A. Br. [12595]
Legal Immigrant Assn. [5808]
Natl. Child Labor Comm. [13500]
Nigerian Social Workers Assn. [24142]
Res. Found. for Jewish Immigration [10469]
U.S. Catholic Conference/Migration and Refugee Services [12823]
Migration; Amer. Comm. on Italian [19159]
Migration Dept. of the Amer. Jewish Joint Distribution Comm. [★12471]
Migration Dept. of the Amer. Jewish Joint Distribution Comm. [★IO]
Migration and Refugee Services [★12823]
Migration and Refugee Services; U.S. Catholic Conference/ [12823]
Migration and Refugee Services; U.S. Catholic Conference/ [★12823]
Migration and Refugee Services; U.S. Catholic Conf. [★12823]
Mikciojimo Problemu Klubas [★IO]
Mike Assn; L. [13124]
Mike Lunsford Fan Club - Address unknown since 2001.
Mike Yager Fan Club - Address unknown since 1999.
Mikes of America - Address unknown since 2003.
Mikita Hockey School for the Hearing Impaired; Stan [★23337]
Milan Cultural Assn. [10222], 75 Ruff Cir., Glastonbury, CT 06033, (860)657-4271
Milano ACM SIGGRAPH Professional Chap. [IO], Milan, Italy
Milano Chamber of Commerce [IO], Milan, Italy
Miler Club; Extra [23013]
Miles Ahead [★18679]
Miles Merwin Assn. [21001], PO Box 35771, Dallas, TX 75235, (214)750-1934
Miles Value Found. [7184], 5505 Connecticut Ave. NW, No. 149, Washington, DC 20015-2601, (202)253-5550
Milestone Car Soc. [21707], 626 N Park Ave., Indianapolis, IN 46204, (317)636-9900
Milieu Information Service - Defunct.
Militar Cubana; Junta Civico- [17366]
Militarism and the Draft; Comm. Opposed to [5669]
Militarism Resource Project - Defunct.
Militarization for Democracy; De [17427]
Military
  2nd Infantry Div. (2id), Korean War Veterans Alliance [21167]
  25th Infantry Div. Assn. [20687]
  29th Infantry Div. Assn. [20679]
  63rd Infantry Div. Assn. [20690]
  80th Fighter Squadron Headhunters' Assn. [5442]
  95th Infantry Div. Assn. [20691]
  187th Airborne Regimental Combat Team Assn. [20697]
  508th Parachute Infantry Regiment Assn. [21379]
  Adjutants Gen. Assn. of the U.S. [6061]
  AdoptaPlatoon [11489]
  African Amer. Post Traumatic Stress Disorder Assn. [21276]
  Air Force Assn. [6062]
  Air Force Sergeants Assn. [6063]
  Aircraft Carrier Indus. Base Coalition [1148]
  Airlift/Tanker Assn. [20646]
  All Navy Women's Natl. Alliance [6144]
  All Ser. Postal Chess Club [21941]
  Amer. Battleship Assn. [21210]
  Amer. Cadet Alliance [20718]

Amer. Civil War Assn. [10087]
Amer. Fighter Aces Assn. [20647]
Amer. History Forum and Civil War Educ. Assn. [8500]
Amer. Legion [20666]
Amer. Legion Auxiliary [21189]
Amer. Logistics Assn. [6064]
Amer. Military Soc. [6065]
Amer. Registry of Pathology [15858]
Amer. Retirees Assn. [21184]
Amer. Soc. of Military Comptrollers [6066]
Amer. Soc. of Military Insignia Collectors [22627]
Amer. Veterans for Equal Rights [12215]
Amer. Veterans Medical Airlift Ser. [6342]
Amer. War Mothers [21190]
Any Soldier [11490]
Armed Forces Communications and Electronics Assn. [6067]
Armed Forces Communications and Electronics Assn. [IO]
Armed Forces Hostess Assn. [6068]
Armed Forces Inst. of Pathology [15261]
Armed Forces Sports [6069]
Armed Forces Stamp Exchange Club [22793]
Armies of Tennessee, CSA and U.S.A. [20722]
Army Aviation Assn. of Am. [6070]
Army Cadet League of Canada [IO]
Army Distaff Foundation/Knollwood [21192]
Army Engineer Assn. [5469]
Army Families Fed. [IO]
Army Nurse Corps Assn. [15262]
Arnold Air Soc. [24546]
Assn. of Amer. Military Uniform Collectors [22628]
Assn. for Counselors and Educators in Govt. [11818]
Assn. of Graduates [8882]
Assn. of Military Banks of Am. [465]
Assn. of Military Colleges and Schools of the U.S. [8883]
Assn. of Military Osteopathic Physicians and Surgeons [15807]
Assn. of Military Surgeons of the U.S. [15263]
Assn. of NROTC Colleges and Universities [8884]
Assn. for the Soldiers of Israel [IO]
Assn. of the U.S. Army [6071]
Australian Inst. of Professional Intelligence Officers [IO]
Auxiliary to Sons of Union Veterans of the Civil War [20723]
Bay of Pigs Veterans Assn. [20717]
Black Military History Inst. of Am. [10472]
Black Veterans for Social Justice [21289]
Books For Soldiers [11491]
Bus. Leaders for Sensible Priorities [18387]
Canadian Assn. for Security and Intelligence Stud. [IO]
Canadian Corps of Commissionaires [IO]
Catholic War Veterans Auxiliary of the U.S.A. [21194]
Catholic War Veterans of the U.S.A. [21290]
Centennial Legion of Historic Military Commands [21240]
Center for Campus Organizing [18195]
Center on Conscience and War [17438]
Center for Defense Info. [17375]
Center for Strategic and Budgetary Assessments [18075]
Central Comm. for Conscientious Objectors [17439]
Challenge Coin Assn. [22731]
Chief Warrant and Warrant Officers Assn., U.S. Coast Guard [6072]
Children of the Confederacy [20724]
Christian Military Fellowship [19782]
Citizen Soldier [6073]
Civil Affairs Assn. [6074]
Civil Affairs Assn. [IO]
Civil War Soc. [10103]
Civil War Token Soc. [22732]
Coalition to Salute America's Heroes [21294]
Coast Defense Study Group [10473]
Colonial Order of the Acorn [20735]
Combat Helicopter Pilots Assn. [20648]
Company of Military Historians [22629]
Congressional Medal of Honor Soc. [20710]

A star before a book entry number signifies that the name is not listed separately, but is mentioned within the entry.

CREDO [19746]
Daedalian Found. [20649]
Daughters of the Cincinnati [20670]
Daughters of Union Veterans of the Civil War, 1861-1865 [20725]
De Re Militari: The Soc. for Medieval Military History [10474]
Defense Advisory Comm. on Women in the Services [6075]
Defense Intel Alumni Assn. [18892]
Defense Orientation Conf. Assn. [18591]
Demilitarization for Democracy [17427]
Descendants of the Signers of the Declaration of Independence [20671]
Desert Storm Veterans Assn. [21298]
Disabled Amer. Veterans [20763]
Disabled Amer. Veterans Auxiliary [20764]
Distinguished Flying Cross Soc. [20711]
EAA Warbirds of Am. [21443]
Emerald Soc. of the Fed. Law Enforcement Agencies [19199]
Empowerment Soc. of the U.S.A. [13425]
Enlisted Assn. of Natl. Guard of the U.S. [6076]
Escort Carrier Sailors and Airmen Assn. [21185]
European Coun. of Conscripts Organisations [IO]
European Org. of Military Associations [IO]
Ex-Partners of Ser. Members for Equality [17437]
F-4 Phantom II Soc. [21445]
Fed. Educ. Assn. [24043]
Fed. of French War Veterans [21416]
Flagon and Trencher - Descendants of Colonial Tavern Keepers [20737]
Forty and Eight [20667]
Freedom Is Not Free [12596]
Gen. Soc. of Colonial Wars [20738]
Gen. Soc., Sons of the Revolution [20672]
Gen. Soc. of the War of 1812 [21354]
German Colonies Collectors Gp. [22822]
GI Joe Collectors' Club [22996]
Give2TheTroops [12597]
GlobalSecurity.org [18208]
Great War Assn. [10475]
Hereditary Order of Descendants of the Loyalists and Patriots of the Amer. Revolution [20673]
Hof Reunion Assn. [20682]
Homefront Hugs USA [13352]
Homes for Our Troops [21302]
Hood's Texas Brigade Assn. [20726]
Huguenot Historical Soc. [21161]
Inter-American Defense Bd. [17378]
Inter-University Seminar on Armed Forces and Soc. [6077]
Intl. Action Center [18076]
Intl. Action Center [IO]
Intl. Assn. of Military Flight Surgeon-Pilots [13541]
Intl. Bird Dog Assn. [21452]
Intl. Comm. of Military Medicine [IO]
Intl. Coun. of Air Shows [21455]
Intl. Soc. for Military Law and Law of War [IO]
Intl. Training and Simulation Alliance [6735]
Iraq and Afghanistan Veterans of Am. [21335]
Iraq War Veterans Org. [21304]
Japanese Amer. Veterans Assn. [21305]
Jewish Community Centers Assn. of North Am. [12473]
Jewish War Veterans of the U.S.A. - Natl. Ladies Auxiliary [21196]
Judge Advocates Assn. [6078]
Korean War Proj. [6344]
Ladies Auxiliary, Military Order of the Purple Heart, U.S.A. [20713]
Legion of Valor of the U.S.A. [20714]
Logistics Officer Assn. [2736]
Logistics Officer Association [IO]
Mackenzie Inst. [IO]
MAPS Air Museum - Military Aviation Preservation Soc. [9342]
Marine Corps Assn. [6079]
Marine Corps Aviation Assn. [6080]
Marine Corps CounterIntelligence Assn. [19224]
Marine Corps Cryptologic Assn. [21174]
Marine Corps Engineer Assn. [6142]
Marine Corps Intelligence Assn. [19225]
Marine Corps League [6081]
Marine Corps Mustang Assn. [21176]

Marine Corps Recruiters Assn. [5799]
Marine Corps Reserve Assn. [6082]
Military Chaplains Assn. of the U.S.A. [19752]
Military Child Educ. Coalition [8886]
Military Families Speak Out [18796]
Military Impacted Schools Assn. [8885]
Military Intelligence Corps Assn. [5862]
Military Law Task Force [6083]
Military Officers Assn. of Am. [21235]
Military Order of the Devil Dog Fleas [21178]
Military Order of the Loyal Legion of the U.S. [20728]
Military Order of the Purple Heart of the U.S.A. [20715]
Military Order of the Stars and Bars [20729]
Military Postal History Soc. [22847]
Military Reporters and Editors [6182]
Military Toxics Proj. [5033]
Military Vehicle Preservation Assn. [22630]
Mine Warfare Assn. [18592]
Montford Point Marine Assn. [6084]
Move Am. Forward [18733]
Natl. Action for Former Military Wives [12012]
Natl. Alliance of Families for the Return of America's Missing Servicemen [21263]
Natl. Assn. of County Veterans Ser. Officers [21309]
Natl. Assn. of Free Will Baptists [19492]
Natl. Assn. of Military Widows [21197]
Natl. Assn. of Superintendents of U.S. Naval Shore Establishments [6085]
Natl. Assn. for Uniformed Services [6086]
Natl. Comm. for Employer Support of the Guard and Reserve [6087]
Natl. Coun. of Indus. Naval Air Stations [6088]
Natl. Counter Intelligence Corps Assn. [21164]
Natl. Defense Indus. Assn. [6089]
Natl. Defense Trans. Assn. [6090]
Natl. Guard Assn. of the U.S. [6091]
Natl. Guard Executive Directors Assn. [6092]
Natl. Huguenot Soc. [21163]
Natl. Indian Wars Assn. [9371]
Natl. Intramural-Recreational Sports Assn. [23842]
Natl. Military Fish and Wildlife Assn. [5342]
Natl. Military Intelligence Assn. [5889]
Natl. Museum of Amer. Jewish Military History [21312]
Natl. Naval Officers Assn. [6093]
Natl. Order of Trench Rats [20766]
Natl. Soc. of the Children of the Amer. Revolution [20674]
Natl. Soc., Daughters of the Amer. Colonists [20746]
Natl. Soc., Daughters of the Amer. Revolution [20675]
Natl. Soc. of Pershing Rifles [24547]
Natl. Soc. of Scabbard and Blade [24548]
Natl. Soc., Sons of the Amer. Revolution [20676]
Natl. Soc., U.S. Daughters of 1812 [21355]
Natl. Soc. Women Descendants of the Ancient and Honorable Artillery Company [20749]
Natl. Training and Simulation Assn. [6738]
Natl. World War II Glider Pilots Assn. [21468]
Naval Airship Assn. [6379]
Naval Civilian Managers Assn. [6094]
Naval Enlisted Reserve Assn. [6095]
Naval Intelligence Professionals [6096]
Naval Reserve Assn. [6097]
Naval Sea Cadet Corps [6098]
Navy Club of the U.S.A. [6099]
Navy Club of the U.S.A. Auxiliary [6100]
Navy League of the U.S. [6101]
Navy League of the U.S. [IO]
Navy Seabee Veterans of Am. [21217]
Navy Wifeline Assn. [21199]
Nine Lives Associates [3540]
Non Commissioned Officers Assn. of the U.S.A. [6102]
North-South Skirmish Assn. [23727]
Nurses Org. of Veterans Affairs [15519]
Oper. AC [11492]
Oper. Gratitude [11493]
Oper. Homelink [11494]
Oper. Sandbox [11495]
Oper. ShoeBox [11496]

Oper. Soldier Support [11497]
Oper.: Take a Soldier to the Movies [11498]
Oper. Truth [21317]
Oper. We Do Care [11499]
Order of Americans of Armorial Ancestry [20750]
Order of Daedalians [20650]
Order of the Founders and Patriots of Am. [20755]
Orders and Medals Soc. of Am. [22631]
Orders and Medals Society of America [IO]
Paralyzed Veterans of Am. [20768]
Patriotic Order Sons of Am. [21242]
Patton Soc. [11141]
PEF Israel Endowment Funds [12461]
Professional Armed Forces Rodeo Assn. [23693]
Proj. Blue Book [7483]
Proj. on Govt. Oversight [18077]
Res. and Development Associates for Military Food and Packaging Systems [7096]
Reserve Officers Assn. of the U.S. [6103]
Retired Activities Br. [6104]
Rolling Thunder [21265]
Royal British Legion Women's Sect. [IO]
Salute Our Services [11500]
SATS/EAF Assn. [21179]
Save the Battlefield Coalition [10061]
Sew Much Comfort [11739]
Sharkhunters Intl. [10480]
Silver Wings [24549]
Soc. of the 3rd Infantry Div. [21186]
Soc. of Air Force Physicians [15264]
Soc. of the Ark and the Dove [20758]
Soc. of the Cincinnati [20677]
Soc. of Civil War Historians [10151]
Soc. of Daughters of Holland Dames [20759]
Soc. of the Descendants of the Colonial Clergy [20760]
Soc. of the Descendants of Washington's Army at Valley Forge [20678]
Soc. of the Fifth Div. [21187]
Soc. of Medical Consultants to the Armed Forces [15265]
Soc. of Military Orthopaedic Surgeons [15266]
Soc. of Military Otolaryngologists - Head and Neck Surgeons [15267]
Soldiers' Angels [19259]
Soldiers Overseas Family Gateway [12598]
Soldiers for the Truth [20683]
A Soldier's Wish List [11501]
Sons of the Amer. Legion [21201]
Sons of Confederate Veterans [20730]
Sons and Daughters In Touch [12599]
Sons of Union Veterans of the Civil War [20731]
Special Forces Assn. [21270]
STAMP - Survivors Take Action Against Abuse by Military Personnel [11507]
Star-Spangled Banner Flag House Assn. [21095]
Stars for Stripes [20770]
State Guard Assn. of the U.S. [6105]
Submarine Indus. Base Coun. [1149]
Support Our Soldiers Am. [11502]
Tailhook Assn. [6106]
Tee it up for the Troops [13357]
Tin Can Sailors - The Natl. Assn. of Destroyer Veterans [21220]
Tragedy Assistance Prog. for Survivors [11503]
Uniformed Services Acad. of Family Physicians [15268]
United Daughters of the Confederacy [20732]
United Spouses Assn. [21202]
U.S. Airsoft Corps [23620]
U.S. Armor Assn. [6107]
U.S. Army Warrant Officers Assn. [6108]
U.S. Coast Guard Chief Petty Officers Assn. [20734]
U.S. Marine Corps Drill Instructors Assn. [6109]
U.S. Marine Corps Scout/Sniper Assn. [21181]
U.S. Naval Inst. [6110]
U.S. War Dogs Assn. [20769]
United We Serve [21203]
USAF Medical Ser. Corps Assn. [13590]
USMC Vietnam Tankers Assn. [21337]
Veterans' Widows Intl. Network [21357]
Vietnam Era Seabees [21339]
Vietnam Veteran Wives [21332]

Reference to "IO" in place of a book number signifies that the association may be found in the 45th edition of International Organizations.

Women Against Military Madness [18078]
Women Marines Assn. [21182]
Women in Military Ser. for Am. Memorial Found. [6360]
Women Veterans of Am. [21333]
Women's Army Corps Veterans' Assn. [20708]
World War I Aeroplanes [21490]
Military Accessories Service Assn. - Address unknown since 1999.
Military Active Retired Travel Club; Special [21271]
Military Aircraft Pilots Assn. - Defunct.
Military Audiology Assn. [13717], 1720 Republic Rd., Silver Spring, MD 20902-3357
Military Aviation Preservation Soc. [★9342]
Military Aviation Preservation Soc; MAPS Air Museum - [9342]
Military Aviation Preservation Soc. and Museum [★9342]
Military Banks of Am; Assn. of [465]
Military Benefit Assn. [18959], PO Box 221110, Chantilly, VA 20153-1110, (703)968-6200
Military Benefits
 Ex-Partners of Servicemembers for Equality [12009]
 Laptops for the Wounded [11741]
 Natl. Org. of Veterans' Advocates [6348]
 Oper. Truth [21317]
 Soldiers for the Truth [20683]
 U.S. Marine Corps Scout/Sniper Assn. [21181]
 Veterans' Widows Intl. Network [21357]
 Women Veterans of Am. [21333]
Military Boot Mfrs. Assn. - Address unknown since 2001.
Military Chaplains Assn. of the U.S.A. [19752], PO Box 7056, Arlington, VA 22207-7056, (703)533-5890
Military Child Educ. Coalition [8886], PO Box 2519, Harker Heights, TX 76548-2519, (254)953-1923
Military Child Educ. Coalition [IO], Harker Heights, TX, United States
Military Collectors and Historians; Company of [★22629]
Military Colleges and Schools of the U.S; Assn. of [★8883]
Military Commands; Centennial Legion of Historic [21240]
Military Equipment
 Aerospace Indus. Assn. of Am. [130]
 Assn. of Amer. Military Uniform Collectors [22628]
 Company of Military Historians [22629]
 Laptops for the Wounded [11741]
 Military Vehicle Preservation Assn. [22630]
 Orders and Medals Soc. of Am. [22631]
 Soldiers for the Truth [20683]
Military Families
 107th Engineer Assn. [5467]
 AdoptaPlatoon [11489]
 Amer. Gold Star Mothers [21188]
 Amer. Legion Auxiliary [21189]
 Amer. War Mothers [21190]
 Ancient and Honorable Artillery Company of Massachusetts [21191]
 Army Distaff Foundation/Knollwood [21192]
 Army Widows' Assn. [IO]
 Assn. for Counselors and Educators in Govt. [11818]
 Auxiliary to Sons of Union Veterans of the Civil War [20723]
 Blue Star Mothers of Am. [21193]
 Catholic War Veterans Auxiliary of the U.S.A. [21194]
 Catholic War Veterans of the U.S.A. [21290]
 Children of the Confederacy [20724]
 Colonial Order of the Acorn [20735]
 Daughters of the Cincinnati [20670]
 Daughters of Union Veterans of the Civil War, 1861-1865 [20725]
 Descendants of the Signers of the Declaration of Independence [20671]
 Disabled Amer. Veterans [20763]
 Disabled Amer. Veterans Auxiliary [20764]
 Ex-Partners of Ser. Members for Equality [17437]
 Fed. Educ. Assn. [24043]
 Flagon and Trencher - Descendants of Colonial Tavern Keepers [20737]

Freedom Is Not Free [12596]
Gen. Soc. of Colonial Wars [20738]
Gen. Soc., Sons of the Revolution [20672]
Gen. Soc. of the War of 1812 [21354]
Give2TheTroops [12597]
Gold Star Wives of Am. [21195]
Hereditary Order of Descendants of the Loyalists and Patriots of the Amer. Revolution [20673]
Homefront Hugs USA [13352]
Hood's Texas Brigade Assn. [20726]
Jewish War Veterans of the U.S.A. - Natl. Ladies Auxiliary [21196]
Ladies Auxiliary, Military Order of the Purple Heart, U.S.A. [20713]
Ladies Auxiliary to the Veterans of Foreign Wars of the U.S. [21307]
Military Child Educ. Coalition [8886]
Military Child Educ. Coalition [IO]
Military Order of the Loyal Legion of the U.S. [20728]
Natl. Alliance of Families for the Return of America's Missing Servicemen [21263]
Natl. Assn. of County Veterans Ser. Officers [21309]
Natl. Assn. of Military Widows [21197]
Natl. Military Family Assn. [21198]
Natl. Soc. of the Children of the Amer. Revolution [20674]
Natl. Soc., Daughters of the Amer. Revolution [20675]
Natl. Soc., Sons of the Amer. Revolution [20676]
Natl. Soc., U.S. Daughters of 1812 [21355]
Navy Wifeline Assn. [21199]
Oper. Sandbox [11495]
Order of Americans of Armorial Ancestry [20750]
Salute Our Services [11500]
Soc. of the Cincinnati [20677]
Soc. of the Descendants of Washington's Army at Valley Forge [20678]
Soc. of Military Widows [21200]
Soldiers' Angels [19259]
Soldiers Overseas Family Gateway [12598]
A Soldier's Wish List [11501]
Sons of the Amer. Legion [21201]
Sons of Confederate Veterans [20730]
Sons and Daughters In Touch [12599]
Sons of Union Veterans of the Civil War [20731]
Tee it up for the Troops [13357]
Tragedy Assistance Prog. for Survivors [11503]
United Daughters of the Confederacy [20732]
United Spouses Assn. [21202]
U.S. Marine Corps Scout/Sniper Assn. [21181]
United We Serve [21203]
Veteran Corps of Artillery, State of New York, Constituting the Military Soc. of the War of 1812 [21204]
Vietnam Veteran Wives [21332]
World War II War Brides [21205]
World War II War Brides [IO]
Military Families Speak Out [18796], PO Box 300549, Jamaica Plain, MA 02130, (617)983-0710
Military Fellowship; Christian [19782]
Military Fish and Wildlife Assn; Natl. [5342]
Military Food and Packaging Systems; Res. and Development Associates for [7096]
Military Geographic Inst. [IO], Santiago, Chile
Military Govt. Assn. [★IO]
Military Govt. Assn. [★6074]
Military Heraldry Soc. [IO], Telford, United Kingdom
Military Historians; Company of [22629]
Military Historical Soc. of Australia [IO], Garran, Australia
Military Historical Soc. - Defunct.
Military History
 25th Infantry Div. Assn. [20687]
 80th Fighter Squadron Headhunters' Assn. [5442]
 107th Engineer Assn. [5467]
 187th Airborne Regimental Combat Team Assn. [20697]
 508th Parachute Infantry Regiment Assn. [21379]
 Air Force Historical Found. [10470]
 Airlift/Tanker Assn. [20646]
 Amer. Civil War Assn. [10087]
 Amer. Civil War Round Table - United Kingdom [IO]

Amer. Fighter Aces Assn. [20647]
Amer. History Forum and Civil War Educ. Assn. [8500]
Amer. Legion [20666]
Amer. Legion Auxiliary [21189]
Amer. Military Medical Impression [6111]
Amer. Soc. of Military Insignia Collectors [22627]
Armies of Tennessee, CSA and U.S.A. [20722]
Army Historical Found. [10471]
Army Records Soc. [IO]
Assn. of Amer. Military Uniform Collectors [22628]
Auxiliary to Sons of Union Veterans of the Civil War [20723]
Bay of Pigs Veterans Assn. [20717]
Black Military History Inst. of Am. [10472]
Black Veterans for Social Justice [21289]
Catholic War Veterans Auxiliary of the U.S.A. [21194]
Catholic War Veterans of the U.S.A. [21290]
Centennial Legion of Historic Military Commands [21240]
Challenge Coin Assn. [22731]
Children of the Confederacy [20724]
Civil War Soc. [10103]
Civil War Token Soc. [22732]
Coast Defense Study Group [10473]
Colonial Order of the Acorn [20735]
Combat Helicopter Pilots Assn. [20648]
Company of Military Historians [22629]
Congressional Medal of Honor Soc. [20710]
Coun. on America's Military Past [10021]
Daedalian Found. [20649]
Daughters of the Cincinnati [20670]
Daughters of Union Veterans of the Civil War, 1861-1865 [20725]
De Re Militari: The Soc. for Medieval Military History [10474]
Descendants of the Signers of the Declaration of Independence [20671]
Disabled Amer. Veterans [20763]
Disabled Amer. Veterans Auxiliary [20764]
Distinguished Flying Cross Soc. [20711]
Fed. of French War Veterans [21416]
Flagon and Trencher - Descendants of Colonial Tavern Keepers [20737]
Fortress Study Group [IO]
Forty and Eight [20667]
Gen. Soc. of Colonial Wars [20738]
Gen. Soc., Sons of the Revolution [20672]
Gen. Soc. of the War of 1812 [21354]
Great War Assn. [10475]
Hereditary Order of Descendants of the Loyalists and Patriots of the Amer. Revolution [20673]
Hof Reunion Assn. [20682]
Hood's Texas Brigade Assn. [20726]
Huguenot Historical Soc. [21161]
Intl. Naval Res. Org. [10476]
Intl. Naval Res. Org. [IO]
Jewish War Veterans of the U.S.A. - Natl. Ladies Auxiliary [21196]
John Pelham Historical Assn. [11131]
Ladies Auxiliary, Military Order of the Purple Heart, U.S.A. [20713]
Legion of Valor of the U.S.A. [20714]
MAPS Air Museum - Military Aviation Preservation Soc. [9342]
Marine Corps Engineer Assn. [6142]
Marine Corps Heritage Found. [10477]
Military Historical Soc. of Australia [IO]
Military History Soc. of Ireland [IO]
Military Order of the Loyal Legion of the U.S. [20728]
Military Order of the Purple Heart of the U.S.A. [20715]
Military Order of the Stars and Bars [20729]
Military Vehicle Preservation Assn. [22630]
Napoleonic Assn. [IO]
Natl. Counter Intelligence Corps Assn. [21164]
Natl. Huguenot Soc. [21163]
Natl. Indian Wars Assn. [9371]
Natl. Museum of Amer. Jewish Military History [21312]
Natl. Order of Trench Rats [20766]
Natl. Soc. of the Children of the Amer. Revolution [20674]

A star before a book entry number signifies that the name is not listed separately, but is mentioned within the entry.

Natl. Soc., Daughters of the Amer. Colonists [20746]
Natl. Soc., Daughters of the Amer. Revolution [20675]
Natl. Soc., Sons of the Amer. Revolution [20676]
Natl. Soc., U.S. Daughters of 1812 [21355]
Natl. Soc. Women Descendants of the Ancient and Honorable Artillery Company [20749]
Naval Historical Found. [10478]
Naval Historical Soc. of Australia [IO]
Navy and Marine Living History Assn. [21206]
North-South Skirmish Assn. [23727]
Order of Americans of Armorial Ancestry [20750]
Order of Daedalians [20650]
Order of the Founders and Patriots of Am. [20755]
Order of the Indian Wars [10479]
Orders and Medals Res. Soc. [IO]
Orders and Medals Soc. of Am. [22631]
Paralyzed Veterans of Am. [20768]
Patriots of Fort McHenry-Living Classrooms [10057]
SATS/EAF Assn. [21179]
Save the Battlefield Coalition [10061]
Sharkhunters Intl. [10480]
Sharkhunters Intl. [IO]
Soc. of the 3rd Infantry Div. [21186]
Soc. of Ancient Military Historians [10481]
Soc. of the Ark and the Dove [20758]
Soc. of the Cincinnati [20677]
Soc. of Civil War Historians [10151]
Soc. of Daughters of Holland Dames [20759]
Soc. of the Descendants of the Colonial Clergy [20760]
Soc. of the Descendants of Washington's Army at Valley Forge [20678]
Soc. for Military History [10482]
Sons of the Amer. Legion [21201]
Sons of Confederate Veterans [20730]
Sons of Union Veterans of the Civil War [20731]
Star-Spangled Banner Flag House Assn. [21095]
Trireme Trust U.S.A. [10483]
Ulysses S. Grant Assn. [11154]
United Daughters of the Confederacy [20732]
U.S. Cavalry Assn. and Memorial Res. Lib. [10484]
USMC Vietnam Tankers Assn. [21337]
USS Constellation Museum [10449]
Victorian Military Soc. [IO]
Vietnam Era Seabees [21339]
Western Front Assn. - U.S. Br. [10485]
Women's Army Corps Veterans' Assn. [20708]
Military History; Center for [★10471]
Military History Found; Amer. [★10482]
Military History; Natl. Museum of Amer. Jewish [21312]
Military History Soc. of Ireland [IO], Dublin, Ireland
Military Impacted Schools Assn. [8885], 1600 Hwy. 370, Bellevue, NE 68005, (402)293-4000
Military Information Center - Defunct.
Military Inst; Amer. [★10482]
Military Intelligence Assn; Natl. [5889]
Military Intelligence Corps Assn. [5862], PO Box 13020, Fort Huachuca, AZ 85670-3020, (520)456-6232

Military Law
Alliance Against the Uniformed Services Former Spouses Protection Act (USFSPA) Law [6112]
Amer. Veterans for Equal Rights [12215]
Judge Advocates Assn. [6078]
Military Law Task Force [6083]
Servicemembers Legal Defense Network [6113]
Military Law Task Force [6083], 318 Ortega St., San Francisco, CA 94122, (619)233-1701
Military Officers Assn. of Am. [21235], 201 N Washington St., Alexandria, VA 22314-2520, (703)549-2311
Military Operations Res. Soc. [7406], 1703 N Beauregard St., Ste. 450, Alexandria, VA 22311-1717, (703)933-9070
Military Order of the Carabao [21246], c/o The Army and Navy Club, 901 17th St. NW, Farragut Sq., Washington, DC 20006-2503
Military Order of Columbia's Shield - Address unknown since 1999.

Military Order of the Cootie; Supreme Pup Tent, [21323]
Military Order of Crusades; Baronial Order of Magna Charta and the [10096]
Military Order of the Devil Dog Fleas [21178], 10620 N McGee St., Kansas City, MO 64155, (816)734-5579
Military Order of Devil Dogs - Address unknown since 1995.
Military Order of Foreign Wars of the U.S. [21236], c/o Col. Duane H. Bartrem, Commander Gen., 5985 Austin Way, Grand Ledge, MI 48837, (517)627-9072
Military Order of the Loyal Legion of the U.S. [20728], c/o Mr. Keith G. Harrison, Junior Vice Commander-in-Chief, 4209 Santa Clara Dr., Holt, MI 48842-1868, (517)694-9394
Military Order of the Mosquito [★21320]
Military Order of the Purple Heart of the U.S.A. [20715], 5413-B Backlick Rd., Springfield, VA 22151-3915, (703)642-5360
Military Order of the Purple Heart, U.S.A; Ladies Auxiliary, [20713]
Military Order of the Stars and Bars [20729], PO Box 100, Daphne, AL 36526, (251)626-0151
Military Order of the World Wars [21417], 435 N Lee St., Alexandria, VA 22314, (703)683-4911
Military Order of the World Wars [IO], Alexandria, VA, United States
Military Order of Zouaves, Militia and Volunteers of the U.S. - Address unknown since 1999.
Military Otolaryngologists; Soc. of [★15267]
Military Past; Coun. on America's [10021]
Military Police
CID Agents Assn. [21207]
Military Police Regimental Assn. [21208]
Retired Military Police Assn. [21209]
Military Police Assn. [★21208]
Military Police Regimental Assn. [21208], PO Box 2182, Fort Leonard Wood, MO 65473, (573)329-6772
Military Postal History Soc. [22847], c/o Ed Dubin, Sec., PO Box 586, Belleville, MI 48112
Military Procurement; Proj. on [★18077]
Military Railway Service Veterans - Defunct.
Military Reform Caucus - Address unknown since 2001.
Military Reporters and Editors [6182], c/o Medill School of Journalism, 1325 G St. NW, Ste. 730, Washington, DC 20005, (202)661-0141
Military Retirees Assn; Amer. [21282]
Military School Band Assn. - Address unknown since 1991.
Military Schools; Natl. Assn. of [★8883]
Military Ser. for Am. Memorial Found; Women in [6360]
Military and Soc; European Res. Gp. on [IO]
Military Soc. War of 1812 [★21204]
Military Sports
U.S. Airsoft Corps [23620]
Military Studies Center - Defunct.
Military Survivors - Defunct.
Military Tax Campaign- U.S; Conscience and [★18716]
Military Toxics Proj. [5033], PO Box 558, Lewiston, ME 04243, (207)783-5091
Military Vehicle Collectors Club [★22630]
Military Vehicle Preservation Assn. [22630], PO Box 520378, Independence, MO 64052, (816)833-6872
Military, Veterans and Patriotic Ser. Organizations of Am. [21245], 1100 Larkspur Landing, Ste. 340, Larkspur, CA 94939, (800)626-6526
Military Wives Assn; Natl. [★21198]
Military Wives; Natl. Action for Former [12012]
Militia Immaculata [★19660]
Militia of the Immaculata Movement [19660], 1600 W Park Ave., Libertyville, IL 60048, (847)367-7800
Miljoforbundet Jordens Vanner [★IO]
Milk; Amer. Dry [★1130]
Milk Assn; Evaporated [★1130]
Milk Bottle Collectors; Natl. Assn. of [22076]
Milk Bottle Crate Mfrs. Coun. - Defunct.
Milk Can Inst. - Defunct.
Milk Carton Quality Performing Coun. - Defunct.
Milk Commissions; Amer. Assn. of Medical [16384]

Milk Control Boards of Am; Natl. Assn. of [★5740]
Milk Dealers Assn; Intl. [★1135]
Milk, Food and Environmental Sanitarians; Intl. Assn. of [★5739]
Milk and Food Sanitarians; Intl. Assn. of [★5739]
Milk Glass Collectors Soc; Natl. [22566]
Milk Indus. Center [IO], Buenos Aires, Argentina
Milk Indus. Found. [IO], Washington, DC, United States
Milk Indus. Found. [1135], c/o Intl. Dairy Foods Assn., 1250 H St. NW, Ste. 900, Washington, DC 20005-3952, (202)737-4332
Milk Inspectors; Intl. Assn. of Dairy and [★5739]
Milk and Lactation; Intl. Soc. for Res. in Human [13776]
Milk Producers Fed; Natl. [4489]
Milk Producers Fed; Natl. Cooperative [★4489]
Milk Sanitarians; Intl. Assn. of [★5739]
Milk Shipments; Natl. Conf. on Interstate [4493]
Milkbottles Only Org. - Defunct.
Milking Devon Cattle Assn; Amer. [4235]
Milking Shorthorn Junior Soc; Amer. [4236]
Milking Shorthorn Soc; Amer. [4237]
Mill Mutual Fire Prevention Bur. - Defunct.
Mill and Smelter Workers; Intl. Union of Mine, [★24137]
Mill Superintendents Assn; Amer. Pulp and Paper [★2893]
Millard Fillmore, Last of the Whigs; Soc. for the Preservation and Enhancement of the Recognition of [22601]
Millard Fillmore Natl. Soc. - Defunct.
Millard Fillmore Soc. [★22601]
Millennium Guild - Address unknown since 2004.
Millennium Inst. [17647], 2200 Wilson Blvd., Ste. 650, Arlington, VA 22201-3357, (703)841-0048
Millennium Promise [11485], 432 Park Ave. S, 13th Fl., New York, NY 10016, (212)584-5710
Millennium Soc. - Address unknown since 2006.
Miller Birthplace Soc; Glenn [24902]
Miller Family Org; James Redman [20958]
Miller Syndromes; Found. for Nager and [14452]
Millers
Asbestos Info. Association/North Am. [2740]
European Flour Milling Assn. [IO]
Flour Advisory Bur. [IO]
Grain Milling Fed. [IO]
Hardwood Coun. [4056]
Intl. Assn. of Operative Millers [2737]
Intl. Assn. of Operative Millers [IO]
Iran's Assn. of Flour Producers [IO]
Natl. Assn. of British and Irish Millers [IO]
North Amer. Millers' Assn. [2738]
Rice Millers' Assn. [2739]
Spanish Assn. of Flour and Semolina Mfrs. [IO]
Millers' Natl. Fed. [★2738]
Millinery Credit Assn. - Defunct.
Millinery Displayers Assn. - Defunct.
Millinery Info. Bur. [★238]
Millinery Inst. of Am. [★238]
Milling and Baking Division of AACC Intl. [7095], 3340 Pilot Knob Rd., St. Paul, MN 55121, (651)454-7250
Milling and Baking Division of Amer. Assn. of Cereal Chemists [★7095]
Milling and Baking Tech; Amer. Soc. of [★6660]
Million Dollar Round Table [2199], 325 W Touhy Ave., Park Ridge, IL 60068-4265, (847)692-6378
Million Mom March [17596], 1225 Eye St. NW, Ste. 1100, Washington, DC 20005, (202)898-0792
Millionaires Inst. - Address unknown since 2002.
Milliron - Millison - Muhleisen Family Exchange [21002]
Millison - Muhleisen Family Exchange; Milliron - [21002]
Mills
Assn. of Coffee Mill Enthusiasts [21973]
Soc. for the Preservation of Old Mills [10065]
Steel Mfrs. Assn. [2732]
Mills Brothers Soc. - Address unknown since 2008.
Mills; Soc. for the Preservation of Old [10065]
Mills; Steel Bar [★2732]
Millwork Cost Bur. [★593]
Millwork Producers Assn; Wood Moulding and [688]
Millwork Producers; Wood Moulding and [★688]

Reference to "IO" in place of a book number signifies that the association may be found in the 45th edition of International Organizations.

Millwright Gp. [24102], c/o Specialized Carriers and Rigging Assn., 2750 Prosperity Ave., Ste. 620, Fairfax, VA 22031-4312, (703)698-0291

Milo's Bali Orchids [IO], Denpasar, Indonesia

Milpas de Oaxaca [IO], Oaxaca, Mexico

Milton H. Erickson Found. [16221], 3606 N 24th St., Phoenix, AZ 85016, (602)956-6196

Milton Helpern Inst. of Forensic Medicine - Address unknown since 2008.

Milton Keynes and North Buckinghamshire Chamber of Commerce [IO], Milton Keynes, United Kingdom

Milton S. Eisenhower Found. [11839], 1875 Connecticut Ave. NW, Ste. 410, Washington, DC 20009-5737, (202)234-8104

Milton Soc. of Am. [9693], Duquesne Univ., English Dept., Pittsburgh, PA 15282, (412)396-6420

Milwaukee Grain Exchange - Defunct.

Milwaukee; Railway Historical Soc. of [★22934]

Mime Assn; Natl. [★11028]

Minato Intl. Assn. [IO], Tokyo, Japan

Mind Acad; Opening [15955]

Mind Control and Ritual Abuse; S.M.A.R.T. Secretive Societies, [13296]

Mind Development Assn. [★7447]

Mind Development Association/U.S. Psi Squad [7447], PO Box 21741, St. Louis, MO 63109

Mind Development and Control; Amer. Inst. of [★7447]

Mind Development and Control Assn. [★7447]

Mind Justice [17775], c/o Cheryl Welsh, Dir., 915 Zaragoza St., Davis, CA 95618, (530)758-1626

Mind Justice [IO], Davis, CA, United States

Mind - Natl. Assn. for Mental Hea. [IO], London, United Kingdom

Mind Sci. Found. [7448], 117 W El Prado Dr., San Antonio, TX 78212, (210)821-6094

MindFreedom Intl. [17776], PO Box 11284, Eugene, OR 97440, (541)345-9106

Minds; Proj.: Hearts and [12538]

Mindszenty Found; Cardinal [16989]

Mine Inspectors' Inst. of Am. [6117], 319 Painterville Rd., Hunker, PA 15639, (724)925-5150

Mine, Mill and Smelter Workers; Intl. Union of [★24137]

Mine Tool Assn. - Defunct.

Mine Warfare Assn. [18592], c/o Mr. Lee Hunt, VP, 7715 Lookout Ct., Alexandria, VA 22306-2520

Mine Workers of Am; Intl. Union United [★24139]

Mineral Economics and Mgt. Soc. [6139], c/o Lisa Morrison, Treas., PO Box 656, Kennett Square, PA 19348, (610)925-1860

Mineral Economics and Management Society [IO], Kennett Square, PA, United States

Mineral Feed Assn; Natl. [★1357]

Mineral Indus. Consultants Assn. [IO], Carlton, Australia

Mineral Indus. Res. Org. [IO], Birmingham, United Kingdom

Mineral Info. Inst. [7343], 505 Violet St., Golden, CO 80401-6714, (303)277-9190

Mineral Insulation Manufacturers Assn. [★659]

Mineral Law Found; Energy and [6136]

Mineral Law Found; Rocky Mountain [6141]

Mineral Policy Center [★6115]

Mineral Res; Amer. Soc. for Bone and [15787]

Mineralogical Assn. of Canada [IO], Quebec, QC, Canada

Mineralogical Assn. of Korea [★IO]

Mineralogical Soc. [IO], Twickenham, United Kingdom

Mineralogical Soc. of Am. [7344], 3635 Concorde Pkwy., Ste. 500, Chantilly, VA 20151-1125, (703)652-9950

Mineralogical Soc. of Denmark [IO], Copenhagen, Denmark

Mineralogical Soc. of Egypt [IO], Cairo, Egypt

Mineralogical Soc. of Finland [IO], Helsinki, Finland

Mineralogical Soc. of Great Britain and Ireland [★IO]

Mineralogical Soc. of Korea [IO], Seoul, Republic of Korea

Mineralogical Soc. of Poland [IO], Krakow, Poland

Mineralogical Soc. of Russia [IO], Moscow, Russia

Mineralogical Soc. of Slovakia [IO], Bratislava, Slovakia

Mineralogical Soc. of South Africa [IO], Helderkruin, Republic of South Africa

Mineralogiese Assosiasie van Suid Afrika [★IO]

Mineralogists; Soc. of Economic Paleontologists and [★7432]

Mineralogy

Amer. Fed. of Mineralogical Societies [7339]

Amer. Lands Access Assn. [22937]

Australian Clay Minerals Soc. [IO]

Bulgarian Mineralogical Soc. [IO]

Canadian Micro Mineral Assn. [IO]

Canadian Mineral Analysts [IO]

Chinese Soc. of Mineralogy, Petrology, and Geochemistry [IO]

Circum-Pacific Council for Energy and Mineral Resources [IO]

Circum-Pacific Coun. for Energy and Mineral Resources [7340]

Clay Minerals Soc. [7341]

Croatian Mineralogical Assn. [IO]

Deutsche Mineralogische Gesellschaft [IO]

European Salt Producers' Assn. [IO]

Fluorescent Mineral Soc. [IO]

Fluorescent Mineral Soc. [7342]

French Assn. of Amateurs in Micromineralogy [IO]

Gem and Mineral Fed. of Canada [IO]

Gemmological Assn. and Gem Testing Lab. of Great Britain [IO]

German Gemmological Assn. [IO]

Intl. Assn. on the Genesis of Ore Deposits [IO]

Intl. Assn. for the Stud. of Clays [IO]

Intl. Coun. for Applied Mineralogy [IO]

Intl. Mineralogical Assn. [IO]

Intl. Sand Collectors Soc. [22056]

Mineral Info. Inst. [7343]

Mineralogical Assn. of Canada [IO]

Mineralogical Soc. [IO]

Mineralogical Soc. of Am. [7344]

Mineralogical Soc. of Denmark [IO]

Mineralogical Soc. of Egypt [IO]

Mineralogical Soc. of Finland [IO]

Mineralogical Soc. of Korea [IO]

Mineralogical Soc. of Poland [IO]

Mineralogical Soc. of Russia [IO]

Mineralogical Soc. of Slovakia [IO]

Mineralogical Soc. of South Africa [IO]

Planetary Gemologists Assn. [IO]

Societa Italiana di Mineralogia e Petrologia [IO]

Soc. for Geology Applied to Mineral Deposits [IO]

Soc. of Mineral Analysts [7345]

South Pacific Applied Geoscience Commn. [IO]

Swedish Mineralogical Soc. [IO]

Ukrainian Mineralogical Soc. [IO]

Mineralolwirtschaftsverband e.V. [★IO]

Minerals

Acad. of Natural Sciences [7356]

Amer. Assn. for Crystal Growth [6851]

Amer. Crystallographic Assn. [6852]

Amer. Fed. of Mineralogical Societies [7339]

Amer. Inst. of Mining, Metallurgical, and Petroleum Engineers [7346]

Amer. Soc. for Bone and Mineral Res. [15787]

Asbestos Info. Association/North Am. [2740]

Asbestos Removal Contractors Assn. [IO]

Assn. of Amer. Ceramic Component Manufacturers [785]

Assn. of European Assay Offices [IO]

Assn. of European Gypsum Indus. [IO]

British Lime Assn. [IO]

Chrysotile Inst. [IO]

Clay Minerals Soc. [7341]

EURISOL, The UK Mineral Wool Assn. [IO]

European Aggregates Assn. [IO]

European Assn. of Feldspar Producers [IO]

European Assn. of Indus. Silica Producers [IO]

European Bentonite Producers Assn. [IO]

European Borates Assn. [IO]

European Calcium Carbonate Assn. - Europe [IO]

European Indus. Minerals Assn. [IO]

European Lime Assn. [IO]

Gems, Minerals and Jewelry Stud. Unit [22821]

Gypsum Assn. [2741]

Gypsum Products Development Assn. [IO]

Indus. Minerals Assn. - North Am. [IO]

Indus. Minerals Assn. - North Am. [2742]

Intl. BioIron Soc. [15269]

Intl. BioIron Soc. [IO]

Intl. Marine Minerals Soc. [5009]

Intl. Sand Collectors Soc. [22056]

Mineral Indus. Res. Org. [IO]

Mineral Info. Inst. [7343]

Mineralogical Soc. of Am. [7344]

Minerals, Metals, and Materials Soc. [7320]

Natl. Indus. Sand Assn. [2743]

Natl. Speleological Soc. [7693]

Northwest Mining Assn. [2753]

Resource Policy Inst. [4603]

Salt Inst. [2744]

Salt Mfrs'. Assn. [IO]

Salters' Company [IO]

Sci. Assn. of European Talc Indus. [IO]

Silica and Moulding Sands Assn. [IO]

Soc. of Economic Geologists [7134]

Soc. of Mineral Analysts [7345]

Sorptive Minerals Inst. [2745]

Southern and Eastern African Mineral Centre [IO]

World Gold Coun. [IO]

World Gold Coun. [2746]

Minerals Coun. of Australia [IO], Kingston, Australia

Minerals Engg. Soc. [IO], Worksop, United Kingdom

Minerals and Jewelry Stud. Unit; Gems, [22821]

Minerals, Metals, and Materials Soc. [7320], 184 Thorn Hill Rd., Warrendale, PA 15086-7514, (724)776-9000

Minerals of the Natl. Acad. of Sciences—National Res. Coun; Comm. on Clay [7341]

Miner's Legal Defense Comm. - Defunct.

Mini-America's Cup Assn. - Defunct.

Mini-Basketball England [IO], Northampton, United Kingdom

Mini-Bike Assn. of America - Address unknown since 1995.

Mini Car Club, U.S.A. [21708], 172 Park St., Montclair, NJ 07042, (973)746-8165

Mini License Plate Collectors Club; License Plate Key Chain and [★22011]

Mini Lop Rabbit Club of Am. [5149], c/o Pennie Grotheer, Sec.-Treas., PO Box 17, Pittsburg, KS 66762, (417)842-3317

Mini/Micro Special Interest Group - Defunct.

Mini Moke Registry; North Amer. [21745]

Mini Owners - Defunct.

Mini Registry - Address unknown since 1999.

Miniature Aircraft Assn; Intl. [22938]

Miniature Armoured Fighting Vehicle Assn. [IO], Crewe, United Kingdom

Miniature Arms Collectors/Makers Society [IO], Plainfield, IL, United States

Miniature Arms Collectors/Makers Soc. [21538], c/o William Adrian, Pres., 2502 Fresno Ln., Plainfield, IL 60544, (815)254-8692

Miniature Arms Soc. [★21538]

Miniature Arms Soc. [★IO]

Miniature Artisans; Intl. Guild of [22159]

Miniature Australian Shepherd Club of Am. [22306], PO Box 1692, Winter Park, FL 32790-1692

Miniature Book Soc. [9752], c/o Kathy King, Treas., 402 York Ave., Delaware, OH 43015, (877)627-1983

Miniature Book Soc. [IO], Delaware, OH, United States

Miniature Bull Terrier Club of Am. [22307], c/o Kathy Flaugh, Membership Chair, 9224 Kinlock Dr., Indianapolis, IN 46256-2242, (317)849-0929

Miniature Cattle Breeders Soc. and Registry; Intl. [4267]

Miniature Donkey Assn; Natl. [5004]

Miniature Donkey Registry [4137], c/o Amer. Donkey and Mule Soc., PO Box 1210, Lewisville, TX 75067, (972)219-0781

Miniature Donkey Registry of the U.S. [★4137]

Miniature Enthusiasts; Natl. Assn. of [22077]

Miniature Figure Collectors of America - Address unknown since 1991.

Miniature Golf Assn. of the U.S. [23829], 1113 Belle Pl., Fort Worth, TX 76107, (817)738-5522

Miniature Golf Development of Am. - Address unknown since 2003.

Miniature Hereford Breeders Assn. [4272], 31270 Private Rd. 23, Elizabeth, CO 80107

Miniature Horse Assn; Amer. [4830]

Miniature Horse Assn. of Australia [IO], Emerald, Australia

A star before a book entry number signifies that the name is not listed separately, but is mentioned within the entry.

Miniature Horse Club of Southland [IO], Invercargill, New Zealand
Miniature Horse Registry; Amer. Shetland Pony Club/American [4845]
Miniature Intl. Racing Assn. - Defunct.
Miniature Jersey Cattle Registry; Amer. [4238]
Miniature Llama Assn; Amer. [21513]
Miniature and Novelty Sheep Breeders Assn. and Registry [5204], 113 Blake Rd., Toledo, WA 98591, (360)864-6116
Miniature Piano Enthusiast Club [22072], 633 Pennsylvania Ave., Hagerstown, MD 21740, (301)797-7675
Miniature Piano Enthusiast Club [IO], Hagerstown, MD, United States
Miniature Pinscher Club of Am. [22308], c/o Christine Filler, Sec., 35038 N 10th St., Desert Hills, AZ 85086, (602)717-7909
Miniature Schnauzer
    Amer. Miniature Schnauzer Club [22205]
Miniature Schnauzer Club; Amer. [22205]
Miniature Truck Assn. - Defunct.
Miniature Warbird Assn; World [22662]
Miniature Zebu Assn; Intl. [4268]
Miniatures Industry Assn. of America - Defunct.
Miniaturists Trade Assn; Cottage Indus. [1162]
Miniaturists Trade Assn., Inc; Cottage Indus. [★858]
Minicar Club; Microcar and [21703]
Minicar and Microcar Club - Address unknown since 1995.
Minicomputer Users; Assn. of [6784]
Minimum Wage Coalition to Save Jobs - Defunct.
Minimums Found; Families Against Mandatory [11864]
Mining
    ADSC: Intl. Assn. of Found. Drilling [2747]
    ADSC: Intl. Assn. of Found. Drilling [IO]
    Amer. Inst. of Mining, Metallurgical, and Petroleum Engineers [7346]
    Amer. Lands Access Assn. [22937]
    Amer. Soc. of Mining and Reclamation [6114]
    Asbestos Info. Association/North Am. [2740]
    Assoc. Equip. Distributors [2000]
    Assn. of Mining Analysts [IO]
    Australasian Inst. of Mining and Metallurgy [IO]
    Australian Mines and Metals Assn. [IO]
    Australian Mining and Petroleum and Law Assn. [IO]
    Black Lung Assn. [13323]
    British Assn. of Colliery Mgt. - Tech., Energy and Administrative Mgt. [IO]
    Canadian Assn. of Mining Equip. and Services for Export [IO]
    Canadian Diamond Drilling Assn. [IO]
    Canadian Inst. of Mining, Metallurgy, and Petroleum [IO]
    Canadian Land Reclamation Assn. [IO]
    Chamber of Mines of Namibia [IO]
    Chamber of Mines of South Africa [IO]
    China Clay Producers Assn. [2748]
    Citizens Coal Coun. [4299]
    Colorado Mining Assn. [2749]
    Copper Development Assn. [2750]
    Earthworks [6115]
    Equip. Managers Coun. of Am. [943]
    European Assn. of Mining Indus., Metals Ores and Indus. Minerals [IO]
    German Mining Assn. [IO]
    Ghana Chamber of Mines [IO]
    Gold Prospectors Assn. of Am. [22913]
    Gypsum Assn. [2741]
    Hungarian Mining and Metallurgical Soc. [IO]
    Indus. Minerals Assn. - North Am. [2742]
    Inst. of Materials, Minerals, and Mining [IO]
    Inst. of Mine Surveyors of South Africa [IO]
    Intl. Mine Water Assn. [IO]
    Intl. Precious Metals Inst. [7318]
    Intl. Soc. of Mine Safety Professionals [15270]
    Intl. Soc. of Mine Safety Professionals [IO]
    Interstate Mining Compact Commn. [6116]
    Irish Mining and Quarrying Soc. [IO]
    Malaysian Chamber of Mines [IO]
    Mine Inspectors' Inst. of Am. [6117]
    Mineral Indus. Consultants Assn. [IO]
    Minerals Coun. of Australia [IO]

Mining Assn. of Canada [IO]
Mining Assn. of the United Kingdom [IO]
Mining Elecl. Maintenance and Safety Assn. [2751]
Mining Found. of the Southwest [2752]
Mining Inst. of Scotland [IO]
Mining and Metallurgical Soc. of Am. [7347]
Natl. Assn. of State Land Reclamationists [6118]
Natl. Mine Rescue Assn. [7348]
Natl. Mining, Petroleum and Energy Soc. [IO]
Natl. Union of Mine Workers [IO]
Natl. Union of Mineworkers - United Kingdom [IO]
North of England Inst. of Mining and Mech. Engineers [IO]
Northwest Mining Assn. [2753]
Papua New Guinea Chamber of Mines and Petroleum [IO]
Perlite Inst. [2754]
Proj. Underground [18079]
Prospectors and Developers Assn. of Canada [IO]
Rocky Mountain Mineral Law Found. [6141]
Royal Geological and Mining Soc. of the Netherlands [IO]
Silver Inst. [2727]
Soc. for Mining, Metallurgy, and Exploration [7349]
Soc. for Mining, Metallurgy, Rsrc. and Environmental Tech. [IO]
Solution Mining Res. Inst. [2755]
South African Inst. of Mining and Metallurgy [IO]
Swedish Assn. of Mines, Minerals and Metal Producers [IO]
United Engg. Found. [7051]
United Mine Workers of Am. [24139]
U.S. Mine Rescue Assn. [12600]
U.S. Mine Rescue Assn. [IO]
The Vermiculite Assn. [IO]
Women in Mining [2756]
Women's Assn. of the Mining Indus. of Canada Found. [IO]
Mining Assn. of Canada [IO], Ottawa, ON, Canada
Mining Assn. Educational Found; Colorado [★2749]
Mining Assn; Natl. [846]
Mining Assn; Pennsylvania Coal [★847]
Mining Assn. of the United Kingdom [IO], Lichfield, United Kingdom
Mining Br., Amer. Inst. of Mining, Metallurgical and Petroleum Engineers [★7349]
Mining, Chem., and Energy Indus. Union [IO], Hannover, Germany
Mining Club [★19374]
Mining Club of the Southwest [★2752]
Mining Development Policy; Center for Alternative [4536]
Mining Elecl. Maintenance and Safety Assn. [2751], c/o Bill Collins, Sec.-Treas., PO Box 7163, Lakeland, FL 33807
Mining Engineers; Soc. of [★7349]
Mining Found. of the Southwest [2752], PO Box 42317, Tucson, AZ 85733, (520)577-7519
Mining History Assn. [10131], PO Box 552, Sedalia, CO 80135, (707)785-3814
Mining History Organisations; Natl. Assn. of [IO]
Mining Inst; Rocky Mountain Coal [848]
Mining Inst. of Scotland [IO], Dunfermline, United Kingdom
Mining and Metallurgical Engineers; Amer. Inst. of [★7346]
Mining, Metallurgical and Petroleum Engineers; Mining Br., Amer. Inst. of [★7349]
Mining and Metallurgical Soc. of Am. [7347], 476 Wilson Ave., Novato, CA 94947-4236, (415)897-1380
Mining, Metallurgy, and Exploration; Soc. for [7349]
Mining and Reclamation; Amer. Soc. for Surface [★6114]
Mining and Reclamation Coun. [★846]
Mining; Women in [★2756]
Ministerial Assn; Fundamental [★19977]
Ministero de Deporte y Juventud [IO], Montevideo, Uruguay
Ministers and Acolytes; Intl. Guild of Lay [★19963]
Ministers Assn; Divine Sci. [19881]
Ministers; Assn. of Southern Baptist Campus [19474]

Ministers Assn; Unitarian Universalist [20602]
Ministers and Certified Mediums Soc; Licentiate [20450]
Ministers; Intl. Convention of Faith, Churches and [★19807]
Ministers Leadership Training Program - Defunct.
Ministers; Natl. Assn. of Catholic Diocesan Family Life [★20288]
Ministers Org; Divine Sci. [★19881]
Ministers for Racial and Social Justice; United Church of Christ [★20608]
Ministers Wives and Ministers' Widows; Natl. Assn. of [★19897]
Ministers' Wives; Natl. Assn. of [★19897]
Ministries Abroad U.S.A; Sharing of [20393]
Ministries; ABW [19468]
Ministries; Alliance for Life [19760]
Ministries; Amer. Baptist Natl. [★19484]
Ministries to Blacks in Higher Education - Address unknown since 1990.
Ministries; Bd. of Natl. [19484]
Ministries; Care [19532]
Ministries; CBM [19995]
Ministries; Chosen People [19998]
Ministries; Christ in Action [19999]
Ministries; Christ Truth [19514]
Ministries in Christian Educ; Natl. Coun. of Churches, [★19935]
Ministries; Christian Motorsports [21610]
Ministries; Christian Reformed Church World Literature [★19832]
Ministries; CityTeam [12844]
Ministries; Clearer Vision [13378]
Ministries; Confessing Synod [20561]
Ministries; CRISTA [13166]
Ministries; Damien [19866]
Ministries; Disability [20216]
Ministries; Division of Homeland [★19856]
Ministries; Division of Overseas [★19856]
Ministries in Educ; United [★19938]
Ministries/Episcopal Church Center; Off. of Black [19968]
Ministries; Episcopal Commn. for Black [★19968]
Ministries of the Gospel; Advancing the [★20298]
Ministries; Hea. [20241]
Ministries; Hea. and Healing [★20241]
Ministries; HealthCare [20076]
Ministries in Higher Educ; United [★19938]
Ministries in Higher Educ; United [★19938]
Ministries; HMI [20597]
Ministries; Inspiration [11952]
Ministries; Intl. Liaison, U.S. Catholic Coordinating Center for Lay Volunteer [★19602]
Ministries Intl; Nazarene Compassionate [19818]
Ministries Intl; Presbyterian and Reformed Renewal [★20474]
Ministries; Lederer Messianic [20019]
Ministries; Life Action [★20020]
Ministries; Life Action Revival [20020]
Ministries Mgt. Assn; Christian [★20511]
Ministries; Metanoia [19869]
Ministries; Moody Literature [★20368]
Ministries; Natl. Coun. for Telephone [★19865]
Ministries; Natl. Episcopal Hea. [14584]
Ministries; Natl. Inst. for Campus [★19916]
Ministries; Natl. Off. of Jesuit Social [★13172]
Ministries; Nations [20370]
Ministries Network; Reconciling [20065]
Ministries; O.C. [★20377]
Ministries in Public Educ. [★19938]
Ministries; Searching Together Educational [19909]
Ministries Team/United Ministries in Higher Educ; Higher Educ. [★19938]
Ministries of the United Methodist Church; Women's Division of the Gen. Bd. of Global [20269]
Ministries U.S.A; CONTACT Tele [★19865]
Ministries; WEF [★19991]
Ministries; Wheat Ridge [20233]
Ministry
    Acad. of Parish Clergy [20274]
    All Roads Ministry [19564]
    Amer. Acad. of Ministry [19914]
    Amer. Missionary Fellowship [20296]
    ASGM [19506]
    Assn. of Christian Church Educators [19842]

Reference to "IO" in place of a book number signifies that the association may be found in the 45th edition of International Organizations.

Assn. for Clinical Pastoral Educ. **[19915]**
Assn. of Full Gospel Women Clergy **[20275]**
Assn. of Grace Brethren Ministers **[19533]**
Assn. of Reformed Baptist Churches of Am.
   [19473]
Assn. of Southern Baptist Campus Ministers
   [19474]
Aurora Ministries **[20276]**
Baptist Women in Ministry/Folio **[19481]**
Bibles for the Blind and Visually Handicapped
   [19511]
Bd. of Intl. Ministries **[19483]**
Braille Bible Found. **[19513]**
Bros. and Sisters in Christ **[19767]**
Campus Ministry Women **[19918]**
Canadian Assn. for Pastoral Practice and Educ.
   [IO]
Canadian Churches' Forum for Global Ministries
   [IO]
Canadian Coun. of Christian Charities **[IO]**
Catholic Campus Ministry Assn. **[19595]**
Center for Organizational and Ministry Develop-
   ment **[19769]**
Children's HopeChest **[11578]**
Christ for the City Intl. **[20277]**
Christ for the City Intl. **[IO]**
Christian Aid Ministries **[18570]**
Christian Community Development Assn. **[20278]**
Christian Coun. on Persons with Disabilities
   [11931]
Christian Educators Assn. Intl. **[19922]**
Church of the Brethren Gen. Bd. Global Mission
   Partnership **[19535]**
Church Growth Center **[20279]**
Concordia Deaconess Conf. **[20213]**
Confessing Synod Ministries **[20561]**
Congregation of the Blessed Sacrament **[19617]**
Conservative Baptist Assn. of Am. **[19485]**
Disciple Nations Alliance **[19847]**
Divine Sci. Ministers Assn. **[19881]**
EAPE/Campolo Ministries - Evangelical Assn. for
   the Promotion of Educ. **[20330]**
Ecumenical Theological Seminary **[19924]**
Episcopal Women's Caucus **[19956]**
Equestrian Ministries Intl. **[20082]**
Evangelical Free Church of Am. - Intl. Mission
   [20333]
First Fruit **[20009]**
FutureChurch **[19627]**
Glenmary Res. Center **[19628]**
Global Hea. Ministries **[14630]**
Harvest **[20280]**
Harvest **[IO]**
HealthCare Ministries **[20076]**
Inst. of Singles Dynamics **[20281]**
Intl. Assn. of Christian Chaplains **[19748]**
Intl. Assn. of Women Ministers **[20619]**
Intl. Christian Technologists Assn. **[20282]**
Intl. Christian Technologists Assn. **[IO]**
Intl. Convention of Faith Ministries **[19807]**
Intl. Network of Children's Ministry **[19758]**
Intl. Network of Prison Ministries **[20283]**
Intl. Network of Prison Ministries **[IO]**
LifeWind Intl. **[20284]**
Lutheran Volunteer Corps **[20228]**
Media in Ministry Assn. **[20285]**
Medical Ambassadors Intl. **[IO]**
Mexican Amer. Cultural Center **[20286]**
Mission Am. Coalition **[19813]**
Mission Builders Intl. **[19814]**
Mission: Moving Mountains **[20287]**
Mission: Moving Mountains **[IO]**
Natl. Assn. of Catholic Family Life Ministers
   [20288]
Natl. Assn. of Free Will Baptists **[19492]**
Natl. Assn. of Hispanic Priests of the USA **[19665]**
Natl. Campus Ministry Assn. **[19933]**
Natl. Coalition of Men's Ministries **[19816]**
Natl. Coun. of Churches **[19852]**
Natl. Coun. of Churches, Educ. and Leadership
   Ministries Commn. **[19935]**
Natl. Evangelization Teams **[19687]**
Natl. Network of Youth Ministries **[20641]**
Native Amer. Church of North Am. of the Cowlitz
   Indians **[19447]**

Paraclete **[20381]**
Pocket Testament League **[19529]**
Progressive, Radically Inclusive Student Ministry
   [19938]
St. Anthony's Guild **[20388]**
Samaritan's Purse **[20289]**
Soc. for the Increase of the Ministry **[20290]**
Soc. of Our Lady of the Most Holy Trinity **[19722]**
Soc. of St. Andrew **[20088]**
Survivors Network of Those Abused by Priests
   [13372]
United Christian Missionary Soc. **[19856]**
United Methodist Assn. of Hea. and Welfare
   Ministries **[14602]**
United Methodist Youth Org. **[20268]**
Wesleyan/Holiness Women Clergy **[20291]**
Wesleyan/Holiness Women Clergy **[IO]**
Women's Division of the Gen. Bd. of Global
   Ministries of the United Methodist Church
   [20269]
World Hope Intl. **[20292]**
World Hope Intl. **[IO]**
World Literature Ministries **[19832]**
Ministry; All Roads **[19564]**
Ministry; Amer. Acad. of **[19914]**
Ministry Assn; Assn. of Presbyterian Univ. Pastors
   and Campus **[★19933]**
Ministry Assn; Catholic Campus **[19595]**
Ministry Assn; Lutheran Outdoors **[★20231]**
Ministry Assn; Natl. Campus **[19933]**
Ministry Assn; Natl. Lutheran Outdoors **[20231]**
Ministry of Concern for Public Health - Address
   unknown since 2003.
Ministry Coordinators; Natl. Assn. of Lay **[★20204]**
Ministry/Folio; Baptist Women in **[19481]**
Ministry; Friends of Israel Gospel **[20010]**
Ministry; Good News Jail and Prison **[★11869]**
Ministry Gp; Natl. Coun. of Churches - Women in
   [20622]
Ministry of Hotels and Tourism **[IO]**, Yangon, Myan-
   mar
Ministry, Inc; CONTACT Tele **[★19865]**
Ministry; Jesuit Off. of Social **[★13172]**
Ministry; Liberty Godparent **[★12918]**
Ministry; Methodist Coun. on Youth **[★20268]**
Ministry; Natl. Apostolate for Inclusion **[20026]**
Ministry; Natl. Assn. for Lay **[20204]**
Ministry; Natl. Coun. of Churches Commn. on
   Women in **[★20622]**
Ministry; Natl. Farm Worker **[12594]**
Ministry in the Natl. Parks; A Christian **[19783]**
Ministry; New Ways **[20064]**
Ministry Org; Natl. Youth **[★20268]**
Ministry with Persons with Disabilities **[★20216]**
Ministry Strategy; Denominational **[★20561]**
Ministry of Teaching; Center for the **[19920]**
Ministry; United Methodist Coun. on Youth **[★20268]**
Ministry Women; Campus **[19918]**
Mink Assn; Great Lakes **[★4129]**
Mink Breeders Assn; Emba **[★4129]**
Minneapolis Grain Exchange **[4329]**, 400 S 4th St.,
   130 Grain Exchange Bldg., Minneapolis, MN
   55415, (612)321-7101
Minnesota Beer Wholesalers Assn. **[204]**, 701 4th
   Ave. S, Ste. 1710, Minneapolis, MN 55415,
   (612)604-4400
Minnesota - Crookston Alumni Assn; Univ. of **[18936]**
Minnesota Groundswell **[★16954]**
Minnesota; Natl. Soc. - First Families of **[21253]**
Minnesota North Stars Booster Club - Defunct.
Minor Breeds Conservancy; Amer. **[★4994]**
A Minor Consideration **[11826]**, 14530 Denker Ave.,
   Gardena, CA 90247
Minor Family Soc; Thomas **[★21071]**
Minor Found. for Major Challenges **[IO]**, Vika,
   Norway
Minor League Baseball **[★IO]**
Minor League Baseball **[★23116]**
Minor Metals Trade Assn. **[IO]**, London, United
   Kingdom
Minor Metals Traders Assn. **[★IO]**
Minor Soc; Thomas **[21071]**
Minorities
   Afghan Women's Assn. Intl. **[13416]**
   AFNA Natl. Educ. and Res. Fund **[8045]**

African Amer. Alliance for Homeownership **[1975]**
African Amer. Art Song Alliance **[10520]**
African-Amer. Assn. of Fitness Professionals
   [15957]
African Amer. Criminal Justice Soc. **[17359]**
African Amer. Environmentalist Assn. **[4529]**
African-American Female Entrepreneurs Alliance
   [4033]
African Amer. Holiday Assn. **[22974]**
African Amer. Literature and Culture Soc. **[8798]**
African Amer. Museum **[9352]**
African Amer. Post Traumatic Stress Disorder
   Assn. **[21276]**
African Amer. Visual Arts Assn. **[9409]**
African-Americans for Democracy **[16936]**
African Asian Latina Lesbians United **[17649]**
Alliance of Minority Medical Associations **[14607]**
Alliance of Minority Women for Bus. and Political
   Development **[2759]**
Alpha Iota Omicron **[24611]**
Amer. Assn. for Affirmative Action **[12066]**
Amer. Assn. of Blacks in Energy **[6936]**
Amer. Assn. of Minority Businesses **[2760]**
Amer. Citizens for Justice **[17083]**
Amer. Hea. and Beauty Aids Inst. **[1841]**
Amer. Indian Higher Educ. Consortium **[8935]**
Amer. Indian Philosophy Assn. **[19268]**
Amer. Indian Res. and Development **[8464]**
Amer. Indian Sci. and Engg. Soc. **[6987]**
Amer. Iranian Coun. **[17926]**
Amer. Jewish World Ser. **[12829]**
Amer. Muslim Alliance **[18083]**
Amer. Soc. for Jewish Heritage in Poland **[10273]**
Amer. Soc. for Muslim Advancement **[10245]**
Amer. Telugu Assn. **[9848]**
Andolan - Organizing South Asian Workers
   [24138]
APPEAL: Asian Pacific Partners for Empowerment
   and Leadership **[11760]**
Arab Amer. Assn. of Engineers and Architects
   [6467]
Asian Amer. Architects and Engineers **[6470]**
Asian Amer. Center for Justice of the Amer.
   Citizens for Justice **[17094]**
Asian Amer. Govt. Executives Network **[5704]**
Asian Amer. Journalists Assn. **[3088]**
Asian Amer. MultiTechnology Assn. **[1204]**
Asian Amer. Music Soc. **[10556]**
Asian Amer./Pacific Islander Nurses Assn. **[15463]**
Asian Amer. Real Estate Assn. **[3299]**
Asian Americans/Pacific Islanders in Philanthropy
   [12710]
Asian Pacific Americans for Progress **[17012]**
Asian and Pacific Islander Amer. Vote **[18345]**
Assn. for the Advancement of Mexican Americans
   [11763]
Assn. of African Amer. Financial Advisors **[1455]**
Assn. of Black Anthropologists **[6409]**
Assn. of Black Nursing Faculty **[8848]**
Assn. of Black Psychologists **[16138]**
Assn. of Black Sociologists **[7659]**
Assn. of Chinese Amer. Physicians **[15991]**
Assn. of Kannada Kootas of Am. **[19111]**
Assn. of Latina and Latino Anthropologists **[6410]**
Assn. of Minority Hea. Professions Schools **[8850]**
Assn. of Nepalis in the Americas **[19286]**
Assn. for the Stud. of African-American Life and
   History **[9356]**
Assn. for Women in Psychology **[16145]**
Assyrian Chaldean Athletics of North Am. **[23062]**
Bear Butte Intl. Alliance **[19446]**
Before Columbus Found. **[10416]**
Bhojpuri Assn. of North Am. **[10299]**
Bihar Assn. of North Am. **[10220]**
Black Alliance for Educational Options **[8322]**
Black Culinarian Alliance **[1122]**
Black and Indian Mission Off. **[19587]**
Black Mental Hea. Alliance **[15193]**
Black Methodists for Church Renewal **[20260]**
Black Veterans for Social Justice **[21289]**
Black Women in Church and Soc. **[20617]**
Black Women United for Action **[13423]**
Black World Found. **[9357]**
Brahman Samaj of North Am. **[9998]**
Catching the Dream **[8427]**

A star before a book entry number signifies that the name is not listed separately, but is mentioned within the entry.

Catholic Negro-Amer. Mission Bd. [19601]
Center for Advancement of Racial and Ethnic
  Equity [8887]
Center for Reflective Community Practice [17211]
Center for Third World Organizing [17099]
Champa Cultural Preservation Assn. of USA
  [11082]
Charles H. Wright Museum of African Amer. His-
  tory [9358]
Charlotte W. Newcombe Found. [12749]
Chinese Amer. Food Soc. [7092]
Chinese Amer. Semiconductor Professional Assn.
  [1208]
Chinese Law Soc. of Am. [5933]
Coalition of Asian Pacifics in Entertainment [1300]
Coalition of Black Trade Unionists [24202]
Conf. of Minority Public Administrators [6191]
Cong. of Natl. Black Churches [19890]
Coun. on Career for Minorities [8047]
Croatian Amer. Assn. [17868]
Croatian Amer. Bar Assn. [5489]
Delta Phi Omega Sorority [24705]
Delta Tau Lambda Sorority [24707]
Dialogue on Diversity [8888]
Diversity Info. Resources [2761]
Emerald Soc. of the Fed. Law Enforcement Agen-
  cies [19199]
Episcopal Women's Caucus [19956]
Equal Employment Advisory Coun. [12079]
Ethiopian Pharmacists Assn. in North Am. [15932]
Ethnic Minorities Development Assn. [IO]
Ethnic and Multicultural Info. Exchange Round-
  table [10354]
European-American Unity and Rights Org.
  [17114]
Executive Leadership Coun. [2762]
Fed. Hispanic Law Enforcement Officers Assn.
  [5969]
Fed. of Chinese Amer. and Chinese Canadian
  Medical Societies [13985]
Ford Motor Minority Dealers Assn. [413]
Gamma Alpha Omega Sorority [24599]
Gamma Gamma Chi Sorority [24711]
German Professional Women's Assn. [4039]
GesherCity [19183]
Gonja Assn. of North Am. [11779]
Hellenic Amer. Natl. Coun. [9995]
Helping Our Teen Girls in Real Life Situations
  [12261]
Hispanas Organized for Political Equality [17703]
Hispanic Amer. Police Command Officers Assn.
  [5970]
Hispanic Coun. on Intl. Relations [17869]
Hispanic Marketing and Commun. Assn. [2628]
Hispanic Neuropsychological Soc. [15388]
Hispanic Professional Women's Assn. [4041]
Hmong Natl. Development [17815]
Honor the Earth [19272]
Igorot Global Org. [10225]
Ijaw Natl. Alliance of the Americas [12639]
INCITE! Women of Color Against Violence
  [18788]
Indigenous Peoples Coun. on Biocolonialism
  [12407]
Indo-American Arts Coun. [9570]
INROADS [8749]
Inst. for Diversity in Hea. Mgt. [14704]
InterAmerican Travel Agents Soc. [3920]
Intercultural Cancer Coun. [13830]
Intl. Alumni Assn. of Shri Mahavir Jain Vidyalaya
  [19346]
Intl. Assn. of African-American Music [10613]
Intl. Assn. of Black Actuaries [2186]
Intl. Assn. of Hispanic Meeting Professionals
  [2684]
Intl. Fed. of Black Prides [12238]
Intl. Native Amer. Flute Assn. [10622]
Intl. Org. of Black Security Executives [3533]
Intl. Possibilities Unlimited [18642]
Iranian Amer. Bar Assn. [5504]
Iranian Amer. Tech. Coun. [2352]
Jack and Jill of Am. Found. [11703]
Jackie Robinson Found. [13491]
Joint Center for Political and Economic Stud.
  [7526]

Just Transition Alliance [24105]
Kappa Phi Gamma Sorority [24712]
Kiribati and Tungaru Assn. [IO]
Korean Amer. Soc. of Entrepreneurs [773]
Laotian Amer. Natl. Alliance [19192]
Laotian Amer. Soc. [19193]
Latin Amer. Art Song Alliance [10636]
Latino Amer. Mgt. Assn. [24288]
Latino Org. for Liver Awareness [14811]
Latinos in Info. Sciences and Tech. Assn. [7201]
Lawyers for One Am. [6028]
Leadership Enterprise for a Diverse Am. [9183]
Lebanese Amer. Professional Soc. [19205]
Leuva Patidar Samaj of USA [10221]
Lithuanian-American Bar Assn. [5507]
Malayalee Engineers Assn. in North Am. [7026]
Mgt. Educ. Alliance [8029]
Mexican Amer. Music Assn. [10647]
Milan Cultural Assn. [10222]
Milton S. Eisenhower Found. [11839]
Minorities in Agriculture, Natural Resources and
  Related Sciences [10486]
Minority Corporate Counsel Assn. [5615]
Minority Hea. Professions Found. [18080]
Minority Peace Corps Assn. [18261]
Minority Student Achievement Network [8401]
Minority Women In Sci. [7615]
Multicultural Educ., Training, and Advocacy
  [11625]
Multicultural Golf Assn. of Am. [23455]
Muslim Amer. Soc. [20440]
Natl. Action Coun. for Minorities in Engg. [8369]
Natl. Adoption Center [11254]
Natl. African Amer. Drug Policy Coalition [17440]
Natl. African-American Insurance Assn. [2202]
Natl. Alliance of Black Interpreters [3854]
Natl. Alliance of Black School Educators [9217]
Natl. Alliance of Vietnamese Amer. Ser. Agencies
  [19423]
Natl. Amer. Arab Nurses Assn. [15490]
Natl. Asian Amer. Pacific Islander Mental Hea.
  Assn. [15215]
Natl. Asian Amer. Soc. of Accountants [42]
Natl. Assn. for the Advancement of Colored
  People Legal Defense and Educational Fund
  [17130]
Natl. Assn. for the Advancement of Haitian
  Descendents [19097]
Natl. Assn. of Black Accountants [44]
Natl. Assn. of Black Citizens Action [16942]
Natl. Assn. of Black Hotel Owners, Operators and
  Developers [1950]
Natl. Assn. of Black Journalists [3129]
Natl. Assn. of Black Owned Broadcasters [568]
Natl. Assn. of Blacks in Criminal Justice [11877]
Natl. Assn. for Direct Care Workers of Color
  [14709]
Natl. Assn. for the Educ. of African Amer. Children
  with Learning Disabilities [12493]
Natl. Assn. for Equal Opportunity in Higher Educ.
  [8109]
Natl. Assn. of Hispanic Journalists [3130]
Natl. Assn. of Hispanic Nurses [15494]
Natl. Assn. of Hispanic Priests of the USA [19665]
Natl. Assn. of Latina Leaders [2411]
Natl. Assn. of Latino Independent Producers
  [1390]
Natl. Assn. of Medical Minority Educators [8868]
Natl. Assn. of Minority Women in Business [2766]
Natl. Assn. for Multi-Ethnicity in Communications
  [2757]
Natl. Assn. for Multicultural Educ. [8582]
Natl. Assn. of Multicultural Engg. Prog. Advocates
  [8370]
Natl. Assn. of Muslim Lawyers [5511]
Natl. Assn. for the Stud. and Performance of
  African-American Music [8922]
Natl. Assn. of Vietnamese Nurses [15504]
Natl. Bar Assn. [5515]
Natl. Black Assn. for Speech-Language and Hear-
  ing [16448]
Natl. Black Bridal Assn. [535]
Natl. Black Catholic Clergy Caucus [19669]
Natl. Black Farmers Assn. [12189]
Natl. Black Herstory Task Force [11089]

Natl. Black Justice Coalition [18643]
Natl. Black Law Students Assn. [8771]
Natl. Black MBA Assn. [8035]
Natl. Black McDonald's Operators Assn. [1955]
Natl. Black Nurses Assn. [15505]
Natl. Black Public Relations Soc. [3194]
Natl. Black Sisters' Conf. [19671]
Natl. Brotherhood of Skiers [23752]
Natl. Center for Urban Ethnic Affairs [11753]
Natl. Coalition of Advocates for Students [8328]
Natl. Coalition of Black Meeting Planners [2687]
Natl. Coalition of Ethnic Minority Nurse Associa-
  tions [15507]
Natl. Comm. for Amish Religious Freedom
  [19448]
Natl. Community for Latino Leadership [19203]
Natl. Cong. of Black Women [6119]
Natl. Cong. of Vietnamese Americans [19425]
Natl. Consortium of Arts and Letters for Histori-
  cally Black Colls. and Universities [8111]
Natl. Consortium for Black Professional Develop-
  ment [8049]
Natl. Coun. of Asian Amer. Bus. Associations
  [774]
Natl. Coun. of Asian Pacific Americans [17013]
Natl. Coun. of Urban Indian Hea. [15277]
Natl. Economic Assn. [6888]
Natl. Fed. of Croatian Americans [17362]
Natl. Fed. of Hispanic Owned Newspapers [3240]
Natl. Haitian Soc. [17817]
Natl. Hispanic Bus. Assn. [8039]
Natl. Iranian Amer. Coun. [19151]
Natl. Latina/Latino Law Student Assn. [17996]
Natl. Latino Alliance for the Elimination of
  Domestic Violence [12037]
Natl. Latino Coun. on Alcohol and Tobacco
  Prevention [12269]
Natl. Latino Officers Assn. [5921]
Natl. Legal Sanctuary for Community Advance-
  ment [6015]
Natl. Medical Assn. [15176]
Natl. Medical Fellowships [8871]
Natl. Minority AIDS Coun. [13580]
Natl. Mobilization Against Sweatshops [17975]
Natl. MultiCultural Inst. [11829]
Natl. Network for Minority Women in Sci. [7350]
Natl. Off. for Black Catholics [19691]
Natl. Org. of African Americans in Housing
  [12331]
Natl. Org. for Mexican Amer. Rights [17709]
Natl. Org. for People of Color Against Suicide
  [13289]
Natl. Org. for the Professional Advancement of
  Black Chemists and Chem. Engineers [6689]
Natl. Podiatric Medical Assn. [16047]
Natl. Soc. of Black Engineers [7034]
Natl. Soc. of Hispanic MBAs [754]
Natl. Soc. of Hispanic Physicists [7505]
Natl. Soc. for Hispanic Professionals [1908]
Natl. South Asian Bar Assn. [6018]
Natl. Tribal Child Support Assn. [11713]
Natl. Urban Fellows [18775]
Natl. Urban League [17138]
Native Amer. Fatherhood and Families Assn.
  [12681]
Native Amer. Leadership Alliance [20455]
Native Amer. Water Assn. [4012]
Native Financial Educ. Coalition [8442]
Negro Airmen Intl. [6380]
Nepalese Americas Coun. [19287]
Nepali Amer. Friendship Assn. [19288]
New Am. Alliance [1169]
New Zealand Fed. of Ethnic Councils [IO]
Nigerian Lawyers Assn. [5526]
Nigerian Social Workers Assn. [24142]
North Am. Taiwanese Engineers' Assn. [7036]
North Amer. Alliance for the Advancement of Na-
  tive Peoples [12631]
North Amer. Sankethi Assn. [9802]
North Amer. South Asian Bar Assn. [5527]
North Amer. South Asian Law Student Assn.
  [8773]
NuBian Exchange News [2770]
Off. for the Advancement of Public Black Colleges
  of the Natl. Assn. of State Universities and
  Land-Grant Colleges [8112]

Reference to "IO" in place of a book number signifies that the association may be found in the 45th edition of International Organizations.

Off. of Women in Higher Educ., Amer. Coun. on Educ. [9324]
Oper. HOPE, Inc. [11787]
Org. of Black Airline Pilots [164]
Org. of Black Screenwriters [1323]
Pacific Islanders in Communications [10455]
Plan of Action for Challenging Times [8331]
PolicyLink [18276]
Polish Amer. Golf Assn. [23462]
Poverty and Race Res. Action Coun. [12781]
Praxis Proj. [17204]
Puerto Rican Legal Defense and Educ. Fund [17149]
Punjabi-American Cultural Assn. [10223]
Quality Educ. for Minorities Network [8303]
Rainbow/PUSH Coalition [13185]
Salvadoran Amer. Leadership and Educational Fund [17484]
SER - Jobs for Progress Natl. [12100]
Serbian Bar Assn. of Am. [5531]
Sigma Beta Rho Fraternity [24656]
Sikh Amer. Legal Defense and Educ. Fund [18600]
Sino-American Pharmaceutical Professionals Assn. [15951]
SisterSong Women of Color Reproductive Hea. Collective [18826]
Slavic Heritage Coalition [10969]
Soc. for the Anal. of African-American Public Hea. Issues [16253]
Soc. of Hispanic Professional Engineers [7042]
Soc. for Indonesian-Americans [19116]
Soc. for the Psychological Stud. of Ethnic Minority Issues [16179]
Somali Family Care Network [19392]
South Asian Amer. Voting Youth [18366]
Sphinx Org. [10710]
Student African Amer. Brotherhood [19444]
Swedish-American Bar Assn. [5532]
Swiss-American Coun. of Women [18815]
Taiwanese Amer. Lawyers Assn. [5533]
Turkish Amer. Alliance for Fairness [19410]
Turkish Coalition of Am. [18754]
Ugbajo Itsekiri USA [19260]
Ulster-Scots Soc. of Am. [21154]
Union of North Amer. Vietnamese Students Assn. [19426]
United Black Fund [12204]
United Church of Christ Justice and Witness Ministries [20608]
United Negro Coll. Fund [8437]
U.S. Hispanic Chamber of Commerce [24327]
USA Sanatan Sports and Cultural Assn. [23787]
Uttaranchal Assn. of North Am. [10219]
Voices in the Wilderness [18253]
Welfare Res., Inc. [13193]
Wimbum Cultural and Development Assn. in the U.S.A. [9344]
World Pen Pals [8636]
Youth Organizations U.S.A. [13523]
Minorities in Agriculture, Natural Resources and Related Sciences [10486], PO Box 381017, Germantown, TN 38183-1017; (901)757-9700
Minorities in Cable - Defunct.
Minorities; Coun. on Career for [8047]
Minorities; Coun. on Career Development for [★8047]
Minorities in Engg; Natl. Advisory Coun. for [★8369]
Minorities in Engg; Natl. Consortium for Graduate Degrees for [★8372]
Minorities in Engg. and Sci; Natl. Consortium for Graduate Degrees for [8372]
Minorities; Intl. Fed. for the Protection of the Rights of Ethnic, Religious, Linguistic and Other [17768]
Minorities Intl. Network for Trade - Address unknown since 2004.
Minorities in Media - Address unknown since 2007.
Minorities Network; Quality Educ. for [8303]
Minorities Proj; Quality Educ. for [★8303]
Minorities in Sci. and Engg; Natl. Consortium for Graduate Degrees for [★8372]
Minority Achievement Program - Defunct.
Minority AIDS Coun.; Natl. [13580]
Minority Architects; Natl. Org. of [6478]
Minority Business
African Amer. Alliance for Homeownership [1975]

Airport Minority Advisory Coun. [2758]
Alliance of Minority Women for Bus. and Political Development [2759]
Amer. Assn. of Minority Businesses [2760]
Asian Amer. Real Estate Assn. [3299]
Diversity Info. Resources [2761]
Executive Leadership Coun. [2762]
Hispanic Marketing and Commun. Assn. [2628]
Hispanic Professional Women's Assn. [4041]
Minority Bus. Enterprise Legal Defense and Educ. Fund [2763]
Natl. Assn. of Investment Companies [2764]
Natl. Assn. of Latina Leaders [2411]
Natl. Assn. of Minority Auto. Dealers [2765]
Natl. Assn. of Minority Women in Business [2766]
Natl. Business League [2767]
Natl. Minority Bus. Coun. [2768]
Natl. Minority Supplier Development Coun. [2769]
NuBian Exchange News [2770]
U.S. Hispanic Chamber of Commerce [24327]
Minority Bus. Campaign; Natl. [★2761]
Minority Bus. Directories; Natl. [★2761]
Minority Bus. Enterprise Legal Defense and Educ. Fund [2763], 1100 Mercantile Ln., Ste. 115-A, Largo, MD 20774, (301)583-4648
Minority Business Information Inst. - Defunct.
Minority Business Opportunity Comm. - Defunct.
Minority Coalition - Address unknown since 1995.
Minority Contractors of Am; Assoc. [★1036]
Minority Corporate Counsel Assn. [5615], 1111 Pennsylvania Ave. NW, Washington, DC 20004, (202)739-5901
Minority Dealers Assn; Ford, Lincoln, Mercury [★413]
Minority Dealers Assn; Ford Motor [413]
Minority Educators; Natl. Assn. of Medical [8868]
Minority Engg. Educ. Effort [★8369]
Minority Engg. Students; Natl. Fund for [★8369]
Minority Enterprise Small Bus. Investment Companies; Amer. Assn. of [★2764]
Minority Golf Assn. of Am. [★23455]
Minority Graphic Arts Org. - Address unknown since 1989.
Minority Hea. Assn; Natl. [14590]
Minority Hea. Professionals Found. [★18080]
Minority Hea. Professions Found. [18080], 100 Edgewood Ave., Ste. 1020, Atlanta, GA 30303, (678)904-4217
Minority Hea. Professions Schools; Assn. of [8850]
Minority Media Executives; Natl. Assn. of [882]
Minority Peace Corps Assn. [18261], PO Box 244, New York, NY 10014, (212)352-5452
Minority Political Families USA; Natl. Assn. of [18357]
Minority Purchasing Coun; Natl. [★2769]
Minority Res. Center - Defunct.
Minority Rights Gp. Intl. [IO], London, United Kingdom
Minority Rights Group U.S.A. - Defunct.
Minority Student Achievement Network [8401], 1600 Dodge Ave., Evanston, IL 60204, (847)424-7185
Minority Students
Ability Soc. [IO]
Active Living Alliance for Canadians with a Disability [IO]
Alberta Assn. for Community Living [IO]
Am. Coun. on Educ., Center for Advancement of Racial and Ethnic Equity [8889]
Amer. Indian Bus. Leaders [2830]
A Better Chance [8321]
Intl. Alumni Assn. of Shri Mahavir Jain Vidyalaya [19346]
Jack and Jill of Am. Found. [11703]
Leadership Enterprise for a Diverse Am. [9183]
Learning Disabilities Assn. of Alberta [IO]
Learning Disabilities Assn. of Alberta - Calgary Chap. [IO]
Learning Disabilities Assn. of Alberta - Edmonton Chap. [IO]
Learning Disabilities Assn. of Alberta - Red Deer Chap. [IO]
Learning Disabilities Assn. of Halton [IO]
Learning Disabilities Assn. of Kingston [IO]
Learning Disabilities Assn. of Kitchener - Waterloo [IO]

Learning Disabilities Assn. of Lambton County [IO]
Learning Disabilities Assn. - London Region [IO]
Learning Disabilities Assn. of Manitoba [IO]
Learning Disabilities Assn. - Mississauga Chap. [IO]
Learning Disabilities Assn. of New Brunswick [IO]
Learning Disabilities Assn. of Newfoundland and Labrador [IO]
Learning Disabilities Assn. - North Peel Chap. [IO]
Learning Disabilities Assn. of Nova Scotia [IO]
Learning Disabilities Assn. of the NWT [IO]
Learning Disabilities Assn. of Ontario [IO]
Learning Disabilities Assn. of Ontario - Durham Region [IO]
Learning Disabilities Assn. of Ontario - Niagara Chap. [IO]
Learning Disabilities Assn. of Ontario - Thunder Bay Chap. [IO]
Learning Disabilities Assn. of Ottawa - Carleton [IO]
Learning Disabilities Assn. of PEI [IO]
Learning Disabilities Assn. of Quebec [IO]
Learning Disabilities Assn. of Quebec - Laval Sect. [IO]
Learning Disabilities Assn. of Saskatchewan [IO]
Learning Disabilities Assn. of Saskatchewan - Prince Albert Br. [IO]
Learning Disabilities Assn. of Saskatchewan - Regina Br. [IO]
Learning Disabilities Assn. of Sault Ste. Marie [IO]
Learning Disabilities Assn. of Simcoe County [IO]
Learning Disabilities Assn. - South Vancouver Island Chap. [IO]
Learning Disabilities Assn. of Sudbury [IO]
Learning Disabilities Assn. of Toronto District [IO]
Learning Disabilities Assn. of Vancouver [IO]
Learning Disabilities Assn. of Wellington County [IO]
Learning Disabilities Assn. of York Region [IO]
Learning Disabilities Assn. of Yukon Territory [IO]
Mgt. Educ. Alliance [8029]
Minorities in Agriculture, Natural Resources and Related Sciences [10486]
Minority Student Achievement Network [8401]
Natl. Hispanic Bus. Assn. [8039]
Natl. Latina/Latino Law Student Assn. [17996]
North Amer. South Asian Law Student Assn. [8773]
Student African Amer. Brotherhood [19444]
Turkish Physiotherapy Assn. [IO]
Union of North Amer. Vietnamese Students Assn. [19426]
Minority Trans. Officials; Conf. of [3866]
Minority Women In Sci. [7615], c/o Amer. Assn. for the Advancement of Sci., Directorate for Educ. and Human Resources Programs, 1200 New York Ave. NW, Washington, DC 20005, (202)326-7019
Minority Women in Sci; Natl. Network of [★7615]
Minsaki Katende Found. [IO], Kampala, Uganda
Minute Women of the U.S.A. - Address unknown since 1995.
Minuteman Civil Defense Corps [17077], 6501 Greenway Pkwy., Ste. 103-640, Scottsdale, AZ 85254, (520)829-3112
Mir Pace Intl. [12872], 1173 Nantasket Ave., Unit C-6, Hull, MA 02045, (781)925-0090
Mir Pace Intl. [IO], Hull, MA, United States
MIRA [IO], Nuneaton, United Kingdom
Miracle Flights for Kids [14319], 2756 N Green Valley Pkwy., No. 115, Green Valley, NV 89014-2120, (702)261-0494
Miracles; Found. for a Course in [20571]
Miracles of Hope Network [11623], 12064 Ulrich Rd., Losantville, IN 47354, (765)381-1112
Miracles of Hope Network [IO], Las Vegas, NV, United States
Miraculous Medal; Assn. of the [19577]
Miraculous Medal; Central Assn. of the [19609]
Mirage Gp. [10864], PO Box 803282, Santa Clarita, CA 91380-3282, (661)799-0694
Miresevini ne Dhomen e Tregtise dhe Industrise se Tiranes [★IO]
Mirinda's Fan Club - Address unknown since 1995.
Mirrer Yeshiva Central Inst. [12477], 1791-5 Ocean Pkwy., Brooklyn, NY 11223, (718)645-0536

A star before a book entry number signifies that the name is not listed separately, but is mentioned within the entry.

Mirrer Yeshiva Central Inst. [IO], Brooklyn, NY, United States
Mirror Class Assn; U.S. [23229]
Mirror Mfrs; North Amer. Assn. of [★1728]
Miscarriage
Amer. Pregnancy Assn. [15588]
Assn. for Recognizing the Life of Stillborns [12661]
Fairview Pregnancy and Newborn Loss Information [12668]
Miscarriage Assn. [IO]
Miscarriage Assn. of Ireland [IO]
Miscarriage Assn. [IO], Wakefield, United Kingdom
Miscarriage Assn. of Ireland [IO], Dublin, Ireland
Miscarriage Infant Death and Stillbirth Support Gp. [16540], PO Box 6345, Parsippany, NJ 07054, (973)884-1016
Miso Music Portugal [IO], Cascais, Portugal
Miss Am. Org. [22135], 222 New Rd., Ste. 700, Linwood, NJ 08221, (609)653-8700
Miss Mom/Mister Mom - Address unknown since 2001.
Missao Para o Interior da Africa [★IO]
Missile Assn; Model [★22650]
Missile Defense Advocacy Alliance [17382], 515 King St., Ste. 320, Alexandria, VA 22314, (703)299-0060
Missile and Space Coun. - Defunct.
Missile, Space and Range Pioneers - Address unknown since 2001.
Missileers; Assn. of Air Force [20662]
Missing Children
Amer. Assn. for Lost Children [12607]
Amer. Rescue Dog Assn. [12889]
Assn. of Missing and Exploited Children's Organizations [12601]
The Child Connection [12602]
Child Find of Am. [11566]
Children's Rights of America [11582]
Commn. on Missing and Exploited Children [11586]
Comm. for Missing Children [12603]
Find the Children [11591]
Hug-A-Tree and Survive [11600]
Jacob Wetterling Found. [11608]
Natl. Center for Missing and Exploited Children [11630]
Nationwide Patrol [11640]
Outpost for Hope [12610]
Polly Klaas Found. [12604]
Sales Assn. of the Chem. Indus. [819]
Search Reports, Inc./Central Registry of the Missing [12611]
Take Root [12605]
Team H.O.P.E (Help Offering Parents Empowerment) [12606]
Vanished Children's Alliance [11659]
Missing Children of America - Address unknown since 1999.
Missing Children Center - Defunct.
Missing Children Network - Defunct.
Missing Children...HELP Center - Defunct. Missing-Missing and Exploited Children; Commn. on [11586]
Missing and Exploited Children; Natl. Center for [11630]
Missing-in-Action
Natl. League of Families of Amer. Prisoners and Missing in Southeast Asia [18081]
Natl. League of Families of Amer. Prisoners and Missing in Southeast Asia [IO]
Rolling Thunder [21265]
VietNow Natl. [13359]
Missing People - Worldwide - Address unknown since 1999.
Missing Persons
Amer. Assn. for Lost Children [12607]
Amer. Rescue Dog Assn. [12889]
Assn. of Missing and Exploited Children's Organizations [12601]
Assn. of Missing and Exploited Children's Organizations [IO]
Chicos Perdidos in Argentina and Latin Am. and Europe [IO]
The Child Connection [IO]

The Child Connection [12602]
Child Find Canada [IO]
Comm. for Missing Children [IO]
Comm. for Missing Children [12603]
Doe Network [12608]
Doe Network [IO]
Intl. Commn. on Missing Persons [IO]
Intl. Fed. of Family Associations of Missing Persons from Armed Conflicts [IO]
Intl. Fed. of Family Associations of Missing Persons from Armed Conflicts [12609]
Intl. Tracing Ser. [IO]
Latin Amer. Fed. of Associations for Relatives of the Detained-Disappeared [IO]
Mothers of the Plaza de Mayo [IO]
Natl. Centre for Missing Children [IO]
North Am. Missing Children Assn. [IO]
Outpost for Hope [12610]
Prisoners Abroad [IO]
Reunite - Intl. Child Abduction Centre [IO]
Search Reports, Inc./Central Registry of the Missing [12611]
Sons and Daughters In Touch [12599]
Take Root [12605]
Team H.O.P.E (Help Offering Parents Empowerment) [12606]
Missing Pet Partnership [12707], PO Box 2457, Clovis, CA 93613-2457, (559)292-4385
Missing Teens and Young Adults - Defunct.
Missiological Soc; Evangelical [20334]
Missiology; Amer. Soc. of [20297]
Mission
ABW Ministries [19468]
Advancing Churches in Missions Commitment [20293]
Advent Christian Gen. Conf. of Am. [19442]
Aetherius Soc. [20568]
Africa - Europe Faith and Justice Network [IO]
Africa Inland Mission Intl. [IO]
Africa Inland Mission Intl. [20294]
Africa Inland Mission Intl. - Brazil [IO]
Africa Inland Mission Intl. - Canada [IO]
Africa Inland Mission Intl. - France [IO]
Africa Inland Mission Intl. Hong Kong Comm. [IO]
Africa Inland Mission Intl. - Netherlands [IO]
Africa Inland Mission Intl. - South Africa [IO]
Africa Inland Mission Intl. - United Kingdom [IO]
Africa Inland Mission New Zealand [IO]
African Enterprise Canada [IO]
Agricultural Missions [20295]
AIM Intl. - Australia [IO]
All-Ukrainian Evangelical Baptist Fellowship [19469]
Amer. and Foreign Christian Union [19762]
Amer. Missionary Fellowship [20296]
Amer. Soc. of Missiology [20297]
AMF Intl. [19988]
AMG Intl. [20298]
AMG Intl. [IO]
Apostleship of the Sea in the U.S.A. [19570]
Apostolate for Family Consecrations [19571]
ARISE Intl. Mission [20299]
ARISE Intl. Mission [IO]
Armenian Church Youth Org. of Am. [19458]
Armenian Missionary Assn. of Am. [19459]
ASGM [19506]
Associate Missionaries of the Assumption [20300]
Associate Missionaries of the Assumption [IO]
Assoc. Comm. of Friends on Indian Affairs [20039]
Assn. of Baptists for World Evangelism [19472]
Assn. of Marian Helpers [19576]
Assn. of North Amer. Missions [20301]
Assn. of Professors of Mission [20302]
Assn. of Reformed Baptist Churches of Am. [19473]
Assn. of Romanian Catholics of America [19579]
Avant Ministries [20303]
Awana Clubs Intl. [20639]
Baptist Bible Fellowship Intl. [19477]
Baptist Joint Comm. for Religious Liberty [19479]
Baptist Mid-Missions [19480]
Baptist World Alliance [19482]
BCM Intl. [19508]
Berean Bible Soc. [19509]

Bethany Intl. Missions [20304]
Bethany Intl. Missions [IO]
Bethlehem Mission Immensee [IO]
Bibles For The World [IO]
Bibles For The World [20305]
Biblical Ministries Worldwide [19991]
BLI [19512]
Bd. of Intl. Ministries [19483]
Bread on the Waters [19993]
Brethren in Christ World Missions [20306]
Brethren in Christ World Missions [IO]
Brethren Church Missionary Ministries [IO]
Brethren Church Missionary Ministries [20307]
Bruderhof Communities [20481]
Bur. of Catholic Indian Missions [19591]
Cabrini Mission Corps [20308]
Call and Response [20309]
CAM Intl. [20310]
CAM Intl. [IO]
Campus Crusade for Christ Intl. [19994]
Canadian Baptist Ministries [IO]
Capuchin-Franciscans (Province of Saint Joseph) [19594]
Catholic Campus Ministry Assn. [19595]
Catholic Church Extension Soc. of the U.S.A. [19596]
Catholic Comm. of Appalachia [20311]
Catholic Negro-Amer. Mission Bd. [19601]
Catholic Network of Volunteer Ser. [19602]
Catholic Pamphlet Soc. of the U.S. [19603]
CCVI Incarnate Word Missionaries - Congregation of the Sisters of Charity of the Incarnate Word [19607]
Ce.L.I.M. Milano Volunteers for Intl. Ser. [IO]
Center for Applied Res. in the Apostolate [19608]
Central Bur., Catholic Central Union of Am. [19610]
Champions for Life Intl. [19996]
Children Intl. [20312]
Children Intl. [IO]
Chinese Christian Mission [20313]
CHOSEN [12516]
Christ for the Nations [20314]
Christ for the Nations [IO]
Christ Truth Ministries [19514]
CHRISTAR [20315]
CHRISTAR [IO]
Christian Aid Mission [IO]
Christian Aid Mission [20316]
Christian Aid Mission - Canada [IO]
Christian Chiropractors Assn. [19773]
Christian Forum Res. Found. [20560]
Christian Found. for Children and Aging [13159]
Christian Literature and Bible Center [20317]
Christian Literature and Bible Center [IO]
Christian Medical and Dental Associations [20238]
Christian Mission for the Deaf [20318]
Christian Missionary Fellowship [20319]
Christian Missionary Fellowship [IO]
Christian Missions in Many Lands [20320]
Christian Pilots Assn. [20321]
Christian TV Mission [19536]
Christians for Peace in El Salvador [20322]
The Christophers [19611]
Church of the Brethren Gen. Bd. Global Mission Partnership [19535]
Church of God World Missions [20323]
Church of God World Missions [IO]
Church Mission Soc. [IO]
Church Periodical Club [19949]
Church Planting Intl. [20324]
Church Planting Intl. [IO]
Church of Sweden Mission [IO]
Claretian Volunteers and Lay Missionaries [19612]
Comm. on Missionary Evangelism [20001]
Commun. Commn. [19537]
Community of Celebration [19790]
Concordia Gospel Outreach [20214]
Congregation of Sisters of Saint Agnes [19618]
Conservative Baptist Assn. of Am. [19485]
Continental Baptist Missions [19486]
Crosier Missions [20325]
Crosier Missions [IO]
Crossworld [IO]

Reference to "IO" in place of a book number signifies that the association may be found in the 45th edition of International Organizations.

Crossworld [20326]
Danish Missionary Coun. [IO]
Domestic/Foreign Missionary Soc. of the
    Protestant Episcopal Church [IO]
Domestic/Foreign Missionary Soc. of the
    Protestant Episcopal Church [20327]
Dominican Mission Found. [20328]
Dominican Volunteers USA [20329]
EAPE/Campolo Ministries - Evangelical Assn. for
    the Promotion of Educ. [20330]
EAPE/Campolo Ministries - Evangelical Assn. for
    the Promotion of Educ. [IO]
Episcopal Evangelical Educ. Soc. [19955]
The Evangelical Alliance Mission [20331]
Evangelical Fellowship of Mission Agencies
    [20332]
Evangelical Free Church of Am. - Intl. Mission
    [20333]
Evangelical Free Church of Am. - Intl. Mission
    [IO]
Evangelical Friends Intl. - North Amer. Region
    [20040]
Evangelical Missiological Soc. [20334]
Evangelism and Home Missions Assn. [20006]
Evangelism and Missions Info. Ser. [20335]
Evangelistic Faith Missions [20336]
Evangelistic Faith Missions [IO]
Evangelize China Fellowship [IO]
Evangelize China Fellowship [20337]
Family Life Mission [IO]
Fed. of Protestant Welfare Agencies [20482]
Fellowship Intl. Mission [20338]
Fellowship Intl. Mission [IO]
Fellowship of Missions [20339]
Found. for Christian Theology [19960]
Found. of Compassionate Amer. Samaritans
    [20340]
Found. of Compassionate Amer. Samaritans [IO]
Friends of the Western Buddhist Order [19551]
Gen. Assn. of Regular Baptist Churches [19489]
Gen. Bd. of Church and Soc. of the United
    Methodist Church [20263]
Glenmary Res. Center [19628]
Global Economic Outreach [20341]
Global Economic Outreach [IO]
Global MissionAir [20487]
Global Teams [19961]
Global Univ. [19802]
Gospel Literature Intl. [20342]
Gospel Literature Intl. [IO]
Gospel Recordings [20343]
HCJB World Radio [20344]
HCJB World Radio [IO]
Hea. Ministries [20241]
Helps Intl. Ministries [20345]
Helps Intl. Ministries [IO]
Holy Childhood Assn. [19632]
Holy Cross Foreign Mission Soc. [19633]
Humility of Mary Ser. [19636]
IFCA Intl. [19849]
IHM Volunteer Prog. of the Sisters, Servants of
    the Immaculate Heart of Mary [20346]
Independent Bd. for Presbyterian Foreign Mis-
    sions [20467]
Inst. of Apostolic Oblates [19638]
Inter Varsity Christian Fellowship [20347]
Interact Ministries [20348]
Interact Ministries [IO]
Interchurch Medical Assistance [20242]
Interdenominational Foreign Missions Assn.
    [20349]
Intl. Assn. for Mission Stud. [IO]
Intl. Bd. of Jewish Missions [20014]
Intl. Catholic Deaf Assn. - U.S. Sect. [19641]
Intl. Christian Media Commn. [19538]
Intl. Convention of Faith Ministries [19807]
Intl. Lutheran Deaf Assn. [20217]
Intl. Mission Bd. [20350]
Intl. Mission Bd. [IO]
Intl. Order of Saint Luke the Physician [20499]
InterServe U.S.A. [20351]
InterServe U.S.A. [IO]
Irish Missionary Union [IO]
Islamic Correctional Reunion Assn. [20105]
Jesuit Conf. [19643]

Jesuit Volunteer Corps: Northwest [19644]
John La Farge Inst. [19645]
Lasallian Volunteers [20352]
Latin Am. Mission [20353]
Latin Am. Mission [IO]
Lay Mission-Helpers Assn. [19648]
Laymen's Home Missionary Movement [20018]
League of St. Dymphna [19650]
Lithuanian Catholic Religious Aid [19653]
Little Flower Mission League [19654]
Lutheran Bible Translators [19524]
Lutheran Mission Societies [20225]
Lutheran Volunteer Corps [20228]
Lutheran Women's Missionary League [20229]
MAP Intl. [20243]
Mariannhill Mission Soc. [19655]
Maryheart Crusaders [19657]
Maryknoll Fathers and Bros. [19658]
Maryknoll Mission Assn. of the Faithful [20354]
Maryknoll Mission Assn. of the Faithful [IO]
Maryknoll Sisters of Saint Dominic [20355]
Media Associates Intl. [19981]
Medical Mission Sisters [20356]
Medical Mission Sisters [IO]
Medical Missions Response [20246]
Men for Missions Intl. [20357]
Men for Missions Intl. [IO]
Mennonite Voluntary Ser. [20251]
Mission Advanced Res. and Commun. Center
    [20358]
Mission Aviation Fellowship [20359]
Mission Builders Intl. [19814]
Mission Doctors Assn. [12532]
Mission to Haiti [12267]
Mission Services Assn. [20360]
Mission Training Intl. [20361]
Mission Training Intl. [IO]
Mission to the World [20468]
Missionary Church [20362]
Missionary Church [IO]
Missionary Gospel Fellowship [20363]
Missionary Sisters of St. Peter Claver [20364]
Missionary Sisters of the Soc. of Mary - Marist
    Missionary Sisters [20365]
Missionary Soc. of Saint Columban [19662]
Missionary Soc. of Saint Paul the Apostle [19663]
Missionary TECH Team [20366]
Missionary Vehicle Assn. [20367]
Missions Door [19491]
Missions Intl. [20037]
Moody Bible Inst. [20368]
More Light Presbyterians for Lesbian, Gay,
    Bisexual and Transgender Concerns [20063]
Morris Cerullo World Evangelism [20025]
Mustard Seed Found. [20369]
Narramore Christian Found. [19815]
Natl. Assn. of Free Will Baptists [19492]
Natl. Baptist Convention, U.S.A. [19493]
Natl. Catholic Women's Union [19678]
Natl. Christ Child Soc. [19679]
Natl. Christian Life Community of the U.S.A.
    [19680]
Natl. Coun. of Catholic Women [19684]
Natl. Coun. of Churches of Christ in the U.S.A.
    [19905]
Natl. Cursillo Movement [19685]
Natl. Ghost Ranch Found. [20469]
Natl. Lutheran Outdoors Ministry Assn. [20231]
Natl. Religious Broadcasters [19539]
Natl. Ser. Committee/Chariscenter USA [19693]
Nations Ministries [20370]
Nazarene Missions Intl. [20371]
Nazarene Missions Intl. [IO]
Neighborhood Bible Stud. [19526]
New Hope Intl. [20372]
New Hope Intl. [IO]
New Life League Intl. [IO]
New Life League Intl. [20373]
New Tribes Mission [20374]
New Tribes Mission [IO]
New Wineskins Missionary Network [20375]
North Am. Indigenous Ministries [20376]
Northern Far East Returned Missionaries Assn.
    [20504]
O.C. Intl. [20377]

O.C. Intl. [IO]
OMF Intl. - Singapore [IO]
OMF Intl. - USA [IO]
OMF Intl. - USA [20378]
OMS Intl. [20379]
OMS Intl. [IO]
Our Little Bros. and Sisters [20380]
Paraclete [20381]
Paulist Memorial Soc. [19699]
Paulist Natl. Catholic Evangelization Assn.
    [19700]
Pentecostal Assemblies of the World [20463]
Pentecostal Charismatic Churches of North Am.
    [20464]
Pilgrim Fellowship [20382]
Pocket Testament League [19529]
Pontifical Coun. for the Pastoral Care of Migrants
    and Itinerant People [IO]
Pontifical Mission Societies in the U.S. [19703]
Presbyterian Evangelistic Fellowship [20471]
Presbyterian Frontier Fellowship [20383]
Presbyterian Lay Comm. [20472]
Presbyterian Men [20473]
Presbyterian-Reformed Ministries Intl. [20474]
Presbyterian Women [20475]
Prison Fellowship Scotland [IO]
Prison Mission Assn. [20384]
Pro Sanctity Movement [19705]
Red Sea Team Intl. [20385]
Red Sea Team Intl. [IO]
Response-Ability [20386]
Revival Fires (Christian Evangelizers Assn.)
    [20031]
Romanian Missionary Soc. [20387]
Rosedale Mennonite Missions [20253]
Royal Natl. Mission to Deep Sea Fishermen [IO]
Sacred Heart League [19711]
St. Anthony's Guild [20388]
St. Martin De Porres Guild [20389]
St. Vincent Pallotti Center for Apostolic Develop-
    ment [20390]
Salesian Missioners [20391]
Salesian Missioners [IO]
Samaritans Intl. [IO]
Samaritans Intl. [20392]
Secular Inst. of Saint Francis de Sales [19716]
Serra Intl. [19717]
Servants in Faith and Tech. [17001]
Seventh Day Baptist Missionary Soc. [19496]
Sharing of Ministries Abroad U.S.A. [20393]
Side by Side Lay Volunteer Prog. [20394]
Side by Side Lay Volunteer Prog. [IO]
Slavic Gospel Assn. [IO]
Slavic Gospel Assn. [20395]
SMA Lay Missionaries [20396]
Soc. of African Missions [19719]
Soc. of the Companions of the Holy Cross
    [19971]
Soc. of Missionaries of Africa [19721]
Soc. of Our Lady of the Most Holy Trinity [19722]
Soc. for Pentecostal Stud. [20465]
Soc. for Promoting Christian Knowledge [IO]
South Am. Mission [20397]
South Amer. Missionary Soc. - USA [20398]
Spanish World Ministries [20399]
Spanish World Ministries [IO]
Sports Ambassadors [20400]
STEER [20401]
STEER [IO]
Teen Missions Intl. [IO]
Teen Missions Intl. [20402]
Trans World Radio [20403]
Trans World Radio [IO]
Transport for Christ, Intl. [IO]
Transport for Christ, Intl. [20404]
United Christian Missionary Soc. [19856]
United Indian Missions, Intl. [20405]
United Indian Missions, Intl. [IO]
United Methodist Comm. on Relief [20267]
United Sisters of Charity [20406]
United Soc. for the Propagation of the Gospel [IO]
United World Mission [IO]
United World Mission [20407]
Ursuline Companions in Mission [20408]
Voice of China and Asia Missionary Soc. [20409]

A star before a book entry number signifies that the name is not listed separately, but is mentioned within the entry.

Voice of China and Asia Missionary Soc. [IO]
Voice of the Martyrs [20410]
Volunteer Missionary Movement - Europe [IO]
Volunteer Missionary Movement - U.S. Off.
[19736]
The Way Intl. [20411]
The Way Intl. [IO]
WEC Intl. [20034]
Woman's Home and Foreign Mission Soc.
[19443]
Woman's Missionary Union, SBC [19501]
Women Nationally Active for Christ [19502]
Women's Alliance for Theology, Ethics and Ritual
[20626]
World for Christ Crusade [20412]
World for Christ Crusade [IO]
World Gospel Mission [IO]
World Gospel Mission [20413]
World Impact [20414]
World Impact [IO]
World Medical Mission [20245]
World Mission Prayer League [20234]
World Opportunities [20415]
World Opportunities [IO]
World Relief [19985]
World Salt Found. [20416]
World Salt Found. [IO]
World Team [IO]
World Team [20417]
World Vision [20418]
World-Wide Missions [20419]
World-Wide Missions [IO]
World Witness, Foreign Bd. of the Associate
Reformed Presbyterian Church
World Witness, Foreign Bd. of the Associate
Reformed Presbyterian Church [20420]
World's Christian Endeavor Union [19829]
WorldVenture [19503]
Wycliffe Bible Translators [19531]
Xaverian Missionaries of the U.S. [20421]
Xaverian Missionaries of the U.S. [IO]
Youth Ministry [20235]
Youth With a Mission [20422]
Zarathushtrian Assembly [20510]
Mission Advanced Res. and Commun. Center
[20358], c/o World Vision Intl., 800 W Chestnut
Ave., Monrovia, CA 91016-3198, (909)463-2998
Mission Air Ministries - Defunct.
Mission; Alaska [★20348]
Mission Am. Coalition [19813], PO Box 13930, Palm
Desert, CA 92255, (760)200-2707
Mission in Am; Ephphatha Services - Div. for
Services and [★20216]
Mission of America; Islamic [20107]
Mission; Amer. Santal [★20234]
Mission to the Americas [★19491]
Mission to the Americas [IO], Denver, CO, United
States
Mission; Assoc. Parishes for Liturgy and [19945]
Mission Assn; U.S. Catholic [19734]
Mission Aviation Fellowship [20359], PO Box 47,
Nampa, ID 83653, (208)498-0800
Mission Bd; Catholic Negro-Amer. [19601]
Mission Bd; Foreign [★20350]
Mission Builders Intl. [19814], PO Box 406, Lake-
side, MT 59922, (406)844-2683
Mission; Central Amer. [★20310]
Mission; Chicago Hebrew [★19988]
Mission; Christian TV [19536]
Mission; COAR Peace [17482]
Mission Commn; Evangelism and Home [★20006]
Mission; Companions in [★20408]
Mission; Comunidad Oscar A. Romero Peace
[★17482]
Mission Convention; Baptist Foreign [★19493]
Mission Coun; U.S. Catholic [★19734]
Mission for Deaf Africans; Christian [★20318]
Mission Doctors Assn. [12532], 3435 Wilshire Blvd.,
Ste. 1035, Los Angeles, CA 90010, (213)368-1875
Mission Doctors Assn. [IO], Los Angeles, CA, United
States
Mission; Eastern European Bible [★20372]
Mission; Episcopal World [★19961]
Mission for Est. of Human Rights in Iran [17777],
PO Box 2037, Palos Verdes Peninsula, CA 90274,
(310)377-4590

Mission for Est. of Human Rights in Iran [IO], Palos
Verdes Peninsula, CA, United States
Mission; Evangelical Free Church [★20333]
Mission; Good News [★11869]
Mission to Greeks; Amer. [★20298]
Mission to Haiti [12267], PO Box 523157, Miami, FL
33152-3157, (305)823-7516
Mission to Haiti [IO], Miami, FL, United States
Mission; Heart of Africa [★20034]
Mission Helpers of the Sacred Heart - Defunct.
Mission; Holy Land Christian [★20312]
Mission, Inc; Children's Bible [★19995]
Mission; The India [★20315]
Mission; Indo-Burma Pioneer [★20305]
Mission Inst. [★20355]
Mission Intl; Holy Land Christian [★20312]
Mission; Iran Interior [★20315]
Mission League; Little Flower [19654]
Mission; Lutheran Men in [20224]
Mission of Mercy [12779], PO Box 62600, 15475
Gleneagle Dr., Colorado Springs, CO 80962,
(719)481-0400
Mission of Mercy [IO], Colorado Springs, CO, United
States
Mission; Moody Literature [★20368]
Mission Movement; Peace [19823]
Mission: Moving Mountains [20287], PO Box 6000,
Colorado Springs, CO 80934, (719)594-2727
Mission: Moving Mountains [IO], Burnsville, MN,
United States
Mission Off; Black and Indian [19587]
Mission; Oriental Boat [★20315]
Mission; Partnership [★20305]
Mission Philafricaine en Angola [★IO]
Mission Prayer League; South Amer. [★20234]
Mission Programs; Intl. Liaison of Lay Volunteers in
Mission U.S. Catholic Network of Lay [★19602]
Mission Proj; CHOSEN [★12516]
Mission; Salem Hebrew Lutheran [★20019]
Mission Sans Frontieres [★IO]
Mission to Seafarers [IO], London, United Kingdom
Mission Secretariat - Defunct.
Mission Services Assn. [20360], PO Box 13111,
Knoxville, TN 37920-0111, (865)577-9740
Mission Societies; Amer. Baptist Home [★19484]
Mission Societies; Lutheran [20225]
Mission Societies in the U.S; Pontifical [19703]
The Mission Soc. [★20265]
Mission Society; American Advent [★19442]
Mission Society; American Advent [★IO]
Mission Soc; Amer. Baptist Foreign [★19483]
Mission Soc; Amer. Baptist Home [★19484]
Mission Soc; Holy Cross Foreign [19633]
Mission Soc; Nazarene World [★20371]
Mission Soc. for United Methodists [20265], 6234
Crooked Creek Rd., Norcross, GA 30092-3106,
(770)446-1381
Mission Soc; Woman's Amer. Baptist Foreign
[★19483]
Mission Soc; Woman's Amer. Baptist Home
[★19484]
Mission Soc; Woman's Home and Foreign [19443]
Mission; Spanish World Gospel [★20399]
Mission Training Intl. [20361], PO Box 1220, Palmer
Lake, CO 80133, (719)487-0111
Mission Training Intl. [IO], Palmer Lake, CO, United
States
Mission Vie et Famillie [★IO]
Mission; West Indies [★20417]
Mission Without Borders - Australia [IO], Bankstown,
Australia
Mission Without Borders - Canada [IO], Abbotsford,
BC, Canada
Mission Without Borders - South Africa [IO], Orange
Grove, Republic of South Africa
Mission Without Borders - United Kingdom [IO],
London, United Kingdom
Mission: Wolf [5340], PO Box 1211, Westcliffe, CO
81252, (719)859-2157
Mission Work Among the Colored People; Catholic
Bd. for [★19601]
Mission to the World [20468], 1600 N Brown Rd.,
Lawrenceville, GA 30043-8141, (678)823-0004
Mission to the World [IO], Lawrenceville, GA, United
States

Mission for Youth Rights [IO], Kampala, Uganda
Missionaries of Africa - Defunct.
Missionaries of Africa; Soc. of [19721]
Missionaries Chap. of Positive Accord; Truth [20585]
Missionaries; Claretian Volunteers and Lay [19612]
Missionaries of the Eternal Word - Defunct.
Missionaries; U.S. Province of Congregation of Mari-
annhill [★19655]
Missionaries; U.S. Region of Congregation of Mari-
annhill [★19655]
Missionary Assn. of Am; Armenian [19459]
Missionary Assn. of Catholic Women - Defunct.
Missionary Church [20362], PO Box 9127, Fort
Wayne, IN 46899-9127, (260)747-2027
Missionary Church [IO], Fort Wayne, IN, United
States
Missionary Church Assn. [★IO]
Missionary Church Assn. [★20362]
Missionary Church Historical Soc. [19851], c/o
Timothy Erdel, Bethel Coll., 1001 W McKinley Ave.,
Mishawaka, IN 46545-5509, (574)257-2570
Missionary Church; United [★20362]
Missionary Comm; Presbyterian [★14147]
Missionary Coun. of the Christian Methodist
Episcopal Church; Women's [20270]
Missionary Dentists [★12525]
Missionary Dentists [★IO]
Missionary Engg. [★20359]
Missionary Evangelism; Comm. on [20001]
Missionary Fathers; Xaverian [★20421]
Missionary Fellowship; China Inland Mission
Overseas [★20378]
Missionary Fellowship; United [★19991]
Missionary Fellowship; World Radio [★20344]
Missionary Flight Training Found. - Defunct.
Missionary Gospel Fellowship [20363], PO Box
1535, Turlock, CA 95381, (209)634-8575
Missionary Internship [★20361]
Missionary Internship [★IO]
Missionary League; Intl. Lutheran Women's
[★20229]
Missionary League; Lutheran Women's [★20229]
Missionary League; Lutheran Women's [20229]
Missionary Movement; Laymen's Home [20018]
Missionary Movement - U.S. Off; Volunteer [19736]
Missionary Pilots Assn. - Defunct.
Missionary and Relief SOC; Friends of Israel
[★20010]
Missionary Sisters of the Catholic Apostolate [IO],
Rome, Italy
Missionary Sisters of the Immaculate Heart of Mary
[IO], Rome, Italy
Missionary Sisters of Our Lady of the Holy Rosary
[IO], Bryn Mawr, PA, United States
Missionary Sisters of Our Lady of the Holy Rosary
[19661], c/o Sister Bernie Murdoch, 205 Cricket
Ave., Ardmore, PA 19003, (610)896-1786
Missionary Sisters of the Precious Blood [IO], Rome,
Italy
Missionary Sisters of Saint Peter Claver [IO], Milton,
ON, Canada
Missionary Sisters of St. Peter Claver [20364], 667
Woods Mill Rd., Chesterfield, MO 63017-5825,
(314)434-8084
Missionary Sisters of the Soc. of Mary - Marist Mis-
sionary Sisters [20365], 349 Grove St., Waltham,
MA 02453
Missionary Soc. AME Church; Women's [20627]
Missionary Soc; Amer. Christian [★19856]
Missionary Soc; China Peniel [★20409]
Missionary Soc. of the Church of God; Natl.
Woman's [★19835]
Missionary Soc; The Foreign Christian [★19856]
Missionary Soc; Oriental [★20379]
Missionary Soc. of Saint Columban [19662], PO Box
10, St. Columbans, NE 68056, (402)291-1920
Missionary Soc. of Saint Columban [IO], Navan,
Ireland
Missionary Soc. of Saint Paul the Apostle [19663],
3015 4th St. NE, Washington, DC 20017-1102,
(202)269-2521
Missionary Soc; Seventh Day Baptist [19496]
Missionary Soc; United Christian [19856]
Missionary Soc; Women's Home and Foreign
[★20627]

Reference to "IO" in place of a book number signifies that the association may be found in the 45th edition of International Organizations.

Missionary Soc; Women's Parent Mite [★20627]
Missionary Soc; Young Men's Auxiliary Educ. and [★19970]
Missionary TECH Team [20366], 25 FRJ Dr., Long- view, TX 75602-4703, (903)757-4530
Missionary Union; Amer. Baptist [★19483]
Missionary Union of the Clergy in U.S.A. [★19703]
Missionary Union; Pontifical [★19703]
Missionary Union of Priests and Religious; Pontifical [★19703]
Missionary Union, SBC; Woman's [19501]
Missionary Vehicle Assn. [20367]
Missionary Vehicle Assn. of America [★20367]
Missionary Women Intl. - Address unknown since 1999.
Missione Bethleem Immense [★IO]
Missioners; Glenmary Home [★19628]
Missioners; Intl. Liaison U.S. Catholic Coordinating Center for Lay [★19602]
Missioners; Salesian Lay [★20391]
Missions; Arctic [★20348]
Missions Assn; Evangelical Foreign [★20332]
Missions Assn; Evangelism and Home [20006]
Missions; Baptist Mid- [19480]
Missions; Bd. of Trustees and Directors of [★19496]
Missions; Brethren in Christ [★20306]
Missions; Bur. of Catholic Indian [19591]
Missions Catholiques au Canada [★IO]
Missions and Charities; Conservative Mennonite Bd. of [★20253]
Missions; Christian Woman's Bd. of [★19856]
Missions to the Communist World; Christian [★20410]
Missions; Continental Baptist [19486]
Missions Door [19491], 2530 Washington St., Denver, CO 80205-3142, (303)308-1818
Missions Fellowship; Inter Varsity [★20347]
Missions Fellowship; Natl. Home [★20301]
Missions Fellowship; Student [★20347]
Missions Fellowship; Student Foreign [★20347]
Missions Found; Agricultural [★20295]
Missions; Gen. Convention of the Baptist Denomina- tion in the U.S. for Foreign [★19483]
Missions; Gen. Coun. of Cooperating Baptist [★19480]
Missions; Independent Bd. for Presbyterian Foreign [20467]
Missions Intl. [20037], PO Box 93235, Southlake, TX 76092-3235, (817)410-7706
Missions; Intl. [★20315]
Missions Intl. [IO], Southlake, TX, United States
Missions; Jesuit [★19643]
Missions to the Jews; Amer. Bd. of [★19998]
Missions of the Natl. Assn. of Free Will Baptists; Bd. of Home [★19492]
Missions; Sacred Heart Southern [★19711]
Missions to Seamen [★IO]
Missions; Unevangelized Fields [★20326]
Mississippi Freedom Democratic Party - Defunct.
Mississippi River Conservation Comm; Upper [4463]
Mississippi Surveillance Proj. of the Amer. Friends Ser. Comm. [★17093]
Mississippi Valley Historical Assn. [★10142]
Mississippi Valley Medical Editors' Assn. [★3082]
Missouri Fox Trotting Horse Breed Assn. [4913], PO Box 1027, Ava, MO 65608-1027, (417)683-2468
Mister Ed Fan Club - Address unknown since 2001.
Mistral Class Assn. [★23710]
Mistral Class Org; Intl. [23710]
Mistresses Anonymous - Address unknown since 1995.
Misuse of Pesticides; Beyond Pesticides - Natl. Coalition Against the [13322]
Misuse of Pesticides; Natl. Coalition Against the [★13322]
Mita Society for Library and Information Science [IO], Tokyo, Japan
Mitchell Assn; Maria [6509]
Mite Missionary Soc; Women's Parent [★20627]
Mitochondria Res. Soc. [14275], PO Box 1952, Buf- falo, NY 14221-1952, (716)845-8017
Mitochondria Research Society [IO], Buffalo, NY, United States
Mitochondrial Disease Found; United [16363]
Mitochondrial Medicine Soc. [14078], Univ. of California San Diego Medical Center, Box 8467, 225 Dickinson St., San Diego, CA 92103-8467

MIVA Am. [★20367]
Mix Intl. Fan Club; Tom [24775]
Mixed Harmony Barbershop Quartet Assn. [10648], c/o Kim Orloff, Coor./Co-Founder, PO Box 1209, Aptos, CA 95001
Mixer Mfrs. Bur. - Defunct.
Mixer Mfrs. Bur; Truck [400]
Mizrachi Hatzair - Defunct.
Mizrachi Palestine Fund - Defunct.
Mizrachi Women; Amer. [★20119]
Mizrachi Women's Org. of Amer. [★20119]
MLRC Institute [★6045]
Mo Time - Address unknown since 1991.
MOA Nature Farming and Culture Agency [IO], Shi- zuoka, Japan
Mobile Air Conditioning Soc. [★IO]
Mobile Air Conditioning Soc. [★1893]
Mobile Air Conditioning Soc. Worldwide [1893], PO Box 88, Lansdale, PA 19446, (215)631-7020
Mobile Air Conditioning Soc. Worldwide [IO], Lans- dale, PA, United States
Mobile Alliance; Open [7781]
Mobile Communications
  Mobile Marketing Assn. [110]
Mobile Communications Coun; Land [3751]
Mobile Data Assn. [IO], Cambridge, United Kingdom
Mobile Electronics Assn. - Defunct.
Mobile Entertainers; Natl. Assn. of [1314]
Mobile Healthcare Alliance [14646], 2100 M St. NW, 170-343, Washington, DC 20037, (202)452-0889
Mobile Home Mfrs. Assn. [★2527]
Mobile Home Owners Fed. [★12323]
Mobile Home Window Mfrs. Inst. - Defunct.
Mobile Homes
  Natl. Found. of Manufactured Home Owners [12323]
  Teton Club Intl. [22632]
  Teton Club Intl. [IO]
Mobile Housing Carriers Conf. - Defunct.
Mobile Indus. Caterers' Assn. [★1938]
Mobile/Manufactured Home Owners Found; Natl. [★12323]
Mobile Manufacturers Forum [IO], Brussels, Belgium
Mobile Marketing Assn. [IO], Boulder, CO, United States
Mobile Marketing Assn. [110], 75 Manhattan Dr., Ste. 204, Boulder, CO 80303, (303)415-2550
Mobile Modular Off. Assn. [★2848]
Mobile Operators Assn. [IO], London, United Kingdom
Mobile and Outside Caterers Assn. (Great Britain) [★IO]
Mobile Payment Forum [IO], Wakefield, MA, United States
Mobile Payment Forum [6816], 401 Edgewater Pl., Ste. 600, Wakefield, MA 01880, (781)876-8840
Mobile Post Off. Soc. [22848], c/o Douglas N. Clark, Sec., PO Box 427, Marstons Mills, MA 02648-0427
Mobile Press Assn. - Defunct.
Mobile Radio Sys; Natl. [★3752]
Mobile Riverine Force Assn. [21346], c/o Albert B. Moore, Pres., 106 Belleview Dr. NE, Conover, NC 28613, (828)464-7228
Mobile Satellite Users Assn. [7591], 1350 Beverly Rd., Ste. 115-341, McLean, VA 22101, (650)839- 0376
Mobile Telecommunications Assn; Amer. [★3742]
Mobile Voter [18032], 44 Elsie St., San Francisco, CA 94110, (415)641-4921
Mobilehome Dealers Natl. Assn. - Defunct.
Mobilehome Parkowners Assn; Western [★2532]
Mobility; Americans for Trans. [6315]
Mobility Intl. USA [11961], 132 E Broadway, Ste. 343, Eugene, OR 97401, (541)343-1284
Mobility Intl. USA [IO], Eugene, OR, United States
Mobility Opportunities Via Educ. - USA; MOVE Intl.: [11962]
Mobility of Systems Users, Data, and Computing; Special Interest Gp. on [6825]
Mobilization Against AIDS [★16966]
Mobilization Against AIDS [16966], c/o Hea. Gap, 429 W 127th St., 2nd Fl., New York, NY 10027, (212)537-0575
Mobilization Against the Draft and Student Peace Mobilization - Defunct.

Mobilization for Animals - Defunct.
Mobilization Proj; Human Rights Campaign Fund's [★17653]
Mobilization for Spiritual Ideals - Defunct.
Mobilization for Youth - Defunct.
Mobius Soc. - Address unknown since 1999.
Mobjack Assn; Intl. [23189]
Moby Dick Acad. - Defunct.
Model A 68-B Cabriolet Club [★21709]
Model A Drivers - Defunct.
Model A Ford Cabriolet Club [21709], PO Box 1487, Conroe, TX 77305, (936)441-8209
Model A Ford Club of Am. [21710], 250 S Cypress, La Habra, CA 90631-5515, (562)697-2712
Model A Ford Found. [21711], PO Box 95151, Nonantum, MA 02495-0151
Model "A" Restorers Club [21712], 6721 Merriman Rd., Garden City, MI 48135, (734)427-9050
Model A Restorers Club of Southern California [★21710]
Model Aeronautical Assn. of Australia [IO], West Pennant Hills, Australia
Model Aeronautical Assn. of Queensland [IO], Salis- bury, Australia
Model Aeronautics; Acad. of [21421]
Model Boating; Western Coun. of [★22654]
Model Car Collectors Assn. - Address unknown since 2007.
Model Cities Community Development Directors Assn; Natl. [★17228]
Model Cities Directors Assn; Natl. [★17228]
Model Code Standardization Coun. - Defunct.
Model Indus. Assn. [★1911]
Model Makers; Assn. of Professional [7006]
Model Missile Assn. [★22650]
Model Pilots Assn; Precision Aerobatics [21473]
Model Racing Assn; Northern Late [23084]
Model Railroad Indus. Assn. [1912]
Model Railroaders; Teen Assn. of [22637]
Model Railroading; Teen Assn. of [★22637]
Model Secondary School for the Deaf [14766], Gal- laudet Univ., 800 Florida Ave. NE, Washington, DC 20002, (202)651-5031
Model "T" Ford Club of Am. [21713], PO Box 126, Centerville, IN 47330-0126, (765)855-5248
Model "T" Ford Club Intl. [21714], PO Box 276236, Boca Raton, FL 33427-6236, (561)750-7170
Model "T" Ford Club Intl. Boca Raton, FL, United StatesIO
Model Trains
  Lionel Collectors Club of Am. [22633]
  Lionel Railroader Club [22634]
  Marklin Digital Special Interest Gp. [22635]
  Natl. Model Railroad Assn. [22636]
  New Zealand Model Railway Guild [IO]
  Teen Assn. of Model Railroaders [22637]
  Toy Train Collectors Soc. [22638]
  Toy Train Operating Soc. [22639]
  Train Collectors Assn. [22640]
  Train Collectors Assn. [IO]
Model United Nations; Natl. [8661]
Model Yacht Racing Assn. of America - Address unknown since 1995.
Modelers Assn. of North Am; Scale Ship [22656]
Modelers; Soc. of Antique [21477]
Modelers Society/United States Br; Intl. Plastic [22646]
Modeling
  Natl. Assn. of Scale Aeromodelers [22651]
Modeling Assn. of America Intl. - Address unknown since 1995.
Modell Found; Jeffrey [14939]
Modellfluggruppe Liechtenstein [IO], Schaan, Liecht- enstein
Models
  1/87 Vehicle Club [22641]
  Acad. of Model Aeronautics [21421]
  Air Mail Pioneers [21425]
  Aircraft Engine Historical Soc. [9364]
  Amer. Aviation Historical Soc. [21426]
  Amer. Bonanza Soc. [21427]
  Amer. Coaster Enthusiasts [22970]
  Amer. Model Yachting Assn. [22642]
  Amer. Navion Soc. [21428]
  Antique Airplane Assn. [21430]

A star before a book entry number signifies that the name is not listed separately, but is mentioned within the entry.

British Model Soldier Soc. [IO]
Canadian Assn. of Rocketry [IO]
Circus Model Builders, Intl. [IO]
Circus Model Builders, Intl. [22643]
EAA Vintage Aircraft Assn. [21442]
EAA Warbirds of Am. [21443]
First Flight Soc. [21447]
Giant Scale Warbirds Assn. [22644]
Giant Scale Warbirds Association [IO]
Helicopter Club of America [21450]
Intl. Cessna 120/140 Assn. [21453]
The Intl. Cessna 170 Assn. [21454]
Intl. Coun. of Air Shows [21455]
Intl. Miniature Aircraft Assn. [22938]
Intl. Model Power Boat Assn. [22645]
Intl. Model Power Boat Assn. [IO]
Intl. Pietenpol Assn. [21456]
Intl. Plastic Modelers Society/United States Br. [22646]
Intl. R/C Helicopter Assn. [22647]
Intl. Scale Soaring Assn. [22648]
Intl. Scale Soaring Assn. [IO]
Kit Collectors Intl. [IO]
Kit Collectors Intl. [22649]
Lighter-Than-Air Soc. [21460]
Lionel Railroader Club [22634]
Man Will Never Fly Memorial Soc. Internationale [22598]
Miniature Armoured Fighting Vehicle Assn. [IO]
Model Aeronautical Assn. of Australia [IO]
Natl. Assn. of Miniature Enthusiasts [22077]
Natl. Assn. of Rocketry [22650]
Natl. Assn. of Scale Aeromodelers [22651]
Natl. Assn. of Scale Aeromodelers [IO]
Natl. Intercollegiate Flying Assn. [21466]
Natl. Model Railroad Assn. [22636]
Natl. Org. for Racing Radio Control Autos [22652]
Natl. World War II Glider Pilots Assn. [21468]
Nautical Res. Guild [21880]
Navy Carrier Soc. [22653]
North Amer. Model Boat Assn. [22654]
North Amer. Model Boat Assn. [IO]
North Amer. Model Horse Shows Assn. [22587]
OX5 Aviation Pioneers [21469]
Popular Rotorcraft Assn. [21471]
Precision Aerobatics Model Pilots Assn. [21473]
R/C Quarter Scale Assn. of Am. [22655]
RC-Unionen [IO]
Scale Ship Modelers Assn. of North Am. [22656]
Scale Warbird Racing Assn. [22657]
Scottish Fed. of Model Boat Clubs [IO]
Ships-in-Bottles Assn. of Am. [22658]
Silver Wings Fraternity [21476]
Soc. of Antique Modelers [21477]
Swift Museum Found. [21481]
Teen Assn. of Model Railroaders [22637]
Toy Train Collectors Soc. [22638]
Toy Train Operating Soc. [22639]
Train Collectors Assn. [22640]
Unlimited Scale Racing Assn. [22659]
US Scale Masters Assn. [22660]
Western Assoc. Modelers [22661]
Whirly-Girls - Intl. Women Helicopter Pilots [21487]
World Airline Historical Soc. [21488]
World Miniature Warbird Assn. [22662]
World Miniature Warbird Association [IO]
World Org. for Modelship Building and Modelship Sport [IO]
World War I Aeroplanes [21490]
The Models Guild - Defunct.
Models and Photographers of America - Address unknown since 1990.
Moderata Samlingspartiet [★IO]
Moderata Ungdomsforbundet [IO], Stockholm, Sweden
Moderate Party [IO], Stockholm, Sweden
Moderaterna [★IO]
Moderation Mgt. [16507], 22 W 27th St., 5th Fl., New York, NY 10001, (212)871-0974
Modern Churchpeople's Union [IO], Liverpool, United Kingdom
Modern Courts; Fund for [5901]
Modern Courts Fund; Comm. for [★5901]
Modern Foods Coun. - Defunct.

Modern Free and Accepted Masons of the World [19243], PO Box 1072, Columbus, GA 31902, (706)322-3326
Modern Free and Accepted Masons of the World [IO], Columbus, GA, United States
Modern Greek Stud. Assn. [IO], Kent, OH, United States
Modern Greek Stud. Assn. [9996], Box 622, Kent, OH 44240, (330)672-0910
Modern Humanities Res. Assn. [IO], Bath, United Kingdom
Modern Humanities Res. Assn., Amer. Br. - Defunct.
Modern Language Assn. of Am. [8735], 26 Broadway, 3rd Fl., New York, NY 10004-1789, (646)576-5000
Modern Language Assn. of Am. [IO], New York, NY, United States
Modern Language Teachers Associations; Natl. Fed. of [8739]
Modern Music Masters [★10713]
Modern Painters and Sculptors; Fed. of [9502]
Modern Pentathlon Assn. of Great Britain [IO], Bath, United Kingdom
Modern Pentathlon Assn; U.S. [23925]
Modern Poetry Assn. [★10867]
Modern Poetry Assn. [★IO]
Modern Transport Tech. and Historical Soc. [★10922]
Modern Woodmen of Am. [19439], PO Box 2005, Rock Island, IL 61204-2005, (309)786-6481
Modernist Stud. Assn. [8780], c/o The Johns Hopkins Univ. Press, PO Box 19966, Baltimore, MD 21211-0966, (800)548-1784
Modernization Comm; Medical Res. [15109]
Modernized Chinese Medicine Intl. Assn. [IO], Hong Kong, People's Republic of China
Modification Assn; Weather [7330]
Modified Owners and Drivers Corp. for the Advancement of Racing - Defunct.
Modular Building Inst. [2848], 944 Glenwood Sta. Ln., Ste. 204, Charlottesville, VA 22901-1480, (434)296-3288
Modular Building Standards Assn. - Defunct.
Modular Building Systems Coun. [2529], c/o Natl. Assn. of Home Builders, 1201 15th St. NW, Washington, DC 20005, (202)266-8200
Modular Off. Assn; Mobile [★2848]
Modular and Portable Building Assn. [IO], Caersws, United Kingdom
Moe Bandy Fan Club - Address unknown since 1999.
Moffitt Memorial Fund for Human Rights; Letelier- [17993]
Mohair Coun. of Am. [4138], 233 W Twohig Ave., PO Box 5337, San Angelo, TX 76903, (325)655-3161
Mohn Family History Soc. of Eastern Pennsylvania - Address unknown since 2007.
Mohs Micrographic Surgery and Cutaneous Oncology; Amer. Coll. of [15636]
Moise Fan Club; Elton Sawyer - Patty [★25005]
Moisture Seekers [★16376]
Moisture Seekers [★IO]
Mojo Nixon World Headquarters - Address unknown since 1995.
Mokanna; Daughters of [19231]
Mokanna; Supreme Cauldron, Daughters of [★19231]
Moke Registry; North Amer. Mini [21745]
Molasses Information Network - Address unknown since 1994.
Mold Builders Assn; Amer. [1996]
Mold Makers Guild; Tool, Die and [★24100]
Mold Makers; Intl. Union of Tool, Die and [24100]
Mold Professionals; Natl. Assn. of [1330]
Moldavian League Against Epilepsy [IO], Chisinau, Moldova
Moldavian League Against Rheumatism [IO], Chisinau, Moldova
Moldavian Soc. of Cardiology [IO], Chisinau, Moldova
Moldavian Squash Fed. [IO], Chisinau, Moldova
Molders' and Allied Workers' Union; Intl. [★24066]
Molders Assn; EPS [3050]
Molders Intl; Assn. of Rotational [3046]

Molders, Pottery, Plastics, and Allied Workers Intl. Union; Glass [24066]
Molding Assn; Metal Injection [2713]
Moldova Dance Sport Fed. [IO], Chisinau, Moldova
Moldova Republic Tennis Fed. [IO], Chisinau, Moldova
Mole Day Found; Natl. [6688]
Molecular Biology; Amer. Soc. for Biochemistry and [6546]
Molecular Imaging; Acad. of [15150]
Molecular Mfg; Inst. for [7263]
Molecular Pathology; Assn. for [15862]
Molecular Plant Microbe Interactions; Intl. Soc. for [6641]
The Moles [19381], 577 Chestnut Ridge Rd., Woodcliff Lake, NJ 07677, (201)930-1923

Molestation
LifeWorks Inst. [12551]
Male Survivor: The Natl. Org. Against Male Sexual Victimization [13077]
Molesters Anonymous [13024]
Stop it Now! [11653]
Molesters Anonymous [13024]
Molluscan Shellfish Inst. [3494], c/o Natl. Fisheries Inst., 7918 Jones Br. Dr., Ste. 700, McLean, VA 22102, (703)752-8880

Mollusks
Amer. Malacological Soc. [7254]
Conchological Soc. of Great Britain and Ireland [IO]
Freshwater Mollusk Conservation Soc. [5034]
Soc. for Experimental and Descriptive Malacology [7256]
Western Soc. of Malacologists [7257]
Molyneux Family Assn; Intl. [20953]
Momazons - Address unknown since 2008.
Moments With Meredith - Meredith Baxter-Birney Fan Club - Defunct.
MOMMA - Address unknown since 1995.
Moms of America - Address unknown since 1995.
MOMS in Touch Intl. [20621], PO Box 1120, Poway, CA 92074-1120, (858)486-4065
MOMS in Touch Intl. [IO], Poway, CA, United States
Mona Lisas and Mad Hatters - Defunct.
Monaco DanceSport Assn. Stade Louis II [IO], Monaco, Monaco
Monaco Red Cross [IO], Monaco, Monaco
Monaco Sci. Center [IO], Monte Carlo, Monaco
Monaghan Photographic Soc. [IO], Monaghan, Ireland
Monarchist League of Canada [IO], Oakville, ON, Canada
Monarchist League - Defunct.

Monarchy
Amer. Coll. of Heraldry [21099]
Amer. Heraldry Soc. [21102]
Amer. Soc. of Genealogists [21103]
Augustan Soc. [21107]
Free Territory of Ely-Chatelaine [18351]
Monarchist League of Canada [IO]
Richard III Soc., Amer. Br. [11145]
Royal Soc. of Canada [IO]
Soc. of Amer. Royalty [18082]
Monarchy; U.S. Comm. to Promote Stud. of the History of the Hapsburg [★9628]
Monash Dance Sport [IO], Clayton, Australia
Moncton Fish and Game Assn. [IO], Riverview, NB, Canada
Mondiale ORT [★IO]
Monegasque Tennis Fed. [IO], Monaco, Monaco
Monell Found; Ambrose [13110]
Money Advice Scotland [IO], Glasgow, United Kingdom
Money Collectors; Dedicated Wooden [22736]
Money Collectors; Soc. of Paper [22757]
Money Coun; Electronic [★471]
Money Guild; Amer. Wooden [22728]
Money Laundering Specialists; Assn. of Certified Anti- [463]
Money is Like Yeast; Early [★18294]
Money Mgt. Assn; Amer. [★1454]
Money Mgt. Gp; Amer. [1454]
Money Mgt. Intl. [12190], 9009 W Loop S, 7th Fl., Houston, TX 77096-1719, (866)889-9347
Money Managers; Amer. Assn. of Daily [1453]

Reference to "IO" in place of a book number signifies that the association may be found in the 45th edition of International Organizations.

Money Network; HOUR [17218]
Money Soc; Latin Amer. Paper [22741]
Mongolia Fed. of Disabled Persons [IO], Ulan Bator, Mongolia
Mongolia Soc. [10487], Indiana Univ., 322 Goodbody Hall, 1011 E 3rd St., Bloomington, IN 47405-7005, (812)855-4078
Mongolian
China Stamp Soc. [22803]
Mongolia Soc. [10487]
North America-Mongolia Bus. Coun. [2310]
Mongolian Acad. of Sciences [IO], Ulan Bator, Mongolia
Mongolian Advt. Assn. [IO], Ulan Bator, Mongolia
Mongolian Assn. of Free and Independent Publishers [IO], Ulan Bator, Mongolia
Mongolian Assn. of Univ. Women [IO], Ulan Bator, Mongolia
Mongolian Athletic Fed. [IO], Ulan Bator, Mongolia
Mongolian Badminton Assn. [IO], Erdenet, Mongolia
Mongolian Dancesport Assn. [IO], Ulan Bator, Mongolia
Mongolian Epilepsy Soc. [IO], Ulan Bator, Mongolia
Mongolian Family Welfare Assn. [IO], Ulan Bator, Mongolia
Mongolian Fed. of Draughts [IO], Ulan Bator, Mongolia
Mongolian Junior Chamber [IO], Ulaanbaatar, Mongolia
Mongolian Natl. Chamber of Commerce and Indus. [IO], Ulan Bator, Mongolia
Mongolian Natl. Fed. of Baseball [IO], Ulan Bator, Mongolia
Mongolian Natl. Soc. for Photogrammetry and Remote Sensing [IO], Ulan Bator, Mongolia
Mongolian Squash Fed. [IO], Ulan Bator, Mongolia
Mongolian Taekwondo Fed. [IO], Ulan Bator, Mongolia
Mongolian Tennis Assn. [IO], Ulan Bator, Mongolia
Mongolian Volunteers Assn. [IO], Ulan Bator, Mongolia
Mongolian Women Lawyers Assn. [IO], Ulan Bator, Mongolia
Mongoliin Deed Bolobsroltoi Emegteichuudiin Holboo [★IO]
Mongoloids; Mothers of Young [★12579]
Monitor Consortium - Address unknown since 1999.
Monkee Headquarters - Defunct.
Monkee Lovers Unlimited - Address unknown since 2001.
Monkeein' Around - Defunct.
Monkees
Purple Flower Gang [24962]
Monkees Anonymous - Defunct.
Monkees, Boyce and Hart Photo Fan Club - Address unknown since 2000.
Monkees Buttonmania Club - Defunct.
Monkey
Great Ape Proj. [11400]
Intl. Primate Protection League [11418]
Save the Chimps [4298]
Simian Soc. of Am. [11457]
Monmouth Antiquarian Soc. - Address unknown since 2003.
Monocoupe Club [21462], 1218 Kingstowne Pl., St. Charles, MO 63304
Monorail Mfrs. Assn. [2046], 8720 Red Oak Blvd., Ste. 201, Charlotte, NC 28217, (704)676-1190
The Monorail Soc. [23007], 36193 Carnation Way, Fremont, CA 94536-2641
Monoski Assn; U.S. [23863]
Monosomy 9P; Support Groups for [★14443]
Monroe Freedom Scholarship Program; James [★11128]
The Monroe Inst. [7378], 365 Roberts Mountain Rd., Faber, VA 22938-2318, (434)361-1252
Monroe Inst. of Applied Sciences [★7378]
Monroe Law Off. Museum and Memorial Lib; James [★11128]
Monroe Memorial Found; James [11128]
Monster In My Pocket Collector's Club - Defunct.
Monster Truck Racing Assn. [23958], 947 Crider Ln., Union, MO 63084, (636)234-6162
Monster Truck Racing Association [IO], Loxahatchee, FL, United States

Montadale Sheep Breeders Assn. [5205], 2514 Willow Rd. NE, Fargo, ND 58102, (701)297-9199
Montana Coun. for Indian Educ. [★8937]
Montana Outfitters and Dude Ranchers Assn. [★23944]
Montana Outfitters and Guides Assn. [23944], 2033 11th Ave., No. 8, Helena, MT 59601, (406)449-3578
Montbrun Heritage Soc; Jacques Timothe Boucher Sieur de [20741]
Monte Carlo Owners Assn; Natl. [21735]
Monte Jade Sci. and Tech. Assn. [7749], c/o Judy Chu, Exec. Sec., 2870 Zanker Rd., Ste. 140, San Jose, CA 95134, (408)428-0388
Montenegrin P.E.N. Centre [IO], Cetinje, Montenegro
Monterey County Vintners and Growers Assn. [5414], PO Box 1793, Monterey, CA 93942-1793, (831)375-9400
Monterey Wine Country Assn. [★5414]
Montessori
Amer. Montessori Consulting [8890]
Amer. Montessori Soc. [8891]
Assn. Montessori International-U.S.A. [8892]
Canadian Coun. of Montessori Administrators [IO]
Intl. Montessori Accreditation Coun. [IO]
Intl. Montessori Accreditation Coun. [8893]
Intl. Montessori Assn. [IO]
Intl. Montessori Soc. [IO]
Intl. Montessori Soc. [8894]
Montessori Accreditation Coun. for Teacher Educ. [8278]
Montessori Assn. of New Zealand [IO]
Montessori Educational Programs Intl. [IO]
Montessori Educational Programs Intl. [8895]
Montessori Accreditation Coun. for Teacher Educ. [8278], 524 Main St., Ste. 202, Monument Sq., Racine, WI 53403, (262)898-1846
Montessori Accreditation Coun. for Teacher Educ. [IO], Racine, WI, United States
Montessori Assn. of New Zealand [IO], Nelson, New Zealand
Montessori Educational Programs Intl. [IO], Gray, GA, United States
Montessori Educational Programs Intl. [8895], PO Box 2199, Gray, GA 31032, (478)986-2768
Montessori Inst. of Am. [8279], 3410 S 272nd, Kent, WA 98032, (888)564-9556
Montford Point Marine Assn. [6084], 27 Red Tail Ct., Limerick, PA 19468
Montgomery Cotton Exchange - Defunct.
Montgomery Family Org; Joseph Goodbrake [20968]
Montgomery Intl; Clan [★20854]
Montgomery Medical and Psychological Inst. - Address unknown since 2001.
Montgomery Soc. Intl; Clan [20854]
Montreat Coll. Alumni Assn. [18909], PO Box 1267, Montreat, NC 28757, (828)669-8012
Montserrat Amateur Radio Soc. [IO], Plymouth, Montserrat
Montserrat Progressive Soc. of New York [19433], 207 W 137th St., New York, NY 10030-2425, (212)283-3346
Monty Python Special Interest Group - Address unknown since 2001.
Monument Assn; Amer. [2772]
Monument Builders of Am. [★2785]
Monument Builders of Canada [★2785]
Monument Builders of North Am. [2785], PO Box 917525, Longwood, FL 32791, (800)233-4472
Monument Soc; Amer. Historic [★2785]
Monumental Brass Soc. [IO], Stratford St. Mary, United Kingdom
Monuments Assn; Southwest Parks and [★7365]
Monuments Assn; Southwestern [★7365]
Moo Montana's Posse - Defunct.
Moody Bible Inst. [20368], 820 N LaSalle Blvd., Chicago, IL 60610, (312)329-4000
Moody Family Assn. [21003]
Moody Literature Ministries [★20368]
Moody Literature Mission [★20368]
Mookee Assn; Amer. [4191]
Moon Soc. [7684], PO Box 940825, Plano, TX 75094-0825
Mooncircles [20577], c/o Dana Gerhardt, MA, 397 Arnos St., Talent, OR 97540

Mooney Aircraft Pilots Assn. - Address unknown since 2001.
Moore 24 Natl. Assn. - Address unknown since 1999.
Moore River Olive Assn. [IO], Gingin, Australia
Moore Stephens North Am. [41], One Penn Plz., 250 W 34th St., 36th Fl., New York, NY 10119, (212)896-3946
Moorhead Kennedy Gp. [8666], 114 Clinton St., Brooklyn, NY 11201, (718)858-2528
Moorish Divine and Natl. Movement in North Am. - Address unknown since 2003.
Moose Intl. [19058], 155 S Intl. Dr., Mooseheart, IL 60539-1169, (630)966-2209
Moose Intl. [IO], Mooseheart, IL, United States
Moose; Supreme Lodge of the World, Loyal Order of [★19058]
Mopar Club; United [21806]
Mopar Muscle Club Intl. - Address unknown since 2001.
Mopar Scat Pack Club [21715]
Mopar Trans-Am Assn. [★21806]
Moped Assn. of America - Defunct.
Morab Breeders' Assn; Intl. [4900]
Morab Breeders Consortium [4914], c/o Donna Lassanske, PO Box 203, Hodgenville, KY 42748-0203, (270)358-8727
Morab Community Network [★4900]
Morab Community Network [★IO]
Morab Horse Association/Registry; North Amer. [★4947]
Morab Horse Association/Registry; Purebred [4947]
Morab Horse Registry of America - Address unknown since 1987.
The Morab Registry [★4901]
Morab Registry; Intl. [4901]
Moral Alternatives [★17143]
Moral Critique; Center for Critical Thinking and [★8179]
Moral Democracy; Center for [★17090]
Moral Development; Center for Res. in Faith and [20534]
Moral Educ; Assn. for [8233]
Moral Re-Armament [★17734]
Moral Re-Armament [★IO]
Moral Re-Armament [★IO]
Moral Support; Mothers United for [★16541]
Morality; Jews for [20154]
Morality in Media [18373], 475 Riverside Dr., Ste. 239, New York, NY 10115, (212)870-3222
Moralogy Intl. Relief Comm. [IO], Chiba, Japan
Moravian
Moravian Historical Soc. [20423]
Moravian Music Found. [10649]
Moravian Historical Soc. [20423], 214 E Center St., Nazareth, PA 18064, (610)759-5070
Moravian Music Found. [10649], 457 S Church St., Winston-Salem, NC 27101, (336)725-0651
Moray Wheels, Adaptive Scuba Assn. - Address unknown since 2006.
Mordechai Anielewicz Circle of Amers. for Progressive Israel - Address unknown since 1999.
Mordechai Bernstein Literary Prizes Assn. [IO], Tel Aviv, Israel
More Assn; John [20964]
More Effective Schools Program - Defunct.
More Game Birds in Am. [★5311]
More Light Presbyterians for Lesbian, Gay, Bisexual and Transgender Concerns [20063], PMB 246, 4737 County Rd. 101, Minnetonka, MN 55345-2634, (505)820-7082
More Than Money [17471], PO Box 1002, Concord, MA 01742, (978)371-1726
Moreno Memorial Assn; Gabriel Garcia [11117]
Morgan 3/4 Gp. [21716], c/o Dean Meyer, Membership Dir., 233 Mountain Rd., Ridgefield, CT 06877, (917)880-2962
Morgan 4/4 Club [★IO]
Morgan Breeders Assn; Lippitt [4912]
Morgan Car Club [21717], 616 Gist Ave., Silver Spring, MD 20910, (301)585-0121
Morgan Cutting Horse Assn. - Defunct.
Morgan Family Club [19053], 3120 6th Ave., Columbus, GA 31904
Morgan Horse Assn; Amer. [4831]

A star before a book entry number signifies that the name is not listed separately, but is mentioned within the entry.

Morgan Horse Breeders Assn. - Defunct.
Morgan Horse Club [★4831]
Morgan Horse Development Inst. - Defunct.
Morgan Intl. Fan Club; Lorrie [24940]
Morgan Memorial and Cooperative Indus. and Stores [★11949]
Morgan Memorial and Cooperative Indus. and Stores [★IO]
Morgan Owners Gp. [★21716]
Morgan Owners Register - Defunct.
Morgan Plus Four Club [21718], 5073 Melbourne Dr., Cypress, CA 90630, (714)828-3127
Morgan Reining Horse Assn; Natl. [4920]
Morgan Shepherd Fan Club - Address unknown since 2000.
Morgan Single-Footing Horse Found. [4915], c/o Ken Thomas, Pres., 650 E 1070 N, Richfield, UT 84701, (435)896-6824
Morgan Sports Car Club [IO], Petersfield, United Kingdom
Morgan Three-Wheeler Club [IO], Loughton, United Kingdom
Morgan Three-Wheeler Club - USA Gp. [21719], c/o Chris Towner, 56 Brick Hill Rd., Orleans, MA 02653-2711, (508)255-6432
Morley Knothole Assn; Christopher [9643]
Mormon Counselors and Psychotherapists; Assn. of [16212]
Mormon History Assn. [20208], 581 S 630 E, Orem, UT 84097, (801)224-0241
Mormon Miner Family Org. - Address unknown since 2002.
Mormonism; Recovery from [12888]
Mormons; Affirmation/Gay and Lesbian [20046]
Morning Bird Social Welfare Org. [IO], Sylhet, Bangladesh
Morningside House [★11271]
Morningstar Found. - Address unknown since 1991.
Mornington Peninsula Olive Assn. [IO], Red Hill South, Australia
Moroccan Amer. Bus. Coun. [IO], Boston, MA, United States
Moroccan Amer. Bus. Coun. [2287], 1085 Commonwealth Ave., Ste. 194, Boston, MA 02215, (508)230-9943
Moroccan Automotive Indus. Assn. [IO], Casablanca, Morocco
Moroccan Exporters' Assn. [IO], Casablanca, Morocco
Moroccan Soc. of Chemotherapy [IO], Casablanca, Morocco
Moroccan Soc. of Dermatology [IO], Rabat, Morocco
Moroccan Soc. for Rheumatology [IO], Rabat, Morocco
Morocco
  Friends of Morocco [IO]
  Friends of Morocco [19261]
  Intl. Workcamps Morocco [IO]
Morocco Baseball Fed. [IO], Rabat, Morocco
Morocco Mfrs. Natl. Assn. [★2416]
Morocco Spotted Horse Assn. of America - Defunct.
Morocco-U.S. Coun. on Trade and Investment [3843]
Morphological Soc; Amer. [★7867]
Morphology and Physiology; Soc. for Plant [★6632]
Morris Animal Found. [11428], 45 Inverness Dr. E, Englewood, CO 80112, (303)790-2345
Morris Animal Found. [IO], Englewood, CO, United States
Morris Cerullo World Evangelism [IO], San Diego, CA, United States
Morris Cerullo World Evangelism [20025], PO Box 85277, San Diego, CA 92186-5277, (858)277-2200
Morris Fan Club; Gary [24897]
Morris Fed. [IO], Suffolk, United Kingdom
Morris-Jumel Mansion [11137], 65 Jumel Terr., New York, NY 10032, (212)923-8008
Morris Minor Registry [21720], c/o Tony Burgess, Exec. Off., 318 Hampton Park, Westerville, OH 43081-5723, (614)899-2394
Morris Plan Bankers Assn. [★470]
Morris Pratt Inst. [★20453]
Morris Pratt Inst. Assn. [20451], 11811 Watertown Plank Rd., Milwaukee, WI 53226-3342, (414)774-2994

Morris Register [IO], London, United Kingdom
Morris Soc. in the U.S; William [9725]
Morrison Commemorative Stamp Comm. - Address unknown since 2000.
Morrocan League Against Epilepsy [IO], Rabat, Morocco
Morrow Lindbergh Found; Charles A. and Anne [4539]
Morse Code - Barry Morse Fan Club - Address unknown since 1989.
Morse Radio Programs for the Blind and Handicapped; Carleton E. [★22929]
Morse Soc. [21131], 3 Poplar Rd., Beacon, NY 12508
Morse Telegraph Club [22984], c/o Roger Reinke, Intl. Sec.-Treas., 5301 Neville Ct., Alexandria, VA 22310, (703)971-4095
Morse Telegraph Club [IO], Alexandria, VA, United States
Morse Telegraph Club [IO], Port Coquitlam, BC, Canada
Morse Telegraph Club, Edmonton Chap. [IO], Port Coquitlam, BC, Canada
Mortar Battalion Assn; 86th Chem. [21368]
Mortar Bd. [24509], 1200 Chambers Rd., Ste. 201, Columbus, OH 43212, (800)989-6266
Mortar Indus. Assn. [IO], London, United Kingdom
Mortar Mfrs. Standards Assn. [★636]
Mortgage Assn; Amer. Credit Union [1103]
Mortgage Assn. and Amer. CU Housing Alliance; Amer. Credit Union [★1103]
Mortgage Bankers Assn. [485], 1919 Pennsylvania Ave. NW, Washington, DC 20006-3404, (202)557-2700
Mortgage Bankers Assn. of Am. [★485]
Mortgage Banking Attorneys; USFN-America's [325]
Mortgage Banking; School of [★485]
Mortgage Brokers; Amer. Inst. of [★489]
Mortgage Brokers; Natl. Assn. of [489]
Mortgage Coalition; Consumer [2424]
Mortgage Consultants; Soc. of [★489]
Mortgage and Finance Assn. of Australia [IO], Neutral Bay, Australia
Mortgage Indus. Assn. of Australia [★IO]
Mortgage Insurance Companies of Am. [2200], 1425 K St. NW, Ste. 210, Washington, DC 20005, (202)682-2683
Mortgage Lenders; Coun. of [IO]
Mortgage Planners; Natl. Assn. of [490]
Mortgage Securities Assn; Commercial [3304]
Mortgage Underwriters; Natl. Assn. of Rev. Appraisers and [3329]
Mortgage Women; Natl. Assn. of Professional [491]
Morticians Assn; Natl. Funeral Directors and [2789]
Morticians Assn; Natl. Negro Funeral Directors and [★2789]
Morticians; Natl. Selected [★2791]
Mortuary Educ; Joint Comm. on [★8896]
Mortuary Science
  Amer. Bd. of Funeral Ser. Educ. [8896]
  Amer. Soc. of Embalmers [2773]
  Intl. Conf. of Funeral Ser. Examining Boards of the U.S. [6120]
Mortuary Services
  Accredited Pet Cemetery Soc. [2953]
  Alberta Funeral Ser. Assn. [IO]
  Amer. Inst. of Commemorative Art [2771]
  Amer. Monument Assn. [2772]
  Amer. Soc. of Embalmers [2773]
  Assoc. Funeral Directors Intl. [2774]
  Associated Funeral Directors International [IO]
  Australasian Cemeteries and Crematoria Assn. [IO]
  Australian Funeral Directors Assn. [IO]
  Casket and Funeral Supply Assn. of Am. [2775]
  Catholic Cemetery Conf. [2776]
  Cremation Assn. of North Am. [2777]
  Cremation Soc. of Great Britain [IO]
  Federated Funeral Directors of Am. [2778]
  Flying Funeral Directors of America [2779]
  Funeral Consumers Alliance [2780]
  Funeral Directors Assn. of New Zealand [IO]
  Funeral Furnishing Mfrs. Assn. [IO]
  Funeral Ser. Assn. of Canada [IO]
  Intl. Cemetery and Funeral Assn. [IO]

  Intl. Cemetery and Funeral Assn. [2781]
  Intl. Cremation Fed. [IO]
  Intl. Fed. of Thanatologists Assn. [IO]
  Intl. Memorialization Supply Assn. [IO]
  Intl. Memorialization Supply Assn. [2782]
  Intl. Order of the Golden Rule [IO]
  International Order of the Golden Rule [IO]
  Jewish Funeral Directors of Am. [2784]
  Monument Builders of North Am. [2785]
  Natl. Assn. of Funeral Directors [IO]
  Natl. Assn. of Memorial Masons [IO]
  Natl. Assn. for Pre-Paid Funeral Plans [IO]
  Natl. Casket Retailers Assn. [2786]
  Natl. Concrete Burial Vault Assn. [2787]
  Natl. Funeral Directors Assn. [2788]
  Natl. Funeral Directors Assn. of Southern Africa [IO]
  Natl. Funeral Directors and Morticians Assn. [2789]
  Natl. Soc. of Allied and Independent Funeral Directors [IO]
  Preferred Funeral Directors Intl. [IO]
  Preferred Funeral Directors Intl. [2790]
  Selected Independent Funeral Homes [2791]
  Sveriges Begravningsbyraers Forbund [IO]
  Telophase Soc. [2792]
  WTC Families For Proper Burial [13312]
Mosaic Artists; Soc. of Amer. [9525]
Mosaic Assn. of Australia [IO], Sydney, Australia
Mosaic Assn; Natl. Terrazzo and [1052]
Mosaism
  United Israel World Union [20424]
  United Israel World Union [IO]
Moscow ACM SIGDA [IO], Moscow, Russia
Moscow ACM SIGMOD [IO], Moscow, Russia
Moscow; Independent Univ., Washington-Paris- [★8597]
Moscow Intl. Bus. Assn. [IO], Moscow, Russia
Moses Collins Family Org. - Defunct.
Moslem Mosque - Defunct.
Mosquito Assn. [20663], c/o Jack Fisher, Pres., 274 Belleman's Church Rd., Dauberville, PA 19533, (610)926-3588
Mosquito Control Assn; Amer. [5072]
Mosquito Control Assn. of Australia [IO], Cleveland, Australia
Mosquito Historical Found. [★20663]
Mosquito; Military Order of the [★21320]
Moss Regional Rsrc. and Info. Center for individuals with Disabilities [★13345]
Mossberg Collectors Assn; Natl. [22430]
MossRehab ResourceNet; Travel Info. Service/ [13345]
Most Worshipful Natl. Grand Lodge Free and Accepted Ancient York Masons - Address unknown since 1999.
Motel Assn; Amer. Hotel and [★1927]
Motel Brokers of Am; Hotel [★3311]
Motel Brokers; Amer. Hotel and [★3311]
Motel Brokers Assn. of Am. [★3311]
Motel Brokers Assn. of Am. [★IO]
Moth Coun; Natl. Gypsy [★5078]
Moth Mgt. Bd; Natl. Gypsy [5078]
Mother and Child Intl. [★IO]
Mother and Child Rights; Comm. for [11689]
Mother is a Working Mother Network; Every [18810]
Mothers' Access to Careers at Home - Defunct.
Mothers Against Drunk Drivers [★12969]
Mothers Against Drunk Driving [12969], 511 E John Carpenter Fwy., Ste. 700, Irving, TX 75062, (214)744-6233
Mothers Against Drunk Driving - Canada [IO], Oakville, ON, Canada
Mothers Against Misuse and Abuse [16508], 5217 SE 28th Ave., Portland, OR 97202, (503)233-4202
Mothers Against Munchausen Syndrome by Proxy Allegations [13968], 1407 Ranch Dr., Senatobia, MS 38668
Mothers Against Sexual Abuse [13078], PO Box 371, Huntersville, NC 28070
Mothers Against Sexual Predators At Large [13079], PO Box 7247, Missoula, MT 59807-7247
Mothers Against Violence in Am. [13375]
Mothers Against War [18221], PO Box 3048, Amherst, MA 01004, (413)253-3354

Reference to "IO" in place of a book number signifies that the association may be found in the 45th edition of International Organizations.

Mothers; Aid to Incarcerated [11851]
Mothers of AIDS Patients - Address unknown since 1994.
Mothers; Am; Blue Star [21193]
Mothers; Amer. Gold Star [21188]
Mothers; Amer. War [21190]
Mothers And More [12086], PO Box 31, Elmhurst, IL 60126, (630)941-3553
Mothers Anonymous [★11645]
Mothers; Archconfraternity of Christian [19572]
Mothers Are People Too - Defunct.
Mothers Arms [13011], 4757 E Greenway Rd., 107B No. 124, Phoenix, AZ 85032, (800)464-4840
Mothers of Asthmatics [★16352]
Mothers of Asthmatics; Allergy and Asthma Network [16352]
Mothers By Choice; Single [12692]
Mothers' Center Development Proj. [★12676]
Mothers' Centers; Natl. Assn. of [12676]
Mothers Comm; Amer. [★12139]
Mothers Counsel; Nursing [12414]
Mother's Day Comm; Natl. [18675]
Mother's Day Coun. [★18671]
Mother's Day Coun; Father's Day/ [18671]
Mother's Day; Natl. Comm. for the Observance of [★18675]
Mothers and Fathers Aligned Saving Kids [17059], 2566 Nostrand Ave., Brooklyn, NY 11210, (718)758-0400
Mothers and Fathers Experiencing Neonatal Death; Aiding [11907]
Mothers, Healthy Babies Coalition; Natl. Healthy [15612]
Mothers at Home [★12669]
Mothers' Home Bus. Network [1920], PO Box 423, East Meadow, NY 11554
Mothers-in-Law Club Intl. - Defunct.
Mothers, Inc; Amer. [12139]
Mothers at the Leading Edge; Formerly Employed [★12086]
Mothers Matter - Defunct.
Mothers of Murdered Youth [11710], PO Box 17516, Colorado Springs, CO 80935, (719)231-8234
Mothers; Natl. Assn. of At-Home [12674]
Mothers; Natl. Cong. of [★8954]
Mothers; Natl. Org. of Single [13108]
Mothers' Network - Address unknown since 2002.
Mothers Organized for Morality - Defunct.
Mothers and Parent-Teachers Associations; Natl. Cong. of [★8954]
Mothers for Peace - Address unknown since 2003.
Mothers of the Plaza de Mayo [IO], Buenos Aires, Argentina
Mothers in Prison Projects - Defunct.
Mother's Right Found. [IO], Moscow, Russia
Mothers Supporting Daughters with Breast Cancer [13844], c/o Charmayne Dierker, Pres., 25235 Fox Chase Dr., Chestertown, MD 21620, (410)778-1982
Mothers of Twins Clubs; Natl. Org. of [12613]
Mothers' Union Australia [IO], Goondiwindi, Australia
Mothers' Union - England [IO], London, United Kingdom
Mothers United for Moral Support [★16541]
Mothers' Voices [13574], 150 W Flagler St., Ste. 1820, Miami, FL 33130, (305)347-5467
Mothers Without Borders [11624], 125 E Main St., Ste. 402, American Fork, UT 84003, (801)796-5535
Mothers Without Borders [IO], American Fork, UT, United States
Mothers Without Custody - Address unknown since 2001.
Mothers of World War II - Address unknown since 1995.
Mothers of Young Mongoloids [★12579]
Motility Disorders Soc; Pediatric Digestion and [15893]
Motility Soc; Amer. [★14407]

Motion Picture
Acad. of Motion Picture Arts and Sciences [1374]
Acad. of Sci. Fiction, Fantasy, and Horror Films [9925]
Acad. of TV Arts and Sciences [542]
African Amer. Cinema Soc. [9926]

Alberta Motion Picture Industries Assn. [IO]
Alliance of Motion Picture and TV Producers [1375]
Amateur Movie Makers Assn. [22418]
Amer. Cinema Editors [1376]
Amer. Film Inst. [9927]
Amer. Guild of Variety Artists [24151]
Amer. Soc. of Camera Collectors [10844]
Amer. Soc. of Cinematographers [1377]
Anthology Film Archives [9928]
Art Directors Guild [9929]
Assn. of Cinema and Video Labs. [1367]
Assn. of Film Commissioners Intl. [1368]
Assn. of Independent Commercial Producers [90]
Assn. of Independent Video and Filmmakers [9931]
Assn. of Moving Image Archivists [9932]
Audio Engg. Soc. [6909]
Black Awareness in TV [17164]
Black Filmmaker Found. [9933]
Black Stuntmen's Assn. [1379]
Broadcast Designer's Assn. [554]
Coun. on Intl. Nontheatrical Events [9935]
Digital Cinema Soc. [1380]
Film Advisory Bd. [9936]
Film Arts Found. [9937]
Film/Video Arts [9938]
Gale Storm Appreciation Soc. [24744]
German Directors Guild [IO]
German Soc. of Cinematographers [IO]
Golden Raspberry Award Found. [22419]
Hollywood Radio and TV Soc. [559]
Hong Kong Film Awards Assn. [IO]
Independent Feature Proj. [1381]
Independent Film and TV Alliance [1382]
Intl. Animated Film Soc., ASIFA - Hollywood [1383]
Intl. Assn. of Audio Visual Communicators [1384]
Intl. Fed. of Film Producers Associations [IO]
Intl. Film Seminars [9940]
Intl. Motion Picture and Lecturers Assn. [1386]
Jane Powell Fan Club [24747]
Japan Audio Soc. [IO]
Jon-Erik Hexum Fan Club [24749]
Junior Hollywood Radio and TV Soc. [564]
The Lambs [11019]
Large Format Cinema Assn. [1387]
Lindsay Wagner's Official Fan Club [24754]
Location Managers Guild of Am. [2522]
Louise Brooks Soc. [24755]
Media Communications Assn. Intl. [1388]
Motion Picture Assn. of Am. [1389]
Motion Picture Producers Assn. of Japan [IO]
Motion Picture and TV Fund [12115]
Natl. Assn. of Theatre Owners [1315]
Natl. Bd. of Rev. of Motion Pictures [9941]
Natl. Center for Film and Video Preservation [9942]
Natl. Center for Jewish Film [9943]
The Official Austin Powers Collector's Club [24826]
Old Time Western Film Club [24827]
Outfest [9944]
Peter Sellers Appreciation Soc. [24767]
Popular Culture Assn. [10888]
Producers Guild of Am. [1392]
Production Equip. Rental Assn. [2793]
Screen Producers Ireland [IO]
Soc. for Cinema and Media Stud. [9946]
Soc. of Motion Picture and TV Engineers [7044]
Stuntmen's Assn. of Motion Pictures [1393]
Stuntwomen's Assn. of Motion Pictures [1394]
Sundance Inst. [9948]
United Drive-In Theatre Owners Assn. [2794]
U.S.A. Film Festival [9949]
Women in Film [1396]
World Chap. of Disneyana Enthusiasts [22132]
Writers Guild of Am., East [24220]
Writers Guild of Am., West [24221]
Motion Picture Art Directors; Soc. of [★9929]
Motion Picture Arts and Sciences; Acad. of [1374]
Motion Picture Assn. of Am. [1389], 15503 Ventura Blvd., Encino, CA 91436, (818)995-6600
Motion Picture Exhibitors; Allied States Assn. of [★1315]

Motion Picture Film Editors - Defunct.
Motion Picture Industry Controllers - Address unknown since 1995.
Motion Picture Industry Coun. - Defunct.
Motion Picture and Lecturers Assn; Travelogues by IMPALA Intl. [★1386]
Motion Picture Pioneers - Defunct.
Motion Picture Producers Assn. of Japan [IO], Tokyo, Japan
Motion Picture Producers and Distributors of Am. [★1389]
Motion Picture Relief Fund [★12115]
Motion Picture Sound Editors [1371], 10061 Riverside Dr., PMB Box 751, Toluca Lake, CA 91602-2560, (818)506-7731
Motion Picture and TV Conf. Unions; Conf. of [★24056]
Motion Picture and TV Credit Assn. [1434], 4102 W Magnolia Blvd., Ste. A, Burbank, CA 91505, (818)729-0220
Motion Picture and TV Credit Managers Assn. [★1434]
Motion Picture and TV Engineers; Soc. of [7044]
Motion Picture and TV Fund [12115], 22212 Ventura Blvd., Ste. 300, Woodland Hills, CA 91364, (818)876-1900
Motion Picture and TV Producers; Alliance of [1375]
Motion Picture and TV Unions; New York Coun. of [24056]
Motion Picture Theatre Associations of Canada [IO], Toronto, ON, Canada
Motion Pictures; Natl. Bd. of Rev. of [9941]
Motion Pictures; Stuntmen's Assn. of [1393]
Motion Pictures; Stuntwomen's Assn. of [1394]
Motion Tech. Representatives Assn; Power- [2059]
Motivation; Inst. of Athletic [★23665]
Motivation and Inst. of Athletic Motivation; Inst. for the Stud. of Athletic [★23665]
Motivation; Inst. for the Stud. of Athletic [★23665]
Motley Crue Fan Club - Address unknown since 1989.
Moto Morini Club of North America - Address unknown since 2001.
Motor Bike Club; Vintage [22699]
Motor Bus Assn; Natl. [★21896]
Motor Bus Division of Amer. Auto. Assn. [★3859]
Motor Bus Soc. [21896], PO Box 261, Paramus, NJ 07653-0261
Motor Bus Soc. [IO], Paramus, NJ, United States
Motor Car Club of Am; Veteran [21808]
Motor Car Collectors of America - Defunct.
Motor Carrier Lawyers Assn. [★6326]
Motor Carriers Tariff Service - Address unknown since 2006.
Motor Club; Antique Outboard [23158]
Motor Coach Assn; Family [22949]
Motor Coach Employees of Am; Amalgamated Assn. of St., Elec. Railway and [★24197]
Motor Contest Assn; Intl. [23078]
Motor-Cycle Club of America; Indian [22682]
Motor and Equip. Manufacturers Assn. [392], 10 Lab. Dr., PO Box 13966, Research Triangle Park, NC 27709-3966, (919)549-4800
Motor and Equip. Manufacturers Assn. [IO], Research Triangle Park, NC, United States
Motor Factors Assn. (MFA) [★IO]
Motor Fleet Supervisor Training and Certification; Natl. Comm. for [★8212]
Motor Freight Carriers Assn. [★3898]
Motor Freight Traffic Assn; Natl. [3577]
Motor, Hearse and Car Owners Assn. - Address unknown since 1995.
Motor Indsutries' Fed. [★IO]
Motor Indus. Assn. [IO], Lower Hutt, New Zealand
Motor Indus. Res. Assn. [★IO]
Motor Maids [23625], PO Box 157, Erie, MI 48133, (419)290-3126
Motor Mfr. Assn; Small [★1198]
Motor Mfrs. Assn; Outboard [★2587]
Motor and Motion Assn; SMMA - The [1198]
Motor Neurone Disease Assn. of Australia [IO], Gladesville, Australia
Motor Neurone Disease Assn; Irish [IO]
Motor Neurone Disease Assn. of New Zealand [IO], Wellington, New Zealand

A star before a book entry number signifies that the name is not listed separately, but is mentioned within the entry.

Motor Neurone Disease Assn. of NSW [IO], Gladesville, Australia
Motor Neurone Disease Assn. of Queensland [IO], Brisbane, Australia
Motor Neurone Disease Assn. of South Africa [IO], Western Cape, Republic of South Africa
Motor Neurone Disease Assn. of South Australia [IO], Unley, Australia
Motor Neurone Disease Assn. of the United Kingdom [IO], Northampton, United Kingdom
Motor Neurone Disease Assn. of Western Australia [IO], Nedlands, Australia
Motor Neurone Disease Res. Inst. of Australia [IO], Gladesville, Australia
Motor Racing; Eastern Museum of [21634]
Motor Schools Assn. of Great Britain [IO], Stockport, United Kingdom
Motor Sports Assn. [IO], Slough, United Kingdom
Motor Sports Assn; Historic [21657]
Motor Sports Assn; Intl. [23079]
Motor Trades Assn. of Australia [IO], Kingston, Australia
Motor Transport Assn; USMC [2599]
Motor Truck, Bus and Fire Engine Club - Defunct.
Motor Vehicle Administrators; Amer. Assn. of [5535]
Motor Vehicle Dismantlers' Assn. of Great Britain [IO], Lichfield, United Kingdom
Motor Vehicle Mfrs. Assn. [★IO]
Motor Voters - Address unknown since 2001.
Motor Wheel and Flyer Club of America - Defunct.
Motorama Corp; California [★23623]
Motorbranschens Riksfoerbund [★IO]
Motorcar Owners Registry; Elgin [21638]
Motorcoach Assn; United [3900]
Motorcoach Therapy; Natl. Coalition of Psychiatrists Against [15222]
Motorcycle
  All-American Indian Motorcycle Club [22663]
  Amateur Motorcycle Assn. [IO]
  Amer. Fed. of Motorcyclists [22664]
  Amer. Historic Racing Motorcycle Assn. [22665]
  Amer. Motorcycle Heritage Found. [23621]
  Amer. Motorcyclist Assn. [23622]
  Amer. Voyager Assn. [22666]
  Amer. Voyager Assn. [IO]
  Antique Motorcycle Club of America [IO]
  Antique Motorcycle Club of Am. [22667]
  Ariel Motorcycle Club North Am. [22668]
  Assn. of Recovering Motorcyclists [13225]
  Automotive Recyclers Assn. [3988]
  Blue Knights Intl. Law Enforcement Motorcycle Club [22669]
  Blue Knights Intl. Law Enforcement Motorcycle Club [IO]
  BlueRibbon Coalition [23680]
  BMW Motorcycle Owners of Am. [22670]
  BMW Riders Assn. Intl. [22671]
  BMW Riders Assn. Intl. [IO]
  British Biker Cooperative [IO]
  British Biker Cooperative [22672]
  British Intl. Motorcycle Assn. [22673]
  British Intl. Motorcycle Assn. [IO]
  British Motorcyclists Fed. [IO]
  Canadian Motorcycle Assn. [IO]
  Christian Motorcyclists Assn. [22674]
  Combat Veterans Motorcycle Assn. [22675]
  Continental Motosport Club [23623]
  Cushman Club of Am. [22676]
  Deutsches Motorrad Register [22677]
  Downed Bikers Assn. [12612]
  Gold Wing Road Riders Assn. [22678]
  Harley Hummer Club [22679]
  Harley Owners Gp. [22680]
  Honda Sport Touring Assn. [22681]
  Indian Motor-Cycle Club of America [22682]
  Intl. Brotherhood of Motorcycle Campers [23624]
  Intl. Brotherhood of Motorcycle Campers [IO]
  Intl. CBX Owners Assn. [IO]
  Intl. CBX Owners Assn. [22683]
  Intl. Motorcycling Fed. [IO]
  Intl. Norton Owners' Assn. [IO]
  Intl. Norton Owners' Assn. [22684]
  Intl. Star Riders Assn. [22685]
  LeMans Am. [22686]
  Motor Maids [23625]

Motorcycle Events Assn. [22687]
Motorcycle Indus. Coun. [2795]
Motorcycle Retailers Assn. [IO]
Motorcycle Riders Found. [22688]
Motorcycle Safety Found. [3447]
Motorcycle Touring Assn. [23626]
New England Trail Rider Assn. [23947]
Norwegian Route 66 Assn. [IO]
Rickman Owners Club Intl. [IO]
Rickman Owners Club Intl. [22689]
Riders for Hea. [15271]
Riders for Justice [22690]
Royal Enfield Owners Club of North Am. [IO]
Rudge Enthusiasts Club [IO]
Rudge Enthusiasts Club [22691]
Scoot-Tours Touring Scooter Riders Assn. [23627]
Triumph Intl. Owners Club [22692]
Triumph Intl. Owners Club [IO]
United Sidecar Assn. [22693]
U.S. Classic Racing Assn. [22694]
Velocette Owners Club of North Am. [22695]
Vespa Club of Am. [22696]
Vincent Owners Club - Keystone Sect. [22697]
Vintage BMW Motorcycle Owners [22698]
Vintage BMW Motorcycle Owners [IO]
Vintage Motor Bike Club [22699]
Virago Owners Club [22700]
WERA Motorcycle Roadracing [23628]
Wheelchair Motorcycle Assn. [23370]
White Plate Flat Trackers Assn. [23629]
Women On Wheels Motorcycle Assn. [23630]
Women in the Wind [22701]
Women's Intl. Motorcycle Assn. [IO]
Women's Intl. Motorcycle Assn. - Australia [IO]
Women's Intl. Motorcycle Assn. - New South Wales [IO]
Women's Intl. Motorcycle Assn. - Queensland [IO]
Women's Intl. Motorcycle Assn. - South Australia [IO]
Women's Intl. Motorcycle Assn. - Tasmania [IO]
Women's Intl. Motorcycle Assn. - Victoria [IO]
Women's Intl. Motorcycle Assn. - Western Australia [IO]
Women's Intl. Motorcycling Assn. - New Zealand [IO]
Women's Motorcyclist Found. [22702]
Yamaha 650 Soc. [22703]
Yamaha 650 Soc. [IO]
Motorcycle and Allied Trades Assn. [★2795]
Motorcycle Assn; Amer. [★23622]
Motorcycle Assn; British Intl. [★22673]
Motorcycle Assn; Wheelchair [23370]
Motorcycle Assn; Women On Wheels [23630]
Motorcycle Club; Ariel Owners' [★22668]
Motorcycle Club; Knights of Life [12968]
Motorcycle Events Assn. [22687], 2993 Tyrone Blvd. N, St. Petersburg, FL 33710, (727)343-1049
Motorcycle Indus. Assn. [IO], Coventry, United Kingdom
Motorcycle Indus. Coun. [2795], 2 Jenner St., Ste. 150, Irvine, CA 92618-3806, (949)727-4211
Motorcycle Indus. Coun. Safety and Educ. Found. [★3447]
Motorcycle Indus. in Europe [IO], Brussels, Belgium
Motorcycle Owners of Am; BMW [22670]
Motorcycle Owners; Vintage BMW [22698]
Motorcycle Retailers Assn. [IO], Rugby, United Kingdom
Motorcycle Riders Found. [22688], 236 Massachusetts Ave. NE, Ste. 510, Washington, DC 20002-4980, (202)546-0983
Motorcycle Safety Administrators; Natl. Assn. of State [6253]
Motorcycle Safety Found. [3447], 2 Jenner St., Ste. 150, Irvine, CA 92618-3806, (949)727-3227
Motorcycle, Scooter and Allied Trades Assn. [★2795]
Motorcycle Touring Assn. [23626], N7068 County Rd. C, Casco, WI 54205, (920)837-7325
Motorcycle Touring Soc. [★23626]
Motorcycling Doctors Assn. - Address unknown since 1994.
Motorcyclists; Assn. of Recovering [13225]
Motorhome Travelers Assn. - Defunct.
Motoring in Miniature Assn. - Defunct.

Motorist Info. and Services Assn. [13344], c/o Cheryl Gribskov, Exec. Dir., 229 Madrona Ave. SE, Salem, OR 97302, (503)373-0864
Motorists Assn; Natl. [13340]
Motorists Information - Defunct.
Motorized Div; Natl. Assn. of the Sixth Infantry/ [★20704]
Motormaids of Am. [★23625]
Motorrad Register; Deutsches [22677]
Motors Owners Assn; Amer. [21576]
Motorsport Indus. Assn. [IO], Stoneleigh, United Kingdom
Motorsports Club; Opel [21752]
Motorsports Marketing Assn. - Defunct.
Motorsports Ministries; Christian [21610]
Motosport Club; Continental [23623]
Motree Family Assn. - Defunct.
Mott Found; Charles Stewart [13113]
Moulding and Millwork Producers Assn; Wood [688]
Moulding and Millwork Producers; Wood [★688]
Moulding Producers; Western Wood [★688]
Mt. Diablo Peace Center [18222], 55 Eckley Ln., Walnut Creek, CA 94596, (925)933-7850
Mt. Marty Coll. Alumni Assn. [24399], 1105 W 8th St., Yankton, SD 57078, (605)668-1232
Mount Rushmore Natl. Memorial Soc. [10046], 13000 Hwy. 244, Bldg. 31, Ste. 1, Keystone, SD 57751-0268, (605)574-2523
Mount Rushmore Soc. [★10046]
Mount Vernon Estate and Gardens [★11138]
Mount Vernon Ladies' Assn. [11138], PO Box 110, Mount Vernon, VA 22121, (703)780-2000
Mount Vernon Ladies' Assn. of the Union [★11138]
Mountain Bicycling Assn; Intl. [23310]
Mountain Bike Assn; Intl. Police [6172]
Mountain Bike Orienteering Australia [IO], Ballarat, Australia
Mountain Bike and Tea Soc; Women's [23323]
Mountain Club; Appalachian [23936]
Mountain Dog Club of Am; Bernese [22230]
Mountain Historical Soc; Superstition [9383]
Mountain Horse Assn; Rocky [4949]
The Mountain Inst. [9960], 1707 L St. NW, Ste. 1030, Washington, DC 20036, (202)452-1636
Mountain Inst; Woodlands [★9960]
Mountain Lion Found. [5341], PO Box 1896, Sacramento, CA 95812, (916)442-2666
Mountain Lion Preservation Found. [★5341]
Mountain Pleasure Horse Assn. [4916], PO Box 112, Mount Olivet, KY 41064, (606)724-2961
Mountain Press Res. Center [21132], PO Box 400, Signal Mountain, TN 37377-0400, (423)886-6369
Mountain Rescue Assn. [12890], c/o Monty Bell, Membership Chm., PO Box 880868, San Diego, CA 92168-0868, (619)884-9456
Mountain Sanctuary; Hawk [5324]
Mountain State Organic Growers and Buyers Assn. [5068], c/o Scott Snyder, Pres., Healing Hills Herb Farm, HC 83, Box 79, Ellenboro, WV 26346, (304)684-5585
Mountain States Genetics Network [14504], c/o Joyce Hooker, Exec. Dir., 8129 W Fremont Ave., Littleton, CO 80128, (303)978-0125
Mountain Travel - Sobek - Defunct.
Mountain Vintners; Santa Cruz [★5420]
Mountaineering Coun; British [IO]
Mountaineering Coun. of Ireland [IO], Dublin, Ireland
Mountaineering Coun. of Scotland [IO], Perth, United Kingdom
Mountaineers [23945], 300 3rd Ave. W, Seattle, WA 98119, (206)284-6310
Mountains and Plains Booksellers Assn. [741], 19 Old Town Sq., Ste. 238, Fort Collins, CO 80524, (970)484-5856
Mountains Winegrowers Assn; Santa Cruz [5420]
Mounted Games Across Am. [23830], 15710 Union Chapel Rd., Woodbine, MD 21797
Mounted Games Assn. of Ireland [IO], Cashel, Ireland
Mounted Orienteering; Natl. Assn. of Competitive [23640]
Moursund Family History Assn. - Address unknown since 2007.
Mouse
  Amer. Fancy Rat and Mouse Assn. [22704]

Reference to "IO" in place of a book number signifies that the association may be found in the 45th edition of International Organizations.

Fitzgerald's Fancys: Rat and Mouse Info. [22705]
Rat Fan Club [22706]
Rat and Mouse Club of Am. [22707]
Rat, Mouse, and Hamster Fanciers [22708]
The Mouse Club - Address unknown since 2001.
Mouse Club of Am; Rat and [22707]
Mouser Family Org; Johann Frederick [20959]
Mouvement Chretien pour la Paix [★IO]
Mouvement Contre le Racisme et pour l'Amitie Entre les Peuples [★IO]
Mouvement Ecologique [★IO]
Mouvement des Entreprises de France [★IO]
Mouvement Francais pour le Planning Familial [IO], Paris, France
Mouvement Haitien de Liberation [★17682]
Mouvement Intl. de la Jeunesse Agricole et Rurale Catholique [★IO]
Mouvement Intl. de la Reconciliation [★IO]
Mouvement Mondial des Meres [★IO]
Mouvement Mondial des Travailleurs Chretiens [★IO]
Mouvement Natl. Contre le Racisme [★IO]
Mouvement du Nid [IO], Clichy, France
Mouvement de Saintete Biblique [★IO]
Mouvement Soufi Intl. [★IO]
MOVE - Address unknown since 1997.
Move Am. Forward [18733], PO Box 1497, Sacramento, CA 95812, (916)441-6197
MOVE Intl.: Mobility Opportunities Via Educ. - USA [11962], 1300 17th St., City Centre, Bakersfield, CA 93301-4504, (800)397-6683
MOVE International: Mobility Opportunities Via Education - USA [IO], Bakersfield, CA, United States
Movement Against Racism and for Friendship Between Peoples [IO], Paris, France
Movement to Arrest Oppressors - Address unknown since 1995.
Movement Assn; Early Childhood Music and [12618]
Movement for a Better World - Defunct.
Movement for a Democratic Military - Address unknown since 1995.
Movement Disorder Soc. [14647], 555 E Wells St., Ste. 1100, Milwaukee, WI 53202-3823, (414)276-2145
Movement Disorder Soc. [IO], Milwaukee, WI, United States
Movement for Economic Justice - Defunct.
Movement for Fed. of the Americas - Defunct.
Movement for a Free Philippines - Address unknown since 1991.
Movement of French Businesses [IO], Paris, France
Movement for the Handicapped; Adventures in [16597]
Movement for Human Rights in Vietnam - Defunct.
Movement for an Independent and Democratic Cuba [17367], 10020 SW 37th Terr., Miami, FL 33165, (305)221-3820
Movement for an Independent and Democratic Cuba [IO], Miami, FL, United States
Movement for a New Soc. - Defunct.
Movement Shorthand Soc. [★11208]
Movement Stud; Laban/Bartenieff Inst. of [9891]
Movement Stud; Laban Inst. of [★9891]
Movement Theatre Assn; Natl. [11028]
Movement Theatre Intl. [11025], 50 Bernard Dr., Yardley, PA 19067, (215)519-0321
Movement Theatre Intl. [IO], Yardley, PA, United States
Movement Writing; Center for Sutton [11208]
Movers Conf; Amer. [★3559]
Movers Inst. [★IO]
Movers Inst; Amer. [★3559]
Movers' and Warehousemen's Assn. of America - Defunct.
Movie Collectors; Valley Camera and [★10844]
Movie Makers Guild - Defunct.
Movie Star Club - Defunct.
Movies; Women Make [11094]
Moviment ghall-Ambjent [★IO]
Movimento Cristiano per la Pace [★IO]
Movimento dei Focolari [★IO]
Movimiento Familiar Cristiano - Address unknown since 2001.
Movimiento Internacional de Estudiantes Catolicos - Pax Romana [★IO]

Movimiento Mundial en favor de la infancia [★IO]
Movimiento Popular Peru - Address unknown since 2002.
Movimiento Pro Independencia de Puerto Rico - Address unknown since 1995.
Moving Ideas Network [18460], 1100 15th St. NW, Ste. 600, Washington, DC 20005, (202)465-3777
Moving Image Archivists; Assn. of [9932]
Moving and Storage Assn; Amer. [3559]
Movius, Mevius, Mobius Family Assn. - Address unknown since 2007.
Mower Inst; Lawn [★1294]
Mower Racing Assn; U.S. Lawn [23673]
Mozambique
    Amer. Refugee Comm. [12805]
Mozambique Chamber of Commerce [IO], Maputo, Mozambique
Mozambique News Agency [IO], Maputo, Mozambique
Mozambique Solidarity Office - Address unknown since 2001.
Mozambique Support Network - Address unknown since 2001.
Mozart Soc. of Am. [9814], Univ. of Nevada, Dept. of Music, 4505 S Maryland Pkwy., Las Vegas, NV 89154-5025, (702)732-4391
MPLS Forum [★6714]
MPLS Forum [★IO]
MPLS and Frame Relay Alliance [IO], Fremont, CA, United States
MPLS and Frame Relay Alliance [6714], 39355 California St., Ste. 307, Fremont, CA 94538, (510)608-5910
MPS Australia [IO], Sydney, Australia
MPS Austria [IO], Graz, Austria
MPS Brazil [IO], Porto Alegre, Brazil
MPS; Parents for [★15253]
MPS Soc. [★15253]
MPS Soc; Natl. [15253]
Mr. Holland's Opus Found. [8914], 15125 Ventura Blvd., Ste. 204, Sherman Oaks, CA 91403, (818)784-6787
Mr. V Fan Club - Defunct.
MRA-The Mgt. Assn. [2502], PO Box 911, Pewaukee, WI 53072-0911, (262)523-9090
MS - Danish Assn. for Intl. Co-operation [IO], Dar es Salaam, United Republic of Tanzania
MS Felag Islands [IO], Reykjavik, Iceland
Ms. Found. for Women [17549], 120 Wall St., 33rd Fl., New York, NY 10005, (212)742-2300
MS Nepal: Danish Assn. for Intl. Cooperation [IO], Kathmandu, Nepal
MS-Training Center for Development Co-operation [IO], Arusha, United Republic of Tanzania
MSG
    The Glutamate Assn. - U.S. [1516]
MSPCA-Angell [11429], 350 S Huntington Ave., Boston, MA 02130, (617)522-7400
MSUD Family Support Gp. [★15250]
MSV - Ennio Morricone Soc. [IO], Alkmaar, Netherlands
MTM Assn. for Standards and Res. [7165], 1111 E Touhy Ave., Des Plaines, IL 60018, (847)299-1111
Mu Alpha Theta [24538], c/o Univ. of Oklahoma, 601 Elm Ave., Rm. 1102, Norman, OK 73019-3103, (405)325-4489
Mu Beta Psi [24552], c/o Megan Roble, Ed., 1211 Ben Avon St., Indiana, PA 15701
Mu Kappa Tau [24535], 1200 Grainger Hall, Univ. of Wisconsin-Madison, 975 Univ. Ave., Madison, WI 53706
Mu Phi Epsilon [★24553]
Mu Phi Epsilon Intl. [24553], 4705 N Sonora Ave., Ste. 114, Fresno, CA 93722-3947, (559)277-1898
Mu Sigma - Address unknown since 1995.
MU-YAP Baglantili Hak Sahibi Fonogram Yapimcilari Meslek Birligi [★IO]
MU-YAP Turkish Phonographic Indus. Soc. [IO], Istanbul, Turkey
Muay Thai Assn; U.S. [23608]
Mucolipidoses
    Natl. MPS Soc. [15253]
Mucopolysaccharidoses
    Canadian Soc. for Mucopolysaccharide and Related Diseases [IO]

Natl. MPS Soc. [15253]
Mucosal Immunology; Soc. for [14943]
Mudgee Olives Assn. [IO], Mudgee, Australia
Muffy VanderBear Club - Defunct.
Mug Collectors of Am; Advt. Cup and [21956]
Muhleisen Family Exchange; Milliron - Millison - [21002]
Muhyiddin Ibn Arabi Soc. [20578], PO Box 45, Berkeley, CA 94701-0045, (510)653-2201
Mujeres Activas en Letras Y Cambio Social [8497], 1404 66th St., Berkeley, CA 94704, (510)926-4021
Mukono Multi-Purpose Youth Org. [IO], Kampala, Uganda
Mulch and Soil Coun. [1651], 10210 Leatherleaf Ct., Manassas, VA 20111-4245, (703)257-0111
Mule Assn; Amer. [4131]
Mule Assn; North Amer. Saddle [21520]
Mule Racing Assn; Amer. [23668]
Mule Soc; Amer. Donkey and [4127]
Mule Soc; British [IO]
Mule Soc; Southwestern Donkey and [21521]
Multi-Bank Data Processing Org. [★61]
Multi-Faith Gp. for Healthcare Chaplaincy [IO], London, United Kingdom
Multi-Handicapped Blind Children; Keren-Or Center for [★IO]
Multi-Handicapped Blind Children; Keren-Or Center for [★16863]
Multi-Housing Laundry Assn. [2406], 1500 Sunday Dr., Ste. 102, Raleigh, NC 27607, (919)861-5579
Multi-Level Marketing Intl. Assn. [2638], 119 Stanford Ct., Irvine, CA 92612, (949)854-0484
Multi-Level Marketing Intl. Assn. [IO], Irvine, CA, United States
Multi-Tenant Telecommunications Assn. - Address unknown since 1991.
Multi Users Group - Address unknown since 2003.
Multi-Vendor Integration Protocol; Global Org. for [18681]
Multicultural
    Alpha Iota Omicron [24611]
    Alpha Rho Lambda Sorority [24703]
    AMISTAD Am. [8502]
    Delta Gamma Pi Multicultural Sorority [24704]
    Delta Phi Omega Sorority [24705]
    Delta Sigma Chi Sorority [24706]
    Delta Xi Nu Multicultural Sorority [24708]
    Delta Xi Phi Multicultural Sorority [24685]
    DIVAS of Lambda Fe Uson Sorority [24709]
    Gamma Alpha Omega Sorority [24599]
    Gamma Delta Pi [24710]
    Intercultural Cancer Coun. [13830]
    Kappa Phi Gamma Sorority [24712]
    Lambda Psi Delta Sorority [24713]
    Mid-American Greek Coun. Assn. [24483]
    Natl. Org. for Diversity in Sales and Marketing [2644]
    Phi Sigma Nu Native Amer. Fraternity [24647]
    Pi Delta Psi Fraternity [24649]
    Proj. RACE [19047]
    Psi Sigma Phi Multicultural Fraternity [24594]
    Sigma Beta Rho Fraternity [24656]
    Sigma Lambda Alpha Sorority [24714]
    Sigma Lambda Gamma Natl. Sorority [24715]
    Theta Chi Omega Multicultural Sorority [24716]
    Zeta Chi Phi Multicultural Sorority [24717]
Multicultural Counseling and Development; Assn. for [11819]
Multicultural Educ; Natl. Assn. for [8582]
Multicultural Educ., Training, and Advocacy [11625], 240A Elm St., Ste. 22, Somerville, MA 02144, (617)628-2226
Multicultural Engg. Prog. Advocates; Natl. Assn. of [8370]
Multicultural Foodservice and Hospitality Alliance [1586], PO Box 25661, Providence, RI 02905, (401)461-6342
Multicultural Forum of the Amer. Soc. for Training and Development - Defunct.
Multicultural Golf Assn. of Am. [23455], 43 Main St., PO Box 1081, Westhampton Beach, NY 11978, (631)288-8255
Multicultural Info. Exchange; Ethnic and [★10354]
Multicultural Info. Exchange Roundtable; Ethnic and [10354]

A star before a book entry number signifies that the name is not listed separately, but is mentioned within the entry.

Multicultural Inst. of the Intl. Counseling Center [★11829]

Multicultural Publishers and Education Consortium - Address unknown since 2007.

Multicultural Rehabilitation Concerns; Natl. Assn. of [16323]

Multicultural Sci. Educ; Assn. for [9097]

Multidisciplinary Assn. for Psychedelic Stud. [15942], 10424 Love Creek Rd., Ben Lomond, CA 95005, (831)336-4325

Multidisciplinary Inst. for Neuropsychological Development - Address unknown since 2003.

Multiemployer Plans; Natl. Coordinating Comm. for [1242]

MultiEthnic Americans; Assn. of [12141]

Multiethnic/Multicultural Christian Education Resources Center - Defunct.

Multifamily Housing Industry; National Coun. of the [★1035]

Multimedia; Assn. for Applied Interactive [2666]

Multimedia Publishers Group - Address unknown since 2003.

Multimedia Telecommunications Consortium; Intl. [7775]

MultiMediaCard Assn. [7305], 3855 SW 153rd Dr., Beaverton, OR 97006, (503)619-0691

MultiMediaCard Assn. [IO], Beaverton, OR, United States

Multipartisan Coalition - Address unknown since 1999.

Multipel Sklerose Forbundet I Norge [IO], Oslo, Norway

Multipel Sklerose Forbundet i Norge [★IO]

Multiple Assn. Mgt. Inst. [★IO]

Multiple Assn. Mgt. Inst. [★314]

Multiple Birth
  Australian Multiple Birth Assn. [IO]
  Center for the Stud. of Multiple Birth [15272]
  Multiple Births Canada [IO]
  Natl. Org. of Mothers of Twins Clubs [12613]
  The Triplet Connection [12614]
  Twinless Twins Support Gp. Intl. [12615]
  Twinless Twins Support Group International [IO]
  Twins Found. [12616]
  Twins and Multiple Births Assn. [IO]
  Twins, Triplets, and More Assn. of Calgary [IO]

Multiple Birth; Center for Loss in [12665]

Multiple Births Canada [IO], Toronto, ON, Canada

Multiple Gestation; Center for Stud. of [★15272]

Multiple Myeloma Res. Found. [13845], 383 Main Ave., 5th Fl., Norwalk, CT 06851, (203)229-0464

Multiple Personalities and Dissociation; Intl. Soc. for the Stud. of [★15210]

Multiple Sclerosis; Assn. for Advancement of Res. on [★15349]

Multiple Sclerosis Assn. of Am. [14276], 706 Haddonfield Rd., Cherry Hill, NJ 08002-2652, (856)488-4500

Multiple Sclerosis Assn; Cyprus [IO]

Multiple Sclerosis Australia [IO], Lidcombe, Australia

Multiple Sclerosis Found. [15338], 6350 N Andrews Ave., Fort Lauderdale, FL 33309-2130, (954)776-6805

Multiple Sclerosis Intl. Fed. [IO], London, United Kingdom

Multiple Sclerosis Soc. of Canada [IO], Toronto, ON, Canada

Multiple Sclerosis Soc; Czech [IO]

Multiple Sclerosis Soc; Danish [IO]

Multiple Sclerosis Soc; Greek [IO]

Multiple Sclerosis Soc; Hungarian [IO]

Multiple Sclerosis Soc. of India [IO], Bombay, India

Multiple Sclerosis Soc. of Ireland [IO], Dublin, Ireland

Multiple Sclerosis Soc. of Malta [IO], B'Kara, Malta

Multiple Sclerosis Soc; Natl. [15349]

Multiple Sclerosis Soc. of New Zealand [IO], Wellington, New Zealand

Multiple Sclerosis Soc; Norwegian [IO]

Multiple Sclerosis Soc. - United Kingdom [IO], London, United Kingdom

Multiple Sclerosis Soc. of Zimbabwe [IO], Harare, Zimbabwe

Multiple Sclerosis South Africa [IO], London, United Kingdom

Multiple V-Belt Drive and Mech. Power Transmission Assn. [★2045]

Multiracial Amer. Scholarship Fund - Address unknown since 2003.

Multiracial Amers. of Philadelphia - Address unknown since 2001.

MultiService Assn. [IO], Desborough, United Kingdom

MultiService Forum [881], 48377 Fremont Blvd., Ste. 117, Fremont, CA 94538, (510)492-4050

Multiservice Switching Forum [★881]

Multisport Assn. of Russia [IO], Moscow, Russia

Multistate Tax Commn. [6297], 444 N Capitol St. NW, Ste. 425, Washington, DC 20001-1512, (202)624-8699

Multivariate Experimental Psychology; Soc. of [16174]

Mumford Family Assn. - Address unknown since 2007.

Mumpower Family Assn. [21004]

MUMS Natl. Parent-to-Parent Network [16541], c/o Julie Gordon, Pres., 150 Custer Ct., Green Bay, WI 54301-1243, (920)336-5333

Munchausen Syndrome by Proxy Allegations; Mothers Against [13968]

Mundo Atraves Dos Meus Olhos [★IO]

Mundo Negro [★IO]

Municipal Analysts; Natl. Fed. of [749]

Municipal Arborists and Urban Foresters Soc. [★6121]

Municipal Assn; Amer. [★6130]

Municipal Bond Women's Club of New York - Address unknown since 2001.

Municipal Consulting - Inst. for Org. and Economic Consulting [IO], Herne, Germany

Municipal Employees
  95th Infantry Div. Assn. [20691]
  Australian Municipal, Administrative, Clerical and Services Union [IO]
  Soc. of Municipal Arborists [6121]

Municipal Employees; Amer. Fed. of State, County and [24069]

Municipal Engineers; Amer. Soc. of [★6233]

Municipal Environmental Assn. - Defunct.

Municipal Finance Officers Assn. of U.S. and Canada [★6204]

Municipal Finance Officers Assn. of U.S. and Canada [★IO]

Municipal Government
  Amer. Fed. of State, County and Municipal Employees [24069]
  Arab Towns Org. [IO]
  Assn. of Civilian Technicians [24072]
  Assn. of County Chief Executives [IO]
  Assn. of Local Authority Chief Executives [IO]
  Assn. of London Govt. [IO]
  Assn. of Metropolitan Water Agencies [6135]
  Assn. of Municipal Equip. Professionals [IO]
  Chief Cultural and Leisure Officers Assn. [IO]
  City Planning Inst. of Japan [IO]
  Civil Ser. Employees Assn. [24073]
  Commn. for Local Admin. in England [IO]
  Commn. for Local Admin. in Wales [IO]
  Convention of Scottish Local Authorities [IO]
  Coun. of European Municipalities and Regions [IO]
  Equip. Managers Coun. of Am. [943]
  Federacion Latinoamericana de Ciudades, Municipios y Asociaciones [IO]
  Hispanic Elected Local Officials [6122]
  Intl. Assn. of Cities and Ports [IO]
  Intl. Assn. of Mayors Responsible for Capital Cities or Metropolises Partially or Entirely French-Speaking [IO]
  Intl. City/County Mgt. Assn. [IO]
  Intl. City/County Mgt. Assn. [6123]
  Intl. Inst. of Municipal Clerks [6124]
  Intl. Inst. of Municipal Clerks [IO]
  Local Authorities Res. and Intelligence Assn. [IO]
  Natl. Assn. of Govt. Employees [24075]
  Natl. Assn. of Local Councils [IO]
  Natl. Assn. of Local Govt. Environmental Professionals [6125]
  Natl. Assn. of Towns and Townships [6126]
  Natl. Black Caucus of Local Elected Officials [6127]

  Natl. Civic League [6128]
  Natl. Conf. of Black Mayors [6129]
  Natl. Fed. of Fed. Employees [24077]
  Natl. League of Cities [6130]
  NLRB Professional Assn. [24081]
  Northern Ireland Local Govt. Assn. [IO]
  Org. of Islamic Capitals and Cities [IO]
  Reason Public Policy Inst. [6131]
  Soc. of Local Authority Chief Executives and Senior Managers [IO]
  Soc. of Procurement Officers in Local Govt. [IO]
  U.S. Conf. of Mayors [6132]
  Women in Govt. [6133]
  Women in Govt. [IO]
  Women in Municipal Govt. [6134]

Municipal Law Officers; Natl. IST of [★5500]

Municipal League; Natl. [★6128]

Municipal Parking Cong; Institutional and [★2899]

Municipal Parking Cong; Intl. [★2899]

Municipal Public Hea. Engineers; Conf. of [★16246]

Municipal Res; Bur. of [★6192]

Municipal Res; Rochester Bur. of [★18427]

Municipal Treasurers Assn. of the U.S. and Canada [★6203]

Municipal Waste Mgt. Assn. [6354], 1620 Eye St. NW, Ste. 600, Washington, DC 20006, (202)861-6775

Munitions Carriers Conf. - Address unknown since 2003.

Munro Assn; Clan [20855]

Muntz Jet Registry [21721], 21303 NE 151st St., Woodinville, WA 98077-7612, (425)788-6587

Muntz Registry [★21721]

Muotikaupan Liitto [★IO]

Muoviyhdistys [★IO]

Mural Painters; Natl. Soc. of [9517]

Murder Victims' Families Against the Death Penalty [★17032]

Murder Victims' Families for Reconciliation [17032], 2100 M St. NW, Ste. 170-296, Washington, DC 20037, (877)896-4702

Murdered Children; Parents of [12685]

Murdered Youth; Mothers of [11710]

Murray Clan Soc. North Am. [21005], c/o Charles D. Murray, Pres., 112 Ruth Ln., La Vergne, TN 37086

Murray Grey Assn; Amer. [4239]

Muscular Atrophy; Natl. Found. for Peroneal [★15313]

Muscular Dystrophy Assn. [15339], 3300 E Sunrise Dr., Tucson, AZ 85718, (520)529-2000

Muscular Dystrophy Assn. [IO], Auckland, New Zealand

Muscular Dystrophy Assn; Brazilian [IO]

Muscular Dystrophy Assn. Singapore [IO], Singapore, Singapore

Muscular Dystrophy Canada [IO], Toronto, ON, Canada

Muscular Dystrophy Info. Intl; Soc. for [IO]

Muscular Dystrophy Ireland [IO], Dublin, Ireland

Muscular and Electrodiagnostic Medicine; Amer. Assn. of Neuro [15303]

Musculo-Skeletal Disorders Found; Jaw Joints and Allied [15773]

Musculoskeletal Disorders
  Coun. of Musculoskeletal Specialty Societies [15273]
  Facioscapulohumeral (FSH) Soc. [15320]
  Intl. Fed. for Manual/Musculoskeletal Medicine [IO]
  Jaw Joints and Allied Musculo-Skeletal Disorders Found. [15773]
  Musculoskeletal Tumor Soc. [15274]
  Musculoskeletal Ultrasound Soc. [16696]
  Natl. Ankylosing Spondylitis Soc. [IO]

Musculoskeletal and Skin Diseases Info. CH; Natl. Inst. of Arthritis and [16372]

Musculoskeletal Tumor Soc. [15274], c/o Marla Holderby, Vanderbilt Orthopaedic Inst., Medical Center East, South Tower, Ste. 4200, 1215 21st Ave. S, Nashville, TN 37232-8774, (615)343-4400

Musculoskeletal Ultrasound Soc. [16696], 3588 Plymouth Rd., No. 249, Ann Arbor, MI 48105, (734)973-7462

Musculoskeletal Ultrasound Soc. [IO], Ann Arbor, MI, United States

---

Reference to "IO" in place of a book number signifies that the association may be found in the 45th edition of International Organizations.

Musee canadien de la nature [★IO]
Museum of African Amer. History [★IO]
Museum of African Amer. History [9360], 14 Beacon
St., Ste. 719, Boston, MA 02108, (617)725-0022
Museum of African Amer. History [★9358]
Museum of African Art - Frederick Douglass Inst. -
Defunct.
Museum of Am; Lock [9835]
Museum of Am; Polish [10882]
Museum of Amer. Finance [10508], 26 Broadway,
Ste. 947, New York, NY 10004, (212)908-4110
Museum of Amer. Financial History [★10508]
Museum of Amer. Jewish Military History; Natl.
[21312]
Museum; Amer. Swedish Historical [10987]
Museum Assn. [★IO]
Museum Assn. of Am; Art [★9541]
Museum Assn. of the Amer. Frontier [★10132]
Museum Assn. of the Amer. Frontier [★IO]
Museum Assn; Custer Battlefield Historical and
[10106]
Museum Assn; Natl. Maritime [★10513]
Museum Assn; Transport [10926]
Museum Assn; Yosemite [★7367]
Museum Cmpt. Network [IO], Ottawa, ON, Canada
Museum and Cultural Center; Swedish [★IO]
Museum and Cultural Center; Swedish [★10990]
Museum of the Earth; Paleontological Res. Institu-
tion/ [7429]
Museum Educ. Roundtable [10509], PO Box 15727,
Washington, DC 20003, (202)547-8378
Museum Found; Swift [21481]
Museum; Friends of the Abraham Lincoln [11113]
Museum of the Fur Trade [10132], 6321 Hwy. 20,
Chadron, NE 69337, (308)432-3843
Museum of the Fur Trade [IO], Chadron, NE, United
States
Museum Hall of Fame; Water Ski [★23975]
Museum; Heisey Collectors of America/National
Heisey Glass [22558]
Museum of Independent Telephony [★22985]
Museum; Intl. Boxing Hall of Fame [23261]
Museum and Memorial Lib; James Monroe Law Off.
[★11128]
Museum of Menstruation and Women's Hea.
[15611], PO Box 2398, Landover Hills Br., Hyatts-
ville, MD 20784-0398, (301)459-4450
Museum of Motor Racing; Eastern [21634]
Museum; Natl. Building [6477]
Museum; National Capital Trolley [★10133]
Museum; Natl. Liberty [17723]
Museum of Natural History; Amer. [7357]
Museum of Negro History; Amer. [★9360]
Museum; Peace [18234]
Museum; Penobscot Marine [10445]
Museum of the Polish Catholic Union of Am;
Archives and [★10882]
Museum of Racing and Hall of Fame; Natl. [23508]
Museum Res. Associates [★6801]
Museum; San Diego County Railway [★10918]
Museum; San Diego Railroad [★10918]
Museum Soc; Tangier Amer. Legation [10068]
Museum; South St. Seaport [10446]
Museum of Sport; Natl. Art [9457]
Museum Store Assn. [3414], 4100 E Mississippi
Ave., Ste. 800, Denver, CO 80246-3055, (303)504-
9223
Museum; Superstition Mountain/Lost Dutchman
[★9383]
Museum of Transport [★10926]
Museum of Trans; Natl. Capital Historical [10133]
Museum; Trotting Horse [★23498]
Museum Trustee Assn. [10510], 4633 E Broadway
Blvd., Ste. 101, Tucson, AZ 85711, (520)322-5555
Museum Trustee Comm. for Res. and Development
[★10510]
Museum; Uncle Remus [9717]
Museum Volunteers; U.S. Assn. of [★10489]
Museum and White House of the Confederacy
[★10105]
Museums
African Amer. Museums Assn. [10488]
Afro-American Historical Soc. Museum [9354]
Aircraft Engine Historical Soc. [9364]
Amer. Assn. for Museum Volunteers [10489]

Amer. Assn. of Museums [10490]
Amer. Assn. for Zoological Nomenclature [7859]
Amer. Aviation Historical Soc. [21426]
Amer. Fed. of Arts [9541]
Amer. Friends of Beth Hatefutsoth [10253]
Amer. Friends of the Israel Museum [10491]
Amer. Friends of the Natl. Gallery of Australia
[10492]
Amer. Inst. of Baking [445]
Amer. Oil and Gas Historical Soc. [2915]
Assn. of Art Museum Curators [10493]
Assn. of Art Museum Curators [IO]
Assn. of Art Museum Directors [10494]
Assn. of Children's Museums [10495]
Assn. of Coll. and Univ. Museums and Galleries
[10496]
Assn. of Independent Museums [IO]
Assn. for Living History, Farm and Agricultural
Museums [10497]
Assn. of Sci. Museum Directors [10498]
Assn. of Science-Technology Centers [10499]
Assn. of Zoological Horticulture [4974]
Australian Fed. of Friends of Museums [IO]
British Assn. of Friends of Museums [IO]
Canadian Art Museum Directors' Org. [IO]
Canadian Conservation Inst. [IO]
Canadian Fed. of Friends of Museums [IO]
Canadian Football Hall of Fame and Museum [IO]
Canadian Museums Assn. [IO]
Coll. Art Assn. [7969]
Commonwealth Assn. of Museums [IO]
Coun. of Amer. Jewish Museums [10500]
Coun. of Amer. Maritime Museums [10501]
Coun. for Museum Anthropology [10502]
Danish Museums Assn. of Cultural History [IO]
Edna Hibel Soc. [10503]
European Assn. of Museums of the History of
Medical Sciences [IO]
Exhibit Designers and Producers Assn. [1337]
Finnish Museums Assn. [IO]
Friends of Fiber Art Intl. [9441]
Friends of the Louvre Museum [IO]
Fudan Museum Found. [IO]
Fudan Museum Found. [10504]
Gay, Lesbian, Bisexual, Transgender Historical
Soc. [10078]
German Museums Assn. [IO]
Historic Naval Ships Assn. [10440]
Hong Kong Museum of Medical Sciences Soc.
[IO]
Independent Curators Intl. [9444]
Intermuseum Conservation Assn. [10505]
Intl. Assn. of Agricultural Museums [IO]
Intl. Confed. of Architectural Museums [IO]
Intl. Cong. of Maritime Museums [IO]
Intl. Cong. of Maritime Museums [10506]
Intl. Coun. of Museums [IO]
Intl. Garden Club [10040]
Intl. Museum Theatre Alliance [10507]
International Museum Theatre Alliance [IO]
Intl. Sports Heritage Assn. [23827]
Mamie Doud Eisenhower Birthplace Found.
[10044]
Maritime Fiddlers Assn. [IO]
Morris-Jumel Mansion [11137]
Museum of Amer. Finance [10508]
Museum Cmpt. Network [IO]
Museum Educ. Roundtable [10509]
Museum Store Assn. [3414]
Museum Trustee Assn. [10510]
Museums Assn. - England [IO]
Museums Australia [IO]
Natl. Assn. of Auto. Museums [10511]
Natl. Assn. for Interpretation [7363]
Natl. Automotive and Truck Museum of U.S.
[10512]
Natl. Historical Fire Found. [22422]
Natural Sci. Collections Alliance [6590]
Org. of Military Museums of Canada [IO]
Pacific Islands Museums Assn. [IO]
Pony Express Historical Assn. [10145]
Pres. Benjamin Harrison Found. [11142]
San Francisco Maritime Natl. Park Assn. [10513]
Scandinavian Union of Museums Danish Sect.
[IO]

Scottish Museums Coun. [IO]
Small Museum Assn. [10514]
Soc. for Indus. Archeology [6458]
South African Museums Assn. [IO]
Swedish Museums Assn. [IO]
Swedish Travelling Exhibitions [IO]
Swift Museum Found. [21481]
Swiss Museums Assn. [IO]
U.S. Natl. Comm. of the Intl. Coun. of Museums
[10515]
Volunteer Committees of Art Museums of Canada
and the U.S. [10516]
Volunteers' Circle of the Natl. Gallery of Canada
[IO]
Western Assn. for Art Conservation [304]
World Antique Dealers Assn. [219]
Wyckoff House and Assn. [10517]
Museums; Amer. Assn. of Youth [★10495]
Museums Assn. - England [IO], London, United
Kingdom
Museums; Assn. for Living Historical Farms and
Agricultural [★10497]
Museums; Assn. of Railway [10908]
Museums; Assn. of Women's Committees of Art
[★10516]
Museums; Assn. of Youth [★10495]
Museums Australia [IO], Civic Square, Australia
Museums; Intl. Assn. of Medical [★15868]
Mushroom Caucus - Address unknown since 1999.
Mushroom Coun. [5035], 2880 Zanker Rd., Ste. 203,
San Jose, CA 95134, (408)432-7210
Mushroom Growers Assn. [★4742]
Mushroom Growers Assn. [IO], Stamford, United
Kingdom
Mushroom Growers' Assn; Natl. [4742]
Mushroom Growers Cooperative Assn. - Defunct.
Mushroom Inst; Amer. [4703]
Mushrooms
Mushroom Coun. [5035]
Music
Academia Musicale Chigiana [IO]
Acad. of Country Music [10518]
Accordion Fed. of North Am. [10519]
Accordion Soc. of Australia [IO]
Accordionists and Teachers Guild, Intl. [IO]
Accordionists and Teachers Guild, Intl. [8897]
Aerosmith's Official Fan Club [24836]
African Amer. Art Song Alliance [10520]
African-American Music Soc. [10521]
African Heritage Center for African Dance and
Music [9347]
Air Supply Fan Club [24837]
Alabama Fan Club [24838]
Alan Jackson Fan Club [24839]
Alliance of Artists and Recording Companies
[3346]
Alliance for Canadian New Music Proj. [IO]
Alternative Hea. and Fitness Assn. [10522]
Always Patsy Cline World Wide Fan Org. [24840]
Amateur Chamber Music Players [10523]
Amateur Chamber Music Players [IO]
Am. Sings! [10524]
Amer. Acad. of Teachers of Singing [8898]
Amer. Accordion Musicological Soc. [10525]
Amer. Accordionists' Assn. [10526]
Amer. Bandmasters Assn. [10527]
Amer. Bandstand Fan Club [25024]
Amer. Banjo Fraternity [10528]
Amer. Berlin Opera Found. [10529]
Amer. Bop Assn. [9863]
Amer. Brahms Soc. [9804]
Amer. Children of SCORE [10530]
Amer. Choral Directors Assn. [10531]
Amer. Coll. of Musicians [8899]
Amer. Composers Alliance [10532]
Amer. Composers Forum [9805]
Amer. Disc Jockey Assn. [2796]
Amer. Fed. of Jazz Societies [10270]
Amer. Fed. of Musicians of the U.S. and Canada
[24149]
Amer. Fed. of Violin and Bow Makers [2797]
Amer. Festival of Microtonal Music [10533]
Amer. Flute Guild [10534]
Amer. Friends of Julio Iglesias Fan Club [24833]
Amer. Guild of English Handbell Ringers [10535]

A star before a book entry number signifies that the name is not listed separately, but is mentioned within the entry.

Amer. Guild of Music [10536]
Amer. Guild of Musical Artists [24150]
Amer. Guild of Organists [10537]
Amer. Harp Soc. [10538]
Amer. Inst. of Musical Stud. [8900]
Amer. Inst. of Musical Stud. [IO]
Amer. Inst. of Organbuilders [2798]
Amer. Inst. for Verdi Stud. [10539]
Amer. Lithuanian Musicians Alliance [10540]
Amer. Matthay Assn. [8901]
Amer. Music Center [10541]
Amer. Music Conf. [10542]
Amer. Music Festival Assn. [10543]
Amer. Music Therapy Assn. [16205]
Amer. Musical Instrument Soc. [10544]
Amer. Musicians Union [24152]
Amer. Musicological Soc. [10545]
Amer. Nyckelharpa Assn. [10546]
American Nyckelharpa Association [IO]
Amer. Orff-Schulwerk Assn. [10547]
Amer. Pianists Assn. [22709]
Amer. Recorder Soc. [10548]
Amer. Recorder Teachers Assn. [8902]
Amer. School Band Directors' Assn. [8903]
American-Slovenian Polka Found. [10549]
Amer. Soc. of Composers, Authors and Publishers [5836]
Amer. Soc. for Jewish Music [10550]
Amer. Soc. of Music Arrangers and Composers [10551]
Amer. String Teachers Assn. [8904]
Amer. Symphony Orchestra League [10552]
Amer. Theatre Organ Soc. [10553]
Amer. Viola Soc. [10554]
Americana Music Assn. [10555]
Amis de Cliff Richard and The Shadows [IO]
Amy Beth Fan Club [24841]
Anglo-Austrian Music Soc. [IO]
Anne Murray Intl. Fan Club [IO]
Annie Sims Intl. Fan Club [24842]
Anthropology Film Center [6407]
Antique Phonograph Collectors Club [22710]
Art Greenhaw Official Intl. Fan Club [24843]
Arthur Rubinstein Intl. Music Soc. [IO]
Asian Amer. Music Soc. [10556]
Asian Worldwide Elvis Fan Club [24805]
Asian Youth Orchestra [IO]
Asiatic Philharmonia Soc. [10557]
Asleep At The Wheel Fan Club [24844]
Asociacion Colombiana de Musica Electroacustica [IO]
Asociacion de Musica Electroacustica de Espana [IO]
Assoc. Male Choruses of Am. [IO]
Assoc. Pipe Organ Builders of Am. [2799]
Assn. for the Advancement of Creative Musicians [10558]
Assn. of Anglican Musicians [20425]
Assn. of Armenian Church Choirs of Am. [10559]
Assn. of British Choral Directors [IO]
Assn. of British Orchestras [IO]
Assn. of Concert Bands [10560]
Assn. of Conductors in the Netherlands [IO]
Assn. of Festival Organisers [IO]
Assn. of Finnish Music Schools [IO]
Assn. of Finnish Symphony Orchestras [IO]
Assn. of German Concert Choirs [IO]
Assn. of German Music Dealers [IO]
Assn. of German Music Publishers [IO]
Assn. of Independent Music Publishers [2800]
Assn. of Irish Musical Societies [IO]
Assn. for Korean Music Res. [IO]
Assn. for Korean Music Res. [10561]
Assn. of Music Producers [2801]
Assn. of Music Writers and Photographers [10562]
Assn. of Music Writers and Photographers [IO]
Assn. of Performing Arts Presenters [7968]
Assn. for the Preservation and Presentation of the Arts [9355]
Assn. of Teachers of Singing [IO]
Assn. for Tech. in Music Instruction [8905]
Assn. of Woodwind Teachers [IO]
Astromusic [6492]
Austin Cody's Official Intl. Fan Club [24845]

Australasian Performing Rights Assn. [IO]
Australian Assn. of Men Barbershop Singers [IO]
Australian Music Centre [IO]
Australian Music Retailers Assn. [IO]
Australian Soc. for Music Educ. [IO]
Austrian Assn. of Music [IO]
Axis of Justice [18640]
Bach Elgar Choir [IO]
Bagpipe Soc. [IO]
Balalaika and Domra Assn. of Am. [10563]
Bands of Am. [10564]
Beach Boys Fan Club [24846]
Beatles Connection [24785]
Beatles Fan Club: Good Day Sunshine [24786]
Beatles Info. Center [IO]
Beatles Unlimited [IO]
Belgian Centre for Music Documentation [IO]
Bessie Smith Soc. [24847]
Better World Chorus [12617]
Better World Chorus [IO]
Big Band Acad. of Am. [10565]
Bill Deal and the Rhondels Fan Club [24848]
Billy "Crash" Craddock Fan Club [24849]
Billy Ray Cyrus Spirit [24850]
Bing's Friends and Collectors Soc. [24851]
Black Rock Coalition [17499]
The Blues Found. [10566]
Blues Heaven Found. [10567]
Blues Music Assn. [2802]
Blur Fan Club [IO]
Bob Homan Fan Club [24852]
Bohemia Ragtime Soc. [10568]
Bonnie Lou Bishop Intl. Fan Club [24853]
Branscombe Richmond Fan Club [24779]
British Acad. of Composers and Songwriters [IO]
British Assn. of Barbershop Singers [IO]
British Assn. of Symphonic Bands and Wind Ensembles [IO]
British Beatles Fan Club [IO]
British Bluegrass Music Assn. [IO]
British Fed. of Brass Bands [IO]
British Flute Soc. [IO]
British Horn Soc. [IO]
British Inst. of Organ Stud. [IO]
British Music Hall Soc. [IO]
British Music Info. Centre [IO]
British Music Rights [IO]
British Organ Grinders Assn. [IO]
British Suzuki Inst. [IO]
British Trombone Soc. [IO]
Broadcast Music, Inc. [10569]
Brooks and Dunn Fan Club [24854]
Bryan Adams BadNews [IO]
Butimar Productions [9849]
Caledonian Found. USA [10570]
Caledonian Found. USA [IO]
Calgary Musicians' Assn. [IO]
Canadian Amateur Musicians [IO]
Canadian Band Assn. [IO]
Canadian Country Music Assn. [IO]
Canadian Educational Ensembles [IO]
Canadian Fed. of Music Teachers' Associations [IO]
Canadian Grand Masters Fiddling Championship [IO]
Canadian Music Centre [IO]
Canadian Music Educators Assn. [IO]
Canadian Music Publishers Assn. [IO]
Canadian Opera Volunteer Comm. [IO]
Canadian Soc. for Traditional Music [IO]
Canadian Univ. Music Soc. [IO]
Canadian Viola Soc. [IO]
Carl Orff Canada - Music for Children [IO]
Carla Riggs-Hall Intl. Fan Club [24855]
Carousel Organ Assn. of Am. [22711]
CAS Forum of the Violin Soc. of Am. [10571]
Cecilia Lee Intl. Fan Club [24856]
Center for Contemporary Opera [10572]
Certification Bd. for Music Therapists [16213]
Chamber Music Am. [10573]
Charles Ives Soc. [10574]
Charley Pride Fan Club [24857]
Chet Atkins Appreciation Soc. [24858]
Chicago Fan Club [24859]
Chicago True Advocates [24860]

Children of the Earth - Italian Michael Jackson Fan Club [IO]
Chinese Music Soc. of North Am. [10575]
Choir Schools Assn. [IO]
Chopin Found. of the U.S. [10576]
Chopin Soc. [IO]
Choristers Guild [20426]
Chorus Am. [10577]
Chris LeDoux Intl. Fan Club [24861]
Chris Young Fan Club [24862]
Christian Instrumentalists and Directors Assn. [20427]
Chuck Negron Fan Club [24863]
Church Music Assn. of Am. [20428]
Church Music Publishers Assn. [20429]
Circle Club - The Official Fan Club of the Grand Ole Opry [24864]
Clarinet and Saxophone Soc. of Great Britain [IO]
Clarsach Soc. [IO]
Classical Music Lovers' Exchange [10578]
Clay Underwood Fan Club [24865]
Cliff Richard Fan Club of Am. [24866]
Cliff Richard Movement of New Zealand [IO]
Coalition of Asian Pacifics in Entertainment [1300]
Cobbett Assn. for Chamber Music Res. [10579]
Collectors Record Club [22712]
Coll. Band Directors Natl. Assn. [8906]
Coll. Music Soc. [8907]
Colm Wilkinson Appreciation Soc. [IO]
Commn. for Music Res. of the Austrian Acad. of Sciences [IO]
Company of Fifers and Drummers [10580]
Comunidad Electroacustica de Chile [IO]
Conductors Guild [10581]
Connie Francis Intl. Fan Club [24867]
Connie Stevens Fan Club [24868]
Contemporary A Cappella Soc. of Am. [10582]
Corps of Drums Soc. [IO]
Coun. for Music in Hospitals [IO]
Coun. for Res. in Music Educ. [IO]
Coun. for Res. in Music Educ. [8908]
Country Legends Assn. [10583]
Country Music Assn. [10584]
Country Music Assn. of Australia [IO]
Country Music Found. [10585]
Country Music Showcase Intl. [10586]
Cowsills Fan Club [24869]
Cowsills Fan Club [IO]
Creative Music Found. [10587]
Creative Musicians Coalition [2827]
Croatian Rock-n-Roll Assn. [IO]
Danish Musicological Soc. [IO]
David Allan Coe Fan Club [24870]
David Ball Intl. Fan Club [24871]
Debbie Harry Collector's Soc. [24872]
Debbie Myers Intl. Fan Club [IO]
Del Shannon Appreciation Soc. [24873]
Delbert McClinton Intl. Fan Club [24874]
Delta Omicron [24550]
Deutscher Allgemeiner Sangerbund [IO]
Diamond Connection [IO]
Diamond Rio Fan Club [24875]
Dinah Shore Fan Club [24876]
Dinah Shore Memorial Fan Club [24738]
Dolly Parton's Fan Club [24877]
Dollywood Found. [24878]
Donna Fargo Intl. Fan Club [24879]
Donny Osmond Intl. Network [24880]
Doors Collectors Club [24881]
Downhill Battle [2803]
Drinker Lib. of Choral Music [10588]
Drum Corps Intl. [10589]
Drum Corps Intl. [IO]
Duane Eddy Circle [IO]
The Duke Ellington Soc. [10590]
Early Childhood Music and Movement Assn. [12618]
Early Music Am. [8909]
Early Music Network [10591]
East Anglian Traditional Music Trust [IO]
East Coast Music Assn. [IO]
Eddy Raven Fan Club [24882]
Electronic Music Found. [10592]
Elvis' Angels Fan Club [24806]
Elvis Costello Info. Ser. [IO]

Reference to "IO" in place of a book number signifies that the association may be found in the 45th edition of International Organizations.

Elvis Forever TCB Fan Club [24808]
Elvis Presley Memorial Soc. [24809]
Elvis Teddy Bears [24810]
Elvisly Yours [IO]
Engelbert's "Goils" [24883]
Engelbert's Golden Eagles [24884]
Engel's Angels in Humperdinck Heaven Fan Club [24885]
Engel's Angels in Humperdinck Heaven Fan Club [IO]
Ernst Bacon Soc. [10593]
Ethel Delaney Intl. Fan Club [24886]
Europa Cantat - European Fed. of Young Choirs [IO]
European Amer. Musical Alliance [10594]
European Assn. of Artists' Managers [IO]
European Assn. of Music Academies [IO]
European Assn. of Music Conservatories, Academies, and High Schools [IO]
European Assn. of Youth Orchestras [IO]
European Conf. of Promoters of New Music [IO]
European Festivals Assn. [IO]
European Music Festival for Young People [IO]
European Music School Union [IO]
European Piano Teachers Assn. [IO]
European Soc. for the Cognitive Sciences of Music [IO]
European String Teachers Assn. [IO]
European Suzuki Assn. [IO]
European Union Choir [IO]
European Union of Music Competition for Youth [IO]
European Union Youth Orchestra [IO]
Everly Bros. Intl. [IO]
Face the Music Fan Club [24887]
Fair Organ Preservation Soc. [IO]
Federacion Argentina de Musica Electroacustica [IO]
Fed. Belge de Musique Electroacoustique [IO]
Fed. of Canadian Music Festivals [IO]
Fed. Nationale Hogroise [IO]
Fed. of Recorded Music Societies [IO]
Fed. Suisse de Musique Electroacoustique [IO]
Federazione CEMAT [IO]
Fellowship of Amer. Baptist Musicians [20430]
Fellowship of Makers and Researchers of Historical Instruments [IO]
Fellowship of United Methodists in Music and Worship Arts [20261]
Film Music Soc. [10595]
Finnish Amateur Musicians' Assn. [IO]
Finnish Music Publishers' Assn. [IO]
Fischoff Natl. Chamber Music Assn. [10596]
Florence Ballard Fan Club [24888]
Florence Ballard Fan Club [IO]
Folk Alliance [9955]
Folk Music Soc. of Ireland [IO]
Found. for the Promotion of Finnish Music [IO]
FR-ENGE Intl. [IO]
FR-ENGE Intl. [24889]
Frankie Laine Soc. of Am. [24890]
French Soc. of Musicology [IO]
Fretted Instrument Guild of Am. [10597]
Friends of the Cassidys [24891]
Friends of Dennis Lee Fan Club [24780]
Friends of Dennis Wilson [24892]
Friends of Guy Clark [24893]
Friends of Julio Intl. [24894]
Friends of Paul Overstreet [24895]
Friends of Ty Herndon Fan Club [24896]
Future of Music Coalition [10598]
Gale Storm Appreciation Soc. [24744]
Galpin Soc. [IO]
Game Audio Network Guild [1715]
Gary Morris Fan Club [24897]
Gathering of Nations [10742]
Gaudeamus Found. [IO]
Gay and Lesbian Assn. of Choruses [10599]
Gene Pitney Intl. Fan Club [24898]
Gene Summers Intl. Fan Club [24899]
Gene Summers Intl. Fan Club [IO]
Genesis Info. [24900]
George Strait Fan Club [24901]
German Soc. of School Music Educators [IO]
Gilbert and Sullivan Soc. [IO]

Glenn Miller Birthplace Soc. [24902]
Global Alliance of Performers [10773]
Global Mobile Entertainers Assn. [1302]
Gordon Inst. for Music Learning [8910]
Gospel Music Assn. [10600]
Gospel Music Assn. Canada [IO]
Gospel Music Workshop of Am. [10601]
Gram Parsons Found. [24903]
GRAMMY Found. [10602]
The Grascals Fan Club [24904]
Groovy Mondays [IO]
Guam Symphony Soc. [10603]
Guild of Amer. Luthiers [2804]
Guild of American Luthiers [IO]
Guild of Carillonneurs in North America [IO]
Guild of Carillonneurs in North Am. [10604]
Guild of Church Musicians [IO]
Guild of Intl. Songwriters and Composers [IO]
Guild of Temple Musicians [20431]
Guitar and Accessories Marketing Assn. [2805]
Guitar Found. of Am. [10605]
Guitars Not Guns [18114]
Hamilton Acoustic Music Club [IO]
Handbell Ringers of Great Britain [IO]
Hank Williams Intl. Fan Club [24905]
Hank Williams Jr. Fan Club [24906]
Hardanger Fiddle Assn. of Am. [10606]
Harmony Found. [10607]
Harry Connick, Jr. Fan Club [24907]
Harry Connick, Jr. Fan Club [IO]
Heart of Texas Country Music Assn. [24908]
Hearts in Harmony - World Family of John Denver [24909]
Helen Forrest Fan Club [24910]
Hercules Intl. - Elton John Fan Club [IO]
Hip-Hop Assn. [10887]
Hispanic Org. of Latin Actors [10001]
Historic Brass Soc. [10608]
Historical Harp Soc. [10609]
Hong Kong Philharmonic Soc. [IO]
Hong Kong Sinfonietta [IO]
Hymn Soc. of Great Britain and Ireland [IO]
Hymn Soc. in the U.S. and Canada [20432]
Iceland Music Info. Centre [IO]
IMZ Intl. Music Media Centre [IO]
Incorporated Assn. of Organists [IO]
Incorporated Soc. of Musicians [IO]
Incorporated Soc. of Organ Builders - England [IO]
Independent Music Retailers Assn. [2806]
Infinite Dreams [IO]
Inst. of the Amer. Musical [10610]
Inst. for Expressive Anal. [16217]
Inst. of Musical Instrument Tech. [IO]
Inst. for Stud. in Amer. Music [8911]
Interactive Audio Special Interest Gp. [2807]
Intercollegiate Men's Choruses, An Intl. Assn. of Male Choruses [10611]
Intercollegiate Men's Choruses, An Intl. Assn. of Male Choruses [IO]
Interlochen Center for the Arts [9571]
Intl. Agnetha Benny Bjorn Frida Fan Club [IO]
Intl. Al Jolson Soc. [IO]
Intl. Al Jolson Soc. [24911]
Intl. Alliance for Women in Music [10612]
Intl. Alliance for Women in Music [IO]
Intl. Assn. of African-American Music [IO]
Intl. Assn. of African-American Music [10613]
Intl. Assn. of Electronic Keyboard Mfrs. [2808]
Intl. Assn. of Electronic Keyboard Mfrs. [IO]
Intl. Assn. of Jazz Appreciation [22713]
Intl. Assn. for Jazz Educ. [8912]
Intl. Assn. for Jazz Educ. [IO]
Intl. Assn. of Jazz Record Collectors [IO]
Intl. Assn. of Jazz Record Collectors [22714]
Intl. Assn. of Music Info. Centres [IO]
Intl. Assn. of Music Libraries, Archives and Documentation Centers (Australia Br.) [IO]
Intl. Assn. of Music Libraries Archives and Documentation Centres [IO]
Intl. Assn. of Piano Builders and Technicians [IO]
Intl. Assn. of Piano Builders and Technicians [2809]
Intl. Assn. for Res. in Vietnamese Music [10614]
Intl. Assn. for Res. in Vietnamese Music [IO]

Intl. Assn. for the Stud. of Popular Music [IO]
Intl. Band and Orchestral Products Assn. [IO]
Intl. Band and Orchestral Products Assn. [2810]
Intl. Bluegrass Music Assn. [10615]
International Bluegrass Music Association [IO]
Intl. Choral Network [IO]
Intl. Clarinet Assn. [IO]
Intl. Clarinet Assn. [10616]
Intl. Cliff Richard Movement [IO]
Intl. Cmpt. Music Assn. [IO]
Intl. Cmpt. Music Assn. [2811]
Intl. Concert Alliance [10617]
Intl. Confed. of Accordionists [IO]
Intl. Confed. for Electroacoustic Music [IO]
Intl. Conf. of Symphony and Opera Musicians [IO]
Intl. Conf. of Symphony and Opera Musicians [10618]
Intl. DJ Guild [2812]
Intl. Double Reed Soc. [10619]
Intl. Double Reed Soc. [IO]
Intl. Elvis Presley Fan Club (Hong Kong) [IO]
Intl. Fan Club Org. [IO]
Intl. Fan Club Org. [24912]
Intl. Fed. for Choral Music [IO]
Intl. Guild of Musicians in Dance [10774]
Intl. Horn Soc. [10620]
Intl. Horn Soc. [IO]
Intl. Manuel Ponce Soc. [IO]
Intl. Manuel Ponce Soc. [10621]
Intl. Music Coun. [IO]
Intl. Musicological Soc. [IO]
International Native American Flute Association [IO]
Intl. Native Amer. Flute Assn. [10622]
Intl. Organ Festival at St. Albans [IO]
Intl. Percy Grainger Soc. [9810]
Intl. Petula Clark Soc. [IO]
Intl. Piano Guild [IO]
Intl. Piano Guild [10623]
Intl. Polka Assn. [10624]
Intl. Polka Assn. [IO]
Intl. Sinatra Soc. [24913]
Intl. Soc. of Bassists [10625]
Intl. Soc. of Bassists [IO]
Intl. Soc. for Contemporary Music - Netherlands [IO]
Intl. Soc. for Contemporary Music - Uruguayan Sect. [IO]
Intl. Soc. for Contemporary Music - USA [IO]
Intl. Soc. for Contemporary Music - USA [10626]
Intl. Soc. of Folk Harpers and Craftsmen [10627]
Intl. Soc. of Folk Harpers and Craftsmen [IO]
Intl. Soc. for Hildegard Von Bingen Stud. [11124]
Intl. Soc. for Music Educ. - Australia [IO]
Intl. Soc. for Music and Educ. - Germany [IO]
Intl. Soc. for Organ History and Preservation [10628]
Intl. Soc. of Organbuilders [IO]
Intl. Soc. for Systematic and Comparative Musicology [IO]
Intl. Songwriters Assn. [IO]
Intl. Songwriters' Assn. - Ireland [IO]
Intl. Steel Guitar Convention [IO]
Intl. Steel Guitar Convention [10629]
Intl. Traditional Country Music Fan Club [24914]
Intl. Trombone Assn. [IO]
Intl. Trumpet Guild [IO]
Intl. Trumpet Guild [10630]
Intl. Tuba-Euphonium Assn. [10631]
Intl. Tuba-Euphonium Assn. [IO]
International Willie Nelson Fan Club [IO]
Intl. Willie Nelson Fan Club [24915]
Iron Maiden Fan Club [IO]
Israel Music Inst. [IO]
Israel Musicological Soc. [IO]
Italian Folk Art Fed. of Am. [10259]
Italian Independent Record Producers' Assn. [IO]
Jana Jae Fan Club [24916]
Japan Fed. of Composers [IO]
Japan Recording Media Indus'. Assn. [IO]
Jazz Nation [22715]
Jazz World Soc. [10632]
Jazz World Soc. [IO]
Jazzmobile [10633]
Jeanette MacDonald Intl. Fan Club [24748]

A star before a book entry number signifies that the name is not listed separately, but is mentioned within the entry.

Jeannie Seely's Circle of Friends [24917]
Jeff Carson Intl. Fan Club [24918]
Jerry Jeff Walker Fan Club [24919]
Jeunesses Musicales Intl. [IO]
Jeunesses Musicales de Suisse [IO]
Jew's Harp Guild [10634]
Jim Hubbard Fan Club [24920]
Jimi Hendrix Info. Mgt. Inst. [24921]
Jimmy Kish "The Flying Cowboy" Fan Club
   [24922]
Joe Diffie Fan Club [24923]
John Berry's Fan Club [24924]
John Gary Intl. Fan Club [24925]
John Gary International Fan Club [IO]
John Mellencamp Official Intl. Fan Club [IO]
John Mellencamp Official Intl. Fan Club [24926]
Johnnie Ray Intl. Fan Club [24927]
Johnny Len Fan Club [24928]
Johnny Mathis East Coast Fan Club [24929]
Julio - Am. Fan Club [24834]
Junior Shag Assn. [9890]
Jussi Bjorling Soc. - USA [9508]
Just Plain Folks Songwriting/Musician Networking
   Org. [2829]
Kappa Kappa Psi [24551]
Kate Smith Commemorative Soc. [24930]
Kate Smith Commemorative Society [IO]
Kathy Mattea Fan Club [24931]
Kelly Lang Fan Club [24932]
Kenny Chesney Fan Club [24933]
Kingston Korner [24934]
KISS Rocks Fan Club [24935]
KISS Rocks Fan Club [IO]
Kitty Wells-Johnny Wright-Bobby Wright Intl. Fan
   Club [24936]
Korea Musical Instrument Indus. Assn. [IO]
Kurt Weill Foundation for Music [IO]
Kurt Weill Found. for Music [10635]
Labor Heritage Found. [9578]
Latin Amer. Art Song Alliance [10636]
Latvian Choir Assn. of the U.S. [10637]
LE TRIPTYQUE [IO]
Lee's Familee [24937]
Lesbian and Gay Band Assn. [10638]
Leschetizky Assn. [10639]
Lesley Gore Fan Club [24938]
Liederkranz Found. [10640]
Light Music Soc. [IO]
Linda Davis Fan Club [24939]
Lorrie Morgan Intl. Fan Club [24940]
Lou Christie Intl. Fan Club [24941]
Lucio Fan Club [24942]
Lute Soc. [IO]
Lute Soc. of Am. [10641]
Lyre Assn. of North Am. [22716]
Making Music [IO]
Maple Leaf Club [10642]
Mariah Carey French Fan Club [IO]
Mariah Carey Official Intl. Fan Club [IO]
Mariah Carey Official Intl. Fan Club [24943]
Martina McBride Fan Club [24944]
Marty Stuart Fan Club [24945]
Meat Loaf UK Fanclub [IO]
Media in Ministry Assn. [20285]
Meet the Composer [10643]
Mel Tillis Fan Club [24946]
Mel Tillis Fan Club [IO]
Melodious Accord [10644]
MENC: The Natl. Assn. for Music Educ. [8913]
Metropolitan Opera Assn. [10645]
Metropolitan Opera Guild [10646]
Mexican Amer. Music Assn. [10647]
Michael Bolton Platinum Club [24947]
Michael Crawford Intl. Fan Assn. [24760]
Michael Jackson Fan Club [24948]
Michael Jackson Fan Club 3 Generations [IO]
MIDI Mfrs. Assn. [2813]
Midori and Friends [7976]
Midwestern Gilbert and Sullivan Soc. [9813]
Miso Music Portugal [IO]
Mixed Harmony Barbershop Quartet Assn.
   [10648]
Moravian Music Found. [10649]
Mozart Soc. of Am. [9814]
Mr. Holland's Opus Found. [8914]

Mu Beta Psi [24552]
Mu Phi Epsilon Intl. [24553]
Music Assn. of Korea [IO]
Music BC [IO]
Music Critics Assn. of North Am. [10650]
Music Distributors Assn. [2814]
Music Educ. Coun. [IO]
Music EdVentures [8915]
Music and Entertainment Indus. Educators Assn.
   [8916]
Music Indus. Assn. of Canada [IO]
Music Indus. Assn. - England [IO]
Music Info. Centre Norway [IO]
Music Lib. Assn. [10374]
Music Masters' and Mistresses' Assn. [IO]
Music Network [IO]
Music Notation Modernization Assn. [8917]
Music Performance Fund [10651]
Music Publishers' Assn. of the U.S. [2815]
Music Teachers Natl. Assn. [8918]
Musical Box Soc. of Great Britain [IO]
Musical Box Soc. Intl. [IO]
Musical Box Soc. Intl. [22717]
Musical Dog Sport Assn. [23385]
Musical Heritage Soc. [10928]
Musical Instrument Technicians Assn., Intl. [2816]
Musical Instrument Technicians Assn., Intl. [IO]
Musicians' Alliance for Peace [18223]
Musicians Found. [10652]
Musicians Union [IO]
Musicians Without Borders [IO]
Musicological Soc. of Australia [IO]
Musicological Soc. of Japan [IO]
Musik Remaja Indonesia [IO]
NAMM Found. Res. Div. [10653]
NAMM, the Intl. Music Products Assn. [2817]
Nashville Songwriters Assn. Intl. [10654]
Nashville Songwriters Assn. Intl. [IO]
Natl. Acad. of Music, Dance and Drama [IO]
Natl. Acad. of Popular Music [10655]
Natl. Acad. of Recording Arts and Sciences
   [10929]
Natl. Acad. of TV Arts and Sciences [567]
Natl. Alliance for Musical Theatre [10656]
Natl. Assn. of Brass Band Conductors [IO]
Natl. Assn. of Choirs [IO]
Natl. Assn. of Coll. Wind and Percussion Instruc-
   tors [8919]
Natl. Assn. of Composers, U.S.A. [10657]
Natl. Assn. of Mobile Entertainers [1314]
Natl. Assn. of Music Educators [IO]
Natl. Assn. of Negro Musicians [10658]
Natl. Assn. of Orchestra Leaders [17981]
Natl. Assn. of Pastoral Musicians [8920]
Natl. Assn. of Professional Band Instrument
   Repair Technicians [2818]
Natl. Assn. of Recording Merchandisers [3349]
Natl. Assn. of Rhythm and Blues Dee Jay's
   [10659]
Natl. Assn. of School Music Dealers [2819]
Natl. Assn. of Schools of Music [8921]
Natl. Assn. for the Stud. and Performance of
   African-American Music [8922]
Natl. Assn. of Teachers of Singing [8923]
Natl. Assn. of Youth Orchestras [IO]
Natl. Band Assn. [10660]
Natl. Catholic Band Assn. [10661]
Natl. Christian Choir [20433]
Natl. Club Indus. Assn. of Am. [1320]
Natl. Fastdance Assn. [9894]
Natl. Fed. of Music Clubs [10662]
Natl. Fed. of State High School Associations
   [23841]
Natl. Flute Assn. [10663]
Natl. Forum of Greek Orthodox Church Musicians
   [20434]
Natl. Found. for Advancement in the Arts [9587]
Natl. Fraternity of Student Musicians [8924]
Natl. Guild of Piano Teachers [8925]
Natl. Harmonica League [IO]
Natl. High School Band Directors Hall of Fame
   [8926]
Natl. Music Coun. [10664]
Natl. Music Coun. of The United Kingdom [IO]
Natl. Music Publishers' Assn. [2820]

Natl. Musicamp Assn. of Zimbabwe [IO]
Natl. Oldtime Fiddlers' Assn. [10665]
Natl. Opera Assn. [10666]
Natl. Orchestral Assn. [10667]
Natl. Pat Boone Fan Club [24949]
Natl. Performance Network [11031]
Natl. Piano Found. [8927]
Natl. Sheet Music Soc. [10668]
Natl. Symphony Orchestra Assn. [10669]
Natl. Traditional Country Music Assn. [10670]
Natl. Union of Phonographic Publishing [IO]
Natl. Youth Orchestra Assn. of Canada [IO]
New Edinburgh Folk Club [IO]
New Orleans Jazz Club [10671]
New Violin Family Assn. [10672]
New Wilderness Found. [10673]
New York Coun. of Motion Picture and TV Unions
   [24056]
New Zealand Accordion Assn. [IO]
NFHS Music Assn. [8928]
Nordic Coun. of Conservatories [IO]
Nordic Music Comm. [IO]
Nordic Symposium for Church Music [IO]
Norma Zimmer Natl. Fan Club [24950]
Norske Symfoni-Orkestres Landsforbund [IO]
North Am. Country Music Associations, Intl.
   [10674]
North Amer. Brass Band Assn. [10675]
North Amer. British Music Stud. Assn. [10676]
North Amer. British Music Stud. Assn. [IO]
North Amer. Dhrupad Assn. [IO]
North Amer. Dhrupad Assn. [10677]
North Amer. Folk Music and Folk Dance Alliance
   [22718]
North Amer. Guild of Change Ringers [10678]
North Amer. Saxophone Alliance [10679]
North Amer. Singers Assn. [10680]
North Amer. Toyah Fan Club [24951]
North Coast Region Music Teachers Assn. [IO]
Norwegian Sect. of the Intl. Confed. for Electroa-
   coustic Music [IO]
Oak Ridge Boys Intl. Fan Club [IO]
Oak Ridge Boys Intl. Fan Club [24952]
Official Dutch Jackson Fanclub [IO]
Official Elvis Presley Fan Club of Great Britain
   [IO]
Official Julio Iglesias Intl. Fan Club [24835]
Official Lane Brody and Eleni Global Fan Club
   [24953]
Official Lane Brody and Eleni Global Fan Club
   [IO]
Official Mary Wilson Message Bd. and Fan Club
   [24954]
One World Beat [IO]
OPERA Am. [10681]
Opera.ca [IO]
Orchestras Canada [IO]
Organ CH LLC [10682]
Organ Historical Soc. [10683]
Organ Historical Trust of Australia [IO]
Org. of Amer. Kodaly Educators [8929]
Original Four Aces and Al Alberts Archv. [24955]
Other Minds [10684]
Pam Tillis Fan Club [24956]
Pat Compton Fan Club [24957]
Pat Shea Intl. Fan Club [24958]
Pat Shea Intl. Fan Club [IO]
Patti Page Appreciation Soc. [IO]
Patti Page Appreciation Soc. [24959]
Pedal Steel Guitar Assn. [10685]
Percussion Marketing Coun. [1165]
Percussive Arts Soc. [10686]
Perry Como Circle [24960]
Peter Sellers Appreciation Soc. [24767]
Phantom Blue Phan Club [24961]
Phi Beta Mu [24554]
Phi Beta Mu [IO]
Phi Mu Alpha Sinfonia Fraternity and Found. Natl.
   HQ [24555]
Pi Kappa Lambda [24556]
Piano Mfrs. Assn. Intl. [2821]
Piano Mfrs. Assn. Intl. [IO]
Piano Technicians Guild [2822]
Pianoforte Tuners' Assn. [IO]
Player Piano Gp. [IO]
Polish Composers Union [IO]

Reference to "IO" in place of a book number signifies that the association may be found in the 45th edition of International Organizations.

Polish Singers Alliance of America [IO]
Polish Singers Alliance of Am. [10687]
Polish Soc. for Contemporary Music [IO]
Portuguese Assn. of Music Educ. [IO]
Positive Music Assn. [IO]
Presbyterian Assn. of Musicians [20435]
Presley-ites Fan Club Intl. [24813]
Producers and Composers of Applied Music [IO]
Professional Women Singers Assn. [10689]
Purple Flower Gang [24962]
Raissa Tselentis Memorial Johann Sebastian
    Bach Intl. Competitions [10690]
Raissa Tselentis Memorial Johann Sebastian
    Bach Intl. Competitions [IO]
Ray Price Intl. Fan Club [24963]
Razzy Bailey Fan Club [24964]
Recording Indus. Assn. of Am. [3350]
Reed Organ Soc. [10691]
REG - The Intl. Roger Waters Fan Club [24965]
Retail Print Music Dealers Assn. [2823]
Reunion pour la Promotion et l'Enseignement de
    la Musique Electroacoustique [IO]
Rhythm and Blues Rock and Roll Soc., Inc.
    [10692]
Rick Springfield Support Club: Human Touch
    [24966]
Rick's Loyal Supporters [24967]
Ricky Martin Worldwide Fan Club [22719]
Ricky Martin Worldwide Fan Club [IO]
Ricky Skaggs Intl. Fan Club [24968]
Rock the Earth [4604]
Rock Out Censorship [17044]
The Rock Poster Soc. [9469]
Rockapella Center [24969]
Roger Sessions Soc. [9815]
Rolling Stones Fan Club Off. [IO]
Ronald Stevenson Soc. [IO]
Ronny and the Daytonas Fan Club [24970]
Roy Rogers - Dale Evans Collectors Assn.
    [24971]
Royal Academy of Music [IO]
Royal Canadian Coll. of Organists [IO]
Royal Choral Soc. [IO]
Royal Coll. of Organists [IO]
Royal Conservatory of Music [IO]
Royal Irish Acad. of Music [IO]
Royal Musical Assn. [IO]
Royal Philharmonic Soc. [IO]
Royal Scottish Acad. of Music and Drama [IO]
Royal Soc. for Music History of the Netherlands
    [IO]
Royal Soc. of Musicians of Great Britain [IO]
Rustie Blue Intl. Fan Club [24972]
Sammy Kershaw Fan Club [24973]
Saskatchewan Music Festival Assn. [IO]
Sawyer Brown Intl. Fan Club [24974]
Schools Music Assn. [IO]
Schubert Soc. of the USA [9816]
Sci. Songwriters' Assn. [10693]
Sci. Songwriters' Assn. [IO]
Scott Joplin Intl. Ragtime Found. [IO]
Scott Joplin Intl. Ragtime Found. [10694]
Scottish Amateur Music Assn. [IO]
Scottish Harp Soc. of Am. [10695]
Scriabin Soc. of Am. [10696]
Sect. Nationale de la CIME [IO]
Sigma Alpha Iota Intl. Music Fraternity [24557]
Sinatra Music Soc. [IO]
Sinatra Soc. of Am. [24995]
Sir Thomas Beecham Soc. [10697]
SMV Fan Club [24975]
Societe Francaise d'Acoustique [IO]
Soc. for Amer. Music [10698]
Soc. for Asian Music [10699]
Soc. for Asian Music [IO]
Soc. for Educ., Music and Psychology Res. [IO]
Soc. for Electro-Acoustic Music in the U.S.
    [10700]
Soc. for Ethnomusicology [10701]
Soc. for Gen. Music [8930]
Soc. for Music Anal. [IO]
Soc. for Music Teacher Educ. [8931]
Soc. for Music Theory [10702]
Soc. for Music Theory [IO]
Society for the Preservation and Advancement of
    the Harmonica [IO]

Soc. for the Preservation and Advancement of the
    Harmonica [10703]
Soc. for the Preservation and Encouragement of
    Barber Shop Quartet Singing in Am. [10704]
Soc. for the Promotion of New Music [IO]
Soc. for the Publication of Danish Music [IO]
Soc. of Recorder Players [IO]
Soc. for Self-Playing Musical Instruments [IO]
Soc. for Seventeenth-Century Music [10705]
Soc. for Strings [10706]
Soc. for Traditional Music in Switzerland [IO]
Songwriters, Composers And Lyricists Assn. [IO]
Songwriters Guild of Am. [5859]
Sonic Arts Network [IO]
South African Music Rights Org. [IO]
South African Soc. of Music Teachers [IO]
Southeastern Composers' League [10707]
Southeastern Historical Keyboard Soc. [22720]
Southern Appalachian Dulcimer Assn. [10708]
Southern Songwriters Guild [2824]
Southwest Bluegrass Assn. [10709]
Southwest Celtic Music Assn. [9779]
Sparks Intl. Official Fan Club [24976]
Sparks Intl. Official Fan Club [IO]
Sphinx Org. [10710]
Spirit of Drum Corps Alumni Assn. [IO]
Spolecnost pro Elektroakustickou Hudbu [IO]
Surfun: The Official Jan and Dean Fan Club
    [24977]
Suzuki Assn. of the Americas [8932]
Suzy Bogguss Fan Club [24978]
Swedish Choral Assn. [IO]
Swedish Soc. for Musicology [IO]
Swedish Soc. of Organbuilding [IO]
Sweet Adelines Intl. [IO]
Sweet Adelines Intl. [10711]
Swiss Musicians' Assn. [IO]
Tamburitza Assn. of Am. [10712]
Tamizdat [9853]
Tammy Wynette Intl. Fan Club [24979]
Tanya Tucker Fan Club [24980]
Tanya Tucker Fan Club [IO]
Tau Beta Sigma [24558]
TCB for Elvis Fan Club [24814]
Tech. Inst. for Music Educators [8933]
Terri Clark Fan Club [24981]
Tex Ritter Fan Club [24982]
Tex Ritter Fan Club [IO]
Texas Intl. Theatrical Arts Soc. [11045]
T.G. Sheppard Intl. Fan Club [24983]
Theater of Dreams [IO]
Three Dog Night Fan Club [24984]
Toby Keith Intl. Fan Club [24985]
Tom Jones "Tom Terrific" Fan Club [24986]
Tom Lee Music Found. [IO]
Tracy Byrd Online Fan Club [24987]
Traditional Irish Music, Singing and Dancing Soc.
    [IO]
TRI-M Music Honor Soc. [10713]
Trisha Yearwood Fan Club [24988]
Ulster Soc. of Organists and Choirmasters [IO]
The Unconservatory [10714]
Union Suisse des Chorales [IO]
Unitarian Universalist Musicians' Network [20436]
United Catholic Music and Video Assn. [19731]
United in Gp. Harmony Assn. [10715]
U.S. Online Disc Jockey Assn. [2825]
U.S. Scottish Fiddling Revival [10716]
Villa-Lobos Music Soc. [10717]
Villa-Lobos Music Soc. [IO]
Vince Gill Fan Club [24989]
Viola d'Amore Soc. of Am. [10718]
Viola da Gamba Soc. of Am. [10719]
Violin Soc. of Am. [10720]
Violoncello Soc. [10721]
Wade Hayes Fan Network [24990]
Wagner Soc. of New York [10722]
We Remember Elvis Fan Club [24815]
Welsh Amateur Music Fed. [IO]
Welsh Music Guild [IO]
Western Music Assn. [10723]
Wilhelm Furtwangler Soc. of Am. [9819]
Wolfpack Fan Club [24991]
Women Band Directors Intl. [8934]
Women Band Directors Intl. [IO]

Women in Music Natl. Network [10724]
Workers' Music Assn. [IO]
Working Class Hero Beatles Club [24788]
World Assn. of Marching Show Bands [IO]
World Fed. of Amateur Orchestras [10766]
World Fed. of Intl. Music Competitions [IO]
World Folk Music Assn. [IO]
World Folk Music Assn. [10725]
World Music Contest Found., Kerkrade [IO]
World Piano Competition [10726]
World Rock 'n' Roll Confed. [IO]
World Swing Dance Coun. [9902]
Worshipful Company of Musicians [IO]
Wynonna Intl. Fan Club [IO]
Wynonna Intl. Fan Club [24992]
Young Concert Artists [10727]
Youngchoirs [IO]
Youth and Music of Germany [IO]
Yrjo Kilpinen Soc. of North Am. [9820]
ZZ Top Intl. Fan Club, Inc. [24993]
Music; Acad. of Country and Western [★10518]
Music Adjudicator Assn; Natl. Fed. [★8928]
Music Advisers Natl. Assn. [★IO]
Music Alliance - Defunct.
Music Arrangers; Amer. Soc. of [★10551]
Music and the Arts; Lutheran Soc. for Worship,
    [★19900]
Music and Arts Soc. of America - Address unknown
    since 1994.
Music Assn; Intl. Western [★10723]
Music Assn. of Korea [IO], Seoul, Republic of Korea
Music Assn; Nashville [★9579]
Music Assn; Natl. Fed. Interscholastic [★8928]
Music Assn; Natl. Traditional [★10670]
Music Assn; Natl. Traditional Country [★10670]
Music Assn; Southwest Celtic [9779]
Music Assn; Traditional Country [★10670]
Music Assn; Western [★10723]
Music; Astro [6492]
Music BC [IO], Vancouver, BC, Canada
Music for the Blind - Defunct.
Music Caucus of the Music Educators Natl. Conf;
    Natl. Black [★8922]
Music for Children; Carl Orff Canada - [IO]
Music Club; Cornhusker Country [★10670]
Music Composers; Christian Fellowship of Art [9808]
Music Critics Assn. [★10650]
Music Critics Assn. of North Am. [10650], 722 Du-
    laney Valley Rd., No. 259, Baltimore, MD 21204,
    (410)435-3881
Music Critics Circle of New York - Defunct.
Music and Dance Alliance; North Amer. Folk
    [★9955]
Music Distributors Assn. [2814], 1026 Northwood
    Dr., Effingham, IL 62401, (217)347-6699
Music Editors Assn. - Defunct.
Music Educ. Coun. [IO], Altrincham, United Kingdom
Music Education League - Defunct.
Music Educators Assn; Natl. Catholic [★8920]
Music Educators Natl. Conf. [★8913]
Music Educators Natl. Conf; Natl. Black Music
    Caucus of the [★8922]
Music EdVentures [8915], c/o Betty Hoffmann, 807
    Montana, Deer Lodge, MT 59722, (406)846-1317
Music and Entertainment Indus. Educators Assn.
    [8916], c/o Ms. Suzanne Clement, Admin. Asst.,
    1900 Belmont Blvd., Nashville, TN 37212-3758,
    (615)460-6946
Music and Folk Dance Alliance; North Amer. Folk
    [22718]
Music; Friends of Folk [★10725]
Music; Friends of Folk [★IO]
Music Indus. Assn. of Canada [IO], Toronto, ON,
    Canada
Music Indus. Assn. - England [IO], Surrey, United
    Kingdom
Music Industry Conf. - Defunct.
Music Industry Educators Assn. - Address unknown
    since 1988.
Music Industry Mfrs. Assn. - Defunct.
Music Info. Centre Norway [IO], Oslo, Norway
Music Instruction; Natl. Consortium for Computer-
    Based [★8905]
Music Jobbers Assn. - Defunct.
Music; Joint Commn. on Church [★19973]

A star before a book entry number signifies that the name is not listed separately, but is mentioned within the entry.

Music Libraries, Archives and Documentation Centers, U.S. Br; Intl. Assn. of [10362]
Music Lib. Assn. [10374], 8551 Res. Way, Ste. 180, Middleton, WI 53562-3567, (608)836-5825
Music Managers Forum [IO], London, United Kingdom
Music Marketing Assn; Guitar and Accessories [★2805]
Music Masters' and Mistresses' Assn. [IO], Cardiff, United Kingdom
Music Masters; Modern [★10713]
Music Merchants; Natl. Assn. of [★2817]
Music Network [IO], Dublin, Ireland
Music Notation Modernization Assn. [8917], c/o Thomas Reed, Founder, PO Box 241, Kirksville, MO 63501, (660)665-8098
Music Operators of Am. [★1299]
Music Operators Assn; Amusement and [1299]
Music Performance Fund [10651], 1501 Broadway, Ste. 518, New York, NY 10036, (212)391-3950
Music Performance Trust Funds [★10651]
Music Performance Trust Funds; Recording Indus. [★10651]
Music Producers Guild [IO], London, United Kingdom
Music Publishers Assn. [IO], London, United Kingdom
Music Publishers Assn; Church and Sunday School [★20429]
Music Publishers' Assn. of the U.S. [2815], 243 5th Ave., Ste. 236, New York, NY 10016, (212)327-4044
Music Publishers Protective Assn. [★2820]
Music Res. Found. - Defunct.
Music for the Rights of Man - Defunct.
Music Scholarship Assn; Cincinnati [★10726]
Music Schools; Natl. Guild of Community [★7979]
Music; Soc. for the Preservation of Film [★10595]
Music; Standing Commn. on Church [19973]
Music Supervisors Natl. Conf. [★8913]
Music Teacher Educ; Coun. on [★8931]
Music Teachers Natl. Assn. [8918], 441 Vine St., Ste. 3100, Cincinnati, OH 45202-3004, (513)421-1420
Music Theater Network; Natl. [11029]
Music Therapists; Certification Bd. for [16213]
Music Therapy; Amer. Assn. for [★16205]
Music Therapy Assn; Amer. [16205]
Music Therapy Assn. of British Columbia [IO], North Vancouver, BC, Canada
Music Therapy; Natl. Assn. for [★16205]
Music Trust Fund; Bluegrass [★10615]
Music Trust Fund; Bluegrass [★IO]
Music; U.S. Info. Center for Amer. [★10541]
Music, U.S. Sect; League of Composers - Intl. Soc. for Contemporary [★10626]
Music Video Assn. - Address unknown since 1987.
Music and Video Assn; United Catholic [19731]
Music Women Intl. - Defunct.
Music and Worship Arts; Fellowship of United Methodists in [20261]
Musica Nostra et Vostra, Natl. Corp. of America - Defunct.
Musica Sul Velluto [★IO]
Musical Arena Theatres Assn. [★9594]
Musical Artists; Amer. Guild of [24150]
Musical Box Hobbyists [★22717]
Musical Box Hobbyists [★IO]
Musical Box Soc. of Great Britain [IO], Welwyn, United Kingdom
Musical Box Soc. Intl. [IO], Springfield, MO, United States
Musical Box Soc. Intl. [22717], PO Box 10196, Springfield, MO 65808-0196, (417)886-8839
Musical Coun., A Natl. Assn. of Male Choruses; Intercollegiate [★10611]
Musical Dog Sport Assn. [23385], 9211 West Rd., No. 143-104, Houston, TX 77064
Musical Heritage Soc. [10928], 1710 Hwy. 35, Oakhurst, NJ 07755, (732)531-7003
Musical Instrument Technicians Assn., Intl. [2816], c/o Fran Hellmann, Treas./Office Mgr., 376 Old Woodbury Rd., Southbury, CT 06488
Musical Instrument Technicians Assn., Intl. [IO], Southbury, CT, United States

Musical Majority - Defunct.
Musical Merchandise Mfrs; Natl. Assn. of [★2805]
Musical Merchandise Wholesalers; Natl. Assn. of [★2814]
Musical Theatres Assn. - Defunct.
Musician Coalition; Cmpt. [★2827]
Musician Networking Org; Just Plain Folks Songwriting/ [2829]

Musicians
Accordian Professionals Intl. [2826]
African Amer. Art Song Alliance [10520]
Alliance of Artists and Recording Companies [3346]
Amer. Children of SCORE [10530]
Amer. Fed. of Musicians of the U.S. and Canada [24149]
Amer. Festival of Microtonal Music [10533]
Amer. Flute Guild [10534]
Amer. Guild of Musical Artists [24150]
Amer. Liszt Soc. [9807]
Amer. Musicians Union [24152]
Amer. Pianists Assn. [22709]
Americana Music Assn. [10555]
Art Greenhaw Official Intl. Fan Club [24843]
Asian Amer. Music Soc. [10556]
Asiatic Philharmonia Soc. [10557]
Assn. of Anglican Musicians [20425]
Assn. of Armenian Church Choirs of Am. [10559]
Austin Cody's Official Intl. Fan Club [24845]
Axis of Justice [18640]
Balalaika and Domra Assn. of Am. [10563]
Branscombe Richmond Fan Club [24779]
Choristers Guild [20426]
Chris Blair Fan Club [24802]
Chris Young Fan Club [24862]
Christian Instrumentalists and Directors Assn. [20427]
Church Music Assn. of Am. [20428]
Church Music Publishers Assn. [20429]
Classical Music Lovers' Exchange [10578]
Clay Underwood Fan Club [24865]
Cobbett Assn. for Chamber Music Res. [10579]
Country Legends Assn. [10583]
Country Music Showcase Intl. [10586]
Creative Musicians Coalition [2827]
Delbert McClinton Intl. Fan Club [24874]
Delta Omicron [24550]
Ernst Bacon Soc. [10593]
European Amer. Musical Alliance [10594]
Fellowship of Amer. Baptist Musicians [20430]
Friends of Josh Groban Fan Club [24994]
Friends of Ty Herndon Fan Club [24896]
Future of Music Coalition [10598]
The Grascals Fan Club [24904]
Guitar and Accessories Marketing Assn. [2805]
Hearing Educ. and Awareness for Rockers [16056]
Hymn Soc. in the U.S. and Canada [20432]
Intl. Artists Network [9506]
Intl. Assn. of African-American Music [10613]
Intl. Assn. of Jazz Appreciation [22713]
Intl. Bluegrass Music Assn. [10615]
Intl. Concert Alliance [10617]
Intl. Crosby Circle [24804]
Intl. Guild of Musicians in Dance [10774]
Intl. Horn Soc. [10620]
Intl. Native Amer. Flute Assn. [10622]
Intl. Percy Grainger Soc. [9810]
Intl. Piano Guild [10623]
Intl. Soc. of Bassists [10625]
Intl. Songwriters Guild [2828]
Intl. Traditional Country Music Fan Club [24914]
Intl. Trumpet Guild [10630]
Jeannie Seely's Circle of Friends [24917]
Jew's Harp Guild [10634]
Jim Hubbard Fan Club [24920]
Johnnie Ray Intl. Fan Club [24927]
Just Plain Folks Songwriting/Musician Networking Org. [2829]
Kelly Lang Fan Club [24932]
Kurt Weill Found. for Music [10635]
Labor Heritage Found. [9578]
Latin Amer. Art Song Alliance [10636]
Lee's Familee [24937]
Lyre Assn. of North Am. [22716]

Melodious Accord [10644]
Mexican Amer. Music Assn. [10647]
Michael Jackson Fan Club [24948]
Mozart Soc. of Am. [9814]
Mu Beta Psi [24552]
Mu Phi Epsilon Intl. [24553]
Musicians' Alliance for Peace [18223]
Musicians' Assistance Prog. [12619]
Musicians' Assistance Prog. Alumni Assn. [12620]
Musicians Found. [10652]
Natl. Assn. of Negro Musicians [10658]
Natl. Forum of Greek Orthodox Church Musicians [20434]
New Violin Family Assn. [10672]
New York Coun. of Motion Picture and TV Unions [24056]
North Am. Country Music Associations, Intl. [10674]
North Am. British Music Stud. Assn. [10676]
North Am. Dhrupad Assn. [10677]
North Am. Saxophone Alliance [10679]
Other Minds [10684]
Phi Mu Alpha Sinfonia Fraternity and Found. Natl. HQ [24555]
Positive Music Assn. [10688]
Presbyterian Assn. of Musicians [20435]
Recording Indus. Assn. of Am. [3350]
REG - The Intl. Roger Waters Fan Club [24965]
Ricky Martin Worldwide Fan Club [22719]
Rock the Earth [4604]
Roger Sessions Soc. [9815]
Rustie Blue Intl. Fan Club [24972]
Sci. Songwriters' Assn. [10693]
Scott Joplin Intl. Ragtime Found. [10694]
Sigma Alpha Iota Intl. Music Fraternity [24557]
Soc. of Singers [12621]
Songwriters Guild of Am. [5859]
Southeastern Historical Keyboard Soc. [22720]
Southern Songwriters Guild [2824]
Sphinx Org. [10710]
Tamizdat [9853]
Three Dog Night Fan Club [24984]
The Unconservatory [10714]
Unitarian Universalist Musicians' Network [20436]
U.S. Scottish Fiddling Revival [10716]
World Fed. of Amateur Orchestras [10766]
World Folk Music Assn. [10725]
World Piano Competition [10726]
Yrjo Kilpinen Soc. of North Am. [9820]
Musicians Against Nuclear Arms - Defunct.
Musicians Alliance; Amer. Lithuanian Organist [★10540]
Musicians' Alliance for Peace [18223], PO Box 1645, New York, NY 10021
Musicians' Alliance for Peace [IO], Stony Brook, NY, United States
Musicians' Assistance Prog. [12619], 322 W 48th St., New York, NY 10036, (212)397-4802
Musicians' Assistance Prog. Alumni Assn. [12620], c/o MAP, 817 Vine St., No. 219, Hollywood, CA 90038, (323)933-3197
Musicians Club of America - Address unknown since 1995.
Musicians Cooperative; Cmpt. [★2827]
Musicians; Fellowship of Christian [★20427]
Musicians; Fellowship of United Methodist [★20261]
Musicians Found. [10652], 875 6th Ave., Ste. 2303, New York, NY 10001-3507, (212)239-9137
Musicians; Intl. Guild of Symphony, Opera and Ballet [24157]
Musicians; Natl. Fellowship of Methodist [★20261]
Musicians; Natl. Hot Line Assn. - Defunct.
Musicians for Social Responsibility - Address unknown since 1995.
Musicians Union [IO], London, United Kingdom
Musicians Union; Amer. [24152]
Musicians United for Safe Energy - Defunct.
Musicians United to Stop Exclusion - Defunct.
Musicians Without Borders [IO], Alkmaar, Netherlands
Musiciens Amateurs du Canada [★IO]
Musicological Soc. of Australia [IO], Canberra, Australia
Musicological Soc. of Japan [IO], Tokyo, Japan
Musik Remaja Indonesia [IO], Jakarta, Indonesia

Reference to "IO" in place of a book number signifies that the association may be found in the 45th edition of International Organizations.

Musikkinformasjonssenteret [★IO]
Muskellunge
  Muskies Inc. [4177]
Muskelsvindfonden [IO], Arhus, Denmark
Muskies Inc. [4177], 14257 Waters Edge Trail, New Berlin, WI 53151-9508, (262)789-1255
Muskoka and District Chefs Assn. [IO], Orillia, ON, Canada
Muslim
  Amer. Muslim Alliance [18083]
  Amer. Muslim Coun. [19262]
  Amer. Muslims Intent on Learning and Activism [10728]
  Amer. Soc. for Muslim Advancement [10245]
  Assn. of Muslim Professionals [IO]
  Assn. of Muslim Scientists and Engineers [7005]
  Assn. of Muslim Social Scientists [7646]
  Assn. for Religion and Intellectual Life [19916]
  Coun. on American-Islamic Relations [19156]
  Coun. on Islamic Educ. [8669]
  Coun. of Masajid of U.S. [20097]
  Fed. of Islamic Associations in the U.S. and Canada [20098]
  Free Muslims Coalition [18084]
  Free Muslims Coalition [IO]
  Gamma Gamma Chi Sorority [24711]
  Human Assistance and Development Intl. [20437]
  Human Assistance and Development Intl. [IO]
  Indian Muslim Relief Comm. of ISNA [12860]
  Intl. Inst. of Islamic Thought [10247]
  Iranian Muslim Assn. of North Am. [20438]
  Iranian Muslim Assn. of North Am. [IO]
  Islamic Center of New York [20104]
  Islamic Circle of North Am. [20439]
  Islamic Correctional Reunion Assn. [20105]
  Islamic Food and Nutrition Coun. of Am. [2353]
  Islamic Info. Center of Am. [20106]
  Islamic Medical Assn. of North Am. [16003]
  Islamic Soc. of North Am. [10249]
  Muslim Amer. Soc. [20440]
  Muslim Assn. of Britain [IO]
  Muslim Public Affairs Coun. [18085]
  Natl. Assn. of Muslim Lawyers [5511]
  Natl. Legal Sanctuary for Community Advancement [6015]
  Natl. Young Adult Assn. [13504]
  Red Sea Team Intl. [20385]
  United Amer. Muslim Assn. [20441]
  Universal Muslim Assn. of Am. [20442]
Muslim Amer. Lawyers; Association of [★20097]
Muslim Amer. Soc. [20440], PO Box 1896, Falls Church, VA 22041, (703)998-6525
Muslim Arab Youth Assn. - Address unknown since 2004.
Muslim Assn. of Britain [IO], Wembley, United Kingdom
Muslim Public Affairs Coun. [18085], 110 Maryland Ave. NE, Ste. 210, Washington, DC 20002, (202)547-7701
Muslim Relations; Duncan Black Macdonald Center for the Stud. of Islam and Christian/ [★20100]
Muslim Scientists and Engineers; Assn. of [7005]
Muslim Social Scientists; Assn. of [7646]
Muslim Students Assn. of the U.S. and Canada [9184], PO Box 1096, Falls Church, VA 22041, (703)820-7900
Muslim Students Assn. of the U.S. and Canada [IO], Falls Church, VA, United States
Muslim Women's Natl. Network of Australia [IO], Granville, Australia
Muslim World League [IO], Makkah, Saudi Arabia
Muslim Writers Guild - Defunct.
Muslim Youth Movement of South Africa [IO], Durban, Republic of South Africa
Muslims of Am; Assn. of Indian [19109]
Muslims; Assn. of Indian [★19109]
Musser Intl. Turfgrass Found. [6644], PO Box 124, Sharon Center, OH 44274, (330)239-2458
Musser Intl. Turfgrass Found. [IO], Sharon Center, OH, United States
Mustang Assn; Amer. [4832]
Mustang Assn; Marine Corps [21176]
Mustang Assn; Natl. [4921]
Mustang Assn. and Registry; North Amer. [4933]
Mustang Assn; Southwest Spanish [4951]

Mustang and Burro Assn; Amer. [4833]
Mustang Club of Am. [21722], 4051 Barrancas Ave., PMB 102, Pensacola, FL 32507, (850)438-0626
Mustang Club; Intl. [★5330]
Mustang II Network [21723], 115 McDonald Dr., Houghton Lake, MI 48629, (313)475-4231
Mustang Motorcycle Registry - Defunct.
Mustang Owners Club [★21724]
Mustang Owners Club Intl. [21724]
Mustang Registry; 71 429 [21551]
Mustang Registry; 66,67,68 High Country Special [21561]
Mustang Registry; Spanish [4953]
Mustang Restorers and Collectors of America - Defunct.
Mustard Information Bur. - Defunct.
The Mustard Seed [★20369]
Mustard Seed Found. [20369], 3330 N Washington Blvd., Ste. 100, Arlington, VA 22201, (703)524-5620
Muszaki Koltsegtervez Klub [★IO]
Mutagen Societies; Intl. Assn. of Environmental [6578]
Mutagen Soc; Environmental [6575]
Mutagenes Presents dans l'Environnement; Assn. Internationale de Societes s'Occupant des Agents [★6578]
Mutilators Support Gp; Self- [★12557]
Mutism Found; Selective [15233]
Mutism, Inc; Found. for Elective [★15233]
Mutual Adjustment Bur. of Cloth and Garment Trades - Defunct.
Mutual Advt. Agency Network [★109]
Mutual Advt. Agency Network [★IO]
Mutual Advertising Agency Network - Address unknown since 2003.
Mutual Aid
  Artists' Fellowship [19263]
  Fed. Employee Educ. and Assistance Fund [19264]
  Gen. Grand Chap. of Royal Arch Masons Intl. [19235]
  Independent United Order of Mechanics - Western Hemisphere [19265]
  Riot Relief Fund [19266]
Mutual Aid Assn; Army [★18957]
Mutual Aid Assn; Army and Air Force [18957]
Mutual Aid Assn; Navy [18961]
Mutual Aid Assn. of the New Polish Immigration - Address unknown since 2000.
Mutual Aid Soc. of U.S.A; Russian Orthodox Catholic [19341]
Mutual Aircraft Conf. [★2131]
Mutual Assistance Assn; Cambodian [19422]
Mutual Assistance of the Latin Amer. Oil Companies [★IO]
Mutual Atomic Energy Liability Underwriters [2201]
Mutual Benefit and Aid Soc. [★19146]
Mutual Benefit Assn; Slovenian [★19368]
Mutual Benefit Assn; U.S. Letter Carriers [19142]
Mutual Benefit Dept. of the Order of Railroad Telegraphers [★19441]
Mutual Fire Insurance Engineers; Assn. of [★2178]
Mutual Fund Assn; No-Load [★3516]
Mutual Fund Educ. Alliance [3516], 100 NW Englewood Rd., Ste. 130, Kansas City, MO 64118, (816)454-9422
Mutual Fund Plan Sponsors; Assn. of [★3515]
Mutual Guild of Grand Secretaries - Address unknown since 1995.
Mutual Help Assn; Southern [11790]
Mutual Improvement Assn; Young Women's [★20209]
Mutual Insurance Advisory Assn. - Defunct.
Mutual Insurance Comm. on Federal Taxation - Defunct.
Mutual Insurance Companies; Natl. Assn. of [2214]
Mutual Insurance Engineers; Assn. of [★2178]
Mutual Insurance Rating Bur. - Defunct.
Mutual Insurance Societies; Americas Assn. of Cooperative/ [2141]
Mutual Israelite Assn. - Argentina [IO], Buenos Aires, Argentina
Mutual Life Assn; Amer. [19368]
Mutual Loss Res. Bur. [★2233]

Mutual Marine Conf. [★2131]
Mutual Musicians Found. - Address unknown since 2001.
Mutual Sewing Machine Dealers Assn. - Address unknown since 1995.
Mutual Soc. of French Colonials - Address unknown since 1995.
Mutual UFO Network [7481], c/o James Carrion, Intl. Dir., PO Box 279, Bellvue, CO 80512-0279, (888)817-2220
Mutualista Obrera Mexicana - Address unknown since 1995.
Mutually Owned Soc. for Songwriters - Defunct.
Muzzaki es Termeszettudomanyi Egyesuletek Szovetsege [★IO]
Muzzle Loaders Assn. of Great Britain [IO], Cambridge, United Kingdom
Muzzle Loading Rifle Assn; Natl. [23722]
MX Campaign - Defunct.
MX Information Center - Defunct.
My Good Deed [13308], 244 Madison Ave., No. 382, New York, NY 10016-2817, (212)613-4979
My Own Bus., Inc. [8030], 13181 Crossroads Pkwy. N, Ste. 190, City of Industry, CA 91746, (562)463-1800
My Travel Bug [9279], 60 Elm St., Westerly, RI 02891
My Travel Bug [IO], Westerly, RI, United States
Myanmar Badminton Fed. [IO], Yangon, Myanmar
Myanmar Customs Brokers Assn. [IO], Yangon, Myanmar
Myanmar Maternal and Child Welfare Assn. [IO], Yangon, Myanmar
Myanmar Medical Assn. [IO], Yangon, Myanmar
Myanmar Taekwondo Fed. [IO], Yangon, Myanmar
Myanmar Track and Field Fed. [IO], Yangon, Myanmar
Myanmar Weightlifting Fed. [IO], Yangon, Myanmar
Myanmar Yachting Fed. [IO], Yangon, Myanmar
Myasthenia Gravis Assn. [IO], Derby, United Kingdom
Myasthenia Gravis Found. [★15340]
Myasthenia Gravis Found. of Am. [15340], 1821 Univ. Ave. W, Ste. S256, St. Paul, MN 55104, (651)917-6256
MYCCI [IO], Huddersfield, United Kingdom
Mycenaean Commn. [IO], Vienna, Austria
Mycological Sect., Botanical Soc. of Am. [★IO]
Mycological Sect., Botanical Soc. of Am. [★7352]
Mycological Soc. of Am. [7352], PO Box 1897, Lawrence, KS 66044-8897, (785)843-1235
Mycological Soc. of Am. [IO], Lawrence, KS, United States
Mycological Soc; Amer. [★6632]
Mycological Soc. of Japan [IO], Tokyo, Japan
Mycologie; Assn. Internationale de [★7351]
Mycology
  British Mycological Soc. [IO]
  British Soc. for Medical Mycology [IO]
  Intl. Mycological Assn. [IO]
  Intl. Mycological Assn. [7351]
  Intl. Soc. for Human and Animal Mycology [IO]
  Medical Mycological Soc. of the Americas [15275]
  Mycological Soc. of Am. [7352]
  Mycological Soc. of Am. [IO]
  Netherlands Mycological Soc. [IO]
  North Amer. Mycological Assn. [7353]
  North Amer. Truffling Soc. [7354]
Myelitis Assn; Transverse [15368]
Myeloma Res. Found; Multiple [13845]
Mykenische Kommission [★IO]
Myoclonus Families United - Address unknown since 2002.
MYOPAIN Soc; Intl. [15842]
Myopia Intl. Res. Found. - Defunct.
The Myositis Assn. [15341], 1233 20th St. NW, Ste. 402, Washington, DC 20036, (202)887-0088
Myositis Assn. of Am. [★15341]
Myotubular Myopathy Rsrc. Gp. [16542], 2602 Quaker Dr., Texas City, TX 77590, (409)945-8569
Myron Floren Fan Club - Defunct.
Myrtle Soc. of Am; Crape [4976]
Myrtle Soc; Amer. Crape [★4976]
Mysore Resettlement and Development Agency [IO], Bangalore, India

A star before a book entry number signifies that the name is not listed separately, but is mentioned within the entry.

Mysteries
Dark Shadows Official Fan Club [25026]
Intl. Thriller Writers [11179]
London Club [11900]
Mystery Readers Intl. [24823]
Mystery Writers of Am. [11181]
Sisters in Crime [4069]
Mystery Readers Intl. [24823], PO Box 8116,
Berkeley, CA 94707-8116, (510)845-3600
Mystery Shopping Providers Assn. [2639], 12300
Ford Rd., Ste. 135, Dallas, TX 75234, (972)406-1104
Mystery Shopping Providers Assn. - Europe [IO],
The Hague, Netherlands
Mystery Writers of Am. [11181], 17 E 47th St., 6th
Fl., New York, NY 10017, (212)888-8171
Mystic Light; Aladdin Knights of the [22617]
Mystic Order of Veiled Prophets of the Enchanted
Realm; Supreme Coun., [19253]
Mystic Seaport [10441], PO Box 6000, Mystic, CT
06355-0990, (860)572-0711
Mystic Seaport Museum [★10441]
Mystic Shrine; Ancient Egyptian Arabic Order Nobles
of the [19227]
Mystic Shrine for North Am; Imperial Coun. of the
Ancient Arabic Order of the Nobles of the [19238]
Mystic Valley Railway Soc. [10914], PO Box
365486, Hyde Park, MA 02136-0009, (617)361-4445
Mysticism
Aetherius Soc. - United Kingdom [IO]
Astara [20443]
Cross-Cultural Shamanism Network [20444]
Earthspirit Community [20445]
Found. for Shamanic Stud. [20446]
Intl. Anchoritic Soc. [10460]
Intl. Assn. of Sufism [20101]
Intl. Soc. for Hildegard Von Bingen Stud. [11124]
Muhyiddin Ibn Arabi Soc. [20578]
Peyote Way Church of God [20447]
Soc. of Pragmatic Mysticism [20448]
Soc. of Pragmatic Mysticism [IO]
MythAdventures Fan Club - Address unknown since
1999.
Mythology
Alexandria Soc. and Educal. Found. [8161]
Mythopoeic Soc. [10427]
Natl. Assn. of Black Storytellers [10981]
Pagan/Occult/Witchcraft Special Interest Gp.
[10768]
Soc. for the Stud. of Myth and Tradition [10729]
Mythopoeic Linguistic Fellowship [★10402]
Mythopoeic Linguistic Fellowship [★IO]
Mythopoeic Soc. [IO], San Francisco, CA, United
States
Mythopoeic Soc. [10427], PO Box 320486, San
Francisco, CA 94132-0486
Myvesta - Defunct.

N

N-X-211 Collectors Soc; C.A.L./ [11106]
N3N Restorers Assn. - Defunct.
NA Cotton Compress and Cotton Warehouse Assn.
[★1093]
NAACCR [★13859]
NAACCR [★IO]
NAACOG Certification Corp. [★15506]
NAACP [★17129]
NAACP Natl. Housing Corp. [★17129]
NAACP Survey and Analysis of Minority Group
Building Contractors - Defunct.
NAADAC The Assn. for Addiction Professionals
[16509], 1001 N Fairfax St., Ste. 201, Alexandria,
VA 22314, (703)741-7686
NA'AMAT Canada [IO], Montreal, QC, Canada
NA'AMAT Pioneras [IO], Buenos Aires, Argentina
Na'amat U.S.A. [20162], 350 5th Ave., Ste. 4700,
New York, NY 10118-4700, (212)563-5222
Na'amat, the Women's Labor Zionist Org. of Am;
Pioneer Women/ [★20162]
NABAC, The Assn. for Bank Audit, Control and
Oper. [★467]
NAC - Environmental Info. Assn. [★620]
NACCA Bar Assn. [★6328]

NACCC [★19861]
NACE Intl. [★6840]
NACE Intl. [★7027]
NACE Intl. [★IO]
NACE Intl. - Brazil Sect. [IO], Rio de Janeiro, Brazil
NACE Intl. - Chile Sect. [IO], Santiago, Chile
NACE Intl. - Colombia Sect. [IO], Bogota, Colombia
NACE Intl. - India Sect. [IO], Bombay, India
NACE Intl. - Israel Sect. [IO], Haifa, Israel
NACE Intl. - Italian Sect. [IO], Milan, Italy
NACE Intl. - Kuwait Sect. [IO], Safat, Kuwait
NACE Intl. - Mainland China Sect. [IO], Beijing,
People's Republic of China
NACE Intl. - Mexico Sect. [IO], Mexico City, Mexico
NACE Intl. - Montreal Sect. [IO], Laval, QC, Canada
NACE Intl. - Oman Sect. [IO], Muscat, Oman
NACE Intl. - Pakistan Sect. [IO], Islamabad,
Pakistan
NACE Intl. - Peru Sect. [IO], Lima, Peru
NACE Intl. - Qatar Sect. [IO], Doha, Qatar
NACE Intl. - Saskatchewan Sect. [IO], Saskatoon,
SK, Canada
NACE Intl. - Saudi Arabia Sect. [IO], Dhahran, Saudi
Arabia
NACE Intl. - Singapore Sect. [IO], Singapore, Sin-
gapore
NACE International: The Corrosion Society [IO],
Houston, TX, United States
NACE Intl.: The Corrosion Soc. [7027], 1440 S
Creek Dr., Houston, TX 77084-4906, (281)228-6200
NACE Intl. - Toronto Sect. [IO], Burlington, ON,
Canada
NACE Intl. - Trinidad and Tobago Sect. [IO], Port of
Spain, Trinidad and Tobago
NACE Intl. - United Arab Emirates Sect. [IO], Abu
Dhabi, United Arab Emirates
NACE Intl. - United Kingdom Sect. [IO], London,
United Kingdom
NACE Intl. - West Asia/Africa Region [IO], Dhahran,
Saudi Arabia
NACEL Open Door [8625], 1536 Hewitt Ave., Box
268, St. Paul, MN 55104, (651)686-0080
NACHA: The Electronic Payments Assn. [486],
13450 Sunrise Valley Dr., Ste. 100, Herndon, VA
20171, (703)561-1100
Nacionalno udruzenje studenata agronomije [★IO]
Nacionalno Turisticne Zdruzenje [★IO]
Naciones Unidas sobre el Cambio Climatico [★IO]
NACM North Central [★1422]
NACORE Intl. [★3305]
NACORE Intl. [★IO]
NACRA Class Racing Assn; Intl. [★23192]
Nacro [IO], London, United Kingdom
NACSCORP [★3415]
NACYP - Clubs for Young People [★IO]
NADD - An Assn. for Persons with Developmental
Disabilities and Mental Hea. Needs [12552], c/o
Dr. Robert J. Fletcher, CEO/Founder, 132 Fair St.,
Kingston, NY 12401-4802, (845)331-4336
NADEC and Inter-Agencies Gp. [★IO]
Nady Eltayaran Elmasry [★IO]
NAE World Relief Commn. [★IO]
NAE World Relief Commn. [★19985]
NAED Educ. and Res. Found. [2503], c/o Natl.
Assn. of Elecl. Distributors, 1100 Corporate Square
Dr., Ste. 100, St. Louis, MO 63132, (314)991-9000
NAEM - Natl. Assn. for Environmental Mgt. [4588],
1612 K St. NW, Ste. 1102, Washington, DC 20006-2830, (202)986-6616
Naeringslivets Hovedorganisasjon [★IO]
Naeseth Lib; Vesterheim Genealogical Center and
[21155]
N.A.F. Intl. A.M.B.A. [IO], Copenhagen, Denmark
NAFSA/Association of Intl. Educators [IO],
Washington, DC, United States
NAFSA/Association of Intl. Educators [8445], 1307
New York Ave. NW, 8th Fl., Washington, DC
20005-4701, (202)737-3699
Nagasaki; Comm. for U.S. Veterans of Hiroshima
and [★13353]
Nager and Miller Syndromes; Found. for [14452]
NAGMR [2541], c/o Ron Otto, 1421 Ridgetree Trails,
St. Louis, MO 63021-5944, (636)527-7115
NAGMR Consumer Products Broker [★2541]

NAGMR Consumer Products Sales Agencies
[★2541]
NAGWS Athletic Training Comm. [★8987]
NAHB; Building Systems Councils of [2524]
NAHB; Home Mfrs. Councils of [★2524]
NAHB Res. Center [★1035]
Nail Collectors Assn; Texas Date [22121]
Nail Mfrs. Coun. [1082], c/o Professional Beauty
Assn., 15825 N 71st St., Scottsdale, AZ 85254,
(312)245-1575
Nail Patella Syndrome Worldwide [14467], 25826
Norrington Sq., South Riding, VA 20152
Nailing Tech. Assn; Indus. Stapling and [★1825]
NAIOP - The Assn. for Commercial Real Estate
[★3320]
Naisjarjestojen Keskusliitto - Kvinnoorganisationer-
nas Centralforbund Ry [★IO]
Naismith Memorial Basketball Hall of Fame [23132],
1000 W Columbus Ave., Springfield, MA 01105,
(413)781-6500
Naissances Multiples [★IO]
Najda: Women Concerned About the Middle East -
Address unknown since 2001.
Nakovammaisten Keskusliitto [★IO]
NALS [6013], 314 E 3rd St., Ste. 210, Tulsa, OK
74120, (918)582-5188
NALS, the Assn. for Legal Professionals [71], 8159
E 41st St., Tulsa, OK 74120, (918)582-5188
NALS, the Association for Legal Professionals [IO],
Tulsa, OK, United States
NAMBA Intl. [★IO]
NAMBA Intl. [★22654]
NAMDRC [15068], 8618 Westwood Center Dr., Ste.
210, Vienna, VA 22182-2222, (703)752-4359
NAMDRC: Physician Advocacy for Excellence in the
Delivery of Pulmonary and Critical Care [★15068]
Name Plate Mfrs; Natl. Assn. of Metal [★2720]
Name Soc; Amer. [10764]
Names Proj. [★13575]
Names Proj. Found. - AIDS Memorial Quilt [13575],
637 Hoke St. NW, Atlanta, GA 30318-4315,
(404)688-5500
Names Soc. - Defunct.
Namesake Towns Assn. - Address unknown since
1995.
NAMI [★15214]
Namibia Agricultural Union [IO], Windhoek, Namibia
Namibia Assn. of Occupational Therapists [IO],
Windhoek, Namibia
Namibia Baseball Assn. [IO], Windhoek, Namibia
Namibia Inst. of Architects [IO], Windhoek, Namibia
Namibia Sailing Assn. [IO], Windhoek, Namibia
Namibia Sports Fed. of the Disabled [IO], Windhoek,
Namibia
Namibia Tennis Assn. [IO], Windhoek, Namibia
Namibian Chef Assn. [IO], Swakopmund, Namibia
Namibian Economic Policy Res. Unit [IO], Wind-
hoek, Namibia
Namibian Food and Catering Assn. [★IO]
Namibian Soc. of Physiotherapy [IO], Windhoek,
Namibia
Namibian Squash Assn. [IO], Windhoek, Namibia
NAMM Found. Res. Div. [10653], 5790 Armada Dr.,
Carlsbad, CA 92008
NAMM, the Intl. Music Products Assn. [2817], 5790
Armada Dr., Carlsbad, CA 92008, (760)438-8001
Nanaimo Brain Injury Soc. [IO], Nanaimo, BC,
Canada
Nancy Fisher Fan Club - Address unknown since
1989.
Nancy Sinatra Fan Club - Address unknown since
1999.
NANDA Intl. [15489], 100 N 20th St., 4th Fl.,
Philadelphia, PA 19103, (215)545-8105
NANDA Intl. [IO], Philadelphia, PA, United States
Nanmin Wo Tasukeru Kai [★IO]
Nannies; Natl. Assn. of [829]
Nanny Acad. of America - Defunct.
Nanny Pop-Ins Assn. - Defunct.
NanoBusiness Alliance [7750], 4901 Searle Pkwy.,
Ste. Q2608, Skokie, IL 60077, (847)568-8415
Nanoose Conversion Campaign [IO], Vancouver,
BC, Canada
Nanzan Inst. for Religion and Culture [IO], Nagoya,
Japan

Reference to "IO" in place of a book number signifies that the association may be found in the 45th edition of International Organizations.

Napa Valley Grape Growers Assn. [★5415]
Napa Valley Grapegrowers [5415], 811 Jefferson St., Napa, CA 94559, (707)944-8311
Napa Valley Vintners Assn. [5416], PO Box 141, St. Helena, CA 94574, (707)963-3388
Napa Valley Wine Lib. Assn. [23027], PO Box 328, St. Helena, CA 94574-0328, (707)963-5145
NAPAEO The Assn. for Land Based Colleges [IO], Beverley, United Kingdom
NAPE, Inc. [★14207]
Napier in North America; Clan [20856]
Naples Alcofuel Club - Defunct.
Naples Sabot Assn; Intl. [23190]
Naples Sabot One—Design Assn. [23190]
Napoleon
    Napoleonic Age Philatelists [22849]
    Napoleonic Historical Soc. [11139]
Napoleonic Age Philatelists [22849], 7513 Clayton Dr., Oklahoma City, OK 73132-5636, (405)721-0044
Napoleonic Assn. [IO], Wokingham, United Kingdom
Napoleonic Historical Soc. [11139], 6000A W Irving Park Rd., Chicago, IL 60634, (610)581-0280
Napoleonic Soc. [★11139]
Napoleonic Soc. of Am. [★11139]
Naprapathic Educ. and Res. Foundation [★15276]
Naprapathy
    Amer. Naprapathic Assn. [15276]
NAQP Cmpt. Users Gp. [★6798]
NAQP Cmpt. Users Gp. [6798], c/o PrintImage Intl., 2250 E Devon Ave., Ste. 245, Des Plaines, IL 60018, (847)298-8680
NAQP Mgt. Systems Gp. [★6798]
NARAL Pro-Choice Am. [18518], 1156 15th St. NW, Ste. 700, Washington, DC 20005, (202)973-3000
NarAnon - Address unknown since 1999.
Narcolepsy Assn. United Kingdom [IO], Penicuik, United Kingdom
Narcolepsy and Cataplexy Found. of America - Defunct.
Narcolepsy Network [16427], PO Box 294, Pleasantville, NY 10570, (914)667-2523
Narcotic Detector Dog Assn; Natl. [5997]
Narcotic Educational Found. of Am. [13256], 28245 Ave. Crocker, Ste. 230, Santa Clarita, CA 91355-1201, (661)775-6960
Narcotic Enforcement Officers Assn; Natl. [★5741]
Narcoticos Anonimos de Argentina [IO], Buenos Aires, Argentina
Narcoticos Anonimos Region Mexico [★IO]
Narcotics Anonymous [IO], Van Nuys, CA, United States
Narcotics Anonymous [13257], c/o World Ser. Off., PO Box 9999, Van Nuys, CA 91409, (818)773-9999
Narcotics Anonymous Berlin [IO], Berlin, Germany
Narcotics Anonymous Bombay, India [IO], Bombay, India
Narcotics Anonymous British Columbia Region [IO], Vancouver, BC, Canada
Narcotics Anonymous Gebeit Berlin [★IO]
Narcotics Anonymous - Hamilton Area [IO], Hamilton, ON, Canada
Narcotics Anonymous Ireland [IO], Dublin, Ireland
Narcotics Anonymous Malta [IO], St. Julian's, Malta
Narcotics Anonymous Mexico Region [IO], Mexico City, Mexico
Narcotics Anonymous Omrade Sor Servicekomite [★IO]
Narcotics Anonymous Polish Region [IO], Torun, Poland
Narcotics Anonymous Southern Area Ser. Comm. [IO], Kristiansand, Norway
Narcotics Anonymous UK Region [IO], London, United Kingdom
Narcotics Anonymous - Victoria Area [IO], Melbourne, Australia
Narcotics Control Bd; Intl. [IO]
Narcotics Educ. [★13245]
Narcotics; Natl. Assn. for the Prevention of Addiction to [★13262]
NARGON, the Grocery Retailers Assn. [IO], Wellington, New Zealand
NARMIC/Amer. Friends Service Comm. - Defunct.
Narodna Asociacia Realitnych Kancelarii Slovenska [★IO]

Narramore Christian Found. [19815], 250 W Colorado Blvd., Ste. 200, Arcadia, CA 91007-9877, (626)821-8400
Narrow Fabrics Inst. [3792], 1801 County Rd. B W, Roseville, MN 55113-4061, (651)222-2508
Narrow Fabrics Institute [IO], Roseville, MN, United States
NARSAD: Mental Hea. Res. Assn. [15213], 60 Cutter Mill Rd., Ste. 404, Great Neck, NY 11021, (516)829-0091
NARTE Inc. [★7773]
NASBA - The Assn. of Sys. Builders and Integrators [3706], 19 Corporate Plz., Ste. 200, Newport Beach, CA 92660, (949)729-2259
NASBITE Intl. [8031], c/o Mr. Archie Pitsilides, Exec. Dir., Texas Tech Univ., Rawls Coll. of Bus., Box 42101, Lubbock, TX 79409-2101, (806)742-1827
NASBITE Intl. [IO], Lubbock, TX, United States
NASCA, Inc [★IO]
NASCA, Inc [★13097]
NASCA Intl. [13097], PO Box 7128, Buena Park, CA 90622-7128, (714)229-4870
NASCA Intl. [IO], Buena Park, CA, United States
NASD [3517], 1735 K St. NW, Washington, DC 20006-1500, (301)590-6500
NASEN [IO], Tamworth, United Kingdom
Nash Car Club of Am. [21725], c/o Jim Bracewell, Membership Chm., 1N274 Prarie Ave., Glen Ellyn, IL 60137, (630)469-5848
Nash-Healey Car Club - Address unknown since 1995.
Nashville Bullfron Fan Club - Defunct.
Nashville Entertainment Assn. [9579]
Nashville Music Assn. [★9579]
Nashville Songwriters Assn. [★10654]
Nashville Songwriters Assn. [★IO]
Nashville Songwriters Assn. Intl. [IO], Nashville, TN, United States
Nashville Songwriters Assn. Intl. [10654], 1710 Roy Acuff Pl., Nashville, TN 37203, (615)256-3354
Nashwaak Watershed Assn. Inc. [IO], Fredericton, NB, Canada
Nasionale Begrafnisondernemersvereniging Van Suider-Afrika [★IO]
Nasionale Wolkwekersvereeniging van Suid-Afrika [★IO]
NASIRE [★5821]
Nasjonalforeningen for Folkehelsen [★IO]
NaSPA, Inc. [★IO]
NaSPA, Inc. [★6799]
NASSCO - Setting the Indus. Standards for the Rehabilitation of Underground Utilities [3959], 1314 Bedford Ave., Ste. 201, Baltimore, MD 21208, (410)486-3500
NASSTRAC [3574], 9382 Oak Ave., Waconia, MN 55387, (952)442-8850
Nast Soc; Thomas [9477]
NASW - Social Work Vocational Bur. - Defunct.
Nat Stuckey Fan Club - Defunct.
Nat-War Alliance - Defunct.
Natal Death; Aiding Mothers and Fathers Experiencing Neo [11907]
Natal Nursing Specialties; Natl. Certification Corp. for the Obstetric, Gynecologic and Neo [15506]
Natal Psychology and Hea; Assn. for Pre- and Peri [13979]
Natal Sharks Bd. [IO], Durban, Republic of South Africa
NATESLA [★IO]
Nathan Cummings Found. [13125], 475 10th Ave., 14th Fl., New York, NY 10018-9715, (212)787-7300
Nathan Hale Inst. [17822]
Nathan W. Ackerman Family Inst. [★12134]
Nathaniel Hawthorne Soc. [9694], c/o Mr. Leland S. Person, Treas., Dept. of English, Univ. of Cincinnati, Cincinnati, OH 45221-0069, (513)556-5924
Nation Inst. [18461], 116 E 16th St., 8th Fl., New York, NY 10003
Nation of Ishmael - Address unknown since 2001.
Nation-Wide Comm. on Import-Export Policy - Defunct.
Nationaal Verbond der Kristelijke Arbeidersvrouwenbeweging [IO], Brussels, Belgium
Natl. 4-H Coun. [13494], 7100 Connecticut Ave., Chevy Chase, MD 20815, (301)961-2800

Natl. 4-H Found. of Am. [★13494]
Natl. 4-H Ser. Comm. [★13494]
Natl. 4 Wheel Drive Assn. - Address unknown since 1999.
Natl. 4th Infantry (Ivy) Div. Assn. [20703], c/o Gregory A. Rollinger, Exec. Dir., 8891 Aviary Path, Inver Grove Heights, MN 55077, (651)322-5736
Natl. 42 Players Assn. [22899], c/o Dennis Roberson, Treas., 8124 Island Park Dr., Fort Worth, TX 76137, (817)927-4278
Natl. 210 Owners Assn. [21463], PO Box 1065, La Canada Flintridge, CA 91011, (818)952-6212
Natl. AAU Taekwondo Union of the U.S.A. [★23610]
Natl. Abandoned Infants Assistance Rsrc. Center [12412], Univ. of California, Berkeley, 1950 Addison St., Ste. 104, No. 7402, Berkeley, CA 94720-7402, (510)643-8390
Natl. Ability Center [23347], PO Box 682799, Park City, UT 84068, (435)649-3991
Natl. Aboriginal Achievement Found. [IO], Ohsweken, ON, Canada
Natl. Aboriginal Capital Corp. Assn. [IO], Ottawa, ON, Canada
Natl. Aboriginal Hea. Org. [IO], Ottawa, ON, Canada
Natl. Aboriginal Islander Skills Development Assn. [IO], Kariong, Australia
Natl. Aboriginal Lands Managers Assn. [IO], Curve Lake, ON, Canada
Natl. Abortion Coun. [★11223]
Natl. Abortion Fed. [11223], 1660 L St. NW, Ste. 450, Washington, DC 20036, (202)667-5881
Natl. Abortion and Reproductive Action League [★18518]
Natl. Abortion Rights Action League [16913], 1156 15th St. NW, Ste. 700, Washington, DC 20005, (202)973-3000
Natl. Abortion Rights Action League [★18518]
Natl. Abstinence Educ. Assn. [9123], 1701 Pennsylvania Ave. NW, Ste. 300, Washington, DC 20006, (202)248-5420
Natl. Academic Advising Assn. [8170], Kansas State Univ., 2323 Anderson Ave., Ste. 225, Manhattan, KS 66502-2912, (785)532-5717
National Academic Advising Association [IO], Manhattan, KS, United States
Natl. Academies of Emergency Dispatch [14348], 139 E South Temple, Ste. 200, Salt Lake City, UT 84111, (801)359-6916
Natl. Academies of Practice [14648], PO Box 1037, Edgewood, MD 21040, (410)676-3390
Natl. Acad. of Amer. Scholars [8356], PO Box 337380, North Las Vegas, NV 89031-7380, (760)488-9673
Natl. Acad. of Arbitrators [5459], 1 N Main St., Ste. 412, Cortland, NY 13045, (607)756-8363
Natl. Acad. of Astrology - Defunct.
Natl. Acad. of Building Inspection Engineers [640], PO Box 522158, Salt Lake City, UT 84152, (800)294-7729
Natl. Acad. of Clinical Biochemistry [13748], 1850 K St. NW, Ste. 625, Washington, DC 20006, (202)857-0717
Natl. Acad. of Clinicians and Holistic Health - Address unknown since 1988.
Natl. Acad. of Code Administration - Address unknown since 2005.
Natl. Acad. of Conciliators - Address unknown since 2003.
Natl. Acad. of Counselors and Family Therapists [★12137]
Natl. Acad. of Economics and Political Science - Defunct.
Natl. Acad. of Educ. [8280], 500 Fifth St. NW, No. 333, Washington, DC 20001, (202)334-2341
Natl. Acad. of Elder Law Attorneys [6029], 1604 N Country Club Rd., Tucson, AZ 85716-3102, (520)881-4005
Natl. Acad. of Emergency Medical Dispatch [★14348]
Natl. Acad. of Engg. [7028], 500 Fifth St. NW, Washington, DC 20001, (202)334-3200
Natl. Acad. of Exact, Physical and Natural Sciences [IO], Buenos Aires, Argentina
Natl. Acad. of Geo-sciences - Address unknown since 2003.

A star before a book entry number signifies that the name is not listed separately, but is mentioned within the entry.

Natl. Acad. of Geography [IO], Buenos Aires, Argentina

Natl. Acad. of History [IO], Buenos Aires, Argentina

Natl. Acad. of Hospital Inservice Education - Defunct.

Natl. Acad. of Jazz - Address unknown since 1995.

Natl. Acad. of Medicine [IO], Bogota, Colombia

Natl. Acad. of Music, Dance and Drama [IO], New Delhi, India

Natl. Acad. of Nannies, Inc. - Address unknown since 2001.

Natl. Acad. of Needlearts [22165], c/o Carlene Harwick, E 9526 E Munising Ave., Munising, MI 49862, (906)387-5162

National Academy of Needlearts [IO], Munising, MI, United States

Natl. Acad. of Neuropsychology [16158], 2121 S Oneida St., Ste. 550, Denver, CO 80224-2594, (303)691-3694

National Acad. for Nuclear Training [★7392]

Natl. Acad. of Opticianry [15707], 8401 Corporate Dr., Ste. 605, Landover, MD 20785, (301)577-4828

Natl. Acad. of Popular Music [10655], 330 W 58th St., Ste. 411, New York, NY 10019-1827, (212)957-9230

Natl. Acad. of Public Admin. [6193], 900 7th St. NW, Ste. 600, Washington, DC 20001, (202)347-3190

Natl. Acad. of Public Admin. [IO], Washington, DC, United States

Natl. Acad. of Recording Arts and Sciences [10929], 3402 Pico Blvd., Santa Monica, CA 90405, (310)392-3777

Natl. Acad. of Sciences [7616], 500 Fifth St. NW, Washington, DC 20001, (202)334-2000

Natl. Acad. of Sciences of Armenia [IO], Yerevan, Armenia

Natl. Acad. of Sciences of Belarus [IO], Minsk, Belarus

Natl. Acad. of Sciences of Bolivia [IO], La Paz, Bolivia

Natl. Acad. of Sciences, Natl. Acad. of Engg., and Inst. of Medicine; Comm. on Human Rights of the U.S. [★17753]

Natl. Acad. of Sciences of the Republic of Korea [IO], Seoul, Republic of Korea

Natl. Acad. of Social Insurance [18647], 1776 Massachusetts Ave. NW, Ste. 615, Washington, DC 20036-1904, (202)452-8097

Natl. Acad. of Songwriters [★5859]

Natl. Acad. of Songwriters - Defunct.

Natl. Acad. of Sports [23831]

Natl. Acad. for State Hea. Policy [14649], 50 Monument Sq., Ste. 502, Portland, ME 04101, (207)874-6524

Natl. Acad. of Surgery [IO], Paris, France

Natl. Acad. of Teaching - Address unknown since 2004.

Natl. Acad. for Teaching and Learning About Aging [11297], PO Box 310919, Denton, TX 76203-0919, (940)565-3450

Natl. Acad. of TV Arts and Sciences [567], 5220 Lankershim Blvd., North Hollywood, CA 91601-3109, (818)754-2810

Natl. Acad. of TV Journalists [3128], PO Box 31, Salisbury, MD 21803, (410)546-9333

Natl. Acad. of Visual Instruction [★8551]

National Acad. for Voluntarism [★12205]

Natl. Acad. of Western Art - Defunct.

Natl. Access Center - Defunct.

Natl. Accessible Apartment CH [11963], 4300 Wilson Blvd., Ste. 400, Arlington, VA 22203, (703)518-6141

Natl. Account Mgt. Assn. [★2650]

Natl. Account Mgt. Assn. [★IO]

Natl. Account Marketing Assn. [★IO]

Natl. Account Marketing Assn. [★2650]

Natl. Accounting and Finance Coun. [3876], 950 N Glebe Rd., Ste. 210, Arlington, VA 22203-4181, (703)838-1700

Natl. Accreditation Commn. for Schools and Colleges of Acupuncture and Oriental Medicine [★15739]

Natl. Accreditation Coun. for Agencies Serving the Blind and Visually Handicapped [★16870]

Natl. Accreditation Coun. for Agencies Serving the Blind and Visually Impaired [16870], 21475 Lorain Rd., Cleveland, OH 44126, (440)409-0340

Natl. Accreditation Coun. for Environmental Hea. Curricula [★14368]

Natl. Accreditation Coun. for Environmental Hea. Sci. and Protection [★14368]

Natl. Accrediting Agency for Clinical Lab. Sciences [15141], 8410 W Bryn Mawr Ave., Ste. 670, Chicago, IL 60631, (773)714-8880

Natl. Accrediting Commn. of Cosmetology Arts and Sciences [7877], 4401 Ford Ave., Ste. 1300, Alexandria, VA 22302, (703)600-7600

Natl. Accrediting Commn. for Cosmetology Schools [★7877]

Natl. Achievement Clubs - Address unknown since 1995.

Natl. Acoustical Contractors Assn. [★1008]

Natl. Acoustical Suppliers Assn. - Defunct.

Natl. Acrylic Painters' Assn. [IO], Wallasey, United Kingdom

Natl. Action Comm. on the Status of Women [IO], Toronto, ON, Canada

Natl. Action Coun. for Minorities in Engg. [8369], 440 Hamilton Ave., Ste. 302, White Plains, NY 10601-1813, (914)539-4010

Natl. Action for Former Military Wives [12012], 2090 N Atlantic Ave., Apt. P-2, Cocoa Beach, FL 32931-5010, (321)783-2101

Natl. Action Forum for Midlife and Older Women - Defunct.

Natl. Action Group for the Prevention and Treatment of Decubitus Ulcers - Address unknown since 1995.

Natl. Action Network [17127], 106 W 145th St., New York, NY 10039, (212)690-3070

Natl. Active and Retired Fed. Employees Assn. [5710], 606 N Washington St., Alexandria, VA 22314-1914, (703)838-7760

Natl. Acupuncture Detoxification Assn. [16510], PO Box 1927, Vancouver, WA 98668-1927, (360)254-0186

National Acupuncture Detoxification Association [IO], Vancouver, WA, United States

Natl. Addison's Disease Found. [★14358]

Natl. Adoption Assistance Center - Address unknown since 2001.

Natl. Adoption Center [11254], 1500 Walnut St., Ste. 701, Philadelphia, PA 19102, (800)TO-ADOPT

Natl. Adoption Information Exchange System - Defunct.

Natl. Adrenal Diseases Found. [14358], 505 Northern Blvd., Ste. 200, Great Neck, NY 11021, (516)487-4992

Natl. Adult Day Services Assn. [11298], 2519 Connecticut Ave. NW, Washington, DC 20008, (202)508-1205

Natl. Adult Education Clearinghouse - Defunct.

Natl. Adult Educ. Honor Soc. [24392], PO Box 76571, Highland Heights, KY 41076, (859)685-8559

Natl. Adult Educ. Professional Development Consortium [7917], c/o Dr. Lennox L. McLendon, Exec. Dir., 444 N Capitol St. NW, Ste. 422, Washington, DC 20001, (202)624-5250

Natl. Adult School Org. [IO], Leicester, United Kingdom

Natl. Adult Vocational Education Assn. - Address unknown since 2006.

Natl. Advertisers; Assn. of [91]

Natl. Advt. Assn. - Mexico [IO], Mexico City, Mexico

Natl. Advt. Assn. - Venezuela [IO], Caracas, Venezuela

Natl. Advt. Div. Coun. of Better Bus. Bureaus [111], 70 W 36th St., 13th Fl., New York, NY 10018, (212)705-0120

Natl. Advt. Golf Assn. [23456], c/o John Black, Dir., 207 Chestnut Oaks Cir., Simpsonville, SC 29681, (864)573-8653

Natl. Advt. Network, Inc. [★88]

Natl. Advt. Network, Inc. [★IO]

Natl. Advt. Newspaper Assn. [★3259]

Natl. Advt. Rev. Bd. [112], 70 W 36th St., 13th Fl., New York, NY 10018, (212)705-0114

Natl. Advt. Rev. Coun. [★112]

Natl. Advisory Comm. on Farm Labor - Defunct.

Natl. Advisory Comm. on Highway Beautification - Defunct.

Natl. Advisory Comm. on Scouting with Special Needs - Defunct.

Natl. Advisory Coun. on the Employment of Women [IO], Wellington, New Zealand

Natl. Advisory Coun. for Minorities in Engg. [★8369]

Natl. Advisory Coun. for South Asian Affairs [17008], 3105 Beaverwood Ln., Silver Spring, MD 20906, (301)460-7090

Natl. Advisory Coun. for South Asian Affairs [IO], Silver Spring, MD, United States

Natl. Advisory Gp., Convenience Stores/Petroleum Companies [★3420]

Natl. Advisory Gp., Convenience Stores/Petroleum Marketers Assn. [★3420]

Natl. Advocates Soc. - Address unknown since 2005.

Natl. Aerial Applicators Assn. [★4188]

Natl. Aerial Applicators Assn. [★IO]

Natl. Aero Club of Bulgaria [IO], Sofia, Bulgaria

Natl. Aero Club of Ireland [IO], Narraghmore, Ireland

Natl. Aeronautic Assn. [158], 1737 King St., Ste. 220, Alexandria, VA 22314, (703)527-0226

Natl. Aeronautic Assn. of the U.S.A. [★158]

Natl. Aeronca Assn. [21464], 304 Adda St., Roberts, IL 60962-8049

Natl. Aerosol Assn. - Address unknown since 2002.

Natl. Aerospace Education Assn. - Defunct.

Natl. Aerospace Services Assn. - Defunct.

Natl. Affiliation of Concerned Business Students - Defunct.

Natl. Affiliation of Durable Medical Equip. Companies [★14670]

Natl. Affordable Housing Mgt. Assn. [1977], 400 N Columbus St., Ste. 203, Alexandria, VA 22314, (703)683-8630

Natl. Affordable Housing Network [12318], PO Box 3706, Butte, MT 59702, (406)782-8145

Natl. AFL-CIO COPE Retiree Program - Address unknown since 2001.

Natl. African Amer. Drug Policy Coalition [17440], Howard Univ., Center for Drug Abuse Res., 2900 Van Ness St. NW, Ste. 400, Washington, DC 20008, (202)806-8600

Natl. African-American Insurance Assn. [2202], 1718 M St. NW, Box No. 1110, Washington, DC 20036, (866)566-2242

Natl. African-American RV'ers Assn. [22958], 1426 W 29th St., Ste. 201, Indianapolis, IN 46208, (877)221-2238

Natl. African Amer. Speakers Assn. - Address unknown since 2008.

Natl. Afro-Amer. Labor Coun. - Address unknown since 1995.

Natl. AfterSchool Assn. [11528], 529 Main St., Ste. 214, Charlestown, MA 02129, (617)778-6020

Natl. Aggregates Assn. [★3699]

Natl. Agri-Marketing Assn. [2640], 11020 King St., Ste. 205, Overland Park, KS 66210, (913)491-6500

Natl. AgriChemical Retailers Assn. [★1363]

Natl. Agricultural Advt. and Marketing Assn. [★2640]

Natl. Agricultural Aviation Assn. [4188], 1005 E St. SE, Washington, DC 20003-2847, (202)546-5722

National Agricultural Aviation Association [IO], Washington, DC, United States

Natl. Agricultural Aviation Assn; Women of the [4189]

Natl. Agricultural Chemicals Assn. [★807]

Natl. Agricultural Communicators of Tomorrow [8714], c/o Deb Dunsford, PhD, Advisor, 127 Scoates Hall, MS 2116, Texas A&M Univ., College Station, TX 77843

Natl. Agricultural Legal Fund - Defunct.

Natl. Agricultural Marketing Officials [★5025]

Natl. Agricultural Plastics Assn. [★4097]

Natl. Agricultural Press Assn. - Address unknown since 1997.

Natl. Agricultural Transportation League - Defunct.

Natl. Agricultural Workers Union - Address unknown since 1995.

Natl. Aid to Visually Handicapped [★16874]

Natl. AIDS CH [★13563]

Natl. AIDS Comm. - Mexico [IO], Mexico City, Mexico

Natl. AIDS Control Org. [IO], New Delhi, India

Reference to "IO" in place of a book number signifies that the association may be found in the 45th edition of International Organizations.

Natl. AIDS Fund **[13576]**, 729 15th St. NW, 9th Fl., Washington, DC 20005-1511, (202)408-4848

Natl. AIDS Housing Coalition **[12319]**, 727 15th St. NW, 6th Fl., Washington, DC 20005, (202)347-0333

Natl. AIDS Info. CH **[★13563]**

Natl. AIDS Network - Defunct.

Natl. AIDS Res. Found. **[★13557]**

Natl. AIDS Res. Found. **[★IO]**

Natl. AIDS/STD Prevention and Control Prog. **[★IO]**

Natl. AIDS Treatment Advocacy Proj. **[IO]**, New York, NY, United States

Natl. AIDS Treatment Advocacy Proj. **[13577]**, 580 Broadway, Ste. 1010, New York, NY 10012, (212)219-0106

Natl. AIDS Trust **[IO]**, London, United Kingdom

Natl. Air Carrier Assn. **[159]**, 1000 Wilson Blvd., Ste. 1700, Arlington, VA 22209, (703)358-8060

National Air Conditioning, Heating, Ventilating and Refrigeration Officials **[★5549]**

National Air Conditioning, Heating, Ventilating and Refrigeration Officials **[★IO]**

Natl. Air Disaster Alliance **[11510]**, 2020 Pennsylvania Ave., No. 315, Washington, DC 20006-1846, (336)643-8516

Natl. Air Duct Cleaners Assn. **[2470]**, 1518 K St. NW, Ste. 503, Washington, DC 20005, (202)737-2926

Natl. Air Filtration Assn. **[1894]**, PO Box 68639, Virginia Beach, VA 23471, (757)313-7400

Natl. Air-Racing Gp. **[23041]**, c/o Betty Sherman, Treas., 1932 Mahan, Richland, WA 99352-2121, (509)946-5690

Natl. Air Traffic Controllers Assn. **[24013]**, 1325 Massachusetts Ave. NW, Washington, DC 20005, (202)628-5451

Natl. Air Transport Coordinating Comm. **[★140]**

Natl. Air Trans. Assn. **[160]**, 4226 King St., Alexandria, VA 22302, (703)845-9000

Natl. Air Trans. Conferences **[★160]**

Natl. Aircraft Appraisers Assn. **[188]**, 7 W Square Lake Rd., Bloomfield Hills, MI 48302, (248)758-2333

Natl. Aircraft Finance Assn. **[2425]**, PO Box 1570, Edgewater, MD 21037, (410)571-1740

Natl. Aircraft Noise Abatement Coun. - Defunct.

Natl. Aircraft Resale Assn. **[189]**, 320 King St., Ste. 250, Alexandria, VA 22314, (703)671-8273

Natl. Airfreight Trucking Alliance - Address unknown since 1994.

Natl. Alarm Assn. of Am. **[3536]**, PO Box 3409, Dayton, OH 45401, (937)461-2208

Natl. Albanian Amer. Coun. **[18870]**, 2021 L St. NW, Ste. 402, Washington, DC 20036, (202)466-6900

Natl. Alcohol Beverage Control Assn. **[★5445]**

Natl. Alcohol Beverage Control Assn. **[5446]**, 4401 Ford Ave., Ste. 700, Alexandria, VA 22302-1473, (703)578-4200

Natl. Alcohol Fuels Producers Assn. - Defunct.

Natl. Alcohol Tax Coalition **[★18703]**

Natl. Aldrich Assn. **[★21006]**

Natl. Aldrich Family Assn. **[21006]**, c/o Ms. Bettina Benoit, Pres., 847 S Main St., Bellingham, MA 02019

Natl. Alfalfa Alliance **[★1358]**

Natl. Alfalfa and Forage Alliance **[1358]**, 4630 Churchill St., No. 1, St. Paul, MN 55126, (651)484-3888

National All-Jersey **[★4230]**

Natl. All States Hobby Club - Defunct.

Natl. Allergy and Asthma Network **[★16352]**

Natl. Alliance **[18800]**, PO Box 90, Hillsboro, WV 24946, (304)653-4600

Natl. Alliance for Accessible Golf **[23348]**, 12100 Sunset Hills Rd., Ste. 130, Reston, VA 20190, (703)234-4136

Natl. Alliance for the Advancement of Nodnarbism - Address unknown since 1999.

Natl. Alliance of Advocates for Buprenorphine Treatment **[16511]**, PO Box 333, Farmington, CT 06034, (860)269-4391

National Alliance Against Blacklisting - Address unknown since 2004.

Natl. Alliance Against Racist and Political Repression **[17128]**, 1325 S Wabash Ave., Ste. 105, Chicago, IL 60605, (312)939-2750

Natl. Alliance for Animal Legislation - Defunct.

Natl. Alliance of Athletic Assns. - Defunct.

Natl. Alliance for Autism Res. **[13726]**, 99 Wall St., Res. Park, Princeton, NJ 08540, (609)430-9160

Natl. Alliance of Black Americans - Address unknown since 1995.

Natl. Alliance of Black Interpreters **[3854]**, PO Box 2777, North Canton, OH 44720-0777

Natl. Alliance of Black Orgs. - Address unknown since 2001.

Natl. Alliance of Black Salesmen and Black Saleswomen **[3469]**

Natl. Alliance of Black School Educators **[9217]**, 310 Pennsylvania Ave., Washington, DC 20003, (202)608-6310

Natl. Alliance of Black School Superintendents **[★9217]**

Natl. Alliance of Blind Students **[16871]**, c/o Amer. Coun. of the Blind, 1155 15th St. NW, Ste. 1004, Washington, DC 20005, (202)467-5081

Natl. Alliance of Breast Cancer Orgs. **[13846]**

Natl. Alliance for Breastfeeding Advocacy **[13777]**, c/o Marsha Walker, RN, Exec. Dir., 254 Conant Rd., Weston, MA 02493-1756

Natl. Alliance of Burmese Breeders **[4210]**, c/o Prudence Dorazio, Sec., 40 Morgan Point, Groton, CT 06340

Natl. Alliance of Business - Address unknown since 2006.

Natl. Alliance of Cardiovascular Technologists **[★13885]**

Natl. Alliance for Caregiving **[12163]**, 4720 Montgomery Ln., 5th Fl., Bethesda, MD 20814

Natl. Alliance for Civic Educ. **[8091]**, Inst. for Philosophy and Public Policy, Maryland School of Public Affairs, 3111 Van Munching, College Park, MD 20742

Natl. Alliance of Clean Energy Bus. Incubators **[1287]**, c/o Lawrence M. Murphy, PhD, 1617 Cole Blvd., Golden, CO 80401-3393, (303)275-3050

Natl. Alliance of Cleaning Distributors - Address unknown since 1987.

Natl. Alliance Concerned With School-Age Parents - Defunct.

Natl. Alliance of Covenanting Congregations **[IO]**, North Vancouver, BC, Canada

Natl. Alliance of Czech Catholics **[19029]**, PO Box 159, Berwyn, IL 60402, (630)766-0462

Natl. Alliance Daughters of Veterans **[★20725]**

Natl. Alliance for Direct Support Professionals **[1986]**, PO Box 13447, Minneapolis, MN 55414, (952)920-0855

Natl. Alliance to End Homelessness **[12294]**, 1518 K St. NW, Ste. 410, Washington, DC 20005, (202)638-1526

Natl. Alliance for Eye and Vision Res. **[16872]**, 12300 Twinbrook Pkwy., Ste. 250, Rockville, MD 20852, (240)221-2905

Natl. Alliance for Fair Competition **[3613]**, 3 Bethesda Metro Center, Ste. 1100, Bethesda, MD 20814, (410)235-7116

Natl. Alliance for Fair Contracting **[24030]**, 905 16th St. NW, 4th Fl., Washington, DC 20006, (866)523-NAFC

Natl. Alliance of Families for the Return of America's Missing Servicemen **[21263]**, PO Box 40327, Bellevue, WA 98015-0327, (425)881-1499

Natl. Alliance for Family Court Justice **[5904]**, c/o Elisabeth Richards, Natl. Dir., 4309 Greenberry Ln., Annandale, VA 22003, (703)658-2308

National Alliance for Family Court Justice **[IO]**, Annandale, VA, United States

Natl. Alliance for Family Life **[★12137]**

Natl. Alliance for Food Safety and Security **[1537]**, c/o James H. Denton, Sec., 1260 W Maple Ave., Rm. 0-114, Univ. of Arkansas, Fayetteville, AR 72701, (501)575-3699

Natl. Alliance of Gang Investigators Associations **[5638]**, c/o Rusty Keeble, Pres., PO Box 608628, Orlando, FL 32860-8628, (321)388-8694

Natl. Alliance for Hea. Info. Tech. **[15142]**, 1 N Franklin St., 27th Fl., Chicago, IL 60606, (312)422-2181

Natl. Alliance for Hispanic Hea. **[13176]**, 1501 16th St. NW, Washington, DC 20036, (202)387-5000

Natl. Alliance of Homebased Businesswomen - Defunct.

Natl. Alliance of HUD Tenants **[18514]**, 42 Seaverns Ave., Boston, MA 02130, (617)267-9564

Natl. Alliance for Hydroelectric Energy - Defunct.

Natl. Alliance of Independent Crop Consultants **[4078]**, 349 E Nolley Dr., Collierville, TN 38017, (901)861-0511

Natl. Alliance for Infusion Therapy **[14839]**, 901 New York Ave. NW, 3rd Fl., Washington, DC 20001, (202)347-0066

Natl. Alliance for Insurance Educ. and Res. **[2203]**, PO Box 27027, Austin, TX 78755-2027, (800)633-2165

Natl. Alliance of Market Developers **[2641]**, c/o Clyde C. Allen, Exec. Dir., 620 Sheridan Ave., Plainfield, NJ 07060, (908)561-4062

Natl. Alliance for Media Arts and Culture **[9580]**, 145 9th St., Ste. 250, San Francisco, CA 94103, (415)431-1391

Natl. Alliance of Medical Researchers and Teaching Physicians **[15143]**, PO Box 19241, Washington, DC 20036-0241, (202)572-6256

Natl. Alliance of Medicare Set-Aside Professionals **[17697]**, 341 N Maitland Ave., Maitland, FL 32751, (407)647-8839

Natl. Alliance on Mental Illness **[15214]**, Colonial Pl. Three, 2107 Wilson Blvd., Ste. 300, Arlington, VA 22201-3042, (703)524-7600

Natl. Alliance for the Mentally Ill **[★15214]**

Natl. Alliance of Methadone Advocates **[14293]**, 435 2nd Ave., New York, NY 10010, (212)595-6262

National Alliance of Methadone Advocates **[IO]**, New York, NY, United States

Natl. Alliance for Migrant and Seasonal Farmworker Vocational Rehabilitation **[12591]**, c/o Noemi Ortega, Pres., 105-B S 6th St., Sunnyside, WA 98944, (509)837-2525

Natl. Alliance for Model State Drug Laws **[5671]**, 700 N Fairfax St., Ste. 550, Alexandria, VA 22314, (703)836-6100

Natl. Alliance for Musical Theatre **[10656]**, 520 8th Ave., 3rd Fl., Ste. 301, New York, NY 10018, (212)714-6668

Natl. Alliance of Nurse Practitioners - Address unknown since 2008.

Natl. Alliance to Nurture the Aged and the Youth **[12358]**, 659 NE 125th St., North Miami, FL 33161-3231, (305)981-3232

Natl. Alliance for Optional Parenthood - Defunct.

Natl. Alliance for Oral Hea. - Defunct.

Natl. Alliance of Police, Security and Corrections Organizations **[24165]**, 25510 Kelly Rd., Ste. 100, Roseville, MI 48066-4932, (866)627-7260

Natl. Alliance of Postal Employees **[★24167]**

Natl. Alliance of Postal and Fed. Employees **[24167]**, 1628 11th St. NW, Washington, DC 20001, (202)939-6325

Natl. Alliance of Preservation Commissions **[5786]**, Founders Garden House, 325 S Lumpkin St., Athens, GA 30602, (706)542-4731

Natl. Alliance of Primary Care Informatics **[14956]**, 4915 St. Elmo Ave., Ste. 401, Bethesda, MD 20814, (301)657-1291

Natl. Alliance for the Primary Prevention of Sharps Injuries **[16381]**, 126 Main St., PO Box 10, Milner, GA 30257, (770)358-7860

Natl. Alliance of Professional and Executive Women's Networks **[★728]**

Natl. Alliance of Professional and Executive Women's Networks **[★IO]**

Natl. Alliance for Public Charter Schools **[9037]**, 1101 14th St. NW, Ste. 801, Washington, DC 20005, (202)289-2700

Natl. Alliance for Reduction of Imprisonment - Defunct.

National Alliance Res. Academy **[★8577]**

Natl. Alliance for Res. on Schizophrenia and Depression **[★15213]**

Natl. Alliance for Rural Action - Defunct.

Natl. Alliance for Safe Schools **[9085]**, PO Box 290, Slanesville, WV 25444-0290, (304)496-8100

Natl. Alliance to Save Native Languages **[10305]**, 1455 Pennsylvania Ave. NW, Washington, DC 20004, (206)420-4638

A star before a book entry number signifies that the name is not listed separately, but is mentioned within the entry.

Natl. Alliance of Senior Citizens [11299]

Natl. Alliance of Sentencing Advocates and Mitigation Specialists [5645], c/o Maureen B. James, 1140 Connecticut Ave. NW, Ste. 900, Washington, DC 20036, (202)452-0620

Natl. Alliance of Short Fiction Authors [11182], c/o Timson Edwards, Co., PO Box 58-0898, Jacksonville, FL 32255-0898

Natl. Alliance of Spanish-Speaking People for Equality - Address unknown since 2007.

Natl. Alliance for Spiritual Growth - Defunct.

Natl. Alliance of State Pharmacy Associations [15943], 5501 Patterson Ave., Ste. 202, Richmond, VA 23226, (804)285-4431

Natl. Alliance of State Sci. and Mathematics Coalitions [9106], 1840 Wilson Blvd., Ste. 200, Arlington, VA 22201-3000, (703)516-5970

Natl. Alliance of State and Territorial AIDS Directors [16967], 444 N Capitol St. NW, Ste. 339, Washington, DC 20001, (202)434-8090

Natl. Alliance of Statewide Preservation Organizations [★5785]

Natl. Alliance of Supermarket Shoppers - Address unknown since 2001.

Natl. Alliance of Third World Journalists - Defunct.

Natl. Alliance for Thrombosis and Thrombophilia [13931], 120 White Plains Rd., Ste. 100, Tarrytown, NY 10591, (914)220-5040

Natl. Alliance of Vietnamese Amer. Ser. Agencies [19423], 1010 Wayne Ave., Ste. 310, Silver Spring, MD 20910, (301)587-2781

Natl. Alliance for Worker and Employer Rights [24110], 122 C St. NW., Ste. 220, Washington, DC 20001, (202)393-1185

Natl. Alliance for Youth Sports [23290], 2050 Vista Pkwy., West Palm Beach, FL 33411, (561)684-1141

Natl. Aloe Sci. Coun. [★1863]

Natl. Aloe Sci. Coun. [★IO]

Natl. Alopecia Areata Found. [16386], 14 Mitchell Blvd., San Rafael, CA 94903, (415)472-3780

Natl. Alpha Lambda Delta [24510], Box 4403, Macon, GA 31208-4403, (478)744-9595

Natl. ALS Found. [★15306]

Natl. Alternative Schools Program - Defunct.

Natl. Alumni Coun. of the UNCF [★18910]

Natl. Alumni Coun. of the United Negro Coll. Fund [18910], c/o United Negro Coll. Fund, PO Box 10444, Fairfax, VA 22031-8044, (703)205-3400

Natl. Amateur Athletic Assn. of Trinidad and Tobago [IO], Port of Spain, Trinidad and Tobago

Natl. Amateur Baseball Fed. [23115], c/o Charles M. Blackburn, Jr., Exec. Dir., PO Box 705, Bowie, MD 20715, (301)464-5460

Natl. Amateur Basketball Assn. - Address unknown since 2004.

Natl. Amateur Body Builders Assn. USA [23244], PO Box 531, Bronx, NY 10469, (718)882-6413

Natl. Amateur Dodgeball Assn. [23091], c/o Schaumburg Park District, 1223 W Sharon Ln., Schaumburg, IL 60193, (847)985-2141

National Amateur Dodgeball Association [IO], Schaumburg, IL, United States

Natl. Amateur Press Assn. [22911], c/o William E. Boys, Sec.-Treas., 6507 Westland Dr., Knoxville, TN 37919

Natl. Amateur Radio Assn. - Address unknown since 1999.

Natl. Amateur Retriever Club [22309], c/o Retriever Field Trial News, 4379 S Howell Ave., Ste. 17, Milwaukee, WI 53207-5053, (414)481-2760

Natl. AMBUCS [11964], 4285 Regency Ct., High Point, NC 27265, (800)838-1845

Natl. Ambulance and Medical Services Assn. [★14313]

Natl. Amer. Arab Nurses Assn. [15490], PO Box 43, Dearborn Heights, MI 48127, (313)680-5049

Natl. Amer. Eskimo Dog Assn. [22310], c/o Sally Bedow, Treas., 1978 School Rd., Port Lavaca, TX 77979, (361)655-8042

Natl. Amer. Farmers Assn. - Defunct.

Natl. Amer. Glass Club [22560], PO Box 489, Millburn, NJ 07041

Natl. Amer. Hispanic Women's Caucus - Defunct.

Natl. Amer. Indian Cattlemen's Assn. [4273]

Natl. Amer. Indian Court Clerks Assn. - Address unknown since 2004.

Natl. Amer. Indian Court Judges Assn. [5905], 4410 Arapahoe Ave., Ste. 135, Boulder, CO 80303, (303)245-0786

Natl. Amer. Indian Housing Coun. [5791], 50 F St. NW, Ste. 3300, Washington, DC 20001, (202)789-1754

Natl. Amer. Indian Safety Coun. - Address unknown since 1985.

Natl. Amer. Legion Press Assn. [20668], PO Box 1055, Indianapolis, IN 46206

Natl. Amer. Motors Drag Racing Assn. [★23080]

Natl. Amer. Motors Drivers and Racers Assn. [23080], PO Box 987, Twin Lakes, WI 53181-0987, (262)843-4326

Natl. Amer. Pit Bull Terrier Assn. [22311], c/o Michael Snyder, Pres., 239 SW 118th St., Seattle, WA 98146, (206)244-5055

Natl. Amer. Studies Faculty of the Amer. Studies Assn. - Defunct.

National-American Wholesale Lumber Assn. [★1611]

Natl. Amputation Found. [11965], 40 Church St., Malverne, NY 11565, (516)887-3600

Natl. Amputee Golf Assn. [23349], 11 Walnut Hill Rd., Amherst, NH 03031-1713, (603)672-6444

Natl. Amputee Skiers Assn. [★23343]

Natl. Amusement Park Historical Assn. [21512], PO Box 871, Lombard, IL 60148-0871

Natl. Anemia Action Coun. [14794], 555 E Wells St., Ste. 1100, Milwaukee, WI 53202, (414)225-0138

Natl. Angora Rabbit Breeders Club [5150], c/o Margaret Bartold, VP, 909 Hwy. E, Silex, MO 63377, (573)384-5866

Natl. Animal Control Assn. [11430], PO Box 480851, Kansas City, MO 64148-0851, (913)768-1319

Natl. Animal Damage Control Assn. [5076], c/o Art Smith, Pres., Dept. of Game, Fish and Parks, 523 E Capitol Ave., Pierre, SD 57501, (402)472-8961

Natl. Animal Interest Alliance [11431], PO Box 66579, Portland, OR 97266, (503)761-1139

Natl. Animal Supplement Coun. [4152], PO Box 2568, Valley Center, CA 92082, (760)751-3360

Natl. Animal Welfare Trust [IO], Watford, United Kingdom

Natl. Ankylosing Spondylitis Soc. [IO], Richmond, United Kingdom

Natl. Anti-Drug Coalition - Defunct.

Natl. Anti-Dumping Comm. - Address unknown since 1995.

Natl. Anti-Hunger Coalition - Defunct.

Natl. Anti-Imperialist Movement in Solidarity With African Liberation - Address unknown since 1989.

Natl. Anti-Klan Network [★17098]

Natl. Anti-Vivisection Soc. [11432], 53 W Jackson Blvd., Ste. 1552, Chicago, IL 60604, (312)427-6065

Natl. Anti-Vivisection Soc. [IO], London, United Kingdom

Natl. Antique and Art Dealers Assn. of Am. [300], 220 E 57th St., New York, NY 10022, (212)826-9707

Natl. Antique Doll Dealers Assn. [22402], PO Box 462, Natick, MA 01760-0005, (508)545-1424

National Antique Doll Dealers Association [IO], Natick, MA, United States

Natl. Antique Oldsmobile Club [21726], 4 Lindworth Dr., St. Louis, MO 63124-1454

Natl. Antique Tractor Pullers Assn. [23004], c/o Dan Paumier, Sec., PO Box 248, Hanoverton, OH 44423-0248, (330)223-1691

Natl. Anxiety Center [18416], 28 W 3rd St., Ste. 1321, South Orange, NJ 07079, (973)763-6392

Natl. Apartment Assn. [3317], 4300 Wilson Blvd., Ste. 400, Arlington, VA 22203-4168, (703)518-6141

Natl. Apartment Owners Assn. [★3317]

Natl. Aphasia Assn. [13705], 350 Seventh Ave., Ste. 902, New York, NY 10001, (800)922-4622

Natl. Apostolate for Inclusion Ministry [20026], PO Box 218, Riverdale, MD 20738-0218, (301)699-9500

Natl. Apostolate for the Mentally Retarded [★20026]

Natl. Apostolate with Mentally Retarded Persons [★20026]

Natl. Apostolate with People with Mental Retardation [★20026]

Natl. Appaloosa Pony [★4945]

Natl. Apple Inst. [★4768]

Natl. Apple Inst. [★IO]

Natl. AppleWorks Users Group - Defunct.

Natl. Appliance Parts Suppliers Assn. [266], c/o Sherry Harrell, Pres., 4015 W Marshall Ave., Longview, TX 75604-4916, (903)759-3983

Natl. Appliance Ser. Assn. [267], PO Box 2514, Kokomo, IN 46904, (765)453-1820

National Apprenticeship Prog. for Cooks and pastry cooks [★790]

Natl. Appropriate Tech. Assistance Ser. [★6951]

Natl. Aquaculture Assn. [4178], 111 W Washington St., Ste. 1, Charles Town, WV 25414, (304)728-2167

National Aquaculture Assn. [★4026]

Natl. Aquaculture Coun. [4179]

Natl. Aquarium Soc. [10442], U.S. Department of Commerce Bldg., Rm. B-077, 14th St. and Constitution Ave. NW, Washington, DC 20230, (202)482-2825

Natl. Aquatic Sports Camps - Defunct.

Natl. Arab Amer. Medical Assn. [14707], 801 S Adams Rd., Ste. 208, Birmingham, MI 48009, (248)646-3661

Natl. Arbor Day; Comm. for [18670]

Natl. Arbor Day Found. [18673], 100 Arbor Ave., Nebraska City, NE 68410, (402)873-8733

Natl. Arborist Assn. [★5262]

Natl. Arborist Assn. [★IO]

Natl. Archery Assn. of the U.S. [23052], 1 Olympic Plz., Colorado Springs, CO 80909-5778, (719)866-4576

Natl. Architect-Engineer Liaison Commn. - Defunct.

Natl. Architects Chamber [★IO]

Natl. Architectural Accrediting Bd. [7962], 1735 New York Ave. NW, Washington, DC 20006, (202)783-2007

Natl. Archives and Historical Found. of the Amer. GI Forum - Address unknown since 1999.

Natl. Archives and Record Ser. Volunteer Assn. [★9402]

Natl. Archives and Records Admin. Volunteer Assn. [9402], 8601 Adelphi Rd., College Park, MD 20740-6001, (301)837-0482

Natl. Archives Volunteers Constitution Study Group - Defunct.

Natl. Armored Cable Mfrs. Assn. - Address unknown since 1994.

Natl. Armored Car Assn. [3575], c/o Larry Sabbath, Exec. Dir., 9532 Stevebrook Rd., Fairfax, VA 22032, (703)426-1976

Natl. Arson Prevention and Action Coalition - Address unknown since 1999.

Natl. Art Educ. Assn. [7977], 1916 Assn. Dr., Reston, VA 20191-1502, (703)860-8000

Natl. Art Exhibitions by the Mentally Ill [9581], PO Box 350891, Miami, FL 33135, (954)922-8692

Natl. Art Materials Trade Assn. [1802], 15806 Brookway Dr., Ste. 300, Huntersville, NC 28078, (704)892-6244

National Art Materials Trade Association [IO], Huntersville, NC, United States

Natl. Art Museum of Sport [9457], Univ. Pl. - IUPUI, 850 W Michigan St., Indianapolis, IN 46202, (317)274-3627

Natl. Arthritis and Musculoskeletal and Skin Diseases Info. CH (NAMSIC) [★16372]

Natl. Artists Equity Assn. [9511], c/o Artists Equity, PO Box HG, Pacific Grove, CA 93950, (831)479-7226

Natl. Arts Coun. of Zimbabwe [IO], Harare, Zimbabwe

Natl. Arts Coun. of Zimbabwe - Masvingo [IO], Masvingo, Zimbabwe

Natl. Arts Coun. of Zimbabwe - Matabeleland North [IO], Bulawayo, Zimbabwe

Natl. Arts Found. [IO], Buenos Aires, Argentina

Natl. Arts Found. [9582], 4444 Oakton St., Skokie, IL 60076, (847)674-7990

Natl. Arts Stabilization Fund - Defunct.

Natl. Asbestos Coun. [★620]

Natl. Ash Assn. [★3986]

Natl. Asian Amer. Pacific Islander Mental Hea. Assn. [15215], 1215 19th St., Ste. A, Denver, CO 80202, (303)298-7910

Reference to "IO" in place of a book number signifies that the association may be found in the 45th edition of International Organizations.

Natl. Asian Amer. Soc. of Accountants [42], c/o Marc Bernardo, CPA, Treas., PO Box 8689, New York, NY 10116

Natl. Asian Amer. Telecommunications Assn. [★17166]

Natl. Asian Pacific Amer. Bar Assn. [5947], 910 17th St. NW, Ste. 315, Washington, DC 20006, (202)775-9555

Natl. Asian Pacific Amer. Families Against Substance Abuse [13258], 340 E Second St., Ste. 409, Los Angeles, CA 90012, (213)625-5795

Natl. Asian Pacific Amer. Legal Consortium [★5470]

Natl. Asian Pacific Center on Aging [11300], 1511 3rd Ave., Ste. 914, Seattle, WA 98101, (206)624-1221

Natl. Asian Peace Officers' Assn. [5983], PO Box 50973, Washington, DC 20091-0973, (202)431-2175

Natl. Asian Women's Hea. Org. [16901], 1 Embarcadero Ctr., Ste. 500, San Francisco, CA 94111, (415)773-2838

Natl. Asian Women's Hea. Org. [IO], San Francisco, CA, United States

Natl. Asphalt Pavement Assn. [641], 5100 Forbes Blvd., Lanham, MD 20706, (301)731-4748

Natl. Assault Prevention Center [★12032]

Natl. Assembly of Chief Livestock Hea. Officials [★16811]

Natl. Assembly of Community Arts Agencies [★9546]

Natl. Assembly of Hea. and Human Ser. Organizations [★13400]

Natl. Assembly of Local Arts Agencies [★9546]

Natl. Assembly of Natl. Hea. and Social Welfare Organizations [★13400]

Natl. Assembly of Natl. Voluntary Hea. and Social Welfare Organizations [★13400]

Natl. Assembly of Religious Bros. [★19707]

Natl. Assembly of Religious Women - Address unknown since 2003.

Natl. Assembly of Rollerbladers - Defunct.

Natl. Assembly for Social Policy and Development [★13400]

Natl. Assembly of State Arts Agencies [9583], 1029 Vermont Ave. NW, 2nd Fl., Washington, DC 20005, (202)347-6352

Natl. Assembly of Women [IO], Tynemouth, United Kingdom

Natl. Assessment of Educational Progress [9253], Assessment Div., 8th Fl., 1990 K St. NW, Washington, DC 20006, (202)502-7300

Natl. Assessment of Educational Progress [★9253]

Natl. Assessment of Educational Progress, The Nation's Rpt. Card [★9253]

Natl. Assistance League [★13035]

Natl. Assistance Mgt. Assn. [★2507]

Natl. Assoc. CPA Firms [43], 136 S Keowee St., Dayton, OH 45402, (937)222-1024

Natl. Assoc. Marine Suppliers [★2584]

Natl. Associates for Informed Depressives - Defunct.

Natl. Assn. of Abortion Facilities [★11223]

Natl. Assn. of Academic Advisors [★8171]

Natl. Assn. of Academic Advisors for Athletics [8171], NC State Univ., Campus Box 8509, Raleigh, NC 27695, (919)513-1007

Natl. Assn. of Academies of Sci. [7617], c/o Dr. Michael Strauss, Pres., 4918 King Richard Dr., Annandale, VA 22003, (703)323-7810

Natl. Assn. of Accident and Hea. Underwriters [★2208]

Natl. Assn. of Accompanists and Coaches - Defunct.

Natl. Assn. of Accordion Wholesalers - Defunct.

Natl. Assn. of Accountants [★34]

Natl. Assn. of Accountants in Insolvencies [★15]

Natl. Assn. for the Accreditation of Colleges and Secondary Schools - Defunct.

Natl. Assn. for the Accreditation of Martial Arts Colleges and Curriculum - Address unknown since 1985.

Natl. Assn. of Activity Professionals - Address unknown since 2004.

Natl. Assn. of ADA Coordinators [11966], PO Box 958, Rancho Mirage, CA 92270, (800)722-4232

Natl. Assn. of Addiction Treatment Providers [13259], 313 W Liberty St., Ste. 129, Lancaster, PA 17603-2748, (717)392-8480

Natl. Assn. of Administrators of State and Fed. Educ. Programs [★7900]

Natl. Assn. of Adult Coll. Students - Address unknown since 1999.

Natl. Assn. of Adult Educ. [IO], Dublin, Ireland

Natl. Assn. for Adults with Special Learning Needs [8204], c/o Correctional Educ. Assn., 8182 Lark Brown Rd., Ste. 202, Elkridge, MD 21075-6332, (888)562-2756

Natl. Assn. to Advance Fat Acceptance [12647], PO Box 22510, Oakland, CA 94609, (916)558-6880

Natl. Assn. for the Advancement of Aardvarks in America - Defunct.

Natl. Assn. for the Advancement of the Black Aged - Address unknown since 1991.

Natl. Assn. for the Advancement of Black Amers. in Vocational Education - Defunct.

Natl. Assn. for the Advancement of Caring Teachers [9218], c/o Sindi D. Wasserman, PO Box 1282, Chino, CA 91708

Natl. Assn. for the Advancement of Colored People [17129], 4805 Mt. Hope Dr., Baltimore, MD 21215, (410)580-5777

Natl. Assn. for the Advancement of Colored People Legal Defense and Educational Fund [17130], 99 Hudson St., Ste. 1600, New York, NY 10013, (212)965-2200

Natl. Assn. for the Advancement of Haitian Descendents [19097], 74 Trinity Pl., Wall St., New York, NY 10006, (212)566-4919

Natl. Assn. for the Advancement of Hispanic People - Address unknown since 2006.

Natl. Assn. for the Advancement of Humane Educ. [★11433]

Natl. Assn. for the Advancement of Leboyer's Birth Without Violence - Defunct.

Natl. Assn. for the Advancement of Native Amer. Composers and Musicians - Address unknown since 1995.

Natl. Assn. for the Advancement of Older People - Address unknown since 1995.

Natl. Assn. for the Advancement of Orthodox Judaism - Address unknown since 2002.

Natl. Assn. for the Advancement of Orthotics and Prosthetics [15786], 1875 Eye St. NW, 12th Fl., Washington, DC 20006-5409, (202)624-0064

Natl. Assn. for the Advancement of Perry Mason - Defunct.

Natl. Assn. for the Advancement of Psychoanalysis [16110], 80 8th Ave., Ste. 1501, New York, NY 10011-7158, (212)741-0515

Natl. Assn. for the Advancement of Psychoanalysis [IO], New York, NY, United States

Natl. Assn. for the Advancement of Psychoanalysis and the Amer. Bd. for Accreditation in Psychoanalysis [★IO]

Natl. Assn. for the Advancement of Psychoanalysis and the Amer. Bd. for Accreditation in Psychoanalysis [★16110]

Natl. Assn. for the Advancement of Time - Address unknown since 2002.

Natl. Assn. for the Advancement of White People Natl. [18801], PO Box 1727, Callahan, FL 32011, (530)733-3119

Natl. Assn. of Advisors for the Hea. Professions [8866], PO Box 1518, Champaign, IL 61824-1518, (217)355-0063

Natl. Assn. of Aeronautical Examiners - Address unknown since 2003.

Natl. Assn. of Affordable Housing Lenders [487], 1300 Connecticut Ave. NW, Washington, DC 20036, (202)293-9850

National Association of African American Chambers of Commerce - Address unknown since 2004.

Natl. Assn. for African-Amer. Education Clearinghouse - Address unknown since 1995.

Natl. Assn. of African-Amer. Sportswriters and Broadcasters - Address unknown since 2008.

Natl. Assn. of African Amer. Students of Law - Address unknown since 1995.

Natl. Assn. of African Amer. Stud. [7931], PO Box 6670, Scarborough, ME 04070-6670, (207)839-8004

Natl. Assn. of African Americans in Human Resources [1982], PO Box 11467, Washington, DC 20008, (404)346-1245

Natl. Assn. of African Americans for Positive Imagery [16941], 1231 N Broad St., Philadelphia, PA 19122, (215)235-6488

Natl. Assn. of African Palm Growers [IO], Quito, Ecuador

Natl. Assn. Agricultural Contractors [IO], Peterborough, United Kingdom

Natl. Assn. of Agricultural Educators [7938], Univ. of Kentucky, 300 Garrigus Bldg., Lexington, KY 40546-0215, (859)257-2224

Natl. Assn. of Agricultural Engineers [IO], Bruckberg, Germany

Natl. Assn. of Agricultural Fair Agencies - Address unknown since 2002.

Natl. Assn. of Agricultural Journalists - Address unknown since 2001.

Natl. Assn. of Agricultural Produce Trading Companies [IO], Mexico City, Mexico

Natl. Assn. of Agriculture Employees [5437], c/o Mike Randall, Pres., PO Box 31143, Honolulu, HI 96820-1143, (808)861-8449

Natl. Assn. to Aid Fat Americans [★12647]

Natl. Assn. of Air Medical Commun. Specialists [13542], PO Box 121822, Nashville, TN 37212-1822, (877)396-2227

Natl. Assn. of Air Natl. Guard Health Technicians - Defunct.

Natl. Assn. of Air Traffic Specialists [24014], PO Box 2550, Landover Hills, MD 20784-0550, (301)459-5595

Natl. Assn. of Aircraft and Communications Suppliers - Defunct.

Natl. Assn. on Alcohol, Drugs and Disability [16512], 2165 Bunker Hill Dr., San Mateo, CA 94402-3801, (650)578-8047

Natl. Assn. of Alcoholic Beverage Importers [★206]

Natl. Assn. of Alcoholism and Drug Abuse Counselors [★16509]

Natl. Assn. of Alcoholism Treatment Programs [★13259]

Natl. Assn. of Alternative Benefits Consultants [1867], 435 Pennsylvania Ave., Glen Ellyn, IL 60137-4401, (800)627-0552

Natl. Assn. for Alternative Certification [8360], PO Box 5750, Washington, DC 20016, (202)277-3600

Natl. Assn. of Alternative Medicines [13641], PO Box 35215, Chicago, IL 60707-0215, (708)453-0080

Natl. Assn. for Alternative Staffing [1268], 3535 S Woodland Cir., Quinton, VA 23141, (804)932-9159

Natl. Assn. of Amateur Oarsmen [★23704]

Natl. Assn. for Ambulatory Care Medicine [★13663]

Natl. Assn. Amer. Balloon Corps Veterans - Defunct.

Natl. Assn. of Amer. Bus. Clubs [★13034]

Natl. Assn. of Amer. Community Orgs. - Address unknown since 1995.

Natl. Assn. of Amer. Granite Producers [★2772]

Natl. Assn. of Amer. School Employees and Retirees - Address unknown since 1995.

Natl. Assn. of Amer. School Employees and Retirees Legal Defense Counsel - Address unknown since 1999.

Natl. Assn. of Amer. Wineries; WineAmerica [4032]

Natl. Assn. of Amers. of Asian Indian Descent - Address unknown since 2001.

Natl. Assn. of Amusement Parks [★1303]

Natl. Assn. of Amusement Parks [★IO]

Natl. Assn. of Amusement Parks; Mfrs. Div., [★1298]

Natl. Assn. of Amusement Parks, Pools, and Beaches [★1303]

Natl. Assn. of Amusement Parks, Pools, and Beaches [★IO]

Natl. Assn. of Amusement Ride Safety Officials [214], PO Box 638, Brandon, FL 33509-0638, (813)661-2779

Natl. Assn. of Animal Breeders [5002], PO Box 1033, Columbia, MO 65205, (573)445-4406

Natl. Assn. of Anorexia Nervosa and Assoc. Disorders [14301], PO Box 7, Highland Park, IL 60035, (847)831-3438

Natl. Assn. of Apnea Professionals - Defunct.

Natl. Assn. for Applied Arts, Science, and Education - Address unknown since 1999.

Natl. Assn. of Appointment Secretaries [★8961]

Natl. Assn. of Arab Amers. - Address unknown since 2002.

A star before a book entry number signifies that the name is not listed separately, but is mentioned within the entry.

Natl. Assn. of Arab-Chaldean Bus. Women - Address unknown since 2003.

Natl. Assn. of Architectural Metal Mfrs. **[2719]**, 800 Roosevelt Rd., Bldg. C, Ste. 312, Glen Ellyn, IL 60137, (630)942-6591

Natl. Assn. of Area Agencies on Aging **[11301]**, 1730 Rhode Island Ave. NW, Ste. 1200, Washington, DC 20036, (202)872-0888

Natl. Assn. for Areas of Outstanding Natural Beauty **[IO]**, Northleach, United Kingdom

Natl. Assn. for Armenian Stud. and Res. **[9406]**, 395 Concord Ave., Belmont, MA 02478, (617)489-1610

Natl. Assn. of Art and Design Companies - Address unknown since 1986.

Natl. Assn. of Art Services - Address unknown since 1995.

Natl. Assn. of Artificial Breeders **[★5002]**

Natl. Assn. of Artists and Crafters **[301]**, c/o Founding Comm., 8630-M Guilford Rd., PMB No. 300, Columbia, MD 21046, (410)744-2296

Natl. Assn. of Artists' Organizations **[9512]**, 308 Prince St., Ste. 270, St. Paul, MN 55101, (651)294-0907

Natl. Assn. of ASCS County Office Employees - Address unknown since 1999.

Natl. Assn. of Asian Amer. Law Enforcement Commanders **[5984]**, PO Box 131672, Houston, TX 77219

Natl. Assn. of Asian Amer. Professionals **[9623]**, PO Box 52030, Boston, MA 02205, (206)619-8427

Natl. Assn. for Asian and Pacific Amer. Educ. **[7988]**, PO Box 280346, Northridge, CA 91328-0346, (818)677-2500

Natl. Assn. of Assessing Officers **[★6296]**

Natl. Assn. of Assessing Officers **[★IO]**

Natl. Assn. of Asst. U.S. Attorneys **[5508]**, 12427 Hedges Run Dr., Ste. 104, Lake Ridge, VA 22192-1715, (703)426-4266

Natl. Assn. for Assn. Political Action Committees - Defunct.

Natl. Assn. of At-Home Mothers **[12674]**, 406 E Buchanan Ave., Fairfield, IA 52556, (515)472-3202

Natl. Assn. of Athletes Against Drugs **[13260]**, 2481 Pacific Ave., Ste. C, Long Beach, CA 90806-2953, (562)989-9692

Natl. Assn. of Athletic Development Directors **[23832]**, PO Box 16428, Cleveland, OH 44116, (440)892-4000

Natl. Assn. of Atomic Veterans **[13353]**, 11214 Sageland, Houston, TX 77089, (281)481-1357

Natl. Assn. of Attorneys Gen. **[6276]**, 2030 M St. NW, 8th Fl., Washington, DC 20036-3306, (202)326-6000

Natl. Assn. of Auto Racing Memorabilia Collectors - Defunct.

Natl. Assn. of Auto Trim and Restyling Shops - Address unknown since 2004.

Natl. Assn. of Auto. Dealers **[IO]**, Mexico City, Mexico

Natl. Assn. of Auto. Mfrs. of South Africa **[IO]**, Pretoria, Republic of South Africa

Natl. Assn. of Auto. Museums **[10511]**, PO Box 271, Auburn, IN 46706, (260)925-1444

Natl. Assn. of Automotive Component and Allied Mfrs. **[IO]**, Johannesburg, Republic of South Africa

Natl. Assn. of Automotive Components Mfrs. **[IO]**, Sao Paulo, Brazil

Natl. Assn. of Automotive Dealers, Repair Outlets and Component Retailers **[IO]**, Madrid, Spain

Natl. Assn. of Avon Clubs **[★22073]**

Natl. Assn. of Avon Collectors **[22073]**, PO Box 7006, Kansas City, MO 64113

Natl. Assn. of Baby Boomer Women **[13431]**, 714 York Rd., Ste. 955, Towson, MD 21204

Natl. Assn. of Bail Insurance Companies **[★442]**

Natl. Assn. of Bakery Products **[IO]**, Mexico City, Mexico

Natl. Assn. of Bakery Sanitarians **[★2463]**

Natl. Assn. of Band Instrument Mfrs. **[★2810]**

Natl. Assn. of Band Instrument Mfrs. **[★IO]**

Natl. Assn. for Bank Auditors and Controllers **[★467]**

Natl. Assn. of Bank Club Orgs. - Address unknown since 2003.

Natl. Assn. for Bank Cost Anal. **[★464]**

Natl. Assn. for Bank, Cost, and Mgt. Accounting **[★464]**

Natl. Assn. of Bank Servicers **[★61]**

Natl. Assn. of Bank Women **[★478]**

Natl. Assn. of Bank Women **[★IO]**

Natl. Assn. of Bankruptcy Trustees **[5578]**, 1 Windsor Cove, Ste. 305, Columbia, SC 29223, (803)252-5646

Natl. Assn. of Bankshot Operators **[3667]**, 785F Rockville Pike, PMB 504, Rockville, MD 20852, (301)309-0260

Natl. Assn. of Baptist Professors of Religion **[9277]**, c/o Danny S. Mynatt, Exec. Sec.-Treas., PO Box 1123, Anderson Coll., Anderson, SC 29621

Natl. Assn. of Bar Executives **[5948]**, c/o Allan Head, Pres., PO Box 3688, Cary, NC 27519, (919)677-0561

Natl. Assn. of Bar-Related Title Insurers **[2204]**, 1430 Lee St., Des Plaines, IL 60018, (847)298-8300

Natl. Assn. of Bar and Tavern Owners **[205]**, PO Box 11578, Fort Lauderdale, FL 33339, (954)776-7017

Natl. Assn. of Barbados Organizations **[9731]**, PO Box 11764, Atlanta, GA 30355, (954)917-5469

Natl. Assn. of Barber Boards **[★1083]**

Natl. Assn. of Barber Boards of Am. **[1083]**, c/o Charles Kirkpatrick, Exec. Off., 2708 Pine St., Arkadelphia, AR 71923, (501)682-2806

Natl. Assn. of Barber Styling Schools - Defunct.

Natl. Assn. of Basketball Coaches **[23133]**, 1111 Main St., Ste. 1000, Kansas City, MO 64105-2136, (816)878-6222

Natl. Assn. of Basketball Coaches of the U.S. **[★23133]**

Natl. Assn. of Bedding Mfrs. **[★1974]**

Natl. Assn. of Bedding Mfrs. **[★IO]**

Natl. Assn. of Beginning Teachers **[9219]**, c/o Warren-Walker Upper School, 1165 Sandy Ridge Ave., Henderson, NV 89052, (702)616-3027

Natl. Assn. of Bench and Bar Spouses **[5509]**, c/o Lyla R. Coleman, Pres., 6837 Lakeshore Dr., Raytown, MO 64133, (816)353-4899

Natl. Assn. for Better Broadcasting - Address unknown since 1999.

Natl. Assn. of Beverage Importers **[206]**, 932 Hungerford Dr., Unit 12A, Rockville, MD 20850, (240)453-9998

Natl. Assn. of Beverage Retailers **[★193]**

Natl. Assn. of Biblical Constitutionalists - Defunct.

Natl. Assn. of Biblical Instructors **[★8223]**

Natl. Assn. of Bicentennial $2 Cancellation Collectors - Defunct.

Natl. Assn. of Bicycle and Sports Retailers **[IO]**, Stockholm, Sweden

Natl. Assn. for Bilingual Educ. **[7999]**, 1313 L St. NW, Ste. 210, Washington, DC 20005, (202)898-1829

Natl. Assn. of Bioengineers - Defunct.

Natl. Assn. of Biology Teachers **[8000]**, 12030 Sunrise Valley Dr., Ste. 110, Reston, VA 20191, (703)264-9696

Natl. Assn. for Biomedical Res. **[13700]**, 818 Connecticut Ave. NW, Ste. 900, Washington, DC 20006, (202)857-0540

Natl. Assn. of Black Accountants **[44]**, 7249-A Hanover Pkwy., Greenbelt, MD 20770, (301)474-6222

Natl. Assn. of Black Catholic Administrators - Address unknown since 2001.

Natl. Assn. of Black Citizens Action **[16942]**, PO Box 182, St. Martinville, LA 70582-0182

Natl. Assn. of Black Consulting Engineers - Address unknown since 2002.

Natl. Assn. of Black County Officials **[5617]**, 440 1st St. NW, Ste. 410, Washington, DC 20001, (202)347-6953

Natl. Assn. of Black Customs Enforcement Officers - Address unknown since 2006.

Natl. Assn. of Black Female Executives in Music and Entertainment **[12117]**, 59 Maiden Ln., 27th Fl., New York, NY 10038, (212)424-9568

Natl. Assn. of Black Geologists and Geophysicists - Address unknown since 1999.

Natl. Assn. of Black Hospitality Professionals - Defunct.

Natl. Assn. of Black Hotel Owners, Operators and Developers **[1950]**, 3520 W Broward Blvd., Ste. 218B, Fort Lauderdale, FL 33312, (954)797-7102

Natl. Assn. of Black Journalists **[3129]**, Univ. of Maryland, 8701-A Adelphi Rd., Adelphi, MD 20783-1716, (301)445-7100

Natl. Assn. of Black Mfrs. - Defunct.

Natl. Assn. of Black Media Workers - Address unknown since 1995.

Natl. Assn. of Black Owned Broadcasters **[568]**, 1155 Connecticut Ave. NW, Ste. 600, Washington, DC 20036, (202)463-8970

Natl. Assn. of Black Professors - Address unknown since 2001.

Natl. Assn. of Black Real Estate Professionals - Address unknown since 2003.

Natl. Assn. of Black Scuba Divers **[23711]**, PO Box 91630, Washington, DC 20090-1630, (800)521-NABS

Natl. Assn. of Black Social Workers **[13204]**, 2305 Martin Luther King Ave. SE, Washington, DC 20020-5813, (202)678-4570

Natl. Assn. of Black Storytellers **[10981]**, PO Box 67722, Baltimore, MD 21215, (410)947-1117

Natl. Assn. of Black Students - Address unknown since 1995.

Natl. Assn. of Black Telecommunications Professionals **[7778]**, 2020 Pennsylvania Ave. NW, Box 735, Washington, DC 20006, (877)349-8869

Natl. Assn. for Black Veterans **[21308]**, PO Box 11432, Milwaukee, WI 53211, (877)622-8387

Natl. Assn. of Black Women Attorneys - Address unknown since 2000.

Natl. Assn. of Black Women Entrepreneurs - Address unknown since 2003.

Natl. Assn. of Blacks in Criminal Justice **[11877]**, 1801 Fayetteville St., Durham, NC 27707-3129, (919)683-1801

Natl. Assn. for the Blind, India **[IO]**, Bombay, India

Natl. Assn. of Blind Merchants **[525]**, 1223 Lake Plaza Dr., Ste. D, Colorado Springs, CO 80906, (719)527-0488

Natl. Assn. of Blind Teachers **[9220]**, c/o Amer. Coun. of the Blind, 1155 15th St. NW, Ste. 1004, Washington, DC 20005, (202)467-5081

Natl. Assn. of Blind and Visually Impaired Computer Users - Defunct.

Natl. Assn. of Blouse Mfrs. **[245]**

Natl. Assn. of Blue Badge Holders **[IO]**, Brandon, United Kingdom

Natl. Assn. of Blueprint and Diazotype Coaters **[★1800]**

Natl. Assn. of Boards of Barbers Examiners of Am. **[★1083]**

Natl. Assn. of Boards, Commissions, and Councils of Catholic Educ. **[8056]**, Natl. Catholic Educational Assn., 1077 30th St. NW, Ste. 100, Washington, DC 20007-3852, (202)337-6232

Natl. Assn. of Boards of Educ. **[★8056]**

Natl. Assn. of Boards of Examiners of Long Term Care Administrators **[15538]**, 1444 I St. NW, No. 700, Washington, DC 20005-6542, (202)712-9040

Natl. Assn. of Boards of Examiners of Nursing Home Administrators **[★15538]**

Natl. Assn. of Boards of Pharmacy **[15944]**, 1600 Feehanville Dr., Mount Prospect, IL 60056, (847)391-4406

Natl. Assn. of Boat Mfrs. - Defunct.

Natl. Assn. of Boating Magazines - Defunct.

Natl. Assn. of Bond Lawyers **[6255]**, 230 W Monroe St., Ste. 320, Chicago, IL 60606-4715, (312)648-9590

Natl. Assn. of Book Editors **[IO]**, Montreal, QC, Canada

Natl. Assn. of Book Editors - Defunct.

Natl. Assn. of Book Mfrs. - Defunct.

Natl. Assn. of Brass Band Conductors **[IO]**, Waterlooville, United Kingdom

Natl. Assn. of Brattice Cloth Mfrs. - Address unknown since 1995.

Natl. Assn. of Breweriana Advt. **[22074]**, PO Box 64, Chapel Hill, NC 27514

Natl. Assn. of Brick Distributors **[★604]**

Natl. Assn. of British and Irish Millers **[IO]**, London, United Kingdom

Natl. Assn. Broadcast Employees and Technicians - Communications Workers of Am. **[24024]**, 501 3rd St. NW, Washington, DC 20001-2797, (202)434-1254

Reference to "IO" in place of a book number signifies that the association may be found in the 45th edition of International Organizations.

Natl. Assn. of Broadcast Unions and Guilds - Address unknown since 1995.

Natl. Assn. of Broadcasters [569], 1771 N St. NW, Washington, DC 20036, (202)429-5300

Natl. Assn. of Broadcasters of South Africa [IO], Craighall, Republic of South Africa

Natl. Assn. of Building Cooperatives Soc. [IO], Dublin, Ireland

Natl. Assn. of Building Mfrs. [★2524]

Natl. Assn. of Building Owners and Managers [★3301]

Natl. Assn. of Building Owners and Managers [★IO]

Natl. Assn. of Building Ser. Contractors [★IO]

Natl. Assn. of Building Ser. Contractors [★2459]

Natl. Assn. of Bur. of Animal Indus. Veterinarians [★16799]

Natl. Assn. of Bus. Brokers [★3322]

Natl. Assn. of Bus. Consultants [IO], Hudson, FL, United States

Natl. Assn. of Bus. Consultants - Defunct.

Natl. Assn. for Bus. Economics [6886], 1233 20th St. NW, Ste. 505, Washington, DC 20036, (202)463-6223

Natl. Assn. of Bus. Economists [★6886]

Natl. Assn. of Bus. and Educational Radio and Assn. of Communications Technicians [★3752]

Natl. Assn. of Bus. and Educational Radio and Assn. of Communications Technicians [★IO]

Natl. Assn. of Business and Industrial Saleswomen - Address unknown since 2001.

Natl. Assn. of Business Leaders [3614]

Natl. Assn. for Bus. Organizations [3615], 3 Woodthorne Ct., No. 12, Owings Mills, MD 21117, (410)363-3698

Natl. Assn. of Bus. Political Action Committees [18300], 101 Constitution Ave. NW, Ste. 800-West, Washington, DC 20001, (202)341-3780

Natl. Assn. of Business Services - Address unknown since 1997.

Natl. Assn. for Bus. Teacher Educ. [8032], c/o Natl. Bus. Educ. Assn., 1914 Assn. Dr., Reston, VA 20191-1596, (703)860-8300

Natl. Assn. of Business Travel Agents - Address unknown since 2007.

Natl. Assn. of Button Mfrs. - Defunct.

Natl. Assn. for Campus Activities [9169], 13 Harbison Way, Columbia, SC 29212-3401, (803)732-6222

Natl. Assn. of Campus Card Users [3707], 9201 N 25th Ave., Ste. 188, Phoenix, AZ 85021, (602)395-8989

Natl. Assn. of Campus and Univ. Ministers - Defunct.

Natl. Assn. of Canada Dry Franchise Bottlers - Defunct.

Natl. Assn. of Canadians of Origins in India [IO], Ottawa, ON, Canada

Natl. Assn. for Cancer Detection - Defunct.

Natl. Assn. of Car Mfrs. [IO], Turin, Italy

Natl. Assn. for the Care and Resettlement of Offenders [★IO]

Natl. Assn. of Career Colleges [IO], Brantford, ON, Canada

Natl. Assn. for Career Education - Defunct.

Natl. Assn. of Careers and Guidance Teachers [★IO]

Natl. Assn. of Carpet Retailers - Defunct.

Natl. Assn. of Carpet Specialists - Defunct.

Natl. Assn. of Casino Party Operators [1313], PO Box 2165, Poulsbo, WA 98370, (800)355-8259

Natl. Assn. of Casino and Theme Party Operators [★1313]

Natl. Assn. of Casual Furniture Retailers [★1693]

Natl. Assn. of Casualty and Surety Agents [★2159]

Natl. Assn. of Casualty and Surety Agents [★IO]

Natl. Assn. of Casualty and Surety Executives - Defunct.

Natl. Assn. of Catalog Showroom Merchandisers - Address unknown since 2001.

Natl. Assn. of Catastrophe Adjusters [2205], PO Box 821864, North Richland Hills, TX 76182, (817)498-3466

Natl. Assn. of Catering Butchers [IO], London, United Kingdom

National Association of Catering Executives [IO], Columbia, MD, United States

Natl. Assn. of Catering Executives [1951], 9881 Broken Land Pkwy., Ste. 101, Columbia, MD 21046, (410)290-5410

Natl. Assn. of Catholic Chaplains [19753], 5007 S Howell Ave., Ste. 120, Milwaukee, WI 53207-6159, (414)483-4898

Natl. Assn. of Catholic Diocesan Family Life Ministers [★20288]

Natl. Assn. of Catholic Family Life Ministers [20288], c/o David Abele, Exec. Dir., 300 Coll. Park, Dayton, OH 45469-2512, (937)431-5443

Natl. Assn. of Catholic Homes and Educators [8057], 7517 Dogwood Rd., Sykesville, MD 21784

Natl. Assn. of Catholic Nurses - USA [15491]

Natl. Assn. of Catholic School Teachers [8058], 1700 Sansom St., Ste. 903, Philadelphia, PA 19103, (215)568-4175

Natl. Assn. for Cave Diving [23962], PO Box 14492, Gainesville, FL 32604, (352)583-5652

Natl. Assn. of Cellular Agents [★3765]

Natl. Assn. of Cement Users [★6832]

Natl. Assn. of Cemeteries [★2781]

Natl. Assn. of Cemeteries [★IO]

Natl. Assn. of Centers for Urgent Treatment [★13663]

Natl. Assn. of Certified Dental Labs. [★14170]

Natl. Assn. of Certified Fraud Examiners [★2084]

Natl. Assn. of Certified Fraud Examiners [★IO]

National Association of Certified Home Inspectors [IO], Boulder, CO, United States

Natl. Assn. of Certified Home Inspectors [2121], 1750 30th St., Boulder, CO 80301

Natl. Assn. of Certified Valuation Analysts [45], 1111 Brickyard Rd., Ste. 200, Salt Lake City, UT 84106-5401, (801)486-0600

National Association of Certified Valuation Analysts [IO], Salt Lake City, UT, United States

Natl. Assn. of Chain Drug Stores [2985], 413 N Lee St., Alexandria, VA 22314, (703)549-3001

Natl. Assn. of Chain Mfrs. - Address unknown since 2003.

Natl. Assn. of Chamber Ambassadors [789], PO Box 1198, Seminole, TX 79360, (800)411-6222

Natl. Assn. of Chap. 13 Trustees [★5578]

Natl. Assn. of Charter School Authorizers [8281], 105 W Adams St., Ste. 1430, Chicago, IL 60603-6253, (312)376-2300

Natl. Assn. of Charterboat Operators [2582], PO Box 2990, Orange Beach, AL 36561, (251)981-5136

Natl. Assn. of Chem. Distributors [815], 1560 Wilson Blvd., Ste. 1250, Arlington, VA 22209, (703)527-6223

Natl. Assn. of Chewing Gum Mfrs. [1538], 15000 Commerce Pkwy., Ste. C, Mount Laurel, NJ 08054, (856)439-0500

Natl. Assn. for Chicana and Chicano Stud. [8498], PO Box 720052, San Jose, CA 95172-0052, (408)924-5310

Natl. Assn. for Chicano Stud. [★8498]

Natl. Assn. of Chiefs of Police [★5972]

Natl. Assn. of Chiefs of Police [6173], 6350 Horizon Dr., Titusville, FL 32780, (321)264-0911

Natl. Assn. of Chiefs of Police [★IO]

Natl. Assn. of Child Advocates [★11662]

Natl. Assn. for Child Care Mgt. - Defunct.

Natl. Assn. of Child Care Professionals [11529], PO Box 90723, Austin, TX 78709, (512)301-5557

Natl. Assn. of Child Care Rsrc. and Referral Agencies [11530], 3101 Wilson Blvd., Ste. 350, Arlington, VA 22201, (703)341-4100

Natl. Assn. for Child Development [13943], 549 25th St., Ogden, UT 84401, (801)621-8606

Natl. Assn. of Childbearing Centers [★15580]

Natl. Assn. of Childbirth Education - Defunct.

Natl. Assn. for Children of Alcoholics [13261], 11426 Rockville Pike, Ste. 301, Rockville, MD 20852, (301)468-0985

Natl. Assn. for Children's Behavioral Hea. [16090], 1025 Connecticut Ave. NW, Ste. 1012, Washington, DC 20036-3536, (202)857-9735

Natl. Assn. for Children's Heart Disorders; Kids With Heart [13915]

Natl. Assn. of Children's Hospitals and Related Institutions [14889], 401 Wythe St., Alexandria, VA 22314, (703)684-1355

Natl. Assn. of Chimney Engineers [IO], Lincoln, United Kingdom

Natl. Assn. of Chimney Sweeps [IO], Stone, United Kingdom

Natl. Assn. of Chiropodists [★16037]

Natl. Assn. for Chiropractic Medicine [14009], 15427 Baybrook Dr., Houston, TX 77062, (281)280-8262

Natl. Assn. of Choirs [IO], Stoke-On-Trent, United Kingdom

Natl. Assn. of Christian Colleges and Universities - Defunct.

Natl. Assn. of Christian Financial Consultants [1465], 1055 Maitland Center Commons Blvd., Maitland, FL 32751, (407)644-9793

Natl. Assn. of Christian Marriage Counselors - Defunct.

Natl. Assn. of Christian Singles - Defunct.

Natl. Assn. of Christians in the Arts - Address unknown since 1987.

Natl. Assn. of Christians in Social Work [★13208]

Natl. Assn. of Church Bus. Admin. [20513], 100 N Central Expy., Ste. 914, Richardson, TX 75080-5326, (972)699-7555

Natl. Assn. of Church Bus. Administrators [★20513]

Natl. Assn. of Church Design Builders [831], 1000 Ballpark Way, Arlington, TX 76011, (817)200-2622

Natl. Assn. of Church Facilities Managers [20514], c/o Ms. Victoria Hardy, Wentworth Inst. of Tech., Dept. of Design and Facilities, 550 Huntington Ave., Boston, MA 02115, (616)956-9377

Natl. Assn. of Church Food Ser. [1587], PO Box 550413, Atlanta, GA 30355, (404)261-1794

Natl. Assn. of Church and Institutional Financing Organizations [2426], c/o Ms. Kerrie Bernardo, Sec.-Treas., Reliance Financial Corp., 1100 Abernathy Rd., 500 Northpark, Atlanta, GA 30328, (404)266-0663

Natl. Assn. for Church Mgt. Consultants - Address unknown since 2001.

Natl. Assn. of Church Personnel Administrators [20515], 100 E 8th St., Cincinnati, OH 45202, (513)421-3134

Natl. Assn. of the Cigar Indus. [IO], Bonn, Germany

Natl. Assn. of Citizens Advice Bureaux [IO], London, United Kingdom

Natl. Assn. of Citizens Crime Commissions [★11840]

Natl. Assn. Citizens on Patrol [12970], PO Box 727, Corona, CA 92878-0727, (951)898-8551

Natl. Assn. of Citrus Juice Processors [★510]

Natl. Assn. for City Drug and Alcohol Coordination - Defunct.

Natl. Assn. of Civic Secretaries - Address unknown since 1995.

Natl. Assn. of Civil Service Employees [5568]

Natl. Assn. of Civilian Conservation Corps Alumni [19082], 16 Hancock Ave., St. Louis, MO 63125, (314)487-8666

Natl. Assn. for Civilian Oversight of Law Enforcement [5985], c/o Charles Reynolds, Sec., PO Box 396, Dover, NH 03821, (866)462-2653

Natl. Assn. of Claimants Compensation Attorneys [★6328]

Natl. Assn. of Claims Assistance Professionals - Address unknown since 2002.

Natl. Assn. of Classroom Educators in Business Education - Address unknown since 2002.

Natl. Assn. of Clean Air Agencies [5696], 444 N Capitol St. NW, Ste. 307, Washington, DC 20001, (202)624-7864

Natl. Assn. of Clean Water Agencies [6237], 1816 Jefferson Pl. NW, Washington, DC 20036-2505, (202)833-2672

Natl. Assn. of Clergy Hypnotherapists [★14926]

Natl. Assn. of Clergy Hypnotherapists - Defunct.

Natl. Assn. of Clinical Managers [★15067]

Natl. Assn. of Clinical Nurse Specialists [15492], 2090 Linglestown Rd., Ste. 107, Harrisburg, PA 17110, (717)234-6799

Natl. Assn. of Clothing Designers [★241]

Natl. Assn. of Clothing Designers [★IO]

Natl. Assn. of Clothing Mfrs. [IO], Lisbon, Portugal

Natl. Assn. of Clubs for Young People [★IO]

Natl. Assn. of Co-op Advertising Professionals - Defunct.

A star before a book entry number signifies that the name is not listed separately, but is mentioned within the entry.

Natl. Assn. of Coal Haulers - Defunct.

Natl. Assn. of the Coat and Dress Industry - Address unknown since 1997.

Natl. Assn. of Cocoa Exporters [IO], Guayaquil, Ecuador

Natl. Assn. of the Coffee Indus. - Mexico [IO], Mexico City, Mexico

Natl. Assn. of Cognitive-Behavioral Therapists [16193], PO Box 2195, Weirton, WV 26062, (304)723-3982

Natl. Assn. of Coin Laundry Equip. Operators [★2406]

Natl. Assn. of Cold Storage Contractors [★1886]

Natl. Assn. of Cold Storage Contractors [★IO]

Natl. Assn. of Cold Storage Insulation Contractors [★IO]

Natl. Assn. of Cold Storage Insulation Contractors [★1886]

Natl. Assn. of Colitis and Crohn's Disease [IO], St. Albans, United Kingdom

Natl. Assn. of Collectors [22075], 18222 Flower Hill Way, No. 299, Gaithersburg, MD 20879, (301)926-8663

Natl. Assn. for Coll. Admission Counseling [7912], 1631 Prince St., Alexandria, VA 22314-2818, (703)836-2222

Natl. Assn. of Coll. Admission Counselors [★7912]

Natl. Assn. of Coll. Admissions Counselors [★7912]

Natl. Assn. of Coll. Automotive Teachers [★7993]

Natl. Assn. of Coll. Auxiliary Services [3478], 7 Boar's Head Ln., Charlottesville, VA 22903-4610, (434)245-8425

Natl. Assn. of Coll. Broadcasters - Address unknown since 2004.

Natl. Assn. of Coll. Deans, Registrars, and Admissions Officers - Address unknown since 2002.

Natl. Assn. of Coll. Stores [3415], 500 E Lorain St., Oberlin, OH 44074, (440)775-7777

Natl. Assn. of College Students - Address unknown since 2005.

Natl. Assn. of Coll. Teachers of Agriculture [★7942]

Natl. Assn. of Coll. and Univ. Attorneys [5677], 1 Dupont Cir., Ste. 620, Washington, DC 20036, (202)833-8390

Natl. Assn. of Coll. and Univ. Bus. Officers [7897], 1110 Vermont Ave. NW, Ste. 800, Washington, DC 20005, (202)861-2500

National Assn. of Coll. and Univ. Chaplains and Directors of Religious Life [★9168]

Natl. Assn. of Coll. and Univ. Food Services [1588], 2525 Jolly Rd., Ste. 280, Okemos, MI 48864-3680, (517)332-2494

Natl. Assn. of Coll. and Univ. Security Directors [★9084]

Natl. Assn. of Coll. and Univ. Security Directors [★IO]

Natl. Assn. of Coll. and Univ. Summer Sessions [★IO]

Natl. Assn. of Coll. and Univ. Summer Sessions [★9200]

Natl. Assn. of Coll. Wind and Percussion Instructors [8919], c/o Dr. Richard K. Weerts, Exec. Sec.-Treas., 308 Hillcrest Dr., Kirksville, MO 63501, (660)785-4442

Natl. Assn. of Coll. Women [★9320]

Natl. Assn. of Colleges and Departments of Educ. [★9208]

Natl. Assn. of Colleges and Employers [8995], 62 Highland Ave., Bethlehem, PA 18017-9481, (610)868-1421

Natl. Assn. of Colleges and Teachers of Agriculture [★7942]

Natl. Assn. of Colls. and Universities [★8225]

Natl. Assn. of Collegiate Commissioners [★23815]

Natl. Assn. of Collegiate Directors of Athletics [23833], PO Box 16428, Cleveland, OH 44116, (440)892-4000

Natl. Assn. of Collegiate Gymnastics Coaches/ Women [23476], c/o Mike Lorenzen, Pres., Stanford Univ., Arrillaga Family Sports Center, Stanford, CA 94305-6150, (650)724-0457

Natl. Assn. of Collegiate Marketing Administrators [23834], PO Box 16428, Cleveland, OH 44116, (440)892-4000

Natl. Assn. of Collegiate Secretaries [★66]

Natl. Assn. of Collegiate Secretaries [★IO]

Natl. Assn. of Collegiate Women Athletics Administrators [8982], 5018 Randall Pkwy., Ste. 3, Wilmington, NC 28403, (910)793-8244

Natl. Assn. of Colored Women's Clubs [13051], 1601 R St. NW, Washington, DC 20009, (202)667-4080

Natl. Assn. of Comics Art Educators [8115], PO Box 125, White River Junction, VT 05001

Natl. Assn. of Commercial Broadcasters in Japan [IO], Tokyo, Japan

Natl. Assn. of Commercial Finance Brokers [IO], Exeter, United Kingdom

Natl. Assn. of Commercial Org. Secretaries [★24251]

Natl. Assn. of Commissioned Travel Agents [3927], 1101 King St., Ste. 200, Alexandria, VA 22314, (703)739-6826

Natl. Assn. of Commissioners, Secretaries and Directors of Agriculture [★5439]

Natl. Assn. of Commissions for Women [17550], 401 N Washington St., Ste. 100, Rockville, MD 20850-1737, (240)777-8308

Natl. Assn. of Commun. Systems Engineers [6715], 18029 E Dorado Ave., Centennial, CO 80015, (720)269-4777

Natl. Assn. of Community Action Agencies [★12770]

Natl. Assn. for Community Coll. Entrepreneurship [8033], Bldg. 101-R, 1 Fed. St., Springfield, MA 01105, (413)755-6102

Natl. Assn. of Community Coll. Teacher Educ. Programs [9221], c/o Dr. Cheri St. Arnauld, Exec. Dir., 2411 W 14th St., Tempe, AZ 85281-6942, (480)731-8760

Natl. Assn. for Community Development - Defunct.

Natl. Assn. of Community Development Extension Professionals [11784], PO Box 4033, Bismarck, ND 58502-4033, (701)526-3556

Natl. Assn. of Community Development Loan Funds [★17233]

Natl. Assn. of Community Hea. Centers [14574], 7200 Wisconsin Ave., Ste. 210, Bethesda, MD 20814, (301)347-0400

Natl. Assn. for Community Leadership [★11795]

Natl. Assn. for Community Leadership [★IO]

Natl. Assn. of Community Leadership Organizations [★IO]

Natl. Assn. of Community Leadership Organizations [★11795]

Natl. Assn. for Community Mediation [5460], PO Box 3263, Washington, DC 20010, (202)545-8866

Natl. Assn. of Competitive Mounted Orienteering [23640], 503 171st Ave. SE, Tenino, WA 98589-9711, (360)264-2727

National Association of Competitive Mounted Orienteering [IO], Tenino, WA, United States

Natl. Assn. for Composers and Conductors [★10657]

Natl. Assn. of Composers, U.S.A. [10657], PO Box 49256, Barrington Sta., Los Angeles, CA 90049, (818)274-6048

Natl. Assn. of Cmpt. Consultant Businesses [968], 1420 King St., Ste. 610, Alexandria, VA 22314, (703)838-2050

Natl. Assn. of Cmpt. Consulting Businesses Canada [IO], Kanata, ON, Canada

Natl. Assn. of Computer Stores - Defunct.

Natl. Assn. of Computerized Tax Processors [6298], c/o Jamie Stiles, Pres., 235 E Palmer St., Franklin, NC 28734, (828)524-8020

Natl. Assn. of Concerned Veterans - Defunct.

Natl. Assn. of Concessionaires [1589], 35 E Wacker Dr., Ste. 1816, Chicago, IL 60601, (312)236-3858

Natl. Assn. of Condo Hotel Owners [1952], 8151 E Evans Rd., Ste. 4, Scottsdale, AZ 85260, (480)905-2374

Natl. Assn. of Congregational Christian Churches [19861], 8473 S Howell Ave., PO Box 288, Oak Creek, WI 53154-0288, (414)764-1620

Natl. Assn. of Conservation Districts [4420], c/o Krysta Harden, CEO, 509 Capitol Ct. NE, Washington, DC 20002-4937, (202)547-6223

Natl. Assn. of Consulting Engineers of Slovenia [IO], Ljubljana, Slovenia

Natl. Assn. of Consumer Advocates [17334], 1730 Rhode Island Ave. NW, Ste. 710, Washington, DC 20036, (202)452-1989

Natl. Assn. of Consumer Agency Administrators [5609], 2 Brentwood Commons, Ste. 150, 750 Old Hickory Blvd., Brentwood, TN 37027, (615)371-6125

Natl. Assn. of Consumer Agency Administrators [IO], Brentwood, TN, United States

National Association of Consumer Bankruptcy Attorneys [IO], Washington, DC, United States

Natl. Assn. of Consumer Bankruptcy Attorneys [5510], 2300 M St., Ste. 800, Washington, DC 20037, (202)331-8005

Natl. Assn. of Consumer Credit Administrators [5610], PO Box 20871, Columbus, OH 43220-0871, (614)326-1165

Natl. Assn. of Consumer Orgs. - Defunct.

Natl. Assn. of Consumer Shows [1346], 2300 SW 102nd Ave., Portland, OR 97216, (503)253-0832

Natl. Assn. of Consumers and Travelers [★3931]

Natl. Assn. of Container Distributors [986], 1601 Bond St., Ste. 101, Naperville, IL 60563, (630)544-5052

Natl. Assn. for Continence [16709], PO Box 1019, Charleston, SC 29402-1019, (843)377-0900

National Association for Continence [IO], Charleston, SC, United States

Natl. Assn. of Continuing Medical Education Meetings and Seminars - Defunct.

Natl. Assn. of Convenience Stores [3416], 1600 Duke St., Alexandria, VA 22314, (703)684-3600

National Association of Convenience Stores [IO], Alexandria, VA, United States

Natl. Assn. of Coordinators of State Programs for the Mentally Retarded [★12576]

Natl. Assn. for Core Curriculum - Defunct.

Natl. Assn. for Corporate Art Mgt. [★24002]

Natl. Assn. for Corporate Art Mgt. [★IO]

Natl. Assn. of Corporate Directors [2504], 2 Lafayette Centre, 1133 21st St. NW, Ste. 700, Washington, DC 20036, (202)775-0509

Natl. Assn. of Corporate and Professional Recruiters [★1265]

Natl. Assn. of Corporate and Professional Recruiters [★IO]

Natl. Assn. of Corporate Real Estate Executives [★IO]

Natl. Assn. of Corporate Real Estate Executives [★3305]

Natl. Assn. for Corporate Speaker Activities - Address unknown since 1999.

Natl. Assn. of Corporate Treasurers [1435], 12100 Sunset Hills Rd., Ste. 130, Reston, VA 20190, (703)437-4377

Natl. Assn. of Corp. Schools [★2481]

Natl. Assn. of Corp. Schools [★IO]

Natl. Assn. of Corrosion Engineers [★IO]

Natl. Assn. of Corrosion Engineers [★7027]

Natl. Assn. of Corrosion Engineers [6840], 1440 S Creek Dr., Houston, TX 77084-4906, (281)228-6200

Natl. Assn. of Cosmetic Boutique Owners - Defunct.

Natl. Assn. of Cosmetology Schools; Teachers' Division of [★8160]

Natl. Assn. of Cost Accountants [★34]

Natl. Assn. of Costume Jewelers - Defunct.

Natl. Assn. for the Cottage Industry - Address unknown since 2002.

Natl. Assn. of Cotton Cloth Glove Mfrs. [★2030]

Natl. Assn. of Cotton Cloth Glove Mfrs. [★IO]

Natl. Assn. of Cotton Mfrs. [★3795]

Natl. Assn. of Councils on Developmental Disabilities [12575], 225 Reinekers Ln., Ste. 650-B, Alexandria, VA 22314, (703)739-4400

Natl. Assn. of Counsel for Children [11711], 1825 Marion St., Ste. 242, Denver, CO 80218, (303)864-5320

Natl. Assn. of Counsellors, Hypnotherapists and Psychotherapists [IO], Cambridge, United Kingdom

Natl. Assn. of Counselors [3318], 303 W Cypress St., PO Box 12528, San Antonio, TX 78212-0528, (210)271-0781

Natl. Assn. of Counties [5618], 25 Massachusetts Ave. NW, Washington, DC 20001, (202)393-6226

Natl. Assn. of Country Sales and Promotion Executives - Defunct.

Natl. Assn. of County 4-H Club Agents [★13495]

Reference to "IO" in place of a book number signifies that the association may be found in the 45th edition of International Organizations.

Natl. Assn. of County Administrators - Defunct.

Natl. Assn. of County Aging Programs [11302], c/o Marilina Sanz, Assoc. Legislative Dir., 25 Massachusetts Ave. NW, Washington, DC 20001-1430, (202)942-4260

Natl. Assn. of County Agricultural Agents [5438], 252 N Park St., Decatur, IL 62523, (217)424-5144

Natl. Assn. of County Behavioral Hea. Directors [14708], 25 Massachusetts Ave., Ste. 500, Washington, DC 20001, (202)661-8816

Natl. Assn. of County and City Hea. Officials [6217], 1100 17th St. NW, 2nd Fl., Washington, DC 20036, (202)783-5550

Natl. Assn. of County Civil Attorneys [5619], c/o Robert Spence, Pres., 2501 7th St., Ste. 300, Tuscaloosa, AL 35401-1801, (205)349-3870

Natl. Assn. of County Club Agents [★13495]

Natl. Assn. of County Community Development Directors [★17225]

Natl. Assn. for County Community and Economic Development [17225], 2025 M St. NW, Ste. 800, Washington, DC 20036-3309, (202)367-1149

Natl. Assn. of County of Employment and Training Administrators [★5618]

Natl. Assn. of County Engineers [7029], 25 Massachusetts Ave. NW, Ste. 580, Washington, DC 20001-1430, (202)393-5041

Natl. Assn. of County Hea. Fac. Administrators [15069], c/o Natl. Assn. of Counties, 25 Massachusetts Ave. NW, Washington, DC 20001-1430, (202)942-4234

Natl. Assn. of County Hea. Officers [★6217]

Natl. Assn. of County Hea. Officials [★6217]

Natl. Assn. of County Human Services Administrators [★5618]

Natl. Assn. of County Info. Officers [5620], c/o Tom Goodman, Public Affairs Dir., 440 1st St. NW, Washington, DC 20001, (913)715-8572

Natl. Assn. of County Off. Employees [★5779]

Natl. Assn. of County Officials [★5618]

Natl. Assn. of County Park and Recreation Officials [6155], 16 W 284-97th St., Burr Ridge, IL 60527

Natl. Assn. of County Planners [5589], c/o Natl. Assn. of Counties, 440 1st St. NW, 8th Fl., Washington, DC 20001, (202)661-8807

Natl. Assn. of County Planning Directors [★5589]

Natl. Assn. of County and Prosecuting Attorneys [★5668]

Natl. Assn. of County Recorders and Clerks [★5621]

Natl. Assn. of County Recorders, Election Officials, and Clerks [5621], 2501 Aerial Center Pkwy., Ste. 103, Morrisville, NC 27560, (919)459-2080

Natl. Assn. of County Relations Officials [5622], c/o Diane Hutchins, Pres., 141 Pryor St. SW, Atlanta, GA 30303-3444, (404)730-7375

Natl. Assn. of County Surveyors [5623], c/o R. Charles Pearson, Sec.-Treas., County Surveyor, Clackamas County, 9101 SE Sunnybrook Blvd., Ste. 428, Clackamas, OR 97015-6612, (503)353-4499

Natl. Assn. of County Training and Employment Professionals [★5618]

Natl. Assn. of County Treasurers and Finance Officers [6205], c/o Kim Reynolds, Treas., PO Box 157, Osceola, IA 50213, (641)342-3311

Natl. Assn. of County Veteran Ser. Officers [21309], c/o Jim Golgart, Treas., LeSueur County Veteran Services, 88 S Park Ave., Le Center, MN 56057-1600, (507)357-2251

Natl. Assn. of County Welfare Directors [★5618]

Natl. Assn. for Court Admin. [★5627]

Natl. Assn. for Court Admin. [★IO]

Natl. Assn. for Court Mgt. [IO], Williamsburg, VA, United States

Natl. Assn. for Court Mgt. [5627], c/o Assn. of Mgt., 300 Newport Ave., Natl. Center for State Courts, Williamsburg, VA 23185-4147, (757)259-1841

Natl. Assn. for the Craniofacially Handicapped [★14061]

Natl. Assn. for Creative Children and Adults - Address unknown since 2003.

Natl. Assn. for Credential Evaluation Services [8409], c/o IERF, PO Box 3665, Culver City, CA 90231-3665, (310)258-9451

Natl. Assn. of Credit Mgt. [1436], 8840 Columbia 100 Pkwy., Columbia, MD 21045, (410)740-5560

Natl. Assn. of Credit Mgt. North Central [★1422]

Natl. Assn. of Credit Union Chairmen [1112], PO Box 160, Del Mar, CA 92014-0160, (858)792-3883

Natl. Assn. of Credit Union Presidents [★1112]

Natl. Assn. of Credit Union Services Organizations [1113], PMB 3419 Via Lido, No. 135, Newport Beach, CA 92663, (949)645-5296

Natl. Assn. of Credit Union Supervisory and Auditing Committees [1114], PO Box 160, Del Mar, CA 92014, (800)287-5949

Natl. Assn. of Crime Commissions [11840], c/o Mr. Bobby Stout, Treas., Wichita Crime Commn., 125 N Market, Ste. 115, Wichita, KS 67202, (316)267-1235

Natl. Assn. of Crime Victim Compensation Boards [13364], PO Box 16003, Alexandria, VA 22302, (703)780-3200

Natl. Assn. for Crime Victims Rights - Defunct.

Natl. Assn. of Criminal Defense Lawyers [5656], 1150 18th St. NW, Ste. 950, Washington, DC 20036, (202)872-8600

Natl. Assn. of Criminal Justice Planners - Defunct.

Natl. Assn. of Cruise Only Agencies [★3928]

Natl. Assn. of Cruise-Oriented Agencies [3928], 7378 Atlantic Blvd., No. 115, Margate, FL 33063, (305)663-5626

Natl. Assn. of Cuban-Amer. Women of the U.S.A. - Address unknown since 2007.

Natl. Assn. of Cuban Architects (in Exile) - Defunct.

Natl. Assn. of Cuban Economists [IO], Havana, Cuba

Natl. Assn. of Cultured Marble Mfrs. [★IO]

Natl. Assn. of Cultured Marble Mfrs. [★630]

Natl. Assn. of Cycle and Motorcycle Traders [★IO]

Natl. Assn. of Cytologist [IO], Brighton, United Kingdom

Natl. Assn. of Dairy Producers [IO], Harare, Zimbabwe

Natl. Assn. of Dairy Prdt. Wholesalers and Exporters [★IO]

Natl. Assn. of Daytime Dress Mfrs. - Defunct.

Natl. Assn. of the Deaf [14767], 8630 Fenton St., Ste. 820, Silver Spring, MD 20910-3819, (301)587-1788

Natl. Assn. for the Deaf in Denmark [★IO]

Natl. Assn. for Deaf People [IO], Dublin, Ireland

Natl. Assn. of Deafened People [IO], Amersham, United Kingdom

Natl. Assn. of Dealer Counsel [361], 7250 Parkway Dr., Ste. 510, Hanover, MD 21076-1343, (410)712-4037

Natl. Assn. of Dealers in Antiques - Defunct.

Natl. Assn. of Deans and Advisers of Men [★7904]

Natl. Assn. of Deans of Women and Advisers to Girls in Negro Schools - Defunct.

Natl. Assn. of Decorative Architectural Finishes - Defunct.

Natl. Assn. of Decorative Fabric Distributors [3793], 1 Windsor Cove, Ste. 305, Columbia, SC 29223-1833, (800)445-8629

Natl. Assn. of Decorative and Fine Arts Societies [IO], London, United Kingdom

Natl. Assn. of Defense Lawyers in Criminal Cases [★5656]

Natl. Assn. of Demolition Contractors [★1043]

Natl. Assn. of Dental Assistants [14169], 900 S Washington St., No. G-13, Falls Church, VA 22046, (703)237-8616

Natl. Assn. of Dental Examiners [★14112]

Natl. Assn. of Dental Labs. [14170], 325 John Knox Rd., No. L103, Tallahassee, FL 32303, (850)205-5626

Natl. Assn. of Dental Plans [14962], 8111 Lyndon B. Johnson Fwy., Ste. 935, Dallas, TX 75251-1347, (972)458-6998

Natl. Assn. of Dental Ser. Plans [★14687]

Natl. Assn. of Deputy U.S. Marshals - Address unknown since 1995.

Natl. Assn. of Desktop Publishers - Address unknown since 2002.

Natl. Assn. of Destroyer Veterans; Tin Can Sailors - The [21220]

Natl. Assn. of Development Companies [2427], 6764 Old McLean Village Dr., McLean, VA 22101, (703)748-2575

Natl. Assn. of Development Educ. Centres [★IO]

Natl. Assn. of Development Organizations [5590], 400 N Capitol St. NW, Ste. 390, Washington, DC 20001, (202)624-7806

Natl. Assn. of Development Organizations Res. Found. [17226], 400 N Capitol St. NW, Ste. 390, Washington, DC 20001, (202)624-7806

Natl. Assn. of Developmental Disabilities Councils [★12575]

Natl. Assn. of Developmental Disabilities Managers - Defunct.

Natl. Assn. for Developmental Educ. [8200], 500 N Estrella Pkwy., Ste. B2, PMB 412, Goodyear, AZ 85338, (877)233-9455

Natl. Assn. of Diaconate Directors [19664], 2136 12th St., Ste. 105, Rockford, IL 61104, (815)965-2100

Natl. Assn. of Diaper Services [2389], 994 Old Eagle School Rd., Ste. 1019, Wayne, PA 19087, (610)971-4850

Natl. Assn. of Diemakers and Diecutters [★2029]

Natl. Assn. of Diemakers and Diecutters [★IO]

Natl. Assn. for the Diffusion of Fertilizers [IO], Sao Paulo, Brazil

Natl. Assn. of Diocesan Altar Guilds of the Protestant Episcopal Church - Address unknown since 1995.

Natl. Assn. of Diocesan Ecumenical Officers [19901], c/o Rev. Robert B. Flannery, Pres., St. Francis Xavier Catholic Church, 303 S Poplar St., Carbondale, IL 62901, (618)457-4556

Natl. Assn. for Direct Care Workers of Color [14709]

Natl. Assn. of Direct Mail Writers - Address unknown since 1995.

Natl. Assn. of Direct Sellers [★1684]

Natl. Assn. of Direct Selling Companies [★3465]

Natl. Assn. of Directors and Administrators [★14574]

Natl. Assn. of Directors of Christian Education [★19937]

Natl. Assn. of Directors of Christian Education [★IO]

Natl. Assn. of Directors of Nursing Admin. in Long Term Care [15493], 11353 Reed Hartman Hwy., Ste. 210, Reed Hartman Tower, Cincinnati, OH 45241, (513)791-3679

Natl. Assn. of Disability Evaluating Professionals [14575], c/o Dr. Virgil R. May, III, Exec. Dir., 13801 Village Mill Dr., Ste. 204, Midlothian, VA 23113, (804)378-7275

Natl. Assn. of Disability Examiners [14034], c/o Georgina Huskey, Pres.-Elect, 3435 Wilshire Blvd., Ste. 1600, Los Angeles, CA 90010, (213)736-7088

Natl. Assn. of Disability Representatives [18648], 1901 Pennsylvania Ave. Nw, Ste. 607, Washington, DC 20006, (202)822-2155

Natl. Assn. for Disabled Athletes - Address unknown since 1995.

Natl. Assn. of Disco Disc Jockeys - Defunct.

Natl. Assn. of Discount Merchants - Defunct.

Natl. Assn. of Display Indus. [2642], 4651 Sheridan St., Ste. 470, Hollywood, FL 33021, (954)893-7300

Natl. Assn. of Distance Educ. and Open Learning in South Africa [IO], Braamfontein, Republic of South Africa

Natl. Assn. of Distance Educ. Organisations of South Africa [★IO]

Natl. Assn. of Distributive Educ. Local Supervisors [★8818]

Natl. Assn. for Distributive Educ. Teachers [★8818]

Natl. Assn. of Diversified Manufacturers Representatives [★2541]

Natl. Assn. of Div. I-A (NCAA Football) Independents - Defunct.

Natl. Assn. of Div. Order Analysts [2934], 2805 Oak Trail Ct., No. 6312, Arlington, TX 76016, (405)749-6601

Natl. Assn. for Divorced Women - Defunct.

Natl. Assn. of Doctors in the U.S. - Defunct.

Natl. Assn. of Document Examiners [5765], c/o Barbara Downer, CDE, Pres., 1734 E 30th Ave. N, Oxford, KS 67119, (620)455-9910

Natl. Assn. of Dog Obedience Instructors [22312], PMB 369, 729 Grapevine Hwy., Hurst, TX 76054-2085

Natl. Assn. of Doll and Stuffed Toy Mfrs. - Address unknown since 2003.

A star before a book entry number signifies that the name is not listed separately, but is mentioned within the entry.

Natl. Assn. of Dome Home Mfrs. [★2530]

Natl. Assn. of Domestic Elecl. Appliance Manufactures [IO], Madrid, Spain

Natl. Assn. for Drama Educ. [IO], Brisbane, Australia

Natl. Assn. for Drama Therapy [16222], 15 Post Side Ln., Pittsford, NY 14534, (585)381-5618

Natl. Assn. of Dramatic and Speech Arts [11026], c/o Dr. Wendy R. Coleman, VP, 504 Coll. Dr., Albany, GA 31705, (229)430-4840

Natl. Assn. of Dredging Contractors [★2576]

Natl. Assn. on Drug Abuse Problems [13262], 355 Lexington Ave., New York, NY 10017, (212)986-1170

Natl. Assn. Drug and Allied Sales Orgs. - Address unknown since 1991.

Natl. Assn. of Drug Court Professionals [6289], 4900 Seminary Rd., Ste. 320, Alexandria, VA 22311, (703)575-9400

National Association of Drug Court Professionals [IO], Alexandria, VA, United States

Natl. Assn. of Drug Diversion Investigators [5986], PO Box 611, Manchester, MD 21102-0611, (443)398-6257

Natl. Assn. of Drug Manufacturers Representatives [★2541]

Natl. Assn. for the Dually Diagnosed [14243], 132 Fair St., Kingston, NY 12401, (845)331-4336

Natl. Assn. for the Dually Diagnosed [★12552]

Natl. Assn. of Early Childhood Teacher Educators [9222], c/o Anne Dorsey, 1082 Witt Rd., Cincinnati, OH 45255

Natl. Assn. of Ecumenical and Interreligious Staff [19902], PO Box 7093, Tacoma, WA 98406-0093, (253)759-0141

Natl. Assn. of Ecumenical Staff [★19902]

Natl. Assn. of the Edible Oils and Fats Indus. [IO], Mexico City, Mexico

Natl. Assn. for the Educ. and Advancement of Cambodian, Laotian, and Vietnamese Americans [19424], c/o Phouang Sixiengmay-Hamilton, 7424 Chinook St. NE, Olympia, WA 98516, (360)725-6152

Natl. Assn. for the Educ. of African Amer. Children with Learning Disabilities [12493], PO Box 9521, Columbus, OH 43209, (614)237-6021

Natl. Assn. for the Educ. of Young Children [8069], 1313 L St. NW, Ste. 500, Washington, DC 20005, (202)232-8777

Natl. Assn. of Educational Broadcasters - Defunct.

Natl. Assn. of Educational Buyers [★7899]

Natl. Assn. for Educational Computing - Defunct.

Natl. Assn. for Educational Guidance for Adults [IO], Glasgow, United Kingdom

Natl. Assn. of Educational Negotiators [★24046]

Natl. Assn. of Educational Off. Personnel [★7898]

Natl. Assn. of Educational Off. Professionals [7898], PO Box 12619, Wichita, KS 67277-2619, (316)942-4822

Natl. Assn. of Educational Procurement [7899], 5523 Res. Park Dr., Ste. 340, Baltimore, MD 21228, (443)543-5540

Natl. Assn. of Educational Secretaries [★7898]

Natl. Assn. for Educational TV - Defunct.

Natl. Assn. of Elec. Companies [★3956]

Natl. Assn. of Elec. Companies [★IO]

Natl. Assn. of Elecl. Distributors [1190], 1100 Corporate Square Dr., Ste. 100, St. Louis, MO 63132, (314)991-9000

Natl. Assn. of Electronic Keyboard Mfrs. [★2808]

Natl. Assn. of Electronic Keyboard Mfrs. [★IO]

Natl. Assn. of Electronic Organ Mfrs. [★IO]

Natl. Assn. of Electronic Organ Mfrs. [★2808]

Natl. Assn. of Elementary School Principals [9014], 1615 Duke St., Alexandria, VA 22314, (703)684-3345

Natl. Assn. of Elevator Contractors [1034], 1298 Wellbrook Cir., Ste. A, Conyers, GA 30012, (770)760-9660

Natl. Assn. of Elevator Safety Authorities Intl. - Defunct.

Natl. Assn. of Emergency Medical Technicians [14335], PO Box 1400, Clinton, MS 39060-1400, (601)924-7744

National Association of Emergency Medical Technicians [IO], Clinton, MS, United States

Natl. Assn. of Emergency Vehicle Technicians [418], 151 Lexington Rd., Shirley, NY 11967, (800)466-2388

Natl. Assn. for Employee Recognition [★17492]

Natl. Assn. of Employees of Collectors of Internal Revenue [★24080]

Natl. Assn. of Employers on Health Care Action - Defunct.

Natl. Assn. of Employment Agencies [★1272]

Natl. Assn. for the Employment of Amers. [1269]

Natl. Assn. of Employment Managers [★2481]

Natl. Assn. of Employment Managers [★IO]

Natl. Assn. of EMS Educators [8867], Foster Plz. 6, 681 Anderson Dr., Pittsburgh, PA 15220-2766, (412)920-4775

National Association of EMS Educators [IO], Pittsburgh, PA, United States

Natl. Assn. of EMS Physicians [14336], PO Box 15945-281, Lenexa, KS 66285-5945, (913)895-4611

Natl. Assn. of Energy Ser. Companies [6960], 1615 M St. NW, Ste. 900, Washington, DC 20036-3224, (202)822-0950

Natl. Assn. of Engine and Boat Mfrs. [★2587]

Natl. Assn. of Engineering Companies - Defunct.

Natl. Assn. of Engg. Student Councils [7030], c/o Natl. Soc. of Professional Engineers, 1420 King St., Alexandria, VA 22314-2794, (480)231-8054

Natl. Assn. of Enrolled Agents [6299], 1120 Connecticut Ave. NW, Ste. 460, Washington, DC 20036-3953, (202)822-6232

Natl. Assn. of Enrolled Federal Tax Accountants - Address unknown since 2001.

Natl. Assn. of Entrepreneurial Parents [12675], PO Box 320722, Fairfield, CT 06825, (203)371-6212

Natl. Assn. for Environmental Educ. [IO], Walsall, United Kingdom

Natl. Assn. of Environmental Law Societies [5697], c/o Dan Worth, Exec. Dir., 1227 Olivia Ave., Ann Arbor, MI 48104, (734)709-8794

Natl. Assn. for Environmental Mgt. [★4588]

Natl. Assn. for Environmental Mgt; NAEM - [4588]

Natl. Assn. of Environmental Professionals [4589], 389 Main St., Ste. 202, Malden, MA 02148, (781)397-8870

Natl. Assn. of Environmental Risk Auditors - Address unknown since 2004.

Natl. Assn. of Episcopal Schools [8398], 815 2nd Ave., Ste. 819, New York, NY 10017-4594, (212)716-6134

Natl. Assn. for Equal Educational Opportunities - Defunct.

Natl. Assn. for Equal Opportunity in Higher Educ. [8109], 209 Third St. SE, Washington, DC 20003, (202)552-3300

Natl. Assn. of Equip. Leasing Brokers [3382], 455 S Fourth St., Ste. 650, Louisville, KY 40202, (502)583-3783

Natl. Assn. of Equity Source Banks [488], 10451 Mill Run Cir., Ste. 400, Owings Mills, MD 21117, (410)363-3698

Natl. Assn. of ESOP Companies [★1248]

Natl. Assn. of Estate Agents [IO], Warwick, United Kingdom

Natl. Assn. of Estate Planners and Councils [1466], 1120 Chester Ave., Ste. 470, Cleveland, OH 44114, (866)226-2224

Natl. Assn. of Estate Planning Councils [★1466]

Natl. Assn. for Ethnic Stud. [9919], Western Washington Univ., 516 High St., MS 9113, Bellingham, WA 98225, (360)650-2349

Natl. Assn. of Evangelicals [19982], PO Box 23269, Washington, DC 20026, (202)789-1011

Natl. Assn. of Evangelicals; World Relief Commn. of the [★19985]

Natl. Assn. for the Exchange of Indus. Resources [8336], 560 McClure St., Galesburg, IL 61401, (309)343-0704

Natl. Assn. of Exclusive Buyer Agents [18495], 929 S 20th St., Arlington, VA 22202, (703)920-1095

Natl. Assn. of Executive Recruiters [1270], c/o Hall and Associates, 1 E Wacker Dr., Ste. 2600, Chicago, IL 60601, (847)885-1453

Natl. Assn. of Executive Secretaries [★72]

Natl. Assn. of Executive Secretaries and Administrative Assistants [72], 900 S Washington St., Ste. G-13, Falls Church, VA 22046, (703)237-8616

Natl. Assn. Executives Club - Address unknown since 1994.

Natl. Assn. of Exotic Pest Plant Councils [5077], c/o Tony Pernas, Chm., Natl. Park Ser., Florida/Caribbean EPMT, 18001 Old Cuttler Rd., Ste. 419, Palmetto Bay, FL 33157, (305)252-0347

Natl. Assn. of Export Companies [2307], c/o Ms. Gerri Cristantiello, Exec. Dir., PO Box 3949, Grand Central Sta., New York, NY 10163, (877)291-4901

Natl. Assn. of Exporters and Importers of Fruit, Vegetables and Citrus Fruits [IO], Rome, Italy

Natl. Assn. of Exposition Managers [★IO]

Natl. Assn. of Exposition Managers [★2682]

Natl. Assn. of Extension 4-H Agents [13495], 1800 Camden Rd., Ste. 107, No. 213, Charlotte, NC 28203, (704)333-3234

Natl. Assn. of Extension Home Economists [★5612]

Natl. Assn. of Exterminators and Fumigators [★2910]

Natl. Assn. of Exterminators and Fumigators [★IO]

Natl. Assn. of Extradition Officials - Address unknown since 1999.

Natl. Assn. for Families and Addiction Res. and Education - Defunct.

Natl. Assn. for Family and Child Care [12171], 5202 Pinemont Dr., Salt Lake City, UT 84123-4607, (801)269-9338

Natl. Assn. for Family and Community Educ. [8513], 73 Cavalier Blvd., Ste. 106, Florence, KY 41042, (859)525-6401

Natl. Assn. of Fan Clubs - Defunct.

Natl. Assn. of Fan Manufacturers [★1876]

Natl. Assn. of Fan Manufacturers [★IO]

Natl. Assn. of Farm Broadcasters [★570]

Natl. Assn. of Farm Broadcasting [570], PO Box 500, Platte City, MO 64079, (816)431-4032

Natl. Assn. of Farm and Ranch Trailer Mfrs. - Defunct.

Natl. Assn. of Farm Ser. Agency County Off. Employees [5779], c/o Jeanne Monday, Membership Chair, PO Box 336, Charleston, MS 38921, (662)647-8857

Natl. Assn. of Farmer Elected Committeemen - Address unknown since 2004.

Natl. Assn. of Farmers' Market Nutrition Programs [4648], PO Box 9080, Alexandria, VA 22304, (703)837-0451

Natl. Assn. of Farmworker Orgs. - Defunct.

Natl. Assn. of Farriers, Blacksmiths and Agricultural Engineers [IO], Kenilworth, United Kingdom

Natl. Assn. of Fashion and Accessory Designers [246]

Natl. Assn. of Federal Career Employers - Defunct.

Natl. Assn. of Fed. Credit Unions [1115], 3138 10th St. N, Arlington, VA 22201-2149, (703)522-4770

Natl. Assn. of Fed. Defenders [5646], PO Box 22223, Nashville, TN 37202

Natl. Assn. of Fed. Educ. Prog. Administrators [7900], c/o Bobby Burns, Pres., PO Box 2084, Anniston, AL 36202, (256)741-7453

Natl. Assn. of Fed. Prog. Administrators [★7900]

Natl. Assn. of Fed. Veterinarians [16799], 1101 Vermont Ave. NW, Ste. 170, Washington, DC 20005, (202)842-4360

Natl. Assn. of Federally Impacted Schools [8349], Hall of States, 444 N Capitol St. NW, Ste. 419, Washington, DC 20001, (202)624-5455

Natl. Assn. of Federally Licensed Firearms Dealers [1478], 2400 E Las Olas Blvd., No. 397, Fort Lauderdale, FL 33301, (954)467-9994

Natl. Assn. of Federations of Syrian and Lebanese Amer. Clubs - Address unknown since 1995.

Natl. Assn. of Fellowships Advisors [9080], c/o John Richardson, Treas., Univ. of Louisville, Louisville, KY 40292

Natl. Assn. for Female Executives [742], 60 E 42nd St., Ste. 2700, New York, NY 10165, (212)351-6451

Natl. Assn. of Field Training Officers [5987], PO Box 3236, Evansville, IN 47731, (812)436-7951

Natl. Assn. of Finance Institutions [IO], Madrid, Spain

Natl. Assn. of Financial and Estate Planning [1437], 525 E 4500 S, No. F-100, Salt Lake City, UT 84107, (801)266-9900

Reference to "IO" in place of a book number signifies that the association may be found in the 45th edition of International Organizations.

Natl. Assn. of Financial Services [IO], Berlin, Germany

Natl. Assn. of Fine Art Dealers [★298]

Natl. Assn. of Fine Arts - Defunct.

Natl. Assn. of Finishers of Textile Fabrics [★3772]

Natl. Assn. of Fire Equip. Distributors [3448], 104 S Michigan Ave., Ste. 300, Chicago, IL 60603, (312)263-8100

Natl. Assn. of Fire Investigators [2206], 857 Tallevast Rd., Sarasota, FL 34243, (941)359-2800

Natl. Assn. of Fire Science and Administration - Defunct.

Natl. Assn. of Firearms Retailers [1479], 11 Mile Hill Rd., Newtown, CT 06470, (203)426-1320

Natl. Assn. of First Responders [14320]

Natl. Assn. of Fiscally Responsible Cities - Defunct.

Natl. Assn. of the Fish Indus. [★IO]

Natl. Assn. of Fisheries Commissioners [★IO]

Natl. Assn. of Fisheries Commissioners [★7255]

Natl. Assn. of Flavors and Food-Ingredient Systems [1539], 3301 Rte. 66, Bldg. C, Ste. 205, Neptune, NJ 07753, (732)922-3218

Natl. Assn. of Fleet Administrators [362], 125 Village Blvd., Ste. 200, Princeton Forrestal Village, Princeton, NJ 08540, (609)720-0882

Natl. Assn. of Fleet Resale Dealers [419], 396 Clarkston Dr., Smyrna, TN 37167, (615)355-5225

Natl. Assn. of Fleet Tug Sailors [21213], 19416 Mohawk Rd., Bend, OR 97702-8908, (541)410-0297

Natl. Assn. of Flight Instructors [161], EAA Aviation Ctr., PO Box 3086, Oshkosh, WI 54903-3086, (920)426-6801

Natl. Assn. of Flood and Storm Water Mgt. Agencies [6140], 1301 K St. NW, Ste. 800 E, Washington, DC 20005, (202)218-4122

Natl. Assn. of Floor Covering Distributors [★657]

Natl. Assn. of Flour Distributors [1540], c/o Jean La Corte, Pres., PO Box 610, Montville, NJ 07045, (973)402-1801

Natl. Assn. of Flower Arrangement Societies [IO], London, United Kingdom

Natl. Assn. of Food and Beverage Recruiters - Address unknown since 2003.

Natl. Assn. of Food Chains [★3406]

Natl. Assn. of Food and Dairy Equip. Manufacturers [★1133]

Natl. Assn. of Food and Dairy Equip. Manufacturers [★IO]

Natl. Assn. of Food Equip. Mfrs. [★1576]

Natl. Assn. of Food Indus. [IO], Paris, France

Natl. Assn. of Food Products Retailers and Manufacturers [IO], Lisbon, Portugal

Natl. Assn. of Football Commissioners [★23815]

Natl. Assn. of Footwear Suppliers [IO], Leon, Mexico

Natl. Assn. of Foreign Medical Graduates [★IO]

Natl. Assn. of Foreign Medical Graduates [★14973]

Natl. Assn. of Foreign Student Advisors [★8445]

Natl. Assn. of Foreign Student Advisors [★IO]

Natl. Assn. for Foreign Student Affairs [★IO]

Natl. Assn. for Foreign Student Affairs [★8445]

Natl. Assn. of Foreign-Trade Zones [2308], 1001 Connecticut Ave. NW, Ste. 350, Washington, DC 20036, (202)331-1950

Natl. Assn. of Foremen [★2509]

Natl. Assn. of Forensic Accountants [46], 2455 E Sunrise Blvd., Ste. 1201, Fort Lauderdale, FL 33304-3115, (954)535-5556

Natl. Assn. of Forensic Counselors [5647], PO Box 8827, Fort Wayne, IN 46898-8827, (260)426-7234

Natl. Assn. of Forensic Economics [6044], PO Box 394, Mount Union, PA 17066, (814)542-3253

Natl. Assn. of Forensic Economists [★6044]

Natl. Assn. of Forest Indus. [IO], Deakin West, Australia

Natl. Assn. of Form 1099 Filers [18711], PQ Box 130053, Ann Arbor, MI 48113-0053, (734)327-9593

Natl. Assn. of Former Foster Care Children of Am. [11626], 5505 5th St. NW, Washington, DC 20011, (202)291-1603

Natl. Assn. of Foster Care Reviewers - Address unknown since 1991.

Natl. Assn. of Foster Grandparent Program Directors - Address unknown since 2002.

Natl. Assn. of Franchise Companies - Address unknown since 1999.

Natl. Assn. of Franchised Businessmen - Defunct.

Natl. Assn. of Fraternal Insurance Counsellors [2207], c/o Anna Maenner, Exec. Sec., 211 Canal Rd., Waterloo, WI 53594, (866)478-3880

Natl. Assn. of Free Clinics [14727], 1140 19th St. NW, Ste. 900, Washington, DC 20036, (202)223-5120

Natl. Assn. for Free Enterprise - Defunct.

Natl. Assn. of Free Will Baptists [19492], 5233 Mt. View Rd., Antioch, TN 37013-2306, (615)731-6812

Natl. Assn. of Free Will Baptists; Master's Men of the [19490]

Natl. Assn. of Freestanding Emergency Centers [★13663]

Natl. Assn. of Freight Payment Banks - Address unknown since 2004.

Natl. Assn. Friends of Rare Porcelain - Defunct.

Natl. Assn. of Frozen Food Packers [★1496]

Natl. Assn. of Fruits, Flavors and Syrups [★1539]

Natl. Assn. of Full Figured Women - Address unknown since 1994.

Natl. Assn. of Fundholding Practices [★IO]

Natl. Assn. of Funeral Directors [IO], Solihull, United Kingdom

Natl. Assn. of Furniture Mfrs. [★1690]

Natl. Assn. of Furniture Repair and Refinishing Specialists - Address unknown since 2004.

Natl. Assn. of Future Doctors of Audiology [13718], c/o Vicky Moore, Treas., 8264 Deerbrook Cir., Sarasota, FL 34238, (817)403-8575

Natl. Assn. of Gagwriters - Defunct.

Natl. Assn. of Gambling Regulatory Agencies [★5772]

Natl. Assn. for Gambling Stud. [IO], Alphington, Australia

Natl. Assn. of Game Commissioners and Wardens [★IO]

Natl. Assn. of Game Commissioners and Wardens [★4360]

Natl. Assn. of Garage Door Mfrs. - Defunct.

Natl. Assn. of Gardeners [★4803]

Natl. Assn. of Gas Chlorinators [★825]

Natl. Assn. of Gay Alcoholism Professionals [★13263]

Natl. Assn. Gen. Merchandise Representatives Consumer Prdt. Brokers [★2541]

Natl. Assn. of Gen. Practitioner Veterinarians [IO], Frankfurt am Main, Germany

Natl. Assn. of Generation X'ers - Address unknown since 2002.

Natl. Assn. of Geoscience Teachers [8459], 31 Crestview Dr., Napa, CA 94558, (707)427-8864

Natl. Assn. of Geriatric Educ. Centers [14513], c/o Edwin Olsen, Pres., PO Box 016960, Miami, FL 33101, (305)243-6270

National Assn. of Geriatric Nursing Assistants [★14514]

Natl. Assn. of German Bus. Consultants [IO], Bonn, Germany

Natl. Assn. of the German Cement Indus. [IO], Berlin, Germany

Natl. Assn. of German Dentists [★IO]

Natl. Assn. of German Export Trade [★IO]

Natl. Assn. of the German Food Indus. [IO], Berlin, Germany

Natl. Assn. of the German Gravel and Sand Indus. [IO], Duisburg, Germany

Natl. Assn. of German Non-Alcoholic Beverage Indus. [IO], Berlin, Germany

Natl. Assn. of the German Soft Drink Indus. [★IO]

Natl. Assn. of German Stamp Dealers [IO], Cologne, Germany

Natl. Assn. of the German Tallow and Lard Indus. [IO], Bonn, Germany

Natl. Assn. of German Tobacco Wholesalers and Vending Machine Installers [IO], Cologne, Germany

Natl. Assn. for Gifted Children [IO], Milton Keynes, United Kingdom

Natl. Assn. for Gifted Children [8466], 1707 L St. NW, Ste. 550, Washington, DC 20036, (202)785-4268

Natl. Assn. of Girl Scout Executives [★12996]

Natl. Assn. of Girls Clubs [★13498]

Natl. Assn. for Girls and Women in Sport [8983], c/o Amer. Alliance for Hea., Physical Educ., Recreation and Dance, 1900 Assn. Dr., Reston, VA 20191-1598, (703)476-3400

Natl. Assn. of the Glass Indus. [IO], Dusseldorf, Germany

Natl. Assn. of Glass Manufacturers [IO], Rome, Italy

Natl. Assn. of Glove Mfrs. [★IO]

Natl. Assn. of Glove Mfrs. - Defunct.

Natl. Assn. of Glue Mfrs. - Defunct.

Natl. Assn. of Goldsmiths [IO], London, United Kingdom

Natl. Assn. of Golf Coach Educators [★23291]

Natl. Assn. of Golf Coaches and Educators [23291]

Natl. Assn. of Golf Tournament Directors [23457]

Natl. Assn. of Goodwill Indus. [★11949]

Natl. Assn. of Goodwill Indus. [★IO]

Natl. Assn. of Govt. Archives and Records Administrators [5820], 90 State St., Ste. 1009, Albany, NY 12207, (518)463-8644

Natl. Assn. of Govt. Communicators [5583], 201 Park Washington Ct., Falls Church, VA 22046-4527, (703)538-1787

Natl. Assn. of Govt. Deferred Compensation Administrators [★2340]

Natl. Assn. of Govt. Defined Contribution Administrators [2340], 201 E Main St., Ste. 1405, Lexington, KY 40507, (859)514-9161

Natl. Assn. of Govt. Employees [24075], 159 Burgin Pkwy., Quincy, MA 02169, (617)376-0220

Natl. Assn. of Govt. Engineers - Defunct.

Natl. Assn. of Govt. Guaranteed Lenders [6039], 215 E 9th Ave., Stillwater, OK 74074, (405)377-4022

Natl. Assn. of Govt. Inspectors and Quality Assurance Personnel - Address unknown since 2001.

Natl. Assn. of Govt. Secretaries - Defunct.

Natl. Assn. of Govt. Service Contractors - Defunct.

Natl. Assn. for Govt. Training and Development [2904], 2516 Wertherson Ln., Raleigh, NC 27613-1700, (919)306-1787

Natl. Assn. of Governmental Labor Officials [5917], PO Box 11910, Lexington, KY 40578-1910, (859)244-8221

Natl. Assn. of Governor's Councils on Physical Fitness and Sport [★15967]

Natl. Assn. of Governors' Highway Safety Representatives [★6317]

Natl. Assn. of Graduate Admissions Professionals [7913], c/o Mr. Michael P. Flanagan, Exec. Dir., PO Box 14605, Lenexa, KS 66285-4605, (913)895-4616

Natl. Assn. of Graduate-Professional Students [9185], 209 Pennsylvania Ave. SE, Washington, DC 20003, (202)543-0812

Natl. Assn. of Graphic and Prdt. Identification Mfrs. [2720], 1300 Sumner Ave., Cleveland, OH 44115-2851, (216)241-7333

Natl. Assn. of Greeting Card Publishers [★3682]

Natl. Assn. of Gun and Knife Shows [★17105]

Natl. Assn. for the Habilitation of the Mentally Handicapped in Israel [IO], Tel Aviv, Israel

Natl. Assn. of Handcraftsmen - Defunct.

Natl. Assn. of Handwriting Analysts - Address unknown since 1995.

Natl. Assn. of Hardwood Wholesalers - Defunct.

Natl. Assn. of Head Teachers [IO], Haywards Heath, United Kingdom

Natl. Assn. of Hea. Care Assistants [14514], 1201 L St. NW, Washington, DC 20005, (202)454-1288

Natl. Assn. of Health Career Schools - Address unknown since 2006.

Natl. Assn. of Hea. Data Organizations [14576], 448 E 400 S, Ste. 301, Salt Lake City, UT 84111, (801)532-2299

Natl. Assn. of Hea. Educ. Centers [14675], 1533 N River Center Dr., Milwaukee, WI 53212-3913, (414)390-2187

Natl. Assn. for Hea. and Fitness [15967], c/o Be Active New York State, 65 Niagara Sq., Rm. 607, Buffalo, NY 14202, (716)583-0521

Natl. Assn. of Hea. Sci. Educ. Partnership [9107], c/o Erin Dolan, PhD, Pres., Biochemistry, Falin Center, Virginia Tech., West Campus Dr., MC 0346, Blacksburg, VA 24061, (540)231-2692

Natl. Assn. of Hea. Services Executives [14577], 8630 Fenton St., Ste. 126, Silver Spring, MD 20910, (202)628-3953

Natl. Assn. of Hea. Underwriters [2208], 2000 N 14th St., Ste. 450, Arlington, VA 22201, (703)276-0220

A star before a book entry number signifies that the name is not listed separately, but is mentioned within the entry.

Natl. Assn. of Hea. Unit Clerks-Coordinators [★14578]

Natl. Assn. of Hea. Unit Coordinators [14578], 1947 Madron Rd., Rockford, IL 61107-1716, (815)633-4351

Natl. Assn. of Hea. and Welfare Ministries of The United Methodist Church [★14602]

Natl. Assn. of Healthcare Access Mgt. [14890], 2025 M St. NW, Ste. 800, Washington, DC 20036, (202)367-1125

Natl. Assn. for Healthcare Quality [16264], 4700 W Lake Ave., Glenview, IL 60025, (847)375-4720

Natl. Assn. of Healthcare Recruiters [★15070]

Natl. Assn. of Healthcare Recruitment [15070], 1401 S Primrose Dr., Orlando, FL 32806, (407)843-6981

Natl. Assn. of Healthcare Transport Mgt. [14579], c/o Cathleen Thom, Sec., PO Box 409, Twin Falls, ID 83303, (208)737-2929

Natl. Assn. of Hearing Officials [5906], PO Box 4999, Midlothian, VA 23112, (360)664-7268

Natl. Assn. for Hearing and Speech Action [★16442]

Natl. Assn. of Hearing and Speech Agencies [★16442]

Natl. Assn. of Hebrew Day School Administrators [7901]

Natl. Assn. of Hebrew Day School PTAs [8953], 160 Broadway, 4th Fl., New York, NY 10038, (212)227-1000

Natl. Assn. of Hepatitis Task Forces [14812], PO Box 66, Miller, NE 68858, (308)457-2641

Natl. Assn. of High School Teachers of Journalism [★8713]

Natl. Assn. for Hispanic Elderly [19100], 234 E Colorado Blvd., Ste. 300, Pasadena, CA 91101, (626)564-1988

Natl. Assn. of Hispanic Fed. Executives [5711], PO Box 23270, Washington, DC 20026-3270, (202)315-3942

Natl. Assn. of Hispanic Firefighters [5721], 2821 McKinney Ave., Ste. 7, Dallas, TX 75204, (972)223-5033

Natl. Assn. of Hispanic Journalists [3130], 1000 Natl. Press Bldg., 529 14th St. NW, Washington, DC 20045-2001, (202)662-7145

Natl. Assn. of Hispanic and Latino Stud. [9920], c/o Natl. Assn. of African Amer. Stud. and Affiliates, PO Box 6670, Scarborough, ME 04070-6670, (207)839-8004

Natl. Assn. of Hispanic Nurses [15494], 1501 Sixteenth St. NW, Washington, DC 20036, (202)387-2477

Natl. Assn. of Hispanic Priests of the USA [19665], 1120 52nd St., Lubbock, TX 79412, (806)763-0710

Natl. Assn. of Hispanic Publications [3237], 8201 Greensboro Dr., Ste. 300, McLean, VA 22102, (703)610-0205

Natl. Assn. of Hispanic Real Estate Professionals [3319], 1150 17th St. NW, Ste. 504, Washington, DC 20036, (800)964-5373

Natl. Assn. of Hispanic-Serving Hea. Professions Schools [★8864]

Natl. Assn. on HIV Over Fifty [14952], 23 Miner St., Boston, MA 02215-3318, (617)233-7107

Natl. Assn. for Holistic Aromatherapy [14830], 3327 W Indian Trail Rd., PMB 144, Spokane, WA 99208, (509)325-3419

Natl. Assn. for Holocaust Education - Address unknown since 2004.

Natl. Assn. of the Holy Name Soc. [19666], c/o Gerard F. Novak, Dir., PO Box 12012, Baltimore, MD 21281-2012, (410)325-1523

Natl. Assn. of Home Based Businesses [1921], 10451 Mill Run Cir., Ste. 400, Owings Mills, MD 21117, (410)363-3698

Natl. Assn. of Home Builders [1035], 1201 15th St. NW, Washington, DC 20005, (202)266-8200

Natl. Assn. of Home Builders of the U.S. [★1035]

Natl. Assn. for Home Care [★14840]

Natl. Assn. for Home Care and Hospice [14840], 228 7th St. SE, Washington, DC 20003, (202)547-7424

Natl. Assn. of Home Delivered and Congregate Meal Providers [★12284]

Natl. Assn. of Home Economics Supervisors [★8514]

Natl. Assn. of Home Hea. Agencies [★14840]

Natl. Assn. of Home Inspectors [2122], 4248 Park Glen Rd., Minneapolis, MN 55416, (952)928-4641

Natl. Assn. of Home Mfrs. [★2524]

Natl. Assn. of Home and Workshop Writers [3131], PO Box 12, Baker, NV 89311, (847)255-0210

Natl. Assn. of Homes for Boys [★13501]

Natl. Assn. of Homes for Children [★12136]

Natl. Assn. of Homes for Children [★IO]

Natl. Assn. of Homes and Services for Children [★IO]

Natl. Assn. of Homes and Services for Children [★12136]

Natl. Assn. of Horological Schools - Defunct.

Natl. Assn. of Horseradish Packers - Defunct.

Natl. Assn. of Horseshoe and Quoit Pitchers [★23540]

Natl. Assn. of Hose and Accessories Distribution [2047], 105 Eastern Ave., Ste. 104, Annapolis, MD 21403-3300, (410)263-1014

Natl. Assn. of Hosiery Manufacturers [★239]

Natl. Assn. of Hosp. Admitting Managers [★14890]

Natl. Assn. of Hosp. Central Ser. Personnel [★14886]

Natl. Assn. of Hosp. Central Ser. Personnel [★IO]

Natl. Assn. of Hosp. and Community Friends [★IO]

Natl. Assn. for Hosp. Development [★IO]

Natl. Assn. for Hosp. Development [★14871]

Natl. Assn. of Hosp. Fire Officers [IO], Bolton, United Kingdom

Natl. Assn. of Hosp. Hospitality Houses [14891], PO Box 18087, Asheville, NC 28814-0087, (828)253-1188

Natl. Assn. of Hospital Purchasing Materials Mgt. - Address unknown since 1995.

Natl. Assn. of Hotel Accountants [★32]

Natl. Assn. of Hotel Accountants [★IO]

Natl. Assn. of the Hotel Indus. [IO], Casablanca, Morocco

Natl. Assn. of Hotel and Motel Accountants [★IO]

Natl. Assn. of Hotel and Motel Accountants [★32]

Natl. Assn. of Hotel and Restaurant Meat Purveyors [★IO]

Natl. Assn. of Hotel and Restaurant Meat Purveyors [★2663]

Natl. Assn. of Household Cleaning Products [IO], Milan, Italy

Natl. Assn. of Housing Cooperatives [12320], 1444 I St. NW, Ste. 700, Washington, DC 20005-6542, (202)737-0797

Natl. Assn. of Housing Info. Managers [5792], 134 S 13th St., Ste. 701, Lincoln, NE 68508, (402)476-9424

Natl. Assn. of Housing Officials [★5793]

Natl. Assn. of Housing and Redevelopment Officials [5793], 630 Eye St. NW, Washington, DC 20001, (202)289-3500

Natl. Assn. for Human Development [11303]

Natl. Assn. of Human Rights Workers - Address unknown since 2001.

Natl. Assn. of Human Services Technologies - Defunct.

Natl. Assn. for Humane and Environmental Educ. [11433], 67 Norwich Essex Tpke., East Haddam, CT 06423-1736, (860)434-8666

Natl. Assn. for Humanities Educ. [8531], c/o Prof. Fred Thompson, Treas., Peninsula College, 1502 E Lauridsen Blvd., Port Angeles, WA 98362

Natl. Assn. of Ice Cream Vendors - Defunct.

Natl. Assn. of the Ice Indus. [★1891]

Natl. Assn. of Importers and Exporters [IO], Mexico City, Mexico

Natl. Assn. for an Inclusive Priesthood; CORPUS - [19619]

Natl. Assn. of Income Tax Practitioners [★10]

Natl. Assn. of Income Tax Preparers - Defunct.

Natl. Assn. of Independent Artists [9513], 72 Douglas St., Homosassa, FL 34446

Natl. Assn. of Independent Business - Defunct.

Natl. Assn. of Independent Christian Colls. and Private Schools - Address unknown since 1995.

Natl. Assn. of Independent Colls. and Private Schools - Address unknown since 1999.

Natl. Assn. of Independent Colleges and Universities [8539], 1025 Connecticut Ave. NW, Ste. 700, Washington, DC 20036, (202)785-8866

Natl. Assn. of Independent Fee Appraisers [284], 401 N Michigan Ave., Ste. 2200, Chicago, IL 60611, (312)321-6830

Natl. Assn. of Independent Food Retailers - Defunct.

Natl. Assn. of Independent Insurance Adjusters [2209], c/o Mr. Dave Mehren, Exec. VP, 825 W State St., Ste. 117 C and B, Geneva, IL 60134, (630)397-5012

Natl. Assn. of Independent Insurance Auditors and Engineers [2210], PO Box 794, Clifton Park, NY 12065, (800)243-0337

Natl. Assn. of Independent Insurers [★2232]

National Assn. of Independent Insurers Safety Association [★12964]

Natl. Assn. of Independent Life Brokerage Agencies [2211], 12150 Monument Dr., Ste. 125, Fairfax, VA 22033, (703)383-3081

Natl. Assn. of Independent Lighting Distributors [2434], 2207 Elmwood Ave., Buffalo, NY 14216-1009, (716)875-3670

Natl. Assn. for Independent Living - Defunct.

Natl. Assn. of Independent Lubes [★408]

Natl. Assn. of Independent Lumbermen - Defunct.

Natl. Assn. of Independent Maritime Educators [★8813]

Natl. Assn. of Independent Music Dealers - Defunct.

Natl. Assn. of Independent Nurses [2839], 1125 E Broadway Rd., Ste. 116, Tempe, AZ 85282, (480)894-6060

Natl. Assn. of Independent Public Finance Advisors [1467], PO Box 304, Montgomery, IL 60538-0304, (630)896-1292

Natl. Assn. of Independent Publishers [3238], PO Box 430, Highland City, FL 33846-0430, (813)648-4420

Natl. Assn. of Independent Publishers Representatives [3239], PMB 157, 111 E 14th St., New York, NY 10003-4103, (646)414-2993

Natl. Assn. of Independent Rebuilders and Parts Suppliers - Defunct.

Natl. Assn. of Independent Resurfacers [642], 5806 W 127th St., Alsip, IL 60803, (708)371-8237

Natl. Assn. of Independent Schools [8540], 1620 L St. NW, Ste. 1100, Washington, DC 20036-5695, (202)973-9700

Natl. Assn. of Independent TV Producers and Distributors - Defunct.

Natl. Assn. of Independent Tire Dealers [★3814]

Natl. Assn. for Independent Truckers - Defunct.

Natl. Assn. of Indian Affairs [★18092]

Natl. Assn. for Indiana Limestone [★3694]

National Assn. of Individual Investors [★2342]

Natl. Assn. of Indonesian Consultants [IO], Jakarta, Indonesia

Natl. Assn. of Indus. and Off. Parks [★3320]

Natl. Assn. of Indus. and Off. Properties [3320], 2201 Cooperative Way, 3rd Fl., Herndon, VA 20171-3034, (703)904-7100

Natl. Assn. of Indus. Parks [★3320]

Natl. Assn. of Indus. Security Companies [IO], Sofia, Bulgaria

Natl. Assn. of Indus. Teacher Educators [★8544]

Natl. Assn. of Indus. Teacher Trainers [★8544]

Natl. Assn. of Indus. and Tech. Teacher Educators [8544], c/o Danny C. Brown, Pres., Illinois State Univ., 210E Turner Hall, Campus Box 5100, Normal, IL 61790-5100, (309)438-2695

Natl. Assn. of Indus. Tech. [8545], 3300 Washtenaw Ave., Ste. 220, Ann Arbor, MI 48104, (734)677-0720

Natl. Assn. for Industry-Education Cooperation [8048], 235 Hendricks Blvd., Buffalo, NY 14226-3304, (716)834-7047

Natl. Assn. for Info. Destruction [2106], 3420 E Shea Blvd., Ste. 115, Phoenix, AZ 85028, (602)788-6243

Natl. Assn. for Info. Destruction [IO], Phoenix, AZ, United States

Natl. Assn. of Inpatient Physicians [★14897]

Natl. Assn. of Insect Electrocutor Mfrs. - Address unknown since 1994.

Natl. Assn. Insecticide and Disinfectant Manufacturers [★806]

Natl. Assn. of Installation Developers [★5811]

Natl. Assn. of Installment Companies - Defunct.

Natl. Assn. of Institutional Laundry Managers [★2401]

Reference to "IO" in place of a book number signifies that the association may be found in the 45th edition of International Organizations.

Natl. Assn. of Institutional Linen Mgt. [★2401]
Natl. Assn. of Instructional Leaders in Technical Education - Defunct.
Natl. Assn. of Insurance Agents [★2169]
Natl. Assn. of Insurance Commissioners [5830], 2301 McGee St., Ste. 800, Kansas City, MO 64108-2662, (816)842-3600
Natl. Assn. of Insurance and Financial Advisors [2212], PO Box 12012, Falls Church, VA 22042-1205, (703)770-8100
Natl. Assn. of Insurance Women [★2213]
Natl. Assn. of Insurance Women Intl. [2213], 6528 E 101st St., Ste. D-1, PMB No. 750, Tulsa, OK 74133, (800)766-6249
Natl. Assn. of Insured Persons - Defunct.
Natl. Assn. of Intellectual Property Assistants - Address unknown since 2003.
Natl. Assn. for Interactive Services [★737]
Natl. Assn. for Interactive Services [★IO]
Natl. Assn. of Intercollegiate Athletics [23835], 1200 Grand Blvd., Kansas City, MO 64106, (816)595-8000
Natl. Assn. of Intercollegiate Basketball [★23835]
Natl. Assn. of Intercollegiate Commissioners - Defunct.
Natl. Assn. of Interdisciplinary Ethnic Stud. [★9919]
Natl. Assn. of Interdisciplinary Stud. for Native Amer., Black, Chicano, Puerto Rican, Asian Americans [★9919]
Natl. Assn. of Intergovernmental Relations Officials [★5622]
Natl. Assn. of Interior Designers - Defunct.
Natl. Assn. of Internal Revenue Employees [★24080]
Natl. Assn. of Internet Ser. Providers of Romania [IO], Bucharest, Romania
Natl. Assn. for Interpretation [7363], PO Box 2246, Fort Collins, CO 80522, (970)484-8283
Natl. Assn. of Investigative Specialists [2325], PO Box 82148, Austin, TX 78708, (512)719-3595
Natl. Assn. of the Investment Advisory Publishers [★3258]
Natl. Assn. of the Investment Advisory Publishers [★IO]
Natl. Assn. of Investment Clubs [★2342]
Natl. Assn. of Investment Companies [★3515]
Natl. Assn. of Investment Companies [2764], 1300 Pennsylvania Ave. NW, Ste. 700, Washington, DC 20004, (202)204-3001
Natl. Assn. of Investment Professionals [2341], 12664 Emmer Pl., Ste. 201, St. Paul, MN 55124, (952)322-4322
Natl. Assn. of Investors Corp. [2342], PO Box 220, Royal Oak, MI 48068, (248)583-6242
Natl. Assn. for Irish Freedom - Defunct.
Natl. Assn. of Italian Shoe Mfrs. [IO], Milan, Italy
Natl. Assn. of Jai Alai Frontons - Address unknown since 1995.
Natl. Assn. of Japan-America Societies [19171], 1150 Connecticut Ave. NW, Ste. 1050, Washington, DC 20036, (202)429-5545
Natl. Assn. of Jazz Educators [★8912]
Natl. Assn. of Jazz Educators [★IO]
Natl. Assn. of JD/MBA Professionals - Defunct.
Natl. Assn. of Jewelry Appraisers [2380], PO Box 18, Rego Park, NY 11374-0018, (718)896-1536
Natl. Assn. of Jewish Center Workers [★12466]
Natl. Assn. of Jewish Homes for the Aged [★11277]
Natl. Assn. of Jewish Vocational Services [★9305]
Natl. Assn. of Jewish Vocational Services [★IO]
Natl. Assn. of Jim Beam Bottle and Specialties Clubs [★IO]
Natl. Assn. of Jim Beam Bottle and Specialties Clubs [★21889]
Natl. Assn. of Journalism Directors [★8713]
Natl. Assn. of Judiciary Interpreters and Translators [5628], 603 Stewart St., Ste. 610, Seattle, WA 98101, (206)267-2300
Natl. Assn. of Junior Auxiliaries [13052], PO Box 1873, Greenville, MS 38702-1873, (662)332-3000
Natl. Assn. for Justice - Address unknown since 1995.
Natl. Assn. for Justice Info. Systems [5648], c/o Jim Parsons, Pres., PO Box 410, Vancouver, WA 98666, (360)397-2113

Natl. Assn. of Juvenile Correctional Agencies - Defunct.
Natl. Assn. of Karate and Martial Arts Schools [IO], Herne Bay, United Kingdom
Natl. Assn. to Keep and Bear Arms - Address unknown since 2001.
Natl. Assn. for Kinesiology and Physical Educ. in Higher Educ. [8984], c/o Ginny Overdorf, Exec. Sec.-Treas., William Paterson Univ., Dept. of Exercise and Movement Sciences, 300 Pompton Rd., Wayne, NJ 07470, (973)720-2419
Natl. Assn. of the Knights of Scorpius, Honorary Leadership Soc. [24511], PO Box 656513, Fresh Meadows, NY 11365-6513, (718)357-7075
Natl. Assn. of Korean Americans [17131], 3883 Plaza Dr., Fairfax, VA 22030, (703)267-2388
National Association of Labor-Management Committees [★24119]
Natl. Assn. of Laboratory Suppliers - Defunct.
Natl. Assn. of Labour Banks [IO], Tokyo, Japan
Natl. Assn. of Lace Curtain Mfrs. - Defunct.
Natl. Assn. of Ladies' Circles of Great Britain and Ireland [IO], Birmingham, United Kingdom
Natl. Assn. of Laity - Address unknown since 2001.
Natl. Assn. of Landowners - Defunct.
Natl. Assn. of Language Advisers [IO], Wigton, United Kingdom
Natl. Assn. of Language Lab. Directors [★IO]
Natl. Assn. of Large City Directors of Vocational Education - Address unknown since 2001.
Natl. Assn. of Laryngectomy Clubs [IO], London, United Kingdom
Natl. Assn. of Latina Leaders [2411], 1230 6th Ave., Ste. 700, New York, NY 10020
Natl. Assn. of Latino Appointed Democratic Officials [★17706]
Natl. Assn. of Latino Arts and Culture [9584], 1204 Buena Vista St., San Antonio, TX 78207, (210)432-3982
Natl. Assn. of Latino Elected and Appointed Officials [17706], 1122 W Washington Blvd., 3rd Fl., Los Angeles, CA 90015-3316, (213)747-7606
Natl. Assn. of Latino Fraternal Organizations [19059], PO Box 27322, Tempe, AZ 85285-7322
Natl. Assn. of Latino Independent Producers [1390], PO Box 1247, Santa Monica, CA 90406, (310)395-8880
Natl. Assn. of the Launderette Indus. [IO], Welling, United Kingdom
Natl. Assn. of Law Firm Marketing Administrators [★IO]
Natl. Assn. of Law Firm Marketing Administrators [★2632]
Natl. Assn. for Law Placement [8770], 1025 Connecticut Ave. NW, Ste. 1110, Washington, DC 20036-5413, (202)835-1001
Natl. Assn. of Lawn and Garden Mfrs. - Defunct.
Natl. Assn. for Lay Ministry [20204], 6896 Laurel St. NW, Washington, DC 20012, (202)291-4100
Natl. Assn. of Lay Ministry Coordinators [★20204]
Natl. Assn. of Leadership for Student Assistance Programs [★9171]
Natl. Assn. of Leagues of Hosp. Friends [★IO]
Natl. Assn. of Leagues, Umpires and Scorers - Defunct.
Natl. Assn. of Learning Lab Directors [★IO]
Natl. Assn. of Left-Handed Golfers [23458], 3249 Hazelwood Dr. SW, Atlanta, GA 30311-3035
Natl. Assn. of Legal Assistants [6150], 1516 S Boston, Ste. 200, Tulsa, OK 74119, (918)587-6828
National Association of Legal Fee Analysis [2409], 10275 W. Higgins Rd., Ste. 420, Rosemont, IL 60018, (312)907-7275
Natl. Assn. of Legal Investigators [5885], c/o Alan E. Goodman, Natl. Dir., PO Box 8479, Portland, ME 04104, (888)244-5685
Natl. Assn. of Legal Search Consultants [2326], 1525 N Park Dr., Ste. 102, Weston, FL 33326, (954)349-4428
Natl. Assn. of Legal Secretaries Intl. [★71]
Natl. Assn. of Legal Secretaries Intl. [★IO]
Natl. Assn. for Legal Support of Alternative Schools [7946], PO Box 2823, Santa Fe, NM 87504, (505)474-0300
Natl. Assn. of Legal Vendors - Defunct.

Natl. Assn. Legions of Honor - Address unknown since 1995.
Natl. Assn. of the Legitimate Theatre - Defunct.
Natl. Assn. of Lesbian/Gay Addiction Professionals [13263], 901 N Washington St., Ste. 600, Alexandria, VA 22314, (703)465-0539
Natl. Assn. of Lesbian/Gay Alcoholism Professionals [★13263]
Natl. Assn. of Lesbian, Gay, Bisexual and Transgender Community Centers [11804], c/o Terry Stone, Exec. Dir., 1325 Massachusetts Ave. NW, Ste. 700, Washington, DC 20005, (202)824-0450
Natl. Assn. of Letter Carriers [★24168]
Natl. Assn. of Letter Carriers of the U.S.A. [24168], 100 Indiana Ave. NW, Washington, DC 20001-2144, (202)393-4695
Natl. Assn. of Licensed Paralegals [IO], Bristol, United Kingdom
Natl. Assn. of Licensed Practical Nurses [★8869]
Natl. Assn. of Life Science Industries - Defunct.
Natl. Assn. of Life Underwriters [★2212]
Natl. Assn. of Lift Makers [★IO]
Natl. Assn. of Lighting Representatives - Address unknown since 2001.
Natl. Assn. of Limited Edition Dealers [862], 332 Hurst Mill N, Bremen, GA 30110, (770)537-1970
Natl. Assn. for Literature Development [IO], London, United Kingdom
Natl. Assn. of Litho Clubs [1779], PO Box 6190, Shallotte, NC 28470, (910)575-0399
Natl. Assn. of Lithographic Plate Mfrs. - Defunct.
Natl. Assn. of Litigation Support Managers [6014], c/o Chad M. Papenfuss, Pres., Fredrikson & Byron, P.A., 200 S 6th St., Ste. 4000, Minneapolis, MN 55402, (612)492-7815
Natl. Assn. of Lively Families [21007], c/o Russell Lively, Treas., 172 Fireside Ln., Ringgold, GA 30736, (706)291-2307
Natl. Assn. of Livestock Trailer Mfrs. [★393]
Natl. Assn. of Local Boards of Hea. [16244], 1840 E Gypsy Lane Rd., Bowling Green, OH 43402, (419)353-7714
Natl. Assn. of Local Councils [IO], London, United Kingdom
Natl. Assn. of Local Govt. Auditors [★5429]
Natl. Assn. of Local Govt. Environmental Professionals [6125], 1333 New Hampshire Ave. NW, 2nd Fl., Washington, DC 20036, (202)638-6254
Natl. Assn. of Local Govts. on Hazardous Wastes - Address unknown since 1990.
Natl. Assn. of Local Housing Finance Agencies [5794], 2025 M St. NW, Ste. 800, Washington, DC 20036-3309, (202)367-1197
Natl. Assn. of Local Supervisors of Vocational Home Economics - Address unknown since 2002.
Natl. Assn. of Location Analysts and Negotiators [★3305]
Natl. Assn. of Location Analysts and Negotiators [★IO]
Natl. Assn. of Locum Tenens Org. [16004], 222 S Westmonte Dr., Ste. 101, Altamonte Springs, FL 32714, (407)774-7880
Natl. Assn. of Louisiana Catahoulas [22313]
Natl. Assn. of Magazine Publishers [★3235]
Natl. Assn. of Mail Ser. Pharmacies [★2988]
Natl. Assn. of Major Mail Users [IO], Toronto, ON, Canada
Natl. Assn. of Managed Care Physicians [16005], 4435 Waterfront Dr., Ste. 101, PO Box 4765, Glen Allen, VA 23058, (804)527-1905
Natl. Assn. of Mgt./Marketing Educators - Defunct.
Natl. Assn. of Mgt. and Tech. Assistance Centers [★9309]
Natl. Assn. of Manufacturers [★565]
Natl. Assn. of Mfrs. [2561], 1331 Pennsylvania Ave. NW, Washington, DC 20004-1790, (202)637-3000
Natl. Assn. of Mfrs. Coun. of Mfg. Associations [2562], 1331 Pennsylvania Ave. NW, Washington, DC 20004-1790, (202)637-3000
Natl. Assn. of Mfrs. and Installers of Security Systems [IO], Brucken, Germany
Natl. Assn. of Mfrs. of Pressed and Blown Glassware - Defunct.
Natl. Assn. of Manufacturing Opticians - Defunct.
Natl. Assn. of Marble Dealers [★3696]

A star before a book entry number signifies that the name is not listed separately, but is mentioned within the entry.

Natl. Assn. of Marble Dealers [★IO]

Natl. Assn. of Marble Producers - Address unknown since 1995.

Natl. Assn. of Margarine Mfrs. [2853], 1156 15th St. NW, Ste. 900, Washington, DC 20005, (202)785-3232

Natl. Assn. of Marinas and Marine Dealers - Address unknown since 1995.

Natl. Assn. of Marine Labs. [7274], c/o Dr. Anthony Michaels, Pres., Wrigley Inst. for Environmental Stud., Univ. of Southern California, PO Box 5069, Avalon, CA 90704-5069, (213)740-6780

Natl. Assn. of Marine Products and Services [2583], 200 E Randolph Dr., Ste. 5100, Chicago, IL 60601, (312)946-6200

Natl. Assn. of Marine Services [2584], 5458 Wagon Master Dr., Colorado Springs, CO 80917, (719)573-5946

Natl. Assn. of Marine Surveyors [7275], PO Box 9306, Chesapeake, VA 23321-9306, (757)638-9638

Natl. Assn. of Maritime Educators [8813], c/o Richard A. Block, Newsl. Ed., 124 North Van Ave., Houma, LA 70363, (985)879-3866

Natl. Assn. of Market Developers [★2641]

Natl. Assn. of Marketing Officials [★5025]

Natl. Assn. of Marketing Teachers [★2613]

Natl. Assn. of Mass Merchandisers - Defunct.

Natl. Assn. of Master Appraisers [3321], 303 W Cypress St., San Antonio, TX 78212, (800)229-6262

Natl. Assn. of Master Bakers - England [IO], Ware, United Kingdom

Natl. Assn. of Master Masons [★IO]

Natl. Assn. of Master Mechanics and Foreman of Naval Shore Establishments [★6085]

Natl. Assn. of Master Monumental Masons [★IO]

Natl. Assn. of Master Plumbers [★1059]

Natl. Assn. of Master Steam and Hot Water Fitters [★1033]

Natl. Assn. of Master Workmen of Navy Yards and Naval Stations [★6085]

National Assn. of Mathematicians [★7289]

Natl. Assn. of Mathematics Advisers [IO], Wotton-under-Edge, United Kingdom

Natl. Assn. of Meal Programs [★12284]

Natl. Assn. of Meat and Food Seasoning Mfrs. [★1552]

Natl. Assn. of Meat Processors - Address unknown since 1995.

Natl. Assn. of Meat Processors and Wholesalers - Defunct.

Natl. Assn. of Meat Purveyors [★2663]

Natl. Assn. of Meat Purveyors [★IO]

Natl. Assn. of Meat Seasoning Mfrs. [★1552]

Natl. Assn. of Media Brokers [3322], 5074 Dorsey Hall Dr., Ste. 205, Ellicott City, MD 21042-7793, (410)740-0250

Natl. Assn. of Media Educators - Address unknown since 1995.

Natl. Assn. of Media and Tech. Centers [2669], PO Box 9844, Cedar Rapids, IA 52409-9844, (319)654-0608

Natl. Assn. of Media Women - Defunct.

Natl. Assn. for Medical Direction of Respiratory Care [★15068]

Natl. Assn. for Medical Equip. Services [★14670]

Natl. Assn. of Medical Equip. Suppliers [★14670]

Natl. Assn. of Medical Examiners [15094], 430 Pryor St. SW, Atlanta, GA 30312, (404)730-4781

Natl. Assn. of Medical Minority Educators [8868], c/o Dr. Dorothy C. Dobbins, Budget and Finance Chair, East Tennessee State Univ., Off. of Cultural Affairs, Division of Hea. Sciences, Box 70599, Johnson City, TN 37614-0734, (423)439-2144

Natl. Assn. Medical Staff Services [15071], 2025 M St. NW, Ste. 800, Washington, DC 20036, (202)367-1196

Natl. Assn. for Membership Development [319]

Natl. Assn. of Membership Directors of Chambers of Commerce [★319]

Natl. Assn. of Memorial Masons [IO], Rugby, United Kingdom

Natl. Assn. of Men's Sportswear Buyers [247], c/o Theresa Ochs, Exec. Dir., NAMSB Found., PO Box 227, Millwood, NY 10546, (212)685-4550

Natl. Assn. for Mental Hea. [★15211]

Natl. Assn. of Mental Health Planning and Advisors Coun. - Address unknown since 2002.

Natl. Assn. of Mental Hea. Planning and Advisory Councils [15216], 2000 N Beauegard St., 6th Fl., Alexandria, VA 22311, (703)797-2595

Natl. Assn. for the Mentally Handicapped of Ireland [★IO]

Natl. Assn. of Metal Cans, Packagings, and Closures Mfrs. [IO], Clichy, France

Natl. Assn. of Metal Name Plate Mfrs. [★2720]

Natl. Assn. for Middle Class Amers. - Address unknown since 1999.

Natl. Assn. of Midwifery Practitioners - Defunct.

Natl. Assn. for Migrant Education - Defunct.

Natl. Assn. of Military Schools [★8883]

Natl. Assn. of Military Spouses - Address unknown since 1999.

Natl. Assn. of Military Widows [21197], 5535 Hempstead Way, Springfield, VA 22151-4094, (703)750-1342

Natl. Assn. of Milk Bottle Collectors [22076], c/o The Milkroute (T.M.R.), 18 Pond Pl., Cos Cob, CT 06807

Natl. Assn. of Milk Control Boards of Am. [★5740]

Natl. Assn. of Milk Control Boards of Am. [★IO]

Natl. Assn. of Milliners, Dressmakers and Tailors - Address unknown since 1999.

Natl. Assn. of Miniature Enthusiasts [22077], PO Box 69, Carmel, IN 46082-0069, (317)571-8094

Natl. Assn. of Mining Groups - Address unknown since 1995.

Natl. Assn. of Mining History Organisations [IO], Matlock, United Kingdom

Natl. Assn. of Ministers' Wives [★IO]

Natl. Assn. of Ministers' Wives [★19897]

Natl. Assn. of Ministers Wives and Ministers' Widows [★19897]

Natl. Assn. of Ministers Wives and Ministers' Widows [★IO]

Natl. Assn. of Minorities in Communications [★2757]

Natl. Assn. of Minority Auto. Dealers [2765], 8201 Corporate Dr., Ste. 190, Lanham, MD 20785, (301)306-1614

Natl. Assn. of Minority Consultants and Urbanologists - Defunct.

Natl. Assn. of Minority Contractors [1036], 1300 Pennsylvania Ave. NW, Ste. 700, Washington, DC 20004, (202)347-8259

Natl. Assn. of Minority Engg. Prog. Administrators [★8370]

Natl. Assn. of Minority Entrepreneurs - Address unknown since 1991.

Natl. Assn. of Minority Media Executives [882], 7950 Jones Br. Dr., McLean, VA 22107, (703)854-7178

Natl. Assn. of Minority Political Families [★18357]

Natl. Assn. of Minority Political Families USA [18357]

Natl. Assn. of Minority Students and Educators in Higher Education - Address unknown since 1989.

Natl. Assn. of Minority Women in Business [2766]

Natl. Assn. of Miscellaneous, Ornamental and Architectural Products Contractors [1037], 10382 Main St., Ste. 200, PO Box 280, Fairfax, VA 22038, (703)591-1870

Natl. Assn. of Missing Persons Investigators - Defunct.

Natl. Assn. of Mobile Entertainers [1314], PO Box 144, Willow Grove, PA 19090, (215)658-1193

Natl. Assn. of Modeling and Entertainment - Address unknown since 1995.

Natl. Assn. of Mold Professionals [1330], 3250 Old Farm Ln., Ste. 1, Walled Lake, MI 48390, (248)669-5673

Natl. Assn. of Mortgage Brokers [489], 7900 Westpark Dr., Ste. T309, McLean, VA 22102, (703)342-5900

Natl. Assn. of Mortgage Planners [490]

Natl. Assn. of Mothers' Centers [12676], 1740 Old Jericho Tpke., Jericho, NY 11753, (516)939-MOMS

Natl. Assn. of Motor Bus Operators [★3859]

Natl. Assn. of Motor Bus Owners [★3859]

Natl. Assn. for Multi-Ethnicity in Communications [2757], 336 W 37th St., Ste. 302, New York, NY 10018, (212)594-5985

Natl. Assn. for Multicultural Educ. [8582], 5272 River Rd., Ste. 430, Bethesda, MD 20816, (301)951-0022

National Association for Multicultural Education [IO], Bethesda, MD, United States

Natl. Assn. of Multicultural Engg. Prog. Advocates [8370], 341 N Maitland Ave., Ste. 130, Maitland, FL 32751, (407)647-8839

Natl. Assn. of Multicultural Rehabilitation Concerns [16323], c/o Chandra M. Donnell, PhD, Pres., Michigan State Univ., Dept. of Counseling, Educational Psychology and Special Educ., 459 Erickson Hall, East Lansing, MI 48824

Natl. Assn. of Multifamily Owners - Address unknown since 1995.

Natl. Assn. of Municipal Judges [★5892]

Natl. Assn. for Music Educ; MENC: The [8913]

Natl. Assn. of Music Educators [IO], Matlock, United Kingdom

Natl. Assn. of Music Executives in State Universities - Defunct.

Natl. Assn. of Music Merchants [★2817]

Natl. Assn. for Music Therapy [★16205]

Natl. Assn. of Musical Instruments Mechanics - Address unknown since 1995.

Natl. Assn. of Musical Merchandise Mfrs. [★2805]

Natl. Assn. of Musical Merchandise Wholesalers [★2814]

Natl. Assn. of Muslim Lawyers [5511], c/o Sadia Ali, Treas., 3225 Woodland Park Dr., Apt. 1562, Houston, TX 77082, (202)448-9978

Natl. Assn. of Mutual Casualty Companies - Defunct.

Natl. Assn. of Mutual Insurance Agents [★2215]

Natl. Assn. of Mutual Insurance Companies [2214], 3601 Vincennes Rd., Indianapolis, IN 46268, (317)875-5250

Natl. Assn. of Myofascial Trigger Point Therapists [16624], PO Box 42446, Pittsburgh, PA 15223, (412)303-5889

Natl. Assn. of Nameplate Mfrs. [★2720]

Natl. Assn. of Nannies [829], PMB 2004, 25 Rte. 31 S, Ste. C, Pennington, NJ 08534, (800)344-6266

Natl. Assn. for Nanny Care [11531], PO Box 23387, Federal Way, WA 98003, (202)318-9156

Natl. Assn. for Native Amer. Children of Alcoholics [11627], c/o White Bison, Inc., 6145 Lehman Dr., Ste. 200, Colorado Springs, CO 80918, (719)548-1000

Natl. Assn. of Native Amer. Stud. [8940], PO Box 6670, Scarborough, ME 04070-6670, (207)839-8004

Natl. Assn. of Naturopathic Physicians - Defunct.

Natl. Assn. of Naval Technical Supervisors - Address unknown since 1995.

Natl. Assn. of Navy and Marine Veterans of the Spanish-Amer. War, 1898-1902 - Defunct.

Natl. Assn. of Negotiated Commissioned Brokers - Defunct.

Natl. Assn. of Negro Bus. and Professional Women's Clubs [13053], 1806 New Hampshire Ave. NW, Washington, DC 20009, (202)483-4206

Natl. Assn. of Negro Musicians [10658], PO Box 43053, Chicago, IL 60643, (773)568-3818

Natl. Assn. of Negro Tailors, Designers, Dressmakers and Dry Cleaners - Address unknown since 1995.

Natl. Assn. of Neighborhood Hea. Centers [★14574]

Natl. Assn. for Neighborhood Schools [17820], PO Box 14883, Columbus, OH 43214, (216)398-4667

Natl. Assn. of Neighborhoods [11752], 1300 Pennsylvania Ave. NW, Ste. 700, Washington, DC 20004, (202)332-7766

Natl. Assn. of Neonatal Nurses [15495], 4700 W Lake Ave., Glenview, IL 60025-1485, (847)375-3660

Natl. Assn. of Nephrology Technicians/Technologists [15293], PO Box 2307, Dayton, OH 45401-2307, (937)586-3705

Natl. Assn. of Nephrology Technologists [★15293]

Natl. Assn. of New Careerists - Address unknown since 1995.

Natl. Assn. of NIDS Users - Address unknown since 1999.

Natl. Assn. of Noise Control Officials [7383], c/o Edward J. DiPolvere, Admin., 53 Cubberley Rd., West Windsor, NJ 08550-3400, (609)586-2684

Natl. Assn. of Non-Custodial Moms [11538], 614 E Hwy. 50, PMB 246, Clermont, FL 34711, (352)241-0046

Reference to "IO" in place of a book number signifies that the association may be found in the 45th edition of International Organizations.

Natl. Assn. of Nonprofit Housing Orgs. - Address unknown since 1995.

Natl. Assn. of Norwegian Architects [IO], Oslo, Norway

Natl. Assn. of Nurse Massage Therapists [15496], 6749 Willow Creek Dr., PO Box 24004, Huber Heights, OH 45424, (937)235-0872

Natl. Assn. of Nurse Practitioners in Reproductive Hea. [★15497]

Natl. Assn. of Nurse Practitioners in Women's Hea. [15497], 505 C St. NE, Washington, DC 20002, (202)543-9693

Natl. Assn. of Nurse Recruiters [★15070]

Natl. Assn. for Nursery Educ. [★8069]

Natl. Assn. of Nutrition and Aging Services Programs [15566], 1612 K St. NW, Ste. 400, Washington, DC 20006, (202)682-6899

Natl. Assn. of OEW Contractors [★1038]

Natl. Assn. of Off-Track Betting [23505], 978 Park Pl., Box 3000, Pomona, NY 10970, (845)362-0400

Natl. Assn. of Official Prison Visitors [IO], Bedford, United Kingdom

Natl. Assn. of Oil Equip. Jobbers [★IO]

Natl. Assn. of Oil Equip. Jobbers [★2941]

Natl. Assn. of Older Worker Employment Services - Defunct.

Natl. Assn. for Olmsted Parks [5591], 1111 16th St. NW, Ste. 310, Washington, DC 20036, (202)223-9113

Natl. Assn. of ONAP Urban Indian Grantees - Defunct.

Natl. Assn. of Oncology Social Workers [★13199]

Natl. Assn. of Optical Goods Manufacturers [IO], Milan, Italy

Natl. Assn. of Optometrists and Opticians [15721], PO Box 459, Marblehead, OH 43440, (419)798-2031

Natl. Assn. of Orchestra Leaders [17981]

Natl. Assn. of Ordnance and Explosive Waste Contractors [1038], c/o Suzy McKinney, Sec., Zapata Engg., 6302 Fairview Rd., Ste. 600, Charlotte, NC 28210, (704)378-4910

Natl. Assn. of Ornamental Metal Mfrs. [★2719]

Natl. Assn. of Orthopaedic Nurses [15498], 401 N Michigan Ave., Ste. 2200, Chicago, IL 60611, (800)289-6266

Natl. Assn. of Orthopaedic Technologists [15144], 8365 Keystone Crossing, Ste. 107, Indianapolis, IN 46240, (317)205-9484

Natl. Assn. of OTC Pharmaceutical Products [IO], Madrid, Spain

Natl. Assn. for Outlaw and Lawman History [9380], c/o Paula Miller, Membership Sec., 1917 Sutton Place Trail, Harker Heights, TX 76548-6043, (254)698-6518

Natl. Assn. of Ovulation Method Instructors UK [IO], Crawley, United Kingdom

Natl. Assn. of the Ovulation Method of Ireland [IO], Dublin, Ireland

Natl. Assn. of Packaged Fuel Mfrs. - Defunct.

Natl. Assn. of Paper and Advt. Collectors [22412]

Natl. Assn. of Paper Merchants [IO], Nottingham, United Kingdom

Natl. Assn. of Paperstock Women [2890], PO Box 826, Williamsville, NY 14221, (630)585-7604

Natl. Assn. of Para-Legals Personnel - Address unknown since 2003.

Natl. Assn. of Paralegals [★IO]

Natl. Assn. of Parents - Address unknown since 2006.

Natl. Assn. for Parents of Children With Visual Impairments [16873], PO Box 317, Watertown, MA 02471, (617)972-7441

Natl. Assn. of Parents and Friends of Mentally Retarded Children [★12561]

Natl. Assn. of Parents and Professionals for Safe Alternatives in Childbirth [★15603]

Natl. Assn. of Parents and Professionals for Safe Alternatives in Childbirth [★IO]

Natl. Assn. for Parents Rights - Address unknown since 2004.

Natl. Assn. for Parents of the Visually Impaired [★16873]

Natl. Assn. of Parish Catechetical Directors [19932], c/o Natl. Catholic Educational Assn., 1077 30th St. NW, Ste. 100, Washington, DC 20007-3852, (202)337-6232

Natl. Assn. of Parish Coordinators/Directors of Religious Educ. [★19932]

Natl. Assn. of Parliamentarians [10771], 213 S Main St., Independence, MO 64050-3850, (816)833-3892

National Association of Parliamentarians [IO], Independence, MO, United States

Natl. Assn. of Part-Time and Temporary Employees [1271], 5800 Barton, Ste. 201, PO Box 3805, Shawnee, KS 66203, (913)962-7740

Natl. Assn. of the Partners of the Alliance [★16980]

Natl. Assn. of the Partners of the Alliance [★IO]

Natl. Assn. of Partners in Education - Defunct.

Natl. Assn. of Party Plan Companies - Defunct.

Natl. Assn. of Passenger Vessel Owners [★2591]

Natl. Assn. for Pastoral Care in Educ. [IO], Coventry, United Kingdom

Natl. Assn. of Pastoral Counselors - Defunct.

Natl. Assn. of Pastoral Musicians [8920], 962 Wayne Ave., Ste. 210, Silver Spring, MD 20910-4461, (240)247-3000

Natl. Assn. for Pastoral Renewal - Defunct.

Natl. Assn. of Pat Boone Fan Clubs [★24949]

Natl. Assn. of Pat Boone Fan Clubs [★24949]

Natl. Assn. of Patent Practitioners [6167], 4680-18i Monticello Ave., PMB 101, Williamsburg, VA 23188, (800)216-9588

Natl. Assn. of Patients on Hemodialysis [★15283]

Natl. Assn. of Patients on Hemodialysis and Transplantation [★15283]

Natl. Assn. of Payment Professionals [1438], c/o Steve Schwimmer, Pres., PO Box 324, Syosset, NY 11791-0324, (516)746-6363

Natl. Assn. of Payment Professionals [IO], Syosset, NY, United States

Natl. Assn. of Peace Educ. - Address unknown since 2008.

Natl. Assn. of Pediatric Nurse Practitioners [15499], 20 Brace Rd., Ste. 200, Cherry Hill, NJ 08034-2634, (856)857-9700

Natl. Assn. of Peer Programs [11827], PO Box 10627, Kansas City, MO 64188-0627, (877)314-7337

Natl. Assn. of Pension Consultants and Administrators [★17350]

Natl. Assn. of Pension Funds [IO], London, United Kingdom

Natl. Assn. for People with Disabilities - Address unknown since 1999.

Natl. Assn. of People Living With HIV/AIDS [IO], Sydney, Australia

Natl. Assn. of People With AIDS [13578], 8401 Colesville Rd., Ste. 750, Silver Spring, MD 20910, (240)247-0880

Natl. Assn. of Percussion Teachers [IO], Basingstoke, United Kingdom

Natl. Assn. Performing Arts Managers and Agent [★175]

Natl. Assn. of Periodical Publishers [★3235]

Natl. Assn. of Permanent Diaconate Directors [★19664]

Natl. Assn. of Personal Financial Advisors [1468], 3250 N Arlington Heights Rd., Ste. 109, Arlington Heights, IL 60004, (847)483-5400

Natl. Assn. of Personnel Consultants [★1272]

Natl. Assn. of Personnel Services [1272], The Village at Banner Elk, Ste. 108, PO Box 2128, Banner Elk, NC 28604, (828)898-4929

Natl. Assn. of Personnel Workers [★7903]

Natl. Assn. for Persons with Intellectual Disabilities of Germany [IO], Marburg, Germany

Natl. Assn. for Persons with Mental Handicap in Germany [★IO]

Natl. Assn. of Pet Cemeteries [★IO]

Natl. Assn. of Pet Cemeteries [★2959]

Natl. Assn. for PET Container Resources [3997], PO Box 1327, Sonoma, CA 95476, (707)996-4207

Natl. Assn. of Pet Food and Animal Feed Manufacturers and Producers [IO], Rome, Italy

Natl. Assn. of the Pet Industry - Defunct.

Natl. Assn. of Pet Sitters [★2961]

Natl. Assn. of the Pharmaceutical Indus. - Italy [IO], Rome, Italy

Natl. Assn. of the Pharmaceutical Indus. - Spain [IO], Madrid, Spain

Natl. Assn. of the Phonographic Indus. [IO], Berlin, Germany

Natl. Assn. of Photographic Equip. Technicians [3004], c/o PMA - The Worldwide Community of Imaging Associations, 3000 Picture Pl., Jackson, MI 49201, (517)788-8100

Natl. Assn. of Photographic Mfrs. [★3002]

Natl. Assn. of Photographic Mfrs. [★IO]

Natl. Assn. of Photography Wholesalers and Distributors [IO], Milan, Italy

National Association of Photoshop Professionals [IO], Oldsmar, FL, United States

Natl. Assn. of Photoshop Professionals [1808], 333 Douglas Rd. E, Oldsmar, FL 34677, (813)433-5006

Natl. Assn. of Physical Administrators of Universities and Colleges [★8333]

Natl. Assn. of Physical Administrators of Universities and Colleges [★IO]

Natl. Assn. for Physical Educ. of Coll. Women [★8985]

Natl. Assn. for Physical Educ. in Higher Educ. [8985], c/o Gail Evans, Dept. of Human Performance, San Jose State Univ., San Jose, CA 95192-0054, (765)285-4217

Natl. Assn. of Physical Therapists - Address unknown since 1988.

Natl. Assn. of the Physically Handicapped [11967], 1375 Dewitt Dr., Akron, OH 44313, (330)724-1994

Natl. Assn. of Physician Nurses [15500], 900 S Washington St., No. G-13, Falls Church, VA 22046, (703)237-8616

Natl. Assn. of Physician Recruiters [16006], 222 S Westmonte Dr., Ste. 101, Altamonte Springs, FL 32714, (407)774-7880

Natl. Assn. of Physicians for the Env. - Defunct.

Natl. Assn. of Piano Tuners [★2822]

Natl. Assn. of Pipe Coating Applicators [852], c/o Merritt B. Chastain, Jr., Managing Dir., 8570 Bus. Park Dr., Shreveport, LA 71105, (318)227-2769

National Association of Pipe Coating Applicators [IO], Shreveport, LA, United States

Natl. Assn. of Pipe Fabricators [3031], 1901 NW 161st St., Edmond, OK 73013, (888)798-1924

Natl. Assn. of Pipe Nipple Mfrs. [★3025]

Natl. Assn. of Pipe Nipple Mfrs. - Defunct.

Natl. Assn. of Pizzeria Operators [1953], 908 S 8th St., Ste. 200, Louisville, KY 40203, (502)736-9532

Natl. Assn. of Placement Personnel Officers [★8961]

Natl. Assn. of Planners - Defunct.

Natl. Assn. of Planners, Estimators and Progressmen - Address unknown since 2004.

Natl. Assn. of Planning Councils [18275], 11118 Ferndale Rd., Dallas, TX 75238, (214)342-2638

Natl. Assn. of Plant Patent Owners [5046], c/o Amer. Nursery and Landscape Assn., 1000 Vermont Ave. NW, Ste. 300, Washington, DC 20005, (202)789-2900

Natl. Assn. for Plastic Container Recovery [★3997]

Natl. Assn. of Plastics Distributors [★3051]

Natl. Assn. of Plastics Distributors [★IO]

Natl. Assn. of Plumbing Contractors [★1059]

Natl. Assn. of Plumbing-Heating-Cooling Contractors [★1059]

Natl. Assn. of Plumbing, Heating and Mech. Services Contractors [★IO]

Natl. Assn. of Plumbing Specialty Distributors [3063]

Natl. Assn. for Poetry Therapy [16223], c/o Lauren Keller, Admin. Asst., 777 E Atlantic Ave., No. 243, Delray Beach, FL 33483, (561)498-8334

Natl. Assn. of Police Athletic Leagues [13496], 658 W Indiantown Rd., Ste. 201, Jupiter, FL 33458, (561)745-5535

Natl. Assn. of Police Community Relations Officers - Address unknown since 1988.

Natl. Assn. of Police and Fire Surgeons - Address unknown since 1995.

Natl. Assn. of Police Laboratories - Address unknown since 1995.

Natl. Assn. of Police Organizations [5988], 317 S Patrick St., Alexandria, VA 22314, (703)549-0775

Natl. Assn. of Polish Americans - Address unknown since 1995.

Natl. Assn. of Pool Owners - Defunct.

Natl. Assn. of Popcorn Mfrs. [★1589]

Natl. Assn. of Post Off. and Postal Trans. Ser. Mail Handlers, Watchmen and Messengers [★24171]

A star before a book entry number signifies that the name is not listed separately, but is mentioned within the entry.

Natl. Assn. of Postal Supervisors [24169], 1727 King St., Ste. 400, Alexandria, VA 22314-2700, (703)836-9660

Natl. Assn. of Postmasters of the U.S. [6178], 8 Herbert St., Alexandria, VA 22305-2600, (703)683-9027

Natl. Assn. of Postpartum Care Services [16902]

Natl. Assn. of Postsecondary and Adult Vocational Home Economics Educators - Address unknown since 1988.

Natl. Assn. of Power Engineers [7532], 1 Springfield St., Chicopee, MA 01013, (413)592-6273

Natl. Assn. for Practical Nurse Educ. and Ser. [8869], PO Box 25647, Alexandria, VA 22314, (703)933-1003

Natl. Assn. Practical Refrigerating Engineers [★7037]

Natl. Assn. for the Practice of Anthropology [6422], c/o Amer. Anthropological Assn., 2200 Wilson Blvd., Ste. 600, Arlington, VA 22201, (703)528-1902

Natl. Assn. for Pre-Paid Funeral Plans [IO], Solihull, United Kingdom

Natl. Assn. of Precancel Collectors - Address unknown since 2003.

Natl. Assn. of PreCollege Directors [8371], c/o Dr. Eugene M. Deloatch, Pres., 1818 N St. NW, Ste. 600, Washington, DC 20036, (202)331-3500

Natl. Assn. of Pregnancy Massage Therapy - Address unknown since 2007.

Natl. Assn. of Premenstrual Syndrome [IO], Kent, United Kingdom

Natl. Assn. of Presbyterian Scouters [13000], c/o Programs of Religious Activities with Youth, 8520 MacKenzie Rd., St. Louis, MO 63123, (636)391-0734

Natl. Assn. for the Preservation of Baseball - Address unknown since 1999.

Natl. Assn. for the Preservation and Perpetuation of Storytelling [★10983]

Natl. Assn. of Preserved Vegetable Indus. [IO], Naples, Italy

Natl. Assn. of Presort Mailers [2452], c/o Joel J. Thomas, Exec. Dir./CEO, PO Box 3295, Annapolis, MD 21403-0295, (877)620-6276

Natl. Assn. of Press Agencies [IO], Leamington Spa, United Kingdom

Natl. Assn. for the Prevention of Addiction to Narcotics [★13262]

Natl. Assn. of Prevention Professionals and Advocates - Address unknown since 2003.

Natl. Assn. of Priest Pilots [19667], c/o Rev. Mel Hemann, Treas., 127 Kaspend Pl., Cedar Falls, IA 50613-1683, (319)266-3889

Natl. Assn. of Primary Care [IO], London, United Kingdom

Natl. Assn. for Primary Educ. [IO], Northampton, United Kingdom

Natl. Assn. of Principal Agricultural Educ. Officers [★IO]

Natl. Assn. of Principals of Schools for Girls [9015], 23490 Caraway Lakes Dr., Bonita Springs, FL 34135-8441, (239)947-6196

Natl. Assn. of Printers and Lithographers [★1780]

Natl. Assn. of Printing Ink Makers [★1803]

Natl. Assn. of Printing Ink Mfrs. [1803], 581 Main St., Woodbridge, NJ 07095-1148, (732)855-1525

Natl. Assn. for Printing Leadership [1780], 75 W Century Rd., Paramus, NJ 07652-1408, (201)634-9600

Natl. Assn. of Printing Purchasers - Defunct.

Natl. Assn. of Private Ambulance Services [IO], Peterborough, United Kingdom

Natl. Assn. of Private Art Founds. - Defunct.

Natl. Assn. of Private Catholic and Independent Schools [7878], 2640 3rd Ave., Sacramento, CA 95818, (916)451-4963

Natl. Assn. of Private Enterprise [3616]

Natl. Assn. of Private Enterprise [IO], San Salvador, El Salvador

Natl. Assn. of Private Geriatric Care Managers [★15539]

Natl. Assn. of Private Indus. Councils [★12087]

Natl. Assn. of Private, Nontraditional Schools and Colleges [7947], 182 Thompson Rd., Grand Junction, CO 81503, (970)243-5441

Natl. Assn. of Private Psychiatric Hospitals [★16091]

Natl. Assn. of Private Residential Facilities for the Mentally Retarded [★12560]

Natl. Assn. of Private Residential Resources [★12560]

Natl. Assn. of Private Schools for Exceptional Children [★9147]

Natl. Assn. of Private Special Educ. Centers [9147], 1522 K St. NW, Ste. 1032, Washington, DC 20005, (202)408-3338

Natl. Assn. of Pro America - Defunct.

Natl. Assn. of Pro-Life Nurses [18378], PO Box 8236, Hot Springs Village, AR 71910-8236, (501)992-5905

Natl. Assn. of Probation Executives [5649], c/o Ms. Christine Davidson, Exec. Dir., Sam Houston State Univ., Correctional Mgt. Inst. of Texas, George J. Beto Criminal Justice Center, Huntsville, TX 77341-2296, (936)294-3757

Natl. Assn. of Probation Officers [IO], London, United Kingdom

Natl. Assn. of Produce Market Managers [5022], PO Box 291284, Columbia, SC 29229, (410)379-5760

Natl. Assn. of Prdt. Fund Raisers [★1684]

Natl. Assn. of Professional Accident Reconstructionists [6252], PO Box 65, Brandywine, MD 20613-0065, (301)843-0048

Natl. Assn. of Professional Asian Amer. Women [743], 304 Oak Knoll Terr., Rockville, MD 20850, (301)785-8585

Natl. Assn. for Professional Assns. and Corporations - Address unknown since 1995.

Natl. Assn. of Professional Background Screeners [1983], PO Box 3159, Durham, NC 27715, (919)433-0123

Natl. Assn. of Professional Band Instrument Repair Technicians [2818], PO Box 51, Normal, IL 61761, (309)452-4257

Natl. Assn. of Professional Baseball Leagues [23116], PO Box A, St. Petersburg, FL 33731, (727)822-6937

National Association of Professional Baseball Leagues [IO], St. Petersburg, FL, United States

Natl. Assn. of Professional Bureaucrats [★IO]

Natl. Assn. of Professional Bureaucrats [★22595]

Natl. Assn. of Professional Contracts Administrators [★1744]

Natl. Assn. for Professional Development Schools [9091], Univ. of South Carolina, College of Educ., Wardlaw 201, Columbia, SC 29208, (803)777-1515

Natl. Assn. of Professional Educators [9223], 900 17th St., Ste. 300, Washington, DC 20006, (202)848-8969

Natl. Assn. of Professional Employer Organizations [1273], 901 N Pitt St., Ste. 150, Alexandria, VA 22314, (703)836-0466

Natl. Assn. of Professional Engravers - Defunct.

Natl. Assn. of Professional Geriatric Care Managers [15539], 1604 N Country Club Rd., Tucson, AZ 85716, (520)881-8008

Natl. Assn. for Professional Inspectors and Testers [IO], Mansfield, United Kingdom

Natl. Assn. of Professional Insurance Agents [2215], 400 N Washington St., Alexandria, VA 22314, (703)836-9340

Natl. Assn. of Professional Martial Artists [23598], 5601 116th Ave. N, Clearwater, FL 33760, (727)540-0500

Natl. Assn. of Professional Mortgage Women [491], PO Box 2016, Edmonds, WA 98020-9516, (425)775-6589

Natl. Assn. of Professional Organizers [7166], 4700 W Lake Ave., Glenview, IL 60025, (847)375-4746

Natl. Assn. of Professional Pet Sitters [2961], 15000 Commerce Pkwy., Ste. C, Mount Laurel, NJ 08054, (856)439-0324

Natl. Assn. of Professional Print Buyers - Address unknown since 1999.

Natl. Assn. of Professional Process Servers [6184], PO Box 4547, Portland, OR 97208-4547, (503)222-4180

Natl. Assn. for Professional Saleswomen - Defunct.

Natl. Assn. of Professional Surplus Lines Offices [2216], 200 NE 54th St., No. 200, Kansas City, MO 64118, (816)741-3910

Natl. Assn. of Professional Upholsterers - Defunct.

Natl. Assn. of Professional Word Processing Technicians - Address unknown since 2003.

Natl. Assn. of Professional Workers of the YWCA - Defunct.

Natl. Assn. of Professionals in Energy Conservation [★6942]

Natl. Assn. of Professionals in Energy Conservation [★IO]

Natl. Assn. of Professionals with Language Impairment in Children [IO], London, United Kingdom

Natl. Assn. of Professionals in Women's Hea. [★16903]

Natl. Assn. of the Professions [19324], Hillsboro Executive Center North, 350 Fairway Dr., Ste. 200, Deerfield Beach, FL 33441-1834, (954)571-1877

Natl. Assn. of Professors of Christian Educ. [★8088]

Natl. Assn. of Professors of Hebrew [8695], Univ. of Wisconsin-Madison, 1346 Van Hise Hall, 1220 Linden Dr., Madison, WI 53706-1525, (608)262-2997

Natl. Assn. for Proficiency Testing [7792], 8100 Wayzata Blvd., St. Louis Park, MN 55426, (763)525-1488

Natl. Assn. of Progressive Radio Announcers - Address unknown since 1995.

Natl. Assn. to Promote Lib. Services to the Spanish-Speaking; REFORMA: [10384]

Natl. Assn. for Promotional and Advt. Allowances [★122]

Natl. Assn. of Property and Casualty Reinsurers [★2234]

Natl. Assn. of Property Inspectors [2123], 303 W Cypress St., San Antonio, TX 78212, (800)486-3676

Natl. Assn. of Property Owners - Defunct.

Natl. Assn. of Property Recovery Investigators [5886], 5715 Will Clayton, No. 1503, Humble, TX 77338, (386)479-5329

National Association of Property Recovery Investigators [IO], Humble, TX, United States

Natl. Assn. of Property Tax Representatives - Defunct.

Natl. Assn. of Property Tax Representatives - Transportation, Energy and Communications - Defunct.

Natl. Assn. to Protect Children [11628], 46 Haywood St., Ste. 315, Asheville, NC 28801, (828)350-9350

Natl. Assn. to Protect Individual Rights - Address unknown since 2006.

Natl. Assn. of Protection and Advocacy Systems [★11970]

Natl. Assn. for Proton Therapy [15649], 1301 Highland Dr., Silver Spring, MD 20910, (301)587-6100

Natl. Assn. for Pseudoxanthoma Elasticum [14207], 8760 Manchester Rd., St. Louis, MO 63144-2724, (314)962-0100

Natl. Assn. of Psychiatric Hea. Systems [16091], 701 13th St. NW, Ste. 950, Washington, DC 20005-3995, (202)393-6700

Natl. Assn. of Psychiatric Survivors - Defunct.

Natl. Assn. of Psychiatric Treatment Centers for Children [★16090]

Natl. Assn. of Psychometrists [16159], c/o April German, Membership Chair, Cincinnati Children's Hosp. Medical Center, Dept. of Behavioral Medicine and Clinical Psychology, MLC 3015, 3333 Burnet Ave., Cincinnati, OH 45229, (513)636-2092

Natl. Assn. of Public Affairs Networks [17026], 21 Oak St., Ste. 605, Hartford, CT 06106, (860)246-1553

Natl. Assn. of Public Child Welfare Administrators [11629], 810 1st St. NE, Ste. 500, Washington, DC 20002, (202)682-0100

Natl. Assn. for Public Continuing Adult Educ. [★8146]

Natl. Assn. of Public Golf Courses [IO], Redditch, United Kingdom

Natl. Assn. for Public Hea. Info. Tech. [7203], c/o Yvonne Claudio, Exec. Dir., 1 Res. Ct., Ste. 450, Rockville, MD 20850-6222, (301)216-3825

Natl. Assn. for Public Hea. Statistics and Info. Systems [6218], 962 Wayne Ave., Ste. 701, Silver Spring, MD 20910, (301)563-6001

Reference to "IO" in place of a book number signifies that the association may be found in the 45th edition of International Organizations.

Natl. Assn. of Public Hospitals [★14892]

Natl. Assn. of Public Hospitals and Hea. Systems [14892], 1301 Pennsylvania Ave. NW, Ste. 950, Washington, DC 20004, (202)585-0100

Natl. Assn. of Public Information Officers for Civil Defense - Defunct.

Natl. Assn. of Public Insurance Adjusters [2217], 21165 Whitfield Pl., No. 105, Potomac Falls, VA 20165, (703)433-9217

Natl. Assn. for Public Interest Law [★5898]

Natl. Assn. of Public and Private Employer Negotiators and Administrators - Defunct.

Natl. Assn. of Public Relations Counsel [★3195]

Natl. Assn. of Public Sector Equal Opportunity Officers [1274], c/o Sharon Ofuani, City of Tallahassee Equal Opportunity Dept., 300 S Adams St., Tallahassee, FL 32301, (850)891-8290

Natl. Assn. of Public Service Org. Executives - Defunct.

Natl. Assn. of Public TV Stations [★547]

Natl. Assn. Publications; Soc. of [321]

Natl. Assn. of Publicly Funded Truck Driving Schools [3877], c/o Chuck Collins, Exec. Dir., 1109 E Park Ridge Ave., Appleton, WI 54911, (920)739-9786

Natl. Assn. of Publicly Traded Partnerships [2343], 1801 K St. NW, Ste. 500, Washington, DC 20006, (202)973-3150

Natl. Assn. of Publishers - Defunct.

Natl. Assn. of Publishers' Representatives [113], 54 Cove Rd., Huntington, NY 11743, (631)223-2200

Natl. Assn. for Puerto Rican Civil Rights - Address unknown since 1999.

Natl. Assn. of Puerto Rican Hispanic Social Workers [13205], PO Box 651, Brentwood, NY 11717, (631)864-1536

Natl. Assn. of Punch Mfrs. [★2055]

Natl. Assn. of Pupil Personnel Administrators [★7902]

Natl. Assn. of Pupil Services Administrators [7902], Box 113, Williamsport, PA 17701, (570)323-2050

Natl. Assn. for Pupil Trans. [6320], 1840 Western Ave., Albany, NY 12203-4624, (518)452-3611

Natl. Assn. of Purchasing Agents [★3263]

Natl. Assn. of Purchasing Card Professionals [3264], 10520 Wayzata Blvd., Minnetonka, MN 55305, (952)546-1880

Natl. Assn. of Purchasing Mgt. [★2718]

Natl. Assn. of Purchasing Mgt. [★3263]

Natl. Assn. of Purchasing and Payables [3265], c/o Larry Kreider, Treas., 1570 Doxee Terr., Marco Island, FL 34145

Natl. Assn. of Qualified Mental Retardation Professionals [15241], 100 N Gougar, Joliet, IL 60432, (815)485-6197

Natl. Assn. of Quality Assurance Professionals [★16264]

Natl. Assn. Quick Printers [★1785]

Natl. Assn. Quick Printers [★IO]

Natl. Assn. of Radiation Survivors [18129], PO Box 1587, Marysville, CA 95901-0047, (530)741-9654

Natl. Assn. of Radio Farm Directors [★570]

Natl. Assn. of Radio News Directors [★581]

Natl. Assn. of Radio Reading Services [★16856]

Natl. Assn. of Radio Reading Services [★IO]

Natl. Assn. of Radio Talk Show Hosts [★IO]

Natl. Assn. of Radio and Telecommunications Engineers [★7773]

Natl. Assn. of Radio Telephone Systems [★3752]

Natl. Assn. of Radio Telephone Systems [★IO]

Natl. Assn. of Radio and TV Broadcasters [★569]

Natl. Assn. of Rail Shippers [★3885]

Natl. Assn. of Rail Shippers Advisory Boards [★3885]

Natl. Assn. of Railroad Enthusiasts [★10919]

Natl. Assn. of Railroad Passengers [3284], 900-2nd St. NE, Ste. 308, Washington, DC 20002, (202)408-8362

Natl. Assn. of Railroad Tie Producers [★3292]

Natl. Assn. of Railroad Trial Counsel [6321], 1430 E Missouri, Ste. B200, Phoenix, AZ 85014, (602)265-2700

Natl. Assn. of Railway Bus. Women [3285], c/o Cynthia Chandler, Natl. 3rd VP, 16507 Hilo Cir., Papillion, NE 68046-5602, (610)328-2975

Natl. Assn. of Railway Commissioners [★6339]

Natl. Assn. of Railway and Utilities Commissioners [★6339]

Natl. Assn. Rainbow Div. Veterans [★21419]

Natl. Assn. of Real Estate Appraisers [285], 1224 N Nokomis NE, Alexandria, MN 56308, (320)763-7626

Natl. Assn. of Real Estate Boards [★3328]

Natl. Assn. of Real Estate Brokers [3323], c/o Clifford Turner, Pres., 225 S 42nd St., Ste. 303-A, Louisville, KY 40212, (502)774-8909

Natl. Assn. of Real Estate Buyer Brokers [3324], 2704 Wemberly Dr., Belmont, CA 94002, (650)655-2500

Natl. Assn. of Real Estate Companies [3325], 216 W Jackson Blvd., Ste. 625, Chicago, IL 60606, (312)263-1755

Natl. Assn. of Real Estate Editors [3132], 1003 NW 6th Terr., Boca Raton, FL 33486-3455, (561)391-3599

Natl. Assn. of Real Estate Exchanges [★3328]

Natl. Assn. of Real Estate Investment Funds [★3327]

Natl. Assn. of Real Estate Investment Managers [3326], 11755 Wilshire Blvd., Ste. 1380, Los Angeles, CA 90025-1539, (310)479-2219

Natl. Assn. of Real Estate Investment Trusts [3327], 1875 I St. NW, Ste. 600, Washington, DC 20006-5413, (202)739-9400

Natl. Assn. of Real Estate License Law Officials [★6243]

Natl. Assn. of Real Estate License Law Officials [★IO]

Natl. Assn. of Real Estate Offices of Slovakia [IO], Bratislava, Slovakia

Natl. Assn. of Realtors [3328], 430 N Michigan Ave., Chicago, IL 60611-4088, (800)874-6500

Natl. Assn. of Record Indus. Professionals [3348], PO Box 2446, Toluca Lake, CA 91610-2446, (818)769-7007

Natl. Assn. of Record Merchandisers [★3349]

Natl. Assn. of Record Retailer Dealers - Address unknown since 1995.

Natl. Assn. of Recording Merchandisers [3349], 9 Eves Dr., Ste. 120, Marlton, NJ 08053, (856)596-2221

Natl. Assn. of Recovered Alcoholics - Defunct.

Natl. Assn. of Recreation Rsrc. Planners [6156], PO Box 221, Marienville, PA 16239, (814)927-8212

Natl. Assn. of Recreation Therapists [★16628]

Natl. Assn. for Recreational Equality [23836], c/o Bankshot Sports, 785 E Rockville Pike, PMB 504, Rockville, MD 20852, (301)309-0260

Natl. Assn. of Recruitment Advertising Agencies - Defunct.

Natl. Assn. Recycling Indus. [★3995]

Natl. Assn. Recycling Indus. [★IO]

Natl. Assn. to Reform State Drinking Ages - Defunct.

Natl. Assn. of Refunders and Shoppers - Defunct.

Natl. Assn. for Regional Ballet - Defunct.

Natl. Assn. for Regional Councils [6244], 1666 Connecticut Ave. NW, Ste. 300, Washington, DC 20009-1039, (202)986-1032

Natl. Assn. of Regional Game Councils [IO], Dublin, Ireland

Natl. Assn. of Regional Media Centers [7204], Oneida Herkimer Co. BOCES, Box 70, Middle Settlement Rd., New Hartford, NY 13413, (315)793-8566

Natl. Assn. of Registered Nurses - Address unknown since 2006.

Natl. Assn. of Registered Nursing Homes [★14540]

Natl. Assn. of Registered Plans - Address unknown since 1994.

Natl. Assn. for Regulatory Admin. [15011], 910 Glen Falls Ct., Newark, DE 19711, (302)234-4152

Natl. Assn. of Regulatory Utility Commissioners [6339], 1101 Vermont NW, Ste. 200, Washington, DC 20005-3553, (202)898-2200

Natl. Assn. of Rehabilitation Facilities [★16312]

Natl. Assn. of Rehabilitation Instructors [16324], c/o Nancy Pendegraph, 3000 Johnson Rd. SW, Huntsville, AL 35805-5844, (800)671-6840

Natl. Assn. for Rehabilitation Leadership [16325], c/o Natl. Rehabilitation Assn., 633 S Washington St., Alexandria, VA 22314, (703)836-0850

Natl. Assn. of Rehabilitation Professionals in the Private Sector [★16322]

Natl. Assn. of Rehabilitation Providers and Agencies [16326], PO Box 1440, Oldsmar, FL 34677-1440, (813)855-9168

Natl. Assn. of Rehabilitation Secretaries - Address unknown since 2002.

Natl. Assn. of Rehabilitation Support Staff [16327], c/o Natl. Rehabilitation Assn., 633 S Washington St., Alexandria, VA 22314, (703)836-0850

Natl. Assn. of Reimbursement Officers - Address unknown since 1997.

Natl. Assn. of Reinforcing Steel Contractors [1039], PO Box 280, Fairfax, VA 22038, (703)591-1870

Natl. Assn. of Relay Manufacturers [★1197]

Natl. Assn. of Religious Bros. [★19707]

Natl. Assn. for Remedia/Developmental Stud. in Postsecondary Educ. [★8200]

Natl. Assn. for Remedial Teachers [★9043]

Natl. Assn. for Remedial Teachers [★IO]

Natl. Assn. of the Remodeling Indus. [643], 780 Lee St., Ste. 200, Des Plaines, IL 60016, (847)298-9200

Natl. Assn. for Remotely Piloted Vehicles [★7580]

Natl. Assn. for Remotely Piloted Vehicles [★IO]

Natl. Assn. of Removal Contractors - Defunct.

Natl. Assn. for Repeal of Abortion Laws [★18518]

Natl. Assn. of Reporter Training Schools - Defunct.

Natl. Assn. of Republican Attorneys [5512], PO Box 656513, Fresh Meadows, NY 11365-6513, (718)357-7075

Natl. Assn. of Resale and Thrift Shops [3417], PO Box 80707, St. Clair Shores, MI 48080-5707, (586)294-6700

Natl. Assn. for Res. in Sci. Teaching [9108], 12100 Sunset Hills Rd., Ste. 130, Reston, VA 20190-3221, (703)437-4377

Natl. Assn. for Res. and Therapy of Homosexuality [14434], 16633 Ventura Blvd., Ste. 1340, Encino, CA 91436-1801, (818)789-4440

Natl. Assn. for the Res. and Treatment of Homosexuality [★14434]

Natl. Assn. of Resident Mgt. Corporations - Address unknown since 2003.

Natl. Assn. of Residential Property Managers [3189], 638 Independence Pkwy., Chesapeake, VA 23320, (800)782-3452

Natl. Assn. of Residents and Interns [15175], Hillsboro Executive Center N, 350 Fairway Dr., Ste. 200, Deerfield Beach, FL 33441-1834, (954)571-1877

Natl. Assn. of Rsrc. Conservation and Development Councils [4421], 444 N Capitol St. NW, Ste. 345, Washington, DC 20001, (202)434-4780

Natl. Assn. of Responsible Loan Officers [1978], 335 Beard St., Tallahassee, FL 32303, (850)222-6000

Natl. Assn. Restaurant Internal Audit Group - Defunct.

Natl. Assn. of Restaurant Managers - Address unknown since 1994.

Natl. Assn. of Retail Coll. Attorneys [5513], 1620 I St. NW, Ste. 615, Washington, DC 20006, (202)861-0706

Natl. Assn. of Retail Druggists [★2986]

Natl. Assn. of Retail Grocers of Australia [IO], Hurstville, Australia

Natl. Assn. of Retail Grocers and Supermarkets of New Zealand [IO], Wellington, New Zealand

Natl. Assn. of Retail Grocers of the U.S. [★3421]

Natl. Assn. of Retail Ice Cream Manufacturers [★1137]

Natl. Assn. for Retail Marketing Services [3418], PO Box 906, Plover, WI 54467-0906, (715)342-0948

Natl. Assn. for Retail Merchandising Services [★3418]

Natl. Assn. of Retail Record Dealers - Defunct.

Natl. Assn. of Retailers' Co-operatives [IO], Rome, Italy

Natl. Assn. of Retailers and Wholesalers of Dairy Products [IO], Milan, Italy

Natl. Assn. for Retarded Children [★12561]

Natl. Assn. for Retarded Citizens [★12561]

Natl. Assn. of Retired Civil Employees [★5710]

Natl. Assn. of Retired Fed. Employees [★5710]

Natl. Assn. of Retired Senior Volunteer Program Directors - Address unknown since 2001.

A star before a book entry number signifies that the name is not listed separately, but is mentioned within the entry.

Natl. Assn. of Retired and Veteran Railway Employees [★3286]

Natl. Assn. of Retired and Veteran Railway Employees [3286], 300 Cedar Blvd., Ste. 201-A, Pittsburgh, PA 15228-1155, (763)757-1501

Natl. Assn. of Reunion Managers [3184], PO Box 59713, Renton, WA 98058-2713, (800)654-2776

Natl. Assn. of Reversionary Property Owners [18380], 227 Bellevue Way NE, Ste. 719, Bellevue, WA 98004, (425)646-8812

Natl. Assn. of Rev. Appraisers and Mortgage Underwriters [3329], 1224 N Nokomis NE, Alexandria, MN 56308-5072, (320)763-6870

Natl. Assn. of Rhythm and Blues Dee Jay's [10659], c/o Berni McKenna, Sec., 3331 Saratoga Dr., Belleville, IL 62221-6633, (618)257-9638

Natl. Assn. for Rights Protection and Advocacy [17132], PO Box 40585, Tuscaloosa, AL 35404, (205)464-0101

Natl. Assn. of Rocketry [22650], PO Box 407, Marion, IA 52302, (800)262-4872

Natl. Assn. of Rotary Clubs [★13060]

Natl. Assn. of Rotary Clubs [★IO]

Natl. Assn. of Royalty Owners [2935], 15 W 6th St., Ste. 2626, Tulsa, OK 74119, (918)794-1660

Natl. Assn. of Rudimental Drummers - Defunct.

Natl. Assn. of Rural Hea. Clinics [16245], 2 E Main St., Fremont, MI 49412, (866)306-1961

Natl. Assn. for Rural Mental Hea. [15217], 300 33rd Ave. S, Ste. 101, Waite Park, MN 56387, (320)202-1820

Natl. Assn. of RV Parks and Campgrounds [3357], 113 Park Ave., Falls Church, VA 22046, (703)241-8801

Natl. Assn. for Safety and Health in the Arts and Crafts - Defunct.

Natl. Assn. of Sailing Instructors and Sailing Schools - Defunct.

Natl. Assn. of Sales Managers [★2481]

Natl. Assn. of Sales Managers [★IO]

Natl. Assn. of Sales and Marketing Professionals - Defunct.

Natl. Assn. of Sales Professionals [3470], 8300 N Hayden Rd., Ste. 207, Scottsdale, AZ 85258, (480)951-4311

Natl. Assn. of Salespeople - Defunct.

Natl. Assn. of Sandwich Mfrs. - Defunct.

Natl. Assn. of Sanitarians [★14367]

Natl. Assn. of Sanitary Milk Bottle Closure Mfrs. - Defunct.

Natl. Assn. of Satellite Equipment Mfrs. - Defunct.

Natl. Assn. of Saw Shops [★2390]

Natl. Assn. of Saw Shops [★IO]

Natl. Assn. of Scale Aeromodelers [IO], Moon Township, PA, United States

Natl. Assn. of Scale Aeromodelers [22651], c/o Bonnie Rediske, Sec.-Treas., 128 Darnley Dr., Moon Township, PA 15108

Natl. Assn. of Scale Mfrs. [★4017]

Natl. Assn. of Scholars [8490], 221 Witherspoon St., 2nd Fl., Princeton, NJ 08542-3215, (609)683-7878

Natl. Assn. of School Accounting and Bus. Officials of Public Schools [★7892]

Natl. Assn. of School Accounting and Bus. Officials of Public Schools [★IO]

Natl. Assn. of School Accounting Officers [★IO]

Natl. Assn. of School Accounting Officers [★7892]

Natl. Assn. of School Affiliates - Address unknown since 1995.

Natl. Assn. of School Building Officials [★7892]

Natl. Assn. of School Building Officials [★IO]

Natl. Assn. of School Bus Contract Operators [★3882]

Natl. Assn. of School Bus. Officials [★7892]

Natl. Assn. of School Bus. Officials [★IO]

Natl. Assn. of School Counselors - Defunct.

Natl. Assn. of School Music Dealers [2819], 14070 Proton Rd., Ste. 100, Dallas, TX 75244-3601, (972)233-9107

Natl. Assn. of School Nurses [15501], 8484 Georgia Ave., Ste. 420, Silver Spring, MD 20910, (240)821-1130

Natl. Assn. of School Nurses for the Deaf [14768], c/o Virginia Muraoka-Meyer, CID, 4560 Clayton Ave., St. Louis, MO 63110

Natl. Assn. of School Psychologists [16160], 4340 E West Hwy., Ste. 402, Bethesda, MD 20814, (301)657-0270

Natl. Assn. of School Rsrc. Officers [9086], 1951 Woodlane Dr., St. Paul, MN 55125, (651)209-3153

Natl. Assn. of School Safety and Law Enforcement Officers [9087], PO Box 210079, Milwaukee, WI 53221, (315)529-4858

Natl. Assn. of School Secretaries [★7898]

Natl. Assn. of School Security Directors [★9087]

Natl. Assn. of School Social Workers [★13206]

Natl. Assn. of School Superintendents [★7882]

Natl. Assn. of Schoolmasters [★IO]

Natl. Assn. of Schoolmasters and Union of Women Teachers [IO], Birmingham, United Kingdom

Natl. Assn. of Schools of Art [★7978]

Natl. Assn. of Schools of Art and Design [7978], 11250 Roger Bacon Dr., Ste. 21, Reston, VA 20190-5248, (703)437-0700

Natl. Assn. of Schools and Colleges [★7947]

Natl. Assn. of Schools, Colleges and Universities of the United Methodist Church [8879], PO Box 340007, Nashville, TN 37203-0007, (615)340-7399

Natl. Assn. of Schools of Dance [8188], 11250 Roger Bacon Dr., Ste. 21, Reston, VA 20190-5248, (703)437-0700

Natl. Assn. of Schools of Design [★7978]

Natl. Assn. of Schools of Music [8921], 11250 Roger Bacon Dr., Ste. 21, Reston, VA 20190-5248, (703)437-0700

Natl. Assn. of Schools of Public Affairs and Admin. [6194], 1029 Vermont Ave. NW, Ste. 1100, Washington, DC 20005, (202)628-8965

Natl. Assn. of Schools of Theatre [9265], 11250 Roger Bacon Dr., Ste. 21, Reston, VA 20190-5248, (703)437-0700

Natl. Assn. for Sci., Tech. and Soc. [★7608]

Natl. Assn. of Sci. Writers [3133], PO Box 890, Hedgesville, WV 25427, (304)754-5077

National Association of Science Writers [IO], Hedgesville, WV, United States

Natl. Assn. of Sci. Materials Managers [3487], c/o Amy Aldrige, Treas., Florida State Univ., Chemistry Dept., 106 DLC, Tallahassee, FL 32306

Natl. Assn. of Scissors and Shears Mfrs. - Address unknown since 2000.

Natl. Assn. of Scorers - Address unknown since 2002.

Natl. Assn. of Screening Agencies [3330], 3337 Duke St., Alexandria, VA 22314, (703)370-7436

Natl. Assn. for Search and Rescue [12891], PO Box 232020, Centreville, VA 20120-2020, (703)222-6277

Natl. Assn. of Search and Rescue Coordinators [★12891]

Natl. Assn. of Secondary School Principals [9016], 1904 Assn. Dr., Reston, VA 20191-1537, (703)860-0200

Natl. Assn. of Secondary School Teachers [★IO]

Natl. Assn. of Secretaries of State [6277], c/o Hall of States, 444 N Capitol St. NW, Ste. 401, Washington, DC 20001-1557, (202)624-3525

Natl. Assn. of Secretaries of State Teachers Associations [★7906]

Natl. Assn. of Securities and Commercial Law Attorneys [★5579]

Natl. Assn. of Securities Commissioners [★3521]

Natl. Assn. of Securities Dealers [★3517]

Natl. Assn. of Securities Professionals [3518], 1212 New York Ave. NW, Ste. 950, Washington, DC 20005-3987, (202)371-5535

Natl. Assn. of Security Companies [3537], 1625 Prince St., Ste. 225-B, Alexandria, VA 22314, (703)519-0912

Natl. Assn. of Security and Data Vaults [★2109]

Natl. Assn. of Security and Data Vaults [★IO]

Natl. Assn. of Selective Distributors - Defunct.

Natl. Assn. for the Self-Employed [3617], PO Box 612067, DFW Airport, Dallas, TX 75261-2067, (800)232-6273

Natl. Assn. for Self Esteem [15218], PO Box 597, Fulton, MD 20759-0597

Natl. Assn. of Self-Instructional Language Programs [8736], Critical Languages Prog., Univ. of Arizona, 1717 E Speedway Blvd., Ste. 3312, Tucson, AZ 85721-0151, (520)626-5258

Natl. Assn. of Self-Service and Dept. Stores [IO], Mexico City, Mexico

Natl. Assn. for the Self-Supporting Active Ministry - Address unknown since 1999.

Natl. Assn. of Senior Companion Proj. Directors [11304], c/o Camellia Pisegna, Pres., Region IV Area Agency on Aging, 2900 Lakeview Ave., St. Joseph, MI 49085, (269)983-7058

Natl. Assn. for Senior Living Industries - Address unknown since 2000.

Natl. Assn. of Senior Meals Organizers [★IO]

Natl. Assn. of Senior Move Managers [2523], 911 N Elm St., Ste. 228, Hinsdale, IL 60521, (877)606-2766

National Assn. of Sentencing Advocates [★5645]

Natl. Assn. of Ser. and Conservation Corps [13497], 666 11th St. NW, Ste. 1000, Washington, DC 20001, (202)737-6272

Natl. Assn. of Service Contractors - Defunct.

Natl. Assn. of Ser. Dealers [3389], c/o North Amer. Retail Dealers Assn., 4700 W Lake Ave., Glenview, IL 60025, (847)375-4713

Natl. Assn. of Ser. Managers [3552], PO Box 250796, Milwaukee, WI 53225, (414)466-6060

Natl. Assn. of Service Merchandising - Defunct.

Natl. Assn. of Ser. Providers in Private Rehabilitation [16328], c/o Natl. Rehabilitation Assn., 633 S Washington St., Alexandria, VA 22314, (703)836-0850

Natl. Assn. of Settlement Purchasers [1439], c/o Peachtree Settlement Funding, 3301 Quantum Blvd., 2nd Fl., Boynton Beach, FL 33426, (800)821-7773

Natl. Assn. of Seventh-day Adventist Dentists [14171], PO Box 101, Loma Linda, CA 92354, (909)558-8187

Natl. Assn. of Sewer Ser. Companies [★3959]

Natl. Assn. of Sewing Machine Dealers - Defunct.

Natl. Assn. of Sewing Machine Distributors - Defunct.

Natl. Assn. of Shareholder and Consumer Attorneys [5579], c/o Barry A. Weprin, Treas., One Pennsylvania Plz., 49th Fl., New York, NY 10119, (212)946-9312

Natl. Assn. of Shell Marketers [2936], 6551 Loisdale Ct., Ste. 100, Springfield, VA 22150, (703)922-9784

Natl. Assn. of Shellfish Commissioners [★7255]

Natl. Assn. of Shellfish Commissioners [★IO]

Natl. Assn. of Sheltered Workshops and Homebound Programs [★16312]

Natl. Assn. of Shippers Advisory Boards [★3885]

Natl. Assn. of Shoe Chain Stores [★1597]

Natl. Assn. of Shooting Range Owners - Address unknown since 1990.

Natl. Assn. of Shooting Ranges [3599], c/o Richard Patterson, Exec. Dir., Flintlock Ridge Off. Ctr., 11 Mile Hill Rd., Newtown, CT 06470-2359, (203)426-1320

Natl. Assn. of Shooting Sports Athletes [23720], 2103 Wheaton Dr., Richardson, TX 75081

Natl. Assn. of Shopfitters [IO], Warlingham, United Kingdom

Natl. Assn. for Shoplifting Prevention [13025], 380 N Broadway, Ste. 306, Jericho, NY 11753, (516)932-0165

Natl. Assn. of Shortwave Broadcasters [541], 10400 NW 240th St., Okeechobee, FL 34972, (863)763-0281

Natl. Assn. for Sick Child Daycare [11532], 1716 5th Ave. N, Birmingham, AL 35203, (205)324-8447

Natl. Assn. for Sickle Cell Disease [★14797]

Natl. Assn. of Sign and Display Advertisers - Defunct.

Natl. Assn. of Sign Supply Distributors [4023], 5024-R Campbell Blvd., Baltimore, MD 21236-5975, (410)931-8100

Natl. Assn. of Silo Manufacturers [★181]

Natl. Assn. of Silo Manufacturers [★IO]

Natl. Assn. of Single People [13107], 380 E Yale Loop, Irvine, CA 92614, (714)756-1000

Natl. Assn. for Single Sex Public Educ. [9038], PO Box 108, Poolesville, MD 20837, (301)461-5065

Natl. Assn. of Sitter Registries - Defunct.

Natl. Assn. of the Sixth Infantry Div. [20704], c/o Thomas E. Price, 317 Court St. NE, Ste. 203, Salem, OR 97301, (503)363-7334

Reference to "IO" in place of a book number signifies that the association may be found in the 45th edition of International Organizations.

Natl. Assn. of the Sixth Infantry Div. [★20704]

Natl. Assn. of the Sixth Infantry Div. [★20704]

Natl. Assn. of the Sixth Infantry/Motorized Div. [★20704]

Natl. Assn. of the Sixth Infantry/Motorized Div. [★20704]

Natl. Assn. of Skirt, Pajama and Sportswear Manufacturers [★221]

Natl. Assn. of Small Bus. Intl. Trade Educators [★8031]

Natl. Assn. of Small Bus. Intl. Trade Educators [★IO]

Natl. Assn. of Small Bus. Investment Companies [3618], 666 11th St. NW, Ste. 750, Washington, DC 20001, (202)628-5055

Natl. Assn. of Small Loan Supervisors [★5610]

Natl. Assn. for Small Schools [IO], Banbury, United Kingdom

Natl. Assn. of Smaller Communities [★6126]

Natl. Assn. of Soap Opera Fans - Address unknown since 2003.

Natl. Assn. of Social Workers [13206], 750 First St. NE, Ste. 700, Washington, DC 20002-4241, (202)408-8600

Natl. Assn. of Social Workers Comm. on Lesbian and Gay Issues [★12245]

Natl. Assn. of Social Workers Natl. Comm. on Lesbian, Gay and Bisexual Issues [12245], 750 First St. NE, Ste. 700, Washington, DC 20002-4241, (202)408-8600

Natl. Assn. of Social Workers- Natl. Comm. on Lesbian and Gay Issues [★12245]

Natl. Assn. of Societies for Care of the Handicapped [IO], Harare, Zimbabwe

Natl. Assn. of Software and Ser. Companies [IO], New Delhi, India

Natl. Assn. of Soil Conservation Districts [★4420]

Natl. Assn. of Soil and Water Conservation Districts [★4420]

Natl. Assn. for the Southern Poor [★11798]

Natl. Assn. of Spanish Broadcasters - Defunct.

Natl. Assn. of Spanish Speaking-Spanish Surnamed Nurses [★15494]

Natl. Assn. of Special Educ. Teachers [9148], 1250 Connecticut Ave. NW, Ste. 200, Washington, DC 20036, (800)754-4421

Natl. Assn. for Special Educational Needs [★IO]

Natl. Assn. of Special Needs State Administrators - Address unknown since 2007.

Natl. Assn. of Special Police and Security Officers [24122], 1101 30th St. NW, Ste. 500, Washington, DC 20007, (202)625-8306

Natl. Assn. of Special and Reserve Police - Defunct.

Natl. Assn. of Specialized Carriers - Defunct.

Natl. Assn. of Specialized Schools - Defunct.

Natl. Assn. of Specialty Food and Confection Brokers - Address unknown since 2003.

Natl. Assn. for the Specialty Food Trade [1541], 120 Wall St., 27th Fl., New York, NY 10005, (212)482-6440

Natl. Assn. of Specialty Hea. Organizations [14650], 222 S First St., Ste. 303, Louisville, KY 40202, (502)403-1122

Natl. Assn. of Sport Aircraft Designers - Address unknown since 1991.

Natl. Assn. for Sport and Physical Educ. [8986], 1900 Assn. Dr., Reston, VA 20191-1598, (703)476-3400

Natl. Assn. of Sporting Goods Wholesalers [3644], c/o Wayne Smith, Pres., PO Box 881525, Port St. Lucie, FL 34988-1525, (772)621-7162

Natl. Assn. of Sports for Cerebral Palsy [★23353]

Natl. Assn. of Sports Commissions [23871], 9916 Carver Rd., Ste. 100, Cincinnati, OH 45242, (513)281-3888

Natl. Assn. of Sports Officials [23872], 2017 Lathrop Ave., Racine, WI 53405, (262)632-5448

Natl. Assn. of Sports Officials - Organizations Network [23873], 2017 Lathrop Ave., Racine, WI 53405, (262)632-5448

Natl. Assn. on Standard Medical Vocabulary - Address unknown since 1985.

Natl. Assn. of State Administrators for Family Consumer Sciences [8514], c/o Robin Harris, Treas., State Dept. of Educ., 120 SE 10th Ave., Topeka, KS 66612-1182, (785)296-4912

Natl. Assn. for State Administrators of Hea. Occupations Educ. [★8870]

Natl. Assn. of State Administrators and Supervisors of Private Schools [9021], c/o Teri Candelaria, Pres., Arizona State Bd. for Private Postsecondary Educ., 1400 W Washington St., Rm. 260, Phoenix, AZ 85007, (602)542-5709

Natl. Assn. State Agencies for Surplus Property [6185], c/o Doug Coleman, Admin., 2301 C St., Auburn, WA 98001-7401

Natl. Assn. of State Alcohol and Drug Abuse Directors [13264], 1025 Connecticut Ave. NW, Ste. 605, Washington, DC 20036, (202)293-0090

Natl. Assn. of State Approved Colls. and Universities - Address unknown since 1999.

Natl. Assn. of State Approving Agencies [6345], c/o Joan L. Ryan, Pres., Dept. of Veterans' Affairs, PO Box 19432, Springfield, IL 62794-9432, (217)782-7838

Natl. Assn. of State Aquaculture Coordinators [4180], c/o Florida Dept. of Agriculture and Consumer Services, Division of Aquaculture, 1203 Governor's Square Blvd., Fifth Fl., Tallahassee, FL 32301, (850)488-4033

Natl. Assn. of State Archaeologists [6450], c/o Arthur E. Spiess, Sec.-Treas., Maine Historic Preservation Commn., 65 State House Sta., Augusta, ME 04333-0065, (207)287-2132

Natl. Assn. of State Archives and Records Administrators [★5820]

Natl. Assn. of State Auditors, Comptrollers, and Treasurers [6206], 449 Lewis Hargett Cir., Ste. 290, Lexington, KY 40503-3669, (859)276-1147

Natl. Assn. of State Aviation Officials [5540], 1010 Wayne Ave., Ste. 930, Silver Spring, MD 20910, (301)588-0587

Natl. Assn. of State Aviation Officials Center for Aviation Res. and Educ. [★5537]

Natl. Assn. of State-Based Child Advocacy Organizations [★11662]

Natl. Assn. of State Beer Assn. Secretaries [★204]

Natl. Assn. of State Boards of Accountancy [5428], 150 4th Ave. N, Ste. 700, Nashville, TN 37219, (615)880-4200

Natl. Assn. of State Boards of Educ. [9082], 277 S Washington St., Ste. 100, Alexandria, VA 22314, (703)684-4000

Natl. Assn. of State Boards of Geology [7133], PO Box 11591, Columbia, SC 29211-1591, (803)739-5676

Natl. Assn. of State Boating Law Administrators [5545], 1500 Leestown Rd., Ste. 330, Lexington, KY 40511, (859)225-9487

Natl. Assn. of State Budget Officers [6207], Hall of the States Bldg., 444 N Capitol St. NW, Ste. 642, Washington, DC 20001-1511, (202)624-5382

Natl. Assn. of State Cable Agencies - Address unknown since 1999.

Natl. Assn. of State Catholic Conf. Directors [19668], c/o Ronald G. Jackson, Pres., PO Box 29260, Washington, DC 20017, (301)853-5342

Natl. Assn. of State Charity Officials [5769], c/o Jody Wahl, Pres., Off. of the Attorney Gen., Bremer Tower, 445 Minnesota St., 12th Fl., St. Paul, MN 55101-2131, (651)297-4607

Natl. Assn. of State Chief Administrators [6278], c/o Coun. of State Governments, PO Box 11910, Lexington, KY 40578-1910, (859)244-8181

Natl. Assn. of State Chief Info. Officers [5821], c/o AMR Mgt. Services, 201 E Main St., Ste. 1405, Lexington, KY 40507, (859)514-9212

Natl. Assn. of State Civil Defense Directors [★5565]

Natl. Assn. for State Community Services Programs [6279], 400 N Capitol St. NW, Ste. 395, Washington, DC 20001, (202)624-5866

Natl. Assn. of State Comprehensive Hea. Insurance Plans [14691], 5775 Wayzata Blvd., Ste. 910, St. Louis Park, MN 55416, (952)593-9609

Natl. Assn. of State Contractors Licensing Agencies [1040], PO Box 14941, Scottsdale, AZ 85267, (602)485-3941

Natl. Assn. of State Controlled Substances Authorities [5672], c/o Katherine Keough, Exec. Dir., 72 Brook St., Quincy, MA 02170, (617)472-0520

Natl. Assn. of State Credit Union Supervisors [5633], 1655 N Ft. Myer Dr., Ste. 300, Arlington, VA 22209, (703)528-8351

Natl. Assn. of State Departments of Agriculture [5439], 1156 15th St. NW, Ste. 1020, Washington, DC 20005, (202)296-9680

Natl. Assn. of State Development Agencies [5592], 10900 Univ. Blvd. MSN 1J2, Bull Run Hall Rm., Manassas, VA 20110-2201, (703)993-9411

Natl. Assn. of State Directors of Admin. and Gen. Ser. Officers [★6278]

Natl. Assn. of State Directors of Developmental Disabilities Services [12576], 113 Oronoco St., Alexandria, VA 22314, (703)683-4202

Natl. Assn. of State Directors for Disaster Preparedness [★5565]

Natl. Assn. of State Directors of Migrant Educ. [12592], 1001 Connecticut Ave. NW, Ste. 915, Washington, DC 20036, (202)775-7780

Natl. Assn. of State Directors of Special Educ. [9149]

Natl. Assn. of State Directors of Teacher Educ. and Certification [9224], 1225 Providence Rd., PMB 116, Whitinsville, MA 01588, (508)380-1202

Natl. Assn. of State Directors of Veterans Affairs [6346], 107 S West St., No. 570, Alexandria, VA 22314, (505)827-6312

Natl. Assn. of State Directors of Vocational Tech. Educ. Consortium [9307], 444 N Capitol St. NW, Ste. 830, Washington, DC 20001, (202)737-0303

Natl. Assn. of State Drug Abuse Prog. Coordinators [★13264]

Natl. Assn. of State Economic Development Agencies [★5592]

Natl. Assn. for State Economic Opportunity Off. Directors [★6279]

Natl. Assn. of State Educational Media Professionals [8568], c/o Frances Roscello, Pres., Off. of New York City School and Community Services, New York State Educ. Dept., Rm. 375 EBA, 89 Washington Ave., Albany, NY 12205, (518)474-8485

Natl. Assn. of State Election Directors [1176], 12543 Westella, Ste. 100, Houston, TX 77077-3929, (281)752-6200

Natl. Assn. of State EMS Officials [14337], 201 Park Washington Ct., Falls Church, VA 22046-4527, (703)538-1799

Natl. Assn. of State Energy Officials [5685], 1414 Prince St., Ste. 200, Alexandria, VA 22314, (703)299-8800

Natl. Assn. of State Facilities Administrators [6195], PO Box 11910, Lexington, KY 40578-1910, (859)244-8181

Natl. Assn. of State Farm Agents [2218], 8015 Corporate Dr., Ste. A, Baltimore, MD 21236, (410)931-3332

Natl. Assn. of State Fire Marshals [5722], 1319 F St. NW, Ste. 301, Washington, DC 20004, (202)737-1226

Natl. Assn. of State Foresters [4689], 444 N Capitol St. NW, Ste. 540, Washington, DC 20001, (202)624-5415

Natl. Assn. of State Head Injury Administrators [14529], 4330 EW Hwy., Ste. 301, Bethesda, MD 20814, (301)656-3500

Natl. Assn. of State Human Resources Directors - Address unknown since 1995.

Natl. Assn. of State Info. Rsrc. Executives [★5821]

Natl. Assn. for State Info. Systems [★5821]

Natl. Assn. of State Land Reclamationists [6118], c/o Anna Harrington, Coal Res. Center, Southern Illinois Univ., Carbondale, IL 62901-4623, (618)536-5521

Natl. Assn. for State and Local River Conservation Programs - Address unknown since 2002.

Natl. Assn. of State Lotteries [★6048]

Natl. Assn. of State Lotteries [★IO]

Natl. Assn. of State Medicaid Directors [14692], 810 1st St. NE, Ste. 500, Washington, DC 20002-4207, (202)682-0100

Natl. Assn. of State Mental Hea. Prog. Directors [15219], 66 Canal Center Plz., Ste. 302, Alexandria, VA 22314, (703)739-9333

Natl. Assn. of State Militia - Address unknown since 1995.

Natl. Assn. of State Motorcycle Safety Administrators [6253], c/o Ruth Wilson, Bus. Mgr., 7881 S Wellington St., Centennial, CO 80122, (303)797-2318

A star before a book entry number signifies that the name is not listed separately, but is mentioned within the entry.

Natl. Assn. of State Outdoor Recreation Liaison Officers [6157], c/o Yvonne S. Ferrell, Exec. Dir., 3116 Woodbrook Pl., Boise, ID 83706, (208)384-5421

Natl. Assn. of State Park Directors [6158], c/o Philip K. McKnelly, Exec. Dir., 8829 Woodyhill Rd., Raleigh, NC 27613, (919)676-8365

Natl. Assn. of State Personnel Executives [6280], c/o Coun. of State Governments, PO Box 11910, Lexington, KY 40578-1910, (859)244-8182

Natl. Assn. of State Procurement Officials [6238], 201 E Main St., Ste. 1405, Lexington, KY 40507-2004, (859)514-9159

Natl. Assn. of State Public Hea. Veterinarians [★16747]

Natl. Assn. of State Purchasing Officials [★6238]

Natl. Assn. of State Racing Commissioners [★6240]

Natl. Assn. of State Racing Commissioners [★IO]

Natl. Assn. of State Radio Networks - Address unknown since 2003.

Natl. Assn. of State Recreation Planners [★6156]

Natl. Assn. of State Retirement Administrators [5569], PO Box 14117, Baton Rouge, LA 70898, (225)757-9558

Natl. Assn. of State Savings and Loan Supervisors [★458]

Natl. Assn. of State School Nurse Consultants [15502], PO Box 708, Kent, OH 44240-0013

Natl. Assn. of State Sentencing Commissions [5650], c/o Lynda Flynt, 300 Dexter Ave., Montgomery, AL 36104-3741, (334)353-4830

Natl. Assn. of State Social Security Administrators [★6259]

Natl. Assn. of State Supervisors and Directors of Secondary Education - Defunct.

Natl. Assn. of State Supervisors of Distributive Educ. [★8818]

Natl. Assn. of State Supervisors of Vocational Home Economics [★8514]

Natl. Assn. of State Telecommunications Directors [6306], 2760 Res. Park Dr., Lexington, KY 40511-8482, (859)244-8187

Natl. Assn. of State and Territorial Public Hea. Veterinarians [★16747]

Natl. Assn. of State Textbook Administrators [9260], c/o Ann Asbeck, Instructional Resources Consultant, Kentucky Dept. of Educ., 500 Mero St., 17th Fl., Frankfort, KY 40601, (502)564-2106

Natl. Assn. of State Textbook Administrators [★9261]

Natl. Assn. of State Textbook Directors [★9261]

Natl. Assn. of State Treasurers [6208], PO Box 11910, Lexington, KY 40578-1910, (859)244-8175

Natl. Assn. of State Units on Aging [11305], 1201 15th St. NW, Ste. 350, Washington, DC 20005, (202)898-2578

Natl. Assn. of State Universities and Land-Grant Colleges [8110], 1307 New York Ave. NW, Ste. 400, Washington, DC 20005-4722, (202)478-6040

Natl. Assn. of State Universities and Land-Grant Colleges; Off. for the Advancement of Public Black Colleges of the [8112]

Natl. Assn. of State Utility Consumer Advocates [6340], 8380 Colesville Rd., Ste. 101, Silver Spring, MD 20910-6267, (301)589-6313

Natl. Assn. of State Veterans Homes [13354], 5211 Auth Rd., Suitland, MD 20746, (301)899-7908

Natl. Assn. of State VOCAL Orgs. [13365]

Natl. Assn. of State Workforce Agencies [5680], 444 N Capitol St. NW, Ste. 142, Washington, DC 20001, (202)434-8020

Natl. Assn. for Statewide Health and Welfare - Defunct.

Natl. Assn. of Stationery Manufacturers [IO], Milan, Italy

Natl. Assn. of Steam and Fluid Specialty Mfrs. [★2018]

Natl. Assn. of Steel and Copper Plate Engravers [★3680]

Natl. Assn. of Steel Exporters - Defunct.

Natl. Assn. of Steel Pipe Distributors [3032], 1501 E Mockingbird Ln., Ste. 307, Victoria, TX 77904, (361)574-7878

Natl. Assn. of Steel Stockholders [IO], Birmingham, United Kingdom

Natl. Assn. of Stevedoves [★2609]

Natl. Assn. for Stock Car Auto Racing [23081], PO Box 2875, Daytona Beach, FL 32120, (386)253-0611

Natl. Assn. of Stock Plan Professionals [1469], PO Box 21639, Concord, CA 94521-0639, (925)685-9271

Natl. Assn. of Stockholders and Traders in Iron and Steel, Non-Ferrous Metals, Ferros and Non-Ferros Scrap [IO], Milan, Italy

Natl. Assn. to Stop Guardian Abuse [12059], 365 E Avenida De Los Arboles, Ste. 102, Thousand Oaks, CA 91360, (805)402-7106

Natl. Assn. of Store Fixture Manufacturers [644], 4651 Sheridan St., Ste. 470, Hollywood, FL 33021, (954)893-7300

Natl. Assn. of Storm Chasers and Spotters [13413], c/o Weatherstock Inc., PO Box 31808, Tucson, AZ 85751

Natl. Assn. of St. Entertainers [IO], Brighton, United Kingdom

Natl. Assn. of St. Schools [9337], 1567 Marion St., Denver, CO 80218, (303)830-8213

Natl. Assn. of Student Activity Advisers - Defunct.

Natl. Assn. of Student Affairs Professionals [7903], c/o Dr. Terrance D. Smith, Financial Sec., Fort Valley State Univ., 1005 State Univ. Dr., Fort Valley, GA 31030

Natl. Assn. of Student Anthropologists [7953], c/o Amer. Anthropological Assn., 2200 Wilson Blvd., Ste. 600, Arlington, VA 22201, (703)528-1902

Natl. Assn. of Student Assistance Professionals [★9171]

Natl. Assn. of Student Councils [9186], 1904 Assn. Dr., Reston, VA 20191-1537, (703)860-0200

Natl. Assn. of Student Employment Administrators [★8996]

Natl. Assn. of Student Employment Services [IO], Liverpool, United Kingdom

Natl. Assn. of Student Financial Aid Administrators [8350], 1129 20th St. NW, Ste. 400, Washington, DC 20036-3453, (202)785-0453

Natl. Assn. of Student Loan Administrators [8432], c/o Paul J. Thornburgh, 2401 Intl. Ln., Madison, WI 53704-3121, (608)246-1403

Natl. Assn. of Student Personnel Administrators [7904], 1875 Connecticut Ave. NW, Ste. 418, Washington, DC 20009, (202)265-7500

Natl. Assn. of Students Against Violence Everywhere [18117], 322 Chapanoke Rd., Ste. 110, Raleigh, NC 27603, (919)661-7800

National Association of Students Against Violence Everywhere [IO], Raleigh, NC, United States

Natl. Assn. for the Stud. and Performance of African-American Music [8922], c/o Mark Philips, Financial Sec., 1225 W High St., Petersburg, VA 23803, (901)396-2913

Natl. Assn. for the Stud. and Prevention of Tuberculosis [★16354]

Natl. Assn. for the Stud. of Snow and Avalanches [IO], Grenoble, France

Natl. Assn. of Subacute and Post-Acute Care [14728], PO Box 65085, Washington, DC 20035, (202)429-2700

Natl. Assn. of Subacute and Post Acute Care [★14728]

Natl. Assn. of Subrogation Professionals [3185], PO Box 390197, Edina, MN 55439-0197, (952)835-8700

Natl. Assn. of Substance Abuse Trainers and Educators [9198], 6400 Press Dr., Southern Univ. at New Orleans, New Orleans, LA 70126, (504)286-5234

Natl. Assn. of Sugar, Alcohol and Yeast Manufacturers [IO], Rome, Italy

Natl. Assn. of Suggestion Systems [★IO]

Natl. Assn. of Suggestion Systems [★1260]

Natl. Assn. of Summer Sessions [★9200]

Natl. Assn. of Summer Sessions [★IO]

Natl. Assn. for the Superconducting Supercollider - Address unknown since 2003.

Natl. Assn. of Superintendents of U.S. Naval Shore Establishments [6085], c/o Mr. Larry Sands, Pres., 89 Pine Legde Dr., Wells, ME 04090, (207)646-7316

Natl. Assn. of Supermarkets and Related Businesses [IO], Caracas, Venezuela

Natl. Assn. of Supervisors [★5708]

Natl. Assn. of Supervisors and Administrators of Hea. Occupations Educ. [8870]

Natl. Assn. of Supervisors of Agricultural Educ. [7939], c/o Dr. Jay Jackman, CAE, Exec. Treas., 300 Garrigus Bldg., Univ. of Kentucky, Lexington, KY 40546-0215, (859)257-2224

Natl. Assn. of Supervisors of Bus. Educ. [8034], c/o Colleen Hunt, Treas., Iowa Dept. of Education, 12528 525th St., Elliott, IA 51532, (515)281-0319

Natl. Assn. of Supervisors of Bus. and Off. Educ. [★8034]

Natl. Assn. of Supervisors, Dept. of Defense [★5708]

Natl. Assn. of Supervisors, Fed. Govt. [★5708]

Natl. Assn. of Supervisors of State Banks [★5544]

Natl. Assn. of Supervisors of Student Training [★9212]

Natl. Assn. of Supervisors and Teachers of High School Journalism [★8713]

Natl. Assn. of Suppliers for the Footwear and Leather Indus. [IO], Leon, Mexico

Natl. Assn. for the Support of Long Term Care [14651], 1321 Duke St., Ste. 304, Alexandria, VA 22314, (703)549-8500

Natl. Assn. of Surety Bond Producers [2219], 1828 L St. NW, Ste. 720, Washington, DC 20036-5104, (202)686-3700

Natl. Assn. for Surface Finishing [1474], 1155 15th St. NW, Ste. 500, Washington, DC 20005, (202)457-8404

Natl. Assn. for Surrogate Mothers - Defunct.

Natl. Assn. for Sustainable Agriculture Australia [IO], Stirling, Australia

Natl. Assn. of Swedish Architects [IO], Stockholm, Sweden

Natl. Assn. of the Swedish Joinery Factories [IO], Stockholm, Sweden

Natl. Assn. of Swine Records [5235], c/o Natl. Swine Registry, PO Box 2417, West Lafayette, IN 47996, (765)463-3594

Natl. Assn. of Synagogue Administrators - Address unknown since 2001.

Natl. Assn. of Tanners [★2416]

Natl. Assn. of Tanning Center Owners - Defunct.

Natl. Assn. of Taurine Clubs - Address unknown since 1995.

Natl. Assn. of Tax Accountants - Defunct.

Natl. Assn. of Tax Administrators [★6292]

Natl. Assn. of Tax Advisors [IO], Cologne, Germany

Natl. Assn. of Tax Consultants [6300], PO Box 90276, Portland, OR 97290-0276, (503)261-0878

Natl. Assn. of Tax Practitioners [★6301]

Natl. Assn. of Tax Professionals [6301], PO Box 8002, Appleton, WI 54914-8002, (800)558-3402

Natl. Assn. of Taxicab Owners [★3894]

Natl. Assn. of Taxicab Owners [★IO]

Natl. Assn. of Teacher Educ. Institutions of Metropolitan Districts [★9208]

Natl. Assn. of Teacher Educators for Business Education - Address unknown since 1999.

Natl. Assn. of Teacher Educators for Family and Consumer Sciences [8515], c/o Debra DeBates, Pres., College of Family and Consumer Sciences, NFA 305, Box 2275A, South Dakota State Univ., Brookings, SD 57007, (605)688-4666

Natl. Assn. of Teacher Educators for Home Economics [★8515]

Natl. Assn. of Teacher Educators for Vocational Home Economics [★8515]

Natl. Assn. of Teachers' Agencies [1275]

Natl. Assn. of Teachers of Electronics - Defunct.

Natl. Assn. of Teachers of Singing [8923], 9957 Moorings Dr., Ste. 401, Jacksonville, FL 32257, (904)992-9101

Natl. Assn. for the Teaching of English [IO], Sheffield, United Kingdom

Natl. Assn. for Teaching English and other Community Languages to Adults [IO], Birmingham, United Kingdom

Natl. Assn. for Tech Prep Leadership [9239], c/o KS Bd. of Regents, 1000 SW Jackson St., Ste. 520, Topeka, KS 66612-1368, (785)296-3958

Natl. Assn. of Telecommunications Dealers - Address unknown since 1994.

Reference to "IO" in place of a book number signifies that the association may be found in the 45th edition of International Organizations.

Natl. Assn. of Telecommunications Officers and Advisors [6307], 1800 Diagonal Rd., Ste. 495, Alexandria, VA 22314, (703)519-8035

Natl. Assn. of Telemarketing Consultants - Defunct.

Natl. Assn. for Telematics for Transport and Safety [IO], Rome, Italy

Natl. Assn. of TV and Electronic Servicers of Am. [★1224]

Natl. Assn. of TV Prog. Executives [571], 5757 Wilshire Blvd., Penthouse 10, Los Angeles, CA 90036-3681, (310)453-4440

National Association of Television Program Executives [IO], Los Angeles, CA, United States

Natl. Assn. of TV and Radio Artists - Defunct.

Natl. Assn. of Television-Radio Farm Directors [★570]

Natl. Assn. of Temple Administrators [20163], PO Box 936, Ridgefield, WA 98642, (360)887-0464

Natl. Assn. of Temple Educators [20164], 633 Third Ave., 7th Fl., New York, NY 10017-6778, (212)452-6510

National Association of Temple Educators [IO], New York, NY, United States

Natl. Assn. of Temple Secretaries [★20163]

Natl. Assn. of Temporary Services [★1254]

Natl. Assn. of Temporary and Staffing Services [★1254]

Natl. Assn. of Tenants' Organisations [IO], Dublin, Ireland

Natl. Assn. of Test Directors [9254], c/o Sherry Rose Bond, 1091 King Ave., Columbus, OH 43212, (614)365-5786

Natl. Assn. of Texaco Consignees [★2936]

Natl. Assn. of Texaco and Shell Marketers [★2936]

Natl. Assn. of Texaco Wholesalers [★2936]

Natl. Assn. of Textile and Apparel Distributors - Defunct.

Natl. Assn. of Textile Machinery Mfrs. [★1997]

Natl. Assn. of Textile Supervisors - Address unknown since 2007.

Natl. Assn. of Theatre Nurses [★IO]

National Association of Theatre Owners [IO], Washington, DC, United States

Natl. Assn. of Theatre Owners [1315], PO Box 77318, Washington, DC 20013-7318, (202)962-0054

Natl. Assn. of Therapeutic Schools and Programs [13738], 126 N Marina, Prescott, AZ 86301, (928)443-9505

Natl. Assn. of Therapeutic Wilderness Camps [23276], 264 Brown Hill Rd., Marklysburg, PA 15459, (724)329-1098

Natl. Assn. of Ticket Brokers [1316], 214 N Hale St., Wheaton, IL 60187, (630)510-4594

Natl. Assn. of Tile Distributors [★IO]

Natl. Assn. of Timetable Collectors [23008], PO Box 446, Georgetown, TX 78627-0446

Natl. Assn. of Tire and Renovating Plants Distributors [IO], Mexico City, Mexico

Natl. Assn. of Tire Specialists [IO], Bologna, Italy

Natl. Assn. of Title Seven Directors [★11315]

Natl. Assn. of Tobacco Distributors [★1500]

Natl. Assn. of Tobacco Outlets [3820], 15560 Boulder Pointe Rd., Minneapolis, MN 55437, (866)869-8888

Natl. Assn. of Tower Erectors [6653], 8 2nd St. SE, Watertown, SD 57201-3624, (605)882-5865

Natl. Assn. of Town Watch [11841], PO Box 303, Wynnewood, PA 19096, (610)649-7055

Natl. Assn. of Towns and Townships [6126], 1130 Connecticut Ave. NW, Ste. 300, Washington, DC 20036, (202)454-3954

Natl. Assn. of Trade Exchanges [3844], c/o Tom McDowell, Exec. Dir., 8836 Tyler Blvd., Mentor, OH 44060, (440)205-5378

Natl. Assn. for Trade and Indus. Educ. and Natl. Assn. of State Supervisors for Trade and Indus. Educ. [★8542]

Natl. Assn. of Trade and Indus. Instructors [9233], PO Box 1665, Leesburg, VA 20177, (703)777-1740

Natl. Assn. of Trade Press Publishers [IO], Milan, Italy

Natl. Assn. of Trade and Tech. Schools and the Assn. of Independent Colleges and Schools [★9303]

Natl. Assn. of Traffic Accident Reconstructionists and Investigators [5887], PO Box 2588, West Chester, PA 19382, (610)696-1919

Natl. Assn. of Trailer Mfrs. [393], 1320 SW Topeka Blvd., Topeka, KS 66612-1817, (785)272-4433

Natl. Assn. of Trailer Owners [22959]

Natl. Assn. of Training Officers in Personal Social Services [★IO]

Natl. Assn. of Transit Consumer Orgs. [13339]

Natl. Assn. of Trap and Skeet Clubs - Address unknown since 1995.

Natl. Assn. of Travel Agents Singapore [IO], Singapore, Singapore

Natl. Assn. of Traveling Nurses [15503]

Natl. Assn. for Treasurers of Religious Institutes [20516], 8824 Cameron St., Silver Spring, MD 20910, (301)587-7776

Natl. Assn. of Trial Court Administrators [★5627]

Natl. Assn. of Trial Court Administrators [★IO]

Natl. Assn. of Tribal Historic Preservation Officers [10047], PO Box 19189, Washington, DC 20036-9189, (202)628-8476

Natl. Assn. of Truck Driving Schools - Address unknown since 1989.

Natl. Assn. of Truck Stop Operators [★3424]

Natl. Assn. of Tutoring [★9283]

Natl. Assn. of Unclaimed Property Administrators [6186], c/o NAST, PO Box 11910, Lexington, KY 40578-1910, (859)244-8150

Natl. Assn. of Underwater Instructors [23963], PO Box 89789, Tampa, FL 33689-0413, (813)628-6284

Natl. Assn. of Unemployed Persons - Defunct.

Natl. Assn. of Unemployment Insurance Appellate Boards [5831], c/o Alice S. Mitchell, Treas., UI Appeals Tribunal, Georgia Dept. of Labor, 1630 Phoenix Blvd., Ste. 201, College Park, GA 30349, (770)994-2220

Natl. Assn. of Uniform Manufacturers and Distributors [248], 16 E 41st St., Ste. 700, New York, NY 10017, (212)869-0670

Natl. Assn. for Uniformed Services [6086], 5535 Hempstead Way, Springfield, VA 22151-4094, (703)750-1342

Natl. Assn. for Uniformed Services Retirees [★6086]

Natl. Assn. of Univ. Fisheries and Wildlife Programs [8391], c/o Thomas Franklin, Liaison/Wildlife Policy Dir., Wildlife Soc., 5410 Grosvenor Ln., Bethesda, MD 20814, (301)897-9770

Natl. Assn. of Univ. Women [9320], 1001 E St. SE, Washington, DC 20003-2847, (202)547-3967

Natl. Assn. of Univ. Women (Moldova) [IO], Balti, Moldova

Natl. Assn. of Upholstery Fabric Distributors [★3793]

Natl. Assn. of Urban Bankers [★499]

Natl. Assn. of Urban Debate Leagues [9155], 332 S Michigan Ave., Ste. 500, Chicago, IL 60604, (312)427-0175

Natl. Assn. of Urban Flood Mgt. Agencies [★6140]

Natl. Assn. of Urban Hospitals [14893], 21351 Gentry Dr., Ste. 210, Sterling, VA 20166, (703)444-0989

Natl. Assn. of USS LCS(L) 1-130 - Address unknown since 2002.

Natl. Assn. of Utilization Rev. Coordinators [★16264]

Natl. Assn. of VA Physicians and Dentists [16007], PO Box 15458, Arlington, VA 22215, (202)414-0782

Natl. Assn. of Van Pool Operators [★13334]

Natl. Assn. of Van Pool Operators [★IO]

Natl. Assn. of the Van Valkenburg Family [21008], PO Box 313, Carson City, NV 89702

Natl. Assn. for Variable Annuities [2220], 11710 Plaza Am. Dr., Ste. 100, Reston, VA 20190, (703)707-8830

Natl. Assn. of Variety Stores - Defunct.

Natl. Assn. of Vascular Access Networks [★16722]

Natl. Assn. of Vehicle Rental Dealers [IO], Mexico City, Mexico

Natl. Assn. for Ventilator Dependent Individuals - Address unknown since 1994.

Natl. Assn. of Vertical Trans. Professionals [2048], c/o Curtis E. Forney, Exec. Dir., 2107 Pounge Ave., Cincinnati, OH 45208-3267, (513)533-3500

Natl. Assn. of Veterans Prog. Administrators [9292], 2020 Pennsylvania Ave. NW, Ste. 1975, Washington, DC 20006-1846, (480)461-7428

Natl. Assn. of Veterans' Res. and Educ. Foundations [6347], 5480 Wisconsin Ave., Ste. 214, Chevy Chase, MD 20815, (301)656-5005

Natl. Assn. for Veterinary Acupuncture - Defunct.

Natl. Assn. of Veterinary Assistants - Defunct.

Natl. Assn. of Veterinary Technicians in Am. [16800], PO Box 224, Battle Ground, IN 47920, (765)742-2216

Natl. Assn. of Victims Support Schemes [★IO]

Natl. Assn. of Video Distributors [1391], 1092 N Forest Oak, Henderson, KY 42420, (270)826-9423

Natl. Assn. of Videographers - Defunct.

Natl. Assn. for Vietnamese Amer. Educ. [★19424]

Natl. Assn. of Vietnamese Nurses [15504], PO Box 9692, Fountain Valley, CA 92728-9692, (714)330-1243

Natl. Assn. of Vision Professionals [15693], 1775 Church St. NW, Washington, DC 20036, (202)234-1010

Natl. Assn. of Vision Prog. Consultants [★15693]

Natl. Assn. for the Visual Arts [IO], Potts Point, Australia

Natl. Assn. of Visual Educ. Dealers [★IO]

Natl. Assn. of Visual Educ. Dealers [★331]

Natl. Assn. of Visual Merchandisers [1153], 15304 Rainbow 1, Ste. 201, Austin, TX 78734

Natl. Assn. for Visually Handicapped [16874], 22 W 21st St., 6th Fl., New York, NY 10010, (212)889-3141

Natl. Assn. of Vocational Educ. Special Needs Personnel - Defunct.

Natl. Assn. of Vocational Home Economics Teachers - Address unknown since 2002.

Natl. Assn. of Vocational-Technical Education Communicators - Address unknown since 2002.

Natl. Assn. for Voluntary and Community Action [IO], Sheffield, United Kingdom

Natl. Assn. of Volunteer Programs in Local Govt. [6352], c/o Natl. Assn. of Counties, 440 First St. NW, Washington, DC 20001

Natl. Assn. of Volvo Owners - Defunct.

Natl. Assn. of Waste Material Producers - Defunct.

Natl. Assn. of Wastewater Transporters [3998], 336 Chestnut Ln., Ambler, PA 19002-1001, (215)643-6798

Natl. Assn. of Watch and Clock Collectors [22990], 514 Poplar St., Columbia, PA 17512-2124, (717)684-8261

Natl. Assn. of Water Companies [4010], 1725 K St. NW, Ste. 200, Washington, DC 20006, (202)833-8383

Natl. Assn. of Water Inst. Directors [★7836]

Natl. Assn. of Waterfront Employers [2609]

Natl. Assn. of Waterproofing and Structural Repair Contractors [645], c/o Claudia J. Clemons, Exec. Dir., 8015 Corporate Dr., Ste. A, Baltimore, MD 21236, (410)931-3332

Natl. Assn. of Webmasters [★2114]

Natl. Assn. of Webmasters [★IO]

Natl. Assn. of Wheat Growers [4309], 415 2nd St. NE, Washington, DC 20002-4993, (202)547-7800

Natl. Assn. of Wheat Weavers [22166], c/o Mary Thrower, Treas., 1299 Granite Rd., Minneapolis, KS 67467

National Association of Wheat Weavers [IO], Formoso, KS, United States

Natl. Assn. of Wholesale Butchers and Meat Merchants [IO], Bonn, Germany

Natl. Assn. of Wholesale Fur Cleaners - Defunct.

Natl. Assn. of Wholesale Independent Distributors [★3686]

Natl. Assn. of Wholesale Pie Bakers - Address unknown since 1995.

Natl. Assn. of Wholesaler-Distributors [4024], 1725 K St. NW, Ste. 300, Washington, DC 20006-1419, (202)872-0885

Natl. Assn. of Wholesalers [★4024]

Natl. Assn. of WIC Directors [★6262]

Natl. Assn. of Widows - England [IO], Coventry, United Kingdom

Natl. Assn. of Women Artists [9514], 80 5th Ave., Ste. 1405, New York, NY 10011, (212)675-1616

Natl. Assn. of Women Bus. Owners [744], 8405 Greensboro Dr., Ste. 800, McLean, VA 22102, (703)506-3268

A star before a book entry number signifies that the name is not listed separately, but is mentioned within the entry.

Natl. Assn. for Women in Careers - Address unknown since 2001.

Natl. Assn. of Women in Chambers of Commerce - Address unknown since 2004.

Natl. Assn. of Women in Constr. **[1041]**, 327 S Adams St., Fort Worth, TX 76104, (817)877-5551

Natl. Assn. of Women in Constr. **[IO]**, Fort Worth, TX, United States

Natl. Assn. of Women in Constr. - Australia **[IO]**, Broadway, Australia

Natl. Assn. of Women in Criminal Justice - Address unknown since 1995.

Natl. Assn. for Women in Education - Defunct.

Natl. Assn. of Women Govt. Contractors - Defunct.

Natl. Assn. of Women Highway Safety Leaders **[12971]**, c/o Suzanne M. Tye, PhD, Pres., 6513 Golf Village St., No. 1, St. Thomas, VI 00802, (340)777-6278

Natl. Assn. of Women in Horticulture - Defunct.

Natl. Assn. of Women Judges **[5907]**, 1341 Connecticut Ave. NW, Ste. 4.2, Washington, DC 20036, (202)393-0222

Natl. Assn. of Women and the Law **[IO]**, Ottawa, ON, Canada

Natl. Assn. of Women Law Enforcement Executives **[5989]**, 3 Dunham St., Carver, MA 02330, (781)789-9500

Natl. Assn. of Women Lawyers **[5514]**, Amer. Bar Center 15.2, 321 N Clark St., Chicago, IL 60610, (312)988-6186

Natl. Assn. of Women MBAs **[745]**, c/o Rice Univ., PO Box 2932, Houston, TX 77252

Natl. Assn. of Women Organizations in Uganda **[IO]**, Kampala, Uganda

Natl. Assn. of Women Pharmacists **[IO]**, London, United Kingdom

Natl. Assn. of Women Writers **[11183]**, 24165 IH-10 W, Ste. 217-637, San Antonio, TX 78257, (866)821-5829

Natl. Assn. of Women's Centers - Address unknown since 2001.

Natl. Assn. of Women's Gymnastic's Judges **[23477]**, c/o Carole Ide, Pres., 26 Country Club Ct., Hilton Head, SC 29926, (843)682-2652

Natl. Assn. for Women's Hea. **[16903]**, 300 W Adams St., Ste. 328, Chicago, IL 60606-5101, (312)786-1468

Natl. Assn. of Women's Yellow Pages **[★4053]**

Natl. Assn. of Woodskills **[★IO]**

Natl. Assn. of Woodworkers New Zealand **[IO]**, Christchurch, New Zealand

Natl. Assn. of Wool Mfrs. **[★3772]**

Natl. Assn. of Wool Producers **[IO]**, Covilha, Portugal

Natl. Assn. on Work and the Coll. Student **[★8996]**

Natl. Assn. of Workforce Boards **[12087]**, 4350 N Fairfax Dr., Ste. 220, Arlington, VA 22203, (703)778-7900

Natl. Assn. of Workforce Development Professionals **[12088]**, c/o Mr. Billy Wooten, Chm., 810 1st St. NE, Ste. 525, Washington, DC 20002-4282, (202)589-1790

Natl. Assn. of Working Women; 9 to 5, **[17512]**

Natl. Assn. of Writers in Educ. **[IO]**, York, United Kingdom

Natl. Assn. of Writing Instrument Distributors **[★3686]**

Natl. Assn. for Year-Round Educ. **[8282]**, PO Box 711386, San Diego, CA 92171-1386, (619)276-5296

Natl. Assn. of Yoruba Descendants in North America; Egbe Omo Yoruba: **[19289]**

Natl. Assn. of Young Asian Professionals **[★9623]**

Natl. Assn. for Young Writers - Defunct.

Natl. Assn. of Youth Clubs **[13498]**, c/o Natl. Assn. of Colored Women's Clubs, 1601 R St. NW, Washington, DC 20009, (202)667-4080

Natl. Assn. for Youth Drama **[IO]**, Dublin, Ireland

Natl. Assn. of Youth Orchestras **[IO]**, Edinburgh, United Kingdom

Natl. Assn. of Youth Theatres **[IO]**, Darlington, United Kingdom

Natl. Associations of Canoe Liveries and Outfitters **[★3650]**

Natl. Asthma Center **[★16361]**

National Asthma Center; Natl. Jewish Hospital/ **[★16361]**

Natl. Astrological Lib. **[★6488]**

Natl. Astrological Soc. - Defunct.

National Astronomy and Ionosphere Center **[★7622]**

Natl. At-Risk Educ. Assn. **[8327]**

Natl. Ataxia Found. **[15342]**, 2600 Fernbrook Ln., No. 119, Minneapolis, MN 55447, (763)553-0020

Natl. Athletic and Cultural Assn. of Ireland **[IO]**, Navan, Ireland

Natl. Athletic and Cycling Assn. **[★IO]**

Natl. Athletic Steering Comm. - Address unknown since 2002.

Natl. Athletic Trainers' Assn. **[23954]**, 2952 Stemmons Fwy., No. 200, Dallas, TX 75247-6196, (214)637-6282

Natl. Athletics Assn. of Zimbabwe **[IO]**, Harare, Zimbabwe

Natl. Attention Deficit Disorder Assn. **[15343]**, 15000 Commerce Pkwy., Ste. C, Mount Laurel, NJ 08054, (856)439-9099

Natl. Auctioneers Assn. **[326]**, 8880 Ballentine, Overland Park, KS 66214, (913)541-8084

Natl. Audio-Visual Assn. **[★331]**

Natl. Audio-Visual Assn. **[★IO]**

Natl. Audubon Soc. **[4422]**, 700 Broadway, New York, NY 10003, (212)979-3000

Natl. Aural Gp. **[★IO]**

Natl. Auricula and Primula Soc. **[IO]**, Loughborough, United Kingdom

Natl. Auricula and Primula Soc. Midland and West Sect. **[IO]**, Loughborough, United Kingdom

Natl. Australia Day Coun. **[IO]**, Parkes, Australia

Natl. Autism Assn. **[13727]**, 1330 W Schatz Rd., Nixa, MO 65714, (866)622-6733

Natl. Autism Hotline **[★13722]**

Natl. Autism Soc. of Malaysia **[IO]**, Kuala Lumpur, Malaysia

Natl. Autism Soc. of Sweden **[IO]**, Stockholm, Sweden

Natl. Autistic Soc. **[IO]**, London, United Kingdom

Natl. Auto Auction Assn. **[327]**, 5320 Spectrum Dr., Ste. D, Frederick, MD 21703, (301)696-0400

Natl. Auto Body Coun. **[363]**, PO Box 3007, Mechanicsville, VA 23116, (888)667-7433

Natl. Auto and Flat Glass Dealers Assn. **[★1732]**

Natl. Auto Racing Historical Soc. **[23082]**, 121 Mt. Vernon, Boston, MA 02108, (617)723-2661

Natl. Auto and Truck Wreckers Assn. **[★3988]**

Natl. Auto Wreckers Assn. **[★3988]**

Natl. Automated CH Assn. **[★486]**

Natl. Automatic Laundry and Cleaning Coun. **[★2402]**

Natl. Automatic Merchandising Assn. **[3971]**, 20 N Wacker Dr., Ste. 3500, Chicago, IL 60606-3102, (312)346-0370

Natl. Automatic Pistol Collectors Assn. **[21539]**, PO Box 15738, St. Louis, MO 63163, (314)638-6505

Natl. Automatic Sprinkler Assn. **[★3449]**

Natl. Automatic Sprinkler and Fire Control Assn. **[★3449]**

Natl. Automatic Vendors' Trade Assn. - Defunct.

Natl. Auto. Dealers Assn. **[420]**, 8400 Westpark Dr., McLean, VA 22102, (703)821-7000

Natl. Automobile Education Assn. - Defunct.

Natl. Auto. Theft Bur. **[★2224]**

Natl. Automobile Transporters Assn. - Address unknown since 2003.

Natl. Automotive Finance Assn. **[421]**, 7250 Parkway Dr., Ste. 510, Hanover, MD 21076-1343, (410)712-4036

Natl. Automotive Muffler Assn. - Defunct.

Natl. Automotive Parts Assn. **[394]**, 2999 Circle 75 Pkwy., Atlanta, GA 30339, (877)805-6272

Natl. Automotive Radiator Ser. Assn. **[422]**, 15000 Commerce Pkwy., Ste. C, Mount Laurel, NJ 08054, (856)439-1575

Natl. Automotive Technicians Educ. Found. **[7992]**, 101 Blue Seal Dr. SE, Ste. 101, Leesburg, VA 20175, (703)669-6650

Natl. Automotive and Truck Museum of U.S. **[10512]**, 1000 Gordon M. Buehrig Pl., Auburn, IN 46706, (260)925-9100

Natl. Autosound Challenge Assn. **[★1219]**

Natl. Autumn Leaf Collectors Club **[22078]**, PO Box 7929, Moreno Valley, CA 92552-7929, (951)653-6308

Natl. Auxiliary of Goodwill Indus. **[★11950]**

Natl. Aviation Club - Defunct.

Natl. Aviation Maintenance Coun. - Defunct.

Natl. Aviation and Space Educ. Alliance **[7994]**, 23 Nutmeg Dr., Enfield, CT 06082, (505)774-0029

Natl. Aviation Trades Assn. **[★160]**

Natl. Avionics Soc. - Address unknown since 1994.

Natl. Award and Trophy Mfrs. Assn. - Defunct.

Natl. Ayurvedic Medical Assn. **[13642]**, 620 Cabrillo Ave., Santa Cruz, CA 95065

National B-Body Owners Assn; Winged Warriors/ **[21820]**

Natl. Baby Care Coun. - Defunct.

Natl. Back Pain Assn. **[★IO]**

Natl. Bakery Suppliers Assn. - Address unknown since 1994.

Natl. Ballroom and Entertainment Assn. **[1317]**, c/o John Matter, Exec. Dir., 2799 Locust Rd., Decorah, IA 52101-7600, (563)382-3871

Natl. Ballroom Operators Assn. **[★1317]**

Natl. Band Assn. **[10660]**, PO Box 25136, Baton Rouge, LA 70894, (225)578-2259

Natl. Band and Choral Directors Hall of Fame **[★8926]**

Natl. Bandage and Medical Products Assn. **[★IO]**

Natl. Bankers Assn. **[492]**, 1513 P St. NW, Washington, DC 20005, (202)588-5432

Natl. Baptist Convention **[★19493]**

Natl. Baptist Convention, U.S.A. **[19493]**, World Center HQ, 1700 Baptist World Center Dr., Nashville, TN 37207, (615)228-6292

Natl. Baptist Deacons Convention of America - Address unknown since 2002.

Natl. Baptist Educational Convention **[★19493]**

Natl. Bar Assn. **[5515]**, 1225 11th St. NW, Washington, DC 20001, (202)842-3900

Natl. Bar Assn. **[★IO]**

Natl. Bar Assn. - Women Lawyers Div. - Address unknown since 1994.

Natl. Barbecue Assn. **[1542]**, 1306-A W Anderson Ln., Austin, TX 78757, (512)454-8626

Natl. Barber Career Center - Address unknown since 1995.

Natl. Bark Producers Assn. **[★1651]**

Natl. Bark and Soil Producers Assn. **[★1651]**

Natl. Barley Foods Coun. **[1751]**, 905 W Riverside, Ste. 501, Spokane, WA 99201, (509)456-4400

Natl. Barley Growers Assn. **[4663]**, c/o Dale Thorenson, 600 Pennsylvania Ave., Washington, DC 20003, (202)969-8900

Natl. Barrel and Drum Assn. **[★994]**

Natl. Barrel Horse Assn. **[23506]**, PO Box 1988, Augusta, GA 30903-1988, (706)722-7223

Natl. Barristers' Wives **[★5509]**

Natl. Baseball Cong. **[23117]**, PO Box 1420, Wichita, KS 67201, (316)267-3372

Natl. Baseball Fan Assn. - Address unknown since 1999.

Natl. Baseball Fed. **[★23115]**

Natl. Baseball Hall of Fame and Museum **[23118]**, 25 Main St., Cooperstown, NY 13326, (607)547-7200

Natl. Basketball Assn. **[23134]**, 645 5th Ave., 10th Fl., New York, NY 10022, (212)826-7000

Natl. Basketball Athletic Trainers Assn. **[23135]**, c/o Rollin Mallernee, Gen. Counsel, 400 Colony Sq., Ste. 1750, Atlanta, GA 30361, (404)892-8919

Natl. Basketball League **[★23134]**

Natl. Basketball Players Assn. **[24192]**, 310 Lenox Ave., New York, NY 10027, (212)655-0880

Natl. Basketball Referees Assn. - Address unknown since 2002.

Natl. Basketball Trainers Assn. **[★23135]**

Natl. Basketry Org. **[22167]**, 475 Rivercane Rd., Brasstown, NC 28902, (828)837-1280

Natl. Bath, Bed and Linen Assn. - Address unknown since 1994.

Natl. Baton Twirling Assn. **[★23142]**

Natl. Baton Twirling Assn. Intl. **[23142]**, PO Box 266, Janesville, WI 53547, (608)754-2238

Natl. Battery Manufacturers Assn. **[★380]**

Natl. Battery Manufacturers Assn. **[★IO]**

Natl. Beagle Club of Am. **[22314]**, c/o Dr. Emily Southgate, Sec., PO Box 642, Middleburg, VA 20118

Reference to "IO" in place of a book number signifies that the association may be found in the 45th edition of International Organizations.

Natl. Beauty and Barber Mfrs. Assn. [★1086]
Natl. Beauty Career Center - Address unknown since 1994.
Natl. Beauty Culturists' League [1084], 25 Logan Cir. NW, Washington, DC 20005-3725, (202)332-2695
Natl. Beauty Salon Chain Assn. [★1081]
Natl. Beauty Salon Chain Assn. [★IO]
Natl. Bed-and-Breakfast Assn. [1954], PO Box 332, Norwalk, CT 06852, (203)847-6196
Natl. Bed Fed. [IO], Skipton, United Kingdom
Natl. Beef Assn. [IO], Hexham, United Kingdom
Natl. Beef Cong. - Defunct.
Natl. Beef Coun. [★5023]
Natl. Beefmaster Assn. - Address unknown since 1999.
Natl. Beekeepers Assn. of New Zealand [IO], Otaki, New Zealand
Natl. Beep Baseball Assn. [23350], c/o Stephen Guerra, Sec., 60 East Ave., Freeport, NY 11520, (516)551-2148
Natl. Beer Wholesalers Assn. [207], 1101 King St., Ste. 600, Alexandria, VA 22314-2944, (703)683-4300
Natl. Beer Wholesalers' Assn. of Am. [★207]
Natl. Begonia Soc. [IO], Rutland, United Kingdom
Natl. Belgian Hare Club of America - Defunct.
Natl. Bench Rest Shooters Assn. [23721], c/o Mrs. Pat Ferrell, Bus. Mgr., 2835 Guilford Ln., Oklahoma City, OK 73120-4404, (405)842-9585
Natl. Benevolent Assn. [★13177]
Natl. Benevolent Assn. of the Christian Church [13177], 149 Weldon Pkwy., Ste. 115, Maryland Heights, MO 63043-3103, (314)993-9000
Natl. Beta Club [24592], 151 Beta Club Way, Spartanburg, SC 29306-3012, (800)845-8281
Natl. Better Bus. Bur. [★17309]
Natl. Better Bus. Bur. [★IO]
Natl. Beverage Dispensing Equip. Assn. [★IO]
Natl. Beverage Dispensing Equip. Assn. [★507]
Natl. Beverage Packaging Assn. [★508]
Natl. Bible Assn. [20205], 405 Lexington Ave., 26th Fl., New York, NY 10174, (212)907-6427
Natl. Bicycle Dealers Assn. [3645], 777 W 19th St., Ste. O, Costa Mesa, CA 92627, (949)722-6909
Natl. Bicycle League [23313], 3958 Brown Park Dr., Ste. D, Hilliard, OH 43026-1160, (614)777-1625
Natl. Bicycle Tour Directors Assn. [23314], PO Box 155, Lanesboro, MN 55949, (507)467-3321
Natl. Biographical Assn. - Defunct.
Natl. Biographysics Conf. [★6612]
Natl. Biosolids Partnership [5096], 601 Wythe St., Alexandria, VA 22314, (703)684-2400
Natl. Biplane Assn. [21465], PO Box 470350, Tulsa, OK 74147-0350, (918)665-0755
Natl. Bird Dog Challenge Assn. [22315], 32 County Rd., 30 SW, Montrose, MN 55363, (866)909-THTV
Natl. Bird-Feeding Soc. - Defunct.
Natl. Birman Fanciers [21913], c/o Joann Lamb, Sec., 7 Cornwall Ct., Hamburg, NJ 07419
Natl. Birth Defects Prevention Network [13757], c/o Prof. Lowell E. Sever, PhD, Convener, Intl. and Family Hea., Univ. of Texas School of Public Hea., 1200 Herman Pressler, Ste. E1023, Houston, TX 77030, (404)498-3918
Natl. Bison Assn. [4139], 8690 Wolff Ct., No. 200, Westminster, CO 80031, (303)292-2833
Natl. Bituminous Concrete Assn. [★641]
Natl. Black Alcoholism and Addiction Coun. [13265], 5104 N Orange Blossom Trail, Ste. 111, Orlando, FL 32810-1013, (407)532-2747
Natl. Black Alcoholism Coun. [★13265]
Natl. Black Alliance for Graduate Level Education - Defunct.
Natl. Black Anti-War Anti-Draft Union - Address unknown since 1995.
Natl. Black Assn. for Speech-Language and Hearing [16448], 800 Perry Hwy., Ste. 3, Pittsburgh, PA 15229, (412)366-1177
Natl. Black on Black Love Campaign [11842], 9535 S Cottage Grove Ave., Chicago, IL 60628-1508, (773)978-0868
Natl. Black Bridal Assn. [535], c/o Dion Magee, Pres., 3401 Ramey Dr., Arlington, TX 76014, (817)784-8515
Natl. Black Business Alliance - Address unknown since 2003.

Natl. Black Bus. Coun. [170], 600 Corporate Pointe, Ste. 1010, Culver City, CA 90230, (310)568-5000
Natl. Black Catholic Clergy Caucus [19669], 440 W 36th St., New York, NY 10018, (212)868-1847
Natl. Black Catholic Cong. [19670], 320 Cathedral St., Baltimore, MD 21201, (410)547-8496
Natl. Black Catholic Seminarians Assn. - Address unknown since 1999.
Natl. Black Caucus of Local Elected Officials [6127], c/o Natl. League of Cities, 1301 Pennsylvania Ave. NW, Washington, DC 20004-1763, (202)626-3169
Natl. Black Caucus of State Legislators [6281], 444 N Capitol St. NW, Ste. 622, Washington, DC 20001, (202)624-5457
Natl. Black Chamber of Commerce [24250], 1350 Connecticut Ave. NW, Ste. 405, Washington, DC 20036, (202)466-6888
Natl. Black Child Development Inst. [11542], 1313 L St. NW, Ste. 110, Washington, DC 20005-4110, (202)833-2220
Natl. Black Coalition of Fed. Aviation Employees [5541], 77 Southgate Rd., Valley Stream, NY 11581, (516)245-3104
Natl. Black Coll. Alumni Hall of Fame Found. [18911], 230 Peachtree St., No. 530, Atlanta, GA 30303, (404)524-1106
Natl. Black Communicators Soc. - Defunct.
Natl. Black Consumers Union [IO], Johannesburg, Republic of South Africa
Natl. Black Deaf Advocates [17418], c/o Cory L. Parker, Sec., PO Box 1126, Asheville, NC 28802-1126
Natl. Black Evangelical Assn. - Defunct.
Natl. Black Farmers Assn. [12189], PO Box 74433, Richmond, VA 23236, (434)848-1592
Natl. Black Feminist Org. - Address unknown since 1995.
Natl. Black Graduate Student Assn. [18869], 2400 6th St. NW, Washington, DC 20059, (800)471-4102
Natl. Black Health Planners Assn. - Address unknown since 1991.
Natl. Black Herstory Task Force [11089], PO Box 55021, Atlanta, GA 30308, (770)369-2700
Natl. Black Home Educators [8519], c/o Eric Burges, Co-Founder, 13434 Plank Rd., PMB 110, Baker, LA 70714
Natl. Black Home Educators Rsrc. Assn. [★8519]
Natl. Black Justice Coalition [18643], 700 12th St. NW, Ste. 700, Washington, DC 20005, (202)349-3756
Natl. Black Langshan Club [★5105]
Natl. Black Law Students Assn. [8771], 1225 11th St. NW, Washington, DC 20001-4217, (202)210-6556
Natl. Black Lay Catholic Caucus - Address unknown since 1995.
Natl. Black Leadership Initiative on Cancer [13847], c/o Robin Mitchell, Res. Specialist, 311 SPWH m/c 922, 2121 W Taylor St., Chicago, IL 60612, (312)996-8046
Natl. Black Leadership Roundtable - Address unknown since 2006.
Natl. Black Liberation Alliance - Address unknown since 1995.
Natl. Black MBA Assn. [8035], 180 N Michigan Ave., Ste. 1400, Chicago, IL 60601, (312)236-2622
Natl. Black McDonald's Operators Assn. [1955], PO Box 820668, South Florida, FL 33082-0668, (954)389-4487
Natl. Black Media Coalition - Address unknown since 2002.
Natl. Black Meeting Planners Coalition [★2687]
Natl. Black Music Caucus of the Music Educators Natl. Conf. [★8922]
Natl. Black Nurses Assn. [15505], 8630 Fenton St., Ste. 330, Silver Spring, MD 20910-3803, (301)589-3200
Natl. Black Organizing Comm. - Defunct.
Natl. Black Owned Broadcasters Assn. [★568]
Natl. Black Police Assn. [5990], 3251 Mt. Pleasant St. NW, Washington, DC 20010-2103, (202)986-2070
Natl. Black Police Assn. - UK [IO], London, United Kingdom

Natl. Black Programming Consortium [9764], 68 E 131st St., 7th Fl., New York, NY 10037, (212)234-8200
Natl. Black Public Relations Soc. [3194], 4929 Wilshire Blvd., Ste. 245, Los Angeles, CA 90010, (323)857-1171
Natl. Black Republican Assn. [18524], 601 Pennsylvania Ave. NW, Ste. 900-S, Washington, DC 20004, (202)638-6940
Natl. Black Republican Coun. - Address unknown since 1999.
Natl. Black Science Students Org. - Address unknown since 1995.
Natl. Black Sisters' Conf. [19671], c/o Sister Patricia Chappell, Pres., 3027 4th St. NE, Washington, DC 20017, (202)529-9250
Natl. Black State Troopers Coalition [5430], c/o Kim Hoffman-Davis, Treas., PO Box 2661, Joliet, IL 60434-2661, (866)363-0467
Natl. Black Survival Fund [12780], PO Box 3005, Lafayette, LA 70502-3005, (337)942-2392
Natl. Black United Fed. of Charities [16943], 40 Clinton St., 5th Fl., Newark, NJ 07102, (973)648-3767
Natl. Black United Front - Address unknown since 1995.
Natl. Black United Fund [12656], 40 Clinton St., Newark, NJ 07102, (973)643-5122
Natl. Black Veterans Org. - Defunct.
Natl. Black Women's Consciousness Raising Assn. [17551], 1906 N Charles St., Baltimore, MD 21218, (410)727-8900
Natl. Black Women's Hea. Proj. [★16895]
Natl. Black Women's Political Leadership Caucus - Address unknown since 2001.
Natl. Black Youth Leadership Coun. - Address unknown since 2003.
Natl. Blacksmiths and Weldors Assn. [524], c/o James E. Holman, Info. Off., PO Box 123, Arnold, NE 69120, (308)848-2913
Natl. Blind Children's Soc. [IO], Birmingham, United Kingdom
National Blindness Info. Center [★16877]
Natl. Block and Bridle Club [24401], c/o Dr. Cindy Wood, Natl. Pres., Dept. of Animal and Poultry Sciences, 3400 Litton Reaves Hall, 0306, Virginia Tech, Blacksburg, VA 24061, (540)231-6936
Natl. Blonde D'Aquitaine Found. [★4215]
Natl. Blood Found. [13764], 8101 Glenbrook Rd., Bethesda, MD 20814-2749, (301)215-6552
Natl. Blue Crab Industry Assn. [3495]
Natl. Bd. of Accreditation in Concrete Construction - Defunct.
Natl. Bd. of Boiler and Pressure Vessel Inspectors [5824], 1055 Crupper Ave., Columbus, OH 43229-1183, (614)888-8320
Natl. Bd. for Cardiopulmonary Credentialing [★13898]
Natl. Bd. for Cardiopulmonary Credentialing [★IO]
Natl. Bd. for Cardiovascular and Pulmonary Credentialing [★IO]
Natl. Bd. for Cardiovascular and Pulmonary Credentialing [★13898]
Natl. Bd. of Cardiovascular Tech. [★13898]
Natl. Bd. of Cardiovascular Tech. [★IO]
Natl. Bd. for Certification in Dental Lab. Tech. [14172], 325 John Knox Rd., No. L103, Tallahassee, FL 32303, (850)205-5627
Natl. Bd. for Certification in Dental Tech. [14173], 325 John Knox Rd., No. L103, Tallahassee, FL 32303, (850)205-5627
Natl. Bd. for Certification in Occupational Therapy [16625], The Eugene B. Casey Bldg., 800 S Frederick Ave., Ste. 200, Gaithersburg, MD 20877-4150, (301)990-7979
Natl. Bd. for Certification of Orthopaedic Technologists [15774], 4736 Onondaga Blvd., No. 166, Syracuse, NY 13219, (866)466-2268
Natl. Bd. for Certified Clinical Hypnotherapists [14925], 1110 Fidler Ln., Ste. 1218, Silver Spring, MD 20910, (301)608-0123
Natl. Bd. for Certified Counselors [★11828]
Natl. Bd. for Certified Counselors and Affiliates [11828], 3 Terrace Way, Greensboro, NC 27403-3660, (336)547-0607
Natl. Bd. of Chiropractic Examiners [14010], 901 54th Ave., Greeley, CO 80634, (970)356-9100

A star before a book entry number signifies that the name is not listed separately, but is mentioned within the entry.

Natl. Bd. of the Coat and Suit Industry - Defunct.

National Bd. Examination Comm. [★16755]

Natl. Bd. of Examiners in Optometry [15722], 200 S Coll. St., No. 1920, Charlotte, NC 28202, (704)332-9565

Natl. Bd. of Examiners for Osteopathic Physicians and Surgeons [★15812]

Natl. Bd. of the Fac. Mgt. Assn. of Australia [IO], Carlton, Australia

Natl. Bd. of Fire Underwriters [★2139]

Natl. Board of Forensic Chiropractors [14011]

Natl. Bd. of Hypnosis Educ. & Certification [★14926]

Natl. Bd. of Medical Examiners [15095], 3750 Market St., Philadelphia, PA 19104-3102, (215)590-9500

Natl. Bd. of Naturopathic Examiners - Address unknown since 2006.

Natl. Bd. of Osteopathic Medical Examiners [15812], 8765 W Higgins Rd., Ste. 200, Chicago, IL 60631-4174, (773)714-0622

Natl. Bd. of Pediatric Nurse Practitioners and Associates [★15522]

Natl. Bd. of Physical Therapy Examiners - Address unknown since 1988.

Natl. Bd. of Podiatric Medical Examiners [16046], PO Box 510, Bellefonte, PA 16823, (814)357-0487

Natl. Bd. of Podiatry Examiners [★16046]

Natl. Bd. for Professional Teaching Standards [9225], 1525 Wilson Blvd., Ste. 500, Arlington, VA 22209, (703)465-2700

Natl. Bd. for the Promotion of Rifle Practice - Address unknown since 1999.

Natl. Bd. for Respiratory Care [16626], 18000 W 105th St., Olathe, KS 66061-7543, (913)895-4900

Natl. Bd. for Respiratory Therapy [★16626]

Natl. Bd. for the Retail Trade [IO], The Hague, Netherlands

Natl. Bd. of Rev. of Motion Pictures [9941], 40 W 37th St., Ste. 501, New York, NY 10018, (212)465-9166

Natl. Bd. of Surgical Tech. and Surgical Assisting [13534], 6 W Dry Creek Cir., Ste. 100, Littleton, CO 80120, (800)707-0057

Natl. Bd. of Trial Advocacy [6333], 200 Stonewall Blvd., Ste. 1, Wrentham, MA 02093-2210, (508)384-6565

Natl. Boat Assn. - Address unknown since 1995.

Natl. Boating Fed. [23201], PO Box 4111, Annapolis, MD 21403-6111

Natl. Boating Safety Advisory Coun. [5546], c/o Jeffrey N. Hoedt, Exec. Dir., U.S. Coast Guard G-0PB-1, Washington, DC 20593-0001, (202)267-0950

Natl. Bobsled Fed. [★23767]

Natl. Bone Marrow Donor Registry [★14292]

Natl. Bone Marrow Donor Registry [★IO]

Natl. Bone Marrow Transplant Link [16676], 20411 W 12 Mile Rd., Ste. 108, Southfield, MI 48076, (248)358-1886

Natl. Book Comm. - Defunct.

Natl. Book Critics Circle [9753], 360 Park Ave. S, New York, NY 10010, (973)744-9045

Natl. Book Development Coun. of Singapore [IO], Singapore, Singapore

Natl. Book Trust India [IO], New Delhi, India

Natl. Bookkeepers' Soc. - Address unknown since 1995.

Natl. Border Patrol Coun. [24123], PO Box 678, Campo, CA 91906, (619)478-5145

Natl. Botanical Inst. [★IO]

Natl. Bottlers Assn. [★503]

Natl. Bottlers Protective Assn. [★503]

Natl. Bowhunter Educ. Found. [23053], PO Box 180757, Fort Smith, AR 72918, (479)649-9036

The Natl. Bowling Assn. [23252], c/o Ms. Annette R. Samuel, Exec. Sec.-Treas., 9944 Reading Rd., Cincinnati, OH 45241-3106, (513)769-1985

Natl. Bowling Coun. - Defunct.

Natl. Bowling Pro Shop and Instructors Assn. [★531]

Natl. Bowling Writer's Assn. [★3101]

Natl. Brachial Plexus-Erb's Palsy Assn. [14277]

Natl. Braille Assn. [16875], 3 Townline Cir., Rochester, NY 14623-2513, (585)427-8260

Natl. Braille Club [★16875]

Natl. Braille Press [16876], 88 St. Stephen St., Boston, MA 02115-4302, (617)266-6160

Natl. Brain Injury Res. Found. - Address unknown since 1999.

Natl. Brain Tumor Found. [15344], 22 Battery St., Ste. 612, San Francisco, CA 94111-5520, (415)834-9970

Natl. Brands Soft Drinks Inst. - Defunct.

Natl. Breast Cancer Centre [IO], Camperdown, Australia

Natl. Breast Cancer Coalition [13848], 1101 17th St. NW, Ste. 1300, Washington, DC 20036, (202)296-7477

Natl. Breeders and Fanciers Assn. [★5139]

Natl. Bridal Ser. [536], 1004 W Thompson St., Ste. 205, Richmond, VA 23230, (804)342-0055

Natl. Broadcast Assn. for Community Affairs [572]

Natl. Broadcast Editorial Assn. [★3136]

Natl. Broadcasting Soc. - Alpha Epsilon Rho [24411], c/o Jim Wilson, Exec. Dir., PO Box 4206, Chesterfield, MO 63006, (314)469-1943

Natl. Broiler Assn. [★5111]

Natl. Broiler Coun. [★5111]

Natl. Broom Corn and Supply Dealers Assn. - Defunct.

Natl. Brotherhood of Packinghouse and Industrial Workers - Address unknown since 2001.

Natl. Brotherhood of Skiers [23752], 1525 E 53rd St., Ste. 418, Chicago, IL 60615, (773)955-4100

Natl. Brownfield Assn. [3191], 5440 N Cumberland Ave., Ste. 155, Chicago, IL 60656, (773)714-0407

Natl. Buck Jones Rangers of America - Address unknown since 2007.

Natl. Bucker Club - Defunct.

Natl. Bucking Bull Assn. [23687], PO Box 577, Whitesboro, TX 76273, (903)564-5649

Natl. Budget and Consultation Comm. - Defunct.

Natl. Buffalo Assn. [★4139]

Natl. Buffalo Assn. Juniors - Defunct.

Natl. Builders' Hardware Assn. [★1821]

Natl. Builders' Hardware Assn. [★IO]

Natl. Building Granite Quarries Assn. [3697], 1220 L St. NW, Ste. 100-167, Washington, DC 20005, (800)557-2848

Natl. Building Material Distributors Assn. [★658]

Natl. Building Museum [6477], 401 F St. NW, Washington, DC 20001, (202)272-2448

Natl. Building Products Assn. - Defunct.

Natl. Bulk Vendors Assn. [3972], 191 N Wacker Dr., Ste. 1800, Chicago, IL 60606-1615, (312)521-2400

Natl. Bur. of Certified Consultants [2505], c/o Peter A. Land Associates, 4210 Lomac St., Montgomery, AL 36106, (334)271-2639

Natl. Bur. of Document Examiners - Defunct.

Natl. Bur. of Economic Res. [6887], 1050 Massachusetts Ave., Cambridge, MA 02138, (617)868-3900

Natl. Bur. of Federated Jewish Women's Orgs. - Address unknown since 1990.

Natl. Bur. of Professional Mgt. Consultants [★2505]

Natl. Burglar and Fire Alarm Assn. [3538], 2300 Valley View Ln., Ste. 230, Irving, TX 75062, (214)260-5970

Natl. Burlap Bag Dealers Assn. [★999]

Natl. Burn Fed. - Defunct.

Natl. Burn Information Exchange - Defunct.

Natl. Burn Victim Found. [13784]

Natl. Bus Traffic Assn. [3878], 700 13th St. NW, Ste. 575, Washington, DC 20005-5923, (202)898-2700

Natl. Bus. Aircraft Assn. [★162]

Natl. Bus. Assn. [3619], PO Box 700728, Dallas, TX 75370, (972)458-0900

Natl. Bus. Aviation Assn. [162], 1200 18th St. NW, Ste. 400, Washington, DC 20036-2527, (202)783-9000

Natl. Business Career Center - Defunct.

Natl. Bus. Circulation Assn. [★3242]

Natl. Bus. Coalition on Hea. [14580], 1015 18th St. NW, Ste. 730, Washington, DC 20036-5214, (202)775-9300

Natl. Business Consortium for the Gifted and Talented - Defunct.

Natl. Bus. and Disability Coun. [12089], 201 I.U. Willets Rd., Albertson, NY 11507, (516)465-1516

Natl. Bus. Educ. Assn. [8036], 1914 Assn. Dr., Reston, VA 20191-1596, (703)860-8300

Natl. Bus. Forms Assn. [★3679]

Natl. Bus. Incubation Assn. [746], 20 E Circle Dr., No. 37198, Athens, OH 45701-3571, (740)593-4331

Natl. Bus. Initiative [IO], Auckland Park, Republic of South Africa

Natl. Business Law Coun. - Defunct.

Natl. Business League [2767]

Natl. Bus. Officers Assn. [8009], c/o Sarah P. Daignault, Exec. Dir., PO Box 4576, Boulder, CO 80306-4576, (720)564-0475

Natl. Bus. Owners Assn. [3620], PO Box 111, Stuart, VA 24171-0111, (276)251-7500

Natl. Bus. Publications [★3201]

Natl. Bus. Teachers Assn. [★8036]

Natl. Bus. Travel Assn. [3929], 110 N Royal St., 4th Fl., Alexandria, VA 22314, (703)684-0836

Natl. Businessmen's Coun. - Defunct.

Natl. Businesswomen's Leadership Assn. - Defunct.

Natl. Butterfly Assn. [23202], c/o Windwards Boatworks, 7005 Hubbard Ave., Middleton, WI 53562, (608)831-8771

Natl. Button Soc. [22079], c/o Lois Pool, Sec., 2733 Juno Pl., Akron, OH 44333-4137

Natl. Buy-Black Campaign [★2761]

Natl. C Scow Sailing Assn. [23203], PO Box 473, Pewaukee, WI 53072

National C Scow Sailing Association [IO], Pewaukee, WI, United States

Natl. Cable and Telecommunications Assn. [573], 25 Massachusetts Ave. NW, Ste. 100, Washington, DC 20001, (202)222-2300

Natl. Cable TV Assn. [★573]

Natl. Cable TV Assn. [IO], Mexico City, Mexico

Natl. Cable TV Cooperative [781], 11200 Corporate Ave., Lenexa, KS 66219-1392, (913)599-5900

Natl. Cable TV Inst. [574], 9697 E Mineral Ave., Centennial, CO 80112, (303)797-9393

Natl. Cage Bird Show [21851], c/o Bonnie Williams-Cain, Pres., 3866 Orders Rd., Grove City, OH 43123, (614)871-5445

Natl. Cage Bird Week Assn. - Defunct.

Natl. Cambodia Crisis Comm. - Defunct.

Natl. Cambridge Collectors [22561], PO Box 416, Cambridge, OH 43725-0416, (740)432-4245

Natl. Camp Assn. [23277], PO Box 5371, New York, NY 10185-5371, (212)645-0653

Natl. Campaign for Freedom of Expression - Defunct.

Natl. Campaign for a Peace Tax Fund [18712], 2121 Decatur Pl. NW, Washington, DC 20008, (202)483-3751

Natl. Campaign to Prevent Teen Pregnancy [13499], 1776 Massachusetts Ave. NW, Ste. 200, Washington, DC 20036, (202)478-8500

Natl. Campaign for Public School Improvement; Proj. Appleseed: The [8332]

Natl. Campaign for Radioactive Waste Safety [18130], c/o Southwest Res. and Info. Center, PO Box 4524, Albuquerque, NM 87106, (505)262-1862

Natl. Campaign for Real Nursery Educ. [IO], London, United Kingdom

Natl. Campaign to Save the ABM Treaty - Defunct.

Natl. Campaign to Stop the MX - Defunct.

Natl. Campaign for a World Peace Tax Fund [★18712]

Natl. Campers and Hikers Assn. [★23271]

Natl. Campground Owners Assn. [★3357]

Natl. Camping Assn. [★23277]

Natl. Campus Antiwar Network - Address unknown since 2008.

Natl. Campus Ministry Assn. [19933], c/o Bob Turner, Admin. Off., PO Box 101, Paoli, IN 47454, (502)314-5445

Natl. Cancer Care Found. [★13803]

Natl. Cancer Center [15650], 88 Sunnyside Blvd., Ste. 307, Plainview, NY 11803-1507, (516)349-0610

Natl. Cancer Coun. [IO], Kuala Lumpur, Malaysia

Natl. Cancer Cytology Center [★15650]

Natl. Cancer Found. [★13803]

National Cancer Institute [★13807]

National Cancer Inst. [★15637]

Natl. Cancer Inst. of Canada [IO], Toronto, ON, Canada

Natl. Cancer Registrars Assn. [15651], 1340 Braddock Pl., Ste. 203, Alexandria, VA 22314, (703)299-6640

Reference to "IO" in place of a book number signifies that the association may be found in the 45th edition of International Organizations.

Natl. Candle Assn. [2268], 1156 15th St., Ste. 900, Washington, DC 20005, (202)393-2210

Natl. Candlewick Collector's Club - Defunct.

Natl. Candy Brokers Assn. - Address unknown since 2002.

Natl. Candy Wholesalers Assn. [★1500]

Natl. Canine Defence League [★IO]

Natl. Canned Tomato Coun. - Defunct.

Natl. Canvas Goods Mfrs. Assn. [★3787]

Natl. Canvas Goods Mfrs. Assn. [★IO]

Natl. Cap and Cloth Hat Inst. - Address unknown since 1995.

Natl. Cap and Patch Assn. [22080]

Natl. Capital FreeNet [IO], Ottawa, ON, Canada

Natl. Capital Historical Museum of Trans. [10133], c/o Natl. Capital Trolley Museum, 1313 Bonifant Rd., Colesville, MD 20905-5955, (301)384-6088

Natl. Capital Speakers Assn. [10902], 2020 Pennsylvania Ave. NW, Washington, DC 20006, (301)459-0738

National Capital Trolley Museum [★10133]

Natl. Capon Coun. - Defunct.

Natl. Captioning Inst. [14769], 1900 Gallows Rd., Ste. 3000, Vienna, VA 22182, (703)917-7600

Natl. Captive Nations Comm. [18088]

Natl. Captive Nations Comm. [IO], Washington, DC, United States

Natl. Caravan Coun. [IO], Aldershot, United Kingdom

Natl. Career Center - Address unknown since 1988.

Natl. Career Development Assn. [12090], 305 N Beech Cir., Broken Arrow, OK 74012, (918)663-7060

Natl. Career Information Center - Defunct.

Natl. Cargo Bur. [3576], 17 Battery Pl., Ste. 1232, New York, NY 10004-1110, (212)785-8300

Natl. Caricaturist Network [1318], c/o Tracey Iverson, Mgr., 922 W Dayton St., Ferndale, MI 48220

Natl. Carl Schurz Assn. - Defunct.

Natl. Carousel Assn. [21897], c/o Barbara May, Exec. Sec., PO Box 19039, Baltimore, MD 21284-9039

Natl. Carousel Roundtable [★21897]

Natl. Carpenters Craft Bd. - Defunct.

Natl. Cartoonists Soc. [9515], 341 N Maitland Ave., Ste. 130, Maitland, FL 32751, (407)647-8839

Natl. Carvers Museum Found. - Defunct.

Natl. Carwash Coun. [★416]

Natl. Carwash Coun. [★IO]

Natl. CASA Assn. [★11636]

Natl. Cashmere Assn. - Defunct.

Natl. Casket Retailers Assn. [2786], c/o Dean Magliocca, Chm., 403 E Hallandale Beach Blvd., Hallandale, FL 33009, (954)454-7474

Natl. Cast Iron Implement Seat Collectors [★22607]

Natl. Castings Coun. - Defunct.

Natl. Cat Protection Soc. [11434], 6904 W Coast Hwy., Newport Beach, CA 92663-1306, (949)650-1232

Natl. Catalog Managers Assn. [3134], c/o Automotive Aftermarket Indus. Assn., 7101 Wisconsin Ave., Ste. 1300, Bethesda, MD 20814-3415, (301)654-6664

Natl. Catfishing Assn. - Address unknown since 2006.

Natl. Cathedral Assn. [19903], Washington Natl. Cathedral, 3101 Wisconsin Ave. NW, Washington, DC 20016, (202)537-6200

Natl. Catholic Action Coalition - Defunct.

Natl. Catholic AIDS Network [13579], 10 E Pearson St., 4th Fl., Chicago, IL 60611-2052, (312)915-7790

Natl. Catholic Assn. for Communicators; UNDA U.S.A. [★9761]

Natl. Catholic Band Assn. [10661], c/o John Badsing, Sec.-Treas., 3334 N Normandy Ave., Chicago, IL 60634-3716

Natl. Catholic Bandmasters' Assn. [★10661]

Natl. Catholic Business Education Assn. - Address unknown since 1999.

Natl. Catholic Camping - Defunct.

National Catholic Cemetery Conf. [★2776]

Natl. Catholic Coalition for Responsible Investment - Address unknown since 2001.

Natl. Catholic Coll. Admission Assn. [19672], 10 W Hubbard 2C, Chicago, IL 60610, (312)321-2726

Natl. Catholic Comm. on Scouting [13001], PO Box 152079, Irving, TX 75015-2079, (972)580-2114

Natl. Catholic Community Service - Defunct.

Natl. Catholic Conf. of Airport Chaplains [19754], c/o U.S. Conf. of Catholic Bishops, 3211 4th St. NE, Washington, DC 20017-1194, (202)541-3352

Natl. Catholic Conf. on Family Life [★12167]

Natl. Catholic Conf. for Interracial Justice [17133], c/o The White House, 1600 Pennsylvania Ave. NW, Washington, DC 20500, (202)456-1414

Natl. Catholic Conf. for Seafarers - Address unknown since 1995.

Natl. Catholic Conf. for Total Stewardship [19673], 405 Pinella Cir., No. 539, Palm Beach Gardens, FL 33410, (561)248-9431

Natl. Catholic Coun. on Alcoholism and Related Drug Problems [13266], 1601 Joslyn Rd., Lake Orion, MI 48360, (248)391-4445

National Catholic Council on Alcoholism and Related Drug Problems [IO], Lake Orion, MI, United States

Natl. Catholic Development and Caritas [IO], Freetown, Sierra Leone

Natl. Catholic Development Conf. [19674], 86 Front St., Hempstead, NY 11550-3667, (516)481-6000

Natl. Catholic Educ. Assn; Coll. and Univ. Dept. of the [★8051]

Natl. Catholic Educational Assn. [8059], 1077 30th St. NW, Ste. 100, Washington, DC 20007, (202)337-6232

Natl. Catholic Educational Exhibitors [1347], 2621 Dryden Rd., Ste. 300, Dayton, OH 45439, (937)293-1415

Natl. Catholic Forensic League [9156], c/o Richard Gaudette, Exec. Sec.-Treas., 21 Nancy Rd., Milford, MA 01757

Natl. Catholic Guidance Conf. [★8166]

Natl. Catholic Music Educators Assn. [★8920]

Natl. Catholic News Ser. [★3103]

Natl. Catholic Off. for the Deaf [19675], 7202 Buchanan St., Landover Hills, MD 20784-2236, (301)577-1684

Natl. Catholic Off. for Persons With Disabilities [★19676]

Natl. Catholic Partnership on Disability [19676], 415 Michigan Ave. NE, Ste. 95, Washington, DC 20017-4501, (202)529-2933

Natl. Catholic Pharmacists Guild of the U.S. [15945]

Natl. Catholic Preschool Assn. - Defunct.

Natl. Catholic Resettlement Coun. - Defunct.

Natl. Catholic Rural Life Conf. [19677], 4625 Beaver Ave., Des Moines, IA 50310-2145, (515)270-2634

National Catholic Rural Life Conference [IO], Des Moines, IA, United States

Natl. Catholic Social Action Conf. - Defunct.

Natl. Catholic Soc. for Animal Welfare [★11419]

Natl. Catholic Soc. for Animal Welfare [★IO]

Natl. Catholic Soc. of Foresters [19007], 320 S School St., Mount Prospect, IL 60056-3334, (800)344-6273

Natl. Catholic Stewardship Coun. [★19642]

Natl. Catholic Stewardship Coun. [★IO]

Natl. Catholic Vocation Coun. - Defunct.

Natl. Catholic Women's Union [19678], c/o Social Justice Rev., 3835 Westminster Pl., St. Louis, MO 63108-3409, (314)371-1653

Natl. Cattlemen's Beef Assn. [5023], 9110 E Nichols Ave., Ste. 300, Centennial, CO 80112, (303)694-0305

Natl. Caucus on the Black Aged [★11306]

Natl. Caucus and Center on Black Aged [11306], 1220 L St. NW, Ste. 800, Washington, DC 20005, (202)637-8400

Natl. Caucus of Gay and Lesbian Counselors [★12216]

Natl. Caves Assn. [1319], PO Box 280, Park City, KY 42160, (270)749-2228

Natl. Cavity Insulation Assn. [★IO]

Natl. Cedar Chest Assn. - Defunct.

Natl. Census of the Deaf - Defunct.

Natl. Center for Administrative Justice - Defunct.

Natl. Center for the Advancement of Blacks in the Health Professions - Address unknown since 2001.

Natl. Center of Afro-American Artists [9361], 300 Walnut Ave., Boston, MA 02119, (617)442-8614

Natl. Center for Amer. Indian and Alaska Native Mental Hea. Res. [15220], UCDHSC Psychiatry Dept., Nighthorse Campbell Native Hea. Bldg., PO Box 6508, Mail Stop F800, Aurora, CO 80045-0508, (303)724-1414

Natl. Center for Amer. Indian Enterprise Development [12628], 953 E Juanita Ave., Mesa, AZ 85204, (480)545-1298

Natl. Center for the Amer. Revolution [10134], 435 Devon Park Dr., Wayne, PA 19087, (610)975-4939

Natl. Center for Appropriate Tech. [16998], PO Box 3838, Butte, MT 59702, (406)494-4572

Natl. Center on Arts and the Aging - Defunct.

Natl. Center for Assault Prevention [12032], 606 Delsea Dr., Sewell, NJ 08080, (856)582-8282

Natl. Center for Assisted Living [14652], 1201 L St. NW, Washington, DC 20005, (202)842-4444

Natl. Center for Assn. Resources - Address unknown since 1994.

National Center for Atmospheric Research [★7622]

Natl. Center for Audio Experimentation - Defunct.

Natl. Center for Audio Tapes Archive - Defunct.

Natl. Center for Automated Information Res. - Defunct.

Natl. Center for a Barrier Free Environment - Defunct.

Natl. Center for Bicycling and Walking [23315], 8120 Woodmont Ave., Ste. 650, Bethesda, MD 20814, (301)656-4220

National Center for Bioethics - Address unknown since 2007.

Natl. Center on Black Aged [★11306]

Natl. Center for Business and Economic Communication - Address unknown since 2003.

Natl. Center for Charitable Statistics [12731], c/o The Urban Inst., 2100 M St. NW, 5th Fl., Washington, DC 20037, (866)518-3874

National Center on Child Abuse Prevention Research [★11647]

National Center on Child Abuse Prevention Research [★IO]

Natl. Center for Children in Poverty [11712], 215 W 125th St., 3rd Fl., New York, NY 10027, (646)284-9600

Natl. Center for Citizens in Education - Defunct.

Natl. Center for Clinical Infant Programs [★13944]

Natl. Center of Communication Arts and Sciences - Defunct.

Natl. Center for Community Action - Defunct.

Natl. Center for Community Crime Prevention - Defunct.

Natl. Center for Community Educ. [8125], 1017 Avon St., Flint, MI 48503, (810)238-0463

Natl. Center for Complementary and Alternative Medicine [13643], PO Box 7923, Gaithersburg, MD 20898-7923, (301)519-3153

Natl. Center for Computer Crime Data [2091]

Natl. Center for Constitutional Stud. [17297], 37777 W Juniper Rd., Malta, ID 83342, (208)645-2625

Natl. Center for Constr. Educ. and Res. [17632], 3600 NW 43rd St., Bldg. G, Gainesville, FL 32606, (352)334-0911

Natl. Center for Creativity [17356]

Natl. Center; Death with Dignity [17109]

Natl. Center for the Development of Bilingual Curriculum - Defunct.

Natl. Center for the Diaconate [★19967]

Natl. Center for Disability Services [★11913]

Natl. Center for the Dissemination of Disability Res. [14244], c/o Southwest Educational Development Lab., 211 E 7th St., Ste. 448, Austin, TX 78701-3253, (512)476-6861

Natl. Center for the Early Childhood Workforce [★12072]

Natl. Center for Economic and Security Alternatives [18409], 2000 P St. NW, Ste. 330, Washington, DC 20036, (202)986-1373

Natl. Center on Educ. and the Economy [8283], 555 13th St. NW, Ste. 500 W, Washington, DC 20004, (202)783-3668

Natl. Center for Educ. in Maternal and Child Hea. [13969], Georgetown Univ., PO Box 571272, Washington, DC 20057-1272, (202)784-9770

Natl. Center for Education in Politics - Defunct.

Natl. Center for Educ. Statistics [★8284]

Natl. Center for Educ. Statistics [8284], 1990 K St. NW, Washington, DC 20006, (202)502-7300

Natl. Center for Educational Brokering - Defunct.

Natl. Center, Educational Media and Materials for the Handicapped - Defunct.

A star before a book entry number signifies that the name is not listed separately, but is mentioned within the entry.

Natl. Center on Elder Abuse **[12033]**, 1201 15th St. NW, Ste. 350, Washington, DC 20005-2800, (202)898-2586

Natl. Center for Employee Ownership **[1250]**, 1736 Franklin St., 8th Fl., Oakland, CA 94612, (510)208-1300

Natl. Center on Employment of the Deaf **[★12095]**

Natl. Center for Environmental Hea. Strategies **[14366]**, c/o Mary Lamielle, Exec. Dir., 1100 Rural Ave., Voorhees, NJ 08043, (856)429-5358

National Center for ESL Literacy Education **[★10401]**

Natl. Center for the Exploration of Human Potential **[★14826]**

Natl. Center for Fair Competition **[3621]**

Natl. Center for Fair and Open Testing **[9255]**, 342 Broadway, Cambridge, MA 02139, (617)864-4810

Natl. Center for Family Literacy **[8793]**, 325 W Main St., Ste. 300, Louisville, KY 40202-4237, (502)584-1133

Natl. Center for Farmworker Hea. **[14581]**, 1770 FM 967, Buda, TX 78610, (512)312-2700

Natl. Center for Fathering **[18181]**, PO Box 413888, Kansas City, MO 64141, (913)384-4661

National Center for Fathering **[IO]**, Kansas City, MO, United States

Natl. Center for Film Study - Address unknown since 1995.

Natl. Center for Film and Video Preservation **[9942]**, c/o Amer. Film Inst., 2021 N Western Ave., Los Angeles, CA 90027-1657, (323)856-7600

Natl. Center for Financial Educ. **[★8424]**

Natl. Center for Food Safety and Tech. **[1543]**, 6502 S Archer Rd., Summit, IL 60501-1957, (708)563-1576

Natl. Center For Advanced Technologies **[7751]**, 1000 Wilson Blvd., Ste. 1700, Arlington, VA 22209-3901, (703)358-1000

Natl. Center for Freedom of Information Studies - Address unknown since 2006.

Natl. Center for Hea. Educ. **[14582]**, 375 Hudson St., New York, NY 10014, (212)463-4053

Natl. Center for Hea. Promotion and Aging **[★11288]**

Natl. Center for Hearing Dog Info. **[★14774]**

Natl. Center for Higher Educ. Mgt. Systems **[7905]**, 3035 Center Green Dr., Ste. 150, Boulder, CO 80301-2251, (303)497-0301

Natl. Center for Historical Res. - Defunct.

Natl. Center for Home Equity Conversion **[1470]**, 360 N Robert St., No. 403, St. Paul, MN 55101

Natl. Center for Homecare Education and Res. - Defunct.

Natl. Center for Homeless Educ. **[12295]**, PO Box 5367, Greensboro, NC 27435, (800)755-3277

Natl. Center for Homeopathy **[14850]**, 801 N Fairfax St., Ste. 306, Alexandria, VA 22314, (703)548-7790

Natl. Center for Housing Mgt. **[12321]**, 12021 Sunset Hills Rd., Ste. 210, Reston, VA 20190, (703)435-9393

Natl. Center for Immigrants' Rights **[★17807]**

Natl. Center for Immigrants' Rights **[★IO]**

Natl. Center for Improving Sci. Educ. **[9109]**, 1840 Wilson Blvd., Ste. 201A, Arlington, VA 22201-3000, (703)875-0496

Natl. Center for Infants, Toddlers and Families **[★13944]**

Natl. Center for Infants, Toddlers and Families; Zero to Three: **[13944]**

Natl. Center for Initiative Review Found. - Defunct.

Natl. Center on Institutions and Alternatives **[11878]**, 7222 Ambassador Rd., Baltimore, MD 21244, (410)265-1490

Natl. Center for Jewish Film **[9943]**, Brandeis Univ., Lown 102 MS053, Waltham, MA 02454, (781)899-7044

Natl. Center for Jewish Healing **[10287]**, 120 W 57th St., New York, NY 10019, (212)399-2320

Natl. Center for Job Market Studies - Address unknown since 2003.

Natl. Center for Jobs and Justice - Address unknown since 1988.

Natl. Center for Juvenile Justice **[11879]**, 3700 S Water St., Ste. 200, Pittsburgh, PA 15203, (412)227-6950

Natl. Center for the Laity **[20206]**, c/o Bill Droel, Ed., PO Box 291102, Chicago, IL 60629

Natl. Center for Law and Deafness - Address unknown since 2000.

Natl. Center for Law and Economic Justice **[6232]**, 275 7th Ave., Ste. 1506, New York, NY 10001-6708, (212)633-6967

Natl. Center for Law and the Handicapped - Defunct.

Natl. Center for Learning Disabilities **[12494]**, 381 Park Ave. S, Ste. 1401, New York, NY 10016, (212)545-7510

Natl. Center for Legislative Res. - Defunct.

Natl. Center for Lesbian Rights **[12246]**, 870 Market St., Ste. 370, San Francisco, CA 94102, (415)392-6257

Natl. Center for Mediation Educ. **[5461]**, 1160 Spa Rd., No. 1B, Annapolis, MD 21403-1022, (410)280-8888

Natl. Center for Men **[18042]**, PO Box 555, Old Bethpage, NY 11804, (516)938-3075

Natl. Center for Minority Business Research and Development - Address unknown since 2002.

Natl. Center for Missing and Exploited Children **[11630]**, Charles B. Wang International Children's Bldg., 699 Prince St., Alexandria, VA 22314-3175, (703)274-3900

Natl. Center for Montessori Educ. and Amer. Montessori Soc. **[★8891]**

Natl. Center for Municipal Development - Defunct.

Natl. Center for Neighborhood Enterprise **[★17208]**

Natl. Center for Neurogenic Commun. Disorders **[16449]**, Univ. of Arizona, PO Box 210071, Tucson, AZ 85721-0071, (520)621-1472

Natl. Center for Nonprofit Boards **[★12651]**

Natl. Center on Nonprofit Enterprise **[12642]**, 205 S Patrick St., Alexandria, VA 22314, (703)548-7978

Natl. Center on Occupational Readjustment - Defunct.

Natl. Center for Policy Alternatives **[★18429]**

Natl. Center for Policy Anal. **[18462]**, Dallas HQ, 12770 Coit Rd., Ste. 800, Dallas, TX 75251-1339, (972)386-6272

Natl. Center for Post Traumatic Stress Disorder **[16490]**, VA Medical Center 116D, 215 N Main St., White River Junction, VT 05009, (802)296-5132

Natl. Center on Poverty Law **[6030]**, 50 E Washington St., Ste. 500, Chicago, IL 60602, (312)263-3830

Natl. Center for Preservation Law - Address unknown since 2004.

Natl. Center for Preservation Tech. and Training **[7161]**, 645 Univ. Pkwy., Natchitoches, LA 71457, (318)356-7444

Natl. Center for Privatization **[★17665]**

Natl. Center for Prosecution of Child Abuse **[11631]**, 99 Canal Center Plz., Ste. 510, Alexandria, VA 22314, (703)549-4253

Natl. Center for Public Policy Res. **[18463]**, 501 Capitol Ct. NE, Washington, DC 20002, (202)543-4110

Natl. Center for Public Ser. Internship Programs **[★8414]**

Natl. Center for Res. on Evaluation, Standards, and Student Testing **[8285]**, UCLA CSE/CRESST, GSE and IS Bldg., 3rd Fl., 300 Charles E. Young Dr. N, Mailbox 951522, Los Angeles, CA 90095-1522, (310)206-1532

Natl. Center for Res. in Vocational Educ. **[★9304]**

Natl. Center for Resource Recovery - Defunct.

Natl. Center on Rural Aging **[★11307]**

Natl. Center for Sci. Educ. **[9110]**, 420 40th St., Ste. 2, Oakland, CA 94609-2688, (510)601-7203

Natl. Center for Service-Learning - Defunct.

Natl. Center for Smoking and Weight Control - Defunct.

Natl. Center for Social Policy and Practice **[★13206]**

Natl. Center for State Courts **[5908]**, 300 Newport Ave., Williamsburg, VA 23185-4147, (757)259-1857

Natl. Center for the Stud. of Collective Bargaining in Higher Educ. **[★24036]**

Natl. Center for the Stud. of Collective Bargaining in Higher Educ. and the Professions **[24036]**, 425 E 25th St., Box 615, New York, NY 10010-2590, (212)481-7550

Natl. Center for the Stud. of Corporal Punishment and Alternatives **[8206]**, Temple Univ., 253 Ritter Annex, Philadelphia, PA 19122, (215)204-6091

Natl. Center for the Study of Wilson's Disease **[15251]**

Natl. Center for Stuttering **[16450]**, 200 E 33rd St., New York, NY 10016, (212)532-1460

Natl. Center for Therapeutic Riding **[23351]**

Natl. Center for Tobacco-Free Kids **[16433]**, 1400 Eye St. NW, Ste. 1200, Washington, DC 20005, (202)296-5469

Natl. Center for Urban Environmental Studies - Defunct.

Natl. Center for Urban Ethnic Affairs **[11753]**, PO Box 20, Cardinal Sta., Washington, DC 20064, (202)319-6188

Natl. Center for Victims of Crime **[13366]**, 2000 M St. NW, Ste. 480, Washington, DC 20036-3398, (202)467-8700

Natl. Center for Voice and Speech **[16451]**, c/o The Denver Center for the Performing Arts, 1101 13th St., Denver, CO 80204-5319, (303)446-4834

Natl. Center for Voluntary Action **[★13401]**

Natl. Center on Women and Family Law - Defunct.

Natl. Center for Women and Policing **[5991]**, 433 S Beverly Dr., Beverly Hills, CA 90212, (310)556-2526

Natl. Center for the Workplace - Defunct.

National Center for Youth with Disabilities - Defunct.

Natl. Center for Youth Law **[5700]**, 405 14th St., 15th Fl., Oakland, CA 94612-2701, (510)835-8098

Natl. Central America Health Rights Network - Address unknown since 1995.

Natl. Centre for Audiology **[IO]**, London, ON, Canada

Natl. Centre for Missing Children **[IO]**, Indore, India

Natl. Centre for the Performing Arts **[IO]**, Bombay, India

Natl. Centre for Res. **[IO]**, Khartoum, Sudan

Natl. Centre for Trade Info. **[IO]**, New Delhi, India

Natl. Ceramic Assn. **[★IO]**

Natl. Ceramic Assn. **[★787]**

Natl. Ceramic Dealers Assn. **[★1911]**

Natl. Ceramic Mfrs. Assn. **[★1911]**

Natl. Ceramic Mold Mfrs. Assn. - Defunct.

Natl. Ceramic Teachers Assn. **[★1911]**

Natl. Certification Agency for Medical Lab Personnel **[★15145]**

Natl. Certification Bd. for Diabetes Educators **[14229]**, 330 E Algonquin Rd., Ste. 4, Arlington Heights, IL 60005, (847)228-9795

Natl. Certification Bd. of Pediatric Nurse Practitioners and Nurses **[★15522]**

Natl. Certification Bd. Perioperative Nursing **[★14878]**

Natl. Certification Bd. for Therapeutic Massage and Bodywork **[15032]**, 1901 S Meyers Rd., Ste. 240, Oakbrook Terrace, IL 60181, (630)627-8000

Natl. Certification Commn. **[8037]**, PO Box 15282, Chevy Chase, MD 20825, (847)847-0102

Natl. Certification Commn. for Acupuncture and Oriental Medicine **[15747]**, 76 S Laura St., Ste. 1290, Jacksonville, FL 32202, (904)598-1005

National Certification Commn. in Chemistry and Chem. Engg. **[★6666]**

Natl. Certification Corp. for the Obstetric, Gynecologic and Neonatal Nursing Specialties **[15506]**, PO Box 11082, Chicago, IL 60611-0082, (312)951-0207

Natl. Certification Coun. for Activity Professionals **[1849]**, PO Box 62589, Virginia Beach, VA 23466, (757)552-0653

National Certification of Family Law, Criminal and Civil Trial Advocates Program **[★6333]**

Natl. Certification Reciprocity Consortium/Alcoholism and Other Drug Abuse - Address unknown since 1994.

Natl. Certified Pipe Welding Bur. **[3033]**, 1385 Piccard Dr., Rockville, MD 20850, (301)869-5800

Natl. Cervical Cancer Coalition **[13849]**, 7247 Hayvenhurst Ave., Ste. A-7, Van Nuys, CA 91406, (818)909-3849

Natl. Cesky Terrier Club of Am. **[22316]**, c/o Sharon Lesniak, Pres., 5275 Crestway Dr., Bay City, MI 48706, (989)686-2044

Natl. CFIDS Found. **[15345]**, 103 Aletha Rd., Needham, MA 02492, (781)449-3535

Natl. Challenge Comm. on Disability **[★17415]**

Natl. Challenge Comm. on Disability **[★IO]**

Reference to "IO" in place of a book number signifies that the association may be found in the 45th edition of International Organizations.

Natl. Challenge Comm. of the Disabled [★IO]

Natl. Challenge Comm. of the Disabled [★17415]

Natl. Challenged Homeschoolers Assoc. Network [8520], PO Box 310, Moyie Springs, ID 83845, (208)267-6246

Natl. Chamber of Agriculture and Agro-Industry [IO], San Jose, Costa Rica

Natl. Chamber of Commerce - Algeria [IO], Algiers, Algeria

Natl. Chamber of Commerce - Bolivia [IO], La Paz, Bolivia

Natl. Chamber of Commerce and Indus. of Malaysia [IO], Kuala Lumpur, Malaysia

Natl. Chamber of Commerce and Ser. of Uruguay [IO], Montevideo, Uruguay

Natl. Chamber of Commerce of Sri Lanka [IO], Colombo, Sri Lanka

Natl. Chamber of Commerce for Women [24388], 10 Waterside Plz., Ste. 6H, New York, NY 10010, (212)889-3806

Natl. Chamber of Consultancy Businesses [IO], Mexico City, Mexico

Natl. Chamber of Elec. Manufactures [IO], Mexico City, Mexico

Natl. Chamber of the Fish Indus. [IO], Mexico City, Mexico

Natl. Chamber of Fisheries [IO], Guayaquil, Ecuador

Natl. Chamber Found. [18464], 1615 H St. NW, Washington, DC 20062-2000, (202)463-5500

Natl. Chamber of Insurance Businesses [IO], San Jose, Costa Rica

Natl. Chamber Litigation Center [6223], 1615 H St. NW, Washington, DC 20062-2000, (202)463-5337

Natl. Chamber of Mfrs. [IO], Mexico City, Mexico

Natl. Chamber of the Mexican Publishing Indus. [IO], Mexico City, Mexico

Natl. Chamber of Milk Producers [IO], San Jose, Costa Rica

Natl. Chamber of the Perfume and Cosmetics Indus. [★IO]

Natl. Chamber of the Perfume and Cosmetics, Toiletries and Hygiene Prdt. [IO], Mexico City, Mexico

Natl. Chamber of the Pharmaceutical Indus. [IO], Mexico City, Mexico

Natl. Chamber of Radio and TV Indus. [IO], Mexico City, Mexico

Natl. Chamber of the Restaurant and Food Seasoning Indus. [★IO]

Natl. Chamber of the Restaurant and Seasoned Food Indus. [IO], Mexico City, Mexico

Natl. Chamber of the Sugar and Alcohol Indus. [IO], Mexico City, Mexico

Natl. Chamber of Sugar Confectionery Mfrs. [IO], Paris, France

Natl. Chambers of Commerce [★IO]

Natl. Championship Racing Assn. [23670], c/o C. Ray Hall, Pres., 7700 N Broadway, Wichita, KS 67219, (316)755-1781

Natl. Change of Address Assn. - Address unknown since 1989.

Natl. Chaplains Assn. [19855], PO Box 635, Groveland, FL 34736, (352)394-6311

Natl. Chaplains Assn. for Youth Rehabilitation - Defunct.

Natl. Chap. of Canada IODE [IO], Toronto, ON, Canada

Natl. Character Lab. [6536], c/o Col. A.J. Stuart, Jr., Pres., 4635 Leeds Ave., El Paso, TX 79903, (915)562-5046

Natl. Charities Info. Bur. [★17309]

Natl. Charities Info. Bur. [★IO]

Natl. Chastity Assn. - Address unknown since 1994.

Natl. Checker Assn. [★22457]

Natl. Checker Assn. [★IO]

Natl. Cheese Inst. [1136], c/o Intl. Dairy Foods Assn., 1250 H St. NW, Ste. 900, Washington, DC 20005-3952, (202)737-4332

Natl. Cheese Seminar [★1522]

Natl. Cheese Seminar [★IO]

Natl. Chem. Credit Assn. [1440], c/o Michael Meyers, Servicing Sec., 1100 Main St., Buffalo, NY 14209-2356, (716)878-2807

Natl. Chem. Indus. Assn. [IO], Mexico City, Mexico

Natl. Chemical Stabilization Assn. - Defunct.

Natl. Cherry Growers and Indus. Found. [4741], 2667 Reed Rd., Hood River, OR 97031, (541)386-5761

Natl. Chevelle Owners Assn. - Address unknown since 2008.

Natl. Chevrolet Restorers Club - Defunct.

Natl. Chevy Assn. [21727], 947 Arcade St., St. Paul, MN 55106-3850, (651)778-9522

Natl. Chevy/GMC Truck Assn. [★21609]

Natl. Chevy/GMC Truckin' Club - Defunct.

Natl. Chicano Coun. for Higher Education - Defunct.

Natl. Chicano Health Org. - Address unknown since 1995.

Natl. Chicken Coun. [5111], 1015 15th St. NW, Ste. 930, Washington, DC 20005-2622, (202)296-2622

Natl. Chief Petty Officers' Assn. [21214], c/o Gary Williams, Membership Dir., 301 Birchwood Blvd., Baldwinsville, NY 13027-3102, (830)537-4899

Natl. Chiefs of Police Union [★5972]

Natl. Chiefs of Police Union [★IO]

Natl. Child Abuse Defense and Rsrc. Center [13367], PO Box 638, Holland, OH 43528, (419)865-0513

Natl. Child Care Assn. [11533], 2025 M St. NW, Ste. 800, Washington, DC 20036-3309, (202)367-1133

Natl. Child Care Development Assn. [11632], 51 Main St., Enterprise, FL 32725, (800)777-0219

Natl. Child Care and Family Development [11534], 1501 Benning Rd. NE, Washington, DC 20002-4599, (202)397-3800

Natl. Child Day Care Assn. [★11534]

Natl. Child Labor Comm. [13500], 1501 Broadway, Ste. 1908, New York, NY 10036, (212)840-1801

Natl. Child Labor Comm; Natl. Comm. on the Educ. of Migrant Children of the [12593]

Natl. Child Nutrition Coalition - Defunct.

Natl. Child Nutrition Project - Address unknown since 1995.

Natl. Child Safety Coun. [12972]

Natl. Child Support Advocacy Coalition - Address unknown since 2003.

Natl. Child Support Enforcement Assn. [5701], 444 N Capitol St., Ste. 414, Washington, DC 20001-1512, (202)624-8180

Natl. Childbirth Trust [IO], London, United Kingdom

Natl. Childcare Campaign/Daycare Trust [★IO]

Natl. Childhood Cancer Found. [13850], 4600 E West Hwy., Ste. 600, Bethesda, MD 20814-3457, (800)458-6223

Natl. Childhood Cancer Found. [★13850]

Natl. Childminding Assn. [IO], Bromley, United Kingdom

Natl. Children's Alliance [11633], 516 C St. NE, Washington, DC 20002, (202)548-0090

Natl. Children's Book and Literacy Alliance - Address unknown since 2002.

Natl. Children's Bur. [IO], London, United Kingdom

Natl. Children's Cancer Soc. [13851], 1015 Locust, Ste. 600, St. Louis, MO 63101, (314)241-1600

Natl. Children's Eye Care Found. [★15679]

Natl. Children's Nurseries Assn. [IO], Dublin, Ireland

Natl. Childrenswear Assn. [IO], London, United Kingdom

Natl. Chimney Sweep Guild [2471], 2155 Commercial Dr., Plainfield, IN 46168, (317)837-1500

Natl. Chincoteague Pony Assn. [4917], 2595 Jensen Rd., Bellingham, WA 98226, (360)671-8338

Natl. Chinese Honor Soc. [24432], c/o Diane Mammone, Chair, PO Box 249, Barre, MA 01005

Natl. Chinese Wushu Assn. - Address unknown since 2002.

Natl. Chiropractic Assn. [★13988]

Natl. Chocolate and Confectionery Producers' Assn. [IO], Mexico City, Mexico

National Choreography Project [★9865]

Natl. Christ Child Soc. [19679], 4340 E West Hwy., Ste. 202, Bethesda, MD 20814, (301)718-0220

Natl. Christian Action Coalition - Defunct.

Natl. Christian Assn. - Address unknown since 2002.

Natl. Christian Barrel Racers Assn. [23507], 3531 W Topeka Dr., Glendale, AZ 85308, (623)879-9288

Natl. Christian Choir [20433], 17B Firstfield Rd., Ste. 108, Gaithersburg, MD 20878, (301)670-6331

Natl. Christian Coll. Athletic Assn. [23837], 302 W Washington St., Greenville, SC 29601-1919, (864)250-1199

Natl. Christian Coun. in Japan [IO], Tokyo, Japan

Natl. Christian Education Assn. - Defunct.

Natl. Christian Forensics and Communications Assn. [8521], PO Box 212, Mountlake Terrace, WA 98043-0212, (425)776-3620

Natl. Christian Leadership Conf. for Israel [17939], 43422 W Oaks Dr., No. 300, Novi, MI 48377, (248)557-4540

Natl. Christian Leadership Conf. for Israel [IO], Novi, MI, United States

Natl. Christian Leadership Fed. - Address unknown since 2004.

Natl. Christian Life Community of the U.S.A. [19680], 3601 Lindell Blvd., No. 421, St. Louis, MO 63108-3301, (314)977-7370

Natl. Christian Network [★12917]

Natl. Christian School Educ. Assn. [★8081]

Natl. Christian School Educ. Assn. [★IO]

Natl. Christian Secretaries Assn. - Address unknown since 1995.

Natl. Christmas Tree Assn. [5261], 16020 Swingley Ridge Rd., Ste. 300, Chesterfield, MO 63017, (636)449-5070

Natl. Christmas Tree Growers Assn. [★5261]

Natl. Chronic Care Consortium - Defunct.

Natl. Chronic Epstein-Barr Virus Assn. [★14278]

Natl. Chronic Fatigue Syndrome Assn. [★14278]

Natl. Chronic Fatigue Syndrome and Fibromyalgia Assn. [14278], PO Box 18426, Kansas City, MO 64133-8426, (816)737-1343

Natl. Chronic Pain Outreach Assn. [15844], PO Box 274, Millboro, VA 24460, (540)862-9437

Natl. Chronic Pain Soc. [15845], 10700 Fuqua St., No. 194, Houston, TX 77082, (281)357-4673

Natl. Chrysanthemum Soc. [22526], 10107 Homar Pond Dr., Fairfax Station, VA 22039-1650, (703)978-7981

Natl. Chrysanthemum Soc. [IO], Blyth, United Kingdom

Natl. Chrysler Products Club - Address unknown since 1999.

Natl. Church Conf. of the Blind [13380], PO Box 196, Grover, CO 80729, (970)895-2352

Natl. Church Goods Assn. [3374], 800 Roosevelt Rd., Bldg. C, Ste. 312, Glen Ellyn, IL 60137, (630)942-6599

Natl. Church Lib. Assn. [10375], 275 S 3rd St., Ste. 101A, Stillwater, MN 55082-4996, (651)430-0770

Natl. Church Music Fellowship - Defunct.

Natl. Church Secretaries Assn. - Defunct.

Natl. Cigar Leaf Tobacco Assn. - Defunct.

Natl. Cinder Concrete Products Assn. - Address unknown since 1995.

National Circus Acad. [★9796]

Natl. Circus Fund [★9799]

Natl. Circus Preservation Soc. [9799], c/o Cheryl Deptula, Exec. Sec.-Treas., 2704 Marshall Ave., Lorain, OH 44052, (440)960-2811

Natl. Circus Proj. [8286], 56 Lion Ln., Westbury, NY 11590, (516)334-2123

Natl. Citizen Communication Lobby - Defunct.

Natl. Citizens Coalition for Nursing Home Reform [17335], 1828 L St. NW, Ste. 801, Washington, DC 20036, (202)332-2275

Natl. Citizens Comm. for Community Relations - Defunct.

Natl. Citizens Comm. for Educational TV - Defunct.

Natl. Citizens Comm. for Fairness to the Presidency - Defunct.

Natl. Citizens Comm. for Food and Shelter [★12294]

Natl. Citizens Comm. for the Right to Keep and Bear Arms [★17105]

Natl. Citizens Participation Coun. - Address unknown since 1990.

Natl. Civic Coun. [IO], North Melbourne, Australia

Natl. Civic League [6128], 1445 Market St., Ste. 300, Denver, CO 80202, (303)571-4343

Natl. Civil Liberties Clearing House - Defunct.

Natl. Civil Liberties Legal Found. - Defunct.

Natl. Civil Service League - Defunct.

Natl. Class E Scow Assn. [23204], PO Box 3022, Madison, WI 53704-0022, (608)347-1480

Natl. Classics Honorary Soc; Eta Sigma Phi, [24433]

Natl. Classification Mgt. Soc. [★2092]

Natl. Classified Network [★3226]

A star before a book entry number signifies that the name is not listed separately, but is mentioned within the entry.

Natl. Clay Pipe Inst. [3034], PO Box 759, Lake Geneva, WI 53147, (262)248-9094

Natl. Clay Pipe Mfrs. [★3034]

Natl. Clay Pot Mfrs. [183], PO Box 485, Jackson, MO 63755, (573)243-3138

Natl. Clean Air Coalition - Defunct.

Natl. Clean Cities [6399], 1735 20th St. NW, Washington, DC 20009

Natl. Clean Up-Paint Up-Fix Up Bur. - Defunct.

Natl. CH for Alcohol and Drug Info. [16513], PO Box 2345, Rockville, MD 20847-2345, (301)468-2600

Natl. CH for Bilingual Educ. [★8287]

Natl. CH on Child Abuse and Neglect Info. and Natl. Adoption Info. CH [★11570]

Natl. CH for Commuter Programs [9187], c/o Jennifer Bonnet, Coor., Univ. of Maryland, 0110 Stamp Student Union, College Park, MD 20742, (301)405-0986

Natl. CH for Corporate Matching Gift Info. [★12199]

Natl. Clearinghouse for Criminal Justice Planning and Architecture - Defunct.

Natl. CH for English Language Acquisition and Language Instruction Educational Programs [8287], 2121 K St. NW, Ste. 260, Washington, DC 20037, (202)467-0867

Natl. CH for Legal Services [★6030]

Natl. CH on Licensure, Enforcement, and Regulation [★6271]

Natl. CH on Marital and Date Rape [12790], 2325 Oak St., Berkeley, CA 94708, (800)656-4673

National CH for Professions in Special Education [★11998]

National CH for Professions in Special Education [★9141]

National CH for Professions in Special Education [★IO]

Natl. Clearinghouse on Revenue Sharing - Defunct.

Natl. CH on Satanic Crime in Am; USCCCN [11848]

Natl. Clergy Conf. on Alcoholism [★13266]

Natl. Clergy Conf. on Alcoholism [★IO]

Natl. Clergy Coun. on Alcoholism and Related Drug Problems [★IO]

Natl. Clergy Coun. on Alcoholism and Related Drug Problems [★13266]

Natl. Client Protection Org. [5949], c/o A. Root Edmonson, Pres., North Carolina Client Security Fund, PO Box 25908, Raleigh, NC 27611, (919)828-4620

National Client Protection Organization [IO], Raleigh, NC, United States

Natl. Clients Coun. - Address unknown since 2001.

National Climatic Data Center [★4590]

Natl. Clogging and Hoedown Coun. - Address unknown since 2002.

Natl. Clogging Org. [9892], c/o David Phillips, Co.-Exec. Dir., 2986 Mill Park Ct., Dacula, GA 30019, (770)985-5557

Natl. Club Assn. [835], 1201 15th St., Ste. 450, Washington, DC 20005, (202)822-9822

Natl. Club Indus. Assn. of Am. [1320], 67 Wall St., 22nd Fl., New York, NY 10005, (917)779-0496

Natl. Club Indus. Assn. of Am. [IO], New York, NY, United States

Natl. Club Sports Assn. - Defunct.

Natl. Coaching Found. [★IO]

Natl. Coal Assn. [★846]

Natl. Coal Policy Center - Defunct.

Natl. Coal Trans. Assn. [844], 4 W Meadow Lark Ln., Ste. 100, Littleton, CO 80127-5718, (303)979-2798

Natl. Coalition of 100 Black Women [17552], 1925 Adam C. Powell Jr. Blvd., Ste. 1L, New York, NY 10026, (212)222-5660

Natl. Coalition to Abolish Corporal Punishment in Schools [8207], 155 W Main St., No. 1603, Columbus, OH 43215, (614)221-8829

Natl. Coalition to Abolish the Death Penalty [17033], 1705 DeSales St. NW, 5th Fl., Washington, DC 20036, (202)331-4090

Natl. Coalition of Abortion Providers [13529], 1625 K St., Ste. 1020, Washington, DC 20006, (202)419-1444

Natl. Coalition for Adequate Alcoholism Programs - Defunct.

Natl. Coalition for Adult Immunization [14583]

Natl. Coalition for Advanced Mfg. [★2563]

Natl. Coalition of Advanced Tech. Centers [9240], c/o Moraine Valley Community Coll., 9000 W Coll. Pkwy., Palos Hills, IL 60465, (708)326-2509

Natl. Coalition of Advanced Tech. Centers [IO], Palos Hills, IL, United States

Natl. Coalition of Advocates for Students [8328]

Natl. Coalition Against Censorship [17042], 275 7th Ave., No. 1504, New York, NY 10001, (212)807-6222

Natl. Coalition Against the Death Penalty [★17033]

Natl. Coalition Against Domestic Violence [12034], 1120 Lincoln St., Ste. 1603, Denver, CO 80203, (303)839-1852

Natl. Coalition Against Legalized Gambling [17648], 100 Maryland Ave. NE, Rm. 311, Washington, DC 20002, (505)899-2599

Natl. Coalition Against the Misuse of Pesticides [★13322]

Natl. Coalition Against the Misuse of Pesticides; Beyond Pesticides - [13322]

Natl. Coalition Against Pornography [★18374]

Natl. Coalition Against Sexual Assault - Defunct.

Natl. Coalition Against Surrogacy - Defunct.

Natl. Coalition of Alternative Community Schools [7948], PO Box 6009, Ann Arbor, MI 48106-6009, (734)483-7040

Natl. Coalition of Amer. Nuns - Address unknown since 2002.

Natl. Coalition of Anti-Deportation Campaigns [IO], Birmingham, United Kingdom

Natl. Coalition of Arts Therapy Associations [★16224]

Natl. Coalition for Asian Pacific Amer. Community Development [11785], 1001 Connecticut Ave. NW, Ste. 730, Washington, DC 20036, (202)223-2442

Natl. Coalition Associates of Mgt. Consultants - Address unknown since 2004.

Natl. Coalition for Aviation Educ. [7995], c/o M.A. Thomson, Member of the Bd., 3146 Valentino Ct., Oakton, VA 22124

Natl. Coalition to Ban Handguns [★17590]

Natl. Coalition on Black Civic Participation [18358], 1900 L St. NW, Ste. 700, Washington, DC 20036, (202)659-4929

Natl. Coalition of Black Lesbians and Gays - Address unknown since 1989.

Natl. Coalition of Black Lung and Respiratory Disease Clinics - Address unknown since 1999.

Natl. Coalition of Black Meeting Planners [2687], 8630 Fenton St., Ste. 126, Silver Spring, MD 20910, (202)628-3952

Natl. Coalition on Black Voter Participation [★18358]

Natl. Coalition of Blacks for Reparations in Am. [16944], PO Box 90604, Washington, DC 20090, (202)291-8400

Natl. Coalition Building Inst. [17227], 1120 Connecticut Ave. NW, Ste. 450, Washington, DC 20036, (202)785-9400

Natl. Coalition for Campus Child Care [★11535]

Natl. Coalition for Campus Children's Centers [11535], 4 Schindler Educ. Ctr., Univ. of Northern Iowa, Cedar Falls, IA 50614, (319)273-3113

Natl. Coalition for Cancer Res. [17691]

Natl. Coalition for Cancer Survivorship [13852], 1010 Wayne Ave., Ste. 770, Silver Spring, MD 20910, (301)650-9127

Natl. Coalition for Child Protection Reform [11634], 53 Skyhill Rd., Ste. 202, Alexandria, VA 22314-4997, (703)212-2006

Natl. Coalition for Children's Centers [★11535]

Natl. Coalition of Concerned Legal Professionals [12501], 25 Chapel St., Ste. 601, Brooklyn, NY 11201, (718)522-1619

Natl. Coalition for Consumer Educ. [17336], c/o Natl. Consumers League, 1701 K St. NW, Ste. 1200, Washington, DC 20006, (202)835-3323

Natl. Coalition of Creative Arts Therapies Associations [16224], c/o AMTA, 8455 Colesville Rd., Ste. 1000, Silver Spring, MD 20910, (703)250-3414

Natl. Coalition for Democracy in Education - Defunct.

Natl. Coalition for Domestic Abuse Awareness - Address unknown since 2008.

Natl. Coalition of Education Activists [9039]

Natl. Coalition for Electronics Educ. [8364], c/o Ed Clingman, I.S.C.E.T., 3608 Pershing Ave., Fort Worth, TX 76107, (817)921-9101

Natl. Coalition to End Racism in America's Child Care System - Defunct.

Natl. Coalition for Enterprise Zones - Address unknown since 2002.

Natl. Coalition of ESEA Title I Parents [★8289]

Natl. Coalition of Ethnic Minority Nurse Associations [15507], c/o Dr. Betty Smith Williams, RN, Pres., 6101 W Centinela Ave., Ste. 378, Culver City, CA 90230, (310)258-9515

Natl. Coalition to Expand Charitable Giving - Defunct.

Natl. Coalition of Free Men [18043], PO Box 582023, Minneapolis, MN 55458-2023, (516)482-6378

Natl. Coalition of Gay Activists - Defunct.

Natl. Coalition of Gay Sexually Transmitted Disease Services - Defunct.

Natl. Coalition of Girls' Schools [8288], 57 Main St., Concord, MA 01742, (978)287-4485

Natl. Coalition for Haitian Refugees [★18499]

Natl. Coalition for Haitian Rights [18499], 275 7th Ave., New York, NY 10001, (212)337-0005

Natl. Coalition on the Hanigan Case - Defunct.

Natl. Coalition on Hea. Care [17698], 1200 G St. NW, Ste. 750, Washington, DC 20005, (202)638-7151

Natl. Coalition for Hea. Professional Educ. in Genetics [14505], 2360 W Joppa Rd., Ste. 320, Lutherville, MD 21093, (410)583-0600

Natl. Coalition of Hispanic Hea. and Human Services Organizations [★13176]

Natl. Coalition for History [10135], 400 A St. SE, Washington, DC 20003, (202)544-2422

Natl. Coalition for the Homeless [12296], 2201 P St. NW, Washington, DC 20037-1033, (202)462-4822

Natl. Coalition for Homeless Veterans [21310], 333 1/2 Pennsylvania Ave. SE, Washington, DC 20003-1148, (800)VET-HELP

Natl. Coalition of Homicide Survivors [13368], c/o Pima County Attorney, 32 N Stone, 11th Fl., Tucson, AZ 85701, (520)740-5729

Natl. Coalition on Immune System Disorders - Address unknown since 1994.

Natl. Coalition of Independent Coll. and Univ. Students - Defunct.

Natl. Coalition of Independent Living Programs [★11968]

Natl. Coalition of Independent Scholars [8491], PO Box 838, St. Helena, CA 94574

Natl. Coalition for Indian Education - Address unknown since 2002.

Natl. Coalition of IRS Whistleblowers - Address unknown since 1994.

Natl. Coalition for Jail Reform - Defunct.

Natl. Coalition for a Just Draft [★18041]

Natl. Coalition for Land Reform - Address unknown since 1995.

Natl. Coalition for LGBT Hea. [12247], 1325 Massachusetts Ave. NW, Ste. 705, Washington, DC 20005, (202)558-6828

Natl. Coalition for Literacy [8794], PO Box 11592, Washington, DC 20008, (202)244-0732

Natl. Coalition for Marine Conservation [4423], 4 Royal St. SE, Leesburg, VA 20175, (703)777-0037

Natl. Coalition of Men's Ministries [19816], 9900 Willows Rd. NE, Redmond, WA 98052, (425)284-2541

Natl. Coalition of Mental Hea. Professionals and Consumers [15221], PO Box 438, Commack, NY 11725, (631)979-5307

Natl. Coalition Party [IO], Helsinki, Finland

Natl. Coalition of Patriotic Amers. - Defunct.

Natl. Coalition for a Policy of No-First-Use of Nuclear Weapons - Defunct.

Natl. Coalition to Preserve Scenic Beauty [★4606]

Natl. Coalition to Prevent Shoplifting - Defunct.

Natl. Coalition for Promoting Physical Activity [23653], 1100 H St. NW, Ste. 510, Washington, DC 20005, (202)454-7521

Natl. Coalition for the Protection of Children and Families [18374], 800 Compton Rd., Ste. 9224, Cincinnati, OH 45231, (513)521-6227

Natl. Coalition of Psychiatrists Against Motorcoach Therapy [15222], c/o Dr. Anne Rose, 4909 Briarwood Ave., No. 7, Royal Oak, MI 48073-1318

Natl. Coalition for Public Education and Religious Liberty - Address unknown since 1999.

Reference to "IO" in place of a book number signifies that the association may be found in the 45th edition of International Organizations.

Encyclopedia of Associations, 46th Edition

3867

Natl. Coalition for Quality Integrated Education - Address unknown since 1994.

Natl. Coalition of Redevelopment Agencies - Address unknown since 1989.

Natl. Coalition for Res. in Neurological and Communicative Disorders [★15346]

Natl. Coalition for Res. in Neurological Disorders [15346]

Natl. Coalition on Rural Aging [11307], c/o Natl. Coun. on Aging, 1901 L St. NW, 4th Fl., Washington, DC 20036, (202)479-1200

Natl. Coalition for School Bus Safety - Defunct.

Natl. Coalition for Science and Technology - Defunct.

Natl. Coalition for Sex Equity in Educ. [★8399]

Natl. Coalition for Sexual Freedom [18599], 822 Guilford Ave., Box 127, Baltimore, MD 21202-3707, (410)539-4824

Natl. Coalition to Stop Food and Water Irradiation [★17328]

Natl. Coalition for Students with Disabilities [★13212]

Natl. Coalition to Support Indian Treaties - Defunct.

Natl. Coalition for Tech. in Educ. and Training [9241], c/o Ann M. Dorman, Meetings and Events of Distinction, LLC, 2724 Kenwood Ave., Alexandria, VA 22302, (703)626-1266

Natl. Coalition on TV Violence - Defunct.

Natl. Coalition of Title I/Chapter 1 Parents [8289], 310 Pennsylvania Ave. SE, 3rd Fl., Washington, DC 20003, (202)547-3135

Natl. Coalition for Universities in the Public Interest - Address unknown since 2003.

Natl. Coalition for Women and Girls in Educ. [9321], c/o Amer. Assn. of Univ. Women, 1111 16th St. NW, Washington, DC 20036, (202)785-7745

Natl. Coalition for Women with Heart Disease; WomenHeart: [13929]

Natl. Coalition for Women's Enterprise - Defunct.

Natl. Coalition for Women's Ordination - Defunct.

Natl. Cochlear Implant Users Assn. [IO], High Wycombe, United Kingdom

Natl. Cockatiel Soc. [21852], c/o Laura Rudman-Robie, Membership Sec., 78 Horace Greely Rd., Amherst, NH 03031, (603)673-4600

Natl. Coffee Assn. of U.S.A. [511], 15 Maiden Ln., Ste. 1405, New York, NY 10038-4003, (212)766-4007

Natl. Coffee Ser. Assn. [★3971]

Natl. Coil Coating Assn. [853], 1300 Sumner Ave., Cleveland, OH 44115-2851, (216)241-7333

Natl. Coin Machine Distributors Assn. - Address unknown since 1995.

Natl. Coin Machine Inst. - Address unknown since 1990.

Natl. Collaboration for Youth [11635], 1319 F St. NW, Ste. 402, Washington, DC 20004, (202)347-2080

Natl. Collaboration for Youth [★13400]

Natl. Collective of Rape Crisis and Related Groups of Aotearoa [IO], Auckland, New Zealand

Natl. Collectors Assn. of Die Doubling [22746], c/o Brian Ribar, Sec./Membership Chm., 2053 Edith Pl., Merrick, NY 11566-3306

Natl. Coll. Alumni Assn. - Address unknown since 2000.

Natl. Coll. for Criminal Defense [★5657]

Natl. Coll. of District Attorneys [5667], Univ. of South Carolina Law School, 1600 Hampton St., Ste. 414, Columbia, SC 29208, (803)705-5005

Natl. Coll. Education and Admissions Found. - Address unknown since 1995.

Natl. Coll. of Foot Surgeons - Address unknown since 2004.

Natl. Coll. of Hypnosis and Psychotherapy [IO], Nelson, United Kingdom

Natl. Coll. Physical Educ. Assn. for Men [★8985]

Natl. Coll. of the State Judiciary [★5914]

Natl. Coll. of State Trial Judges [★5914]

Natl. Coll. Student Found. - Defunct.

Natl. Collegiate Assn. for Res. of Principles [8087], 481 8th Ave., D-10, New York, NY 10001, (212)382-2402

Natl. Collegiate Assn. for Secretaries - Defunct.

Natl. Collegiate Athletic Assn. [23838], PO Box 6222, Indianapolis, IN 46206-6222, (317)917-6222

Natl. Collegiate Athletic Assn. of Wrestling Coaches and Officials [★23987]

Natl. Collegiate Baseball Writers Assn. [3135], c/o Russell Anderson, Assoc. Exec. Dir., Conf. USA, 5201 N O'Connor, Ste. 300, Irving, TX 75039, (214)774-1351

Natl. Collegiate Cross Country Coaches Assn. [★23924]

Natl. Collegiate Div. 1 Track Coaches Assn. - Address unknown since 2002.

Natl. Collegiate EMS Found. [14338], PO Box 93, West Sand Lake, NY 12196, (208)728-7342

Natl. Collegiate Football Assn. - Defunct.

Natl. Collegiate Honors Coun. [8290], 1100 Neihardt Residence Ctr., Univ. of Nebraska-Lincoln, 540 N 16th St., Lincoln, NE 68588-0627, (402)472-9150

Natl. Collegiate Honors Soc. for Anthropology [★24402]

Natl. Collegiate Inventors and Innovators Alliance [7218], 100 Venture Way, 3rd Fl., Hadley, MA 01035, (413)587-2172

Natl. Collegiate Licensing Assn. [★2630]

Natl. Collegiate Paintball Assn. [23646], c/o Chris Raehl, Pres., 530 E South Ave., Chippewa Falls, WI 54729, (612)605-8323

Natl. Collegiate Parachuting Championships - Defunct.

Natl. Collegiate Players - Defunct.

Natl. Collegiate Poultry Club - Address unknown since 1995.

Natl. Collegiate Roller Hockey Assn. [23487], 4151 W 182nd St., No. B, Torrance, CA 90504, (310)753-7285

Natl. Collegiate Ski Assn. [★23760]

Natl. Collegiate Table Tennis Assn. [23895], 2322 5th St., No. 204, Santa Monica, CA 90405

Natl. Collegiate Tennis Assn. [★23902]

Natl. Collegiate Water Ski Assn. [23977], c/o USA Water Ski, 1251 Holy Cow Rd., Polk City, FL 33868-8200, (800)533-2972

Natl. Color-Bred Assn. [21853], c/o Henry Vela, Treas., 109 Neece Dr., Irving, TX 75060

Natl. Colored Women's League [★13051]

Natl. Columbia Challenger Assn. - Address unknown since 1995.

Natl. Combination Storm Window and Door Inst. - Defunct.

Natl. Comedians' Assn. - Address unknown since 2003.

Natl. Coming Out Day [12248], c/o Human Rights Campaign, 1640 Rhode Island Ave. NW, Washington, DC 20036-3200, (202)628-4160

Natl. Commemorative Soc. - Defunct.

National Commercial Builders Council [★1035]

Natl. Commercial Finance Assn. [★2423]

Natl. Commercial Finance Assn. [★IO]

Natl. Commercial Finance Conf. [★IO]

Natl. Commercial Finance Conf. [★2423]

Natl. Commn. on Accreditation of Alcoholism and Drug Abuse Counselor Credentialing Bodies - Defunct.

Natl. Commn. Against Drunk Driving [12973], 8403 Colesville Rd., Ste. 370, Silver Spring, MD 20910, (240)247-6004

Natl. Commn. for the Certification of Acupuncturists [★15747]

Natl. Commn. on Certification of Physician Assistants [15975], 12000 Findley Rd., Ste. 200, Duluth, GA 30097, (678)417-8100

Natl. Commn. on Certification of Physician's Assistants [★15975]

Natl. Commn. on Confidentiality of Health Records - Defunct.

Natl. Commn. for Cooperative Educ. [8159], 360 Huntington Ave., 384CP, Boston, MA 02115-5096, (617)373-3770

Natl. Commn. on Correctional Hea. Care [14729], 1145 W Diversey Pkwy., Chicago, IL 60614, (773)880-1460

Natl. Commission for Culture and the Arts [IO], Manila, Philippines

Natl. Commn. for Electrologist Certification - Address unknown since 2003.

Natl. Commn. for Fraudulent Financial Reporting - Defunct.

Natl. Commn. on a Free and Responsible Media - Defunct.

Natl. Commn. for Hea. Certifying Agencies [★14591]

Natl. Commn. on Human Life, Reproduction and Rhythm [16008], PO Box 101501, Pittsburgh, PA 15237, (724)444-8045

Natl. Commn. on Jobs and Small Business - Defunct.

Natl. Commn. on Nuclear Safety and Safeguards [IO], Mexico City, Mexico

Natl. Commn. on the Public Service - Defunct.

Natl. Commn. on Res. - Defunct.

Natl. Commn. on Resources for Youth [★8408]

Natl. Commn. on the Role and Future of State Colleges and Universities - Defunct.

Natl. Commn. on Safety Education - Defunct.

National Commn. on Secondary Schooling for Hispanics [★17704]

National Commn. on Secondary Schooling for Hispanics [★IO]

Natl. Commn. on Taxes and the Internal Revenue Service - Defunct.

Natl. Commn. on Teacher Education and Professional Standards - Defunct.

Natl. Commn. for Women's Equality [★17522]

Natl. Commn. on Working Women - Defunct.

Natl. Comm. to Abolish the Federal Death Penalty - Defunct.

Natl. Comm. to Abolish HUAC [★17134]

Natl. Comm. on Accounting [★3876]

Natl. Comm. for an Adequate Overseas U.S. Information Program - Defunct.

Natl. Comm. for Adoption [★11255]

Natl. Comm. Against Discrimination in Housing - Defunct.

Natl. Comm. Against Fluoridation [★14587]

Natl. Comm. Against Mental Illness - Defunct.

Natl. Comm. Against Repressive Legislation [17134], 3321 12th St. NE, Washington, DC 20017, (202)529-4225

Natl. Comm. on Aging of Natl. Social Welfare Assembly [★11309]

Natl. Comm. on Alcoholism [★13268]

Natl. Comm. for Amateur Baseball [★23127]

Natl. Comm. on Amer. Foreign Policy [17615], 320 Park Ave., 8th Fl., New York, NY 10022-6839, (212)224-1120

Natl. Comm. on Amer. Foreign Policy [IO], New York, NY, United States

Natl. Comm. for Amish Religious Freedom [19448], 15343 Susanna Cir., Livonia, MI 48154, (734)464-3908

Natl. Comm. for Amnesty Now - Defunct.

Natl. Comm. on Art Education for the Elderly - Defunct.

Natl. Comm. for the Berne Convention - Defunct.

Natl. Comm. of Black Churchmen - Address unknown since 1995.

Natl. Comm. for Careers in the Medical Laboratory - Defunct.

Natl. Comm. of Catholic Laymen [19681]

Natl. Comm. on Central America - Address unknown since 1991.

Natl. Comm. for Certifying Agencies [16916], 2025 M St. NW, Ste. 800, Washington, DC 20036-3309, (202)367-1165

Natl. Comm. for Child Nutrition - Defunct.

Natl. Comm. for Clinical Lab. Standards [★14994]

Natl. Comm. for Clinical Lab. Standards [★14994]

Natl. Comm. for Clinical Lab. Standards [★IO]

Natl. Comm. for Clinical Lab. Standards [★IO]

Natl. Comm. to Commemorate Genocide Victims in Ukraine 1932-33 - Defunct.

Natl. Comm. to Commemorate the Millenium of Christianity in the Ukraine - Defunct.

Natl. Comm. of Communications Supervisors [★3748]

Natl. Comm. of Communications Supervisors [★IO]

Natl. Comm. on Concerns of Hispanics and Blacks - Defunct.

Natl. Comm. on Crime and the Elderly - Defunct.

Natl. Comm. in Deafness and Other Commun. Disorders [★14773]

Natl. Comm. for the Defense of Democracy in Bolivia - Defunct.

A star before a book entry number signifies that the name is not listed separately, but is mentioned within the entry.

Natl. Comm. for Economic Freedom [★17296]

Natl. Comm. for Educ. on Alcoholism [★13268]

Natl. Comm. on the Educ. of Migrant Children (of the Natl. Child Labor Comm.) [12593], 1501 Broadway, Ste. 1908, New York, NY 10036, (212)840-1801

Natl. Comm. for an Effective Cong. [17252], 122 C St. NW, Ste. 650, Washington, DC 20001, (202)639-8300

Natl. Comm. for Effective Design Legislation - Defunct.

Natl. Comm. on the Emeriti - Address unknown since 1995.

Natl. Comm. for Employer Support of the Guard and Reserve [6087], 1555 Wilson Blvd., Ste. 200, Arlington, VA 22209-2405, (703)696-1386

Natl. Comm. on Ethics of the Hearing Aid Industry - Defunct.

Natl. Comm. for Fair Divorce and Alimony Laws [★18045]

Natl. Comm. of the Fed. Ser. Campaign for Natl. Hea. Agencies [★12200]

Natl. Comm. on Films for Safety - Defunct.

Natl. Comm. on Foundations and Trusts for Community Welfare [★12652]

Natl. Comm. for a Freedom Now Party - Defunct.

Natl. Comm. for Full Employment - Defunct.

Natl. Comm. for the Furtherance of Jewish Educ. [8696], c/o Chabad of Mineola, NY, 261 Willis Ave., Mineola, NY 11501, (516)739-3636

Natl. Comm. on the Homeless and Institutional Alcoholic - Defunct.

Natl. Comm. on Household Employment - Defunct.

Natl. Comm. for a Human Life Amendment [18557], 1500 Massachusetts Ave. NW, Ste. 24, Washington, DC 20005, (202)393-0703

Natl. Comm. for the Improvement of Nursing Services [★15510]

Natl. Comm. for Independent Political Action - Address unknown since 2006.

Natl. Comm. for Insurance Taxation - Address unknown since 1995.

Natl. Comm. of the Jewish Folk Schools of the Labor Zionist Movement - Defunct.

Natl. Comm. for Judicial Reform [17963]

Natl. Comm. for Labor Israel [12460], 275 7th Ave., Rm. 1501, New York, NY 10001, (212)647-0300

National Committee for Labor Israel [IO], New York, NY, United States

Natl. Comm. for Labor Palestine [★IO]

Natl. Comm. for Labor Palestine [★12460]

Natl. Comm. for Latin and Greek [9800], c/o Nancy McKee, Chair, 239 Eacker Dr., Jeffersonville, VT 05464, (802)644-6434

Natl. Comm. to Liberalize the Tariff Laws for Art - Defunct.

Natl. Comm. for Liberation of Slovakia - Defunct.

Natl. Comm. for Limited Profit Housing - Defunct.

Natl. Comm. for Medical Res. Ethics [IO], Oslo, Norway

Natl. Comm. for Mental Hygiene [★15211]

Natl. Comm. for Motor Fleet Supervisor Training and Certification [★8212]

Natl. Comm. for a Non-Subsidized Seaway - Defunct.

Natl. Comm. for the Observance of Mother's Day [★18675]

Natl. Comm. on Pay Equity [17553], 555 New Jersey Ave. NW, Washington, DC 20001-2029, (703)920-2010

Natl. Comm. for Peace in Central America - Defunct.

Natl. Comm. for Physics [★IO]

Natl. Comm. on Planned Giving [1689], 233 McCrea St., Ste. 400, Indianapolis, IN 46225, (317)269-6274

Natl. Comm. for a Political Settlement in Vietnam - Defunct.

Natl. Comm. on Pot Bellied Pigs [4140]

Natl. Comm. for Preservation of U.S. Capitol - Defunct.

Natl. Comm. to Preserve Social Security [★18649]

Natl. Comm. to Preserve Social Security and Medicare [18649], 10 G St. NE, Ste. 600, Washington, DC 20002-4215, (202)216-0420

Natl. Comm. for the Prevention of Alcoholism [★13267]

Natl. Comm. for the Prevention of Alcoholism [★IO]

National Committee for the Prevention of Alcoholism and Drug Dependency [IO], Silver Spring, MD, United States

Natl. Comm. for the Prevention of Alcoholism and Drug Dependency [13267], c/o Intl. Commn. for the Prevention of Alcoholism and Drug Dependency, 12501 Old Columbia Pike, Silver Spring, MD 20904-6600, (301)680-6719

Natl. Comm. for the Prevention of Blindness [★16882]

Natl. Comm. for the Prevention of Elder Abuse [11308], 1612 K St. NW, Washington, DC 20006, (202)682-4140

Natl. Comm. on Property Insurance [★2171]

Natl. Comm. on Public Employee Pension Systems - Address unknown since 2003.

Natl. Comm. on Public Polls [★18370]

Natl. Comm. for Quality Assurance [16265], 1100 13th St. NW, Ste. 1000, Washington, DC 20005, (202)955-3500

Natl. Comm. on Radiation Protection [★6242]

Natl. Comm. on Radiation Protection and Measurements [★6242]

Natl. Comm. for Radiation Victims - Address unknown since 2000.

Natl. Comm. for Recording for the Blind [★16885]

Natl. Comm. of Regional Accrediting Agencies - Defunct.

Natl. Comm. Relations Advisory Coun. [★12474]

Natl. Comm. to Reopen the Rosenberg Case [17135], c/o Richard Corey, Co-Dir., PO Box 1100, New York, NY 10113-1100, (718)667-4740

Natl. Comm. to Repeal 55 MPH Speed Limit - Defunct.

Natl. Comm. to Repeal the Federal Reserve Act [18410]

Natl. Comm. for a Representative Cong. - Address unknown since 1985.

Natl. Comm. for Res. in Neruological and Communicative Disorders [★15346]

Natl. Comm. for Res. in Neurological Disorders [★15346]

Natl. Comm. for Res. in Ophthalmology and Blindness - Defunct.

Natl. Comm. for Responsible Family Life and Sex Education - Defunct.

Natl. Comm. for Responsive Philanthropy [12732], 2001 S St. NW, Ste. 620, Washington, DC 20009, (202)387-9177

Natl. Comm. to Restore Internal Security - Defunct.

Natl. Comm. for Rural Schools - Defunct.

Natl. Comm. for Senior Amers. - Address unknown since 2003.

Natl. Comm. for Sexual Civil Liberties - Address unknown since 2007.

Natl. Comm. of Shatnez Testers and Researchers - Address unknown since 1999.

Natl. Comm. for Small Bus. Mgt. Development [★3611]

Natl. Comm. for Small Bus. Mgt. Development [★IO]

Natl. Comm. on the Treatment of Intractable Pain - Defunct.

Natl. Comm. for UHF Television - Address unknown since 2000.

Natl. Comm. on Uniform Traffic Accidents Statistics [★12993]

Natl. Comm. on Uniform Traffic Laws and Ordinances [6309], 107 S West St., No. 110, Alexandria, VA 22314-2824, (800)807-5290

Natl. Comm. on United States-China Relations [17064], 71 W 23rd St., Ste. 1901, New York, NY 10010-4102, (212)645-9677

National Committee on United States-China Relations [IO], New York, NY, United States

Natl. Comm. for Urban Transportation - Defunct.

Natl. Comm. for Utilities Radio [★3762]

Natl. Comm. for Wild Flowers of the U.S. - Defunct.

Natl. Comm. for Women in Public Admin. [★6198]

Natl. Comm. of YMCAs of China [IO], Shanghai, People's Republic of China

Natl. Commodity and Barter Assn. [18411]

Natl. Commun. Assn. [9157], 1765 N St. NW, Washington, DC 20036, (202)464-4622

Natl. Commun. Coun. for Human Services [★3195]

Natl. Communications Club - Defunct.

Natl. Communications Network for the Elimination of Violence Against Women [★12034]

Natl. Community Action Agency Directors Assn. [★12770]

Natl. Community Action Agency Executive Directors Assn. [★12770]

Natl. Community Action Found. [11754], 810 1st St., Ste. 530, Washington, DC 20002, (202)842-2092

Natl. Community Building Network [11786]

Natl. Community Capital Assn. [★17233]

Natl. Community Development Assn. [17228], 522 21st St. NW, No. 120, Washington, DC 20006, (202)293-7587

Natl. Community Development Org. [11798]

Natl. Community Educ. Assn. [8126], 3929 Old Lee Hwy., No. 91-A, Fairfax, VA 22030-2421, (703)359-8973

Natl. Community Energy Mgt. Center - Defunct.

Natl. Community Land Trust Center [★17221]

Natl. Community for Latino Leadership [19203], 1701 K St. NW, Ste. 301, Washington, DC 20006, (202)721-8290

Natl. Community Mental Healthcare Coun. [★15223]

Natl. Community Pharmacists Assn. [2986], 100 Daingerfield Rd., Alexandria, VA 22314, (703)683-8200

National Community Pharmacists Assn. Foundation [★2986]

Natl. Community Radio Forum [IO], Johannesburg, Republic of South Africa

Natl. Community Reinvestment Coalition [17229], 727 15th St. NW, Ste. 900, Washington, DC 20005, (202)628-8866

Natl. Community School Educ. Assn. [★8126]

Natl. Community TV Assn. [★573]

Natl. Compadres Network [12545], PO Box 2007, Santa Ana, CA 92707, (714)745-8718

Natl. Company of Crossbowmen - Defunct.

Natl. Composition and Prepress Assn. - Defunct.

Natl. Comprehensive Cancer Network [13853], 500 Old York Rd., Ste. 250, Jenkintown, PA 19046, (215)690-0300

Natl. Computer Assn. - Address unknown since 1999.

National Computer Crime Data Center [★2091]

Natl. Computer Dealer Assn. - Defunct.

Natl. Cmpt. Graphics Assn. [★894]

Natl. Cmpt. Graphics Assn. [★IO]

Natl. Computer Service Network - Address unknown since 1994.

Natl. Concierge Assn. [1956], c/o Sara-ann G. Kasner, Pres., 2920 Idaho Ave. N, Minneapolis, MN 55427, (612)317-2932

Natl. Concilio of America - Address unknown since 2001.

Natl. Concrete Burial Vault Assn. [2787], PO Box 917525, Longwood, FL 32791-7525, (407)788-1996

Natl. Concrete Contractors Assn. [★1001]

Natl. Concrete Masonry Assn. [929], 13750 Sunrise Valley Dr., Herndon, VA 20171-4662, (703)713-1900

Natl. Condominium Owners Assn. - Defunct.

Natl. Confectioners Assn. of the U.S. [1544], 8320 Old Courthouse Rd., Ste. 300, Vienna, VA 22182, (703)790-5750

Natl. Confectionary Sales Assn. [3419], c/o Teresa M. Tarantino, Co-Exec. Dir., 10225 Berea Rd., Ste. B, Cleveland, OH 44102, (216)631-8200

Natl. Confectionery Sales Assn. of Am. [★3419]

Natl. Confed. of Bakers [IO], Paris, France

Natl. Confed. of Commerce [IO], Rio de Janeiro, Brazil

Natl. Confed. of Hungarian Trade Unions [IO], Budapest, Hungary

Natl. Confed. of Ice Cream Producers [IO], Paris, France

Natl. Confed. of Workers in Educ. [IO], Brasilia, Brazil

Natl. Conf. on the Advancement of Res. - Defunct.

Natl. Conf. of Appellate Court Clerks [5629], c/o Sandra L. Skinner, Pres., Missouri Court of Appeals, Southern Dist., 300 Hammons Pkwy., Springfield, MO 65806, (417)895-6811

Reference to "IO" in place of a book number signifies that the association may be found in the 45th edition of International Organizations.

Natl. Conf. of Artists - Address unknown since 1994.

Natl. Conf. of Bankruptcy Judges [5909], c/o Ms. Christine J. Molick, Exec. Dir., 241 Aristides Dr., Irmo, SC 29063, (803)749-4115

Natl. Conf. of Bar Examiners [5950], 402 W Wilson St., Madison, WI 53703-3614, (608)280-8550

Natl. Conf. of Bar Executives [★5948]

Natl. Conf. of Bar Foundations [5951], c/o Amer. Bar Assn., Div. for Bar Services, 321 N Clark St., Ste. 2000, Chicago, IL 60610, (312)988-6008

Natl. Conf. of Bar Foundations [IO], Chicago, IL, United States

Natl. Conf. of Bar Presidents [5516], c/o Pamela Robinson, Assoc. Dir., Div. for Bar Services, 321 N Clark St., 20th Fl., Chicago, IL 60610, (312)988-5345

Natl. Conf. of Bar-Related Title Insurers [★2204]

Natl. Conf. of Bar Secretaries [★5948]

Natl. Conf. of the Bishop of Brazil-Pastoral of the Child [IO], Curitiba, Brazil

Natl. Conf. of Black Lawyers [IO], Lansing, MI, United States

Natl. Conf. of Black Lawyers [5517], PO Box 80043, Lansing, MI 48908-0043, (866)266-5091

National Conference of Black Lawyers [★5519]

Natl. Conf. of Black Mayors [6129], 1151 Cleveland Ave., Bldg. D, East Point, GA 30344, (404)765-6444

Natl. Conf. of Black Political Scientists - Address unknown since 1995.

Natl. Conf. for Catechetical Leaders [★19934]

Natl. Conf. for Catechetical Leadership [19934], 125 Michigan Ave. NE, Washington, DC 20017, (202)884-9753

Natl. Conf. of Catholic Bishops [★19735]

Natl. Conf. of Catholic Charities [★13158]

Natl. Conf. of Catholic Guidance Councils [★8166]

Natl. Conf. of Catholics in Youth Serving Agencies - Defunct.

Natl. Conf. of Christian Employers and Managers - Address unknown since 1995.

Natl. Conf. of Christians and Jews [★19904]

Natl. Conf. on Citizenship [17073], PO Box 15129, Chevy Chase, MD 20825, (202)467-8833

Natl. Conf. on City Planning [★5586]

Natl. Conf. of Commercial Receivable Companies [★2423]

Natl. Conf. of Commercial Receivable Companies [★IO]

Natl. Conf. of Commissioners on Uniform State Laws [6282], 211 E Ontario St., Ste. 1300, Chicago, IL 60611-3261, (312)915-0195

Natl. Conf. for Community and Justice [19904], 760 N Frontage Rd., Ste. 105, Willowbrook, IL 60527, (630)789-6709

Natl. Conf. of County Development Coordinators [★5622]

Natl. Conf. of Court Administrative Officers [★5625]

Natl. Conf. of CPA Practitioners [47], 22 Jericho Tpke., Mineola, NY 11501, (516)333-8282

Natl. Conf. on Developmental Disabilities [★12575]

Natl. Conf. of Diocesan Guidance Councils [★8166]

Natl. Conf. of Diocesan Vocation Directors [19682], 450 Hewett St., Neillsville, WI 54456, (715)254-0830

Natl. Conf. of Directors of Religious Educ. [★19934]

Natl. Conf. of Editorial Writers [3136], 3899 N Front St., Harrisburg, PA 17110, (717)703-3015

Natl. Conf. of Executives of the Arc [2506], 1010 Wayne Ave., Ste. 650, Silver Spring, MD 20910, (301)565-5475

Natl. Conf. of Executives of Higher Educ. Loan Plans [★8351]

Natl. Conf. of Family Relations [★12164]

Natl. Conf. of Fed. Trial Judges [5910], c/o Amer. Bar Assn., 321 N Clark St., 19th Fl., Chicago, IL 60610, (312)988-5689

Natl. Conf. of Firemen and Oilers [24058], 1023 15th St. NW, 10th Fl., Washington, DC 20005-2630, (202)962-0981

Natl. Conf. on Fluid Power [7085], 3333 N Mayfair Rd., Ste. 211, Milwaukee, WI 53222-3219, (414)778-3344

Natl. Conf. of Forty Plus Clubs of the U.S. - Defunct.

Natl. Conf. of Governmental Indus. Hygienists [★15625]

Natl. Conf. of Hospital Administrators - Defunct.

Natl. Conf. of Insurance Legislators [5832], 385 Jordan Rd., Troy, NY 12180, (518)687-0178

Natl. Conf. on Interstate Milk Shipments [4493], c/o Leon Townsend, Exec. Sec., 123 Buena Vista Dr., Frankfort, KY 40601, (502)695-0253

Natl. Conf. of Jewish Communal Ser. [★12472]

Natl. Conf. of Jewish Communal Ser. [★IO]

Natl. Conf. of Judicial Councils - Defunct.

Natl. Conf. of Law Historians of America - Address unknown since 1989.

Natl. Conf. of Lawyers and Social Workers - Defunct.

Natl. Conf. of Lieutenant Governors [★6285]

Natl. Conf. of Local Environmental Hea. Administrators [16246], c/o Univ. of Washington, Dept. of Environmental Hea., PO Box 357234, Seattle, WA 98195-7234, (206)616-2097

Natl. Conf. of the Methodist Student Movement - Defunct.

Natl. Conf. on Ministry to the Armed Forces - Defunct.

Natl. Conf. of Non-Profit Shipping Assns. - Address unknown since 1995.

Natl. Conf. on Parent Involvement - Address unknown since 2004.

Natl. Conf. on Peacemaking and Conflict Resolution [18118], 1718 E Speedway Blvd., No. 305, Tucson, AZ 85719, (520)670-1541

Natl. Conf. of Personal Managers [174], PO Box 50008, Henderson, NV 89016-0008, (702)837-1170

Natl. Conf. on Power Transmission - Defunct.

Natl. Conf. of Professors of Educational Administration - Address unknown since 1995.

Natl. Conf. on Public Employee Retirement Systems [5570], 444 N Capitol St. NW, Ste. 221, Washington, DC 20001-1512, (877)202-5706

Natl. Conf. of Public Youth Agencies - Defunct.

Natl. Conf. of Puerto Rican Women [17554], 1220 L St. NW, Ste. No. 177, Washington, DC 20005-4018

Natl. Conf. of Real Estate Editors [★3132]

Natl. Conf. of Religious Vocation Directors [★19692]

Natl. Conf. for Repeal of Taxes on Transportation - Defunct.

Natl. Conf. on Res. in Language and Literacy - Address unknown since 2002.

Natl. Conf. of Schools of Design [★7978]

Natl. Conf. of Shomrim Societies [12478], c/o Martin Turetzky, Treas., 264 E Broadway, No. C1905, New York, NY 10002, (212)777-7809

Natl. Conf. on Social Welfare - Defunct.

Natl. Conf. on Soviet Jewry [★17448]

Natl. Conf. on Soviet Jewry [★IO]

Natl. Conf. of Special Court Judges [★5911]

Natl. Conf. of Specialized Court Judges [5911], c/o ABA Judicial Div., 321 N Clark St., 19th Fl., Chicago, IL 60610, (312)988-5705

Natl. Conf. of Standards Labs. [★7698]

Natl. Conf. of Standards Labs. [★IO]

Natl. Conf. of State Court Administrators [★5625]

Natl. Conf. of State Criminal Justice Planning Administrators [★11881]

Natl. Conf. of State Fleet Administrators [6322], 1544 W 6785 S, West Jordan, UT 84084, (801)685-3040

Natl. Conf. of State Gen. Ser. Officers [★6278]

Natl. Conf. of State Historic Preservation Officers [5787], 444 N Capitol St. NW, Hall of States, Ste. 342, Washington, DC 20001-1512, (202)624-5465

Natl. Conf. of State Legislative Leaders [★6283]

Natl. Conf. of State Legislatures [6283], 700 E First Pl., Denver, CO 80230-7143, (303)364-7700

Natl. Conf. of State Liquor Administrators [★5445]

Natl. Conf. of State Liquor Administrators [5447], c/o Ms. Pamela D. Salario, Exec. Dir., 6183 Beau Douglas Ave., Gonzales, LA 70737, (225)473-7209

Natl. Conf. on State Parks [★6161]

Natl. Conf. of State Pharmaceutical Assn. Secretaries [★15943]

Natl. Conf. of State Social Security Administrators [6259], Social Security Div., 2 Northside 75, Ste. 300, Atlanta, GA 30318-7778, (404)603-5608

Natl. Conf. of State Societies [19382], 237 Hall of States, 444 N Capitol St. NW, Washington, DC 20001

Natl. Conf. of State Trans. Specialists [6323], c/o Mr. Terry Willert, Pres., Public Utilities Commn., 1560 Broadway, Ste. 250, Denver, CO 80202, (303)894-2850

Natl. Conf. of States on Building Codes and Standards [5552], 505 Huntmar Park Dr., Ste. 210, Herndon, VA 20170, (703)437-0100

Natl. Conf. on St. and Highway Safety [★6309]

Natl. Conf. on Student Leadership [9188], 2718 Dryden Dr., Madison, WI 53704-3086, (608)246-3590

Natl. Conf. on Student Services [★9188]

Natl. Conf. on Synagogue Youth [20165], 11 Broadway, New York, NY 10004, (212)613-8233

National Conf. on Trusteeship [★7889]

Natl. Conf. on Tuberculosis Secretaries [★16357]

Natl. Conf. on Tuberculosis Workers [★16357]

Natl. Conf. on Uniform Reciprocal Enforcement of Support [★5701]

Natl. Conf. of Vicars for Religious - Address unknown since 2002.

Natl. Conf. on Weights and Measures [6269], 15245 Shady Grove Rd., Ste. 130, Rockville, MD 20850-6240, (240)632-9454

Natl. Conf. of Women's Bar Associations [5518], PO Box 82366, Portland, OR 97282-0366, (503)657-3813

Natl. Conf. of Yeshiva Principals [9017]

Natl. Conferences on Undergraduate Res. [9062], c/o Janet Stocks, Chair, Center for Academic and Professional Success, Baldwin-Wallace Coll., 275 Eastland Rd., 201 Bonds, Berea, OH 44017-2088, (440)826-2379

Natl. Congenital Port Wine Stain Found. - Defunct.

Natl. Cong. of Amer. Indians [18096], 1301 Connecticut Ave. NW, Ste. 200, Washington, DC 20036, (202)466-7767

Natl. Cong. of Animal Trainers and Breeders [11435]

Natl. Cong. of Black Faculty - Address unknown since 2001.

Natl. Cong. of Black Women [6119], 1224 W St. SE, Ste. 200, Washington, DC 20020, (202)678-6788

Natl. Cong. of Colored Parents and Teachers [★8954]

Natl. Cong. for Community Economic Development - Defunct.

Natl. Cong. for Educational Excellence - Defunct.

Natl. Cong. for Fathers and Children [12172], 9454 Wilshire Blvd., Ste. 907, Beverly Hills, CA 90212, (310)247-6051

Natl. Cong. of Floor Covering Assns. - Defunct.

Natl. Cong. of Hispanic Amer. Citizens - Defunct.

Natl. Cong. of Inventors Organizations [7230], 8306 Wilshire Blvd., Ste. 391, Beverly Hills, CA 90211, (323)878-6952

Natl. Cong. of Jewish Deaf - Address unknown since 2001.

Natl. Cong. for Men - Address unknown since 2001.

Natl. Cong. of Mothers [★8954]

Natl. Cong. of Mothers and Parent-Teachers Associations [★8954]

Natl. Cong. of Neighborhood Women - Defunct.

Natl. Cong. of Parents and Teachers [★8954]

Natl. Cong. of Parents and Teachers; Natl. PTA - [8954]

Natl. Cong. of Patriotic Organizations [18185]

Natl. Cong. of Petroleum Retailers [★2946]

Natl. Cong. for Puerto Rican Rights - Address unknown since 1995.

Natl. Cong. of Puerto Rican Veterans - Address unknown since 2001.

National Cong. Recreation and Parks [★6161]

Natl. Cong. on Rights and Responsibilities of the Public in Commercial Broadcasting - Defunct.

Natl. Cong. on Surveying and Mapping [★7717]

Natl. Cong. of Vietnamese Americans [19425], 6433 Northanna Dr., Springfield, VA 22150, (703)971-9178

National Congressional Club - Address unknown since 2001.

Natl. Conservation Bur. - Defunct.

Natl. Conservation District Employees Assn. [24209], 1607 W Jackson St., Macomb, IL 61455, (309)833-1711

Natl. Conservative Congressional Comm. - Address unknown since 1987.

A star before a book entry number signifies that the name is not listed separately, but is mentioned within the entry.

Natl. Conservative Found. - Address unknown since 1999.

Natl. Conservative Political Action Comm. - Address unknown since 1999.

Natl. Consortium on Alternatives for Youth at Risk - Address unknown since 2008.

Natl. Consortium of Arts and Letters for Historically Black Colls. and Universities [8111]

Natl. Consortium for Black Professional Development [8049]

Natl. Consortium of Breast Centers [13773], PO Box 1334, Warsaw, IN 46581-1334, (574)267-8058

Natl. Consortium of Chem. Dependency Nurses [★15474]

Natl. Consortium for Child Mental Health Services - Address unknown since 1999.

Natl. Consortium for Computer-Based Music Instruction [★8905]

Natl. Consortium for Educational Access - Address unknown since 2000.

Natl. Consortium for Graduate Degrees for Minorities in Engg. [★8372]

Natl. Consortium for Graduate Degrees for Minorities in Engg. and Sci. [8372], 1800 K St. NW, Ste. 900, Washington, DC 20006, (202)457-8672

Natl. Consortium for Graduate Degrees for Minorities in Sci. and Engg. [★8372]

Natl. Consortium on Hea. Sci. and Tech. Educ. [8473], c/o Michigan Hea. Coun., 2410 Woodlake Dr., Okemos, MI 48864-3997, (517)347-3332

Natl. Consortium for Justice Info. and Statistics; SEARCH - The [11892]

Natl. Consortium for Plant Conservation - Defunct.

Natl. Consortium of the Rubber Indus. [IO], Madrid, Spain

Natl. Consortium of Universities Preparing Rural Special Educators - Defunct.

Natl. Constables Assn. [5992], 16 Stonybrook Dr., Levittown, PA 19055-2217, (215)547-6400

Natl. Construction Employers Coun. - Defunct.

Natl. Construction Industry Coun. - Address unknown since 1988.

Natl. Constr. Investigators Assn. [5606]

Natl. Construction Software Assn. - Address unknown since 1995.

Natl. Constructors Assn. - Address unknown since 2003.

Natl. Consultation on Pornography and Obscenity [★18374]

Natl. Consumer Affairs Internship Program [17337]

Natl. Consumer Bd. for Stuttering - Defunct.

Natl. Consumer Center for Legal Services [★6022]

Natl. Consumer Center for Legal Services [★IO]

Natl. Consumer Finance Assn. [★2422]

Natl. Consumer Forum [IO], Johannesburg, Republic of South Africa

Natl. Consumer Fraud Task Force - Address unknown since 2004.

Natl. Consumer Law Center [5611], 77 Summer St., 10th Fl., Boston, MA 02110-1006, (617)542-8010

Natl. Consumer Res. Inst. - Address unknown since 1995.

Natl. Consumer's Assn. of Swaziland [IO], Mbabane, Swaziland

Natl. Consumers Coun. [★13342]

Natl. Consumers League [17338], 1701 K St. NW, Ste. 1200, Washington, DC 20006, (202)835-3323

Natl. Contact Lens Examiners [15723], 6506 Loisdale Rd., Ste. 209, Springfield, VA 22150-1815, (703)719-5800

Natl. Contesters Assn. - Defunct.

Natl. Contract Mgt. Assn. [1744], 21740 Beaumeade Cir., Ste. 125, Ashburn, VA 20147, (571)382-0082

Natl. Contract Sweepers Inst. - Address unknown since 1994.

Natl. Convenience Store Advisory Gp. [3420], 2063 Oak St., Jacksonville, FL 32204, (904)384-1010

Natl. Convenience Store Distributors Assn. [IO], Laval, QC, Canada

Natl. Convention Assn. [2688], 1560 Broadway, 46th St., Times Sq., New York, NY 10036-1518, (212)555-8665

Natl. Convention of Gospel Choirs and Choruses - Address unknown since 1995.

Natl. Convention of Insurance Commissioners [★5830]

Natl. Cooperative Bus. Assn. [1073], 1401 New York Ave. NW, Ste. 1100, Washington, DC 20005, (202)638-6222

Natl. Cooperative Grocers Assn. [1074], 389 E Coll. St., Iowa City, IA 52240, (319)466-9029

National Cooperative Highway Res. Program [★6312]

Natl. Cooperative Milk Producers Fed. [★4489]

Natl. Cooperatives [★4484]

Natl. Coordinating Comm. of the Beverage Industry - Defunct.

Natl. Coordinating Comm. to End the War in Vietnam - Defunct.

Natl. Coordinating Comm. for Multiemployer Plans [1242], 815 16th St. NW, Washington, DC 20006, (202)737-5315

Natl. Coordinating Comm. for the Promotion of History [★10135]

Natl. Coordinating Coun. on Drug Education - Defunct.

Natl. Coordinating Coun. on Emergency Mgt. [★5563]

Natl. Coordinating Coun. on Emergency Mgt. [★IO]

Natl. Coordinating Coun. for Medication Error Reporting and Prevention [14653], c/o Deborah Nadzam, PhD, Chair, One Renaissance Blvd., Oakbrook Terrace, IL 60181, (630)261-5048

Natl. Coordinating Off. for Latin and Greek [★9800]

Natl. Cops for Life [18558], PO Box 267, Cutchogue, NY 11935

Natl. Corn Growers Assn. [4310], 632 Cepi Dr., Chesterfield, MO 63005-1221, (636)733-9004

Natl. Corporate Cash Mgt. Assn. [★1403]

National Corporate Leadership Program [★12205]

Natl. Corporate Theatre Fund [11027], 505 8th Ave., Ste. 2303, New York, NY 10018, (212)750-6895

Natl. Correctional Indus. Assn. [11880], 1202 N Charles St., Baltimore, MD 21201, (410)230-3972

Natl. Correctional Recreational Assn. - Defunct.

Natl. Corrugated Metal Pipe Assn. [★3035]

Natl. Corrugated Steel Pipe Assn. [3035], 14070 Proton Rd., Ste. 100, LB 9, Dallas, TX 75244, (972)850-1907

Natl. Corvette Owners Assn. [21728], 900 S Washington St., Ste. G-13, Falls Church, VA 22046, (703)533-7222

Natl. Corvette Restorers Soc. [21729], 6291 Day Rd., Cincinnati, OH 45252-1334, (513)385-8526

Natl. Cosmetology Assn. [1085], 401 N Michigan Ave., 22nd Fl., Chicago, IL 60611, (312)527-6765

Natl. Costumers Assn. [249], 121 N Bosart Ave., Indianapolis, IN 46201, (317)351-1940

Natl. Cotton Batting Inst. [1094], 4322 Bloombury St., Southaven, MS 38672, (662)449-0000

Natl. Cotton Coun. of Am. [1095], PO Box 820285, Memphis, TN 38182-0285, (901)274-9030

Natl. Cotton Ginners' Assn. [1096], PO Box 820285, Memphis, TN 38182-0285, (901)274-9030

Natl. Cottonseed Products Assn. [2854], 104 Timber Creek Dr., Ste. 200, PO Box 172267, Cordova, TN 38018-4234, (901)682-0800

Natl. Coun. for Accreditation of Teacher Educ. [7879], 2010 Massachusetts Ave. NW, Ste. 500, Washington, DC 20036, (202)466-7496

Natl. Coun. of Acoustical Consultants [646], 7150 Winton Dr., Ste. 300, Indianapolis, IN 46268, (317)328-0642

Natl. Coun. of Acupuncture Schools and Colleges [★15743]

Natl. Coun. of Administrative Women in Education - Address unknown since 2001.

Natl. Coun. of Administrators of Adult Education - Address unknown since 2002.

Natl. Coun. for Adoption [11255], 225 N Washington St., Alexandria, VA 22314, (703)299-6633

Natl. Coun. on Adult Jewish Education - Defunct.

Natl. Coun. for Advanced Mfg. [2563], 2000 L St. NW, Ste. 807, Washington, DC 20036, (202)429-2220

Natl. Coun. for the Advancement of Educ. Writing [★3112]

Natl. Coun. of African-Amer. Men - Address unknown since 2001.

Natl. Coun. Against Compulsory Service - Defunct.

Natl. Coun. Against Hea. Fraud [★17692]

Natl. Coun. Against Hea. Fraud [17692], 119 Foster St., Bldg. R, 2nd Fl., Peabody, MA 01960, (978)532-9383

Natl. Coun. Against Illegal Liquor - Defunct.

Natl. Coun. on the Aging [11309], 1901 L St. NW, 4th Fl., Washington, DC 20036, (202)479-1200

Natl. Coun. for Agricultural Educ. [4091], 1410 King St., Ste. 400, Alexandria, VA 22314, (703)838-5882

Natl. Coun. of Agricultural Employers [4079], 1112 16th St. NW, Ste. 920, Washington, DC 20036, (202)728-0300

Natl. Coun. on Agricultural Life and Labor - Defunct.

Natl. Coun. on Agricultural Life and Labor Res. Fund [12322], 363 Saulsbury Rd., Dover, DE 19904, (302)678-9400

Natl. Coun. for Air and Stream Improvement [4690], PO Box 13318, Research Triangle Park, NC 27709-3318, (919)941-6400

Natl. Coun. on Alcoholism [★13268]

Natl. Coun. on Alcoholism and Drug Dependence [13268], 244 E 58th St., 4th Fl., New York, NY 10022, (212)269-7797

Natl. Coun. on Alternative Health Care Policy - Defunct.

Natl. Coun. for Alternative Work Patterns - Defunct.

Natl. Coun. of Amer. Baptist Women [★19468]

Natl. Coun. of Amer. Importers [★2297]

Natl. Coun. of Amer. Shipbuilders [★2592]

Natl. Coun. of Applied Economic Res. [IO], New Delhi, India

Natl. Coun. of Architectural Registration Boards [IO], Washington, DC, United States

Natl. Coun. of Architectural Registration Boards [5466], 1801 K St. NW, Ste. 1100-K, Washington, DC 20006-1310, (202)783-6500

Natl. Coun. on Art in Jewish Life - Defunct.

Natl. Coun. on the Arts and Govt. - Defunct.

Natl. Coun. of Asian Amer. Bus. Associations [774], PO Box 2157, Walnut, CA 91789, (831)425-4502

Natl. Coun. of Asian Indian Organizations in North America [★19114]

Natl. Coun. of Asian Pacific Americans [17013], c/o Lisa Hasegawa, Chair, 1001 Connecticut Ave. NW, Ste. 730, Washington, DC 20036, (202)223-2442

Natl. Coun. of Athletic Training [8987], c/o Natl. Assn. for Sport and Physical Educ., 1900 Assn. Dr., Reston, VA 20191-1598, (703)476-3410

Natl. Coun. for Better Education - Address unknown since 1994.

Natl. Coun. of BIA Educators [★8938]

Natl. Coun. of Bishops, USA [19683], PO Box 1403, Green Cove Springs, FL 32043, (863)802-4536

Natl. Coun. on Black Aging - Address unknown since 2000.

Natl. Coun. of Black Engineers and Scientists [7618], 1525 Aviation Blvd., Ste. C-424, Redondo Beach, CA 90278, (213)896-9779

Natl. Coun. for Black Studies - Address unknown since 2002.

Natl. Coun. for the Blind of Ireland [IO], Drumcondra, Ireland

Natl. Coun. of Boards of Beauty Culture [★5616]

Natl. Coun. of Brown Swiss Cattle Breeders of Australia [IO], Leura, Australia

Natl. Coun. of Building Material Producers [★IO]

Natl. Coun. for Bus. Educ. [★8036]

Natl. Coun. on Business Mail - Address unknown since 1995.

Natl. Coun. of the Canadian-Soviet Friendship [★IO]

Natl. Coun. of Career Women - Address unknown since 1999.

Natl. Coun. of Catholic Laity - Defunct.

Natl. Coun. of Catholic Men - Defunct.

Natl. Coun. of Catholic Nurses - Defunct.

Natl. Coun. of Catholic Women [19684], 200 N Glebe Rd., Ste. 703, Arlington, VA 22203, (703)224-0990

Natl. Coun. of Catholic Youth - Defunct.

Natl. Coun. for Cement and Building Materials [IO], New Delhi, India

Natl. Coun. of Chain Restaurants [1957], 325 7th St. NW, Ste. 1100, Washington, DC 20004, (202)626-8183

Natl. Coun. of Chief State School Officers [★8246]

Natl. Coun. on Child Abuse and Family Violence [12035], 1025 Connecticut Ave. NW, Ste. 1000, Washington, DC 20036, (202)429-6695

Reference to "IO" in place of a book number signifies that the association may be found in the 45th edition of International Organizations.

Natl. Coun. for Children and TV [★17186]
Natl. Coun. for Children's Rights [★12007]
Natl. Coun. of Chiropractic Hosp. and Sanitaria [★13988]
Natl. Coun. of Chiropractic Roentgenologists [★16288]
Natl. Coun. for the Church and Social Action - Address unknown since 1991.
Natl. Coun. of Churches [★19905]
Natl. Coun. of Churches [★19935]
Natl. Coun. of Churches [19852], 475 Riverside Dr., Ste. 880, New York, NY 10115, (212)870-2227
Natl. Coun. of Churches of Burundi [IO], Bujumbura, Burundi
Natl. Coun. of Churches of Christ in the U.S.A. [19905], 475 Riverside Dr., Ste. 880, New York, NY 10115, (212)870-2227
Natl. Coun. of Churches Commn. on Women in Ministry [★20622]
Natl. Coun. of Churches; Dept. of United Church Women of the [★20618]
Natl. Coun. of Churches, Educ. and Leadership Ministries Commn. [19935], 475 Riverside Dr., Ste. 880, New York, NY 10115-0500, (212)870-2141
Natl. Coun. of Churches Energy Project - Defunct.
Natl. Coun. of Churches, Ministries in Christian Educ. [★19935]
Natl. Coun. of Churches; Professors and Res. Sect. of the Division of Christian Educ. of the [★19939]
Natl. Coun. of Churches - Women in Ministry Gp. [20622]
Natl. Coun. for Civic Responsibility - Defunct.
Natl. Coun. of Coal Lessors [845], 902 Oakbridge Dr., Hurricane, WV 25526
Natl. Coun. of Coll. Publications Advisers [★8708]
Natl. Coun. of Columbia Assns. in Civil Service - Address unknown since 1995.
Natl. Coun. of Commercial Plant Breeders [5175], 225 Reinekers Ln., Ste. 650, Alexandria, VA 22314, (703)837-8140
Natl. Coun. of Community Bankers [★461]
Natl. Coun. for Community Behavioral Healthcare [15223], 12300 Twinbrook Pkwy., Ste. 320, Rockville, MD 20852, (301)984-6200
Natl. Coun. of Community Churches [★19850]
Natl. Coun. of Community Churches [★19850]
Natl. Coun. of Community Churches [★IO]
Natl. Coun. of Community Churches [★IO]
Natl. Coun. on Community Foundations [★12652]
Natl. Coun. of Community Hospitals - Defunct.
Natl. Coun. on Community Mental Hea. Centers [★15223]
Natl. Coun. for Community Relations [★9032]
Natl. Coun. on Community Services and Continuing Educ. [★8152]
Natl. Coun. for Community Services to Intl. Visitors [★17903]
Natl. Coun. for Community Services to Intl. Visitors [★IO]
Natl. Coun. of Community World Affairs Organizations [★IO]
Natl. Coun. of Community World Affairs Organizations [★18843]
Natl. Coun. on Compensation Insurance [2221], 901 Peninsula Corporate Cir., Boca Raton, FL 33487, (561)893-1000
Natl. Coun. on Compulsive Gambling [★12212]
Natl. Coun. for Computer Based Training - Defunct.
Natl. Coun. for the Conservation of Plants and Gardens [IO], Woking, United Kingdom
Natl. Coun. for Continuing Educ. and Training [8152], PO Box 820062, Portland, OR 97282-1062, (503)233-1842
Natl. Coun. to Control Handguns [★17588]
Natl. Coun. of Corvette Clubs [21730], c/o Rhonda Higgins, 907 Oakcrest Dr., Champaign, IL 61821-4167, (800)245-8388
Natl. Coun. of County Assn. Executives [5624], c/o Kaye Braaten, 503 4th Ave. N, Wahpeton, ND 58075-4405, (701)642-2237
Natl. Coun. on Crime and Delinquency [11843], 1970 Broadway, Ste. 500, Oakland, CA 94612, (510)208-0500
Natl. Coun. for Critical Analysis - Defunct.
Natl. Coun. for Culture and Art - Address unknown since 2001.

Natl. Coun. of Dance Teacher Organizations [★8189]
Natl. Coun. of Dance Teachers Organizations [★23325]
Natl. Coun., Daughters of America [19132]
Natl. Coun. of Development Commun. [IO], Varanasi, India
Natl. Coun. for Developmental Commun. [★IO]
Natl. Coun. for Drama Training [IO], London, United Kingdom
Natl. Coun. on Drug Abuse - Defunct.
Natl. Coun. on Drugs - Defunct.
Natl. Coun. on Economic Educ. [8217], 1140 Ave. of the Americas, 2nd Fl., New York, NY 10036, (212)730-7007
Natl. Coun. on Educ. for the Ceramic Arts [9836], 77 Erie Village Sq., Ste. 280, Erie, CO 80516-6996, (303)828-2811
Natl. Coun. of Educ. Providers [8329], 1001 Connecticut Ave. NW, Ste. 216, Washington, DC 20036, (202)822-5076
Natl. Coun. for Educational Awards [★IO]
Natl. Coun. of Educational Opportunity Associations [★8324]
Natl. Coun. of Educational Res. and Training [IO], New Delhi, India
Natl. Coun. for Educational Tech. [★IO]
Natl. Coun. of Elected County Executives - Defunct.
Natl. Coun. for Elementary Sci. [★9100]
Natl. Coun. for Elementary Sci. [★IO]
Natl. Coun. on Employment Policy - Address unknown since 1999.
Natl. Coun. for the Encouragement of Patriotism - Defunct.
Natl. Coun. of Engg. Examiners [★7031]
Natl. Coun. of Engineers and Technicians [★IO]
Natl. Coun. for Equal Business Opportunity - Defunct.
Natl. Coun. of Erectors, Fabricators and Riggers [1042], 10382 Main St., Ste. 200, PO Box 3687, Fairfax, VA 22038, (703)591-1870
Natl. Coun. on Ethics in Human Res. [IO], Ottawa, ON, Canada
Natl. Coun. for Eurasian and East European Res. [10968], 2601 4th Ave., Ste. 310, Seattle, WA 98121, (206)441-6433
Natl. Coun. on the Evaluation of Foreign Educational Credentials - Address unknown since 2002.
Natl. Coun. of Examiners for Engg. and Surveying [7031], 280 Seneca Creek Rd., PO Box 1686, Clemson, SC 29633-1686, (864)654-6824
Natl. Coun. of Exchangors [3331], PO Box 668, Morro Bay, CA 93443-0668, (800)324-1031
Natl. Coun. for Families and TV [17186], c/o Leo Burnett Advt., 6500 Wilshire Blvd., Ste. 1950, Los Angeles, CA 90048, (323)866-6020
Natl. Coun. for Family Reconciliation - Address unknown since 1988.
Natl. Coun. on Family Relations [12164], 3989 Central Ave. NE, Ste. 550, Minneapolis, MN 55421, (763)781-9331
Natl. Coun. on Family Relations; Educ. and Enrichment Sect. of the [12151]
Natl. Coun. on Family Relations; Family and Hea. Sect. of the [14385]
Natl. Coun. on Family Relations; Family Therapy Sect. of the [16612]
Natl. Coun. on Family Relations Family Therapy Sect. [★16612]
Natl. Coun. on Family Relations; Feminism and Family Stud. Sect. of the [12156]
Natl. Coun. of Family Relations Feminism and Family Stud. Sect. [★12156]
Natl. Coun. of Farmer Cooperatives [4483], 50 F St. NW, Ste. 900, Washington, DC 20001, (202)626-8700
Natl. Coun. for Fishing Vessel Safety and Insurance - Defunct.
Natl. Coun. on Foreign Language and Intl. Stud. [★8593]
Natl. Coun. of Forestry Assn. Executives - Address unknown since 2002.
Natl. Coun. on Gene Resources [7118], 1738 Thousand Oaks Blvd., Berkeley, CA 94707, (510)524-8973

Natl. Coun. for GeoCosmic Res. [6841], c/o Liane Thomas Wade, Exec. Sec., 531 Main St., No. 1612, New York, NY 10044, (212)838-6247
Natl. Coun. for Geographic Educ. [8457], 206A Martin Hall, Jacksonville State Univ., Jacksonville, AL 36265-1602, (256)782-5293
Natl. Coun. of Geography Teachers [★8457]
Natl. Coun. for the Gifted - Defunct.
Natl. Coun. on Governmental Accounting [★5427]
Natl. Coun. for Graduate Entrepreneurship [IO], Birmingham, United Kingdom
Natl. Coun. on Harness Racing - Defunct.
Natl. Coun. of Hea. Centers [★14540]
Natl. Coun. of Hea. Facilities Finance Authorities [1850], 2211 Clermont St., Denver, CO 80207
Natl. Coun. on Health Laboratory Services - Defunct.
Natl. Coun. of Higher Educ. Loan Programs [8351], 1100 Connecticut Ave. NW, Ste. 1200, Washington, DC 20036-4110, (202)822-2106
Natl. Coun. of Hispanic Women - Address unknown since 2004.
Natl. Coun. for Historic Sites and Buildings [★10051]
Natl. Coun. for History Educ. [8508], 26915 Westwood Rd., Ste. B-2, Westlake, OH 44145, (440)835-1776
Natl. Coun. for Hospice and Specialist Palliative Care Services [★IO]
Natl. Coun. on Hotel and Restaurant Educ. [★IO]
Natl. Coun. on Hotel and Restaurant Educ. [★8525]
Natl. Coun. of the Housing Indus. [647], 1201 15th St. NW, Washington, DC 20005, (202)266-8200
Natl. Coun. on Hunger and Malnutrition in the U.S. - Defunct.
Natl. Coun. on Illegitimacy - Defunct.
Natl. Coun. of Independent Colleges and Universities [★8539]
Natl. Coun. of Independent Junior Colleges - Defunct.
Natl. Coun. on Independent Living [11968], 1710 Rhode Island Ave. NW, 5th Fl., Washington, DC 20036, (202)207-0334
Natl. Coun. of Independent Petroleum Assn. [★2943]
Natl. Coun. of Independent Schools [★8540]
Natl. Coun. of Independent Schools' Associations [★IO]
Natl. Coun. of Independent Truckers - Defunct.
Natl. Coun. for Industrial Defense - Defunct.
Natl. Coun. for Industrial Innovation - Address unknown since 1995.
Natl. Coun. of Indus. Naval Air Stations [6088]
Natl. Coun. on Infant and Child Care - Defunct.
Natl. Coun. of Innovation, Sci. and Tech. [IO], Montevideo, Uruguay
Natl. Coun. on Inordinacy - Address unknown since 1995.
Natl. Coun. on Intellectual Disability [IO], Mawson, Australia
Natl. Coun. of Intellectual Property Law Assns. [5855]
Natl. Coun. for Interior Design Qualification [2269], 1200 18th St. NW, Ste. 1001, Washington, DC 20036-2506, (202)721-0220
Natl. Coun. for Interior Design Qualification [IO], Washington, DC, United States
Natl. Coun. for Interior Horticultural Certification - Address unknown since 1995.
Natl. Coun. for Intl. Hea. [★14979]
Natl. Coun. for Intl. Hea. [★IO]
Natl. Coun. on Intl. Trade Development [IO], Washington, DC, United States
Natl. Coun. on Intl. Trade Development [2288], 1707 L St. NW, Ste. 570, Washington, DC 20036, (202)872-9280
Natl. Coun. for Intl. Visitors [17903], 1420 K St. NW, Ste. 800, Washington, DC 20005, (202)842-1414
Natl. Coun. for Intl. Visitors [IO], Washington, DC, United States
Natl. Coun. on Interpreting in Hea. Care [1851], 270 W Lawrence St., Albany, NY 12208
Natl. Coun. of Investigation and Security Services [3539], 7501 Sparrows Point Blvd., Baltimore, MD 21219-1927, (800)445-8408
Natl. Coun. for Japanese Amer. Redress - Defunct.

A star before a book entry number signifies that the name is not listed separately, but is mentioned within the entry.

Natl. Coun. of Japanese Language Teachers [9226], PO Box 3719, Boulder, CO 80307-3719

Natl. Coun. on Jewish Audio-Visual Materials - Defunct.

Natl. Coun. for Jewish Educ. [★8690]

Natl. Coun. for Jewish Educ. [★IO]

Natl. Coun. of Jewish Women [20166], 53 W 23rd St., 6th Fl., New York, NY 10010-4237, (212)645-4048

Natl. Coun. of Jewish Women in Australia [IO], Caulfield Junction, Australia

Natl. Coun. of Junior Outdoorsmen - Address unknown since 1995.

Natl. Coun. of Juvenile Court Judges [★5912]

Natl. Coun. of Juvenile and Family Court Judges [5912], PO Box 8970, Reno, NV 89507, (775)784-6012

Natl. Coun. of La Raza [12278], Raul Yzaguirre Bldg., 1126 16th St. NW, Washington, DC 20036, (202)785-1670

National Council of La Raza [IO], Washington, DC, United States

Natl. Coun. for Labor Reform - Address unknown since 1994.

Natl. Coun. for Languages and Intl. Stud. [10306], 4646 40th St. NW, Ste. 310, Washington, DC 20016, (202)966-8477

Natl. Coun. for Languages and Intl. Stud. [IO], Washington, DC, United States

Natl. Coun. of Legislators from Gaming States - Address unknown since 2003.

Natl. Coun. of Less Commonly Taught Languages [8737], c/o Antonia Folarin Schleicher, PhD, Exec. Dir., Natl. African Language Rsrc. Ctr., 4231 Humanities Bldg., 455 N Park St., Madison, WI 53706, (608)265-7905

Natl. Coun. of Less Commonly Taught Languages [IO], Madison, WI, United States

Natl. Coun. of Local Public Human Ser. Administrators [13178], c/o Amer. Public Human Services Assn., 810 1st St. NE, Ste. 500, Washington, DC 20002, (202)682-0100

Natl. Coun. of Local Public Welfare Administrators [★13178]

Natl. Coun. of Maori Nurses [IO], Tauranga, New Zealand

Natl. Coun. of Marine Trade Assns. - Defunct.

Natl. Coun. for Marketing and Public Relations [9032], c/o Becky Olson, Exec. Dir., PO Box 336039, Greeley, CO 80633, (970)330-0771

Natl. Coun. of Marriage and Divorce Law Reform and Justice Orgs. - Defunct.

Natl. Coun. on Measurement in Educ. [9256], 2810 Crossroads Dr., Ste. 3800, Madison, WI 53718, (608)443-2487

Natl. Coun. on Measurements Used in Educ. [★9256]

Natl. Coun. on Medical Technology Education - Defunct.

Natl. Coun. of Millinery Assns. - Defunct.

Natl. Coun. on Minority Educ. in Transplantation [16677], c/o Diana Carter, Pres./Founder, PO Box 7401, Freeport, NY 11520

National Coun. of the Multifamily Housing Industry [★1035]

Natl. Coun. of Music Importers and Exporters - Address unknown since 2006.

Natl. Coun. of Mustang Clubs - Defunct.

Natl. Coun. of Naval Air Stations Employee Organizations [★6088]

Natl. Coun. of Negro Women [17555], 633 Pennsylvania Ave. NW, Washington, DC 20004, (202)737-0120

Natl. Coun. on Noise Abatement - Address unknown since 1995.

Natl. Coun. of Nonprofit Associations [320], 1101 Vermont Ave. NW, Ste. 1002, Washington, DC 20005-1525, (202)962-0322

Natl. Coun. of Obesity - Address unknown since 1995.

Natl. Coun. for the Observance of Grandparent's Day - Address unknown since 1988.

Natl. Coun. for Occupational Educ. [★8361]

Natl. Coun. on Occupational Licensing - Defunct.

Natl. Coun. of Officers of State Teachers Assns. - Address unknown since 1995.

Natl. Coun. On Bible Curriculum In Public Schools [9052], PO Box 9743, Greensboro, NC 27429, (336)272-3799

Natl. Coun. of Organizations of Less Commonly Taught Languages [★8737]

Natl. Coun. of Organizations of Less Commonly Taught Languages [★IO]

Natl. Coun. for Palliative Care [IO], London, United Kingdom

Natl. Coun. on Participative Mgt. - Defunct.

Natl. Coun. of Patent Law Assns. [★5855]

Natl. Coun. on Patient Info. and Educ. [15946], 4915 St. Elmo Ave., Ste. 505, Bethesda, MD 20814-6082, (301)656-8565

Natl. Coun. on Philanthropy [★12725]

Natl. Coun. of Physical Distribution Mgt. [★4018]

Natl. Coun. of Postal Credit Unions [1116], PO Box 160, Del Mar, CA 92014-0160, (858)792-3883

Natl. Coun. for Prescription Drug Programs [2987], 9240 E Raintree Dr., Scottsdale, AZ 85260-7518, (480)477-1000

Natl. Coun. of Preservation Executives - Defunct.

Natl. Coun. of Primary Educ. [★8064]

Natl. Coun. of Primary Educ. [★IO]

Natl. Coun. of Private Enterprises - Dominican Republic [IO], Santo Domingo, Dominican Republic

Natl. Coun. of Private Enterprises - Panama [IO], Panama City, Panama

Natl. Coun. on Private Forests [4691], c/o Ian Mac-Farlane, Chm., 444 N Capitol St. NW, Washington, DC 20001, (202)624-5977

Natl. Coun. for Private School Accreditation [7880], PO Box 13686, Seattle, WA 98198-1010, (253)874-3408

Natl. Coun. on Problem Gambling [12212], 216 G St. NE, Ste. 200, Washington, DC 20002, (202)547-9204

Natl. Coun. for the Professional Development of Nursing and Midwifery [IO], Dublin, Ireland

Natl. Coun. of Professional Services Firms [★17636]

Natl. Coun. of Psychotherapists [★IO]

Natl. Coun. of Psychotherapists and Hypnotherapy Register [★IO]

Natl. Coun. for the Public Assessment of Technology - Defunct.

Natl. Coun. on Public History [10136], 327 Cavanaugh Hall - IUPUI, 425 Univ. Blvd., Indianapolis, IN 46202, (317)274-2716

Natl. Coun. on Public Policy - Address unknown since 1990.

Natl. Coun. on Public Polls [18370], c/o Dr. Barbara L. Carvalho, Sec.-Treas., Marist Inst. for Public Opinion, Marist Coll., Poughkeepsie, NY 12601, (845)575-5050

Natl. Coun. for Public-Private Partnerships [17633], 1660 L St. NW, Ste. 510, Washington, DC 20036, (202)467-6800

Natl. Coun. of Puerto Rican Volunteers - Defunct.

Natl. Coun. on Qualifications for the Lighting Professions [2435], PO Box 142729, Austin, TX 78714-2729, (512)973-0042

Natl. Coun. on Radiation Protection and Measurements [6242], 7910 Woodmont Ave., Ste. 400, Bethesda, MD 20814-3076, (301)657-2652

Natl. Coun. of Real Estate Investment Fiduciaries [2344], 2 Prudential Plz., 180 N Stetson Ave., Ste. 2515, Chicago, IL 60601, (312)819-5890

Natl. Coun. on Rehabilitation Educ. [16329], c/o Sharon Benshoff, Admin. Sec., 2012 W Norwood Dr., Carbondale, IL 62901, (618)549-3267

Natl. Coun. for Reliable Hea. Info. [★17692]

Natl. Coun. on Religion in Higher Educ. [★19940]

Natl. Coun. on Religion and Public Education - Address unknown since 2002.

Natl. Coun. to Repeal the Draft - Defunct.

Natl. Coun. of Republican Workshops - Address unknown since 1995.

Natl. Coun. for Res. and Planning [8121], c/o Richard C. Rindone, Membership Coor., Santa Fe Community Coll., 6401 Richards Ave., Santa Fe, NM 87508-4887, (505)428-1658

Natl. Coun. for Res. on Women [17556], 11 Hanover Sq., 24th Fl., New York, NY 10005, (212)785-7335

Natl. Coun. of Resistance of Iran [IO], London, United Kingdom

Natl. Coun. for a Responsible Firearms Policy - Defunct.

Natl. Coun. of Returned Peace Corps Volunteers [★18262]

Natl. Coun. of Salesmen's Orgs. - Defunct.

Natl. Coun. of Savings Institutions [★461]

Natl. Coun. for School Sport [IO], Loughborough, United Kingdom

Natl. Coun. for School Sport [★IO]

Natl. Coun. on Schoolhouse Constr. [★IO]

Natl. Coun. on Schoolhouse Constr. [★8335]

Natl. Coun. for Sci. and the Env. [7067], 1707 H St. NW, Ste. 200, Washington, DC 20006-3918, (202)530-5810

Natl. Coun. for Sci. Res. - Lebanon [IO], Beirut, Lebanon

Natl. Coun. of Sci. and Technological Development [IO], Brasilia, Brazil

Natl. Coun. for Scientific and Technological Research [IO], Caracas, Venezuela

Natl. Coun. of Seamen's Agencies [★IO]

Natl. Coun. of Seamen's Agencies [★13007]

Natl. Coun. of Secondary School Athletic Directors [8988], 1900 Assn. Dr., Reston, VA 20191-1598, (703)476-3400

Natl. Coun. of Self-Insurers [2222], 1253 Springfield Ave., PMB 345, New Providence, NJ 07974, (908)665-2152

Natl. Coun. of Senior Citizens - Defunct.

Natl. Council for Single Adoptive Parents [11256]

Natl. Coun. of Small Federal Contractors - Address unknown since 2003.

Natl. Coun. of Social Security Mgt. Associations [6260], AJC Federal Bldg., 1240 E 9th St., Rm. 793, Cleveland, OH 44199, (216)522-3204

Natl. Coun. of Social Ser. [★IO]

Natl. Coun. of Social Ser. [IO], Singapore, Singapore

Natl. Coun. for the Social Stud. [9128], 8555 16th St., Ste. 500, Silver Spring, MD 20910, (301)588-1800

Natl. Coun., Sons and Daughters of Liberty - Address unknown since 1995.

Natl. Coun. for Soviet and East European Res. [★10968]

Natl. Coun. of Specialty Contractors' Assn. - Defunct.

Natl. Coun. of State Agencies for the Blind - Address unknown since 2002.

Natl. Coun. of State Assn. Presidents [★7906]

Natl. Coun. of State Boards of Engg. Examiners [★7031]

Natl. Coun. of State Boards of Nursing [15508], 111 E Wacker Dr., Ste. 2900, Chicago, IL 60601, (312)525-3600

Natl. Coun. of State Committees for Children and Youth - Address unknown since 1995.

Natl. Coun. of State Consultants in Elementary Education - Defunct.

Natl. Coun. of State Directors of Community Colleges [8122], 1 Dupont Cir. NW, Ste. 410, Washington, DC 20036-1176, (202)728-0200

Natl. Coun. of State Educ. Associations [7906], 1201 16th St. NW, Washington, DC 20036-3290, (202)833-4000

Natl. Coun. of State Emergency Medical Services Training Coordinators [★14345]

Natl. Coun. of State Garden Clubs [★22528]

Natl. Coun. of State Good Roads Assn. - Defunct.

Natl. Coun. of State Housing Agencies [5795], 444 N Capitol St., Ste. 438, Washington, DC 20001, (202)624-7710

Natl. Coun. of State Human Ser. Administrators [13179], c/o Amer. Public Human Services Assn., 810 1st St. NE, Ste. 500, Washington, DC 20002, (202)682-0100

Natl. Coun. of State Pharmaceutical Assn. [★15943]

Natl. Coun. of State Pharmacy Assn. Executives [★15943]

Natl. Coun. of State Public Welfare Administrators [★13179]

Natl. Coun. of State School Boards Assn. [★9083]

Natl. Coun. of State Self-Insurers' Associations [★2222]

Natl. Coun. of State Sociological Associations [7665], c/o Susan Webb, Pres., PO Box 261954, Conway, SC 29528-6054, (843)349-2933

Reference to "IO" in place of a book number signifies that the association may be found in the 45th edition of International Organizations.

Natl. Coun. of State Supervisors of Foreign Languages **[8738]**, c/o Ryan Wertz, Treas., 1265 Millington Ct., Columbus, OH 43235

Natl. Coun. of State Supervisors of Music - Address unknown since 2008.

Natl. Coun. of State Tourism Directors **[24385]**, c/o Travel Indus. Assn. of Am., 1100 New York Ave. NW, Ste. 450, Washington, DC 20005-3934, (202)408-8422

Natl. Coun. of State Travel Directors **[★24385]**

Natl. Coun. on Strength and Fitness **[23955]**, PO Box 163908, Miami, FL 33116, (305)668-8705

Natl. Coun. of Structural Engineers Associations **[7032]**, 645 N Michigan Ave., Ste. 540, Chicago, IL 60611, (312)649-4600

Natl. Coun. on Student Development **[9170]**, c/o Dr. Ron Opp, Univ. of Toledo, Judith Herb Coll. of Educ., MS 921, Dept. of Educational Leadership, 2801 W Bancroft St., Toledo, OH 43606-3390, (419)530-4947

Natl. Coun. on Stuttering - Address unknown since 1994.

Natl. Coun. of Supervisors of Mathematics **[8826]**, 6000 E Evans Ave., No. 3-205, Denver, CO 80222, (303)758-9611

Natl. Coun. for Support of Disability Issues **[13212]**, Mountain Rd., Haymarket, VA 20169, (703)753-9148

Natl. Coun. of Swedish Youth Organisations **[IO]**, Stockholm, Sweden

Natl. Coun. of Synthetic Fuels Production **[★IO]**

Natl. Coun. of Synthetic Fuels Production **[★1677]**

Natl. Coun. for Taekwondo Masters Certification **[23599]**, 501 W Glenoaks Blvd., No. 336, Glendale, CA 91202, (213)219-3583

Natl. Coun. of Tanzania YMCA **[IO]**, Moshi, United Republic of Tanzania

Natl. Coun. on Teacher Retirement **[24044]**, 7600 Greenhaven Dr., Ste. 302, Sacramento, CA 95831, (916)394-2075

Natl. Coun. of Teachers of English **[8380]**, 1111 Kenyon Rd., Urbana, IL 61801-1096, (217)328-3870

Natl. Coun. of Teachers of Mathematics **[8827]**, 1906 Assn. Dr., Reston, VA 20191-1502, (703)620-9840

Natl. Coun. of Technical Schools - Address unknown since 1995.

Natl. Coun. of Tech. Ser. Indus. **[★1743]**

Natl. Coun. for Telephone Ministries **[★19865]**

Natl. Coun. for Textile Education - Address unknown since 2004.

Natl. Coun. for Therapeutic Recreation Certification **[16627]**, 7 Elmwood Dr., New City, NY 10956, (845)639-1439

Natl. Coun. for Torah Education - Defunct.

Natl. Coun. for the Traditional Arts **[9961]**, 1320 Fenwick Ln., Ste. 200, Silver Spring, MD 20910, (301)565-0654

Natl. Coun. for the Training of Journalists **[IO]**, Saffron Walden, United Kingdom

Natl. Coun. for Uniform Interest Compensation **[★486]**

Natl. Coun. of United Presbyterian Men **[★20473]**

Natl. Coun. on U.S.-Arab Relations **[18066]**, 1730 M St. NW, Ste. 503, Washington, DC 20036, (202)293-6466

Natl. Coun. on U.S.-Arab Relations **[IO]**, Washington, DC, United States

Natl. Coun. of the U.S., Intl. Org. of Good Templars **[19081]**, Natl. HQ, IOGT-USA, PO Box 202238, Minneapolis, MN 55420-7238, (952)210-0382

Natl. Coun. for Universal and Unconditional Amnesty - Defunct.

Natl. Coun. of Univ. Res. Administrators **[9063]**, 1225 19th St. NW, Ste. 850, Washington, DC 20036, (202)466-3894

Natl. Coun. of Urban Educ. Associations **[9290]**, c/o Natl. Educ. Assn., 1201 16th St. NW, Ste. 410, Washington, DC 20036, (202)822-7155

Natl. Coun. of Urban Indian Hea. **[15277]**, 501 Capitol Ct. NE, Ste. 100, Washington, DC 20002, (202)544-0344

Natl. Coun. for US-China Trade **[★2319]**

Natl. Coun. of Voluntary Child Care Organisations **[IO]**, London, United Kingdom

Natl. Coun. for Voluntary Organisations **[IO]**, London, United Kingdom

Natl. Coun. on Wholistic Therapeutics and Medicine - Defunct.

Natl. Coun. of Woman of Malta **[IO]**, Blata I-Bajda, Malta

Natl. Coun. of Women of Australia **[IO]**, Deakin, Australia

Natl. Coun. of Women of Canada **[IO]**, Ottawa, ON, Canada

Natl. Coun. of Women of Finland **[IO]**, Helsinki, Finland

Natl. Coun. of Women of Free Czechoslovakia - Address unknown since 1999.

Natl. Coun. of Women of Kenya **[IO]**, Nairobi, Kenya

Natl. Coun. of Women of New Zealand **[IO]**, Wellington, New Zealand

Natl. Coun. of Women of Switzerland **[IO]**, Bern, Switzerland

Natl. Coun. of Women of Thailand **[IO]**, Bangkok, Thailand

Natl. Coun. of Women of the U.S. **[17557]**, 777 United Nations Plz., New York, NY 10017, (212)697-1278

Natl. Coun. on Women's Hea. **[16904]**, 1300 York Ave., New York, NY 10065-4805, (212)746-6967

Natl. Coun. of Women's Organizations **[17558]**, 1050 17th St. NW, Ste. 250, Washington, DC 20036, (202)293-4505

Natl. Coun. for Workforce Educ. **[8361]**, 410 Oak St., ALU 113, Big Rapids, MI 49307, (231)591-3534

Natl. Coun. on Workmen's Compensation Insurance **[★2221]**

Natl. Coun. of World Affairs Organizations **[★18843]**

Natl. Coun. of World Affairs Organizations **[★IO]**

Natl. Coun. for a World Peace Tax Fund **[★18712]**

Natl. Coun. on Writing Prog. Administrators **[★9333]**

Natl. Coun. of Yacht Clubs - Address unknown since 1995.

Natl. Coun. of the YMCAs of Australia **[IO]**, South Melbourne, Australia

Natl. Coun. of YMCA's of Bangladesh **[IO]**, Dhaka, Bangladesh

Natl. Coun. of YMCA's of Ghana **[IO]**, Accra, Ghana

Natl. Coun. of YMCA's of Greece **[IO]**, Athens, Greece

Natl. Coun. of YMCA's of Ireland **[IO]**, Belfast, United Kingdom

Natl. Coun. of YMCA's of Jamaica **[IO]**, Kingston, Jamaica

Natl. Coun. of YMCAs of Japan **[IO]**, Tokyo, Japan

Natl. Coun. of YMCA's of Liberia **[IO]**, Monrovia, Liberia

Natl. Coun. of YMCA's of Malaysia **[IO]**, Kuala Lumpur, Malaysia

Natl. Coun. of YMCA's of Myanmar **[IO]**, Yangon, Myanmar

Natl. Coun. of YMCA's of New Zealand **[IO]**, Wellington, New Zealand

Natl. Coun. of YMCA's of Pakistan **[IO]**, Lahore, Pakistan

Natl. Coun. of YMCA's of Sri Lanka **[IO]**, Colombo, Sri Lanka

Natl. Coun. of YMCA's of Sudan **[IO]**, Khartoum, Sudan

Natl. Coun. of YMCA's - Zambia **[IO]**, Lusaka, Zambia

Natl. Coun. of YMCA's of Zimbabwe **[IO]**, Harare, Zimbabwe

Natl. Coun. of Young Israel **[20167]**, 111 John St., Ste. 450, New York, NY 10038, (212)929-1525

Natl. Coun. of Youth Organizations in Korea **[IO]**, Seoul, Republic of Korea

Natl. Coun. of Youth Sports **[23839]**, 7185 SE Seagate Ln., Stuart, FL 34997, (772)781-1452

Natl. Counsel of Black Lawyers **[5519]**

Natl. Counter Intelligence Corps Assn. **[21164]**, c/o Jerry Malme, Chm., 6198 Morris Rd., Geneseo, NY 14454, (585)243-0819

Natl. Country Ham Assn. **[1545]**, PO Box 948, Conover, NC 28613, (828)466-2760

Natl. Country Party of Australia **[★IO]**

Natl. Courier Assn. **[IO]**, Milton Keynes, United Kingdom

Natl. Courier Network **[★IO]**

Natl. Court Appointed Special Advocate Assn. **[11636]**, 100 W Harrison St., Ste. 500, North Tower, Seattle, WA 98119, (206)270-0072

Natl. Court Clubs Assn. **[★3021]**

Natl. Court Clubs Assn. **[★IO]**

Natl. Court Reporters Assn. **[5630]**, 8224 Old Courthouse Rd., Vienna, VA 22182-3808, (703)556-6272

Natl. Cowboy Hall of Fame and Western Heritage Center **[★9381]**

Natl. Cowboy and Western Heritage Museum **[9381]**, 1700 NE 63rd St., Oklahoma City, OK 73111, (405)478-2250

Natl. CPA Gp. **[★18]**

Natl. CPA Gp. **[★IO]**

Natl. CPA Hea. Care Advisors Assn. **[13530]**, 1 Valmont Plz., 4th Fl., Omaha, NE 68154, (402)778-7922

Natl. Crafts Assn. - Defunct.

Natl. Crafts Found. - Address unknown since 1995.

Natl. Creameries Assn. **[★4489]**

Natl. Creamery Buttermakers' Assn. - Defunct.

Natl. Credentialing Agency for Lab. Personnel **[15145]**, PO Box 15945-289, Lenexa, KS 66285, (913)895-4613

Natl. Credit Union Mgt. Assn. **[1117]**, 4989 Rebel Trail, Atlanta, GA 30327, (404)255-6828

Natl. Crime Prevention Assn. - Defunct.

Natl. Crime Prevention Coun. **[11844]**, 1000 Connecticut Ave. NW, 13th Fl., Washington, DC 20036, (202)466-6272

Natl. Crime Prevention Inst. **[11845]**, c/o Dr. Deborah Wilson, Advisor, Univ. of Louisville, Justice Admin., Louisville, KY 40292, (502)852-6567

Natl. Crime Stop Program - Address unknown since 1995.

Natl. Crime Victim Bar Assn. **[6349]**, 2000 M St. NW, Ste. 480, Washington, DC 20036, (202)467-8753

Natl. Criminal Defense Coll. **[5657]**, c/o Mercer Law School, 343 Orange St., Macon, GA 31207, (478)746-4151

Natl. Criminal Justice Assn. **[11881]**, 720 7th St. NW, 3rd Fl., Washington, DC 20001, (202)628-8550

Natl. Cristina Found. **[11969]**, 500 W Putnam Ave., Greenwich, CT 06830, (203)863-9100

National Cristina Foundation **[IO]**, Greenwich, CT, United States

Natl. Critics Inst. **[★11036]**

Natl. Croatian Soc. **[★19022]**

Natl. Crop Insurance Assn. **[★2223]**

Natl. Crop Insurance Coun. - Defunct.

Natl. Crop Insurance Services **[2223]**, 8900 Indian Creek Pkwy., Ste. 600, Overland Park, KS 66210-1567, (913)685-2767

Natl. Crossbow Hunters Assn. - Defunct.

Natl. Crossbowmen of the U.S.A., Inc. **[★23054]**

The Natl. Crossbowmen of the U.S.A. **[23054]**, c/o Patricia Copley, Sec.-Treas., 38 B Ave., Richwood, WV 26261, (304)846-6420

Natl. Crusaders Youth Fed. - Address unknown since 1995.

Natl. Crushed Stone Assn. **[★3699]**

Natl. Cued Speech Association/Deaf Children's Literacy Proj. **[16452]**, 5619 McLean Dr., Bethesda, MD 20814-1021, (301)915-8009

Natl. Cuff Link Soc. - Address unknown since 2006.

Natl. Cursillo Movement **[19685]**, PO Box 210226, Dallas, TX 75211, (214)339-6321

Natl. Customs Brokers and Forwarders Assn. of Am. **[2309]**, 1200 18th St. NW, No. 901, Washington, DC 20036, (202)466-0222

Natl. Customs Ser. Assn. **[★24080]**

Natl. Cutting Horse Assn. **[4918]**, 260 Bailey Ave., Fort Worth, TX 76107-1862, (817)244-6188

Natl. Cycle League - Address unknown since 1999.

Natl. Cylinder Grinders Assn. **[★375]**

Natl. Cylinder Grinders Assn. **[★IO]**

Natl. CYO Fed. **[★19688]**

Natl. Cystic Fibrosis Res. Found. **[★16358]**

Natl. Dairy Coun. **[4494]**, 10255 W Higgins Rd., Ste. 900, Rosemont, IL 60018, (312)240-2880

Natl. Dairy Coun. **[★1132]**

Natl. Dairy Coun. **[IO]**, Dublin, Ireland

Natl. Dairy Herd Improvement Assn. **[4274]**, PO Box 930399, Verona, WI 53593-0399, (608)848-6455

A star before a book entry number signifies that the name is not listed separately, but is mentioned within the entry.

Natl. Dairy Shrine [4488], c/o Mr. Maurice E. Core, Exec. Dir., 1224 Alton Darby Creek Rd., Columbus, OH 43228-9792, (614)878-5333

Natl. Dance Assn. [9893], 1900 Assn. Dr., Reston, VA 20191, (703)476-3400

Natl. Dance Coun. of Am. [8189], c/o Eleanor Wiblin, Registrar, PO Box 22018, Provo, UT 84602-2018, (801)422-8124

Natl. Dance Educ. Assn. [23324], c/o Jane Bonbright, Exec. Dir., 8609 Second Ave., Ste. 203-B, Silver Spring, MD 20910, (301)585-2880

Natl. Dance Exercise Instructors Training Assn; NDEITA - [★23037]

Natl. Dance Guild [★9866]

Natl. Dance Inst. [8190], 594 Broadway, Rm. 805, New York, NY 10012, (212)226-0083

Natl. Dance Teacher's Assn. [23325], c/o Ronnie Gardner, Pres., 2309 E Atlantic Blvd., Pompano Beach, FL 33062, (954)782-7760

Natl. Dance Teachers Guild [★9866]

Natl. DanceSport Fed. of Greece [IO], Piraeus, Greece

Natl. Dart Assn; AMOA [23329]

Natl. Day of Bread Comm. - Defunct.

Natl. Day Laborer Organizing Network [24111], 675 S Park View St., Ste. B, Los Angeles, CA 90057, (213)380-2784

Natl. Day Nurseries Assn. [IO], Huddersfield, United Kingdom

Natl. Days Fan Club - Address unknown since 2001.

Natl. Deaf Bowling Assn. - Address unknown since 1999.

Natl. Deaf Children's Soc. [IO], London, United Kingdom

Natl. Deaf Educ. Network and CH [11906], c/o Laurent Clerc Natl. Deaf Educ. Center, 800 Florida Ave. NE, Washington, DC 20002, (202)651-5051

Natl. Deaf Women's Bowling Assn. [23352], c/o Sandy Heston, Sec.-Treas., 3314 64th St., Urbandale, IA 50322

Natl. Deafblind and Rubella Assn. [★IO]

Natl. Debt Repayment Found. - Defunct.

Natl. Decorated Packaging Assn. - Address unknown since 1995.

Natl. Decorating Products Assn. [★2274]

Natl. Decorating Products Assn. [★IO]

Natl. Defeat Dukakis Campaign - Address unknown since 1989.

Natl. Defender 12 Class Assn. - Address unknown since 1995.

Natl. Defender Investigator Assn. [5888], 460 Smith St., Ste. K, Middletown, CT 06457, (860)635-5533

Natl. Defense Coun. Found. [18465], 1220 King St., Ste. No. 230, Alexandria, VA 22314, (703)836-3443

Natl. Defense Found. [★20767]

Natl. Defense Indus. Assn. [6089], 2111 Wilson Blvd., Ste. 400, Arlington, VA 22201-3061, (703)522-1820

Natl. Defense Preparedness Assn. [★6089]

Natl. Defense Trans. Assn. [6090], 50 S Pickett St., Ste. 220, Alexandria, VA 22304-7296, (703)751-5011

Natl. Defined Contribution Coun. - Defunct.

Natl. Democratic Club [17407], 30 Ivy St. SE, Washington, DC 20003, (202)543-2035

Natl. Democratic Forum [★18428]

Natl. Democratic Front - Address unknown since 1994.

Natl. Democratic Inst. [★17870]

Natl. Democratic Inst. [★IO]

Natl. Democratic Inst. for Intl. Affairs [IO], Washington, DC, United States

Natl. Democratic Inst. for Intl. Affairs [17870], 2030 M St. NW, 5th Fl., Washington, DC 20036-3306, (202)728-5500

Natl. Democratic Policy Comm. - Address unknown since 1995.

Natl. Democratic Pro-Life Comm. - Defunct.

Natl. Demolition Assn. [1043], 16 N Franklin St., Ste. 203, Doylestown, PA 18901-3536, (215)348-4949

Natl. Demolition Derby Assn. - Defunct.

Natl. Demonstration Water Proj. [★7841]

Natl. Dental Assistants Assn. [14174], c/o Natl. Dental Assn., 3517 16th St. NW, Washington, DC 20010, (202)588-1697

Natl. Dental Assn. [14175], 3517 16th St. NW, Washington, DC 20010, (202)588-1697

Natl. Dental Assn. [★14131]

Natl. Dental EDI Coun. [14176], 2020 W Indian School Rd., Ste. F44, Phoenix, AZ 85015-5040, (602)266-7740

Natl. Dental Hygiene Honor Soc. [★24441]

Natl. Dental Hygienists' Assn. [14177], PO Box 22463, Tampa, FL 33622, (800)234-1096

Natl. Dental Technicians Assn. - Defunct.

Natl. Denturist Assn. [14178], PO Box 308, Towanda, PA 18848, (570)265-0238

Natl. Depression Glass Assn. [22562], PO Box 8264, Wichita, KS 67208-0264

Natl. Depressive and Manic Depressive Assn. [★15196]

Natl. Derby Rallies [23771], 6644 Switzer Ln., Shawnee, KS 66203, (913)962-6360

Natl. DeSoto Club [21731], c/o Barrett Taft, Membership Sec., 1323 W Beach Rd., Oak Harbor, WA 98277, (360)720-2465

Natl. Determination Party - Address unknown since 1994.

Natl. Development Coun. [17463], 708 Third Ave., Ste. 710, New York, NY 10017, (212)682-1106

Natl. Diabetes Info. CH [14230], 1 Info. Way, Bethesda, MD 20892-3560, (301)654-3327

Natl. Dialysis Registry - Defunct.

Natl. Dietary Foods Assn. [★3425]

Natl. Digestive Diseases Educ. and Info. CH [★14422]

Natl. Digestive Diseases Info. CH [14422], 2 Info. Way, Bethesda, MD 20892-3570, (800)891-5389

Natl. Dimension Mfrs. Assn. [★1656]

Natl. Ding-A-Ling Club - Defunct.

Natl. Diocesan Press [★19953]

Natl. Directors of Educational Res. [★9053]

Natl. Directory Publishing Assn. - Defunct.

Natl. Disability Rights Network [11970], 900 2nd St. NE, Ste. 211, Washington, DC 20002, (202)408-9514

Natl. Disability Services [IO], Deakin West, Australia

Natl. Disability Sports Alliance [23353], 25 W Independence Way, Kingston, RI 02881, (401)792-7130

Natl. Disabled Law Officers Assn. - Defunct.

Natl. Disabled Police Assn. [IO], Ashford, United Kingdom

Natl. Disaster Search Dog Found. [12892], 206 N Signal St., Ste. R, Ojai, CA 93023, (888)459-4376

Natl. Displaced Homemakers Network [★18819]

Natl. Disposal Services Assn. - Address unknown since 1995.

Natl. Dissemination Assn. [8291], c/o Max McConkey, Exec. Dir., 4732 N Oracle Rd., Ste. 217, Tucson, AZ 85705, (602)888-2838

Natl. Dissemination Center for Children with Disabilities [11971], PO Box 1492, Washington, DC 20013-1492, (202)884-8200

National Distinguished Principals Program [★9014]

Natl. Distribution Union [IO], Auckland, New Zealand

Natl. Distributors Assn. of Constr. Equip. [★2000]

Natl. District Attorneys Assn. [5668], 99 Canal CN Plz., Ste. 510, Alexandria, VA 22314, (703)549-9222

Natl. District Attorneys Assn. Found. [★5668]

Natl. District Heating Assn. [★1888]

Natl. District Heating Assn. [★IO]

Natl. Dog Groomers Assn. of Am. [2962], PO Box 101, Clark, PA 16113-0101, (724)962-2711

Natl. Dog Registry [11436], PO Box 51105, Mesa, AZ 85208, (800)NDR-DOGS

Natl. Dog Wardens Assn. [IO], Gloucester, United Kingdom

Natl. Dog Week Assn. - Defunct.

Natl. Doll and Toy Collectors [★22407]

Natl. Dome Assn. [★2530]

Natl. Dome Comm. [★2530]

Natl. Dome Coun. [★2530]

Natl. Dome Coun. [2530], c/o Building Systems Councils of NAHB, 1201 15th St. NW, Washington, DC 20005, (202)266-8200

Natl. Domestic Violence Hotline [12036], PO Box 161810, Austin, TX 78716, (512)794-1133

Natl. Domestic Workers Union - Address unknown since 2000.

Natl. Door Assn. - Defunct.

Natl. Door Manufacturers Assn. [★686]

Natl. Down Syndrome Cong. [12577], 1370 Center Dr., Ste. 102, Atlanta, GA 30338, (770)604-9500

Natl. Down Syndrome Soc. [12040], 666 Broadway, New York, NY 10012, (212)460-9330

Natl. Down's Syndrome Assn. [★12577]

Natl. Draft Information Center - Defunct.

Natl. Drain Tile Mfrs. Assn. - Defunct.

Natl. Dress Mfrs. Assn. [★225]

Natl. Dried Fruit Trade Assn. [IO], London, United Kingdom

National Drilling Association [IO], Brunswick, OH, United States

Natl. Drilling Assn. [1044], 3511 Center Rd., Ste. 8, Brunswick, OH 44212, (330)220-6436

Natl. Drilling Contractors Assn. [★1044]

Natl. Drilling Contractors Assn. [★IO]

Natl. Drivers Assn. for the Prevention of Traffic Accidents - Defunct.

Natl. Dropout Prevention Center/Network [8330], Clemson Univ., 209 Martin St., Clemson, SC 29631-1555, (864)656-2599

Natl. Drowning Prevention Alliance [12974], c/o Kim Tyson, Pres.-Elect, Univ. of Texas, Austin, Coll. of Educ., Dept. of Kinesiology and Hea. Educ., 1102 Twin Creek Dr., Pflugerville, TX 78660, (512)431-0332

Natl. Drowning Prevention Coalition - Address unknown since 1994.

Natl. Drug Abuse Found. - Defunct.

Natl. Drug Enforcement Officers Assn. [5993], Off. of Training/TRDS, FBI Acad., PO Box 1475, Quantico, VA 22134-1475, (202)298-9653

Natl. Drug Strategy Network [17136], c/o Criminal Justice Policy Found., 8730 Georgia Ave., Ste. 400, Silver Spring, MD 20910, (301)589-6020

Natl. Drug Trade Conf. - Address unknown since 2001.

Natl. Dry Bean Coun. [★4769]

Natl. Duck Stamp Collectors Soc. [22850], PO Box 43, Harleysville, PA 19438-0043

Natl. Duckling Coun. - Defunct.

Natl. Duckpin Bowling Cong. [23253], c/o Sue Burucker, Exec. Dir./Sec., 4991 Fairview Ave., Linthicum, MD 21090, (410)636-2695

Natl. Duncan Glass Soc. [22563], 525 Jefferson Ave., Washington, PA 15301, (724)225-9950

Natl. Dysautonomia Res. Found. [14279], PO Box 301, Red Wing, MN 55066-0301, (651)267-0525

Natl. Eagle Scout Assn. [13002], c/o Boy Scouts of Am., 1325 W Walnut Hill Ln., PO Box 152079, Irving, TX 75015-2079, (972)580-2000

Natl. Early Amer. Glass Club [★22560]

Natl. Earth Sci. Teachers Assn. [9111], c/o Dr. Roberta Johnson, Exec. Dir., PO Box 3000, Boulder, CO 80307-3000, (303)497-2591

Natl. Earth Shelter Builders Assn. - Defunct.

Natl. Easter Seal Soc. [★11944]

Natl. Eating Disorder Info. Centre [IO], Toronto, ON, Canada

Natl. Eating Disorders Assn. [14302], 603 Stewart St., Ste. 803, Seattle, WA 98101, (206)382-3587

Natl. Eating Disorders Org. [★14302]

Natl. Eclectic Medical Assn. - Defunct.

Natl. Economic Assn. [6888], c/o Kwabena Gyimah-Brempong, Pres., Univ. of South Florida, Coll. of Bus. Admin., 4202 E Fowler Ave., BSN 3403, Tampa, FL 33620

Natl. Economic Coun. - Defunct.

Natl. Economic Development and Law Center [17464], 2201 Broadway, Ste. 815, Oakland, CA 94612, (510)251-2600

Natl. Economic and Social Planning Assn. [★5593]

Natl. Economic and Social Rights Initiative [17778], 90 John St., Ste. 308, New York, NY 10038, (212)253-1710

Natl. Economists Club [6889], PO Box 19281, Washington, DC 20036, (703)493-8824

National Economists Club Educ. Foundation [★6889]

Natl. Ecumenical Coalition - Address unknown since 1999.

Natl. Eczema Assn. [14208], 4460 Redwood Hwy., Ste. 16-D, San Rafael, CA 94903-1953, (415)499-3474

Reference to "IO" in place of a book number signifies that the association may be found in the 45th edition of International Organizations.

Natl. Eczema Assn. for Sci. and Educ. [★14208]

Natl. Eczema Soc. [IO], London, United Kingdom

Natl. Editorial Assn. [★3140]

Natl. Editorial Found. [★8715]

Natl. Educ. Alliance for Borderline Personality Disorder [15224], PO Box 974, Rye, NY 10580, (914)835-9011

Natl. Educ. for Assistance Dog Services [14770], PO Box 213, West Boylston, MA 01583, (978)422-9064

Natl. Educ. Assn. [24045], 1201 16th St. NW, Washington, DC 20036-3290, (202)833-4000

Natl. Education Center for Paraprofessionals in Mental Health - Defunct.

Natl. Educ. Center for Women in Bus. [★8040]

Natl. Educ. Coun. of the Christian Bros. [★8060]

Natl. Educ. Fed. [IO], Bucharest, Romania

Natl. Educ. Fed. [★IO]

Natl. Education Field Service Assn. - Defunct.

Natl. Educ., Hea. and Allied Workers' Union [IO], Johannesburg, Republic of South Africa

Natl. Educ. Knowledge Indus. Assn. [★9061]

Natl. Educational Assn. of Disabled Students [IO], Ottawa, ON, Canada

Natl. Educational Found. for Individual Rights - Defunct.

Natl. Educational Inst. for Economic Development - Address unknown since 1995.

Natl. Educational Mgt. Assn. - Address unknown since 1995.

Natl. Educational Task Force de La Raza - Defunct.

Natl. Educational Telecommunications Assn. [8337], PO Box 50008, Columbia, SC 29250, (803)799-5517

Natl. Educational TV [★9763]

Natl. Educators Fellowship [★19922]

Natl. Educators Fellowship [★IO]

Natl. Electric Comfort Trade Assn. - Defunct.

Natl. Elec. Drag Racing Assn. [23396], 3200 Dutton Ave., No. 220, Santa Rosa, CA 95407

Natl. Elec. Reliability Coun. [★1195]

Natl. Elec. Sign Assn. [★1189]

Natl. Elec. Sign Assn. [★IO]

Natl. Elec. Wholesalers Assn. [★1190]

Natl. Elecl. and Communications Assn. [IO], St. Leonards, Australia

Natl. Elecl. Contractors Assn. [1045], 3 Bethesda Metro Ctr., Ste. 1100, Bethesda, MD 20814, (301)657-3110

Natl. Elecl. Contractors Coun. [1046], c/o Assoc. Builders and Contractors, 4250 N Fairfax Dr., 9th Fl., Arlington, VA 22203, (703)812-2000

Natl. Elecl. Engg. Dept. Heads Assn. [★7011]

Natl. Elecl. Manufacturers Assn. [1191], 1300 N 17th St., Ste. 1752, Rosslyn, VA 22209, (703)841-3200

National Electrical Manufacturers Association [IO], Rosslyn, VA, United States

Natl. Elecl. Manufacturers Assn; Consumer Products Division of the [★264]

Natl. Elecl. Manufacturers Representatives Assn. [1192], 660 White Plains Rd., Ste. 600, Tarrytown, NY 10591-5172, (914)524-8650

Natl. Elecl. Testing Assn. [★1187]

Natl. Elecl. Testing Assn. [★IO]

Natl. Electrolysis Org. [★14310]

Natl. Electronic Associations [★1224]

Natl. Electronic Distributors Assn. [1223], 1111 Alderman Dr., Ste. 400, Alpharetta, GA 30005, (678)393-9990

Natl. Electronic Ser. Dealers Assn. [★1224]

Natl. Electronics Conf. [★6928]

Natl. Electronics Conf. [★IO]

Natl. Electronics Mfg. Initiative [★7265]

Natl. Electronics Ser. Dealers Assn. [1224], 3608 Pershing Ave., Fort Worth, TX 76107-4527, (817)921-9061

Natl. Electronics Teachers' Service - Defunct.

Natl. Elementary Education Assn. - Defunct.

Natl. Elementary School Center - Address unknown since 2004.

Natl. Elementary Schools Press Assn. [9012], 1345 Hendersonville Rd., Asheville, NC 28803, (828)210-9164

Natl. Elephant Collectors Soc. [22081]

Natl. Elevator Indus., Inc. [2049], 1677 County Rte. 64, PO Box 838, Salem, NY 12865-0838, (518)854-3100

Natl. Elevator Mfg. Indus. [★2049]

Natl. Emergency Civil Liberties Comm. [★17097]

Natl. Emergency Coalition for Haitian Refugees [★18499]

Natl. Emergency Dept. Nurses Assn. [★14333]

Natl. Emergency Equip. Dealers Assn. [14339], 8421 Frost Way, Annandale, VA 22003, (703)280-4622

Natl. Emergency Mgt. Assn. [5565], PO Box 11910, Lexington, KY 40578-1910, (859)244-8000

Natl. Emergency Medicine Assn. [14340], 306 W Joppa Rd., Baltimore, MD 21204-4048, (410)494-0300

Natl. Emergency Mobilization on the Right to Vote - Defunct.

Natl. Emergency Number Assn. [14321], 4350 N Fairfax Dr., Ste. 750, Arlington, VA 22203-1695, (703)812-4600

Natl. Emphysema Found. [13932], 128 East Ave., Norwalk, CT 06851, (203)866-5000

Natl. Employee Benefits Inst. [1243]

Natl. Employee Rights Inst. [★12064]

Natl. Employee Services and Recreation Assn. [★12796]

Natl. Employee Union Information Center [24076]

Natl. Employer Coun. - Address unknown since 2004.

Natl. Employers' Resource Alliance - Address unknown since 2004.

Natl. Employment Assn. [★1272]

Natl. Employment Bd. [★1272]

Natl. Employment Counseling Assn. [12091], PO Box 791006, Baltimore, MD 21279-1006, (800)347-6647

Natl. Employment Law Proj. [12092], 80 Maiden Ln., Ste. 509, New York, NY 10038, (212)285-3025

Natl. Employment Lawyers Assn. [5520], 44 Montgomery St., Ste. 2080, San Francisco, CA 94104, (415)296-7629

Natl. Employment Services Assn. [IO], South Melbourne, Australia

Natl. Employment and Training Assn. - Address unknown since 2001.

Natl. EMS Pilots Assn. [14322], 526 King St., Ste. 415, Alexandria, VA 22314-3143, (703)836-8930

Natl. EMS Pilots Assn. - Defunct.

Natl. Endangered Species Act Reform Coalition [17504], 1050 Thomas Jefferson St., 7th Fl., Washington, DC 20007, (202)333-7481

Natl. Endometriosis Soc. [IO], London, United Kingdom

Natl. Endowment for the Animals [11437], PO Box 1161, Boulder, CO 80306, (720)252-8449

Natl. Endowment for the Arts [9585], 1100 Pennsylvania Ave. NW, Washington, DC 20004, (202)682-5400

Natl. Endowment for the Christian Arts [9586], 13222 Park Ln., Fort Washington, MD 20744, (301)203-8789

Natl. Endowment for Democracy [17397], 1025 F St. NW, Ste. 800, Washington, DC 20004, (202)293-9700

National Endowment for the Humanities [★11129]

Natl. Endowment for the Humanities [5805], 1100 Pennsylvania Ave. NW, Washington, DC 20506, (202)606-8400

National Endowment for Liberty [★17293]

Natl. Energy Assistance Directors' Assn. [1987], 1615 M St. NW, Ste. 800, Washington, DC 20036, (202)237-5199

Natl. Energy Educ. Day Proj. [★17497]

Natl. Energy Educ. Development Proj. [17497], 8408 Kao Cir., Manassas, VA 20110, (703)257-1117

Natl. Energy Found. [8392], 3676 California Ave., Ste. A117, Salt Lake City, UT 84104, (801)908-5800

Natl. Energy Found. [IO], Milton Keynes, United Kingdom

Natl. Energy Mgt. Inst. [6961], 601 N Fairfax St., Ste. 250, Alexandria, VA 22314, (703)739-7100

Natl. Energy Marketers Assn. [1288], 3333 K St. NW, Ste. 110, Washington, DC 20007, (202)333-3288

National Energy Marketers Association [IO], Washington, DC, United States

Natl. Energy Resources Org. - Address unknown since 2000.

Natl. Energy Services Assn. [6962], 6430 FM 1960 W, No. 213, Houston, TX 77069, (713)856-6525

Natl. Energy Specialist Assn. - Address unknown since 1994.

Natl. Engine Parts Mfrs. Assn. - Address unknown since 2006.

Natl. Engine Use Coun. - Defunct.

Natl. Engg. Consortium [★6928]

Natl. Engg. Consortium [★IO]

Natl. Engg. Coun. for Guidance [★8368]

Natl. Entertainment Agents Coun. [IO], Seaford, United Kingdom

Natl. Entertainment and Campus Activities Assn. [★9169]

Natl. Entertainment Conf. [★9169]

Natl. Entertainment Journalists Assn. - Defunct.

Natl. Entertainment Service Comm. - Defunct.

Natl. Enthronement Center [19686], PO Box 111, Fairhaven, MA 02719-0111, (508)999-2680

Natl. Entlebucher Mountain Dog Assn. [22317], c/o Mike Roberts, Membership Chm., PO Box 385144, Waikoloa, HI 96738

Natl. Entlebucher Mountain Dog Assn. [IO], Sandy, UT, United States

Natl. Enuresis Soc. [★15294]

Natl. Environmental Balancing Bur. [1895], 8575 Grovement Cir., Gaithersburg, MD 20877-4121, (301)977-3698

Natl. Environmental Coalition of Native Americans [5037], c/o Claremore Veterans Center, PO Box 988, Claremore, OK 74018, (918)342-3041

Natl. Environmental Development Assn. - Address unknown since 2001.

Natl. Environmental Development Assn./Ground Water Project [★7835]

Natl. Environmental Development Assn./Resource Conservation and Recovery Act Project [7835]

Natl. Environmental Education Development Program - Defunct.

Natl. Environmental Educ. Found. [8395], 4301 Connecticut Ave. NW, Ste. 160, Washington, DC 20008, (202)833-2933

Natl. Environmental Educ. and Training Found. [★8395]

Natl. Environmental Hea. Assn. [14367], 720 S Colorado Blvd., Ste. 1000-N, Denver, CO 80246-1926, (303)756-9090

Natl. Environmental Hea. Sci. and Protection Accreditation Coun. [14368], 2632 SE 25th Ave., Ste. D, Portland, OR 97202, (503)235-6047

Natl. Environmental Hea. Sci. and Protection Accreditation Coun. [★14368]

Natl. Environmental Law Soc. - Defunct.

Natl. Environmental, Safety and Hea. Training Assn. [5097], PO Box 10321, Phoenix, AZ 85064-0321, (602)956-6099

National Environmental, Safety and Health Training Association [IO], Phoenix, AZ, United States

Natl. Environmental Satellite, Data, and Info. Ser. [4590], 1335 East-West Hwy., SSMC1, 8th Fl., Silver Spring, MD 20910, (301)713-3578

Natl. Environmental Societies Trust [IO], Kingston, Jamaica

Natl. Environmental Studies Project - Defunct.

Natl. Environmental Study Areas Program - Defunct.

Natl. Environmental Systems Contractors Assn. [★1872]

Natl. Environmental Training Assn. [★5097]

Natl. Environmental Training Assn. [★IO]

Natl. Environmental Trust [4591], 1200 18th St. NW, 5th Fl., Washington, DC 20036, (202)887-8800

Natl. Eosinophilia-Myalgia Syndrome Network [16662], c/o Jann Heston, Pres., 155 Delaware Ave., Lexington, OH 44904-1212

Natl. Episcopal AIDS Coalition [11332], 520 Clinton Ave., Brooklyn, NY 11238-2211, (718)857-9445

Natl. Episcopal Coalition on Alcohol and Drugs [★13279]

Natl. Episcopal Hea. Ministries [14584], 6050 N Meridian St., Indianapolis, IN 46208, (317)253-1277

Natl. Equipment Distributors Assn. - Defunct.

Natl. Equipment Servicing Dealers Assn. - Defunct.

Natl. Erectors Assn. [★1056]

Natl. Estimating Soc. [★1448]

A star before a book entry number signifies that the name is not listed separately, but is mentioned within the entry.

Natl. Ethanol Vehicle Coalition [4776], 3216 Emerald Ln., Ste. C, Jefferson City, MO 65109, (573)635-8445

Natl. Ethiopian Cycling Fed. [IO], Addis Ababa, Ethiopia

Natl. Ethnic Coalition of Organizations [19046], 232 Madison Ave., Ste. 900, New York, NY 10016-2901, (212)755-1492

Natl. Euchre Players Assn. - Address unknown since 2002.

Natl. Evangelization Teams [19687], 110 Crusader Ave. W, West St. Paul, MN 55118-4427, (651)450-6833

Natl. Ex-Offender Grant Alliance - Defunct.

Natl. Examining Bd. of Ocularists [15694], c/o David M. Bulgarelli, Exec. Dir., 625 1st Ave., Ste. 220, Coralville, IA 52241-2101, (319)339-1125

Natl. Exchange Carrier Assn. [3960], 80 S Jefferson Rd., Whippany, NJ 07981-1009, (800)228-8597

Natl. Exchange Club [13054], 3050 Central Ave., Toledo, OH 43606-1700, (419)535-3232

Natl. Exchange Club Found. [11637], 3050 Central Ave., Toledo, OH 43606-1700, (419)535-3232

Natl. Exchange Club Found. for the Prevention of Child Abuse [★11637]

Natl. Execution Alert Network [★17033]

Natl. Executive Housekeepers Assn. [★2464]

Natl. Executive Housekeepers Assn. [★IO]

National Executive Placement Comm. [★19202]

Natl. Executive Ser. Corps [747], 29 W 38th St., 8th Fl., New York, NY 10018, (212)269-1234

Natl. Exercise Trainers Assn; NETA - [23037]

Natl. Exhaust Distributors Assn./Undercar Specialists Assn. - Defunct.

Natl. Explorers and Collectors Assn. - Defunct.

Natl. Export Traffic League - Address unknown since 2002.

Natl. Extension Assn. of Family and Consumer Sciences [5612], 14070 Proton Rd., Ste. 100, Dallas, TX 75244-3601, (800)808-9133

Natl. Extension Assn. of Family and Consumer Services [★5612]

Natl. Extension Homemakers Coun. [★8513]

Natl. Eye Care Proj. [★15701]

Natl. Eye Res. Found. [15724]

Natl. Fac. Mgt. Assn. [★3188]

Natl. Fac. Mgt. Assn. [★IO]

Natl. Faculty of Humanities, Arts, and Sciences - Address unknown since 2005.

Natl. Fair Housing Alliance [17733], 1212 New York Ave. NW, Ste. 525, Washington, DC 20005, (202)898-1661

Natl. Families in Action [13269], 2957 Clairmont Rd. NE, Ste. 150, Atlanta, GA 30329, (404)248-9676

Natl. Family Assn. for Deaf-Blind [14771], 141 Middle Neck Rd., Sands Point, NY 11050, (800)255-0411

Natl. Family Business Assn. - Defunct.

Natl. Family Bus. Coun. [748], 1640 W Kennedy Rd., Lake Forest, IL 60045, (847)295-1040

Natl. Family Caregivers Assn. [14841], 10400 Connecticut Ave., Ste. 500, Kensington, MD 20895-3944, (301)942-6430

Natl. Family Coun. on Drug Addiction - Defunct.

Natl. Family Farm Coalition [16956], 110 Maryland Ave. NE, Ste. 307, Washington, DC 20002, (202)543-5675

Natl. Family Life Found. - Address unknown since 1995.

Natl. Family Partnership [13270], c/o Informed Families Educ. Center, 2490 Coral Way, Ste. 501, Miami, FL 33145, (305)856-4886

Natl. Family Planning Forum [★12185]

Natl. Family Planning and Reproductive Hea. Assn. [12185], 1627 K St. NW, 12th Fl., Washington, DC 20006, (202)293-3114

Natl. Fantasy Fan Club for Disneyana Enthusiasts [24791], PO Box 19212, Irvine, CA 92623-9212, (714)731-4705

Natl. Fantasy Fan Fed. [10946], c/o Dennis L. Davis, Chm./Sec., 25549 Byron St., San Bernardino, CA 92404-6403

Natl. Farm Borrowers Assn. - Address unknown since 1995.

Natl. Farm-City Comm. [★4649]

Natl. Farm-City Coun. [4649], 600 Maryland Ave. SW, Ste. 1000W, Washington, DC 20024, (202)406-3706

Natl. Farm Coalition - Defunct.

Natl. Farm Home Editors Assn. - Defunct.

Natl. Farm and Power Equip. Dealers Assn. [★185]

Natl. Farm and Ranch Bus. Mgt. Educ. Assn. [4639], 6540 65th St. NE, Rochester, MN 55906-1911, (507)252-6928

Natl. Farm Worker Ministry [12594], 438 N Skinker Blvd., St. Louis, MO 63130, (314)726-6470

Natl. Farm Workers Assn. [★23999]

Natl. Farmers' Fed. [IO], Kingston, Australia

Natl. Farmers Org. [4650], 528 Billy Sunday Rd., Ste. 100, Ames, IA 50010-2000, (800)247-2110

Natl. Farmers Union [4651], 5619 DTC Pkwy., Ste. 300, Greenwood Village, CO 80111-3136, (303)337-5500

Natl. Farmers Union - Canada [IO], Saskatoon, SK, Canada

Natl. Farmers' Union - England [IO], Stoneleigh, United Kingdom

Natl. Fashion Accessories Assn. [250], 350 5th Ave., Ste. 2030, New York, NY 10118, (212)947-3424

Natl. Fashion Accessories Salesmen's Guild - Defunct.

Natl. Fastdance Assn. [9894], c/o Bill Maddox, Pres., 3371 Debussy Rd., Jacksonville, FL 32277, (904)744-2424

Natl. Fastener Distributors Assn. [1828], 401 N Michigan Ave., Chicago, IL 60611, (312)527-6671

Natl. Fastpitch Coaches Assn. [23840], 100 G T Thames Dr., Ste. D, Starkville, MS 39759, (662)320-2155

Natl. Fatherhood Initiative [17510], 101 Lake Forest Blvd., Ste. 360, Gaithersburg, MD 20877, (301)948-0599

Natl. Father's Day Comm. [18674], 47 W 34th St., Ste. 534, New York, NY 10001, (212)594-5977

Natl. Fats and Oils Brokers Assn. - Defunct.

Natl. Fauna Preservation Soc. [★IO]

Natl. Federated Craft [19244], 11 Country Arrow Dr., Lafayette, IN 47905-8753, (765)447-7972

Natl. Fed. of 18 Plus Groups [★IO]

Natl. Fed. of Abstracting and Indexing Services [★IO]

Natl. Fed. of Abstracting and Indexing Services [★7205]

Natl. Fed. of Abstracting and Info. Services [7205], 1518 Walnut St., Ste. 1004, Philadelphia, PA 19102-3403, (215)893-1561

Natl. Fed. of Abstracting and Info. Services [IO], Philadelphia, PA, United States

Natl. Fed. of Advt. Agencies [IO], Madrid, Spain

Natl. Fed. of Afro-American Women [★13051]

Natl. Fed. of Agricultural Cooperative Associations [IO], Tokyo, Japan

Natl. Fed. of Agricultural Cooperators and Producers [IO], Budapest, Hungary

Natl. Fed. of American Hungarians [19108]

Natl. Fed. of Anglers [IO], Nottingham, United Kingdom

Natl. Fed. of Arch Clubs [IO], Dublin, Ireland

Natl. Fed. of Asian-Amer. United Methodists [20266]

Natl. Fed. of Asian Indian Organizations in Am. [★19114]

Natl. Fed. of Beekeepers Associations [★502]

Natl. Fed. for Biblio/Poetry Therapy [16225], c/o Linda Hendrick, Admin., 7857 S Univ. Way, Centennial, CO 80122, (720)200-1015

Natl. Fed. of the Blind [16877], 1800 Johnson St., Baltimore, MD 21230, (410)659-9314

Natl. Fed. of Buddhist Women's Associations [★19543]

Natl. Fed. of Builders [IO], London, United Kingdom

Natl. Fed. of Bus Users [★IO]

Natl. Fed. of Bus. and Professional Women's Clubs [★17515]

Natl. Fed. of Catholic Coll. Students - Defunct.

Natl. Fed. of Catholic Physicians Guilds [★15996]

Natl. Fed. of Catholic Seminarians - Defunct.

Natl. Fed. for Catholic Youth Ministry [19688], 415 Michigan Ave. NE, Ste. 40, Washington, DC 20017-4503, (202)636-3825

Natl. Fed. of Cemetery Friends [IO], South Croydon, United Kingdom

Natl. Fed. of Citizen Band Radio Operators - Defunct.

Natl. Fed. of City Farms [★IO]

Natl. Fed. of Clinical Social Workers [★13201]

Natl. Fed. Coaches Assn. [★23294]

Natl. Fed. of Coffee Growers of Colombia [IO], Bogota, Colombia

Natl. Fed. of Coll. and Univ. Bus. Officers Associations [★7897]

Natl. Fed. of Community Broadcasters [575], 1970 Broadway, Ste. 1000, Oakland, CA 94612, (510)451-8200

Natl. Fed. of Community Development Credit Unions [1118], 116 John St., 33rd Fl., New York, NY 10038, (212)809-1850

Natl. Fed. of Community Organizations [★IO]

Natl. Fed. of Consulting Service - Defunct.

Natl. Fed. of Credit Guarantee Corporations [IO], Tokyo, Japan

Natl. Fed. of Croatian Americans [17362], 2401 Res. Blvd., Ste. 115, Rockville, MD 20850, (301)208-6650

Natl. Fed. of Dairy Cooperatives [IO], Paris, France

Natl. Fed. of the Dairy Indus. [IO], Paris, France

Natl. Fed. of Dairy Producers [IO], Paris, France

Natl. Fed. for Decency [★17162]

Natl. Fed. of Democratic Women [17408], c/o Helen Knetzer, Pres., 7211 E Lincoln, Wichita, KS 67210, (316)612-9709

Natl. Fed. of Demolition Contractors [IO], Staines, United Kingdom

Natl. Fed. of Diocesan Catholic Youth Councils [★19688]

Natl. Fed. of the Disabled Nepal [IO], Kathmandu, Nepal

Natl. Fed. of Disabled Persons Associations [IO], Budapest, Hungary

Natl. Fed. of Edible Oil Traders [IO], Rome, Italy

Natl. Fed. of Electrotechnical and Electronic Indus. [IO], Milan, Italy

Natl. Fed. of Enterprise Agencies [IO], Bedford, United Kingdom

Natl. Fed. of Export Assns. - Defunct.

Natl. Fed. of Fed. Employees [24077], 805 15th St. NW, Ste. 500, Washington, DC 20005, (202)862-4420

Natl. Fed. of Filipino Amer. Associations [10780], 2607 24th St. NW, Ste. 4, Washington, DC 20008-2600, (202)986-1153

Natl. Fed. of Fish Friers [IO], Leeds, United Kingdom

Natl. Fed. of Fishermen - Defunct.

Natl. Fed. of Fishermen's Organisations [IO], Grimsby, United Kingdom

Natl. Fed. of Fishing Companies [IO], Rome, Italy

Natl. Fed. of Fishmongers [IO], Colchester, United Kingdom

Natl. Fed. of Flemish Giant Breeders [★5151]

Natl. Fed. of Flemish Giant Rabbit Breeders [5151], c/o Judith Welch, Sec.-Treas., 1460 McGill Hollow Rd., Linden, PA 17744-7722, (570)321-1013

Natl. Fed. of French-Canadian Women [IO], Ottawa, ON, Canada

Natl. Fed. of French Hairdressers [IO], Paris, France

Natl. Fed. of Furniture Traders [IO], Milan, Italy

Natl. Fed. of Goldsmiths [IO], Milan, Italy

Natl. Fed. of Grain Cooperatives [★4483]

Natl. Fed. of Grain Growers [IO], Bogota, Colombia

Natl. Fed. of the Grand Order of Pachyderm Clubs [18359], PO Box 1602, Great Falls, MT 59403-1602, (888)GOPACHY

Natl. Fed. of Grandmother Clubs of Am. [19383], c/o Cure Childhood Cancer, 1835 Savoy Dr., Ste. 317, Atlanta, GA 30341-1000, (770)986-0035

Natl. Fed. of Grange Mutual Insurance Companies - Defunct.

Natl. Fed. of Hebrew Teachers and Principals - Defunct.

Natl. Fed. of Hispanic Owned Newspapers [3240], 20 W 22nd St., Ste. 808, New York, NY 10010-5804, (708)652-6397

Natl. Fed. of Hispanic Publications [★3240]

Natl. Fed. of Hispanics in Communications - Defunct.

Natl. Fed. of Housestaff Orgs. - Defunct.

Reference to "IO" in place of a book number signifies that the association may be found in the 45th edition of International Organizations.

Encyclopedia of Associations, 46th Edition

3877

Natl. Fed. of Housing Counselors - Address unknown since 2008.

Natl. Federation of Hungarian-Americans [★19108]

Natl. Fed. of Independent Bus. [3622], 53 Century Blvd., Ste. 250, Nashville, TN 37214, (615)872-5800

Natl. Fed. of Independent Scrap Yard Dealers - Address unknown since 1995.

Natl. Fed. of Independent Unions [24210], 1166 S 11th St., Philadelphia, PA 19147, (215)336-3300

Natl. Fed. of Indian Amer. Associations [19114], 319 Summit Hall Rd., Gaithersburg, MD 20877, (301)926-3013

Natl. Fed. Interscholastic Music Assn. [★8928]

Natl. Fed. Interscholastic Officials Assn. [★23874]

Natl. Fed. Interscholastic Speech and Debate Assn. [★9161]

National Fed. Interscholastic Spirit Association [★23841]

Natl. Fed. Interscholastic Spirit Assn. [★23295]

Natl. Fed. of Italian Perfume Retailers [IO], Milan, Italy

Natl. Fed. of Jewish Men's Clubs [★20137]

Natl. Fed. of Licensed Practical Nurses [15509], 605 Poole Dr., Garner, NC 27529, (919)779-0046

Natl. Fed. of Local Cable Programmers [★17161]

Natl. Fed. of Master Steeplejacks and Lightning Conductor Engineers [★IO]

Natl. Fed. of Meat and Food Traders [IO], Tunbridge Wells, United Kingdom

Natl. Fed. of Milk Hauler Assns. - Address unknown since 2001.

Natl. Fed. of Mobile Home Owners [★12323]

Natl. Fed. of Modern Language Teachers Associations [8739], c/o Dr. Gerard L. Ervin, Treas., 7841 E Camino Montaraz, Tucson, AZ 85715-3713, (520)885-2663

Natl. Fed. of Municipal Analysts [749], PO Box 14893, Pittsburgh, PA 15234-0893, (412)341-4898

Natl. Fed. Music Adjudicator Assn. [★8928]

Natl. Fed. of Music Clubs [10662], 1336 N Delaware St., Indianapolis, IN 46202-2481, (317)638-4003

Natl. Fed. of Music Societies [★IO]

Natl. Fed. of Nonprofits [★317]

Natl. Fed. of Officers for Life [18559]

Natl. Fed. Officials Assn. [★23874]

Natl. Fed. of Opticianry Schools [15708], c/o Randall L. Smith, Exec. Mgr., 2800 Springport Rd., Jackson, MI 49202, (517)990-6945

Natl. Fed. of Paralegal Associations [6151], PO Box 2016, Edmonds, WA 98020, (425)967-0045

Natl. Fed. of Parents for Drug-Free Youth [★13270]

Natl. Fed. of Parents and Friends of Gays - Address unknown since 1999.

Natl. Fed. of Pentecostal Churches - Defunct.

Natl. Fed. of Plus Areas of Great Britain [IO], Sutton Coldfield, United Kingdom

Natl. Fed. of Preserved Vegetable Indus. Associations [IO], Madrid, Spain

Natl. Fed. of Press Women [3137], PO Box 5556, Arlington, VA 22205, (703)812-9487

Natl. Fed. of Priests' Councils [19689], 333 N Michigan Ave., Ste. 1205, Chicago, IL 60601-4002, (312)442-9700

Natl. Fed. of Professional Bullriders [23688], 2222 Hwy. F, Mansfield, MO 65704, (417)924-3591

Natl. Fed. of Professional Orgs. - Address unknown since 1999.

Natl. Fed. of Professional Trainers [23956], PO Box 4579, Lafayette, IN 47903-4579, (765)471-4514

Natl. Fed. of Professors [IO], Lisbon, Portugal

Natl. Fed. of Republican Women [18525], 124 N Alfred St., Alexandria, VA 22314, (703)548-9688

Natl. Fed. of Residential Landlords [IO], Brighton, United Kingdom

Natl. Fed. of Retail Newsagents [IO], London, United Kingdom

Natl. Fed. of Roofing Contractors [IO], London, United Kingdom

Natl. Fed. of Sci. Abstracting and Indexing Services [★IO]

Natl. Fed. of Sci. Abstracting and Indexing Services [★7205]

Natl. Fed. of Sea Anglers [IO], Buckfastleigh, United Kingdom

Natl. Fed. of Seed Potato Growers [IO], Beaurains, France

Natl. Fed. of Services for Unmarried Parents and Their Children [IO], Dublin, Ireland

Natl. Fed. of Settlements [★11792]

Natl. Fed. of Settlements and Neighborhood Centers [★11792]

Natl. Fed. of Shoe Traders [IO], Trieste, Italy

Natl. Fed. of Societies for Clinical Social Work [★13201]

Natl. Fed. of Specialized Press [IO], Paris, France

Natl. Fed. for Specialty Nursing Orgs. - Defunct.

Natl. Fed. of Spiritual Healers [IO], Sunbury-On-Thames, United Kingdom

Natl. Fed. of Stamp Clubs - Defunct.

Natl. Fed. of State High School Associations [23841], PO Box 690, Indianapolis, IN 46206, (317)972-6900

Natl. Fed. of State High School Athletic Associations [★23841]

Natl. Fed. of State Humanities Councils [★10198]

Natl. Fed. of State Poetry Societies [10865], c/o Ms. Doris Stengel, Pres., 1510 S 7th St., Brainerd, MN 56401, (218)829-9072

Natl. Fed. of SubPostmasters [IO], Shoreham-by-Sea, United Kingdom

Natl. Fed. TARGET Program - Defunct.

Natl. Fed. of Taxicab Associations [★IO]

Natl. Fed. of Temple Brotherhoods [★20160]

Natl. Fed. of Temple Sisterhoods [★20192]

Natl. Fed. of Terrazzo, Marble and Mosaic Specialists [IO], London, United Kingdom

Natl. Fed. of Textiles [★3772]

Natl. Fed. of Tire Retailers [IO], Bologna, Italy

Natl. Fed. of Tourism Chambers of Ecuador [IO], Quito, Ecuador

Natl. Fed. of Tourist Guide Associations-USA [24380], c/o Bobbie Gattuso, Pres., 121 Commerce St., Gretna, LA 70056, (504)367-8162

Natl. Fed. of the Travel and Tourism Indus. [IO], Rome, Italy

Natl. Fed. of UNESCO Associations in Japan [IO], Tokyo, Japan

Natl. Fed. of Vegetable Producers [IO], Paris, France

Natl. Fed. of Wholesale Distributors of Elec. Materials [IO], Milan, Italy

Natl. Fed. of Women's Institutes [IO], London, United Kingdom

Natl. Fed. of Women's Republican Clubs [★18525]

Natl. Fed. of Young Farmers' Clubs [IO], Kenilworth, United Kingdom

Natl. Feed Ingredients Assn. [★1357]

Natl. Feeder Pig Marketing Assn. - Defunct.

Natl. Fellowship of Child Care Executives [13501], c/o Gregg Dowty, The Children's Home of Easton, 2000 S 25th St., Easton, PA 18042

Natl. Fellowship of Disciple Directors [★19842]

Natl. Fellowship of Grace Brethren Ministries [★19533]

Natl. Fellowship of Methodist Musicians [★20261]

Natl. Feminist Therapist Assn. - Defunct.

Natl. Fencing Coaches Assn. of Am. [★23403]

Natl. Fenestration Rating Coun. [648], 6305 Ivy Ln., Ste. 140, Greenbelt, MD 20770, (301)589-1776

Natl. Fenton Glass Soc. [22564], PO Box 4008, Marietta, OH 45750, (740)374-3345

Natl. Ferret Welfare Soc. [IO], Coventry, United Kingdom

Natl. Fertilizer Solutions Assn. [★1363]

Natl. FFA [★7940]

Natl. FFA [★7940]

Natl. FFA [★IO]

Natl. FFA [★IO]

National FFA Alumni Assn. [★IO]

National FFA Alumni Assn. [★7940]

Natl. FFA Org. [7940], PO Box 68960, Indianapolis, IN 46268-0960, (317)802-6060

National FFA Organization [IO], Indianapolis, IN, United States

Natl. Fibre Can and Tube Assn. [★IO]

Natl. Fibre Can and Tube Assn. [★976]

Natl. Fibromyalgia Assn. [14397], 2121 S Towne Centre Pl., Ste. 300, Anaheim, CA 92806, (714)921-0150

Natl. Fibromyalgia Awareness Campaign [★14397]

Natl. Fibromyalgia Partnership [14398], PO Box 160, Linden, VA 22642-0160, (866)725-4404

Natl. Fibromyalgia Res. Assn. [15347], PO Box 500, Salem, OR 97308, (503)315-7257

Natl. Field Archery Assn. [23055], 31407 Outer I-10, Redlands, CA 92373, (909)794-2133

Natl. Field Archery Soc. [IO], Chorley, United Kingdom

Natl. Field Hockey Coaches Assn. [23404], 11921 Meadow Ridge Terr., Glen Allen, VA 23059, (804)364-8700

Natl. Field Selling Assn. [3471], 100 N 20th St., 4th Fl., Philadelphia, PA 19103-1443, (215)564-1627

Natl. Film Bd. of Canada [IO], Montreal, QC, Canada

Natl. Film Music Coun. - Defunct.

Natl. Film Soc. - Defunct.

Natl. Finals Rodeo Commn. [★23689]

Natl. Finals Rodeo Comm. [23689], 101 Pro Rodeo Dr., Colorado Springs, CO 80919, (719)593-8840

Natl. Finance Adjusters [493], PO Box 3855, Baltimore, MD 21217, (410)728-2400

Natl. Financial Institutions' Assn. [IO], Bogota, Colombia

Natl. Finch Soc. [★21854]

Natl. Finch and Softbill Soc. [21854], c/o Ms. Rebecca Mikel, Exec. Sec., 13779 US 12 E, Union, MI 49130, (269)641-7209

Natl. Fire Indus. Assn. [IO], Melbourne, Australia

Natl. Fire Protection Assn. [12975], 1 Batterymarch Park, Quincy, MA 02169-7471, (617)770-3000

Natl. Fire Sprinkler Assn. [3449], 40 Jon Barret Rd., Patterson, NY 12563, (845)878-4200

Natl. Firearms Act Trade and Collectors Assn. [1480], PO Box 855, Winchester, KY 40392, (703)263-7676

Natl. Firebird Club [★21732]

Natl. Firebird and T/A Club [21732], PO Box 11238, Chicago, IL 60611, (773)769-6262

Natl. Fireplace Assn. [IO], Wycombe, United Kingdom

Natl. Fireproofing Contractors Assn. [1476], PO Box 1571, Westford, MA 01886, (866)250-4111

Natl. Fireworks Assn. [1352], 8224 NW Bradford Ct., Kansas City, MO 64151, (816)505-3589

Natl. Fish Meal and Oil Assn. [2855], c/o Natl. Fisheries Inst., 7918 Jones Br. Dr., Ste. 700, McLean, VA 22102-3319, (703)524-8884

Natl. Fisheries Contaminant Res. Center [★7172]

Natl. Fisheries Education and Res. Found. - Defunct.

Natl. Fisheries Inst. [3496], 7918 Jones Br. Dr., Ste. 700, McLean, VA 22102, (703)752-8880

Natl. Fishing Lure Collectors Club [22082], c/o Colby Sorrells, Sec.-Treas., PO Box 509, Mansfield, TX 76063, (817)473-6748

Natl. Fitness Assn. [★3670]

Natl. Fitness Found. - Address unknown since 1991.

Natl. Fitness Therapy Assn. [15968], PO Box 522, Winter Park, CO 80482, (970)726-0697

Natl. Flag Celebration - Address unknown since 2007.

Natl. Flag Day Found. [21094], PO Box 55, Waubeka, WI 53021-0055, (262)692-9111

Natl. Flag Found. [11076], Flag Plz., 1275 Bedford Ave., Pittsburgh, PA 15219, (412)261-1776

Natl. Flexible Packaging Assn. [★2875]

Natl. Flight Nurses Assn. [★15427]

Natl. Flight Paramedics Assn. [★14334]

Natl. Flood Insurers Assn. - Defunct.

Natl. Floor Covering Assn. [IO], Mississauga, ON, Canada

Natl. Floor Safety Inst. [3450], PO Box 92607, Southlake, TX 76092, (817)749-1700

Natl. Florist Assn. - Defunct.

Natl. Fluid Power Assn. [2050], 3333 N Mayfair Rd., Ste. 211, Milwaukee, WI 53222-3219, (414)778-3344

Natl. Fluid Power Assn. [IO], Milwaukee, WI, United States

Natl. Flute Assn. [10663], 26951 Ruether Ave., Ste. H, Santa Clarita, CA 91351, (661)713-6013

Natl. Flying Farmers Assn. [★4646]

Natl. Flying Farmers Assn. [★IO]

Natl. Folk Festival Assn. [★9961]

A star before a book entry number signifies that the name is not listed separately, but is mentioned within the entry.

Natl. Food Conf. Assn. - Defunct.

Natl. Food and Conservation Through Swine - Defunct.

Natl. Food, Drug and Cosmetic Assn. of Mfrs. and Distributors - Defunct.

Natl. Food and Energy Coun. [6963], PO Box 309, Wilmington, OH 45177-0309, (937)383-0001

Natl. Food Service Assn. - Defunct.

Natl. Food Ser. Mgt. Inst. [1590], PO Drawer 188, Univ. of Mississippi, 6 Jeanette Philips Dr., University, MS 38677-0188, (662)915-7658

Natl. Foodservice Marketing Associates [★3467]

Natl. Foodservice Marketing Associates [★IO]

Natl. Foot Health Coun. - Defunct.

National Football Conf. [★23432]

Natl. Football Found. and Coll. Hall of Fame [23431], 433 E Las Colinas Blvd., Ste. 1130, Irving, TX 75039, (972)556-1000

Natl. Football League [23432], 280 Park Ave., New York, NY 10017, (212)655-5665

Natl. Football League Alumni [23433], 3696 N Fed. Hwy., Ste. 202, Fort Lauderdale, FL 33308-6262, (954)630-2100

Natl. Football League Alumni, Inc. [★23433]

Natl. Football League Players Assn. [23434], 2021 L St. NW, Ste. 600, Washington, DC 20036, (202)463-2200

Natl. Football Shrine and Hall of Fame [★23431]

Natl. Footwear Assn. of Russia [IO], Moscow, Russia

Natl. Foreign Language Center [8740], 5201 Paint Br. Pkwy., Patapsco Bldg., Ste. 2132, College Park, MD 20742-6715, (301)405-9828

Natl. Foreign Trade Coun. [2289], 1625 K St. NW, Ste. 200, Washington, DC 20006, (202)887-0278

Natl. Foreign Trade Coun. [IO], Washington, DC, United States

Natl. Forensic Assn. [9158], c/o Prof. Larry Schnoor, Pres., 107 Agency Rd., Mankato, MN 56001-5053, (507)387-3010

Natl. Forensic Center [5766], PO Box 270529, San Diego, CA 92198-2529, (800)735-6660

Natl. Forensic League [9159], 125 Watson St., PO Box 38, Ripon, WI 54971, (920)748-6206

Natl. Forest Found. [4424], Bldg. 27, Ste. 3, Ft. Missoula Rd., Missoula, MT 59804, (406)542-2805

Natl. Forest Products Assn. [★4679]

Natl. Forest Protection Alliance [4592], 423 W 1st Ave., Ste. 240, Spokane, WA 99201, (509)838-4912

Natl. Forest Recreation Assn. [3358], PO Box 488, Woodlake, CA 93286, (559)564-2365

Natl. Forest Workers' Union of Japan [IO], Tokyo, Japan

Natl. Fort Daughters of '98, Auxiliary United Spanish War Veterans [21267], c/o Mrs. Berna Mae Reinwald, Natl. Sec./Quartermaster, 32028 Mt. Vernon, Rockwood, MI 48173-9650, (313)379-4996

Natl. Forum for the Advancement of Aquatics - Defunct.

Natl. Forum API [IO], Plovdiv, Bulgaria

Natl. Forum for Black Public Administrators [6196], 777 N Capitol St. NE, Ste. 807, Washington, DC 20002, (202)408-9300

Natl. Forum of Catholic Parent Orgs. - Defunct.

Natl. Forum for Executive Women - Defunct.

Natl. Forum of Greek Orthodox Church Musicians [20434], c/o Dr. Vicki Pappas, Natl. Chair, 3814 Regents Cir., Bloomington, IN 47401, (812)855-8248

Natl. Forum for Hea. Care Quality Measurement and Reporting [★14658]

Natl. Foster Care Assn. [★IO]

Natl. Foster Parent Assn. [12677], 7512 Stanich Ave., Ste. 6, Gig Harbor, WA 98335, (253)853-4000

Natl. Found. for Advancement in the Arts [9587], 444 Brickell Ave., P-14, Miami, FL 33131, (305)377-1140

Natl. Found. for Australian Women [IO], Sydney, Australia

Natl. Found. for Brain Res. [15397], c/o BrainNet. org, PO Box 390, Solomons, MD 20688, (202)250-3845

Natl. Found. for Cancer Res. [15652], 4600 E West Hwy., Ste. 525, Bethesda, MD 20814, (301)654-1250

Natl. Found. for Cancer Res. [IO], Bethesda, MD, United States

Natl. Found. for the Chemically Hypersensitive - Address unknown since 2008.

Natl. Found. for Children's Hearing Education and Res. - Address unknown since 1999.

Natl. Found. for Conservation and Environmental Officers - Defunct.

Natl. Found. for Credit Counseling [2428], 801 Roeder Rd., Ste. 900, Silver Spring, MD 20910, (301)589-5600

Natl. Found. of Dentistry for the Handicapped [14179], 1800 15th St., Ste. 100, Denver, CO 80202, (303)534-5360

Natl. Found. for Depressive Illness [15225]

Natl. Found. for Ectodermal Dysplasias [14468], 410 E Main St., PO Box 114, Mascoutah, IL 62258, (618)566-2020

Natl. Found. for Education in Amer. Citizenship - Address unknown since 1995.

Natl. Found. for Educational Res. [IO], Slough, United Kingdom

Natl. Found. for Environmental Control - Address unknown since 1995.

Natl. Found. for Eye Res. - Address unknown since 1995.

Natl. Found. for Facial Reconstruction [14065], 317 E 34th St., Rm. 901, New York, NY 10016, (212)263-6656

Natl. Found. of Funeral Service - Address unknown since 2002.

Natl. Found. for the Handicapped and Disabled - Defunct.

Natl. Found. for Happy Horsemanship for the Handicapped - Address unknown since 1994.

Natl. Found. for Health, Physical Education and Recreation - Defunct.

Natl. Found. of Hea., Welfare and Pension Plans [★1240]

Natl. Found. of Hea., Welfare and Pension Plans [★IO]

Natl. Found. of Hea., Welfare and Pension Plans, Trustees and Administrators [★IO]

Natl. Found. of Hea., Welfare and Pension Plans, Trustees and Administrators [★1240]

Natl. Found. for History of Chemistry [★10101]

Natl. Found. for Ileitis and Colitis [★14414]

Natl. Found. for the Improvement of Educ. [★8294]

Natl. Found. of Indian Engineers [IO], New Delhi, India

Natl. Found. for Infantile Paralysis [★13756]

Natl. Found. for Infectious Diseases [14953], 4733 Bethesda Ave., Ste. 750, Bethesda, MD 20814, (301)656-0003

Natl. Found. for Jewish Genetic Diseases - Defunct.

Natl. Found. for Long Term Health Care - Defunct.

Natl. Found. of Manufactured Home Owners [12323], c/o Deborah Chapman, Chair, 62 Hawthorne Cir., Willow Street, PA 17584, (717)284-4520

Natl. Found. - March of Dimes [★13756]

Natl. Found. for Metabolic Res. - Defunct.

Natl. Found. for Non-Invasive Diagnostics - Defunct.

Natl. Found. for Peroneal Muscular Atrophy [★15313]

Natl. Found. for the Prevention of Oral Disease - Defunct.

Natl. Found. for Professional Legal Assistants - Address unknown since 1999.

Natl. Found. for Res. in Medicine - Address unknown since 2001.

Natl. Found. for Rural Medical Care - Defunct.

Natl. Found. for the Study of Employment Policy [★12077]

Natl. Found. for the Study of Equal Employment [★12077]

Natl. Found. for the Study and Treatment of Pathological Gambling - Defunct.

Natl. Found. for Teaching Entrepreneurship [8038], 120 Wall St., 29th Fl., New York, NY 10005, (212)232-3333

Natl. Found. for Transplants [16678], 5350 Poplar Ave., Ste. 430, Memphis, TN 38119, (901)684-1697

Natl. Found. for Unemployment Compensation and Workers Compensation [5681], 910 17th St., Ste. 315, Washington, DC 20006, (202)223-8902

Natl. Found. of Wheelchair Tennis - Address unknown since 2003.

Natl. Found. for Wholistic Medicine - Defunct.

Natl. Found. for Women Bus. Owners [★4037]

Natl. Found. for Women Legislators [6359], 910 16th St., Ste. 100, Washington, DC 20006, (202)293-3040

Natl. Found. of Zoological Parks and Aquaria [IO], Caracas, Venezuela

Natl. Fox Hunters Assn. - Address unknown since 1990.

Natl. Fragile X Found. [14469], PO Box 190488, San Francisco, CA 94119, (925)938-9300

Natl. Frame Builders Assn. [1047], 4840 Bob Billings Pkwy., Lawrence, KS 66049-3862, (785)843-2444

Natl. Franchise Assn. [★1669]

Natl. Franchise Assn. [★IO]

Natl. Franchise Assn. Coalition - Defunct.

Natl. Franchisee Assn. [1669], 1201 Roberts Blvd., Ste. 100, Kennesaw, GA 30144, (678)797-5160

Natl. Franchisee Assn. [IO], Kennesaw, GA, United States

Natl. Fraternal Cong. [★19133]

Natl. Fraternal Cong. of Am. [19133], 1315 W 22nd St., Ste. 400, Oak Brook, IL 60523, (630)522-6322

Natl. Fraternal Flag Day Found. - Defunct.

Natl. Fraternal Soc. of the Deaf [19134], 1118 S 6th St., Springfield, IL 62703-2406, (217)789-7429

Natl. Fraternity of Student Musicians [8924], c/o Amer. Coll. of Musicians, PO Box 1807, Austin, TX 78767, (512)478-5775

Natl. Fraud Info. Center/Internet Fraud Watch [17339], c/o Natl. Consumers League, 1701 K St. NW, Ste. 1200, Washington, DC 20006, (202)835-3323

Natl. Free Clinic Found. of Am. [14585]

Natl. Free Lance Photographers Assn. - Address unknown since 2001.

Natl. Freedom Acad. - Address unknown since 1995.

Natl. Freedom Fund for Librarians [★17040]

Natl. Freedom of Info. Coalition [5822], c/o Missouri School of Journalism, 133 Neff Annex, Univ. of Missouri-Columbia, Columbia, MO 65211, (573)882-5736

Natl. Freedom Shrine Found. - Defunct.

Natl. Freight Transportation Assn. - Defunct.

Natl. French Honor Soc. [★24490]

Natl. Friends of the Arts - Defunct.

Natl. Friends of Public Broadcasting - Address unknown since 1999.

Natl. Front for the Liberation of Angola - Address unknown since 1989.

Natl. Frozen Dessert and Fast Food Assn. [1958]

Natl. Frozen Food Assn. [★1547]

Natl. Frozen Food Distributors Assn. [★1547]

Natl. Frozen Food Locker Assn. [★2656]

Natl. Frozen Food Locker Inst. [★2656]

Natl. Frozen Pizza Inst. [1546], 2000 Corporate Ridge, Ste. 1000, McLean, VA 22102, (703)821-0770

Natl. Frozen and Refrigerated Foods Assn. [1547], PO Box 6069, Harrisburg, PA 17112, (717)657-8601

Natl. Fructose Center - Defunct.

Natl. Fruit and Syrup Manufacturers Assn. [★1539]

Natl. Frumps of America - Defunct.

Natl. Fuchsia Soc. [22527]

Natl. Fuel Credit Assn. - Defunct.

Natl. Fund for Graduate Nursing Education - Defunct.

Natl. Fund for Medical Education - Address unknown since 1994.

Natl. Fund for Minority Engg. Students [★8369]

Natl. Funeral Directors Assn. [2788], 13625 Bishop's Dr., Brookfield, WI 53005-6607, (262)789-1880

Natl. Funeral Directors Assn. of Southern Africa [IO], Germiston, Republic of South Africa

Natl. Funeral Directors and Morticians Assn. [2789], 3951 Snapfinger Pkwy., Ste. 570, Omega World Center, Decatur, GA 30035, (800)434-0958

Natl. Furniture Traffic Conf. [★3570]

Natl. Furniture Traffic Conf. [★IO]

Natl. Futures Assn. [1713], 200 W Madison St., No. 1600, Chicago, IL 60606-3447, (312)781-1300

Natl. Gaming Coun. [★8455]

Reference to "IO" in place of a book number signifies that the association may be found in the 45th edition of International Organizations.

Natl. Garden Bur. [4982], 1311 Butterfield Rd., Ste. 310, Downers Grove, IL 60515, (630)963-0770

Natl. Garden Clubs [22528], 4401 Magnolia Ave., St. Louis, MO 63110, (314)776-7574

Natl. Gardening Assn. [22529], 1100 Dorset St., South Burlington, VT 05403, (802)863-5251

Natl. Gardens Scheme [IO], Guildford, United Kingdom

Natl. Gardens Scheme Charitable Trust [★IO]

Natl. Gas Measurement Assn. - Address unknown since 1994.

Natl. Gasohol Commn. - Defunct.

Natl. Gastroenterological Assn. [★14405]

Natl. Gaucher Found. [15252], 2227 Idlewood Rd., Ste. 12, Tucker, GA 30084, (800)504-3189

Natl. Gay Alliance for Young Adults - Defunct.

Natl. Gay and Lesbian Chamber of Commerce [24321], Dupont Cir., 2000 P St. NW, Ste. 300, Washington, DC 20036, (202)419-0440

Natl. Gay and Lesbian Domestic Violence Victims' Network - Address unknown since 2003.

Natl. Gay and Lesbian Task Force [12249], 1325 Massachusetts Ave. NW, Ste. 600, Washington, DC 20005, (202)393-5177

Natl. Gay/Lesbian Travel Desk [24322], 2790 Wrondel Way, PMB No. 444, Reno, NV 89502

Natl. Gay Pilot's Assn. [439], PO Box 7271, Dallas, TX 75209-0271, (214)336-0873

Natl. Gay Rights Advocates - Defunct.

Natl. Gay Student Center - Defunct.

Natl. Gay Task Force [★12249]

Natl. Gay Youth Network - Address unknown since 2001.

Natl. Gender Selection Center - Address unknown since 1995.

Natl. Genealogical Soc. [21133], 3108 Columbia Pike, Ste. 300, Arlington, VA 22204-4304, (703)525-0050

Natl. Genetics Found. - Defunct.

Natl. Geographic Soc. [7123], 1145 17th St. NW, Washington, DC 20036, (202)857-7000

Natl. Geographic Soc. Educ. Found. [8458], 1145 17th St. NW, Washington, DC 20036-4688, (202)857-7310

National Geographic Soc. Geography Educ. Prog. [★7123]

National Geophysical Data Center [★4590]

Natl. Geriatrics Soc. - Address unknown since 1994.

Natl. Gerontological Nursing Assn. [14515], 7794 Grow Dr., Pensacola, FL 32514, (850)473-1174

Natl. Ghost Ranch Found. [20469], Ghost Ranch Educ. and Retreat Center, HC77, Box 11, Abiquiu, NM 87510, (505)685-4327

Natl. GI Pipe Smokers Club of America - Address unknown since 1995.

Natl. Gift and Art Assn. - Defunct.

National Gifts in Kind [★8336]

Natl. Girls Athletic Assn. - Defunct.

Natl. Glass Assn. [1732], 8200 Greensboro Dr., Ste. 302, McLean, VA 22102-3881, (703)442-4890

Natl. Glass Clubs Affl. [★22554]

Natl. Glass Dealers Assn. [★1732]

Natl. Glaucoma Trust and The Glaucoma Found. [★15682]

Natl. Gliding Assn. [★23043]

Natl. Gloster Club - Address unknown since 1995.

Natl. Gold Star Mothers - Defunct.

Natl. Goldfish Soc. - Address unknown since 1995.

Natl. Golf Clubs' Advisory Assn. [IO], Worcester, United Kingdom

Natl. Golf Course Owners Assn. [3668], 291 Seven Farms Dr., Charleston, SC 29492, (843)881-9956

Natl. Golf Found. [3669], 1150 S U.S. Hwy. 1, Ste. 401, Jupiter, FL 33477, (561)744-6006

Natl. Golf Salesmen Assn. - Defunct.

Natl. Good Roads Assn. - Defunct.

Natl. Govt. Publishing Assn. [1781], 207 3rd Ave., Hattiesburg, MS 39401, (601)582-3330

Natl. Governors Assn. [6284], Hall of States, 444 N Capitol St., Ste. 267, Washington, DC 20001-1512, (202)624-5300

Natl. Governors' Conf. [★6284]

Natl. Grain and Feed Assn. [1359], 1250 Eye St. NW, Ste. 1003, Washington, DC 20005-3922, (202)289-0873

Natl. Grain Sorghum Producers [★4311]

Natl. Grain Suppliers Credit Assn. - Defunct.

National Grain Trade Coun. [★1748]

Natl. Grand Lodge, Intl. Order of Good Templars [★19081]

Natl. Grange [4652], 1616 H St. NW, Washington, DC 20006, (202)628-3507

Natl. Graniteware Soc. [22083], PO Box 9248, Cedar Rapids, IA 52409-9248, (616)361-8697

Natl. Grants Mgt. Assn. [2507], 11654 Plaza Am. Dr., No. 609, Reston, VA 20190-4700, (703)648-9023

Natl. Graphic Artists Guild [★9505]

Natl. Graphic Artists Guild [★IO]

Natl. Graphic Arts Dealers Assn. [★1804]

Natl. Graphic Arts Educ. Assn. [★8470]

Natl. Graphic Arts Educ. Assn. [★IO]

Natl. Graphic Arts Guild [★IO]

Natl. Graphic Arts Guild [★8470]

Natl. Grassroots Peace Network - The Natl. Network to End the War Against Iraq - Defunct.

Natl. Graves Assn. [IO], Dublin, Ireland

Natl. Graves' Disease Found. [16647], PO Box 1969, Brevard, NC 28712, (828)877-5251

Natl. Greek-Amer. Restaurant Assn. - Address unknown since 2002.

Natl. Greenhouse Manufacturers Assn. [184], 4305 N Sixth St., Ste. A, Harrisburg, PA 17110, (717)238-4530

Natl. Greenkeeping Superintendents Assn. [★3663]

Natl. Greentown Glass Assn. - Address unknown since 1995.

Natl. Greyhound Adoption Prog. [11438], 10901 Dutton Rd., Philadelphia, PA 19154, (215)331-7918

Natl. Greyhound Assn. [22318], PO Box 543, Abilene, KS 67410, (785)263-4660

Natl. Grigsby Family Soc. [21009], 4418 Kiowa St., Pasadena, TX 77504-3544, (281)998-8594

Natl. Grocers Assn. [3421], 1005 N Glebe Rd., Ste. 250, Arlington, VA 22201-5758, (703)516-0700

Natl. Ground Water Assn. [4011], 601 Dempsey Rd., Westerville, OH 43081-8978, (614)898-7791

National Ground Water Association [IO], Westerville, OH, United States

Natl. Group Rides and Designated Drivers - Defunct.

Natl. Guard Assn. of the U.S. [6091], 1 Massachusetts Ave. NW, Washington, DC 20001, (202)789-0031

Natl. Guard Civilian Employees Assn. [★24072]

Natl. Guard Executive Directors Assn. [6092], 3706 Crawford Ave., Austin, TX 78731, (512)454-7300

Natl. Guard of the U.S; Enlisted Assn. of [6076]

Natl. Guardianship Assn. [1813], 174 Crestview Dr., Bellefonte, PA 16823, (877)326-5992

Natl. Guideline CH [14654], c/o Vivian Coates, Proj. Dir., ECRI, 5200 Butler Pike, Plymouth Meeting, PA 19462

Natl. Guild of Catholic Psychiatrists - Defunct.

Natl. Guild of Churchmen [19965], PO Box 34548, San Diego, CA 92163, (619)542-8660

Natl. Guild of Community Music Schools [★7979]

Natl. Guild of Community Schools of the Arts [7979], 520 8th Ave., Ste. 302, New York, NY 10018, (212)268-3337

Natl. Guild of Decoupeurs [22168], 1017 Pucker St., Stowe, VT 05672, (802)253-3903

Natl. Guild of Hypnotists [14926], PO Box 308, Merrimack, NH 03054, (603)429-9438

Natl. Guild of Master Craftsmen [IO], Dublin, Ireland

Natl. Guild of Piano Teachers [8925], c/o Amer. Coll. of Musicians, PO Box 1807, Austin, TX 78767, (512)478-5775

Natl. Guild of Professional Paperhangers [2270], 136 S Keowee St., Dayton, OH 45402, (937)222-6477

Natl. Guilds of St. Paul - Address unknown since 1999.

Natl. Gulf War Rsrc. Center [21311], 1403 Southwest Blvd., Ste. 2B, Kansas City, KS 66103, (913)831-7183

National Gulf War Resource Center [IO], Kansas City, MO, United States

Natl. Gym Assn. [23654], PO Box 970579, Coconut Creek, FL 33097-0579, (954)344-8410

Natl. Gymanfa GANU Assn. of U.S. and Canada [★19432]

Natl. Gymanfa GANU Assn. of U.S. and Canada [★IO]

Natl. Gymnastics Judges Assn. [23478], c/o Butch Zunich, Pres., 2302 Sand Point, Champaign, IL 61822, (217)359-4866

Natl. Gypsy Moth Coun. [★5078]

Natl. Gypsy Moth Mgt. Bd. [5078]

Natl. Hacky Sack Footbag Players Assn. [★23426]

Natl. Hacky Sack Footbag Players Assn. [★IO]

Natl. Hair Sys. Culture League [★1084]

Natl. Hairdressers and Cosmetologists Assn. [★1085]

Natl. Hairdressers' Fed. [IO], Bedford, United Kingdom

Natl. Haitian Soc. [IO], Garden City, NY, United States

Natl. Haitian Soc. [17817]

Natl. Half-Tennessee Walking Horse Registry - Address unknown since 2002.

Natl. Hall-Davis Campaign '84 - Defunct.

Natl. Hamburger Coun. - Defunct.

Natl. Hamiltonian Party [18328], 1901 Montclair Ave., Flint, MI 48503, (810)234-3771

Natl. Hand Embroidery and Novelty Mfrs. Assn. - Defunct.

Natl. Handbag Assn. [★250]

Natl. Handcraft Inst. - Defunct.

Natl. Handcraft Soc. - Address unknown since 1995.

Natl. Handicapped Found. - Defunct.

Natl. Handicapped Sports [★23343]

Natl. Handicapped Sports and Recreation Assn. [★23343]

Natl. Handle Mfrs. Assn. - Defunct.

Natl. Hardwood Lumber Assn. [1652], 6830 Raleigh LaGrange Rd., Memphis, TN 38134, (901)377-1818

Natl. Hardwood Lumber Assn. [IO], Memphis, TN, United States

Natl. Harmonica League [IO], Maidenhead, United Kingdom

Natl. Harry Benjamin Gender Dysphoria Assn. [★IO]

Natl. Harry Benjamin Gender Dysphoria Assn. [★13103]

Natl. Havurah Comm. [20168], 7135 Germantown Ave., 2nd Fl., Philadelphia, PA 19119-1842, (215)248-1335

Natl. Havurah Coordinating Comm. [★20168]

Natl. Hay Assn. [1360], 102 Treasure Island Causeway, St. Petersburg, FL 33706, (727)367-9702

Natl. Hay Fever Relief Assn. - Defunct.

Natl. Head Injury Found. [★14528]

Natl. Head Start Assn. [9006], 1651 Prince St., Alexandria, VA 22314, (703)739-0875

National Head Start Directors Association [★9006]

National Head Start Friends Association [★9006]

National Head Start Parent Association [★9006]

National Head Start Staff Association [★9006]

Natl. Headache Found. [14533], 820 N Orleans St., Ste. 217, Chicago, IL 60610-3498, (888)NHF-5552

Natl. Hea. Agencies Comm. for the Combined Fed. Campaign [★12200]

Natl. Hea. Assn. [15279], PO Box 30630, Tampa, FL 33630, (813)961-6100

Natl. Hea. Care Anti-Fraud Assn. [14963], 1201 New York Ave. NW, Ste. 1120, Washington, DC 20005-4006, (202)659-5955

Natl. Health Care Campaign - Defunct.

Natl. Hea. Care Found. for the Deaf [★14752]

Natl. Hea. Care for the Homeless Coun. [14730], PO Box 60427, Nashville, TN 37206-0427, (615)226-2292

Natl. Health Career Assn. - Address unknown since 1999.

National Health Careers Program [★8231]

Natl. Hea. Club Assn. [3670], 640 Plaza Dr., Ste. 300, Highlands Ranch, CO 80129, (800)765-6422

Natl. Hea. Coun. [14586], 1730 M St. NW, Ste. 500, Washington, DC 20036, (202)785-3910

Natl. Hea. Fed. [14587], PO Box 688, Monrovia, CA 91017, (626)357-2181

Natl. Hea. Info. Center [14588], PO Box 1133, Washington, DC 20013-1133, (301)565-4167

Natl. Hea. Info. CH [★14588]

Natl. Hea. Law Prog. [5784], 2639 S La Cienega Blvd., Los Angeles, CA 90034-2675, (310)204-6010

A star before a book entry number signifies that the name is not listed separately, but is mentioned within the entry.

Natl. Health Lawyers Assn. - Defunct.

Natl. Hea. and Medical Res. Coun. [IO], Canberra, Australia

Natl. Hea. Policy Forum [17693], 2131 K St. NW, Ste. 500, Washington, DC 20037, (202)872-1390

Natl. Hea. Prog; Physicians for a [18313]

Natl. Health and Safety Awareness Center - Defunct.

Natl. Hea. Ser. Consultants Assn. [★IO]

Natl. Health Standards and Quality Information Clearinghouse - Defunct.

Natl. Healthcare Collectors Assn. [1869], 1502 Williamson Rd. NE, Ste. 100, Roanoke, VA 24012, (888)698-8022

Natl. Healthcare Cost & Quality Assn. - Defunct.

Natl. Healthy Mothers, Healthy Babies Coalition [15612], 2000 N Beauregard St., 6th Fl., Alexandria, VA 22311, (703)837-4792

Natl. Healthy Start Assn. [15613], PO Box 25227, Baltimore, MD 21229-0327, (410)525-1600

Natl. Hearing Aid Soc. [★14763]

Natl. Hearing Aid Soc. [★IO]

Natl. Hearing Assn. - Address unknown since 1989.

Natl. Hearing Conservation Assn. [14772], 7995 E Prentice Ave., Ste. 100, Greenwood Village, CO 80111, (303)224-9022

Natl. Heart Assn. of Malaysia [IO], Petaling Jaya, Malaysia

Natl. Heart Coun. [13918], c/o Natl. Emergency Medicine Assn., 306 W Joppa Rd., Baltimore, MD 21204-4048, (410)494-0300

Natl. Heart Education Res. Soc. - Address unknown since 1995.

Natl. Heart Forum [IO], London, United Kingdom

Natl. Heart Res. [★13918]

Natl. Heart Savers Assn. [13919], c/o Am. Heart Assn., 16817 Holmes Cir., Omaha, NE 68135-1455, (402)398-1993

Natl. Heartburn Alliance [14423], 303 E Wacker Dr., Ste. 440, Chicago, IL 60601, (877)471-2081

Natl. Hebrew Culture Coun. - Address unknown since 1995.

Natl. Hedgelaying Soc. [IO], Toddington, United Kingdom

National Heisey Glass Museum; Heisey Collectors of America/ [22558]

Natl. Hemi Owners Assn. - Address unknown since 1999.

Natl. Hemophilia Found. [14795], 116 W 32nd St., 11th Fl., New York, NY 10001, (212)328-3700

Natl. Hepatitis C Advocacy Coun. [14813], c/o Missouri Hepatitis C Alliance, 10800 E Walnut Dr., Centralia, MO 65240, (877)737-4372

Natl. Hepatitis C Coalition [14814], PO Box 5058, Hemet, CA 92544, (951)658-4414

Natl. Herb Study Soc. - Address unknown since 1995.

Natl. Herbalist Assn. - Defunct.

Natl. Herbalists Assn. of Australia [IO], Concord West, Australia

Natl. Herbart Soc. for the Sci. Stud. of Educ. [★8293]

Natl. Hereford Hog Record Assn. [5236]

Natl. Hide Assn. [★2421]

Natl. High School Athletic Coaches Assn. [23292], c/o Gelaine Orvik, Exec. Dir., PO Box 10065, Fargo, ND 58106, (701)293-2099

Natl. High School Band and Choral Directors Hall of Fame [★8926]

Natl. High School Band Directors Hall of Fame [8926], c/o Dr. Oliver C. Boone, Exec. Dir., 4166 Will Rhoades Dr., Columbus, GA 31909

Natl. High School Band Inst. [★8926]

Natl. High School Baseball Coaches Assn. [23119], PO Box 12843, Tempe, AZ 85284, (602)615-0571

Natl. High School Boys Volleyball Assn. - Defunct.

Natl. High School and Junior Coll. Mathematics Club [★24538]

Natl. High School Rodeo Assn. [23690], 12001 Tejon St., Ste. 128, Denver, CO 80234, (303)452-0820

Natl. High School Slavic Honor Soc. - SLAVA - Defunct.

Natl. Higher Education Conf. on Students of Color - Defunct.

Natl. Higher Education Staff Assn. - Defunct.

Natl. Highway Post Off. Soc. [★22848]

Natl. Hire Amer. Citizens Soc. [1276]

Natl. Hispana Leadership Inst. [17707], 1601 N Kent St., Ste. 803, Arlington, VA 22209, (703)527-6007

Natl. Hispanic Assn. of Construction Enterprises - Address unknown since 1991.

Natl. Hispanic Bus. Assn. [8039], 5766 Balcones Dr., Ste. 203, Austin, TX 78731, (512)380-7575

Natl. Hispanic Cong. on Alcoholism - Defunct.

Natl. Hispanic Corporate Coun. [750], 1530 Wilson Blvd., Ste. 110, Arlington, VA 22209, (703)807-5137

Natl. Hispanic Coun. on Aging [11310], 734 15th St. NW, Ste. 1050, Washington, DC 20005, (202)347-9733

Natl. Hispanic Employee Assn. [12279], 25A Crescent Dr., No. 312, Pleasant Hill, CA 94523, (202)842-4812

Natl. Hispanic Family - Address unknown since 2006.

Natl. Hispanic Found. for the Arts [19101], 1010 Wisconsin Ave. NW, Ste. 650, Washington, DC 20007-3676, (202)293-8330

Natl. Hispanic Housing Coalition - Defunct.

Natl. Hispanic Inst. [10004], PO Box 220, Maxwell, TX 78656-0020, (512)357-6137

Natl. Hispanic Inst. of Public Policy - Defunct.

Natl. Hispanic Leadership Agenda [17708], c/o Natl. Puerto Rican Coalition, Inc., 1901 L St. NW, Ste. 802, Washington, DC 20036, (202)223-3915

Natl. Hispanic Leadership Conf. - Defunct.

Natl. Hispanic Media Coalition [17187], 1201 W 5th St., Ste. T-205, Los Angeles, CA 90017-2019, (213)534-3026

Natl. Hispanic Medical Assn. [14820], 1411 K St. NW, Ste. 1100, Washington, DC 20005, (202)628-5895

Natl. Hispanic Psychological Assn. - Defunct.

Natl. Hispanic Quincentennial Commn. - Address unknown since 2003.

Natl. Historic Communal Societies Assn. [★10020]

Natl. Historic Route 66 Fed. [24328], PO Box 1848, Dept. WS, Lake Arrowhead, CA 92352-1848, (909)336-6131

Natl. Historic Shrines Found. - Defunct.

Natl. Historical Fire Found. [22422], c/o Hall of Flame Museum, 6101 E Van Buren St., Phoenix, AZ 85008, (602)275-3473

National Historical Publications and Records Commission [★11129]

Natl. Historical Soc.- Address unknown since 1995.

Natl. History Club [8509], The Concord Rev., Inc., 730 Boston Post Rd., Ste. 24, Sudbury, MA 01776, (978)443-0022

Natl. History Day [8510], Univ. of Maryland, 0119 Cecil Hall, College Park, MD 20742, (301)314-9739

Natl. HIV Nurses Assn. [IO], London, United Kingdom

Natl. Hobby Inst. - Defunct.

Natl. Hobo Assn. - Defunct.

Natl. Hockey League Booster Clubs Assn. [25008], PO Box 805, St. Louis, MO 63188, (314)895-9466

Natl. Hockey League Players' Assn. [IO], Toronto, ON, Canada

Natl. Hockey League Writers' Assn. [★3156]

Natl. Holography and Imaging Assn. - Defunct.

Natl. Home Buyers and Home Owners Assn. - Defunct.

Natl. Home Demonstration Agents' Assn. [★5612]

Natl. Home Demonstration Coun. [★8513]

Natl. Home Educ. Res. Inst. [8522], PO Box 13939, Salem, OR 97309, (503)364-1490

National Home Education Research Institute [IO], Salem, OR, United States

Natl. Home Equity Mortgage Assn. [494], 1301 Pennsylvania Ave. NW, Ste. 500, Washington, DC 20004, (202)347-1210

Natl. Home Fashions League [★2264]

Natl. Home Fashions League [★IO]

National Home Furnishings Association [IO], High Point, NC, United States

Natl. Home Furnishings Assn. [1703], 3910 Tinsley Dr., Ste. 101, High Point, NC 27265-3610, (336)886-6100

Natl. Home Furnishings Representatives Assn. [★1702]

Natl. Home Furnishings Representatives Assn. [★IO]

Natl. Home Improvement Coun. [IO], London, United Kingdom

Natl. Home Improvement Coun. [★643]

Natl. Home Infusion Assn. [15043], 100 Daingerfield Rd., Alexandria, VA 22314, (703)549-3740

Natl. Home Missions Fellowship [★20301]

Natl. Home Oxygen Patients Assn. [14404], 8618 Westwood Center Dr., Ste. 210, Vienna, VA 22182-2222, (888)646-7244

Natl. Home Service Assn. - Defunct.

Natl. Home Sewing Assn. [★3784]

Natl. Home Stud. Coun. [★8517]

Natl. Homeowners Assn. [12324]

Natl. Homeschool Assn. - Defunct.

Natl. Honey Bd. [1548], 11409 Bus. Park Cir., Ste. 210, Firestone, CO 80504, (303)776-2337

Natl. Honey Packers and Dealers Assn. [1549], 3301 Rte. 66, Ste. 205, Bldg. C, Neptune, NJ 07753, (732)922-3008

Natl. Honor Soc. [24512], 1904 Assn. Dr., Reston, VA 20191-1537, (703)860-0200

Natl. Hook-Up of Black Women [17559], 1809 E 71st St., Ste. 205, Chicago, IL 60649-2000, (773)667-7061

Natl. Hop Assn. of England [IO], Faversham, United Kingdom

Natl. Hormone and Pituitary Prog. [16021], Harbor - UCLA Medical Ctr., 1000 W Carson St., Torrance, CA 90509, (310)222-3537

Natl. Horse Protection Coalition [11439], PO Box 1252, Alexandria, VA 22313, (703)836-4300

Natl. Horse Show Assn. of America - Address unknown since 2001.

Natl. Horse Show Commn. [4919], PO Box 167, 1021 Colloredo Rd., Shelbyville, TN 37162, (931)684-9506

Natl. Horse Show Found. - Address unknown since 1999.

Natl. Horsemen's Benevolent and Protective Assn. [12301], 4063 Ironworks Pkwy., Ste. 2, Lexington, KY 40511-8905, (859)259-0451

Natl. Horseracing [IO], Budapest, Hungary

Natl. Horseracing Authority of Southern Africa [IO], Turffontein, Republic of South Africa

Natl. Horseshoe Pitchers Assn. of Am. [23540], c/o Dick Hansen, Sec.-Treas., 3085 S 76th St., Franksville, WI 53126, (262)835-9108

Natl. HOSA [★8863]

Natl. Hose Assemblies Mfrs. Assn. - Defunct.

Natl. Hospice Org. [★14856]

Natl. Hospice and Palliative Care Org. [14856], 1700 Diagonal Rd., Ste. 625, Alexandria, VA 22314-2848, (703)837-1500

Natl. Hospital Assn. - Defunct.

Natl. Hospitality Mgt. Club [IO], Sofia, Bulgaria

Natl. Hot Dog and Sausage Coun. - Defunct.

Natl. Hot Rod Assn. [23083], 2035 Financial Way, Glendora, CA 91741, (626)914-4761

Natl. Hotels' and Restaurants' Assn. - Dominican Republic [IO], Santo Domingo, Dominican Republic

Natl. House-Building Coun. [IO], Amersham, United Kingdom

Natl. House Buyers Assn. [IO], Kuala Lumpur, Malaysia

Natl. Household Hazardous Waste Forum [IO], Leeds, United Kingdom

Natl. Housewares Mfrs. Assn. [★IO]

Natl. Housewares Mfrs. Assn. [★1972]

Natl. Housewives' League of America for Economic Security - Defunct.

Natl. Housing Center Coun. [★647]

Natl. Housing Conf. [12325], 1801 K St. NW, Ste. M-100, Washington, DC 20006-1301, (202)466-2121

Natl. Housing Endowment [649], 1201 15th St. NW, Washington, DC 20005, (202)266-8483

Natl. Housing Inst. [12326], 460 Bloomfield Ave., Ste. 211, Montclair, NJ 07042-3552, (973)509-2888

Natl. Housing Law Proj. [5796], 614 Grand Ave., Ste. 320, Oakland, CA 94610, (510)251-9400

Natl. Housing and Rehabilitation Assn. [12327], 1400 16th St. NW, Ste. 420, Washington, DC 20036-2244, (202)939-1750

Reference to "IO" in place of a book number signifies that the association may be found in the 45th edition of International Organizations.

Natl. Housing Rehabilitation Assn. [★12327]

Natl. Housing and Town Planning Coun. [★IO]

Natl. Huguenot Soc. [21163], 9033 Lyndale Ave. S, Ste. 108, Bloomington, MN 55420-3535, (952)885-9776

Natl. Human Resources Assn. [2905], PO Box 7326, Nashua, NH 03060-7326, (866)523-4417

National Human Rights Committee [★19337]

Natl. Human Rights Comm. for POW/MIA'S - Defunct.

Natl. Human Services Assembly [13400], 1319 F St. NW, Ste. 402, Washington, DC 20004, (202)347-2080

Natl. Humane Educ. Soc. [11440], PO Box 340, Charles Town, WV 25414-0340, (304)725-0506

Natl. Humanitarian League [★11471]

National Humanitarian Proj. for the Physically Challenged Child [★19231]

Natl. Humanities Alliance [10199], 21 Dupont Cir. NW, Ste. 800, Washington, DC 20036, (202)296-4994

Natl. Humanities Center [10200], PO Box 12256, Research Triangle Park, NC 27709-2256, (919)549-0661

Natl. Humanities Inst. [8532], PO Box 1387, Bowie, MD 20718-1387, (301)464-4277

Natl. Hunter Jumper Assn. [23530], c/o W. Gary Baker, Pres., PO Box 2122, Middleburg, VA 20118, (203)869-1225

Natl. Hunter/Jumper Coun. [23531], 4047 Ironworks Pkwy., Lexington, KY 40511-8483, (859)258-2472

Natl. Hunters Assn. [23547]

Natl. Huntington's Disease Assn. [★15329]

Natl. Hydrocephalus Found. [14280], 12413 Centralia Rd., Lakewood, CA 90715-1623, (562)924-6666

Natl. Hydrogen Assn. [7619], 1211 Connecticut Ave. NW, Ste. 600, Washington, DC 20036-2705, (202)223-5547

Natl. Hydropower Assn. [6964], One Massachusetts Ave. NW, Ste. 850, Washington, DC 20001, (202)682-1700

Natl. Hypertension Assn. [14910], 324 E 30th St., New York, NY 10016, (212)889-3557

Natl. Hypoglycemia Assn. - Address unknown since 2003.

Natl. Ice Assn. [★1891]

Natl. Ice Carving Assn. [9458], PO Box 2664, Glen Ellyn, IL 60138, (630)871-8431

Natl. Ice Cream Retailers Assn. [★1137]

Natl. Ice Cream Retailers Assn. [1137], 1028 W Devon Ave., Elk Grove Village, IL 60007, (847)301-7500

Natl. Ice Cream and Yogurt Retailers Assn. [★1137]

Natl. Ice Skating Assn. of the United Kingdom [IO], Nottingham, United Kingdom

Natl. Iceboat Authority - Address unknown since 1995.

Natl. Ichthyosis Found. [★14201]

Natl. Identification Prog. for the Advancement in Higher Educ. Admin. [★9324]

Natl. Illumination Comm. of Great Britain [IO], London, United Kingdom

Natl. Image [19102], PO Box 1368, Bonita, CA 91908-1368, (619)934-5277

Natl. Immigration Forum [17806], 50 F St. NW, Ste. 300, Washington, DC 20001, (202)347-0040

Natl. Immigration Forum [IO], Washington, DC, United States

National Immigration Law Center [IO], Los Angeles, CA, United States

Natl. Immigration Law Center [17807], 3435 Wilshire Blvd., Ste. 2850, Los Angeles, CA 90010, (213)639-3900

Natl. Immigration Proj. of the Natl. Lawyers Guild [5810], 14 Beacon St., Ste. 602, Boston, MA 02108, (617)227-9727

Natl. Immigration Refugee Citizenship Forum [★17806]

Natl. Immigration Refugee Citizenship Forum [★IO]

Natl. Immunotherapy Cancer Res. Found. [14940], PO Box 1027, Flemington, NJ 08822, (908)806-4300

Natl. Impala Assn. [21733], PO Box 968, 2928 4th Ave., Spearfish, SD 57783-0968, (605)642-5864

Natl. Impeachment Coalition - Defunct.

Natl. Imperial Glass Collectors Soc. [22565], PO Box 534, Bellaire, OH 43906

Natl. Imported Car Dealers Assn. - Address unknown since 1995.

Natl. Incontinentia Pigmenti Found. [14470], c/o Susanne Bross Emmerich, Exec. Dir., 30 E 72nd St., 16th Fl., New York, NY 10021, (212)452-1231

Natl. Incontinentia Pigmenti Found. [★14455]

Natl. Incontinentia Pigmenti Found. [★IO]

Natl. Inconvenienced Sportsmen's Assn. [★23343]

Natl. Independent Auto. Dealers Assn. [423], 2521 Brown Blvd., Arlington, TX 76006, (817)640-3838

Natl. Independent Bank Equip. Suppliers Assn. [★476]

Natl. Independent Bank Equip. and Systems Assn. [★476]

Natl. Independent Bicycle Rep Assn. - Defunct.

Natl. Independent Coal Operators Assn. - Defunct.

Natl. Independent Concessionaires Assn. [1591], 6671 13th Ave. N, Ste. 1B, St. Petersburg, FL 33710, (727)346-9302

Natl. Independent Dairy-Food Assn. - Defunct.

Natl. Independent Energy Producers [★6950]

Natl. Independent Flag Dealers Assn. [1488], 214 N Hale St., Wheaton, IL 60187, (630)510-4528

Natl. Independent Nursery Furniture Retailers Assn. - Address unknown since 1999.

Natl. Independent Poultry and Food Distributors Assn. [★1551]

Natl. Independent Telephone Assn. [★3965]

Natl. Independent Truckers Unity Coun. - Defunct.

Natl. Independent Union Coun. [★24210]

Natl. Independent Vendors Assn. - Defunct.

Natl. Indian AIDS Hotline [★16968]

Natl. Indian Athletic Assn. - Address unknown since 1985.

Natl. Indian Bus. Assn. [751], 1730 Rhode Island Ave. NW, Ste. 501, Washington, DC 20036, (202)223-3766

Natl. Indian Child Welfare Assn. [19277], 5100 SW Macadam Ave., Ste. 300, Portland, OR 97239, (503)222-4044

Natl. Indian Coun. on Aging [11311], 10501 Montgomery Blvd. NE, Ste. 210, Albuquerque, NM 87111-3846, (505)292-2001

Natl. Indian Counselors Assn. - Defunct.

Natl. Indian Educ. Assn. [8941], 110 Maryland Ave. NE, Ste. 104, Washington, DC 20002, (202)544-7290

Natl. Indian Festival Assn. - Address unknown since 2006.

Natl. Indian Gaming Assn. [5771], 224 Second St. SE, Washington, DC 20003, (202)546-7711

Natl. Indian Hea. Bd. [12629], 1940 Duke St., Ste. 200, Alexandria, VA 22314, (703)486-5706

Natl. Indian Justice Center [19278], 5250 Aero Dr., Santa Rosa, CA 95403, (707)579-5507

Natl. Indian Social Workers Assn. - Address unknown since 1994.

Natl. Indian Training and Res. Center - Address unknown since 2006.

Natl. Indian Wars Assn. [9371], 1707 Bates Ct., Thousand Oaks, CA 91362

Natl. Indian Youth Coun. [10749], c/o Norman Ration, Exec. Dir., 318 Elm St. SE, Albuquerque, NM 87102, (505)247-2251

Natl. Indirect Air Carrier Assn. - Defunct.

Natl. Indoor Tennis Assn. [★3021]

Natl. Indoor Tennis Assn. [★IO]

Natl. Indoor Track Meet Directors Assn. - Defunct.

Natl. Indus. Advertisers Assn. [★94]

Natl. Indus. Advertisers Assn. [★IO]

Natl. Industrial Basketball League - Address unknown since 1995.

Natl. Indus. Belting Assn. [2051], N19 W24400 Riverwood Dr., Waukesha, WI 53188, (262)523-9090

Natl. Indus. Coalition [IO], Moscow, Russia

Natl. Indus. Conf. Bd. [★IO]

Natl. Indus. Conf. Bd. [★6877]

Natl. Indus. Coun. [★2555]

Natl. Industrial Glove Distributors Assn. - Defunct.

Natl. Indus. Leather Assn. [★2051]

Natl. Indus. Property Mgt. Assn. [★3190]

Natl. Indus. Recreation Assn. [★12796]

Natl. Indus. Sand Assn. [2743], 2011 Pennsylvania Ave., Ste. 301, Washington, DC 20006, (202)457-0200

Natl. Indus. Ser. Assn. [★1180]

Natl. Indus. Ser. Assn. [★IO]

Natl. Industrial Stores Assn. - Defunct.

Natl. Indus. TV Assn. [★1388]

Natl. Indus. TV Assn. [★IO]

Natl. Indus. Traffic League [★3879]

Natl. Indus. Trans. League [3879], 1700 N Moore St., Ste. 1900, Arlington, VA 22209, (703)524-5011

Natl. Industrial Workers Union - Address unknown since 2003.

Natl. Industrial Zoning Comm. - Defunct.

Natl. Indus. for the Blind [16878], 1310 Braddock Pl., Alexandria, VA 22314-1691, (703)310-0500

Natl. Indus. for the Severely Handicapped [★11976]

Natl. Indus. Assn. [IO], Tegucigalpa, Honduras

Natl. Indy 500 Collectors Club [21734], 1920 Patton Dr., Speedway, IN 46224

Natl. Infant Torticollis Assn. [14945], 200 Crestview Dr., Springville, AL 35146, (205)467-0353

Natl. Infertility Network Exchange [12678], PO Box 204, East Meadow, NY 11554, (516)794-5772

Natl. Infomercial Marketing Assn. [★2626]

Natl. Infomercial Marketing Assn. [★IO]

Natl. Information Bur. for Jewish Life - Address unknown since 1995.

Natl. Info. Center for Children and Youth with Disabilities [★11971]

Natl. Info. Center for Children and Youth with Handicaps [★11971]

Natl. Information Center on Deafness - Defunct.

Natl. Info. Center for Educational Media [8569], PO Box 8640, Albuquerque, NM 87198-8640, (505)998-0800

Natl. Info. Center for the Handicapped [★11971]

Natl. Info. Center for Handicapped Children and Youth [★11971]

Natl. Information Center on Health for the Aging - Defunct.

Natl. Info. Center on Volunteerism [★13401]

Natl. Info. CH for Infants with Disabilities and Life-Threatening Conditions - Defunct.

Natl. Info. CH On Children Who Are Deaf-Blind; DB-Link: The [16845]

Natl. Info. and Communications Tech. Indus. Alliance [IO], Canberra, Australia

Natl. Info. Officers Assn. [6231], PO Box 10125, Knoxville, TN 37939, (865)389-8736

Natl. Info. Ser. for Earthquake Engg. [7641], Univ. of California, Berkeley, 1301 S 46th St., RFS 453, Richmond, CA 94804-4698, (510)665-3419

Natl. Info. Standards Org. [7206], 1 N Charles St., Ste. 1905, Baltimore, MD 21201, (301)654-2512

Natl. Info. Standards Org. - Z39 [★7206]

Natl. Ingredient Marketing Specialists [★1554]

Natl. Inhalant Prevention Coalition [16514], 322-A Thompson St., Chattanooga, TN 37405, (423)265-4662

Natl. Inholders Assn. [★6187]

Natl. Initiative for Children's Healthcare Quality [13970], 20 Univ. Rd., 7th Fl., Cambridge, MA 02138, (617)301-4900

Natl. Initiative for a Networked Cultural Heritage [9858], 21 Dupont Cir., NW, Washington, DC 20036, (202)296-5346

Natl. Innkeeping Assn. - Defunct.

Natl. Inspection Coun. for Elecl. Installation Contracting [IO], Dunstable, United Kingdom

Natl. InStar Users Gp. [7221], PO Box 41368, Raleigh, NC 27629, (800)549-2515

Natl. Institut voor de Statistiek - Institut Natl. de Statistique [★IO]

Natl. Inst. of Adult Continuing Educ. [IO], Leicester, United Kingdom

Natl. Inst. for the Advancement of Career Education - Defunct.

Natl. Inst. Against Prejudice and Violence [★17146]

Natl. Inst. on Age, Work and Retirement - Defunct.

Natl. Inst. on Aging [14516], 31 Center Dr., MSC 2292, Bldg. 31, Rm. 5C27, Bethesda, MD 20892, (301)496-1752

Natl. Inst. of Agricultural Botany [IO], Cambridge, United Kingdom

Natl. Inst. of Amer. Doll Artists [22403], c/o Diana Rew, Treas., 8320 Maplewood St., Lenexa, KS 66215, (913)894-2382

A star before a book entry number signifies that the name is not listed separately, but is mentioned within the entry.

Natl. Inst. for Animal Agriculture [5003], 1910 Lyda Ave., Bowling Green, KY 42104-3326, (270)782-9798

Natl. Inst. for Applied Behavioral Sci. [★8415]

Natl. Inst. for Applied Behavioral Sci. [★IO]

Natl. Inst. for Architectural Educ. [★7963]

Natl. Inst. of Arthritis and Musculoskeletal and Skin Diseases Info. CH [16372], c/o Natl. Institutes of Hea., 1 AMS Cir., Bethesda, MD 20892-3675, (301)495-4484

National Inst. for Automotive Ser. Excellence [★1290]

Natl. Inst. for Automotive Ser. Excellence [424], 101 Blue Seal Dr. SE, Ste. 101, Leesburg, VA 20175, (703)669-6600

National Inst. for Automotive Ser. Excellence [★IO]

Natl. Inst. of Bank Mgt. [IO], Pune, India

Natl. Inst. for Biological Standards and Control [IO], Potters Bar, United Kingdom

Natl. Inst. for the Blind - Address unknown since 1995.

Natl. Inst. of Building Sciences [6838], 1090 Vermont Ave. NW, Ste. 700, Washington, DC 20005-4950, (202)289-7800

Natl. Inst. for Burn Medicine - Address unknown since 2003.

Natl. Inst. for Campus Ministries [★19916]

Natl. Inst. for Carpet Fitters [★IO]

Natl. Inst. of Carpet and Floorlayers [IO], Nottingham, United Kingdom

Natl. Inst. for Ceramic Engineers [6658], c/o Greg Geiger, Admin., 735 Ceramic Pl., Ste. 100, Westerville, OH 43081-8728, (614)794-5858

Natl. Inst. for Certification in Engg. Technologies [7033], 1420 King St., Alexandria, VA 22314-2794, (703)548-1518

Natl. Inst. for the Certification of Healthcare Sterile Processing and Distribution Personnel [★15119]

Natl. Inst. for Chem. Stud. [13326], 2300 MacCorkle Ave. SE, Charleston, WV 25304, (304)346-6264

Natl. Inst. of Child Hea. and Human Development [13971], PO Box 3006, Rockville, MD 20847, (800)370-2943

Natl. Inst. for Child Support Enforcement - Address unknown since 1999.

Natl. Inst. for Citizen Educ. in the Law [★6035]

Natl. Inst. for the Clinical Application of Behavioral Medicine [13739], PO Box 523, Mansfield Center, CT 06250, (860)456-1153

Natl. Inst. on Community-Based Long-Term Care [11312], c/o Natl. Coun. on Aging, 1901 L St. NW, 4th Fl., Washington, DC 20036, (202)479-1200

Natl. Inst. for Compilation and Translation [IO], Taipei, Taiwan

National Inst. for Computer-Assisted Reporting [★IO]

National Inst. for Computer-Assisted Reporting [★3126]

Natl. Inst. for Computers in Engineering - Defunct.

Natl. Inst. for Consumer Justice - Address unknown since 1995.

Natl. Inst. for Continuing Education in Developmental Disabilities - Address unknown since 1995.

National Inst. of Cosmetology [★1084]

Natl. Inst. for Creativity - Defunct.

Natl. Inst. of Credit [★1436]

Natl. Inst. on Deafness and Other Commun. Disorders Info. CH [14773], 1 Commun. Ave., Bethesda, MD 20892-3456, (800)241-1044

Natl. Inst. of Dental and Craniofacial Res. [14180], c/o Natl. Institutes of Hea., 45 Center Dr., MSC-6400, Bethesda, MD 20892, (301)496-4261

Natl. Inst. of Diaper Services - Defunct.

Natl. Inst. for Disaster Mobilization - Address unknown since 1995.

Natl. Inst. for Dispute Resolution - Defunct.

Natl. Inst. on Drug Abuse [5670], c/o Natl. Institutes of Hea., 6001 Executive Blvd., Rm. 5213, Bethesda, MD 20892, (301)443-1124

Natl. Inst. of Drycleaning [★2405]

Natl. Inst. of Drycleaning [★IO]

Natl. Inst. of Dyslexia - Defunct.

Natl. Inst. of Economic and Social Res. [IO], London, United Kingdom

Natl. Inst. of Education for Overseas Koreans - Address unknown since 1994.

Natl. Inst. of Electromedical Info. [14311], PO Box 4633, Bay Terrace, NY 11360-4633, (718)849-1044

Natl. Inst. for the Family - Address unknown since 2001.

Natl. Inst. of Farm and Land Brokers [★3342]

Natl. Inst. for Farm Safety [12976], c/o Chip Petrea, PhD, Interim Sec., 1304 W Pennsylvania Ave., Urbana, IL 61801, (217)333-5035

Natl. Inst. for Farm Safety [IO], Urbana, IL, United States

Natl. Inst. for the Foodservice Indus. [★1960]

Natl. Inst. for Gay, Lesbian, Bisexual and Transgender Educ. - Address unknown since 2006.

National Inst. of Golf Management [★3669]

Natl. Inst. of Governmental Purchasing [6239], 151 Spring St., Herndon, VA 20170-5223, (703)736-8900

Natl. Inst. of Governmental Purchasing [IO], Herndon, VA, United States

Natl. Inst. for Hea. Care Mgt. Res. and Educational Found. [14655], 1225 19th St. NW, Ste. 710, Washington, DC 20036, (202)296-4426

Natl. Inst. of Hispanic Liturgy [★19640]

Natl. Inst. on the Holocaust [★17723]

Natl. Inst. on the Holocaust [★IO]

Natl. Inst. of Hypertension Studies - Inst. of Hypertension School of Res. - Address unknown since 2005.

Natl. Inst. of Independent Colleges and Universities [★8539]

Natl. Inst. of Independent Colls. and Universities - Defunct.

Natl. Inst. for Infant Services [★2389]

Natl. Inst. for Jewish Hospice [14857], 732 Univ. St., Valley Stream, NY 11581, (516)791-9888

Natl. Inst. of Judicial Dynamics - Defunct.

Natl. Inst. for Labor Education - Defunct.

Natl. Inst. for Lay Training - Defunct.

Natl. Inst. for Leadership Development [2412], 1202 W Thomas Rd., Phoenix, AZ 85013, (602)285-7727

Natl. Inst. of Locker and Freezer Provisioners [★2656]

Natl. Inst. for Low Power TV - Defunct.

Natl. Inst. for Mgt. Counsellors [2508]

Natl. Inst. for Materials Sci. [IO], Ibaraki, Japan

Natl. Inst. of Medical Herbalists [IO], Exeter, United Kingdom

Natl. Inst. of Mental Hea. [15226], 6001 Executive Blvd., Rm. 8184, MSC 9663, Bethesda, MD 20892-9663, (301)443-4513

Natl. Inst. for Metalworking Skills [7321], 3251 Old Lee Hwy., Ste. 205, Fairfax, VA 22030, (703)352-4971

Natl. Inst. of Metrology, Standardization and Indus. Quality [IO], Rio de Janeiro, Brazil

Natl. Inst. for Multicultural Education - Defunct.

Natl. Inst. for Music Theater - Defunct.

Natl. Inst. of Neurological Disorders and Stroke [15348], PO Box 5801, Bethesda, MD 20824, (301)496-5751

Natl. Inst. of Oilseed Products [2856], 1156 15th St. NW, Ste. 900, Washington, DC 20005-1717, (202)785-8450

Natl. Inst. of Oilseed Products [IO], Washington, DC, United States

Natl. Inst. of Ophthalmology [IO], Pune, India

Natl. Inst. on Out-of-School Time [11543], 106 Central St., Wellesley Centers for Women, Waban House, Wellesley, MA 02481, (781)283-2547

Natl. Inst. of Packaging, Handling and Logistics Engineers [7427], 177 Fairsom Ct., Lewisburg, PA 17837-6844, (570)523-6475

Natl. Inst. on Park and Grounds Mgt. [4801]

Natl. Inst. of Pension Administrators [1244], 401 N Michigan Ave., Ste. 2200, Chicago, IL 60611, (800)999-6472

National Inst. for People with Disabilities; Young Adult Institute/ [12584]

Natl. Inst. of Prdt. Coding [IO], Milan, Italy

Natl. Inst. of Public Admin. [★IO]

Natl. Inst. of Public Admin. [★6192]

Natl. Inst. of Public Mgt. - Defunct.

Natl. Inst. for Public Policy [18466], 9302 Lee Hwy., Ste. 750, Fairfax, VA 22031, (703)293-9181

Natl. Inst. of Red Orange Canaries and All Other Cage Birds [21855]

Natl. Inst. for Rehabilitation Engg. [11972], PO Box T, Hewitt, NJ 07421, (973)853-6585

National Inst. of Relationship Enhancement; Inst. for the Development of Emotional and Life Skills/ [15201]

Natl. Inst. for Res. in Cmpt. Sci. and Control [IO], Le Chesnay, France

Natl. Inst. for Resources in Science and Engineering - Address unknown since 2002.

National Inst. of Safety and Health [★9101]

Natl. Inst. of Science - Address unknown since 2002.

Natl. Inst. for Sci., Law and Public Policy [4105], 1400 16th St. NW, Ste. 101, Washington, DC 20036, (202)462-8800

Natl. Inst. of Senior Centers [11313], c/o Natl. Coun. on the Aging, 1901 L St. NW, 4th Fl., Washington, DC 20036, (202)479-1200

Natl. Inst. of Senior Housing [12328], c/o Natl. Coun. on the Aging, 1901 L St. NW, 4th Fl., Washington, DC 20036, (202)479-1200

Natl. Inst. of Social and Behavioral Science - Address unknown since 1995.

Natl. Inst. of Social Sciences - Address unknown since 2001.

Natl. Inst. for State Credit Union Examination [★5633]

Natl. Inst. of Statistical Sciences [7711], PO Box 14006, 19 T.W. Alexander Dr., Research Triangle Park, NC 27709-4006, (919)685-9300

Natl. Inst. of Steel Detailing [2721], 7700 Edgewater Dr., Ste. 670, Oakland, CA 94621-3022, (510)568-3741

National Institute of Steel Detailing [IO], Oakland, CA, United States

Natl. Inst. of Student Governments - Defunct.

Natl. Inst. of Transplantation [16679], 2200 W 3rd St., Ste. 100, Los Angeles, CA 90057, (213)413-2779

Natl. Inst. for Trial Advocacy [6334], 361 Centennial Pkwy., Ste. 220, Louisville, CO 80027, (800)225-6482

Natl. Inst. for Urban Wildlife - Address unknown since 1995.

Natl. Inst. of Victimology - Address unknown since 1999.

Natl. Inst. of Womanhood [13432]

Natl. Inst. for Women of Color [★17541]

Natl. Inst. for Women of Color [★IO]

Natl. Inst. for Wood Kitchen Cabinets [★2267]

Natl. Inst. for the Word of God [19690], 487 Michigan Ave. NE, Washington, DC 20017-1518, (202)529-0001

Natl. Inst. for Work and Learning [17974], 1825 Connecticut Ave. NW, Washington, DC 20009, (202)884-8185

Natl. Inst. on Workshop Standards - Defunct.

Natl. Institutes for Water Resources [7836], c/o Dr. Anders Andren, Pres.-Elect, Water Resources Inst., 1975 Willow Dr., 2nd Fl., The Univ. of Wisconsin - Madison, Madison, WI 53706-1177, (608)262-0591

Natl. Institutional Food Distributors Assn. [★1566]

Natl. Institutional Res. Forum [★8997]

Natl. Institutional Teacher Placement Assn. [★8994]

Natl. Instructional TV Lib. [★8549]

Natl. Insulation and Abatement Contractors Assn. [★1048]

Natl. Insulation Assn. [1048], 99 Canal Center Plz., Ste. 222, Alexandria, VA 22314, (703)683-6422

Natl. Insulation Assn. [IO], Leighton Buzzard, United Kingdom

Natl. Insulation Certification Inst. - Defunct.

Natl. Insulation Contractors Assn. [★1048]

Natl. Insulator Assn. [22408], c/o Donald Briel, Membership Dir., PO Box 188, Providence, UT 84332

Natl. Insurance Assn. - Address unknown since 2007.

Natl. Insurance Brokers Assn. - Defunct.

Natl. Insurance Buyers Assn. [★2235]

Natl. Insurance Consumer Org. - Address unknown since 1999.

Natl. Insurance Crime Bur. [2224], 1111 E Touhy Ave., Ste. 400, Des Plaines, IL 60018, (847)544-7000

Reference to "IO" in place of a book number signifies that the association may be found in the 45th edition of International Organizations.

National Insurance Educ. Scholarship Program [★8577]

Natl. Intelligence Study Center - Defunct.

Natl. Inter-religious Conf. on Peace [★18257]

Natl. Inter-religious Conf. on Peace [★IO]

Natl. Interagency Coun. on Smoking and Health - Defunct.

Natl. InterAssociation Comm. on Internships [★8872]

Natl. Intercollegiate Boxing Coaches Assn. - Defunct.

Natl. Intercollegiate Flying Assn. [21466], PO Box 15081, Monroe, LA 71207, (318)325-6156

Natl. Intercollegiate Flying Club [★21466]

Natl. Intercollegiate Rodeo Assn. [23691], 2316 Eastgate N, Ste. 160, Walla Walla, WA 99362, (509)529-4402

Natl. Intercollegiate Running Club Assn. [23707], c/o Julia Stulock, 35241 Rosslyn St., Westland, MI 48185-3686

Natl. Intercollegiate Soccer Officials Assn. [23778], 541 Woodview Dr., Longwood, FL 32779-2614, (407)862-3305

Natl. Intercollegiate Squash Racquets Assn. - Address unknown since 1999.

Natl. Intercollegiate Women's Fencing Assn. - Address unknown since 1999.

Natl. Interest; Coun. for the [18056]

Natl. Interfaith Coalition on Aging [11314], c/o Natl. Coun. on the Aging, 1901 L St. NW, 4th Fl., Washington, DC 20036, (202)479-6655

Natl. Interfaith Comm. for Worker Justice [★20092]

Natl. Interfaith Hospitality Network [★12290]

Natl. Interfraternity Conf. [★24487]

Natl. Interfraternity Found. [★24486]

Natl. Intern Matching Prog. [★8872]

Natl. Intern and Resident Matching Prog. [★8872]

Natl. and Intl. Energy Programs - Defunct.

National/International Safe Transit Assn. [★3571]

National/International Safe Transit Assn. [★IO]

Natl. Interpreter Training Consortium - Defunct.

Natl. Interprofessional Off. of Cognac [IO], Cognac, France

Natl. Interprofessional Off. of Fruit, Vegetables and Horticulture [IO], Paris, France

Natl. Interprofessional Off. of Wine [IO], Paris, France

Natl. Interreligious Ser. Bd. for Conscientious Objectors [★IO]

Natl. Interreligious Ser. Bd. for Conscientious Objectors [★17438]

Natl. Interreligious Task Force - Address unknown since 1999.

Natl. Interscholastic Athletic Administrators Assn. [8989], 9100 Keystone Crossing, Ste. 650, Indianapolis, IN 46240, (317)587-1450

Natl. Interscholastic Music Activities Commn. - Defunct.

Natl. Interscholastic Swimming Coaches Assn. of Am. [23887], c/o Tom Wojslawowicz, Treas./ Membership Chm., 93 Kennedy Blvd., Bayonne, NJ 07002

Natl. - Interstate Coun. of State Boards of Cosmetology [5616], 7622 Briarwood Cir., Little Rock, AR 72205, (501)227-8262

Natl. Intervenors - Defunct.

Natl. Intramural Assn. [★23842]

Natl. Intramural-Recreational Sports Assn. [23842], 4185 SW Res. Way, Corvallis, OR 97333-1067, (541)766-8211

Natl. Introducing Brokers Assn. [1714], 55 W Monroe St., Ste. 3330, Chicago, IL 60603, (312)977-0598

Natl. Inventors Found. [7231], c/o Inventors Assistance League, 1053 Colorado Blvd., Los Angeles, CA 90041, (818)246-6546

Natl. Inventors Hall of Fame Found. [★5855]

Natl. Investigation Comm. on Aerial Phenomena [★7479]

Natl. Investigations Comm. on Unidentified Flying Objects [7482], 21601 Devonshire St., Ste. 217, Chatsworth, CA 91311-8415, (818)882-0052

National Investigations Committee on Unidentified Flying Objects [IO], Chatsworth, CA, United States

Natl. Investment Company Ser. Assn. [2345], 2 Mt. Royal Ave., 3rd Fl., Marlborough, MA 01752, (508)485-1500

Natl. Investor Relations Inst. [2346], 8020 Towers Crescent Dr., Ste. 250, Vienna, VA 22182, (703)506-3570

Natl. Involvement Assn. - Address unknown since 1995.

Natl. Iranian Amer. Coun. [19151], 1411 K St. NW, Ste. 600, Washington, DC 20005, (202)386-6325

Natl. Iridology Res. Assn. [★15687]

Natl. Iridology Res. Assn. [★IO]

Natl. Irish Safety Org. [IO], Dublin, Ireland

Natl. Issues Forums [★18467]

Natl. Issues Forums Inst. [18467], PO Box 41626, Dayton, OH 45441, (937)434-7300

Natl. IST of Municipal Law Officers [★5500]

Natl. IST of Municipal Law Officers [★IO]

Natl. Italian Amer. Bar Assn. [5952], PMB 932, 2020 Pennsylvania Ave. NW, Washington, DC 20006-1846, (212)269-1400

Natl. Italian Amer. Found. [19166], 1860 19th St. NW, Washington, DC 20009, (202)387-0600

Natl. Italian Amer. Found. [IO], Washington, DC, United States

Natl. Italian Amer. Foundation; Affiliates of the [★IO]

Natl. Italian Amer. Foundation; Affiliates of the [★19166]

Natl. Italian Civic League [★19169]

Natl. Jail Assn. [★11856]

Natl. Jail Managers Assn. [★11856]

Natl. Japanese Amer. Historical Soc. [10267], 1684 Post St., San Francisco, CA 94115, (415)921-5007

Natl. Jazz Service Org. - Address unknown since 2000.

Natl. Jersey Wooly Rabbit Club [5152], c/o Amanda Pitsch, Sec., PO Box 264, Marne, MI 49435, (616)498-2330

Natl. Jersey Wooly Rabbit Club [IO], San Jose, CA, United States

Natl. Jewish Artisans Guild - Defunct.

Natl. Jewish Center for Immunology and Respiratory Medicine [★16361]

Natl. Jewish Center for Learning and Leadership; CLAL: [20132]

Natl. Jewish Civil Service Employees - Address unknown since 1995.

Natl. Jewish Coalition [★18530]

Natl. Jewish Coalition for Literacy [8795], 134 Beach St., Boston, MA 02111, (617)423-0063

Natl. Jewish Comm. on Scouting [13003], PO Box 152079, Irving, TX 75015-2091, (201)836-7019

Natl. Jewish Girl Scout Comm. [13004], 33 Central Dr., Bronxville, NY 10708-4603, (914)738-3986

Natl. Jewish Girl Scout Comm. of the Synagogue Coun. of Amer. [★13004]

Natl. Jewish Hospital/National Asthma Center [★16361]

Natl. Jewish Hosp. and Res. Center [★16361]

Natl. Jewish Hospitality Comm. - Address unknown since 2003.

Natl. Jewish Information Service (for the Propagation of Judaism) - Defunct.

Natl. Jewish Law Students Assn. - Address unknown since 2007.

Natl. Jewish Medical and Res. Center [16361], 1400 Jackson St., Denver, CO 80206, (303)388-4461

Natl. Jewish Welfare Bd. [★12473]

Natl. Job Corps Alumni Assn. [12093], PO Box 1885, Gresham, OR 97030, (800)424-2866

Natl. Jobbers Coun. [★2943]

Natl. Jobs With Peace Campaign - Address unknown since 1999.

Natl. Jogging Assn. [★23651]

Natl. Joint Heavy and Highway Construction Comm. - Address unknown since 1999.

Natl. Joint Painting, Decorating, and Drywall Apprenticeship and Training Comm. [★12082]

Natl. Joint Painting, Decorating, and Drywall Apprenticeship and Training Comm. [★IO]

Natl. Joint Practice Commn. - Defunct.

Natl. Journalism Center [17634], 110 Elden St., Herndon, VA 20170, (800)872-1776

Natl. Jousting Assn. [23551], PO Box 14, Mount Solon, VA 22843, (434)983-2989

Natl. Judges Assn. [5913], c/o Ralph J. Zeller, Exec. Dir., PO Box 160, Maud, OK 74854-0160, (405)374-2896

National Judges Educ. and Res. Foundation [★5913]

Natl. Judicial Coll. [5914], Univ. of Nevada, Judicial Coll. Bldg., MS 358, Reno, NV 89557, (775)784-6747

Natl. Judicial Educ. Prog. [17964], 395 Hudson St., New York, NY 10014-3669, (212)925-6635

Natl. Judicial Educ. Prog. to Promote Equality for Women and Men in the Courts [★17964]

National Judo Hall of Fame [★23555]

Natl. Juice Products Assn. and Processed Apples Inst. [★510]

Natl. Juneteenth Observance Found. [16945], 1100-15th St. NW, Ste. 300, Washington, DC 20005, (202)331-8864

Natl. Junior Angus Assn. [4275], 3201 Frederick Ave., St. Joseph, MO 64506, (816)383-5100

Natl. Junior Baseball League [23120], c/o Jan Rosenblum, 2800 Coyle St., Apt. 205, Brooklyn, NY 11235, (631)582-5191

Natl. Junior Classical League [8095], Miami Univ., 422 Wells Mill Dr., Oxford, OH 45056, (513)529-7741

Natl. Junior Coll. Athletic Assn. [23843], 1755 Telstar Dr., Ste. 103, Colorado Springs, CO 80920, (719)590-9788

Natl. Junior Hereford Assn. [4276], c/o Amer. Hereford Assn., PO Box 014059, Kansas City, MO 64101, (816)842-3757

Natl. Junior Honor Soc. [24513], 1904 Assn. Dr., Reston, VA 20191-1537, (703)860-0200

Natl. Junior Horticultural Assn. [22530], c/o Carole S. Carney, Exec. Sec., 15 Railroad Ave., Homer City, PA 15748-1378, (724)479-3254

Natl. Junior Polled Hereford Coun. - Address unknown since 2003.

Natl. Junior Santa Gertrudis Assn. [4277], PO Box 1257, Kingsville, TX 78364, (361)592-9357

Natl. Junior Swine Assn. [5237], PO Box 2417, West Lafayette, IN 47996-2417, (765)463-3594

Natl. Junior Vegetable Growers Assn. [★22530]

Natl. Justice Found. of Am. [17298]

Natl. Juvenile Court Services Assn. [5702], c/o Ian Curley, Staff Liaison, Univ. of Nevada, PO Box 8970, Reno, NV 89507, (775)784-6895

Natl. Juvenile Detention Assn. [11882], c/o Eastern Kentucky Univ., 300 Perkins Bldg., 521 Lancaster Ave., Richmond, KY 40475-3102, (859)622-6259

Natl. Kappa Kappa Iota [24454], 1875 E 15th St., Tulsa, OK 74104-4610, (918)744-0389

Natl. Karting Assn. [IO], Colchester, United Kingdom

Natl. Kerosene Heater Assn. [1896]

Natl. Kidney Disease Found. [★15294]

Natl. Kidney Found. [15294], 30 E 33rd St., New York, NY 10016, (212)889-2210

Natl. Kidney and Urologic Diseases Info. CH [16710], 3 Info. Way, Bethesda, MD 20892-3580, (800)891-5390

Natl. Kindergarten Alliance [9007], PO Box 309, Agua Dulce, TX 78330, (361)998-2240

Natl. Kindergarten Assn. - Defunct.

Natl. Kitchen and Bath Assn. [2271], 687 Willow Grove St., Hackettstown, NJ 07840, (908)852-0033

Natl. Kitchen Cabinet Assn. [★2267]

Natl. Knife Collectors Assn. [22616], PO Box 21070, Chattanooga, TN 37424-0070, (423)875-6009

Natl. Knitted Outerwear Assn. [★251]

Natl. Knitwear and Sportswear Assn. [251]

Natl. Korean Amer. Bilingual Educators Assn. - Defunct.

Natl. Kosher Food Trade Assn. - Defunct.

Natl. Kraut Packers Assn. - Defunct.

Natl. Labor Alliance of Hea. Care Coalitions [24091], PO Box 6858, Edison, NJ 08818-6858, (800)427-9005

Natl. Labor Comm. for the Jewish Workers in Palestine [★12460]

Natl. Labor Comm. for the Jewish Workers in Palestine [★IO]

Natl. Labor Comm. in Support of Democracy and Human Rights in El Salvador [★IO]

Natl. Labor Comm. in Support of Democracy and Human Rights in El Salvador [★17049]

Natl. Labor Comm. in Support of Worker and Human Rights in Central Am. [★17049]

A star before a book entry number signifies that the name is not listed separately, but is mentioned within the entry.

Natl. Labor Comm. in Support of Worker and Human Rights in Central Am. [★IO]

National Labor Committee for Worker and Human Rights [IO], New York, NY, United States

Natl. Labor Comm. for Worker and Human Rights [17049], 75 Varick St., Ste. 1500, New York, NY 10013, (212)242-3002

Natl. Labor Law Center - Defunct.

Natl. Labor-Management Assn. [24119]

Natl. Labor-Mgt. Conference - Address unknown since 2003.

Natl. Labor Policy; Center on [17980]

Natl. Labrador Retriever Club [22319], c/o Leigh Green, Membership Chair, 1408 Bel Air Blvd., Sanford, FL 32771-4616

Natl. Ladies Auxiliary to Veterans of World War I of the U.S.A. [21359], 767 SW 4th St., Rm. 101, Forest Lake, MN 55025-1547, (651)775-2180

National Ladies Auxiliary to Veterans of World War I of the U.S.A. [IO], Forest Lake, MN, United States

Natl. Lakes and Rivers Assn. - Defunct.

Natl. Lamb Feeders Assn. [5206], 1270 Chemeketa St. NE, Salem, OR 97301-4145, (503)370-7024

Natl. Land for People [★4656]

Natl. Land Title Reclamation Assn. - Defunct.

Natl. Land Use Planning Commn. [IO], Dar es Salaam, United Republic of Tanzania

Natl. Landlords Assn. [IO], London, United Kingdom

Natl. Landscape Assn. [2396], c/o Amer. Nursery and Landscape Assn., 1000 Vermont Ave. NW, Ste. 300, Washington, DC 20005-4914, (202)789-2900

Natl. Landscape Nurserymen's Assn. [★2396]

Natl. Latin Amer. Fed. - Address unknown since 1995.

Natl. Latina Hea. Network [14589], 2201 Wisconsin Ave. NW, Ste. 340, Washington, DC 20007, (202)965-9633

Natl. Latina Health Org. [14983]

Natl. Latina Health Org. [IO], Oakland, CA, United States

Natl. Latina/Latino Law Student Assn. [17996], c/o Andrea Maldonado, Treas., 535 S Curson Ave., Apt. 6B, Los Angeles, CA 90036

Natl. Latina/o Lesbian, Gay, Bisexual, and Transgender Org. [9972]

Natl. Latinas Caucus - Defunct.

Natl. Latino Alliance for the Elimination of Domestic Violence [12037], PO Box 672, New York, NY 10035, (646)672-1404

Natl. Latino Behavioral Hea. Assn. [15227], c/o A. Marie Sanchez, BSW, Exec. Dir., PO Box 387, Berthoud, CO 80513, (970)532-7210

Natl. Latino Communications Center - Address unknown since 2004.

Natl. Latino Coun. on Alcohol and Tobacco Prevention [12269], 1875 Connecticut Ave. NW, Ste. 1012, Washington, DC 20009, (202)265-8054

Natl. Latino Officers Assn. [5921], PO Box 02-0120, Brooklyn, NY 11201, (866)579-5809

Natl. Latino Peace Officers Assn. [19195], PO Box 8986, Emeryville, CA 94662-8986, (702)355-8704

Natl. Laundry Allied Trades Assn. [★2407]

Natl. Law Center for Children and Families [5703], 225 N Fairfax St., Alexandria, VA 22314, (703)548-5522

Natl. Law Center on Homelessness and Poverty [12297], 1411 K St. NW, Ste. 1400, Washington, DC 20005, (202)638-2535

Natl. Law Enforcement Coun. [5994], 1620 Eye St. NW, Ste. 210, Washington, DC 20006, (202)331-1275

Natl. Law Enforcement Officers Memorial Fund [5995], 400 7th St. NW, Ste. 300, Washington, DC 20004, (202)737-3400

Natl. Law Firm Marketing Assn. [★2632]

Natl. Law Firm Marketing Assn. [★IO]

Natl. Lawn and Garden Distributors Assn. [★2395]

Natl. Lawyers Assn. [5521], 17201 E 40 Hwy., Ste. 207, Independence, MO 64055, (800)471-2994

Natl. Lawyers Club - Defunct.

Natl. Lawyers Comm. for Soviet Jewry - Address unknown since 2000.

Natl. Lawyers Guild [5522], 132 Nassau St., Rm. 922, New York, NY 10038, (212)679-5100

Natl. Lawyers Guild Gay Caucus - Defunct.

Natl. Lawyers Guild; Natl. Immigration Proj. of the [5810]

Natl. Lawyer's Guild Peace and Disarmament Soc. - Address unknown since 2003.

Natl. Lawyers Wines [★5480]

Natl. Lead Burning Assn. [★2052]

Natl. Leadership Coun. - Defunct.

National Leadership Development Program [★24456]

National Leadership Development Program [★IO]

Natl. Leadership Inst. - Defunct.

Natl. League of Amer. Pen Women [9588], Pen Arts Bldg., 1300 17th St. NW, Washington, DC 20036-1973, (202)785-1997

Natl. League of the Blind and Disabled [IO], London, United Kingdom

Natl. League of Cities [6130], 1301 Pennsylvania Ave. NW, Ste. 550, Washington, DC 20004-1747, (202)626-3000

National League of Cities Institute [★6130]

Natl. League for the Control of Cardiovascular Disease [IO], Rabat, Morocco

Natl. League of Cuban Amer. Community-Based Centers - Address unknown since 2003.

Natl. League of Disabled Voters - Defunct.

Natl. League of Families of Amer. Prisoners and Missing in Southeast Asia [18081], 1005 N Glebe Rd., Ste. 170, Arlington, VA 22201, (703)465-7432

Natl. League of Families of Amer. Prisoners and Missing in Southeast Asia [IO], Arlington, VA, United States

Natl. League of Masonic Clubs [19245], 2244 Locust Ln., York, PA 17404

Natl. League for Nursing [15510], 61 Broadway, 33rd Fl., New York, NY 10006, (212)363-5555

Natl. League of Nursing Educ. [★15510]

Natl. League of Postmasters; Retired League Postmasters of the [6180]

Natl. League of Postmasters of the U.S. [24170], One Beltway Ctr., 5904 Richmond Hwy., Ste. 500, Alexandria, VA 22303-1864, (703)329-4550

Natl. League of POW/MIA Families [★18081]

Natl. League of POW/MIA Families [★IO]

Natl. League of Professional Baseball Clubs - Defunct.

Natl. League to Promote School Attendance [★8326]

Natl. League to Promote School Attendance [★IO]

Natl. League for the Separation of Church and State [19838], 239 S Juniper St., Escondido, CA 92025, (760)489-5211

Natl. League for Social Understanding - Address unknown since 2006.

Natl. League of Spanish Speaking Elected Officials [★6122]

Natl. League of Teachers' Assns. - Defunct.

Natl. League of Wholesale Fresh Fruit and Vegetable Distributors [★4766]

Natl. League of Women Voters [★18355]

Natl. Leased Housing Assn. [12329], 1900 L St. NW, Ste. 300, Washington, DC 20036, (202)785-8888

Natl. Leather Assn. [★13098]

Natl. Leather Assn. - Intl. [13098], PO Box 423, Blacklick, OH 43004-0423, (780)454-1992

Natl. Leather Coun. [IO], Paris, France

Natl. Leather and Shoe Finders Assn. [★1600]

Natl. Left-Handers Racquet Sports Assn. - Address unknown since 1989.

Natl. Legal Aid and Defender Assn. [6031], 1140 Connecticut Ave. NW, Ste. 900, Washington, DC 20036, (202)452-0620

Natl. Legal Center for the Medically Dependent and Disabled [6032], 3 S 6th St., Terre Haute, IN 47807, (812)232-2434

Natl. Legal Center for the Public Interest [6224], 1776 K St. NW, 8th Fl., Washington, DC 20006-2844, (202)466-9360

Natl. Legal Data Center - Defunct.

Natl. Legal Found. [6225], PO Box 64427, Virginia Beach, VA 23467-4427, (757)463-6133

Natl. Legal Found. for the Protection of Parents and Children's Rights - Defunct.

Natl. Legal and Policy Center [17671], 107 Park Washington Ct., Falls Church, VA 22046, (703)237-1970

Natl. Legal Rsrc. Center for Child Advocacy and Protection [11555]

Natl. Legal Sanctuary for Community Advancement [6015], 444 DeHaro St., Ste. 205, San Francisco, CA 94107, (415)553-7100

Natl. Legal Video Assn. [6016], 80 Bloomfield Ave., Ste. 104, Caldwell, NJ 07006, (973)228-8872

Natl. Legion of Greek-Amer. War Veterans in America - Address unknown since 1995.

Natl. Legislation; Friends Comm. on [20041]

Natl. Legislative Conf. [★6283]

Natl. Legislative Coun. for the Disabled and Senior Citizens of the Democratic Party - Defunct.

Natl. Legislative Education Found. - Address unknown since 2004.

Natl. Leigh's Disease Found. - Address unknown since 2000.

Natl. Lesbian and Gay Health Assn. - Address unknown since 2003.

Natl. Lesbian and Gay Journalists Assn. [3138], 1420 K St. NW, Ste. 910, Washington, DC 20005, (202)588-9888

Natl. Lesbian and Gay Law Assn. [5523], 601 Thirteenth St. NW, Ste. 1170 S, Washington, DC 20005-3823, (202)607-6384

Natl. Lesbian and Gay Lawyers Assn. [★5523]

Natl. Leukemia Assn. [★13813]

Natl. Liberal League [★19838]

Natl. Liberty Museum [17723], 321 Chestnut St., Philadelphia, PA 19106, (215)925-2800

National Liberty Museum [IO], Philadelphia, PA, United States

Natl. Librarians Assn. - Defunct.

Natl. Lib. and Documentation Services Bd. [IO], Colombo, Sri Lanka

Natl. Lib. of Medicine; Friends of the [15167]

Natl. Lib. of Uganda [IO], Kampala, Uganda

Natl. Licensed Beverage Assn. [★193]

Natl. Licensed Beverage Assn. - Defunct.

Natl. Licensed Practical Nurses Educational Found. - Defunct.

Natl. Lieutenant Governors Assn. [6285], 71 Cavalier Blvd., Ste. 124, Florence, KY 41042-5168, (859)283-1400

Natl. Life Center [12922], 686 N Broad St., Woodbury, NJ 08096, (856)848-1819

Natl. Life Share Found. - Defunct.

Natl. Lighting Bur. [2436], 8811 Colesville Rd., Ste. G106, Silver Spring, MD 20910, (301)587-9572

Natl. Lighting Bur. [IO], Silver Spring, MD, United States

Natl. Lilac Rabbit Club of Am. [5153], c/o Chris Schmidt, Sec.-Treas., 771 E-1000S, Warren, IN 46792, (260)375-2892

Natl. Lime Assn. [816], 200 N Glebe Rd., Ste. 800, Arlington, VA 22203, (703)243-5463

Natl. Limestone Inst. [★3699]

Natl. Limousine Assn. [3880], 49 S Maple Ave., Marlton, NJ 08053, (856)596-3344

Natl. Lincoln Civil War Coun. [★11113]

Natl. Lincoln Sheep Breeders' Assn. [5207], 15603 173rd Ave., Milo, IA 50166, (608)437-5086

Natl. Liquor Law Enforcement Assn. [5996], 11710 Beltsville Dr., Ste. 300, Beltsville, MD 20705-3102, (301)755-2795

Natl. Liquor Stores Assn. [★193]

Natl. Listen America Club - Defunct.

Natl. Literatures; Coun. on [10419]

Natl. Lithuanian Soc. of Am. [19215]

Natl. Litigation Support Services Assn. [IO], Mississauga, ON, Canada

Natl. Little Britches Rodeo Assn. [23692], 5050 Edison Ave., Ste. 105, Colorado Springs, CO 80915, (719)389-0333

Natl. Little Coll. Athletic Assn. [★23859]

Natl. Live Stock Marketing Assn. [★5024]

Natl. Live Stock and Meat Bd. [★5023]

Natl. Livestock Brand Conf. [★4998]

Natl. Livestock Dealers Assn. [★5021]

Natl. Livestock Exchange - Defunct.

Natl. Livestock Loss Prevention Bd. [★5003]

Natl. Livestock Producers Assn. [5024], 660 Southpointe Ct., Ste. 314, Colorado Springs, CO 80906, (719)538-8843

Natl. Livestock Sanitary Comm. [★5003]

Reference to "IO" in place of a book number signifies that the association may be found in the 45th edition of International Organizations.

Natl. Locksmith Suppliers Assn. [★1834]

Natl. Locksmiths Assn. - Defunct.

Natl. Low Income Housing Coalition [12330], 727 15th St. NW, 6th Fl., Washington, DC 20005, (202)662-1530

Natl. LP-Gas Coun. [★1681]

Natl. LSM Assn. [★21228]

Natl. Lubricating Grease Inst. [2937], 4635 Wyandotte St., Kansas City, MO 64112-1509, (816)931-9480

National Lubricating Grease Inst. Res. Fund [★2937]

Natl. Luggage Dealers Assn. [2418], 1817 Elmdale Ave., Glenview, IL 60025-1355, (847)998-6869

Natl. Lum and Abner Soc. [22925], c/o Tim Hollis, Sec., 81 Sharon Blvd., Dora, AL 35062, (205)674-0101

Natl. Lumber and Building Material Dealers Assn. [1653], 900 2nd St. NE, Ste. 305, Washington, DC 20002, (202)547-2230

Natl. Lumber Exporters Assn. [★1603]

Natl. Lung Cancer Partnership [13854], 222 N Midvale Blvd., Ste. 6, Madison, WI 53705, (608)233-7905

Natl. Lupron Victims Network - Address unknown since 2006.

Natl. Lupus Erythematosus Found. - Defunct.

Natl. Lutheran Commn. on Scouting - Defunct.

Natl. Lutheran Editors and Managers Assn. - Defunct.

Natl. Lutheran Educ. Conf. [★8804]

Natl. Lutheran Outdoors Ministry Assn. [20231], c/o Kevin Hall, Pres., 275 N Syndicate St., St. Paul, MN 55104, (651)603-6165

Natl. Lymphedema Network [15018], Latham Sq., 1611 Telegraph Ave., Ste. 1111, Oakland, CA 94612-2138, (510)208-3200

Natl. Macaroni Manufacturers Assn. [★1550]

Natl. Machine Accountants Assn. [★8128]

Natl. Machine Embellishment Instructors and Artists - Defunct.

Natl. Magazine, Book and Film Carriers Conf. - Address unknown since 2003.

Natl. Mah Jongg League [22468], 250 W 57th St., New York, NY 10107, (212)246-3052

Natl. Maier Musical Assn. - Defunct.

Natl. Mail Order Assn. [2643], 2807 Polk St. NE, Minneapolis, MN 55418-2954, (612)788-1673

Natl. Main St. Center [17237], 1785 Massachusetts Ave. NW, Washington, DC 20036, (202)588-6219

Natl. Maintenance Mgt. Assn. - Defunct.

Natl. Major Gang Task Force [5651], 338 S Arlington Ave., Ste. 112, Indianapolis, IN 46219, (317)322-0537

Natl. Malaria Soc. [★16693]

Natl. Male Nurse Assn. [★15431]

Natl. Mgt. Assn. [2509], 2210 Arbor Blvd., Dayton, OH 45439, (937)294-0421

Natl. Manpower Coun. - Address unknown since 1995.

Natl. Manpower Inst. [★17974]

Natl. Manufactured Housing Fed. [★2527]

Natl. Manufactured Housing Finance Assn. - Defunct.

Natl. Mfrs. of Beverage Flavors - Defunct.

Natl. Marble Club of America [22084]

Natl. Marfan Found. [16652], 22 Manhasset Ave., Port Washington, NY 11050-2023, (516)883-8712

Natl. Marina Assn. - Defunct.

Natl. Marina Mfrs. Consortium - Defunct.

Natl. Marine Bankers Assn. [495], 200 E Randolph Dr., Ste. 5100, Chicago, IL 60601, (312)946-6260

Natl. Marine Charter Assn. [2610], 1600 Duke St., Ste. 400, Alexandria, VA 22314, (800)745-6094

Natl. Marine Distributors Assn. [2585], 37 Pratt St., Essex, CT 06426-1159, (860)767-7898

Natl. Marine Educ. Assn. [★8810]

Natl. Marine Educators Assn. [8810], c/o Johnette Bosarge, Admin. Asst., PO Box 1470, Ocean Springs, MS 39566-1470, (228)818-8893

Natl. Marine Electronics Assn. [2586], Seven Riggs Ave., Severna Park, MD 21146, (410)975-9425

Natl. Marine Mfrs. Assn. [2587], 200 E Randolph Dr., Ste. 5100, Chicago, IL 60601, (312)946-6200

Natl. Marine Representatives Assn. [2588], PO Box 360, Gurnee, IL 60031, (847)662-3167

Natl. Maritime Coun. - Defunct.

Natl. Maritime Historical Soc. - Address unknown since 2002.

Natl. Maritime Museum Assn. [★10513]

Natl. Maritime Union of Am. - Address unknown since 2008.

Natl. Market Traders' Fed. [IO], Barnsley, United Kingdom

Natl. Marriage Encounter [12507], c/o Jeannette Babcock, Bus. Admin., 3922 77th St., Urbandale, IA 50322, (515)278-8458

Natl. Marriage Guidance [★IO]

National Marrow Donor Program [IO], Minneapolis, MN, United States

Natl. Marrow Donor Prog. [14292], 3001 Broadway St. NE, Ste. 500, Minneapolis, MN 55413-1753, (612)627-5800

Natl. Mass Retailing Inst. [★3427]

Natl. Master Farm Homemakers' Guild - Address unknown since 2006.

Natl. Master Shoe Rebuilders Assn. - Defunct.

Natl. Mastitis Coun. [★16802]

Natl. Materials Advisory Bd. [7284], c/o The Natl. Academies, 500 5th St. NW, Keck WS938, Washington, DC 20001, (202)334-3505

National Materials Properties Data Network [★7319]

Natl. Maternal and Child Health Clearinghouse - Defunct.

Natl. Maternity Care Reform Movement - Address unknown since 1995.

Natl. Meals on Wheels Found. [11315]

Natl. Meat Assn. [2662], c/o NMA West, 1970 Broadway, Ste. 825, Oakland, CA 94612, (510)763-1533

Natl. Meat Assn. [★2658]

Natl. Meat Assn. of Australia [★IO]

Natl. Meat Canners Assn. [★2664]

Natl. Meat Industry Coun. - Defunct.

Natl. Mech. Contractors Coun. [1049], c/o Assoc. Builders and Contractors, 4250 N Fairfax Dr., 9th Fl., Arlington, VA 22203-1607, (703)812-2000

Natl. Mech. Trade Coun. [★1049]

Natl. Medic-Card Systems - Defunct.

Natl. Medical Assn. [15176], 1012 10th St. NW, Washington, DC 20001, (202)347-1895

Natl. Medical Assn; Auxiliary to the [15161]

Natl. Medical Assn. Found. - Defunct.

Natl. Medical Assn; Women's Auxiliary to the [★15161]

Natl. Medical and Dental Assn. [19305], c/o Dorothy Czarnecki, MD, Exec. Sec., 9412 Acad. Rd., Philadelphia, PA 19114

Natl. Medical Fellowships [8871], 5 Hanover Sq., 15th Fl., New York, NY 10004, (212)483-8880

Natl. MedPeds Residents' Assn. [14969], c/o Cheryl Dempsey, Exec. Asst., Dept. of Pediatrics, 1430 Tulane Ave., SL-37, New Orleans, LA 70112

Natl. Memorial Inst. for the Prevention of Terrorism [18734], PO Box 889, Oklahoma City, OK 73101, (405)278-6300

Natl. Meningitis Assn. [14281], 738 Robinson Farms Dr., Marietta, GA 30068, (866)366-3662

Natl. Men's Rsrc. Center [18044], PO Box 1080, Brookings, OR 97415-0024

Natl. Mental Hea. Assn. [★15211]

Natl. Mental Health Consumers' Assn. - Address unknown since 1994.

Natl. Mental Hea. Consumers' Self-Help CH [12553], 1211 Chestnut St., Ste. 1207, Philadelphia, PA 19107, (215)751-1810

Natl. Mental Hea. Found. [★15211]

Natl. Merchants' Fed. [IO], Bogota, Colombia

Natl. Metal Awning Assn. - Defunct.

Natl. Metal Decorators Assn. [★1775]

Natl. Metal Spinners Assn. - Address unknown since 2007.

Natl. Metal Trades Assn. [★2480]

Natl. Metal Trades Fed. [IO], Glasgow, United Kingdom

Natl. Microfilm Assn. [★2095]

Natl. Micrographics Assn. [★2095]

Natl. Midas Dealers Assn. [★417]

Natl. Midas Dealers Assn. [★IO]

Natl. Middle Level Sci. Teachers' Assn. [9112], c/o Dale Rosene, Founding Pres., 548 N Linden St., Marshall, MI 49068

Natl. Middle School Assn. [8881], 4151 Executive Pkwy., Ste. 300, Westerville, OH 43081, (614)895-4730

Natl. Middle School Resource Center - Defunct.

Natl. Migraine Found. [★14533]

Natl. Migrant Referral Proj. [★14581]

Natl. Migrant Workers Coun. [★12590]

Natl. Migrant Workers Coun. [★12590]

Natl. Military Family Assn. [21198], 2500 N Van Dorn St., Ste. 102, Alexandria, VA 22302-1601, (703)931-6632

Natl. Military Fish and Wildlife Assn. [5342], c/o Terry Bashore, Pres., 2220 Somerset Pl., Newport News, VA 23602, (757)225-4965

Natl. Military Guidance Assn. - Address unknown since 1995.

Natl. Military Intelligence Assn. [5889], PO Box 479, Hamilton, VA 20159, (540)338-1143

Natl. Military Vehicle Collectors Assn. - Defunct.

Natl. Military Wives Assn. [★21198]

Natl. Milk Glass Collectors Soc. [22566], c/o Barb Pinkston, Membership Sec., 1306 Stowe St., Inverness, FL 34450-6853, (937)666-5011

Natl. Milk Producers Fed. [4489], 2101 Wilson Blvd., Ste. 400, Arlington, VA 22201, (703)243-6111

Natl. Millinery Planning Bd. - Defunct.

Natl. Mime Assn. [★11028]

Natl. Mine Rescue Assn. [7348], c/o Robert Gross, Pres., 145 High St., Waynesburg, PA 15370

Natl. Mineral Feed Assn. [★1357]

Natl. Mini Rex Rabbit Club [5154], c/o Doug King, Sec.-Treas., 2719 Terrace Ave., Sanger, CA 93657, (559)787-2588

Natl. Mini Rex Rabbit Club [IO], Sanger, CA, United States

Natl. Mini-Storage Inst. - Defunct.

Natl. Miniature Donkey Assn. [5004], c/o Lynn Gattari, Gen. Mgr., 6450 Dewey Rd., Rome, NY 13440, (315)336-0154

Natl. Mining Assn. [846], 101 Constitution Ave. NW, Ste. 500 E, Washington, DC 20001-2133, (202)463-2600

Natl. Mining, Petroleum and Energy Soc. [IO], Lima, Peru

Natl. Ministries; Bd. of [19484]

Natl. Minority AIDS Coun. [13580], 1931 13th St. NW, Washington, DC 20009-4432, (202)483-6622

Natl. Minority Bus. Campaign [★2761]

Natl. Minority Bus. Coun. [2768], 120 Broadway, 19th Fl., New York, NY 10271, (212)693-5050

Natl. Minority Bus. Directories [★2761]

Natl. Minority Hea. Assn. [14590], 10 E Baltimore St., Ste. 1404, Baltimore, MD 21202, (866)347-9959

Natl. Minority Purchasing Coun. [★2769]

Natl. Minority Supplier Development Coun. [2769], 1040 Ave. of the Americas, 2nd Fl., New York, NY 10018, (212)944-2430

Natl. MIS User Gp. [7207], c/o Mary Prolux, Chair, 23 Bank St., Lebanon, NH 03766, (603)520-5327

Natl. Mitigation Banking Assn. [4425], PO Box 547881, Orlando, FL 32854-7881, (888)272-6622

Natl. Mobile/Manufactured Home Owners Found. [★12323]

Natl. Mobile Radio Assn. - Defunct.

Natl. Mobile Radio Sys. [★3752]

Natl. Mobile Radio Sys. [★IO]

Natl. Mobility Equip. Dealers Assn. [IO], Tampa, FL, United States

Natl. Mobility Equip. Dealers Assn. [2542], 3327 W Bearss Ave., Tampa, FL 33618, (813)264-2697

Natl. Mobilization Against AIDS [★16966]

Natl. Mobilization Against Sweatshops [17975], PO Box 130293, New York, NY 10013-0995, (718)625-9091

Natl. Mobilization for Survival - Defunct.

Natl. Model Cities Community Development Directors Assn. [★17228]

Natl. Model Cities Directors Assn. [★17228]

Natl. Model League of Nations - Defunct.

Natl. Model Railroad Assn. [22636], 4121 Cromwell Rd., Chattanooga, TN 37421-2119, (423)892-2846

Natl. Model United Nations [★8661]

Natl. Model United Nations [8661], 3489 Valento Cir., St. Paul, MN 55127, (651)493-4404

A star before a book entry number signifies that the name is not listed separately, but is mentioned within the entry.

Natl. Mole Day Found. **[6688]**, PO Box 602, Millersport, OH 43046, (740)928-8455

Natl. Monte Carlo Owners Assn. **[21735]**, 204 Shelby Dr., Greensburg, PA 15601-4974

National Monuments
Mount Rushmore Natl. Memorial Soc. **[10046]**

Natl. Moratorium on Prison Construction - Defunct.

Natl. Morgan Cutting and Stock Horse Assn. - Defunct.

Natl. Morgan Pony Registry - Address unknown since 2006.

Natl. Morgan Reining Horse Assn. **[4920]**, 7701 Olivas Ln., Vacaville, CA 95688, (608)835-7442

Natl. Mosquito Control - Fish and Wildlife Mgt. Coordination Comm. - Defunct.

Natl. Mossberg Collectors Assn. **[22430]**, PO Box 487, Festus, MO 63028, (636)937-6401

Natl. Mother's Day Comm. **[18675]**, 47 W 34th St., Ste. 534, New York, NY 10001, (212)594-6421

Natl. Motor Bus Assn. **[★21896]**

Natl. Motor Bus Assn. **[★IO]**

Natl. Motor Bus Division of Amer. Auto. Assn. **[★3859]**

Natl. Motor Freight Traffic Assn. **[3577]**, 1001 N Fairfax, Ste. 600, Alexandria, VA 22314, (703)838-1810

Natl. Motor Vehicle Assn. **[IO]**, Porto, Portugal

Natl. Motor Vehicle Res. Safety Found. - Defunct.

Natl. Motorcycle Commuter Assn. - Defunct.

Natl. Motorcycle Dealers Assn. - Defunct.

Natl. Motorcycle Dismantelers Assn. - Address unknown since 1994.

Natl. Motorcycle Racing Assn. - Defunct.

Natl. Motorcycle Retailers Assn. - Defunct.

Natl. Motorists Assn. **[13340]**, 402 W 2nd St., Waunakee, WI 53597-1342, (608)849-6000

Natl. Motorists Assn. Australia **[IO]**, Clayfield, Australia

Natl. Motorsports Comm. - Address unknown since 2003.

Natl. Motorsports Press Assn. - Address unknown since 2001.

Natl. Mounted Services Org. - Address unknown since 2004.

Natl. Movement Ekoglasnost **[IO]**, Sofia, Bulgaria

Natl. Movement Theatre Assn. **[11028]**

Natl. Moving and Storage Assn. **[★3559]**

Natl. Moving and Storage Assn. **[★IO]**

Natl. Moving and Storage Assn. - Defunct.

Natl. MPS Soc. **[15253]**, PO Box 736, Bangor, ME 04402-0736, (207)947-1445

Natl. Mule Memorial Assn. - Address unknown since 1995.

Natl. Multi Housing Coun. **[3332]**, 1850 M St. NW, Ste. 540, Washington, DC 20036-5803, (202)974-2300

Natl. MultiCultural Inst. **[11829]**, 3000 Connecticut Ave. NW, Ste. 438, Washington, DC 20008-2556, (202)483-0700

Natl. Multiple Sclerosis Soc. **[15349]**, 733 3rd Ave., 3rd Fl., New York, NY 10017, (212)986-3240

Natl. Multiple Sclerosis Soc. Australia **[★IO]**

Natl. Municipal League **[★6128]**

Natl. Muscle Car Assn. - Address unknown since 2006.

Natl. Museum of Amer. Jewish Military History **[21312]**, 1811 R St. NW, Washington, DC 20009, (202)265-6280

Natl. Museum and Gallery Registration Assn. - Address unknown since 1994.

Natl. Museum of Racing and Hall of Fame **[23508]**, 191 Union Ave., Saratoga Springs, NY 12866-3566, (518)584-0400

Natl. Museum of Transport **[★10926]**

Natl. Mushroom Growers' Assn. **[4742]**, c/o Mushroom Info. Center, 35 E 21st St., New York, NY 10010

Natl. Music Camp **[★9571]**

Natl. Music Camp **[★IO]**

Natl. Music Coun. **[10664]**, 425 Park St., Upper Montclair, NJ 07043, (973)655-7974

Natl. Music Coun. of The United Kingdom **[IO]**, London, United Kingdom

Natl. Music League - Address unknown since 1995.

Natl. Music Printers and Allied Trades Assn. - Address unknown since 1995.

Natl. Music Publishers' Assn. **[2820]**, 101 Constitution Ave. NW, Ste. 705 E, Washington, DC 20001, (202)742-4375

Natl. Music Theater Network **[11029]**, 242 W 38th St., No. 1102, New York, NY 10018, (212)664-0979

Natl. Musicamp Assn. of Zimbabwe **[IO]**, Harare, Zimbabwe

Natl. Mustang Assn. **[4921]**, PO Box 1367, Cedar City, UT 84721, (888)867-8662

Natl. Mutual Fund Managers Assn. - Defunct.

Natl. Muzzle Loading Rifle Assn. **[23722]**, PO Box 67, Friendship, IN 47021, (812)667-5131

Natl. Myoclonus Found. - Defunct.

Natl. Narcotic Detector Dog Assn. **[5997]**, 379 CR 105, Carthage, TX 75633, (888)289-0070

Natl. Narcotic Enforcement Officers Assn. **[★5741]**

Natl. Narcotic Enforcement Officers Assn. **[★IO]**

Natl. Native Amer. AIDS Prevention Center **[16968]**, 436-14th St., Ste. 100, Oakland, CA 94612, (510)444-2051

Natl. Native Amer. Chamber of Commerce - Defunct.

Natl. Native Amer. EMS Assn. **[14341]**, c/o Chebon Tiger, PO Box 80, Maricopa, AZ 85239, (602)361-2099

Natl. Native Amer. (Indian) Cooperative **[10750]**, c/o Carole J. Garcia, Intl. Rep., PO Box 27626, Tucson, AZ 85726-7626, (520)622-4900

Natl. Native Amer. Law Enforcement Assn. **[5998]**, PO Box 171, Washington, DC 20044, (800)948-3863

Natl. Native Amer. Law Students Assn. **[8772]**, c/o Marilyn Phelps, Treas., UCLA School of Law, 2L, Los Angeles, CA 90095

Natl. Native Amer. Veterans Assn. **[21313]**, PO Box 761475, San Antonio, TX 78245

National Native Arts Network **[★9557]**

Natl. Naval Officers Assn. **[6093]**, PO Box 10871, Alexandria, VA 22310-0871, (703)997-1068

Natl. Neckwear Assn. - Address unknown since 2004.

Natl. Necrotizing Fasciitis Found. **[16543]**, c/o Donna Batdorff, Co-Founder, 2731 Porter SW, Grand Rapids, MI 49509, (616)261-2538

The Natl. Needle Arts Assn. **[3794]**, 1100-H Brandywine Blvd., Zanesville, OH 43701-7303, (740)455-6773

Natl. Needlecraft Bur. - Address unknown since 1995.

The Natl. Needlework Assn. **[★3794]**

Natl. Negro Bankers Assn. **[★492]**

Natl. Negro Business League **[★2767]**

Natl. Negro Business and Professional Comm. for the Legal Defense Fund - Address unknown since 1995.

Natl. Negro Funeral Directors and Morticians Assn. **[★2789]**

Natl. Negro Newspaper Publishers Assn. **[★3241]**

Natl. Negro Press Assn. - Defunct.

Natl. Negro Republican Assembly - Defunct.

Natl. Neighborhood Coalition **[17230]**, 1221 Connecticut Ave. NW, 2nd Fl., Washington, DC 20036, (202)429-0790

Natl. Neighbors - Address unknown since 1995.

Natl. Nephrosis Found. **[★15294]**

Natl. Network **[★12935]**

Natl. Network of Abortion Funds **[16914]**, 42 Seaverns Ave., Boston, MA 02130-2865, (617)524-6040

Natl. Network of Asian and Pacific Women - Address unknown since 1989.

Natl. Network of Bilingual Centers - Address unknown since 1997.

Natl. Network of Commercial Real Estate Women **[★3309]**

Natl. Network of Courier Companies **[★IO]**

Natl. Network for Curriculum Coordination in Vocational and Technical Education - Defunct.

Natl. Network for the Disabled **[11973]**, PO Box 3574, Gardena, CA 90247-7274, (310)638-5717

Natl. Network to End Domestic Violence **[12038]**, 2001 S St. NW, Ste. 400, Washington, DC 20009, (202)543-5566

Natl. Network to End Violence Against Immigrant Women **[13433]**, c/o Family Violence Prevention Fund, 383 Rhode Island St., Ste. 304, San Francisco, CA 94103, (415)252-8900

Natl. Network of Episcopal Clergy Associations **[19966]**, c/o Ken Beason, 514-14th St., Paso Robles, CA 93446, (805)238-0819

Natl. Network of Estate Planning Attorneys **[5524]**, 3500 DePauw Blvd., Ste. 2090, Indianapolis, IN 46268, (800)638-8681

Natl. Network of Forest Practitioners **[4692]**, 8 N Court St., Ste. 411, Athens, OH 45701, (740)593-8733

Natl. Network of Graduate Business School Women - Address unknown since 1989.

Natl. Network of Grantmakers **[12202]**, 2801 21st Ave. S, Ste. 132, Minneapolis, MN 55407-1227, (612)724-0702

Natl. Network of Hispanic Women - Address unknown since 2003.

Natl. Network for Immigrant and Refugee Rights **[17808]**, 310 8th St., Ste. 303, Oakland, CA 94607, (510)465-1984

Natl. Network for Immunization Info. **[14941]**, 301 Univ. Blvd., Galveston, TX 77555-0351, (409)772-0199

Natl. Network for Learning Disabled Adults **[★12495]**

Natl. Network for Minority Women in Sci. **[7350]**, 1200 New York Ave. NW, Washington, DC 20005, (202)326-6670

Natl. Network for Minority Women in Sci. **[★7615]**

Natl. Network for Social Work Managers **[13207]**, c/o Jane Addams Coll. of Social Work, M/C 309, 1040 W Harrison St., Chicago, IL 60607-7129, (312)413-2302

Natl. Network in Solidarity With the Nicaraguan People **[★18105]**

Natl. Network in Solidarity With the Nicaraguan People **[★IO]**

Natl. Network for Women Leaders **[★9324]**

Natl. Network of Women in Sales - Defunct.

National Network of Women's Caucuses and Committees in the Disciplinary and Professional Associations **[★17556]**

Natl. Network of Women's Funds **[★13450]**

Natl. Network for Youth **[12935]**, 1319 F St. NW, Ste. 401, Washington, DC 20004-1106, (202)783-7949

Natl. Network of Youth Advisory Bds. - Address unknown since 2000.

Natl. Network of Youth Ministries **[20641]**, 12335 World Trade Dr., Ste. 16, San Diego, CA 92128, (858)451-1111

Natl. Networker **[12495]**

Natl. Neurofibromatosis Found. **[★15315]**

Natl. Neurological Res. Found. - Address unknown since 1995.

Natl. Neurotrauma Soc. **[15398]**, 8032 SW 45 Ln., Gainesville, FL 32608, (352)271-1169

Natl. New Deal Preservation Assn. **[10775]**, PO Box 602, Santa Fe, NM 87504-0602, (505)473-3985

Natl. New England Lead Burning Assn. **[2052]**, c/o Karl Weiss, CEO, 800 W Cummings Park, Ste. 3950, Woburn, MA 01801, (781)933-1941

Natl. New Play Network **[11030]**, c/o David Golston, Gen. Mgr., InterAct Theatre, 2030 Sansom St., Philadelphia, PA 19103, (215)568-8077

Natl. Newman Alumni Assn. - Defunct.

Natl. Newman Assn. of Faculty and Staff - Defunct.

Natl. Newman Chaplains Assn. **[★19595]**

Natl. Newman Club Fed. - Defunct.

Natl. Newman Found. - Defunct.

Natl. News Bur. **[3139]**, PO Box 43039, Philadelphia, PA 19129, (215)849-9016

Natl. News Coun. - Defunct.

Natl. Newspaper Assn. **[3140]**, PO Box 7540, Columbia, MO 65205-7540, (573)882-5800

Natl. Newspaper Assn. Found. **[8715]**, Univ. of Missouri, Columbia, 129 Neff Annex, Columbia, MO 65211, (573)882-5800

Natl. Newspaper Found. **[★8715]**

Natl. Newspaper Publishers Assn. **[3241]**, 3200 13th St. NW, Washington, DC 20010, (202)588-8764

Natl. Newspapers of Ireland **[IO]**, Dublin, Ireland

Natl. Niemann Pick Disease Found. **[15254]**, PO Box 49, 401 Madison Ave., Ste. B, Fort Atkinson, WI 53538, (920)563-0930

Natl. Nitrogen Solutions Assn. **[★1363]**

Natl. No-Nukes Prison Support Collective **[18160]**, c/o Felice Cohen-Joppa, Co-Ed., PO Box 43383, Tucson, AZ 85733, (520)323-8697

Reference to "IO" in place of a book number signifies that the association may be found in the 45th edition of International Organizations.

National No-Nukes Prison Support Collective [IO], Tucson, AZ, United States

Natl. Noise Abatement Coun. - Defunct.

Natl. Nomad Club - Defunct.

Natl. Noriance for Safer Cities - Defunct.

Natl. Norwegian Forest Cat Breed Club - Address unknown since 2001.

Natl. Nostalgic Nova [21736], PO Box 2344, York, PA 17405, (717)252-4192

Natl. Notary Assn. [6147], 9350 DeSoto Ave., PO Box 2402, Chatsworth, CA 91313-2402, (800)876-6827

Natl. Nothing Found. - Defunct.

Natl. Notions Wholesaler-Distributor Assn. - Defunct.

Natl. Nubian Club [★4135]

Natl. Nubian Club [★IO]

Natl. Nudist Coun. - Defunct.

Natl. Nurses in Bus. Assn. [752], PO Box 561081, Rockledge, FL 32956-1081, (321)633-4610

Natl. Nurses Soc. on Addictions [★15484]

Natl. Nurses Soc. on Addictions [★IO]

Natl. Nurses Soc. on Alcoholism [★IO]

Natl. Nurses Soc. on Alcoholism [★15484]

Natl. Nursing Accrediting Ser. [★15510]

Natl. Nursing Staff Development Org. [15511], 7794 Grow Dr., Pensacola, FL 32514, (850)474-0995

Natl. Nutrition Consortium - Defunct.

National Nutritional Foods Assn. [★3425]

Natl. Oak Flooring Manufacturers Assn. [★656]

Natl. Ocean Access Project - Address unknown since 1999.

Natl. Ocean Indus. Assn. [7400], 1120 G St. NW, Ste. 900, Washington, DC 20005, (202)347-6900

National Oceanographic Data Center [★4590]

Natl. Oceanography Assn. [★7400]

Natl. Odd Shoe Exchange [11974], PO Box 1120, Chandler, AZ 85244-1120, (480)892-3484

National Odd Shoe Exchange [IO], Chandler, AZ, United States

Natl. Off-Campus Housing Assn. - Defunct.

Natl. Off-Road Bicycling Assn. [★23320]

Natl. Off. for Black Catholics [19691], c/o Archdiocese of Washington Pastoral Center, PO Box 29620, Washington, DC 20017-0260, (301)853-4500

Natl. Off. of Jesuit Social Ministries [★13172]

Natl. Off. of Jesuit Social Ministries [★IO]

Natl. Off. Machine Dealers Assn. [★2844]

Natl. Office Machine Service Assn. - Address unknown since 1994.

Natl. Off. Paper Recycling Proj. [3999], c/o U.S. Conf. of Mayors, 1620 Eye St. NW, Washington, DC 20006, (202)293-7330

Natl. Off. Products Alliance [3685], 301 N Fairfax St., Alexandria, VA 22314, (703)549-9040

Natl. Off. for the Rights of the Indigent [★17130]

Natl. Office for Social Responsibility - Defunct.

Natl. Office Systems Assn. - Defunct.

Natl. Officers Assn. - Address unknown since 2004.

Natl. Offshore Coun. [★23205]

Natl. Offshore Dept. [23205], c/o U.S. Sailing Assn., PO Box 1260, 15 Maritime Dr., Portsmouth, RI 02871-0907, (401)683-0800

Natl. Oil and Acrylic Painters' Soc. [9459], PO Box 676, Osage Beach, MO 65065-0676, (573)348-1764

Natl. Oil Fuel Inst. [★2943]

Natl. Oil Marketers Assn. - Defunct.

Natl. Oil Recyclers Assn. [2938], c/o Scott D. Parker, Exec. Dir., 5965 Amber Ridge Rd., Haymarket, VA 20169, (703)753-4277

Natl. Oil Scouts and Landmen's Assn. [★2932]

Natl. Oil Scouts and Landmen's Assn. [★IO]

Natl. Oilseed Processors Assn. [2857], 1300 L St. NW, Ste. 1020, Washington, DC 20005-4168, (202)842-0463

Natl. Old Lacers [★22161]

Natl. Old Lacers [★IO]

Natl. Old Timers' Assn. of the Energy Indus. [6965]

Natl. Old Timers Auto Racing Club [21737], c/o Pete Poodiack, Exec. Dir., 4 Rita Dr., Bethel, CT 06801-3025, (203)791-8536

Natl. Oldtime Fiddlers' Assn. [10665], c/o Natl. Old-time Fiddlers' Contest and Festival, 115 W Idaho St., Weiser, ID 83672, (208)414-0255

Natl. Oleander Soc. [★22523]

Natl. Oleander Soc. [★IO]

Natl. Olympic Comm. of Armenia [IO], Yerevan, Armenia

Natl. Olympic Comm. of Azerbaijan [IO], Baku, Azerbaijan

Natl. Olympic Comm. for Germany [IO], Frankfurt, Germany

Natl. Olympic Comm. of Iraq [IO], Baghdad, Iraq

Natl. Olympic Comm. of the Islamic Republic of Iran [IO], Tehran, Iran

Natl. Olympic Comm. of Lithuania [IO], Vilnius, Lithuania

Natl. Olympic Comm. of the Republic of Belarus [IO], Minsk, Belarus

Natl. Olympic Comm. of the Republic of Kazakhstan [IO], Almaty, Kazakhstan

Natl. Olympic Comm. of Solomon Islands [IO], Honiara, Solomon Islands

Natl. Olympic Comm. of South Africa [★IO]

Natl. Olympic Comm. and Sports Confed. of Denmark [IO], Brondby, Denmark

Natl. Olympic Comm. of Turkey [IO], Istanbul, Turkey

Natl. Olympic Comm. of Ukraine [IO], Kiev, Ukraine

Natl. One Coat Stucco Assn. [650], 1615 W Abram St., Ste. L, Arlington, TX 76013, (817)461-3351

Natl. One Design Racing Assn. [23206], c/o Jolly Booth, Sec.-Treas., 1225 E Bronson St., South Bend, IN 46615, (330)644-9305

Natl. One-Liners Club - Address unknown since 1995.

Natl. Onion Assn. [4743], 822 7th St., Ste. 510, Greeley, CO 80631-3941, (970)353-5895

Natl. Online Circuit - Defunct.

Natl. Onsite Wastewater Recycling Assn. [5271], PO Box 1270, Edgewater, MD 21037, (410)798-1697

Natl. Opera Assn. [10666], c/o Robert Hansen, Exec. Dir., PO Box 60869, Canyon, TX 79016-0869, (806)651-2857

Natl. Operatic and Dramatic Assn. [IO], Peterborough, United Kingdom

Natl. Operating Comm. on Standards for Athletic Equip. [3451], 11020 King St., Ste. 215, Overland Park, KS 66210, (913)888-1340

Natl. Operations Analysts Assn. - Defunct.

Natl. Opossum Soc. [4160], PO Box 21197, Catonsville, MD 21228, (410)233-1102

Natl. Opportunity Camps for the Pre-Teen Child - Address unknown since 1987.

Natl. Optical Assn. [★15721]

National Optical Astronomy Observatory [★7622]

Natl. Option and Futures Soc. - Defunct.

Natl. Optometric Assn. [15725], c/o Dr. Charles Comer, Mgr., 3723 Main St., PO Box F, East Chicago, IN 46312, (219)398-4483

Natl. Optometric Soc. for Developmental Vision Care [★15718]

Natl. Optometry Assn. [15726], PO Box 35215, Chicago, IL 60707-0215, (708)453-0080

Natl. Oral Hea. Info. CH [14181], 1 NOHIC Way, Bethesda, MD 20892-3500, (301)402-7364

Natl. Orange Juice Assn. [★510]

Natl. Oratorio Soc. - Defunct.

Natl. Orchestral Assn. [10667], PO Box 7016, New York, NY 10150-7016, (212)208-4691

Natl. Order of Battlefield Commissions [21237], c/o Robert C. Evans, Natl. Commander, 2506 King St., Alexandria, VA 22301, (703)838-5548

Natl. Order of the Blue and Gray - Defunct.

Natl. Order of Trench Rats [20766], PO Box 1068, Kingston, PA 18704-0068, (570)714-2554

Natl. Order of Women Legislators [6038], 910 16th St., Ste. 100, Washington, DC 20006, (202)293-3040

Natl. Organ Transplant Education Found. - Address unknown since 1991.

Natl. Org. for Motor Retail Trade and Repairs [IO], Stockholm, Sweden

Natl. Org. of Trade Unions [IO], Kampala, Uganda

Natl. Org. of Adolescent Pregnancy and Parenting [★12182]

Natl. Org. on Adolescent Pregnancy, Parenting and Prevention [★12182]

Natl. Org. for Advancement of Associate Degree Nursing [★15512]

Natl. Org. of African Americans in Housing [12331], 507 Capitol Ct. NE, Ste. 300, Washington, DC 20002, (202)544-1058

Natl. Org. Against Male Sexual Victimization; Male Survivor: The [13077]

Natl. Org. for Albinism and Hypopigmentation [15255], PO Box 959, East Hampstead, NH 03826-0959, (603)887-2310

Natl. Org. of Alternative Programs [16382], PO Box 10703, Austin, TX 78766, (512)467-7027

Natl. Org. for an Amer. Revolution - Address unknown since 1994.

Natl. Org. for Apraxia and Dyspraxia - Address unknown since 1996.

Natl. Org. for Associate Degree Nursing [15512], 7794 Grow Dr., Pensacola, FL 32514, (850)484-6948

Natl. Org. of Bar Counsel [5953], c/o Nancy L. Cohen, Pres., 1560 Broadway, Ste. 1800, Denver, CO 80210, (303)866-6577

Natl. Org. for Birthfathers and Adoption Reform - Defunct.

Natl. Org. of Black Architects [★6478]

Natl. Org. of Black Chemists and Chem. Engineers [★6689]

Natl. Org. of Black Coll. Alumni - Address unknown since 2002.

Natl. Org. of Black County Officials [★5617]

Natl. Org. of Black Law Enforcement Executives [5999], 4609-F Pinecrest Off. Park Dr., Alexandria, VA 22312-1442, (703)658-1529

Natl. Org. of Blacks in Govt. [5571], 3005 Georgia Ave. NW, Washington, DC 20001-3807, (202)667-3280

Natl. Org. Caring for Kids [11638], PO Box 1822, Tacoma, WA 98401, (253)851-6625

Natl. Org. for Changing Men [★17779]

Natl. Org. for Changing Men - Address unknown since 1994.

Natl. Org. for Chronically Ill Kids [★11638]

Natl. Org. of Circumcision Info. Rsrc. Centers [11732], PO Box 2512, San Anselmo, CA 94979-2512, (415)488-9883

Natl. Org. of Circumcision Info. Rsrc. Centers [IO], San Anselmo, CA, United States

Natl. Org. for Competency Assurance [14591], 2025 M St. NW, Ste. 800, Washington, DC 20036, (202)367-1165

Natl. Org. for Continuing Educ. of Roman Catholic Clergy [19936], 333 N Michigan Ave., Ste. 1205, Chicago, IL 60601, (312)781-9450

Natl. Org. on Disability [17419], 910 16th St. NW, Ste. 600, Washington, DC 20006, (202)293-5960

Natl. Org. on Disability [IO], Washington, DC, United States

Natl. Org. for Disorders of the Corpus Callosum [15350], PMB 363, 18032-C Lemon Dr., Yorba Linda, CA 92886, (714)747-0063

Natl. Org. for Diversity in Sales and Marketing [2644], PO Box 61118, Raleigh, NC 27661, (888)689-8896

Natl. Org. of Downsized Employees - Defunct.

Natl. Org. of Episcopalians for Life [★12905]

Natl. Org. of Fed. Employees Against Abuse and Retaliation [24078], PO Box 94, Brooklyn, NY 11234, (718)377-0249

Natl. Org. on Fetal Alcohol Syndrome [16515], 900 17th St. NW, Ste. 910, Washington, DC 20006, (202)785-4585

Natl. Org. For Empowering Caregivers [13295], 425 W 23rd St., Ste. 9B, New York, NY 10011, (212)807-1204

National Organization For Empowering Caregivers [IO], New York, NY, United States

Natl. Org. For River Sports [★23683]

Natl. Org. of Forensic Social Work [8446], 460 Smith St., Ste. K, Middletown, CT 06457, (860)613-0254

Natl. Org. of Gay and Lesbian Scientists and Tech. Professionals [7620], PO Box 91803, Pasadena, CA 91109, (626)791-7689

Natl. Org. to Halt the Abuse and Routine Mutilation of Males [11733], PO Box 460795, San Francisco, CA 94146, (415)826-9351

Natl. Org. of HIV over Fifty - Address unknown since 2002.

A star before a book entry number signifies that the name is not listed separately, but is mentioned within the entry.

Natl. Org. of Hospital Schools of Nursing - Defunct.

Natl. Org. for Human Ser. Educ. [★9131]

Natl. Org. of Human Ser. Educators [★9131]

Natl. Org. for Human Services [9131], 90 Madison St., Ste. 206, Denver, CO 80206, (303)320-5430

Natl. Org. of Human Services - Defunct.

Natl. Org. of Immigrants and Visible Minority Women of Canada [IO], Ottawa, ON, Canada

Natl. Org. for Improving School Environments - Defunct.

Natl. Org. of Indus. Trade Unions [24103], 148-06 Hillside Ave., Jamaica, NY 11435, (718)291-3434

Natl. Org. to Insure a Sound-Controlled Environment - Address unknown since 1995.

Natl. Org. to Insure Survival Economics - Address unknown since 2003.

Natl. Org. of Italian-American Women [19167], 25 W 43rd St., 10th Fl., New York, NY 10036, (212)642-2003

Natl. Org. on Legal Problems of Educ. [★5676]

Natl. Org. on Legal Problems of Educ. [★IO]

Natl. Org. of Legal Services Workers [★24079]

Natl. Org. of Legal Services Workers, UAW Local 2320 [24079], 113 Univ. Pl., 5th Fl., New York, NY 10003, (212)228-0992

Natl. Org. for Lesbians of Size; NOLOSE - The [12250]

Natl. Org. of Life and Hea. Insurance Guaranty Associations [1852], 13873 Park Center Rd., Ste. 329, Herndon, VA 20171, (703)481-5206

Natl. Org. on Male Sexual Victimization [★13077]

Natl. Org. for Men [18045], 30 Besey St., New York, NY 10007, (760)753-5000

Natl. Org. for Men Against Sexism [17779], PO Box 455, Louisville, CO 80027-0455, (303)666-7043

Natl. Org. for Men Legal Defense and Education Fund - Address unknown since 2006.

Natl. Org. for Mentally Ill Children [★15211]

Natl. Org. for Mexican Amer. Rights [17709], c/o Mary Louise Garcia, Sec., PO Box 4468, Fairview, NM 87533, (505)852-2278

Natl. Org. of Miniaturists and Dollers - Defunct.

Natl. Org. of Minority Architects [6478], Howard Univ., Coll. of Engg., Architecture and Cmpt. Sciences, School of Architecture and Design, 2366 Sixth St. NW, Rm. 100, Washington, DC 20059, (202)686-2780

Natl. Org. of Mothers of Twins Clubs [12613], PO Box 700860, Plymouth, MI 48170-0955, (248)231-4480

Natl. Org. for Non-Enumeration - Address unknown since 2006.

Natl. Org. of Nurse Practitioners Faculties [15513], 1522 K St. NW, Ste. 702, Washington, DC 20005, (202)289-8044

Natl. Org. of Nurses with Disabilities [15514], 1640 W Roosevelt Rd., Rm. 736, Chicago, IL 60608

Natl. Org. of Parents of Blind Children [16879], 1800 Johnson St., Baltimore, MD 21230-4998, (410)659-9314

Natl. Org. for People of Color Against Suicide [13289], PO Box 75571, Washington, DC 20017, (202)549-6039

Natl. Org. of Poll-ettes - Address unknown since 2004.

Natl. Org. for the Professional Advancement of Black Chemists and Chem. Engineers [6689], PO Box 77040, Washington, DC 20013, (800)776-1419

Natl. Org. for Public Hea. Nursing [★15510]

Natl. Org. for Racing Radio Control Autos [22652]

Natl. Org. for Rare Disorders [14282], PO Box 1968, Danbury, CT 06813-1968, (203)744-0100

Natl. Org. for Raw Materials [16957], 680 E 5 Point Hwy., Charlotte, MI 48813, (517)543-0111

Natl. Org. for the Reform of Marijuana Laws [17137], 1600 K St. NW, Ste. 501, Washington, DC 20006-2832, (202)483-5500

Natl. Org. of Remediators and Mold Inspectors [1331], 22174 Prats Rd., Abita Springs, LA 70420, (877)251-2296

Natl. Org. for the Repeal of the Fed. Reserve Act and the Internal Revenue Code [★17666]

Natl. Org. of Responsible Animal Owners - Defunct.

Natl. Org. of Restoring Men [11734], c/o Mr. R. Wayne Griffiths, Exec. Dir., 3205 Northwood Dr., Ste. 209, Concord, CA 94520-4506, (925)827-4077

Natl. Org. of Restoring Men - UK [IO], Stone, United Kingdom

Natl. Org. for the Rights of Guide Dogs - Address unknown since 1994.

Natl. Org. for Rivers [23683], 212 W Cheyenne Mountain Blvd., Colorado Springs, CO 80906-3712, (719)579-8759

Natl. Org. for Seasonal Affective Disorder - Address unknown since 1999.

Natl. Org. of Single Mothers [13108], PO Box 68, Midland, NC 28107

Natl. Org. of Social Security Claimants' Representatives [18650], 560 Sylvan Ave., Englewood Cliffs, NJ 07632, (562)868-5886

Natl. Org. Taunting Safety and Fairness Everywhere [22599], PO Box 5743, Montecito, CA 93150, (805)969-6217

Natl. Org. of Test, Res., and Training Reactors [7388], c/o Steve Reese, Chm., Oregon State Univ., Radiation Center, Corvallis, OR 97331, (541)737-2341

Natl. Org. of Travelers Aid Societies [★13191]

Natl. Org. of Travelers Aid Societies [★IO]

Natl. Org. of Tutoring and Mentoring Centers [★9283]

Natl. Org. of Veterans' Advocates [6348], PO Box 65876, Washington, DC 20035-5876, (480)838-6566

Natl. Org. for Victim Assistance [13369], 510 King St., Ste. 424, Alexandria, VA 22314, (703)535-6682

Natl. Org. of I Walkers [23971], PO Box 191, Hermann, MO 65041

Natl. Org. for Water Awareness [5277]

Natl. Org. for Women [17560], 1100 H St. NW, 3rd Fl., Washington, DC 20005, (202)628-8669

Natl. Org. for Women's Shelters and Young Women's Shelters in Sweden [IO], Stockholm, Sweden

Natl. Org. of World War Nurses - Address unknown since 2003.

Natl. Organizations for Youth Safety [13502], c/o Sandy Spavone, Exec. Dir., 7371 Atlas Walk Way, No. 109, Gainesville, VA 20155, (703)981-0264

Natl. Organizers Alliance [13136], 2307 Martin Luther King Jr. Ave. SE, Washington, DC 20020, (202)543-6603

Natl. Orientation Directors Assn. [7907], c/o Univ. of Michigan, 375 Univ. Center, Flint, MI 48502-1950, (810)424-5513

Natl. Orientation Directors Conf. [★7907]

Natl. Ornament and Electric Lights Christmas Assn. - Address unknown since 2003.

Natl. Ornamental Glass Mfrs. Assn. [★1736]

Natl. Ornamental Goldfish Growers Assn. [4181]

Natl. Ornamental Iron Mfrs. Assn. [★2722]

Natl. Ornamental Metal Mfrs. Assn. [★2722]

Natl. Ornamental and Miscellaneous Metals Assn. [2722], 1535 Pennsylvania Ave., McDonough, GA 30253, (770)288-2004

Natl. ORT League - Defunct.

Natl. Orthotic and Prosthetic Res. Inst. - Address unknown since 2003.

Natl. Osteopathic Found. [★15806]

Natl. Osteopathic Guild Assn. - Address unknown since 2002.

Natl. Osteopathic Interfraternity Coun. - Address unknown since 1995.

Natl. Osteopathic Women Physician's Assn. [24564], ATSU - Kirksville Coll. of Osteophatic Medicine, 800 W Jefferson St., Kirksville, MO 63501

Natl. Osteoporosis Found. [15775], 1232 22nd St. NW, Washington, DC 20037-1202, (202)223-2226

Natl. Osteoporosis Soc. [IO], Bath, United Kingdom

Natl. Outboard Assn. - Defunct.

Natl. Outdoor Advertising Bur. - Defunct.

Natl. Outdoor Drama Assn. - Defunct.

Natl. Outdoor Events Assn. [IO], Wallington, United Kingdom

Natl. Outdoor Showmen's Assn. [★IO]

Natl. Outdoor Showmen's Assn. [★1303]

Natl. Outdoor Volleyball Assn. - Defunct.

Natl. Outdoorsmen's Assn. - Defunct.

Natl. Outerwear and Sportswear Assn. [★221]

Natl. Ovarian Cancer Assn. [IO], Toronto, ON, Canada

Natl. Ovarian Cancer Coalition [13855], 500 NE Spanish River Blvd., Ste. 8, Boca Raton, FL 33431, (561)393-0005

Natl. PAC [18067], 600 Pennsylvania Ave. SE, Ste. 207, Washington, DC 20003, (202)879-7710

Natl. PAC [★18067]

Natl. PACE Assn. [12272], 801 N Fairfax St., Ste. 309, Alexandria, VA 22314, (703)535-1565

Natl. Pacific/Asian Rsrc. Center on Aging [★11300]

Natl. Paddleball Assn. [23092], 7642 Kingston Dr., Portage, MI 49002, (269)323-0121

Natl. Paideia Center [8357], 400 Silver Cedar Ct., Ste. 200, Chapel Hill, NC 27514, (919)962-3128

Natl. Pain Educ. Coun. [15846], c/o CME Scholar, 1010 Washington Blvd., 7th Fl., Stamford, CT 06901, (888)536-7545

Natl. Paint and Coatings Assn. [2884], 1500 Rhode Island Ave. NW, Washington, DC 20005, (202)462-6272

Natl. Paint Distributors - Address unknown since 1994.

Natl. Paint and Ink Mfrs'. Assn. [IO], Mexico City, Mexico

Natl. Paint, Oil and Varnish Assn. [★2884]

Natl. Paint, Varnish and Lacquer Assn. [★2884]

Natl. Painting, Decorating, and Drywall Apprenticeship and Manpower Training Fund [★12082]

Natl. Painting, Decorating, and Drywall Apprenticeship and Manpower Training Fund [★IO]

Natl. PAL [★13496]

Natl. Palliative Care Nursing Org. [IO], Eltham, Australia

Natl. Palm Oil Growers' Fed. [IO], Bogota, Colombia

Natl. Palomino Breeders Assn. - Defunct.

Natl. Pan-American Junior Golf Assn. [23459], c/o Natl. Pan-American Golf Assn., PO Box 7211, Corpus Christi, TX 78467-7211, (903)569-2638

Natl. Pan-Hellenic Conf; Central Off. Executives Assn. of [24477]

Natl. Pan-Hellenic Coun. [24484], 3951 Snapfinger Pkwy., Ste. 218, Decatur, GA 30035, (404)592-6145

Natl. Pan-Hellenic Editors Conf. [24448], 8777 Purdue Rd., Ste. 117, Indianapolis, IN 46268, (317)872-3185

Natl. Panhellenic Assn. of Central Off. Executives [★24477]

Natl. Panhellenic Conf. [24485], 8777 Purdue Rd., Ste. 117, Indianapolis, IN 46268-3000, (317)872-3185

Natl. Panhellenic Conf. of Central Off. Executives [★24477]

Natl. Paper Box Assn. [★987]

Natl. Paper Box Manufacturers Assn. [★987]

Natl. Paper Box and Packaging Assn. [★987]

Natl. Paper Box Suppliers Assn. - Defunct.

Natl. Paper Trade Assn. [★2891]

Natl. Paperbox Assn. [987], 113 S West St., 3rd Fl., Alexandria, VA 22314, (703)684-2212

Natl. Parachute Jumpers-Riggers Assn. [★23648]

Natl. Paralegal Assn. [6152], Box 406, Solebury, PA 18963, (215)297-8333

Natl. Paralegal Inst. - Defunct.

Natl. Paralympic Comm. Germany [IO], Duisburg, Germany

Natl. Paralympic Comm. Islamic Republic of Iran [IO], Tehran, Iran

Natl. Paralympic Comm. of Turkey [IO], Istanbul, Turkey

Natl. Paraplegia Found. [★16468]

Natl. Parent Info. Network - Defunct.

Natl. Parent Network on Disabilities [14245]

Natl. Parent-to-Parent Support and Info. Sys. - Address unknown since 2004.

Natl. Parenting Assn. [12679]

Natl. Parents Assn. [12680], Main Sta., Box 1993, Valparaiso, IN 46384-1993

Natl. Park Acad. of the Arts [9460], PO Box 608, Jackson Hole, WY 83001, (307)690-0055

Natl. Park Found. [6159], 1201 Eye St. NW, Ste. 550B, Washington, DC 20005, (202)354-6460

Natl. Park Hospitality Assn. [1321], 129 Park St. NE, Ste. B, Vienna, VA 22180, (703)242-1999

Natl. Park Trust [5071], 51 Monroe St., Ste. 110, Rockville, MD 20850, (301)279-PARK

Reference to "IO" in place of a book number signifies that the association may be found in the 45th edition of International Organizations.

Natl. Park Trust Fund Bd. [★6159]

Natl. Parking Assn. [2900], 1112 16th St. NW, Ste. 300, Washington, DC 20036, (202)296-4336

Natl. Parkinson Found. [15351], 1501 NW 9th Ave., Bob Hope Rd., Miami, FL 33136-1494, (305)243-6666

National Parkinson Institute [★15351]

Natl. Parks Assn. [★6160]

Natl. Parks and Conservation Assn. [★6160]

Natl. Parks Conservation Assn. [6160], 1300 19th St. NW, Ste. 300, Washington, DC 20036, (202)223-6722

Natl. Parks Inholders Assn. [★6187]

Natl. Parliamentary Debate Assn. [9160], c/o Prof. Brent Northup, Treas., Carroll Coll., 1601 N Benton, Helena, MT 59625, (406)447-5400

Natl. Parrot Sanctuary [IO], Friskney, United Kingdom

Natl. Particleboard Assn. [★IO]

Natl. Particleboard Assn. [★1643]

Natl. Partnership for Community Leadership [11805], PO Box 5719, Washington, DC 20037, (202)429-2027

Natl. Partnership for Immunization [14942], c/o Natl. Immunization Prog., Centers for Disease Control and Prevention, 1600 Clifton Rd., Mailstop E-05, Atlanta, GA 30333

Natl. Partnership for Social Enterprise [18623]

Natl. Partnership for Women and Families [17561], 1875 Connecticut Ave. NW, Ste. 650, Washington, DC 20009, (202)986-2600

Natl. Party of Australia [★IO]

Natl. Party Boat Owners Alliance [3359], 181 Thames St., Groton, CT 06340, (860)535-2066

Natl. Passenger Safety Assn. - Defunct.

Natl. Passenger Traffic Assn. [★3929]

Natl. Pasta Assn. [1550], 1156 15th St. NW, Ste. 900, Washington, DC 20005, (202)637-5888

Natl. Pat Boone Fan Club [24949]

Natl. Patent Coun. - Address unknown since 1999.

Natl. Patient Safety Found. [14656], 1120 MASS MoCA Way, North Adams, MA 01247, (413)663-8900

Natl. Patio Enclosure Assn. - Address unknown since 2007.

Natl. Patriot Plan - Defunct.

Natl. Pavement Contractors Assn. [651], PO Box 57, Mineral Wells, TX 76068-0057, (940)327-8041

Natl. Paving Brick Assn. [★604]

Natl. Pawnbrokers Assn. [2429], PO Box 1040, Roanoke, TX 76262-1040, (817)491-4554

Natl. Pawnbrokers Assn. [IO], Reading, United Kingdom

Natl. Payphone Assn. [★3733]

Natl. PC Users Group - Address unknown since 2001.

Natl. Peace Acad. Campaign [★18224]

Natl. Peace Acad. Found. [★18224]

Natl. Peace Acad. Fund [★18224]

Natl. Peace Corps Assn. [18262], 1900 L St. NW, Ste. 205, Washington, DC 20036-5028, (202)293-7728

Natl. Peace Corps Assn. [★18262]

Natl. Peace Coun. of Norway [★IO]

Natl. Peace Day Celebrations - Defunct.

Natl. Peace Found. [18224], 666 11th St. NW, Ste. 202, Washington, DC 20001, (202)783-7030

Natl. Peace Garden [★18225]

Natl. Peace Garden Foundation [18225]

Natl. Peace Inst. Found. [★18224]

Natl. Peach Coun. [4744], 12 Nicklaus Ln., Ste. 101, Columbia, SC 29229, (803)788-7101

Natl. Peach Partners [4745], c/o Maple Lawn Farms, 251 E Maple Lawn Rd., New Park, PA 17352, (717)382-4878

Natl. Peanut Buying Points Assn. [5057], PO Box 314, 115 W 2nd St., Tifton, GA 31793, (229)386-1716

Natl. Peanut Coun. [★5049]

Natl. Peanut Festival Assn. [5058], 5622 Hwy. 231 S, Dothan, AL 36301, (334)793-4323

Natl. Pearson Yacht Owners Assn. [21878], c/o William J. Lawrence, 28 Vesey St., Ste. 2172, New York, NY 10007

Natl. Pecan Marketing Coun. - Defunct.

Natl. Pecan Shellers Assn. [5059], 1100 Johnson Ferry Rd., Ste. 300, Atlanta, GA 30342, (404)252-3663

Natl. Pediatric and Family HIV Rsrc. Center [13581], Univ. of Medicine & Dentistry of New Jersey, 30 Bergen St., ADMC No. 4, Newark, NJ 07103, (973)972-0410

Natl. Pediatrics AIDS Network [15890], c/o Gary Gale, Dir., PO Box 1032, Boulder, CO 80306, (800)646-1001

Natl. Pediculosis Assn. [16247], PO Box 610189, Newton, MA 02461

Natl. Pedigreed Livestock Coun. [4141], c/o Zane Akins, Sec.-Treas., 177 Palermo Pl., The Villages, FL 32159, (352)259-6005

Natl. Peer Helpers Assn. [★11827]

Natl. Pell Grant Coalition [8433]

Natl. Pemphigus Found. [★14268]

Natl. Pensioners and Senior Citizens Fed. [IO], Trenton, ON, Canada

Natl. People's Action [11755], 810 Milwaukee Ave., Chicago, IL 60622, (312)243-3038

Natl. Performance Network [11031], 900 Camp St., 2nd Fl., New Orleans, LA 70130, (504)595-8008

Natl. Perinatal Assn. [15900], 2090 Linglestown Rd., Ste. 107, Harrisburg, PA 17110, (888)971-3295

Natl. Perinatal Bereavement Assn. - Defunct.

Natl. Perinatal Info. Center [15901], 225 Chapman St., Ste. 200, Providence, RI 02905, (401)274-0650

Natl. Perishable Logistics Assn. - Defunct.

Natl. Personal Fitness Trainers Assn. - Address unknown since 1989.

Natl. Personnel Assn. [★2481]

Natl. Personnel Assn. [★IO]

Natl. Personnel Consultants - Defunct.

Natl. Pest Control Assn. [★2910]

Natl. Pest Control Assn. [★IO]

Natl. Pest Mgt. Assn. Intl. [IO], Fairfax, VA, United States

Natl. Pest Mgt. Assn. Intl. [2910], 9300 Lee Hwy., Ste. 301, Fairfax, VA 22031, (703)352-6762

Natl. Pest Technicians Assn. [IO], Nottingham, United Kingdom

Natl. Pesticide Info. Center [13327], Oregon State Univ., 333 Weniger Hall, Corvallis, OR 97331-8574, (800)858-7378

Natl. Pesticide Info. CH [★13327]

Natl. Pesticide Telecommunications Network [★13327]

Natl. Pet Alliance [11441], PO Box 53385, San Jose, CA 95153, (408)363-0700

Natl. Pet Assn. - Defunct.

Natl. Pet Dealers and Breeders Assn. - Defunct.

Natl. Petrochemical and Refiners Assn. [2939], 1899 L St. NW, Ste. 1000, Washington, DC 20036-3810, (202)457-0480

Natl. Petroleum Assn. [★2939]

Natl. Petroleum Coun. [5686], 1625 K St. NW, Ste. 600, Washington, DC 20006, (202)393-6100

Natl. Petroleum Refiners Assn. [★2939]

Natl. Pharmaceutical Alliance [★2975]

Natl. Pharmaceutical Assn. [15947], 107 Kilmayne Dr., Ste. C, Cary, NC 27511, (800)944-NPHA

Natl. Pharmaceutical Assn. [★IO]

Natl. Pharmaceutical Coun. [2978], 1894 Preston White Dr., Reston, VA 20191-5433, (703)620-6390

Natl. Pharmaceutical Direct Advertising Assn. - Defunct.

Natl. Pharmaceutical Found. - Address unknown since 1990.

Natl. Pharmacies' Assn. [IO], Lisbon, Portugal

Natl. Pharmacy Assn. [IO], St. Albans, United Kingdom

Natl. Pharmacy Insurance Coun. - Defunct.

Natl. Philatelic Soc. [IO], London, United Kingdom

Natl. Philatelic Soc. - Defunct.

Natl. Phlebotomy Assn. [14796], 1901 Brightseat Rd., Landover, MD 20785, (301)386-4200

Natl. Phobics Soc. [IO], Manchester, United Kingdom

Natl. Photographic Dealers Assn. [★IO]

Natl. Photographic Dealers Assn. [★3009]

Natl. Photography Instructors Assn. [8973], 1255 Hill Dr., Eagle Rock, CA 90041, (323)254-1549

Natl. Phyllis Diller Fan Club [24799]

Natl. Physicians Alliance [16009], 1902 Assn. Dr., Ste. 200, Reston, VA 20191, (703)254-8972

Natl. Physicians Assn. [16010], PO Box 35215, Chicago, IL 60707-0215, (708)453-0080

Natl. Piano Found. [8927], 5960 W Parker Rd., Ste. 278, No. 233, Plano, TX 75093-7792, (972)625-0110

Natl. Piano Mfrs. Assn. of Am. [★2821]

Natl. Piano Mfrs. Assn. of Am. [★IO]

Natl. Piano Travelers Assn. - Address unknown since 2001.

Natl. Pickle Packers Assn. [★1557]

Natl. Pickle Packers Assn. [★IO]

Natl. Piers Soc. [IO], Benfleet, United Kingdom

Natl. Pig Carvers Assn. [22169]

Natl. Pigeon Assn. [21856], c/o Stephen St. Clair, Co-Sec.-Treas., 1717 SE 43rd Terr., Topeka, KS 66609-1728, (785)267-5732

Natl. Pigeon Assn. - Defunct.

Natl. Piggly Wiggly Operators Assn. [3422], Piggly Wiggly, LLC, 2605 Sagebrush Dr., Ste. 200, Flower Mound, TX 75028-2739, (972)906-7191

Natl. Pilots Assn. - Defunct.

Natl. Pinochle Bugs Social and Civic Club [13055], c/o Millie Boatright, Prog. Chair, 5201 Arlington St., Philadelphia, PA 19131, (215)477-3617

Natl. Pipeline Reform Coalition - Defunct.

Natl. Pitching Assn. [23121], PO Box 2350, Del Mar, CA 92014, (866)977-4824

Natl. Pituitary Agency [★16021]

Natl. Pizza and Pasta Assn. - Address unknown since 2003.

A Natl. Plan for Arts in Small Communities - Defunct.

Natl. Planning Assn. [★5593]

Natl. Plant Bd. [5440], c/o Aurelio Posadas, PO Box 847, Elk Grove, CA 95759, (916)709-3484

Natl. Plant, Flower and Fruit Guild - Address unknown since 1995.

Natl. Plant Food Inst. [★1365]

Natl. Plastercraft Assn. [1913], 0465 N 300 E, Albion, IN 46701, (219)636-7552

Natl. Plasterers Coun. [3043], 2811-D Tamiami Trail, Port Charlotte, FL 33952, (941)766-0634

Natl. Plastics Indus. Assn. [IO], Mexico City, Mexico

Natl. Playing Fields Assn. [★IO]

Natl. Playwrights Conf. [★11039]

Natl. Pledge of Allegiance Found. [21241]

Natl. Plott Hound Assn. - Address unknown since 1995.

Natl. Pocket Billiard Assn. - Defunct.

Natl. Podiatric Medical Assn. [16047], 1706 E 87th St., Chicago, IL 60617, (773)374-5300

Natl. Podiatry Assn. [★16047]

Natl. Poetry Day Comm. - Defunct.

Natl. Poetry Found. [10866], c/o Univ. of Maine, 5752 Neville Hall, Rm. 400, Orono, ME 04469-5752, (207)581-3814

Natl. Poison Center Network - Defunct.

Natl. Poker Assn. [22900]

Natl. Police Accountability Proj. [6174], 14 Beacon St., Ste. 701, Boston, MA 02108, (617)227-6015

Natl. Police Athletic League [★13496]

Natl. Police Bloodhound Assn. [6000]

Natl. Police Constables Assn. [★5992]

Natl. Police and Fire Fighters Assn. [★5962]

Natl. Police Officers Assn. of Am. [6001], c/o Natl. Police and Security Officers Assn. of Am., PO Box 663, South Plainfield, NJ 07080-0663, (908)226-8715

Natl. Policewomen Information Center - Defunct.

Natl. Policy Assn. [5593]

Natl. Policy; Center for [18428]

Natl. Political Button Exchange - Defunct.

Natl. Political Cong. of Black Women [★6119]

Natl. Pollution Control Found. - Address unknown since 1995.

Natl. Pollution Prevention Roundtable [5098], 11 Dupont Cir. NW, Ste. 201, Washington, DC 20036, (202)299-9701

Natl. Polymer Clay Guild [22579], PMB 345, 1350 Beverly Rd., 115, McLean, VA 22101

Natl. Pond Soc. - Address unknown since 2008.

Natl. Pony Soc. [IO], Alton, United Kingdom

Natl. Poodle Assn. - Defunct.

A star before a book entry number signifies that the name is not listed separately, but is mentioned within the entry.

Natl. Pop Can Collectors [22085], c/o Lance Meade, Treas., 335 Dellwood St. S, Cambridge, MN 55008

Natl. Pork Coun. Women [★5238]

Natl. Pork Producers Coun. [5238], 122 C St. NW, Ste. 875, Washington, DC 20001, (202)347-3600

Natl. Poro Beautician Assn. - Defunct.

Natl. Portage Assn. [IO], Yeovil, United Kingdom

Natl. Portraiture Assn. [IO], London, United Kingdom

Natl. Post Off. Mail Handlers, Watchmen, Messengers, and Gp. Leaders [★24171]

Natl. Postal Arts Assn. [22139]

Natl. Postal Comm. for Educational and Cultural Materials - Defunct.

Natl. Postal Forum [6179], 3998 Fair Ridge Dr., Ste. 300, Fairfax, VA 22033, (703)218-5015

Natl. Postal Mail Handlers Union [24171], 1101 Connecticut Ave. NW, Ste. 500, Washington, DC 20036-4325, (202)833-9095

Natl. Postdoctoral Assn. [9064], 1200 New York Ave. NW, Ste. 635, Washington, DC 20005, (202)326-6424

Natl. Postsecondary Agricultural Student Org. [7941], PO Box 68960, Indianapolis, IN 46278-1370, (317)802-4214

The Natl. Potato Bd. [★4770]

Natl. Potato Chip Inst. [★1562]

Natl. Potato Coun. [4746], 1300 L St. NW, No. 910, Washington, DC 20005-4107, (202)682-9456

Natl. Potato Promotion Bd. [★4770]

Natl. Potato Res. and Education Found. - Defunct.

Natl. Potter Syndrome Support Gp. [16544], c/o Delores Schlegel, 8221 Township Rd. 323, Holmesville, OH 44633, (330)279-4374

Natl. Poultry, Butter and Egg Assn. - Defunct.

Natl. Poultry and Food Distributors Assn. [1551], 958 McEver Rd. Extension, Unit B-8, Gainesville, GA 30504, (770)535-9901

Natl. Poultry Improvement Plan [5112], 1498 Klondike Rd., Ste. 101, Conyers, GA 30094-5169, (770)922-3496

Natl. Poultry Producers Fed. - Defunct.

Natl. Poultry Union [IO], Rome, Italy

Natl. PR1ME User Group - Defunct.

Natl. Prairie Grouse Technical Coun. - Address unknown since 2001.

Natl. Precast Concrete Assn. [930], 10333 N Meridian St., Ste. 272, Indianapolis, IN 46290-1081, (317)571-9500

Natl. Precast Concrete Assn. Australia [IO], Summer Hill, Australia

Natl. Precinct Workers - Defunct.

Natl. Precure Retread Dealers Assn. - Defunct.

Natl. Prefab. Building Assn. [★IO]

Natl. Premium Mfrs. Representatives [★2536]

Natl. Prepared Food Assn. - Address unknown since 2004.

Natl. Presbyterian Hea. and Welfare Assn. [★13184]

Natl. Preservation Inst. [10048], PO Box 1702, Alexandria, VA 22313, (703)765-0100

Natl. Preservers Assn. [★1530]

Natl. Preservers Assn. [★IO]

Natl. Press Club [3141], Natl. Press Bldg., 529 14th St. NW, 13th Fl., Washington, DC 20045, (202)662-7500

Natl. Press Found. [3142], 1211 Connecticut Ave. NW, Ste. 310, Washington, DC 20036, (202)663-7280

Natl. Press Photographers Assn. [3005], 3200 Croasdaile Dr., Ste. 306, Durham, NC 27705-2588, (919)383-7246

Natl. Pressure Ulcer Advisory Panel [14657], 1255 23rd St. NW, Ste. 200, Washington, DC 20037, (202)521-6789

Natl. Pretzel Bakers Inst. - Defunct.

Natl. Printing Equip. Assn. [★1782]

Natl. Printing Equip. and Supply Assn. [★1782]

National Printing Ink Res. Institute [★1803]

Natl. Priorities Proj. [17511], 17 New South St., Ste. 302, Northampton, MA 01060, (413)584-9556

Natl. Prison Assn. [★11854]

Natl. Prison Hospice Assn. [14858], PO Box 4623, Boulder, CO 80306-4623, (303)447-8051

Natl. Prison Proj. of the ACLU [11883], 915 15th St. NW, 7th Fl., Washington, DC 20005, (202)393-4930

Natl. Private Court Div. Paralegal Inst. - Defunct.

Natl. Private Duty Assn. [14842], 941 E 86th St., Ste. 270, Indianapolis, IN 46240, (317)663-3637

Natl. Private Truck Coun. [3881], 950 N Gelebe Rd., Ste. 530, Arlington, VA 22203-4183, (703)683-1300

Natl. Private Trucking Assn. [★3881]

Natl. Privy Diggers Assn. - Defunct.

Natl. Pro-Family Coalition - Address unknown since 1995.

Natl. Pro-Life Democrats - Address unknown since 2003.

Natl. Pro-Life Information Service - Defunct.

Natl. Pro-Life Political Action Comm. - Defunct.

Natl. Pro-Life Religious Coun. [18560], PO Box 61838, Staten Island, NY 10306, (718)980-4400

Natl. Probation Assn. [★11843]

Natl. Probation and Parole Assn. [★11843]

Natl. Proctologic Assn. - Defunct.

Natl. Product Liability Coun. - Defunct.

Natl. Productivity Coun. [IO], New Delhi, India

Natl. Professional Anglers' Assn. [23420], c/o Mr. Cody Roswick, Dir., 4030 Sheyenne Valley Estates, Valley City, ND 58072, (701)845-0381

Natl. Professional Colorists of Am. [★2990]

Natl. Professional Honorary Agricultural Educ. Fraternity [★24394]

Natl. Professional Soccer League - Address unknown since 2003.

Natl. Professional Squash Racquets Assn. - Address unknown since 1995.

Natl. Prog. for Playground Safety [18578], Scholarship of HPELS, WRC 205, Univ. of Northern Iowa, Cedar Falls, IA 50614-0618, (800)554-PLAY

Natl. Progress Assn. for Economic Development - Defunct.

Natl. Progress; Found. for [18446]

Natl. Progressive Broadcast Coalition - Defunct.

Natl. Progressive Consumers Alliance - Address unknown since 2002.

Natl. Propane Gas Assn. [1681], 1150 17th St. NW, Ste. 310, Washington, DC 20036-4623, (202)466-7200

Natl. Property Mgt. Assn. [3190], 28100 US Hwy. 19 N, Ste. 400, Clearwater, FL 33761, (727)736-3788

Natl. Prostate Cancer Coalition [13856], 1154 15th St. NW, Washington, DC 20005, (202)463-9455

Natl. and Provincial Parks Assn. of Canada [★IO]

Natl. Prune Juice Packers Assn. - Defunct.

Natl. Psoriasis Found. [★14203]

Natl. Psoriasis Found. [★IO]

Natl. Psoriasis Foundation/USA [14209], 6600 SW 92nd Ave., Ste. 300, Portland, OR 97223-7195, (503)244-7404

Natl. Psychic Science Assn. - Address unknown since 1999.

Natl. Psychological Assn. - Defunct.

Natl. Psychological Assn. for Psychoanalysis [16111], 150 W 13th St., New York, NY 10011-7891, (212)924-7440

Natl. PTA - Natl. Cong. of Parents and Teachers [8954], 541 N Fairbanks Ct., Ste. 1300, Chicago, IL 60611-3396, (312)670-6782

Natl. Public Affairs Center for TV - Defunct.

Natl. Public Employee Union Information Center [★24076]

Natl. Public Employer Labor Relations Assn. [5918], 1012 S Coast Hwy., Ste. M, Oceanside, CA 92054, (760)433-1686

Natl. Public Housing Conf. [★12325]

Natl. Public Interest Res. Group - Defunct.

Natl. Public Law Training Center - Address unknown since 1995.

Natl. Public Parks Tennis Assn. [23906], c/o USTA Northern, 1001 W 98th St., No. 101, Bloomington, MN 55431, (952)887-5001

Natl. Public Radio [9765], 635 Massachusetts Ave. NW, Washington, DC 20001, (202)513-2000

Natl. Public Records Res. Assn. [2107], 2501 Aerial Center Pkwy., Ste. 103, Morrisville, NC 27560, (919)459-2078

Natl. Public Relations Roundtable - Defunct.

Natl. Public School ABC Prog. [★8321]

Natl. Publishers Assn. [★3235]

Natl. Puerto Rican Business and Marketing Assn. - Defunct.

Natl. Puerto Rican Coalition [18491], 1901 L St. NW, Ste. 802, Washington, DC 20036, (202)223-3915

Natl. Puerto Rican Coalition [IO], Washington, DC, United States

Natl. Puerto Rican Forum [12280], 1910 Webster Ave., Bronx, NY 10457, (718)466-3992

Natl. Puerto Rican Women's Caucus - Defunct.

Natl. Purchasing Inst. [3266], PO Box 370192, Las Vegas, NV 89137-0192, (702)989-8095

Natl. Puzzlers' League [22469], c/o Joseph J. Adamski, Treas., 2507 Almar St., Jenison, MI 49428

Natl. Pygmy Goat Assn. [4142], 1932 149th Ave. SE, Snohomish, WA 98290, (425)334-6506

Natl. Pyrotechnic Distributors Assn. [★3267]

Natl. Qigong (Chi Kung) Assn. [13644], PO Box 252, Lakeland, MN 55043, (888)815-1893

Natl. QSS Dealers Assn. - Defunct.

Natl. Quality Forum [14658], 601 13th St. NW, Ste. 500 N, Washington, DC 20005, (202)783-1300

Natl. Quality Forum and Natl. Comm. for Quality Hea. Care [★14658]

Natl. Quarter Horse Registry [4922], PO Box 716, New Harmony, UT 84757-0716, (435)251-7224

Natl. Quarter Pony Assn. [4923], 3232 U.S. 42 S, Delaware, OH 43015

Natl. Quartz Producers Coun. [3698], PO Box 1719, Wheat Ridge, CO 80034, (303)432-0044

Natl. Quilting Assn. [22170], PO Box 12190, Columbus, OH 43212-0190, (614)488-8520

Natl. Racquetball Assn. of the Deaf - Address unknown since 2001.

Natl. Racquetball Club - Defunct.

Natl. Radiator Core Mfg. Credit Assn. [★1422]

Natl. Radiator Mfg. Credit Assn. [★1422]

National Radio Astronomy Observatory [★7622]

Natl. Radio Broadcasters Assn. [★569]

Natl. Radio Club - Defunct.

Natl. Radio Heritage Assn. - Defunct.

Natl. Radio Parts Distributors [★1223]

Natl. Railroad Constr. and Maintenance Assn. [3287], 500 New Jersey Ave. NW, Ste. 400, Washington, DC 20001, (202)715-2920

Natl. Railroad Freight Comm. - Address unknown since 1999.

Natl. Railroad Intermodal Assn. - Defunct.

Natl. Railroad Pension Forum - Defunct.

Natl. Railway Historical Soc. [10915], 100 N 17th St., Ste. 1203, Philadelphia, PA 19103-2767, (215)557-6606

Natl. Railway Labor Conf. [3288], 1901 L St. NW, Ste. 500, Washington, DC 20036, (202)862-7200

Natl. Ramah Commn. [8697], 3080 Broadway, New York, NY 10027, (212)678-8881

Natl. Ramah Commn. [IO], New York, NY, United States

Natl. Rare Blood Club - Defunct.

Natl. Reading Conf. [9044], 7044 S 13th St., Oak Creek, WI 53154, (414)908-4924

Natl. Reading Coun. - Address unknown since 1995.

Natl. Ready Mixed Concrete Assn. [931], 900 Spring St., Silver Spring, MD 20910, (301)587-1400

Natl. Real Estate Investors Assn. [2347], 525 W 5th St., Ste. 230, Covington, KY 41011, (859)261-3335

Natl. Realty Club - Address unknown since 2001.

Natl. Reamer Collectors Assn. [22609], c/o Pat Carberry, 4612 Charles Pl., Plano, TX 75093

Natl. Rebel Class Assn. - Address unknown since 1999.

Natl. Reciprocal and Family Support Enforcement Assn. [★5701]

Natl. Reclamation Assn. [★7838]

Natl. Records Mgt. Coun. - Defunct.

Natl. Recovery and Collection Assn. - Defunct.

Natl. Recreation Assn. of Japan [IO], Tokyo, Japan

Natl. Recreation and Park Assn. [6161], 22377 Belmont Ridge Rd., Ashburn, VA 20148-4501, (703)858-0784

Natl. Recreational Vehicle Owners Club [22960], Jack's Br. Rd., PO Box 520, Gonzalez, FL 32560-0520, (850)937-8354

Natl. Recycling Coalition [4000], 805 15th St. NW, Ste. 425, Washington, DC 20005, (202)789-1430

Natl. Recycling Policy; Assn. for a [★4000]

Natl. Red Cherry Inst. [★4723]

Natl. Redbone Coonhound Assn. - Address unknown since 1995.

Reference to "IO" in place of a book number signifies that the association may be found in the 45th edition of International Organizations.

Natl. Referral Center - Defunct.

Natl. Reform Assn. **[20485]**, PO Box 8741-WP, Pittsburgh, PA 15221

Natl. Refrigeration Contractors Assn. - Defunct.

Natl. Refuse Sack Coun. - Defunct.

Natl. Regap Network **[1193]**, PO Box 454, Cary, IL 60013-0454, (847)217-1836

Natl. Register Assn. **[★11140]**

Natl. Register Assn. **[★IO]**

Natl. Register of Hea. Ser. Providers in Psychology **[16161]**, 1120 G St. NW, Ste. 330, Washington, DC 20005, (202)783-7663

Natl. Register of Hypnotherapists and Psychotherapists **[IO]**, Nelson, United Kingdom

Natl. Register of Personal Fitness Trainers **[★IO]**

Natl. Register of Personal Trainers **[IO]**, Marlow, United Kingdom

Natl. Register of Prominent Americans and Intl. Notables **[IO]**, Washington, DC, United States

Natl. Register of Prominent Americans and Intl. Notables **[11140]**, Drawer 1375, Washington, DC 20013-1375, (301)565-5155

Natl. Register of Warranted Builders **[IO]**, London, United Kingdom

Natl. Registration Center for Stud. Abroad **[IO]**, Milwaukee, WI, United States

Natl. Registration Center for Stud. Abroad **[8626]**, PO Box 1393, Milwaukee, WI 53201, (414)278-0631

Natl. Registry of Ambulatory Surgical Facilities - Defunct.

Natl. Registry of Certified Chemists **[13939]**, c/o Gilbert E. Smith, PhD, Exec. Dir., 927 S Walter Reed Dr., No. 11, Arlington, VA 22204, (703)979-9001

Natl. Registry in Clinical Chemistry **[★13939]**

Natl. Registry of Emergency Medical Technicians **[14342]**, Rocco V. Morando Bldg., 6610 Busch Blvd., PO Box 29233, Columbus, OH 43229, (614)888-4484

Natl. Registry of Environmental Professionals **[4593]**, PO Box 2099, Glenview, IL 60025, (847)724-6631

Natl. Registry of Environmental Professionals **[IO]**, Glenview, IL, United States

Natl. Registry for Librarians - Defunct.

Natl. Registry of Medical Secretaries - Defunct.

National Registry of Microbiologists **[★6559]**

National Registry of Microbiologists **[★IO]**

Natl. Registry of Professional Interpreters and Translators for the Deaf **[★14778]**

Natl. Registry of Willys - Knight Automobiles **[★21819]**

Natl. Registry of Willys - Knight Automobiles **[★IO]**

Natl. Rehabilitation Admin. Assn. **[★16325]**

Natl. Rehabilitation Assn. **[16330]**, 633 S Washington St., Alexandria, VA 22314, (703)836-0850

Natl. Rehabilitation Counseling Assn. **[16331]**, PO Box 4480, Manassas, VA 20108, (703)361-2077

Natl. Rehabilitation Info. Center **[16332]**, 8201 Corporate Dr., Ste. 600, Landover, MD 20785, (301)459-5900

Natl. Rehabilitation and Service Found. - Address unknown since 2003.

Natl. Rehabilitation Training Inst. - Defunct.

Natl. Reined Cow Horse Assn. **[22586]**, 13181 US Hwy. 177, Byars, OK 74831, (580)759-4949

Natl. Reining Horse Assn. **[4924]**, 3000 NW 10th St., Oklahoma City, OK 73107-5302, (405)946-7400

National Reining Horse Association **[IO]**, Oklahoma City, OK, United States

Natl. Relief Network **[12873]**, PO Box 125, Greenville, MI 48838-0125, (616)225-2525

Natl. Religious Affairs Assn. **[19872]**, PO Box 77075, Washington, DC 20013-7075

Natl. Religious Broadcasters **[19539]**, 9510 Tech. Dr., Manassas, VA 20110, (703)330-7000

Natl. Religious Broadcasters **[IO]**, Manassas, VA, United States

Natl. Religious Liberty Assn. **[★IO]**

Natl. Religious Liberty Assn. **[★18512]**

Natl. Religious Partnership for the Env. **[19941]**, 49 S Pleasant St., Ste. 301, Amherst, MA 01002, (413)253-1515

Natl. Religious Publicity Coun. **[★20483]**

Natl. Religious Vocation Conf. **[19692]**, 5401 S Cornell Ave., Ste. 207, Chicago, IL 60615-5604, (773)363-5454

Natl. Reloading Mfrs. Assn. **[1481]**, 1 Centerpointe Dr., Ste. 550, Lake Oswego, OR 97035

Natl. Remodelers Assn. **[★643]**

Natl. Remotivation Technique Org. **[★16226]**

Natl. Remotivation Therapy Org. **[16226]**, PO Box 440, York Harbor, ME 03911, (207)363-7577

Natl. Renal Administrators Assn. **[15072]**, 100 N 20th St., 4th Fl., Philadelphia, PA 19103, (215)320-4655

Natl. Renderers Assn. **[2858]**, 801 N Fairfax St., Ste. 205, Alexandria, VA 22314-1776, (703)683-0155

Natl. Rental Housing Coun. **[★3332]**

Natl. Rental Ser. Assn. **[★3377]**

Natl. Rep/Wholesaler Assn. - Address unknown since 2004.

Natl. Repertory Theatre Found. - Defunct.

Natl. Reprographic Centre for Documentation **[★IO]**

Natl. Republican Club **[18526]**, 300 1st St. SE, Washington, DC 20003, (202)484-4590

Natl. Republican Coalition for Choice - Address unknown since 1999.

Natl. Republican Congressional Comm. **[18527]**, 320 1st St. SE, Washington, DC 20003, (202)479-7000

Natl. Republican Found. - Address unknown since 1988.

Natl. Republican Heritage Groups Nationalities Coun. - Address unknown since 1999.

Natl. Republican Inst. for Intl. Affairs **[★17396]**

Natl. Republican Inst. for Intl. Affairs **[★IO]**

Natl. Republican Senatorial Comm. **[18528]**, c/o Ronald Reagan Republican Center, 425 2nd St. NE, Washington, DC 20002, (202)675-6000

National Republican Senatorial Inner Circle **[★18528]**

Natl. Res. Coun. **[7621]**, c/o Natl. Acad. of Sciences, 500 5th St. NW, Washington, DC 20001, (202)334-2000

Natl. Res. Coun. **[IO]**, Rome, Italy

Natl. Res. Coun. **[★IO]**

Natl. Res. Coun. **[★IO]**

Natl. Res. Coun. of Canada **[IO]**, Ottawa, ON, Canada

Natl. Res. Coun. for Health - Address unknown since 2003.

Natl. Res. Coun. on Peace Strategy - Address unknown since 1999.

Natl. Res. Coun. of the Philippines **[IO]**, Taguig, Philippines

Natl. Res. Council's Inst. for Res. in Constr. **[IO]**, Ottawa, ON, Canada

Natl. Res. Found. **[IO]**, Pretoria, Republic of South Africa

Natl. Res. Found. for Business Statistics - Address unknown since 1995.

Natl. Res. Found. for Fertility - Address unknown since 1990.

Natl. Resident Matching Prog. **[8872]**, 2450 N St. NW, Washington, DC 20037-1118, (202)828-0566

Natl. Residential Appraisers Inst. **[3333]**, 2001 Cooper Foster Park Rd., Amherst, OH 44001, (440)282-7925

Natl. Resistance Comm. - Address unknown since 1994.

National Rsrc. Center **[★5594]**

Natl. Rsrc. Center for Consumers of Legal Services **[★6022]**

Natl. Rsrc. Center for Consumers of Legal Services **[★IO]**

Natl. Rsrc. Center for Hea. and Safety in Child Care **[★11536]**

Natl. Rsrc. Center for Hea. and Safety in Child Care and Early Educ. **[11536]**, c/o UCHSC at Fitzsimons, Campus Mail Stop F541, PO Box 6508, Aurora, CO 80045-0508, (303)724-0658

Natl. Rsrc. Center on Homelessness and Mental Illness **[12298]**, c/o The CDM Gp., 7500 Old Georgetown Rd., Ste. 900, Bethesda, MD 20814, (301)654-6740

Natl. Rsrc. Center for Paraprofessionals in Educ. and Related Services **[9150]**, Utah State Univ., 6526 Old Main Hill, Logan, UT 84322-6526, (435)797-4242

Natl. Rsrc. Center for Paraprofessionals in Educ. and Related Services **[★9150]**

Natl. Rsrc. Center for Paraprofessionals in Special Educ. and Related Human Services **[★9150]**

Natl. Rsrc. Center for Youth Services **[11639]**, 4502 E 41st St., Bldg. 4W, Tulsa, OK 74135-2512, (918)660-3700

Natl. Rsrc. and Info. Center **[18814]**, U.S. Dept. of Labor, 200 Constitution Ave. NW, Rm. S-3002, Washington, DC 20210-0002, (202)693-6710

Natl. Resource Inst. on Children and Youth with Handicaps - Defunct.

Natl. Resource Network - Defunct.

Natl. Respiratory Disease Conf. **[★16357]**

Natl. Restaurant Assn. **[1959]**, 1200 17th St. NW, Washington, DC 20036, (202)331-5900

Natl. Restaurant Assn. Educational Found. **[1960]**, 175 W Jackson Blvd., Ste. 1500, Chicago, IL 60604-2702, (312)715-1010

Natl. Restaurant Assn. Financial Officers - Defunct.

Natl. Restaurant Assn. Foodservice Purchasing Managers Group - Defunct.

Natl. Restaurant Assn. Foodservice Security Coun. - Defunct.

Natl. Restaurant Assn. Labor Relations Group - Defunct.

Natl. Restaurant Assn. Large Independent Operators - Defunct.

Natl. Restaurant Assn. Mgt. Information Services - Defunct.

Natl. Restaurant Assn. Market Research Group - Defunct.

Natl. Restaurant Assn. Marketing Executives Group - Defunct.

Natl. Restaurant Assn. Multi-Unit Architects, Engineers and Constr. Officers **[1050]**, c/o Natl. Restaurant Assn., 1200 17th St. NW, Washington, DC 20036, (202)973-3678

Natl. Restaurant Assn. Quality Assurance Study Group **[16385]**, c/o Natl. Restaurant Assn., 1200 17th St. NW, Washington, DC 20036, (202)331-5900

Natl. Restaurant Assn. Risk and Safety Managers - Defunct.

Natl. Restaurant Assn. Tax Executives - Defunct.

Natl. Resume Writers' Assn. **[4063]**, PO Box 475, Tuckahoe, NY 10707, (631)930-6287

National Resume Writers' Association **[IO]**, Tuckahoe, NY, United States

Natl. Resuscitation Soc. - Address unknown since 1995.

Natl. Retail Farm Equip. Assn. **[★185]**

Natl. Retail Fed. **[3423]**, 325 7th St. NW, Ste. 1100, Washington, DC 20004, (202)783-7971

Natl. Retail Floor Coverings Coun. - Defunct.

Natl. Retail Florists Assn. - Defunct.

Natl. Retail Furniture Assn. **[★1703]**

Natl. Retail Furniture Assn. **[★IO]**

Natl. Retail Grocers Secretaries Assn. **[★3405]**

Natl. Retail Hardware Assn. **[★1829]**

Natl. Retail Hobby Stores Assn. **[753]**, 214 N Hale St., Wheaton, IL 60187, (630)510-4596

Natl. Retail Hobby Stores Assn. **[IO]**, Wheaton, IL, United States

Natl. Retail Liquor Package Stores Assn. **[★193]**

Natl. Retail Lumber Dealers Assn. **[★1653]**

Natl. Retail Merchants Assn. **[★3423]**

Natl. Retail Pet Supply Assn. - Defunct.

Natl. Retail Sales Tax Alliance **[18696]**, 2897 N Druid Hills Rd., No. 258, Atlanta, GA 30329, (404)438-9832

Natl. Retail Tenants Assn. **[3383]**, 60 Shaker Rd., East Longmeadow, MA 01028-2760, (413)525-4565

Natl. Retinoblastoma Parents Group - Address unknown since 2001.

Natl. Retired Teachers Assn., Division of AARP **[9065]**, c/o Amer. Assn. of Retired Persons, 601 E St. NW, Washington, DC 20049, (202)434-2560

Natl. Retreat Assn. **[★IO]**

Natl. Retriever Club **[23386]**, 4379 S Howell Ave., Ste. 17, Milwaukee, WI 53207-5053, (414)481-2760

Natl. Reverse Mortgage Lenders Assn. **[2430]**, 1400 16th St. NW, Ste. 420, Washington, DC 20036, (202)939-1760

Natl. Review Bd. for the Center for Cultural and Technical Interchange Between East and West - Defunct.

A star before a book entry number signifies that the name is not listed separately, but is mentioned within the entry.

Natl. Rex Rabbit Club [5155], c/o Arlyse DeLoyola, Sec.-Treas., 117 Allegheny Ct., San Marcos, TX 78666, (512)392-6033

Natl. Reye's Syndrome Found. [16366], 426 N Lewis, PO Box 829, Bryan, OH 43506, (419)636-2679

Natl. Rheumatoid Arthritis Soc. [IO], Maidenhead, United Kingdom

Natl. Rice Growers' Assn. [IO], Bogota, Colombia

Natl. Rice Growers Assn. - Defunct.

Natl. Rice Producers' Assn. [IO], Lisbon, Portugal

Natl. Rick Nelson Fan Club - Address unknown since 2006.

Natl. Rifle Assn. [IO], Brookwood, United Kingdom

Natl. Rifle Assn. of Am. [23723], 11250 Waples Mill Rd., Fairfax, VA 22030, (703)267-1600

Natl. Rifle Assn. of New Zealand [IO], Upper Hutt, New Zealand

Natl. Rifle and Pistol Assn. of Ireland [IO], Blackrock, Ireland

Natl. Right to Life Comm. [12923], 512 10th St. NW, Washington, DC 20004, (202)626-8800

Natl. Right to Life Educational Trust Fund [18561], 512 10th St. NW, Washington, DC 20004, (202)626-8800

Natl. Right to Read Found. [9045], PO Box 560, Strasburg, VA 22657, (540)465-2349

Natl. Right to Work Comm. [17982], 8001 Braddock Rd., Ste. 500, Springfield, VA 22160, (703)321-9820

Natl. Right to Work Found. [★17983]

Natl. Right to Work Legal Defense and Educ. Found. [17983], 8001 Braddock Rd., Springfield, VA 22160, (703)321-8510

Natl. Right to Work Legal Defense Found. [★17983]

Natl. Right to Work Legal Defense Found; Concerned Educators Against Forced Unionism - A Special Proj. of the [17971]

Natl. Risk Retention Assn. [2225], 4248 Park Glen Rd., Minneapolis, MN 55416, (952)928-4656

Natl. Road Carriers [IO], Auckland, New Zealand

Natl. Road Runners Club [★23923]

Natl. Road Transport Assn. [IO], Rome, Italy

Natl. Roadside Vegetation Mgt. Assn. [4802], c/o John Reynolds, Exec. Dir., 5616 Lynchburg Cir., Hueytown, AL 35023, (205)491-7574

Natl. Rocket Club [★6377]

Natl. Roller Hockey Assn. of England [IO], Farnham, United Kingdom

Natl. Roller Hockey Assn. U.K. [★IO]

Natl. Roof Deck Contractors Assn. - Defunct.

Natl. Roofing Contractors Assn. [1051], 10255 W Higgins Rd., Ste. 600, Rosemont, IL 60018-5607, (847)299-9070

Natl. Roofing Educ. Found. [★8144]

Natl. Roofing Found. [8144], 10255 W Higgins Rd., Ste. 600, Rosemont, IL 60018-5607, (847)299-9070

Natl. Roommate Assn. [★12305]

Natl. Roque Assn. [★23090]

Natl. Rosacea Soc. [14210], 800 S Northwest Hwy., Ste. 200, Barrington, IL 60010

Natl. Rose O'Neill Club [★22399]

Natl. Rose O'Neill Club [★IO]

Natl. ROTC Band Assn. - Address unknown since 1995.

Natl. Rounders Assn. [IO], Sheffield, United Kingdom

Natl. Roundtable of State P2 Programs [★5098]

Natl. Rowing Found. [23702], c/o W. Hart Perry, Exec. Dir., 67 Mystic Rd., North Stonington, CT 06359, (860)535-0634

Natl. RSD Assistance Center - Address unknown since 2007.

Natl. Runaway Switchboard [12936], 3080 N Lincoln Ave., Chicago, IL 60657, (773)880-9860

Natl. Running Data Center - Defunct.

Natl. Rural Center - Defunct.

Natl. Rural Development Inst. - Address unknown since 1994.

Natl. Rural Economic Developers Assn. [18574], 100 E Grand Ave., Ste. 330, Des Moines, IA 50309, (515)284-1421

Natl. Rural Educ. Advocacy Coalition [9068], 22 S 22nd St., Harrisburg, PA 17104, (717)236-7180

Natl. Rural Educ. Assn. [9069], c/o Dr. Bob Mooney-ham, Exec. Dir., Univ. of Oklahoma, 112 4th St., Box 2, Norman, OK 73019, (405)325-7959

Natl. Rural Education Res. Consortium - Defunct.

Natl. Rural Elec. Cooperative Assn. [1194], 4301 Wilson Blvd., Arlington, VA 22203, (703)907-5500

Natl. Rural Elec. Cooperative Assn. [IO], Arlington, VA, United States

Natl. Rural Fellows [★18775]

Natl. Rural Fire Defense Comm. - Defunct.

Natl. Rural Hea. Assn. [16248], Administrative Off., 521 E 63rd St., Kansas City, MO 64110-3329, (816)756-3140

Natl. Rural Hea. Care Assn. [★16248]

Natl. Rural Housing Coalition [12332], 1250 Eye St. NW, Ste. 902, Washington, DC 20005, (202)393-5229

Natl. Rural Letter Carriers' Assn. [24172], 1630 Duke St., 4th Fl., Alexandria, VA 22314-3426, (703)684-5545

Natl. Rural Recruitment and Retention Network [14710], 2004 King St., La Crosse, WI 54601, (608)782-0660

Natl. Rural and Small Schools Consortium - Defunct.

Natl. Rural Utilities Cooperative Finance Corp. [1441], 2201 Cooperative Way, Herndon, VA 20171, (703)709-6700

Natl. Rural Water Assn. [12939], 2915 S 13th St., Duncan, OK 73533, (580)252-0629

Natl. RV Owners Club [★22960]

National RV Park and Campground Indus. Educ. Found. [★3357]

Natl. Saanen Breeders Assn. [4143], c/o Lisa Shep-ard, Sec.-Treas., PO Box 315, Santa Margarita, CA 93453, (805)461-5547

Natl. Saanen Club [★4143]

Natl. Saddleball Assn. - Address unknown since 1995.

Natl. Safe Boating Comm. [★12977]

Natl. Safe Boating Coun. [12977], c/o Virgil Chambers, Exec. Dir., PO Box 509, Bristow, VA 20136, (703)361-4294

Natl. Safe Boating Week Comm. [★12977]

Natl. Safe Deposit Advisory Coun. [★460]

Natl. Safe Kids Campaign [★11651]

Natl. Safe Skies Alliance [18748], McGhee Tyson Airport, 2057 Alcoa Hwy., Alcoa, TN 37701-3163, (865)970-0515

Natl. Safe Transit Assn. [★3571]

Natl. Safe Transit Assn. [★IO]

Natl. Safe Transit Comm. [★IO]

Natl. Safe Transit Comm. [★3571]

Natl. Safe Waterways and Seaports Alliance [18749], c/o McGhee Tyson Airport, 2057 Alcoa Hwy., Alcoa, TN 37701, (865)970-0515

Natl. Safe Workplace Institute/SafeSpaces.com [12978]

Natl. Safety Coun. [12979], 1121 Spring Lake Dr., Itasca, IL 60143-3201, (630)285-1121

Natl. Safety Coun. of Australia [IO], Malvern, Australia

Natl. Safety Coun. of Ireland [IO], Dublin, Ireland

Natl. Safety Coun. of Singapore [IO], Singapore, Singapore

Natl. Safety Mgt. Soc. [12980], PO Box 4460, Walnut Creek, CA 94596-0460, (800)321-2910

Natl. Safflower Coun. - Defunct.

Natl. Sailing Industry Assn. - Address unknown since 2001.

National Sales and Marketing Council [★1035]

Natl. Samuel de Champlain Soc. - Defunct.

Natl. Sanitary Supply Assn. [★2466]

Natl. Sanitary Supply Assn. [★IO]

Natl. Sanitation Found. [★IO]

Natl. Sanitation Found. [★16249]

Natl. Sash and Door Jobbers Assn. [★600]

Natl. Satellite Cable Assn. - Address unknown since 2003.

Natl. Save-a-Life League - Defunct.

Natl. Save the Family Farm Coalition [★16956]

Natl. Scale Men's Assn. [★4016]

Natl. Scale Men's Assn. [★IO]

Natl. Schizophrenia Fellowship [★IO]

Natl. Scholarship Providers Assn. [9074], 101 Monroe St., Denver, CO 80206, (720)941-4498

Natl. Scholarship Ser. and Fund for Negro Students [★8435]

Natl. Scholarship Ser. and Fund for Negro Students; Southeastern Regional Off. [8435]

Natl. Scholastic Press Assn. [9013], 2221 Univ. Ave. SE, Ste. 121, Univ. of Minnesota, Minneapolis, MN 55414, (612)625-8335

Natl. Scholastic Surfing Assn. [23880], PO Box 495, Huntington Beach, CA 92648, (714)378-0899

Natl. School-Age Care Alliance [★11528]

Natl. School Boards Assn. [9083], 1680 Duke St., Alexandria, VA 22314-3493, (703)838-6722

Natl. School Calendar Study Comm. - Address unknown since 1995.

Natl. School Curriculum Center for Educational Computing - Defunct.

Natl. School Development Coun. [8292], c/o Dr. John R. Sullivan, Jr., Sec.-Treas., 28 Lord Rd., No. 210, Marlborough, MA 01752, (508)481-9444

Natl. School Orchestra Assn. [★8904]

Natl. School Public Relations Assn. [9033], 15948 Derwood Rd., Rockville, MD 20855-2123, (301)519-0496

Natl. School Resource Network - Defunct.

Natl. School Safety Center [9088], 141 Duesenberg Dr., Ste. 11, Westlake Village, CA 91362-3480, (805)373-9977

Natl. School Sailing Assn. [IO], Windermere, United Kingdom

Natl. School Ser. Inst. [★3479]

Natl. School Supply and Equip. Assn. [3479], 8380 Colesville Rd., Ste. 250, Silver Spring, MD 20910, (301)495-0240

Natl. School Trans. Assn. [3882], 113 S West St., 4th Fl., Alexandria, VA 22314, (703)684-3200

Natl. School Yearbook/Newspaper Assn. - Defunct.

Natl. Schools Comm. for Economic Educ. [8218], 250 E 73rd St., Ste. 12G, New York, NY 10021-8641, (212)535-9534

Natl. Sci. Coun. [IO], Taipei, Taiwan

Natl. Sci. Educ. Leadership Assn. [9113], 2011 Holly Dr., Prescott, AZ 86305, (928)771-1030

Natl. Sci. Found. [7622], 4201 Wilson Blvd., Arlington, VA 22230, (703)292-5111

Natl. Sci. Supervisors Assn. [★9113]

Natl. Sci. Teachers Assn. [9114], 1840 Wilson Blvd., Arlington, VA 22201-3000, (703)243-7100

Natl. Sci. and Tech. Educ. Partnership [13126], 2500 Wilson Blvd., Ste. 300, Arlington, VA 22201-3834, (703)907-7400

Natl. Scoliosis Found. [16393], 5 Cabot Pl., Stough-ton, MA 02072-4624, (800)673-6922

Natl. Score Found. - Defunct.

Natl. Scouting Collectors Soc. - Defunct.

Natl. Scouts Assn. of Panama [IO], Panama City, Panama

Natl. Scrabble Assn. [22470], PO Box 700, 403 Front St., Greenport, NY 11944, (631)477-0033

Natl. Screw Machine Products Assn. [★1832]

Natl. Scrip Collectors Assn. - Address unknown since 2000.

Natl. Sculpture Soc. [10959], 237 Park Ave., New York, NY 10017, (212)764-5645

National Sea Grant Program [★7276]

Natl. Seafood Educators [3497], PO Box 60006, Seattle, WA 98160, (206)546-6410

Natl. Seasoning Mfrs. Assn. [1552], c/o Dr. Richard H. Alsmeyer, Exec. Dir., 2527 Mill Race Rd., Fred-erick, MD 21701, (301)694-0419

Natl. Secretarial Assn. [73], PO Box 35215, Chicago, IL 60707-0215, (708)453-0080

Natl. Secretaries Assn. (Intl.) [★66]

Natl. Secretaries Assn. (Intl.) [★IO]

Natl. Secular Soc. [IO], London, United Kingdom

Natl. Security; Bus. Executives for [18587]

Natl. Security Caucus Inst. - Address unknown since 1999.

Natl. Security; Center for New [17864]

Natl. Security Indus. Assn. [★6089]

Natl. Security Inspectorate [IO], Maidenhead, United Kingdom

Natl. Security Political Action Comm. - Defunct.

Natl. Security Stud; Center for [18588]

Natl. Security Task Force - Defunct.

Natl. Security Traders Assn. [★3525]

Natl. Selected Morticians [★2791]

Natl. Self Govt. Comm. - Address unknown since 1995.

Natl. Self-Help Action Center - Food Program - Address unknown since 1995.

Natl. Self-Help CH [13026], c/o Graduate School & Univ. Center of the City Univ. of New York, 365 5th Ave., Ste. 3300, New York, NY 10016, (212)817-1822

Natl. Self-Help Resource Center - Defunct.

Natl. Semi-Professional Baseball Assn. [23122], c/o Tim Turpin, Dir., 2609 Vista View Dr., Evansville, IN 47711, (812)430-2725

Natl. Senior Citizens Assn. - Address unknown since 1989.

Natl. Senior Citizens Law Center [11316], 1101 14th St. NW, Ste. 400, Washington, DC 20005, (202)289-6976

Natl. Senior Games Assn. [23655], PO Box 82059, Baton Rouge, LA 70884-2059, (225)766-6316

Natl. Senior Golf Assn. [23460], 3673 Nottingham Way, Hamilton Square, NJ 08690, (609)631-8145

Natl. Senior Service Corps Directors Assns. - Address unknown since 2002.

Natl. Senior Sports Assn. - Defunct.

Natl. Senior Women's Tennis Assn. [23907], PO Box 7115, West Palm Beach, FL 33405, (561)307-8026

Natl. Serials Data Prog. [10376], Lib. of Cong., 101 Independence Ave. SE, Washington, DC 20540-4160, (202)707-6452

Natl. Seriograph Soc. - Defunct.

Natl. Ser. Agencies [★12196]

Natl. Ser. Bd. for Religious Objectors [★17438]

Natl. Ser. Bd. for Religious Objectors [★IO]

Natl. Ser. Committee/Chariscenter USA [19693], PO Box 628, Locust Grove, VA 22508-0628, (540)972-0225

Natl. Ser. Dog Center [14774], c/o Delta Soc., 875 124th Ave. NW, Ste. 101, Bellevue, WA 98005, (425)679-5500

Natl. Service League - Address unknown since 1999.

Natl. Service-Learning CH [9092], c/o ETR Associates, 4 Carbonero Way, Scotts Valley, CA 95066, (831)438-4060

Natl. Service-Learning Partnership [9120], c/o Acad. for Educational Development, 1825 Connecticut Ave. NW, Ste. 800, Washington, DC 20009-5721, (202)884-8356

Natl. Ser. Org. - COSA [★13072]

Natl. Ser. Org. - COSA [★IO]

Natl. Ser. to Regional Councils [★6244]

Natl. Service Secretariat - Address unknown since 1999.

Natl. Service Star Legion - Address unknown since 2001.

Natl. Settlement Purchasers Assn. [★1439]

Natl. Sewerage Assn. [IO], New Malden, United Kingdom

Natl. Sex Forum [★16401]

Natl. Sex Information Network - Address unknown since 1999.

Natl. Sexual Violence Rsrc. Center [13080], 123 N Enola Dr., Enola, PA 17025, (717)909-0710

Natl. Shade Tree Evaluation [★5259]

Natl. Shade Tree Evaluation [★IO]

Natl. Sharecroppers Fund - Address unknown since 1995.

Natl. Shared Housing Rsrc. Center [12333], c/o Laura Fanucchi, Treas., 364 S Railroad Ave., San Mateo, CA 94401, (650)348-6660

Natl. Shared Housing Rsrc. Center [★12333]

Natl. Shaving Mug Collectors Assn. [22086], c/o Dick Leidlein, VP, 3443 Boston Twp Line Rd., Richmond, IN 47374, (765)935-7736

Natl. Sheep Assn. [IO], Malvern, United Kingdom

Natl. Sheet Music Soc. [10668]

Natl. Shelley China Club [22087], 591 W 67th Ave., Anchorage, AK 99518-1555, (907)562-2124

Natl. Shellfisheries Assn. [7255], c/o Linda Kallansrude, 14 Carter Ln., East Quogue, NY 11942, (631)653-6327

Natl. Shellfisheries Assn. [IO], Accomac, VA, United States

Natl. Sheriffs' Assn. [6002], 1450 Duke St., Alexandria, VA 22314-3490, (703)836-7827

Natl. Shiba Club of Am. [22320], c/o Sue Thomas, 1210 W Indian Hills Dr., No. 24, St. George, UT 84770-6376

Natl. Shippers Strategic Trans. Coun. [3578], 9382 Oak Ave., Waconia, MN 55387, (952)442-8850

Natl. Shipyard Assn. [★2592]

Natl. Shoe Retailers Assn. [1598], 7150 Columbia Gateway Dr., Ste. G, Columbia, MD 21046-1151, (410)381-8282

Natl. Shoe Traveler's Assn. - Address unknown since 2003.

Natl. Shooting Sports Found. [23724], Flintlock Ridge Off. Ctr., 11 Mile Hill Rd., Newtown, CT 06470-2359, (203)426-1320

Natl. Shorthand Reporters Assn. [★5630]

Natl. Show Horse Registry [4925], 10368 Bluegrass Pkwy., Louisville, KY 40299, (502)266-5100

Natl. Show Pig Assn. [22982], c/o Jeff Langemeier, Sec.-Treas., 8737 E 2700th Rd., Sidell, IL 61876, (217)493-8037

Natl. Showmen's Assn. - Address unknown since 2003.

Natl. Shrimp Breaders and Processors Assn. [★3498]

Natl. Shrimp Canners Assn. - Defunct.

Natl. Shrimp Cong. - Defunct.

Natl. Shrimp Indus. Assn. [3498], c/o Beth Dancy, 1520 Berkeley Rd., Highland Park, IL 60035, (847)831-2030

Natl. Shrimp Processors Assn. [★3498]

Natl. Shrine to the Jewish War Dead [★21312]

Natl. Shrine of St. Elizabeth Ann Seton [19694], Seton Shrine Center, 333 S Seton Ave., Emmitsburg, MD 21727, (301)447-6606

Natl. Shuffleboard Assn. - Address unknown since 2001.

Natl. Shut-In Day Soc. [★18651]

Natl. Shut-In Soc. - Address unknown since 1995.

Natl. Siamese Cat Club - Address unknown since 1994.

Natl. Sickle Cell Disease Res. Found. - Defunct.

Natl. SIDS/Infant Death Rsrc. Center [16526], 8280 Greensboro Dr., Ste. 300, McLean, VA 22102, (703)821-8955

Natl. Silo Assn. [★181]

Natl. Silo Assn. [★IO]

Natl. Silver Dollar Roundtable - Defunct.

Natl. Silver-Haired Cong. - Defunct.

Natl. Silver Rabbit Club [5156], c/o Laura Atkins, Sec.-Treas., 1030 SW KK Hwy., Holden, MO 64040, (816)732-6208

Natl. Single Parent Coalition [★12693]

Natl. Single Service Food Assn. - Defunct.

Natl. Singles Registry - Address unknown since 1991.

Natl. Sisters Vocation Conf. [★19692]

Natl. Sjogren's Syndrome Assn. [16373], PO Box 22066, Beachwood, OH 44122, (216)292-3866

Natl. Skeet Shooting Assn. [23725], 5931 Roft Rd., San Antonio, TX 78253, (210)688-3371

Natl. Ski Areas Assn. [1961], 133 S Van Gordon St., Ste. 300, Lakewood, CO 80228, (303)987-1111

Natl. Ski Assn. of Am. [★23760]

Natl. Ski Patrol Sys. [23753], 133 S Van Gordon St., Ste. 100, Lakewood, CO 80228, (303)988-1111

Natl. Ski Retailers Asso. [★3646]

Natl. Ski and Snowboard Retailers Assn. [3646], 1601 Feehanville Dr., Ste. 300, Mount Prospect, IL 60056-6035, (847)391-9825

Natl. Ski Study Group - Defunct.

Natl. Ski Touring Assn. [★23934]

Natl. Ski Touring Operators' Assn. [★3660]

Natl. Skin Cancer Found. [★13874]

Natl. Skirt and Sportswear Assn. [★254]

Natl. Slag Assn. [652], 25 Stevens Ave., Bldg. A, West Lawn, PA 19609, (610)670-0701

Natl. Slate Assn. - Address unknown since 1995.

Natl. Slavic Convention [19360], c/o Slavic Amer. Natl. Convention, 603 S Ann St., Baltimore, MD 21221, (410)276-7676

Natl. Sleep Found. [16428], 1522 K St. NW, Ste. 500, Washington, DC 20005, (202)347-3471

Natl. Slovak Soc. of the U.S.A. [19363], 351 Valley Brook Rd., McMurray, PA 15317-3337, (724)731-0094

Natl. Small-Bore Rifle Assn. [IO], Woking, United Kingdom

Natl. Small Bus. Assn. [3623], 1156 15th St. NW, Ste. 1100, Washington, DC 20005, (202)293-8830

Natl. Small Bus. Assn. [★3623]

Natl. Small Business Benefits Assn. - Defunct.

Natl. Small Business Govt. Contractors Assn. - Defunct.

Natl. Small Bus. United [★3623]

Natl. Small Coll. Athletic Assn. [★23859]

Natl. Small Sailing Yacht Assn. - Defunct.

Natl. Small Shipments Traffic Conf. [★3574]

Natl. Small Shipments Traffic Conf. [★3578]

Natl. Snaffle Bit Assn. [4926], 4845 S Sheridan, Ste. 515, Tulsa, OK 74145, (918)270-1469

Natl. Snapdragon Soc. - Defunct.

Natl. Snow Indus. Assn. [IO], Westmount, QC, Canada

Natl. Snurfing Assn. - Defunct.

Natl. Soaring Found. [23042], PO Box 684, Hobbs, NM 88240, (505)392-6032

Natl. Soccer Assn. - Address unknown since 1994.

Natl. Soccer Coaches Assn. of Am. [23779], 6700 Squibb Rd., Ste. 215, Mission, KS 66202-3252, (913)362-1747

Natl. Soccer League - Address unknown since 2001.

Natl. Social Sci. Honor Soc. [★24672]

Natl. Social Sci. Honor Soc. [★IO]

Natl. Social Science and Law Center - Address unknown since 1989.

Natl. Social Welfare Assembly [★13400]

Natl. Social Work Coun. [★13400]

National Socialism

New Order [18805]

Natl. Socialist Amer. Workers Freedom Movement [★18802]

Natl. Socialist Amer. Workers Freedom Movement [★IO]

National Socialist Movement [IO], Minneapolis, MN, United States

Natl. Socialist Movement [18802], PO Box 580669, Minneapolis, MN 55458-0669, (651)659-6307

Natl. Socialist Party of America - Defunct.

Natl. Socialist Union Green Political Party - Address unknown since 2002.

Natl. Socialist Vanguard [18803]

Natl. Socialist White Americans Party [★18798]

Natl. Socialist White Americans Party [★IO]

Natl. Socialist White People's Party [★IO]

Natl. Socialist White People's Party [★18805]

Natl. Soc. of Accountants [48], 1010 N Fairfax St., Alexandria, VA 22314, (703)549-6400

Natl. Soc. of Accountants for Cooperatives [49], 136 S Keowee St., Dayton, OH 45402, (937)222-6707

Natl. Soc. of Allied and Independent Funeral Directors [IO], Sawbridgeworth, United Kingdom

Natl. Soc. of Allotment and Leisure Gardeners [IO], Corby, United Kingdom

Natl. Soc. for Amer. Indian Elderly [19279], 200 E Filmore St., No. 151, Phoenix, AZ 85004, (602)424-0542

Natl. Soc. of Andersonville - Address unknown since 2003.

Natl. Soc. for Animal Protection - Address unknown since 1991.

Natl. Soc. of Appraiser Specialists [286], 303 W Cypress St., PO Box 12528, San Antonio, TX 78212-0528, (210)271-0781

Natl. Soc. of Architectural Administrators - Address unknown since 1999.

Natl. Soc. of Architectural Engineers [★6468]

Natl. Soc. of Architectural Engineers [★IO]

Natl. Soc. of Arkansas Pottery Collectors [22088], 2006 Beckenham Cove, Little Rock, AR 72212

Natl. Soc. of Art Directors - Address unknown since 1995.

Natl. Soc. for Art Educ. [★IO]

Natl. Soc. of Artists [9516], PO Box 1885, Dickinson, TX 77539-1885, (281)337-4232

Natl. Soc. of Arts and Letters [10201], 4227 46th St. NW, Washington, DC 20016, (202)363-5443

Natl. Soc. for Autistic Children [★13723]

Natl. Soc. of Black Engineers [7034], 205 Daingerfield Rd., Alexandria, VA 22314, (703)549-2207

Natl. Soc. of Black Physicists [7504], 6704G Lee Hwy., Arlington, VA 22205, (703)536-4207

A star before a book entry number signifies that the name is not listed separately, but is mentioned within the entry.

Natl. Soc. of Cardiology of the Former Yugoslav Republic of Macedonia [IO], Skopje, Macedonia

Natl. Soc. of Cardiopulmonary Technologists [★13885]

Natl. Soc. for Cardiopulmonary Tech. [★13885]

Natl. Soc. for Cardiovascular Tech. [★13885]

Natl. Soc. of Certified Healthcare Bus. Consultants [14711], 12100 Sunset Hills Rd., Ste. 130, Reston, VA 20190, (703)234-4099

Natl. Soc. of Certified Public Accountants - Address unknown since 1995.

Natl. Soc. of Chemotherapy of the Russian Fed. [IO], Moscow, Russia

Natl. Soc. of Chief Executive Officers - Defunct.

Natl. Soc. of the Children of the Amer. Revolution [20674], 1776 D St. NW, Rm. 224, Washington, DC 20006-5303, (202)638-3153

Natl. Soc. for Clean Air and Environmental Protection [IO], Brighton, United Kingdom

Natl. Soc. of Coll. Teachers of Educ. [★8307]

Natl. Soc. of Collegiate Scholars [9075], 1900 K St. NW, Ste. 890, Washington, DC 20006, (202)265-9000

Natl. Soc. of the Colonial Dames of Am. [20743], 2715 Que St. NW, Washington, DC 20007-3071, (202)337-2288

Natl. Soc. Colonial Dames XVII Century [20744], 1300 New Hampshire Ave. NW, Washington, DC 20036-1595, (202)293-1700

Natl. Soc. Colonial Daughters of the 17th Century [20745], c/o Mrs. Donald Zimmerman, PO Box 200, Harvel, IL 62538, (217)526-4530

Natl. Soc. of Compliance Professionals [1745], 22 Kent Rd., Cornwall Bridge, CT 06754, (860)672-0843

Natl. Soc. for Computer Applications in Engineering, Planning, and Architecture - Defunct.

Natl. Soc. of Computer/Genealogists - Defunct.

Natl. Soc. of Conservationists [IO], Budapest, Hungary

Natl. Soc. of Consulting Soil Scientists [5222], PO Box 1724, Sandpoint, ID 83864, (800)535-7148

Natl. Soc. of Controllers and Financial Officers of Savings Institutions [★1418]

Natl. Soc. of Cwens - Address unknown since 1995.

Natl. Soc. of Dames of the Court of Honor - Address unknown since 2002.

Natl. Soc., Daughters of the Amer. Colonists [20746], 2205 Massachusetts Ave. NW, Washington, DC 20008, (202)667-3076

Natl. Soc., Daughters of the Amer. Revolution [20675], 1776 D St. NW, Washington, DC 20006-5303, (202)628-1776

Natl. Soc., Daughters of the British Empire in the U.S.A. [18985], 3312 Edloe, Houston, TX 77027

Natl. Soc. Daughters of Founders and Patriots of America - Address unknown since 2000.

Natl. Soc. Daughters of the Revolution of 1776 - Defunct.

Natl. Soc. Daughters of Utah Pioneers [★21252]

Natl. Soc. Daughters of Utah Pioneers [★IO]

Natl. Soc. Descendants of Colonial Hispanics - Defunct.

Natl. Soc. Descendants of Early Quakers [21134], PO Box 453, Abingdon, MD 21009-0453, (301)262-1019

Natl. Soc. of Descendants of Lords of the Maryland Manors [20747]

Natl. Soc. for Educ. in Art and Design [IO], Corsham, United Kingdom

Natl. Soc. of Electronic Data Processing Machine Operators and Programmers - Defunct.

Natl. Soc. of Environmental Consultants [3334], PO Box 12528, San Antonio, TX 78212-0528, (210)271-0781

Natl. Soc. for Epilepsy [IO], Aylesbury, United Kingdom

Natl. Soc. for Experiential Educ. [8414], c/o Talley Mgt. Gp., Inc., 19 Mantua Rd., Mount Royal, NJ 08061, (856)423-3427

Natl. Soc. of Film Critics - Address unknown since 1995.

Natl. Soc. - First Families of Minnesota [21253]

Natl. Soc. of Fund Raisers [★12197]

Natl. Soc. of Fund Raising Executives [★12197]

Natl. Soc. of Genetic Counselors [14506], 401 N Michigan Ave., Ste. 2200, Chicago, IL 60611, (312)321-6834

Natl. Soc. for Graphology [11212], 250 W 57th St., Ste. 1228A, New York, NY 10107, (212)265-1148

Natl. Soc. of Guide Dog Users [★16850]

Natl. Soc. for Healthcare Foodservice Mgt. [1592], 355 Lexington Ave., 15th Fl., New York, NY 10017, (212)297-2166

Natl. Soc. of High School Scholars [9076], 1936 N Druid Hills Rd., Atlanta, GA 30319, (866)343-1800

Natl. Soc. of Hispanic MBAs [754], 1303 Walnut Hill Ln., Ste. 100, Irving, TX 75038, (214)596-9338

Natl. Soc. of Hispanic Physicists [7505], c/o David J. Ernst, Admin. Exec. Off., Vanderbilt Univ., Physics and Astronomy Dept., 1807 Sta. B, Nashville, TN 37235, (615)343-0483

Natl. Soc. for Hispanic Professionals [1908], 1835 NE Miami Gardens Dr., No. 33, Miami, FL 33179

Natl. Soc. for Histotechnology [15146], 10320 Little Patuxent Pkwy., Ste. 804, Columbia, MD 21044, (443)535-4060

Natl. Soc. of Hypnotherapists - Address unknown since 2001.

Natl. Soc. of Insurance Premium Auditors [2226], PO Box 1896, Columbus, OH 43216-1896, (888)846-7472

Natl. Soc. of Interior Designers [★2251]

Natl. Soc. for Internships and Experiential Educ. [★8414]

Natl. Soc. of Leadership and Success [9189], 50 Harrison St., Ste. 308, Hoboken, NJ 07030, (201)222-6544

Natl. Soc. of Lefton Collectors - Address unknown since 2003.

Natl. Soc. of Literature and the Arts - Defunct.

Natl. Soc. of Live Stock Record Associations [★4141]

Natl. Soc. of Madison Family Descendants [21135], c/o John F. Macon, Pres., PO Box 2272, Palm Springs, CA 92263, (760)408-2625

Natl. Soc. of Master Thatchers [IO], Oxford, United Kingdom

Natl. Soc. for Medical Res. [★13700]

Natl. Soc. of Mural Painters [9517], 450 W 31st St., 7th Fl., New York, NY 10001, (212)244-2800

Natl. Soc. of New England Women - Address unknown since 1995.

Natl. Soc. of Newspaper Columnists [3143], PO Box 411532, San Francisco, CA 94141, (415)722-7030

Natl. Soc. of Old Plymouth Colony Descendants - Address unknown since 1995.

Natl. Soc. of Painters in Casein and Acrylic [9518], 969 Catasauqua Rd., Whitehall, PA 18052, (610)264-7472

Natl. Soc. of Patient Representation and Consumer Affairs of the Amer. Hosp. Assn. [★15005]

Natl. Soc. of Patient Representatives of the Amer. Hosp. Assn. [★15005]

Natl. Soc. of Penal Info. [★11885]

Natl. Soc. for Performance and Instruction [★9252]

Natl. Soc. for Performance and Instruction [★IO]

Natl. Soc. of Pershing Rifles [24547], PO Box 25057, Baton Rouge, LA 70894

Natl. Soc. of Persons with disAbilities [IO], Kingstown, St. Vincent and the Grenadines

Natl. Soc. of Pharmaceutical Sales Trainers [★3475]

Natl. Soc. for Phenylketonuria [IO], London, United Kingdom

Natl. Soc. for the Preservation of Covered Bridges [10049], PO Box 267, Jericho, VT 05465-0267, (802)899-2093

Natl. Soc. to Prevent Blindness [★16882]

Natl. Soc. for the Prevention of Blindness [★16882]

Natl. Soc. for the Prevention of Cruelty to Children [IO], London, United Kingdom

Natl. Soc. for Prevention of Cruelty to Mushrooms - Address unknown since 1995.

Natl. Soc. of Professional Engineers [7035], 1420 King St., Alexandria, VA 22314-2794, (703)684-2800

Natl. Soc. of Professional Insurance Investigators [2227], PO Box 88, Delaware, OH 43015, (888)677-4498

Natl. Soc. of Professional Resident Managers - Address unknown since 1994.

Natl. Soc. of Professional Sanitarians - Defunct.

Natl. Soc. of Professional Surveyors [7719], 6 Montgomery Village Ave., Ste. 403, Gaithersburg, MD 20879-3557, (240)632-9716

Natl. Soc. for Programmed Instruction [★9252]

Natl. Soc. for Programmed Instruction [★IO]

Natl. Soc. for the Promotion of Occupational Therapy [★16602]

Natl. Soc. of Public Accountants [★48]

Natl. Soc. for Pulmonary Tech. [★13885]

National Soc. of Real Estate Appraisers [★3323]

Natl. Soc. for Real Estate Finance - Address unknown since 2003.

Natl. Soc. for Res. into Allergy [IO], Hinckley, United Kingdom

Natl. Soc. of Saint Vincent de Paul - Malaysia [IO], Petaling Jaya, Malaysia

Natl. Soc. of Sales Training Executives [★3472]

Natl. Soc. of Scabbard and Blade [24548], 1018 S Lewis St., Stillwater, OK 74074-4622, (405)377-2237

Natl. Soc. for Shut-Ins [18651]

Natl. Soc., Sons of the Amer. Colonists [20748], c/o Arthur Louis Finnell, Natl. Registrar, 7501 W 101th St., No. 204, Minneapolis, MN 55438-2521

Natl. Soc., Sons of the Amer. Revolution [20676], 1000 S 4th St., Louisville, KY 40203, (502)589-1776

Natl. Soc. Sons and Daughters of the Pilgrims - Defunct.

Natl. Soc. of the Sons of Utah Pioneers [21254], 3301 E 2920 S, Salt Lake City, UT 84109, (801)484-4441

Natl. Soc. of State Legislators [★6283]

Natl. Soc. of Stress Analysts [★5764]

Natl. Soc. of Stress Analysts [★IO]

Natl. Soc. of Student Film Critics - Defunct.

Natl. Soc. of Student Keyboardists - Address unknown since 2002.

Natl. Soc. for the Stud. of Commun. [★3748]

Natl. Soc. for the Stud. of Commun. [★IO]

Natl. Soc. for the Stud. of Educ. [8293], Univ. of Illinois at Chicago, Coll. of Educ. (M/C 147), 1040 W Harrison St., Chicago, IL 60607-7133, (312)996-4529

Natl. Soc. of Tole and Decorative Painters [★22175]

Natl. Soc., U.S. Daughters of 1812 [21355], 1461 Rhode Island Ave. NW, Washington, DC 20005-5402, (202)745-1812

Natl. Soc. for Vision and Perception Training [★15718]

Natl. Soc. for Vocational Educ. [★9300]

Natl. Soc. Women Descendants of the Ancient and Honorable Artillery Company [20749], c/o Mrs. Daniel P. Moroney, Pres. Gen., 49 Carriage Hill Dr., Windham, ME 04062-4927, (207)893-0175

Natl. Soda Dispensing Equip. Assn. [★507]

Natl. Soda Dispensing Equip. Assn. [★IO]

Natl. Soft Drink Assn. [★503]

Natl. Soft Drink Manufacturers' Assn. [IO], Madrid, Spain

National Soft Serve and Fast Food Association [★1958]

Natl. Soft Wheat Assn. [★2738]

Natl. Softball Assn. [23792], PO Box 7, Nicholasville, KY 40340, (859)887-4114

Natl. Sojourners [19246], 8301 E Boulevard Dr., Alexandria, VA 22308-1316, (703)765-5000

Natl. Solar Energy Education Campaign - Address unknown since 1995.

Natl. Solar Heating and Cooling [★6951]

Natl. Solid Waste Assn. of India [IO], Bombay, India

Natl. Solid Wastes Mgt. Assn. [3579], 4301 Connecticut Ave. NW, Ste. 300, Washington, DC 20008-2304, (202)244-4700

Natl. Sorghum Producers [4311], 4201 N Interstate 27, Lubbock, TX 79403-7507, (806)749-3478

Natl. Sorority of Phi Delta Kappa [24455], 8233 S King Dr., Chicago, IL 60619, (773)783-7379

Natl. Sound and Communications Assn. [★1225]

Natl. Soup Mix Assn. - Defunct.

Natl. South Asian Bar Assn. [6018], c/o Bharati Sharma, VP of Individual Membership, Schiffrin and Barroway, LLP, 280 King of Prussia Rd., Radnor, PA 19087, (484)270-1456

Reference to "IO" in place of a book number signifies that the association may be found in the 45th edition of International Organizations.

National Sovereignty

Armenian Revolutionary Fed. [18086]

Armenian Revolutionary Fed. [IO]

Armenian Youth Fed. - Youth Org. of the ARF [18087]

Assn. des Amis de la Republique Arabe Sahraouie Democratique [IO]

Australia Tibet Coun. [IO]

Escarre Intl. Center for the Ethnic Minorities and Nations [IO]

Israeli Coun. for Israeli-Palestinian Peace [IO]

Natl. Captive Nations Comm. [IO]

Natl. Captive Nations Comm. [18088]

Sovereignty Intl. [17873]

Natl. Sovereignty; Walter Bagehot Res. Coun. on [7528]

Natl. Soy Ink Info. Center - Defunct.

Natl. Soybean Crop Improvement Coun. - Defunct.

Natl. Soybean Processors Assn. [★2857]

Natl. Spa and Pool Inst. [★3353]

Natl. Spa and Pool Inst. [★IO]

Natl. Space Club [6377], 2025 M St. NW, Ste. 800, Washington, DC 20036-2422, (202)973-8661

Natl. Space Inst. [★6378]

Natl. Space Soc. [6378], 1620 I St. NW, Ste. 615, Washington, DC 20006, (202)429-1600

Natl. Space Soc. of Australia [IO], Sydney, Australia

Natl. Spasmodic Dysphonia Assn. [15352], 300 Park Blvd., Ste. 415, Itasca, IL 60143, (800)795-6732

Natl. Spasmodic Torticollis Assn. [15353], 9920 Talbert Ave., Fountain Valley, CA 92708, (714)378-9837

Natl. Speakers Assn. [10903], 1500 S Priest Dr., Tempe, AZ 85281, (480)968-2552

Natl. Speakers Assn. of Australia [IO], Adelaide, Australia

Natl. Speakers Assn. of New Zealand [IO], Auckland, New Zealand

Natl. Special Educ. Info. Center [★11971]

Natl. Special Needs Network [★14232]

Natl. Special Needs Network Found. [14232], c/o Jeffrey H Minde, Pres., 4613 N Univ. Dr., No. 242, Coral Springs, FL 33067, (954)345-6465

Natl. Specialist Contractors Coun. [IO], London, United Kingdom

Natl. Specialty Beverage Retailers Marketing Assn. - Defunct.

Natl. Specialty Gift Assn. [1724], 7238 Bucks Ford Dr., Riverview, FL 33569, (813)671-4757

Natl. Speleological Soc. [7693], 2813 Cave Ave., Huntsville, AL 35810-4431, (256)852-1300

Natl. Spinach Assn. [★4738]

Natl. Spinal Cord Injury Assn. [16468], 1 Church St., No. 600, Rockville, MD 20850, (301)214-4006

Natl. Spinal Cord Injury Found. [★16468]

Natl. Spirit, Metropolitan Club of America - Address unknown since 1999.

The Natl. Spiritual Alliance [20452], PO Box 88, Lake Pleasant, MA 01347

Natl. Spiritual Assembly of the Baha'is of India [IO], New Delhi, India

Natl. Spiritual Assembly of the Baha'is of New Zealand [IO], Auckland, New Zealand

Natl. Spiritual Assembly of the Baha'is of the U.S. [19467], 1233 Central St., Evanston, IL 60201, (847)733-3559

Natl. Spiritual Assembly of the Baha'is of the U.S. and Canada [★19467]

Natl. Spiritual Assembly of the Baha'is of Vanuatu [IO], Port Vila, Vanuatu

National Spiritualist

Healers League of the Natl. Spiritualist Assn. of Churches [20449]

Licentiate Ministers and Certified Mediums Soc. [20450]

Morris Pratt Inst. Assn. [20451]

The Natl. Spiritual Alliance [20452]

Natl. Spiritualist Assn. of Churches [20453]

Natl. Spiritualist Teachers Club [20454]

Natl. Spiritualist Assn. of Churches [20453], PO Box 217, Lily Dale, NY 14752, (716)595-2000

Natl. Spiritualist Assn. of Churches; Healers League of the [20449]

Natl. Spiritualist Teachers Club [20454], c/o Rev. E. Ann Otzelberger, NST, Pres., 4332 Woodlynne Ln., Orlando, FL 32812

Natl. Split Pea Assn. - Defunct.

Natl. Sport Aviation Coun. - Defunct.

Natl. Sport Custom Registry - Defunct.

Natl. Sporting Clays Assn. [23726], 5931 Roft Rd., San Antonio, TX 78253, (210)688-3371

Natl. Sporting Goods Assn. [3647], 1601 Feehanville Dr., Ste. 300, Mount Prospect, IL 60056, (847)296-6742

Natl. Sports Assn. - Address unknown since 1989.

Natl. Sports and Fitness Assn. - Address unknown since 2004.

Natl. Sportscasters and Sportswriters Assn. [3144], PO Box 1545, Salisbury, NC 28145, (704)633-4275

Natl. Spotted Poland China Record [★5239]

Natl. Spotted Saddle Horse Assn. [4927], PO Box 898, Murfreesboro, TN 37133-0898, (615)890-2864

Natl. Spotted Swine Record [5239], PO Box 9758, Peoria, IL 61612-9758, (309)693-1804

Natl. Spray Equipment Mfrs. Assn. - Defunct.

Natl. Sprayer and Duster Assn. - Defunct.

Natl. Sprouting Assn. - Defunct.

Natl. Spurs - Address unknown since 1995.

Natl. Square Dance Convention [9895], c/o Jack Cauble, Registration and Housing Chm., 3430 Statesville Blvd., Salisbury, NC 28145, (704)633-9147

Natl. Squash Tennis Assn. - Address unknown since 1995.

Natl. Staff Development Coun. [7908], 5995 Fairfield Rd., Ste. 4, Oxford, OH 45056, (513)523-6029

Natl. Staff Development and Training Assn. [13180], c/o Dee Gross, Conf. Coor., Amer. Public Human Services Assn., 810 First St. NE, Ste. 500, Washington, DC 20002-4207, (202)682-0100

Natl. Staff Leasing Assn. [★1273]

Natl. Stamp Dealers Assn. [22851], 2916 NW Bucklin Hill Rd., No. 136, Silverdale, WA 98383-8514, (800)875-6633

Natl. Standard Plumbing Code Comm. [5553], 180 S Washington St., PO Box 6808, Falls Church, VA 22046, (703)237-8100

Natl. Standards Authority of Ireland [IO], Dublin, Ireland

Natl. Standards Educators Assn. [7697], PO Box 773, Placentia, CA 92871, (909)930-3835

Natl. Star Route Mail Carriers Assn. [★2453]

Natl. Star Route Mail Contractors Assn. [2453], 324 E Capitol St., Washington, DC 20003-3897, (202)543-1661

Natl. Starwind/Spindrift Class Assn. [23207], PO Box 21262, Columbus, OH 43221

Natl./State Leadership Training Inst. on the Gifted and the Talented - Defunct.

Natl. State Printing Assn. [★1781]

Natl. State Publishing Assn. [★1781]

Natl. States Conf. on Alcoholism [★13216]

Natl. States Rights Party - Address unknown since 1999.

Natl. Statistical Onion Assn. [★4743]

Natl. Steam Specialty Club [★2018]

Natl. Steel Bridge Alliance [539], 1 E Wacker Dr., Ste. 700, Chicago, IL 60601-1802, (312)670-7010

Natl. Steel Door and Frame Assn. [★2719]

Natl. Steel Producers Assn. [★2732]

Natl. Steeplechase Assn. [23509], 400 Fair Hill Dr., Elkton, MD 21921, (410)392-0700

Natl. Steeplechase and Hunt Assn. [★23509]

Natl. Steinbeck Center [9695], 1 Main St., Salinas, CA 93901, (831)796-3833

Natl. Stepfamily Assn. [★IO]

Natl. Stereoscopic Assn. [10853], PO Box 86708, Portland, OR 97286, (951)736-8918

Natl. Stigma CH [15228], 245 8th Ave., No. 213, New York, NY 10011, (212)255-4411

Natl. Stinson Club [21467], c/o Intl. Stinson Club, PO Box 3311, San Jose, CA 95157-3311, (408)272-8120

Natl. Stinson Club - 108 Series - Defunct.

Natl. Stock Horse Assn. - Address unknown since 1995.

Natl. Stone Assn. [★3699]

Natl. Stone, Sand and Gravel Assn. [3699], 1605 King St., Alexandria, VA 22314, (703)525-8788

Natl. Stop the Violence Alliance - Address unknown since 2001.

Natl. Storage Indus. Consortium [★903]

Natl. Storm Shelter Assn. [2831], PO Box 41023, Lubbock, TX 79409, (806)742-6773

Natl. Story League [10982]

Natl. Storytelling Assn. [★10983]

Natl. Storytelling Network [10983], 132 Boone St., Ste. 5, Jonesborough, TN 37659, (423)913-8201

Natl. Strategy Info. Center [17383], 1730 Rhode Island Ave. NW, Ste. 500, Washington, DC 20036-3117

Natl. St. Law Inst. [★6035]

Natl. St. Rod Assn. [21738], 4030 Park Ave., Memphis, TN 38111, (901)452-4030

Natl. Strength Coaches Assn. [★23957]

Natl. Strength and Conditioning Assn. [23957], 1885 Bob Johnson Dr., Colorado Springs, CO 80906, (719)632-6722

Natl. Stripper Well Assn. [2940]

Natl. Stroke Assn. [16494], 9707 E Easter Ln., Bldg. B, Centennial, CO 80112, (303)649-9299

Natl. Stroke Assn. of Malaysia [IO], Petaling Jaya, Malaysia

Natl. Stroke Recovery Found. - Address unknown since 1988.

Natl. Structured Settlements Trade Assn. [6033], 1800 K St. NW, Ste. 718, Washington, DC 20006, (202)466-2714

Natl. Student Action Center - Address unknown since 1989.

Natl. Student Aid Coalition - Defunct.

Natl. Student Assistance Assn. [9171], 4200 Wisconsin Ave. NW, Ste. 106-118, Washington, DC 20016, (800)257-6310

Natl. Student Campaign Against Hunger [★12396]

Natl. Student Campaign Against Hunger and Homelessness [12396], 407 S Dearborn, Ste. 701, Chicago, IL 60605, (312)291-0349

Natl. Student Campaign for Voter Registration [18360]

Natl. Student Comm. for the Loyalty Oath - Defunct.

Natl. Student Consumer Protection Coun. - Address unknown since 2001.

Natl. Student Educational Fund [★9196]

Natl. Student Employment Assn. [8996], c/o Joan Adams, Off. Mgr., PO Box 23606, Eugene, OR 97402, (541)484-6935

Natl. Student Exchange [9172], 4656 W Jefferson Blvd., Ste. 140, Fort Wayne, IN 46804, (260)436-2634

Natl. Student Involvement Assistance Center - Defunct.

Natl. Student Lobby [★9195]

Natl. Student Nurses' Assn. [8873], 45 Main St., Ste. 606, Brooklyn, NY 11201, (718)210-0705

Natl. Student Safety Prog. [18579], Highway Safety Center, Indiana Univ. of Pennsylvania, R&P Bldg., Indiana, PA 15705, (724)357-4051

Natl. Student Speech and Hearing Assn. [★16453]

Natl. Student Speech Language Hearing Assn. [16453], c/o Dawn D. Dickerson, Dir. of Operations, 10801 Rockville Pike, Rockville, MD 20852, (800)498-2071

National Student Trial Advocacy Competition [★6328]

Natl. Student Union of Macedonia [IO], Skopje, Macedonia

Natl. Students Comm. on Cold War Education - Defunct.

Natl. Study Group on Chronic Disorganization [1979], 4728 Hedgemont Dr., St. Louis, MO 63128, (314)416-2236

Natl. Stud. of School Evaluation [8410], 1699 E Woodfield Rd., Ste. 406, Schaumburg, IL 60173-4958, (847)995-9080

Natl. Stud. of Secondary School Evaluation [★8410]

Natl. Study Service - Defunct.

Natl. Stuttering Assn. [16454], 119 W 40th St., 14th Fl., New York, NY 10018, (212)944-4050

Natl. Subacute Care Assn. [★14728]

Natl. Submetering and Utility Allocation Assn. [3961], 6757 Arapaho Rd., Ste. 711-145, Dallas, TX 75248-4005, (972)392-9619

Natl. Sudden Infant Death Syndrome CH [★16526]

Natl. Sudden Infant Death Syndrome Found. [★16525]

A star before a book entry number signifies that the name is not listed separately, but is mentioned within the entry.

Natl. Suffolk Sheep Assn. [★5219]

Natl. Sugar Ingredient Marketing Assn. [1553]

Natl. Sugarbeet Growers Fed. - Defunct.

Natl. Sunday School Assn. - Defunct.

Natl. Sunflower Assn. [4312], 4023 State St., Bismarck, ND 58503-0690, (701)328-5100

Natl. Sunroom Assn. [653], 1300 Sumner Ave., Cleveland, OH 44115-2851, (216)241-7333

Natl. Suppliers to Food Processors Assn. - Defunct.

Natl. Supply Distributors Assn. - Address unknown since 2001.

Natl. Support Center for Families of the Aging - Defunct.

Natl. Support Gp. for Arthrogryposis Multiplex Congenita; Avenues, [15309]

Natl. Support Group for PM/DM - Address unknown since 1999.

Natl. Surf Life Saving Assn. of Am. [★12894]

Natl. Surgical Asst. Assn. [16585], 2615 Amesbury Rd., Winston-Salem, NC 27103, (336)768-4443

Natl. Sweet Sorghum Producers and Processors Assn. [871], c/o Morris Bitzer, Exec. Sec., 2049 Rebel Rd., Lexington, KY 40503, (859)806-3358

Natl. Swim School Assn. [★23892]

Natl. Swimming Pool Found. [3360], 4775 Granby Cir., Colorado Springs, CO 80919-3131, (719)540-9119

Natl. Swimming Pool Inst. [★3353]

Natl. Swimming Pool Inst. [★IO]

Natl. Swine Growers Coun. [★5238]

Natl. Swine Improvement Fed. [5240], c/o Kenneth J. Stalder, PhD, Sec.-Treas., Iowa State Univ., Dept. of Animal Sci., 109 Kildee Hall, Ames, IA 50011-3150, (515)294-4683

Natl. Swine Registry [5241], PO Box 2417, West Lafayette, IN 47996, (765)463-3594

Natl. Symphony Orchestra Assn. [10669], John F. Kennedy Center for the Performing Arts, 2700 F St. NW, Washington, DC 20566, (202)416-8000

Natl. Systems Contractors Assn. [1225], 625 1st St. SE, Ste. 420, Cedar Rapids, IA 52401, (319)366-6722

Natl. Systems Programmers Assn. [★6799]

Natl. Systems Programmers Assn. [★IO]

Natl. T-Shirt Assn. - Address unknown since 1990.

Natl. T. T. T. Soc. - Address unknown since 1995.

Natl. Tabletop Assn. [★3711]

Natl. Tabletop and Giftware Assn. [3711], 112 Adrossan Ct., Deptford, NJ 08096, (856)227-6802

Natl. Tactical Officers Assn. [6175], PO Box 797, Doylestown, PA 18901, (800)279-9127

Natl. Tank Mfrs. Assn. - Defunct.

Natl. Tank Truck Carriers [3580], 2200 Mill Rd., Alexandria, VA 22314, (703)838-1960

Natl. Task Force on Autocratic Options - Defunct.

Natl. Task Force on Education for Economic Growth - Defunct.

Natl. Task Force on Prostitution - Address unknown since 1995.

Natl. Task Force on Sexuality and Disability - Defunct.

Natl. Tattoo Assn. [10994], 485 Bus. Park Ln., Allentown, PA 18109-9120, (610)433-7261

Natl. Tattoo Assn. [IO], Allentown, PA, United States

Natl. Tattoo Club of the World [★IO]

Natl. Tattoo Club of the World [★10994]

Natl. Tax Assn. [★6302]

Natl. Tax Assn. - Tax Inst. of Am. [6302], 725 15th St. NW, No. 600, Washington, DC 20005-2109, (202)737-3325

Natl. Tax Equality Assn. - Address unknown since 2003.

Natl. Tax-Limitation Comm. [18713], 151 N Sunrise Ave., Ste. 901, Roseville, CA 95661, (916)786-9400

National Tax Practice Institute [★6299]

Natl. Tax Strike Coalition - Address unknown since 1995.

Natl. Taxicab Assn. [IO], Carlisle, United Kingdom

Natl. Taxidermists Assn. [3718], 108 Br. Dr., Slidell, LA 70461, (985)641-4682

Natl. Taxpayers' Investigative Fund - Defunct.

Natl. Taxpayers Union [18714], 108 N Alfred St., Alexandria, VA 22314, (703)683-5700

Natl. Tay-Sachs and Allied Diseases Assn. [15354], 2001 Beacon St., Ste. 204, Boston, MA 02135, (617)277-4463

National Tay-Sachs and Allied Diseases Association [IO], Boston, MA, United States

Natl. Tay-Sachs Assn. [★IO]

Natl. Tay-Sachs Assn. [★15354]

Natl. Teachers Assn. [★24045]

Natl. Teachers' Union [IO], Luxembourg, Luxembourg

Natl. Teaching-Family Assn. [★12169]

Natl. Tech Prep Network [8358], PO Box 21689, Waco, TX 76702-1689, (254)772-5095

Natl. Technical Assistance Center on Family Violence - Defunct.

Natl. Tech. Assn. [7752], 1200 G St. NW, Ste. 800, Washington, DC 20005, (216)289-4682

Natl. Tech. Honor Soc. [24725], PO Box 1336, Flat Rock, NC 28731, (828)698-8011

National Tech. Inst. for the Deaf [★12095]

Natl. Technical Services Assn. [7753]

Natl. Teen Age Republican HQ [18529], PO Box 1896, Manassas, VA 20108-1896, (703)368-4214

Natl. Teen Anglers [22454], 1177 Bayshore Dr., No. 207, Fort Pierce, FL 34949, (772)519-0482

Natl. Teen Challenge [★20643]

Natl. Teen Challenge [★IO]

Natl. Teens for Life [12924], 419 7th St. NW, Ste. 500, Washington, DC 20004

Natl. Telecommunications Cooperative Assn. [3962], 4121 Wilson Blvd., Ste. 1000, Arlington, VA 22203, (703)351-2000

Natl. Telemedia Coun. [9766], c/o Marieli Rowe, Exec. Dir., 120 E Wilson St., Madison, WI 53703, (608)257-7712

Natl. Telephone Cooperative Assn. [★3962]

Natl. TV Film Coun. - Address unknown since 1995.

Natl. TV and Video Assn. of South Africa [IO], Cape Town, Republic of South Africa

Natl. Temperance League [★13220]

Natl. Temperance and Prohibition Coun. [13305], PO Box 532, Richardson, TX 75083-0532, (972)235-4960

Natl. Temple Hill Assn. [10050], PO Box 315, Vails Gate, NY 12584, (845)561-5073

Natl. Temporal Bone Banks Prog. of The DRF [★15121]

Natl. Temporal Bone, Hearing and Balance Pathology Registry [★15121]

Natl. Temporal Bone, Hearing and Balance Pathology Rsrc. Registry [★15121]

Natl. Temporal Bone, Hearing and Balance Pathology Rsrc. Registry; NIDCD - [15121]

Natl. Temporal Bone Registry [★15121]

Natl. Tenants Org. - Defunct.

Natl. Tenants Union - Defunct.

Natl. Tennis Acad. [★23913]

Natl. Tennis Assn. [★3021]

Natl. Tennis Assn. [★IO]

Natl. Tennis Educational Found. [★IO]

Natl. Tennis Educational Found. [★23903]

Natl. Tennis Fed. of Republic of Tajikistan [IO], Dushanbe, Tajikistan

Natl. Tennis Found. and Hall of Fame [★IO]

Natl. Tennis Found. and Hall of Fame [★23903]

Natl. Terrazzo and Mosaic Assn. [1052], 201 N Maple Ave., Ste. 208, Purcellville, VA 20132, (540)751-0930

Natl. Tertiary Educ. Union [IO], South Melbourne, Australia

Natl. Textile Assn. [3795], 6 Beacon St., Ste. 1125, Boston, MA 02108, (617)542-8220

Natl. Textile Processors Guild - Defunct.

Natl. Textile Rsrc. and Res. Center [★22165]

Natl. Textile Rsrc. and Res. Center [★IO]

Natl. Thanksgiving Commn. [★IO]

Natl. Thanksgiving Commn. [★18676]

Natl. Theatre Arts Conf. - Defunct.

Natl. Theatre Conf. [11032], c/o Jack B. Wright, Pres., 4513 Turnberry Dr., Lawrence, KS 66047, (785)864-4110

Natl. Theatre of the Deaf [IO], West Hartford, CT, United States

Natl. Theatre Inst. [★9266]

Natl. Theatre Workshop of the Handicapped [11033], 535 Greenwich St., New York, NY 10013, (212)206-7789

Natl. Therapeutic Recreation Soc. [16628], 22377 Belmont Ridge Rd., Ashburn, VA 20148-4501, (703)858-0784

Natl. Thespian Soc. [★9264]

Natl. Thoroughbred Racing Assn. [23510], 2525 Harrodsburg Rd., Lexington, KY 40504, (859)223-5444

Natl. Threshers Assn. [9484], c/o David Schramm, Pres., 22343 Lemoyne Rd., Luckey, OH 43443, (419)833-6371

Natl. Thrift Comm. - Defunct.

Natl. Throws Coaches Assn. [23293], PO Box 14114, Palm Desert, CA 92255-4114, (888)527-6772

Natl. Tile Contractors Assn. [1053], PO Box 13629, Jackson, MS 39236, (601)939-2071

Natl. Tile Promotion Fed. - Defunct.

Natl. Tile Roofing Manufacturers Assn. [★681]

Natl. Timberwolf Assn; 104th Infantry Div. [20695]

Natl. Time Equip. Assn. [3812], PO Box 27399, Memphis, TN 38167-0399, (800)235-6832

Natl. Tire Dealers and Retreaders Assn. [★3814]

Natl. Toggenburg Club [4787], c/o Tracey Jones, Specialty Show Chair, 2754 Crooked Finger Rd., Scotts Mills, OR 97375-9640, (503)873-8512

Natl. Token Collectors Assn. [21954], c/o Clark Rohmer, Sec., PO Box 281, Ormond Beach, FL 32175, (386)677-4206

Natl. Tool and Die Mfrs. Assn. [★2031]

Natl. Tool and Die Mfrs. Assn. [★IO]

Natl. Tool, Die and Precision Machining Assn. [★IO]

Natl. Tool, Die and Precision Machining Assn. [★2031]

Natl. Toothpick Holder Collectors' Soc. [22089], PO Box 852, Archer City, TX 76351

Natl. Tots and Teens [13503], 16555 Wyoming Ave., Detroit, MI 48221, (313)863-1705

Natl. Touch Football Leagues - Address unknown since 2001.

Natl. Tour Assn. [3930], 546 E Main St., Lexington, KY 40508, (859)226-4444

Natl. Tour Brokers Assn. [★3930]

Natl. Tourism Org. Malta [★IO]

Natl. Tourism Org. of Serbia [IO], Belgrade, Serbia

Natl. Town Builders' Assn. [654], 3220 N St. NW, No. 238, Washington, DC 20007, (202)333-1902

Natl. Town Class Assn. - Address unknown since 2001.

Natl. Toxics Campaign - Address unknown since 1994.

Natl. Toy Fox Terrier Assn. [22321], c/o Patricia Johnson, Pres., 51215 Sand Song Ave., Johnson Valley, CA 92285-2961, (760)364-3130

Natl. Toy Libraries Assn. [★IO]

Natl. Track and Field Assn. - Defunct.

Natl. Tractor Pullers Assn. [23928], 6155-B Huntley Rd., Columbus, OH 43229, (614)436-1761

Natl. Trade Circulation Found., Inc. [3242], c/o JoAnn Binz, PO Box 515, Swiftwater, PA 18370-0515, (570)839-2708

Natl. Trade Press Assn. [IO], Milan, Italy

Natl. Trade Show Exhibitors Assn. [★1349]

Natl. Trades Union Cong. [IO], Singapore, Singapore

Natl. Traditional Country Music Assn. [★10670]

Natl. Traditional Country Music Assn. [10670], PO Box 492, Anita, IA 50020, (712)762-4363

Natl. Traditional Music Assn. [★10670]

Natl. Traditionalist Caucus [17276], PO Box 971, New York, NY 10116-0971, (212)685-4689

National Traffic System [★21494]

Natl. Trail Ride Assn. [23946], PO Box 379, Big Sandy, TN 38221, (731)593-5139

Natl. Trailer Dealers Assn. [3883], 37400 Hills Tech Dr., Farmington Hills, MI 48331, (800)800-4552

Natl. Trailer Rental Assn. - Address unknown since 1995.

Natl. Trails Coun. [★23935]

Natl. Trainers Fed. [IO], Hungerford, United Kingdom

Natl. Training and Info. Center [11799], 810 N Milwaukee Ave., Chicago, IL 60622, (312)243-3035

Natl. Training Labs. [★8415]

Natl. Training Labs. [★IO]

Natl. Training Lab. in Gp. Development [★IO]

Natl. Training Lab. in Gp. Development [★8415]

Natl. Training and Simulation Assn. [6738], 2111 Wilson Blvd., Ste. 400, Arlington, VA 22201-3061, (703)247-9471

Natl. Training Systems Assn. [★6089]

Natl. Transgender Advocacy Coalition [13333], PO Box 76027, Washington, DC 20013, (978)373-8898

Reference to "IO" in place of a book number signifies that the association may be found in the 45th edition of International Organizations.

Natl. Transit Benefit Assn. **[6324]**, PO Box 25, Clifton, VA 20124, (703)222-9373

Natl. Translation Center - Defunct.

Natl. Translator Assn. **[576]**, 5611 Kendall Ct., Ste. 2, Arvada, CO 80002, (303)465-5742

Natl. Translator LPTV Assn. **[★576]**

Natl. Transplant Information Center - Defunct.

Natl. Transplant Soc. **[16680]**, 3149 Dundee Rd., Ste. 314, Northbrook, IL 60062, (847)962-3441

Natl. Transportation Safety Assn. - Defunct.

Natl. Transsexual - Transvestite Feminization Union - Defunct.

Natl. Trappers Assn. **[5251]**, 2815 Washington Ave., Bedford, IN 47421, (812)277-9670

Natl. Travel Club **[3931]**

Natl. Treasure Hunters League - Defunct.

Natl. Treasury Employees Union **[24080]**, 1750 H St. NW, Ste. 600, Washington, DC 20006, (202)572-5500

Natl. Treatment Consortium for Alcohol and Other Drugs - Defunct.

National Tree Fund **[★4594]**

Natl. Tree Soc. **[4594]**, PO Box 10808, Bakersfield, CA 93389, (805)589-6912

Natl. Tribal Chairman's Assn. - Defunct.

Natl. Tribal Child Support Assn. **[11713]**, PO Box 154, Ada, OK 74820, (580)436-7016

Natl. Tribal Development Assn. **[19280]**, RR1, Box 694, Box Elder, MT 59521-9722, (406)395-4095

Natl. Tribal Environmental Coun. **[18097]**, 2501 Rio Grande Blvd. NW, Ste. A, Albuquerque, NM 87104, (505)242-2175

Natl. Triton Assn. - Address unknown since 2001.

National Troopers Coalition **[★5995]**

Natl. Trotting Assn. **[★23519]**

Natl. Trotting and Pacing Assn. **[★23501]**

Natl. Trotting and Pacing Assn. **[★IO]**

Natl. Truck Equip. Assn. **[395]**, 37400 Hills Tech Dr., Farmington Hills, MI 48331-3414, (248)489-7090

Natl. Truck and Heavy Equip. Claims Coun. **[2228]**, c/o Tom Fergus, Admin., PO Box 27, Wolfeboro Falls, NH 03896-0027, (603)569-8910

Natl. Truck Leasing Sys. **[3384]**, 1S450 Summit Ave., Ste. 300, Oakbrook Terrace, IL 60181, (800)729-6857

Natl. Truck Tank Assn. **[★998]**

Natl. Truck Tank and Trailer Tank Inst. **[★998]**

Natl. Truckdrivers Safety Assn. **[2843]**

Natl. Truckers Assn. **[3884]**, 3131 Turtle Creek Blvd., Ste. 910, Dallas, TX 75219, (800)823-8454

Natl. Trucking Industrial Relations Assn. **[★2906]**

Natl. Trust **[IO]**, Warrington, United Kingdom

Natl. Trust of Australia **[IO]**, Civic Square, Australia

Natl. Trust, Central Volunteering Team **[IO]**, Swindon, United Kingdom

Natl. Trust Closely Held Business Assn. - Address unknown since 1990.

Natl. Trust for the Development of African Amer. Men **[16946]**, 1608 Nordic Hill Cir., Silver Spring, MD 20906, (301)933-6151

Natl. Trust for Historic Preservation **[10051]**, 1785 Massachusetts Ave. NW, Washington, DC 20036-2117, (202)588-6000

Natl. Trust for Ireland **[IO]**, Dublin, Ireland

Natl. Trust Main St. Center **[17231]**, 1785 Massachusetts Ave. NW, Washington, DC 20036, (202)588-6219

National Trust for Scotland **[★19356]**

Natl. Trust for Scotland **[IO]**, Edinburgh, United Kingdom

Natl. Trust Volunteering and Community Involvement Off. **[★IO]**

Natl. Tuberculosis Assn. **[★16354]**

Natl. Tuberculosis Controllers Assn. **[14283]**, 2452 Spring Rd. SE, Smyrna, GA 30080, (877)503-0806

Natl. Tuberculosis and Respiratory Disease Assn. **[★16354]**

Natl. Tuberous Sclerosis Assn. **[★15371]**

Natl. Tulip Soc. - Defunct.

Natl. Tumor Registrars Assn. **[★15651]**

Natl. Tung Oil Marketing Cooperative - Defunct.

Natl. Tunis Sheep Registry, Inc. **[5208]**, c/o Barbara Cassell, Sec., 15603 173rd Ave., Milo, IA 50166, (641)942-6402

Natl. Turf Writers Assn. **[3145]**, 3920 Grassy Creek Dr., Lexington, KY 40514, (859)219-9437

Natl. Turkey Fed. **[5113]**, 1225 New York Ave., Ste., 400, Washington, DC 20005, (202)898-0100

Natl. Turnpike Assn. - Defunct.

Natl. Tutoring Assn. **[9283]**, PO Box 6840, Lakeland, FL 33807-6840, (863)529-5206

Natl. Typewriter and Off. Machine Dealers Assn. **[★2844]**

Natl. Tyre Distributors Assn. **[IO]**, Aylesbury, United Kingdom

Natl. UHF Broadcasters Assn. - Address unknown since 1988.

Natl. Ulcer Found. - Address unknown since 1999.

Natl. UNESCO Club for Sci. Expeditions **[IO]**, Sofia, Bulgaria

Natl. Unfinished Furniture Inst. - Defunct.

Natl. Uniform Certification of Building Operators **[2472]**

Natl. Union of Associated Employees - Address unknown since 2000.

Natl. Union of Automotive Distributors **[IO]**, Rome, Italy

Natl. Union of Christian Schools **[★IO]**

Natl. Union of Christian Schools **[★8083]**

Natl. Union of Czechoslovak Protestants in Amer. and Canada - Defunct.

Natl. Union of Czechoslovak Students in Exile - Address unknown since 1995.

Natl. Union of Disabled Persons of Uganda **[IO]**, Kampala, Uganda

Natl. Union of Domestic Appliances and Gen. Operatives **[IO]**, Rotherham, United Kingdom

Natl. Union of Eritrean Women - North America - Address unknown since 1999.

Natl. Union of Eritrean Youth and Students **[IO]**, Asmara, Eritrea

Natl. Union of Eritrean Youth and Students **[★IO]**

Natl. Union for the Homeless - Address unknown since 2000.

Natl. Union of Israel Students **[IO]**, Tel Aviv, Israel

Natl. Union of Journalists - England **[IO]**, London, United Kingdom

Natl. Union of Journalists (India) **[IO]**, New Delhi, India

Natl. Union of Law Enforcement Associations **[24124]**, 3150 Monroe St. NE, Washington, DC 20018-4026, (202)635-4206

Natl. Union of the Leather Indus. **[IO]**, Milan, Italy

Natl. Union of Marine, Aviation and Shipping Transport Officers **[★IO]**

Natl. Union of Metalworkers of South Africa **[IO]**, Excom, Republic of South Africa

Natl. Union of Mine Workers **[IO]**, Johannesburg, Republic of South Africa

Natl. Union of Mineworkers - United Kingdom **[IO]**, Barnsley, United Kingdom

Natl. Union of Olive Growers Associations **[IO]**, Rome, Italy

Natl. Union of Pharmacies **[IO]**, Paris, France

Natl. Union of Phonographic Publishing **[IO]**, Paris, France

Natl. Union of Public and Gen. Employees **[IO]**, Nepean, ON, Canada

Natl. Union of Publishing **[IO]**, Paris, France

Natl. Union of Rail, Maritime and Transport Workers **[IO]**, London, United Kingdom

Natl. Union of Rubber and Polymers **[IO]**, Vitry-sur-Seine, France

Natl. Union of School Workers **[IO]**, Rome, Italy

Natl. Union of Small and Medium-Sized Textile and Clothing Companies **[IO]**, Rome, Italy

Natl. Union of Students - Australia **[IO]**, Carlton South, Australia

Natl. Union of Students - United Kingdom **[IO]**, London, United Kingdom

Natl. Union of Teachers in Sweden **[IO]**, Stockholm, Sweden

Natl. Union of the Teaching Profession **[IO]**, Kuala Lumpur, Malaysia

Natl. Union of Tenants of Nigeria **[IO]**, Port Harcourt, Nigeria

Natl. Union of the Toast Indus. **[IO]**, Paris, France

Natl. Union of Tourism Hospitality **[IO]**, Neuilly-sur-Seine, France

Natl. Union of Tourism and Outdoor Associations **[IO]**, Paris, France

Natl. Union of Townswomen's Guilds **[★IO]**

Natl. Union of Tunisian Women **[IO]**, Tunis, Tunisia

Natl. Union of Workers **[IO]**, North Melbourne, Australia

Natl. United Affiliated Beverage Assn. - Address unknown since 1994.

Natl. United Church Ushers Assn. **[★20609]**

Natl. United Church Ushers Assn. of Am. **[20609]**, PO Box 363863, North Las Vegas, NV 89036-7863, (206)240-1174

Natl. United Front for the Liberation of Vietnam - Address unknown since 2007.

Natl. United Italian Assns. - Address unknown since 1995.

Natl. United Licensees Beverage Assn. - Address unknown since 1995.

Natl. United States-Arab Chamber of Commerce **[24290]**, 1023 15th St. NW, Ste. 400, Washington, DC 20005, (202)289-5920

Natl. United Women's Societies of the Adoration of the Most Blessed Sacrament - Address unknown since 2004.

National UNITY Council **[★10756]**

Natl. Unity Party - Address unknown since 2006.

Natl. Univ. Consortium for Telecommunications in Teaching **[★8566]**

Natl. Univ. Consortium for Telecommunications in Teaching **[★IO]**

Natl. Univ. Continuing Educ. Assn. **[★IO]**

Natl. Univ. Continuing Educ. Assn. **[★8154]**

Natl. Univ. Extension Assn. **[★8154]**

Natl. Univ. Extension Assn. **[★IO]**

Natl. Upper Cervical Chiropractic Assn. **[14012]**, c/o Ms. Lesley Louvar, Exec. Dir., 2608 W Kenosha St., Ste. 224, Broken Arrow, OK 74012-8952, (800)541-5799

Natl. Urban Affairs Coun. **[★IO]**

Natl. Urban Affairs Coun. - Address unknown since 2001.

Natl. Urban Agriculture Coun. **[4113]**, 1015 18th St. NW, No. 600, Washington, DC 20036, (202)429-4344

Natl. Urban Alliance for Effective Educ. **[9291]**, 33 Queens St., Ste. 100, Syosset, NY 11791, (516)802-4192

Natl. Urban Coalition - Address unknown since 2003.

Natl. Urban Fellows **[★18775]**

Natl. Urban Fellows **[18775]**, 102 W 38th St., Ste. 700, New York, NY 10018, (212)730-1700

Natl. Urban Indian Coun. - Address unknown since 1999.

Natl. Urban League **[17138]**, 120 Wall St., 8th Fl., New York, NY 10005, (212)558-5300

Natl. Urban/Rural Fellows **[★18775]**

Natl. Urban Tech. Center **[7754]**, 80 Maiden Ln., Ste. 606, New York, NY 10038, (212)528-7350

Natl. Used Car Dealers Assn. **[★423]**

Natl. Utility Contractors Assn. **[1054]**, 4301 N Fairfax Dr., Ste. 360, Arlington, VA 22203-1627, (703)358-9300

Natl. Utility Locating Contractors Assn. **[1055]**, 2563 Capital Medical Blvd., Tallahassee, FL 32308, (850)531-8352

Natl. Utility Training and Safety Educ. Assn. **[3963]**, c/o Melissa Robokoff, 8240 Resurrection Dr., Anchorage, AK 99504, (907)563-2551

Natl. Vaccine Info. Center **[13972]**, 204 Mill St., Ste. B1, Vienna, VA 22180, (703)938-0342

Natl. Valedictorian Honor Soc. **[24514]**, PO Box 3, Redmond, WA 98073, (425)836-1000

Natl. Valedictorian Soc. **[9077]**, PO Box 3, Redmond, WA 98073, (425)836-1000

Natl. Valentine Collectors' Assn. **[22090]**, c/o Nancy Rosin, VP, PO Box 1404, Santa Ana, CA 92702

Natl. Variety Artists - Defunct.

Natl. Vascular Malformations Found. - Address unknown since 2001.

Natl. Vaudeville Artists - Defunct.

Natl. Vegetable Soc. **[IO]**, Stockport, United Kingdom

Natl. Vehicle Conversion Assn. - Address unknown since 1999.

Natl. Vehicle Leasing Assn. **[3385]**, 1199 N Fairfax St., Ste. 400, Alexandria, VA 22314, (800)225-NVLA

A star before a book entry number signifies that the name is not listed separately, but is mentioned within the entry.

Natl. Vehicle Safety-Check for Communities - Defunct.

Natl. Velthrow Assn. - Address unknown since 1990.

Natl. Vending Machine Assn. [IO], Madrid, Spain

Natl. Vendors Assn. [★3972]

Natl. Venture Capital Assn. [2348], 1655 N Ft. Myer Dr., Ste. 850, Arlington, VA 22209, (703)524-2549

Natl. Verbatim Reporters Assn. [4064], 207 3rd Ave., Hattiesburg, MS 39401, (601)582-4345

Natl. Veteran Boxers Assn. - Address unknown since 1994.

Natl. Veterans Assn. [★21315]

Natl. Veterans Law Center - Defunct.

Natl. Veterans Legal Services Prog. [21314], PO Box 65762, Washington, DC 20035, (202)265-8305

Natl. Veterans Org. of Am. [21315], PO Box 2510, Victoria, TX 77902-2510, (210)200-8756

Natl. Veterans Outreach Prog. [13355], c/o Amer. GI Forum, 5038 W 127th St., Alsip, IL 60803, (708)371-9800

Natl. Veterans Services Fund [13356], PO Box 2465, Darien, CT 06820-0465, (203)656-0003

Natl. Veterinarian Ser. Assn. [16801], PO Box 35215, Chicago, IL 60707-0215, (708)453-0080

Natl. Veterinary Medical Assn. [★IO]

Natl. Viatical Assn. - Defunct.

Natl. Victim Advocacy Center; Sunny Von Bulow [★13366]

Natl. Victims' Constitutional Amendment Network [18779], 789 Sherman St., Ste. 670, Denver, CO 80203, (303)832-1522

Natl. Victims of Crime - Defunct.

Natl. Victims of Crime Found. - Defunct.

Natl. Video Clearinghouse - Defunct.

Natl. Vietnam and Gulf War Veterans Coalition [18781], 2020 Pennsylvania Ave., No. 961, Washington, DC 20006

Natl. Vietnam Veterans Coalition [★18781]

Natl. Viewers and Listeners Assn. [★IO]

Natl. Vintage Tractor and Engine Club [IO], Retford, United Kingdom

Natl. Viral Hepatitis Roundtable [14815], 750 Commerce Dr., Ste. 400, Decatur, GA 30030, (404)483-2826

Natl. Visiting Teachers Assn. [8955]

Natl. VISTA Alliance - Defunct.

Natl. Visual Communication Assn. - Defunct.

Natl. Vitamin Distributors Assn. - Address unknown since 1995.

Natl. Vitamin Found. - Address unknown since 1995.

Natl. Viticulture Inst. [IO], Mendoza, Argentina

Natl. Vitiligo Found. [14211], 76 Garden Rd., Columbus, OH 43214, (614)261-8145

Natl. Vocational Agricultural Teachers Assn. [★7938]

Natl. Vocational Educational Found. [★9308]

Natl. Vocational Educational Professional Development Found. [★9308]

Natl. Vocational Guidance Assn. [★12090]

Natl. Vocational Technical Education Found. [9308]

Natl. Vocational-Technical Honor Soc. [★24725]

Natl. Voice [17076]

Natl. Volkswagen Assn. - Address unknown since 1987.

Natl. Voluntary Groups Inst. - Defunct.

Natl. Voluntary Hea. Agencies [★12200]

Natl. Voluntary Organizations Active in Disaster [12874], 1720 I St. NW, Ste. 700, Washington, DC 20006, (202)955-8396

Natl. Voluntary Orgs. for Independent Living for the Aging - Defunct.

Natl. Volunteer Center [★13401]

Natl. Volunteer Clearinghouse for the Homeless - Defunct.

Natl. Volunteer Fire Coun. [5723], 1050 17th St. NW, Ste. 490, Washington, DC 20036, (202)887-5700

Natl. Voter Mobilization - Defunct.

Natl. Vulvodynia Assn. [16905], PO Box 4491, Silver Spring, MD 20914-4491, (301)299-0775

Natl. Waco Club - Address unknown since 2006.

Natl. Walking Horse Assn. [4928], 4059 Iron Works Pkwy., Ste. 4, Lexington, KY 40511, (859)252-6942

Natl. Wallpaper Wholesalers Assn. [★2278]

Natl. War Dog Memorial Fund [21347], c/o Bank of Am., 5101 Pennsylvania Ave. NW, Washington, DC 20005

Natl. War Tax Resistance Coordinating Comm. [18715], PO Box 150553, Brooklyn, NY 11215, (718)768-3420

Natl. Wargaming Alliance [★22475]

Natl. Warm Air Heating and Air Conditioning Assn. [★1872]

Natl. Waste Prevention Coalition [4001], c/o King County Solid Waste Div., 201 S Jackson St., No. 701, Seattle, WA 98104-3855, (206)296-4481

National Watch Mark Identification Bureau [★2359]

Natl. Water Alliance - Defunct.

Natl. Water Carriers Assn. - Defunct.

Natl. Water Center [★7837]

Natl. Water Center [7837], 5473 Hwy. 23 N, Eureka Springs, AR 72631, (479)253-9431

Natl. Water Company Conf. [★4010]

Natl. Water Purification Found. - Address unknown since 1995.

Natl. Water Resources Assn. [7838], 3800 N Fairfax Dr., Ste. 4, Arlington, VA 22203, (703)524-1544

Natl. Water Safety Cong. [12981], c/o Cecilia Duer, Exec. Dir., PO Box 1632, Mentor, OH 44061, (440)209-9805

National Water Safety Congress [IO], Mentor, OH, United States

Natl. Water Slide Assn. - Defunct.

Natl. Water Supply Improvement Assn. [★7824]

Natl. Water Supply Improvement Assn. [★IO]

Natl. Water Well Assn. [★IO]

Natl. Water Well Assn. [★4011]

Natl. Waterbed Retailers Assn. [★1705]

Natl. Watercolor Soc. [9461], 915 S Pacific Ave., San Pedro, CA 90731, (310)831-1099

Natl. Waterfowl Alliance, Waterfowl U.S.A. [★4465]

Natl. Waterfowl Coun. - Defunct.

Natl. Watermelon Assn. [4747], c/o Bob Morrissey, Exec. Dir., 1305 W Martin Luther King, Jr. Blvd., Ste. 1, Plant City, FL 33563, (813)754-7575

Natl. Watershed Cong. - Defunct.

Natl. Waterways Conf. [3581], 4650 Washington Blvd., No. 608, Arlington, VA 22201, (703)243-4090

Natl. Weather Assn. [7327], 228 W Millbrook Rd., Raleigh, NC 27609-4304, (919)845-1546

Natl. Weather Ser. Employees Org. [6357], 601 Pennsylvania Ave. NW, Ste. 900, Washington, DC 20004, (703)293-9651

Natl. Weightlifting Fed. of Georgia [IO], Tbilisi, Georgia

Natl. Welding Supply Assn. [★2021]

Natl. Welfare Rights Org. - Defunct.

Natl. Well Spouse Found. [★16553]

Natl. Wellness Inst. [16057], PO Box 827, Stevens Point, WI 54481-0827, (715)342-2969

National Wellness Institute [IO], Stevens Point, WI, United States

Natl. Welsh-American Found. [19430], 143 Sunny Hillside Rd., Benton, PA 17814-7822, (570)925-6923

Natl. Wetlands Coalition [5284], 1050 Thomas Jefferson St. NW, Ste. 700, Washington, DC 20007, (202)298-1800

Natl. Wetlands Conservation Project - Defunct.

Natl. Wetlands Technical Coun. - Defunct.

Natl. Wheelchair Athletic Assn. [★23371]

Natl. Wheelchair Basketball Assn. [23354], 6165 Lehman Dr., Ste. 101, Colorado Springs, CO 80918, (719)266-4082

Natl. Wheelchair Poolplayer Assn. [23355], 9651 Halekulani Dr., Garden Grove, CA 92841-4911, (703)817-1215

National Wheelchair Poolplayer Association [IO], Garden Grove, CA, United States

Natl. Wheelchair Softball Assn. [23356], c/o Mike Wheaton, Commissioner, 6000 W Floyd Ave., No. 110, Denver, CO 80227, (303)842-1229

Natl. Whistleblower Center [12982], PO Box 3768, Washington, DC 20027, (202)342-1903

Natl. White Collar Crime Center of Canada [IO], Ottawa, ON, Canada

Natl. White Wyandotte Club - Defunct.

Natl. Wholesale Druggists' Assn. [★2984]

Natl. Wholesale Frozen Food Distributors Assn. [★1547]

Natl. Wholesale Furniture Assn. [★1700]

Natl. Wholesale Furniture Assn. [★IO]

Natl. Wholesale Furniture Salesmen's Assn. [★IO]

Natl. Wholesale Furniture Salesmen's Assn. [★1702]

Natl. Wholesale Garment Assn. - Defunct.

Natl. Wholesale Liquor Dealers Assn. - Defunct.

Natl. Wholesale Lumber Dealers Assn. [★1611]

Natl. Wholesale Lumber Distributing Yard Assn. [★1647]

Natl. WIC Assn. [6262], 2001 S St. NW, Ste. 580, Washington, DC 20009, (202)232-5492

Natl. Wild Horse and Burro Prog; Bur. of Land Mgt. [4868]

Natl. Wild Turkey Fed. [5343], PO Box 530, Edgefield, SC 29824-0530, (803)637-3106

Natl. Wilderness Inst. [5344], PO Box 25766, Washington, DC 20007, (703)836-7404

Natl. Wildlife Control Operators Assn. [4027], PO Box 402, Neotsu, OR 97364, (541)994-8900

Natl. Wildlife Fed. [4426], 11100 Wildlife Center Dr., Reston, VA 20190-5362, (800)822-9919

Natl. Wildlife Fed. Corporate Conservation Coun. - Defunct.

Natl. Wildlife Health Found. - Address unknown since 2007.

Natl. Wildlife Refuge Assn. [5345], 1901 Pennsylvania Ave. NW, Ste. 407, Washington, DC 20006, (202)333-9075

Natl. Wildlife Rehabilitators Assn. [5346], 2625 Clearwater Rd., Ste. 110, St. Cloud, MN 56301, (320)230-9920

Natl. Wildlife Rescue Team - Address unknown since 1995.

Natl. Windshield Repair Assn. [425], PO Box 569, Garrisonville, VA 22463, (540)720-7484

Natl. Wine Assn. - Defunct.

Natl. Wine Distribution Assn. - Defunct.

Natl. Wine Trade Fed. [IO], Milan, Italy

Natl. Winter Sports - Defunct.

Natl. Wiring Bur. - Defunct.

Natl. Woman Abuse Prevention Project - Address unknown since 1994.

Natl. Woman's Christian Temperance Union [13306], c/o Frances Williard Memorial Lib. Archives, 1730 Chicago Ave., Evanston, IL 60201-4585, (847)864-1397

Natl. Woman's Forum - Address unknown since 1995.

Natl. Woman's Missionary Soc. of the Church of God [★19835]

Natl. Woman's Party [17562], Sewall-Belmont House & Museum, 144 Constitution Ave. NE, Washington, DC 20002-5608, (202)546-1210

Natl. Woman's Relief Corps, Auxiliary to the Grand Army of the Republic - Address unknown since 1992.

Natl. Woman's Suffrage Assn. [★18459]

Natl. Women and the Law Assn. - Address unknown since 1995.

Natl. Women Law Students Assn. [9322], PO Box 60727, Oklahoma City, OK 73146-0727, (417)425-7832

Natl. Women Student's Coalition - Address unknown since 2001.

Natl. Women's Assn. of Allied Beverage Indus. [★213]

Natl. Women's Assn. of Allied Beverage Indus. [★IO]

Natl. Women's Automotive Assn. - Defunct.

Natl. Women's Auxiliary to the Goodwill Indus. [★11950]

Natl. Women's Bus. Coun. [4044], 409 3rd St. SW, Ste. 210, Washington, DC 20024, (202)205-3850

Natl. Women's Coalition - Defunct.

Natl. Women's Conf. [17563], 2020 Pennsylvania Ave., No. 267, Washington, DC 20006, (703)922-4468

Natl. Women's Conf. Center [17564]

Natl. Women's Conf. Comm. [★17563]

Natl. Women's Conf; Continuing Comm. of the [★17563]

Natl. Women's Coun. of Ireland [IO], Dublin, Ireland

Natl. Women's Coun. of the New Zealand Coun. of Trade Unions [IO], Wellington, New Zealand

Natl. Women's Economic Alliance Found. - Address unknown since 2004.

Natl. Women's Employment and Education - Defunct.

Reference to "IO" in place of a book number signifies that the association may be found in the 45th edition of International Organizations.

Natl. Women's Employment Proj. [★17512]
Natl. Women's Forum [★13429]
Natl. Women's Forum [★IO]
Natl. Women's Hall of Fame [20716], PO Box 335, Seneca Falls, NY 13148, (315)568-8060
Natl. Women's Hea. Coalition [★16899]
Natl. Women's Hea. Coalition [★IO]
Natl. Women's Hea. Network [16906], 514 10th St. NW, Ste. 400, Washington, DC 20004, (202)347-1140
Natl. Women's Hea. Rsrc. Center [16907], 157 Broad St., Ste. 315, Red Bank, NJ 07701, (732)530-3425
Natl. Women's History Proj. [11090], 3343 Indus. Dr., Ste. 4, Santa Rosa, CA 95403, (707)636-2888
Natl. Women's History Week Proj. [★11090]
Natl. Women's Insurance Center - Defunct.
Natl. Women's Justice Coalition [IO], Canberra, Australia
Natl. Women's Law Center [17565], 11 Dupont Cir. NW, Ste. 800, Washington, DC 20036, (202)588-5180
Natl. Women's League of the United Synagogue of Am. [★20193]
Natl. Women's Martial Arts Fed. [23600], 100 Bush St., Ste. 1500, San Francisco, CA 94104, (415)982-9200
Natl. Women's Neckwear and Scarf Assn. - Defunct.
Natl. Women's Political Caucus [17566], PO Box 50476, Washington, DC 20091, (202)785-1100
Natl. Women's Register [IO], Norwich, United Kingdom
Natl. Women's Rowing Assn. [★23704]
Natl. Women's Sailing Assn. [21879], 98 Washington St., Marblehead, MA 01945, (866)631-6972
Natl. Women's Scuba Soc. - Address unknown since 1999.
Natl. Women's Stud. Assn. [9323], c/o Univ. of Maryland, 7100 Baltimore Ave., Ste. 502, College Park, MD 20740, (301)403-0525
Natl. Women's Trucking Assn. - Defunct.
Natl. Wood Carvers Assn. [22171], PO Box 43218, Cincinnati, OH 45243, (513)561-0627
National Wood Carvers Association [IO], Cincinnati, OH, United States
National Wood Flooring Association [IO], Chesterfield, MO, United States
Natl. Wood Flooring Assn. [655], 111 Chesterfield Indus. Blvd., Chesterfield, MO 63005, (636)519-9663
Natl. Wood Tank Inst. [988], PO Box 2755, Philadelphia, PA 19120, (215)329-9022
Natl. Wood Window and Door Assn. [★686]
Natl. Wooden Box Assn. [★989]
Natl. Wooden Pallet and Container Assn. [989], 1421 Prince St., Ste. 340, Alexandria, VA 22314-2805, (703)519-6104
Natl. Wooden Pallet Manufacturers Assn. [★989]
Natl. Woodie Club [21739], c/o John Lee, Ed., PO Box 6134, Lincoln, NE 68506, (402)488-0990
Natl. Woodland Owners Assn. [4693], 374 Maple Ave. E, Ste. 310, Vienna, VA 22180, (703)255-2700
Natl. Woodwork Manufacturers Assn. [★686]
Natl. Wool Growers Assn. [★5194]
Natl. Wool Growers' Assn. of South Africa [IO], Port Elizabeth, Republic of South Africa
Natl. Wool Marketing Corp. - Defunct.
Natl. Wool Trade Assn. - Defunct.
Natl. Work at Home Mom Assn. [1922]
Natl. Work at Home Mom Assn. [IO], Rocky Mount, VA, United States
Natl. Workers Network - Defunct.
Natl. Workforce Assn. [1739], 810 1st St. NE, Ste. 530, Washington, DC 20002, (202)842-4004
Natl. World War II Glider Pilots Assn. [21468], 21 Phyllis Rd., Freehold, NJ 07728, (732)462-1838
Natl. World War II Glider Pilots Assn. [IO], Freehold, NJ, United States
Natl. Wrestling Coaches Assn. [23987], PO Box 254, Manheim, PA 17545-0254, (717)653-8009
Natl. Write Your Congressman [18361], PO Box 830308, Richardson, TX 75083-0308, (214)342-0299
Natl. Write Your Congressman Club [★18361]

Natl. Writers Assn. [3146], 10940 S Parker Rd., No. 508, Parker, CO 80134, (303)841-0246
Natl. Writers Union [24219], 113 Univ. Pl., 6th Fl., New York, NY 10003, (212)254-0279
Natl. Writing Centers Assn. - Address unknown since 2002.
Natl. Writing Proj. [9334], Univ. of California, 2105 Bancroft Way, Berkeley, CA 94720, (510)642-0963
Natl. Xeriscape Coun. - Defunct.
Natl. Yellow Pages Agency Assn. - Address unknown since 1994.
Natl. Yellow Pages Ser. Assn. [★3261]
Natl. Yeomen F - Defunct.
Natl. Yiddish Book Center [10288], Harry and Jeanette Weinberg Bldg., 1021 West St., Amherst, MA 01002-3375, (413)256-4900
Natl. Yiddish Book Exchange [★10288]
Natl. Yogurt Assn. [1138], 2000 Corporate Ridge, Ste. 1000, McLean, VA 22102, (703)821-0770
Natl. Young Adult Assn. [13504], 938 E Swan Creek Rd., Box 283, Fort Washington, MD 20744
Natl. Young Buddhist Assn. - Defunct.
Natl. Young Farmer Educational Assn. [4653], PO Box 20326, Montgomery, AL 36120, (334)213-3276
Natl. Young Professionals Forum - Address unknown since 1999.
Natl. Youth Advocacy Alliance - Address unknown since 2001.
Natl. Youth Advocacy Coalition [13505], 1638 R St. NW, Ste. 300, Washington, DC 20009, (202)319-7596
Natl. Youth Agency [IO], Leicester, United Kingdom
Natl. Youth Alliance [★18800]
Natl. Youth Coun. of Ireland [IO], Dublin, Ireland
Natl. Youth Court Center [18854], c/o Amer. Probation and Parole Assn., PO Box 11910, Lexington, KY 40578-1910, (859)244-8193
Natl. Youth Development Found. - Defunct.
Natl. Youth Employment Coalition [13506], 1836 Jefferson Pl. NW, Washington, DC 20036, (202)659-1064
Natl. Youth Leadership Coun. [8754], 1667 Snelling Ave. N, Ste. D300, St. Paul, MN 55108, (651)631-3672
Natl. Youth Ministry Org. [★20268]
Natl. Youth Orchestra Assn. of Canada [IO], Toronto, ON, Canada
Natl. Youth Pro-Life Coalition - Address unknown since 1995.
Natl. Youth Rights Assn. [18855], 1133 19th St. NW, 9th Fl., Washington, DC 20036, (202)833-1200
Natl. Youth Sports Coaches Assn. [★23290]
Natl. Youth Sports Found. for the Prevention of Athletic Injuries [★16484]
Natl. Youth Sports Safety Found. [16484], 1 Beacon St., Ste. 3333, Boston, MA 02108, (617)367-6677
Natl. Youth and Student Peace Coalition [18226], PO Box 3674, Washington, DC 20027-0174, (800)228-1228
Natl. Zoo; Friends of the [7858]
NationaLease [★3384]
Nationales Olympisches Komitee fur Deutschland [★IO]
Nationalism
  League of the South [17125]
  Soc. for the Promotion of Educ. and Res. [IO]
Nationalist Chams Org. - Address unknown since 1989.
Nationalist Found. - Address unknown since 2008.
Nationalist Movement; The [18804]
The Nationalist Movement [18804], PO Box 2000, Learned, MS 39154, (601)885-2288
Nationalist Observer - Defunct.
Nationalist Party [IO], Pieta, Malta
Nationality Lawyers; Assn. of Immigration and [★5807]
Nationals [IO], Kingston, Australia
Nationless Worldwide Assn. [IO], Paris, France
Nations Assn; League of Free [★17610]
Nations; Gathering of [10742]
Nations Ministries [20370], PO Box 620, Springtown, TX 76082, (302)729-0835
Nations; Natl. Model United [8661]
Nation's Rpt. Card [★9253]
Nations Unies Commn. Economique pour l'Afrique [★IO]

Nations Unies pour l'Enfance; Fonds des [★11658]
Nationwide Action for a Fair Budget - Defunct.
Nationwide Caterers Assn. [IO], Solihull, United Kingdom
Nationwide Patrol [11640]
Native American
  Advancing Native Missions [19833]
  All Indian Pueblo Coun. [18089]
  Alliance of Tribal Tourism Advocates [19267]
  Amer. Indian Arts Coun. [10730]
  Amer. Indian Bus. Leaders [2830]
  Amer. Indian Culture Res. Center [10731]
  Amer. Indian Graduate Center [8426]
  Amer. Indian Heritage Found. [10732]
  Amer. Indian Higher Educ. Consortium [8935]
  Amer. Indian Inst. [10733]
  Amer. Indian Law Alliance [16973]
  Amer. Indian Liberation Crusade [12622]
  Amer. Indian Lib. Assn. [10319]
  Amer. Indian Movement [18090]
  Amer. Indian Philosophy Assn. [19268]
  Amer. Indian Res. and Development [8464]
  Amer. Indian Ritual Object Repatriation Found. [18091]
  Amer. Indian Sci. and Engg. Soc. [6987]
  Amer. Indian Youth Running Strong [12623]
  Americans for Indian Opportunity [12624]
  Assembly of First Nations [IO]
  Assn. on Amer. Indian Affairs [18092]
  Assn. of Amer. Indian Physicians [15989]
  Assn. of Community Tribal Schools [8936]
  Assn. of Native Amer. Medical Students [15087]
  Assn. for the Stud. of Amer. Indian Literatures [10734]
  Atlatl [9557]
  Authentic Artifact Collectors Assn. [21543]
  Bear Butte Intl. Alliance [19446]
  Before Columbus Found. [10416]
  Black and Indian Mission Off. [19587]
  Black Indians and Intertribal Native Amer. Assn. [19269]
  Catching the Dream [8427]
  Center for Third World Organizing [17099]
  Cherokee Natl. Historical Soc. [10735]
  Citizens Equal Rights Alliance [5800]
  Comanche Language and Cultural Preservation Comm. [10736]
  Consortia of Administrators for Native Amer. Rehabilitation [19270]
  Continental Confed. of Adopted Indians [10737]
  Coun. on Career for Minorities [8047]
  Coun. of Energy Rsrc. Tribes [18093]
  Coun. for Indian Educ. [8937]
  Coun. for Native Amer. Indians [10738]
  Crazy Horse Memorial Found. [10739]
  Creek Indian Memorial Assn. [10740]
  Cultural Conservancy [10741]
  First Nations Development Inst. [12625]
  For Mother Earth [17813]
  Gamma Delta Pi [24710]
  Gathering of Nations [10742]
  Great Lakes Indian Fish and Wildlife Commn. [5323]
  Heritage Inst. [19271]
  Honor the Earth [19272]
  Indian Arts and Crafts Assn. [10743]
  Indian Defense League of Am. [19273]
  Indian Educators Fed. [8938]
  Indian Heritage Coun. [10744]
  Indian Law Rsrc. Center [18094]
  Indian Youth of Am. [12626]
  Indians Into Medicine [8865]
  INROADS [8749]
  Inst. of Amer. Indian Arts [10745]
  Inst. for the Development of Indian Law [18095]
  Inst. for the Stud. of Amer. Cultures [10746]
  Inst. for Tribal Environmental Professionals [19274]
  Inter-Tribal Indian Ceremonial Assn. [10747]
  Intl. Assn. of Native Amer. Stud. [8939]
  Intl. Native Amer. Flute Assn. [10622]
  Intertribal Bison Cooperative [5036]
  Iroquois Stud. Assn. [10748]
  Lakota Student Alliance [19275]
  Leadership Enterprise for a Diverse Am. [9183]

A star before a book entry number signifies that the name is not listed separately, but is mentioned within the entry.

Maniilaq Assn. [12627]
Midwest Treaty Network [19276]
Natl. Alliance to Save Native Languages [10305]
Natl. Assn. of Native Amer. Stud. [8940]
Natl. Assn. of PreCollege Directors [8371]
Natl. Assn. of Tribal Historic Preservation Officers [10047]
Natl. Center for Amer. Indian Enterprise Development [12628]
Natl. Center for Neurogenic Commun. Disorders [16449]
Natl. Cong. of Amer. Indians [18096]
Natl. Coun. of Urban Indian Hea. [15277]
Natl. Environmental Coalition of Native Americans [5037]
Natl. Indian Bus. Assn. [751]
Natl. Indian Child Welfare Assn. [19277]
Natl. Indian Coun. on Aging [11311]
Natl. Indian Educ. Assn. [8941]
Natl. Indian Hea. Bd. [12629]
Natl. Indian Justice Center [19278]
Natl. Indian Youth Coun. [10749]
Natl. Native Amer. AIDS Prevention Center [16968]
Natl. Native Amer. EMS Assn. [14341]
Natl. Native Amer. (Indian) Cooperative [10750]
Natl. Native Amer. Law Enforcement Assn. [5998]
Natl. Native Amer. Law Students Assn. [8772]
Natl. Native Amer. Veterans Assn. [21313]
Natl. Soc. for Amer. Indian Elderly [19279]
Natl. Tribal Child Support Assn. [11713]
Natl. Tribal Development Assn. [19280]
Natl. Tribal Environmental Coun. [18097]
Native Amer. Bus. Alliance [19281]
Native Amer. Church of North Am. of the Cowlitz Indians [19447]
Native Amer. Community Bd. [12630]
Native Amer. Fatherhood and Families Assn. [12681]
Native Amer. Finance Officers Assn. [1442]
Native Amer. Fish and Wildlife Soc. [4595]
Native Amer. Indian Info. and Trade Center [24358]
Native Amer. Inst. [10751]
Native Amer. Leadership Alliance [20455]
Native Amer. Recreation and Sport Inst. [23631]
Native Amer. Rights Fund [18098]
Native Amer. Sports Coun. [23632]
Native Amer. Water Assn. [4012]
Native Americans in Philanthropy [12733]
Native Elder Hea. Care Rsrc. Center [19282]
Native Financial Educ. Coalition [8442]
Native Tourism Alliance [24381]
Native Writers' Circle of the Americas [19283]
Navajo Area School Bd. Assn. [8942]
North Am. Indigenous Ministries [20376]
North Am. Native Amer. (Indian) Info. and Trade Center [10752]
North Am. Alliance for the Advancement of Native Peoples [12631]
North Am. Alliance for the Advancement of Native Peoples [IO]
Old Sleepy Eye Collectors' Club of Am. [21934]
Order of the Indian Wars [10479]
Oyate [19284]
Pan Amer. Indian Assn. [10753]
Phi Sigma Nu Native Amer. Fraternity [24647]
Punjabi-American Cultural Assn. [10223]
Quality Educ. for Minorities Network [8303]
Red Earth [19285]
Seventh Generation Fund for Indian Development [18099]
Soc. of Amer. Royalty [18082]
Tekakwitha Conf. Natl. Center [19727]
Thunderbird Amer. Indian Dancers [10754]
Trail of Tears Assn. [11057]
Tree of Peace Soc. [9913]
Tribal Preservation Prog. [10755]
United Indian Missions, Intl. [20405]
United Indians of All Tribes Found. [18100]
United Natl. Indian Tribal Youth [10756]
United South and Eastern Tribes [12632]
UNITY: Journalists of Color [3172]
White Bison [10757]
Wordcraft Circle of Native Writers and Storytellers [9859]

World Emergency Relief [12885]
Native Amer. AIDS Prevention Center; Natl. [16968]
Native Amer. Art Stud. Assn. [7965], Arizona State Univ., School of Art, Tempe, AZ 85287-1505
Native Amer., Black, Chicano, Puerto Rican, Asian Americans; Natl. Assn. of Interdisciplinary Stud. for [★9919]
Native Amer. Bus. Alliance [19281], 30700 Telegraph Rd., Ste. 1675, Bingham Farms, MI 48025-4566, (248)988-9344
Native Amer. Cancer Res. [13857], 3022 S Nova Rd., Pine, CO 80470-7830, (303)838-9359
Native Amer. Children of Alcoholics; Natl. Assn. for [11627]
Native Amer. Church of North Am. of the Cowlitz Indians [19447]
Native Amer. Community Bd. [12630], PO Box 572, Lake Andes, SD 57356-0572, (605)487-7072
Native Amer. Fatherhood and Families Assn. [12681], 123 N Centennial Way, Ste. 150, Mesa, AZ 85201, (480)833-5007
Native Amer. Finance Officers Assn. [1442], PO Box 50637, Phoenix, AZ 85076-0637, (928)567-1007
Native Amer. Fish and Wildlife Soc. [4595], 8333 Greenwood Blvd., Ste. 260, Denver, CO 80221, (303)466-1725
Native Amer. Heritage Found. [★10732]
Native Amer. Indian Info. and Trade Center [24358], c/o Reservation Creation Women's Charitable Trust, PO Box 27626, Tucson, AZ 85726-7626, (520)622-4900
Native Amer. Inst. [10751], 220 W Central Ave., No. 314, Brea, CA 92821, (714)256-4945
Native Amer. Journalists Assn. [3147], Univ. of Oklahoma, Gaylord Coll., Norman, OK 73019-0001, (405)436-3744
Native Amer. Law Students Assn. [★8772]
Native Amer. Leadership Alliance [20455], 3600 New York Ave. NE, 3rd Fl., Washington, DC 20002, (503)490-8535
Native Amer. Medical Students; Assn. of [15087]
Native Amer. Policy Network - Address unknown since 2003.
Native Amer. Press Assn. [★3147]
Native Amer. Press Assn. - Address unknown since 1990.
Native Amer. Public Broadcasting Consortium [★9767]
Native Amer. Public Telecommunications [9767], 1800 N 33rd St., Lincoln, NE 68503, (402)472-3522
Native Amer. Recreation and Sport Inst. [23631], c/o Judith G. Shepherd, Founder, 116 W Osage, Greenfield, IN 46140, (317)462-4245
Native Amer. Res. Inst. - Defunct.
Native Amer. Rights Fund [18098], 1506 Broadway, Boulder, CO 80302, (303)447-8760
Native Amer. Scholarship Fund [★8427]
Native Amer. Science Education Assn. - Defunct.
Native Amer. Sports Coun. [23632], 1235 Lake Plaza Dr., Ste. 221, Colorado Springs, CO 80906, (719)632-5282
Native Amer. Stud; Natl. Assn. of [8940]
Native Amer. Water Assn. [4012], 1662 Hwy. 395, Ste. 212, Minden, NV 89423, (775)782-6636
Native Amer. Women Hea. Educ. Rsrc. Center [★12630]
Native Amer. Women's Hea. Educ. Rsrc. Center [16908], PO Box 572, Lake Andes, SD 57356-0572, (605)487-7072
Native Amer. Women's Hea. Educ. Rsrc. Center [IO], Lake Andes, SD, United States
Native Amer. Women's Leadership Proj. [★IO]
Native Amer. Women's Leadership Proj. [★13448]
Native Amer. Youth Initiative [★13448]
Native Amer. Youth Initiative [★IO]
Native Amers. for a Clean Environment - Address unknown since 1999.
Native Americans in Philanthropy [12733], 2801 21st Ave. S, Ste. 132 D, Minneapolis, MN 55407, (612)724-8798
Native Americans in Sci; Soc. for Advancement of Chicanos and [7630]
Native Bison; Northwest Alaska [★12627]
Native Clergy; Soc. of St. Peter the Apostle for [★19725]

Native Daughters of the Golden West [18986], 543 Baker St., San Francisco, CA 94117, (415)563-9091
Native Elder Hea. Care Rsrc. Center [19282], PO Box 6508, Mailstop F800, Aurora, CO 80045-0508, (303)724-1414
Native Financial Educ. Coalition [8442], c/o Joanna Donohoe, Coor., PO Box 32188, Palm Beach Gardens, FL 33420, (561)626-9700
Native Fish Australia [IO], Doncaster, Australia
Native Fish Soc. [5347], PO Box 19570, Portland, OR 97280, (503)977-3133
Native Forest Coun. [4427], PO Box 2190, Eugene, OR 97402, (541)688-2600
Native Forest Network [4428], PO Box 8251, Missoula, MT 59807, (406)542-7343
Native Forest Network Australia [IO], Deloraine, Australia
Native Forest Network - Australia [★IO]
Native Habitat Org. [4596], c/o Nol Ward, Pres., PO Box 101071, Fort Worth, TX 76185, (817)396-4370
Native Hawaiian Culture and Arts Prog. [10884], Bishop Museum, 1525 Bernice St., Honolulu, HI 96817, (808)847-3511
Native Indian/Inuit Photographers' Assn. [IO], Hamilton, ON, Canada
Native Preacher Company - Defunct.
Native Seeds/SEARCH [4429], 526 N 4th Ave., Tucson, AZ 85705-8450, (520)622-5561
Native Seeds/Southwestern Endangered Arid-Land Rsrc. Clearing House [★4429]
Native Sons of the Golden State [★19013]
Native Sons of the Golden West [18987], 414 Mason St., Ste. 300, San Francisco, CA 94102, (800)337-1875
Native Tourism Alliance [24381], 1900 Wazee St., Ste. 100, Denver, CO 80202, (303)661-9819
Native Women's Assn. of Canada [IO], Ottawa, ON, Canada
Native Writers' Circle of the Americas [19283], c/o Native Amer. Stud., Univ. of Oklahoma, 633 Elm Ave., 216 Ellison Hall, Norman, OK 73019-3119, (405)325-2312
Natives of the Four Directions Cultural Center - Address unknown since 2003.
NATO Consultation, Command and Control Agency [IO], Brussels, Belgium
NATO Parliamentarians' Conf. [★IO]
NATO Parliamentary Assembly [IO], Brussels, Belgium
NATO Tattoo Assn. - Address unknown since 1995.
NATOPSS - Learn to Care [IO], Birmingham, United Kingdom
NATPAC [★18067]
NATPE Educational Foundation [★571]
NATPE Educational Foundation [★IO]
NATSO [3424], 1737 King St., Ste. 200, Alexandria, VA 22314, (703)549-2100
NATSO Found. [8948], 1737 King St., Ste. 200, Alexandria, VA 22314, (703)549-2100
NATSO, Representing the Travel Plaza and Truckstop Indus. [★3424]
Natur og Ungdom [★IO]
Natural Area Coun. - Defunct.
Natural Areas Assn. [4430], PO Box 1504, Bend, OR 97709, (541)317-0199
Natural Biocontrol Producers; Assn. of [5074]
Natural Casing Inst. [★2659]
Natural Casing Inst. [★IO]
Natural Colored Wool Growers Association [IO], Valparaiso, IN, United States
Natural Colored Wool Growers Assn. [5209], 429 W US30, Valparaiso, IN 46385, (219)759-9665
Natural Conditions Ecological Soc. of Am; Comm. on Preservation of [★4433]
Natural Cork Quality Coun. [★1645]
Natural Disaster Hospitals - Address unknown since 1995.
Natural Disasters
Floodplain Mgt. Assn. [5038]
GeoHazards Intl. [12633]
GeoHazards Intl. [IO]
Mir Pace Intl. [12872]
Natl. Assn. of Storm Chasers and Spotters [13413]

Reference to "IO" in place of a book number signifies that the association may be found in the 45th edition of International Organizations.

Natl. Storm Shelter Assn. [2831]
Natural Hazards Res. and Applications Info. Center [7355]
Natural Dyes Intl. [8213], Box 21912, El Prado, NM 87529, (505)751-1596

Natural Family Planning
Amer. Acad. of Fertility Care Professionals [12634]
Billings Ovulation Method Assn. - USA [12635]
Couple to Couple League [12636]
EngenderHealth [12180]
Family of the Americas Found. [12637]
Healthy Teen Network [12182]
Intl. Planned Parenthood Fed., Western Hemisphere Region [12184]
Natl. Abortion Fed. [11223]
Natl. Commn. on Human Life, Reproduction and Rhythm [16008]
Natl. Family Planning and Reproductive Hea. Assn. [12185]
Pathfinder Intl. [12186]
Planned Parenthood Fed. of Am. [12187]
Wellstart Intl. [14666]
World Org. Ovulation Method Billings, Argentina [IO]
World Org. Ovulation Method Billings, Canada [IO]
World Org. Ovulation Method Billings, Italy [IO]
Natural Family Planning; Amer. Acad. of [★12634]
Natural Fertility New Zealand [IO], Wellington, New Zealand
Natural Figure Art Assn. [9462]
Natural Food Associates - Address unknown since 2001.
Natural Food Inst. - Defunct.
Natural Gas Assn. of Am; Independent [★1680]
Natural Gas Assn. of Am; Interstate [1680]
Natural Gas Consumers Information Center - Defunct.
Natural Gas Processors Assn. [★2924]
Natural Gas Processors Supplier's Assn. [★2925]
Natural Gas Supply Assn. [1682], 805 15th St. NW, Ste. 510, Washington, DC 20005, (202)326-9300
Natural Gas Supply Comm. [★1682]
Natural Gas Vehicle for Am. [6519], 400 N Capitol St. NW, Washington, DC 20001, (202)824-7366
Natural Gas Vehicle Assn. [★6519]
Natural Gas Vehicle Assn. [IO], Leamington Spa, United Kingdom
Natural Gas Vehicle Coalition [★6519]
Natural Gasoline Assn. of Am. [★2924]
Natural Gasoline Supply Men's Assn. [★2925]
Natural Guard Fund - Defunct.
Natural Hazards Res. and Applications Info. Center [7355], Univ. of Colorado, 482 UCB, Boulder, CO 80309-0482, (303)492-6818
Natural Helping Networks Project - Defunct.
Natural Heritage Trust; Big Thicket [4368]
Natural and Historical Anomalies; Center for the Stud. of [7862]
Natural History Assn; Shenandoah [★10062]
Natural History Assn; Yosemite [★7367]
Natural History Collections; Soc. for the Preservation of [10064]

Natural Hygiene
British Natural Hygiene Soc. [IO]
Intl. Assn. of Hygienic Physicians [IO]
Intl. Assn. of Hygienic Physicians [15278]
Natl. Hea. Assn. [15279]
Natural Hygiene Soc; Amer. [★15279]
Natural Hygiene Soc; Amer. Physiological and [★15279]
Natural Hygienists; Intl. Assn. of Professional [★15278]
Natural Law Soc. [10813], c/o Dr. Robert L. Chapman, Ed., Dept. of Philosophy and Religious Stud., Pace Univ., 41 Park Row, Rm. 310, New York, NY 10038, (212)346-1460
Natural Law Society [IO], New York, NY, United States
Natural Marketing Assn. [★13609]
Natural Medicine Pharmacists; Assn. of [15282]
Natural Philosophy; Soc. for [7295]
Natural Product Broker Assn. - Defunct.
Natural Products Assn. [3425], 2112 E 4th St., Ste. 200, Santa Ana, CA 92705, (714)460-7732

Natural Products Marketing Coun. [IO], Truro, NS, Canada

Natural Resources
African Amer. Environmentalist Assn. [4529]
Alliance for Intl. Reforestation [4344]
Amer. Exploration and Production Coun. [2914]
Amer. Forests [4347]
Amer. Land Conservancy [4348]
Amer. Lands Alliance [4533]
Amer. Soc. of Mining and Reclamation [6114]
Animals as Intermediaries [4157]
Aquaculture Intl. [4169]
Aquatic Resources Educ. Assn. [7956]
Assn. of Fish and Wildlife Agencies [4360]
Assn. of Metropolitan Water Agencies [6135]
Assn. to Preserve Cape Cod [4361]
Assn. for Professional Observers [4667]
Camp Fire Club of Am. [4369]
Camp Fire Conservation Fund [4370]
Center for Commun. Programs [12755]
Center for Rsrc. Mgt. [4373]
Children of the Earth United [4621]
Clean Beaches Coun. [4540]
Clean Energy Gp. [6948]
Clean Energy States Alliance [6949]
Coastal Conservation Assn. [4376]
Connecticut River Watershed Coun. [4377]
ConservAmerica [4378]
Conservation and Res. Found. [4383]
Conservation Tech. Info. Center [4384]
Conservation Treaty Support Fund [4385]
Delta Waterfowl Found. [5308]
Desert Fishes Coun. [4388]
EarthEcho Intl. [4391]
EarthWave Soc. [4556]
Energy and Mineral Law Found. [6136]
Environmental Entrepreneurs [4392]
Forest Stewardship Coun. - U.S. [4684]
Freshwater Mollusk Conservation Soc. [5034]
Freshwater Soc. [5091]
Future Nepal [IO]
Geode Rsrc., Conservation, and Development [4077]
Grassland Heritage Found. [4404]
Great Lakes Commn. [6137]
Henry M. Jackson Found. [17480]
Intl. Assn. of Natural Rsrc. Pilots [4187]
Intl. Assn. for Soc. and Natural Resources [5039]
Intl. Assn. for Soc. and Natural Resources [IO]
Intl. Joint Commn. [IO]
Intl. Joint Commn. [5040]
Intl. Ranger Fed. [IO]
Intl. Union for the Conservation of Nature and Natural Resources U.S. [4412]
Interstate Coun. on Water Policy [6138]
Izaak Walton League of Am. [4413]
Izaak Walton League of Am. Endowment [4414]
Keepers of the Waters [5273]
Marine Fish Conservation Network [4419]
Mineral Economics and Mgt. Soc. [6139]
Mineral Economics and Management Society [IO]
Minorities in Agriculture, Natural Resources and Related Sciences [10486]
Natl. Assn. of Exotic Pest Plant Councils [5077]
Natl. Assn. of Flood and Storm Water Mgt. Agencies [6140]
Natl. Assn. of Rsrc. Conservation and Development Councils [4421]
Natl. Assn. of State Land Reclamationists [6118]
Natl. Conservation District Employees Assn. [24209]
Natl. Forest Protection Alliance [4592]
Natl. Mitigation Banking Assn. [4425]
Natl. Religious Partnership for the Env. [19941]
Natl. Rural Water Assn. [12939]
Natl. Soc. of Consulting Soil Scientists [5222]
Natl. Wilderness Inst. [5344]
Natl. Wildlife Fed. [4426]
Native Amer. Fish and Wildlife Soc. [4595]
Natural Areas Assn. [4430]
Natural Resources Coun. of Am. [4431]
Natural Resources Defense Coun. [4432]
Negative Population Growth [12756]
New Water Supply Coalition [7839]
Ocean Res. and Conservation Assn. [4436]

Outfitters Assn. of Am. [23642]
Ozark Soc. [4438]
Population Action Intl. [12758]
Population Commun. [12759]
Population Connection [12761]
Population Coun. [12762]
Population-Environment Balance [12763]
Population Inst. [12764]
Population Rsrc. Center [12765]
Public Lands Coun. [5127]
Rachel Carson Coun. [13330]
Renewable Natural Resources Found. [4443]
Resource Policy Inst. [4603]
River of Words [4186]
Rock the Earth [4604]
Rocky Mountain Inst. [18101]
Rocky Mountain Mineral Law Found. [6141]
Rocky Mountain Mineral Law Foundation [IO]
Save Our Seas [4449]
School of Living [10178]
Sierra Club [4520]
SkyTruth [4637]
Soc. for Conservation GIS [6831]
Soc. for Range Mgt. [5166]
Student Conservation Assn. [4455]
Sustainable Obtainable Solutions [5129]
Telapak [IO]
Theodore Roosevelt Conservation Partnership [4458]
Trees, Water and People [4610]
Turner Found. [4611]
U.S. Aquaculture Soc. [4183]
U.S. Consortium of Soil Sci. Associations [5223]
U.S. Dept. of Agriculture - Forest Ser. Volunteers Prog. [4699]
Upper Mississippi River Conservation Comm. [4463]
World Bamboo Org. [5041]
World Bamboo Org. [IO]
World Environmental Org. [4475]
World Parks [4617]
World Preserve [4476]
World Resources Inst. [4477]
WorldWIDE Network, Women in Development and Environment [4618]
Natural Resources Coun. of Am. [4431], 1616 P St. NW, Ste. 340, Washington, DC 20036, (202)232-6531
Natural Resources Defense Coun. [4432], 40 W 20th St., New York, NY 10011, (212)727-2700
Natural Resources Found; Renewable [4443]
Natural Resources Info. Coun. [10377], c/o Beth Thomsett-Scott, Sci. Librarian, Sci. and Tech. Lib., Univ. of North Texas, PO Box 305190, Denton, TX 76203-5190
Natural Resources Info. Coun. [IO], Denton, TX, United States
Natural Resources, and Life and Human Sciences; Assn. for Commun. Excellence in Agriculture, [4098]
Natural Rights Center [★6235]
Natural Rights Center [★IO]
Natural Rubber Shippers Assn. - Defunct.
Natural Sci. Collections Alliance [6590], 1313 Dolley Madison Blvd., Ste. 402, McLean, VA 22101, (703)790-1745
Natural Sci. Illustrators; Guild of [7153]
Natural Sci. for Youth Found. - Defunct.

Natural Sciences
Acad. of Natural Sciences [7356]
Acad. of Natural Sciences [IO]
Amer. Exploration and Production Coun. [2914]
Amer. Museum of Natural History [7357]
Amer. Nature Stud. Soc. [7358]
Amer. Quaternary Assn. [7359]
Amer. Soc. of Naturalists [7360]
Big Bend Natural History Assn. [7361]
Birmingham Natural History Soc. [IO]
Bombay Natural History Soc. [IO]
Canadian Quaternary Assn. [IO]
Centre for Res. Ethics [IO]
European Nature Heritage Fund [IO]
Field Stud. Coun. [IO]
Green Leaf Natl. Honor Soc. [24471]
HOPOS - The Intl. Soc. for the History of Philosophy of Sci. [9103]

A star before a book entry number signifies that the name is not listed separately, but is mentioned within the entry.

Intl. Assn. for Soc. and Natural Resources [5039]
Internet Infidels [7490]
Interspecies [7223]
John Burroughs Assn. [7362]
Linnean Soc. of London [IO]
Luxembourg Naturalist Soc. [IO]
Maria Mitchell Assn. [6509]
Natl. Assn. for Interpretation [7363]
Natl. Tech. Assn. [7752]
Natural Dyes Intl. [8213]
Nature Kenya: the East Africa Natural History Soc. [IO]
Oceanic Soc. Expeditions [23016]
Paleontological Res. Institution/Museum of the Earth [7429]
Ray Soc. [IO]
Royal Soc. [IO]
Royal Soc. of South Australia [IO]
Sigma Xi, The Sci. Res. Soc. [24588]
Soc. for Evolutionary Anal. in Law [6539]
Soc. for the History of Natural History [IO]
Soc. for Molecular Biology and Evolution [6601]
Soc. for Northwestern Vertebrate Biology [7364]
Turkish Amer. Scientists and Scholars Assn. [7636]
U.S. Soc. for Ecological Economics [6865]
Western Natl. Parks Assn. [7365]
Western Soc. of Naturalists [7366]
World Acad. of Art and Sci. [9612]
Yosemite Assn. [7367]
Natural Soda Ash Corp; Amer. [1725]
Natural-Source Vitamin E Assn. - Address unknown since 2004.
Natural Waters; Coun. of [★509]
Naturalist Soc. of the Central Atlantic States; Audubon [4364]
Naturalists; Amer. Soc. of [7360]
Naturalists; Assn. of Interpretive [★7363]
The Naturalists - Defunct.
Naturalists; Western Soc. of [7366]
Nature Canada [IO], Ottawa, ON, Canada
Nature Center Design Network - Address unknown since 2004.
Nature Conservancy [4433], 4245 Fairfax Dr., Ste. 100, Arlington, VA 22203-1606, (703)841-5300
Nature Conservation Soc. of Japan [IO], Tokyo, Japan
Nature and Environmental Writers - Coll. and Univ. Educators [8362], c/o St. Thomas Aquinas Coll., 125 Rte. 340, Sparkill, NY 10976, (845)398-4247
Nature Farming Intl. Res. Found. [★IO]
Nature; Interfaith Coun. for the Protection of Animals and [4409]
Nature Kenya [IO], Nairobi, Kenya
Nature Kenya: the East Africa Natural History Soc. [IO], Nairobi, Kenya
Nature of Man; Found. for Res. on the [★7452]
Nature; People, Animals, [13319]
Nature Photography Assn; North Amer. [3006]
Nature Religions
  Hedonic Soc. of Am. [10758]
  Universal Pantheist Soc. [20586]
Nature; Second [8495]
Nature Stud. Soc; Amer. [7358]
Nature of Wellness [13701], PO Box 10400, Glendale, CA 91209-3400, (818)790-6384
Nature of Wellness [IO], Glendale, CA, United States
Nature and Youth [IO], Oslo, Norway
Naturfreunde Osterreich [★IO]
The Naturist Soc. [10763], PO Box 132, Oshkosh, WI 54903, (920)426-5009
The Naturists [★10763]
Naturists; The [★10763]
Naturopathic Medicine; Canadian Coll. of [IO]
Naturopaths; Gen. Coun. and Register of [IO]
Naturopathy
  Alberta Assn. of Naturopathic Practitioners [IO]
  Amer. Assn. of Naturopathic Physicians [15280]
  Amer. Naturopathic Medical Assn. [15281]
  Assn. of Accredited Naturopathic Medical Colleges [8943]
  Assn. of Natural Medicine Pharmacists [15282]
  Canadian Coll. of Naturopathic Medicine [IO]
  Nova Scotia Assn. of Naturopathic Doctors [IO]

  Ontario Assn. of Naturopathic Doctors [IO]
NAUCRATES [IO], Cori, Italy
NAUGAS [★2143]
Nauru Badminton Assn. [IO], Nauru, Nauru
Nauru Olympic Comm. [IO], Nauru, Nauru
Nauru Tennis Assn. [IO], Aiwo, Nauru
Nautical Archaeology Soc. [IO], Portsmouth, United Kingdom
Nautical Inst. [IO], London, United Kingdom
Nautical Research Guild [IO], Cuba, NY, United States
Nautical Res. Guild [21880], 31 Water St., Ste. 7, Cuba, NY 14727, (585)968-8111
Nautilus Inst. [18593], Univ. of San Francisco, 2130 Fulton St., LM200, San Francisco, CA 94117-1080, (415)422-5523
Nautilus Inst. [IO], San Francisco, CA, United States
Nautilus UK [IO], London, United Kingdom
Navajo Area School Bd. Assn. [8942], PO Box 3719, Window Rock, AZ 86515-0578, (928)871-5225
Navajo-Churro Sheep Assn. [5210], PO Box 94, Ojo Caliente, NM 87549, (505)737-0488
Navajo Code Talkers Assn. [21396], PO Box 1182, Window Rock, AZ 86515, (520)871-5468
Navajo Gospel Crusade [★20405]
Navajo Gospel Crusade [★IO]
Navajo Natl. Coun. [★8942]
Naval Air Stations Employee Organizations; Natl. Coun. of [★6088]
Naval Air Stations; Natl. Coun. of Indus. [6088]
Naval Airship Assn. [6379], c/o Peter F. Brouwer, Treas., 1950 SW Cycle St., Port St. Lucie, FL 34953-1778, (772)871-9379
Naval Aviation Museum Found. [★6379]
Naval Civilian Administrators Assn. [★6094]
Naval Civilian Managers Assn. [6094], PO Box 215, Portsmouth, VA 23705, (757)396-2265
Naval Commandery of Am. [★21215]
Naval Engineering
  Inst. of Marine Engg., Sci. and Tech. [IO]
  Marine Corps Engineer Assn. [6142]
  Pan-American Inst. of Naval Engg. [IO]
  Royal Institution of Naval Architects [IO]
  Soc. of Naval Architects and Marine Engineers [7368]
  Trireme Trust U.S.A. [10483]
Naval Engineers; Amer. Soc. of [7270]
Naval Enlisted Reserve Assn. [6095], 6703 Farragut Ave., Falls Church, VA 22042-2189, (703)534-1329
Naval Historical Collectors and Res. Assn. [IO], North Walsham, United Kingdom
Naval Historical Found. [10478], 1306 Dahlgren Ave. SE, Washington Navy Yard, Washington, DC 20374-5055, (202)678-4333
Naval Historical Soc. of Australia [IO], Garden Island, Australia
Naval Intelligence Professionals [6096], PO Box 11579, Burke, VA 22009-1579, (703)250-6765
Naval Legion of the U.S. [★21215]
Naval and Marine Scouts; Amer. [★20718]
Naval and Military Order of the Spanish Amer. War - Address unknown since 1995.
Naval Militia; New York Junior [★20718]
Naval Oceanographic Off; Ocean Floor Anal. Div. of U.S. [★7404]
Naval Officers' Assn. of Canada [IO], Ottawa, ON, Canada
Naval Officers Assn; Natl. [6093]
Naval Order of the U.S. [21215], PO Box 2714, Merrifield, VA 22116-2714, (703)323-0929
Naval Records Club [★10476]
Naval Records Club [★IO]
Naval Reserve of Am; Junior [★20718]
Naval Reserve Assn. [6097], 1619 King St., Alexandria, VA 22314-2793, (703)548-5800
Naval Reserve Officers Assn. [★6103]
Naval ROTC Colleges and Universities; Assn. of [★8884]
Naval Sailing Assn; Annapolis [21867]
Naval Sea Cadet Corps [6098], 2300 Wilson Blvd., Arlington, VA 22201-3308, (703)243-6910
Naval Services; Reserve Officers of the [★6103]
Naval Ships Assn; Historic [10440]
Naval Shore Establishments; Natl. Assn. of Master Mechanics and Foreman of [★6085]

Naval Shore Establishments; Natl. Assn. of Superintendents of U.S. [6085]
Naval Submarine League [17384], PO Box 1146, Annandale, VA 22003, (877)280-7827
Navigation
  Arab Inst. of Navigation [IO]
  Canadian Navigation Soc. [IO]
  DBA - The Barge Assn. [IO]
  European Barge Union [IO]
  German Inst. of Navigation [IO]
  Inst. of Navigation [7369]
  Intl. Assn. of Marine Aids to Navigation and Lighthouse Authorities [IO]
  Intl. Loran Assn. [IO]
  Intl. Loran Assn. [7370]
  Intl. Navigation Assn. - Belgium [IO]
  Intl. Navigation Assn. - USA [IO]
  Japan Inst. of Navigation [IO]
  Netherlands Inst. of Navigation [IO]
  Oceanic Navigation Res. Soc. [10444]
  Royal Inst. of Navigation [IO]
  USS Wainwright Veterans Assn. [21329]
Navigation Res. Soc; Oceanic [10444]
The Navigators [19817], PO Box 6000, Colorado Springs, CO 80934, (719)598-1212
Navigators; Guild of Air Pilots and Air [IO]
Navigators Observer Assn; Air Force [20659]
Navigators Observers Assn; Ellington [★20659]
Navion Soc; Amer. [21428]
Navy
  AdoptaPlatoon [11489]
  AE Sailors Assn. [6143]
  Aircraft Carrier Indus. Base Coalition [1148]
  All Navy Women's Natl. Alliance [6144]
  Amer. Battleship Assn. [21210]
  Annapolis Naval Sailing Assn. [21867]
  Any Soldier [11490]
  Armed Forces Sports [6069]
  Assn. of Amer. Military Uniform Collectors [22628]
  Assn. of Military Surgeons of the U.S. [15263]
  Battle of Ormoc Bay Assn. [21390]
  Beirut Veterans of Am. [21287]
  Books For Soldiers [11491]
  Escort Carrier Sailors and Airmen Assn. [21185]
  Fleet Air Arm Officers Assn. [IO]
  Fleet Reserve Assn. [21211]
  Force Recon Assn. [21212]
  Indian Navy Found. [IO]
  Intl. Naval Res. Org. [10476]
  Judge Advocates Assn. [6078]
  Marine Corps Cryptologic Assn. [21174]
  Marine Corps Engineer Assn. [6142]
  Marine Corps Recruiters Assn. [5799]
  Military Officers Assn. of Am. [21235]
  Mobile Riverine Force Assn. [21346]
  Natl. Assn. of Fleet Tug Sailors [21213]
  Natl. Chief Petty Officers' Assn. [21214]
  Natl. Coun. of Indus. Naval Air Stations [6088]
  Natl. Counter Intelligence Corps Assn. [21164]
  Natl. Naval Officers Assn. [6093]
  Naval Airship Assn. [6379]
  Naval Civilian Managers Assn. [6094]
  Naval Enlisted Reserve Assn. [6095]
  Naval Historical Found. [10478]
  Naval Officers' Assn. of Canada [IO]
  Naval Order of the U.S. [21215]
  Naval Reserve Assn. [6097]
  Navy Club of the U.S.A. [6099]
  Navy Club of the U.S.A. Auxiliary [6100]
  Navy League of the U.S. [6101]
  Navy Mail Ser. Veterans Assn. [21216]
  Navy and Marine Living History Assn. [21206]
  Navy Nurse Corps Assn. [2832]
  Navy Records Soc. [IO]
  Navy Seabee Veterans of Am. [21217]
  Navy Wifeline Assn. [21199]
  Oper. AC [11492]
  Oper. Homelink [11494]
  Oper. Sandbox [11495]
  Oper. ShoeBox [11496]
  Oper. Soldier Support [11497]
  Oper.: Take a Soldier to the Movies [11498]
  Oper. We Do Care [11499]
  Orders and Medals Soc. of Am. [22631]
  Patrol Craft Sailors Assn. [21218]

Reference to "IO" in place of a book number signifies that the association may be found in the 45th edition of International Organizations.

Proj. Handclasp [17911]
Retired Activities Br. [6104]
Salisbury Sound Assn. [21219]
Salute Our Services [11500]
Sea Ser. Leadership Assn. [21238]
Sino-American Cooperative Org. [21405]
Soc. of Medical Consultants to the Armed Forces [15265]
Soc. of Military Otolaryngologists - Head and Neck Surgeons [15267]
Soc. of U.S. Naval Flight Surgeons [13544]
Submarine Indus. Base Coun. [1149]
Support Our Soldiers Am. [11502]
Swift Boat Veterans for Truth [21324]
Tailhook Assn. [6106]
Tin Can Sailors - The Natl. Assn. of Destroyer Veterans [21220]
Tragedy Assistance Prog. for Survivors [11503]
Trireme Trust U.S.A. [10483]
U.S. Naval Cryptologic Veterans Assn. [21327]
U.S. Naval Inst. [6110]
U.S. Navy Memorial Found. [21221]
U.S. Navy Salvage Divers Reunited [21409]
U.S. Navy TACAMO Survivors [21222]
U.S. Submarine Veterans of World War II [21410]
Universal Ship Cancellation Soc. [22889]
USMC Vietnam Tankers Assn. [21337]
USS (BB-42) Idaho Assn. [21223]
USS Chilton Assn. [21224]
USS Constellation Museum [10449]
USS Intrepid Assn. of Former Crew Members [21225]
U.S.S. LCI Natl. Assn. [21328]
USS Leyte CV32 Assn. [21226]
USS Liberty Veterans Assn. [21227]
USS LSM-LSMR Assn. [21228]
USS Nevada Assn. (BB-36/SSBN-733) [21229]
USS Nimitz (CVN-68) Assn. [21230]
USS North Carolina Battleship Assn. [21411]
USS Pyro AE-1 and AE-24 Assn. [21231]
USS St. Louis CL-49 Assn. [10450]
USS Wainwright Veterans Assn. [21329]
USS Wisconsin Assn. [21232]
Veteran's Assn. of the USS Iowa [21233]
Vietnam Era Seabees [21339]
WAVES Natl. [21234]
Women of Naval Special Warfare [6145]
Navy, and Air Force Veterans in Canada; Army, [IO]
Navy Anesthesia Soc. [13687], c/o LCDR David G. Elkins, Sec., Dept. of Anesthesiology, Naval Medical Ctr., 34800 Bob Wilson Dr., San Diego, CA 92134-5000, (619)532-8943
Navy Carrier Soc. [22653], 225 W Orchid Ln., Phoenix, AZ 85021
Navy Club of the U.S.A. [6099], 6134 S 375 W, Lafayette, IN 47909, (800)628-7265
Navy Club of the U.S.A. Auxiliary [6100], 124 E Front St., Delphi, IN 46923-1508, (765)564-6147
Navy League [★IO]
Navy League Cadet Corps. [★6098]
Navy League of the U.S. [6101], 2300 Wilson Blvd., Ste. 200, Arlington, VA 22201-3308, (703)528-1775
Navy League of the U.S. [IO], Arlington, VA, United States
Navy Mail Ser. Veterans Assn. [21216], 2768 State Rte. 29, Dolgeville, NY 13329, (315)429-8645
Navy-Marine Corps Coun. - Defunct.
Navy-Marine Corps Relief Soc. [18960], 875 N Randolph St., Ste. 225, Arlington, VA 22203, (703)696-4904
Navy and Marine Living History Assn. [21206], 422 Clay St., Erlanger, KY 41018-1466
Navy Mothers' Clubs of America - Address unknown since 2001.
Navy Mutual Aid Assn. [18961], Henderson Hall, 29 Carpenter Rd., Arlington, VA 22212, (703)614-1638
Navy Nurse Corps Assn. [2832], PO Box 1229, Oak Harbor, WA 98277-1229, (360)678-0825
Navy Records Soc. [IO], Petersfield, United Kingdom
Navy Relief Soc. [★18960]
Navy Salvage Divers Reunited; U.S. [21409]
Navy Seabee Veterans of Am. [21217], c/o Mel Ramige, Natl. Sec., 555 Fairview Ave., Creve Coeur, IL 61610-3237, (309)699-7344

Navy Union, U.S.A; Army and [21286]
Navy Wifeline Assn. [21199], Washington Navy Yard, Bldg. 120, Washington, DC 20374, (202)433-2332
Navy Wives Clubs of America - Address unknown since 2002.
Navy Yards and Naval Stations; Natl. Assn. of Master Workmen of [★6085]
NAWE: Advancing Women in Higher Education - Defunct.
Nazarene Compassionate Ministries Intl. [19818], 6401 The Paseo, Kansas City, MO 64131-1213, (877)626-4145
Nazarene Compassionate Ministries International [IO], Kansas City, MO, United States
Nazarene Foreign Missionary Soc. [★IO]
Nazarene Foreign Missionary Soc. [★20371]
Nazarene Missions Intl. [20371], 6401 The Paseo, Kansas City, MO 64131, (816)333-7000
Nazarene Missions Intl. [IO], Kansas City, MO, United States
Nazarene Univ. Alumni Assn; Northwest [18916]
Nazarene World Mission Soc. [★20371]
Nazarene World Mission Soc. [★IO]
Nazarene World Missionary Soc. [★IO]
Nazarene World Missionary Soc. [★20371]
Nazi Party; Amer. [★18805]
Nazi War Criminals to Justice; Ad Hoc Comm. to Bring [★17719]
Nazism
Anti-Repression Rsrc. Team [17093]
The Blue Card [12468]
Conf. on Jewish Material Claims Against Germany [12470]
Intl. Network of Children of Jewish Holocaust Survivors [17720]
Jewish Philanthropic Fund of 1933 [12475]
Res. Found. for Jewish Immigration [10469]
Warsaw Ghetto Resistance Org. [20191]
Nazism, Anti-
Conf. on Jewish Material Claims Against Germany [12470]
Intl. Network of Children of Jewish Holocaust Survivors [17720]
NBIA Disorders Assn. [15355], 2082 Monaco Ct., El Cajon, CA 92019-4235, (619)588-2315
NBLC Dutch Assn. of Public Libraries [IO], The Hague, Netherlands
NCAA Golf Coaches Assn. [★23448]
NCAI Fund [★18096]
NCCLS: The Clinical Lab. Standards Org. [★14994]
NCCLS: The Clinical Lab. Standards Org. [★IO]
NCCPG [★IO]
NCI Alliance for Nanotechnology in Cancer [15110], c/o Natl. Cancer Inst., Off. of Tech. & Indus. Relations, Bldg. 31, Rm. 10A49, 31 Center Dr., MSC 2580, Bethesda, MD 20892-2580
NCITD - The Intl. Trade Facilitation Coun. - Address unknown since 1999.
NCMS — Soc. of Indus. Security Professionals [2092], 994 Old Eagle School Rd., Ste. 1019, Wayne, PA 19087-1866, (610)971-4856
NCO Assn. [★21316]
NCO Assn. [★6102]
NCPG [★1689]
NCSJ: Advocates on Behalf of Jews in Russia, Ukraine, the Baltic States and Eurasia [17448], 2020 K St. NW, Ste. 7800, Washington, DC 20006, (202)898-2500
NCSJ: Advocates on Behalf of Jews in Russia, Ukraine, the Baltic States and Eurasia [IO], Washington, DC, United States
NCSL Intl. [IO], Boulder, CO, United States
NCSL Intl. [7698], 2995 Wilderness Pl., Ste. 107, Boulder, CO 80301-5404, (303)440-3339
NDEITA - Natl. Dance Exercise Instructors Training Assn. [★23037]
NDT Soc. of Great Britain [★IO]
NEA Bricklin Club [★IO]
NEA Bricklin Club [★21598]
NEA; Dept. of Elementary School Principals, [★9014]
NEA Found. for the Improvement of Educ. [8294], 1201 16th St. NW, Washington, DC 20036-3207, (202)822-7840
NEA Hea. Info. Network [8474], 1201 16th St. NW, Ste. 216, Washington, DC 20036, (202)822-7570

NEA Higher Educ. Coun. [★24045]
NEA Search - Defunct.
NEA - The Assn. of Union Constructors [1056], 1501 Lee Hwy., Ste. 202, Arlington, VA 22209-1109, (703)524-3336
Neal Dougan-Theodorus Scowden Family Org. [21010], 165 4th St., Aultman, PA 15713-9605, (724)726-5653
Near Death Experience Res. Found. [14904], PO Box 23367, Federal Way, WA 98093
Near East Archaeological Soc. [6451], Horn Archaeological Museum, Andrews Univ., Berrien Springs, MI 49104-0990, (269)471-3273
Near East Archaeological Society [IO], Berrien Springs, MI, United States
Near East Coll. Assn. - Address unknown since 2001.
Near East Found. [18068], 90 Broad St., 15th Fl., New York, NY 10004, (212)425-2205
Near East Found. [IO], New York, NY, United States
Near East Relief [★IO]
Near East Relief [★18068]
Near Eastern Soc. - Address unknown since 1999.
Nebraska Christian Coll. Alumni Assn. [18912], 12550 S 114th St., Papillion, NE 68046, (402)935-9400
Neck and Facial Pain; Amer. Acad. of Head, [★15751]
Neck Nurses; Soc. of Otorhinolaryngology and Head/ [15526]
Neck Radiology; Amer. Soc. of Head and [16279]
Neck Soc; Amer. Head and [15819]
Neck Surgeons; Amer. Soc. of Head and [★15819]
Neck Surgeons; Soc. of Head and [★15819]
Neck Surgeons; Soc. of Military Otolaryngologists - Head and [15267]
Neck Surgeons; Soc. of Univ. Otolaryngologists - Head and [15828]
Neck Surgery; Amer. Acad. of Otolaryngology - Head and [15817]
Neckwear Assn. of America [252]
Necrotizing Fasciitis Found; Natl. [16543]
NEDA/Clean Air Act Project - Defunct.
Nederlands Antilliaans Olympisch Comite [★IO]
Nederlands Antilliaanse Atletiek Unie [IO], Curacao, Netherlands Antilles
Nederlands Atoomforum [★IO]
Nederlands Bijbelgenootschap [★IO]
Nederlands Centrum voor Inheemse Volken [★IO]
Nederlands akoestisch Genootschap [★IO]
Nederlands Genootschap van Abortusartsen [★IO]
Nederlands Genootschap voor Japanse Studien [★IO]
Nederlands Helsinki Comite [★IO]
Nederland's Instituut voor Navigatie [★IO]
Nederlands Instituut voor Zorg en Welzijn [★IO]
Nederlands Instituut voor Zuidelijk Afrika [★IO]
Nederlands Juristen Comite voor de Mensenrechten [★IO]
Nederlands Nationaal Comite van de Internationale Zuivelbond [★IO]
Nederlands Normalisatie-instituut [★IO]
Nederlands Olympisch Comite [★IO]
Nederlands forum voor Techniek en Wetenschap [★IO]
Nederlands Textielinstituut [★IO]
Nederlands Uitgeversverbond [★IO]
Nederlands Verbond van de Groothandel [★IO]
Nederlandsch Economisch-Historisch Archief [★IO]
Nederlandsche Maatschappij tot Bevordering des Tandheelkunde [★IO]
Nederlandsche Maatschappij voor Nijverheid en Handel [★IO]
Nederlandse Algemene Danssport Bond [IO], Rotterdam, Netherlands
Nederlandse Badminton Bond [IO], Nieuwegein, Netherlands
Nederlandse Bakkerij Centrum [★IO]
Nederlandse Beroepsvereniging Tolken Gebarentaal [★IO]
Nederlandse vereniging voor Biomaterialen en Tissue Engg. [★IO]
Nederlandse Biotechnologische Vereniging [★IO]
Nederlandse Boekverkopersbond [★IO]
Nederlandse Bond van Handelaren in Vee [★IO]

A star before a book entry number signifies that the name is not listed separately, but is mentioned within the entry.

Nederlandse Cosmetica Vereniging [★IO]
Nederlandse Culturele Aikikai Federatie [IO], Berg-schenhoek, Netherlands
Nederlandse Federatie van Ouders van Dove Kinderen [★IO]
Nederlandse Franchise Vereniging [★IO]
Nederlandse Frisbee Bond [★IO]
Nederlandse Fruittelers Organisatie [★IO]
Nederlandse Juweliers- en Uurwerkenbranche [★IO]
Nederlandse Kring voor Joodse Genealogie [★IO]
Nederlandse Mycologische Vereniging [★IO]
Nederlandse Natuurkundige Vereniging [★IO]
Nederlandse Organisatie voor Internationale Ontwikkelingssamenwerking [★IO]
Nederlandse Organisatie voor Internationale Samenwerking in het Hoger Onderwijs [★IO]
Nederlandse Organisatie voor toegepast-Natuurwetenschappelijk onderzoek [★IO]
Nederlandse Patienten Consumenten Federatie [★IO]
Nederlandse Stichting Voor Kostentechniek [★IO]
Nederlandse Taalunie [★IO]
Nederlandse Triathlon Bond [IO], Nieuwegein, Netherlands
Nederlandse Vereiniging voor Psychiatrie [★IO]
Nederlandse Vereniging voor Addison en Cushing Patienten [★IO]
Nederlandse Vereniging Algemene Toelevering [★IO]
Nederlandse Vereniging voor Calcium en Botstofwisseling [★IO]
Nederlandse Vereniging voor Cardiologie [★IO]
Nederlandse Vereniging van Dietisten [★IO]
Nederlandse Vereniging voor Endocrinologie [★IO]
Nederlandse Vereniging voor Fysiologie [★IO]
Nederlandse Vereniging voor Fysiologie [★IO]
Nederlandse Vereniging van Journalisten [★IO]
Nederlandse Vereniging voor Kwaliteit en Zorg [★IO]
Nederlandse Vereniging voor Medische Milieukunde [★IO]
Nederlandse Vereniging voor Microscopie [★IO]
Nederlandse Vereniging van Producenten en Importeurs van Beeld- en Geluidsdragers [★IO]
Nederlandse Vereniging voor Psychiatrische Verpleegkunde [★IO]
Nederlandse Vereniging van de Research-georienteerde Farmaceutische Industrie [★IO]
Nederlandse Vereniging voor Reumatologie [★IO]
Nederlandse Vereniging Techniek in de Landbouw [★IO]
Nederlandse Vereniging voor Tuin en Landschapsarchitektuur [★IO]
Nederlandse Vereniging Van Huisvrouwen [IO], Amersfoort, Netherlands
Nederlandse Vereniging Voor Farmacologie [★IO]
Nederlandse Vereniging Voor Gerontologie [★IO]
Nederlandse Vereniging Voor Vrouwenbelangen [★IO]
Nederlandse Vereniging voor Weer- en Sterrenkunde [IO], Utrecht, Netherlands
Nederlandse Vereniging van Zeepfabrikanten [★IO]
Nederlandse Vrouwen Raad [★IO]
Nederlandse Woonbond [★IO]
Nederlanse Floorball en Unihockey Bond [★IO]
Need [IO], Phoenix, AZ, United States
Need [12875], PO Box 54541, Phoenix, AZ 85078, (623)879-9676
Need Proj. [★17497]
Needle Arts Assn; The Natl. [3794]
Needlearts; Natl. Acad. of [22165]
Needleloom Underlay Mfrs. Assn. [IO], Bury, United Kingdom
Needlepoint Guild; Amer. [22148]
Needlework
    Amer. Bunka Embroidery Assn. [22721]
    Amer. Bunka Embroidery Assn. [IO]
    Amer. Needlepoint Guild [22148]
    Amer. Sewing Guild [22150]
    Brazilian Dimensional Embroidery Intl. Guild [22987]
    Charted Designers Assn. [2833]
    Crochet Assn. Intl. [22154]
    Crochet Guild of Am. [22722]
    Embroiderers' Guild of Am. [22155]

Embroidery Trade Assn. [3781]
    Handweavers Guild of Am. [22158]
    Intl. Machine Quilters Assn. [22160]
    Intl. Old Lacers, Inc. [22161]
    Natl. Acad. of Needlearts [22165]
    The Natl. Needle Arts Assn. [3794]
    Natl. Quilting Assn. [22170]
    Sewing Educator Alliance [9121]
    Smocking Arts Guild of Am. [22174]
Needlework Assn; The Natl. [★3794]
Needlework Guild of Am. [★13056]
Needlework; Pomegranate Guild of Judaic [9837]
Needmor Fund [13127], 42 S St. Clair St., Toledo, OH 43602, (419)255-5560
Needy; New Eyes for the [12533]
Negative Population Growth [12756], 2861 Duke St., Ste. 36, Alexandria, VA 22314, (703)370-9510
Negev; Amer. Associates, Ben-Gurion Univ. of the [8673]
Negev; Amer. Friends of the Univ. of the [★8673]
Neglect Info; CH on Child Abuse and [★11570]
Neglect Info. and Natl. Adoption Info. CH; Natl. CH on Child Abuse and [★11570]
Negotiators; Assn. of Educational [★24046]
Negotiators; Natl. Assn. of Educational [★24046]
Negotiators; North Amer. Assn. of Educational [24046]
Negro Actors Guild of America - Address unknown since 1995.
Negro Affairs Natl. Educ. and Res. Fund; American Found. for [★8045]
Negro Airmen Intl. [6380], PO Box 23911, Savannah, GA 31403, (912)964-6523
Negro-Amer. Mission Bd; Catholic [19601]
Negro Bankers Assn; Natl. [★492]
Negro Business League; Natl. [★2767]
Negro Bus. and Professional Women's Clubs; Natl. Assn. of [13053]
Negro Coll. Comm. on Adult Education - Address unknown since 1995.
Negro Coll. Fund; Natl. Alumni Coun. of the United [18910]
Negro Coll. Fund; United [8437]
Negro Colleges; Comm. for the Development of Art in [★7969]
Negro Colleges - of the Natl. Assn. of State Universities and Land-Grant Colleges; Off. for Advancement of Public [★8112]
Negro Funeral Directors and Morticians Assn; Natl. [★2789]
Negro Historical Soc. of America - Defunct.
Negro History; Amer. Museum of [★9360]
Negro Labor Comm. - Defunct.
Negro Leagues Baseball Museum [23123], 1616 E 18th St., Kansas City, MO 64108-1610, (816)221-1920
Negro Life and History; Assn. for the Stud. of [★9356]
Negro Musicians; Natl. Assn. of [10658]
Negro Natl. Bowling Assn. [★23252]
Negro Newspaper Publishers Assn; Natl. [★3241]
Negro Radio Assn. - Defunct.
Negro Students; Natl. Scholarship Ser. and Fund for [★8435]
Negro Students; Southeastern Regional Off. Natl. Scholarship Ser. and Fund for [8435]
Negro Women; Natl. Coun. of [17555]
Negron Fan Club; Chuck [24863]
Negros; Consortium for Graduate Stud. in Bus. for [★8806]
Neighbor to Neighbor [17050], 1550 Blue Spruce Dr., Fort Collins, CO 80524, (970)484-7498
Neighbor to Neighbor [IO], Fort Collins, CO, United States
Neighbor to Neighbor Political Action Comm. [★IO]
Neighbor to Neighbor Political Action Comm. [★17050]
Neighborhood Arts Programs Natl. Org. Comm. [★9536]
Neighborhood Bible Stud. [19526], 56 Main St., Dobbs Ferry, NY 10522, (914)693-3273
Neighborhood Centers of Am; United [11792]
Neighborhood Centers; Natl. Fed. of Settlements and [★11792]
Neighborhood Coalition [★17230]

Neighborhood Coalition; Natl. [17230]
Neighborhood Councils; Independence Plan for [17219]
Neighborhood Enterprise; Center for [17208]
Neighborhood Enterprise; Natl. Center for [★17208]
Neighborhood Funders Gp. [12734], 1301 Connecticut Ave. NW, Ste. 500, Washington, DC 20036, (202)833-4690
Neighborhood Govt; Alliance for [★11752]
Neighborhood Hea. Centers; Natl. Assn. of [★14574]
Neighborhood Housing Services of Am. [12334], 1970 Broadway, Ste. 470, Oakland, CA 94612, (510)832-5542
Neighborhood Info Centers Project - Defunct.
Neighborhood Information Sharing Exchange - Defunct.
Neighborhood Prevention Network [★13262]
Neighborhood Reinvestment Corp. [★12335]
Neighborhood Salon Assn. - Address unknown since 1999.
Neighborhood Schools; Natl. Assn. for [17820]
Neighborhood Tech; Center for [17209]
Neighborhoods Everyday; Seeking Harmony in [18857]
Neighborhoods-in-Action - Defunct.
Neighborhoods; Natl. Assn. of [11752]
Neighborhoods U.S.A. - Address unknown since 1995.
Neighbors of Am; Royal [19137]
Neighbors of Woodcraft [★19441]
NeighborWorks Am. [12335], 1325 G St. NW, Ste. 800, Washington, DC 20005-3100, (202)220-2300
NEIGHBOURS [IO], London, United Kingdom
Neighbours of the Roundtable - Address unknown since 1995.
Nelson Charlmers; Intersure - Singer [2191]
Nelson Fan Club; Intl. Willie [24915]
Nelson Jack Edwards Educational Centre [★17158]
Nematological Soc. of Southern Africa [IO], Potchefstroom, Republic of South Africa
Nematologiese Vereniging van Suidelike Afrika [★IO]
Nematology
    Afro-Asian Soc. of Nematologists [IO]
    Chinese Soc. of Plant Nematologists [IO]
    European Soc. of Nematologists [IO]
    Intl. Fed. of Nematology Societies [IO]
    Nematological Soc. of Southern Africa [IO]
    Russian Soc. of Nematologists [IO]
    Soc. of Nematologists [7371]
Nemzeti Loverseny [★IO]
Nemzetkozi Adoszakertok Magyarorszagi Tarsasaga [★IO]
Neo-American Church [★20456]
Neo-American Church, The Original Kleptonian [20456], c/o NeoACT, Inc., PO Box 3473, Austin, TX 78764, (512)443-8464
Neo-Hellenic Stud; Amer. Soc. for [★9770]
Neo-American
    Neo-American Church, The Original Kleptonian [20456]
Neonatal Death; Aiding Mothers and Fathers Experiencing [11907]
Neonatal Death Soc; Stillbirth and [IO]
Neonatal Hea; Intl. Assn. for Maternal and [IO]
Neonatal Nurses; Assn. of Women's Hea., Obstetric and [15470]
Neonatal Nurses; Natl. Assn. of [15495]
Neonatal Nursing Specialties; Natl. Certification Corp. for the Obstetric, Gynecologic and [15506]
Neo-Nazi
    The Generation After [17119]
Neot Kedumim [★19505]
Neot Kedumim [★IO]
Nepal Airsport Assn. [IO], Kathmandu, Nepal
Nepal Assn. of Tour and Travel Agents [IO], Kathmandu, Nepal
Nepal Assn. of Univ. Women [IO], Kathmandu, Nepal
Nepal Athletics Assn. [IO], Lalitpur, Nepal
Nepal Badminton Assn. [IO], Kathmandu, Nepal
Nepal Bible Soc. [IO], Kathmandu, Nepal
Nepal Carpet Exporters' Assn. [IO], Kathmandu, Nepal

Reference to "IO" in place of a book number signifies that the association may be found in the 45th edition of International Organizations.

Nepal Chamber of Commerce [IO], Kathmandu, Nepal
Nepal Dental Assn. [IO], Lalitpur, Nepal
Nepal Epilepsy Soc. [IO], Kathmandu, Nepal
Nepal Geotechnical Soc. [IO], Kathmandu, Nepal
Nepal Habitat for Humanity [IO], Kathmandu, Nepal
Nepal Hastakala Udhyog Sangh [★IO]
Nepal Medical Assn. [IO], Kathmandu, Nepal
Nepal Olympic Comm. [IO], Kathmandu, Nepal
Nepal Physiotheraphy Assn. [IO], Kathmandu, Nepal
Nepal Press Inst. [IO], Kathmandu, Nepal
Nepal Red Cross Soc. [IO], Kathmandu, Nepal
Nepal Reliance Org. [IO], Kathmandu, Nepal
Nepal Remote Sensing and Photogrammetric Soc. [IO], Kathmandu, Nepal
Nepal Squash Rackets Assn. [IO], Kathmandu, Nepal
Nepal Stationery and Educational Materials Indus. Assn. [IO], Kathmandu, Nepal
Nepal Stationery Indus. Assn. [★IO]
Nepal Stud. Assn. [★IO]
Nepal Stud. Assn. [★8944]
Nepal Taekwondo Assn. [IO], Kathmandu, Nepal
Nepal and Tibet Philatelic Stud. Circle [22852], 6 Rainbow Ct., Warwick, RI 02889-1118, (401)738-0466
Nepal Weight Lifting Assn. [IO], Kathmandu, Nepal
Nepalese
  Assn. of Nepal and Himalayan Stud. [IO]
  Assn. of Nepal and Himalayan Stud. [8944]
  Assn. of Nepalis in the Americas [19286]
  Assn. of Nepalis in the Americas [IO]
  Hands for Help Nepal [IO]
  INFO Nepal [IO]
  Nepal and Tibet Philatelic Stud. Circle [22852]
  Nepalese Americas Coun. [19287]
  Nepali Amer. Friendship Assn. [19288]
  Non-Resident Nepali Assn. [IO]
  Tibetan Aid Proj. [12822]
Nepalese Americas Coun. [19287], 3077 N Foxridge Ct., Ann Arbor, MI 48105, (734)663-7225
Nepali Amer. Friendship Assn. [19288], 408 Midland Ln., Monona, WI 53716
Nephrology
  Amer. Assn. of Kidney Patients [15283]
  Amer. Kidney Fund [15284]
  Amer. Lithotripsy Soc. [15285]
  Amer. Nephrology Nurses' Assn. [15286]
  Amer. Soc. of Diagnostic and Interventional Nephrology [15287]
  Amer. Soc. of Nephrology [15288]
  Amer. Soc. of Pediatric Nephrology [15289]
  Asian-Pacific Soc. of Nephrology [IO]
  Bd. of Nephrology Examiners Nursing and Tech. [15290]
  British Assn. for Paediatric Nephrology [IO]
  Canadian Assn. of Nephrology Nurses and Technologists [IO]
  DaVita Patient Citizens [15291]
  Egyptian Soc. of Nephrology [IO]
  European Dialysis and Transplant Nurses Association/European Renal Care Assn. [IO]
  European Soc. for Pediatric Nephrology [IO]
  Hong Kong Soc. of Nephrology [IO]
  Indian Soc. of Nephrology [IO]
  Intl. Pediatric Nephrology Assn. [IO]
  Intl. Pediatric Nephrology Assn. [15292]
  Intl. Soc. of Nephrology [IO]
  Intl. Soc. for Peritoneal Dialysis [IO]
  Irish Kidney Assn. [IO]
  Japanese Soc. for Dialysis Therapy [IO]
  Japanese Soc. of Nephrology [IO]
  Latin Amer. Soc. of Nephrology and Hypertension [IO]
  Malaysian Soc. of Nephrology [IO]
  Natl. Assn. of Nephrology Technicians/Technologists [15293]
  Natl. Kidney Found. [15294]
  Natl. Kidney and Urologic Diseases Info. CH [16710]
  North Amer. Soc. for Dialysis and Transplantation [15295]
  Oxalosis and Hyperoxaluria Found. [15296]
  Rainbow Celebration of Hope Network [15297]
  Renal Assn. [IO]

  Renal Pathology Soc. [15872]
  Renal Physicians Assn. [15298]
  Renal Support Network [15299]
Nephrology; Amer. Soc. of Pediatric [15289]
Nephrology Examiners - Nursing and Tech; Bd. of [★15290]
Nephrology Nurses and Technicians; Amer. Assn. of [★15286]
Nephrology Technicians/Technologists; Natl. Assn. of [15293]
Nephrology Technologists; Natl. Assn. of [★15293]
Nephrosis Found; Natl. [★15294]
Nepisiguit Salmon Assn. [IO], Bathurst, NB, Canada
Nerine Soc. - Defunct.
Nero Wolfe
  Wolfe Pack [9727]
Neruological and Communicative Disorders; Natl. Comm. for Res. in [★15346]
The Nerve Center - Address unknown since 1994.
Nervosa and Related Eating Disorders; Anorexia [14298]
Nervous and Former Mental Patients; Recovery, Inc., The Assn. of [★16230]
Nervous and Mental Disease; Assn. for Res. in [16082]
Nesbitt-Nisbet Soc.: A Worldwide Clan Soc. [21011], c/o Diana Hawkins, Sec., 5930 Creekside Ln., Hoschton, GA 30548-8232
Nesbitt-Nisbet Soc.: A Worldwide Clan Soc. [IO], Zelienople, PA, United States
Net Assn; Amer. Power [★3780]
NET Ministries, Inc. [★19687]
NETA - Natl. Exercise Trainers Assn. [23037], 5955 Golden Valley Rd., Ste. 240, Minneapolis, MN 55422-4472, (763)545-2505
NetAction [17242], PO Box 6739, Santa Barbara, CA 93160, (415)215-9392
NetAid [11486], 75 Broad St., Ste. 2410, New York, NY 10004, (212)537-0500
Netball
  All England Netball Assn. [IO]
  Caribbean Amer. Netball Assn. [23633]
  Intl. Fed. of Netball Associations [IO]
  Netball New Zealand [IO]
  U.S.A. Netball Assn. [23634]
Netball New Zealand [IO], Auckland, New Zealand
NetGALA [★18913]
Netherland-Amer. Univ. League - Defunct.
Netherland Dwarf Rabbit Club; Amer. [5138]
Netherlands
  Assn. for the Advancement of Dutch-American Stud. [9908]
  Netherlands Bd. of Tourism and Conventions [24359]
  Netherlands Chamber of Commerce in the U.S. [24360]
  North Amer. Dept. of the Royal Warmblood Studbook of the Netherlands [4931]
Netherlands ACM SIGCHI [IO], Amsterdam, Netherlands
Netherlands Aerospace Gp. [IO], Zoetermeer, Netherlands
Netherlands Amer. Stud. Assn. [IO], Middelburg, Netherlands
Netherlands Antillean Baseball Fed. [IO], Curacao, Netherlands Antilles
Netherlands Antilles
  Bonaire Govt. Tourist Off. [24361]
  Curacao Convention Bureau/Tourist Bd. [24362]
Netherlands Antilles Olympic Comm. [IO], Curacao, Netherlands Antilles
Netherlands Antilles Tennis Fed. [IO], Curacao, Netherlands Antilles
Netherlands Assn. of Intl. Dutch Contractors [IO], Gouda, Netherlands
Netherlands Assn. for Japanese Stud. [IO], Leiden, Netherlands
Netherlands Assn. of Journalists [IO], Amsterdam, Netherlands
Netherlands Assn. for Landscape Architecture [IO], Amsterdam, Netherlands
Netherlands Assn. for Lib., Info. and Knowledge Professionals [IO], Utrecht, Netherlands
Netherlands Assn. of Sports Medicine [IO], Bilthoven, Netherlands

Netherlands Assn. for Women's Interests, Women's Work and Equal Citizenship [IO], The Hague, Netherlands
Netherlands Atlantic Assn. [IO], The Hague, Netherlands
Netherlands Atomic Forum [IO], Petten, Netherlands
Netherlands Bible Soc. [IO], Haarlem, Netherlands
Netherlands Bio-Energy Assn. [IO], Arnhem, Netherlands
Netherlands Biotechnological Soc. [IO], Vlaardingen, Netherlands
Netherlands Bd. of Tourism [★24359]
Netherlands Bd. of Tourism [★24359]
Netherlands Bd. of Tourism and Conventions [24359], 355 Lexington Ave., 19th Fl., New York, NY 10017, (212)370-7360
Netherlands Bd. of Tourism and Conventions [IO], Leidschendam, Netherlands
Netherlands British Chamber of Commerce [IO], London, United Kingdom
Netherlands Centre Alternatives to Animal Use [IO], Utrecht, Netherlands
Netherlands Centre for Indigenous Peoples [IO], Amsterdam, Netherlands
Netherlands Chamber of Commerce Australia [IO], Hampton, Australia
Netherlands Chamber of Commerce in the U.S. [24360], 267 5th Ave., Ste. 301, New York, NY 10016, (212)265-6460
Netherlands and Colonial Philately - Defunct.
Netherlands Comm. of Jurists for Human Rights [IO], Leiden, Netherlands
Netherlands Convention Bur. [★IO]
Netherlands Convention Bur. [★24359]
Netherlands Convention and Visitors Bur. [★24359]
Netherlands Coun. for Libraries and Info. Services [★IO]
Netherlands Coun. of Women [IO], The Hague, Netherlands
Netherlands Defence Mfrs. Assn. [IO], The Hague, Netherlands
Netherlands Development Org. [IO], The Hague, Netherlands
Netherlands Development Org. - Burkina Faso [IO], Ouagadougou, Burkina Faso
Netherlands Development Org. - Cameroon [IO], Yaounde, Cameroon
Netherlands Development Org. - Mali [IO], Bamako, Mali
Netherlands Dietetic Assn. [IO], Houten, Netherlands
Netherlands Economic History Archv. [IO], Amsterdam, Netherlands
Netherlands Economic Inst. [IO], Rotterdam, Netherlands
Netherlands Fed. of Film Professionals [IO], Amsterdam, Netherlands
Netherlands Floorball and Unihockey Assn. [IO], Groningen, Netherlands
Netherlands Flower-Bulb Inst. - Defunct.
Netherlands Franchise Assn. [IO], Hilversum, Netherlands
Netherlands Helsinki Comm. [IO], The Hague, Netherlands
Netherlands Industrial Inst. - Defunct.
Netherlands Inst. for Care and Welfare [IO], Utrecht, Netherlands
Netherlands Inst. of Navigation [IO], Pernis, Netherlands
Netherlands Inst. for Southern Africa [IO], Amsterdam, Netherlands
Netherlands Museum [★IO]
Netherlands Museum [★9909]
Netherlands Mycological Soc. [IO], Utrecht, Netherlands
Netherlands Natl. Comm. of the Intl. Dairy Fed. [IO], Zoetermeer, Netherlands
Netherlands Olympic Comm. [IO], Arnhem, Netherlands
Netherlands Org. for Hea. Res. and Development [IO], The Hague, Netherlands
Netherlands Org. for Applied Sci. Res. [IO], Delft, Netherlands
Netherlands Org. for Intl. Cooperation in Higher Educ. [IO], The Hague, Netherlands
Netherlands Org. for Intl. Development Cooperation [IO], The Hague, Netherlands

A star before a book entry number signifies that the name is not listed separately, but is mentioned within the entry.

Netherlands Org. for Small- and Medium-Sized Mfrs. of Metal [★IO]

Netherlands Paralympic Comm. [IO], Bunnik, Netherlands

Netherlands Physical Soc. [IO], Amsterdam, Netherlands

Netherlands Pioneer and Historical Found. [★IO]

Netherlands Pioneer and Historical Found. [★9909]

Netherlands Psychiatric Assn. [IO], Utrecht, Netherlands

Netherlands Red Cross Soc. [IO], The Hague, Netherlands

Netherlands' Shipbuilding Indus. Assn. [IO], Zoetermeer, Netherlands

Netherlands Soc. of Agricultural Engineers [IO], Wageningen, Netherlands

Netherlands Soc. for Agricultural Sciences [★IO]

Netherlands Soc. of Cardiology [IO], Utrecht, Netherlands

Netherlands Soc. for Endocrinology [IO], Haren, Netherlands

Netherlands Soc. for English Stud. [IO], Amsterdam, Netherlands

Netherlands Soc. of Gerontology [IO], Lelystad, Netherlands

Netherlands Soc. of Hypertension [IO], Rotterdam, Netherlands

Netherlands Soc. for Indus. and Trade [IO], The Hague, Netherlands

Netherlands Soc. for Intl. Affairs [IO], The Hague, Netherlands

Netherlands Soc. for Nature and Env. [IO], Utrecht, Netherlands

Netherlands Soc. of Parents with Nepalese Children [IO], Diemen, Netherlands

Netherlands Soc. for Statistics and Operations Res. [IO], Barendrecht, Netherlands

Netherlands Soc. of Technological Sciences and Engg. [IO], Amsterdam, Netherlands

Netherlands Standardization Inst. [IO], Delft, Netherlands

Netherlands Wholesale and Intl. Trade Fed. [IO], The Hague, Netherlands

Netting Manufacturers; Amer. Cordage and [★1075]

Neturei Karta of U.S.A. - Address unknown since 1994.

NetWare Users Intl. [★3725]

NetWare Users Intl. [★IO]

Network [IO], Swanmore, United Kingdom

NETWORK [8295], 136 Fenno Dr., Rowley, MA 01969-1004, (978)948-7764

NETWORK [★18624]

Network 20/20 [18004], 850 Seventh Ave., Ste. 1200, New York, NY 10019, (212)582-1870

NETWORK, A Natl. Catholic Social Justice Lobby [18624], 25 E St. NW, Ste. 200, Washington, DC 20001-1630, (202)347-9797

Network Against Coercive Psychiatry [12554], c/o Seth Farber, PhD, 172 W 79th St., No. 2E, New York, NY 10024, (212)560-7288

Network Against Psychiatric Assault - Address unknown since 1990.

Network of Alternative Tech. and Tech. Assessment [IO], Milton Keynes, United Kingdom

Network for Analysis of Fireball Trajectories - Defunct.

Network for Better Nutrition - Defunct.

Network Branded Prepaid Card Assn. [1443], PO Box 180, Sherborn, MA 01770, (508)655-6107

Network; Communitarian [18437]

Network of Communities for Peacemaking and Conflict Resolution [★18118]

Network of Concerned Correspondents - Address unknown since 1999.

Network for Continuing Medical Educ. [15177], 1 Harmon Plz., Secaucus, NJ 07094, (201)867-3550

Network on Disabilities; Natl. Parent [14245]

Network for Economic Rights - Defunct.

Network for Educ. and Academic Rights [IO], London, United Kingdom

Network of Educators on the Americas [★8359]

Network of Employers for Traffic Safety [18746], 8150 Leesburg Pike, Ste. 410, Vienna, VA 22182, (703)891-6005

Network for Environmental Policy Awareness [17501], c/o Paula P. Easley, Coor., 2134 Crataegus Ave., Anchorage, AK 99508-4028, (907)274-6800

Network of European Agricultural (Tropically and Sub-tropically Oriented) Universities and Sci. Complexes Related with Agricultural Development [IO], Prague, Czech Republic

Network of European Foundations for Innovative Cooperation [IO], Brussels, Belgium

Network on Feminist Approaches to Bioethics [★IO]

Network on Feminist Approaches to Bioethics [★12126]

Network of Gay and Lesbian Alumni/ae Associations [18913], PO Box 53188, Washington, DC 20009

Network of Govt. Lib. and Info. Specialists [IO], London, United Kingdom

Network of Indian Professionals [19115], c/o North Am. Chap. Development, PO Box 06362, Chicago, IL 60606, (312)952-0254

Network of Ingredient Marketing Specialists [1554], c/o Mr. Kenneth W. Reynolds, Exec. Dir., 630 Village Trace NE, Bldg. 15, Ste. A, Marietta, GA 30067, (770)989-0049

Network of Innovative Schools [★8295]

The Network: Interaction for Conflict Resolution [★IO]

Network Intl. [★13479]

Network of Iranian Amer. Soc. [13507], 14252 Culver Dr., No. 406, Irvine, CA 92604, (949)651-8454

Network of NGOs of Trinidad and Tobago for the Advancement of Women [IO], Port of Spain, Trinidad and Tobago

Network for Online Commerce [IO], London, United Kingdom

Network for Organ Sharing; United [16684]

Network; Planners [18476]

Network Professional Assn. [6739], 1401 Hermes Ln., San Diego, CA 92154, (888)672-6720

Network for Professional Women - Address unknown since 2003.

Network of Single Adult Leaders - Defunct.

Network for Size Esteem; Largesse, the [12646]

Network in Solidarity With the People of Guatemala [17681], 1830 Connecticut Ave. NW, Washington, DC 20009, (202)518-7638

Network and Systems Professionals Assn. [6799], 7044 S 13th St., Oak Creek, WI 53154, (414)908-4945

Network and Systems Professionals Assn. [IO], Oak Creek, WI, United States

Network TV Assn; Syndicated [120]

Network on Thinking; Engg. and Sci. [7217]

Network of Trial Law Firms [5525], 303 S Broadway, Ste. 222, Tarrytown, NY 10591, (914)332-4400

Network Users Assn. - Defunct.

Network of Utility Professionals; Women's Intl. [1200]

Network Women in Development Europe [IO], Brussels, Belgium

Network of Women in Trade and Technical Jobs - Defunct.

Networked Info; Coalition for [7191]

Networking
  10 Gigabit Ethernet Alliance [7372]
  Assn. for Community Networking [8124]
  Atlatl [9557]
  Australian Public Access Network Assn. [IO]
  Benchmarking Network [2834]
  Caucus-Association of High Tech Procurement Professionals [7373]
  Coun. of Regional Info. Tech. Associations [7192]
  GesherCity [19183]
  Intl. Assn. of Outsourcing Professionals [2871]
  Intl. Assn. of Space Entrepreneurs [3634]
  League of Professional Sys. Administrators [6815]
  Metro Ethernet Forum [7748]
  Natl. Community Building Network [11786]
  Natl. Soc. for Hispanic Professionals [1908]
  POWERLUNCH! [759]
  Soc. for Organizational Learning [2868]
  Virtual Private Network Consortium [2320]
  Young Women Social Entrepreneurs [770]

Networking Alternatives for Publishers, Retailers and Artists [3243], c/o Marilyn McGuire, Founder, PO Box 9, Eastsound, WA 98245-0009, (360)376-2001

Networking Alternatives for Publishers, Retailers and Artists [IO], Eastsound, WA, United States

Networking Inst; Gazette Intl. [★11981]

Networking Project; Local Alliance [★9116]

Networking Proj. for Young Adults with Disabilities [11975], 50 Broadway, 13th Fl., New York, NY 10004, (212)755-4500

Networks Unlimited, Inc. - Defunct.

Neumann Janos Szamitogep-tudomanyi Tarsasag [★IO]

Neural Networks Coun; IEEE [★7009]

Neural Transplantation; Amer. Soc. for [★15380]

Neural Transplantation and Repair; Amer. Soc. for [15380]

Neuralgia Assn; Trigeminal [15370]

Neuro-Developmental Treatment Assn. [15399], 1540 S Coast Hwy., Ste. 203, Laguna Beach, CA 92651, (800)869-9295

Neuro-Linguistic Programming; Assn. for [IO]

Neuro-Linguistic Programming; Intl. Assn. of [★16219]

Neuro-Linguistic Programming; Intl. Assn. for [★16219]

Neuro-Linguistic Programming; Intl. Assn. of [★16219]

Neuro-Linguistic Programming; North Amer. Assn. of [★16219]

Neuro-Linguistic Programming; Soc. of [15012]

Neuro-Ophthalmology
  Neuro-Optometric Rehabilitation Assn., Intl. [15300]
  Neuro-Optometric Rehabilitation Assn., Intl. [IO]

Neuro-Optometric Rehabilitation Assn., Intl. [IO], Irvine, CA, United States

Neuro-Optometric Rehabilitation Assn., Intl. [15300], PO Box 14934, Irvine, CA 92623-4934, (866)222-3887

Neuro Therapeutics; Amer. Soc. for Experimental [15379]

Neurobehavioral Teratology Soc. [15356], c/o Susan M. Melnick, PhD, Sec., SK Bio-Pharmaceuticals, 22-10 State Rte. 208 S, Fair Lawn, NJ 07410, (201)796-4288

Neurobiology and Cell Biology; Canadian Assn. for Anatomy, [IO]

Neuroblastoma Children's Cancer Soc. [13858], PO Box 957672, Hoffman Estates, IL 60195, (800)532-5162

Neurochemistry; Amer. Soc. for [7374]

Neurochemistry; European Soc. for [IO]

Neurochemistry; Intl. Soc. for [IO]

Neurocritical Care Soc. [IO], Minneapolis, MN, United States

Neurocritical Care Soc. [14070], 5841 Cedar Lake Rd., Ste. 204, Minneapolis, MN 55416, (952)646-2034

Neuroelectric Soc. - Defunct.

Neuroendocrinology; Intl. Soc. of Psycho [15108]

Neuroendocrinology; Soc. for Behavioral [13741]

Neurofibromatosis [14471], PO Box 18246, Minneapolis, MN 55418, (301)918-4600

Neurofibromatosis Assn. of Australia [IO], Lindfield, Australia

Neurofibromatosis Assn. of Ireland [IO], Dublin, Ireland

Neurofibromatosis Assn. of the United Kingdom [IO], Kingston Upon Thames, United Kingdom

Neurofibromatosis Found; Natl. [★15315]

Neurogenic Commun. Disorders; Natl. Center for [16449]

Neuroimaging; Amer. Soc. of [16281]

Neuroimaging; Soc. for Computerized Tomography and [★16281]

Neuroleptic Malignant Syndrome Info. Ser. [15357], PO Box 1069, Sherburne, NY 13460-1069, (607)674-7920

Neuroleptic Malignant Syndrome Info. Ser. [IO], Sherburne, NY, United States

Neurological and Communicative Disorders; Natl. Coalition for Res. in [★15346]

Neurological Coun. of Western Australia [IO], Nedlands, Australia

Neurological Disorders
  Acad. of Aphasia [13704]
  Accelerated Cure Proj. for Multiple Sclerosis [15301]
  Acoustic Neuroma Assn. of Canada [IO]
  ADHD-foreningen [IO]

Reference to "IO" in place of a book number signifies that the association may be found in the 45th edition of International Organizations.

ALS Diagnostic Support Gp. **[IO]**
ALS Res. Fund **[IO]**
ALS Support Gp. - Belgium **[IO]**
Alternating Hemiplegia of Childhood Vereniging Nederland **[IO]**
Amer. Acad. of Hea. Care Providers in the Addictive Disorders **[15302]**
Amer. Acad. of Neurology **[15376]**
Amer. Assn. of Neurological Surgeons **[15410]**
Amer. Assn. of Neuromuscular and Electrodiagnostic Medicine **[15303]**
Amer. Assn. of Neuropathologists **[15853]**
Amer. Bd. of Neurological Surgery **[15411]**
Amer. Coll. of Neuropsychopharmacology **[15915]**
Amer. Nystagmus Network **[16828]**
Amer. Parkinson Disease Assn. **[15304]**
Amer. Soc. for Neural Transplantation and Repair **[15380]**
Amer. Soc. for Stereotactic and Functional Neurosurgery **[15412]**
Amer. Syringomyelia Alliance Proj. **[15305]**
Amyotrophic Lateral Sclerosis Assn. **[15306]**
Amyotrophic Lateral Sclerosis Soc. of Canada **[IO]**
Angioma Alliance **[IO]**
Angioma Alliance **[15307]**
Asociacion Distrofia Muscular **[IO]**
Asociacion Espanola de Esclerosis Lateral Amiotrofica **[IO]**
Asociacion Mexicana De la Enfermedad De Huntington I.A.P. **[IO]**
Asociacion Venezolana de Huntington **[IO]**
Associacao Brasil Huntington **[IO]**
Associacao Brasileira de Esclerose Multipla **[IO]**
Associacao Portuguesa de Doentes de Huntington **[IO]**
Assn. of Child Neurology Nurses **[15465]**
Assn. Huntington France **[IO]**
Assn. of Neuromuscular Disorders **[IO]**
Assn. pour la Recherche sur la Sclerose Laterale Amyotrophique **[IO]**
Assn. de la Suisse Romande et Italienne Contre les Myopathies **[IO]**
Associazione Italian Sclerosi Laterale Amiotrofica **[IO]**
Associazione Italiana Sclerosi Multipla **[IO]**
Ataxia-Telangiectasia Soc. **[IO]**
Ataxia - UK **[IO]**
Attention Deficit Info. Network **[15308]**
Australian Huntington Disease Assn. - New South Wales **[IO]**
Australian Huntington Disease Assn. - Victoria **[IO]**
Australian Huntington Disease Assn. - Western Australia **[IO]**
Australian Huntington's Disease Assn. **[IO]**
Austrian Huntington Assn. **[IO]**
Avenues, Natl. Support Gp. for Arthrogryposis Multiplex Congenita **[15309]**
Batten Disease Support and Res. Assn. **[15310]**
Batten Disease Support and Res. Assn. - Australia **[IO]**
Benign Essential Blepharospasm Res. Found. **[15311]**
Beyondblue **[IO]**
Brain Injury Assn. of Alberta **[IO]**
Brain Injury Assn. of Am. **[14528]**
Brain Injury Assn. of Chatham-Kent **[IO]**
Brain Injury Assn. of London and Region **[IO]**
Brain Injury Assn. of New South Wales **[IO]**
Brain Injury Assn. of New Zealand **[IO]**
Brain Injury Assn. of New Zealand - Auckland **[IO]**
Brain Injury Assn. of New Zealand - Bay of Plenty **[IO]**
Brain Injury Assn. of New Zealand - Canterbury **[IO]**
Brain Injury Assn. of New Zealand - Central Districts **[IO]**
Brain Injury Assn. of New Zealand - Eastern Bay of Plenty **[IO]**
Brain Injury Assn. of New Zealand - Gisborne **[IO]**
Brain Injury Assn. of New Zealand - Hawkes Bay **[IO]**
Brain Injury Assn. of New Zealand - Nelson **[IO]**
Brain Injury Assn. of New Zealand - Northland **[IO]**

Brain Injury Assn. of New Zealand - Rotorua **[IO]**
Brain Injury Assn. of New Zealand - Taranaki **[IO]**
Brain Injury Assn. of New Zealand - Waikato **[IO]**
Brain Injury Assn. of New Zealand - Wellington **[IO]**
Brain Injury Assn. of New Zealand - Whanganui **[IO]**
Brain Injury Assn. of Niagara **[IO]**
Brain Injury Assn. of North Bay **[IO]**
Brain Injury Assn. of Peel and Halton **[IO]**
Brain Injury Assn. of Queensland **[IO]**
Brain Injury Assn. of Sarnia and Lambton **[IO]**
Brain Injury Assn. of Sault Ste. Marie and District **[IO]**
Brain Injury Assn. of Southeastern Ontario **[IO]**
Brain Injury Assn. of Sudbury and District **[IO]**
Brain Injury Assn. of Tasmania **[IO]**
Brain Injury Assn. of Waterloo-Wellington **[IO]**
Brain Injury Assn. of Windsor-Essex County **[IO]**
Brain Injury Australia **[IO]**
Brain Injury Network of South Australia **[IO]**
Brain Injury Soc. of Toronto **[IO]**
BrainTrust Canada Assn. **[IO]**
Brazilian Assn. of Amyotrophic Lateral Sclerosis **[IO]**
Brazilian Muscular Dystrophy Assn. **[IO]**
British Assn. of Brain Injury Case Managers **[IO]**
British Neuropathological Soc. **[IO]**
Cajal Club **[15385]**
Canadian Assn. for Familial Ataxia **[IO]**
Care4Dystonia **[15312]**
Central Alberta Brain Injury Soc. **[IO]**
Centro de Informacao Lisboa **[IO]**
Charcot-Marie-Tooth Assn. **[15313]**
Children and Adults With Attention Deficit/Hyperactivity Disorder **[15314]**
Children's Hemiplegia and Stroke Assn. **[16493]**
Children's Tumor Found. **[15315]**
Chronic Syndrome Support Assn. **[14259]**
Collegium Internationale Neuro-Psychopharmacologicum **[15929]**
Commun. Independence for the Neurologically Impaired **[15316]**
Cyprus Multiple Sclerosis Assn. **[IO]**
Czech Multiple Sclerosis Soc. **[IO]**
Dana Alliance for Brain Initiatives **[15387]**
Danish Acoustic Neuroma Assn. **[IO]**
Danish Brain Injury Assn. **[IO]**
Danish Huntington Assn. **[IO]**
Danish Multiple Sclerosis Soc. **[IO]**
Dementia Advocacy and Support Network Intl. **[IO]**
Dementia Advocacy and Support Network Intl. **[12638]**
Deutsche Gesellschaft fur Muskelkranke **[IO]**
Deutsche Multiple Sklerose Gesellschaft Bundesverband e.V. **[IO]**
Devereux Natl. **[13734]**
Dutch Tourette Syndrome Assn. **[IO]**
Dysautonomia Found. **[15317]**
Dysautonomia Youth Network of Am. **[15318]**
Dyspraxia Assn. of Ireland **[IO]**
Dystonia Medical Res. Found. **[15319]**
Dystonia Soc. **[IO]**
The Erythromelalgia Assn. **[14261]**
Esclerosis Multiple Argentina **[IO]**
European Alliance of Neuromuscular Disorders Associations **[IO]**
European Charcot Found. **[IO]**
European Parkinson's Disease Assn. **[IO]**
Facioscapulohumeral (FSH) Soc. **[15320]**
Familiares y Amigos de Enfermos de la Neurona Motora **[IO]**
Families of Adults Afflicted with Asperger's Syndrome **[16531]**
Families of S.M.A. **[15321]**
Fibromuscular Dysplasia Soc. of Am. **[15322]**
Finnish Huntington Assn. **[IO]**
Finnish MS Soc. **[IO]**
Finnish Parkinson's Disease Assn., Huntington Disease Br. **[IO]**
Forbes Norris MDA/ALS Res. Center **[15323]**
Four Counties Brain Injury Assn. **[IO]**
Friedreich's Ataxia Res. Alliance **[14403]**
Friedreichs Ataxia Soc. of Ireland **[IO]**

German Huntington Help **[IO]**
Global Neuro Rescue **[IO]**
Global Neuro Rescue **[15324]**
Global and Regional Asperger Syndrome Partnership **[15325]**
Global and Regional Asperger Syndrome Partnership **[IO]**
Greek Multiple Sclerosis Soc. **[IO]**
Grupo Multidisciplinario Para la Atencion a Pacientes y Familiares con Diagnostico de Enfermedad de Huntington **[IO]**
Guardians of Hydrocephalus Res. Found. **[15326]**
Guillain-Barre Syndrome Found. Intl. **[15327]**
Guillain-Barre Syndrome Found. Intl. **[IO]**
Head Injury Assn. of Ottawa Valley **[IO]**
Headway Victoria **[IO]**
Hereditary Disease Found. **[15328]**
Hungarian Multiple Sclerosis Soc. **[IO]**
Huntington Assn. of Russia **[IO]**
Huntington Assn. of Slovenia **[IO]**
Huntington Disease Care and Cure Soc. of Pakistan **[IO]**
Huntington Disease Soc. of Argentina **[IO]**
Huntington Disease Soc. of Colombia **[IO]**
Huntington Espoir **[IO]**
Huntington Foreningen I Sverige **[IO]**
Huntington Liga **[IO]**
Huntington Self Support Gp. Malta **[IO]**
Huntington Soc. of Canada **[IO]**
Huntington's Assn. of South Africa **[IO]**
Huntington's Disease Assn. **[IO]**
Huntington's Disease Assn. - Canterbury, New Zealand **[IO]**
Huntington's Disease Soc. of Am. **[15329]**
Huntington's Org. **[IO]**
Huntington's United Gp. South Africa **[IO]**
Hydrocephalus Assn. **[15330]**
Inter-American Conductive Educ. Assn. **[9146]**
Intl. Alliance of ALS/MND Associations **[IO]**
International Essential Tremor Foundation **[IO]**
Intl. Essential Tremor Found. **[15331]**
Intl. Functional Elecl. Stimulation Soc. **[15390]**
Intl. Huntington Assn. - Chile **[IO]**
Intl. Huntington Assn. - Ecuador **[IO]**
Intl. Huntington Assn. - Egypt **[IO]**
Intl. Huntington Assn. - Hungary **[IO]**
Intl. Huntington Assn. - Iceland **[IO]**
Intl. Huntington Assn. - Korea **[IO]**
Intl. Huntington Assn. - Lebanon **[IO]**
Intl. Huntington Assn. - Lithuania **[IO]**
Intl. Huntington Assn. - Moldova **[IO]**
Intl. Huntington Assn. - Oman **[IO]**
Intl. Huntington Assn. - Paraguay **[IO]**
Intl. Huntington Assn. - Peru **[IO]**
Intl. Huntington Assn. - Philippines **[IO]**
Intl. Huntington Assn. - Taiwan **[IO]**
Intl. Huntington Assn. - Thailand **[IO]**
Intl. Huntington Assn. - Tunisia **[IO]**
Intl. Huntington Assn. - Uruguay **[IO]**
Intl. Huntington Assn. - Zimbabwe **[IO]**
Intl. Huntington Org. - Iran **[IO]**
International Organization of Glutaric Acidemia **[IO]**
Intl. Org. of Glutaric Acidemia **[15332]**
Intl. Org. of Multiple Sclerosis Nurses **[15486]**
Intl. Pompe Assn. **[IO]**
Intl. Post Polio Support Org. **[16048]**
Intl. Rett Syndrome Assn. **[15333]**
Intl. Rett Syndrome Assn. **[IO]**
Irish Motor Neurone Disease Assn. **[IO]**
Israeli Support Gp. for HD Families **[IO]**
Italian Assn. for the Fight against Parkinson's Disease, Extrapyramidal Disorders and Dementia **[IO]**
Italian Moebius Syndrome Assn. **[IO]**
Japan Amyotrophic Lateral Sclerosis Assn. **[IO]**
Japanese Huntington's Disease Network **[IO]**
Kennedy's Disease Assn. **[15334]**
Kent Waldrep Natl. Paralysis Found. **[16467]**
Lansforeningen for Huntington's Sykdom **[IO]**
Latvian Multiple Sclerosis Assn. **[IO]**
Lewy Body Dementia Assn. **[IO]**
Lewy Body Dementia Assn. **[15335]**
Ligue Francaise contre la Sclerose En Plaques **[IO]**

A star before a book entry number signifies that the name is not listed separately, but is mentioned within the entry.

Ligue Huntington Francophone Belge [IO]
Ligue Nationale Belge de la Sclerose en Plaques [IO]
Lissencephaly Network [IO]
Lissencephaly Network [15336]
MAAP Services for Autism and Asperger Syndrome [15337]
Motor Neurone Disease Assn. of Australia [IO]
Motor Neurone Disease Assn. of New Zealand [IO]
Motor Neurone Disease Assn. of NSW [IO]
Motor Neurone Disease Assn. of Queensland [IO]
Motor Neurone Disease Assn. of South Africa [IO]
Motor Neurone Disease Assn. of South Australia [IO]
Motor Neurone Disease Assn. of the United Kingdom [IO]
Motor Neurone Disease Assn. of Western Australia [IO]
Motor Neurone Disease Res. Inst. of Australia [IO]
MS Felag Islands [IO]
Multipel Sklerose Forbundet I Norge [IO]
Multiple Sclerosis Australia [IO]
Multiple Sclerosis Found. [15338]
Multiple Sclerosis Intl. Fed. [IO]
Multiple Sclerosis Soc. of Canada [IO]
Multiple Sclerosis Soc. of India [IO]
Multiple Sclerosis Soc. of Ireland [IO]
Multiple Sclerosis Soc. of Malta [IO]
Multiple Sclerosis Soc. of New Zealand [IO]
Multiple Sclerosis Soc. - United Kingdom [IO]
Multiple Sclerosis Soc. of Zimbabwe [IO]
Multiple Sclerosis South Africa [IO]
Muscular Dystrophy Assn. [15339]
Muscular Dystrophy Assn. Singapore [IO]
Muscular Dystrophy Ireland [IO]
Muskelsvindfonden [IO]
Myasthenia Gravis Found. of Am. [15340]
The Myositis Assn. [15341]
Nanaimo Brain Injury Soc. [IO]
Narcolepsy Assn. United Kingdom [IO]
Natl. Acad. of Neuropsychology [16158]
Natl. Assn. for Child Development [13943]
Natl. Ataxia Found. [15342]
Natl. Attention Deficit Disorder Assn. [15343]
Natl. Brain Tumor Found. [15344]
Natl. Center for Neurogenic Commun. Disorders [16449]
Natl. Center for Voice and Speech [16451]
Natl. CFIDS Found. [15345]
Natl. Coalition for Res. in Neurological Disorders [15346]
Natl. Fibromyalgia Res. Assn. [15347]
Natl. Found. for Brain Res. [15397]
Natl. Inst. of Neurological Disorders and Stroke [15348]
Natl. Multiple Sclerosis Soc. [15349]
Natl. Org. for Disorders of the Corpus Callosum [15350]
Natl. Parkinson Found. [15351]
Natl. Spasmodic Dysphonia Assn. [15352]
Natl. Spasmodic Torticollis Assn. [15353]
Natl. Tay-Sachs and Allied Diseases Assn. [15354]
National Tay-Sachs and Allied Diseases Association [IO]
NBIA Disorders Assn. [15355]
Neurobehavioral Teratology Soc. [15356]
Neurocritical Care Soc. [14070]
Neurofibromatosis [14471]
Neurofibromatosis Assn. of Australia [IO]
Neurofibromatosis Assn. of Ireland [IO]
Neurofibromatosis Assn. of the United Kingdom [IO]
Neuroleptic Malignant Syndrome Info. Ser. [IO]
Neuroleptic Malignant Syndrome Info. Ser. [15357]
Neurologiskt Handikappades Riksforbund [IO]
Neuromuscular Diseases Assn. of Romania [IO]
Neurosurgeons to Preserve Hea. Care Access [15414]
Newfoundland Brain Injury Assn. [IO]
Northern Alberta Brain Injury Soc. [IO]
Norwegian Multiple Sclerosis Soc. [IO]

Norwegian Parkinson Assn. [IO]
Ontario Brain Injury Assn. [IO]
Org. of Huntington in Greece [IO]
Pakistan Huntington Disease Soc. [IO]
Parents of Infants and Children with Kernicterus [15358]
Parkinson Alliance [15359]
Parkinson Soc. of Canada [IO]
Parkinson Soc. Canada - Maritime Region [IO]
Parkinson Soc. Canada - Southwestern Ontario Region [IO]
Parkinson Soc. Manitoba [IO]
Parkinson Soc. Newfoundland and Labrador [IO]
Parkinson Soc. Ottawa [IO]
Parkinson Soc. Quebec [IO]
Parkinson's Action Network [14285]
Parkinson's Assn. of Ireland [IO]
Parkinson's Australia [IO]
Parkinson's Disease Found. [15360]
Parkinson's New South Wales [IO]
Parkinsons New Zealand [IO]
Parkinson's Soc. of Alberta [IO]
Parkinson's Soc. of Southern Alberta [IO]
Parkinson's Victoria [IO]
Parkinson's Western Australia [IO]
Pediatric Neurotransmitter Disease Assn. [15361]
Polio Soc. [15362]
Polosh Soc. of Multiple Sclerosis [IO]
Portuguesa Multiple Sclerosis Soc. [IO]
Prince George Brain Injured Gp. Soc. [IO]
Progressive Supranuclear Palsy Assn. - Europe [IO]
Purine Res. Soc. [15258]
Reflex Sympathetic Dystrophy Syndrome Assn. of Am. [15363]
Res. Center Against Meningitis and Schistosomiasis [IO]
Ryan's Reach [16550]
Schweizerische Huntington Vereinigung [IO]
Scottish Huntington's Assn. [IO]
Scottish Motor Neurone Disease Assn. [IO]
Scottish Spina Bifida Assn. [IO]
Shy Drager Syndrome/Multiple Sys. Atrophy Support Gp. [15364]
Simcoe County Brain Injury Assn. [IO]
Slovak Multiple Sclerosis Soc. [IO]
Soc. for Behavioral Neuroendocrinology [13741]
South Okanagan Similkameen Brain Injury Soc. [IO]
Southern Alberta Brain Injury Soc. [IO]
Spanish ALS Assn. [IO]
Spanish Assn. of Multiple Sclerosis [IO]
Stowarzyszenie na Rzecz Osob z Choroba Huntingtona w Polsce [IO]
Sturge-Weber Found. [15365]
Take Charge! Cure Parkinson's [15366]
Tourette Syndrome Assn. [15367]
Tourette Syndrome Assn. of Australia [IO]
Transverse Myelitis Association [IO]
Transverse Myelitis Assn. [15368]
Tremor Action Network [15369]
Tremor Action Network [IO]
Trigeminal Neuralgia Assn. [15370]
Tuberous Sclerosis Alliance [15371]
United Brachial Plexus Network [15403]
United Leukodystrophy Found. [15372]
United Leukodystrophy Foundation [IO]
Vereniging van Huntington [IO]
Vereniging Spierziekten Nederland [IO]
VOICES Assn. [13211]
West Kootenay Brain Injury Assn. [IO]
World Fed. of Neurology Res. Gp. on Motor Neuron Diseases [IO]
World Fed. of Neurology Res. Gp. on Motor Neuron Diseases [15373]
World Soc. for Stereotactic and Functional Neurosurgery [15418]
Young Onset Parkinson's Assn. [15374]
Yugoslav MND Assn. [IO]
Zdruzenje Multiple Sklerose Slovenie [IO]
Neurological Disorders; Natl. Comm. for Res. in [★15346]
Neurological and Orthopaedic Surgeons; Amer. Acad. of [15409]
Neurological Surgeons; Amer. Assn. of [15410]

Neurological Surgeons; Soc. of [15416]
Neurological Surgery; Amer. Bd. of [15411]
Neurologiskt Handikappades Riksforbund [★IO]
Neurologiskt Handikappades Riksforbund [IO], Stockholm, Sweden
Neurology
Acad. of Aphasia [13704]
Accelerated Cure Proj. for Multiple Sclerosis [15301]
Amer. Acad. of Clinical Neurophysiology [15375]
Amer. Acad. of Neurological and Orthopaedic Surgeons [15409]
Amer. Acad. of Neurology [15376]
Amer. Assn. of Neurological Surgeons [15410]
Amer. Assn. of Neuromuscular and Electrodiagnostic Medicine [15303]
Amer. Assn. of Neuropathologists [15853]
Amer. Assn. of Neuroscience Nurses [15436]
Amer. Autonomic Soc. [15406]
Amer. Bd. of Neurological Surgery [15411]
Amer. Bd. of Psychiatry and Neurology [16071]
Amer. Clinical Neurophysiology Soc. [14306]
Amer. Coll. of Neuropsychiatrists [16072]
Amer. Coll. of Neuropsychopharmacology [15915]
Amer. Coll. of Osteopathic Neurologists and Psychiatrists [15377]
Amer. Coll. of Veterinary Internal Medicine [16767]
Amer. Neuroendocrine Soc. [15035]
Amer. Neurological Assn. [15378]
Amer. Parkinson Disease Assn. [15304]
Amer. Soc. for Experimental Neuro Therapeutics [15379]
Amer. Soc. of Interventional and Therapeutic Neuroradiology [16280]
Amer. Soc. for Neural Transplantation and Repair [15380]
Amer. Soc. of Neuroimaging [16281]
Amer. Soc. of Neurophysiological Monitoring [15381]
Amer. Soc. of Neuroradiology [16282]
Amer. Soc. of Neurorehabilitation [15382]
Amer. Soc. for Stereotactic and Functional Neurosurgery [15412]
Amer. Syringomyelia Alliance Proj. [15305]
Amyotrophic Lateral Sclerosis Assn. [15306]
Angioma Alliance [15307]
Argentinian Soc. of EEG and Clinical Neurophysiology [IO]
ASEAN Neurological Assn. [IO]
Assn. of British Neurologists [IO]
Assn. of Child Neurology Nurses [15465]
Assn. for Comprehensive NeuroTherapy [15383]
Assn. des Neurologues Liberaux de Langue Francaise [IO]
Assn. of Neuroscience Departments and Programs [15384]
Assn. for Res. in Nervous and Mental Disease [16082]
Attention Deficit Info. Network [15308]
Australian Soc. of Clinical Neurophysiologists [IO]
Austrian Soc. for Clinical Neurophysiology [IO]
Avenues, Natl. Support Gp. for Arthrogryposis Multiplex Congenita [15309]
Belgian EMG and Clinical Neurophysiology Soc. [IO]
Belgian Neurological Soc. [IO]
Belgian Soc. of Clinical Neurophysiology [IO]
Benign Essential Blepharospasm Res. Found. [15311]
Bolivian Soc. of Clinical Neurophysiology [IO]
Brain Injury Assn. of Am. [14528]
Brazilian Soc. of Clinical Neurophysiology [IO]
British Soc. for Clinical Neurophysiology [IO]
Cajal Club [15385]
Canadian Assn. for Child Neurology [IO]
Canadian Brain Tissue Bank [IO]
Canadian Neurological Sciences Fed. [IO]
Canadian Neuropathy Assn. [IO]
Canadian Soc. of Clinical Neurophysiologists [IO]
Care4Dystonia [15312]
Child Neurology Soc. [15386]
Children's Hemiplegia and Stroke Assn. [16493]
Children's Tumor Found. [15315]
Chilean Soc. of Clinical Neurophysiology [IO]

Reference to "IO" in place of a book number signifies that the association may be found in the 45th edition of International Organizations.

Chinese Soc. of EMG and Clinical Neurophysiology [IO]
Chronic Syndrome Support Assn. [14259]
Cognitive Neuroscience Soc. [15407]
Collegium Internationale Neuro-Psychopharmacologicum [15929]
Colombian Assn. of Clinical Neurophysiology [IO]
Croatian Fed. for EEG and Neurophysiology [IO]
Cuban Clinical Neurophysiology Soc. [IO]
Czech Soc. for Clinical Neurophysiology [IO]
Dana Alliance for Brain Initiatives [15387]
Danish Soc. of Clinical Neurophysiology [IO]
Dominican Soc. of EEG and Clinical Neurophysiology [IO]
Dysautonomia Youth Network of Am. [15318]
Dystonia Medical Res. Found. [15319]
Estonian Soc. of Clinical Neurophysiology [IO]
European Brain and Behaviour Soc. [IO]
European Brain Coun. [IO]
European Brain Injury Soc. [IO]
European Fed. of Neurological Societies [IO]
European Neural Network Soc. [IO]
European Neuroendocrine Assn. [IO]
European Neurological Soc. [IO]
European Paediatric Neurology Soc. [IO]
European Soc. for Neurochemistry [IO]
European Soc. of Neuroradiology [IO]
European Soc. of Neurosonology and Cerebral Hemodynamics [IO]
Facioscapulohumeral (FSH) Soc. [15320]
Fibromuscular Dysplasia Soc. of Am. [15322]
Forbes Norris MDA/ALS Res. Center [15323]
Friedreich's Ataxia Res. Alliance [14403]
German Soc. of Neurogenetics [IO]
Global Neuro Rescue [15324]
Guardians of Hydrocephalus Res. Found. [15326]
Hispanic Neuropsychological Soc. [15388]
Huntington's Disease Soc. of Am. [15329]
Hydrocephalus Assn. [15330]
Indian Acad. of Neurology - Clinical Neurophysiology [IO]
Indonesian Soc. for Clinical Neurophysiology [IO]
Intl. Acad. for Child Brain Development [IO]
Intl. Acad. for Child Brain Development [15389]
Intl. Behavioral Neuroscience Soc. [15408]
Intl. Brain Res. Org. [IO]
Intl. Child Neurology Assn. [IO]
Intl. Fed. of Clinical Neurophysiology [IO]
Intl. Functional Elecl. Stimulation Soc. [IO]
Intl. Functional Elecl. Stimulation Soc. [15390]
Intl. Neural Network Soc. [15391]
Intl. Neural Network Soc. [IO]
International Neuromodulation Society [IO]
Intl. Neuromodulation Soc. [15392]
Intl. Neuropsychological Soc. [15393]
Intl. Neuropsychological Soc. [IO]
Intl. Org. of Glutaric Acidemia [15332]
Intl. Org. of Multiple Sclerosis Nurses [15486]
Intl. Post Polio Support Org. [16048]
Intl. Rett Syndrome Assn. [15333]
Intl. Soc. for the History of the Neurosciences [7376]
Intl. Soc. of Motor Control [7377]
Intl. Soc. of Neuro-Semantics [16396]
Intl. Soc. for Neurofeedback and Res. [15394]
Intl. Soc. for Neuroimmunomodulation [15395]
Intl. Soc. for Neuroimmunomodulation [IO]
Intl. Soc. for Neuronal Regulation [IO]
Intl. Soc. of Neuropathology [IO]
Intl. Soc. of NeuroVirology [IO]
Intl. Soc. of NeuroVirology [15396]
Intl. Soc. of Psychoneuroendocrinology [15108]
Japanese Soc. of Clinical Neurophysiology [IO]
Japanese Soc. of Neurology [IO]
Kennedy's Disease Assn. [15334]
Lewy Body Dementia Assn. [15335]
Lissencephaly Network [15336]
Multiple Sclerosis Found. [15338]
Myasthenia Gravis Found. of Am. [15340]
The Myositis Assn. [15341]
Natl. Acad. of Neuropsychology [16158]
Natl. Ataxia Found. [15342]
Natl. Coalition for Res. in Neurological Disorders [15346]
Natl. Dysautonomia Res. Found. [14279]

Natl. Found. for Brain Res. [15397]
Natl. Infant Torticollis Assn. [14945]
Natl. Multiple Sclerosis Soc. [15349]
Natl. Neurotrauma Soc. [15398]
Natl. Org. for Disorders of the Corpus Callosum [15350]
Natl. Parkinson Found. [15351]
Natl. Spasmodic Dysphonia Assn. [15352]
Natl. Spasmodic Torticollis Assn. [15353]
Natl. Tay-Sachs and Allied Diseases Assn. [15354]
NBIA Disorders Assn. [15355]
Neuro-Developmental Treatment Assn. [15399]
Neurobehavioral Teratology Soc. [15356]
Neurocritical Care Soc. [14070]
Neurofibromatosis [14471]
Neurological Coun. of Western Australia [IO]
The Neuropathy Assn. [15400]
Neurosurgeons to Preserve Hea. Care Access [15414]
Neurosurgery Intl. [15415]
North Amer. Skull Base Soc. [15401]
North Amer. Spine Soc. [15402]
North American Spine Society [IO]
Org. for Human Brain Mapping [7379]
Pan-African Assn. of Neurological Sciences [IO]
Parkinson Alliance [15359]
Parkinson's Disease Found. [15360]
Pediatric Brain Tumor Found. of the U.S. [13863]
Pediatric Neurotransmitter Disease Assn. [15361]
Peruvian Soc. of Clinical Neurophysiology [IO]
Philippine Soc. of Clinical Neurophysiology [IO]
Purine Res. Soc. [15258]
Ryan's Reach [16550]
Shy Drager Syndrome/Multiple Sys. Atrophy Support Gp. [15364]
Societa Italiana di Neurofisiologia Clinica [IO]
Spanish Neuromodulation Soc. [IO]
Taiwan Soc. of Clinical Neurophysiology [IO]
Take Charge! Cure Parkinson's [15366]
Thai Soc. of Clinical Neurophysiology [IO]
Tourette Syndrome Assn. [15367]
Transverse Myelitis Assn. [15368]
Tremor Action Network [15369]
Tuberous Sclerosis Alliance [15371]
United Brachial Plexus Network [15403]
Uruguayan Soc. of Clinical Neurophysiology [IO]
William H. Donner Found. [13880]
Women in Neurotrauma Res. [15404]
World Fed. of Neurology [IO]
World Fed. of Neurology Res. Gp. on Motor Neuron Diseases [15373]
World Fed. of Neuroradiological Societies [16306]
World Soc. for Stereotactic and Functional Neurosurgery [15418]
World Spine Soc. [15405]
World Spine Soc. [IO]
Young Onset Parkinson's Assn. [15374]
Neurology; Amer. Bd. of Psychiatry and [16071]
Neuroma Assn; Acoustic [15816]
Neuromodulation Soc; Amer. [★15847]
Neuromodulation Soc; Intl. [15392]
Neuromodulation Soc; North Amer. [15847]
Neuromuscular Diseases Assn. of Romania [IO], Arad, Romania
Neuromuscular Disorders Associations; European Alliance of [IO]
Neuromuscular and Electrodiagnostic Medicine; Amer. Assn. of [15303]
Neuromuscular Res. Found; ALS and [★15323]
Neuronal Regulation; Soc. for [★15394]
Neurone Disease Assn; Scottish Motor [IO]
NeuroOncology; European Assn. for [IO]
Neuropathologists; Amer. Assn. of [15853]
Neuropathologists; Canadian Assn. of [IO]
Neuropathologists; Club of [★15853]
The Neuropathy Assn. [15400], 60 E 42 St., Ste. 942, New York, NY 10165, (212)692-0662
Neurophysiology; Amer. Acad. of Clinical [15375]
Neurophysiology; Intl. Fed. of Clinical [IO]
Neuropsychiatric Assn; Amer. [16074]
Neuropsychiatric Res. Soc. [★16082]
Neuropsychiatrists; Amer. Coll. of [16072]
Neuropsychology; Amer. Bd. of Professional [16120]
Neuropsychology; Natl. Acad. of [16158]

Neuropsychopharmacology; Amer. Coll. of [15915]
Neuroradiology; Amer. Soc. of [16282]
Neuroradiology; Amer. Soc. of Interventional and Therapeutic [16280]
Neuroradiology; Amer. Soc. of Pediatric [16283]
Neuroradiology; European Soc. of [IO]
Neurorehabilitation; Amer. Soc. of [15382]
Neuroscience
Amer. Assn. of Neurological Surgeons [15410]
Amer. Assn. of Neuroscience Nurses [15436]
Amer. Autonomic Soc. [15406]
Amer. Bd. of Neurological Surgery [15411]
Amer. Bd. of Professional Neuropsychology [16120]
Amer. Neuropsychiatric Assn. [16074]
Amer. Soc. for Neural Transplantation and Repair [15380]
Amer. Soc. for Neurochemistry [7374]
Amer. Soc. of Neuroimaging [16281]
Amer. Soc. for Stereotactic and Functional Neurosurgery [15412]
Australian Neuroscience Soc. [IO]
Austrian Neuroscience Assn. [IO]
Brain Res. Soc. of Finland [IO]
British Neuroscience Assn. [IO]
British Soc. for Neuroendocrinology [IO]
Canadian Soc. for Brain, Behaviour and Cognitive Sci. [IO]
Cognitive Neuroscience Soc. [IO]
Cognitive Neuroscience Soc. [15407]
Danish Soc. for Neuroscience [IO]
Fed. of European Neuroscience Societies - Milan [IO]
German Neuroscience Soc. [IO]
Global Assn. for Interpersonal Neurobiology Stud. [IO]
Global Assn. for Interpersonal Neurobiology Stud. [7375]
Hispanic Neuropsychological Soc. [15388]
Intl. Behavioral Neuroscience Soc. [15408]
Intl. Behavioral Neuroscience Soc. [IO]
Intl. Behavioural and Neural Genetics Soc. [IO]
Intl. Neuroendocrine Fed. [IO]
Intl. Soc. for Developmental Neuroscience [IO]
Intl. Soc. for the History of the Neurosciences [IO]
Intl. Soc. for the History of the Neurosciences [7376]
Intl. Soc. of Motor Control [7377]
Intl. Soc. of Motor Control [IO]
Intl. Soc. of Neuro-Semantics [16396]
Intl. Soc. for Neurochemistry [IO]
Intl. Soc. for Neurofeedback and Res. [15394]
Israel Soc. for Neuroscience [IO]
Italian Neuroscience Soc. [IO]
Japan Neuroendocrine Soc. [IO]
Japan Neuroscience Soc. [IO]
The Monroe Inst. [7378]
Neurocritical Care Soc. [14070]
Neurosurgeons to Preserve Hea. Care Access [15414]
Neurosurgery Intl. [15415]
Norwegian Neuroscience Soc. [IO]
Org. for Human Brain Mapping [7379]
Societe de Neuroendocrinologie [IO]
Soc. for Neuroscience [7380]
Whitehall Found. [7381]
World Soc. for Stereotactic and Functional Neurosurgery [15418]
Neuroscience Nurses; British Assn. of [IO]
Neuroscience Nursing; Amer. Bd. of [15443]
Neurosurgeons to Preserve Hea. Care Access [15414], 5550 Meadowbrook Dr., Rolling Meadows, IL 60008, (202)628-2883
Neurosurgery
Amer. Acad. of Neurological and Orthopaedic Surgeons [15409]
Amer. Assn. of Neurological Surgeons [15410]
American Association of Neurological Surgeons [IO]
Amer. Bd. of Neurological Surgery [15411]
Amer. Soc. of Neuroimaging [16281]
Amer. Soc. for Stereotactic and Functional Neurosurgery [15412]
American Society for Stereotactic and Functional Neurosurgery [IO]

A star before a book entry number signifies that the name is not listed separately, but is mentioned within the entry.

Asian - Australasian Soc. of Neurological Surgeons **[IO]**
Cong. of Neurological Surgeons **[IO]**
Cong. of Neurological Surgeons **[15413]**
European Assn. of Neurosurgical Societies **[IO]**
European Soc. for Stereotactic and Functional Neurosurgery **[IO]**
Japan Neurosurgical Soc. **[IO]**
Neurosurgeons to Preserve Hea. Care Access **[15414]**
Neurosurgery Intl. **[15415]**
Neurosurgery Intl. **[IO]**
Neurosurgical Assn. of Malaysia **[IO]**
Neurosurgical Soc. of Australasia **[IO]**
Scandinavian Neurosurgical Soc. **[IO]**
Soc. of British Neurological Surgeons **[IO]**
Soc. of Neurological Surgeons **[15416]**
Soc. of Neurosurgical Anesthesia and Critical Care **[15417]**
World Fed. of Neurosurgical Societies **[IO]**
World Soc. for Stereotactic and Functional Neurosurgery **[IO]**
World Soc. for Stereotactic and Functional Neurosurgery **[15418]**
World Soc. for Stereotactic and Functional Neurosurgery - Canada **[IO]**
Neurosurgery; Amer. Soc. for Stereotactic and Functional **[15412]**
Neurosurgery Intl. **[15415]**, c/o Seattle Neuroscience Inst., 1600 E Jefferson, Ste. 200, Seattle, WA 98122, (206)320-2028
Neurosurgery Intl. **[IO]**, Seattle, WA, United States
Neurosurgery; Intl. Soc. for Pediatric **[IO]**
Neurosurgical Assn. of Malaysia **[IO]**, Kelantan, Malaysia
Neurosurgical Assn. of Thailand **[IO]**, Bangkok, Thailand
Neurosurgical Nurses **[★15443]**
Neurosurgical Physician Assistants; Assn. of **[15974]**
Neurosurgical Soc. of America - Address unknown since 2001.
Neurosurgical Soc. of Australasia **[IO]**, Melbourne, Australia
Neurosurgical Soc; Canadian **[IO]**
NeuroTherapy; Assn. for Comprehensive **[15383]**
Neurotics Anonymous Intl. Liaison - Address unknown since 2003.
Neurotology Soc; Amer. **[16441]**
Neurowissenschaftliche Gesellschaft e.V. **[★IO]**
NEUS, Inc. - Defunct.
Neutron Scattering Soc. of Am. **[7506]**, c/o Dr. Greg S. Smith, Membership Sec., PO Box 2008, MS6393, Oak Ridge, TN 37831-6393, (865)241-1742
Neutropenia Support Assn. **[IO]**, Winnipeg, MB, Canada
Nevada Assn. (BB-36/SSBN-733); USS **[21229]**
Nevada Assn. Race and Sports Book Operators - Defunct.
Nevada COBOL Users Group - Defunct.
Nevada Desert Experience **[18161]**, 1420 W Bartlett Ave., Las Vegas, NV 89106-2226, (702)646-4814
Nevada Test Site Radiation Victim Assn. - Address unknown since 1999.
Never Again Campaign **[18162]**, c/o Prof. Donald N. Lathrop, Coor., Berkshire Community Coll., 1350 West St., Pittsfield, MA 01201-5720, (413)499-4660
Never Again Campaign **[IO]**, Pittsfield, MA, United States
Never More War **[IO]**, Tarm, Denmark
Nevil Inst. for Rehabilitation and Ser. **[★16831]**
Nevil Shute Soc. - Defunct.
Nevis Historical and Conservation Soc. **[IO]**, Charlestown, St. Kitts and Nevis
Nevis Island Cultural Center of the U.S. - Defunct.
Nevis Tourist Off; Saint Kitts- **[★24254]**
Nevus Network **[16545]**, c/o The Congenital Nevus Support Gp., PO Box 305, West Salem, OH 44287, (419)853-4525
Nevus Network **[IO]**, West Salem, OH, United States
Nevus Outreach **[14284]**, 600 SE Delaware Ave., Ste. 200, Bartlesville, OK 74003, (918)331-0595
New Afrikan People's Org. - Address unknown since 1995.

New Age **[★11294]**
New Age
Coalition of Visionary Resources **[2835]**
Friends of Falun Gong **[17061]**
Networking Alternatives for Publishers, Retailers and Artists **[3243]**
Unarius Acad. of Sci. **[12366]**
New Age Citizen **[17139]**, PO Box 419, Dearborn Heights, MI 48127, (313)704-0021
New Age Learning Center - Defunct.
New Age Patriot **[★17139]**
New Age Publishing and Retailing Alliance **[★3243]**
New Age Publishing and Retailing Alliance **[★IO]**
New Age World Religious and Scientific Res. Found. - Defunct.
New Alchemy Inst. - Defunct.
New Am. Alliance **[1169]**, 6688 N Central Expy., Ste. 625, Dallas, TX 75206, (214)466-6410
New Am. Found. **[18468]**, 1630 Connecticut Ave. NW, 7th Fl., Washington, DC 20009, (202)986-2700
New Am. Movement **[★18652]**
New Atlantean Res. Soc. - Defunct.
New Avenues to Independence **[12578]**, c/o Debbie Dombek, Human Resources Asst., 17608 Euclid Ave., Cleveland, OH 44112-1216, (216)481-1909
New Bedford Glass Soc. - Defunct.
New Believer Lib. Program **[★20368]**
New Brunswick Coun. of the Atlantic Salmon Fed. **[IO]**, Fredericton, NB, Canada
New Brunswick Fed. of Woodlot Owners **[IO]**, Fredericton, NB, Canada
New Brunswick Wheelchair Sports Assn. **[IO]**, St. John, NB, Canada
New Brunswick Wildlife Fed. **[IO]**, Moncton, NB, Canada
New Brunswick Women's Inst. **[IO]**, Fredericton, NB, Canada
New Buildings Inst. **[5554]**, PO Box 2349, White Salmon, WA 98672, (509)493-4468
New Call to Peacemaking - Address unknown since 2002.
New Canaan Historical Soc. **[10137]**, 13 Oenoke Ridge, New Canaan, CT 06840, (203)966-1776
New Century Policies Educational Programs **[18469]**, c/o Carla Brooks Johnston, Pres., One Percy Pl., Cambridge, MA 02139, (617)354-5811
New Civilization **[★12359]**
New Civilization Network **[12359]**, PO Box 260433, Encino, CA 91316, (818)774-1462
New Communities Program - Defunct.
New Dawn **[22140]**, PO Box 11462, Takoma Park, MD 20913
New Deal Preservation Assn; Natl. **[10775]**
New Democratic Dimensions **[17409]**, 152 Madison Ave., Ste. 804, New York, NY 10016-5424, (212)481-7251
New Democratic Movement - Address unknown since 1989.
New Democratic Party of Canada **[IO]**, Ottawa, ON, Canada
New Dimensions Found. **[★IO]**
New Dimensions Found. **[★17738]**
New Dimensions Radio **[17738]**, PO Box 569, Ukiah, CA 95482, (707)468-5215
New Dimensions Radio **[IO]**, Ukiah, CA, United States
New Directions Educational Fund - Defunct.
New Dramatists **[11034]**, 424 W 44th St., New York, NY 10036, (212)757-6960
New Dramatists Comm. **[★11034]**
New Economics Found. **[IO]**, London, United Kingdom
New Edinburgh Folk Club **[IO]**, Dunedin, New Zealand
New El Salvador Today **[★IO]**
New El Salvador Today **[★17485]**
New El Salvador Today - Address unknown since 1999.
New England
Bostonian Soc. **[10097]**
Colonial Soc. of Massachusetts **[10104]**
Historic New England **[10035]**
New England Antiquities Res. Assn. **[6452]**
New England Wild Flower Soc. **[4434]**

New England Advisory Bd. for Fish and Game Problems - Defunct.
New England Antiquities Res. Assn. **[6452]**, 94 Cross Point Rd., Edgecomb, ME 04556, (207)882-9425
New England Antiquities; Soc. for the Preservation of **[★10035]**
New England Assistance Dog Prog. **[★14770]**
New England Assistance Dog Ser. **[★14770]**
New England Assn. of Colleges and Secondary Schools **[★8296]**
New England Assn. of Graduate Admissions Professionals **[★7913]**
New England Assn. of Schools and Colleges **[8296]**, 209 Burlington Rd., Bedford, MA 01730-1433, (781)271-0022
New England Assn. of Soldiers of the War of 1812 **[★21354]**
New England Camping Assn. **[★23273]**
New England Center for Organizational Effectiveness - Address unknown since 2001.
New England Congressional Caucus - Defunct.
New England Family Campers Assn. **[★23273]**
New England Fish Exchange **[4330]**
New England Fisheries Development Assn. **[3499]**, c/o Kenelm W. Coons, Exec. Dir., PO Box 5307, Annapolis, MD 21403-0702, (443)482-9889
New England Fisheries Development Found. **[★3499]**
New England Found. for Cooperative Living **[★18011]**
New England Gerontological Assn. **[14517]**, 1 Cutts Rd., Durham, NH 03824-3102, (603)868-5757
New England Historic Genealogical Soc. **[21136]**, 101 Newbury St., Boston, MA 02116, (617)536-5740
New England Kiln Drying Assn. **[1610]**, c/o Scott Ferland, Pres., 36 Frost St., Brattleboro, VT 05301
New England Knitted Outerwear Assn. **[★20816]**
New England Knitted Outerwear Manufacturers Assn. **[★20816]**
New England Knitwear and Sportswear Assn. - Defunct.
New England Lumber Women's Assn. - Defunct.
New England; Maryknoll Mission Center of **[8660]**
New England M.G. "T" Register Limited **[21740]**, PO Box 1957, Cary, NC 27512-1957, (704)544-1253
New England Natl. Soc; Sons of Colonial **[20761]**
New England Order of Protection **[★19441]**
New England Project on Education of the Aging - Defunct.
New England Rainwear Manufacturers Assn. **[★221]**
New England Rubber Club **[★3434]**
New England Soc. of Open Salts Collectors - Address unknown since 2003.
New England Theatre Conf. **[11035]**, 215 Knob Hill Dr., Hamden, CT 06518, (617)851-8535
New England Trail Rider Assn. **[23947]**, PO Box 469, Collinsville, CT 06022, (860)693-9111
New England Trails Conf. **[23948]**, c/o Marsha Towns, PO Box 550, Charlestown, NH 03603, (603)543-1700
New England Wild Flower Preservation Soc. **[★4434]**
New England Wild Flower Soc. **[4434]**, 180 Hemenway Rd., Framingham, MA 01701, (508)877-7630
New England and World Missions - Address unknown since 1994.
New English Art Club **[IO]**, London, United Kingdom
New Env. Assn. **[4597]**, 821 Euclid Ave., Syracuse, NY 13210, (315)446-8009
New ERA Education/Child Care Parent Advocacy Program - Defunct.
New Eyes for the Needy **[12533]**, PO Box 332, Short Hills, NJ 07078, (973)376-4903
New Farmers of Am. **[★7940]**
New Farmers of Am. **[★IO]**
New Feminist Talent Associates - Address unknown since 1995.
New Flemish Alliance **[IO]**, Brussels, Belgium
New Forest Pony Assn. **[★4929]**
New Forest Pony Assn. and Registry **[4929]**, c/o Lucille Guilbault, VP, PO Box 206, Pascoag, RI 02859-0206, (401)568-8238
New Forest Pony Breeding and Cattle Soc. **[IO]**, Bransgore, United Kingdom

Reference to "IO" in place of a book number signifies that the association may be found in the 45th edition of International Organizations.

New Forests Fund [★12436]
New Forests Proj. [12436], 1025 Vermont Ave. NW, 7th Fl., Washington, DC 20005, (202)547-3800
New Frontiers of Medicine [★12834]
New Games Found. - Defunct.
New Gnostics Special Interest Group - Address unknown since 1995.
New Hampshire; Acadian Genealogical and Historical Assn. of [★21098]
New Homemakers of Am. [★8417]
New Hope Found. [13271], PO Box 66, Marlboro, NJ 07746, (732)946-3030
New Hope Intl. [20372], PO Box 25490, Colorado Springs, CO 80936, (719)577-4450
New Hope Intl. [IO], Colorado Springs, CO, United States
New Hope Ministries [★IO]
New Hope Ministries [★20372]
New Horizon World Center [19527]
New Horizons Arts Initiative [9589]
New Israel Fund [17940], 1101 14th St. NW, 6th Fl., Washington, DC 20005-5639, (202)842-0900
New Jersey Asparagus Indus. Coun. [4748], PO Box 330, Trenton, NJ 08625-0330, (609)292-8853
New Jersey; Assoc. Humane Societies of [★11366]
New Jersey; Coun. on Compulsive Gambling of [12209]
New Jersey; Descendants of Founders of [20736]
New Jersey Devils Fan Club [★25004]
New Jersey Foreign Freight Forwarders and Brokers Assn; New York/ [3582]
New Jersey; Maritime Assn. of the Port of New York/ [3572]
New Jersey Midland Historical Soc. - Address unknown since 2001.
New Jersey; Seamen's Church Inst. of New York and [19970]
New Jersey Sect. of the Microchemical Soc; New York- [★6668]
New Jetsons Fan Club [25037], PO Box 02222, Detroit, MI 48202
New Jewish Agenda - Address unknown since 1994.
New Komeito [IO], Tokyo, Japan
New Kuban; All Cossack Assn. [★19019]
New Kuban Educ. and Welfare Assn. [19019], 228 Don Rd., Buena, NJ 08310-1615
New Kuban Historical Museum [★19019]
New Leaders for New Schools [8755], 30 W 26th St., 2nd Fl., New York, NY 10010, (646)792-1070
New Leadership Fund - Address unknown since 1999.
New Libertarian Alliance - Address unknown since 1997.
New Life Inst. - Address unknown since 1995.
New Life League [★20373]
New Life League [★IO]
New Life League Intl. [IO], Houston, TX, United States
New Life League Intl. [20373], PO Box 35857, Houston, TX 77235-5857, (832)242-7750
New Mgt. Era [IO], Tirana, Albania
New Media Development Assn. [IO], Tokyo, Japan
New Mexico Barbed Wire Collectors Assn. [22091], PO Box 102, Stanley, NM 87056, (505)832-4339
New Mexico People and Energy [★16976]
New Mexico People and Energy [★IO]
New Mexico Philatelic Assn. - Defunct.
New Mexico Univ. Alumni Assn; Western [18944]
New Mexico Vine and Wine Soc. - Address unknown since 2004.
New Millenium Global Outreach - Address unknown since 2007.
New Moon Matchbox and Label Club - Address unknown since 1990.
New Music Distribution Service - Address unknown since 2001.
New Options - Defunct.
New Order [18805], Box 270486, Milwaukee, WI 53227
New Order [IO], Milwaukee, WI, United States
New Order Legion [18806], PO Box 15259, Portland, OR 97293
New Orleans Bd. of Trade [4331], 316 Bd. of Trade Pl., New Orleans, LA 70130, (504)262-0412
New Orleans Jazz Club [10671], 828 Royal St., Ste. 265, New Orleans, LA 70116, (504)887-9839

New Orleans Produce Exchange [★4331]
New Orleans Steamship Assn. [★3591]
New Parents Network [8956], PO Box 64237, Tucson, AZ 85728-4237, (520)327-1451
New Party [18338]
New Paths Unlimited - Address unknown since 2007.
New Political Sci. [★7523]
New Political Sci; Caucus for a [7523]
New Populist Action - Defunct.
New Producers Alliance [IO], London, United Kingdom
New Professionals Sect. of the Amer. Public Health Assn. - Address unknown since 2002.
New Right Coalition - Address unknown since 1995.
New Right Watch [★18789]
New Road Map Found. [12360], PO Box 15320, Seattle, WA 98115, (206)527-0437
New Roots for Young America - Defunct.
New School for Democratic Mgt. - Defunct.
New School of Family Birthing - Defunct.
New Schools Exchange - Defunct.
New Schools Movement - Defunct.
New Socialist Network [IO], Bury St. Edmunds, United Kingdom
New Soc. Educational Found. - Address unknown since 1995.
New South Wales Assn. for Adolescent Hea. [IO], Strawberry Hills, Australia
New South Wales Dental Therapists' Assn. [IO], Sydney, Australia
New South Wales Farmers' Assn. [IO], Sydney, Australia
New South Wales Secondary Principals Assn. [IO], Ryde, Australia
New South Wales Wheelchair Sports Assn. [IO], Putney, Australia
New South Wales Women's Bowling Assn. [IO], Sydney, Australia
New Testament Colloquium - Defunct.
New Thing Art and Architecture Center - Address unknown since 1995.
New Thought Alliance; Intl. [10802]
New Tide [★4376]
New Transport for Christ [★20404]
New Transport for Christ [★IO]
New Tribes Mission [IO], Sanford, FL, United States
New Tribes Mission [20374], 1000 E 1st St., Sanford, FL 32771-1441, (407)323-3430
New Univ. Conf. - Address unknown since 1995.
New Uses Coun. [4080], c/o Dan Manternach, Exec. Dir., 91 W Galloway, Memphis, TN 38111, (901)309-1668
New Uses Council [IO], Memphis, TN, United States
New Violin Family Assn. [10672], 42 Taylor Dr., Wolfeboro, NH 03894, (603)569-7946
New Water Supply Coalition [7839], 1750 H St. NW, Ste. 600, Washington, DC 20006, (202)737-0700
New Ways Ministry [20064], 4012 29th St., Mount Rainier, MD 20712, (301)277-5674
New Ways to Work [12094], 103 Morris St., Ste. A, Sebastopol, CA 95472, (707)824-4000
New Wilderness Found. [10673], c/o Charles Morrow Associates, Inc., 307 Seventh Ave., Ste. 1402, New York, NY 10001, (212)989-2400
New Wineskins Missionary Network [20375], PO Box 278, Ambridge, PA 15003, (724)266-2810
New World [IO], Tirunelveli, India
New World Alliance - Defunct.
New World Club - Defunct.
New World Coalition - Address unknown since 1995.
New World Found. - Defunct.
New World Soc. - Defunct.
New York Acad. of Sciences [7623], 7 World Trade Ctr., 250 Greenwich St., 40th Fl., New York, NY 10007-2157, (212)298-8600
New York; Advt. Club of [77]
New York Advertising Media Planners - Defunct.
New York; Advt. Women of [81]
New York Alliance for the Eradication of Venereal Disease, Inc. [★16409]
New York Alumni Assn; Brooklyn Coll. of the City Univ. of [18880]
New York; Architectural League of [17235]
New York; Assn. of Commercial Finance Companies of [★2423]

New York Assn. for New Americans [12479], 2 Washington St., New York, NY 10004, (212)425-2900
New York Assn. of Wine Producers [★5417]
New York Bible Soc. [★19520]
New York Bible Soc. [★IO]
New York Bible Soc. Intl. [★IO]
New York Bible Soc. Intl. [★19520]
New York Bd. of Trade [3845], World Financial Center, 1 N End Ave., 13th Fl., New York, NY 10282-1101, (212)748-4000
New York; Boot and Shoe Travelers Assn. of [1596]
New York British Merchant Navy Clubs - Defunct.
New York; British Schools and Universities Club of [18984]
New York Browning Soc. - Address unknown since 2003.
New York Business Press Editors - Address unknown since 1995.
New York; Butter, Cheese, and Egg Exchange of the City of [★4333]
New York; Canadian Club of [18988]
New York; Carnegie Corp. of [8239]
New York Children's Aid Soc. [★21140]
New York; China Medical Bd. of [14976]
New York Cipher Soc. [6850], 17 Alfred Rd. W, Merrick, NY 11566, (516)378-0263
New York City Commn. for the United Nations, Consular Corps, and Intl. Business - Address unknown since 2001.
New York City Intl. Bible Soc. [★19520]
New York City Intl. Bible Soc. [★IO]
New York City Medical Soc. on Alcoholism [★16501]
New York Clothing Mfrs. Assn. - Address unknown since 2003.
New York Coat and Suit Assn. [253]
New York Comm. for All Amer. Hungarian Churches and Societies - Defunct.
New York Comm., General Strike for Peace - Defunct.
New York, Constituting the Military Soc. of the War of 1812; Veteran Corps of Artillery, State of [21204]
New York Constitution Study Group - Address unknown since 1995.
New York Correspondence School [★9506]
New York Corset Club - Address unknown since 1994.
New York Cotton Exchange [4332], 1 N End Ave., New York, NY 10282-1101, (212)748-4094
New York Cotton Exchange; Citrus Associates of the [★4332]
New York Coun. for Foreign Students -English in Action; Greater [★17885]
New York Coun. of Motion Picture and TV Unions [24056]
New York Couture Business Coun. - Defunct.
New York C.S. Lewis Soc. [9696], c/o Clara Sarrocco, Sec., 84-23 77th Ave., Glendale, NY 11385-7706, (718)846-7858
New York Curb Agency [★3507]
New York Curb Exchange [★3507]
New York Curb Market [★3507]
New York Curb Market Assn. [★3507]
New York Curtain and Drapery Club - Address unknown since 1995.
New York Customs Brokers Assn. [★2309]
New York Drama Critics Circle - Address unknown since 2004.
New York; Dried Fruit Assn. of [★1503]
New York Exchange for Woman's Work - Address unknown since 2007.
New York Fashion Designers and Found. - Defunct.
New York; The Feminist Press at the City Univ. of [9317]
New York Fertility Inst. [★14391]
New York Fertility Res. Found. [★14391]
New York Film Bd. of Trade - Defunct.
New York Film Critics - Address unknown since 1995.
New York; Financial Women's Assn. of [1421]
New York Financial Writers' Assn. [3148], PO Box 338, Ridgewood, NJ 07451-0338, (201)612-0100
New York Foreign Freight Forwarders and Brokers Assn. [★3582]

A star before a book entry number signifies that the name is not listed separately, but is mentioned within the entry.

New York Fund/United Way; Greater [★12479]
New York Genealogical and Biographical Soc.
  [21137], 122 E 58th St., New York, NY 10022-
  1939, (212)755-8532
New York; Gen. Soc. of Mechanics and Tradesmen
  of the City of [9229]
New York; German Soc. of the City of [19075]
New York Guild for the Jewish Blind [★16862]
New York Inst. of Clinical Oral Pathology - Address
  unknown since 1995.
New York; Insurance Soc. of [2184]
New York Iroquois Conf. - Defunct.
New York; Islamic Center of [20104]
New York Islanders Booster Club [25009], PO Box
  502, Hicksville, NY 11802-0502, (631)547-6942
New York; Japanese Chamber of Commerce of
  [★24346]
New York; Japanese Chamber of Commerce and
  Indus. of [24346]
New York Jazz Museum - Defunct.
New York Junior Naval Militia [★20718]
New York; Marine Soc. of the City of [2581]
New York Mathematical Soc. [★7286]
New York Mercantile Exchange [4333], World
  Financial Ctr., 1 N End Ave., New York, NY 10282-
  1101, (212)299-2000
New York Microscopical Soc. [7336], 30 N Mountain
  Ave., Montclair, NJ 07042, (973)744-0043
New York; Montserrat Progressive Soc. of [19433]
New York Mounters Assn. - Defunct.
New York/New Jersey DreamSharing Network
  [★16425]
New York and New Jersey Dry Dock Assn. -
  Defunct.
New York/New Jersey Foreign Freight Forwarders
  and Brokers Assn. [3582], PO Box 8217, Red
  Bank, NJ 07701, (732)747-1936
New York/New Jersey; Maritime Assn. of the Port of
  [3572]
New York and New Jersey; Seamen's Church Inst.
  of [19970]
New York-New Jersey Sect. of the Microchemical
  Soc. [★6668]
New York New Visions [17232], c/o AIA New York
  Chapter, 536 LaGuardia Pl., New York, NY 10012,
  (212)683-0023
New York Newspaper Women's Club [★3150]
New York; Newspaper Women's Club of [★3150]
New York; Newswomen's Club of [3150]
New York Pigment Club - Address unknown since
  2001.
New York; Press Div., Taipei Economic and Cultural
  Off. in [9792]
New York Pro Musica Antiqua - Defunct.
New York Produce Exchange - Defunct.
New York Publishing Soc. - Defunct.
New York Raincoat Mfrs. Assn. - Defunct.
New York Rainforest Alliance [★4442]
New York Rainforest Alliance [★IO]
New York Rangers Fan Club [25010], GPO Box
  8713, New York, NY 10116-8713
New York Road Runners Club [23921], 9 E 89th St.,
  New York, NY 10128, (212)860-4455
New York; Rubber Trade Assn. of [★3435]
New York; Saint Andrew's Soc. of the State of
  [19355]
New York; Saint Nicholas Soc. of the City of [21148]
New York; Seaman's Church Inst. of [★19970]
New York Security Dealers Assn. - Address unknown
  since 1995.
New York Shipping Assn. [3583], 100 Wood Ave. S,
  Ste. 304, Iselin, NJ 08830-2716, (732)452-7800
New York Skirt and Sportswear Assn. [254]
New York Soc. of Anesthetists [★13674]
New York; Soc. of the Friendly Sons of St. Patrick in
  the City of [19155]
New York Soc. of Security Analysts [3519], 1177
  Ave. of the Americas, 2nd Fl., New York, NY
  10036-2714, (212)541-4530
New York Soc. for the Stud. of Orthodontics
  [★14144]
New York Southern Soc. - Defunct.
New York State Assn. of Ser. Stations [★426]
New York State Assn. of Ser. Stations [★426]
New York State Assn. of Ser. Stations and Repair
  Shops [426], 6 Walker Way, Albany, NY 12205,
  (518)452-4367

New York State; Canal Soc. of [9773]
New York State Colonization Soc. - Defunct.
New York State Comm. for the Prevention of Blind-
  ness [★16882]
New York State Intl. Official Visitors Office - Defunct.
New York State Turf and Landscape Assn. [2397], 1
  Prospect Ave., White Plains, NY 10607, (914)993-
  9455
New York State Wine Grape Growers [★5417]
New York State Wines; Women for [★5417]
New York Stock Exchange [3520], c/o The
  Corporate Secretary, 11 Wall St., New York, NY
  10005, (212)656-3000
New York Stock Transfer Assn. [★3524]
New York Triathlon Club [23922], PO Box 50,
  Saugerties, NY 12477-0050, (845)247-0271
New York Turkish Students Assn. - Address
  unknown since 1995.
New York Turtle and Tortoise Soc. [5348], PO Box
  878, Orange, NJ 07051-0878
New York; Twenty-Four Karat Club of the City of
  [2383]
New York; Watchtower Bible and Tract Soc. of
  [20109]
New York; Welfare League Assn. of [★11885]
New York Wine Coun. [★5417]
New York Wine/Grape Found. [5417], 800 S Main
  St., Ste. 200, Canandaigua, NY 14424, (585)394-
  3620
New York Women in Communications, Inc. Found.
  [883], 355 Lexington Ave., 15th Fl., New York, NY
  10017-6603, (212)297-2133
New York Women's League for Animals [★11353]
New York Workshop in Nonviolence [★18123]
New York Zoological Soc. [★4469]
New Zealand
  Australian New Zealand - Amer. Chambers of
    Commerce [24248]
  Australian and New Zealand Stud. Assn. of North
    Amer. [8484]
  New Zealand Tourism Bd. [24363]
  Soc. of Australasian Specialists/Oceania [22871]
New Zealand Acad. of Fine Arts [IO], Wellington,
  New Zealand
New Zealand Accordion Assn. [IO], Auckland, New
  Zealand
New Zealand ACM SIGCHI [IO], Auckland, New
  Zealand
New Zealand Aikido Fed. [IO], Auckland, New
  Zealand
New Zealand Air Line Pilots' Assn. [IO], Auckland,
  New Zealand
New Zealand Antique Dealers Assn. [IO], Auckland,
  New Zealand
New Zealand Archaeological Assn. [IO], Dunedin,
  New Zealand
New Zealand Asian Stud. Soc. [IO], Wellington, New
  Zealand
New Zealand Assn. for Adolescent Hea. and
  Development [IO], Wellington, New Zealand
New Zealand Assn. for Adolescent Hea. and
  Development Otago/Southland [IO], Invercargill,
  New Zealand
New Zealand Assn. for Adolescent Hea. and
  Development - Wellington [IO], Wellington, New
  Zealand
New Zealand Assn. for Comparative Law [IO], Well-
  ington, New Zealand
New Zealand Assn. of Credit Unions [IO], Auckland,
  New Zealand
New Zealand Assn. for Environmental Educ. [IO],
  Wellington, New Zealand
New Zealand Assn. of Events Professionals [IO],
  Christchurch, New Zealand
New Zealand Assn. of Gerontology [IO], Wellington,
  New Zealand
New Zealand Assn. for Gifted Children [IO],
  Waitomo Caves, New Zealand
New Zealand Assn. of Optometrists [IO], Wellington,
  New Zealand
New Zealand Assn. of Orthodontics [IO],
  Christchurch, New Zealand
New Zealand Assn. of Plastic Surgeons [IO], Well-
  ington, New Zealand
New Zealand Assn. for Psychological Type [IO],
  Wellington, New Zealand

New Zealand Assn. of Radio Transmitters [IO], Up-
  per Hutt, New Zealand
New Zealand Assn. of Rationalists and Humanists
  [IO], Auckland, New Zealand
New Zealand Assn. of Rsrc. Mgt. [IO], Palmerston
  North, New Zealand
New Zealand Assn. of Sci. Educators [IO], Welling-
  ton, New Zealand
New Zealand Assn. of Scientists [IO], Wellington,
  New Zealand
New Zealand Assn. of Soil Conservators [★IO]
New Zealand Assn. for the Teaching of English [IO],
  Christchurch, New Zealand
New Zealand Assn. for Training and Development
  [IO], Lower Hutt, New Zealand
New Zealand Atomic Energy Advocacy Coun. [IO],
  Wellington, New Zealand
New Zealand Audiological Soc. [IO], Auckland, New
  Zealand
New Zealand Auto. Assn. [IO], Auckland, New
  Zealand
New Zealand Avocado Growers Assn. [IO], Tau-
  ranga, New Zealand
New Zealand Badminton Fed. [IO], Wellington, New
  Zealand
New Zealand Bankers' Assn. [IO], Wellington, New
  Zealand
New Zealand Baptist Missionary Soc. [IO], South
  Auckland, New Zealand
New Zealand Baseball Fed. [IO], Auckland, New
  Zealand
New Zealand Biological Producers and Consumers
  Coun. [★IO]
New Zealand Biological Producers Coun. Inc. [★IO]
New Zealand Bonsai Assn. [IO], Dunedin, New
  Zealand
New Zealand Book Coun. [IO], Wellington, New
  Zealand
New Zealand Buick Enthusiasts [IO], North Shore
  City, New Zealand
New Zealand Building Trades Union [IO],
  Christchurch, New Zealand
New Zealand Bus. Coun. for Sustainable Develop-
  ment [IO], Auckland, New Zealand
New Zealand Canoeing Assn. [★IO]
New Zealand Cartographic Soc. [IO], Auckland, New
  Zealand
New Zealand Chambers of Commerce and Indus.
  [IO], Wellington, New Zealand
New Zealand Chefs Assn. [IO], Auckland, New
  Zealand
New Zealand Chem. Indus. Coun. [IO], Wellington,
  New Zealand
New Zealand Childcare Assn. [IO], Wellington, New
  Zealand
New Zealand Christian Counsellors Assn. [IO], Auck-
  land, New Zealand
New Zealand Coastal Soc. [IO], Hamilton, New
  Zealand
New Zealand Coll. of Midwives [IO], Christchurch,
  New Zealand
New Zealand Comm. for the Sci. Investigation of
  Claims of the Paranormal [IO], Christchurch, New
  Zealand
New Zealand Community Newspapers Assn. [IO],
  Ashburton, New Zealand
New Zealand Cmpt. Soc. [IO], Wellington, New
  Zealand
New Zealand Continence Assn. [IO], Auckland, New
  Zealand
New Zealand Coun. of Christian Social Services
  [IO], Wellington, New Zealand
New Zealand Coun. for Educational Res. [IO], Well-
  ington, New Zealand
New Zealand Coun. of Trade Unions [IO], Welling-
  ton, New Zealand
New Zealand Coun.; United States- [2318]
New Zealand Croquet Coun. [IO], Wellington, New
  Zealand
New Zealand Curling Assn. [IO], Central Otago, New
  Zealand
New Zealand Dairy Goat Breeders Assn. [IO], Gis-
  borne, New Zealand
New Zealand Dairy Workers' Union [IO], Hamilton,
  New Zealand

Reference to "IO" in place of a book number signifies that the association may be found in the 45th edition of International Organizations.

New Zealand Dancesport Assn. [IO], Auckland, New Zealand

New Zealand Deer Farmers Assn. [IO], Wellington, New Zealand

New Zealand Democratic Party [IO], Christchurch, New Zealand

New Zealand Dental Assn. [IO], Auckland, New Zealand

New Zealand Dental Hygienists Assn. [IO], Christchurch, New Zealand

New Zealand Dental Therapists Assn. [IO], Auckland, New Zealand

New Zealand Dermatological Soc. [IO], Auckland, New Zealand

New Zealand Dietetic Assn. [IO], Wellington, New Zealand

New Zealand Direct Marketing Assn. [IO], Auckland, New Zealand

New Zealand Down Syndrome Assn. [IO], Auckland, New Zealand

New Zealand Ecological Soc. [IO], Christchurch, New Zealand

New Zealand Educational Inst. [IO], Wellington, New Zealand

New Zealand Educational Inst. - Women's Network [IO], Wellington, New Zealand

New Zealand Employers Fed. [★IO]

New Zealand Endometriosis Found. [IO], Christchurch, New Zealand

New Zealand Engg., Printing and Mfg. Union [IO], Wellington, New Zealand

New Zealand Ergonomics Soc. [IO], Palmerston North, New Zealand

New Zealand Ex-Wrens Assn. [IO], Paihia, New Zealand

New Zealand Fed. of Ethnic Councils [IO], Wellington, New Zealand

New Zealand Fed. of Graduate Women [IO], North Shore City, New Zealand

New Zealand Fed. of Univ. Women [★IO]

New Zealand Ferret Protection and Welfare Soc. [IO], Auckland, New Zealand

New Zealand Film Commn. [IO], Wellington, New Zealand

New Zealand First [IO], Wellington, New Zealand

New Zealand Fishing Indus. Bd. [★IO]

New Zealand Fishing Industry Bd. - Defunct.

New Zealand Flower Exporters Assn. [IO], Auckland, New Zealand

New Zealand Flying Disc Assn. [IO], Auckland, New Zealand

New Zealand Forest Owners Assn. [IO], Auckland, New Zealand

New Zealand Franchise Assn. [IO], Auckland, New Zealand

New Zealand Freshwater Sciences Soc. [IO], Christchurch, New Zealand

New Zealand; Friends of [★2318]

New Zealand Fruitgrowers' Fed. [IO], Wellington, New Zealand

New Zealand Geographical Soc. [IO], Auckland, New Zealand

New Zealand Geotechnical Soc. [IO], Wellington, New Zealand

New Zealand Gift Trade Assn. [IO], Auckland, New Zealand

New Zealand Golf [IO], Wellington, New Zealand

New Zealand Green Building Coun. [IO], Auckland, New Zealand

New Zealand Guidelines Gp. [IO], Wellington, New Zealand

New Zealand Guild of Agricultural Journalists and Communicators [IO], Wellington, New Zealand

New Zealand Guild of Storytellers [IO], Invercargill, New Zealand

New Zealand Heavy Engg. Res. Assn. [IO], Manukau City, New Zealand

New Zealand Historic Places Trust [IO], Wellington, New Zealand

New Zealand Historical Assn. [IO], Wellington, New Zealand

New Zealand Holstein Friesian Assn. [IO], Hamilton, New Zealand

New Zealand Hydrological Soc. [IO], Wellington, New Zealand

New Zealand Ice Cream Mfrs'. Assn. [IO], Wellington, New Zealand

New Zealand Ice Skating Assn. [IO], Auckland, New Zealand

New Zealand Inst. of Agricultural and Horticultural Sci. [IO], Auckland, New Zealand

New Zealand Inst. of Agricultural Sci. [IO], Auckland, New Zealand

New Zealand Inst. of Architects [IO], Auckland, New Zealand

New Zealand Inst. of Chartered Accountants [★IO]

New Zealand Inst. of Chemistry [IO], Christchurch, New Zealand

New Zealand Inst. of Economic Res. [IO], Wellington, New Zealand

New Zealand Inst. of Food Sci. and Tech. [IO], Palmerston North, New Zealand

New Zealand Inst. of Forestry [IO], Christchurch, New Zealand

New Zealand Inst. of Intl. Affairs [IO], Wellington, New Zealand

New Zealand Inst. of Landscape Architects [IO], Wellington, New Zealand

New Zealand Inst. of Mgt. [IO], Wellington, New Zealand

New Zealand Inst. of Medical Radiation Tech. [IO], Auckland, New Zealand

New Zealand Inst. of Physics [IO], Dunedin, New Zealand

New Zealand Inst. of Quantity Surveyors [IO], Wellington, New Zealand

New Zealand Inst. of Travel and Tourism [IO], Wellington, New Zealand

New Zealand Ireland Assn. [IO], Dublin, Ireland

New Zealand Juice and Beverage Assn. [IO], Auckland, New Zealand

New Zealand Kennel Club [IO], Porirua, New Zealand

New Zealand Kiwifruit Marketing Bd. [★IO]

New Zealand Labour Party [IO], Wellington, New Zealand

New Zealand Ladies Golf Union [★IO]

New Zealand Law Soc. [IO], Wellington, New Zealand

New Zealand Leather and Shoe Res. Assn. [IO], Palmerston North, New Zealand

New Zealand Lib. and Info. Assn. [★IO]

New Zealand Limnological Soc. [★IO]

New Zealand Maori Arts and Crafts Inst. [IO], Rotorua, New Zealand

New Zealand Marching Assn. [★IO]

New Zealand Marine Sciences Soc. [IO], Dunedin, New Zealand

New Zealand Masonry Trades Registration Bd. [IO], Wellington, New Zealand

New Zealand Mathematical Soc. [IO], Auckland, New Zealand

New Zealand Meat Bd. [★IO]

New Zealand Medical Assn. [IO], Wellington, New Zealand

New Zealand Merchant Ser. Guild [IO], Wellington, New Zealand

New Zealand Microbiological Soc. [IO], Dunedin, New Zealand

New Zealand Miniature Horse Assn. [IO], Invercargill, New Zealand

New Zealand Model Railway Guild [IO], Auckland, New Zealand

New Zealand Mortgage Brokers Assn. [IO], Auckland, New Zealand

New Zealand Mounted Games Assn. [IO], Caterton, New Zealand

New Zealand Natl. Party [IO], Wellington, New Zealand

New Zealand Native Freshwater Fish Soc. [IO], Auckland, New Zealand

New Zealand Natural Medicine Assn. [IO], Auckland, New Zealand

New Zealand Naturist Fed. [IO], Auckland, New Zealand

New Zealand Nga Herenga Tatai o AFS [★IO]

New Zealand Nurses Assn. (NZNA) [★IO]

New Zealand Nurses Org. [IO], Wellington, New Zealand

New Zealand Olympic Comm. [IO], Wellington, New Zealand

New Zealand Olympic and Commonwealth Games Assn. [★IO]

New Zealand Orienteering Fed. [IO], Christchurch, New Zealand

New Zealand Pacific Bus. Coun. [IO], Auckland, New Zealand

New Zealand Pain Soc. [IO], Wellington, New Zealand

New Zealand Photovoltaic Assn. [IO], Rangiora, New Zealand

New Zealand Plant Protection Soc. [IO], Hastings, New Zealand

New Zealand Playcentre Fed. [IO], Hamilton, New Zealand

New Zealand Police Assn. [IO], Wellington, New Zealand

New Zealand Pork Indus. Bd. [IO], Wellington, New Zealand

New Zealand Press Assn. [IO], Wellington, New Zealand

New Zealand Press Coun. [IO], Wellington, New Zealand

New Zealand Professional Firefighters Union [IO], Petone, New Zealand

New Zealand Professional Fishing Guides Assn. [IO], Gisborne, New Zealand

New Zealand Property Investors Fed. [IO], Bishopdale, New Zealand

New Zealand Psychological Soc. [IO], Wellington, New Zealand

New Zealand Public Ser. Assn. [IO], Wellington, New Zealand

New Zealand Publishers Assn. [★IO]

New Zealand Rabbit Breeders; Amer. Fed. of [5135]

New Zealand Railway and Locomotive Soc. [IO], Wellington, New Zealand

New Zealand Recreation Assn. [IO], Wellington, New Zealand

New Zealand Recreational Canoeing Assn. [IO], Wellington, New Zealand

New Zealand Red Cross [IO], Wellington, New Zealand

New Zealand Resident Doctors' Assn. [IO], Auckland, New Zealand

New Zealand Retailers Assn. [IO], Wellington, New Zealand

New Zealand Rodeo Cowboys Assn. [IO], Outram, New Zealand

New Zealand Rugby Players Assn. [IO], Auckland, New Zealand

New Zealand Sci. Fiction and Fantasy Writers' Assn. [IO], Auckland, New Zealand

New Zealand Seafarers' Union [★IO]

New Zealand Seafood Indus. Coun. [IO], Wellington, New Zealand

New Zealand Secondary Schools Sports Coun. [IO], Christchurch, New Zealand

New Zealand Shipping Fed. [IO], Wellington, New Zealand

New Zealand Sign Language Tutors Assn. [IO], Auckland, New Zealand

New Zealand Skeptics [★IO]

New Zealand Ski Assn. [★IO]

New Zealand Snowsports Coun. [IO], Wellington, New Zealand

New Zealand Soc. of Accountants [★IO]

New Zealand Soc. of Animal Production [IO], Hamilton, New Zealand

New Zealand Soc. of Authors [IO], Auckland, New Zealand

New Zealand Soc. of Contact Lens Practitioners [★IO]

New Zealand Soc. of Diversional Therapists [IO], Christchurch, New Zealand

New Zealand Soc. for Earthquake Engg. [IO], Wellington, New Zealand

New Zealand Soc. for Electron Microscopy [★IO]

New Zealand Soc. of Gastroenterology [IO], Wellington, New Zealand

New Zealand Soc. of Genealogists [IO], Auckland, New Zealand

New Zealand Soc. of Genealogists - Auckland Br. [IO], Auckland, New Zealand

New Zealand Soc. of Genealogists - Cambridge Br. [IO], Cambridge, New Zealand

A star before a book entry number signifies that the name is not listed separately, but is mentioned within the entry.

New Zealand Soc. of Genealogists - Coromandel **[IO]**, Coromandel, New Zealand

New Zealand Soc. of Genealogists - Far North **[IO]**, Kaitaia, New Zealand

New Zealand Soc. of Genealogists - Hamilton Br. **[IO]**, Hamilton, New Zealand

New Zealand Soc. of Genealogists - Hibiscus Coast Br. **[IO]**, Orewa, New Zealand

New Zealand Soc. of Genealogists - Howick Br. **[IO]**, Auckland, New Zealand

New Zealand Soc. of Genealogists - Matamata Br. **[IO]**, Matamata, New Zealand

New Zealand Soc. of Genealogists - North Shore Br. **[IO]**, North Shore City, New Zealand

New Zealand Soc. of Genealogists - Northern Wairoa Br. **[IO]**, Dargaville, New Zealand

New Zealand Soc. of Genealogists - Onehunga Br. **[IO]**, Auckland, New Zealand

New Zealand Soc. of Genealogists - Papakura Br. **[IO]**, Papakura, New Zealand

New Zealand Soc. of Genealogists - Rotorua Br. **[IO]**, Rotorua, New Zealand

New Zealand Soc. of Genealogists - St. Johns Br. **[IO]**, Auckland, New Zealand

New Zealand Soc. of Genealogists - Taupo Br. **[IO]**, Taupo, New Zealand

New Zealand Soc. of Genealogists - Tauranga Br. **[IO]**, Tauranga, New Zealand

New Zealand Soc. of Genealogists - Waitakere Br. **[IO]**, Auckland, New Zealand

New Zealand Soc. of Genealogists - Wanganui Br. **[IO]**, Wanganui, New Zealand

New Zealand Soc. of Genealogists - Wellsford Br. **[IO]**, Wellsford, New Zealand

New Zealand Soc. of Genealogists - Whakatane Br. **[IO]**, Whakatane, New Zealand

New Zealand Soc. of Genealogists - Whangarei Br. **[IO]**, Whangarei, New Zealand

New Zealand Soc. for Music Therapy **[IO]**, Wellington, New Zealand

New Zealand Soc. of Physiotherapists **[IO]**, Wellington, New Zealand

New Zealand Soc. of Plant Biologists **[IO]**, TePuke, New Zealand

New Zealand Soc. of Plant Physiologists **[★IO]**

New Zealand Soc. of Soil Sci. **[IO]**, Christchurch, New Zealand

New Zealand Soc. for Sustainability Engg. and Sci. **[IO]**, Auckland, New Zealand

New Zealand Soc. of Translators and Interpreters **[IO]**, Auckland, New Zealand

New Zealand Specialist Cheesemakers Assn. **[IO]**, Auckland, New Zealand

New Zealand Stainless Steel Development Assn. **[IO]**, Manukau City, New Zealand

New Zealand Standards Inst. **[★IO]**

New Zealand Statistical Assn. **[IO]**, Mosgiel, New Zealand

New Zealand Stock Exchange **[★IO]**

New Zealand Taekwondo Coun. **[IO]**, Auckland, New Zealand

New Zealand Taxi Fed. **[IO]**, Wellington, New Zealand

New Zealand Theatre Fed. **[IO]**, Christchurch, New Zealand

New Zealand Thoroughbred Racing **[IO]**, Wellington, New Zealand

New Zealand Timber Indus. Fed. **[IO]**, Wellington, New Zealand

New Zealand Touch Assn. **[IO]**, Christchurch, New Zealand

New Zealand Tourism Bd. **[24363]**, 501 Santa Monica Blvd., Ste. 300, Santa Monica, CA 90401, (310)395-7480

New Zealand Tourism Indus. Assn. **[★IO]**

New Zealand Tourist and Publicity Off. **[★24363]**

New Zealand Trade and Enterprise **[IO]**, Auckland, New Zealand

New Zealand Vegetable and Potato Growers' Fed. **[IO]**, Wellington, New Zealand

New Zealand Vegetarian Soc. **[IO]**, Auckland, New Zealand

New Zealand Veterinary Assn. **[IO]**, Wellington, New Zealand

New Zealand Water Safety Coun. **[★IO]**

New Zealand Water Ski Racing Assn. **[IO]**, Auckland, New Zealand

New Zealand Water and Wastes Assn. **[IO]**, Wellington, New Zealand

New Zealand Wind Energy Assn. **[IO]**, Wellington, New Zealand

New Zealand Writers Guild **[IO]**, Auckland, New Zealand

New Zealand's Biotech Indus. Org. **[IO]**, Wellington, New Zealand

Newborn Rights Soc. **[IO]**, St. Peters, PA, United States

Newborn Rights Soc. **[12413]**, PO Box 48, St. Peters, PA 19470-0048, (610)323-6061

Newcastle Cycleways Movement **[IO]**, New Lambton, Australia

Newcastle Master Builders Assn. **[IO]**, Hunter, Australia

Newcombe Found; Charlotte W. **[12749]**

Newcomen; Amer. **[★10138]**

Newcomen Soc. in North Am. **[★10138]**

Newcomen Soc. for the Stud. of the History of Engg. and Tech. **[IO]**, London, United Kingdom

Newcomen Soc. of the U.S. **[10138]**, 211 Welsh Pool Rd., Ste. 240, Exton, PA 19341-1321, (610)363-6600

Newfoundland Brain Injury Assn. **[IO]**, St. John's, NL, Canada

Newfoundland Club of Am. **[22322]**, PO Box 2614, Cheyenne, WY 82003-2614, (716)683-1578

Newfoundland and Labrador Assn. of Social Workers **[IO]**, St. John's, NL, Canada

Newfoundland and Labrador Palliative Care Assn. **[IO]**, St. John's, NL, Canada

Newport Inst. for Ethics, Law and Public Policy **[18470]**, PO Box 9044, Newport Beach, CA 92658, (800)811-4770

Newport Restoration Found. **[10052]**, 51 Touro St., Newport, RI 02840, (401)849-7300

News Agency; People's **[3155]**

News Assn; Online **[3151]**

News Broadcasters Assn; Economics **[★3164]**

News Brunswick Advisory Coun. on the Status of Women **[IO]**, Fredericton, NB, Canada

News Bur; Natl. **[3139]**

News Design; Soc. for **[3163]**

News Directors Assn; Radio-Television **[581]**

News Directors; Natl. Assn. of Radio **[★581]**

News Distributors; Amer. Assn. of Independent **[3078]**

News and Info. Bur; Guatemala **[17680]**

News Intl. - Address unknown since 1991.

News and Letters Comm. **[18656]**, 36 S Wabash, Rm. 1440, Chicago, IL 60603, (312)236-0799

News Media Seminar at the United Nations - Defunct.

News Mission; Good **[★11869]**

News Network; Inter **[18027]**

News Ombudsmen; Org. of **[3152]**

News Photographers Assn; White House **[3018]**

News Publications Assn; Red Tag **[2456]**

News Publications; Red Tag **[★2456]**

News Reporting; Fund for Objective **[17179]**

News Ser; Africa **[16921]**

News Ser; Catholic **[3103]**

News Ser; Intl. **[★3169]**

News Ser; Religion **[3158]**

News Women's Club; Amer. **[3083]**

Newsboys; Good Fellows Old **[13042]**

Newsl. Assn. **[★3258]**

Newsl. Assn. **[★IO]**

Newsl. Assn. of Am. **[★IO]**

Newsl. Assn. of Am. **[★3258]**

Newsl. and Electronic Publishers Assn. **[★3258]**

Newsl. and Electronic Publishers Assn. **[IO]**, Arlington, VA, United States

Newsl. Publishers Assn. **[★IO]**

Newsl. Publishers Assn. **[★3258]**

Newsline II Fan Club - Address unknown since 2003.

Newspaper Advt. Bur. **[★3244]**

Newspaper Advt. Co-Op Network **[★3244]**

Newspaper Advt. Executives Assn. **[★IO]**

Newspaper Advt. and Marketing Executives; Intl. **[★3244]**

Newspaper Advertising Sales Assn. - Address unknown since 2004.

Newspaper Assn. of Am. **[3244]**, 4401 Wilson Blvd., Ste. 900, Arlington, VA 22203-1867, (571)366-1000

Newspaper Assn. Found; Natl. **[8715]**

Newspaper Assn. Managers **[3149]**, 70 Washington St., Ste. 214, Salem, MA 01970, (978)744-8940

Newspaper Assn. of Mongolia **[IO]**, Ulan Bator, Mongolia

Newspaper Assn; Natl. **[3140]**

Newspaper Assn; Natl. Advt. **[★3259]**

Newspaper Assn; Suburban Sect. of the Natl. **[★3259]**

Newspaper Assn. of the United Kingdom; Talking **[IO]**

Newspaper Classified Advt. Managers; Assn. of **[★3244]**

Newspaper Collectors Soc. of Am. **[22092]**, c/o Rick Brown, 6031 Winterset Dr., Lansing, MI 48911-4860, (517)887-1255

Newspaper Conf. **[IO]**, London, United Kingdom

Newspaper Design; Soc. of **[★3163]**

Newspaper Editors; Amer. Soc. of **[3086]**

Newspaper Features Coun. - Address unknown since 2006.

Newspaper Food Editors and Writers Assn. **[★3094]**

Newspaper Food Editors and Writers Assn. **[★IO]**

Newspaper Found; Natl. **[★8715]**

Newspaper Fund **[★8711]**

Newspaper Fund; Dow Jones **[8711]**

Newspaper Gp; Intl. **[3121]**

The Newspaper Guild **[24140]**, 501 3rd St. NW, Ste. 250, Washington, DC 20001-2760, (202)434-7177

Newspaper Guild; Amer. **[★24140]**

The Newspaper Guild - Canada/CWA **[★IO]**

Newspaper and Magazine Wholesalers; Assn. of **[IO]**

Newspaper Ombudsmen; Org. of **[★3152]**

Newspaper Personnel Relations Assn. **[★2903]**

Newspaper Personnel Relations Assn. **[★IO]**

Newspaper Promotion Assn. **[★IO]**

Newspaper Promotion Assn. **[★3230]**

Newspaper Promotion Assn; Intl. **[★3230]**

Newspaper Publishers Assn; Amer. **[★3244]**

Newspaper Publishers' Assn; European **[IO]**

Newspaper Publishers Assn; Natl. **[3241]**

Newspaper Publishers Assn; Natl. Negro **[★3241]**

Newspaper Publishers' Assn. of New Zealand **[IO]**, Wellington, New Zealand

Newspaper Publishers Assn; Scottish **[IO]**

Newspaper Purchasing Mgt. Assn. - Address unknown since 2000.

Newspaper Res. Coun. **[★3244]**

Newspaper Soc. **[IO]**, London, United Kingdom

Newspaper Soc. of England **[★IO]**

Newspaper Soc; Scottish Daily **[IO]**

Newspaper Soc. of Sri Lanka **[IO]**, Colombo, Sri Lanka

Newspaper Systems Group - Address unknown since 2005.

Newspaper Women's Club; Amer. **[★3083]**

Newspaper Women's Club; New York **[★3150]**

Newspaper Women's Club of New York **[★3150]**

Newspapers

   Africa News Ser. **[16921]**

   Alternative Press Center **[10892]**

   Amer. Assn. of Independent News Distributors **[3078]**

   Amer. Court and Commercial Newspapers **[3202]**

   Amer. Horse Publications **[3203]**

   Amer. News Women's Club **[3083]**

   Amer. Soc. of Bus. Publication Editors **[3084]**

   Amer. Soc. of Newspaper Editors **[3086]**

   Asian Amer. Journalists Assn. **[3088]**

   Assoc. Church Press **[3205]**

   Assoc. Press **[3089]**

   Assoc. Press Managing Editors **[3090]**

   Assn. of Young Journalists **[3098]**

   Audit Bur. of Circulations - United Kingdom **[IO]**

   Boating Writers Intl. **[3100]**

   Brazilian Assn. of Media Companies Representatives **[IO]**

   Catholic Press Assn. **[3215]**

   Dog Writers' Assn. of Am. **[3110]**

Reference to "IO" in place of a book number signifies that the association may be found in the 45th edition of International Organizations.

Ecuadorian Assn. of Newspaper Publishers [IO]
Finnish Newspapers Assn. [IO]
Football Writers Assn. of Am. [23430]
Golf Writers Assn. of Am. [23450]
Good Fellows (Old Newsboys) [13042]
Hollywood Foreign Press Assn. [3115]
Independent Free Papers of Am. [3226]
Intl. Newspaper Gp. [3121]
Intl. Newspaper Marketing Assn. [3230]
Intl. Press Inst., Amer. Comm. [3123]
Intl. Soc. of Weekly Newspaper Editors [3125]
Investigative Reporters and Editors [3126]
Italian Newspaper Publishers' Assn. [IO]
Media Action Network for Asian Americans
   [18029]
Media Human Resources Assn. [2903]
Midwest Free Community Papers [3236]
Natl. Acad. of Sports [23831]
Natl. Assn. of Hispanic Journalists [3130]
Natl. Conf. of Editorial Writers [3136]
Natl. Fed. of Hispanic Owned Newspapers [3240]
Natl. News Bur. [3139]
Natl. Newspaper Assn. [3140]
Natl. Newspaper Publishers Assn. [3241]
Natl. Newspapers of Ireland [IO]
Natl. Press Club [3141]
Natl. Scholastic Press Assn. [9013]
Newspaper Assn. of Am. [3244]
Newspaper Assn. Managers [3149]
Newspaper Collectors Soc. of Am. [22092]
Newspaper Conf. [IO]
The Newspaper Guild [24140]
Newswomen's Club of New York [3150]
North Amer. St. Newspaper Assn. [18102]
Norwegian Media Businesses' Assn. [IO]
Org. of News Ombudsmen [3152]
Outdoor Writers Assn. of Am. [3153]
Overseas Press Club of Am. [3154]
Print Media South Africa [IO]
Red Tag News Publications Assn. [2456]
Religion News Ser. [3158]
Religion Newswriters Assn. [3159]
Soc. for News Design [3163]
Southern Newspaper Publishers Assn. [3257]
Suburban Newspapers of Am. [3259]
Swedish Newspapers' Assn. [IO]
Trade Press Assn. [IO]
United Press Intl. [3169]
White House Correspondents' Assn. [3173]
Wire Ser. Guild [24141]
Newspapers of Am; Accredited Home [★3259]
Newspapers of Am; Suburban [3259]
Newspapers; Amer. Assn. of English Jewish [★3081]
Newspapers; Amer. Court and Commercial [3202]
Newspapers; Assoc. Court and Commercial [★3202]
Newspapers Assn; New Zealand Community [IO]
Newspapers; Natl. Fed. of Hispanic Owned [3240]
Newsprint Information Comm. - Defunct.
Newsweeklies; Assn. of Alternative [3091]
Newswomen's Club of New York [3150], 15
   Gramercy Park S, New York, NY 10003, (212)777-
   1610
Newswriters Assn; Religion [3159]
NewTithing Gp. [18742], c/o Jamie Anderson, Web-
   ster Systems, LLC, 1 Maritime Plz., Ste. 1400, San
   Francisco, CA 94111, (415)733-9722
Next Stop - New Life [IO], Minsk, Belarus
Next Urban Form - Address unknown since 1995.
NextGen Energy Coun. [6966], 350 Indiana St., Ste.
   640, Golden, CO 80401, (303)577-4611
NEXUS - Intl. Broadcasting Assn. [IO], Milan, Italy
Neylan Commission [★8051]
NF Assn. [★1648]
NFHS Coaches Assn. [23294], c/o Natl. Fed. of
   State High Schools, PO Box 690, Indianapolis, IN
   46206, (317)972-6900
NFHS Music Assn. [8928], PO Box 690,
   Indianapolis, IN 46206, (317)972-6900
NFHS Officials Assn. [23874], PO Box 690,
   Indianapolis, IN 46206, (317)972-6900
NFHS Speech, Debate and Theatre Assn. [9161],
   PO Box 690, Indianapolis, IN 46206, (317)972-
   6900
NFHS Spirit Assn. [23295], c/o Natl. Fed. of State
   High School Associations, PO Box 690,
   Indianapolis, IN 46206, (317)972-6900

NGA [13056], 822 Veterans Way, Warminster, PA
   18974, (215)682-9183
Nga Kaikorero Purakau O Aotearoa [★IO]
Nga Whare Takiura o Aotearoa [★IO]
Nga Whiitiki Whanau Ahuru Mowai o Aotearoa [★IO]
NgaKohine Whakamahiri o Aotecroa [★IO]
NGLTF Policy Inst. [★12249]
NGO Comm. on Disarmament [★17432]
NGO Comm. on Disarmament [★IO]
NGO Comm. on Disarmament, Peace and Security
   [IO], New York, NY, United States
NGO Comm. on Disarmament, Peace and Security
   [17432], 777 UN Plz., Ste. 3-B, New York, NY
   10017, (212)687-5340
NGO Comm. on Human Rights - Address unknown
   since 2001.
NGO Coordination for Development [IO], Madrid,
   Spain
NGO Volunteer Gp. Khoop Khun Maak [★IO]
NHS Consultants Assn. [IO], Oxon, United Kingdom
Niagara Inst. [IO], Niagara-on-the-Lake, ON, Canada
Niagara Network for Freedom from Weight Preoc-
   cupation and Eating Disorders [IO], St. Catharines,
   ON, Canada
Niatrek Intl. - Defunct.
NIBA - The Belting Assn. [★2051]
Nic-Anon - Defunct.

Nicaragua
   Alliance for Intl. Reforestation [4344]
   Bikes Not Bombs [18103]
   Bikes Not Bombs [IO]
   Bridges to Community [13389]
   Center for Religious Freedom, Freedom House
      [17749]
   Intermed Intl. [14982]
   Latinas and Latinos for Social Change [18104]
   Latinas and Latinos for Social Change [IO]
   MADRE [12529]
   Nicaragua Network Educ. Fund [18105]
   Nicaragua Network Educ. Fund [IO]
   Quest for Peace [IO]
   Quest for Peace [18106]
   Witness for Peace [18107]
   Witness for Peace [IO]
Nicaragua Chap. of the ILAE [IO], Managua,
   Nicaragua
Nicaragua-Honduras Educ. Proj. [★IO]
Nicaragua-Honduras Educ. Proj. [★8662]
Nicaragua Interfaith Comm. for Action - Address
   unknown since 2003.
Nicaragua Medical Aid - Address unknown since
   2004.
Nicaragua Mobile Education Project - Defunct.
Nicaragua Network [★18105]
Nicaragua Network [★IO]
Nicaragua Network Educ. Fund [IO], Washington,
   DC, United States
Nicaragua Network Educ. Fund [18105], 1247 E St.
   SE, Washington, DC 20003, (202)544-9355
Nicaragua Solidarity Campaign [IO], London, United
   Kingdom
Nicaraguan
   Bridges to Community [13389]
Nicaraguan Assn. for Human Rights - Address
   unknown since 1995.
Nicaraguan Information Center - Defunct.
Nicaraguan People; Natl. Network in Solidarity With
   the [★18105]
Nicaraguan Relief Comm. - Defunct.
Nicaraguan Resistance - Address unknown since
   1989.
Nichidoku-Shakaikagaku-Gakkai [★IO]
Nichiren Buddhist Assn. of Am. [19555], PO Box
   340953, Sacramento, CA 95834-0953
Nichiren Shoshu Soka Gakkai of Am. [★19556]
Nichiren Shoshu Soka Gakkai of Am. [★IO]
Nicholas Soc. of the City of New York; Saint [21148]
Nicholas Thomas Pittenger Family Org. - Address
   unknown since 2003.
Nick Mancuso Fan Network [24762], c/o Arrista
   Pottle, Pres., 116 Sharon Ave., Sebring, FL 33872
Nick Mancuso Fan Network [IO], Sebring, FL, United
   States
Nickel Development Inst. [★IO]
Nickel Development Inst. - UK [★IO]

Nickel Inst. - North Am. [IO], Toronto, ON, Canada
Nickel Inst. - UK [IO], Birmingham, United Kingdom
Nicotine Anonymous World Services [IO], Huntington
   Beach, CA, United States
Nicotine Anonymous World Services [13027], 419
   Main St., PMB No. 370, Huntington Beach, CA
   92648, (415)750-0328
Nicotine and Tobacco; Soc. for Res. on [5249]
NICRO Women's Support Centre [IO], Cape Town,
   Republic of South Africa
NICUFO [★IO]
NICUFO [★7482]
NIDCD - Natl. Temporal Bone, Hearing and Balance
   Pathology Rsrc. Registry [15121], Massachusetts
   Eye and Ear Infirmary, 243 Charles St., Boston,
   MA 02114-3002, (617)573-3711
Nielsen/Wilson/Willson Family Org; Brough/
   [★20810]
Nieman Found. [8716], Harvard Univ., Lippmann
   House, 1 Francis Ave., Cambridge, MA 02138,
   (617)495-2237
Nieman Found. for Journalism [★8716]
Niemann Pick Disease Found; Natl. [15254]
Nietzsche Soc. [10814], c/o Babette E. Babich,
   Exec. Sec., Fordham Univ., Dept. of Philosophy,
   113 W 60th St., New York, NY 10023, (212)636-
   6297
Nietzsche Soc; North Amer. [10818]
Nieuw-Vlaamse Alliantie [★IO]
Niger Delta Women for Justice [IO], Port Harcourt,
   Nigeria
Niger Junior Chamber [IO], Niamey, Niger
Nigeria Assn. of Univ. Women [IO], Nsukka, Nigeria
Nigeria Employers' Consultative Assn. [IO], Lagos,
   Nigeria
Nigeria Org. of Volunteers for the Preservation of the
   Env. [IO], Niamey, Niger
Nigeria Scripture Union [IO], Niamey, Nigeria
Nigeria Taekwondo Fed. [IO], Lagos, Nigeria
Nigeria Tennis Fed. [IO], Lagos, Nigeria
Nigeria War Victims Relief Found. - Defunct.
Nigerian
   Egbe Omo Yoruba: Natl. Assn. of Yoruba
      Descendants in North America [19289]
   Egbe Omo Yoruba: National Association of Yoruba
      Descendants in North America [IO]
   Friends of Nigeria [IO]
   Friends of Nigeria [19290]
   Ijaw Natl. Alliance of the Americas [12639]
   Nigerian Lawyers Assn. [5526]
   Nigerian Social Workers Assn. [24142]
   Nigerian Women Leadership Coun. Intl. [12640]
   Ogwashi-Uku Assn., USA [19291]
   Ugbajo Itsekiri USA [19260]
Nigerian-Amer. Alliance - Address unknown since
   2000.
Nigerian Assn. of Chambers of Commerce, Indus.,
   Mines, and Agriculture [IO], Lagos, Nigeria
Nigerian Assn. of Occupational Therapists [IO], La-
   gos, Nigeria
Nigerian Assn. of Sports Medicine [IO], Lagos,
   Nigeria
Nigerian Baseball and Softball Assn. [IO], Lagos,
   Nigeria
Nigerian Dwarf Goat Assn. [4788], c/o Jim Mannos,
   Pres., 1414 Wilson Rd., Lancaster, TX 75146,
   (972)227-7311
Nigerian Economic Soc. [IO], Ibadan, Nigeria
Nigerian Fertility Soc. [IO], Lagos, Nigeria
Nigerian Gas Assn. [IO], Lagos, Nigeria
Nigerian Geotechnical Assn. [IO], Port Harcourt,
   Nigeria
Nigerian Hypertension Soc. [IO], Enugu, Nigeria
Nigerian Integrated Rural Accelerated Development
   Org. [IO], Lagos, Nigeria
Nigerian Lawyers Assn. [5526], 321 Broadway, 3rd
   Fl., New York, NY 10007, (212)566-9926
Nigerian Medical Assn. [IO], Lagos, Nigeria
Nigerian Red Cross Soc. [IO], Lagos, Nigeria
Nigerian School Sports Fed. [IO], Osogbo, Nigeria
Nigerian Social Workers Assn. [24142], PO Box
   3295, New York, NY 10008-3295, (646)460-2324
Nigerian Soc. of Engineers [IO], Lagos, Nigeria
Nigerian Soc. for Photogrammetry and Remote
   Sensing [IO], Lagos, Nigeria

A star before a book entry number signifies that the name is not listed separately, but is mentioned within the entry.

Nigerian Squash Rackets Assn. [IO], Lagos, Nigeria

Nigerian Students Union in the Americas - Address unknown since 2003.

Nigerian Weightlifting Fed. [IO], Lagos, Nigeria

Nigerian Women Leadership Coun. Intl. [12640], 6523 Hwy. 85, Ste. 101, Riverdale, GA 30274, (678)777-3322

Night Adoration in the Home [19695], c/o Natl. Enthronement Center, PO Box 111, Fairhaven, MA 02719-0111, (508)999-2680

Night Adoration in the Home; League of [★19695]

Nightingale Res. Found. [IO], Ottawa, ON, Canada

NIH Black Scientists Assn. [6395], PO Box 2262, Kensington, MD 20891-2262, (301)435-4568

Nihilism Assn; Amer. [8966]

Nihon Afurika Gakkai [★IO]

Nihon Arerugi Gakkai [★IO]

Nihon Bengoshi Rengokai [★IO]

Nihon Boseki Kyokai [★IO]

Nihon Boueki Shinkou Kai, Ajia Keizai Kenkyusho [★IO]

Nihon Bunseki Kagaku-Kai [★IO]

Nihon Do Senta [★IO]

Nihon Doro Kensetsugyo Kyokai [★IO]

Nihon Electronics Show Kyokai [★IO]

Nihon Gakujutsu Shinko-kai [★IO]

Nihon Gazo Jyohou Manejimento Kyokai [★IO]

Nihon Genshiryoku Gakkai [★IO]

Nihon Gomu Kyokai [★IO]

Nihon Hinyokika Gakkai [★IO]

Nihon Ishi-Kai [★IO]

Nihon Jidosha Yunyu Kumiai [★IO]

Nihon Jui Gakkai [★IO]

Nihon Kagakushi Gakkai [★IO]

Nihon Kairui Gakkai [★IO]

Nihon Kensetsu Kikai-ka Kyokai [★IO]

Nihon Kikai Gakkai [★IO]

Nihon Kikaku Kyokai Gaikoku Kikaku Raiburari [★IO]

Nihon Koku Eisei Gakkai [★IO]

Nihon Kokusai Koryu Center [★IO]

Nihon Kokusai Mondai Kenkyusho [★IO]

Nihon Kokusai Volunteer Center [★IO]

Nihon Kyoiku Gakkai [★IO]

Nihon Maku Gakkai [★IO]

Nihon Masuka Gakkai [★IO]

Nihon Naika Gakkai [★IO]

Nihon Nettai Igakkai [★IO]

Nihon Noritsu Kyokai [★IO]

Nihon Oyo Toshitsu Kagaku Kai [★IO]

Nihon Recreation Kyokai [★IO]

Nihon Reito Kucho Gakkai [★IO]

Nihon Ronen Igakukai [★IO]

Nihon Ryukoshoku Kyokai [★IO]

Nihon Sakumotsu Gakkai [★IO]

Nihon Sangyo Kikai Kogyo-kai [★IO]

Nihon Seikatsu Kyodo Kumiai Rengokai [★IO]

Nihon Seishin Shinkei Gakkai [★IO]

Nihon Seitai Gakkai [★IO]

Nihon Shakai Shinri Gakkai [★IO]

Nihon Shichokaku Kyoiku Kyokai [★IO]

Nihon Shinbun Kyokai [★IO]

Nihon Shinju Yushutsu Kumiai [★IO]

Nihon Shinri Gakkai [★IO]

Nihon Shokaki Naishikyo Gakkai [★IO]

Nihon Shonika Gakkai [★IO]

Nihon Shutei Kogyo-kai [★IO]

Nihon Syoyakuga Gakkai [★IO]

Nihon Takkyu Kyokai [★IO]

Nihon Tanners Kyokai [★IO]

Nihon Tenmon Gakkai [★IO]

Nihon Tokei Gakkai [★IO]

Nihon Toshokan Kyokai [★IO]

Nihon Tsushin Hanbai Kyokai [★IO]

Nihon UNESCO Kyokai Renmei [★IO]

Nihon YMCA Domei [★IO]

Nikon Historical Soc. [10854], RJR Publishing Inc., PO Box 3213, Munster, IN 46321

Nile Children and Family Support Org. [IO], Addis Ababa, Ethiopia

Nile, Supreme Temple; Daughters of the [19232]

NIMA Intl. [★2626]

NIMA Intl. [★IO]

Nimitz (CVN-68) Assn; USS [21230]

Nimoy and DeForest Kelley; Fans of Leonard [24739]

Nims Family Assn. [21012], PO Box 99, Deerfield, MA 01342-0099

Nine Lives Associates [3540], Executive Protection Inst., PO Box 802, Berryville, VA 22611-0802, (540)554-2540

Nine Lives Associates [IO], Berryville, VA, United States

Nine-Pin Assn. [★IO]

Nineteen Thirty-Two Buick Registry [21741], 3000 Warren Rd., Indiana, PA 15701, (412)463-3372

Nineteenth-Century Art; Assn. of Historians of [9431]

Ninety-Nines, Intl. Org. of Women Pilots [163], 4300 Amelia Earhart Rd., Oklahoma City, OK 73159, (405)685-7969

Ninety-Nines, Intl. Org. of Women Pilots [IO], Oklahoma City, OK, United States

Ninety-Nines Intl. Women Pilots [★IO]

Ninety-Nines Intl. Women Pilots [★163]

NIPPA - Early Years Org. [IO], Belfast, United Kingdom

Nipple Mfrs; Natl. Assn. of Pipe [★3025]

Nippon Badminton Assn. [IO], Tokyo, Japan

Nippon Bitamin Gakkai [★IO]

Nippon Butsuri Gakkai [★IO]

Nippon Byori Gakkai [★IO]

Nippon Chiri Gakkai [★IO]

Nippon Chishitsu Gakkai [★IO]

Nippon Cho Gakkai [★IO]

Nippon Club [19172], 145 W 57th St., New York, NY 10019, (212)581-2223

Nippon Dai-Yonki Gakkai [★IO]

Nippon Dam Kyokai [★IO]

Nippon Dobutsu Gakkai [★IO]

Nippon Dojo-Hiryo Gakkai [★IO]

Nippon Engeki Gakkai [★IO]

Nippon Ganka Gakkai [★IO]

Nippon Ganseki Kobutsu Kosho Gakkai [★IO]

Nippon Geka Gakkai [★IO]

Nippon Hifuka Gakkai [★IO]

Nippon Hoshasen Eikyo Gakkai [★IO]

Nippon Hotetsu Gakkai [★IO]

Nippon Iden Gakkai [★IO]

Nippon Igaku Hoshasen Gakkai [★IO]

Nippon Indus. Mgt. Assn. [★IO]

Nippon Interior Fabrics Assn. [IO], Tokyo, Japan

Nippon Junkatsu Gakkai [★IO]

Nippon Kaiji Kyokai [IO], Tokyo, Japan

Nippon Kaiyo Gakkai [★IO]

Nippon Kazan Gakkai [★IO]

Nippon Keidanren [★IO]

Nippon Keiei Gakkai [★IO]

Nippon Keiho Gakkai [★IO]

Nippon Keizai Seisaku Gakkai [★IO]

Nippon Ketsueki Gakkai [★IO]

Nippon Kin Gakkai [★IO]

Nippon Kinzoku Gakkai [★IO]

Nippon Kisho Gakkai [★IO]

Nippon Kodo Bunseki Gakkai [★IO]

Nippon Kokai Gakkai [★IO]

Nippon Koseibutsu Gakkai [★IO]

Nippon Koshu-Eisei Kyokai [★IO]

Nippon Mokuzai Gakkai [★IO]

Nippon No-Shinkei Gek Gakkai [★IO]

Nippon Nogei Kagaku Kai [★IO]

Nippon Nogyo-Kisho Gakkai [★IO]

Nippon Ongaku Gakkai [★IO]

Nippon Rikusui Gakkai [★IO]

Nippon Ringyo Gijutsu Kyokai [★IO]

Nippon Sci. Mgt. Fed. [★IO]

Nippon Sei Ko Kai [★IO]

Nippon Seikei Geka Gakkai [★IO]

Nippon Seiri Gakkai [★IO]

Nippon Seramikkusu Kyokai [★IO]

Nippon Shakai Gakkai [★IO]

Nippon Shashin Gakkai [★IO]

Nippon Shashin Sokuryo Gakkai [★IO]

Nippon Shinkeikagaku Gakkai [★IO]

Nippon Shokubutsu Gakkai [★IO]

Nippon Sokuchi Gakkai [★IO]

Nippon Suisan Gakkai [★IO]

Nippon Toshi Keikaku Gakkai [★IO]

Nippon Yakugakkai [★IO]

NIRA; SEMAA - The Safety Affiliate of [3456]

Nirnaya [IO], Secunderabad, India

Nisaa Inst. for Women's Development [IO], Johannesburg, Republic of South Africa

NISH [11976], 8401 Old Courthouse Rd., Ste. 200, Vienna, VA 22182, (571)226-4660

Nissan Infiniti Car Owners Club [21742], 237 Fernwood Blvd., Ste. 111, Fern Park, FL 32730-2116, (407)828-8908

Nitro (AE-2/AE-23) Assn; USS [5468]

Nitrobenzene Assn. - Defunct.

Nitrogen Fixing Tree Assn. - Defunct.

Nitrogen Inst; Agricultural [★1365]

Nitrogen Solutions Assn; Natl. [★1363]

Nitty Gritty Dirt Band Fan Club - Address unknown since 1989.

Niue Touch Assn. [IO], Alofi, Niue

NiUG Intl. [7208], 208 Eagle Valley Mall, No. 124, East Stroudsburg, PA 18301, (908)459-7889

Niwano Heiwa Zaidan [★IO]

Niwano Peace Found. [IO], Tokyo, Japan

Nixon Center [17616], 1615 L St. NW, Ste. 1250, Washington, DC 20036, (202)887-1000

Nixon Center for Peace and Freedom [★17616]

Nixon Family Assn. [21013], 5817 144th St. E, Puyallup, WA 98375-5221, (253)537-8288

NKS - Nordic Nuclear Safety Res. [IO], Roskilde, Denmark

NLDA Associates [★2418]

NLRB Professional Assn. [24081], 1099 14th St. NW, Ste. 6604, Washington, DC 20570, (202)273-1928

NLRB Watch [★17980]

NMC [16802], 421 S Nine Mound Rd., Verona, WI 53593, (608)848-4615

NMTBA (Natl. Machine Tool Builders' Assn.) [★7262]

No Business As Usual - Address unknown since 1995.

No-Code Intl. [21506], c/o Carl R. Stevenson, Exec. Dir., 4991 Shimerville Rd., Emmaus, PA 18049

No Compromise Majority - Defunct.

No Greater Love [13370], 1750 New York Ave. NW, Ste. 1971, Washington, DC 20006, (202)637-0776

No Kidding! [IO], Vancouver, BC, Canada

No-Load Mutual Fund Assn. [★3516]

No More War Movement [★IO]

No-Nukes Prison Support Collective; Natl. [18160]

No Peace Without Justice [18227], c/o United Nations, 866 UN Plz., No. 408, New York, NY 10017, (212)980-2558

No Peace Without Justice [IO], New York, NY, United States

NOAH Friends of the Earth - Denmark [IO], Copenhagen, Denmark

Noah Webster Found. [★10053]

Noah Webster House [10053], 227 S Main St., West Hartford, CT 06107, (860)521-5362

Noah Worcester Dermatological Soc. - Address unknown since 1995.

Nobel Found. [IO], Stockholm, Sweden

Nobel Laureates
    Standing Comm. for Nobel Prize Winners' Congresses [IO]

Nobelstiftelsen [★IO]

Nobility Assn. in Am; Russian [21147]

Nobility Assn. Found; Polish [19313]

Nobility in North Am; Assn. of the German [21105]

Noble Found; Samuel Roberts [4082]

Noble Order, Descendants of the Conqueror and His Companions - Address unknown since 1995.

Nobles; Intl. Guild of [19056]

Nock, Albert Jay
    Nockian Soc. [9697]

Nockian Soc. [9697], 42 Leathers Rd., Fort Mitchell, KY 41017

Nocturnal Adoration Soc. [19696], c/o Saint Jean Baptiste Catholic Church, 184 E 76th St., New York, NY 10021, (212)288-5082

Noer Res. Found; O.J. [4796]

Noetic Sciences; IONS - Inst. of [10976]

Noetic Soc. [★9986]

NOF [IO], Washington, United Kingdom

NOFMA: The Wood Flooring Manufacturers Assn. [656], 22 N Front St., Ste. 660, Memphis, TN 38103, (901)526-5016

Noise
    Citizens Aviation Watch Assn. [11509]
    Educators for Social Responsibility [17883]

Reference to "IO" in place of a book number signifies that the association may be found in the 45th edition of International Organizations.

Intl. Commn. on Biological Effects of Noise [IO]
Noise Control
Assn. of Noise Consultants [IO]
Aviation Env. Fed. [IO]
Citizens Aviation Watch Assn. [11509]
Inst. of Noise Control Engg. [7382]
Natl. Assn. of Noise Control Officials [7383]
Noise Control Assn; Community Indus. [★7383]
Noise Control Assn. - Defunct.
Noles Family Assn; Knowles/Knoles/ [21129]
NOLOSE - The Natl. Org. for Lesbians of Size [12250], PO Box 7522, Ann Arbor, MI 48107, (510)541-5948
Nomad Assn; Chevrolet [21607]
Nomads Outdoor Gp. [IO], Melbourne, Australia
Nomads of the Time Streams - Intl. Michael Moorcock Appreciation Soc. - Defunct.
Nomenclature; Amer. Assn. for Zoological [7859]
Nominating Convention; Republican Natl. [★18534]
Non-Administrative Receivers Assn. [IO], Worcester, United Kingdom
Non-Circumcision Educational Found. [11735], PO Box 251, Oxford, PA 19363, (717)529-2561
Non-Circumcision Info. Center [11736], 82 Lexington St., Weston, MA 02493-2146, (617)489-4530
Non Commissioned Officers Assn. [21316], 10635 IH 35 N, San Antonio, TX 78233, (703)549-0311
Non Commissioned Officers Assn. of the U.S.A. [6102], 10635 IH 35 N, San Antonio, TX 78233, (210)653-6161
Non-Denominational Bible Prophecy Stud. Assn. [19528], c/o Dr. Patricia H. Burns, Founder, 339 E Laguna Dr., Tempe, AZ 85282, (480)967-3066
Non-Denominational Bible Prophecy Study Association [IO], Tempe, AZ, United States
Non-Executive Directors Assn. [IO], Woking, United Kingdom
Non-Ferrous Founders' Soc. [2053], 1480 Renaissance Dr., Ste. 310, Park Ridge, IL 60068, (847)299-0950
Non-Ferrous Metals Producers Comm. [2723], 2030 M St. NW, Ste. 800, Washington, DC 20036, (202)466-7720
Non-Governmental Org. Comm. on Disarmament [★17432]
Non-Governmental Org. Comm. on Disarmament [★IO]
Non-Governmental Organizations Committee on UNICEF [IO], New York, NY, United States
Non-Governmental Organizations Comm. on UNICEF [18766], 3 UN Plz., New York, NY 10017, (212)824-6394
Non Guvernamental Org. BIOS [IO], Chisinau, Moldova
Non-Heatset Web Sect. [★1795]
Non-Heatset Web Sect. [★1795]
Non-Intervention in Chile - Defunct.
Non-Partisan Political League; Machinists [24101]
Non-Powder Gun Products Assn. - Defunct.
Non Profit Assn. for Sporting Goods [★3648]
Non-profit Mgt. Assn. and Support Centers of Am. [★313]
Non-Resident Nepali Assn. [IO], Kathmandu, Nepal
Non-Sectarian Anti-Nazi League - Address unknown since 1995.
Non-Traditional Casting Proj. [★10996]
Non-Violence; Community for Creative [12288]
Non-Violent Action Community of Cascadia and the CMTC Escrow Fund [18716], 4554 12th Ave. NE, Seattle, WA 98105, (206)547-0952
Non-Violent Alternatives - Defunct.
Non-Violent Food; Coalition for [11377]
Non-Woven Fabrics Inst. - Defunct.
Nondestructive Testing; Amer. Soc. for [7787]
Nondestructive Testing; Soc. for [★7787]
The Nonferrous Metals Soc. of China [★IO]
Nonferrous Metals Soc. of China [IO], Beijing, People's Republic of China
Nongovernmental Organizations Comm. on Youth [13508], c/o Conf. of NGOs, 777 United Nations Plz., 6th Fl., New York, NY 10017, (212)986-8557
Nonprescription Drug Mfrs. Assn. [★2973]
Nonprescription Drug Mfrs. Assn. of Canada [IO], Ottawa, ON, Canada
Nonprofit Associations; Natl. Coun. of [320]

Nonprofit Australia [IO], Royal Exchange, Australia
Nonprofit Boards; Natl. Center for [★12651]
Nonprofit Mailers; Alliance of [2445]
Nonprofit Mailers Fed. [★317]
Nonprofit Mgt; Alliance for [313]
Nonprofit Marketing Forum - Address unknown since 1994.
Nonprofit Organizations
Advocacy Inst. [12650]
Alliance for Advancing Nonprofit Hea. Care [14606]
Alliance of Nonprofit Mailers [2445]
Alliance for Nonprofit Mgt. [313]
Amer. Charities for Reasonable Fundraising Regulation [12195]
Amer. Inst. for Shippers' Associations [3558]
Amer. News Women's Club [3083]
Assn. Chief Executives Coun. [698]
Assn. of Professional Researchers for Advancement [12198]
Assn. of PVO Financial Managers [1458]
Assn. for Res. on Nonprofit Organizations and Voluntary Action [13387]
Assn. for Strategic Alliance Professionals [2521]
Believe In Tomorrow Natl. Children's Found. [11674]
BoardSource [12651]
CASE Matching Gifts CH [12199]
Center for Mgt. Effectiveness [2489]
Commonwealth Assn. of Non-Governmental Organisations [IO]
CompuMentor [7728]
Coun. of Institutional Investors [3512]
Coun. of Protocol Executives [2677]
DMA Nonprofit Fed. [317]
DOCHAS, The Irish Assn. of Non-Governmental Development Organisations [IO]
Economic Justice Inst. [6221]
European Assn. of Consultants to and about Not-for-Profit Organisations [IO]
First Nations Development Inst. [12625]
HandsNet [12641]
Harry S. Truman Lib. Inst. for Natl. and Intl. Affairs [11120]
Independent Charities of Am. [1688]
Independent Educational Services [1263]
Independent Sector [12725]
Intl. Engg. Consortium [6928]
Justice Res. Assn. [5655]
Mgt. Assistance Gp. [12655]
Marketing Sci. Inst. [2635]
Milton S. Eisenhower Found. [11839]
Natl. Bus Traffic Assn. [3878]
Natl. Center for Charitable Statistics [12731]
Natl. Center for Fair Competition [3621]
Natl. Center on Nonprofit Enterprise [12642]
Natl. Comm. for Responsive Philanthropy [12732]
Natl. Executive Ser. Corps [747]
Natl. Partnership for Community Leadership [11805]
Natl. Voice [17076]
Nonprofit Australia [IO]
Oak Ridge Assoc. Universities [7625]
OMB Watch [17672]
Professional Convention Mgt. Assn. [2689]
Public Relations Soc. of Am. [3195]
Social Enterprise Alliance [3633]
Soc. for Info. Mgt. [2516]
Soc. for Nonprofit Organizations [322]
Southeastern Fisheries Assn. [3504]
Synergos Inst. [12784]
Tech. Assistance Collaborative [13145]
Theatre Communications Gp. [11047]
Theatre Development Fund [11048]
Transnational Diplomatic Network [17874]
United Black Fund [12204]
Volunteer Trustees of Not-for-Profit Hospitals [14902]
Women in Govt. Relations [17676]
Women in Govt. Relations LEADER Found. [17677]
Nonprofit Organizations; Soc. for [322]
Nonprofit Organizations and Voluntary Action; Assn. for Res. on [13387]
Nonsmokers' Rights; Americans for [16432]

Nonsmokers' Rights; Californians for [★16432]
Nonsmokers' Travel Club - Defunct.
Nontraditional Schools and Colleges; Natl. Assn. of Private, [7947]
Nonverbal Learning Disorders Assn. [14998], 507 Hopmeadow St., Simsbury, CT 06070, (860)658-5522
Nonverbal Learning Disorders Assn. [IO], Simsbury, CT, United States
Nonviolence
A.J. Muste Memorial Inst. [18188]
Albert Einstein Institution [18108]
Amer. Friends Ser. Comm. [13148]
Amer. Patriots Assn. [21239]
Americans United for Israel [19157]
Anglican Pacifist Fellowship [IO]
Anuvrat Global Org. [IO]
Axis of Justice [18640]
Benedictines for Peace [19582]
Brethren Peace Fellowship [19534]
Canadian Inst. for Conflict Resolution [IO]
Canadian Intl. Inst. of Applied Negotiation [IO]
Catholic Worker Movement [18109]
CAVEAT BC (Canadians Against Violence) [IO]
Center for Nonviolent Commun. [18110]
Conflict Resolution Prog. [18111]
Daphne Inst. of Applied Ecology [IO]
Empower Prog. [8945]
European Bur. for Conscientious Objection [IO]
Fed. of Jain Associations in North America [20495]
Fourth Freedom Forum [18112]
Fourth Freedom Forum [IO]
Friends of Sabeel - North Am. [18205]
Global Action to Prevent War [18113]
Global Action to Prevent War [IO]
Global Majority [17249]
Grace Contrino Abrams Peace Educ. Found. [8139]
Greenaction for Hea. and Environmental Justice [17699]
Guitars Not Guns [18114]
Intl. Nonviolent Initiatives [18115]
Justice Stud. Assn. [13109]
Martin Luther King, Jr. Center for Nonviolent Social Change [18116]
Mediators Without Borders [5458]
Men Stopping Violence [12643]
Mercy For Animals [11336]
Natl. Assn. of Students Against Violence Everywhere [18117]
National Association of Students Against Violence Everywhere [IO]
Natl. Conf. on Peacemaking and Conflict Resolution [18118]
Natl. Endowment for the Animals [11437]
Native Amer. Leadership Alliance [20455]
Nonviolence Intl. [18119]
Nonviolence Intl. [IO]
Nonviolence.Org [18228]
Nonviolent Peaceforce [18120]
Nonviolent Peaceforce [IO]
Partners for Peace [18230]
Pax Christi - U.S.A. [18121]
Peace Brigades Intl. - U.S.A. [18231]
Peace X Peace [18237]
Physicians for a Violence-Free Soc. [12985]
Play for Peace [12699]
Rsrc. Center for Nonviolence [18122]
Rsrc. Center for Nonviolence [IO]
Rsrc. Centre on Nonviolence [IO]
September Eleventh Families for Peaceful Tomorrows [12701]
Soc. for the Stud. of Peace, Conflict, and Violence: Peace Psychology Div. of the Amer. Psychological Assn. [16185]
Southern Christian Leadership Conf. [17154]
Teachers Resisting Unhealthy Children's Entertainment [11657]
Tuesday's Children [12003]
Voices in the Wilderness [18253]
War Resisters' Intl. [IO]
War Resisters League [18123]
Win Without War [18124]
Women in Black [18255]

A star before a book entry number signifies that the name is not listed separately, but is mentioned within the entry.

Nonviolence Intl. **[18119]**, PO Box 39127, Washington, DC 20016, (202)244-0951

Nonviolence Intl. **[IO]**, Washington, DC, United States

Nonviolence; New York Workshop in **[★18123]**

Nonviolence.Org **[18228]**, c/o Martin Kelley, Founder, PO Box 38504, Philadelphia, PA 19104, (215)681-0783

Nonviolent Action; Comm. for **[★18123]**

Nonviolent Action; Intl. Seminars on Training for **[★18115]**

Nonviolent Peaceforce **[18120]**, 425 Oak Grove St., Minneapolis, MN 55403, (612)871-0005

Nonviolent Peaceforce **[IO]**, Minneapolis, MN, United States

Nonviolent Persuasion; Center for **[★18110]**

Nonviolent Techniques Against Rape - Address unknown since 1995.

Nonwoven Fabrics Indus; INDA, Assn. of the **[3785]**

Nonwovens and Disposables Assn; Intl. **[★3785]**

NOPA Norwegian Soc. of Composers and Lyricists **[IO]**, Oslo, Norway

NOPA Soc. of Norwegian Composers and Lyricists **[★IO]**

NOPE: No Pornographic Exploitation - Address unknown since 2006.

NORAID

Irish Northern Aid Comm. **[17934]**

Norbert Barrie Family Org. - Address unknown since 2007.

Norcross Wildlife Found. **[5349]**, 250 W 88th St., No. 806, New York, NY 10024, (212)362-4831

Nord Amerikanischer Sangerbund **[★10680]**

Nordens Fackliga Samorganisation **[★IO]**

Nordens Institut pa Aland **[★IO]**

Nordic Africa Inst. **[IO]**, Uppsala, Sweden

Nordic Alcohol and Drug Policy Network **[IO]**, Copenhagen, Denmark

Nordic Amateur Theatre Coun. **[IO]**, Helsinki, Finland

Nordic Assn. of Agricultural Scientists **[IO]**, Stockholm, Sweden

Nordic Assn. for Amer. Stud. **[IO]**, Frederiksberg, Denmark

Nordic Assn. for Andrology **[IO]**, Copenhagen, Denmark

Nordic Assn. for Canadian Stud. **[IO]**, Arhus, Denmark

Nordic Assn. for China Stud. **[IO]**, Stockholm, Sweden

Nordic Assn. for Computational Mechanics **[IO]**, Stockholm, Sweden

Nordic Assn. for Hydrology **[IO]**, Norrkoping, Sweden

Nordic Assn. of Lexicography **[IO]**, Oslo, Norway

Nordic Assn. for Palliative Care **[IO]**, Copenhagen, Denmark

Nordic Assn. for Psychiatric Epidemiology **[IO]**, Bronshoj, Denmark

Nordic Assn. for Semiotic Stud. **[IO]**, Lund, Sweden

Nordic Assn. for South Asian Stud. **[IO]**, Bergen, Norway

Nordic Assn. of Univ. Administrators **[IO]**, Stockholm, Sweden

Nordic Assn. for Women's Stud. and Gender Res. **[IO]**, Tromso, Norway

Nordic Audiological Soc. **[IO]**, Copenhagen, Denmark

Nordic Church Coun. for Seamen **[IO]**, Copenhagen, Denmark

Nordic Coll. of Caring Sciences **[IO]**, Oslo, Norway

Nordic Comm. on Food Anal. **[IO]**, Oslo, Norway

Nordic Comm. of Schools of Social Work **[IO]**, Frederiksberg, Denmark

Nordic Cooperation on Disability **[IO]**, Vallingby, Sweden

Nordic Coun. **[IO]**, Copenhagen, Denmark

Nordic Coun. for Alcohol and Drug Res. **[IO]**, Helsinki, Finland

Nordic Coun. for Arctic Medical Res. **[★IO]**

Nordic Coun. of Conservatories **[IO]**, Helsinki, Finland

Nordic Coun. of Ministers **[IO]**, Copenhagen, Denmark

Nordic Coun. for Reindeer Husbandry Res. **[IO]**, Tromso, Norway

Nordic Coun. for Tax Res. **[IO]**, Arhus, Denmark

Nordic Educational Res. Assn. **[IO]**, Orebro, Sweden

Nordic Fed. of Res. Libraries Associations **[IO]**, Copenhagen, Denmark

Nordic Fed. of Societies of Obstetrics and Gynecology **[IO]**, Reykjavik, Iceland

Nordic Forest Res. Cooperation Comm. **[IO]**, Helsinki, Finland

Nordic Geodetic Commn. **[IO]**

Nordic Gerontological Fed. **[IO]**, Norrkoping, Sweden

Nordic Immigration Comm. **[IO]**, Norrkoping, Sweden

Nordic IN **[IO]**, Stockholm, Sweden

Nordic Info. Center for Media and Commun. Res. **[IO]**, Goteborg, Sweden

Nordic Info. Center for Media and Commun. Res. - Denmark **[IO]**, Goteborg, Sweden

Nordic Info. Center for Media and Commun. Res. - Sweden **[★IO]**

Nordic Inst. of Advanced Occupational Env. Stud. **[★IO]**

Nordic Inst. for Advanced Training in Occupational Hea. **[IO]**, Helsinki, Finland

Nordic Inst. on Aland **[IO]**, Mariehamn, Finland

Nordic Inst. of Asian Stud. **[IO]**, Copenhagen, Denmark

Nordic Inst. of Dental Materials **[IO]**, Haslum, Norway

Nordic Inst. for Theoretical Physics **[IO]**, Copenhagen, Denmark

Nordic Inst. for Women's Stud. and Gender Res. **[IO]**, Oslo, Norway

Nordic Intl. Stud. Assn. **[IO]**, Helsinki, Finland

Nordic Joint Comm. for Agricultural Res. **[IO]**, Ruukki, Finland

Nordic Lichen Soc. **[IO]**, Helsinki, Finland

Nordic Metal and Nordic Indus. Workers Fed. **[★IO]**

Nordic Microscopy Soc. **[IO]**, Jyvaskyla, Finland

Nordic Music Comm. **[IO]**, Stockholm, Sweden

Nordic Proj. Fund **[IO]**, Helsinki, Finland

Nordic Rheuma Coun. **[IO]**, Reykjavik, Iceland

Nordic Soc. for Aerosol Res. **[IO]**, Goteborg, Sweden

Nordic Soc. of Clinical Chemistry **[IO]**, Malmo, Sweden

Nordic Soc. for Middle Eastern Stud. **[IO]**, Bergen, Norway

Nordic Soc. for Radiation Protection **[IO]**, Osteras, Norway

Nordic Swimming Federations Assn. **[IO]**, Helsinki, Finland

Nordic Symposium for Church Music **[IO]**, Vejle, Denmark

Nordic Telemedicine Assn. **[IO]**, Odense, Denmark

Nordic Temperance Coun. **[★IO]**

Nordic Women's Peace Network **[IO]**, Sandefjord, Norway

Nordic Wood Preservation Coun. **[IO]**, Stockholm, Sweden

Nordisk Arbetsmiljoutbildning **[★IO]**

Nordisk Audiologisk Selskab **[★IO]**

Nordisk Copyright Bur. **[IO]**, Copenhagen, Denmark

Nordisk Forening For Fysiologi **[★IO]**

Nordisk Forening for Leksikografi **[★IO]**

Nordisk Forening for Obstetrik och Gynekologi **[★IO]**

Nordisk Forening for Pedagogisk Forskning **[★IO]**

Nordisk Furening fur Klinisk Kemi **[★IO]**

Nordisk Gerontologisk Forening **[★IO]**

Nordisk Herpetologisk Forening **[★IO]**

Nordisk Hydrologisk Forening **[★IO]**

Nordisk Institut for Asienstudier **[★IO]**

Nordisk Institut for Odontologisk MaterialprEovning **[★IO]**

Nordisk Institut for Teoretisk Fysik **[★IO]**

Nordisk Institutt for Kvinne- og Kjonnsforskning **[★IO]**

Nordisk Institutt for Sjorett **[★IO]**

Nordisk Kernesikkerhedsforskning **[★IO]**

Nordisk Kirkemusik Symposium **[★IO]**

Nordisk Konservatorierad **[★IO]**

Nordisk Kontaktorgan for Jordbrugsforskning **[★IO]**

Nordisk Lichenologisk Forening **[★IO]**

Nordisk Metodikkommitte for Livsmedel **[★IO]**

Nordisk Ministerrad **[★IO]**

Nordisk Musikkomite **[★IO]**

Nordisk Neurokirurgisk Forening **[★IO]**

Nordisk Organ for Reindriftsforskning **[★IO]**

Nordisk Selskap for Midtaustenstudiar **[★IO]**

Nordisk Skattevitenskapelig Forskningsrad **[★IO]**

Nordisk Skibsrederforening **[★IO]**

Nordisk Thoraxkirurgisk Forening **[★IO]**

Nordisk Urologisk Forening **[★IO]**

Nordiska Afrikainstitutet **[★IO]**

Nordiska Biskopskonferensen **[★IO]**

Nordiska Finansanstalldas Union **[★IO]**

Nordiska Glastekniska Foreningen **[★IO]**

Nordiska Jordbruksforskares Foerening **[★IO]**

Nordiska foreningen for Kinastudier **[★IO]**

Nordiska Namnden for Alkohol- och Drogforskning **[★IO]**

Nordiska Nykterhetsradet **[★IO]**

Nordiska Projektexportfonden **[★IO]**

Nordiska Radet **[★IO]**

Nordiska Sallskapet for Stralskydd **[★IO]**

Nordiska Samarbetsorganet for Handikappfragor **[★IO]**

Nordiska Samarbetsradet for Kriminologi **[★IO]**

Nordiska Traskyddsradet **[★IO]**

Nordiska Universitets Administrators-Samarbetet **[★IO]**

Nordiska Vetenskapliga Biblioteksforeningarnas Forbund **[★IO]**

Nordiske Kvinners Fredsnettverk **[★IO]**

Nordiske Laererorganisationers Samrad **[★IO]**

Nordiskt Amatorteaterrad **[★IO]**

Nordiskt Informationscenter for Medie- och Kommunikationsforskning **[★IO]**

Nordiskt Reumarad **[★IO]**

Nordmanns-Forbundet **[★IO]**

NORDTEST **[IO]**, Oslo, Norway

Norfolk Chamber of Commerce and Indus. **[IO]**, Norwich, United Kingdom

Norfolk Sample Drug Program - Defunct.

Norfolk Terrier Club; Norwich and **[22333]**

Norge-Amerika Foreningen **[★IO]**

Norges Aikidoforbund **[★IO]**

Norges Ake-, Bob- og skeleton Forbund **[★IO]**

Norges Astma- og Allergiforbund **[★IO]**

Norges Bandyforbund/Innebandyseksjonen **[★IO]**

Norges Bondelag **[★IO]**

Norges Danseforbund **[IO]**, Oslo, Norway

Norges Diabetesforbund **[★IO]**

Norges Fibromyalgi Forbund **[★IO]**

Norges Fotballforbund **[★IO]**

Norges Fredslag **[★IO]**

Norges Fredsraad **[★IO]**

Norges Fri-Idrettsforbund **[★IO]**

Norges Geotekniske Institutt **[★IO]**

Norges Idrettsforbund og Olympiske Komite **[★IO]**

Norges Ingeniororganisasjon **[★IO]**

Norges Kunst - og Antikvitetshandleres Forening **[IO]**, Oslo, Norway

Norges Kvinne og Familieforbund **[★IO]**

Norges Luftsportsforbund **[★IO]**

Norges Miljovernforbund **[★IO]**

Norges Naturvernforbund **[★IO]**

Norges Padleforbund **[★IO]**

Norges Parkinsonforbund **[★IO]**

Norges Pelsdyralslag **[★IO]**

Norges Rafisklags **[★IO]**

Norges Rederiforbund **[★IO]**

Norges Sildesalgslag **[★IO]**

Norges Squashforbund **[★IO]**

Norges Taekwondo Forbund **[★IO]**

Norges Tekniske Vitenskapsakademi **[★IO]**

Norges Tennisforbund **[★IO]**

Norks Virologisk Forening **[★IO]**

Norma Jean Fan Club - Address unknown since 1989.

Norma Terris Humane Educ. Center **[★11433]**

Norma Zimmer Natl. Fan Club **[24950]**

Norman Found. **[13128]**, 147 E 48th St., New York, NY 10017, (212)230-9830

Norman Horse Registry; Spanish- **[4954]**

Norman Rockwell Memorial Soc. - Defunct.

Normande Assn; Amer. **[★4281]**

Normande Assn; North Amer. **[4281]**

Normes Canadiennes de la Publicite **[★IO]**

Norris MDA/ALS Res. Center; Forbes **[15323]**

NORSAR **[IO]**, Kjeller, Norway

Norse

Asatru Alliance **[19461]**

Reference to "IO" in place of a book number signifies that the association may be found in the 45th edition of International Organizations.

Nordic Intl. Stud. Assn. [IO]
Norse Fed. [IO], Oslo, Norway
Norsemen's Fed. [★IO]
Norsk lokalhistorisk institutt [★IO]
Norsk forening for internasjonal rett [★IO]
Norsk fagbibliotekforening [★IO]
Norsk Astronautisk Forening [★IO]
Norsk Bibliotekforening [★IO]
Norsk Biokjemisk Selskap [★IO]
Norsk Botanisk Forening [IO], Oslo, Norway
Norsk institutt for by- og regionforskning [★IO]
Norsk Cardiologisk Selskap [★IO]
Norsk Dermatologisk Selskap [★IO]
Norsk Dykkenhistorisk Forening [★IO]
Norsk Elektroteknisk Komite [★IO]
Norsk Epilepsiforbund [★IO]
Norsk Ergoterapeutforbund [★IO]
Norsk Faglitterae Forfatter- og Oversetterforening [★IO]
Norsk Forening for Cystisk Fibrose [★IO]
Norsk Forening for Ernaering og Dietetikk [★IO]
Norsk Forening for Klassisk Akupunktur [★IO]
Norsk Forening for Kvalitet i Helsetjenesten [★IO]
Norsk Forening fur Landbruksteknikk [★IO]
Norsk Forening for Norske Komponister og Tekstforfattere [★IO]
Norsk Forening for Osteogenesis Imperfecta [★IO]
Norsk Forening for Prosjektledelse [★IO]
Norsk Forening for Signalbehandling [★IO]
Norsk Forening for Stomi-og Reservoaropererte [★IO]
Norsk Forskerforbund [★IO]
Norsk Fysioterapeutforbund [★IO]
Norsk Fysisk Selskap [★IO]
Norsk Geoteknisk Forening [★IO]
Norsk Heraldisk Forening [★IO]
Norsk Immunsviktforening [★IO]
Norsk gren av Intl. Fellowship Reconciliation [★IO]
Norsk Jockey Club [IO], Osteras, Norway
Norsk Journalistag [★IO]
Norsk Kabel-TV Forbund [★IO]
Norsk Kjemisk Selskap [★IO]
Norsk Kommunalteknisk Forening [★IO]
Norsk Komponistforening [★IO]
Norsk Kulturrad [★IO]
Norsk Oppfinnerforening [★IO]
Norsk Oversetterforening [★IO]
Norsk PEN [★IO]
Norsk Presseforbund [★IO]
Norsk Psykologforening [★IO]
Norsk Revmatikerforbund [IO], Oslo, Norway
Norsk Roseforening [★IO]
Norsk Selskap for Farmakologi og Toksikologi [★IO]
Norsk Selskap for Immunologi [★IO]
Norsk Skuespillerforbund [★IO]
Norsk Slektshistorisk Forening [★IO]
Norsk Student Pugwash [★IO]
Norsk Sykepleierforbund [★IO]
Norsk Utenrikspolitisk Institutt [★IO]
Norsk Venturkapitalforeningen [★IO]
Norsk Yngling Klubb [IO], Kolsas, Norway
Norske interiorarkitekters og mobeldesigneres landsforening [★IO]
Norske Arbeiderparti [★IO]
Norske Arkitekters Landsforbund [★IO]
Norske Barne-og Ungdomsbokforfattere [★IO]
Norske Billedkunstnere [★IO]
Norske Dramatikeres Forbund [★IO]
Norske Finansanalytikeres Forening [★IO]
Norske Landskapsarkitekters Forening [★IO]
Norske Sjomatbedrifters Landsforening [★IO]
Norske Symfoni-Orkestres Landsforbund [IO], Oslo, Norway
Norske Vandrerhjem [★IO]
North America
Amer. Culture Assn. [10886]
Assn. for the Advancement of Dutch-American Stud. [9908]
Before Columbus Found. [10416]
Czech-North Amer. Chamber of Commerce [24274]
Filipinas Americas Sci. and Art Found. [9609]
Hemispheric Cong. of Latin Chambers of Commerce [24281]
Inter-American Commn. on Human Rights [17765]

Leif Ericson Viking Ship [11134]
Mexican Epigraphic Soc. [10130]
North Amer. South Asian Bar Assn. [5527]
Powys Soc. of North Am. [9705]
Soc. for the Anthropology of North Am. [6425]
Wales North Am. Bus. Chamber [24306]
North Am; Assn. of Record Librarians of [★15097]
North Am; Bnei Akiva of [★20178]
North Am. Chinese Semiconductor Assn. [1226], PO Box 61086, Sunnyvale, CA 94088-1086, (408)428-5112
North America Chinese Semiconductor Association [IO], Sunnyvale, CA, United States
North America Coordinating Center for Responsible Tourism - Defunct.
North Am. Country Music Associations, Intl. [10674], PO Box 1145, Maynardville, TN 37807
North Am. - Ecological and Toxicological Assn. of Dyes and Organic Pigments Mfrs; ETAD [5089]
North Am; Hockey [23486]
North Am. Indian Ministries [★20376]
North Am. Indian Mission [★20376]
North Am. Indigenous Ministries [20376], PO Box 151, Point Roberts, WA 98281, (604)946-1227
North Am; Islamic Medical Assn. of [16003]
North Am; Lipizzan Assn. of [4911]
North Am. Missing Children Assn. [IO], Dartmouth, NS, Canada
North America-Mongolia Bus. Coun. [IO], Alexandria, VA, United States
North America-Mongolia Bus. Coun. [2310], 1015 Duke St., Alexandria, VA 22314, (703)549-8444
North Am. Native Amer. (Indian) Info. and Trade Center [10752], PO Box 27626, Tucson, AZ 85726-7626, (520)622-4900
North Am. Taiwanese Engineers' Assn. [7036], PO Box 360776, Milpitas, CA 95036
North Am. Taiwanese Engineers' Assn. [IO], Milpitas, CA, United States
North Am. Taiwanese Professors' Assn. [IO], Gaithersburg, MD, United States
North Am. Taiwanese Professors' Assn. [19402], c/o Dr. Ken Lin, Membership Chm., 4135 Creekpoint Ct., Danville, CA 94506, (510)559-5764
North America Trail Complex - Defunct.
North Am. Wu(Hao) Taiji Fed. [23601], 1350 E Arapaho Rd., No. 110, Richardson, TX 75081, (972)680-7888
North Am. Wu(Hao) Taiji Fed. [IO], Richardson, TX, United States
North Amer. Acad. of Ecumenists [19906], c/o Rev. Russell L. Meyer, Membership Sec.-Treas., 5025 Southampton Cir., Tampa, FL 33647-2031, (813)910-1532
North Amer. Acad. of Musculoskeletal Medicine - Address unknown since 1999.
North Amer. Acad. of the Spanish Language - Address unknown since 2002.
North Amer. Advertising Agency Network - Address unknown since 2000.
North Amer. Agricultural Marketing Officials [5025], c/o Mary Jordan, Sec.-Treas., 251 Causeway St., Ste. 500, Boston, MA 02114-2151, (617)626-1750
North Amer. Aliyah Movement - Defunct.
North Amer. Alliance for the Advancement of Native Peoples [12631], 29780 Hwy. UU, Keytesville, MO 65261
North Amer. Alliance for the Advancement of Native Peoples [IO], Keytesville, MO, United States
North Amer. Alliance of Chem. Engineers [6690], 3 Park Ave., New York, NY 10016
North Amer. Alliance for Fair Employment [1277], 30 Harrison Ave., 4th Fl., Boston, MA 02111, (617)482-6300
North Amer. Amateur Paintball Sports Assn. - Defunct.
North Amer. Apio-Therapy Soc. [★13614]
North Amer. Araucanian Royalist Soc. [10054], c/o Daniel Morrison, Gen. Sec., 205 Loetscher Pl., Ste. 1-A, Princeton, NJ 08540
North Amer. Assn. of Alcoholism Programs [★13216]
North Amer. Assn. for Ambulatory Urgent Care [13663], c/o Yvette Harvieux, Dir. of Development, 600 S Hwy. 169, Ste. 1585, Minneapolis, MN 55426, (952)767-2403

North Amer. Assn. for Belarusian Stud. [9735], c/o Curt Woolhiser, Sec.-Treas., Dept. of Slavic Languages and Literatures, Harvard Univ., Barker Ctr. 327, 12 Quincy St., Cambridge, MA 02138-3804
North Amer. Assn. for Belarusian Stud. [IO], Cambridge, MA, United States
North Amer. Assn. for the Catechumenate [IO], Portland, OR, United States
North Amer. Assn. for the Catechumenate [19697], c/o Rev. Bryon Hansen, Pres., 1279 High St., Auburn, CA 95603, (503)885-4515
North Amer. Assn. for Celtic Language Teachers [8741], c/o John J. Morrissey, Sec.-Treas., 647 Maybell Ave., Palo Alto, CA 94306-3817
North Amer. Assn. of Central Cancer Registries [13859], 2121 W White Oaks Dr., Ste. C, Springfield, IL 62704-7412, (217)698-0800
North Amer. Assn. of Central Cancer Registries [IO], Springfield, IL, United States
North Amer. Assn. of Christians in Social Work [13208], PO Box 121, Botsford, CT 06404-0121, (888)426-4712
North Amer. Assn. of Commencement Officers [8492], 1901 N Roselle Rd., Ste. 920, Schaumburg, IL 60195, (877)622-2606
North Amer. Assn. for the Diaconate [19967], Executive Off., 815 2nd Ave., New York, NY 10017, (646)486-7672
North Amer. Assn. of Educational Negotiators [24046], c/o OSBA, PO Box 1068, Salem, OR 97308, (503)588-2800
North Amer. Assn. for Environmental Educ. [8393], 2000 P St. NW, Ste. 540, Washington, DC 20036, (202)419-0412
North Amer. Assn. of Fisheries Economists [1485], c/o IIFET, Dept. of Agriculture and Rsrc. Economics, Oregon State Univ., Corvallis, OR 97331-3601, (541)737-1416
North Amer. Assn. of Floor Covering Distributors [657], 401 N Michigan Ave., Ste. 2200, Chicago, IL 60611, (312)321-6836
North Amer. Assn. of Food Equip. Mfrs. [1576], 161 N Clark St., Ste. 2020, Chicago, IL 60601, (312)821-0201
North Amer. Assn. of Hunter Safety Coordinators [★23545]
North Amer. Assn. of Hunter Safety Coordinators [★IO]
North Amer. Assn. of the Intl. Constantinian Order - Address unknown since 1995.
North Amer. Assn. of the Intl. Cooperative Insurance Fed. [★2141]
North Amer. Assn. of Inventory Services [755], PO Box 120145, St. Paul, MN 55112, (888)529-DATA
North Amer. Assn. of Jewish High Schools [8698], Akiba Hebrew Acad., 223 N Highland Ave., Merion Station, PA 19066
North Amer. Assn. of Jewish High Schools [IO], Merion Station, PA, United States
North Amer. Assn. of Jewish Homes and Housing for the Aging [★11277]
North Amer. Assn. of Medical Educ. and Commun. Companies [8874], 3416 Primm Ln., Birmingham, AL 35216, (205)824-7612
North Amer. Assn. of Mirror Mfrs. [★1728]
North Amer. Assn. of Mirror Mfrs. - Defunct.
North Amer. Assn. of Neuro-Linguistic Programming [★16219]
North Amer. Assn. of Neuro-Linguistic Programming [★IO]
North Amer. Assn. of Professors of Christian Educ. [★8088]
North Amer. Assn. of State and Provincial Lotteries [6048], 6 N Broadway, Geneva, OH 44041, (440)466-5630
North Amer. Assn. of State and Provincial Lotteries [IO], Geneva, OH, United States
North Amer. Assn. for the Stud. of Jean-Jacques Rousseau [★IO]
North Amer. Assn. for the Stud. of Jean-Jacques Rousseau [★9708]
North Amer. Assn. for the Stud. of Obesity [15576], c/o Ann Kenworthy, Interim Exec. Dir., 8630 Fenton St., Ste. 918, Silver Spring, MD 20910, (301)563-6526

A star before a book entry number signifies that the name is not listed separately, but is mentioned within the entry.

North Amer. Assn. for the Stud. of Obesity [IO], Silver Spring, MD, United States

North Amer. Assn. for the Stud. of Welsh Culture and History [IO], Flint, MI, United States

North Amer. Assn. for the Stud. of Welsh Culture and History [11083], c/o John S. Ellis, Sec.-Treas., Dept. of History, Univ. of Michigan, Flint, MI 48502, (810)762-3366

North Amer. Assn. of Subway Franchisees [1670], 95 Merrick Way, Ste. 710, Coral Gables, FL 33134, (305)448-8553

North Amer. Assn. of Summer Sessions [9200], c/o Michael U. Nelson, Exec. Sec., 43 Belanger Dr., Dover, NH 03820-4602, (603)740-9880

North Amer. Assn. of Summer Sessions [IO], Dover, NH, United States

North Amer. Assn. of Synagogue Executives [20517], Rapport House, 155 Fifth Ave., New York, NY 10010, (646)519-9385

North Amer. Assn. of Teachers of Czech [★9861]

North Amer. Assn. of Teachers of Czech [★IO]

North Amer. Assn. of Telecommunications Dealers [7779], 131 NW 1st Ave., Delray Beach, FL 33444, (561)266-9440

North Amer. Assn. of Urgent Care Medicine [★13663]

North Amer. Assn. of Ventriloquists [1322], c/o Maher Ventriloquists Studios, PO Box 420, Littleton, CO 80160-0420, (303)346-6819

North Amer. Assn. of Wardens and Superintendents [11884], PO Box 11037, Albany, NY 12211-0037, (518)786-6801

North Amer. Assn. of Wardens and Superintendents [IO], Albany, NY, United States

North Amer. Auto Union Register [21743]

North Amer. Babydoll Southdown Sheep Assn. and Registry [5211], PO Box 146, Wellsville, KS 66092, (785)883-4774

North Amer. Babydoll Southdown Sheep Assn. and Registry [IO], Wellsville, KS, United States

North Amer. Ballet Assn. - Defunct.

North Amer. Band Directors Coordinating Comm. - Defunct.

North Amer. Banding Coun. [7421], c/o Linda L. Long, USFS Redwood Sci. Lab., 1700 Bayview Dr., Arcata, CA 95521, (707)825-2947

North American Banding Council [IO], Arcata, CA, United States

North Amer. Bear Center [5350], 1926 Hwy. 169, Ely, MN 55731, (218)365-7879

North Amer. Bear Soc. [5351]

North Amer. Benefit Assn. [★19145]

North Amer. Benthological Soc. [4516], PO Box 1897, Lawrence, KS 66044-8897, (785)843-1235

North American Benthological Society [IO], Lawrence, KS, United States

North Amer. Bicycle Exhibitor Assn. - Defunct.

North Amer. Blueberry Coun. [4749], PO Box 1036, Folsom, CA 95763, (916)983-2279

North Amer. Bluebird Soc. [5352], PO Box 43, Miamiville, OH 45147, (812)988-1876

North American Bluebird Society [IO], Miamiville, OH, United States

North Amer. Bd. of Certified Energy Practitioners [6967], Saratoga Tech. Energy Park, 10 Hermes Rd., Ste. 400, Malta, NY 12020, (518)899-8186

North Amer. Border Terrier Welfare [12019], c/o Jo Ellen Wolf, U.S. Coor., 132 Buckboard Dr., Martinez, GA 30907, (706)863-0951

North Amer. Bowhunter [★23542]

North Amer. Bowhunting Coalition [22606], PO Box 493, Chatfield, MN 55923

North Amer. Boxing Fed. [23266], c/o Rex Ross Walker, Pres., 3300 Airport Rd., Boulder, CO 80301, (303)442-0258

North Amer. Boxing Fed. [IO], Edmonton, AB, Canada

North Amer. Brain Tumor Coalition [13860], c/o Elizabeth Goss, Esq., Counsel, 1 Metro Ctr., 700 12th St. NW, Ste. 900, Washington, DC 20005, (202)508-4670

North Amer. Bramble Growers Res. Found. [1675], c/o Debby Wechsler, Exec. Sec., 1138 Rock Rest Rd., Pittsboro, NC 27312, (919)542-3687

North Amer. Br. (1940) Dunkirk Veterans Assn. - Defunct.

North Amer. Br. of Intl. Life Sciences Inst. [★15561]

North Amer. Br. of Intl. Life Sciences Inst. [★IO]

North Amer. Brass Band Assn. [10675], c/o Rusty Morris, Pres., 5 Big Stone Ct., Little Rock, AR 72227

North Amer. Brewers' Assn. [208], 601 W 19th St., Idaho Falls, ID 83402, (208)705-2667

North Amer. British Music Stud. Assn. [10676], c/o Deborah Heckert, Sec., Music Dept., 3304 Staller Ctr., SUNY Stony Brook, Stony Brook, NY 11794-5475

North Amer. British Music Stud. Assn. [IO], Stony Brook, NY, United States

North Amer. Broadcasters Assn. [IO], Toronto, ON, Canada

North Amer. Building Material Distribution Assn. [658], 401 N Michigan Ave., Chicago, IL 60611, (312)321-6845

North American-Bulgarian Chamber of Commerce [24291], 851 Irwin St., Ste. 200, San Rafael, CA 94901, (415)738-3481

North Amer. Bungee Assn. [23844], PO Box 121, Fairview, OR 97024, (503)520-0303

North Amer. Bungee Assn. [IO], Fairview, OR, United States

North Amer. Butterfly Assn. [7249], 4 Delaware Rd., Morristown, NJ 07960, (973)285-0907

North Amer. Canon Law Soc. [★19593]

North Amer. Canon Law Soc. [★IO]

North Amer. Cartographic Info. Soc. [6656], c/o AGS Lib., PO Box 399, Milwaukee, WI 53201-0399, (414)229-6282

North Amer. Case Res. Assn. [4065], c/o Bob Crowner, Sec.-Treas., 466 Owen Bldg., Ypsilanti, MI 48197, (734)487-2215

North Amer. Catalysis Soc. [7624], c/o John N. Armor, Pres., 7201 Hamilton Blvd., Allentown, PA 18195-1501, (610)481-5792

North Amer. Celtic Buyers Assn. [784], 27 Addison Ave., Rutherford, NJ 07070, (201)842-9922

North Amer. Celtic Buyers Assn. [IO], Rutherford, NJ, United States

North Amer. Center on Adoption - Defunct.

North Amer. Center for Emergency Communications - Defunct.

North Amer. Chap. of the Assn. for Computational Linguistics [10408], c/o Lillian Lee, Sec., Dept. of Cmpt. Sci., Cornell Univ., 4152 Upson Hall, Ithaca, NY 14853, (607)255-8119

North Amer. Chap. of the Assn. for Computational Linguistics [IO], Ithaca, NY, United States

North American-Chilean Chamber of Commerce [24307], 30 Vasay St., Ste. 506, New York, NY 10007, (212)233-7776

North Amer. Chinese Clinical Chemists Assn. [6691], c/o Run-Zhang Shi, PhD, Treas., Medical Coll. of Wisconsin, Dept. of Pathology, 8701 Watertown Plank Rd., Milwaukee, WI 53226, (414)805-1524

North American Chinese Clinical Chemists Association [IO], Milwaukee, WI, United States

North Amer. Chinese Soccer League [IO], Landenberg, PA, United States

North Amer. Chinese Soccer League [23780], 1 Cronssan Ct., Landenberg, PA 19350, (302)831-0625

North Amer. Christian Peace Conf. - Address unknown since 2004.

North Amer. Clinical Dermatologic Soc. [14212], c/o Judith A. Koperski, MD, Membership Chair, Dermatologist Medical Gp. of North County, 9850 Genesee Ave., Ste. 530, La Jolla, CA 92037, (858)558-0677

North Amer. Clinical Dermatologic Soc. [IO], La Jolla, CA, United States

North Amer. Clun Forest Assn. [5212], c/o Bets Reedy, Sec.-Treas., Bramble Hill, 21727 Randall Dr., Houston, MN 55943, (507)864-7585

North Amer. Coalition for Christian Admissions Professionals [7914], c/o Chant Thompson, Exec. Dir., PO Box 5211, Huntington, IN 46750-5211, (260)356-5211

North Amer. Coalition for Christianity and Ecology [4517], 866 Park Pl., Brooklyn, NY 11216-4004, (718)496-5139

North Amer. Coalition for Human Rights in Korea [★17966]

North Amer. Coalition for Human Rights in Korea [★IO]

North Amer. Coalition on Religion and Ecology [4598]

North Amer. Cockatiel Soc. [21857], c/o Renee Martin, Band/Membership Chair, PO Box 143, Bethel, CT 06801-0143

North American Cockatiel Society [IO], Bethel, CT, United States

North Amer. Collectors [22747], 16000 Ventura Blvd., Ste. 1000, Encino, CA 91436, (818)370-4020

North Amer. Coll. of Botanical Medicine [14819]

North Amer. Colleges and Teachers of Agriculture [7942], c/o Marilyn B. Parker, Sec.-Treas., 151 W 100 S, Rupert, ID 83350, (208)436-0692

North Amer. Comm. - Defunct.

North Amer. Comm. of Enamel Creators - Address unknown since 2001.

North Amer. Comm. for IME (Institut Medical Evangelique) - Defunct.

North Amer. Comm. for Reconciliation in Ulster - Defunct.

North Amer. Computational Social and Org. Sciences [6740], c/o Janice Kusmierek, Carnegie Mellon Univ., ISRI, Wean Hall 1325, 5000 Forbes Ave., Pittsburgh, PA 15213, (412)268-3163

North Amer. Computer Service Assn. [907]

North Amer. Confed. of the Red Dragon [22479], c/o Mark Edwards, 5559K Southfield Dr., St. Louis, MO 63129

North Amer. Conf. on British Stud. [9760], c/o Dr. Andrew August, Exec. Sec., Pennsylvania State Univ., 1600 Woodland Rd., Abington, PA 19001, (215)881-7584

North Amer. Conf. on Christianity and Ecology [★4517]

North Amer. Conf. on Ethiopian Jewry [17953], 132 Nassau St., Ste. 412, New York, NY 10038-2434, (212)233-5200

North Amer. Conf. on Ethiopian Jewry [IO], New York, NY, United States

North Amer. Conf. of Separated and Divorced Catholics [12013], PO Box 10, Hancock, MI 49930-0010, (906)482-0494

North Amer. Cong. on Latin Am. [16977], 38 Greene St., 4th Fl., New York, NY 10013, (646)613-1440

North Amer. Connection [IO], West Midlands, United Kingdom

North Amer. Coordinating Coun. on Japanese Lib. Resources [IO], Cambridge, MA, United States

North Amer. Coordinating Coun. on Japanese Lib. Resources [8781], c/o Victoria Lyon Bestor, Exec. Dir., 149 Upland Rd., Cambridge, MA 02140, (617)945-7294

North Amer. Corriente Assn. [4278], c/o James Spawn, Sec.-Treas./Exec. Dir., PO Box 12359, North Kansas City, MO 64116, (816)421-1992

North Amer. Cottage Garden Soc. and North Amer. Dianthus Soc; Combined [22507]

North Amer. Coun. on Adoptable Children [11257], 970 Raymond Ave., Ste. 106, St. Paul, MN 55114, (651)644-3036

North Amer. Coun. of Automotive Teachers [7993], PO Box 80010, Charleston, SC 29416, (843)556-7068

North Amer. Coun. for Muslim Women - Defunct.

North Amer. Coun. for Online Learning [7949], 1934 Old Gallows Rd., Ste. 350, Vienna, VA 22182-4040, (703)752-6216

North Amer. Coun. for Online Learning [IO], Vienna, VA, United States

North Amer. Crane Working Group [5353], PO Box 566, Gambier, OH 43022, (206)286-8607

North Amer. Currach Assn. - Address unknown since 2002.

North Amer. Dairy Sheep Assn. - Defunct.

North Amer. Danish Warmblood Assn. [4930], c/o Karin Dilou, Pres., PO Box 536, Nicasio, CA 94946, (415)662-9555

North Amer. Danish Warmblood Assn. [IO], Nicasio, CA, United States

North Amer. Deer Farmers Assn. [4654], 1215 N 7th St., Ste. 104, Lake City, MN 55041, (651)345-5600

North Amer. Dept. of the Royal Warmblood Studbook of the Netherlands [4931], PO Box 0, Sutherlin, OR 97479, (541)459-3232

Reference to "IO" in place of a book number signifies that the association may be found in the 45th edition of International Organizations.

North Amer. Deutsch Kurzhaar Club [22323], c/o Rich Dobey, Treas., 1017 S Fourth Ave., Libertyville, IL 60048

North Amer. Dhrupad Assn. [10677], PO Box 361, Agoura Hills, CA 91376, (818)991-0825

North Amer. Dhrupad Assn. [IO], Agoura Hills, CA, United States

North Amer. Dianthis Soc. [★22507]

North Amer. Dianthis Soc; Combined North Amer. Cottage Garden Soc. and [22507]

North Amer. Die Casting Assn. [2054], 241 Holbrook Dr., Wheeling, IL 60090-5809, (847)279-0001

North Amer. Diecast Toy Collectors Assn. [★22997]

North Amer. Diecast Toy Collectors Assn. [★IO]

North Amer. District of the Belgian Warmblood Breeding Assn. - Address unknown since 2001.

North Amer. District Heating and Cooling Inst. - Defunct.

North Amer. Dog Agility Coun. [23387], PO Box 1206, Colbert, OK 74733

North Amer. Dostoevsky Soc. - Defunct.

North Amer. Draft Cross Assn. - Defunct.

North Amer. Economic Stud. Assn. [★6890]

North Amer. Economics and Finance Assn. [6890], c/o Harvey Rosenblum, Exec. Dir., Fed. Reserve Bank of Dallas, Dallas, TX 75201, (214)922-5055

North Amer. Edged Weapon Collectors Assn. - Defunct.

North Amer. Elec. Reliability Coun. [1195], 116-390 Village Blvd., Princeton, NJ 08540-5721, (609)452-8060

North Amer. Elk Breeders Assn. [4028], PO Box 1640, Platte City, MO 64079, (816)431-3605

North Amer. English and European Ford Registry [21744], PO Box 11415, Olympia, WA 98508, (360)754-9585

North Amer. Equine Ranching Info. Coun. [1926], PO Box 43968, Louisville, KY 40253-0968, (502)245-0425

North Amer. Equip. Dealers Assn. [185], 1195 Smizer Mill Rd., Fenton, MO 63026-3480, (636)349-5000

North Amer. Export Grain Assn. [1752], 1250 I St. NW, Ste. 1003, Washington, DC 20005, (202)682-4030

North Amer. Export Grain Assn. [IO], Washington, DC, United States

North Amer. Falconers Assn. [23398], c/o Bridget Rocheford-Kearney, Corresponding Sec., 59311 Hwy. 78, Burns, OR 97720-9500, (253)572-0194

North Amer. Family Campers Assn. [23273], PO Box 318, Lunenburg, MA 01462, (508)867-3215

North Amer. Farm Alliance - Address unknown since 1995.

North Amer. Farm Show Coun. [4114], c/o R. Craig Fendrick, Exec. Coor., 11240 Beacom Rd., Sunbury, OH 43074, (740)524-0658

North Amer. Farmers' Direct Marketing Assn. [5026], 62 White Loaf Rd., Southampton, MA 01073, (413)529-0386

North Amer. Fastpitch Assn. [23793], PO Box 566, Dayton, OR 97114, (503)864-4487

North American Fastpitch Association [IO], Dayton, OR, United States

North Amer. Fed. of German Folk Dance Groups [IO], San Antonio, TX, United States

North Amer. Fed. of German Folk Dance Groups [9965], c/o Doug Hall, Treas., 515 Marquis St., San Antonio, TX 78216-5217

North Amer. Fed. of Temple Brotherhoods [★20160]

North Amer. Fed. of Temple Youth [19185], c/o Union for Reform Judaism - Youth Division, 633 3rd Ave., 7th Fl., New York, NY 10017, (212)650-4070

North Amer. Fichte Soc. [10815], c/o Daniel Breazeale, Ed./Co-Founder, Dept. of Philosophy, Univ. of Kentucky, Lexington, KY 40506, (859)257-4376

North Amer. Fish Breeders Guild [22444], c/o D.L. Sponenberg, RR 2, Box 67-L, Orangeville, PA 17859, (717)683-6126

North American Fish Breeders Guild [IO], Orangeville, PA, United States

North Amer. Fishing Club [23421], 12301 Whitewater Dr., Minnetonka, MN 55343

North Amer. Flowerbulb Wholesalers Assn. [4983], c/o Marlboro Bulb Company, 2424 Hwy. 72/221 E, Greenwood, SC 29649, (864)229-1618

North Amer. Folk Music and Dance Alliance [★9955]

North Amer. Folk Music and Dance Alliance [★IO]

North Amer. Folk Music and Folk Dance Alliance [22718], 510 S Main St., 1st Fl., Memphis, TN 38103, (901)522-1170

North Amer. Foodservice Companies [★1566]

North Amer. Football League [23435], 250 Prairie Center Dr., No. 217, Eden Prairie, MN 55344, (952)829-7999

North Amer. Football League [IO], Eden Prairie, MN, United States

North Amer. Forensic Entomology Assn. [IO], Davis, CA, United States

North Amer. Forensic Entomology Assn. [7064], c/o Rebecca O'Flaherty Bullard, Treas., Univ. of California, Dept. of Entomology, One Shields Ave., Davis, CA 95616

North Amer. Formula 18 Assn. [23208], 7505 Elkmont Ct., Wilmington, NC 28411

North Amer. Forum on the Catechumenate [19698], 125 Michigan Ave. NE, Washington, DC 20017, (202)884-9758

North Amer. Free Trade Assn. - Address unknown since 2001.

North Amer. Friends of Palestinian Universities - Defunct.

North Amer. Fruit Explorers [22531], 1716 Apples Rd., Chapin, IL 62628-4048, (217)245-7589

North Amer. Fur Trade [IO], Powassan, ON, Canada

North Amer. Fuzzy Info. Processing Soc. [6741], c/o Dr. Bill Tastle, Treas., Ithaca Coll., Scholarship of Bus., 424 Smiddy Hall, Ithaca, NY 14850, (607)274-3669

North Amer. Game Breeders and Shooting Preserve Assn. [★4144]

North Amer. Gamebird Assn. [4144], 201 N Main, Eureka, KS 67045, (620)583-8779

North Amer. Gaming Regulators Assn. [5772], 1000 Westgate Dr., Ste. 252, St. Paul, MN 55114, (651)203-7244

North Amer. Geosynthetics Soc. [6701], PO Box 12063, Albany, NY 12212-2063, (518)869-2917

North American Geosynthetics Society [IO], Albany, NY, United States

North Amer. Ginseng Assn. - Defunct.

North Amer. Gladiolus Coun. [22532], 14625 E C Ave., Augusta, MI 49012-9652, (616)731-4259

North Amer. Gladiolus Coun., Commercial Growers Div. - Defunct.

North Amer. Graphic Arts Suppliers Assn. [1804], PO Box 934483, Margate, FL 33093, (954)971-1383

North Amer. Grouse Partnership [5354], c/o C. Sealing, 1670 N 1/2 Rd., Fruita, CO 81521, (970)858-9659

North Amer. Guild of Change Ringers [10678], c/o A. Thomas Miller, Membership Sec., 229 Howard Ave., Woodstown, NJ 08098-1249, (856)769-7264

North Amer. Hardwood Preservation Soc. - Defunct.

North Amer. Hazardous Materials Mgt. Assn. [4806], 3030 W 81st Ave., Westminster, CO 80031-4111, (303)433-4446

North Amer. Heather Soc. [22533], c/o Mario A. Abreu, Pres., PO Box 673, Albion, CA 95410-0673, (707)937-3155

North Amer. Heather Soc. [IO], Albion, CA, United States

North Amer. Horsemen's Assn. [4932], PO Box 223, Paynesville, MN 56362, (320)243-7250

North Amer. Horticultural Supply Assn. [4984], 100 N 20th St., 4th Fl., Philadelphia, PA 19103-1443, (215)564-3484

North Amer. Hunting Club [23548], 12301 Whitewater Dr., PO Box 3401, Minnetonka, MN 55343, (952)988-9333

North Amer. Hyperthermia Soc. [★16639]

North Amer. Importers Assn. [2311], Empire State Bldg., 350 5th Ave., Manhattan, New York, NY 10118, (716)989-4234

North Amer. Importers Assn. [IO], New York, NY, United States

North Amer. Indian Assn. - Address unknown since 2002.

North Amer. Indian Chamber of Commerce of North Am. [★24358]

North Amer. Indian Museums Assn. - Defunct.

North Amer. Indian Trade and Info. Center [★10750]

North Amer. Indian Women's Assn. - Address unknown since 1994.

North Amer. Indus. Hemp Coun. [7079], PO Box 259329, Madison, WI 53725-9329, (608)835-0428

North Amer. Industrial Representatives Assn. [2543]

North Amer. Insulation Manufacturers Assn. [659], 44 Canal Center Plz., Ste. 310, Alexandria, VA 22314, (703)684-0084

North Amer. Interfraternal Found. [24486], 1750 Royalton Dr., Carmel, IN 46032-9620, (317)595-9613

North-American Interfraternity Conf. [24487], 3901 W 86th St., Ste. 390, Indianapolis, IN 46268-1791, (317)872-1112

North Amer. Islamic Trust [10250], 745 McClintock Dr., Ste. 114, Burr Ridge, IL 60527, (630)789-9191

North Amer. Jack Russell Terrier Assn. [22324], c/o Nan Owen, Treas., 415 Walker Hollow Dr., Monterey, TN 38574, (931)839-7462

North Amer. Jack Russell Terrier Assn. [IO], Monterey, TN, United States

North Amer. Jewish Students Appeal - Address unknown since 2001.

North Amer. Jewish Students' Network - Address unknown since 1995.

North Amer. Jewish Youth Coun. - Defunct.

North Amer. Judges Assn. [★5892]

North Amer. Jules Verne Soc. [11184], c/o Brian Kutzera, Sec.-Treas., 1632 N 54th St., Seattle, WA 98103-6120

North Amer. Jules Verne Soc. [IO], Seattle, WA, United States

North Amer. Kai Assn. [22325], 3410 Galbraith Line Rd., Yale, MI 48097

North Amer. Kant Soc. [10816], c/o Patricia Kitcher, Pres., Columbia Univ., Dept. of Philosophy, 708 Philosophy Hall, 1150 Amsterdam Ave., New York, NY 10027, (314)935-6670

North Amer. Kettlebell Fed. [23984], c/o Lorraine Patten, Treas., PO Box 478, Pleasant Valley, NY 12569

North Amer. Kettlebell Fed. [IO], Pleasant Valley, NY, United States

North Amer. Lake Mgt. Soc. [7241], PO Box 5443, Madison, WI 53705-0443, (608)233-2836

North Amer. Laminate Flooring Assn. [660], 1747 Pennsylvania Ave. NW, Ste. 1000, Washington, DC 20006, (202)785-9500

North Amer. Laminate Flooring Assn. [IO], Washington, DC, United States

North Amer. Levinas Soc. [10817], c/o Sol Neely, Sec./Webmaster, Dept. of English, Purdue Univ., 500 Oval Dr., West Lafayette, IN 47907-2038

North Amer. Lily Soc. [22534], c/o Stephanie Sims, Exec. Sec., PO Box W, Bonners Ferry, ID 83805

North American Lily Society [IO], Beaufort, MO, United States

North Amer. Limousin Found. [4279], 7383 S Alton Way, Ste. 100, Englewood, CO 80112, (303)220-1693

North Amer. Limousin Junior Assn. [4280], c/o North Amer. Limousin Found., 7383 S Alton Way, Ste. 100, Centennial, CO 80112, (303)220-1693

North Amer. Lionhead Rabbit Club [5157], c/o Arden Wetzel, Sec., 23657 140th Ave., Milaca, MN 56353, (320)983-5715

North Amer. Lionhead Rabbit Club [IO], Milaca, MN, United States

North Amer. Llewellin Breeders Assn. [IO], Waco, TX, United States

North Amer. Llewellin Breeders Assn. [22326], 3413 Forrester Ln., Waco, TX 76708, (254)752-1526

North Amer. Loon Fund [5355]

North Amer. Lumbar Spine Assn. [★15402]

North Amer. Lumbar Spine Assn. [★IO]

North Amer. Man/Boy Love Assn. [13099], PO Box 174, New York, NY 10018, (212)631-1194

North Amer. Mfg. Res. Institution of the Soc. of Mfg. Engineers [7266], 1 SME Dr., PO Box 930, Dearborn, MI 48121-0930, (313)271-1500

North Amer. Manx Assn. [19223], c/o Mr. Bradley E. Prendergast, Pres., 6135 N Glenwood Ave., No. 1-W, Chicago, IL 60660

A star before a book entry number signifies that the name is not listed separately, but is mentioned within the entry.

North Amer. Manx Assn. **[IO]**, Chicago, IL, United States

North Amer. Maple Syrup Coun. - Address unknown since 2001.

North Amer. Maritime Ministry Assn. **[13007]**, c/o Rev. Lloyd Burghart, Exec. Sec., PO Box 2434, Niagara Falls, NY 14302, (905)892-8818

North Amer. Maritime Ministry Assn. **[IO]**, Niagara Falls, NY, United States

North Amer. Marten Rabbit Club - Address unknown since 1995.

North Amer. Masonic Historical Assn. - Defunct.

North Amer. Meat Processors Assn. **[2663]**, 1910 Assn. Dr., Reston, VA 20191, (703)758-1900

North Amer. Meat Processors Assn. **[IO]**, Reston, VA, United States

North Amer. Medical/Dental Assn. - Defunct.

North Amer. Membrane Soc. **[7307]**, c/o Chem. and Env. Engg., Univ. of Toledo, Mail Stop 305, Toledo, OH 43606-3390, (419)530-8088

North Amer. Menopause Soc. **[15614]**, PO Box 94527, Cleveland, OH 44101, (440)442-7550

North Amer. Meteor Network **[7328]**, c/o Mark Davis, Coor., 101 Margate Cir., Goose Creek, SC 29445

North Amer. Meteor Network **[IO]**, Goose Creek, SC, United States

North Amer. MGA Register - Address unknown since 1991.

North Amer. Millers' Assn. **[2738]**, 600 Maryland Ave. SW, Ste. 825 W, Washington, DC 20024, (202)484-2200

North Amer. Mini Champ Racing Assn. - Address unknown since 1985.

North Amer. Mini Moke Registry **[21745]**, c/o Sherry Chandler, Ed., 1779 Kickapoo St., South Lake Tahoe, CA 96150, (530)577-7895

North Amer. Model Boat Assn. **[22654]**, c/o Ms. Cathie Galbraith, Exec. Sec., 1815 Halley St., San Diego, CA 92154, (619)424-6380

North Amer. Model Boat Assn. **[IO]**, San Diego, CA, United States

North Amer. Model Horse Shows Assn. **[22587]**, PO Box 55815, Portland, OR 97238-5815, (518)862-2294

North Amer. Monogrammers and Embroiderers - Defunct.

North Amer. Morab Horse Association/Registry **[★4947]**

North Amer. Morab Horse Association/Registry **[★IO]**

North Amer. Multihull Sailing Assn. - Address unknown since 1995.

North Amer. Mustang Assn. and Registry **[4933]**

North Amer. Mycological Assn. **[7353]**, c/o Judy Roger, Exec. Sec., 6615 Tudor Ct., Gladstone, OR 97027-1032, (503)657-7358

North Amer. Natl. Broadcasters Assn. **[★IO]**

North Amer. Native Bankers Assn. - Address unknown since 2004.

North Amer. Native Fishes Assn. **[7175]**, c/o Christopher Scharpf, Ed./Membership Coor., 1107 Argonne Dr., Baltimore, MD 21218, (410)243-9050

North Amer. Native Fishes Assn. **[IO]**, Baltimore, MD, United States

North Amer. Native Plant Soc. **[IO]**, Etobicoke, ON, Canada

North Amer. Natural Bodybuilding Fed. **[23245]**, 7026 Alden, Shawnee, KS 66216, (913)268-4133

North Amer. Natural Casing Assn. **[1555]**, c/o Leon Van Leeuwen Corp., 494 8th Ave., Ste. 805, New York, NY 10001, (212)695-4980

North Amer. Natural Casing Assn. **[IO]**, New York, NY, United States

North Amer. Nature Photography Assn. **[3006]**, 10200 W 44th Ave., Ste. 304, Wheat Ridge, CO 80033-2840, (303)422-8527

North Amer. NCR Financial Users Group - Address unknown since 2004.

North Amer. Network of Women Runners **[23656]**, PO Box 2736, Bala Cynwyd, PA 19004, (610)668-9886

North Amer. Neuro-Ophthalmology Soc. **[15695]**, 5841 Cedar Lake Rd., Ste. 204, Minneapolis, MN 55416, (952)646-2037

North Amer. Neuro-Ophthalmology Soc. **[IO]**, Minneapolis, MN, United States

North Amer. Neuromodulation Soc. **[15847]**, 4700 W Lake Ave., Glenview, IL 60025, (847)375-4714

North Amer. Nietzsche Soc. **[10818]**, Univ. of Illinois, Dept. of Philosophy, 105 Gregory Hall, 810 S Wright St., Urbana, IL 61801, (217)333-1939

North American Nietzsche Society **[IO]**, Urbana, IL, United States

North Amer. Normande Assn. **[4281]**, c/o Michael Mueller, Treas./Registry Sec., 748 Enloe Rd., Re-wey, WI 53580, (608)943-6091

North Amer. Nursing Diagnosis Assn. **[★15489]**

North Amer. Nursing Diagnosis Assn. **[★IO]**

North Amer. Nutrition and Preventive Medicine Assn. - Address unknown since 1995.

North Amer. Offshore One-Design Assn. - Defunct.

North Amer. Olive Oil Assn. **[2859]**, 3301 Rte. 66, Bldg. C, Ste. 205, Neptune, NJ 07753-2705, (732)922-3008

North American Olive Oil Association **[IO]**, Neptune, NJ, United States

North Amer. Opel GT Club - Address unknown since 2006.

North Amer. Parrot Soc. **[21858]**, c/o Gary Morgan, Pres./Chm., 15341 Kingston St., Brighton, CO 80602-7439, (303)659-9544

North Amer. Patristics Soc. **[20460]**, c/o Clayton N. Jefford, Sec.-Treas., St. Meinrad School of Theology, 200 Hill Dr., St. Meinrad, IN 47577, (812)357-6631

North Amer. Peregrine Found. **[★23398]**

North Amer. Performing Arts Managers and Agents **[175]**, 459 Columbus Ave., No. 133, New York, NY 10024, (888)745-8759

North Amer. Peruvian Horse Assn. **[4934]**, 3095 Burleson Retta Rd., Ste. B, Burleson, TX 76028, (817)447-7574

North Amer. Peruvian Horse Assn. **[IO]**, Burleson, TX, United States

North Amer. Photonics Assn. - Defunct.

North Amer. Piedmontese Assn. **[4282]**, PO Box 330, Valleyford, WA 99036-0330, (306)329-8600

North American Piedmontese Association **[IO]**, Valleyford, WA, United States

North Amer. Plant Preservation Coun. **[5356]**, c/o Barry Glick, Exec. Dir., HC 67 Box 539B, Renick, WV 24966, (304)497-2208

North Amer. Plant Protection Org. **[IO]**, Ottawa, ON, Canada

North Amer. Poetry Network - Defunct.

North Amer. Police Work Dog Assn. **[6003]**, 4222 Manchester Ave., Perry, OH 44081-9611, (440)259-3169

North Amer. Potbellied Pig Assn. **[4145]**, c/o Jamie Holley, Pres., 3850 Dacy Ln., Kyle, TX 78640, (512)295-7897

North Amer. Poultry Cooperative Assn. - Defunct.

North Amer. Power Sweeping Assn. **[2473]**, PO Box 2114, Kalamazoo, MI 49003-2114, (269)383-6993

North Amer. Powerlifting Fed. **[23662]**, c/o Robert Keller, Gen. Sec.-Treas., PO Box 291571, Davie, FL 33329-1571, (954)384-4472

North Amer. Predatory Animal Center - Defunct.

North Amer. Primary Care Res. Gp. **[13664]**, 11400 Tomahawk Creek Pkwy., Ste. 540, Leawood, KS 66211-2672, (913)906-6000

North Amer. Professional Driver Education Assn. - Defunct.

North Amer. Professional Driver's Assn. - Defunct.

North Amer. Professors of Christian Educ. **[8088]**, 2825 Lexington Rd., Louisville, KY 40280, (502)649-3726

North Amer. Pt-to-Pt Assn. **[23511]**, PO Box 102, Butler, MD 21023, (410)329-3749

North Amer. Punch Mfrs. Assn. **[2055]**, 21 Turquoise Ave., Naples, FL 34114, (239)775-7245

North Amer. Quilling Guild **[21541]**, PO Box 1575, Salina, KS 67402

North Amer. Radio Archives **[22926]**, c/o Don Aston, Sec.-Treas., PO Box 1392, Lake Elsinore, CA 92531, (888)33-AVPRO

North Amer. Radon Assn. - Defunct.

North Amer. Rail Shippers Assn. **[3885]**, 2115 Portsmouth Dr., Richardson, TX 75082-4839, (972)690-4740

North Amer. Railcar Operators Assn. **[3886]**, c/o Joel Williams, Sec., PO Box 802, Lock Haven, PA 17745, (570)893-1610

North Amer. Reggio Emilia Alliance **[11641]**, c/o Cheryl Rapaport, Admin. Coor., Inspired Practices in Early Educ., Inc., 2040 Wilson Ridge Ct., Roswell, GA 30075, (770)552-0179

North Amer. Regional Alliance of IATA - Address unknown since 1994.

North Amer. Registry of Midwives **[13983]**, 5257 Rosestone Dr., Lilburn, GA 30047, (888)842-4784

North Amer. Restaurant and Tavern Alliance - Address unknown since 1987.

North Amer. Retail Dealers Assn. **[1227]**, 4700 W Lake Ave., Glenview, IL 60025, (847)375-4713

North Amer. Retail Hardware Assn. **[1829]**, 5822 W 74th St., Indianapolis, IN 46278-1787, (317)290-0338

North Amer. Rhea Assn. **[5005]**

North Amer. Riders Club - Address unknown since 1985.

North Amer. Riding for the Handicapped Assn. **[23357]**, PO Box 33150, Denver, CO 80233, (303)452-1212

North Amer. Ring Assn. **[22327]**, c/o Jennifer Sunga, Treas., PO Box 175, Ryde, CA 95680-0175, (707)746-8584

North Amer. Ring Assn. **[IO]**, Ryde, CA, United States

North American Rock Garden Society **[IO]**, Millwood, NY, United States

North Amer. Rock Garden Soc. **[22535]**, c/o Jacques Mommens, Exec. Sec., PO Box 67, Millwood, NY 10546, (914)762-2948

North Amer. Romagnola and RomAngus Assn. **[4283]**, 14305 W 379th St., LaCygne, KS 66040-4077, (913)594-1080

North Amer. Saddle Mule Assn. **[21520]**

North Amer. Sankethi Assn. **[9802]**, 34 Longwood Dr., Clifton Park, NY 12065

North Amer. Sartre Soc. **[10819]**, c/o Berghahn Books, 150 Broadway, Ste. 812, New York, NY 10038

North Amer. Sawing Assn. **[1830]**, 1300 Sumner Ave., Cleveland, OH 44115-2851, (216)241-7333

North Amer. Saxophone Alliance **[10679]**, c/o Kenneth Tse, Membership Dir., Univ. of Iowa, School of Music, 2046 Voxman Music Bldg., Iowa City, IA 52242

North Amer. Schweizer Bund **[★19399]**

North Amer. Sea Plant Soc. - Defunct.

North Amer. Securities Administrators Assn. **[3521]**, 750 1st St. NE, Ste. 1140, Washington, DC 20002-8034, (202)737-0900

North Amer. Selle Francais Assn. **[4935]**, PO Box 579, Waynesboro, VA 22980, (540)932-9160

North Amer. Serials Interest Gp. **[10378]**, c/o Ms. Joyce Tenney, Sec., PMB 214, 2103 N Decatur Rd., Decatur, GA 30033

North Amer. Shagya-Arabian Soc. **[4936]**, c/o Gwyn Davis, VP/Information Off., 9797 S Rangeline Rd., Clinton, IN 47842, (765)665-3851

North Amer. Sheep Dog Soc. **[22328]**

North Amer. Shetland Sheepbreeders Assn. **[5213]**, c/o Karey Claghorn, NASSA Registry, 15603 173rd Ave., Milo, IA 50166, (641)942-6402

North Amer. Shippers Assn. **[3584]**, 1600 St. Georges Ave., PO Box 249, Rahway, NJ 07065, (732)680-4535

North Amer. Shortwave Assn. **[21507]**, 45 Wildflower Rd., Levittown, PA 19057, (215)945-0543

North Amer. Sikh Medical and Dental Assn. **[16416]**, c/o Dr. Baljit Singh Sidhu, MD, Sec., 13801 Allied Rd., Chester, VA 23836, (804)691-1906

North Amer. Sikh Medical and Dental Assn. **[IO]**, Chester, VA, United States

North Amer. Simulation and Gaming Assn. **[8455]**, PO Box 78636, Indianapolis, IN 46278, (317)387-1424

North Amer. Singer Owners Club - Address unknown since 1994.

North Amer. Singers Assn. **[10680]**, c/o Mrs. Lois Lynch, Sec., 1828 Pinecrest Dr., Dayton, OH 45414, (937)278-4606

North Amer. Singers Union **[★10680]**

North Amer. Single-Footed Horse Assn. **[★4937]**

North Amer. Single-footing Horse Assn. **[4937]**, PO Box 3170, Carefree, AZ 85377, (480)488-7169

Reference to "IO" in place of a book number signifies that the association may be found in the 45th edition of International Organizations.

North Amer. Singlefooting Horse Assn. [★4937]

North Amer. Ski Joring Assn. [23845], PO Box 1745, Red Lodge, MT 59068

North Amer. Ski Journalists Assn. [★IO]

North Amer. Skull Base Soc. [15401], 12100 Sunset Hills Rd., Ste. 130, Reston, VA 20190, (703)437-4377

North Amer. Small Bus. Intl. Trade Educators [★8031]

North Amer. Small Bus. Intl. Trade Educators [★IO]

North Amer. Snowsports Journalists Assn. [IO], Kelowna, BC, Canada

North Amer. Soccer Found. - Address unknown since 2002.

North Amer. Soccer League - Defunct.

North Amer. Soccer League Players Assn. - Defunct.

North Amer. Soc. of Adlerian Psychology [16162], 614 Old W Chocolate Ave., Hershey, PA 17033, (717)579-8795

North Amer. Soc. of Ancient and Medieval Wargamers [22471], c/o Michael Byrne, Sec., 18344 Gardenia Way, Gaithersburg, MD 20879

North Amer. Soc. for Cardiac Imaging [13920], 1500 Sunday Dr., Ste. 102, Raleigh, NC 27607, (919)861-4544

North American Society for Cardiac Imaging [IO], Raleigh, NC, United States

North Amer. Soc. for Childhood Onset Schizophrenia [15229], 88 Briarwood Dr. E, Berkeley Heights, NJ 07922

North Amer. Soc. for Dialysis and Transplantation [15295], c/o Laura Brazill-Nichols, Exec. Dir., 4010 Bentley Dr., Pearland, TX 77584, (281)997-1944

North Amer. Soc. of Homeopaths [14851], PO Box 450039, Sunrise, FL 33345-0039, (206)720-7000

North Amer. Soc. of Obstetric Medicine [15615], c/o Sandra Justa, Women and Infants' Hosp., 101 Dudley St., Providence, RI 02905, (401)274-1122

North Amer. Soc. for Oceanic History [10443], Dept. of History, Texas Christian Univ., Box 297260, Fort Worth, TX 76129

North Amer. Soc. for Oceanic History [IO], Fort Worth, TX, United States

North Amer. Soc. of Pacing and Electrophysiology [★IO]

North Amer. Soc. of Pacing and Electrophysiology [★13907]

North Amer. Soc. of Pacing and Electrophysiology/ Heart Rhythm Assn. [★13907]

North Amer. Soc. of Pacing and Electrophysiology/ Heart Rhythm Assn. [★IO]

North Amer. Soc. for Pediatric Gastroenterology [★14424]

North Amer. Soc. for Pediatric Gastroenterology, Hepatology and Nutrition [14424], PO Box 6, Flourtown, PA 19031, (215)233-0808

North Amer. Soc. for Pediatric Medicine [15891], c/o Pat Nixon, PhD, Pres., Exercise Sci. Dept., Syracuse Univ., Women's Bldg., Rm. 201, 820 Comstock Ave., Syracuse, NY 13244-5040, (336)758-4642

North Amer. Soc. of Phlebology [★16720]

North Amer. Soc. of Pipe Collectors [22093], PO Box 9642, Columbus, OH 43209-0642

North Amer. Soc. of Pipe Collectors [IO], Columbus, OH, United States

North Amer. Soc. for the Psychology of Sport and Physical Activity [23666], c/o Ann L. Smiley-Oyen, Sec.-Treas., Iowa State Univ., Dept. of Kinesiology, 244 Forker, Ames, IA 50011, (515)294-8261

North Amer. Soc. for Social Philosophy [10820], c/o Philosophy Documentation Center, PO Box 7147, Charlottesville, VA 22906-7147, (434)220-3300

North Amer. Soc. for the Sociology of Sport [7666], c/o Dean A. Purdy, Treas., PO Box 291, Bowling Green, OH 43403, (419)352-1928

North Amer. Soc. for Sport History [10139], c/o Ronald A. Smith, Sec.-Treas., PO Box 1026, 121 Dale St., Lemont, PA 16851-1026

North Amer. Soc. for Sport Mgt. [8990], W Gym 014, Slippery Rock Univ., Slippery Rock, PA 16057, (724)738-4812

North Amer. Soc. for Sport Mgt. [IO], Slippery Rock, PA, United States

North Amer. Soc. for the Stud. of Hypertension in Pregnancy [16342], c/o Chaur-Dong Hsu, MD, 7 Colvin Rd., Scarsdale, NY 10583, (914)593-5888

North Amer. Soc. for Trenchless Tech. [7819], 1655 N Ft. Myer Dr., Ste. 700, Arlington, VA 22209, (703)351-5252

North Amer. South Asian Bar Assn. [5527], c/o Bharati Sharma, VP-Individual Membership, Schiffrin amd Barroway, LLP, 280 King of Prussia Rd., Radnor, PA 19087, (484)270-1456

North Amer. South Asian Law Student Assn. [8773], c/o Shaheen Karolia, Treas., 1901 Minnehaha Ave., Apt. 419, Minneapolis, MN 55404

North Amer. South Asian Law Student Assn. [IO], Minneapolis, MN, United States

North Amer. South Devon Assn. [4284], 19590 E Main St., Ste. 202, Parker, CO 80138, (303)770-3130

North Amer. Spanish Language Acad. - Address unknown since 2002.

North Amer. Specialized Coagulation Lab. Assn. [14996], c/o Elizabeth Van Cott, MD, VP, Massachusetts Gen. Hosp., Gray-Jackson 235, 55 Fruit St., Boston, MA 02114, (617)726-9468

North Amer. Spine Soc. [15402], 7075 Veterans Blvd., Burr Ridge, IL 60527, (630)230-3600

North American Spine Society [IO], Burr Ridge, IL, United States

North Amer. Sport Lib. Network [IO], Calgary, AB, Canada

North Amer. Sports Fed. [IO], Drifton, PA, United States

North Amer. Sports Fed. [23065], Box K, Drifton, PA 18221, (570)454-1952

North Amer. Spotted Draft Horse Assn. [4938], c/o Sherry Shank, Sec.-Treas./Registrar, 17420 US Hwy. 20, Goshen, IN 46528, (574)825-1924

North American Spotted Draft Horse Association [IO], Goshen, IN, United States

North Amer. Squirrel Assn. [22773], c/o Bob Bandoli, Financial Mgr., PO Box 186, Holmen, WI 54636, (608)781-3100

North Amer. Steam Boat Assn. [21881], c/o Earle Jones, Ed., 1876 Lakeland Dr., Finksburg, MD 21048, (410)549-3446

North Amer. Steam Boat Assn. [IO], Finksburg, MD, United States

North Amer. Steel Alliance [2724], 2266 N State College Blvd., Fullerton, CA 92831, (714)256-8707

North Amer. Stone Skipping Assn. [22939], PO Box 189, Driftwood, TX 78619

North Amer. Stone Skipping Assn. [IO], Driftwood, TX, United States

North American Strawberry Growers Association [IO], Fremont, OH, United States

North Amer. Strawberry Growers Assn. [4750], c/o Steve Polter, Pres., Polter Berry Farm Inc., 2275 CR 239, Fremont, OH 43420, (419)332-5890

North Amer. St. Newspaper Assn. [18102], c/o Timothy Harris, Pres., 2129 2nd Ave., Seattle, WA 98121, (206)441-3247

North Amer. Strongman [23246], 11676 Mark Twain Ln., Bridgeton, MO 63044, (314)770-9279

North Amer. Student Cooperative Org. [★9190]

North Amer. Student Humanist Organizing Comm. - Defunct.

North Amer. Students of Cooperation [9190], PO Box 7715, Ann Arbor, MI 48107, (734)663-0889

North Amer. Sundial Soc. [9278], c/o Frederick W. Sawyer, III, Pres./Ed., 8 Sachem Dr., Glastonbury, CT 06033

North Amer. Sundial Soc. [IO], Glastonbury, CT, United States

North Amer. Super Sports - Defunct.

North Amer. Swing Club Assn. [★13097]

North Amer. Swing Club Assn. [★IO]

North Amer. Swiss Alliance [19399]

North Amer. Sys. Builders Assn. [★3706]

North Amer. Taiwan Stud. Assn. [9205], c/o Huey-Tyng Gau, Treas., Educ., UW-Madison, 4723 Sheboygan Ave., No. 221, Madison, WI 53705

North Amer. Taiwan Stud. Assn. [IO], Madison, WI, United States

North Amer. Taiwanese Medical Assn. [14712], 7923 Garden Grove Blvd., Garden Grove, CA 92841, (714)898-2275

North Amer. Tang Shou Tao Assn. [13645], PO Box 36235, Tucson, AZ 85740, (520)498-0678

North Amer. Tasar Assn. [IO], Vancouver, BC, Canada

North Amer. Technician Excellence [1897], 4100 N Fairfax Dr., Ste. 210, Arlington, VA 22203, (703)276-7247

North Amer. Teckel Club [22329], c/o Carrie Hamilton, Sec., 9621 Bachelor Rd., Kutztown, PA 19530

North Amer. Thermal Anal. Soc. [7797], c/o Lois Hall, Staff Mgt. Dir., Thermal Anal. Lab., Western Kentucky Univ., Center for Res. and Development, 2413 Nashville Rd., Bowling Green, KY 42101, (270)745-2220

North Amer. Thoroughbred Soc. [23538], 79 Brittin St., Madison, NJ 07940-2138

North Amer. Tiddlywinks Assn. [22472], c/o Rick Tucker, PO Box 1701, Falls Church, VA 22041-0701, (703)671-7098

North Amer. Tornado Assn. [23209], c/o James Young, USA Measurer, 401 County Rd. 413, Granby, CO 80446, (562)431-9930

North Amer. Torquay Soc. [22094], 136007 Maxson Ct., Spotsylvania, VA 22553

North Amer. Torquay Soc. [IO], Spotsylvania, VA, United States

North Amer. Toyah Fan Club [24951]

North Amer. Trackless Trolley Assn. - Address unknown since 1995.

North Amer. Trail Ride Conf. [23949], PO Box 224, Sedalia, CO 80135, (303)688-1677

North Amer. Trakehner Assn. [★4848]

North Amer. Trakehner Assn. [★IO]

North Amer. Transplant Coordinators Org. [16681], PO Box 15384, Lenexa, KS 66285-5384, (913)492-3600

North Amer. Trans. Mgt. Inst. [8212], 2460 W 26th Ave., Ste. 17-C, Denver, CO 80211, (303)952-4013

North Amer. Transvestite/Transsexual Soc. - Defunct.

North Amer. Trap Collector Assn. [22095], PO Box 94, Galloway, OH 43119, (614)878-6011

North Amer. Travel Assn. - Defunct.

North Amer. Travel Journalist Assn. [4066], 531 Main St., No. 902, El Segundo, CA 90245, (310)836-8712

North Amer. Truck Camper Owners Assn. [23025], PO Box 30408, Bellingham, WA 98228

North Amer. Trucking Industrial Relations Assn. [2906]

North Amer. Truffling Soc. [7354], PO Box 296, Corvallis, OR 97339, (541)752-2243

North Amer. Tug of War Fed. [★23959]

North Amer. Tuli Assn. [4285], c/o Ray E. Record, Exec. Sec., 10853 Forest Dr., College Station, TX 77845, (979)774-9095

North Amer. UFO Fed. - Defunct.

North Amer. Union Life Assurance Soc. [★19010]

North Amer. Union Life Assurance Soc. - Defunct.

North Amer. Vascular Biology Org. [16728], 18501 Kingshill Rd., Germantown, MD 20874-2211, (301)760-7745

North Amer. Vegetarian Soc. [11070], PO Box 72, Dolgeville, NY 13329, (518)568-7970

North Amer. Vexillological Assn. [11077], 1977 N Olden Ave. Extension, PMB 225, Trenton, NJ 08618-2193

North Amer. Victorian Stud. Assn. [11079], c/o Prof. Dino Franco Felluga, Chm., Purdue Univ., Dept. of English, 500 Oval Dr., West Lafayette, IN 47907

North Amer. Vodder Assn. of Lymphatic Therapy [15019], c/o Bonnie Peterson, Membership Comm. Chm., 833 Independence Dr., Longmont, CO 80501, (303)702-0557

North Amer. Vodder Assn. of Lymphatic Therapy [IO], Longmont, CO, United States

North Amer. Voyageur Coun. [10055], c/o Northwest Co. Fur Post, PO Box 51, Pine City, MN 55063

North Amer. Warmblood Assn. [★4852]

North Amer. Waterfowlers [★4465]

North Amer. Weed Mgt. Assn. [4106], PO Box 687, Meade, KS 67864, (620)873-8730

North American Weed Management Association [IO], Granby, CO, United States

North Amer. Wensleydale Sheep Assn. [5214], 4589 Fruitland Rd., Loma Rica, CA 95901, (530)743-5262

A star before a book entry number signifies that the name is not listed separately, but is mentioned within the entry.

North Amer. Wholesale Lumber Assn. [1611], 3601 Algonquin Rd., Ste. 400, Rolling Meadows, IL 60008, (847)870-7470

North Amer. Wild Sheep; Found. for [5318]

North Amer. Wildlife Enforcement Officers Assn. [5357], c/o Steve Kleiner, Sec.-Treas., PO Box 22, Hollidaysburg, PA 16648, (801)942-9432

North Amer. Wildlife Found. [★5308]

North Amer. Wildlife Park Found. [5358], Wolf Park, 4012 E 800 N, Battle Ground, IN 47920, (765)567-2265

North Amer. Wolf Assn. [5359], 23214 Tree Bright, Spring, TX 77373, (281)821-4439

North Amer. Working Bouvier Assn. [22330], 426 3rd Ave., West Haven, CT 06516, (203)241-6574

North Amer. Working Dog Assn. - Address unknown since 1989.

North Amer. Yacht Racing Union [★23232]

North Amer. YMCA Development Org. [13461], c/o Mary Zoller, 21 Chateau Trianon, Kenner, LA 70065, (504)464-7845

North American YMCA Development Organization [IO], Kenner, LA, United States

North Amer. Yngling Assn. [★23237]

North Amer. Yoga Fed. [11219], 114 E 28th St., 2A, New York, NY 10016, (212)696-9642

North Amer. Yoga Fed. [IO], New York, NY, United States

North America's SuperCorridor Coalition [3887], 901 Main St., Ste. 4400, Dallas, TX 75202, (214)744-1042

North Atlantic Assembly [★IO]

North Atlantic Coun. [IO], Brussels, Belgium

North Atlantic Network/U.S.A. - Defunct.

North Atlantic Ports Assn. - Address unknown since 1994.

North Atlantic Salmon Conservation Org. [IO], Edinburgh, United Kingdom

North Atlantic Seafood Assn. - Defunct.

North Atlantic Treaty Org. [IO], Brussels, Belgium

North Carolina Battleship Assn; USS [21411]

North Central Assn. of Colleges and Schools [★8297]

North Central Assn. of Colleges and Schools Commn. on Accreditation and School Improvement [8297], Arizona State Univ., PO Box 871008, Tempe, AZ 85287-1008, (480)773-6900

North Central Assn. Commn. on Accreditation and School Improvement [9093], Arizona State Univ., PO Box 871008, Tempe, AZ 85287-1008, (480)773-6900

North Central Conf. on Summer Schools [9201], c/o Jon C. Neidy, Pres., Bradley Univ., 1501 W Bradley Ave., Peoria, IL 61625, (309)677-2374

North Central Name Soc. - Defunct.

North Central Wholesalers Assn. [3064], 3271 Springcrest Dr., Hamilton, OH 45011, (513)895-0695

North Coast Export Company - Defunct.

North Coast Railroad Historical Soc. - Address unknown since 1999.

North Coast Region Music Teachers Assn. [IO], Sawtell, Australia

North Conway Inst. - Address unknown since 2001.

North Country Trail Assn. [23950], 229 E Main St., Lowell, MI 49331-1711, (616)897-5987

North Dakota Historical Soc. of Germans from Russia [★19078]

North Dakota Historical Soc. of Germans from Russia [★IO]

North Dakota State Univ. Alumni Assn. [18914], PO Box 5144, Fargo, ND 58105-5144, (701)231-6800

North-East Atlantic Fisheries Commn. [IO], London, United Kingdom

North East Chamber of Commerce [IO], Durham, United Kingdom

North Eastern Counties Welsh Pony and Cob Assn. [IO], Durham, United Kingdom

North of England Inst. of Mining and Mech. Engineers [IO], Newcastle upon Tyne, United Kingdom

North of England Zoological Soc. [IO], Chester, United Kingdom

North Hampshire Chamber of Commerce and Indus. [IO], Basingstoke, United Kingdom

North of Ireland Family History Soc. [IO], Belfast, United Kingdom

North Manchester Fellowship of Reconciliation [★18723]

North Pacific Anadromous Fish Commn. [IO], Vancouver, BC, Canada

North Pacific Fur Seal Commn. - Defunct.

North Sea Mine Force Assn. - Address unknown since 1995.

North/South Development Partnership; Katalysis [★17048]

North-South Inst. [IO], Ottawa, ON, Canada

North South Roundtable - Defunct.

North-South Skirmish Assn. [23727], PO Box 361, Bloomfield Hills, MI 48303-0361, (248)258-9007

North Staffordshire Chamber of Commerce and Indus. [IO], Stoke-On-Trent, United Kingdom

North Star Computer Soc. - Address unknown since 1995.

North Star Fund [12657], 520 8th Ave., 22nd Fl., 36th and 37th St., New York, NY 10018, (212)620-9110

North Star Network - Defunct.

North Vietnamese and Viet Cong Collecting Group - Defunct.

North West England and North Wales Narcotics Anonymous [IO], Manchester, United Kingdom

North West Frontier Fellowship - Address unknown since 1988.

North Yorkshire AIDS Action [IO], York, United Kingdom

Northamerican Assn. of Masters in Psychology [IO], Norman, OK, United States

Northamerican Assn. of Masters in Psychology [9030], PO Box 721270, Norman, OK 73070, (405)329-3030

Northamerican Heating, Refrigeration, and Airconditioning Wholesalers Assn. [★1882]

Northamerican Heating, Refrigeration, and Airconditioning Wholesalers Assn. [★IO]

Northamerican Heating, Refrigeration, and Airconditioning Wholesalers Assn. - Defunct.

Northamerican Ingredient Marketing Specialists [★1554]

Northamptonshire Chamber of Commerce [IO], Northampton, United Kingdom

Northeast Conf. on the Teaching of Foreign Languages [8742], c/o Dickinson Coll., PO Box 1773, Carlisle, PA 17013-2896, (717)245-1977

Northeast Dairy Cooperative Fed. - Defunct.

Northeast-Midwest Congressional Coalition - Address unknown since 1999.

Northeast-Midwest Inst. [18471], 50 F St. NW, No. 950, Washington, DC 20001, (202)544-5200

Northeast-Midwest Senate Coalition [18472], c/o Northeast Midwest Inst., 50 F St. NW, No. 950, Washington, DC 20001; (202)544-5200

Northeast Organic Farming Assn. - Defunct.

Northeast Sustainable Energy Assn. [6968], 50 Miles St., Greenfield, MA 01301, (413)774-6051

Northeast Waterfowl Comm. [★5295]

Northeastern Bird-Banding Assn. [★7413]

Northeastern Gay and Lesbian Alumni/ae Assn. [★18913]

Northeastern Loggers Assn. [1612], PO Box 69, Old Forge, NY 13420, (315)369-3078

Northeastern Lumber Mfrs. Assn. [1654], 272 Tuttle Rd., Cumberland, ME 04021, (207)829-6901

Northeastern Retail Lumber Assn. [1655], 585 N Greenbush Rd., Rensselaer, NY 12144, (518)286-1010

Northeastern Retail Lumberman's Assn. [★1655]

Northeastern Sangerbund of America - Address unknown since 2002.

Northeastern Spoon Collectors Guild [22096], PO Box 12072, Albany, NY 12212

Northeastern Weed Sci. Soc. [4990], c/o Jerry J. Baron, Pres.-Elect, IR-4, Rutgers Univ., 681 US Hwy. 1 S, North Brunswick, NJ 08902-3390, (732)932-4605

Northeastern Wood Utilization Coun. [★1612]

Northern Alberta Brain Injury Soc. [IO], Edmonton, AB, Canada

Northern Cross Soc. - Address unknown since 2000.

Northern Environmental Comm. - Defunct.

Northern Far East Returned Missionaries Assn. [20504], PO Box 94342, Las Vegas, NV 89193-4342, (801)964-2825

Northern Far East Returned Missionaries Assn. [IO], Las Vegas, NV, United States

Northern Fishing Vessel Owners Assn. - Defunct.

Northern Forest Products Assn. [★IO]

Northern Fraternal Life Insurance - Address unknown since 1999.

Northern Frontier Visitors Assn. [IO], Yellowknife, NT, Canada

Northern Hardwood and Pine Mfrs. Assn. - Defunct.

Northern Heraldic Assn. [★IO]

Northern Illinois Citizens Against the Antiballistic Missile - Defunct.

Northern Indiana Muck Crop Growers Assn. - Defunct.

Northern Ireland

Children's Friendship Proj. for Northern Ireland [13478]

Doors of Hope [17931]

Proj. Children [11717]

Northern Ireland Archery Soc. [IO], Craigavon, United Kingdom

Northern Ireland Assn. of Chefs and Cooks [IO], Dungannon, United Kingdom

Northern Ireland Assn. for Mental Hea. [IO], Belfast, United Kingdom

Northern Ireland Bankers' Assn. [IO], Belfast, United Kingdom

Northern Ireland Bat Gp. [IO], Belfast, United Kingdom

Northern Ireland Chamber of Commerce and Indus. [IO], Belfast, United Kingdom

Northern Ireland Chest Heart and Stroke Assn. [IO], Belfast, United Kingdom

Northern Ireland; Children's Friendship Proj. for [13478]

Northern Ireland Fed. of Housing Associations [IO], Belfast, United Kingdom

Northern Ireland Food and Drink Assn. [IO], Belfast, United Kingdom

Northern Ireland Grain Trade Assn. [IO], Moira, United Kingdom

Northern Ireland Hotels and Caterers Assn. [★IO]

Northern Ireland Hotels Fed. [IO], Belfast, United Kingdom

Northern Ireland Human Rights Commn. [IO], Belfast, United Kingdom

Northern Ireland Local Govt. Assn. [IO], Belfast, United Kingdom

Northern Ireland Meat Exporters Assn. [IO], Lisburn, United Kingdom

Northern Ireland Mixed Marriage Assn. [IO], Belfast, United Kingdom

Northern Ireland Orienteering Assn. [IO], Lisburn, United Kingdom

Northern Ireland Pre-School Playgroups Assn. (NIPPA) [★IO]

Northern Ireland Public Ser. Alliance [IO], Belfast, United Kingdom

Northern Late Model Racing Assn. [23084], c/o Harold Schill, Jr., Pres., 1817 8th Ave. N, Grand Forks, ND 58203, (701)356-5320

Northern Libraries Colloquy [★10380]

Northern Libraries Colloquy [★IO]

Northern Mariana Islands Swimming Fed. [IO], Saipan, Northern Mariana Islands

Northern Mariana Islands Tennis Assn. [IO], Saipan, Northern Mariana Islands

Northern Marianas Islands Track and Field Fed. [IO], Saipan, Northern Mariana Islands

Northern Masonic Jurisdiction; Supreme Coun., Ancient Accepted Scottish Rite of Free-Masonry [19252]

Northern Michigan Univ. Alumni Assn. [18915], 603 Cohodas, Marquette, MI 49855, (906)227-2610

Northern Nut Growers Assn. [2842], c/o Mr. Thomas Molnar, PhD, Sec., 59 Dudley Rd., Foran Hall, New Brunswick, NJ 08901, (732)932-9711

Northern Nut Growers Assn. [IO], Niagara-on-the-Lake, ON, Canada

Northern Offshore Fed. [★IO]

Northern Rhodesian Game Preservation and Hunting Assn. [★IO]

Reference to "IO" in place of a book number signifies that the association may be found in the 45th edition of International Organizations.

Northern Rockies Alaska Highway Tourism Assn. [IO], Fort St. John, BC, Canada
Northern Sash and Door Jobbers Assn. [★600]
Northern Shipowners' Defence Club [IO], Oslo, Norway
Northern Student Movement - Defunct.
Northern Textile Assn. [★3795]
Northern Trail Horse Riders Club [IO], Spalding, Australia
Northern Virginia Functional Jaw Stud. Club [★14115]
Northern Woods Logging Assn. - Address unknown since 2001.
Northhamptonshire Chamber of Commerce, Training and Enterprise [★IO]
Northland Miniature Horse Club [IO], Whangarei, New Zealand
Northridge Alumni Assn; California State Univ. - [18883]
Northwest Alaska Native Assn. [★12627]
Northwest Assn. of Accredited Schools [8298], 1910 Univ. Dr., Boise, ID 83706-3007, (208)426-5727
Northwest Assn. of Accredited Schools [IO], Boise, ID, United States
Northwest Assn. of Animal Protective Agencies - Defunct.
Northwest Assn. of Horticulturists, Entomologists and Plant Pathologists - Defunct.
Northwest Assn. of Private Colleges and Universities - Address unknown since 1995.
Northwest Assn. of Schools and Colleges [★8298]
Northwest Assn. of Schools and Colleges [★IO]
Northwest Assn. of Schools and Colleges Commn. on Schools [★IO]
Northwest Assn. of Schools and Colleges Commn. on Schools [★8298]
Northwest Assn. of Secondary and Higher Schools [★8298]
Northwest Assn. of Secondary and Higher Schools [★IO]
Northwest Atlantic Fisheries Org. [IO], Dartmouth, NS, Canada
Northwest Bird and Mammal Soc; Pacific [★7364]
Northwest Cartoonists Assn. [★9561]
Northwest Cherry Briners - Address unknown since 2007.
Northwest Cherry Growers [4751], 105 S 18th St., Ste. 205, Yakima, WA 98901-2149, (509)453-4837
Northwest Coalition for Alternatives to Pesticides [13328], PO Box 1393, Eugene, OR 97440-1393, (541)344-5044
Northwest Drama Conf. - Address unknown since 2007.
Northwest Dried Fruit Export Assn. - Defunct.
Northwest Ecosystem Alliance [★4546]
Northwest Energy Efficiency Alliance [4528], 529 SW 3rd Ave., Ste. 600, Portland, OR 97204, (503)827-8416
Northwest Farm Managers Assn. [4640], c/o Inst. for Regional Stud. and Univ. Archives, PO Box 5599, Fargo, ND 58105-5599, (701)231-8914
Northwest Festivals Assn. - Address unknown since 2002.
Northwest Fisheries Assn. [3500], 2208 NW Market St., Ste. 318, Seattle, WA 98107, (206)789-6197
Northwest Forest Workers Assn. - Defunct.
Northwest Forestry Assn. [1613], 1500 SW 1st Ave., Ste. 700, Portland, OR 97201, (503)222-9505
Northwest Fruit Exporters [4752], 105 S 18th St., Ste. 227, Yakima, WA 98901, (509)576-8004
Northwest Furniture Mfrs. Assn. - Defunct.
Northwest Grain Dealers; Pacific [★4314]
Northwest Guides Assn. - Defunct.
Northwest Hardwood Assn. [★1630]
Northwest Horticultural Coun. [4753], 105 S 18th St., Ste. 105, Yakima, WA 98901, (509)453-3193
Northwest Marine Indus. [★2589]
Northwest Marine Trade Assn. [2589], 1900 N Northlake Way, No. 233, Seattle, WA 98103-9087, (206)634-0911
Northwest Medical Teams Intl. [★12869]
Northwest Medical Teams Intl. [IO], Portland, OR, United States
Northwest Mining Assn. [2753], 10 N Post St., Ste. 220, Spokane, WA 99201, (509)624-1158

Northwest Nazarene Univ. Alumni Assn. [18916], 623 Holly St., Nampa, ID 83686, (208)467-8011
Northwest Pea Growers and Dealers; Pacific [★4314]
Northwest; Pear Bur. [4755]
Northwest Pine Assn. [★1613]
Northwest Quoin Key Assn. - Defunct.
Northwest Regional Spinners' Assn. [22172], c/o Kris Heidner, Membership Chair, 3300 166th Pl. SW, Lynnwood, WA 98037, (425)741-2774
Northwest Salmon Canners Assn. - Address unknown since 1995.
Northwest Schooner Soc. [21882], PO Box 9504, Seattle, WA 98109, (800)551-NWSS
Northwest Ski Assn; Pacific [23754]
Northwest Steam Soc. [22978], PO Box 9639, Seattle, WA 98109, (206)310-4565
Northwest Stud; Center for Pacific [7647]
Northwest Territory Alliance [9374], c/o Robin Klepfer, Adjutant Gen., 11405 E 63rd St., Indianapolis, IN 46236-3925, (317)823-4556
Northwest Territory, Canadian and French Heritage Center [★20720]
Northwest Territory, Canadian and French Heritage Center [★IO]
Northwest Territory Genealogical Soc. [IO], Yellowknife, NT, Canada
North West Token Kai - Defunct.
Northwestern Lumber Assn. [1614], 1405 Lilac Dr. N, No. 130, Minneapolis, MN 55422, (763)544-6822
Northwestern Lumbermen's Assn. [★1614]
Northwestern Vertebrate Biology; Soc. for [7364]
Norton Owners' Assn; U.S. [★22684]
Norvell Family Org. [21014]

Norway
　Norwegian Lundehund Assn. of Am. [22332]
　Scandinavian Tourist Boards [24372]
　Vesterheim Genealogical Center and Naeseth Lib. [21155]
Norway-America Assn. [IO], Oslo, Norway
Norway; Daughters of [★19293]
Norway; Trade Commn. of [★24283]

Norwegian
　Innovation Norway - U.S. [24283]
　Norse Fed. [IO]
　Norway-America Assn. [IO]
　Norwegian Amer. Chamber of Commerce - New York City [24292]
　Norwegian-American Historical Assn. [10759]
　Norwegian-American Historical Association [IO]
　Norwegian Club/Det Norske Selskab [19292]
　Norwegian Coun. for Cultural Affairs [IO]
　Norwegian Elkhound Assn. of Am. [22331]
　Norwegian Forest Cat Breed Coun. [21914]
　Norwegian Lundehund Assn. of Am. [22332]
　Sons of Norway [19293]
　Sons of Norway [IO]
　Vesterheim Genealogical Center and Naeseth Lib. [21155]
Norwegian Acad. of Sci. and Letters [IO], Oslo, Norway
Norwegian Acad. of Technological Sciences [IO], Trondheim, Norway
Norwegian ACM Chap. [IO], Oslo, Norway
Norwegian Actors' Equity Assn. [IO], Oslo, Norway
Norwegian Acupuncture Assn. [IO], Oslo, Norway
Norwegian Aero Club [IO], Oslo, Norway
Norwegian Aikido Fed. [IO], Broettum, Norway
Norwegian Amer. Chamber of Commerce - New York City [IO], New York, NY, United States
Norwegian Amer. Chamber of Commerce - New York City [24292], 800 3rd Ave., New York, NY 10022, (212)421-1655
Norwegian-American Historical Assn. [10759], 1510 St. Olaf Ave., Northfield, MN 55057-1097, (507)646-3221
Norwegian-American Historical Association [IO], Northfield, MN, United States
Norwegian Assn. of Advertisers [IO], Oslo, Norway
Norwegian Assn. of Agricultural Journalists [IO], Hamar, Norway
Norwegian Assn. of Authors of Light Music and Texts [★IO]
Norwegian Assn. for Energy Economics [IO], Oslo, Norway

Norwegian Assn. of Geomorphologists [IO], Blindern, Norway
Norwegian Assn. of Landscape Architects [IO], Oslo, Norway
Norwegian Assn. of Literary Translators [IO], Oslo, Norway
Norwegian Assn. of Municipal Engineers [IO], Oslo, Norway
Norwegian Assn. of Occupational Therapists [IO], Oslo, Norway
Norwegian Assn. of Pharmaceutical Manufacturers [IO], Oslo, Norway
Norwegian Assn. of Res. Workers [IO], Oslo, Norway
Norwegian Assn. of Special Libraries [IO], Oslo, Norway
Norwegian Asthma and Allergy Assn. [IO], Oslo, Norway
Norwegian Astronautical Soc. [IO], Oslo, Norway
Norwegian Athletics Fed. [IO], Oslo, Norway
Norwegian Authors' Union [IO], Oslo, Norway
Norwegian Bandy Federation/Floorball Sect. [IO], Oslo, Norway
Norwegian Bible Soc. [IO], Oslo, Norway
Norwegian Billiard Fed. [IO], Oslo, Norway
Norwegian Biochemical Soc. [IO], Oslo, Norway
Norwegian Bioindustry Assn. [IO], Oslo, Norway
Norwegian Botanical Soc. [★IO]
Norwegian Brewers and Soft Drink Producers [IO], Oslo, Norway
Norwegian Cable-TV Assn. [IO], Fetsund, Norway
Norwegian Canoe Assn. [IO], Oslo, Norway
Norwegian Chem. Soc. [IO], Oslo, Norway
Norwegian Church Aid [IO], Oslo, Norway
Norwegian Club/Det Norske Selskab [19292]
Norwegian Coun. for Cultural Affairs [IO], Oslo, Norway
Norwegian Coun. On Cardiovascular Diseases [IO], Oslo, Norway
Norwegian Coun. for Sci. and Indus. Res. [★IO]
Norwegian Cricket Bd. [IO], Oslo, Norway
Norwegian Cystic Fibrosis Assn. [IO], Oslo, Norway
Norwegian Defence and Security Indus. Assn. [IO], Oslo, Norway
Norwegian Dental Assn. [IO], Oslo, Norway
Norwegian Dermatological Soc. [IO], Oslo, Norway
Norwegian Diabetes Assn. [IO], Oslo, Norway
Norwegian Dietetics Assn. [IO], Oslo, Norway
Norwegian Dyslexia Assn. [IO], Oslo, Norway
Norwegian Electrotechnical Comm. [IO], Lysaker, Norway
Norwegian Elkhound Assn. of Am. [22331], c/o Karen Elvin, Corresponding Sec., 14465 St. Croix Trail N, Marine on St. Croix, MN 55047, (651)433-4666
Norwegian Epilepsy Assn. [IO], Oslo, Norway
Norwegian Farmers' Union [IO], Oslo, Norway
Norwegian Fed. of Organisations of Disabled People [IO], Oslo, Norway
Norwegian Fibromyalgia Patients' Assn. [IO], Lysaker, Norway
Norwegian Fishermen's Sales Org. for Pelagic Fish [IO], Bergen, Norway
Norwegian Fjord Assn. of North America - Address unknown since 2008.
Norwegian Fjord Horse Registry [4939], 1203 Appian Dr., Webster, NY 14580, (585)872-4114
Norwegian Football Assn. [IO], Oslo, Norway
Norwegian Forest Cat Breed Coun. [21914], c/o Cat Fanciers' Assn., PO Box 1005, Manasquan, NJ 08736-0805
Norwegian Formation Evaluation Soc. [IO], Hafrsfjord, Norway
Norwegian Fur Breeders' Assn. [IO], Oslo, Norway
Norwegian Gastroenterological Assn. [IO], Fredrikstad, Norway
Norwegian Genealogical Soc. [IO], Oslo, Norway
Norwegian Geotechnical Inst. [IO], Oslo, Norway
Norwegian Geotechnical Soc. [IO], Oslo, Norway
Norwegian Gerontological Soc. [IO], Oslo, Norway
Norwegian Heraldic Assn. [IO], Oslo, Norway
Norwegian Heraldry Soc. [★IO]
Norwegian Hospitality Assn. [IO], Oslo, Norway
Norwegian Hotel and Restaurant Assn. [★IO]
Norwegian Immune Deficiency Found. [IO], Alesund, Norway

A star before a book entry number signifies that the name is not listed separately, but is mentioned within the entry.

Norwegian Independent Meat Assn. [IO], Oslo, Norway

Norwegian Inst. of Intl. Affairs [IO], Oslo, Norway

Norwegian Inst. of Local History [IO], Oslo, Norway

Norwegian Inst. of Public Accountants [IO], Oslo, Norway

Norwegian Inst. of State Authorized Public Accountants [★IO]

Norwegian Inst. for Urban and Regional Res. [IO], Oslo, Norway

Norwegian Inventors' Assn. [IO], Stavanger, Norway

Norwegian Labour Party [IO], Oslo, Norway

Norwegian League of Handicap Organizations [★IO]

Norwegian Lib. Assn. [IO], Oslo, Norway

Norwegian Literature Abroad [IO], Oslo, Norway

Norwegian Luge, Bobsleigh and Skeleton Fed. [IO], Oslo, Norway

Norwegian Lundehund Assn. of Am. [22332], PO Box 301, Tomales, CA 94971

Norwegian Lutheran Young People's Societies of America; Federated [★20225]

Norwegian Martial Arts Fed. [IO], Oslo, Norway

Norwegian Media Businesses' Assn. [IO], Oslo, Norway

Norwegian Medical Assn. [IO], Oslo, Norway

Norwegian Mountain Touring Assn. [IO], Oslo, Norway

Norwegian Multiple Sclerosis Soc. [IO], Oslo, Norway

Norwegian Natl. Meat Assn. [★IO]

Norwegian Neuroscience Soc. [IO], Oslo, Norway

Norwegian Non-Fiction Writers and Translators Assn. [IO], Oslo, Norway

Norwegian Nurses Org. [IO], Oslo, Norway

Norwegian Oil Indus. Assn. [IO], Stavanger, Norway

Norwegian Oil Spill Control Assn. [IO], Horten, Norway

Norwegian Olympic Comm. [★IO]

Norwegian Olympic Comm. and Confed. of Sports [IO], Oslo, Norway

Norwegian Operations Res. [IO], Sandvika, Norway

Norwegian Org. for Children and Youth with Rheumatism [IO], Oslo, Norway

Norwegian Org. of Interior Architects and Furniture Designers [IO], Oslo, Norway

Norwegian Osteogenesis Imperfecta Found. [IO], Oslo, Norway

Norwegian Ostomy Assn. [IO], Oslo, Norway

Norwegian Parkinson Assn. [IO], Oslo, Norway

Norwegian Peace Alliance [IO], Oslo, Norway

Norwegian Peace Assn. [IO], Oslo, Norway

Norwegian PEN [IO], Oslo, Norway

Norwegian Physical Soc. [IO], Trondheim, Norway

Norwegian Physiotherapist Assn. [IO], Oslo, Norway

Norwegian Playwrights' Assn. [IO], Oslo, Norway

Norwegian Press Assn. [IO], Oslo, Norway

Norwegian Proj. Mgt. Assn. [IO], Oslo, Norway

Norwegian Psoriasis Assn. [IO], Oslo, Norway

Norwegian Psychological Assn. [IO], Oslo, Norway

Norwegian Publishers' Assn. [IO], Oslo, Norway

Norwegian Pulp and Paper Indus. Assn. [IO], Oslo, Norway

Norwegian Raw Fish Org. [IO], Tromso, Norway

Norwegian Rose Soc. [IO], Holmsbu, Norway

Norwegian Route 66 Assn. [IO], Radal, Norway

Norwegian Seafood Assn. [IO], Trondheim, Norway

Norwegian Seafood Export Coun. [IO], Charlestown, MA, United States

Norwegian Seafood Export Coun. [1486]

Norwegian Seafood Fed. [IO], Oslo, Norway

Norwegian Seamen's Assn., U.S. Br. - Defunct.

Norwegian Sect. of the Intl. Confed. for Electroacoustic Music [IO], Oslo, Norway

Norwegian Shipowners' Assn. [IO], Oslo, Norway

Norwegian Signal Processing Soc. [IO], Stavanger, Norway

Norwegian Singers Assn. of America - Address unknown since 2001.

Norwegian Soc. of Agricultural Engg. [IO], Aas, Norway

Norwegian Soc. for Autism [★IO]

Norwegian Soc. for Biomedical Engg. [IO], Gjovik, Norway

Norwegian Soc. of Cardiology [IO], Oslo, Norway

Norwegian Soc. of Chartered Tech. and Sci. Professionals [IO], Oslo, Norway

Norwegian Soc. of Composers [IO], Oslo, Norway

Norwegian Soc. for the Conservation of Nature/ Friends of the Earth Norway [IO], Oslo, Norway

Norwegian Soc. of Dermatology [IO], Bergen, Norway

Norwegian Soc. of Engineers [IO], Oslo, Norway

Norwegian Soc. of Financial Analysts [IO], Oslo, Norway

Norwegian Soc. for Image Processing and Pattern Recognition [IO], Oslo, Norway

Norwegian Soc. for Immunology [IO], Oslo, Norway

Norwegian Soc. for Medical Informatics [IO], Oslo, Norway

Norwegian Soc. of Pharmacology and Toxicology [IO], Oslo, Norway

Norwegian Soc. for Quality in Healthcare [IO], Vennesla, Norway

Norwegian Soc. for Rheumatology [IO], Oslo, Norway

Norwegian Soc. for Virology [IO], Bergen, Norway

Norwegian Squash Assn. [IO], Stavanger, Norway

Norwegian Tenants Assn. [★IO]

Norwegian Tennis Assn. [IO], Oslo, Norway

Norwegian Trade Coun. [★IO]

Norwegian Trade Coun. [★24283]

Norwegian Trade Coun. - London Br. [IO], London, United Kingdom

Norwegian Trade Coun. - U.S. [★IO]

Norwegian Trade Coun. - U.S. [★24283]

Norwegian Union of Journalists [IO], Oslo, Norway

Norwegian Venture Capital and Private Equity Assn. [IO], Oslo, Norway

Norwegian Veterinary Assn. [IO], Oslo, Norway

Norwegian Women and Family Assn. [IO], Oslo, Norway

Norwegian Wood - The Beatles Fan Club of Norway [IO], Kristiansund, Norway

Norwegian Writers for Children [IO], Oslo, Norway

Norweigan Cancer Registry [★IO]

Norweigan Luge and Bob Fed. [★IO]

Norwich Campaign for Nuclear Disarmament [IO], Norwich, United Kingdom

Norwich, Connecticut; Soc. of the Founders of [★10063]

Norwich, Connecticut; Soc. of the Founders and Friends of [10063]

Norwich and Norfolk Terrier Club [22333], c/o Carol Jordan, Membership Chair, 604 Old Fritztown Rd., Reading, PA 19607-1016, (610)775-0792

Norwich Terrier Club [★22333]

Nose, and Throat Advances in Children; Soc. for Ear, [15827]

Nostalgia Drag Racing Assn. - Address unknown since 1999.

Nostalgiana Collectors Club - Defunct.

Nostalgic Nova; Natl. [21736]

Not-for-Profit Hospitals; Volunteer Trustees of [14902]

Not-For-Profit Services Assn. [50], One Valmont Plz., 4th Fl., Omaha, NE 68154, (402)964-3805

Not Forgotten Assn. [IO], London, United Kingdom

Notaries Public
   Amer. Soc. of Notaries [6146]
   Luxembourg Chamber of Notaries [IO]
   Natl. Notary Assn. [6147]

Notation Bur; Dance [9878]

Notch - Address unknown since 1999.

Notion Round Table - Defunct.

Notions
   Belt and Button Assn. [2836]
   Graphic Products Assn. [2837]
   Home Sewing Assn. [3784]

Notions and Crafts Assn; Southeastern Fabric, [3798]

Nottinghamshire Chamber of Commerce and Indus. [IO], Nottingham, United Kingdom

Nouveau Parti Democratique du Canada [★IO]

Nova; Natl. Nostalgic [21736]

Nova Scotia Arm Wrestling Assn. [IO], Lower Sackville, NS, Canada

Nova Scotia Assn. of Naturopathic Doctors [IO], Wolfville, NS, Canada

Nova Scotia Curling Assn. [IO], Halifax, NS, Canada

Nova Scotia Equestrian Fed. [IO], Halifax, NS, Canada

Nova Scotia Hospice Palliative Care Assn. [IO], Truro, NS, Canada

Nova Scotia Salmon Assn. [IO], Chester, NS, Canada

Nova Scotia Snowboard Assn. [IO], Middle Sackville, NS, Canada

Nova Scotia Snowboarding Assn. [IO], Halifax, NS, Canada

Nova Scotia Trails Fed. [IO], Halifax, NS, Canada

Nova Scotia Wheelchair Sports Fed. [IO], Centreville, NS, Canada

Novelists, Inc. [4067], PO Box 2037, Manhattan, KS 66505

Novell Users Intl. [3725], c/o Brent Sharp, Exec. Dir., 1800 S Novell Pl., MS/H-811, Provo, UT 84606, (800)228-4684

Novelties and Allied Prdts. of the U.S. and Canada; Intl. Union of Dolls, Toys, Playthings, [★24196]

Novelty and Prdt.ion Workers; Intl. Union of Allied [24196]

Novelty Salt and Pepper Shakers Club [22097], PO Box 416, Gladstone, OR 97027-0416

Novelty Trade Assn; Souvenir and [★861]

Novelty Trade Assn; Souvenir and Gift [★861]

November Coalition [18690], 282 W Astor Ave., Colville, WA 99114, (509)684-1550

Now Christian Freedom Intl. [★20521]

Now Christian Freedom Intl. [★IO]

NOW Legal Comm. [★17546]

NOW Legal Defense and Educ. Fund [★17546]

NOWZUWAN [IO], Chittagong, Bangladesh

Noyes Found; Jessie Smith [4583]

NPES - The Assn. for Suppliers of Printing, Publishing and Converting Technologies [1782], 1899 Preston White Dr., Reston, VA 20191-5468, (703)264-7200

NPTA Alliance [2891], 500 Bi-County Blvd., Ste. 200E, Farmingdale, NY 11735, (631)777-2223

NRH Center for Hea. and Disability Res. [14233], c/o Natl. Rehabilitation Hosp., 102 Irving St. NW, Washington, DC 20010, (202)466-1900

NROTC Colleges and Universities; Assn. of [8884]

NSAC Ministerial Assn. - Defunct.

NSAC, The Natl. Soc. for Children and Adults with Autism [★13723]

NSDAP Auslands-Und Aufbauorganisation [18329], Box 6414, Lincoln, NE 68506

NSDAP Auslands-Und Aufbauorganisation [IO], Lincoln, NE, United States

NSDAP Auslandsorganisation [★IO]

NSDAP Auslandsorganisation [★18329]

NSF Intl. [16249], 789 N Dixboro Rd., PO Box 130140, Ann Arbor, MI 48113-0140, (734)769-8010

NSF Intl. [IO], Ann Arbor, MI, United States

NSGA Team Dealer Div. [3648], 1601 Feehanville Dr., Ste. 300, Mount Prospect, IL 60056-6042, (847)296-6742

NSO of COSA [★13072]

NSO of COSA [★IO]

NSU Club of America - Defunct.

NSU Enthusiasts U.S.A. [21746], 2909 Utah Pl., Alton, IL 62002, (618)462-9195

NSU Register [★22677]

NSU/U.S.A. Enthusiasts' Club [★21746]

NSW Dept. of Primary Indus. Rural Women's Network [IO], Orange, Australia

NSW Fed. of Housing Associations [IO], Surry Hills, Australia

NSW Ferret Welfare Soc. [IO], Dee Why, Australia

NSW Right to Life Assn. [IO], Sydney, Australia

NSX Club of Am. [21747], PO Box A3416, Chicago, IL 60690-3416, (877)679-2582

NTID's Center on Employment [12095], Lyndon Baines Johnson Bldg., Rochester Inst. of Tech., 52 Lomb Memorial Dr., Rochester, NY 14623-5604, (585)475-6219

NTL Inst. [★8415]

NTL Inst. [★IO]

NTL Institute for Applied Behavioral Sciences [IO], Alexandria, VA, United States

NTL Inst. for Applied Behavioral Sciences [8415], 300 N Lee St., Ste. 300, Alexandria, VA 22314-2630, (703)548-8840

Nu Sigma Nu - Defunct.

Nu-Trans Cooperative - Address unknown since 2000.

Reference to "IO" in place of a book number signifies that the association may be found in the 45th edition of International Organizations.

Nubian Club; Natl. [★4135]
NuBian Exchange News [2770]
Nuclear
Amer. Bd. of Nuclear Medicine [15419]
Amer. Coll. of Nuclear Medicine [15421]
Amer. Coll. of Nuclear Physicians [15422]
Amer. Glovebox Soc. [7384]
Amer. Nuclear Soc. [7385]
Bulletin of the Atomic Scientists [7603]
Canadian Nuclear Soc. [IO]
Chinese Nuclear Soc. [IO]
Commn. on Nuclear Physics [IO]
Comm. to Bridge the Gap [18145]
Croatian Nuclear Soc. [IO]
Egyptian Nuclear Physics Assn. [IO]
IEEE Nuclear and Plasma Sciences Soc. [7386]
Inst. of Nuclear Materials Mgt. [7387]
Joint Inst. for Nuclear Res. [IO]
Korean Nuclear Soc. [IO]
Malaysian Nuclear Soc. [IO]
Natl. Environmental Coalition of Native Americans [5037]
Natl. Org. of Test, Res., and Training Reactors [7388]
Natl. Whistleblower Center [12982]
Nuclear Info. and Records Mgt. Assn. [7389]
Nuclear Medicine Tech. Certification Bd. [15423]
Nuclear Suppliers Assn. [7390]
Preparatory Commn. for the Comprehensive Nuclear-Test-Ban Treaty Org. [IO]
Professional Reactor Operator Soc. [7391]
Soc. of Nuclear Medicine [15424]
Soc. of Nuclear Medicine Technologist Sect. [15425]
Thermal and Nuclear Power Engg. Soc. [IO]
Utilities Ser. Alliance [3966]
Women in Nuclear Global [IO]
Women in Nuclear Korea [IO]
Nuclear Action Project - Address unknown since 2001.
Nuclear Age Peace Found. [18229], PMB 121, 1187 Coast Village Rd., Ste. 1, Santa Barbara, CA 93108-2794, (805)965-3443
Nuclear Age Peace Found. [IO], Santa Barbara, CA, United States
Nuclear Age Rsrc. Center [★18151]
Nuclear Arms Alert Network - Defunct.
Nuclear Arms Control; Lawyers Alliance for [★18158]
Nuclear Arms; Intl. Assn. of Lawyers Against [IO]
Nuclear Attack; Assn. for Community-Wide Protection from [★5559]
Nuclear Club [★18163]
Nuclear Compact; Western Interstate [★18139]
Nuclear Control Inst. [18163], 1000 Connecticut Ave. NW, Ste. 400, Washington, DC 20036, (202)822-8444
Nuclear Disarmament; Women's Action for [★18175]
Nuclear Energy
Alliance for Nuclear Accountability [18125]
Arab Atomic Energy Agency [IO]
Atomic Energy Soc. of Japan [IO]
Australian Inst. of Nuclear Sci. and Engg. [IO]
Australian Nuclear Assn. [IO]
Australian Nuclear Sci. and Tech. Org. [IO]
British Nuclear Energy Soc. [IO]
Campaign for Nuclear Phaseout [IO]
Canadian Coalition for Nuclear Responsibility [IO]
Canadian Nuclear Assn. [IO]
CANDU Owners Gp. [IO]
Comm. of Atomic Bomb Survivors in the U.S. [18144]
Comm. for Nuclear Responsibility [18126]
Comm. for Nuclear Responsibility [IO]
Environmental Coalition on Nuclear Power [18127]
European Atomic Forum [IO]
European Nuclear Soc. [IO]
European Org. for Nuclear Res. [IO]
Friends of Hibakusha [IO]
Friends of Hibakusha [18128]
German Atomic Forum [IO]
Global Issues Rsrc. Center [18151]
Global Village Inst. [6235]
Inst. of Nuclear Power Operations [7392]

Intl. Atomic Energy Agency [IO]
Intl. Nuclear Law Assn. [IO]
Mutual Atomic Energy Liability Underwriters [2201]
Natl. Assn. of Radiation Survivors [18129]
Natl. Campaign for Radioactive Waste Safety [18130]
Natl. Commn. on Nuclear Safety and Safeguards [IO]
Natl. Org. of Test, Res., and Training Reactors [7388]
Netherlands Atomic Forum [IO]
NKS - Nordic Nuclear Safety Res. [IO]
Nuclear Energy Info. Ser. [18131]
Nuclear Energy Inst. [6969]
Nuclear Info. and Records Mgt. Assn. [7389]
Nuclear Info. and Rsrc. Ser. [18132]
Nuclear Safety Standards Commn. [IO]
Nuclear Suppliers Assn. [7390]
Nukewatch [18133]
OECD Nuclear Energy Agency [IO]
Professional Reactor Operator Soc. [7391]
Public Citizen's Critical Mass Energy and Env. Prog. [18134]
Swedish Anti-Nuclear Movement [IO]
Task Force Against Nuclear Pollution [18135]
Three Mile Island Alert [18136]
Union of Concerned Scientists [18137]
Utilities Ser. Alliance [3966]
We the People [18138]
Western Interstate Energy Board/WINB [18139]
World Info. Ser. on Energy [IO]
Nuclear Energy Info. Ser. [18131], 3411 W Diversey Ave., No. 16, Chicago, IL 60647, (773)342-7650
Nuclear Energy Inst. [6969], 1776 I St. NW, Ste. 400, Washington, DC 20006-3708, (202)739-8000
Nuclear Energy Women - Defunct.
Nuclear Engineers; Institution of [IO]
Nuclear Free America - Address unknown since 2003.
Nuclear Free Philippines Coalition [IO], Quezon City, Philippines
Nuclear Free Zone Registry - Defunct.
Nuclear Freeze Found. - Defunct.
Nuclear Freeze Political Action Comm. - Defunct.
Nuclear Info. and Records Mgt. Assn. [7389], 10 Almas Rd., Windham, NH 03087-1105, (603)432-6476
Nuclear Info. and Rsrc. Ser. [18132], 6930 Carroll Ave., Ste. 340, Takoma Park, MD 20912, (301)270-6477
Nuclear Insurers; Amer. [3948]
Nuclear Issues Education Project - Defunct.
Nuclear Mgt. and Resources Coun. [★6969]
Nuclear Medicine
Amer. Assn. for Women Radiologists [16271]
Amer. Bd. of Nuclear Medicine [15419]
Amer. Bd. of Sci. in Nuclear Medicine [15420]
Amer. Coll. of Nuclear Medicine [15421]
Amer. Coll. of Nuclear Physicians [15422]
Amer. Soc. of Radiologic Technologists [15131]
Argentine Assn. of Biology and Nuclear Medicine [IO]
Australian and New Zealand Assn. of Physicians in Nuclear Medicine [IO]
Australian and New Zealand Soc. of Nuclear Medicine [IO]
British Nuclear Medicine Soc. [IO]
Canadian Soc. of Nuclear Medicine [IO]
European Assn. of Nuclear Medicine [IO]
European Soc. for Therapeutic Radiology and Oncology [IO]
Intl. Assn. of Radiopharmacology [IO]
Intl. Coll. of Nuclear Medicine Physicians [IO]
Japanese Soc. of Nuclear Medicine [IO]
Nuclear Medicine Soc. of Thailand [IO]
Nuclear Medicine Tech. Certification Bd. [15423]
Soc. of Nuclear Medicine [15424]
Soc. of Nuclear Medicine Technologist Sect. [15425]
Nuclear Medicine Soc. of Thailand [IO], Chiang Mai, Thailand
Nuclear Medicine; Technologist Sect. of the Soc. of [★15425]
Nuclear Medicine Tech. Certification Bd. [15423], 3558 Habersham at Northlake, Bldg. I, Tucker, GA 30084, (404)315-1739

Nuclear Network [★18595]
Nuclear Network [★IO]
Nuclear Policy; Comm. for a SANE [★18166]
Nuclear Reactors; Assn. of Swedish Municipalities with [IO]
Nuclear Records Mgt. Assn. [★7389]
Nuclear Recycling Consultants - Address unknown since 2002.
Nuclear Resistance Life Force - Defunct.
Nuclear Safety Standards Commn. [IO], Salzgitter, Germany
Nuclear Steam Sys. Supply [★7389]
Nuclear Stud; Oak Ridge Inst. of [★7625]
Nuclear Suppliers Assn. [7390], PO Box 2038, Springfield, VA 22152, (703)451-1912
Nuclear Threat Initiative [18164], 1747 Pennsylvania Ave. NW, 7th Fl., Washington, DC 20006, (202)296-4810
Nuclear Threat Reduction Campaign [18165], c/o Veterans for Am., 1025 Vermont Ave. NW, 7th Fl., Washington, DC 20006-2412, (202)483-9222
Nuclear Training; National Acad. for [★7392]
Nuclear Transportation Project - Defunct.
Nuclear War Graphics Project - Defunct.
Nuclear War Prevention Proj; Accidental [★18229]
Nuclear War Study Group - Address unknown since 1995.
Nuclear War and Weapons
Accidental Nuclear War Prevention Proj. [18140]
Acronym Inst. for Disarmament Diplomacy [IO]
ALEPH: Alliance for Jewish Renewal [IO]
ALEPH: Alliance for Jewish Renewal [18141]
Architects/Designers/Planners for Social Responsibility [18142]
Campaign to Boycott SDI [18143]
Comm. of Atomic Bomb Survivors in the U.S. [18144]
Comm. to Bridge the Gap [18145]
Cmpt. Professionals for Social Responsibility [18146]
Concerned Citizens for Nuclear Safety [18147]
Concerned Educators Allied for a Safe Env. [18148]
Corporate Accountability Intl. [18149]
Corporate Accountability Intl. [IO]
Coun. for a Livable World Educ. Fund [17426]
Downwinders [18150]
Downwinders [IO]
Global Issues Rsrc. Center [18151]
Global Network Against Weapons and Nuclear Power in Space [18152]
Global Security Inst. [18153]
Global Security Inst. [IO]
Grandmothers for Peace Intl. [IO]
Grandmothers for Peace Intl. [18154]
Greenpeace U.S.A. [4571]
High Frontier Org. [18686]
Inst. for Space and Security Stud. [18155]
Intl. Philosophers for the Prevention of Nuclear Omnicide [18156]
Intl. Philosophers for the Prevention of Nuclear Omnicide [IO]
Intl. Physicians for the Prevention of Nuclear War [IO]
Intl. Physicians for the Prevention of Nuclear War [18157]
Intl. Student/Young Pugwash - Netherlands [IO]
Japan Coun. Against A and H Bombs [IO]
Kazakhstan Assn. Inst. of Non-Proliferation [IO]
Lawyers Alliance for World Security [IO]
Lawyers Alliance for World Security [18158]
Lawyers' Comm. on Nuclear Policy [18159]
Medical Assn. for Prevention of War - Australia [IO]
Natl. Memorial Inst. for the Prevention of Terrorism [18734]
Natl. No-Nukes Prison Support Collective [18160]
National No-Nukes Prison Support Collective [IO]
Nevada Desert Experience [18161]
Never Again Campaign [18162]
Never Again Campaign [IO]
Nuclear Control Inst. [18163]
Nuclear Threat Initiative [18164]
Nuclear Threat Reduction Campaign [18165]
Nukewatch [18133]

A star before a book entry number signifies that the name is not listed separately, but is mentioned within the entry.

Parliamentarians For Global Action [17433]
Peace Action [18166]
Peace Action Educ. Fund [18167]
Peace Pac [18168]
Physicians for Social Responsibility [18169]
Physicians for Social Responsibility [IO]
Progressive Found. [18170]
Psychologists for Social Responsibility [18171]
Reaching Critical Will [17436]
Students for Social Responsibility [18172]
UrgentCall.org [18173]
WAND Educ. Fund [18174]
Western States Legal Found. [6148]
Women's Action for New Directions [18175]
World Peacemakers [18176]
World Peacemakers [IO]
Nuclear Waste Project - Defunct.
Nuclear Weapons Freeze Campaign [★18166]
Nude Recreation; Amer. Assn. for [10760]
Nudism
Amer. Assn. for Nude Recreation [10760]
Australian Nudist Fed. [IO]
Australian Nudist Fed. Supporter Club [IO]
Beach Educ. Advocates for Culture, Hea., Env.
and Safety [10761]
BeachFront USA [10762]
British Naturism [IO]
Intl. Naturist Fed. [IO]
Intl. Naturist Org. for Esperanto [9916]
Natural Figure Art Assn. [9462]
The Naturist Soc. [10763]
New Zealand Naturist Fed. [IO]
Nudist Information Center - Defunct.
Nuestros Pequenos Hermanos [★20380]
Nuestros Pequenos Hermanos [IO], Milan, Italy
Nuffield Coun. on Bioethics [IO], London, United
Kingdom
Nukes Prison Support Collective; Natl. No- [18160]
Nukewatch [18133], PO Box 649, Luck, WI 54853,
(715)472-4185
Numerical Control Soc./AIM Tech - Defunct.
Numismatic
American-Israel Numismatic Assn. [22723]
Amer. Numismatic Assn. [22724]
Amer. Numismatic Soc. [22725]
Amer. Soc. of Check Collectors [22726]
Amer. Tax Token Soc. [22727]
Amer. Wooden Money Guild [22728]
Ancient Coin Collectors Guild [22729]
Armenian Numismatic Soc. [22730]
Armenian Numismatic Soc. [IO]
Australian Numismatic Soc. [IO]
British Assn. of Numismatic Societies [IO]
British Numismatic Soc. [IO]
British Numismatic Trade Assn. [IO]
Canadian Assn. of Numismatic Dealers [IO]
Canadian Assn. of Wooden Money Collectors [IO]
Canadian Numismatic Assn. [IO]
Canadian Numismatic Res. Soc. [IO]
Canadian Paper Money Soc. [IO]
Casino Chip and Gaming Token Collectors Club
[21989]
Challenge Coin Assn. [22731]
Civil War Token Soc. [22732]
Colonial Coin Collectors Club [22733]
Combined Organizations of Numismatic Error Col-
lectors of Am. [22734]
Cuban Numismatic Assn. [22735]
Cuban Numismatic Assn. [IO]
Dedicated Wooden Money Collectors [22736]
Early Amer. Coppers [22737]
The Elongated Collectors [22738]
Indus. Coun. for Tangible Assets [3713]
Inter-Governmental Philatelic Corp. [22829]
Intl. Assn. of Professional Numismatists [IO]
Intl. Bank Note Soc. [IO]
Intl. Bank Note Soc. [22739]
Intl. Banknotes Soc. - England [IO]
Intl. Numismatic Commn. [IO]
John Reich Collectors Soc. [22740]
Latin Amer. Paper Money Soc. [22741]
Liberty Seated Collectors Club [22742]
Lithuanian Numismatic Assn. [22743]
Lithuanian Numismatic Assn. [IO]
Love Token Soc. [22744]

Mathematical Stud. Unit [22842]
Mech. Bank Collectors of Am. [21826]
Medal Collectors of Am. [22745]
Natl. Collectors Assn. of Die Doubling [22746]
Natl. Token Collectors Assn. [21954]
North Amer. Collectors [22747]
Numismatic Bibliomania Soc. [22748]
Numismatic Literary Guild [22749]
Numismatics Intl. [22750]
Numismatics Intl. [IO]
One Cent Intl. [IO]
One Cent Intl. [22751]
Oriental Numismatic Soc. [IO]
Original Hobo Nickel Soc. [22752]
Professional Currency Dealers Assn. [22753]
Professional Numismatists Guild [22754]
Royal Numismatic Soc. [IO]
Russian Numismatic Soc. [22755]
Societe Royale de Numismatique de Belgique
[IO]
Soc. of Lincoln Cent Collectors [22756]
Soc. of Paper Money Collectors [22757]
Soc. of Private and Pioneer Numismatists [22758]
Soc. of Ration Token Collectors [22759]
Soc. for U.S. Commemorative Coins [22760]
Soc. of U.S. Pattern Collectors [22761]
Solano Silver Round Club [22762]
Token and Medal Soc. [22763]
Toned Coin Collectors Soc. [22764]
Ukrainian Philatelic and Numismatic Soc. [22883]
U.S. Mexican Numismatic Assn. [22765]
Unrecognised States Numismatic Soc. [22766]
Women in Numismatics [22767]
World Internet Numismatic Soc. [22768]
World Internet Numismatic Soc. [IO]
World Proof Numismatic Assn. [IO]
World Proof Numismatic Assn. [22769]
Young Numismatists of Am. [22770]
Numismatic and Archaeological Soc; Amer.
[★22725]
Numismatic Bibliomania Soc. [22748], c/o David M.
Sundman, Sec.-Treas., PO Box 82, Littleton, NH
03561
Numismatic Error Collectors of Am. [★22734]
Numismatic Errors; Collectors of [★22734]
Numismatic Guild; Professional [★22754]
Numismatic Literary Guild [22749], c/o Ed Reiter,
Exec. Dir., 12 Abbington Terr., Glen Rock, NJ
07452
Numismatics and Artifact Soc; Armenian [★22730]
Numismatics Intl. [22750], PO Box 570842, Dallas,
TX 75357-0842, (940)440-2213
Numismatics Intl. [IO], Dallas, TX, United States
Numismatists Guild; Professional [22754]
Nunavut Tourism [IO], Nunavut, NT, Canada
Nuorten Naisten Kristillinen Yhdistys [★IO]
Nuova Lamborghini Club [★21684]
Nurse Advocates for Childbirth Solutions; Assn. of
[13978]
Nurse Anesthesia Educational Programs; Coun. on
Accreditation of [8835]
Nurse Anesthesia Overseas [★15778]
Nurse Anesthesia Overseas [★IO]
Nurse Assessment Coordinators; Amer. Assn. of
[14608]
Nurse Assn; Natl. Male [★15431]
Nurse Attorneys; Amer. Assn. of [15000]
Nurse Consultants; Amer. Assn. of Legal [14999]
Nurse Consultants Assn. - Address unknown since
1994.
Nurse Corps Assn; Army [15262]
Nurse Corps Assn; Navy [2832]
Nurse Corps Assn; Retired Army [★15262]
Nurse Educ. and Ser; Natl. Assn. for Practical [8869]
Nurse Healers Professional Associates [★14831]
Nurse Healers Professional Associates Intl. [14831],
PO Box 419, Craryville, NY 12521, (518)325-1185
Nurse-Midwifery; Amer. Coll. of [★15447]
Nurse-Midwives; Amer. Assn. of [★15447]
Nurse Practitioner Associates for Continuing Educ.
[15515], 209 W Central St., Ste. 228, Natick, MA
01760, (508)907-6424
Nurse Practitioners and Associates; Natl. Bd. of
Pediatric [★15522]
Nurse Practitioners in Reproductive Hea; Natl. Assn.
of [★15497]

Nurse Recruiters; Natl. Assn. of [★15070]
Nurse Task Force; Lipid [★15523]
Nurseries
African Violet Soc. of Am. [22480]
All-America Gladiolus Selections [22481]
Amer. Begonia Soc. [22482]
Amer. Bonsai Soc. [22483]
Amer. Boxwood Soc. [22484]
Amer. Community Gardening Assn. [22486]
Amer. Daffodil Soc. [22487]
Amer. Fuchsia Soc. [22488]
Amer. Gourd Soc. [22489]
Amer. Hemerocallis Soc. [22490]
Amer. Hibiscus Soc. [22491]
Amer. Horticultural Soc. [22492]
Amer. Hosta Soc. [22493]
Amer. Iris Soc. [22495]
Amer. Ivy Soc. [22496]
Amer. Nursery and Landscape Assn. [5042]
Amer. Penstemon Soc. [22497]
Amer. Peony Soc. [22498]
Amer. Primrose Soc. [22499]
Amer. Rhododendron Soc. [22500]
Amer. Rose Soc. [22501]
Aril Soc. Intl. [22502]
Bonsai Clubs Intl. [22504]
Bromeliad Soc. Intl. [22505]
Cactus and Succulent Soc. of Am. [22506]
Cymbidium Soc. of Am. [22508]
Epiphyllum Soc. of Am. [22510]
Garden Centers of Am. [5043]
Garden Club of Am. [22511]
Garden Conservancy [4402]
Garden Writers Assn. [22512]
The Gardeners of Am. [22513]
Gesneriad Hybridizers Assn. [22514]
Gesneriad Soc. [22515]
Heritage Roses Gp. [22517]
Horticultural Res. Inst. [5044]
Indoor Gardening Soc. of Am. [22519]
Intl. Aroid Soc. [22520]
Intl. Carnivorous Plant Soc. [22521]
Intl. Lilac Soc. [22522]
Intl. Oleander Soc. [22523]
Landscape Nursery Coun. [5045]
Median Iris Soc. [22525]
Metropolitan Tree Improvement Alliance [5260]
Natl. Assn. of Plant Patent Owners [5046]
Natl. Chrysanthemum Soc. [22526]
Natl. Day Nurseries Assn. [IO]
Natl. Fuchsia Soc. [22527]
Natl. Garden Clubs [22528]
Natl. Gardening Assn. [22529]
North Amer. Fruit Explorers [22531]
North Amer. Gladiolus Coun. [22532]
North Amer. Heather Soc. [22533]
North Amer. Lily Soc. [22534]
North Amer. Rock Garden Soc. [22535]
Nursery and Landscape Assn. Executives of North
Am. [5047]
Pacific Orchid Soc. of Hawaii [22536]
Plumeria Soc. of Am. [22537]
Reblooming Iris Soc. [22538]
Rose Hybridizers Assn. [22539]
Seed Savers Exchange [22540]
Soc. for Japanese Irises [22541]
Soc. for Louisiana Irises [22542]
Soc. for Pacific Coast Native Iris [22543]
Soc. for Siberian Irises [22544]
Species Iris Gp. of North Am. [22545]
Terrarium Assn. [22548]
Nursery Assn. Executives [★5047]
Nursery Assn. Executives of North Am. [★5047]
Nursery Assn. Secretaries [★5047]
Nursery Educ; Natl. Assn. for [★8069]
Nursery and Garden Indus. Australia [IO], Epping,
Australia
Nursery Indus. Assn. of Australia [★IO]
Nursery Landscape Assn; Canadian [IO]
Nursery and Landscape Assn. Executives of North
Am. [5047], c/o Beverly Gelvin, Exec. Dir., 968
Trinity Rd., Raleigh, NC 27607, (919)816-9120
Nurserymen; Amer. Assn. of [★5042]
Nurserymen, Florists and Seedsmen; Amer. Assn. of
[★5042]

Reference to "IO" in place of a book number signifies that the association may be found in the 45th edition of International Organizations.

Encyclopedia of Associations, 46th Edition   3929

Nurserymen's Assn; Florida Citrus [4728]
Nurserymen's Assn; Natl. Landscape [★2396]
Nurses Against Misrepresentation - Address
  unknown since 1995.
Nurses in AIDS Care; Assn. of [13559]
Nurses Alliance for the Prevention of Nuclear War -
  Defunct.
Nurses; Amer. Assn. of Cardiovascular [★15433]
Nurses; Amer. Assn. of Indus. [★15439]
Nurses; Amer. Soc. of Plastic and Reconstructive
  Surgical [★15461]
Nurses; Amer. Soc. of Post Anesthesia [★15460]
Nurses Anonymous; Intl. [16505]
Nurses Assoc. Alumnae of U.S. and Canada
  [★15451]
Nurses and Associates; Certification Bd. for Urologic
  [16706]
Nurses and Associates; Soc. of Gastroenterology
  [14429]
Nurses Assn. of the Amer. Coll. of Obstetricians and
  Gynecologists [★15470]
Nurses Assn. of the Amer. Coll. of Obstetricians and
  Gynecologists [★IO]
Nurses' Assn; Amer. Holistic [14825]
Nurses' Assn; Amer. Nephrology [15286]
Nurses; Assn. of Child and Adolescent Psychiatric
  [★15487]
Nurses Assn; Emergency [14333]
Nurses Assn; Emergency Dept. [★14333]
Nurses' Assn. in memory of Frances Tompkins;
  Foundation of the Natl. Student [★8873]
Nurses Assn; Hospice [★15482]
Nurses Assn; Natl. Emergency Dept. [★14333]
Nurses Assn; Natl. Flight [★15427]
Nurses' Assn; Natl. Student [8873]
Nurses; Assn. of Operating Room [★15468]
Nurses Associations and Services; Amer. Affiliation
  of Visiting [★15532]
Nurses in Bus. Assn; Natl. [752]
Nurses Christian Fellowship [19819], PO Box 7895,
  Madison, WI 53707-7895, (608)274-9001
Nurses Credentialing Center; Amer. [2838]
Nurses Educational Funds [15516], 304 Park Ave.
  S, 11th Fl., New York, NY 10010, (212)590-2443
Nurses Endorsing Transplantation; Assn. of [15670]
Nurses for Eye Acquisition; Consortium of
  Registered [★15670]
Nurses in Genetics; Intl. Soc. of [14501]
Nurses and Hea. Professionals; Fed. of [★24087]
Nurses for a Healthier Tomorrow [15517], Honor
  Soc. of Nursing, Sigma Theta Tau Intl., 550 W
  North St., Indianapolis, IN 46202
Nurses' House [15518], Veronica M. Driscoll Center
  for Nursing, 2113 Western Ave., Ste. 2, Guilder-
  land, NY 12084-9559, (518)456-7858
Nurses' Hypertension Assn. [IO], London, United
  Kingdom
Nurses for Laughter - Defunct.
Nurses; Natl. Assn. of Licensed Practical [★8869]
Nurses; Natl. Assn. of Orthopaedic [★15498]
Nurses; Natl. Assn. of Spanish Speaking-Spanish
  Surnamed [★15494]
Nurses; Natl. Consortium of Chem. Dependency
  [★15474]
Nurses/NEA; Dept. of School [★15501]
Nurses; Neurosurgical [★15443]
Nurses Org. of the Veterans Admin. [★15519]
Nurses Org. of Veterans Affairs [15519], 1726 M St.
  NW, Ste. 1101, Washington, DC 20036, (202)296-
  0888
Nurses for the Rights of the Child [11737], 369 Mon-
  tezuma, No. 354, Santa Fe, NM 87501, (505)989-
  7377
Nurses Soc. on Addictions; Natl. [★15484]
Nurses Soc. on Alcoholism; Natl. [★15484]
Nurses Soc., An Assn. of E.T. Nurses; Wound, Os-
  tomy and Continence [★15533]
Nurses Soc; Endocrine [14354]
Nurses Soc; Infusion [16614]
Nurses Soc; Intravenous [★16614]
Nurses in Substance Abuse Intl; Consolidated Assn.
  of [★15484]
Nurses and Technicians; Amer. Assn. of Nephrology
  [★15286]
Nurses in Transition - Address unknown since 1994.

Nursing
Aboriginal Nurses Assn. of Canada [IO]
Acad. of Canadian Executive Nurses [IO]
Acad. of Medical Surgical Nurses [15426]
AFT Healthcare [24087]
Air and Surface Transport Nurses Assn. [15427]
Alpha Tau Delta [24559]
Amer. Acad. of Ambulatory Care Nursing [15428]
Amer. Acad. of Nurse Practitioners [15429]
Amer. Acad. of Nursing [15430]
Amer. Assembly for Men in Nursing [15431]
Amer. Assisted Living Nurses Assn. [15432]
Amer. Assn. of Colleges of Nursing [8842]
Amer. Assn. of Critical-Care Nurses [15433]
Amer. Assn. of Heart Failure Nurses [15434]
Amer. Assn. for the History of Medicine [10082]
Amer. Assn. for the History of Nursing [10083]
Amer. Assn. of Legal Nurse Consultants [14999]
Amer. Assn. of Managed Care Nurses [15435]
Amer. Assn. of Neuroscience Nurses [15436]
Amer. Assn. of Neuroscience Nurses [IO]
Amer. Assn. of Nurse Anesthetists [15437]
Amer. Assn. of Nurse Assessment Coordinators
  [14608]
Amer. Assn. of Nurse Attorneys [15000]
Amer. Assn. of Nurse Life Care Planners [15438]
Amer. Assn. of Occupational Hea. Nurses [15439]
Amer. Assn. of Off. Nurses [15440]
Amer. Assn. of Spinal Cord Injury Nurses [15441]
Amer. Bd. of Managed Care Nursing [15442]
Amer. Bd. of Neuroscience Nursing [15443]
Amer. Bd. of Nursing Specialties [15444]
Amer. Bd. for Occupational Hea. Nurses [15445]
Amer. Bd. of Perianesthesia Nursing Certification
  [15446]
Amer. Coll. of Hea. Care Administrators [15535]
Amer. Coll. of Nurse-Midwives [15447]
Amer. Coll. of Nurse Practitioners [15448]
Amer. Forensic Nurses [15449]
Amer. Holistic Nurses' Assn. [14825]
Amer. Licensed Practical Nurses Assn. [15450]
Amer. Nephrology Nurses' Assn. [15286]
Amer. Nurses Assn. [15451]
Amer. Nurses Credentialing Center [2838]
Amer. Nurses Found. [15452]
Amer. Nursing Informatics Assn. [15453]
Amer. Org. of Nurse Executives [15454]
Amer. Pediatric Surgical Nurses Assn. [15455]
Amer. Psychiatric Nurses Assn. [15456]
Amer. Radiological Nurses Assn. [15457]
Amer. Soc. of Ophthalmic Registered Nurses
  [15458]
Amer. Soc. for Pain Mgt. Nursing [15459]
Amer. Soc. of PeriAnesthesia Nurses [15460]
American Society of PeriAnesthesia Nurses [IO]
Amer. Soc. of Plastic Surgical Nurses [15461]
Anthroposophical Nurses Assn. of Am. [15462]
Army Distaff Foundation/Knollwood [21192]
Army Nurse Corps Assn. [15262]
Asian Amer./Pacific Islander Nurses Assn. [15463]
Asian Amer./Pacific Islander Nurses Assn. [IO]
Assn. of Black Nursing Faculty [8848]
Assn. of Camp Nurses [15464]
Assn. of Camp Nurses [IO]
Assn. of Child Neurology Nurses [IO]
Assn. of Child Neurology Nurses [15465]
Assn. for Common European Nursing Diagnoses,
  Interventions and Outcomes [IO]
Assn. of Community Hea. Nursing Educators
  [15466]
Assn. of Hong Kong Nursing Staff [IO]
Assn. of Military Surgeons of the U.S. [15263]
Assn. of Nurse Advocates for Childbirth Solutions
  [13978]
Assn. of Nurses in AIDS Care [13559]
Assn. of Pediatric Hematology/Oncology Nurses
  [15467]
Assn. for Perioperative Practice [IO]
Association of PeriOperative Registered Nurses
  [IO]
Assn. of PeriOperative Registered Nurses [15468]
Assn. of Rehabilitation Nurses [15469]
Assn. of Women's Hea., Obstetric and Neonatal
  Nurses [15470]
Association of Women's Health, Obstetric and
  Neonatal Nurses [IO]

Australian Coll. of Occupational Hea. Nurses [IO]
Australian Dermatology Nurses Assn. [IO]
Australian Nurses' Cardiovascular and Hyperten-
  sion Assn. [IO]
Australian Nursing Fed. [IO]
Baromedical Nurses Assn. [15471]
British Assn. of Dental Nurses [IO]
British Assn. of Neuroscience Nurses [IO]
Canadian Assn. of Advanced Practice Nurses [IO]
Canadian Assn. of Burn Nurses [IO]
Canadian Assn. of Critical Care Nurses [IO]
Canadian Assn. of Neuroscience Nurses [IO]
Canadian Assn. of Nurses in AIDS Care [IO]
Canadian Assn. of Nurses in Oncology [IO]
Canadian Coun. of Cardiovascular Nurses [IO]
Canadian Fed. of Mental Hea. Nurses [IO]
Canadian Fed. of Nurses Unions [IO]
Canadian Gerontological Nursing Assn. [IO]
Canadian Holistic Nurses Assn. [IO]
Canadian Intravenous Nurses Assn. [IO]
Canadian Nurses Assn. [IO]
Canadian Nurses Found. [IO]
Canadian Nurses Protective Soc. [IO]
Canadian Nurses Respiratory Soc. [IO]
Canadian Nursing Students' Assn. [IO]
Canadian Occupational Hea. Nurses Assn. [IO]
Canadian Orthopaedic Nurses Assn. [IO]
Canadian Soc. of Gastroenterology Nurses and
  Associates [IO]
Certification Bd. for Urologic Nurses and Associ-
  ates [16706]
Certifying Bd. of Gastroenterology Nurses and
  Associates [15472]
Chi Eta Phi Sorority [24560]
Children of Aging Parents [11282]
Children's Hospice Intl. [14853]
Clinicians for Choice [13528]
Coll. and Assn. of Registered Nurses of Alberta
  [IO]
Commn. on Collegiate Nursing Educ. [8859]
Commn. on Graduates of Foreign Nursing
  Schools [15473]
Commonwealth Nurses Fed. [IO]
Community and District Nursing Assn. [IO]
Community Hea. Nurses Assn. of Canada [IO]
Consortium of Behavioral Hea. Nurses and As-
  sociates [15474]
Coun. on Accreditation of Nurse Anesthesia
  Educational Programs [8835]
Coun. on Certification of Nurse Anesthetists
  [15475]
Danish Nurses' Org. [IO]
Democratic Nursing Org. of South Africa [IO]
Dermatology Nurses' Assn. [15476]
Developmental Disabilities Nurses Assn. [15477]
Dutch Assn. of Paediatric Nurses [IO]
Dutch Assn. of Psychiatric Nursing [IO]
Emergency Nurses Assn. [14333]
Endocrine Nurses Soc. [14354]
European Fed. of Critical Care Nursing Associa-
  tions [IO]
European Oncology Nursing Soc. [IO]
European Union of Independent Hospitals [IO]
Fed. for Accessible Nursing Educ. and Licensure
  [15478]
Fed. of European Nurses in Diabetes [IO]
Frontier Nursing Ser. [15479]
Genito-Urinary Nurses Assn. [IO]
Helene Fuld Hea. Trust [15480]
Home Healthcare Nurses Assn. [15481]
Homeopathic Nurses Assn. [14846]
Hong Kong Assn. of Critical Care Nurses [IO]
Hong Kong Soc. for Nursing Educ. [IO]
Hospice and Palliative Nurses Assn. [15482]
Icelandic Nurses' Assn. [IO]
Infection Control Nurses' Assn. [IO]
Infusion Nurses Soc. [16614]
Interagency Coun. on Info. Resources for Nursing
  [10360]
Intl. Assn. of Forensic Nurses [15483]
Intl. Assn. of Forensic Nurses [IO]
Intl. Assn. for Human Caring [14640]
Intl. Assn. of Sickle Cell Nurses And Physician
  Assistants [14706]
Intl. Coun. of Nurses [IO]

A star before a book entry number signifies that the name is not listed separately, but is mentioned within the entry.

Intl. Nurses Soc. on Addictions [IO]
Intl. Nurses Soc. on Addictions [15484]
Intl. Nursing Assn. for Clinical Simulation and Learning [15485]
International Nursing Association for Clinical Simulation and Learning [IO]
Intl. Nursing Coalition for Mass Casualty Educ. [IO]
Intl. Nursing Coalition for Mass Casualty Educ. [8946]
Intl. Org. of Multiple Sclerosis Nurses [15486]
Intl. Org. of Multiple Sclerosis Nurses [IO]
Intl. Skin Care Nursing Gp. [IO]
Intl. Soc. of Nurses in Cancer Care [IO]
Intl. Soc. of Nurses in Genetics [14501]
Intl. Soc. of Psychiatric-Mental Hea. Nurses [15487]
Intl. Soc. of Psychiatric-Mental Hea. Nurses [IO]
Intl. Transplant Nurses Soc. [IO]
Intl. Transplant Nurses Soc. [15488]
Irish Hosp. Consultants Assn. [IO]
Japanese Midwives' Assn. [IO]
Japanese Nursing Assn. [IO]
Luxembourg Fed. of Hospitals [IO]
NANDA Intl. [IO]
NANDA Intl. [15489]
Natl. Amer. Arab Nurses Assn. [15490]
Natl. Assn. of Catholic Nurses - USA [15491]
Natl. Assn. of Clinical Nurse Specialists [15492]
Natl. Assn. for Direct Care Workers of Color [14709]
Natl. Assn. of Directors of Nursing Admin. in Long Term Care [15493]
Natl. Assn. of Hea. Care Assistants [14514]
Natl. Assn. of Hea. Unit Coordinators [14578]
Natl. Assn. of Hispanic Nurses [15494]
Natl. Assn. for Home Care and Hospice [14840]
Natl. Assn. of Independent Nurses [2839]
Natl. Assn. of Neonatal Nurses [15495]
Natl. Assn. of Nurse Massage Therapists [15496]
Natl. Assn. of Nurse Practitioners in Women's Hea. [15497]
Natl. Assn. of Orthopaedic Nurses [15498]
Natl. Assn. of Pediatric Nurse Practitioners [15499]
Natl. Assn. of Physician Nurses [15500]
Natl. Assn. for Practical Nurse Educ. and Ser. [8869]
Natl. Assn. of Pro-Life Nurses [18378]
Natl. Assn. of School Nurses [15501]
Natl. Assn. of School Nurses for the Deaf [14768]
Natl. Assn. of State School Nurse Consultants [15502]
Natl. Assn. of Traveling Nurses [15503]
Natl. Assn. of Vietnamese Nurses [15504]
Natl. Black Nurses Assn. [15505]
Natl. Certification Corp. for the Obstetric, Gynecologic and Neonatal Nursing Specialties [15506]
Natl. Coalition of Ethnic Minority Nurse Associations [15507]
Natl. Coun. of Maori Nurses [IO]
Natl. Coun. of State Boards of Nursing [15508]
Natl. Fed. of Licensed Practical Nurses [15509]
Natl. HIV Nurses Assn. [IO]
Natl. Hospice and Palliative Care Org. [14856]
Natl. League for Nursing [15510]
Natl. Nursing Staff Development Org. [15511]
Natl. Org. for Associate Degree Nursing [15512]
Natl. Org. of Nurse Practitioners Faculties [15513]
Natl. Org. of Nurses with Disabilities [15514]
Natl. Student Nurses' Assn. [8873]
Navy Anesthesia Soc. [13687]
New Zealand Nurses Org. [IO]
Norwegian Nurses Org. [IO]
Nurse Practitioner Associates for Continuing Educ. [15515]
Nurses Educational Funds [15516]
Nurses for a Healthier Tomorrow [15517]
Nurses' House [15518]
Nurses Org. of Veterans Affairs [15519]
Nurses for the Rights of the Child [11737]
Oncology Nursing Certification Corp. [15520]
Oncology Nursing Soc. [15521]
Parkinson's Disease Nurse Specialist Assn. [IO]

Pediatric Endocrinology Nursing Soc. [15894]
Pediatric Nursing Certification Bd. [15522]
Philippine Nurses Assn. of Am. [2840]
Preventive Cardiovascular Nurses Assn. [15523]
Professional Assn. of Nursery Nurses [IO]
Psychiatric Nurses Assn. of Ireland [IO]
Respiratory Nursing Soc. [15524]
Royal Coll. of Nursing [IO]
Royal Coll. of Nursing - Australia [IO]
School Nurse Achievement Prog. [15525]
Sigma Theta Tau Intl. [24561]
Sigma Theta Tau Intl. [IO]
Soc. of Critical Care Medicine [14071]
Soc. of Gastroenterology Nurses and Associates [14429]
Soc. of Otorhinolaryngology and Head/Neck Nurses [15526]
Soc. of Pediatric Nurses [15527]
Soc. of Trauma Nurses [15528]
Soc. of Urologic Nurses and Associates [15529]
Soc. for Vascular Nursing [15530]
Tissue Viability Nurses Assn. [IO]
Transcultural Nursing Soc. [IO]
Transcultural Nursing Soc. [15531]
United Kingdom Multiple Sclerosis Specialist Nurse Assn. [IO]
Univ. of Colorado Hea. Sciences Center Alumni Assn. [24494]
Visiting Nurse Associations of Am. [15532]
World Homecare and Hospice Org. [14844]
Wound, Ostomy and Continence Nurses Soc.: An Assn. of E.T. Nurses [15533]
Wound, Ostomy and Continence Nurses Soc.: An Assn. of E.T. Nurses [IO]
Wound, Ostomy and Continence Nursing Certification Bd. [15534]
Nursing Admin; Amer. Acad. of Ambulatory [★15428]
Nursing; Advocates for Child Psychiatric [★15487]
Nursing Alumni Assn; Columbia Coll. of [18891]
Nursing Alumni Assn. U.S.A; UERMMMC [18928]
Nursing; Amer. Assn. of Colleges of [8842]
Nursing; Amer. Assn. for the History of [10083]
Nursing Assn; British Veterinary [IO]
Nursing Assn; Natl. Gerontological [14515]
Nursing Diagnosis Assn; North Amer. [★15489]
Nursing Faculty; Assn. of Black [8848]
Nursing Found; Rehabilitation [★15469]
Nursing; Frontier School of Midwifery and Family [★15479]
Nursing Home Administrators; Amer. Coll. of [★15535]
Nursing Home Administrators; Natl. Assn. of Boards of Examiners of [★15538]
Nursing Home Advisory and Res. Coun. - Address unknown since 1999.
Nursing Home Reform; Amer. [★14540]
Nursing Home Information Service - National Council of Senior Citizens - Defunct.
Nursing Home Reform Coalition [★17335]
Nursing Home Reform; Natl. Citizens Coalition for [17335]
Nursing Homes
Alliance for Healthcare Strategy and Marketing [2612]
Amer. Assisted Living Nurses Assn. [15432]
Amer. Assn. of Caregiving Youth [13466]
Amer. Assn. of Homes and Services for the Aging [11273]
Amer. Assn. for Intl. Aging [11274]
Amer. Baptist Homes and Hospitals Assn. [19471]
Amer. Coll. of Hea. Care Administrators [15535]
Amer. Disabled for Attendant Prog. Today [17413]
Amer. Hea. Care Assn. [14540]
Amer. Medical Directors Assn. [15536]
Amer. Soc. of Consultant Pharmacists [15922]
Assn. of Jewish Aging Services [11277]
Center for the Stud. of Aging of Albany [11281]
Children of Aging Parents [11282]
Consultant Dietitians in Hea. Care Facilities [15554]
Consumer Consortium on Assisted Living [11283]
Found. Aiding the Elderly [17329]
Intl. Assn. of Homes and Services for the Ageing [11289]
Legal Counsel for the Elderly [12497]

Lemko Housing Org. [15537]
Natl. Assn. of Boards of Examiners of Long Term Care Administrators [15538]
Natl. Assn. of Hea. Care Assistants [14514]
Natl. Assn. of Professional Geriatric Care Managers [15539]
Natl. Citizens Coalition for Nursing Home Reform [17335]
Natl. Inst. on Community-Based Long-Term Care [11312]
Natl. Inst. of Senior Housing [12328]
Registered Nursing Home Assn. [IO]
Relatives and Residents Assn. [IO]
United Methodist Assn. of Hea. and Welfare Ministries [14602]
Nursing Homes; Amer. Assn. of [★14540]
Nursing Homes; Natl. Assn. of Registered [★14540]
Nursing; Interagency Coun. on Info. Resources for [10360]
Nursing Mother's Assn. of Australia [★IO]
Nursing Mothers Counsel [12414], PO Box 50063, Palo Alto, CA 94303, (650)327-6455
Nursing; Natl. Certification Bd. Perioperative [★14878]
Nursing; Natl. Org. for Advancement of Associate Degree [★15512]
Nursing Overseas [★15778]
Nursing Overseas [★IO]
Nursing Ser. Administrators; Amer. Soc. for [★15454]
Nursing Ser. Administrators; Amer. Soc. for Hosp. [★15454]
Nursing Services Assn; Intl. [★14978]
Nursing Soc; Pediatric Endocrinology [15894]
Nursing; Soc. for Peripheral Vascular [★15530]
Nursing and Tech; Bd. of Nephrology Examiners [15290]
Nursing and Tech; Bd. of Nephrology Examiners - [★15290]
Nursing Touch and Massage Therapy Assn. Intl. - Address unknown since 2005.
NURTUREart Non-Profit [9519], 910 Grand St., Brooklyn, NY 11211, (718)782-7755
NURTUREart Non-Profit [IO], New York, NY, United States
The Nurturing Network [13434], Development Off., PO Box 1489, White Salmon, WA 98672, (509)493-4026
Nut Processors Assn; Peanut Butter and [★1556]
Nut Processors Assn; Peanut and Tree [1556]
Nut and Rivet Mfrs; Amer. Inst. of Bolt, [★1823]
Nut Salters Assn; Peanut and [★1556]
Nut Salters Assn; Peanut Butter Manufacturers and [★1556]
Nutmeg Forum - Defunct.
Nutraceutical Assn; Amer. [14612]
Nutrition
Action for Healthy Kids [13945]
Amer. Assn. of Clinical Endocrinologists [14350]
Amer. Assn. of Nutritional Consultants [15540]
Amer. Bd. of Nutrition [15541]
Amer. Bd. of Physician Nutrition Specialists [15542]
Amer. Celiac Society/Dietary Support Coalition [15543]
Amer. Coll. of Gastroenterology [14405]
Amer. Coll. of Nutrition [15544]
Amer. Coll. of Nutrition [IO]
Amer. Coun. of Applied Clinical Nutrition [15545]
Amer. Coun. for Fitness and Nutrition [15959]
Amer. Coun. on Sci. and Hea. [14539]
Amer. Dietetic Assn. [15546]
Amer. Gastroenterological Assn. [14406]
Amer. Nutraceutical Assn. [14612]
Amer. School Hea. Assn. [14718]
Amer. Soc. for Clinical Nutrition [15547]
Amer. Soc. for Nutrition [15548]
Amer. Soc. for Parenteral and Enteral Nutrition [15549]
America's Second Harvest [12388]
Angelcare [11672]
Assn. of Nutrition Departments and Programs [8947]
Assn. of Nutrition Services Agencies [14720]
Assn. for the Stud. of Food and Soc. [7090]

Reference to "IO" in place of a book number signifies that the association may be found in the 45th edition of International Organizations.

Encyclopedia of Associations, 46th Edition

3931

Benjamin Franklin Literary and Medical Soc. [14549]
British Assn. for Nutritional Therapy [IO]
British Dietetic Assn. [IO]
British Nutrition Found. [IO]
Canadian Found. for Dietetic Res. [IO]
Canadian Soc. for Nutritional Sciences [IO]
Chicano Family Center [17701]
Coeliac UK [IO]
Commn. on Dietetic Registration [IO]
Commn. on Dietetic Registration [15550]
Community Food Security Coalition [12192]
Community Nutrition Inst. [15551]
Community Systems Found. [15552]
Comparative Nutrition Soc. [15553]
Compassionate Cooks [13350]
Concern Am. [12845]
Consultant Dietitians in Hea. Care Facilities [15554]
Coun. on Hea. Info. and Educ. [14553]
Coun. for Responsible Nutrition [2841]
Dietary Managers Assn. [15555]
Dietitians Assn. of Australia [IO]
Dietitians of Canada [IO]
Digestive Disease Natl. Coalition [14416]
EarthSave Intl. [4504]
Egg Nutrition Center [15556]
European Acad. of Nutritional Sciences [IO]
European Assn. for Stud. on Nutrition and Child Development [IO]
European Fed. of the Associations of Dietitians [IO]
Feingold Assn. of the U.S. [15557]
Food and Nutrition Bd. [15558]
Freedom from Hunger [12394]
French Soc. for Vitamins and Biofactors [IO]
German Assn. of Dietitians [IO]
German Nutrition Soc. [IO]
German Org. of Nutrition [IO]
German Soc. of Nutrition [IO]
Gerson Inst. [13632]
Gluten Intolerance Gp. [15559]
God's Love We Deliver [12283]
Greek Dietetic Assn. [IO]
Holt Intl. Children's Services [11698]
Indian Soc. for Parenteral and Enteral Nutrition [IO]
Inst. of Nutrition of Central Am. and Panama [IO]
Intl. and Amer. Assn. of Clinical Nutritionists [IO]
Intl. and Amer. Associations of Clinical Nutrition- ists [15560]
Intl. Assn. for Surgical Metabolism and Nutrition [IO]
The Intl. Found. [12434]
Intl. Life Sciences Inst. - North Am. [15561]
Intl. Life Sciences Inst. - North Am. [IO]
Intl. Maillard Reaction Soc. [6683]
Intl. Soc. for Behavioral Nutrition and Physical Activity [13745]
Intl. Soc. of Sports Nutrition [15562]
Intl. Soc. of Sports Nutrition [IO]
Intl. Union of Nutritional Sciences [IO]
Intl. Union of Nutritional Sciences [15563]
Intl. Vitamin A Consultative Gp. [15564]
Intl. Vitamin A Consultative Gp. [IO]
Intersociety Professional Nutrition Educ. Consortium [15565]
Irish Nutrition and Dietetic Inst. [IO]
Islamic Food and Nutrition Coun. of Am. [2353]
Kids With Food Allergies [13603]
Life Extension Soc. [14074]
Lifegain Inst. [14573]
Los Ninos [12589]
Luxembourg Dietetic Assn. [IO]
Malaysian Dietitians Assn. [IO]
Meals4Israel [12459]
Natl. Alliance for Infusion Therapy [14839]
Natl. Assn. of Farmers' Market Nutrition Programs [4648]
Natl. Assn. of Nutrition and Aging Services Programs [15566]
Natl. Dairy Coun. [4494]
Natl. Hea. Assn. [15279]
Natl. Meals on Wheels Found. [11315]
Netherlands Dietetic Assn. [IO]

New Zealand Dietetic Assn. [IO]
North Amer. Soc. for Pediatric Gastroenterology, Hepatology and Nutrition [14424]
Norwegian Dietetics Assn. [IO]
Nutrition Australia [IO]
Nutrition Found. of the Philippines [IO]
Nutrition for Optimal Hea. Assn. [15567]
Nutrition Soc. [IO]
Nutrition Soc. of Australia [IO]
Nutrition Soc. of Southern Africa [IO]
Oley Found. for Home Parenteral and Enteral Nutrition [14843]
Parenteral and Enteral Nutrition Soc. of Asia [IO]
Peanut Inst. [5061]
Presbyterian Hunger Prog. [12397]
Price-Pottenger Nutrition Found. [15568]
Protein Foods and Nutrition Development Assn. of India [IO]
Self Help Intl. [12442]
Seventh-Day Adventist Dietetic Assn. [15569]
Shape Up Am. [15969]
Soc. for the Anthropology of Food and Nutrition [6424]
Soc. for Nutrition Educ. [15570]
Sports Dietitians Australia [IO]
Swedish Assn. of Dietitians [IO]
Swiss Assn. for Nutrition [IO]
Swiss Dietetic Assn. [IO]
Task Force for Child Survival and Development [12542]
TOPS Club (Take Off Pounds Sensibly) [12649]
Truth in Fitness [15970]
Vegan Action [11071]
Vegetarian Awareness Network [11072]
Vegetarian Rsrc. Gp. [11073]
Vitamin Angel Alliance [15571]
Vitamin Angel Alliance [IO]
Weight-Control Info. Network [15578]
Weight Watchers Intl. [14603]
Wellstart Intl. [14666]
Weston A. Price Found. [15572]
Nutrition; Amer. Acad. of Veterinary [16737]
Nutrition; Amer. Inst. of [★15548]
Nutrition Assn. of Canada; Animal [IO]
Nutrition Assn; School [9173]
Nutrition Australia [IO], Northcote, Australia
Nutrition Education Assn. - Defunct.
Nutrition; Families, 4-H, and [13483]
Nutrition, Food Safety and Consumer Hea; Comm. of Experts on [IO]
Nutrition Found. [★IO]
Nutrition Found. [★15561]
Nutrition; Found. for Digestive Hea. and [14417]
Nutrition Found; Intl. Life Sciences Inst. - [★15561]
Nutrition Found. of the Philippines [IO], Quezon City, Philippines
Nutrition; Intl. Coll. of Applied [★15560]
Nutrition; North Amer. Soc. for Pediatric Gastroenterology, Hepatology and [14424]
Nutrition; Oley Found. for Home Parenteral and En- teral [14843]
Nutrition for Optimal Hea. Assn. [15567], PO Box 380, Winnetka, IL 60093, (847)604-3258
Nutrition Soc. [IO], London, United Kingdom
Nutrition; Soc. for the Anthropology of Food and [6424]
Nutrition Soc. of Australia [IO], Kent Town, Australia
Nutrition Soc. of Southern Africa [IO], Brits, Republic of South Africa
Nutrition Today Soc. - Defunct.
Nutritional Consultants; Intl. Acad. of [★15540]
Nutritional Foods Assn; National [★3425]
Nutritional Sciences; Canadian Soc. for [IO]
Nutritionists; Amer. Assn. of Veterinary [★16737]
Nuts
African Groundnut Coun. [IO]
Almond Bd. of California [5048]
Amer. Peanut Coun. [5049]
Amer. Peanut Coun. - European Off. [IO]
Amer. Peanut Res. and Educ. Soc. [5050]
Amer. Peanut Shellers Assn. [5051]
Australian Macadamia Soc. [IO]
Blue Diamond Growers [5052]
British Peanut Coun. [IO]
California Macadamia Soc. [5053]

California Pistachio Commn. [5054]
Cashew Export Promotion Coun. of India [IO]
Combined Edible Nut Trade Assn. [IO]
Diamond Walnut Growers [5055]
European Nut Assn. [IO]
Georgia Peanut Commn. [5056]
Hazelnut and Products Exporters Union [IO]
Intl. Tree Nut Coun. [IO]
Natl. Peanut Buying Points Assn. [5057]
Natl. Peanut Festival Assn. [5058]
Natl. Pecan Shellers Assn. [5059]
Northern Nut Growers Assn. [2842]
Northern Nut Growers Assn. [IO]
Peanut Advisory Bd. [5060]
Peanut Inst. [5061]
Southwestern Peanut Growers Assn. [5062]
Specialty Crop Trade Coun. [4761]
Virginia-Carolina Peanut Assn. [5063]
Virginia-Carolina Peanut Promotions [5064]
Walnut Coun. [5065]
Walnut Marketing Bd. [5066]
Nuttall Ornithological Club [7422], c/o Museum of Comparative Zoology, 26 Oxford St., Harvard Univ., Cambridge, MA 02138, (617)495-2471
NWS Artists Referral Program [★9461]
Nyckelharpa Assn; Amer. [10546]
Nystagmus Network; Amer. [16828]
NYU School of Law; Brennan Center for Justice at [6176]
NYZS/The Wildlife Conservation Soc. [★4469]
NZ Amateur DanceSport Assn. [★IO]
NZX [IO], Wellington, New Zealand

O

O-Anon General Service Office - Address unknown since 2008.
Oak Flooring Indus; Southern [★656]
Oak Flooring Manufacturers Assn; Natl. [★656]
Oak Flooring Manufacturers of U.S. [★656]
Oak Ridge Assoc. Universities [7625], PO Box 117, Oak Ridge, TN 37831-0117, (865)576-3146
Oak Ridge Boys Intl. Fan Club [24952], 88 New Shackle Island Rd., Hendersonville, TN 37075, (615)824-4924
Oak Ridge Boys Intl. Fan Club [IO], Hendersonville, TN, United States
Oak Ridge Inst. of Nuclear Stud. [★7625]
Oak Soc; Intl. [5258]
Oak Soc; Live [4688]
Oakeshott Assn; Michael [7491]
Oakland-Pontiac Enthusiast Org. [21748]
Oaktree Found. [IO], Melbourne, Australia
Oarsmen; Natl. Assn. of Amateur [★23704]
OAS Staff Assn. [24144], 1889 F St. NW, No. 694C, Washington, DC 20006, (202)458-6230
Oasis [IO], London, United Kingdom
OASIS PKI Member Sect. [7780], c/o OASIS, PO Box 455, Billerica, MA 01821, (978)667-5115
Obec Architektu [★IO]
Obedience Instructors; Natl. Assn. of Dog [22312]
Obedience Stewards Club - Address unknown since 2004.
Oberhasli Breeders of Am. [4146], c/o Elise Shope Anderson, Sec.-Treas., 1035 Bardin Rd., Palatka, FL 32177
Obesity
Action for Healthy Kids [13945]
Amer. Assn. of Clinical Endocrinologists [14350]
Amer. Bd. of Bariatric Medicine [15573]
Amer. Obesity Assn. [15574]
Amer. Soc. of Bariatric Physicians [15575]
Asia-Oceania Assn. for the Stud. of Obesity [IO]
Australasian Soc. for the Stud. of Obesity [IO]
Belgian Assn. for the Stud. of Obesity [IO]
British Obesity Surgery Patient Assn. [IO]
Coun. on Size and Weight Discrimination [12644]
Fed. of Latin Amer. Societies of Obesity [IO]
Intl. Assn. for the Stud. of Obesity [IO]
Intl. Fed. for the Surgery of Obesity [IO]
International Size Acceptance Association [IO]
Intl. Size Acceptance Assn. [12645]
Israeli Soc. for Res. and Treatment of Obesity [IO]
Largely Positive [18177]

A star before a book entry number signifies that the name is not listed separately, but is mentioned within the entry.

Largesse, the Network for Size Esteem [12646]
Largesse, the Network for Size Esteem [IO]
Natl. Assn. to Advance Fat Acceptance [12647]
NOLOSE - The Natl. Org. for Lesbians of Size [12250]
North Amer. Assn. for the Stud. of Obesity [15576]
North Amer. Assn. for the Stud. of Obesity [IO]
Obesity Action Coalition [15577]
Overeaters Anonymous World Ser. Off. [12648]
Overeaters Anonymous World Ser. Off. [IO]
Prader-Willi Syndrome Assn. (U.S.A.) [14475]
Sociedad Espanola para el Estudio de la Obesidad [IO]
TOPS Club (Take Off Pounds Sensibly) [12649]
Truth in Fitness [15970]
Weight-Control Info. Network [15578]
Weight Watchers Intl. [14603]
Yugoslav Assn. for the Stud. of Obesity [IO]
Obesity Action Coalition [15577], 4511 N Himes Ave., Ste. 250, Tampa, FL 33614, (813)872-7835
Obesity; Assn. for the Stud. of [IO]
The Obesity Found. - Defunct.
Objective News Reporting; Fund for [17179]
Objectivism
Ayn Rand Inst. [10787]
The Objectivist Center [10821]
The Objectivist Center [10821], 1001 Connecticut Ave. NW, Ste. 425, Washington, DC 20036, (202)296-7263
Objectivist Stud; Inst. for [★10821]
Objectors; Natl. Interreligious Ser. Bd. for Conscientious [★17438]
Oblate Conf. of the U.S. - Defunct.
Oblate Education Assn. - Defunct.
Oblates; Inst. of Apostolic [19638]
Oblinger/Oplinger Family Assn. [21015], c/o Richard H. Oplinger, Pres., 1535 Morning Star Dr., Allentown, PA 18106-8760, (610)336-9330
O'Brian Youth Leadership; Hugh [8748]
Obscenity; Natl. Consultation on Pornography and [★18374]
Observatoire des Fonctions Publiques Africaines [★IO]
Observatoire du Sahara et du Sahel [★IO]
Observatory; National Optical Astronomy [★7622]
Observatory; National Radio Astronomy [★7622]
Observer Assn; Air Force Navigators [20659]
Observers Assn; Ellington Navigators [★20659]
Obsessive-Compulsive Anonymous [12555], PO Box 215, New Hyde Park, NY 11040, (516)739-0662
Obsessive Compulsive Disorder Found. [★15230]
Obsessive-Compulsive Found. [15230], 676 State St., New Haven, CT 06511, (203)401-2070
Obstetric Anaesthetists' Assn. [IO], London, United Kingdom
Obstetric Anesthesia and Perinatology; Soc. for [15903]
Obstetric, Gynecologic and Neonatal Nursing Specialties; Natl. Certification Corp. for the [15506]
Obstetric and Neonatal Nurses; Assn. of Women's Hea., [15470]
Obstetrical and Gynaecological Soc. of Hong Kong [IO], Hong Kong, People's Republic of China
Obstetrical and Gynaecological Soc. of Singapore [IO], Singapore, Singapore
Obstetricians and Gynecologists; Amer. Assn. of [★15587]
Obstetricians and Gynecologists; Amer. Assn. of Pro Life [18545]
Obstetricians and Gynecologists; Nurses Assn. of the Amer. Coll. of [★15470]
Obstetricians; Soc. of Perinatal [★15902]
Obstetrics; Amer. Soc. for Psychoprophylaxis in [★15608]
Obstetrics and Gynecology
Amer. Acad. of Husband-Coached Childbirth [15579]
Amer. Assn. of Birth Centers [15580]
Amer. Assn. of Gynecologic Laparoscopists [15581]
Amer. Bd. of Obstetrics and Gynecology [15582]
Amer. Coll. of Domiciliary Midwives [15583]
Amer. Coll. of Nurse-Midwives [15447]
Amer. Coll. of Obstetricians and Gynecologists [15584]

Amer. Coll. of Osteopathic Obstetricians and Gynecologists [15585]
Amer. Found. for Maternal and Child Health [15586]
Amer. Gynecological and Obstetrical Soc. [15587]
Amer. Pregnancy Assn. [15588]
Amer. Soc. of Breast Disease [13772]
Amer. Soc. of Childbirth Educators [15589]
Amer. Soc. for Colposcopy and Cervical Pathology [15590]
Amer. Soc. for Reproductive Medicine [14389]
Argentine Soc. of Psychosomatic Obstetrics and Gynaecology [IO]
Assn. for Childbirth at Home, Intl. [IO]
Assn. for Childbirth at Home, Intl. [15591]
Assn. of Professors of Gynecology and Obstetrics [15592]
Assn. of Radical Midwives [IO]
Assn. of Supervisors of Midwives [IO]
Assn. of Women's Hea., Obstetric and Neonatal Nurses [15470]
Australasian Menopause Soc. [IO]
Australian Gynaecological Endoscopy Soc. [IO]
British Soc. of Psychosomatic Obstetrics, Gynaecology and Andrology [IO]
C/SEC [15593]
Canadian Assn. of Midwives [IO]
Center for Humane Options in Childbirth Experiences [15594]
Childbirth Connection [15595]
Childbirth and Postpartum Professional Assn. [13980]
Chilean Soc. of Obstetrics and Gynecology [IO]
Coalition for Improving Maternity Services [15596]
Coun. on Resident Educ. in Obstetrics and Gynecology [15597]
Czech Gynecological and Obstetrical Soc. [IO]
Danish Soc. of Obstetrics and Gynaecology [IO]
Depression After Delivery [12667]
DONA Intl. [15598]
Dutch Soc. of Psychosomatic Obstetrics and Gynaecology [IO]
Endometriosis Assn. [IO]
Endometriosis Assn. [15599]
European Assn. of Perinatal Medicine [IO]
European Bd. and Coll. of Obstetrics and Gynaecology [IO]
European Soc. for Gynaecological Endoscopy [IO]
European Soc. of Gynecology [IO]
Fed. of Obstetric and Gynecological Societies of India [IO]
Fertility Res. Found. [14391]
French Soc. of Psychosomatic Obstetrics and Gynaecology [IO]
German Assn. of Self-Employed Midwives [IO]
Gp. B Strep Assn. [13962]
Gynecologic Oncology Gp. [15646]
Gynecologic Surgery Soc. [15600]
Hong Kong Coll. of Obstetricians and Gynaecologists [IO]
Hong Kong Gynaecological Endoscopy Soc. [IO]
Hong Kong Soc. for Colposcopy and Cervical Pathology [IO]
Hungarian Soc. of Psychosomatic Obstetrics and Gynaecology [IO]
Hysterectomy Educational Resources and Services Foundation [IO]
Hysterectomy Educational Resources and Services Found. [15601]
Independent Midwives Assn. [IO]
Indian Soc. of Psychosomatic Obstetrics and Gynaecology [IO]
Informed Homebirth/Informed Birth and Parenting [15602]
Inst. for Female Alternative Medicine [16345]
Intl. Assn. for Maternal and Neonatal Hea. [IO]
Intl. Assn. of Parents and Professionals for Safe Alternatives in Childbirth [IO]
Intl. Assn. of Parents and Professionals for Safe Alternatives in Childbirth [15603]
Intl. Cesarean Awareness Network [15604]
Intl. Cesarean Awareness Network [IO]
Intl. Childbirth Educ. Assn. [IO]
Intl. Childbirth Educ. Assn. [15605]

Intl. Confed. of Midwives [IO]
Intl. Coun. on Infertility Info. Dissemination [14392]
Intl. Fed. for Cervical Pathology and Colposcopy [IO]
Intl. Fed. of Gynecology and Obstetrics [IO]
Intl. Fed. of Pediatric and Adolescent Gynecology [IO]
Intl. Pelvic Pain Soc. [15843]
Intl. Premature Ovarian Failure Assn. [15606]
Intl. Soc. for Gynaecologic Endoscopy [IO]
Intl. Soc. of Psychosomatic Obstetrics and Gynaecology [IO]
Intl. Soc. of Ultrasound in Obstetrics and Gynecology [IO]
Intl. Stillbirth Alliance [13982]
Israeli Soc. of Psychosomatic Obstetrics and Gynaecology [IO]
Italian Soc. of Psychosomatic Obstetrics and Gynaecology [IO]
Japan Soc. of Obstetrics and Gynecology [IO]
La Leche League [IO]
Lamaze Birth Without Pain Educ. Assn. [15607]
Lamaze Intl. [15608]
Lamaze Intl. [IO]
Malaysian Menopause Soc. [IO]
Maternity Coalition [IO]
Midwest Parentcraft Center [15609]
Midwifery Educ. Accreditation Coun. [8063]
Midwives Alliance of North Am. [15610]
Midwives Info. and Rsrc. Ser. [IO]
Museum of Menstruation and Women's Hea. [15611]
Natl. Assn. of Nurse Practitioners in Women's Hea. [15497]
Natl. Certification Corp. for the Obstetric, Gynecologic and Neonatal Nursing Specialties [15506]
Natl. Coun. on Women's Hea. [16904]
Natl. Endometriosis Soc. [IO]
Natl. Healthy Mothers, Healthy Babies Coalition [15612]
Natl. Healthy Start Assn. [15613]
Natl. Perinatal Assn. [15900]
New Zealand Coll. of Midwives [IO]
Nordic Fed. of Societies of Obstetrics and Gynecology [IO]
North Amer. Menopause Soc. [15614]
North Amer. Soc. of Obstetric Medicine [15615]
North Amer. Soc. for the Stud. of Hypertension in Pregnancy [16342]
Obstetrical and Gynaecological Soc. of Hong Kong [IO]
Obstetrical and Gynaecological Soc. of Singapore [IO]
Org. Gestosis - Soc. for the Stud. of Pathophysiology of Pregnancy [IO]
Polycystic Ovarian Syndrome Assn. [IO]
Polycystic Ovarian Syndrome Assn. [15616]
Polycystic Ovarian Syndrome Assn. of Australia [IO]
Postpartum Support Intl. [12689]
Pregnant With Cancer Network [13865]
Premenstrual Soc. [IO]
Resolve, The Natl. Infertility Assn. [14394]
Royal Australian and New Zealand Coll. of Obstetricians and Gynaecologists [IO]
Royal Coll. of Midwives [IO]
Royal Coll. of Obstetricians and Gynaecologists - United Kingdom [IO]
Russian Gestosis Assn. [IO]
Sidelines Natl. High-Risk Pregnancy Support Network [15617]
Sociedad de Obstetricia y Ginecologia de Venezuela [IO]
Societa Italiana di Ginecologia ed Ostetricia [IO]
Soc. for Assisted Reproductive Tech. [16346]
Soc. for Gynecologic Investigation [15618]
Soc. of Gynecologic Oncologists [15654]
Soc. for Menstrual Cycle Res. [15619]
Soc. for Obstetric Anesthesia and Perinatology [15903]
Soc. of Obstetricians and Gynaecologists of Canada [IO]
Soc. of Psychosomatic Obstetrics and Gynaecology, Brazil [IO]

Reference to "IO" in place of a book number signifies that the association may be found in the 45th edition of International Organizations.

Soc. of Reproductive Surgeons [16349]
Soc. for the Stud. of Reproduction [16350]
Spanish Soc. of Psychosomatic Obstetrics and Gynaecology [IO]
Swedish Soc. of Psychosomatic Obstetrics and Gynaecology [IO]
Vulvar Pain Foundation [IO]
Vulvar Pain Found. [15620]
Waterbirth Intl. [13984]
Yugoslav Soc. of Cervical Pathology and Colposcopy [IO]
Obstetrics and Gynecology; Amer. Acad. of [★15584]
O.C. Intl. [20377], PO Box 36900, Colorado Springs, CO 80936, (719)592-9292
O.C. Intl. [IO], Colorado Springs, CO, United States
O.C. Ministries [★IO]
O.C. Ministries [★20377]
OCADES - Caritas Burkina Faso [IO], Ouagadougou, Burkina Faso
O'Carragher Clan Assn.: Caraher Family History Soc. - Address unknown since 2004.
Occidental Soc. of Metempiric Analysis - Address unknown since 2003.
Occipital Res. Soc; Sacro [★14013]
Occult
Christian Res. Inst. [19785]
USCCCN Natl. CH on Satanic Crime in Am. [11848]
Watchman Fellowship [19877]
Occult Stud. Found. [★7446]
Occult/Witchcraft Special Interest Gp; Pagan/ [10768]
Occupational Coun; Jewish [★9305]
Occupational Educ; Coun. on [8248]
Occupational Educ; Natl. Coun. for [★8361]
Occupational Education Project - Defunct.
Occupational and Environmental Diseases Assn. [IO], Enfield, United Kingdom
Occupational and Environmental Medical Assn. of Canada [IO], Oakville, ON, Canada
Occupational Health
Abilities! [11913]
Alberta Occupational Hea. Nurses Assn. [IO]
Amer. Acad. of Physical Medicine and Rehabilitation [16307]
Amer. Assn. of Occupational Hea. Nurses [15439]
Amer. Bd. for Occupational Hea. Nurses [15445]
Amer. Bd. of Physical Medicine and Rehabilitation [16309]
Amer. Conf. of Governmental Indus. Hygienists [15625]
Amer. Cong. of Rehabilitation Medicine [16310]
Amer. Industrial Health Coun. [15626]
Amer. Indus. Hygiene Assn. [15627]
Amer. Kinesiotherapy Assn. [16311]
Amer. Medical Rehabilitation Providers Assn. [16312]
Amer. Occupational Therapy Assn. [16602]
Amer. Physical Therapy Assn. [16603]
Amer. Rehabilitation Counseling Assn. [16313]
Amer. Soc. of Hand Therapists [14524]
Assn. of Academic Physiatrists [16316]
Bangladesh Occupational Therapy Assn. [IO]
Canadian Soc. of Occupational Scientists [IO]
Continuing Care Accreditation Commn. [16318]
Coun. of State Administrators of Vocational Rehabilitation [16320]
Hospitalized Veterans Writing Proj. [16321]
Inst. for Labor and Mental Health [15202]
Intl. Assn. of Rehabilitation Professionals [16322]
Intl. Sharps Injury Prevention Soc. [16380]
Natl. Assn. of Rehabilitation Instructors [16324]
Natl. Bd. for Certification in Occupational Therapy [16625]
Natl. Coun. on Rehabilitation Educ. [16329]
Natl. Rehabilitation Assn. [16330]
Natl. Rehabilitation Info. Center [16332]
Rehabilitation Intl. [16333]
Sheet Metal Occupational Hea. Inst. Trust [12991]
Singapore Assn. of Occupational Therapists [IO]
Sister Kenny Rehabilitation Inst. [16335]
Soc. for Occupational and Environmental Hea. [15633]
Soc. for Vocational Psychology [7551]

South African Soc. of Occupational Hea, Nursing Practitioners [IO]
Vocational Evaluation and Career Assessment Professionals [16337]
Occupational Health Inst. - Defunct.
Occupational Hea. Inst; Sheet Metal [★12991]
Occupational Hea. Inst. Trust; Sheet Metal [12991]
Occupational Hea; Intl. Commn. on [IO]
Occupational Hea; Nordic Inst. for Advanced Training in [IO]
Occupational Hea. Nurses; Amer. Assn. of [15439]
Occupational Hea. Nurses; Amer. Bd. for [15445]
Occupational Hea. Nurses Assn; Canadian [IO]
Occupational Knowledge International [IO], San Francisco, CA, United States
Occupational Knowledge Intl. [5099], 220 Montgomery St., Ste. 1027, San Francisco, CA 94104, (415)362-9898
Occupational Medical Administrators' Assn. - Address unknown since 1990.
Occupational Medical Assn; Amer. [★15624]
Occupational Medicine
Abilities! [11913]
Acad. of Organizational and Occupational Psychiatry [15621]
Acad. of Organizational and Occupational Psychiatry [IO]
Amer. Acad. of Physical Medicine and Rehabilitation [16307]
Amer. Acad. of Physician Assistants in Occupational Medicine [15622]
Amer. Bd. of Indus. Hygiene [15623]
Amer. Bd. of Physical Medicine and Rehabilitation [16309]
Amer. Coll. of Occupational and Environmental Medicine [15624]
Amer. Conf. of Governmental Indus. Hygienists [15625]
Amer. Cong. of Rehabilitation Medicine [16310]
Amer. Industrial Health Coun. [15626]
Amer. Indus. Hygiene Assn. [15627]
Amer. Kinesiotherapy Assn. [16311]
Amer. Medical Rehabilitation Providers Assn. [16312]
Amer. Occupational Therapy Assn. [16602]
Amer. Occupational Therapy Found. [15628]
Amer. Osteopathic Coll. of Occupational and Preventive Medicine [15802]
Amer. Physical Therapy Assn. [16603]
Amer. Rehabilitation Counseling Assn. [16313]
Amer. Soc. of Hand Therapists [14524]
Assn. of Academic Physiatrists [16316]
Assn. of Occupational and Environmental Clinics [16329]
Assn. of Occupational Hea. Professionals in Healthcare [16330]
Assn. for Repetitive Motion Syndromes [16331]
British Occupational Hygiene Soc. [IO]
Canadian Occupational Therapy Found. [IO]
Continuing Care Accreditation Commn. [16318]
Coun. for Accreditation in Occupational Hearing Conservation [15632]
Coun. of State Administrators of Vocational Rehabilitation [16320]
European Assn. of Schools of Occupational Medicine [IO]
European Centre for Occupational Hea., Safety and the Env. [IO]
European Network for Workplace Hea. Promotion [IO]
Faculty of Occupational Medicine [IO]
Hospitalized Veterans Writing Proj. [16321]
Inst. of Occupational Medicine [IO]
Intl. Assn. of Rehabilitation Professionals [16322]
Intl. Commn. on Occupational Hea. [IO]
Intl. Hea. and Safety Assn. for Radio and TV [IO]
Intl. Soc. for the Stud. of Tension in Performance [IO]
Irish Soc. of Occupational Medicine [IO]
Natl. Assn. of Rehabilitation Instructors [16324]
Natl. Assn. of Rehabilitation Providers and Agencies [16326]
Natl. Bd. for Certification in Occupational Therapy [16625]
Natl. Coun. on Rehabilitation Educ. [16329]

Natl. Rehabilitation Assn. [16330]
Natl. Rehabilitation Info. Center [16332]
Occupational and Environmental Diseases Assn. [IO]
Occupational and Environmental Medical Assn. of Canada [IO]
Occupational Therapy Assn. of South Africa [IO]
OT Australia: Australian Assn. of Occupational Therapists [IO]
Private Practice Section/American Physical Therapy Assn. [16633]
Rehabilitation Intl. [16333]
Sister Kenny Rehabilitation Inst. [16335]
Soc. for Occupational and Environmental Hea. [15633]
Soc. of Occupational Medicine [IO]
Swedish Assn. for the Electrosensitive [IO]
Vocational Evaluation and Career Assessment Professionals [16337]
Occupational Medicine; Amer. Acad. of [★15624]
Occupational Medicine; Amer. Coll. of [★15624]
Occupational and Preventive Medicine; Amer. Osteopathic Coll. of [15802]
Occupational Program Consultants Assn. - Address unknown since 2001.
Occupational Res. and Development; Center for [8354]
Occupational Safety and Health
Amer. Assn. of Safety Councils [12947]
Amer. Lung Assn. [16354]
Asia Pacific Occupational Safety and Hea. Org. [IO]
Assn. of Societies for Occupational Safety and Hea. [IO]
Canadian Centre for Occupational Hea. and Safety [IO]
Cong. of Lung Assn. Staff [16357]
Coun. for Accreditation in Occupational Hearing Conservation [15632]
Cystic Fibrosis Found. [16358]
European Found. for the Improvement of Living and Working Conditions [IO]
European Safety Fed. [IO]
Indus. Accident Prevention Assn. [IO]
Intl. Sharps Injury Prevention Soc. [16380]
Intl. Soc. of Mine Safety Professionals [15270]
Korea Indus. Safety Assn. [IO]
Natl. Jewish Medical and Res. Center [16361]
Natl. Safety Coun. of Australia [IO]
Natl. Safety Coun. of Singapore [IO]
Natl. Truckdrivers Safety Assn. [2843]
NATSO Found. [8948]
Sheet Metal Occupational Hea. Inst. Trust [12991]
Site Safe New Zealand [IO]
Voluntary Protection Programs Participants' Assn. [15634]
Occupational Therapists Assn. Mauritius [IO], Port Louis, Mauritius
Occupational Therapists Assn., Tanzania [IO], Moshi, United Republic of Tanzania
Occupational Therapists Assn. of Thailand [IO], Chiang Mai, Thailand
Occupational Therapists; Canadian Assn. of [IO]
Occupational Therapists for the European Countries; Coun. of [IO]
Occupational Therapy Assn; Amer. [16602]
Occupational Therapy Assn. of the Philippines [IO], Quezon City, Philippines
Occupational Therapy Assn. of South Africa [IO], Hatfield, Republic of South Africa
Occupational Therapy Certification Bd; Amer. [★16625]
Occupational Therapy Found; Amer. [15628]
Occupational Therapy Found; Canadian [IO]
Occupational Therapy; Natl. Bd. for Certification in [16625]
Occupational Therapy; Natl. Soc. for the Promotion of [★16602]
Occupied Japan Club [22098], c/o Florence Archambault, Sec./Ed., 29 Freeborn St., Newport, RI 02840-1821, (401)846-9024
Ocean Conservancy [4435], 2029 K St. NW, Washington, DC 20006, (202)429-5609
Ocean Conservancy [IO], Washington, DC, United States

A star before a book entry number signifies that the name is not listed separately, but is mentioned within the entry.

Ocean Education Project - Defunct.
Ocean Floor Anal. Div. (of U.S. Naval Oceanographic Off.) [★7404]
Ocean Floor Anal. and Res. Center; Global [★7404]
Ocean Futures [★5280]
Ocean Futures [★IO]
Ocean Futures Soc. [IO], Santa Barbara, CA, United States
Ocean Futures Soc. [5280], 325 Chapala St., Santa Barbara, CA 93101, (805)899-8899
Ocean Living Inst. - Defunct.
Ocean Outlook - Address unknown since 1995.
Ocean Pearl Button Mfrs. Assn. - Defunct.
Ocean Racing Club; Midget [23200]
Ocean Res. and Conservation Assn. [4436], Duerr Lab. for Marine Conservation, 1420 Seaway Dr., 2nd Fl., Fort Pierce, FL 34949, (772)467-1600
Ocean Resources Inst. - Defunct.
Ocean Soc. [7401], 441 Ridgewater Dr., Marietta, GA 30068-4071, (770)977-1838
Ocean Youth Club Scotland [★IO]
Ocean Youth Trust Scotland [IO], Glasgow, United Kingdom
Oceana [IO], Washington, DC, United States
Oceana [4437], 2501 M St. NW, Ste. 300, Washington, DC 20037-1311, (202)833-3900
Oceania; Assn. for Social Anthropology in Eastern [★6413]
Oceania Basketball Confed. [★IO]
Oceania Natl. Olympic Committees [IO], Suva, Fiji
Oceania Philatelic Soc. [★IO]
Oceania Philatelic Soc. [★22871]
Oceania Tennis Fed. [IO], Auckland, New Zealand
Oceania Weightlifting Fed. [IO], Apia, Western Samoa
Oceanic Educational Found. - Defunct.
Oceanic Engg. Soc; IEEE [7397]
Oceanic Navigation Res. Soc. [10444], PO Box 1641, Palm Springs, CA 92263-1641, (760)325-5398
Oceanic Soc. [★4397]
Oceanic Soc. [7402], Quarters 35 N, Ft. Mason, San Francisco, CA 94123, (415)441-1106
Oceanic Soc. Expeditions [23016], Ft. Mason, Quarters 35 N, San Francisco, CA 94123-1394, (415)441-1106
Oceanic Soc. Expeditions [IO], San Francisco, CA, United States
Oceanographic Data Center; National [★4590]
Oceanographic Off; Ocean Floor Anal. Div. of U.S. Naval [★7404]
Oceanographic Soc. of Japan [IO], Tokyo, Japan
Oceanographic Soc. of the Pacific [★IO]
Oceanographic Soc. of the Pacific [★7393]
Oceanography
Amer. Meteorological Soc. [7325]
Amer. Soc. of Limnology and Oceanography [7393]
American Society of Limnology and Oceanography [IO]
Center for Oceans Law and Policy [7394]
Clean Beaches Coun. [4540]
The Coastal Soc. [7395]
Coastal States Org. [7396]
Cushman Found. for Foraminiferal Res. [7428]
Estuarine and Coastal Sciences Assn. [IO]
IEEE Oceanic Engg. Soc. [7397]
Intergovernmental Oceanographic Commn. [IO]
Intl. Assn. for Biological Oceanography [IO]
Intl. Assn. for the Physical Sciences of the Oceans [IO]
Intl. Assn. for the Physical Sciences of the Oceans [7398]
Intl. Ocean Inst. [IO]
Intl. Oceanographic Found. [IO]
Intl. Oceanographic Found. [7399]
Intl. SeaKeepers Soc. [5010]
Natl. Ocean Indus. Assn. [7400]
North Amer. Soc. for Oceanic History [10443]
Ocean Res. and Conservation Assn. [4436]
Ocean Soc. [7401]
Oceanic Soc. [7402]
Oceanographic Soc. of Japan [IO]
The Oceanography Soc. [IO]
The Oceanography Soc. [7403]

Permanent Ser. for Mean Sea Level [IO]
Sea Grant Assn. [7276]
Seafloor Geosciences Div. [7404]
SeaWeb [5015]
Soc. for Underwater Tech. [IO]
Soc. of Woman Geographers [7124]
Oceanography; Amer. Soc. for [★7273]
Oceanography; Amer. Soc. of Limnology and [7393]
Oceanography Assn; Natl. [★7400]
Oceanography; Assn. of Physical [★7398]
Oceanography; Intl. Assn. of Physical [★7398]
Oceanography of the Intl. Union of Geodesy and Geophysics; Sect. of Physical [★7398]
Oceanography and Marine Meteorology; Tech. Commn. for [IO]
The Oceanography Soc. [IO], Rockville, MD, United States
The Oceanography Soc. [7403], PO Box 1931, Rockville, MD 20849-1931, (301)251-7708
Ockenden Intl. - England [IO], Woking, United Kingdom
Octaves Beyond Silence - Address unknown since 2005.
Octavian Soc. - Address unknown since 2001.
Octogenarians; United Flying [21485]
Ocular Implant Soc; Amer. Intra- [★15665]
Ocularists; Amer. Soc. of [15118]
Ocularists; Natl. Examining Bd. of [15694]
Oculo-Cerebro-Renal Syndrome
Lowe Syndrome Assn. [14462]
O'Day Owners Assn. - Address unknown since 1991.
Odborovy svaz Unios [IO], Prague, Czech Republic
Odd Fellows
Grand United Order of Odd Fellows [19294]
Independent Order of Odd Fellows [19295]
Intl. Assn. of Rebekah Assemblies, IOOF [19296]
Intl. Assn. of Rebekah Assemblies, IOOF [IO]
Junior Lodge, Independent Order of Odd Fellows [19297]
Odd Shoe Exchange; Natl. [11974]
Oddities; Registry of Italian [★21673]
Odell Family Assn. - Address unknown since 2005.
ODF Alliance [7209], 1090 Vermont Ave. NW, 6th Fl., Washington, DC 20005, (202)789-4450
Odinism
Asatru Alliance [19461]
O'Dochartaigh Clann Assn. [IO], Buncrana, Ireland
Odontology; Amer. Bd. of Forensic [14401]
Odontology; Amer. Soc. of Forensic [14142]
ODPHP Hea. Info. Center [★14588]
ODPHP Natl. Hea. Info. Center [★14588]
Odyssey Fringe Science Res. Network - Address unknown since 1999.
Odyssey Inst. Corp. - Address unknown since 2007.
OECD Nuclear Energy Agency [IO], Issy-les-Moulineaux, France
OECD; U.S.A. - Bus. and Indus. Advisory Comm. to the [17466]
Oekologischer Aerztebund [★IO]
Oesterreichische Akademie der Wissenschaften [★IO]
Oesterreichische Forschungsstiftung fuer Entwicklungshilfe [★IO]
Oesterreichische Gesellschaft fur Musik [★IO]
Oesterreichische Theatertechnische Gesellschaft [★IO]
Oesterreichischer Astronomischer Verein [★IO]
Oesterreichischer Kaffee- und Tee-Verband [★IO]
Oesterreichischer Tennisverband [★IO]
Oesterreichischer Zeitschriften-und Fachmedien-Verband [★IO]
Oesterreichisches Nord-Sud Institut fur Entwicklungszusammenarbeit [★IO]
OEW Contractors; Natl. Assn. of [★1038]
Of a Like Mind [★20623]
Of the People Found. - Address unknown since 2004.
Off-Off Broadway Assn. - Defunct.
Off-Road Bicycling Assn; Natl. [★23320]
Off-Track Betting; Natl. Assn. of [23505]
Offender Aid and Restoration - Defunct.
Offender Counselors; Intl. Assn. of Addictions and [11824]
Offenders; Assn. on Programs for Female [11857]

Office
British Coun. for Offices [IO]
Early Typewriter Collectors Assn. [22015]
Independent Off. Products and Furniture Dealers Assn. [1698]
Off. Furniture Recyclers Forum [1704]
Off. and Professional Employees Intl. Union [23995]
SEIU, District 925, AFL-CIO [23996]
Office for the Advancement of Public Black Colleges [★8110]
Off. for the Advancement of Public Black Colleges of the Natl. Assn. of State Universities and Land-Grant Colleges [8112], c/o Natl. Assn. of State Universities and Land-Grant Colleges, 1307 New York Ave. NW, Ste. 400, Washington, DC 20005-4722, (202)478-6040
Off. for Advancement of Public Negro Colleges - of the Natl. Assn. of State Universities and Land-Grant Colleges [★8112]
Off. of the Americas [17051], 8124 W 3rd St., Ste. 202, Los Angeles, CA 90048, (323)852-9808
Off. of the Americas [IO], Los Angeles, CA, United States
Office Automation Mgt. Assn. - Address unknown since 1988.
Office Automation Soc. Intl. - Defunct.
Off. Automation Specialists; Assn. of Mailing, Shipping, and [2448]
Office-Based Surgery; Soc. for [★16558]
Off. of Black Ministries/Episcopal Church Center [19968], c/o Episcopal Church, 815 2nd Ave., New York, NY 10017, (212)716-6084
Off. of Black and Urban Ministries/Episcopal Church Center [★19968]
Off. Bus. Center Assn. Intl. [74], 15000 Commerce Pkwy., Ste. C, Mount Laurel, NJ 08054, (856)439-1076
Off. Canadien de Commercialisation du Dindon [★IO]
Off. Canadien de Commercialisation des Oeufs [★IO]
Office for Church in Soc. - Defunct.
Office of Communication - Defunct.
Off. for the Coordination of Humanitarian Affairs - Geneva [IO], Geneva, Switzerland
Off. Directors; Natl. Assn. for State Economic Opportunity [★6279]
Office of Domestic Social Development [★19613]
Office of Domestic Social Development [★IO]
Off. Du Haut Commissaire Aux Droits de l'Homme [★IO]
Off. Educ. Assn. [★9302]
Off. Educ; Natl. Assn. of Supervisors of Bus. and [★8034]
Off. on Educational Credit [★8406]
Off. on Educational Credit and Credentials [★8406]
Off. Employees Intl. Union [★23995]
Off. Employees; Natl. Assn. of Farm Ser. Agency County [5779]
Office Equipment
British Off. Supplies and Services Fed. [IO]
Bus. Tech. Assn. [2844]
Canadian Off. Products Assn. [IO]
Copier Dealers Assn. [2845]
Document Mgt. Indus. Assn. [3679]
Dvorak Intl. [2846]
Dvorak Intl. [IO]
Early Typewriter Collectors Assn. [22015]
ISDA - Assn. of Storage and Retrieval Professionals [2847]
Japan Bus. Machine and Info. Sys. Indus. Assn. [IO]
Modular Building Inst. [2848]
Natl. Assn. of Graphic and Prdt. Identification Mfrs. [2720]
Off. Furniture Distribution Assn. [4025]
Off. Products Wholesalers Assn. [3686]
Operations Mgt. Education and Res. Found. [7167]
School and Home Off. Products Assn. [2849]
Tag and Label Mfrs. Inst. [3687]
Writing Instrument Mfrs. Assn. [3688]
Off. Equip. Mfrs. Inst. [★904]
Off. Furniture Dealers Alliance [★1698]

Reference to "IO" in place of a book number signifies that the association may be found in the 45th edition of International Organizations.

Off. Furniture Distribution Assn. [4025], 739 Daniel Shays Hwy., D-16, Athol, MA 01331, (978)249-0303

Off. Furniture Forum; Retail [★1704]

Off. Furniture Recyclers Forum [1704], c/o Off. Furniture Dealers Alliance, 301 N Fairfax St., Alexandria, VA 22314, (703)549-9040

Off. of Hea. Economics [IO], London, United Kingdom

Off. of the High Commissioner for Human Rights [IO], Geneva, Switzerland

Off. for Intellectual Freedom [6047], c/o Judith F. Krug, Dir., Amer. Lib. Assn., 50 E Huron St., Chicago, IL 60611, (800)545-2433

Off. Intl. des Epizooties [★IO]

Office of Intl. Justice and Peace [★IO]

Office of Intl. Justice and Peace [★19613]

Off. Intl. de l'Eau [★IO]

Off. Intl. de l'Enseignement Catholique [★IO]

Office for Jewish Population Res. - Defunct.

Off. Machine Dealers Assn; Natl. [★2844]

Off. Machine Dealers Assn; Natl. Typewriter and [★2844]

Off. Mgt. Assn; Life [★2196]

Off. Mgt; Professional Assn. of Hea. Care [15073]

Off. Managers; Professional Assn. of Hea. Care [★15073]

Off. of Minorities in Higher Educ. [★8887]

Off. of the Natl. Bibliography [★IO]

Off. Natl. Du Film Du Canada [★IO]

Off. Natl. Interprofessionnel des Fruits, des Legumes et de l'Horticulture [★IO]

Off. Natl. Interprofessionnel des Vins [★IO]

Off. Paper Recycling Proj; Natl. [3999]

Off. of Paranormal Investigation and Res. Intl. - Defunct.

Off. Parks; Natl. Assn. of Indus. and [★3320]

Off. Personnel; Natl. Assn. of Educational [★7898]

Office Planners and Users Group - Address unknown since 2007.

Off. of Population Affairs CH [12757], PO Box 30686, Bethesda, MD 20824, (866)640-7827

Off. Products Alliance; Natl. [3685]

Off. Products of the Bus. Products Indus. Assn. Dealers Alliance [★3685]

Off. Products and Furniture Dealers Assn; Independent [1698]

Office Products Mfrs. Alliance - Defunct.

Office Products Representatives Alliance - Defunct.

Off. Products Wholesalers Assn. [3686], 5024 Campbell Blvd., Ste. R, Baltimore, MD 21236-5943, (410)931-8100

Off. and Professional Employees Intl. Union [23995], 265 W 14th St., 6th Fl., New York, NY 10011, (212)675-3210

Off. Professionals; Natl. Assn. of Educational [7898]

Off. Properties; Natl. Assn. of Indus. and [3320]

Off. Realtors; Soc. of Indus. and [3343]

Office of State-Federal Relations [★6283]

Off. Systems Cooperative; ISDA - The [★2847]

Off. Systems Res. Assn. [★9234]

Office Technology Mgt. Assn. - Defunct.

Office Technology Res. Group - Defunct.

Off. Underwriters; Assn. of Home [2148]

Off. of the United Nations Disaster Relief Coordinator [★IO]

Off. of Women in Higher Educ., Amer. Coun. on Educ. [9324], c/o Amer. Coun. on Educ., 1 Dupont Cir. NW, Washington, DC 20036, (202)939-9300

Officer Assn; Logistics [2736]

Officer Training School Assn. - Address unknown since 1999.

Officers

Amer. Heraldry Soc. [21102]

Assn. of Inspectors Gen. [5777]

European Reserve Noncommissioned Officers Assn. [IO]

Fed. Hispanic Law Enforcement Officers Assn. [5969]

Hispanic Amer. Police Command Officers Assn. [5970]

Military Officers Assn. of Am. [21235]

Military Order of Foreign Wars of the U.S. [21236]

Natl. Assn. of Responsible Loan Officers [1978]

Natl. Assn. of Tribal Historic Preservation Officers [10047]

Natl. Chief Petty Officers' Assn. [21214]

Natl. Info. Officers Assn. [6231]

Natl. Order of Battlefield Commissions [21237]

North Amer. Assn. of Commencement Officers [8492]

Private Equity CFO Assn. [1445]

SATS/EAF Assn. [21179]

Sea Ser. Leadership Assn. [21238]

Women in Fed. Law Enforcement [6010]

Officers' Action League; Gay [12231]

Officers; Amer. Fed. of Security [24184]

Officers Assn; Employed Coun. [★19902]

Officers' Assn; Marine Corps Reserve [★6082]

Officers Assn; Natl. Bus. [8009]

Officers' Assn; Natl. Chief Petty [21214]

Officers Assn; Natl. Drug Enforcement [5993]

Officers Assn; Natl. Latino Peace [19195]

Officers Assn; Natl. Narcotic Enforcement [★5741]

Officers Assn; Natl. Naval [6093]

Officers Assn; Native Amer. Finance [1442]

Officers Assn; Naval Reserve [★6103]

Officers Assn; Non Commissioned [21316]

Officers Assn; North Amer. Wildlife Enforcement [5357]

Officers Assn; The Retired [★21235]

Officers Assn. of the U.S.A; Non Commissioned [6102]

Officers Assn; U.S. Army Warrant [6108]

Officers Assn; U.S. Coast Guard Chief Petty [20734]

Officers Assn. of the U.S. Public Hea. Ser; Commissioned [6214]

Officers Assn. of the U.S; Reserve [6103]

Officers' Christian Fellowship of the U.S.A. [19820], 3784 S Inca, Englewood, CO 80110-3405, (800)424-1984

Officers; Community Coll. Bus. [8020]

Officers for Life; Natl. Fed. of [18559]

Officers; Natl. Assn. of Placement Personnel [★8961]

Officers; Natl. Assn. of Special Police and Security [24122]

Officers of the Naval Services; Reserve [★6103]

Officers; Retired Affairs [★6104]

Officers Ser; Amer. Maritime [6058]

Official 3 Stooges Fan Club - Defunct.

Official Aerrage Fan Club - Defunct.

Official All-4-One Intl. Fan Club - Defunct.

The Official Austin Powers Collector's Club [24826]

Official Betty Boop Fan Club [24792], 10550 Western Ave., No. 133, Stanton, CA 90680-6909, (714)816-0717

Official Betty Boop Fan Club [IO], Stanton, CA, United States

Official Bobby Hart Fan Club - Address unknown since 1989.

Official Centennial Olympic Games Club - Address unknown since 1999.

Official David McCallum Fan Club - Defunct.

Official Dutch Jackson Fanclub [IO], Nijmegen, Netherlands

Official Elvis Presley Fan Club of Great Britain [IO], Leicester, United Kingdom

Official Gary Lewis and the Playboys Fan Club - Defunct.

Official Gilligan's Island Fan Club [25038], 12429 Dormouse Rd., San Diego, CA 92129

Official Gumby Fan Club [24793], c/o Toon's Sta., Inc., 5 Hanley Ct., Tabernacle, NJ 08088, (609)268-6680

Official Intl. Dave Prowse Fan Club - Address unknown since 2004.

Official Intl. Michael York Fan Club [24763], c/o Alexandria Banevicius, 3424 Knox Pl., Apt. 3G, Bronx, NY 10467

Official Intl. Peter Coyote Fan Club - Address unknown since 2007.

Official Intl. Robert Trebor Fan Club - Defunct.

Official International Toy Center Dir. - Defunct.

Official Jan and Dean Authorized Intl. Collectors' Club - Address unknown since 1989.

Official Julio Iglesias Intl. Fan Club [24835], PO Box 611930, Miami, FL 33161, (305)940-8449

Official Kate Linder Fan Club - Address unknown since 2001.

Official Lane Brody and Eleni Global Fan Club [24953], c/o Eddie Bayers, Gen. Mgr., PO Box 24775, Nashville, TN 37202

Official Lane Brody and Eleni Global Fan Club [IO], Nashville, TN, United States

Official Lane Brody Global Fan Club [★IO]

Official Lane Brody Global Fan Club [★24953]

Official Leonard Nimoy Fan Club [IO], Coventry, United Kingdom

Official Mail Study Group - Defunct.

Official Martha Hackett Fan Club - Defunct.

Official Mary Wilson Message Bd. and Fan Club [24954], 2305 W Ruthrauff Rd., No. L-14, Tucson, AZ 85705-1985

Official Michael Biehn Fan Club [24764], c/o Ed Limato, 8942 Wilshire Blvd., Beverly Hills, CA 90211

Official Red Dwarf Fan Club [25039], c/o Jupiter Mining Company, PO Box 13097, Coyote, CA 95013

Official Robert Newman Fan Club [24765], PO Box 102, Hope Mills, NC 28348

Official Rocky Horror Fan Club - Address unknown since 1995.

Official Secretariat Fan Club - Defunct.

Official Sybil Jason Fan Club [★24746]

Official Tim Topper Fan Club - Defunct.

Official Valentine's Day Coun. - Defunct.

Officials Assn; Amer. Wrestling Coaches and [★23987]

Officials Assn; Natl. Fed. [★23874]

Officials Assn; Natl. Fed. Interscholastic [★23874]

Officials Assn; Natl. Intercollegiate Soccer [23778]

Officials Assn; NFHS [23874]

Officials Bur; Eastern Coll. Soccer [★23776]

Officials Bur; Eastern Soccer [★23776]

Officials of Bureaus of Labor; Assn. of Chiefs and [★5917]

Officials Conf. of Am; Building [★5548]

Officials; Elected Spanish Speaking [★6122]

Officials; Natl. Assn. of County [★5618]

Officials; Natl. Assn. of Sports [23872]

Officials; Natl. Assn. of State Procurement [6238]

Officials; Natl. Assn. of State Purchasing [★6238]

Officials; Natl. Collegiate Athletic Assn. of Wrestling Coaches and [★23987]

Officials; Natl. League of Spanish Speaking Elected [★6122]

Offset Assn; Web [1794]

Offshore Contractors Assn. [IO], Aberdeen, United Kingdom

Offshore Coun; Natl. [★23205]

Offshore Dept; Natl. [23205]

Offshore Fish and Lobster Assn; Atlantic [★5728]

Offshore Fishermen's Assn; Atlantic [★5728]

Offshore Lobstermen's Assn; Atlantic [5728]

Offshore Marine Ser. Assn. [2590], 990 N Corporate Dr., Ste. 210, Harahan, LA 70123, (504)734-7622

Offshore Pollution Liability Assn. [IO], Ewell, United Kingdom

Offshore Rescue and Towing; Comm. for Private [2574]

Offshore Valve Assn. - Address unknown since 2003.

Ogden House Seniors 50 Club [IO], Calgary, AB, Canada

Ogolnopolskie Porozumienie Zwiazkow Zawodowych [★IO]

OGR [★IO]

OGR [★2783]

Ogwashi-Uku Assn., USA [19291], 10575 Westpark Dr., No. 424, Houston, TX 77042

Oh Ji Ho Intl. Fan Club [24781], PO Box 894045, Mililani, HI 96789

O'Hare Family Assn. [21016], 7472 Whistlestop Way, Roseville, CA 95747, (916)791-0405

Ohashi Inst. [15748], 147 W 25th St., 6th Fl., New York, NY 10001, (646)486-1187

Ohashi Inst. [IO], New York, NY, United States

Ohio Assn. of Christian Schools [★IO]

Ohio Assn. of Christian Schools [★8081]

Ohio Ceramics Assn. [★786]

Ohio Farm and Rural Vacation Assn. - Defunct.

Ohio Genealogical Soc. [21138], 713 S Main St., Mansfield, OH 44907-1644, (419)756-7294

Ohio Herpetological Soc. [★7160]

Ohio Historical Soc; Chesapeake and [10910]

Ohio Longrifle Collectors; Assn. of [22425]

Ohio Org. Development Network [★2866]

A star before a book entry number signifies that the name is not listed separately, but is mentioned within the entry.

Ohio Org. Development Network [★IO]
Ohio Penal Racing Assn. - Defunct.
Ohio Standard Breeding Assn. Youth Found.
[★23496]
Ohio Wage and Salary Assn. [★1283]
Ohio Wage and Salary Assn. [★IO]
Ohr Torah Institutions of Israel [8678], 49 W 45th
St., Ste. 701, New York, NY 10036-4603,
(212)935-8672
OIC Swine Breeders Assn. - Defunct.
An Oige [★IO]
Oil
   Amer. Exploration and Production Coun. [2914]
   Amer. Oil and Gas Historical Soc. [2915]
   Assn. for the Stud. of Peak Oil and Gas - USA
   [7461]
   Completion Engg. Assn. [7182]
   Energy Future Coalition [6952]
   Flight Safety Found. [148]
   Intl. Coun. for Machinery Lubrication [7253]
   Interstate Oil and Gas Compact Commn. [5684]
   Natl. Petroleum Coun. [5686]
   Used Oil Mgt. Assn. [1903]
Oil and Acrylic Painters' Soc; Natl. [9459]
Oil Assn. of Am; Olive [★1503]
Oil Assn; Amer. Olive [★2859]
Oil Assn; North Amer. Olive [2859]
Oil Assn; Olive [★2859]
Oil Assn; Tall [★818]
Oil Assn. of the U.S.A; Essential [★1662]
Oil Change Assn; Automotive [408]
Oil, Chemical and Atomic Workers Intl. Union -
Defunct.
Oil Chemists' Soc; Amer. [6669]
Oil and Colour Chemists' Assn. [IO], Wembley,
United Kingdom
Oil Compact Commn; Interstate [★5684]
Oil Companies' European Org. for Environmental
and Hea. Protection [IO], Brussels, Belgium
Oil Companies Intl. Marine Forum [IO], London,
United Kingdom
Oil Company Cooperative; Union [★4482]
Oil Compounders Assn; Independent [★2927]
Oil Equip. Jobbers; Natl. Assn. of [★2941]
Oil Field Haulers Assn. - Defunct.
Oil Firing Tech. Assn. for the Petroleum Indus. [IO],
Ipswich, United Kingdom
Oil Fuel Inst; Natl. [★2943]
Oil and Gas Assn; Mid-Continent [★2950]
Oil and Gas Assn; Western [★2951]
Oil and Gas Associations; Liaison Comm. of
Cooperating [2933]
Oil and Gas Compact Commn; Interstate [5684]
Oil Heat Inst. of Am. [★2943]
Oil Heating Mfrs. Assn; Waste [★1903]
Oil Industry Information Comm. - Defunct.
Oil Investment Inst. - Address unknown since 1989.
Oil Mgt. Assn; Used [1903]
Oil Marketers Assn; BP and Amoco [★2920]
Oil Men's Assn. of America - Defunct.
Oil Out!; Get [5092]
Oil Painters of Am. [9520], PO Box 2488, Crystal
Lake, IL 60039-2488, (815)356-5987
Oil Pastel Assn. Intl. - Defunct.
Oil Pipe Lines; Assn. of [2919]
Oil Pipe Lines; Comm. for [★2919]
Oil Recyclers Assn; Natl. [2938]
Oil Scouts and Landmen's Assn; Natl. [★2932]
Oil Spill Control Assn. of Amer. [★3073]
Oil Spills
   Norwegian Oil Spill Control Assn. [IO]
Oil Trades Assn. of New York - Address unknown
since 1991.
Oil and Varnish Assn; Natl. Paint, [★2884]
Oil Wholesale Marketers Assn; Gulf [★2920]
Oilers; Natl. Conf. of Firemen and [24058]
Oilers and Watertenders of the Pacific; Marine Fire-
men, [★24130]
Oilers, Watertenders and Wipers Assn; Pacific Coast
Marine Firemen, [24130]
Oilfield Production Equipment Mfrs. Assn. - Defunct.
Oilfields Workers' Trade Union [IO], San Fernando,
Trinidad and Tobago
Oils and Fats
   Amer. Oil Chemists' Soc. [6669]

Andhra Pradesh Oil Millers' Assn. [IO]
Argentina Oils and Fats Assn. [IO]
Argentine Oil Indus. Chamber [IO]
ASEAN Vegetable Oils Club [IO]
Assn. of Danish Oil and Oilseed Processors [IO]
Assn. of the German Margarine Indus. [IO]
Associazione Italiana dell' Industria Olearia [IO]
Australian Oilseeds Fed. [IO]
Australian Olive Oil Assn. [IO]
Austrian Oil Crushers and Processors [IO]
Canadian Oilseed Processors Assn. [IO]
Canola Assn. of Australia [IO]
Canola Coun. of Canada [IO]
EC Seed Crushers' and Oil Processors' Fed. [IO]
European Petroleum Indus. Assn. [IO]
Fats and Proteins Research Foundation [IO]
Fats and Proteins Res. Found. [2850]
Federacion de Asociaciones Molturadores y Refi-
nadores de Aceites Vegetales del Reino de Es-
pana [IO]
Fed. of Oils, Seeds, and Fats Associations [IO]
Federative van Belgische Fabrikanten van Vetten
en Olien [IO]
Finnish Oil Millers' Assn. [IO]
Greek Assn. of Indus. and Processors of Olive Oil
[IO]
Huileries de France [IO]
Inst. of Shortening and Edible Oils [2851]
Intl. Castor Oil Assn. [2852]
Intl. Castor Oil Assn. [IO]
Intl. Fish Meal and Fish Oil Org. [IO]
Intl. Olive Oil Coun. [IO]
International Society for Fat Research [IO]
Intl. Soc. for Fat Res. [7405]
Margarine and Spreads Assn. [IO]
Natl. Assn. of the Edible Oils and Fats Indus. [IO]
Natl. Assn. of the German Tallow and Lard Indus.
[IO]
Natl. Assn. of Margarine Mfrs. [2853]
Natl. Cottonseed Products Assn. [2854]
Natl. Fed. of Edible Oil Traders [IO]
Natl. Fish Meal and Oil Assn. [2855]
Natl. Inst. of Oilseed Products [2856]
Natl. Inst. of Oilseed Products [IO]
Natl. Oilseed Processors Assn. [2857]
Natl. Renderers Assn. [2858]
North Amer. Olive Oil Assn. [2859]
North American Olive Oil Association [IO]
Olajmagfeldolgozok Magyarorszagi Egyesulete
[IO]
Philippine Coconut Oil Producers Assn. [IO]
Seed Crushers' and Oil Processors' Assn. [IO]
Spanish Olive Oil Exporters Assn. [IO]
Taiwan Margarine Indus. Assn. [IO]
Verband Deutscher Oelmuhlen e.v. [IO]
Vereniging van Nederlandse Fabrikanten van Eet-
bare Olien en Vetten [IO]
Oilwatch Network [IO], Quito, Ecuador
Oilwell Drilling Contractors; Amer. Assn. of [★2930]
Oilwell Servicing Contractors; Assn. of [★2918]
OISTAT Centre of Great Britain [IO], London, United
Kingdom
OISTAT Japan Centre [IO], Tokyo, Japan
Oita Sports Assn. for the Disabled [IO], Oita, Japan
O.J. Club [★22098]
O.J. Noer Res. Found. [4796], PO Box 94, Juneau,
WI 53039-0094, (863)619-9822
OK Kosher Certification [20169], 391 Troy Ave.,
Brooklyn, NY 11213, (718)756-7500
OK Labs - Kosher Certification [★20169]
Oklahoma Assn; Univ. of [★18919]
Oklahoma Baptist Univ. Alumni Assn. [18917],
Oklahoma Baptist Univ., 500 W Univ., Shawnee,
OK 74804, (405)275-2850
Oklahoma City Univ. Alumni Off. [18918], 2501 N
Blackwelder, Oklahoma City, OK 73106-1493,
(405)521-5117
Oklahoma Univ. Alumni Assn. [18919], 900 Asp
Ave., Ste. 427, Norman, OK 73019-4051,
(405)325-1710
Okologischer Arztebund eV Ecological Physicians
Assn. [★IO]
Okologisk Landslag [★IO]
Okruzhajuschaya steda i Ya [★IO]
Oksana Baiul Official Intl. Fan Club - Address
unknown since 2006.

Olajmagfeldolgozok Magyarorszagi Egyesulete [IO],
Budapest, Hungary
The Old Appliance Club [21535], PO Box 65, Ven-
tura, CA 93002, (805)643-3532
Old Boys Network Turtle Club - Address unknown
since 1999.
Old Crows; Assn. of [6908]
Old English Game Club of America - Address
unknown since 1995.
Old English Sheepdog Club of Am. [22334], c/o Col-
leen Allen Grady, Pres., 3643 N Pearl St., Tacoma,
WA 98407, (253)262-1797
Old Fishes; Soc. for the Protection of [7177]
Old Guard Soc. [★1519]
Old House Lovers; Victorian Homeowner's Assn.
and [10075]
Old Ivory Porcelain Soc. - Address unknown since
2004.
Old Lesbians Organizing [★11317]
Old Lesbians Organizing for Change [11317], PO
Box 5853, Athens, OH 45701, (740)448-6424
Old Mills; Soc. for the Preservation of [10065]
Old Mine Lamp Collectors Soc. of America -
Defunct.
Old Newsboys; Good Fellows [13042]
Old Old Timers Club [21508], c/o Milbert Wells,
Exec. Sec., 3191 Darvany Dr., Dallas, TX 75220-
1611, (214)352-4743
Old Old Timers Club [IO], Dallas, TX, United States
Old Radio Program Collectors Club - Defunct.
Old Reel Collectors Assn. [22099], c/o Roger
Schulz, Sec.-Treas., 160 Shoreline Walk, Al-
pharetta, GA 30022
Old Reel Collectors Association [IO], Alpharetta, GA,
United States
Old Settlers and Threshers Assn; Midwest [9483]
Old Sleepy Eye Collectors' Club of Am. [21934],
1405 10th Ave. SE, Rochester, MN 55904-5369,
(507)254-3024
Old Time Dance Soc. [IO], East Yorkshire, United
Kingdom
Old Time Radio Club [22927], 56 Christen Ct., Lan-
caster, NY 14086, (716)683-6199
Old-time Radio-Show Collectors Assn. [IO], Shef-
field, United Kingdom
Old Time Western Film Club [24827]
Old Timer Assay Commissioners Soc. - Defunct.
Old Timers' Assn. of the Energy Indus; Natl. [6965]
Old Timers' Club - Defunct.
Old Timers' Club of the Oilburners Indus. [★6965]
Old Timers; Williams Grove [★21634]
Old World Archaeological Study Unit - Defunct.
Oldenburg Registry N.A. [4940], 517 DeKalb Ave.,
Sycamore, IL 60178, (815)899-7803
Older Men; Wives of [12509]
Older Women's League [13435], 3300 N Fairfax Dr.,
Ste. 218, Arlington, VA 22201, (703)812-7990
Older Women's League Task Force on Care Givers -
Defunct.
Older Women's Liberation - Defunct.
Older Women's Network NSW [IO], Millers Point,
Australia
Olds Club of Am; Hurst/ [21661]
Oldsmobile Club of Am. [21749]
Oldsmobile Club; Natl. Antique [21726]
Oldsmobile Performance Chap. - Address unknown
since 1994.
Oldtime Fiddlers' Assn; Natl. [10665]
Oldtime Radio Collectors and Traders Soc. -
Defunct.
Oleander Soc; Natl. [★22523]
O'Leary Brothers Fan Club - Address unknown since
2004.
Oleochemicals Assn; Glycerine and [★822]
Oley Found. for Home Parenteral and Enteral Nutri-
tion [14843], 214 Hun Memorial, MC-28, Albany
Medical Ctr., Albany, NY 12208-3478, (518)262-
5079
Olfactory Res. Fund [★1664]
Olfactory Res. Fund [★IO]
Olimpiadas Especiales de Hondras [★IO]
Olimpiadas Especiales de Paraguay [★IO]
Olimpiadas Especiales de Uruguay [★IO]
Olimpiady Specjalne Polska [★IO]
Olimpijiski komite slovenijie zdruzenje sportnih zvez
[★IO]

Reference to "IO" in place of a book number signifies that the association may be found in the 45th edition of International Organizations.

Encyclopedia of Associations, 46th Edition

3937

Olimpijski komite slovenije [★IO]
Olin Found; John M. [12047]
Olive Advisory Bd. - Defunct.
Olive Assn; California [1504]
Olive Assn. Midnorth South Australia [IO], Adelaide, Australia
Olive Oil Assn. [★IO]
Olive Oil Assn. [★2859]
Olive Oil Assn. of Am. [★1503]
Olive Oil Assn; Amer. [★2859]
Olive Oil Assn; North Amer. [2859]
Olive Oil Gp. [★2859]
Olive Oil Gp. [★IO]
Olive Producers (North East Victoria) [IO], Wangaratta, Australia
Oliver Wendell Holmes Assn. - Defunct.
Olives South Australia [IO], Adelaide, Australia
Oljeindustriens Landsforening [★IO]
Ollier's Disease Self-Help Gp. [★15749]
Ollier's/Maffucci Self-Help Gp. [★15749]
Olmsted Parks; Natl. Assn. for [5591]
Olodaryngologists; Soc. of Univ. [★15828]
Olson 30 Class Assn. [23210], 12 La Linda Dr., Long Beach, CA 90807
Oluklu Mukavva Sanayicileri Dernegi [★IO]
Olympian Intl. - Defunct.
Olympic Assn; U.S. [★23637]
Olympic Comm. of the Former Yugoslav Republic of Macedonia [IO], Skopje, Macedonia
Olympic Comm. of Israel [IO], Tel Aviv, Israel
Olympic Comm. of Portugal [IO], Lisbon, Portugal
Olympic Comm. of Serbia and Montenegro [IO], Belgrade, Serbia
Olympic Comm. of Slovenia [IO], Ljubljana, Slovenia
Olympic Comm. of Slovenia Assn. of Sports Federations [IO], Ljubljana, Slovenia
Olympic Coun. of Asia [IO], Hawalli, Kuwait
Olympic Coun. of Ireland [IO], Dublin, Ireland
Olympic Coun. of Malaysia [IO], Kuala Lumpur, Malaysia
Olympic Educ. Center [★23637]
Olympic Games
  Amer. Samoa Natl. Olympic Comm. [IO]
  Assn. of Natl. Olympic Committees [IO]
  Assn. of Natl. Olympic Committees of Africa [IO]
  Assn. of Summer Olympic Intl. Federations [IO]
  Austrian Olympic Comm. [IO]
  Bahamas Olympic Assn. [IO]
  Barbados Olympic Assn. [IO]
  Bermuda Olympic Assn. [IO]
  Brazilian Olympic Comm. [IO]
  British Olympic Assn. [IO]
  Bulgarian Olympian Comm. [IO]
  Canadian Olympic Comm. [IO]
  Chinese Olympic Comm. [IO]
  Chinese Taipei Olympic Comm. [IO]
  Colombian Olympic Comm. [IO]
  Comitato Olimpico Nazionale Sammarinese [IO]
  Cook Island Sports and Natl. Olympic Comm. [IO]
  Croatian Olympic Comm. [IO]
  Cyprus Olympic Comm. [IO]
  Czech Olympic Comm. [IO]
  Ecuadorian Olympic Comm. [IO]
  Egyptian Olympic Comm. [IO]
  Estonian Olympic Comm. [IO]
  Federated States of Micronesia Natl. Olympic Comm. [IO]
  Fed. of Intl. Polo [23819]
  Finnish Olympic Comm. [IO]
  Gambia Natl. Olympic Comm. [IO]
  Greek Olympic Soc. [IO]
  Greek Olympic Soc. [23635]
  Guam Natl. Olympic Comm. [23636]
  Guatemalan Olympic Comm. [IO]
  Hellenic Olympic Comm. [IO]
  Hungarian Olympic Comm. [IO]
  Indian Olympic Assn. [IO]
  Intl. Acad. of Olympic Chiropractic Officers [14006]
  Intl. Olympic Comm. [IO]
  Intl. Soc. of Olympic Historians [IO]
  Intl. Unicycling Fed. [23311]
  Jamaica Olympic Assn. [IO]
  Japanese Olympic Comm. [IO]
  Kiribati Natl. Olympic Comm. [IO]

Korean Olympic Comm. [IO]
Kuwait Olympic Comm. [IO]
Lebanese Olympic Comm. [IO]
Macedonian Olympic Comm. [IO]
Malta Olympic Comm. [IO]
Mexican Olympic Comm. [IO]
Natl. Olympic Comm. of Armenia [IO]
Natl. Olympic Comm. of Azerbaijan [IO]
Natl. Olympic Comm. for Germany [IO]
Natl. Olympic Comm. of Iraq [IO]
Natl. Olympic Comm. of the Islamic Republic of Iran [IO]
Natl. Olympic Comm. of Lithuania [IO]
Natl. Olympic Comm. of the Republic of Belarus [IO]
Natl. Olympic Comm. of the Republic of Kazakhstan [IO]
Natl. Olympic Comm. of Solomon Islands [IO]
Natl. Olympic Comm. and Sports Confed. of Denmark [IO]
Natl. Olympic Comm. of Turkey [IO]
Natl. Olympic Comm. of Ukraine [IO]
Native Amer. Sports Coun. [23632]
Nauru Olympic Comm. [IO]
Nepal Olympic Comm. [IO]
Netherlands Antilles Olympic Comm. [IO]
Netherlands Olympic Comm. [IO]
New Zealand Olympic Comm. [IO]
Norwegian Olympic Comm. and Confed. of Sports [IO]
Oceania Natl. Olympic Committees [IO]
Olympic Comm. of the Former Yugoslav Republic of Macedonia [IO]
Olympic Comm. of Israel [IO]
Olympic Comm. of Portugal [IO]
Olympic Comm. of Serbia and Montenegro [IO]
Olympic Comm. of Slovenia [IO]
Olympic Comm. of Slovenia Assn. of Sports Federations [IO]
Olympic Coun. of Asia [IO]
Olympic Coun. of Ireland [IO]
Olympic Coun. of Malaysia [IO]
Papua New Guinea Natl. Olympic Comm. [IO]
Philippine Olympic Comm. [IO]
Polish Olympic Comm. [IO]
Qatar Natl. Olympic Comm. [IO]
Romanian Olympic and Sports Comm. [IO]
St. Kitts and Nevis Olympic Assn. [IO]
St. Vincent and the Grenadines Natl. Olympic Comm. [IO]
Saudi Arabian Olympic Comm. [IO]
Singapore Natl. Olympic Coun. [IO]
Slovak Olympic Comm. [IO]
South African Sports Confed. and Olympic Comm. [IO]
Sports Fed. and Olympic Comm. of Hong Kong, China [IO]
Suriname Olympic Comm. [IO]
Swaziland Olympic and Commonwealth Games Assn. [IO]
Swedish Olympic Comm. [IO]
Swiss Olympic Assn. [IO]
Tonga Amateur Sports Assn. and Natl. Olympic Comm. [IO]
Trinidad and Tobago Olympic Comm. [IO]
U.S. Amateur Tug of War Assn. [23959]
U.S. Biathlon Assn. [23756]
U.S. Bobsled and Skeleton Fed. [23767]
U.S. Modern Pentathlon Assn. [23925]
U.S. Olympic Comm. [23637]
U.S. Speedskating [23745]
U.S. Squash Racquets Assn. [23876]
USA Badminton [23089]
USA Canoe/Kayak [23280]
USA Shooting [23732]
Vanuatu Natl. Olympic Comm. [IO]
Vietnam Olympic Comm. [IO]
Virgin Islands Olympic Comm. [IO]
Virgin Islands Olympic Comm. [23638]
World Olympians Assn. [23639]
World Olympians Assn. [IO]
Olympic Sailing Committee; U.S. [★23238]
Olympics; AAU/U.S.A. Junior [★23797]
Olympiques Speciaux Canada [★IO]
Omaha Grain Exchange - Defunct.

Omaha Woodmen Life Insurance Soc; Woodmen of the World/ [19441]
Oman Athletic Assn. [IO], Muscat, Oman
Oman Chamber of Commerce and Indus. [IO], Muscat, Oman
Oman Tennis Assn. [IO], Muscat, Oman
Omar Khayyam Club - Address unknown since 1995.
OMB Watch [17672], 1742 Connecticut Ave. NW, Washington, DC 20009, (202)234-8494
The Ombudsman Assn. [★736]
Ombudsman Assn; Corporate [★736]
Ombudsman Assn; Intl. [736]
Ombudsmen; Org. of News [3152]
Ombudsmen; Org. of Newspaper [★3152]
Omega 7 - Address unknown since 1997.
Omega Arts Network [★9590]
Omega Chi Epsilon [24462], c/o Richard A. Davis, Exec. Sec., Univ. Minnesota-Duluth, Chem. Engg. Dept., 176 Engg. Bldg., 1303 Ordean Ct., Duluth, MN 55812-3025, (218)726-6162
Omega Delta [24563], Southern Coll. of Optometry, 1245 Madison Ave., Memphis, TN 38104, (901)722-3200
Omega Epsilon Phi - Address unknown since 1999.
Omega First Amendment Legal Fund [17140], c/o Mark H. Carson and Associates, P.C., 1790 30th St., Ste. 418, Boulder, CO 80301, (303)449-3060
Omega Gamma Delta [24638], 89 Longview Rd., Port Washington, NY 11050-3039, (516)883-0159
Omega Project - Address unknown since 1995.
Omega Psi Phi Fraternity [24639], 3951 Snapfinger Pkwy., Decatur, GA 30035, (404)284-5533
Omega Tau Sigma - Address unknown since 2002.
Omega Theatre and the Omega Arts Network [9590], 41 Greenough Ave., Jamaica Plain, MA 02130, (617)522-8300
OMF Intl. - Singapore [IO], Singapore, Singapore
OMF Intl. - USA [IO], Littleton, CO, United States
OMF Intl. - USA [20378], 10 W Dry Creek Cir., Littleton, CO 80120-4413, (303)730-4160
Omicron Chi Epsilon [★24446]
Omicron Delta Epsilon [24446], PO Box 1486, Hattiesburg, MS 39402, (601)264-3115
Omicron Delta Gamma [★24446]
Omicron Delta Kappa Foundation [★24515]
Omicron Delta Kappa Soc. [24515], 300 N. Broadway, Lexington, KY 40508, (859)455-8870
Omicron Kappa Upsilon [24439], c/o Ms. Jan John, Corresponding Sec., Univ. of Nebraska, Coll. of Dentistry, 40th and Holdrege St., Rm. 105, Lincoln, NE 68583-0740, (402)472-1345
Omicron Nu [★24496]
OMNI Learning Inst. [8299], 135 Verrill Rd., Poland Spring, ME 04274-5316, (207)865-1611
Omnibus Soc. [IO], Bromley, United Kingdom
Omnibus Soc. of America - Address unknown since 2004.
Omohundro Inst. of Early Amer. History and Culture [10140], PO Box 8781, Williamsburg, VA 23187-8781, (757)221-1114
Omospondia Ergodoton ke Biomichanon Kyprou [★IO]
Omowale Educational Fund - Address unknown since 2007.
OMS Intl. [20379], PO Box A, Greenwood, IN 46142, (317)881-6751
OMS Intl. [IO], Greenwood, IN, United States
Omslag Werkplaats voor Duurzame Ontwikkeling [★IO]
Omslag Workshop for Sustainable Development [IO], Eindhoven, Netherlands
On the Lighter Side, International Lighter Collectors [IO], Quitman, TX, United States
On the Lighter Side, Intl. Lighter Collectors [22100], PO Box 1733, Quitman, TX 75783-2733, (903)763-2795
On-line Audiovisual Catalogers [★10379]
On-the-Job Training - Address unknown since 1995.
Once Upon A Time (The Prisoner Fan Club) [25040], 515 Ravenel Cir., Seneca, SC 29678
Oncologists; Canadian Assn. of Radiation [IO]
Oncology
  Acoustic Neuroma Assn. [15816]
  Alliance for Childhood Cancer [13787]

A star before a book entry number signifies that the name is not listed separately, but is mentioned within the entry.

Amer. Assn. for Cancer Educ. [13789]
Amer. Assn. for Cancer Res. [15635]
Amer. Assn. for Cancer Res. [IO]
Amer. Brain Tumor Assn. [13791]
Amer. Coll. of Mohs Micrographic Surgery and
  Cutaneous Oncology [15636]
Amer. Coll. of Radiation Oncology [16267]
Amer. Coll. of Veterinary Internal Medicine
  [16767]
Amer. Joint Comm. on Cancer [15637]
Amer. Psychosocial Oncology Soc. [15638]
Amer. Radium Soc. [15639]
Amer. Soc. of Breast Disease [13772]
Amer. Soc. of Clinical Oncology [15640]
Amer. Soc. for Mohs Surgery [15641]
Amer. Soc. for Mohs Surgery [IO]
Amer. Soc. of Preventive Oncology [15642]
Amer. Soc. for Therapeutic Radiology and Oncol-
  ogy [16285]
Assn. of Amer. Cancer Institutes [13794]
Assn. of Community Cancer Centers [13797]
Assn. for Directors of Radiation Oncology
  Programs [3271]
Assn. of Oncology Social Work [13199]
Assn. of Pediatric Hematology/Oncology Nurses
  [15467]
Assn. of Pediatric Oncology Social Workers
  [15885]
Assn. for Res. of Childhood Cancer [13798]
Assn. of Residents in Radiation Oncology [15643]
Assn. of Univ. Radiologists [16286]
Bladder Cancer Advocacy Network [13799]
British Oncology Data Managers' Assn. [IO]
British Psychosocial Oncology Soc. [IO]
Canadian Assn. of Psychosocial Oncology [IO]
Canadian Assn. of Radiation Oncologists [IO]
Canadian Urologic Oncology Gp. [IO]
Cancer Care [13803]
Cancer Control Soc. [13804]
Cancer Fed. [13805]
Cancer Info. Ser. [13807]
Cancer Prevention Coalition [13808]
Cancer Quality Alliance [13809]
Candlelighters Childhood Cancer Found. [13810]
Chemotherapy Found. [15644]
Children's Blood Found. [14786]
Children's Cause for Cancer Advocacy [13812]
Children's Leukemia Res. Assn. [13813]
Coalition of Cancer Cooperative Groups [13814]
Computerized Medical Imaging Soc. [16287]
Connective Tissue Oncology Soc. [15645]
Connective Tissue Oncology Soc. [IO]
Corporate Angel Network [13817]
Coun. on Diagnostic Imaging [16288]
Damon Runyon Cancer Res. Found. [13819]
DES Action, U.S.A. [13821]
Esophageal Cancer Awareness Assn. [13822]
European Assn. for NeuroOncology [IO]
European Soc. of Gynaecological Oncology [IO]
European Soc. for Hyperthermic Oncology [IO]
European Soc. for Medical Oncology [IO]
European Soc. of Surgical Oncology [IO]
Fed. of European Cancer Societies [IO]
Found. for Advancement in Cancer Therapy
  [13824]
Gynecologic Oncology Gp. [15646]
Hereditary Colon Cancer Assn. [13829]
Histiocytosis Assn. of Am. [14790]
Indian Assn. of Surgical Oncology [IO]
Intl. Assn. of Cancer Victors and Friends [13831]
Intl. Assn. for Comparative Res. on Leukemia and
  Related Diseases [15647]
Intl. Assn. for Comparative Res. on Leukemia and
  Related Diseases [IO]
Intl. Psycho-Oncology Soc. [13834]
Intl. Skeletal Soc. [16289]
Intl. Soc. for Biological Therapy of Cancer [13835]
Intl. Soc. of Oncology Pharmacy Practitioners
  [15937]
Intl. Soc. of Paediatric Oncology [IO]
Intl. Soc. for Preventive Oncology [IO]
Intl. Soc. for Preventive Oncology [15648]
Irish Assn. for Nurses in Oncology [IO]
Japan Soc. of Clinical Oncology [IO]
Leukemia and Lymphoma Soc. [13837]

Make Today Count [13841]
Natl. Assn. for Proton Therapy [15649]
Natl. Cancer Center [15650]
Natl. Cancer Registrars Assn. [15651]
Natl. Coalition for Cancer Survivorship [13852]
Natl. Found. for Cancer Res. [15652]
Natl. Found. for Cancer Res. [IO]
Neuroblastoma Children's Cancer Soc. [13858]
Neurofibromatosis [14471]
Oncology Nursing Certification Corp. [15520]
Oncology Nursing Soc. [15521]
Pituitary Network Assn. [16022]
Pregnant With Cancer Network [13865]
R.A. Bloch Cancer Found. [13867]
Radiation Therapy Oncology Gp. [15653]
Radiological Soc. of North Am. [16293]
Radiology Mammography Intl. [13774]
Retinoblastoma Intl. [13869]
Rose Kushner Breast Cancer Advisory Center
  [13870]
Scandinavian Soc. for Head and Neck Oncology
  [IO]
Skin Cancer Found. [13874]
Soc. of Gynecologic Oncologists [15654]
Soc. of Gynecologic Oncologists of Canada [IO]
Soc. of Interventional Radiology [16300]
Soc. for Melanoma Res. [13875]
Soc. for Radiation Oncology Administrators
  [16302]
Soc. of Surgical Oncology [15655]
Oncology Administrators; Amer. Coll. of [15055]
Oncology Administrators; Radiation [★16302]
Oncology Administrators; Soc. for Radiation [16302]
Oncology; Amer. Coll. of Radiation [16267]
Oncology; Amer. Soc. of Pediatric Hematology/
  [14784]
Oncology; Amer. Soc. for Therapeutic Radiology and
  [16285]
Oncology; Canadian Assn. of Pharmacy in [IO]
Oncology Centers; Assn. of Freestanding Radiation
  [16268]
Oncology Gp; Found. for the Children's [★13850]
Oncology Nurses; Assn. of Pediatric [★15467]
Oncology Nursing Certification Corp. [15520], 125
  Enterprise Dr., Pittsburgh, PA 15275-1214,
  (412)859-6104
Oncology Nursing Soc. [15521], 125 Enterprise Dr.,
  Pittsburgh, PA 15275, (412)859-6100
Oncology Nursing Soc; European [IO]
Oncology Social Work; Assn. of [13199]
Oncology Social Workers; Assn. of Pediatric [15885]
Oncology Social Workers; Natl. Assn. of [★13199]
Oncology Study Group; Hong Kong Paediatric Hae-
  matology and [IO]
One-Arm Dove Hunt Assn. [23358], PO Box 582,
  Olney, TX 76374, (940)564-8867
One Cent Intl. [22751], 334 W Magnolia St., Durant,
  MS 39063, (662)653-3262
One Cent Intl. [IO], Durant, MS, United States
One Child at a Time [11642], c/o AIAA/Corporate
  Off., 2151 Livernois, Ste. 200, Troy, MI 48083,
  (248)362-1207
One-Design Class Coun. [23211], c/o U.S. Sailing
  Assn., 15 Maritime Dr., PO Box 1260, Portsmouth,
  RI 02871-0907, (401)683-0800
One Design Racing Assn; Natl. [23206]
One Earth One Justice [12437], 4343 Clairemont
  Mesa Blvd., San Diego, CA 92117, (619)223-3482
One Economy [7755], 1220 19th St. NW, Ste. 610,
  Washington, DC 20036, (202)393-0051
One Family [IO], Dublin, Ireland
One/Fourth, The Alliance for Cancer Patients and
  Their Families - Defunct.
One-in-a-Million Soc. [★9986]
One-in-a-Thousand Soc. [★9985]
ONE, Inc. [12251], c/o Inst. for the Stud. of Human
  Resources, PO Box 191728, Los Angeles, CA
  90019-1028, (323)737-1066
The One and Only Tom Jones Fan Club - Defunct.
One Parent Families Scotland [IO], Edinburgh,
  United Kingdom
One Percent Soc; Top [★9985]
One Person's Impact - Address unknown since
  1994.
The One Shoe Crew [11977], PO Box 285, Rio
  Linda, CA 95673, (916)991-0412

One-Time Carbon Paper Mfrs. Assn. - Defunct.
One Village [IO], Chipping Norton, United Kingdom
One Voice, Natl. Alliance for Abuse Awareness -
  Defunct.
One World Action [IO], London, United Kingdom
One World Beat [IO], Lausanne, Switzerland
One World: For Children - Address unknown since
  2001.
O'Neill Club; Natl. Rose [★22399]
O'Neill Critics Inst. [11036], c/o Dan Sullivan, Dir.,
  Eugene O'Neill Theater Ctr., 305 Great Neck Rd.,
  Waterford, CT 06385, (860)443-5378
O'Neill Memorial Theater Center; Eugene [11014]
O'Neill Memorial Theater Found; Eugene [★11014]
O'Neill Natl. Theater Inst. [9266], Eugene O'Neill
  Theater Center, 305 Great Neck Rd., Waterford,
  CT 06385, (860)443-7139
O'Neill Soc; Eugene [9648]
O'Neill Theater Center [★11014]
OneWorld Intl. Found. [17780], c/o OneWorld U.S.,
  3201 New Mexico Ave. NW, Ste. 395, Washington,
  DC 20016, (202)885-2679
OneWorld Intl. Found. [IO], Washington, DC, United
  States
Onion Assn; Natl. [4743]
Onion Assn; Natl. Statistical [★4743]
Onion Commn; Idaho Potato and [★4735]
Onion Ring Packers Coun; Frozen [★1496]
Online Audiovisual Catalogers [10379], c/o Vicki
  Toy-Smith, Pres., Univ. of Nevada, Mail Stop 322,
  Reno, NV 89557-0044, (775)682-5601
Online Booksellers Assn; Independent [530]
Online Imperial Club [21750], c/o Elijah Scott, 40
  Signal Hill Ct., Rock Spring, GA 30739
Online Insurance Agents; Assn. of [2149]
Online News Assn. [3151], PO Box 2022, New York,
  NY 10101, (646)290-7900
Online Policy Gp. [17243], 1800 Market St., No.
  123, San Francisco, CA 94102
Online Privacy Alliance [17141], c/o Christine Var-
  ney, Pres., Hogan and Hartson, 555 13th St. NW,
  Washington, DC 20004, (202)637-5600
Online Publishers Assn. [3245], 249 W 17th St.,
  New York, NY 10011, (212)204-1488
Online Publishers Assn. Europe [IO], Paris, France
Online Resources; Assn. of Cancer [13796]
Online Scholarship; Commun. Inst. for [6899]
Online Users' Group/Ireland [★IO]
Online/Women Organizing For Change; Women
  Leaders [18818]
Only a Child [11643], PO Box 990885, Boston, MA
  02199, (617)848-8940
Only a Child [IO], Boston, MA, United States
Only Official Peggy Lee Fan Club and Archives -
  Address unknown since 1994.
Onomatology
  Amer. Name Soc. [10764]
  American Name Society [IO]
Ontario Arts Council/Ontario Arts Coun. Found. [IO],
  Toronto, ON, Canada
Ontario Assn. for the Application of Personality Type
  [IO], Concord, ON, Canada
Ontario Assn. of Naturopathic Doctors [IO], Toronto,
  ON, Canada
Ontario Assn. of Social Workers [IO], Toronto, ON,
  Canada
Ontario Assn. of Social Workers - Eastern Br. [IO],
  Ottawa, ON, Canada
Ontario Assn. of Social Workers - Hamilton Area and
  District Br. [IO], Hamilton, ON, Canada
Ontario Assn. of Youth Employment Centres [IO],
  Toronto, ON, Canada
Ontario Brain Injury Assn. [IO], St. Catharines, ON,
  Canada
Ontario Conf. of Catholic Bishops [IO], Toronto, ON,
  Canada
Ontario Fabricare Assn. [IO], Toronto, ON, Canada
Ontario Lawn Bowls Assn. [IO], Uxbridge, ON,
  Canada
Ontario Mining Equip. and Services for Export [★IO]
Ontario Native Educ. Counselling Assn. [IO], Naugh-
  ton, ON, Canada
Ontario Nature [IO], Toronto, ON, Canada
Ontario Psychological Assn. [IO], Toronto, ON,
  Canada

Reference to "IO" in place of a book number signifies that the association may be found in the 45th edition of International Organizations.

Encyclopedia of Associations, 46th Edition

3939

Ontario Recreational Canoeing Assn. **[IO]**, Toronto, ON, Canada

Ontario School Counsellor's Assn. **[IO]**, Bridgenorth, ON, Canada

Ontario Soc. of Psychotherapists **[IO]**, Toronto, ON, Canada

Ontario and Western Railroad Historical Soc. **[★10916]**

Ontario and Western Railway Historical Soc. **[10916]**, PO Box 713, Middletown, NY 10940

Ontario Wheelchair Sports Assn. **[IO]**, Toronto, ON, Canada

OPAM America - Address unknown since 2003.

OPEC Fund for Intl. Development **[IO]**, Vienna, Austria

OPEC News Agency **[IO]**, Vienna, Austria

OPEC Special Fund **[★IO]**

Opel Assn. of North Am. **[21751]**, 630 Watch Hill Rd., Midlothian, VA 23113, (804)379-9737

Opel Motorsports Club **[21752]**, c/o Dick Counsil, Treas., 3824 Franklin St., La Crescenta, CA 91214

Opel Motorsports Club **[IO]**, La Crescenta, CA, United States

Opel Motorsports Club AG **[★IO]**

Opel Motorsports Club AG **[★21752]**

Open Air Campaigners, U.S.A. **[20027]**, PO Box D, Nazareth, PA 18064, (610)746-0508

Open Applications Gp. **[890]**, PO Box 4897, Marietta, GA 30061, (678)715-7588

Open Channel - Address unknown since 1995.

Open Data Acquisition Assn. **[891]**

Open Data Acquisition Assn. **[IO]**, Stamford, CT, United States

Open Debates **[17488]**, PO Box 18881, Washington, DC 20036, (703)299-6045

Open DeviceNet Vendor Assn. **[892]**, c/o Tech. and Training Center, 4220 Varsity Dr., Ste. A, Ann Arbor, MI 48108-5006, (734)975-8840

Open DeviceNet Vendor Association **[IO]**, Ann Arbor, MI, United States

Open Die Forging Inst. - Defunct.

Open and Distance Learning Assn. of Australia **[IO]**, Bondi Junction, Australia

Open and Distance Learning Quality Coun. **[IO]**, London, United Kingdom

Open Door Educ. Found. **[9242]**, 1420 King St., Ste. 610, Alexandria, VA 22314, (703)838-2050

Open Door Student Exchange **[★8625]**

Open Geospatial Consortium **[6817]**, 35 Main St., Ste. 5, Wayland, MA 01778-5037, (508)655-5858

Open GIS Consortium **[★6817]**

The Open Gp. **[2108]**, 44 Montgomery St., Ste. 960, San Francisco, CA 94104-4704, (415)374-8280

Open Heart World Mission - Address unknown since 1999.

Open Housing Investment; Sponsors of **[★17819]**

Open Minded Comics Club - Defunct.

Open Mobile Alliance **[7781]**, 4275 Executive Sq., Ste. 240, La Jolla, CA 92037, (858)623-0742

Open Mobile Architecture Initiative **[★7781]**

OPEN Mortgage **[★17819]**

Open Pit Mining Assn. **[★2751]**

Open Road "See America" Club - Defunct.

Open Soc. Found. for Albania **[IO]**, Tirana, Albania

Open Soc. Found. - Romania **[IO]**, Bucharest, Romania

Open Soc. Found. - Sofia (Bulgaria) **[IO]**, Sofia, Bulgaria

OPEN Soc; Fund for an **[17819]**

Open Soc. Inst. **[17871]**, 400 W 59th St., New York, NY 10019, (212)548-0600

Open Soc. Inst. **[IO]**, New York, NY, United States

Open Space Action Comm. **[★4599]**

Open Space Inst. **[4599]**, 1350 Broadway, Ste. 201, New York, NY 10018-7799, (212)290-8200

Open Spaces Soc. **[IO]**, Henley-On-Thames, United Kingdom

Open Systems Alliance; Machinery Info. Mgt. **[2560]**

Open Systems Professionals; Intl. Assn. of **[★6805]**

Open Testing; Natl. Center for Fair and **[9255]**

Open Voting Consortium **[17489]**, 9560 Windrose Ln., Granite Bay, CA 95746, (916)791-0456

Open Voting Consortium **[IO]**, Granite Bay, CA, United States

Openers; Just for **[22062]**

Opening Door **[3932]**, 8049 Ormesby Ln., Woodford, VA 22580, (804)633-6752

Opening Mind Acad. **[15955]**, PO Box 444, Huntington Beach, CA 92648, (714)379-4911

OpenView Forum Intl. **[★6807]**

Opera
Amer. Friends of the Paris Opera and Ballet **[9543]**
Asian Amer. Music Soc. **[10556]**
Center for Contemporary Opera **[10572]**
Gerda Lissner Found. **[10765]**
Jussi Bjorling Soc. - USA **[9508]**
Metropolitan Opera Assn. **[10645]**
Metropolitan Opera Guild **[10646]**
Midwestern Gilbert and Sullivan Soc. **[9813]**
Natl. Opera Assn. **[10666]**
OPERA Am. **[10681]**
Wagner Soc. of New York **[10722]**
Wolf Trap Found. for the Performing Arts **[9602]**

OPERA Am. **[10681]**, 330 Seventh Ave., 16th Fl., New York, NY 10001, (212)796-8620

Opera; Amer. Friends of Scottish **[★10570]**

Opera Assn; Metropolitan **[10645]**

Opera Assn; Natl. **[10666]**

Opera and Ballet; Amer. Friends of the Paris **[9543]**

Opera and Ballet Musicians; Intl. Guild of Symphony, **[24157]**

Opera; Center for Contemporary **[10572]**

Opera Company; Wolf Trap **[★9602]**

Opera Found; Amer. Berlin **[10529]**

Opera Guild; Metropolitan **[10646]**

Opera Ser; Central **[★10681]**

Opera for Youth **[★10666]**

Opera for Youth - Defunct.

Operability; Intl. Alliance for Inter **[7018]**

Opera.ca **[IO]**, Toronto, ON, Canada

Operacion Sonrisa **[★IO]**

Operacion Sonrisa Peru **[★IO]**

Operacion Sonrisa Venezuela **[★IO]**

Operasionele Navorsingsvereniging van Suid-Afrika **[★IO]**

Operating Engineers; Intl. Union of **[24028]**

Operating Personnel; Assn. of Boards of Certification for **[★6337]**

Operating Personnel in Water and Wastewater Utilities; Assn. of Boards of Certification for **[★6337]**

Operating Room Technicians; Assn. of **[★15133]**

Oper. AC **[11492]**, 560 Peoples Plz., No. 121, Newark, DE 19702, (302)836-1008

Oper. Appreciation **[20767]**, c/o Non-Commissioned Officers Assn. of the U.S.A., 10635 1H 35 N, San Antonio, TX 78233, (703)549-0311

Oper. Big Vote **[18362]**, c/o Natl. Coalition on Black Civic Participation, 1900 L St. NW, Ste. 700, Washington, DC 20036, (202)659-4929

Operation Big Vote Rap **[★18362]**

Oper. Blessing Intl. **[19821]**, 977 Centerville Tpke., Virginia Beach, VA 23463, (757)226-3401

Oper. Blessing Intl. **[IO]**, Virginia Beach, VA, United States

Oper. Blessing Intl. Relief and Development Corp. **[★IO]**

Oper. Blessing Intl. Relief and Development Corp. **[★19821]**

Oper. Brother's Keeper **[★12837]**

Oper. Brother's Keeper **[★IO]**

Oper. California **[★12535]**

Operation Child Identification - Defunct.

Operation Connection - Defunct.

Operation CORK - Defunct.

Oper. Crossroads Africa **[16932]**, PO Box 5570, New York, NY 10027, (212)289-1949

Oper. Crossroads-Africa **[★IO]**

Operation Crossroads Africa **[IO]**, New York, NY, United States

Oper. Enterprise **[8808]**, c/o Amer. Mgt. Assn., 1601 Broadway, New York, NY 10019-7420, (212)903-8038

Oper. Eyesight Universal **[IO]**, Calgary, AB, Canada

Oper. Gratitude **[IO]**, Encino, CA, United States

Oper. Gratitude **[11493]**, c/o Carolyn Blashek, Founder, 16444 Refugio Rd., Encino, CA 91436, (818)789-0123

Operation Help Org. - Address unknown since 2002.

Oper. Homelink **[11494]**, 25 E Washington, Ste. 1735, Chicago, IL 60602, (312)863-6336

Oper. HOPE, Inc. **[11787]**, 707 Wilshire Blvd., 30th Fl., Los Angeles, CA 90017, (213)891-2900

Oper. Identity **[11258]**, 7045 Maynardville Pike, Knoxville, TN 37918, (865)922-9099

Oper. Joshua **[★12457]**

Oper. K.I.D. - Keeping Ill Children Dreaming - Address unknown since 2006.

Oper. Kid-To-Kid **[19757]**, 1820 Jet Stream Dr., Colorado Springs, CO 80921

Oper. Lifesaver **[12983]**, 1420 King St., Ste. 401, Alexandria, VA 22314, (703)739-0308

Operation Lifesaver **[IO]**, Alexandria, VA, United States

Operation Liftoff - Defunct.

Operation Mailcall - Address unknown since 1995.

Operation Monkees - Address unknown since 1999.

Operation Morning Star **[★18992]**

Oper. Pass-Along; Anglican Bookstore, **[★19972]**

Oper. PUSH **[★13185]**

Oper. Rainbow **[15077]**, PMB 157, 4200 Park Blvd., Oakland, CA 94602, (510)273-2485

Oper. Rescue **[★18562]**

Oper. Sandbox **[11495]**, PO Box 163, Sarahsville, OH 43779, (740)732-0130

Oper. Save Am. **[18562]**, PO Box 740066, Dallas, TX 75374, (704)933-3414

Oper. SER **[★12100]**

Oper. ShoeBox **[11496]**, PO Box 1465, Belleview, FL 34421-1465, (352)553-9362

Operation Sisters United - Address unknown since 2003.

Oper. Smile **[12534]**, 6435 Tidewater Dr., Norfolk, VA 23509, (757)321-7645

Oper. Smile **[★12534]**

Oper. Smile **[★IO]**

Oper. Smile **[IO]**, Norfolk, VA, United States

Oper. Smile - Australia **[IO]**, Stafford, Australia

Oper. Smile - Bolivia **[IO]**, Santa Cruz, Bolivia

Oper. Smile - Colombia **[IO]**, Bogota, Colombia

Oper. Smile - Ecuador **[IO]**, Quito, Ecuador

Oper. Smile - Hangzhou **[IO]**, Hangzhou, People's Republic of China

Oper. Smile - Honduras **[IO]**, Tegucigalpa, Honduras

Oper. Smile - Hong Kong **[IO]**, Hong Kong, People's Republic of China

Oper. Smile - India **[IO]**, Bombay, India

Oper. Smile Intl. **[★IO]**

Oper. Smile Intl. **[★12534]**

Oper. Smile Intl. - Vietnam **[IO]**, Hanoi, Vietnam

Oper. Smile - Ireland **[IO]**, Dublin, Ireland

Oper. Smile - Italy **[IO]**, Rome, Italy

Oper. Smile - Jordan **[IO]**, Amman, Jordan

Oper. Smile - Mission in Kenya **[IO]**, Nairobi, Kenya

Oper. Smile - Morocco **[IO]**, Casablanca, Morocco

Oper. Smile - Nicaragua **[IO]**, Managua, Nicaragua

Oper. Smile - Panama **[IO]**, Panama City, Panama

Oper. Smile - Peru **[IO]**, Lima, Peru

Oper. Smile - Philippines **[IO]**, Makati City, Philippines

Oper. Smile - Russia **[IO]**, Moscow, Russia

Oper. Smile - Thailand **[IO]**, Bangkok, Thailand

Oper. Smile - United Kingdom **[IO]**, London, United Kingdom

Oper. Smile - Venezuela **[IO]**, Caracas, Venezuela

Oper. Soldier Support **[11497]**

Oper. Sourire Morocco **[★IO]**

Operation Suburbia - Defunct.

Oper.: Take a Soldier to the Movies **[11498]**, c/o Hintzke and Associates, Inc., 14775 W Natl. Ave., New Berlin, WI 53151-4434, (262)754-4300

Operation Town Affiliations - Address unknown since 1995.

Oper. Truth **[21317]**, 770 Broadway, 2nd Fl., New York, NY 10003, (212)982-9699

Oper. U.S.A. **[12535]**, 3617 Hayden Ave., Ste. A, Culver City, CA 90232, (310)838-3455

Operation Venus - Address unknown since 2001.

Oper. We Do Care **[11499]**, PO Box 604, Holloman AFB, NM 88330, (866)447-3665

Operational Res. Soc. of Hong Kong **[IO]**, Hong Kong, People's Republic of China

Operational Res. Soc. of India **[IO]**, Calcutta, India

Operational Res. Soc. of New Zealand **[IO]**, Auckland, New Zealand

Operational Res. Soc. of Singapore **[IO]**, Singapore, Singapore

---

A star before a book entry number signifies that the name is not listed separately, but is mentioned within the entry.

Operational Res. Soc. of Turkey [IO], Ankara, Turkey
Operational Res. Soc. of the United Kingdom [IO], Birmingham, United Kingdom
Operations Mgt. Education and Res. Found. [7167]
Operations Mgt. Soc; Production and [2512]

Operations Research
Assn. of Polish Operational Res. Societies [IO]
Assn. Suisse de Recherche Operationnelle [IO]
Australian Soc. for Operations Res. [IO]
Australian Soc. for Operations Res. - ACT Chap. [IO]
Australian Soc. for Operations Res. - Melbourne Chap. [IO]
Australian Soc. for Operations Res. - Queensland Chap. [IO]
Australian Soc. for Operations Res. - South Australia Chap. [IO]
Australian Soc. for Operations Res. - Sydney Chap. [IO]
Australian Soc. for Operations Res. - Western Australia Chap. [IO]
Austrian Soc. of Operations Res. [IO]
Belgian Operations Res. Soc. [IO]
Brazilian Soc. of Operational Res. [IO]
Bulgarian Operational Res. Soc. [IO]
Byelorussian Operational Res. Soc. [IO]
Canadian Operational Res. Soc. [IO]
Canadian Professional Logistics Inst. [IO]
Chartered Inst. of Logistics and Transport [IO]
Croatian Operational Res. Soc. [IO]
Czech Operational Res. Soc. [IO]
Danish Operations Res. Soc. [IO]
Finnish Operations Res. Soc. [IO]
German Soc. of Operations Res. [IO]
Hellenic Operational Res. Soc. [IO]
Hungarian Operational Res. Soc. [IO]
Intl. Fed. for Systems Res. [IO]
Korean Operations Res. and Mgt. Sci. Soc. [IO]
Machinery Info. Mgt. Open Systems Alliance [2560]
Mgt. Sci. Soc. of Ireland [IO]
Mfg. Enterprise Solutions Assn. Intl. [7722]
Military Operations Res. Soc. [7406]
Norwegian Operations Res. [IO]
Operational Res. Soc. of Hong Kong [IO]
Operational Res. Soc. of India [IO]
Operational Res. Soc. of Singapore [IO]
Operational Res. Soc. of Turkey [IO]
Operational Res. Soc. of the United Kingdom [IO]
Operations Res. and Decision Making Soc. of Egypt [IO]
Operations Res. Soc. of China [IO]
Operations Res. Soc. of Israel [IO]
Operations Res. Soc. of Japan [IO]
Operations Res. Soc. of the Philippines [IO]
Operations Res. Soc. of South Africa [IO]
Portuguese Operations Res. Soc. [IO]
Slovak Soc. for Operations Res. [IO]
Supply Chain and Logistics Canada [IO]
Swedish Operations Res. Soc. [IO]
Operations Res. and Decision Making Soc. of Egypt [IO], Cairo, Egypt
Operations Res; Netherlands Soc. for Statistics and [IO]
Operations Res. Soc. of China [IO], Beijing, People's Republic of China
Operations Res. Soc. of Israel [IO], Haifa, Israel
Operations Res. Soc. of Japan [IO], Tokyo, Japan
Operations Res. Soc. of the Philippines [IO], Quezon City, Philippines
Operations Res. Soc. of South Africa [IO], Sasolburg, Republic of South Africa
Operations Soc; Exposition [1339]
Operative Dentistry; Acad. of [14089]
Operative Millers; Assn. of [★2737]
Operative Plasterers and Cement Masons Intl. Assn. of U.S. and Canada [24031], 14405 Laurel Pl., Ste. 300, Laurel, MD 20707, (301)470-4200
Operative Plasterers and Cement Masons Intl. Assn. of U.S. and Canada [IO], Laurel, MD, United States
Operative Registered Nurses; Assn. of Peri [15468]
Operative Res. Org; Global Peri [14026]
Operator Dealers Assn; Door and [★631]

Operators Assn. of Am; Roller Skating [★3601]
Operators Assn; Amusement and Music [1299]
Operators Assn; Archery Lane [★3657]
Operators Assn; Natl. Black McDonald's [1955]
Operators Assn; Roller Skating Rink [★3601]
Operators Caucus; TV [583]
Operators; Natl. Assn. of Casino Party [1313]
Operators; Natl. Assn. of Casino and Theme Party [★1313]
Opetusalan Ammattijarjesto [★IO]
Ophelia Proj. [IO], Erie, PA, United States
Ophelia Proj. [13509], 718 Nevada Dr., Erie, PA 16505, (814)456-5437
Ophthalmic Administrators; Amer. Soc. of [15058]
Ophthalmic Care for Underserved Sectors; Interprofessional Fostering of [16859]
Ophthalmic Cooperation to Asia; Assn. for [IO]
Ophthalmic Examinations; Amer. Bd. for [★15661]
Ophthalmic Photographers' Soc. [15696], c/o Barbara S. McCalley, Exec. Dir., 1887 W Ranch Rd., Nixa, MO 65714-8262, (417)725-0181
Ophthalmic Plastic and Reconstructive Surgery; Amer. Soc. of [14043]
Ophthalmic Plastic and Reconstructive Surgery; European Soc. of [IO]
Ophthalmic Registered Nurses; Amer. Soc. of [15458]
Ophthalmic Res. Inst. - Address unknown since 2001.
Ophthalmic Surgery Soc; Outpatient [15698]
Ophthalmologic and Otolaryngologic Allergy; Amer. Soc. of [★13593]
Ophthalmological Found. [★16882]
Ophthalmological Org. of Egypt [★IO]
Ophthalmological Soc. of the Republic of China [★IO]
Ophthalmological Soc. of Taiwan [IO], Taipei, Taiwan
Ophthalmologists; Amer. Coll. of Veterinary [16768]
Ophthalmologists; Contact Lens Assn. of [15680]

Ophthalmology
Accreditation Coun. on Optometric Educ. [15710]
Achromatopsia Network [16820]
All India Ophthalmological Soc. [IO]
Amer. Acad. of Ophthalmology [15656]
Amer. Acad. of Optometry [15711]
Amer. Assn. of Certified Orthoptists [15657]
Amer. Assn. of Dispensing Ophthalmologists [15658]
Amer. Assn. of Eye and Ear Hospitals [14859]
Amer. Assn. for Ophthalmic Standardized Echography [15659]
Amer. Assn. for Pediatric Ophthalmology and Strabismus [15660]
Amer. Bd. of Ophthalmology [15661]
Amer. Bd. of Opticianry [15704]
Amer. Coll. of Veterinary Ophthalmologists [16768]
Amer. Nystagmus Network [16828]
Amer. Ophthalmological Soc. [15662]
Amer. Optometric Assn. [15712]
Amer. Optometric Found. [15713]
Amer. Optometric Student Assn. [15714]
Amer. Orthoptic Coun. [15663]
Amer. Osteopathic Colleges of Ophthalmology and Otolaryngology-Head and Neck Surgery [15664]
Amer. Soc. of Cataract and Refractive Surgery [15665]
Amer. Soc. of Contemporary Medicine, Surgery, and Ophthalmology [15666]
Amer. Soc. of Ophthalmic Administrators [15058]
Amer. Soc. of Ophthalmic Registered Nurses [15458]
Amer. Soc. for Ophthalmic Ultrasonography [15667]
Amer. Soc. of Veterinary Ophthalmology [16775]
Amer. Uveitis Soc. [15668]
Applied Vision Assn. [IO]
Argentine Soc. of Ophthalmology [IO]
Assn. for Macular Diseases [15669]
Assn. of Nurses Endorsing Transplantation [15670]
Assn. for Ocular Pharmacology and Therapeutics [15671]
Assn. for Ocular Pharmacology and Therapeutics [IO]

Assn. of Regulatory Boards of Optometry [15716]
Assn. for Res. in Vision and Ophthalmology [15672]
Association for Research in Vision and Ophthalmology [IO]
Assn. for Retinopathy of Prematurity and Related Diseases [15673]
Assn. of Schools and Colleges of Optometry [15717]
Assn. of Tech. Personnel in Ophthalmology [15674]
Assn. of Univ. Professors of Ophthalmology [15675]
Assn. of Veterans Affairs Ophthalmologists [15676]
Assn. of Veterans Affairs Ophthalmologists [IO]
Assn. of Vision Educators [IO]
Assn. of Vision Educators [15677]
Australasian Soc. of Cataract and Refractive Surgeons [IO]
Better Vision Inst. [15678]
BiOptic Driving Network - USA [15705]
British and Irish Orthoptic Soc. [IO]
British Retinitis Pigmentosa Soc. [IO]
Bulgarian Soc. of Ophthalmology [IO]
Canadian Ophthalmological Soc. [IO]
Canadian Orthoptic Coun. [IO]
Children's Eye Found. [15679]
Christian Record Services [16842]
Coll. of Optometrists in Vision Development [15718]
Comm. on Opticianry Accreditation [15706]
Comm. on Accreditation for Opthalmic Medical Personnel [8834]
Contact Lens Assn. of Ophthalmologists [15680]
Cornea and Contact Lens Soc. of New Zealand [IO]
Danish Ophthalmological Soc. [IO]
Egyptian Ophthalmological Soc. [IO]
European Bd. of Ophthalmology [IO]
European Contact Lens Soc. of Ophthalmologists [IO]
European Soc. for Cataract and Refractive Surgeons [IO]
European Strabismological Assn. [IO]
Eye Bank Assn. of Am. [14288]
Eye-Bank for Sight Restoration [14289]
Focus [15681]
Found. Fighting Blindness [16847]
German Ophthalmological Soc. [IO]
The Glaucoma Found. [15682]
Glaucoma Res. Found. [15683]
Helen Keller Intl. [16854]
Inst. of Ophthalmology [IO]
Intercontinental Fed. of Behavioral Optometry [15719]
Intl. Assn. of Ocular Surgeons [15684]
Intl. Assn. of Optometric Executives [15720]
Intl. Children's Anophthalmia Network [16857]
Intl. Color Vision Soc. [IO]
Intl. Eye Found. [IO]
Intl. Eye Found. [15685]
Intl. Fed. of Ophthalmological Societies [15686]
Intl. Fed. of Ophthalmological Societies [IO]
Intl. Glaucoma Assn. [IO]
International Iridology Practitioners Association [IO]
Intl. Iridology Practitioners Assn. [15687]
Intl. Orthoptic Assn. [IO]
Intl. Perimetric Soc. [IO]
Intl. Perimetric Soc. [15688]
Intl. Refractive Surgery Club [15689]
Intl. Refractive Surgery Club [IO]
Intl. Soc. for Clinical Electrophysiology of Vision [IO]
Intl. Soc. of Geographical and Epidemiological Ophthalmology [IO]
Intl. Soc. for Imaging in the Eye [IO]
Intl. Soc. for Imaging in the Eye [15690]
Intl. Soc. on Metabolic Eye Disease [15691]
Intl. Soc. on Metabolic Eye Disease [IO]
Intl. Soc. on Ultrasonic Diagnostics in Ophthalmology [IO]
Intl. Trachoma Initiative [16858]
Japanese Ophthalmological Soc. [IO]

Reference to "IO" in place of a book number signifies that the association may be found in the 45th edition of International Organizations.

Joint Commn. on Allied Hea. Personnel in Ophthalmology **[15692]**
MAB Community Services **[16868]**
Natl. Acad. of Opticianry **[15707]**
Natl. Alliance for Eye and Vision Res. **[16872]**
Natl. Assn. of Optometrists and Opticians **[15721]**
Natl. Assn. of Vision Professionals **[15693]**
Natl. Bd. of Examiners in Optometry **[15722]**
Natl. Contact Lens Examiners **[15723]**
Natl. Examining Bd. of Ocularists **[15694]**
Natl. Eye Res. Found. **[15724]**
Natl. Inst. of Ophthalmology **[IO]**
Natl. Optometric Assn. **[15725]**
Neuro-Optometric Rehabilitation Assn., Intl. **[15300]**
New Eyes for the Needy **[12533]**
North Amer. Neuro-Ophthalmology Soc. **[15695]**
North Amer. Neuro-Ophthalmology Soc. **[IO]**
Ophthalmic Photographers' Soc. **[15696]**
Ophthalmological Soc. of Taiwan **[IO]**
Optical Labs. Assn. **[1864]**
Optical Storage Tech. Assn. **[2860]**
Optician Assn. **[IO]**
Opticians Assn. of Am. **[15709]**
Optometric Extension Prog. Found. **[15727]**
ORBIS Intl. **[15697]**
ORBIS Intl. **[IO]**
Outpatient Ophthalmic Surgery Soc. **[15698]**
Pan-American Assn. of Ophthalmology **[15699]**
Pan-American Assn. of Ophthalmology **[IO]**
Pediatric Keratoplasty Assn. **[15700]**
Prevent Blindness Am. **[16882]**
Res. to Prevent Blindness **[16886]**
Royal Australian and New Zealand Coll. of Ophthalmologists **[IO]**
Royal Coll. of Ophthalmologists **[IO]**
Scandinavian Soc. of Cataract and Refractive Surgery **[IO]**
Seniors EyeCare Prog. **[15701]**
Sociedad Venezolana de Oftalmologia **[IO]**
Soc. for Excellence in Eyecare **[15702]**
Soc. of Eye Surgeons **[15703]**
Tear Film and Ocular Surface Soc. **[15729]**
Thyroid Eye Disease Assn. **[IO]**
Vision World Wide **[16890]**
VOSH Intl. **[12543]**
Ophthalmology; Amer. Acad. of **[15656]**
Ophthalmology; Amer. Assn. of Certified Allied Hea. Personnel in **[★15674]**
Ophthalmology; Amer. Assn. of Pediatric **[★15660]**
Ophthalmology; Amer. Bd. of **[15661]**
Ophthalmology; Amer. Soc. of Veterinary **[16775]**
Ophthalmology; Assn. for Res. in **[★15672]**
Ophthalmology; Assn. for Res. in Vision and **[15672]**
Ophthalmology; Assn. of Tech. Personnel in **[15674]**
Ophthalmology; Assn. of Univ. Professors of **[15675]**
Ophthalmology; Joint Commn. on Allied Hea. Personnel in **[15692]**
Ophthalmology Matching Prog. **[★15675]**
Ophthalmology and Otolaryngology-Head and Neck Surgery; Amer. Osteopathic Colleges of **[15664]**
Ophthalmology and Otorhinolaryngology; Osteopathic Coll. of **[★15664]**
Ophthalmology; Soc. for Cryo- **[★15666]**
Ophthalmology and Strabismus; Amer. Assn. for Pediatric **[15660]**
Opimian, the Wine Soc. of Canada **[IO]**, Montreal, QC, Canada
Opinion Res; Amer. Assn. for Public **[18368]**
Opinion Res; Coun. for Marketing and **[2622]**
Opintotoiminnan Keskusliitto **[★IO]**
Opioid Dependence; Amer. Assn. for the Treatment of **[16499]**
Oplinger Family Assn; Oblinger/ **[21015]**
Opossum Soc; Natl. **[4160]**
OPP Concerned Sheep Breeders Soc. **[16803]**, c/o Jean T. Walsh, Treas., 228 Main St., Jordanville, NY 13361
Opportunities Industrialization Centers of Am. **[12096]**, 1415 N Broad St., Philadelphia, PA 19122-3323, (215)236-4500
Opportunities Industrialization Centers Intl. **[13181]**, 240 W Tulpehocken St., Philadelphia, PA 19144, (215)842-0220
Opportunities Industrialization Centers International **[IO]**, Philadelphia, PA, United States

Opportunities for Professional Transition - Address unknown since 1995.
Opportunity Finance Network **[17233]**, Public Ledger Bldg., 620 Chestnut St., Ste. 572, Philadelphia, PA 19106, (215)923-4754
Opportunity International-USA **[12384]**, 2122 York Rd., Ste. 340, Oak Brook, IL 60523, (630)242-4100
Opportunity League; Campus Outreach **[★17640]**
Opportunity Off. Directors; Natl. Assn. for State Economic **[★6279]**
Opportunity Plus **[11978]**
Opposed to Militarism and the Draft; Comm. **[5669]**
Opry; Circle Club - The Official Fan Club of the Grand Ole **[24864]**
Opry Fan Club; Grand Ole **[★24864]**
OPSEC Professionals Soc. **[18594]**, PO Box 489, Hamilton, VA 20159, (540)338-3048
Opthalmic Medical Asst; Joint Rev. Comm. for the **[★8834]**
Opthalmic Medical Personnel; Comm. on Accreditation for **[8834]**
Opthalmic Medical Personnel; Joint Rev. Commn. for the **[★8834]**
Opthalmic Medical Personnel; Joint Rev. Comm. for **[★8834]**
Optical Assn; Amer. **[★15712]**
Optical Assn; Natl. **[★15721]**
Optical Equipment
    Amer. Precision Optics Mfrs. Assn. **[3480]**
    Contact Lens Mfrs. Assn. **[1856]**
    Found. Fighting Blindness **[16847]**
    Intl. Fed. of Ophthalmological Societies **[15686]**
    Intl. Photonics Commercialization Alliance **[2862]**
    New Eyes for the Needy **[12533]**
    Optical Labs. Assn. **[1864]**
    Optical Storage Tech. Assn. **[2860]**
    Optical Storage Tech. Assn. **[IO]**
    Optoelectronics Indus. Development Assn. **[IO]**
    Optoelectronics Indus. Development Assn. **[2861]**
    VOSH Intl. **[12543]**
    Zeiss Historical Soc. of Am. **[22133]**
Optical Imaging Assn. **[2735]**, 225 Reinekers Ln., Ste. 625, Alexandria, VA 22314, (703)836-1360
Optical Industry Assn. - Defunct.
Optical Instrumentation Engineers; Soc. of Photo- **[★7408]**
Optical Internetworking Forum **[3726]**, 48377 Fremont Blvd., Ste. 117, Fremont, CA 94538, (510)492-4040
Optical Labs. Assn. **[1864]**, 11096 Lee Hwy., Ste. A-101, Fairfax, VA 22030-5039, (703)359-2830
Optical Laboratories Association **[IO]**, Fairfax, VA, United States
Optical Media Manufacturers and Related Indus; ITA - Intl. Assn. of Magnetic and **[★1370]**
Optical Prdt. Code Coun. **[339]**, 1700 Diagonal Rd., Ste. 500, Alexandria, VA 22314, (703)548-4560
Optical Publishing Assn. - Address unknown since 1999.
Optical Soc. of Am. **[7407]**, 2010 Massachusetts Ave. NW, Washington, DC 20036-1023, (202)223-8130
Optical Soc. of India **[IO]**, Calcutta, India
Optical Storage Tech. Assn. **[IO]**, Cupertino, CA, United States
Optical Storage Tech. Assn. **[2860]**, 19925 Stevens Creek Blvd., Cupertino, CA 95014, (408)253-3695
Optical Video Disc Assn. - Defunct.
Optical Wholesalers Assn. **[★1864]**
Optical Wholesalers Assn. **[★IO]**
Optical Wholesalers; Assn. of Independent **[★1864]**
Optical Wholesalers Natl. Assn. **[★1864]**
Optical Wholesalers Natl. Assn. **[★IO]**
Optician Assn. **[IO]**, Dusseldorf, Germany
Opticianry
    Accreditation Coun. on Optometric Educ. **[15710]**
    Amer. Acad. of Ophthalmology **[15656]**
    Amer. Acad. of Optometry **[15711]**
    Amer. Assn. of Dispensing Ophthalmologists **[15658]**
    Amer. Assn. for Ophthalmic Standardized Echography **[15659]**
    Amer. Assn. for Pediatric Ophthalmology and Strabismus **[15660]**

Amer. Bd. of Ophthalmology **[15661]**
Amer. Bd. of Opticianry **[15704]**
Amer. Bd. of Opticianry **[IO]**
Amer. Ophthalmological Soc. **[15662]**
Amer. Optometric Assn. **[15712]**
Amer. Optometric Found. **[15713]**
Amer. Optometric Student Assn. **[15714]**
Amer. Orthoptic Coun. **[15663]**
Amer. Osteopathic Colleges of Ophthalmology and Otolaryngology-Head and Neck Surgery **[15664]**
Amer. Soc. of Cataract and Refractive Surgery **[15665]**
Amer. Soc. of Contemporary Medicine, Surgery, and Ophthalmology **[15666]**
Amer. Soc. for Ophthalmic Ultrasonography **[15667]**
Assn. of British Dispensing Opticians **[IO]**
Assn. for Macular Diseases **[15669]**
Assn. of Nurses Endorsing Transplantation **[15670]**
Assn. for Ocular Pharmacology and Therapeutics **[15671]**
Assn. of Regulatory Boards of Optometry **[15716]**
Assn. for Res. in Vision and Ophthalmology **[15672]**
Assn. of Tech. Personnel in Ophthalmology **[15674]**
Assn. of Univ. Professors of Ophthalmology **[15675]**
Assn. of Veterans Affairs Ophthalmologists **[15676]**
Benevolent Fund of the Coll. of Optometrists and the Assn. of Optometrists **[IO]**
Better Vision Inst. **[15678]**
BiOptic Driving Network - USA **[15705]**
Children's Eye Found. **[15679]**
China Optical Goods' Indus. Assn. **[IO]**
Coll. of Optometrists in Vision Development **[15718]**
Commn. on Opticianry Accreditation **[15706]**
Contact Lens Assn. of Ophthalmologists **[15680]**
Fed. of Ophthalmic and Dispensing Opticians **[IO]**
Focus **[15681]**
Found. Fighting Blindness **[16847]**
Gen. Optical Coun. **[IO]**
Glaucoma Res. Found. **[15683]**
Hong Kong Optical Mfrs. Assn. **[IO]**
Intercontinental Fed. of Behavioral Optometry **[15719]**
Intl. Assn. of Ocular Surgeons **[15684]**
Intl. Assn. of Optometric Executives **[15720]**
Intl. Eye Found. **[15685]**
Intl. Fed. of Ophthalmological Societies **[15686]**
Intl. Opticians Assn. **[IO]**
Intl. Refractive Surgery Club **[15689]**
Intl. Soc. on Metabolic Eye Disease **[15691]**
Intl. Trachoma Initiative **[16858]**
Japan Optical Measuring Instrument Mfrs'. Assn. **[IO]**
Japan Telescope Mfrs. Assn. **[IO]**
Joint Commn. on Allied Hea. Personnel in Ophthalmology **[15692]**
Natl. Acad. of Opticianry **[15707]**
Natl. Assn. of Optical Goods Manufacturers **[IO]**
Natl. Assn. of Optometrists and Opticians **[15721]**
Natl. Assn. of Vision Professionals **[15693]**
Natl. Bd. of Examiners in Optometry **[15722]**
Natl. Contact Lens Examiners **[15723]**
Natl. Eye Res. Found. **[15724]**
Natl. Fed. of Opticianry Schools **[15708]**
Natl. Optometric Assn. **[15725]**
Ophthalmic Photographers' Soc. **[15696]**
Opticians Assn. of Am. **[15709]**
Opticians Assn. of Canada **[IO]**
Optometric Extension Prog. Found. **[15727]**
ORBIS Intl. **[15697]**
Outpatient Ophthalmic Surgery Soc. **[15698]**
Pan-American Assn. of Ophthalmology **[15699]**
Soc. of Eye Surgeons **[15703]**
Tear Film and Ocular Surface Soc. **[15729]**
Opticianry; Amer. Bd. of **[★15707]**
Opticianry; Intl. Acad. of **[★15707]**
Opticians of Am; Guild of Prescription **[★15709]**
Opticians Assn. of Am. **[15709]**, 441 Carlisle Dr., Herndon, VA 20170, (703)437-8780

A star before a book entry number signifies that the name is not listed separately, but is mentioned within the entry.

Opticians Assn. of Canada [IO], Winnipeg, MB, Canada
Opticians; Natl. Assn. of Optometrists and [15721]
Optics
   Amer. Bd. of Opticianry [15704]
   Australian Optical Soc. [IO]
   BiOptic Driving Network - USA [15705]
   Commn. on Opticianry Accreditation [15706]
   Danish Optical Soc. [IO]
   Fiber Optic Assn. [9238]
   Found. Fighting Blindness [16847]
   French Optics Mfrs. Assn. [IO]
   The Glaucoma Found. [15682]
   Intercontinental Fed. of Behavioral Optometry [15719]
   Intl. Assn. of Optometric Executives [15720]
   Intl. Commn. for Optics [IO]
   Intl. Comm. on Ultra-High Intensity Lasers [7245]
   Intl. Fed. of Ophthalmological Societies [15686]
   Intl. Perimetric Soc. [15688]
   Intl. Photonics Commercialization Alliance [2862]
   Intl. Photonics Commercialization Alliance [IO]
   Intl. Soc. on Optics within Life Sciences [IO]
   Natl. Acad. of Opticianry [15707]
   New Eyes for the Needy [12533]
   Optical Soc. of Am. [7407]
   Optical Soc. of India [IO]
   Opticians Assn. of Am. [15709]
   Optoelectronics Indus. Development Assn. [2861]
   Plastic Optical Fiber Trade Org. [2863]
   SPIE - The Intl. Soc. for Optical Engg. [7408]
   SPIE - The Intl. Soc. for Optical Engg. [IO]
   Swedish Optical Soc. [IO]
   VOSH Intl. [12543]
Optics Mfrs. Assn; Amer. Precision [3480]
Optics Mfrs. Assn; Laser and Electro- [7246]
Optics Soc; IEEE Lasers and Electro- [6920]
Optimal Hea. Assn; Nutrition for [15567]
Optimist Dinghy Assn; U.S. [23230]
Optimist Intl. [13057], 4494 Lindell Blvd., St. Louis, MO 63108, (314)371-6000
Optimist Intl. [IO], St. Louis, MO, United States
Optimist Octagon Intl; Junior [13045]
Optimum Population Trust [IO], Manchester, United Kingdom
Option Inst. and Fellowship [★IO]
Option Inst. and Fellowship [★16629]
Option Inst. Intl. Learning and Training Center [16629], 2080 S Undermountain Rd., Sheffield, MA 01257-9643, (413)229-2100
Option Inst. Intl. Learning and Training Center [IO], Sheffield, MA, United States
Options - Address unknown since 2006.
Options for Animals [★16804]
Options for Animals Found. [★16804]
Options for Animals Intl. [16804], 4267 Virginia Rd., Wellsville, KS 66092, (309)658-2920
Options; Center for Population [★12173]
Options Exchange; Chicago Bd. [3509]
OPTIONS Service of Project Concern - Defunct.
Opto-Precision Instruments Association [★3488]
Optoelectronics Indus. Development Assn. [2861], 1133 Connecticut Ave. NW, Ste. 600, Washington, DC 20036, (202)785-4426
Optoelectronics Indus. Development Assn. [IO], Washington, DC, United States
Optometric Assn; Fiji [IO]
Optometric Editors Assn. - Defunct.
Optometric Educ; Coun. on [★15710]
Optometric Educators; Assn. of [8851]
Optometric Executives; Soc. of Assn. [★15720]
Optometric Extension Prog. Found. [15727], 1921 E Carnegie Ave., Ste. 3L, Santa Ana, CA 92705-5510, (949)250-8070
Optometric Historical Soc. [15728], 243 N Lindbergh Blvd., St. Louis, MO 63141, (800)365-2219
Optometric Services to Humanity/International; Volunteer [★12543]
Optometric Soc. for Developmental Vision Care; Natl. [★15718]
Optometrists Assn. Australia [IO], Carlton South, Australia
Optometrists; New Zealand Assn. of [IO]
Optometry
   Accreditation Coun. on Optometric Educ. [15710]

Amer. Acad. of Ophthalmology [15656]
Amer. Acad. of Optometry [15711]
Amer. Acad. of Optometry [IO]
Amer. Acad. of Optometry - British Chap. [IO]
Amer. Assn. of Dispensing Ophthalmologists [15658]
Amer. Assn. for Ophthalmic Standardized Echography [15659]
Amer. Assn. for Pediatric Ophthalmology and Strabismus [15660]
Amer. Bd. of Ophthalmology [15661]
Amer. Ophthalmological Soc. [15662]
Amer. Optometric Assn. [15712]
Amer. Optometric Found. [15713]
Amer. Optometric Student Assn. [15714]
Amer. Orthoptic Coun. [15663]
Amer. Osteopathic Colleges of Ophthalmology and Otolaryngology-Head and Neck Surgery [15664]
Amer. Soc. of Cataract and Refractive Surgery [15665]
Amer. Soc. of Contemporary Medicine, Surgery, and Ophthalmology [15666]
Amer. Soc. for Ophthalmic Ultrasonography [15667]
Amer. Uveitis Soc. [15668]
Asia-Pacific Coun. of Optometry [15715]
Asia-Pacific Coun. of Optometry [IO]
Assn. for Macular Diseases [15669]
Assn. of Nurses Endorsing Transplantation [15670]
Assn. for Ocular Pharmacology and Therapeutics [15671]
Assn. of Optometric Educators [8851]
Assn. of Optometrists [IO]
Assn. Professionnelle des Opticiens et Optometristes de Belgique [IO]
Assn. of Regulatory Boards of Optometry [IO]
Assn. of Regulatory Boards of Optometry [15716]
Assn. for Res. in Vision and Ophthalmology [15672]
Assn. of Schools and Colleges of Optometry [15717]
Assn. of Tech. Personnel in Ophthalmology [15674]
Assn. of Univ. Professors of Ophthalmology [15675]
Assn. of Veterans Affairs Ophthalmologists [15676]
Assn. of Vision Educators [15677]
Beta Sigma Kappa [24562]
Better Vision Inst. [15678]
BiOptic Driving Network - USA [15705]
British Assn. of Behavioral Optometrists [IO]
Canadian Assn. of Optometrists [IO]
Children's Eye Found. [15679]
China Optometric and Optical Assn. [IO]
Coll. of Optometrists [IO]
Coll. of Optometrists in Vision Development [15718]
Commn. on Opticianry Accreditation [15706]
Contact Lens Assn. of Ophthalmologists [15680]
Contact Lens Mfrs. Assn. [1856]
Cornea Res. Found. of Am. [15105]
European Assn. of Universities, Schools and Colleges of Optometry [IO]
European Glaucoma Soc. [IO]
European Optical Soc. [IO]
Eyecare Trust [IO]
Fiji Optometric Assn. [IO]
Focus [15681]
Found. Fighting Blindness [16847]
The Glaucoma Found. [15682]
Glaucoma Res. Found. [15683]
Hong Kong Soc. of Professional Optometrists [IO]
Intercontinental Fed. of Behavioral Optometry [IO]
Intercontinental Fed. of Behavioral Optometry [15719]
Intl. Assn. of Ocular Surgeons [15684]
Intl. Assn. of Optometric Executives [15720]
Intl. Assn. of Optometric Executives [IO]
Intl. Eye Found. [15685]
Intl. Fed. of Ophthalmological Societies [15686]
Intl. Perimetric Soc. [15688]
Intl. Refractive Surgery Club [15689]

Intl. Soc. for Imaging in the Eye [15690]
Intl. Soc. on Metabolic Eye Disease [15691]
Intl. Trachoma Initiative [16858]
Joint Commn. on Allied Hea. Personnel in Ophthalmology [15692]
Natl. Assn. of Optometrists and Opticians [15721]
Natl. Assn. of Vision Professionals [15693]
Natl. Bd. of Examiners in Optometry [15722]
Natl. Contact Lens Examiners [15723]
Natl. Eye Res. Found. [15724]
Natl. Optometric Assn. [15725]
Natl. Optometry Assn. [15726]
Neuro-Optometric Rehabilitation Assn., Intl. [15300]
New Eyes for the Needy [12533]
New Zealand Assn. of Optometrists [IO]
Omega Delta [24563]
Ophthalmic Photographers' Soc. [15696]
Optical Labs. Assn. [1864]
Optical Storage Tech. Assn. [2860]
Optometric Extension Prog. Found. [15727]
Optometric Historical Soc. [15728]
Optometrists Assn. Australia [IO]
ORBIS Intl. [15697]
Outpatient Ophthalmic Surgery Soc. [15698]
Pan-American Assn. of Ophthalmology [15699]
Scottish Comm. of Optometrists [IO]
Soc. of Eye Surgeons [15703]
South African Optometric Assn. [IO]
Swiss Soc. of Optometry [IO]
Tear Film and Ocular Surface Soc. [IO]
Tear Film and Ocular Surface Soc. [15729]
Vision Coun. of Am. [1866]
Vision USA [15730]
Vision World Wide [16890]
VOSH Intl. [12543]
World Coun. of Optometry [15731]
World Coun. of Optometry [IO]
Ora Gp. NA'AMAT [IO], Melbourne, Australia
Oracle Applications Users Gp. [6773], 3525 Piedmont Rd. NE, Bldg. 5, Ste. 300, Atlanta, GA 30305, (404)240-0897
Oracle Development Tools User Gp. [6774], 3208 Oleander Dr., Ste. C, Wilmington, NC 28403, (910)452-7444
ORACLE Religious Assn. [20070], c/o Sr. Dr. Oralisa Martin, Founder, PO Box 697, Beltsville, MD 20705, (202)635-2672
Oracle Users Gp. - Americas; Intl. [★6796]
Oral Biology; Amer. Inst. of [14137]
Oral Contraceptive Coun. - Defunct.
Oral Deaf Adults Sect. [★14775]
Oral Deaf Adults Sect. [★IO]
Oral Diagnosis; Org. of Teachers of [8197]
Oral Dynamics; Acad. of [14090]
Oral Dynamics; Intl. Acad. of [★14090]
Oral Hea. Am. [8196], 410 N Michigan Ave., Ste. 352, Chicago, IL 60611-4211, (312)836-9900
Oral Hea. Info. CH; Natl. [14181]
Oral Hearing-Impaired Sect. [14775], 3417 Volta Pl. NW, Washington, DC 20007, (202)337-5220
Oral Hearing-Impaired Sect. [IO], Washington, DC, United States
Oral History Assn. [10141], c/o Madelyn Campbell, Exec. Sec., Dickinson Coll., PO Box 1773, Carlisle, PA 17013-2896, (717)245-1036
Oral History Soc. [IO], Colchester, United Kingdom
Oral Implantologists; Intl. Coll. of [★14165]
Oral and Maxillofacial Pathology; Amer. Acad. of [15852]
Oral and Maxillofacial Pathology; Amer. Bd. of [15855]
Oral and Maxillofacial Radiology; Amer. Acad. of [14104]
Oral and Maxillofacial Surgery
   Acad. for Implants and Transplants [14087]
   Acad. of Oral Dynamics [14090]
   Amer. Acad. of Dental Gp. Practice [14094]
   Amer. Acad. of Dental Practice Admin. [14095]
   Amer. Acad. of Esthetic Dentistry [14096]
   Amer. Acad. of Fixed Prosthodontics [14097]
   Amer. Acad. of Gnathologic Orthopedics [14098]
   Amer. Acad. of the History of Dentistry [14100]
   Amer. Acad. of Implant Dentistry [14101]
   Amer. Acad. of Oral and Maxillofacial Pathology [15852]

Reference to "IO" in place of a book number signifies that the association may be found in the 45th edition of International Organizations.

Amer. Acad. of Oral and Maxillofacial Radiology [14104]
Amer. Acad. of Oral Medicine [14105]
Amer. Acad. of Orofacial Pain [14106]
Amer. Acad. of Orthodontics for the Gen. Practitioner [14107]
Amer. Acad. of Pediatric Dentistry [14108]
Amer. Acad. of Periodontology [14109]
Amer. Acad. of Restorative Dentistry [14110]
Amer. Assn. of Dental Examiners [14112]
Amer. Assn. for Dental Res. [14113]
Amer. Assn. of Endodontists [14114]
Amer. Assn. for Functional Orthodontics [14115]
Amer. Assn. of Hosp. Dentists [14116]
Amer. Assn. of Oral and Maxillofacial Surgeons [15732]
Amer. Assn. of Orthodontists [14117]
Amer. Assn. of Public Hea. Dentistry [14118]
Amer. Assn. of Women Dentists [14119]
Amer. Bd. of Dental Public Hea. [14120]
Amer. Bd. of Endodontics [14121]
Amer. Bd. of Oral and Maxillofacial Pathology [15855]
Amer. Bd. of Oral and Maxillofacial Surgery [15733]
Amer. Bd. of Orthodontics [14124]
Amer. Bd. of Periodontology [14125]
Amer. Bd. of Prosthodontics [14126]
Amer. Coll. of Dentists [14128]
Amer. Coll. of Oral and Maxillofacial Surgeons [15734]
American College of Oral and Maxillofacial Surgeons [IO]
Amer. Coll. of Prosthodontists [14129]
Amer. Dental Assistants Assn. [14130]
Amer. Dental Assn. [14131]
Amer. Dental Hygienists' Assn. [14132]
Amer. Dental Soc. of Anesthesiology [14133]
Amer. Endodontic Soc. [14134]
Amer. Equilibration Soc. [14135]
Amer. Inst. of Oral Biology [14137]
Amer. Orthodontic Soc. [14138]
Amer. Prosthodontic Soc. [14139]
Amer. Soc. for Dental Aesthetics [14140]
Amer. Soc. of Forensic Odontology [14142]
Amer. Soc. of Master Dental Technologists [14143]
Amer. Soc. of Maxillofacial Surgeons [15735]
Amer. Soc. for the Stud. of Orthodontics [14144]
Assn. of Oral and Maxillofacial Surgeons of India [IO]
Assn. of State and Territorial Dental Directors [14146]
Australian and New Zealand Assn. of Oral and Maxillofacial Surgeons [IO]
British Assn. of Oral and Maxillofacial Surgeons [IO]
Canadian Assn. of Oral and Maxillofacial Surgeons [IO]
Christian Dental Soc. [14147]
Delta Dental Plans Assn. [14687]
Dental Assisting Natl. Bd. [14151]
Dental Hea. Intl. [14152]
European Assn. for Cranio-Maxillofacial Surgery [IO]
Flying Dentists Assn. [14153]
Holistic Dental Assn. [14156]
Intl. Acad. of Myodontics [14159]
Intl. Assn. for Dental Res. [14161]
Intl. Assn. of Dental Traumatology [IO]
Intl. Assn. of Oral and Maxillofacial Surgeons [IO]
Intl. Assn. of Oral and Maxillofacial Surgeons [15736]
Intl. Assn. for Orthodontics [14162]
Intl. Coll. of Dentists [14163]
Intl. Cong. of Oral Implantologists [14165]
Intl. Fed. of Esthetic Dentistry [14167]
Natl. Assn. of Dental Assistants [14169]
Natl. Assn. of Dental Labs. [14170]
Natl. Bd. for Certification in Dental Lab. Tech. [14172]
Natl. Dental Assn. [14175]
Natl. Dental Hygienists' Assn. [14177]
Natl. Denturist Assn. [14178]
Natl. Found. of Dentistry for the Handicapped [14179]

Orthodontic Education and Res. Found. [14183]
Pierre Fauchard Acad. [14184]
Uplift Internationale [15737]
Uplift Internationale [IO]
Oral and Maxillofacial Surgery Overseas [★IO]
Oral and Maxillofacial Surgery Overseas [★15778]
Oral Medicine; Amer. Acad. of [14105]
Oral Medicine; American Bd. of [★8197]
Oral Pathology; Amer. Acad. [★15852]
Oral Pathology; Amer. Bd. of [★15855]
Oral and Performing Literature; Conf. for Chinese [9790]
Oral and Plastic Surgeons; Amer. Assn. of [★14040]
Oral Roberts Univ. Educational Fellowship [8089], Oral Roberts Univ., 7777 S Lewis Ave., Tulsa, OK 74171, (918)495-6163
Oral Roentgenology; Amer. Acad. of [★14104]
Oral Surgeons; Amer. Soc. of [★15732]
Oral Surgery; Amer. Bd. of [★15733]
Oral Surgery; Assn. of Diplomates of the Amer. Bd. of [★15734]
Orange Juice Assn; Natl. [★510]
Orangeburgh German Swiss Genealogical Soc. [21139], PO Box 974, Orangeburg, SC 29116-0974
ORBEL [★IO]
Orbilian Soc. - Defunct.
ORBIS Intl. [15697], 520 8th Ave., 11th Fl., New York, NY 10018, (646)674-5500
ORBIS Intl. [IO], New York, NY, United States
Orbis; Proj. [★15697]
Orchard House [★9682]
Orchard Soc; Home [4734]
Orchestra Assn; Natl. Symphony [10669]
Orchestra Leaders; Natl. Assn. of [17981]
Orchestra League; Amer. Symphony [10552]
Orchestra Librarians' Assn; Major [10371]
Orchestral Assn; Natl. [10667]
Orchestras
    Amer. Symphony Orchestra League [10552]
    Asiatic Philharmonia Soc. [10557]
    Intl. Conf. of Symphony and Opera Musicians [10618]
    Natl. Orchestral Assn. [10667]
    Natl. Symphony Orchestra Assn. [10669]
    World Fed. of Amateur Orchestras [10766]
    World Fed. of Amateur Orchestras [IO]
Orchestras Canada [IO], Toronto, ON, Canada
Orchestras; Natl. Assn. of Youth [IO]
Orchestre national des jeunes du Canada [★IO]
Orchestre des Jeunes de l'Union Europeenne [★IO]
Orchestres Canada [★IO]
Orchid Soc; Amer. [6625]
Orchid Soc; French [IO]
Orchid Soc. of Hawaii; Pacific [22536]
Orchids
    South African Orchid Coun. [IO]
Orchids - Defunct.
Orchids Dominican, S.A. [IO], Santo Domingo, Dominican Republic
Orde Van Nederalndse Raadgevende Ingenieurs [★IO]
Orde Van Raadgevende Ingenieurs in Suriname [★IO]
Ordem dos Medicos [IO], Lisbon, Portugal
The Order - Address unknown since 1997.
Order of AHEPA [★19083]
Order of the Alhambra [★19001]
Order of Alhambra [★19001]
Order of the Alhambra [★IO]
Order of Alhambra [★IO]
Order of Alhambra; Intl. [19001]
Order of the Amaranth; Supreme Coun. [19254]
Order of Americans of Armorial Ancestry [20750], PO Box 453, Abingdon, MD 21009-0453, (410)515-1824
Order of Architects and Consulting Engineers [IO], Luxembourg, Luxembourg
Order of the Arrow [13005], 1325 W Walnut Hill Ln., PO Box 152079, Irving, TX 75015-2079, (972)580-2438
Order of the Canons Regular of Premontre [IO], Rome, Italy
Order of the Coif [24516], Univ. of North Carolina, Law Lib., CB No. 3385, Chapel Hill, NC 27599-3385, (919)962-8501

Order of the Compassionate Heart - Address unknown since 1999.
Order of the Cross Soc. - Address unknown since 2003.
Order of Daedalians [20650], PO Box 249, Universal City, TX 78148-0249, (210)945-2111
Order of the Daughters of the King [19969], 101 Weatherstone Dr., Ste. 870, Woodstock, GA 30188, (770)517-8552
Order of DeMolay [★19375]
Order of DeMolay [★IO]
Order of DeMolay; International Supreme Coun. [★IO]
Order of DeMolay; International Supreme Coun. [★19375]
Order of Descendants of the Ancient and Honorable Artillery Company [20751], 300 N Hill Rd., Sutton, WV 26601, (304)765-0321
Order of Descendants of Colonial Physicians and Chirurgiens [20752]
Order of the Eastern Star; Gen. Grand Chap., [19234]
Order of Fifinella [★21413]
Order of First Families of Connecticut 1631-1662 [20753], 300 N Hill Rd., Sutton, WV 26601, (304)765-0321
Order of First Families of Rhode Island and Providence Plantations [20754], 300 N Hill Rd., Sutton, WV 26601, (304)765-0321
Order of the Flaming Cross - Defunct.
Order of the Fleur de Lis - Defunct.
Order of the Founders and Patriots of Am. [20755], c/o Natl. Soc., Daughters of Founders and Patriots of Am., The Woodward Bldg., 733 15th St. NW, No. 915, Washington, DC 20005-2112
Order of Friars Minor [IO], Rome, Italy
Order of the Golden Chain - Address unknown since 1999.
Order of the Golden Eagle [★21320]
Order of Good Templars; Natl. Grand Lodge, Intl. [★19081]
Order of the Indian Wars [10479], PO Box 1650, Johnstown, CO 80534
Order of Indian Wars of the U.S. [★10482]
Order of Lafayette [21418], c/o Bruce A. Laue, Pres. Gen., 243 W 70th St., Apt. 6f, New York, NY 10023-4321
Order of Military Wine Tasters - Address unknown since 1995.
Order of the Noble Companions of the Swan [9969], c/o William de Alabona-Ostrogojsk, Exec. Off., PO Box 404, Milltown, NJ 08850
Order of the Noble Companions of the Swan [IO], Milltown, NJ, United States
Order of Owls - Defunct.
Order of Pachyderms; Grand [★18359]
Order of Railway Conductors and Brakemen [★24181]
Order of Saint Andrew the Apostle [20073], 8 E 79th St., New York, NY 10021, (212)570-3550
Order of Saint Augustine [IO], Rome, Italy
Order of St. Lazarus [IO], Ottawa, ON, Canada
Order of St. Vincent Soc. [★IO]
Order of St. Vincent Soc. [★19963]
Order Selection, Staging and Storage Coun. of the Material Handling Indus. of Am. [3980], 8720 Red Oak Blvd., Ste. 201, Charlotte, NC 28217-3992, (704)676-1190
Order of Seville - Address unknown since 1995.
Order of Shepherds of Bethlehem - Address unknown since 1995.
Order of Skeletons - Address unknown since 1995.
Order Sons of Italy in Am. [19168], 219 E St. NE, Washington, DC 20002, (202)547-2900
Order of Sons of Zion [★19177]
Order of the Stars and Bars [★20729]
Order of United Commercial Travelers of Am. [19135], 632 N Park St., Columbus, OH 43215-8619, (614)228-3276
Order of United Commercial Travelers of Am. - Canadian Off. [IO], Calgary, AB, Canada
Orders and Medals Res. Soc. [IO], High Wycombe, United Kingdom
Orders and Medals Society of America [IO], San Ramon, CA, United States

A star before a book entry number signifies that the name is not listed separately, but is mentioned within the entry.

Orders and Medals Soc. of Am. **[22631]**, PO Box 198, San Ramon, CA 94583

Ordinances; Natl. Comm. on Uniform Traffic Laws and **[6309]**

Ordinary Assembly of Catholics of the Holy Land **[IO]**, Jerusalem, Israel

Ordination Conf; Women's **[19740]**

Ordine Secolare dei Carmelitani Scalzi **[★IO]**

Ordnance and Explosive Waste Contractors; Natl. Assn. of **[1038]**

Ordo Fratrum Excalceatorum Beatissimae Mariae Virginis de Monte Carmelo **[★IO]**

Ordo Fratrum Sancti Augustini **[★IO]**

Ordre des Architectes et des Ingenieurs-Conseils **[★IO]**

L'Ordre de Bienfaisance et de Protection de l'Ordre des Elans **[★IO]**

Ordre des Experts Comptables Agrees au Liban **[★IO]**

Ordre de Premontre **[★IO]**

Ordre de Saint-Lazare au Canada **[★IO]**

L'Ordre Souverain Militaire Hospitalier de Malte Assn. Canadienne **[★IO]**

Ore Assn; Lake Superior Iron **[★2696]**

Ore Assn; Western Iron **[★2696]**

Oregon-California Trails Assn. **[10056]**, PO Box 1019, Independence, MO 64051-0519, (816)252-2276

Oregon Highland Bentgrass Commn. **[4797]**, PO Box 3366, Salem, OR 97302-0366, (503)364-2944

Oregon Horsemen's Benevolent Protective Assn. **[23512]**, 10350 N Vancouver Way, No. 351, Portland, OR 97217-7530, (503)285-4941

Oregon Pioneers; Sons and Daughters of **[21257]**

Oregon Ryegrass Growers Seed Commn. **[4798]**, PO Box 3366, Salem, OR 97302-0366, (503)364-2944

Orff-Schulwerk Assn; Amer. **[10547]**

Organ

Amer. Assn. of Blood Banks **[13761]**

Amer. Guild of Organists **[10537]**

Amer. Inst. of Organbuilders **[2798]**

Amer. Soc. of Transplant Surgeons **[16667]**

Amer. Theatre Organ Soc. **[10553]**

Assoc. Pipe Organ Builders of Am. **[2799]**

Assn. of Anglican Musicians **[20425]**

Assn. of Organ Procurement Organizations **[14287]**

Center for Organ Recovery and Educ. **[16670]**

Choristers Guild **[20426]**

Church Music Assn. of Am. **[20428]**

Church Music Publishers Assn. **[20429]**

Fellowship of Amer. Baptist Musicians **[20430]**

Hymn Soc. in the U.S. and Canada **[20432]**

Intl. Liver Transplantation Soc. **[16672]**

Intl. Soc. for Heart and Lung Transplantation **[16674]**

Intl. Soc. for Organ History and Preservation **[10628]**

LifeBanc **[14290]**

The Living Bank Intl. **[14291]**

Natl. Coun. on Minority Educ. in Transplantation **[16677]**

Natl. Forum of Greek Orthodox Church Musicians **[20434]**

North Amer. Transplant Coordinators Org. **[16681]**

Organ CH LLC **[10682]**

Organ Historical Soc. **[10683]**

Presbyterian Assn. of Musicians **[20435]**

Reed Organ Soc. **[10691]**

Southeastern Historical Keyboard Soc. **[22720]**

Transplant Recipients Intl. Org. **[16682]**

Unitarian Universalist Musicians' Network **[20436]**

United Network for Organ Sharing **[16684]**

Organ Builders of Am; Assoc. Pipe **[2799]**

Organ Center **[★16684]**

Organ CH LLC **[10682]**, PO Box 290786, Charlestown, MA 02129-0214, (617)241-8550

Organ Enthusiasts; Amer. Assn. of Theatre **[★10553]**

Organ Enthusiasts; Amer. Theatre **[★10553]**

Organ Historical Soc. **[10683]**, PO Box 26811, Richmond, VA 23261, (804)353-9226

Organ Historical Trust of Australia **[IO]**, Camberwell, Australia

Organ Inst. - Defunct.

Organ Literature Found. - Defunct.

Organ Mfrs; Natl. Assn. of Electronic **[★2808]**

Organ and Piano Teachers Assn. - Defunct.

Organ Procurement Organizations; Assn. of **[14287]**

Organ Recovery **[★14290]**

Organ Recovery and Educ; Center for **[16670]**

Organ Sharing; United Network for **[16684]**

Organ Soc. of Am; Reed **[★10691]**

Organ Soc; Amer. Theatre **[10553]**

Organ Soc; Reed **[10691]**

Organ Transplant Assn; Amer. **[16664]**

Organ Transplant Assn; Children's **[13956]**

Organ Transplant Fund **[★16678]**

Organbuilders; Amer. Inst. of **[2798]**

Organic Acidemia Assn. **[14472]**, c/o Kathy Stagni, Exec. Dir., 13210 35th Ave. N, Plymouth, MN 55441-2227, (763)559-1797

Organic Agriculture Assn. **[IO]**, Tirana, Albania

Organic Certifiers Caucus **[★5027]**

Organic Chem. Manufacturers Assn; Synthetic **[827]**

Organic Consumers Assn. **[5069]**, 6771 S Silver Hill Dr., Finland, MN 55603, (218)226-4164

Organic Crop Improvement Assn. **[4655]**, 1340 N Cotner, Lincoln, NE 68505, (402)477-2323

Organic Crop Improvement Assn. **[IO]**, Lincoln, NE, United States

Organic Exchange **[2864]**, 5332 Coll. Ave., Ste. 203, Oakland, CA 94618, (510)597-9949

Organic Farming

Assn. of Natural Biocontrol Producers **[5074]**

Ecological Farming Assn. **[4100]**

European Network for Sci. Res. Coordination in Organic Farming **[IO]**

Henry Doubleday Res. Assn. **[IO]**

Independent Organic Inspectors Assn. **[5067]**

Intl. Fed. of Organic Agriculture Movements **[IO]**

Irish Organic Farmers and Growers Assn. **[IO]**

Japanese Organic Inspectors Assn. **[IO]**

Kitchen Gardeners Intl. **[9966]**

MOA Nature Farming and Culture Agency **[IO]**

Mountain State Organic Growers and Buyers Assn. **[5068]**

Organic Consumers Assn. **[5069]**

Organic Crop Improvement Assn. **[4655]**

Organic Exchange **[2864]**

Organic Grapes Into Wine Alliance **[5418]**

Organic Growers Assn. Western Australia **[IO]**

Organic Growers and Buyers Assn. **[5070]**

Permaculture Assn. **[IO]**

Permaculture Intl. **[IO]**

Permaculture Trust of Botswana **[IO]**

Price-Pottenger Nutrition Found. **[15568]**

School of Living **[10178]**

Soil Assn. **[IO]**

Soil and Hea. Assn. of New Zealand **[IO]**

Universal Proutist Farmers Fed. **[4659]**

Willing Workers on Organic Farms **[IO]**

Organic Food Alliance **[★5027]**

Organic Food Fed. **[IO]**, Norfolk, United Kingdom

Organic Grapes Into Wine Alliance **[5418]**

Organic Growers Assn. Western Australia **[IO]**, Forrestfield, Australia

Organic Growers of Australia **[IO]**, South Lismore, Australia

Organic Growers and Buyers Assn. **[5070]**

Organic Herb Growers of Australia **[★IO]**

Organic Inspectors Assn; Independent **[5067]**

Organic Pigments Mfrs; ETAD North Am. - Ecological and Toxicological Assn. of Dyes and **[5089]**

Organic Reactions Catalysis Soc. **[6692]**, c/o Michael L. Prunier, Chm., Lilly Corporate Ctr., DC 1940, Indianapolis, IN 46285, (317)433-0372

Organic Trade Assn. **[5027]**, PO Box 547, Greenfield, MA 01302, (413)774-7511

Organisatie Van Advies en Ingenieursbureaus **[★IO]**

Org. mondiale des personnes handicapees **[★IO]**

Org. humanitaire de rehabilitation pour les pauvres et les necceiteux **[★IO]**

Org. mondiale des douanes **[★IO]**

L'Organisation pour les carrieres en environnement **[★IO]**

Org. Africaine de la Propriete Intellectuelle **[★IO]**

Org. Afro-Asiatique pour la Developpement Rural **[★IO]**

Org. of Asia Pacific News Agencies **[IO]**, Jakarta, Indonesia

Org. des Assurances Africaines **[★IO]**

Org. Canadienne pour l'Education au Ser. du Developpement **[★IO]**

Org. Catholique pour la Promotion Humaine - Caritas Rep. de Guinee **[IO]**, Conakry, Guinea

Org. de la Charite pour un Developpement Integral - Caritas Togo **[IO]**, Lome, Togo

Org. Clandestine de Resistance **[★IO]**

Org. for the Collaboration of Railways **[★IO]**

Org. Cooperation et de Developpement Economiques **[★IO]**

Org. for the Cooperation of Railways **[IO]**, Warsaw, Poland

Org. mondiale d'endoscopie digestive **[★IO]**

Org. mondiale d'Etudes Specialisees pour les Maladies de l'Oesophage **[★IO]**

Org. of Eastern Caribbean States **[IO]**, Castries, St. Lucia

Org. for Economic Co-Operation and Development **[IO]**, Paris, France

Org. of European Aluminium Refiners and Remelters **[IO]**, Dusseldorf, Germany

Org. of European Aluminium Smelters **[★IO]**

Org. for European Economic Co-operation **[★6866]**

Org. of European Indus. Transforming Fruit and Vegetables **[IO]**, Brussels, Belgium

Org. Europeenne pour l'Equipement de l'Aviation Civile **[★IO]**

Org. Europeenne pour l'Exploitation de Satellites Meteorologiques **[★IO]**

Org. Europeenne et Mediterraneenne pour la Protection des Plantes **[★IO]**

Org. Europeenne pour la Qualite **[★IO]**

Org. Europeenne pour la Recherche Nucleaire **[★IO]**

Org. Europeenne pour la Recherche et le Traitement du Cancer **[★IO]**

Org. Europeenne pour des Recherches Astronomiques dans l'Hemisphere Austral **[★IO]**

Org. Europeenne pour les Recherches Chimiosensorielles **[★IO]**

Org. Europeenne de Telecommunications par Satellite **[★IO]**

Org. Gestosis - Soc. for the Stud. of Pathophysiology of Pregnancy **[IO]**, Basel, Switzerland

Org. of Huntington in Greece **[IO]**, Athens, Greece

Org. Interafricaine du Cafe **[★IO]**

Org. Intergouvernementale pour les Transports Internationaux Ferroviaires **[★IO]**

Org. Internationale de Biophysique Pure et Appliquee **[★IO]**

Org. Internationale du Cafe **[★IO]**

Org. Internationale des Commissions de Valeurs **[★IO]**

Org. Internationale des Constructeurs d'Automobiles **[★IO]**

Org. Internationale des Femmes Sionistes **[★IO]**

Org. Internationale des Institutions Superieures de Control des Finances Publiques **[★IO]**

Org. Internationale pour l'Elimination de Toutes les Formes de Discrimination Raciale **[★IO]**

Org. Internationale de Lutte Biologique contre les Animaux et les Plantes Nuisibles **[★IO]**

Org. Internationale de Lutte Biologique Contre les Animaux et les Plantes Nuisibles **[★IO]**

Org. Internationale de Metrologie Legale **[★IO]**

Org. Internationale de Normalisation **[★IO]**

Org. Internationale de Police Criminelle **[★IO]**

Org. Internationale pour le Progres **[★IO]**

Org. Internationale de Psychophysiologie **[★IO]**

Org. Internationale de Recherche sur la Cellule **[★IO]**

Org. Internationale de Recherche sur le Cerveau **[★IO]**

Org. Internationale des scenographes, architectes et techniciens de theatre **[★IO]**

Org. Internationale des Telecommunications Spatiales **[★IO]**

Org. Internationale du Travail **[★IO]**

Org. Internationale de la Vigne et du Vin **[★IO]**

Org. Islamique pour l'Education, les Sciences et la Culture **[★IO]**

Org. de l'Aviation Civile Internationale **[★IO]**

Reference to "IO" in place of a book number signifies that the association may be found in the 45th edition of International Organizations.

Org. pour l'Etude Phyto-Taxonomique de la Region Mediterraneenne [★IO]
Org. pour l'histoire du Canada [★IO]
Org. Maritime Internationale [★IO]
Org. Meteorologique Mondiale [★IO]
Org. Mondiale Contre la Torture/SOS-Torture [★IO]
Org. Mondiale de Gastroenterologie [★IO]
Org. Mondiale de Labourage [★IO]
Org. Mondiale pour l'Education Prescolaire [★IO]
Org. Mondiale de la Propriete Intellectuelle [★IO]
Org. Mondiale de la Sante [★IO]
Org. Mondiale pour la Systemique et la Cybernet-ique [★IO]
L'Organisation des Musees Militaires du Canada [★IO]
Org. Nationale de la sante autochtone [★IO]
Org. Nationale des Femmes Immigrantes et des Femmes Appartement a une Minorite Visible du Canada [★IO]
Org. des Nations Unies pour le Developpement In-dustriel [★IO]
Org. des Nations Unies pour l'Education, la Sci. et la Culture [★IO]
Org. Neederlandaise de Developpement - Mali [★IO]
Org. Neerlandaise de Developpement - Cameroon [★IO]
Org. Nord Americaine Pour La Protection des Plan-tes [★IO]
Org. for Nordic Elecl. Cooperation [IO], Helsinki, Finland
Org. des Pays Exportateurs de Petrole [★IO]
Org. des Peches de l'Atlantique Nord-Ouest [★IO]
Org. of Pharmaceutical Producers of India [IO], Bombay, India
L'Organisation Pour La Conservation Du Saumon De l'Atlantique Nord [★IO]
Org. de Producteurs dans le Secteur de la Peche Belge [★IO]
Org. of Professional Users of Statistics [IO], Esher, United Kingdom
Org. for Professionals in Regulatory Affairs [IO], London, United Kingdom
Org. des Radiodiffusions des Etats Islamiques [★IO]
Org. Regionale Africaine De Communications Par Satellite [★IO]
Org. Regionale Africaine de Normalisation [★IO]
Org. pour la Sauvegarde des Droits des Enfants [★IO]
Org. Suisse pour l'Information Geographique [★IO]
Org. of Swedish-Speaking Teachers in Finland [IO], Helsinki, Finland
Org. for Timeshare in Europe [IO], Brussels, Belgium
Org. du Traite de l'Atlantique Nord [★IO]
Org. Universitaire Interamericaine [★IO]
Org. Werbungtreibende im Markenverband [IO], Berlin, Germany
Org. fur die Zusammenarbeit der Eisenbahnen [★IO]
Organisme Europeen de Recherche sur la Carie [★IO]
Organisme de Liaison des Indus. Mecaniques, Elec-triques, Electroniques, et des Metaux en Europe [★IO]
Organismo Internacional Regional de Sanidad Agropecuaria [★IO]
Organismo para la Proscripcion de las Armas Nucle-ares en la Am. Latin y el Caribe [★IO]
Organist Alliance; Amer. Lithuanian Roman Catholic [★10540]
Organist Musicians Alliance; Amer. Lithuanian [★10540]
Organists; Amer. Guild of [10537]
Organists; Royal Coll. of [IO]
Organizacion Arabe de Derchos Humanos [★IO]
Organizacion de las Ciudades del Patrimonio Mun-dial [★IO]
Organizacion Democrata Cristiana de Am. [★IO]
Organizacion Empresarial Espanola de la Peleteria [IO], Madrid, Spain
Organizacion de las Entidades Fiscalizadoras Supe-riores de Europa [★IO]
Organizacion de Entidades Fiscalizadoras Superiors de Africa [★IO]

Organizacion de Estados Iberoamericanos para la Educacion, la Ciencia y la Cultura [★IO]
Organizacion para Estudios Tropicales [★IO]
Organizacion para Estudios Tropicales [★IO]
Organizacion para Estudios Tropicales [★7816]
Organizacion Internacional del Azucar [★IO]
Organizacion Internacional para las Migraciones [★IO]
Organizacion Internacional para las Migraciones - Guatemala [★IO]
Organizacion Intl. para las Migraciones - Costa Rica [★IO]
Organizacion Internationale del Cacao [★IO]
Organizacion Latinoamericana de Energia [★IO]
Organizacion Mundial del Comercio [★IO]
Organizacion Mundial de Peronas con Discapacidad [★IO]
Organizacion Mundial del Turismo [★IO]
Organizacion de la Naciones Unidas para La Agri-cultura y la Alimentacion [★IO]
Organizacion PROFAUNA [IO], Buenos Aires, Argentina
Organizacion Regional del Oriente para la Adminis-tracion Publica [★IO]
Organizatia neguvernamentala BIOS [★IO]
Org. for the Advancement of Knowledge [4313], c/o Richard Alan Miller, Dir., 1212 SW 5th St., Grants Pass, OR 97526-6104, (541)476-5588
Org. for the Advancement of Structured Info. Standards [7756], PO Box 455, Billerica, MA 01821, (978)667-5115
Org. for African-Amer. Veterans - Address unknown since 2006.
Org. of Amer. Historians [10142], PO Box 5457, Bloomington, IN 47407-5457, (812)855-9852
Org. of Amer. Kodaly Educators [8929], 1612 29th Ave. S, Moorhead, MN 56560, (218)227-6253
Org. for Amer.-Soviet Exchanges [★17905]
Org. of Amer. States [16978], 17th St. and Constitu-tion Ave. NW, Washington, DC 20006, (202)458-3000
Org. of Amer. States [IO], Washington, DC, United States
Org. of Arab Petroleum Exporting Countries [IO], Safat, Kuwait
Org. of Arab Students in the U.S. and Canada - Ad-dress unknown since 1995.
Org. of Athletic Administrators - Defunct.
Org. for Attempters and Survivors of Suicide in Interfaith Services [13290], 211 Russell Ave., Apt. 71, Gaithersburg, MD 20877, (240)361-3171
Org. for Autism Res. [13728], 2000 N 14th St., Ste. 480, Arlington, VA 22201, (703)243-9710
Org. of Biological Field Stations [6591], c/o Dr. Shorty Boucher, Univ. California - Davis, Environmental Sci. and Policy, 1 Shields Ave., Davis, CA 95616, (707)875-2020
Org. of Black Airline Pilots [164], 8630 Fenton St., Ste. 126, Silver Spring, MD 20910, (703)753-2047
Org. of Black Designers [9907], 300 M St. SW, Ste. N110, Washington, DC 20024, (202)659-3918
Org. of Black Screenwriters [1323]
Org. of Black Screenwriters [IO], Los Angeles, CA, United States
Org. of the Black Sea Economic Cooperation [IO], Istanbul, Turkey
Org. for Bodywork Therapies of Asia; Amer. [15024]
Org. of Bricklin Owners [21753], PO Box 24775, Rochester, NY 14624-0775, (585)247-1575
Org. of CANDU Indus. [IO], Toronto, ON, Canada
Org. Central Amer. States [★IO]
Org. of Chinese Amer. Women [17567], 4641 Montgomery Ave., Ste. 208, Bethesda, MD 20814, (301)907-3898
Org. of Chinese Americans [17065], 1322 18th St. NW, Washington, DC 20036, (202)223-5500
Org. of Chinese Americans [IO], Washington, DC, United States
Org. for Collectors of Covered Bridge Postcards - Address unknown since 2001.
Org. for Competitive Markets [4081], PO Box 6486, Lincoln, NE 68506, (402)817-4443
Org. of Country Radio Broadcasters [★557]
Org. for Defending Victims of Violence [IO], Tehran, Iran

Org. for Defense of Four Freedoms for Ukraine - Address unknown since 1995.
Org. Design; Assn. for the Mgt. of [★2510]
Org. Design Forum [2510], 5713 Carriage House Ct., Apex, NC 27539, (919)662-8548
Organization Design Forum [IO], Apex, NC, United States

Organization Development
Assn. for Strategic Alliance Professionals [2521]
Assn. for Strategic Planning [3042]
Center for Organizational and Ministry Develop-ment [19769]
Chaordic Commons [7409]
European Gp. for Organizational Stud. [IO]
Intl. Coach Fed. [836]
Intl. Registry of Org. Development Professionals [2865]
Intl. Registry of Org. Development Professionals [IO]
Org. Development Inst. [IO]
Org. Development Inst. [2866]
Org. Development Network [2867]
Ruckus Soc. [18178]
Soc. for Organizational Learning [2868]
Society for Organizational Learning [IO]

Org. Development Coun. - Defunct.
Org. Development Inst. [2866], 11234 Walnut Ridge Rd., Chesterland, OH 44026, (440)729-7419
Org. Development Inst. [IO], Chesterland, OH, United States
Org. Development Network [2867], 71 Valley St., Ste. 301, South Orange, NJ 07079-2825, (973)763-7337
Org. des Directeurs des Musees d'art du Canada [★IO]
Org. for Economic Cooperation and Development [6866], 2001 L St. NW, Ste. 650, Washington, DC 20036-4922, (202)785-6323
Org. for the Enforcement of Child Support - Defunct.
Org. for Equal Education of the Sexes [8402]
Org. of European Cancer Institutes [IO], Brussels, Belgium
Org. for European Economic Cooperation [★IO]
Org. of Facility Managers and Planners [★7167]
Org. for Fair Treatment of Intl. Investment [★18473]
Org. for Fair Treatment of Intl. Investment [★IO]
Org. of Fitness and Personal Care Professionals - Defunct.
Org. for Flora Neotropica [6645], New York Botanical Garden, Bronx, NY 10458-5126, (718)817-8625
Org. for Flora Neotropica [IO], Bronx, NY, United States
Org. of Historical Studies - Defunct.
Org. for the History of Canada [IO], Ottawa, ON, Canada
Org. for Human Brain Mapping [7379], 5841 Cedar Lake Rd., Ste. 204, Minneapolis, MN 55416, (952)646-2029
Org. for Human Rights in Iraq [★12374]
Org. of Ibero-American States for Educ., Sci. and Culture - Spain [IO], Madrid, Spain
Org. for Indus., Spiritual and Cultural Advancement Intl. [IO], Tokyo, Japan
Org. of Inland Biological Field Stations [★6591]
Org. for Intl. Cooperation [17904], 100 Conestoga Dr., Bldg. C, Ste. 196, Marlton, NJ 08053, (856)596-6679
Org. for Intl. Investment [18473], 1225 Nineteenth St. NW, Ste. 501, Washington, DC 20036, (202)659-1903
Org. for Intl. Investment [IO], Washington, DC, United States
Org. for Intl. Professional Exchanges [17905]
Org. Intl. de Protection Civile [★IO]
Org. Internationale du Travail Bur. de l'OIT pour l'Union Europeenne et le Benelux [★IO]
Org. of Islamic Capitals and Cities [IO], Jeddah, Saudi Arabia
Org. for the Lifelong Establishment of Paternity [11714]
Org. Mgt; Institutes for [★24301]
Org. for Mayan and Indigenous Spiritual Bodies; Saq' Be': [10226]
Org. of Military Museums of Canada [IO], Ottawa, ON, Canada

A star before a book entry number signifies that the name is not listed separately, but is mentioned within the entry.

Org. for Myelin Disorders Research and Support - Address unknown since 2002.

Organization; Natl. Study Group on Chronic Dis [1979]

Org. of News Ombudsmen [3152], c/o Gina Lubrano, Exec. Sec., PO Box 120191, San Diego, CA 92123, (858)292-1594

Organization of News Ombudsmen [IO], San Diego, CA, United States

Org. of Newspaper Ombudsmen [★IO]

Org. of Newspaper Ombudsmen [★3152]

Org. of Nigerian Citizens - Address unknown since 1999.

Org. of North Amer. Indian Students - Defunct.

Org. de Paises Arabes Exportadores de Petroleo [★IO]

Org. of Pakistani Entrepreneurs of North Am. [756], 4 Maxwell Cir., Hudson, MA 01749, (781)266-2141

Org. of Pan Asian Amer. Women - Address unknown since 1999.

Org. of Parents Through Surrogacy [13299], PO Box 611, Gurnee, IL 60031, (847)782-0224

Org. of the Petroleum Exporting Countries [IO], Vienna, Austria

Org. for the Phyto-Taxonomic Investigation of the Mediterranean Area [IO], Madrid, Spain

The Org. of Plastics Processors - Defunct.

Org. of Professional Acting Coaches and Teachers [9267], 3968 Eureka Dr., Studio City, CA 91604, (323)877-4988

Org. for Professional Astrology [6495], c/o Bob Mulligan, Pres., PO Box 9237, Naples, FL 34101, (239)261-2840

Org. of Professional Employees of the U.S. Dept. of Agriculture [5441], c/o U.S. Department of Agriculture, PO Box 381, Washington, DC 20044, (202)720-4898

Org. of Professional Immigration Consultants [★IO]

Org. for the Promotion and Advancement of Small Telecommunications Companies [3964], 21 Dupont Cir. NW, Ste. 700, Washington, DC 20036, (202)659-5990

Org. for the Protection and Advancement of Small Telephone Companies [★3964]

Org. for the Protection of Children's Rights [IO], St.-Leonard, QC, Canada

Org. for Rebirth of Ukraine - Address unknown since 1995.

Org. of Regulatory and Clinical Associates [521], PO Box 3490, Redmond, WA 98073, (206)464-0825

Org. for the Relief of Underprivileged Women and Children in Africa [12876], PO Box 278, Waldorf, MD 20604, (301)685-6561

The Org. for the Rights of Amer. Workers [1278], PO Box 2354, Meriden, CT 06450-1454

Org. for Safety and Asepsis Procedures [14182], PO Box 6297, Annapolis, MD 21401, (410)571-0003

Org. Secretaries; Natl. Assn. of Commercial [★24251]

Org. for Security and Co-operation in Europe [IO], Vienna, Austria

Org. for Social Development of Unemployed Youth [IO], Dhaka, Bangladesh

Org. for Social Sci. Res. in Eastern and Southern Africa [IO], Addis Ababa, Ethiopia

Org. for the Support of Democratic Movement of Taiwan - Address unknown since 2002.

Org. of Teachers of Oral Diagnosis [8197], c/o William Garbee, DDS, Sec.-Treas., LSU School of Dentistry, 1100 Florida Ave., Box 140, New Orleans, LA 70119-2799

Org. of Teratology Info. Services [13758], Univ. of Arizona, Drachman Hall, PO Box 210202, Tucson, AZ 85721-0202, (520)626-3547

Org. for Tropical Stud. [7816], North Amer. Off., Box 90630, Durham, NC 27708-0630; (919)684-5774

Org. for Tropical Stud. [IO], Durham, NC, United States

Org. for Tropical Stud. - Costa Rica [IO], San Pedro, Costa Rica

Org. of Wildlife Planners [5360], c/o Andrea Crews, Treas., PO Box 53465, Oklahoma City, OK 73152, (405)522-0769

Org. of Women in Intl. Trade [2290]

Org. of Women in Intl. Trade Alberta [IO], Calgary, AB, Canada

Org. of Women for Legal Awareness - Defunct.

Org. of Women Writers Australia - Victorian Br. [★IO]

Org. of World Heritage Cities [IO], Quebec, QC, Canada

Organizational Behavior Teaching Soc. [6537], c/o Dr. Cynthia Krom, Treas., Mt. Saint Mary Coll., 330 Powell Ave., Newburgh, NY 12550

Organizational Development Network in Higher Educ; Professional and [8494]

Organizational Systems Res. Assn. [9234], c/o Dr. Donna R. Everett, Exec. Dir., Morehead State Univ., 150 Univ. Blvd., Box 2478, Morehead, KY 40351-1689, (606)783-2718

Organizations

  Advocacy Inst. [12650]

  Assn. of Fundraising Professionals [12197]

  Assn. of Professional Researchers for Advancement [12198]

  BoardSource [12651]

  Chaordic Commons [7409]

  Coun. on Foundations [12652]

  Evergreen Freedom Found. [6230]

  Found. Center [12653]

  Grantmakers Without Borders [12724]

  Interaction/American Coun. for Voluntary Intl. Action [12433]

  Intl. Soc. for Third-Sector Res. [12654]

  Intl. Soc. for Third-Sector Res. [IO]

  Italian Soc. for Intl. Org. [IO]

  Mgt. Assistance Gp. [12655]

  Natl. Black United Fund [12656]

  Natl. Network of Grantmakers [12202]

  Nongovernmental Organizations Comm. on Youth [13508]

  North Star Fund [12657]

  OAS Staff Assn. [24144]

  Social Contract Press [12658]

  Soc. for Organizational Learning [2868]

  United Way of Am. [12205]

  United Way Intl. [12206]

Organizations; Coun. of [★18771]

Organizations; Soc. for Nonprofit [322]

Organizations Staff

  Assn. of Former Intl. Civil Servants [IO]

  European Civil Ser. Fed. [IO]

  European Fed. of Employees in Public Services [IO]

  Fed. of Intl. Civil Servants' Associations [IO]

  Intl. Civil Ser. Commn. [IO]

  Intl. Civil Ser. Commn. [24143]

  OAS Staff Assn. [24144]

  Staff Union of the Intl. Labour Org. [IO]

  United Nations Staff Union [IO]

  United Nations Staff Union [24145]

Organize, Inc. [★11800]

Organize Training Center [11800], 508 Johnson Ave., Pacifica, CA 94044, (650)557-9720

Organized Adoption Search Info. Services [11259], PO Box 53-0761, Miami Shores, FL 33153, (305)947-8788

Organized Fandom of Harrison Ford - Defunct.

Organized Flying Adjusters [2229], c/o Donald H. Hendricks, Exec. Sec., 1501 Bluff Dr., Round Rock, TX 78681, (512)255-2740

Organized Migrants in Community Action - Defunct.

Organized Resistance to Capture in Alaska - Defunct.

Organizers; Assn. of Professional [★7166]

Organizers' Collaborative [17244], 14 Beacon St., Ste. 707, Boston, MA 02108, (617)720-6190

Organizers; Natl. Assn. of Professional [7166]

Organizing Bur. of European School Student Unions [IO], Brussels, Belgium

Organizing Comm. for a Natl. Writers Union [★24219]

Organizzazione Internazionale del Lavoro Ufficio per Italia e San Marino [★IO]

Orgonomy

  Amer. Coll. of Orgonomy [15738]

Orient; Assn. of Baptists for Evangelism in the [★19472]

Orient Crusades-Gospel Outreach [★20377]

Orient Crusades-Gospel Outreach [★IO]

Orientacijska Zveza Slovenije [★IO]

Oriental Actors of America - Defunct.

Oriental Boat Mission [★20315]

Oriental Boat Mission [★IO]

Oriental Bodywork Therapy Assn; Amer. [★15024]

Oriental Ceramic Soc. [IO], Cambridge, United Kingdom

Oriental Healing

  Accreditation Commn. for Acupuncture and Oriental Medicine [15739]

  Acupuncture and Oriental Medicine Alliance [13607]

  Acupuncturists Without Borders [13536]

  Amer. Acad. of Acupuncture and Oriental Medicine [13611]

  Amer. Acad. of Medical Acupuncture [15740]

  Amer. Acupuncture Assn. [15741]

  Amer. Assn. of Oriental Medicine [15742]

  American Association of Oriental Medicine [IO]

  Amer. Org. for Bodywork Therapies of Asia [15024]

  Amer. Qigong Assn. [13620]

  Coun. of Colleges of Acupuncture and Oriental Medicine [15743]

  East West Acad. of Healing Arts [15744]

  G-Jo Inst. [15745]

  Intl. Assn. of Reiki Professionals [13637]

  Intl. Fed. of Martial Arts and Oriental Medicine [15021]

  Intl. Yan Xin Qigong Assn. [13640]

  Jin Shin Do Found. for Bodymind Acupressure [15746]

  Jin Shin Do Foundation for Bodymind Acupressure [IO]

  Natl. Certification Commn. for Acupuncture and Oriental Medicine [15747]

  Natl. Qigong (Chi Kung) Assn. [13644]

  Ohashi Inst. [15748]

  Ohashi Inst. [IO]

  Patience T'ai Chi Assn. [23897]

  QiGong Res. Soc. [13647]

  Reiki Alliance [13651]

  Soc. for Acupuncture Res. [13537]

Oriental Healing Arts; Amer. Assn. of [★15024]

Oriental Medicine Alliance; Acupuncture and [13607]

Oriental Medicine; Amer. Acad. of Acupuncture and [13611]

Oriental Medicine; Amer. Assn. of [15742]

Oriental Medicine; Coun. of Colleges of Acupuncture and [15743]

Oriental Medicine; Natl. Accreditation Commn. for Schools and Colleges of Acupuncture and [★15739]

Oriental Merchants Assn. - Defunct.

Oriental Missionary Soc. [★20379]

Oriental Missionary Soc. [★IO]

Oriental Numismatic Soc. [IO], Bergambacht, Netherlands

Oriental Rug Importers Assn. [2272], 100 Park Plaza Dr., Secaucus, NJ 07094, (201)866-5054

Oriental Rug Retailers of Am. [2273], c/o Elizabeth Arnold, Exec. Dir., PO Box 71831, Richmond, VA 23255, (804)270-3195

Oriental Shorthairs Intl. - Address unknown since 1989.

Oriental Shrine of North Am; Ladies [19241]

Oriental Stud. Inst. [IO], Louvain-la-Neuve, Belgium

Orientation Directors Conf. [★7907]

Orientation Directors Conf; Natl. [★7907]

Orientation Program; Corporate [★8047]

Orienteering

  Alberta Orienteering Assn. [IO]

  British Orienteering Fed. [IO]

  Bulgarian Orienteering Fed. [IO]

  Canadian Orienteering Fed. [IO]

  Chinese Orienteering Comm. [IO]

  Croatian Orienteering Fed. [IO]

  Danish Orienteering Fed. [IO]

  Estonian Orienteering Fed. [IO]

  Federacion del Deporte de Orientacion de la Republica Argentina [IO]

  French Orienteering Fed. [IO]

  German Gymnastics Fed. - Orienteering Dept. [IO]

  Hong Kong Orienteering Club [IO]

  Intl. Orienteering Fed. [IO]

Reference to "IO" in place of a book number signifies that the association may be found in the 45th edition of International Organizations.

Irish Orienteering Assn. [IO]
Israel Sport Orienteering Assn. [IO]
Korea Orienteering Fed. [IO]
Lithuanian Orienteering Fed. [IO]
National Association of Competitive Mounted Orienteering [IO]
Natl. Assn. of Competitive Mounted Orienteering [23640]
New Zealand Orienteering Fed. [IO]
Northern Ireland Orienteering Assn. [IO]
Orienteering Assn. of Hong Kong [IO]
Orienteering Australia [IO]
Orienteering Fed. of Serbia and Montenegro [IO]
Polish Orienteering Assn. [IO]
Portuguese Orienteering Fed. [IO]
Slovak Orienteering Assn. [IO]
Slovenian Orienteering Fed. [IO]
Swedish Orienteering Fed. [IO]
U.S. Adventure Racing Assn. [23672]
U.S. Orienteering Fed. [23641]
Orienteering Assn. of Hong Kong [IO], Hong Kong, People's Republic of China
Orienteering Australia [IO], Mitchell, Australia
Orienteering Fed. of Australia [★IO]
Orienteering Fed. of Serbia and Montenegro [IO], Belgrade, Serbia
Orienteering; Natl. Assn. of Competitive Mounted [23640]
Origami
Origami USA [22771]
Origami USA [22771], 15 W 77th St., New York, NY 10024-5192, (212)769-5635
Original Cosmopolitans - Defunct.
Original Doll Artists Coun. of Am. [22404], c/o Myra Sherrod, 2nd VP, 1251 Garden Circle Dr., St. Louis, MO 63125, (314)894-1489
Original Equip. Suppliers Assn. [777], 1301 W Long Lake Rd., Ste. 225, Troy, MI 48098, (248)952-6401
Original Four Aces and Al Alberts Archv. [24955], c/o Walt Gollender, PO Box 1655, Orange, NJ 07051, (973)868-1995
Original Gilligan's Island Fan Club [★25038]
Original Hobo Nickel Soc. [22752], c/o Verne Walrafen, Sec./Webmaster, 12000 Sunset Ridge Dr., Ozawkie, KS 66070-6045
Original Kleptonian; Neo-American Church, The [20456]
Original Paper Doll Artists Guild [22405], PO Box 14, Kingfield, ME 04947, (207)265-2500
Original Print Collectors Group - Address unknown since 1995.
Original Westmoreland Glass Collector's Newsl. and Org. - Defunct.
ORIGINS [11260], c/o Mary Anne Cohen, Co-Founder, PO Box 556, Whippany, NJ 07981, (973)428-9683
Orillia Against Drunk Driving [IO], Orillia, ON, Canada
Orioles
Fraternal Order Orioles [19298]
Orion [★20066]
Orion [★IO]
Ormoc Bay Assn; Battle of [21390]
Ornamental Aquatic Trade Assn. [IO], Westbury, United Kingdom
Ornamental and Architectural Products Contractors; Natl. Assn. of Miscellaneous, [1037]
Ornamental Concrete Producers Assn. [932], 502 Kay Ave. SE, Bemidji, MN 56601, (218)751-1982
Ornamental Distributors Assn; Independent Turf and [2394]
Ornamental Fish Intl. - Defunct.
Ornamental Glass Mfrs. Assn; Natl. [★1736]
Ornamental Goldfish Growers Assn; Natl. [4181]
Ornamental Horticulturists; Soc. of Amer. Florists and [★1493]
Ornamental Iron Mfrs. Assn; Natl. [★2722]
Ornamental Metal Mfrs. Assn; Natl. [★2722]
Ornamental Metal Mfrs; Natl. Assn. of [★2719]
Ornamental and Miscellaneous Metals Assn; Natl. [2722]
Ornamental Plant Conservation Assn. [IO], South Yarra, Australia
Ornamental and Reinforcing Iron Workers; Intl. Assn. of Bridge, Structural, [24134]

Ornithological Club; Cooper [★7415]
Ornithological Societies of North Am. [7423], 5400 Bosque Blvd., Ste. 680, Waco, TX 76710, (254)399-9636
Ornithological Soc. of Japan [IO], Tokyo, Japan
Ornithological Soc. of the Middle East [IO], Sandy, United Kingdom
Ornithological Soc. of New Zealand [IO], Wellington, New Zealand
Ornithological Soc; Wilson [7424]
Ornithology
The Amazona Soc. [7410]
Amer. Birding Assn. [7411]
American Birding Association [IO]
Amer. Ornithologists' Union [7412]
Assn. of Field Ornithologists [7413]
Avicultural Advancement Coun. of Canada [IO]
Avicultural Soc. [IO]
Avicultural Soc. of Am. [IO]
Avicultural Soc. of Am. [7414]
Bird Stud. Canada [IO]
BirdLife Cyprus [IO]
BirdLife Intl. [IO]
British Ornithologists' Union [IO]
British Trust for Ornithology [IO]
Cooper Ornithological Soc. [IO]
Cooper Ornithological Soc. [7415]
Cornell Lab. of Ornithology [7416]
Eastern Bird Banding Assn. [7417]
Falklands Conservation [IO]
German Ornithologists' Soc. [IO]
Gothenburg Ornithological Soc. [IO]
Hartz Club of Am. [22772]
Hawk Migration Assn. of North Am. [7418]
Hawkwatch Intl. [7419]
Hawkwatch Intl. [IO]
Inland Bird Banding Assn. [7420]
The Intl. Osprey Found. [5328]
Latvian Ornithological Soc. [IO]
North American Banding Council [IO]
North Amer. Banding Coun. [7421]
Nuttall Ornithological Club [7422]
Ornithological Societies of North Am. [7423]
Ornithological Soc. of Japan [IO]
Ornithological Soc. of the Middle East [IO]
Parrot Soc. - U.K. [IO]
Seabird Gp. [IO]
Soc. for Northwestern Vertebrate Biology [7364]
South African Bird Ringing Unit [IO]
Wilson Ornithological Soc. [7424]
Ornithology; Cornell Univ. Lab. of [★7416]
Orofacial Pain; Amer. Acad. of [14106]
Orphan Car Club Intl. - Defunct.
Orphan Care Intl; Warm Blankets [11727]
Orphan Drugs
Natl. Org. for Rare Disorders [14282]
Orphan Found. [★11715]
Orphan Found. of Am. [11715], 21351 Gentry Dr., Ste. 130, Sterling, VA 20166, (571)203-0270
Orphan Resources Intl. [11644], 550 W Trout Run Rd., Ephrata, PA 17522, (717)733-7444
Orphan Resources Intl. [IO], Ephrata, PA, United States
Orphan Train Heritage Soc. of Am. [21140], PO Box 322, Concordia, KS 66901, (785)243-4471
Orphan Train Riders Res. Center [★21140]
Orphan Voyage [11261], c/o Gay Swearington, 13906 Pepperrell Dr., Tampa, FL 33624, (813)961-1393
Orphans, Inc; Intl. [★11680]
Orphans of Italy - Address unknown since 1995.
Orphans; World [11667]
Orquidario Quinta do Lago [IO], Petropolis, Brazil
Orquideas Del Valle [IO], Cali, Colombia
Orr Shalom Children's Homes [IO], Tzfone Yehuda, Israel
Orsagos Magyar Banyaszati Es Kohaszati Egyesulet [★IO]
ORT Am. [IO], New York, NY, United States
ORT Am. [12480], 75 Maiden Ln., 10th Fl., New York, NY 10038, (212)505-7700
ORT Canada [IO], Toronto, ON, Canada
Ortho-Bionomy Intl; Soc. of [13767]
Orthodontia; Amer. Bd. of [★14124]
Orthodontic Education and Res. Found. [14183]

Orthodontic Soc; Amer. [14138]
Orthodontic Soc; British [IO]
Orthodontic Soc; European [IO]
Orthodontic Soc. of Ireland [IO], Dublin, Ireland
Orthodontics; Amer. Assn. for Functional [14115]
Orthodontics; Amer. Bd. of [14124]
Orthodontics; Amer. Soc. for the Stud. of [14144]
Orthodontics; Coll. of Diplomates of the Amer. Bd. of [14149]
Orthodontics for the Gen. Practitioner; Amer. Acad. of [14107]
Orthodontics; Intl. Acad. of [★14162]
Orthodontics; New York Soc. for the Stud. of [★14144]
Orthodontists; Amer. Assn. of [14117]
Orthodontists; Amer. Assn. of Functional [★14115]
Orthodontists; Amer. Soc. of [★14117]
Orthodontists; Canadian Assn. of [IO]
Orthodox and Anglican Fellowship - Defunct.
Orthodox Catholic Church; Canon Law Soc. of the [19593]
Orthodox Christian Assn. of Medicine, Psychology and Religion [16163], 50 Goddard Ave., Brookline, MA 02445, (904)396-5383
Orthodox Christians in Am; Fellowship of [20542]
Orthodox Christians for Life [20478], PO Box 805, Melville, NY 11747, (631)271-4408
Orthodox Church and the Hellenic Language; Pan Amer. Coun. for the Preservation of the Hellenic [20074]
Orthodox Church Musicians; Natl. Forum of Greek [20434]
Orthodox Clubs; Federated Russian [★20542]
Orthodox Jewish Congregations of Am; Orthodox Union - Union of [20170]
Orthodox Jewish Scientists; Assn. of [7601]
Orthodox Jewish Teachers; Assn. of [9210]
Orthodox Ladies Philoptochos Soc; Greek [20071]
Orthodox People in Am. [19884], 7061 Itaska Dr., St. Louis, MO 63123, (314)351-0404
Orthodox Rabbis of the U.S. and Canada; Union of [20183]
Orthodox Soc. of Am. [19339], 29510 Lorain Rd., North Olmsted, OH 44070-3909, (440)716-2360
Orthodox Theological Soc. in Am. [19885], 50 Goddard Ave., Brookline, MA 02445-7415
Orthodox Union - Union of Orthodox Jewish Congregations of Am. [20170], 11 Broadway, New York, NY 10004, (212)613-8123
Orthodox Young Adult League; Greek [20072]
Orthodox Youth of Am; Greek [★20072]
Orthodox Youth; Amer. Romanian [20540]
Orthodox Youth Org; Syrian [★19882]
Orthodox Youth Organizations; Soc. of [★19882]
Orthography; Comm. for the Implementation of the Standardized Yiddish [10276]
Orthological Club; Wilson [★7424]
Orthopaedic Chairmen; Assn. of [★15750]
Orthopaedic Physician's Assistants; Amer. Soc. of [15760]
Orthopaedic Res. and Educ. Found. [8949], 6300 N River Rd., Ste. 700, Rosemont, IL 60018, (847)698-9980
Orthopaedic Res. Soc. [15776], 6300 N River Rd., Ste. 727, Rosemont, IL 60018-4226, (847)698-1625
Orthopaedic Sect., Amer. Physical Therapy Assn. [16630], 2920 East Ave. S, Ste. 200, La Crosse, WI 54601, (608)788-3982
Orthopaedic Soc; Amer. [★15750]
Orthopaedic Soc. for Sports Medicine; Amer. [16476]
Orthopaedic Surgeons; Amer. Acad. of Neurological and [15409]
Orthopaedic Surgeons; Soc. of Military [15266]
Orthopaedic Technologists; Natl. Assn. of [15144]
Orthopaedic Trauma Assn. [15777], 6300 N River Rd., Ste. 727, Rosemont, IL 60018-4226, (847)698-1631
Orthopaedics Overseas [15778], 1900 L St. NW, Ste. 310, Washington, DC 20036, (202)296-0928
Orthopaedics Overseas [IO], Washington, DC, United States
Orthopaedics and Traumatology; European Soc. of Veterinary [IO]
Orthopedic Appliance and Limb Mfrs. Assn. [★1855]

A star before a book entry number signifies that the name is not listed separately, but is mentioned within the entry.

Orthopedic Found. for Animals [16805], 2300 E Nifong Blvd., Columbia, MO 65201-3806, (573)442-0418
Orthopedic Resident Educ; Advisory Coun. for [★15752]
Orthopedic Soc; Veterinary [16816]
Orthopedic Surgical Mfrs. Assn. [1865], PO Box 38805, Germantown, TN 38183, (901)754-8097
Orthopedics
  AAMED - The Amer. Assn. of Multiple Enchondroma Diseases [15749]
  Academic Orthopaedic Soc. [15750]
  Acad. of Ambulatory Foot and Ankle Surgery [16023]
  Amer. Acad. of Craniofacial Pain [15751]
  Amer. Acad. of Neurological and Orthopaedic Surgeons [15409]
  Amer. Acad. of Orthopaedic Surgeons [15752]
  American Academy of Orthopaedic Surgeons [IO]
  Amer. Assn. of Colleges of Podiatric Medicine [16025]
  Amer. Assn. of Hosp. Podiatrists [16026]
  Amer. Assn. of Orthopedic Medicine [15753]
  Amer. Back Soc. [15754]
  Amer. Bd. of Orthopaedic Surgery [15755]
  Amer. Bd. of Podiatric Orthopedics and Primary Podiatric Medicine [16030]
  Amer. Bd. of Podiatric Surgery [16031]
  Amer. Coll. of Foot and Ankle Orthopedics and Medicine [16032]
  Amer. Coll. of Foot and Ankle Pediatrics [16033]
  Amer. Coll. of Foot and Ankle Surgeons [16034]
  Amer. Fracture Assn. [15756]
  Amer. Orthopaedic Assn. [15757]
  Amer. Orthopaedic Foot and Ankle Soc. [15758]
  Amer. Orthopaedic Soc. for Sports Medicine [16476]
  Amer. Osteopathic Acad. of Orthopedics [15759]
  Amer. Podiatric Medical Assn. [16037]
  Amer. Shoulder and Elbow Surgeons [16567]
  Amer. Soc. of Orthopaedic Physician's Assistants [15760]
  Amer. Soc. of Orthopedic Professionals [15761]
  Amer. Soc. of Podiatric Medical Assistants [16040]
  Argentine Orthopedic and Traumatology Assn. [IO]
  Arthroscopy Assn. of North Am. [15762]
  Asia Pacific Orthopaedic Assn. [IO]
  Asian Assn. for Dynamic Osteosynthesis [IO]
  Asian Pacific Fed. of Societies for Surgery of the Hand [IO]
  Assn. of Bone and Joint Surgeons [15763]
  Australian Orthopaedic Assn. [IO]
  Australian Orthopaedic Foot and Ankle Soc. [IO]
  Bones Soc. [15764]
  Brazilian Assn. of Orthodontics and Facial Orthopedics [IO]
  British Inst. of Musculoskeletal Medicine [IO]
  British Orthopaedic Assn. [IO]
  British Orthopaedic Foot and Ankle Soc. [IO]
  British Soc. for Surgery of the Hand [IO]
  Canadian Orthopaedic Assn. [IO]
  Canadian Orthopaedic Found. [IO]
  Canadian Soc. of Orthopaedic Technologists [IO]
  Christian Orthopaedic Partners [IO]
  Christian Orthopaedic Partners [15765]
  Clinical Orthopaedic Soc. [15766]
  Conservative Orthopedics Intl. Assn. [15767]
  Coun. on Chiropractic Orthopedics [15768]
  Coun. on Podiatric Medical Educ. [16042]
  Danish Orthopedic Soc. [IO]
  Egyptian Orthopaedic Assn. [IO]
  European Fed. of Natl. Associations of Orthopaedics and Traumatology [IO]
  European Soc. for Movement Anal. for Adults and Children [IO]
  French Soc. of Orthopedic and Osteopathic Manual Medicine [IO]
  Hip Soc. [15769]
  Intl. Coll. of Cranio-Mandibular Orthopedics [15770]
  International College of Cranio-Mandibular Orthopedics [IO]
  Intl. Fed. of Foot and Ankle Societies [16045]

  Intl. Soc. of Arthroscopy, Knee Surgery and Orthopaedic Sports Medicine [15771]
  Intl. Soc. of Arthroscopy, Knee Surgery and Orthopaedic Sports Medicine [IO]
  Intl. Soc. for Cmpt. Assisted Orthopaedic Surgery [IO]
  Intl. Soc. for Cmpt. Assisted Orthopaedic Surgery [15772]
  Intl. Soc. of Orthopaedic Surgery and Traumatology [IO]
  Japanese Orthopaedic Assn. [IO]
  Jaw Joints and Allied Musculo-Skeletal Disorders Found. [15773]
  Natl. Assn. of Orthopaedic Nurses [15498]
  Natl. Assn. of Orthopaedic Technologists [15144]
  Natl. Bd. for Certification of Orthopaedic Technologists [15774]
  Natl. Bd. of Podiatric Medical Examiners [16046]
  Natl. Osteoporosis Found. [15775]
  Natl. Podiatric Medical Assn. [16047]
  North Amer. Spine Soc. [15402]
  Norwegian Osteogenesis Imperfecta Found. [IO]
  Orthopaedic Res. and Educ. Found. [8949]
  Orthopaedic Res. Soc. [15776]
  Orthopaedic Sect., Amer. Physical Therapy Assn. [16630]
  Orthopaedic Trauma Assn. [15777]
  Orthopaedics Overseas [15778]
  Orthopaedics Overseas [IO]
  Orthopedic Surgical Mfrs. Assn. [1865]
  Osteogenesis Imperfecta Found. [15779]
  Pediatric Orthopedic Soc. of North Am. [15780]
  Ruth Jackson Orthopaedic Soc. [15781]
  Shriners Hospitals for Children [13973]
  Soc. of Military Orthopaedic Surgeons [15266]
  South African Orthopaedic Assn. [IO]
  Turkish Soc. of Orthopaedic Surgery and Traumatology [IO]
  Veterinary Orthopedic Soc. [16816]
  World Spine Soc. [15405]
Orthopedics; Amer. Acad. of Craniomandibular [★14106]
Orthopedics; Amer. Acad. of Gnathologic [14098]
Orthopedics; Amer. Bd. of Podiatric [★16030]
Orthopedics and Medicine; Amer. Coll. of Foot and Ankle [16032]
Orthopedics and Primary Medicine; Amer. Bd. of Podiatric [★16030]
Orthopedics and Primary Podiatric Medicine; Amer. Bd. of Podiatric [16030]
Orthopedists; Amer. CLG of Foot [★16032]
Orthopedists; Amer. Coll. of Chiropractic [13992]
Orthopic Technicians; Amer. Assn. of [★15657]
Orthopsychiatric Assn; Amer. [16075]
Orthopterists' Soc. [7065], c/o Dr. Charles Bomar, Exec. Dir., Univ. of Wisconsin - Stout, Biology Dept., 203A Sci. Wing, Menomonie, WI 54751, (715)232-2562
Orthopterists' Soc. [IO], Menomonie, WI, United States
Orthoptic Coun; Amer. [15663]
Orthoptists; Amer. Assn. of Certified [15657]
Orthospinology; Soc. of Chiropractic [14014]
Orthostatic Intolerance; Pediatric Network for Chronic Fatigue Syndrome, Fibromyalgia, and [15895]
Orthotic and Prosthetic Assn; Amer. [1855]
Orthotics and Prosthetics
  Amer. Acad. of Orthotists and Prosthetists [15782]
  Amer. Bd. for Certification in Orthotics, Prosthetics and Pedorthics [15783]
  Assn. of Children's Prosthetic-Orthotic Clinics [15784]
  Bd. for Orthotist/Prosthetist Certification [15785]
  British Assn. of Prosthetists and Orthotists [IO]
  Canadian Assn. for Prosthetics and Orthotics [IO]
  Hong Kong Soc. of Certified Prosthetist-Orthotists [IO]
  Intl. Campaign to Ban Landmines [17431]
  Intl. Soc. for Prosthetics and Orthotics [IO]
  Intl. Soc. for Prosthetics and Orthotics - United Kingdom [IO]
  A Leg To Stand On [12659]
  Natl. Assn. for the Advancement of Orthotics and Prosthetics [15786]

  World Community Chaplains [12884]
Orton Dyslexia Soc. [★14295]
Orton Dyslexia Soc. [★IO]
Orton Soc. [★IO]
Orton Soc. [★14295]
Osaka Chamber of Commerce and Indus. [IO], Osaka, Japan
Osborne Assn. [11885], 809 Westchester Ave., Bronx, NY 10455, (718)707-2600
Osho Chidvilas - Defunct.
Osler Soc; Amer. [15157]
Oslo Chamber of Commerce [IO], Oslo, Norway
Osmond Fan Club; Donny [★24880]
Osmond Intl. Network; Donny [24880]
Osmonds Intl. Fan Club - Address unknown since 1999.
OSPAR Commn. [IO], London, United Kingdom
Osprey Found; The Intl. [5328]
Osseointegration; Acad. of [14091]
Osseous Heteroplasia Assn; Progressive [14477]
OsteoArthritis Res. Soc. Intl. [16374], 15000 Commerce Pkwy., Ste. C, Mount Laurel, NJ 08054, (856)439-1385
OsteoArthritis Res. Soc. Intl. [IO], Mount Laurel, NJ, United States
Osteogenesis Imperfecta
  Osteogenesis Imperfecta Found. [15779]
Osteogenesis Imperfecta Found. [15779], 804 W Diamond Ave., Ste. 210, Gaithersburg, MD 20878, (301)947-0083
Osteogenesis Imperfecta Found; Norwegian [IO]
Osteology
  Aktion Gesunde Knochen [IO]
  Amer. Soc. for Bone and Mineral Res. [15787]
  Asociacion Argentina de Osteologia y Metabolismo Mineral [IO]
  Asociacion Colombiana de Osteologia y Metabolismo Mineral [IO]
  Associacion Colombiana de Endocrinologia [IO]
  Assn. des Femmes contre l'Osteoporose [IO]
  Assn. Luxembourg Osteoporose [IO]
  Australian and New Zealand Bone and Mineral Soc. [IO]
  Austrian Soc. for Bone and Mineral Res. [IO]
  Belgian Assn. for Osteoporosis Patients [IO]
  Belgian Bone Club [IO]
  Belgian Royal Soc. of Rheumatology [IO]
  Bone Res. Soc. [IO]
  Brazilian Soc. of Osteoporosis [IO]
  Bulgarian League for the Prevention of Osteoporosis [IO]
  Bulgarian Soc. for Clinical Densitometry [IO]
  Chilean Soc. of Osteology and Mineral Metabolism [IO]
  Chinese Taiwan Osteoporosis Assn. [IO]
  Consejo Dominicano Contra la Osteoporosis [IO]
  Croatian Osteoporosis Soc. [IO]
  Cyprus Soc. Against Osteoporosis and Myoskeletal Diseases [IO]
  Czech Osteoporosis League [IO]
  Czech Soc. for Metabolic Skeletal Diseases [IO]
  Dachverband der Osterreichischen Osteoporose-Selbsthilfegruppen [IO]
  Danish Bone Soc. [IO]
  Dutch Soc. for Calcium and Bone Metabolism [IO]
  Egyptian Osteoporosis Prevention Soc. [IO]
  Estonian Osteoporosis Soc. [IO]
  European Calcified Tissue Soc. [IO]
  Finnish Osteoporosis Soc. [IO]
  Hungarian Osteoporosis Patients Assn. [IO]
  Hungarian Soc. for Osteoporosis and Osteoarthrology [IO]
  Indonesian Osteoporosis Soc. [IO]
  Intl. Soc. for Clinical Densitometry [IO]
  Intl. Soc. for Clinical Densitometry [15788]
  Italian Assn. of Osteoporosis Patients [IO]
  Jordanian Osteoporosis Prevention Soc. [IO]
  Latvian Soc. of Osteoporosis [IO]
  Lebanese Osteoporosis Prevention Soc. [IO]
  Lega Italiana Osteoporosi [IO]
  Liga Colombiana de Lucha contra la Osteoporosis [IO]
  Malaysian Osteoporosis Soc. [IO]
  Osteoporosis Comm. of China Gerontological Soc. [IO]

Reference to "IO" in place of a book number signifies that the association may be found in the 45th edition of International Organizations.

Osteoporosis New Zealand [IO]
Osteoporosis Soc. of Hong Kong [IO]
Osteoporosis Soc. of India [IO]
Osteoporosis Soc. of Pakistan [IO]
Osteoporosis Soc. of Singapore [IO]
Osteoporosis Soc. of Sri Lanka [IO]
Pan Arab Osteoporosis Soc. [IO]
Polish Osteoarthrology Soc. [IO]
Portugese Soc. of Metabolic Bone Disease [IO]
Portuguese Assn. of Osteoporosis [IO]
Romanian Soc. of Osteoporosis [IO]
Russian Assn. on Osteoporosis [IO]
Saudi Osteoporosis Soc. [IO]
Sci. Coun. for Osteoporosis and Skeletal
  Diseases [IO]
Slovak Union against Osteoporosis [IO]
Slovene Bone Soc. [IO]
Slovene Osteoporosis Patient Soc. [IO]
Sociedad Argentina de Osteoporosis [IO]
Sociedad Boliviana de Osteologia y Metabolismo
  Mineral [IO]
Sociedad Espanola de Investigaciones Oseas y
  Metabolismo Mineral [IO]
Societe Congolaise d'Osteoporose [IO]
Societe Francaise d'Osteodensitometrie Clinic
  [IO]
Soc. of Life with Osteoporosis [IO]
Spanish Assn. Against Osteoporosis [IO]
Swedish Osteoporosis Soc. [IO]
Swiss Assn. against Osteoporosis [IO]
Swiss Bone and Mineral Soc. [IO]
Turkish Osteoporosis Soc. [IO]
Ukrainian Assn. on Osteoporosis [IO]
Woman and Family [IO]
Women Without Osteoporosis [IO]
Osteopathic Acad. of Addiction Medicine; Amer.
  [16500]
Osteopathic Acad. of Orthopedics; Amer. [15759]
Osteopathic Acad. of Physical Medicine and
  Rehabilitation; Amer. [★15805]
Osteopathic Acad. of Public Hea. and Preventive
  Medicine; Amer. [★15802]
Osteopathic Acad. of Sclerotherapy; Amer. [★15814]
Osteopathic Acad. of Sports Medicine; Amer.
  [16477]
Osteopathic Bd. of Emergency Medicine; Amer.
  [14328]
Osteopathic Bd. of Gen. Practice; Amer. [★15799]
Osteopathic Bd. of Rehabilitation Medicine;
  American [★15805]
Osteopathic Coll. of Anesthesiologists; Amer.
  [13672]
Osteopathic Coll. of Dermatology; Amer. [14194]
Osteopathic Coll. of Ophthalmology and Otorhino-
  laryngology [★15664]
Osteopathic Coll. of Physical Medicine and
  Rehabilitation; Amer. [★15805]
Osteopathic Coll. of Preventive Medicine; Amer.
  [★15802]
Osteopathic Coll. of Radiology; Amer. [16276]
Osteopathic Coll. of Rehabilitation Medicine; Amer.
  [★15805]
Osteopathic Colleges; Amer. Assn. of [★15791]
Osteopathic Cranial Assn. [★15811]
Osteopathic Emergency Physicians; Amer. Coll. of
  [14327]
Osteopathic Found. [★15806]
Osteopathic Found; Natl. [★15806]
Osteopathic Healthcare Executives; Coll. of [14876]
Osteopathic Herniologists; Central States [★15814]
Osteopathic Hosp. Administrators; Amer. Coll. of
  [★14876]
Osteopathic Intl. Alliance [15813], c/o Amer.
  Osteopathic Assn., 142 E Ontario St., Chicago, IL
  60611
Osteopathic Libraries Assn. - Defunct.
Osteopathic Manipulative Therapeutic and Clinical
  Res. Assn. [★15790]
Osteopathic Medicine
  Advocates for the Amer. Osteopathic Assn.
    [15789]
  Amer. Acad. of Osteopathy [15790]
  Amer. Assn. of Colleges of Osteopathic Medicine
    [15791]
  Amer. Assn. of Physician Specialists [15792]

Amer. Coll. of Osteopathic Emergency Physicians
  [14327]
Amer. Coll. of Osteopathic Family Physicians
  [15793]
Amer. Coll. of Osteopathic Internists [15794]
Amer. Coll. of Osteopathic Neurologists and
  Psychiatrists [15377]
Amer. Coll. of Osteopathic Pediatricians [15795]
Amer. Coll. of Osteopathic Sclerotherapeutic Pain
  Mgt. [15796]
Amer. Coll. of Osteopathic Surgeons [15797]
Amer. Osteopathic Acad. of Sports Medicine
  [16477]
Amer. Osteopathic Assn. [15798]
Amer. Osteopathic Bd. of Emergency Medicine
  [14328]
Amer. Osteopathic Bd. of Family Physicians
  [15799]
Amer. Osteopathic Bd. of Pediatrics [15800]
Amer. Osteopathic Bd. of Preventive Medicine
  [15801]
Amer. Osteopathic Coll. of Dermatology [14194]
Amer. Osteopathic Coll. of Occupational and
  Preventive Medicine [15802]
Amer. Osteopathic Coll. of Ophthalmology and the
  Amer. Osteopathic Coll. of Otolaryngology-
  Head and Neck Surgery [15803]
Amer. Osteopathic Coll. of Pathologists [15804]
Amer. Osteopathic Coll. of Physical Medicine and
  Rehabilitation [15805]
Amer. Osteopathic Coll. of Radiology [16276]
Amer. Osteopathic Colleges of Ophthalmology
  and Otolaryngology-Head and Neck Surgery
  [15664]
Amer. Osteopathic Found. [15806]
Assn. of Military Osteopathic Physicians and
  Surgeons [15807]
Assn. of Osteopathic Directors and Medical
  Educators [15808]
Assn. of Osteopathic State Executive Directors
  [15809]
British Osteopathic Assn. [IO]
Bur. of Professional Educ. of the Amer.
  Osteopathic Assn. [15810]
Canadian Osteopathic Aid Soc. [IO]
Canadian Osteopathic Assn. [IO]
Coll. of Osteopathic Healthcare Executives
  [14876]
Cranial Acad. [15811]
Fed. of State Medical Boards of the U.S. [15165]
Gen. Osteopathic Coun. [IO]
Intl. Acad. of Osteopathy [IO]
Natl. Bd. of Osteopathic Medical Examiners
  [15812]
Osteopathic Intl. Alliance [15813]
Pain Mgt. and Sclerotherapy [15814]
Student Osteopathic Medical Assn. [15815]
Osteopathic Medicine; Center for Sports and [16055]
Osteopathic Medicine and Surgery; Amer. Coll. of
  Gen. Practitioners in [★15793]
Osteopathic Neurologists and Psychiatrists; Amer.
  Coll. of [15377]
Osteopathic Obstetricians and Gynecologists; Amer.
  Coll. of [15585]
Osteopathic Occupational Medical Assn; Amer.
  [★15802]
Osteopathic Physicians and Surgeons; Natl. Bd. of
  Examiners for [★15812]
Osteopathic Soc. of Anesthesiologists; Amer.
  [★13672]
Osteopathic Soc. of Herniologists; Amer. [★15814]
Osteopathic Specialists; Amer. Assn. of [★15792]
Osteopathic Surgeons; Amer. Acad. of [★15792]
Osteopathy
  Advocates for the Amer. Osteopathic Assn.
    [15789]
  Amer. Coll. of Osteopathic Emergency Physicians
    [14327]
  Amer. Osteopathic Acad. of Orthopedics [15759]
  Amer. Osteopathic Bd. of Emergency Medicine
    [14328]
  Amer. Osteopathic Coll. of Dermatology [14194]
  Amer. Osteopathic Found. [15806]
  Assn. of Military Osteopathic Physicians and
    Surgeons [15807]

Bay Area Physicians for Human Rights [12218]
Bur. of Professional Educ, of the Amer.
  Osteopathic Assn. [15810]
Conservative Orthopedics Intl. Assn. [15767]
Cranial Acad. [15811]
Natl. Bd. of Osteopathic Medical Examiners
  [15812]
Natl. Osteopathic Women Physician's Assn.
  [24564]
Osteopathic Intl. Alliance [15813]
Sigma Sigma Phi [24565]
Theta Psi [24566]
Osteopathy; Acad. of Applied [★15790]
Osteoporose Canada [★IO]
Osteoporosis Australia [IO], Sydney, Australia
Osteoporosis Australian Capital Territory [IO],
  Weston, Australia
Osteoporosis Canada [IO], Toronto, ON, Canada
Osteoporosis Canada - Ottawa Chap. [IO], Ottawa,
  ON, Canada
Osteoporosis Comm. of China Gerontological Soc.
  [IO], Beijing, People's Republic of China
The Osteoporosis Found. [★15775]
Osteoporosis Found; Natl. [15775]
Osteoporosis New South Wales [IO], North Parra-
  matta, Australia
Osteoporosis New Zealand [IO], Wellington, New
  Zealand
Osteoporosis Northern Territory [IO], Nightcliff,
  Australia
Osteoporosis Soc. of Canada [★IO]
Osteoporosis Soc. of Canada - British Columbia Div.
  [IO], Vancouver, BC, Canada
Osteoporosis Soc. of Canada - Eastern Ontario
  Chap. [★IO]
Osteoporosis Soc. of Canada - Hamilton Chap. [IO],
  Hamilton, ON, Canada
Osteoporosis Soc. of Canada - Kelowna Chap. [IO],
  Kelowna, BC, Canada
Osteoporosis Soc. of Canada - London and Thames
  Valley Chap. [IO], London, ON, Canada
Osteoporosis Soc. of Canada - Manitoba Chap. [IO],
  Winnipeg, MB, Canada
Osteoporosis Soc. of Canada - New Brunswick
  Chap. [IO], Cambridge-Narrows, NB, Canada
Osteoporosis Soc. of Canada - Niagara Chap. [IO],
  St. Catharines, ON, Canada
Osteoporosis Soc. of Canada - North Shore Chap.
  [IO], North Vancouver, BC, Canada
Osteoporosis Soc. of Canada - Nova Scotia Chap.
  [IO], Halifax, NS, Canada
Osteoporosis Soc. of Canada - Peterborough Chap.
  [IO], Peterborough, ON, Canada
Osteoporosis Soc. of Canada - Quebec City Chap.
  [IO], Ste.-Foy, QC, Canada
Osteoporosis Soc. of Canada - Regina Chap. [IO],
  Regina, SK, Canada
Osteoporosis Soc. of Canada - Saskatoon Chap.
  [IO], Saskatoon, SK, Canada
Osteoporosis Soc. of Canada - Sudbury Chap. [IO],
  Sudbury, ON, Canada
Osteoporosis Soc. of Canada - Toronto Chap. [IO],
  Toronto, ON, Canada
Osteoporosis Soc. of Hong Kong [IO], Hong Kong,
  People's Republic of China
Osteoporosis Soc. of India [IO], New Delhi, India
Osteoporosis Soc; Natl. [IO]
Osteoporosis Soc. of Pakistan [IO], Karachi,
  Pakistan
Osteoporosis Soc. of Singapore [IO], Singapore,
  Singapore
Osteoporosis Soc. of Sri Lanka [IO], Nugegoda, Sri
  Lanka
Osteoporosis South Australia [IO], Fullarton,
  Australia
Osteoporosis Tasmania [IO], Hobart, Australia
Osteoporosis Victoria [IO], Caulfield South, Australia
Osteoporosis Western Australia [IO], Wembley,
  Australia
Osterreichische Arbeitsgemeinschaft fur Mus-
  tererkennung [★IO]
Osterreichische Arztekammer [★IO]
Osterreichische Bundes Sportorganisation [★IO]
Osterreichische Cmpt. Gesellschaft [★IO]
Osterreichische Gesellschaft fur Akupunktur [★IO]

A star before a book entry number signifies that the name is not listed separately, but is mentioned within the entry.

Osterreichische Gesellschaft fur Amerikastudien [★IO]

Osterreichische Gesellschaft fur Angewandte Forschung in der Tourismusund Freizeitwirtschaft [★IO]

Osterreichische Gesellschaft fur Antimikrobielle Chemotherapie [★IO]

Osterreichische Gesellschaft fur Dermatologie und Venerologie [★IO]

Osterreichische Gesellschaft fur Familienplanung [IO], Vienna, Austria

Osterreichische Gesellschaft fur Geriatrie and Gerontologie [★IO]

Osterreichische Gesellschaft fur Landschaftsplanung und Landschaftsarchitektur [IO], Vienna, Austria

Osterreichische Gesellschaft fuer Neurowissenschaften [★IO]

Osterreichische Gesellschaft fur Operations Res. [★IO]

Osterreichische Gesellschaft fur Rheumatologie [IO], Vienna, Austria

Osterreichische Hochschulerschaft [★IO]

Osterreichische Huntington Hilfe [★IO]

Osterreichische Kommission Iustitia Et Pax [IO], Vienna, Austria

Osterreichische Landjugend [IO], Vienna, Austria

Osterreichische Pharmakologische Gessellschaft [★IO]

Osterreichische Physiologische Gesellschaft [★IO]

Osterreichische Psysikalische Gesellschaft [★IO]

Osterreichische Rheumaliga [IO], Vienna, Austria

Osterreichische Rosenfreunde in der Osterreichischen Gartenbau-Gessellschaft [IO], Vienna, Austria

Osterreichische Statistische Gesellschaft [★IO]

Osterreichische Werbewissenschaftliche Gesellschaft [★IO]

Osterreichischen Rollsport und Inline-Skate Verband [★IO]

Osterreichischer Aero Club [IO], Vienna, Austria

Osterreichischer Automobil-, Motorrad-, und Touring Club [★IO]

Osterreichischer Badminton Verband [★IO]

Osterreichischer Baseball- und Softballverband [★IO]

Osterreichischer Cricket Verband [★IO]

Osterreichischer Dachverband fur Geographische Info. [★IO]

Osterreichischer Eishockey-Verband [★IO]

Osterreichischer Floorball Verband [★IO]

Osterreichischer Frisbee-Sport Verband [★IO]

Osterreichischer Golf-Verband [★IO]

Osterreichischer Judo Verband [IO], Vienna, Austria

Osterreichischer Jugendherbergsverband [★IO]

Osterreichischer Komponistenbund [★IO]

Osterreichischer P.E.N-Club [★IO]

Osterreichischer Squash Rackets Verband [IO], Vienna, Austria

Osterreichischer Taekwondo Verband [★IO]

Osterreichischer Tennisverband [IO], Vosendorf, Austria

Osterreichischer Verein fur Kraftfahrzeugtechnik [★IO]

Osterreichischer Wasserskiverband [★IO]

Osterreichischer Wasserskiverband [★IO]

Osterreichisches Institut fur Wirtschaftsforschung [★IO]

Osterreichisches Komitee fur UNICEF [★IO]

Osterreichisches Kuratorium fur Landtechnik und Landentwicklung [★IO]

Osterreichisches Olympisches Comite [★IO]

Osterreichisches Paralympisches Comm. [★IO]

Ostomy
 Algerian Ostomy Assn. [IO]
 European Ostomy Assn. [IO]
 Ileostomy and Internal Pouch Support Gp. [IO]
 Intl. Ostomy Assn. [IO]
 Lebanese Ostomy Assn. [IO]
 Norwegian Ostomy Assn. [IO]
 Ostomy Assn. of China [IO]
 Stoma Care Soc. [IO]
 United Ostomy Assn. of Canada [IO]
 World Coun. of Enterostomal Therapists [IO]
 Wound, Ostomy and Continence Nurses Soc.: An Assn. of E.T. Nurses [15533]
Ostomy Assn. of China [IO], Shanghai, People's Republic of China

Ostomy Assn; Intl. [IO]

Ostomy and Continence Nurses Soc., An Assn. of E.T. Nurses; Wound, [★15533]

Ostomy and Continence Nursing Certification Bd; Wound, [15534]

Ostrich Assn; Amer. [4132]

OT Australia: Australian Assn. of Occupational Therapists [IO], Fitzroy, Australia

Otesha Proj. [IO], Ottawa, ON, Canada

Othello Assn. Singapore [IO], Singapore, Singapore

Othello Assn; U.S. [22477]

The Other Economic Summit of North Am. [★6891]

The Other Economic Summit of the U.S. [6891], 777 UN Plz., Ste. 3C, New York, NY 10017, (212)972-9877

Other Minds [10684], 333 Valencia St., Ste. 303, San Francisco, CA 94103-3552, (415)934-8134

The Other "NBA" [13177]

The Other Victims of Alcoholism - Address unknown since 2002.

Otolaryngic Allergy and Found; Amer. Acad. of [13593]

Otolaryngologic Allergy; Amer. Soc. of Ophthalmologic and [★13593]

Otolaryngologists - Head and Neck Surgeons; Soc. of Military [15267]

Otolaryngologists - Head and Neck Surgeons; Soc. of Univ. [15828]

Otolaryngologists; Soc. of Military [★15267]

Otolaryngology Administrators; Assn. of [15062]

Otolaryngology; Amer. Bd. of [15818]

Otolaryngology; Assn. for Res. in [15824]

Otolaryngology - Head and Neck Surgery; Amer. Acad. of [15817]

Otolaryngology-Head and Neck Surgery; Amer. Osteopathic Colleges of Ophthalmology and [15664]

Otolaryngology - Head and Neck Surgery; Canadian Soc. of [IO]

Otological Soc; Amer. [15822]

Otological Soc; Amer. Laryngological, Rhinological and [15821]

Otomotiv Sanayii Dernegi [★IO]

Otorhinolaryngology
 Acoustic Neuroma Assn. [15816]
 Amer. Acad. of Otolaryngology - Head and Neck Surgery [15817]
 Amer. Bd. of Otolaryngology [15818]
 Amer. Head and Neck Soc. [15819]
 Amer. Laryngological Assn. [15820]
 Amer. Laryngological, Rhinological and Otological Soc. [15821]
 Amer. Otological Soc. [15822]
 Amer. Rhinologic Soc. [15823]
 Assn. of Otolaryngology Administrators [15062]
 Assn. for Res. in Otolaryngology [15824]
 Australian Soc. of Otolaryngology Head and Neck Surgery [IO]
 British Assn. of Otorhinolaryngologists - Head and Neck Surgeons [IO]
 Canadian Soc. of Otolaryngology - Head and Neck Surgery [IO]
 Ear Found. [15825]
 European Laryngological Soc. [IO]
 European Rhinologic Soc. [IO]
 Intl. Fed. of Oto-Rhino-Laryngological Societies [IO]
 Intl. Meniere Fed. [IO]
 Meniere's Network [15826]
 Natl. Assn. of Laryngectomy Clubs [IO]
 Politzer Soc. - Intl. Soc. for Otological Surgery [IO]
 Soc. for Ear, Nose, and Throat Advances in Children [15827]
 Soc. of Military Otolaryngologists - Head and Neck Surgeons [15267]
 Soc. of Otorhinolaryngology and Head/Neck Nurses [15526]
 Soc. of Univ. Otolaryngologists - Head and Neck Surgeons [15828]
 Vestibular Disorders Assn. [15829]
 Vestibular Disorders Assn. [IO]
Otorhinolaryngology; Osteopathic Coll. of Ophthalmology and [★15664]

Otorhinologic Soc. for Plastic Surgery; Amer. [★14038]

Otosclerosis Study Group - Defunct.

Otter; Friends of the Sea [5320]

Otterhound Club of Am. [22335], c/o Ron Abernathy, Sec., PO Box 61068, Fairbanks, AK 99706, (907)490-5996

Ouachita Baptist Univ. Alumni Assn. [18920], 410 Ouachita St., OBU Box 3762, Arkadelphia, AR 71998, (870)245-5506

Ouderkerk Family Genealogical Assn. [21017], 700 Atlanta Country Club Dr., Marietta, GA 30067

Ouellette Family Assn. of Am. [IO], La Pocatiere, QC, Canada

Oughtred Soc. [22101], c/o Clark McCoy, Membership Sec., PO Box 69, Pleasanton, CA 94566

Our Bodies, Ourselves [16909], 34 Plympton St., Boston, MA 02118, (617)451-3666

Our Developing World [17906], 13004 Paseo Presada, Saratoga, CA 95070-4125, (408)379-4431

Our Developing World [IO], Saratoga, CA, United States

Our Global Heritage [IO], Ho, Ghana

Our Lady of the Cenacle; Auxiliaries of [19581]

Our Lady of Fatima, U.S.A; Blue Army of [19589]

Our Lady of the Most Holy Trinity; Soc. of [19722]

Our Little Bros. and Sisters [20380], PO Box 3134, Alexandria, VA 22302, (703)836-1233

Our Voices Together [13309], 1730 Rhode Island Ave. NW, Ste. 712, Washington, DC 20036, (202)223-0080

Our World-Underwater Scholarship Soc. - Defunct.

Our Youths Found. [IO], San Antonio de Pichincha, Ecuador

Ourobourus Inst. - Address unknown since 1986.

Out/Look Found. - Address unknown since 1999.

Out-of-Home Measurement Bur. [★123]

Out-of-School Time; Natl. Inst. on [11543]

!Out Proud! The Natl. Coalition for Gay, Lesbian, Bisexual and Transgender Youth [★12252]

Out on the Screen [★9944]

Out to Swim London [IO], London, United Kingdom

Outagamie County Historical Soc; Houdini Historical Center/ [11123]

Outboard Boating Club of America - Defunct.

Outboard Motor Club; Antique [23158]

Outboard Motor Mfrs. Assn. [★2587]

Outdoor Advt. Assn. of Am. [114], 1850 M St. NW, Ste. 1040, Washington, DC 20036, (202)833-5566

Outdoor Advt. Assn; Eight Sheet [99]

Outdoor Advt. Assn. of Great Britain [IO], London, United Kingdom

Outdoor Advt. Assn; Junior Panel [★99]

Outdoor Amusement Bus. Assn. [1324], 1035 S Semoran Blvd., Ste. 1045A, Winter Park, FL 32792, (407)681-9444

Outdoor Drama; Inst. of [11018]

Outdoor Education
 Amer. Camp Assn. [23268]
 Assn. of Outdoor Recreation and Educ. [8950]
 Boy Scouts of Am. [12997]
 Equine Guided Educ. Assn. [8524]
 Hungarian Scouts Assn. [12999]
 Natl. Assn. of Therapeutic Wilderness Camps [23276]
 Natl. Eagle Scout Assn. [13002]
 Natl. Jewish Comm. on Scouting [13003]
 Order of the Arrow [13005]
 Tread Lightly! [5167]
 Wilderness Classroom Org. [8951]
 Wilderness Educ. Assn. [8952]
 Wilderness Medical Soc. [15184]
Outdoor Education Assn. - Defunct.

Outdoor Entertainment
 Darkride and Funhouse Enthusiasts [21511]
 Intl. Assn. of Haunted Attractions [1304]
Outdoor Ethics [★4413]

Outdoor Ethics Guild - Defunct.

Outdoor Indus. Assn. [IO], South Ruislip, United Kingdom

Outdoor Indus. Assn. [2870], 4909 Pearl East Cir., Ste. 200, Boulder, CO 80301, (303)444-3353

Outdoor Leisure Development; Blind [★23342]

Outdoor Power Equip. Aftermarket Assn. [1292], 1726 M St. NW, Ste. 1101, Washington, DC 20036, (202)775-8605

Outdoor Power Equipment Aftermarket Association [IO], Washington, DC, United States

---

Reference to "IO" in place of a book number signifies that the association may be found in the 45th edition of International Organizations.

Outdoor Power Equip. Distributors Assn. [★1293]
Outdoor Power Equipment Distributors Assn. -
Defunct.
Outdoor Power Equip. and Engine Ser. Assn.
[1293], c/o Nancy Cueroni, Exec. Dir., 37 Pratt St.,
Essex, CT 06426-1159, (860)767-1770
Outdoor Power Equip. Inst. [1294], 341 S Patrick
St., Old Town, Alexandria, VA 22314, (703)549-
7600
Outdoor Recreation
Adirondack Forty-Sixers [23930]
Adirondack Mountain Club [23931]
Adirondack Trail Improvement Soc. [23932]
Adventure Cycling Assn. [23304]
All-American Indian Motorcycle Club [22663]
Am. Outdoors [23681]
Amer. Blind Golf Assn. [23335]
Amer. Camp Assn. [23268]
Amer. Canoe Assn. [23278]
Amer. Canyoneering Assn. [21949]
Amer. Carp Soc. [22448]
Amer. Casting Assn. [23406]
Amer. Endurance Ride Conf. [23933]
Amer. Hiking Soc. [23934]
Amer. Kitefliers Assn. [23569]
Amer. Mountain Guides Assn. [23284]
Amer. Safe Climbing Assn. [21950]
Amer. Ski-Bike Assn. [23801]
Amer. Sports Org. [23993]
Amer. Trails [23935]
Amer. Whitewater [23682]
Antique Motorcycle Club of Am. [22667]
Appalachian Mountain Club [23936]
Appalachian Trail Conservancy [23937]
Archery Shooters Assn. [23050]
Ariel Motorcycle Club North Am. [22668]
Assn. for Challenge Course Tech. [2869]
Assn. of Girl Scout Executive Staff [12996]
Assn. of Jewish Sponsored Camps [23275]
Assn. of Northwest Steelheaders [23409]
Assn. of Outdoor Recreation and Educ. [8950]
Athletic Success Inst. [23665]
Bass Anglers Sportsman Soc. [23410]
Bicycle Ride Directors' Assn. of Am. [23308]
Bikes Belong Coalition [21831]
Black Farmers and Agriculturists Assn. [4111]
Blue Knights Intl. Law Enforcement Motorcycle
Club [22669]
BlueRibbon Coalition [23680]
Bowfishing Assn. of Am. [23411]
Boy Scouts of Am. [12997]
Brotherhood of the Jungle Cock [23412]
Camping Women [23269]
Carp Anglers Gp. [22450]
Centered Riding [22584]
Challenge Aspen at Snowmass [23342]
Chinese-American Golf Assn. [23445]
Christian Camping International/U.S.A. [23270]
Christian Golfers' Assn. [23283]
Continental Divide Trail Soc. [23938]
Croquet Found. of Am. [23300]
Darkride and Funhouse Enthusiasts [21511]
Disabled Sports USA [23343]
Dream Catchers, USA [11943]
Family Campers and RVers [23271]
Fed. of Fly Fishers [23413]
Fishing Has No Boundaries [23414]
Florida Trail Assn. [23939]
Future Fisherman Found. [23415]
Giant Scale Warbirds Assn. [22644]
Girl Scouts of the U.S.A. [12998]
Great Lakes Sport Fishing Coun. [23416]
Highpointers Club [23014]
Hungarian Scouts Assn. [12999]
Intercollegiate Outing Club Assn. [23941]
Intl. Assn. of Fly Fishing Veterinarians [22451]
Intl. Assn. of Haunted Attractions [1304]
Intl. Bonefishing Soc. [22452]
Intl. Bowhunting Org. [23544]
Intl. Brotherhood of Motorcycle Campers [23624]
Intl. Fellowship of Fishing Rotarians [22453]
Intl. Hunter Educ. Assn. [23545]
Intl. Playground Contractors Assn. [1028]
Intl. Scale Soaring Assn. [22648]
Intl. Underwater Spearfishing Assn. [23418]

Intl. Unicycling Fed. [23311]
Intl. Women's Fishing Assn. [23419]
IOCALUM [23942]
League of Amer. Bicyclists [23312]
Lincoln Heritage Trail Found. [23943]
Masters of Foxhounds Assn. of Am. [23546]
Montana Outfitters and Guides Assn. [23944]
Mountaineers [23945]
Natl. African-American RV'ers Assn. [22958]
Natl. Archery Assn. of the U.S. [23052]
Natl. Assn. of Therapeutic Wilderness Camps
[23276]
Natl. Bicycle League [23313]
Natl. Bicycle Tour Directors Assn. [23314]
Natl. Bowhunter Educ. Found. [23053]
Natl. C Scow Sailing Assn. [23203]
Natl. Camp Assn. [23277]
Natl. Center for Bicycling and Walking [23315]
The Natl. Crossbowmen of the U.S.A. [23054]
Natl. Eagle Scout Assn. [13002]
Natl. Field Archery Assn. [23055]
Natl. Hunters Assn. [23547]
Natl. Intramural-Recreational Sports Assn. [23842]
Natl. Jewish Comm. on Scouting [13003]
Natl. Lutheran Outdoors Ministry Assn. [20231]
Natl. Org. for Rivers [23683]
Natl. Senior Golf Assn. [23460]
Natl. Trail Ride Assn. [23946]
Natl. Wheelchair Basketball Assn. [23354]
Natl. Wheelchair Softball Assn. [23356]
New England Trails Conf. [23948]
Nomads Outdoor Gp. [IO]
North Amer. Bowhunting Coalition [22606]
North Amer. Family Campers Assn. [23273]
North Amer. Fastpitch Assn. [23793]
North Amer. Fishing Club [23421]
North Amer. Hunting Club [23548]
North Amer. Riding for the Handicapped Assn.
[23357]
North Amer. Ski Joring Assn. [23845]
North Amer. Squirrel Assn. [22773]
North Amer. Stone Skipping Assn. [22939]
North Amer. Trail Ride Conf. [23949]
North Country Trail Assn. [23950]
Norwegian Mountain Touring Assn. [IO]
One-Arm Dove Hunt Assn. [23358]
Order of the Arrow [13005]
Outdoor Indus. Assn. [2870]
Outfitters Assn. of Am. [23642]
Pope and Young Club [23056]
Prairie Club [12799]
Professional Bowhunter's Soc. [23057]
Rails-to-Trails Conservancy [23952]
Randonneurs USA [23316]
Recreational Fishing Alliance [17603]
Ride and Tie Assn. [23849]
Salmon Unlimited [23422]
Scale Ship Modelers Assn. of North Am. [22656]
Scale Warbird Racing Assn. [22657]
Sheclimbs [23285]
Shore Fishing and Casting Club Intl. [23423]
Ski for Light [23361]
Soccer in the Streets [11789]
Special Olympics [23362]
Tandem Club of Am. [23317]
Toyota Territory Off-Roaders Assn. [22965]
Tread Lightly! [5167]
Tugboat Enthusiasts Soc. of the Americas [21886]
Unicycling Soc. of Am. [23319]
United Sportsmans Assn. of North Am. [23058]
U.S.A. Cricket Assn. [23299]
U.S. Assn. for Blind Athletes [23363]
U.S. Canoe Assn. [23279]
U.S. Croquet Assn. [23301]
U.S. Cycling Fed. [23320]
U.S. Fastpitch Assn. [23794]
U.S. Handcycling Fed. [23321]
U.S. Hang Gliding and Paragliding Assn. [23044]
U.S. Lawn Bowls Assn. [23256]
U.S. Monoski Assn. [23863]
U.S. Orienteering Fed. [23641]
U.S. Powered Paragliding Assn. [23643]
U.S. Shore Angling Assn. [23425]
U.S. Ski Mountaineering Assn. [23759]
US Scale Masters Assn. [22660]

USA Climbing [23286]
USGA Green Sect. [23470]
Wheelchair Motorcycle Assn. [23370]
Wheelchair Sports, USA [23371]
Wilderness Classroom Org. [8951]
Wilderness Medical Soc. [15184]
Wilderness Volunteers [22774]
Women Outdoors [23644]
World Miniature Warbird Assn. [22662]
World Senior Golf Fed. [23472]
Outdoor Recreation Coalition of Am. [★2870]
Outdoor Recreation and Educ; Assn. of [8950]
Outdoor Recreation Inst. - Address unknown since
1995.
Outdoor Recreation Liaison Officers; Natl. Assn. of
State [6157]
Outdoor Women - Defunct.
Outdoor Writers Assn. of Am. [3153], 121 Hickory
St., Ste. 1, Missoula, MT 59801, (406)728-7434
Outdoor Writers of Canada [IO], Kitchener, ON,
Canada
Outdoor Writers' Guild [IO], Preston, United
Kingdom
Outdoors; Am. [23681]
Outdoors Ministry Assn; Lutheran [★20231]
Outdoors Ministry Assn; Natl. Lutheran [20231]
Outdoors Unlimited - Address unknown since 2001.
Outer Critics Circle [11037], c/o Marjorie Gunner,
Pres. Emerita, 101 W 57th St., New York, NY
10019, (212)765-8557
Outerwear Assn; Natl. Knitted [★251]
Outerwear Assn; New England Knitted [★20816]
Outerwear Manufacturers Assn; New England Knit-
ted [★20816]
Outerwear and Sportswear Assn; Natl. [★221]
Outfest [9944], 3470 Wilshire Blvd., Ste. 1022, Los
Angeles, CA 90010, (213)480-7088
Outfitters Assn. of Am. [23642], Rte. 1, Box 3255,
Old Valdosta Rd., Ray City, GA 31645, (229)686-
7621
Outfitters Assn; Eastern Professional River [★23681]
Outfitters; Bitterroot [★23944]
Outfitters and Dude Ranchers Assn; Montana
[★23944]
Outfitters and Guides Assn; Montana [23944]
Outfitters; Natl. Associations of Canoe Liveries and
[★3650]
Outfitters; Treasure State [★23944]
Outing Club Assn; Intercollegiate [23941]
Outlaw and Lawman History; Natl. Assn. for [9380]
Outlet and Switch Box Assn. - Defunct.
Outlets; Natl. Assn. of Tobacco [3820]
Outpatient Intravenous Infusion Therapy Assn.
[16631]
Outpatient Ophthalmic Surgery Soc. [15698], c/o
Ms. Claudia A. McDougal, Exec. Dir., 6564 Umbers
Cir., Arvada, CO 80007, (866)892-1001
Outpatient Surgeons; Amer. Soc. of [★16558]
Outplacement Consulting Firms; Assn. of [★1255]
Outplacement Consulting Firms Intl; Assn. of
[★1255]
Outpost [19870], PO Box 22429, Robbinsdale, MN
55422-0429, (763)592-4700
Outpost for Hope [12610], 7405 Greenback Ln., No.
147, Citrus Heights, CA 95610-5603, (916)965-
4673
OutProud [12252], 369 3rd St., Ste. B-362, San
Rafael, CA 94901-3581
Outreach Assn; Amer. [13223]
Outreach Inc; Aneurysm [14544]
Outreach Intl; Life [20021]
Outreach Program; Midtown [★13277]
Outreach and Synagogue Community; Commn. on
[20133]
Outsiders Club [IO], London, United Kingdom
Outsourcing
Fabless Semiconductor Assn. [1215]
Human Resources Outsourcing Assn. [1981]
Intl. Assn. of Outsourcing Professionals [2871]
Intl. Assn. of Outsourcing Professionals [IO]
Outsourcing Assn; Human Resources [1981]
Outsourcing Inst. [757], Jericho Atrium, 500 N
Broadway, Ste. 141, Jericho, NY 11753, (516)681-
0066
Outstretched Hands [IO], Milan, Italy

A star before a book entry number signifies that the name is not listed separately, but is mentioned within the entry.

Outward Bound [9204], 100 Mystery Point Rd., Garrison, NY 10524, (845)424-4000
Oval Track Equipment Assn. - Defunct.
Ovarian Cancer Coalition; Natl. [13855]
Ovarian Cancer Natl. Alliance [13861], 910 17th St. NW, Ste. 1190, Washington, DC 20006, (202)331-1332
Ovarian Cancer Prevention and Early Detection Foundation - Address unknown since 1999.
Ovarian Cancer Registry; Gilda Radner Familial [13826]
Over the Front [★21459]
Over the Front [★IO]
Over the Hill Gang, Intl. [IO], Colorado Springs, CO, United States
Over the Hill Gang, Intl. [23846], 1515 N Tejon St., Colorado Springs, CO 80907, (719)389-0022
Overachievers Anonymous - Address unknown since 2003.
Overcoming Mobility Barriers Intl. - Address unknown since 2006.
Overeaters Anonymous World Ser. Off. [12648], PO Box 44020, Rio Rancho, NM 87174-4020, (505)891-2664
Overeaters Anonymous World Ser. Off. [IO], Rio Rancho, NM, United States
Overhead Components Mfrs. Prdt. Sect. of the Material Handling Inst. [★2042]
Overhead Components Mfrs. Production Sect. of the Material Handling Inst. of Am. [★2042]
Overland Jeepster Club; Willys [21818]
Overland-Knight Registry; Willys- [21819]
Overseas Ambassadors - Defunct.
Overseas Assistance; Volunteers in [★4481]
Overseas Assn; Amer. [★12831]
Overseas Assn; Amer. Red Cross [12831]
Overseas Automotive Club [★364]
Overseas Automotive Coun. [364], PO Box 13966, 10 Lab. Dr., Research Triangle Park, NC 27709-3966, (919)406-8810
Overseas Blind; Amer. Found. for [★16854]
Overseas Brats [19384], PO Box 47112, Wichita, KS 67201, (316)269-9610
Overseas Chinese Physics Assn. [7507], c/o Sun-Yiu Fung, Treas., PO Box 8743, Newport Beach, CA 92658, (949)721-8812
Overseas Constr. Assn. of Japan, Inc. [IO], Tokyo, Japan
Overseas Crusades [★IO]
Overseas Crusades [★20377]
Overseas Development Admin. [★IO]
Overseas Development Coun. - Address unknown since 2005.
Overseas Development Inst. [IO], London, United Kingdom
Overseas Development Network [★IO]
Overseas Development Network [★12435]
Overseas Development Network [★18853]
Overseas EDU Assn. [★24043]
Overseas Educational Service - Defunct.
Overseas Indian Cong. of North America - Defunct.
Overseas Investors Chamber of Commerce and Indus. [IO], Karachi, Pakistan
Overseas Jazz Club - Defunct.
Overseas Liaison Comm. of Amer. Coun. on Education - Defunct.
Overseas Ministries; Division of [★19856]
Overseas Mission Soc. - Defunct.
Overseas Missionary Fellowship Canada [IO], Mississauga, ON, Canada
Overseas Missionary Fellowship, U.S.A. [★IO]
Overseas Missionary Fellowship, U.S.A. [★20378]
Overseas Press Club of Am. [3154], 40 W 45 St., New York, NY 10036, (212)626-9220
Overseas Press Club of Am. [IO], New York, NY, United States
Overseas Press and Media Assn. [IO], Cambridge, United Kingdom
Overseas Prog; Christian Rural [★12842]
Overseas Relief; Methodist Comm. for [★20267]
Overseas Relief; United Methodist Comm. on [★20267]
Overseas Res. Centers; Coun. of Amer. [7566]
Overseas Sales and Marketing Assn. of Am. [2312], 1S132 Summit Ave., Ste. 202D, Oakbrook Terrace, IL 60181-3940, (630)424-0600

Overseas Ser. League; Women's [21334]
Overseas Teachers Assn. [★24043]
Overseas Writers - Defunct.
Overspenders Anonymous - Defunct.
Overstreet; Friends of Paul [24895]
Overstress/Electrostatic Discharge Assn; Elecl. [6910]
Overview Latin America - Defunct.
Ovulation Method Assn. - USA; Billings [12635]
Ovulation Method-Billings, U.S.A; World Org. of the [★12637]
Ovulation Method Billings; World Org. [IO]
Ovulation Method Instructors UK; Natl. Assn. of [IO]
Ovulation Method of Ireland; Natl. Assn. of the [IO]
Ovulation Method Res. and Reference Centre of Australia [IO], North Fitzroy, Australia
Ovulation Method Teachers Assn. - Address unknown since 1999.
Owen Family Assn. [21018], 1478 Dallas Cir., Marietta, GA 30064
Owen Hart Fan Club - Address unknown since 1994.
Owen M. Kupferschmid Holocaust and Human Rights Proj. [17781], c/o Maria Stookey, Pres., Boston Coll. Law School, 885 Centre St., Newton, MA 02459, (617)552-8285
Owen M. Kupferschmid Holocaust and Human Rights Proj. [IO], Newton, MA, United States
Owls
Hawk and Owl Trust [IO]
Owner Handler Assn. of America - Address unknown since 1999.
Owner-Operator Independent Drivers Assn. [3888], 1 NW OOIDA Dr., Grain Valley, MO 64029-7903, (816)229-5791
Owner Operators of America - Address unknown since 2002.
Owner Soc; Piper [21470]
Owners Assn; Amer. Thoroughbred [★23515]
Owners Assn; Cleveland Vessel [★2606]
Owners Assn; Natl. Apartment [★3317]
Owners and Breeders of Peruvian Paso Horses; Amer. Assn. of [4810]
Owners Club; FoMoCo [21646]
Owners; League of Private Property [★6187]
Owners and Managers Inst. Intl; Building [9027]
Owners and Pilots Assn; Aircraft [135]
Owsley Family Historical Soc. [21019], 916 N Ridge Dr., Columbus, GA 31904, (706)324-7237
OX5 Aviation Pioneers [21469], PO Box 7974, Pittsburgh, PA 15216-7974, (412)341-5650
OX5 Club of Am. [★21469]
Oxalosis and Hyperoxaluria Found. [15296], 201 E 19th St., Ste. 12E, New York, NY 10003, (212)777-0470
OXFAM Am. [12438], 226 Causeway St., 5th Fl., Boston, MA 02114-2206, (617)482-1211
OXFAM Am. [IO], Boston, MA, United States
Oxfam Australia [IO], Fitzroy, Australia
Oxfam Australia [IO], Carlton, Australia
OXFAM - Canada [IO], Ottawa, ON, Canada
OXFAM - GB in Vietnam [IO], Hanoi, Vietnam
Oxfam - Germany [IO], Berlin, Germany
OXFAM - Hong Kong [IO], Hong Kong, People's Republic of China
Oxfam Intl. Advocacy Off. [IO], Washington, DC, United States
Oxfam Intl. Advocacy Off. [12877], 1100 15th St. NW, Ste. 600, Washington, DC 20005, (202)496-1170
OXFAM - Ireland [IO], Dublin, Ireland
Oxfam-Magasins du monde [★IO]
Oxfam - New Zealand [IO], Auckland, New Zealand
OXFAM - Projects [★IO]
Oxfam - Quebec [IO], Montreal, QC, Canada
OXFAM - Solidarity [IO], Brussels, Belgium
OXFAM - U.K. [IO], Oxford, United Kingdom
Oxfam World Shops [IO], Bierges, Belgium
Oxford Comm. for Famine Relief [★IO]
Oxford Comm. for Famine Relief [★12438]
Oxford Down Record Assn; Amer. [★5190]
Oxford Gp. - Moral Re-Armament [★17734]
Oxford Gp. - Moral Re-Armament [★IO]
Oxford Sheep Assn; Amer. [5190]
Oxide Sterilization Assn; Ethylene [808]
Oxychloride Cement Assn. - Defunct.

Oxygen Soc. [★6613]
Oxygen Soc. [★IO]
Oxygenated Fuels Assn. - Address unknown since 2006.
Oyate [19284], 2702 Mathews St., Berkeley, CA 94702, (510)848-6700
Oyo-buturi Gakkai [★IO]
Oyster Growers Assn; Pacific Coast [★3501]
Oyster Inst. of North Am. [★3494]
Oyster Shell Inst. - Defunct.
Oz; Fans of [25048]
Oz GREEN - Global Rivers Environmental Educ. Network - Australia [IO], Dee Why, Australia
Oz ve Shalom [★IO]
Oz Veshalom-Netivot Shalom [IO], Jerusalem, Israel
Ozar Hatorah [20171]
Ozark Inst. - Defunct.
Ozark Soc. [4438], PO Box 2914, Little Rock, AR 72203, (501)847-3738

P

P-47 Thunderbolt Pilots Assn. [21397], PO Box 1266, Ridgewood, NJ 07451-1266
P-51 Mustang Pilots Assn. [21398], 1040 SE 58th Ave., Hillsboro, OR 97123-6326, (503)591-9312
P-51 Mustang Pilots Assn. [IO], Hillsboro, OR, United States
P. J. Allman Fan Club - Defunct.
P. N. Elrod Fan Club [IO], Fort Worth, TX, United States
P6 Rover Owners Club [IO], Newmarket, United Kingdom
PAC; BANK [18281]
PAC Charitable Found. [★19306]
PAC; Natl. [18067]
PACE Assn; Natl. [12272]
Pace Car Soc. - Defunct.
Pace Intl. Union - Defunct.
PACER Center - Parent Advocacy Coalition for Educational Rights [14246], 8161 Normandale Blvd., Minneapolis, MN 55437, (952)838-9000
Paceship Py 23 Class Assn. - Defunct.
Pachamama Alliance [5163], PO Box 29191, San Francisco, CA 94129-9191, (415)561-4522
Pachyderm Clubs; Natl. Fed. of the Grand Order of [18359]
Pachyderms; Grand Order of [★18359]
Pacific
APPEAL: Asian Pacific Partners for Empowerment and Leadership [11760]
The Asia Found. [17005]
Asia Pacific - USA Chamber of Commerce [24264]
Asia Soc. [9616]
Asian Americans/Pacific Islanders in Philanthropy [12710]
Asian/Pacific Amer. Heritage Assn. [18972]
Asian Pacific Amer. Labor Alliance [24003]
Asian Pacific Americans for Progress [17012]
Asian and Pacific Islander Amer. Vote [18345]
Asian and Pacific Islander Inst. on Domestic Violence [12022]
Circum-Pacific Coun. for Energy and Mineral Resources [7340]
Conservation Northwest [4546]
East-West Center [17882]
Gay Asian Pacific Support Network [12229]
Honolulu Japanese Chamber of Commerce [24348]
Inst. for the Advancement of Hawaiian Affairs [10883]
Japanese Chamber of Commerce and Industry of Hawaii [24345]
Law Enforcement Assn. of Asian Pacifics [19201]
Natl. Asian Amer. Pacific Islander Mental Hea. Assn. [15215]
Natl. Coalition for Asian Pacific Amer. Community Development [11785]
Natl. Coun. of Asian Pacific Americans [17013]
Native Hawaiian Culture and Arts Prog. [10884]
Pacific Arts Assn. [9463]
Pacific Dermatologic Assn. [14213]
Pacific Islanders in Communications [10455]
Pacific Islanders' Cultural Assn. [10767]

Reference to "IO" in place of a book number signifies that the association may be found in the 45th edition of International Organizations.

Pacific Sci. Assn. [7626]
Pacific Seabird Gp. [5362]
Pacifica Found. [18179]
Polynesian Voyaging Soc. [22775]
RARE [5373]
U.S. Natl. Comm. for Pacific Economic Cooperation [17465]
Pacific 10 Conf. [23847], 1350 Treat Blvd., Ste. 500, Walnut Creek, CA 94597-8853, (925)932-4411
Pacific Agricultural Cooperative for Export - Address unknown since 1991.
Pacific Amer. Educ; Natl. Assn. for Asian and [7988]
Pacific Amer. Families Against Substance Abuse; Natl. Asian [13258]
Pacific Amer. Flag Berth Operators; Trans-Atlantic Amer. Flag Liner Operators/Trans- [3592]
Pacific Amer. Heritage Coun; Asian [18973]
Pacific Amer. Inst. - Address unknown since 2003.
Pacific Amer. Labor Alliance; Asian [24003]
Pacific Amer. Steamship Assn. [★6059]
Pacific Amer. Tankship Assn. - Defunct.
Pacific Antique Label Soc. [★21995]
Pacific Area Newspaper Publishers' Assn. [IO], Ultimo, Australia
Pacific Area Travel Assn. [★IO]
Pacific Area Travel Assn. [★3933]
Pacific Arts Assn. [9463], c/o Hilary Scothorn, Treas., PO Box 6061-120, Sherman Oaks, CA 91413
Pacific Arts Assn. [IO], Sherman Oaks, CA, United States
Pacific Asia Travel Assn. [IO], Bangkok, Thailand
Pacific Asia Travel Assn. [IO], Oakland, CA, United States
Pacific Asia Travel Assn. [3933], Latham Square Bldg., 1611 Telegraph Ave., Ste. 550, Oakland, CA 94612, (510)625-2055
Pacific Asia Travel Assn. - Singapore [IO], Singapore, Singapore
Pacific Asian Coalition - Defunct.
Pacific/Asian Rsrc. Center on Aging; Natl. [★11300]
Pacific Assn. of Quantity Surveyors [IO], Tokyo, Japan
Pacific Assn; Wabash, Frisco and [10927]
Pacific Associations of Optometrists; Intl. Fed. of Asian and [★15715]
Pacific; Astronomical Soc. of the [6503]
Pacific Bantam Austin Club [★21583]
Pacific Bantam Austin Club [★IO]
Pacific Basin Development Coun. [17843], 711 Kapiolana Blvd., Ste. 1075, Honolulu, HI 96813-5214, (808)596-7229
Pacific Basin Economic Coun. - Canadian Comm. [IO], Vancouver, BC, Canada
Pacific Basin (Honolulu) [★17071]
Pacific Broadcasting Assn. [IO], Tokyo, Japan
Pacific Center on Aging; Natl. Asian [11300]
Pacific Christian Coll. Alumni Assn. [★18898]
Pacific Class Catamaran Assn. - Defunct.
Pacific Coast Building Officials Conf. [★5551]
Pacific Coast Building Officials Conf. [★IO]
Pacific Coast Canned Pear Service - Address unknown since 2001.
Pacific Coast Cichlid Assn. [22445], PO Box 28145, San Jose, CA 95159-8145
Pacific Coast Clam Canners Assn. - Defunct.
Pacific Coast Economics Assn. [6897]
Pacific Coast Economics Assn. [★IO]
Pacific Coast Fed. of Fishermen's Associations [4669], PO Box 29370, San Francisco, CA 94129-0370, (415)561-5080
Pacific Coast Garment Manufacturers Assn. [★221]
Pacific Coast Marine Firemen, Oilers, Watertenders and Wipers Assn. [24130], 240 2nd St., San Francisco, CA 94105, (415)362-4592
Pacific Coast Marine Firemen's Union [★24130]
Pacific Coast Meat Assn. [★2662]
Pacific Coast Native Iris; Soc. for [22543]
Pacific Coast Oyster Growers Assn. [★3501]
Pacific Coast Paper Box Mfrs'. Assn. [990], c/o Paperboard Packaging Coun., 201 N Union St., Ste. 220, Alexandria, VA 22314, (703)836-3300
Pacific Coast Rugby Union [★23706]
Pacific Coast Shellfish Growers Assn. [3501], 120 State Ave. NE, PMB No. 142, Olympia, WA 98501, (360)754-2744

Pacific Coast Shippers Advisory Bd. - Address unknown since 1995.
Pacific Coast Stock Exchange [★3522]
Pacific Community Hea. Organizations; Assn. of Asian [14719]
Pacific Cruise Conf. [★3915]
Pacific Cruise Conf. [★IO]
Pacific Dance Assn. [★IO]
Pacific Dance Assn. [★9882]
Pacific Dance; Found. for [9882]
Pacific Dermatologic Assn. [14213], 100 Meadowcreek Dr., Ste. 150, Corte Madera, CA 94925, (415)927-5729
Pacific Dermatologic Assn. [IO], Corte Madera, CA, United States
Pacific Dragon Boat Assn. [21883], c/o Diane McCabe, Treas., 607 30th St., Hermosa Beach, CA 90254
Pacific Economic Cooperation Coun. [IO], Singapore, Singapore
Pacific Fisheries Conf. - Defunct.
Pacific Fisheries Development Found. - Defunct.
Pacific Fishery Mgt. Coun. [5732], 7700 NE Ambassador Pl., Ste. 200, Portland, OR 97220-1384, (503)820-2280
Pacific; Found. for the Peoples of the South [★12426]
Pacific Gamefish Res. Found. [★7176]
Pacific Gender and Trade Network [IO], Suva, Fiji
Pacific Herring Packers Assn. - Defunct.
Pacific; Inlandboatman's Union of the [2605]
Pacific Inst. [★12120]
Pacific Inst. [★18474]
Pacific Inst. of Gemmology [★IO]
Pacific Inst. for Stud. in Development, Env., and Security [12120], 654 13th St., Preservation Park, Oakland, CA 94612, (510)251-1600
Pacific Intellectual Property Assn. - Address unknown since 2003.
Pacific Intl. Trapshooting Assn. [23728], PO Box 770, Lebanon, OR 97355, (541)258-8766
Pacific International Trapshooting Association [IO], Lebanon, OR, United States
Pacific Islander Amer. Hea. Forum; Asian and [14545]
Pacific Islander Inst. on Domestic Violence; Asian and [12022]
Pacific Islanders in Communications [10455], 1221 Kapiolani Blvd., Ste. 6A-4, Honolulu, HI 96814, (808)591-0059
Pacific Islanders' Cultural Assn. [10767], 1016 Lincoln Blvd., No. 5, San Francisco, CA 94129, (415)281-0221
Pacific Islands Assn. - Address unknown since 2003.
Pacific Islands Museums Assn. [IO], Suva, Fiji
Pacific Islands News Assn. [IO], Suva, Fiji
Pacific Legal Found. [6226], 3900 Lennane Dr., Ste. 200, Sacramento, CA 95834-2918, (916)419-7111
Pacific Logging Cong. [1615], PO Box 1281, Maple Valley, WA 98038, (425)413-2808
Pacific Logging Cong. [IO], Maple Valley, WA, United States
Pacific Lumber Exporters Association [IO], Beaverton, OR, United States
Pacific Lumber Exporters Assn. [1616], 1260 NW Waterhouse Ave., Ste. 150, Beaverton, OR 97006, (503)439-6000
Pacific Lumber Inspection Bur. [1617], 33442 First Way S, Ste. 300, Federal Way, WA 98003, (253)835-3344
Pacific Lumber Inspection Bur. [IO], Federal Way, WA, United States
Pacific; Marine Firemen, Oilers and Watertenders of the [★24130]
Pacific Marine Fisheries Commn. [★5733]
Pacific Marine Mammal Center [5361], 20612 Laguna Canyon Rd., Laguna Beach, CA 92651, (949)494-3050
Pacific Maritime Assn. [3585], 555 Market St., San Francisco, CA 94105-2800, (415)576-3200
Pacific Music Indus. Assn. [★IO]
Pacific Northwest Bird and Mammal Soc. [★7364]
Pacific Northwest Christmas Tree Assn. [3947], PO Box 3366, Salem, OR 97302, (503)364-2942
Pacific Northwest Grain Dealers [★4314]

Pacific Northwest Grain and Feed Assn. [4314], 200 SW Market St., Ste. 190, Portland, OR 97201, (503)227-0234
Pacific Northwest Heather Soc. [★22533]
Pacific Northwest Heather Soc. [★IO]
Pacific Northwest Loggers Assn. - Address unknown since 1995.
Pacific Northwest Pea Growers and Dealers [★4314]
Pacific Northwest Region of the Lincoln and Continental Owners Club [21754], c/o Becky D'Ambrosia, 21920 SE Mark Rd., Damascus, OR 97089-8756
Pacific Northwest Region of the Lincoln and Continental Owners Club [IO], Snohomish, WA, United States
Pacific Northwest Ski Assn. [23754], PO Box 1278, Snoqualmie Pass, WA 98068, (425)434-0014
Pacific Northwest Ski Educ. Found. [★23754]
Pacific Northwest Stud; Center for [7647]
Pacific Northwest Trail Assn. [23951], North Cascades Gateway Center, 24854 Charles Jones Memorial Cir., Unit 4, Sedro Woolley, WA 98284, (877)854-9417
Pacific Ocean Res. Found. [7176], PO Box 4800, Kailua-Kona, HI 96740, (808)329-6105
Pacific; Oceanographic Soc. of the [★7393]
Pacific Orchid Soc. of Hawaii [22536], PO Box 1091, Honolulu, HI 96808
Pacific Peacemaker Project - Defunct.
Pacific Peoples' Partnership [IO], Victoria, BC, Canada
Pacific Post Partum Support Soc. [IO], Vancouver, BC, Canada
Pacific Printing and Imaging Assn. [1783], 1400 SW 5th Ave., Ste. 815, Portland, OR 97201, (877)762-7742
Pacific Railroad Soc. [10917], PO Box 80726, San Marino, CA 91118-8726, (562)692-4858
Pacific Regional Br. of the Intl. Coun. on Archives [IO], Wellington, New Zealand
Pacific Regional Env. Programme [IO], Apia, Western Samoa
Pacific Res. Inst. for Public Policy [18474], 755 Sansome St., Ste. 450, San Francisco, CA 94111, (415)989-0833
Pacific Riding for the Disabled Assn. [IO], Langley, BC, Canada
Pacific Rim Consortium [★IO]
Pacific Rim Consortium [★13427]
Pacific Rocket Soc. [6381], PO Box 662, Mojave, CA 93502, (661)824-1662
Pacific; Sailors' Union of the [24131]
Pacific Salmon Commn. [IO], Vancouver, BC, Canada
Pacific Sci. Assn. [IO], Honolulu, HI, United States
Pacific Sci. Assn. [7626], c/o Bishop Museum, 1525 Bernice St., Honolulu, HI 96817, (808)848-4124
Pacific Seabird Gp. [5362], c/o Ron LeValley, Treas., 920 Samoa Blvd., Ste. 210, Arcata, CA 95521, (707)826-0300
Pacific Seafood Processors Assn. [3502], 1900 W Emerson Pl., No. 205, Seattle, WA 98119, (206)281-1667
Pacific Shellfish Inst. [4182], 120 State Ave. NE, No. 142, Olympia, WA 98501, (360)754-2741
Pacific Soc. for Women in Philosophy [10822], c/o Amy Coplan, Exec. Sec., California State Univ. Fullerton, Dept. of Philosophy, PO Box 6868, Fullerton, CA 92834-6868
Pacific and Southeast Asia Women's Assn. of the U.S.A.; Pan- [17907]
Pacific Southwest Railway Museum [10918], 4695 Nebo Dr., La Mesa, CA 91941-5259, (619)465-7776
Pacific States Marine Fisheries Commn. [5733], 205 SE Spokane St., Ste. 100, Portland, OR 97202, (503)595-3100
Pacific Stock Exchange [3522]
Pacific Stud. Center [6892], 278 Hope St., No. A, Mountain View, CA 94041-1367, (650)969-1545
Pacific Telecommunications Coun. [7782], 2454 S Beretania St., Ste. 302, Honolulu, HI 96826-1524, (808)941-3789
Pacific Telecommunications Coun. [IO], Honolulu, HI, United States

---

A star before a book entry number signifies that the name is not listed separately, but is mentioned within the entry.

Pacific Whale Found. [5363], 300 Maalaea Rd., Ste. 211, Wailuku, HI 96793, (808)249-8811

Pacific Women's Rsrc. Bur. [IO], Noumea, New Caledonia

Pacific Women's Resources [★12244]

Pacifica Found. [18179], 1925 Martin Luther King Jr. Way, Berkeley, CA 94704, (510)849-2590

Pacifics; Leadership Educ. for Asian [9621]

Pacificulture Found. - Address unknown since 1995.

Pacifism

  Amer. Vegan Soc. [11067]

Pacifist Fellowship; Episcopal [★18614]

Pacifist Party; U.S. [18337]

Pacing and Electrophysiology; North Amer. Soc. of [★13907]

Pack Collectors Assn; Cigarette [21994]

Package Design Coun. Intl. - Address unknown since 2004.

Package Stores Assn; Natl. Retail Liquor [★193]

Packaged Ice Assn. [★1891]

Packaging

  Argentine Packaging Inst. [IO]

  Aseptic Packaging Coun. [2872]

  Australian Inst. of Packaging [IO]

  Australian Packaging Machinery Assn. [IO]

  Belgian Packaging Inst. [IO]

  BPIF Cartons [IO]

  Brazilian Packaging Assn. [IO]

  British Packaging Assn. [IO]

  Can Makers [IO]

  Canadian Corrugated Case Assn. [IO]

  Canned Vegetable Coun. [3969]

  Center for Electronic Packaging Res. [7425]

  China Packaging Fed. [IO]

  Contract Packaging Assn. [2873]

  Coopers' Company [IO]

  Corrugated Packaging Coun. [2874]

  Corrugated Sector of the Confed. of Paper Indus. [IO]

  European Assn. of Makers of Packaging Papers [IO]

  European Fed. for the Flexible Packaging Indus. [IO]

  European Food Ser. and Packaging Assn. [IO]

  European Mfrs. of Expanded Polystyrene [IO]

  European Org. for Packaging and the Env. [IO]

  Flexible Packaging Assn. [2875]

  Flexible Packaging Europe [IO]

  Fluid Sealing Assn. [2020]

  French Plastic Packaging Manufacturer's Trade Assn. [IO]

  Gift Packaging and Greeting Card Assn. of Canada [IO]

  Hong Kong Packaging Inst. [IO]

  Hungarian Assn. of Packaging and Materials Handling [IO]

  Indian Inst. of Packaging [IO]

  Indus. Coun. for Packaging and the Env. [IO]

  Inst. of Packaging Professionals [7426]

  Inst. of Packaging - South Africa [IO]

  Intl. Assn. of Diecutting and Diemaking [2029]

  Intl. Corrugated Packaging Found. [12726]

  Intl. Safe Transit Assn. [3571]

  IoP: The Packaging Soc. [IO]

  Italian Inst. of Packaging [IO]

  Lithuanian Packaging Assn. [IO]

  Metal Packaging Mfrs. Assn. [IO]

  Natl. Assn. of Metal Cans, Packagings, and Closures Mfrs. [IO]

  Natl. Inst. of Packaging, Handling and Logistics Engineers [7427]

  Packaging Assn. of Canada [IO]

  Packaging Coun. of Australia [IO]

  Packaging Coun. of Malaysia [IO]

  Packaging Coun. of South Africa [IO]

  Packaging Fed. [IO]

  Packaging and Label Gravure Assn. Global [1784]

  Packaging Machinery Mfrs. Inst. [2876]

  Paperboard Packaging Coun. [2877]

  Petroleum Packaging Coun. [2878]

  Plastics Foodservice Packaging Gp. [2879]

  Retail Packaging Assn. [2880]

  Scandinavian Packaging Assn. [IO]

  TAPPI - Tech. Assn. of the Pulp and Paper Indus. [2895]

  Thai Packaging Assn. [IO]

  Timber Packaging and Pallet Confed. [IO]

  Tube Coun. of North Am. [2881]

  Union of the Mfrs. and Consumers of Packages and Packaging Products [IO]

  Western Growers Assn. [4774]

  Women in Packaging [2882]

Packaging Assn; Brewers and Beverage [★508]

Packaging Assn. of Canada [IO], Toronto, ON, Canada

Packaging Assn; Contract [★2873]

Packaging Assn; Egg [★1157]

Packaging Assn; Intl. Beverage [508]

Packaging Assn; Natl. Flexible [★2875]

Packaging Assn; Natl. Paper Box and [★987]

Packaging Assn; Produce [★5028]

Packaging Assn; Reusable Indus. [994]

Packaging Assn; Textile Bag and [999]

Packaging and Containerization Inst; Bulk [★978]

Packaging Coun. of Australia [IO], South Melbourne, Australia

Packaging Coun; HealthCare Compliance [15934]

Packaging Coun. of Malaysia [IO], Kuala Lumpur, Malaysia

Packaging Coun. of North Am; Metal Tube [★2881]

Packaging Coun. of South Africa [IO], Sandton, Republic of South Africa

Packaging Distributors Assn. [★IO]

Packaging Education Forum - Address unknown since 2008.

Packaging Electronic Circuits; Inst. for Interconnecting and [★1221]

Packaging Fed. [IO], London, United Kingdom

Packaging and Indus. Films Assn. [IO], Nottingham, United Kingdom

Packaging; Inst. for Better [★2877]

Packaging Inst; Foodservice and [1157]

Packaging Inst; Glass [982]

Packaging Inst. Intl. [★7426]

Packaging and Label Gravure Assn. Global [1784], c/o Jim Lepp, Exec. Dir., 18481 Royal Hammock Blvd., Naples, FL 34114, (920)217-6059

Packaging and Label Gravure Association Global [IO], Naples, FL, United States

Packaging Machinery Mfrs. Inst. [2876], 4350 N Fairfax Dr., Ste. 600, Arlington, VA 22203-1632, (703)243-8555

Packaging and Marketing Assn; Produce [★5028]

Packaging Professionals; SPHE - The Soc. of [★7426]

Packaging Recyclers; Alliance of Foam [5265]

Packaging Systems; Res. and Development Associates for Military Food and [7096]

Packard and Allied Families Assn. - Address unknown since 1995.

Packard Auto. Classics [21755], PO Box 360806, Columbus, OH 43236-0806, (614)478-4946

Packard Club [21756], PO Box 360806, Columbus, OH 43236-0806, (614)478-4946

Packard Club [IO], Columbus, OH, United States

Packard Club; Eastern [21635]

Packard Convertible Roster; 1948-50 [21553]

Packard Data Bank - Address unknown since 2004.

Packard Truck Org. - Defunct.

Packard V-8 Roster, '55-'56 [21757], 84 Hoy Ave., Fords, NJ 08863, (732)738-7859

Packards Intl. Motor Car Club [21758], 302 French St., Santa Ana, CA 92701, (714)541-8431

Packards Intl. Motor Car Club [IO], Santa Ana, CA, United States

Packers Assn; Amer. Meat [★2658]

Packers Coun; Frozen Onion Ring [★1496]

Packers and Dealers Assn; Natl. Honey [1549]

Packers; Inst. of Amer. Meat [★2658]

Packet Communications Consortium; Intl. [★7771]

Packing Assn; Mech. [★2020]

Packing Soc; Intl. Microelectric and [★6930]

PACON Intl. [5011], 2525 Correa Rd., HIG 407A, Honolulu, HI 96822, (808)956-6163

PACON Intl. [IO], Honolulu, HI, United States

PACT [12439], 1200 18th St. NW, Ste. 350, Washington, DC 20036, (202)466-5666

Pact Training [11830], PO Box 106, New Kingston, NY 12459-0106, (845)586-3992

Paddle Assn; Intl. [★23678]

Paddle Canada [IO], Kingston, ON, Canada

Paddle Manitoba [IO], Winnipeg, MB, Canada

Paddle Rackets Assn; Intl. [★23678]

Paddle Steamer Preservation Soc. [IO], Worcester, United Kingdom

Paddle Tennis

  Natl. Paddleball Assn. [23092]

Paddleball Assn; Natl. [23092]

Paddlesports Assn; Professional [3650]

PADI Travel Network [★23964]

PADI Travel Network [★IO]

Padrewski Found. - Defunct.

Paediatric Dentistry; Intl. Assn. of [IO]

Paediatric Nephrology; British Assn. for [IO]

Paediatric Oncology; Intl. Soc. of [IO]

PAF Users Unlimited - Defunct.

Pagan Fed. [IO], London, United Kingdom

Pagan/Occult/Witchcraft Special Interest Gp. [10768], c/o Amer. Mensa, Ltd., 1229 Corporate Dr. W, Arlington, TX 76006-6103, (817)607-0060

Paganism

  Alternative Religions Educational Network [20457]

  Circle of Earth [20458]

  Circle Sanctuary [20570]

  Covenant of Unitarian Universalist Pagans [20459]

  Pagan Fed. [IO]

  Pagan/Occult/Witchcraft Special Interest Gp. [10768]

Pagayer Canada [★IO]

Pageant Pacifica - Defunct.

Pageant for Peace [★17916]

Pageant for Peace [★IO]

Paget Found. for Paget's Disease of Bone and Related Disorders [15256], 120 Wall St., Ste. 1602, New York, NY 10005-4001, (212)509-5335

Paget's Disease of Bone and Related Disorders; Paget Found. for [15256]

Paget's Disease Found. [★15256]

Paging Carriers; Amer. Assn. of [872]

PAHAL [IO], Jalandhar, India

Paid Circulation Comm. [★2455]

Paid Circulation Coun. [★2455]

Paid Circulation Publications; Assn. of [★2455]

Paideia Center; Natl. [8357]

Pain

  Albanian Pain Assn. [IO]

  Alliance of State Pain Initiatives [15830]

  Amer. Acad. of Craniofacial Pain [15751]

  Amer. Acad. of Pain Mgt. [15831]

  Amer. Acad. of Pain Medicine [15832]

  Amer. Bd. of Pain Medicine [15833]

  Amer. Chronic Pain Assn. [15834]

  Amer. Headache Soc. [14531]

  Amer. Pain Found. [15835]

  Amer. Pain Soc. [15836]

  Amer. Soc. of Interventional Pain Physicians [15837]

  Amer. Soc. of Pain Educators [15838]

  Asociacion Argentina para el Estudio del Dolor [IO]

  Asociacion Boliviana para Estudio and Tratamiento del Dolor [IO]

  Asociacion Chilena para el Estudio del Dolor [IO]

  Asociacion Colombiana para el Estudio del Dolor [IO]

  Asociacion Peruana para el Estudio del Dolor [IO]

  Asociacion Uruguaya para el Estudio del Dolor [IO]

  Asociacion Venezolana para el Estudio del Dolor [IO]

  Australian Pain Soc. [IO]

  BackCare, The Charity for Healthier Backs [IO]

  Bangladesh Soc. for Stud. of Pain [IO]

  Belgian Pain Soc. [IO]

  Canadian Pain Soc. [IO]

  Chinese Assn. for the Stud. of Pain, People's Republic of China [IO]

  Chinese Assn. for the Stud. of Pain, Taiwan [IO]

  Chronic Pain Assn. of Canada [IO]

  Chronic Pain Support Gp. [15839]

  Croatian Assn. for the Treatment of Pain [IO]

  Czech Pain Soc. [IO]

  Estonian Pain Soc. [IO]

  Hellenic Pain Soc. [IO]

Reference to "IO" in place of a book number signifies that the association may be found in the 45th edition of International Organizations.

Hungarian Pain Soc. [IO]
Inst. for the Stud. and Treatment of Pain (iSTOP) [IO]
International Adhesions Society [IO]
Intl. Adhesions Soc. [15840]
Intl. Assn. for the Stud. of Pain [15841]
Intl. Assn. for the Stud. of Pain [IO]
Intl. Medical and Dental Hypnotherapy Assn. [14924]
Intl. MYOPAIN Soc. [15842]
Intl. Pelvic Pain Soc. [15843]
International Pelvic Pain Society [IO]
Intl. Spine Intervention Soc. [16466]
Iranian Pain Soc. [IO]
Irish Pain Soc. [IO]
Israel Pain Assn. [IO]
Korean Pain Res. Soc. [IO]
Latvian Assn. for the Stud. of Pain [IO]
Lebanese Soc. for the Stud. of Pain [IO]
Middle East Assn. for the Stud. of Pain [IO]
Migraine Action Assn. [IO]
Natl. Assn. of Myofascial Trigger Point Therapists [16624]
Natl. Chronic Pain Outreach Assn. [15844]
Natl. Chronic Pain Soc. [15845]
Natl. Headache Found. [14533]
Natl. Pain Educ. Coun. [15846]
New Zealand Pain Soc. [IO]
North Amer. Neuromodulation Soc. [15847]
Pain Assn. of Singapore [IO]
Pain Soc. of the Philippines [IO]
Polish Soc. for the Stud. of Pain [IO]
RSDHope Gp. [15848]
Scandinavian Assn. for the Stud. of Pain [IO]
Slovenian Assn. for Pain Mgt. [IO]
Soc. of Chest Pain Centers and Providers [15849]
Soc. of Interventional Pain Mgt. Surgery Centers [16588]
Soc. for the Stud. of Pain, Nigeria [IO]
Swiss Assn. for the Stud. of Pain [IO]
Thai Assn. for the Stud. of Pain [IO]
TMJ Assn. [15850]
Tunisian Chap. of IASP [IO]
Vulval Pain Soc. [IO]
Vulvar Pain Found. [15620]
World Spine Soc. [15405]
Pain; Amer. Acad. of Craniofacial [15751]
Pain; Amer. Acad. of Orofacial [14106]
Pain Assn. of Singapore [IO], Singapore, Singapore
Pain Educ. Assn; Childbirth Without [★15607]
Pain Educ. Assn; Lamaze Birth Without [15607]
Pain Found; Vulvar [15620]
Pain Mgt; Amer. Coll. of Osteopathic Sclerotherapeutic [15796]
Pain Mgt. and Sclerotherapy [15814], 303 S Ingram Ct., Middletown, DE 19709-7935, (302)376-8080
Pain Mgt. and Sclerotherapy; Amer. Coll. of Osteopathic [★15796]
Pain Soc. [★IO]
Pain Soc. of the Philippines [IO], Quezon City, Philippines
Paine Natl. Historical Assn; Thomas [11153]
Paint, Body and Equipment Assn. - Defunct.
Paint and Decorating Retailers Assn. [2274], 403 Axminister Dr., Fenton, MO 63026-2941, (636)326-2636
Paint and Decorating Retailers Assn. [IO], Fenton, MO, United States
Paint Horse Assn; Amer. [4834]
Paint Horse Assn; Amer. Junior [4828]
Paint Mfrs. Assn; Amer. [★2884]
Paint, Oil and Varnish Assn; Natl. [★2884]
Paint Quarter Horse Assn; Amer. [★4834]
Paint Res. Assn. [★IO]
Paint Research Inst. - Defunct.
Paint Stock Horse Assn; Amer. [★4834]
Paint Tech; Fed. of Societies for [★6704]
Paint, Varnish and Lacquer Assn; Natl. [★2884]
Paint and Varnish Production Clubs; Fed. of [★6704]
Paint and Wallcovering Dealers Assn; Southern [★2274]
Paint and Wallpaper Assn. of Am. [★2274]
Paint and Wallpaper Assn. of Am. [★IO]
Paint and Wallpaper Distributors of Am; Retail [★2274]

Paintball
Amer. Paintball Players Assn. [23645]
Natl. Collegiate Paintball Assn. [23646]
United Kingdom Paintball Sports Fed. [IO]
Painted Desert Sheep Soc. [5215], c/o Anita Garza, Founder/Registrar, 11819 Puska Rd., Needville, TX 77461, (979)793-4207
Painted Soda Bottles Collectors Assn. - Address unknown since 1999.
Painter of America - Defunct.
Painter-Stainers' Company [IO], London, United Kingdom
Painters and Allied Trades; Intl. Brotherhood of [★12082]
Painters; British Soc. of Master Glass [IO]
Painters in Casein and Acrylic; Natl. Soc. of [9518]
Painters, Decorators and Paperhangers of Am; Brotherhood of [★12082]
Painters of Glass; Worshipful Company of Glaziers' and [IO]
Painters; Natl. Soc. of Mural [9517]
Painters and Sculptors; Assn. of Women [★9514]
Painters and Sculptors; Fed. of Modern [9502]
Painters, Sculptors and Gravers; Royal Soc. of Miniature [IO]
Painters; Soc. of Decorative [22175]
Painters' Soc; Natl. Oil and Acrylic [9459]
Painters in Water Colours; Royal Inst. of [IO]
Painting; Amer. Artists of Chinese Brush [9538]
Painting Coun; Steel Structures [★2885]
Painting Craft Teachers; Assn. of [IO]
Painting and Decorating Assn. of Great Britain [IO], Nuneaton, United Kingdom
Painting and Decorating Contractors of Am. [1057], 1801 Park 270 Dr., Ste. 220, St. Louis, MO 63146, (314)514-7322
Painting, Decorating and Drywall Apprenticeship and Manpower Training Fund; Intl. Joint [★12082]
Painting, Decorating, and Drywall Apprenticeship and Manpower Training Fund; Natl. [★12082]
Painting, Decorating, and Drywall Apprenticeship and Training Comm; Natl. Joint [★12082]
Paintmakers Assn. [★IO]
Paints and Finishes
Amer. Artists of Chinese Brush Painting [9538]
Assn. of Dutch Wholesalers in Paint [IO]
Australian Paint Mfrs. Fed. [IO]
British Coatings Fed. [IO]
Color Guild Associates [2883]
European Coun. of the Paint, Printing Ink and Artists' Colours Indus. [IO]
Fed. of the Associations of Technicians of the Paint, Varnish, Enamel, and Printing Ink Indus. of Continental Europe [IO]
Fed. of Paints, Inks, Glues and Adhesives Indus. [IO]
Independent Professional Painting Contractors Assn. of Am. [1019]
Intl. Union of Painters and Allied Trades [24146]
Intl. Union of Painters and Allied Trades/Joint Apprenticeship and Training Fund [12082]
Japan Paint Mfrs. Assn. [IO]
Master Painters Assn. of Finland [IO]
Natl. Acrylic Painters' Assn. [IO]
Natl. Guild of Decoupeurs [22168]
Natl. Paint and Coatings Assn. [2884]
Natl. Paint and Ink Mfrs'. Assn. [IO]
Oil and Colour Chemists' Assn. [IO]
Painter-Stainers' Company [IO]
Painting and Decorating Contractors of Am. [1057]
PRA Coatings Tech. Centre [IO]
Set Decorators Soc. of Am. [2276]
Shellac Export Promotion Coun. [IO]
Soc. of Decorative Painters [22175]
South African Paint Mfrs. Assn. [IO]
Spanish Paint and Printing Inks Manufactures' Assn. [IO]
SSPC: The Society for Protective Coatings [IO]
SSPC: The Soc. for Protective Coatings [2885]
Swedish Paint Trade Fed. [IO]
Transocean Marine Paint Assn. [IO]
Pairing Proj; Ground Zero [17894]
Pairpoint Cup Plate Collectors of America - Defunct.
Pairti Soisialta Daonlathach an Lucht Oibre [★IO]

Paisley Family Soc. [21020], c/o Martha Pasley Milam Brown, USA Commissioner, 2205 Pine Knoll Cir., Conyers, GA 30013
Pajama and Sportswear Manufacturers; Natl. Assn. of Skirt, [★221]
Pakistan
Assn. of Pakistani Physicians of North Am. [15993]
Kashmiri Amer. Coun. [12753]
Pakistan Chamber of Commerce USA [24364]
Pakistan Chamber of Commerce USA [IO]
Pakistan Welfare Org. [13182]
Pakistani Amer. Bus. Executives Assn. [758]
REFORMERS, Pakistan [IO]
Rising Leaders [18005]
Pakistan Acad. of Sciences [IO], Islamabad, Pakistan
Pakistan Advertisers Soc. [IO], Karachi, Pakistan
Pakistan Advt. Assn. [IO], Karachi, Pakistan
Pakistan - Amer. Businesses Assn. - Address unknown since 2002.
Pakistan Assn. of Automotive Parts and Accessories Manufacturers [IO], Lahore, Pakistan
Pakistan Assn. of Dermatologists [IO], Karachi, Pakistan
Pakistan Assn. for Small and Medium Enterprises [IO], Karachi, Pakistan
Pakistan Banks' Assn. [IO], Karachi, Pakistan
Pakistan Cardiac Soc. [IO], Karachi, Pakistan
Pakistan Chamber of Commerce USA [IO], Houston, TX, United States
Pakistan Chamber of Commerce USA [24364], 9700 Club Creek Dr., Ste. E, Houston, TX 77036, (713)771-9628
Pakistan Comm. for Democracy and Justice - Defunct.
Pakistan Cotton Ginners' Assn. [IO], Multan, Pakistan
Pakistan Coun. of Appropriate Tech. [★IO]
Pakistan Coun. of Renewable Energy Tech. [IO], Karachi, Pakistan
Pakistan Cricket Bd. [IO], Lahore, Pakistan
Pakistan DanceSport Fed. [IO], Lahore, Pakistan
Pakistan Fed. Baseball and Softball [IO], Lahore, Pakistan
Pakistan Fed. of Floorball [IO], Faisalabad, Pakistan
Pakistan Fed. of Univ. Women [IO], Karachi, Pakistan
Pakistan Flying Disc Fed. [IO], Gujranwala, Pakistan
Pakistan Footwear Mfrs. Assn. [IO], Lahore, Pakistan
Pakistan Geotechnical Engg. Soc. [IO], Lahore, Pakistan
Pakistan Hosiery Manufacturers Assn. [IO], Karachi, Pakistan
Pakistan Huntington Disease Soc. [IO], Peshawar, Pakistan
Pakistan Hypertension League [IO], Karachi, Pakistan
Pakistan Inst. of Intl. Affairs [IO], Karachi, Pakistan
Pakistan Natl. Rose Soc. [IO], Islamabad, Pakistan
Pakistan Occupational Therapy Assn. [IO], Karachi, Pakistan
Pakistan Physiological Soc. [IO], Karachi, Pakistan
Pakistan Press Found. [IO], Karachi, Pakistan
Pakistan Readymade Garments Mfrs'. and Exporters' Assn. [IO], Karachi, Pakistan
Pakistan Red Crescent Soc. [IO], Islamabad, Pakistan
Pakistan Sailing Fed. [IO], Karachi, Pakistan
Pakistan School Sports Assn. [IO], Karachi, Pakistan
Pakistan Ship's Agents Assn. [IO], Karachi, Pakistan
Pakistan Small Indus'. Assn. [IO], Karachi, Pakistan
Pakistan Soc. of Gastroenterology and G.I. Endoscopy [IO], Karachi, Pakistan
Pakistan Software Export Bd. [IO], Islamabad, Pakistan
Pakistan Software Houses Assn. [IO], Islamabad, Pakistan
Pakistan Sports Medicine Assn. [IO], Karachi, Pakistan
Pakistan Squash Fed. [IO], Islamabad, Pakistan
Pakistan Student's Assn. of America - Address unknown since 1995.
Pakistan Sugar Mills Assn. [IO], Islamabad, Pakistan

A star before a book entry number signifies that the name is not listed separately, but is mentioned within the entry.

Pakistan Taekwondo Fed. [IO], Lahore, Pakistan
Pakistan Tennis Fed. [IO], Islamabad, Pakistan
Pakistan Touch Ball Fed. [IO], Faisalabad, Pakistan
Pakistan Tourism Development Corp. [IO], Islamabad, Pakistan
Pakistan Voluntary Hea. and Nutrition Assn. [IO], Karachi, Pakistan
Pakistan Welfare Org. [IO], Houston, TX, United States
Pakistan Welfare Org. [13182], PO Box 20328, Houston, TX 77025-0328, (713)851-0834

Pakistani
Assn. of Pakistani Physicians of North Am. [15993]
Org. of Pakistani Entrepreneurs of North Am. [756]
Pakistan Chamber of Commerce USA [24364]
Pakistan Welfare Org. [13182]
Pakistani Amer. Bus. Executives Assn. [758]
Rising Leaders [18005]
Pakistani Amer. Bus. Executives Assn. [758], 23105 Kashiwa Ct., Torrance, CA 90505, (310)534-1505
Pakistani Amer. Bus. Executives Assn. [IO], Torrance, CA, United States
Pakistani Physicians; Assn. of [★15993]
Pakistani Physicians of North Am; Assn. of [15993]
Pakolaisneuvonta [★IO]
Palaeontographical Soc. - United Kingdom [IO], London, United Kingdom
Palaeontological Assn. [IO], Aberystwyth, United Kingdom
Palaeontological Soc. of Japan [IO], Tokyo, Japan
Palate Assn; Amer. Cleft [★14055]
Palate-Craniofacial Assn; Amer. Cleft [14055]
Palate Prosthesis; Amer. Acad. of Cleft [★14055]
Palate Rehabilitation; Amer. Assn. for Cleft [★14055]
Palatines to Am.: Researching German-Speaking Ancestry [21141], 611 E Weber Rd., Columbus, OH 43211-1097, (614)267-4700
Palatines to Am.: Researching German-Speaking Ancestry [IO], Columbus, OH, United States
Palau Evangelistic Team; Luis [★20022]
Palau Tennis Fed. [IO], Koror, Palau
Palau Weightlifting Assn. [IO], Koror, Palau
Paleontological Res. Institution/Museum of the Earth [7429], 1259 Trumansburg Rd., Ithaca, NY 14850, (607)273-6623
Paleontological Soc. [7430], c/o Prof. Roger D.K. Thomas, Sec., PO Box 3003, Lancaster, PA 17604-3003, (717)291-4135
Paleontological Soc. [IO], Lancaster, PA, United States
Paleontological Society [IO], Munich, Germany
Paleontologists and Mineralogists; Soc. of Economic [★7432]

Paleontology
Amer. Elasmobranch Soc. [7278]
Amer. Teilhard Assn. [9632]
Argentine Paleontological Assn. [IO]
Assn. of Australasian Palaeontologists [IO]
Cushman Found. for Foraminiferal Res. [7428]
Dinosaur Soc. [IO]
Evolutionary Anthropology Soc. [6416]
Intl. Assn. for the Stud. of Fossil Cnidaria and Porifera [IO]
Intl. Biogeography Soc. [7122]
Palaeontographical Soc. - United Kingdom [IO]
Palaeontological Assn. [IO]
Palaeontological Soc. of Japan [IO]
Paleontological Res. Institution/Museum of the Earth [7429]
Paleontological Soc. [7430]
Paleontological Society [IO]
Paleontological Soc. [IO]
Paleopathology Assn. [7431]
Soc. for Sedimentary Geology [7432]
Soc. of Vertebrate Paleontology [7433]
Society of Vertebrate Paleontology [IO]
Paleontology; French Amateur Fed. of Mineralogy and [IO]
Paleontology and Systematics of Natl. Res. Coun; Comm. on Common Problems of Genetics, [★7073]
Paleopathology Assn. [7431], c/o Ann L.W. Stodder, Treas., Dept. of Anthropology, Univ. of Wisconsin Milwaukee, PO Box 413, Milwaukee, WI 53201

Paleopathology Club [★7431]
Palestine
Amer. Task Force on Palestine [17860]
Birzeit Soc. [9394]
Friends of Sabeel - North Am. [18205]
Jewish Peace Lobby [17614]
A Jewish Voice for Peace [19184]
Jews Against the Occupation [17952]
Middle East Children's Alliance [17774]
Palestine Liberation Org. [18069]
Rebuilding Alliance [12336]
Palestine Affairs Center [★18069]
Palestine Aid Soc. of Am. - Address unknown since 2004.
Palestine Arab Delegation - Defunct.
Palestine Badminton Fed. [IO], Palestine, Israel
Palestine Center [8627], 2425 Virginia Ave. NW, Washington, DC 20037, (202)338-1290
Palestine; Center for Policy Anal. on [★8627]
Palestine Cong. of North America - Defunct.
Palestine Fund; Amer. [★10251]
Palestine Human Rights Information Center Intl. - Address unknown since 1999.
Palestine Info. Off. [★18069]
Palestine Institutions; Amer. Fund for [★10251]
Palestine/Israel; Search for Justice and Equality in [18071]
Palestine Liberation Org. [18069], c/o Fed. of Amer. Scientists, 1717 K St. NW, Ste. 209, Washington, DC 20036, (202)546-3300
Palestine; Natl. Comm. for Labor [★12460]
Palestine; Natl. Labor Comm. for the Jewish Workers in [★12460]
Palestine Philatelic Soc. of Am; Israel- [★22874]
Palestine Pioneer Found. - Address unknown since 1995.
Palestine Res. and Educational Center - Defunct.
Palestine; Search for Justice and Equality in [★18071]
Palestine Solidarity Comm. - Address unknown since 1999.
Palestine Study Group [22853]
Palestine Symphonic Choir Project - Address unknown since 1995.
Palestine; Women's League for [★20194]
Palestinian
Amer. Fed. of Ramallah, Palestine [9392]
Amer. Near East Refugee Aid [12804]
Partners for Peace [18230]
Rebuilding Alliance [12336]
Scholars for Peace in the Middle East [18070]
StandWithUs [17941]
Palestinian Academic Soc. for the Stud. of Intl. Affairs [IO], Jerusalem, Israel
Palestinian Agricultural Relief Comm. [IO], Jerusalem, Israel
Palestinian Family Planning and Protection Assn. [IO], Jerusalem, Israel
Palestinian Hydrology Gp. [★IO]
Palestinian Hydrology Gp. for Water and Environmental Resources Development [IO], Ramallah, Israel
Palestinian Info. Tech. Assn. of Companies [IO], Jerusalem, Israel
Palestinian Peace; America-Israel Coun. for Israeli- [18047]
Palestinian Tennis Assn. [IO], Palestine, Israel
Pali Text Soc. [IO], Lancaster, United Kingdom
Pallet and Container Assn; Natl. Wooden [989]
Pallet Manufacturers Assn; Natl. Wooden [★989]
Palliative Care Assn. of Alberta [IO], Stony Plain, AB, Canada
Palliative Care Assn. of NSW [IO], Kings Cross, Australia
Palliative Care; Center to Advance [14875]
Palliative Care Org; Natl. Hospice and [14856]
Palliative Care Policy Center [14082], RAND Hea., 1200 S Hayes St., Ste. 6402, Arlington, VA 22202-5050, (703)413-1100
Palliative Care Victoria [IO], Melbourne, Australia
Palliative Medicine; Amer. Acad. of Hospice and [15985]
Palliative Nurses Assn; Hospice and [15482]
Pallotti Center [★20390]
Pallotti Center for Apostolic Development; St. Vincent [20390]

Palm Soc. [★6640]
Palm Soc. [★IO]
Palmtherapy Assn; Intl. [16621]
Palomino Horse Assn. [4941], Rte. 1, Box 125, Nelson, MO 65347, (660)859-2064
Palomino Horse Breeders of Am. [4942], 15253 E Skelly Dr., Tulsa, OK 74116-2637, (918)438-1234
Palomino Rabbit Co-Breeders Assn. [5158], c/o Deb Morrison, Sec., 396202 W 4000 Rd., Skiatook, OK 74070, (918)396-3587
Palsy Assn; Natl. Brachial Plexus-Erb's [14277]
Palsy Athletic Assn; U.S. Cerebral [★23353]
Palsy and Developmental Medicine; Amer. Acad. for Cerebral [13934]
Palsy Res. and Educational Found; United Cerebral [★13935]
Palsy; Soc. for Progressive Supranuclear [14286]
PALTEX - Expanded Textbook and Instructional Materials Prog. [9261], 525 23rd St. NW, Washington, DC 20037, (202)974-3451
Palynology
Amer. Assn. of Stratigraphic Palynologists [7434]
Amer. Assn. of Stratigraphic Palynologists [IO]
Canadian Assn. of Palynologists [IO]
Commn. Internationale de Microflore du Paleozoique [IO]
Pam Tillis Fan Club [24956], PO Box 128575, Nashville, TN 37212
Pambansang Sanggunian sa Pananaliksik ng Pilipinas [★IO]
Pamphlet Soc. of the U.S; Catholic [19603]
Pamunkey Project - Defunct.
Pan-African Assn. of Neurological Sciences [IO], Nairobi, Kenya
Pan-African Assn. of Plastic and Reconstructive Surgeons [IO], Johannesburg, Republic of South Africa
Pan African Business Information Center - Address unknown since 1995.
Pan African Chiropractic Assn. [★IO]
Pan African Fed. of the Disabled [IO], Zanzibar, United Republic of Tanzania
Pan African Inst. for Development - Burkina Faso [IO], Ouagadougou, Burkina Faso
Pan African Postal Union [IO], Arusha, United Republic of Tanzania
Pan African Resource Center - Address unknown since 1995.
Pan-African Soc. of Cardiology [IO], Yaounde, Cameroon
Pan African Students Org. in the Americas - Address unknown since 1995.
Pan-American Acridological Soc. [★7065]
Pan-American Acridological Soc. [★IO]
Pan Amer. Aero Collectors Club - Defunct.
Pan-American Aerobiology Assn. [6592], c/o Michael L. Muilenberg, Membership Sec.-Treas., Harvard School of Public Hea., SPH-1, G-33, 665 Huntington Ave., Boston, MA 02115, (617)432-0642
Pan-American Aerobiology Assn. [IO], Boston, MA, United States
Pan-Amer. Airmail Collectors Club - Address unknown since 2007.
Pan-American Allergy Soc. [13604], PO Box 700587, San Antonio, TX 78270-0587, (210)495-9853
Pan-American Alumni Assn; Univ. of Texas - [18939]
Pan Amer. Assn. of Anatomy [13669]
Pan Amer. Assn. of Biochemical Societies [★6551]
Pan Amer. Assn. of Biochemical Societies [★IO]
Pan-American Assn. for Biochemistry and Molecular Biology [IO], East Lansing, MI, United States
Pan-American Assn. for Biochemistry and Molecular Biology [6551], c/o Dr. Jack Preiss, Michigan State Univ., Dept. of Biochemistry and Molecular, East Lansing, MI 48824-1319, (517)353-3137
Pan-American Assn. of Educational Credit Institutions [IO], Bogota, Colombia
Pan-American Assn. of Ophthalmology [IO], Arlington, TX, United States
Pan-American Assn. of Ophthalmology [15699], 1301 S Bowen Rd., Ste. 365, Arlington, TX 76013, (817)275-7553
Pan-Amer. Biodeterioration Soc. - Address unknown since 2003.

Reference to "IO" in place of a book number signifies that the association may be found in the 45th edition of International Organizations.

Pan Amer. Cancer Cytology Soc. - Defunct.

Pan Amer. Center for Sanitary Engg. and Environmental Sciences [IO], Lima, Peru

Pan Amer. Coffee Bur. - Defunct.

Pan Amer. Coun. for the Preservation of the Hellenic Orthodox Church and the Hellenic Language [20074]

Pan Amer. Development Found. [16979], 1889 F St. NW, Washington, DC 20006, (202)458-3969

Pan Amer. Development Found. [IO], Washington, DC, United States

Pan-American Fed. of Consultants [IO], Rio de Janeiro, Brazil

Pan Amer. Found. - Defunct.

Pan Amer. Hea. and Educ. Found. [12536], 525 23rd St. NW, Washington, DC 20037, (202)974-3416

Pan Amer. Hea. and Educ. Found. [IO], Washington, DC, United States

Pan Amer. Hea. Org. [IO], Washington, DC, United States

Pan Amer. Hea. Org. [14592], 525 23rd St. NW, Washington, DC 20037, (202)974-3000

Pan Amer. Highway Congresses - Defunct.

Pan Amer. Indian Assn. [10753], c/o Loving Hands Inst., 639 11th St., Fortuna, CA 95540, (707)725-9627

Pan Amer. Inst. of Geography and History [IO], Mexico City, Mexico

Pan Amer. Inst. of Mining, Engineering and Geology, U.S. Sect. - Defunct.

Pan-American Inst. of Naval Engg. [IO], Rio de Janeiro, Brazil

Pan-American Junior Golf Assn; Natl. [23459]

Pan Amer. Liaison Comm. of Women's Orgs. - Address unknown since 2001.

Pan Amer. Medical Assn. - Address unknown since 2006.

Pan Amer. Odontological Assn. - Defunct.

Pan Amer. Round Tables in the U.S. - Defunct.

Pan Amer. Sanitary Bur. [14593], c/o Pan Amer. Hea. Org., 525 23rd St. NW, Washington, DC 20037, (202)974-3000

Pan Amer. Sanitary Bur. [IO], Washington, DC, United States

Pan Amer. Standards Commn. [IO], Caracas, Venezuela

Pan Amer. Taekwondo Union [IO], Colorado Springs, CO, United States

Pan Amer. Taekwondo Union [23602], c/o Mr. David Askinas, Co-VP, One Olympic Plz., Ste. 104C, Colorado Springs, CO 80909, (719)866-4632

Pan Amer. Tung Res. and Development League - Defunct.

Pan Amer. Union [★16978]

Pan Amer. Union [★IO]

Pan Amer. Union of Baptist Men - Defunct.

Pan-American Union of Karatedo Organizations [23564], 1300 Kenmore Blvd., Akron, OH 44314, (330)753-3114

Pan-American Union of Karatedo Organizations [IO], Akron, OH, United States

Pan-Amer. Weightlifting Confed. - Address unknown since 1999.

Pan Amer. Women's Assn. - Address unknown since 1994.

Pan Arab Osteoporosis Soc. [IO], Dubai, United Arab Emirates

Pan Arcadian Fed. of Am. [19090], 880 N York Rd., Elmhurst, IL 60126, (630)833-1900

Pan-Dodecanesian Assn. of Am. "Xanthos O Philikos" 19091

Pan-Hellenic Conf; Central Off. Executives Assn. of Natl. [24477]

Pan-Hellenic Coun; Natl. [24484]

Pan-Hellenic Editors Conf; Natl. [24448]

Pan Hellenic Soc. Inventors of Greece in U.S.A. - Defunct.

Pan Mac Junior Chamber [★IO]

Pan-Macedonian Assn. - Address unknown since 2002.

Pan Pacific Centers - Defunct.

Pan Pacific Public Relations Fed. - Defunct.

Pan-Pacific and South-East Asia Women's Assn. [IO], Turramurra, Australia

Pan-Pacific and Southeast Asia Women's Assn. of the U.S.A. [17907], PO Box 1531, Madison Sq. Sta., New York, NY 10159

Pan-Pacific Surgical Assn. - Address unknown since 2000.

Pan-Rhodian Soc. of America - Address unknown since 1988.

PanAfrican Assn; Panamerican/ [17371]

Pan-Albanian Fed. of America, VATRA - Address unknown since 1995.

Panama League Against Epilepsy [IO], Panama City, Panama

Panamanian Assn. for Planned Parenthood [IO], Panama City, Panama

Panamanian Comm. for Human Rights - Address unknown since 1994.

Panamanian Food Retailers and Distributors Assn. [IO], Panama City, Panama

Panamerican Cultural Circle [IO], Cedar Grove, NJ, United States

Panamerican Cultural Circle [10312], PO Box 469, Cedar Grove, NJ 07009-0469, (973)239-3125

Panamerican Dairy Fed. [IO], Montevideo, Uruguay

Panamerican/PanAfrican Assn. [17371], London Park Towers, 5375 Duke St., Ste. 1210, Alexandria, VA 22304, (703)567-1441

PanAmerican Soc. for Pigment Cell Res. [15111], c/o Dr. Raymond E. Boissy, Sec.-Treas., Dept. of Dermatology, Univ. of Cincinnati, 231 Bethesda Ave., Cincinnati, OH 45267-0592

Pancreatic Assn; Intl. Hepato-Biliary [★14802]

Pancreatic Cancer Action Network [15851], 2141 Rosecrans Ave., Ste. 7000, El Segundo, CA 90245, (310)725-0025

Pancreatic Diseases

   European Pancreatic Club [IO]

   Indian Chap. of Intl. Hepato Pancreato Biliary Assn. [IO]

   Pancreatic Cancer Action Network [15851]

Pancreato-Biliary Assn; Intl. Hepato- [★14802]

Pancretan Assn. of America - Address unknown since 1988.

Pancyprian Assn. of America - Defunct.

Pancyprian Assn. for the Mentally Handicapped Persons [★IO]

Pancyprian Fed. of Labor [IO], Nicosia, Cyprus

Pancyprian Veterinary Assn. [IO], Nicosia, Cyprus

Panel on Alternate Approaches to Graduate Education - Defunct.

Panel Assn; Radiant [1898]

Panel Assn; Structural Insulated [675]

Panel Outdoor Advt. Assn; Junior [★99]

Panel Report - Address unknown since 2003.

Panel on Santa Barbara Oil Spill - Defunct.

Panel on World Data Centers [7210], 325 Broadway, Boulder, CO 80305

Panel on World Data Centers [IO], Boulder, CO, United States

Panelized Building Systems Coun. [2531], c/o Natl. Assn. of Home Builders, 1201 15th St. NW, Washington, DC 20005, (202)266-8200

Panepirotic Fed. of America, Canada, and Australia - Address unknown since 2002.

Panetics; Intl. Soc. for [18621]

Paneuropean Union [★IO]

PANGEA - Comunicacio per a la Cooperacio [IO], Barcelona, Spain

Panhard and Deutsch Bonnet; Les Amis de [21686]

Panhellenic Assn. of Central Off. Executives; Natl. [★24477]

Panhellenic Assn. of Landscape Architects [IO], Athens, Greece

Panhellenic Assn; Professional [★24488]

Panhellenic Conf. of Central Off. Executives; Natl. [★24477]

Panhellenic Conf; Natl. [24485]

Panhellenic Physiotherapists Assn. [IO], Athens, Greece

Panic, Anxiety, and Depression Assistance [IO], Glen Iris, Australia

Panic Anxiety Disorder Assn. [IO], Adelaide, Australia

Panic Anxiety Disorder Assn. (Queensland) [IO], Stafford, Australia

Panic Attack Syndrome

   Anxiety Disorders Assn. of Am. [12743]

TERRAP Programs [12748]

Panimo-ja Virvoitusjuomateollisuusliitto [★IO]

Pankration Athlima; USA Fed. of [23066]

Pankypria Ergatiki Omospondia [★IO]

Pannellinios Syllogos Epikiaston [IO], Athens, Greece

Panos Inst. [IO], Washington, DC, United States

Panos Inst. [12440], Webster House, 1718 P St. NW, Ste. T-6, Washington, DC 20036, (202)429-0730

Panos Inst. - London [IO], London, United Kingdom

Panos Inst. - Western Africa [IO], Dakar, Senegal

Pansophic Inst. - Defunct.

Pantera Intl. [21759], 330 Central Ave., No. 25, Fillmore, CA 93015, (805)524-5248

Pantera Intl. [IO], Fillmore, CA, United States

Pantera Intl. - Defunct.

Pantera Owners Club of Am. [21760], PO Box 3574, San Dimas, CA 91773, (714)897-6964

Pantheist Soc; Universal [20586]

Pantheon de l'Aviation de Canada [★IO]

Panthers Proj. Fund; Gray [★11287]

Panthessalonikan Athletic Org. of Konstantinople [IO], Melbourne, Australia

Pantone Color Inst. [★6707]

Papal Volunteers for Latin America - Defunct.

Paper

   100% Recycled Paperboard Alliance [2886]

   Amer. Forest and Paper Assn. [4679]

   Amer. Soc. of Check Collectors [22726]

   Appita [IO]

   Appita - Tech. Assn. for the Australian and New Zealand Pulp and Paper Indus. [IO]

   ASSOCARTA - Italian Assn. of Paper, Cardboard and Pulp Mfrs. [IO]

   Assn. of the Austrian Paper Indus. [IO]

   Assn. of Belgian Pulp, Paper and Bd. Producers [IO]

   Assn. of Makers of Printings and Writings [IO]

   Assn. of Nordic Paper Historians [IO]

   Assn. of Polish Papermakers [IO]

   Assn. of the Pulp and Paper Indus. [IO]

   Assn. of Spanish Pulp and Paper Manufactures [IO]

   Assn. of Suppliers to the Paper Indus. [2003]

   Assn. of Western Pulp and Paper Workers [24064]

   Brazilian Corrugated Bd. Assn. [IO]

   British Assn. of Paper Historians [IO]

   British Wood Pulp Assn. [IO]

   Canadian Paper Box Mfrs. Assn. [IO]

   Center for Book Arts [9745]

   Confed. of European Paper Indus. [IO]

   Confed. of Paper Indus. [IO]

   Corrugated Bd. Manufacturers Assn. [IO]

   Corrugated Packaging Coun. [2874]

   Environmental and Tech. Assn. for the Paper Sack Indus. [IO]

   European Carton Makers Assn. [IO]

   European Liaison Comm. for Pulp and Paper [IO]

   Fed. of the Paper and Bd. Converting Indus. [IO]

   Fibre Box Assn. [2887]

   Finnish Paper Engineers' Assn. [IO]

   Forest Products Assn. of Canada [IO]

   French Confed. of the Paper, Cardboard and Cellulose Indus. [IO]

   German Pulp and Paper Assn. [IO]

   German Pulp and Paper Chemists and Engineers Assn. [IO]

   Guild of Amer. Papercutters [22157]

   Guild of Book Workers [9750]

   Independent Waste Paper Processors Assn. [IO]

   Indonesian Pulp and Paper Assn. [IO]

   Inst. of Paper [IO]

   Inst. of Paper Conservation [IO]

   Institute of Paper Science and Technology [IO]

   Inst. of Paper Sci. and Tech. [7435]

   Intl. Assn. of Hand Papermakers and Paper Artists [IO]

   Intl. Assn. of Paper Historians [IO]

   Intl. Assn. of Papyrologists [IO]

   Intl. Bond and Share Soc. [22046]

   Intl. Gonfed. of Paper and Bd. Converters in Europe [IO]

   Intl. Molded Pulp Environmental Packaging Assn. [IO]

A star before a book entry number signifies that the name is not listed separately, but is mentioned within the entry.

Intl. Molded Pulp Environmental Packaging Assn. [2888]
Intl. Paperweight Soc. [22776]
Intl. Thermographers Assn. [2889]
Intl. Vintage Poster Dealers Assn. [106]
Korea Paper Manufacturers' Assn. [IO]
Mfrs. of Educational and Commercial Stationery European Assn. [IO]
Manuscript Soc. [22068]
Mexican Pulp and Paper Indus'. Assn. [IO]
Natl. Assn. of Paper and Advt. Collectors [22412]
Natl. Assn. of Paper Merchants [IO]
Natl. Assn. of Paperstock Women [2890]
Natl. Coun. for Air and Stream Improvement [4690]
Natl. Guild of Decoupeurs [22168]
Natl. Guild of Professional Paperhangers [2270]
Natl. Off. Paper Recycling Proj. [3999]
Natl. Valentine Collectors' Assn. [22090]
North Amer. Quilling Guild [21541]
Norwegian Pulp and Paper Indus. Assn. [IO]
NPTA Alliance [2891]
Origami USA [22771]
Painting and Decorating Contractors of Am. [1057]
Paper Agents' Assn. [IO]
Paper, Allied-Indus., Chem. and Energy Workers Intl. Union [24211]
Paper Distribution Coun. [2892]
Paper Fed. of Great Britain [IO]
Paper Indus. Mgt. Assn. [2893]
Paper Indus. Tech. Assn. [IO]
Paper Machine Clothing Coun. [2056]
Paper and Pulp Processing Indus. Assn. [IO]
Paper Shipping Sack Manufacturers' Assn. [991]
Paper Stock Indus. Chap. of ISRI [4002]
Paperboard Packaging Coun. [2877]
PIRA Intl. [IO]
Portuguese Assn. for Technicians of the Pulp and Paper Indus. [IO]
Portuguese Paper Indus. Assn. [IO]
Professional Currency Dealers Assn. [22753]
Pulp and Paper Indus. Fed. of the Slovak Republic [IO]
Pulp and Paper Res. and Tech. Center [IO]
Pulp and Paper Safety Assn. [7436]
Recycled Paperboard Tech. Assn. [993]
Sales Assn. of the Paper Indus. [2894]
Slovenian Assn. of Pulp and Paper Engineers and Technicians [IO]
Spanish Paper Inst. [IO]
Swiss Pulp, Paper and Cardboard Indus. Assn. [IO]
TAPPI - Tech. Assn. of the Pulp and Paper Indus. [2895]
Tissue Sector [IO]
United Paperworkers Intl. Union [24104]
Universal Autograph Collectors Club [22126]
Venezuelan Assn. of Paper, Pulp and Carton Producers [IO]
Paper and Advt. Collectors; Natl. Assn. of [22412]
Paper Agents' Assn. [IO], Fleet, United Kingdom
Paper, Allied-Indus., Chem. and Energy Workers Intl. Union [24211]
Paper Assn; Amer. Forest and [4679]
Paper Bag Inst. - Defunct.
Paper Box Assn. of Am; Folding [★2877]
Paper Box Assn; Natl. [★987]
Paper Box Manufacturers Assn; Natl. [★987]
Paper Box Mfrs'. Assn; Pacific Coast [990]
Paper Box and Packaging Assn; Natl. [★987]
Paper Can Assn. - Defunct.
Paper Converters Assn. - Defunct.
Paper Cup and Container Inst. [★1157]
Paper Distribution Coun. [2892], c/o NPTA Alliance, 500 Bi-County Blvd., Ste. 200E, Farmingdale, NY 11735, (631)777-2223
Paper Doll Artists Guild; Original [22405]
Paper Express [★2895]
Paper Fed. of Great Britain [IO], Swindon, United Kingdom
Paper Indus; Assn. of Suppliers to the [2003]
Paper Indus. Mgt. Assn. [2893], 15 Tech. Pkwy. S, Norcross, GA 30092, (770)209-7230
Paper Indus; Sales Assn. of the [2894]

Paper Indus; Salesmen's Assn. of the [★2894]
Paper Indus. Tech. Assn. [IO], Bury, United Kingdom
Paper Inst; Linen and Lace [★1157]
Paper Inst; Waxed [★2875]
Paper Machine Clothing Coun. [2056]
Paper Machinery Assn; Amer. [★2003]
Paper Machinery Assn; Pulp and [★2003]
Paper Machinery Mfrs. Assn; Pulp and [★2003]
Paper Makers Advertising Assn. - Defunct.
Paper Mill Fourdrinier Wire Cloth Mfrs. Assn. [★2056]
Paper Mill Superintendents Assn; Amer. Pulp and [★2893]
Paper Money Collectors; Soc. of [22757]
Paper Money Soc; Latin Amer. [22741]
Paper Pail Assn. - Defunct.
Paper and Plastic Representatives Mgt. Coun. [2645], PO Box 150229, Arlington, TX 76015, (682)518-6008
Paper Plate Assn. [★1157]
Paper and Pulp Processing Indus. Assn. [IO], Vienna, Austria
Paper Recycling Proj; Natl. Off. [3999]
Paper Safety Assn; Pulp and [7436]
Paper Safety Assn; Southern Pulp and [★7436]
Paper Shipping Sack Manufacturers' Assn. [991], 520 E Oxford St., Coopersburg, PA 18036, (610)282-6845
Paper Soc. for the Overseas Blind - Defunct.
Paper Stock Indus. Chap. of ISRI [4002], 3300 PGA Blvd., Ste. 635, Palm Beach Gardens, FL 33410-2811, (561)627-9191
Paper Stock Inst. of Am; PSI Chap. [★4002]
Paper and Twine Assn. - Address unknown since 1995.
Paper Workers; Assn. of Western Pulp and [24064]
Paperback Assn; Educational [3221]
Paperboard Packaging Coun. [2877], 201 N Union St., Ste. 220, Alexandria, VA 22314-2651, (703)836-3300
Paperboard Tech. Assn; Recycled [993]
Paperbox Assn; Natl. [987]
Papercutters; Guild of Amer. [22157]
Paperhangers of Am; Brotherhood of Painters, Decorators and [★12082]
Paperhangers; Guild of Professional [★2270]
Paperhangers; Natl. Guild of Professional [2270]
Paperless Entry Processing User Group - Defunct.
Papermakers Felt Assn. - Address unknown since 1995.
Papers of Am; Independent Free [3226]
Papers; Assn. of Free Community [88]
The Papers of Jefferson Davis [★11129]
Papers; Midwest Free Community [3236]
Paperweight Collectors' Assn. [22102], PO Box 4153, Emerald Isle, NC 28594, (336)869-2769
Paperweight Soc; Intl. [22776]

Paperweights
    Intl. Paperweight Soc. [22776]
    Paperweight Collectors' Assn. [22102]
Papillon Club of Am. [22336], c/o Paula Botwinick, Recording Sec., 4 Carstairs St., East Patchogue, NY 11772
Papua New Guinea Assn. of Accountants [★IO]
Papua New Guinea Athletic Union [IO], Lae, Papua New Guinea
Papua New Guinea Baseball Fed. [IO], Boroko, Papua New Guinea
Papua New Guinea Chamber of Commerce and Indus. [IO], Port Moresby, Papua New Guinea
Papua New Guinea Chamber of Mines and Petroleum [IO], Port Moresby, Papua New Guinea
Papua New Guinea Cricket Bd. [IO], Port Moresby, Papua New Guinea
Papua New Guinea Inst. of Accountants [★IO]
Papua New Guinea Lawn Tennis Assn. [IO], Boroko, Papua New Guinea
Papua New Guinea Natl. Olympic Comm. [IO], Boroko, Papua New Guinea
Papua New Guinea Olympic Comm. [★IO]
Papua New Guinea Squash Rackets Fed. [IO], Boroko, Papua New Guinea
Papua New Guinea Tourism Promotion Authority [IO], Port Moresby, Papua New Guinea
Papua New Guinea Yachting Assn. [IO], Port Moresby, Papua New Guinea

Papyrologists; Intl. Assn. of [IO]
Papyrology
    Amer. Soc. of Papyrologists [10769]
    Assn. for Convulsive Therapy [15192]
PAR Leadership Training Found. - Defunct.
Para-Amps - Defunct.
Parachute Club of Am. [★23648]
Parachute Infantry Assn; 509th [21380]
Parachute Infantry Regiment Assn; 504th [21378]
Parachute Infantry Regiment Assn; 508th [21379]
Parachute Jumpers-Riggers Assn; Natl. [★23648]
Parachute Medical Rescue Ser. [★12540]
Parachute Medical Rescue Ser. [★IO]
Parachute Regimental Combat Team Assn; 517th [21381]
Parachute Study Group - Address unknown since 2002.
Parachuting
    508th Parachute Infantry Regiment Assn. [21379]
    Canadian Sport Parachuting Assn. [IO]
    Caterpillar Club [146]
    U.S. BASE Assn. [23647]
    U.S. Parachute Assn. [23648]
Paraclete [20381], PO Box 623, Gilbert, AZ 85296, (480)854-4444
Paraffin Safety Assn. of Southern Africa [IO], Clareinch, Republic of South Africa
Paraffins Indus. Assn; Chlorinated [804]
Paragliding Assn; British Hang Gliding and [IO]
Paraguay Squash Assn. [IO], Asuncion, Paraguay
Paraguay Watch - Address unknown since 1995.
Paraguayan-American Chamber of Commerce [IO], Asuncion, Paraguay
Paraguayan Bible Soc. [IO], Asuncion, Paraguay
Paraguayan Chamber of Cereals and Oilseed Exporters [IO], Asuncion, Paraguay
Paraguayan Indus. Union [IO], Asuncion, Paraguay
Paraguayan League Against Epilepsy [IO], Asuncion, Paraguay
Paraguayan Soc. of Dermatology [IO], Asuncion, Paraguay
Paraguayan Soc. of Hypertension [IO], Asuncion, Paraguay
Parakeet Soc; Quaker [4200]
Paralegal Educ; Amer. Assn. for [8759]
Paralegal Patriots - Defunct.
Paralegals
    Amer. Alliance of Paralegals, Inc. [6149]
    Global Village Inst. [6235]
    Intl. Paralegal Mgt. Assn. [5944]
    Natl. Assn. of Legal Assistants [6150]
    Natl. Assn. of Licensed Paralegals [IO]
    Natl. District Attorneys Assn. [5668]
    Natl. Fed. of Paralegal Associations [6151]
    Natl. Hea. Law Prog. [5784]
    Natl. Paralegal Assn. [6152]
Parallax Soc. [10947], 744 Arkansas St., Tallahassee, FL 32304-2060
Parallax Soc. [IO], Tallahassee, FL, United States
Paralympic Comm. of Azerbaijan Republic [IO], Baku, Azerbaijan
Paralympic Comm. of Moldova [IO], Chisinau, Moldova
Paralympic Comm. of Moscow [IO], Moscow, Russia
Paralympic Comm. of the Republic of Belarus [IO], Minsk, Belarus
Paralympic Comm. of Russia [IO], Moscow, Russia
Paralympic Comm. of Serbia and Montenegro [IO], Belgrade, Serbia
Paralympic Coun. of Ireland [IO], Dublin, Ireland
Paralympic Sports Assn. [IO], Edmonton, AB, Canada
Paralympics New Zealand [IO], Auckland, New Zealand
Paralysis Assn; Amer. [★16463]
Paralysis Assn; Periodic [15122]
Paralysis Cure Res. Found. [★16463]
Paralysis Found; Christopher Reeve [★16463]
Paralysis Found; Kent Waldrep Natl. [16467]
Paralysis; Natl. Found. for Infantile [★13756]
Paralyzed Veterans of Am. [20768], 801 18th St. NW, Washington, DC 20006-3517, (202)872-1300
Paramedic; Joint Rev. Comm. on Educational Programs for the EMT- [★8833]
Paramedics Assn; Natl. Flight [★14334]

Reference to "IO" in place of a book number signifies that the association may be found in the 45th edition of International Organizations.

Paramount Orchids [IO], Calgary, AB, Canada
Paranormal
   Amer. Assn. for Critical Sci. Investigation into Claimed Hauntings [7437]
   Amer. Assn. of Paranormal Investigators [2896]
   Amer. Ghost Soc. [7438]
   Amer. Soc. for Psychical Res. [7442]
   Assn. for Res. and Enlightenment [7443]
   Comm. for the Sci. Investigation of Claims of the Paranormal [7444]
   Consciousness Res. and Training Project [12343]
   Ghost Res. Soc. [7475]
   Intl. Soc. for a Complete Earth [12354]
   Intl. Soc. for Paranormal Res. [2897]
   International Society for Paranormal Research [IO]
   Intl. Soc. for the Stud. of Ghosts and Apparitions [7445]
   MetaScience Found. [7446]
   Mind Development Association/U.S. Psi Squad [7447]
   Mind Sci. Found. [7448]
   Mutual UFO Network [7481]
   Natl. Investigations Comm. on Unidentified Flying Objects [7482]
   Paranormal Solutions [2898]
   Parapsychology Found. [7450]
   Parapsychology Inst. of Am. [7451]
   Rhine Res. Center - Inst. for Parapsychology [7452]
   Soc. for Sci. Exploration [7485]
   Survival Res. Found. [7453]
   UFO Info. Retrieval Center [7486]
   U.S. Psychotronics Assn. [7454]
   Vampire Info. Exchange [7455]
Paranormal; Comm. for the Sci. Investigation of Claims of the [7444]
Paranormal; New Zealand Comm. for the Sci. Investigation of Claims of the [IO]
Paranormal Solutions [2898]
Paraplegia Found; Natl. [★16468]
Paraplegia Soc; Amer. [16460]
Paraprofessional Healthcare Inst. [1853], 349 E 149th St., 10th Fl., Bronx, NY 10451, (718)402-7766
Paraprofessionals in Educ. and Related Services; Natl. Rsrc. Center for [9150]
Parapsychological Assn. [7449], 1390 N McDowell Blvd., Ste. G-208, Petaluma, CA 94954
Parapsychological Res. Assn; Amer. [★7441]
Parapsychological Services Inst. - Defunct.
Parapsychology
   Acad. of Psychic Arts and Sciences [7439]
   Acad. of Spirituality and Paranormal Stud., Inc. [7440]
   Acad. of Spirituality and Paranormal Stud., Inc. [IO]
   Aloha Intl. [12340]
   Amer. Assn. of Electronic Voice Phenomena [7469]
   Amer. Assn. of Paranormal Investigators [2896]
   Amer. Assn. for Parapsychology [7441]
   Amer. Ghost Soc. [7438]
   Amer. Soc. for Psychical Res. [7442]
   Assn. for Res. and Enlightenment [7443]
   Assn. for Res. and Enlightenment [IO]
   Assn. for the Sci. Stud. of Anomalous Phenomena [IO]
   Assn. for Skeptical Enquiry [IO]
   Borderland Sciences Res. Found. [7471]
   British Soc. of Dowsers [IO]
   Comite Belge pour l'Investigation Scientifique des Phenomenes Reputes Pananormaux [IO]
   Comm. for the Sci. Investigation of Claims of the Paranormal [7444]
   Consciousness Res. and Training Project [12343]
   Earthstewards Network [12344]
   The FORUM [12346]
   Freedom of Thought Found. [18616]
   Ghost Club [IO]
   HUNA Res. [12349]
   Intl. Assn. for Religion and Parapsychology [IO]
   Intl. Inst. for the Stud. of Death [13315]
   Intl. Soc. for Paranormal Res. [2897]
   Intl. Soc. for the Stud. of Ghosts and Apparitions [7445]

   Intl. Soc. for the Stud. of Ghosts and Apparitions [IO]
   MetaScience Found. [7446]
   Mind Development Association/U.S. Psi Squad [7447]
   Mind Sci. Found. [7448]
   Parapsychological Assn. [7449]
   Parapsychology Found. [7450]
   Parapsychology Inst. of Am. [7451]
   Radionic Assn. [IO]
   Rhine Res. Center - Inst. for Parapsychology [7452]
   Soc. for Psychical Res. [IO]
   Soc. for Sci. Exploration [7485]
   Survival Res. Found. [7453]
   U.S. Psychotronics Assn. [7454]
   Vampire Info. Exchange [7455]
Parapsychology Found. [7450], PO Box 1562, New York, NY 10021-0043, (212)628-1550
Parapsychology Inst. of Am. [7451], PO Box 5442, Babylon, NY 11707, (631)321-9362
Parapsychology Lab. of Duke Univ. [★7452]
Parasitological Soc. of Southern Africa [IO], Isando, Republic of South Africa
Parasitologie Veterinaire; Assn. Mondiale pour l'Advancement de [★16818]
Parasitologiese Vereniging van Suidelike Afrika [★IO]
Parasitologists; Amer. Assn. of Veterinary [16754]
Parasitology
   Amer. Heartworm Soc. [16772]
   Australian Soc. for Parasitology [IO]
   British Soc. for Parasitology [IO]
   European Fed. of Parasitologists [IO]
   Georgian Soc. of Parasitologists [IO]
   Parasitological Soc. of Southern Africa [IO]
   Scandinavian-Baltic Soc. for Parasitology [IO]
   World Assn. for the Advancement of Veterinary Parasitology [16818]
Paratransit Assn; Taxicab, Limousine and [3894]
Paratuberculosis Awareness and Res. Assn. [14425], PO Box 16219, Temple Terrace, FL 33687-6219
Paratuberculosis Awareness and Res. Assn. [IO], Temple Terrace, FL, United States
Parbatya Bouddha Mission [IO], Khagrachari, Bangladesh
Parcel Centers; Assoc. Mail and [2446]
Parcel Post Assn. [★2454]
Parcel Shippers Assn. [2454], 1211 Connecticut Ave. NW, Ste. 620, Washington, DC 20036-2701, (202)296-3690
Parent Advocacy Coalition for Educational Rights; PACER Center - [14246]
Parent Association; National Head Start [★9006]
Parent Coalition; Natl. Single [★12693]
Parent Cooperative Preschools Intl. [8070], 1401 New York Ave. NW, Ste. 1100, Natl. Cooperative Bus. Center, Washington, DC 20005
Parent Cooperative Preschools Intl. [IO], Washington, DC, United States
Parent Education and Monitoring Program - Defunct.
Parent Finders of Canada [IO], Delta, BC, Canada
Parent Found; Surrogate [★13297]
Parent Gp. U.S.A; Rubinstein-Taybi [13759]
Parent Mite Missionary Soc; Women's [★20627]
Parent Network [8957], c/o The Montessori Acad., 530 E Day Rd., Mishawaka, IN 46545, (574)255-1703
Parent Network on Disabilities; Natl. [14245]
Parent Networking Prog. [★11973]
Parent Resources and Info. on Drug Educ. [★13276]
Parent Support Assn. of Calgary [IO], Calgary, AB, Canada
Parent Support Gp; Because I Love You: The [13293]
Parent Support Gp; Freeman-Sheldon [14063]
Parent Support Network; Adoptee-Birth [11228]
Parent-Teachers Associations; Natl. Cong. of Mothers and [★8954]
Parent-to-Parent Network; MUMS Natl. [16541]
Parent Training and Info. Proj. [★12569]
Parentcraft Center; Midwest [15609]
Parenteral Drug Assn. [★2979]

Parenteral Drug Assn. [★IO]
Parenteral and Enteral Nutrition; Amer. Soc. for [15549]
Parenteral and Enteral Nutrition; Oley Found. for Home [14843]
Parenteral and Enteral Nutrition Soc. of Asia [IO], Bangkok, Thailand
Parenteral Soc. [★IO]
Parenthood Fed. of Am; Planned [12187]
Parenthood Fed. of Am; Res. and Development Division of Planned [★12175]
Parenthood Physicians; Amer. Assn. of [★12177]
Parenthood Physicians; Assn. of Planned [★12177]
Parenthood Professionals; Assn. of Planned [★12177]
Parenthood/World Population; Planned [★12187]
Parenting; Center for Surrogate [13297]
Parenting; Informed Homebirth/Informed Birth and [15602]
Parenting Materials Information Center - Defunct.
Parenting; Natl. Org. of Adolescent Pregnancy and [★12182]
Parenting in a Nuclear Age - Address unknown since 2001.
Parenting and Prevention; Natl. Org. on Adolescent Pregnancy, [★12182]
Parenting Publications of Am. [3246], 4929 Wilshire Blvd., Ste. 428, Los Angeles, CA 90010, (323)937-5514
Parentless Children's Comm. [IO], Yerevan, Armenia
Parentline Plus [IO], London, United Kingdom
Parents
   Adopt Am. Network [11227]
   Adoptee-Birthparent Support Network [11228]
   Adoption Info. Services [11230]
   Adoptions Together [11231]
   Advocates for Youth [12173]
   Aid to Incarcerated Mothers [11851]
   Aiding Mothers and Fathers Experiencing Neonatal Death [11907]
   Alan Guttmacher Inst. [12175]
   Alliance for Children and Families [12136]
   ALMA Soc. - Adoptees' Liberty Movement Assn. [11232]
   Amer. Adoption Cong. [11234]
   Amer. Fathers Coalition [12660]
   Amer. Fertility Assn. [14388]
   Amer. Mothers, Inc. [12139]
   America's Angel [12140]
   Archconfraternity of Christian Mothers [19572]
   Assn. for Recognizing the Life of Stillborns [12661]
   Assn. for Shared Parenting [IO]
   Attachment Parenting Intl. [IO]
   Attachment Parenting Intl. [12662]
   Because I Love You: The Parent Support Gp. [13293]
   Bereaved Parents of the USA [11512]
   Bereavement Services [12663]
   Better World J. L. Inst. [12142]
   Black Mental Hea. Alliance [15193]
   Bonus Families [12143]
   Catholic Parents Network [12664]
   Center for Commercial-Free Public Educ. [8241]
   Center for Loss in Multiple Birth [12665]
   Center for Surrogate Parenting [13297]
   Child-Friendly Initiative [11678]
   Child Support Resistance [12006]
   Child Welfare Inst. [11571]
   CHOICE [12178]
   Christian Family Life [12146]
   Citizenship Through Sports Alliance [23812]
   Coll. Parents of Am. [8485]
   Comm. for Missing Children [12603]
   Comm. for Mother and Child Rights [11689]
   The Compassionate Friends [12666]
   Concerned Persons for Adoption [11240]
   Concerned United Birthparents [11241]
   Coun. on Contemporary Families [12149]
   Coun. of Parent Attorneys and Advocates [9142]
   Dads Rights [12008]
   Depression After Delivery [12667]
   Designs for Change [9035]
   Educ. and Enrichment Sect. of the Natl. Coun. on Family Relations [12151]

A star before a book entry number signifies that the name is not listed separately, but is mentioned within the entry.

Every Person Influences Children [11540]
Fairview Pregnancy and Newborn Loss Information [12668]
Families Adopting Children Everywhere [11242]
Families for Natural Living [8416]
Families for Private Adoption [11244]
Family and Home Network [12669]
Family Pride Coalition [12227]
Family Res. Coun. [12153]
Family Support Am. [12154]
Family Supports [12155]
Father Matters [18180]
Fatherhood Proj. [12670]
Fed. Suisse des Familles Monoparentales [IO]
First Sunday [12671]
Friends in Adoption [11245]
Generation Green [17054]
Generations [IO]
Great Dads [12672]
GreatSchools [8066]
Guardian Assn. of Pinellas County [12266]
Hispanic Coun. for Reform and Educational Options [8260]
Holistic Moms Network [12673]
Home School Legal Defense Assn. [8339]
Inst. in Basic Life Principles [13489]
Intl. Reading Assn. [9043]
Intl. Soundex Reunion Registry [11248]
Intl. Stillbirth Alliance [13982]
Jack and Jill of Am. [11702]
Jack and Jill of Am. Found. [11703]
Kids First Parent Assn. of Canada [IO]
Kids Fund [11704]
Kids Konnected [11706]
Kids Need Both Parents [17509]
KIDSCOPE [11518]
Latin Am. Parents Assn. [11252]
Liberal Educ. for Adoptive Families [11253]
Mothers Against Sexual Abuse [13078]
Mothers Against Sexual Predators At Large [13079]
Mother's Right Found. [IO]
Natl. Adoption Center [11254]
Natl. Assn. of At-Home Mothers [12674]
Natl. Assn. of Entrepreneurial Parents [12675]
Natl. Assn. of Hebrew Day School PTAs [8953]
Natl. Assn. of Mothers' Centers [12676]
Natl. Assn. of Non-Custodial Moms [11538]
Natl. Assn. of Students Against Violence Everywhere [18117]
Natl. Black Home Educators [8519]
National Center for Fathering [IO]
Natl. Center for Fathering [18181]
Natl. Childbirth Trust [IO]
Natl. Coun. for Adoption [11255]
Natl. Council for Single Adoptive Parents [11256]
Natl. Exchange Club Found. [11637]
Natl. Fatherhood Initiative [17510]
Natl. Fed. of Services for Unmarried Parents and Their Children [IO]
Natl. Foster Parent Assn. [12677]
Natl. Head Start Assn. [9006]
Natl. Home Educ. Res. Inst. [8522]
Natl. Infertility Network Exchange [12678]
Natl. Org. of Mothers of Twins Clubs [12613]
Natl. Org. of Parents of Blind Children [16879]
Natl. Org. of Single Mothers [13108]
Natl. Parenting Assn. [12679]
Natl. Parents Assn. [12680]
Natl. PTA - Natl. Cong. of Parents and Teachers [8954]
Natl. Rural Educ. Assn. [9069]
Natl. Visiting Teachers Assn. [8955]
Native Amer. Fatherhood and Families Assn. [12681]
Netherlands Soc. of Parents with Nepalese Children [IO]
New Parents Network [8956]
North Amer. Coun. on Adoptable Children [11257]
The Nurturing Network [13434]
One Family [IO]
One Parent Families Scotland [IO]
Org. for the Lifelong Establishment of Paternity [11714]
Org. of Parents Through Surrogacy [13299]

Organized Adoption Search Info. Services [11259]
ORIGINS [11260]
Orphan Voyage [11261]
Parent Cooperative Preschools Intl. [8070]
Parent Network [8957]
Parentline Plus [IO]
Parents' Action For Children [12682]
Parents Against Childhood Epilepsy [14382]
Parents Against Tired Truckers [12984]
Parents Centres New Zealand [IO]
Parents' Choice Found. [12683]
Parents in Control [8340]
Parents Helping Parents [12684]
Parents of Infants and Children with Kernicterus [15358]
Parents of Kids with Infectious Diseases [14954]
Parents of Murdered Children [12685]
Parents of Premature Babies [12686]
Parents for Public Schools [12052]
Parents Rights Coalition [12687]
Parents Without Partners [12688]
Parents Without Partners - Australia [IO]
Partners in Foster Care [12193]
Pilot Parents of Southern Arizona [12581]
Postpartum Support Intl. [12689]
Postpartum Support Intl. [IO]
Prepare Tomorrow's Parents [13511]
Reading Is Fundamental [9047]
Sallie Mae Fund [8434]
SHARE-Pregnancy and Infant Loss Support [12690]
Single and Custodial Fathers Network [12691]
Single Mothers By Choice [12692]
Single Parent Rsrc. Center [12693]
Slowlane/Stay At Home Dads [18182]
Social Policy Action Network [13138]
Soc. of Special Needs Adoptive Parents [IO]
Special Needs Advocate for Parents [11652]
Stillbirth and Neonatal Death Soc. [IO]
Supporting Our Sons [11547]
Sweet Mother Intl. [IO]
Take Root [12605]
Toughlove Intl. [12694]
Toughlove Intl. [IO]
The Triplet Connection [12614]
Twins Found. [12616]
UNITE [12695]
United Fathers of Am. [12014]
U.S.A. Toy Lib. Assn. [11548]
Welfare Warriors [18183]
Windward Found. [13195]
World Movement of Mothers [IO]
Parents' Action For Children [12682], PO Box 2096, Culver City, CA 90231, (310)285-2385
Parents Active for Vision Educ. [16880], 4135 54th Pl., San Diego, CA 92105-2303, (619)287-0081
Parents Against Childhood Epilepsy [14382], 7 E 85th St., Ste. A3, New York, NY 10028, (212)665-7223
Parents Against Molesters - Address unknown since 2003.
Parents Against Subliminal Seduction - Defunct.
Parents Against Tired Truckers [12984], PO Box 209, Lisbon Falls, ME 04252-0209, (888)353-4572
Parents' Alliance to Protect Our Children - Defunct.
Parents; Amer. Coun. of the Blind [★16844]
Parents Anonymes [★IO]
Parents Anonymous [11645], 675 W Foothill Blvd., Ste. 220, Claremont, CA 91711-3475, (909)621-6184
Parents Are Also People - Defunct.
Parents Assn. for Children with Retarded Mental Development [★12572]
Parents Assn. for Jewish Residential Care [★12570]
Parents Assn; Latin Am. [11252]
Parents Campaign for Handicapped Children and Youth [★11971]
Parents Centres New Zealand [IO], Wellington, New Zealand
Parents; Children of Aging [11282]
Parents of Children with Down Syndrome [★12579]
Parents of Children With Visual Impairments; Natl. Assn. for [16873]
Parents and Children's Equality [★18040]
Parents and Children's Equality [★IO]

Parents' Choice Found. [12683], 201 W Padonia Rd., Ste. 303, Timonium, MD 21093, (410)308-3858
Parents; Comm. of Concerned [★5869]
Parents Comm. for Jewish Refugee Children - Address unknown since 1995.
Parents Comm; Single [★11256]
Parents; Comm. for Single Adoptive [★11256]
Parents; Concerned United Birth [11241]
Parents in Control [8340], c/o Jeff Barclay, Interim Exec. Dir., 2511 Jasu Dr., Lawrence, KS 66046, (785)749-0083
Parents of the Deaf; Intl. Assn. of [★14742]
Parents of Down Syndrome [12579], PO Box 10416, Rockville, MD 20849, (301)916-4985
Parents of Down Syndrome Children [★12579]
Parents for Drug-Free Youth; Natl. Fed. of [★13270]
Parents Educational Rsrc. Center [★12496]
Parents Empowerment; Team H.O.P.E Help Offering [12606]
Parents, Families, and Friends of Lesbians and Gays [12253], 1726 M St. NW, Ste. 400, Washington, DC 20036, (202)467-8180
Parents and Friends of Ex-Gays and Gays [12254], c/o Regina Griggs, Exec. Dir., PO Box 561, Fort Belvoir, VA 22060-0561, (703)360-2225
Parents and Friends of Lesbians and Gays [★12253]
Parents of Galactosemic Children [15257], c/o Michelle Fowler, Pres., PO Box 2401, Mandeville, LA 70470, (866)900-7421
Parents; Grandparents as [12263]
Parents Gp; Cornelia de Lange [★13754]
Parents Helping Parents [12684], 3041 Olcott St., Santa Clara, CA 95054-3222, (408)727-5775
Parents of Hippies - Defunct.
Parents of Infants and Children with Kernicterus [15358], One W Superior St., Ste. 2410, Chicago, IL 60610, (312)274-9695
Parents of Kids with Infectious Diseases [14954], PO Box 5666, Vancouver, WA 98668, (360)695-0293
Parents League of Amer. Students of Medicine Abroad - Defunct.
Parents for MPS [★15253]
Parents of Murdered Children [12685], 100 E 8th St., Ste. 202, Cincinnati, OH 45202, (513)721-5683
Parents' Music Resource Center - Address unknown since 2002.
Parents; Natl. Coalition of Title I/Chapter 1 [8289]
Parents; Natl. Council for Single Adoptive [11256]
Parents of Near Drownings - Defunct.
Parents Network for the Post Institutionalized Child [16546], PO Box 613, Meadow Lands, PA 15347, (724)222-1766
Parents' Org; Intl. [★14776]
Parents; Partnership [★20305]
Parents; Partnership [★IO]
PARENTS - People of America Responding to Educational Needs of Today's Soc. - Defunct.
Parents Plan - U.S.A; Foster [★11681]
Parents of Premature Babies [12686], 21 Lansing Ln., East Northport, NY 11731
Parents for Private Adoption - Defunct.
Parents and Professionals and Autism Northern Ireland [IO], Belfast, United Kingdom
Parents for Public Schools [12052], 3252 N State St., Jackson, MS 39216, (601)713-3229
Parents of Punkers - Address unknown since 1987.
Parents for Quality Education - Defunct.
Parents and Researchers Interested in Smith-Magenis Syndrome; PRISMS [14476]
Parents Rights Coalition [12687], PO Box 1612, Waltham, MA 02454, (781)899-4905
Parents Rights, Inc. [★7950]
Parents' Rights Org. [7950], 9333 Clayton Rd., St. Louis, MO 63124-1511, (314)997-6361
Parents' Sect. of the Alexander Graham Bell Assn. for the Deaf [★14776]
Parents' Sect. of the Alexander Graham Bell Assn. for the Deaf and Hard of Hearing [14776], 3417 Volta Pl. NW, Washington, DC 20007, (202)337-5220
Parents Sharing Custody - Defunct.
Parents of Southern Arizona; Pilot [12581]

Reference to "IO" in place of a book number signifies that the association may be found in the 45th edition of International Organizations.

Parents of Surrogate-Borne Infants and Toddlers in Verbal Exchange - Defunct.

Parents and Teachers Against Violence in Educ. **[8208]**, PO Box 1033, Alamo, CA 94507-7033, (925)831-1661

Parents as Teachers Intl. - Address unknown since 2002.

Parents and Teachers in Lutheran Schools - Defunct.

Parents and Teachers; Natl. Cong. of **[★8954]**

Parents and Teachers; Natl. Cong. of Colored **[★8954]**

Parents Through Surrogacy; Org. of **[13299]**

Parents United **[13081]**, 615 15th St., Modesto, CA 95354, (209)572-3446

Parents of the Visually Impaired; Natl. Assn. for **[★16873]**

Parents Volunteer Assn. **[★12578]**

Parents With a Purpose **[★12566]**

Parents Without Partners **[12688]**, 1650 S Dixie Hwy., Ste. 510, Boca Raton, FL 33432, (561)391-8833

Parents Without Partners - Australia **[IO]**, Dickson, Australia

Pareveh, the Alliance for Adult Children of Jewish-Gentile Intermarriage - Defunct.

Paris Chamber of Commerce and Indus. **[IO]**, Paris, France

Paris-Moscow; Independent Univ., Washington- **[★8597]**

Paris Opera and Ballet; Amer. Friends of the **[9543]**

Parish Catechetical Directors; Natl. Assn. of **[19932]**

Parish Clergy; Acad. of **[20274]**

Parish Coordinators/Directors of Religious Educ; Natl. Assn. of **[★19932]**

Parishes for Liturgy and Mission; Assoc. **[19945]**

Parity Found. - Defunct.

Park Acad. of the Arts; Natl. **[9460]**

Park Assn; San Francisco Maritime Natl. **[10513]**

Park Concessionaires; Conf. of Natl. **[★1321]**

Park Executives; Amer. Inst. of **[★6153]**

Park Found; North Amer. Wildlife **[5358]**

Park Gallatin Hereford Assn. - Address unknown since 2002.

Park and Grounds Mgt; Natl. Inst. on **[4801]**

Park Historical Assn; Natl. Amusement **[21512]**

Park Hospitality Assn; Natl. **[1321]**

Park Law Enforcement Assn. **[6162]**, c/o Steve Newsom, Pres., Hamilton County Park District, 10245 Winton Rd., Cincinnati, OH 45231, (513)521-3980

Park Ridge Center - Defunct.

Park Safety and Security; Amer. Soc. for Amusement **[3526]**

Parke Soc. **[21021]**, 710 7th St., Huntingdon, PA 16652-2424

Parker Chiropractic Resource Found. - Address unknown since 2005.

Parker-Coltrane Political Action Comm. - Defunct.

Parking

European Parking Assn. **[IO]**

Intl. Parking Inst. **[IO]**

Intl. Parking Inst. **[2899]**

Natl. Parking Assn. **[2900]**

Natl. Time Equip. Assn. **[3812]**

Parking Assn. of Australia **[IO]**

Parking Assn. of Australia **[IO]**, North Beach, Australia

Parking Cong; Institutional and Municipal **[★2899]**

Parking Cong; Intl. Municipal **[★2899]**

Parking Found; Bicycling **[★23307]**

Parking Indus. Institute **[★2900]**

Parking Proj; Bicycle **[23307]**

Parking Proj; Bicycling **[★23307]**

Parkinson Alliance **[15359]**, PO Box 308, Kingston, NJ 08528-0308, (609)688-0870

Parkinson Assn; Norwegian **[IO]**

Parkinson Disease Assn; Amer. **[15304]**

Parkinson Found; Natl. **[15351]**

Parkinson Found; United **[★15360]**

Parkinson Soc. of Canada **[IO]**, Toronto, ON, Canada

Parkinson Soc. Canada - Maritime Region **[IO]**, Halifax, NS, Canada

Parkinson Soc. Canada - Southwestern Ontario Region **[IO]**, London, ON, Canada

Parkinson Soc. Manitoba **[IO]**, Winnipeg, MB, Canada

Parkinson Soc. Newfoundland and Labrador **[IO]**, St. John's, NL, Canada

Parkinson Soc. Ottawa **[IO]**, Ottawa, ON, Canada

Parkinson Soc. Quebec **[IO]**, Montreal, QC, Canada

Parkinson Support Groups of America - Address unknown since 2002.

Parkinson's Action Network **[14285]**, 1025 Vermont Ave. NW, Ste. 1120, Washington, DC 20005, (202)638-4101

Parkinson's Assn. of Ireland **[IO]**, Dublin, Ireland

Parkinson's Australia **[IO]**, Calwell, Australia

Parkinson's Disease Found. **[15360]**, 1359 Broadway, Ste. 1509, New York, NY 10018, (212)923-4700

Parkinson's Disease Nurse Specialist Assn. **[IO]**, Aberdeen, United Kingdom

Parkinson's Disease Soc. of the United Kingdom **[IO]**, London, United Kingdom

Parkinson's Educational Program - U.S.A. - Defunct.

Parkinson's New South Wales **[IO]**, North Ryde, Australia

Parkinsons New Zealand **[IO]**, Wellington, New Zealand

Parkinson's Soc. of Alberta **[IO]**, Edmonton, AB, Canada

Parkinson's Soc. of Southern Alberta **[IO]**, Calgary, AB, Canada

Parkinson's Victoria **[IO]**, Cheltenham, Australia

Parkinson's Western Australia **[IO]**, Nedlands, Australia

Parks; Arts for the **[★9460]**

Parks Assn; Natl. **[★6160]**

Parks Assn; Western Natl. **[7365]**

Parks and Campgrounds; Natl. Assn. of RV **[3357]**

Parks; A Christian Ministry in the Natl. **[19783]**

Parks and Conservation Assn; Natl. **[★6160]**

Parks Inholders Assn; Natl. **[★6187]**

Parks; Intl. Assn. of Amusement **[★1303]**

Parks and Monuments Assn; Southwest **[★7365]**

Parks; Natl. Assn. of Amusement **[★1303]**

Parks; Natl. Assn. for Olmsted **[5591]**

Parks; Natl. Conf. on State **[★6161]**

Parks; National Cong. Recreation and **[★6161]**

Parks; Partners in **[4439]**

Parks, Pools, and Beaches; Natl. Assn. of Amusement **[★1303]**

Parks and Recreation

The Adirondack Coun. **[4340]**

Alliance for Am. **[11807]**

Alliance of Marine Mammal Parks and Aquariums **[5006]**

Alliance of Natl. Heritage Areas **[9856]**

Amer. Assn. for Physical Activity and Recreation **[12793]**

Amer. Park and Recreation Soc. **[6153]**

Assn. of Natl. Park Authorities **[IO]**

Assn. of Natl. Park Rangers **[6154]**

Assn. of Univ. Res. Parks **[9054]**

Big Bend Natural History Assn. **[7361]**

Big Thicket Assn. **[4367]**

Big Thicket Natural Heritage Trust **[4368]**

Canadian Parks and Recreation Assn. **[IO]**

Canadian Parks and Wilderness Soc. **[IO]**

A Christian Ministry in the Natl. Parks **[19783]**

City Parks Alliance **[18184]**

Coalition to Protect Animals in Parks and Refuges **[11379]**

Coun. for Natl. Parks **[IO]**

Darkride and Funhouse Enthusiasts **[21511]**

Death Valley '49ers **[4807]**

European Fed. of Campingsite Organisations and Holiday Park Associations **[IO]**

Greater Yellowstone Coalition **[4406]**

Greensward Found. **[4407]**

Intl. Assn. of Haunted Attractions **[1304]**

Intl. Fed. of Park and Recreation Admin. **[IO]**

Intl. Playground Contractors Assn. **[1028]**

Natl. Amusement Park Historical Assn. **[21512]**

Natl. Assn. of County Park and Recreation Officials **[6155]**

Natl. Assn. for Olmsted Parks **[5591]**

Natl. Assn. of Recreation Rsrc. Planners **[6156]**

Natl. Assn. of State Outdoor Recreation Liaison Officers **[6157]**

Natl. Assn. of State Park Directors **[6158]**

Natl. Forest Found. **[4424]**

Natl. Inst. on Park and Grounds Mgt. **[4801]**

Natl. Park Acad. of the Arts **[9460]**

Natl. Park Found. **[6159]**

Natl. Park Trust **[5071]**

Natl. Parks Conservation Assn. **[6160]**

Natl. Public Parks Tennis Assn. **[23906]**

Natl. Recreation and Park Assn. **[6161]**

New Zealand Recreation Assn. **[IO]**

North Amer. Wildlife Park Found. **[5358]**

Park Law Enforcement Assn. **[6162]**

Partners in Parks **[4439]**

Prairie Club **[12799]**

Proj. for Public Spaces **[17238]**

Public Art Fund **[17239]**

Sci. Park Assn. **[IO]**

Sculpture in the Env. **[17240]**

Shenandoah Natl. Park Assn. **[10062]**

Soc. of Park and Recreation Educators **[6163]**

Trail of Tears Assn. **[11057]**

Tread Lightly! **[5167]**

Western Natl. Parks Assn. **[7365]**

World Commn. on Protected Areas **[IO]**

Yosemite Assn. **[7367]**

Parks Tennis Assn; Natl. Public **[23906]**

Parkside Alcoholic Res. Foundation **[★14821]**

Parliamentarians; Amer. Inst. of **[10770]**

Parliamentarians For Global Action **[17433]**, 211 E 43rd St., Ste. 1604, New York, NY 10017, (212)687-7755

Parliamentarians For Global Action **[IO]**, New York, NY, United States

Parliamentarians Global Action for Disarmament, Development, and World Reform **[★IO]**

Parliamentarians Global Action for Disarmament, Development, and World Reform **[★17433]**

Parliamentarians; Natl. Assn. of **[10771]**

Parliamentarians for World Order **[★17433]**

Parliamentarians for World Order **[★IO]**

Parliamentary Centre **[IO]**, Ottawa, ON, Canada

Parliamentary Gp. of the Party of European Socialists **[★IO]**

Parliamentary on Human Rights - Address unknown since 2000.

Parliaments

Amer. Inst. of Parliamentarians **[10770]**

Amer. Parliamentary Debate Assn. **[9153]**

ASEAN Inter-Parliamentary Assembly **[IO]**

Assn. of Secretaries Gen. of Parliaments **[IO]**

Canadian Assn. of Former Parliamentarians **[IO]**

Canadian Stud. of Parliament Gp. **[IO]**

Commonwealth Parliamentary Assn. **[IO]**

Commonwealth Speakers and Presiding Officers Conf. **[IO]**

European Parliamentarians for Africa **[IO]**

Hansard Soc. **[IO]**

Inter-Parliamentary Consultative Coun. of Benelux **[IO]**

Inter-Parliamentary Union **[IO]**

National Association of Parliamentarians **[IO]**

Natl. Assn. of Parliamentarians **[10771]**

Natl. Parliamentary Debate Assn. **[9160]**

Parliamentary Centre **[IO]**

Programme for the Stud. and Promotion of Representative Institutions **[IO]**

Parole

Alston Wilkes Veterans Home **[11852]**

Amer. Assn. for Correctional and Forensic Psychology **[11853]**

Amer. Correctional Assn. **[11854]**

Amer. Criminal Justice Assn. (Lambda Alpha Epsilon) **[11855]**

Amer. Jail Assn. **[11856]**

Amer. Probation and Parole Assn. **[6164]**

Amer. Soc. of Criminology **[11899]**

Assn. of Paroling Authorities Intl. **[6165]**

Assn. of Paroling Authorities Intl. **[IO]**

Assn. on Programs for Female Offenders **[11857]**

Assn. of State Correctional Administrators **[11858]**

Center for Stud. in Criminal Justice **[11859]**

Correctional Educ. Assn. **[11862]**

Family Justice **[11865]**

Fortune Soc. **[11867]**

Friends Outside **[11868]**

A star before a book entry number signifies that the name is not listed separately, but is mentioned within the entry.

Intl. Assn. of Correctional Officers [11870]

Intl. Assn. of Correctional Training Personnel [11871]

Intl. Assn. of Reentry [17355]

Intl. Community Corrections Assn. [11872]

John Howard Assn. [11874]

Justice Res. and Statistics Assn. [11876]

London Club [11900]

Natl. Center on Institutions and Alternatives [11878]

Natl. Center for Juvenile Justice [11879]

Natl. Correctional Indus. Assn. [11880]

Natl. Criminal Justice Assn. [11881]

Natl. Juvenile Detention Assn. [11882]

Natl. Prison Proj. of the ACLU [11883]

Natl. Youth Court Center [18854]

North Amer. Assn. of Wardens and Superintendents [11884]

Osborne Assn. [11885]

Parole and Probation Compact Administrators' Assn. [6166]

Prison Fellowship Intl. [11887]

Prison Fellowship Ministries [11888]

Prison Ministry of Yokefellow's Intl. [11889]

Prisoners' Rights Union [11890]

Safer Soc. Found. [11891]

Volunteers in Prevention, Probation, Prisons [11896]

We Care Prog. [11897]

Women's Prison Assn. [11898]

Parole Assn; Amer. [★11843]

Parole Assn; Natl. Probation and [★11843]

Parole and Probation Compact Administrators' Assn. [6166], c/o Karen Tucker, Treas., 2601 Blair Stone Rd., Tallahassee, FL 32399, (850)410-4324

Parolees and Probationers; Assn. of Administrators of the Interstate Compact for the Supervision of [★6166]

Parrot Breeders and Exhibitors; Soc. of [21860]

Parrot Soc; African [21833]

Parrot Soc. of Australia [IO], Brisbane, Australia

Parrot Soc; North Amer. [21858]

Parrot Soc. - U.K. [IO], Berkhamsted, United Kingdom

Parrotlet Soc; Intl. [21850]

Parrots and People [11516], 3930 Glade Rd., No. 108-130, Colleyville, TX 76034, (817)498-9636

Parson Russell Terrier Assn. of Am. [22337], c/o Marcia Walsh, Pres., 839 Canada Rd., Woodside, CA 94062, (650)851-4044

Parsons Found; Gram [24903]

Parsons Memorial Found; Gram [★24903]

Part-Blooded Horse Registry; Amer. [4835]

Part-Time and Temporary Employees; Natl. Assn. of [1271]

partei des Demokratischen Sozialismus [★IO]

Parthenais Cattle Breeders Assn. [4286], 982 Hutchins Ln., Chipley, FL 32428, (800)762-0164

Parti Abolitionniste du Canada [★IO]

Parti liberal du Canada [★IO]

Parti Chretien Social [★IO]

Parti Europeen des Liberaux Democrates et Reformateurs [★IO]

Parti Gerakan Rakyat Malaysia [IO], Kuala Lumpur, Malaysia

Parti Islam Se Malaysia [★IO]

Parti de L'Heritage Chretien [★IO]

Parti Ouvrier Socialiste Luxembourgeois [★IO]

Parti Populaire Europeen [★IO]

Parti Socialiste [★IO]

Parti Socialiste Progressiste [★IO]

Partial Hospitalization; Amer. Assn. for [★16080]

Partial Hospitalization Study Group [★16080]

Partially Sighted Soc. [IO], Doncaster, United Kingdom

Participa [IO], Santiago, Chile

Participatory Ecological Land Use Mgt. Assn. [IO], Chimanimani, Zimbabwe

Particleboard Assn; Natl. [★1643]

Partij van de Arbeid [★IO]

Partisan Prohibition Historical Soc. [22103], PO Box 2635, Denver, CO 80201, (303)237-4947

Partit Laburista [★IO]

Partit Nazzjonalista [★IO]

Partitioning and Interiors Assn. [★IO]

PARTIZANS [IO], London, United Kingdom

Partners [★17844]

Partners of the Americas [16980], 1424 K St. NW, Ste. 700, Washington, DC 20005, (202)628-3300

Partners of the Americas [IO], Washington, DC, United States

Partners for Christian Development [★19822]

Partners in Community Development Fiji [IO], Suva, Fiji

Partners for Democratic Change [17844], 2121 K St. NW, Ste. 700, Washington, DC 20037, (202)942-2166

Partners for Development/Cambodia [IO], Phnom Penh, Cambodia

Partners for Effective Parenting - Defunct.

Partners in Faith; Equal [20494]

Partners in Foster Care [12193], c/o Cora E. White, Pres., PO Box 2534, Madison, WI 53701, (608)274-9111

Partners in Friendship - Address unknown since 2004.

Partners in Harmony, World Family of John Denver [★24909]

Partners in Hea. [12270], 641 Huntington Ave., 1st Fl., Boston, MA 02115, (617)432-5256

Partners in Hea. [IO], Boston, MA, United States

Partners Intl. - Defunct.

Partners for Livable Communities [5594], 1429 21st St. NW, Washington, DC 20036, (202)887-5990

Partners for Livable Places [★5594]

Partners in Parks [4439], PO Box 130, Paonia, CO 81428-0130, (970)527-6675

Partners for Peace [18230], 1250 4th St. SW, Ste. WG-1, Washington, DC 20024, (202)863-2951

Partners in Peace [★12696]

Partners in Peace [★IO]

Partners for Peace [IO], Washington, DC, United States

Partners in Politics - Address unknown since 2007.

Partners; Rights Action/Guatemala [12819]

Partners for Sacred Places [20505], 1700 Sansom St., 10th Fl., Philadelphia, PA 19103, (215)567-3234

Partners Task Force for Gay and Lesbian Couples [17654], Box 9685, Seattle, WA 98109-0685, (206)935-1206

Partners Worldwide [19822], 2850 Kalamazoo Ave. SE, Grand Rapids, MI 49560-0600, (616)224-5874

Partnership for Civil Justice Legal Defense and Educ. Fund [17142], c/o Partnership for Civil Justice, 10 G St. NE, Ste. 650, Washington, DC 20002, (202)789-4330

Partnership for Democracy - Address unknown since 2003.

Partnership for a Drug-Free Am. [13272], 405 Lexington Ave., Ste. 1601, New York, NY 10174, (212)922-1560

Partnership for a Drug-Free Am; Media-Advertising [★13272]

Partnership for Employment and Training Careers [★12088]

Partnership for Food Safety Educ. [14399], 655 15th St. NW, 7th Fl., Washington, DC 20005, (202)220-0651

Partnership for Human Res. Protection - Defunct.

Partnership Mission [★20305]

Partnership Mission [★IO]

Partnership Parents [★IO]

Partnership Parents [★20305]

Partnership for Patient Safety [14659], 1 W Superior St., Ste. 2410, Chicago, IL 60610, (312)274-9695

Partnership for Prevention [14594], 1015 18th St. NW, Ste. 200, Washington, DC 20036, (202)833-0009

Partnership for Quality Medical Donations [12537], 146 Koenig Rd., Bernville, PA 19506, (610)488-8303

Partnership for Quality Medical Donations [IO], Bernville, PA, United States

Partnership for Research Integrity in Science and Medicine [18489], c/o Professional & Scholarly Publishing, Association of American Publishers, 71 Fifth Ave., 2nd Fl., New York, NY 10003, (212)255-0200

Partnership for Sri Lanka/USA - Address unknown since 2004.

Partnership for Sustainable Development - Nepal [IO], Kathmandu, Nepal

Partnerships Data Net - Defunct.

Partnerships; Natl. Coun. for Public-Private [17633]

Parton Fan Club; Dolly [★24878]

Parton's Fan Club; Dolly [24877]

Parts Distributors Assn; Aftermarket Body [★405]

Parts Distributors Assn; Appliance [263]

Parts Distributors; Natl. Radio [★1223]

Parts for Import Cars Coalition - Defunct.

Parts Jobbers Assn; Appliance [★263]

Parts Manufacturers; Representatives of Radio [★1213]

Parts Plus; Assn. of Automotive Aftermarket Distributors/ [370]

Parts Rebuilders Assn; Automotive [★409]

Parts Remanufacturers Assn; Automotive [409]

Parts Suppliers Assn; Natl. Appliance [266]

Party Boat Owners Alliance; Natl. [3359]

Party; Comm. for a Unified Independent [18321]

Party of Democratic Socialism [IO], Berlin, Germany

Party of European Socialists [IO], Brussels, Belgium

An Party Kenethlegek Kernow - Address unknown since 1995.

Party Operators; Natl. Assn. of Casino [1313]

Party Operators; Natl. Assn. of Casino and Theme [★1313]

Pascal/MT Users Group - Defunct.

Pascal Users' Group - Defunct.

Paso Fino Fed. of Am; Pure Puerto Rican [4946]

Paso Fino Horse Assn. [4943], 101 N Collins St., Plant City, FL 33563-3311, (813)719-7777

Paso Fino Horse Assn. [IO], Plant City, FL, United States

Paso Fino Horse Assn; Amer. [4836]

Paso Fino Owners and Breeders Assn. [★4943]

Paso Fino Owners and Breeders Assn. [★IO]

Paso Horse Assn; Intl. Peruvian [★4934]

Paso Horse Registry; Amer. Peruvian [★4934]

Paso Horses; Amer. Assn. of Owners and Breeders of Peruvian [4810]

Paso Part-Blood Registry; Peruvian [★4934]

Pass-Gp. [12747]

Passaic River Coalition [7840], 94 Mt. Bethel Rd., Warren, NJ 07059, (908)222-0315

Passenger Ship Assn; Intl. [★3915]

Passenger Shipping Assn. [IO], London, United Kingdom

Passenger Traffic Assn; Natl. [★3929]

Passenger Vessel Assn. [2591], 901 N Pitt St., Ste. 100, Alexandria, VA 22314, (703)518-5005

Passenger Vessel Owners; Natl. Assn. of [★2591]

Passengers Assn; Airline [★23015]

Passengers; Natl. Assn. of Railroad [3284]

Passiflora Soc. Intl. [4673], c/o Butterfly World, 3600 W Sample Rd., Coconut Creek, FL 33073

Passionists Intl. [IO], Rome, Italy

Passionists - Southern Baptists United for Lesbian/Gay Concerns - Defunct.

Passive Solar Found. - Defunct.

Passive Solar Inst. - Defunct.

Past-Life Res. and Therapies; Assn. for [★16617]

Past Life Res. and Therapies; Assn. for [★16617]

Past Preservation Network; Recent [7162]

Past in Review - Address unknown since 1999.

Past Savio Movement - Defunct.

Pasta Assn; Natl. [1550]

Pasteef Youth Assn. for Development [IO], Dakar, Senegal

Pastel Artists Canada [IO], Flesherton, ON, Canada

Pastel Societies; Intl. Assn. of [9445]

Pastel Soc. [IO], London, United Kingdom

Pastel Soc. of Am. [IO], New York, NY, United States

Pastel Soc. of Am. [9464], 15 Gramercy Park S, New York, NY 10003, (212)533-6931

Pastel Soc. of Australia [IO], Moorooka, Australia

Pastel Soc. of Eastern Canada [IO], St.-Hyacinthe, QC, Canada

Pastoral Care; Inst. of [★19915]

Pastoral Counseling; Amer. Bd. of Examiners in [19864]

Pastoral Counselors; Amer. Assn. of [19863]

Pastoral da Crianca - Organismo de Agao Social da Conferencia Nacionaldos bispos do Brasil [★IO]

Reference to "IO" in place of a book number signifies that the association may be found in the 45th edition of International Organizations.

Pastoral Educ; Assn. for Clinical [19915]
Pastoral Educators; Assn. of Clinical [★19915]
Pastoral Musicians; Natl. Assn. of [8920]
Pastoral Stud; Inst. for Advanced [★19924]
Pastors Anonymous Recovery Directed Order for Newness - Defunct.
Pastors and Campus Ministry Assn; Assn. of Presbyterian Univ. [★19933]
Pat Boone Fan Club; Natl. [24949]
Pat Boone Fan Clubs; Natl. Assn. of [★24949]
Pat Compton Fan Club [24957]
Pat Shea Intl. Fan Club [24958], PO Box 991, Orchard Park, NY 14127, (888)862-7107
Pat Shea Intl. Fan Club [IO], Orchard Park, NY, United States
Patch Assn; Natl. Cap and [22080]
Patee House Museum [★10145]
Patent and Enamelled Leather Mfrs. Assn. [★2416]
Patent Law
　Intl. Intellectual Property Assn. [5848]
　Intl. Trademark Assn. [5850]
　Inventors Workshop Intl. Educ. Foundation/ Entrepreneurs Workshop [5851]
　IP Justice [5852]
　Natl. Assn. of Patent Practitioners [6167]
　Natl. Assn. of Plant Patent Owners [5046]
　Natl. Inventors Found. [7231]
　Patent Off. Professional Assn. [5856]
　Patent and Trademark Depository Lib. Prog. [6168]
　Patent and Trademark Off. Soc. [5857]
　Trademark Soc. [5860]
Patent Law Assn; Amer. [★5835]
Patent Law Assn. of Washington [★5835]
Patent Law Assns; Natl. Coun. of [★5855]
Patent Model Found; U.S. [★7227]
Patent Off. Professional Assn. [5856], PO Box 2745, Arlington, VA 22202, (571)272-0897
Patent Off. Soc. [★5857]
Patent Owners; Natl. Assn. of Plant [5046]
Patent and Trademark Assn; Intl. [★5848]
Patent and Trademark Depository Lib. Prog. [6168], U.S. Patent & Trademark Off., PO Box 1450, Alexandria, VA 22313-1450, (703)308-4357
Patent and Trademark Off. Soc. [5857], PO Box 2089, Arlington, VA 22202, (571)272-4190
Paternity; Org. for the Lifelong Establishment of [11714]
Path-Finder Guide Dogs [★16864]
Path-Finder Guide Dogs [★IO]
Pathfinder do Brasil [★IO]
Pathfinder Intl. [IO], Watertown, MA, United States
Pathfinder Intl. [12186], 9 Galen St., Ste. 217, Watertown, MA 02472, (617)924-7200
Pathfinder Intl. - Brazil [IO], Salvador, Brazil
Pathological Assn; Amer. Psycho [16190]
Pathological Soc. of Great Britain and Ireland [IO], London, United Kingdom
Pathologists; Amer. Assn. of [★15860]
Pathologists; Amer. Assn. of Avian [16740]
Pathologists; Amer. Coll. of Veterinary [16769]
Pathologists; Amer. Osteopathic Coll. of [15804]
Pathologists; Amer. Soc. of Clinical [★15859]
Pathologists and Bacteriologists; Amer. Assn. of [★15860]
Pathologists; Intl. Assn. of Oral [IO]
Pathologists; Soc. of Toxicologic [★15876]
Pathology
　Amer. Acad. of Oral and Maxillofacial Pathology [15852]
　Amer. Assn. of Avian Pathologists [16740]
　Amer. Assn. of Neuropathologists [15853]
　Amer. Assn. of Pathologists' Assistants [15854]
　Amer. Bd. of Oral and Maxillofacial Pathology [15855]
　Amer. Bd. of Pathology [15856]
　Amer. Coll. of Veterinary Pathologists [16769]
　Amer. Neurotology Soc. [16441]
　Amer. Pathology Found. [15857]
　Amer. Registry of Pathology [15858]
　Amer. Soc. for Clinical Pathology [15859]
　Amer. Soc. for Colposcopy and Cervical Pathology [15590]
　Amer. Soc. for Investigative Pathology [15860]
　Amer. Speech Language Hearing Assn. [16442]

Armed Forces Inst. of Pathology [15261]
Assn. of Clinical Pathologists [IO]
Assn. of Indian Pathologists in North Am. [15861]
Assn. for Molecular Pathology [15862]
Assn. of Pathology Chairs [15863]
Assn. for Pathology Informatics [15864]
British Soc. of Toxicological Pathologists [IO]
Canadian Assn. of Neuropathologists [IO]
Canadian Assn. of Pathologists [IO]
Clinical Cytometry Soc. [15865]
Clinical Pathology Accreditation [IO]
Coll. of Amer. Pathologists [15866]
Consortium for Conservation Medicine [15164]
Dept. of Environmental and Toxicologic Pathology [15867]
Department of Environmental and Toxicologic Pathology [IO]
European Found. for Plant Pathology [IO]
European Ophthalmic Pathology Soc. [IO]
European Soc. of Pathology [IO]
French Assn. for Quality Assurance in Pathology [IO]
German Soc. of Speech, Language, and Voice-Pathology [IO]
House Ear Inst. [16446]
Intl. Acad. of Pathology [15868]
Intl. Acad. of Pathology [IO]
Intl. Assn. of Coroners and Medical Examiners [15093]
Intl. Assn. of Oral Pathologists [IO]
Intl. Assn. of Orofacial Myology [15869]
Intl. Soc. for Plastination [15870]
International Society for Plastination [IO]
Intl. Soc. of Veterinary Dermatopathology [16795]
Intersociety Coun. for Pathology Info. [15871]
Italian Soc. for Plant Pathology [IO]
Japanese Soc. of Pathology [IO]
Natl. Assn. of Medical Examiners [15094]
Natl. Bd. of Medical Examiners [15095]
Natl. Center for Stuttering [16450]
Natl. Student Speech Language Hearing Assn. [16453]
North Amer. Vascular Biology Org. [16728]
Pathological Soc. of Great Britain and Ireland [IO]
Renal Pathology Soc. [IO]
Renal Pathology Soc. [15872]
Royal Coll. of Pathologists of Australasia [IO]
Royal Coll. of Pathologists - United Kingdom [IO]
Sociedad Argentina de Patologia [IO]
Societe de Pathologie Exotique [IO]
Soc. for Applied Immunohistochemistry [15873]
Soc. for Cardiovascular Pathology [13925]
Soc. for Colposcopy and Cervical Pathology of Singapore [IO]
Soc. for Hematopathology [15874]
Soc. for Pediatric Pathology [15875]
Soc. of Toxicologic Pathology [15876]
Soc. for Ultrastructural Pathology [15877]
U.S. and Canadian Acad. of Pathology [15878]
U.S. and Canadian Acad. of Pathology [IO]
World Assn. of Societies of Pathology and Lab. Medicine [IO]
Pathology; Amer. Acad. Oral [★15852]
Pathology; Amer. Assn. of Chairmen of Medical School Departments of [★15863]
Pathology; Amer. Soc. for Colposcopy and Cervical [15590]
Pathology; Amer. Soc. of Dermato [14198]
Pathology; Amer. Soc. for Experimental [★15860]
Pathology; Armed Forces Inst. of [15261]
Pathology Chairmen; Assn. of [★15863]
Pathology; Dept. of Environmental and Drug-Induced [★15867]
Pathology Found; Private Practitioners of [★15857]
Pathology Practice Assn. - Defunct.
Pathology Soc; Australasian Plant [IO]
Pathology; Soc. for Cardiovascular [13925]
Pathology Soc; Exotic [IO]
Pathways to Coll. Network [8493], c/o Aimee McCarron, Admin. Asst., The Educ. Resources Inst., 31 St. James Ave., 4th Fl., Boston, MA 02116, (617)535-6829
Pathways to Peace [12698], PO Box 1057, Larkspur, CA 94977, (415)461-0500
Pathways To Peace [IO], Larkspur, CA, United States

Pathwork Helpers Assn. of North Am. [20565], c/o Jan Rigsby, Chair, 301 E 4th St., Apt. 328, Austin, TX 78701, (512)215-2544
Patidar Cultural Assn. of USA [10218], 32 Stevenson Dr., Marlboro, NJ 07746, (732)761-9829
Patience T'ai Chi Assn. [23897], PO Box 350-532, Brooklyn, NY 11235, (718)332-3477
Patient Account Managers; Amer. Guild of [★15047]
Patient Advocacy; Center for [14620]
Patient Advocacy Legal Service - Defunct.
Patient Advocate Found. [14660], 700 Thimble Shoals Blvd., Ste. 200, Newport News, VA 23606, (800)532-5274
Patient Advocates for Advanced Cancer Treatments [13862], 1143 Parmelee NW, PO Box 141695, Grand Rapids, MI 49514-1695, (616)453-1477
Patient Info. and Educ; Natl. Coun. on [15946]
Patient Representation and Consumer Affairs of the Amer. Hosp. Assn; Natl. Soc. of [★15005]
Patient Representatives of the Amer. Hosp. Assn; Natl. Soc. of [★15005]
Patient Representatives; Soc. of [★15005]
Patient Safety Found; Natl. [14656]
Patient Safety Inst. [14661], 555 Republic Dr., Ste. 200, Plano, TX 75074, (972)444-9800
Patients' Aid Soc. - Defunct.
Patients; Amer. Assn. of Kidney [15283]
Patients Assn. for Pulmonary Hypertension; United [★14911]
Patients on Hemodialysis; Natl. Assn. of [★15283]
Patients on Hemodialysis and Transplantation; Natl. Assn. of [★15283]
Patients; Recovery, Inc., The Assn. of Nervous and Former Mental [★16230]
Patinage Canada [★IO]
Patinage de Vitesse Canada [★IO]
Patriarch Athenagoras Natl. Inst. - Address unknown since 2004.
Patrice Lumumba Coalition - Address unknown since 1989.
Patrick in the City of New York; Soc. of the Friendly Sons of St. [19155]
Patrick Henry Found. - Address unknown since 1990.
Patrick Henry; Friends of [11115]
Patriot Network - The Natl. Assn. of Independent Patriot Clubs - Defunct.
Patriot; New Age [★17139]
Patriotic Educ. Inc. [8092], 1926 Hidden Creek Dr., Kingwood, TX 77339, (713)906-3649
Patriotic Majority - Address unknown since 1999.
Patriotic Order Sons of Am. [21242], 3368 Memphis St., Philadelphia, PA 19134-4510, (215)634-2546
Patriotic Pets [11442], PO Box 95706, Atlanta, GA 30347, (404)879-1053
Patriotism
　107th Engineer Assn. [5467]
　Air Distribution Inst. [1875]
　Amer. Patriots Assn. [21239]
　Amer. Rosie the Riveter Assn. [21388]
　Centennial Legion of Historic Military Commands [21240]
　Christian-Patriots Defense League/Citizen's Emergency Defense Sys. [17263]
　Indicorps [12406]
　Iraq and Afghanistan Veterans of Am. [21335]
　Japanese Amer. Veterans Assn. [21305]
　Junior Amer. Citizens [11335]
　Marine Embassy Guard Assn. [21177]
　Military, Veterans and Patriotic Ser. Organizations of Am. [21245]
　Minuteman Civil Defense Corps [17077]
　Natl. Cong. of Patriotic Organizations [18185]
　Natl. Flag Day Found. [21094]
　Natl. Graves Assn. [IO]
　Natl. Pledge of Allegiance Found. [21241]
　Natl. Traditionalist Caucus [17276]
　Oper. Gratitude [11493]
　Oper.: Take a Soldier to the Movies [11498]
　Oper. Truth [21317]
　Patriotic Educ. Inc. [8092]
　Patriotic Order Sons of Am. [21242]
　Patriots for the Defense of Am. [18186]
　Red River Valley Fighter Pilots Assn. [21318]
　Soldiers' Angels [19259]

A star before a book entry number signifies that the name is not listed separately, but is mentioned within the entry.

A Soldier's Wish List [11501]

Patriots of Am; Order of the Founders and [20755]

Patriots of the Amer. Revolution; Hereditary Order of Descendants of the Loyalists and [20673]

Patriots for the Defense of Am. [18186]

Patriots Defense League/Citizen's Emergency Defense Sys; Christian- [17263]

Patriots of Fort McHenry [★10057]

Patriots of Fort McHenry-Living Classrooms [10057], Ft. McHenry Natl. Monument and Historic Shrine, 802 S Caroline St., Baltimore, MD 21231, (410)396-3453

The Patriots Found. [★20669]

Patriots Found; Black Revolutionary War [20669]

Patriots Information Network - Defunct.

Patriots Network - Defunct.

Patristics

North Amer. Patristics Soc. [20460]

Patrol Craft Sailors Assn. [21218], c/o Jim Heywood, 7005 Bridge Rd., Cincinnati, OH 45230, (315)487-2623

Patrolmen's Intl. Union; Railway [★24180]

Patrons of the Arts in the Vatican Museum - Address unknown since 1999.

Patrouille canadienne de ski [★IO]

Pat's Peace Kids Intl. Peace Clubs [★IO]

Pat's Peace Kids Intl. Peace Clubs [★18196]

Patsy Cline World Wide Fan Org; Always [24840]

Patsy Montana Fan Club - Address unknown since 2002.

Patt Family Assn. - Defunct.

Patterdale Terrier Club of Am. [22338], 108 Olde Towne Rd., Paradise, TX 76073

Pattern Glass Soc; Early Amer. [22014]

Pattern Makers Assn. of New York - Address unknown since 1995.

Pattern Makers' League of North Am. [★24012]

Pattern, Model, and Mould Mfrs. Assn. [IO], West Bromwich, United Kingdom

Pattern and Plastic Tool Builders Assn. - Defunct.

Pattern Recognition

Associacao Portuguesa de Reconhecimento de Padroes [IO]

Assn. for Image Anal. and Recognition [IO]

Assn. for Image Processing [IO]

Australian Pattern Recognition Soc. [IO]

Austrian Assn. for Pattern Recognition [IO]

British Machine Vision Assn. and Soc. for Pattern Recognition [IO]

Bulgarian Assn. of Pattern Recognition [IO]

Canadian Image Processing and Pattern Recognition Soc. [IO]

Classification Soc. of North Am. [7456]

Cmpt. Vision and Pattern Recognition Gp. of Korea Info. Sci. Soc. [IO]

Cuban Assn. for Pattern Recognition [IO]

Czechoslovak Pattern Recognition Soc. [IO]

Danish Pattern Recognition Soc. [IO]

Deutsche Arbeitsgemeinschaft fur Mustererkennung [IO]

French Assn. for Pattern Recognition and Interpretation [IO]

Hong Kong Soc. for Multimedia and Image Computing [IO]

Indian Unit for Pattern Recognition and Artificial Intelligence [IO]

Intl. Assn. for Pattern Recognition [IO]

Irish Pattern Recognition and Classification Soc. [IO]

Israel Assn. for Cmpt. Vision and Pattern Recognition [IO]

Italian Assn. for Pattern Recognition [IO]

Mexican Assn. for Cmpt. Vision, Neurocomputing and Robotics [IO]

Norwegian Soc. for Image Processing and Pattern Recognition [IO]

Pattern Recognition Assn. of South Africa [IO]

Pattern Recognition and Machine Intelligence Assn. [IO]

Pattern Recognition Soc. [7457]

Pattern Recognition Soc. of Finland [IO]

Russian Fed. Assn. for Pattern Recognition and Image Anal. [IO]

Slovenian Soc. for Pattern Recognition [IO]

Spanish Assn. for Pattern Recognition and Image Anal. [IO]

Swedish Soc. for Automated Image Anal. [IO]

Swiss Assn. for Pattern Recognition [IO]

Turkish Soc. for Image Anal. and Pattern Recognition [IO]

Pattern Recognition Assn. of South Africa [IO], Matieland, Republic of South Africa

Pattern Recognition and Machine Intelligence Assn. [IO], Singapore, Singapore

Pattern Recognition Soc. [7457], c/o Natl. Biomedical Res. Found., 3900 Reservoir Rd. NW, Washington, DC 20007, (202)687-2121

Pattern Recognition Soc. of Finland [IO], Oulu, Finland

Patti Page Appreciation Soc. [IO], Ponce Inlet, FL, United States

Patti Page Appreciation Soc. [24959], c/o Rene Paquette, Pres., 4565 S Atlantic Ave., Ste. 5103, Ponce Inlet, FL 32127, (386)756-6682

Patton, Jr. Historical Soc; George Smith [★11141]

Patton Soc. [11141], c/o Charles M. Province, Pres./ Founder, 17010 S Potter Rd., Oregon City, OR 97045

Patty Moise Fan Club; Elton Sawyer - [★25005]

Pauktuutit Inuit Women's Assn. [IO], Ottawa, ON, Canada

Paul Andrew Dawkins Children's Project [★11690]

Paul Anka Fan Club - Address unknown since 1999.

Paul the Apostle; Missionary Soc. of Saint [19663]

Paul Casey Fan Club - Address unknown since 2000.

Paul Claudel Soc. [9698]

Paul Claudel Society [IO], Athens, GA, United States

Paul; Company of Saint [19614]

Paul-Ehrlich-Gesellschaft fur Chemotherapie [IO], Rheinbach, Germany

Paul; Fellowship of Saint [19958]

Paul and Lisa Found. [★13082]

Paul and Lisa Prog. [13082], PO Box 348, Westbrook, CT 06498, (860)767-7660

Paul Revere Soc. [18301], 150 Shoreline Hwy., Bldg. E, Mill Valley, CA 94941

Paul VI Inst. for the Arts [9591], 619 10th St. NW, Washington, DC 20001-4532, (202)347-2714

Pauline Pinkney Intl. Fan Club - Defunct.

Paulist Fathers [★19663]

Paulist League [★19699]

Paulist Memorial Soc. [19699], Paulist Fathers, 3015 4th St. NE, Washington, DC 20017-1102, (202)269-2521

Paulist Natl. Catholic Evangelization Assn. [19700], 3031 4th St. NE, Washington, DC 20017-1102, (202)832-5022

Paved Arts New Media [IO], Saskatoon, SK, Canada

Pavement Assn; Amer. Concrete [913]

Pavement Assn; Natl. Asphalt [641]

Pavement Contractors Assn; Natl. [651]

Pavement Inst; Interlocking Concrete [926]

Pavement Preservation; Found. for [945]

Paving Brick Assn; Natl. [★604]

Paving Moratorium; Alliance for a [17234]

Paving Technologists; Assn. of Asphalt [6835]

Paviors' Company [IO], Enfield, United Kingdom

Paw Paw Found. [4754], c/o Paw Paw Res., 129 Atwood Res. Fac., Kentucky State Univ., Frankfort, KY 40601-2355, (502)597-6174

Pawnbrokers Assn; Natl. [2429]

PAWS For A Cause [11443], 2708 Freeman Mill Rd., Suffolk, VA 23438, (757)986-2287

Paws With a Cause [11979], 4646 South Div., Wayland, MI 49348, (616)877-7297

Pax Assn; Amer. [★18121]

Pax Christi Aotearoa New Zealand [IO], Auckland, New Zealand

Pax Christi - Australia [IO], Carlton, Australia

Pax Christi Australia (New South Wales Br.) [IO], Sydney, Australia

Pax Christi - Austria [IO], Linz, Austria

Pax Christi - Denmark [IO], Copenhagen, Denmark

Pax Christi Flanders [IO], Antwerp, Belgium

Pax Christi - France [IO], Paris, France

Pax Christi - Germany [IO], Bad Vilbel, Germany

Pax Christi Goma [IO], Goma, Democratic Republic of the Congo

Pax Christi - Great Britain [IO], London, United Kingdom

Pax Christi Groupe de Paroisse Busogo [IO], Ruhengeri, Rwanda

Pax Christi - Hungary [IO], Szeged, Hungary

Pax Christi Intl. [IO], Brussels, Belgium

Pax Christi - Ireland [IO], Dublin, Ireland

Pax Christi - Italy [IO], Florence, Italy

Pax Christi Kikwit [IO], Kikwit, Democratic Republic of the Congo

Pax Christi - Luxembourg [IO], Luxembourg, Luxembourg

Pax Christi - Netherlands [IO], Utrecht, Netherlands

Pax Christi Osterreich [★IO]

Pax Christi - Philippines [IO], Bacolod City, Philippines

Pax Christi Port-au-Prince [IO], Port-au-Prince, Haiti

Pax Christi - Portugal [IO], Lisbon, Portugal

Pax Christi Queensland Br. [IO], Lutwyche, Australia

Pax Christi - Sect. Francaise [★IO]

Pax Christi - Switzerland [IO], Villars-sur-Glane, Switzerland

Pax Christi - U.S.A. [18121], 532 W 8th St., Erie, PA 16502, (814)453-4955

Pax Christi Vlaanderen [★IO]

Pax Christi Wallonie-Bruxelles [IO], Brussels, Belgium

Pax Christi Warsaw [IO], Warsaw, Poland

Pax Romana, Intl. Catholic Movement for Intellectual and Cultural Affairs [IO], Geneva, Switzerland

Pax Romana, Movimento Internacional de Intelectuales Catolicos [★IO]

Pax World Found. [★IO]

Pax World Found. [★17845]

Pax World Ser. [17845], c/o Mercy Corps., Dept. W, PO Box 2669, Portland, OR 97208-2669, (800)292-3355

Pax World Ser. [IO], Portland, OR, United States

Pay Equity; Natl. Comm. on [17553]

Pay for Schools by Regulating Cannabis [18302], PO Box 86741, Portland, OR 97286, (503)229-0428

Payasos Sin Fronteras [★IO]

Payload Prog; Student Experimental [6390]

Payments Alliance; Western [1451]

Payments Assn; NACHA: The Electronic [486]

Payments Assn. of South Africa [IO], Marshalltown, Republic of South Africa

Payments and Electronic Commerce Inst; sponsors Accredited ACH Professional (AAP) program [★486]

Payphone Assn; Natl. [★3733]

Payroll Assn; Amer. [1253]

Paz y Cooperacion [★IO]

Pazarlama ve Kamuoyu Arastirmacilari Dernegi [★IO]

PBCers Org. [14816], 1430 Garden Rd., Pearland, TX 77581

PBR Forces Veterans Assn. [21348], c/o Robert Gray, Membership Chm., 1600 Township Rd. 395, Jeromesville, OH 44840-9712, (419)281-4711

PC/104 Consortium [3727], 1712 Devonshire Rd., Sacramento, CA 95864, (916)270-2016

PC Hackers - Defunct.

PC-SIG - Defunct.

PCI Indus. Cmpt. Mfrs. Gp. [6818], c/o Virtual, Inc., 401 Edgewater Pl., Ste. 600, Wakefield, MA 01880, (781)246-9318

PCIA - The Wireless Infrastructure Assn. [3752], 500 Montgomery St., Ste. 700, Alexandria, VA 22314-1560, (703)535-7447

PCIA - The Wireless Infrastructure Association [IO], Alexandria, VA, United States

PCPCI-The Transformer Assn. [★IO]

PCPCI-The Transformer Assn. [★1836]

PDA [2979], 4350 E West Hwy., Ste. 200, Bethesda, MD 20814-4426, (301)656-5900

PDA [IO], Bethesda, MD, United States

PDCI [★17844]

PDO Infosources - Defunct.

PE4life [8991], 810 Baltimore, Ste. 100, Kansas City, MO 64105-1706, (816)472-7345

Pea Growers and Dealers; Pacific Northwest [★4314]

Peace

A. J. Muste Memorial Inst. [IO]

Acad. for Peace Res. [18187]

Reference to "IO" in place of a book number signifies that the association may be found in the 45th edition of International Organizations.

Action Comm. Ser. for Peace [IO]
Action from Ireland [IO]
Afghanistan Peace Assn. [16917]
African Peace Support Trainers' Assn. [IO]
A.J. Muste Memorial Inst. [18188]
Alliance for Peacebuilding [17248]
Ambedkar Center for Justice and Peace [IO]
Amer. Comm. for Peace in Chechnya [18189]
American Committee for Peace In Chechnya [IO]
Amer. Task Force on Palestine [17860]
Americans for Peace Now [17935]
Americans United for Israel [19157]
Amnesty Intl. of the U.S.A. [17746]
Asia Pacific Peace Res. Assn. [IO]
Assn. for Peace [IO]
Athletes United for Peace [18190]
Axis of Justice [18640]
Baptist Peace Fellowship of North Am. [18191]
Baptist Peace Fellowship of North Am. [IO]
Boise Peace Quilt Proj. [18192]
Brethren Peace Fellowship [19534]
Buddhist Peace Fellowship [18193]
Buddhist Peace Fellowship [IO]
Campaign for the Accountability of Amer. Bases
   [IO]
Canadian Friends of Peace Now [IO]
Canadian Friends of Soviet People [IO]
Canadian Peace Alliance [IO]
Canadian Peace Res. and Educational Assn. [IO]
Canadian Peacebuilding Coordinating Comm. [IO]
Canadian Voice of Women for Peace [IO]
Carnegie Coun. for Ethics in Intl. Affairs [20093]
Carnegie Endowment for Intl. Peace [17863]
Catholic Peace Fellowship [18194]
Catholic Worker Movement [18109]
Center for Campus Organizing [18195]
Center on Conscience and War [17438]
Center for Documentation and Res. of Peace and
   Conflicts [IO]
Center for Intl. Policy [17748]
Center for Nonviolent Commun. [18110]
Central Comm. for Conscientious Objectors
   [17439]
Children of the Earth [12696]
Children of the Earth [IO]
Children as the Peacemakers [IO]
Children as the Peacemakers [18196]
The Children of War [18197]
The Children of War [IO]
Christian Peace Conf. [IO]
Christians Assoc. for Relationships with Eastern
   Europe [IO]
Church and Peace [IO]
Coalition for Harmony of Races in the U.S.
   [18198]
Code Pink Women's Pre-Emptive Strike for Peace
   [18199]
Code Pink Women's Pre-Emptive Strike for Peace
   [IO]
Coexistence Intl. [IO]
Coexistence Intl. [12697]
Concerned Philosophers for Peace [7489]
Conscience Canada [IO]
Consistent Life [18200]
Cross-Cultural Solutions [11901]
Disciples Peace Fellowship [18201]
Do Right Found. [20492]
Educ. for Peace in Iraq Center [17927]
European Peace Res. Assn. [IO]
European Univ. Center for Peace Stud. [IO]
Fellowship of Reconciliation - USA [IO]
Fellowship of Reconciliation - USA [18202]
Found. for Global Community [18203]
Found. for P.E.A.C.E. [18204]
Found. for P.E.A.C.E. [IO]
Found. for Peace - Spain [IO]
Friends of Peace Pilgrim [11116]
Friends of Sabeel - North Am. [18205]
Friends of Sabeel - North Am. [IO]
Friends World Comm. for Consultation [IO]
Friends World Comm. for Consultation [18206]
German Peace Soc. - United War Resisters [IO]
Global Majority [17249]
Global Vision for Peace [18207]
Global Youth Connect [18851]

GlobalSecurity.org [18208]
Henry L. Stimson Center [17824]
Historians Against the War [18795]
Hong Kong Network on Religion and Peace [IO]
Horn Relief [IO]
Initiatives of Change - Switzerland [IO]
Inst. for Global Communications [7772]
Inst. for Individual and World Peace [12352]
Inst. for Peace and Justice [18209]
Inter-American Conf. of Ministers of Labor [17394]
Intl. Alliance of Holistic Lawyers [5498]
Intl. A.N.S.W.E.R. Coalition - Act Now to Stop War
   and End Racism [18210]
Intl. A.N.S.W.E.R. Coalition - Act Now to Stop War
   and End Racism [IO]
Intl. Assn. of Educators for World Peace - Canada
   [IO]
Intl. Assn. of Educators for World Peace - USA
   [IO]
Intl. Assn. of Educators for World Peace - USA
   [18211]
Intl. Christian Ser. for Peace [IO]
Intl. Fellowship of Reconciliation - Austria [IO]
Intl. Fellowship of Reconciliation - Bangladesh
   [IO]
Intl. Fellowship of Reconciliation - Belgium [IO]
Intl. Fellowship of Reconciliation - England [IO]
Intl. Fellowship of Reconciliation - France [IO]
Intl. Fellowship of Reconciliation - Germany [IO]
Intl. Fellowship of Reconciliation - India [IO]
Intl. Fellowship of Reconciliation - Italy [IO]
Intl. Fellowship of Reconciliation - Japan [IO]
Intl. Fellowship of Reconciliation - Madagascar
   [IO]
Intl. Fellowship of Reconciliation - Netherlands
   [IO]
Intl. Fellowship of Reconciliation - Norway [IO]
Intl. Fellowship of Reconciliation - Sweden [IO]
Intl. Fellowship of Reconciliation - Uganda [IO]
Intl. Fellowship of Reconciliation - Wales [IO]
Intl. Fellowship of Reconciliation - Zimbabwe [IO]
Intl. Inst. of Peace Stud. and Global Philosophy
   [IO]
Intl. Mothers' Peace Day Comm. [IO]
Intl. Mothers' Peace Day Comm. [18212]
Intl. Peace Bur. [IO]
Intl. Peace Operations Assn. [IO]
Intl. Peace Operations Assn. [18213]
Intl. Soc. for a Complete Earth [12354]
Interreligious and Intl. Fed. for World Peace [IO]
Iraq Action Coalition [17928]
Irish Amer. Unity Conf. [17932]
Jane Addams Peace Assn. [18214]
Jane Addams Peace Assn. [IO]
Jewish Peace Fellowship [18215]
Joan B. Kroc Inst. for Intl. Peace Stud. [18216]
Joan B. Kroc Institute for International Peace
   Studies [IO]
Lentz Peace Res. Assn. [18217]
Lutheran Peace Fellowship [18218]
Mediators Without Borders [5458]
Medicine for Peace [12789]
Mennonite Central Comm. Overseas Peace Off.
   [18219]
Mennonite Central Comm. Overseas Peace Off.
   [IO]
Men's Intl. Peace Exchange [IO]
Men's Intl. Peace Exchange [18220]
Middle East Children's Alliance [17774]
Middle East Nonviolence and Democracy [IO]
Military Families Speak Out [18796]
Mothers Against War [18221]
Mt. Diablo Peace Center [18222]
Move Am. Forward [18733]
Musicians' Alliance for Peace [18223]
Musicians' Alliance for Peace [IO]
Natl. Asian Peace Officers' Assn. [5983]
Natl. Assn. Citizens on Patrol [12970]
Natl. Peace Found. [18224]
Natl. Peace Garden Foundation [18225]
Natl. Pledge of Allegiance Found. [21241]
Natl. Youth and Student Peace Coalition [18226]
Native Amer. Leadership Alliance [20455]
Never Again Campaign [18162]
Never More War [IO]

Niwano Peace Found. [IO]
No Peace Without Justice [IO]
No Peace Without Justice [18227]
Nonviolence.Org [18228]
Nordic Women's Peace Network [IO]
Norwegian Peace Alliance [IO]
Norwegian Peace Assn. [IO]
Nuclear Age Peace Found. [IO]
Nuclear Age Peace Found. [18229]
Oz Veshalom-Netivot Shalom [IO]
Partners for Peace [IO]
Partners for Peace [18230]
Pathways to Peace [12698]
Pathways To Peace [IO]
Pax Christi Aotearoa New Zealand [IO]
Pax Christi - Australia [IO]
Pax Christi Australia (New South Wales Br.) [IO]
Pax Christi - Austria [IO]
Pax Christi - Denmark [IO]
Pax Christi Flanders [IO]
Pax Christi - France [IO]
Pax Christi - Germany [IO]
Pax Christi Goma [IO]
Pax Christi - Great Britain [IO]
Pax Christi Groupe de Paroisse Busogo [IO]
Pax Christi - Hungary [IO]
Pax Christi Intl. [IO]
Pax Christi - Ireland [IO]
Pax Christi - Italy [IO]
Pax Christi Kikwit [IO]
Pax Christi - Luxembourg [IO]
Pax Christi - Netherlands [IO]
Pax Christi - Philippines [IO]
Pax Christi Port-au-Prince [IO]
Pax Christi - Portugal [IO]
Pax Christi Queensland Br. [IO]
Pax Christi - Switzerland [IO]
Pax Christi Wallonie-Bruxelles [IO]
Pax Christi Warsaw [IO]
Pax World Ser. [17845]
Peace Brigade Intl. - Australia [IO]
Peace Brigade Intl. - Belgium [IO]
Peace Brigade Intl. - Canada [IO]
Peace Brigade Intl. - Luxembourg [IO]
Peace Brigade Intl. - Netherlands [IO]
Peace Brigade Intl. - Switzerland [IO]
Peace Brigade Intl. - United Kingdom [IO]
Peace Brigades Intl. - Aotearoa/New Zealand [IO]
Peace Brigades Intl. - Italy [IO]
Peace Brigades Intl. - U.S.A. [IO]
Peace Brigades Intl. - U.S.A. [18231]
Peace Child Intl. [IO]
Peace and Cooperation [IO]
Peace Development Fund [18232]
Peace and Justice Stud. Assn. [18233]
Peace Movement of Esbjerg [IO]
Peace Museum [18234]
Peace and Neutrality Alliance [IO]
Peace Now [IO]
Peace Pledge Union [IO]
Peace Res. Center [IO]
Peace Sci. Soc. (Intl.) [IO]
Peace Sci. Soc. (Intl.) [18235]
Peace Through Law Educ. Fund [18236]
Peace X Peace [18237]
Peacefund Canada [IO]
PeaceJam [8958]
Peacework Volunteer Org. [18238]
Peacework Volunteer Org. [IO]
Peaceworkers Nonviolent Peaceforce [IO]
Peaceworkers Nonviolent Peaceforce [18239]
People's Rights Fund [17144]
Physicians for Peace [15078]
Play for Peace [12699]
Play for Peace [IO]
Plowshares Inst. [18240]
Poets Against the War [11189]
Potters for Peace [9838]
Presbyterian Peace Fellowship [18241]
Prog. on the Anal. and Resolution of Conflicts
   [18242]
Proj. Ploughshares [IO]
Promoting Enduring Peace [18243]
Pugwash Conferences on Sci. and World Affairs
   [17247]

A star before a book entry number signifies that the name is not listed separately, but is mentioned within the entry.

Pups for Peace [12700]
Pups for Peace [IO]
Quaker Peace and Social Witness [IO]
Reaching Critical Will [17436]
Roots of Peace [18244]
Sasakawa Peace Found. [IO]
Scherman Found. [13189]
Scholars for Peace in the Middle East [18070]
Seeds of Peace [18245]
Seeking Common Ground [13514]
September Eleventh Families for Peaceful Tomorrows [12701]
Serendipity Assn. [14832]
Ser. Civil Intl. - Germany [IO]
Ser. for Peace [18246]
Ser. of Peace and Justice, Chile [IO]
Soc. for the Stud. of Peace, Conflict, and Violence: Peace Psychology Div. of the Amer. Psychological Assn. [16185]
Spirit of Am. [18488]
StandWithUs [17941]
Stop the War Coalition [IO]
Students for Social Responsibility [18172]
Swedish Fellowship of Reconciliation [IO]
Swedish Peace and Arbitration Soc. [IO]
Swiss Peace Coun. [IO]
Temple of Understanding [20583]
Transnational Found. for Peace and Future Res. [IO]
Traprock Peace Center [18247]
Tree of Peace Soc. [9913]
Tuesday's Children [12003]
United for Peace and Justice [18248]
United for Peace and Justice [IO]
United States Canada Peace Anniversary Association [IO]
U.S. Canada Peace Anniversary Assn. [19299]
U.S. Farmers Assn. [16958]
U.S. Indus. Coalition [7637]
U.S. Inst. of Peace [18249]
U.S. Inst. of Peace [IO]
U.S. Peace Govt. [18250]
Unity Coalition for Israel [8672]
Unity Corps [19017]
Universal Peace Fed. [18251]
Veterans for Peace [18252]
Veterans for Peace [IO]
Voices in the Wilderness [IO]
Voices in the Wilderness [18253]
Volunteers for Peace [17919]
WAND Educ. Fund [18174]
War and Peace Found. [18254]
War and Peace Found. [IO]
West Africa Network for Peacebuilding [IO]
Win Without War [18124]
Women in Black [18255]
Women for Peace - Switzerland [IO]
Women's Alliance for Peace and Human Rights in Afghanistan [12380]
Women's Intl. League for Peace and Freedom - Albania [IO]
Women's Intl. League for Peace and Freedom - Australia [IO]
Women's Intl. League for Peace and Freedom - Belarus [IO]
Women's Intl. League for Peace and Freedom - Bolivia [IO]
Women's Intl. League for Peace and Freedom - Burundi [IO]
Women's Intl. League for Peace and Freedom - Canada [IO]
Women's Intl. League for Peace and Freedom - Chile [IO]
Women's Intl. League for Peace and Freedom - Colombia [IO]
Women's Intl. League for Peace and Freedom - Costa Rica [IO]
Women's Intl. League for Peace and Freedom - Denmark [IO]
Women's Intl. League for Peace and Freedom - Finland [IO]
Women's Intl. League for Peace and Freedom - France [IO]
Women's Intl. League for Peace and Freedom - French Polynesia [IO]

Women's Intl. League for Peace and Freedom - Germany [IO]
Women's Intl. League for Peace and Freedom - India [IO]
Women's Intl. League for Peace and Freedom - Ireland [IO]
Women's Intl. League for Peace and Freedom - Israel [IO]
Women's Intl. League for Peace and Freedom - Italy [IO]
Women's Intl. League for Peace and Freedom - Japan [IO]
Women's Intl. League for Peace and Freedom - Lebanon [IO]
Women's Intl. League for Peace and Freedom - Nepal [IO]
Women's Intl. League for Peace and Freedom - Netherlands [IO]
Women's Intl. League for Peace and Freedom - New Zealand [IO]
Women's Intl. League for Peace and Freedom - Norway [IO]
Women's Intl. League for Peace and Freedom - Peru [IO]
Women's Intl. League for Peace and Freedom - Philippines [IO]
Women's Intl. League for Peace and Freedom - Russia [IO]
Women's Intl. League for Peace and Freedom - Sierra Lone [IO]
Women's Intl. League for Peace and Freedom - Sri Lanka [IO]
Women's Intl. League for Peace and Freedom - Sweden [IO]
Women's Intl. League for Peace and Freedom - Switzerland [IO]
Women's Intl. League for Peace and Freedom - United Kingdom [IO]
Women's Intl. League for Peace and Freedom, U.S. Sect. [IO]
Women's Intl. League for Peace and Freedom, U.S. Sect. [18256]
Women's Intl. League for Peace and Freedom - Venezuela [IO]
Women's Learning Partnership for Rights, Development, and Peace [13452]
World Assn. for the School as an Instrument of Peace [IO]
World Conf. of Religions for Peace [IO]
World Conf. of Religions for Peace [18257]
World Coun. of Religious Leaders [20519]
World Peace Prayer Soc. [18258]
World Peace Prayer Soc. [IO]
World Peace Through Tech. Org. [IO]
World Peace Through Tech. Org. [7458]
World Without War Coun. [18259]
Worldwide Forgiveness Alliance [8959]
Worldwide Forgiveness Alliance [IO]
Young Koreans United [12485]
Youth Action for Peace [IO]
Youth Action for Peace - Italy [IO]
Peace Acad. Campaign; Natl. [★18224]
Peace Acad. Found; Natl. [★18224]
Peace Acad. Fund; Natl. [★18224]
Peace Action [18166], 1100 Wayne Ave., Ste. 1020, Silver Spring, MD 20910, (301)565-4050
Peace Action Center - Defunct.
Peace Action Educ. Fund [18167], 1100 Wayne Ave., Ste. 1020, Silver Spring, MD 20910-5643, (301)565-4050
Peace Activists East and West Coordinating Comm. - Address unknown since 2003.
Peace; Acts for [★18259]
Peace; America-Israel Coun. for Israeli-Palestinian [18047]
Peace; Benedictines for [19582]
Peace Brigade Intl. - Australia [IO], Fitzroy, Australia
Peace Brigade Intl. - Belgium [IO], Brussels, Belgium
Peace Brigade Intl. - Canada [IO], Ottawa, ON, Canada
Peace Brigade Intl. - Luxembourg [IO], Luxembourg, Luxembourg
Peace Brigade Intl. - Netherlands [IO], Amsterdam, Netherlands

Peace Brigade Intl. - Switzerland [IO], Bern, Switzerland
Peace Brigade Intl. - United Kingdom [IO], London, United Kingdom
Peace Brigades Intl. - Aotearoa/New Zealand [IO], Wanganui, New Zealand
Peace Brigades Intl. - Italy [IO], Bollate, Italy
Peace Brigades Intl. - U.S.A. [IO], Washington, DC, United States
Peace Brigades Intl. - U.S.A. [18231], 1326 9th St. NW, Washington, DC 20001, (202)232-0142
Peace Builders [★17914]
Peace Builders [★IO]
Peace & Carrots Caucus - Defunct.
Peace Child Intl. [IO], Buntingford, United Kingdom
Peace; Children as Teachers of [★18196]
Peace Clubs; Pat's Peace Kids Intl. [★18196]
Peace Clubs; Pat's Peace Kids Intl. [★IO]
Peace and Common Security - Defunct.
Peace; Concerned Philosophers for [7489]
Peace and Cooperation [IO], Madrid, Spain
Peace Corps [18263], c/o Paul D. Coverdell Peace Corps HQ, 1111 20th St. NW, Washington, DC 20526, (202)692-2170

Peace Corps
Aprovecho Res. Center [16993]
Lesbian, Gay, Bisexual and Transgender US Peace Corps Alumni [18260]
Minority Peace Corps Assn. [18261]
Natl. Peace Corps Assn. [18262]
Peace Corps [18263]
Peace Corps Partnership Prog. [18264]
Peace Corps Assn; Natl. [★18262]
Peace Corps Inst. - Defunct.
Peace Corps Partnership Prog. [18264], 1111 20th St. NW, 8th Fl., Washington, DC 20526, (202)692-2170
Peace Corps School Partnership Prog. [★18264]
Peace Corps School to School Prog. [★18264]
Peace Corps of the U.S. [★18263]
Peace Corps; U.S. [★18263]
Peace Corps Volunteers; Natl. Coun. of Returned [★18262]
Peace and Democracy in the Middle East; Youth Comm. for [★18073]
Peace; Department of Social Development and World [★19613]
Peace; Department of Social Development and World [★IO]
Peace Development Fund [18232], 44 N Prospect St., PO Box 1280, Amherst, MA 01004, (413)256-8306
Peace Educ. Found. [★8139]
Peace Educ. Found; Grace Contrino Abrams [8139]
Peace Education Network (K-12) - Address unknown since 1999.
Peace through Educ. Project - Address unknown since 2004.
Peace in El Salvador; Christians for [20322]
Peace Fellowship; Brethren [19534]
Peace Fellowship; Episcopal [18614]
Peace Fellowship; Southern Presbyterian [★18241]
Peace Fellowship; United Presbyterian [★18241]
Peace Found. [★IO]
Peace; Found. for Middle East [18058]
Peace, and Freedom in the Americas; Coalition for Jobs, [★18463]
Peace and Freedom Party [18330], PO Box 24764, Oakland, CA 94623, (510)465-9414
Peace; Fund for [18834]
Peace Garden; Natl. [★18225]
Peace Garden Project [★18225]
Peace; Grandmothers for [★18154]
PEACE for Guatemala [★12819]
Peace, Hea. and Human Development Found. [IO], Kobe, Japan
Peace History Soc. [10143], c/o Christy Snider, Treas., Dept. of History, Berry Coll., 5010 Mt. Berry Sta., Mount Berry, GA 30149, (706)368-5652
Peace; Hoover Institution on War, Revolution and [18836]
Peace Hostage Exchange Found. [★17370]
Peace Hostage Exchange Found. [★IO]
Peace and Human Rights; Commn. on [★18242]
Peace Inst. Found; Natl. [★18224]

Reference to "IO" in place of a book number signifies that the association may be found in the 45th edition of International Organizations.

Encyclopedia of Associations, 46th Edition

3967

Peace Inst; Korean Amer. [17966]

Peace, Justice and Reunification; Korea Church Coalition for [★17966]

Peace and Justice Ser. in Argentina [IO], Buenos Aires, Argentina

Peace and Justice Stud. Assn. [18233], Univ. Ctr., 5th Fl., 2130 Fulton St., San Francisco, CA 94117-1080, (402)533-2615

Peace; Kids [11615]

Peace Links - Address unknown since 2002.

Peace Lobby; Jewish [17614]

A Peace of Love - Defunct.

Peace in the Middle East; Writers and Artists for [18072]

Peace in the Middle East; Youth Inst. for [18073]

Peace Mission [★18196]

Peace Mission [★IO]

Peace Mission; COAR [17482]

Peace Mission; Comunidad Oscar A. Romero [★17482]

Peace Mission Movement [19823], c/o Palace Mission Church Inc., 1622 Spring Mill Rd., Gladwyne, PA 19035-1021, (610)525-5598

Peace Movement of Esbjerg [IO], Esbjerg, Denmark

Peace Movement of Ethiopia - Address unknown since 1995.

Peace Movement; Inner [10173]

Peace Museum [18234], PO Box 803887, Chicago, IL 60680-3887, (773)638-6450

Peace and Neutrality Alliance [IO], Dalkey, Ireland

Peace Now [★IO]

Peace Now [IO], Jerusalem, Israel

Peace Now [★17935]

Peace Now; Americans for [17935]

Peace Now; Friends of [★17935]

Peace; Office of Intl. Justice and [★19613]

Peace; Office of Intl. Justice and [★IO]

Peace Officers for Christ Intl. [IO], Santa Ana, CA, United States

Peace Officers for Christ Intl. [19824], 3000 W Mac-Arthur Blvd., Ste. 426, Santa Ana, CA 92704-6962, (714)426-7632

Peace Officers; Fellowship of Christian [★19798]

Peace Officers - U.S.A; Fellowship of Christian [19798]

Peace Pac [18168], c/o Coun. for a Livable World, 322 4th St. NE, Washington, DC 20002, (202)543-4100

Peace; Pageant for [★17916]

Peace Party; Women's [★18256]

Peace Pilgrim; Friends of [11116]

Peace Pledge Union [IO], London, United Kingdom

Peace Race Comm. - Defunct.

Peace Res. Center [IO], Madrid, Spain

Peace Res., Educ. and Development; Consortium on [★18233]

Peace Res. in History; Coun. on [★10143]

Peace Res. Inst. [★18455]

Peace Res. Inst. [★IO]

Peace Res. Lab. [★18217]

Peace Res. Network [★18233]

Peace Res. Soc. - Intl. [★18235]

Peace Res. Soc. - Intl. [★IO]

Peace Rsrc. Proj. [18625], PO Box 1122, Arcata, CA 95518-1122, (707)822-4229

Peace and Reunification of Korea; Campaign for the [★17966]

Peace Run - Address unknown since 2008.

Peace Scholarship Fund; International [★9325]

Peace Scholarship Fund; International [★IO]

Peace Sci. Soc. (Intl.) [IO], University Park, PA, United States

Peace Sci. Soc. (Intl.) [18235], c/o Prof. Glenn Palmer, Exec. Dir., Dept. of Political Sci., 202 Pond Bldg., Pennsylvania State Univ., University Park, PA 16802, (814)865-5594

Peace; Serendipity Assn. for Res. and Implementation of Holistic Hea. and World [★14832]

Peace Soc; Amer. [17858]

Peace; Soc. of Prayer for World [★18258]

Peace and Solidarity Alliance - Address unknown since 1991.

Peace Stud; Center for War/ [17865]

Peace Tax Fund; Natl. Campaign for a [18712]

Peace Tax Fund; Suffolk County Comm. for a World [★18716]

Peace Taxpayers - Defunct.

Peace Through Law Center; World [★5875]

Peace Through Law Educ. Fund [18236], PO Box 44354, Washington, DC 20026-4354, (202)686-4600

Peace Tour [★7458]

Peace Tour [★IO]

Peace; Turn Toward [★18259]

Peace Union; Church [★20093]

Peace Villages Found. Venezuela [IO], Bolivar, Venezuela

Peace; Weave a Real [11505]

Peace X Peace [18237], 1601 Connecticut Ave. NW, Washington, DC 20009, (703)391-8932

Peacebuilder Movement - Defunct.

Peaceful Beginnings [11669], c/o Kari Niedermaier, 18119 S Prairie Ave., No. 116, Torrance, CA 90504, (310)793-1050

Peaceful Env. Among Communities Everywhere; Found. for a [★18204]

Peacefund Canada [IO], Ottawa, ON, Canada

PeaceJam [8958], 5605 Yukon St., Arvada, CO 80002, (303)455-2099

Peacemakers - Address unknown since 2003.

Peacemakers Found; Children as the [★18196]

Peacemaking and Conflict Resolution; Natl. Conf. on [18118]

Peacemaking; Training Inst. for Conflict Resolution, Mediation, and [★8139]

PeaceNet - Address unknown since 2003.

PeaceQuest Intl. - Address unknown since 2003.

PeaceQuest - Sweden [IO], Stockholm, Sweden

PeaceWeb [★18118]

Peacework Volunteer Org. [18238], 209 Otey St., Blacksburg, VA 24060-7426, (540)953-1376

Peacework Volunteer Org. [IO], Blacksburg, VA, United States

Peaceworkers [★IO]

Peaceworkers [★18239]

Peaceworkers Nonviolent Peaceforce [18239], 425 Oak Grove St., Minneapolis, MN 55403, (612)871-0005

Peaceworkers Nonviolent Peaceforce [IO], Minneapolis, MN, United States

Peach Advisory Bd; California Cling [★4710]

Peach Advisory Bd; Cling [★4710]

Peach Assn; California Canning [4709]

Peach Bd; California Cling [4710]

Peach Coun; Natl. [4744]

Peach Partners; Natl. [4745]

Peale Center for Christian Living [19825], c/o Guideposts, 39 Seminary Hill Rd., Carmel, NY 10512, (971)221-1100

Peanut

Amer. Peanut Coun. [5049]

Amer. Peanut Res. and Educ. Soc. [5050]

Amer. Peanut Shellers Assn. [5051]

Georgia Peanut Commn. [5056]

Natl. Peanut Buying Points Assn. [5057]

Natl. Peanut Festival Assn. [5058]

Peanut Advisory Bd. [5060]

Peanut Inst. [5061]

Peanut Pals [22104]

Southwestern Peanut Growers Assn. [5062]

Virginia-Carolina Peanut Assn. [5063]

Virginia-Carolina Peanut Promotions [5064]

Peanut Advisory Bd. [5060], 1025 Sugar Pike Way, Canton, GA 30115, (770)998-7311

Peanut Assn; Southeastern [★5051]

Peanut Assn; Virginia-Carolina [5063]

Peanut Butter Manufacturers Assn. [★1556]

Peanut Butter Manufacturers and Nut Salters Assn. [★1556]

Peanut Butter and Nut Processors Assn. [★1556]

Peanut Butter Sandwich and Cookie Manufacturers Assn. [★1556]

Peanut Buying Points Assn; Natl. [5057]

Peanut Commn; Georgia [5056]

Peanut Coun; Amer. [5049]

Peanut Coun; Natl. [★5049]

Peanut Festival Assn; Natl. [5058]

Peanut Growers Assn; Southwestern [5062]

Peanut Improvement Working Group [★5050]

Peanut Inst. [5061], PO Box 70157, Albany, GA 31708-0157, (229)888-0216

Peanut and Nut Salters Assn. [★1556]

Peanut Pals [22104], PO Box 113, Nesquehoning, PA 18240

Peanut Promotions; Virginia-Carolina [5064]

Peanut Res. and Educ. Assn; Amer. [★5050]

Peanut Res. and Educ. Soc; Amer. [5050]

Peanut Shellers Assn; Amer. [5051]

Peanut and Tree Nut Processors Assn. [1556], PO Box 59811, Potomac, MD 20859-9811, (301)365-2521

Pear Bur. Northwest [4755], 4382 SE Intl. Way, Ste. A, Milwaukie, OR 97222-4635, (503)652-9720

Pearl Harbor History Associates [10144], PO Box 1007, Stratford, CT 06615, (203)378-2353

Pearl Harbor Survivors Assn. [21399], PO Box 1816, Carlsbad, CA 92018-1816, (760)727-9027

Pearl S. Buck Birthplace Found. [9699], c/o Pearl S. Buck Museum, PO Box 126, Hillsboro, WV 24946, (304)653-4430

Pearl S. Buck Found. [★11646]

Pearl S. Buck Found. [★IO]

Pearl S. Buck Intl. [IO], Perkasie, PA, United States

Pearl S. Buck Intl. [11646], 520 Dublin Rd., Perkasie, PA 18944, (215)249-0100

Peat

Estonian Peat Assn. [IO]

U.S. Natl. Comm. of the Intl. Peat Soc. [7459]

Peat Moss Assn. - Address unknown since 1995.

Peat Producers Assn. of the U.S. - Defunct.

Peat Soc. of Belarus [IO], Minsk, Belarus

Peat Soc. of Czech Republic [IO], Prague, Czech Republic

Peat Soc. of Latvia [IO], Riga, Latvia

Peat Soc. of Lithuania [IO], Taurage, Lithuania

Peat Soc. of Netherlands [IO], Coevorden, Netherlands

Peat Soc. of Poland [IO], Olsztyn, Poland

Peat Soc. of Russia [IO], Moscow, Russia

Peat Soc. of Ukraine [IO], Kiev, Ukraine

Pecan Shellers Assn; Natl. [5059]

Peck Pioneers - Defunct.

Peckglo Org. [IO], Uyo, Nigeria

Pedal Power ACT [IO], Canberra, Australia

Pedal Steel Guitar Assn. [10685], PO Box 20248, Floral Park, NY 11002-0248, (516)616-9214

Pedestrians

Am. Bikes [17022]

Amer. Coll. of Osteopathic Pediatricians [15795]

Amer. Osteopathic Bd. of Pediatrics [15800]

Assn. of Pedestrian and Bicycle Professionals [18747]

Assn. of Pediatric Hematology/Oncology Nurses [15467]

Children's Hospice Intl. [14853]

Living Streets [IO]

North Amer. Soc. for Pediatric Gastroenterology, Hepatology and Nutrition [14424]

Pediatric Nursing Certification Bd. [15522]

Thunderhead Alliance [18751]

Pedestrians' Assn. [★IO]

Pediatric/Adolescent Gastroesophageal Reflux Association [IO], Buckeystown, MD, United States

Pediatric/Adolescent Gastroesophageal Reflux Assn. [14426], PO Box 486, Buckeystown, MD 21717-0486, (301)601-9541

Pediatric AIDS Coalition - Defunct.

Pediatric AIDS Found. [13582], 2950 31st St., No. 125, Santa Monica, CA 90405, (310)314-1459

Pediatric Anesthesia; Soc. for [13691]

Pediatric Brain Tumor Found. of the U.S. [13863], 302 Ridgefield Ct., Asheville, NC 28806, (828)665-6891

Pediatric Cardiac Intensive Care Soc. [15892], c/o Anthony C. Chang, MD, Pres., CHOC Heart Inst., 455 S Main St., LLW-108, Orange, CA 92868, (714)532-7576

Pediatric Cardiac Intensive Care Soc. [IO], Orange, CA, United States

Pediatric Chaplains Network [19755], c/o Chaplain Karen Black, Sec.-Treas., Our Children's House at Baylor, 3301 Swiss Ave., Dallas, TX 75204

Pediatric Dentistry; Amer. Acad. of [14108]

Pediatric Dermatology; Soc. for [14215]

Pediatric Digestion and Motility Disorders Soc. [15893], PO Box 1360, Buffalo, NY 14205

A star before a book entry number signifies that the name is not listed separately, but is mentioned within the entry.

Pediatric Endocrinology Nursing Soc. [15894], 7794 Grow Dr., Pensacola, FL 32514, (850)484-5223
Pediatric Gastroenterology, Hepatology and Nutrition; North Amer. Soc. for [14424]
Pediatric Gastroenterology; North Amer. Soc. for [★14424]
Pediatric Hematology/Oncology; Amer. Soc. of [14784]
Pediatric Infectious Diseases Soc. [14955], 66 Canal Center Plz., Ste. 600, Alexandria, VA 22314, (703)299-6764
Pediatric Infectious Diseases Soc. [IO], Alexandria, VA, United States
Pediatric Keratoplasty Assn. [15700], c/o Dr. Gerald W. Zaidman, MD, Assoc. Dir., Westchester Medical Ctr., Dept. of Ophthalmology, Valhalla, NY 10595, (914)493-1599
Pediatric Liver Res. Found. - Defunct.
Pediatric Nephrology; Amer. Soc. of [15289]
Pediatric Network for Chronic Fatigue Syndrome, Fibromyalgia, and Orthostatic Intolerance [15895], c/o Mary Robinson, Co-Founder, 507 Park Ave., Medina, NY 14103-1519
Pediatric Neuroradiology; Amer. Soc. of [16283]
Pediatric Neurotransmitter Disease Assn. [15361], c/o Nancy Speller, Pres., 6 Nathan Dr., Plainview, NY 11803, (516)937-0049
Pediatric Nurse Practitioners and Associates; Natl. Bd. of [★15522]
Pediatric Nurse Practitioners; Natl. Assn. of [15499]
Pediatric Nurse Practitioners and Nurses; Natl. Certification Bd. of [★15522]
Pediatric Nurses; Soc. of [15527]
Pediatric Nursing Certification Bd. [15522], 800 S Frederick Ave., Ste. 204, Gaithersburg, MD 20877-4152, (301)330-2921
Pediatric Oncology Nurses; Assn. of [★15467]
Pediatric Ophthalmology; Amer. Assn. of [★15660]
Pediatric Ophthalmology and Strabismus; Amer. Assn. for [15660]
Pediatric Orthopedic Soc. of North Am. [15780], 6300 N River Rd., Ste. 727, Rosemont, IL 60018-4226, (847)698-1692
Pediatric Pathology; Soc. for [15875]
Pediatric Pharmacy Advocacy Gp. [15896], 7975 Stage Hills Blvd., Ste. No. 6, Memphis, TN 38133, (901)380-3617
Pediatric Prog. Directors; Assn. of [8852]
Pediatric Projects - Defunct.
Pediatric Psychology; Soc. for [16175]
Pediatric Radiology; Soc. for [16301]
Pediatric Services; Assn. for Ambulatory [★15879]
Pediatric Therapists; Assn. of [16606]
Pediatric Urology; Soc. for [16715]
Pediatricians; Amer. Assn. of Pro-Life [18546]
Pediatricians; Amer. Coll. of Osteopathic [15795]
Pediatrics
Acoustic Neuroma Assn. [15816]
Alliance for Childhood Cancer [13787]
ALSAC/Saint Jude Children's Res. Hosp. [13946]
Ambulatory Pediatric Assn. [15879]
Amer. Acad. of Child and Adolescent Psychiatry [16063]
Amer. Acad. of Pediatric Dentistry [14108]
Amer. Acad. of Pediatrics [15880]
Amer. Bd. of Pediatrics [15881]
Amer. Bd. of Psychiatry and Neurology [16071]
Amer. Coll. of Foot and Ankle Pediatrics [16033]
Amer. Coll. of Osteopathic Pediatricians [15795]
Amer. Orthodontic Soc. [14138]
Amer. Osteopathic Bd. of Pediatrics [15800]
Amer. Otological Soc. [15822]
Amer. Pediatric Soc. [15882]
Amer. Pediatric Surgical Assn. [15883]
Amer. Soc. for Adolescent Psychiatry [16078]
Amer. Sudden Infant Death Syndrome Inst. [16523]
Argentine Soc. of Pediatrics [IO]
Asian Pan-Pacific Soc. for Pediatric Gastroenterology, Hepatology and Nutrition [IO]
Assn. for Child Psychoanalysis [16106]
Assn. of Maternal and Child Hea. Programs [13947]
Assn. of Medical School Pediatric Dept. Chairs [15884]

Assn. for Pediatric Educ. in Europe [IO]
Assn. of Pediatric Oncology Social Workers [15885]
Assn. of Pediatric Therapists [16606]
Assn. for Res. of Childhood Cancer [13798]
Assn. of SIDS and Infant Mortality Programs [16524]
Brave Kids [13949]
British Assn. of Paediatric Surgeons of England [IO]
Canadian Found. for the Stud. of Infant Deaths [IO]
Canadian Paediatric Soc. [IO]
Childhood Arthritis and Rheumatology Res. Alliance [16371]
Children's Cause for Cancer Advocacy [13812]
Children's Hea. Fund [13954]
Children's Hemiplegia and Stroke Assn. [16493]
CityMatch [13957]
Congenital Heart Defects Awareness [13900]
Coun. on Medical Student Educ. in Pediatrics [8861]
Coun. of Pediatric Subspecialties [15886]
Docs for Tots [13958]
Ear Found. [15825]
Epilepsy Therapy Development Proj. [14381]
European Club for Paediatric Burns [IO]
European Soc. for Paediatric Infectious Diseases [IO]
European Soc. of Paediatric and Neonatal Intensive Care [IO]
European Soc. for Paediatric Res. [IO]
Fed. of Pediatric Organizations [15887]
German Soc. of Pediatrics and Adolescent Medicine [IO]
Global Neuro Rescue [15324]
Hong Kong Paediatric Haematology and Oncology Study Group [IO]
Intl. Assn. of Pediatric Lab. Medicine [IO]
Intl. Assn. of Pediatric Lab. Medicine [15888]
Intl. Pediatric Endosurgery Gp. [15889]
Intl. Pediatric Endosurgery Gp. [IO]
Intl. Pediatric Nephrology Assn. [15292]
Intl. Pediatric Transplant Assn. [16673]
Intl. Soc. for Adolescent Psychiatry and Psychology [16087]
Intl. Soc. for Pediatric Neurosurgery [IO]
Japan Pediatric Soc. [IO]
Juvenile Diabetes Res. Found. Intl. [14228]
Natl. Assn. of Pediatric Nurse Practitioners [15499]
Natl. Center for Educ. in Maternal and Child Hea. [13969]
Natl. Pediatrics AIDS Network [15890]
Neuroblastoma Children's Cancer Soc. [13858]
North Amer. Soc. for Pediatric Gastroenterology, Hepatology and Nutrition [14424]
North Amer. Soc. for Pediatric Medicine [15891]
Parents Against Childhood Epilepsy [14382]
Parents of Infants and Children with Kernicterus [15358]
Pediatric Brain Tumor Found. of the U.S. [13863]
Pediatric Cardiac Intensive Care Soc. [15892]
Pediatric Cardiac Intensive Care Soc. [IO]
Pediatric Digestion and Motility Disorders Soc. [15893]
Pediatric Endocrinology Nursing Soc. [15894]
Pediatric Infectious Diseases Soc. [14955]
Pediatric Keratoplasty Assn. [15700]
Pediatric Network for Chronic Fatigue Syndrome, Fibromyalgia, and Orthostatic Intolerance [15895]
Pediatric Neurotransmitter Disease Assn. [15361]
Pediatric Orthopedic Soc. of North Am. [15780]
Pediatric Pharmacy Advocacy Gp. [15896]
Puerto Rico Assn. of Pediatric Surgeons [15897]
Royal Coll. of Paediatrics and Child Hea. [IO]
Saudi Pediatric Assn. [IO]
Shriners Hospitals for Children [13973]
Sociedad Mexicana de Pediatria [IO]
Sociedad Venezolana de Puericultura y Pediatria [IO]
Societa Italiana di Pediatria [IO]
Soc. for Developmental and Behavioral Pediatrics [15898]

Soc. for Ear, Nose, and Throat Advances in Children [15827]
Soc. for Pediatric Dermatology [14215]
Soc. of Pediatric Nurses [15527]
Soc. for Pediatric Psychology [16175]
Soc. for Pediatric Radiology [16301]
Soc. for Pediatric Res. [15899]
Soc. for Pediatric Urology [16715]
Soc. of Professors of Child and Adolescent Psychiatry [16096]
Soc. of Univ. Otolaryngologists - Head and Neck Surgeons [15828]
South African Assn. of Paediatric Surgeons [IO]
Taiwan Pediatric Assn. [IO]
World Assn. for Infant Mental Hea. [16098]
Pediatrics; Amer. Coll. of Foot and Ankle [16033]
Pediatrics; Amer. Coll. of Podo [★16033]
Pediatrics; Amer. Osteopathic Bd. of [15800]
Pediatrics Overseas [★15778]
Pediatrics Overseas [★IO]
Pediatrics; Soc. for Physician Assistants in [15980]
Pediculosis Assn; Natl. [16247]
Pedigreed Livestock Coun; Natl. [4141]
Pedodontics; Amer. Acad. of [★14108]
Pedorthic Footwear Assn. [1599], 2025 M St. NW, Ste. 800, Washington, DC 20036, (202)367-1145
Peel Olive Assn. [IO], Mandurah, Australia
Peer Hea. Exchange [9338], 1460 Broadway, Ste. 5-24D, New York, NY 10036, (212)735-2844
Peer Helpers Assn; Natl. [★11827]
Peer Programs; Natl. Assn. of [11827]
Peer Rev. Assn; Amer. Medical [★16262]
Peer Tech. Assistance Network [★11968]
Peerless Motor Car Club - Defunct.
PEF Israel Endowment Funds [12461], 317 Madison Ave., Ste. 607, New York, NY 10017, (212)599-1260
PEF Israel Endowment Funds [IO], New York, NY, United States
Pegasus Found; United [17732]
Peggy Browning Fund [6362], 1818 Market St., Ste. 2300, Philadelphia, PA 19103-3648, (215)665-6815
Peggy Sue and Sonny Wright Fan Club - Defunct.
Pekinese
Pekingese Club of Am. [22339]
Pekingese Club of Am. [22339], c/o T. Diane Renihan, Sec., 9161 159th Ct. N, Jupiter, FL 33478-6313, (561)743-0888
Pelastakaa Lapset [★IO]
Pele Defense Fund [4440], PO Box 404, Volcano, HI 96785
Pelham Historical Assn; John [11131]
Pelican Man's Bird Sanctuary [5364], 1708 Ken Thompson Pkwy., Sarasota, FL 34236-1000, (941)388-4444
Pell Grant Coalition; Natl. [8433]
Pellet Fuels Inst. [1683], 1901 N Moore St., Ste. 600, Arlington, VA 22209-1708, (703)522-6778
Pellien/Jaeger/Loretan/Steiner/Ross Soc. [21022], 10435 W Concordia Ave., Milwaukee, WI 53222, (414)259-1315
Pelsinform [IO], Oslo, Norway
Peltier Defense Comm; Leonard [17381]
Pelvic Pain Soc; Intl. [15843]
Pembina Inst. for Appropriate Development [IO], Drayton Valley, AB, Canada
Pembroke Welsh Corgi Club of Am. [22340], c/o Anne H. Bowes, Corresponding Sec., PO Box 2141, Duxbury, MA 02331-2141, (781)934-0110
Pemphigus Found; Intl. [14268]
Pemphigus Found; Natl. [★14268]
PEN Amer. Center [11185], 588 Broadway, Ste. 303, New York, NY 10012, (212)334-1660
Pen and Brush [9521], 16 E 10th St., New York, NY 10003, (212)475-3669
PEN Canada [IO], Toronto, ON, Canada
PEN Center U.S.A. [11186], c/o Antioch Univ., 400 Corporate Pointe, Culver City, CA 90230, (310)862-1555
PEN Club Italiano [★IO]
PEN Club Liechtenstein [IO], Vaduz, Liechtenstein
P.E.N. Club - Poland [IO], Warsaw, Poland
P.E.N. Club of Puerto Rico - Address unknown since 1994.
Pen Collectors of Am. [22105], PO Box 174, Garden Prairie, IL 61038-0174, (319)372-3730

Reference to "IO" in place of a book number signifies that the association may be found in the 45th edition of International Organizations.

Pen Fanciers Club - Defunct.

Pen Friends - Defunct.

Pen and Mech. Pencil Mfrs. Assn; Fountain [★3688]

P.E.N New Zealand [★IO]

Pen Pal Network; Vampire [25022]

Pen Pals; Prison [22141]

Pen-Parents - Address unknown since 2005.

PEN - U.S.A West; Intl. [★11186]

Pen Women; Natl. League of Amer. [9588]

Penal Info; Natl. Soc. of [★11885]

Penal Reform Intl. [IO], London, United Kingdom

Penalty Fund; Tax Resister's [★18723]

Penalty Fund; War Tax Resister's [18723]

Penance; Bros. and Sisters of [19590]

Penance of St. Francis; Bros. and Sisters of [19590]

Penang Turf Club [IO], Penang, Malaysia

Pencil Collectors Soc; Amer. [21964]

Pencil Industry Export Assn. - Defunct.

Pencil Makers Assn. [★3688]

Pencil Mfrs. Assn; Fountain Pen and Mech. [★3688]

Pencil Soc. of Am; Colored [9436]

PenDelfin; Family Circle of [22020]

Penelope; Daughters of [19087]

Penelope Foundation; Daughters of [★19087]

Penguins Booster Club; Pittsburgh [25012]

Peniel Missionary Soc; China [★20409]

Peninsula Hang Glider Club [★23044]

Peninsula Woodturners Guild [IO], Frankston, Australia

Penis; RECAP Recover a [★11734]

Penitents; Confraternity of [19616]

Penland Historical Soc. - Address unknown since 2001.

Penn Assn; William [19144]

Penn Fraternal Assn; William [★19144]

Penn House; William [17619]

Penn State Alumni Assn. - Austria [IO], Vienna, Austria

Penn State Alumni Assn. - Brazil [IO], Ribeirao Preto, Brazil

Penn State Alumni Assn. - Canada [IO], Edmonton, AB, Canada

Penn State Alumni Assn. - Caracas [IO], Caracas, Venezuela

Penn State Alumni Assn. - Chiba [IO], Chiba, Japan

Penn State Alumni Assn. - Chile [IO], Santiago, Chile

Penn State Alumni Assn. - China [IO], Beijing, People's Republic of China

Penn State Alumni Assn. - Congo [IO], Brazzaville, Republic of the Congo

Penn State Alumni Assn. - Cyprus [IO], Nicosia, Cyprus

Penn State Alumni Assn. - Fiji [IO], Lautoka, Fiji

Penn State Alumni Assn. - Greece [IO], Athens, Greece

Penn State Alumni Assn. - Hong Kong [IO], Hong Kong, People's Republic of China

Penn State Alumni Assn. - India [IO], Bombay, India

Penn State Alumni Assn. - Indonesia [IO], Jakarta, Indonesia

Penn State Alumni Assn. - Iran [IO], Mashhad, Iran

Penn State Alumni Assn. - Japan [IO], Tokyo, Japan

Penn State Alumni Assn. - Karachi [IO], Karachi, Pakistan

Penn State Alumni Assn. - Kiev [IO], Kiev, Ukraine

Penn State Alumni Assn. - Korea [IO], Seoul, Republic of Korea

Penn State Alumni Assn. - Lesotho [IO], Maseru, Lesotho

Penn State Alumni Assn. - Malaysia [IO], Kuala Lumpur, Malaysia

Penn State Alumni Assn. - Morocco [IO], Casablanca, Morocco

Penn State Alumni Assn. - Moscow [IO], Moscow, Russia

Penn State Alumni Assn. - New Zealand [IO], Palmerston North, New Zealand

Penn State Alumni Assn. - Pakistan [IO], Islamabad, Pakistan

Penn State Alumni Assn. - Philippines [IO], Caloocan City, Philippines

Penn State Alumni Assn. - Russia [IO], Moscow, Russia

Penn State Alumni Assn. - St. Petersburg [IO], St. Petersburg, Russia

Penn State Alumni Assn. - Saudi Arabia [IO], Riyadh, Saudi Arabia

Penn State Alumni Assn. - Slovakia [IO], Bratislava, Slovakia

Penn State Alumni Assn. - Spain [IO], Madrid, Spain

Penn State Alumni Assn. - Sweden [IO], Stockholm, Sweden

Penn State Alumni Assn. - Taiwan [IO], Taipei, Taiwan

Penn State Alumni Assn. - Thailand [IO], Bangkok, Thailand

Penn State Alumni Assn. - Trinidad [IO], Port of Spain, Trinidad and Tobago

Penn State Alumni Assn. - Turkey [IO], Istanbul, Turkey

Penn Univ. Alumni Assn; William [18945]

Penning Assn; U.S. Team [23518]

Pennsylvania Coal Assn. [847], 212 N 3rd St., Ste. 102, Harrisburg, PA 17101-1588, (717)233-7909

Pennsylvania Coal Mining Assn. [★847]

Pennsylvania Dog Owners Protective Assn. - Address unknown since 1995.

Pennsylvania Dutch

    Folk Heritage Inst. [10772]

    Pennsylvania German Soc. [21243]

    Pennsylvania German Soc. [IO]

    Quiet Valley Living Historical Farm [10147]

    Soc. of the Descendants of the Schwenkfeldian Exiles [21244]

Pennsylvania German Folklore Soc. [★21243]

Pennsylvania German Folklore Soc. [★IO]

Pennsylvania German Soc. [IO], Kutztown, PA, United States

Pennsylvania German Soc. [21243], PO Box 244, Kutztown, PA 19530, (484)646-4227

Pennsylvania; German Soc. of [19076]

Pennsylvania Grade Crude Oil Assn. - Defunct.

Pennsylvania Labor History Soc. - Address unknown since 1999.

Pennsylvania Mfg. Confectioner's Assn. [★1558]

Pennsylvania Mfg. Confectioner's Assn. [★IO]

Pennsylvania; Philomathean Soc. of the Univ. of [10429]

Pennsylvania Railroad Technical and Historical Soc. - Address unknown since 1995.

Pennsylvania Scotch-Irish Soc. [★21151]

Pennsylvania; Soc. of the War of 1812 in [★21354]

Penny Resistance - Defunct.

Penobscot Marine Museum [10445], PO Box 498, Searsport, ME 04974-0498, (207)548-2529

Pension Actuaries; Amer. Soc. of [★1233]

Pension Actuaries; Japanese Soc. of Certified [IO]

Pension Administrators; Natl. Inst. of [1244]

Pension Consultants and Administrators; Natl. Assn. of [★17350]

Pension Fund; Church [19948]

Pension Funds; Irish Assn. of [IO]

Pension Mgt; Assn. of Canadian [IO]

Pension Plans; Natl. Found. of Hea., Welfare and [★1240]

Pension Real Estate Assn. [3335], 100 Pearl St., 13th Fl., Hartford, CT 06103, (860)692-6341

Pension Res. Coun. [12702], The Wharton School of the Univ. of Pennsylvania, 3620 Locust Walk, 3000 Steinberg Hall - Dietrich Hall, Philadelphia, PA 19104-6302, (215)898-7620

Pension Res. Coun. [IO], Philadelphia, PA, United States

Pension Rights Center [12703], 1350 Connecticut Ave. NW, Ste. 206, Washington, DC 20036-1739, (202)296-3776

Pension Supervisory Authorities; Canadian Assn. of [IO]

Pension and Welfare Plans; Assn. of Private [★6169]

Pensions

    Alliance for Worker Retirement Security [18544]

    Amer. Benefits Coun. [6169]

    Assn. of Public Pension Fund Auditors [24147]

    Canadian Assn. of Pension Supervisory Authorities [IO]

    Canadian Pensioners Concerned [IO]

    Church Benefits Assn. [20461]

    Coun. of Institutional Investors [3512]

    ESOP Assn. Canada [IO]

    Fund for Assuring an Independent Retirement [5709]

    Inst. of Payroll and Pensions Mgt. [IO]

    Irish Assn. of Pension Funds [IO]

    Kristelijke Beweging van Gepensioneerden [IO]

    Natl. Assn. of Pension Funds [IO]

    Natl. Coun. of Real Estate Investment Fiduciaries [2344]

    Natl. Org. of Veterans' Advocates [6348]

    Pension Real Estate Assn. [3335]

    Pension Res. Coun. [12702]

    Pension Res. Coun. [IO]

    Pension Rights Center [12703]

    Pensions Mgt. Inst. [IO]

    Retirement Indus. Trust Assn. [497]

    Soc. of Pension Consultants [IO]

    Union Chretienne des Pensionnes [IO]

Pensions Conf; Church [★20461]

Pensions Mgt. Inst. [IO], London, United Kingdom

Pensions for Professionals - Address unknown since 1995.

Penstemon Soc; Amer. [22497]

Penta Users Group - Address unknown since 2001.

Pentathlon

    Canadian Modern Pentathlon Assn. [IO]

    Modern Pentathlon Assn. of Great Britain [IO]

    U.S. Modern Pentathlon Assn. [23925]

Pentathlon Assn; Canadian Modern [IO]

Pentathlon Assn; U.S. Modern [23925]

Pentathlon and Biathlon Assn; U.S. Modern [★23925]

Pentecostal

    Crusaders for Christ [20462]

    European Pentecostal Theological Assn. [IO]

    Intl. Pentecostal Press Assn. [3122]

    Pentecostal Assemblies of the World [20463]

    Pentecostal Assemblies of the World [IO]

    Pentecostal Charismatic Churches of North Am. [IO]

    Pentecostal Charismatic Churches of North Am. [20464]

    Soc. for Pentecostal Stud. [20465]

Pentecostal Assemblies of the World [20463], 3939 N Meadows Dr., Indianapolis, IN 46205, (317)547-9541

Pentecostal Assemblies of the World [IO], Indianapolis, IN, United States

Pentecostal Charismatic Churches of North Am. [IO], Hayward, CA, United States

Pentecostal Charismatic Churches of North Am. [20464], c/o Church of God in Christ, 1027 W Tennyson Rd., Hayward, CA 94544, (510)783-9377

Pentecostal Coalition for Human Rights - Defunct.

Pentecostal Faith Missions [★20336]

Pentecostal Faith Missions [★IO]

Pentecostal Fellowship of North Am. [★IO]

Pentecostal Fellowship of North Am. [★20464]

PEO Intl. [9325], 3700 Grand Ave., Des Moines, IA 50312, (515)255-3153

PEO Intl. [IO], Des Moines, IA, United States

PEO Sisterhood [★IO]

PEO Sisterhood [★9325]

Peony Soc; Amer. [22498]

People Against Cancer [13864], 604 East St., PO Box 10, Otho, IA 50569, (515)972-4444

People Against Chlordane - Address unknown since 1990.

People Against Impaired Driving [IO], Edmonton, AB, Canada

People Against Racism in Education - Defunct.

People Against Racist Terror [★17092]

People Against Racist Terror [★IO]

People Against Racist Terror; Anti-Racist Action-Los Angeles/ [17092]

People Against Rape [13083], 2154 N Centre St., Ste. 302-C, North Charleston, SC 29406, (843)745-0144

People Against Telephone Terrorism and Harassment - Address unknown since 1999.

People for the Amer. Way [17143], 2000 M St. NW, Ste. 400, Washington, DC 20036, (202)467-4999

People-Animals-Love [16632], 4900 Massachusetts Ave. NW, Ste. 330, Washington, DC 20016, (202)966-2171

People, Animals, Nature [13319], 1820 Princeton Cir., Naperville, IL 60565

A star before a book entry number signifies that the name is not listed separately, but is mentioned within the entry.

People Before Lawyers [5528], c/o Marc Perkel, 309 N Jefferson, No. 220, Springfield, MO 65802, (417)866-1222

People for Better TV - Address unknown since 2006.

People for a Change - Defunct.

People for Children [11716], PO Box 13534, San Juan, PR 00908-3534

People for Children [IO], San Juan, PR, United States

People; Christians Helping Animals and [19456]

People for Constiutional Rights - Defunct.

People with Disabilities; Amer. Assn. of [11917]

People and Dogs Soc. [IO], Normanton, United Kingdom

People of the Earth [★IO]

People of the Earth [★4441]

People for Energy Progress - Defunct.

People for the Ethical Treatment of Animals [11444], 501 Front St., Norfolk, VA 23510, (757)622-7382

People for the Ethical Treatment of Animals Europe [IO], London, United Kingdom

People of Faith Against the Death Penalty [17034], 110 W Main St., Ste. 2-G, Carrboro, NC 27510, (919)933-7567

People First Intl. [12580], PO Box 12642, Salem, OR 97309, (503)362-0336

People First Intl. [IO], Salem, OR, United States

People Food and Land Found. [4656], 35751 Oak Springs Dr., Tollhouse, CA 93667-9611, (559)855-3710

People Helping People [12385], c/o Andrea Clinton, Pres., 53 Watson Ave., East Orange, NJ 07018, (973)676-4292

People In Aid [IO], London, United Kingdom

People for Internet Responsibility [12453], c/o Peter G. Neumann, SRI Intl. EL-243, 333 Ravenswood Ave., Menlo Park, CA 94025-3493, (818)225-2800

People for Latin America Now - Defunct.

People for Life [12925], PO Box 1126, Erie, PA 16512, (814)459-1333

People Living with HIV/AIDS (SA) [IO], Adelaide, Australia

People; Natl. Land for [★4656]

People for a New System - Address unknown since 2004.

People Opposing Women Abuse [IO], Yeoville, Republic of South Africa

People Organized to Stop Rape of Imprisoned Persons [★11894]

People Organized to Win Employment Rights; POWER [17494]

People; Parrots and [11516]

People to People Ambassador Prog. [17908], 1956 Ambassador Way, Dwight D. Eisenhower Bldg., Spokane, WA 99224-4004, (509)534-0430

People to People Ambassador Prog. [IO], Spokane, WA, United States

People to People Citizen Ambassador Prog. [★IO]

People to People Citizen Ambassador Prog. [★17908]

People to People Comm. on Fungi [★7353]

People to People Intl. [17909], 501 E Armour Blvd., Kansas City, MO 64109-2200, (816)531-4701

People to People Intl. [IO], Kansas City, MO, United States

People to People Music Comm. - Defunct.

People and Planet [IO], Oxford, United Kingdom

People-Plant Coun. [4518], 2021 Throckmorton Plant Sciences Ctr., Manhattan, KS 66506-5501, (785)532-6170

People Protecting Animals and Their Habitats [11445], 373 Moreland Ave. NE, Ste. 303, Atlanta, GA 30307, (617)354-2826

People Protecting Animals and Their Habitats [IO], New Orleans, LA, United States

People-to-People Comm. on Disability [11980], c/o Marc L. Bright, Deputy CEO/Exec.VP, 510 E Armour Blvd., Kansas City, MO 64109-2200, (816)531-4701

People-to-People Comm. for the Handicapped [★11980]

People-to-People Hea. Found. [14984], 255 Carter Hall Ln., Millwood, VA 22646, (540)837-2100

People-to-People Hea. Found. [IO], Millwood, VA, United States

People-to-People Sports Comm. - Address unknown since 2002.

People; United Confed. of Taino [18989]

People United to Fight Frustrations - Address unknown since 1987.

People United for Rural Education - Address unknown since 1999.

People United to Serve Humanity [★13185]

People; Up With [8311]

People With AIDS Coalition - Defunct.

People With Disabilities - Uganda [IO], Kampala, Uganda

People's Action for Comprehensive Test Ban - Defunct.

People's Action; Natl. [11755]

People's Alliance to Reform, Transform and Improve Everything - Address unknown since 1994.

People's Anti-War Mobilization - Address unknown since 2003.

Peoples Assembly for the United Nations [18767]

People's Business Commn. - Defunct.

People's Center for Housing Change - Address unknown since 2001.

People's Coalition for Peace and Justice - Defunct.

People's Comm. on Env. and Development India [IO], New Delhi, India

People's Comm. for Libyan Students - Address unknown since 1991.

People's Decade of Human Rights Educ. [17782], 526 W 111th St., Ste. 4E, New York, NY 10025, (212)749-3156

People's Decade of Human Rights Educ. [IO], New York, NY, United States

Peoples Dispensary for Sick Animals [IO], Telford, United Kingdom

Peoples; Found. for Emerging [★12426]

People's Inst. for Survival and Beyond [18626], 601 N Carrollton, New Orleans, LA 70119, (504)301-9292

People's Involvement Corp. [13183]

People's Law School - Defunct.

People's Librarian Task Force - Defunct.

People's Lobby [18363], 359 Jean St., Mill Valley, CA 94941, (415)383-7880

People's Mandate Comm. - Defunct.

People's Medical Soc. [17694], PO Box 868, Allentown, PA 18105-0868, (610)770-1670

People's Multipurpose Development Soc. [IO], Villupuram District, India

People's Music Network for Songs of Freedom and Struggle - Address unknown since 2002.

People's News Agency [3155], c/o Proutist Universal New York Sector, 6310 Tilden Ln., Rockville, MD 20852, (301)231-0110

People's Party - Defunct.

People's Peace and Prosperity Party - Defunct.

People's Progressive Party of Guyana [IO], Georgetown, Guyana

People's Relief Comm. [★IO]

People's Relief Comm. [★12464]

People's Revolutionary Party; All-African [16925]

People's Rights Fund [17144], 39 W 14th St., No. 206, New York, NY 10011, (212)633-6646

Peoples Rights Org. [17145], 4444 Indianola Ave., Columbus, OH 43214-2226, (614)268-0122

Peoples of the South Pacific; Found. for the [★12426]

People's Trust for Endangered Species [IO], London, United Kingdom

Peoplesmedia Cooperative - Address unknown since 1995.

Peoria Bd. of Trade - Defunct.

Peperomia and Exotic Plant Soc. - Defunct.

Pepper Bottlers Assn; Dr [506]

Pepper Community [★IO]

Pepper Marketing Bd. Malaysia [★IO]

Pepper Shakers Club; Novelty Salt and [22097]

Pepsi-Cola Collectors Club [22106], PO Box 817, Claremont, CA 91711, (909)946-6026

Per Scholas [8300], 1231 Lafayette Ave., Bronx, NY 10474, (718)991-8400

Perahia Funds for the Needy Committee; Henry J. [★20179]

Perbutuhan Kebangsaan St. Vincent de Paul [★IO]

Percussion Arts; Academy of Wind and [★10660]

Percussion Instructors; Natl. Assn. of Coll. Wind and [8919]

Percussion Marketing Coun. [1165], PO Box 33252, Cleveland, OH 44133, (440)582-7006

Percussive Arts Soc. [10686], 32 E Washington, Ste. 1400, Indianapolis, IN 46204, (317)974-4488

Percy Grainger Lib. Soc. [★9810]

Percy Grainger Lib. Soc. [★IO]

Percy Grainger Soc. [IO], Aylesbury, United Kingdom

Pere Marquette Memorial Assn. - Address unknown since 2002.

Peregrine Found; North Amer. [★23398]

The Peregrine Fund [5365], 5668 W Flying Hawk Ln., Boise, ID 83709, (208)362-3716

The Peregrine Fund [IO], Boise, ID, United States

Perennial Plant Assn. [4985], 3383 Schirtzinger Rd., Hilliard, OH 43026, (614)771-8431

Perfins Club [22854], c/o Ken Rehfield, Sec., PO Box 125, Greenacres, WA 99016-0125, (509)924-6375

Perforators Assn; Indus. [2709]

Performance of African-American Music; Natl. Assn. for the Stud. and [8922]

Performance Automotive Advertising Assn. - Defunct.

Performance Ford Club of America - Defunct.

Performance Fund; Music [10651]

Performance and Instruction; Natl. Soc. for [★9252]

Performance Mgt. Assn. [★2491]

Performance Mgt. Assn. [★IO]

Performance Network; Natl. [11031]

Performance Textiles Assn. [IO], Tamworth, United Kingdom

Performance Trust Funds; Music [★10651]

Performance Trust Funds; Recording Indus. Music [★10651]

Performance Warehouse Assn. [3981], 41-701 Corporate Way, Ste. 1, Palm Desert, CA 92260, (760)346-5647

Performers Assn; Comedy Writers and [★10211]

Performers; Canadian Soc. of Children's Authors, Illustrators and [IO]

Performing Animal Welfare Soc. [11446], PO Box 849, Galt, CA 95632, (209)745-2606

Performing Artists for Nuclear Disarmament - Address unknown since 1995.

Performing Arts

Actors' Equity Assn. [24148]

Alliance of Artists and Recording Companies [3346]

Alliance of Canadian Cinema, TV and Radio Artists [IO]

Amer. Arts Alliance [9539]

Amer. Assn. of Community Theatre [10999]

Amer. Ballet Competition [9862]

Amer. Bop Assn. [9863]

Amer. Coll. Dance Festival Assn. [9864]

Amer. Dance Festival [9865]

Amer. Dance Guild [9866]

Amer. Fed. of Musicians of the U.S. and Canada [24149]

Amer. Fed. of Musicians of the U.S. and Canada [IO]

Amer. Friends of the Paris Opera and Ballet [9543]

Amer. Guild of Musical Artists [24150]

Amer. Guild of Variety Artists [24151]

Amer. Musicians Union [24152]

Amer. Russian Theatrical Alliance [11001]

Amer. Theatre Arts for Youth [11003]

Amer. Theatre and Drama Soc. [11005]

Amer. Youth Circus Org. [9795]

Americans for the Arts [9546]

Art Resources in Collaboration [9867]

Artists Helping Artists [9498]

Arts and Bus. Coun. [9550]

Arts Intl. [9551]

Assoc. Actors and Artistes of Am. [24153]

Assoc. Actors and Artistes of Am. [IO]

Assn. of Asian Performing Arts Festivals [IO]

Assn. of British Jazz Musicians [IO]

Assn. of Hispanic Arts [9999]

Assn. for Korean Music Res. [10561]

Assn. for the Preservation and Presentation of the Arts [9355]

Reference to "IO" in place of a book number signifies that the association may be found in the 45th edition of International Organizations.

Assn. of Theatrical Press Agents and Managers [24154]
Audience Development Comm. [11006]
Austin Cody's Official Intl. Fan Club [24845]
Austrian Assn. for Theatre Technics [IO]
Ballet Theatre Found. [9868]
Better World Chorus [12617]
Beyond Baroque Literary/Arts Center [9559]
Blues Heaven Found. [10567]
Bohemia Ragtime Soc. [10568]
Branscombe Richmond Fan Club [24779]
Burlesque Historical Soc. [11009]
Bus. Comm. for the Arts [9560]
Butimar Productions [9849]
Canadian Actors' Equity Assn. [IO]
Canadian Inst. for Theatre Tech. [IO]
Chinese-American Arts Coun. [9608]
Chris Blair Fan Club [24802]
Chris Young Fan Club [24862]
Circus Educ. Specialists [9796]
Circus Fans Assn. of Am. [9797]
Clay Underwood Fan Club [24865]
Clowns of Am., Intl. [21951]
Conf. for Chinese Oral and Performing Literature [9790]
Cong. on Res. in Dance [9871]
Costume Coll. [9821]
Dance/Drill Team Directors of Am. [9876]
Dance Heritage Coalition [9877]
Dance Theater Workshop [9566]
Dance/U.S.A. [9879]
Danish Actors' Assn. [IO]
Delbert McClinton Intl. Fan Club [24874]
Drs. for Artists [12520]
Drama Desk [11010]
Dramatists Guild of Am. [11012]
Episcopal Actors' Guild of Am. [11013]
Equity [IO]
Eugene O'Neill Memorial Theater Center [11014]
European Amer. Musical Alliance [10594]
European Network of Info. Centres for the Performing Arts [IO]
Film Artistes Assn. [IO]
Fine Arts Philatelists [22819]
Finnish Musicians Union [IO]
Folk Alliance [9955]
Fractured Atlas [9503]
Friars Club [11016]
Friends of Dennis Lee Fan Club [24780]
Friends of Ty Herndon Fan Club [24896]
Global Alliance of Performers [10773]
Global Alliance of Performers [IO]
Grantmakers in the Arts [12722]
The Grascals Fan Club [24904]
Guild of Italian Amer. Actors [24155]
Hispanic Org. of Latin Actors [10001]
Homowo African Arts and Cultures [9350]
Hosp. Audiences [11017]
Interlochen Center for the Arts [9571]
Intl. Alliance of Theatrical Stage Employees, Moving Picture Technicians, Artists and Allied Crafts of the U.S., Its Territories and Canada [24156]
Intl. Alliance of Theatrical Stage Employees, Moving Picture Technicians, Artists and Allied Crafts of the U.S., Its Territories and Canada [IO]
Intl. Brotherhood of Magicians [22620]
Intl. Concert Alliance [10617]
Intl. Fed. of Actors [IO]
Intl. Fed. of Musicians [IO]
Intl. Guild of Musicians in Dance [IO]
Intl. Guild of Musicians in Dance [10774]
Intl. Guild of Symphony, Opera and Ballet Musicians [24157]
Intl. Jugglers' Assn. [23557]
Intl. Order of E.A.R.S. [10979]
Intl. Org. of Scenographers, Theatre Architects, and Technicians [IO]
Intl. Shrine Clown Assn. [21952]
Intl. Soc. for the Performing Arts [9575]
Intl. Tap Assn. [9888]
Irish Arts Center - An Claidheamh Soluis [10243]
Jeannie Seely's Circle of Friends [24917]
Jim Hubbard Fan Club [24920]
Johnnie Ray Intl. Fan Club [24927]
Junior Shag Assn. [9890]

Jussi Bjorling Soc. - USA [9508]
Kelly Lang Fan Club [24932]
League of Historic Amer. Theatres [11021]
Lee's Familee [24937]
Magic Collectors' Assn. [22621]
Magic Youth Intl. [22622]
Magicians Without Borders [12503]
Media, Entertainment and Arts Alliance [IO]
Mexican Amer. Music Assn. [10647]
Michael Jackson Fan Club [24948]
Mixed Harmony Barbershop Quartet Assn. [10648]
Movement Theatre Intl. [11025]
Music Performance Fund [10651]
Musicians' Alliance for Peace [18223]
Natl. Alliance for Media Arts and Culture [9580]
Natl. Assembly of State Arts Agencies [9583]
Natl. Center of Afro-American Artists [9361]
Natl. Circus Preservation Soc. [9799]
Natl. Clogging Org. [9892]
Natl. Coun. for the Traditional Arts [9961]
Natl. Dance Assn. [9893]
Natl. Fastdance Assn. [9894]
Natl. Found. for Advancement in the Arts [9587]
Natl. Movement Theatre Assn. [11028]
Natl. New Deal Preservation Assn. [10775]
Natl. New Play Network [11030]
Natl. Theatre Conf. [11032]
Natl. Theatre Workshop of the Handicapped [11033]
New Dramatists [11034]
New England Theatre Conf. [11035]
New Horizons Arts Initiative [9589]
New York Coun. of Motion Picture and TV Unions [24056]
North Amer. Fed. of German Folk Dance Groups [9965]
Norwegian Actors' Equity Assn. [IO]
Official Robert Newman Fan Club [24765]
Oh Ji Ho Intl. Fan Club [24781]
OISTAT Centre of Great Britain [IO]
OISTAT Japan Centre [IO]
O'Neill Critics Inst. [11036]
Performing Arts Found. [9592]
Performing Arts Medicine Assn. [16164]
Phi Beta [24405]
The Players [11038]
Playwrights Conf. [11039]
Polish Actors Assn. [IO]
Professional Arts Mgt. Inst. [9594]
Puerto Rican Traveling Theatre Company [11040]
Return to Unity [18265]
Richard Burgi Fan Club [24768]
Roger Sessions Soc. [9815]
Royal Netherlands Assn. of Musicians [IO]
Rustie Blue Intl. Fan Club [24972]
Screen Actors Guild [24158]
Shakespeare Theatre Assn. of Am. [11042]
Sino-Amer. Cultural Soc. [9793]
Soc. of Amer. Magicians [22623]
Soc. for Applied Psychological Res. in the Performing Arts [16170]
Soc. of Finnish Composers [IO]
Soc. for Seventeenth-Century Music [10705]
Soc. of Stage Directors and Choreographers [24159]
Southeastern Theatre Conf. [11043]
Spellbinders [10984]
Subud Intl. Cultural Assn. - U.S.A. [9600]
Swedish Musicians' Union [IO]
Swedish Theater Union - Swedish ITI [IO]
Sword Swallowers Assn. Intl. [10776]
Theatre Communications Gp. [11047]
Theatre Development Fund [11048]
Theatre Guild [11049]
Theatre Inst. [IO]
Theatre Lib. Assn. [10391]
Theatre for Young Audiences/USA [11051]
Three Dog Night Fan Club [24984]
UNIMA-U.S.A., Amer. Center of the Union Internationale de la Marionnette [22916]
Union of Brazilian Composers [IO]
United Scenic Artists [24160]
U.S. Inst. for Theatre Tech. [11052]
U.S. Natl. Inst. of Dance [9899]

U.S. Scottish Fiddling Revival [10716]
William and Flora Hewlett Found. [13194]
Wolf Trap Found. for the Performing Arts [9602]
World Juggling Fed. [23558]
World Piano Competition [10726]
World Swing Dance Coun. [9902]
Yiddish Theatrical Alliance [11053]
Young Audiences [9603]
Youth Educ. in the Arts [9604]
Ziegfeld Club [11054]
Performing Arts Administrators; Intl. Soc. of [★9575]
Performing Arts for Crisis Training [★11830]
Performing Arts Found. [9592], 401 N 4th St., Wausau, WI 54403, (715)842-0988
Performing Arts; GALA [★10599]
Performing Arts Mgt. Inst. [★9594]
Performing Arts Managers and Agent; Natl. Assn. [★175]
Performing Arts Managers and Agents; North Amer. [175]
Performing Arts Medicine Assn. [16164], c/o Mary Fletcher, Exec. Dir., PO Box 61228, Denver, CO 80206, (303)632-9255
Performing Arts Presenters; Assn. of [7968]
Performing Arts Resources [9593], 88 E 3rd St., No. 19, New York, NY 10003, (212)673-6343
Performing Arts Study Unit - Address unknown since 1990.
Performing Arts; Tibetan Inst. of [★11055]
Performing Arts; Wolf Trap Found. for the [9602]
Performing Literature; Conf. for Chinese Oral and [9790]
Performing Right Soc. [IO], London, United Kingdom
Performing Rights Soc. [★IO]
Performing and Visual Arts Soc. - Defunct.
Perfume and Scent Bottle Collectors [★22054]
Perfume and Scent Bottle Collectors [★IO]
Perfume and Scent Bottle Collectors Assn; Intl. [★22054]
Perfumers; Amer. Soc. of [1659]
Perfumers Assn. of the U.S; Mfg. [★1845]
Perfumery Importers Assn. - Defunct.
Perfusion; Amer. Bd. of Cardiovascular [13887]
Perfusion Prog. Directors' Coun. [13921], c/o Bruce Searles, CCP, Pres., SUNY Upstate Medical Univ., Dept. of Cardiovascular Perfusion, 750 E Adams St., Syracuse, NY 13210, (315)464-6932
Perhaps Kids Meeting Kids Can Make a Difference [17910], 380 Riverside Dr., Box 8H, New York, NY 10025, (212)662-2327
Perhaps Kids Meeting Kids Can Make a Difference [IO], New York, NY, United States
Perhimpunan Pembina Kesehatan Olahraga Indonesia [★IO]
PeriAnesthesia Nurses; Amer. Soc. of [15460]
Perianesthesia Nursing Certification; Amer. Bd. of [15446]
Pericles; Sons of [19093]
Perinatal Psychology and Hea; Assn. for Pre- and [13979]
Perinatology
  Amer. Assn. of Birth Centers [15580]
  Amer. Assn. of Gynecologic Laparoscopists [15581]
  Amer. Bd. of Obstetrics and Gynecology [15582]
  Amer. Coll. of Domiciliary Midwives [15583]
  Amer. Coll. of Nurse-Midwives [15447]
  Amer. Coll. of Obstetricians and Gynecologists [15584]
  Amer. Coll. of Osteopathic Obstetricians and Gynecologists [15585]
  Amer. Found. for Maternal and Child Health [15586]
  Amer. Gynecological and Obstetrical Soc. [15587]
  Amer. Soc. of Childbirth Educators [15589]
  Amer. Soc. for Colposcopy and Cervical Pathology [15590]
  Amer. Soc. for Reproductive Medicine [14389]
  Assn. for Childbirth at Home, Intl. [15591]
  Assn. of Professors of Gynecology and Obstetrics [15592]
  Assn. of Women's Hea., Obstetric and Neonatal Nurses [15470]
  British Assn. of Perinatal Medicine [IO]
  C/SEC [15593]

A star before a book entry number signifies that the name is not listed separately, but is mentioned within the entry.

Center for Humane Options in Childbirth Experiences [15594]
Childbirth Connection [15595]
CityMatch [13957]
Coun. on Resident Educ. in Obstetrics and Gynecology [15597]
Endometriosis Assn. [15599]
Fertility Res. Found. [14391]
Informed Homebirth/Informed Birth and Parenting [15602]
Intl. Assn. of Parents and Professionals for Safe Alternatives in Childbirth [15603]
Intl. Cesarean Awareness Network [15604]
Intl. Childbirth Educ. Assn. [15605]
Intl. Soc. of Prenatal and Perinatal Psychology and Medicine [IO]
Lamaze Birth Without Pain Educ. Assn. [15607]
Midwives Alliance of North Am. [15610]
Natl. Healthy Start Assn. [15613]
Natl. Perinatal Assn. [15900]
Natl. Perinatal Info. Center [15901]
Purine Res. Soc. [15258]
Resolve, The Natl. Infertility Assn. [14394]
Soc. for Fetal Urology [16713]
Soc. for Gynecologic Investigation [15618]
Soc. for Maternal-Fetal Medicine [15902]
Soc. for Menstrual Cycle Res. [15619]
Soc. for Obstetric Anesthesia and Perinatology [15903]
Period Furniture Makers; Soc. of Amer. [9970]
Periodic Paralysis Assn. [15122], 1101 Douglas Dr., Tracy, CA 95304-5879, (626)638-3326
Periodical and Book Assn. of Am. [3247], 481 8th Ave., Ste. 826, New York, NY 10001, (212)563-6502
Periodical Club; Church [19949]
Periodical Publications Assn. [2455], c/o Kimberly Scott, Exec. Dir., PO Box 10669, Rockville, MD 20849-0669, (301)260-0929
Periodical Publishers Assn. [★1432]
Periodical Publishers Assn. [IO], London, United Kingdom
Periodical Publishers Assn. of Ireland [IO], Dublin, Ireland
Periodical Publishers; Natl. Assn. of [★3235]
Periodical Wholesalers of North Am. - Defunct.
Periodical Writers' Assn. of Canada [★IO]
Periodicals
ReREAD [12299]
Res. Soc. for Victorian Periodicals [11080]
Periodicals Inst. - Address unknown since 1994.
Periodontists; Amer. Soc. of [★14109]
Periodontology; Amer. Acad. of [14109]
Periodontology; Amer. Bd. of [14125]
Periodontology; British Soc. of [IO]
Periodontology; Canadian Acad. of [IO]
Periodontology; Western Soc. of [14187]
Perioperative Nursing; Natl. Certification Bd. [★14878]
Perioperative Res. Org; Global [14026]
Peripheral Arterial Disease Coalition [13922], 1075 S Yukon St., Ste. 320, Lakewood, CO 80226, (301)524-1535
Peripheral Vascular Nursing; Soc. for [★15530]
Peripheral Vascular Soc. of America - Defunct.
Perkehner Soc; Universal [22602]
Perkumpulan Keluarga Berencana Indonesia [★IO]
Perlite Inst. [2754], 4305 N 6th St., Ste. A, Harrisburg, PA 17110, (717)238-9723
Permaculture Assn. [IO], London, United Kingdom
Permaculture Intl. [IO], Maleny, Australia
Permaculture Trust of Botswana [IO], Serowe, Botswana
Permanent Blind Relief War Fund [★IO]
Permanent Blind Relief War Fund [★16854]
Permanent Charities Comm. of the Entertainment Indus. [★12114]
Permanent Commn. for the South Pacific [IO], Guayaquil, Ecuador
Permanent Commn. for the Stud. of Building Indus. Problems in the European Common Market [★IO]
Permanent Cosmetic Professionals; Soc. of [1087]
Permanent Court of Arbitration [IO], The Hague, Netherlands
Permanent End Intl. [IO], Hamilton, ON, Canada

Permanent European Conf. on Probation and Aftercare [IO], Utrecht, Netherlands
Permanent Executive Comm. of the Inter-Amer. Economic and Social Coun. - Address unknown since 1999.
Permanent Families for Children - Defunct.
Permanent Intl. Altaistic Conf. [7989], Indiana Univ., GoodBody Hall 157, Bloomington, IN 47405-7005, (812)855-0959
Permanent Intl. Altaistic Conf. [IO], Bloomington, IN, United States
Permanent Intl. Assn. of Navigation Congresses [★IO]
Permanent Intl. Assn. of Road Congresses [★IO]
Permanent Intl. Commn. for the Proof of Small-Arms [IO], Liege, Belgium
Permanent Intl. Comm. for Intl. Congresses of Administrative Sciences [★IO]
Permanent Magnet Producers Assn. [★IO]
Permanent Magnet Producers Assn. [★1824]
Permanent Magnet Users Inst. - Defunct.
Permanent Secretariat of the Hemispheric Cong. of Latin C.O.C. and Indiana [★24281]
Permanent Secretariat of the Hemispheric Cong. of Latin C.O.C. and Indiana [★IO]
Permanent Ser. for Mean Sea Level [IO], Liverpool, United Kingdom
Permanent Ware Inst. - Defunct.
Permanent Way Institution [IO], Stoke-On-Trent, United Kingdom
Permanent Working Group of European Junior Doctors [IO], Lisbon, Portugal
Permit Imprint Collectors Soc. - Address unknown since 1999.
Peroneal Muscular Atrophy
Pacific Ocean Res. Found. [7176]
Peroneal Muscular Atrophy; Natl. Found. for [★15313]
Perry Como Circle [24960]
Persatuan Ahli-Ahli Sains Malaysia [★IO]
Persatuan Alergi and Imunologi Malaysia [★IO]
Persatuan Bagi Orang Buta Malaysia [★IO]
Persatuan Bantuan Perubatan Malaysia [★IO]
Persatuan Bulan Sabit Merah Malaysia [★IO]
Persatuan Dermatologi Malaysia [★IO]
Persatuan Ekonomi Malaysia [★IO]
Persatuan Elektrik Dan Elektronik Malaysia [★IO]
Persatuan Farmakologi dan Fisiologi Malaysia [★IO]
Persatuan Farmaseutikal Malaysia [★IO]
Persatuan Floorball Malaysia [★IO]
Persatuan Geologi Malaysia [★IO]
Persatuan Gerontologi Malaysia [★IO]
Persatuan Hosp. Swasta Malaysia [★IO]
Persatuan Hotel Budget Malaysia [★IO]
Persatuan Industri Komputer Dan Multimedia Malaysia [★IO]
Persatuan Juru X-Ray Malaysia [★IO]
Persatuan Jurupulih Carakerja Malaysia [★IO]
Persatuan Jurutera Perunding Malaysia [★IO]
Persatuan Kebangsaan Pembeli Rumah [★IO]
Persatuan Nuklear Malaysia [★IO]
Persatuan Olahraga Amatur Brunei [★IO]
Persatuan Panahan Indonesia [★IO]
Persatuan Pandu Puteri Malaysia [★IO]
Persatuan Pejenamaan Malaysia [★IO]
Persatuan Pemborong Binaan Malaysia [★IO]
Persatuan Pengilang-Pengilang Tekstil Malaysia [★IO]
Persatuan Perancang Keluarga Sabah [★IO]
Persatuan Perubatan Malaysia [★IO]
Persatuan Perusahaan Periklanan Indonesia [★IO]
Persatuan Pustakawan Malaysia [★IO]
Persatuan Squash Indonesia [IO], Jakarta, Indonesia
Persatuan Teknopreneur Malaysia [★IO]
Persatuan Tenis Seluruh Indonesia [★IO]
Persatuan Transplan Malaysia [★IO]
Persatuan Wanita Keristian Malaysia [★IO]
Persatuan Warga Emas Malaysia [★IO]
Persekutuan Sukan Udara Malaysia [IO], Petaling Jaya, Malaysia
Pershing Rifles; Natl. Soc. of [24547]
Persian Bicolor and Calico Soc. - Defunct.
Persian Greyhounds
Saluki Club of Am. [22353]

Personal Assistants; Assn. of Celebrity [59]
Personal Chef Assn; Amer. [★791]
Personal Chef Assn; U.S. [793]
Personal Communications Indus. Assn. [★3752]
Personal Communications Indus. Assn. [★IO]
Personal Cmpt. Assn. [★IO]
Personal Cmpt. Direct Marketers' Assn. [★IO]
Personal Computer Mgt. Assn. - Defunct.
Personal Cmpt. Memory Card Intl. Assn. [6742], 2635 N First St., Ste. 218, San Jose, CA 95134, (408)433-2273
Personal Cmpt. Memory Card Intl. Assn. [IO], San Jose, CA, United States
Personal Computers
Amer. Assn. of Cmpt. Rental Professionals [895]
Assn. of Macintosh Trainers [6810]
Capital PC User Gp. [6788]
E-quip Africa [12704]
E-quip Africa [IO]
Personal Development
African-American Women in Tech. [6394]
Alliance for Tech. Access [11915]
Assn. for Res. in Personality [7543]
Career Gear [12705]
Combat Martial Art Practitioners Assn. [23587]
Delancey St. Found. [13018]
Dress for Success Worldwide [13424]
Intl. Center for Reiki Training [22969]
Intl. Center for Spirit at Work [20575]
Intl. Coach Fed. [836]
Intl. Enneagram Assn. [15904]
Intl. Enneagram Assn. [IO]
Intl. Soc. for Self and Identity [7546]
MOVE Intl.: Mobility Opportunities Via Educ. - USA [11962]
Soc. for Personal Growth [IO]
Society for Research on Identity Formation [IO]
Soc. for Res. on Identity Formation [8960]
Women's Learning Partnership for Rights, Development, and Peace [13452]
Youth Impact Intl. [13521]
Personal Economics Program [★457]
Personal Engineering Computer User's Soc. - Defunct.
Personal Financial Advisors; Natl. Assn. of [1468]
Personal Freedom Outreach [19875], PO Box 26062, St. Louis, MO 63136-0062, (314)921-9800
Personal Managers' Assn. [IO], East Molesey, United Kingdom
Personal Managers; Natl. Conf. of [174]
Personal Power Development Corp. - Defunct.
Personal Protective Armor Assn. - Address unknown since 2001.
Personal Radio Operators Fed. - Defunct.
Personal Retirement Alliance Ltd. - Defunct.
Personal Watercraft Assn. of Bermuda [IO], Hamilton, Bermuda
Personal Watercraft Indus. Assn. [3369], 444 N Capitol St., Ste. 645, Washington, DC 20001, (202)737-9768
Personalist Group - Western Div. - Address unknown since 1995.
Personalistic Discussion Group - Eastern Div. - Address unknown since 2008.
Personality Assessment; Soc. for [16176]
Personality and Social Psychology; Soc. for [7549]
Personalization Consortium [6800]
Personalization and Identification Assn. [★2837]
Personalized and ID Products Assn. [★2837]
Personnel
Agricultural Personnel Mgt. Assn. [4638]
Amer. Coll. Personnel Assn. [8961]
ARTDO Intl. [IO]
Assn. of Staff Physician Recruiters [15995]
Black Human Resources Network [2901]
Cable and Telecommunications Human Resources Assn. [1980]
Canadian Trucking Human Resources Coun. [IO]
Coll. and Univ. Professional Assn. for Human Resources [8962]
German Assn. for Personnel Mgt. [IO]
Human Rsrc. Certification Inst. [2902]
Human Resources Benchmarking Assn. [723]
Human Resources Outsourcing Assn. [1981]
Intl. Fed. of Training and Development Organizations [IO]

Reference to "IO" in place of a book number signifies that the association may be found in the 45th edition of International Organizations.

Intl. Personnel Mgt. Assn. - Canada **[IO]**
Intl. Public Mgt. Assn. for Human Resources **[1267]**
Marine Corps Recruiters Assn. **[5799]**
Media Human Resources Assn. **[2903]**
Media Human Resources Assn. **[IO]**
Natl. Alliance for Direct Support Professionals **[1986]**
Natl. Assn. for Govt. Training and Development **[2904]**
Natl. Assn. of Healthcare Transport Mgt. **[14579]**
Natl. Assn. of State Personnel Executives **[6280]**
Natl. Human Resources Assn. **[2905]**
North Amer. Trucking Industrial Relations Assn. **[2906]**
SHRM Global Forum **[2907]**
SHRM Global Forum **[IO]**
Soc. for Human Rsrc. Mgt. **[2908]**
Personnel Accreditation Inst. **[★2902]**
Personnel Admin; Amer. Soc. for **[★2908]**
Personnel Admin. Intl; Amer. Soc. for **[★2907]**
Personnel Admin; Soc. for **[★1267]**
Personnel Administrators; Conf. on Jesuit Student **[★7896]**
Personnel Administrators; Jesuit Assn. of Student **[7896]**
Personnel Administrators; Natl. Assn. of Church **[20515]**
Personnel Administrators; Natl. Assn. of Pupil **[★7902]**
Personnel Administrators; Natl. Assn. of Student **[7904]**
Personnel Assn; Amer. Coll. **[8961]**
Personnel; Assn. of Boards of Certification for Operating **[★6337]**
Personnel Assn; Coll. and Univ. **[★8962]**
Personnel Assn; Public **[★1267]**
Personnel Assn. for Teacher Educ; Student **[★8527]**
Personnel/Burden Carrier Mfrs. Assn. - Defunct.
Personnel Executives; Natl. Assn. of State **[6280]**
Personnel and Guidance Assn; Amer. **[★11815]**
Personnel; Natl. Assn. of Educational Off. **[★7898]**
Personnel Officers; Natl. Assn. of Placement **[★8961]**
Personnel in Ophthalmology; Joint Commn. on Allied Hea. **[15692]**
Personnel Relations Assn; Newspaper **[★2903]**
Personnel Res; Special Interest Gp. for Cmpt. **[★6824]**
Personnel Resources - Address unknown since 2001.
Personnel Services; Natl. Assn. of **[1272]**
Personnel in Water and Wastewater Utilities; Assn. of Boards of Certification for Operating **[★6337]**
Personnel Women; Intl. Assn. for **[★2905]**
Persons Conf. Bd. of Assoc. Res. Councils; Comm. on Intl. Exchange of **[★8609]**
Persons with disAbilities; World Assn. of **[14247]**
Persons Responsive to Educational Problems - Address unknown since 1995.
Perspectives in Communication - Address unknown since 1995.
Perspectives in Educ; Global **[★8593]**
Perth Australia ACM SIGGRAPH **[IO]**, Nedlands, Australia
Pertubuhan Akitek Malaysia **[★IO]**
Pertubuhan Pertolongan Wanita **[★IO]**
Peru
    Peruvian Heart Assn. **[13923]**
Peru; Comm. to Support the Revolution in **[18341]**
Peruvian
    Peruvian Heart Assn. **[13923]**
    U.S. Peruvian Horse Assn. **[4964]**
Peruvian Amer. Assn. - Address unknown since 1994.
Peruvian Assn. of Advt. Agencies **[IO]**, Lima, Peru
Peruvian Assn. for Conservation of Nature **[IO]**, Lima, Peru
Peruvian Bible Soc. **[IO]**, Lima, Peru
Peruvian Constr. Indus. Chamber **[IO]**, Lima, Peru
Peruvian Heart Assn. **[IO]**, Fabens, TX, United States
Peruvian Heart Assn. **[13923]**, PO Box 797, Fabens, TX 79838, (915)764-4321
Peruvian Horse Assn. of Canada **[IO]**, Lyalta, AB, Canada

Peruvian Inca Orchid Dog Club of Am. **[22341]**, c/o Jean Schroeder, AKC Liaison, 17502 S 750 W, Wanatah, IN 46390, (219)733-9480
Peruvian Inst. for Educ. in Human Rights and Peace **[IO]**, Lima, Peru
Peruvian League Against Epilepsy **[IO]**, Lima, Peru
Peruvian Paso Horse Assn; Intl. **[★4934]**
Peruvian Paso Horse Registry; Amer. **[★4934]**
Peruvian Paso Horse Registry of North Am. **[★4934]**
Peruvian Paso Horse Registry of North Am. **[★IO]**
Peruvian Paso Horses; Amer. Assn. of Owners and Breeders of **[4810]**
Peruvian Paso Part-Blood Registry **[★4934]**
Peruvian Paso Part-Blood Registry **[★IO]**
Peruvian Soc. of Arterial Hypertension **[IO]**, Lima, Peru
Peruvian Soc. of Cardiology **[IO]**, Lima, Peru
Peruvian Soc. of Clinical Neurophysiology **[IO]**, Lima, Peru
Peruvian Soc. of Dermatology **[IO]**, Lima, Peru
Pessimists; Benevolent and Loyal Order of **[22591]**
Pest Control
    Amer. Assn. of Pesticide Safety Educators **[4627]**
    Amer. Mosquito Control Assn. **[5072]**
    American Mosquito Control Association **[IO]**
    Assn. of Amer. Pesticide Control Officials **[6170]**
    Assn. of Applied IPM Ecologists **[5073]**
    Assn. of Natural Biocontrol Producers **[5074]**
    Australian Environmental Pest Managers Assn. **[IO]**
    Beyond Pesticides - Natl. Coalition Against the Misuse of Pesticides **[13322]**
    Bio-Integral Rsrc. Center **[5075]**
    British Pest Control Assn. **[IO]**
    CABI Bioscience **[IO]**
    CABI Bioscience Pakistan Centre **[IO]**
    CABI Bioscience Switzerland Centre **[IO]**
    Canadian Pest Mgt. Assn. **[IO]**
    Chem. Producers and Distributors Assn. **[803]**
    Confed. of European Pest Control Associations **[IO]**
    Indian Pest Control Assn. **[IO]**
    Intl. Assn. for the Plant Protection Sciences **[6397]**
    Intl. Org. for Biological Control of Noxious Animals and Plants **[IO]**
    Intl. Org. for Biological Control of Noxious Animals and Plants **[IO]**
    Intl. Red Locust Control Org. for Central and Southern Africa **[IO]**
    Interstate Professional Applicators Assn. **[2909]**
    Natl. Animal Damage Control Assn. **[5076]**
    Natl. Assn. of Exotic Pest Plant Councils **[5077]**
    Natl. Gypsy Moth Mgt. Bd. **[5078]**
    Natl. Pest Mgt. Assn. Intl. **[2910]**
    Natl. Pest Mgt. Assn. Intl. **[IO]**
    Natl. Pest Technicians Assn. **[IO]**
    Natl. Pesticide Info. Center **[13327]**
    North Amer. Horticultural Supply Assn. **[4984]**
    Northwest Coalition for Alternatives to Pesticides **[13328]**
    Pesticide Action Network North Am. Regional Center **[13329]**
    Pesticide Applicators Professional Assn. **[2911]**
    The Pesticide Stewardship Alliance **[7068]**
    Rachel Carson Coun. **[13330]**
    Responsible Indus. for a Sound Env. **[2912]**
    Soc. for Vector Ecology **[5079]**
Pest Control Assn; Natl. **[★2910]**
Pesticide Action Network North Am. Regional Center **[13329]**, 49 Powell St., Ste. 500, San Francisco, CA 94102, (415)981-1771
Pesticide Action Network UK **[IO]**, London, United Kingdom
Pesticide Applicators Professional Assn. **[2911]**, PO Box 80095, Salinas, CA 93912-0095, (831)442-3536
Pesticide Educ. and Action Proj. **[★13329]**
Pesticide Info. Center; Natl. **[13327]**
Pesticide Info. CH; Natl. **[★13327]**
Pesticide Producers Assn. - Defunct.
Pesticide Res. Lab; Fish **[★7172]**
Pesticide Safety Educators; Amer. Assn. of **[4627]**
The Pesticide Stewardship Alliance **[7068]**, PO Box 5204, Takoma Park, MD 20913, (877)920-6772

Pesticides; Beyond Pesticides - Natl. Coalition Against the Misuse of **[13322]**
Pesticides; Natl. Coalition Against the Misuse of **[★13322]**
Pesticides - Natl. Coalition Against the Misuse of Pesticides; Beyond **[13322]**
Pet Care Trust **[11447]**, c/o Debbie Mazur, Admin., 135 W Lemon Ave., Monrovia, CA 91016, (626)447-2222
Pet Care Trust **[IO]**, Bedford, United Kingdom
Pet Cemeteries; Natl. Assn. of **[★2959]**
PET Container Resources; Natl. Assn. for **[3997]**
Pet Dog Trainers; Assn. of **[1160]**
Pet Food Assn. of Canada **[IO]**, Toronto, ON, Canada
Pet Food Inst. **[2963]**, 2025 M St. NW, Ste. 800, Washington, DC 20036-2422, (202)367-1120
Pet Food Mfrs'. Assn. **[IO]**, London, United Kingdom
Pet; Ident-A- **[★11463]**
Pet Indus. Distributors Assn. **[2964]**, 2105 Laurel Bush Rd., Ste. 200, Bel Air, MD 21015-5200, (443)640-1060
Pet Indus. Joint Advisory Coun. **[2965]**, 1220 19th St. NW, Ste. 400, Washington, DC 20036-2438, (202)452-1525
Pet Lovers Assn. **[2966]**, PO Box 145, Joppa, MD 21085, (410)679-0978
Pet Pride **[11448]**, PO Box 1055, Pacific Palisades, CA 90272, (310)836-5427
Pet Producers of America - Defunct.
Pet Professional Retailers Org. - Defunct.
Pet Professionals; California Assn. of **[★2968]**
PET Resin Assn. **[3054]**, 355 Lexington Ave., Ste. 1500, New York, NY 10017-6603, (212)297-2125
Pet Savers Found. **[11449]**, 59 S Bayles Ave., Port Washington, NY 11050-3728, (516)944-5025
Pet Sitters Intl. **[2967]**, 201 E King St., King, NC 27021, (336)983-9222
Pet Sitters Intl. **[IO]**, King, NC, United States
Pet Sitters; Natl. Assn. of **[★2961]**
Pet Soc; Amer. **[11349]**
Pet Stock Assn; Amer. **[★5139]**
Pet Supply Assn; Western Wholesale **[★2968]**
Pet Supply Assn; Western World **[★2968]**
Pet Switchboard - Defunct.
Pet; Tattoo-a- **[11463]**
Pet Therapy Soc. of Northern Alberta **[IO]**, Edmonton, AB, Canada
PETA India **[IO]**, Bombay, India
Petanque
    Fed. of Petanque U.S.A. **[23649]**
Petanque Assn. U.S.A; Amer. **[★23649]**
Petanque of U.S.A; Fed. of **[★23649]**
Peter Alrichs Found. - Address unknown since 2001.
Peter the Apostle for Native Clergy; Soc. of St. **[★19725]**
Peter Apostle; Soc. of Saint **[19725]**
Peter Breck Fan Club **[24766]**, Box 70, Mecklenburg, NY 14863-0070
Peter Burwash Intl. Special Tennis Programs **[23908]**, 4200 Res. Forest Dr., Ste. 250, The Woodlands, TX 77381, (281)363-4707
Peter Burwash Intl. Special Tennis Programs **[IO]**, The Woodlands, TX, United States
Peter Claver; Junior Daughters of **[19002]**
Peter Claver; Junior Knights of **[19003]**
Peter Claver; Knights of **[19005]**
Peter Claver; Missionary Sisters of St. **[20364]**
Peter Crapo Descendants (France-Massachusetts) - Defunct.
Peter Deuel Remembrance Club - Address unknown since 2002.
Peter Noone Just A Little Bit Better Promotion Club - Address unknown since 2002.
Peter Sellers Appreciation Soc. **[24767]**, c/o Jason Simos, US Rep., 221 E 50th St., Apt. No. 7E, New York, NY 10022
Peter Warlock Soc. **[IO]**, London, United Kingdom
Petfood and Accessories Mfrs. Assn. **[IO]**, Bremen, Germany
Petite World - Defunct.
Petites Soeurs de Jesus **[★IO]**
Petites Soeurs de l'Assomption **[★IO]**
Petrified Wood Soc. - Defunct.
Petrochemical Energy Group - Address unknown since 2003.

A star before a book entry number signifies that the name is not listed separately, but is mentioned within the entry.

Petrochemical Indus. Assn. of Taiwan [IO], Taipei, Taiwan
Petrochemical and Refiners Assn; Natl. [2939]
Petroglyphs and Pictographs; Amer. Comm. to Advance the Study of [6437]
Petrol Pump Mfrs. Assn. [★IO]

Petroleum
Amer. Assn. of Drilling Engineers [7460]
Amer. Assn. of Petroleum Geologists [7125]
Amer. Assn. of Professional Landmen [2913]
Amer. Exploration and Production Coun. [2914]
Amer. Oil and Gas Historical Soc. [2915]
Amer. Petroleum Inst. [2916]
ASEAN Coun. on Petroleum - Indonesia [IO]
Assn. of British Offshore Indus. [IO]
Assn. of Desk and Derrick Clubs [2917]
Assn. of Energy Ser. Companies [2918]
Assn. of the German Petroleum Indus. [IO]
Assn. of Oil and Gas Producing Companies [IO]
Assn. of Oil Pipe Lines [2919]
Assn. for Petroleum and Explosives Admin. [IO]
Assn. for the Stud. of Peak Oil and Gas - USA [7461]
Assn. for Women Geoscientists [7139]
Atlantic Independent Union [24161]
Australian Inst. of Petroleum [IO]
Australian Petroleum Production and Exploration Assn. [IO]
BP Amoco Marketers Assn. [2920]
British Drilling Assn. [IO]
British Rig Owners' Assn. [IO]
Canadian Assn. of Drilling Engineers [IO]
Canadian Assn. of Oilwell Drilling Contractors [IO]
Canadian Assn. of Petroleum Landmen [IO]
Canadian Assn. of Petroleum Producers [IO]
Clean Harbors Cooperative [3070]
Colombian Petroleum Assn. [IO]
Completion Engg. Assn. [7182]
Coordinating Res. Coun. [2921]
Danish Petroleum Indus. Assn. [IO]
Distribution Contractors Assn. [24162]
Drilling Engg. Assn. [2922]
Energy Inst. [IO]
Energy Policy Res. Found., Inc. [7462]
Energy Security Coun. [2089]
Energy Traffic Assn. [2923]
Estonian Oil Assn. [IO]
European Bitumen Assn. [IO]
European Liquefied Petroleum Gas Assn. [IO]
European Petrochemical Assn. [IO]
Fed. of Petroleum Suppliers [IO]
Finnish Fed. of Petrol Retailers [IO]
Finnish Oil and Gas Fed. [IO]
French Petroleum Inst. [IO]
French Union of Petroleum Indus. [IO]
Gas Processors Assn. [2924]
Gas Processors Suppliers Assn. [2925]
Gasoline Pump Mfrs. Assn. [2926]
Independent Lubricant Mfrs. Assn. [2927]
Independent Lubricant Mfrs. Assn. [IO]
Independent Petroleum Assn. of Am. [2928]
Independent Terminal Operators Assn. [2929]
Indus. Tech. Facilitator [IO]
Intl. Assn. of Drilling Contractors [IO]
Intl. Assn. of Drilling Contractors [2930]
Intl. Assn. of Geophysical Contractors [2931]
Intl. Assn. of Geophysical Contractors [IO]
Intl. Coun. for Machinery Lubrication [7253]
Intl. Oil Scouts Assn. [2932]
Intl. Oil Scouts Assn. [IO]
Intl. Pipe Line and Offshore Contractors Assn. [IO]
Intl. Union of Petroleum and Indus. Workers [24163]
Intl. Well Control Forum [IO]
Irish Offshore Operators' Assn. [IO]
Japan Petroleum Development Assn. [IO]
Japanese Assn. for Petroleum Tech. [IO]
Korea Petrochemical Indus. Assn. [IO]
Latin Amer. Petrochemical Assn. [IO]
Liaison Comm. of Cooperating Oil and Gas Associations [2933]
LPG Australia [IO]
LPG Australia [IO]
Natl. Assn. of Div. Order Analysts [2934]

Natl. Assn. of Royalty Owners [2935]
Natl. Assn. of Shell Marketers [2936]
Natl. Convenience Store Advisory Gp. [3420]
Natl. Lubricating Grease Inst. [2937]
Natl. Oil Recyclers Assn. [2938]
Natl. Petrochemical and Refiners Assn. [2939]
Natl. Stripper Well Assn. [2940]
NOF [IO]
Norwegian Oil Indus. Assn. [IO]
Offshore Contractors Assn. [IO]
Oil Companies Intl. Marine Forum [IO]
Oil Firing Tech. Assn. for the Petroleum Indus. [IO]
Org. of Arab Petroleum Exporting Countries [IO]
Org. of the Petroleum Exporting Countries [IO]
Petrochemical Indus. Assn. of Taiwan [IO]
Petroleum Assn. of Japan [IO]
Petroleum Equipment Institute [IO]
Petroleum Equip. Inst. [2941]
Petroleum Equip. Suppliers Assn. [2942]
Petroleum Exploration Soc. of Australia [IO]
Petroleum Exploration Soc. of Great Britain [IO]
Petroleum Joint Venture Assn. [IO]
Petroleum Marketers Assn. of Am. [2943]
Petroleum Services Assn. of Canada [IO]
Petroleum Tech. Alliance Canada [IO]
Petroleum Tech. Transfer Coun. [2944]
Pigging Products and Services Assn. [IO]
Pipe Line Contractors Assn. [2945]
Pipeline Indus. Guild [IO]
Portuguese Petroleum Enterprises' Assn. [IO]
Production Engg. Assn. [IO]
Regional Assn. of Oil and Natural Gas Companies in Latin Am. and the Caribbean [IO]
Ser. Sta. Dealers of America/National Coalition of Petroleum Retailers and Allied Trades [2946]
Small Explorers and Producers Assn. of Canada [IO]
Soc. for Environmental Exploration [IO]
Soc. of Independent Gasoline Marketers of Am. [2947]
Soc. of Independent Professional Earth Scientists [7135]
Soc. for Mining, Metallurgy, and Exploration [7349]
The Soc. for Organic Petrology [7463]
The Soc. for Organic Petrology [IO]
Soc. of Petroleum Engineers [IO]
Soc. of Petroleum Engineers [7464]
Soc. of Petroleum Engineers - London Off. [IO]
Soc. of Petroleum Evaluation Engineers [7465]
Soc. of Petrophysicists and Well Log Analysts [7466]
Soc. of Professional Women in Petroleum [2948]
Soc. of Professional Women in Petroleum [IO]
South African Petroleum Indus. Assn. [IO]
Spanish Assn. of Petroleum Products Operators [IO]
Swedish Petroleum Inst. [IO]
Texas Independent Producers and Royalty Owners Assn. [2949]
Union Petroliere Europeenne Independante [IO]
Unione Petrolifera [IO]
United Engg. Found. [7051]
United Kingdom Offshore Operators' Assn. [IO]
United Kingdom Petroleum Indus. Assn. [IO]
U.S. Oil and Gas Assn. [2950]
Venezuelan Chamber of Petroleum Indus. [IO]
Well Drillers Assn. [IO]
Well Services Contractors Assn. [IO]
Western States Petroleum Assn. [2951]
World Fed. of Pipe Line Contractors Associations [2952]
World Fed. of Pipe Line Contractors Associations [IO]
World LP Gas Assn. [IO]
World Petroleum Coun. - The Global Forum for Oil and Gas Sci., Tech., Economics and Mgt. [IO]
Petroleum Accountants Societies; Coun. of [23]
Petroleum Assn. [★IO]
Petroleum Assn. of Japan [IO], Tokyo, Japan
Petroleum Assn; Natl. Coun. of Independent [★2943]
Petroleum Br. of AIME [★7464]

Petroleum Br. of AIME [★IO]
Petroleum; Canadian Inst. of Mining, Metallurgy, and [IO]
Petroleum Companies; Natl. Advisory Gp., Convenience Stores/ [★3420]
Petroleum Coun; Natl. [5686]
Petroleum Credit Assn; Amer. [★1427]
Petroleum Credit Assn; Intl. [★1427]
Petroleum Electric Supply Assn. - Defunct.
Petroleum Engineers; Amer. Inst. of Mining, Metallurgical, and [7346]
Petroleum Engineers; Mining Br., Amer. Inst. of Mining, Metallurgical and [★7349]
Petroleum Equipment Contractors Assn. - Address unknown since 1995.
Petroleum Equip. Inst. [2941], PO Box 2380, Tulsa, OK 74101-2380, (918)494-9696
Petroleum Equipment Institute [IO], Tulsa, OK, United States
Petroleum Equip. Suppliers; Amer. [★2942]
Petroleum Equip. Suppliers Assn. [2942], 9225 Katy Fwy., Ste. 310, Houston, TX 77024-1510, (713)932-0168
Petroleum Exploration Soc. of Australia [IO], Perth, Australia
Petroleum Exploration Soc. of Great Britain [IO], London, United Kingdom
Petroleum Gas Assn; Liquefied [★1681]
Petroleum Geologists; Amer. Assn. of [7125]
Petroleum Geologists; Canadian Soc. of [IO]
Petroleum Geologists; Southwest Assn. of [★7125]
Petroleum Geophysicists; Soc. of [★7149]
Petroleum Indus. Elecl. Assn. [★1185]
Petroleum Indus. Res. Found. [★7462]
Petroleum Indus. Security Coun. [★2089]
Petroleum Joint Venture Assn. [IO], Calgary, AB, Canada
Petroleum Landmen; Amer. Assn. of [★2913]
Petroleum and Law Assn; Australian Mining and [IO]
Petroleum Marketers Assn. of Am. [2943], 1901 N Ft. Myer Dr., Ste. 500, Arlington, VA 22209-1604, (703)351-8000
Petroleum Marketers Assn; Natl. Advisory Gp., Convenience Stores/ [★3420]
Petroleum Marketers; Coun. of Independent [★2943]
Petroleum Marketing Education Found. - Address unknown since 1994.
Petroleum and Natural Gas Extraction Assn. [★IO]
Petroleum Packaging Coun. [2878], c/o ATD Mgt. Inc., 1219 Ganado, San Clemente, CA 92673, (949)369-7102
Petroleum Refiners Assn; Natl. [★2939]
Petroleum Retailers; Natl. Cong. of [★2946]
Petroleum Services Assn. of Canada [IO], Calgary, AB, Canada
Petroleum Tech. Alliance Canada [IO], Calgary, AB, Canada
Petroleum Tech. Transfer Coun. [2944], c/o E. Lance Cole, Exec. Dir., PO Box 246, Sand Springs, OK 74063, (918)241-5801
Petroleum Workers; Independent Union of [★24163]
Petroleum Workers; Intl. Union of [★24163]
Petrophysicists and Well Log Analysts; Soc. of [7466]

Pets
2nd Chance 4 Pets [11481]
Accredited Pet Cemetery Soc. [2953]
Actors and Others for Animals [11339]
Afghan Hound Club of Am. [22179]
African Parrot Soc. [21833]
Airedale Terrier Club of Am. [22180]
Akita Club of Am. [22181]
Alaskan Malamute Club of Am. [22182]
All Amer. Premier Breeds Admin. [22183]
Alley Cat Allies [11343]
Alliance for Animals [11344]
Amateur Field Trial Clubs of Am. [22184]
Amer. Assn. of Black Russian Terriers [22185]
Amer. Assn. of Cat Enthusiasts [21899]
Amer. Assn. of Food Hygiene Veterinarians [16745]
Amer. Assn. of Housecall Veterinarians [16746]
Amer. Assn. of Spanish Timbrado Breeders [21834]
Amer. Boarding Kennels Assn. [2954]

Reference to "IO" in place of a book number signifies that the association may be found in the 45th edition of International Organizations.

Amer. Bouvier des Flandres Club [22188]
Amer. Boxer Club [22189]
Amer. Boxer Rescue Assn. [11346]
Amer. Brittany Club [22190]
Amer. Brussels Griffon Assn. [22191]
Amer. Bullmastiff Assn. [22192]
Amer. Canary Fanciers Assn. [21837]
Amer. Canine Educ. Found. [22193]
Amer. Cat Assn. [21900]
Amer. Cat Fanciers Assn. [21901]
Amer. Chesapeake Club [22195]
Amer. Dobermann Assn. [22196]
Amer. Dog Owner's Assn. [11347]
Amer. Dog Show Judges [22198]
Amer. Eskimo Dog Club of Am. [22199]
Amer. Fancy Rat and Mouse Assn. [22704]
Amer. Ferret Assn. [22415]
Amer. Fox Terrier Club [22200]
Amer. Gerbil Soc. [21515]
Amer. Guinea Hog Assn. [5231]
Amer. Kennel Club [22201]
Amer. Keuda Cat Assn. [4204]
Amer. Killifish Assn. [22434]
Amer. Kuvasz Assn. [12015]
Amer. Lhasa Apso Club [22202]
Amer. Maltese Assn. [22203]
Amer. Manchester Terrier Club [22204]
Amer. Miniature Schnauzer Club [22205]
Amer. Mobile Groomers Assn. [2955]
Amer. Mookee Assn. [4191]
Amer. Pet Products Mfrs. Assn. [2956]
Amer. Pet Soc. [11349]
Amer. Pointer Club [22206]
Amer. Pomeranian Club [22207]
Amer. Rare Breed Assn. [4496]
Amer. Rottweiler Club [22208]
Amer. Sealyham Terrier Club [22209]
Amer. Shetland Sheepdog Assn. [22210]
Amer. Shih Tzu Club [22211]
Amer. Soc. for the Prevention of Cruelty to
    Animals [11350]
Amer. Spaniel Club [22213]
Amer. Toy Fox Terrier Club [22214]
Amer. Veterinary Distributors Assn. [2957]
Amer. Water Spaniel Club [22215]
Amer. Waterslager Soc. [21842]
Amer. Whippet Club [22216]
Amer. White Shepherd Assn. [22217]
Amer. Working Collie Assn. [22218]
Amer. Working Dog Fed. [21516]
Amer. Working Malinois Assn. [21517]
Animal Medical Center [11353]
Animal Rights Coalition [11356]
Anti-Cruelty Soc. [11364]
Arizona Canine Acad. [22219]
Assoc. Koi Clubs of Am. [22437]
Assn. for People with Dogs Named Marty [22220]
Assn. of Pet Behavior Counsellors [IO]
Assn. for Pet Loss and Bereavement [12706]
Australian Cattle Dog Club of Am. [22221]
Australian Shepherd Club of Am. [22222]
Australian Terrier Club of Am. [22223]
Authentic Hovawarts of North Am. [22224]
Avian Welfare Coalition [4193]
Basenji Club of Am. [22225]
Basset Hound Club of Am. [22226]
Bearded Collie Club of Am. [22227]
Belgian Sheepdog Club of Am. [22228]
Berger Picard Club of Am. [22229]
Bernese Mountain Dog Club of Am. [22230]
Bichon Frise Club of Am. [22231]
Bide-A-Wee Home Assn. [11371]
Bird Clubs of Am. [21843]
Black Russian Terrier Club of Am. [22232]
Bluetick Breeders of Am. [22233]
Border Terrier Club of Am. [22234]
Borzoi Club of Am. [22235]
Boston Terrier Club of Am. [22236]
Brotogeris Soc. Intl. [4194]
Bull Terrier Club of Am. [22237]
Cairn Terrier Club of Am. [22238]
Canine Cancer Awareness [16788]
Canine Defense Fund [11373]
Cardigan Welsh Corgi Club of Am. [22240]
Carver-Scott Humane Soc. [11374]

Cat Fanciers' Assn. [21903]
Cat Fanciers' Fed. [21904]
Cats on Stamps Stud. Unit [22801]
Caucasian Ovcharka Club of Am. [22241]
Cavalier King Charles Spaniel Club of Am.
    [22242]
Chihuahua Club of Am. [22243]
Chinese Shar-Pei Club of Am. [22244]
Chow Chow Club, Inc. [22245]
Clumber Spaniel Club of Am. [22246]
Coalition to Protect Animals in Entertainment
    [11378]
Cockapoo Club of Am. [22247]
Collie Club of Am. [22248]
Continental Mi-Ki Assn. [22250]
Cow Observers Worldwide [22002]
Curly-Coated Retriever Club of Am. [22252]
Dachshund Club of Am. [22253]
Dalmatian Club of Am. [22254]
Dandie Dinmont Terrier Club of Am. [22255]
Delta Soc. Australia [IO]
Desert German Shorthaired Pointer Club [22256]
The Designer Cat Assn. [21906]
Doberman Pinscher Club of Am. [22257]
Dog Scouts of Am. [12016]
Dogs Deserve Better [12017]
Dogs on Stamps Stud. Unit [22815]
Dogue de Bordeaux Soc. of Am. [22258]
Doing Things for Animals [11386]
Doris Day Animal League [11387]
English Cocker Spaniel Club of Am. [22259]
English Setter Assn. of Am. [22260]
English Shepherd Club [22261]
English Springer Spaniel Field Trial Assn. [22262]
English Toy Spaniel Club of Am. [22263]
Epagneul Breton USA [22264]
Estrela Mountain Dog Assn. of Am. [22265]
European Pet Food Indus. Fed. [IO]
Fed. for the Amer. Staffordshire Terrier [21518]
Ferret Fanciers Club [22416]
Field Spaniel Soc. of Am. [22266]
Fitzgerald's Fancys: Rat and Mouse Info. [22705]
Flat-Coated Retriever Soc. of Am. [22268]
Fox Terrier Network [22269]
French Brittany Gun Dog Assn. [22270]
French Bull Dog Club of Am. [22271]
Fur Commn. U.S.A. [11399]
German Shepherd Dog Club of Am. [22272]
German Shepherd Dog Club of Am. - Working
    Dog Assn. [22273]
German Shorthaired Pointer Club of Am. [22274]
German Wirehaired Pointer Club of Am. [22275]
Golden Retriever Club of Am. [22277]
Goldfish Soc. of Am. [22439]
Gordon Setter Club of Am. [22278]
Great Dane Club of Am. [22279]
Great Pyrenees Club of Am. [22280]
GREY2K USA [4800]
Greyhound Club of Am. [22281]
Happy Household Pet Cat Club [21909]
Hartz Club of Am. [22772]
Havana Silk Dog Assn. of Am. [22282]
Heart Bandits Amer. Eskimo Dog Rescue [12018]
Hikers Against Doo Doo [4572]
Hovawart Club of Am. [22283]
Humane Soc. of the U.S. [11412]
Hungarian Pumi Club of Am. [22284]
Hunting Retriever Club [22285]
Icelandic Sheepdog Assn. of Am. [22286]
Independent Pet and Animal Trans. Assn. Intl.
    [2958]
Intl. Alliance for Animal Therapy and Healing
    [13703]
Intl. Assn. of Canine Professionals [1161]
Intl. Assn. of Pet Cemeteries and Crematories
    [2959]
Intl. Assn. of Pet Cemeteries and Crematories
    [IO]
The Intl. Bengal Breeders' Assn. [4205]
The Intl. Bengal Cat Soc. [4206]
Intl. Borzoi Coun. [22287]
The Intl. Cat Assn. [21910]
Intl. Conure Assn. [21848]
Intl. Defenders of Animals [11414]
Intl. Desert Lynx Cat Assn. [4207]

Intl. French Brittany Club of Am. [22288]
Intl. Kennel Club of Chicago [22289]
Intl. Modena Club [22896]
Intl. Professional Groomers [2960]
The Intl. Savannah Breeders' Assn. [4208]
Intl. Seppala Assn. [22291]
Intl. Soc. of Animal License Collectors [22058]
Intl. Veterinary Assistance [11420]
Intl. Weight Pull Assn. [23384]
Irish Terrier Club of Am. [22293]
Irish Water Spaniel Club of Am. [22294]
Irish Wolfhound Club of Am. [22295]
Jack Russell Terrier Club of Am. [22297]
Japanese Akita Club of Am. [22298]
Japanese Chin Club of Am. [22299]
Jews for Animal Rights [11422]
Keeshond Club of Am. [22300]
Kuvasz Club of Am. [22302]
Ladies Kennel Assn. of Am. [22303]
LaPerm Soc. of Am. [21912]
Maremma Sheepdog Club of Am. [22304]
Mastiff Club of Am. [22305]
Mercy For Animals [11336]
Miniature Australian Shepherd Club of Am.
    [22306]
Miniature Bull Terrier Club of Am. [22307]
Miniature Pinscher Club of Am. [22308]
Missing Pet Partnership [12707]
Musical Dog Sport Assn. [23385]
Natl. Alliance of Burmese Breeders [4210]
Natl. Amateur Retriever Club [22309]
Natl. Amer. Eskimo Dog Assn. [22310]
Natl. Amer. Pit Bull Terrier Assn. [22311]
Natl. Assn. of Dog Obedience Instructors [22312]
Natl. Assn. of Louisiana Catahoulas [22313]
Natl. Assn. of Professional Pet Sitters [2961]
Natl. Beagle Club of Am. [22314]
Natl. Bird Dog Challenge Assn. [22315]
Natl. Birman Fanciers [21913]
Natl. Cat Protection Soc. [11434]
Natl. Cesky Terrier Club of Am. [22316]
Natl. Cockatiel Soc. [21852]
Natl. Comm. on Pot Bellied Pigs [4140]
Natl. Cong. of Animal Trainers and Breeders
    [11435]
Natl. Dog Groomers Assn. of Am. [2962]
Natl. Dog Registry [11436]
Natl. Entlebucher Mountain Dog Assn. [22317]
Natl. Greyhound Assn. [22318]
Natl. Humane Educ. Soc. [11440]
Natl. Pet Alliance [11441]
Natl. Pigeon Assn. [21856]
Natl. Toy Fox Terrier Assn. [22321]
North Amer. Border Terrier Welfare [12019]
North Amer. Cockatiel Soc. [21857]
North Amer. Deutsch Kurzhaar Club [22323]
North Amer. Dog Agility Coun. [23387]
North Amer. Fish Breeders Guild [22444]
North Amer. Jack Russell Terrier Assn. [22324]
North Amer. Kai Assn. [22325]
North Amer. Lionhead Rabbit Club [5157]
North Amer. Llewellin Breeders Assn. [22326]
North Amer. Potbellied Pig Assn. [4145]
North Amer. Sheep Dog Soc. [22328]
North Amer. Teckel Club [22329]
North Amer. Working Bouvier Assn. [22330]
Norwegian Elkhound Assn. of Am. [22331]
Norwegian Forest Cat Breed Coun. [21914]
Norwegian Lundehund Assn. of Am. [22332]
Norwich and Norfolk Terrier Club [22333]
Old English Sheepdog Club of Am. [22334]
Patriotic Pets [11442]
Patterdale Terrier Club of Am. [22338]
Pekingese Club of Am. [22339]
Pembroke Welsh Corgi Club of Am. [22340]
People-Animals-Love [16632]
Performing Animal Welfare Soc. [11446]
Peruvian Inca Orchid Dog Club of Am. [22341]
Pet Care Trust [11447]
Pet Care Trust [IO]
Pet Food Inst. [2963]
Pet Food Mfrs'. Assn. [IO]
Pet Indus. Distributors Assn. [2964]
Pet Indus. Joint Advisory Coun. [2965]
Pet Lovers Assn. [2966]

A star before a book entry number signifies that the name is not listed separately, but is mentioned within the entry.

Pet Pride [11448]
Pet Savers Found. [11449]
Pet Sitters Intl. [2967]
Pet Sitters Intl. [IO]
Pet Therapy Soc. of Northern Alberta [IO]
Petfood and Accessories Mfrs. Assn. [IO]
PIGS - A Sanctuary [4147]
PIJAC Canada [IO]
Pionus Breeders Assn. [21859]
Polish Tatra Sheepdog Club of Am. [22342]
Poodle Club of Am. [22343]
Portuguese Podengo Club of Am. [22344]
Portuguese Water Dog Club of Am. [22345]
Prevent a Litter Coalition [11451]
Professional Handlers Assn. [22346]
Pug Dog Club of Am. [22347]
Pyrenean Mastiff Club of Am. [22349]
RagaMuffin Cat Lovers Soc. [22777]
Rat Assistance and Teaching Soc. [22778]
Rat Fan Club [22706]
Rat, Mouse, and Hamster Fanciers [22708]
Rat Terrier Club of Am. [22350]
Rex Breeders United [21915]
Rhodesian Ridgeback Club of the U.S. [22351]
Sacred Cat of Burma Fanciers [21916]
Saint Bernard Club of Am. [22352]
Samoyed Club of Am. [22354]
Savannah Cat Club [4211]
Scottish Deerhound Club of Am. [22356]
Scottish Terrier Club of Am. [22357]
Selkirk Rex Breed Club [21917]
Senior Conformation Judges Assn. [22358]
Siberian Husky Club of Am. [22359]
Silky Terrier Club of Am. [22360]
Skye Terrier Club of Am. [22361]
Soc. Against Vivisection [11458]
Soc. of Parrot Breeders and Exhibitors [21860]
Somali Cat Club of Am. [21918]
Somali Intl. Cat Club [21919]
Soul Friends [16637]
Spanish Water Dog Assn. of Am. [22362]
Stafford Canary Club of Am. [21861]
Staffordshire Terrier Club of Am. [22364]
Standard Schnauzer Club of Am. [22365]
Tattoo-a-Pet [11463]
Therapy Dogs Intl. [16638]
Tibetan Spaniel Club of Am. [22366]
Tibetan Terrier Club of Am. [22367]
Traditional Cat Assn. [21920]
Traditional and Classic Cat Intl. [21921]
Tree House Animal Found. [11464]
Treeing Walker Breeders and Fanciers Assn. [22368]
United Action for Animals [11468]
United Activists for Animal Rights [11469]
United Animal Nations [11470]
United Burmese Cat Fanciers [21922]
United Cat Fed. [21923]
United Doberman Club [22369]
United Gloster Breeders [21863]
United Humanitarians [11471]
United Kennel Club [22370]
United Silver Fanciers [21924]
U.S. Border Collie Club [22372]
U.S. Boxer Assn. [22373]
U.S. Dog Agility Assn. [23388]
U.S. Kerry Blue Terrier Club [22374]
U.S. Lakeland Terrier Club [22375]
U.S. Mondioring Assn. [23389]
U.S. Neapolitan Mastiff Club [22376]
U.S. Rottweiler Club [22377]
Vizsla Club of Am. [22378]
Weimaraner Club of Am. [22379]
Welsh Springer Spaniel Club of Am. [22380]
West Highland White Terrier Club of Am. [22381]
Westminster Kennel Club [22382]
White German Shepherd Dog Club of Am. [22383]
Wirehaired Vizsla Club of Am. [22384]
Working Pit Bull Terrier Club of Am. [22385]
Working Riesenschnauzer Fed. [22386]
World Bulldog Alliance [22387]
World Canine Freestyle Org. [23390]
World Wide Kennel Club [22388]
World Wide Pet Indus. Assn. [2968]

World Wide Pet Indus. Assn. [IO]
WTCARES [22389]
Yorkshire Terrier Club of Am. [22390]
Pets of Am; Greyhound [★11401]
Pets; Retired Greyhounds As [★11473]
Petty Officers' Assn; Natl. Chief [21214]
Petty Officers Assn; U.S. Coast Guard Chief [20734]
Peugeot Owners' Club - Defunct.
Pew Charitable Trusts [13129], 2005 Market St., Ste. 1700, Philadelphia, PA 19103-7077, (215)575-9050
PEWSACTION Fellowship - Address unknown since 2000.
Pewter Collectors Club of Am. [22107], c/o Wayne Hilt, 176 Injun Hollow Rd., Haddam Neck, CT 06424-3022
Pewter Soc. [IO], Monmouth, United Kingdom
Pewterers' Company [IO], London, United Kingdom
P'eylim - Amer. Yeshiva Student Union - Address unknown since 1999.
The Peyote Way Church [★20447]
Peyote Way Church of God [20447], 30800 W Klondyke Rd., Willcox, AZ 85643, (928)828-3444
PF [★12186]
PF [★IO]
PFB Project - Address unknown since 1999.
PGA Tour Directors Assn. [★23461]
PGA TOUR Tournaments Assn. [23461], 13000 Sawgrass Village Cir., Ste. 36, Ponte Vedra Beach, FL 32082, (904)285-4222
PGAA - Defunct.
PGI [396]
Phantom Blue Phan Club [24961], PMB No. 1674, 8306 Wilshire Blvd., Beverly Hills, CA 90211
Phantom Class Racing Assn. - Address unknown since 1988.
Phantom Friends; Soc. of [9739]
Phantom II Soc; F-4 [21445]
Pharma Indus. Finland [IO], Helsinki, Finland
Pharmaceutica Intl. - Defunct.
Pharmaceutical Advt. Club [★100]
Pharmaceutical Advt. Coun. [★100]
Pharmaceutical Alliance; Natl. [★2975]
Pharmaceutical Assn; Amer. Chinese [15911]
Pharmaceutical Assn. of Malaysia [IO], Kuala Lumpur, Malaysia
Pharmaceutical Assn; Natl. [15947]
Pharmaceutical Assn; Natl. Coun. of State [★15943]
Pharmaceutical Assn. Secretaries; Natl. Conf. of State [★15943]
Pharmaceutical Assn; Student Amer. [★15919]
Pharmaceutical Assn. Student Sect; Amer. [★15919]
Pharmaceutical and Biotech Trainers; Soc. of [3475]
Pharmaceutical Care Mgt. Assn. [2988], 601 Pennsylvania Ave. NW, 7th Fl., Washington, DC 20004-2601, (202)207-3610
Pharmaceutical Educ; Amer. Coun. on [★15907]
Pharmaceutical Educ; Amer. Found. for [15916]
Pharmaceutical Engineers; Intl. Soc. of [★7468]
Pharmaceutical Excipients Coun; Intl. [★2977]
Pharmaceutical Faculties; Amer. Conf. of [★15909]
Pharmaceutical Gp. of the European Community [★IO]
Pharmaceutical Gp. of the European Union [IO], Brussels, Belgium
Pharmaceutical and Healthcare Assn. of the Philippines [IO], Makati City, Philippines
Pharmaceutical and Healthcare Sciences Soc. [IO], Swindon, United Kingdom
Pharmaceutical Info. and Pharmacovigilance Assn. [IO], Haslemere, United Kingdom
Pharmaceutical Manufacturers Assn. [★2980]
Pharmaceutical Mfrs. Assn; Amer. [★2980]
Pharmaceutical Mfrs. Assn. of Canada [★IO]
Pharmaceutical Mfrs. Assn. Found. [★2980]
Pharmaceutical Manufacturers' Assn. of South Africa [IO], Johannesburg, Republic of South Africa
Pharmaceutical Physicians Educ. Found; Amer. Acad. of [★8840]
Pharmaceutical Res. and Manufacturers of Am. [2980], 950 F St. NW, Washington, DC 20004, (202)835-3400
Pharmaceutical Res. and Sci; Acad. of [15906]
Pharmaceutical Sales Trainers; Natl. Soc. of [★3475]

Pharmaceutical Sciences; Acad. of [★15906]
Pharmaceutical Soc. of Australia [IO], Deakin, Australia
Pharmaceutical Soc. of Denmark [IO], Copenhagen, Denmark
Pharmaceutical Soc. of Ireland [IO], Dublin, Ireland
Pharmaceutical Soc. of Japan [IO], Tokyo, Japan
Pharmaceutical Soc. of Namibia [IO], Windhoek, Namibia
Pharmaceutical Soc. of New Zealand [IO], Wellington, New Zealand
Pharmaceutical Soc. of Northern Ireland [IO], Belfast, United Kingdom
Pharmaceutical Soc. of Singapore [IO], Singapore, Singapore
Pharmaceutical Soc. of South Africa [IO], Arcadia, Republic of South Africa
Pharmaceutical Students' Fed; Intl. [IO]
Pharmaceuticals
Acad. of Pharmaceutical Res. and Sci. [15906]
Accreditation Coun. for Pharmacy Educ. [15907]
Alliance for the Prudent Use of Antibiotics [15908]
Alpha Zeta Omega [24567]
Amer. Acad. of Clinical Toxicology [16657]
Amer. Acad. of Veterinary Pharmacology and Therapeutics [16738]
Amer. Assn. of Colleges of Pharmacy [15909]
Amer. Assn. of Pharmaceutical Scientists [7467]
American Association of Pharmaceutical Scientists [IO]
Amer. Assn. of Poison Control Centers [16658]
Amer. Coll. of Apothecaries [15912]
Amer. Coll. of Clinical Pharmacology [15913]
Amer. Coll. of Clinical Pharmacy [15914]
Amer. Coll. of Medical Toxicology [16660]
Amer. Coll. of Neuropsychopharmacology [15915]
Amer. Found. for Pharmaceutical Educ. [15916]
Amer. Inst. of the History of Pharmacy [15917]
Amer. Pharmacists Assn. - Acad. of Pharmacy Practice and Mgt. [15918]
Amer. Pharmacists Assn. Acad. of Student Pharmacists [15919]
Amer. Soc. for Automation in Pharmacy [2969]
Amer. Soc. for Clinical Pharmacology and Therapeutics [15920]
Amer. Soc. of Consultant Pharmacists [15922]
Amer. Soc. of Hea. Sys. Pharmacists [15923]
Amer. Soc. of Pharmacognosy [15924]
Amer. Soc. for Pharmacology and Experimental Therapeutics [15925]
Amer. Soc. for Pharmacy Law [15003]
Animal Hea. Inst. [2970]
Argentine Chamber of Producers of Pharmaceutical Chemicals [IO]
ASHP Found. [15926]
Aspirin Found. of Am. [2971]
Assn. of the British Pharmaceutical Indus. [IO]
Assn. for Clinical Data Mgt. [IO]
Assn. of Finnish Pharmacies [IO]
Assn. of Intl. Pharmaceutical Mfrs. [IO]
Assn. of Pharmaceutical Distributors - Italy [IO]
Assn. of Pharmaceutical Manufacturers [IO]
Assn. of Regulatory and Clinical Scientists Australia [IO]
Australasian Pharmaceutical Sci. Assn. [IO]
Belgian Pharmaceutical Indus. Assn. [IO]
Brazilian Pharmaceutical Assn. [IO]
British Assn. of Pharmaceutical Physicians [IO]
British Assn. of Pharmaceutical Wholesalers [IO]
British Soc. for the History of Pharmacy [IO]
Brother's Brother Found. [12837]
Bulk Drug Manufacturers' Assn. [IO]
Canada's Research-Based Pharmaceutical Companies [IO]
Canadian Assn. for Pharmacy Distribution Mgt. [IO]
Canadian Generic Pharmaceutical Assn. [IO]
Chain Drug Marketing Assn. [IO]
Chain Drug Marketing Assn. [2972]
Chem. Pharmaceutical Generic Assn. [IO]
CIIT Centers for Hea. Res. [7801]
Collegium Internationale Neuro-Psychopharmacologicum [15929]
Consumer Healthcare Prdt. Assn. [2973]
Croatian Pharmaceutical Soc. [IO]

Reference to "IO" in place of a book number signifies that the association may be found in the 45th edition of International Organizations.

Danish Assn. of the Pharmaceutical Indus. [IO]
Drug, Chem. and Assoc. Technologies Assn. [2974]
Drug Info. Assn. [15931]
Dutch Assn. of the Research-based Pharmaceutical Indus. [IO]
European Behavioral Pharmacology Soc. [IO]
European Fed. of Pharmaceutical Indus. and Associations [IO]
European Fed. for Pharmaceutical Sciences [IO]
European Fed. of Statisticians in the Pharmaceutical Indus. [IO]
European Forum for Good Clinical Practice [IO]
European Generic Medicines Assn. [IO]
Fed. of Drug and Alcohol Professionals [IO]
Fed. of Pharmaceutical Mfrs'. Associations of Japan [IO]
Foreign Pharmacy Graduate Examination Comm. [15933]
French Pharmaceutical Distribution Assn. [IO]
Generic Pharmaceutical Assn. [2975]
German Assn. of Pharmaceutical Medicine [IO]
Hea. Prdt. Wholesalers' and Manufacturers' Assn. in Finland [IO]
Hea. Products Assn. of Southern Africa [IO]
Hellenic Assn. of Pharmaceutical Companies [IO]
Hong Kong Assn. of the Pharmaceutical Indus. [IO]
Indian Drug Mfrs'. Assn. [IO]
Indian Pharmaceutical Assn. [IO]
INFARMA - Employers' Union of Innovative Pharmaceutical Companies [IO]
Inst. of Clinical Res. [IO]
Inst. of Pharmacy Mgt. Intl. [IO]
Intl. Aloe Sci. Coun. [1863]
Intl. Fed. of Pharmaceutical Mfrs. and Associations [IO]
International Federation of Pharmaceutical Wholesalers [IO]
Intl. Fed. of Pharmaceutical Wholesalers [2976]
Intl. Pharmaceutical Excipients Coun. of the Americas [2977]
Intl. Pharmaceutical Excipients Coun. of the Americas [IO]
Intl. Soc. for Pharmaceutical Engg. [IO]
Intl. Soc. for Pharmaceutical Engg. [7468]
Intl. Tech. Caramel Assn. [1532]
Irish Pharmaceutical Healthcare Assn. [IO]
Italian Pharmacists' Fed. [IO]
Japan Pharmaceutical Mfrs'. Assn. [IO]
Japanese Soc. of Pharmacognosy [IO]
Kappa Psi [24568]
Korea Pharmaceutical Manufacturers Assn. [IO]
Lambda Kappa Sigma [24569]
Latin Amer. Fed. of the Pharmaceutical Indus. [IO]
Malaysian Org. of Pharmaceutical Indus. [IO]
Medical Letter [15940]
Medical Marketing Assn. [2637]
Medicines Australia [IO]
Mexican Pharmaceutical Assn. [IO]
Natl. Alliance of State Pharmacy Associations [15943]
Natl. Assn. of Boards of Pharmacy [15944]
Natl. Assn. of OTC Pharmaceutical Products [IO]
Natl. Assn. of the Pharmaceutical Indus. - Italy [IO]
Natl. Assn. of the Pharmaceutical Indus. - Spain [IO]
Natl. Catholic Pharmacists Guild of the U.S. [15945]
Natl. Chamber of the Pharmaceutical Indus. [IO]
Natl. Coun. on Patient Info. and Educ. [15946]
Natl. Found. for Depressive Illness [15225]
Natl. Hea. Fed. [14587]
Natl. Org. for Rare Disorders [14282]
Natl. Pharmaceutical Assn. [15947]
Natl. Pharmaceutical Coun. [2978]
Natl. Pharmacies' Assn. [IO]
Natl. Pharmacy Assn. [IO]
Natl. Union of Pharmacies [IO]
Nonprescription Drug Mfrs. Assn. of Canada [IO]
Norwegian Assn. of Pharmaceutical Manufacturers [IO]
Org. of Pharmaceutical Producers of India [IO]
PDA [IO]

PDA [2979]
Pharma Indus. Finland [IO]
Pharmaceutical Assn. of Malaysia [IO]
Pharmaceutical and Healthcare Assn. of the Philippines [IO]
Pharmaceutical Info. and Pharmacovigilance Assn. [IO]
Pharmaceutical Manufacturers' Assn. of South Africa [IO]
Pharmaceutical Res. and Manufacturers of Am. [2980]
Pharmaceutical Soc. of Australia [IO]
Pharmaceutical Soc. of Denmark [IO]
Pharmaceutical Soc. of Ireland [IO]
Pharmaceutical Soc. of Japan [IO]
Pharmaceutical Soc. of Namibia [IO]
Pharmaceutical Soc. of New Zealand [IO]
Pharmachemical Ireland [IO]
Phi Delta Chi [24570]
Polish Chamber of Pharmaceutical Indus. and Medical Devices [IO]
Portuguese Assn. of the Pharmaceutical Indus. [IO]
Proj. Inform [13583]
Proprietary Assn. of Great Britain [IO]
Regulatory Affairs Professionals Soc. [14599]
Researched Medicines Indus. Assn. of New Zealand [IO]
Returns Indus. Assn. [2981]
Singapore Assn. of Pharmaceutical Indus. [IO]
Soc. for Applied Pharmacological Sciences [IO]
Soc. For Clinical Data Mgt. [2982]
Soc. of Pharmaceutical and Biotech Trainers [3475]
Soc. of Pharmaceutical Medicine [IO]
Swedish Assn. of the Pharmaceutical Indus. [IO]
Swiss Retail Chemists' Assn. [IO]
U.S. Pharmacopeia [15953]
Pharmachemical Ireland [IO], Dublin, Ireland
Pharmacies; Natl. Assn. of Mail Ser. [★2988]
Pharmacists Against Drug Abuse - Address unknown since 2000.
Pharmacists; Amer. Soc. of Consultant [15922]
Pharmacists; Amer. Soc. of Hea. Sys. [15923]
Pharmacists Assn. Foundation; National Community [★2986]
Pharmacists; Assn. of Natural Medicine [15282]
Pharmacists Guild of the U.S; Natl. Catholic [15945]
Pharmacists; Intl. Acad. of Compounding [15935]
Pharmacists for Life [★18563]
Pharmacists for Life [★IO]
Pharmacists for Life Intl. [IO], Powell, OH, United States
Pharmacists for Life Intl. [18563], PO Box 1281, Powell, OH 43065-1281, (740)881-5520
Pharmacists in Ophthalmic Practice - Address unknown since 2001.
Pharmacists Res. and Educ. Found; Amer. Soc. of Hosp. [★15926]
Pharmacists; Soc. of Infectious Diseases [15952]
Pharmacoeconomics and Outcomes Res; Intl. Soc. for [15938]
Pharmacognosy; Amer. Soc. of [15924]
Pharmacokinetics Group - Defunct.
Pharmacological Soc. of Canada [IO], London, ON, Canada
Pharmacology; Amer. Coll. of Clinical [15913]
Pharmacology; Amer. Coll. of Neuropsycho [15915]
Pharmacology; Canadian Soc. for Clinical [IO]
Pharmacology and Chemotherapy; Amer. Soc. of Clinical [★15920]
Pharmacology and Experimental Therapeutics; Amer. Soc. for [15925]
Pharmacology; Intl. Soc. for Anaesthetic [13685]
Pharmacology and Therapeutics; Amer. Acad. of Veterinary [16738]
Pharmacology and Therapeutics; Amer. Soc. for Clinical [15920]
Pharmacopeia; U.S. [15953]
Pharmacopoeia of the U.S; Homeopathic [14847]
Pharmacy
  AARP Pharmacy Services [2983]
  Acad. of Managed Care Pharmacy [15905]
  Acad. of Pharmaceutical Res. and Sci. [15906]
  Accreditation Coun. for Pharmacy Educ. [15907]

Alliance for the Prudent Use of Antibiotics [15908]
Alpha Zeta Omega [24567]
Amer. Acad. of Clinical Toxicology [16657]
Amer. Acad. of Veterinary Pharmacology and Therapeutics [16738]
Amer. Assn. of Colleges of Pharmacy [15909]
Amer. Assn. for the History of Medicine [10082]
Amer. Assn. of Pharmacy Technicians [15910]
Amer. Assn. of Poison Control Centers [16658]
Amer. Chinese Pharmaceutical Assn. [15911]
Amer. Coll. of Apothecaries [15912]
Amer. Coll. of Clinical Pharmacology [15913]
Amer. Coll. of Clinical Pharmacy [15914]
Amer. Coll. of Medical Toxicology [16660]
Amer. Coll. of Neuropsychopharmacology [15915]
Amer. Found. for Pharmaceutical Educ. [15916]
Amer. Inst. of the History of Pharmacy [15917]
Amer. Osteopathic Acad. of Sports Medicine [16477]
Amer. Pharmacists Assn. - Acad. of Pharmacy Practice and Mgt. [15918]
Amer. Pharmacists Assn. Acad. of Student Pharmacists [15919]
Amer. Soc. for Clinical Pharmacology and Therapeutics [15920]
Amer. Soc. of Clinical Psychopharmacology [15921]
Amer. Soc. of Consultant Pharmacists [15922]
Amer. Soc. of Hea. Sys. Pharmacists [15923]
Amer. Soc. of Pharmacognosy [15924]
American Society of Pharmacognosy [IO]
Amer. Soc. for Pharmacology and Experimental Therapeutics [15925]
Amer. Soc. for Pharmacy Law [15003]
ASHP Found. [15926]
Assn. of Clinical Res. Professionals [15927]
Assn. of Clinical Res. Professionals [IO]
Assn. of Deans of Pharmacy of Canada [IO]
Assn. of Democratic Pharmacists [IO]
Assn. of the European Self-Medication Indus. [IO]
Assn. of Faculties of Pharmacy of Canada [IO]
Assn. of Natural Medicine Pharmacists [15282]
Assn. of Pharmacy Technicians of United Kingdom [IO]
Australasian Soc. of Clinical and Experimental Pharmacologists and Toxicologists [IO]
Australian Assn. of Consultant Pharmacy [IO]
Australian Coll. of Pharmacy Practice [IO]
Australian Self-Medication Indus. [IO]
Austrian Pharmacological Soc. [IO]
Belgian Soc. of Fundamental and Clinical Physiology and Pharmacology [IO]
Biomedical Res. and Experimental Therapeutics Soc. of Singapore [IO]
Brazilian Soc. of Pharmacology and Experimental Therapeutics [IO]
British Assn. for Psychopharmacology [IO]
British Pharmacological Soc. [IO]
Canadian Assn. of Pharmacy in Oncology [IO]
Canadian Assn. of Pharmacy Technicians [IO]
Canadian Pharmacists Assn. [IO]
Canadian Soc. for Clinical Pharmacology [IO]
Canadian Soc. of Hosp. Pharmacists [IO]
Chilean Soc. of Pharmacology [IO]
Chinese Pharmaceutical Soc. [IO]
Christian Pharmacists Fellowship Intl. [IO]
Christian Pharmacists Fellowship Intl. [15928]
Collegium Internationale Neuro-Psychopharmacologicum [15929]
Collegium Internationale Neuro-Psychopharmacologicum [IO]
Commn. for Certification in Geriatric Pharmacy [15930]
Commonwealth Pharmaceutical Assn. [IO]
Croatian Pharmacological Soc. [IO]
Czech Soc. for Experimental and Clinical Pharmacology and Toxicology [IO]
Danish Soc. of Pharmacology and Toxicology [IO]
Drug Info. Assn. [IO]
Drug Info. Assn. [15931]
Dutch Pharmacological Soc. [IO]
Estonian Soc. of Pharmacology [IO]
Ethiopian Pharmacists Assn. in North Am. [IO]
Ethiopian Pharmacists Assn. in North Am. [15932]
European Assn. of Hosp. Pharmacists [IO]

A star before a book entry number signifies that the name is not listed separately, but is mentioned within the entry.

European Coll. of Neuropsychopharmacology **[IO]**
European Fed. for Medicinal Chemistry **[IO]**
European Soc. of Clinical Pharmacy **[IO]**
Fed. of European Pharmacological Societies **[IO]**
Finnish Pharmacological Soc. **[IO]**
Foreign Pharmacy Graduate Examination Comm. **[15933]**
French Pharmacology Soc. **[IO]**
German Soc. for Experimental and Clinical Pharmacology and Toxicology **[IO]**
HealthCare Compliance Packaging Coun. **[15934]**
Healthcare Distribution Mgt. Assn. **[2984]**
HIV Pharmacy Assn. **[IO]**
Hong Kong Pharmacology Soc. **[IO]**
Indian Pharmacological Soc. **[IO]**
Intl. Acad. of Compounding Pharmacists **[15935]**
Intl. Biopharmaceutical Assn. **[15936]**
Intl. Biopharmaceutical Assn. **[IO]**
Intl. Fed. of Associations of Pharmaceutical Physicians **[IO]**
Intl. Pharmaceutical Fed. **[IO]**
The Intl. Publication Planning Assn. **[3231]**
Intl. Soc. for Anaesthetic Pharmacology **[13685]**
Intl. Soc. for the History of Pharmacy **[IO]**
Intl. Soc. of Oncology Pharmacy Practitioners **[15937]**
Intl. Soc. for Pharmacoeconomics and Outcomes Res. **[15938]**
International Society for Pharmacoeconomics and Outcomes Research **[IO]**
Intl. Soc. for Pharmacoepidemiology **[15939]**
Intl. Soc. of Regulatory Toxicology and Pharmacology **[14570]**
Iranian Soc. of Physiology and Pharmacology **[IO]**
Italian Pharmacological Soc. **[IO]**
Italian Soc. for Hosp. Pharmacy **[IO]**
Japanese Pharmacological Soc. **[IO]**
Kappa Psi **[24568]**
Korean Soc. of Pharmacology **[IO]**
Lambda Kappa Sigma **[24569]**
Latvian Soc. of Pharmacology **[IO]**
Malaysian Soc. of Pharmacology and Physiology **[IO]**
Medical Letter **[15940]**
Medication Compliance Inst. **[15941]**
Medication Compliance Inst. **[IO]**
Multidisciplinary Assn. for Psychedelic Stud. **[15942]**
Natl. Alliance of State Pharmacy Associations **[15943]**
Natl. Assn. of Boards of Pharmacy **[15944]**
Natl. Assn. of Chain Drug Stores **[2985]**
Natl. Assn. of Women Pharmacists **[IO]**
Natl. Catholic Pharmacists Guild of the U.S. **[15945]**
Natl. Community Pharmacists Assn. **[2986]**
Natl. Coordinating Coun. for Medication Error Reporting and Prevention **[14653]**
Natl. Coun. on Patient Info. and Educ. **[15946]**
Natl. Coun. for Prescription Drug Programs **[2987]**
Natl. Hea. Fed. **[14587]**
Natl. Pharmaceutical Assn. **[15947]**
Norwegian Soc. of Pharmacology and Toxicology **[IO]**
Pediatric Pharmacy Advocacy Gp. **[15896]**
Pharmaceutical Care Mgt. Assn. **[2988]**
Pharmaceutical Gp. of the European Union **[IO]**
Pharmaceutical Soc. of Northern Ireland **[IO]**
Pharmaceutical Soc. of Singapore **[IO]**
Pharmaceutical Soc. of South Africa **[IO]**
Pharmacological Soc. of Canada **[IO]**
Pharmacy Benefit Mgt. Inst. **[15948]**
Pharmacy Defence Assn. **[IO]**
Pharmacy Guild of Australia **[IO]**
Pharmacy Guild of New Zealand **[IO]**
Pharmacy Technician Educators Coun. **[IO]**
Pharmacy Technician Educators Coun. **[8963]**
Phi Delta Chi **[24570]**
Portuguese Soc. of Pharmacology **[IO]**
Proj. Inform **[13583]**
Public Hosp. Pharmacy Coalition **[15949]**
Regulatory Affairs Professionals Soc. **[14599]**
Rho Chi - Alpha Beta Chap. **[24571]**
Royal Pharmaceutical Soc. of Great Britain **[IO]**
Russian Sci. Soc. of Pharmacology **[IO]**

Safety Pharmacology Soc. **[15950]**
Scottish Pharmaceutical Fed. **[IO]**
Scottish Pharmaceutical Gen. Coun. **[IO]**
Sino-American Pharmaceutical Professionals Assn. **[15951]**
Slovak Pharmacological Soc. **[IO]**
Slovenian Pharmaceutical Soc. **[IO]**
Slovenian Pharmacological Soc. **[IO]**
Soc. of Infectious Diseases Pharmacists **[15952]**
Soc. for Medicinal Plant Res. **[IO]**
Soc. for Medicines Res. **[IO]**
South African Pharmacology Soc. **[IO]**
Spanish Soc. of Pharmacology **[IO]**
Swedish Acad. of Pharmaceutical Sciences **[IO]**
Swiss Soc. of Pharmacology and Toxicology **[IO]**
Turkish Pharmacological Soc. **[IO]**
United States Pharmacopeia **[IO]**
U.S. Pharmacopeia **[15953]**
Venezuelan Soc. of Pharmacology **[IO]**
Worshipful Soc. of Apothecaries of London **[IO]**
Pharmacy; Acad. of Gen. Practice of **[★15918]**
Pharmacy; Acad. of Students of **[★15919]**
Pharmacy Advocacy Gp; Pediatric **[15896]**
Pharmacy; Amer. Pharmaceutical Assn. Acad. of Students of **[★15919]**
Pharmacy; Amer. Soc. for Automation in **[2969]**
Pharmacy Benefit Mgt. Inst. **[15948]**, 8679 E San Alberto Dr., Ste. 101, Scottsdale, AZ 85258-4368, (480)730-0814
Pharmacy; Canadian Coun. on Continuing Educ. in **[IO]**
Pharmacy Defence Assn. **[IO]**, Wellington, New Zealand
Pharmacy Graduate Examination Commn; Foreign **[★15933]**
Pharmacy Guild of Australia **[IO]**, Canberra, Australia
Pharmacy Guild of New Zealand **[IO]**, Wellington, New Zealand
Pharmacy Law; Amer. Soc. for **[15003]**
Pharmacy Practice; Acad. of **[★15918]**
Pharmacy Practice and Mgt; Acad. of **[★15918]**
Pharmacy Practice and Mgt; Amer. Pharmaceutical Assn. - Acad. of **[★15918]**
Pharmacy Students and Interns; Canadian Assn. of **[IO]**
Pharmacy Technician Educators Coun. **[IO]**, Pittsburgh, PA, United States
Pharmacy Technician Educators Coun. **[8963]**, c/o Dolores Sewchok, Pres., Bidwell Training Center, Inc., 1650 Metropolitan St., Ste. 200, Pittsburgh, PA 15233, (412)323-4000
Pheasant Soc; Amer. **[★5292]**
Pheasant and Waterfowl Soc; Amer. **[5292]**
Pheasants Forever **[5366]**, 1783 Buerkle Cir., St. Paul, MN 55110, (651)773-2000
Phelps Family Assn. of America - Address unknown since 2002.
Phelps-Stokes Fund **[8301]**, 1400 Eye St. NW, Ste. 750, Washington, DC 20005, (202)371-9544
Phelps-Stokes Fund **[IO]**, Washington, DC, United States
Phenix Soc. - Defunct.
Phenomena
    Amer. Assn. of Electronic Voice Phenomena **[7469]**
    American Association of Electronic Voice Phenomena **[IO]**
    Amer. Soc. of Dowsers **[7470]**
    Archives for UFO Res. **[IO]**
    Australian Skeptics - NSW Br. **[IO]**
    Borderland Sciences Res. Found. **[7471]**
    British UFO Res. Assn. **[IO]**
    Canadian Found. for the Awareness of Miracles **[IO]**
    Center for Bigfoot Stud. **[7472]**
    Central Bur. for Astronomical Telegrams **[6504]**
    Citizens Against UFO Secrecy **[7473]**
    Fund for UFO Res. **[7474]**
    Ghost Res. Soc. **[7475]**
    Intl. Assn. for Near-Death Stud. **[7476]**
    Intl. Assn. for Near-Death Stud. **[IO]**
    Intl. Fortean Org. **[IO]**
    Intl. Fortean Org. **[7477]**
    Intl. UFO Museum and Res. Center at Roswell, New Mexico **[7478]**

    Intl. UFO Museum and Res. Center at Roswell, New Mexico **[IO]**
    J. Allen Hynek Center for UFO Stud. **[7479]**
    Michigan/Canadian Bigfoot Info. Center **[7480]**
    Michigan/Canadian Bigfoot Info. Center **[IO]**
    Mutual UFO Network **[7481]**
    Natl. Investigations Comm. on Unidentified Flying Objects **[7482]**
    National Investigations Committee on Unidentified Flying Objects **[IO]**
    New Zealand Comm. for the Sci. Investigation of Claims of the Paranormal **[IO]**
    Proj. Blue Book **[7483]**
    Sasquatch Investigations of Mid-America **[7484]**
    Soc. for Sci. Exploration **[7485]**
    Soc. for the Sci. Investigation of Para-Sciences **[IO]**
    UFO Information Retrieval Center **[IO]**
    UFO Info. Retrieval Center **[7486]**
Phenomena; Amer. Assn. - Electronic Voice **[★7469]**
Phenomena; Natl. Investigation Comm. on Aerial **[★7479]**
Phenomenology and Existential Philosophy; Soc. for **[10834]**
Phenomenology and the Human Sciences; Intl. Soc. for **[★10807]**
Phenomenon of Man Project - Defunct.
Phenylketonuria
    Children's PKU Network **[15245]**
    Natl. Soc. for Phenylketonuria **[IO]**
Phi Alpha Delta **[24528]**, 345 N Charles St., Baltimore, MD 21201, (410)347-3118
Phi Alpha Epsilon **[24463]**, c/o Prof. Brian A. Rock, PhD, Faculty Advisor, Univ. of Kansas, Architectural Engg. Prog., CEAE Dept., Learned Hall, 1530 W 15th St., Rm. 2150, Lawrence, KS 66045-7609, (785)864-3603
Phi Alpha Sigma **[24543]**, 313 S 10th St., Philadelphia, PA 19107
Phi Alpha Theta **[24495]**, Univ. of South Florida, 4202 E Fowler Ave., SOC107, Tampa, FL 33620-8100, (813)974-8212
Phi Beta **[24405]**, c/o Cora Willett, Treas., 377 Pearl St., Jackson, OH 45640-1756
Phi Beta Chi **[24691]**, PO Box 65426, West Des Moines, IA 50265
Phi Beta Delta **[24517]**, c/o Yvonne Captain-Hidalgo, PhD, Exec. Dir., 1527 New Hampshire Ave. NW, Washington, DC 20036, (202)483-2512
Phi Beta Gamma - Address unknown since 1995.
Phi Beta Kappa **[24406]**, 1606 New Hampshire Ave. NW, Washington, DC 20009, (202)265-3808
Phi Beta Kappa Foundation **[★24406]**
Phi Beta Lambda; Future Bus. Leaders of Am. - **[24420]**
Phi Beta Mu **[24554]**, c/o David Willson, Pres., 7 Surrey Run Pl., The Woodlands, TX 77384-4786, (936)321-8946
Phi Beta Mu **[IO]**, The Woodlands, TX, United States
Phi Beta Pi - Theta Kappa Psi - Address unknown since 1999.
Phi Beta Sigma Fraternity **[24593]**, 145 Kennedy St. NW, Washington, DC 20011-5294, (202)726-5434
Phi Chi **[★24544]**
Phi Chi Medical Fraternity **[24544]**, Jefferson Medical Coll., 1025 Spruce St., Philadelphia, PA 19107
Phi Chi Theta **[24422]**, c/o Saundra Finley, Exec. Dir., 1508 E Beltline Rd., Ste. 104, Carrollton, TX 75006, (972)245-7202
Phi Chi Welfare Association **[★24544]**
Phi Delta Chi **[24570]**, PO Box 83250, Conyers, GA 30013, (800)PDC-1883
Phi Delta Delta **[★24528]**
Phi Delta Epsilon Medical Fraternity **[24540]**, 2655 Collins Ave., Ste. 912, Miami Beach, FL 33140, (305)531-1929
Phi Delta Epsilon Medical Fraternity **[IO]**, Miami Beach, FL, United States
Phi Delta Gamma **[24577]**, 1201 Red Mile Rd., PO Box 4599, Lexington, KY 40544-4599, (859)255-1848
Phi Delta Kappa **[24578]**, 408 N Union St., PO Box 789, Bloomington, IN 47402-0789, (812)339-1156
Phi Delta Kappa; Natl. Sorority of **[24455]**

Reference to "IO" in place of a book number signifies that the association may be found in the 45th edition of International Organizations.

Phi Delta Phi Intl. Legal Fraternity [24530], 1426 21st St. NW, Washington, DC 20036, (800)368-5606

Phi Delta Phi Intl. Legal Fraternity [IO], Washington, DC, United States

Phi Delta Phi Legal Inst. [★IO]

Phi Delta Phi Legal Inst. [★24530]

Phi Delta Pi [★24573]

Phi Delta Theta Intl. Fraternity [24640], 2 S Campus Ave., Oxford, OH 45056-1801, (513)523-6345

Phi Epsilon - Address unknown since 1999.

Phi Epsilon Kappa [24574], 901 W New York St., Indianapolis, IN 46202, (317)637-8431

Phi Epsilon Phi [24692], c/o Bernice O'Leary, Exec. Sec., PO Box 4096, Burlingame, CA 94011-4096, (650)347-1765

Phi Eta - Defunct.

Phi Gamma Delta [24641], 1201 Red Mile Rd., PO Box 4599, Lexington, KY 40544-4599, (859)255-1848

Phi Gamma Nu [24423], 6745 Cheryl Ann Dr., Seven Hills, OH 44131-3720, (216)524-0019

Phi Kappa [★24644]

Phi Kappa Epsilon [★24422]

Phi Kappa Kaze - Address unknown since 1995.

Phi Kappa Phi [24518], PO Box 16000, Baton Rouge, LA 70893-6000, (225)388-4917

Phi Kappa Pi - Address unknown since 1995.

Phi Kappa Sigma [24642], 2 Timber Dr., Chester Springs, PA 19425, (610)469-3282

Phi Kappa Sigma [IO], Chester Springs, PA, United States

Phi Kappa Tau [24643], 5221 Morning Sun Rd., Oxford, OH 45056-8928, (513)523-4193

Phi Kappa Theta Natl. [24644], 9640 N Augusta Dr., Ste. 420, Carmel, IN 46032-9602, (317)872-9934

Phi Kappa Upsilon Fraternity [24464], 21000 W 9 Mile Rd., Southfield, MI 48075, (734)775-3164

Phi Lambda Kappa Medical Fraternity - Defunct.

Phi Lambda Pi - Address unknown since 1997.

Phi Lambda Upsilon [24430], c/o Dr. Manuel P. So-riaga, Pres., Texas A&M Univ., Dept. of Chemistry, College Station, TX 77842-3012, (979)845-1846

Phi Mu Alpha Sinfonia Fraternity and Found. Natl. HQ [24555], 10600 Old State Rd., Evansville, IN 47711, (812)867-2433

Phi Mu Delta [24645], 316 Cherry Hill Blvd., Cherry Hill, NJ 08002, (888)401-2213

Phi Mu Fraternity [24693], 400 Westpark Dr., Peachtree City, GA 30269, (770)632-2090

Phi Mu Gamma - Address unknown since 1995.

Phi Omega Pi [★24686]

Phi Pi Epsilon [★13102]

Phi Pi Phi [★24616]

Phi Psi - Address unknown since 1995.

Phi Rho Sigma Medical Soc. [24545], PO Box 90264, Indianapolis, IN 46290-0264

Phi Sigma [24409], c/o Henry R. Owen, PhD, Pres., Eastern Illinois Univ., 600 Lincoln Ave., Charleston, IL 61920, (217)581-3126

Phi Sigma Delta [★24670]

Phi Sigma Epsilon [★24646]

Phi Sigma Gamma - Address unknown since 1995.

Phi Sigma Iota [24526], World Language Educ., CPR 107, Univ. of South Florida, 4202 E Fowler Ave., Tampa, FL 33620-5500, (813)974-3658

Phi Sigma Kappa [24646], 2925 E 96th St., Indianapolis, IN 46240, (317)573-5420

Phi Sigma Nu Native Amer. Fraternity [24647], PO Box 2040, Pembroke, NC 28372

Phi Sigma Pi Natl. Honor Fraternity [24531], 2119 Ambassador Cir., Lancaster, PA 17603-2391, (717)299-4710

Phi Sigma Sigma [24694], 8178 Lark Brown Rd., Ste. 202, Elkridge, MD 21075-6424, (410)799-1224

Phi Sigma Tau [24572], PO Box 1881, Milwaukee, WI 53201-1881, (414)288-6857

Phi Tau Phi Scholastic Honor Soc. of America - Address unknown since 1991.

Phi Theta Epsilon - Address unknown since 1995.

Phi Theta Kappa [★24456]

Phi Theta Kappa [★24422]

Phi Theta Kappa [★IO]

Phi Theta Kappa Intl. [★IO]

Phi Theta Kappa Intl. [★24456]

Phi Theta Kappa, Intl. Honor Soc. [24456], PO Box 13729, Jackson, MS 39236-3729, (601)984-3504

Phi Theta Kappa, Intl. Honor Soc. [IO], Jackson, MS, United States

Phi Theta Pi [24424], 6552 Bradford Dr., West Des Moines, IA 50266-2308, (515)440-2045

Phi Upsilon Omicron [24497], PO Box 329, Fairmont, WV 26555-0329, (304)368-0612

Phi Zeta [24723], c/o Dr. James E. Smallwood, Sec.-Treas., APR Dept., Coll. of Veterinary Medicine, North Carolina State Univ., Raleigh, NC 27606, (919)513-6223

Phil Collins Information - Address unknown since 2008.

Phil Esposito Found. - Defunct.

Philadelphia; Athenaeum of [10342]

Philadelphia; Carpenters' Company of the City and County of [★10018]

Philadelphia Flyers Fan Club [25011], 3601 S Broad St., Philadelphia, PA 19148, (215)451-PUCK

Philadelphia Inst. - Address unknown since 2001.

Philadelphia Soc. [18475], 11620 Rutan Cir., Jerome, MI 49249, (517)688-5111

Philalethes Soc. [19247], 800 S 15th St., No. 1803, Sebring, OH 44672

Philangeli (Friends of the Angels) - Defunct.

Philanthropic Counsel; Assn. of [958]

Philanthropic Fund of 1933; Jewish [12475]

Philanthropic Fund; Amer. Jewish [12803]

Philanthropic Roundtable [★12735]

Philanthropic Societies of New York; Fed. for the Support of Jewish [★12482]

Philanthropies of Greater New York; Fed. of Jewish [★12482]

Philanthropies of New York; United Jewish Appeal - Fed. of Jewish [12482]

Philanthropique; Societe Culinaire [19138]

Philanthropy

Active 20-30 Assn. of U.S./Canada [13032]

Albert Schweitzer Fellowship [11101]

Altrusa Intl. [13033]

Amer. Assn. of Grant Professionals [12708]

Amer. Inst. of Philanthropy [12709]

Amer. Jewish Philanthropic Fund [12803]

Amer. Jewish World Ser. [12829]

America's Charities [12196]

AmeriCorps VISTA [13383]

Andrew W. Mellon Found. [10777]

Angelcare [11672]

Arcus Found. [18266]

Asian Americans/Pacific Islanders in Philanthropy [12710]

Assn. of Charity Officers [IO]

Assn. of Fundraising Professionals [12197]

Assn. for Healthcare Philanthropy [14871]

Assn. of Professional Researchers for Advancement [12198]

Assn. for Res. on Nonprofit Organizations and Voluntary Action [13387]

Assn. of Small Foundations [18267]

Assn. of Superannuation Funds of Australia [IO]

BAPS Care Intl. [IO]

BAPS Charities [18268]

Believe In Tomorrow Natl. Children's Found. [11674]

Brass Ring Soc. [11677]

Bread for the Journey Intl. [12711]

Bread for the Journey Intl. [IO]

Bread and Roses [12113]

Brethren Volunteer Ser. [13388]

Canadian Progress Club [IO]

Caring Voice Coalition [12712]

CASE Matching Gifts CH [12199]

Catholic Campaign for Human Development [12713]

Catholic Charities USA [13158]

Catholic Relief Services (U.S. Catholic Conf.) [12807]

Christian Children's Fund [11688]

Circle K Intl. [13037]

Civitan Intl. [13038]

Comm. to Encourage Corporate Philanthropy [12714]

Community Hea. Charities [12200]

Corporate Angel Network [13817]

Cosmopolitan Intl. [13039]

Coun. on Foundations [12652]

Coun. of Religious Volunteer Agencies [13391]

David and Lucile Packard Found. [11808]

Downed Bikers Assn. [12612]

Dream Factory [11691]

Dyson Found. [12715]

East West Educ. Development Found. [12716]

East West Educ. Development Found. [IO]

Entertainment Indus. Found. [12114]

Famous Fone Friends [11692]

Feed the Children [12854]

First Foundations [13169]

Forum of Regional Associations of Grantmakers [12717]

Found. of Compassionate Amer. Samaritans [20340]

Funders' Collaborative on Youth Organizing [12718]

G. Unger Vetlesen Found. [12719]

G. Unger Vetlesen Foundation [IO]

Gifts In Kind Intl. [12720]

Giraffe Heroes Proj. [10185]

Giving U.S.A. Found. [12721]

Good Bears of the World [13041]

Good Fellows (Old Newsboys) [13042]

Grantmakers in the Arts [12722]

Grantmakers for Children, Youth, and Families [12723]

Grantmakers in Hea. [15954]

Grantmakers Without Borders [12724]

Grantmakers Without Borders [IO]

Healing the Children [11697]

Holiday Proj. [13395]

Hunters Helping Hunters [22604]

Imagine Canada [IO]

Independent Sector [12725]

Intl. Corrugated Packaging Found. [12726]

Intl. Corrugated Packaging Found. [IO]

Intimate Apparel Square Club [12201]

Israel Humanitarian Found. [12458]

Jessie Ball duPont Fund [12727]

Jewish Philanthropic Fund of 1933 [12475]

John S. and James L. Knight Found. [12484]

Joygerms Unlimited [10190]

Just Act: Youth Action for Global Justice [12435]

Kettering Family Found. [12728]

Ladies of Charity of the U.S.A. [13173]

Local Independent Charities of Am. [12729]

Makassed Found. of Am. [12730]

Makassed Found. of Am. [IO]

Make-A-Wish Found. of Am. [11707]

Marine Toys for Tots Found. [11709]

Matrix Found. [18813]

Military, Veterans and Patriotic Ser. Organizations of Am. [21245]

Natl. AMBUCS [11964]

Natl. Black United Fund [12656]

Natl. Center for Charitable Statistics [12731]

Natl. Comm. for Responsive Philanthropy [12732]

Natl. Human Services Assembly [13400]

Natl. Network of Grantmakers [12202]

Natl. Women's Hall of Fame [20716]

Native Americans in Philanthropy [12733]

Neighborhood Funders Gp. [12734]

New Horizons Arts Initiative [9589]

NewTithing Gp. [18742]

North Amer. YMCA Development Org. [13461]

North Star Fund [12657]

PEF Israel Endowment Funds [12461]

Philanthropy Roundtable [12735]

Pollock-Krasner Found. [17004]

Rebuilding Together [12337]

Retired and Senior Volunteer Prog. [13403]

The Revitalization Corps [12782]

Rockefeller Bros. Fund [12736]

Rockefeller Bros. Fund [IO]

Rockefeller Family Fund [12737]

St. Paul Soc. [IO]

SCI - Intl. Voluntary Ser. [13404]

Senior Companion Prog. [13405]

Senior Gleaners [12398]

Soc. of St. Vincent de Paul Coun. of the U.S. [13190]

A Special Wish Found. [11723]

A star before a book entry number signifies that the name is not listed separately, but is mentioned within the entry.

Starlight Starbright Children's Found. [11724]
Step Up Women's Network [13440]
Sunshine Found. [11726]
Support Our Aging Religious [11321]
Surdna Found. [12738]
Synergos Inst. [12784]
Trull Found. [12739]
Twenty-First Century Found. [12740]
United Black Fund [12204]
United Charity Institutions of Jerusalem [12462]
United Jewish Appeal - Fed. of Jewish
   Philanthropies of New York [12482]
United Sisters of Charity [20406]
U.S. Natl. Comm. for World Food Day [12401]
United Way of Am. [12205]
United Way Intl. [12206]
U.S.A. Harvest [12402]
Variety Intl. - The Children's Charity [11660]
Veterans Bedside Network [12116]
A Wish With Wings [11728]
Women in Philanthropy [18269]
Women's Philanthropy Inst. [12741]
Philanthropy; Comm. for Responsive [★12732]
Philanthropy; Natl. Coun. on [★12725]
Philanthropy Roundtable [12735], 1150 17th St. NW,
   Ste. 503, Washington, DC 20036, (202)822-8333
Philanthropy; Women and [17575]
Philanthropy; Women and Foundations/Corporate
   [★17575]
Philatelic
Alaska Collectors' Club [22779]
Amer. Air Mail Soc. [22780]
Amer. First Day Cover Soc. [22781]
Amer. Helvetia Philatelic Soc. [22782]
Amer. Helvetia Philatelic Soc. [IO]
Amer. Philatelic Cong. [22783]
Amer. Philatelic Res. Lib. [22784]
Amer. Philatelic Soc. [22785]
Amer. Philatelic Soc. Writers Unit [22786]
American Philatelic Society Writers Unit [IO]
Amer. Plate Number Single Soc. [22787]
Amer. Revenue Assn. [22788]
American Revenue Association [IO]
Amer. Soc. of Polar Philatelists [22789]
Amer. Stamp Dealers Assn. [1910]
Amer. Tax Token Soc. [22727]
Amer. Topical Assn. [22790]
Amer. Topical Assn. [IO]
Amer. Topical Assn., Americana Unit [22791]
Amer. Topical Assn., Biology Unit [22792]
Armed Forces Stamp Exchange Club [22793]
Assoc. Collectors of El Salvador [22794]
Assn. of British Philatelic Societies [IO]
Astronomy Stud. Unit [22795]
Bicycle Stamps Club [22796]
Brazil Philatelic Assn. [22797]
Brazil Philatelic Assn. [IO]
British North Am. Philatelic Soc. [IO]
British Thematic Assn. [IO]
Bullseye Cancel Collectors' Club [22798]
Canadian Aerophilatelic Soc. [IO]
Canadian Air Mail Collectors Club [IO]
CartoPhilatelic Soc. [22799]
Casey Jones Railroad Unit - ATA [22800]
Cats on Stamps Stud. Unit [22801]
Chemistry and Physics on Stamps Stud. Unit
   [22802]
China Stamp Soc. [22803]
China Stamp Soc. [IO]
Christmas Philatelic Club [22804]
Christopher Columbus Philatelic Soc. [22805]
Cinderella Stamp Club [IO]
Citizens' Stamp Advisory Comm. [22806]
Civil Censorship Study Group [22807]
Civil Censorship Study Group [IO]
Collectors Club [22808]
Collectors of Religion on Stamps [22809]
Concorde Collectors Club [22810]
Confederate Stamp Alliance [22811]
Cover Collectors Circuit Club [22812]
Croatian Philatelic Soc. [22813]
Disabled Collectors' Correspondence Club
   [22814]
Dogs on Stamps Stud. Unit [22815]
Earth's Physical Features Stud. Unit [22816]

Eire Philatelic Assn. [22817]
Emirates Philatelic Assn. [IO]
Errors, Freaks and Oddities Collector's Club
   [22818]
Falkland Islands Philatelic Study Group [IO]
Fed. of European Philatelic Associations [IO]
Fine Arts Philatelists [IO]
Fine Arts Philatelists [22819]
France and Colonies Philatelic Soc. [22820]
France and Colonies Philatelic Soc. [IO]
Gems, Minerals and Jewelry Stud. Unit [22821]
German Colonies Collectors Gp. [22822]
German Colonies Collectors Gp. [IO]
Germany Philatelic Soc. [22823]
Germany Philatelic Soc. [IO]
Graphics Philately Assn. [22824]
Great Britain Collectors Club [22032]
Haiti Philatelic Soc. [22825]
Hellenic Philatelic Soc. of Am. [22826]
Humor Stamp Club [22827]
India Stud. Circle for Philately [22828]
India Stud. Circle for Philately [IO]
Indus. Coun. for Tangible Assets [3713]
Inter-Governmental Philatelic Corp. [22829]
Intl. Assn. of Philatelic Experts [IO]
Intl. Fed. of Stamp Dealers' Associations [IO]
Intl. Philatelic Fed. [IO]
Intl. Soc. for Japanese Philately [IO]
Intl. Soc. for Japanese Philately [22830]
Intl. Soc. of Worldwide Stamp Collectors [22831]
Intl. Soc. of Worldwide Stamp Collectors [IO]
Intl. Stamp and Coin Collectors Soc. [IO]
Intl. Stamp and Coin Collectors Soc. [22832]
Israel Plate Block Soc. [22833]
Jack Knight Air Mail Soc. [22834]
Jack Knight Air Mail Soc. [IO]
Japan Philatelic Soc. [IO]
John F. Kennedy First Day Cover Stud. Unit
   [22835]
Journalists, Authors and Poets on Stamps Stud.
   Unit [10778]
Journalists, Authors and Poets on Stamps Study
   Unit [IO]
Jugoslavia Study Group [22836]
Junior Philatelists of Am. [22837]
Korea Stamp Soc. [22838]
Korea Stamp Soc. [IO]
Machine Cancel Soc. [22839]
Mailer's Postmark Permit Club [22840]
Mailer's Postmark Permit Club [IO]
Maritime Postmark Society [IO]
Maritime Postmark Soc. [22841]
Mathematical Stud. Unit [22842]
Medical Subjects Unit [22843]
Medical Subjects Unit [IO]
Meter Stamp Soc. [22844]
Metropolitan Air Post Soc. [22845]
Metropolitan Air Post Society [IO]
Mexico Elmhurst Philatelic Soc. Intl. [IO]
Mexico Elmhurst Philatelic Soc. Intl. [22846]
Military Postal History Soc. [22847]
Mobile Post Off. Soc. [22848]
Napoleonic Age Philatelists [22849]
Natl. Assn. of German Stamp Dealers [IO]
Natl. Duck Stamp Collectors Soc. [22850]
Natl. Philatelic Soc. [IO]
Natl. Stamp Dealers Assn. [22851]
Nepal and Tibet Philatelic Stud. Circle [22852]
Palestine Study Group [22853]
Perfins Club [22854]
Philatelic Found. [22855]
Philatelic Friends Exchange Circuit [22856]
Philatelic Friends Exchange Circuit [IO]
Philatelic Traders' Soc. [IO]
Polonus Philatelic Soc. [22857]
Post Mark Collectors Club [22858]
Postal Commemorative Soc. [22859]
Postal History Soc. [22860]
Postal History Soc. of Canada [IO]
Postcard History Soc. [22909]
Precancel Stamp Soc. [22861]
Rossica Soc. of Russian Philately [22862]
Rossica Soc. of Russian Philately [IO]
Rotary on Stamps Fellowship [IO]
Rotary on Stamps Fellowship [22863]

Royal Philatelic Soc. [IO]
Royal Philatelic Soc. of Canada [IO]
Russian Zone Handoverprint Stud. and Res. Gp.
   [22864]
Ryukyu Philatelic Specialist Soc. [22865]
Ryukyu Philatelic Specialist Soc. [IO]
St. Helena, Ascension, and Tristan da Cunha
   Philatelic Soc. [22866]
Samuel Gompers Stamp Club [22867]
Scandinavian Collectors Club [22868]
Scandinavian Collectors Club [IO]
Scouts on Stamps Soc. Intl. [IO]
Scouts on Stamps Soc. Intl. [22869]
Ships on Stamps Unit [22870]
Ships on Stamps Unit [IO]
Soc. of Australasian Specialists/Oceania [IO]
Soc. of Australasian Specialists/Oceania [22871]
Soc. for Costa Rica Collectors [22872]
Soc. for Hungarian Philately [22873]
Society for Hungarian Philately [IO]
Soc. of Israel Philatelists [22874]
Soc. for Polish Philately [IO]
Soc. of the Postal History of Eretz Israel [IO]
Soc. for Thai Philately [22875]
Space Topic Stud. Unit [22876]
Space Topic Stud. Unit [IO]
Sports Philatelists International [IO]
Sports Philatelists Intl. [22877]
Stamps on Stamps Collectors Club [22878]
Stamps on Stamps Collectors Club [IO]
Stamps for the Wounded [22879]
State Revenue Soc. [22880]
Tannu Tuva Collectors' Soc. [22881]
Tannu Tuva Collectors' Soc. [IO]
Third Reich Study Group [IO]
Third Reich Study Group [22882]
Ukrainian Philatelic and Numismatic Soc. [22883]
Ukrainian Philatelic and Numismatic Soc. [IO]
United Nations Philatelists, Inc. [22884]
United Postal Stationery Soc. [22885]
U.S. Cancellation Club [22886]
U.S. Philatelic Classics Soc. [22887]
U.S. Stamp Soc. [22888]
Universal Ship Cancellation Soc. [22889]
Universal Ship Cancellation Society [IO]
Western Cover Soc. [22890]
Windmill Stud. Unit [IO]
Young Stamp Collectors of Am. [22891]
Zeppelin Collectors Club [22892]
Philatelic Assn. of Govt. Employees - Address
   unknown since 1995.
Philatelic Found. [22855], 70 W 40th St., 15th Fl.,
   New York, NY 10018, (212)221-6555
Philatelic Friends Exchange Circuit [22856], PO Box
   93006, Austin, TX 78709-3006
Philatelic Friends Exchange Circuit [IO], Austin, TX,
   United States
Philatelic Hobbies for the Wounded - Defunct.
Philatelic Lib. Assn. [★22784]
Philatelic Literature Assn. [★22784]
Philatelic Music Circle - Defunct.
Philatelic Numismatic Combination Producers Assn.
   - Defunct.
Philatelic Soc. of Am; Hellenic [22826]
Philatelic Soc. of Am; Israel-Palestine [★22874]
Philatelic Soc. of Am; Junior [★22837]
Philatelic Soc. of Egypt - Defunct.
Philatelic Soc; Helvetia [★22782]
Philatelic Soc; Sta. Helena and Dependencies
   [★22866]
Philatelic Specialists Stud. Club; Intl. Japanese
   [★22830]
Philatelic Traders' Soc. [IO], Fleet, United Kingdom
Philatelists; Aero [★22780]
Philatelists of Am; Junior [22837]
Philatelists; Amer. Soc. of Polar [22789]
Philatelists; Fine Arts [22819]
Philatelists, Inc; United Nations [22884]
Philatelists Intl; Sports [22877]
Philatelists; Soc. of Israel [22874]
Philatelists; Soc. of Ukrainian [★22883]
Philately
Alaska Collectors' Club [22779]
Amer. Air Mail Soc. [22780]
Amer. First Day Cover Soc. [22781]

Reference to "IO" in place of a book number signifies that the association may be found in the 45th edition of International Organizations.

Amer. Helvetia Philatelic Soc. **[22782]**
Amer. Philatelic Cong. **[22783]**
Amer. Philatelic Res. Lib. **[22784]**
Amer. Philatelic Soc. **[22785]**
Amer. Philatelic Soc. Writers Unit **[22786]**
Amer. Plate Number Single Soc. **[22787]**
Amer. Racing Pigeon Union **[22894]**
Amer. Revenue Assn. **[22788]**
Amer. Soc. of Polar Philatelists **[22789]**
Amer. Tax Token Soc. **[22727]**
Amer. Topical Assn. **[22790]**
Amer. Topical Assn., Americana Unit **[22791]**
Amer. Topical Assn., Biology Unit **[22792]**
Armed Forces Stamp Exchange Club **[22793]**
Assoc. Collectors of El Salvador **[22794]**
Astronomy Stud. Unit **[22795]**
Bicycle Stamps Club **[22796]**
Brazil Philatelic Assn. **[22797]**
Carriers and Locals Soc. **[22904]**
CartoPhilatelic Soc. **[22799]**
Casey Jones Railroad Unit - ATA **[22800]**
Cats on Stamps Stud. Unit **[22801]**
Chemistry and Physics on Stamps Stud. Unit
  [22802]
China Stamp Soc. **[22803]**
Christmas Philatelic Club **[22804]**
Christopher Columbus Philatelic Soc. **[22805]**
Citizens' Stamp Advisory Comm. **[22806]**
Civil Censorship Study Group **[22807]**
Collectors Club **[22808]**
Collectors of Religion on Stamps **[22809]**
Confederate Stamp Alliance **[22811]**
Cover Collectors Circuit Club **[22812]**
Croatian Philatelic Soc. **[22813]**
Dogs on Stamps Stud. Unit **[22815]**
Earth's Physical Features Stud. Unit **[22816]**
Eire Philatelic Assn. **[22817]**
Errors, Freaks and Oddities Collector's Club
  [22818]
Fine Arts Philatelists **[22819]**
France and Colonies Philatelic Soc. **[22820]**
Gems, Minerals and Jewelry Stud. Unit **[22821]**
German Colonies Collectors Gp. **[22822]**
Germany Philatelic Soc. **[22823]**
Graphics Philately Assn. **[22824]**
Haiti Philatelic Soc. **[22825]**
Hellenic Philatelic Soc. of Am. **[22826]**
Humor Stamp Club **[22827]**
India Stud. Circle for Philately **[22828]**
Inter-Governmental Philatelic Corp. **[22829]**
Intl. Fed. of Amer. Homing Pigeon Fanciers
  [22895]
Intl. Soc. for Japanese Philately **[22830]**
Intl. Soc. of Worldwide Stamp Collectors **[22831]**
Intl. Stamp and Coin Collectors Soc. **[22832]**
Jack Knight Air Mail Soc. **[22834]**
John F. Kennedy First Day Cover Stud. Unit
  [22835]
Junior Philatelists of Am. **[22837]**
Korea Stamp Soc. **[22838]**
Machine Cancel Soc. **[22839]**
Mailer's Postmark Permit Club **[22840]**
Maritime Postmark Soc. **[22841]**
Mathematical Stud. Unit **[22842]**
Medical Subjects Unit **[22843]**
Meter Stamp Soc. **[22844]**
Metropolitan Air Post Soc. **[22845]**
Mexico Elmhurst Philatelic Soc. Intl. **[22846]**
Military Postal History Soc. **[22847]**
Mobile Post Off. Soc. **[22848]**
Napoleonic Age Philatelists **[22849]**
Natl. Duck Stamp Collectors Soc. **[22850]**
Nepal and Tibet Philatelic Stud. Circle **[22852]**
Perfins Club **[22854]**
Philatelic Found. **[22855]**
Philatelic Friends Exchange Circuit **[22856]**
Polonus Philatelic Soc. **[22857]**
Post Mark Collectors Club **[22858]**
Postal Commemorative Soc. **[22859]**
Postal History Soc. **[22860]**
Postcard History Soc. **[22909]**
Precancel Stamp Soc. **[22861]**
Rossica Soc. of Russian Philately **[22862]**
Rotary on Stamps Fellowship **[22863]**
Russian Zone Handoverprint Stud. and Res. Gp.
  [22864]

Ryukyu Philatelic Specialist Soc. **[22865]**
St. Helena, Ascension, and Tristan da Cunha
  Philatelic Soc. **[22866]**
Samuel Gompers Stamp Club **[22867]**
Scandinavian Collectors Club **[22868]**
Scouts on Stamps Soc. Intl. **[22869]**
Ships on Stamps Unit **[22870]**
Soc. of Australasian Specialists/Oceania **[22871]**
Soc. for Hungarian Philately **[22873]**
Soc. of Israel Philatelists **[22874]**
Soc. for Thai Philately **[22875]**
Space Topic Stud. Unit **[22876]**
Sports Philatelists Intl. **[22877]**
Stamps on Stamps Collectors Club **[22878]**
Stamps for the Wounded **[22879]**
State Revenue Soc. **[22880]**
Ukrainian Philatelic and Numismatic Soc. **[22883]**
United Nations Philatelists, Inc. **[22884]**
United Postal Stationery Soc. **[22885]**
U.S. Cancellation Club **[22886]**
U.S. Stamp Soc. **[22888]**
Universal Ship Cancellation Soc. **[22889]**
Western Cover Soc. **[22890]**
Young Stamp Collectors of Am. **[22891]**
Zeppelin Collectors Club **[22892]**
Philately; Amer. Acad. of **[★22783]**
Philately Assn; Graphics **[22824]**
Philately; Soc. for Hungarian **[22873]**
Philately; Soc. for Thai **[22875]**
Philip Boileau Collectors' Soc. **[21542]**, c/o Karen
  Gamlin, 1025 Redwood Blvd., Redding, CA 96003-
  1905
Philip Jose Farmer Soc. **[9700]**
Philip K. Dick Soc. - Defunct.
Philip Larkin Soc. **[IO]**, Hornsea, United Kingdom
Philip Randolph Educal. Fund; A. **[17078]**
Philip Randolph Inst; A. **[18604]**
Philip Roth Soc. **[11187]**, c/o Derek Parker Royal,
  Pres./Exec. Ed., Texas A&M University-Commerce,
  Dept. of Literature and Languages, 2600 S Neal
  St., Commerce, TX 75429-3011, (903)886-5260
Philippine
  Filipinas Americas Sci. and Art Found. **[9609]**
  Filipino Amer. Coalition for Environmental Solidar-
    ity **[4634]**
  Filipino Amer. Natl. Historical Soc. **[10779]**
  Filipino American National Historical Society **[IO]**
  Igorot Global Org. **[10225]**
  Natl. Fed. of Filipino Amer. Associations **[10780]**
  Philippine-Amer. Chamber of Commerce **[24365]**
  Philippine Workers Support Comm. **[24212]**
Philippine Airlines Mountaineering Club **[IO]**, Makati
  City, Philippines
Philippine Amateur Baseball Assn. **[IO]**, Makati City,
  Philippines
Philippine Amateur Track and Field Assn. **[IO]**,
  Manila, Philippines
Philippine-Amer. Chamber of Commerce **[24365]**
Philippine Amer. Writers and Artists **[11188]**, PO Box
  31928, San Francisco, CA 94131-0928
Philippine Article Numbering Coun. **[★IO]**
Philippine Assn. - Address unknown since 1999.
Philippine Assn. of Entomologists **[IO]**, Los Banos,
  Philippines
Philippine Assn. of Gerontology **[IO]**, Valenzuela
  City, Philippines
Philippine Assn. of the Record Indus. **[IO]**, Manila,
  Philippines
Philippine Assn. of Secretaries and Administrative
  Professionals **[IO]**, Makati City, Philippines
Philippine Assn. of Ser. Exporters **[IO]**, Mandaluyong
  City, Philippines
Philippine Assn. of Univ. Women **[IO]**, Manila, Philip-
  pines
Philippine Badminton Assn. **[IO]**, Manila, Philippines
Philippine Bible Soc. **[IO]**, Manila, Philippines
Philippine Chamber of Commerce of America - Ad-
  dress unknown since 1995.
Philippine Chamber of Commerce and Indus. **[IO]**,
  Makati City, Philippines
Philippine Coconut Oil Producers Assn. **[IO]**, Pasig
  City, Philippines
Philippine Collectors Soc. - Address unknown since
  2008.
Philippine Convention and Visitors Corp. **[IO]**,
  Manila, Philippines

Philippine Dermatological Soc. **[IO]**, Quezon City,
  Philippines
Philippine Diabetes Assn. **[IO]**, Mandaluyong City,
  Philippines
Philippine Electronics and Telecommunications Fed.
  [IO], Makati City, Philippines
Philippine Exporters Confed. **[IO]**, Pasay City, Philip-
  pines
Philippine League Against Epilepsy **[IO]**, Iloilo City,
  Philippines
Philippine Leprosy Mission **[★IO]**
Philippine Leprosy Mission **[★15010]**
Philippine Ling Ming Martial Arts Assn. **[IO]**, Manila,
  Philippines
Philippine Mahogany Assn. - Defunct.
Philippine Medical Assn. **[IO]**, Quezon City, Philip-
  pines
Philippine Medical Informatics Soc. **[IO]**, Manila,
  Philippines
Philippine Natl. AIDS Coun. **[IO]**, Manila, Philippines
Philippine Natl. Red Cross **[IO]**, Manila, Philippines
Philippine Natl. Sci. Soc. **[★IO]**
Philippine Nurses Assn. of Am. **[2840]**, 333 E 14th
  St., Apt. 8G, New York, NY 10003-4212, (212)677-
  2261
Philippine Olympic Comm. **[IO]**, Pasay City, Philip-
  pines
Philippine Partnership for the Development of Hu-
  man Resources in Rural Areas **[IO]**, Quezon City,
  Philippines
Philippine Physical Therapy Assn. **[IO]**, Quezon City,
  Philippines
Philippine Physicians in Am; Assn. of **[15994]**
Philippine Plastics Indus. Assn. **[IO]**, Caloocan City,
  Philippines
Philippine Practicing Physicians in Am; Assn. of
  [★15994]
Philippine Resource Center - Address unknown
  since 1999.
Philippine Retailers Assn. **[IO]**, Pasig City, Philip-
  pines
Philippine Sailing Assn. **[IO]**, Makati City, Philippines
Philippine Skating Union **[IO]**, Pasay City, Philip-
  pines
Philippine Social Sci. Coun. **[IO]**, Quezon City,
  Philippines
Philippine Soc. of Anesthesiologists **[IO]**, Quezon
  City, Philippines
Philippine Soc. of Clinical Neurophysiology **[IO]**, Qu-
  ezon City, Philippines
Philippine Soc. of Gastrointestinal Endoscopy **[IO]**,
  Quezon City, Philippines
Philippine Soc. of Hypertension **[IO]**, Pasig City,
  Philippines
Philippine Soc. for Microbiology and Infectious
  Diseases **[IO]**, Quezon City, Philippines
Philippine Soc. of Photogrammetry and Remote
  Sensing **[IO]**, Quezon City, Philippines
Philippine Software Indus. Assn. **[IO]**, Makati City,
  Philippines
Philippine Sports Assn. of the Differently Abled **[IO]**,
  Pasig City, Philippines
Philippine Statehood U.S.A. Movement - Address
  unknown since 1999.
Philippine Sugar Millers Assn. **[IO]**, Makati City,
  Philippines
Philippine Taekwondo Assn. **[IO]**, Manila, Philippines
Philippine Tennis Assn. **[IO]**, Manila, Philippines
Philippine Travel Agencies Assn. **[IO]**, Pasay City,
  Philippines
Philippine Tropical Fish Exporters Assn. **[IO]**,
  Paranaque, Philippines
Philippine Urological Assn. **[IO]**, Quezon City, Philip-
  pines
Philippine Workers Support Comm. **[IO]**, Honolulu,
  HI, United States
Philippine Workers Support Comm. **[24212]**, 2252
  Puna St., Honolulu, HI 96817, (808)595-7362
Philippines
  Books for the Barrios **[12049]**
  Fed. of Philippine Amer. Chambers of Commerce
    [24277]
  Filipino Amer. Coalition for Environmental Solidar-
    ity **[4634]**
  Filipino Amer. Medical Inc. **[14722]**

A star before a book entry number signifies that the name is not listed separately, but is mentioned within the entry.

Filipinos for Affirmative Action [18270]
Igorot Global Org. [10225]
Intl. Inst. of Rural Reconstruction, U.S. Chap.
  [12938]
Military Order of the Carabao [21246]
Philippine-Amer. Chamber of Commerce [24365]
Philippine Amer. Writers and Artists [11188]
Physicians for Human Rights [17783]
Rizal-MacArthur Memorial Found. [12541]
Solidarity Philippines Australia Network [IO]
Philippines; Army of the [★21331]
Philippines Assn. of Landscape Architects [IO],
  Pasig City, Philippines
Philippines Cricket Assn. [IO], Makati City, Philip-
  pines
Phillipe du Trieux Descendants Assn. - Address
  unknown since 2000.
Philolexian Soc. [10428], Columbia Univ., 515
  Lerner Hall, 2920 Broadway, New York, NY 10027
Philological Assn; Amer. [10296]
Philological Soc. [IO], London, United Kingdom
Philomathean Soc. of the Univ. of Pennsylvania
  [10429], Coll. Hall, Box H, Philadelphia, PA 19104,
  (215)898-8907
Philoptochos Soc; Greek Orthodox Ladies [20071]
Philosophical Association; Canadian [★10785]
Philosophical Assn; Jesuit [9778]
Philosophical Assn. of the U.S. and Canada; Jesuit
  [★9778]
Philosophical Res. Soc. [10823], 3910 Los Feliz
  Blvd., Los Angeles, CA 90027, (323)663-2167
Philosophical Soc; Amer. [7598]
Philosophical Soc; Evangelical [19979]
Philosophical Stud. of Marxism; Soc. for the [10452]
Philosophy
  Acad. of Spirituality and Paranormal Stud., Inc.
    [7440]
  Aesthetic Realism Found. [10781]
  Afro-Asian Philosophy Assn. [IO]
  Agni Yoga Soc. [20632]
  Alexandria Soc. and Educal. Found. [8161]
  Amer. Assn. of Philosophy Teachers [8964]
  Amer. Catholic Philosophical Assn. [8965]
  Amer. Ethical Union [20083]
  Amer. Humanist Assn. [20084]
  Amer. Indian Philosophy Assn. [19268]
  Amer. Inst. for Patristic and Byzantine Stud.
    [9770]
  Amer. Maritain Assn. [10782]
  Amer. Nihilism Assn. [8966]
  Amer. Philosophical Assn. [10783]
  Amer. Philosophical Soc. [7598]
  Amer. Soc. for Philosophy Counseling and
    Psychotherapy [16209]
  Amer. Soc. for Value Inquiry [10784]
  Ananda Yoga Teachers Assn. [11217]
  Argentinian Assn. of Ethical Investigations [IO]
  Aristotelian Soc. [IO]
  Asociacion Filosofica de Mexico [IO]
  Association for the Advancement of Philosophy
    and Psychiatry [IO]
  Assn. for the Advancement of Philosophy and
    Psychiatry [7487]
  Assn. of Himalayan Yoga Meditation Societies
    [11218]
  Assn. for Informal Logic and Critical Thinking
    [10785]
  Assn. for Philosophy of the Unconscious [10786]
  Assn. for Practical and Professional Ethics [8967]
  Assn. for Social Economics [6873]
  Australasian Assn. of Philosophy [IO]
  Australian Soc. of Legal Philosophy [IO]
  Austrian Ludwig Wittgenstein Soc. [IO]
  Ayn Rand Inst. [10787]
  Ayn Rand Soc. [10788]
  Bernard Shaw Soc. [9636]
  Bertrand Russell Soc. [9637]
  British Philosophical Assn. [IO]
  Cambridge Philosophical Soc. [IO]
  Camus Stud. Assn. [7488]
  Canadian Philosophical Assn. [IO]
  Canadian Soc. for Aesthetics [IO]
  Canadian Soc. for Neoplatonic Stud. [IO]
  Center For Inquiry [17643]
  Center for Philosophy, Law, Citizenship [18271]

Center for Process Stud. [10789]
Concerned Philosophers for Peace [7489]
Conf. of Philosophical Societies [10790]
Coun. for Res. in Values and Philosophy [10791]
Coun. for Res. in Values and Philosophy [IO]
Coun. for Secular Humanism [20085]
Deutsche Gesellschaft fuer Philosphie e.V. [IO]
East-West Cultural Center [9619]
ERIS Roundtable for Independent Study [10792]
European Soc. for Analytic Philosophy [IO]
Found. for Philosophy of Creativity [10793]
Francis Bacon Found. [9650]
Gabriel Marcel Soc. [10794]
Hedonic Soc. of Am. [10758]
Hegel Soc. of Am. [9657]
Himalayan Intl. Inst. of Yoga Sci. and Philosophy
  of the U.S.A. [12348]
HOPOS - The Intl. Soc. for the History of
  Philosophy of Sci. [9103]
Hume Soc. [IO]
Inst. of Advanced Philosophic Res. [10795]
Inst. for the Advancement of Philosophy for
  Children [10796]
Institute for the Advancement of Philosophy for
  Children [IO]
Inst. for Axiomatic Knowledge and Educ. [7606]
Inst. of Speculative Philosophy [IO]
Intl. Assn. for Greek Philosophy [IO]
Intl. Assn. for Philosophy and Literature [IO]
Intl. Assn. for Philosophy and Literature [10797]
Intl. Berkeley Soc. [10798]
Intl. Boethius Soc. [10799]
Intl. Coun. for Philosophy and Humanistic Stud.
  [IO]
Intl. Fed. for Gerda Alexander Eutony [IO]
Intl. Fed. of Philosophical Societies [IO]
Intl. Fed. of Philosophical Societies [10800]
Intl. Fortean Org. [7477]
Intl. Gottfried Wilhelm Leibniz Soc. [IO]
Intl. Husserl and Phenomenological Res. Soc.
  [IO]
Intl. Husserl and Phenomenological Res. Soc.
  [10801]
Intl. Inst. for Field-Being [8968]
Intl. Inst. for the Stud. of Death [13315]
Intl. New Thought Alliance [10802]
Intl. Phenomenological Soc. [10803]
Intl. Phenomenological Soc. [IO]
Intl. Plato Soc. [IO]
Intl. Soc. for the History, Philosophy, and Social
  Stud. of Biology [8507]
Intl. Soc. for Neoplatonic Stud. [IO]
Intl. Soc. for Neoplatonic Stud. [10804]
Intl. Soc. for New Institutional Economics [6885]
Intl. Soc. for Phenomenological Stud. [10805]
Intl. Soc. for Phenomenological Stud. [IO]
Intl. Soc. for Phenomenology and Literature [IO]
Intl. Soc. for Phenomenology and Literature
  [10806]
Intl. Soc. for Phenomenology and the Sciences of
  Life [10807]
Intl. Soc. for Phenomenology and the Sciences of
  Life [IO]
Intl. Soc. for the Stud. of Human Ideas on
  Ultimate Reality and Meaning [IO]
Intl. Soc. for Utilitarian Stud. [IO]
Internationale Hegel-Gesellschaft [IO]
Internationale Hegel-Vereinigung [IO]
Internet Infidels [7490]
IONS - Inst. of Noetic Sciences [10976]
Jagannath Org. for Global Awareness [20527]
Japan Assn. of Legal Philosophy [IO]
Japan Assn. for Philosophy of Sci. [IO]
Jesuit Philosophical Assn. [9778]
Kahlil Gibran Memorial Found. [11132]
Karl Jaspers Soc. of North Am. [10808]
Leeds Philosophical and Literary Soc. [IO]
Leibniz Soc. of North Am. [10809]
Lessing Soc. [9680]
Libertarian SIG [10810]
Lonergan Philosophical Soc. [18272]
Lonergan Philosophical Soc. [IO]
Louisa May Alcott Memorial Assn. [9682]
Merleau-Ponty Circle [10811]
Metaphysical Soc. of Am. [10812]

Metapsychic Investigations and Sci. Res. Soc.
  [IO]
Michael Oakeshott Assn. [7491]
Natural Law Soc. [10813]
Natural Law Society [IO]
Nietzsche Soc. [10814]
North Amer. Fichte Soc. [10815]
North Amer. Kant Soc. [10816]
North Amer. Levinas Soc. [10817]
North Amer. Nietzsche Soc. [10818]
North American Nietzsche Society [IO]
North Amer. Sartre Soc. [10819]
North Amer. Soc. for Social Philosophy [10820]
North Amer. Yoga Fed. [11219]
The Objectivist Center [10821]
Opening Mind Acad. [15955]
Pacific Soc. for Women in Philosophy [10822]
Phi Sigma Tau [24572]
Philosophical Res. Soc. [10823]
Philosophy Documentation Center [10824]
Philosophy of Educ. Soc. [8969]
Philosophy of Educ. Soc. of Australasia [IO]
Philosophy of Sci. Assn. [10825]
Polanyi Soc. [10826]
Radical Philosophy Assn. [18273]
Resources for Independent Thinking [10827]
Rosicrucian Fellowship [20541]
Royal Inst. of Philosophy [IO]
Royal Philosophical Soc. of Glasgow [IO]
Soc. for the Advancement of Amer. Philosophy
  [10828]
Soc. for Analytical Feminism [10829]
Soc. for Ancient Greek Philosophy [10830]
Soc. for Applied Philosophy [IO]
Soc. for Asian and Comparative Philosophy
  [10831]
Soc. for Bus. Ethics [12127]
Soc. of Christian Philosophers [10832]
Society of Christian Philosophers [IO]
Soc. for Exact Philosophy [IO]
Soc. for Exact Philosophy [10833]
Soc. for Existential and Phenomenological Theory
  and Culture [IO]
Soc. for Medieval and Renaissance Philosophy
  [10464]
Soc. of Metaphysicians [IO]
Soc. for Natural Philosophy [7295]
Soc. for New Language Stud. [10307]
Soc. for Phenomenology and Existential
  Philosophy [10834]
Soc. for the Philosophical Stud. of Genocide and
  the Holocaust [10835]
Soc. for the Philosophical Stud. of Genocide and
  the Holocaust [IO]
Soc. for the Philosophical Stud. of Marxism
  [10452]
Society for Philosophy in the Contemporary World
  [IO]
Soc. for Philosophy in the Contemporary World
  [18274]
Soc. for Philosophy and Psychology [7492]
Soc. for Philosophy of Religion [8970]
Soc. for the Philosophy of Sex and Love [10836]
Soc. for Philosophy and Tech. [10837]
Society for Philosophy and Technology [IO]
Soc. for Skeptical Stud. [7493]
Soc. for the Stud. of Process Philosophies
  [10838]
Soc. for Theoretical and Philosophical Psychology
  [16186]
Soc. for Utopian Stud. [10839]
Soc. for Utopian Stud. [IO]
Southern Soc. for Philosophy and Psychology
  [7494]
Swedenborg Assn. [9164]
Theosophical Book Assn. for the Blind [20592]
Theosophical Soc. in Am. [20593]
Theosophical Soc. in England [IO]
Thomas Paine Natl. Historical Assn. [11153]
Undergraduate Philosophy Assn. [8971]
United Lodge of Theosophists [20594]
Universal White Brotherhood [IO]
Univ. Philosophical Soc. [IO]
Urania Trust [IO]
Washington Ethical Soc. [20087]

Reference to "IO" in place of a book number signifies that the association may be found in the 45th edition of International Organizations.

World Inst. for Advanced Phenomenological Res. and Learning [IO]

World Inst. for Advanced Phenomenological Res. and Learning [10840]

World Union of Catholic Philosophical Societies [IO]

Yoga Alliance [11220]

Yves R. Simon Inst. [10841]

Philosophy in the Contemporary World; Soc. for [18274]

Philosophy Counseling and Psychotherapy; Amer. Soc. for [16209]

Philosophy Documentation Center [10824], PO Box 7147, Charlottesville, VA 22906-7147, (434)220-3300

Philosophy of Educ. Soc. [8969], c/o Dr. Alexander Sidorkin, Exec. Dir., Univ. of Northern Colorado, McKee 208, Greeley, CO 80639, (970)351-2701

Philosophy of Educ. Soc. of Australasia [IO], Perth, Australia

Philosophy and Literature; Intl. Assn. for [★10806]

Philosophy and Literature; Intl. Assn. of [★10840]

Philosophy and Public Policy; Center for [★18454]

Philosophy and Public Policy; Inst. for [18454]

Philosophy of Sci. Assn. [10825], c/o Univ. of Chicago Press, Journals Div., PO Box 37005, Chicago, IL 60637, (773)753-3347

Philosophy of Sci; Canadian Soc. for the History and [IO]

Philosophy in Ser. to Humanity; Realia - [★10795]

Philosophy; Soc. for Medieval and Renaissance [10464]

Philosophy; Soc. for Natural [7295]

Phlebology; Amer. Coll. of [16720]

Phlebology Soc. of Am. [★16732]

Phlebotomy Assn; Natl. [14796]

Phobia Clinic [★12745]

Phobia Clinic; Anxiety and [★12745]

Phobia Soc. of Am. [★12743]

Phobias

ABIL - Agoraphobics Building Independent Lives [12546]

Agoraphobics in Motion [12742]

Anxiety Disorders Assn. of Am. [12743]

Anxiety Disorders Special Interest Gp. [12744]

Anxiety and Phobia Treatment Center [12745]

Dental Anxiety and Phobia Assn. [IO]

Fly Without Fear [12746]

Natl. Phobics Soc. [IO]

Pass-Gp. [12747]

Social Anxiety Australia [IO]

TERRAP Programs [12748]

Triumph Over Phobia [IO]

Phoenix Bird Collectors of Am. [21935], 1107 Deerfield Ln., Marshall, MI 49068, (269)781-9791

Phoenix Center [★13785]

Phoenix House [13273], 164 W 74th St., New York, NY 10023, (212)595-5810

Phoenix House Found. [★13273]

Phoenix Proj. [★16317]

Phoenix Soc. for Burn Survivors [13785], 1835 R W Berends Dr. SW, Grand Rapids, MI 49519-4955, (616)458-2773

Phoenix Theatre - of Theatre Incorporated - Defunct.

Phone-TTY [14777], 1246 Rte., 46 W, Parsippany, NJ 07054-2121, (973)229-6627

Phonemic Spelling Coun. [★8785]

Phonemic Spelling Coun. - Defunct.

Phonetics

Amer. Assn. of Phonetic Sciences [10842]

Intl. Phonetic Assn. [IO]

Phonics Inst. [9046], PO Box 98785, Tacoma, WA 98498-0785, (253)588-3436

Phonograph Collectors Club; Antique [22710]

Phonograph Mfrs. Assn. - Defunct.

Phonograph Soc; Southwest Vintage Radio and [★22931]

Phonograph Soc; Vintage Radio and [22931]

Phonographic Performances New Zealand [IO], Auckland, New Zealand

Phosphate Chemicals Export Assn. [817], c/o Chris Reynolds, PO Box 3320, Northbrook, IL 60062, (847)849-4305

Phosphate Inst; Potash and [4107]

Phosphate Rock Inst. - Defunct.

Phosphate Task Force; Tributyl [828]

Phosphoric Acid and Phosphates Producers Assn. [IO], Brussels, Belgium

Photios Found; Saint [20075]

Photo Art Assn. of Singapore [IO], Singapore, Singapore

Photo-Chemical Machining Institute [IO], East Dennis, MA, United States

Photo-Chemical Machining Inst. [2725], PO Box 739, 38 Strawberry Ln., East Dennis, MA 02641-0739, (508)385-0085

Photo Dealers' and Finishers' Assn; Master [★3009]

Photo Engravers Bd. of Trade - Defunct.

Photo Finishers and Dealers Assn; Master [★3009]

Photo Finishing Inst. - Defunct.

Photo Imagers; Independent [2998]

Photo Imaging Coun. [IO], Caterham, United Kingdom

Photo Imaging Educ. Assn. [8974], c/o Mark Murray, Consultant, Arlington Independent School District, 1203 W Pioneer Pkwy., Arlington, TX 76013, (817)229-2237

Photo Marketing Assn. - Australia [IO], Rosebery, Australia

Photo Marketing Assn. - Canada [IO], Ancaster, ON, Canada

Photo Marketing Association International [IO], Jackson, MI, United States

Photo Marketing Assn. Intl. [IO], Welwyn Garden City, United Kingdom

Photo Marketing Assn. Intl. [★3009]

Photo Marketing Assn. - New Zealand [IO], Auckland, New Zealand

Photo-Optical Instrumentation Engineers; Soc. of [★7408]

Photobiology; Amer. Soc. for [6566]

Photobiology; European Soc. for [IO]

Photocopiers

Bus. Tech. Assn. [2844]

Copier Dealers Assn. [2845]

Copyright Clearance Center [5842]

Copyright Soc. of the U.S.A. [5843]

Intl. Soc. of Copier Artists [9507]

Photoelectric Photometry; Intl. Amateur-Professional [6505]

Photogrammetry

Argentine Assn. for Photogrammetry and Related Sciences [IO]

ASPRS - The Imaging and Geospatial Info. Soc. [7495]

Associacao Portuguesa de Fotogrammetria e Deteccao Remote [IO]

Canadian Remote Sensing Soc. [IO]

Chinese Taipei Soc. of Photogrammetry and Remote Sensing [IO]

European Assn. of Remote Sensing Labs. [IO]

German Soc. for Photogrammetry and Remote Sensing [IO]

Hellenic Soc. for Photogrammetry and Remote Sensing [IO]

Hungarian Soc. of Surveying, Mapping and Remote Sensing [IO]

Intl. Inst. for Geo-Information Sci. and Earth Observation [IO]

Intl. Soc. for Photogrammetry and Remote Sensing [IO]

Irish Soc. of Surveying, Photogrammetry and Remote Sensing [IO]

Israeli Soc. of Photogrammetry and Remote Sensing [IO]

Italian Remote Sensing Assn. [IO]

Korean Soc. of Geodesy, Photogrammetry and Cartography [IO]

Korean Soc. of Remote Sensing [IO]

Latvian Soc. of Geodesy and Photogrammetry [IO]

Mgt. Assn. for Private Photogrammetric Surveyors [7496]

Mongolian Natl. Soc. for Photogrammetry and Remote Sensing [IO]

Nepal Remote Sensing and Photogrammetric Soc. [IO]

Nigerian Soc. for Photogrammetry and Remote Sensing [IO]

Philippine Soc. of Photogrammetry and Remote Sensing [IO]

Polish Soc. for Photogrammetry and Remote Sensing [IO]

Remote Sensing and Photogrammetry Soc. [IO]

Romanian Soc. of Photogrammetry and Remote Sensing [IO]

Sociedad Chilena de Fotogrametria y Percepcion Remota [IO]

Sociedad Colombiana de Percepcion Remota y Sistemas de Informacion Geografica [IO]

Societa Italiana di Fotogrammetria e Topografia [IO]

Societe Belge de Photogrammetrie, de Teledetection et de Cartographie [IO]

Soc. of Photographic Sci. and Tech. of Japan [IO]

Spanish Soc. of Cartography, Photogrammetry and Remote Sensing [IO]

Swiss Soc. of Photogrammetry Image Anal. and Remote Sensing [IO]

Ukrainian Soc. of Photogrammetry and Remote Sensing [IO]

United Kingdom Remote Sensing and Photogrammetry Soc. [IO]

Photogrammetry; Amer. Soc. of [★7495]

Photogrammetry; Legislative Coun. for [★7496]

Photogrammetry and Remote Sensing; Amer. Soc. for [★7495]

Photographers; Amer. Assn. of School [★3012]

Photographers; Amer. Soc. of Magazine [★2992]

Photographers' Assn. of Am. [★3011]

Photographers, Collectors and Enthusiasts Club; Stereo [★10853]

Photographers in Communications; ASMP - The Soc. of [★2992]

Photographers Gallery Assn. [★IO]

Photographers Intl; Wedding [★3017]

Photographers; Soc. of Magazine [★2992]

Photographers' Soc; Ophthalmic [15696]

Photographers Telegraph Assn. - Address unknown since 1995.

Photographes Professionnels du Canada [★IO]

Photographic Administrators - Address unknown since 1994.

Photographic Art and Sci. Found. [8975], c/o Intl. Photography Hall of Fame and Museum, 2100 NE 52nd St., Kirkpatrick Ctr., Oklahoma City, OK 73111, (405)424-4055

Photographic Art and Science Foundation [IO], Oklahoma City, OK, United States

Photographic Artists Guild; Amer. [★2990]

Photographic Assn; Biological [★14031]

Photographic Credit Inst. - Address unknown since 1995.

Photographic Dealers Assn; Natl. [★3009]

Photographic Engg; Soc. of [★7497]

Photographic Equip. Technicians; Natl. Assn. of [3004]

The Photographic Historical Soc. [10855], 350 Whiting Rd., Webster, NY 14580

Photographic Historical Soc. of Canada [IO], Toronto, ON, Canada

Photographic Historical Soc. of New York [★10843]

Photographic and Imaging Mfrs. Assn. [★3002]

Photographic and Imaging Mfrs. Assn. [★IO]

Photographic Industry Coun. - Defunct.

Photographic Instrumentation Engineers; Soc. of [★7408]

Photographic Mfrs. and Distributors Assn. [★3007]

Photographic Mfrs; Natl. Assn. of [★3002]

Photographic Merchandising and Distributing Assn. [★3007]

Photographic Scientists and Engg; Soc. of [★7497]

Photographic Soc. of Am. [22893], 3000 United Founders Blvd., Ste. 103, Oklahoma City, OK 73112-3940, (405)843-1437

Photographic Soc. Intl. - Defunct.

Photographic Soc. of Southern Africa [IO], Gauteng, Republic of South Africa

Photographic Stereoview and Slide Collectors Assn. - Address unknown since 1995.

Photographic Stud. Workshop [★9950]

Photographica Assn; Bay Area [★10851]

Photography

Advt. and Illustrative Photographers Assn. [IO]

Advt. Photographers of Am. [2989]

Affiliation of Honourable Photographers [IO]

A star before a book entry number signifies that the name is not listed separately, but is mentioned within the entry.

Amer. Photographic Artists Guild [2990]
Amer. Photographic Historical Soc. [10843]
Amer. Professional Wedding Photographers Assn.
  [2991]
Amer. Soc. of Camera Collectors [10844]
Amer. Soc. of Cinematographers [1377]
Amer. Soc. of Media Photographers [2992]
Amer. Soc. of Photographers [10845]
Amer. Soc. of Picture Professionals [2993]
Anthropology Film Center [6407]
Antique and Amusement Photographers Intl.
  [2994]
Architectural League of New York [17235]
Asociacion de fotografos profesionales de Espana
  [IO]
Assn. of Advt., Commercial and Magazine
  Photographers of Australia [IO]
Assn. of Commercial Stock Image Licensors
  [1378]
Assn. of Intl. Photography Art Dealers [10846]
Assn. of Intl. Photography Art Dealers [IO]
Assn. of Intl. Trading Companies in Audio-Visual
  Equip. and Public Info. Services [IO]
Assn. of Music Writers and Photographers
  [10562]
Assn. of Photographers [IO]
Associazione Nazionale Fotografi Professionisti
  [IO]
Australian Inst. of Professional Photography [IO]
BioCommunications Assn. [14031]
Blue Earth Alliance [10847]
Boating Writers Intl. [3100]
British Inst. of Professional Photography [IO]
British Press Photographers Assn. [IO]
Broadcast Designer's Assn. [554]
Bund Freischaffender Foto-Designer [IO]
Bur. of Freelance Photographers [IO]
Canadian Assn. for Photographic Art [IO]
Centre for Photographic Conservation [IO]
Commercial Photographers Intl. [2995]
Daguerreian Soc. [10848]
Disabled Photographers' Soc. [IO]
Dutch Assn. for Producers and Importers of Audio,
  Video and Multimedia [IO]
Editorial Photographers [2996]
En Foco [10849]
Evidence Photographers Intl. Coun. [5759]
Fed. of European Professional Photographers [IO]
Fed. Internationale de l'Art Photographique [IO]
Glamour Photographers Intl. [IO]
Glamour Photographers Intl. [2997]
Green Destiny [IO]
Guild of British Camera Technicians [IO]
Hong Kong Inst. of Professional Photographers
  [IO]
Independent Photo Imagers [2998]
Inst. of Photographic Tech. [IO]
Intl. Artists Network [9506]
Intl. Assn. of Architectural Photographers [2999]
Intl. Assn. of Architectural Photographers [IO]
Intl. Assn. of Panoramic Photographers [IO]
Intl. Assn. of Panoramic Photographers [3000]
Intl. Center of Photography [8972]
Intl. Center of Photography [IO]
Intl. Coun. of the Museum of Modern Art [9448]
Intl. Fed. of Photographic Art [IO]
Intl. Fire Photographers Assn. [IO]
Intl. Fire Photographers Assn. [3001]
Intl. Hologram Mfrs. Assn. [IO]
Intl. Imaging Indus. Assn. [IO]
Intl. Imaging Indus. Assn. [3002]
Intl. Indus. Photographers Assn. [IO]
Intl. Inst. of Photographic Arts [IO]
Intl. Inst. of Photographic Arts [3003]
Intl. Kodak Historical Soc. [10850]
International Kodak Historical Society [IO]
Intl. League of Conservation Photographers [IO]
Intl. League of Conservation Photographers
  [5080]
Intl. Photographic Historical Org. [10851]
International Photographic Historical Organization
  [IO]
Intl. Soc. of Fine Art Photographers [IO]
Intl. Soc. of Fine Art Photographers [10852]
Japan Image and Info. Mgt. Assn. [IO]

Japan Light Machinery Info. Center of Central
  New York [24343]
Kappa Pi Intl. Honorary Art Fraternity [24404]
Location Managers Guild of Am. [2522]
Master Photographers Assn. [IO]
Monaghan Photographic Soc. [IO]
Natl. Assn. of Photographic Equip. Technicians
  [3004]
Natl. Assn. of Photography Wholesalers and
  Distributors [IO]
Natl. Found. for Advancement in the Arts [9587]
Natl. Geographic Soc. [7123]
Natl. Photography Instructors Assn. [8973]
Natl. Press Photographers Assn. [3005]
Natl. Stereoscopic Assn. [10853]
Native Indian/Inuit Photographers' Assn. [IO]
Natural Figure Art Assn. [9462]
Nikon Historical Soc. [10854]
North Amer. Cartographic Info. Soc. [6656]
North Amer. Nature Photography Assn. [3006]
Ophthalmic Photographers' Soc. [15696]
Overseas Press Club of Am. [3154]
Photo Art Assn. of Singapore [IO]
Photo Imaging Coun. [IO]
Photo Imaging Educ. Assn. [8974]
Photo Marketing Assn. - Australia [IO]
Photo Marketing Assn. - Canada [IO]
Photo Marketing Association International [IO]
Photo Marketing Assn. - New Zealand [IO]
Photographic Art and Science Foundation [IO]
Photographic Art and Sci. Found. [8975]
The Photographic Historical Soc. [10855]
Photographic Historical Soc. of Canada [IO]
Photographic Soc. of Am. [22893]
Photographic Soc. of Southern Africa [IO]
Photoimaging Mfrs. and Distributors Assn. [3007]
Pictorial Photographers of Am. [10856]
Picture Archv. Coun. of Am. [3008]
PMA - The Worldwide Community of Imaging As-
  sociations [3009]
The Print Center [9522]
Print Coun. of Am. [9466]
Professional Aerial Photographers Assn. [3010]
Professional Aerial Photographers Association
  [IO]
Professional Photographers of Am. [3011]
Professional Photographers of Canada [IO]
Professional Photographic Labs. Assn. [IO]
Professional School Photographers Assn. Intl. [IO]
Professional School Photographers Assn. Intl.
  [3012]
Professional Women Photographers [3013]
Royal Photographic Soc. of Great Britain [IO]
Scottish Photographic Fed. [IO]
Silver Users Assn. [2728]
Soc. for Imaging Sci. and Tech. [7497]
Soc. of Photo-Technologists [3014]
Soc. of Photo-Technologists [IO]
Soc. for Photographic Educ. [8976]
Soc. of Sport and Event Photographers [3015]
Soc. of Sport and Event Photographers [IO]
South Australian Photographic Fed. [IO]
Stereoscopic Soc. [IO]
Student Photographic Soc. [10857]
Svenska Fotografers Forbund [IO]
Travel Journalists Guild [3167]
United Press Intl. [3169]
U.S. Marine Corps Combat Correspondents Assn.
  [3171]
U.S. Senate Press Photographers Gallery [3016]
Univ. Photographers Assn. of Am. [8977]
Visual Artists and Galleries Assn. [5861]
Wedding and Portrait Photographers Intl. [3017]
Wedding and Portrait Photographers Intl. [IO]
White House News Photographers Assn. [3018]
Women in Photography Intl. [3019]
Photography; Intl. Fund for Concerned [★8972]
Photoimaging Mfrs. and Distributors Assn. [3007],
  109 White Oak Ln., Ste. 72F, Old Bridge, NJ
  08857-1981, (732)679-3460
Photoluminescent Safety Products Assn. [IO], Brain-
  tree, United Kingdom
Photometry; Intl. Amateur-Professional Photoelectric
  [6505]
Photoplatemakers Assn; Amer. [★7154]

Photoplatemakers; Intl. Assn. of [★7154]
Photoshop Professionals; Natl. Assn. of [1808]
Photosynthesis Res; Intl. Soc. of [IO]
Phototherapy Assn; Intl. [IO]
Phrenocon [★24643]
Phycological Soc. of Am. [6646], c/o Blackwell
  Publishing, Inc., 350 Main St., Malden, MA 02148,
  (781)388-8599
Phycological Soc. of Am. [IO], Malden, MA, United
  States
Phycological Soc; British [IO]
Phylaxis Soc. - Address unknown since 1995.
Phyllis' Collectors Club - Defunct.
Phyllis Diller Fan Club; Natl. [24799]
Phylloxera and Grape Indus. Bd. of South Australia
  [IO], Stepney, Australia
Physiatrists; Assn. of Academic [16316]
Physical Activity; North Amer. Soc. for the Psychol-
  ogy of Sport and [23666]
Physical Anthropologists; Amer. Assn. of [6403]
Physical Culture Org; Amer. Sokol Educational and
  [19025]
Physical Disability Coun. of Australia [IO], Willawar-
  rin, Australia
Physical Disability Law; Amer. Bar Assn. - Commn.
  on Mental and [5781]
Physical Distribution Mgt; Natl. Coun. of [★4018]
Physical Education
  Amer. Acad. of Kinesiology and Physical Educ.
    [8978]
  Amer. Alliance for Hea., Physical Educ.,
    Recreation and Dance [8979]
  Amer. Assn. for Physical Activity and Recreation
    [12793]
  Amer. Kinesiotherapy Assn. [16311]
  Amer. Senior Fitness Assn. [15961]
  Athletic Equip. Managers Assn. [23805]
  Canadian Assn. for Hea., Physical Educ.,
    Recreation and Dance [IO]
  Delta Psi Kappa [24573]
  Deutscher Sportlehrerverband [IO]
  European Physical Educ. Assn. [IO]
  The Fitness League [IO]
  Intl. Assn. of Physical Educ. and Sport for Girls
    and Women [IO]
  Intl. Assn. of Physical Educ. and Sport for Girls
    and Women [8980]
  Intl. Coun. for Hea., Physical Educ., Recreation,
    Sport, and Dance [8981]
  Intl. Coun. for Hea., Physical Educ., Recreation,
    Sport, and Dance [IO]
  Intl. Fed. for Physical Educ. [IO]
  Intl. Soc. for Aging and Physical Activity [13545]
  Natl. Assn. of Collegiate Women Athletics
    Administrators [8982]
  Natl. Assn. for Girls and Women in Sport [8983]
  Natl. Assn. for Kinesiology and Physical Educ. in
    Higher Educ. [8984]
  Natl. Assn. for Physical Educ. in Higher Educ.
    [8985]
  Natl. Assn. for Sport and Physical Educ. [8986]
  Natl. Coalition for Promoting Physical Activity
    [23653]
  Natl. Coun. of Athletic Training [8987]
  Natl. Coun. of Secondary School Athletic Directors
    [8988]
  Natl. Gym Assn. [23654]
  Natl. High School Athletic Coaches Assn. [23292]
  Natl. Interscholastic Athletic Administrators Assn.
    [8989]
  NFHS Coaches Assn. [23294]
  North Amer. Soc. for Sport Mgt. [8990]
  North Amer. Soc. for Sport Mgt. [IO]
  PE4life [8991]
  Phi Epsilon Kappa [24574]
  Physical Educ. Assn. of Ireland [IO]
  Physical Educ. Assn. of the United Kingdom [IO]
  Scottish Local Authority Network of Physical Educ.
    [IO]
  Soc. of State Directors of Hea., Physical Educ.
    and Recreation [8992]
  Sport and Recreation Law Assn. [23870]
  U.S. High School Tennis Assn. [23912]
Physical Educ; Amer. Acad. of [★8978]
Physical Educ; Amer. Assn. for Advancement of
  [★8979]

Reference to "IO" in place of a book number signifies that the association may be found in the 45th edition of International Organizations.

Physical Educ. Assn; Amer. [★8979]
Physical Educ. Assn. of Ireland [IO], Limerick, Ireland
Physical Educ. Assn. for Men; Natl. Coll. [★8985]
Physical Educ. Assn. of the United Kingdom [IO], Reading, United Kingdom
Physical Educ. of Coll. Women; Natl. Assn. for [★8985]
Physical Educ. in Israel; Wingate Inst. for [★23828]
Physical Educ. and Recreation; Amer. Alliance for Hea., [★8979]
Physical Educ. and Recreation; Amer. Assn. for Hea., [★8979]
Physical Educ., and Recreation; Division of Girl's and Women's Sports of the Amer. Assn. of Hea., [★8983]
Physical Educ. and Recreation; Recreation Division of the Amer. Alliance for Hea., [★12793]
Physical Educ. and Recreation; School Hea. Division of Amer. Assn. for Hea., [★16234]
Physical Features Stud. Unit; Earth's [22816]
Physical Fitness
  Achilles Track Club [23331]
  Action for Healthy Kids [13945]
  Adirondack Forty-Sixers [23930]
  Adirondack Mountain Club [23931]
  Adirondack Trail Improvement Soc. [23932]
  Aerobics and Fitness Assn. of Am. [15956]
  Aerobics and Fitness Association of America [IO]
  African-Amer. Assn. of Fitness Professionals [15957]
  Aikido Yoshokai Assn. of North Am. [7943]
  Am. on the Move Found. [14537]
  Am. Outdoors [23681]
  Amer. Armsport Assn. [23059]
  Amer. Assn. of adaptedSPORTS Programs [23333]
  Amer. Athletic Trainers Assn. and Certification Bd. [23953]
  Amer. Barefoot Club [23974]
  Amer. Bicycle Assn. [23305]
  Amer. Center for the Alexander Technique [13617]
  Amer. Chiropractic Assn. Coun. on Sports Injuries and Physical Fitness [13989]
  Amer. Coll. of Sports Medicine [16473]
  Amer. Coun. on Exercise [15958]
  Amer. Coun. for Fitness and Nutrition [15959]
  Amer. Double Dutch League [23697]
  Amer. Endurance Ride Conf. [23933]
  Amer. Hiking Soc. [23934]
  Amer. Hot Rod Assn. [23071]
  Amer. Junior Rodeo Assn. [23684]
  Amer. Kenpo Karate Intl. [23560]
  Amer. Medical Athletic Assn. [23650]
  Amer. Medical Tennis Assn. [23898]
  Amer. Motorcycle Heritage Found. [23621]
  Amer. Nordic Walking Assn. [15960]
  Amer. Platform Tennis Assn. [23899]
  Amer. Running Assn. [23651]
  Amer. Sambo Assn. [23580]
  Amer. Self-Protection Assn. [23712]
  Amer. Senior Fitness Assn. [15961]
  Amer. Soc. of Exercise Physiologists [16019]
  Amer. Swimming Coaches Assn. [23882]
  Amer. Tai Chi Assn. [16593]
  Amer. Teachers Assn. of the Martial Arts [23582]
  Amer. Tennis Assn. [23900]
  Amer. Trails [23935]
  Amer. Turners [23802]
  Amer. Vaulting Assn. [23967]
  Amer. Volleyball Coaches Assn. [23969]
  Amer. Water Ski Educational Found. [23975]
  Amer. Whitewater [23682]
  Amer. Yangjia Michuan Taijiquan Assn. [23584]
  AMOA Natl. Dart Assn. [23329]
  Appalachian Mountain Club [23936]
  Appalachian Trail Conservancy [23937]
  Aquatic Exercise Assn. [23652]
  Arabian Jockey Club [23494]
  Assn. of Commercial Diving Educators [23960]
  Assn. of Northwest Steelheaders [23409]
  Assn. of Surfing Professionals [23877]
  Athletic Equip. Managers Assn. [23805]
  Athletic Inst. [3658]
  Australian Assn. for Exercise and Sport Sci. [IO]

Australian Parkour Assn. [IO]
Babe Ruth Birthplace/Sports Legends at Camden Yards [23107]
Bicycle Parking Proj. [23307]
Bicycle Ride Directors' Assn. of Am. [23308]
Big West Conf. [23809]
BlueRibbon Coalition [23680]
Canadian Fitness and Lifestyle Res. Inst. [IO]
Catalina 22 Natl. Sailing Assn. [23162]
Center for the Stud. of Aging of Albany [11281]
Central Collegiate Hockey Assn. [23483]
Championship Assn. of Mechanics [23075]
Choy Lee Fut Martial Arts Fed. of Am. [23586]
Cinderella Softball Leagues [23789]
Coll. Gymnastics Assn. [23474]
Coll. Swimming Coaches Assn. of Am. [23883]
Collegiate Soaring Assn. [23039]
Combat Martial Art Practitioners Assn. [23587]
Continental Divide Trail Soc. [23938]
Cooper Inst. [15962]
Cooper Inst. [IO]
Divers Alert Network [23378]
Eastern Surfing Assn. [23878]
Employee Services Mgt. Assn. [12796]
Exercise Safety Assn. [15963]
Fitness Indus. Assn. [IO]
Fitness Indus. Suppliers Assn. - North Am. [IO]
Fitness Indus. Suppliers Assn. - North Am. [3020]
Fitness for Life [15964]
Florida Trail Assn. [23939]
Free Throwers Boomerang Soc. [23247]
Future Fisherman Found. [23415]
Great Lakes Sport Fishing Coun. [23416]
Hampton One-Design Class Racing Assn. [23173]
Harness Horse Youth Found. [23496]
Heritage Trails Fund [23940]
Highpointers Club [23014]
IDEA Hea. and Fitness Assn. [15965]
Inland Lake Yachting Assn. [23175]
Inst. of Diving [23961]
Intercollegiate Outing Club Assn. [23941]
Intercollegiate Tennis Assn. [23902]
Intl. 210 Assn. [23179]
Intl. 505 Yacht Racing Assn., Amer. Sect. [23180]
Intl. Acad. of Aquatic Art [23884]
Intl. Assn. of Gay and Lesbian Martial Artists [23588]
Intl. Boxing Fed. [23260]
Intl. Boxing Hall of Fame Museum [23261]
Intl. Coun. for Physical Activity and Fitness Res. [IO]
Intl. Fed. of Sleddog Sports [23393]
Intl. Female Boxers Assn. [23263]
Intl. Hea., Racquet and Sportsclub Assn. [3021]
Intl. Hea., Racquet and Sportsclub Assn. [IO]
Intl. Hunter Educ. Assn. [23545]
Intl. J/22 Class Assn. [23187]
Intl. Lacrosse Fed. [23570]
Intl. Martial Arts League [23589]
Intl. Mental Game Coaching Assn. [23289]
Intl. Mountain Bicycling Assn. [23310]
Intl. Naples Sabot Assn. [23190]
Intl. Natural Bodybuilding and Fitness Fed. [23243]
Intl. Okinawa Kobudo Assn. [23590]
Intl. Physical Fitness Assn. [3665]
Intl. Racquetball Fed. [23677]
Intl. Senior Softball Assn. [23790]
Intl. Soc. for Aging and Physical Activity [13545]
Intl. Soc. for Behavioral Nutrition and Physical Activity [13745]
Intl. Soc. of Sports Nutrition [15562]
Intl. Sports Exchange [23826]
Intl. Sports Heritage Assn. [23827]
Intl. Sungja-Do Assn. [23593]
Intl. Swimming Hall of Fame [23886]
Intl. Tennis Hall of Fame [23903]
Intl. Thunderbird Class Assn. [23195]
Intl. Track and Field Coaches Assn. [23919]
Intl. Vaulting Club [23968]
IOCALUM [23942]
Japan Aikido Assn. U.S.A. [23595]
Keep Fit Assn. [IO]
Korean Amer. Professional Tennis Assn. [23904]
Lifegain Inst. [14573]

Light Living Library [23272]
Lincoln Heritage Trail Found. [23943]
Maccabi USA/Sports for Israel [23828]
Major Wingfield Historical Soc. [23905]
Martial Arts USA [23597]
Medical Fitness Assn. [15966]
Montana Outfitters and Guides Assn. [23944]
Mountaineers [23945]
Multicultural Golf Assn. of Am. [23455]
Natl. Ability Center [23347]
Natl. Acad. of Sports [23831]
Natl. Assn. of Athletic Development Directors [23832]
Natl. Assn. of Collegiate Marketing Administrators [23834]
Natl. Assn. for Hea. and Fitness [15967]
Natl. Assn. for Human Development [11303]
Natl. Assn. for Kinesiology and Physical Educ. in Higher Educ. [8984]
Natl. Assn. of Police Athletic Leagues [13496]
Natl. Assn. of Sports Commissions [23871]
Natl. Assn. of Sports Officials [23872]
Natl. Assn. of Sports Officials - Organizations Network [23873]
Natl. Assn. of Underwater Instructors [23963]
Natl. Athletic Trainers' Assn. [23954]
Natl. Baseball Hall of Fame and Museum [23118]
Natl. Basketball Athletic Trainers Assn. [23135]
Natl. Camp Assn. [23277]
Natl. Coalition for Promoting Physical Activity [23653]
Natl. Collegiate Table Tennis Assn. [23895]
Natl. Disability Sports Alliance [23353]
Natl. Fed. of Professional Trainers [23956]
Natl. Fitness Therapy Assn. [15968]
Natl. Football League Players Assn. [23434]
Natl. Gym Assn. [23654]
Natl. Hea. Club Assn. [3670]
Natl. Interscholastic Swimming Coaches Assn. of Am. [23887]
Natl. Junior Baseball League [23120]
Natl. Org. for Rivers [23683]
Natl. Org. of I Walkers [23971]
Natl. Public Parks Tennis Assn. [23906]
Natl. Register of Personal Trainers [IO]
Natl. Scholastic Surfing Assn. [23880]
Natl. Senior Games Assn. [23655]
Natl. Softball Assn. [23792]
Natl. Sporting Clays Assn. [23726]
Natl. Starwind/Spindrift Class Assn. [23207]
Natl. Strength and Conditioning Assn. [23957]
Natl. Thoroughbred Racing Assn. [23510]
Natl. Throws Coaches Assn. [23293]
Natl. Tractor Pullers Assn. [23928]
Natl. Wellness Inst. [16057]
Natl. Women's Martial Arts Fed. [23600]
Natl. Wrestling Coaches Assn. [23987]
NETA - Natl. Exercise Trainers Assn. [23037]
New England Trails Conf. [23948]
New York Triathlon Club [23922]
NFHS Officials Assn. [23874]
North Am. Wu(Hao) Taiji Fed. [23601]
North Amer. Fishing Club [23421]
North Amer. Kettlebell Fed. [23984]
North Amer. Natural Bodybuilding Fed. [23245]
North Amer. Network of Women Runners [23656]
North Amer. Powerlifting Fed. [23662]
North Amer. Soc. for Pediatric Medicine [15891]
North Amer. Strongman [23246]
North Amer. Trail Ride Conf. [23949]
North Country Trail Assn. [23950]
Olson 30 Class Assn. [23210]
Over the Hill Gang, Intl. [23846]
Pan-American Union of Karatedo Organizations [23564]
Patience T'ai Chi Assn. [23897]
PE4life [8991]
Professional Assn. of Diving Instructors [23964]
Professional Assn. of Volleyball Officials [23875]
Professional Baseball Athletic Trainers Soc. [23125]
Professional Tennis Registry [23909]
Rails-to-Trails Conservancy [23952]
Recreational Scuba Training Coun. [23965]
Running USA [23708]

A star before a book entry number signifies that the name is not listed separately, but is mentioned within the entry.

San Juan 21 Class Assn. [23215]
Scoot-Tours Touring Scooter Riders Assn. [23627]
Shape Up Am. [15969]
Shudokan Martial Arts Assn. [23603]
Sony Ericsson WTA Tour [23910]
Sports Hall of Oblivion [23855]
Sportscar Vintage Racing Assn. [23085]
Surfrider Found. [23881]
Synchro Swimming U.S.A. [23889]
Tandem Club of Am. [23317]
Truth in Fitness [15970]
Ultimate Players Assn. [23375]
Underwater Soc. of Am. [23966]
United Fly Tyers [23424]
U.S. Adult Soccer Assn. [23857]
U.S. Amateur Tug of War Assn. [23959]
U.S. Apnea Assn. [23380]
U.S. Aquatic Sports [23890]
U.S. ArmSports [23991]
U.S. Blind Golf Assn. [23364]
U.S. Bobsled and Skeleton Fed. [23767]
U.S. Bocce Fed. [23241]
U.S. Competitive Aerobics Fed. [23038]
U.S. Cultural Exchange and Sports Soc. [23861]
U.S. Dental Tennis Assn. [23911]
U.S. Disc Sports [23376]
U.S. Flag and Touch Football League [23441]
U.S. Football Alliance [23442]
U.S. Futsal Fed. [23862]
U.S. Girls' Wrestling Assn. [23988]
U.S. Hapki Hae [23606]
U.S. Isshinryu Karate Assn. [23565]
U.S. Judo [23554]
U.S. Judo Assn. [23555]
U.S. Masters Swimming [23891]
U.S. Mirror Class Assn. [23229]
U.S. Natl. Tennis Acad. [23913]
U.S. Professional Diving Coaches Assn. [23381]
U.S. Professional Tennis Assn. [23914]
U.S. Running Streak Assn. [23709]
U.S. Ski and Snowboard Assn. [23760]
U.S. Ski Team Found. [23761]
U.S. Soling Assn. [23234]
U.S. Sport Jujitsu Assn. [23609]
U.S. Sports Acad. [23864]
U.S. Squash Racquets Assn. [23876]
U.S. Swim School Assn. [23892]
U.S. Tennis Assn. [23915]
U.S. Volleyball Association/USA Volleyball [23970]
U.S. Water Fitness Assn. [23657]
U.S. Yngling Assn. [23237]
U.S. Yudo Assn. [23611]
Universal Martial Arts Brotherhood [23612]
Univ. Athletic Assn. [23865]
USA Canoe/Kayak [23280]
USA Diving [23382]
U.S.A. Karate Fed. [23566]
USA Powerlifting [23664]
USA Pulling [23929]
USA Swimming [23893]
U.S.A. Table Tennis [23896]
USA Tennis - NJTL [23916]
U.S.A. Track and Field [23926]
USA Triathlon [23927]
USA Water Ski [23979]
USA Weightlifting [23985]
U.S.A. Wrestling [23989]
USGA Green Sect. [23470]
Weight-Control Info. Network [15578]
Weight Watchers Intl. [14603]
Western Athletic Conf. [23866]
Western Collegiate Hockey Assn. [23489]
Western Women Premier Bowlers [23257]
Women Outdoors [23644]
Women's All-Star Assn. [23258]
Women's Sports Found. [23867]
World Aquatic Babies and Children [23894]
World Armsport Fed. [23060]
World Diving Coaches Assn. [23383]
World Fast-Draw Assn. [23733]
World Head of Family Sokeship Coun. [23614]
World Jeet Kune Do Fed. [23615]
World Masters Cross-Country Ski Assn. [23763]
World Modern Arnis Alliance [23617]
World Traditional Karate Org. [23567]

WTA Tour Players Assn. [23917]
Physical Fitness; Amer. Chiropractic Assn. Coun. on Sports Injuries and [13989]
Physical Fitness Assn; Intl. [3665]
Physical and Hea. Educ; Soc. of State Directors of [★8992]
Physical Medicine and Rehabilitation; Amer. Acad. of [16307]
Physical Medicine and Rehabilitation; Amer. Bd. of [16309]
Physical Medicine and Rehabilitation; Amer. Osteopathic Acad. of [★15805]
Physical Medicine and Rehabilitation; Amer. Osteopathic Coll. of [★15805]
Physical Medicine and Rehabilitation; Amer. Soc. of [★16307]
Physical Medicine and Rehabilitation; Canadian Assn. of [IO]
Physical and Mental Rehabilitation; Assn. for [★16311]
Physical, and Natural Sciences; Colombian Acad. of Exact, [IO]

Physical Science
   Alliance for Sci. and Tech. Res. in Am. [7595]
   Assn. of Sci. Museum Directors [10498]
   Intl. Assn. of Nanotechnology [7741]
   Lambda Delta Lambda [24586]
   Natl. Soc. of Hispanic Physicists [7505]
   Neutron Scattering Soc. of Am. [7506]
Physical Soc. [★IO]
Physical Soc. of China [★IO]
Physical Soc. of Japan [IO], Tokyo, Japan
Physical Soc. of Republic of China [IO], Taipei, Taiwan
Physical Therapeutic Assn; Amer. Women's [★16603]

Physical Therapy
   Abilities! [11913]
   Amer. Acad. of Orthopaedic Manual Physical Therapists [15971]
   Amer. Acad. of Physical Medicine and Rehabilitation [16307]
   Amer. Bd. of Physical Medicine and Rehabilitation [16309]
   Amer. Cong. of Rehabilitation Medicine [16310]
   Amer. Hippotherapy Assn. [16600]
   Amer. Kinesiotherapy Assn. [16311]
   Amer. Medical Rehabilitation Providers Assn. [16312]
   Amer. Occupational Therapy Assn. [16602]
   Amer. Physical Therapy Assn. [16603]
   Amer. Rehabilitation Counseling Assn. [16313]
   Amer. Soc. of Hand Therapists [14524]
   Amer. Spinal Injury Assn. [16461]
   Assn. of Academic Physiatrists [16316]
   Assn. of Pediatric Therapists [16606]
   Christopher and Dana Reeve Found. [16463]
   Conservative Orthopedics Intl. Assn. [15767]
   Continuing Care Accreditation Comm. [16318]
   Coun. of State Administrators of Vocational Rehabilitation [16320]
   Hospitalized Veterans Writing Proj. [16321]
   Intl. Assn. of Rehabilitation Professionals [16322]
   Intl. Private Practitioners Assn. [IO]
   Natl. Assn. of Rehabilitation Instructors [16324]
   Natl. Assn. of Rehabilitation Providers and Agencies [16326]
   Natl. Coun. on Rehabilitation Educ. [16329]
   Natl. Rehabilitation Assn. [16330]
   Natl. Rehabilitation Info. Center [16332]
   Natl. Spinal Cord Injury Assn. [16468]
   Orthopaedic Sect., Amer. Physical Therapy Assn. [16630]
   Private Practice Section/American Physical Therapy Assn. [16633]
   Rehabilitation Intl. [16333]
   Sect. for Long Term Care and Rehabilitation [14894]
   Sister Kenny Rehabilitation Inst. [16335]
   Soc. of Ortho-Bionomy Intl. [13767]
   Spinal Cord Soc. [16469]
   Univ. of Colorado Hea. Sciences Center Alumni Assn. [24494]
   Vocational Evaluation and Career Assessment Professionals [16337]

Physical Therapy Assn; Amer. [16603]
Physical Therapy Assn; Orthopaedic Sect., Amer. [16630]
Physical Therapy Assn; Private Practice Section/American [16633]
Physical Therapy Assn. of Thailand [IO], Chiang Mai, Thailand
Physical Therapy; Found. for [16613]
Physical Therapy Overseas [★15778]
Physical Therapy Overseas [★IO]
Physically Challenged Bowhunters of Am. [23549], 2152 Rte. 981, New Alexandria, PA 15670-2592, (724)668-7439
Physically Challenged Child; National Humanitarian Proj. for the [★19231]
Physically Challenged Golf Assn. [23359], 10 E View Dr., Farmington, CT 06032, (860)676-2035
Physically Challenged Golf Assn. [IO], Farmington, CT, United States
Physically Handicapped; Div. for [★11998]
Physically Handicapped; Div. for [★9141]
Physically Handicapped, Homebound and Hospitalized; Div. on [★9141]
Physically Handicapped, Homebound and Hospitalized; Div. on [★11998]
Physically Handicapped; Natl. Assn. of the [11967]
Physically Handicapped; Special Interest Comm. for Computers and the [★6803]
Physically Handicapped; Special Interest Gp. for Computers and the [★6803]

Physically Impaired
   Accessible Housing Soc. [IO]
   Alliance for Tech. Access [11915]
   Amer. Amputee Found. [11916]
   Amer. Amputee Hockey Assn. [23799]
   Amer. Amputee Soccer Assn. [23773]
   Amer. Assn. on Hea. and Disability [14235]
   Amer. Assn. of People with Disabilities [11917]
   Amer. Bd. of Disability Analysts [16308]
   Amer. Competition Opportunities for Riders with Disabilities [23330]
   Amer. Disability Assn. [11918]
   Amer. Friends of ALYN Hosp. [12825]
   Amer. Soc. of Handicapped Physicians [11919]
   Americans With Disabilities Act [11920]
   America's Athletes with Disabilities [23340]
   Amputees in Motion, Intl. [11921]
   Assistance Dogs of Am., Inc. [11922]
   Assn. of Assistive Tech. Act Programs [14237]
   Assn. of Disabled Amer. Golfers [23341]
   Assn. of Rehabilitation Programs in Cmpt. Tech. [11924]
   B'nai B'rith Senior Citizens Housing Comm. [12469]
   Canine Assistants [11925]
   Canine Companions for Independence [11926]
   Canines for Disabled Kids [11927]
   Center on Human Policy [11928]
   Charlotte W. Newcombe Found. [12749]
   Christian Coun. on Persons with Disabilities [11931]
   Christian Overcomers [11932]
   CH on Disability Info. [11933]
   DateAble [11936]
   Disability Resources [11938]
   Disability Rights Educ. and Defense Fund [11940]
   Disabled and Alone/Life Services for the Handicapped [11941]
   Easter Seals [11944]
   Extensions for Independence [11945]
   Found. for Sci. and Disability [11946]
   Free Wheelchair Mission [11947]
   Friends of Libraries for Blind and Physically Handicapped Individuals in North America [10357]
   Global Deaf Connection [12274]
   Goodwill Indus. Intl. [11949]
   Goodwill Indus. Volunteer Services [11950]
   Gospel Assn. for the Blind [16848]
   Indoor Sports Club [11951]
   Intl. Child Amputee Network [11954]
   Intl. Post Polio Support Org. [16048]
   Job Accommodation Network [11955]
   Just One Break [11957]
   A Leg To Stand On [12659]

Reference to "IO" in place of a book number signifies that the association may be found in the 45th edition of International Organizations.

Manitoba Wheelchair Sports Assn. [IO]
Mobility Intl. USA [11961]
MOVE Intl.: Mobility Opportunities Via Educ. -
  USA [11962]
NADD - An Assn. for Persons with Developmental
  Disabilities and Mental Hea. Needs [12552]
Natl. Alliance for Accessible Golf [23348]
Natl. AMBUCS [11964]
Natl. Amputation Found. [11965]
Natl. Assn. of ADA Coordinators [11966]
Natl. Assn. of the Physically Handicapped [11967]
Natl. Coun. on Independent Living [11968]
Natl. Disability Rights Network [11970]
Natl. Dissemination Center for Children with Dis-
  abilities [11971]
Natl. Inst. for Rehabilitation Engg. [11972]
Natl. Odd Shoe Exchange [11974]
Natl. Org. Caring for Kids [11638]
Natl. Theatre Workshop of the Handicapped
  [11033]
Natl. Wheelchair Poolplayer Assn. [23355]
Networking Proj. for Young Adults with Disabilities
  [11975]
New Brunswick Wheelchair Sports Assn. [IO]
NISH [11976]
North Amer. Squirrel Assn. [22773]
Nova Scotia Wheelchair Sports Fed. [IO]
The One Shoe Crew [11977]
Ontario Wheelchair Sports Assn. [IO]
Opportunity Plus [11978]
Paws With a Cause [11979]
People-to-People Comm. on Disability [11980]
Post-Polio Hea. Intl. [11981]
P.R.I.D.E. Found. - Promote Real Independence
  for the Disabled and Elderly [11982]
Quebec Wheelchair Assn. [IO]
Rehabilitation Engg. and Assistive Tech. Soc. of
  North Am. [11983]
Res. and Training Center on Independent Living
  [11984]
Saskatchewan Wheelchair Sports Assn. [IO]
Siblings for Significant Change [11987]
Soc. for Disability Stud. [11988]
Special Recreation for disABLED Intl. [11989]
Support Dogs, Inc. [11990]
Tech. Assistance Collaborative [13145]
U.S. Handcycling Fed. [23321]
U.S. Power Soccer Assn. [23783]
Universal Wheelchair Football Assn. [23368]
VSA arts [11993]
Wheelchair Sports Alberta [IO]
Wheelchair Sports Assn. of Newfoundland and
  Labrador [IO]
World Ability Fed. [11995]
World Inst. on Disability [11996]
World Rehabilitation Fund [11997]
Yukon Wheelchair Recreation Soc. [IO]
Physician Advocacy for Excellence in the Delivery of
  Pulmonary and Critical Care; NAMDRC: [★15068]
Physician Analysts; Amer. Soc. of [★16104]
Physician Art Assn; Amer. [9415]
Physician Asst. Educ. Assn. [15976], 300 N
  Washington St., Ste. 505, Alexandria, VA 22314-
  2544, (703)548-5538

Physician Assistants
Accreditation Rev. Commn. on Educ. for the
  Physician Asst. [15972]
Amer. Acad. of Physician Assistants [15973]
Amer. Assn. of Pathologists' Assistants [15854]
Amer. Bd. of Cardiovascular Perfusion [13887]
Amer. Soc. of Podiatric Medical Assistants
  [16040]
Assn. of Family Practice Physician Assistants
  [14698]
Assn. of Neurosurgical Physician Assistants
  [15974]
Assn. of Physician Assistants in Cardiovascular
  Surgery [13895]
Clinicians for Choice [13528]
Natl. Commn. on Certification of Physician As-
  sistants [15975]
Physician Asst. Educ. Assn. [15976]
Soc. of Air Force Physician Assistants [20665]
Soc. of Army Physician Assistants [15977]
Soc. of Dermatology Physician Assistants [15978]

Soc. of Emergency Medicine Physician Assistants
  [15979]
Soc. for Physician Assistants in Pediatrics [15980]
Physician Assistants; Accreditation Rev. Comm. on
  Educ. for [★15972]
Physician Assistants in Cardiovascular Surgery;
  Assn. of [13895]
Physician Assistants in Dermatology [★15978]
Physician Assistants; Joint Rev. on Educational
  Programs for [★15972]
Physician Assistants; Soc. of Air Force [20665]
Physician Executives; Amer. Coll. of [15056]
Physician-Hospital Organizations; Amer. Assn. of
  [★15048]
Physician Insurers Assn. of Am. [14964], 2275 Res.
  Blvd., Ste. 250, Rockville, MD 20850, (301)947-
  9000
Physician Nurses; Natl. Assn. of [15500]
Physician Prog; Impaired [13246]
Physician Specialists; Amer. Assn. of [15792]
Physician Task Force on Hunger in America -
  Defunct.

Physicians
Academic Orthopaedic Soc. [15750]
Acad. of Ambulatory Foot and Ankle Surgery
  [16023]
Acad. of Clinical Lab. Physicians and Scientists
  [15981]
Academy of Clinical Laboratory Physicians and
  Scientists [IO]
Acad. on Mental Retardation [15238]
Acad. of Scientific Hypnotherapy [14913]
Accreditation Commn. for Acupuncture and
  Oriental Medicine [15739]
Accreditation Rev. Commn. on Educ. for the
  Physician Asst. [15972]
Adopt a Dr. [12750]
Advocates for the Amer. Osteopathic Assn.
  [15789]
Aerospace Medical Assn. [13538]
Aesculapian Club [15982]
African Medical and Res. Found. [14971]
Aid for Intl. Medicine [14972]
Air Charity Network [14312]
Air Medical Physician Assn. [15983]
Air and Surface Transport Nurses Assn. [15427]
Airlines Medical Directors Assn. [13539]
Alliance of Minority Medical Associations [14607]
Amer. Acad. of Allergy, Asthma and Immunology
  [13592]
Amer. Acad. of Ambulatory Care Nursing [15428]
Amer. Acad. of Child and Adolescent Psychiatry
  [16063]
Amer. Acad. on Commun. in Healthcare [15984]
Amer. Acad. of Dermatology [14189]
Amer. Acad. of Disability Evaluating Physicians
  [14033]
Amer. Acad. of Environmental Medicine [14360]
Amer. Acad. of Facial Plastic and Reconstructive
  Surgery [14038]
Amer. Acad. of Family Physicians [14383]
Amer. Acad. of Hospice and Palliative Medicine
  [15985]
Amer. Acad. of Medical Administrators [15045]
Amer. Acad. of Medical Administrators Res. and
  Educational Found. [15046]
Amer. Acad. of Neurological and Orthopaedic
  Surgeons [15409]
Amer. Acad. of Neurology [15376]
Amer. Acad. of Nursing [15430]
Amer. Acad. of Ophthalmology [15656]
Amer. Acad. of Orofacial Pain [14106]
Amer. Acad. of Orthopaedic Surgeons [15752]
Amer. Acad. of Osteopathy [15790]
Amer. Acad. of Otolaryngic Allergy and Found.
  [13593]
Amer. Acad. of Physician Assistants [15973]
Amer. Acad. of Sports Physicians [16472]
Amer. Acad. of Tropical Medicine [16692]
Amer. Assembly for Men in Nursing [15431]
Amer. Assn. of Ambulatory Surgery Centers
  [16558]
Amer. Assn. of Birth Centers [15580]
Amer. Assn. of Certified Allergists [13594]
Amer. Assn. of Clinical Directors [15986]

Amer. Assn. of Colleges of Osteopathic Medicine
  [15791]
Amer. Assn. of Colleges of Podiatric Medicine
  [16025]
Amer. Assn. of Genito-Urinary Surgeons [16699]
Amer. Assn. of Gynecologic Laparoscopists
  [15581]
Amer. Assn. for Hand Surgery [14522]
Amer. Assn. of Hosp. Podiatrists [16026]
Amer. Assn. of Immunologists [14929]
Amer. Assn. of Integrated Healthcare Delivery
  Systems [15048]
Amer. Assn. on Intellectual and Developmental
  Disabilities [15239]
Amer. Assn. of Kidney Patients [15283]
Amer. Assn. of Medical Assistants [15081]
Amer. Assn. of Medical Milk Commissions [16384]
Amer. Assn. of Medical Soc. Executives [15153]
Amer. Assn. of Neuromuscular and Electrodiag-
  nostic Medicine [15303]
Amer. Assn. of Neuropathologists [15853]
Amer. Assn. of Neuroscience Nurses [15436]
Amer. Assn. of Nurse Anesthetists [15437]
Amer. Assn. of Nurse Attorneys [15000]
Amer. Assn. of Nutritional Consultants [15540]
Amer. Assn. of Occupational Hea. Nurses [15439]
Amer. Assn. of Off. Nurses [15440]
Amer. Assn. of Oriental Medicine [15742]
Amer. Assn. of Orthopedic Medicine [15753]
Amer. Assn. of Pathologists' Assistants [15854]
Amer. Assn. of Physician Offices and Labs.
  [14990]
Amer. Assn. of Physician Specialists [15792]
Amer. Assn. of Physicians of Indian Origin
  [15987]
Amer. Assn. of Professional Hypnotherapists
  [14915]
Amer. Assn. of Professional Ringside Physicians
  [15988]
Amer. Assn. of Psychiatric Administrators [14861]
Amer. Assn. of Spinal Cord Injury Nurses [15441]
Amer. Assn. for the Stud. of Liver Diseases
  [14801]
Amer. Bd. of Abdominal Surgery [16561]
Amer. Bd. of Anesthesiology [13671]
Amer. Bd. of Cardiovascular Perfusion [13887]
American Bd. of Clinical Metal Toxicology [16659]
Amer. Bd. of Dermatology [14190]
Amer. Bd. of Family Medicine [14384]
Amer. Bd. of Genetic Counseling [14492]
Amer. Bd. of Indus. Hygiene [15623]
Amer. Bd. of Internal Medicine [14965]
Amer. Bd. of Medical Specialties [15117]
Amer. Bd. of Nuclear Medicine [15419]
Amer. Bd. of Nutrition [15541]
Amer. Bd. of Obstetrics and Gynecology [15582]
Amer. Bd. of Ophthalmology [15661]
Amer. Bd. of Orthopaedic Surgery [15755]
Amer. Bd. of Physician Nutrition Specialists
  [15542]
Amer. Bd. of Podiatric Orthopedics and Primary
  Podiatric Medicine [16030]
Amer. Bd. of Podiatric Surgery [16031]
Amer. Bd. of Preventive Medicine [16050]
Amer. Bd. of Professional Disability Consultants
  [6040]
Amer. Bd. of Psychiatry and Neurology [16071]
Amer. Bd. of Psychological Hypnosis [14917]
Amer. Bd. of Quality Assurance and Utilization
  Rev. Physicians [16260]
Amer. Bd. of Radiology [16272]
Amer. Bd. of Surgery [16563]
Amer. Bd. of Urology [16700]
Amer. Celiac Society/Dietary Support Coalition
  [15543]
Amer. Cleft Palate-Craniofacial Assn. [14055]
Amer. Clinical Lab. Assn. [14991]
Amer. Coll. for Advancement in Medicine [16051]
Amer. Coll. of Allergy, Asthma and Immunology
  [13596]
Amer. Coll. of Cardiology [13888]
Amer. Coll. of Chest Physicians [13889]
Amer. Coll. of Domiciliary Midwives [15583]
Amer. Coll. of Emergency Physicians [14326]
Amer. Coll. of Foot and Ankle Orthopedics and
  Medicine [16032]

A star before a book entry number signifies that the name is not listed separately, but is mentioned within the entry.

Amer. Coll. of Foot and Ankle Pediatrics [16033]
Amer. Coll. of Foot and Ankle Surgeons [16034]
Amer. Coll. of Gastroenterology [14405]
Amer. Coll. Hea. Assn. [14714]
Amer. Coll. of Hea. Care Administrators [15535]
Amer. Coll. of Healthcare Executives [14862]
Amer. Coll. of Intl. Physicians [14973]
Amer. Coll. of Legal Medicine [15001]
Amer. Coll. of Medical Quality [16261]
Amer. Coll. of Nuclear Medicine [15421]
Amer. Coll. of Nuclear Physicians [15422]
Amer. Coll. of Nurse-Midwives [15447]
Amer. Coll. of Nutrition [15544]
Amer. Coll. of Obstetricians and Gynecologists [15584]
Amer. Coll. of Occupational and Environmental Medicine [15624]
Amer. Coll. of Oral and Maxillofacial Surgeons [15734]
Amer. Coll. of Orgonomy [15738]
Amer. Coll. of Osteopathic Emergency Physicians [14327]
Amer. Coll. of Osteopathic Family Physicians [15793]
Amer. Coll. of Osteopathic Internists [15794]
Amer. Coll. of Osteopathic Obstetricians and Gynecologists [15585]
Amer. Coll. of Osteopathic Pediatricians [15795]
Amer. Coll. of Osteopathic Surgeons [15797]
Amer. Coll. of Physician Executives [15056]
Amer. Coll. of Physicians-American Soc. of Internal Medicine [14966]
Amer. Coll. of Preventive Medicine [16052]
Amer. Coll. of Radiology [16274]
Amer. Coll. of Sports Medicine [16473]
Amer. Coll. of Surgeons [16565]
Amer. Conf. of Governmental Indus. Hygienists [15625]
Amer. Coun. of Applied Clinical Nutrition [15545]
Amer. Dietetic Assn. [15546]
Amer. Epilepsy Soc. [14379]
Amer. Found. for Maternal and Child Health [15586]
Amer. Fracture Assn. [15756]
Amer. Gastroenterological Assn. [14406]
Amer. Guild of Hypnotherapists [14919]
Amer. Gynecological and Obstetrical Soc. [15587]
Amer. Head and Neck Soc. [15819]
Amer. Hea. Care Assn. [14540]
Amer. Healthcare Radiology Administrators [16275]
Amer. Holistic Nurses' Assn. [14825]
Amer. Industrial Health Coun. [15626]
Amer. Indus. Hygiene Assn. [15627]
Amer. Inst. of Homeopathy [14845]
Amer. Kidney Fund [15284]
Amer. Laryngological, Rhinological and Otological Soc. [15821]
Amer. Liver Found. [14803]
Amer. Massage Therapy Assn. [15022]
Amer. Medical Assn. [15155]
Amer. Medical Assn. Alliance [15156]
Amer. Medical Athletic Assn. [23650]
Amer. Medical Directors Assn. [15536]
Amer. Medical Fly Fishing Assn. [4349]
Amer. Medical Gp. Assn. [14717]
Amer. Medical Tennis Assn. [23898]
Amer. Mental Hea. Alliance [15188]
Amer. Mental Hea. Counselors Assn. [15189]
Amer. Naprapathic Assn. [15276]
Amer. Nephrology Nurses' Assn. [15286]
Amer. Nurses Assn. [15451]
Amer. Nurses Found. [15452]
Amer. Ophthalmological Soc. [15662]
Amer. Org. of Nurse Executives [15454]
Amer. Orthopaedic Assn. [15757]
Amer. Orthopaedic Foot and Ankle Soc. [15758]
Amer. Orthopaedic Soc. for Sports Medicine [16476]
Amer. Orthoptic Coun. [15663]
Amer. Osler Soc. [15157]
Amer. Osteopathic Acad. of Orthopedics [15759]
Amer. Osteopathic Acad. of Sports Medicine [16477]
Amer. Osteopathic Assn. [15798]

Amer. Osteopathic Bd. of Emergency Medicine [14328]
Amer. Osteopathic Bd. of Family Physicians [15799]
Amer. Osteopathic Bd. of Pediatrics [15800]
Amer. Osteopathic Coll. of Anesthesiologists [13672]
Amer. Osteopathic Coll. of Dermatology [14194]
Amer. Osteopathic Coll. of Physical Medicine and Rehabilitation [15805]
Amer. Osteopathic Coll. of Radiology [16276]
Amer. Osteopathic Found. [15806]
Amer. Parkinson Disease Assn. [15304]
Amer. Physician Art Assn. [9415]
Amer. Physicians Fellowship for Medicine in Israel [12456]
Amer. Podiatric Medical Assn. [16037]
Amer. Professional Practice Assn. [14697]
Amer. Radium Soc. [15639]
Amer. Registry of Medical Assistants [15082]
Amer. Roentgen Ray Soc. [16277]
Amer. Shoulder and Elbow Surgeons [16567]
Amer. Soc. of Abdominal Surgeons [16568]
Amer. Soc. for Adolescent Psychiatry [16078]
Amer. Soc. of Anesthesiologists [13674]
Amer. Soc. of Bariatric Physicians [15575]
Amer. Soc. of Cataract and Refractive Surgery [15665]
Amer. Soc. of Childbirth Educators [15589]
Amer. Soc. of Clinical Hypnosis [14921]
Amer. Soc. of Clinical Hypnosis - Educ. and Res. Found. [14922]
Amer. Soc. for Clinical Nutrition [15547]
Amer. Soc. of Clinical Oncology [15640]
Amer. Soc. for Colposcopy and Cervical Pathology [15590]
Amer. Soc. of Contemporary Medicine, Surgery, and Ophthalmology [15666]
Amer. Soc. of Cytopathology [14075]
Amer. Soc. for Cytotechnology [14076]
Amer. Soc. for Dermatologic Surgery [14196]
Amer. Soc. for Echocardiography [13891]
Amer. Soc. of Exercise Physiologists [16019]
Amer. Soc. for Gastrointestinal Endoscopy [14409]
Amer. Soc. of Hand Therapists [14524]
Amer. Soc. of Handicapped Physicians [11919]
Amer. Soc. for Healthcare Central Ser. Professionals [14864]
Amer. Soc. for Healthcare Engg. of the Amer. Hosp. Assn. [14865]
Amer. Soc. for Healthcare Risk Mgt. [14869]
Amer. Soc. for Histocompatibility and Immunogenetics [14931]
Amer. Soc. of Interventional Pain Physicians [15837]
Amer. Soc. for Laser Medicine and Surgery [14997]
Amer. Soc. of Law, Medicine and Ethics [15002]
Amer. Soc. of Lipo-Suction Surgery [16572]
Amer. Soc. of Maxillofacial Surgeons [15735]
Amer. Soc. for Mohs Surgery [15641]
Amer. Soc. of Nephrology [15288]
Amer. Soc. of Neuroimaging [16281]
Amer. Soc. of Neuroradiology [16282]
Amer. Soc. for Nutrition [15548]
Amer. Soc. of Ophthalmic Registered Nurses [15458]
Amer. Soc. for Parenteral and Enteral Nutrition [15549]
Amer. Soc. for Pharmacy Law [15003]
Amer. Soc. of Plastic Surgeons [14044]
Amer. Soc. of Plastic Surgical Nurses [15461]
Amer. Soc. of Podiatric Medical Assistants [16040]
Amer. Soc. for Reconstructive Microsurgery [16573]
Amer. Soc. of Regional Anesthesia and Pain Medicine [13676]
Amer. Soc. for Surgery of the Hand [14525]
Amer. Soc. for Therapeutic Radiology and Oncology [16285]
Amer. Surgical Assn. [16575]
Amer. Urological Assn. [16704]
Amyloidosis Support Network [14251]

Amyotrophic Lateral Sclerosis Assn. [15306]
Army Nurse Corps Assn. [15262]
Arthroscopy Assn. of North Am. [15762]
Asian Amer./Pacific Islander Nurses Assn. [15463]
Assn. for Academic Surgery [16576]
Assn. of Air Medical Services [14314]
Assn. of Amer. Indian Physicians [15989]
Assn. of Amer. Physicians and Surgeons [15990]
Assn. of Behavioral Healthcare Mgt. [15191]
Assn. of Bone and Joint Surgeons [15763]
Assn. for Childbirth at Home, Intl. [15591]
Assn. of Chinese Amer. Physicians [15991]
Assn. of Family Practice Administrators [15060]
Assn. of Forensic Physicians [IO]
Assn. of French-Speaking Physicians of Canada [IO]
Assn. for Healthcare Documentation Integrity [15084]
Assn. for Healthcare Philanthropy [14871]
Assn. for Healthcare Rsrc. and Materials Mgt. [14872]
Assn. for Hosp. Medical Educ. [14873]
Assn. for Macular Diseases [15669]
Assn. of Medical Directors of Info. Systems [14957]
Assn. of Medical Doctors of Asia [IO]
Assn. of Medical Illustrators [13707]
Assn. of Medicine and Psychiatry [16081]
Assn. of Military Osteopathic Physicians and Surgeons [15807]
Assn. of Nigerian Physicians in the Americas [15992]
Assn. of Nigerian Physicians in the Americas [IO]
Assn. of Nurses Endorsing Transplantation [15670]
Assn. of Osteopathic State Executive Directors [15809]
Assn. of Otolaryngology Administrators [15062]
Assn. of Pakistani Physicians of North Am. [15993]
Assn. of Pakistani Physicians and Surgeons of the United Kingdom [IO]
Assn. of PeriOperative Registered Nurses [15468]
Assn. of Philippine Physicians in Am. [15994]
Assn. of Physician Assistants in Cardiovascular Surgery [13895]
Assn. for Prevention Teaching and Res. [16054]
Assn. for Professionals in Infection Control and Epidemiology [14947]
Assn. of Professors of Gynecology and Obstetrics [15592]
Assn. of Prog. Directors in Internal Medicine [14967]
Assn. of Prog. Directors in Vascular Surgery [16578]
Assn. of Rehabilitation Nurses [15469]
Assn. for Res. in Vision and Ophthalmology [15672]
Assn. of Staff Physician Recruiters [15995]
Association of Staff Physician Recruiters [IO]
Assn. of Surgeons of Great Britain and Ireland [IO]
Assn. of Tech. Personnel in Ophthalmology [15674]
Assn. of Uganda Women Medical Doctors [IO]
Assn. of Univ. Anesthesiologists [13680]
Assn. of Univ. Professors of Ophthalmology [15675]
Assn. of Univ. Radiologists [16286]
Assn. of Veterans Affairs Anesthesiologists [13681]
Assn. of Women's Hea., Obstetric and Neonatal Nurses [15470]
Assyrian Medical Soc. [13715]
Asthma and Allergy Found. of Am. [13598]
Auxiliary to the Natl. Medical Assn. [15161]
Avenues, Natl. Support Gp. for Arthrogryposis Multiplex Congenita [15309]
Bangladesh Medical Assn. of North Am. [15162]
Bay Area Physicians for Human Rights [12218]
Behavior Genetics Assn. [14498]
Benign Essential Blepharospasm Res. Found. [15311]
Better Vision Inst. [15678]
Bones Soc. [15764]

Reference to "IO" in place of a book number signifies that the association may be found in the 45th edition of International Organizations.

Brain Injury Assn. of Am. **[14528]**
Bur. of Professional Educ. of the Amer. Osteopathic Assn. **[15810]**
C/SEC **[15593]**
Cajal Club **[15385]**
Canadian Assn. of Emergency Physicians **[IO]**
Canadian Assn. of Interns and Residents **[IO]**
Canadian Soc. of Plastic Surgeons **[IO]**
Cardiovascular Credentialing Intl. **[13898]**
Catholic Hea. Assn. of the U.S. **[14874]**
Catholic Medical Assn. **[15996]**
Center for Humane Options in Childbirth Experiences **[15594]**
Center for Professional Well-Being **[14700]**
Center for Sports and Osteopathic Medicine **[16055]**
Certification Bd. for Urologic Nurses and Associates **[16706]**
Childbirth Connection **[15595]**
Children's Tumor Found. **[15315]**
Chinese Amer. Medical Soc. **[15163]**
Christian Medical and Dental Associations **[20238]**
Christian Medical and Dental Soc. **[IO]**
Civil Aviation Medical Assn. **[13540]**
Clinical Lab. Mgt. Assn. **[14993]**
Clinical and Lab. Standards Inst. **[14994]**
Clinical Ligand Assay Soc. **[14995]**
Coll. of Amer. Pathologists **[15866]**
Coll. of Operating Dept. Practitioners **[IO]**
Coll. of Osteopathic Healthcare Executives **[14876]**
Community Systems Found. **[15552]**
Computerized Medical Imaging Soc. **[16287]**
Congenital Cardiac Anesthesia Soc. **[13682]**
Conservative Orthopedics Intl. Assn. **[15767]**
Contact Lens Assn. of Ophthalmologists **[15680]**
Coun. on Arteriosclerosis, Thrombosis and Vascular Biology of the Amer. Heart Assn. **[13902]**
Coun. on Chiropractic Orthopedics **[15768]**
Coun. of Colleges of Acupuncture and Oriental Medicine **[15743]**
Coun. on Diagnostic Imaging **[16288]**
Coun. of Medical Specialty Societies **[15120]**
Coun. of Pediatric Subspecialties **[15886]**
Coun. on Podiatric Medical Educ. **[16042]**
Coun. on Resident Educ. in Obstetrics and Gynecology **[15597]**
Coun. of State and Territorial Epidemiologists **[14374]**
Coun. of Teaching Hospitals **[14879]**
Cranial Acad. **[15811]**
Crohn's and Colitis Found. of Am. **[14414]**
CTSNet: Cardiothoracic Surgery Network **[16643]**
Cure Res. Found. **[13818]**
CyberKnife Soc. **[16581]**
Danish Medical Assn. **[IO]**
Dannemiller Memorial Educational Found. **[13683]**
Dermatology Found. **[14199]**
Dermatology Nurses' Assn. **[15476]**
Dietary Managers Assn. **[15555]**
Digestive Disease Natl. Coalition **[14416]**
Docs for Tots **[13958]**
Drs. for Artists **[12520]**
Doctors Ought to Care **[14554]**
Dystonia Medical Res. Found. **[15319]**
Dystrophic Epidermolysis Bullosa Res. Assn. of Am. **[14200]**
Educational Commn. for Foreign Medical Graduates **[15997]**
Educational Commn. for Foreign Medical Graduates **[IO]**
Emergency Medicine Found. **[14331]**
Emergency Medicine Residents' Assn. **[14332]**
Emergency Nurses Assn. **[14333]**
Endometriosis Assn. **[15599]**
Epilepsy Found. **[14380]**
Estonian Medical Assn. **[IO]**
European Assn. of Senior Hosp. Physicians **[IO]**
European Coun. of Doctors for Plurality in Medicine **[IO]**
European Fed. of Salaried Doctors **[IO]**
European Union of Gen. Practitioners **[IO]**
Fed. Physicians Assn. **[15998]**
Federated Ambulatory Surgery Assn. **[16582]**

Fed. for Accessible Nursing Educ. and Licensure **[15478]**
Fed. of Amer. Hospitals **[14881]**
Fed. of Chinese Amer. and Chinese Canadian Medical Societies **[13985]**
Fed. of Pediatric Organizations **[15887]**
Fed. of State Physician Hea. Programs **[15999]**
Flower Essence Soc. **[14818]**
Flying Chiropractors Assn. **[14002]**
Flying Physicians Assn. **[13731]**
Focus **[15681]**
Food and Nutrition Bd. **[15558]**
Forbes Norris MDA/ALS Res. Center **[15323]**
Found. for Advancement in Cancer Therapy **[13824]**
Found. for Ichthyosis and Related Skin Types **[14201]**
Found. for Innovation in Medicine **[15166]**
Found. for the Support of Intl. Medical Training **[14977]**
Frederick A. Cook Soc. **[11112]**
Frontier Nursing Ser. **[15479]**
Gay and Lesbian Medical Assn. **[14431]**
Glaucoma Res. Found. **[15683]**
Global Hea. Coun. **[14979]**
Global Lawyers and Physicians **[14558]**
Global Perioperative Res. Org. **[14026]**
Gluten Intolerance Gp. **[15559]**
Harvey Soc. **[15168]**
Hea. Acad. **[14883]**
Hea. Res. and Educational Trust **[14884]**
Healthcare Info. and Mgt. Systems Soc. **[14885]**
Heart Disease Res. Found. **[13905]**
Heart Rhythm Soc. **[13907]**
Hemochromatosis Found. **[14799]**
Hepatitis Rsrc. Network **[14810]**
Hesperian Found. **[14980]**
Histochemical Soc. **[15692]**
Human Ecology Action League **[14364]**
Huntington's Disease Soc. of Am. **[15329]**
Informed Homebirth/Informed Birth and Parenting **[15602]**
Inst. for the Development of Emotional and Life Skills/National Inst. of Relationship Enhancement **[15201]**
Inst. for Labor and Mental Health **[15202]**
Interamerican Coll. of Physicians and Surgeons **[16000]**
Interamerican Coll. of Physicians and Surgeons **[IO]**
InterAmerican Heart Found. **[13909]**
Interchurch Medical Assistance **[20242]**
Intercontinental Fed. of Behavioral Optometry **[15719]**
Intermed Intl. **[14982]**
Intl. and Amer. Associations of Clinical Nutritionists **[15560]**
Intl. Anesthesia Res. Soc. **[13684]**
Intl. Assn. of Coroners and Medical Examiners **[15093]**
Intl. Assn. of Healthcare Central Ser. Materiel Mgt. **[14886]**
Intl. Assn. for Healthcare Security and Safety **[14887]**
Intl. Assn. of Hygienic Physicians **[15278]**
Intl. Assn. of Ocular Surgeons **[15684]**
Intl. Assn. of Optometric Executives **[15720]**
Intl. Assn. of Pediatric Lab. Medicine **[15888]**
Intl. Assn. of Physicians in AIDS Care **[16001]**
Intl. Assn. of Physicians in AIDS Care **[IO]**
International Association of Physicians and Health Care Professionals **[IO]**
Intl. Assn. of Physicians and Hea. Care Professionals **[16002]**
Intl. Assn. of Sickle Cell Nurses And Physician Assistants **[14706]**
Intl. Assn. of Transpersonal Therapists and Physicians **[15205]**
Intl. Bundle Br. Block Assn. **[13911]**
Intl. Center for Attitudinal Healing **[15206]**
Intl. Cesarean Awareness Network **[15604]**
Intl. Childbirth Educ. Assn. **[15605]**
Intl. Coll. of Surgeons **[16583]**
Intl. Comm. Against Mental Illness **[15207]**
Intl. Correspondence Soc. of Allergists and Clinical Immunologists **[13601]**

Intl. Doctors in Alcoholics Anonymous **[13252]**
Intl. Eye Found. **[15685]**
Intl. Fed. of Foot and Ankle Societies **[16045]**
Intl. Fed. of Psoriasis Associations **[14203]**
Intl. Found. for Homeopathy **[14849]**
Intl. Hea. Evaluation Assn. **[14568]**
Intl. Hyperhidrosis Soc. **[14357]**
Intl. Life Sciences Inst. - North Am. **[15561]**
Intl. Mobile Hea. Assn. **[14724]**
Intl. Pediatric Transplant Assn. **[16673]**
Intl. Refractive Surgery Club **[15689]**
Intl. Skeletal Soc. **[16289]**
Intl. Soc. of Arthroscopy, Knee Surgery and Orthopaedic Sports Medicine **[15771]**
Intl. Soc. for Clinical Densitometry **[15788]**
Intl. Soc. for Cmpt. Assisted Orthopaedic Surgery **[15772]**
Intl. Soc. of Cosmetic and Laser Surgeons **[14048]**
Intl. Soc. for Dermatologic Surgery **[14204]**
Intl. Soc. of Dermatology **[14205]**
Intl. Soc. of Doctors for the Env. - Germany **[IO]**
Intl. Soc. for Imaging in the Eye **[15690]**
Intl. Soc. of Oncology Pharmacy Practitioners **[15937]**
Intl. Vitamin A Consultative Gp. **[15564]**
Intersociety Professional Nutrition Educ. Consortium **[15565]**
Interstate Postgraduate Medical Assn. of North Am. **[14386]**
The IPA Assn. of Am. **[3022]**
Iraqi Medical Sciences Assn. **[14987]**
Islamic Medical Assn. of North Am. **[16003]**
Joint Commn. on Accreditation of Healthcare Organizations **[14888]**
Joint Commn. on Allied Hea. Personnel in Ophthalmology **[15692]**
Joint Commn. on Sports Medicine and Sci. **[16483]**
Joint Coun. of Allergy, Asthma and Immunology **[13602]**
Korean-American Medical Assn. **[15174]**
Lamaze Birth Without Pain Educ. Assn. **[15607]**
Lesbian, Gay, Bisexual, and Transgender People in Medicine **[12243]**
Lupus Found. of Am. **[15014]**
Malignant Hyperthermia Assn. of the U.S. **[14464]**
MAP Intl. **[20243]**
Medical Gp. Mgt. Assn. **[15067]**
Medical Women's Fed. **[IO]**
Mended Hearts, Inc. **[13916]**
Mental Hea. Am. **[15211]**
Michael E. DeBakey Intl. Surgical Soc. **[13917]**
Midwives Alliance of North Am. **[15610]**
Mission Doctors Assn. **[12532]**
Myasthenia Gravis Found. of Am. **[15340]**
Natl. Alliance of Medical Researchers and Teaching Physicians **[15143]**
Natl. Alliance on Mental Illness **[15214]**
Natl. Assn. of County Hea. Fac. Administrators **[15069]**
Natl. Assn. of Disability Examiners **[14034]**
Natl. Assn. of Free Clinics **[14727]**
Natl. Assn. for Healthcare Quality **[16264]**
Natl. Assn. for Healthcare Recruitment **[15070]**
Natl. Assn. of Hispanic Nurses **[15494]**
Natl. Assn. for Home Care and Hospice **[14840]**
Natl. Assn. of Locum Tenens Org. **[16004]**
Natl. Assn. of Managed Care Physicians **[16005]**
Natl. Assn. of Medical Examiners **[15094]**
Natl. Assn. of Orthopaedic Nurses **[15498]**
Natl. Assn. of Physician Nurses **[15500]**
Natl. Assn. of Physician Recruiters **[16006]**
Natl. Assn. of Public Hospitals and Hea. Systems **[14892]**
Natl. Assn. of Residents and Interns **[15175]**
Natl. Assn. for Rural Mental Hea. **[15217]**
Natl. Assn. of School Nurses **[15501]**
Natl. Assn. of State EMS Officials **[14337]**
Natl. Assn. of State Mental Hea. Prog. Directors **[15219]**
Natl. Assn. of VA Physicians and Dentists **[16007]**
Natl. Assn. of Vision Professionals **[15693]**
Natl. Ataxia Found. **[15342]**
Natl. Black Nurses Assn. **[15505]**

A star before a book entry number signifies that the name is not listed separately, but is mentioned within the entry.

Natl. Bd. of Medical Examiners [15095]
Natl. Bd. of Osteopathic Medical Examiners [15812]
Natl. Bd. of Podiatric Medical Examiners [16046]
Natl. Certification Commn. for Acupuncture and Oriental Medicine [15747]
Natl. Coalition for Res. in Neurological Disorders [15346]
Natl. Commn. on Certification of Physician Assistants [15975]
Natl. Commn. on Human Life, Reproduction and Rhythm [16008]
Natl. Contact Lens Examiners [15723]
Natl. Coun. of State Boards of Nursing [15508]
Natl. Digestive Diseases Info. CH [14422]
Natl. Environmental Hea. Assn. [14367]
Natl. Eye Res. Found. [15724]
Natl. Fed. of Licensed Practical Nurses [15509]
Natl. Found. for Ectodermal Dysplasias [14468]
Natl. Found. for Infectious Diseases [14953]
Natl. Free Clinic Found. of Am. [14585]
Natl. Gaucher Found. [15252]
Natl. Hea. Assn. [15279]
Natl. Hospice and Palliative Care Org. [14856]
Natl. Kidney Found. [15294]
Natl. League for Nursing [15510]
Natl. Medical Assn. [15176]
Natl. Multiple Sclerosis Soc. [15349]
Natl. Pain Educ. Coun. [15846]
Natl. Parkinson Found. [15351]
Natl. Perinatal Assn. [15900]
Natl. Physicians Alliance [16009]
Natl. Physicians Assn. [16010]
Natl. Podiatric Medical Assn. [16047]
Natl. Postdoctoral Assn. [9064]
Natl. Registry of Emergency Medical Technicians [14342]
Natl. Scoliosis Found. [16393]
Natl. Soc. of Certified Healthcare Bus. Consultants [14711]
Natl. Soc. of Genetic Counselors [14506]
Natl. Spasmodic Torticollis Assn. [15353]
Natl. Tay-Sachs and Allied Diseases Assn. [15354]
Navy Anesthesia Soc. [13687]
Neurosurgery Intl. [15415]
New Zealand Resident Doctors' Assn. [IO]
North Amer. Assn. for Ambulatory Urgent Care [13663]
North Amer. Clinical Dermatologic Soc. [14212]
North Amer. Sikh Medical and Dental Assn. [16416]
North Amer. Soc. for Dialysis and Transplantation [15295]
North Amer. Soc. of Obstetric Medicine [15615]
Nuclear Medicine Tech. Certification Bd. [15423]
Nurses Educational Funds [15516]
Nurses' House [15518]
Nurses Org. of Veterans Affairs [15519]
Nutrition for Optimal Hea. Assn. [15567]
Ohashi Inst. [15748]
Oncology Nursing Soc. [15521]
Ophthalmic Photographers' Soc. [15696]
ORBIS Intl. [15697]
Orthopaedic Res. Soc. [15776]
Osteopathic Intl. Alliance [15813]
Outpatient Intravenous Infusion Therapy Assn. [16631]
Outpatient Ophthalmic Surgery Soc. [15698]
Pacific Dermatologic Assn. [14213]
Pain Mgt. and Sclerotherapy [15814]
Pan-American Allergy Soc. [13604]
Pan-American Assn. of Ophthalmology [15699]
Parkinson's Disease Found. [15360]
Pediatric Infectious Diseases Soc. [14955]
Pediatric Orthopedic Soc. of North Am. [15780]
Perfusion Prog. Directors' Coun. [13921]
Physician Asst. Educ. Assn. [15976]
Physicians for Global Survival [IO]
Physicians for Peace [15078]
Physicians for a Violence-Free Soc. [12985]
Price-Pottenger Nutrition Found. [15568]
Qualified Private Medical Practitioners' and Hospitals' Assn. [IO]
Radiological Soc. of North Am. [16293]

Ray Helfer Soc. [13976]
Renal Physicians Assn. [15298]
Royal Australasian Coll. of Physicians - Australia [IO]
Royal Australasian Coll. of Surgeons [IO]
Royal Coll. of Physicians [IO]
Royal Coll. of Physicians of Edinburgh [IO]
Royal Coll. of Physicians of Ireland [IO]
Royal Coll. of Physicians and Surgeons of Canada [IO]
Royal Coll. of Physicians and Surgeons of Glasgow [IO]
Rural Doctors Assn. of Australia [IO]
Rural Doctors Assn. of Southern Africa [IO]
Russian Amer. Medical Assn. [16378]
Scoliosis Assn., Inc. [16394]
Scoliosis Res. Soc. [16395]
Sect. for Long Term Care and Rehabilitation [14894]
Sect. for Metropolitan Hospitals [14895]
Simon Found. for Continence [16711]
Soc. for Academic Emergency Medicine [14344]
Soc. for the Advancement of Women's Imaging [16294]
Soc. of Air Force Physicians [15264]
Soc. of Amer. Gastrointestinal and Endoscopic Surgeons [14428]
Soc. for Assisted Reproductive Tech. [16346]
Soc. of Cardiovascular Anesthesiologists [13689]
Soc. for Clinical and Experimental Hypnosis [14927]
Soc. of Correctional Physicians [16011]
Soc. for Epidemiologic Res. [14377]
Soc. of Eye Surgeons [15703]
Soc. of Gastroenterology Nurses and Associates [14429]
Soc. for Gynecologic Investigation [15618]
Soc. for Healthcare Consumer Advocacy of the Amer. Hosp. Assn. [15005]
Soc. for Healthcare Strategy and Market Development of the Amer. Hosp. Assn. [14896]
Soc. of Interventional Pain Mgt. Surgery Centers [16588]
Soc. of Interventional Radiology [16300]
Soc. for Investigative Dermatology [14214]
Soc. of Medical Consultants to the Armed Forces [15265]
Soc. of Medical Friends of Wine [23028]
Soc. of Medical Jurisprudence [15006]
Soc. for Menstrual Cycle Res. [15619]
Soc. of Military Orthopaedic Surgeons [15266]
Soc. of Nuclear Medicine [15424]
Soc. of Nuclear Medicine Technologist Sect. [15425]
Soc. for Obstetric Anesthesia and Perinatology [15903]
Soc. for Occupational and Environmental Hea. [15633]
Soc. of Otorhinolaryngology and Head/Neck Nurses [15526]
Soc. for Pediatric Dermatology [14215]
Soc. for Pediatric Urology [16715]
Soc. for Radiation Oncology Administrators [16302]
Soc. of Reproductive Surgeons [16349]
Soc. of Rural Physicians of Canada [IO]
Soc. of Surgical Oncology [15655]
Soc. of Teachers of Family Medicine [14387]
Soc. for Tech. in Anesthesia [13692]
Soc. of Univ. Surgeons [16591]
Soc. of Univ. Urologists [16716]
State EMS Training Coordinators Coun. of NASEMSO [14345]
Thai Physicians Assn. of Am. [16012]
Tourette Syndrome Assn. [15367]
Tremor Action Network [15369]
Trinity Medical Center [14900]
Tuberous Sclerosis Alliance [15371]
Ukrainian Medical Assn. of North Am. [15182]
Union of Amer. Physicians and Dentists [24092]
Velo-Cardio-Facial Syndrome [14488]
Visiting Nurse Associations of Am. [15532]
Volunteer Trustees of Not-for-Profit Hospitals [14902]
Western Surgical Assn. [16592]

World Allergy Org. [13605]
World Fed. of Doctors Who Respect Human Life (U.S. Sect.) [16013]
World Fed. of Doctors Who Respect Human Life (U.S. Sect.) [IO]
World Fed. for Mental Hea. [15237]
World Homecare and Hospice Org. [14844]
World Medical Mission [20245]
World Spine Soc. [15405]
Physicians Abroad; Assn. of Haitian [15159]
Physicians Against Landmines [17434], c/o Center for Intl. Rehabilitation, 333 E Huron St., Ste. 225, Chicago, IL 60611, (312)926-0030
Physicians in Am; Assn. of Philippine Practicing [★15994]
Physicians; Amer. Acad. of Disability Evaluating [14033]
Physicians; Amer. Acad. of Family [14383]
Physicians; Amer. Acad. of Sports [16472]
Physicians; Amer. Assn. of Naturopathic [15280]
Physicians; Amer. Assn. of Parenthood [★12177]
Physicians; Amer. Assn. of Psychoanalytic [★16104]
Physicians; Amer. Assn. of Public Hea. [16235]
Physicians; Amer. Assn. of School [★14718]
Physicians; Amer. Assn. of Senior [★15155]
Physicians; Amer. Assn. of Women Emergency [14324]
Physicians; Amer. Bd. of Quality Assurance and Utilization Rev. [16260]
Physicians; Amer. Coll. of [★14966]
Physicians; Amer. Coll. of Emergency [14326]
Physicians; Amer. Coll. of Nuclear [15422]
Physicians; Amer. Coll. of Osteopathic Emergency [14327]
Physicians; Amer. Coll. of Osteopathic Family [15793]
Physicians; Amer. Osteopathic Bd. of Family [15799]
Physicians; Amer. Soc. of Bariatric [15575]
Physicians; Amer. Soc. of Handicapped [11919]
Physicians-American Soc. of Internal Medicine; Amer. Coll. of [14966]
Physicians; Amer. Soc. of Psychoanalytic [16104]
Physicians Assistants; Accreditation Comm. on Educ. for [★15972]
Physician's Assistants; Amer. Soc. of Orthopaedic [15760]
Physician's Assistants; Joint Rev. Comm. on Educational Programs for [★15972]
Physician's Assistants; Natl. Commn. on Certification of [★15975]
Physicians Assoc. for AIDS Care [★16001]
Physicians Assoc. for AIDS Care [★IO]
Physicians' Assn. for Anthroposophical Medicine [13646], 1923 Geddes Ave., Ann Arbor, MI 48104-1797, (734)930-9462
Physicians Assn; Flying [13731]
Physician's Assn; Natl. Osteopathic Women [24564]
Physicians; Assn. of Pakistani [★15993]
Physicians; Assn. of Planned Parenthood [★12177]
Physicians Assn; Renal [15298]
Physicians Assn. of Uzbekistan [IO], Tashkent, Uzbekistan
Physicians; Australasian Coll. of Sexual Hea. [IO]
Physicians for Automotive Safety - Defunct.
Physicians and Chirurgiens; Order of Descendants of Colonial [20752]
Physicians for Choice - Defunct.
Physicians Commn; Intl. [★17444]
Physicians' Comm; Amer. Jewish [★8676]
Physicians Comm. for Responsible Medicine [14595], 5100 Wisconsin Ave. NW, Ste. 400, Washington, DC 20016, (202)686-2210
Physicians' Coun. - Defunct.
Physicians and Dentists; Union of Amer. [24092]
Physicians Educ. Found; Amer. Acad. of Pharmaceutical [★8840]
Physicians Education Network - Address unknown since 1999.
Physicians Fellowship for the Israel Medical Assn; Amer. [★12456]
Physicians Forum - Address unknown since 2001.
Physicians for Global Survival [IO], Ottawa, ON, Canada
Physicians Guilds; Natl. Fed. of Catholic [★15996]
Physicians for Human Rights [17783], 2 Arrow St., Ste. 301, Cambridge, MA 02138, (617)301-4200

Reference to "IO" in place of a book number signifies that the association may be found in the 45th edition of International Organizations.

Physicians for Human Rights [IO], Cambridge, MA, United States
Physicians for Human Rights; Amer. Assn. of [★14431]
Physicians for Human Rights; Bay Area [12218]
Physicians for Human Rights - Israel [IO], Tel Aviv, Israel
Physicians for Human Rights (UK) [IO], Dundee, United Kingdom
Physicians for Moral Responsibility - Defunct.
Physicians; Natl. Assn. of EMS [14336]
Physicians for a Natl. Hea. Prog. [18313], 29 E Madison St., Ste. 602, Chicago, IL 60602, (312)782-6006
Physicians Natl. Housestaff Assn. - Defunct.
Physicians for Peace [15078], 229 W Bute St., Ste. 200, Norfolk, VA 23510, (757)625-7569
Physicians for Peace [IO], Norfolk, VA, United States
Physicians for Res. in Cost-Effectiveness - Address unknown since 1999.
Physicians for Social Responsibility [18169], 1875 Connecticut Ave. NW, Ste. 1012, Washington, DC 20009, (202)667-4260
Physicians for Social Responsibility [IO], Washington, DC, United States
Physicians for Social Responsibility - Finland [IO], Helsinki, Finland
Physicians; Soc. of Air Force [15264]
Physicians and Surgeons; Natl. Bd. of Examiners for Osteopathic [★15812]
Physicians and Surgeons of the U.S.A; Royal Coll. of [16694]
Physicians; Uniformed Services Acad. of Family [15268]
Physicians for a Violence-Free Soc. [12985]
Physicians Who Care - Defunct.
Physicists in Medicine; Amer. Assn. of [16014]
Physicists; Natl. Soc. of Black [7504]
Physicists; Soc. of Exploration Geo- [7149]
Physicists and Well Log Analysts; Soc. of Petro [7466]

Physics
Abdus Salam Intl. Centre for Theoretical Physics [IO]
Acoustical Soc. of Am. [6364]
Adhesion Soc. [6661]
Amer. Assn. for Crystal Growth [6851]
Amer. Assn. of Physicists in Medicine [16014]
American Association of Physicists in Medicine [IO]
Amer. Assn. of Physics Teachers [8993]
Amer. Bd. of Hea. Physics [16015]
Amer. Bd. of Radiology [16272]
Amer. Carbon Soc. [6663]
Amer. Center for Physics [7498]
Amer. Coll. of Medical Physics [16016]
Amer. Crystallographic Assn. [6852]
Amer. Inst. of Physics [7499]
Amer. Nuclear Soc. [7385]
Amer. Physical Soc. [7500]
Amer. Physical Soc. [IO]
Armenian Physical Soc. [IO]
Asian Physics Educ. Network - UNESCO Representative [IO]
Assn. of Asia Pacific Physical Societies [IO]
Assn. of Medical Physicists of India [IO]
Assn. of Physical Scientists in Medicine [IO]
Australasian Coll. of Physical Scientists and Engineers in Medicine [IO]
Australian Inst. of Physics [IO]
Austrian Physical Soc. [IO]
Balkan Physical Union [IO]
Belarusian Physical Soc. [IO]
Belgian Physical Soc. [IO]
British Soc. of Rheology [IO]
British Vacuum Coun. [IO]
Canadian Assn. of Physicists [IO]
Canadian Coll. of Physicists in Medicine [IO]
Carnegie Institution of Washington [7564]
Chemistry and Physics on Stamps Stud. Unit [22802]
Colombian Soc. of Physics [IO]
Combustion Inst. [6709]
Coun. on Ionizing Radiation Measurements and Standards [7556]

Coun. on Undergraduate Res. [9059]
Croatian Physical Soc. [IO]
Cryogenic Engg. Conf. [6843]
Danish Physical Soc. [IO]
Danish Soc. for Medical Physics [IO]
Electrochemical Soc. [6680]
Environmental and Engg. Geophysical Soc. [7140]
Estonian Physical Soc. [IO]
Euler Soc. [10453]
European Physical Soc. [IO]
European Physics Educ. Network [IO]
Fiber Soc. [7078]
Finnish Physical Soc. [IO]
Found. for Fundamental Res. on Matter [IO]
French Physical Soc. [IO]
Geochemical Soc. [7141]
German Physical Soc. [IO]
Hea. Physics Soc. [16017]
Hellenic Physical Soc. [IO]
Icelandic Physical Soc. [IO]
Indian Physics Assn. [IO]
Inst. of Physics [IO]
Inst. of Physics [7501]
Inst. of Physics, Singapore [IO]
Intl. Assn. of Mathematical Physics [IO]
Intl. Assn. of Nanotechnology [7741]
Intl. Assn. of Physics Students [IO]
Intl. Comm. on Ultra-High Intensity Lasers [7245]
Intl. Cryogenic Materials Conf. [6846]
Intl. Gravity Bur. [IO]
Intl. Liquid Crystal Soc. [6853]
Intl. Org. for Medical Physics [16018]
Intl. Org. for Medical Physics [IO]
Intl. Quantum Structure Assn. [IO]
Intl. Soc. for Gen. Relativity and Gravitation [IO]
Intl. Soc. for Theoretical Chem. Physics [IO]
Intl. Union of Pure and Applied Physics [IO]
Intl. Union of Pure and Applied Physics - USA [IO]
Intl. Union of Pure and Applied Physics - USA [7502]
Israel Physical Soc. [IO]
Italian Assn. of Medical Physics [IO]
Italian Physical Soc. [IO]
Japan Soc. of Applied Physics [IO]
Japan Soc. of Microgravity Application [IO]
JILA [7503]
Latin Amer. Center of Physics [IO]
Latvian Physical Soc. [IO]
Lithuanian Physical Soc. [IO]
Natl. Soc. of Black Physicists [7504]
Natl. Soc. of Hispanic Physicists [7505]
Netherlands Physical Soc. [IO]
Neutron Scattering Soc. of Am. [7506]
New Zealand Inst. of Physics [IO]
Nordic Inst. for Theoretical Physics [IO]
Norwegian Physical Soc. [IO]
Overseas Chinese Physics Assn. [7507]
Physical Soc. of Japan [IO]
Physical Soc. of Republic of China [IO]
Polish Physical Soc. [IO]
Radiation Res. Soc. [7557]
Radiological Soc. of North Am. [16293]
Sci. Comm. on Solar Terrestrial Physics [7508]
Sci. Comm. on Solar Terrestrial Physics [IO]
Sigma Pi Sigma [24575]
Slovak Physical Soc. [IO]
Soc. of Exploration Geo-physicists [7149]
Soc. of Mathematicians, Physicists and Astronomers of Slovenia [IO]
Soc. of Physicists of the Republic of Macedonia [IO]
Soc. of Physics Students [7509]
Soc. of Rheology [7579]
Soil Sci. Soc. of Am. [7674]
South African Medical Physics Soc. [IO]
Spanish Royal Soc. of Physics [IO]
Spanish Soc. of Gravitation and Relativity [IO]
Swedish Physical Soc. [IO]
Swiss Physical Soc. [IO]
Turkish Physical Soc. [IO]
Ukrainian Physical Soc. [IO]
Union of Czech Mathematicians and Physicists [IO]
Union of the Physicists in Bulgaria [IO]

Physics Gp; Women in [IO]
Physics; Inter-Union Commn. on Solar Terrestrial [★7508]
Physics on Stamps Stud. Unit; Chemistry and [22802]
Physics Stud. Unit; Chemistry and [★22802]
Physiological and Natural Hygiene Soc; Amer. [★15279]
Physiological and Pharmacological Soc. - Belgium [IO], Gent, Belgium
Physiological Res; Soc. for Psycho [16183]
Physiological Soc. - France [IO], Angers, France
Physiological Soc. - Ghana [IO], Accra, Ghana
Physiological Soc. - Hungary [IO], Debrecen, Hungary
Physiological Soc. - Italy [IO], Catania, Italy
Physiological Soc. - Japan [IO], Tokyo, Japan
Physiological Soc. - Latvia [IO], Riga, Latvia
Physiological Soc. - Lithuania [IO], Kaunas, Lithuania
Physiological Soc. - Netherlands [IO], Maastricht, Netherlands
Physiological Soc. of New Zealand [IO], Auckland, New Zealand
Physiological Soc. of Nigeria [IO], Lagos, Nigeria
Physiological Soc. - Poland [IO], Krakow, Poland
Physiological Soc. - Romania [IO], Targu Mures, Romania
Physiological Soc. - Spain [IO], Santa Cruz de Tenerife, Spain
Physiological Soc. of Thailand [IO], Bangkok, Thailand
Physiological Soc. - Turkey [IO], Konya, Turkey
Physiological Soc. - UK [IO], London, United Kingdom
Physiological Soc. - Ukraine [IO], Kiev, Ukraine
Physiological Stud. of Sleep; Assn. for the Psycho [★16429]
Physiological Therapeutics and Rehabilitation; Coun. of Chiropractic [13999]
Physiologists; Soc. of Gen. [7511]

Physiology
African Assn. of Physiological Sciences [IO]
Amer. Physiological Soc. [7510]
Amer. Soc. of Exercise Physiologists [16019]
Amer. Soc. of Neurophysiological Monitoring [15381]
Archaeus Proj. [13625]
Assn. for Applied Psychophysiology and Biofeedback [13749]
Assn. of Polysomnographic Technologists [16423]
Australian Physiological Soc. [IO]
Australian Soc. of Plant Scientists [IO]
Austrian Physiological Soc. [IO]
Belarussian Physiological Soc. [IO]
Beritashvili Physiological Soc. of Georgia [IO]
Brazilian Soc. of Physiology [IO]
Cameroon Soc. of Physiological Sciences [IO]
Canadian Alliance of Physiotherapy Regulators [IO]
Canadian Physiological Soc. [IO]
Canadian Soc. of Plant Physiologists [IO]
Chilean Soc. of Physiological Sciences [IO]
Chinese Assn. for Physiological Sciences [IO]
Croatian Physiological Soc. [IO]
Cuban Soc. of Physiological Sciences [IO]
Czech Physiological Soc. [IO]
Deutsche Physiologische Gesellschaft [IO]
Dutch Physiological Soc. [IO]
Estonia Physiological Soc. [IO]
European Soc. of Comparative Physiology and Biochemistry [IO]
Fed. of Amer. Societies for Experimental Biology [6576]
Fed. of European Physiological Societies [IO]
Fed. of European Physiological Societies [IO]
Fed. of European Societies of Plant Biology [IO]
Finnish Physiological Soc. [IO]
German Soc. of Physiology [IO]
Hellenic Soc. of Physiology [IO]
Human Anatomy and Physiology Soc. [7951]
Hungarian Physiological Soc. [IO]
Indonesian Physiological Soc. [IO]
Intl. Assn. for the Stud. of Dreams [16426]
Intl. Cell Death Soc. [6854]

A star before a book entry number signifies that the name is not listed separately, but is mentioned within the entry.

Intl. Soc. for Developmental Psychobiology [16153]
Intl. Soc. for Interferon and Cytokine Res. [16351]
Intl. Soc. for Pathophysiology [IO]
Intl. Union of Physiological Sciences [IO]
Israel Soc. for Physiology and Pharmacology [IO]
Kazakh Physiology Soc. [IO]
Kenyan Physiological Soc. [IO]
Korean Physiological Soc. [IO]
Latvian Physiological Soc. [IO]
Lithuanian Physiological Soc. [IO]
North Amer. Soc. for Pediatric Medicine [15891]
Norwegian Physiotherapist Assn. [IO]
Pakistan Physiological Soc. [IO]
Physiological and Pharmacological Soc. - Belgium [IO]
Physiological Soc. - France [IO]
Physiological Soc. - Ghana [IO]
Physiological Soc. - Hungary [IO]
Physiological Soc. - Italy [IO]
Physiological Soc. - Japan [IO]
Physiological Soc. - Latvia [IO]
Physiological Soc. - Lithuania [IO]
Physiological Soc. - Netherlands [IO]
Physiological Soc. of New Zealand [IO]
Physiological Soc. of Nigeria [IO]
Physiological Soc. - Poland [IO]
Physiological Soc. - Romania [IO]
Physiological Soc. - Spain [IO]
Physiological Soc. of Thailand [IO]
Physiological Soc. - Turkey [IO]
Physiological Soc. - UK [IO]
Physiological Soc. - Ukraine [IO]
Physiology Soc. of the Philippines [IO]
Physiology Soc. of Southern Africa [IO]
Physiology Soc. of Sri Lanka [IO]
Polish Physiological Soc. [IO]
Portuguese Physiological Soc. [IO]
Romanian Soc. of Physiological Sciences [IO]
Royal Academies for Sci. and the Arts of Belgium [IO]
Russian Physiological Soc. [IO]
Scandinavian Physiological Soc. [IO]
Scandinavian Soc. of Clinical Physiology and Nuclear Medicine [IO]
Serbian Physiological Soc. [IO]
Slovak Physiological Soc. [IO]
Slovakian Physiological Soc. [IO]
Slovene Physiological Soc. [IO]
Sociedad Argentina de Fisiologica [IO]
Sociedad Mexicana de Ciencias Fisiologicas, A.C. [IO]
Soc. of Biological Psychiatry [16095]
Soc. of Gen. Physiologists [7511]
Soc. for Male Reproduction and Urology [16343]
Sport Physiotherapy Canada [IO]
Swedish Natl. Comm. on Physiology [IO]
Swiss Physiological Soc. [IO]
Turkish Soc. of Physiological Sciences [IO]
Ukraine Physiological Soc. [IO]
Venezuelan Physiological Soc. [IO]
Yoga Alliance [11220]
Physiology; North Amer. Soc. of Pacing and Electro [★13907]
Physiology Soc; Human Anatomy and [7951]
Physiology Soc. of the Philippines [IO], Quezon City, Philippines
Physiology; Soc. for Plant Morphology and [★6632]
Physiology Soc. of Southern Africa [IO], Matieland, Republic of South Africa
Physiology Soc. of Sri Lanka [IO], Nugegoda, Sri Lanka
Physiotherapeuten Verband Furstentum Liechtenstein [IO], Schaan, Liechtenstein
Physiotherapists; Irish Soc. of Chartered [IO]
Physiotherapists; Swedish Assn. of Registered [IO]
Physiotherapy; Amer. Coun. on Chiropractic [★13999]
Physiotherapy Assn; Amer. [★16603]
Physiotherapy Assn; Australian [IO]
Physiotherapy Assn; Canadian [IO]
Physiotherapy Assn. of Malawi [IO], Lilongwe, Malawi
Physiotherapy Assn. of Trinidad and Tobago [IO], Port of Spain, Trinidad and Tobago

Physiotherapy; Chartered Soc. of [IO]
Physiotherapy; German Assn. for [IO]
Physiotherapy and Rehabilitation Support for Afghanistan [IO], Kabul, Afghanistan
Phytochemical Gp. [★IO]
Phytochemical Soc. [★IO]
Phytochemical Soc. of Europe [IO], Pulawy, Poland
Phytochemical Soc. of Europe - United Kingdom [IO], London, United Kingdom
Phytopathological Soc; Amer. [6626]
Phytopathological Soc; Canadian [IO]
Phytopathological Soc. of Japan [IO], Tokyo, Japan
Phytopathology Assn; Latin Amer. [IO]
Pi Alpha Alpha [24581], c/o NASPAA, 1029 Vermont Ave. NW, Ste. 1100, Washington, DC 20005, (202)628-8965
Pi Alpha Kappa - Address unknown since 1999.
Pi Alpha Mu - Address unknown since 1995.
Pi Alpha Nu - Defunct.
Pi Beta Alpha - Defunct.
Pi Beta Phi [24648], 1154 Town and Country Commons Dr., Town and Country, MO 63017-8200, (636)256-0680
Pi Delta Phi [24490], c/o Dr. Pamela Park, Exec. Dir., Idaho State Univ., Dept. of Foreign Languages, Box 8350, Pocatello, ID 83209, (208)282-3740
Pi Delta Psi Fraternity [24649], PO Box 2920, New York, NY 10008-2920
Pi Gamma Mu [24672], 1001 Millington St., Ste. B, Winfield, KS 67156, (620)221-3128
Pi Gamma Mu [IO], Winfield, KS, United States
Pi Kappa Alpha [24650], 8347 W Range Cove, Memphis, TN 38125, (901)748-1868
Pi Kappa Delta - Address unknown since 2002.
Pi Kappa Lambda [24556], c/o Mark Lochstampfor, Exec. Dir., Capital Univ., Conservatory of Music, 1 Coll. and Main, Columbus, OH 43209, (614)236-7211
Pi Kappa Phi [24651], PO Box 240526, Charlotte, NC 28224, (704)504-0888
Pi Kappa Sigma [★24696]
Pi Lambda Phi Fraternity [24652], 304 Fed. Rd., Ste. 113, Brookfield, CT 06804-2420, (203)740-1044
Pi Lambda Theta [24457], 4101 E 3rd St., PO Box 6626, Bloomington, IN 47407-6626, (800)487-3411
Pi Mu Epsilon [24539], c/o Leo J. Schneider, Sec.-Treas., John Carroll Univ., Dept. of Mathematics and Cmpt. Sci., University Heights, OH 44118-4581, (216)397-4481
Pi Omega Pi [24427], c/o Dr. Lana Carnes, Pres., Coll. of Bus. and Tech., Eastern Kentucky Univ., 521 Lancaster Ave., Bus. and Tech. Center 011, Richmond, KY 40475, (859)622-8005
Pi Omicron Natl. Sorority [24601]
Pi Sigma Alpha [24576], 1527 New Hampshire Ave. NW, Washington, DC 20036-1203, (202)483-2512
Pi Sigma Alpha, the Natl. Political Sci. Honor Soc. [★24576]
Pi Sigma Epsilon [24536], 3747 S Howell Ave., Milwaukee, WI 53207-3870, (414)328-1952
Pi Tau Delta - Address unknown since 1989.
Pi Tau Sigma [24465], c/o Dr. Farrokh Mistree, Natl. Sec.-Treas., Georgia Inst. of Tech., Woodruff School of Mech. Engg., Systems Realization Lab, Atlanta, GA 30332-0405, (404)894-8412
Pi Tau Sigma [IO], Atlanta, GA, United States
PIA Natl. [★2215]
Pia Zadora Fan Club - Address unknown since 1995.
Piaget Soc; Jean [★16156]
Piaget Soc.: Soc. for the Stud. of Knowledge and Development; Jean [16156]
Pianists Assn; Amer. [22709]
Pianists Found. of America - Defunct.
Piano Enthusiast Club; Miniature [22072]
Piano Found; Natl. [8927]
Piano Mfrs. Assn. of Am; Natl. [★2821]
Piano Mfrs. Assn. Intl. [2821], c/o Donald W. Dillon, Exec. Dir., 5960 W Parker Rd., Ste. 278, No. 233, Plano, TX 75093-7792, (972)625-0110
Piano Mfrs. Assn. Intl. [IO], Plano, TX, United States
Piano Teachers; Natl. Guild of [8925]
Piano Technicians; Amer. Soc. of [★2822]

Piano Technicians Guild [2822], 4444 Forest Ave., Kansas City, KS 66106-3750, (913)432-9975
Piano Tuners; Natl. Assn. of [★2822]
Pianoforte Tuners' Assn. [IO], Herne Bay, United Kingdom
Piccole Apostole della Carita [★IO]
Pickard Collectors Club [22108], 300 E Grove St., Bloomington, IL 61701, (309)828-5533
Pickle Packers Assn; Natl. [★1557]
Pickle Packers Intl. [1557], 1620 I St. NW, Ste. 925, Washington, DC 20006, (202)331-2456
Pickle Packers Intl. [IO], Washington, DC, United States
Picon [IO], Godalming, United Kingdom
Pictographs; Amer. Comm. to Advance the Study of Petroglyphs and [6437]
Pictorial Res. Associates; U.S. 1869 [★22887]
Pictorial Cancellation Soc. - Defunct.
Pictorial Photographers of Am. [10856], c/o Jack Levy, Treas., 300 E 74th St., Apt. 35G, New York, NY 10021-3717, (212)243-0273
Picture Agency Coun. of Am. [★3008]
Picture Archv. Coun. of Am. [3008], c/o Cathy Aron, Exec. Dir., 23046 Avenida de la Carlota, Ste. 600, Laguna Hills, CA 92653-1537, (949)282-5065
Picture Art Directors; Soc. of Motion [★9929]
Picture Exhibitors; Allied States Assn. of Motion [★1315]
Picture and Frame Inst. - Defunct.
Picture Framers Assn; Professional [9467]
Picture Peace - Defunct.
Picture Professionals; Amer. Soc. of [2993]
Picture and TV Credit Managers Assn; Motion [★1434]
Pie Coun; Amer. [446]
Pie Filling Inst. - Defunct.
Piece Goods Buyers Assn. - Defunct.
Piece Goods Salesmen's Assn. [★3782]
Piedmontese Assn; Amer. [★4287]
Piedmontese Assn; North Amer. [4282]
Piedmontese Assn. of the U.S. [4287], 343 Barrett Rd. 1, Elsberry, MO 63343-4137, (573)384-5685
Pierce-Arrow Soc. [21761], PO Box 16022, Oakland, CA 94610-6022
Pierce-Arrow Soc. [IO], Oakland, CA, United States
Pierce Brosnan Fan Club - Defunct.
Pierce Butler, Jr. Found. for Educ. in World Law [★18834]
Piercers; Assn. of Professional [3715]
Pierre Bowdoin/Baudoin Family Assn. - Address unknown since 2003.
Pierre Chastain Family Assn. [21023], c/o Susan Slape-Hoysagk, Membership Chair/Ed., 92012 Hagen Dr., Astoria, OR 97103
Pierre Fauchard Acad. [14184], PO Box 3718, Mesquite, NV 89024-3718, (702)345-4450
Pierre Robin Network [14473], 3604 Biscayne St., Quincy, IL 62305
Piezoceramic Mfrs. Assn. - Defunct.
Pig Assn; Natl. Show [22982]
Pig Assn; North Amer. Potbellied [4145]
Pig Carvers Assn; Natl. [22169]
Pig Refuge; Safe Harbour [★11454]
Pig Rescue; Pot Belly [11450]
Pig Res. Coun. [★IO]
Pig Res. and Development Corp. [★IO]
Pigeon Assn; Natl. [21856]
Pigeons
Amer. Racing Pigeon Union [22894]
Dove Sportsman's Soc. [11515]
Intl. Fed. of Amer. Homing Pigeon Fanciers [22895]
Intl. Fed. of Amer. Homing Pigeon Fanciers [IO]
Intl. Modena Club [22896]
Pigging Products and Services Assn. [IO], Stroud, United Kingdom
Piggly Wiggly Operators Assn; Natl. [3422]
Pigment Cell Res; PanAmerican Soc. for [15111]
Pigments Manufacturers Assn; Color [868]
Pigments Mfrs; ETAD North Am. - Ecological and Toxicological Assn. of Dyes and Organic [5089]
PIGS - A Sanctuary [4147], 1112 Persimmon Ln., Shepherdstown, WV 25443, (304)262-0080
Pigs; Natl. Comm. on Pot Bellied [4140]
PIJAC Canada [IO], Ottawa, ON, Canada

Reference to "IO" in place of a book number signifies that the association may be found in the 45th edition of International Organizations.

Pile Driving Contractors Assn. **[1058]**, PO Box 66208, Orange Park, FL 32065, (904)215-4771
Pilgrim; The **[★20382]**
The Pilgrim **[★20382]**
Pilgrim Adventure **[IO]**, Tenby, United Kingdom
Pilgrim Edward Doty Soc. **[20756]**, c/o Mary Lee Merrill, Membership Chair, 52 Cushing Rd., PO Box 45, Warren, ME 04864
Pilgrim Fellowship **[20382]**
Pilgrim; Friends of Peace **[11116]**
Pilgrim Soc. **[21249]**, Pilgrim Hall Museum, 75 Court St., Plymouth, MA 02360, (508)746-1620
Pilgrims
  Gen. Soc. of Mayflower Descendants **[21247]**
  General Society of Mayflower Descendants **[IO]**
  Governor William Bradford Compact **[21248]**
  Pilgrim Soc. **[21249]**
  Pilgrims of the U.S. **[21250]**
  Pilgrims of the U.S. **[IO]**
Pilgrims of the U.S. **[IO]**, New York, NY, United States
Pilgrims of the U.S. **[21250]**
Pilipinas Aikido Propagation Assn. **[IO]**, Quezon City, Philippines
Pill Addicts Anonymous **[13274]**
Pillar Voluntary Sector Network **[IO]**, London, ON, Canada
Pills Anonymous **[13275]**, c/o CFR, 2740 Grant St., Concord, CA 94520
Pills Anonymous **[★13275]**
Pilot Assn; China-Burma-India Hump **[21391]**
Pilot Class 43-D Assn. **[21400]**, c/o Francis J. Dutko, 316 Florida Ave., Gulf Breeze, FL 32561, (850)932-3467
Pilot District Project - Defunct.
Pilot Dogs **[16881]**, 625 W Town St., Columbus, OH 43215, (614)221-6367
Pilot Intl. Found. **[★13058]**
Pilot Intl. Found. **[★IO]**
Pilot Intl. and Pilot Intl. Found. **[IO]**, Macon, GA, United States
Pilot Intl. and Pilot Intl. Found. **[13058]**, PO Box 4844, Macon, GA 31208-4844, (478)477-1208
Pilot Parents of Southern Arizona **[12581]**, 2600 N Wyatt Dr., Tucson, AZ 85712, (520)324-3150
Pilots of Am; Black **[435]**
Pilots Assn; Aircraft Owners and **[135]**
Pilots Assn; Allied **[24007]**
Pilots' Assn; Amer. **[2571]**
Pilots Assn; Canadian Air Line **[★24005]**
Pilots Assn; Cessna **[21436]**
Pilots' Assn; Cherokee **[21437]**
Pilots Assn; Christian **[20321]**
Pilots Assn; Independent **[24000]**
Pilots Assn; Natl. EMS **[14322]**
Pilots Assn; P-47 Thunderbolt **[21397]**
Pilots Assn; Precision Aerobatics Model **[21473]**
Pilots Assn; Seaplane **[167]**
Pilots Assn; Steward/Stewardess Div., Air Line **[★24009]**
Pilots Assn; U.S. **[168]**
Pilots Assn; U.S. Seaplane **[★167]**
Pilots Assn; Vietnam Helicopter **[21351]**
Pilots Bar Assn; Lawyer- **[5539]**
Pilots for Christ Intl. **[20028]**, 7869 Meadowgate Dr., Manassas, VA 20112, (540)439-0940
Pilots for Christ Intl. **[IO]**, Manassas, VA, United States
Pilots, ILA, AFL-CIO; Intl. Org. of Masters, Mates and **[24128]**
Pilots Intl. Assn. - Address unknown since 2008.
Pilots; Intl. Assn. of Military Flight Surgeon- **[13541]**
Pilots; Intl. Social Affiliation of Women Airline **[★157]**
Pilots; Natl. Assn. of Priest **[19667]**
Pilots; Org. of Black Airline **[164]**
Pilots and Passengers Assn. - Defunct.
Pilots Rights Assn. - Address unknown since 2003.
Pilots Security Alliance; Airline **[432]**
Pilots; Soc. of Experimental Test **[6384]**
Pilots WWII; Women Airforce Ser. **[21413]**
Pilsudski Inst. of Am. for Res. in the Modern History of Poland; Jozef **[10878]**
PIMA - Agricultural Manufacturers of Canada **[IO]**, Regina, SK, Canada
Pin, Clip and Fastener Services - Address unknown since 1999.

Pinball Owner's Assn. **[IO]**, Cambridge, United Kingdom
Pine Assn; Northwest **[★1613]**
Pine Assn; Western **[★1631]**
Pine Bluff Cotton Exchange - Defunct.
Pine Chemicals Assn. **[818]**, 3350 Riverwood Pkwy. SE, Ste. 1900, Atlanta, GA 30339, (770)984-5340
Pine Coun; Southern **[4057]**
Pine Creek Railroad **[22935]**, c/o N.J. Museum of Trans., PO Box 622, Farmingdale, NJ 07727-0622, (732)938-5524
Pine Inspection Bur; Southern **[1623]**
Pine Lumber Manufacturers; Southern **[★1623]**
Pine Woodwork Assn; Ponderosa **[★686]**
Pineapple
  Pineapple Growers Assn. of Hawaii **[4756]**
Pineapple Growers Assn. of Hawaii **[4756]**
Pineapple Producers Cooperative Assn. **[★4756]**
Pineapple Res. Inst. of Hawaii - Defunct.
Pinellas County; Guardian Assn. of **[★12266]**
Pinnatus; Soc. of Tympanuchus Cupido **[5383]**
Pinscher Club of Am; Doberman **[22257]**
Pinscher Club of Am; Miniature **[22308]**
Pinto Arabian Registry; Amer. **[4837]**
Pinto Horse Assn. of Am. **[4944]**, 7330 NW 23rd St., Bethany, OK 73008, (405)491-0111
Pinzgauer Assn; Amer. **[4241]**
Pioneer America Soc. - Address unknown since 2002.
Pioneer Auto. Touring Club **[21762]**
Pioneer Buttermakers' Club of America - Address unknown since 1995.
Pioneer Centennial Comm; Swedish **[★10989]**
Pioneer Clubs **[20642]**, PO Box 788, Wheaton, IL 60189-0788, (630)293-1600
Pioneer Dairymen's Club of Am. **[4490]**, 3097 145th St. NW, Monticello, MN 55362, (763)878-2636
Pioneer Fraternal Assn. - Address unknown since 1995.
Pioneer Girls **[★20642]**
Pioneer Girls, Pioneer Boys **[★20642]**
Pioneer Historical Soc; Swedish **[★10989]**
Pioneer Memorial and Educational Found; Willa Cather **[9722]**
Pioneer Numismatists; Soc. of Private and **[22758]**
Pioneer Rivermen; Sons and Daughters of **[21258]**
Pioneer TV and Electronic Technicians Soc. - Defunct.
Pioneer Total Abstinence Assn. **[IO]**, Dublin, Ireland
Pioneer Women/Na'amat, the Women's Labor Zionist Org. of Am, **[★20162]**
Pioneer Women, The Women's Labor Zionist Org. of Am. **[★20162]**
Pioneer Youth - Address unknown since 1995.
Pioneers
  Alaska Yukon Pioneers **[21251]**
  Intl. Soc. Daughters of Utah Pioneers **[21252]**
  Intl. Soc. Daughters of Utah Pioneers **[IO]**
  Midwest Old Settlers and Threshers Assn. **[9483]**
  Natl. Cowboy and Western Heritage Museum **[9381]**
  Natl. Soc. - First Families of Minnesota **[21253]**
  Natl. Soc. of the Sons of Utah Pioneers **[21254]**
  Pennsylvania German Soc. **[21243]**
  Soc. of California Pioneers **[21255]**
  Soc. of Indiana Pioneers **[21256]**
  Sons and Daughters of Oregon Pioneers **[21257]**
  Sons and Daughters of Pioneer Rivermen **[21258]**
Pioneers of Am; Telephone **[★12203]**
Pioneers; Amer. **[★21067]**
Pioneers; Lutheran Girl **[20221]**
Pioneers; Natl. Soc. Daughters of Utah **[★21252]**
Pioneers; Soc. of Indiana **[21256]**
Pioneers; Sons of Utah **[★21254]**
Pioneers; Telecom **[12203]**
Pionus Breeders Assn. **[21859]**, c/o Larry Ring, Chm., PO Box 150, Pilot Hill, CA 95664, (530)885-7868
Pionus Breeders Assn. **[IO]**, Pilot Hill, CA, United States
Pious Union of the Holy Spirit - Defunct.
Pious Union of Prayer **[19701]**
Pious Union of St. Joseph for the Dying - Defunct.
Pipe Assn; Corrugated Metal **[★3035]**
Pipe Assn; Corrugated Polyethylene **[3049]**

Pipe Assn; Natl. Corrugated Metal **[★3035]**
Pipe Coating Applicators; Natl. Assn. of **[852]**
Pipe Collectors Club of America - Defunct.
Pipe Division of the Soc. of the Plastics Indus; Thermoplastic **[★3038]**
Pipe Fabrication Inst. **[3036]**, 511 Ave. of the Americas, No. 601, New York, NY 10011, (514)634-3434
Pipe Fabricators Assn., Intl; Amer. Tube Assn. and Tube and **[★3040]**
Pipe Fitting Indus. of the U.S. and Canada; United Assn. of Journeymen and Apprentices of the Plumbing and **[★24164]**
Pipe Fitting, Sprinkler Fitting Indus. of the U.S. and Canada; United Assn. of Journeymen and Apprentices of the Plumbing, **[24164]**
Pipe Fittings Mfrs. Assn. **[★3025]**
Pipe Inst; Cast Iron **[★3029]**
Pipe Inst; Fiberglass Tank and **[979]**
Pipe Jacking Assn. **[IO]**, London, United Kingdom
Pipe Line Companies; Comm. for **[★2919]**
Pipe Line Contractors Assn. **[2945]**, 1700 Pacific Ave., Ste. 4100, Dallas, TX 75201-4675, (214)969-2700
Pipe Line Insurance Managers Conf. - Defunct.
Pipe Lines; Assn. of Oil **[2919]**
Pipe Mfrs; Natl. Clay **[★3034]**
Pipe Nipple Mfrs; Natl. Assn. of **[★3025]**
Pipe Organ Builders of Am; Assoc. **[2799]**
Pipe Plug Producers Coun. - Address unknown since 1995.
Pipe Producers; Assn. of Asbestos Cement **[★3026]**
Pipe Publicity Bur; Cast Iron **[★3029]**
Pipe Smoking
  Intl. Assn. of Pipe Smokers Clubs **[22897]**
  Intl. Assn. of Pipe Smokers Clubs **[IO]**
  North Amer. Soc. of Pipe Collectors **[22093]**
  The Universal Coterie of Pipe Smokers **[22898]**
Pipe Tobacco Coun. **[3821]**, 1707 H St. NW, Ste. 800, Washington, DC 20006, (202)223-8207
Pipe and Tobacco Coun. of America - Defunct.
Pipeline Indus. Guild **[IO]**, London, United Kingdom
Piper Club; Short Wing **[21475]**
Piper Owner Soc. **[21470]**, PO Box 5000, Iola, WI 54945, (715)445-5006
Pipes
  Amer. Concrete Pipe Assn. **[3023]**
  Amer. Concrete Pressure Pipe Assn. **[3024]**
  Amer. Pipe Fittings Assn. **[3025]**
  Assn. of Asbestos Cement Prdt. Producers **[3026]**
  Assn. of Steam Boiler, Pressure Vessel and Piping Manufacturers **[IO]**
  Canadian Concrete Pipe Assn. **[IO]**
  Cast Iron Soil Pipe Inst. **[3027]**
  Concrete Pipe Assn. of Australasia **[IO]**
  Concrete Pipe Associations **[3028]**
  Concrete Pipeline Systems Assn. **[IO]**
  Corrugated Polyethylene Pipe Assn. **[3049]**
  Distribution Contractors Assn. **[24162]**
  Ductile Iron Pipe Res. Assn. **[3029]**
  European Tube Mfrs. Assn. **[IO]**
  Expansion Joint Mfrs. Assn. **[3030]**
  Intl. Assn. of Pipe Smokers Clubs **[22897]**
  Intl. Tube Assn. **[IO]**
  Intervention and Coiled Tubing Assn. **[7512]**
  Mfrs. Standardization Soc. of the Valve and Fittings Indus. **[2040]**
  Natl. Assn. of Pipe Fabricators **[3031]**
  Natl. Assn. of Steel Pipe Distributors **[3032]**
  Natl. Certified Pipe Welding Bur. **[3033]**
  Natl. Clay Pipe Inst. **[3034]**
  Natl. Coil Coating Assn. **[853]**
  Natl. Corrugated Steel Pipe Assn. **[3035]**
  North Amer. Soc. of Pipe Collectors **[22093]**
  Pipe Fabrication Inst. **[3036]**
  Plastic Pipe and Fittings Assn. **[3037]**
  Plastics Pipe Inst. **[3038]**
  Pressure Vessel Res. Coun. **[3039]**
  Tube and Pipe Assn., Intl. **[3040]**
  Tube and Pipe Assn., Intl. **[IO]**
  Uni-Bell PVC Pipe Association **[IO]**
  Uni-Bell PVC Pipe Assn. **[3041]**
  United Assn. of Journeymen and Apprentices of the Plumbing, Pipe Fitting, Sprinkler Fitting Indus. of the U.S. and Canada **[24164]**

A star before a book entry number signifies that the name is not listed separately, but is mentioned within the entry.

The Universal Coterie of Pipe Smokers [22898]
Piping and Air Conditioning Contractors Natl. Assn;
Heating and [★1033]
Piping Contractors Natl. Assn; Heating and [★1033]
Piping Engineers and Designers; Soc. of [7045]
PIRA Intl. [IO], Leatherhead, United Kingdom
Pirandello Soc. of Am. [9701], CNL Anne and Henry
Paolucci Intl. Conf. Center, 68-02 Metropolitan
Ave., Middle Village, NY 11379, (718)821-3916
Pirchei Agudath Israel [8699]
Piscataqua Pioneers - Address unknown since 2008.
Pisces Soc. of America - Defunct.
Pistachio Commn; California [5054]
Pistol Assn; Intl. Defensive [23718]
Pistol Collectors Assn; Natl. Automatic [21539]
Pit Bull Terrier
Amer. Dog Breeders Assn. [22197]
Natl. Amer. Pit Bull Terrier Assn. [22311]
Pit Bull Terrier Assn; Natl. Amer. [22311]
Pitcairn Islands Study Group - Defunct.
Pitch Assn; North Amer. Fast [23793]
Pitch-In Canada [IO], White Rock, BC, Canada
Pitch and Putt Union of Ireland [IO], Dublin, Ireland
Pitcher Collectors Assn. of Am; Whisky [22130]
Pitchers; Grand League of Amer. Horseshoe
[★23540]
Pitchers; Natl. Assn. of Horseshoe and Quoit
[★23540]
Pitless Adapter Division of Water Systems Coun.
[★4014]
Pitney Fan Club; Gene [★24898]
Pitney Intl. Fan Club; Gene [24898]
Pittsburgh Coal Mining Inst. of America - Address
unknown since 1994.
Pittsburgh Hornets Booster Club [★25012]
Pittsburgh Penguins Booster Club [25012], PO Box
903, Pittsburgh, PA 15230
Pittsburgh Transplant Found. [★16670]
Pituitary
Endocrine Soc. [14355]
Human Growth Found. [16020]
Natl. Hormone and Pituitary Prog. [16021]
Pituitary Found. [IO]
Pituitary Network Assn. [16022]
Pituitary Agency; Natl. [★16021]
Pituitary Found. [IO], Bristol, United Kingdom
Pituitary Network Assn. [16022], PO Box 1958,
Thousand Oaks, CA 91358, (805)499-9973
Pituitary Tumor Network Assn. [★16022]
Pius X Secular Inst. [19702], 27 Cove St., Manches-
ter, NH 03104, (603)622-4849
Pius X Secular Inst. [IO], Manchester, NH, United
States
Pizza Assn. [★IO]
Pizza Delivery Drivers; Assn. of [1579]
Pizza Inst; Natl. Frozen [1546]
Pizza, Pasta and Italian Food Assn. [IO], Chepstow,
United Kingdom
Pizzeria Operators; Natl. Assn. of [1953]
PKA Fighters Assn. - Defunct.
PKI Forum [★7780]
PKI Member Sect; OASIS [7780]
PKU Network; Children's [15245]
PKU Parents - Address unknown since 2001.
Placement
Amer. Assn. for Employment in Educ. [8994]
Aviation Maintenance Found. Intl. [143]
Employee Relocation Council/Worldwide ERC
[1261]
Intl. Assn. of Employment Web Sites [1266]
Natl. Assn. of Black Accountants [44]
Natl. Assn. of Colleges and Employers [8995]
Natl. Student Employment Assn. [8996]
Placement of Children; Assn. of Administrators of the
Interstate Compact on the [11559]
Placement; Natl. Assn. for Law [8770]
Placement Personnel Officers; Natl. Assn. of
[★8961]
Placement Services; Coll. [★8047]
Placename Survey of the U.S. - Address unknown
since 1990.
Plagiocephaly Support; Craniosynostosis and
Positional [14060]
Plaid Cymru - The Party of Wales [IO], Cardiff,
United Kingdom

Plain Managers; Assn. of State Flood [4362]
Plain Talk - Defunct.
Plains Booksellers Assn; Mountains and [741]
Plains Cotton Growers [4315], 4517 W Loop 289,
Lubbock, TX 79414, (806)792-4904
Plains Historical Assn; Great [★9994]
Plaintiff Employment Lawyers Assn. [★5520]
Plan of Action for Challenging Times [8331], 635
Divisadero St., San Francisco, CA 94117,
(415)922-2550
Plan Intl. [IO], Woking, United Kingdom
Plan Intl. Deutschland e.V. [★IO]
PLAN Intl. - U.S.A. [★IO]
PLAN Intl. - U.S.A. [★11681]
Plan Japan [IO], Tokyo, Japan
Plan Netherlands [IO], Amsterdam, Netherlands
Plan - United Kingdom [IO], London, United
Kingdom
Plane Assn; Natl. Bi [21465]
Planet 21 [IO], Bern, Switzerland
Planet Aid [IO], Holliston, MA, United States
Planet Aid [13144], One Cross St., Holliston, MA
01746, (508)893-0644
Planet Ark [IO], Sydney, Australia
Planet Ark Environmental Found. [★IO]
Planet Club [IO], Budapest, Hungary
Planet Drum Found. [IO], San Francisco, CA, United
States
Planet Drum Found. [16999], PO Box 31251,
Shasta Bioregion, USA, San Francisco, CA 94131,
(415)285-6556
Planet Peace - Address unknown since 2004.
Planeta Sustenable [IO], Mexico City, Mexico
Planetarium Educators; Intl. Soc. of [★6508]
Planetarium Soc; Middle Atlantic [9105]
Planetary Assn. for Clean Energy [IO], Ottawa, ON,
Canada
Planetary Citizens [IO], Mount Shasta, CA, United
States
Planetary Citizens [18838], PO Box 1056, Mount
Shasta, CA 96067, (530)926-6424
Planetary Gemologists Assn. [IO], Bangkok,
Thailand
Planetary Observers; Assn. of Lunar and [21550]
The Planetary Soc. [6382], 65 N Catalina Ave.,
Pasadena, CA 91106-2301, (626)793-5100
The Planetary Soc. [IO], Pasadena, CA, United
States
The Planetary Soc. of Youth [IO], Bagalkot, India
PlanetMUG [6819], PO Box 1264, Fremont, CA
94538-0126
PlanetRead [8796], 26 Manor Dr., Piedmont, CA
94611, (510)435-3175
PlanetRead [IO], Piedmont, CA, United States
Planetree [14596], 130 Div. St., Derby, CT 06418,
(203)732-1365
Planets; Intl; United Fed. of [25020]
Planned Giving; Natl. Comm. on [1689]
Planned Parenthood [★12187]
Planned Parenthood Assn. of Sierra Leone [IO],
Freetown, Sierra Leone
Planned Parenthood Assn. of South Africa [IO], Sax-
onwold, Republic of South Africa
Planned Parenthood Assn. of Thailand [IO],
Bangkok, Thailand
Planned Parenthood Edmonton [IO], Edmonton, AB,
Canada
Planned Parenthood Fed. of Am. [12187], 434 W
33rd St., New York, NY 10001, (212)541-7800
Planned Parenthood Fed. of Am; Res. and Develop-
ment Division of [★12175]
Planned Parenthood Fed. of Canada [★IO]
Planned Parenthood Fed. of Nigeria [IO], Lagos,
Nigeria
Planned Parenthood/World Population [★12187]
Planners; Amer. Inst. of [★5586]
Planners; Amer. Inst. of Certified [5585]
Planners; Amer. Soc. of Consulting [5587]
Planners and Councils; Natl. Assn. of Estate [1466]
Planners for Equal Opportunity - Defunct.
Planners Inst; Registered Financial [1471]
Planners Intl; Meeting [★2686]
Planners; Natl. Assn. of County [5589]
Planners; Natl. Assn. of Mortgage [490]
Planners; Natl. Assn. of Recreation Rsrc. [6156]

Planners; Natl. Assn. of State Recreation [★6156]
Planners Network [18476], Cornell Univ., 106 W Sib-
ley Hall, Ithaca, NY 14853, (607)254-8890
Planners; Org. of Facility Managers and [★7167]
Planners for Social Responsibility; Architects/Design-
ers/ [18142]
Planning
Amer. Assn. of Cmpt. Rental Professionals [895]
Amer. Assn. of Wedding Planners [2654]
Amer. Inst. of Certified Planners [5585]
Amer. Planning Assn. [5586]
Amer. Soc. of Consulting Planners [5587]
Arab Planning Inst. [IO]
Asian Planning Schools Assn. [IO]
Assn. of European Schools of Planning [IO]
Assn. for Institutional Res. [8997]
Assn. of Metropolitan Planning Organizations
[17207]
Assn. for Strategic Planning [3042]
Capitol Hill Restoration Soc. [10017]
Center for Design Planning [5588]
Educational Planning Inst. [8998]
European Coun. of Town Planners [IO]
Genesis Fac. Found. [IO]
Inst. for Urban Design [6475]
Intl. Inst. of Site Planning [5465]
Intl. Production Planning and Scheduling Assn.
[8809]
The Intl. Publication Planning Assn. [3231]
Intl. Soc. for Educational Planning [8999]
Intl. Soc. for Educational Planning [IO]
Natl. Assn. of County Planners [5589]
Natl. Assn. of Development Organizations [5590]
Natl. Assn. of Financial and Estate Planning
[1437]
Natl. Assn. of Mental Hea. Planning and Advisory
Councils [15216]
Natl. Assn. of Mobile Entertainers [1314]
Natl. Assn. for Olmsted Parks [5591]
Natl. Assn. of Planning Councils [18275]
Natl. Assn. of Recreation Rsrc. Planners [6156]
Natl. Black Bridal Assn. [535]
Natl. Policy Assn. [5593]
Partners for Livable Communities [5594]
Rural Planning Organizations of Am. [6247]
Soc. for Coll. and Univ. Planning [9000]
State Higher Educ. Executive Officers [9001]
Value Engg. Soc. Intl. [7052]
Weddings Beautiful Worldwide [537]
Planning Administrators; Natl. Conf. of State Criminal
Justice [★11881]
Planning and Adult Development Network; Career
[12070]
Planning Advisory Service [★5586]
Planning Assistance [17846], 50 F St. NW, Ste.
1100, Washington, DC 20001, (202)879-0247
Planning Assistance [IO], Washington, DC, United
States
Planning Assn; Amer. [5586]
Planning; Assn. of Collegiate Schools of [9285]
Planning Assn; Natl. [★5593]
Planning Assn; Natl. Economic and Social [★5593]
Planning Attorneys; Natl. Network of Estate [5524]
Planning and the Black Community - Address
unknown since 2000.
Planning; Center for Design [5588]
Planning Councils; Natl. Assn. of Estate [★1466]
Planning and Development Agencies; Assn. of State
[★5592]
Planning and Development Collaborative Intl.
[18776], 1025 Thomas Jefferson St. NW, Ste. 170,
Washington, DC 20007, (202)337-2326
Planning and Development Collaborative Intl. [IO],
Washington, DC, United States
Planning Directors; Natl. Assn. of County [★5589]
Planning; Educational [★8999]
Planning Engineers Desktop Computer Users Group
- Defunct.
Planning Inst. Australia [IO], Kingston, Australia
Planning; Intl. Soc. for Educational [★8999]
Planning and Mgt. Assistance Proj. of the Center for
Community Change [★12655]
Planning; Natl. Conf. on City [★5586]
Planning; Natl. Coun. for Res. and [8121]
Planning Officials; Amer. Soc. of [★5586]

Reference to "IO" in place of a book number signifies that the association may be found in the 45th edition of International Organizations.

Planning Prog. Development; Center for Family [★12175]

Planning; Soc. for Coll. and Univ. [9000]

Planning Soc; Human Rsrc. [2496]

Planning and Visual Educ. Partnership [3426], 4651 Sheridan St., Ste. 470, Hollywood, FL 33021, (954)893-7225

Plans; Alliance of Community Hea. [14678]

Plant Anal. Coun; Soil and [7673]

Plant Anal. Coun. on Soil Testing and [★7673]

Plant Assn; Perennial [4985]

Plant Biologists; Amer. Soc. of [6628]

Plant Bd; Natl. [5440]

Plant Breeders; Natl. Coun. of Commercial [5175]

Plant Breeding Res. Forum - Defunct.

Plant Conservation; Center for [4372]

Plant Coun; People- [4518]

Plant Engg. and Maintenance Assn. of Canada [IO], Mississauga, ON, Canada

Plant Engineers; Amer. Inst. of [★7003]

Plant Food Control Officials; Assn. of Amer. [5433]

Plant Food Inst; Natl. [★1365]

Plant Growth Regulation Soc. of Am. [6647], c/o Mr. Charles Hall, Exec. Sec., PO Box 2945, LaGrange, GA 30241, (706)845-9085

Plant Growth Regulator Soc. of Am. [★6647]

Plant Growth Regulator Working Group [★6647]

Plant Mgt. Soc; Aquatic [6630]

Plant Microbe Interactions; Intl. Soc. for Molecular [6641]

Plant Molecular Biology Assn. [★6589]

Plant Molecular Biology Assn. [★IO]

Plant Morphology and Physiology; Soc. for [★6632]

Plant Patent Owners; Natl. Assn. of [5046]

Plant Pathology; Chinese Soc. for [IO]

Plant Phenolics Gp. [★IO]

Plant Preservation Coun; North Amer. [5356]

Plant Propagators Soc; Intl. [4981]

Plant Protection Assn. [24188], 302 N Huron, Ypsilanti, MI 48197, (734)487-5522

Plant Protection Comm. for the Southeast Asia and Pacific Region [★IO]

Plant Protection Employees; Independent Union of [★24188]

Plant Protection Sciences; Intl. Assn. for the [6397]

Plant Quarantine Inspectors Natl. Assn; Fed. [★5437]

Plant Savers; United [13655]

Plant Sci. Seminar [★15924]

Plant Sci. Seminar [★IO]

Plant Seeds of Hope [★19135]

Plant Taxonomists; Amer. Soc. of [6629]

Plant Yng Nghymru [★IO]

Planters Assn., Amer. Cane Growers Assn. and; Louisiana Sugar [★5225]

Planters' Labor and Supply Company [★5228]

Plantio La Orquidea [IO], Caracas, Venezuela

Plasma Protein Therapeutics Assn. [13765], 147 Old Solomons Island Rd., Ste. 100, Annapolis, MD 21401, (410)263-8296

Plasma Sciences Soc; IEEE Nuclear and [7386]

Plast, Ukrainian Scouting Org. - U.S.A. [19412], 144 2nd Ave., New York, NY 10003, (212)475-6960

Plaster

Natl. Plasterers Coun. [3043]

Plaster; Assoc. Institutes for Lath and [★1026]

Plaster; Intl. Inst. for Lath and [1026]

Plastercraft Assn. [★1913]

Plastercraft Assn; Natl. [1913]

Plasterers Intl. of Amer; Bricklayers, Masons and [★24027]

Plastering; Intl. Coun. for Lathing and [★1026]

Plastic Adhesive and Sealant Manufacturers Coun; Rubber and [★56]

Plastic Bag Assn. [★980]

Plastic Bottle Inst. - Defunct.

Plastic Coatings and Film Assn. [★3048]

Plastic Coatings and Film Assn. [★IO]

Plastic Container Mfrs. Inst. - Defunct.

Plastic Container Recovery; Natl. Assn. for [★3997]

Plastic Food Container Assn. - Defunct.

Plastic Lumber Trade Assn. [3055], PO Box 211, Worthington, MN 56187, (507)372-5558

Plastic and Metal Products Mfrs. Assn. [3056], 145 W 45th St., Ste. 800, New York, NY 10036, (212)398-5400

Plastic Modelers Society/United States Br; Intl. [22646]

Plastic Optical Fiber Trade Org. [2863], c/o Richard Beach, Dir., Beach Communications, 674 High St., Santa Cruz, CA 95060, (831)426-1424

Plastic Pipe and Fittings Assn. [3037], 800 Roosevelt Rd., Bldg. C, Ste. 312, Glen Ellyn, IL 60137, (630)858-6540

Plastic Products Mfrs. Assn. [★3056]

Plastic and Reconstructive Surgeons; Educ. Found. of Amer. Soc. of [★14051]

Plastic and Reconstructive Surgery; Amer. Acad. of Facial [14038]

Plastic and Reconstructive Surgery; Amer. Bd. of Facial [16562]

Plastic and Reconstructive Surgery; Amer. Soc. of Ophthalmic [14043]

Plastic and Reconstructive Surgical Nurses; Amer. Soc. of [★15461]

Plastic Representatives Mgt. Coun; Paper and [2645]

Plastic Shipping Container Inst. [992], 1700 Pennsylvania Ave. NW, Ste. 400, Washington, DC 20006, (202)349-4190

Plastic Soft Materials Mfrs. Assn. - Address unknown since 2003.

Plastic Surgeons; Amer. Assn. of [14040]

Plastic Surgeons; Amer. Assn. of Oral and [★14040]

Plastic Surgeons; Amer. Soc. of [14044]

Plastic Surgeons; Canadian Soc. of [IO]

Plastic Surgeons and Plastic Surgery Educ. Found; Amer. Soc. of [14045]

Plastic Surgery Administrative Assn. [14050], 6324 Fairview Ave. N, Crystal, MN 55428, (800)373-0302

Plastic Surgery; Amer. Bd. of [14041]

Plastic Surgery; Amer. Otorhinologic Soc. for [★14038]

Plastic Surgery; Amer. Soc. for Aesthetic [14042]

Plastic Surgery; Amer. Soc. of Facial [★14038]

Plastic Surgery; Assn. of Academic Chairmen of [14046]

Plastic Surgery Educational Found. [14051], 444 E Algonquin Rd., Arlington Heights, IL 60005, (847)228-9900

Plastic Surgery Facilities; Amer. Assn. for Accreditation of Ambulatory [★16557]

Plastic Surgery Res. Coun. [14052], 45 Lyme Rd., Ste. 304, Hanover, NH 03755, (603)643-2325

Plastic Surgery Research Council [IO], Hanover, NH, United States

Plastic Surgical Nurses; Amer. Soc. of [15461]

Plastica Infantil con Excelencia en el Logro [IO], Buenos Aires, Argentina

Plastics

All India Plastics Mfrs. Assn. [IO]

Alliance of Foam Packaging Recyclers [5265]

Amer. Collectors of Infant Feeders [21959]

Amer. Plastics Coun. [3044]

Assn. of Japan Plastics Machinery [IO]

Assn. of Postconsumer Plastic Recyclers [3045]

Assn. of Rotational Molders Intl. [3046]

Association of Rotational Molders International [IO]

Belgian Assn. of Plastics and Rubber Converters [IO]

British Laminate Fabricators Assn. [IO]

British Plastics Fed. [IO]

Canadian Plastics Indus. Assn. [IO]

Canadian Urethane Foam Contractors Assn. [IO]

Canadian Urethane Mfrs. Assn. [IO]

Center for the Polyurethanes Indus. [3047]

Chamber of Argentine Plastics Indus. [IO]

Chemical Fabrics and Film Association [IO]

Chem. Fabrics and Film Assn. [3048]

Construction and Agricultural Film Mfrs. Assn. [1369]

Corrugated Polyethylene Pipe Assn. [3049]

Corrugated Polyethylene Pipe Association [IO]

Costa Rican Assn. of the Plastic Indus. [IO]

Danish Plastics Fed. [IO]

EPS Molders Assn. [3050]

Euromoulders [IO]

European Assn. of Mfrs. of Moulded Polyurethane Parts for the Automotive Indus. [IO]

European Comm. of Machinery Mfrs. for the Plastics and Rubber Indus. [IO]

European Coun. for Plasticisers and Intermediates [IO]

European Coun. of Vinyl Manufacturers [IO]

European Plastics Converters [IO]

European Plastics Distributors Assn. [IO]

Fed. of European Rigid Polyurethane Foam Associations [IO]

Figures Collectors Club [22024]

Film and Bag Fed. [980]

Finnish Plastics Assn. [IO]

Glass Molders, Pottery, Plastics, and Allied Workers Intl. Union [24066]

Hong Kong Plastics Mfrs. Assn. [IO]

Indian Polyurethane Assn. [IO]

Intl. Assn. of Plastics Distributors [IO]

Intl. Assn. of Plastics Distributors [3051]

Intl. Assn. of Used Equip. Dealers [3052]

International Association of Used Equipment Dealers [IO]

Intl. Card Manufacturers Assn. [IO]

Intl. Card Mfrs. Assn. [3053]

Intl. Comm. of Plastics in Agriculture [IO]

Malaysian Plastic Manufacturers Assn. [IO]

Malaysian Plastics Manufacturers Assn. [IO]

Packaging and Indus. Films Assn. [IO]

PET Resin Assn. [3054]

Philippine Plastics Indus. Assn. [IO]

Plastic Lumber Trade Assn. [3055]

Plastic and Metal Products Mfrs. Assn. [3056]

Plastic Optical Fiber Trade Org. [2863]

Plastic Pipe and Fittings Assn. [3037]

Plastic Shipping Container Inst. [992]

Plastics and Chemicals Indus. Assn. [IO]

Plastics Export Promotion Coun. [IO]

Plastics Fed. [IO]

Plastics Historical Soc. [IO]

Plastics Injection Moulders Assn. [IO]

Plastics Inst. of Am. [7513]

Plastics Pipe Inst. [3038]

PlasticsEurope [IO]

Polymer Machinery Mfrs. and Distributors Assn. [IO]

Polyurethane Foam Assn. [3057]

Polyurethane Mfrs. Assn. [3058]

Portuguese Plastics Manufacturers' Assn. [IO]

Singapore Plastic Indus. Assn. [IO]

Society of Plastics Engineers [IO]

Soc. of Plastics Engineers [7514]

Soc. of the Plastics Indus. [3059]

Spanish Confed. of Plastics Indus. [IO]

Swedish Plastics and Chem. Fed. [IO]

Taiwan Plastics Indus. Assn. [IO]

Taiwan Regional Assn. of Synthetic Leather Indus. [IO]

Union of the Plastics and Rubber Indus. [IO]

United Steel Workers of Am., Rubber/Plastics Indus. Conf. [24183]

Verband der Polyurethan-Weichschaum Industrie [IO]

Vinyl Coun. of Australia [IO]

Plastics, and Allied Workers Intl. Union; Glass Molders, Pottery, [24066]

Plastics Assn; Natl. Agricultural [★4097]

Plastics and Bd. Indus. Fed. [IO], Devon, United Kingdom

Plastics and Chemicals Indus. Assn. [IO], Abbotsford, Australia

Plastics Distributors Assn; United [★3051]

Plastics Distributors; Natl. Assn. of [★3051]

Plastics Education Found. - Defunct.

Plastics Engineers Assn. - Defunct.

Plastics Engineers; Soc. of [7514]

Plastics Export Promotion Coun. [IO], Bombay, India

Plastics Fed. [IO], Paris, France

Plastics Fed. of South Africa [IO], Halfway House, Republic of South Africa

Plastics Foodservice Packaging Gp. [2879], c/o Amer. Chemistry Coun., 1300 Wilson Blvd., 8th Fl., Arlington, VA 22209, (703)741-5000

Plastics Historical Soc. [IO], Sidcup, United Kingdom

Plastics Indus. Conf; United Steel Workers of Am., Rubber/ [24183]

Plastics Indus; Polyurethane Div., Soc. of the [★3047]

A star before a book entry number signifies that the name is not listed separately, but is mentioned within the entry.

Plastics Indus. Polyurethane Div; Urethane Inst., Soc. of the [★3047]

Plastics Indus; Thermoplastic Exterior Building Division of the Soc. of the [★685]

Plastics Indus; Thermoplastic Pipe Division of the Soc. of the [★3038]

Plastics Injection Moulders Assn. [IO], Sydney, Australia

Plastics Inst. of Am. [7513], 600 Suffolk St., CVIP, 2nd Fl. S, Lowell, MA 01854, (978)934-3130

Plastics and Linoleums Export Promotion Coun. [★IO]

Plastics Pipe Inst. [3038], 105 Decker Ct., Ste. 825, Irving, TX 75062, (469)499-1044

Plastics Recycling Found. - Address unknown since 1999.

Plastics Res. in Dentistry; Amer. Acad. for [★14084]

Plastics Window Fed. [IO], Luton, United Kingdom

PlasticsEurope [IO], Brussels, Belgium

Plasticulture; Amer. Soc. for [4097]

Plastination; Intl. Soc. for [15870]

Plastindustrien i Danmark [★IO]

Plate Block Soc; Israel [22833]

Plate, Cup, Container, and Doily Inst. [★1157]

Plate, Cup, and Container Inst. [★1157]

Plate Inst; Truss [683]

Plate Number Single Soc; Amer. [22787]

Plate Number Soc. - Defunct.

Plate Printers, Die Stampers, and Engravers' Union of North Am; Intl. [24085]

Plate Soc; Intl. Gold and Silver [18977]

Platelet Disorder Support Assn. [13730], PO Box 61533, Potomac, MD 20859, (301)770-6636

Platemakers Educational and Res. Inst. [★7154]

Platemakers Educational and Res. Inst. [★IO]

Platemakers Guild; Collectibles and [★860]

Platemakers Guild; Collector [★860]

Platers and Allied Workers Intl. Union; Metal Polishers, Buffers, [★24021]

Platform Assn; Intl. [10901]

Platform for Peace - Defunct.

Platform Tennis Assn; Amer. [23899]

Platinum Guild Intl. USA [2381], 620 Newport Center Dr., Ste. 800, Newport Beach, CA 92660, (714)760-8279

Platinum Guild Intl. USA [IO], Newport Beach, CA, United States

Platinumsmiths Assn. of New York - Address unknown since 1995.

Platslageriernas Riksforbund [★IO]

Platt Family Assn. [21024], c/o Theodore Penick, Treas., 226 Birnam Rd., Northfield, MA 01360

Plattelands Jongeren Nederland [IO], Arnhem, Netherlands

The Platters Fan Club - Defunct.

Platteville Alumni Assn; Univ. of Wisconsin - [18941]

Play

Arthur Miller Soc. [11159]

The Assn. for the Stud. of Play [10858]

Boardgame Players Assn. [22461]

Collegiate Assn. of Table Top Gamers [22462]

Cormac McCarthy Soc. [11168]

Intl. Play Equip. Manufacturers Assn. [3060]

Intl. Play Equip. Manufacturers Assn. [IO]

Intl. Playground Contractors Assn. [1028]

KaBOOM! [12751]

Natl. Prog. for Playground Safety [18578]

Play for Peace [12699]

Playing for Keeps [11544]

Teachers Resisting Unhealthy Children's Entertainment [11657]

Thornton Wilder Soc. [11200]

U.S.A. Toy Lib. Assn. [11548]

Writers Workshop [11203]

Play; Assn. for the Anthropological Stud. of [★10858]

Play for Peace [12699], 1 E Superior St., Ste. 304, Chicago, IL 60611, (773)275-0077

Play for Peace [IO], Chicago, IL, United States

Play Schools Assn. - Address unknown since 2000.

Play Therapy; Assn. for [16607]

Play Therapy Intl. [IO], Uckfield, United Kingdom

Player Piano Gp. [IO], Hillesley, United Kingdom

The Players [11038], 16 Gramercy Park S, New York, NY 10003, (212)475-6116

Players Assn. of Am; Domino [22465]

Players Assn; Amer. Football League [★23434]

Players Assn; Ultimate [23375]

Players Assn; WTA Tour [23917]

Playground Safety; Natl. Prog. for [18578]

Playing 2 Win [8570], 1330 5th Ave., New York, NY 10026, (212)369-4077

Playing Card Collectors' Assn. - Defunct.

Playing Card Collectors; Chicago [21992]

Playing Card Collector's Club; Amer. Antique [★21955]

Playing Cards

52 Plus Joker [21955]

Cribbage Bd. Collectors Soc. [22004]

Natl. 42 Players Assn. [22899]

Playing for Keeps [11544], 116 W Illinois St., Ste. 5E, Chicago, IL 60610, (312)222-0982

Playing to Win [★8570]

PLAYLINK [IO], London, United Kingdom

Playthings, Novelties and Allied Prdts. of the U.S. and Canada; Intl. Union of Dolls, Toys, [★24196]

Playwrights Conf. [11039]

Playwrights Conf; Natl. [★11039]

Playwrights Guild of Canada [IO], Toronto, ON, Canada

Playwrights Union of Canada [★IO]

Pleasure Horse Assn; Amer. Saddlebred [★4842]

Pleasure Horse Assn; Intl. Amer. Saddlebred [★4842]

Pleasure Horse Assn; Mountain [4916]

Pleasure Horse Club of America - Defunct.

Pleaters, Stitchers and Embroiderers Assn. - Address unknown since 2006.

Pledge of Allegiance Found; Natl. [21241]

Pleiades Found. for Peace and Space Education - Defunct.

Plenty [★12878]

Plenty [★IO]

Plenty Canada [IO], Lanark, ON, Canada

Plenty Intl. [IO], Summertown, TN, United States

Plenty Intl. [12878], PO Box 394, Summertown, TN 38483, (931)964-4323

Plenty - U.S.A. [★12878]

Plenty - U.S.A. [★IO]

Plesna Zveza Slovenije [★IO]

Plesni Sporstki Savez Bosne I Hercegovine [★IO]

Plexus-Erb's Palsy Assn; Natl. Brachial [14277]

Plowing Org; U.S.A. [4660]

Plowshares Inst. [18240], 809 Hopmeadow St., PO Box 243, Simsbury, CT 06070-0243, (860)651-4304

Plum Bd; California Dried [4712]

Plumbers' Company [IO], London, United Kingdom

Plumbing

Amer. Soc. of Plumbing Engineers [6996]

Amer. Soc. of Sanitary Engg. [7590]

Amer. Supply Assn. [3061]

Assn. of Independent Manufacturers'/Representatives [2534]

Bath Enclosure Mfrs. Assn. [3062]

Bathroom Mfrs. Assn. [IO]

Building and Constr. Trades Dept. - AFL-CIO [24025]

Intl. Assn. of Plumbing and Mech. Officials [5549]

Natl. Assn. of Plumbing Specialty Distributors [3063]

Natl. Standard Plumbing Code Comm. [5553]

North Central Wholesalers Assn. [3064]

Plumbing Distributors Assn. of New Zealand [IO]

Plumbing and Drainage Inst. [3065]

Plumbing Mfrs. Inst. [3066]

Plumbing Manufacturers Institute [IO]

United Assn. of Journeymen and Apprentices of the Plumbing, Pipe Fitting, Sprinkler Fitting Indus. of the U.S. and Canada [24164]

Wholesale Distributors Assn. [3067]

World Plumbing Coun. [IO]

Plumbing Brass Inst. [★IO]

Plumbing Brass Inst. [★3066]

Plumbing Code Comm; Natl. Standard [5553]

Plumbing Distributors Assn. of New Zealand [IO], Auckland, New Zealand

Plumbing and Drainage Inst. [3065], 800 Turnpike St., Ste. 300, North Andover, MA 01845, (978)557-0720

Plumbing and Drainage Mfrs. Assn. [★3065]

Plumbing Employers' Fed; Scottish and Northern Ireland [IO]

Plumbing Engineers; Amer. Soc. of [6996]

Plumbing Engineers Res. Foundation; American Soc. of [★6996]

Plumbing Fixture Mfrs. Assn. - Defunct.

Plumbing and Heating; Canadian Inst. of [IO]

Plumbing-Heating-Cooling Contractors Assn. [1059], PO Box 6808, Falls Church, VA 22046, (703)237-8100

Plumbing-Heating-Cooling Contractors; Natl. Assn. of [★1059]

Plumbing, Heating and Cooling Information Bur. - Defunct.

Plumbing Mfrs. Inst. [3066], 1921 Rohlwing Rd., Unit G, Rolling Meadows, IL 60008, (847)481-5500

Plumbing Manufacturers Institute [IO], Schaumburg, IL, United States

Plumbing Officials Assn; Western [★5549]

Plumbing and Pipe Fitting Indus. of the U.S. and Canada; United Assn. of Journeymen and Apprentices of the [★24164]

Plumbing and Sanitary Engg; Amer. Soc. of Inspectors of [★7590]

Plumeria Soc. of Am. [22537], PO Box 22791, Houston, TX 77227-2791, (713)946-9175

Plunkett Found. [IO], Oxford, United Kingdom

Plymouth Barracuda/Cuda Owners Club [21763], c/o Ann M. Curman, Sec., 36 Woodland Rd., East Greenwich, RI 02818-3430

Plymouth Four Cylinder Owners Club [★21764]

Plymouth Four and Six Cylinder Owners Club [★21764]

Plymouth Historical Soc. [20757], 155 S Main St., Plymouth, MI 48170-1635, (734)455-8940

Plymouth Owners Club [21764], PO Box 416, Cavalier, ND 58220-0416, (701)549-3746

Plymouth Rock Club; Amer. Barred [★5114]

Plymouth Rock Fanciers Club [5114], c/o Pat Horstman, Sec.-Treas., 5 S Kings Creek Rd., Burgettstown, PA 15021, (856)825-2484

Plymouth Rock Found. [8302], 1120 Long Pond Rd., Plymouth, MA 02360, (508)833-1189

Plywood Assn. of Am; Imported Hardwood [★1609]

Plywood Assn; Amer. [★1637]

Plywood Assn; Douglas Fir [★1637]

Plywood Assn; Imported Hardwood [★1609]

Plywood Inst; Hardwood [★1649]

Plywood Intl. - Defunct.

Plywood Mfrs. Assn; Hardwood [★1649]

Plywood Mfrs. Assn; Southern [★1649]

Plywood Res. Found. [★1646]

Plywood and Veneer Assn; Hardwood [1649]

PM - Greece [IO], Athens, Greece

PMA - Independent Book Publishers Assn. [3248], 627 Aviation Way, Manhattan Beach, CA 90266, (310)372-2732

PMA - The Worldwide Community of Imaging Associations [3009], 3000 Picture Pl., Jackson, MI 49201-8853, (517)788-8100

PMC Sect. of the Sci. Apparatus Makers Assn. [★3485]

PMCA: An Intl. Assn. of Confectioners [1558], 2980 Linden St., Ste. E3, Bethlehem, PA 18017, (610)625-4655

PMCA: An Intl. Assn. of Confectioners [IO], Bethlehem, PA, United States

P.N. Elrod Fan Club [9702], c/o The Teeth in the Neck Gang, PO Box 60391, Fort Worth, TX 76115

Poale Agudath Israel of America - Address unknown since 2003.

Poale Zion - United Labor Zionist Org. of Am. [★19174]

Pocahontas, Improved Order of Red Men; Degree of [19327]

Pocket Testament League [19529], PO Box 800, Lititz, PA 17543-7026, (866)636-8106

Pocket Testament League [IO], Lititz, PA, United States

POD Network [★IO]

POD Network [★8494]

Podiatric Mgt; Amer. Acad. of [★16024]

Podiatric Medical Assn; Canadian [IO]

Podiatric Multiple Specialties Bd; Amer. [★16029]

Reference to "IO" in place of a book number signifies that the association may be found in the 45th edition of International Organizations.

Encyclopedia of Associations, 46th Edition

3997

Podiatric Orthopedics; Amer. Bd. of [★16030]
Podiatric Orthopedics and Primary Medicine; Amer. Bd. of [★16030]
Podiatric Sports Medicine; Amer. Acad. of [16471]
Podiatric Students Assn; Amer. [★16038]

Podiatry
Acad. of Ambulatory Foot and Ankle Surgery [16023]
Acad. of Ambulatory Foot and Ankle Surgery [IO]
Amer. Acad. of Podiatric Practice Mgt. [16024]
Amer. Acad. of Podiatric Sports Medicine [16471]
Amer. Assn. of Colleges of Podiatric Medicine [16025]
Amer. Assn. of Hosp. Podiatrists [16026]
Amer. Assn. for Women Podiatrists [16027]
Amer. Bd. of Lower Extremities Surgery [16028]
Amer. Bd. of Multiple Specialties in Podiatry [16029]
Amer. Bd. of Podiatric Orthopedics and Primary Podiatric Medicine [16030]
Amer. Bd. of Podiatric Surgery [16031]
Amer. Coll. of Foot and Ankle Orthopedics and Medicine [16032]
Amer. Coll. of Foot and Ankle Pediatrics [16033]
Amer. Coll. of Foot and Ankle Surgeons [16034]
Amer. Coll. of Podiatric Medical Rev. [16035]
Amer. Podiatric Circulatory Soc. [16036]
Amer. Podiatric Medical Assn. [16037]
Amer. Podiatric Medical Students' Assn. [16038]
Amer. Podiatric Medical Writers Assn. [16039]
Amer. Soc. of Podiatric Medical Assistants [16040]
Amer. Soc. of Podiatrists and Chiropractors [16041]
Bay Area Physicians for Human Rights [12218]
Canadian Podiatric Medical Assn. [IO]
Coun. on Podiatric Medical Educ. [16042]
Fed. of Podiatric Medical Boards [16043]
Fund for Podiatric Medical Educ. [16044]
Intl. Fed. of Foot and Ankle Societies [16045]
Intl. Fed. of Foot and Ankle Societies [IO]
Natl. Bd. of Podiatric Medical Examiners [16046]
Natl. Podiatric Medical Assn. [16047]
Soc. of Chiropodists and Podiatrists [IO]
Podiatry; Amer. Acad. of Practice Mgt. in [★16024]
Podiatry; Amer. Assn. of Colleges of [★16025]
Podiatry Assn; Amer. [★16037]
Podiatry Assn; Natl. [★16047]
Podiatry Bibliographical Soc. - Defunct.
Podiatry Boards; Fed. of [★16043]
Podiatry Educ; Coun. on [★16042]
Podiatry Examiners; Natl. Bd. of [★16046]
Podiatry Medical Boards; Fed. of [★16043]
Podopediatrics; Amer. Coll. of [★16033]
Poe Found. [9703], c/o Poe Museum, 1914-16 Main St., Richmond, VA 23223, (804)648-5523
Poe Shrine; The [★9703]
The Poe Shrine [★9703]
Poe Soc. of Baltimore; Edgar Allan [9647]
Poe Stud. Assn. [9704], c/o Paul C. Jones, Sec.-Treas., Dept. of English, 360 Ellis Hall, Ohio Univ., Athens, OH 45701
Poetics and Linguistics Assn. [IO], Middelburg, Netherlands

Poetry
Acad. of Amer. Poets [10859]
Assn. for Applied Poetry [16211]
August Derleth Soc. [9634]
Bread Loaf Writers Conf. [11163]
Canadian Fed. of Poets [IO]
Canadian Poetry Assn. [IO]
Dante Soc. of Am. [9644]
Edgar Allan Poe Soc. of Baltimore [9647]
English Poetry and Song Soc. [IO]
Friends of Robert Frost [10860]
Haiku Soc. of Am. [10861]
Hans Christian Andersen Soc. of Copenhagen [IO]
Intl. Artists Network [9506]
Intl. Brecht Soc. [9661]
Intl. Poetry Forum [10862]
International Poetry Forum [IO]
Intl. Spenser Soc. [9663]
Intl. Vladimir Nabokov Soc. [9667]
James Dickey Soc. [10875]

Jargon Soc. [9958]
Jesse Stuart Found. [9674]
Keats-Shelley Assn. of Am. [9677]
Langston Hughes Soc. [9678]
League of Canadian Poets [IO]
Longfellow Soc. [10863]
Lowell Celebrates Kerouac! [9683]
Marlowe Lives! Assn. [9689]
Milton Soc. of Am. [9693]
Mirage Gp. [10864]
Natl. Assn. for Poetry Therapy [16223]
Natl. Fed. for Biblio/Poetry Therapy [16225]
Natl. Fed. of State Poetry Societies [10865]
Natl. Poetry Found. [10866]
PEN Center U.S.A. [11186]
Philip Larkin Soc. [IO]
Poe Found. [9703]
Poe Stud. Assn. [9704]
Poetry Found. [10867]
Poetry Found. [IO]
Poetry Ireland [IO]
Poetry Proj. [10868]
Poetry Soc. [IO]
Poetry Soc. of Am. [10869]
Poets Against the War [11189]
Poets and Writers [10870]
River of Words [4186]
Robinson Jeffers Assn. [11190]
Shakespeare Oxford Soc. [9709]
Shakespeare Soc. [9710]
Shakespeare Theatre Assn. of Am. [11042]
Tanka Soc. of Am. [10871]
Theodore Roethke Memorial Found. [10872]
Vachel Lindsay Assn. [9718]
W. T. Bandy Center for Baudelaire and Modern French Stud. [9720]
Walt Whitman Birthplace Assn. [9721]
William Morris Soc. in the U.S. [9725]
World Congress of Poets [10873]
World Cong. of Poets [IO]
Yuki Teikei Haiku Soc. [10874]
Poetry; Assn. for Applied [16211]
Poetry Assn; Modern [★10867]
Poetry Assn; Sci. Fiction [10948]
Poetry Forum; Intl. [10862]
Poetry Found. [10867], 444 N Michigan Ave., Ste. 1850, Chicago, IL 60611-4034, (312)787-7070
Poetry Found. [IO], Chicago, IL, United States
Poetry Ireland [IO], Dublin, Ireland
Poetry Proj. [10868], St. Mark's Church, 131 E 10th St., New York, NY 10003, (212)674-0910
Poetry Soc. [IO], London, United Kingdom
Poetry Soc. of Am. [10869], 15 Gramercy Park, New York, NY 10003, (212)254-9628
Poetry Therapy; Assn. for [★16223]
Poetry Therapy Assn; World [★16223]
Poetry Therapy; Natl. Assn. for [16223]
Poetry Therapy; Natl. Fed. for Biblio/ [16225]
Poetry Treasury - Defunct.

Poets
Acad. of Amer. Poets [10859]
Assn. for Applied Poetry [16211]
Dante Soc. of Am. [9644]
Edgar Allan Poe Soc. of Baltimore [9647]
Friends of Robert Frost [10860]
Intl. Artists Network [9506]
Intl. Brecht Soc. [9661]
Intl. Poetry Forum [10862]
Intl. Spenser Soc. [9663]
Intl. Vladimir Nabokov Soc. [9667]
James Dickey Soc. [10875]
Jesse Stuart Found. [9674]
Journalists, Authors and Poets on Stamps Stud. Unit [10778]
Kahlil Gibran Memorial Found. [11132]
Keats-Shelley Assn. of Am. [9677]
Lowell Celebrates Kerouac! [9683]
Marlowe Lives! Assn. [9689]
Milton Soc. of Am. [9693]
Mirage Gp. [10864]
Natl. Fed. of State Poetry Societies [10865]
Natl. Poetry Found. [10866]
Natl. Writers Union [24219]
Nietzsche Soc. [10814]
North Amer. Nietzsche Soc. [10818]

PEN Center U.S.A. [11186]
Poe Found. [9703]
Poe Stud. Assn. [9704]
Poetry Proj. [10868]
Poetry Soc. of Am. [10869]
Poets and Writers [10870]
Shakespeare Oxford Soc. [9709]
Shakespeare Soc. [9710]
Shakespeare Theatre Assn. of Am. [11042]
Tanka Soc. of Am. [10871]
Theodore Roethke Memorial Found. [10872]
Vachel Lindsay Assn. [9718]
W. T. Bandy Center for Baudelaire and Modern French Stud. [9720]
Walt Whitman Birthplace Assn. [9721]
William Morris Soc. in the U.S. [9725]
Women's Interart Center [11096]
Poets Against the War [11189], Box 1614, Port Townsend, WA 98368
Poets for Christ - Address unknown since 2001.
Poets on Stamps Stud. Unit; Journalists, Authors and [10778]
Poets; World Cong. of [IO]
Poets and Writers [10870], 72 Spring St., Ste. 301, New York, NY 10012, (212)226-3586
Pogo Fan Club and Walt Kelly Soc. [24794], c/o Spring Hollow Books, 6908 Wentworth, Richfield, MN 55423
Pogranicze Found. [IO], Sejny, Poland
POINT [★IO]
POINT [★21144]
Point Found. [4519], 5757 Wilshire Blvd., Ste. 370, Los Angeles, CA 90036, (866)337-6468
Point-of-Purchase Advt. Inst. [★115]
Point-of-Purchase Advt. Intl. [115], 1600 Duke St., Ste. 400, Alexandria, VA 22314, (703)373-8800
Pointer Club of Am; German Shorthaired [22274]
Pointer Club of Am; German Wirehaired [22275]
Pointer Club; Amer. [22206]
Pointer Club Francais [IO], St. Vincent-de-Tyrosse, France
POINTers [★IO]
POINTers [★21144]
Points of Light Found. [13401], 1400 I St. NW, Ste. 800, Washington, DC 20005-2208, (202)729-8000
Poison Control Centers; Amer. Assn. of [16658]
Poisoning; Alliance to End Childhood Lead [★13320]
Poisoning Assn; Citizens United to Reduce Emissions of Formaldehyde [★13324]
Poisoning Assn; CURE Formaldehyde [13324]
Poisoning Surveillance and Epidemiology Br. - Defunct.
Poisons Control Officials; Assn. of Economic [★6170]

Poker
Natl. Poker Assn. [22900]
U.S. Poker Assn. [22901]
World Poker Assn. [22902]

Poland
Amer. Soc. for Jewish Heritage in Poland [10273]
Jozef Pilsudski Inst. of Am. for Res. in the Modern History of Poland [10878]
Kosciuszko Found. [10879]
Polish Amer. Chamber of Commerce [24293]
Polish Amer. Golf Assn. [23462]
Polish Amer. Historical Assn. [10880]
Polish Genealogical Soc. of Am. [21142]
Polish Inst. of Arts and Sciences of Am. [10881]
Polish Museum of Am. [10882]
Polish-U.S. Bus. Coun. [24366]
Polonus Philatelic Soc. [22857]
Poland ACM Chap. [IO], Wroclaw, Poland
Poland China Record; Amer. Spotted [★5239]
Poland China Record Assn. [5242], PO Box 9758, Peoria, IL 61612-9758, (309)691-6301
Poland China Record; Natl. Spotted [★5239]
Poland; Institute for Res. in Modern History of [★10878]
Poland; Institute for Res. in Modern History of [★IO]
Poland Sports Medicine Assn. [IO], Warsaw, Poland
Poland Watch Center - Defunct.
Polanyi Soc. [10826], c/o Phil Mullins, Ed., Missouri Western State Univ., 4525 Downs Dr., St. Joseph, MO 64507, (816)271-4386
Polar Bear Assn. - Defunct.

A star before a book entry number signifies that the name is not listed separately, but is mentioned within the entry.

Polar Bear Assn. of World War II [**21401**], 448 Princeton Dr., Costa Mesa, CA 92626-6129
Polar Bear Club; Coney Island [★**23888**]
Polar Bear Club - U.S.A. [**23888**], Coney Island, Staten Island, NY 10305, (718)356-7741
Polar Bear Club - Winter Swimmers [★**23888**]
Polar Bears Intl. [**5367**], PO Box 66142, Baton Rouge, LA 70896, (225)923-3114
Polar Bears International [**IO**], Baton Rouge, LA, United States
Polar Libraries Colloquy [**IO**], Pullman, WA, United States
Polar Libraries Colloquy [**10380**], c/o Betty Galbraith, Sec.-Treas., 1915 NW Valhalla Dr., Washington State Univ., Pullman, WA 99163, (509)335-7930
Polar Philatelists; Amer. Soc. of [**22789**]
Polar Studies
  Amer. Polar Soc. [**7515**]
  Amer. Polar Soc. [**IO**]
  Amer. Soc. of Polar Philatelists [**22789**]
  Antarctic Inst. of Canada [**IO**]
  Antarctic and Southern Ocean Coalition [**IO**]
  Antarctic and Southern Ocean Coalition [**7516**]
  The Antarctica Proj. [**7517**]
  The Antarctica Proj. [**IO**]
  Arctic Inst. of North Am. [**IO**]
  Arctic Monitoring and Assessment Programme [**IO**]
  Assn. of Canadian Universities for Northern Stud. [**IO**]
  Danish Arctic Inst. [**IO**]
  Frederick A. Cook Soc. [**11112**]
  Intl. Arctic Sci. Comm. [**IO**]
  Intl. Soc. for a Complete Earth [**12354**]
  Intl. Soc. of Offshore and Polar Engineers [**7021**]
  Sci. Comm. on Antarctic Res. [**IO**]
  U.S. Antarctic Prog. [**7518**]
  World Glacier Monitoring Ser. [**IO**]
Polaris Intl. North Amer. Network [**IO**], Duluth, GA, United States
Polaris Intl. North Amer. Network [**51**], 3700 Crestwood Pkwy., Ste. 350, Duluth, GA 30096, (770)279-4560
Polaris Proj. Combating Trafficking of Women and Children [**17784**], PO Box 77892, Washington, DC 20013, (202)745-1001
Polarity Therapy Assn; Amer. [**13619**]
Police
  Amer. Assn. of State Troopers [**5960**]
  Amer. Fed. of Security Officers [**24184**]
  Anti-Repression Rsrc. Team [**17093**]
  Assn. of European Police Colleges [**IO**]
  Assn. of Police Authorities [**IO**]
  Assn. of Retired Hispanic Police [**6171**]
  Blue Knights Intl. Law Enforcement Motorcycle Club [**22669**]
  Community Policing Consortium [**3068**]
  Concerns of Police Survivors [**12752**]
  Gay Officers' Action League [**12231**]
  Hispanic Amer. Police Command Officers Assn. [**5970**]
  Intl. Assn. of Undercover Officers [**5976**]
  Intl. Brotherhood of Police Officers [**24120**]
  Intl. Conf. of Police Chaplains [**19749**]
  Intl. Guards Union of Am. [**24185**]
  Intl. Homicide Investigators Assn. [**5883**]
  Intl. Police and Fire Chaplain's Assn. [**19750**]
  Intl. Police Mountain Bike Assn. [**6172**]
  Intl. Police Work Dog Assn. [**5979**]
  Intl. Union of Police Associations [**24121**]
  Intl. Union of Security Officers [**24186**]
  Natl. Alliance of Gang Investigators Associations [**5638**]
  Natl. Alliance of Police, Security and Corrections Organizations [**24165**]
  Natl. Assn. of Chiefs of Police [**6173**]
  Natl. Assn. for Civilian Oversight of Law Enforcement [**5985**]
  Natl. Assn. of Field Training Officers [**5987**]
  Natl. Assn. of Police Athletic Leagues [**13496**]
  Natl. Assn. of Police Organizations [**5988**]
  Natl. Assn. of School Rsrc. Officers [**9086**]
  Natl. Black Police Assn. [**5990**]
  Natl. Black State Troopers Coalition [**5430**]
  Natl. Constables Assn. [**5992**]

  Natl. Disabled Police Assn. [**IO**]
  Natl. Major Gang Task Force [**5651**]
  Natl. Narcotic Detector Dog Assn. [**5997**]
  Natl. Police Accountability Proj. [**6174**]
  Natl. Tactical Officers Assn. [**6175**]
  Natl. Union of Law Enforcement Associations [**24124**]
  Police Assn. for Coll. Educ. [**6004**]
  Police Executive Res. Forum [**6005**]
  Police Found. [**6006**]
  Police Marksman Assn. [**6007**]
  Public Safety Writers Assn. [**4068**]
  Riot Relief Fund [**19266**]
  U.S. Police Canine Assn. [**6008**]
  U.S. Secret Ser. Uniformed Div. Retirement Assn. [**6009**]
  Vietnam Security Police Assn. [**21340**]
Police; Amer. Fed. of [★**5962**]
Police Assn. for Coll. Educ. [**6004**], 63 Lake Forest Dr., Mineral, VA 23117, (540)894-8781
Police Assn; Intl. [**IO**]
Police Assn; Military [★**21208**]
Police Assn; Natl. Black [**5990**]
Police Associations; Intl. Union of [**24121**]
Police Athletic League; Natl. [★**13496**]
Police Athletic Leagues; Natl. Assn. of [**13496**]
Police Bloodhound Assn; Eastern [★**6000**]
Police Bloodhound Assn; Natl. [**6000**]
Police; Canadian Assn. of Chiefs of [**IO**]
Police Canine Assn; U.S. [**6008**]
Police Car Collectors Assn. - Defunct.
Police Car Owners of Am. [**21765**], 172 County Rd. 136, Eureka Springs, AR 72631-9138, (479)253-2364
Police Car Owners of America [**IO**], Eureka Springs, AR, United States
Police; CB Radio Patrol of Amer. Fed. of [★**5962**]
Police Chaplains; Intl. Conf. of [**19749**]
Police Chiefs Spouses - Worldwide - Address unknown since 2004.
Police Communications Officers; Assoc. [★**6248**]
Police-Community Relations Projects - Defunct.
Police and Concerned Citizens; Amer. Fed. of [**5962**]
Police Constables Assn; Natl. [★**5992**]
Police and Criminal Psychology; Soc. for [**16177**]
Police Educators; Canadian Assn. of [**IO**]
Police Executive Res. Forum [**6005**], 1120 Connecticut Ave. NW, Ste. 930, Washington, DC 20036, (202)466-7820
Police Fed. of England and Wales [**IO**], Surbiton, United Kingdom
Police Fed; Scottish [**IO**]
Police and Fire Fighters Assn; Natl. [★**5962**]
Police and Fire Professionals of Am; Intl. Union, Security, [**24187**]
Police and Firemen's Insurance Assn. [**19136**], 101 E 116th St., Carmel, IN 46032, (317)581-1913
Police Found. [**6006**], 1201 Connecticut Ave. NW, Washington, DC 20036, (202)833-1460
Police, Grand Lodge; Fraternal Order of [**19200**]
Police History Soc. [**IO**], Altrincham, United Kingdom
Police; Intl. Assn. of Airport and Seaport [**IO**]
Police K-9 Assn. [★**6008**]
Police Mgt. Assn. - Defunct.
Police Marksman Assn. [**6007**], 200 Green St., Ste. 200, San Francisco, CA 94111, (888)765-4231
Police Martial Arts Assn. [**IO**], Riverview, NB, Canada
Police; Natl. Assn. of Chiefs of [★**5972**]
Police Officers Assn. of Am; Natl. [**6001**]
Police Officers; Intl. Brotherhood of [**24120**]
Police Organizations; Natl. Assn. of [**5988**]
Police Polygraphists; Amer. Assn. of [**5748**]
Police Professors; Intl. Assn. of [★**11850**]
Police Regimental Assn; Military [**21208**]
Police Safety Ser. [★**12972**]
Police and Security Officers; Natl. Assn. of Special [**24122**]
Police; Senior Mgt. Inst. for [★**6005**]
Police Superintendents' Assn. of England and Wales [**IO**], Pangbourne, United Kingdom
Police Training Officials; Assn. of Coll. [★**11899**]
Police Union; Natl. Chiefs of [★**5972**]
Police of the U.S. and Canada; Chiefs of [★**5972**]
Police; U.S. Fed. of [★**5962**]

Police Work Dog Assn; North Amer. [**6003**]
Policemen; Fellowship of Christian [★**19798**]
Policies; Intl. Center for Alcohol [**203**]
Policing; Natl. Center for Women and [**5991**]
Policy
  50 Years is Enough: U.S. Network for Global Economic Justice [**18829**]
  Amer. Comm. for Peace in Chechnya [**18189**]
  Amer. Mfg. Trade Action Coalition [**2547**]
  Americans for Informed Democracy [**5660**]
  Bridging Nations [**17861**]
  Center for Economic and Policy Res. [**17469**]
  Coalition to Keep Am. Connected [**18724**]
  Conf. of Peripheral Maritime Regions of Europe [**IO**]
  Consuming Indus. Trade Action Coalition [**771**]
  League of Private Property Voters [**17985**]
  Mediascope [**18031**]
  Moving Ideas Network [**18460**]
  Natl. Acad. for State Hea. Policy [**14649**]
  Natl. African Amer. Drug Policy Coalition [**17440**]
  Natl. Alliance for Model State Drug Laws [**5671**]
  PolicyLink [**18276**]
  Soc. of Primary Care Policy Fellows [**14664**]
  Tech. Assistance Collaborative [**13145**]
Policy Alliance; Drug [**17112**]
Policy Alternatives for the Caribbean and Central America - Address unknown since 2002.
Policy Alternatives; Center for [**18429**]
Policy Alternatives; Natl. Center for [★**18429**]
Policy Anal; Inst. for Foreign [**17612**]
Policy Anal. and Mgt; Assn. for Public [**18423**]
Policy Anal; Natl. Center for [**18462**]
Policy Anal. on Palestine; Center for [★**8627**]
Policy Assn; Domestic [★**18467**]
Policy Assn; HR [**17972**]
Policy Assn; Labor [★**17972**]
Policy Assn; Natl. [**5593**]
Policy; Assn. for Trans. Law, Logistics and [★**6316**]
Policy Awareness; Network for Environmental [**17501**]
Policy; Center for Alternative Mining Development [**4536**]
Policy; Center for Clean Air [**5083**]
Policy; Center for Development [★**17613**]
Policy Center; Ethics and Public [**18444**]
Policy; Center for Natl. [**18428**]
Policy Center; Natl. Legal and [**17671**]
Policy; Center for Oceans Law and [**7394**]
Policy; Center for Philosophy and Public [★**18454**]
Policy; Center for Religion, Ethics and Social [**18609**]
Policy; Center for Reproductive Law and [★**18516**]
Policy; Center for the Stud. of Social [**18432**]
Policy; Center for the Stud. of Welfare [★**18432**]
Policy Center; Violence [**18789**]
Policy; Churches' Center for Theology and Public [**18434**]
Policy; Common Sense for Drug [**18436**]
Policy Development Proj; Hispanic [**17704**]
Policy Forum; Amer. Youth [**13468**]
Policy Forum; European [**IO**]
Policy Forum; Global [**17839**]
Policy Forum; Natl. Hea. [**17693**]
Policy Found; Drug [★**17112**]
Policy Gp; Online [**17243**]
Policy Inst; Economic [**18441**]
Policy Inst; Genetics [**14499**]
Policy; Inst. for Philosophy and Public [**18454**]
Policy Inst; Reason Public [**6131**]
Policy Inst; Resource [**4603**]
Policy Inst; Youth [**18486**]
Policy; Intl. Center for Development [★**17613**]
Policy; Lawyers' Comm. on Nuclear [**18159**]
Policy Leadership Program; Aspira Public [★**8231**]
Policy; Lincoln Inst. of Land [**5920**]
Policy; Natl. Inst. for Public [**18466**]
Policy Network; Electronic [★**18460**]
Policy; Newport Inst. for Ethics, Law and Public [**18470**]
Policy Priorities; Center on Budget and [**18403**]
Policy Res; Amer. Enterprise Inst. for Public [**18420**]
Policy Res; Center for Economic and [**17469**]
Policy Res; Centre for Economic [**IO**]
Policy Res; Manhattan Inst. for [**18408**]

Reference to "IO" in place of a book number signifies that the association may be found in the 45th edition of International Organizations.

Policy Res; Natl. Center for Public [18463]
Policy Stud; Center for Women [17518]
Policy Stud. Gp. (of the Amer. Political Sci. Assn.)
 [★18477]
Policy Stud; Intl. Center for Economic [★18408]
Policy Stud. Org. [18477], 1527 New Hampshire
 Ave. NW, Washington, DC 20036, (202)483-2512
Policy and Taxation Gp. [18697], 141 Kalmus Dr.,
 Ste. J-1, Costa Mesa, CA 92626, (714)641-6913
Policyholders Protective Assn. Intl. - Address
 unknown since 1995.
PolicyLink [18276], 1438 Webster St., Ste. 303,
 Oakland, CA 94612, (510)663-2333
Polio
 Global Polio Eradication Initiative [IO]
 Intl. Post Polio Support Org. [IO]
 Intl. Post Polio Support Org. [16048]
 Polio Fellowship of Ireland [IO]
 Polio Soc. [15362]
 Post-Polio Hea. Intl. [11981]
Polio Fellowship of Ireland [IO], Dublin, Ireland
Polio Found; Korea [IO]
Polio League for Info. and Outreach; Post- [★15362]
Polio Network; Intl. [★11981]
Polio Soc. [15362], PMB 106-273, 4200 Wisconsin
 Ave. NW, Washington, DC 20016, (301)897-8180
Polis '76 - Defunct.
Polish
 Alliance of Poles of Am. [19300]
 Amer. Coun. for Polish Culture [19301]
 Amer. Fed. of Polish Jews [19302]
 Amer. Inst. of Polish Culture [10876]
 Amer. Inst. of Polish Culture [IO]
 American-Slovenian Polka Found. [10549]
 Assn. of the Sons of Poland [19303]
 Canadian Polish Cong. [IO]
 Fed. of Polish Americans [IO]
 Fed. of Polish Americans [10877]
 Intl. Polka Assn. [10624]
 Jozef Pilsudski Inst. of Am. for Res. in the Modern
  History of Poland [10878]
 Jozef Pilsudski Institute of America for Research
  in the Modern History of Poland [IO]
 Kosciuszko Found. [IO]
 Kosciuszko Found. [10879]
 Legion of Young Polish Women [19304]
 Leschetizky Assn. [10639]
 Natl. Medical and Dental Assn. [19305]
 Polish Amer. Chamber of Commerce [24293]
 Polish Amer. Cong. [19306]
 Polish Amer. Golf Assn. [23462]
 Polish Amer. Historical Assn. [10880]
 Polish Amer. Historical Assn. [IO]
 Polish-American-Jewish Alliance for Youth Action
  [13510]
 Polish Army Veterans Assn. of Am. [21259]
 Polish Arts and Culture Found. [19307]
 Polish Assistance, Inc. [19308]
 Polish Beneficial Assn. [19309]
 Polish Falcons of Am. [19310]
 Polish Genealogical Soc. of Am. [21142]
 Polish Inst. of Arts and Sciences of Am. [10881]
 Polish Legion of Amer. Veterans, U.S.A., Ladies
  Auxiliary [21260]
 Polish Museum of Am. [10882]
 Polish Natl. Alliance of the U.S. of North Am.
  [19311]
 Polish Natl. Union of Am. [19312]
 Polish Nobility Assn. Found. [19313]
 Polish Roman Catholic Union of Am. [19314]
 Polish Singers Alliance of Am. [10687]
 Polish Social and Cultural Assn. [IO]
 Polish Tatra Sheepdog Club of Am. [22342]
 Polish Union of Am. [19315]
 Polish Union of the U.S. of North Am. [19316]
 Polish-U.S. Bus. Coun. [24366]
 Polish Women's Alliance of Am. [19317]
 Polonus Philatelic Soc. [22857]
 Soc. of Polish-American Travel Agents [3936]
 Union of Poles in Am. [19318]
 Union of Polish Women in Am. [19319]
Polish Acad. of Sciences [IO], Warsaw, Poland
Polish Actors Assn. [IO], Warsaw, Poland
Polish Actors Union [★IO]
Polish Air Force Veterans Assn. - Address unknown
 since 1999.

Polish Airclub [★IO]
Polish Alma Mater of Am. [★19311]
Polish Alzheimer's Assn. [IO], Warsaw, Poland
Polish Amateur Radio Union [IO], Bydgoszcz,
 Poland
Polish Amer. Chamber of Commerce [24293], 4800
 N Milwaukee Ave., Ste. No. 206, Chicago, IL
 60630, (773)205-1998
Polish Amer. Cong. [19306], 5711 N Milwaukee
 Ave., Chicago, IL 60646-6215, (773)763-9944
Polish-American Cultural Inst. of Miami [★10876]
Polish-American Cultural Inst. of Miami [★IO]
Polish-Amer. Enterprise Fund - Address unknown
 since 2007.
Polish-Amer. Golf Assn. [23462], 616 Manhattan
 Ave., Brooklyn, NY 11222, (718)389-8536
Polish-Amer. Guardian Soc. - Defunct.
Polish Amer. Historical Assn. [10880], Central Con-
 necticut State Univ., 1615 Stanley St., New Britain,
 CT 06050, (860)832-3010
Polish Amer. Historical Assn. [IO], New Britain, CT,
 United States
Polish Amer. Historical Commn. of the Polish Inst. of
 Arts and Sciences in Am. [★IO]
Polish Amer. Historical Commn. of the Polish Inst. of
 Arts and Sciences in Am. [★10880]
Polish Amer. Immigration and Relief Comm. -
 Defunct.
Polish-American-Jewish Alliance for Youth Action
 [13510], 13B Pipe Hill Ct., Baltimore, MD 21209,
 (410)486-0698
Polish-American-Jewish Alliance for Youth Action
 [IO], Silver Spring, MD, United States
Polish-Amer. Librarians Assn. - Defunct.
Polish-Amer. Numismatic Assn. - Address unknown
 since 1999.
Polish-American Travel Agents; Soc. of [3936]
Polish Americans for the Statue of Liberty - Defunct.
Polish Army Veterans Assn. of Am. [21259]
Polish Arts and Culture Found. [19307], 4077 Water-
 house Rd., Oakland, CA 94602, (510)599-2244
Polish Assistance, Inc. [19308], 15 E 65th St., New
 York, NY 10021-6501, (212)570-5560
Polish Assn. for Amer. Stud. [IO], Poznan, Poland
Polish Assn. of Dermatology [IO], Warsaw, Poland
Polish Assn. of Former Political Prisoners - Address
 unknown since 1995.
Polish Assn. for Landscape Ecology [★IO]
Polish Assn. for Landscape Ecology [IO], Warsaw,
 Poland
Polish Assn. of Meat Producers, Exporters and
 Importers [IO], Warsaw, Poland
Polish Assn. of People Suffering From Epilepsy [IO],
 Bialystok, Poland
Polish Assn. for Spina Bifida and Hydrocephalus
 [IO], Lublin, Poland
Polish Assn. of Tenants [IO], Krakow, Poland
Polish Auto. and Motorcycle Fed. [IO], Warsaw,
 Poland
Polish Baseball and Softball Fed. [IO], Warsaw,
 Poland
Polish Beneficial Assn. [19309], 2595 Orthodox St.,
 Philadelphia, PA 19137, (215)535-2626
Polish Canoe Fed. [IO], Warsaw, Poland
Polish Cardiac Soc. [IO], Warsaw, Poland
Polish Catholic Union of Am; Archives and Museum
 of the [★10882]
Polish Chamber of Books [IO], Warsaw, Poland
Polish Chamber of the Chem. Indus. [IO], Warsaw,
 Poland
Polish Chamber of the Chem. Indus. - Employers'
 Org. [★IO]
Polish Chamber of Commerce [IO], Warsaw, Poland
Polish Chamber of Commerce of Importers, Export-
 ers and Cooperation [IO], Poznan, Poland
Polish Chamber of Pharmaceutical Indus. and Medi-
 cal Devices [IO], Warsaw, Poland
Polish Chem. Soc. [IO], Warsaw, Poland
Polish Commn. for Electron Microscopy [IO],
 Poznan, Poland
Polish Composers' Union [IO], Warsaw, Poland
Polish Composers Union [IO], Warsaw, Poland
Polish Corp. of Trade Fairs and Economic Exhibi-
 tions Organizers [★IO]
Polish Coun. of Unity in the U.S. - Defunct.

Polish Culture; Amer. Center for [★10879]
Polish Democratic Union [★IO]
Polish Draughts Fed. [IO], Minsk Mazowiecki,
 Poland
Polish Economic Soc. [IO], Warsaw, Poland
Polish Entomological Soc. [IO], Poznan, Poland
Polish Falcons of Am. [19310], 615 Iron City Dr.,
 Pittsburgh, PA 15205-4397, (412)922-2244
Polish Figure Skating Assn. [IO], Warsaw, Poland
Polish Floorball Fed. [IO], Gdynia, Poland
Polish Football Assn. [IO], Warsaw, Poland
Polish Fur Fed. [IO], Grodzisk Wielkopolski, Poland
Polish Genealogical Soc. [★IO]
Polish Genealogical Soc. [★21142]
Polish Genealogical Soc. of Am. [21142], 984 N
 Milwaukee Ave., Chicago, IL 60622
Polish Genealogical Soc. of Am. [IO], Chicago, IL,
 United States
Polish Geographical Soc. [IO], Warsaw, Poland
Polish Geological Soc. [IO], Krakow, Poland
Polish Geotechnical Soc. [IO], Warsaw, Poland
Polish Independent Student Assn. - Defunct.
Polish Info. Processing Soc. [IO], Warsaw, Poland
Polish Inst. [★IO]
Polish Inst. of Arts and Sci. of Am. [★10881]
Polish Inst. of Arts and Sciences of Am. [10881],
 208 E 30th St., New York, NY 10016, (212)686-
 4164
Polish Inst. of Arts and Sciences in Am; Polish Amer.
 Historical Commn. of the [★10880]
Polish Jet Sports Boating Assn. [IO], Gdansk,
 Poland
Polish Jews, Amer. Sect; World Fed. of [★19302]
Polish Jews in the U.S; Fed. of [★19302]
Polish Journalists' Assn. [IO], Warsaw, Poland
Polish Legion of Amer. Veterans, U.S.A. - Address
 unknown since 1995.
Polish Legion of Amer. Veterans, U.S.A., Ladies
 Auxiliary [21260]
Polish Librarians Assn. [IO], Warsaw, Poland
Polish Medical Assn. [IO], Warsaw, Poland
Polish Medical Assn., Sect. of Chemotherapy [IO],
 Warsaw, Poland
Polish Military History Soc. of America - Address
 unknown since 2002.
Polish Motorcycle Fed. [★IO]
Polish Museum of Am. [10882], 984 N Milwaukee
 Ave., Chicago, IL 60622-4101, (773)384-3352
Polish Mutual Assistance [★19308]
Polish Natl. Alliance of Brooklyn, U.S.A. - Address
 unknown since 1995.
Polish Natl. Alliance of the U.S. of North Am.
 [19311], 6100 N Cicero Ave., Chicago, IL 60646,
 (773)286-0500
Polish Natl. Union of Am. [19312], 1002 Pittston
 Ave., Scranton, PA 18505, (800)724-6352
Polish Nobility Assn. [★19313]
Polish Nobility Assn. Found. [19313], Villa Anneslie,
 529 Dunkirk Rd., Baltimore, MD 21212-2014
Polish Olympic Comm. [IO], Warsaw, Poland
Polish Orienteering Assn. [IO], Warsaw, Poland
Polish Orthodontic Soc. [IO], Lublin, Poland
Polish Osteoarthrology Soc. [IO], Krakow, Poland
Polish Paralympic Comm. [IO], Warsaw, Poland
Polish Philatelic Fed. in Great Britain [★IO]
Polish Philatelists Assn. in United Kingdom [★IO]
Polish Phonetic Assn. [IO], Poznan, Poland
Polish Physical Soc. [IO], Warsaw, Poland
Polish Physiological Soc. [IO], Krakow, Poland
Polish POW Camps Philatelic Study Group -
 Defunct.
Polish Private Equity Assn. [IO], Warsaw, Poland
Polish Psychological Assn. [IO], Warsaw, Poland
Polish Roman Catholic Union of Am. [19314], 984 N
 Milwaukee Ave., Chicago, IL 60622-4101,
 (773)782-2600
Polish Sea League of America - Address unknown
 since 1995.
Polish Seed Trade Assn. [IO], Poznan, Poland
Polish Singers Alliance of America [IO], Williamsville,
 NY, United States
Polish Singers Alliance of Am. [10687], c/o Mrs. Ter-
 esa Krenglicki, Pres., 208 Caesar Blvd., Williams-
 ville, NY 14221, (716)827-1722
Polish Social and Cultural Assn. [IO], London,
 United Kingdom

A star before a book entry number signifies that the name is not listed separately, but is mentioned within the entry.

Polish Socialist Alliance of U.S.A. - Address unknown since 1995.
Polish Soc. of Agricultural Engg. [IO], Warsaw, Poland
Polish Soc. for Contemporary Music [IO], Warsaw, Poland
Polish Soc. of Gerontology [IO], Warsaw, Poland
Polish Soc. of Hypertension [IO], Poznan, Poland
Polish Soc. of the Phonographic Indus. [IO], Warsaw, Poland
Polish Soc. for Photogrammetry and Remote Sensing [IO], Warsaw, Poland
Polish Soc. of Physiotherapy [IO], Pabianice, Poland
Polish Soc. of Rose Fanciers [IO], Warsaw, Poland
Polish Soc. for the Stud. of Pain [IO], Krakow, Poland
Polish Soc. of Veterinary Sci. [IO], Warsaw, Poland
Polish Sociological Assn. [IO], Warsaw, Poland
Polish Speed Skating Assn. [IO], Warsaw, Poland
Polish Surname Network - Defunct.
Polish Taekwondo Fed. [IO], Warsaw, Poland
Polish Tatra Sheepdog Club of Am. [22342], c/o Pat Kolakowski, Sec., 7 Deer Run Rd., Stafford, VA 22556, (540)752-1135
Polish Tourist Country-Lovers' Soc. [IO], Warsaw, Poland
Polish Trade Fair Corp. [IO], Poznan, Poland
Polish Trade and Indus. Assn. [IO], Poznan, Poland
Polish Underground Movement (1939-1945) Stud. Trust [IO], London, United Kingdom
Polish Union of Am. [19315], 745 Center Rd., West Seneca, NY 14224-2108, (716)677-0220
Polish Union of the U.S. of North Am. [19316], PO Box 660, Wilkes-Barre, PA 18703-0660, (570)823-1611
Polish-U.S. Bus. Coun. [24366], c/o Chamber of Commerce of the U.S., 1615 H St. NW, Washington, DC 20062-2000, (202)659-6000
Polish-U.S. Economic Coun. [★24366]
Polish Western Assn. of America - Defunct.
Polish Women in Am; Assn. of [★19311]
Polish Women of Am; United [★19311]
Polish Women's Alliance of Am. [19317], 6643 N Northwest Hwy., 2nd Fl., Chicago, IL 60631, (847)384-1200
Polish Workers' Aid Fund - Defunct.
Polish Youth Hostels Assn. [IO], Warsaw, Poland
Polishers, Buffers, Platers and Allied Workers Intl. Union; Metal [★24021]
Political Action
20/20 Vision Natl. Proj. [18277]
African-Americans for Democracy [16936]
AIDS Action Coun. [18278]
Alcohol Beverage Legislative Coun. [5444]
Amer. Medical Political Action Comm. [18279]
Amer. Renewal Found. [18280]
Aouon Archv. [9418]
Asian Pacific Americans for Progress [17012]
Assn. of Community Organizations for Reform Now [11749]
Australians for Constitutional Monarchy [IO]
BANKPAC [18281]
Better Govt. Assn. [18282]
Black Sash Trust [IO]
Bus. Alliance for Commerce in Hemp [18283]
Business-Industry Political Action Comm. [18284]
Campaign for America [18285]
Campaign for Working Families [18286]
Center for the Stud. of Political Graphics [9434]
Citizens for Legitimate Govt. [17663]
Common Cause [18287]
Congressional Agenda: Millennium [18288]
Constitutional Rights Proj. [IO]
Consumers United for Rail Equity [18289]
Cosmic Baseball Assn. [23108]
Coun. of Canadians [IO]
The Creative Coalition [18290]
Debts AIDS Trade Africa [16928]
Democracy for Am. [18291]
Democracy Intl. [18292]
Democracy Intl. [IO]
Dredging Industry Size Standard Comm. [18293]
EMILY's List [18294]
European Movement [IO]
Free Cong. Res. and Educ. Found. [18295]

FreedomWorks [18296]
Fund for New Priorities in Am. [18297]
Hate Free Zone [17392]
Human Rights Campaign [17653]
Intl. Union, UAW - Community Action Prog. [18298]
Jaan Tonisson Inst. [IO]
Kashmiri Amer. Coun. [12753]
League of Revolutionaries for a New Am. [18299]
Natl. Action Network [17127]
Natl. Assn. of Bus. Political Action Committees [18300]
Natl. Law Center on Homelessness and Poverty [12297]
Netherlands Inst. for Southern Africa [IO]
Paul Revere Soc. [18301]
Pay for Schools by Regulating Cannabis [18302]
Peace Pac [18168]
Political Dept. of the AFL-CIO [18303]
ReclaimDemocracy.org [17398]
Refuse and Resist [18304]
Resist [18305]
Sam Adams Alliance [17673]
Social Democrats, U.S.A. [18306]
Terror Free Tomorrow [18736]
U.S.English [18307]
Uyghur Amer. Assn. [17788]
Voters for Choice/Friends of Family Planning [18521]
Women's Electoral Lobby - Australia [IO]
Political Action Comm. [★18303]
Political Action Comm; Bankers [★18281]
Political Action Comm; Banking Profession [★18281]
Political Action Comm; Free Cong. [17268]
Political Action Comm. of Young Americans for Freedom [★17261]
Political Assn. for Animal Rights in Europe [IO], Dusseldorf, Germany
Political Asylum Project - Defunct.
Political Campaign Inst. - Defunct.
Political Caucus; Natl. Women's [17566]
Political Dept. of the AFL-CIO [18303], 815 16th St. NW, 7th Fl., Washington, DC 20006, (202)637-5000
Political Development; Alliance of Minority Women for Bus. and [2759]
Political Ecology Group [17502]
Political Economics; Union for Radical [6896]
Political Economy and Economic History Soc. [IO], Tokyo, Japan
Political Economy Res. Center - The Center for Free Market Environmentalism [4600], 2048 Anal. Dr., Ste. A, Bozeman, MT 59718, (406)587-9591
Political Education
Amer. Soc. of Contrarian Speakers and Writers [5601]
Democracy for Am. [18291]
Jefferson Legacy Found. [9002]
Kashmiri Amer. Coun. [12753]
Kashmiri Amer. Coun. [IO]
ReclaimDemocracy.org [17398]
Robert H. Smith Intl. Center for Jefferson Stud. [9003]
Terror Free Tomorrow [18736]
VoterWatch [5600]
Political Educ., AFL-CIO; Comm. on [★18303]
Political Educ. Comm. [★18762]
Political Educ; Labor's League for [★18303]
Political Equality; Hispanas Organized for [17703]
Political Federations
Ashburn Inst. for Global Stud. in Federalism and Democracy [18308]
Ashburn Institute for Global Studies in Federalism and Democracy [IO]
Center of the Amer. Experiment [17262]
Center for Democracy [5932]
Christian Democrat Intl. [IO]
Christian Democrat Org. of Am. [IO]
CIVICUS: World Alliance for Citizen Participation [18340]
Coun. of Volunteer Americans [18309]
Crusade to Abolish War and Armaments by World Law [18310]
European Fed. of Green Parties [IO]
European Liberal Democrat and Reform Party [IO]

European Peoples' Party [IO]
European Senior Citizens Union [IO]
Freedom Union [IO]
Gen. Assembly Binding Women for Reforms, Integrity, Equality, Leadership, and Action [IO]
Independent Women's Forum [18311]
Intl. Democrat Union [IO]
Intl. Network of Liberal Women [IO]
Intl. Young Democrat Union [IO]
League of Conservation Voters [18312]
Liberal Intl. [IO]
Mouvement du Nid [IO]
Natl. Parenting Assn. [12679]
Party of European Socialists [IO]
Physicians for a Natl. Hea. Prog. [18313]
Semisocialist Coalition of Earth [18314]
Semisocialist Coalition of Earth [IO]
Socialist Gp. in the European Parliament [IO]
Socialist Intl. [IO]
United Fascist Union [18315]
U.S. Term Limits Found. [18316]
Unrepresented Nations and Peoples Org. [IO]
World Constitution and Parliament Assn. [IO]
World Constitution and Parliament Assn. [18317]
World Ser. Authority [18318]
World Ser. Authority [IO]
Youth of the European People's Party [IO]
Political Graphics; Center for the Stud. of [9434]
Political Integration
Dialogue on Diversity [8888]
VoterWatch [5600]
Political Items
Amer. Political Items Collectors [22903]
Inst. for Foreign Policy Anal. [17612]
Political League; Machinists Non-Partisan [24101]
Political League; Responsible Citizens [★24180]
Political Parties
Abolitionist Party of Canada [IO]
ACT New Zealand [IO]
Alliance of Free Democrats [IO]
Alliance New Zealand [IO]
Alliance Party of Northern Ireland [IO]
Amer. Muslim Alliance [18083]
Amer. Nationalist Union [18319]
Australian Democrats [IO]
Australian Labor Party [IO]
Barbados Labour Party [IO]
Bharatiya Janata Party [IO]
Breton Democratic Union [IO]
Cambodian People's Party [IO]
Campus Greens [18320]
Christian Democratic Union [IO]
Christian Heritage Party of Canada [IO]
Christian Social Party [IO]
Comm. for a Unified Independent Party [18321]
Communist Party of Australia [IO]
Communist Party of Bangladesh [IO]
Communist Party of Canada (Marxist-Leninist) [IO]
Communist Party of India [IO]
Communist Party of Nepal (Unified Marxist-Leninist) [IO]
Communist Party of the U.S.A. [18322]
Conservative Party [18323]
Conservative Party Central Off. [IO]
Conservative Party of Norway [IO]
Conservative People's Party [IO]
Danish Social-Liberal Party [IO]
Democratic Party of Hong Kong [IO]
Democratic Party of Japan [IO]
Democratic Progressive Party [IO]
Democratic Rally [IO]
EMILY'S List [IO]
Estonian Reform Party [IO]
Expansionist Party of the U.S. [IO]
Expansionist Party of the U.S. [18324]
Finnish Social Democratic Party [IO]
Free Democratic Party [IO]
Free Democratic Party of Switzerland [IO]
Green Party of Aotearoa - New Zealand [IO]
Green Party - Taiwan [IO]
Green Party of the U.S. [18325]
Hong Kong Democratic Found. [IO]
Islamic Party of Malaysia [IO]
Japanese Communist Party [IO]

Reference to "IO" in place of a book number signifies that the association may be found in the 45th edition of International Organizations.

La Raza Unida Party **[18326]**
Labour Party - Britain **[IO]**
Labour Party - Ireland **[IO]**
Labour Party - Netherlands **[IO]**
Labour Women's Network **[IO]**
Latvian Social Democratic Workers' Party **[IO]**
Liberal Democratic Party of Japan **[IO]**
Liberal Party of Australia **[IO]**
Liberal Party of Canada **[IO]**
Liberal Party of Norway **[IO]**
Libertarian Natl. Comm. **[18327]**
Luxembourg Socialist Workers' Party **[IO]**
Malaysian Chinese Assn. **[IO]**
Malta Labour Party **[IO]**
Moderate Party **[IO]**
Natl. Coalition Party **[IO]**
Natl. Hamiltonian Party **[18328]**
Nationalist Party **[IO]**
Nationals **[IO]**
New Democratic Party of Canada **[IO]**
New Flemish Alliance **[IO]**
New Komeito **[IO]**
New Zealand Democratic Party **[IO]**
New Zealand First **[IO]**
New Zealand Labour Party **[IO]**
New Zealand Natl. Party **[IO]**
Norwegian Labour Party **[IO]**
NSDAP Auslands-Und Aufbauorganisation **[IO]**
NSDAP Auslands-Und Aufbauorganisation
  [18329]
Open Debates **[17488]**
Parti Gerakan Rakyat Malaysia **[IO]**
Party of Democratic Socialism **[IO]**
Peace and Freedom Party **[18330]**
People's Progressive Party of Guyana **[IO]**
Plaid Cymru - The Party of Wales **[IO]**
Political Party Democrats 66 **[IO]**
Progressive Labor Party **[18331]**
Progressive Socialist Party **[IO]**
Prohibition Natl. Comm. **[18332]**
Refounded Natl. Party of South Africa **[IO]**
Republicans Abroad Intl. **[IO]**
Republicans Abroad Intl. **[18333]**
Sarawak United People's Party **[IO]**
Scottish Natl. Party **[IO]**
Scottish Natl. Party - Women's Forum **[IO]**
Social Democratic and Labour Party **[IO]**
Social Democratic Party of Austria **[IO]**
Social Democratic Party of Denmark **[IO]**
Social Democratic Party of Germany **[IO]**
Socialist Alliance **[IO]**
Socialist Labor Party of Am. **[18334]**
Socialist Party **[IO]**
Socialist Party of Canada **[IO]**
Socialist Party - France **[IO]**
Socialist Party U.S.A. **[18335]**
Socialist Workers Party **[18336]**
Swedish People's Party of Finland **[IO]**
Swiss Christian Democratic Party **[IO]**
Trotskyist League of Canada **[IO]**
United Civil Party **[IO]**
United Future New Zealand **[IO]**
United Liberal Democrats **[IO]**
U.S. Pacifist Party **[18337]**
Vrouwen in de Volkspartij voor Vrijheid en
  Democratie **[IO]**
Welsh Liberal Democrats **[IO]**
Women's Org. of the Social Democratic Party of
  Austria **[IO]**
Working Families Party **[18338]**
World Socialist Party - New Zealand **[IO]**
World Socialist Party of the U.S. **[18339]**
Political Party Democrats 66 **[IO]**, The Hague,
  Netherlands
Political Prisoners
Chicago Action for Jews in the Former Soviet
  Union **[17444]**
Comm. on Human Rights **[17753]**
Falun Data Info. Center **[17757]**
Friends of Falun Gong **[17061]**
Irish Northern Aid Comm. **[17934]**
Raoul Wallenberg Comm. **[IO]**
Women's Org. for Political Prisoners **[IO]**
Political Prisoners; Amer. Assn. of Former Soviet
  [★17766]

Political Products
Amer. Political Items Collectors **[22903]**
Political Products Mfrs. Assn. **[3069]**
Political Products Mfrs. Assn. **[3069]**
Political Reform
Aouon Archv. **[9418]**
Brennan Center for Justice at NYU School of Law
  [6176]
Canadian Friends of Burma **[IO]**
Center for the Stud. of Political Graphics **[9434]**
CIVICUS: World Alliance for Citizen Participation
  [18340]
CIVICUS: World Alliance for Citizen Participation
  [IO]
Comm. to Support the Revolution in Peru **[18341]**
Debts AIDS Trade Africa **[16928]**
Inst. for Democracy in Eastern Europe **[17446]**
Latvian Natl. Found. **[IO]**
Lithuanian Natl. Union **[IO]**
Natl. Action Network **[17127]**
Nicaragua Solidarity Campaign **[IO]**
ReclaimDemocracy.org **[17398]**
Servicio Colombiano de Comunicacion **[IO]**
Special Interest Gp. on Mgt. Info. Systems **[6824]**
Uyghur Amer. Assn. **[17788]**
Veterans for Common Sense **[21330]**
Women's Org. of the Swedish People's Party in
  Finland **[IO]**
Political Repression; Natl. Alliance Against Racist
  and **[17128]**
Political Res. Associates **[6177]**, 1310 Broadway,
  Ste. 201, Somerville, MA 02144, (617)666-5300
Political Res. Found. **[★18349]**
Political Rights Defense Fund - Defunct.
Political Science
Academia a Ciencias Politicas y Sociales **[IO]**
Acad. of Political Sci. **[7519]**
African Assn. of Political Sci. **[IO]**
Albanian Political Sci. Assn. **[IO]**
Amer. Acad. of Political and Social Sci. **[7520]**
Amer. Muslim Alliance **[18083]**
Amer. Political Sci. Assn. **[7521]**
Assn. for Politics and the Life Sciences **[7522]**
Assn. for the Stud. of Free Institutions **[8481]**
Assn. for the Stud. of German Politics **[IO]**
Australasian Political Stud. Assn. **[IO]**
Brookings Institution **[18424]**
Canadian Political Sci. Assn. **[IO]**
Caucus for a New Political Sci. **[7523]**
Centre for Sci. and Indus. Policy Res. **[IO]**
Conf. Gp. on French Politics and Soc. **[17621]**
Conf. for the Stud. of Political Thought **[7524]**
European Consortium for Political Res. **[IO]**
German Political Sci. Assn. **[IO]**
German Politics Assn. **[17662]**
Hong Kong Political Sci. Assn. **[IO]**
Inst. of European Politics **[IO]**
Inst. for Intl. Political Stud. **[IO]**
Inter-University Consortium for Political and Social
  Res. **[7525]**
Intl. Soc. for Human Ethology **[6534]**
Jefferson Legacy Found. **[9002]**
Joint Center for Political and Economic Stud.
  [7526]
Konrad Adenauer Found. - Germany **[IO]**
Konrad Adenauer Found. - South Africa **[IO]**
North Amer. Conf. on British Stud. **[9760]**
Pi Sigma Alpha **[24576]**
Political Stud. Assn. **[IO]**
Political Stud. Assn. of Ireland **[IO]**
Public Choice Soc. **[7527]**
Robert H. Smith Intl. Center for Jefferson Stud.
  [9003]
Social Sciences Services and Resources **[7656]**
Soc. for Cross-Cultural Res. **[10230]**
Southern Africa Political Economy Series Trust
  [IO]
Trans European Policy Stud. Assn. **[IO]**
Ukrainian Center for Independent Political Res.
  [IO]
Walter Bagehot Res. Coun. on Natl. Sovereignty
  [7528]
Women's Caucus for Political Sci. **[7529]**
Political Sci. Assn; Policy Stud. Gp. of the Amer.
  [★18477]

Political Scientists' Comm. for Human Rights -
  Defunct.
Political Stud. Assn. **[IO]**, Newcastle upon Tyne,
  United Kingdom
Political Stud. Assn. of Ireland **[IO]**, Dublin, Ireland
Political Stud; Center for **[★7650]**
Political Stud; Joint Center for **[★7526]**
Politics
Aaron Burr Accord **[11097]**
Aaron Burr Assn. **[11098]**
Abigail Adams Historical Soc. Inc. **[11099]**
Abraham Lincoln Assn. **[11100]**
Academie des Sciences Morales et Politiques **[IO]**
Acad. of Political Sci. **[7519]**
African-Americans for Democracy **[16936]**
Alliance of Minority Women for Bus. and Political
  Development **[2759]**
Amer. Acad. of Political and Social Sci. **[7520]**
Amer. Assn. of Political Consultants **[18342]**
Amer. Conservative Union **[17261]**
Amer. League of Lobbyists **[18343]**
Amer. Muslim Alliance **[18083]**
Amer. Political Items Collectors **[22903]**
Amer. Political Sci. Assn. **[7521]**
Arab Amer. Inst. **[18344]**
Arab Amer. Inst. **[IO]**
Arab Amer. Leadership Coun. **[17003]**
Asian Pacific Americans for Progress **[17012]**
Asian and Pacific Islander Amer. Vote **[18345]**
Assn. of Community Organizations for Reform
  Now **[11749]**
Assn. for Political and Legal Anthropology **[6411]**
Black Women's Roundtable on Voter Participation
  [18346]
Brennan Center for Justice at NYU School of Law
  [6176]
Calvin Coolidge Memorial Found. **[11107]**
Center of Concern **[17747]**
Center for Public Integrity **[17667]**
Center for Responsive Politics **[18347]**
Center for the Stud. of Political Graphics **[9434]**
Center for the Stud. of the Presidency **[17069]**
Center for Voting and Democracy **[18348]**
Churchill Centre **[11109]**
Citizens for Legitimate Govt. **[17663]**
Citizens' Res. Found. **[18349]**
Citizens United **[17664]**
Coalition for Women's Appointments **[17520]**
Commn. on Presidential Debates **[18350]**
Comm. for the Advancement of Stem Cell Res.
  [18542]
Comm. on the Constitutional Sys. **[17289]**
Common Dreams **[16972]**
Conf. for the Stud. of Political Thought **[7524]**
Consumers Educ. and Protective Assn. **[17323]**
Democracy Intl. **[18292]**
Eugene V. Debs Found. **[10295]**
Fair Elections Legal Network **[5491]**
Franklin and Eleanor Roosevelt Inst. **[11111]**
Free Territory of Ely-Chatelaine **[18351]**
GenerationEngage **[18848]**
Guatemala News and Info. Bur. **[17680]**
Henry Clay Memorial Found. **[11121]**
Herbert Hoover Presidential Lib. Assn. **[11122]**
Hereditary Order of the Families of the Presidents
  and First Ladies of Am. **[21261]**
Independent Americans **[17294]**
Indian Amer. Forum for Political Educ. **[18352]**
Indus. Areas Found. **[17220]**
Inst. for Advanced Strategic and Political Stud.
  [IO]
Inst. for America's Future **[18353]**
Inter-University Consortium for Political and Social
  Res. **[7525]**
Intl. League for Human Rights **[17769]**
Intl. Soc. of Political Psychology **[16154]**
James Buchanan Found. for the Preservation of
  Wheatland **[11126]**
James K. Polk Memorial Assn. **[11127]**
James Monroe Memorial Found. **[11128]**
Jefferson Davis Assn. **[11129]**
John M. Olin Found. **[12047]**
Joint Center for Political and Economic Stud.
  [7526]
Judson Welliver Soc. **[10127]**

A star before a book entry number signifies that the name is not listed separately, but is mentioned within the entry.

Laborers' Political League [18354]
League of Conservation Voters [18312]
League of Women Voters of the U.S. [18355]
League of Young Voters [18356]
Martin Van Buren Fan Club [11136]
Mobile Voter [18032]
Mount Vernon Ladies' Assn. [11138]
Move Am. Forward [18733]
Natl. Assn. of Minority Political Families USA [18357]
Natl. Coalition on Black Civic Participation [18358]
Natl. Coun. of Asian Pacific Americans [17013]
Natl. Fed. of the Grand Order of Pachyderm Clubs [18359]
Natl. Student Campaign for Voter Registration [18360]
Natl. Write Your Congressman [18361]
Oper. Big Vote [18362]
People's Lobby [18363]
Philadelphia Soc. [18475]
Political Economy Res. Center - The Center for Free Market Environmentalism [4600]
Political Res. Associates [6177]
Politics Assn. [IO]
Pres. Benjamin Harrison Found. [11142]
Progressive Policy Inst. [18478]
Proj. on Govt. Oversight [18077]
Proj. Vote! [18364]
Reagan Alumni Assn. [18365]
Ronald Reagan Home Preservation Found. [11147]
Rutherford B. Hayes Presidential Center [11148]
Sam Adams Alliance [17673]
South Asian Amer. Voting Youth [18366]
Southwest Voter Registration Educ. Proj. [18367]
Special Interest Gp. on Mgt. Info. Systems [6824]
Terror Free Tomorrow [18736]
Theodore Roosevelt Assn. [11152]
Thomas Jefferson's Poplar Forest [10069]
Thomas Paine Natl. Historical Assn. [11153]
Toward Freedom [17645]
Ulysses S. Grant Assn. [11154]
United Black Republican Coalition [18538]
UrgentCall.org [18173]
Uyghur Amer. Assn. [17788]
VoterWatch [5600]
Walter Bagehot Res. Coun. on Natl. Sovereignty [7528]
The Woman Activist [17573]
Women in Govt. Relations [17676]
Women in Govt. Relations LEADER Found. [17677]
Women Leaders Online [18817]
Women Leaders Online/Women Organizing For Change [18818]
Women's Caucus for Political Sci. [7529]
Woodrow Wilson Presidential Lib. Found. [11155]
Working Families Party [18338]
Politics Assn. [IO], Manchester, United Kingdom
Politics; Assn. for Sciences and [IO]
Politics; Center for Amer. Women and [17516]
Politics; Center for the Stud. of Law and [★5693]
Politics and the Life Sciences; Assn. for [7522]
Politics and Soc; Conf. Gp. on French [17621]
Politieke Partij Democraten 66 [★IO]
Politischer Arbeitskreis fur Tierrechte in Europa [★IO]
Politzer Soc. - Intl. Soc. for Otological Surgery [IO], Ankara, Turkey
Polk Memorial Assn; James K. [11127]
Polka Found; American-Slovenian [10549]
Polka Lovers Klub of America - Address unknown since 2001.
Pollock; Clan [20857]
Pollock-Krasner Found. [17004], 863 Park Ave., New York, NY 10021, (212)517-5400
Pollock-Krasner Foundation [IO], New York, NY, United States

Polls
Amer. Assn. for Public Opinion Res. [18368]
Coun. of Amer. Survey Res. Organizations [18369]
Natl. Coun. on Public Polls [18370]
World Assn. for Public Opinion Res. [18371]
World Assn. for Public Opinion Res. [IO]

Polls; Natl. Coun. on Public [18370]
Pollution Control
Advisory Comm. on Protection of the Sea [IO]
Air and Waste Mgt. Assn. [IO]
Air and Waste Mgt. Assn. [5081]
Amer. Assn. for Aerosol Res. [6662]
Amer. Backflow Prevention Assn. [7818]
Amer. Decentralized Wastewater Assn. [4006]
Amer. Indoor Air Quality Coun. [5082]
Assn. for the Prevention of Atmospheric Pollution [IO]
Basel Action Network [18797]
British Oil Spill Control Assn. [IO]
British Water [IO]
Canadian Assn. on Water Quality [IO]
Canadian Centre for Pollution Prevention [IO]
Center for Clean Air Policy [5083]
Center For Hea., Env. and Justice [5266]
Centre for Documentation, Res. and Experimenta-tion on Accidental Water Pollution [IO]
Citizens for Alternatives to Chem. Contamination [5084]
Clean Air Trust [5085]
Clean Fuels Development Coalition [5086]
Clean Harbors Cooperative [3070]
Clean Production Action [4631]
Clean Water Action [5087]
Clean Water Fund [5088]
Commn. on Air Pollution Prevention of VDI and DIN - Standards Comm. [IO]
Contaminated Land: Applications in Real Environ-ments [IO]
Ecological and Toxicological Assn. of Dyes and Organic Pigments Mfrs. [IO]
Environmental Defense [4562]
Environmental Working Group [4564]
ETAD North Am. - Ecological and Toxicological Assn. of Dyes and Organic Pigments Mfrs. [5089]
European Assn. for the Sci. of Air Pollution [IO]
European Fed. of Clean Air and Environmental Protection Associations [IO]
European Ozone Res. Coordinating Unit [IO]
Fed. of Environmental Technologists [5090]
Freshwater Soc. [5091]
Gaia Inst. [4509]
German Assn. for Water, Wastewater and Waste [IO]
Get Oil Out! [5092]
Global Alliance for Incinerator Alternatives [5268]
Greenaction for Hea. and Environmental Justice [17699]
Greenpeace U.S.A. [4571]
Helsinki Commn. - Baltic Marine Env. Protection Commn. [IO]
Indoor Air Quality Assn. [5093]
Inst. of Clean Air Companies [3071]
Intl. Assn. of Classification Societies [IO]
Intl. Assn. of Waterworks in the Rhine Basin Area [IO]
Intl. Commn. on Atmospheric Chemistry and Global Pollution [IO]
Intl. Commn. on Atmospheric Chemistry and Global Pollution [5094]
Intl. Commn. for the Protection of the Rhine [IO]
Intl. Dark-Sky Assn. [6506]
Intl. Oil Pollution Compensation Funds [IO]
Intl. Petroleum Indus. Environmental Conservation Assn. [IO]
Intl. SeaKeepers Soc. [5010]
Intl. Tanker Owners Pollution Fed. [IO]
Intl. Union of Air Pollution Prevention and Environmental Protection Associations [IO]
Intl. Water Assn. [IO]
Legambiente [IO]
Mfrs. of Emission Controls Assn. [3072]
Midwest Center for Environmental Sci. and Public Policy [5095]
Military Toxics Proj. [5033]
Natl. Assn. of Clean Air Agencies [5696]
Natl. Biosolids Partnership [5096]
Natl. Environmental, Safety and Hea. Training Assn. [5097]
National Environmental, Safety and Health Train-ing Association [IO]

Natl. Pollution Prevention Roundtable [5098]
New Zealand Water and Wastes Assn. [IO]
NOAH Friends of the Earth - Denmark [IO]
Occupational Knowledge International [IO]
Occupational Knowledge Intl. [5099]
Ocean Conservancy [4435]
Offshore Pollution Liability Assn. [IO]
Passaic River Coalition [7840]
Regional Org. for the Protection of the Marine Env. [IO]
Save Our Seas [4449]
Seacoast Anti-Pollution League [4451]
Singapore Natl. Comm. of the Intl. Water Assn. [IO]
Soc. Promoting Environmental Conservation [IO]
Solar Cookers Intl. [IO]
Solar Cookers Intl. [5100]
Spill Control Assn. of Am. [3073]
Surfers Against Sewage [IO]
Swedish NGO Secretariat on Acid Rain [IO]
Thai Natl. Comm. of the Intl. Assn. on Water Quality [IO]
United Kingdom Comm. of Intl. Water Assn. [IO]
Water Env. Fed. [IO]
Water Env. Fed. [5101]
Pollution Control Administrators; Assn. of State and Interstate Water [5688]
Pollution Control Assn; Air [★5081]
Pollution Control Fed; Water [★5101]
Pollution League; Seacoast Anti- [4451]
Pollution Liability Insurance Assn. - Defunct.
Pollution Probe [IO], Toronto, ON, Canada
Pollution Prog. Administrators and Assn. of Local Air Pollution Control Officials; State and Territorial Air [★5696]
Pollution; Task Force Against Nuclear [18135]
Polly Klaas Found. [12604], PO Box 800, Petaluma, CA 94953, (707)769-1334
Polo
Amer. Bicycle Polo Assn. [23658]
Canadian Polo Assn. [IO]
Collegiate Equestrian Polo Assn. [23659]
Fed. of Intl. Polo [23819]
Hurlingham Polo Assn. [IO]
Movement for an Independent and Democratic Cuba [17367]
Schools and Universities Polo Assn. [IO]
United Kingdom Polocrosse Assn. [IO]
U.S. Bicycle Polo Assn. [23660]
U.S. Polo Assn. [23661]
Polo Assn; Collegiate Water [23972]
Polo Comm. of the Amateur Athletic Union; Water [★23973]
Polo; U.S. Water [23973]
Polocrosse Assn; Amer. [23338]
Polonus Philatelic Soc. [22857], PO Box 489, Maryville, IL 62062
Polosh Soc. of Multiple Sclerosis [IO], Warsaw, Poland
Polska Akademia Nauk [★IO]
Polska Asocjacja Ekologii Krajobrazu [★IO]
Polska Federacja Aikido [IO], Warsaw, Poland
Polska Federacja Squasha [IO], Warsaw, Poland
Polska Federacja Unihokeja - Floorball [★IO]
Polska Izba Ksiazki [★IO]
Polska Izba Nasienna [★IO]
Polska Izba Przemyslu Chemicznego [★IO]
Polska Izba Przemyslu Farmaceutycznego i Wy-robow Medycznych [★IO]
Polska Korporacja Targowa [★IO]
Polska Unia W Ameryce [★19315]
Polski Komitet Olimpijski [★IO]
Polski Komitet Paraolimpijski [★IO]
Polski Komitet Swiatowej Rady Energetycznej [★IO]
Polski Osrodek Spoleczno Kulturalny [★IO]
Polski Towarzystwo Milosnikow Roz [★IO]
Polski Towarzystwo Taneczne [IO], Krakow, Poland
Polski Zwiazek Badmintona [IO], Warsaw, Poland
Polski Zwiazek Biegu na Orientacje [★IO]
Polski Zwiazek Kajakowy [★IO]
Polski Zwiazek Krotkofalowcow [★IO]
Polski Zwiazek Lekkiej Atletyki [IO], Warsaw, Poland
Polski Zwiazek Lyzwiarstwa Szybkiego [★IO]
Polski Zwiazek Lyzwiarswa Figurowego [★IO]
Polski Zwiazek Motorowy [★IO]

Reference to "IO" in place of a book number signifies that the association may be found in the 45th edition of International Organizations.

Polski Zwiazek Pilki Noznej [★IO]
Polski Zwiazek Producentow, Eksporterow i Import-
erow Miesa [★IO]
Polski Zwiazek Taekwondo [★IO]
Polskie Stowarzyszenie Inwestorow Kapitalowych
[★IO]
Polskie Stowarzysznie Ludzi Cierpiacych na Padac-
zke [★IO]
Polskie Towarzystwo Badania Bolu [★IO]
Polskie Towarzystwo Chemiczne [★IO]
Polskie Towarzystwo Entomologiczne [★IO]
Polskie Towarzystwo Fizyczne [★IO]
Polskie Towarzystwo Geograficzne [★IO]
Polskie Towarzystwo Geologiczne [★IO]
Polskie Towarzystwo Informatyczne [★IO]
Polskie Towarzystwo Inzynierii Rolniczej [★IO]
Polskie Towarzystwo Kardiologiczne [★IO]
Polskie Towarzystwo Lekarskie [★IO]
Polskie Towarzystwo Mineralogiczne [★IO]
Polskie Towarzystwo Nauk Weterynaryjnych [★IO]
Polskie Towarzystwo Psychologiczne [★IO]
Polskie Towarzystwo Schronisk Mlodziezowych
[★IO]
Polskie Towarzystwo Socjologiczne [★IO]
Polskie Towarzystwo Stwardnienia Rozsianego
[★IO]
Polskie Towarzystwo Turystyczno-Krajoznawcze
[★IO]
Polskie Zrzeszenie Lokatorow [★IO]
Polskiego Towarzystwo Ekonomicznego [★IO]
Polyacrylate Absorbents; Inst. for [811]
Polycystic Ovarian Syndrome Assn. [15616], PO
Box 3403, Englewood, CO 80111
Polycystic Ovarian Syndrome Assn. [IO], Engle-
wood, CO, United States
Polycystic Ovarian Syndrome Assn. of Australia [IO],
Dapto, Australia
Polyethylene Pipe Assn; Corrugated [3049]
Polygraph Assn; Amer. [5753]
Polygraphists; Amer. Assn. of Police [5748]
Polyisocyanurate Insulation Mfrs. Assn. [661], 7315
Wisconsin Ave., Ste. 400E, Bethesda, MD 20814,
(301)654-0000
Polymer Clay Guild; Natl. [22579]
Polymer Machinery Mfrs. and Distributors Assn. [IO],
Rugby, United Kingdom
Polymers Inst; Emulsion [6681]
Polymers Liaison Program; Emulsion [★6681]
Polynesian
Inst. for the Advancement of Hawaiian Affairs
[10883]
Native Hawaiian Culture and Arts Prog. [10884]
Polynesian Cultural Center [10885]
Polynesian Cultural Center [IO]
Polynesian Cultural Center [IO], Laie, HI, United
States
Polynesian Cultural Center [10885], 55-370 Kame-
hameha Hwy., Laie, HI 96762, (808)293-3333
Polynesian Soc. [IO], Auckland, New Zealand
Polynesian Soc. - Address unknown since 1995.
Polynesian Studies; Institute for [★10885]
Polynesian Studies; Institute for [★IO]
Polynesian Voyaging Soc. [22775], 191 Ala Moana
Blvd., Pier 7, Honolulu, HI 96813, (808)536-8405
Polypay Sheep Assn; Amer. [5191]
Polysomnographic Technologists; Assn. of [16423]
Polysomnographic Technologists; Bd. of Registered
[15134]
Polystyrene Packaging Coun. [★2879]
Polyurethane Div., Soc. of the Plastics Indus.
[★3047]
Polyurethane Foam Assn. [3057], c/o Robert J.
Luedeka, Exec. Dir., 9724 Kingston Pike, Ste. 503,
Knoxville, TN 37922, (865)690-4648
Polyurethane Foam Mfrs. Assn; Flexible [★3057]
Polyurethane Mfrs. Assn. [3058], 6737 W
Washington Ave., Ste. 1420, Milwaukee, WI 53214,
(414)431-3094
Pomegranate Guild of Judaic Needlework [9837],
c/o Randy Paul Heskins, Membership VP, PO Box
132, Fair Lawn, NJ 07410, (856)667-5609
Pomeranian Club; Amer. [22207]
Pomological Soc; Amer. [4704]
Pompeiiana, Inc. - Defunct.
Pompe's Disease
Assn. for Glycogen Storage Disease [15244]

Muscular Dystrophy Assn. [15339]
Pond Restoration Comm; Walden [★4464]
Ponderosa Pine Woodwork Assn. [★686]
Ponies Assn. - UK [IO], Huntingdon, United Kingdom
Pontiac
Fiero Owners Club of Am. [21645]
GTO Assn. of Am. [21651]
The Judge GTO Intl. [21678]
Natl. Firebird and T/A Club [21732]
Oakland-Pontiac Enthusiast Org. [21748]
Pontiac-Oakland Club Intl. [21766]
Pontiac Drag Sports - Address unknown since 2002.
Pontiac Enthusiast Org; Oakland- [21748]
Pontiac-Oakland Club Intl. [21766], PO Box 539,
Victor, NY 14564, (816)554-2099
Pontiac-Oakland Club Intl. [IO], Victor, NY, United
States
Pontifica Academia delle Scienze [★IO]
Pontifical Acad. of Sciences [IO], Vatican City, Vati-
can City
Pontifical Assn. of the Holy Childhood [★19632]
Pontifical Coun. for Culture [IO], Rome, Italy
Pontifical Coun. for the Pastoral Care of Migrants
and Itinerant People [IO], Vatican City, Vatican City
Pontifical Mission for Palestine [IO], New York, NY,
United States
Pontifical Mission for Palestine [12816], c/o Catholic
Near East Welfare Assn., 1011 1st Ave., New York,
NY 10022-4195, (212)826-1480
Pontifical Mission Societies - Canada [IO], Toronto,
ON, Canada
Pontifical Mission Societies in the U.S. [19703], 366
5th Ave., 12th Fl., New York, NY 10001, (212)563-
8700
Pontifical Mission Soc. [IO], Aachen, Germany
Pontifical Missionary Union [★19703]
Pontifical Missionary Union of Priests and Religious
[★19703]
Pontificia Academia dei Nuovi Lincei [★IO]
Pontificium Consilium de Cultura [★IO]
Pontius Family Assn. [21025], c/o B.J. Bongo,
Treas., 21810 Fairmont Blvd., Shaker Heights, OH
44118-4816
Ponty Circle; Merleau- [10811]
Pony of the Americas Club [4945], 3828 S Emerson
Ave., Indianapolis, IN 46203, (317)788-0107
Pony Assn; Amer. Quarter [4840]
Pony Assn; Amer. Walking [4850]
Pony Assn; Intl. Quarter [4904]
Pony Assn; Natl. Chincoteague [4917]
Pony Assn; Natl. Quarter [4923]
Pony Assn. of North Am; Dales [4875]
Pony Baseball and Softball [23124], PO Box 225,
Washington, PA 15301, (724)225-1060
Pony Club [IO], Kenilworth, United Kingdom
Pony Club/American Miniature Horse Registry; Amer.
Shetland [4845]
Pony Club Australia [IO], Fortitude Valley, Australia
Pony Club; British Horse Soc. - [★23537]
Pony Clubs; U.S. [23537]
Pony and Cob Soc. of Am; Welsh [4969]
Pony and Cob Soc. of Am; Welsh [★4969]
Pony and Colt Boys Baseball [★23124]
Pony Express Historical Assn. [10145], 1202 Penn
St., PO Box 1022, St. Joseph, MO 64502,
(816)232-8206
Pony League [★23124]
Pony; Natl. Appaloosa [★4945]
Pony Registry; Gliding Horse and [4884]
Pony Soc. of Am; Dales [4876]
Pony Soc. of Am; Welsh [★4969]
Pony Soc; Amer. Connemara [4815]
Pony Soc; Amer. Kerry Bog [4829]
Pony Soc; Amer. Welara [4854]
Pony Soc. and Conservancy of the Americas; Fell
[4878]
Pony Soc. of North Am; Fell [4879]
Poodle
Poodle Club of Am. [22343]
Poodle Club of Am. [22343], c/o Ms. Peggy McDill,
Corresponding Sec., 24922 Las Marias Ln., Mis-
sion Viejo, CA 92691-5119, (949)378-6701
Poodle Club of Am. Foundation [★22343]
Pool Found; Natl. Swimming [3360]
Pool Inst; Natl. Spa and [★3353]

Pool Inst; Natl. Swimming [★3353]
Pool and Spa Professionals; Assn. of [3353]
Poolplayer Assn; Natl. Wheelchair [23355]
Pools, and Beaches; Natl. Assn. of Amusement
Parks, [★1303]
Poor Cleric Regulars of the Mother of God of the
Pious Schools [IO], Rome, Italy
Poor; Consultative Gp. to Assist the [17833]
Poor; Legal Sers. for the Elderly [★12499]
Poor; Sisters Concerned for the Rural [★12590]
Pop Can Collectors; Natl. [22085]
Pop Music
Air Supply Fan Club [24837]
Beach Boys Fan Club [24846]
Cecilia Lee Intl. Fan Club [24856]
Chicago Fan Club [24859]
Cliff Richard Fan Club of Am. [24866]
Connie Stevens Fan Club [24868]
Dinah Shore Fan Club [24876]
Donny Osmond Intl. Network [24880]
Engelbert's "Goils" [24883]
Engelbert's Golden Eagles [24884]
Engel's Angels in Humperdinck Heaven Fan Club
[24885]
FR-ENGE Intl. [24889]
Friends of the Cassidys [24891]
Friends of Debbie Reynolds Fan Club [24741]
Friends of Dennis Wilson [24892]
Gene Pitney Intl. Fan Club [24898]
Harry Connick, Jr. Fan Club [24907]
Hip-Hop Assn. [10887]
John Gary Intl. Fan Club [24925]
Kate Smith Commemorative Soc. [24930]
Lesley Gore Fan Club [24938]
Natl. Acad. of Popular Music [10655]
Norma Zimmer Natl. Fan Club [24950]
Patti Page Appreciation Soc. [24959]
REG - The Intl. Roger Waters Fan Club [24965]
Tom Jones "Tom Terrific" Fan Club [24986]
Pop-Rock Music
John Mellencamp Official Intl. Fan Club [24926]
Mariah Carey Official Intl. Fan Club [24943]
Michael Bolton Platinum Club [24947]
Rockapella Center [24969]
Pop Warner Football [23436], 586 Middletown Blvd.,
Ste. C-100, Langhorne, PA 19047, (215)752-2691
Pop Warner Junior League Football [★23436]
Popcorn Assn; Intl. [★1589]
Popcorn and Concessions Assn. [★1589]
Popcorn Inst. [1559], 401 N Michigan Ave., Ste.
2200, Chicago, IL 60611-4267, (312)644-6610
Popcorn Mfrs; Natl. Assn. of [★1589]
Popcorn Processors Assn. [★1559]
Pope and Young Club [23056], PO Box 548, Chat-
field, MN 55923-0548, (507)867-4144
Poplar Coun. of Canada [IO], Edmonton, AB,
Canada
Poplar and Fast Growing Forest Trees Res. Inst.
[IO], Izmit-Kocaeli, Turkey
Poplar Forest; Thomas Jefferson's [10069]
Popotnisko zdruzenje Slovenije [★IO]
POPS, Preserve Our Presidential Sites - Defunct.
Popular Culture
Amer. Culture Assn. [10886]
Hip-Hop Assn. [10887]
Popular Culture Assn. [10888]
Popular Culture Assn. [10888], c/o Michael K.
Schoenecke, Exec. Dir., Texas Tech Univ., English
Dept., Box 43091, Lubbock, TX 79409-3091,
(806)742-2500
Popular Economics; Center for [6875]
Popular Flying Assn. [IO], Brackley, United Kingdom
Popular Flying Assn. [IO], London, United Kingdom
Popular Music; Natl. Acad. of [10655]
Popular Price Dress Contractors Assn. [★244]
Popular Price Shoe Retailer Assn. [★1597]
Popular Priced Dress Mfrs. Gp. [★225]
Popular Rotorcraft Assn. [21471], PO Box 68, Men-
tone, IN 46539-0068, (574)353-7227
Population
Action Canada for Population and Development
[IO]
Amer. Inst. for Managing Diversity [17369]
Anita Borg Inst. for Women and Tech. [12754]
Anita Borg Inst. for Women and Tech. [IO]

A star before a book entry number signifies that the name is not listed separately, but is mentioned within the entry.

Asia-Pacific Population Info. Network **[IO]**
Asian Forum of Parliamentarians on Population and Development **[IO]**
Assn. for Population/Family Planning Libraries and Info. Centers-International **[10336]**
Australian Population Assn. **[IO]**
Canadian Population Soc. **[IO]**
Center for Commun. Programs **[IO]**
Center for Commun. Programs **[12755]**
Eugenics Special Interest Gp. **[7114]**
Forum Intl.: Intl. Ecosystems Univ. **[18833]**
Inter-American Parliamentary Gp. on Population and Development **[12432]**
Interact Worldwide **[IO]**
Negative Population Growth **[12756]**
Off. of Population Affairs CH **[12757]**
Optimum Population Trust **[IO]**
Population Action Intl. **[IO]**
Population Action Intl. **[12758]**
Population Assn. of Am. **[6860]**
Population Assn. of New Zealand **[IO]**
Population Assn. of Pakistan **[IO]**
Population Commun. **[IO]**
Population Commun. **[12759]**
Population Communications Intl. **[12760]**
Population Communications Intl. **[IO]**
Population Connection **[12761]**
Population Coun. **[12762]**
Population Coun. **[IO]**
Population and Development Intl. - Vietnam **[IO]**
Population-Environment Balance **[12763]**
Population Inst. **[12764]**
Population Inst. **[IO]**
Population Reference Bur. **[6861]**
Population Rsrc. Center **[12765]**
Population Rsrc. Center **[IO]**
Population and Social Development Stud. Center **[IO]**
Soc. of Population Ecology **[IO]**
Soc. for the Stud. of Reproduction **[16350]**
Sustainable Population Australia **[IO]**
Thai Population Assn. **[IO]**
United Nations Population Fund - Afghanistan **[IO]**
United Nations Population Fund - Albania **[IO]**
United Nations Population Fund - Algeria **[IO]**
United Nations Population Fund - Angola **[IO]**
United Nations Population Fund - Argentina **[IO]**
United Nations Population Fund - Armenia **[IO]**
United Nations Population Fund - Azerbaijan **[IO]**
United Nations Population Fund - Bahrain **[IO]**
United Nations Population Fund - Bangladesh **[IO]**
United Nations Population Fund - Barbados **[IO]**
United Nations Population Fund - Belarus **[IO]**
United Nations Population Fund - Belgium **[IO]**
United Nations Population Fund - Benin **[IO]**
United Nations Population Fund - Bhutan **[IO]**
United Nations Population Fund - Bolivia **[IO]**
United Nations Population Fund - Bosnia and Herzegovina **[IO]**
United Nations Population Fund - Brazil **[IO]**
United Nations Population Fund - Bulgaria **[IO]**
United Nations Population Fund - Burkina Faso **[IO]**
United Nations Population Fund - Burundi **[IO]**
United Nations Population Fund - Cambodia **[IO]**
United Nations Population Fund - Cameroon **[IO]**
United Nations Population Fund - Cape Verde **[IO]**
United Nations Population Fund - Central African Republic **[IO]**
United Nations Population Fund - Chad **[IO]**
United Nations Population Fund - Chile **[IO]**
United Nations Population Fund - China **[IO]**
United Nations Population Fund - Colombia **[IO]**
United Nations Population Fund - Comoros **[IO]**
United Nations Population Fund - Costa Rica **[IO]**
United Nations Population Fund - Cote d'Ivoire **[IO]**
United Nations Population Fund - Cuba **[IO]**
United Nations Population Fund - Cyprus **[IO]**
United Nations Population Fund - Democratic People's Republic of Korea **[IO]**
United Nations Population Fund - Democratic Republic of Congo **[IO]**
United Nations Population Fund - Djibouti **[IO]**

United Nations Population Fund - Dominican Republic **[IO]**
United Nations Population Fund - Ecuador **[IO]**
United Nations Population Fund - Egypt **[IO]**
United Nations Population Fund - El Salvador **[IO]**
United Nations Population Fund - Estonia **[IO]**
United Nations Population Fund - Ethiopia **[IO]**
United Nations Population Fund - Fiji **[IO]**
United Nations Population Fund - Gabon **[IO]**
United Nations Population Fund - Gambia **[IO]**
United Nations Population Fund - Georgia **[IO]**
United Nations Population Fund - Ghana **[IO]**
United Nations Population Fund - Guatemala **[IO]**
United Nations Population Fund - Guinea **[IO]**
United Nations Population Fund - Guyana **[IO]**
United Nations Population Fund - Haiti **[IO]**
United Nations Population Fund - Honduras **[IO]**
United Nations Population Fund - India **[IO]**
United Nations Population Fund - Indonesia **[IO]**
United Nations Population Fund - Iran **[IO]**
United Nations Population Fund - Iraq **[IO]**
United Nations Population Fund - Jamaica **[IO]**
United Nations Population Fund - Japan **[IO]**
United Nations Population Fund - Jordan **[IO]**
United Nations Population Fund - Kazakhstan **[IO]**
United Nations Population Fund - Kenya **[IO]**
United Nations Population Fund - Kuwait **[IO]**
United Nations Population Fund - Kyrgyzstan **[IO]**
United Nations Population Fund - Latvia **[IO]**
United Nations Population Fund - Lebanon **[IO]**
United Nations Population Fund - Lesotho **[IO]**
United Nations Population Fund - Liberia **[IO]**
United Nations Population Fund - Lithuania **[IO]**
United Nations Population Fund - Madagascar **[IO]**
United Nations Population Fund - Malawi **[IO]**
United Nations Population Fund - Malaysia **[IO]**
United Nations Population Fund - Maldives **[IO]**
United Nations Population Fund - Mali **[IO]**
United Nations Population Fund - Mauritania **[IO]**
United Nations Population Fund - Mauritius **[IO]**
United Nations Population Fund - Mexico **[IO]**
United Nations Population Fund - Mongolia **[IO]**
United Nations Population Fund - Morocco **[IO]**
United Nations Population Fund - Mozambique **[IO]**
United Nations Population Fund - Myanmar **[IO]**
United Nations Population Fund - Namibia **[IO]**
United Nations Population Fund - Nepal **[IO]**
United Nations Population Fund - Nicaragua **[IO]**
United Nations Population Fund - Niger **[IO]**
United Nations Population Fund - Nigeria **[IO]**
United Nations Population Fund - Pakistan **[IO]**
United Nations Population Fund - Palestine **[IO]**
United Nations Population Fund - Panama **[IO]**
United Nations Population Fund - Papua New Guinea **[IO]**
United Nations Population Fund - Paraguay **[IO]**
United Nations Population Fund - Peru **[IO]**
United Nations Population Fund - Philippines **[IO]**
United Nations Population Fund - Poland **[IO]**
United Nations Population Fund - Republic of Korea **[IO]**
United Nations Population Fund - Republic of Moldova **[IO]**
United Nations Population Fund - Romania **[IO]**
United Nations Population Fund - Rwanda **[IO]**
United Nations Population Fund - Samoa **[IO]**
United Nations Population Fund - Sao Tome and Principe **[IO]**
United Nations Population Fund - Saudi Arabia **[IO]**
United Nations Population Fund - Senegal **[IO]**
United Nations Population Fund - Sierra Leone **[IO]**
United Nations Population Fund - South Africa **[IO]**
United Nations Population Fund - Sri Lanka **[IO]**
United Nations Population Fund - Sudan **[IO]**
United Nations Population Fund - Swaziland **[IO]**
United Nations Population Fund - Syrian Arab Republic **[IO]**
United Nations Population Fund - Tajikistan **[IO]**
United Nations Population Fund - Tanzania **[IO]**
United Nations Population Fund - Thailand **[IO]**

United Nations Population Fund - Togo **[IO]**
United Nations Population Fund - Trinidad and Tobago **[IO]**
United Nations Population Fund - Tunisia **[IO]**
United Nations Population Fund - Turkey **[IO]**
United Nations Population Fund - Turkmenistan **[IO]**
United Nations Population Fund - Uganda **[IO]**
United Nations Population Fund - Ukraine **[IO]**
United Nations Population Fund - United Arab Emirates **[IO]**
United Nations Population Fund - Uruguay **[IO]**
United Nations Population Fund - Uzbekistan **[IO]**
United Nations Population Fund - Venezuela **[IO]**
United Nations Population Fund - Yemen **[IO]**
Population Action Intl. **[IO]**, Washington, DC, United States
Population Action Intl. **[12758]**, 1300 19th St. NW, Ste. 200, Washington, DC 20036, (202)557-3400
Population Activities; Centre for Development and **[12422]**
Population Assn. of Am. **[6860]**, 8630 Fenton St., Ste. 722, Silver Spring, MD 20910-3812, (301)565-6710
Population Assn. of New Zealand **[IO]**, Auckland, New Zealand
Population Assn. of Pakistan **[IO]**, Islamabad, Pakistan
Population Commun. **[IO]**, Pasadena, CA, United States
Population Commun. **[12759]**, 1250 E Walnut St., Ste. 220, Pasadena, CA 91106, (626)793-4750
Population Communications Intl. **[12760]**, 777 United Nations Plz., 5th Fl., 44th St. at 1st Ave., New York, NY 10017, (212)687-3366
Population Communications Intl. **[IO]**, New York, NY, United States
Population and Community Development Assn. **[IO]**, Bangkok, Thailand
Population Concern **[★IO]**
Population Connection **[12761]**, 2120 L St. NW, Ste. 500, Washington, DC 20037, (202)332-2200
Population Coun. **[12762]**, 1 Dag Hammarskjold Plz., New York, NY 10017, (212)339-0500
Population Coun. **[IO]**, New York, NY, United States
Population Countdown **[★IO]**
Population Crisis Comm. **[★IO]**
Population Crisis Comm. **[★12758]**
Population and Development Intl. - Vietnam **[IO]**, Hanoi, Vietnam
Population Emergency Campaign; World **[★12187]**
Population-Environment Balance **[12763]**, 2000 P St. NW, Ste. 600, Washington, DC 20036, (202)955-5700
Population Growth - Seattle Chap; Zero **[★12761]**
Population Inst. **[12764]**, 107 2nd St. NE, Washington, DC 20002, (202)544-3300
Population Inst. **[IO]**, Washington, DC, United States
Population Inst. Advocates, Inc. **[★IO]**
Population Inst. Advocates, Inc. **[★12764]**
Population; Intl. Union for the Sci. Stud. of **[IO]**
Population Options; Center for **[★12173]**
Population Options' Media Proj; Center for **[★12174]**
Population; Planned Parenthood/World **[★12187]**
Population Reference Bur. **[6861]**, 1875 Connecticut Ave. NW, Ste. 520, Washington, DC 20009-5728, (202)483-1100
Population Reference Bur. **[IO]**, Washington, DC, United States
Population Renewal Office - Address unknown since 2005.
Population Rsrc. Center **[12765]**, 1725 K St. NW, Ste. 1102, Washington, DC 20006, (202)467-5030
Population Rsrc. Center **[IO]**, Washington, DC, United States
Population and Responsible Parenthood Stud. Center **[★IO]**
Population and Social Development Stud. Center **[IO]**, Quito, Ecuador
Populist Party of Am. **[★18319]**
Porcelain
  Belleek Collectors' Intl. Soc. **[21925]**
  Doll Artisan Guild **[22394]**
  Hummel Collectors Club **[22040]**
  Intl. Assn. of R.S. Prussia Collectors **[22043]**

Reference to "IO" in place of a book number signifies that the association may be found in the 45th edition of International Organizations.

Intl. Doll Makers Assn. [22397]
Little Elegance Memories of Yesterday [22065]
Lladro Soc. [21930]
McCoy Pottery Collectors' Soc. [21932]
Natl. Inst. of Amer. Doll Artists [22403]
Pickard Collectors Club [22108]
Porcelain Enamel Inst. [662]
United Fed. of Doll Clubs [22407]
World Org. of China Painters [22177]
Porcelain Enamel Inst. [662], PO Box 920220, Norcross, GA 30010, (770)281-8980
Porcelain on Steel Coun. - Defunct.
Pork Coun. Women; Natl. [★5238]
Pork Producers Coun; Natl. [5238]
Porlock Soc. - Address unknown since 2003.
Pornography
Amer. Decency Assn. [17281]
Americans for Decency [17282]
Anti-Child Pornography Org. [12766]
Anti-Child Pornography Org. [IO]
Children of the Night [12933]
Conservative Majority for Citizen's Rights [17266]
DC Feminists Against Pornography [17527]
Enough Is Enough [17923]
Found. for Moral Restoration [18372]
Morality in Media [18373]
Natl. Coalition for the Protection of Children and Families [18374]
Natl. Network for Youth [12935]
Natl. Runaway Switchboard [12936]
Pornography; Citizens Against [★18372]
Pornography; DC Feminists Against [17527]
Pornography; Natl. Coalition Against [★18374]
Pornography and Obscenity; Natl. Consultation on [★18374]
Porphyria Found; Amer. [15243]
Porpoise Rescue Found. - Defunct.
Porpoise School; Santini's [★7261]
Porsche 356 Registry - Defunct.
Porsche 914 Owners Assn. - Address unknown since 1989.
Porsche Club of Am. [21767], PO Box 1347, Springfield, VA 22151-0347, (703)321-2111
Porsche Owners Club - Address unknown since 1994.
Port Douglas Daintree Tourism Assn. [IO], Port Douglas, Australia
Port and Douro Wines Inst. [IO], Porto, Portugal
Port Engineers; Soc. of Marine [3588]
Port of New York; Customs Clerks Assn. of the [★2309]
Port of New York/New Jersey; Maritime Assn. of the [3572]
Port Resources Information Comm. - Defunct.
Portable Cmpt. and Communications Assn. [908], PO Box 680, Hood River, OR 97031, (541)490-5140
Portable Drilling Rig Mfrs. Assn. - Defunct.
Portable Power Equipment Mfrs. Assn. - Address unknown since 2005.
Portable Rechargeable Battery Assn. [501], 1776 K St., 4th Fl., Washington, DC 20006, (202)719-4978
Portable Sanitation Assn. [★4003]
Portable Sanitation Assn. [★IO]
Portable Sanitation Assn. Intl. [IO], Bloomington, MN, United States
Portable Sanitation Assn. Intl. [4003], 7800 Metro Pkwy., Ste. 104, Bloomington, MN 55425, (952)854-8300
Porter Inst. for Applied Bio-Dynamics; Josephine [4104]
Porter Memorial Soc; Gene Stratton [9651]
Porter Wagoner Intl. Fan Club - Defunct.
Porterfield Airplane Club [21472]
Porters; Brotherhood of Sleeping Car [★24180]
Portland Cement Alliance; Amer. [★915]
Portland Cement Assn. [933], 5420 Old Orchard Rd., Skokie, IL 60077-1053, (847)966-6200
Portland Cement Assn; Amer. [915]
Portland Cement Mfrs'. Assn. [IO], Buenos Aires, Argentina
Portland Grain Exchange - Defunct.
Portland and Seattle Railway Historical Soc; Spokane, [10924]
Portmarnock Sub-Aqua Club [IO], Portmarnock, Ireland

Portobello Antique Dealers Assn. [IO], London, United Kingdom
Portrait Artists; Amer. Soc. of [9495]
Portrait Soc. of Am. [9465], PO Box 11272, Tallahassee, FL 32302, (850)878-9996
Ports and Terminals; Inland Rivers [2604]
Portsmouth and South East Hampshire Chamber of Commerce and Indus. [IO], Havant, United Kingdom
Portugal
Amer. Portuguese Soc. [10889]
Luso-American Educ. Found. [10890]
Portuguese Natl. Tourist Off. [24367]
Portuguese Podengo Club of Am. [22344]
Portuguese Trade Commn. [24368]
Portugal Information Center - Defunct.
Portugese Info., Tourist and Trade Off. [★24367]
Portugese Soc. of Metabolic Bone Disease [IO], Lisbon, Portugal
Portugese Tourist and Info. Off. [★24367]
Portuguesa Continental do Estado da California; Uniao [★19131]
Portuguesa Multiple Sclerosis Soc. [IO], Lisbon, Portugal
Portuguese
Amer. Assn. of Teachers of Spanish and Portuguese [8725]
Amer. Portuguese Engg. and Architecture Soc. [7530]
Amer. Portuguese Soc. [10889]
Amer. Portuguese Soc. [IO]
Amer. Portuguese Stud. Assn. [9004]
Luso-American Educ. Found. [10890]
Portuguese Amer. Leadership Coun. of the U.S. [19320]
Portuguese Historical and Cultural Soc. [19321]
Portuguese Natl. Tourist Off. [24367]
Portuguese Podengo Club of Am. [22344]
Portuguese Soc. Queen St. Isabel [19322]
Portuguese Trade Commn. [24368]
Portuguese Water Dog Club of Am. [22345]
Seminar on the Acquisition of Latin Amer. Lib. Materials [10386]
Portuguese Acad. of History [IO], Lisbon, Portugal
Portuguese-American Chamber of Commerce [★IO]
Portuguese Amer. Leadership Coun. of the U.S. [19320], 1316 Pennsylvania Ave. SE, Capitol Hill, Washington, DC 20003, (202)466-4664
Portuguese Assn. of Animal Feed Mfrs. [IO], Lisbon, Portugal
Portuguese Assn. of Automotive Suppliers [IO], Porto, Portugal
Portuguese Assn. of Booksellers and Publishers [IO], Lisbon, Portugal
Portuguese Assn. of Car Components Mfrs. [★IO]
Portuguese Assn. of Music Educ. [IO], Lisbon, Portugal
Portuguese Assn. of Osteoporosis [IO], Porto, Portugal
Portuguese Assn. of the Pharmaceutical Indus. [IO], Lisbon, Portugal
Portuguese Assn. of Pulp and Paper Technicians [★IO]
Portuguese Assn. of Restaurants and Bars [IO], Lisbon, Portugal
Portuguese Assn. of Supermarkets [IO], Lisbon, Portugal
Portuguese Assn. for Technicians of the Pulp and Paper Indus. [IO], Tomar, Portugal
Portuguese Assn. for Telework [IO], Lisbon, Portugal
Portuguese Broadcasting Assn. [IO], Lisbon, Portugal
Portuguese Cancer Soc. [IO], Porto, Portugal
Portuguese Chamber [IO], London, United Kingdom
Portuguese Chamber of Commerce in Britain [IO], London, United Kingdom
Portuguese Confed. of Bus. and Services [IO], Lisbon, Portugal
Portuguese Continental Union of the U.S.A. [★19131]
Portuguese Coun. of Shopping Centers [IO], Lisbon, Portugal
Portuguese Fiscal Assn. [IO], Lisbon, Portugal
Portuguese Football Fed. [IO], Lisbon, Portugal
Portuguese Footwear, Components, Leather Goods Manufacturer's Assn. [IO], Porto, Portugal

Portuguese Govt. Trade Off. [★24368]
Portuguese Gp. of the Intl. Assn. of Hydrogeologists [IO], Aveiro, Portugal
Portuguese Historical and Cultural Soc. [19321], PO Box 161990, Sacramento, CA 95816, (916)392-1048
Portuguese Hotel Assn. [IO], Lisbon, Portugal
Portuguese League Against Epilepsy [IO], Porto, Portugal
Portuguese League Against Hypertension [IO], Lisbon, Portugal
Portuguese Leather Indus. Assn. [IO], Porto, Portugal
Portuguese Mineral Water Producers' Assn. [IO], Lisbon, Portugal
Portuguese Natl. Tourist Off. [24367], 590 5th Ave., 4th Fl., New York, NY 10036-4702, (212)354-4403
Portuguese Operations Res. Soc. [IO], Lisbon, Portugal
Portuguese Orienteering Fed. [IO], Mafra, Portugal
Portuguese Paper Indus. Assn. [IO], Lisbon, Portugal
Portuguese Petroleum Enterprises' Assn. [IO], Lisbon, Portugal
Portuguese Physiological Soc. [IO], Carcavelos, Portugal
Portuguese Plastics Manufacturers' Assn. [IO], Lisbon, Portugal
Portuguese Podengo Club of Am. [22344], 76-2 River St. W, Old Saybrook, CT 06475, (401)374-5364
Portuguese Soc. of Cardiology [IO], Lisbon, Portugal
Portuguese Soc. of Dermatology and Venereology [IO], Lisbon, Portugal
Portuguese Soc. of Digestive Endoscopy [IO], Lisbon, Portugal
Portuguese Soc. of Hypertension [★IO]
Portuguese Soc. of Infectious Diseases [IO], Lisbon, Portugal
Portuguese Soc. of Pharmacology [IO], Coimbra, Portugal
Portuguese Soc. Queen St. Isabel [19322]
Portuguese Soc. of Rheumatology [IO], Lisbon, Portugal
Portuguese Soc. of Stomatology and Dental Medicine [IO], Lisbon, Portugal
Portuguese Squash Assn. [IO], Corroios, Portugal
Portuguese Trade Commn. [24368], 590 5th Ave., 3rd Fl., New York, NY 10036, (212)354-4610
Portuguese Water Dog Club of Am. [22345], c/o Pat Qvigstad, Membership Chair, 111 Foxtail Cir., Golden, CO 80403-8861, (303)582-5009
Positional Plagiocephaly Support; Craniosynostosis and [14060]
Positive Accord; Truth Missionaries Chap. of [20585]
Positive Coaching Alliance [23296], 3430 W Bayshore Rd., Ste. 104, Palo Alto, CA 94303, (650)354-0909
Positive Futures Network [18839], PO Box 10818, Bainbridge Island, WA 98110-0818, (206)842-0216
Positive Imagery; Natl. Assn. of African Americans for [16941]
Positive Music Assn. [10688], c/o Scott Johnson, 4593 Maple Ct., Boulder, CO 80301, (303)581-9083
Positive Pregnancy and Parenting Fitness - Address unknown since 2003.
Positive Sexuality; Coalition for [13480]
Positive Thinkers Club [★19825]
Positive Youth Found. [18856], PO Box 64, Greencastle, PA 17225, (717)597-9065
Positively Addictive Dog Sports [IO], Brisbane, Australia
Positively Women [IO], London, United Kingdom
Possum Growers and Breeders Assn. - Address unknown since 1995.
Post Anesthesia Nurses; Amer. Soc. of [★15460]
Post and Antenatal Depression Assn. [IO], Richmond, Australia
Post Assn; Parcel [★2454]
Post Card Collectors Club [22908]
Post Card Distributors Assn. of North Am. [★3074]
Post Card Mfrs. Assn. - Defunct.
Post Card and Souvenir Distributors Assn. [3074], 2105 Laurel Bush Rd., Ste. 200, Bel Air, MD 21015, (443)640-1055

A star before a book entry number signifies that the name is not listed separately, but is mentioned within the entry.

Post Institutionalized Child; Parents Network for the [16546]
Post Mark Collectors Club [22858], c/o Robert J. Milligan, Membership Mgr., 7014 Woodland Oaks Dr., Magnolia, TX 77354-4898
Post-Mortem Club - Defunct.
Post Natal Depression Support Assn. [IO], Subiaco, Australia
Post Natal Depression Support Assn. South Africa [IO], Kenilworth, Republic of South Africa
Post Off. Mail Handlers, Watchmen, Messengers, and Gp. Leaders; Natl. [★24171]
Post Off. and Postal Trans. Ser. Mail Handlers, Watchmen and Messengers; Natl. Assn. of [★24171]
Post Office Regional Employees' Assn. - Address unknown since 1995.
Post Off. Soc; Mobile [22848]
Post Off. Soc; Natl. Highway [★22848]
Post-Polio Hea. Intl. [11981], 4207 Lindell Blvd., No. 110, St. Louis, MO 63108-2930, (314)534-0475
Post-Polio Hea. Intl. [IO], St. Louis, MO, United States
Post-Polio League for Info. and Outreach [★15362]
Post Primary Teachers Assn. [IO], Wellington, New Zealand
Post Soc; Metropolitan Air [22845]
Post-Tensioning Inst. [663], 8601 N Black Canyon Hwy., Ste. 103, Phoenix, AZ 85021, (602)870-7540
Post-Traumatic Stress
  African Amer. Post Traumatic Stress Disorder Assn. [21276]
  Armenian Amer. Soc. for Stud. on Stress and Genocide [15190]
  EMDR - Humanitarian Assistance Programs [12767]
  EMDR - Humanitarian Assistance Programs [IO]
  EMDR Intl. Assn. [16215]
  Gift From Within [12768]
  Inst. for Victims of Trauma [13362]
  Vietnam Veteran Wives [21332]
Post Traumatic Stress Disorder; Natl. Center for [16490]
Post War World Coun. - Defunct.
Post World War II Study and Res. Group of the Germany Philatelic Soc. - Defunct.
Postal Arts Assn; Natl. [22139]
Postal Cancellation Soc. [★22858]
Postal Card Soc. of Am. [★22885]
Postal Chess Club; All Ser. [21941]
Postal Chess Tournaments; Amer. [21943]
Postal Clerks; United Fed. of [★24166]
Postal Commemorative Soc. [22859], c/o MBI Inc., 47 Richards Ave., Norwalk, CT 06857, (203)853-2000
Postal Credit Unions; Natl. Coun. of [1116]
Postal Employees; Natl. Alliance of [★24167]
Postal Fairness; Main St. Coalition for [18375]
Postal History Soc. [22860], c/o Kalman V. Illyefalvi, Sec.-Treas., 8207 Daren Ct., Pikesville, MD 21208
Postal History Soc. of Canada [IO], Ottawa, ON, Canada
Postal Satsang - Defunct.
Postal Service
  Air Mail Pioneers [21425]
  Alaska Collectors' Club [22779]
  All Ser. Postal Chess Club [21941]
  Alliance of Nonprofit Mailers [2445]
  Amer. Air Mail Soc. [22780]
  Amer. First Day Cover Soc. [22781]
  Amer. Helvetia Philatelic Soc. [22782]
  Amer. Mailorder Assn. [2457]
  Amer. Philatelic Cong. [22783]
  Amer. Philatelic Res. Lib. [22784]
  Amer. Philatelic Soc. [22785]
  Amer. Philatelic Soc. Writers Unit [22786]
  Amer. Plate Number Single Soc. [22787]
  Amer. Postal Workers Union [24166]
  Amer. Racing Pigeon Union [22894]
  Amer. Revenue Assn. [22788]
  Amer. Soc. of Polar Philatelists [22789]
  Amer. Topical Assn. [22790]
  Amer. Topical Assn., Americana Unit [22791]
  Amer. Topical Assn., Biology Unit [22792]
  Assoc. Collectors of El Salvador [22794]

Assn. of Alternate Postal Systems [2447]
Assn. of European Public Postal Operators [IO]
Assn. for Postal Commerce [2449]
Astronomy Stud. Unit [22795]
Brazil Philatelic Assn. [22797]
Canadian Postmasters and Assistants Assn. [IO]
Carriers and Locals Soc. [22904]
CartoPhilatelic Soc. [22799]
Casey Jones Railroad Unit - ATA [22800]
Chemistry and Physics on Stamps Stud. Unit [22802]
China Stamp Soc. [22803]
Christmas Philatelic Club [22804]
Christopher Columbus Philatelic Soc. [22805]
Citizens' Stamp Advisory Comm. [22806]
Civil Censorship Study Group [22807]
Collectors Club [22808]
Collectors of Religion on Stamps [22809]
Confederate Stamp Alliance [22811]
Cover Collectors Circuit Club [22812]
Croatian Philatelic Soc. [22813]
Dogs on Stamps Stud. Unit [22815]
Earth's Physical Features Stud. Unit [22816]
Eire Philatelic Assn. [22817]
Errors, Freaks and Oddities Collector's Club [22818]
European Conf. of Postal and Telecommunications Administrations [IO]
Fine Arts Philatelists [22819]
France and Colonies Philatelic Soc. [22820]
Gems, Minerals and Jewelry Stud. Unit [22821]
German Colonies Collectors Gp. [22822]
Germany Philatelic Soc. [22823]
Graphics Philately Assn. [22824]
Haiti Philatelic Soc. [22825]
Hellenic Philatelic Soc. of Am. [22826]
Humor Stamp Club [22827]
India Stud. Circle for Philately [22828]
Inter-Governmental Philatelic Corp. [22829]
Intl. Fed. of Amer. Homing Pigeon Fanciers [22895]
Intl. Soc. for Japanese Philately [22830]
Intl. Stamp and Coin Collectors Soc. [22832]
Jack Knight Air Mail Soc. [22834]
John F. Kennedy First Day Cover Stud. Unit [22835]
Junior Philatelists of Am. [22837]
Korea Stamp Soc. [22838]
Machine Cancel Soc. [22839]
Mail Systems Mgt. Assn. [2450]
Mail Users' Assn. [IO]
Mailer's Postmark Permit Club [22840]
Main St. Coalition for Postal Fairness [18375]
Maritime Postmark Soc. [22841]
Mathematical Stud. Unit [22842]
Medical Subjects Unit [22843]
Meter Stamp Soc. [22844]
Metropolitan Air Post Soc. [22845]
Mexico Elmhurst Philatelic Soc. Intl. [22846]
Military Postal History Soc. [22847]
Mobile Post Off. Soc. [22848]
Natl. Alliance of Postal and Fed. Employees [24167]
Natl. Assn. of Letter Carriers of the U.S.A. [24168]
Natl. Assn. of Postal Supervisors [24169]
Natl. Assn. of Postmasters of the U.S. [6178]
Natl. Fed. of SubPostmasters [IO]
Natl. League of Postmasters of the U.S. [24170]
Natl. Mail Order Assn. [2643]
Natl. Postal Forum [6179]
Natl. Postal Mail Handlers Union [24171]
Natl. Rural Letter Carriers' Assn. [24172]
Natl. Star Route Mail Contractors Assn. [2453]
Pan African Postal Union [IO]
Parcel Shippers Assn. [2454]
Perfins Club [22854]
Philatelic Found. [22855]
Polonus Philatelic Soc. [22857]
Post Mark Collectors Club [22858]
Postal Commemorative Soc. [22859]
Postal History Soc. [22860]
Postal Union of the Americas, Spain, and Portugal [IO]
PostEurop [IO]

Postwatch [IO]
Precancel Stamp Soc. [22861]
Retired League Postmasters of the Natl. League of Postmasters [6180]
Rossica Soc. of Russian Philately [22862]
Rotary on Stamps Fellowship [22863]
Russian Zone Handoverprint Stud. and Res. Gp. [22864]
Ryukyu Philatelic Specialist Soc. [22865]
St. Helena, Ascension, and Tristan da Cunha Philatelic Soc. [22866]
Samuel Gompers Stamp Club [22867]
Scandinavian Collectors Club [22868]
Scouts on Stamps Soc. Intl. [22869]
Ships on Stamps Unit [22870]
Soc. of Australasian Specialists/Oceania [22871]
Soc. for Hungarian Philately [22873]
Soc. of Israel Philatelists [22874]
Soc. for Thai Philately [22875]
Space Topic Stud. Unit [22876]
Sports Philatelists Intl. [22877]
Stamps on Stamps Collectors Club [22878]
Stamps for the Wounded [22879]
State Revenue Soc. [22880]
Ukrainian Philatelic and Numismatic Soc. [22883]
United Nations Philatelists, Inc. [22884]
United Postal Stationery Soc. [22885]
U.S. Cancellation Club [22886]
U.S. Stamp Soc. [22888]
Universal Postal Union [IO]
Universal Ship Cancellation Soc. [22889]
Western Cover Soc. [22890]
Zeppelin Collectors Club [22892]
Postal Stationery Soc; United [22885]
Postal Systems; Assn. of Alternate [2447]
Postal Systems; Assn. of Private [★2447]
Postal Trans. Ser. Mail Handlers, Watchmen and Messengers; Natl. Assn. of Post Off. and [★24171]
Postal Union of the Americas and Spain [★IO]
Postal Union of the Americas, Spain, and Portugal [IO], Montevideo, Uruguay
Postal Workers
  Air Mail Pioneers [21425]
  Alaska Collectors' Club [22779]
  Amer. Air Mail Soc. [22780]
  Amer. First Day Cover Soc. [22781]
  Amer. Helvetia Philatelic Soc. [22782]
  Amer. Philatelic Cong. [22783]
  Amer. Philatelic Res. Lib. [22784]
  Amer. Philatelic Soc. [22785]
  Amer. Philatelic Soc. Writers Unit [22786]
  Amer. Plate Number Single Soc. [22787]
  Amer. Postal Workers Union [24166]
  Amer. Racing Pigeon Union [22894]
  Amer. Revenue Assn. [22788]
  Amer. Soc. of Polar Philatelists [22789]
  Amer. Topical Assn. [22790]
  Amer. Topical Assn., Americana Unit [22791]
  Amer. Topical Assn., Biology Unit [22792]
  Assoc. Collectors of El Salvador [22794]
  Assn. of Postal Officials of Canada [IO]
  Astronomy Stud. Unit [22795]
  Brazil Philatelic Assn. [22797]
  Canadian Union of Postal Workers [IO]
  Carriers and Locals Soc. [22904]
  CartoPhilatelic Soc. [22799]
  Casey Jones Railroad Unit - ATA [22800]
  Chemistry and Physics on Stamps Stud. Unit [22802]
  Christmas Philatelic Club [22804]
  Christopher Columbus Philatelic Soc. [22805]
  Citizens' Stamp Advisory Comm. [22806]
  Civil Censorship Study Group [22807]
  Collectors Club [22808]
  Collectors of Religion on Stamps [22809]
  Confederate Stamp Alliance [22811]
  Cover Collectors Circuit Club [22812]
  Dogs on Stamps Stud. Unit [22815]
  Earth's Physical Features Stud. Unit [22816]
  Eire Philatelic Assn. [22817]
  Errors, Freaks and Oddities Collector's Club [22818]
  Fine Arts Philatelists [22819]
  France and Colonies Philatelic Soc. [22820]
  Gems, Minerals and Jewelry Stud. Unit [22821]

Reference to "IO" in place of a book number signifies that the association may be found in the 45th edition of International Organizations.

German Colonies Collectors Gp. **[22822]**
Germany Philatelic Soc. **[22823]**
Graphics Philately Assn. **[22824]**
Haiti Philatelic Soc. **[22825]**
Hellenic Philatelic Soc. of Am. **[22826]**
India Stud. Circle for Philately **[22828]**
Intl. Fed. of Amer. Homing Pigeon Fanciers **[22895]**
Intl. Soc. of Postmasters **[IO]**
Intl. Stamp and Coin Collectors Soc. **[22832]**
Jack Knight Air Mail Soc. **[22834]**
John F. Kennedy First Day Cover Stud. Unit **[22835]**
Junior Philatelists of Am. **[22837]**
Korea Stamp Soc. **[22838]**
Machine Cancel Soc. **[22839]**
Mailer's Postmark Permit Club **[22840]**
Maritime Postmark Soc. **[22841]**
Mathematical Stud. Unit **[22842]**
Medical Subjects Unit **[22843]**
Meter Stamp Soc. **[22844]**
Metropolitan Air Post Soc. **[22845]**
Mexico Elmhurst Philatelic Soc. Intl. **[22846]**
Military Postal History Soc. **[22847]**
Mobile Post Off. Soc. **[22848]**
Natl. Alliance of Postal and Fed. Employees **[24167]**
Natl. Assn. of Letter Carriers of the U.S.A. **[24168]**
Natl. Assn. of Postal Supervisors **[24169]**
Natl. Assn. of Postmasters of the U.S. **[6178]**
Natl. League of Postmasters of the U.S. **[24170]**
Natl. Postal Mail Handlers Union **[24171]**
Natl. Rural Letter Carriers' Assn. **[24172]**
Perfins Club **[22854]**
Philatelic Found. **[22855]**
Polonus Philatelic Soc. **[22857]**
Post Mark Collectors Club **[22858]**
Postal Commemorative Soc. **[22859]**
Postal History Soc. **[22860]**
Precancel Stamp Soc. **[22861]**
Rossica Soc. of Russian Philately **[22862]**
Rotary on Stamps Fellowship **[22863]**
Russian Zone Handoverprint Stud. and Res. Gp. **[22864]**
Ryukyu Philatelic Specialist Soc. **[22865]**
St. Helena, Ascension, and Tristan da Cunha Philatelic Soc. **[22866]**
Samuel Gompers Stamp Club **[22867]**
Scandinavian Collectors Club **[22868]**
Scouts on Stamps Soc. Intl. **[22869]**
Ships on Stamps Unit **[22870]**
Soc. of Australasian Specialists/Oceania **[22871]**
Soc. for Hungarian Philately **[22873]**
Soc. of Israel Philatelists **[22874]**
Soc. for Thai Philately **[22875]**
Space Topic Stud. Unit **[22876]**
Sports Philatelists Intl. **[22877]**
Stamps on Stamps Collectors Club **[22878]**
Stamps for the Wounded **[22879]**
State Revenue Soc. **[22880]**
Ukrainian Philatelic and Numismatic Soc. **[22883]**
United Nations Philatelists, Inc. **[22884]**
United Postal Stationery Soc. **[22885]**
U.S. Cancellation Club **[22886]**
U.S. Stamp Soc. **[22888]**
Universal Ship Cancellation Soc. **[22889]**
Western Cover Soc. **[22890]**
Zeppelin Collectors Club **[22892]**
Postcard Club Fed. - Defunct.
Postcard Collector's Club of America - Defunct.
Postcard Collectors' Club; Better **[★22905]**
Postcard History Soc. **[22909]**, 1795 Kleinfeltersville Rd., Stevens, PA 17578-9669, (717)721-9273
Postcards
Aeronautica and Air Label Collectors Club **[21422]**
Deltiologists of Am. **[22905]**
Golden Glow of Christmas Past **[22975]**
Intl. Fed. of Postcard Dealers **[22906]**
Intl. Fed. of Postcard Dealers **[IO]**
Korea Postcard Collectors Gp. **[22907]**
Post Card Collectors Club **[22908]**
Post Card and Souvenir Distributors Assn. **[3074]**
Postcard History Soc. **[22909]**
Postconsumer Plastic Recyclers; Assn. of **[3045]**

Postdoctoral Assn; Natl. **[9064]**
Postdoctoral and Internship Centers; Assn. of Psychology **[8854]**
Poster Dealers Assn; Intl. Vintage **[106]**
Poster Soc. - Address unknown since 1995.
PostEurop **[IO]**, Brussels, Belgium
Postgraduate Center for Mental Hea. **[16227]**, c/o Vocational Services Dept., 344 W 36th St., New York, NY 10018-1843, (212)560-6720
Postgraduate Center for Psychotherapy **[★16227]**
Postgraduate Medical Assn. of North Am; Interstate **[14386]**
Postmark Soc; Maritime **[22841]**
Postmasters of the U.S; Natl. League of **[24170]**
Postpartum Care Services; Natl. Assn. of **[16902]**
Postpartum Professional Assn; Childbirth and **[13980]**
Postpartum Support Intl. **[12689]**, PO Box 60931, Santa Barbara, CA 93160, (805)967-7636
Postpartum Support Intl. **[IO]**, Santa Barbara, CA, United States
Postsecondary Electronic Standards Coun. **[9165]**, 1 Dupont Cir., Ste. 520, Washington, DC 20036, (202)293-7383
Postwatch **[IO]**, London, United Kingdom
Pot Bellied Pigs; Natl. Comm. on **[4140]**
Pot Belly Pig Rescue **[11450]**, 19025 Parthenia St., Dept. IN, Northridge, CA 91324, (818)701-1534
Pot Mfrs; Natl. Clay **[183]**
Potash Export Assn. - Defunct.
Potash Inst. **[★4107]**
Potash Inst; Amer. **[★4107]**
Potash Inst. of North Am. **[★4107]**
Potash and Phosphate Inst. **[4107]**, 655 Engg. Dr., Ste. 110, Norcross, GA 30092-2837, (770)447-0335
Potato Assn. of Am. **[4757]**, Univ. of Maine, 5715 Coburn Hall, Rm. 6, Orono, ME 04469-5715, (207)581-3042
The Potato Bd. **[★4770]**
Potato Bd; The **[★4770]**
Potato Bd; The Natl. **[★4770]**
Potato Bd; U.S. **[4770]**
Potato Chip Inst., Intl. **[★1562]**
Potato Chip Inst; Natl. **[★1562]**
Potato Chip/Snack Food Assn. **[★1562]**
Potato Commn; Idaho **[4735]**
Potato Coun; Natl. **[4746]**
Potato Coun; U.S. Sweet **[4771]**
Potato Eaters - Defunct.
Potato and Onion Commn; Idaho **[★4735]**
Potato Products Inst; Frozen **[1515]**
Potato Promotion Bd; Natl. **[★4770]**
Potatoes
Idaho Potato Commn. **[4735]**
Natl. Potato Coun. **[4746]**
Potato Assn. of Am. **[4757]**
U.S. Potato Bd. **[4770]**
U.S. Sweet Potato Coun. **[4771]**
Potbellied Pig Assn; North Amer. **[4145]**
Potency Restored - Defunct.
Potentiometer Manufacturers Assn; Precision **[★1230]**
Potomac Antique Tools and Indus. Assn. **[22610]**, c/o Mr. Hugh M. South, Treas., 11166 Wood Elves Way, Columbia, MD 21044, (410)992-1823
Potomac Appalachian Trail Club - Address unknown since 1994.
Potomac Inst. - Defunct.
Potsmokers Anonymous - Address unknown since 2001.
Pottenger Found; Price- **[★15568]**
Pottenger Nutrition Found; Price- **[15568]**
Potter Syndrome Support Gp; Natl. **[16544]**
Potters Coun. **[9780]**, 735 Ceramic Pl., Ste. 100, Westerville, OH 43081, (866)721-3322
Potters Coun. **[IO]**, Westerville, OH, United States
Potters for Peace **[IO]**, Bisbee, AZ, United States
Potters for Peace **[9838]**, PO Box 1043, Bisbee, AZ 85603, (520)432-4616
Potters' Soc. of Australia **[IO]**, Waverley, Australia
Pottery and Allied Workers; Intl. Brotherhood of **[★24066]**
Pottery Assn; Amer. Art **[9411]**
Pottery Assn; Hull **[22039]**

Pottery Club; Abingdon **[21522]**
Pottery Club; Blue/White **[21527]**
Pottery Collectors Soc; Dedham **[22009]**
Pottery Collectors' Soc; Torquay **[IO]**
Pottery Experience - Defunct.
Pottery Mfrs; Assoc. Glass and **[3709]**
Pottery, Plastics, and Allied Workers Intl. Union; Glass Molders, **[24066]**
Poultry
Amer. Assn. of Meat Processors **[2656]**
Amer. Bantam Assn. **[5102]**
Amer. Dutch Bantam Soc. **[5103]**
Amer. Egg Bd. **[5104]**
Amer. Grassfed Assn. **[2438]**
Amer. Langshan Club **[5105]**
Amer. Livestock Breeds Conservancy **[4994]**
Amer. Meat Inst. **[2658]**
Amer. Pastured Poultry Producers Assn. **[5106]**
Amer. Poultry Assn. **[5107]**
Amer. Poultry Intl. **[5108]**
Amer. Poultry Intl. **[IO]**
Amer. Silkie Bantam Club **[5109]**
Assn. of Dutch Poultry Processing Indus. **[IO]**
Australian Chicken Meat Fed. **[IO]**
Brazilian Chicken Producers and Exporters Assn. **[IO]**
British Egg Indus. Coun. **[IO]**
British Poultry Coun. **[IO]**
Canadian Broiler Hatching Eggs Producers' Assn. **[IO]**
Canadian Egg Marketing Agency **[IO]**
Canadian Poultry and Egg Processors Coun. **[IO]**
Canadian Turkey Marketing Agency **[IO]**
Egg CH, Inc. **[5110]**
Food Animal Concerns Trust **[4997]**
Food Safety Consortium **[5031]**
Further Poultry Processors Assn. of Canada **[IO]**
Guinea Fowl Intl. Assn. **[4197]**
Intl. Egg Commn. **[IO]**
Intl. Network on Family Poultry Development **[IO]**
Meat Indus. Suppliers Assn. **[2661]**
Natl. Chicken Coun. **[5111]**
Natl. Poultry Improvement Plan **[5112]**
Natl. Poultry Union **[IO]**
Natl. Turkey Fed. **[5113]**
Plymouth Rock Fanciers Club **[5114]**
Poultry Breeders of Am. **[5115]**
Poultry and Egg Farmers and Processors Assn. **[IO]**
Poultry Indus. Assn. of New Zealand **[IO]**
Poultry Sci. Assn. **[5116]**
Sebright Club of Am. **[5117]**
Serama Coun. of North Am. **[4201]**
Silver Wyandotte Club of Am. **[5118]**
Soc. for the Preservation of Poultry Antiquities **[5119]**
Spanish Assn. of Egg Producers **[IO]**
Swiss Egg Producers' Assn. **[IO]**
Thai Broiler Processing Exporters Assn. **[IO]**
United Egg Assn. Further Processors **[5120]**
United Egg Producers **[5121]**
U.S. Poultry and Egg Assn. **[5122]**
U.S.A. Poultry and Egg Export Coun. **[5123]**
Virginia Poultry Breeders Assn. **[5124]**
World's Poultry Sci. Assn. **[IO]**
World's Poultry Sci. Assn. - The Netherlands **[IO]**
World's Poultry Sci. Assn. - UK **[IO]**
World's Poultry Sci. Assn., U.S.A. Br. **[5125]**
Poultry Breeders of Am. **[5115]**, 1530 Cooledge Rd., Tucker, GA 30084-7303, (770)493-9401
Poultry Breeders Club; Virginia **[★5124]**
Poultry Concerns; United **[11472]**
Poultry and Egg Farmers and Processors Assn. **[IO]**, Buenos Aires, Argentina
Poultry and Egg Inst. of America - Defunct.
Poultry and Egg Natl. Bd. **[★5104]**
Poultry and Food Distributors Assn; Natl. **[1551]**
Poultry and Food Distributors Assn; Natl. Independent **[★1551]**
Poultry Indus. Assn. of New Zealand **[IO]**, Auckland, New Zealand
Poultry Industry Mfrs. Coun. - Defunct.
Poultry Publishers Assn. - Address unknown since 1995.
Poultry Sci. Assn. **[5116]**, 1111 N Dunlap Ave., Savoy, IL 61874, (217)356-5285

A star before a book entry number signifies that the name is not listed separately, but is mentioned within the entry.

Poultry U.S.A; Mgt. Company for Amer. [★5108]
Poultrymen's Cooperative Assn. - Address unknown since 1994.
Pound Civil Justice Inst. [6335], 1054 31st St. NW, Ste. 260, Washington, DC 20007-4453, (202)965-3500
Pound Inst; Roscoe [★6335]
Pounds Sensibly; Take Off [★12649]
Poured Concrete Contractors Assn. [★1011]

Poverty
ACCION Intl. [17205]
Afribike Assn. [IO]
Amer. Bar Assn. Commn. on Homelessness and Poverty [12286]
Amer. Jewish Joint Distribution Comm. [12464]
America's Children Hunger Network [11558]
America's Second Harvest [12388]
Assisted Living Fed. of Am. [12306]
Box Proj. [12836]
Bread for the World [17792]
Bright Hope Intl. [20466]
Bright Hope Intl. [IO]
Call to Renewal [18376]
Caritas Puerto Rico [12839]
Catholic Campaign for Human Development [12713]
Catholic Charities USA [13158]
Catholic Worker Movement [18109]
Center for Community Action of B'Nai B'rith Intl. [11766]
Center for Community Change [12769]
Center on Urban Poverty and Community Development [18377]
Children Now [11575]
China Assn. for NGO Cooperation [IO]
Coalition for Economic Survival [13160]
Coffee Kids [11769]
Community Action Partnership [12770]
Community for Creative Non-Violence [12288]
Concern Am. [12845]
Consultative Gp. to Assist the Poor [17833]
CORSO [IO]
Coun. for Opportunity in Educ. [8324]
CRISTA Ministries [13166]
Debts AIDS Trade Africa [16928]
Development Gp. for Alternative Policies [17835]
Economic Success CH [12771]
Egyptians Relief Assn. [11774]
Env. and Development in Action [IO]
Environmental Development Action in the Third World [IO]
Eurostep: European Solidarity Towards Equal Participation of People [IO]
Find Your Feet [IO]
Flying Doctors of Am. [12523]
Food for the Poor [12772]
Food for the Poor [IO]
Food Providers of Am. [12392]
Food Res. and Action Center [12393]
Found. of Compassionate Amer. Samaritans [20340]
Free Store/Food Bank [12773]
Freedom from Hunger [12394]
Friends of the Third World [12774]
Friends of the Third World [IO]
Global Envision [12194]
Hearts and Minds Network [18730]
Help Darfur Now [12259]
Indus. Areas Found. [17220]
Inst. for Children and Poverty [11602]
Inst. for Food and Development Policy [17795]
Inter-Faith Community Services [12775]
Interreligious Found. for Community Org. [11797]
Jewish Fund for Justice [12776]
Just Act: Youth Action for Global Justice [12435]
Ladies of Charity of the U.S.A. [13173]
Leadership Development Network [17223]
Manpower Demonstration Res. Corp. [12777]
Manpower Demonstration Res. Corp. [IO]
MAZON [12395]
Meals4Israel [12459]
Mercy Corps [12778]
Mercy Corps [IO]
Mexican Amer. Unity Coun. [12277]
Mir Pace Intl. [12872]

Mission of Mercy [12779]
Mission of Mercy [IO]
Mission Without Borders - Australia [IO]
Mission Without Borders - Canada [IO]
Mission Without Borders - South Africa [IO]
Mission Without Borders - United Kingdom [IO]
Multicultural Educ., Training, and Advocacy [11625]
Natl. Black Survival Fund [12780]
Natl. Center for Children in Poverty [11712]
Natl. Coalition of Concerned Legal Professionals [12501]
Natl. Community Action Found. [11754]
Natl. Community Development Org. [11798]
Natl. Immigration Law Center [17807]
Natl. People's Action [11755]
Natl. Student Campaign Against Hunger and Homelessness [12396]
Natl. Training and Info. Center [11799]
Need [12875]
NetAid [11486]
North Amer. St. Newspaper Assn. [18102]
Oper. HOPE, Inc. [11787]
Organize Training Center [11800]
People In Aid [IO]
People's Involvement Corp. [13183]
Poverty Alliance [IO]
Poverty and Race Res. Action Coun. [12781]
POWER: People Organized to Win Employment Rights [17494]
Presbyterian Hunger Prog. [12397]
Rainbow/PUSH Coalition [13185]
Rebuilding Together [12337]
The Revitalization Corps [12782]
Scottish Educ. and Action for Development [IO]
Soc. of St. Vincent de Paul Coun. of the U.S. [13190]
Southern Development Found. [12783]
Southern Mutual Help Assn. [11790]
Southern Poverty Law Center [17155]
Synergos Inst. [12784]
Synergos Inst. [IO]
Tapori Intl. ATD Fourth World [IO]
TechnoServe [17849]
Together, Inc. [12365]
Touching Hearts [11267]
Travelers Aid Intl. [13191]
Trickle Up Prog. [12446]
Union Settlement Assn. [12785]
U.S.A. Harvest [12402]
USC Canada [IO]
War on Want [IO]
Welfare Warriors [18183]
Windward Found. [13195]
Women in Community Ser. [12786]
Work Fairness [12110]
World Concern [12787]
World Concern [IO]
World Hunger Year [17799]
Poverty Alliance [IO], Glasgow, United Kingdom
Poverty; Amer. Bar Assn. Commn. on Homelessness and [12286]
Poverty, Anti-
ActionAid Intl. USA [11758]
Bread for the World [17792]
Catholic Campaign for Human Development [12713]
Center for Community Change [12769]
Community Action Partnership [12770]
Consultative Gp. to Assist the Poor [17833]
Engineers for a Sustainable World [11776]
Free Store/Food Bank [12773]
Friends of the Third World [12774]
Global Envision [12194]
Humanitarian Rehabilitation Org. For The Poor And Needy [IO]
Inst. for Food and Development Policy [17795]
Inter-Faith Community Services [12775]
Jewish Fund for Justice [12776]
Natl. Black Survival Fund [12780]
NetAid [11486]
Sales Exchange for Refugee Rehabilitation and Vocation [3846]
Southern Development Found. [12783]
Union Settlement Assn. [12785]

Women in Community Ser. [12786]
World Concern [12787]
World Hunger Year [17799]
Poverty; Citizens Crusade Against [★12769]
Poverty; Inst. for Children and [11602]
Poverty Law Center; Southern [17155]
Poverty Law; Natl. Center on [6030]
Poverty; Natl. Center for Children in [11712]
Poverty; Natl. Law Center on Homelessness and [12297]
Poverty and Race Res. Action Coun. [12781], 1015 15th St. NW, Ste. 400, Washington, DC 20005, (202)906-8023
Poverty; Western Center on Law and [6037]
P.O.W. Network [21264], PO Box 68, Skidmore, MO 64487-0068, (660)928-3304
POW-WOW - Defunct.
Powder Actuated Systems Assn. [IO], Sheffield, United Kingdom
Powder Actuated Tool Mfrs'. Inst. [2057], 136 S Main St., Ste. 2E, St. Charles, MO 63301, (314)889-7117
Powder Coating Inst. [854], 2121 Eisenhower Ave., Ste. 401, Alexandria, VA 22314, (703)684-1770
Powder Indus. Fed; Metal [2714]
Powder Metallurgy Equip. Association [★2714]
Powder Metallurgy Inst; Amer. [★7310]
Powder Metallurgy Parts Association [★2714]
Powder Producers Assn; Metal [2715]
Powder Sci. and Tech. Res. [★IO]
Powell Fan Club; Jane [24747]
Powell Sport Wagon Registry - Address unknown since 2000.
Power
Ash Development Assn. of Australia [IO]
Elec. Power Res. Inst. [IO]
Elec. Power Res. Inst. [7531]
Electricity Storage Assn. [3957]
Intl. Model Power Boat Assn. [22645]
Natl. Assn. of Power Engineers [7532]
Org. of CANDU Indus. [IO]
Power Sources Mfrs. Assn. [3075]
Solar Elec. Power Assn. [7678]
Tesla Memorial Soc. [11151]
Turbine Inlet Cooling Assn. [7055]
U.S. Combined Heat and Power Assn. [7821]
Utilities Ser. Alliance [3966]
Power Associates; Fusion [6954]
Power Assn; Amer. Public [6336]
Power Bar Assn; Fed. [★5683]
Power Boat Assn; Amer. [23152]
Power Cable Engineers Assn; Insulated [★7017]
Power Club; Elec. [★1191]
Power and Commun. Contractors Assn. [1060], 103 Oronoco St., Ste. 200, Alexandria, VA 22314, (703)212-7734
Power Conversion Products Coun. Intl. [★1836]
Power Conversion Products Coun. Intl. [★IO]
Power Crane and Shovel Assn. [2058], c/o Assn. of Equip. Manufacturers, 6737 W Washington St., Ste. 2400, Milwaukee, WI 53214-5647, (414)272-0943
Power Distributors Assn; Fluid [2019]
Power Electronics Coun; IEEE [★6922]
Power Electronics Soc; IEEE [6922]
Power Engg. Soc; IEEE [6903]
Power Equip. Aftermarket Assn; Outdoor [1292]
Power Equip. Dealers Assn; Natl. Farm and [★185]
Power Equip. Distributors Assn; Outdoor [★1293]
Power Equip. and Engine Ser. Assn; Outdoor [1293]
Power Equip. Inst; Outdoor [1294]
Power Fan Manufacturers Assn. [★1876]
Power Fan Manufacturers Assn. [★IO]
Power Fastenings Assn. [IO], Birmingham, United Kingdom
Power Generation Contractors Assn. [IO], London, United Kingdom
Power Industry Biologists Task Force - Defunct.
Power Industry Laboratory Assn. - Defunct.
Power-Motion Tech. Representatives Assn. [2059], One Spectrum Pointe, Ste. 150, Lake Forest, CA 92630, (949)859-2885
Power; Natl. Conf. on Fluid [7085]
Power Net Assn; Amer. [★3780]
Power Operations; Inst. of Nuclear [7392]

Reference to "IO" in place of a book number signifies that the association may be found in the 45th edition of International Organizations.

POWER: People Organized to Win Employment Rights [17494], 32 7th St., San Francisco, CA 94103, (415)864-8372
Power Res. Inst; Electronic [★7531]
Power Soc; Fluid [★7084]
Power Sources Mfrs. Assn. [3075], PO Box 418, Mendham, NJ 07945-0418, (973)543-9660
Power Sprayer and Duster Coun. - Defunct.
Power Squadrons; U.S. [23231]
Power Sweeping Assn; North Amer. [2473]
Power Tool Inst. [1831], 1300 Sumner Ave., Cleveland, OH 44115-2851, (216)241-7333
Power Transmission Assn; Mech. [2045]
Power Transmission Coun. - Defunct.
Power Transmission Distributors Assn. [2060], 230 W Monroe, Ste. 1410, Chicago, IL 60606-4703, (312)516-2100
Power Transmission Distributors Association [IO], Chicago, IL, United States
Power Transmission Equip. Distributors Assn; Mech. [★2060]
Power Transmission Representatives Assn. [★2059]
Power Washers of North Am. [2474], PO Box 668, Quakertown, PA 18951, (800)393-7962
Power Washers of North Am. [IO], Quakertown, PA, United States
Power for Women [13436], 28 E Jackson Blvd., Ste. 1900, Chicago, IL 60604, (312)957-0195
Power to the Youth - Address unknown since 2007.
Powered Ultralight Mfrs. Assn. - Defunct.
Powerlifting
    Natl. Amateur Body Builders Assn. USA [23244]
    North Amer. Powerlifting Fed. [23662]
    U.S. Powerlifting Fed. [23663]
    United World Powerlifting Fed. [IO]
    USA Powerlifting [23664]
    World Assn. of Benchers and Dead Lifters [23986]
Powerlifting Comm. of the Amateur Athletic Union [★23663]
Powerlifting Fed. of the AAU; U.S. [★23663]
POWERLUNCH! [759], c/o The Employment Support Center, 1556 Wisconsin Ave. NW, Washington, DC 20007, (202)628-2919
Powers' Official Fan Club; Stefanie [24774]
Powys Soc. [IO], Taunton, United Kingdom
Powys Soc. of North Am. [9705], c/o Nicholas Birns, Exec. Sec., 205 E 10th St., New York, NY 10003-7634, (212)533-8397
PPFA Guild [★9467]
PR Comm. for Licensing and Registration - Defunct.
PRA Coatings Tech. Centre [IO], Hampton, United Kingdom
Practical Action [IO], Rugby, United Kingdom
Practical Action - Bangladesh [IO], Dhaka, Bangladesh
Practical Allergy Res. Found. [★13599]
Practical Nurse Educ. and Ser; Natl. Assn. for [8869]
Practical Nurses Assn; Amer. Licensed [15450]
Practical Nurses; Natl. Assn. of Licensed [★8869]
Practical Nurses; Natl. Fed. of Licensed [15509]
Practical Refrigerating Engineers; Natl. Assn. [★7037]
Practical Shooting Assn; U.S. [23730]
Practice; Acad. of Pharmacy [★15918]
Practice and Mgt; Acad. of Pharmacy [★15918]
Practice Mgt. Assn; Emergency Dept. [14330]
Practice Mgt. in Podiatry; Amer. Acad. of [★16024]
Practice; Natl. Academies of [14648]
Practice of Pharmacy; Acad. of Gen. [★15918]
Practice Sect. of APhA; Gen. [★15918]
Practising Law Inst. [8774], 810 7th Ave., New York, NY 10019-5818, (212)824-5710
Practitioners; Amer. Bd. of Veterinary [16758]
Practitioners; Amer. Coll. of Nurse [15448]
Practitioners Assn; Cash Mgt. [★1403]
Practitioners; Assn. of Interstate Commerce Commn. [★6316]
Practitioners Before the Interstate Commerce Commn; Assn. of [★6316]
Practitioners Faculties; Natl. Org. of Nurse [15513]
Practitioners in Osteopathic Medicine and Surgery; Amer. Coll. of Gen. [★15793]
Prader-Willi Connection - Defunct.
Prader-Willi Found. [14474]

Prader-Willi Syndrome Assn. [★14475]
Prader-Willi Syndrome Assn. - South Africa [IO], Pretoria, Republic of South Africa
Prader-Willi Syndrome Assn. (U.S.A.) [14475], 8588 Potter Park Dr., Ste. 500, Sarasota, FL 34238, (941)312-0400
Prader-Willi Syndrome Assn. U.S.A [★14475]
Prader-Willi Syndrome Parents and Friends [★14475]
Prairie Chicken Found. - Address unknown since 1994.
Prairie Club [12799], c/o Jacquie Dziak, 110 E Schiller, Ste. 302, Elmhurst, IL 60126, (630)516-1277
Prairie Found; Tallgrass [★4404]
Prairie Implement Manufacturers' Assn. [★IO]
Prairie Print Makers - Defunct.
Prall Family Assn. [21026], c/o Richard D. Prall, Historian/Ed., 14104 Piedras Rd. NE, Albuquerque, NM 87123
Prang-Mark Soc. - Address unknown since 1999.
Pratt Inst. Assn; Morris [20451]
Pratt Inst; Morris [★20453]
Pravah [IO], New Delhi, India
Praxis Proj. [17204], 1750 Columbia Rd. NW, 2nd Fl., Washington, DC 20009, (202)234-5921
Prayer; Anglican Fellowship of [19452]
Prayer; Apostleship of [19569]
Prayer Center; World [★19553]
Prayer; Fellowship in [19894]
Prayer; Intl. Comm. for World Day of [★20629]
Prayer League; South Amer. Mission [★20234]
Prayer; Pious Union of [19701]
Prayer Team; Presidential [20210]
Prayer for World Peace; Soc. of [★18258]
Prayers for Life [19907], c/o Dr. James F. Nugent, Pres., Salve Regina Univ., Ochre Ct., Newport, RI 02840, (401)849-5421
Praying Hands Ranches [23360], c/o Shirley A. Hanson, Exec. Dir., 4825 E Daley Cir., Parker, CO 80138, (303)841-4043
Pre-Eclampsia Soc. [IO], Caernarfon, United Kingdom
Pre- and Perinatal Psychology and Hea; Assn. for [13979]
Pre-Raphaelite Soc. [IO], Coventry, United Kingdom
Pre-Retirement Assn. [★IO]
Pre-Retirement Assn. - Address unknown since 1995.
Pre-Retirement Assn. of Great Britain and Northern Ireland [★IO]
Pre-school Learning Alliance [IO], London, United Kingdom
Preachers; College of [★19903]
Preamble Center [5664], 2040 S St. NW, Washington, DC 20009, (202)265-3263
Precancel Club; Intl. [★22861]
Precancel Stamp Soc. [22861], c/o James Hirstein, Sec., PO Box 4072, Missoula, MT 59806-4072
Precanceled Envelope Collectors Club - Defunct.
Precast Assn; Architectural [917]
Precast Concrete Assn; Natl. [930]
Precast Concrete Paving and Kerb Assn. [★IO]
Precast Flooring Fed. [IO], Leicester, United Kingdom
Precast/Prestressed Concrete Inst. [934], 209 W Jackson Blvd., No. 500, Chicago, IL 60606-6938, (312)786-0300
Precious Metal Clay Guild [8172], PO Box 3000, Denville, NJ 07834, (859)586-0595
Precious Metal Clay Guild [IO], Denville, NJ, United States
Precision Aerobatics Model Pilots Assn. [21473], 158 Flying Cloud Isle, Foster City, CA 94404, (650)345-0130
Precision Chiropractic Res. Soc. - Defunct.
Precision Engg; Amer. Soc. for [6997]
Precision Instruments Association; Opto- [★3488]
Precision Machined Products Assn. [1832], 6700 W Snowville Rd., Brecksville, OH 44141, (440)526-0300
Precision Measurements Assn. - Defunct.
Precision Metalforming Assn. [2726], 6363 Oak Tree Blvd., Independence, OH 44131-2556, (216)901-8800

Precision Optics Mfrs. Assn; Amer. [3480]
Precision Potentiometer Manufacturers Assn. [★1230]
PreCollege Directors; Natl. Assn. of [8371]
Predator Conservation Alliance [5368], PO Box 6733, Bozeman, MT 59771, (406)587-3389
Predator Proj. [★5368]
Predmore - Pridmore - Pridemore - Prigmore Assn. - Defunct.
Prefab. Home Mfrs. Inst. [★2524]
Preferential Trade Area for Eastern and Southern African States [★IO]
Preferred Funeral Directors Intl. [IO], Indian Rocks Beach, FL, United States
Preferred Funeral Directors Intl. [2790], PO Box 335, Indian Rocks Beach, FL 33785, (888)655-1566
Preferred Hotels Assn. - Defunct.
Preferred Provider Organizations; Amer. Assn. of [14680]
Pregnancy and Infant Loss Center [★12668]
Pregnancy and Infant Loss Support; SHARE- [12690]
Pregnancy; Natl. Campaign to Prevent Teen [13499]
Pregnancy; North Amer. Soc. for the Stud. of Hypertension in [16342]
Pregnancy; Org. Gestosis - Soc. for the Stud. of Pathophysiology of [IO]
Pregnancy and Parenting; Natl. Org. of Adolescent [★12182]
Pregnancy, Parenting and Prevention; Natl. Org. on Adolescent [★12182]
Pregnancy Support Network; Sidelines Natl. High-Risk [15617]
Pregnant With Cancer Network [13865], PO Box 1243, Buffalo, NY 14220, (800)743-4471
Prehistoric Soc. [IO], London, United Kingdom
Prejudice and Ethnoviolence; Center for the Applied Stud. of [★17146]
Prejudice Institute/Center for the Applied Stud. of Ethnoviolence [17146], 2743 Maryland Ave., Baltimore, MD 21218, (410)366-9654
Prejudice and Violence; Natl. Inst. Against [★17146]
Premature Babies; Parents of [12686]
Premature Birth
    Assn. for Retinopathy of Prematurity and Related Diseases [15673]
    Fairview Pregnancy and Newborn Loss Information [12668]
    Parents of Premature Babies [12686]
    Prevent Blindness in Premature Babies [16883]
Premedical Summer Institute [★8437]
Premenstrual Soc. [IO], Addlestone, United Kingdom
Premenstrual Syndrome Action - Defunct.
Premenstrual Syndrome; Natl. Assn. for [IO]
Premier [★14597]
Premier Advocacy [14597], 444 N Capitol St. NW, Ste. 625, Washington, DC 20001-1511, (202)393-0860
Premium Advt. Assn. of Am. [★2647]
Premium Incentive, Travel Suppliers and Agents; Amer. Assn. of [3904]
Premm Family Assn. [21027]
Preoperative Assn. [IO], London, United Kingdom
Prepackaging Assn; Produce [★5028]
Prepaid Communications Assn; Intl. [3767]
Prepaid Legal Services Inst; Amer. [6020]
Preparatory Commn. for the Comprehensive Nuclear-Test-Ban Treaty Org. [IO], Vienna, Austria
Preparatory Comm. for the Second United Nations Development Decade - Defunct.
Prepare Tomorrow's Parents [13511], 454 NE 3rd St., Boca Raton, FL 33432, (561)620-0256
Presbyterian
    Assn. for Interdisciplinary Res. in Values and Social Change [12906]
    Assn. of Presbyterian Colleges and Universities [9005]
    Independent Bd. for Presbyterian Foreign Missions [20467]
    The Interchurch Center [19896]
    Medical Benevolence Found. [14725]
    Mission to the World [20468]
    Mission to the World [IO]
    More Light Presbyterians for Lesbian, Gay, Bisexual and Transgender Concerns [20063]

A star before a book entry number signifies that the name is not listed separately, but is mentioned within the entry.

Natl. Assn. of Presbyterian Scouters [13000]
Natl. Ghost Ranch Found. [20469]
Presbyterian Assn. of Musicians [20435]
Presbyterian Church of Aotearoa New Zealand [IO]
Presbyterian Church Bus. Administrators' Assn. [20470]
Presbyterian Evangelistic Fellowship [20471]
Presbyterian Frontier Fellowship [20383]
Presbyterian Historical Soc. [10891]
Presbyterian Lay Comm. [20472]
Presbyterian Men [20473]
Presbyterian-Reformed Ministries Intl. [20474]
Presbyterian-Reformed Ministries Intl. [IO]
Presbyterian Women [20475]
Presbyterians Pro-Life [12926]
Presbyterians for Renewal [20476]
Progressive, Radically Inclusive Student Ministry [19938]
World Witness, Foreign Bd. of the Associate Reformed Presbyterian Church [20420]
Presbyterian Assn. of Diversified Ministries - Defunct.
Presbyterian Assn. of Musicians [20435], 100 Witherspoon St., Louisville, KY 40202-1396, (502)569-5288
Presbyterian Church of Aotearoa New Zealand [IO], Wellington, New Zealand
Presbyterian Church Bus. Administrators' Assn. [20470], c/o Christopher Nicholas, Pres., The Presbyterian Center, 100 Witherspoon St., Louisville, KY 40202-6300, (888)728-7228
Presbyterian Church of the U.S.A. in 1981; Hunger Prog. Comm. of the United [★12397]
Presbyterian Church in the U.S; Task Force on World Hunger/ [★12397]
Presbyterian Church (U.S.A.); Dept. of History and Records Mgt. Services of the [★10891]
Presbyterian Church, World Witness; Associate Reformed [★20420]
Presbyterian Churchmen United - Address unknown since 1995.
Presbyterian Coll. Union [★9005]
Presbyterian Colleges; Assn. of [★9005]
Presbyterian Educational Assn. of the South - Defunct.
Presbyterian Evangelical Fellowship - Defunct.
Presbyterian Evangelistic Fellowship [20471], 425 State St., Ste. 312, Bristol, VA 24201, (276)591-5335
Presbyterian Frontier Fellowship [20383], c/o Rev. Bill Young, Exec. Dir., 7132 Portland Ave., Ste. 136, Richfield, MN 55423-3264, (612)869-0062
Presbyterian Hea., Educ. and Welfare Assn. [13184], 100 Witherspoon St., Louisville, KY 40202-1396, (502)569-5800
Presbyterian Hea., Educ. and Welfare Assn; United [★13184]
Presbyterian Hea. and Welfare Assn; Natl. [★13184]
Presbyterian Historical Assn. [★10891]
Presbyterian Historical Soc. [10891], 425 Lombard St., Philadelphia, PA 19147-1516, (215)627-1852
Presbyterian Historical Soc. [★10891]
Presbyterian Hunger Prog. [12397], Presbyterian Church (U.S.A.), 100 Witherspoon St., Louisville, KY 40202-1396, (888)728-7228
Presbyterian Interracial Coun. - Address unknown since 1995.
Presbyterian Lay Comm. [20472], PO Box 2210, Lenoir, NC 28645-2210, (828)758-8716
Presbyterian Men [20473], c/o Dr. Kyung-il Ghymn, Pres., 4266 Whistlewood Ct., Reno, NV 89509, (775)825-3104
Presbyterian Men; Natl. Coun. of United [★20473]
Presbyterian Missionary Comm. [★14147]
Presbyterian Missions; World [★20468]
Presbyterian Parents of Gays and Lesbians [17655], 3500 Oak Lawn Ave., Ste. 300, Dallas, TX 75219-4349, (972)219-6063
Presbyterian Peace Fellowship [18241], PO Box 271, Nyack, NY 10960, (520)780-6928
Presbyterian Peace Fellowship; Southern [★18241]
Presbyterian Peace Fellowship; United [★18241]
Presbyterian-Reformed Ministries Intl. [20474], PO Box 429, Black Mountain, NC 28711-0429, (828)669-7373

Presbyterian-Reformed Ministries Intl. [IO], Black Mountain, NC, United States
Presbyterian and Reformed Renewal Ministries Intl. [★IO]
Presbyterian and Reformed Renewal Ministries Intl. [★20474]
Presbyterian Scouters; Natl. Assn. of [13000]
Presbyterian Univ. Pastors and Campus Ministry Assn; Assn. of [★19933]
Presbyterian Women [20475], c/o Ann Ferguson, Coor., 100 Witherspoon St., Louisville, KY 40202, (888)728-7228
Presbyterian Women; United [★20475]
Presbyterians for Biblical Concerns [★20476]
Presbyterians; Covenant Fellowship of [★20476]
Presbyterians for Lesbian, Gay, Bisexual and Trans-gender Concerns; More Light [20063]
Presbyterians for Lesbian and Gay Concerns [★20063]
Presbyterians Pro-Life [12926], 3942 Middle Rd., Allison Park, PA 15101, (412)487-1990
Presbyterians for Renewal [20476], 8134 New LaGrange Rd., Ste. 227, Louisville, KY 40222-4673, (502)425-4630
Preschool Education
  Natl. Head Start Assn. [9006]
  Natl. Jewish Coalition for Literacy [8795]
  Natl. Kindergarten Alliance [9007]
  Waldorf Early Childhood Assn. of North Am. [9008]
Prescott Builders Assn. - Defunct.
Prescott Coll. Alumni Assn. [18921], 220 Grove Ave., Prescott, AZ 86301, (877)350-2100
Prescription Drug Programs; Natl. Coun. for [2987]
Prescription Footwear Assn. [★1599]
Prescription Opticians of Am; Guild of [★15709]
Presentation Bros. of Mary [IO], Cork, Ireland
Preservation Action [10058], 401 F St. NW, Ste. 324, Washington, DC 20001, (202)637-7873
Preservation and Appreciation of Antique Motor Fire Apparatus in Am; Soc. for the [22423]
Preservation Association; American Shore and Beach [4352]
Preservation Assn; Natl. New Deal [10775]
Preservation of Birds of Prey; Soc. for the [5382]
Preservation Charities of Am; Conservation and [4382]
Preservation Commissions; Natl. Alliance of [5786]
Preservation Comm; Comanche Language and Cultural [10736]
Preservation Coun; North Amer. Plant [5356]
Preservation of Covered Bridges; Natl. Soc. for the [10049]
Preservation of Film Music; Soc. for the [★10595]
Preservation of the Greek Heritage; Soc. for the [9997]
Preservation of the Hellenic Orthodox Church and the Hellenic Language; Pan Amer. Coun. for the [20074]
Preservation Inst. [13130], 2140 Shattuck Ave., Ste. 2122, Berkeley, CA 94704, (510)848-7827
Preservation Inst; Natl. [10048]
Preservation; Inst. for Responsible Housing [5790]
Preservation; Intl. Coun. for Bird [★5290]
Preservation of Jewish Holy Sites; Athra Kadisha: The Soc. for the [10274]
Preservation of the Mahayana Tradition; Found. for the [19550]
Preservation; Natl. Trust for Historic [10051]
Preservation of Natural Conditions Ecological Soc. of Am; Comm. on [★4433]
Preservation of New England Antiquities; Soc. for the [★10035]
Preservation Officers; Natl. Conf. of State Historic [5787]
Preservation of Old Mills; Soc. for the [10065]
Preservation of Our Femininity and Finances - Defunct.
Preservation and Presentation of the Arts; Assn. for the [9355]
Preservation Soc; Military Aviation [★9342]
Preservation Soc. and Museum; Military Aviation [★9342]
Preservation Soc; New England Wild Flower [★4434]

Preservation of Square Dancing; Foundation for the Promotion and [★9869]
Preservation of Square Dancing; Foundation for the Promotion and [★IO]
Preservation Tech; Assn. for [★10016]
Preservation Tech. and Training; Natl. Center for [7161]
Preservation Trust; Frank Lloyd Wright [10023]
Preservation Trust Intl; Wildlife [★5402]
Preservation of Virginia Antiquities; Assn. for the [★10013]
Preservation Volunteers [10059], 232 E 11th St., New York, NY 10003, (212)769-2900
Preservation of Wheatland; James Buchanan Found. for the [11126]
Preserve Assn; North Amer. Game Breeders and Shooting [★4144]
Preserve Cape Cod; Assn. to [4361]
Preserve Catacombs in Italy; Intl. Comm. to [★10039]
Preservers Assn; Natl. [★1530]
Preserving Arts and Cultural Environments; Saving and [9470]
Presidency; Center for the Stud. of the [17069]
Pres. Benjamin Harrison Found. [11142], 1230 N Delaware St., Indianapolis, IN 46202, (317)631-1898
Pres. Lincoln's Farm [★23943]
Presidential Center; Rutherford B. Hayes [11148]
Presidential Classroom [8756], 119 Oronoco St., Alexandria, VA 22314-2015, (703)683-5400
Presidential Classroom for Young Americans [★8756]
Presidential Debates; Commn. on [18350]
Presidential and Democratic Party Victory Fund - Defunct.
Presidential Families of Am. [21143], c/o Rev. Barry Christopher Howard, Pres., 10939 W 59th Pl., Arvada, CO 80004-4732
Presidential Lib. Assn; Herbert Hoover [11122]
Presidential Papers; Lib. of [★17069]
Presidential Prayer Team [20210], PO Box 15040, Scottsdale, AZ 85267-5040, (520)219-5400
Presidential Task Force; Republican [18536]
Presidents; Amer. Assn. of Independent Coll. and Univ. [★8534]
Presidents Assn. - Defunct.
President's Award for Educational Excellence [★9014]
President's Commn. on the Holocaust [★17725]
Presidents; Coun. of [★17558]
Presidents; Coun. of Sci. Soc. [7605]
President's Coun. on Youth Opportunity - Defunct.
President's Day Natl. Comm. - Defunct.
Presidents and First Ladies of Am; Hereditary Order of the Families of the [21261]
Presidents Forum [★719]
Presidents of Independent Colleges and Universities; Amer. Assn. of [8534]
Presidents of Major Amer. Jewish Organizations; Conf. of [20134]
Presidents; Natl. Assn. of Credit Union [★1112]
Presidents; Natl. Conf. of Bar [5516]
Presidents' Org; Young [769]
Presidents of Statistical Societies; Comm. of [7704]
Presley, Elvis
  Asian Worldwide Elvis Fan Club [24805]
  Elvis Forever TCB Fan Club [24808]
  Elvis Presley Memorial Soc. [24809]
  Elvis Teddy Bears [24810]
  Presley-ites Fan Club Intl. [24813]
  TCB for Elvis Fan Club [24814]
  We Remember Elvis Fan Club [24815]
Presley Fan Club; ElvisNet Elvis [24812]
Presley-ites Fan Club Intl. [24813], c/o Kathy Ferguson, Pres., 6010 18th St., Zephyrhills, FL 33540-2702, (813)788-9133
Presley Memorial Soc; Elvis [24809]
Presort Mailers; Natl. Assn. of [2452]
Press
  Agricultural Journalists Assn. of Armenia [IO]
  Alternative Press Center [10892]
  Amer. Agricultural Editors' Assn. [3076]
  Amer. Amateur Press Assn. [22910]
  Amer. Assn. of Dental Editors [3077]

Amer. Assn. of Independent News Distributors [3078]
Amer. Assn. of Sunday and Feature Editors [3079]
Amer. Copy Editors Soc. [3080]
Amer. Horse Publications [3203]
Amer. Jewish Press Assn. [3081]
Amer. Medical Writers Assn. [3082]
Amer. News Women's Club [3083]
Amer. Printing History Assn. [9989]
Amer. Soc. of Bus. Publication Editors [3084]
Amer. Soc. of Magazine Editors [3085]
Amer. Soc. of Newspaper Editors [3086]
Arab-American Press Guild [3087]
Asian Amer. Journalists Assn. [3088]
Asociacion de Revistas de Informacion [IO]
Assoc. Press [3089]
Assoc. Press Broadcasters [546]
Assoc. Press Managing Editors [3090]
Assn. of Alternative Newsweeklies [3091]
Assn. of Amer. Editorial Cartoonists [3092]
Assn. of Amer. Univ. Presses [8550]
Assn. of Capitol Reporters and Editors [6181]
Assn. of Christian Journalists [IO]
Association of Earth Science Editors [IO]
Assn. of Earth Sci. Editors [3093]
Assn. of Educational Publishers [9009]
Assn. of European Journalists [IO]
Association of Food Journalists [IO]
Assn. of Food Journalists [3094]
Assn. of Golf Writers [IO]
Assn. of Hea. Care Journalists [IO]
Assn. of Hea. Care Journalists [3095]
Assn. of Music Writers and Photographers [10562]
Assn. of Newspaper and Magazine Wholesalers [IO]
Assn. de Periodistas y Escritores Agrarios Espanoles [IO]
Assn. of Polish Agricultural Journalists [IO]
Assn. of Sports Journalists [IO]
Assn. for Women Journalists [3096]
Assn. for Women in Sports Media [3097]
Assn. of Young Journalists [3098]
Association of Young Journalists [IO]
Australian Coun. of Agricultural Journalists [IO]
Australian Press Coun. [IO]
Austrian Magazines Assn. [IO]
Austrian Newspaper Assn. [IO]
Baseball Writers Assn. of Am. [3099]
Belgium Assn. of Agricultural Journalists [IO]
Boating Writers Intl. [IO]
Boating Writers Intl. [3100]
Bowling Writers Assn. of Am. [3101]
British Guild of Travel Writers [IO]
Canadian Assn. of Journalists [IO]
Canadian Community Newspapers Assn. [IO]
Capital Press Club [3102]
Catholic News Ser. [3103]
Chartered Inst. of Journalists [IO]
Chess Journalists of Am. [3104]
Circle of Wine Writers [IO]
Columbia Scholastic Press Advisers Assn. [9010]
Columbia Scholastic Press Assn. [9011]
Comm. of Concerned Journalists [3105]
Commonwealth Journalists Assn. [IO]
Commonwealth Press Union - New Zealand Sect. [IO]
Commonwealth Press Union - United Kingdom [IO]
Community Newspapers of Australia [IO]
Construction Writers Association [IO]
Constr. Writers Assn. [3106]
Coun. for the Advancement of Sci. Writing [3107]
Coun. of Literary Magazines and Presses [10893]
Coun. of Sci. Editors [3108]
CrossRef [3220]
Czech Publishers Assn. [IO]
Dance Critics Assn. [9875]
Dansk Journalistforbund [IO]
Deadline Club [3109]
Dog Writers' Assn. of Am. [3110]
Dutch Newspaper Publishers Assn. [IO]
Editorial Freelancers Assn. [3111]
Editors' Assn. of Canada [IO]

Educ. Writers Assn. [3112]
EMS/Science Commun. Network [5032]
Estonian Press Coun. [IO]
European Alliance of News Agencies [IO]
European Assn. of Sci. Editors [IO]
European Baptist Press Ser. of the European Baptist Fed. [IO]
European Sports Press Union [IO]
European Union of Sci. Journalists' Associations [IO]
Evangelical Press Assn. [20004]
The Feminist Press at the City Univ. of New York [9317]
Foreign Correspondents' Club, Hong Kong [IO]
Foreign Press Assn. [IO]
Foreign Press Assn. [3113]
Foreign Press Assn. in London [IO]
Freedom to Read Found. [17040]
French Language Press Assn. [IO]
French Specialised Periodical Publishers Fed. [IO]
German Journalists' Fed. [IO]
Graphic Arts Employers of Am. [24082]
Graphics Philately Assn. [22824]
Gridiron Club of Washington, DC [IO]
Guild of Agricultural Journalists [IO]
Guild of Agricultural Journalists of Ireland [IO]
Guild of Motoring Writers [IO]
Hollywood Foreign Press Assn. [3115]
Hong Kong Journalists Assn. [IO]
Hungarian Agricultural Journalists Assn. [IO]
Independent Free Papers of Am. [3226]
Independent Press Assn. [3116]
Independent Schools Coun. Info. Ser. [IO]
Indian Newspaper Soc. [IO]
Inst. of Maltese Journalists [IO]
Inst. of Sci. and Tech. Communicators [IO]
Inter Press Ser. Intl. Assn. [IO]
Intl. Assn. of Obituarists [4062]
Intl. Catholic Union of the Press [IO]
Intl. Center for Journalists [IO]
Intl. Center for Journalists [3117]
Intl. Fed. of Journalists [IO]
Intl. Fed. of Press Cutting Agencies [IO]
Intl. Food, Wine and Travel Writers Assn. [IO]
Intl. Food, Wine and Travel Writers Assn. [3118]
Intl. Foodservice Editorial Coun. [3119]
Intl. Foodservice Editorial Coun. [IO]
Intl. Freedom of Expression Exchange CH [IO]
Intl. Islamic News Agency [IO]
Intl. Motor Press Assn. [IO]
Intl. Motor Press Assn. [3120]
Intl. Newspaper Gp. [3121]
Intl. Newspaper Marketing Assn. [3230]
Intl. Pentecostal Press Assn. [3122]
Intl. Pentecostal Press Assn. [IO]
Intl. Press Inst. [IO]
Intl. Press Inst., Amer. Comm. [3123]
Intl. Sci. Writers Assn. [3124]
Intl. Sci. Writers Assn. [IO]
Intl. Soc. for Augmentative and Alternative Commun. [IO]
Intl. Soc. of Weekly Newspaper Editors [IO]
Intl. Soc. of Weekly Newspaper Editors [3125]
Intl. Sport Press Assn. [IO]
Intl. Union of Francophone Press [IO]
Investigative Reporters and Editors [IO]
Investigative Reporters and Editors [3126]
IPS - Inter Press Ser. Intl. Assn. [IO]
Japanese Agricultural Journalists Assn. [IO]
Jazz Journalists Assn. [IO]
Jazz Journalists Assn. [3127]
Jerusalem Media and Communications Centre [IO]
John S. and James L. Knight Found. [12484]
Livestock Publications Coun. [3233]
Mauritius Union of Journalists [IO]
Media Human Resources Assn. [2903]
Media Rsrc. Ser. [7202]
Military Reporters and Editors [6182]
Millwright Gp. [24102]
Mozambique News Agency [IO]
Natl. Acad. of TV Journalists [3128]
Natl. Amateur Press Assn. [22911]
Natl. Assn. of Black Journalists [3129]

Natl. Assn. of Hispanic Journalists [3130]
Natl. Assn. of Home and Workshop Writers [3131]
Natl. Assn. of Press Agencies [IO]
Natl. Assn. of Real Estate Editors [3132]
Natl. Assn. of Sci. Writers [3133]
National Association of Science Writers [IO]
Natl. Catalog Managers Assn. [3134]
Natl. Collegiate Baseball Writers Assn. [3135]
Natl. Conf. of Editorial Writers [3136]
Natl. Coun. for the Training of Journalists [IO]
Natl. Elementary Schools Press Assn. [9012]
Natl. Fed. of Hispanic Owned Newspapers [3240]
Natl. Fed. of Press Women [3137]
Natl. Fed. of Specialized Press [IO]
Natl. Lesbian and Gay Journalists Assn. [3138]
Natl. News Bur. [3139]
Natl. Newspaper Assn. [3140]
Natl. Newspaper Publishers Assn. [3241]
Natl. Press Club [3141]
Natl. Press Found. [3142]
Natl. Scholastic Press Assn. [9013]
Natl. Soc. of Newspaper Columnists [3143]
Natl. Sportscasters and Sportswriters Assn. [3144]
Natl. Turf Writers Assn. [3145]
Natl. Union of Journalists - England [IO]
Natl. Union of Journalists (India) [IO]
Natl. Writers Assn. [3146]
Native Amer. Journalists Assn. [3147]
Nepal Press Inst. [IO]
Netherlands Assn. of Journalists [IO]
New York Financial Writers' Assn. [3148]
New Zealand Community Newspapers Assn. [IO]
New Zealand Guild of Agricultural Journalists and Communicators [IO]
New Zealand Press Assn. [IO]
New Zealand Press Coun. [IO]
Newspaper Assn. of Am. [3244]
Newspaper Assn. Managers [3149]
Newspaper Publishers' Assn. of New Zealand [IO]
Newswomen's Club of New York [3150]
North Amer. Snowsports Journalists Assn. [IO]
North Amer. St. Newspaper Assn. [18102]
Norwegian Assn. of Agricultural Journalists [IO]
Norwegian Press Assn. [IO]
Norwegian Union of Journalists [IO]
Online News Assn. [3151]
OPEC News Agency [IO]
Organization of News Ombudsmen [IO]
Org. of News Ombudsmen [3152]
Outdoor Writers Assn. of Am. [3153]
Overseas Press Club of Am. [3154]
Overseas Press Club of Am. [IO]
Overseas Press and Media Assn. [IO]
Pacific Islands News Assn. [IO]
Pakistan Press Found. [IO]
Parenting Publications of Am. [3246]
People's News Agency [3155]
Press Complaints Commn. [IO]
Professional Hockey Writers' Assn. [3156]
Professional Writers' Assn. of Canada [IO]
Red Tag News Publications Assn. [2456]
Regional Reporters Assn. [3157]
Religion News Ser. [3158]
Religion News Service [IO]
Religion Newswriters Assn. [3159]
Reporters Network [3160]
Reporters Without Borders - France [IO]
Res. Soc. for Victorian Periodicals [11080]
Reuters Found. [IO]
Schweizer Verband der Journalistinnen und Journalisten [IO]
Singles Press Assn. [3251]
Soc. of Amer. Bus. Editors and Writers [3161]
Soc. of Amer. Travel Writers [3162]
Soc. for News Design [3163]
Society for News Design [IO]
Soc. of Professional Journalists [3164]
Soc. of Publication Designers [1810]
Soc. of the Silurians [3165]
Soc. of Women Writers and Journalists [IO]
South Asian Journalists Assn. [IO]
South Asian Journalists Assn. [3166]
Specialized Info. Publishers Assn. [3258]
Sports Journalists' Assn. of Great Britain [IO]

A star before a book entry number signifies that the name is not listed separately, but is mentioned within the entry.

Student Press Law Center [17194]
TNG Canada/CWA [IO]
Travel Journalists Guild [3167]
Ukrainian Guild of Agri-journalists [IO]
Union of Catholic Asian News [IO]
United Amateur Press Assn. of Am. [22912]
United Nations Correspondents Assn. [3168]
United Nations Correspondents Assn. [IO]
United Press Intl. [IO]
United Press Intl. [3169]
United Press Intl. - Chile [IO]
United Press Intl. - Hong Kong [IO]
United Press Intl. - Japan [IO]
United Press Intl. - Korea [IO]
United Press Intl. - Middle East [IO]
United Press Intl. - UK [IO]
U.S. Harness Writers' Assn. [3170]
U.S. Marine Corps Combat Correspondents Assn.
   [3171]
U.S. Senate Press Photographers Gallery [3016]
UNITY: Journalists of Color [3172]
West African Journalists Assn. [IO]
White House Correspondents' Assn. [3173]
White House News Photographers Assn. [3018]
Women's Natl. Book Assn. [3174]
World Bowling Writers [3175]
World Bowling Writers [IO]
Press Advisers; Columbia School [★9010]
Press Agents and Managers; Assn. of Theatrical
   [24154]
Press of Am; Intl. Labor [★3229]
Press; Amer. Bus. [★3201]
Press; Assoc. Church [3205]
Press; Assoc. Collegiate [8705]
Press Assn. of Am; Educational [★9009]
Press Assn. of Am; United Amateur [★22912]
Press Assn; Amer. Legion [★20668]
Press Assn; Catholic [3215]
Press Assn; Central Inter-Scholastic [★8713]
Press Assn; Evangelical [20004]
Press Assn; Inland [3227]
Press Assn; Intl. Labor [★3229]
Press Assn; Natl. Amer. Legion [20668]
Press Assn; Singles [3251]
Press Assn; Southern Baptist [★19475]
Press Assn; United Amateur [★22912]
Press Associations; United [★3169]
Press Broadcasters; Assoc. [546]
Press Center for Independent Publishing; Small
   [3252]
Press at the City Univ. of New York; The Feminist
   [9317]
Press Club; Washington [★3141]
Press Complaints Commn. [IO], London, United
   Kingdom
Press Div., Taipei Economic and Cultural Off. in New
   York [9792], 1 E 42nd St., 11th Fl., New York, NY
   10017, (212)557-5122
Press; Editorial Coun. of the Religious [★3205]
Press Editors; Amer. Soc. of Bus. [★3084]
Press and Info. Ser; Austrian [24230]
Press Inst; Amer. [8704]
Press Law Center; Student [17194]
Press; Natl. Braille [16876]
Press; Natl. Diocesan [★19953]
Press Photographers Assn; Natl. [3005]
Press Photographers Gallery; U.S. Senate [3016]
Press and Public Affairs; European Community Off.
   of [★17507]
Press and Public Affairs; European Union Off. of
   [★17507]
Press Relations Wire - Address unknown since
   1995.
Press; Reporters Comm. for Freedom of the [17192]
Press Ser; Jewish Student [8694]
Press Soc; Lithuanian Catholic [19213]
Press Specialists; Columbia School [★9010]
Press; United Amateur [★22912]
Press for War and Civilian Blind; Amer. Braille
   [★16854]
Press; Women's Inst. for Freedom of the [17200]
Pressed and Cut Glass Assn. and Collectors Club of
   America - Address unknown since 1995.
Pressed Metal Inst. [★2726]
Presses; Assn. of Amer. Univ. [8550]

Pressure Gauge and Dial Thermometer Assn. [IO],
   Birmingham, United Kingdom
Pressure Pipe Assn; Amer. Concrete [3024]
Pressure Sensitive Manufacturers Assn. [IO], Melton
   Mowbray, United Kingdom
Pressure Sensitive Tape Coun. [57], PO Box 609,
   Northbrook, IL 60062, (847)562-2630
Pressure Treaters' Assn; Southern [1624]
Pressure Ulcer Advisory Panel; Natl. [14657]
Pressure Vessel Inspectors; Natl. Bd. of Boiler and
   [5824]
Pressure Vessel Mfrs. Assn. [2061], 800 Roosevelt
   Rd., Bldg. C, Ste. 312, Glen Ellyn, IL 60137,
   (630)942-6590
Pressure Vessel Res. Coun. [3039], PO Box 1942,
   New York, NY 10156, (216)658-3847
Pressure Washer Mfrs. Assn. [2062], 1300 Sumner
   Ave., Cleveland, OH 44115-2851, (216)241-7333
Prestressed Concrete Assn. [IO], Leicester, United
   Kingdom
Prestressed Concrete Inst; Precast/ [934]
Pretrial Justice Indus. [6034], 927 15th St. NW, 3rd
   Fl., Washington, DC 20005, (202)638-3080
Pretrial Services Rsrc. Center [★6034]
Pretty Things Fan Club - Address unknown since
   1989.
Prevent Blindness Am. [16882], 211 W Wacker Dr.,
   Ste. 1700, Chicago, IL 60606, (800)331-2020
Prevent Blindness; Natl. Soc. to [★16882]
Prevent Blindness in Premature Babies [16883]
Prevent Blindness; Res. to [16886]
Prevent Cancer Found. [13866], 1600 Duke St., Ste.
   500, Alexandria, VA 22314, (703)836-4412
Prevent Child Abuse [11647], 500 N Michigan Ave.,
   Ste. 200, Chicago, IL 60611, (312)663-3520
Prevent Child Abuse [★11647]
Prevent Child Abuse [IO], Chicago, IL, United States
Prevent Child Abuse [★IO]
Prevent Gun Violence; Brady Center to [17589]
Prevent Handgun Violence; Center to [★17589]
Prevent a Litter Coalition [11451], 2579 John Milton
   Dr., Ste. 105 - PMB 143, Herndon, VA 20171,
   (703)818-8009
Prevention of Addiction to Narcotics; Natl. Assn. for
   the [★13262]
Prevention; Aggressive Aids [13546]
Prevention of Alcoholism and Drug Dependency;
   Natl. Comm. for the [13267]
Prevention of Alcoholism; Natl. Comm. for the
   [★13267]
Prevention Assn. of Amer; Smoke [★5081]
Prevention of Blindness; Natl. Comm. for the
   [16882]
Prevention of Blindness; Natl. Soc. for the [★16882]
Prevention of Blindness; New York State Comm. for
   the [★16882]
Prevention Center; Natl. Assault [★12032]
Prevention Center/Network; Natl. Dropout [8330]
Prevention of Child Abuse; Natl. Exchange Club
   Found. for the [★11637]
Prevention and Control of Violence and Extremism;
   Inst. for [★17146]
Prevention Coun; Trans. Claims and [★3595]
Prevention of Cruelty to Animals; Amer. Soc. for the
   [11350]
Prevention and Defense; Prdt. Liability [3453]
Prevention of Deterioration Center - Defunct.
Prevention; Global Strategies for HIV [13566]
Prevention; Inst. for Financial Crime [★2084]
Prevention; Natl. Org. on Adolescent Pregnancy,
   Parenting and [★12182]
Prevention; Partnership for [14594]
Prevention, Probation, Prisons; Volunteers in
   [11896]
Prevention Proj; Accidental Nuclear War [18140]
Prevention Research; National Center on Child
   Abuse [★11647]
Prevention Research; National Center on Child
   Abuse [★IO]
Prevention Res; Soc. for [16520]
Preventive Cardiovascular Nurses Assn. [15523],
   613 Williamson St., Ste. 205, Madison, WI 53703,
   (608)250-2440
Preventive Medicine
   Amer. Assn. for Hea. Freedom [16049]

Amer. Assn. of Nutritional Consultants [15540]
Amer. Bd. of Nutrition [15541]
Amer. Bd. of Preventive Medicine [16050]
Amer. Coll. for Advancement in Medicine [16051]
Amer. Coll. for Advancement in Medicine [IO]
Amer. Coll. of Nutrition [15544]
Amer. Coll. of Preventive Medicine [16052]
Amer. Coun. of Applied Clinical Nutrition [15545]
Amer. Coun. on Exercise [15958]
Amer. Dietetic Assn. [15546]
Amer. Found. for the Prevention of Venereal
   Disease [16409]
Amer. Inst. for Preventive Medicine [16053]
Amer. Inst. for Preventive Medicine [IO]
Amer. Lung Assn. [16354]
Amer. Osteopathic Coll. of Occupational and
   Preventive Medicine [15802]
Amer. Soc. for Clinical Nutrition [15547]
Amer. Soc. for Nutrition [15548]
Amer. Soc. for Parenteral and Enteral Nutrition
   [15549]
Assn. for Applied and Therapeutic Humor [16605]
Assn. for Prevention Teaching and Res. [16054]
Benjamin Franklin Literary and Medical Soc.
   [14549]
Center for Professional Well-Being [14700]
Center for Sports and Osteopathic Medicine
   [16055]
Center for the Well Being of Hea. Professionals
   [14701]
Community Systems Found. [15552]
Cong. of Lung Assn. Staff [16357]
Cystic Fibrosis Found. [16358]
Dietary Managers Assn. [15555]
Food and Nutrition Bd. [15558]
Hearing Educ. and Awareness for Rockers
   [16056]
Inst. for Traditional Medicine and Preventive Hea.
   Care [13635]
Intl. and Amer. Associations of Clinical Nutrition-
   ists [15560]
Intl. Life Sciences Inst. - North Am. [15561]
Intl. Vitamin A Consultative Gp. [15564]
Japan Soc. of Risk Mgt. for Preventive Medicine
   [IO]
Natl. Inst. of Electromedical Info. [14311]
Natl. Jewish Medical and Res. Center [16361]
Natl. Reye's Syndrome Found. [16366]
Natl. Stroke Assn. [16494]
Natl. Wellness Inst. [16057]
National Wellness Institute [IO]
Nutrition for Optimal Hea. Assn. [15567]
Price-Pottenger Nutrition Found. [15568]
San Francisco AIDS Found. [13584]
SMARTRISK [IO]
Trust for America's Hea. [16255]
Wellness Associates [16058]
Preventive Medicine; Amer. Osteopathic Acad. of
   Public Hea. and [★15802]
Preventive Medicine; Amer. Osteopathic Coll. of
   [★15802]
Preventive Medicine; Amer. Osteopathic Coll. of Oc-
   cupational and [15802]
Preventive Medicine; Conf. of Professors of
   [★16054]
Preventive Medicine; Intl. Acad. of [★15560]
Preventive Medicine and Public Hea; Amer. Bd. of
   [★16050]
Preventive Oncology; Amer. Soc. of [15642]
Preventive Psychology; Amer. Assn. of Applied and
   [16119]
Prey Found; Birds of [5300]
Priatelia Zeme - Slovensko [★IO]
Price; Fans and Friends of Ray [★24963]
Price Found; Louis and Harold [13174]
Price Found; Weston A. [15572]
Price Memorial Found; Weston A. [★15568]
Price-Pottenger Found. [★15568]
Price-Pottenger Nutrition Found. [15568], 7890
   Broadway, Lemon Grove, CA 91945, (619)462-
   7600
PRICE Users Assn. [★6734]
PRICE Users Assn. [★IO]
Pride Fan Club; Charley [24857]
Pride Foster Family Agency [★18847]

Reference to "IO" in place of a book number signifies that the association may be found in the 45th edition of International Organizations.

P.R.I.D.E. Found. - Promote Real Independence for the Disabled and Elderly [11982], 391 Long Hill Rd., Groton, CT 06340-1293, (860)445-7320

Pride Prog. [13437], 4123 E Lake St., Minneapolis, MN 55406-2028, (612)728-2062

PRIDE World Drug Conference [★13276]

PRIDE Youth Programs [13276], 4 W Oak St., Fremont, MI 49412, (231)924-1662

Priest Pilots; Natl. Assn. of [19667]

Priesthood; CORPUS - Natl. Assn. for an Inclusive [19619]

Priesthood; CORPUS - Natl. Assn. for a Married [★19619]

Priestly Formation; Bishops' Comm. on [19917]

Priestly Soc. of Saint Pius X [★IO]

Priests' Assn. in Am; Hungarian Catholic [19637]

Priests, Bros., and Priest and Brother Associates; Maryknoll [★19658]

Priests' Councils; Natl. Fed. of [19689]

Priests for Equality [17568], PO Box 5206, Hyattsville, MD 20782, (301)699-0042

Priests Eucharistic League [★19617]

Priests for Life [18564], PO Box 141172, Staten Island, NY 10314, (718)980-4400

Priests and Religious; Pontifical Missionary Union of [★19703]

Priests; Survivors Network of Those Abused by [13372]

Primal Assn. Intl. - Address unknown since 2001.

Primarily Primates, Inc. [11452], 26099 Dull Knife Trail, San Antonio, TX 78255, (830)755-4616

Primary Care Internal Medicine; Soc. for Res. and Educ. in [★14970]

Primary Care Res. Gp; North Amer. [13664]

Primary English Teaching Assn. [IO], Marrickville, Australia

Primary Glass Mfrs. Coun. - Defunct.

Primary Immunodeficiency Assn. [IO], London, United Kingdom

Primary Tungsten Assn. [★IO]

Primate Rescue Center [11453], 5087 Danville Rd., Nicholasville, KY 40356, (859)858-4866

Primate Soc. of Great Britain [IO], Chester, United Kingdom

Primates
  Amer. Assn. of Physical Anthropologists [6403]
  Amer. Soc. of Primatologists [6405]
  European Fed. for Primatology [IO]
  European Marmoset Res. Gp. [IO]
  Gorilla Found. [7533]
  Intl. Primate Protection League [11418]
  Primate Rescue Center [11453]
  Primate Soc. of Great Britain [IO]

Primates, Inc; Primarily [11452]

Primatological Soc; Intl. [6419]

Primatologists; Amer. Soc. of [6405]

Prime Time School TV - Defunct.

Primer [★18585]

Primetimers; Christian Assn. of [★11320]

Primitive Art Soc. of Chicago - Address unknown since 2003.

Primitive Peoples Fund [★IO]

Primrose Soc; Amer. [22499]

Primus Official Fan Club - Address unknown since 2003.

Prince Edward Island 4-H [IO], Charlottetown, PE, Canada

Prince Edward Island Assn. of Chefs and Cooks [IO], Charlottetown, PE, Canada

Prince Edward Island Assn. of Social Workers [IO], Charlottetown, PE, Canada

Prince Edward Island Coun. of the Arts [IO], Charlottetown, PE, Canada

Prince Edward Island Coun. of the Arts [IO], Charlottetown, PE, Canada

Prince Edward Island Recreation and Sports Assn. for the Physically Challenged [IO], Charlottetown, PE, Canada

Prince George Brain Injured Gp. Soc. [IO], Prince George, BC, Canada

Prince Hall Grand Masters; Conf. of [19230]

Prince Henry Sinclair Soc. of the U.S. [9922], c/o Delane Coleman, 5044 W New World Dr., Glendale, AZ 85302-5024

Prince of Wales Intl. Bus. Leaders Forum [IO], London, United Kingdom

Princess Kitty Fan Club [24778], PO Box 430784, Miami, FL 33243-0784, (305)665-1639

Principals
  Australian Principals Assn. Professional Development Coun. [IO]
  Natl. Assn. of Elementary School Principals [9014]
  Natl. Assn. of Principals of Schools for Girls [9015]
  Natl. Assn. of Secondary School Principals [9016]
  Natl. Conf. of Yeshiva Principals [9017]
  New Leaders for New Schools [8755]

Principals of Amer. Schools for the Deaf; Assn. of Superintendents and [★14749]

Principals; Natl. Assn. of Elementary School [9014]

Principals; Natl. Assn. of Secondary School [9016]

Principals, NEA; Dept. of Elementary School [★9014]

Principles; Natl. Collegiate Assn. for Res. of [8087]

Prindle Class Assn. [23212], c/o Performance Catamarans, Inc., 1800 E Borchard Ave., Santa Ana, CA 92705, (714)835-6416

Print Advertising Assn. - Defunct.

Print Alliance; Amer. [9544]

Print Alliance Credit Exchange [1444], c/o ABC - Amega, Inc., 1100 Main St., Buffalo, NY 14209, (716)887-9515

Print Associates Credit Exchange [★1444]

The Print Center [9522], 1614 Latimer St., Philadelphia, PA 19103, (215)735-6090

The Print Center [IO], Philadelphia, PA, United States

Print Club [★IO]

Print Club [★9522]

Print Collectors Soc; Amer. Historical [21523]

Print Coun. of Am. [9466], Dept. of Drawings and Prints, The Metropolitan Museum of Art, 1000 Fifth Ave., New York, NY 10025

Print Dealers Assn; Intl. Fine [309]

Print and Media Assn. Singapore [IO], Singapore, Singapore

Print Media South Africa [IO], Parklands, Republic of South Africa

Print Music Dealers Assn; Retail [2823]

Print Soc; Amer. Color [9412]

Print; Task Force on Alternatives in [★10315]

Printed Circuits; Inst. of [★1221]

Printers; Advt. Specialty Assn. for [80]

Printers of Am; Master [★1765]

Printers' Assn; Amalgamated [1805]

Printers, Die Stampers, and Engravers' Union of North Am; Intl. Plate [24085]

Printers and Lithographers; Natl. Assn. of [★1780]

Printers Natl. Assn; Lithographers and [★1788]

Printers; Natl. Assn. Quick [★1785]

PrintImage Intl. [1785], 2250 E Devon Ave., Ste. 245, Des Plaines, IL 60018, (847)298-8680

PrintImage Intl. [IO], Des Plaines, IL, United States

Printing Accountants Club - Address unknown since 1995.

Printing Assn. of Canada; Screen [★1792]

Printing Assn. Intl; Screen [★1792]

Printing Assn; Natl. State [★1781]

Printing Assn; Screen Process [★1792]

Printing Assn; Waterless [1793]

Printing Brokerage Assn. [★1786]

Printing Brokerage Assn. [★IO]

Printing Brokerage/Buyers Association [IO], Palm Beach, FL, United States

Printing Brokerage/Buyers Assn. [1786], PO Box 744, Palm Beach, FL 33480, (561)546-0116

Printing Brokerage/Buyers Assn. Intl. [★1786]

Printing Brokerage/Buyers Assn. Intl. [★IO]

Printing Equip. and Supply Assn; Natl. [★1782]

Printing Equip. and Supply Dealers' Assn. [IO], Ridgeville, ON, Canada

Printing Estimators and Production Men's Club - Defunct.

Printing and Graphic Communs. Assn. [1787]

Printing and Graphics Communications Union; Intl. [★24083]

Printing and Graphics Indus. Assn. of Alberta [IO], Calgary, AB, Canada

Printing Historical Soc. [IO], London, United Kingdom

Printing History Assn; Amer. [9989]

Printing House for the Blind; Amer. [16829]

Printing and Imaging Assn; Digital [1764]

Printing and Imaging Assn; Pacific [1783]

Printing Indus. of Am. [1788], 200 Deer Run Rd., Sewickley, PA 15143, (412)741-6860

Printing Indus. of Am; Label [3684]

Printing Indus. Fed. of South Africa [IO], Honeydew, Republic of South Africa

Printing Indus. of Am. [★1788]

Printing Indus. Assn. of the Slovak Republic [IO], Bratislava, Slovakia

Printing Industry Credit Exchange/PIA - Defunct.

Printing Indus. Credit Executives [1101], 1100 Main St., Buffalo, NY 14209, (800)226-0722

Printing Ink Makers; Natl. Assn. of [★1803]

Printing Ink Mfrs; Natl. Assn. of [1803]

Printing Ink Res. Institute; National [★1803]

Printing Leadership; Natl. Assn. for [1780]

Printing and Publishing and Converting Technologies; Assn. for Suppliers of [★1782]

Printing, Publishing and Converting Technologies; NPES - The Assn. for Suppliers of [1782]

Printing, Publishing and Media Workers Sector of the CWA [24086], 501 3rd St. NW, Washington, DC 20001-2797, (202)434-1243

Printing; Soc. for Ser. Professionals in [1790]

Printing Tech. Found; Screen [1789]

Printing Trades Assn; Intl. Allied [24084]

Printmakers; Bay Area [★1762]

Printmakers; California Soc. of [1762]

Priorities in Am; Fund for New [18297]

PRISM Intl. - Professional Records and Info. Services Mgt. [2109], 131 US 70 W, Garner, NC 27529, (919)771-0657

PRISM International - Professional Records and Information Services Management [IO], Garner, NC, United States

PRISMS: Parents and Researchers Interested In Smith-Magenis Syndrome [IO], Dallas, TX, United States

PRISMS: Parents and Researchers Interested In Smith-Magenis Syndrome [14476], 21800 Town Center Plz., Ste. No. 266A-633, Sterling, VA 20164, (972)231-0035

Prison-Ashram Proj. [11886], c/o Human Kindness Found., PO Box 61619, Durham, NC 27715, (919)383-5160

Prison Assn; Amer. [★11854]

Prison Assn; Natl. [★11854]

Prison Assn; Women's [11898]

Prison Atheist League of America - Defunct.

Prison Chaplains Assn; Amer. Catholic [★19741]

Prison Families Anonymous - Address unknown since 1995.

Prison Fellowship [★11888]

Prison Fellowship Angel Tree Program [★11888]

Prison Fellowship Intl. [11887], PO Box 17434, Washington, DC 20041, (703)481-0000

Prison Fellowship Intl. [IO], Washington, DC, United States

Prison Fellowship Ministries [11888], PO Box 1550, Merrifield, VA 22116-1550, (703)478-0100

Prison Fellowship Scotland [IO], Glasgow, United Kingdom

Prison Hospice Assn; Natl. [14858]

Prison Ministry; Good News Jail and [★11869]

Prison Ministry of Yokefellow's Intl. [11889], PO Box 482, Rising Sun, MD 21911, (410)658-2661

Prison Ministry of Yokefellow's Intl. [IO], Rising Sun, MD, United States

Prison Ministry; Yokefellowship [★11889]

Prison Mission Assn. [20384], PO Box 2300, Port Orchard, WA 98366, (360)876-0918

Prison Pen Pals [22141], PO Box 120074, Fort Lauderdale, FL 33312

Prison Proj. of the ACLU; Natl. [11883]

Prison Res. Educ. Action Proj. [★11891]

Prison Support Collective; Natl. No-Nukes [18160]

Prisoner Appreciation Soc; Six of One Club: The [25043]

Prisoner Fan Club; Once Upon A Time The [25040]

Prisoner Rape; Stop [11894]

Prisoners
  Acad. of Criminal Justice Sciences [11850]

A star before a book entry number signifies that the name is not listed separately, but is mentioned within the entry.

Aid to Incarcerated Mothers [11851]
All of Us or None [17081]
Alston Wilkes Veterans Home [11852]
Amer. Assn. for Correctional and Forensic Psychology [11853]
Amer. Correctional Assn. [11854]
Amer. Correctional Hea. Services Assn. [14715]
Amer. Criminal Justice Assn. (Lambda Alpha Epsilon) [11855]
Amer. Jail Assn. [11856]
Amer. Soc. of Criminology [11899]
Assn. on Programs for Female Offenders [11857]
Assn. of State Correctional Administrators [11858]
Bible Believers Fellowship [20477]
Center for Stud. in Criminal Justice [11859]
Champions for Life Intl. [19996]
Christ Truth Ministries [19514]
Christian Chaplain Sers. [19745]
Correctional Educ. Assn. [11862]
Death Row Support Proj. [11863]
Families Against Mandatory Minimums Found. [11864]
Fathers Behind Bars [11866]
Fortune Soc. [11867]
Friends Outside [11868]
Intl. Assn. of Correctional Officers [11870]
Intl. Assn. of Correctional Training Personnel [11871]
Intl. Assn. of Reentry [17355]
Intl. Community Corrections Assn. [11872]
Intl. Network of Prison Ministries [20283]
Intl. Prison Ministry [11873]
Islamic Correctional Reunion Assn. [20105]
John Howard Assn. [11874]
Justice Res. and Statistics Assn. [11876]
Life After Exoneration Prog. [17360]
London Club [11900]
Natl. Assn. of State Sentencing Commissions [5650]
Natl. Center on Institutions and Alternatives [11878]
Natl. Center for Juvenile Justice [11879]
Natl. Commn. on Correctional Hea. Care [14729]
Natl. Correctional Indus. Assn. [11880]
Natl. Criminal Justice Assn. [11881]
Natl. Juvenile Detention Assn. [11882]
Natl. Prison Hospice Assn. [14858]
Natl. Prison Proj. of the ACLU [11883]
North Amer. Assn. of Wardens and Superintendents [11884]
November Coalition [18690]
Osborne Assn. [11885]
Prison Fellowship Intl. [11887]
Prison Fellowship Ministries [11888]
Prison Ministry of Yokefellow's Intl. [11889]
Prisoners' Rights Union [11890]
Safer Soc. Found. [11891]
Sentencing Proj. [11893]
Soc. of Correctional Physicians [16011]
Soc. of Saint Stephen [20523]
Southern Center for Human Rights [17036]
Volunteers in Prevention, Probation, Prisons [11896]
Volunteers for Prison Inmates [IO]
We Care Prog. [11897]
Women's Prison Assn. [11898]
Prisoners Abroad [IO], London, United Kingdom
Prisoners; Amer. Assn. of Former Soviet Political [★17766]
Prisoners Bible Broadcast [★19514]
Prisoners' Friends' Assn. [IO], Hong Kong, People's Republic of China
Prisoners' Rights Union [11890], PO Box 161321, Sacramento, CA 95816-1321, (916)422-2240
Prisoner's Union [★11890]
Prisoners of War
Amer. Ex-Prisoners of War [21262]
Natl. Alliance of Families for the Return of America's Missing Servicemen [21263]
P.O.W. Network [21264]
Rolling Thunder [21265]
Sons and Daughters In Touch [12599]
Prisons; Volunteers in Prevention, Probation, [11896]
Privacy Alliance; Online [17141]

Privacy Info. Center; Electronic [7194]
Privacy Intl. [IO], London, United Kingdom
Privacy Rights CH [3176], 3100 5th Ave., Ste. B, San Diego, CA 92103, (619)298-3396
Private Adoption; Families for [11244]
Private Agencies Collaborating Together [★12439]
Private Agencies Collaborating Together [6351], 1200 18th St. NW, Ste. 350, Washington, DC 20036, (202)466-5666
Private Agencies Collaborating Together [IO], Washington, DC, United States
Private Art Dealers Assn. [302], PO Box 872, Lenox Hill Sta., New York, NY 10021, (212)572-0772
Private Care Assn. - Address unknown since 2003.
Private Citizen, Inc. [17147], PO Box 233, Naperville, IL 60566, (630)393-1555
Private Coll. Athletic Conf. - Defunct.
Private Communications Assn. [★9157]
Private Concerns - Defunct.
Private Doctors of America - Defunct.
Private Enterprise; Coun. for [★17636]
Private Enterprise; Natl. Assn. of [3616]
Private Enterprise Res. Center [17635], Texas A&M Univ., 4231 TAMU, College Station, TX 77843-4231, (979)845-7722
Private Equity CFO Assn. [1445], c/o Citizens Bank, 101 Park Ave., 11th Fl., New York, NY 10178, (212)401-3894
Private Forests; Natl. Coun. on [4691]
Private Higher Educ; Consortium for the Advancement of [8105]
Private Higher Educ; Consortium for the Advancement of [★8535]
Private Indus. Councils; Natl. Assn. of [★12087]
Private Investigators; Intl. Assn. [★2325]
Private Label Assn. [IO], Lisbon, Portugal
Private Label Mfrs. Assn. [2646], 630 Third Ave., 4th Fl., New York, NY 10017, (212)972-3131
Private Libraries Assn. [IO], Stroud, United Kingdom
Private Motor Truck Coun. of Canada [IO], Oakville, ON, Canada
Private Network Consortium; Virtual [2320]
Private, Nontraditional Schools and Colleges; Natl. Assn. of [7947]
Private Offshore Rescue and Towing; Comm. for [2574]
Private Partnerships; Natl. Coun. for Public- [17633]
Private Photogrammetric Surveyors; Mgt. Assn. for [7496]
Private and Pioneer Numismatists; Soc. of [22758]
Private Planning Assn. of Canada [★IO]
Private Postal Systems; Assn. of [★2447]
Private Practice Section/American Physical Therapy Assn. [16633], 1055 N Fairfax St., Ste. 100, Alexandria, VA 22314, (703)299-2410
Private Practitioners of Pathology Found. [★15857]
Private Psychiatric Hospitals; Natl. Assn. of [★16091]
Private Radio
Assn. of Clandestine Radio Enthusiasts [21497]
Private Railroad Car Owners; Amer. Assn. of [3276]
Private School Data Educ; Soc. of Independent and [★8132]
Private Schools
The Assn. of Boarding Schools [9018]
Assn. of Private Enterprise Educ. [9019]
Association of Private Enterprise Education [IO]
Coun. for Amer. Private Educ. [9020]
Natl. Assn. of State Administrators and Supervisors of Private Schools [9021]
Natl. Coun. for Private School Accreditation [7880]
Private Schools for Exceptional Children; Natl. Assn. of [★9147]
Private Sector Coun. [17348], c/o Partnership for Public Ser., 1100 New York Ave. NW, Ste. 1090 E, Washington, DC 20005, (202)775-9111
Private Sector Org. of Jamaica [IO], Kingston, Jamaica
Private Security Liaison Coun. - Defunct.
Private Special Educ. Centers; Natl. Assn. of [9147]
Private Truck Coun. of Am. [★3881]
Privatization
Intl. Security, Trust and Privacy Alliance [3535]
Privacy Rights CH [3176]

Privatization Center [★6131]
Privatization Coun., Inc. [★17633]
Privatization; Natl. Center for [★17665]
Pro-Am Skateboard Racing Assn. - Defunct.
Pro-American Books [★19784]
Pro-Amer. Forum - Defunct.
Pro Athletes Outreach [20029], 72 E Sunset Way, Issaquah, WA 98027, (425)392-6300
Pro Bike [★23315]
Pro-Choice Am; NARAL [18518]
Pro-Choice Defense League - Address unknown since 2003.
Pro-Choice Public Educ. Proj. [11224], PO Box 3952, New York, NY 10163, (888)253-CHOICE
Pro Ecclesia Found. - Address unknown since 2006.
Pro Familia: Deutsche Gesellschaft fur Familienplanung, Sexualpadagogik und Sexualberatung [IO], Frankfurt am Main, Germany
Pro Familia Hungarian Sci. Soc. [IO], Budapest, Hungary
Pro-Family Forum - Defunct.
Pro-Family Press Assn. - Defunct.
Pro Helvetia Arts Coun. of Switzerland [IO], Zurich, Switzerland
Pro Legends [★23433]
Pro-Life Action League [18565], 6160 N Cicero Ave., Chicago, IL 60646, (773)777-2900
Pro-Life Action League [IO], Chicago, IL, United States
Pro-Life Alliance of Gays and Lesbians [12927], PO Box 16753, Alexandria, VA 22302-0753, (202)223-6697
Pro-Life Movement of the Czech Republic [IO], Prague, Czech Republic
Pro-Life Nonviolent Action Project - Address unknown since 1995.
Pro Life Obstetricians and Gynecologists; Amer. Assn. of [18545]
Pro-Life Pediatricians; Amer. Assn. of [18546]
Pro-Life; Presbyterians [12926]
Pro-Life Religious Coun; Natl. [18560]
Pro Maria Comm. [19704]
PRO Media Found. - Defunct.
Pro Natura [★IO]
Pro Players Assn. [13402], PO Box 1233, Castle Rock, CO 80104, (720)327-9207
Pro Sanctity Movement [19705], 11002 N 204th St., Elkhorn, NE 68022-3800, (402)289-2670
Pro Se Assn; Amer. [6021]
Pro Stock Owners Assn. - Defunct.
Pro Vita Advisors [20479], PO Box 292813, Dayton, OH 45429, (937)226-1300
Probasco Clearinghouse - Defunct.
Probate Counsel; Amer. Coll. of [★6183]
Probate Law
Amer. Coll. of Trust and Estate Counsel [6183]
Probation and Aftercare; Permanent European Conf. on [IO]
Probation Boards' Assn. [IO], London, United Kingdom
Probation Compact Administrators' Assn; Parole and [6166]
Probation Executives; Natl. Assn. of [5649]
Probation Officers; Natl. Assn. of [IO]
Probation and Parole Assn; Amer. [6164]
Probation and Parole Assn; Natl. [★11843]
Probation, Prisons; Volunteers in Prevention, [11896]
Probationers; Assn. of Administrators of the Interstate Compact for the Supervision of Parolees and [★6166]
Probe Anal. Soc. of Am; Electron [★7334]
Probe Intl. [IO], Toronto, ON, Canada
Probe Ministries Intl. [IO], Richardson, TX, United States
Probe Ministries Intl. [8090], 1900 Firman Dr., Ste. 100, Richardson, TX 75081, (972)480-0240
Problems; Soc. for the Stud. of Social [13133]
Procedural Coders; Amer. Acad. of [★14694]
Procedures for Engineering Consultants; APEC - Automated [6999]
Procedures for Engineering Consultants, Inc; Automated [★6999]
Process Analytical Chemistry; Center for [6675]
Process Engg; Soc. for the Advancement of Material and [7285]

Reference to "IO" in place of a book number signifies that the association may be found in the 45th edition of International Organizations.

Process Engineers; Soc. of Aerospace Material and [★7285]

Process Engineers; Soc. of Aircraft Material and [★7285]

Process Equip. Mfrs. Assn. [2063], 201 Park Washington Ct., Falls Church, VA 22046-4527, (703)538-1796

Process Gas Consumers Gp. [17340], 1275 Pennsylvania Ave., Washington, DC 20004-2415, (202)383-0444

Process Philosophies; Soc. for the Stud. of [10838]

Process Serving

Natl. Assn. of Professional Process Servers [6184]

Process Stud; Center for [10789]
Processed Apples Inst. [★4705]
Processed Apples Inst. [★510]
Processed Vegetable Growers Assn. [IO], Louth, United Kingdom
Processing Machinery Assn; Intl. Assn. of Food Indus. Suppliers and Food [★1133]
Processing Soc; Grain Elevator and [1750]
Processors Assn; Apple [1673]
Processors Assn; At-sea [1483]
Processors Assn; Natl. Soybean [★2857]
Processors' and Growers' Res. Org. [IO], Peterborough, United Kingdom
Processors; United Egg Assn. Further [5120]
ProChiropractic Europe [IO], Copenhagen, Denmark
ProChoice Rsrc. Center - Defunct.
Procicaribe - Caribbean Agricultural Sci. and Tech. Network Sys. [IO], St. Augustine, Trinidad and Tobago
Procrastinators' Club of Am. [IO], Bryn Athyn, PA, United States
Procrastinators' Club of Am. [19385], PO Box 712, Bryn Athyn, PA 19009, (215)947-9020

Proctology

Amer. Bd. of Colon and Rectal Surgery [16059]
Amer. Soc. of Colon and Rectal Surgeons [16060]
C3: Colorectal Cancer Coalition [13802]
Intl. Assn. of Colon Therapy [16061]
Intl. Assn. of Colon Therapy [IO]

Proctology; Amer. Bd. of [★16059]
Procurement Officials; Natl. Assn. of State [6238]
Procurement Organizations; Assn. of Organ [14287]
Procurement; Proj. on Military [★18077]
Procurement Round Table - Address unknown since 2003.
Procurement and Supply Chain Benchmarking Assn. [760], c/o The Benchmarking Network, 4606 FM 1960 W, Ste. 250, Houston, TX 77069-9949, (281)440-5044
Procurers of Painted-Label Sodas - Defunct.
Prodemca: Friends of the Democratic Center in the Americas - Defunct.

Produce

Apple Processors Assn. [1673]
Natl. Assn. of Farmers' Market Nutrition Programs [4648]
Natl. Barley Growers Assn. [4663]

Produce Assn. of the Americas; Fresh [1513]
Produce and Floral Coun; Fresh [1514]
Produce Market Managers; Natl. Assn. of [5022]
Produce Marketing Assn. [5028], 1500 Casho Mill Rd., Newark, DE 19714-6036, (302)738-7100
Produce Marketing Assn. [IO], Newark, DE, United States
Produce Packaging Assn. [★IO]
Produce Packaging Assn. [★5028]
Produce Packaging and Marketing Assn. [★5028]
Produce Packaging and Marketing Assn. [★IO]
Produce Prepackaging Assn. [★IO]
Produce Prepackaging Assn. [★5028]
Producers Alliance for Cinema and TV [IO], London, United Kingdom
Producers; Alliance of Motion Picture and TV [1375]
Producers Assn; Amer. Apparel [★222]
Producers Assn; Music [2801]
Producers Assn; Ornamental Concrete [932]
Producers Assn; Sweet Wine [★5419]
Producers Assn; Wood Moulding and Millwork [688]
Producers Commn. Assn. [★5029]
Producers Comm; Lead-Zinc [★2723]
Producers and Composers of Applied Music [IO], Malvern, United Kingdom

Producers and Distributors of Am; Motion Picture [★1389]
Producers and Distributors Assn; Chem. [803]
Producers Group - Address unknown since 2002.
Producers Guild of Am. [1392], 8530 Wilshire Blvd., Ste. 450, Beverly Hills, CA 90211-3115, (310)358-9020
Producers Guild; Screen [★1392]
Producers; League of Amer. Theatres and [11020]
Producers; League of New York Theatres and [★11020]
Producers Livestock Marketing Assn. [5029], c/o Rick Lovell, Gen. Mgr., PO Box 540477, North Salt Lake, UT 84054-0477, (801)936-2424
Producers and Mfrs. Assn. [★5225]
Producers; Natl. Assn. of Latino Independent [1390]
Producers' Network; Amer. Apparel [222]
Producers and Royalty Owners Assn; Texas Independent [2949]
Producers; United Egg [5121]
Producers, Writers, and Directors; Caucus for TV [17165]

Product Code

Hea. Indus. Bus. Communications Coun. [14080]

Prdt. Code Coun; Optical [339]
Prdt. Code Coun; Uniform [★337]
Prdt. Code Coun; Uniform Grocery [★337]
Prdt. Development and Mgt. Assn. [2511], 15000 Commerce Pkwy., Ste. C, Mount Laurel, NJ 08054, (856)439-9052
Prdt. Fund Raisers; Natl. Assn. of [★1684]
Prdt. Identification Mfrs; Natl. Assn. of Graphic and [2720]
The Prdt. Liability Alliance [3452], c/o Natl. Assn. of Wholesaler-Distributors, 1725 K St. NW, Ste. 300, Washington, DC 20006-1419, (202)872-0885
Prdt. Liability Common Defense [3453]
Prdt. Liability Prevention and Defense [3453], 201 Park Washington Ct., Falls Church, VA 22046-4513, (703)538-1797
Product Safety Assn. - Defunct.
Prdt. Safety Mgt; Bd. of Certified [3441]

Product Testing

Clinical Res. Associates [14148]
Intl. Assn. for Prdt. Development [3177]
Intl. Assn. for Prdt. Development [IO]
International Consumer Product Health and Safety Organization [IO]
Intl. Consumer Prdt. Hea. and Safety Org. [3178]
Kids In Danger [11612]

Production Engine Rebuilders Assn. [★1295]
Production Engine Remanufacturers Assn. [1295], 28203 Woodhaven Rd., Edwards, MO 65326, (417)998-5057
Production Engg. Assn. [IO], Guildford, United Kingdom
Production Engg. Res. Assn. [IO], Melton Mowbray, United Kingdom
Production Equip. Rental Assn. [2793], PO Box 77327, San Francisco, CA 94107-0327, (415)552-2094
Production Guild of Great Britain [IO], Aylesbury, United Kingdom
Production and Inventory Control Soc; Amer. [★7181]
Production Managers Assn. [IO], London, United Kingdom
Production Managers Guild of Hollywood; Unit [★24055]
Production Men's Guild of the Dress Industry of New York City - Address unknown since 1995.
Production Music Library Assn. - Defunct.
Production and Operations Mgt. Soc. [2512], c/o Dr. Sushil K. Gupta, Exec. Dir., Coll. of Bus., Florida Intl. Univ., Miami, FL 33174, (305)348-1413
Production and Operations Management Society [IO], Miami, FL, United States
Production Planning and Scheduling Assn; Intl. [8809]
Production Records Intl. - Address unknown since 1995.
Production Services Assn. [IO], Bath, United Kingdom
Production; Women in [1796]
Productivity Center; Amer. [★2482]

Productivity Communication Center - Defunct.
Productivity Enhancement; Intl. Soc. for [7022]
Productivity and Innovation; Mfrs. Alliance for [★2039]
Productivity & Quality Center; Amer. [★2482]
Productivity Specialists; Assn. of [2486]
Products Assn; Consumer Specialty [806]
Products Assn; Lab. [3484]
Productschap Vis [★IO]
Produits alimentaires et de consommation du Canada [★IO]
ProEnglish [9912], 1601 N Kent St., Ste. 1100, Arlington, VA 22209, (703)816-8821
Prof. Dr. G. A. Lindeboom Inst. [IO], Ede, Netherlands
Prof. Dr. G. A. Lindeboom Instituut [★IO]
Professeurs Francais en Amerique; Societe des [★8450]
Professeurs Francais et Francophones d'Amerique; Societe des [8450]
Professional Accounting Soc. of Am. [1], PO Box 251451, Los Angeles, CA 90025
Professional Acting Coaches and Teachers; Org. of [9267]
Professional Advancement of Black Chemists and Chem. Engineers; Natl. Org. for the [6689]
Professional Aerial Photographers Assn. [3010], c/o Off. of the Sec., 4910 Willowbend, Ste. E, Houston, TX 77035, (713)721-6593
Professional Aerial Photographers Association [IO], Houston, TX, United States
Professional Aeromedical Transport Assn. - Defunct.
Professional Air Traffic Controllers Org. - Defunct.
Professional Airmen; Union of [★24005]
Professional Airways Systems Specialists [24015], 1150 17th St. NW, Ste. 702, Washington, DC 20036-4603, (202)293-7277
Professional and Amateur Horseman's Assn; Arabian [4862]
Professional Anglers Assn. [IO], Stoneleigh, United Kingdom
Professional Anglers' Assn; Natl. [23420]
Professional Apparel Assn. [255], 994 Old Eagle School Rd., Ste. 1019, Wayne, PA 19087-1866, (610)971-4850
Professional Applicators Assn; Interstate [2909]
Professional Archers Assn. - Defunct.
Professional Armed Forces Rodeo Assn. [23693], c/o Chester Howe, Pres., 17054 NE Watts Rd., Fletcher, OK 73541, (580)351-7673
Professional Armed Forces Rodeo Assn. [IO], Tuttle, OK, United States
Professional Art Dealers Assn. of Canada [★IO]
Professional Arts Mgt. Inst. [9594], 110 Riverside Dr., No. 4E, New York, NY 10024, (212)579-2039
Professional Asian Amer. Women; Natl. Assn. of [743]
Professional Assn. of Alexander Teachers [IO], Birmingham, United Kingdom
Professional Assn. of Canadian Theatres [IO], Toronto, ON, Canada
Professional Assn. of Catering and Tourism of Slovenia [★IO]
Professional Association of Christian Educators [IO], Dallas, TX, United States
Professional Assn. of Christian Educators [19937]
Professional Assn. of Comics Entertainment Retailers [9523]
Professional Assn. of Custom Clothiers [256], 56 S 33rd Ave., No. 220, St. Cloud, MN 56301, (320)240-2007
Professional Assn. of Diving Instructors [23964], 30151 Tomas St., Rancho Santa Margarita, CA 92688-2125, (949)858-7234
Professional Assn. of Diving Instructors [IO], Rancho Santa Margarita, CA, United States
Professional Assn. for the Electronics Indus. of Slovenia [★IO]
Professional Assn. of Foreign Ser. Officers [IO], Ottawa, ON, Canada
Professional Assn. of German Yoga Instructors [IO], Gottingen, Germany
Professional Assn. of Hea. Care Off. Mgt. [15073], 461 E Ten Mile Rd., Pensacola, FL 32534, (850)474-9460

A star before a book entry number signifies that the name is not listed separately, but is mentioned within the entry.

Professional Assn. of Hea. Care Off. Managers [★15073]

Professional Assn. Info. Lib. [★IO]

Professional Assn. of Innkeepers Intl. [IO], Haddon Heights, NJ, United States

Professional Assn. of Innkeepers Intl. [1962], 207 White Horse Pike, Haddon Heights, NJ 08035, (856)310-1102

Professional Assn. for Investment Communications Resources [2349], 191 Clarksville Rd., Princeton Junction, NJ 08550, (609)799-4382

Professional Assn; Network [6739]

Professional Assn; NLRB [24081]

Professional Assn. of Nursery Nurses [IO], Derby, United Kingdom

Professional Assn. of Pet Industries - Defunct.

Professional Assn. of Physicians in the Pharmaceutical Indus. [★IO]

Professional Assn. of the Power Indus. [★IO]

Professional Assn. of Practitioners - Address unknown since 1995.

Professional Assn. of Publishers and Booksellers of Slovenia [★IO]

Professional Assn. of Resume Writers and Career Coaches [12097], 1388 Brightwaters Blvd. NE, St. Petersburg, FL 33704-1336, (727)821-2274

Professional Assn. for SQL Server [909], 203 N La-Salle, Ste. 2100, Chicago, IL 60601, (604)899-6009

Professional Assn. of Teachers - UK [IO], Derby, United Kingdom

Professional Assn. of Volleyball Officials [23875], PO Box 780, Oxford, KS 67119, (888)791-2074

Professional Associations on Fed. Statistics; Coun. of [5816]

Professional Audio Recording Services; Soc. of [3351]

Professional Audiovideo Retailers Assn. [★1209]

Professional Audiovideo Retailers Assn. - Defunct.

Professional Autograph Dealers Assn. [865], PO Box 1729W, Murray Hill Sta., New York, NY 10016, (888)338-4338

Professional Autograph Dealers Association [IO], New York, NY, United States

Professional Aviation Maintenance Assn. [165], 400 Commonwealth Dr., Warrendale, PA 15096, (724)772-4092

Professional Bail Agents of the U.S. [5542], 1301 Pennsylvania Ave. NW, Ste. 925, Washington, DC 20004, (202)783-4120

Professional Ball Players of Am; Assn. of [23105]

Professional Band Instrument Repair Technicians; Natl. Assn. of [2818]

Professional Baseball Assn; Natl. Semi- [23122]

Professional Baseball Athletic Trainers Soc. [23125], c/o Brian Ebel, ATC, Baltimore Orioles, 333 W Camden St., Baltimore, MD 21201

Professional Baseball Clubs; Amer. League of [★23113]

Professional Baseball Clubs; Intl. League of [23110]

Professional Baseball Leagues; Natl. Assn. of [23116]

Professional Basketball Writers' Assn. - Defunct.

Professional Beauty Assn. [1086], 15825 N 71st St., Ste. 100, Scottsdale, AZ 85254, (480)281-0424

Professional Benefit Administrators; Soc. of [1245]

Professional Benefits; Web Network of [★1246]

Professional Bicycle Racers Assn. - Defunct.

Professional Billiards Tour - Address unknown since 2002.

Professional Boatman's Assn. [IO], Yapton, United Kingdom

Professional Bodyguard Assn. [IO], London, United Kingdom

Professional Bowhunter's Soc. [23057], PO Box 246, Terrell, NC 28682, (704)664-2534

Professional Bowlers Assn. of Am. [23254], 719 2nd Ave., Ste. 701, Seattle, WA 98104-1747, (206)332-9688

Professional Bowls Assn. [IO], North Shore City, New Zealand

Professional Bridal Consultants; Amer. Assn. of [★533]

Professional Bureaucrats; Intl. Assn. of [22595]

Professional Car Soc. [21768], c/o Jeff Hookway, Sec./Membership Dir., 201 Glenside Trail, Sparta, NJ 07871-1249

Professional Chaplains; Assn. of [19744]

Professional Chess Assn. - Defunct.

Professional Clubmakers' Soc. [3649], 70 Persimmon Ridge Dr., Louisville, KY 40245, (502)241-2816

Professional Coders; Amer. Acad. of [14694]

Professional Commun. Soc; IEEE [6923]

Professional Cmpt. Assn. of Lebanon [IO], Beirut, Lebanon

Professional Computing Assn. [IO], Royston, United Kingdom

Professional Constr. Estimators Assn. of Am. [1061], PO Box 680336, Charlotte, NC 28216, (704)489-1494

Professional Consultants; Amer. Assn. of [★960]

Professional Consultants; Assn. of [960]

Professional Contractors Gp. [IO], West Drayton, United Kingdom

Professional Contracts Administrators; Natl. Assn. of [★1744]

Professional Convention Mgt. Assn. [2689], 2301 S Lake Shore Dr., Ste. 1001, Chicago, IL 60616-1419, (312)423-7262

Professional Currency Dealers Assn. [22753], c/o Mr. James A. Simek, Sec., PO Box 7157, Westchester, IL 60154, (630)889-8207

Professional Dance Teachers Assn. [8191], c/o Hoctor Dance Enterprises, PO Box 38, 157 Franklin Tpke., Waldwick, NJ 07463, (800)462-8679

Professional Dancers Fed. [23326], c/o Richard Booth, Pres., 6830 N Broadway, Ste. D, Denver, CO 80221, (303)412-1213

Professional Development; Engineers' Coun. for [★6979]

Professional Development League [★5714]

Professional Development League; Senior Executives Assn. [5714]

Professional Development; Natl. Consortium for Black [8049]

Professional Disc Golf Assn. [IO], Toronto, ON, Canada

Professional Drag Racing Assn. [★23077]

Professional Drivers Coun. [★24199]

Professional Drivers; Soc. of [3893]

Professional Dyers Guild - Defunct.

Professional Earth Scientists; Soc. of Independent [7135]

Professional Educ; ALI-ABA Comm. on Continuing [8758]

Professional Educ. of the Amer. Osteopathic Assn; Bur. of [15810]

Professional Educ. for Bus; Coun. for [★8010]

Professional Educational Development Corporation - Address unknown since 2003.

Professional Educators; Natl. Assn. of [9223]

Professional Elecl. Apparatus Recyclers League [1196], 4255 S Buckley Rd., No. 118, Aurora, CO 80013, (877)AT-PEARL

Professional Employees; Coun. of AFL-CIO Unions for [★24173]

Professional Employees Intl. Union; Off. and [23995]

Professional Employees of the U.S. Dept. of Agriculture; Org. of [5441]

Professional Employer Organizations; Natl. Assn. of [1273]

Professional Engineers Conf. Bd. for Industry - Defunct.

Professional Enrichment; Inst. for [★7901]

Professional Equestrian Instructors and Trainers Assn. - Defunct.

Professional Ethics; Assn. for Practical and [8967]

Professional Excellence Recognition Prog; Actions for [★14865]

Professional and Executive Women's Networks; Natl. Alliance of [★728]

Professional Farmers of Am. [4657], PO Box 36, Cedar Falls, IA 50613, (319)277-1278

Professional Film and Video Equipment Assn. - Defunct.

Professional Floral Commentators International [★1493]

Professional Football Athletic Trainers Soc. [23437], c/o Steve Antonopulos, Pres., 13655 Broncos Pkwy., Englewood, CO 80112, (303)649-9000

Professional Football Referees Assn. - Address unknown since 2001.

Professional Football Researchers Assn. [23438], 12870 Rte. 30, No. 39, North Huntingdon, PA 15642

Professional Football Writers of Am. [23439], 12030 Cedar Lake Ct., Maryland Heights, MO 63043, (314)453-0755

Professional Footballers' Assn. [IO], Manchester, United Kingdom

Professional Fraternity Assn. [24488], 345 N Charles St., 3rd Fl., Baltimore, MD 21201, (888)771-4PFA

Professional Gardeners Guild [IO], East Cowes, United Kingdom

Professional Geologists; Amer. Inst. of [7127]

Professional Golf Assn; Ladies [23454]

Professional Golf Assn; Women's [★23454]

Professional Golf Club Repairmen's Assn. - Defunct.

Professional Golf Teachers Assn. of Am. [23463], PO Box 912, La Quinta, CA 92247, (760)777-1925

Professional Golf Teachers Assn. of Am. [IO], La Quinta, CA, United States

Professional Golf Tour; Women's [★23451]

Professional Golf Tournaments Assn. [★23461]

Professional Golfers' Assn. of Am. [23464], 100 Ave. of the Champions, Palm Beach Gardens, FL 33418, (561)624-8400

Professional Golfers' Assn. - England [IO], Sutton Coldfield, United Kingdom

Professional Golfers' Associations of Europe [IO], Sutton Coldfield, United Kingdom

Professional Grounds Mgt. Soc. [4803], 720 Light St., Baltimore, MD 21230-3816, (800)609-7467

Professional Handlers Assn. [22346], 17017 Norbrook Dr., Olney, MD 20832-2623, (301)924-0089

Professional Hockey Writers' Assn. [3156], c/o Sherry L. Ross, Sec.-Treas., 1480 Pleasant Valley Way, No. 44, West Orange, NJ 07052, (973)669-8607

Professional Home Inspectors; Examination Bd. of [2118]

Professional Horsemen's Assn. of America - Address unknown since 2001.

Professional Horsemen's Assn; United [4961]

Professional Housing Mgt. Assn. [5797], 154 Ft. Evans Rd. NE, Leesburg, VA 20176, (703)771-1888

Professional Hunters' Assn. of South Africa [IO], Centurion, Republic of South Africa

Professional Hypnotherapists; Amer. Assn. of [14915]

Professional Independent Mass Marketing Administrators [★2230]

Professional Insurance Communicators of Am. [884], PO Box 68700, Indianapolis, IN 46268-0700, (317)875-5250

Professional Insurance Investigators; Natl. Soc. of [2227]

Professional Insurance Marketing Assn. [2230], 230 E Ohio St., Ste. 400, Chicago, IL 60611, (817)569-7462

Professional Insurance Mass-Marketing Assn. [★2230]

Professional Insurance Women; Assn. of [★2142]

Professional Inter-fraternity Conf. [★24488]

Professional Intl. Network Soc. - Defunct.

Professional Investigators; Soc. of [5890]

Professional Italian-Americans; Assn. of Student and [19160]

Professional Journalists; Soc. of [3164]

Professional Karate Assn. - Defunct.

Professional Knifemakers Assn. [9839], 2905 N Montana Ave., Ste. 30027, Helena, MT 59601, (618)753-2147

Professional Knitwear Designers Guild [★228]

Professional Knitwear Designers Guild [★IO]

Professional Lacrosse Players Assn. [24193], 52 Haynes Rd., Sudbury, MA 01776, (401)845-6263

Professional Landcare Network [2398], 950 Herndon Pkwy., Ste. 450, Herndon, VA 20170, (703)736-9666

Professional Lawn Tennis Assn. of U.S. [★23914]

Professional Lawn Tennis Assn. of U.S. [★IO]

Professional Liability Attorneys; Amer. Bd. of [6041]

Professional Liability Underwriting Soc. [2231], c/o Derek B. Hazeltine, Exec. Dir., 5353 Wayzata Blvd., Ste. 600, Minneapolis, MN 55416, (952)746-2580

Reference to "IO" in place of a book number signifies that the association may be found in the 45th edition of International Organizations.

Professional Liability Underwriting Soc. [IO], Minneapolis, MN, United States

Professional Lighting and Sound Assn. [IO], Eastbourne, United Kingdom

Professional Mgt. Consultants; Natl. Bur. of [★2505]

Professional Managers Assn. [5712], PO Box 77235, Washington, DC 20013, (202)874-1508

Professional Mfrs. Agents - Defunct.

Professional Mariners Alliance - Defunct.

Professional Material Handling Consultants; Assn. of [961]

Professional Mediation Assn. [5462], 1645 Martha Leeville Rd., Lebanon, TN 37090

Professional Midwives Assn. of Germany [★IO]

Professional Music Men - Address unknown since 1995.

Professional Numismatic Guild [★22754]

Professional Numismatists Guild [22754], c/o Robert Brueggeman, Exec. Dir., 3950 Concordia Ln., Fallbrook, CA 92028, (760)728-1300

Professional Nutrition Educ. Consortium; Intersociety [15565]

Professional Older Women's Theatre Project - Defunct.

Professional Opera Companies of Canada [★IO]

Professional Opportunities for Women Comm. - of Amer. Inst. of Chemists - Defunct.

Professional and Organizational Development Network in Higher Educ. [8494], PO Box 3318, Nederland, CO 80466, (303)258-9521

Professional and Organizational Development Network in Higher Education [IO], Nederland, CO, United States

Professional Paddlesports Assn. [3650], 7432 Alban Sta. Blvd., Ste. B-232, Springfield, VA 22150, (703)451-3864

Professional Panhellenic Assn. [★24488]

Professional Photographers of Am. [3011], 229 Peachtree St. NE, Ste. 2200, Atlanta, GA 30303-1608, (404)522-8600

Professional Photographers of Canada [IO], Woodstock, ON, Canada

Professional Photographic Labs. Assn. [IO], Welwyn Garden City, United Kingdom

Professional Picture Framers Assn. [9467], 3000 Picture Pl., Jackson, MI 49201, (517)788-8100

Professional Piercers; Assn. of [3715]

Professional Pilots Fed. [24016], c/o Bert Yetman, Pres., PO Box 622, Scranton, PA 18503, (817)481-5318

Professional Plant Users Gp. [IO], London, United Kingdom

Professional Pool Players Assn. - Defunct.

Professional Practice Assn; Amer. [14697]

Professional Process Servers; Natl. Assn. of [6184]

Professional Programmers Assn. - Address unknown since 1995.

Professional Psychics United - Address unknown since 2003.

Professional Publishers Marketing Group - Address unknown since 1991.

Professional Putters Assn. [23465], 5225 28th St., Lubbock, TX 79407

Professional Racing Org. of Am. [★23320]

Professional Reactor Operator Soc. [7391], PO Box 484, Byron, IL 61010-0484, (815)234-8140

Professional Records and Info. Services Mgt; PRISM Intl. - [2109]

Professional Recruiters; Natl. Assn. of Corporate and [★1265]

Professional Recruitment; Intl. Assn. of Corporate and [1265]

Professional Resellers Org. - Defunct.

Professional Resources; Intl. Assn. of Corporate and [★1265]

Professional Responsibility; Amer. Bar Assn. Center for [5476]

Professional Responsibility Lawyers; Assn. of [5487]

Professional Rodeo Assn; Women's [23696]

Professional Rodeo Cowboys Assn. [★23694]

Professional Rodeo Cowboys Assn. [23694], 101 Pro Rodeo Dr., Colorado Springs, CO 80919-2301, (719)593-8840

Professional Rugby Players' Assn. [IO], Twickenham, United Kingdom

Professional Sales Assn. - Address unknown since 2004.

Professional Salespersons of America - Address unknown since 2003.

Professional School Photographers of Am. [★3012]

Professional School Photographers of Am. [★IO]

Professional School Photographers Assn. Intl. [IO], Spokane, WA, United States

Professional School Photographers Assn. Intl. [3012], c/o Robert W. Kerr, Pres., 26 W Broad St., Bethlehem, PA 18018-5732, (610)694-8825

Professional Scripophily Trade Assn. [761], c/o Bob Kerstein, Pres., PO Box 223795, Chantilly, VA 20153, (703)579-4209

Professional Secretaries Intl. [★66]

Professional Secretaries Intl. [★IO]

Professional Ser. Assn. [3553], 71 Columbia St., Cohoes, NY 12047, (518)237-7777

Professional Services Bus. Mgt. Assn. [★2513]

Professional Services Coun. [17636], 2101 Wilson Blvd., Ste. 750, Arlington, VA 22201, (703)875-8059

Professional Services Firms; Natl. Coun. of [★17636]

Professional Services Mgt. Assn. [2513], 99 Canal Center Plz., Ste. 330, Alexandria, VA 22314, (703)739-0277

Professional Skaters Assn. [23738], 3006 Allegro Park SW, Rochester, MN 55902, (507)281-5122

Professional Skaters Guild of Am. [★23738]

Professional Ski Instructors of Am. [23755], 133 S Van Gordon St., Ste. 101, Lakewood, CO 80228, (303)987-9390

Professional Ski Instructors of Am. Educational Foundation [★23755]

Professional Sleep Societies; Assoc. [16422]

Professional Sleep Societies; Assn. of [★16422]

Professional Soccer Reporters Assn. - Address unknown since 2002.

Professional Soc; Directed Energy [6858]

Professional Soc. for Sales and Marketing Training [3472], 5905 NW 54th Cir., Coral Springs, FL 33067, (800)219-0096

Professional Speakers Network - Address unknown since 2001.

Professional Sports Car Racing [★23079]

Professional Squash Assn. [IO], Cardiff, United Kingdom

Professional Standards Rev. Coun. of Am. [★16266]

Professional Stringers Assn. - Defunct.

Professional Surveyors; Natl. Soc. of [7719]

Professional Tattoo Artists Guild [3716]

Professional and Tech. Consultants Assn. [969], PO Box 2261, Santa Clara, CA 95055, (408)971-5902

Professional and Tech. Engineers; Intl. Fed. of [24052]

Professional Tennis Coun; Women's Intl. [★23910]

Professional Tennis Registry [23909], PO Box 4739, Hilton Head Island, SC 29938, (843)785-7244

Professional Tennis Registry; U.S. [★23909]

Professional Tennis Registry - U.S.A. [★23909]

Professional Tour Guide Assn. of Australia [IO], Armidale, Australia

Professional Training; Amer. Inst. for Stuttering Treatment and [16440]

Professional Travelogue Sponsors - Address unknown since 2002.

Professional Truck Driver Inst. [3889], 555 E Braddock Rd., Alexandria, VA 22314-2182, (703)647-7015

Professional Truck Driver Inst. of Am. [★3889]

Professional Trucking Services Assn. [3890], c/o Anthony L. Keenan, Pres., United Truckers Ser., 1385 Iris Dr., Conyers, GA 30013, (770)922-6200

Professional Turf and Landscape Conf. [★2397]

Professional Union of the Building Sector [IO], Brussels, Belgium

Professional Union of Insurance Companies [IO], Brussels, Belgium

Professional Wireless Pioneers; Soc. of [★3757]

Professional Women in Constr. [1062], 315 E 56th St., New York, NY 10022-3730, (212)486-7745

Professional Women Controllers [1446], PO Box 950085, Oklahoma City, OK 73195-0085, (800)232-9792

Professional Women in Healthcare [4045], c/o Lyn Rawdon, 310 Montgomery St., Alexandria, VA 22314, (703)838-6138

Professional Women; The Intl. Alliance, An Assn. of Executive and [★728]

Professional Women Photographers [3013], 511 Ave. of the Americas, No. 138, New York, NY 10011, (212)726-8292

Professional Women Singers Assn. [10689], PO Box 884, New York, NY 10159, (212)969-0590

Professional Women's Appraisal Assn. [287], 1224 N Nokomis NE, Alexandria, MN 56308-5072, (320)763-7626

Professional Women's Bowling Assn. - Defunct.

Professional Women's Caucus. - Address unknown since 1995.

Professional Women's Clubs; Natl. Assn. of Negro Bus. and [13053]

Professional Women's Found; Bus. and [11084]

Professional Women's Rodeo Assn. [★23696]

Professional Writers' Assn. of Canada [IO], Toronto, ON, Canada

Professional Writers Network - Defunct.

Professional Yachtsmen's Assn. [IO], Antibes, France

Professionals

African-American Women in Tech. [6394]

African Language Teachers Assn. [9207]

Alliance of Merger and Acquisition Advisors [54]

Alliance of Professional Consultants [952]

Alliance of Professional Tattooists [3714]

Alliance for Work-Life Progress [3179]

Alpha Kappa Psi [24414]

Amateur Ski Instructors Assn. [23748]

Amer. Acad. of Micropigmentation [14039]

Amer. and African Bus. Women's Alliance [691]

Amer. Alliance of Paralegals, Inc. [6149]

Amer. Assn. of Anger Mgt. Providers [15185]

Amer. Assn. of Christian Counselors [19862]

Amer. Assn. of Cmpt. Rental Professionals [895]

Amer. Assn. of Electronic Reporters and Transcribers [3180]

Amer. Assn. of Equine Veterinary Technicians [16743]

Amer. Assn. of Grant Professionals [12708]

Amer. Assn. of Snowboard Instructors [23765]

Amer. Assn. of Teaching and Curriculum [9209]

Amer. Bus. Assn. of Russian Professionals [3181]

Amer. Commun. Assn. [6710]

Amer. Contract Compliance Assn. [17493]

Amer. Engg. Alliance [6985]

Amer. Escrow Assn. [1398]

Amer. Football Coaches Assn. [23427]

Amer. Guild of Town Criers [10896]

Amer. Hockey League [23482]

Amer. Portuguese Engg. and Architecture Soc. [7530]

Amer. Professional Wedding Photographers Assn. [2991]

Amer. Screenwriters Assn. [4060]

Amer. Soc. of Embalmers [2773]

Amer. Soc. of Professional Communicators [873]

Amer. Soc. of Sugar Cane Technologists [3700]

Amer. Soc. of Tax Problem Solvers [6290]

Amer. Soc. for Training and Development [3182]

American Society for Training and Development [IO]

Amer. Soc. of Validation Engineers [1289]

Amer. Sommelier Assn. [194]

Aquatic Resources Educ. Assn. [7956]

Arab Amer. Assn. of Engineers and Architects [6467]

Arab Amer. Women's Coun. [18951]

Assn. for the Accreditation of Human Res. Protection Programs [11225]

Assn. of African Amer. Financial Advisors [1455]

Assn. of Certified Anti-Money Laundering Specialists [463]

Assn. of Certified Fraud Specialists [2085]

Assn. of Certified Turnaround Professionals [956]

Assn. of Chinese Finance Professionals [1402]

Assn. of Chinese Scientists and Engineers - U.S.A. [6698]

Assn. of Commercial Stock Image Licensors [1378]

A star before a book entry number signifies that the name is not listed separately, but is mentioned within the entry.

Assn. of Family Practice Physician Assistants [14698]
Assn. of Fertilizer and Phosphate Chemists [6673]
Assn. of Intl. Professional and Bus. Women [IO]
Assn. of Jewish Center Professionals [12466]
Assn. of Licensed Architects [290]
Assn. of Lifecasters Intl. [10957]
Assn. Luxembourgeoise de Producteurs Professionnels d'Assurances [IO]
Assn. for Machine Translation in the Americas [7807]
Assn. of Music Writers and Photographers [10562]
Assn. of Pizza Delivery Drivers [1579]
Assn. of Professional Ball Players of Am. [23105]
Assn. of Professional Futurists [7102]
Assn. for Professional Observers [4667]
Assn. of Professors of Human and Medical Genetics [14497]
Assn. for Rehabilitation Marketing [2617]
Assn. of Senior Anthropologists [6412]
Assn. for Strategic Planning [3042]
Assn. of Support Professionals [3546]
Assn. of Thai Professionals in Am. and Canada [19406]
Athletic Equip. Managers Assn. [23805]
Australian Inst. of Company Directors [IO]
Australian Soc. of Assn. Executives [IO]
Automotive Women's Alliance [353]
Beta Alpha Psi [24391]
Bus. and Professional Women's Found. [11084]
Catalyst [11085]
Chartered Alternative Investment Analyst Assn. [2332]
Chinese Amer. Semiconductor Professional Assn. [1208]
Chinese Language Assn. of Secondary-Elementary Schools [8075]
Clarity [6011]
Commercial Photographers Intl. [2995]
Community Built Assn. [11770]
Continental Basketball Assn. [23129]
Coun. of Intl. Restaurant Real Estate Brokers [3392]
Croatian Amer. Bar Assn. [5489]
Delta Omicron [24550]
Delta Sigma Delta [24438]
Delta Theta Phi [24527]
Dominicans on Wall St. [1413]
Editorial Photographers [2996]
Epsilon Pi Tau [24720]
Equip. Appraisers Assn. of North Am. [279]
Fed. of Professional Associations [IO]
Financial Executives Intl. of Australia [IO]
Flair Bartenders' Assn. [201]
Football Writers Assn. of Am. [23430]
Gamma Iota Sigma [24520]
German Professional Women's Assn. [4039]
Glamour Photographers Intl. [2997]
Global Assn. of Risk Professionals [1423]
Global Mobile Entertainers Assn. [1302]
Green Meeting Indus. Coun. [2681]
Gp. Underwriters Assn. of Am. [2167]
Guild of Intl. Butler Administrators and Personal Assistants [IO]
Hastings Center [12125]
Hispanic Amer. Police Command Officers Assn. [5970]
Hispanic Professional Women's Assn. [4041]
Hospitality Asset Managers Assn. [1942]
Human Resources Outsourcing Assn. [1981]
Info. Tech. Professionals Assn. of Am. [7195]
Inst. of Hazardous Materials Mgt. [4805]
Interdisciplinary Environmental Assn. [4988]
Intl. Assn. of Architectural Photographers [2999]
Intl. Assn. of Biblical Counselors [19867]
Intl. Assn. of Black Actuaries [2186]
Intl. Assn. of Canine Professionals [1161]
Intl. Assn. of Employment Web Sites [1266]
Intl. Assn. of Facilitators [3183]
Intl. Assn. of Facilitators [IO]
Intl. Assn. of Financial Engineers [1424]
Intl. Assn. of Fly Fishing Veterinarians [22451]
Intl. Assn. of Hispanic Meeting Professionals [2684]

Intl. Assn. of Home Staging Professionals [2261]
Intl. Assn. of Info. Tech. Asset Managers [2093]
Intl. Assn. of Integrative Coaches [11740]
Intl. Assn. of Messaging Professionals [6711]
Intl. Assn. of Natural Rsrc. Pilots [4187]
Intl. Assn. of Outsourcing Professionals [2871]
Intl. Assn. of Privacy Professionals [2104]
Intl. Assn. of Professional Protection Specialists [13009]
Intl. Assn. of Reiki Professionals [13637]
Intl. Assn. of Software Architects [6770]
Intl. Assn. of Torch Clubs [10894]
Intl. Center for Spirit at Work [20575]
Intl. Certified Floorcovering Installers Assn. [1025]
Intl. Coach Fed. [836]
Intl. Design Guild [2263]
Intl. DJ Guild [2812]
Intl. Doctors Soc. [10895]
Intl. Guild of Professional Butlers [24040]
Intl. Guild of Professional Consultants [966]
Intl. Hot Rod Assn. [23077]
Intl. League of Professional Baseball Clubs [23110]
Intl. Mgt. Development Assn. [735]
Intl. Medical Volunteers Assn. [15075]
Intl. Mentoring Network Org. [11520]
Intl. Motor Sports Assn. [23079]
Intl. Org. of Black Security Executives [3533]
The Intl. Publication Planning Assn. [3231]
Intl. Security, Trust and Privacy Alliance [3535]
Intl. Soc. of Iraqi Scientists [7613]
Intl. Soc. for Law and Tech. [5945]
Intl. Soc. for Medical Publication Professionals [16259]
Intl. Soc. of Mine Safety Professionals [15270]
Intl. Soc. of Nurses in Genetics [14501]
Intl. Soc. of Primerus Law Firms [5503]
Intl. Soc. of Six Sigma Professionals [7534]
Intl. Soc. of Six Sigma Professionals [IO]
Intl. Systems Security Engg. Assn. [7023]
Intl. Veteran Boxers Assn. [23264]
Iota Phi Lambda [24421]
Iranian Amer. Tech. Coun. [2352]
Iranian Chemists' Assn. of the Amer. Chem. Soc. [6687]
Kappa Delta Epsilon [24452]
Korea Info. Tech. Network [6736]
Ladies Professional Golf Assn. [23454]
Lawyers Assoc. Worldwide [5505]
Lawyers for One Am. [6028]
League of Professional Sys. Administrators [6815]
Lebanese Amer. Professional Soc. [19205]
Logistics Officer Assn. [2736]
Major League Baseball [23113]
Malayalee Engineers Assn. in North Am. [7026]
Marine Corps Intelligence Assn. [19225]
Mu Phi Epsilon Intl. [24553]
Musical Instrument Technicians Assn., Intl. [2816]
Natl. Asian Amer. Soc. of Accountants [42]
Natl. Assn. of Alternative Benefits Consultants [1867]
Natl. Assn. of Asian Amer. Professionals [9623]
Natl. Assn. for Beginning Teachers [9219]
Natl. Assn. of Black Telecommunications Professionals [7778]
Natl. Assn. of Chamber Ambassadors [789]
Natl. Assn. of Community Development Extension Professionals [11784]
Natl. Assn. of Disability Representatives [18648]
Natl. Assn. of Forensic Counselors [5647]
Natl. Assn. of Left-Handed Golfers [23458]
Natl. Assn. of Mold Professionals [1330]
Natl. Assn. of Mortgage Planners [490]
Natl. Assn. of Payment Professionals [1438]
Natl. Assn. of Professional Background Screeners [1983]
Natl. Assn. of Professional Baseball Leagues [23116]
Natl. Assn. of Professional Martial Artists [23598]
Natl. Assn. of Psychometrists [16159]
Natl. Assn. of Purchasing Card Professionals [3264]
Natl. Assn. of Purchasing and Payables [3265]
Natl. Assn. of Qualified Mental Retardation Professionals [15241]

Natl. Assn. of Reunion Managers [3184]
Natl. Assn. of Subrogation Professionals [3185]
Natl. Assn. of Women Law Enforcement Executives [5989]
Natl. Basketball Assn. [23134]
Natl. Black Bridal Assn. [535]
Natl. Block and Bridle Club [24401]
Natl. Broadcasting Soc. - Alpha Epsilon Rho [24411]
Natl. Brownfield Assn. [3191]
Natl. Career Development Assn. [12090]
Natl. Certification Coun. for Activity Professionals [1849]
Natl. Coalition for Electronics Educ. [8364]
Natl. Coun. of Black Engineers and Scientists [7618]
Natl. Coun. of Japanese Language Teachers [9226]
Natl. Football League [23432]
Natl. Football League Alumni [23433]
Natl. Gay Pilot's Assn. [439]
Natl. Introducing Brokers Assn. [1714]
Natl. Kindergarten Alliance [9007]
Natl. Lawyers Assn. [5521]
Natl. Liquor Law Enforcement Assn. [5996]
Natl. Org. of Forensic Social Work [8446]
Natl. Org. of Remediators and Mold Inspectors [1331]
Natl. Physicians Alliance [16009]
Natl. Registry of Environmental Professionals [4593]
Natl. Resume Writers' Assn. [4063]
Natl. Semi-Professional Baseball Assn. [23122]
Natl. Soc. for Hispanic Professionals [1908]
Natl. Study Group on Chronic Disorganization [1979]
Natl. Urban Alliance for Effective Educ. [9291]
Network of Trial Law Firms [5525]
New Horizons Arts Initiative [5589]
North Am. Chinese Semiconductor Assn. [1226]
North Amer. Bd. of Certified Energy Practitioners [6967]
North Amer. British Music Stud. Assn. [10676]
North Amer. Coalition for Christian Admissions Professionals [7914]
North Amer. Football League [23435]
Northamerican Assn. of Masters in Psychology [9030]
Nurses for a Healthier Tomorrow [15517]
Org. for Professional Astrology [6495]
Overseas Chinese Physics Assn. [7507]
Partners Worldwide [19822]
PGA TOUR Tournaments Assn. [23461]
Phi Alpha Delta [24528]
Phi Delta Gamma [24577]
Phi Mu Alpha Sinfonia Fraternity and Found. Natl. HQ [24555]
Philippine Nurses Assn. of Am. [2840]
Pictorial Photographers of Am. [10856]
Positive Music Assn. [10688]
Private Equity CFO Assn. [1445]
Professional Accounting Soc. of Am. [1]
Professional Aerial Photographers Assn. [3010]
Professional Bowhunter's Soc. [23057]
Professional Bowlers Assn. of Am. [23254]
Professional Football Researchers Assn. [23438]
Professional Fraternity Assn. [24488]
Professional Golf Teachers Assn. of Am. [23463]
Professional Golfers' Assn. of Am. [23464]
Professional Managers Assn. [5712]
Professional Skaters Assn. [23738]
Professional Women in Healthcare [4045]
Real Estate Services Providers Coun. [3341]
Recruiters Online Network [1281]
Senior Executives Assn. [5713]
Ser. and Support Professionals Assn. [3556]
Sigma Delta Chi Found. [24524]
Sino-American Pharmaceutical Professionals Assn. [15951]
Soc. of Afghan Professionals [9343]
Soc. for Amer. Baseball Res. [23126]
Soc. for Design Admin. [6481]
Soc. for Executive Leadership in Academic Medicine Intl. [15179]
Soc. for the History of Psychology [7548]

Reference to "IO" in place of a book number signifies that the association may be found in the 45th edition of International Organizations.

Soc. for Organizational Learning [2868]
Soc. of Professional Rope Access Technicians [2068]
Soc. of Registered Professional Adjusters [2242]
Soc. of Sport and Event Photographers [3015]
Soc. for Vocational Psychology [7551]
Springboard Enterprises [4046]
Stencil Artisans League, Inc. [9474]
Taiwanese Amer. Lawyers Assn. [5533]
Tau Epsilon Rho Law Soc. [24529]
Theta Tau [24469]
Turkish Amer. Scientists and Scholars Assn. [7636]
U.S. Basketball Writers Assn. [23137]
U.S. Law Firm Gp. [5534]
U.S. Online Disc Jockey Assn. [2825]
U.S. Professional Poolplayers Assn. [23147]
Upwardly Global [3186]
USMC Motor Transport Assn. [2599]
Vietnamese Professionals Soc. [19429]
Women Entrepreneurs in Sci. and Tech. [4050]
Women's Automotive Assn. Intl. [367]
World Coun. for Venue Mgt. [1350]
World Soc. of Mixed Jurisdiction Jurists [5957]
Xi Psi Phi [24442]
Young Women Social Entrepreneurs [770]
Professionals of Am; Bus. [9302]
Professionals; Amer. Soc. for Healthcare Central Ser. [14864]
Professionals; Assn. of Coupon [3399]
Professionals; Assn. of Fundraising [12197]
Professionals; Assn. of Proposal Mgt. [2487]
Professionals; Assn. of Rheumatology Hea. [16370]
Professionals; Assn. of Yachting [23159]
Professionals in Bus; Soc. of Consumer Affairs [3196]
Professionals; Center for the Well-Being of Hea. [★14700]
Professionals; Center for the Well Being of Hea. [14701]
Professionals Coalition for Nuclear Arms Control - Address unknown since 1999.
Professionals in Energy Conservation; Natl. Assn. of [★6942]
Professionals Found; Minority Hea. [★18080]
Professionals with Hearing Losses; Assn. of Medical [14744]
Professionals; IDEA: The Assn. for Fitness [★15965]
Professionals in Infection Control and Epidemiology; Assn. for [14947]
Professionals; Inst. for Retired [12898]
Professionals; Intl. Acad. of Health Care [14705]
Professionals; The Intl. Assn. of Hewlett-Packard Computing [★6795]
Professionals; Natl. Assn. of Asian Amer. [9623]
Professionals; Natl. Assn. of Child Care [11529]
Professionals; Natl. Assn. of Vision [15693]
Professionals; Natl. Certification Coun. for Activity [1849]
Professionals for Natl. Security - Defunct.
Professionals Networking for Excellence in Ser. Delivery with Individuals who are Deaf or Hard of Hearing; ADARA: [14735]
Professionals - Nicaragua - Defunct.
Professionals in the Public Interest - Defunct.
Professionals in Sci. and Tech; Commn. on [7604]
Professionals for Social Responsibility; Cmpt. [18146]
Professionals in Taxation; Inst. for [6294]
Professionals; Total Energy Mgt. [★6942]
Professionels Canadiens du ski et du surf des neiges [★IO]

Professions
Alpha Kappa Psi [24414]
Amateur Movie Makers Assn. [22418]
Amer. Engg. Alliance [6985]
Amer. Guild of Town Criers [10896]
Amer. Professional Wedding Photographers Assn. [2991]
Assn. of Licensed Architects [290]
Assn. of Mgt. and Professional Staffs [IO]
Assn. of Professional Futurists [7102]
Assn. of Women in Environmental Professions [4619]
Beta Alpha Psi [24391]

Beta Pi Sigma Sorority [24417]
Black Career Women [19323]
Canadian Assn. of Professional Employees [IO]
Canadian Coun. of Professional Certification [IO]
Catalyst [11085]
Christelijke Onderwijscentrale [IO]
Commercial Photographers Intl. [2995]
Confed. of Unions for Academic Professionals in Finland [IO]
Delta Omicron [24550]
Delta Sigma Delta [24438]
Delta Theta Phi [24527]
Dept. for Professional Employees, AFL-CIO [24173]
DIK Assn. [IO]
Editorial Photographers [2996]
Epsilon Pi Tau [24720]
Fed. of Lawyers, Economists, Sys. Managers, Human Rsrc. Managers, and Other Social Scientists [IO]
Gamma Iota Sigma [24520]
Intl. Assn. of Torch Clubs [10894]
Intl. Doctors Soc. [10895]
Intl. Doctors Soc. [IO]
Intl. Mentoring Network Org. [11520]
Intl. Soc. of Six Sigma Professionals [7534]
Iota Phi Lambda [24421]
Kappa Delta Epsilon [24452]
Mu Phi Epsilon Intl. [24553]
Musical Instrument Technicians Assn., Intl. [2816]
Natl. Assn. of Asian Amer. Professionals [9623]
Natl. Assn. of the Professions [19324]
Natl. Assn. of Workforce Development Professionals [12088]
Natl. Broadcasting Soc. - Alpha Epsilon Rho [24411]
Natl. Hispanic Employee Assn. [12279]
Natl. Lawyers Assn. [5521]
Natl. Physicians Alliance [16009]
Org. for Professional Astrology [6495]
Phi Alpha Delta [24528]
Phi Delta Gamma [24577]
Phi Delta Kappa [24578]
Phi Mu Alpha Sinfonia Fraternity and Found. Natl. HQ [24555]
Professional Fraternity Assn. [24488]
Prospect [IO]
Schweizerischer Verband Akademischen Volks- und Betriebswirtschafter [IO]
Sigma Delta Chi Found. [24524]
Soc. for Philosophy in the Contemporary World [18274]
Swedish Confed. of Professional Associations [IO]
Swedish Confed. of Professional Employees [IO]
Tau Epsilon Rho Law Soc. [24529]
Theta Tau [24469]
Upwardly Global [3186]
Vietnamese Professionals Soc. [19429]
World Fed. of Clerical Workers [IO]
Xi Psi Phi [24442]
Professions Assn; Arthritis Hea. [★16370]
Professions Found; Minority Hea. [18080]
Professions; Natl. Center for the Stud. of Collective Bargaining in Higher Educ. and the [24036]
Professor Chen Wen-Chen Memorial Found. [18694], PO Box 6223, Lawrenceville, NJ 08648, (609)936-1352
Professors
Amer. Assn. of Teachers of Slavic and East European Languages [9125]
Amer. Assn. of Univ. Professors [9022]
Amer. Real Estate Soc. [9049]
Assn. of Environmental Engg. and Sci. Professors [9023]
Assn. of Professors of Human and Medical Genetics [14497]
Assn. of Specialty Professors [8587]
Center for Commun. [8003]
Coll. Theology Soc. [9273]
Fed. for Unified Sci. Educ. [9102]
Intercollegiate Stud. Inst. [17271]
Intl. Soc. for Educational Planning [8999]
Intl. Textile and Apparel Assn. [3791]
Natl. Assn. of Baptist Professors of Religion [9277]

Natl. Assn. for Beginning Teachers [9219]
Natl. Reading Conf. [9044]
Philosophy of Educ. Soc. [8969]
Soc. of Chinese Amer. Professors and Scientists [9024]
Soc. for Philosophy of Religion [8970]
Univ. Faculty for Life [9025]
Univ. Faculty for Life [IO]
Univ. Professors for Academic Order [9026]
Professors; Assn. of Environmental Engg. and Sci. [9023]
Professors of Cardiology; Assn. of [13896]
Professors of Child and Adolescent Psychiatry; Soc. of [16096]
Professors of Child Psychiatry; Soc. of [★16096]
Professors of Christian Educ; Natl. Assn. of [★8088]
Professors of Christian Educ; North Amer. [8088]
Professors of Christian Educ; North Amer. Assn. of [★8088]
Professors of Curriculum - Address unknown since 2001.
Professors; Ecumenical Assn. of [★19906]
Professors of Educ; Soc. of [8307]
Professors of Gynecology and Obstetrics; Assn. of [15592]
Professors of Hebrew; Natl. Assn. of [8695]
Professors of Higher Educ; Assn. of [★8482]
Professors; Intl. Assn. of Police [★11850]
Professors of Medicine; Assn. of [8853]
Professors of Mission; Assn. of [20302]
Professors of Ophthalmology; Assn. of Univ. [15675]
Professors of Preventive Medicine; Conf. of [★16054]
Professors of Religion; Assn. of Baptist [★9277]
Professors of Religion; Natl. Assn. of Baptist [9277]
Professors and Res. Sect. of the Division of Christian Educ. of the Natl. Coun. of Churches [★19939]
Professors and Scientists; Soc. of Chinese Amer. [9024]
Professors of Textiles and Clothing; Assn. of Coll. [★3791]
Proficiency Testing; Natl. Assn. for [7792]
Proficiency Testing Res. - Defunct.
Profile Automobile League - Address unknown since 2001.
PROFIT Control Users Assn. - Address unknown since 2003.
Profit Sharing/401(k) Coun. of Am. [1279], 20 N Wacker Dr., Ste. 3700, Chicago, IL 60606, (312)419-1863
Profit Sharing/401(k) Educ. Found. [1280], 20 N Wacker Dr., Ste. 3700, Chicago, IL 60606, (312)419-1863
Profit Sharing Coun. of Am. [★1279]
Profit Sharing Indus; Coun. of [★1279]
Profit Sharing Res. Found. [★1280]
Progenitor Genealogical Soc. [★21146]
Progenitor Genealogical Soc. [★IO]
Progeria Res. Found. [IO], Peabody, MA, United States
Progeria Res. Found. [16547], PO Box 3453, Peabody, MA 01961-3453, (978)535-2594
Prog. of Academic Exchange [8628], 242 King St., Port Chester, NY 10573, (914)690-1340
Prog. of Academic Exchange [IO], Port Chester, NY, United States
Prog. Anal; Amer. Assn. for Budget and [6201]
Prog. on the Anal. and Resolution of Conflicts [18242], Syracuse Univ., 400 Eggers Hall, Syracuse, NY 13244-1090, (315)443-2367
Prog. for Appropriate Tech. in Hea. [17000], 1455 NW Leary Way, Seattle, WA 98107-5136, (206)285-3500
Prog. for Appropriate Tech. in Hea. [IO], Seattle, WA, United States
Program for Catalogues of Amer. Fine Arts Collections - Address unknown since 1995.
Prog. Directors in Endocrinology, Diabetes and Metabolism; Assn. of [14351]
Prog. Directors in Endocrinology and Metabolism; Assn. of [★14351]
Prog. Directors in Internal Medicine; Assn. of [14967]
Prog. Directors in Radiology; Assn. of [15088]

A star before a book entry number signifies that the name is not listed separately, but is mentioned within the entry.

Prog. Directors in Surgery; Assn. of [16577]

Prog. in Ethnographic Film [★6436]

Prog. for the Introduction and Adaptation of Contraceptive Tech. [★17000]

Prog. for the Introduction and Adaptation of Contraceptive Tech. [★IO]

Program for New Americans [★17071]

Prog. for Res. on Black Americans [6396], c/o 5062 Inst. for Social Res., PO Box 1248, Ann Arbor, MI 48106-1248, (734)763-0045

Prog. for Res. and Documentation for a Sustainable Soc. [IO], Oslo, Norway

Program Res. in Integrated Multiethnic Education - Defunct.

Program With Developing Institutions - Defunct.

Prog. of World Learning; Delphi Intl. [17881]

Prog; Youth Adult [★8808]

Programa de las Naciones Unidas para el Desarrollo [★IO]

Programa de las Naciones Unidas para el Medio Ambiente [IO], Mexico City, Mexico

Programas Interculturales de Honduras [★IO]

Programme Alimentaire Mondiale [★IO]

Programme for Belize [IO], Belize City, Belize

Programme Intl. sur la Securite des Substances Chimiques [★IO]

Programme sur l'Homme et la Biosphere [★IO]

Programme des Nations Unies pour le developpement [★IO]

Programme des Nations Unies pour le developpment Cote d'Ivoire [★IO]

Programme des Nations Unies pour l'Environnement [★IO]

Programme des Nations Unies pour le developpement - Mali [★IO]

Programme des Nations Unies pour le developpement en Mauritanie [★IO]

Programme des Nations Unies pour le developpement - Togo [★IO]

Programme Parents-Secours du Canada [★IO]

Programme Regional Oceanien de l'Environnement [★IO]

Programme of Res. in Powder Sci. and Tech. [★IO]

Programme for the Stud. and Promotion of Representative Institutions [IO], Geneva, Switzerland

Programmed Instruction; Natl. Soc. for [★9252]

Programmers Assn; Natl. Systems [★6799]

Programmers Guild [7757], PO Box 1250, Summit, NJ 07902-1250

Programmers; Natl. Fed. of Local Cable [★17161]

Programmers and Systems Analysts; Soc. of Educational [★8132]

Programming Consortium; Natl. Black [9764]

Programming Div; Meridian Intl. Center [17902]

Programming Interface Consortium; Biometric Application [6572]

Programming; Intl. Assn. of Neuro-Linguistic [★16219]

Programming Languages

FORTH Interest Gp. [7535]

Intl. Assn. of Webmasters and Designers [888]

Internet Professional Publishers Assn. [1777]

League for Programming Freedom [7536]

Rexx Language Assn. [7537]

Special Interest Gp. on Ada [7538]

Special Interest Gp. on Algorithms and Computation Theory [7539]

Special Interest Gp. on the APL and J Languages [7540]

Special Interest Gp. on Programming Languages [7541]

Programs; Natl. Assn. of Peer [11827]

Progress - Address unknown since 2001.

Progress Campaign for Res. into Human Reproduction [★IO]

Progress Educational Trust [IO], London, United Kingdom

Progress and Freedom Found. [17188], 1444 Eye St. NW, Ste. 500, Washington, DC 20005, (202)289-8928

Progress; SER - Jobs for [★12100]

Progressio [IO], London, United Kingdom

Progressive

Independent Progressive Politics Network [18619]

Progressive Alliance - Defunct.

Progressive Anarchists for the World - Defunct.

Progressive Angus Breeders Assn. - Defunct.

Progressive Communications; Assn. for [17163]

Progressive Found. [18170], PO Box 649, Luck, WI 54853-0649, (715)472-4185

Progressive Jewish Activism List - Address unknown since 2003.

Progressive Jewish Network/New Jewish Agenda - Defunct.

Progressive Labor Party [18331], PO Box 808, Brooklyn, NY 11202, (212)255-3959

Progressive Librarians Guild [10381], Rider Univ. Lib., 2083 Lawrenceville Rd., Lawrenceville, NJ 08648, (425)831-8155

Progressive Order of the West - Defunct.

Progressive Osseous Heteroplasia Assn. [14477], 33 Stonehearth Sq., Indian Head Park, IL 60525, (708)246-9410

Progressive Policy Inst. [18478], 600 Pennsylvania Ave. SE, Ste. 400, Washington, DC 20003, (202)547-0001

Progressive Political Action Comm. - Defunct.

Progressive, Radically Inclusive Student Ministry [19938], 1041 Grandview Ave., Boulder, CO 80302, (303)443-3960

Progressive Socialist Party [IO], Beirut, Lebanon

Progressive Space Forum - Defunct.

Progressive Student Network - Address unknown since 1999.

Progressive Supranuclear Palsy Assn. - Europe [IO], Towcester, United Kingdom

Progressive Tech. Proj. [7758], 2801 21st Ave. S, Ste. 132E, Minneapolis, MN 55407, (612)724-2600

Progressive Youth Org. [IO], Beirut, Lebanon

Progressive Zionist Caucus - Address unknown since 2001.

Prohibition Coun; Natl. Temperance and [13305]

Prohibition Historical Soc; Partisan [22103]

Prohibition; Law Enforcement Against [17999]

Prohibition Natl. Comm. [18332], PO Box 2635, Denver, CO 80201, (303)237-4947

Project 51 - '92 - Address unknown since 1999.

Project '88: Americans for the Reagan Agenda - Defunct.

Proj. 70,001 [★12105]

Proj. Abolition - Address unknown since 2006.

Project ADVOCATE - Defunct.

Project Africa [★24603]

Proj. Africa [★IO]

Proj. Americana [★18632]

Proj. Appleseed: The Natl. Campaign for Public School Improvement [8332], 520 Melville Ave., St. Louis, MO 63130-4506, (314)225-7757

Project Bank [★15156]

Proj. Blue Book [7483], 6214 Carthage St., Fort Smith, AR 72903, (479)484-7512

Project BREED (Breed Rescue Efforts and Education) - Address unknown since 2008.

Project Bridge Program [★11715]

Proj. Censored [17043], Sonoma State Univ., 1801 E Cotati Ave., Rohnert Park, CA 94928, (707)664-2500

Proj. Children [11717], PO Box 933, Greenwood Lake, NY 10925, (845)477-3472

Proj. Children [IO], Greenwood Lake, NY, United States

Proj. Concern, Inc. [★IO]

Proj. Concern, Inc. [★14985]

Proj. Concern Intl. [14985], 5151 Murphy Canyon Rd., Ste. 320, San Diego, CA 92123, (858)279-9690

Proj. Concern Intl. [IO], San Diego, CA, United States

Project Connect - Defunct.

Project on Corporate Responsibility - Defunct.

Proj. Cuddle [11648], 2973 Harbor Blvd., No. 326, Costa Mesa, CA 92626, (714)432-9681

Proj. on Defense Alternatives [17385], c/o The Commonwealth Inst., PO Box 398105, Inman Sq. Post Off., Cambridge, MA 02139, (617)547-4474

Project on Equal Education Rights - Defunct.

Proj. Equality [17148], PO Box 7085, Kansas City, MO 64113-0085, (913)486-7010

Project Equus - Defunct.

Proj. on Ethnic Relations [17785], 15 Chambers St., Princeton, NJ 08542-3707, (609)683-5666

Proj. EverGreen [4991], c/o Den Gardner, Exec. Dir., PO Box 156, New Prague, MN 56071, (952)758-9135

Proj. Exports Promotion Coun. of India [IO], New Delhi, India

Project Focus - Defunct.

Proj. Food, Land and People [4525], c/o John H. Davis, 65 Poinsetta Rd. SE, Scio, OH 43988

Project Forward '76 - Defunct.

Proj. Genesis [8700], 122 Slade Ave., Ste. 250, Baltimore, MD 21208, (410)602-1350

Proj. on Govt. Oversight [18077], 666 11th St. NW, Ste. 500, Washington, DC 20001-4542, (202)347-1122

Proj. Handclasp [17911], c/o Commander M.C. Tevelson, Dir., Naval Base, San Diego, CA 92132, (619)532-1492

Proj. Harmony [8629], 5197 Main St., Unit 6, Waitsfield, VT 05673, (802)496-4545

Project Hea., Educ., and AIDS Leadership [★13580]

Proj.: Hearts and Minds [12538], 599 Crock Ln., Howard, PA 16841

Project HOLD [★13223]

Proj. HOPE [★14984]

Proj. HOPE [14598], 255 Carter Hall Ln., Millwood, VA 22646, (540)837-2100

Proj. HOPE [IO], Millwood, VA, United States

Proj. HOPE [★IO]

Proj. Hope to Abolish the Death Penalty [17035], PO Box 1362, Lanett, AL 36863, (334)499-0003

Proj. Human Aid [IO], Konstanz, Germany

Proj. Inform [13583], 205 13th St., Ste. 2001, San Francisco, CA 94103, (415)558-9051

Project on Information Technology and Education - Defunct.

Project Intrex - Defunct.

Project Jonah - Defunct.

Project LEAD [★13848]

Proj. Lighthawk [★4418]

Project Local - Defunct.

Proj. Magic [16634], c/o Stormont-Vail West, 3707 SW 6th Ave., Topeka, KS 66606, (785)270-4610

Proj. Mgt; Amer. Soc. for the Advancement of [2519]

Proj. Mgt. Assn. of Denmark [IO], Hillerod, Denmark

Proj. Mgt. Assn. of Finland [IO], Espoo, Finland

Proj. Mgt. Assn. of Iceland [IO], Reykjavik, Iceland

Proj. Mgt. Assn. of Slovakia [IO], Trnava, Slovakia

Proj. Mgt. Inst. [IO], Newtown Square, PA, United States

Proj. Mgt. Inst. [2514], 4 Campus Blvd., Newtown Square, PA 19073-3299, (610)356-4600

Proj. Mgt. South Africa [IO], Johannesburg, Republic of South Africa

Project Med-Aid - Defunct.

Proj. on Military Procurement [★18077]

Proj. Mind Found. [IO], Jerusalem, Israel

Project Newgate - Defunct.

Proj. Orbis [★15697]

Proj. Orbis [★IO]

Project Outreach - Defunct.

Project Overcome - Defunct.

Project Peace Pipe - Defunct.

Project Piaxtla [★IO]

Project Pledge [★12139]

Proj. Ploughshares [IO], Waterloo, ON, Canada

Project Pride [★11982]

Project Projimo [★IO]

Project Prometheus and Krishna - Defunct.

Proj. for Public Spaces [17238], 700 Broadway, 4th Fl., New York, NY 10003, (212)620-5660

Proj. RACE [19047], PO Box 2366, Los Banos, CA 93635

Proj. READ Literacy Network [IO], Kitchener, ON, Canada

Project Reassurance [★24603]

Project Release - Address unknown since 1991.

Proj. Renewal [13277], 200 Varick St., New York, NY 10014, (212)620-0340

Project to Res. Objects Theories, Extraterrestrials and Unusual Sightings - Defunct.

Proj. ROSE (Recycled Oil Saves Energy) - Defunct.

Project Safe Run - Address unknown since 2001.

Project Sanguine - Defunct.

Reference to "IO" in place of a book number signifies that the association may be found in the 45th edition of International Organizations.

Project SHARE - Defunct.
Project SMART - Defunct.
Proj. South: Inst. for the Elimination of Poverty and Genocide [17872], 9 Gammon Ave., Atlanta, GA 30315, (404)622-0602
Proj. South: Inst. for the Elimination of Poverty and Genocide [IO], Atlanta, GA, United States
Project Speed - Defunct.
Proj. S.T. [★15353]
Project on Standards for Criminal Justice - Defunct.
Project Starlight Intl. - Address unknown since 1999.
Project Stigma - Address unknown since 2001.
Project SUNSHINE [★18651]
Proj. on Tech., Work and Character [7168], c/o The Maccoby Gp., 4825 Linnean Ave. NW, Washington, DC 20008, (202)895-8922
Proj. Tibet [18739], 403 Canyon Rd., Santa Fe, NM 87501, (505)982-3002
Proj. Tibet [IO], Santa Fe, NM, United States
Project Top Hat - Defunct.
Project Transition - Defunct.
Proj. Trust [IO], Isle of Coll, United Kingdom
Project Tubeflight - Defunct.
Proj. Underground [18079], c/o Carol Zokaites, Natl. Coor., 7516 Lee Hwy., Radford, VA 24141, (540)831-4057
Project US - Address unknown since 2008.
Proj. on the Vietnam Generation [★10122]
Project VISIT - Vehicle Internal Systems Investigative Team - Address unknown since 2003.
Project Volunteer - Address unknown since 2001.
Project Volunteer Info., Tech. Assistance, and Leadership [★13580]
Proj. Vote! [18364], 739 8th St. SE, Ste. 202, Washington, DC 20003, (800)546-8683
Project Watchdog [★24524]
Project With Indus. [★13126]
Project Wolf U.S.A. - Address unknown since 1999.
Project Woodstove [★12081]
Project Yedid - Defunct.
Proj. YES [9339], 5275 Sunset Dr., Miami, FL 33143, (305)663-7195
Project Yield [★5370]
Proj. for Young Adults with Disabilities; Networking [11975]
Projected Books - Defunct.
Projects With Indus. Prog. [★11271]
ProjectUSA [17809], PO Box 15641, Washington, DC 20003, (202)543-2323
Projekt Mgt. Austria [IO], Vienna, Austria
Projektiyhdistys ry [★IO]
ProJet Assn. - Defunct.
Projet Otesha [★IO]
Projets pour une Agriculture Ecologique [★IO]

Pro-Life
African Amer. Life Alliance [11268]
Amer. Center for Law and Justice [12901]
Amer. Life League [12902]
Amer. Victims of Abortion [12903]
Assn. for Interdisciplinary Res. in Values and Social Change [12906]
Black Americans for Life [12909]
Campaign for Working Families [18286]
Catholics United for Life [12910]
Center for Bio-Ethical Reform [18547]
Children of the Rosary [18548]
Healing the Culture [12788]
Heartbeat Intl. [12912]
Liberty Godparent Home [12918]
Life Decisions Intl. [12920]
Natl. Assn. of Pro-Life Nurses [18378]
Natl. Commn. on Human Life, Reproduction and Rhythm [16008]
Natl. Life Center [12922]
Natl. Right to Life Comm. [12923]
Orthodox Christians for Life [20478]
Presbyterians Pro-Life [12926]
Priests for Life [18564]
Pro-Life Alliance of Gays and Lesbians [12927]
Pro Vita Advisors [20479]
Republican Majority for Choice [18533]
Rock for Life [18567]
Sisters of Life [20480]
Students for Life of Am. [12928]
U.S. Coalition for Life [12929]

Women Exploited by Abortion [12932]
Prolifers for Survival - Defunct.
ProLiteracy Worldwide [8797], 1320 Jamesville Ave., Syracuse, NY 13210, (315)422-9121
ProLiteracy Worldwide [IO], Syracuse, NY, United States
ProLitteris [IO], Zurich, Switzerland
Prolotherapy Assn. [★15753]
PROMAX [577], 9000 W Sunset Blvd., Ste. 900, Los Angeles, CA 90069, (310)788-7600
PROMAX [IO], Los Angeles, CA, United States
PROMAX Intl. [★IO]
PROMAX Intl. [★577]
Prometheus Soc. [9987], PO Box 24513, Federal Way, WA 98093
PROMETRA - France [IO], Paris, France
PROMETRA - Spain [IO], Las Palmas, Spain
Promise - Address unknown since 1995.
Promise Keepers [19834], PO Box 11798, Denver, CO 80211-0798, (303)964-7600
Promote Real Independence for the Disabled and Elderly; P.R.I.D.E. Found. - [11982]
Promoting Achievement in School Through Sports [★8229]
Promoting and Encouraging Arts and Knowledge of the Church; Soc. for [19972]
Promoting Enduring Peace [18243], 66 Edgewood Ave., New Haven, CT 06511, (203)624-0339
Promotion Assn; Broadcasters' [★577]
Promotion Assn; Intl. Newspaper [★3230]
Promotion Assn; Newspaper [★3230]
Promotion Fund; Steamfitting Indus. [1901]
Promotion Industry Coun. - Defunct.
Promotion Marketing Assn. [2647], 257 Park Ave. S, 11th Fl., New York, NY 10010-7304, (212)420-1100
Promotion Marketing Assn. of Am. [★2647]
Promotion and Marketing Executives; Broadcast [★577]
Promotion of Medical Res; Comm. for the [15104]
Promotion and Preservation of Square Dancing; Foundation for the [★9869]
Promotion and Preservation of Square Dancing; Foundation for the [★IO]
Promotion and Res. Bd; Beef [★4261]
Promotion and Res. Bd; Cattlemen's Beef [4261]
Promotion of Sci. and Scholarship; Soc. for the [3255]
Promotional and Advt. Allowances; Natl. Assn. for [★122]
Promotional Glass Collectors Assn. [22109], c/o Marilyn Johnston, Treas., 528 Oakley, Central Point, OR 97502, (901)794-8723
Promotional Products Assn. of Canada [IO], Westmount, QC, Canada
Promotional Products Assn. Intl. [IO], Irving, TX, United States
Promotional Products Assn. Intl. [116], 3125 Skyway Cir. N, Irving, TX 75038-3526, (972)252-0404
Promotora de las Comunidades Municipales [IO], Bogota, Colombia
Prompt Pay; Coalition for [1742]
Promusicae [IO], Madrid, Spain
Proofreaders Club of New York - Defunct.
Propagation of the Faith; Soc. for the [19723]
Propagation Soc; IEEE Antennas and [6913]
Propane Gas Assn. of Canada [IO], Calgary, AB, Canada
Propane Gas Assn; Natl. [1681]
Propeller Club of the U.S. [3586], 3927 Old Lee Hwy., No. 101A, Fairfax, VA 22030, (703)691-2777
Properties Data Network; National Materials [★7319]

Property
African Amer. Alliance for Homeownership [1975]
AIR Commercial Real Estate Assn. [3295]
Amer. Intellectual Property Law Assn. [5835]
Amer. Land Title Assn. [3297]
Asian Amer. Real Estate Assn. [3299]
CoreNet Global [3305]
Coun. of Intl. Restaurant Real Estate Brokers [3392]
FIABCI-U.S.A. - U.S. Chap., Intl. Real Estate Fed. [3310]
Forest Landowners Tax Coun. [6293]
Imaging Supplies Coalition [5845]
Inst. of Real Estate Mgt. [3312]

Intl. Assn. of Assessing Officers [6296]
Intl. Assn. for Property and Evidence [5975]
Intl. Real Estate Inst. [3316]
IP Justice [5852]
Natl. Assn. of Indus. and Off. Properties [3320]
Natl. Assn. of Property Inspectors [2123]
Natl. Assn. of Property Recovery Investigators [5886]
Natl. Assn. of Real Estate Brokers [3323]
Natl. Assn. of Real Estate Buyer Brokers [3324]
Natl. Assn. of Real Estate Editors [3132]
Natl. Assn. of Real Estate Investment Trusts [3327]
Natl. Assn. of Realtors [3328]
Natl. Assn. of Rev. Appraisers and Mortgage Underwriters [3329]
Natl. Assn. of Senior Move Managers [2523]
Natl. Assn. State Agencies for Surplus Property [6185]
Natl. Assn. of Unclaimed Property Administrators [6186]
Natl. Brownfield Assn. [3191]
Natl. Multi Housing Coun. [3332]
NeighborWorks Am. [12335]
Pension Real Estate Assn. [3335]
Property Mgt. Assn. [3336]
Property Records Indus. Assn. [3187]
Real Estate Educators Assn. [3338]
Real Estate Services Providers Coun. [3341]
Realtors Land Inst. [3342]
Soc. of Trust and Estate Practitioners USA [1332]
Property Admin. Assn. [★3190]
Property Administrators; Assn. of Unclaimed [★6186]
Property; Amer. Soc. for the Defense of Tradition, Family and [★19763]
Property Casualty Insurers Assn. of Am. [2232], 2600 S River Rd., Des Plaines, IL 60018-3286, (847)297-7800
Property and Casualty Reinsurers; Natl. Assn. of [★2234]
Property and Casualty Underwriters; Soc. of Chartered [★2160]
Property Consultants Soc. [IO], Arundel, United Kingdom
Property Coun. of Australia [IO], Sydney, Australia
Property Inspectors; Natl. Assn. of [2123]
Property Insurance; Natl. Comm. on [★2171]
Property Law Assn; Amer. Intellectual [5835]
Property Law Assns; Natl. Coun. of Intellectual [5855]
Property and Liability Underwriters; Amer. Inst. for [★2137]
Property Loss Reduction; Insurance Inst. for [★2171]
Property Loss Res. Bur. [2233], 3025 Highland Pkwy., Ste. 800, Downers Grove, IL 60515-1291, (630)724-2200

Property Management
African Amer. Alliance for Homeownership [1975]
Assn. of Mgt. Corporations In Singapore [IO]
Building Owners and Managers Inst. Intl. [9027]
European Confed. of Property Managers [IO]
FIABCI-U.S.A. - U.S. Chap., Intl. Real Estate Fed. [3310]
Forest Landowners Tax Coun. [6293]
Hong Kong Assn. of Property Mgt. Companies [IO]
Independent Property Managers' Assn. [IO]
Inst. of Real Estate Mgt. [3312]
Intellectual Property Owners Assn. [5846]
Intl. Fac. Mgt. Assn. [3188]
Intl. Fac. Mgt. Assn. [IO]
Natl. Assn. of Residential Property Managers [3189]
Natl. Assn. of Senior Move Managers [2523]
Natl. Brownfield Assn. [3191]
Natl. Property Mgt. Assn. [3190]
New Zealand Property Investors Fed. [IO]
Non-Administrative Receivers Assn. [IO]
Property Mgt. Assn. [3336]
Real Estate Services Providers Coun. [3341]
Soc. of Trust and Estate Practitioners USA [1332]
Property Mgt. Assn. [3336], 7900 Wisconsin Ave., Ste. 305, Bethesda, MD 20814, (301)657-9200

A star before a book entry number signifies that the name is not listed separately, but is mentioned within the entry.

Property Mgt. Assn. of Am. [★3336]
Property Mgt. Assn; Natl. Indus. [★3190]
Property Owners Assn. of America - Defunct.
Property Owners Assn; Intellectual [5846]
Property Owners; Intellectual [★5846]
Property Owners; League of Private [★6187]
Property Records Indus. Assn. [3187], PO Box
3159, Durham, NC 27715-3159, (919)433-0121
Property Rights
Amer. Assn. of Small Property Owners [18379]
Amer. Land Rights Assn. [6187]
Amer. Land Title Assn. [3297]
Consumer Proj. on Tech. [7542]
Country Land and Bus. Assn. [IO]
Defenders of Property Rights [6188]
European Landowners Org. [IO]
FIABCI-U.S.A. - U.S. Chap., Intl. Real Estate Fed.
[3310]
Forest Landowners Tax Coun. [6293]
Intl. Intellectual Property Assn. [5848]
Natl. Assn. of Patent Practitioners [6167]
Natl. Assn. of Reversionary Property Owners
[18380]
Stewards of the Range [18381]
Property Tax Assn; Canadian [IO]
Property Taxation; Inst. of [★6294]
Prophecy Stud. Assn; Non-Denominational Bible
[19528]
Proportional Representation; Citizens for [★18348]
Proposal Mgt. Professionals; Assn. of [2487]
Proposition One Comm. [17435], PO Box 27217,
Washington, DC 20038, (202)682-4282
Proposition One - Defunct.
The Proprietary Assn. [★2973]
Proprietary Assn. of Great Britain [IO], London,
United Kingdom
Proprietary Medicine Assn. of Australia [★IO]
Proprietors' Assn. of Am; Bowling [3659]
Prosecuting Attorneys; Natl. Assn. of County and
[★5668]
Prosecution of Child Abuse; Natl. Center for [11631]
Prosecutors Res. Inst; Amer. [5481]
ProShare (United Kingdom) [IO], London, United
Kingdom
Prospect [IO], London, United Kingdom
Prospect Hill Found. [11545], 99 Park Ave., Ste.
2220, New York, NY 10016-1601, (212)370-1165
Prospect Park; Friends of [★4407]
Prospectors
Gold Prospectors Assn. of Am. [22913]
Prospectors Club Intl. - Defunct.
Prospectors and Developers Assn. of Canada [IO],
Toronto, ON, Canada
Prospectors and Development Assn. [★IO]
Prospectors and Mine Owners Assn. - Address
unknown since 1995.
Prospectors and Treasure Hunters Guild - Defunct.
The Prosperos - Address unknown since 1997.
Prostate Awareness Week [★16701]
Prostate Cancer Alliance of Canada [IO], Montreal,
QC, Canada
Prostate Cancer Coalition; Natl. [13856]
Prostate Cancer Res. Found. of Canada [IO], Tor-
onto, ON, Canada
Prostate Cancer Support Assn. [IO], London, United
Kingdom
Prostate Soc; Amer. [16701]
Prosthesis; Amer. Acad. of Cleft Palate [★14055]
Prosthetic Assn; Amer. Orthotic and [1855]
Prosthetic Dentistry; British Soc. for the Stud. of [IO]
Prosthetic-Orthotic Clinics; Assn. of Children's
[15784]
Prosthetics; Amer. Acad. of Maxillofacial [14103]
Prosthetics and Orthotics; Intl. Soc. for [IO]
Prosthetics Outreach Found. [16586], 400 E Pine
St., Ste. 225, Seattle, WA 98122, (206)726-1636
Prosthetics Res. Found. [★16586]
Prosthetist Certification; Bd. for Orthotist/ [15785]
Prosthetist-Orthotists; Hong Kong Soc. of Certified
[IO]
Prosthetists; Amer. Acad. of Orthotists and [15782]
Prosthodontic Soc; Amer. [14139]
Prosthodontics; Amer. Acad. of Crown and Bridge
[★14097]
Prosthodontics; Amer. Acad. of Fixed [14097]

Prosthodontics; Amer. Acad. of Implant [14102]
Prosthodontics; Amer. Bd. of [14126]
Prosthodontists; Amer. Coll. of [14129]
Prostitutes Anonymous [★13029]
Prostitution
Assn. of Albanian Girls and Women [18382]
Assn. of Albanian Girls and Women [IO]
Captive Daughters [18383]
Children of the Night [12933]
European Network Male Prostitution [IO]
Intl. Union of Sex Workers [IO]
Johns and Call Girls United Against Repression
[13094]
Love146 [11620]
Natl. Network for Youth [12935]
Natl. Runaway Switchboard [12936]
People for Children [11716]
Pride Prog. [13437]
Shared Hope Intl. [13457]
SW5 [IO]
Protect Adult Welfare [★13028]
Protect All Children's Env. [14369], c/o E.M.T. O'nan,
Dir., 396 Sugar Cove Rd., Marion, NC 28752,
(828)724-4221
Protect Animals in Entertainment; Coalition to
[11378]
Protect Life in All Nations - Address unknown since
2001.
Protect Our Pelicans Soc. [★5364]
Protect Your Environment - Defunct.
Protecting Adult Welfare [13028], c/o William Mar-
gold, 17400 Marilla St., Northridge, CA 91325,
(818)998-5400
Protecting and Caring Together [★11565]
Protection and Advancement of Small Telephone
Companies; Org. for the [★3964]
Protection and Advocacy Systems; Natl. Assn. of
[★11970]
Protection Agency; War Agencies Employee
[★5776]
Protection Alliance; Natl. Forest [4592]
Protection of Animals and Nature; Interfaith Coun.
for the [4409]
Protection Assn; Natl. Fire [12975]
Protection of Children and Families; Natl. Coalition
for the [18374]
Protection Coun; Trans. Consumer [★3595]
Protection Inst. of Am; Animal [11355]
Protection Inst; Lightning [3446]
Protection League; Alaskan Malamute [★11342]
Protection and Measurements; Natl. Coun. on
Radiation [6242]
Protection from Nuclear Attack; Assn. for
Community-Wide [★5559]
Protection Org; Natl. Client [5949]
Protection Proj. [12377], c/o The Paul H. Nitze
School of Advanced Intl. Stud., The Johns Hopkins
Univ., 1717 Massachusetts Ave. NW, Washington,
DC 20036, (202)663-5894
Protection Reform; Natl. Coalition for Child [11634]
Protection Soc. of Am; Animal [★11469]
Protection Soc; Natl. Cat [11434]
Protection Specialists; Intl. Assn. of Professional
[13009]
Protection Sports Assn. [23848], 8481 Kenton Rd.,
Pasadena, MD 21122
Protective Assn; Amer. Foreign Ser. [19118]
Protective Assn; Amer. Game [★5308]
Protective Assn; Animal [★11404]
Protective Assn; Degree of Honor [19121]
Protective Assn; Oregon Horsemen's Benevolent
[23512]
Protective Bur; Thoroughbred Racing [23517]
Protective Coatings; SSPC: The Soc. for [2885]
Protective Coun; Desert [4389]
Protective Coun. Foundation; Desert [★4389]
Protective Glazing Assn. [★1733]
Protective Glazing Coun. [1733], 2945 SW Wana-
maker Dr., Ste. A, Topeka, KS 66614-5321,
(785)271-0208
Protective League; Independent Investor [2334]
Protective Legislation; Soc. for Animal [11459]
Protective Soc; Children's [★11565]
Protein Coun; Intl. Hydrolyzed [1529]
Protein Coun; Soy [1563]

Protein Foods and Nutrition Development Assn. of
India [IO], Bombay, India
Protein Grain Products Intl. [★2738]
Protein Grain Products Intl. - Defunct.
Protein Soc. [6552], 9650 Rockville Pike, Bethesda,
MD 20814-3999, (301)634-7277
Protein Soc. [IO], Bethesda, MD, United States
Protein Soc. of Thailand [IO], Bangkok, Thailand
Proteins Res. Found; Fats and [2850]
Proteome Org; U.S. Human [6604]
Proteome Soc. [7119], PO Box 197, Ross, CA
94957-0197, (415)459-2266
Proteome Soc. [IO], Ross, CA, United States
Protestant
Ancient and Illustrious Order Knights of Malta
[19325]
Assembly of Episcopal Healthcare Chaplains
[19944]
Assoc. Parishes for Liturgy and Mission [19945]
Assn. of Protestant Churches and Missions in
Germany [IO]
Assn. of Theological Schools in the U.S. and
Canada [9270]
Brotherhood of Saint Andrew [19946]
Bruderhof Communities [20481]
Campus Ministry Women [19918]
Children's Friendship Proj. for Northern Ireland
[13478]
China Connection [12423]
Church Army [19947]
Churches Uniting in Christ [19889]
Commn. of the Churches on Intl. Affairs [20094]
Disciples Ecumenical Consultative Coun. [19848]
Fed. of Protestant Welfare Agencies [20482]
Fellowship of Saint James [19800]
Huguenot Soc. of the Founders of Manakin in the
Colony of Virginia [21162]
Interchurch Medical Assistance [20242]
Joint Action in Community Ser. [11803]
Louis Finkelstein Inst. for Religious and Social
Stud. at the Louis Stein Center [19931]
Natl. Coun. of Churches of Burundi [IO]
Natl. Huguenot Soc. [21163]
Protestant Church-Owned Publishers Assn. [3249]
Protestant Center [★19896]
Protestant Children; Fed. of Institutes Caring for
[★20482]
Protestant Church-Owned Publishers Assn. [3249],
2850 Kalamazoo Ave. SE, Grand Rapids, MI
49560, (616)224-0831
Protestant Cinema Guild - Defunct.
Protestant Film Commn. [★19537]
Protestant Guild for the Blind [★16884]
Protestant Guild for Human Services [16884], 411
Waverley Oaks Rd., Ste. 104, Waltham, MA
02452, (781)893-6000
Protestant Health and Human Services Assembly -
Address unknown since 1999.
Protestant Hosp. Assn; Chaplains Assn. of the Amer.
[★19744]
Protestant Motion Picture Coun. - Defunct.
Protestant Radio and TV Commn. [★19537]
Protestantism Study Group, Collectors of Religion on
Stamps Soc. - Defunct.
Protestants and Other Americans United for Separa-
tion of Church and State [★19836]
Protocol Consultants; Intl. Assn. of [965]
Protocol Executives; Coun. of [2677]
Proton Therapy; Natl. Assn. for [15649]
PROTOS [IO], Gent, Belgium
Protozoologists; Soc. of [★7866]
Proust Res. Assn. - Address unknown since 2002.
Prout; Girls' [★18633]
Prout Res. Inst. - Address unknown since 2003.
Proutist Farmers Fed; Universal [4659]
Proutist Intellectual Fed; Universal [★18627]
Proutist Universal [18627], PO Box 56533,
Washington, DC 20040, (301)231-0110
Proutist Youth Fed; Universal [18631]
Proutists; Women [18633]
Proutists Women; Universal [★18633]
Provide Addict Care Today [★13262]
Providence Assn. of Ukrainian Catholics in Am.
[19413], 817 N Franklin St., Philadelphia, PA
19123, (215)627-4984

Reference to "IO" in place of a book number signifies that the association may be found in the 45th edition of International Organizations.

Provident Medical Associates [★8871]
Provider Organizations; Amer. Assn. of Preferred [14680]
Providers Assn; Mystery Shopping [2639]
Province of Saint Joseph; Capuchin-Franciscans [19594]
Provincial Booksellers Fairs Assn. [IO], Royston, United Kingdom
Provincial Tenant's Rights Action Coalition - British Colombia [IO], Vancouver, BC, Canada
Provision Trade Fed. [IO], London, United Kingdom
Provisional Govt. of the Republic of New Africa - Address unknown since 1995.
Pruitt/Prewitt Family Assn. - Address unknown since 2005.
Prune Advisory Bd; California [★4712]
Prune Belly Syndrome Network [14478], PO Box 154, Beloit, WI 53512-0154
Prune Belly Syndrome Network [IO], Beloit, WI, United States
Prune Bd; California [★4712]
Prussia Collectors; Intl. Assn. of R.S. [22043]
Prva Katolicka Slovenska Jednota [★19362]
PRX Intl. [★3193]
P.S.1 Contemporary Art Center [9595], 22-25 Jackson Ave., Long Island City, NY 11101, (718)784-2084
Pseudo-Obstruction; Amer. Soc. of Adults with [★14410]
Pseudo-Obstruction and Hirschsprung's Disease Soc; Amer. [★14419]
Pseudoxanthoma Elasticum; Natl. Assn. for [14207]
Psi Beta [24579], c/o Jerry Rudmann, PhD, Exec. Dir., 8918 W 21st St. N, Ste. 200, No. 179, Wichita, KS 67205, (888)PSI-BETA
Psi Chi, the Natl. Honor Soc. in Psychology [24580], PO Box 709, 825 Vine St., Chattanooga, TN 37401-0709, (423)756-2044
Psi Epsilon Delta - Address unknown since 1999.
PSI Inst. for Contemporary Art [★9595]
Psi Omega [24440], 1040 Savannah Hwy., Charleston, SC 29407-7804, (843)556-0573
Psi Psi Psi - Address unknown since 2002.
PSI Res. - Address unknown since 1994.
Psi Sigma Alpha - Address unknown since 2002.
Psi Sigma Phi Multicultural Fraternity [24594], PO Box 3062, Jersey City, NJ 07303-3062
Psi Squad; Mind Development Association/U.S. [7447]
Psi Upsilon [24653], 3003 E 96th St., Indianapolis, IN 46240, (317)571-1833
Psi Upsilon [IO], Indianapolis, IN, United States
Psi Upsilon Found. [★IO]
Psi Upsilon Found. [★24653]
Psoriasis Assn. [IO], Northampton, United Kingdom
Psoriasis Assn. of Kenya [IO], Nairobi, Kenya
Psoriasis Assn. of New Zealand [IO], Lower Hutt, New Zealand
Psoriasis Found; Natl. [★14203]
Psoriasis Foundation/USA; Natl. [14209]
Psoriasis and Psoriatic Arthritis Alliance [IO], St. Albans, United Kingdom
Psoriasis Res. Assn. - Defunct.
Psoriasis Res. Inst. - Defunct.
Psoriasis Soc. of Canada [IO], Halifax, NS, Canada
Psoriasis Soc. of Lithuania [IO], Kaunas, Lithuania
Psoriatic Arthropathy Alliance [IO], St. Albans, United Kingdom
PSRC of Am. [16266], 200 Madison Ave., Ste. 2108, New York, NY 10016, (646)419-4020
Psychedelic Stud; Multidisciplinary Assn. for [15942]
Psychiatric Administrators; Amer. Assn. of [14861]
Psychiatric Assn; Amer. [16076]
Psychiatric Assn; Canadian [IO]
Psychiatric Assn; Caucus of Gay, Lesbian, and Bisexual Members of the Amer. [★12217]
Psychiatric Assn; Danubian [IO]
Psychiatric Assn; Gay Caucus of Members of the Amer. [★12217]
Psychiatric Assn; Gay, Lesbian, and Bisexual Caucus of the Amer. [★12217]
Psychiatric Day and Evening Clinic [★16231]
Psychiatric Found. [★15211]
Psychiatric Hosp. Sect. [★16093]
Psychiatric Hospitals; Natl. Assn. of Private [★16091]

Psychiatric Nurses Assn; Amer. [15456]
Psychiatric Nurses; Assn. of Child and Adolescent [★15487]
Psychiatric Nurses Assn. of Ireland [IO], Dublin, Ireland
Psychiatric Nursing; Advocates for Child [★15487]
Psychiatric Rehabilitation Services [15231], 500 W Annandale Rd., Falls Church, VA 22046, (703)536-9000
Psychiatric Res. Soc; Neuro [★16082]
Psychiatric Services/American Psychiatric Assn; Inst. on [16085]
Psychiatric Services Sect. [★16093]
Psychiatric Services; Special Constituency Sect. for Mental Hea. and [★16093]
Psychiatric Social Workers; Amer. Assn. of [★13206]
Psychiatric and Substance Abuse Services; Sect. for [16093]
Psychiatric Survivors Using Alternative Methods - Address unknown since 2001.
Psychiatric Treatment Centers for Children; Natl. Assn. of [★16090]
Psychiatrists Against Motorcoach Therapy; Natl. Coalition of [15222]
Psychiatrists; Amer. Acad. of Clinical [16064]
Psychiatrists; The Amer. Coll. of [16073]
Psychiatrists; Amer. Coll. of Osteopathic Neurologists and [15377]
Psychiatrists; Assn. of Gay and Lesbian [12217]
Psychiatry
Acad. on Mental Retardation [15238]
Acad. of Psychosomatic Medicine [16195]
Albert Ellis Inst. [16197]
Alfred Adler Inst. [16117]
Alliance for Eating Disorders Awareness [14297]
Amer. Acad. of Addiction Psychiatry [16062]
Amer. Acad. of Child and Adolescent Psychiatry [16063]
Amer. Acad. of Clinical Psychiatrists [16064]
Amer. Acad. of Medical Hypnoanalysts [14914]
Amer. Acad. of Psychiatry and the Law [5780]
Amer. Acad. of Psychoanalysis and Dynamic Psychiatry [16101]
Amer. Acad. of Psychotherapists [16198]
Amer. Acad. of Sleep Medicine [16418]
Amer. Art Therapy Assn. [16199]
Amer. Assn. of Chairs of Departments of Psychiatry [16065]
Amer. Assn. of Community Psychiatrists [16066]
Amer. Assn. of Directors of Psychiatric Residency Training [16067]
Amer. Assn. for Geriatric Psychiatry [16068]
Amer. Assn. on Intellectual and Developmental Disabilities [15239]
Amer. Assn. for Marriage and Family Therapy [16200]
Amer. Assn. of Psychiatric Administrators [14861]
Amer. Assn. of Psychiatric Technicians [16069]
Amer. Assn. for Tech. in Psychiatry [16070]
Amer. Bd. of Examiners of Psychodrama, Sociometry, and Gp. Psychotherapy [16201]
Amer. Bd. of Medical Psychotherapists and Psychodiagnosticians [16202]
Amer. Bd. of Psychiatry and Neurology [16071]
Amer. Coll. of Forensic Psychiatry [5752]
Amer. Coll. of Neuropsychiatrists [16072]
Amer. Coll. of Osteopathic Neurologists and Psychiatrists [15377]
The Amer. Coll. of Psychiatrists [16073]
Amer. Coun. of Hypnotist Examiners [14918]
Amer. Counseling Assn. [11815]
Amer. Dance Therapy Assn. [16203]
Amer. Gp. Psychotherapy Assn. [16204]
Amer. Hypnosis Assn. [14920]
Amer. Mental Hea. Alliance [15188]
Amer. Mental Hea. Counselors Assn. [15189]
Amer. Music Therapy Assn. [16205]
Amer. Neuropsychiatric Assn. [16074]
Amer. Orthopsychiatric Assn. [16075]
Amer. Psychiatric Assn. [16076]
Amer. Psychiatric Assn. Alliance [16077]
Amer. Psychoanalytic Assn. [16102]
Amer. Psychological Assn. Division of Independent Practice [16126]
Amer. Psychological Assn. of Graduate Students [16129]

Amer. Psychopathological Assn. [16190]
Amer. Psychosocial Oncology Soc. [15638]
Amer. Psychosomatic Soc. [16196]
Amer. Psychotherapy Assn. [16207]
Amer. Soc. for Adolescent Psychiatry [16078]
American Society for Adolescent Psychiatry [IO]
Amer. Soc. of Clinical Psychopharmacology [15921]
Amer. Soc. of Psychoanalytic Physicians [16104]
AMHS [11817]
Antipsychiatry Coalition [16079]
Assn. for Advancement of Psychoanalysis (of the Karen Horney Psychoanalytic Inst. and Center) [16105]
Assn. for the Advancement of Psychotherapy [16210]
Assn. for Ambulatory Behavioral Healthcare [16080]
Assn. for Behavioral and Cognitive Therapies [13733]
Assn. for Child and Adolescent Mental Hea. [IO]
Assn. for Child Psychoanalysis [16106]
Assn. of European Psychiatrists [IO]
Assn. of Gay and Lesbian Psychiatrists [12217]
Assn. of Medicine and Psychiatry [16081]
Assn. for Multicultural Counseling and Development [11819]
Assn. for Psychoanalytic Medicine [16107]
Assn. for Res. in Nervous and Mental Disease [16082]
Assn. for Specialists in Gp. Work [11820]
Assn. of State and Provincial Psychology Boards [16144]
Assn. for Women in Psychology [16145]
Awake In Am. [18601]
Better Sleep Coun. [16424]
Black Mental Hea. Alliance [15193]
British Columbia Psychological Assn. [IO]
British Indian Psychiatric Assn. [IO]
British Neuropsychiatry Assn. [IO]
Canadian Psychiatric Assn. [IO]
Center for Psychological and Spiritual Hea. [15194]
Christian Assn. for Psychological Stud. [16148]
Colombian Assn. of Psychiatry [IO]
Community Dreamsharing Network [16425]
Community Guidance Ser. [16214]
Conservative Orthopedics Intl. Assn. [15767]
Danubian Psychiatric Assn. [IO]
Depression and Bipolar Support Alliance [15196]
Disaster Psychiatry Outreach [16083]
Dr. to Dr. [12519]
Employee Assistance Soc. of North Am. [11823]
European Assn. for Forensic Child and Adolescent Psychiatry, Psychology and other involved Professionals [IO]
European Assn. for Psychotherapy [IO]
European Assn. of Transactional Anal. [IO]
European Soc. of Child and Adolescent Psychiatry [IO]
Families for Depression Awareness [15198]
Global Alliance of Mental Illness Advocacy Networks [15200]
Gp. for the Advancement of Psychiatry [16084]
Independent Psychiatric Assn. of Russia [IO]
Inst. for the Development of Emotional and Life Skills/National Inst. of Relationship Enhancement [15201]
Inst. for Labor and Mental Health [15202]
Inst. on Psychiatric Services/American Psychiatric Assn. [16085]
Inst. of Psychiatry [IO]
Intl. Alliance for Child and Adolescent Mental Hea. and Schools [15204]
Intl. Assn. for Child and Adolescent Psychiatry and Allied Professions [IO]
Intl. Assn. for Child and Adolescent Psychiatry and Allied Professions Germany [IO]
Intl. Assn. for Regression Res. and Therapies [16617]
Intl. Assn. for Relational Psychoanalysis and Psychotherapy [16108]
Intl. Assn. for the Stud. of Dreams [16426]
Intl. Center for Attitudinal Healing [15206]
Intl. Center for the Stud. of Psychiatry and Psychology [16086]

A star before a book entry number signifies that the name is not listed separately, but is mentioned within the entry.

International Center for the Study of Psychiatry and Psychology [IO]
Intl. Comm. Against Mental Illness [15207]
Intl. Fed. for Psychoanalytic Educ. [9028]
Intl. Neuropsychiatric Assn. [IO]
Intl. Psycho-Oncology Soc. [13834]
Intl. REST Investigators Soc. [16220]
Intl. Soc. for Adolescent Psychiatry and Psychology [16087]
Intl. Soc. for Adolescent Psychiatry and Psychology [IO]
Intl. Soc. for Human Ethology [6534]
Intl. Soc. of Psychiatric Genetics [14502]
Intl. Soc. for the Psychological Treatments of the Schizophrenias and Other Psychoses - USA [15209]
Intl. Soc. for Res. on Impulsivity [16088]
Intl. Soc. for Res. on Impulsivity [IO]
Intl. Soc. for the Stud. of Trauma and Dissociation [15210]
Intl. Transactional Anal. Assn. [16089]
Intl. Transactional Anal. Assn. [IO]
Japanese Soc. of Psychiatry and Neurology [IO]
Karen Horney Clinic [16109]
Mental Hea. Am. [15211]
Mental Res. Inst. [13737]
Milton H. Erickson Found. [16221]
NARSAD: Mental Hea. Res. Assn. [15213]
Natl. Alliance on Mental Illness [15214]
Natl. Assn. for the Advancement of Psychoanalysis [16110]
Natl. Assn. for Children's Behavioral Hea. [16090]
Natl. Assn. for Drama Therapy [16222]
Natl. Assn. for Poetry Therapy [16223]
Natl. Assn. of Psychiatric Hea. Systems [16091]
Natl. Assn. of Psychometrists [16159]
Natl. Assn. for Res. and Therapy of Homosexuality [14434]
Natl. Assn. for Rural Mental Hea. [15217]
Natl. Assn. of State Mental Hea. Prog. Directors [15219]
Natl. Autism Assn. [13727]
Natl. Center for Amer. Indian and Alaska Native Mental Hea. Res. [15220]
Natl. Character Lab. [6536]
Natl. Coun. for Community Behavioral Healthcare [15223]
Natl. Eating Disorders Assn. [14302]
Natl. Educ. Alliance for Borderline Personality Disorder [15224]
Natl. Found. for Depressive Illness [15225]
Natl. Guild of Hypnotists [14926]
Natl. Psychological Assn. for Psychoanalysis [16111]
Natl. Remotivation Therapy Org. [16226]
Netherlands Psychiatric Assn. [IO]
Network Against Coercive Psychiatry [12554]
Nordic Assn. for Psychiatric Epidemiology [IO]
Obsessive-Compulsive Found. [15230]
Performing Arts Medicine Assn. [16164]
Postgraduate Center for Mental Hea. [16227]
Psychohistory Forum [16113]
Psychotherapy Network [16228]
Rabbinic Center for Res. and Counseling [16229]
Radical Caucus in Psychiatry [16092]
Recovery, Inc. [16230]
Res. Soc. on Alcoholism [16517]
Royal Australian and New Zealand Coll. of Psychiatrists [IO]
Royal Coll. of Psychiatrists [IO]
Sandplay Therapists of Am. [16635]
Schizophrenia Intl. Res. Soc. [15232]
Sect. for Psychiatric and Substance Abuse Services [16093]
Sigmund Freud Archives [16115]
Sleep Res. Soc. [16429]
Social Psychiatry Res. Inst. [16094]
Social/Vocational Rehabilitation Clinic [16231]
Sociedad de Psiquiatria del Uruguay [IO]
Soc. of Biological Psychiatry [IO]
Soc. of Biological Psychiatry [16095]
Soc. of Clinical Child and Adolescent Psychology [16171]
Soc. for the Exploration of Psychotherapy Integration [16232]

Soc. for Pediatric Psychology [16175]
Soc. for Personality Assessment [16176]
Soc. of Professors of Child and Adolescent Psychiatry [16096]
Soc. for the Psychological Stud. of Men and Masculinity [16181]
Soc. for Psychophysiological Res. [16183]
Soc. for Res. in Child Development [11546]
South African Soc. of Psychiatrists [IO]
Tokyo Inst. of Psychiatry [IO]
Treatment and Res. Advancements Assn. for Personality Disorder [15235]
U.S. Psychiatric Rehabilitation Assn. [16336]
Western Pacific Assn. of Transactional Analysts [IO]
William Glasser Inst. [16233]
World Assn. of Cultural Psychiatry [16097]
World Assn. of Cultural Psychiatry [IO]
World Assn. for Infant Mental Hea. [IO]
World Assn. for Infant Mental Hea. [16098]
World Assn. for Psychosocial Rehabilitation - U.S. Br. [16338]
World Assn. for Social Psychiatry [16099]
World Assn. for Social Psychiatry [IO]
World Fed. for Mental Hea. [15237]
World Psychiatric Assn. [16100]
World Psychiatric Assn. [IO]
Psychiatry; Amer. Acad. of Psychoanalysis and Dynamic [16101]
Psychiatry; Amer. Coll. of Forensic [5752]
Psychiatry; Assn. for the Advancement of Philosophy and [7487]
Psychiatry; Center for the Stud. of [★16086]
Psychiatry; Comm. for Truth in [15195]
Psychiatry; Inst. on Hosp. and Community [★16085]
Psychiatry; Intl. Assn. for Social [★16099]
Psychiatry and the Law; Amer. Acad. of [5780]
Psychiatry; Network Against Coercive [12554]
Psychiatry and Psychology; Center for the Stud. of [★16086]
Psychiatry Seminar; San Francisco Social [★16089]
Psychiatry; Soc. of Professors of Child [★16096]
Psychiatry; World Assn. for Allied Disciplines and Infant [★16098]
Psychic Arts and Sciences; Acad. of [7439]
Psychic Detective Bur. - Address unknown since 1990.
Psychic Rescue Squad [★7447]
Psychic Science Intl. Special Interest Group - Address unknown since 2001.
Psychical Res; Amer. Soc. for [7442]
Psychoactive Drugs; Amer. Coun. on Marijuana and Other [★13222]

Psychoanalysis
Acad. of Psychosomatic Medicine [16195]
Alfred Adler Inst. [16117]
Amer. Acad. of Psychoanalysis and Dynamic Psychiatry [16101]
Amer. Acad. of Psychotherapists [16198]
Amer. Art Therapy Assn. [16199]
Amer. Assn. of Community Psychiatrists [16066]
Amer. Assn. for Marriage and Family Therapy [16200]
Amer. Bd. of Professional Psychology [16121]
Amer. Counseling Assn. [11815]
Amer. Dance Therapy Assn. [16203]
Amer. Gp. Psychotherapy Assn. [16204]
Amer. Music Therapy Assn. [16205]
Amer. Psychoanalytic Assn. [16102]
Amer. Psychoanalytic Found. [16103]
Amer. Psychological Assn. [16122]
Amer. Psychological Assn. - Addictions Div. [16123]
American Psychological Association Division 31 - State, Provincial, and Territorial Psychological Association Affairs [16124]
Amer. Psychological Assn. - Div. of Intl. Psychology [16127]
Amer. Psychological Assn. - Div. of Trauma Psychology [16128]
Amer. Psychological Assn. - Hea. Psychology Div. [16130]
Amer. Psychological Assn. - Media Psychology Div. [16131]
Amer. Psychological Assn. - Psychology of Religion (Division 36) [16132]

Amer. Psychology-Law Soc. [16133]
Amer. Psychopathological Assn. [16190]
Amer. Psychosomatic Soc. [16196]
Amer. Psychotherapy Assn. [16207]
Amer. Soc. for the Advancement of Pharmacotherapy [16134]
Amer. Soc. of Psychoanalytic Physicians [16104]
AMHS [11817]
Assn. for the Advancement of Applied Sport Psychology [16479]
Assn. for Advancement of Psychoanalysis (of the Karen Horney Psychoanalytic Inst. and Center) [16105]
Assn. for the Advancement of Psychology [16136]
Assn. for the Advancement of Psychotherapy [16210]
Assn. for Birth Psychology [16137]
Assn. of Black Psychologists [16138]
Assn. for Child Psychoanalysis [16106]
Assn. for Humanistic Psychology [16140]
Assn. for Multicultural Counseling and Development [11819]
Assn. for Philosophy of the Unconscious [10786]
Assn. for Psychoanalytic Medicine [16107]
Assn. for Psychoanalytic Self Psychology [16141]
Assn. for Psychological Type Intl. [16143]
Assn. for Specialists in Gp. Work [11820]
British Psychoanalytical Soc. [IO]
Canadian Assn. of Psychoanalytic Child Therapists [IO]
Canadian Psychoanalytic Soc. [IO]
Center for Applications of Psychological Type [16146]
C.G. Jung Found. for Analytical Psychology [16147]
Christian Assn. for Psychological Stud. [16148]
Community Dreamsharing Network [16425]
Community Guidance Ser. [16214]
European Fed. for Psychoanalytic Psychotherapy [IO]
European Psychoanalytical Fed. [IO]
German Acad. for Psychoanalysis [IO]
Hispanic Neuropsychological Soc. [15388]
Intl. Assn. for Relational Psychoanalysis and Psychotherapy [16108]
Intl. Assn. for Relational Psychoanalysis and Psychotherapy [IO]
Intl. Fed. for Psychoanalytic Educ. [IO]
Intl. Fed. for Psychoanalytic Educ. [9028]
Intl. Fed. of Psychoanalytic Societies [IO]
Intl. Psychoanalytical Assn. [IO]
Intl. REST Investigators Soc. [16220]
Intl. Soc. for Behavioral Nutrition and Physical Activity [13745]
Intl. Soc. for Dialogical Sci. [7544]
Intl. Soc. of Integral Psychoanalysis [IO]
Israeli Assn. for Psychoanalytic Psychotherapy [IO]
Jean Piaget Soc.: Soc. for the Stud. of Knowledge and Development [16156]
Karen Horney Clinic [16109]
Milton H. Erickson Found. [16221]
Natl. Assn. for the Advancement of Psychoanalysis [16110]
Natl. Assn. for the Advancement of Psychoanalysis [IO]
Natl. Assn. for Drama Therapy [16222]
Natl. Assn. for Poetry Therapy [16223]
Natl. Assn. of School Psychologists [16160]
Natl. Guild of Hypnotists [14926]
Natl. Psychological Assn. for Psychoanalysis [16111]
Natl. Remotivation Therapy Org. [16226]
North Amer. Soc. of Adlerian Psychology [16162]
North Amer. Soc. for Childhood Onset Schizophrenia [15229]
Psychoanalytic Res. Soc. [16112]
Psychohistory Forum [16113]
Psychology Soc. [16165]
Psychometric Soc. [16166]
Psychonomic Soc. [16167]
Psychotherapy Network [16228]
Rabbinic Center for Res. and Counseling [16229]
Radical Psychology Network [16169]
Radix Inst. [13649]

Reference to "IO" in place of a book number signifies that the association may be found in the 45th edition of International Organizations.

Encyclopedia of Associations, 46th Edition

4025

Recovery, Inc. [16230]
Res. Soc. on Alcoholism [16517]
Sandtray Network [16114]
Sandtray Network [IO]
Sigmund Freud Archives [16115]
Social/Vocational Rehabilitation Clinic [16231]
Soc. for Applied Psychological Res. in the Performing Arts [16170]
Soc. of Clinical Child and Adolescent Psychology [16171]
Soc. of Consulting Psychology [16172]
Soc. of Multivariate Experimental Psychology [16174]
Soc. for Pediatric Psychology [16175]
Soc. for Personality Assessment [16176]
Soc. of Psychological Hypnosis [16178]
Soc. for the Psychological Stud. of Ethnic Minority Issues [16179]
Soc. for the Psychological Stud. of Social Issues [16182]
Soc. for Psychophysiological Res. [16183]
Soc. for the Stud. of Peace, Conflict, and Violence: Peace Psychology Div. of the Amer. Psychological Assn. [16185]
Soc. for Theoretical and Philosophical Psychology [16186]
Swedish Psychoanalytical Soc. [IO]
U.S. Psychiatric Rehabilitation Assn. [16336]
William Glasser Inst. [16233]
World Org. and Public Educ. Corp. of the Natl. Assn. for the Advancement of Psychoanalysis [16116]
World Org. and Public Educ. Corp. of the Natl. Assn. for the Advancement of Psychoanalysis [IO]
Psychoanalysis; Acad. of [★16101]
Psychoanalysis; Amer. Acad. of [★16101]
Psychoanalysis; Amer. Assn. for Child [★16106]
Psychoanalysis; Natl. Assn. for the Advancement of Psychoanalysis and the Amer. Bd. for Accreditation in [★16110]
Psychoanalysis and Psychoanalysis in Groups; Amer. Found. for [★16101]
Psychoanalytic Assistance Fund [★16103]
Psychoanalytic Clinic; Karen Horney [★16109]
Psychoanalytic Inst. and Center; Assn. for Advancement of Psychoanalysis of the Karen Horney [16105]
Psychoanalytic Physicians; Amer. Assn. of [★16104]
Psychoanalytic and Psychosomatic Medicine; Assn. for [★16107]
Psychoanalytic Res. Soc. [16112], c/o Pamela A. Foelsch, 600 Mamaroneck Ave., Ste. 400, Harrison, NY 10528, (914)468-0865
Psychodrama; Amer. Soc. of Gp. Psychotherapy and [16208]
Psychohistory; Assn. for [★10123]
Psychohistory Forum [16113]
Psychoholics Unanimous - Address unknown since 2003.
Psychological Assn; Amer. Catholic [★16132]
Psychological Assn. - Division of Psychotherapy; Amer. [16206]
Psychological Assn. for Psychoanalysis; Natl. [16111]
Psychological Astrology; Assn. for [6490]
Psychological, and Cognitive Sciences; Fed. of Behavioral, [6530]
Psychological Hypnosis; Amer. Bd. of [14917]
Psychological Hypnosis; Amer. Bd. of Examiners in [★14917]
Psychological Professions and Sciences; Coun. for the Advancement of [★16136]
Psychological Soc. of Ireland [IO], Dublin, Ireland
Psychological Soc. of Northern Greece [IO], Thessaloniki, Greece
Psychological Soc. of South Africa [IO], Houghton, Republic of South Africa
Psychological and Spiritual Hea; Center for [15194]
Psychologists; Amer. Assn. of Correctional [★11853]
Psychologists' Assn. of Alberta [IO], Edmonton, AB, Canada
Psychologists; Assn. of Black [16138]
Psychologists; Assn. for Women [★16145]
Psychologists for the Ethical Treatment of Animals [★11460]

Psychologists For Legislative Action Now [★16136]
Psychologists Interested in the Advancement of Psychotherapy [★16122]
Psychologists Interested in Religious Issues [★16132]
Psychologists; Natl. Assn. of School [16160]
Psychologists for Social Action - Defunct.
Psychologists for Social Responsibility [18171], 208 I St. NE, Washington, DC 20002-4340, (202)543-5347
Psychologists and Social Workers; Amer. Assn. of Spinal Cord Injury [16459]
Psychology
Abilities! [11913]
Acad. of Psychosomatic Medicine [16195]
Acad. of Scientific Hypnotherapy [14913]
African Amer. Post Traumatic Stress Disorder Assn. [21276]
Alfred Adler Inst. [16117]
Alliance for Eating Disorders Awareness [14297]
Amer. Acad. of Counseling Psychology [16118]
Amer. Acad. of Forensic Psychology [5746]
Amer. Acad. of Medical Hypnoanalysts [14914]
Amer. Acad. of Psychoanalysis and Dynamic Psychiatry [16101]
Amer. Acad. of Psychotherapists [16198]
Amer. Acad. of Sleep Medicine [16418]
Amer. Assn. of Applied and Preventive Psychology [16119]
American Association of Applied and Preventive Psychology [IO]
Amer. Assn. of Behavioral Therapists [13744]
Amer. Assn. of Christian Counselors [19862]
Amer. Assn. of Community Psychiatrists [16066]
Amer. Assn. for Correctional and Forensic Psychology [11853]
Amer. Assn. of Directors of Psychiatric Residency Training [16067]
Amer. Assn. of Mental Hea. Professionals in Corrections [15186]
Amer. Assn. of Professional Hypnotherapists [14915]
Amer. Assn. of Psychiatric Technicians [16069]
Amer. Assn. of Spinal Cord Injury Psychologists and Social Workers [16459]
Amer. Bd. of Examiners of Psychodrama, Sociometry, and Gp. Psychotherapy [16201]
Amer. Bd. of Medical Psychotherapists and Psychodiagnosticians [16202]
Amer. Bd. of Professional Neuropsychology [16120]
Amer. Bd. of Professional Psychology [16121]
Amer. Bd. of Psychological Hypnosis [14917]
Amer. Bd. of Vocational Experts [9299]
Amer. Coll. of Forensic Psychology [14402]
Amer. Correctional Hea. Services Assn. [14715]
Amer. Coun. of Hypnotist Examiners [14918]
Amer. Counseling Assn. [11815]
Amer. Dance Therapy Assn. [16203]
Amer. Gp. Psychotherapy Assn. [16204]
Amer. Guild of Hypnotherapists [14919]
Amer. Hypnosis Assn. [14920]
Amer. Institutes for Res. in the Behavioral Sciences [6523]
Amer. Music Therapy Assn. [16205]
Amer. Psychoanalytic Assn. [16102]
Amer. Psychological Assn. [16122]
Amer. Psychological Assn. - Addictions Div. [16123]
American Psychological Association Division 31 - State, Provincial, and Territorial Psychological Association Affairs [16124]
Amer. Psychological Assn. - Division of Family Psychology [16125]
Amer. Psychological Assn. Division of Independent Practice [16126]
Amer. Psychological Assn. - Div. of Intl. Psychology [16127]
Amer. Psychological Assn. - Div. of Trauma Psychology [16128]
Amer. Psychological Assn. of Graduate Students [16129]
Amer. Psychological Assn. - Hea. Psychology Div. [16130]
Amer. Psychological Assn. - Media Psychology Div. [16131]

Amer. Psychological Assn. - Psychology of Religion (Division 36) [16132]
Amer. Psychology-Law Soc. [16133]
Amer. Psychopathological Assn. [16190]
Amer. Psychosocial Oncology Soc. [15638]
Amer. Psychosomatic Soc. [16196]
Amer. Psychotherapy Assn. [16207]
Amer. Soc. for the Advancement of Pharmacotherapy [16134]
Amer. Soc. of Clinical Hypnosis [14921]
Amer. Soc. of Clinical Hypnosis - Educ. and Res. Found. [14922]
Amer. Soc. of Psychoanalytic Physicians [16104]
AMHS [11817]
Asian Assn. of Social Psychology [IO]
Assoc. Professional Sleep Societies [16422]
Assn. for Advanced Training in the Behavioral Sciences [8878]
Assn. for the Advancement of Gestalt Therapy [16135]
Assn. for Advancement of Psychoanalysis (of the Karen Horney Psychoanalytic Inst. and Center) [16105]
Assn. for the Advancement of Psychology [16136]
Assn. for the Advancement of Psychotherapy [16210]
Assn. for Behavior Anal. [6526]
Assn. for Behavioral and Cognitive Therapies [13733]
Assn. for Birth Psychology [16137]
Assn. of Black Psychologists [16138]
Assn. of Bus. Psychologists [IO]
Assn. for Child Psychoanalysis [16106]
Assn. for Clinical Psychosocial Res. [16139]
Assn. for Death Educ. and Counseling [11909]
Assn. of Himalayan Yoga Meditation Societies [11218]
Assn. for Humanistic Psychology [16140]
Assn. of Humanistic Psychology Practitioners [IO]
Assn. of Lesbian, Gay, and Bisexual Psychologies - Europe [IO]
Assn. of Maternal and Child Hea. Programs [13947]
Assn. of Medicine and Psychiatry [16081]
Assn. for Multicultural Counseling and Development [11819]
Assn. for Pre- and Perinatal Psychology and Hea. [13979]
Assn. for Psychoanalytic Medicine [16107]
Assn. for Psychoanalytic Self Psychology [16141]
Assn. for Psychological Astrology [6490]
Assn. for Psychological Sci. [16142]
Assn. for Psychological Type Intl. [16143]
Assn. of Psychologists of Nova Scotia [IO]
Assn. of Psychology Postdoctoral and Internship Centers [8854]
Assn. for Res. in Personality [7543]
Assn. for Specialists in Gp. Work [11820]
Assn. of State and Provincial Psychology Boards [16144]
Assn. of State and Provincial Psychology Boards [IO]
Assn. for Teaching Psychology [IO]
Assn. for Therapeutic Philosophy [IO]
Assn. for Transpersonal Psychology [10170]
Assn. for Women in Psychology [16145]
Athletic Success Inst. [23665]
Australian Assn. for Cognitive and Behaviour Therapy [IO]
Australian Assn. for Psychological Type [IO]
Australian Psychological Soc. [IO]
Awake In Am. [18601]
Balint Soc. [IO]
Belgian Fed. of Psychologists [IO]
Better Sleep Coun. [16424]
Black Mental Hea. Alliance [15193]
British Psychological Soc. [IO]
Canadian Psychological Assn. [IO]
Canadian Register of Hea. Ser. Providers in Psychology [IO]
Center for Applications of Psychological Type [16146]
Center for Death Educ. and Bioethics [13314]
Center for Psychological and Spiritual Hea. [15194]

A star before a book entry number signifies that the name is not listed separately, but is mentioned within the entry.

C.G. Jung Found. for Analytical Psychology [16147]
Chinese Psychological Soc. [IO]
Christian Assn. for Psychological Stud. [16148]
Cognitive Neuroscience Soc. [15407]
Cognitive Sci. Soc. [6484]
Community Dreamsharing Network [16425]
Community Guidance Ser. [16214]
Comparative Cognition Soc. [6400]
Consciousness-Based Educ. Assn. [9029]
Coun. for the Natl. Register of Hea. Ser. Providers in Psychology [16149]
Create A Smile Dental Found. [13318]
Czech-Moravian Psychological Soc. [IO]
Danish Psychologists' Assn. [IO]
Depression and Bipolar Support Alliance [15196]
Devereux Natl. [13734]
Early Childhood Music and Movement Assn. [12618]
Eiseman Center for Color Info. and Training [6707]
EMDR - Humanitarian Assistance Programs [12767]
EMDR Intl. Assn. [16215]
Employee Assistance Soc. of North Am. [11823]
European Assn. for Aviation Psychology [IO]
European Assn. for Body Psychotherapy [IO]
European Assn. of Experimental Social Psychology [IO]
European Assn. of Personality Psychology [IO]
European Assn. of Psychological Assessment [IO]
European Coll. for the Stud. of Consciousness [IO]
European Fed. of Psychoanalytic Self-Psychology [IO]
European Fed. of Psychology Students' Associations [IO]
European Hea. Psychology Soc. [IO]
European Personal Construct Assn. [IO]
European Soc. for Cognitive Psychology [IO]
European Soc. for Developmental Psychology [IO]
European Soc. of Handwriting Psychology [IO]
European Soc. for Philosophy and Psychology [IO]
Experimental Psychology Soc. [IO]
False Memory Syndrome Found. [16150]
Families for Depression Awareness [15198]
Fed. of Behavioral, Psychological, and Cognitive Sciences [6530]
German Assn. of Sport Psychology [IO]
German Transpersonal Assn. [IO]
Gestalt Australia and New Zealand [IO]
Gift From Within [12768]
Global Alliance of Mental Illness Advocacy Networks [15200]
Global Assn. for Interpersonal Neurobiology Stud. [7375]
Gp. for the Use of Psychology in History [10112]
Himalayan Intl. Inst. of Yoga Sci. and Philosophy of the U.S.A. [12348]
Hispanic Neuropsychological Soc. [15388]
Hong Kong Psychological Soc. [IO]
Human Resources Res. Org. [6532]
Hungarian Psychological Assn. [IO]
Inst. for the Advancement of Human Behavior [13735]
Inst. for Labor and Mental Health [15202]
Inst. for Psychohistory [10123]
Intl. Acad. for Child Brain Development [15389]
Intl. Alliance for Child and Adolescent Mental Hea. and Schools [15204]
Intl. Assn. for Analytical Psychology [IO]
Intl. Assn. of Applied Psychology [IO]
Intl. Assn. for Cognitive Psychotherapy [16218]
Intl. Assn. for Cross-Cultural Psychology [IO]
Intl. Assn. of Individual Psychology [IO]
Intl. Assn. of Jungian Stud. [IO]
Intl. Assn. of Pastoral Psychologists [IO]
Intl. Assn. of Pastoral Psychologists [16151]
Intl. Assn. for Regression Res. and Therapies [16617]
Intl. Assn. for Relational Psychoanalysis and Psychotherapy [16108]
Intl. Assn. for the Stud. of Dreams [16426]

Intl. Assn. of Transpersonal Therapists and Physicians [15205]
Intl. Fed. for Psychoanalytic Educ. [9028]
Intl. Graphological Soc. [11211]
Intl. Inst. for the Stud. of Death [13315]
Intl. Mental Game Coaching Assn. [23289]
Intl. Network on Personal Meaning [IO]
Intl. Neuropsychological Soc. [15393]
Intl. Org. of Psychophysiology [IO]
Intl. Org. for the Stud. of Gp. Tensions [10189]
Intl. Psycho-Oncology Soc. [13834]
Intl. Psychohistorical Assn. [10125]
Intl. REST Investigators Soc. [16220]
Intl. Rorschach Soc. [IO]
Intl. School Psychology Assn. [IO]
Intl. Soc. for Adaptive Behavior [6533]
Intl. Soc. for Adolescent Psychiatry and Psychology [16087]
Intl. Soc. for Behavioral Nutrition and Physical Activity [13745]
Intl. Soc. for Comparative Psychology [16152]
Intl. Soc. for Comparative Psychology [IO]
Intl. Soc. for Developmental Psychobiology [IO]
Intl. Soc. for Developmental Psychobiology [16153]
Intl. Soc. for Dialogical Sci. [7544]
Intl. Soc. for Ecological Psychology [7545]
Intl. Soc. for Ecological Psychology [IO]
Intl. Soc. for Existential Psychology and Psychotherapy [IO]
Intl. Soc. for Human Ethology [6534]
Intl. Soc. of Neuro-Semantics [16396]
Intl. Soc. of Political Psychology [16154]
Intl. Soc. of Political Psychology [IO]
Intl. Soc. for Psychiatric Genetics [14502]
Intl. Soc. for the Psychological Treatments of the Schizophrenias and Other Psychoses - USA [15209]
Intl. Soc. of Psychoneuroendocrinology [15108]
Intl. Soc. for the Psychopathology of Expression and Art Therapy [IO]
Intl. Soc. for Psychophysics [IO]
Intl. Soc. for Res. on Aggression [6535]
Intl. Soc. for Res. on Impulsivity [16088]
Intl. Soc. for Self and Identity [7546]
Intl. Soc. for Self and Identity [IO]
Intl. Soc. of Sports Psychology [IO]
Intl. Soc. of Sports Psychology [16155]
Intl. Soc. for the Stud. of Trauma and Dissociation [15210]
Intl. Transactional Anal. Assn. [16089]
Intl. Union of Psychological Sci. [IO]
Japanese Psychological Assn. [IO]
Japanese Soc. of Adlerian Psychology [IO]
Japanese Soc. of Social Psychology [IO]
Jean Piaget Soc.: Soc. for the Stud. of Knowledge and Development [16156]
Karen Horney Clinic [16109]
Lithuanian Psychological Assn. [IO]
Manitoba Psychological Soc. [IO]
Mental Hea. Workers Without Borders [15212]
Mental Res. Inst. [13737]
Mexican Soc. of Psychology [IO]
Midwestern Psychological Assn. [16157]
Milton H. Erickson Found. [16221]
MTM Assn. for Standards and Res. [7165]
NARSAD: Mental Hea. Res. Assn. [15213]
Natl. Acad. of Neuropsychology [16158]
Natl. Assn. for the Advancement of Psychoanalysis [16110]
Natl. Assn. for Children's Behavioral Hea. [16090]
Natl. Assn. for Drama Therapy [16222]
Natl. Assn. of Mental Hea. Planning and Advisory Councils [15216]
Natl. Assn. for Poetry Therapy [16223]
Natl. Assn. of Psychiatric Hea. Systems [16091]
Natl. Assn. of Psychometrists [16159]
Natl. Assn. for Res. and Therapy of Homosexuality [14434]
Natl. Assn. of School Psychologists [16160]
Natl. Assn. of Therapeutic Schools and Programs [13738]
Natl. Autism Assn. [13727]
Natl. Center for Amer. Indian and Alaska Native Mental Hea. Res. [15220]

Natl. Center for Educ. in Maternal and Child Hea. [13969]
Natl. Character Lab. [6536]
Natl. Comm. for Certifying Agencies [16916]
Natl. Coun. for Community Behavioral Healthcare [15223]
Natl. Eating Disorders Assn. [14302]
Natl. Educ. Alliance for Borderline Personality Disorder [15224]
Natl. Fed. for Biblio/Poetry Therapy [16225]
Natl. Found. for Depressive Illness [15225]
Natl. Guild of Hypnotists [14926]
Natl. Psychological Assn. for Psychoanalysis [16111]
Natl. Register of Hea. Ser. Providers in Psychology [16161]
Natl. Remotivation Therapy Org. [16226]
New Zealand Assn. for Psychological Type [IO]
New Zealand Psychological Soc. [IO]
North Amer. Soc. of Adlerian Psychology [16162]
North Amer. Soc. for Childhood Onset Schizophrenia [15229]
North Amer. Soc. for the Psychology of Sport and Physical Activity [23666]
North Amer. Yoga Fed. [11219]
Northamerican Assn. of Masters in Psychology [9030]
Northamerican Assn. of Masters in Psychology [IO]
Norwegian Psychological Assn. [IO]
Obsessive-Compulsive Found. [15230]
Ontario Assn. for the Application of Personality Type [IO]
Ontario Psychological Assn. [IO]
Ophelia Proj. [13509]
Org. for Professional Astrology [6495]
Orthodox Christian Assn. of Medicine, Psychology and Religion [16163]
Performing Arts Medicine Assn. [16164]
Play Therapy Intl. [IO]
Polish Psychological Assn. [IO]
Psi Beta [24579]
Psi Chi, the Natl. Honor Soc. in Psychology [24580]
Psychohistory Forum [16113]
Psychological Soc. of Ireland [IO]
Psychological Soc. of Northern Greece [IO]
Psychological Soc. of South Africa [IO]
Psychologists' Assn. of Alberta [IO]
Psychology Soc. [16165]
Psychometric Soc. [16166]
Psychonomic Soc. [16167]
Psychosynthesis Intl. [16168]
Psychosynthesis Intl. [IO]
Psychotherapy Network [16228]
Radical Caucus in Psychiatry [16092]
Radical Psychology Network [16169]
Radical Psychology Network [IO]
Radix Inst. [13649]
Recovery, Inc. [16230]
Res. Soc. on Alcoholism [16517]
Romanian Assn. for Transpersonal Psychology [IO]
Sandplay Therapists of Am. [16635]
Sandtray Network [16114]
Schizophrenia Intl. Res. Soc. [15232]
Sculpture in the Env. [17240]
Secret Soc. of Happy People [10212]
Sidran Inst. for Traumatic Stress Educ. [12559]
Sigmund Freud Archives [16115]
Singapore Psychological Soc. [IO]
Sleep Res. Soc. [16429]
S.M.A.R.T. (Secretive Societies, Mind Control and Ritual Abuse) [13296]
Social Psychiatry Res. Inst. [16094]
Social/Vocational Rehabilitation Clinic [16231]
Societa Italiana di Psicologia [IO]
Soc. for Applied Anthropology [6427]
Soc. for Applied Psychological Res. in the Performing Arts [16170]
Soc. of Behavioral Medicine [13740]
Soc. of Biological Psychiatry [16095]
Soc. for Chaos Theory in Psychology and Life Sciences [7547]
Soc. of Clinical Child and Adolescent Psychology [16171]

Reference to "IO" in place of a book number signifies that the association may be found in the 45th edition of International Organizations.

Soc. for Clinical and Experimental Hypnosis [14927]
Soc. of Consulting Psychology [16172]
Soc. for Consumer Psychology [17344]
Soc. for Cross-Cultural Res. [10230]
Soc. for the Exploration of Psychotherapy Integration [16232]
Soc. for the History of Psychology [7548]
Soc. for Human Performance in Extreme Environments [6540]
Soc. for Indus. and Organizational Psychology [16173]
Society for Industrial and Organizational Psychology [IO]
Soc. of Multivariate Experimental Psychology [16174]
Soc. for Pediatric Psychology [16175]
Society for Pediatric Psychology [IO]
Society for Personality Assessment [IO]
Soc. for Personality Assessment [16176]
Soc. for Personality and Social Psychology [7549]
Soc. for Police and Criminal Psychology [16177]
Soc. of Professors of Child and Adolescent Psychiatry [16096]
Soc. for Psychological Anthropology [7550]
Soc. for Psychological Assistance - Croatia [IO]
Soc. of Psychological Hypnosis [16178]
Soc. for the Psychological Stud. of Ethnic Minority Issues [16179]
Soc. for the Psychological Stud. of Lesbian, Gay and Bisexual Issues [16180]
Soc. for the Psychological Stud. of Men and Masculinity [16181]
Soc. for the Psychological Stud. of Social Issues [16182]
Soc. for Psychophysiological Res. [16183]
Society for Psychophysiological Research [IO]
Soc. for Res. in Child Development [11546]
Soc. for Res. on Identity Formation [8960]
Soc. for a Sci. of Clinical Psychology [16184]
Soc. for Sex Therapy and Res. [16408]
Soc. for the Stud. of Ingestive Behavior [13742]
Soc. for the Stud. of Normal Psychology [IO]
Soc. for the Stud. of Peace, Conflict, and Violence: Peace Psychology Div. of the Amer. Psychological Assn. [16185]
Soc. for the Stud. of Social Biology [6862]
Soc. for Theoretical and Philosophical Psychology [16186]
Soc. for Vocational Psychology [7551]
Southern Soc. for Philosophy and Psychology [7494]
Space Settlement Studies Program [6387]
Sri Aurobindo Assn. [20636]
Sufi Psychology Assn. [16187]
Suicide and Mental Hea. Assn. Intl. [15234]
Treatment and Res. Advancements Assn. for Personality Disorder [15235]
Turkish Psychological Assn. [IO]
Union of Estonian Psychologists [IO]
U.S. Assn. for Body Psychotherapy [16188]
Violent Death Bereavement Soc. [11513]
Western Canada Psychoanalytic Psychotherapy Assn. [IO]
William Glasser Inst. [16233]
Workplace Bullying Inst. [16189]
World Assn. of Cultural Psychiatry [16097]
World Assn. for Psychosocial Rehabilitation - U.S. Br. [16338]
World Assn. for Social Psychiatry [16099]
Psychology; Amer. Acad. of Forensic [5746]
Psychology; Amer. Assn. for Correctional and Forensic [11853]
Psychology; Amer. Assn. for Humanistic [★16140]
Psychology; Amer. Soc. of Alderian [★16162]
Psychology; Assn. for the Advancement of Applied Sport [16479]
Psychology; Assn. for Astrological [★6490]
Psychology; Assn. for Aviation [6370]
Psychology; Assn. for Comprehensive Energy [16192]
Psychology; Assn. for Transpersonal [10170]
Psychology; Center for the Stud. of Psychiatry and [★16086]
Psychology in History; Gp. for the Use of [10112]

Psychology in Hypnosis; Amer. Bd. of Professional [★14917]
Psychology; Intl. Center for the Stud. of Psychiatry and [16086]
Psychology Internship Centers; Assn. of [★8854]
Psychology Postdoctoral and Internship Centers; Assn. of [8854]
Psychology Soc. [16165], 100 Beekman St., New York, NY 10038-1810, (212)285-1872
Psychology; Soc. for Computers in [6744]
Psychology; Soc. for Philosophy and [7492]
Psychology; Southern Soc. for Philosophy and [7494]
Psychometric Soc. [16166], c/o Carol Earey, Off. Mgr., Univ. of North Carolina - Greensboro, 210 Curry Bldg., PO Box 26171, Greensboro, NC 27402-6171
Psychoneuroendocrinology; Intl. Soc. of [15108]
Psychonomic Soc. [16167], 1710 Fortview Rd., Austin, TX 78704, (512)462-2442
Psychopathology
  Amer. Bd. of Professional Psychology [16121]
  Amer. Psychological Assn. [16122]
  Amer. Psychological Assn. - Addictions Div. [16123]
  American Psychological Association Division 31 - State, Provincial, and Territorial Psychological Association Affairs [16124]
  Amer. Psychological Assn. - Div. of Intl. Psychology [16127]
  Amer. Psychological Assn. - Div. of Trauma Psychology [16128]
  Amer. Psychological Assn. - Hea. Psychology Div. [16130]
  Amer. Psychological Assn. - Media Psychology Div. [16131]
  Amer. Psychological Assn. - Psychology of Religion (Division 36) [16132]
  Amer. Psychology-Law Soc. [16133]
  Amer. Psychopathological Assn. [16190]
  Amer. Soc. for Philosophy Counseling and Psychotherapy [16209]
  Amer. Soc. of Psychopathology of Expression [16191]
  Assn. for the Advancement of Psychology [16136]
  Assn. for Birth Psychology [16137]
  Assn. of Black Psychologists [16138]
  Assn. for Comprehensive Energy Psychology [16192]
  Assn. for Humanistic Psychology [16140]
  Assn. for Psychological Type Intl. [16143]
  Center for Applications of Psychological Type [16146]
  C.G. Jung Found. for Analytical Psychology [16147]
  Christian Assn. for Psychological Stud. [16148]
  Jean Piaget Soc.: Soc. for the Stud. of Knowledge and Development [16156]
  Natl. Assn. of Cognitive-Behavioral Therapists [16193]
  Natl. Assn. of School Psychologists [16160]
  North Amer. Soc. of Adlerian Psychology [16162]
  Psychology Soc. [16165]
  Psychometric Soc. [16166]
  Psychonomic Soc. [16167]
  Soc. of Multivariate Experimental Psychology [16174]
  Soc. for Personality Assessment [16176]
  Soc. for the Psychological Stud. of Social Issues [16182]
  Soc. for Psychophysiological Res. [16183]
  Soc. for Psychotherapy Res. [16194]
Psychopharmacology; Amer. Coll. of Neuro [15915]
Psychopharmacology; Amer. Soc. of Clinical [15921]
Psychopharmacology; British Assn. for [IO]
Psychophysiological Res; Soc. for [16183]
Psychophysiology and Biofeedback; Assn. for Applied [13749]
Psychophysiology; Intl. Org. of [IO]
Psychoprophylaxis in Obstetrics; Amer. Soc. for [★15608]
Psychosocial Development and Advisory Center [IO], Lima, Peru
Psychosocial Rehabilitation - U.S. Br; World Assn. for [16338]

Psychosocial Res; Assn. for Clinical [16139]
Psychosomatic Medicine
  Acad. of Psychosomatic Medicine [16195]
  Amer. Psychosomatic Soc. [16196]
Psychosomatic Medicine; Assn. for Psychoanalytic and [★16107]
Psychosomatic Problems; Amer. Soc. for Res. in [★16196]
Psychosynthesis Inst. - Defunct.
Psychosynthesis Intl. [16168], PO Box 4237, Oceanside, CA 92052
Psychosynthesis Intl. [IO], Oceanside, CA, United States
Psychotherapists and Counsellors Assn. of Western Australia [IO], Subiaco, Australia
Psychotherapy
  Acad. of Scientific Hypnotherapy [14913]
  Albert Ellis Inst. [16197]
  Alfred Adler Inst. [16117]
  AMEND [12020]
  Amer. Acad. of Psychotherapists [16198]
  Amer. Art Therapy Assn. [16199]
  Amer. Assn. of Anger Mgt. Providers [15185]
  Amer. Assn. of Community Psychiatrists [16066]
  Amer. Assn. for Marriage and Family Therapy [16200]
  Amer. Assn. of Professional Hypnotherapists [14915]
  Amer. Bd. of Examiners of Psychodrama, Sociometry, and Gp. Psychotherapy [16201]
  Amer. Bd. of Medical Psychotherapists and Psychodiagnosticians [16202]
  Amer. Bd. of Professional Psychology [16121]
  Amer. Bd. of Psychological Hypnosis [14917]
  Amer. Dance Therapy Assn. [16203]
  Amer. Gp. Psychotherapy Assn. [16204]
  Amer. Guild of Hypnotherapists [14919]
  Amer. Mental Hea. Alliance [15188]
  Amer. Music Therapy Assn. [16205]
  Amer. Psychological Assn. [16122]
  Amer. Psychological Assn. - Addictions Div. [16123]
  American Psychological Association Division 31 - State, Provincial, and Territorial Psychological Association Affairs [16124]
  Amer. Psychological Assn. - Div. of Intl. Psychology [16127]
  Amer. Psychological Assn. - Division of Psychotherapy [16206]
  Amer. Psychological Assn. - Div. of Trauma Psychology [16128]
  Amer. Psychological Assn. of Graduate Students [16129]
  Amer. Psychological Assn. - Hea. Psychology Div. [16130]
  Amer. Psychological Assn. - Media Psychology Div. [16131]
  Amer. Psychological Assn. - Psychology of Religion (Division 36) [16132]
  Amer. Psychology-Law Soc. [16133]
  Amer. Psychotherapy Assn. [16207]
  Amer. Soc. for the Advancement of Pharmacotherapy [16134]
  Amer. Soc. of Gp. Psychotherapy and Psychodrama [16208]
  Amer. Soc. for Philosophy Counseling and Psychotherapy [16209]
  Amer. Therapeutic Recreation Assn. [16315]
  Animals as Intermediaries [4157]
  The Arts We Need [13710]
  Assn. for the Advancement of Psychology [16136]
  Assn. for the Advancement of Psychotherapy [16210]
  Assn. for Applied Poetry [16211]
  Assn. for Birth Psychology [16137]
  Assn. of Black Psychologists [16138]
  Assn. of Child Psychotherapists [IO]
  Association for Comprehensive Energy Psychology [IO]
  Assn. for Gp. and Individual Psychotherapy [IO]
  Assn. for Humanistic Psychology [16140]
  Assn. of Mormon Counselors and Psychotherapists [16212]
  Assn. for Psychological Type Intl. [16143]
  Athletic Success Inst. [23665]

A star before a book entry number signifies that the name is not listed separately, but is mentioned within the entry.

Australian Assn. of Somatic Psychotherapists [IO]
Australian and New Zealand Assn. of Psychotherapy [IO]
Australian and New Zealand Psychodrama Assn. [IO]
British Assn. for Behavioural and Cognitive Psychotherapies [IO]
British Assn. of Psychotherapists [IO]
British Columbia Assn. for Marriage and Family Therapy [IO]
British Soc. for Clinical Psychophysiology [IO]
Center for Applications of Psychological Type [16146]
Certification Bd. for Music Therapists [16213]
C.G. Jung Found. for Analytical Psychology [16147]
Christian Assn. for Psychological Stud. [16148]
Community Dreamsharing Network [16425]
Community Guidance Ser. [16214]
Counselling and Psychotherapy in Scotland [IO]
EMDR Assn. of Australia [IO]
EMDR Europe [IO]
EMDR - Humanitarian Assistance Programs [12767]
EMDR Intl. Assn. [16215]
EMDR Intl. Assn. [IO]
EMDR Mexico [IO]
EMDR Network Japan [IO]
EMDRIA Latinoamerica Asociacion Civil [IO]
Equine Assisted Growth and Learning Association [IO]
Equine Assisted Growth and Learning Assn. [16216]
Eye Movement Desensitization and Reprocessing Assn. of Canada [IO]
Gen. Hypnotherapy Register [IO]
Group-Analytic Soc. [IO]
Guild of Psychotherapists [IO]
Hispanic Neuropsychological Soc. [15388]
Inst. for Expressive Anal. [16217]
Inst. of Gp. Anal. [IO]
Inst. of Psychosexual Medicine [IO]
Intl. Assn. for Art, Creativity and Therapy [IO]
Intl. Assn. for Cognitive Psychotherapy [IO]
Intl. Assn. for Cognitive Psychotherapy [16218]
Intl. Assn. for Forensic Psychotherapy [IO]
Intl. Assn. of Gp. Psychotherapy [IO]
Intl. Assn. of Pastoral Psychologists [16151]
Intl. Assn. for Relational Psychoanalysis and Psychotherapy [16108]
Intl. Assn. for the Stud. of Dreams [16426]
Intl. Assn. of Transpersonal Therapists and Physicians [15205]
Intl. Assn. for Voice Movement Therapy [13711]
Intl. Expressive Arts Therapy Assn. [13712]
Intl. Neuro-Linguistic Programming Assn. [16219]
Intl. Neuro-Linguistic Programming Assn. [IO]
Intl. Phototherapy Assn. [IO]
Intl. REST Investigators Soc. [16220]
Intl. Soc. for Dialogical Sci. [7544]
Intl. Soc. for the Psychological Treatments of the Schizophrenias and Other Psychoses - USA [15209]
Italian Soc. of Therapeutic Psychosynthesis [IO]
Jean Piaget Soc.: Soc. for the Stud. of Knowledge and Development [16156]
Korean Acad. of Psychotherapists [IO]
Korean EMDR Assn. [IO]
London Assn. of Primal Psychotherapists [IO]
Mental Hea. Workers Without Borders [15212]
Milton H. Erickson Found. [16221]
Natl. Assn. for Drama Therapy [16222]
Natl. Assn. for Poetry Therapy [16223]
Natl. Assn. of School Psychologists [16160]
Natl. Coalition of Creative Arts Therapies Associations [16224]
Natl. Coll. of Hypnosis and Psychotherapy [IO]
Natl. Fed. for Biblio/Poetry Therapy [16225]
Natl. Guild of Hypnotists [14926]
Natl. Register of Hypnotherapists and Psychotherapists [IO]
Natl. Remotivation Therapy Org. [16226]
North Amer. Soc. of Adlerian Psychology [16162]
Ontario Soc. of Psychotherapists [IO]
Performing Arts Medicine Assn. [16164]

Postgraduate Center for Mental Hea. [16227]
Psychology Soc. [16165]
Psychometric Soc. [16166]
Psychonomic Soc. [16167]
Psychotherapy Network [16228]
Rabbinic Center for Res. and Counseling [16229]
Recovery, Inc. [16230]
Recovery, Inc. [IO]
Res. Soc. on Alcoholism [16517]
Sandplay Therapists of Am. [16635]
Sandtray Network [16114]
Social/Vocational Rehabilitation Clinic [16231]
Soc. of Clinical Child and Adolescent Psychology [16171]
Soc. of Counselling and Psychotherapy Educators [IO]
Soc. for the Exploration of Psychotherapy Integration [IO]
Soc. for the Exploration of Psychotherapy Integration [16232]
Soc. of Multivariate Experimental Psychology [16174]
Soc. for Personality Assessment [16176]
Soc. of Psychological Hypnosis [16178]
Soc. for the Psychological Stud. of Men and Masculinity [16181]
Soc. for the Psychological Stud. of Social Issues [16182]
Soc. for Psychophysiological Res. [16183]
Soc. for the Stud. of Peace, Conflict, and Violence: Peace Psychology Div. of the Amer. Psychological Assn. [16185]
Treatment and Res. Advancements Assn. for Personality Disorder [15235]
United Kingdom Coun. for Psychotherapy [IO]
U.S.A. Transactional Anal. Assn. [13743]
U.S. Assn. for Body Psychotherapy [16188]
Uruguayan Assn. of the Analytical Psychotherapy [IO]
William Glasser Inst. [16233]
Psychotherapy; Amer. Psychological Assn. - Division of [16206]
Psychotherapy Assn; Amer. [16207]
Psychotherapy Assn; Amer. Gp. [16204]
Psychotherapy; Center for Expressive [★16217]
Psychotherapy and Counselling Fed. of Australia [IO], Fitzroy, Australia
Psychotherapy; European Assn. for [IO]
Psychotherapy; Inst. for Advanced Stud. in Rational [★16197]
Psychotherapy; Inst. for Res. in [★16227]
Psychotherapy Network [16228], 5135 MacArthur Blvd. NW, Washington, DC 20016, (202)537-8950
Psychotherapy; Postgraduate Center for [★16227]
Psychotherapy and Psychodrama; Amer. Soc. of Gp. [16208]
Psychotherapy; Psychologists Interested in the Advancement of [★16122]
Psychotherapy Res; Soc. for [16194]
Psychotherapy, Transcultural Family Therapy and Psychosomatic Medicine; Intl. Center for Positive [IO]
Psychotronics Assn; U.S. [7454]
Psynetics Found. [★10177]
PT Boats All Hands [★21402]
PT Boats All Hands [★IO]
PT Boats, Bases and Tenders [★IO]
PT Boats, Bases and Tenders [★21402]
PT Boats, Inc. [21402], PO Box 38070, Germantown, TN 38183-0070, (901)755-8440
PT Boats, Inc. [IO], Germantown, TN, United States
Pt-to-Pt Assn; North Amer. [23511]
PTA - Natl. Cong. of Parents and Teachers; Natl. [8954]
PTAs; Natl. Assn. of Hebrew Day School [8953]
Pteridological Soc; British [IO]
PTI [★12569]
PTNA [★16022]
Publi-Cable - Defunct.
Public Accountant Examiners; Assn. of Certified [★5428]
Public Accountants; Amer. Assn. of Attorney-Certified [8]
Public Accountants; Amer. Inst. of Certified [9]
Public Accountants; Amer. Woman's Soc. of Certified [12]

Public Accountants; Assn. of Practicing Certified [17]
Public Accuracy; Inst. for [18456]
Public Action - Defunct.
Public Administration
African-Americans for Democracy [16936]
African Assn. for Public Admin. and Mgt. [IO]
Amer. Assn. of State Ser. Commissions [6189]
Amer. Soc. for Public Admin. [6190]
American Society for Public Administration [IO]
Asian Amer. Govt. Executives Network [5704]
British Coun. [IO]
Commonwealth Assn. for Public Admin. and Mgt. [IO]
Conf. of Minority Public Administrators [6191]
Eastern Regional Org. for Public Admin. [IO]
European Gp. of Public Admin. [IO]
European Inst. of Public Admin. [IO]
Hong Kong Public Admin. Assn. [IO]
Inst. of Public Admin. [IO]
Inst. of Public Admin. Australia [IO]
Inst. of Public Admin. of Canada [IO]
Inst. of Public Admin. - USA [IO]
Inst. of Public Admin. - USA [6192]
Intl. Assn. of Lemon Law Administrators [5536]
Intl. Inst. of Administrative Sciences [IO]
Latin Amer. Centre for Development Admin. [IO]
Law Enforcement Against Prohibition [17999]
Natl. Acad. of Public Admin. [6193]
Natl. Acad. of Public Admin. [IO]
Natl. Assn. of Schools of Public Affairs and Admin. [6194]
Natl. Assn. of State Facilities Administrators [6195]
Natl. Assn. of Urban Hospitals [14893]
Natl. Forum for Black Public Administrators [6196]
Pi Alpha Alpha [24581]
Public Tech. Inst. [6197]
Sect. for Women in Public Admin. [6198]
Southern Public Admin. Educ. Found. [6199]
Student Assn. for Voter Empowerment [17490]
Public Admin; Coun. on Graduate Educ. for [★6194]
Public Admin; Natl. Comm. for Women in [★6198]
Public Admin; Natl. Inst. of [★6192]
Public Administration Service - Address unknown since 2006.
Public Admin; Task Force for Women in [★6198]
Public Advocate - Coalition of Public Interest Professionals - Address unknown since 1995.
Public Advocate of the U.S. [18685], 5613 Leesburg Pike, Ste. 17, Falls Church, VA 22041, (703)845-1808
Public Affairs
9/11 Families for a Secure Am. [18728]
Ad Coun. [18384]
African-Americans for Democracy [16936]
Air Force Public Affairs Alumni Assn. [6200]
Albanian Amer. Civic League [16970]
Alfred P. Sloan Found. [18385]
Alliance for Democracy [18386]
Amer. Muslim Alliance [18083]
Arcus Found. [18266]
Asian and Pacific Islander Amer. Vote [18345]
Assn. of Americans for Civic Responsibility [17074]
Athena Alliance [17468]
Bus. Leaders for Sensible Priorities [18387]
Buying Influence [17310]
Campaign for America's Future [18388]
Campaign to Label Genetically Engineered Foods [17604]
Carter Center [18389]
Center for Applied Christian Ethics [19975]
Center for Strategic and Intl. Stud. [18390]
Center for Strategic and Intl. Stud. [IO]
Citizens Coal Coun. [4299]
Citizens for Consumer Justice [18641]
Citizens for Independent Public Broadcasting [17025]
Citizens for Legitimate Govt. [17663]
Citizens United [17664]
Coalition for Genetic Fairness [17107]
Commercial Alert [18391]
Commn. for the Advancement of Public Interest Orgs. [17317]
Concerned Citizens for Nuclear Safety [18147]

Reference to "IO" in place of a book number signifies that the association may be found in the 45th edition of International Organizations.

Consumer Action [17319]
Consumer Alert [17320]
Consumer Fed. of Am. [17321]
Downwinders [18150]
Eisenhower Inst. [18392]
Emergency Coalition for U.S. Financial Support of the United Nations [18764]
European-American Unity and Rights Org. [17114]
European Union - Delegation of the Commn. to the U.S. [17507]
First Amendment Proj. [18393]
Ford Found. [18394]
Ford Found. [IO]
Free the Grapes! [16971]
Genocide Watch [17660]
Global Network Against Weapons and Nuclear Power in Space [18152]
Global Youth Action Network [18850]
Heart of Am. Northwest [18395]
The Heritage Found. [17631]
Inst. of Public Affairs [IO]
Intl. Assn. of Facilitators [3183]
Intl. Assn. of Genocide Scholars [17661]
Intl. Inst. for Strategic Stud. - US [18396]
Intl. Inst. for Strategic Stud. - US [IO]
Intl. Network of Women Against Tobacco [18744]
Joseph and Edna Josephson Inst. of Ethics [17505]
Latino Issues Forum [19098]
League of Young Voters [18356]
Mainstream Media Proj. [18494]
May I Speak Freely Media [18028]
Mobile Voter [18032]
Move Am. Forward [18733]
Muslim Public Affairs Coun. [18085]
Natl. Action Network [17127]
Natl. Assn. of Public Affairs Networks [17026]
Natl. Assn. of Schools of Public Affairs and Admin. [6194]
Natl. Center for Policy Anal. [18462]
Natl. Civic Coun. [IO]
Natl. Coun. of Asian Pacific Americans [17013]
Natl. Economic and Social Rights Initiative [17778]
Natl. Fed. of Croatian Americans [17362]
Natl. Immigration Law Center [17807]
Natl. Priorities Proj. [17511]
Natl. Voice [17076]
Network 20/20 [18004]
No Peace Without Justice [18227]
North Amer. St. Newspaper Assn. [18102]
Ogwashi-Uku Assn., USA [19291]
Pi Alpha Alpha [24581]
Planet Club [IO]
ProEnglish [9912]
Proj. Underground [18079]
Public Campaign [18397]
Public Educ. Center [18398]
Rising Leaders [18005]
Scholars for Peace in the Middle East [18070]
School of the Americas Watch [18399]
South Asian Amer. Voting Youth [18366]
Southwest Res. and Info. Center [17345]
Spirit of Am. [18488]
US-Azerbaijan Coun. [17876]
Uyghur Amer. Assn. [17788]
What Kids Can Do [18859]
William C. Velasquez Inst. [19197]
William J. Clinton Found. [17855]
W.K. Kellogg Found. [18400]
Public Affairs; Amer. Zionist Comm. for [★18050]
Public Affairs Assn; Cable TV [★5556]
Public Affairs; Baptist Joint Comm. on [★19479]
Public Affairs; Center for Media and [17169]
Public Affairs Comm; Amer. Israel [18050]
Public Affairs Comm. - Defunct.
Public Affairs Coun. [17354], 2033 K St. NW, Ste. 700, Washington, DC 20006, (202)872-1790
Public Affairs; European Community Off. of Press and [★17507]
Public Affairs; European Union Off. of Press and [★17507]
Public Affairs Inst. - Defunct.
Public Agency Risk Managers Assn. [5833], PO Box 6810, San Jose, CA 95150, (888)412-5913

Public Agenda [18479], 6 E 39th St., 9th Fl., New York, NY 10016, (212)686-6610
Public Agenda Found. [★18479]
Public Archives Commn. of the Amer. Historical Assn. [★9403]
Public Art Fund [17239], 1 E 53rd St., New York, NY 10022, (212)980-4575
Public Arts Coun. [★17239]
Public Black Colleges of the Natl. Assn. of State Universities and Land-Grant Colleges; Off. for the Advancement of [8112]
Public Broadcasting; Assn. for [★547]
Public Broadcasting; Citizens for Independent [17025]
Public Broadcasting Consortium; Native Amer. [★9767]
Public Broadcasting; Corp. for [9762]
Public Broadcasting Mgt. Assn. [578], PO Box 50008, Columbia, SC 29250, (803)799-5517
Public Broadcasting Ser. [9768], 2100 Crystal Dr., Arlington, VA 22202, (703)739-5000
Public Campaign [18397], 1320 19th St. NW, Ste. M-1, Washington, DC 20036, (202)293-0222
Public Child Welfare Administrators; Natl. Assn. of [11629]
Public Choice Soc. [7527], c/o Jo Ann S. Burgess, George Mason Univ., Buchanan House MSN 1E6, 4400 Univ. Dr., Fairfax, VA 22030-4444, (703)993-2337
Public Citizen [17341], 1600 20th St. NW, Washington, DC 20009, (202)588-1000
Public Citizen Hea. Res. Gp. [16250], 1600 20th St. NW, Washington, DC 20009, (202)588-1000
Public Citizen Information Center - Defunct.
Public Citizen Litigation Gp. [17342], 1600 20th St. NW, Washington, DC 20009, (202)588-1000
Public Citizen's Cong. Watch [17343], 1600 20th St. NW, Washington, DC 20009, (202)588-1000
Public Citizen's Critical Mass Energy and Env. Prog. [18134], 215 Pennsylvania Ave. SE, Washington, DC 20003, (202)546-4996
Public Citizen's Critical Mass Energy and Env. Proj. [★18134]
Public Citizens Visitor Center - Defunct.
Public and Commercial Services Union [IO], London, United Kingdom
Public Communications Coun; Amer. [3733]
Public Concern Found. - Address unknown since 1990.
Public Continuing Adult Educ; Natl. Assn. for [★8146]
Public Conversations Proj. [17189], 46 Kondazian St., Watertown, MA 02472-2832, (617)923-1216
Public Cryptography Study Group - Defunct.
Public Data Users; Assn. of [7190]
Public Doublespeak; Comm. on [17173]
Public Dreams Soc. [IO], Vancouver, BC, Canada
Public Educ. Center [18398], 1100 Connecticut Ave. NW, Ste. 1310, Washington, DC 20036-4119, (202)466-4310
Public Educ. Corp. of the Natl. Assn. for the Advancement of Psychoanalysis [★16116]
Public Educ. Corp. of the Natl. Assn. for the Advancement of Psychoanalysis [★IO]
Public Educ; Ministries in [★19938]
Public Educ. Network [9040], 601 13th St. NW, Ste. 710 S, Washington, DC 20005, (202)628-7460
Public Education Religion Studies Center - Defunct.
Public Employee Dept. (of AFL-CIO) - Defunct.
Public Employee Retirement Systems; Natl. Conf. on [5570]
Public Employees Roundtable [5572], c/o Coun. for Excellence in Govt., 1301 K St. NW, Ste. 450 W, Washington, DC 20005, (202)728-0418
Public Employer Labor Relations Assn; Natl. [5918]
Public Employment and the Disadvantaged - Defunct.
Public Employment Services; Intl. Assn. of [★5679]
Public Environment Center - Defunct.

Public Finance
    Amer. Assn. for Budget and Prog. Anal. [6201]
    Amer. Soc. of Tax Problem Solvers [6290]
    Assn. for Governmental Leasing and Finance [6202]
    Assn. of Public Treasurers of the U.S. and Canada [6203]

    Bus. Coun. [18401]
    Bus. Roundtable [18402]
    Center on Budget and Policy Priorities [18403]
    Center for Financial Freedom and Accuracy in Financial Reporting [18404]
    Comm. for a Responsible Fed. Budget [18405]
    Consultative Gp. to Assist the Poor [17833]
    Coun. of Development Finance Agencies [17458]
    Found. for Economic Educ. [18406]
    Govt. Finance Officers Assn. of U.S. and Canada [6204]
    Govt. Finance Officers Assn. of U.S. and Canada [IO]
    Intl. Assn. for Res. in Income and Wealth [IO]
    Intl. Assn. for Res. in Income and Wealth [18407]
    Intl. Org. of Supreme Audit Institutions [IO]
    Manhattan Inst. for Policy Res. [18408]
    Natl. Assn. of County Treasurers and Finance Officers [6205]
    Natl. Assn. of State Auditors, Comptrollers, and Treasurers [6206]
    Natl. Assn. of State Budget Officers [6207]
    Natl. Assn. of State Treasurers [6208]
    Natl. Assn. of Urban Hospitals [14893]
    Natl. Center for Economic and Security Alternatives [18409]
    Natl. Comm. to Repeal the Federal Reserve Act [18410]
    Natl. Commodity and Barter Assn. [18411]
    Native Amer. Finance Officers Assn. [1442]
    Professional Accounting Soc. of Am. [1]
    Soc. of County Treasurers [IO]
    Soc. of Financial Examiners [6209]
Public Finance Advisors; Natl. Assn. of Independent [1467]
Public Gas Assn; Amer. [3951]
Public-General Hosp. Sect. [★14895]
Public Golf Mgt. Assn. - Address unknown since 2004.

Public Health
    African Chap. of Intl. Assn. of Agricultural Medicine and Rural Hea. - Egypt [IO]
    African Medical and Res. Found. - Canada [IO]
    African Medical and Res. Found. - France [IO]
    African Medical and Res. Found. - Kenya [IO]
    African Medical and Res. Found. - Sweden [IO]
    African Medical and Res. Found. - Uganda [IO]
    Alliance for Advancing Nonprofit Hea. Care [14606]
    Amer. Acad. of Sanitarians [16383]
    Amer. Assn. for Hea. Educ. [16234]
    Amer. Assn. for the History of Medicine [10082]
    Amer. Assn. of Public Hea. Dentistry [14118]
    Amer. Assn. of Public Hea. Physicians [16235]
    Amer. Assn. of Public Hea. Veterinarians [16747]
    Amer. Bd. of Dental Public Hea. [14120]
    Amer. Manual Medicine Assn. [13618]
    Amer. Public Hea. Assn. [16236]
    Amer. School Hea. Assn. [14718]
    Amer. Social Hea. Assn. [16410]
    Amer. Tai Chi Assn. [16593]
    Amer. Youth Understanding Diabetes Abroad [14219]
    Armenian Amer. Soc. for Stud. on Stress and Genocide [15190]
    Asia Pacific Public Health Nutrition Assn. [16237]
    Asian Hea. Inst. [IO]
    Assn. for Community Affiliated Plans [14617]
    Assn. for Community Hea. Improvement [16238]
    Assn. for Community Hea. Improvement [IO]
    Assn. of Hea. Fac. Survey Agencies [6210]
    Assn. of Korean Agricultural Medicine and Rural Hea. [IO]
    Assn. of Local Public Hea. Agencies [IO]
    Assn. of Port Hea. Authorities [IO]
    Assn. of Public Hea. Labs. [IO]
    Assn. of Public Hea. Labs. [16239]
    Assn. of Schools of Public Hea. [16240]
    Assn. of State Drinking Water Administrators [6211]
    Assn. of State and Territorial Hea. Officials [6212]
    Assn. of State and Territorial Local Hea. Liaison Officials [6213]
    Australian Hea. Promotion Assn. [IO]
    British Fluoridation Soc. [IO]

A star before a book entry number signifies that the name is not listed separately, but is mentioned within the entry.

Canadian Inst. of Public Hea. Inspectors **[IO]**
Canadian Public Hea. Assn. **[IO]**
Chinese Rural Hea. Assn. China **[IO]**
Citizens Alliance for VD Awareness **[16411]**
CityMatch **[13957]**
Commissioned Officers Assn. of the U.S. Public Hea. Ser. **[6214]**
Comm. to Reduce Infection Deaths **[14877]**
Commonwealth Fund **[16241]**
Concern Am. **[12845]**
Coun. on Educ. for Public Hea. **[16242]**
Delta Omega **[24582]**
Directors of Hea. Promotion and Educ. **[6215]**
Eating Disorders Coalition for Res., Policy and Action **[14299]**
Educ., Training and Res. Associates **[8556]**
European Public Hea. Alliance **[IO]**
European Public Hea. Assn. **[IO]**
Faculty of Public Hea. Medicine **[IO]**
Food and Drug Admin. Alumni Assn. **[17606]**
Healing Waters Intl. **[13410]**
Hea. Educ. Coun. **[14562]**
Hea. Educ. Found. **[16243]**
Healthlink Worldwide **[IO]**
Herpes Rsrc. Center - Amer. Social Hea. Assn. **[16412]**
Intl. Assn. of Agricultural Medicine and Rural Hea. **[IO]**
Intl. Assn. for Medicinal Compliance **[15041]**
The Intl. Found. **[12434]**
Intl. Inst. of Concern for Public Hea. **[IO]**
Intl. Medical Equip. Collaborative **[14569]**
Intl. Network for the History of Public Hea. **[IO]**
Intl. Public Hea. Watch **[IO]**
Intl. Relief Teams **[12863]**
Intl. Soc. for Disease Surveillance **[14269]**
Intl. Union Against Sexually Transmitted Infections, Regional Off. for North Am. **[16414]**
IUD Claims Info. Source **[6216]**
Japan Public Hea. Assn. **[IO]**
Japanese Assn. of Rural Medicine **[IO]**
Medicine for Peace **[IO]**
Medicine for Peace **[12789]**
MedShare Intl. **[12531]**
Mental Hea. Media **[IO]**
Mercury Policy Proj. **[18745]**
Mercy-USA for Aid and Development **[12871]**
Natl. Alliance for Food Safety and Security **[1537]**
Natl. Assn. of Community Hea. Centers **[14574]**
Natl. Assn. of County and City Hea. Officials **[6217]**
Natl. Assn. of Hea. Educ. Centers **[14675]**
Natl. Assn. of Local Boards of Hea. **[16244]**
Natl. Assn. for Public Hea. Info. Tech. **[7203]**
Natl. Assn. for Public Hea. Statistics and Info. Systems **[6218]**
Natl. Assn. of Public Hospitals and Hea. Systems **[14892]**
Natl. Assn. of Rural Hea. Clinics **[16245]**
Natl. Assn. of State Head Injury Administrators **[14529]**
Natl. Assn. of Urban Hospitals **[14893]**
Natl. Center for Environmental Hea. Strategies **[14366]**
Natl. Coalition for Promoting Physical Activity **[23653]**
Natl. Conf. of Local Environmental Hea. Administrators **[16246]**
Natl. Hea. Assn. **[15279]**
Natl. Hepatitis C Advocacy Coun. **[14813]**
Natl. Latina Hea. Network **[14589]**
Natl. Latino Coun. on Alcohol and Tobacco Prevention **[12269]**
Natl. Liquor Law Enforcement Assn. **[5996]**
Natl. Meningitis Assn. **[14281]**
Natl. Pediculosis Assn. **[16247]**
Natl. Rural Hea. Assn. **[16248]**
NSF Intl. **[16249]**
NSF Intl. **[IO]**
Occupational Knowledge Intl. **[5099]**
Pakistan Voluntary Hea. and Nutrition Assn. **[IO]**
Physicians for a Violence-Free Soc. **[12985]**
Public Citizen Hea. Res. Gp. **[16250]**
Public Hea. Assn. of Australia **[IO]**
Public Hea. Assn. of Australia - Australian Capital Territory **[IO]**

Public Hea. Assn. of Australia - New South Wales **[IO]**
Public Hea. Assn. of Australia - Northern Territory **[IO]**
Public Hea. Assn. of Australia - South Australia **[IO]**
Public Hea. Assn. of Australia - Tasmania **[IO]**
Public Hea. Assn. of Australia - Victoria **[IO]**
Public Hea. Assn. of Australia - Western Australia **[IO]**
Public Hea. Assn. of New Zealand **[IO]**
Public Hea. Comm. of the Coun. of Europe **[IO]**
Public Hea. Found. **[16251]**
Public Hea. Leadership Soc. **[16252]**
Public Hosp. Pharmacy Coalition **[15949]**
Radiation and Public Hea. Proj. **[16270]**
Royal Inst. of Public Hea. **[IO]**
Royal Soc. for the Promotion of Hea. **[IO]**
Scottish Assn. of Hea. Councils **[IO]**
Sino-American Pharmaceutical Professionals Assn. **[15951]**
Soc. for the Anal. of African-American Public Hea. Issues **[16253]**
Soc. for Public Hea. Educ. **[16254]**
Society for Public Health Education **[IO]**
Soc. for Vector Ecology **[5079]**
South Africa Partners **[18666]**
Swedish Farmers Safety and Preventive Hea. Assn. **[IO]**
Swiss Tropical Inst. **[IO]**
Temas Atuais na Promocao da Saude **[IO]**
Trust for America's Hea. **[16255]**
Truth in Fitness **[15970]**
UK Public Hea. Assn. **[IO]**
Union of Estonian Emergency Medical Services **[IO]**
Unite for Sight **[13381]**
U.S.-Mexico Border Hea. Assn. **[16256]**
U.S.-Mexico Border Hea. Assn. **[IO]**
Water Advocates **[9310]**
Water Missions Intl. **[13411]**
Women's Intl. Public Hea. Network **[16257]**
Women's Intl. Public Hea. Network **[IO]**
Women's Voices for the Earth **[4616]**
World Fed. of Public Hea. Associations **[16258]**
World Fed. of Public Hea. Associations **[IO]**
Public Hea; Amer. Bd. of Dental **[14120]**
Public Hea; Amer. Bd. of Preventive Medicine and **[★16050]**
Public Hea. Assn. of Australia **[IO]**, Curtin, Australia
Public Hea. Assn. of Australia - Australian Capital Territory **[IO]**, Canberra, Australia
Public Hea. Assn. of Australia - New South Wales **[IO]**, Brisbane, Australia
Public Hea. Assn. of Australia - Northern Territory **[IO]**, Bedford Park, Australia
Public Hea. Assn. of Australia - South Australia **[IO]**, Bedford Park, Australia
Public Hea. Assn. of Australia - Tasmania **[IO]**, Bedford Park, Australia
Public Hea. Assn. of Australia - Victoria **[IO]**, Carlton, Australia
Public Hea. Assn. of Australia - Western Australia **[IO]**, Perth, Australia
Public Hea. Assn. of New Zealand **[IO]**, Wellington, New Zealand
Public Health Cancer Assn. of America - Defunct.
Public Hea. Comm. of the Coun. of Europe **[IO]**, Strasbourg, France
Public Hea. Dentistry; Amer. Assn. of **[14118]**
Public Hea. Dentists; Amer. Assn. of **[★14118]**
Public Hea. Educators; Soc. of **[★16254]**
Public Hea. Engineers; Conf. of Municipal **[★16246]**
Public Hea. Found. **[16251]**, 1300 L St. NW, Ste. 800, Washington, DC 20005, (202)218-4400
Public Hea. Leadership Soc. **[16252]**, 1515 Poydras St., Ste. 1200, New Orleans, LA 70112, (504)301-9821
Public Hea. and Preventive Medicine; Amer. Osteopathic Acad. of **[★15802]**
Public Hea. Ser. Clinical Soc; U.S. **[★6214]**
Public Hea. Statistics; Amer. Assn. for Vital Records and **[★6218]**
Public Hea. Veterinarians; Amer. Assn. of **[16747]**
Public Hea. Veterinarians; Assn. of State **[★16747]**

Public Hea. Veterinarians; Assn. of State and Territorial **[★16747]**
Public Hea. Veterinarians; Natl. Assn. of State **[★16747]**
Public Hea. Veterinarians; Natl. Assn. of State and Territorial **[★16747]**
Public History; Natl. Coun. on **[10136]**
Public Hosp. Pharmacy Coalition **[15949]**, 1875 Eye St. NW, 12th Fl., Washington, DC 20006, (202)466-6550
Public Hospitals and Hea. Systems; Natl. Assn. of **[14892]**
Public Hospitals; Natl. Assn. of **[★14892]**
Public Housing Authorities; Coun. of Large **[5788]**
Public Housing Authorities Directors Assn. **[5798]**, 511 Capitol Ct. NE, Washington, DC 20002-4937, (202)546-5445
Public Housing Conf; Natl. **[★12325]**
Public Human Ser. Administrators; Natl. Coun. of Local **[13178]**
Public Human Services Assn; Amer. **[13151]**
Public Human Services Assn. - Info. Systems Mgt; Amer. **[13152]**
Public Information
 Amer. Guild of Town Criers **[10896]**
 Amer. Lib. Assn. - Off. for Res. and Statistics **[10934]**
 Amer. Lib. Assn. - Public Info. Off. **[10897]**
 AMISTAD Am. **[8502]**
 Assn. of Capitol Reporters and Editors **[6181]**
 Athena Alliance **[17468]**
 Buying Influence **[17310]**
 Citizens for Consumer Justice **[18641]**
 DataCenter **[18412]**
 First Amendment Proj. **[18393]**
 Freedom of Info. Center **[18413]**
 Freedom of Info. CH **[18414]**
 Global Alliance of Performers **[10773]**
 Information Coun. of the Americas **[18415]**
 Military Reporters and Editors **[6182]**
 Natl. Anxiety Center **[18416]**
 Natl. Assn. for Public Hea. Info. Tech. **[7203]**
 ODF Alliance **[7209]**
 Property Records Indus. Assn. **[3187]**
Public Integrity; Center for **[17667]**
Public Interest Advocacy Centre **[IO]**, Ottawa, ON, Canada
Public Interest - Alcohol Policies Proj; Center for Sci. in the **[18703]**
Public Interest Campaign - Defunct.
Public Interest; Center for Sci. in the **[17314]**
Public Interest Communications **[★17190]**
Public Interest Computer Assn. - Defunct.
Public Interest Economics Found. - Defunct.
Public Interest Law
 Alliance for Justice **[6219]**
 Center for Law and Social Policy **[6220]**
 Coalition for Genetic Fairness **[17107]**
 Coalition for an Intl. Criminal Court **[17361]**
 Economic Justice Inst. **[6221]**
 Equal Rights Advocates **[6222]**
 First Amendment Proj. **[18393]**
 Intl. Criminal Court Alliance **[5654]**
 Natl. Chamber Litigation Center **[6223]**
 Natl. Legal Center for the Public Interest **[6224]**
 Natl. Legal Found. **[6225]**
 Natl. Liquor Law Enforcement Assn. **[5996]**
 No Peace Without Justice **[18227]**
 Pacific Legal Found. **[6226]**
 Public Justice **[6227]**
 U.S. Justice Found. **[6228]**
 Washington Legal Found. **[6229]**
Public Interest Law; Coun. for **[★6219]**
Public Interest Law; Natl. Assn. for **[★5898]**
Public Interest Orgs; Commn. for the Advancement of **[17317]**
Public Interest Public Relations - Address unknown since 1995.
Public Interest Research; Center for **[★9192]**
Public Interest Satellite Assn. - Defunct.
Public Interest Video Network/New Voices Radio - Address unknown since 1995.
Public Investors Arbitration Bar Assn. **[5891]**, 2415 A Wilcox Dr., Norman, OK 73069, (405)360-8776
Public Justice **[6227]**, 1825 K St. NW, Ste. 200, Washington, DC 20006-1220, (202)797-8600

Reference to "IO" in place of a book number signifies that the association may be found in the 45th edition of International Organizations.

Public Justice Educ. Fund; Assn. for [★18431]
Public Land; Trust for [4461]
Public Land Users Coalition - Defunct.
Public Lands
  Abundant Wildlife Soc. of North Am. [5287]
  Amer. Lands Access Assn. [22937]
  Forest Ser. Employees for Environmental Ethics
    [5126]
  Natl. Brownfield Assn. [3191]
  Natl. Land Use Planning Commn. [IO]
  Proj. for Public Spaces [17238]
  Public Art Fund [17239]
  Public Lands Coun. [5127]
  Public Lands Found. [5128]
  Sculpture in the Env. [17240]
  Sustainable Obtainable Solutions [5129]
Public Lands Coun. [5127], 1301 Pennsylvania Ave.
  NW, Ste. 300, Washington, DC 20004-1701,
  (202)347-0228
Public Lands Found. [5128], PO Box 7226,
  Arlington, VA 22207, (703)790-1988
Public Law Education Inst. - Address unknown since
  2002.
Public Leadership Educ. Network [9326], 1001 Con-
  necticut Ave. NW, Ste. 900, Washington, DC
  20036, (202)872-1585
Public Libraries Bd. [★IO]
Public Libraries Div. [★10382]
Public Lib. Assn. [10382], c/o Amer. Lib. Assn., 50 E
  Huron St., Chicago, IL 60611, (312)280-5028
Public Lib. of the High Seas [★10321]
Public Media Center [17190], 466 Green St., Ste.
  300, San Francisco, CA 94133, (415)434-1403
Public Media Found. [18033], 351 Ryder Hall, Coll.
  of Arts and Sciences, Northeastern Univ., Boston,
  MA 02115-5000, (617)373-4698
Public Members Assn. of the Foreign Service - Ad-
  dress unknown since 1989.
Public Monuments and Sculpture Assn. [IO],
  London, United Kingdom
Public Negro Colleges - of the Natl. Assn. of State
  Universities and Land-Grant Colleges; Off. for
  Advancement of [★8112]
Public Officers Gp. [★IO]
Public Opinion Res; Amer. Assn. for [18368]
Public Parks Tennis Assn; Natl. [23906]
Public Pension Fund Auditors; Assn. of [24147]
Public Personnel Assn. [★1267]
Public Personnel Assn. [★IO]
Public Policy
  9/11 CitizensWatch [18727]
  20/20 Vision Natl. Proj. [18277]
  Acad. for State and Local Govt. [18417]
  Amer. Assembly [18418]
  Amer. Assn. of Family and Consumer Sciences
    [12285]
  Amer. Assn. of Women [18419]
  The Amer. Cause [17642]
  Amer. Enterprise Inst. for Public Policy Res.
    [18420]
  Amer. Entrepreneurs for Economic Growth [695]
  Amer. Freedom Center [18421]
  Amer. Inst. for Full Employment [12068]
  Amer. Lands Access Assn. [22937]
  Amer. Legislative Exchange Coun. [18422]
  Amer. Rights at Work [17968]
  Asian and Pacific Islander Amer. Vote [18345]
  Assn. for Public Policy Anal. and Mgt. [18423]
  Association for Public Policy Analysis and
    Management [IO]
  Assn. of State and Territorial Local Hea. Liaison
    Officials [6213]
  Athena Alliance [17468]
  BoardSource [12651]
  Brookings Institution [18424]
  Canadian Coun. for Public-Private Partnerships
    [IO]
  Cato Inst. [18425]
  C.D. Howe Inst. [IO]
  Center for Advancement of Public Policy [18426]
  Center for the Community Interest [17096]
  Center for Governmental Res. [18427]
  Center for Liberal Strategies [IO]
  Center for Natl. Policy [18428]
  Center for Policy Alternatives [18429]

  Center for Public Dialogue [18430]
  Center for Public Justice [18431]
  Center for Strategic and Intl. Stud. [18390]
  Center for the Stud. of Social Policy [18432]
  Center for Women Policy Stud. [17518]
  The Century Found. [18433]
  Children of Alcoholics Found. [13228]
  Churches' Center for Theology and Public Policy
    [18434]
  Citizens for Consumer Justice [18641]
  CitizensLobby.com [18435]
  Coalition for Genetic Fairness [17107]
  Commercial Alert [18391]
  Common Sense for Drug Policy [18436]
  Communitarian Network [18437]
  Congressional Economic Leadership Inst. [18438]
  Coro [18439]
  Coun. for Social and Economic Stud. [18440]
  Croatian Amer. Assn. [17868]
  Economic Policy Inst. [18441]
  Economic and Social Res. Inst. [IO]
  Economic Success CH [12771]
  Educating for Justice [9126]
  Eisenhower Inst. [18392]
  Eisenhower World Affairs Inst. [18442]
  Eisenhower World Affairs Inst. [IO]
  Emergency Comm. to Defend Constitutional
    Welfare Rights, U.S.A. [18443]
  Equal Justice Soc. [6258]
  Equestrian Land Conservation Rsrc. [5130]
  Essential Info. [17175]
  Ethics and Public Policy Center [18444]
  European Policy Forum [IO]
  Evergreen Freedom Found. [6230]
  Fed. of Amer. Scientists [18445]
  Found. for Natl. Progress [18446]
  Found. for Public Affairs [18447]
  Generations United [13170]
  Genocide Watch [17660]
  Global Options [18448]
  Global Options [IO]
  Governmental Res. Assn. [18449]
  Harry Singer Found. [18450]
  Hispanic Coun. on Intl. Relations [17869]
  HIV/AIDS Prevention Grants Prog. [16964]
  Hudson Inst. [18451]
  The Independent Inst. [18452]
  Innovations in Civic Participation [17075]
  Inst. for Contemporary Stud. [18453]
  Inst. for Justice [5940]
  Inst. for Philosophy and Public Policy [18454]
  Inst. for Policy Stud. [18455]
  Inst. for Policy Stud. [IO]
  Inst. for Public Accuracy [18456]
  Inst. for Res. on Public Policy [IO]
  Inst. for Rsrc. and Security Stud. [18457]
  Inst. for SocioEconomic Stud. [18458]
  Intl. Assn. of Lemon Law Administrators [5536]
  Intl. Coalition for Sustainable Production and
    Consumption [17222]
  Latino Issues Forum [19098]
  Leadership Coun. of Aging Organizations [11293]
  League of Women Voters Educ. Fund [18459]
  League of Young Voters [18356]
  Marijuana Policy Proj. [18024]
  Moving Ideas Network [18460]
  Nation Inst. [18461]
  Natl. Adult Day Services Assn. [11298]
  Natl. Alliance for Civic Educ. [8091]
  Natl. Alliance for Model State Drug Laws [5671]
  Natl. Alliance of Senior Citizens [11299]
  Natl. Assn. of Area Agencies on Aging [11301]
  Natl. Assn. for Civilian Oversight of Law Enforce-
    ment [5985]
  Natl. Assn. of State Units on Aging [11305]
  Natl. Center for Policy Anal. [18462]
  Natl. Center for Public Policy Res. [18463]
  Natl. Chamber Found. [18464]
  Natl. Coalition on Rural Aging [11307]
  Natl. Defense Coun. Found. [18465]
  Natl. Economic and Social Rights Initiative
    [17778]
  Natl. Fair Housing Alliance [17733]
  Natl. Inst. for Public Policy [18466]
  Natl. Issues Forums Inst. [18467]

  Natl. Retail Sales Tax Alliance [18696]
  New Am. Found. [18468]
  New Century Policies Educational Programs
    [18469]
  Newport Inst. for Ethics, Law and Public Policy
    [18470]
  Northeast-Midwest Inst. [18471]
  Northeast-Midwest Senate Coalition [18472]
  Online Privacy Alliance [17141]
  Org. for Intl. Investment [18473]
  Org. for Intl. Investment [IO]
  Pacific Res. Inst. for Public Policy [18474]
  Philadelphia Soc. [18475]
  Planners Network [18476]
  Policy Stud. Org. [18477]
  Policy and Taxation Gp. [18697]
  PolicyLink [18276]
  Praxis Proj. [17204]
  Progressive Policy Inst. [18478]
  Public Affairs Coun. [17354]
  Public Agenda [18479]
  Public Interest Advocacy Centre [IO]
  Public Policy Assessment Soc. [IO]
  Reason Found. [18480]
  RESOLVE [18481]
  Sarah Scaife Found. [18482]
  Sarah Scaife Found. [IO]
  Seat Belt Choice Coalition [17016]
  September Eleventh Families for Peaceful Tomor-
    rows [12701]
  Sharq Informational-Analytical Center [IO]
  Social Policy Assn. [IO]
  South Asian Amer. Voting Youth [18366]
  Tomas Rivera Policy Inst. [19196]
  Unitarian Universalist Assn. of Congregations
    [13135]
  United to Secure Am. [18596]
  U.S. Public Interest Res. Gp. [18483]
  U.S. Soc. for Ecological Economics [6865]
  Voices of September 11th [18737]
  William C. Velasquez Inst. [19197]
  William J. Clinton Found. [17855]
  Women's Economic Round Table [18484]
  Workplace Fairness [12064]
  World Inst. on Disability [11996]
  World Priorities [18485]
  World Priorities [IO]
  Youth Policy Inst. [18486]
Public Policy Assessment Soc. [IO], Woden,
  Australia
Public Policy; Center for Philosophy and [★18454]
Public Policy Education Fund - Address unknown
  since 2001.
Public Policy Inst; Reason [6131]
Public Policy Leadership Program; Aspira [★8231]
Public Policy; Natl. Inst. for Sci., Law and [4105]
Public Policy Stud; Federalist Soc. for Law and
  [5900]
Public Policy Task Force - Defunct.
Public Policy; Tufts Center for Animals and [11466]
Public Power Assn; Amer. [6336]
Public-Private Partnerships; Natl. Coun. for [17633]
Public Radio; Natl. [9765]
Public Radio News Directors Incorporated [579], c/o
  Jonathan Ahl, Treas., 1501 W Bradley Ave.,
  Peoria, IL 61625, (309)677-2773
Public Radio Programmer's Assn. [3272], 517
  Ocean Front Walk, Ste. 10, Venice, CA 90291,
  (310)664-1591
Public Radio Stations; Assn. of [★9765]
Public Radio; Western [3273]
Public Records Res. Assn; Natl. [2107]
Public Relations
  ACCE Communications Coun. [24257]
  Agricultural Relations Coun. [3192]
  Amer. Agri-Women Rsrc. Center [16949]
  Amer. Soc. for Public Admin. [6190]
  Arab-American Press Guild [3087]
  Asian Amer. Govt. Executives Network [5704]
  Austrian Press and Info. Ser. [24230]
  Canadian Public Relations Soc. [IO]
  Center for Defense Info. [17375]
  Challenge Intl. [17415]
  Chartered Inst. of Public Relations [IO]
  Coun. of Public Relations Firms [18487]

A star before a book entry number signifies that the name is not listed separately, but is mentioned within the entry.

Earth Communications Off. [4547]
European Public Relations Confed. [IO]
European Sponsorship Assn. [IO]
German Coun. for Public Relations [IO]
Hea. Acad. [14883]
Inst. for Public Relations [9031]
Intl. Assn. of Bus. Communicators [879]
Intl. Communications Consultancy Org. [IO]
Intl. Public Relations Assn. [IO]
IPREX [3193]
Lib. Public Relations Coun. [10369]
Natl. Assn. of Collegiate Marketing Administrators [23834]
Natl. Black Public Relations Soc. [3194]
Natl. Coun. for Marketing and Public Relations [9032]
Natl. Info. Officers Assn. [6231]
Natl. School Public Relations Assn. [9033]
Natl. Writers Union [24219]
PROMAX [577]
Public Conversations Proj. [17189]
Public Relations Consultants Assn. [IO]
Public Relations Inst. of Australia [IO]
Public Relations Inst. of Southern Africa [IO]
Public Relations Soc. of Am. [3195]
Public Relations Student Soc. of Am. [9034]
Publicity Club of London [IO]
Religion Communicators Coun. [20483]
Slovak Republic Public Relations Assn. [IO]
Soc. of Consumer Affairs Professionals in Bus. [3196]
Soc. for Healthcare Strategy and Market Development of the Amer. Hosp. Assn. [14896]
Soc. of Sport and Event Photographers [3015]
Transworld Advt. Agency Network [124]
Women Executives in Public Relations [3197]
Public Relations; Amer. Coun. on [★3195]
Public Relations; Amer. Soc. for Healthcare Marketing and [★14896]
Public Relations; Amer. Soc. for Hosp. [★14896]
Public Relations; Amer. Soc. for Hosp. Marketing and [★14896]
Public Relations Assn; Amer. [★3195]
Public Relations Assn; Amer. Coll. [★8245]
Public Relations Assn; Baptist [★19478]
Public Relations Assn; Financial [★2611]
Public Relations Assn; Hispanic [17180]
Public Relations Assn; Sports Sect., Amer. Coll. [★23814]
Public Relations; Comm. on Women in [★3197]
Public Relations Conf; CIO Editors and [★3229]
Public Relations Consultants Assn. [IO], London, United Kingdom
Public Relations Coun; Constr. Equip. Advertisers and [★82]
Public Relations Coun; Lib. [10369]
Public Relations Coun; Religious [★20483]
Public Relations Counsel; Natl. Assn. of [★3195]
Public Relations Exchange [★3193]
Public Relations Found. - Defunct.
Public Relations Inst. of Australia [IO], Sydney, Australia
Public Relations Inst. of South Africa [★IO]
Public Relations Inst. of Southern Africa [IO], Pinegowrie, Republic of South Africa
Public Relations and Marketing Assn; Bank [★2611]
Public Relations Res. and Educ; Found. for [★9031]
Public Relations Res. and Educ; Inst. for [★9031]
Public Relations Soc. of Am. [3195], 33 Maiden Ln., 11th Fl., New York, NY 10038-5150, (212)460-1400
Public Relations Student Soc. of Am. [9034], 33 Maiden Ln., 11th Fl., New York, NY 10038-5150, (212)460-1474
Public Representation; Citizens Communications Center Proj. of the Inst. for [17171]
Public Resources Assn. - Defunct.
Public Resources; Center for [★11488]
Public Responsibility in Medicine and Res. [18585], 126 Brookline Ave., Ste. 202, Boston, MA 02215-3920, (617)423-4112
Public Revenue Education Coun. - Address unknown since 2004.
Public Risk Mgt. Assn. [5834], 500 Montgomery St., Ste. 750, Alexandria, VA 22314, (703)528-7701

Public-Safety Communications Officers; Assoc. [★6248]
Public-Safety Communications Officials - Intl; Assn. of [6248]
Public Safety Writers Assn. [4068], 2024 Falcon Ct., Bellingham, WA 98229, (360)647-1785
Public School ABC Prog; Natl. [★8321]
Public School Improvement; Proj. Appleseed: The Natl. Campaign for [8332]
Public Schools
Amer. Assn. of Classified School Employees [24041]
Big Picture Company [8353]
Designs for Change [9035]
Horace Mann League of the U.S.A. [9036]
Learning First Alliance [8273]
Natl. Alliance for Public Charter Schools [9037]
Natl. Assn. for the Advancement of Caring Teachers [9218]
Natl. Assn. of Charter School Authorizers [8281]
Natl. Assn. for Neighborhood Schools [17820]
Natl. Assn. for Single Sex Public Educ. [9038]
Natl. Assn. of Test Directors [9254]
Natl. Coalition of Education Activists [9039]
Natl. Coun. of Educ. Providers [8329]
Natl. Coun. On Bible Curriculum In Public Schools [9052]
Natl. Rural Educ. Advocacy Coalition [9068]
New Leaders for New Schools [8755]
Parents for Public Schools [12052]
Public Educ. Network [9040]
Urban Superintendent's Assn. of Am. [9288]
Public Schools; Natl. Assn. of School Accounting and Bus. Officials of [★7892]
Public Sector Equal Opportunity Officers; Natl. Assn. of [1274]
Public Service
Advt. Club of New York [77]
Amer. Assn. of State Ser. Commissions [6189]
Community Built Assn. [11770]
Consumer Web Watch [17322]
Consumers Union of U.S. [17324]
Doe Network [12608]
George C. Marshall Found. [11118]
Henry M. Jackson Found. [17480]
A Matter of Justice Coalition [6012]
Private Sector Coun. [17348]
Public Employees Roundtable [5572]
Sew Much Comfort [11739]
Southwest Res. and Info. Center [17345]
Vera Inst. of Justice [11895]
Public Ser. Alliance of Canada [IO], Ottawa, ON, Canada
Public Ser; Amer. Inst. for [13150]
Public Ser; Grand Coun. of Hispanic Societies in [12275]
Public Ser. Internship Programs; Natl. Center for [★8414]
Public Ser. Res. Coun. [17976], 320-D Maple Ave. E, Vienna, VA 22180-4742, (703)242-3575
Public Service Satellite Consortium - Address unknown since 1994.
Public Services Intl. [IO], Ferney-Voltaire, France
Public Spaces; Proj. for [17238]
Public Speaking
Amer. Soc. of Professional Communicators [873]
Assn. for Commun. Admin. [9154]
Assn. of Speakers Clubs [IO]
British Professional Toastmasters' Authority [IO]
Canadian Assn. of Professional Speakers [IO]
Citizens for Independent Public Broadcasting [17025]
Gavel Clubs [10898]
Genealogical Speakers Guild [10899]
Intl. Assn. of Speakers Bureaus [10900]
Intl. Assn. of Speakers Bureaus [IO]
Intl. Platform Assn. [10901]
Intl. Public Debate Assn. [9041]
Intl. Public Debate Assn. [IO]
Judson Welliver Soc. [10127]
Natl. Capital Speakers Assn. [10902]
Natl. Catholic Forensic League [9156]
Natl. Christian Forensics and Communications Assn. [8521]
Natl. Commun. Assn. [9157]

Natl. Forensic Assn. [9158]
Natl. Forensic League [9159]
Natl. Speakers Assn. [10903]
Natl. Speakers Assn. of Australia [IO]
Natl. Speakers Assn. of New Zealand [IO]
Open Debates [17488]
Public Conversations Proj. [17189]
Religious Commun. Assn. [8116]
Toastmasters Intl. [10904]
Toastmasters Intl. [IO]
Walters Intl. Speakers Bur. [10905]
Public Speaking and Humor Club - Defunct.
Public Tech; Alliance for [7723]
Public Tech., Inc. [★6197]
Public Tech. Inst. [6197], 1301 Pennsylvania Ave. NW, Ste. 830, Washington, DC 20004, (202)626-2412
Public Telecommunications Financial Mgt. Assn. [★578]
Public Telecommunications; Native Amer. [9767]
Public TV Stations; Assn. of America's [547]
Public TV Stations; Natl. Assn. of [★547]
Public Transit
Alliance for a New Trans. Charter [6311]
Americans for Trans. Mobility [6315]
Carriage Operators of North Am. [783]
Intl. Trans. Mgt. Assn. [6319]
Natl. Transit Benefit Assn. [6324]
North America's SuperCorridor Coalition [3887]
Scottish Assn. for Public Transport [IO]
Public Transit; Amer. Disabled for Accessible [★17413]
Public Trans. Assn; Amer. [3860]
Public Utilities Advt. Assn. [★125]
Public Utilities Advt. Assn. [★IO]
Public Utilities Communicators Assn. [★IO]
Public Utilities Communicators Assn. [★125]
Public Utilities; Inst. of [3958]
Public Voice for Food and Health Policy - Defunct.
Public Welfare
Amer. Public Human Services Assn. [13151]
Amer. Public Human Services Assn. - Info. Systems Mgt. [13152]
Armenian Amer. Soc. for Stud. on Stress and Genocide [15190]
Assn. of Lighting and Mercury Recyclers [5168]
Assn. of Major City/County Building Officials [5547]
Children's Network Intl. [11579]
Citizens Aviation Watch Assn. [11509]
Coalition for Fire-Safe Cigarettes [12191]
Commn. for the Advancement of Public Interest Orgs. [17317]
Common Ground Alliance [12958]
Forensic Sciences Found. [5761]
Hate Free Zone [17392]
Historians Against the War [18795]
Mercury Policy Proj. [18745]
Mercy-USA for Aid and Development [12871]
Mothers Against War [18221]
Natl. Assn. for the Advancement of Haitian Descendents [19097]
Natl. Center for Law and Economic Justice [6232]
Natl. Collegiate Inventors and Innovators Alliance [7218]
Natl. Coun. of Local Public Human Ser. Administrators [13178]
Natl. Coun. of State Human Ser. Administrators [13179]
Proj. Underground [18079]
Russian Amer. Jews for Israel [18576]
Spirit of Am. [18488]
Public Welfare Administrators; Natl. Coun. of Local [★13178]
Public Welfare Administrators; Natl. Coun. of State [★13179]
Public Welfare Assn; Amer. [★13151]
Public Welfare Found. [13131], 1200 U St. NW, Washington, DC 20009-4443, (202)965-1800
Public Welfare Info. Systems Mgt; Amer. Assn. of [★13152]
Public Works
Amer. Public Works Assn. [6233]
Coun. of Infrastructure Financing Authorities [6234]

Reference to "IO" in place of a book number signifies that the association may be found in the 45th edition of International Organizations.

Coun. of Infrastructure Financing Authorities [IO]
European Centre of Enterprises with Public
  Participation and of Enterprises of Gen.
  Economic Interest [IO]
Global Village Inst. [IO]
Global Village Inst. [6235]
Inst. of Public Works Engg. Australia [IO]
Intl. Assn. for Public Participation Practitioners
  [IO]
Intl. Assn. for Public Participation Practitioners
  [6236]
Natl. Assn. of Clean Water Agencies [6237]
Proj. for Public Spaces [17238]
Public Works Historical Soc. [10146]
Restroom Assn. of Singapore [IO]
Public Works and Economic Development Assn.
  [5595]
Public Works Historical Soc. [10146], c/o Amer.
  Public Works Assn., 2345 Grand Blvd., Ste. 700,
  Kansas City, MO 64108, (816)472-6100
Public Works Officials; Intl. Assn. of [★6233]
Publication Designers; Soc. of [1810]
Publication Designers; Soc. of [★1810]
Publication Editors; Amer. Soc. of Bus. [3084]
Publication Soc. of Am; Jewish [★10283]
Publication Soc; Jewish [10283]
Publication Task Force; Alternatives in [10315]
Publications Advisers; Natl. Coun. of Coll. [★8708]
Publications of Am; Parenting [3246]
Publications of Am; Women's Regional [4053]
Publications; Amer. Assn. of Commerce [★24257]
Publications; Amer. Horse [3203]
Publications; Assoc. Bus. [★3201]
Publications; Assn. of Area Bus. [★3199]
Publications; Assn. of Paid Circulation [★2455]
Publications Assn; Red Tag News [2456]
Publications; Assn. of Second Class Mail [★2455]
Publications Audit of Circulation; Bus. [★93]
Publications Coun; Livestock [3233]
Publications; El Cariso [★20484]
Publications; Natl. Assn. of Hispanic [3237]
Publications; Natl. Bus. [★3201]
Publications; Natl. Fed. of Hispanic [★3240]
Publications; Red Tag News [★2456]
Publications; Second Class Mail [★2455]
Publications; Sermon [★19825]
Publications; Soc. of Natl. Assn. [321]
Publicis Dialogue - Address unknown since 2006.
Publicity Bur; Amer. Lutheran [20212]
Publicity Club of London [IO], London, United
  Kingdom
Publicity Coun; Natl. Religious [★20483]
Publicity Off; New Zealand Tourist and [★24363]
Publicly Traded Partnerships; Coalition of [★2343]
Publish; Comm. on Intl. Freedom to [★17041]
Publishers' Advertising and Marketing Assn. - Ad-
  dress unknown since 2004.
Publishers' Alliance - Defunct.
Publishers; Amer. Assn. of Yellow Pages [★3261]
Publishers; Amer. Soc. of Composers, Authors and
  [5836]
Publishers Assn. [IO], London, United Kingdom
Publishers; Assn. of Amer. Medical Book [★3204]
Publishers Assn; Amer. Newspaper [★3244]
Publishers Assn; Audio [3347]
Publishers; Assn. of Bus. [★3201]
Publishers Assn; Church Music [20429]
Publishers Assn; Church and Sunday School Music
  [★20429]
Publishers Assn. for Cultural Exchange, Japan [IO],
  Tokyo, Japan
Publishers; Assn. of Educational [9009]
Publishers; Assn. of Independent Music [2800]
Publishers Assn; Internet Professional [1777]
Publishers Assn; Magazine [★3235]
Publishers Assn; Marin Self- [★3212]
Publishers Assn; Marin Small- [★3212]
Publishers Assn; Natl. [★3235]
Publishers' Assn; Natl. Music [2820]
Publishers Assn; Natl. Negro Newspaper [★3241]
Publishers Assn; Newsl. [★3258]
Publishers; Assn. of North Amer. Dir. [★3208]
Publishers Assn; Periodical [★1432]
Publishers; Assn. of Second Class Mail [★2455]
Publishers' Assn. of South Africa [IO], Cape Town,
  Republic of South Africa

Publishers Assn. of Tanzania [IO], Dar es Salaam,
  United Republic of Tanzania
Publishers' Assn. of the U.S; Music [2815]
Publishers Assn; Yellow Pages [★3261]
Publishers and Booksellers Assn; Hungarian [IO]
Publishers' and Booksellers' Assn. of Macedonia
  [IO], Skopje, Macedonia
Publishers; Classroom Publishers Assn. and Assn.
  of Educational [★9009]
Publishers Comm; Federal [5581]
Publishers; EdPress - The Assn. of Educational
  [★9009]
Publishers Forum [★3206]
Publishers Info. Bur. [128], 810 7th Ave., 24th Fl.,
  New York, NY 10019, (212)872-3722
Publishers Info. Found. [★3243]
Publishers Info. Found. [★IO]
Publishers' Library Marketing Group - Defunct.
Publishers Licensing Soc. [IO], London, United
  Kingdom
Publishers Marketing Assn. [★3248]
Publishers; Natl. Assn. of Greeting Card [★3682]
Publishers; Natl. Assn. of the Investment Advisory
  [★3258]
Publishers; Natl. Assn. of Magazine [★3235]
Publishers; Natl. Assn. of Periodical [★3235]
Publishers for Peace - Defunct.
Publishers Protective Assn; Music [★2820]
Publishers' Publicity Assn. - Address unknown since
  2003.
Publishers Publicity Circle [IO], London, United
  Kingdom
Publishers' Representatives; Assn. of [★113]
Publishers' Representatives; Natl. Assn. of [113]
Publishers; Soc. of Tech. Writers and [★886]
Publishing
About Books, Inc. [3198]
Ad Coun. [18384]
Advt. Club of New York [77]
African Publishers Network [IO]
Alliance of Area Bus. Publications [3199]
Amer. Amateur Press Assn. [22910]
Amer. Book Producers Assn. [3200]
Amer. Bus. Media [3201]
Amer. Christian Fiction Writers [11156]
Amer. Court and Commercial Newspapers [3202]
Amer. Horse Publications [3203]
Amer. Medical Publishers' Assn. [3204]
Amer. Medical Writers Assn. [3082]
Amer. Soc. of Composers, Authors and Publishers
  [5836]
Amer. Soc. of Healthcare Publication Editors
  [14613]
Asociacion de Diarios y Revistas del Peru [IO]
Asociacion Editores de Diarios de la Ciudad de
  Buenos Aires [IO]
Asociacion de Editores de Diarios Espanoles [IO]
Asociacion de Editores de los Estados [IO]
Asociacion de Entidades Periodisticas Argentinas
  [IO]
Asociacion de Entidades Periodisticas del
  Paraguay [IO]
Asociacion Nacional de la Prensa - Chile [IO]
Asociacion Nacional de la Publicidad [IO]
Associacao Nacional de Jornais [IO]
Associacion de Diarios Colombianos [IO]
Assoc. Church Press [3205]
Assn. of Amer. Publishers [3206]
Assn. of Art Editors [3207]
Assn. of Canadian Publishers [IO]
Assn. of Canadian Univ. Presses [IO]
Assn. D'Editeurs de la Press Libre et Indepen-
  dante [IO]
Assn. of Dir. Publishers [3208]
Assn. des Editeurs de la Presse Privee du Mali
  [IO]
Assn. of Educational Publishers [9009]
Assn. for the Export of Canadian Books [IO]
Assn. of Learned and Professional Soc. Publish-
  ers [IO]
Assn. of Local Newspapers [IO]
Assn. of Medical Publications [3209]
Assn. of Printed Media of Macedonia [IO]
Assn. of Publishing Agencies [IO]
Assn. of Subscription Agents and Intermediaries
  [IO]

Assn. of Test Publishers [3210]
Athens Daily Newspaper Publishers Assn. [IO]
Audio Publishers Assn. [3347]
Australian Publishers' Assn. [IO]
Authors' Licensing and Collecting Soc. [IO]
Authors and Publishers Assn. [3211]
Bay Area Independent Publishers Assn. [3212]
Belgian Periodical Press Fed. [IO]
Book Indus. Study Group [IO]
Book Indus. Study Group [3213]
Book and Periodical Coun. [IO]
Book Publishers Assn. of Alberta [IO]
Book Publishers Assn. of Israel [IO]
Book Publishers Assn. of New Zealand [IO]
Book Publishers' Professional Assn. [IO]
Braille Authority of North Am. [16838]
Brazilian Book Chamber [IO]
British Soc. of Magazine Editors [IO]
Bulgarian Book Assn. [IO]
Canadian Assn. of Learned Journals [IO]
Canadian Bus. Press [IO]
Canadian Circulation Mgt. Assn. [IO]
Canadian Newspaper Assn. [IO]
Canadian Printing Ink Mfrs'. Assn. [IO]
Canadian Publishers' Coun. [IO]
Catholic Book Publishers Assn. [3214]
Catholic Press Assn. [3215]
The Christian Sci. Publishing Soc. [3216]
Christian Small Publishers Assn. [3217]
Church Music Publishers Assn. [20429]
City and Regional Magazine Assn. [3218]
Coalition of Asian Pacifics in Entertainment [1300]
Comics Magazine Assn. of America [3219]
Commonwealth Hansard Editors Assn. [IO]
Coun. of Academic and Professional Publishers
  [IO]
CrossRef [3220]
Cyprus Newspaper and Magazines Publishers
  Assn. [IO]
Danish Assn. of the Specialist Press [IO]
Danish Magazine Publishers Assn. [IO]
Data Publishers Assn. [IO]
Digital Printing and Imaging Assn. [1764]
Direct Marketing Assn. [2625]
Distripress - Assn. for the Promotion of the Intl.
  Press Distribution [IO]
Editorial Photographers [2996]
Educational Paperback Assn. [3221]
Educational Publishers Coun. [IO]
Electronic Publishing Assn. [IO]
Engineering Coll. Magazines Associated [3222]
English Westerners Soc. [IO]
EPIC - Electronically Published Internet Connec-
  tion [22914]
Estonian Newspaper Assn. [IO]
European Assn. of Dir. and Database Publishers
  [IO]
European Fed. of Magazine Publishers [IO]
European Newspaper Publishers' Assn. [IO]
European Publishers Coun. [IO]
European Rotogravure Assn. [IO]
Evangelical Christian Publishers Association [IO]
Evangelical Christian Publishers Assn. [3223]
Evangelical Press Assn. [20004]
Fed. Assn. of German Newspaper Publishers [IO]
Federal Publishers Comm. [5581]
Fed. Belge des Magazines [IO]
Fed. of European Publishers [IO]
Fed. of the Printing Indus. in Finland [IO]
Federazione Nazionale della Stampa Italiana [IO]
The Feminist Press at the City Univ. of New York
  [9317]
Finnish Book Publishers Assn. [IO]
Fulfillment Mgt. Assn. [3224]
German Publishers and Booksellers Assn. [IO]
Great Lakes Booksellers Assn. [3225]
Gridiron Club of Washington, DC [3114]
Guild of Food Writers [IO]
Guild of Press Publishers [IO]
Hong Kong Printers' Assn. [IO]
Hong Kong's Women in Publishing Soc. [IO]
Icelandic Publishers' Assn. [IO]
IFRA [IO]
Independent Assn. of Publishers' Employees
  [24174]

A star before a book entry number signifies that the name is not listed separately, but is mentioned within the entry.

Independent Free Papers of Am. [3226]
Independent Press Assn. [IO]
Independent Publishers Guild [IO]
Inland Press Assn. [3227]
Intl. Allied Printing Trades Assn. [24084]
Intl. Assn. of Cross-Reference Dir. Publishers [3228]
Intl. Assn. of Sci., Tech. and Medical Publishers [IO]
Intl. Fed. of Audit Bureaus of Circulations [IO]
Intl. Fed. of the Periodical Press [IO]
Intl. Freedom to Publish Comm. [17041]
Intl. Labor Communications Assn., AFL-CIO/CLC [3229]
Intl. Network for the Availability of Sci. Publications [IO]
Intl. Newspaper Gp. [3121]
Intl. Newspaper Marketing Assn. [3230]
Intl. Newspaper Marketing Assn. [IO]
Intl. Pentecostal Press Assn. [3122]
Intl. Press Telecommunications Coun. [IO]
The Intl. Publication Planning Assn. [IO]
The Intl. Publication Planning Assn. [3231]
Intl. Publishers Assn. [IO]
Intl. Publishing Mgt. Assn. [1776]
Intl. Soc. for Medical Publication Professionals [16259]
Intl. Soc. for Medical Publication Professionals [IO]
Irish Book Publishers' Assn. [IO]
Italian Publishers Assn. [IO]
Japan Book Publishers Assn. [IO]
Japan Newspaper Publishers and Editors Assn. [IO]
Japan Printing Machinery Mfrs'. Assn. [IO]
Jewish Student Press Ser. [8694]
Kenyan Publishers Assn. [IO]
Latvian Press Publishers Assn. [IO]
Listin Diario [IO]
Literary Press Gp. of Canada [IO]
Literary Source [3232]
Lithuanian Printers' Assn. [IO]
Livestock Publications Coun. [3233]
Macrocosm USA [3234]
Magazine Publishers of Am. [3235]
Magazine Publishers of Australia [IO]
Magazines Canada [IO]
Malaysian Printers' Assn. [IO]
Midwest Free Community Papers [3236]
Mongolian Assn. of Free and Independent Publishers [IO]
Music Publishers Assn. [IO]
Natl. Amateur Press Assn. [22911]
Natl. Assn. of Book Editors [IO]
Natl. Assn. of Hispanic Publications [3237]
Natl. Assn. of Independent Publishers [3238]
Natl. Assn. of Independent Publishers Representatives [3239]
Natl. Assn. of Publishers' Representatives [113]
Natl. Assn. of Trade Press Publishers [IO]
Natl. Fed. of Hispanic Owned Newspapers [3240]
Natl. Geographic Soc. [7123]
Natl. Music Publishers' Assn. [2820]
Natl. Newspaper Publishers Assn. [3241]
Natl. Trade Circulation Found., Inc. [3242]
Networking Alternatives for Publishers, Retailers and Artists [3243]
Networking Alternatives for Publishers, Retailers and Artists [IO]
Newsl. and Electronic Publishers Assn. [IO]
Newspaper Assn. of Am. [3244]
Newspaper Assn. Managers [3149]
Newspaper Assn. of Mongolia [IO]
Newspaper Soc. [IO]
Newspaper Soc. of Sri Lanka [IO]
Novelists, Inc. [4067]
NPES - The Assn. for Suppliers of Printing, Publishing and Converting Technologies [1782]
Online Publishers Assn. [3245]
Online Publishers Assn. Europe [IO]
Pacific Area Newspaper Publishers' Assn. [IO]
Parenting Publications of Am. [3246]
Partnership for Research Integrity in Science and Medicine [18489]
Periodical and Book Assn. of Am. [3247]

Periodical Publishers Assn. [IO]
Periodical Publishers Assn. of Ireland [IO]
PMA - Independent Book Publishers Assn. [3248]
Print and Media Assn. Singapore [IO]
Printing Brokerage/Buyers Assn. [1786]
Printing Indus. Fed. of South Africa [IO]
Printing Indus. Assn. of the Slovak Republic [IO]
Printing, Publishing and Media Workers Sector of the CWA [24086]
Professional Assn. of Comics Entertainment Retailers [9523]
Protestant Church-Owned Publishers Assn. [3249]
Public Safety Writers Assn. [4068]
Publishers Assn. [IO]
Publishers' Assn. of South Africa [IO]
Publishers Assn. of Tanzania [IO]
Publishers Licensing Soc. [IO]
Publishers Publicity Circle [IO]
Publishing, Printing and Media Assn. [IO]
Reader's Digest Assn. [3250]
Red Tag News Publications Assn. [2456]
Reporters Network [3160]
Romanian Local Press Editors Assn. [IO]
Romanian Press Club [IO]
Scottish Daily Newspaper Soc. [IO]
Scottish Newspaper Publishers Assn. [IO]
Scottish Publishers Assn. [IO]
Self-Publishers' Assn. of New Zealand [IO]
Singles Press Assn. [3251]
Slovak Union of Newspaper Publishers [IO]
Slovenian Publishers Assn. [IO]
Small Press Center for Independent Publishing [3252]
Small Publishers, Artists and Writers Network [3253]
Small Publishers, Artists and Writers Network [IO]
Small Publishers Assn. of North Am. [3254]
Societe des Editeurs de la Presse Privee [IO]
Soc. of Bookbinders [IO]
Soc. of Editors [IO]
Soc. for the History of Authorship, Reading and Publishing [9754]
Soc. for the Promotion of Sci. and Scholarship [3255]
Soc. of Publishers in Asia [IO]
Soc. for Scholarly Publishing [3256]
Soc. of Young Publishers [IO]
Southern Classified Advt. Managers Assn. [119]
Southern Newspaper Publishers Assn. [3257]
Specialized Info. Publishers Assn. [3258]
Specialized Info. Publishers Assn. [IO]
Suburban Newspapers of Am. [3259]
Swedish Newspaper Publishers Assn. [IO]
Syndicat de la Presse Quotidienne Nationale [IO]
Syndicat de la Presse Quotidienne Regionale [IO]
Theosophical Book Assn. for the Blind [20592]
Turf and Ornamental Communicators Assn. [2400]
Uganda Newspaper Editors and Proprietors Assn. [IO]
UK Assn. of Online Publishers [IO]
Union des Editeurs de la Presse Periodique [IO]
Union of Finnish Writers [IO]
United Amateur Press Assn. of Am. [22912]
Verband Deutscher Zeitschriftenverleger [IO]
What Kids Can Do [18859]
Women in Production [1796]
Women in Publishing [IO]
Women in Scholarly Publishing [3260]
World Assn. of Medical Editors [14303]
World Assn. of Newspapers [IO]
Writers' Guild of Great Britain [IO]
Yachting Journalists' Assn. [IO]
Yellow Pages Assn. [3261]
Publishing Alliance (LEAPA); Legion Amateur [★22042]
Publishing Assn; Natl. Govt. [1781]
Publishing Center for Cultural Resources - Defunct.
Publishing and Converting Technologies; Assn. for Suppliers of Printing and [★1782]
Publishing and Converting Technologies; NPES - The Assn. for Suppliers of Printing, [1782]
Publishing Mfrs. Executive Assn. - Address unknown since 1987.
Publishing and Media Workers Sector of the CWA; Printing, [24086]

Publishing, Printing and Media Assn. [IO], Ljubljana, Slovenia
Publishing and Retailing Alliance; New Age [★3243]
Publishing; Soc. for the History of Authorship, Reading and [9754]
Publishing Soc; Tech. [★886]
Puebla Inst. [★17749]
Puebla Inst. [★IO]
Pueblo Coun; All Indian [18089]
Pueblo Cultural Center; Indian [★18089]
Pueblo to People - Address unknown since 2000.
Puerto Rican
   Natl. Assn. of Puerto Rican Hispanic Social Workers [13205]
   Natl. Puerto Rican Forum [12280]
   Puerto Rican Family Inst. [12281]
   Puerto Rican Stud. Assn. [19326]
   Puerto Rican Traveling Theatre Company [11040]
   Pure Puerto Rican Paso Fino Fed. of Am. [4946]
   Quality Educ. for Minorities Network [8303]
Puerto Rican, Asian Americans; Natl. Assn. of Interdisciplinary Stud. for Native Amer., Black, Chicano, [★9919]
Puerto Rican Assn. for Community Affairs - Address unknown since 2006.
Puerto Rican Bar Assn. - Address unknown since 1995.
Puerto Rican Bd. of Guardians - Defunct.
Puerto Rican Family Inst. [12281], 145 W 15th St., New York, NY 10011, (212)924-6320
Puerto Rican Forum; Natl. [12280]
Puerto Rican Hispanic Genealogical Soc. [9975], PO Box 260118, Bellerose, NY 11426-0118, (914)941-4920
Puerto Rican Hispanic Social Workers; Natl. Assn. of [13205]
Puerto Rican Legal Defense and Educ. Fund [17149], 99 Hudson St., 14th Fl., New York, NY 10013-2815, (212)219-3360
Puerto Rican Legal Project - Defunct.
Puerto Rican Migration Res. Consortium - Defunct.
Puerto Rican Stud. Assn. [19326], c/o Latino Stud. Prog., 434 Rockefeller Hall, Cornell Univ., Ithaca, NY 14853
Puerto Rican Traveling Theatre Company [11040], 304 W 47th St., New York, NY 10036, (212)354-1293
Puerto Rican Women; Natl. Conf. of [17554]
Puerto Rico
   Assn. of Racing Commissioners Intl. [6240]
   Comm. 51st State for Puerto Rico [18490]
   Conf. of Chief Justices [5896]
   Conf. of State Bank Supervisors [5544]
   Conf. of State Court Administrators [5625]
   Fed. of State Humanities Councils [10198]
   Natl. Assn. State Agencies for Surplus Property [6185]
   Natl. Assn. of State Aviation Officials [5540]
   Natl. Coun. of Architectural Registration Boards [5466]
   Natl. Coun. of State Housing Agencies [5795]
   Natl. Guard Assn. of the U.S. [6091]
   Natl. Plant Bd. [5440]
   Natl. Puerto Rican Coalition [18491]
   Natl. Puerto Rican Coalition [IO]
   Natl. Puerto Rican Forum [12280]
   Puerto Rican Family Inst. [12281]
   Puerto Rican Legal Defense and Educ. Fund [17149]
   Puerto Rican Stud. Assn. [19326]
   Puerto Rican Traveling Theatre Company [11040]
   Puerto Rico Golf Assn. [23466]
   Puerto Rico U.S.A. Citizenship Found. [18492]
   Puerto Rico Water and Env. Assn. [5282]
   Southeastern Assn. of Fish and Wildlife Agencies [5734]
Puerto Rico Alpha 1 Support Gp. [★16360]
Puerto Rico Alpha 1 Support Gp. [★IO]
Puerto Rico Assn. of Pediatric Surgeons [15897], PO Box 10426, Caparra Heights Sta., San Juan, PR 00922-0426, (787)777-3535
Puerto Rico Golf Assn. [23466], 264 Matadero St., Ste. 11, San Juan, PR 00920, (787)793-3444
Puerto Rico Mainland U.S. Statehood Students Assn. - Address unknown since 1994.

Reference to "IO" in place of a book number signifies that the association may be found in the 45th edition of International Organizations.

Puerto Rico Rum Producers Assn. - Defunct.
Puerto Rico Soc. of Microbiologists [7331], PO Box 360175, San Juan, PR 00936-0175, (787)751-3057
Puerto Rico Solidarity Day Comm. - Address unknown since 1988.
Puerto Rico Statehood Commn. - Address unknown since 1994.
Puerto Rico U.S.A. Citizenship Found. [18492], 600 13th St. NW, Washington, DC 20005, (202)756-8213
Puerto Rico, U.S.A. Found. [★18492]
Puerto Rico Water and Env. Assn. [5282], PO Box 13702, San Juan, PR 00908-3702
Puff Intl. - Defunct.
Pug
    Pug Dog Club of Am. [22347]
Pug Dog Club of Am. [22347], c/o Donna Manha, Sec., 449 Maar Ave., Fremont, CA 94536
Pugwash Conferences on Sci. and World Affairs [17247], Washington Off., 1111 19th St. NW, No. 1200, Washington, DC 20036, (202)478-3440
Pugwash Conferences on Sci. and World Affairs [IO], Washington, DC, United States
Pugwash Conferences on Sci. and World Affairs; International [★18842]
Pugwash; Intl. Student [★18842]
Pugwash U.S.A; Student [18842]
Puli Club of Am. [22348], c/o Michael Rohe, Corresponding Sec., 5032 Winton Ridge Ln., Cincinnati, OH 45232, (513)541-6819
Pull-thru Network [14427], 2312 Savoy St., Hoover, AL 35226-1528, (205)978-2930
Pulling Foundation [★23928]
Pullman Found; Historic [10036]
Pulmonary and Allergy Patients' Assn. of Slovenia [IO], Ljubljana, Slovenia
Pulmonary Credentialing; Natl. Bd. for Cardiovascular and [★13898]
Pulmonary and Critical Care; NAMDRC: Physician Advocacy for Excellence in the Delivery of [★15068]
Pulmonary Fibrosis; Coalition for [16356]
Pulmonary Hypertension Assn. [14911], 801 Roeder Rd., Ste. 400, Silver Spring, MD 20910, (301)565-3004
Pulmonary Hypertension Assn. - United Kingdom [IO], Rotherham, United Kingdom
Pulmonary Hypertension; United Patients Assn. for [★14911]
Pulmonary Rehabilitation; Amer. Assn. of Cardiovascular and [13886]
Pulmonary Technologists; Natl. Soc. of Cardio [★13885]
Pulmonary Tech; Natl. Soc. for [★13885]
Pulmonary Tech; Natl. Soc. for Cardio [★13885]
Pulp Chemicals Assn. [★818]
Pulp and Paper Indus. Fed. of the Slovak Republic [IO], Banska Bystrica, Slovakia
Pulp and Paper Indus; TAPPI - Tech. Assn. of the [2895]
Pulp and Paper Machinery Assn. [★2003]
Pulp and Paper Machinery Mfrs. Assn. [★2003]
Pulp and Paper Mill Superintendents Assn; Amer. [★2893]
Pulp, Paper and Paperboard Export Assn. of the U.S. - Address unknown since 2002.
Pulp and Paper Res. and Tech. Center [IO], Grenoble, France
Pulp and Paper Safety Assn. [7436], 1370 N Nealon Dr., Portage, IN 46368, (219)764-4787
Pulp and Paper Safety Assn; Southern [★7436]
Pulp and Paper Traffic League - Defunct.
Pulp and Paper Workers; Assn. of Western [24064]
Pulp Refining Equipment Mfrs. Assn. - Address unknown since 1995.
Pulpwood Assn; Amer. [★1607]
P.U.L.S.E. [14662], PO Box 353, Wantagh, NY 11793-0353, (516)579-4711
Pulverized Limestone Assn. [★3699]
Pump Assn; Intl. Ground Source Heat [1889]
Pump Assn; Submersible Wastewater [677]
Pump Bur; Contractors [2011]
Pump Distributors Assn. [IO], Woodbridge, United Kingdom

Pump Indus. Australia [IO], Stuarts Point, Australia
Pump Mfrs. Assn; Gasoline [2926]
Pump Mfrs. Assn; Sump [★678]
Pump Mfrs. Assn; Sump and Sewage [678]
Pumpers Assn. of Southern California; Concrete [★914]
Punch Mfrs. Assn; North Amer. [2055]
Punishment and Alternatives; Natl. Center for the Stud. of Corporal [8206]
Punishment Proj; Capital [17029]
Punishment in Schools; Natl. Coalition to Abolish Corporal [8207]
Punjabi-American Cultural Assn. [10223], 5055 Bus. Center Dr., Ste. 108, No. 165, Fairfield, CA 94534
Puns Corps - Address unknown since 2007.
Pupil Personnel Administrators; Natl. Assn. of [★7902]
Pupil Services Administrators; Natl. Assn. of [7902]
Pupil Trans; Natl. Assn. for [6320]
Puppet Centre Trust [IO], London, United Kingdom
Puppeteers of Am. [22915], c/o Fred Thompson, 26 Howard Ave., New Haven, CT 06519-2809, (203)777-4601
Puppetry
    Clowns of Am., Intl. [21951]
    North Amer. Assn. of Ventriloquists [1322]
    Puppeteers of Am. [22915]
    UNIMA-U.S.A., Amer. Center of the Union Internationale de la Marionnette [22916]
Puppets
    Clowns of Am., Intl. [21951]
    North Amer. Assn. of Ventriloquists [1322]
    Puppeteers of Am. [22915]
    UNIMA-U.S.A., Amer. Center of the Union Internationale de la Marionnette [22916]
    UNIMA-U.S.A., American Center of the Union Internationale de la Marionnette [IO]
Pups for Peace [IO], West Hollywood, CA, United States
Pups for Peace [12700], 8424A Santa Monica Blvd., Ste. 112, West Hollywood, CA 90069-4267, (800)669-8930
Purcell Family of Am. [21028], 2962 Moreland Ave., Oceanside, NY 11572, (516)764-7068
Purchase Applied Honors Soc; Francena [17018]
Purchasing
    Amer. Purchasing Soc. [3262]
    Assn. for Purchasing and Supply [IO]
    Buying Influence [17310]
    Chartered Inst. of Purchasing and Supply [IO]
    European Inst. of Purchasing Mgt. [IO]
    Inst. of Purchasing and Supply of Hong Kong [IO]
    Inst. for Supply Mgt. [3263]
    Intl. Assn. of Home Staging Professionals [2261]
    Intl. Fed. of Purchasing and Supply Mgt. [IO]
    Natl. Assn. of Purchasing Card Professionals [3264]
    Natl. Assn. of Purchasing and Payables [3265]
    Natl. Assn. of State Procurement Officials [6238]
    Natl. Inst. of Governmental Purchasing [6239]
    Natl. Inst. of Governmental Purchasing [IO]
    Natl. Purchasing Inst. [3266]
    Procurement and Supply Chain Benchmarking Assn. [760]
    Purchasing Mgt. Assn. of Canada [IO]
Purchasing Agents; Amer. Soc. for Hosp. [★14872]
Purchasing Agents; Natl. Assn. of [★3263]
Purchasing Assn; Hea. Indus. Gp. [14672]
Purchasing Company; Allied [1127]
Purchasing Coun; Natl. Minority [★2769]
Purchasing Mgt. Assn. of Canada [IO], Toronto, ON, Canada
Purchasing Mgt; Natl. Assn. of [★2718]
Purchasing Mgt; Natl. Assn. of [★3263]
Purchasing and Materials Mgt; Amer. Soc. for Hosp. [★14872]
Purchasing Officials; Natl. Assn. of State [★6238]
Pure Country Velvet Fan Club - Address unknown since 2004.
Pure Puerto Rican Paso Fino Fed. of Am. [4946], PO Box 280444, Columbia, SC 29228, (203)799-9792
Pure Water Assn. of America - Defunct.
Purebred Dairy Cattle Assn. [4288]
Purebred Dexter Cattle Assn. of North Am. [4289], 25979 Hwy. EE, Prairie Home, MO 65068, (660)841-9502

Purebred Hanoverian Assn. of Amer. Breeders and Owners - Address unknown since 2004.
Purebred Morab Horse Association/Registry [4947], PO Box 280, Sherwood, WI 54169, (920)358-8727
Purebred Morab Horse Association/Registry [IO], Sherwood, WI, United States
Purine 24, Inc. [★15258]
Purine Res. Soc. [15258], c/o Tahma Metz, Exec. Dir., 5424 Beech Ave., Bethesda, MD 20814-1730, (301)530-0354
Purple Flower Gang [24962], c/o Cindy Bryant, Pres./Ed., 1803 Lucas St., Muscatine, IA 52761
Purple Heart, U.S.A; Ladies Auxiliary, Military Order of the [20713]
Purple Heart of the U.S.A; Military Order of the [20715]
Purple Loosestrife Task Force - Defunct.
Purple Martin Colony Registry Program [★5369]
Purple Martin Conservation Assn. [5369], 301 Peninsula Dr., Ste. 6, Erie, PA 16505, (814)833-7656
Purple Plum Assn. - Defunct.
Purse Seine Vessel Owners Assn. - Address unknown since 2002.
Pursuing Our Italian Names Together [21144], Box 14966, Las Vegas, NV 89114-4966
Pursuing Our Italian Names Together [IO], Las Vegas, NV, United States
PUSH Coalition; Rainbow/ [13185]
PUSH Commercial Div. [12098], 930 E 50th St., Chicago, IL 60615-2702, (773)373-3366
Push for Excellence Prog. [★13185]
PUSH Intl. Trade Bur. [★12098]
PUSH; Oper. [★13185]
Put and Call Brokers and Dealers Assn. - Defunct.
Putters Assn; Professional [23465]
Putting People First - Address unknown since 1999.
Puu- ja Erityisalojen Liitto [★IO]
Puusepaenteollisuuden Liitto Ry [★IO]
Puzzle Buffs Intl. [22473], 41 Park Dr., Port Clinton, OH 43452, (419)734-2600
Puzzle Collectors; Assn. of Game and [22460]
Puzzlers' League; Natl. [22469]
PVC Belting Mfrs. Assn. - Defunct.
PVC Collectors Club [★22024]
PVC Pipe Assn; Uni-Bell [3041]
PWSA USA [★14475]
PXE Intl. [14479], 4301 Connecticut Ave. NW, Ste. 404, Washington, DC 20008-2369, (202)362-9599
PXI Systems Alliance [6820], c/o Bode Enterprises, LLC, PO Box 1016, Niwot, CO 80544, (619)297-1212
Pygmy Goat Assn; Natl. [4142]
Pyles-Ross-Sellards Family; Bloss- [20798]
Pyramidology
    Life Understanding Found. [20484]
Pyrenean Mastiff Club of Am. [22349], 4083 W Ave. L, No. 107, Quartz Hill, CA 93536, (661)724-0268
Pyrenees
    Friends of the Pyrenees [IO]
Pyrotechnic Distributors Assn; Natl. [★3267]
Pyrotechnic Signal Mfrs. Assn. - Address unknown since 2004.
Pyrotechnics
    Amer. Pyrotechnics Assn. [3267]
    Pyrotechnics Guild Intl. [3268]
    Pyrotechnics Guild Intl. [IO]
    UK Pyrotechnics Soc. [IO]
Pyrotechnics Guild Intl. [IO], Mishawaka, IN, United States
Pyrotechnics Guild Intl. [3268], c/o Bill Bahr, Pres., 19 Yellowbrook Rd., Freehold, NJ 07728, (732)919-1120
Pyrotechnists Assn; British [IO]
Pythian Sisters; Supreme Temple Order [19189]
Pythias; Junior Order, Knights of [19187]
Pythias; Supreme Lodge Knights of [19188]

Q

Qabel Found. - Address unknown since 1995.
Qajaq USA [23981], PO Box 826, Hattiesburg, MS 39403-0826
Qatar Assn. of Athletics Fed. [IO], Doha, Qatar
Qatar Chamber of Commerce and Indus. [IO], Doha, Qatar

A star before a book entry number signifies that the name is not listed separately, but is mentioned within the entry.

Qatar Fencing Fed. [IO], Doha, Qatar
Qatar League Against Epilepsy [IO], Doha, Qatar
Qatar Natl. Olympic Comm. [IO], Doha, Qatar
Qatar Sailing and Rowing Fed. [IO], Doha, Qatar
Qatar Squash Fed. [IO], Doha, Qatar
Qatar Taekwondo and Karate Fed. [IO], Doha, Qatar
Qatar Tennis Fed. [IO], Doha, Qatar
Qatar Weightlifting Fed. [IO], Doha, Qatar
QEM Proj. [★8303]
Qigong (Chi Kung) Assn; Natl. [13644]
QiGong Res. Soc. [13647], 3201 Rte. 38, Ste. 201,
   Mount Laurel, NJ 08054, (856)234-3056
Quacks
   Natl. Coun. Against Hea. Fraud [17692]
Quackwatch [★17692]
Quad Rugby Assn; U.S. [23705]
Quad V - Address unknown since 1999.
Quadex Users' Org. - Defunct.
Quail Unlimited [5370], PO Box 610, Edgefield, SC
   29824, (803)637-5731
Quaker Comm. on Jails and Justice [★IO]
Quaker Coun. for European Affairs [IO], Brussels,
   Belgium
Quaker Fellowship; Wider [20045]
Quaker Parakeet Society [IO], Fiskdale, MA, United
   States
Quaker Parakeet Soc. [4200], PO Box 7241,
   Eugene, OR 97401
Quaker Peace and Social Witness [IO], London,
   United Kingdom
Quaker Peace Tax Fund - Defunct.
Quaker Ser. Australia [IO], Surry Hills, Australia
Quaker Theological Discussion Group - Address
   unknown since 1994.
Quaker United Nations Off. - Switzerland [IO],
   Geneva, Switzerland
Quakers
   Amer. Friends Ser. Comm. [13148]
   Evangelical Friends Intl. - North Amer. Region
      [20040]
   Friends Comm. on Natl. Legislation [20041]
   Friends Disaster Ser. [12856]
   Friends Gen. Conf. [20042]
   Friends Historical Assn. [20043]
   Friends for Lesbian, Gay, Bisexual, Transgender,
      and Queer Concerns [20056]
   Quaker Ser. Australia [IO]
   Wider Quaker Fellowship [20045]
Quakers Fostering Justice [IO], Mission, BC,
   Canada
Quakers; Natl. Soc. Descendants of Early [21134]
Qualifications and Curriculum Authority [IO], London,
   United Kingdom
Qualifications for the Lighting Professions; Natl.
   Coun. on [2435]
Qualified Mental Retardation Professionals; Natl.
   Assn. of [15241]
Qualified Private Medical Practitioners' and
   Hospitals' Assn. [IO], North Paravur, India
Qualitative Res. Consultants Assn. [7573], 1000
   Westgate Dr., Ste. 252, St. Paul, MN 55114,
   (651)290-7491
Quality Assn; Indoor Air [5093]
Quality Assurance
   Amer. Backflow Prevention Assn. [7818]
   Amer. Bd. of Quality Assurance and Utilization
      Rev. Physicians [16260]
   Amer. Bd. of Radiology [16272]
   Amer. Coll. of Medical Quality [16261]
   Amer. Hea. Quality Assn. [16262]
   Amer. Healthcare Radiology Administrators
      [16275]
   Amer. Soc. of Validation Engineers [1289]
   Aquaculture Certification Coun. [4168]
   Assn. of Forensic Quality Assurance Managers
      [5758]
   British Assn. of Res. Quality Assurance [IO]
   Healthcare Quality Certification Bd. [13533]
   Inst. for Medical Quality [16263]
   Intl. Assn. of Ser. Evaluators [3269]
   Intl. Mystery Shopping Alliance [3412]
   Lighting Controls Assn. [2433]
   Natl. Acad. for State Hea. Policy [14649]
   Natl. Assn. for Healthcare Quality [16264]
   Natl. Comm. for Quality Assurance [16265]

Natl. Quality Forum [14658]
Natl. Storm Shelter Assn. [2831]
PSRC of Am. [16266]
Soc. of Quality Assurance [IO]
Soc. of Quality Assurance [3270]
Soc. for Software Quality [6775]
Quality Assurance Professionals; Natl. Assn. of
   [★16264]
Quality Assurance Study Group; Natl. Restaurant
   Assn. [16385]
Quality Bakers of Am. Cooperative [453], 1055 Par-
   sippany Blvd., Ste. 201, Parsippany, NJ 07054,
   (973)263-6970
Quality Brands Associates of America - Defunct.
Quality Center; Amer. Productivity & [★2482]
Quality Certification Bd; Healthcare [13533]
Quality Chekd Dairies [1139], 1733 Park St., Naper-
   ville, IL 60563, (630)717-1110
Quality Chekd Ice Cream Assn. [★1139]
Quality Control
   Amer. Backflow Prevention Assn. [7818]
   Amer. Soc. for Quality [7552]
   Amer. Soc. of Validation Engineers [1289]
   Canadian Process Control Assn. [IO]
   Chartered Quality Inst. [IO]
   Cork Quality Coun. [1645]
   European Found. for Quality Mgt. [IO]
   European Org. for Quality [IO]
   Healthcare Quality Certification Bd. [13533]
   Hong Kong Quality Mgt. Assn. [IO]
   Intl. Acad. for Quality [IO]
   Intl. Acad. for Quality [7553]
   Intl. Soc. of Six Sigma Professionals [7534]
   Israel Soc. for Quality [IO]
   Natl. Assn. for Proficiency Testing [7792]
   Quality Systems Assessment Registrar [IO]
   Statistical Process Controls [IO]
   Statistical Process Controls [7554]
   Team and Workplace Excellence Forum [7555]
Quality Control; Amer. Soc. for [★7552]
Quality Control Coun. of America - Defunct.
Quality Courts Motels - Address unknown since
   1995.
Quality Educ. for Minorities Network [8303], 1818 N
   St. NW, Ste. 350, Washington, DC 20036,
   (202)659-1818
Quality Educ. for Minorities Proj. [★8303]
Quality and Leadership in Supports for People with
   Disabilities; Coun. on [★12567]
Quality Meat Scotland [IO], Edinburgh, United
   Kingdom
Quality-of-Life Stud; Intl. Soc. for [7997]
Quality and Productivity Mgt. Assn. - Defunct.
Quality Scheme for Ready Mixed Concrete [IO],
   Hampton, United Kingdom
Quality Systems Assessment Registrar [IO], Missis-
   sauga, ON, Canada
Quality Tourism Services Assn. [IO], Hong Kong,
   People's Republic of China
Quantitative Analyses of Behavior; Soc. for [6541]
Quantitative Analysts; Soc. of [1450]
Quantum League - Defunct.
Quarab Horse Assn; Intl. [4903]
Quarries Assn; Natl. Building Granite [3697]
Quarry Products Assn. [IO], London, United
   Kingdom
Quarrymen's Assn; Intl. Cut Stone [★3692]
Quarter Century Wireless Assn. [21509], c/o Chuck
   Walbridge, Gen. Mgr., PO Box 3247, Framingham,
   MA 01705-3247, (508)405-1930
Quarter Horse Assn; Amer. [4838]
Quarter Horse Assn; Amer. Junior [★4839]
Quarter Horse Assn; Amer. Paint [★4834]
Quarter Horse Registry; Amer. Half- [4822]
Quarter Horse Registry; Natl. [4922]
Quarter Horse Youth Assn; Amer. [4839]
Quarter Pony Assn; Amer. [4840]
Quarter Pony Assn; Intl. [4904]
Quarter Pony Assn; Natl. [4923]
Quarter Racing Owners of America - Defunct.
Quarter Sport Horse Registry [★4852]
Quartermaster Assn. [★6064]
Quartus Found. for Spiritual Res. [12361], PO Box
   1768, Boerne, TX 78006-6768, (830)249-3985
Quartz Producers Coun; Natl. [3698]

Quartzite Rock Assn. [946], PO Box 661, Sioux
   Falls, SD 57101, (605)339-1520
Quaternary Assn; Amer. [7359]
Quaternary Assn; Canadian [IO]
Quaternary and Geomorphological Assn. of Vietnam
   [IO], Hanoi, Vietnam
Quaternary Res. Assn. [IO], Egham, United Kingdom
Quebec Assn. of Independent Schools [IO], Mont-
   real, QC, Canada
Quebec Assn. of Marriage and Family Therapy [IO],
   Montreal, QC, Canada
Quebec Fed. of Historical Societies [IO], Montreal,
   QC, Canada
Quebec-Labrador Foundation/Atlantic Center for the
   Env. [4601], 55 S Main St., Ipswich, MA 01938,
   (978)356-0038
Quebec-Labrador Foundation/Atlantic Center for the
   Environment [IO], Ipswich, MA, United States
Quebec dans le Monde [IO], Ste.-Foy, QC, Canada
Quebec Stud; Amer. Coun. for [★8044]
Quebec Wheelchair Assn. [IO], Montreal, QC,
   Canada
Quebec Writers' Fed. [IO], Montreal, QC, Canada
Queen Elizabeth II Arts Coun. of New Zealand [★IO]
Queen Fan Club [IO], West Horsley, United
   Kingdom
Queen Isabella Foundation [★IO]
Queen Isabella Foundation [★19000]
Queen Sofia Spanish Inst. [10973], 684 Park Ave.,
   New York, NY 10021, (212)628-0420
Queen Sofia Spanish Inst. [IO], New York, NY,
   United States
Queen's English Soc. [IO], London, United Kingdom
Queensland Chamber of Commerce And Indus.
   [★IO]
Queensland Chamber of Commerce and Indus. [IO],
   Brisbane, Australia
Queensland Counsellors Assn. [IO], Brisbane,
   Australia
Queensland Herb Soc. [IO], Kenmore, Australia
Queensland History Teachers Assn. [IO], New Farm,
   Australia
Queensland Master Builders Assn. [IO], Brisbane,
   Australia
Queensland Olive Coun. [IO], Kingaroy, Australia
Queensland Right To Life [IO], Toowong, Australia
Queensland Secondary Principals Assn. [IO], South-
   port, Australia
Queensland Weightlifting Assn. [IO], Capalaba,
   Australia
Queer Alliance; Columbia [12224]
Queer Nation [17656], c/o The Online Gay Comic,
   PO Box 447, New York, NY 10159-0447
Quekett Microscopical Club [IO], South Ruislip,
   United Kingdom
Quest Books [★20593]
Quest, Inc. [★8199]
Quest Intl. [★8199]
Quest Intl. Users Gp. [6857], 2365 Harrodsburg Rd.,
   Ste. A325, Lexington, KY 40504, (859)226-4307
Quest Natl. Center [★8199]
Quest for Peace [18106], PO Box 5206, Hyattsville,
   MD 20782, (301)699-0042
Quest for Peace [IO], Hyattsville, MD, United States
The Questers [21532], 210 S Quince St.,
   Philadelphia, PA 19107-5534, (215)923-5183
Questioned Document Examiners; Amer. Soc. of
   [5755]
Questioned Document Examiners; Independent
   Assn. of [5762]
Questscope for Social Development in the Middle
   East - Jordan [IO], Amman, Jordan
Questscope for Social Development in the Middle
   East - United Kingdom [IO], Crowborough, United
   Kingdom
Quetzaltrekkers Guatemala [IO], Quetzaltenango,
   Guatemala
Quetzaltrekkers - Nicaragua [IO], Leon, Nicaragua
Quickdraw Animation Soc. [IO], Calgary, AB,
   Canada
Quiet Valley Living Historical Farm [10147], 1000
   Turkey Hill Rd., Stroudsburg, PA 18360, (570)992-
   6161
Quill and Scroll Foundation [★24523]
Quill and Scroll Soc. [24523], Univ. of Iowa, School
   of Journalism and Mass Commun., 100 Adler
   Journalism Bldg., Rm. E346, Iowa City, IA 52242,
   (319)335-3457

Reference to "IO" in place of a book number signifies that the association may be found in the 45th edition of International Organizations.

Quilt Art Assn; Contemporary [22152]
Quilt Associates; Studio Art [21547]
Quilt Assn; Intl. [22162]
Quilt Proj; Boise Peace [18192]
Quilt Study Group; Amer. [9828]
Quilters' Guild of the British Isles [IO], Halifax, United Kingdom
Quilters Hall of Fame [22173], PO Box 681, Marion, IN 46952, (765)664-9333
Quilter's Soc; Amer. [22149]
Quilting Assn; Natl. [22170]
Quilting Cong; Continental [★22173]
Quilts; Alliance for Amer. [9823]
Quilts Projs; ABC [11506]
Quimper Club Intl. [21546], 331 Raven Ct., Healdsburg, CA 95448
Quit [IO], London, United Kingdom
Quivera Soc. - Defunct.
Quixote Center [18628], PO Box 5206, Hyattsville, MD 20782-0206, (301)699-0042
Quixote Center [IO], Hyattsville, MD, United States
Quoit Pitchers; Natl. Assn. of Horseshoe and [★23540]
Quota Club Intl. [★13059]
Quota Club Intl. [★IO]
Quota Intl. [IO], Washington, DC, United States
Quota Intl. [13059], c/o We Share Found., 1420 21st St. NW, Washington, DC 20036, (202)331-9694

R

R. Austin Freeman Soc. - Defunct.
R/C Helicopter Assn; Intl. [22647]
R/C Quarter Scale Assn. of Am. [22655]
R. J. Sutton Fan Club - Address unknown since 1989.
R-T-P - Defunct.
R.A. Bloch Cancer Found. [13867], One H&R Block Way, Kansas City, MO 64105, (816)854-5050
Raad voor Cultuur [★IO]
Rabbinic Center for Res. and Counseling [16229], c/o Rabbinic Center Synagogue, 128 E Dudley Ave., Westfield, NJ 07090, (908)233-0419
Rabbinical Alliance of Am. [20172]
Rabbinical Assembly [20173], 3080 Broadway, New York, NY 10027, (212)280-6000
Rabbinical Assembly [IO], New York, NY, United States
Rabbinical Assembly of Am. [★IO]
Rabbinical Assembly of Am. [★20173]
Rabbinical Assn; Reconstructionist [20175]
Rabbinical Cong. of the U.S.A. and Canada; Central [20130]
Rabbinical Coun. of Am. [20174], 305 7th Ave., 12th Fl., New York, NY 10001, (212)807-9000
Rabbinical and Talmudic Schools; Assn. of Advanced [8683]
Rabbis; Assn. of Humanistic [20120]
Rabbis; Central Conf. of Amer. [20129]
Rabbis; Coun. of Young Israel [★20197]
Rabbis of the U.S. and Canada; Union of Orthodox [20183]
Rabbis - Vaad Harabonim of Am; Amer. Bd. of [20111]
Rabbis; Young Israel Coun. of [20197]
Rabbit Assn; Amer. Standard Chinchilla [★5141]
Rabbit Breeders; Amer. Fed. of New Zealand [5135]
Rabbit Breeders Assn; Amer. [5139]
Rabbit Breeders' Assn; Amer. Satin [5140]
Rabbit Breeders Assn; Cinnamon [5144]
Rabbit Breeders Assn; Havana [5145]
Rabbit Breeders Club; Natl. Angora [5150]
Rabbit Breeders Intl; Hotot [5147]
Rabbit and Cavy Breeders Assn; Amer. [★5139]
Rabbit Club of Am; Lop [5148]
Rabbit Club of Am; Rhinelander [5159]
Rabbit Club; Amer. Checkered Giant [5132]
Rabbit Club; Amer. English Spot [5134]
Rabbit Club; Amer. Harlequin [5136]
Rabbit Club; Natl. Rex [5155]
Rabbit Club; Natl. Silver [5156]
Rabbit Co-Breeders Assn; Palomino [5158]
Rabbit Fed; Champagne d'Argent [5143]
Rabbit Network; House [11409]
Rabbit Soc; House [11410]

Rabbit Specialty Club; Californian [5142]
Rabbits
Amer. Belgian Hare Club [5131]
Amer. Beveren Rabbit Club [22917]
Amer. Checkered Giant Rabbit Club [5132]
Amer. Dutch Rabbit Club [5133]
Amer. English Spot Rabbit Club [5134]
Amer. Fed. of New Zealand Rabbit Breeders [5135]
Amer. Fuzzy Lop Rabbit Club [22918]
Amer. Harlequin Rabbit Club [5136]
Amer. Himalayan Rabbit Assn. [5137]
American Himalayan Rabbit Association [IO]
Amer. Netherland Dwarf Rabbit Club [5138]
Amer. Rabbit Breeders Assn. [5139]
Amer. Satin Rabbit Breeders' Assn. [5140]
Amer. Standard Chinchilla Rabbit Breeders Assn. [5141]
Californian Rabbit Specialty Club [5142]
Champagne d'Argent Rabbit Fed. [5143]
Cinnamon Rabbit Breeders Assn. [5144]
Havana Rabbit Breeders Assn. [5145]
Holland Lop Rabbit Specialty Club [5146]
Hotot Rabbit Breeders Intl. [5147]
Hotot Rabbit Breeders International [IO]
House Rabbit Soc. [11410]
Lop Rabbit Club of Am. [5148]
Mini Lop Rabbit Club of Am. [5149]
Natl. Angora Rabbit Breeders Club [5150]
Natl. Fed. of Flemish Giant Rabbit Breeders [5151]
Natl. Jersey Wooly Rabbit Club [5152]
Natl. Jersey Wooly Rabbit Club [IO]
Natl. Lilac Rabbit Club of Am. [5153]
Natl. Mini Rex Rabbit Club [5154]
Natl. Mini Rex Rabbit Club [IO]
Natl. Rex Rabbit Club [5155]
Natl. Silver Rabbit Club [5156]
North Amer. Lionhead Rabbit Club [5157]
North Amer. Lionhead Rabbit Club [IO]
Palomino Rabbit Co-Breeders Assn. [5158]
Rabbits Unlimited Inc. [4161]
Rhinelander Rabbit Club of Am. [5159]
Silver Marten Rabbit Club [5160]
Rabbits Unlimited Inc. [4161]
Rabbonim Aid Soc. - Address unknown since 1995.
Race Gp; California Vintage [★22665]
Race Horse Club [★4922]
Race Relations Information Center - Defunct.
Race Res. Action Coun; Poverty and [12781]
Race Track Chaplaincy of Am. [19756], PO Box 91640, Los Angeles, CA 90009-1640, (310)419-1640
Racecourse Assn. [IO], Ascot, United Kingdom
Racehorse Owners Assn. of Great Britain [IO], London, United Kingdom
Racers Assn; Midwest United Drag [★23070]
Racers Assn; Natl. Amer. Motors Drivers and [23080]
Races in the U.S; Coalition for Harmony of [18198]
Rachel Carson Coun. [13330], PO Box 10779, Silver Spring, MD 20914-0779, (301)593-7507
Rachel Carson Homestead Assn. [11143], 613 Marion Ave., PO Box 46, Springdale, PA 15144-0046, (724)274-5459
Rachel Carson Trust for the Living Env. [★13330]
Rachel Minke Fan Club - Address unknown since 1999.
Racial and Economic Equality; Fellowship for [★18629]
Racial Equality; Cong. of [16939]
Racial and Ethnic Equity; Am. Coun. on Educ., Center for Advancement of [8889]
Racial Family Alliance of Houston; Inter [12160]
Racial Family Alliance; Inter [★12160]
Racial Family Circle; Inter [12161]
Racial-Intercultural Pride; Inter [12162]
Racial Justice 911 [18493], c/o CAAAV: Organizing Asian Communities, 2473 Valentine Ave., Bronx, NY 10458, (718)220-7391
Racial Justice; Commn. for [★20608]
Racial Justice; Natl. Catholic Conf. for Inter [17133]
Racial Justice; United Church of Christ Commn. for [★20608]
Racial and Social Justice; United Church of Christ Ministers for [★20608]

Racially Free Am; Concerned Citizens for [17754]
Racing
Adventure Cycling Assn. [23304]
Amer. Auto Racing Writers and Broadcasters Assn. [23069]
Amer. Barrel Racing Assn. [23492]
Amer. Bicycle Assn. [23305]
Amer. Bicycle Racing [23667]
Amer. Cmpt. Barrel Racing Assn. [23493]
Amer. Funny Car Series [23070]
Amer. Greyhound Track Operators Assn. [23391]
Amer. Historic Racing Motorcycle Assn. [22665]
Amer. Hot Rod Assn. [23071]
Amer. Model Yachting Assn. [22642]
Amer. Mule Racing Assn. [23668]
Amer. Power Boat Assn. [23152]
Amer. Sail Training Assn. [23153]
Amer. Sailing Assn. [23154]
Amer. Shark Assn. [23156]
Amer. Speed Assn. [23072]
Amer. Swan Boat Assn. [23669]
Amer. Track Racing Assn. [23306]
Antique Auto Racing Assn. [21578]
Antique Snowmobile Club of Am. [22943]
Arabian Jockey Club [23494]
Assn. of Racing Commissioners Intl. [6240]
Assn. of Racing Commissioners Intl. [IO]
Auto. Competition Comm. for the U.S. FIA [23073]
Auto. Racing Club of Am. [23074]
Barrel Futurities of Am. [23495]
Boat Owners Assn. of the U.S. [23160]
Buick St. Rod Assn. [22919]
Bullseye Assn. [23161]
Catalina 22 Natl. Sailing Assn. [23162]
Catboat Assn. [23163]
Championship Assn. of Mechanics [23075]
Championship Auto Racing Teams [23076]
Circuits Intl. [IO]
Coun. of Sailing Associations [23165]
Day Sailer Assn. [23167]
Derrike Cope Fan Club [24783]
East Coast Timing Assn. [22920]
El Toro Intl. Yacht Racing Assn. [23168]
Elec. Boat Assn. of the Americas [21872]
FJ U.S. [23169]
Flying Scot Sailing Assn. [23170]
Force 5 Class Assn. [23171]
Geary 18 Intl. Yacht Racing Assn. [23172]
Godolphin Soc. [10906]
Grand Amer. Road Racing Assn. [23068]
Greyhound Racing Assn. of Am. [23392]
Hampton One-Design Class Racing Assn. [23173]
Harness Horse Youth Found. [23496]
Harness Horsemen Intl. [23497]
Harness Racing Museum and Hall of Fame [23498]
Harness Tracks of Am. [23499]
Highlander Class Intl. Assn. [23174]
Historic Motor Sports Assn. [21657]
Inland Lake Yachting Assn. [23175]
Inter-Collegiate Sailing Assn. of North Am. [23176]
Inter-Lake Yachting Assn. [23177]
Intl. 210 Assn. [23179]
Intl. 505 Yacht Racing Assn., Amer. Sect. [23180]
Intl. Aerobatic Club [23040]
Intl. Barrel Racing Assn. [23500]
Intl. Blue Jay Class Assn. [23181]
Intl. D.N. Ice Yacht Racing Assn. [23183]
Intl. Etchells Class Assn. [23184]
Intl. Fed. of Sleddog Sports [23393]
Intl. Flying Dutchman Class Assn. of the U.S. [23185]
Intl. Gravity Sports Assn. [23823]
Intl. Hobie Class Assn. [23186]
Intl. Hot Rod Assn. [23077]
Intl. J/22 Class Assn. [23187]
Intl. Jet Sports Boating Assn. and Amer. Watercraft Assn. [23976]
Intl. Kart Fed. [23568]
Intl. Lightning Class Assn. [23188]
Intl. Model Power Boat Assn. [22645]
Intl. Motor Contest Assn. [23078]
Intl. Motor Sports Assn. [23079]

A star before a book entry number signifies that the name is not listed separately, but is mentioned within the entry.

Intl. Naples Sabot Assn. [23190]
Intl. Penguin Class Dinghy Assn. [23191]
Intl. Prindle Class Racing Assn. [23192]
Intl. Sled Dog Racing Assn. [23394]
Intl. Soap Box Derby [23770]
Intl. Sunfish Class Assn. [23194]
Intl. Thunderbird Class Assn. [23195]
Intl. Trotting and Pacing Assn. [23501]
Intl. Unicycling Fed. [23311]
Intl. Wheelchair Road Racers Club [23346]
Jet 14 Class Assn. [23196]
The Jockey Club [23502]
Jockeys' Guild [23503]
Johnny Benson Fan Club [24784]
Kustoms of Am. [22921]
Lakes Region Sled Dog Club [23395]
League of Amer. Bicyclists [23312]
Lido 14 Intl. Class Assn. [23198]
Marathon Skating Intl. [23737]
MC Sailing Assn. [23199]
Media Action Network for Asian Americans
    [18029]
MG Vintage Racers [22922]
Natl. Air-Racing Gp. [23041]
Natl. Amer. Motors Drivers and Racers Assn.
    [23080]
Natl. Assn. of Off-Track Betting [23505]
Natl. Assn. for Stock Car Auto Racing [23081]
Natl. Auto Racing Historical Soc. [23082]
Natl. Bicycle League [23313]
Natl. Boating Fed. [23201]
Natl. Butterfly Assn. [23202]
Natl. C Scow Sailing Assn. [23203]
Natl. Center for Bicycling and Walking [23315]
Natl. Championship Racing Assn. [23670]
Natl. Christian Barrel Racers Assn. [23507]
Natl. Class E Scow Assn. [23204]
Natl. Derby Rallies [23771]
Natl. Elec. Drag Racing Assn. [23396]
Natl. Hot Rod Assn. [23083]
Natl. Museum of Racing and Hall of Fame
    [23508]
Natl. Offshore Dept. [23205]
Natl. Old Timers Auto Racing Club [21737]
Natl. One Design Racing Assn. [23206]
Natl. Org. for Racing Radio Control Autos [22652]
Natl. Starwind/Spindrift Class Assn. [23207]
Natl. Thoroughbred Racing Assn. [23510]
North Amer. Formula 18 Assn. [23208]
North Amer. Ski Joring Assn. [23845]
North Amer. Thoroughbred Soc. [23538]
North Amer. Tornado Assn. [23209]
Northern Late Model Racing Assn. [23084]
Olson 30 Class Assn. [23210]
One-Design Class Coun. [23211]
Oregon Horsemen's Benevolent Protective Assn.
    [23512]
Pacific Northwest Ski Assn. [23754]
Prindle Class Assn. [23212]
Professional Ski Instructors of Am. [23755]
Rhodes 19 Class Assn. [23213]
Rhodes Bantam Class Assn. [23214]
Rickman Owners Club Intl. [22689]
San Juan 21 Class Assn. [23215]
Santana 20 Class Assn. [23216]
Scale Warbird Racing Assn. [22657]
Seven Seas Cruising Assn. [23217]
Siberian Husky Club of Am. [22359]
Snipe Class Intl. Racing Assn. [23219]
Sports Car Club of Am. [21787]
Sportscar Vintage Racing Assn. [23085]
Standardbred Owners Assn. [23513]
Swan Owners Assn. of Am. [23221]
Thoroughbred Club of Am. [23514]
Thoroughbred Owners and Breeders Assn.
    [23515]
Thoroughbred Racing Associations [23516]
Thoroughbred Racing Protective Bur. [23517]
Unicycling Soc. of Am. [23319]
United Black Drag Racers Assn. [23397]
United Speedways of North Am. [23671]
U.S. A-Class Catamaran Assn. [23225]
U.S. Adventure Racing Assn. [23672]
U.S. Albacore Assn. [23226]
U.S. Auto Club [23086]

U.S. Classic Racing Assn. [22694]
U.S. Collegiate Ski and Snowboard Assn. [23757]
U.S. Cross Country Snowmobile Racing Assn.
    [23768]
U.S. Cycling Fed. [23320]
U.S. Equestrian Fed. [23534]
U.S. Handcycling Fed. [23321]
U.S. J/24 Class Assn. [23227]
U.S. Late Model Assn. [23087]
U.S. Lawn Mower Racing Assn. [23673]
U.S. Mariner Class Assn. [23228]
U.S. Mirror Class Assn. [23229]
U.S. Power Squadrons [23231]
U.S. Sailing Assn. [23232]
U.S. Sailing Found. [23233]
U.S. Ski Coaches Assn. [23758]
U.S. Ski and Snowboard Assn. [23760]
U.S. Ski Team Found. [23761]
U.S. Snowshoe Assn. [23769]
U.S. Soling Assn. [23234]
U.S. Speedskating [23745]
U.S. Team Penning Assn. [23518]
U.S. Trotting Assn. [23519]
U.S. Wayfarer Assn. [23235]
U.S. Windsurfing Assn. [23236]
U.S. Yngling Assn. [23237]
USA Canoe/Kayak [23280]
U.S.A. Finn Assn. [23238]
Vintage Drivers Club of Am. [21810]
WERA Motorcycle Roadracing [23628]
White Plate Flat Trackers Assn. [23629]
Windmill Class Assn. [23239]
World Championship Cutter and Chariot Racing
    Assn. [23281]
Worldloppet/American Birkebeiner [23764]
Yachting Club of Am. [23240]
Young Racers of Am. [23674]
Racing Assn; Amer. Drag [★23071]
Racing Assn; Amer. Motors Drag [★23080]
Racing Assn., Amer. Sect; Intl. 505 Yacht [23180]
Racing Assn; Amer. Y-Flyer Yacht [23157]
Racing Assn; Antique Auto [21578]
Racing Association; Chesapeake Bay Yacht
    [★23173]
Racing Assn; Coronado 15 Class [★23164]
Racing Assn; El Toro Intl. Yacht [23168]
Racing Assn; Geary 18 Intl. Yacht [23172]
Racing Assn; Hampton One-Design Class [23173]
Racing Assn; Inter-Collegiate Yacht [★23176]
Racing Assn; Intl. Flattie Yacht [★23172]
Racing Assn; Intl. MC Class Sailboat [★23199]
Racing Assn; Intl. NACRA Class [★23192]
Racing Assn; Intl. Prindle Class [23192]
Racing Assn; Intl. Star Class Yacht [23193]
Racing Assn; Monster Truck [23958]
Racing Assn; Natl. Amer. Motors Drag [★23080]
Racing Assn; Natl. One Design [23206]
Racing Assn; Natl. Thoroughbred [23510]
Racing Assn. of North Am; Inter-Collegiate Yacht
    [★23176]
Racing Assn; Professional Drag [★23077]
Racing Assn; Sportscar Vintage [23085]
Racing Assn; United Hunts [★23509]
Racing Assn; U.S. Air [★23041]
Racing Assn; World Championship Cutter and
    Chariot [23281]
Racing Associations Coun; Yacht [★23165]
Racing Associations; Thoroughbred [23516]
Racing Club; Midget Ocean [23200]
Racing Club; Natl. Old Timers Auto [21737]
Racing Commissioners; Natl. Assn. of State [★6240]
Racing Communications; Harness [★23519]
Racing; Eastern Museum of Motor [21634]
Racing Fans Club of America (Milton S. Forman
    Memorial) - Address unknown since 2007.
Racing Gp; Natl. Air- [23041]
Racing and Hall of Fame; Natl. Museum of [23508]
Racing Historical Soc; Natl. Auto [23082]
Racing Motorcycle Assn; Amer. Historic [22665]
Racing Museum and Hall of Fame; Harness [23498]
Racing; Natl. Assn. for Stock Car Auto [23081]
Racing Org. of Am; Professional [★23320]
Racing Pigeon Union; Amer. [22894]
Racing Protective Bur; Thoroughbred [23517]
Racing Radio Control Autos; Natl. Org. for [22652]

Racing Res. Fund - Defunct.
Racing Union; North Amer. Yacht [★23232]
Racing Union; U.S. Yacht [★23232]
Racing Writers and Broadcasters Assn; Amer. Auto
    [23069]
Racism
    Black Holocaust Soc. [16938]
    Call to Renewal [18376]
    Common Destiny Alliance [8244]
    European Network Against Racism [IO]
    Leadership Development Network [17223]
    Natl. Alliance Against Racist and Political Repres-
        sion [17128]
    Natl. Assn. for the Advancement of Colored
        People [17129]
    Natl. Black Justice Coalition [18643]
    Natl. Youth and Student Peace Coalition [18226]
    Positive Youth Found. [18856]
    Poverty and Race Res. Action Coun. [12781]
    Proj. RACE [19047]
    Racial Justice 911 [18493]
    Radical Philosophy Assn. [18273]
    Soc. for Philosophy in the Contemporary World
        [18274]
    Turkish Amer. Alliance for Fairness [19410]
Racism; Artists Against [IO]
Racism and for Friendship Between Peoples; Move-
    ment Against [IO]
Racism Info. Ser; Anti- [IO]
Racism No Way [IO], Darlinghurst, Australia
Racist and Political Repression; Natl. Alliance
    Against [17128]
Racist Terror; Anti-Racist Action-Los Angeles/People
    Against [17092]
Racist Terror; People Against [★17092]
Rack Mfrs. Inst. [2064], c/o John B. Nofsinger, Sr.,
    Managing Dir., 8720 Red Oak Blvd., Ste. 201,
    Charlotte, NC 28217-3992, (704)676-1190
Rack Manufacturers Institute [IO], Charlotte, NC,
    United States
Rack Service Assn. - Defunct.
Racket Sports Assn; Amer. Recreational [3637]
Rackets Assn; Intl. Paddle [★23678]
Rackham Soc; Arthur [9427]
Racking Horse Breeders' Assn. of Am. [4948], 67
    Horse Center Rd., Decatur, AL 35603, (256)353-
    7225
Racquet Sports
    Amer. Medical Tennis Assn. [23898]
    Amer. Platform Tennis Assn. [23899]
    Amer. Tennis Assn. [23900]
    Badminton Pan Amer. Confed. [23088]
    Intercollegiate Tennis Assn. [23902]
    Intl. Racquetball Fed. [23677]
    Intl. Tennis Hall of Fame [23903]
    Korean Amer. Professional Tennis Assn. [23904]
    Major Wingfield Historical Soc. [23905]
    Natl. Collegiate Table Tennis Assn. [23895]
    Natl. Public Parks Tennis Assn. [23906]
    Professional Tennis Registry [23909]
    Sony Ericsson WTA Tour [23910]
    U.S. Dental Tennis Assn. [23911]
    U.S. Natl. Tennis Acad. [23913]
    U.S. Professional Tennis Assn. [23914]
    U.S. Racquetball Assn. [23678]
    U.S. Squash Racquets Assn. [23876]
    U.S. Tennis Assn. [23915]
    USA Badminton [23089]
    USA Tennis - NJTL [23916]
    WTA Tour Players Assn. [23917]
Racquet Sports Assn; Intl. [★3021]
Racquet Stringers Assn; U.S. [3674]
Racquetball
    Guam Racquetball Fed. [23675]
    Guam Racquetball Fed. [IO]
    Intl. Bi-Rak-It Assn. [23676]
    Intl. Racquetball Fed. [23677]
    Intl. Racquetball Fed. [IO]
    Racquetball Assn. of Ireland [IO]
    Racquetball Canada [IO]
    U.S. Racquetball Assn. [23678]
Racquetball Assn; Intl. [★23678]
Racquetball Assn. of Ireland [IO], Dublin, Ireland
Racquetball Assn; U.S. Amateur [★23678]
Racquetball Canada [IO], Winnipeg, MB, Canada

Reference to "IO" in place of a book number signifies that the association may be found in the 45th edition of International Organizations.

Racquetball Mfrs. Assn. - Defunct.
Racquets Assn; U.S. Squash [23876]
Rader Assn. [21029], 2633 Gilbert Way, Rancho
  Cordova, CA 95670-3513, (916)366-6833
Radgivende Ingeniorers Forening [★IO]
Radiance Technique Assn. Intl. [★IO]
Radiance Technique Assn. Intl. [★13648]
The Radiance Technique Intl. Assn. [13648], PO Box
  40570, St. Petersburg, FL 33743-0570
The Radiance Technique Intl. Assn. [IO], St.
  Petersburg, FL, United States
Radiance Technique and Radiant Peace Assn. Intl.
  [★IO]
Radiance Technique and Radiant Peace Assn. Intl.
  [★13648]
Radiant Heating Assn; Hydronic [★1884]
Radiant Panel Assn. [1898], PO Box 717, Loveland,
  CO 80539, (970)613-0100
Radiation
  Algerian Assn. of Medical Physicists [IO]
  Amer. Acad. of Oral and Maxillofacial Radiology
    [14104]
  Amer. Bd. of Hea. Physics [16015]
  Amer. Bd. of Radiology [16272]
  Amer. Coll. of Radiation Oncology [16267]
  Amer. Coll. of Radiology [16274]
  Amer. Coll. of Veterinary Radiology [16770]
  Amer. Healthcare Radiology Administrators
    [16275]
  Amer. Osteopathic Coll. of Radiology [16276]
  Amer. Radiological Nurses Assn. [15457]
  Amer. Radium Soc. [15639]
  Amer. Registry of Radiologic Technologists
    [15128]
  Amer. Roentgen Ray Soc. [16277]
  Amer. Soc. of Neuroimaging [16281]
  Amer. Soc. of Neuroradiology [16282]
  Amer. Soc. for Therapeutic Radiology and Oncol-
    ogy [16285]
  Assn. for Directors of Radiation Oncology
    Programs [3271]
  Assn. of Freestanding Radiation Oncology
    Centers [16268]
  Assn. for Radiation Res. [IO]
  Assn. of Univ. Radiologists [16286]
  Australasian Radiation Protection Soc. [IO]
  Canadian Radiation Protection Assn. [IO]
  Computerized Medical Imaging Soc. [16287]
  Conf. of Radiation Control Prog. Directors [6241]
  Coun. on Diagnostic Imaging [16288]
  Coun. on Ionizing Radiation Measurements and
    Standards [7556]
  CyberKnife Soc. [16581]
  Friends of Hibakusha [18128]
  Hea. Physics Soc. [16017]
  Intl. Commn. on Radiation Units and Measure-
    ments [5161]
  Intl. Commn. on Radiation Units and Measure-
    ments [IO]
  Intl. Isotope Soc. [6548]
  Intl. Radiation Protection Assn. [IO]
  Intl. RadioSurgery Assn. [IO]
  Intl. RadioSurgery Assn. [16269]
  Intl. Skeletal Soc. [16289]
  Japan Indus. Assn. of Radiological Systems [IO]
  Japan Radiation Res. Soc. [IO]
  Japan Radiological Soc. [IO]
  Japan Soc. of Radiological Tech. [IO]
  Joint Rev. Comm. on Educ. in Radiologic Tech.
    [8838]
  Natl. Assn. of Atomic Veterans [13353]
  Natl. Coun. on Radiation Protection and Measure-
    ments [6242]
  Nordic Soc. for Radiation Protection [IO]
  Radiation Effects Res. Found. [IO]
  Radiation and Public Hea. Proj. [16270]
  Radiation Res. Soc. [7557]
  Radiation Safety Inst. of Canada [IO]
  Radiation Therapy Oncology Gp. [15653]
  Radiological Soc. of North Am. [16293]
  Radiological Soc. of the Republic of China [IO]
  RadTech Intl. North Am. [IO]
  RadTech Intl. North Am. [7558]
  Soc. of Interventional Radiology [16300]
  Soc. for Radiation Oncology Administrators
    [16302]

  Soc. for Radiological Protection [IO]
  Soc. for Whole Body Autoradiography [15149]
  World Fed. of Neuroradiological Societies [16306]
Radiation Effects Res. Found. [IO], Hiroshima,
  Japan
Radiation Health Information Project - Defunct.
Radiation Oncology Administrators [★16302]
Radiation Oncology Administrators; Soc. for [16302]
Radiation Oncology; Assn. of Residents in [15643]
Radiation Projects; Health and [★17345]
Radiation Protection and Measurements; Natl.
  Comm. on [★6242]
Radiation Protection; Natl. Comm. on [★6242]
Radiation and Public Hea. Proj. [16270], PO Box 60,
  Unionville, NY 10988, (800)582-3716
Radiation Res. Soc. [7557], PO Box 7050,
  Lawrence, KS 66044, (800)627-0326
Radiation Safety Inst. of Canada [IO], Toronto, ON,
  Canada
Radiation Survivors; Natl. Assn. of [18129]
Radiation Technologists; Canadian Assn. of Medical
  [IO]
Radiation Therapy Oncology Gp. [15653], 1818
  Market St., Ste. 1600, Philadelphia, PA 19103,
  (215)574-3189
Radiator Core Mfg. Credit Assn; Natl. [★1422]
Radiator Manufacturers Assn; Boiler and [IO]
Radiator Mfrs; Inst. of Boiler and [★1884]
Radiator Mfg. Credit Assn; Natl. [★1422]
Radiator Ser. Assn; Natl. Automotive [422]
Radiator Standards Assn; Intl. [★19897]
Radical
  Black Radical Cong. [18868]
  Catholic Worker Movement [18109]
  Oper. Save Am. [18562]
Radical Alliance of Social Service Workers - Defunct.
Radical Biology and Medicine; Soc. for Free [6613]
Radical Caucus [★18273]
Radical Caucus in Psychiatry [16092]
Radical Cong; Black [18868]
Radical Force - Address unknown since 1990.
Radical Historians' Org; MARHO: The [10129]
Radical Historians Org; Mid-Atlantic [★10129]
Radical Libertarian Alliance [★IO]
Radical Philosophy Assn. [18273], c/o Harry van der
  Linden, Treas., Butler Univ., Philosophy and
  Religion Dept., 4600 Sunset Ave., Indianapolis, IN
  46208, (434)220-3300
Radical Political Economics; Union for [6896]
Radical Psychology Network [16169], c/o Dennis
  Fox, Co-Founder/Archivist, PO Box 470783,
  Brookline Village, MA 02447-0783, (650)493-5000
Radical Psychology Network [IO], Brookline, MA,
  United States
Radical Res. Center [★10892]
Radical Women [17569], New Valencia Hall, 1908
  Mission St., San Francisco, CA 94103, (415)864-
  1278
Radicalist Intl. - Defunct.
Radiesthesia
  Borderland Sciences Res. Found. [7471]
Radikale Venstre [★IO]
Radio
  Africa News Ser. [16921]
  Amer. CB Radio Assn. [21493]
  Amer. Fed. of TV and Radio Artists [24022]
  Amer. Indian Liberation Crusade [12622]
  Amer. Lib. Assn. - Public Info. Off. [10897]
  Amer. Psychological Assn. - Media Psychology
    Div. [16131]
  Amer. Radio Assn. [24023]
  Amer. Radio Relay League [21494]
  Amer. Screenwriters Assn. [4060]
  Amer. Shortwave Listeners Club [21495]
  Antique Wireless Assn. [22923]
  Antique Wireless Association [IO]
  ARRL Found. [21496]
  Assoc. Press Broadcasters [546]
  Assn. of Fed. Communications Consulting
    Engineers [7767]
  Assn. of North Amer. Radio Clubs [21498]
  Assn. of Radio Amateurs of Slovenia [IO]
  Audio Engg. Soc. [6909]
  Black Awareness in TV [17164]
  Black Coll. Radio Org. [551]

  Boating Writers Intl. [3100]
  British Vintage Wireless Soc. [IO]
  Broadcast Cable Financial Mgt. Assn. [553]
  Canadian Soc. for Independent Radio Production
    [IO]
  Catholic Acad. for Commun. Arts Professionals
    [9761]
  The Christian Sci. Publishing Soc. [3216]
  Christian TV Mission [19536]
  Collins Collectors Assn. [21499]
  Commun. Commn. [19537]
  Communications Marketing Assn. [3738]
  Community Media Assn. [IO]
  Corp. for Public Broadcasting [9762]
  Educational Broadcasting Corp. [9763]
  Enterprise Wireless Alliance [3742]
  Friends of Old-Time Radio [22924]
  Garden Writers Assn. [22512]
  Geospatial Info. and Tech. Assn. [900]
  Gibraltar Amateur Radio Soc. [IO]
  Hispanic Org. of Latin Actors [10001]
  Historical Radio Soc. of Australia [IO]
  Hollywood Foreign Press Assn. [3115]
  Hollywood Radio and TV Soc. [559]
  Intercollegiate Broadcasting Sys. [8004]
  Intl. Amateur Radio Union [21501]
  Intl. Assn. for Radio, Telecommunications and
    Electromagnetics [7773]
  Intl. Nanocasting Assn. [562]
  Intl. Radio Club of Am. [21503]
  Intl. Soc. of Certified Electronics Technicians
    [1220]
  InTouch Networks [16860]
  Iota Beta Sigma [24410]
  Junior Hollywood Radio and TV Soc. [564]
  The Lambs [11019]
  Land Mobile Communications Coun. [3751]
  Leo Lassen Legacy Proj. [24789]
  Lone Ranger Fan Club [25032]
  Longwave Club of Am. [21505]
  Mainstream Media Proj. [18494]
  Mainstream Media Proj. [IO]
  Manufacturers Radio Frequency Advisory Comm.
    [565]
  Media Access Proj. [17182]
  Media Action Network for Asian Americans
    [18029]
  Media Rating Coun. [566]
  Natl. Assn. of Black Owned Broadcasters [568]
  Natl. Assn. Broadcast Employees and Technicians
    - Communications Workers of Am. [24024]
  Natl. Assn. of Broadcasters [569]
  Natl. Assn. of Commercial Broadcasters in Japan
    [IO]
  Natl. Assn. of Farm Broadcasting [570]
  Natl. Assn. of Shortwave Broadcasters [541]
  Natl. Black Programming Consortium [9764]
  Natl. Black Public Relations Soc. [3194]
  Natl. Broadcast Assn. for Community Affairs [572]
  Natl. Broadcasting Soc. - Alpha Epsilon Rho
    [24411]
  Natl. Conf. of Editorial Writers [3136]
  Natl. Fed. of Community Broadcasters [575]
  Natl. Lum and Abner Soc. [22925]
  Natl. Press Club [3141]
  Natl. Public Radio [9765]
  Natl. Religious Broadcasters [19539]
  New Dimensions Radio [17738]
  Newswomen's Club of New York [3150]
  No-Code Intl. [21506]
  North Amer. Radio Archives [22926]
  North Amer. Shortwave Assn. [21507]
  Old Old Timers Club [21508]
  Old Time Radio Club [22927]
  Other Minds [10684]
  Polish Amateur Radio Union [IO]
  Portuguese Broadcasting Assn. [IO]
  PROMAX [577]
  Public Radio Programmer's Assn. [3272]
  Quarter Century Wireless Assn. [21509]
  Radio Advt. Bur. [117]
  Radio Advisory Bd. of Canada [IO]
  Radio Amateur Satellite Corp. [7783]
  Radio Amateurs of Canada [IO]
  Radio Club of Am. [22928]

A star before a book entry number signifies that the name is not listed separately, but is mentioned within the entry.

Radio Collectors of Am. [22929]
Radio Free Europe/Radio Liberty [17191]
Radio Marketing Bur. [IO]
Radio Soc. of Sri Lanka [IO]
Radio-Television Correspondents Assn. [580]
Radio-Television News Directors Assn. [581]
Radio and TV Res. Coun. [7784]
REACT Intl. [6254]
Soc. for the Eradication of TV [17193]
Soc. to Preserve and Encourage Radio Drama, Variety and Comedy [22930]
Swiss Radio and TV Retailers' Assn. [IO]
Tanzania Amateur Radio Club [IO]
Telecommunications Res. and Action Center [17195]
Traffic Directors Guild of Am. [584]
Trinidad and Tobago Amateur Radio Soc. [IO]
United Elecl., Radio and Machine Workers of Am. [24050]
United Nations Correspondents Assn. [3168]
U.S. Marine Corps Combat Correspondents Assn. [3171]
U.S. Natl. Comm. of the Intl. Union of Radio Sci. [7785]
Veteran Wireless Operators Assn. [3763]
Vintage Radio and Phonograph Soc. [22931]
Western Public Radio [3273]
White House Correspondents' Assn. [3173]
World Miniature Warbird Assn. [22662]
Worldwide Television-FM DX Assn. [21510]
Writers Guild of Am., East [24220]
Writers Guild of Am., West [24221]
Radio Advt. Bur. [117], 1320 Greenway Dr., Ste. 500, Irving, TX 75038-2587, (212)681-7214
Radio Advisory Bd. of Canada [IO], Ottawa, ON, Canada
Radio Amateur Assn. of Greece [IO], Athens, Greece
Radio Amateur Satellite Corp. [7783], 850 Sligo Ave., Ste. 600, Silver Spring, MD 20910-4787, (301)589-6062
Radio Amateur Telecommunications Soc. - Defunct.
Radio Amateurs; ACB [21492]
Radio Amateurs of Canada [IO], Ottawa, ON, Canada
Radio Amateurs du Canada [★IO]
Radio Amateurs; Intl. Order of Handicapped [★21502]
Radio Artists; Amer. Fed. of [★24022]
Radio Artists; Amer. Fed. of TV and [24022]
Radio Assn; Amer. [24023]
Radio Assn; Amer. CB [21493]
Radio and Assn. of Communications Technicians; Natl. Assn. of Bus. and Educational [★3752]
Radio Assn. Defending Airwave Rights - Address unknown since 2000.
Radio Astronomy Observatory; National [★7622]
Radio Broadcasters Assn; Natl. [★569]
Radio Broadcasters; Canadian Assn. of Ethnic [IO]
Radio Broadcasters; Country [557]
Radio Broadcasters; Org. of Country [★557]
Radio Club of Am. [22928], PO Box 621074, Littleton, CO 80162, (303)948-4921
Radio Club of Am; Antique [★22923]
Radio Club of Am; Intl. [21503]
Radio Club; Lambda Amateur [21504]
Radio Club; Worldwide Monitors [★21510]
Radio Clubs; Assn. of North Amer. [21498]
Radio Collectors of Am. [22929], 15 Walden Dr., Walpole, MA 02081, (508)660-0923
Radio Communications Assn; Cellular [★3741]
Radio Communications; Forest Indus. [★1606]
Radio Communications Monitoring Assn. - Address unknown since 1999.
Radio Control Autos; Natl. Org. for Racing [22652]
Radio Control Hobby Trade Assn. [1914], PO Box 315, Butler, NJ 07405-0315, (973)283-9088
Radio Correspondents Assn. [★580]
Radio Creative Fund [★117]
Radio Crusade; Christ Truth [★19514]
Radio Drama, Variety and Comedy; Soc. to Preserve and Encourage [22930]
Radio, Elecl. and TV Retailers' Assn. [IO], Bedford, United Kingdom
Radio Electronics TV Manufacturers Assn. [★1212]

Radio Emergency Assoc. Communications Teams [★6254]
Radio Emergency Assoc. Communications Teams [★IO]
Radio Engineers; Inst. of [★6926]
Radio Enthusiasts; Assn. of Clandestine [21497]
Radio Executives Club [★563]
Radio Farm Directors; Natl. Assn. of [★570]
Radio Farm Directors; Natl. Assn. of Television- [★570]
Radio Free Europe/Radio Liberty [17191], 1201 Connecticut Ave. NW, Washington, DC 20036, (202)457-6947
Radio Free People - Defunct.
Radio Free Women - Defunct.
Radio Frequency Advisory Comm; Manufacturers [565]
Radio Historical Soc. of America - Defunct.
Radio Info. Center for the Blind [★16831]
Radio Internacional Feminista [★IO]
Radio Liberty Comm. [★17191]
Radio Liberty; Radio Free Europe/ [17191]
Radio and Machine Workers of Am; United Elecl., [24050]
Radio and Machine Workers; Intl. Union of Elecl., [★24049]
Radio Manufacturers Assn. [★1212]
Radio Marketing Bur. [IO], Toronto, ON, Canada
Radio Missionary Fellowship; World [★20344]
Radio; Natl. Comm. for Utilities [★3762]
Radio; Natl. Public [9765]
Radio News Directors Incorporated; Public [579]
Radio News Directors; Natl. Assn. of [★581]
Radio-Newsreel-TV Working Press Assn. - Address unknown since 1995.
Radio Org; Black Coll. [551]
Radio Parts Distributors; Natl. [★1223]
Radio Parts Manufacturers; Representatives of [★1213]
Radio Patrol of Amer. Fed. of Police; CB [★5962]
Radio and Phonograph Soc; Southwest Vintage [★22931]
Radio Pioneers Club [★555]
Radio Reading Services; Natl. Assn. of [★16856]
Radio Relay League; Amer. [21494]
Radio Sci; U.S. Natl. Comm. of the Intl. Union of [7785]
Radio Ser. Assn; Special Indus. [★3742]
Radio Shack Computer Alumni Assn. - Address unknown since 1994.
Radio Soc. of Bermuda [IO], Hamilton, Bermuda
Radio Soc. of Great Britain [IO], Potters Bar, United Kingdom
Radio Soc. of Sri Lanka [IO], Colombo, Sri Lanka
Radio Stations; Assn. of Public [★9765]
Radio Sys; Natl. Mobile [★3752]
Radio Talk Show Hosts Assn. [★IO]
Radio Tech. Commn. for Aeronautics [★6308]
Radio Tech. Commn. for Marine Ser. [★3753]
Radio Tech. Commn. for Marine Ser. [★IO]
Radio Tech. Commn. for Maritime Services [IO], Arlington, VA, United States
Radio Tech. Commn. for Maritime Services [3753], 1800 N Kent St., Ste. 1060, Arlington, VA 22209-2109, (703)527-2000
Radio and Telecommunications Engineers; Natl. Assn. of [★7773]
Radio Telephone Systems; Natl. Assn. of [★3752]
Radio and TV; Amer. Women in [545]
Radio-Television Assn; Assoc. Press [★546]
Radio and TV Broadcasters; Natl. Assn. of [★569]
Radio and TV Commn; Protestant [★19537]
Radio-Television Correspondents Assn. [580], c/o Senate Radio-TV Gallery, U.S. Capitol, Rm. S-325, Washington, DC 20510, (202)224-6421
Radio and TV Directors Guild [★24055]
Radio and TV Executive Soc. [★563]
Radio and TV Fed. [IO], Rome, Italy
Radio and TV Guild; Veterans Hosp. [★12116]
Radio and TV; Intl. Hea. and Safety Assn. for [IO]
Radio TV Manufacturers Assn. [★1212]
Radio-Television News Directors Assn. [581], 1600 K St. NW, Ste. 700, Washington, DC 20006-2806, (202)659-6510
Radio-Television News Directors' Assn. [IO], Toronto, ON, Canada

Radio and TV Res. Coun. [7784], c/o Mgt. Solutions for Associations, 234 5th Ave., Ste. 417, New York, NY 10001, (212)481-3038
Radio and TV Soc. Found; Intl. [563]
Radio and TV Soc; Hollywood [559]
Radio and TV Soc; Intl. [★563]
Radio Writers Guild [★24221]
Radioactive Waste
Center for Alternative Mining Development Policy [4536]
Concerned Citizens for Nuclear Safety [18147]
Downwinders [18150]
Military Toxics Proj. [5033]
Radioactive Waste Campaign - Defunct.
Radioactive Waste Mgt. Advisory Comm. [IO], London, United Kingdom
Radioactive Waste Safety; Natl. Campaign for [18130]
Radioassay Soc; Clinical [★14995]
Radiocommunication Bur. [IO], Geneva, Switzerland
Radiographers; Amer. Soc. of [★15131]
Radiographers; Assn. of Vascular and Interventional [16723]
Radiography; Australian Inst. of [IO]
Radiologic Technologists; Amer. Registry of [15128]
Radiologic Technologists; Amer. Soc. of [15131]
Radiologic Tech; Joint Rev. Comm. on Educ. in [8838]
Radiological Nurses Assn; Amer. [15457]
Radiological Sciences; Assn. of Educators in [★9096]
Radiological Soc. of North Am. [16293], 820 Jorie Blvd., Oak Brook, IL 60523, (630)571-2670
Radiological Soc. of the Republic of China [IO], Taipei, Taiwan
Radiological Technicians; Amer. Registry of [★15128]
Radiological Units; Intl. Commn. on [★5161]
Radiological Units; Intl. Comm. for [★5161]
Radiological Units and Measurements; Intl. Commn. on [★5161]
Radiologists; Amer. Soc. of Therapeutic [★16285]
Radiologists Bus. Managers Assn. [★15074]
Radiologists; Hong Kong Coll. of [IO]
Radiologists in Ultrasound; Soc. of [16303]
Radiology
Amer. Acad. of Oral and Maxillofacial Radiology [14104]
Amer. Assn. for Women Radiologists [16271]
Amer. Bd. of Radiology [16272]
Amer. Chiropractic Coll. of Radiology [13990]
Amer. Chiropractic Registry of Radiologic Technologists [16273]
Amer. Coll. of Radiation Oncology [16267]
Amer. Coll. of Radiology [16274]
Amer. Coll. of Veterinary Radiology [16770]
Amer. Healthcare Radiology Administrators [16275]
Amer. Osteopathic Coll. of Radiology [16276]
Amer. Radiological Nurses Assn. [15457]
Amer. Roentgen Ray Soc. [16277]
American Roentgen Ray Society [IO]
Amer. Soc. of Emergency Radiology [16278]
Amer. Soc. of Head and Neck Radiology [16279]
Amer. Soc. of Interventional and Therapeutic Neuroradiology [16280]
Amer. Soc. of Neuroimaging [16281]
Amer. Soc. of Neuroradiology [16282]
Amer. Soc. of Pediatric Neuroradiology [16283]
Amer. Soc. of Spine Radiology [16284]
Amer. Soc. for Therapeutic Radiology and Oncology [16285]
Assn. of Freestanding Radiation Oncology Centers [16268]
Assn. of Univ. Radiologists [16286]
British Inst. of Radiology [IO]
Canadian Assn. of Radiologists [IO]
Computerized Medical Imaging Soc. [16287]
Coun. on Diagnostic Imaging [16288]
Coun. on Ionizing Radiation Measurements and Standards [7556]
CyberKnife Soc. [16581]
Czech Radiological Soc. [IO]
Danish Assn. of Medical Imaging [IO]
European Assn. of Radiology [IO]

Reference to "IO" in place of a book number signifies that the association may be found in the 45th edition of International Organizations.

European Soc. of Head and Neck Radiology [IO]
European Soc. of Paediatric Radiology [IO]
European Soc. of Thoracic Imaging [IO]
European Soc. of Urogenital Radiology [IO]
Hellenic Radiological Soc. [IO]
Hong Kong Coll. of Radiologists [IO]
Indian Soc. of Neuroradiology [IO]
Indian Soc. of Vascular and Interventional Radiology [IO]
Intl. RadioSurgery Assn. [16269]
Intl. Skeletal Soc. [16289]
Intl. Skeletal Soc. [IO]
Intl. Soc. for Magnetic Resonance in Medicine [IO]
Intl. Soc. for Magnetic Resonance in Medicine [16290]
Intl. Soc. of Radiology [16291]
Intl. Soc. of Radiology [IO]
Italian Soc. of Radiology [IO]
Magnetic Resonance Managers Soc. [16292]
Medical Image Perception Soc. [15140]
Musculoskeletal Ultrasound Soc. [16696]
Radiological Soc. of North Am. [16293]
Radiology Bus. Mgt. Assn. [15074]
Radiology Mammography Intl. [13774]
Royal Australian and New Zealand Coll. of Radiologists [IO]
Royal Coll. of Radiologists - United Kingdom [IO]
Singapore Radiological Soc. [IO]
Soc. for the Advancement of Women's Imaging [16294]
Soc. of Breast Imaging [16295]
Soc. of Chairmen of Academic Radiology Departments [16296]
Soc. of Computed Body Tomography and Magnetic Resonance [16297]
Soc. of Gastrointestinal Radiologists [16298]
Soc. for Imaging Informatics in Medicine [16299]
Soc. of Interventional Radiology [16300]
Soc. for Pediatric Radiology [16301]
Soc. for Radiation Oncology Administrators [16302]
Soc. of Radiologists in Ultrasound [16303]
Soc. of Skeletal Radiology [16304]
Soc. of Thoracic Radiology [16305]
Soc. of Uroradiology [16717]
Soc. for Whole Body Autoradiography [15149]
World Fed. of Neuroradiological Societies [16306]
World Fed. of Neuroradiological Societies [IO]
Radiology Administrators; Amer. Hosp. [★16275]
Radiology; Amer. Acad. of Dental [★14104]
Radiology; Amer. Acad. of Oral and Maxillofacial [14104]
Radiology; Amer. Bd. of Veterinary [★16770]
Radiology; Amer. Chiropractic Coll. of [13990]
Radiology; Amer. Coll. of Veterinary [16770]
Radiology; Amer. Osteopathic Coll. of [16276]
Radiology; Amer. Soc. of Interventional and Therapeutic Neuro [16280]
Radiology; British Soc. for Dental and Maxillofacial [IO]
Radiology Bus. Mgt. Assn. [15074], 10300 Eaton Pl., Ste. 460, Fairfax, VA 22030, (703)621-3355
Radiology Info. Sys. Consortium [★16299]
Radiology Mammography Intl. [13774], c/o Dr. Richard N. Hirsh, MD, Founder, 1037 Robinwood Hills Dr., Akron, OH 44333, (330)375-3567
Radiology and Oncology; European Soc. for Therapeutic [IO]
Radiology; Soc. of Cardiovascular and Interventional [★16300]
Radiology Soc; Computerized [★16287]
Radionavigation
Intl. Loran Assn. [7370]
Intl. Miniature Aircraft Assn. [22938]
Radionic Assn. [IO], Banbury, United Kingdom
Radionics Assn; U.S. [★7454]
Radium Protection; Advisory Comm. on X-Ray and [★6242]
Radium Soc; Amer. [15639]
Radium and X-Ray Soc; Amer. Indus. [★7787]
Radix Inst. [13649], 3212 Monte Vista NE, Albuquerque, NM 87106-2120, (888)777-2349
Radix Teachers Assn. - Address unknown since 2000.

Radner Familial Ovarian Cancer Registry; Gilda [13826]
Radon Scientists and Technologists; Amer. Assn. of [7108]
RadTech Intl. North Am. [7558], 7986 Old George-town Rd., Unit 8D, Bethesda, MD 20814, (240)497-1242
RadTech Intl. North Am. [IO], Chevy Chase, MD, United States
RAFAD Found. [IO], Geneva, Switzerland
RAFI-USA [★IO]
RAFI-USA [★4108]
RagaMuffin Cat Lovers Soc. [22777], PO Box 1774, Orange Park, FL 32067-1774
Ragsdales of America - Address unknown since 1995.
Ragtime Festival Comm; Scott Joplin [★10694]
Ragtime Festival; Scott Joplin [★10694]
Ragtime Soc. - Address unknown since 1994.
Ragtime Soc; Bohemia [10568]
RAID Advisory Board - Defunct.
The Rail Archive - Defunct.
Rail Equity; Consumers United for [18289]
Rail Freight Gp. [IO], London, United Kingdom
Rail and Maritime Transport Union [IO], Wellington, New Zealand
Rail Shippers Advisory Boards; Natl. Assn. of [★3885]
Rail Shippers Assn; North Amer. [3885]
Rail Shippers; Natl. Assn. of [★3885]
Rail, Tram and Bus Union [IO], Redfern, Australia
Rail Travel Promotion Agency - Defunct.
Railfuture [IO], Leeds, United Kingdom
Railroad Advancement Through Information and Law Found. - Defunct.
Railroad Assn; Amer. Short Line [★3281]
Railroad Assn; Natl. Model [22636]
Railroad Constr. and Maintenance Assn. [★3287]
Railroad Enthusiasts [10919], PO Box 96, Peabody, MA 01960-0896
Railroad Enthusiasts; Natl. Assn. of [★10919]
Railroad Evangelistic Assn. - Address unknown since 1995.
Railroad Historical Soc; Illinois Central [10120]
Railroad Historical Soc; Ontario and Western [★10916]
Railroad Indus. Assn; Model [1912]
Railroad Insurance Rating Bur. - Defunct.
Railroad Museum; San Diego [★10918]
Railroad Public Relations Assn. - Defunct.
Railroad Res. Information Service - Defunct.
Railroad Sta. Historical Soc. [10920], c/o Jim Dent, Bus. Mgr., 26 Thackeray Rd., Oakland, NJ 07436-3312, (212)818-8085
Railroad Tie Producers; Natl. Assn. of [★3292]
Railroad Trainmen; Brotherhood of [★24181]
Railroad Transportation Insurers - Defunct.
Railroad Trial Counsel; Natl. Assn. of [6321]
Railroad Unit - ATA; Casey Jones [22800]
Railroad Unit; Casey Jones [★22800]
Railroad Yardmasters of Am. [★24181]
Railroader Club; Lionel [22634]
Railroaders; Teen Assn. of Model [22637]
Railroadiana Collectors Assn. Incorporated [22936], c/o Bob James, Pres., 17675 W 113th St., Olathe, KS 66061, (913)541-8568
Railroading; Teen Assn. of Model [★22637]
Railroads
Air Brake Assn. [3274]
All India Railwaymen's Fed. [IO]
Alliance for Rail Competition [3275]
Amer. Assn. of Private Railroad Car Owners [3276]
Amer. Assn. of Railroad Superintendents [3277]
Amer. Railway Car Inst. [3278]
Amer. Railway Development Assn. [3279]
Amer. Railway Development Assn. [IO]
American Railway Engineering and Maintenance of Way Association [IO]
Amer. Railway Engg. and Maintenance of Way Assn. [3280]
Amer. Short Line and Regional Railroad Assn. [3281]
Amer. Train Dispatchers Dept. of the BLE [24175]
Anthracite Railroads Historical Soc. [10907]

Assn. of Amer. Railroads [3282]
Assn. of Community Rail Partnerships [IO]
Assn. of Railway Museums [10908]
Assn. of Railway Training Providers [IO]
Associazione Nazionale Imprese Armamento Fer-roviario [IO]
Baltimore and Ohio Railroad Historical Soc. [10909]
Bluebell Railway Preservation Soc. [IO]
Bridge Line Historical Soc. [22932]
Brotherhood of Locomotive Engineers and Train-men, A Division of the Rail Conf. of the Intl. Brotherhood of Teamsters [24176]
Brotherhood of Locomotive Engineers and Train-men, A Division of the Rail Conf. of the Intl. Brotherhood of Teamsters [IO]
Brotherhood of Maintenance of Way Employees [24177]
Brotherhood of Railroad Signalmen [24178]
Brotherhood Railway Carmen Division/Transporta-tion Communications Union [24179]
Bytown Railway Soc. [IO]
Canadian Northern Soc. [IO]
Casey Jones Railroad Unit - ATA [22800]
Central Elec. Railfans' Assn. [22933]
Chesapeake and Ohio Historical Soc. [10910]
CN Lines Special Interest Gp. [IO]
Community of European Railways [IO]
Elec. Railroaders' Assn. [10911]
Elec. Railway Soc. [IO]
European Fed. of Museum and Tourist Railways [IO]
Forum Train Europe [IO]
Friends of the Valley Railroad [10912]
Fylde Tramway Soc. [IO]
German Assn. for Railroad-History [IO]
Highland Railway Soc. [IO]
Historical Model Railway Soc. [IO]
Horn and Whistle Enthusiasts Gp. [22037]
Intercontainer-Interfrigo [IO]
Intergovernmental Org. for Intl. Carriage by Rail [IO]
Intermodal Assn. of North Am. [3872]
Intl. Assn. of Railway Operations Res. [IO]
Intl. Rail Transport Comm. [IO]
Intl. Railroad and Transportation Postcard Collec-tors Club [22055]
Intl. Union of Private Wagons [IO]
Intl. Union of Railways [IO]
Irish Railway Record Soc. [IO]
Japan Confed. of Railway Workers' Unions [IO]
Japan Overseas Rolling Stock Assn. [IO]
Japan Railway Engineers Assn. [IO]
Latin Amer. Railway Assn. [IO]
Lexington Gp. in Trans. History [10913]
Lionel Railroader Club [22634]
Locomotive and Carriage Institution [IO]
Locomotive Maintenance Officers' Assn. [3283]
Marklin Digital Special Interest Gp. [22635]
Mid-Continent Railway Historical Soc. [22934]
Mobile Post Off. Soc. [22848]
Model Railroad Indus. Assn. [1912]
The Monorail Soc. [23007]
Mystic Valley Railway Soc. [10914]
Natl. Assn. of Railroad Passengers [3284]
Natl. Assn. of Railway Bus. Women [3285]
Natl. Assn. of Retired and Veteran Railway Employees [3286]
Natl. Assn. of Timetable Collectors [23008]
Natl. Model Railroad Assn. [22636]
Natl. Railroad Constr. and Maintenance Assn. [3287]
Natl. Railway Historical Soc. [10915]
Natl. Railway Labor Conf. [3288]
New Zealand Railway and Locomotive Soc. [IO]
North Amer. Rail Shippers Assn. [3885]
North Amer. Railcar Operators Assn. [3886]
Northwest Steam Soc. [22978]
Ontario and Western Railway Historical Soc. [10916]
Oper. Lifesaver [12983]
Org. for the Cooperation of Railways [IO]
Pacific Railroad Soc. [10917]
Pacific Southwest Railway Museum [10918]
Permanent Way Institution [IO]

A star before a book entry number signifies that the name is not listed separately, but is mentioned within the entry.

Pine Creek Railroad [22935]
Rail Freight Gp. [IO]
Rail and Maritime Transport Union [IO]
Railfuture [IO]
Railroad Enthusiasts [10919]
Railroad Sta. Historical Soc. [10920]
Railroadiana Collectors Assn. Incorporated [22936]
Rails-to-Trails Conservancy [23952]
Railtrails Australia [IO]
Railway Assn. of Canada [IO]
Railway Canal Historical Soc. [IO]
Railway Correspondence and Travel Soc. [IO]
Railway Engineering-Maintenance Suppliers Association [IO]
Railway Engineering-Maintenance Suppliers Assn. [3289]
Railway Enthusiasts Soc. [IO]
Railway Indus. Clearance Assn. [3891]
Railway Indus. Assn. [IO]
Railway and Locomotive Historical Soc. [10921]
Railway Supply Inst. [3290]
Railway Systems Suppliers, Inc. [3291]
Railway Tech. Soc. of Australasia [IO]
Railway Tie Assn. [3292]
Rough and Tumble Engineers' Historical Assn. [22979]
Soc. of Freight Car Historians [10922]
Soo Line Historical and Tech. Soc. [10923]
Spokane, Portland and Seattle Railway Historical Soc. [10924]
Steam Plough Club [IO]
Steamship Historical Soc. of Am. [22980]
Stephenson Locomotive Soc. [IO]
Talyllyn Railway Preservation Soc. [IO]
Teen Assn. of Model Railroaders [22637]
Terminal Railroad Assn. Historical and Tech. Soc. [10925]
Texas Date Nail Collectors Assn. [22121]
Tourist Railway Assn. [3293]
Tourist Railway Assn. [IO]
Toy Train Collectors Soc. [22638]
Toy Train Operating Soc. [22639]
Train Collectors Assn. [22640]
Tramway and Light Railway Soc. [IO]
Transport Museum Assn. [10926]
Transport Workers Union of Am. [24200]
Trans. Clubs Intl. [3896]
Trans. Communications Intl. Union [24180]
Truckload Carriers Assn. [3899]
Union of European Railway Indus. [IO]
United Trans. Union [24181]
Wabash, Frisco and Pacific Assn. [10927]
World War Two Railway Study Group [IO]
Rails-to-Trails Conservancy [23952], 1100 17th St. NW, 10th Fl., Washington, DC 20036, (202)331-9696
Railsplitter Soc; 84th Infantry Div., [21367]
Railton Owners Club [IO], Whitstable, United Kingdom
Railtrails Australia [IO], East Melbourne, Australia
Railway, Airline and Steamship Clerks, Freight Handlers, Express and Sta. Employees; Brotherhood of [★24180]
Railway, Airline and Steamship Clerks, Freight Handlers, Express and Sta. Employees; Carmen Division of the Brotherhood of [★24179]
Railway and Airline Supervisors Assn; Amer. [★24180]
Railway Assn. of Canada [IO], Ottawa, ON, Canada
Railway Automotive Mgt. Assn. - Defunct.
Railway Bridge and Building Assn; Amer. [★3280]
Railway Bus. Assn. [★3290]
Railway Bus. Women's Assn. [★3285]
Railway Canal Historical Soc. [IO], Oxford, United Kingdom
Railway Car Mfrs. Assn. [★3278]
Railway Carmen of Am; Brotherhood [★24179]
Railway Carmen; Brotherhood [★24180]
Railway Carmen of the U.S. and Canada; Brotherhood [★24179]
Railway Children [IO], Cheshire, United Kingdom
Railway Commissioners; Natl. Assn. of [★6339]
Railway Communications Suppliers Assn. [★3291]
Railway Conductors and Brakemen; Order of [★24181]

Railway Correspondence and Travel Soc. [IO], Slough, United Kingdom
Railway Development Soc. [★IO]
Railway Employees Dept. of AFL-CIO - Defunct.
Railway Employees; Natl. Assn. of Retired and Veteran [★3286]
Railway Engg. and Maintenance Assn; Amer. [★3280]
Railway Engineering-Maintenance Suppliers Assn. [★3289]
Railway Engineering-Maintenance Suppliers Assn. [3289], 417 W Broad St., Ste. 203, Falls Church, VA 22046, (703)241-8514
Railway Engineering-Maintenance Suppliers Assn. [★IO]
Railway Engineering-Maintenance Suppliers Association [IO], Falls Church, VA, United States
Railway Enthusiasts Soc. [IO], Auckland, New Zealand
Railway Gen. Foremen's Associations; Intl. [★3283]
Railway Historical Soc. of Milwaukee [★22934]
Railway Historical Soc; St. Louis [★10926]
Railway Indus. Clearance Assn. [3891], c/o Michael R. Scott, Sec.-Treas., 6119 Hampton Way Ct., Spring, TX 77389, (832)585-3854
Railway and Industrial Spring Res. Inst. - Defunct.
Railway Indus. Assn. [IO], London, United Kingdom
Railway Indus. Clearance Assn. [★3891]
Railway Insurance Rating Bur. - Defunct.
Railway Labor Executives' Assn. - Defunct.
Railway and Locomotive Historical Soc. [10921], c/o William H. Lugg, Jr., Membership Sec., PO Box 292927, Sacramento, CA 95829-2927, (916)383-4711
Railway and Locomotive Historical Soc; Lancaster (Pennsylvania) [★10915]
Railway and Motor Coach Employees of Am; Amalgamated Assn. of St., Elec. [★24197]
Railway Museum; San Diego County [★10918]
Railway Patrolmen's Intl. Union [★24180]
Railway Preservation Soc. of Ireland [IO], Larne, United Kingdom
Railway Progress Inst. [★3290]
Railway Signal and Communications Suppliers Assn. [★3291]
Railway and Steamship Clerks, Freight Handlers, Express and Sta. Employees; Brotherhood of [★24180]
Railway Supervisors Assn; Western [★24180]
Railway Supply Assn. [★3290]
Railway Supply Inst. [3290], 29W 140 Butterfield Rd., Ste. 103-A, Warrenville, IL 60555, (630)393-0106
Railway Systems and Mgt. Assn. - Defunct.
Railway Systems Suppliers, Inc. [3291], 9304 New LaGrange Rd., Ste. 200, Louisville, KY 40242-3671, (502)327-7774
Railway Tech. Soc. of Australasia [IO], Kingston, Australia
Railway Tie Assn. [3292], 115 Commerce Dr., Ste. C, Fayetteville, GA 30214-7335, (770)460-5553
Railway and Utilities Commissioners; Natl. Assn. of [★6339]
Railway Wheel Assn. - Defunct.

Rain Forests
Africa Rainforest and River Conservation [4341]
Amazon Alliance [4531]
Amazonian Proj. [IO]
Bank Info. Center [468]
Intl. Soc. for Preservation of the Tropical Rainforest [5162]
Intl. Soc. for Preservation of the Tropical Rainforest [IO]
Pachamama Alliance [5163]
Rainforest Action Network [4441]
Rainforest Relief [5164]
Rain and Hail Insurance Bur. - Defunct.
Rainbow Alliance of the Deaf [12255], c/o Steven Schumacher, Sec., 9804 Walker House Rd., No. 4, Montgomery Village, MD 20886-0506
Rainbow Bridge Org. - Address unknown since 1999.
Rainbow Celebration of Hope Network [15297], PO Box 20621, Houston, TX 77225-0621, (866)849-3853

Rainbow Div. Veterans Memorial Found. [21419], c/o Mrs. Suellen McDaniel, Natl. Membership Off., 1400 Knolls Dr., Newton, NC 28658-9452, (828)464-1466
Rainbow Div. Veterans; Natl. Assn. [★21419]
Rainbow Lobby - Defunct.
Rainbow Network - Address unknown since 1999.
Rainbow/PUSH Coalition [13185], 930 E 50th St., Chicago, IL 60615-2702, (773)373-3366
Rainbow Rsrc. Centre: Serving Manitoba's Gay, Lesbian, Bisexual, Transgendered, and Two-Spirited Communities [IO], Winnipeg, MB, Canada
Rainbowfish Study Group of North Am. [IO], Dayton, MN, United States
Rainbowfish Study Group of North Am. [22446], c/o Cary Hostrawser, Show Sanctioning Coor., 12920 Zachary Cir. N; Dayton, MN 55327, (612)422-9446
RAINBOWS [11718], 2100 Golf Rd., No. 370, Rolling Meadows, IL 60008-4231, (847)952-1770
RAINBOWS [IO], Rolling Meadows, IL, United States
Rainbows for All God's Children [★IO]
Rainbows for All God's Children [★11718]
Rainforest Action Gp; Big Island [4366]
Rainforest Action Network [4441], 221 Pine St., 5th Fl., San Francisco, CA 94104, (415)398-4404
Rainforest Action Network [IO], San Francisco, CA, United States
Rainforest Alliance [IO], New York, NY, United States
Rainforest Alliance [4442], 665 Broadway, Ste. 500, New York, NY 10012, (212)677-1900
Rainforest Alliance; New York [★4442]
Rainforest Info. Centre [IO], Lismore, Australia
Rainforest Relief [5164], PO Box 298, New York, NY 10008-0298, (917)543-4064
Rainier Soc. [21145], Chateaux L'Aiglon, 31 rue Royale, Ste. E, Kettering, OH 45429-1474, (937)299-9896
Rainwater Catchment Systems Assn; Amer. [7825]
Rainwater Catchment Systems Assn; Intl. [7832]
Rainwear Manufacturers Assn; New England [★221]
Raisin Administrative Comm. [4758], PO Box 5217, Fresno, CA 93755, (559)225-0520
Raisin Bargaining Assn. [4759], 1300 E Shaw Ave., Ste. 175, Fresno, CA 93710-7911, (559)221-1925
Raising Voices [IO], Kampala, Uganda
Raissa Tselentis Memorial Johann Sebastian Bach Intl. Competitions [IO], Herndon, VA, United States
Raissa Tselentis Memorial Johann Sebastian Bach Intl. Competitions [10690], c/o James Marra, Dir., 569 Legacy Pride Dr., Herndon, VA 20170, (703)787-9652
Raitliuden Ystavat [★IO]
Rajagiri Outreach Ser. Soc. [IO], Kochi, India
Rakennusliitto [★IO]
Rallying Points [14083]
Ralph Shepard Family Org. [21030], 1672 Forests Ct. NE, Atlanta, GA 30341, (770)457-6644
Ralph Waldo Emerson Memorial Assn. [9706]
Ralph Waldo Emerson Study Group - Defunct.
Ralston Family Assn; Holloway - [20943]
Ramakrishna Order of India [★20610]
Ramakrishna - Vivekananda Center [20610], 17 E 94th St., New York, NY 10128, (212)534-9445
Ramallah, Palestine; Amer. Fed. of [9392]
Rambler Club; AMC [21567]
Rambler Recreational Vehicle Club; Holiday [22954]
Ramblers' Assn. [IO], London, United Kingdom
Rambouillet Sheep Breeders' Assn; Amer. [5192]
Rampart Inst. - Address unknown since 2007.
Ramsay Clan Soc. - Address unknown since 1999.
Ramsey Assn. of North Am; Clan [20858]
Ranch Bus. Mgt. Educ. Assn; Natl. Farm and [4639]
Ranch HQ Assn. [★10148]
Ranch Horse Assn; Amer. [4841]
The Ranchero Club - Address unknown since 2001.
Ranchers' Assn; Dude [1940]
Ranchers Assn; Montana Outfitters and Dude [★23944]
Ranchers-Cattlemen Action Legal Fund, United Stockgrowers of Am. [4290], PO Box 30715, Billings, MT 59107, (406)252-2516
Ranchers for Peace - Defunct.
Ranching Heritage Assn. [10148], c/o Whitney Barron, Bus. Mgr., PO Box 43201, Lubbock, TX 79409-3201, (806)742-0497

Reference to "IO" in place of a book number signifies that the association may be found in the 45th edition of International Organizations.

Ranching Heritage Center [★10148]
Ranching Info. Coun; North Amer. Equine [1926]
Rand Inst; Ayn [10787]
Rand Soc; Ayn [10788]
Randolph Educal. Fund; A. Philip [17078]
Randolph Inst; A. Philip [18604]
Randolph Intl. Public Works Fellowship; Eisenhower/
Jennings [★18442]
Randolph Intl. Public Works Fellowship; Eisenhower/
Jennings [★IO]
Randolph-Sheppard Vendors of Am. [3973], 1808
Faith Pl., Ste. B, Terrytown, LA 70056-4104,
(504)368-7785
Randonneurs USA [23316], c/o Mark Thomas,
Pres., 13543 160th Ave. NE, Redmond, WA 98052,
(206)612-4700
Randy Floyd Fan Club - Address unknown since
1989.
Randy Travis Fan Club - Address unknown since
2001.
Randy Wade Fan Club - Address unknown since
2007.
Ranfurly Lib. Ser. [★IO]
Range Assn; Western [5220]
Range Mgt; Amer. Soc. of [★5166]
Range Mgt; Intl. Soc. for [★5166]
Range; Stewards of the [18381]
Rangeland
    Amer. Forage and Grassland Coun. [5165]
    Amer. Wildlands [4354]
    Ecological Soc. of Am. [4506]
    Soc. for Range Mgt. [5166]
    Working Ranch Cowboys Assn. [3294]
Ranger Assn; U.S. Army [20707]
Ranger Horse Assn; Colorado [4873]
Ranger Regimental Assn. - Address unknown since
1995.
Rangerettes; Rangers and [★19440]
Rangers Fan Club [★25010]
Rangers Fan Club; New York [25010]
Rangers and Rangerettes [★19440]
Rangers; Woodmen [19440]
Rangpur Dinajpur Rural Ser. Bangladesh [IO],
Dhaka, Bangladesh
Rank and File [IO], Montreal, QC, Canada
Rannsoknarrad Islands [★IO]
Raoul Wallenberg Comm. [IO], Stockholm, Sweden
Raoul Wallenberg Committee of the United States
[IO], New York, NY, United States
Raoul Wallenberg Comm. of the U.S. [17449], 230
Park Ave., 7th Fl., New York, NY 10169, (212)499-
2695
Raoul Wallenberg Kommitten [★IO]
Raoul Wallenberg Working Group [★IO]
Raoul Wallenberg Working Group [★17449]
Rape
    Canadian Assn. of Sexual Assault Centres [IO]
    Communities Against Violence Network [13374]
    LifeWorks Inst. [12551]
    Male Survivor: The Natl. Org. Against Male
        Sexual Victimization [13077]
    Molesters Anonymous [13024]
    Natl. CH on Marital and Date Rape [12790]
    Natl. Collective of Rape Crisis and Related
        Groups of Aotearoa [IO]
    Natl. Sexual Violence Rsrc. Center [13080]
    Paul and Lisa Prog. [13082]
    People Against Rape [13083]
    Rape, Abuse and Incest Natl. Network [12791]
    Stop it Now! [11653]
    Survivors of Incest Anonymous [13085]
    TransAct - Dutch Center for Gender Issues in
        Healthcare and Prevention of Sexual Violence
        [IO]
    VOICES in Action [13086]
    We Are AWARE [13442]
    Women in Crisis [13443]
    Women in Transition [13447]
    Women for Women [12792]
Rape, Abuse and Incest Natl. Network [12791], 2000
L St. NW, Ste. 406, Washington, DC 20036,
(202)544-1034
Rape of Imprisoned Persons; People Organized to
Stop [★11894]
Rape; People Against [13083]

Rape; Stop Prisoner [11894]
Rapha Intl. [12539], 402 Blue Smoke Ct. W, Fort
Worth, TX 76105, (817)536-3383
Rapid Technologies and Additive Mfg. Community
[7267], c/o SME, PO Box 930, Dearborn, MI
48121, (313)271-1500
Rapid Transit Guerrilla Communications - Defunct.
RapidIO Trade Assn. [889], 12343 Hymeadow Dr.,
Ste. 2R, Austin, TX 78750, (512)401-2900
Rapier Registry of North Am; Sunbeam [★21793]
Rapier Registry; Sunbeam [21793]
RAPRA Tech. [IO], Shrewsbury, United Kingdom
Raptor Conservation; Western Found. for [★7419]
Raptor Educ. Found. [5371], PO Box 200400,
Denver, CO 80220, (303)680-8500
Raptor Rehabilitation and Propagation Proj. [★5403]
Raptor Rehabilitation and Propagation Proj. [★IO]
Raptor Res. Found. [5372], c/o Leonard Young,
Pres., 1640 Oriole Ln. NW, Olympia, WA 98502-
4342, (360)943-7394
RARE [5373], 1840 Wilson Blvd., Ste. 204,
Arlington, VA 22201, (703)522-5070
Rare Animal Relief Effort [★5373]
Rare Breed Assn; Amer. [4496]
Rare Breeds Canada [IO], Castleton, ON, Canada
Rare Breeds Poultry Club of America - Address
unknown since 1995.
RARE Center [★5373]
Rare Center for Tropical Bird Conservation [★5373]
RARE Center for Tropical Conservation [★5373]
Rare Disorders; Natl. Org. for [14282]
Rare-Earth Information Center - Defunct.
Rare Earth Res. Conf. - Address unknown since
2005.
Rare Fruit Coun. [★4760]
Rare Fruit Coun. [★IO]
Rare Fruit Coun. Intl. [IO], Miami Springs, FL, United
States
Rare Fruit Coun. Intl. [4760], PO Box 660506, Miami
Springs, FL 33266, (305)554-1333
Rare Fruit Growers; California [4719]
Raskob Found; Bill [17479]
Raskob Found. for Catholic Activities [19706], PO
Box 4019, Wilmington, DE 19807-0019, (302)655-
4440
Raskob Found. for Catholic Activities [IO], Wilming-
ton, DE, United States
Raspberry Award Found; Golden [22419]
Raspberry Indus. Development Coun. [IO], Abbots-
ford, BC, Canada
Rassemblement des Amateurs de Levriers d'Irlande
et d'Ecosse [IO], Rochegude, France
Rat Assistance and Teaching Soc. [22778], 857
Lindo Ln., Chico, CA 95973, (530)899-0605
Rat Fan Club [22706], 857 Lindo Ln., Chico, CA
95973, (530)899-0605
Rat fur Formgebung [★IO]
Rat and Mouse Assn; Amer. Fancy [22704]
Rat and Mouse Club of Am. [22707], 6082 Modoc
Rd., Westminster, CA 92683
Rat, Mouse, and Hamster Fanciers [22708], 783
Solana Dr., Lafayette, CA 94549
Rat and Mouse Info; Fitzgerald's Fancys: [22705]
Rat Soc; Roo [5375]
Rat Terrier Club of Am. [22350], 47044 5th St. W,
Lancaster, CA 93534-7501, (661)945-5663
Rathkamp Matchcover Soc. [22626], 1509 S Dugan
Rd., Urbana, OH 43078-9209
Rating Bur; Towner [★2245]
Rating and Certification Corp; Solar [7681]
Rating Coun; Broadcast [★566]
Rating Coun; Media [566]
Rating Surveyors' Assn. [IO], Manchester, United
Kingdom
Ration Stamp and Book Collecting [★22759]
Ration Token Collectors; Soc. of [22759]
Rational Community AIDS Partnership [★13576]
Rational Economics and Educ; Found. for [17293]
Rational Living; Inst. for [★16197]
Rational Recovery Systems [16516], PO Box 800,
Lotus, CA 95651, (530)621-2667
Ratisbonne Center - Defunct.
Ratkaisiya Kansainvalistymiseen [★IO]
Raueddi kross Islands [★IO]
Rauma Chamber of Commerce [IO], Rauma,
Finland

Rauman Kauppakamari [★IO]
Rav Tov Comm. to Aid New Immigrants [★IO]
Rav Tov Comm. to Aid New Immigrants [★12817]
Rav Tov Intl. Jewish Rescue Org. [12817], 500 Bed-
ford Ave., Brooklyn, NY 11211, (718)963-1991
Rav Tov Intl. Jewish Rescue Org. [IO], Brooklyn, NY,
United States
Ravan Fan Club - Defunct.
Raven Fan Club; Eddy [24882]
Raw Materials; Natl. Org. for [16957]
Rawalt Rsrc. Center; Marguerite [★11084]
Rawhide and Leather Braiders Assn. - Address
unknown since 1999.
Rawlin(g)s-Rollin(g)s Family History Assn. - Defunct.
Ray Coble Fan Club - Defunct.
Ray Fan Club; Aldo [24726]
Ray Griff Fan Club - Defunct.
Ray Heatherton Irish Friends Club - Defunct.
Ray Helfer Soc. [13976], c/o Kent P. Hymel, MD,
VP, Inova Fairfax Hosp. for Children, The Pediatric
FACT Center, 3300 Gallows Rd., Falls Church, VA
22042-3300, (703)970-2630
Ray of Hope [13291], 2778 Snapfinger Rd., Decatur,
GA 30034, (770)696-5100
Ray Price; Fans and Friends of [★24963]
Ray Price Intl. Fan Club [24963], c/o Sandra Orwig,
Pres., 4205 Catalina Ln., Harrisburg, PA 17109
Ray Soc. [IO], London, United Kingdom
Raymond Intl. Registry; Caitlin [13770]
Raynaud's Assn. Trust [★IO]
Raynaud's and Scleroderma Assn. [IO], Alsager,
United Kingdom
Raynaud's and Scleroderma Soc; Irish [IO]
Raza Unida Party - Address unknown since 1995.
Razor Collectors Guild; Safety [22113]
Razzie Awards [★22419]
Razzy Bailey Fan Club [24964], PO Box 727,
Goodlettsville, TN 37070-0727, (615)884-0901
RC-Unionen [IO], Lystrup, Denmark
RCA Computer Users Assn. - Defunct.
RDMA Consortium [7759], c/o Joseph Mouhanna,
Microsoft Corp., 1 Microsoft Way, Redmond, WA
98052, (425)706-7421
Re-Formed Congregation of the Goddess - Intl.
[20623], PO Box 6677, Madison, WI 53716,
(608)226-9998
Re-Geniusing Project - Defunct.
Re-Solv, the Soc. for the Prevention of Solvent and
Volatile Substance Abuse [IO], Stone, United
Kingdom
REACH: Assn. for Children with Hand or Arm
Deficiency [IO], Cornwall, United Kingdom
Reach the Children [IO], Fairport, NY, United States
Reach the Children [11649], PO Box 1208, Fairport,
NY 14450, (585)223-3344
Reach Ireland [IO], Dublin, Ireland
Reach Out [IO], Buea, Cameroon
Reach-Out Intl. [IO], Baton Rouge, LA, United
States
Reach-Out Intl. [17994], 1968 Wooddale Ct., Baton
Rouge, LA 70806-1526, (225)928-3123
Reach Out To Help [★21200]
Reach Out for Youth with Ileitis and Colitis [16548],
84 Northgate Cir., Melville, NY 11747, (631)293-
3102
Reach to Recovery [13868], c/o Amer. Cancer Soc.,
PO Box 22718, Oklahoma City, OK 73123-1718,
(800)ACS-2345
Reach to Recovery Found. [★13792]
Reaching Critical Will [17436], c/o Women's Intl.
League for Peace and Freedom, 777 UN Plz., New
York, NY 10017, (212)682-1265
ReachOut - A Community Intervention - Address
unknown since 1999.
REACT [★6254]
REACT [★6254]
REACT [★IO]
REACT [★IO]
REACT Intl. [IO], Suitland, MD, United States
REACT Intl. [6254], 5210 Auth Rd., No. 403, Suit-
land, MD 20746-4393, (301)316-2900
REACT Intl.: CB Radio Coalition Against Drunk Driv-
ing - Defunct.
Reaction Missile Res. Soc. - Defunct.
Reactor Operator Soc; Professional [7391]

A star before a book entry number signifies that the name is not listed separately, but is mentioned within the entry.

Reactors; Natl. Org. of Test, Res., and Training [7388]
Read Found; Freedom to [17040]
Read Natural Childbirth Found. - Address unknown since 2005.
Read; Room to [12053]
Reader's Digest Assn. [3250], Reader's Digest Rd., Pleasantville, NY 10570-7000, (914)244-5425
Reader's Digest Funds; Wallace- [12055]
Readers Intl; Mystery [24823]
Reading
    Academic Language Therapy Assn. [12488]
    Assn. of Book Gp. Readers and Leaders [9738]
    Center for the Book [10417]
    Coll. Reading and Learning Assn. [9042]
    Freedom to Read Found. [17040]
    Intl. Reading Assn. [9043]
    Intl. Reading Assn. [IO]
    Natl. Braille Assn. [16875]
    Natl. Reading Conf. [9044]
    Natl. Right to Read Found. [9045]
    Philomathean Soc. of the Univ. of Pennsylvania [10429]
    Phonics Inst. [9046]
    PlanetRead [8796]
    Reading Is Fundamental [9047]
    Reading Recovery Coun. of North Am. [9048]
    Reading Recovery Coun. of North Am. [IO]
    ReREAD [12299]
    Rolling Readers [12502]
    Seedlings Braille Books for Children [9297]
    Single Booklovers [22142]
    Soc. for the History of Authorship, Reading and Publishing [9754]
    Story Circle Network [10985]
Reading Assn; Western Coll. [★9042]
Reading Indus. Assn; Magnetic [★1212]
Reading and Instruction; Intl. Coun. for the Improvement of [★9043]
Reading Is Fundamental [9047], 1825 Connecticut Ave. NW, Ste. 400, Washington, DC 20009, (202)536-3400
Reading and Learning Assn; Coll. [9042]
Reading and Learning Assn; Western Coll. [★9042]
Reading and Publishing; Soc. for the History of Authorship, [9754]
Reading Recovery Coun. of North Am. [9048], 400 W Wilson Bridge Rd., Ste. 250, Worthington, OH 43085-5218, (614)310-7323
Reading Recovery Coun. of North Am. [IO], Worthington, OH, United States
Reading Reform Found. [★9046]
Readjustment Counseling Program [★21308]
Reagan Alumni Assn. [18365], 122 S Royal St., Alexandria, VA 22314-3328, (703)461-7250
Reagan Appointees Alumni Assn. [★18365]
Reagan Home Preservation Found; Ronald [11147]
Reagan Political Items Collectors - Address unknown since 1999.
Reagan Restoration and Preservation Assn; Ronald [★11147]
Reagan for Shah Campaign - Defunct.
Real Americans Buy Amer. Cars - Defunct.
Real Estate
    Accredited Rev. Appraisers Coun. [269]
    AIR Commercial Real Estate Assn. [3295]
    Alberta Real Estate Assn. [IO]
    Amer. Escrow Assn. [1398]
    Amer. Homeowners Found. [3296]
    Amer. Land Title Assn. [3297]
    Amer. Railway Development Assn. [3279]
    Amer. Real Estate Soc. [9049]
    Amer. Real Estate and Urban Economics Assn. [9050]
    Amer. Resort Development Assn. [3298]
    Appraisal Inst. of Canada [IO]
    Architects/Designers/Planners for Social Responsibility [18142]
    Asian Amer. Real Estate Assn. [3299]
    Assn. of Belgian Relocation Agents [IO]
    Assn. of Chief Estate Surveyors and Property Managers in Local Govt. [IO]
    Assn. of Foreign Investors in Real Estate [2328]
    Assn. of Home Info. Pack Providers [IO]
    Assn. of Real Estate Companies of Estonia [IO]

    Assn. of Real Estate License Law Officials [IO]
    Assn. of Real Estate License Law Officials [6243]
    Assn. of Real Estate Women [3300]
    Assn. of Relocation Professionals [IO]
    Assn. of Residential Letting Agents [IO]
    Assn. of Residential Managing Agents [IO]
    Assn. of Valuers of Licensed Property [IO]
    Bahamas Real Estate Assn. [IO]
    British Property Fed. [IO]
    Building Owners and Managers Assn. Intl. [IO]
    Building Owners and Managers Assn. Intl. [3301]
    Building Professionals' Consortium [IO]
    Canadian Real Estate Assn. [IO]
    Cayman Islands Real Estate Brokers Assn. [IO]
    CCIM Inst. [IO]
    CCIM Inst. [3302]
    Certified Exchangors [3303]
    Commercial Mortgage Securities Assn. [3304]
    Community Economics, Inc. [12308]
    CoreNet Global [3305]
    CoreNet Global [IO]
    Coun. of Intl. Restaurant Real Estate Brokers [3392]
    Coun. of Real Estate Brokerage Managers [3306]
    Coun. of Real Estate Brokerage Managers [IO]
    Coun. of Residential Specialists [3307]
    Counselors of Real Estate [3308]
    Counselors of Real Estate [IO]
    CREW Network [3309]
    European Confed. of Real Estate Agents [IO]
    European Real Estate Soc. [IO]
    European Relocation Assn. [IO]
    Fed. of Overseas Property Developers, Agents and Consultants [IO]
    FIABCI - Andorra [IO]
    FIABCI - Argentina [IO]
    FIABCI - Australia [IO]
    FIABCI - Austria [IO]
    FIABCI - Brazil [IO]
    FIABCI - Bulgaria [IO]
    FIABCI - Canada [IO]
    FIABCI - Colombia [IO]
    FIABCI - Costa Rica [IO]
    FIABCI - Cyprus [IO]
    FIABCI - Czech Republic [IO]
    FIABCI - Dominican Republic [IO]
    FIABCI - Finland [IO]
    FIABCI - Georgia [IO]
    FIABCI - German Chap. [IO]
    FIABCI - Greece [IO]
    FIABCI - Hungary [IO]
    FIABCI - Indonesia [IO]
    FIABCI - Ireland [IO]
    FIABCI - Israel [IO]
    FIABCI - Italy [IO]
    FIABCI - Japan [IO]
    FIABCI - Korea [IO]
    FIABCI - Latvia [IO]
    FIABCI - Luxembourg [IO]
    FIABCI - Malaysia [IO]
    FIABCI - Mexico [IO]
    FIABCI - Monaco [IO]
    FIABCI - Netherlands [IO]
    FIABCI - Nigeria [IO]
    FIABCI - Norway [IO]
    FIABCI - Panama [IO]
    FIABCI - Philippines Intl. [IO]
    FIABCI - Portugal [IO]
    FIABCI - Russia [IO]
    FIABCI - Singapore [IO]
    FIABCI - Slovenia [IO]
    FIABCI - Spain [IO]
    FIABCI - Sweden [IO]
    FIABCI - Switzerland [IO]
    FIABCI - Taiwan [IO]
    FIABCI - Thailand [IO]
    FIABCI - Turkey [IO]
    FIABCI - United Kingdom [IO]
    FIABCI - Uruguay [IO]
    FIABCI-U.S.A. - U.S. Chap., Intl. Real Estate Fed. [3310]
    Found. of Real Estate Appraisers [280]
    French Fed. of Building [IO]
    Hong Kong Inst. of Real Estate [IO]
    Hotel Brokers Intl. [IO]

    Hotel Brokers Intl. [3311]
    Hungarian Real Estate Assn. [IO]
    Inst. of Real Estate Mgt. [3312]
    Intl. Accrediting Commn. for Real Estate and Appraisal Educ. and Training [3313]
    Intl. Accrediting Commn. for Real Estate and Appraisal Educ. and Training [IO]
    International Association of Attorneys and Executives in Corporate Real Estate [IO]
    Intl. Assn. of Attorneys and Executives in Corporate Real Estate [3314]
    Intl. Assn. of Home Staging Professionals [2261]
    Intl. Bus. Brokers Assn. [3315]
    Intl. Bus. Brokers Assn. [IO]
    Intl. Real Estate Fed. - France [IO]
    Intl. Real Estate Inst. [IO]
    Intl. Real Estate Inst. [3316]
    Intl. Right of Way Assn. [6246]
    Irish Auctioneers' and Valuers' Inst. [IO]
    Lithuanian Real Estate Development Assn. [IO]
    Natl. Apartment Assn. [3317]
    Natl. Assn. of Certified Home Inspectors [2121]
    Natl. Assn. of Counselors [3318]
    Natl. Assn. of Exclusive Buyer Agents [18495]
    Natl. Assn. of Hispanic Real Estate Professionals [3319]
    Natl. Assn. of Indus. and Off. Properties [3320]
    Natl. Assn. of Master Appraisers [3321]
    Natl. Assn. of Media Brokers [3322]
    Natl. Assn. of Real Estate Appraisers [285]
    Natl. Assn. of Real Estate Brokers [3323]
    Natl. Assn. of Real Estate Buyer Brokers [3324]
    Natl. Assn. of Real Estate Companies [IO]
    Natl. Assn. of Real Estate Editors [3132]
    Natl. Assn. of Real Estate Investment Managers [3326]
    Natl. Assn. of Real Estate Investment Trusts [3327]
    Natl. Assn. of Real Estate Offices of Slovakia [IO]
    Natl. Assn. of Realtors [3328]
    Natl. Assn. of Rev. Appraisers and Mortgage Underwriters [3329]
    Natl. Assn. of Screening Agencies [3330]
    Natl. Assn. of Senior Move Managers [2523]
    Natl. Coun. of Exchangors [3331]
    Natl. Fed. of Residential Landlords [IO]
    Natl. Landlords Assn. [IO]
    Natl. Multi Housing Coun. [3332]
    Natl. Real Estate Investors Assn. [2347]
    Natl. Residential Appraisers Inst. [3333]
    Natl. Retail Tenants Assn. [3383]
    Natl. Soc. of Environmental Consultants [3334]
    Pension Real Estate Assn. [3335]
    Property Consultants Soc. [IO]
    Property Mgt. Assn. [3336]
    Real Estate Buyer's Agent Coun. [3337]
    Real Estate Developers' Assn. of Singapore [IO]
    Real Estate Educators Assn. [3338]
    Real Estate Info. Professionals Assn. [3339]
    Real Estate Inst. of Canada [IO]
    Real Estate Inst. of Zimbabwe [IO]
    Real Estate Roundtable [3340]
    Real Estate Services Providers Coun. [3341]
    Real Property Assn. of Canada [IO]
    Realtors Land Inst. [3342]
    Scottish Rural Property and Bus. Assn. [IO]
    Soc. of Indus. and Off. Realtors [3343]
    Soc. of Trust and Estate Practitioners USA [1332]
    Vacation Rental Managers Assn. [3344]
    Women's Coun. of Realtors [3345]
Real Estate Advisory Coun; Employee Relocation [★1261]
Real Estate Appraisers; Amer. Inst. of [★275]
Real Estate Appraisers; Natl. Assn. of [285]
Real Estate Appraisers; National Soc. of [★3323]
Real Estate Appraisers; Soc. of [★275]
Real Estate; Assn. of Foreign Investors in U.S. [★2328]
Real Estate Aviation Chap. - Defunct.
Real Estate Boards; Natl. Assn. of [★3328]
Real Estate Brokerage Coun. [★3306]
Real Estate Brokerage Coun. [★IO]
Real Estate Brokerage Institute [★3323]
Real Estate Brokerage Managers Coun. [★3306]
Real Estate Brokerage Managers Coun. [★IO]

Reference to "IO" in place of a book number signifies that the association may be found in the 45th edition of International Organizations.

Real Estate Buyer's Agent Coun. [3337], 430 N Michigan Ave., Chicago, IL 60611, (312)329-8656
Real Estate Coun. - Defunct.
Real Estate Counselors; Amer. Soc. of [★3308]
Real Estate Developers' Assn. of Singapore [IO], Singapore, Singapore
Real Estate Editors; Natl. Assn. of [3132]
Real Estate Editors; Natl. Conf. of [★3132]
Real Estate Educators Assn. [3338], 19 Mantua Rd., Mount Royal, NJ 08061, (856)423-3215
Real Estate Exchanges; Natl. Assn. of [★3328]
Real Estate Executives; Intl. Assn. of Corporate [★3305]
Real Estate Executives; Natl. Assn. of Corporate [★3305]
Real Estate Fed; Amer. Chap., Intl. [★3310]
Real Estate Info. Professionals Assn. [3339], c/o InfoMarketing Inc., PO Box 3159, Durham, NC 27715-3159, (919)383-0044
Real Estate Info. Providers Assn. [★3339]
Real Estate Inst. of Canada [IO], Toronto, ON, Canada
Real Estate Inst. of Zimbabwe [IO], Harare, Zimbabwe
Real Estate Investment Fiduciaries; Natl. Coun. of [2344]
Real Estate Investment Funds; Natl. Assn. of [★3327]
Real Estate Investors Assn; Natl. [2347]
Real Estate Law Inst. - Defunct.
Real Estate Lawyers; Amer. Coll. of [5479]
Real Estate Leaders of America - Address unknown since 1988.
Real Estate License Law Officials; Natl. Assn. of [★6243]
Real Estate Mgt. Brokers Institute [★3323]
Real Estate; NAIOP - The Assn. for Commercial [★3320]
Real Estate Res. Institute [★2344]
Real Estate Roundtable [3340], 801 Pennsylvania Ave. NW, Ste. 720, Washington, DC 20004, (202)639-8400
Real Estate Services Providers Coun. [3341], 2000 L St. NW, Ste. 522, Washington, DC 20036, (202)862-2051
Real Estate Trainers Assn.; Intl. - Defunct.
Real Estate; Women in [9329]
Real Estate's Roundtable [★3340]
Real Federacion Espanola de Squash [IO], Madrid, Spain
Real Federacion Espanola de Tenis [IO], Barcelona, Spain
Real Found. [13438], 550 Hinesburg Rd., South Burlington, VT 05403, (802)846-7871
Real Great Soc. - Defunct.
Real Property Assn. of Canada [IO], Toronto, ON, Canada
Real Sociedad Economica de Amigos del Pais de Tenerife [★IO]
Real Sociedad Espanola de Fisica [★IO]
Real Sociedad Espanola de Fisica [★IO]
Real Sociedad Espanola de Historia Natural [IO], Madrid, Spain
Real Sociedad Espanola de Quimica [★IO]
Real Sociedad Matematica Espanola [IO], Madrid, Spain
REAL Women of Canada [IO], Ottawa, ON, Canada
Realia - Philosophy in Ser. to Humanity [★10795]
Realism Found; Aesthetic [10781]
Reality Therapy; Inst. for [★16233]
Reality Therapy, and Quality Mgt; Inst. for Control Therapy, [★16233]
Realm of the Vampire - Address unknown since 2001.
Realtors Land Inst. [3342], 430 N Michigan Ave., Chicago, IL 60611, (800)441-5263
Realtors of the Natl. Assn. of Realtors; Women's Coun. of [★3345]
Realtors Natl. Marketing Inst. - Defunct.
Realtors; Soc. of Indus. [★3343]
Reamer Collectors Assn; Natl. [22609]
REAP Intl. [12940]
REAP Intl. [IO], Cedar Rapids, IA, United States
Rearwin Club [21474], c/o Eric Rearwin, PO Box 70044, Richmond, CA 94807, (510)724-2500

Reason Found. [18480], 3415 S Sepulveda Blvd., Ste. 400, Los Angeles, CA 90034, (310)391-2245
Reason Public Policy Inst. [6131], 3415 S Sepulveda Blvd., Ste. 400, Los Angeles, CA 90034, (310)391-2245
Reasons to Believe [20551], PO Box 5978, Pasadena, CA 91117, (626)335-1480
Reb Meir Baal Haness; Kolel Shomre Hachomos/ [17938]
Reba McEntire Intl. Fan Club - Address unknown since 2003.
Rebel Lee Fan Club - Address unknown since 1995.
Reblooming Iris Soc. [22538], c/o Barbara Aitken, Pres., 608 NW 119th St., Vancouver, WA 98685, (360)573-4472
Rebuild Am. [17349], c/o U.S. Department of Energy, Off. of Energy Efficiency and Renewable Energy, 1000 Independence Ave. SW, Washington, DC 20585-0121, (202)586-9424
Rebuilders Assn; Automotive Parts [★409]
Rebuilders Assn; Production Engine [★1295]
Rebuilders Assn; Western Engine [★1295]
Rebuilding Alliance [12336], 457 Kingsley Ave., Palo Alto, CA 94301, (650)325-4663
Rebuilding Alliance [IO], Palo Alto, CA, United States
Rebuilding Together [12337], 1536 Sixteenth St. NW, Washington, DC 20036-1402, (202)483-9083
Rebuilding Together with Christmas in April - U.S.A. [★12337]
Rebus Inst. - Address unknown since 2000.
RECAP (Recover a Penis) [★11734]
Receivable Companies; Natl. Conf. of Commercial [★2423]
Receivers; Intl. Assn. of Insurance [2187]
Recent Past Preservation Network [7162], PO Box 100505, Arlington, VA 22210, (434)293-2872
Rechargeable Battery Assn; Portable [501]
Reciclanet Hezgarri Elkartea [IO], Bilbao, Spain
Reciprocal Enforcement of Support; Natl. Conf. on Uniform [★5701]
Reciprocal and Family Support Enforcement Assn; Natl. [★5701]
Reciprocal Meat Conf. [★7088]
Reclaim Managers Assn. - Defunct.
ReclaimDemocracy.org [17398], 222 S Black Ave., Bozeman, MT 59715, (406)582-1224
Reclaiming Assn; Asphalt Recycling and [3987]
Reclamation; Amer. Soc. of Mining and [6114]
Reclamation; Amer. Soc. for Surface Mining and [★6114]
Reclamation Assn. [★IO]
Reclamation Assn; Natl. [★7838]
Reclamation Inc. [12556], 2502 Waterford Dr., San Antonio, TX 78217, (210)822-3569
Reclamationists; Natl. Assn. of State Land [6118]
Recognition Assn; Awards and [441]
Recognition; Natl. Assn. for Employee [★17492]
Recognition Professionals Intl. [17492], 1601 N Bond St., Ste. 303, Naperville, IL 60563, (630)369-7783
Recognition Soc; Pattern [7457]
Recognition Technologies Users Assn., OCR/Scanner/Fax Assn. [★6787]
Recon Assn; Force [21212]
Reconciliation; North Manchester Fellowship of [★18723]
Reconciling Congregation Prog. [★20065]
Reconciling Ministries Network [20065], 3801 N Keeler Ave., Chicago, IL 60641-3007, (773)736-5526
Reconditioners; Assn. of Container [★994]
Reconnaissance Assn; Air Weather [21279]
Reconnaissance Assn; Marine Corps Aviation [6052]
Reconnaissance Squadron - Address unknown since 2002.
Reconstruction; Assn. for Crime Scene [5634]
Reconstruction; Natl. Found. for Facial [14065]
Reconstructionist Congregations and Fellowships; Fed. of [★20151]
Reconstructionist Fed. of Congregations and Fellowships [★20151]
Reconstructionist Fed; Jewish [20151]
Reconstructionist Fellowship of Congregations [★20151]

Reconstructionist Found; Jewish [★20151]
Reconstructionist Rabbinical Assn. [20175], 1299 Church Rd., Wyncote, PA 19095, (215)576-5210
Reconstructionists and Investigators; Natl. Assn. of Traffic Accident [5887]
Reconstructionists; Natl. Assn. of Professional Accident [6252]
Reconstructive Microsurgery; Amer. Soc. for [16573]
Reconstructive Surgeons; Educ. Found. of Amer. Soc. of Plastic and [14051]
Reconstructive Surgery; Amer. Acad. of Facial Plastic and [14038]
Reconstructive Surgery; Amer. Bd. of Facial Plastic and [16562]
Reconstructive Surgery; Amer. Soc. for [16574]
Reconstructive Surgery; Amer. Soc. of Ophthalmic Plastic and [14043]
Record Associations; Natl. Soc. of Live Stock [★4141]
Record Benevolent Assn; Christian [★16842]
Record Braille Found; Christian [★16842]
Record Club; Collectors [22712]
Record Collectors' Club - Address unknown since 2003.
Record Examinations Bd; Graduate [9251]
Record Indus. Assn. of Am. [★3350]
Record Librarians; Amer. Assn. of Medical [★15097]
Record Librarians of North Am; Assn. of [★15097]
Record Merchandisers; Natl. Assn. of [★3349]
Record One Stop Assn. - Defunct.
Record Ser. Volunteer Assn; Natl. Archives and [★9402]
Record Services; Christian [16842]
Record and Tape Exchange - Defunct.
Recorded Sound Collections; Assn. for [10337]
Recorder Soc; Amer. [10548]
Recorders and Clerks; Natl. Assn. of County [★5621]
Recorders, Election Officials, and Clerks; Natl. Assn. of County [5621]
The Recording Acad. [★10929]
Recording Artists, Actors and Athletes Against Drink Driving - Australia [IO], North Sydney, Australia
Recording Artists, Actors and Athletes Against Drunk Driving [IO], Studio City, CA, United States
Recording Artists, Actors and Athletes Against Drunk Driving [12986], 4370 Tujunga Ave., Ste. 330, Studio City, CA 91604, (818)752-7799
Recording Artists; Amer. Fed. of TV [★17981]
Recording for the Blind [★16885]
Recording for the Blind and Dyslexic [16885], 20 Roszel Rd., Princeton, NJ 08540, (609)520-8044
Recording for the Blind; Natl. Comm. for [★16885]
Recording Indus. Music Performance Trust Funds [★10651]

Recording Industry
Alliance of Artists and Recording Companies [3346]
Electronic Music Found. [10592]
GRAMMY Found. [10602]
Just Plain Folks Songwriting/Musician Networking Org. [2829]
Natl. Acad. of Recording Arts and Sciences [10929]
Natl. Club Indus. Assn. of Am. [1320]
Tamizdat [9853]
Yrjo Kilpinen Soc. of North Am. [9820]
Recording Indus. Assn. of Am. [3350]
Recording Indus. Assn. of Japan [IO], Tokyo, Japan
Recording Indus. Assn. of Malaysia [IO], Kuala Lumpur, Malaysia
Recording Indus. Assn. of New Zealand [IO], Auckland, New Zealand
Recording Indus. Assn. of Singapore [IO], Singapore, Singapore
Recording Indus. of South Africa [IO], Randburg, Republic of South Africa
Recording Rights Coalition; Home [5844]
Recording Studios; Soc. of Professional Audio [★3351]
Recordings
Antique Phonograph Collectors Club [22710]
Asociacion Colombiana de Productores de Fonogramas [IO]
Asociacion Mexicana de Productores de Fonogramas AC [IO]

A star before a book entry number signifies that the name is not listed separately, but is mentioned within the entry.

Asociacion de Productores Fonograficos de
  Venezuela **[IO]**
Associacao Brasileira dos Produtores de Discos
  [IO]
Associacao Fonografica Portugesa **[IO]**
Assn. of Greek Producers of Phonograms **[IO]**
Assn. of Hungarian Record Companies **[IO]**
Assn. of Independent Music **[IO]**
Assn. of Independent Record Labels **[IO]**
Assn. of Music Producers **[2801]**
Assn. of Professional Recording Services **[IO]**
Assn. of the Recording Indus. of Ghana **[IO]**
Audio Publishers Assn. **[3347]**
Australasian Sound Recordings Assn. **[IO]**
British Assn. of Record Dealers **[IO]**
British Phonographic Indus. **[IO]**
British Sound Recording Assn. **[IO]**
Bulgarian Assn. of Music Producers **[IO]**
Butimar Productions **[9849]**
Canadian Acad. of Recording Arts and Sciences
  [IO]
Canadian Independent Record Production Assn.
  [IO]
Canadian Recording Indus. Assn. **[IO]**
Collectors Record Club **[22712]**
Egyptian Natl. Gp. of IFPI **[IO]**
Federazione Industria Musicale Italiana **[IO]**
Friends of Old-Time Radio **[22924]**
Icelandic Natl. Gp. of IFPI **[IO]**
Independent Music Companies Assn. **[IO]**
Independent Music New Zealand **[IO]**
Indian Music Indus. **[IO]**
Intl. Assn. of Jazz Record Collectors **[22714]**
Intl. Fed. of the Phonographic Indus. - Belgium
  [IO]
Intl. Fed. of the Phonographic Indus. - Chile **[IO]**
Intl. Fed. of the Phonographic Indus. - Czech
  Republic **[IO]**
Intl. Fed. of the Phonographic Indus. - Denmark
  [IO]
Intl. Fed. of the Phonographic Indus. - England
  [IO]
Intl. Fed. of the Phonographic Indus. - Finland
  [IO]
Intl. Fed. of the Phonographic Indus. - Germany
  [IO]
Intl. Fed. of the Phonographic Indus. - Hong Kong
  [IO]
Intl. Fed. of the Phonographic Indus. - Israel **[IO]**
Intl. Fed. of the Phonographic Indus. - Jamaica
  [IO]
Intl. Fed. of the Phonographic Indus. - Nigeria **[IO]**
Intl. Fed. of the Phonographic Indus. - Russia and
  CIS **[IO]**
Intl. Fed. of the Phonographic Indus. - Slovak
  Republic **[IO]**
Intl. Fed. of the Phonographic Indus. - Sweden
  [IO]
Intl. Fed. of the Phonographic Indus. - Switzerland
  [IO]
Intl. Fed. of the Phonographic Indus. - Taiwan **[IO]**
Irish Recorded Music Assn. **[IO]**
Just Plain Folks Songwriting/Musician Networking
  Org. **[2829]**
Kenya Assn. of Producers and Videograms **[IO]**
MU-YAP Turkish Phonographic Indus. Soc. **[IO]**
Music Producers Guild **[IO]**
Musical Heritage Soc. **[10928]**
Natl. Acad. of Recording Arts and Sciences
  [10929]
Natl. Assn. of the Phonographic Indus. **[IO]**
Natl. Assn. of Record Indus. Professionals **[3348]**
Natl. Assn. of Recording Merchandisers **[3349]**
North Amer. British Music Stud. Assn. **[10676]**
Philippine Assn. of the Record Indus. **[IO]**
Polish Soc. of the Phonographic Indus. **[IO]**
Positive Music Assn. **[10688]**
Promusicae **[IO]**
Recording for the Blind and Dyslexic **[16885]**
Recording Indus. Assn. of Am. **[3350]**
Recording Indus. Assn. of Japan **[IO]**
Recording Indus. Assn. of Malaysia **[IO]**
Recording Indus. Assn. of New Zealand **[IO]**
Recording Indus. Assn. of Singapore **[IO]**
Recording Indus. of South Africa **[IO]**

Soc. of Professional Audio Recording Services
  [3351]
Sound Recordings and Multimedia Assn. **[IO]**
Syndicat Natl. de l'Edition Phonographique **[IO]**
Thai Entertainment Content Trade Assn. **[IO]**
The Unconservatory **[10714]**
Verband der Osterreichischen Musikwirtschaft **[IO]**
Yrjo Kilpinen Soc. of North Am. **[9820]**
Zimbabwe Music Rights Assn. **[IO]**
Recordings; Gospel **[20343]**
Records Admin. Volunteer Assn; Natl. Archives and
  [9402]
Records Administrators; Natl. Assn. of Govt.
  Archives and **[5820]**
Records Administrators; Natl. Assn. of State
  Archives and **[★5820]**
Records Executives and Administrators; Assn. of
  [★2096]
Records Indus. Assn; Property **[3187]**
Records Inst; Medical **[15098]**
Records Mgt. Assn; Amer. **[★2096]**
Records Mgt. Assn. of Australasia **[IO]**, Brisbane,
  Australia
Records Mgt. Assn; Nuclear **[★7389]**
Records Mgt. Assn; Nuclear Info. and **[7389]**
Records Mgt. Soc. **[IO]**, Princes Risborough, United
  Kingdom
Records Managers; Inst. of Certified **[2103]**
Records and Public Hea. Statistics; Amer. Assn. for
  Vital **[★6218]**
Recover a Penis; RECAP **[★11734]**
Recovered Alcoholic Clergy Assn. **[13278]**, c/o St.
  David's Episcopal Church, 4700 Roland Ave.,
  Baltimore, MD 21210, (410)467-0476
Recovered Medical Equip. for the Developing World
  [15079], PO Box 208051, New Haven, CT 06520-
  8051, (203)737-5356
Recovered Medical Equip. for the Developing World
  [IO], New Haven, CT, United States
Recovering Motorcyclists; Assn. of **[13225]**
Recovery Assn; Aircraft **[12945]**
Recovery Assn. of Am; Towing and **[429]**
Recovery Assn; Amer. **[1145]**
Recovery Educational Found. - Address unknown
  since 1999.
Recovery Found; Reach to **[★13792]**
Recovery From Depression; Depressives
  Anonymous: **[12547]**
Recovery, Inc. **[16230]**, 802 N Dearborn St.,
  Chicago, IL 60610, (312)337-5661
Recovery, Inc. **[IO]**, Chicago, IL, United States
Recovery, Inc., The Assn. of Nervous and Former
  Mental Patients **[★IO]**
Recovery, Inc., The Assn. of Nervous and Former
  Mental Patients **[★16230]**
Recovery Investigators; Natl. Assn. of Property
  [5886]
Recovery of Male Potency - Address unknown since
  2002.
Recovery Ministries **[13279]**, PO Box 115, Clover-
  dale, IN 46120, (317)797-3813
Recovery from Mormonism **[12888]**, c/o Richard
  Packham, 2145 Melton Rd., Roseburg, OR 97470,
  (541)672-2360
Recovery; SMART **[16519]**
Recovery Soc; Anonymous Arts **[10956]**
Recovery Systems; Rational **[16516]**
RECRA - Address unknown since 2004.
Recreation
  Adventure Cycling Assn. **[23304]**
  Adventure Travel Trade Assn. **[3902]**
  African Amer. Holiday Assn. **[22974]**
  Airline Sports and Cultural Assn. **[IO]**
  Alberg 37 Intl. Owners Assn. **[21866]**
  All-American Indian Motorcycle Club **[22663]**
  Am. Outdoors **[23681]**
  Amer. Assn. for Physical Activity and Recreation
    [12793]
  Amer. Assn. of Riding Schools **[22582]**
  Amer. Assn. of Spanish Timbrado Breeders
    [21834]
  Amer. Blind Bowling Assn. **[23334]**
  Amer. Boat Builders and Repairers Assn. **[2568]**
  Amer. Boat and Yacht Coun. **[2569]**
  Amer. Camp Assn. **[23268]**

  Amer. Canoe Assn. **[23278]**
  Amer. Canyoneering Assn. **[21949]**
  Amer. Carp Soc. **[22448]**
  Amer. Casting Assn. **[23406]**
  Amer. Checker Fed. **[22457]**
  Amer. Coaster Enthusiasts **[22970]**
  Amer. Go Assn. **[22459]**
  Amer. Kitefliers Assn. **[23569]**
  Amer. Lands Access Assn. **[22937]**
  Amer. Mountain Guides Assn. **[23284]**
  Amer. Recreation Coalition **[12794]**
  Amer. Recreational Golf Assn. **[3636]**
  Amer. Safe Climbing Assn. **[21950]**
  Amer. Senior Fitness Assn. **[15961]**
  Amer. Ski-Bike Assn. **[23801]**
  Amer. Spa and Hea. Resort Assn. **[3352]**
  Amer. Sports Org. **[23993]**
  Amer. Trans. Bowling Assn. **[23249]**
  Amer. Whitewater **[23682]**
  America's Athletes with Disabilities **[23340]**
  Antique Motorcycle Club of Am. **[22667]**
  A.R.C.I Nuova Associazione **[IO]**
  Arctic Cat Club of Am. **[22944]**
  Ariel Motorcycle Club North Am. **[22668]**
  Assn. for Challenge Course Tech. **[2869]**
  Assn. of Club Executives **[1932]**
  Assn. of Jewish Sponsored Camps **[23275]**
  Assn. of Natl. Park Rangers **[6154]**
  Assn. of Pool and Spa Professionals **[3353]**
  Association of Pool and Spa Professionals **[IO]**
  Athletic Equip. Managers Assn. **[23805]**
  Athletic Success Inst. **[23665]**
  Badminton Pan Amer. Confed. **[23088]**
  Bass Anglers Sportsman Soc. **[23410]**
  Best Holiday Trav-L-Park Assn. **[3354]**
  Bikes Belong Coalition **[21831]**
  Blue Knights Intl. Law Enforcement Motorcycle
    Club **[22669]**
  BMW Motorcycle Owners of Am. **[22670]**
  BMW Riders Assn. Intl. **[22671]**
  Boardgame Players Assn. **[22461]**
  Bowfishing Assn. of Am. **[23411]**
  Bowlers to Veterans Link **[23250]**
  Boys' and Girls' Clubs of Northern Ireland **[IO]**
  Break Away: The Alternative Break Connection
    [12795]
  British Intl. Spa Assn. **[IO]**
  Brotherhood of the Jungle Cock **[23412]**
  Camping Women **[23269]**
  Carp Anglers Gp. **[22450]**
  Centered Riding **[22584]**
  Challenge Aspen at Snowmass **[23342]**
  Chinese-American Golf Assn. **[23445]**
  Christian Camping International/U.S.A. **[23270]**
  Christian Golfers' Assn. **[23283]**
  Christian Motorcyclists Assn. **[22674]**
  City Parks Alliance **[18184]**
  Collegiate Assn. of Table Top Gamers **[22462]**
  Combat Veterans Motorcycle Assn. **[22675]**
  Comm. for the Advancement of Role-Playing
    Games **[22463]**
  Comm. for the Game **[22464]**
  Crochet Guild of Am. **[22722]**
  Croquet Found. of Am. **[23300]**
  Cruise Club of Am. **[3914]**
  Cruise Lines Intl. Assn. **[3915]**
  Darkride and Funhouse Enthusiasts **[21511]**
  Delta Psi Kappa **[24573]**
  Deutsches Motorrad Register **[22677]**
  Direction Sports **[13482]**
  Disabled Sports USA **[23343]**
  Discovery Owners Assn., Inc. **[22947]**
  Dude Ranchers' Assn. **[1940]**
  Employee Services Mgt. Assn. **[12796]**
  European Fed. for Company Sports **[IO]**
  European Leisure and Recreation Assn. **[IO]**
  Family Campers and RVers **[23271]**
  Fed. of Fly Fishers **[23413]**
  Fed. of Metal Detector and Archaeological Clubs
    [22578]
  Fishing Has No Boundaries **[23414]**
  Game Audio Network Guild **[1715]**
  Gamers Intl. **[22478]**
  Giant Scale Warbirds Assn. **[22644]**
  Harley Hummer Club **[22679]**

Reference to "IO" in place of a book number signifies that the association may be found in the 45th edition of International Organizations.

Hea. Jam [14674]
Help Hospitalized Veterans [13351]
Honda Sport Touring Assn. [22681]
Hostelling International-American Youth Hostels [12797]
Hostelling International-American Youth Hostels [IO]
Indian Motor-Cycle Club of America [22682]
Indonesia Skateboarding Assn. [IO]
Inst. of Leisure and Amenity Mgt. [IO]
Inst. of Sport and Recreation Mgt. [IO]
Intl. Alliance for Youth Sports [23994]
Intl. Assn. of Fly Fishing Veterinarians [22451]
Intl. Assn. of Haunted Attractions [1304]
Intl. Assn. of Skateboard Companies [23679]
Intl. Assn. of Skateboard Companies [IO]
Intl. Bonefishing Soc. [22452]
Intl. Brotherhood of Motorcycle Campers [23624]
Intl. Catalina 400 Assn. [21875]
Intl. Dodge Ball Fed. [23821]
Intl. Family Recreation Assn. [12798]
International Family Recreation Association [IO]
Intl. Fellowship of Fishing Rotarians [22453]
Intl. Medical Spa Assn. [1870]
Intl. Miniature Aircraft Assn. [22938]
International Miniature Aircraft Association [IO]
Intl. Norton Owners' Assn. [22684]
Intl. Playground Contractors Assn. [1028]
Intl. Recreational Go-Kart Assn. [1310]
Intl. Scale Soaring Assn. [22648]
Intl. Snowmobile Mfrs. Assn. [3368]
Intl. Spa Assn. [3355]
Intl. Spa Assn. [IO]
Intl. Unicycling Fed. [23311]
Intl. Women's Fishing Assn. [23419]
KampGround Owners Assn. [3356]
Kite Trade Assn. Intl. [3643]
League of Amer. Bicyclists [23312]
Loners of Am. [22956]
Lyman Boat Owners Assn. [21877]
Masters of Foxhounds Assn. of Am. [23546]
Natl. 42 Players Assn. [22899]
Natl. African-American RV'ers Assn. [22958]
Natl. Amateur Dodgeball Assn. [23091]
Natl. Amusement Park Historical Assn. [21512]
Natl. Antique Tractor Pullers Assn. [23004]
Natl. Assn. of Police Athletic Leagues [13496]
Natl. Assn. of Recreation Rsrc. Planners [6156]
Natl. Assn. for Recreational Equality [23836]
Natl. Assn. of RV Parks and Campgrounds [3357]
Natl. Assn. of State Veterans Homes [13354]
Natl. Assn. of Therapeutic Wilderness Camps [23276]
Natl. Bicycle League [23313]
The Natl. Bowling Assn. [23252]
Natl. C Scow Sailing Assn. [23203]
Natl. Center for Bicycling and Walking [23315]
Natl. Coalition for Promoting Physical Activity [23653]
Natl. Coun. for Therapeutic Recreation Certification [16627]
Natl. Duckpin Bowling Cong. [23253]
Natl. Forest Recreation Assn. [3358]
Natl. Intramural-Recreational Sports Assn. [23842]
Natl. Mah Jongg League [22468]
Natl. Party Boat Owners Alliance [3359]
Natl. Pearson Yacht Owners Assn. [21878]
Natl. Poker Assn. [22900]
Natl. Polymer Clay Guild [22579]
Natl. Puzzlers' League [22469]
Natl. Recreation Assn. of Japan [IO]
Natl. Scrabble Assn. [22470]
Natl. Swimming Pool Found. [3360]
Natl. Teen Anglers [22454]
Natl. Therapeutic Recreation Soc. [16628]
Natl. Trail Ride Assn. [23946]
Natl. Veterans Services Fund [13356]
Natl. Wheelchair Basketball Assn. [23354]
Natl. Wheelchair Softball Assn. [23356]
North Amer. Bowhunting Coalition [22606]
North Amer. Confed. of the Red Dragon [22479]
North Amer. Family Campers Assn. [23273]
North Amer. Model Horse Shows Assn. [22587]
North Amer. Natural Bodybuilding Fed. [23245]
North Amer. Riding for the Handicapped Assn. [23357]

North Amer. Ski Joring Assn. [23845]
North Amer. Squirrel Assn. [22773]
North Amer. Steam Boat Assn. [21881]
North Amer. Stone Skipping Assn. [22939]
North Amer. Stone Skipping Assn. [IO]
North Amer. Tiddlywinks Assn. [22472]
One-Arm Dove Hunt Assn. [23358]
Outfitters Assn. of Am. [23642]
Park Law Enforcement Assn. [6162]
Prairie Club [12799]
Prince Edward Island Recreation and Sports Assn. for the Physically Challenged [IO]
Professional Bowlers Assn. of Am. [23254]
Randonneurs USA [23316]
Recreation Vehicle Indus. Assn. [3371]
Recreation Vehicle Rental Assn. [3372]
Recreational Fishing Alliance [17603]
Resort and Commercial Recreation Assn. [3361]
Rickman Owners Club Intl. [22689]
RollerSoccer Intl. Fed. [23850]
Rudge Enthusiasts Club [22691]
RVing Women [22962]
Salmon Unlimited [23422]
Sauna Soc. of Am. [3362]
Scale Ship Modelers Assn. of North Am. [22656]
Scale Warbird Racing Assn. [22657]
Senior Roller Skaters of Am. [23739]
Sheclimbs [23285]
Shore Fishing and Casting Club Intl. [23423]
Ski for Light [23361]
Soccer in the Streets [11789]
Soc. of Recreation Executives [3363]
Spa Assn. Singapore [IO]
Special Olympics [23362]
Special Recreation for disABLED Intl. [11989]
Sport and Recreation Law Assn. [23870]
Sports Charities USA [23854]
Sports Philatelists Intl. [22877]
Stars for Stripes [20770]
STRIDE: Sports and Therapeutic Recreation Instruction/Developmental Educ. [8205]
Suntanning Assn. for Educ. [3364]
Thai Spa Operators Assn. [IO]
Toyota Territory Off-Roaders Assn. [22965]
Tread Lightly! [5167]
Tugboat Enthusiasts Soc. of the Americas [21886]
Unicycling Soc. of Am. [23319]
United Franchise Benefits Assn. [3365]
United Sidecar Assn. [22693]
U.S.A. Cricket Assn. [23299]
U.S. Assn. for Blind Athletes [23363]
U.S. BASE Assn. [23647]
U.S. Boomerang Assn. [23248]
U.S. Bowling Cong. [23255]
U.S. Broomball Assn. [23858]
U.S. Calf Ropers Assn. [23695]
U.S. Canoe Assn. [23279]
U.S. Croquet Assn. [23301]
U.S. Cycling Fed. [23320]
U.S. Fastpitch Assn. [23794]
U.S. Futsal Fed. [23862]
U.S. Hang Gliding and Paragliding Assn. [23044]
U.S. Lawn Bowls Assn. [23256]
U.S. Monoski Assn. [23863]
U.S. Orienteering Fed. [23641]
U.S. Othello Assn. [22477]
U.S. Parachute Assn. [23648]
U.S. Poker Assn. [22901]
U.S. Powered Paragliding Assn. [23643]
U.S. Shore Angling Assn. [23425]
U.S. Ski Team Found. [23761]
US Scale Masters Assn. [22660]
USA Climbing [23286]
USA Roller Sports [23746]
Valley Intl. Foosball Assn. [1717]
Velocette Owners Club of North Am. [22695]
Veterans Educ. Proj. [13358]
Vincent Owners Club - Keystone Sect. [22697]
Vintage BMW Motorcycle Owners [22698]
Vintage Motor Bike Club [22699]
Wheelchair Motorcycle Assn. [23370]
Wheelchair Sports, USA [23371]
Wilderness Volunteers [22774]
Wood Tank Mfrs. Assn. [3366]
World Miniature Warbird Assn. [22662]

World Poker Assn. [22902]
World Senior Golf Fed. [23472]
World Sport Stacking Assn. [23868]
Yacht Brokers Assn. of Am. [2598]
Recreation; Amer. Alliance for Hea., Physical Educ. and [★8979]
Recreation; Amer. Assn. for Hea., Physical Educ. and [★8979]
Recreation; Amer. Assn. for Nude [10760]
Recreation Assn; Amer. Therapeutic [16315]
Recreation Assn; Natl. Employee Services and [★12796]
Recreation Assn; Natl. Handicapped Sports and [★23343]
Recreation Assn; Natl. Indus. [★12796]
Recreation Certification; Natl. Coun. for Therapeutic [16627]
Recreation Coalition of Am; Outdoor [★2870]
Recreation and Dance; Amer. Alliance for Hea., Physical Educ., [8979]
Recreation for Disabled; Special [★11989]
Recreation Division of the Amer. Alliance for Hea., Physical Educ. and Recreation [★12793]
Recreation; Division of Girl's and Women's Sports of the Amer. Assn. of Hea., Physical Educ., and [★8983]
Recreation Educators; Soc. of Park and [6163]
Recreation Liaison Officers; Natl. Assn. of State Outdoor [6157]
Recreation Managers' Assn. of Great Britain [IO], Kidsgrove, United Kingdom
Recreation Officials; Natl. Assn. of County Park and [6155]
Recreation and Parks; National Cong. [★6161]
Recreation Planners; Natl. Assn. of State [★6156]
Recreation; Recreation Division of the Amer. Alliance for Hea., Physical Educ. and [★12793]
Recreation Rsrc. Planners; Natl. Assn. of [6156]
Recreation; School Hea. Division of Amer. Assn. for Hea., Physical Educ. and [★16234]
Recreation Soc; Amer. [★6153]
Recreation Soc; Amer. Park and [6153]
Recreation Soc; Hosp. Sect. of the Amer. [★16628]
Recreation Soc; Natl. Therapeutic [16628]
Recreation; Soc. of State Directors of Hea., Physical Educ. and [8992]
Recreation Therapists; Natl. Assn. of [★16628]
Recreation Vehicle Aftermarket Div. [★3370]
Recreation Vehicle Dealers Assn. of Am. [3370], 3930 Univ. Dr., Fairfax, VA 22030-2515, (703)591-7130
Recreation Vehicle Dealers Assn. of Canada [IO], Richmond, BC, Canada
Recreation Vehicle Indus. Assn. [3371], 1896 Preston White Dr., Reston, VA 20191, (703)620-6003
Recreation Vehicle Rental Assn. [3372], 3930 Univ. Dr., Fairfax, VA 22030, (703)591-7130
Recreational Canoeing Assn. of British Columbia [IO], Vancouver, BC, Canada
Recreational Equality; Natl. Assn. for [23836]
Recreational Equip. Assn; Amer. [★1298]
Recreational Fishing Alliance [17603], PO Box 3080, New Gretna, NJ 08224, (609)404-1060
Recreational Industries Coun. on Exporting - Defunct.
Recreational Park Trailer Indus. Assn. [3373], 30 Greenville St., 2nd Fl., Newnan, GA 30263-2602, (770)251-2672
Recreational Scuba Training Coun. [23965], PO Box 11083, Jacksonville, FL 32239-1083
Recreational Sports Assn; Natl. Intramural- [23842]
Recreational Vehicle Aftermarket Assn. [3982], c/o Karl J. Etshied, Exec. Dir., 54 Westerly Rd., Camp Hill, PA 17011, (717)730-0300
Recreational Vehicle Club Directors Assn. [★22961]
Recreational Vehicle Division of the Trailer Coach Assn. [★3371]
Recreational Vehicle Inst. [★3371]
Recreational Vehicle Owners Club; Natl. [22960]
Recreational Vehicles
  Alpenlite Travel Club [22940]
  Alpine Coach Assn. [22941]
  Amer. Clipper Owners Club [22942]
  Antique Snowmobile Club of Am. [22943]
  Arctic Cat Club of Am. [22944]

A star before a book entry number signifies that the name is not listed separately, but is mentioned within the entry.

ATV Safety Institute/Division of Specialty Vehicle Inst. of Am. [12952]
Avion Travelcade Club [22945]
Beaver Ambassador Club [22946]
BlueRibbon Coalition [23680]
Bounders United [23010]
Canadian Off-Highway Vehicle Distributors Coun. [IO]
Canadian Recreational Vehicle Assn. [IO]
Carriage Travel Club [23011]
Country Coach Intl. [23012]
Delta Houseboat Rental Assn. [3367]
Discovery Owners Assn., Inc. [22947]
Escapees [22948]
European Caravan Fed. [IO]
Family Campers and RVers [23271]
Family Motor Coach Assn. [22949]
Georgie Boy Owners' Club [22950]
Good Sam Recreational Vehicle Club [22951]
Handicapped Travel Club [22952]
HitchHikers of Am. Intl. [22953]
Holiday Rambler Recreational Vehicle Club [22954]
Intl. Family Recreation Assn. [12798]
Intl. Snowmobile Mfrs. Assn. [3368]
Intl. Snowmobile Mfrs. Assn. [IO]
Jayco Travel Club [22955]
Light Living Library [23272]
Loners of Am. [22956]
Loners on Wheels [22957]
Natl. African-American RV'ers Assn. [22958]
Natl. Assn. of RV Parks and Campgrounds [3357]
Natl. Assn. of Trailer Owners [22959]
Natl. Caravan Coun. [IO]
Natl. Pearson Yacht Owners Assn. [21878]
Natl. Recreational Vehicle Owners Club [22960]
North Amer. Family Campers Assn. [23273]
North Amer. Truck Camper Owners Assn. [23025]
Personal Watercraft Indus. Assn. [3369]
Recreation Vehicle Dealers Assn. of Am. [3370]
Recreation Vehicle Dealers Assn. of Canada [IO]
Recreation Vehicle Indus. Assn. [3371]
Recreation Vehicle Rental Assn. [3372]
Recreational Park Trailer Indus. Assn. [3373]
Roving Volunteers in Christ's Ser. [23017]
RV Mfrs'. Clubs Assn. [22961]
RVing Women [22962]
SunnyTravelers [22963]
Supreme Travel Club [22964]
Teton Club Intl. [22632]
Toyota Territory Off-Roaders Assn. [22965]
Tugboat Enthusiasts Soc. of the Americas [21886]
Vagabundos Del Mar RV, Boat and Travel Club [22966]
Vagabundos Del Mar RV, Boat and Travel Club [IO]
Wally Byam Caravan Club Intl. [22967]
Winnebago-Itasca Travelers [22968]
Yacht Brokers Assn. of Am. [2598]
Recruiters; Assn. of Staff Physician [15995]
Recruiters; Natl. Assn. of Corporate and Professional [★1265]
Recruiters; Natl. Assn. of Executive [1270]
Recruiters; Natl. Assn. of Healthcare [★15070]
Recruiters; Natl. Assn. of Nurse [★15070]
Recruiters; Natl. Assn. of Physician [16006]
Recruiters Online Network [1281], c/o Minnie Ahlstrand, 135 Bishops Curve, Berlin, CT 06037-3703, (800)364-8425
Recruiting and Staffing Focus Area [1984], c/o Soc. for Human Rsrc. Mgt., 1800 Duke St., Alexandria, VA 22314, (703)548-3440
Recruitment and Consulting Services Assn. [IO], Melbourne, Australia
Recruitment and Employment Confed. [IO], London, United Kingdom
Recruitment; Natl. Assn. for Healthcare [15070]
Recruitment and Retention Network; Natl. Rural [14710]
Rectal Cancer Network; Colo [13815]
Rectal Surgeons; Amer. Soc. of Colon and [16060]
Rectal Surgery; Amer. Bd. of Colon and [16059]
ReCycle BiCycle of Sydney Australia [IO], Camperdown, Australia
Recycled Art Assn. [9468]

Recycled Paperboard Alliance; 100% [2886]
Recycled Paperboard Tech. Assn. [993], 920 Davis Rd., Ste. 306, Elgin, IL 60123, (847)622-2544
Recycled Textiles; Shippers of [3587]
Recyclers; Alliance of Foam Packaging [5265]
Recyclers of Am; Automotive Dismantlers and [★3988]
Recyclers Assn. of Australia; Auto Parts [IO]
Recyclers; Assn. of Auto and Truck [★3988]
Recyclers Assn; Automotive [3988]
Recyclers Assn; Natl. Oil [2938]
Recyclers Forum; Off. Furniture [1704]
Recyclers League; Professional Elecl. Apparatus [1196]
Recycling
    Aircraft Fleet Recycling Assn. [12800]
    Aircraft Fleet Recycling Assn. [IO]
    Assn. of Lighting and Mercury Recyclers [5168]
    Australasian Cartridge Remanufacturers Assn. [IO]
    Automotive Recyclers Assn. [3988]
    Building Materials Reuse Assn. [608]
    Compost Tea Indus. Assn. [186]
    Container Recycling Alliance [4479]
    Container Recycling Inst. [4480]
    East West Educ. Development Found. [12716]
    European Battery Recycling Assn. [IO]
    European Toner and Inkjet Remanufacturers Assn. [IO]
    European Tyre Recycling Assn. [IO]
    Global Alliance for Incinerator Alternatives [5268]
    Inst. for Local Self-Reliance [11747]
    Inst. of Scrap Recycling Indus. [3995]
    Intl. Compost Tea Coun. [5244]
    Natl. Off. Paper Recycling Proj. [3999]
    Natl. Recycling Coalition [4000]
    Natl. Waste Prevention Coalition [4001]
    Paper Stock Indus. Chap. of ISRI [4002]
    Plastic Lumber Trade Assn. [3055]
    ReCycle BiCycle of Sydney Australia [IO]
    Recycled Art Assn. [9468]
    Recycled Paperboard Tech. Assn. [993]
    Recycling Coun. of Ontario [IO]
    Secondary Materials and Recycled Textiles [2066]
    Textile Bag and Packaging Assn. [999]
    Tire Soc. [7798]
    Waste Mgt. and Recycling Assn. of Singapore [IO]
Recycling Advisory Comm; Local Authority [IO]
Recycling Assn; Canadian Polystyrene [IO]
Recycling Assn; Natl. Onsite Wastewater [5271]
Recycling; Bur. of Intl. [IO]
Recycling Coalition; Cement Kiln [4337]
Recycling Coalition; Natl. [4000]
Recycling Coordinators; Assn. of Municipal [IO]
Recycling Coun. of Alberta [IO], Bluffton, AB, Canada
Recycling Coun. - Canada [★IO]
Recycling Coun. of Ontario [IO], Toronto, ON, Canada
Recycling Fed; European Ferrous Recovery and [IO]
Recycling Indus; Canadian Assn. of [IO]
Recycling Indus; Inst. of Scrap [3995]
Recycling Indus; Natl. Assn. [★3995]
Recycling; Indus. Coun. for Electronic Equip. [IO]
Recycling Inst; Steel [4004]
Recycling Inst; Steel Can [★4004]
Recycling Legislation Action Coalition - Defunct.
Recycling Org; Aluminium Packaging [IO]
Recycling Policy; Assn. for a Natl. [★4000]
Recycling Proj; Natl. Off. Paper [3999]
Recycling and Reclaiming Assn; Asphalt [3987]
Red Angus Assn. of Am. [4291], 4201 N, Interstate 35, Denton, TX 76207, (940)387-3502
Red des Automatica de Cuba [IO], Havana, Cuba
Red Badge of Courage - Defunct.
Red Bancos [IO], Montevideo, Uruguay
Red Barnet Danmark [★IO]
Red Brangus Assn; Amer. [4242]
Red Cedar Shake Assn; Handsplit [★1640]
Red Cedar Shingle Bur. [★1640]
Red Cedar Shingle Bur. [★IO]
Red Cedar Shingle and Handsplit Shake Bur. [★IO]
Red Cedar Shingle and Handsplit Shake Bur. [★1640]

Red Costarricense de Albergues Juveniles [★IO]
Red Crescent Soc. - Uzbekistan [IO], Tashkent, Uzbekistan
Red Cross
    Amer. Red Cross Natl. HQ [12830]
    Amer. Red Cross Overseas Assn. [12831]
    Amer. Red Magen David for Israel - Amer. Friends of Magen David Adom [12832]
    George C. Marshall Found. [11118]
Red Cross; Armenian [★18966]
Red Cross of Constantine - United Grand Imperial Coun. [19248], c/o Ned E. Dull, Right Illustrious Grand Recorder, PO Box 5716, Springfield, IL 62705-5716, (217)788-5090
Red Cross Natl. HQ; Amer. [12830]
Red Cross Overseas Assn; Amer. [12831]
Red Cross Soc. of China [IO], Beijing, People's Republic of China
Red Cross - Ukraine [IO], Kiev, Ukraine
Red Dwarf Fan Club; Official [25039]
Red Earth [19285], 2100 NE 52nd St., Oklahoma City, OK 73111, (405)427-5228
Red Espanola de Albergues Juveniles [★IO]
Red Hat Soc. [11091], 431 S Acacia Ave., Fullerton, CA 92831, (714)738-0001
Red Hills Conservation Prog. [★4456]
Red Men
    Degree of Pocahontas, Improved Order of Red Men [19327]
    Great Coun. of U.S. Improved Order of Red Men [19328]
Red Men; Degree of Pocahontas, Improved Order of [19327]
Red Men; Great Coun. of U.S. Improved Order of [19328]
Red Mogen David [★12832]
Red Mogen David [★IO]
Red Orange Canaries and All Other Cage Birds; Natl. Inst. of [21855]
Red Poll Assn; Amer. [4243]
Red Poll Beef Breeders Intl. [★4243]
Red Poll Cattle Club of Am. [★4243]
Red Poll Cattle Soc. [IO], Woodbridge, United Kingdom
Red Red Rose - Defunct.
Red River Boys Fan Club - Defunct.
Red River Valley Fighter Pilots Assn. [21318], PO Box 1553, Front Royal, VA 22630-0033, (540)636-9798
Red River Valley Sugarbeet Growers Assn. [5229], 1401 32nd St. SW, Fargo, ND 58103-3428, (701)239-4151
Red Sea Mission Team [★20385]
Red Sea Mission Team [★IO]
Red Sea Team Intl. [IO], Lexington, SC, United States
Red Sea Team Intl. [20385], PO Box 2047, Lexington, SC 29071-2047, (803)358-2330
Red Suspender League - Defunct.
Red Tag News Publications [★2456]
Red Tag News Publications Assn. [2456], c/o Lindsey Klingele, 1415 N Dayton St., Chicago, IL 60622, (312)274-2000
Red and White Dairy Cattle Assn. - Defunct.
Red Wing Collectors Soc. [22110], PO Box 50, Red Wing, MN 55066, (651)388-4004
Red Wing For'em Club [25013], PO Box 230, Eastpointe, MI 48021
Redd Barna [★IO]
Rede Brasileira Agroflorestal [★IO]
Redeem Our Country - Defunct.
Rederscentrale [IO], Ostend, Belgium
Redevelopment Officials; Natl. Assn. of Housing and [5793]
Redford Fan Club; Robert [24770]
Redheads Intl. - Address unknown since 2008.
RedR Australia [IO], Barton, Australia
RedR Canada [IO], Ottawa, ON, Canada
RedR Eastern Africa [IO], Nairobi, Kenya
RedR India [IO], Pune, India
RedR Intl. - Edegem, Belgium
RedR London - Intl. Hea. Exchange [IO], London, United Kingdom
RedR New Zealand [IO], Auckland, New Zealand
REDRESS [IO], London, United Kingdom

Reference to "IO" in place of a book number signifies that the association may be found in the 45th edition of International Organizations.

Reduction of Crime; Inst. for [★9085]

Redundant Churches Fund [★IO]

Redwood Alliance [17498], PO Box 293, Arcata, CA 95518, (707)822-7884

Redwood Assn; California [1639]

Redwood Cultural Work/Redwood Records - Address unknown since 1999.

Redwood Export Company - Defunct.

Redwood Inspection Ser. [1618], c/o California Redwood Assn., 405 Enfrente Dr., Ste. 200, Novato, CA 94949, (415)382-0662

Redwood Region Logging Conf. [4694], 5601 S Broadway, Eureka, CA 95502-7127, (707)443-4091

Redwoods League; Save the [4450]

Reed Organ Soc. [10691], c/o Carol Kuhn, Sec., 70 William Blaydes St., Atoka, TN 38004

Reed Organ Soc. of Am. [★10691]

Reed-Reid CH [21031], 207 Auburn Dr., Dalton, GA 30720, (706)278-1504

Reef Alliance; Global Coral [4403]

Reef Check [5012], PO Box 1057, Pacific Palisades, CA 90272-1057, (310)230-2371

Reef Check [IO], Pacific Palisades, CA, United States

Reef Check Europe [IO], Bremen, Germany

Reef Relief [IO], Key West, FL, United States

Reef Relief [5013], PO Box 430, Key West, FL 33041, (305)294-3100

Reef Stud; Intl. Soc. for [4581]

ReefGuardian Intl. [5014], 2829 Bird Ave., Ste. 5, PMB 162, Miami, FL 33133-4668, (305)358-4600

ReefGuardian Intl. [IO], Miami, FL, United States

Reel Collectors Assn; Old [22099]

Reel Recovery [11519], 160 Brookside Rd., Needham, MA 02492, (800)699-4490

Reeve Found; Christopher [★16463]

Reeve; Christopher and Dana [16463]

Reeve Paralysis Found; Christopher [★16463]

Referees' Assn. [IO], Coventry, United Kingdom

Reference and Adult Services Division of ALA [★10383]

Reference Libraries; Assn. of Coll. and [★10331]

Reference Point Found. - Defunct.

Reference Services Division of ALA [★10383]

Reference and User Services Assn. of Amer. Lib. Assn. [10383], c/o Barbara Macikas, Exec. Dir., 50 E Huron St., Chicago, IL 60611, (312)280-4395

Referral Proj; Natl. Migrant [★14581]

Referral Systems; Alliance of Info. and [7187]

Refined Bitumen Assn. [IO], Wokingham, United Kingdom

Refined Sugar Assn. [IO], London, United Kingdom

Refiners Assn; Corn [1508]

Reflections of Elvis Fan Club - Address unknown since 2001.

Reflex Sympathetic Dystrophy Assn. [★15363]

Reflex Sympathetic Dystrophy Syndrome Assn. of Am. [15363], PO Box 502, Milford, CT 06460, (203)877-3790

Reflexologists; Intl. Coun. of [IO]

Reflexology Assn. of Am. [IO], Columbus, OH, United States

Reflexology Assn. of Am. [13650], PO Box 714, Chepachet, RI 02814, (419)578-6661

Reflexology Assn. of Australia [IO], Wynnum, Australia

Reflexology Assn; British [IO]

Reflexology Assn. of Canada [IO], Winnipeg, MB, Canada

Reflexology Certification Bd; Amer. [13621]

Reflexology; Intl. Inst. of [16620]

Reflux Assn; Pediatric/Adolescent Gastroesophageal [14426]

Reform

Anglicans United [19943]

Coun. for Govt. Reform [17665]

Natl. Alliance for Family Court Justice [5904]

Natl. Endangered Species Act Reform Coalition [17504]

Natl. Reform Assn. [20485]

Reform; Americans for Tax [18702]

Reform; Campaign for U.N. [★18762]

Reform; Coun. for Govt. [17665]

Reform Educ; Center for U.N. [18761]

Reform and Educational Options; Hispanic Coun. for [8260]

Reform; HALT - Americans for Legal [★17961]

Reform; HALT - An Org. of Americans for Legal [17961]

Reform Jewish Appeal [20176], c/o Union for Reform Judaism, 633 3rd Ave., New York, NY 10017-6778, (212)650-4000

Reform Judaism [20177], 2027 Massachusetts Ave. NW, Washington, DC 20036, (202)387-2800

Reform Judaism; Religious Action Center of [17954]

Reform Judaism, The Fed. of Temple Sisterhoods; Women of [20192]

Reform Judaism; Union for [20184]

Reform of Marijuana Laws; Natl. Org. for the [17137]

Reform Movement; FARM Farm Animal [11394]

Reform; Natl. Citizens Coalition for Nursing Home [17335]

Reform; Natl. Coalition for Child Protection [11634]

Reform; Natl. Comm. for Judicial [17963]

Reform Now; Assn. of Community Organizations for [11749]

Reform Zionists of Am; Assn. of [★20122]

REFORMA: Natl. Assn. of Lib. Services to the Spanish-Speaking [★10384]

REFORMA: Natl. Assn. to Promote Lib. Services to the Spanish-Speaking [10384], c/o Sandra Rios Balderrama, PO Box 4386, Fresno, CA 93744, (480)734-4460

REFORMA: Natl. Assn. of Spanish-Speaking Librarians [★10384]

ReformAMT [18698], PO Box 915, Cupertino, CA 95015, (408)482-2400

Reformation

Center for Reformation Res. [10930]

Lollard Soc. [20524]

Soc. for Reformation Res. [10931]

Reformation Res; Amer. Soc. for [★10931]

Reformation Res; Found. for [★10930]

Reformation Res; Soc. for [10931]

Reformed Church Women - Address unknown since 2001.

Reformed Ecumenical Coun. [19908], 2050 Breton Rd. SE, Ste. 102, Grand Rapids, MI 49546-5547, (616)949-2910

Reformed Ecumenical Coun. [IO], Grand Rapids, MI, United States

Reformed Ecumenical Synod [★IO]

Reformed Ecumenical Synod [★19908]

Reformed Historical Soc; Evangelical and [20607]

Reformed Renewal Ministries Intl; Presbyterian and [★20474]

Reformed Young Men Societies; Amer. Fed. of [★19831]

Reformed Young Women Societies; Amer. Fed. of [★19831]

REFORMERS, Pakistan [IO], Faisalabad, Pakistan

Refounded Natl. Party of South Africa [IO], Pretoria, Republic of South Africa

Refractive Surgery; Amer. Soc. of Cataract and [15665]

The Refractories Inst. [6659], Centre City Tower, 650 Smithfield St., Ste. 1160, Pittsburgh, PA 15222-3907, (412)281-6787

Refractory Ceramic Fibers Coalition [788], c/o Dana Bishop, 2300 N St. NW, Washington, DC 20037, (202)663-9188

Refractory Metals Association [★2714]

Refreshments Canada [IO], Toronto, ON, Canada

Refrigerant and Desuperheating Mfg; Assn. of [1877]

Refrigerated Foods Assn. [1560], 2971 Flowers Rd. S, Ste. 266, Atlanta, GA 30341, (770)452-0660

Refrigerated Foods Assn; Natl. Frozen and [1547]

Refrigerating and Air-Conditioning Engineers; Amer. Soc. of Heating, [6995]

Refrigerating Engineers; Amer. Soc. of [★6995]

Refrigerating Engineers; Natl. Assn. Practical [★7037]

Refrigerating Engineers and Technicians Assn. [7037], PO Box 1819, Salinas, CA 93902, (831)455-8783

Refrigeration

Amer. Soc. of Heating, Refrigerating and Air-Conditioning Engineers [6995]

Assn. of Home Appliance Manufacturers [264]

French Refrigeration Assn. [IO]

Japan Refrigeration and Airconditioning Indus. Assn. [IO]

Swedish Soc. of Refrigeration [IO]

Refrigeration, and Airconditioning Wholesalers Assn; Northamerican Heating, [★1882]

Refrigeration Assn; British [IO]

Refrigeration Compressor and Controls Mfrs; Assn. of European [IO]

Refrigeration Compressor Rebuilders Assn. [★IO]

Refrigeration Compressor Rebuilders Assn. [★1887]

Refrigeration Contractors of Am; Air Conditioning and [★1872]

Refrigeration Equip. Manufacturers Assn. [★1873]

Refrigeration European Assn; Air Conditioning and [IO]

Refrigeration; Inst. of [IO]

Refrigeration Inst; Air-Conditioning and [1873]

Refrigeration; Intl. Inst. of [IO]

Refrigeration Machinery Assn; Air-Conditioning and [★1873]

Refrigeration Products Inst; Automotive [378]

Refrigeration Res. and Educ. Found. [★3985]

Refrigeration Res. and Educ. Found. [★IO]

The Refrigeration Res. Found. [IO]

The Refrigeration Res. Found. [★3985]

Refrigeration Ser. Engineers Soc. [1899], 1666 Rand Rd., Des Plaines, IL 60016-3552, (847)297-6464

Refrigeration Service Engineers Society [IO], Des Plaines, IL, United States

Refrigeration Tech; Cambridge [IO]

Refrigeration Wholesalers Intl; Air-Conditioning and [★1882]

Refrigerator Mfrs. Div; Commercial [1878]

Refuge Assn; Natl. Wildlife [5345]

Refuge; Unexpected Wildlife [11467]

Refugee Action Center; Indochina [★12820]

Refugee Advice Centre [IO], Helsinki, Finland

Refugee Citizenship Forum; Natl. Immigration [★17806]

Refugee Coun. of Australia [IO], Surry Hills, Australia

Refugee Coun. of New Zealand [IO], Auckland, New Zealand

Refugee Coun. USA [IO], Washington, DC, United States

Refugee Coun. USA [18500], 3211 4th St. NE, Washington, DC 20017-1194, (202)541-5402

Refugee Fund; World [★18318]

Refugee Fund; World [★IO]

Refugee Legal Support Ser. [★IO]

Refugee Legal Support Ser. [★17989]

Refugee Policy Group - Address unknown since 2002.

Refugee Rehabilitation and Vocation; Sales Exchange for [3846]

Refugee Relief Intl. [12540], 2995 Woodside Rd., No. 400-244, Woodside, CA 94062

Refugee Relief Intl. [IO], Woodside, CA, United States

Refugee Resource Center - Defunct.

Refugee Rights; Natl. Network for Immigrant and [17808]

Refugee Services; Migration and [★12823]

Refugee Services; U.S. Catholic Conference/Migration and [★12823]

Refugee Services; U.S. Catholic Conf. Migration and [★12823]

Refugee Women in Development [18501], Robert S. Strauss Bldg., 1333 New Hampshire Ave. NW, No. 547, Washington, DC 20036-1564, (703)931-6442

Refugee Women in Development [IO], Washington, DC, United States

Refugees

Adventist Development and Relief Agency Intl. [12826]

Afghan Community in Am. [12801]

Afghan Community in Am. [IO]

Afghan Women's Assn. Intl. [13416]

African Refugees Found. [IO]

Al Amel Iraqi Assn. [IO]

Amer. Civic Assn. [12403]

Amer. Fund for Czechoslovak Relief [12802]

American Fund for Czechoslovak Relief [IO]

Amer. Jewish Philanthropic Fund [12803]

Amer. Near East Refugee Aid [12804]

Amer. Near East Refugee Aid [IO]

Amer. Refugee Comm. [IO]

A star before a book entry number signifies that the name is not listed separately, but is mentioned within the entry.

Amer. Refugee Comm. [12805]
Assn. for Aid and Relief, Japan [IO]
Assn. of Cambodian Survivors of America [12806]
Assn. for the Stud. of the World Refugee Problem [IO]
Auckland Refugee Coun. [IO]
Canadian Coun. for Refugees [IO]
Catholic Relief Services (U.S. Catholic Conf.) [IO]
Catholic Relief Services (U.S. Catholic Conf.) [12807]
Center for Migration Stud. of New York [10468]
Center for Women War Victims [IO]
Central American Resource Center [IO]
Central Amer. Rsrc. Center [18496]
Children Out of Detention [IO]
Church World Ser., Immigration and Refugee Prog. [IO]
Church World Ser., Immigration and Refugee Prog. [18497]
Comm. for Humanitarian Assistance to Iranian Refugees [12808]
Cuban Amer. Natl. Coun. [13167]
Danish Refugee Coun. [IO]
El Rescate [12809]
Ethiopian Community Development Coun. [12810]
Ethiopian Community Development Council [IO]
European Coun. on Refugees and Exiles [IO]
Fed. for Amer. Immigration Reform [17805]
FilmAid Intl. [12811]
FilmAid Intl. [IO]
Finnish Refugee Coun. [IO]
Hebrew Immigrant Aid Soc. [12471]
Humanitarian Law Proj. - Intl. Educ. Development [18498]
Humanitarian Law Proj. - Intl. Educ. Development [IO]
Immigration and Refugee Services of Am. [12404]
Interaction/American Coun. for Voluntary Intl. Action [12433]
Intl. Fed. of Iranian Refugees [IO]
Intl. Rescue Comm. - USA [IO]
Intl. Rescue Comm. - USA [12812]
Intl. Social Ser., U.S.A. Br. [12595]
Iranian Refugees' Alliance [12813]
Iranian Refugees' Alliance [IO]
Irish Refugee Coun. [IO]
Japan Intl. Volunteer Center [IO]
Jesuit Refugee Ser. Italy [IO]
Jesuit Refugee Service/U.S.A. [IO]
Jesuit Refugee Service/U.S.A. [12814]
Liberty's Promise [5809]
Lighthouse Intl. - Japan [IO]
Lutheran Immigration and Refugee Service [IO]
Lutheran Immigration and Refugee Ser. [12815]
Magicians Without Borders [12503]
Mapendo Intl. [12868]
Mir Pace Intl. [12872]
Moralogy Intl. Relief Comm. [IO]
Natl. Alliance of Vietnamese Amer. Ser. Agencies [19423]
Natl. Coalition for Asian Pacific Amer. Community Development [11785]
Natl. Coalition for Haitian Rights [18499]
New York Assn. for New Americans [12479]
North Amer. Conf. on Ethiopian Jewry [17953]
Ockenden Intl. - England [IO]
Pontifical Mission for Palestine [IO]
Pontifical Mission for Palestine [12816]
Rav Tov Intl. Jewish Rescue Org. [12817]
Rav Tov Intl. Jewish Rescue Org. [IO]
Red Bancos [IO]
Refugee Advice Centre [IO]
Refugee Coun. of Australia [IO]
Refugee Coun. of New Zealand [IO]
Refugee Coun. USA [IO]
Refugee Coun. USA [18500]
Refugee Women in Development [18501]
Refugee Women in Development [IO]
Refugees Intl. [IO]
Refugees Intl. [12818]
Rights Action/Guatemala Partners [12819]
Scottish Refugee Coun. [IO]
Shelter for Life Intl. [19329]
Somali Family Care Network [19392]
South-East Asia Center [18502]

South-East Asia Center [IO]
Southeast Asia Rsrc. Action Center [12820]
Spanish Refugee Aid [12821]
Sri Lanka Proj. [IO]
Swedish Refugee Aid [IO]
Tibet AID - Japan [IO]
Tibetan Aid Proj. [IO]
Tibetan Aid Proj. [12822]
United Methodist Comm. on Relief [20267]
United Nations High Commissioner for Refugees - Regional Off. Mexico [IO]
United Nations High Commissioner for Refugees - Switzerland [IO]
U.S. Catholic Conference/Migration and Refugee Services [12823]
U.S. Comm. for Refugees and Immigrants [18503]
U.S. Comm. for Refugees and Immigrants [IO]
Upwardly Global [3186]
USA for the United Nations High Commissioner for Refugees [12824]
USA for the United Nations High Commissioner for Refugees [IO]
War Child USA [11663]
Welfare Res., Inc. [13193]
WITNESS [17789]
Working Group on Refugee Resettlement [IO]
World Relief [19985]
ZOA Refugee Care - Netherlands [IO]
Refugees; Amer. Fund for Czechosloval [★12802]
Refugees Fund; Save the [★12778]
Refugees Intl. [12818], 1705 N St. NW, Washington, DC 20036, (202)828-0110
Refugees Intl. [IO], Washington, DC, United States
Refugees; Natl. Emergency Coalition for Haitian [★18499]
Refuse Coll. and Disposal Assn; Governmental [★6355]
Refuse and Resist [18304], 305 Madison Ave., Ste. 1166, New York, NY 10165, (212)713-5657
Refuseniks
   Action for Post-Soviet Jewry [17443]
   Center for Russian and East European Jewry [17946]
   NCSJ: Advocates on Behalf of Jews in Russia, Ukraine, the Baltic States and Eurasia [17448]
   Student Struggle for Soviet Jewry [17451]
   Union of Councils for Jews in the Former Soviet Union [17452]
REG - The Intl. Roger Waters Fan Club [24965], 128 Onyx Dr., Watsonville, CA 95076
REGAP [★11473]
Regap Network; Natl. [1193]
Regatta Assn; Middle States [23701]
Regency Found. Networx [IO], London, United Kingdom
Regeneration [19871], PO Box 9830, Baltimore, MD 21284-9830, (410)661-0284
Regeneration Soc; Earth [4552]
Regent St. Assn. [IO], London, United Kingdom
Regents Coll; Alumni Assn. of [★18896]
Regiment Assn; 504th Parachute Infantry [21378]
Regiment of Foot, Amer. Contingent; H.M. 10th [9373]
Regimental Assn; Signal Corps [20705]
Regimental Combat Team Assn; 187th Airborne [20697]
Regimental Combat Team Assn; 517th Parachute [21381]
Regional African Satellite Communications Org. [IO], Abidjan, Cote d'Ivoire
Regional Airline Assn. [166], 2025 M St. NW, Ste. 800, Washington, DC 20036-3309, (202)367-1170
Regional Anesthesia and Pain Practice; Amer. Soc. of [★13676]
Regional Assn. of Oil and Natural Gas Companies in Latin Am. and the Caribbean [IO], Montevideo, Uruguay
Regional Aviation Assn. of Australia [IO], Mitchell, Australia
Regional Center for Mapping of Resources for Development [★IO]
Regional Centre for Mapping of Resources for Development [IO], Nairobi, Kenya
Regional Centre for Seismology for South Am. [IO], Lima, Peru

Regional Centre for Services in Surveying and Mapping [★IO]
Regional Commn. for Power Integration [★IO]
Regional Cong. of Construction Employers - Defunct.
Regional Councils; Natl. Ser. to [★6244]
Regional Dance America - Defunct.
Regional and Distribution Carriers Conf. [★3564]
Regional and Distribution Carriers Conf. - Address unknown since 1994.
Regional Educ. Bd. of the Christian Bros. [8060], c/o Christian Bros. Conf., Hecker Center, 3025 Fourth St. NE, Ste. 300, Washington, DC 20017, (202)529-0047
Regional Educ. Comm. of the Christian Bros. [★8060]
Regional Educ. Coun. of the Christian Bros. [★8060]
Regional Educational Assn; Rural/ [★9069]
Regional Energy Resources Info. Center [IO], Bangkok, Thailand
Regional Environmental Center for Central and Eastern Europe - Albania [IO], Tirana, Albania
Regional Environmental Center for Central and Eastern Europe - Country Off. Latvia [IO], Riga, Latvia
Regional Environmental Center for Central and Eastern Europe - Hungary [IO], Szentendre, Hungary
Regional Environmental Centre for Central and Eastern Europe - Country Off. Lithuania [IO], Vilnius, Lithuania
Regional Government
   Natl. Assn. of Regional Councils [6244]
Regional Info. Systems Assn; Urban and [7215]
Regional Inst. of Social Welfare Res. - Address unknown since 2004.
Regional Integration Energy Commn. [IO], Montevideo, Uruguay
Regional Magazine Assn; City and [3218]
Regional Org. for the Protection of the Marine Env. [IO], Safat, Kuwait
Regional Publications of Am; Women's [4053]
Regional Reporters Assn. [3157], PO Box 254, Ben Franklin Sta., Washington, DC 20044, (202)408-2705
Regional Sci. Assn. [★5596]
Regional Sci. Assn. [★IO]
Regional Sci. Assn. Intl. [IO], Urbana, IL, United States
Regional Sci. Assn. Intl. [5596], c/o David Boyce, Archivist, 2149 Grey Ave., Evanston, IL 60201
Regional Stud. Assn. [IO], Seaford, United Kingdom
Regional Stud; Center for Urban and [11066]
Regional Trade and Indus. Chamber [★IO]
Regional Victim Assistance Training Prog. [★13369]
Regional Weed Control Conferences; Assn. of [★4109]
Regionalais Vides Centrs Centralai un Austrumeiropai [★IO]
Regioninio Aplinkos Centro Centrinei ir Rytu Europai [★IO]
Regis Coll. Lay Apostolate - Defunct.
Regis Sys. Users' Gp. [6801], 11 Spring St., Hallowell, ME 04347, (207)395-4837
The Register [★21740]
Register of Am; Triumph [21800]
Register Assn; Natl. [★11140]
Register; Brabham [21597]
Register; Brabham Owners [★21597]
Register of Elecl. Contractors of Ireland [IO], Dublin, Ireland
Register; Jordan [21677]
Register of North Am; Topolino [21797]
Register; North Amer. Auto Union [21743]
Register of Professional Archaeologists [6453], 5024-R Campbell Blvd., Baltimore, MD 21236, (410)933-3486
Register of Reclamation Res. and Demonstration Plots on Lands Surface Mined for Coal [★6114]
Register; Road Race Lincoln [21773]
Register; Vintage Triumph [21813]
Registered Architects; Soc. of Amer. [6480]
Registered Bank Holding Companies; Assn. of [★477]
Registered Engineers for Disaster Relief [★IO]

Reference to "IO" in place of a book number signifies that the association may be found in the 45th edition of International Organizations.

Registered Financial Planners Inst. **[1471]**, 2001 Cooper Foster Park Rd., Amherst, OH 44001, (440)282-7176

Registered Master Builders Fed. **[IO]**, Wellington, New Zealand

Registered Nurses; Amer. Soc. of Ophthalmic **[15458]**

Registered Nurses for Eye Acquisition; Consortium of **[★15670]**

Registered Nursing Home Assn. **[IO]**, Birmingham, United Kingdom

Registered Nursing Homes; Natl. Assn. of **[★14540]**

Registered Plumbers Assn. **[★IO]**

Registrars and Admissions Officers; Amer. Assn. of Collegiate **[7910]**

Registrars Assn; Natl. Cancer **[15651]**

Registrars Assn; Natl. Tumor **[★15651]**

Registration Boards; Coun. of Landscape Architectural **[6473]**

Registration of EEG and EP Technologists; Amer. Bd. of **[14305]**

Registro Aprilia **[IO]**, Vicenza, Italy

Registro Aurelia Italiano **[IO]**, Milan, Italy

Registry; 71 429 Mustang **[21551]**

Registry; 1970 Dart Swinger 340s **[21558]**

Registry; 1971 GTO and Judge Convertible **[21559]**

Registry; 66,67,68 High Country Special Mustang **[21561]**

Registry of Am; Standard Jack and Jennet **[★4130]**

Registry; Amer. Mammoth Jack Stock **[★4130]**

Registry of Certified Chemists; Natl. **[13939]**

Registry in Clinical Chemistry; Natl. **[★13939]**

Registry of Comparative Pathology - Defunct.

Registry of Emergency Medical Technicians - Ambulance **[★14342]**

Registry of Emergency Medical Technicians; Natl. **[14342]**

Registry; Intl. Beefalo Breeders **[★4123]**

Registry of Interpreters for the Deaf **[14778]**, 333 Commerce St., Alexandria, VA 22314, (703)838-0030

Registry; Italian Car **[21673]**

Registry of Italian Oddities **[★21673]**

Registry of Medical Assistants; Amer. **[15082]**

Registry; Morris Minor **[21720]**

Registry; Muntz **[★21721]**

Registry; Muntz Jet **[21721]**

Registry; Natl. Bone Marrow Donor **[★14292]**

Registry; Nineteen Thirty-Two Buick **[21741]**

Registry; North Amer. English and European Ford **[21744]**

Registry; North Amer. Mini Moke **[21745]**

Registry Program; Purple Martin Colony **[★5369]**

Registry of Radiologic Technologists; Amer. Chiropractic **[16273]**

Registry; Saxon Owners **[21781]**

Registry of Sidereal Astrologers - Defunct.

Registry; Squire SS-100 **[21788]**

Registry of Tissue Reactions to Drugs **[★15867]**

Registry of Tissue Reactions to Drugs **[★IO]**

Registry; Wild Horses of Am. **[5395]**

Registry; Willys-Overland-Knight **[21819]**

Registry; Zimmerman **[21825]**

Regression Res. and Therapies; Intl. Assn. for **[16617]**

Regroupement pour la surveillance du nucleaire **[★IO]**

Regroupement des consultants canadiens en developpement internationale **[★IO]**

Regular Amer. Veterans **[21319]**

Regular Associated Troupers - Address unknown since 1995.

Regular Baptist Churches; Gen. Assn. of **[19489]**

Regular Common Carrier Conf. **[★3564]**

Regular and Disabled Ser. Assn. **[★21320]**

Regular and Disabled Ser. Assn. **[★21319]**

Regular Veterans Assn. **[21320]**

Regular Veterans Assn. **[★21320]**

Regular Veterans Assn. of the U.S. **[★21320]**

Regulation; Amer. Charities for Reasonable Fundraising **[12195]**

Regulation; American Found. for Res. and Consumer Educ. in Social Work **[★13200]**

Regulation; Coun. on Licensure, Enforcement and **[6271]**

Regulation Found. **[★18420]**

Regulation; Natl. CH on Licensure, Enforcement, and **[★6271]**

Regulation Soc. of Am; Plant Growth **[6647]**

Regulator Soc. of Am; Plant Growth **[★6647]**

Regulators Assn; North Amer. Gaming **[5772]**

Regulatory Admin; Natl. Assn. for **[15011]**

Regulatory Affairs Professionals Soc. **[14599]**, 5635 Fishers Ln., Ste. 550, Rockville, MD 20852, (301)770-2920

Regulatory Affairs Professionals Soc. **[IO]**, Rockville, MD, United States

Regulatory Authority; Tennessee **[6341]**

Regulatory Boards; Fed. of Associations of **[14555]**

Regulatory and Clinical Associates; Org. of **[521]**

Regulatory Examiners Soc; Insurance **[2182]**

Regulatory Reform; Assn. for **[★2526]**

Regulatory Reform; Manufactured Housing Assn. for **[2526]**

Regulatory Toxicology and Pharmacology; Intl. Soc. of **[14570]**

Regulatory Utility Commissioners; Natl. Assn. of **[6339]**

Rehabilitation

Abilities! **[11913]**

Addiction Res. and Treatment Corp. **[13213]**

Adventures in Movement for the Handicapped **[16597]**

Amer. Acad. of Physical Medicine and Rehabilitation **[16307]**

Amer. Assn. for Cancer Educ. **[13789]**

Amer. Assn. of Cardiovascular and Pulmonary Rehabilitation **[13886]**

Amer. Assn. of Mental Hea. Professionals in Corrections **[15186]**

Amer. Assn. of Spinal Cord Injury Psychologists and Social Workers **[16459]**

Amer. Auditory Soc. **[14738]**

Amer. Blind Bowling Assn. **[23334]**

Amer. Blind Skiing Found. **[23336]**

Amer. Bd. of Disability Analysts **[16308]**

Amer. Bd. of Physical Medicine and Rehabilitation **[16309]**

Amer. Coll. of Addiction Treatment Administrators **[13219]**

Amer. Cong. of Rehabilitation Medicine **[16310]**

Amer. Coun. for Drug Educ. **[13222]**

Amer. Friends of ALYN Hosp. **[12825]**

American Friends of ALYN Hospital **[IO]**

Amer. Head and Neck Soc. **[15819]**

Amer. Horticultural Therapy Assn. **[16601]**

Amer. Kinesiotherapy Assn. **[16311]**

Amer. Medical Rehabilitation Providers Assn. **[16312]**

Amer. Osteopathic Coll. of Physical Medicine and Rehabilitation **[15805]**

Amer. Rehabilitation Counseling Assn. **[16313]**

Amer. Rehabilitation Economics Assn. **[16314]**

Amer. Soc. of Exercise Physiologists **[16019]**

Amer. Soc. of Hand Therapists **[14524]**

Amer. Spinal Injury Assn. **[16461]**

Amer. Therapeutic Recreation Assn. **[16315]**

Amer. Wheelchair Bowling Assn. **[23339]**

Amputees in Motion, Intl. **[11921]**

Assoc. Blind **[16830]**

Assoc. Services for the Blind **[16831]**

Assn. of Academic Physiatrists **[16316]**

Assn. of Assistive Tech. Act Programs **[14237]**

Assn. for Educ. and Rehabilitation of the Blind and Visually Impaired **[16833]**

Assn. of Recovering Motorcyclists **[13225]**

Assn. for Rehabilitation Marketing **[2617]**

Assn. of Rehabilitation Nurses **[15469]**

Assn. of Rehabilitation Programs in Cmpt. Tech. **[11924]**

Assn. for the Treatment of Tobacco Use and Dependence **[16653]**

Blue Heron Support Services Assn. **[IO]**

Brain Injury Rsrc. Center **[16317]**

British Soc. of Rehabilitation Medicine **[IO]**

Canadian Assn. of Physical Medicine and Rehabilitation **[IO]**

Canadian Assn. of Rehabilitation Professionals **[IO]**

Canadian Coun. on Rehabilitation and Work **[IO]**

Cancer Info. Ser. **[13807]**

Canine Companions for Independence **[11926]**

Carroll Center for the Blind **[16840]**

Center on Human Policy **[11928]**

Challenge Aspen at Snowmass **[23342]**

Christopher and Dana Reeve Found. **[16463]**

Coma Recovery Assn. **[14029]**

Commn. on Rehabilitation Counselor Certification **[11822]**

Consortia of Administrators for Native Amer. Rehabilitation **[19270]**

Continuing Care Accreditation Commn. **[16318]**

Coun. of Chiropractic Physiological Therapeutics and Rehabilitation **[13999]**

Coun. on Compulsive Gambling of New Jersey **[12209]**

Coun. on Rehabilitation Educ. **[16319]**

Coun. of State Administrators of Vocational Rehabilitation **[16320]**

Covenant World Relief **[12848]**

Disability Rights Educ. and Defense Fund **[11940]**

Disabled Sports USA **[23343]**

Double Trouble in Recovery **[12548]**

Ethos Found. **[13239]**

Faces and Voices of Recovery **[18688]**

Families Worldwide **[13241]**

Found. for Sci. and Disability **[11946]**

Goodwill Indus. Intl. **[11949]**

Goodwill Indus. Volunteer Services **[11950]**

Handicapped Scuba Assn. **[23344]**

Hea. Connection **[13245]**

Helen Keller Intl. **[16854]**

Help Hospitalized Veterans **[13351]**

Hong Kong Assn. of Rehabilitation Medicine **[IO]**

Hong Kong Soc. for Rehabilitation **[IO]**

Hospitalized Veterans Writing Proj. **[16321]**

Inst. for Integral Development **[13249]**

Inter-National Assn. of Bus., Indus. and Rehabilitation **[17417]**

Intl. Assn. of Addictions and Offender Counselors **[11824]**

Intl. Assn. of Laryngectomees **[11953]**

Intl. Assn. of Rehabilitation Professionals **[16322]**

Intl. Rehabilitation Coun. for Torture Victims **[IO]**

Intl. Soc. of Physical and Rehabilitation Medicine **[IO]**

Intl. Wheelchair Road Racers Club **[23346]**

Intl. Wildlife Rehabilitation Coun. **[5333]**

Jewish Guild for the Blind **[16862]**

MAB Community Services **[16868]**

NAADAC The Assn. for Addiction Professionals **[16509]**

Narcotic Educational Found. of Am. **[13256]**

Natl. African Amer. Drug Policy Coalition **[17440]**

Natl. Alliance of Advocates for Buprenorphine Treatment **[16511]**

Natl. Alliance of Methadone Advocates **[14293]**

Natl. Amputation Found. **[11965]**

Natl. Amputee Golf Assn. **[23349]**

Natl. Assn. of Addiction Treatment Providers **[13259]**

Natl. Assn. on Drug Abuse Problems **[13262]**

Natl. Assn. of Housing and Redevelopment Officials **[5793]**

Natl. Assn. of Multicultural Rehabilitation Concerns **[16323]**

Natl. Assn. of Rehabilitation Instructors **[16324]**

Natl. Assn. for Rehabilitation Leadership **[16325]**

Natl. Assn. of Rehabilitation Providers and Agencies **[16326]**

Natl. Assn. of Rehabilitation Support Staff **[16327]**

Natl. Assn. of Ser. Providers in Private Rehabilitation **[16328]**

Natl. Assn. of State Head Injury Administrators **[14529]**

Natl. Assn. of State Veterans Homes **[13354]**

Natl. Black Alcoholism and Addiction Coun. **[13265]**

Natl. Bd. for Certification in Occupational Therapy **[16625]**

Natl. Coalition of Creative Arts Therapies Associations **[16224]**

Natl. Coun. on Rehabilitation Educ. **[16329]**

Natl. Families in Action **[13269]**

Natl. Family Partnership **[13270]**

A star before a book entry number signifies that the name is not listed separately, but is mentioned within the entry.

Natl. Org. of Alternative Programs [16382]
Natl. Rehabilitation Assn. [16330]
Natl. Rehabilitation Counseling Assn. [16331]
Natl. Rehabilitation Info. Center [16332]
Natl. Spinal Cord Injury Assn. [16468]
Natl. Therapeutic Recreation Soc. [16628]
Natl. Veterans Services Fund [13356]
Natl. Wheelchair Basketball Assn. [23354]
Natl. Wheelchair Softball Assn. [23356]
Neuro-Optometric Rehabilitation Assn., Intl. [15300]
North Amer. Riding for the Handicapped Assn. [23357]
One-Arm Dove Hunt Assn. [23358]
Phoenix House [13273]
Praying Hands Ranches [23360]
P.R.I.D.E. Found. - Promote Real Independence for the Disabled and Elderly [11982]
PRIDE Youth Programs [13276]
Private Practice Section/American Physical Therapy Assn. [16633]
Reclamation Inc. [12556]
Reel Recovery [11519]
Rehabilitation Engg. and Assistive Tech. Soc. of North Am. [11983]
Rehabilitation Intl. [16333]
Rehabilitation Intl. [IO]
Rehabilitation Tech. Assn. [16334]
Secular Organizations for Sobriety [13281]
Seventh Step Soc. of Canada [IO]
Sex and Love Addicts Anonymous [13074]
Sister Kenny Rehabilitation Inst. [16335]
Ski for Light [23361]
Social/Vocational Rehabilitation Clinic [16231]
Special Olympics [23362]
Spinal Cord Soc. [16469]
STRIDE: Sports and Therapeutic Recreation Instruction/Developmental Educ. [8205]
Therapy Dogs Intl. [16638]
Torture Abolition and Survivors Support Coalition Intl. [17786]
U.S. Assn. for Blind Athletes [23363]
U.S. Intl. Coun. on Disabilities [11992]
U.S. Psychiatric Rehabilitation Assn. [16336]
U.S. Psychiatric Rehabilitation Assn. [IO]
USA Deaf Sports Fed. [23369]
Veterans Educ. Proj. [13358]
Visually Impaired Veterans of Am. [16891]
Vocational Evaluation and Career Assessment Professionals [16337]
Vocational Evaluation and Career Assessment Professionals [IO]
Wheelchair Motorcycle Assn. [23370]
Wheelchair Sports, USA [23371]
Women's Drug Res. Project [13285]
World Assn. for Psychosocial Rehabilitation - U.S. Br. [16338]
World Association for Psychosocial Rehabilitation - U.S. Branch [IO]
World Coun. for Cardiovascular and Pulmonary Rehabilitation [13930]
Rehabilitation; Amer. Assn. of Cardiovascular and Pulmonary [13886]
Rehabilitation; Amer. Assn. for Cleft Palate [★14055]
Rehabilitation; Amer. Cong. of Physical Medicine and [★16310]
Rehabilitation; Amer. Osteopathic Acad. of Physical Medicine and [★15805]
Rehabilitation; Amer. Osteopathic Coll. of Physical Medicine and [15805]
Rehabilitation; Amer. Osteopathic Coll. of Physical Medicine and [★15805]
Rehabilitation; Amer. Soc. of Neuro [15382]
Rehabilitation; Amer. Soc. of Physical Medicine and [★16307]
Rehabilitation Assn; Amer. [★16312]
Rehabilitation Assn; Amer. Deafness and [★14735]
Rehabilitation Assn; Natl. Housing and [12327]
Rehabilitation Assn; Natl. Housing [★12327]
Rehabilitation; Assn. for Physical and Mental [★16311]
Rehabilitation Center; Florida Keys Wild Bird [5317]
Rehabilitation Center for the Visually Impaired; Carroll [★16840]
Rehabilitation Centers; Assn. of [★16312]

Rehabilitation Clinic; Social [★16231]
Rehabilitation Clinic; Social/Vocational [16231]
Rehabilitation Comm; Amer. [★12075]
Rehabilitation Coun; Wildlife [★5333]
Rehabilitation Counselor Certification; Commn. on [11822]
Rehabilitation Counselor Educators; Coun. of [★16329]
Rehabilitation of the Disabled; Intl. Soc. for [★16333]
Rehabilitation Engg. and Assistive Tech. Soc. of North Am. [11983], 1700 N Moore St., Ste. 1540, Arlington, VA 22209-1903, (703)524-6686
Rehabilitation Engg. Center [★13126]
Rehabilitation Engg; Natl. Inst. for [11972]
Rehabilitation of Errants; Citizens United for [11860]
Rehabilitation of the Facially Disfigured; Soc. for the [★14065]
Rehabilitation Facilities; Assn. of [★16312]
Rehabilitation Facilities; CARF, Commn. on Accreditation of [★16318]
Rehabilitation Facilities; Intl. Assn. of [★16312]
Rehabilitation Facilities; Natl. Assn. of [★16312]
Rehabilitation Found; Amer. [★16335]
Rehabilitation Gazette [★11981]
Rehabilitation Gazette [★IO]
Rehabilitation Hospitals and Services; Center for [★14894]
Rehabilitation Information Round Table - Address unknown since 2002.
Rehabilitation Inst; Voice [★11953]
Rehabilitation Inst; Voice [★IO]
Rehabilitation Intl. [IO], New York, NY, United States
Rehabilitation Intl. [16333], 25 E 21st St., 4th Fl., New York, NY 10010, (212)420-1500
Rehabilitation Medicine; American Osteopathic Bd. of [★15805]
Rehabilitation Medicine; Amer. Osteopathic Coll. of [★15805]
Rehabilitation Nurses; Assn. of [15469]
Rehabilitation Nursing Found. [★15469]
Rehabilitation Programs in Cmpt. Tech; Assn. of [11924]
Rehabilitation Res. Found. - Address unknown since 2003.
Rehabilitation and Rsrc. Centre for Torture Victims [★IO]
Rehabilitation; Sect. for Long Term Care and [14894]
Rehabilitation and Ser; Nevil Inst. for [★16831]
Rehabilitation Services; Psychiatric [15231]
Rehabilitation Tech. Assn. [16334]
Rehabilitation Tech; RESNA: Assn. for the Advancement of [★11983]
Rehabilitation of Underground Utilities; NASSCO - Setting the Indus. Standards for the [3959]
Rehabilitation and Vocation; Sales Exchange for Refugee [3846]
Rehabilitative Audiology; Acad. of [14734]
Rehearsal Club - Defunct.
Reich Collectors Soc; John [22740]
Reid CH; Reed- [21031]

Reiki
Intl. Assn. of Reiki Professionals [13637]
Intl. Center for Reiki Training [22969]
International Center for Reiki Training [IO]

Reiki Alliance [IO], Kellogg, ID, United States
Reiki Alliance Intl. [13651], 204 N Chestnut St., Kellogg, ID 83837, (208)783-3535
The Reiki Assn. [IO], Peel, United Kingdom
Reiki Master Assn; Amer. [13622]
Reiki Training; Intl. Center for [22969]
Reimer Genealogy Center Worldwide - Address unknown since 2002.
Reindeer Husbandry Res; Nordic Coun. for [IO]
Reined Cow Horse Assn; Natl. [22586]
Reinforcement Inst; Wire [687]
Reinforcing Steel Contractors; Natl. Assn. of [1039]
Reinforcing Steel Inst; Concrete [612]
Reining Horse Assn; Natl. [4924]
Reining Horse Assn; Natl. Morgan [4920]
Reinsurance Assn. of Am. [2234], 1301 Pennsylvania Ave. NW, Ste. 900, Washington, DC 20004-1701, (202)638-3690
Reinsurance Brokers' Assn. (Singapore) [IO], Singapore, Singapore

Reinsurance Underwriters Assn; Intermediaries and [2185]
Reinsurers; Natl. Assn. of Property and Casualty [★2234]
Reinvestment Coalition; Natl. Community [17229]
Reiselivsbedriftenes Landsforening [★IO]
Reklamcilar Dernegi [★IO]
Relate [IO], Rugby, United Kingdom
Relate Scotland [IO], Edinburgh, United Kingdom
Relations Res. Assn; Indus. [★24115]
Relationships Australia [IO], Curtin, Australia
Relatives and Residents Assn. [IO], London, United Kingdom
Relax and Rebound Centre [★10179]
Relax Tension Centre [★10179]
Relay Manufacturers; Natl. Assn. of [★1197]
Relay and Switch Indus. Assn. [1197], 2500 Wilson Blvd., Arlington, VA 22201, (703)907-8021
Reliability Engg. and Mgt. Inst. [★7038]
Reliability Engg. and Mgt. Institute/Reliability Testing Inst. [7038], 1130 N Mountain Ave., Bldg. No. 119, PO Box 210119, Rm. N517, Tucson, AZ 85721-0119, (520)297-2679
Reliability Engineers; Soc. of [7046]
Reliability Professionals; Soc. for Maintenance and [2478]
Reliability Soc; IEEE [6924]
Reliability Testing Inst; Reliability Engg. and Mgt. Institute/ [7038]
Reliable and Safe Highways; Citizens for [18577]
Relief
ActionAid Intl. USA [11758]
Adventist Community Services [20552]
Adventist Development and Relief Agency - Canada [IO]
Adventist Development and Relief Agency Intl. [IO]
Adventist Development and Relief Agency Intl. [12826]
Adventist Development and Relief Agency - Japan [IO]
Africa Inland Mission Intl. [20294]
African Medical and Res. Found. [14971]
Agency for Tech. Cooperation and Development [IO]
Air Serv Intl. [IO]
Air Serv Intl. [12827]
Amer. Belarussian Relief Org. [12828]
Amer. Coll. of Intl. Physicians [14973]
Amer. Disaster Reserve [12000]
Amer. Fund for Czechoslovak Relief [12802]
Amer. Jewish World Ser. [12829]
Amer. Jewish World Ser. [IO]
Amer. Red Cross Natl. HQ [12830]
Amer. Red Cross Overseas Assn. [12831]
Amer. Red Magen David for Israel - Amer. Friends of Magen David Adom [12832]
Amer. Red Magen David for Israel - Amer. Friends of Magen David Adom [IO]
AmeriCares Found. [12833]
AMG Intl. [20298]
Ananda Marga Universal Relief Team - Brazil [IO]
Antigua and Barbuda Red Cross Soc. [IO]
Architecture for Humanity [11761]
Armenian Missionary Assn. of Am. [19459]
Armenian Relief Soc. [IO]
Ashoka: Innovators for the Public [12419]
Assn. of Baptists for World Evangelism [19472]
Assn. of Evangelical Relief and Development Organizations [20486]
Assn. to Help Chernobyl [IO]
Assn. for Intl. Medical Study [12834]
Assn. for Ophthalmic Cooperation to Asia [IO]
Assyrian Aid Soc. of Am. [11508]
Australian Red Cross ACT [IO]
Australian Red Cross Soc. [IO]
Aviation Sans Frontieres [IO]
Azerbaijan Red Crescent Soc. [IO]
Bahamas Red Cross Soc. [IO]
Bangladesh Red Crescent Soc. [IO]
Baptist World Alliance [19482]
Basic Human Needs Assn. [IO]
Batey Relief Alliance [IO]
Batey Relief Alliance [12835]
Belize Red Cross [IO]

Reference to "IO" in place of a book number signifies that the association may be found in the 45th edition of International Organizations.

Bd. of Intl. Ministries [19483]
Bosnian-Canadian Relief Assn. [IO]
Box Proj. [IO]
Box Proj. [12836]
British Red Cross [IO]
Brother's Brother Found. [IO]
Brother's Brother Found. [12837]
Bulgarian Red Cross [IO]
Bulgarian Red Cross Youth [IO]
Bur. des Activities Socio-Caritatives - Caritas
    Cameroun [IO]
Canadian Lutheran World Relief [IO]
Canadian Physicians for Aid and Relief [IO]
Canadian Red Cross [IO]
CARE Austria [IO]
CARE Canada [IO]
CARE Danmark [IO]
CARE Deutschland (Germany) [IO]
CARE Egypt [IO]
CARE France [IO]
CARE Guatemala [IO]
CARE Honduras [IO]
CARE India [IO]
CARE Intl. - Belgium [IO]
CARE Intl. UK [IO]
CARE Intl. USA [IO]
CARE Intl. USA [12838]
CARE Japan [IO]
CARE Nepal [IO]
CARE Netherlands [IO]
CARE Norge (Norway) [IO]
CARE Peru [IO]
CARE Philippines [IO]
Caritas Andorrana [IO]
Caritas de Angola [IO]
Caritas Aotearoa New Zealand [IO]
Caritas Argentina [IO]
Caritas Australia [IO]
Caritas Azerbaijan [IO]
Caritas Bangladesh [IO]
Caritas Belarus [IO]
Caritas Benin [IO]
Caritas Bolivia [IO]
Caritas Bulgaria [IO]
Caritas Caboverdeana [IO]
Caritas Cambodia [IO]
Caritas Catholica Belgica [IO]
Caritas Centrafrique [IO]
Caritas Colombia [IO]
Caritas Comores [IO]
Caritas Coreana [IO]
Caritas Cote d'Ivoire [IO]
Caritas Cuba [IO]
Caritas Denmark [IO]
Caritas Djibouti [IO]
Caritas Dominicana [IO]
Caritas Ecuador [IO]
Caritas Egypte [IO]
Caritas El Salvador [IO]
Caritas Eritrea [IO]
Caritas Ethiopia [IO]
Caritas Gabon [IO]
Caritas Gambia [IO]
Caritas Georgia [IO]
Caritas Guinea Ecuatorial [IO]
Caritas Hellas [IO]
Caritas de Honduras [IO]
Caritas Hong Kong [IO]
Caritas Hungarica [IO]
Caritas Iceland [IO]
Caritas Ile Maurice [IO]
Caritas India [IO]
Caritas Indonesia [IO]
Caritas Internationalis - Vatican City [IO]
Caritas Iran [IO]
Caritas Iraq [IO]
Caritas Italiana [IO]
Caritas Jordan [IO]
Caritas Karuna Myanmar [IO]
Caritas Kazakhstan [IO]
Caritas Kenya [IO]
Caritas Latvia [IO]
Caritas Lesotho [IO]
Caritas Liberia [IO]
Caritas Libie [IO]

Caritas Macedonia [IO]
Caritas Maroc [IO]
Caritas Mauritanie [IO]
Caritas Mocambicana [IO]
Caritas Moldova [IO]
Caritas Monaco [IO]
Caritas Mongolia [IO]
Caritas Nepal [IO]
Caritas Nicaragua [IO]
Caritas Niger [IO]
Caritas Nigeria [IO]
Caritas Pakistan [IO]
Caritas Paraguay [IO]
Caritas Puerto Rico [12839]
Caritas Republique du Congo [IO]
Caritas Rwanda [IO]
Caritas Sao Tome and Principe [IO]
Caritas Senegal [IO]
Caritas Seychelles [IO]
Caritas South Africa [IO]
Caritas Swaziland [IO]
Caritas Switzerland [IO]
Caritas Tanzania [IO]
Caritas Tunisie [IO]
Caritas Uganda [IO]
Caritas Ukraine [IO]
Catholic Church Extension Soc. of the U.S.A.
    [19596]
Catholic Development Commn. - Caritas
    Zimbabwe [IO]
Catholic Development Commn. in Malawi - Cari-
    tas Malawi [IO]
Catholic Network of Volunteer Ser. [19602]
Catholic Relief Services - El Salvador [IO]
CED - Caritas Burundi [IO]
Center for Intl. Disaster Info. [12001]
Center of Stud. of Disaster and Prevention [IO]
Change for Good [12840]
Chernobyl Children's Fund - Japan [IO]
Child Relief and You Am. [11569]
Children's Network Intl. [11579]
Children's Relief Network [11581]
Christ for the Nations [20314]
Christian Forum Res. Found. [20560]
Christian Pilots Assn. [20321]
Christian Reformed World Relief Comm. [12424]
Christian Relief Services [12841]
Christian Relief Services [IO]
Church of the Brethren Gen. Bd. Global Mission
    Partnership [19535]
Church World Ser. [12842]
Church World Ser. [IO]
Circle of Hea. Intl. [12268]
CitiHope Intl. [12843]
CitiHope Intl. [IO]
CityTeam Ministries [12844]
Comite de Coordination des Actions des Organi-
    sations Non Gouvernementales [IO]
Commn. de Pastorale Sociale - Caritas Mali [IO]
Comm. on Missionary Evangelism [20001]
Concern Am. [12845]
Concern Am. [IO]
Concern Worldwide [IO]
Concern Worldwide [12846]
Convoy of Hope [12847]
Covenant World Relief [12848]
Covenant World Relief [IO]
Croatian Red Cross [IO]
Danish Red Cross [IO]
Dept. of Socio-Economic Development - Caritas
    Ghana [IO]
Developpement Caritas Republique Democratique
    du Congo Democratic [IO]
Direct Aid Intl. [IO]
Direct Aid Intl. [12849]
Direct Relief Intl. [12517]
DOCARE Intl., N.F.P. [12518]
Doctors Without Borders - Australia [IO]
Doctors Without Borders - Canada [IO]
Doctors Without Borders USA [IO]
Doctors Without Borders USA [12850]
Doctors Worldwide [12851]
Doctors Worldwide [IO]
Doctors Worldwide [IO]
Dominican Mission Found. [20328]

Educational Concerns for Hunger Org. [12389]
Egyptian Red Crescent Soc. [IO]
Emergency Social Services Assn. [IO]
Episcopal Relief and Development [IO]
Episcopal Relief and Development [12852]
Estonian Amer. Fund for Economic Educ. [8215]
Estonian Relief Comm. [12853]
Estonian Relief Comm. [IO]
Evangelical Fellowship of India Commn. on Relief
    [IO]
Evangelical Medical Aid Soc. [IO]
Fed. of Protestant Welfare Agencies [20482]
Feed the Children [12854]
Feed the Children [IO]
Feeding Hungry Children Intl. [12390]
FilmAid Intl. [12811]
Finn Church Aid [IO]
Finnish Red Cross [IO]
Flying Doctors of Am. [12523]
Food for Life Global [12855]
Food for Life Global [IO]
Found. of Compassionate Amer. Samaritans
    [20340]
Found. for the Support of Intl. Medical Training
    [14977]
Free Wheelchair Mission [11947]
Freedom Is Not Free [12596]
Friends Disaster Ser. [12856]
German Medical Aid Org., Action Medeor [IO]
Ghana Red Cross Soc. [IO]
Giving Children Hope [11596]
Global Action Intl. [12857]
Global Action Intl. [IO]
Global Hea. Coun. [14979]
Global MissionAir [20487]
Global MissionAir [IO]
Grassroots Intl. [12428]
Guyana Red Cross Soc. [IO]
Healing Hands Intl. [13141]
Hea. Volunteers Overseas [12526]
Heart to Heart Intl. [12858]
Heart to Heart Intl. [IO]
Hesperian Found. [14980]
Hong Kong Red Cross [IO]
Human Appeal Intl. [IO]
Human Assistance and Development Intl. [20437]
Humanity Intl. [12859]
Humanity Intl. [IO]
Icelandic Church Aid [IO]
Icelandic Red Cross [IO]
Indian Muslim Relief Comm. of ISNA [IO]
Indian Muslim Relief Comm. of ISNA [12860]
Indian Red Cross Soc. [IO]
Interchurch Medical Assistance [20242]
Intl. Aid [12861]
Intl. Aid [IO]
Intl. Aid Services [IO]
Intl. Blue Crescent Relief and Development
    Found. [IO]
Intl. Comm. for the Children of Chechnya [11605]
Intl. Comm. of the Red Cross - Armenia [IO]
Intl. Comm. of the Red Cross - Azerbaijan [IO]
Intl. Comm. of the Red Cross - Switzerland [IO]
Intl. Development and Relief Found. [IO]
Intl. Fed. of Red Cross and Red Crescent Societ-
    ies [IO]
Intl. Fed. of Red Cross and Red Crescent Societ-
    ies - Vietnam [IO]
Intl. Medical Corps [IO]
Intl. Medical Corps [12862]
Intl. Relief And Development [11782]
Intl. Relief Teams [12863]
Intl. Relief Teams [IO]
Intl. Social Ser. - Hong Kong [IO]
InterServe U.S.A. [20351]
Iranian Red Crescent [IO]
Islamic Amer. Relief Agency [IO]
Islamic Amer. Relief Agency [12864]
Islamic Relief USA [12865]
Islamic Relief USA [IO]
Jamaica Red Cross [IO]
Japan Palestine Medical Assn. [IO]
Japanese Red Cross Soc. [IO]
Jesuit Volunteer Corps: Northwest [19644]
Just Act: Youth Action for Global Justice [12435]

A star before a book entry number signifies that the name is not listed separately, but is mentioned within the entry.

Just World Partners **[IO]**
Koinonia Caritas **[IO]**
Korean Red Cross **[IO]**
Lalmba Assn. **[IO]**
Lalmba Assn. **[12866]**
Lay Mission-Helpers Assn. **[19648]**
Lebanese Red Cross **[IO]**
Life for Relief and Development **[IO]**
Life for Relief and Development **[12867]**
Malawi Proj. **[11266]**
Malawi Red Cross Soc. **[IO]**
Malaysian Red Crescent Soc. **[IO]**
Malta Red Cross **[IO]**
MAP Intl. **[20243]**
Mapendo Intl. **[12868]**
Mapendo Intl. **[IO]**
Medecins Sans Frontieres - Hong Kong **[IO]**
Medecins Sans Frontieres - UAE **[IO]**
Medecins Sans Frontieres - UK **[IO]**
Medical Teams Intl. **[12869]**
Medicine for Peace **[12789]**
MediSend Intl. **[12530]**
Mennonite Disaster Ser. **[12870]**
Mennonite Disaster Service **[IO]**
MERCY Malaysia **[IO]**
Mercy Universal **[IO]**
Mercy-USA for Aid and Development **[IO]**
Mercy-USA for Aid and Development **[12871]**
Mir Pace Intl. **[12872]**
Mir Pace Intl. **[IO]**
Mission to Haiti **[12267]**
Monaco Red Cross **[IO]**
Natl. Catholic Development and Caritas **[IO]**
Natl. Christ Child Soc. **[19679]**
Natl. Coun. of Catholic Women **[19684]**
Natl. Coun. of Churches of Christ in the U.S.A.
  [19905]
Natl. Defense Coun. Found. **[18465]**
Natl. Relief Network **[12873]**
Natl. Voluntary Organizations Active in Disaster
  [12874]
Near East Found. **[18068]**
Need **[12875]**
Need **[IO]**
Nepal Red Cross Soc. **[IO]**
Netherlands Red Cross Soc. **[IO]**
New Zealand Red Cross **[IO]**
Nigerian Red Cross Soc. **[IO]**
Northwest Medical Teams Intl. **[IO]**
Norwegian Church Aid **[IO]**
OCADES - Caritas Burkina Faso **[IO]**
Off. for the Coordination of Humanitarian Affairs -
  Geneva **[IO]**
Oper. Smile **[12534]**
Oper. U.S.A. **[12535]**
Org. Catholique pour la Promotion Humaine -
  Caritas Rep. de Guinee **[IO]**
Org. de la Charite pour un Developpement
  Integral - Caritas Togo **[IO]**
Org. for the Relief of Underprivileged Women and
  Children in Africa **[12876]**
Our Little Bros. and Sisters **[20380]**
Oxfam Intl. Advocacy Off. **[12877]**
Oxfam Intl. Advocacy Off. **[IO]**
Pakistan Red Crescent Soc. **[IO]**
Partnership for Quality Medical Donations **[12537]**
PEF Israel Endowment Funds **[12461]**
Philippine Natl. Red Cross **[IO]**
Planet Aid **[13144]**
Plenty Intl. **[12878]**
Plenty Intl. **[IO]**
Pontifical Mission for Palestine **[12816]**
Rapha Intl. **[12539]**
Red Crescent Soc. - Uzbekistan **[IO]**
Red Cross Soc. of China **[IO]**
Red Cross - Ukraine **[IO]**
RedR Canada **[IO]**
RedR Intl. **[IO]**
RedR New Zealand **[IO]**
Refugee Relief Intl. **[12540]**
Refugees Intl. **[12818]**
Relief Interactive **[12879]**
Relief Interactive **[IO]**
Religious Freedom Coalition **[12880]**
Restoration Proj. Intl. **[12441]**

RHEMA Intl. **[12881]**
RHEMA Intl. **[IO]**
Rosedale Mennonite Missions **[20253]**
St. Martin De Porres Guild **[20389]**
Salesian Missioners **[20391]**
Services for the Hea. in Asian and African
  Regions **[IO]**
Share Our Strength **[12399]**
Sierra Leone Red Cross Soc. **[IO]**
Singapore Red Cross **[IO]**
Social Relief Intl. **[12445]**
Soc. of Missionaries of Africa **[19721]**
South African Red Cross Soc. **[IO]**
Sphere Proj. **[IO]**
SUDANAID - Caritas Sudan **[IO]**
Synergos Inst. **[12784]**
Tearfund **[IO]**
Thai Red Cross Soc. **[IO]**
Tibet Soc. of the United Kingdom **[IO]**
Tirisanyo Catholic Commn. - Caritas Botswana
  [IO]
Tunisian Red Crescent **[IO]**
Turkish Red Crescent Soc. **[IO]**
Union Nationale des Associations Diocesaines de
  Secours et de Developpement - Caritas Tchad
  [IO]
United Methodist Comm. on Relief **[20267]**
United Sisters of Charity **[20406]**
U.S. Fund for UNICEF **[11658]**
U.S.A. for Africa **[12882]**
U.S.A. for Africa **[IO]**
Vanuatu Red Cross Soc. **[IO]**
Vietnam Red Cross Soc. **[IO]**
Vitamin Angel Alliance **[15571]**
Voluntary Organisations in Cooperation in
  Emergencies **[IO]**
Water Missions Intl. **[13411]**
We Care Am. **[13210]**
Wings of Hope **[12883]**
Wings of Hope **[IO]**
WishKids Intl. **[11665]**
World Community Chaplains **[12884]**
World Community Chaplains **[IO]**
World Emergency Relief **[IO]**
World Emergency Relief **[12885]**
World Medical Mission **[20245]**
World Medical Relief **[12544]**
World Mercy Fund **[12886]**
World Mercy Fund **[IO]**
World Opportunities **[20415]**
World Rehabilitation Fund **[11997]**
World Relief **[19985]**
World Vision **[20418]**
World Vision **[20488]**
World Vision **[IO]**
World Vision Armenia **[IO]**
World Vision Asia Pacific Region **[IO]**
World Vision Australia **[IO]**
World Vision Colombia **[IO]**
World Vision Hong Kong **[IO]**
World Vision India **[IO]**
World Vision Ireland **[IO]**
World Vision Japan **[IO]**
World Vision Malaysia **[IO]**
World Vision Middle East/Eastern Europe **[IO]**
World Vision Singapore **[IO]**
World Vision Taiwan **[IO]**
Relief for Africans in Need - Defunct.
Relief; Army Emergency **[18958]**
Relief Assn; Egyptians **[11774]**
Relief Assn; Intl. **[★12812]**
Relief Assn. of U.S.A. and Canada; Masonic
  [★19229]
Relief in Belgium; Commission for **[★9736]**
Relief and Benefit Assn; Armed Forces **[★18955]**
Relief Commn; NAE World **[★19985]**
Relief Commn. of the Natl. Assn. of Evangelicals;
  World **[★19985]**
Relief Comm; World **[★19985]**
Relief Comm; Amer. Jewish **[★12464]**
Relief Comm; Central **[★12464]**
Relief Comm; People's **[★12464]**
Relief Comm; United Ukrainian Amer. **[19420]**
Relief Found. **[IO]**, Chennai, India
Relief Found; Direct **[★12517]**

Relief Found; Iuliu Maniu Amer. Romanian **[19332]**
Relief Friendship Found; World **[★13171]**
Relief Fund of Am; United Lithuanian **[19216]**
Relief Fund; Motion Picture **[★12115]**
Relief Fund; Riot **[19266]**
Relief Interactive **[12879]**
Relief Interactive **[IO]**, Vienna, VA, United States
Relief for Italy; Amer. **[★13474]**
Relief of Jewish War Sufferers; Joint Distribution
  Comm. for **[★12464]**
Relief; Methodist Comm. for Overseas **[★20267]**
Relief; Near East **[★18068]**
Relief Services - Natl. Catholic Welfare Conf;
  Catholic **[★12807]**
Relief Services - Natl. Catholic Welfare Conf; War
  [★12807]
Relief SOC; Friends of Israel Missionary and
  [★20010]
Relief Soc; Armenian **[★18966]**
Relief Soc; Army **[★18958]**
Relief Soc. of China **[★IO]**
Relief Soc; Navy-Marine Corps **[18960]**
Relief Soc; United Tiberias Institutions **[12463]**
Relief; United Methodist Comm. on Overseas
  [★20267]
Relief War Fund; Permanent Blind **[★16854]**
Religion
  ABW Ministries **[19468]**
  Acad. of Amer. Franciscan History **[19560]**
  Acad. of Homiletics **[20081]**
  Acad. of Parish Clergy **[20274]**
  Acad. of Spirituality and Paranormal Stud., Inc.
    [7440]
  Acton Inst. for the Stud. of Religion and Liberty
    [20489]
  Adopt-A-Church Intl. **[19839]**
  Adult Christian Educ. Found. **[19913]**
  Advancing Churches in Missions Commitment
    [20293]
  Advancing Native Missions **[19833]**
  Advent Christian Gen. Conf. of Am. **[19442]**
  Adventist Community Services **[20552]**
  Advocates Intl. **[17998]**
  Aetherius Soc. **[20568]**
  Affirmation/Gay and Lesbian Mormons **[20046]**
  Affirmation: United Methodists for Lesbian, Gay
    and Bisexual Concerns **[20047]**
  Africa Faith and Justice Network **[16920]**
  African Amer. Lutheran Assn. **[20211]**
  African-Amer. Women's Clergy Assn. **[20615]**
  Aglow Intl. **[20616]**
  Agni Yoga Soc. **[20632]**
  Agudath Israel of Am. **[20110]**
  Aid to the Church in Need **[19563]**
  All Roads Ministry **[19564]**
  All-Ukrainian Evangelical Baptist Fellowship
    [19469]
  Alliance for Intl. Monasticism **[IO]**
  Alliance for Life Ministries **[19760]**
  Ambassadors of Mary **[19565]**
  Ambrose Monell Found. **[13110]**
  Am. World Adoption Assn. **[11233]**
  Amer. Acad. of Ministry **[19914]**
  Amer. Assn. of Christian Counselors **[19862]**
  Amer. Baptist Historical Soc. **[19470]**
  Amer. Baptist Homes and Hospitals Assn. **[19471]**
  Amer. Baptists Concerned **[20048]**
  Amer. Benedictine Acad. **[19566]**
  Amer. Bible Soc. **[19504]**
  Amer. Bd. of Examiners in Pastoral Counseling
    [19864]
  Amer. Buddhist Assn. **[19540]**
  Amer. Buddhist Movement **[19541]**
  Amer. Buddhist Stud. Center **[19542]**
  Amer. Catholic Lawyers Assn. **[5558]**
  Amer. Coalition of Unregistered Churches **[20520]**
  Amer. Comm. for KEEP **[12418]**
  Amer. Conf. of Cantors **[20112]**
  Amer. Congregational Assn. **[19859]**
  Amer. Coun. of Christian Churches **[19761]**
  Amer. Coun. for Judaism **[20113]**
  Amer. Ethical Union **[20083]**
  Amer. and Foreign Christian Union **[19762]**
  Amer. Forum for Jewish-Christian Cooperation
    [19887]

Reference to "IO" in place of a book number signifies that the association may be found in the 45th edition of International Organizations.

Amer. Freedom Alliance [18507]
Amer. Hindu Assn. [20077]
Amer. Jewish Comm. [20114]
Amer. Jewish Cong. [20115]
Amer. Jewish League for Israel [20116]
Amer. Lutheran Publicity Bur. [20212]
Amer. Missionary Fellowship [20296]
Amer. Psychological Assn. - Psychology of
   Religion (Division 36) [16132]
Amer. Romanian Orthodox Youth [20540]
Amer. Sci. Affiliation [20546]
Amer. Sephardi Fed. [20117]
Amer. Soc. for Church Growth [19841]
Amer. Soc. of Church History [20078]
Amer. Soc. of Missiology [20297]
Amer. Soc. for Muslim Advancement [10245]
Amer. Tract Soc. [19987]
Amer. Vinland Assn. [19460]
Amer. Zionist Movement [20118]
Americans for Religious Liberty [17090]
Americans United for Separation of Church and
   State [19836]
AMG Intl. [20298]
Anabaptist Sociology and Anthropology Assn.
   [7559]
Anglican Assn. of Biblical Scholars [19449]
Anglican Fellowship of Prayer [19452]
Anglican Order of Archbishop Robert Leighton
   [19453]
Anglican Soc. [19942]
Anglican Use Assn. [19450]
Anglicans United [19943]
Anthroposophical Soc. in Am. [19457]
Apostleship of Prayer [19569]
Apostleship of Prayer [IO]
Apostleship of the Sea in the U.S.A. [19570]
Apostolate for Family Consecrations [19571]
Archconfraternity of Christian Mothers [19572]
Archconfraternity of the Holy Ghost [19573]
Armenian Church Youth Org. of Am. [19458]
Armenian Missionary Assn. of Am. [19459]
ASGM [19506]
Assoc. Church Press [3205]
Assoc. Parishes for Liturgy and Mission [19945]
Associates for Biblical Res. [19507]
Assn. of Anglican Musicians [20425]
Assn. of Armenian Church Choirs of Am. [10559]
Assn. of Baptists for World Evangelism [19472]
Assn. of Christian Church Educators [19842]
Assn. for Christian Ethics [19574]
Assn. for Clinical Pastoral Educ. [19915]
Assn. of Coll. and Univ. Religious Affairs [9168]
Assn. of Contemplative Sisters [20563]
Assn. for the Development of Religious Info.
   Systems [20091]
Assn. of Evangelical Relief and Development
   Organizations [20486]
Assn. of Grace Brethren Ministers [19533]
Assn. of Humanistic Rabbis [20120]
Assn. of Islamic Charitable Projects [20096]
Assn. of Life-Giving Churches [19843]
Assn. of Marian Helpers [19576]
Assn. of Mercy Colleges [8053]
Assn. of North Amer. Missions [20301]
Assn. of Professional Chaplains [19744]
Assn. of Professors of Mission [20302]
Assn. of Reformed Baptist Churches of Am.
   [19473]
Assn. for Religion and Intellectual Life [19916]
Assn. for the Restoration of the Church and Home
   [19844]
Assn. pour le Retablissement des Institutions et
   Oeuvres Israelites en France [20121]
Assn. of Romanian Catholics of America [19579]
Assn. for the Sociology of Religion [7661]
Assn. of Southern Baptist Campus Ministers
   [19474]
Assn. for Spiritual, Ethical and Religious Values in
   Counseling [8166]
Assn. of State Baptist Papers [19475]
Assn. of Theological Schools in the U.S. and
   Canada [9270]
Assn. of Welcoming and Affirming Baptists
   [19476]
Assumption Guild [19580]

Astara [20443]
Athletes in Action [19990]
Augustinian Secondary Educational Assn. [8054]
Australian Assn. for the Stud. of Religions [IO]
Auxiliaries of Our Lady of the Cenacle [19581]
Baptist Bible Fellowship Intl. [19477]
Baptist Joint Comm. for Religious Liberty [19479]
Baptist Mid-Missions [19480]
Baptist Women in Ministry/Folio [19481]
Baptist World Alliance [19482]
BCM Intl. [19508]
Bear Butte Intl. Alliance [19446]
Becket Fund for Religious Liberty [18509]
Berean Bible Soc. [19509]
Bible League [19510]
Bible Sabbath Assn. [20543]
Bibles For The World [20305]
Biblical Inst. for Social Change [20490]
Biblical Ministries Worldwide [19991]
Biblical Witness Fellowship [20606]
Billy Graham Evangelistic Assn. [19992]
Bishop Baraga Assn. and Archives [19583]
Bishops' Comm. for Ecumenical and Interreligious
   Affairs [19584]
Bishops' Comm. on the Liturgy [19585]
Bishops' Comm. on Priestly Formation [19917]
Bishops' Comm. on Vocations [19586]
Black Holocaust Soc. [16938]
Black and Indian Mission Off. [19587]
Black Methodists for Church Renewal [20260]
Black Women in Church and Soc. [20617]
Blessed Kateri Tekakwitha League [19588]
BLI [19512]
Blue Army of Our Lady of Fatima, U.S.A. [19589]
B'nai B'rith Intl. [20125]
B'nai B'rith Youth Org. [20126]
Bnos Agudath Israel [20127]
Bd. of Intl. Ministries [19483]
BoardSource [12651]
Boston Theological Inst. [9271]
Bread on the Waters [19993]
Brethren in Christ World Missions [20306]
Brethren/Mennonite Coun. for Lesbian, Gay,
   Bisexual and Transgender Interest [20050]
Brethren Peace Fellowship [19534]
Brotherhood of Saint Andrew [19946]
Bros. and Sisters in Christ [19767]
Bruderhof Communities [20481]
Buddhist Churches of Am. Fed. of Buddhist
   Women's Associations [19543]
Bur. of Catholic Indian Missions [19591]
Burma-America Buddhist Assn. [19546]
Cambridge Buddhist Assn. [19547]
Campus Crusade for Christ Intl. [19994]
Campus Ministry Women [19918]
Canadian Canon Law Soc. [IO]
Canadian Religious Conf. [IO]
Canadian Soc. for the Stud. of Religion [IO]
Canon Law Soc. of Am. [19592]
Cantors Assembly [20128]
Capuchin-Franciscans (Province of Saint Joseph)
   [19594]
Catholic Acad. of Sciences in the U.S.A. [19919]
Catholic Biblical Assn. of Am. [9272]
Catholic Campus Ministry Assn. [19595]
Catholic Church Extension Soc. of the U.S.A.
   [19596]
Catholic Inst. of the Food Indus. [19598]
Catholic Kolping Soc. of Am. [19599]
Catholic League for Religious and Civil Rights
   [19600]
Catholic Negro-Amer. Mission Bd. [19601]
Catholic Network of Volunteer Ser. [19602]
Catholic Pamphlet Soc. of the U.S. [19603]
Catholic Traditionalist Movement [19604]
Catholic War Veterans Auxiliary of the U.S.A.
   [21194]
Catholic War Veterans of the U.S.A. [21290]
Catholics Speak Out [19605]
Catholics United for the Faith [19606]
CBA [3403]
CBM Ministries [19995]
Center for Applied Res. in the Apostolate [19608]
Center for Christian/Jewish Understanding of
   Sacred Heart Univ. [19888]

Center for Confucian Sci. [19879]
Center on Conscience and War [17438]
Center for the Evangelical United Brethren
   Heritage [19976]
Center for Global Educ. [8662]
Center for the Ministry of Teaching [19920]
Center for Reduction of Religious-Based Conflict
   [18504]
Center for Reduction of Religious-Based Conflict
   [IO]
Center on Religion and Soc. [20491]
Center for Res. in Faith and Moral Development
   [20534]
Central Assn. of the Miraculous Medal [19609]
Central Bur., Catholic Central Union of Am.
   [19610]
Central Conf. of Amer. Rabbis [20129]
Central Org. for Jewish Educ. [8688]
Central Rabbinical Cong. of the U.S.A. and
   Canada [20130]
Champions for Life Intl. [19996]
Chatlos Found. [20591]
Child Evangelism Fellowship [19997]
Chinese Christian Mission [20313]
Choristers Guild [20426]
Christ in Action Ministries [19999]
Christ for the Nations [20314]
Christ Truth Ministries [19514]
Christian Aid Mission [20316]
Christian Anti-Defamation League [17102]
Christian Boaters Assn. [20000]
Christian Bus. Men's Comm. [19771]
Christian Camping International/U.S.A. [23270]
Christian Century Found. [19772]
Christian Chaplain Sers. [19745]
Christian Communications, Inc. [19774]
Christian Defense League [19775]
Christian Educators Assn. Intl. [19922]
Christian Educators Fellowship of the United
   Methodist Church [19923]
Christian Family Renewal [19776]
Christian Fencers Assn. [23400]
Christian Forum Res. Found. [20560]
Christian Freedom Intl. [20521]
Christian Friends of Israel - USA [19777]
Christian Holiness Partnership [19779]
Christian Instrumentalists and Directors Assn.
   [20427]
Christian Literature and Bible Center [20317]
Christian Mgt. Assn. [20511]
Christian Media Assn. [20237]
Christian Medical and Dental Associations [20238]
Christian Military Fellowship [19782]
Christian Missionary Fellowship [20319]
Christian Res. [19784]
Christian Res. Assn. [IO]
Christian Res. Inst. [19785]
Christian Ser. Club [19515]
Christian Small Publishers Assn. [3217]
Christian Stewardship Assn. [20512]
Christian TV Mission [19536]
Christians in Crisis [20555]
Christians in Govt. [19516]
Christians for Peace in El Salvador [20322]
The Christophers [19611]
Church Army [19947]
Church Benefits Assn. [20461]
Church of the Brethren Gen. Bd. Global Mission
   Partnership [19535]
Church Growth Center [20279]
Church Growth Inc. [20536]
Church Music Assn. of Am. [20428]
Church Music Publishers Assn. [20429]
Church Periodical Club [19949]
Church of Spiritual Discovery [20569]
Church and Synagogue Lib. Assn. [10348]
Church Universal and Triumphant [19462]
Church Women United [20618]
Churches Uniting in Christ [19889]
Circle of Earth [20458]
CLAL: Natl. Jewish Center for Learning and
   Leadership [20132]
Claretian Volunteers and Lay Missionaries
   [19612]
Collectors of Religion on Stamps [22809]

A star before a book entry number signifies that the name is not listed separately, but is mentioned within the entry.

Coll. Theology Soc. [9273]
Commn. of the Churches on Intl. Affairs [20094]
Commn. on Religious Counseling and Healing [19445]
Comm. on Missionary Evangelism [20001]
Comm. on Social Development and World Peace of the U.S. Catholic Conf. [19613]
Commun. Commn. [19537]
Community of Celebration [19790]
Community for Religious Res. and Education [20537]
Company of Saint Paul [19614]
Concordia Deaconess Conf. [20213]
Concordia Gospel Outreach [20214]
Concordia Historical Inst. [20215]
Conf. for Catholic Lesbians [20051]
Conf. on Faith and History [20079]
Conf. of Presidents of Major Amer. Jewish Organizations [20134]
Confessing Synod Ministries [20561]
Confraternity of the Blessed Sacrament [19951]
Congregation of the Blessed Sacrament [19617]
Congregation Shema Yisrael [20135]
Congregation of Sisters of Saint Agnes [19618]
Cong. of Natl. Black Churches [19890]
Connecting Church Assn. [19846]
Conservative Baptist Assn. of Am. [19485]
Continental Baptist Missions [19486]
CORPUS - Natl. Assn. for an Inclusive Priesthood [19619]
Coun. of Khalistan/International Sikh Org. [20557]
Coun. of Masajid of U.S. [20097]
Coun. of Societies for the Stud. of Religion [9274]
Coun. on Spiritual Practices [20564]
Covenant of Unitarian Universalist Pagans [20459]
Covenant World Relief [12848]
Cowboys for Christ [19792]
Creation Health Found. [20547]
Creation Res. Soc. [20548]
Cross-Cultural Shamanism Network [20444]
Crossworld [20326]
Crusaders for Christ [20462]
CSB Ministries [20640]
CUSA: An Apostolate of the Sick and Disabled [19620]
Dawn Bible Students Assn. [19517]
Dharma Realm Buddhist Assn. [19548]
Dialogue Found. [20207]
Dignity/USA [20053]
Disciples of Christ Historical Soc. [19853]
Disciples Ecumenical Consultative Coun. [19848]
Disciples Justice Action Network [19793]
Divine Sci. Fed. Intl. [19880]
Divine Sci. Ministers Assn. [19881]
Division of Higher Educ., Christian Church-Disciples of Christ [19854]
DMA Nonprofit Fed. [317]
Do Right Found. [20492]
Dominican Mission Found. [20328]
Dynamic Youth Ministries [19831]
EAPE/Campolo Ministries - Evangelical Assn. for the Promotion of Educ. [20330]
East-West Cultural Center [9619]
ECKANKAR [20493]
Ecumenical Theological Seminary [19924]
Edith Stein Guild [19621]
Emunah Women of Am. [20136]
Episcopal Church Building Fund [19952]
Episcopal Evangelical Educ. Soc. [19955]
Episcopal Women's Caucus [19956]
Equal Partners in Faith [20494]
Equestrian Ministries Intl. [20082]
Ethics and Religious Liberty Commn. of the Southern Baptist Convention [19487]
European Soc. for the Stud. of Sci. and Theology [IO]
Evangelical Alliance of the United Kingdom [IO]
Evangelical Christian Publishers Assn. [3223]
Evangelical Church Alliance [19977]
Evangelical Coun. for Financial Accountability [20002]
Evangelical and Ecumenical Women's Caucus [19978]
Evangelical Free Church of Am. - Intl. Mission [20333]

Evangelical Friends Intl. - North Amer. Region [20040]
Evangelical Missiological Soc. [20334]
Evangelical Press Assn. [20004]
Evangelical and Reformed Historical Soc. [20607]
Evangelical Social Action Commn. [20005]
Evangelical Theological Soc. [19980]
Evangelical Training Assn. [19925]
Evangelicals Concerned [20054]
Evangelism and Home Missions Assn. [20006]
Evangelistic Faith Missions [20336]
Faith Alive [19957]
Faith at Work [19893]
FaithWorks Intl. [11777]
Family and Church History Dept. of the Church of Jesus Christ of Latter-Day Saints [21115]
Family Rosary [19622]
Fed. of Fire Chaplains [19747]
Fed. of Islamic Associations in the U.S. and Canada [20098]
Fed. of Jain Associations in North America [20495]
Fed. of Jewish Men's Clubs [20137]
Fellowship of Amer. Baptist Musicians [20430]
Fellowship of Christian Airline Personnel [20007]
Fellowship of Christian Athletes [20008]
Fellowship of Christian Magicians [19797]
Fellowship of Christian Released Time Ministries [19926]
Fellowship of Concerned Churchmen [19454]
Fellowship of Orthodox Christians in Am. [20542]
Fellowship in Prayer [19894]
Fellowship of Saint James [19800]
Fellowship of Saint Paul [19958]
Fellowship of United Methodists in Music and Worship Arts [20261]
Fiqh Coun. of North America [20099]
First Zen Inst. of Am. [19549]
Focolare Movement [19624]
Focus on the Chinese Family [20496]
Forum for Scriptural Christianity [20262]
Forward in Faith North Am. [19959]
Found. for Christian Theology [19960]
Found. for a Course in Miracles [20571]
Found. for the Preservation of the Mahayana Tradition [19550]
Found. for Shamanic Stud. [20446]
Found. for Traditional Values [18505]
Foundations and Donors Interested in Catholic Activities [19625]
Freedom From Religion Found. [19837]
Friends Comm. on Natl. Legislation [20041]
Friends Gen. Conf. [20042]
Friends Historical Assn. [20043]
Friends of Israel Gospel Ministry [20010]
Friends for Lesbian, Gay, Bisexual, Transgender, and Queer Concerns [20056]
Friends of Old St. Ferdinand [19626]
Friends of the Shakers [10963]
Friends of the Western Buddhist Order [19551]
Full Gospel Bus. Men's Fellowship Intl. [19801]
G. Unger Vetlesen Found. [12719]
Gen. Assn. of Regular Baptist Churches [19489]
Gen. Bd. of Church and Soc. of the United Methodist Church [20263]
Gen. Commn. on Archives and History of the United Methodist Church [10467]
The Gideons Intl. [20011]
Glenmary Res. Center [19628]
Global Teams [19961]
Good Tidings [19629]
Grailville [19630]
Graymoor Ecumenical and Interreligious Inst. [19895]
Greek Orthodox Ladies Philoptochos Soc. [20071]
Guild of Catholic Lawyers [19631]
Hadassah, The Women's Zionist Org. of Am. [20139]
Hagiography Soc. [20526]
Hashomer Hatzair Zionist Youth Movement [20140]
Healers League of the Natl. Spiritualist Assn. of Churches [20449]
Hea. Ministries Assn. [16339]
HeartStrong [12232]

Hebrew Christian Fellowship [20012]
Hebrew Free Burial Assn. [20141]
High School Evangelism Fellowship [20013]
Hillel: The Found. for Jewish Campus Life [20142]
Hindustan Bible Inst. [19927]
Historical Soc. of the Episcopal Church [19962]
Historical Soc. of the United Methodist Church [10113]
Holy Childhood Assn. [19632]
Holy Cross Foreign Mission Soc. [19633]
Holy Shroud Guild [19635]
Huguenot Soc. of the Founders of Manakin in the Colony of Virginia [21162]
Hymn Soc. in the U.S. and Canada [20432]
IFCA Intl. [19849]
Independent Bd. for Presbyterian Foreign Missions [20467]
Independent Catholic Churches Intl. [20497]
Independent Catholic Churches Intl. [IO]
Inst. for Advanced Stud. of World Religions [9275]
Inst. of Apostolic Oblates [19638]
Inst. for Biblical Res. [19519]
Inst. for Creation Res. [20538]
Inst. for Jewish Medical Ethics [20143]
Inst. on Religion in an Age of Sci. [20550]
Inst. on Religion and Democracy [17393]
Inst. on Religious Life [19639]
Inst. of Singles Dynamics [20281]
Integrity [20058]
Interact Ministries [20348]
The Interchurch Center [19896]
Intercristo [19804]
Interdisciplinary Biblical Res. Inst. [19928]
InterEuropean Commn. on Church and School [IO]
Interfaith Alliance [20498]
Interfaith Church of Metaphysics [20573]
Interfaith Working Group [12887]
Intl. Alumni Assn. of Shri Mahavir Jain Vidyalaya [19346]
Intl. Anchoritic Soc. [10460]
Intl. Assn. of Biblical Counselors [19867]
Intl. Assn. of Christian Chaplains [19748]
Intl. Assn. of Pastoral Psychologists [16151]
Intl. Assn. for Sci., Tech. and Soc. [7608]
Intl. Assn. of Women Ministers [20619]
Intl. Bible Soc. [19520]
Intl. Bible Students Assn. [19521]
Intl. Bd. of Jewish Missions [20014]
Intl. Book Proj. [8620]
Intl. Catacomb Soc. [10039]
Intl. Catholic Deaf Assn. - U.S. Sect. [19641]
Intl. Christian Media Commn. [19538]
Intl. Christian Stud. Assn. [19806]
Intl. Conf. of Police Chaplains [19749]
Intl. Convention of Faith Ministries [19807]
Intl. Coun. of Christian Churches [20015]
Intl. Coun. of Community Churches [19850]
Intl. Coun. of Iranian Christians [19809]
Intl. Disciples Women's Ministries [20620]
Intl. Fed. of Messianic Jews [20255]
Intl. Fed. of Rabbis [20144]
Intl. Fed. of Secular Humanistic Jews [20086]
Intl. Lutheran Deaf Assn. [20217]
Intl. Lutheran Laymen's League [20218]
Intl. Network of Children's Ministry [19758]
Intl. Order of the King's Daughters and Sons [19810]
Intl. Order of Saint Luke the Physician [20499]
Intl. Order of Saint Luke the Physician [IO]
Intl. Order of St. Vincent [19963]
Intl. Org. for Septuagint and Cognate Stud. [19522]
Intl. Police and Fire Chaplain's Assn. [19750]
Intl. Soc. of Bible Collectors [19523]
Intl. Soc. for the Stud. of Pilgrimage Art [9451]
Intl. Students, Inc. [20017]
InterServe U.S.A. [20351]
Interweave Continental (Unitarian Universalists for Lesbian, Gay, Bisexual and Transgender Concerns) [20059]
Iranian B'nei Torah Movement [20145]
Iranian Muslim Assn. of North Am. [20438]
Islamic Center of New York [20104]
Islamic Correctional Reunion Assn. [20105]

Reference to "IO" in place of a book number signifies that the association may be found in the 45th edition of International Organizations.

Islamic Food and Nutrition Coun. of Am. [2353]
Islamic Info. Center of Am. [20106]
Israel Aliyah Center [20146]
Jagannath Org. for Global Awareness [20527]
Japan Intl. Christian Univ. Found. [19929]
Jesuit Conf. [19643]
Jesuit Volunteer Corps: Northwest [19644]
Jewel Heart [19552]
Jewish Natl. Fund [20150]
Jewish Reconstructionist Fed. [20151]
Jewish Women Intl. [20153]
Jews for Judaism [20500]
Jews for Judaism [IO]
Jews for Morality [20154]
John La Farge Inst. [19645]
John Templeton Found. [20501]
JWB Jewish Chaplains Coun. [19751]
Kadima [20155]
Koinonia Found. [19899]
Kolel Chibas Jerusalem [20156]
Kristana Esperantista Ligo Internacia [19812]
Kunzang Palyul Choling [19553]
Lama Found. [10176]
Latin Am. Mission [20353]
Latin Liturgy Assn. [19646]
Lay Carmelite Order of the Blessed Virgin Mary of
   Mount Carmel [19647]
Lay Mission-Helpers Assn. [19648]
Laymen's Home Missionary Movement [20018]
Leadership Conf. of Women Religious [19649]
League of St. Dymphna [19650]
League of Tarcisians [19651]
League for Yiddish, Inc. [20157]
Legatus [19652]
Liberal Religious Educators Assn. [20599]
Licentiate Ministers and Certified Mediums Soc.
   [20450]
Life Action Revival Ministries [20020]
Life Outreach Intl. [20021]
Life Understanding Found. [20484]
Literacy and Evangelism Intl. [8791]
Lithuanian Catholic Religious Aid [19653]
Little Flower Mission League [19654]
Liturgical Conf. [19900]
Living Church Found. [19964]
Lollard Soc. [20524]
Lord's Day Alliance of the U.S. [20544]
Lord's Day Observance Soc. [IO]
Louis Finkelstein Inst. for Religious and Social
   Stud. at the Louis Stein Center [19931]
Lubavitch Youth Org. [20158]
Luis Palau Assn. [20022]
Lutheran Bible Translators [19524]
Lutheran Deaconess Assn. [20219]
Lutheran Deaconess Conf. [20220]
Lutheran Historical Conf. [20222]
Lutheran Human Relations Assn. [20223]
Lutheran Mission Societies [20225]
Lutheran Student Movement - U.S.A. [20227]
Lutheran Volunteer Corps [20228]
Lutheran Women's Missionary League [20229]
Lutherans Concerned/North Am. [20061]
Macedonian Orthodox Youth Assn. of North Am.
   [19883]
Maclellan Found. [20502]
Maclellan Found. [IO]
The Mailbox Club [19525]
Makatab Tarighat Oveyssi Shahmaghsoudi
   [20576]
Malacological Soc. of London [IO]
Mariannhill Mission Soc. [19655]
Mariological Soc. of Am. [19656]
Maryheart Crusaders [19657]
Maryknoll Fathers and Bros. [19658]
Maryknoll Mission Center of New England [8660]
Master's Men of the Natl. Assn. of Free Will
   Baptists [19490]
Media Associates Intl. [19981]
Men of the Sacred Heart [19659]
Mennonite Church USA Historical Comm. [20248]
Mentalphysics [20503]
A Messianic Jewish Perspective [20259]
Methodist Fed. for Social Action [20264]
Metropolitan Community Churches [20062]
Military Chaplains Assn. of the U.S.A. [19752]

Mission Builders Intl. [19814]
Mission to the World [20468]
Missionary Gospel Fellowship [20363]
Missionary Sisters of St. Peter Claver [20364]
Missionary Soc. of Saint Paul the Apostle [19663]
Missionary TECH Team [20366]
Missions Door [19491]
MOMS in Touch Intl. [20621]
Mooncircles [20577]
Moravian Historical Soc. [20423]
More Light Presbyterians for Lesbian, Gay,
   Bisexual and Transgender Concerns [20063]
Mormon History Assn. [20208]
Morris Cerullo World Evangelism [20025]
Morris Pratt Inst. Assn. [20451]
Muslim Amer. Soc. [20440]
Narramore Christian Found. [19815]
Natl. Apostolate for Inclusion Ministry [20026]
Natl. Assn. of Baptist Professors of Religion
   [9277]
Natl. Assn. of Catholic Family Life Ministers
   [20288]
Natl. Assn. of Catholic Homes and Educators
   [8057]
Natl. Assn. of Church Bus. Admin. [20513]
Natl. Assn. of Church Design Builders [831]
Natl. Assn. of Church Facilities Managers [20514]
Natl. Assn. of Church Personnel Administrators
   [20515]
Natl. Assn. of Ecumenical and Interreligious Staff
   [19902]
Natl. Assn. of Evangelicals [19982]
Natl. Assn. of Free Will Baptists [19492]
Natl. Assn. of Hispanic Priests of the USA [19665]
Natl. Assn. of Parish Catechetical Directors
   [19932]
Natl. Assn. of Priest Pilots [19667]
Natl. Assn. of State Catholic Conf. Directors
   [19668]
Natl. Assn. of Temple Administrators [20163]
Natl. Assn. of Temple Educators [20164]
Natl. Assn. for Treasurers of Religious Institutes
   [20516]
Natl. Baptist Convention, U.S.A. [19493]
Natl. Bible Assn. [20205]
Natl. Black Catholic Clergy Caucus [19669]
Natl. Black Sisters' Conf. [19671]
Natl. Campus Ministry Assn. [19933]
Natl. Cathedral Assn. [19903]
Natl. Catholic Conf. of Airport Chaplains [19754]
Natl. Catholic Conf. for Total Stewardship [19673]
Natl. Catholic Off. for the Deaf [19675]
Natl. Catholic Rural Life Conf. [19677]
Natl. Catholic Women's Union [19678]
Natl. Center for the Laity [20206]
Natl. Christ Child Soc. [19679]
Natl. Christian Life Community of the U.S.A.
   [19680]
Natl. Coalition of Men's Ministries [19816]
Natl. Comm. for Amish Religious Freedom
   [19448]
Natl. Comm. of Catholic Laymen [19681]
Natl. Conf. for Community and Justice [19904]
Natl. Conf. of Diocesan Vocation Directors
   [19682]
Natl. Coun. of Bishops, USA [19683]
Natl. Coun. of Catholic Women [19684]
Natl. Coun. of Churches of Christ in the U.S.A.
   [19905]
Natl. Coun. of Churches, Educ. and Leadership
   Ministries Commn. [19935]
Natl. Coun. of Jewish Women [20166]
Natl. Coun. On Bible Curriculum In Public Schools
   [9052]
Natl. Coun. of Young Israel [20167]
Natl. Cursillo Movement [19685]
Natl. Enthronement Center [19686]
Natl. Episcopal Hea. Ministries [14584]
Natl. Evangelization Teams [19687]
Natl. Fed. of Asian-Amer. United Methodists
   [20266]
Natl. Fed. of Priests' Councils [19689]
Natl. Forum of Greek Orthodox Church Musicians
   [20434]
Natl. Ghost Ranch Found. [20469]

Natl. Guild of Churchmen [19965]
Natl. Havurah Comm. [20168]
Natl. Huguenot Soc. [21163]
Natl. Interfaith Coalition on Aging [11314]
Natl. League for the Separation of Church and
   State [19838]
Natl. Lutheran Outdoors Ministry Assn. [20231]
Natl. Off. for Black Catholics [19691]
Natl. Org. for Continuing Educ. of Roman Catholic
   Clergy [19936]
Natl. Religious Affairs Assn. [19872]
Natl. Religious Broadcasters [19539]
Natl. Religious Partnership for the Env. [19941]
Natl. Religious Vocation Conf. [19692]
Natl. Ser. Committee/Chariscenter USA [19693]
Natl. Shrine of St. Elizabeth Ann Seton [19694]
Natl. Spiritual Assembly of the Baha'is of the U.S.
   [19467]
Natl. Spiritualist Assn. of Churches [20453]
Natl. Spiritualist Teachers Club [20454]
Natl. Temperance and Prohibition Coun. [13305]
Natl. United Church Ushers Assn. of Am. [20609]
Natl. Young Adult Assn. [13504]
The Navigators [19817]
Nazarene Missions Intl. [20371]
Neo-American Church, The Original Kleptonian
   [20456]
New Hope Intl. [20372]
New Wineskins Missionary Network [20375]
Nichiren Buddhist Assn. of Am. [19555]
Night Adoration in the Home [19695]
Nocturnal Adoration Soc. [19696]
Non-Denominational Bible Prophecy Stud. Assn.
   [19528]
North Amer. Acad. of Ecumenists [19906]
North Amer. Assn. for the Catechumenate [19697]
North Amer. Assn. for the Diaconate [19967]
North Amer. Assn. of Synagogue Executives
   [20517]
North Amer. Coalition on Religion and Ecology
   [4598]
North Amer. Forum on the Catechumenate
   [19698]
North Amer. Patristics Soc. [20460]
Northern Far East Returned Missionaries Assn.
   [20504]
Northern Far East Returned Missionaries Assn.
   [IO]
Ohr Torah Institutions of Israel [8678]
OK Kosher Certification [20169]
ORACLE Religious Assn. [20070]
Order of Saint Andrew the Apostle [20073]
Orthodox Theological Soc. in Am. [19885]
Orthodox Union - Union of Orthodox Jewish
   Congregations of Am. [20170]
Our Little Bros. and Sisters [20380]
Ozar Hatorah [20171]
Pan Amer. Coun. for the Preservation of the Hel-
   lenic Orthodox Church and the Hellenic
   Language [20074]
Partners for Sacred Places [20505]
Pathwork Helpers Assn. of North Am. [20565]
Paulist Memorial Soc. [19699]
Paulist Natl. Catholic Evangelization Assn.
   [19700]
Peale Center for Christian Living [19825]
Pele Defense Fund [4440]
Personal Freedom Outreach [19875]
Pew Charitable Trusts [13129]
Peyote Way Church of God [20447]
Pilots for Christ Intl. [20028]
Pioneer Clubs [20642]
Pious Union of Prayer [19701]
Plymouth Rock Found. [8302]
Pocket Testament League [19529]
Polish-American-Jewish Alliance for Youth Action
   [13510]
Pontifical Mission Societies in the U.S. [19703]
Prayers for Life [19907]
Presbyterian Assn. of Musicians [20435]
Presbyterian Church Bus. Administrators' Assn.
   [20470]
Presbyterian Evangelistic Fellowship [20471]
Presbyterian Lay Comm. [20472]
Presbyterian Men [20473]

A star before a book entry number signifies that the name is not listed separately, but is mentioned within the entry.

Presbyterian-Reformed Ministries Intl. [20474]
Presbyterian Women [20475]
Prison Ministry of Yokefellow's Intl. [11889]
Pro Athletes Outreach [20029]
Pro Maria Comm. [19704]
Pro Sanctity Movement [19705]
Progressive, Radically Inclusive Student Ministry [19938]
Promise Keepers [19834]
Punjabi-American Cultural Assn. [10223]
Rabbinical Assembly [20173]
Rabbinical Coun. of Am. [20174]
Ramakrishna - Vivekananda Center [20610]
Raskob Found. for Catholic Activities [19706]
Recovery from Mormonism [12888]
Red Sea Team Intl. [20385]
Reform Jewish Appeal [20176]
Reform Judaism [20177]
Religion Communicators Coun. [20483]
Religion and Family Life Sect. of the Natl. Coun. on Family Relations [12165]
Religion News Ser. [3158]
Religion Newswriters Assn. [3159]
Religious Bros. Conf. [19707]
Religious Coalition for Reproductive Choice [18519]
Religious Commun. Assn. [8116]
Religious Conf. Mgt. Assn. [2690]
Religious Res. Assn. [20539]
Religious Sci. Intl. [20525]
Religious Zionist Youth Movement - Bnei Akiva of the U.S. and Canada [20178]
Reparation Soc. of the Immaculate Heart of Mary [19709]
Response-Ability [20386]
Revival Fires (Christian Evangelizers Assn.) [20031]
Rosedale Mennonite Missions [20253]
Rosicrucian Fellowship [20541]
Roving Volunteers in Christ's Ser. [23017]
Sacred Dance Guild [9897]
Sacred Dance Soc. [19878]
Sacred Heart League [19711]
St. Ansgar's Scandinavian Catholic League [19712]
St. Anthony's Guild [20388]
St. Jude League [19713]
St. Martin De Porres Guild [20389]
Saint Photios Found. [20075]
St. Thomas Aquinas Found. [19714]
Saints Alive in Jesus [20032]
Salesian Missioners [20391]
Samaritans Intl. [20392]
Saq' Be': Org. for Mayan and Indigenous Spiritual Bodies [10226]
Seafarers and Intl. House [20232]
Seamen's Church Inst. of New York and New Jersey [19970]
Searching Together Educational Ministries [19909]
Secretariat for Catholic-Jewish Relations [19910]
Secular Inst. of Saint Francis de Sales [19716]
Sephardic Jewish Brotherhood of Am. [20179]
Serra Intl. [19717]
Seventh Day Adventist Kinship Intl. [20066]
Seventh Day Baptist Gen. Conf. [19494]
Seventh Day Baptist Gen. Conf. of the U.S. and Canada [20545]
Seventh Day Baptist Historical Soc. [19495]
Seventh Day Baptist Missionary Soc. [19496]
Seventh Day Baptist World Fed. [19497]
Sharing of Ministries Abroad U.S.A. [20393]
Shomrim Soc. [12481]
Sikh Coun. on Religion and Educ. [20558]
Sikh Stud. Circle [20559]
Skinner Leadership Inst. [20033]
Slavic Gospel Assn. [20395]
Slovene Franciscan Fathers [19718]
Soc. for the Advancement of Judaism [20180]
Soc. of African Missions [19719]
Soc. for the Anthropology of Religion [6426]
Soc. for the Arts, Religion and Contemporary Culture [9599]
Soc. of Biblical Literature [19530]
Soc. of the Companions of the Holy Cross [19971]

Soc. of the Descendants of the Colonial Clergy [20760]
Soc. for Hindu-Christian Stud. [20528]
Soc. for Humanistic Judaism [20181]
Soc. of Jewish Sci. [20202]
Soc. of Missionaries of Africa [19721]
Soc. for Old Testament Stud. [IO]
Soc. of Our Lady of the Most Holy Trinity [19722]
Soc. for Philosophy of Religion [8970]
Soc. of Pragmatic Mysticism [20448]
Soc. for Promoting and Encouraging Arts and Knowledge of the Church [19972]
Soc. for the Propagation of the Faith [IO]
Soc. of Saint Stephen [20523]
Soc. for the Sci. Stud. of Religion [20506]
Society for the Scientific Study of Religion [IO]
Soc. for the Stud. of Christian Spirituality [19826]
Soc. for the Stud. of Japanese Religions [20529]
Soc. of Traditional Roman Catholics [19726]
Solbrekken Evangelistic Assn. of Canada [IO]
Southern Baptist Found. [19498]
Southern Baptist Historical Lib. and Archives [19499]
Spiritual Directors Intl. [20507]
Spiritual Directors Intl. [IO]
Spiritual Life Inst. [20566]
Spiritual Unity of Nations [20580]
Standing Commn. on Ecumenical Relations of the Episcopal Church [19974]
Standing Conf. of the Canonical Orthodox Bishops in the Americas [19886]
STEER [20401]
Subud U.S.A. [20589]
Support Our Aging Religious [11321]
Supreme Master Ching Hai Meditation Assn. [19557]
Survivors Network of Those Abused by Priests [13372]
Swedenborg Assn. [9164]
Tayu Center [20581]
Teen Challenge Intl. [20643]
Teen Missions Intl. [20402]
Thanks-Giving Square [20584]
Theosophical Book Assn. for the Blind [20592]
Theosophical Soc. in Am. [20593]
Third Order of Mary/Marists [19728]
Tithing Found. [20595]
Toward Tradition [20508]
Truckers for Christ [19828]
Truth Missionaries Chap. of Positive Accord [20585]
Tyndale Soc. [20530]
Union of Orthodox Rabbis of the U.S. and Canada [20183]
Union for Reform Judaism [20184]
Union of Sephardic Congregations [20185]
Union for Traditional Judaism [20186]
Unitarian Universalist Christian Fellowship [20600]
Unitarian Universalist Historical Soc. [20601]
Unitarian Universalist Ministers Assn. [20602]
Unitarian Universalist Musicians' Network [20436]
Unitarian Universalist Ser. Comm. [20603]
Unitarian Universalist Women's Fed. [20604]
United Christian Missionary Soc. [19856]
United Church of Christ Coalition for Lesbian, Gay, Bisexual and Transgender Concerns [20067]
United Church of Christ Justice and Witness Ministries [20608]
United Hasroun Men's and St. Laba Ladies Charity Societies [19732]
United Indian Missions, Intl. [20405]
United Lodge of Theosophists [20594]
United Methodist Comm. on Relief [20267]
United Methodist Youth Org. [20268]
United Religions Initiative [20518]
United Sisters of Charity [20406]
United Sons of Israel [20187]
U.S. Assn. of Consecrated Virgins [19733]
U.S. Conf. of Catholic Bishops [19735]
U.S. Copts Assn. [10192]
United Synagogue of Conservative Judaism [20188]
United Synagogue Youth [20189]
Unity Coalition for Israel [8672]

Universal Muslim Assn. of Am. [20442]
Universal Torah Registry [20190]
URANTIA Assn. of the U.S. [9051]
Urantia Found. [20587]
Ursuline Companions in Mission [20408]
Values and Visions [8155]
Volunteer Missionary Movement - U.S. Off. [19736]
Wainwright House [20588]
Warsaw Ghetto Resistance Org. [20191]
Washington Ethical Soc. [20087]
Watchman Fellowship [19877]
Watchtower Bible and Tract Soc. of New York [20109]
The Way Intl. [20411]
We Believe! [19738]
We Care Am. [13210]
WEC Intl. [20034]
Westar Inst. [20509]
Western Young Buddhist League [19558]
Wider Quaker Fellowship [20045]
William H. Whitsitt Baptist Heritage Soc. [19500]
Woman's Home and Foreign Mission Soc. [19443]
Woman's Missionary Union, SBC [19501]
Women for Faith and Family [19739]
Women Nationally Active for Christ [19502]
Women of Reform Judaism, The Fed. of Temple Sisterhoods [20192]
Women's Alliance for Theology, Ethics and Ritual [20626]
Women's Division of the Gen. Bd. of Global Ministries of the United Methodist Church [20269]
Women's League for Conservative Judaism [20193]
Women's Ordination Conf. [19740]
Women's Spirituality Forum [20628]
World Confed. of United Zionists [20195]
World Cong. of Gay, Lesbian, Bisexual, and Transgender Jews [20069]
World Coun. of Conservative/Masorti Synagogues [20196]
World Coun. of Religious Leaders [20519]
World Evangelical Alliance [19983]
World Fellowship of Slavic Evangelical Christians [19984]
World Impact [20414]
World Jewish Genealogy Org. [21158]
World Literature Ministries [19832]
World Methodist Coun. [20272]
World Methodist Historical Soc. [20273]
World Mission Prayer League [20234]
World Team [20417]
World Union of Deists [20531]
World's Christian Endeavor Union [19829]
WorldVenture [19503]
Wycliffe Bible Translators [19531]
Xaverian Missionaries of the U.S. [20421]
Young Israel Coun. of Rabbis [20197]
Young Judaea [20198]
Young Life [20644]
Young Religious Unitarian Universalists [20605]
Youth for Christ/U.S.A. [20645]
Youth Evangelism Assn. [20036]
Youth Ministry [20235]
Zarathushtrian Assembly [20510]
Zeirei Agudath Israel [20200]
Zen Stud. Soc. [19559]
Zionist Org. of Am. [20201]
Religion in an Age of Sci; Inst. on [20550]
Religion; Amer. Acad. of [8223]
Religion in Amer. Life - Defunct.
Religion; Assn. of Baptist Professors of [★9277]
Religion; Assn. for the Sociology of [7661]
Religion; Committee for the Sci. Examination of [★20085]
Religion; Committee for the Sci. Examination of [★IO]
Religion Communicators Coun. [20483], 475 Riverside Dr., Rm. 1355, New York, NY 10115, (212)870-2985
Religion; Conf. on Sci. and [★17916]
Religion and Contemporary Culture; Soc. for the Arts, [9599]

Reference to "IO" in place of a book number signifies that the association may be found in the 45th edition of International Organizations.

Religion; Coun. of Societies for the Stud. of [9274]
Religion; Coun. on the Stud. of [★9274]
Religion and Culture; Found. for the Arts, [★9599]
Religion and Democracy; Inst. on [17393]
Religion and Ecology; North Amer. Coalition on [4598]
Religion and Ethics Inst. - Address unknown since 2001.
Religion and Ethics Network - Defunct.
Religion, Ethics and Social Policy; Center for [18609]
Religion and Family Life Sect. [★12165]
Religion and Family Life Sect. [★IO]
Religion and Family Life Sect. of the Natl. Coun. on Family Relations [IO], Minneapolis, MN, United States
Religion and Family Life Sect. of the Natl. Coun. on Family Relations [12165], c/o Natl. Coun. on Family Relations, 3989 Central Ave. NE, Ste. 550, Minneapolis, MN 55421, (763)781-9331
Religion Found; Freedom From [19837]
Religion in Higher Educ; Natl. Coun. on [★19940]
Religion in Higher Educ; Soc. for [★19940]
Religion in Independent Schools; Coun. for [★8536]
Religion and Intellectual Life; Assn. for [19916]
Religion and Intl. Affairs; Coun. on [★20093]
Religion and Labor Coun. of America - Defunct.
Religion; Natl. Assn. of Baptist Professors of [9277]
Religion News Ser. [3158], 1101 Connecticut Ave. NW, Ste. 350, Washington, DC 20036, (202)463-8777
Religion News Service [IO], Washington, DC, United States
Religion Newswriters Assn. [3159], PO Box 2037, Westerville, OH 43086-2037, (614)891-9001
Religion Publishing Group - Defunct.
Religion and Socialism Commn. of the Democratic Socialists of Am. [18657], 536 W 111th St., No. 37, New York, NY 10025
Religion and Socialism Comm. of DSA [★18657]
Religion and Soc; Center on [20491]
Religion; Soc. for Philosophy of [8970]
Religion; Soc. for the Sci. Stud. of [20506]
Religion on Stamps; Collectors of [22809]
Religions Educational Network; Alternative [20457]
Religiosos Terciarios Capuchinos de Nuestra Senora de los Dolores [★IO]
Religious Action Center of Reform Judaism [IO], Washington, DC, United States
Religious Action Center of Reform Judaism [17954], Arthur and Sara Jo Kobacker Bldg., 2027 Massachusetts Ave. NW, Washington, DC 20036, (202)387-2800
Religious Action Center of the Union of Amer. Hebrew Congregations [★17954]
Religious Action Center of the Union of Amer. Hebrew Congregations [★IO]
Religious Activities Task Force, Natl. Safety Coun. - Defunct.

Religious Administration
African-Amer. Women's Clergy Assn. [20615]
All-Ukrainian Evangelical Baptist Fellowship [19469]
Amer. Benedictine Acad. [19566]
Amer. Congregational Assn. [19859]
Amer. and Foreign Christian Union [19762]
Amer. Forum for Jewish-Christian Cooperation [19887]
Amer. Freedom Alliance [18507]
Apostleship of the Sea in the U.S.A. [19570]
Assn. of Christian Church Educators [19842]
Assn. of Grace Brethren Ministers [19533]
Assn. of Life-Giving Churches [19843]
Assn. of Professional Chaplains [19744]
Assn. of Southern Baptist Campus Ministers [19474]
Assn. of State Baptist Papers [19475]
Assumption Guild [19580]
Bishop Baraga Assn. and Archives [19583]
Bishops' Comm. for Ecumenical and Interreligious Affairs [19584]
Bishops' Comm. on the Liturgy [19585]
Blessed Kateri Tekakwitha League [19588]
Canon Law Soc. of Am. [19592]
Catholic Church Extension Soc. of the U.S.A. [19596]

Christian Mgt. Assn. [20511]
Christian Stewardship Assn. [20512]
Church Benefits Assn. [20461]
Church of the Brethren Gen. Bd. Global Mission Partnership [19535]
Comm. on Social Development and World Peace of the U.S. Catholic Conf. [19613]
Company of Saint Paul [19614]
CORPUS - Natl. Assn. for an Inclusive Priesthood [19619]
Edith Stein Guild [19621]
Episcopal Women's Caucus [19956]
Fellowship of Concerned Churchmen [19454]
HealthCare Chaplaincy [16340]
Intl. Assn. of Christian Chaplains [19748]
Intl. Catholic Deaf Assn. - U.S. Sect. [19641]
Leadership Conf. of Women Religious [19649]
Maryknoll Fathers and Bros. [19658]
Multi-Faith Gp. for Healthcare Chaplaincy [IO]
Natl. Assn. of Church Bus. Admin. [20513]
Natl. Assn. of Church Facilities Managers [20514]
Natl. Assn. of Church Personnel Administrators [20515]
Natl. Assn. of Hispanic Priests of the USA [19665]
Natl. Assn. of State Catholic Conf. Directors [19668]
Natl. Assn. of Temple Administrators [20163]
Natl. Assn. for Treasurers of Religious Institutes [20516]
Natl. Comm. for Amish Religious Freedom [19448]
Natl. Conf. of Diocesan Vocation Directors [19682]
Natl. Coun. of Bishops, USA [19683]
Natl. Coun. of Catholic Women [19684]
Natl. Fed. of Priests' Councils [19689]
Natl. Org. for Continuing Educ. of Roman Catholic Clergy [19936]
Natl. Religious Affairs Assn. [19872]
Natl. Spiritual Assembly of the Baha'is of the U.S. [19467]
North Amer. Assn. of Synagogue Executives [20517]
Presbyterian Church Bus. Administrators' Assn. [20470]
Seventh Day Baptist Gen. Conf. [19494]
Seventh Day Baptist Historical Soc. [19495]
Seventh Day Baptist Missionary Soc. [19496]
Seventh Day Baptist World Fed. [19497]
Southern Baptist Found. [19498]
Support Our Aging Religious [11321]
Survivors Network of Those Abused by Priests [13372]
United Religions Initiative [20518]
United Religions Initiative [IO]
U.S. Conf. of Catholic Bishops [19735]
Woman's Missionary Union, SBC [19501]
Women Nationally Active for Christ [19502]
Women's Ordination Conf. [19740]
World Coun. of Religious Leaders [20519]
World Coun. of Religious Leaders [IO]
Religious Affairs; Assn. of Coll. and Univ. [9168]
Religious Affairs; Assn. for the Coordination of Univ. [★9168]
Religious Affairs; Bishops' Comm. for Ecumenical and Inter [19584]
Religious Aid; Lithuanian Catholic [19653]
Religious Arts Guild - Defunct.
Religious Booksellers Assn. - Address unknown since 1999.
Religious Bros. Conf. [19707], 5401 S Cornell Ave., Chicago, IL 60615, (773)595-4023
Religious Bros; Natl. Assn. of [★19707]
Religious and Civil Rights; Catholic League for [19600]
Religious Coalition for Abortion Rights [★18519]
Religious Coalition for a Moral Drug Policy - Address unknown since 2002.
Religious Coalition for Reproductive Choice [18519], 1025 Vermont Ave. NW, Ste. 1130, Washington, DC 20005, (202)628-7700
Religious Commun. Assn. [8116], c/o Michael E. Eidenmuller, Coor. of Electronic Commun., Univ. of Texas at Tyler, Dept. of Commun., 3900 Univ. Blvd., Tyler, TX 75799, (903)566-7093

Religious Communities for the Arts - Defunct.
Religious Conf. Mgt. Assn. [2690], 1 RCA Dome, Ste. 120, Indianapolis, IN 46225, (317)632-1888
Religious Conf. Mgt. Assn. [IO], Indianapolis, IN, United States
Religious Convention Managers Assn. [★IO]
Religious Convention Managers Assn. [★2690]
Religious Educ. Assn.: An Assn. of Professors, Practitioners, and Researchers in Religious Educ. [19939], 1107 Waterfall Ln., Lakeland, FL 33803, (863)430-3893
Religious Educ; Natl. Assn. of Parish Coordinators/ Directors of [★19932]
Religious Educ; Natl. Conf. of Directors of [★19934]
Religious Enrichment Development Operation; Chaplains [★19746]
Religious Experience Res. Centre [IO], Lampeter, United Kingdom
Religious Formation Conf. [19708], 8820 Cameron St., Silver Spring, MD 20910-4152, (301)588-4938
Religious Freedom
Acton Inst. for the Stud. of Religion and Liberty [20489]
Albanian Catholic Inst. [18506]
Albanian Catholic Inst. [IO]
Alternative Religions Educational Network [20457]
Amer. Coalition of Unregistered Churches [20520]
Amer. Freedom Alliance [18507]
Americans United for Separation of Church and State [19836]
Appeal of Conscience Found. [18508]
Bear Butte Intl. Alliance [19446]
Becket Fund for Religious Liberty [18509]
Center for Christian/Jewish Understanding of Sacred Heart Univ. [19888]
Center for Law and Religious Freedom [18510]
Center for Religious Freedom, Freedom House [17749]
Children's Healthcare Is a Legal Duty [15004]
Christian Anti-Defamation League [17102]
Christian Forum Res. Found. [20560]
Christian Freedom Intl. [20521]
Christian Freedom Intl. [IO]
Christian Solidarity Intl. [IO]
Christian Solidarity Intl. [20522]
Christian Solidarity Intl. - Switzerland [IO]
Christians in Crisis [20555]
Conquistadores 1492 [18669]
Ethics and Religious Liberty Commn. of the Southern Baptist Convention [19487]
Falun Data Info. Center [17757]
Freedom From Religion Found. [19837]
Huguenot Soc. of the Founders of Manakin in the Colony of Virginia [21162]
IARF - Australian and New Zealand Unitarian Assn. [IO]
IARF - Europe and the Middle East [IO]
IARF - Philippines [IO]
IARF - South Asia [IO]
Interfaith Church of Metaphysics [20573]
Intl. Assn. for Religious Freedom [IO]
Intl. Assn. for Religious Freedom - Japan [IO]
Intl. Coalition for Religious Freedom [IO]
Intl. Coalition for Religious Freedom [18511]
Intl. Religious Liberty Assn. [18512]
Intl. Religious Liberty Assn. [IO]
Jewish Coun. for Public Affairs [12474]
Natl. Comm. for Amish Religious Freedom [19448]
Natl. Huguenot Soc. [21163]
Natl. League for the Separation of Church and State [19838]
Romanian Missionary Soc. [20387]
Rutherford Inst. [18513]
Sikh Coun. on Religion and Educ. [20558]
Soc. of Saint Stephen [20523]
Spiritual Unity of Nations [20580]
U.S. Copts Assn. [10192]
William H. Whitsitt Baptist Heritage Soc. [19500]
World Union of Deists [20531]
Religious Freedom; Coalition for [★18511]
Religious Freedom Coalition [12880], PO Box 77511, Washington, DC 20013, (202)543-0300
Religious Freedom; Comm. for [★18511]
Religious Freedom; Natl. Comm. for Amish [19448]

A star before a book entry number signifies that the name is not listed separately, but is mentioned within the entry.

Religious Heritage of America - Address unknown since 2001.
Religious Info. Systems; Assn. for the Development of [20091]
Religious Inst; Graymoor Ecumenical and Inter [19895]
Religious Issues; Psychologists Interested in [★16132]
Religious; Leadership Conf. of Women [19649]
Religious Liberty; Americans for [17090]
Religious Liberty Assn; Natl. [★18512]
Religious Liberty Commn. of the Southern Baptist Convention; Ethics and [19487]
Religious Liberty Found. - Defunct.
Religious Life; Inst. on [19639]
Religious Life; National Assn. of Coll. and Univ. Chaplains and Directors of [★9168]
Religious, Linguistic and Other Minorities; Intl. Fed. for the Protection of the Rights of Ethnic, [17768]
Religious and Military Order of Knights of the Holy Sepulchre of Jerusalem [19008], c/o The Sovereign Grand Priory, 3620 W 10th St., B-150, Greeley, CO 80634-1821
Religious and Military Order of Knights of the Holy Sepulchre of Jerusalem [IO], Greeley, CO, United States
Religious Network for Equality for Women - Address unknown since 2003.
Religious News Ser. [★3158]
Religious News Ser. [★IO]
Religious Newswriters Assn. [★3159]
Religious Objectors; Natl. Ser. Bd. for [★17438]
Religious; Pontifical Missionary Union of Priests and [★19703]
Religious Press Assns. Postal Coalition - Address unknown since 2004.
Religious Press; Editorial Coun. of the [★3205]
Religious Public Relations Coun. [★20483]
Religious Publicity Coun; Natl. [★20483]
Religious Reform
  Anglicans United [19943]
  Concerned Clergy and Laity of the Episcopal Church [19950]
  Free Muslims Coalition [18084]
  Interfaith Working Group [12887]
  Lollard Soc. [20524]
  Natl. Assn. of Temple Educators [20164]
  Reform Jewish Appeal [20176]
  Union for Reform Judaism [20184]
  Women of Reform Judaism, The Fed. of Temple Sisterhoods [20192]
Religious Res. Assn. [20539], 618 SW 2nd Ave., Galva, IL 61434-1912, (309)932-2727
Religious Res. Center; Town and Country [★19628]
Religious Res. and Education; Community for [20537]
Religious Res. Fellowship [★20539]
Religious Roundtable - Address unknown since 2002.
Religious Science
  Religious Sci. Intl. [20525]
  Religious Sci. Intl. [IO]
Religious Sci. Churches; Intl. Assn. of [★20525]
Religious Sci. Intl. [20525], PO Box 2152, Spokane, WA 99210-2152, (509)624-7000
Religious Sci. Intl. [IO], Spokane, WA, United States
Religious and Social Stud. at the Louis Stein Center; Louis Finkelstein Inst. for [19931]
Religious Soc. of Friends [★18206]
Religious Soc. of Friends [★IO]
Religious Soc. of Friends (Quakers) [★20042]
Religious Speech Commun. Assn. [★8116]
Religious Speech Division of Speech Commun. Assn. [★8116]
Religious Studies
  Acad. of Amer. Franciscan History [19560]
  Acad. of Homiletics [20081]
  Adult Christian Educ. Found. [19913]
  Agni Yoga Soc. [20632]
  Agudath Israel of Am. [20110]
  Amer. Benedictine Acad. [19566]
  Amer. Bible Soc. [19504]
  Amer. Buddhist Assn. [19540]
  Amer. Buddhist Movement [19541]
  Amer. Buddhist Stud. Center [19542]

Amer. Forum for Jewish-Christian Cooperation [19887]
  Amer. Soc. of Church History [20078]
  Anglican Assn. of Biblical Scholars [19449]
  ASGM [19506]
  Assn. for Religion and Intellectual Life [19916]
  Bible League [19510]
  Bishops' Comm. for Ecumenical and Interreligious Affairs [19584]
  Blue Army of Our Lady of Fatima, U.S.A. [19589]
  British Assn. for the Stud. of Religions [IO]
  Buddhist Churches of Am. Fed. of Buddhist Women's Associations [19543]
  Burma-America Buddhist Assn. [19546]
  Center for Applied Res. in the Apostolate [19608]
  Christ Truth Ministries [19514]
  Christian Res. [19784]
  Christian Res. Inst. [19785]
  Christian Ser. Club [19515]
  Community for Religious Res. and Education [20537]
  Conf. on Faith and History [20079]
  Coun. on Spiritual Practices [20564]
  Dawn Bible Students Assn. [19517]
  Disciples of Christ Historical Soc. [19853]
  Dynamic Youth Ministries [19831]
  Edith Stein Guild [19621]
  European Assn. for the Stud. of Religions [IO]
  Fed. of Jain Associations in North America [20495]
  First Zen Inst. of Am. [19549]
  Hagiography Soc. [20526]
  Historical Soc. of the United Methodist Church [10113]
  Holy Shroud Guild [19635]
  Inst. for Biblical Res. [19519]
  Inst. on Religious Life [19639]
  Intl. Bible Soc. [19520]
  Intl. Bible Students Assn. [19521]
  Intl. Catacomb Soc. [10039]
  Intl. Christian Stud. Assn. [19806]
  Intl. Org. for Septuagint and Cognate Stud. [19522]
  Jagannath Org. for Global Awareness [20527]
  Jagannath Org. for Global Awareness [IO]
  Jewel Heart [19552]
  Jews for Judaism [20500]
  Leadership Conf. of Women Religious [19649]
  Life Understanding Found. [20484]
  Lollard Soc. [20524]
  The Mailbox Club [19525]
  Mariological Soc. of Am. [19656]
  Natl. Assn. of Temple Educators [20164]
  Natl. Coun. On Bible Curriculum In Public Schools [9052]
  Natl. Org. for Continuing Educ. of Roman Catholic Clergy [19936]
  Nichiren Buddhist Assn. of Am. [19555]
  Non-Denominational Bible Prophecy Stud. Assn. [19528]
  Northern Far East Returned Missionaries Assn. [20504]
  Orthodox Theological Soc. in Am. [19885]
  Red Sea Team Intl. [20385]
  Reformed Ecumenical Coun. [19908]
  Religious Res. Assn. [20539]
  St. Thomas Aquinas Found. [19714]
  Soc. for the Anthropology of Religion [6426]
  Soc. of Biblical Literature [19530]
  Soc. for Hindu-Christian Stud. [20528]
  Soc. of Jewish Sci. [20202]
  Soc. for the Sci. Stud. of Religion [20506]
  Soc. for the Stud. of Christian Spirituality [19826]
  Soc. for the Stud. of Japanese Religions [20529]
  Spiritual Unity of Nations [20580]
  Theta Chi Beta [24583]
  Tyndale Soc. [20530]
  Westar Inst. [20509]
  William H. Whitsitt Baptist Heritage Soc. [19500]
  World Union of Deists [20531]
  Wycliffe Bible Translators [19531]
  Zen Stud. Soc. [19559]
Religious Superiors of Men's Institutes of the U.S; Conf. of Major [★19615]

Religious Superiors of Women's Institutes of the United States of Am; Conf. of Major [★19649]
Religious Supplies
  Church Universal and Triumphant [19462]
  Natl. Church Goods Assn. [3374]
Religious Task Force on Central Am. [★17052]
Religious Task Force on Central Am. [★IO]
Religious Task Force on Central Am. and Mexico [IO], Washington, DC, United States
Religious Task Force on Central Am. and Mexico [17052], 3053 4th St. NE, Washington, DC 20017-1102, (202)529-0441
Religious Task Force - Defunct.
Religious Task Force on El Salvador [★17052]
Religious Task Force on El Salvador [★IO]
Religious Understanding
  Alliance for Life Ministries [19760]
  Amer. Buddhist Assn. [19540]
  Amer. Buddhist Movement [19541]
  Amer. Buddhist Stud. Center [19542]
  Amer. Clergy Leadership Conf. [19858]
  Amer. Forum for Jewish-Christian Cooperation [19887]
  Amer. Hindu Assn. [20077]
  Amer. Soc. for Muslim Advancement [10245]
  Anabaptist Sociology and Anthropology Assn. [7559]
  Assn. for the Restoration of the Church and Home [19844]
  Buddhist Churches of Am. Fed. of Buddhist Women's Associations [19543]
  Burma-America Buddhist Assn. [19546]
  Center for Christian/Jewish Understanding of Sacred Heart Univ. [19888]
  Center on Religion and Soc. [20491]
  Christian Friends of Israel - USA [19777]
  Christian Res. Inst. [19785]
  Coun. of Masajid of U.S. [20097]
  Coun. for a Parliament of the World's Religions [20532]
  Coun. for a Parliament of the World's Religions [IO]
  Coun. on Spiritual Practices [20564]
  Covenant of Unitarian Universalist Pagans [20459]
  Disciples Ecumenical Consultative Coun. [19848]
  Edith Stein Guild [19621]
  Episcopal Evangelical Educ. Soc. [19955]
  Fed. of Jain Associations in North America [20495]
  First Zen Inst. of Am. [19549]
  Foundations and Donors Interested in Catholic Activities [19625]
  Free Muslims Coalition [18084]
  Hea. Ministries Assn. [16339]
  Inst. on Religious Life [19639]
  Intl. Assn. of Sufism [20101]
  Intl. Center for Spirit at Work [20575]
  Intl. Coun. of Iranian Christians [19809]
  Intl. Fed. of Secular Humanistic Jews [20086]
  Intl. Fellowship of Christians and Jews [20533]
  Intl. Fellowship of Christians and Jews [IO]
  Iranian Muslim Assn. of North Am. [20438]
  Jewel Heart [19552]
  Jews for Judaism [20500]
  Makatab Tarighat Oveyssi Shahmaghsoudi [20576]
  Muslim Amer. Soc. [20440]
  Natl. Org. for Continuing Educ. of Roman Catholic Clergy [19936]
  Natl. Religious Partnership for the Env. [19941]
  New Wineskins Missionary Network [20375]
  Nichiren Buddhist Assn. of Am. [19555]
  Northern Far East Returned Missionaries Assn. [20504]
  Polish-American-Jewish Alliance for Youth Action [13510]
  Recovery from Mormonism [12888]
  Red Sea Team Intl. [20385]
  Scottish Bible Soc. [IO]
  Sikh Coun. on Religion and Educ. [20558]
  Soc. of Jewish Sci. [20202]
  Soc. for the Stud. of Christian Spirituality [19826]
  Soc. for the Stud. of Japanese Religions [20529]
  Soulforce [17657]

Reference to "IO" in place of a book number signifies that the association may be found in the 45th edition of International Organizations.

Toward Tradition [20508]
United Religions Initiative [20518]
Universal Muslim Assn. of Am. [20442]
Western Young Buddhist League [19558]
Women for Faith and Family [19739]
World Coun. of Religious Leaders [20519]
World Literature Ministries [19832]
World Union of Deists [20531]
Zen Stud. Soc. [19559]
Religious Unitarian Universalists; Young [20605]
Religious of the U.S.A; Leadership Conf. of Women
[★19649]
Religious and Value Issues in Counseling; Assn. for
[★8166]
Religious Values in Counseling; Assn. for Spiritual,
Ethical and [8166]
Religious Vocation Conf; Natl. [19692]
Religious Vocation Directors; Natl. Conf. of
[★19692]
Religious Volunteer Agencies; Coun. of [13391]
Religious Zionist Youth Movement - Bnei Akiva of
the U.S. and Canada [20178], 7 Penn Plz., Ste.
205, New York, NY 10001, (212)465-9536
Religious Zionists of America - Defunct.
Reloading Mfrs. Assn; Natl. [1481]
Reloading Tool Collector's Assn; Antique [22424]
Relocation Assistance Assn. of America - Defunct.
Relocation Council/Worldwide ERC; Employee
[1261]
Relocation Real Estate Advisory Coun; Employee
[★1261]
The Remain Intact "ORGAN"ization - Defunct.
Remanufacturers Assn; Production Engine [1295]
Remanufacturers Coun; Valve [★1839]
Remanufacturing Assn; Intl. Computer Products
[★3996]
Remanufacturing Industries Coun. Intl. - Defunct.
The Remanufacturing Inst. [2564], c/o Ron Giuntini,
Exec. Dir., PO Box 48, Lewisburg, PA 17837,
. (570)523-0992
The Remanufacturing Inst. [IO], Lewisburg, PA,
United States
Remarried Parents, Inc. - Defunct.
Remedial Teachers; Natl. Assn. for [★9043]
Remedios AIDS Found. [IO], Manila, Philippines
Remember That Song - Address unknown since
2008.
Remembering ADAM [13280], PO Box 665, Hast-
ings, PA 16646, (877)767-2326
Remembrance of the Holocaust Found. - Address
unknown since 1999.
Remnant Of Israel [20030], PO Box 142633, Irving,
TX 75014-2633, (214)821-0633
Remodelers Assn; Natl. [★643]
Remodeling Indus; Natl. Assn. of the [643]
Remote Sensing
Japan Soc. of Photogrammetry and Remote
Sensing [IO]
SkyTruth [4637]
Remote Sensing; Amer. Soc. for Photogrammetry
and [★7495]
Remote Sensing and Photogrammetry Soc. [IO],
Nottingham, United Kingdom
Remote Sensing Soc. [★IO]
Remote Sensing Soc; IEEE Geoscience and [7144]
Remotivation Technique Org; Natl. [★16226]
Remotivation Therapy Org; Natl. [16226]
Removal Community; Machining and Material [7025]
Remove Intoxicated Drivers - U.S.A. [★12987]
Remus Museum; Uncle [9717]
Renaissance
Amer. Boccaccio Assn. [9629]
Assn. for Renaissance Martial Arts [8820]
Center for Medieval and Renaissance Stud.
[10456]
Center for Medieval and Renaissance Stud.
[10457]
Centers and Regional Associations [10458]
Charles Homer Haskins Soc. [10459]
Medieval Acad. of Am. [10462]
Renaissance Artists and Writers Assn. [10202]
Renaissance English Text Soc. [10932]
Renaissance English Text Society [IO]
Renaissance Lawyer Soc. [5529]
Renaissance Soc. of Am. [10933]

Renaissance Soc. of Am. [IO]
Soc. for Medieval and Renaissance Philosophy
[10464]
Soc. for Renaissance Stud. [IO]
Renaissance Artists and Writers Assn. [10202], c/o
RAWA New York Sector, 97-38 42nd Ave., 1st Fl.,
Corona, NY 11368, (718)898-1603
Renaissance Educ. Assn. [★13100]
Renaissance Educational Associates - Defunct.
Renaissance English Text Soc. [10932], c/o Arthur F.
Kinney, Dir., Univ. of Massachusetts, Dept. of
English, Center for Renaissance Stud., PO Box
2300, Amherst, MA 01004, (413)577-3600
Renaissance English Text Society [IO], Amherst,
MA, United States
Renaissance of Italian Youth - Address unknown
since 1995.
Renaissance Lawyer Soc. [5529], 4905 Glendarion
Dr., Durham, NC 27713
Renaissance Philosophy; Soc. for Medieval and
[10464]
Renaissance Soc. of Am. [10933], c/o CUNY, 365
5th Ave., Rm. 5400, New York, NY 10016-4309,
(212)817-2130
Renaissance Soc. of Am. [IO], New York, NY, United
States
Renaissance Stud; Assn. of Centers of Medieval and
[★10458]
Renaissance Stud; Center for Medieval and [10456]
Renaissance Stud; Center for Medieval and [10457]
Renaissance Stud; Center for Medieval and Early
[★10456]
Renaissance Transgender Assn. [13100], 987 Old
Eagle School Rd., Ste. 719, Wayne, PA 19087,
(610)975-9119
Renaissance Universal [18840], 3001 58th Ave. S,
Apt. 511, St. Petersburg, FL 33712, (727)867-1813
Renaissance Universal [IO], St. Petersburg, Russia
Renal Administrators Assn; Natl. [15072]
Renal Assn. [IO], Petersfield, United Kingdom
Renal Disease Program; End Stage [★15298]
Renal Pathology Soc. [15872], c/o Dr. Helen Liapis,
Sec.-Treas., Dept. of Pathology and Immunology,
Washington Univ. School of Medicine, 660 S Euclid
Ave., St. Louis, MO 63110, (314)362-0136
Renal Pathology Soc. [IO], St. Louis, MO, United
States
Renal Physicians Assn. [15298], 1700 Rockville
Pike, Ste. 220, Rockville, MD 20852, (301)468-
3515
Renal Support Network [15299], 1311 N Maryland
Ave., Glendale, CA 91207, (818)543-0896
Renault Club of America - Defunct.
Renault Owners Club of America - Defunct.
Renault Owners Club of North Am. [21769], c/o Ray
Dietz, New Member Sec., 1250 Lanier Rd., Martin-
sville, VA 24112-5212, (619)561-6687
Renderers Assn; Natl. [2858]
Rene Dubos Center for Human Environments
[4602], The Rene Dubos Ctr., Ste. 387, Bronxville,
NY 10708, (914)337-1636
Rene Dubos Forum [★4602]
Rene Guyon Soc. - Address unknown since 2007.
Renew Am. [4336], PO Box 77636, Washington, DC
20013
Renew Am. [★7677]
Renew Am. [★IO]
Renew the Earth [IO], Reston, VA, United States
Renew the Earth [7677], 1900 Oracle Way, Ste. 717,
Reston, VA 20190, (703)689-4670
Renewable Energy; Amer. Coun. on [6939]
Renewable Energy Assn. [IO], London, United
Kingdom
Renewable Energy Assn. of Swaziland [IO], Mba-
bane, Swaziland
Renewable Energy Congressional Staff Group -
Defunct.
Renewable Energy Coun; Interstate [6959]
Renewable Energy Info Center - Address unknown
since 1991.
Renewable Energy Info. Center; Energy Efficiency
and [6951]
Renewable Energy Inquiry and Referral Ser;
Conservation and [★6951]
Renewable Energy Policy Proj. - Center For Renew-
able Energy and Sustainable Tech. [6970], 1612 K
St. NW, Ste. 202, Washington, DC 20006,
(202)293-2898

Renewable Energy Resources Info. Center [★IO]
Renewable Energy and Sustainable Tech; Renew-
able Energy Policy Proj. - Center For [6970]
Renewable Fuels Assn. [6971], One Massachusetts
Ave. NW, Ste. 820, Washington, DC 20001,
(202)289-3835
Renewable Natural Resources Found. [4443], 5430
Grosvenor Ln., Bethesda, MD 20814-2142,
(301)493-9101
Renewable Power Assn. [★IO]
Renewable Technologies; Center for Energy Ef-
ficiency and [4526]
Rental Assn. of Am; Furniture [★1699]
Rental Assn; Delta Houseboat [3367]
Rental Assn; Production Equip. [2793]
Rental Assn; Recreation Vehicle [3372]
Rental Housing Coun; Natl. [★3332]
Rental Managers Assn; Vacation [3344]
Rental Managers; Assn. of Vacation Home [★3344]
Rental Operators; Amer. Assoc. [★3377]
Rental Ser. Assn; Natl. [★3377]
Renting and Leasing
Amer. Assn. of Cmpt. Rental Professionals [895]
Amer. Automotive Leasing Assn. [3375]
Amer. Car Rental Assn. [3376]
Amer. Rental Assn. [3377]
Amer. Soc. of Roommate Services [12305]
Amtralease [3378]
Assn. of Luxury Suite Directors [3676]
Assn. of Progressive Rental Organizations [3379]
Avis Licensee Assn. [3380]
Calgary Apartment Assn. [IO]
Coalition for Economic Survival [13160]
Coun. of Intl. Restaurant Real Estate Brokers
[3392]
Delta Houseboat Rental Assn. [3367]
Equip. Leasing and Finance Assn. [3381]
Equip. Leasing and Finance Assn. [IO]
Fork Lift Truck Assn. [IO]
Hire Assn. Europe [IO]
Hire Indus. Assn. of New Zealand [IO]
Natl. Alliance of HUD Tenants [18514]
Natl. Assn. of Equip. Leasing Brokers [3382]
Natl. Assn. of Housing Cooperatives [12320]
Natl. Assn. of Tenants' Organisations [IO]
Natl. Caucus and Center on Black Aged [11306]
Natl. Inst. of Senior Housing [12328]
Natl. Retail Tenants Assn. [3383]
Natl. Truck Leasing Sys. [3384]
Natl. Vehicle Leasing Assn. [3385]
Off. Bus. Center Assn. Intl. [74]
Recreation Vehicle Rental Assn. [3372]
Tenants and Residents Org. of England [IO]
Textile Rental Services Assn. of Am. [3386]
Truck Renting and Leasing Assn. [3387]
United Assn. of Equip. Leasing [3388]
Renwick Alliance; James [9452]
REO Club of Am. [21770], c/o Marilyn Cooper, Sec.,
1323 W Maple Ave., Enid, OK 73703-4512,
(651)457-6968
REO Club of Am. [IO], Enid, OK, United States
R.E.O. Pals NW - Address unknown since 2003.
Repair
Intl. Luggage Repair Assn. [2440]
Musical Instrument Technicians Assn., Intl. [2816]
Natl. Assn. of Ser. Dealers [3389]
Professional Ser. Assn. [3553]
Repair Assn; Natl. Windshield [425]
Repair Assn; Truck-Frame and Axle [430]
Repair Coun; Valve [1839]
Repair and Growth Soc; Bioelectrical [★6554]
Repair; Inter-Industry Conf. on Auto Collision [415]
Repair Shops; New York State Assn. of Ser. Stations
and [426]
Repair Specialists; Intl. Assn. of Concrete [★927]
Repair Specialists; Soc. of Collision [428]
Repair Sta. Assn; Aeronautical [129]
Repair Technicians; Natl. Assn. of Professional Band
Instrument [2818]
Repairers Assn; Amer. Boat Builders and [2568]
Reparation Soc. of the Immaculate Heart of Mary
[19709]
Reparations in Am; Natl. Coalition of Blacks for
[16944]
Repatriation Found; Amer. Indian Ritual Object
[18091]

A star before a book entry number signifies that the name is not listed separately, but is mentioned within the entry.

Repeal of the Fed. Reserve Act and the Internal
  Revenue Code; Natl. Org. for the [★17666]
Repertoire Canadien des Psychologues Offrant des
  Services de Sante [★IO]
Repetitive Motion Injury
  Assn. for Repetitive Motion Syndromes [15631]
Rephael Soc. - Defunct.
The Replica - Defunct.
Rpt. Card; Nation's [★9253]
Reporters Assn; Natl. Court [5630]
Reporters Assn; Natl. Shorthand [★5630]
Reporters Assn; Natl. Verbatim [4064]
Reporters Assn; Regional [3157]
Reporters Comm. for Freedom of the Press [17192],
  1101 Wilson Blvd., Ste. 1100, Arlington, VA 22209,
  (703)807-2100
Reporters and Editors; Investigative [3126]
Reporters sans Frontieres [★IO]
Reporters of Judicial Decisions; Assn. of [5895]
Reporters Network [3160], c/o Criminal Justice
  Journalists, Jerry Lee Center of Criminology, 720
  7th St. NW, 3rd Fl., Washington, DC 20001,
  (202)448-1717
Reporters Without Borders - France [IO], Paris,
  France
Reporting; Center for Financial Freedom and Ac-
  curacy in Financial [18404]
Reporting; Center for Investigative [17168]
Reporting; Fairness and Accuracy in [17176]
Reporting; Fund for Objective News [17179]
Reporting; National Inst. for Computer-Assisted
  [★3126]
Reporting; National Inst. for Computer-Assisted
  [★IO]
Reporting; Soc. for the Technological Advancement
  of [5631]
Repossessions Division of Amer. Collectors Assn.
  [★1145]
Repossessors Assn; Amer. [★1145]
Representation; Citizens for Proportional [★18348]
Representation Fund; Taxation With [★18718]
Representation; Taxation With [★18718]
Representative of German Indus. and Trade [762],
  1627 I St. NW, Ste. 550, Washington, DC 20006,
  (202)659-4777
Representative of German Indus. and Trade [IO],
  Washington, DC, United States
Representatives Alliance; Incentive Mfrs. and [2536]
Representatives of Am; Manufacturers [1158]
Representatives Assn; Agricultural and Indus. Mfrs.
  [2533]
Representatives Assn; Incentive Mfrs. and [★2536]
Representatives Assn; Natl. Elecl. Manufacturers
  [1192]
Representatives of Electronic Products Manufactur-
  ers [★1213]
Representatives Org; Independent Professional
  [330]
Representatives of Radio Parts Manufacturers
  [★1213]
Repression Rsrc. Team; Anti- [17093]
Repressive Legislation; Natl. Comm. Against [17134]
Reprint Soc; Augustan [10415]
Reprints for Teaching; Medieval Acad. [★10458]
REPROBEL [IO], Brussels, Belgium
Reproduction and Rhythm; Natl. Commn. on Human
  Life, [16008]
Reproduction Rights Soc. of Nigeria [IO], Ibadan,
  Nigeria
Reproduction; Soc. for the Stud. of [16350]
Reproductive Action League; Natl. Abortion and
  [★18518]
Reproductive and Family Hea. Assn. of Fiji [IO],.
  Suva, Fiji
Reproductive Freedom
  Amer. Center for Law and Justice [12901]
  Amer. Victims of Abortion [12903]
  Assn. for Interdisciplinary Res. in Values and
    Social Change [12906]
  Childbirth and Postpartum Professional Assn.
    [13980]
  Interfaith Working Group [12887]
  Law Students for Choice [18517]
  Liberty Godparent Home [12918]
  Presbyterians Pro-Life [12926]

Reproductive Health
  Advocates for Youth [12173]
  Advocates for Youth's Media Proj. [12174]
  Alan Guttmacher Inst. [12175]
  Amer. Assn. of Birth Centers [15580]
  Amer. Assn. of Gynecologic Laparoscopists
    [15581]
  Amer. Bd. of Obstetrics and Gynecology [15582]
  Amer. Center for Law and Justice [12901]
  Amer. Coll. of Domiciliary Midwives [15583]
  Amer. Coll. of Obstetricians and Gynecologists
    [15584]
  Amer. Coll. of Osteopathic Obstetricians and
    Gynecologists [15585]
  Amer. Coll. of Theriogenologists [16763]
  Amer. Fertility Assn. [14388]
  Amer. Found. for Maternal and Child Health
    [15586]
  Amer. Found. for the Prevention of Venereal
    Disease [16409]
  Amer. Gynecological and Obstetrical Soc. [15587]
  Amer. Pregnancy Assn. [15588]
  Amer. Social Hea. Assn. [16410]
  Amer. Soc. of Breast Disease [13772]
  Amer. Soc. of Childbirth Educators [15589]
  Amer. Soc. for Colposcopy and Cervical Pathol-
    ogy [15590]
  Amer. Victims of Abortion [12903]
  Asociacion Puertorriquena Pro-Bienestar de la
    Familia [12176]
  Assn. for Interdisciplinary Res. in Values and
    Social Change [12906]
  Assn. of Reproductive Hea. Professionals [12177]
  Assn. of Women's Hea., Obstetric and Neonatal
    Nurses [15470]
  Billings Ovulation Method Assn. - USA [12635]
  C/SEC [15593]
  Childbirth Connection [15595]
  CHOICE [12178]
  Citizens Alliance for VD Awareness [16411]
  Coun. on Resident Educ. in Obstetrics and
    Gynecology [15597]
  Couple to Couple League [12636]
  DES Action, U.S.A. [13821]
  Donors' Offspring [13298]
  Endometriosis Assn. [15599]
  EngenderHealth [12180]
  Facing Our Risk of Cancer Empowered [13823]
  Family of the Americas Found. [12637]
  Family Hea. Intl. [12181]
  Fertile Hope [14390]
  Hea. Global Access Proj. [11331]
  Healthy Teen Network [12182]
  Herpes Rsrc. Center - Amer. Social Hea. Assn.
    [16412]
  Hysterectomy Educational Resources and
    Services Found. [15601]
  Informed Homebirth/Informed Birth and Parenting
    [15602]
  Inst. for Female Alternative Medicine [16345]
  Intl. Cesarean Awareness Network [15604]
  Intl. Consortium for Emergency Contraception
    [12183]
  Intl. Dalkon Shield Victims Educ. Assn. [16898]
  Intl. Embryo Transfer Soc. [16794]
  Intl. Planned Parenthood Fed., Western
    Hemisphere Region [12184]
  Intl. Premature Ovarian Failure Assn. [15606]
  Intl. Stillbirth Alliance [13982]
  Intl. Union Against Sexually Transmitted Infec-
    tions, Regional Off. for North Am. [16414]
  Lamaze Birth Without Pain Educ. Assn. [15607]
  Law Students for Choice [18517]
  Liberty Godparent Home [12918]
  Maternal Life Intl. [16341]
  Maternal Life Intl. [IO]
  Midwifery Educ. Accreditation Coun. [8063]
  Midwives Alliance of North Am. [15610]
  Museum of Menstruation and Women's Hea.
    [15611]
  Natl. Abortion Fed. [11223]
  Natl. Assn. of Nurse Practitioners in Women's
    Hea. [15497]
  Natl. Commn. on Human Life, Reproduction and
    Rhythm [16008]

  Natl. Coun. on Women's Hea. [16904]
  Natl. Family Planning and Reproductive Hea.
    Assn. [12185]
  Natl. Healthy Start Assn. [15613]
  Natl. Infertility Network Exchange [12678]
  Natl. Inst. of Child Hea. and Human Development
    [13971]
  Natl. Perinatal Assn. [15900]
  North Amer. Menopause Soc. [15614]
  North Amer. Soc. of Obstetric Medicine [15615]
  North Amer. Soc. for the Stud. of Hypertension in
    Pregnancy [16342]
  Off. of Population Affairs CH [12757]
  Org. of Parents Through Surrogacy [13299]
  Pathfinder Intl. [12186]
  Planned Parenthood Fed. of Am. [12187]
  Pregnant With Cancer Network [13865]
  Presbyterians Pro-Life [12926]
  SisterSong Women of Color Reproductive Hea.
    Collective [18826]
  Soc. of Andrology - India [IO]
  Soc. for Assisted Reproductive Tech. [16346]
  Soc. for Gynecologic Investigation [15618]
  Soc. for Male Reproduction and Urology [16343]
  Soc. for Menstrual Cycle Res. [15619]
  Soc. for Obstetric Anesthesia and Perinatology
    [15903]
  Soc. of Reproductive Surgeons [16349]
  Soc. for Sex Therapy and Res. [16408]
  Soc. for the Stud. of Male Reproduction [16344]
  Soc. for the Stud. of Reproduction [16350]
  Soc. for Theriogenology [16806]
  Waterbirth Intl. [13984]
Reproductive Hea. Assn; Natl. Family Planning and
  [12185]
Reproductive Hea; Natl. Assn. of Nurse Practitioners
  in [★15497]
Reproductive Hea. Professionals; Assn. of [12177]
Reproductive Law and Policy; Center for [★18516]
Reproductive Medicine
  Advocates for Youth [12173]
  Amer. Assn. of Birth Centers [15580]
  Amer. Assn. of Gynecologic Laparoscopists
    [15581]
  Amer. Bd. of Obstetrics and Gynecology [15582]
  Amer. Coll. of Domiciliary Midwives [15583]
  Amer. Coll. of Osteopathic Obstetricians and
    Gynecologists [15585]
  Amer. Coll. of Theriogenologists [16763]
  Amer. Fertility Assn. [14388]
  Amer. Found. for Maternal and Child Health
    [15586]
  Amer. Found. for the Prevention of Venereal
    Disease [16409]
  Amer. Gynecological and Obstetrical Soc. [15587]
  Amer. Social Hea. Assn. [16410]
  Amer. Soc. of Breast Disease [13772]
  Amer. Soc. of Childbirth Educators [15589]
  Asociacion Colombiana De Fertilidad Y Esterilidad
    [IO]
  Asociacion Guatemalteca De Fertilidad Y Repro-
    duccion Humana [IO]
  Assn. of Clinical Embryologists [IO]
  Assn. for Interdisciplinary Res. in Values and
    Social Change [12906]
  Assn. of Reproductive Hea. Professionals [12177]
  Australian Reproductive Hea. Alliance [IO]
  Austrian Soc. of Sterility, Fertility and Endocrinol-
    ogy [IO]
  Bangladesh Fertility Soc. [IO]
  Belgium Soc. for Reproductive Medicine [IO]
  Billings Ovulation Method Assn. - USA [12635]
  British Infertility Counselling Assn. [IO]
  Bulgarian Assn. of Sterility and Reproductive Hea.
    [IO]
  C/SEC [15593]
  Canadian Fertility and Andrology Soc. [IO]
  CHOICE [12178]
  Citizens Alliance for VD Awareness [16411]
  Coun. on Resident Educ. in Obstetrics and
    Gynecology [15597]
  DES Action, U.S.A. [13821]
  Donors' Offspring [13298]
  Egyptian Fertility and Sterility Soc. [IO]
  EngenderHealth [12180]

Reference to "IO" in place of a book number signifies that the association may be found in the 45th edition of International Organizations.

European Acad. of Andrology [IO]
European Soc. of Contraception [IO]
European Soc. of Human Reproduction and
    Embryology [IO]
Family Hea. Intl. [12181]
Fertility Soc. of Australia [IO]
Finnish Gynecological Assn. [IO]
German Soc. of Reproductive Medicine [IO]
German Soc. for Sex Res. [IO]
Guyana Responsible Parenthood Assn. [IO]
Healthy Teen Network [12182]
Hellenic Fertility and Sterility Soc. [IO]
Herpes Rsrc. Center - Amer. Social Hea. Assn.
    [16412]
Hysterectomy Educational Resources and
    Services Found. [15601]
Indian Soc. for Assisted Reproduction [IO]
Infertility Awareness Assn. of Canada [IO]
Infertility Network UK [IO]
Informed Homebirth/Informed Birth and Parenting
    [15602]
Inst. for Female Alternative Medicine [16345]
Intl. Cesarean Awareness Network [15604]
Intl. Dalkon Shield Victims Educ. Assn. [16898]
Intl. Embryo Transfer Soc. [16794]
Intl. Planned Parenthood Fed., Western
    Hemisphere Region [12184]
Intl. Premature Ovarian Failure Assn. [15606]
Intl. Union Against Sexually Transmitted Infec-
    tions, Regional Off. for North Am. [16414]
Intl. Women's Hea. Coalition [16899]
Iranian Soc. of Fertility and Sterility [IO]
Iraqi Fertility Soc. [IO]
Italian Soc. of Fertility, Sterility and Reproductive
    Medicine [IO]
Japan Soc. for Reproductive Medicine [IO]
Jordanian Soc. for Fertility and Genetics [IO]
Korean Soc. of Fertility and Sterility [IO]
Maternal Life Intl. [16341]
Midwifery Educ. Accreditation Coun. [8063]
Museum of Menstruation and Women's Hea.
    [15611]
Natl. Abortion Fed. [11223]
Natl. Assn. of Nurse Practitioners in Women's
    Hea. [15497]
Natl. Campaign to Prevent Teen Pregnancy
    [13499]
Natl. Commn. on Human Life, Reproduction and
    Rhythm [16008]
Natl. Coun. on Women's Hea. [16904]
Natl. Family Planning and Reproductive Hea.
    Assn. [12185]
Natl. Perinatal Assn. [15900]
New Zealand Endometriosis Found. [IO]
Nigerian Fertility Soc. [IO]
North Amer. Menopause Soc. [15614]
North Amer. Soc. of Obstetric Medicine [15615]
Off. of Population Affairs CH [12757]
Org. of Parents Through Surrogacy [13299]
Pathfinder Intl. [12186]
Planned Parenthood Fed. of Am. [12187]
Pregnant With Cancer Network [13865]
Presbyterians Pro-Life [12926]
Sociedad Chilena De Fertilidad [IO]
Sociedad Ecuatoriana De Medicina Reproductiva
    [IO]
Sociedad Paraguaya De Fertilidad [IO]
Sociedad Peruana De Fertilidad [IO]
Sociedad Salvadorena De Endoscopia Gineco-
    logica Y Medicina [IO]
Societe Marcoaine De Fertilite Et De Contracep-
    tion [IO]
Soc. for Assisted Reproductive Tech. [16346]
Soc. for Gynecologic Investigation [15618]
Soc. for Male Reproduction and Urology [16343]
Soc. for Menstrual Cycle Res. [15619]
Soc. for Prevention of Human Infertility [16347]
Soc. for Prevention of Human Infertility [IO]
Soc. for Reproductive Biology [IO]
Soc. for Reproductive Endocrinology and Infertility
    [16348]
Soc. of Reproductive Surgeons [16349]
Soc. for Sex Therapy and Res. [16408]
Soc. for the Stud. of Male Reproduction [16344]
Soc. for the Stud. of Reproduction [16350]

Soc. for Theriogenology [16806]
Waterbirth Intl. [13984]
World Org. Ovulation Method Billings [IO]
Reproductive Medicine; Amer. Soc. for [14389]

Reproductive Rights
Abortion Rights [IO]
Americans for Religious Liberty [17090]
Assn. for Interdisciplinary Res. in Values and
    Social Change [12906]
Assn. for the Legal Right to Abortion [IO]
Catholics for a Free Choice [18515]
Center for Reproductive Rights [18516]
Center for Reproductive Rights [IO]
Childbirth by Choice Trust [IO]
EngenderHealth [12180]
Healthy Teen Network [12182]
Intl. Consortium for Emergency Contraception
    [12183]
Intl. Planned Parenthood Fed., Western
    Hemisphere Region [12184]
Jessie Smith Noyes Found. [4583]
Law Students for Choice [18517]
NARAL Pro-Choice Am. [18518]
Natl. Abortion Fed. [11223]
Natl. Family Planning and Reproductive Hea.
    Assn. [12185]
Off. of Population Affairs CH [12757]
Org. of Parents Through Surrogacy [13299]
Pathfinder Intl. [12186]
Planned Parenthood Fed. of Am. [12187]
Presbyterians Pro-Life [12926]
Progress Educational Trust [IO]
Religious Coalition for Reproductive Choice
    [18519]
Republicans for Choice [18520]
SisterSong Women of Color Reproductive Hea.
    Collective [18826]
Voters for Choice/Friends of Family Planning
    [18521]
Women's Global Network for Reproductive Rights
    - Netherlands [IO]
Reproductive Rights Natl. Network - Defunct.
Reproductive Rights Project [★24204]
Reproductive Tech; Soc. for Assisted [16346]
Reproductive Toxicology Center [14393], 7831
    Woodmont Ave., Ste. 375, Bethesda, MD 20814,
    (301)514-3081
Reproductive Toxicology Center [IO], Bethesda, MD,
    United States

Reptiles
Amer. Soc. of Ichthyologists and Herpetologists
    [7158]
Global Gecko Assn. [5169]
Herpetologists' League [7159]
Soc. for the Stud. of Amphibians and Reptiles
    [7160]
Reptiles; Soc. for the Stud. of Amphibians and
    [7160]
Reptilian and Amphibian Veterinarians; Assn. of
    [16783]
Republic of China Aikido Assn. [IO], Taipei, Taiwan
Republic of China Economic Coun; U.S.A.- [★2294]
Republic of the Congo Information Office - Defunct.
Republic of the Marshall Islands Baseball Fed. [IO],
    Majuro, Marshall Islands
Republic of New Africa - Address unknown since
    1997.
Republic of Texas; Daughters of the [21114]
Republic of Trinidad and Tobago Taekwondo Assn.
    [IO], Port of Spain, Trinidad and Tobago
Republican Attorneys; Natl. Assn. of [5512]
Republican Citizens Comm. of the U.S. - Defunct.
Republican Clubs; Natl. Fed. of Women's [★18525]
Republican Coalition for Choice [★18533]
Republican Communications Assn. - Address
    unknown since 2001.
Republican Congressional Leadership Coun. - Ad-
    dress unknown since 2001.
Republican Coordinating Comm. - Defunct.
Republican Fed; Arab Amer. [★17003]
Republican Governors Assn. [6286], 1747
    Pennsylvania Ave. NW, Ste. 250, Washington, DC
    20006, (202)662-4140
Republican Inst. for Intl. Affairs; Natl. [★17396]
Republican Jewish Coalition [18530], 50 F St. NW,
    Ste. 100, Washington, DC 20001, (202)638-6688

Republican Liberty Caucus [18531], 44 Summerfield
    St., Thousand Oaks, CA 91360, (805)493-4332
Republican Mainstream Comm. [18532], 7620 W
    21st Ave., Kennewick, WA 99338-9163, (509)528-
    1265
Republican Majority for Choice [18533], 1660 L St.
    NW, Ste. 609, Washington, DC 20036-5676,
    (202)887-4786
Republican Natl. Coalition for Life [18566], PO Box
    618, Alton, IL 62002, (214)559-4460
Republican Natl. Comm. [18534], 310 1st St. SE,
    Washington, DC 20003, (202)863-8500
Republican Natl. Fed; Coll. Ser. Comm. of the Young
    [★18522]
Republican Natl. Hispanic Assembly of the U.S.
    [18535], 1717 Pennsylvania Ave. NW, Ste. 650,
    Washington, DC 20006, (202)558-5477
Republican Natl. Nominating Convention [★18534]

Republican Party
Arab Amer. Leadership Coun. [17003]
Coll. Republican Natl. Comm. [18522]
Congressional Automotive Caucus [17255]
Congressional Human Rights Caucus [17755]
Conservative Opportunity Soc. [17257]
Constitution Soc. [5604]
Free Cong. Political Action Comm. [17268]
Log Cabin Republicans [18523]
Madison Proj. [6245]
Natl. Black Republican Assn. [18524]
Natl. Comm. for an Effective Cong. [17252]
Natl. Fed. of Republican Women [18525]
Natl. Republican Club [18526]
Natl. Republican Congressional Comm. [18527]
Natl. Republican Senatorial Comm. [18528]
Natl. Teen Age Republican HQ [18529]
Republican Governors Assn. [6286]
Republican Jewish Coalition [18530]
Republican Liberty Caucus [18531]
Republican Mainstream Comm. [18532]
Republican Majority for Choice [18533]
Republican Natl. Coalition for Life [18566]
Republican Natl. Comm. [18534]
Republican Natl. Hispanic Assembly of the U.S.
    [18535]
Republican Presidential Task Force [18536]
Ripon Soc. [18537]
Senate Tourism Caucus [17259]
United Black Republican Coalition [18538]
U.S. Assn. of Former Members of Cong. [17253]
WISH List [5770]
Women's Natl. Republican Club [18539]
Young Republican Natl. Fed. [18540]
Republican Presidential Task Force [18536], Ronald
    Reagan Republican Center, 425 2nd St. NE,
    Washington, DC 20002, (202)675-6000
Republican Pro-Choice Coalition [★18533]
Republican Senatorial Inner Circle; National
    [★18528]
Republican Women of Capitol Hill - Address
    unknown since 1999.
Republican Youth Public Assn. [★IO]
Republicans Abroad Intl. [IO], Washington, DC,
    United States
Republicans Abroad Intl. [18333], 1275 K St. NW,
    Ste. 102, Washington, DC 20005, (202)608-1423
Republicans for Choice [18520], 205 S Whiting St.,
    Ste. 260, Alexandria, VA 22304, (703)212-0890
Republicans for Choice Emergency Task Force
    [★18520]
Republicans for Environmental Protection [4444],
    3200 Carlisle Blvd., Ste. 114, Albuquerque, NM
    87110, (505)889-4544
Republicans for Equality and Privacy; United
    [★18523]
Republicans for Progress - Defunct.
Republicko Udruzenje Srbije za Pomoc Osobama sa
    Autizmom [★IO]
ReREAD [12299]
ReRun [17731], PO Box 113, Helmetta, NJ 08828,
    (732)521-1370
Rerun Watchers Club; The Andy Griffith Show
    [25025]
Resale Assn; Natl. Aircraft [189]
Resale Dealers; Natl. Assn. of Fleet [419]
Resale and Thrift Shops; Natl. Assn. of [3417]

A star before a book entry number signifies that the name is not listed separately, but is mentioned within the entry.

RESCARE [IO], Stockport, United Kingdom
Rescate Democratico Revolucionario - Address unknown since 1995.
Rescate; El [12809]
Rescue
  Akita Rescue Soc. of Am. [11341]
  Amer. German Shepherd Rescue Assn. [11348]
  Amer. Rescue Dog Assn. [12889]
  Amer. Rescue Dog Assn. [IO]
  Bulldog Club of Am. Rescue Network [11372]
  Canadian Lifeboat Inst. [IO]
  CityTeam Ministries [12844]
  Dogs Deserve Better [12017]
  Echo Dogs White Shepherd Rescue [11388]
  Intl. Commn. for Alpine Rescue [IO]
  Intl. Comm. for the Rescue of KAL 007 Survivors [18541]
  Intl. Maritime Rescue Fed. [IO]
  Last Chance Corral [11425]
  Mountain Rescue Assn. [12890]
  Natl. Assn. for Search and Rescue [12891]
  Natl. Disaster Search Dog Found. [12892]
  Natl. Emergency Equip. Dealers Assn. [14339]
  North Amer. Border Terrier Welfare [12019]
  Pups for Peace [12700]
  Swedish Sea Rescue Soc. [IO]
  U.S. Homeland Emergency Response Org. [12893]
  U.S. Life-Saving Ser. Heritage Assn. [10072]
  U.S. Lifesaving Assn. [12894]
  U.S. Mine Rescue Assn. [12600]
Rescue Am; English Springer [11390]
Rescue Amer. Jobs [17984], c/o United Steelworkers of Am., 5 Gateway Ctr., Pittsburgh, PA 15222, (866)879-2937
Rescue Assn; Natl. Mine [7348]
Rescue Comm; Emergency [★12812]
Rescue Coordinators; Natl. Assn. of Search and [★12891]
Rescue - Defunct.
Rescue Fund; Sea Turtle [★4435]
Rescue Mission; San Jose [★12844]
Rescue; Pot Belly Pig [11450]
Rescue Ser; Parachute Medical [★12540]
Rescue and Towing; Comm. for Private Offshore [2574]
Rescue Workers; Amer. [13153]
RescueNet; Llama [11427]
Research
  AACR-Women in Cancer Res. [16893]
  Acad. of Behavioral Medicine Res. [13732]
  Accelerated Cure Proj. for Multiple Sclerosis [15301]
  Aerospace Indus. Assn. of Am. [130]
  Alliance for Human Res. Protection [17741]
  Alliance for Sci. and Tech. Res. in Am. [7595]
  Alliance in Support of Independent Res. [3390]
  Amer. Acad. of Psychiatry and the Law [5780]
  Amer. Acad. of Sleep Medicine [16418]
  Amer. Acad. of Somnology [16419]
  Amer. Assn. of Behavioral and Social Sciences [6522]
  Amer. Assn. for Dental Res. [14113]
  Amer. Assn. for Medical Chronobiology and Chronotherapeutics [13751]
  Amer. Clinical Lab. Assn. [14991]
  Amer. Coll. of Angiology [16719]
  Amer. Coll. of Medical Genetics [14494]
  Amer. Educational Res. Assn. [9053]
  Amer. Hea. Assistance Found. [15100]
  Amer. Inst. of Stress [16487]
  Amer. Institutes for Res. [7560]
  Amer. Labor Education Center [8720]
  Amer. Lib. Assn. - Off. for Res. and Statistics [10934]
  Amer. Philatelic Res. Lib. [22784]
  Amer. Porphyria Found. [15243]
  Amer. Seed Res. Found. [5173]
  Amer. Soc. of Greek and Latin Epigraphy [11207]
  Amer. Spinal Injury Assn. [16461]
  Amer. Urological Assn. Found. [16705]
  Assoc. Professional Sleep Societies [16422]
  Assn. for the Accreditation of Human Res. Protection Programs [11225]
  Assn. of Amer. Cancer Institutes [13794]

Assn. for Applied Community Researchers [7561]
Assn. of Asian-Pacific Operational Res. Societies [IO]
Assn. of European Operational Res. Societies within IFORS [IO]
Assn. of European Operational Res. Societies within IFORS - France [IO]
Assn. of Former Intelligence Officers [5878]
Assn. of Freestanding Radiation Oncology Centers [16268]
Assn. of Independent Res. Institutes [7562]
Assn. of Independent Res. and Tech. Organisations [IO]
Assn. of Intl. Hea. Researchers [14548]
Assn. for Korean Music Res. [10561]
Assn. of Latina and Latino Anthropologists [6410]
Assn. for Ocular Pharmacology and Therapeutics [15671]
Assn. of Polysomnographic Technologists [16423]
Assn. of Res. Directors [7563]
Assn. of Res. Libraries [10338]
Assn. for Res. in Personality [7543]
Assn. of Researchers in Medicine and Sci. [IO]
Assn. of State Energy Res. and Tech. Transfer Institutions [6945]
Assn. for the Stud. of Free Institutions [8481]
Assn. for the Stud. of the Worldwide African Diaspora [7929]
Assn. of Univ. Res. and Indus. Links [IO]
Assn. of Univ. Res. Parks [9054]
Assn. of Veterans Affairs Ophthalmologists [15676]
Assn. of Zoological Horticulture [4974]
Australian Coun. for Educational Res. [IO]
Australian and New Zealand Stud. Assn. of North Amer. [8484]
Australian Res. Coun. [IO]
Better Sleep Coun. [16424]
The Billfish Found. [5298]
Canadian Inst. for Advanced Res. [IO]
Canadian Institutional Res. and Planning Assn. [IO]
Carnegie Institution of Washington [7564]
Cell Stress Soc. Intl. [16488]
Center for Applied Res. in the Apostolate [19608]
Center for Ergonomic Res. [7565]
Center for Res. in Faith and Moral Development [20534]
Center for Res. Libraries [10345]
Centre for Educational Res. and Innovation [IO]
Chalcedon Found. [20535]
CHERUBS - Assn. of Congenital Diaphragmatic Hernia Res., Advocacy and Support [13753]
Childhood Arthritis and Rheumatology Res. Alliance [16371]
Christopher and Dana Reeve Found. [16463]
Church Growth Inc. [20536]
City of Hope Natl. Medical Center [15102]
Clinical Lab. Mgt. Assn. [14993]
Clinical and Lab. Standards Inst. [14994]
Clinical Ligand Assay Soc. [14995]
Coalition for Hemophilia B [14787]
Cognitive Neuroscience Soc. [15407]
College-University Rsrc. Inst. [9055]
Comm. for the Advancement of Stem Cell Res. [18542]
Comm. on Institutional Cooperation [8104]
Comm. for the Promotion of Medical Res. [15104]
Commonwealth Sci. and Indus. Res. Org. [IO]
Community Info. and Epidemiological Technologies [12121]
Community for Religious Res. and Education [20537]
Comparative Cognition Soc. [6400]
Cmpt. Ethics Inst. [9056]
Conservation and Res. Found. [4383]
Consortium on Financing Higher Educ. [9057]
Corrugated Polyethylene Pipe Assn. [3049]
Coun. of Amer. Overseas Res. Centers [7566]
Coun. of Archives and Res. Libraries in Jewish Stud. [10351]
Coun. on Contemporary Families [12149]
Coun. on Food, Agricultural and Rsrc. Economics [4524]
Coun. on Governmental Relations [9058]

Coun. for Sci. and Indus. Res. [IO]
Coun. on Undergraduate Res. [9059]
Creation Res. Soc. [20548]
CrossRef [3220]
Cure Res. Found. [13818]
Dana Alliance for Brain Initiatives [15387]
Danish Acad. of Tech. Sciences [IO]
Depression and Bipolar Support Alliance [15196]
Diabetes Res. Assn. of Am. [14223]
Diabetes Res. Inst. Found. [14224]
Digital Govt. Soc. of North Am. [7151]
Earthtrust [5312]
Earthwatch Inst. [8413]
ECRI [15136]
Educational Res. Associates [8254]
Elliot Inst. [16911]
Environmental Res. Found. [13599]
Euler Soc. [10453]
EUREKA [IO]
Eureka - Croatia [IO]
Eureka - Ukraine [IO]
European Assn. of Development Res. and Training Institutes [IO]
European Assn. for Institutional Res. [IO]
European Assn. for Res. on Adolescence [IO]
European Biological Rhythms Soc. [IO]
European Cooperation in the Field of Sci. and Tech. Res. [IO]
European Histamine Res. Soc. [IO]
European Indus. Res. Mgt. Assn. [IO]
European Res. Gp. on Military and Soc. [IO]
European Soc. for Pigment Cell Res. [IO]
European Thrombosis Res. Org. [IO]
Evolutionary Anthropology Soc. [6416]
Executive Search Roundtable [7567]
Executive Search Roundtable [IO]
Fanconi Anemia Res. Fund [14450]
Financial Executives Res. Found. [1417]
Financial Services Tech. Consortium [7732]
Foreign Policy Res. Inst. [5743]
Found. for Sci. and Indus. Res. at the Norwegian Inst. of Tech. [IO]
Fraunhofer-Gesellschaft zur Forderung der Angewandten Forschung [IO]
Friedreich's Ataxia Res. Alliance [14403]
Gait and Clinical Movement Anal. Soc. [14557]
German Assn. of Market and Social Researchers [IO]
German Educational Res. Assn. [IO]
German Res. Found. [IO]
German Soc. for Fat Sci. [IO]
Global Applied Disability Res. and Info. Network [14240]
Global Assn. for Interpersonal Neurobiology Stud. [7375]
Global Bus. and Tech. Assn. [778]
Global Perioperative Res. Org. [14026]
Greenpeace U.S.A. [4571]
Guardians of Hydrocephalus Res. Found. [15326]
Hagiography Soc. [20526]
Hawaii Agriculture Res. Center [5228]
Hea. Res. Bd. [IO]
Histochemical Soc. [13938]
Icelandic Center for Res. [IO]
Independent Res. Libraries Assn. [10359]
Indus. Res. Inst. [7568]
Inner Light Found. [7569]
Innovation Mgt. Assn. of Canada [IO]
Inst. for Creation Res. [20538]
Inst. of Environmental Sciences and Tech. [7570]
Institute of Environmental Sciences and Technology [IO]
Inst. for Learning Technologies [8355]
Inst. of Public Admin. - USA [6192]
Inst. for Women's Policy Res. [17539]
Inter-American Inst. for Global Change Res. [IO]
Intl. Anchoritic Soc. [10460]
Intl. Assn. for Dialogue Anal. [7244]
Intl. Assn. for the Evaluation of Educational Achievement [IO]
Intl. Assn. for Game Educ. and Res. [8823]
Intl. Assn. of Genocide Scholars [17661]
Intl. Assn. for Intelligence Educ. [8581]
Intl. Assn. for Paratuberculosis [16793]
Intl. Assn. for the Promotion of Cooperation with Scientists from the New Independent States of the Former Soviet Union [IO]

Reference to "IO" in place of a book number signifies that the association may be found in the 45th edition of International Organizations.

Intl. Assn. for Relationship Res. [IO]
Intl. Assn. for Relationship Res. [7571]
Intl. Assn. of Ser. Evaluators [3269]
Intl. Assn. of Word and Image Stud. [9060]
Intl. Assn. of Word and Image Stud. [IO]
Intl. Atherosclerosis Soc. [13910]
Intl. Behavioral Neuroscience Soc. [15408]
Intl. Biopharmaceutical Assn. [15936]
Intl. Cell Death Soc. [6854]
Intl. Comm. on Ultra-High Intensity Lasers [7245]
Intl. Criminal Court Alliance [5654]
Intl. Development Res. Centre - Canada [IO]
Intl. Economics and Finance Soc. [6884]
Intl. Endotoxin and Innate Immunity Soc. [7803]
Intl. Experimental Aerospace Soc. [6375]
Intl. Fed. of Latin Amer. Stud. Centers [IO]
Intl. Fed. of Nonlinear Analysts [7609]
Intl. Guild of Lamp Researchers [22618]
Intl. High IQ Soc. [19149]
Intl. Humic Substances Soc. [7610]
Intl. Hyperhidrosis Soc. [14357]
Intl. Inst. for Applied Systems Anal. [IO]
Intl. Intelligence Network [3532]
Intl. Leptospirosis Soc. [14950]
Intl. Mystery Shopping Alliance [3412]
Intl. Pedigree Assignment and Bloodline Res.
   Assn. [4902]
Intl. Permafrost Assn. - Argentina [IO]
Intl. Permafrost Assn. - Austria [IO]
Intl. Permafrost Assn. - Belgium [IO]
Intl. Permafrost Assn. - Canada [IO]
Intl. Permafrost Assn. - China [IO]
Intl. Permafrost Assn. - Finland [IO]
Intl. Permafrost Assn. - France [IO]
Intl. Permafrost Assn. - Germany [IO]
Intl. Permafrost Assn. - Iceland [IO]
Intl. Permafrost Assn. - Japan [IO]
Intl. Permafrost Assn. - Kazakhstan [IO]
Intl. Permafrost Assn. - Mongolia [IO]
Intl. Permafrost Assn. - Netherlands [IO]
Intl. Permafrost Assn. - Norway [IO]
Intl. Permafrost Assn. - Poland [IO]
Intl. Permafrost Assn. - Russia [IO]
Intl. Permafrost Assn. - South Africa [IO]
Intl. Permafrost Assn. - Spain [IO]
Intl. Permafrost Assn. - Sweden [IO]
Intl. Permafrost Assn. - Switzerland [IO]
Intl. Permafrost Assn. - United Kingdom [IO]
Intl. Proteolysis Soc. [6549]
Intl. Sand Collectors Soc. [22056]
Intl. Soc. for Behavioral Nutrition and Physical
   Activity [13745]
Intl. Soc. for Bioluminescence and Chemilumines-
   cence [7612]
Intl. Soc. for Biosafety Res. [6586]
Intl. Soc. for Complementary Medicine Res.
   [13639]
Intl. Soc. for Computational Biology [2094]
Intl. Soc. of Dynamic Games [IO]
Intl. Soc. of Environmental Forensics [7098]
Intl. Soc. for Fat Res. [7405]
Intl. Soc. for Gesture Stud. [6712]
Intl. Soc. for the History of the Neurosciences
   [7376]
Intl. Soc. for Interferon and Cytokine Res. [16351]
International Society for Interferon and Cytokine
   Research [IO]
Intl. Soc. of Iraqi Scientists [7613]
Intl. Soc. for Language Stud. [10302]
Intl. Soc. of Lymphology [15016]
Intl. Soc. of Motor Control [7377]
Intl. Soc. for Nanoscale Sci., Computation and
   Engg. [7614]
Intl. Soc. for Neuroimmunomodulation [15395]
Intl. Soc. for New Institutional Economics [6885]
Intl. Soc. for Presence Res. [7572]
Intl. Soc. for Res. on Impulsivity [16088]
Intl. Soc. for the Sociology of Religion [IO]
Intl. Soc. for the Stud. of Pilgrimage Art [9451]
Intl. Spinal Res. Trust [IO]
Intl. Tech. Inst. [7744]
Irish Res. Scientists' Assn. [IO]
Istituto Paolo VI: Intl. Centre for Stud. and
   Documentation [IO]
Italian Natl. Res. Coun. [IO]

Japan Assn. for Quaternary Res. [IO]
Kennedy's Disease Assn. [15334]
The Keystone Center [7746]
Knowledge Alliance [9061]
Lab. Animal Mgt. Assn. [13699]
Latin Amer. Inst. for Social Res. [IO]
League of European Res. Universities [IO]
Lincoln Inst. for Res. and Educ. [16940]
Ludwig Boltzmann Assn. - Austrian Soc. for the
   Promotion of Sci. Res. [IO]
Malaysia/Singapore/Brunei Stud. Gp. of the
   Southeast Asia Coun. Assn. for Asian Stud.
   [7987]
Mariological Soc. of Am. [19656]
The Media Inst. [17184]
Medical Image Perception Soc. [15140]
Medical Res. Modernization Comm. [15109]
Mental Res. Inst. [13737]
Mozart Soc. of Am. [9814]
MTM Assn. for Standards and Res. [7165]
Multiple Sclerosis Found. [15338]
NAMM Found. Res. Div. [10653]
NARSAD: Mental Hea. Res. Assn. [15213]
Natl. Alliance for Thrombosis and Thrombophilia
   [13931]
Natl. Amer. Indian Court Judges Assn. [5905]
Natl. Assn. for Res. in Sci. Teaching [9108]
Natl. Assn. for Res. and Therapy of Homosexual-
   ity [14434]
Natl. Assn. of Sci. Materials Managers [3487]
Natl. Assn. of Univ. Fisheries and Wildlife
   Programs [8391]
Natl. Black Herstory Task Force [11089]
Natl. Center for the Dissemination of Disability
   Res. [14244]
Natl. Coalition of Advanced Tech. Centers [9240]
Natl. Conferences on Undergraduate Res. [9062]
Natl. Coun. of Educational Res. and Training [IO]
Natl. Coun. for Sci. and the Env. [7067]
Natl. Coun. of Univ. Res. Administrators [9063]
Natl. Dairy Coun. [4494]
Natl. Eye Res. Found. [15724]
Natl. Found. for Brain Res. [15397]
Natl. Inst. of Electromedical Info. [14311]
Natl. Inst. for Hea. Care Mgt. Res. and
   Educational Found. [14655]
Natl. Memorial Inst. for the Prevention of Terror-
   ism [18734]
Natl. Military Intelligence Assn. [5889]
Natl. Mitigation Banking Assn. [4425]
Natl. Ornamental Goldfish Growers Assn. [4181]
Natl. Postdoctoral Assn. [9064]
Natl. Res. Coun. [IO]
Natl. Res. Found. [IO]
Natl. Spinal Cord Injury Assn. [16468]
Natl. Stroke Assn. [16494]
NATO Consultation, Command and Control
   Agency [IO]
Natural Dyes Intl. [8213]
Netherlands Org. for Applied Sci. Res. [IO]
Neurofibromatosis [14471]
Neutron Scattering Soc. of Am. [7506]
North Am. Taiwanese Engineers' Assn. [7036]
North Amer. Assn. for Belarusian Stud. [9735]
North Amer. Assn. for the Stud. of Welsh Culture
   and History [11083]
North Amer. Coordinating Coun. on Japanese Lib.
   Resources [8781]
North Amer. Fuzzy Info. Processing Soc. [6741]
North Amer. Meteor Network [7328]
North Amer. Taiwan Stud. Assn. [9205]
Norwegian Inst. for Urban and Regional Res. [IO]
NRH Center for Hea. and Disability Res. [14233]
Operational Res. Soc. of New Zealand [IO]
Org. for Autism Res. [13728]
Paratuberculosis Awareness and Res. Assn.
   [14425]
Parents Against Childhood Epilepsy [14382]
Pathways to Coll. Network [8493]
Peanut Inst. [5061]
Professional Football Researchers Assn. [23438]
Proteome Soc. [7119]
Public Responsibility in Medicine and Res.
   [18585]
QiGong Res. Soc. [13647]

Qualitative Res. Consultants Assn. [7573]
Raptor Res. Found. [5372]
Religious Experience Res. Centre [IO]
Religious Res. Assn. [20539]
Reproductive Toxicology Center [14393]
Res. Chefs Assn. [1124]
Res. and Development Soc. [IO]
Res. Libraries Gp. [10385]
Res. Prog. at Earthwatch Inst. [7574]
Res. Prog. at Earthwatch Inst. [IO]
Res. Soc. on Alcoholism [16517]
ResearchChannel [7575]
Rudjer Boskovic Inst. [IO]
Schizophrenia Intl. Res. Soc. [15232]
Schubert Soc. of the USA [9816]
Scottish Soc. for Psychical Res. [IO]
Shareholders Res. Alliance [3391]
Shark Res. Inst. [IO]
Slavic and East European Folklore Assn. [9962]
Sleep Res. Soc. [16429]
Social Psychiatry Res. Inst. [16094]
Soc. for Acupuncture Res. [13537]
Soc. for Amateur Scientists [7631]
Soc. for the Anal. of African-American Public Hea.
   Issues [16253]
Soc. for the Anthropology of North Am. [6425]
Soc. for Applied Psychological Res. in the
   Performing Arts [16170]
Soc. of Clinical Res. Associates [14027]
Soc. for Clinical Trials [14028]
Soc. of Govt. Ser. Urologists [16714]
Soc. for Hindu-Christian Stud. [20528]
Soc. for the History of Psychology [7548]
Soc. for Melanoma Res. [13875]
Soc. for Molecular Imaging [15181]
Soc. for Organizational Learning [2868]
Soc. of Psychological Hypnosis [16178]
Soc. for the Psychological Stud. of Ethnic Minority
   Issues [16179]
Soc. for Psychotherapy Res. [16194]
Soc. of Res. Administrators [7576]
Soc. for Res. on Nicotine and Tobacco [5249]
Soc. for Simulation in Healthcare [15148]
Soc. for Social Work and Res. [9135]
Soc. for the Stud. of Early Modern Women [9331]
Soc. for the Stud. of Peace, Conflict, and
   Violence: Peace Psychology Div. of the Amer.
   Psychological Assn. [16185]
Soc. for Whole Body Autoradiography [15149]
Soc. for Women's Hea. Res. [16910]
Software and Info. Indus. Assn. [5858]
South East Asian Assn. for Institutional Res. [IO]
Space Stud. Bd. [7687]
Spencer Found. [12054]
Spinal Cord Soc. [16469]
Syrian Stud. Assn. [8880]
Tanzania Indus. Res. and Development Org. [IO]
Thyroid Soc. for Educ. and Res. [16650]
Transworld Advt. Agency Network [124]
Treatment and Res. Advancements Assn. for
   Personality Disorder [15235]
Undersea and Hyperbaric Medical Soc. [16697]
UNESCO Regional Bur. for Sci. in Europe [IO]
United Nations Inst. for Training and Res. [IO]
U.S. Permafrost Assn. [7675]
Universities Res. Assn. [7577]
Universities Res. Assn. [IO]
Urban Affairs Assn. [9287]
William T. Grant Found. [11549]
Williams Syndrome Assn. [14490]
Women Educators [9328]
Women in Neurotrauma Res. [15404]
World Assn. for Case Method Res. and Applica-
   tion [7578]
World Assn. for Case Method Res. and Applica-
   tion [IO]
World Assn. of Indus. and Technological Res.
   Organizations [IO]
World Assn. of Sleep Medicine [16430]
World Assn. for Vedic Stud. [9854]
World Fed. of Neurology Res. Gp. on Motor
   Neuron Diseases [15373]
Res; Acad. for Peace [18187]
Res. and Action Center; Food [12393]
Res. Action and Info. Network for the Bodily Integrity
   of Women [IO], London, United Kingdom

A star before a book entry number signifies that the name is not listed separately, but is mentioned within the entry.

Res. on Adolescence; Soc. for [13515]
Res. Advisory Coun; All-Industry [★2183]
Res. in Ambulatory Hea. Care Admin; Center for [15064]
Res.! Am. [15112], 1101 King St., Ste. 520, Alexandria, VA 22314-2960, (703)739-2577
Res; Amer. Assn. for Dental [14113]
Res; Amer. Assn. for Public Opinion [18368]
Res; Amer. Enterprise Inst. for Public Policy [18420]
Res; Amer. Fed. for Medical [14019]
Res; Amer. Found. for Mgt. [★2481]
Res; Amer. Soc. for Bone and Mineral [15787]
Res; Amer. Soc. for Psychical [7442]
Res; Amer. Soc. for Reformation [★10931]
Res; Amer. Soc. for Theatre [11002]
Res., Anal. and Educ. Found; The Conservative Caucus [17265]
Res. Analysts; Educational [9259]
Res; Andrew Furuseth Found. for Maritime [★3593]
Res. in the Apostolate; Center for Applied [19608]
Res. and Applications of Alternative Financing for Development [★IO]
Res. and Applications Info. Center; Natural Hazards [7355]
Res. Applied to Natl. Needs Program - Defunct.
Res. Applied to World Needs Committee; Chemical [★6697]
Res. Applied to World Needs Committee; Chemical [★IO]
Res. Assessment Consultants; Training [★6528]
Res. Assistance Program; Royal Arch [★19235]
Res. Assistance Program; Royal Arch [★IO]
Res. Associates of Am. [24060], 1420 K St. NW, Ste. 300, Washington, DC 20005, (202)737-7200
Res. Associates; Educ., Training and [8556]
Res. Associates; U.S. 1869 Pictoral [★22887]
Res. Assn. of Am; Dystrophic Epidermolysis Bullosa [14200]
Res. Assn; Amer. Rock Art [6438]
Res. Assn; Amer. Vocational Educ. [★9301]
Res. Assn. for Arts and Culture [★IO]
Res; Assn. for Biomedical [★13700]
Res. Assn. of British Rubber Mfrs. [★IO]
Res; Assn. for Clinical Psychosocial [16139]
Res. Assn; Computing [6725]
Res; Assn. for Consumer [17306]
Res. Assn; Environmental Design [5464]
Res. Assn; German [21120]
Res. Assn. of the German Glass Indus. [IO], Offenbach, Germany
Res. Assn; Governmental [18449]
Res; Assn. for Hea. Services [★14535]
Res; Assn. for Indus. Relations [★24115]
Res; Assn. for Institutional [8997]
Res; Assn. for Investment Mgt. and [★2331]
Res. Assn; Labor [24118]
Res. Assn; Lentz Peace [18217]
Res. Assn; Life Insurance Marketing and [★2195]
Res. Assn; Minority Professors - Address unknown since 2003.
Res. Assn; Natl. Public Records [2107]
Res. Assn; New England Antiquities [6452]
Res. Assn; North Amer. Case [4065]
Res. Assn; Organizational Systems [9234]
Res. Assn; Osteopathic Manipulative Therapeutic and Clinical [★15790]
Res. Assn; Sociological [7671]
Res. Assn; Universities Space [6392]
Res. Assn. Women's Caucus; Amer. Educational [★9328]
Res.-Based Dietary Ingredient Assn. - Address unknown since 2006.
Res. in the Behavioral Sciences; Amer. Institutes for [6523]
Res; Biologists; Amer. Inst. of Fishery [7170]
Res. on Black Americans; Prog. for [6396]
Res. Bd; California Melon [4718]
Res. Bd; Maritime Trans. [★7272]
Res. Bd; Trans. [7814]
Res. and Breeding Inst. of Pomology Holovousy [IO], Horice v Podkrkonosi, Czech Republic
Res. Bur; Crop Insurance [2161]
Res; Bur. of Municipal [★6192]
Res. Bur; Property Loss [2233]
Res; Californians for Responsible [★11413]

Res. Center Against Meningitis and Schistosomiasis [IO], Niamey, Niger
Res. Center of Am; Slovenian [10972]
Res. Center; Assassination Archives and [18787]
Res. Center; Chabad [★8688]
Res. Center for Economic Growth and Bus. Development [IO], Paris, France
Res. Center; Flag [11074]
Res. Center; FSC Rural Training and [★12937]
Res. Center; Glenmary [19628]
Res; Center for Governmental [18427]
Res. Center - Inst. for Parapsychology; Rhine [7452]
Res. Center; Jack London [9669]
Res. Center for Labor and Community [17970]
Res. Center; Mountain Press [21132]
Res. Center; Natl. Fisheries Contaminant [★7172]
Res. Center; Natl. Jewish Hosp. and [★16361]
Res. Center; Private Enterprise [17635]
Res. Center; Radical [★10892]
Res; Center for Reformation [10930]
Res. Center for Religion and Human Rights in Closed Societies - Defunct.
Res. Center; Sultan Qaboos bin Said [★18062]
Res. Center; Sultan Qaboos bin Said [★IO]
Res. Center; Sun Mountain [★4656]
Res; Center for Whale [7260]
Res. Center; Wild Canid Survival and [5393]
Res. Centers; Assn. of Ecosystem [4499]
Res; Central Soc. for Clinical [14023]
Res. Centre for Islamic History, Art and Culture [IO], Istanbul, Turkey
Res. Chefs Assn. [1124], 1100 Johnson Ferry Rd., Ste. 300, Atlanta, GA 30342, (404)252-3663
Res. in Child Development; Soc. for [11546]
Res. of Childhood Cancer; Assn. for [13798]
Res; Christian [19784]
Res; Coalition of Labor Union Women Center for Educ. and [24204]
Res; Commn. of Natl. Sunday School [★8088]
Res; Comm. for the Promotion of Medical [15104]
Res; Comm; University [★7851]
Res. and Commun. Center; Mission Advanced [20358]
Research and Community Development Institute [★18840]
Res. and Conservation Center; Animal [★4469]
Res. and Consumer Educ. in Social Work Regulation; American Found. for [★13200]
Res; Cooper Inst. for Aerobics [★15962]
Res. Coun. of Am; Family [★12153]
Res. Coun. of Am; Jesuit [★8052]
Res. Coun; Automotive Market [347]
Res. Coun; Building [7960]
Res; Coun. for Chem. [6679]
Res; Coun. on Communications [★8706]
Res. Coun; Coordinating [2921]
Res. Coun. of the Great Cities Prog. for School Improvement [★9289]
Res. Coun; Insurance [2183]
Res. Coun; Natl. [7621]
Res. Coun. on Natl. Sovereignty; Walter Bagehot [7528]
Res. Coun; Newspaper [★3244]
Res. Coun. of Norway/Norsar [★IO]
Res. Coun; Public Ser. [17976]
Res. Coun; Radio and TV [7784]
Res. Coun. on Riveted and Bolted Structural Joints [★7712]
Res. Coun; Social Sci. [7655]
Res. Coun. on Structural Connections [7712], c/o Rex Owen, Chm., 7269 S Sundown Cir., Littleton, CO 80120, (303)797-1956
Res. Coun; Structural Stability [7714]
Res. Coun; Warehousing Educ. and [3984]
Res. and Counseling; Rabbinic Center for [16229]
Res. and Demonstration Center for the Education of Handicapped Children and Youth - Defunct.
Res. and Development; Amer. Indian [8464]
Res. and Development Associates [★7096]
Res. and Development Associates for Military Food and Packaging Systems [7096], 16607 Blanco Rd., Ste. 1506, San Antonio, TX 78232, (210)493-8024
Res. and Development Center; Caribbean Tourism [★24252]
Res. and Development Division of Planned Parenthood Fed. of Am. [★12175]

Res. and Development Soc. [IO], London, United Kingdom
Res. Discussion Group - Defunct.
Res. and Documentation Center; Ukrainian [★11065]
Res. and Documentation Center; Ukrainian [★IO]
Res. at Earthwatch Inst; Center for Field [★7574]
Res., Educ., and Conservation; Jane Goodall Inst. for Wildlife [5334]
Res. and Education Found. for Chest Disease - Defunct.
Res. and Educ. Found; Cooking Advancement [★8174]
Res. and Educ. Found; Free Cong. [18295]
Res. and Educ. Found; Orthopaedic [8949]
Res. and Educ. Foundation; Solar Energy [★7679]
Res. and Educ. Foundations; Natl. Assn. of Veterans' [6347]
Res. and Educ. Inst; Women's [17580]
Res. and Educ; Lincoln Inst. for [16940]
Res. and Educ. Soc; Amer. Peanut [5050]
Res. and Educational Found; Amer. Acad. of Medical Administrators [15046]
Res. and Educational Found; College Stores [★3415]
Res. and Educational Found; United Cerebral Palsy [★13935]
Res. and Educational Trust; Hea. [14884]
Res. and Educational Trust; Hosp. [★14884]
Res. Fed; Estuarine [7271]
Res; Fisher Inst. for Medical [17628]
Res. Forum; Trans. [7815]
Res. Found; African [★14971]
Res. Found; Amer. Bus. Men's [★13217]
Res. Found; Amer. Hearing [14740]
Res. Found; Amer. Medical [★8843]
Res. Found; Amer. Seed [5173]
Res. Found; Aquarian [18606]
Res. Found; Atlas Economic [6874]
Res. Found; AVKO Dyslexia [9138]
Res. Found; Benign Essential Blepharospasm [15311]
Res. Found; Borderland Sciences [7471]
Res. Found. for Children; Cooley's Anemia Blood and [★14788]
Res. Found; Chiropractic [★14004]
Res; Found. for Chiropractic Educ. and [14004]
Res. Found; Citizens' [18349]
Res. Found; Consumer Energy Coun. of Am. [17496]
Res. Found; Credit [1412]
Res. Found; Damon Runyon Cancer [13819]
Res. Found; Dystonia Medical [15319]
Res. Found; Engineered Wood [★1646]
Res. Found; Environmental [13599]
Res. Found; Family Law [★12138]
Res. Found; Fats and Proteins [2850]
Res. Found; Financial Executives [1417]
Res. Found; Guardians of Hydrocephalus [15326]
Res; Found. for Interior Design Educ. [★8584]
Res. Found; Intl. Chiropractors [★14003]
Res. Found. for Jewish Immigration [10469], 570 7th Ave., New York, NY 10018, (212)921-3871
Res. Found; Kent Waldrep Intl. Spinal Cord [★16463]
Res. Found; Mfrs. Representatives Educational [2539]
Res. Found; Mark Twain [9688]
Res. Foundation; Medical Educ. and [★14549]
Res. Found; Natl. AIDS [★13557]
Res. Found; Natl. Eye [15724]
Res. Foundation; National Judges Educ. and [★5913]
Res. Found; North Amer. Bramble Growers [1675]
Res. Found; O.J. Noer [4796]
Res. Found; Operations Mgt. Education and [7167]
Res. Found; Orthodontic Education and [14183]
Res. Found; Paralysis Cure [★16463]
Res. Foundation; Parkside Alcoholic [★14821]
Res. Found; Petroleum Indus. [★7462]
Res. Found; Plywood [★1646]
Res. Found; Practical Allergy [★13599]
Res. Found; Raptor [5372]
Res; Found. for Reformation [★10930]
Res. Found; Retirement [11318]

Reference to "IO" in place of a book number signifies that the association may be found in the 45th edition of International Organizations.

Res. Found; Scleroderma [16390]
Res. Found. for the Study of Degenerative Diseases; Independent Citizens [14263]
Res. Found; Tuna [★3506]
Res; Friends of the Natl. Inst. of Dental and Cranio-facial [14154]
Res. Fund; Natl. Coun. on Agricultural Life and Labor [12322]
Res. Fund; Olfactory [★1664]
Res. Funding; Ad Hoc Gp. for Medical [17686]
Res. Gp. on African Development Perspectives [★IO]
Res. Gp; Family [★12153]
Res. Gp; Public Citizen Hea. [16250]
Res. Gp; U.S. Public Interest [18483]
Res. Guild; Nautical [21880]
Res. and Hea. Policy; Acad. for Hea. Services [★14535]
Res. Hosp; ALSAC/Saint Jude Children's [13946]
Res. in Human Milk and Lactation; Intl. Soc. for [13776]
Res; HUNA [12349]
Res. on Identity Formation; Soc. for [8960]
Res., Inc; Welfare [13193]
Res. and Indus. Development; Maritime Inst. for [6060]
Res. and Info. Center; Southwest [17345]
Res. and Information Centre of Eritrea - Address unknown since 1995.
Res. Info. Ser; Alcohol [13217]
Res. Institute; ADA Found. [★14131]
Res. Inst; ADC [★17082]
Res. Inst. of Advanced Philosophic [10795]
Res. Inst. of African and African Diaspora Arts - Address unknown since 2003.
Res. Inst; Amaryllis [★6637]
Res. Inst. of Am; Ginseng [1905]
Res. Inst; Amer. Cocoa [★6545]
Res. Inst; Amer. Prosecutors [5481]
Res. Inst. of Andean [9386]
Res. Inst. for Animal Hea. [IO], Teramo, Italy
Res. Inst; Aquatic [7171]
Res. Inst. of the Assn. of the Austrian Cement Indus. [IO], Vienna, Austria
Res; Inst. for Biblical [19519]
Res. Inst. of Chem. Processing and Utilization of Forest Products [IO], Nanjing, People's Republic of China
Res. Inst; Chihuahuan Desert [4374]
Res. Inst; Do-It-Yourself [★1159]
Res. Inst; Earthquake Engg. [7638]
Res. Inst; Educ. and [★17634]
Res. Inst; Electronic Power [★7531]
Res. Inst; Elm [4682]
Res. Inst. of Forestry, Policy and Info. [IO], Beijing, People's Republic of China
Res. Inst. for Fragrance Materials [1663], 50 Tice Blvd., Woodcliff Lake, NJ 07677, (201)689-8089
Res. Inst; Gas [★1678]
Res. Inst; Genealogy [★21146]
Res. Inst; Gray Iron [★2033]
Res. Inst; Home Improvement [1159]
Res. Inst; IBEC [★4103]
Res. Inst; Interdisciplinary Biblical [19928]
Res. Inst. Intl; Christian [★19785]
Res. Inst; Interscience [★13649]
Res. Inst. of Investment Analysts Malaysia [IQ], Kuala Lumpur, Malaysia
Res. Inst; IRI [4103]
Res. Inst; Iron Casting [2033]
Res. Inst; Kundalini [★20631]
Res. Inst; Mental [13737]
Res. Institute; National Printing Ink [★1803]
Res. Inst. for Public Policy; Pacific [18474]
Res. Institute; Real Estate [★2344]
Res. Inst. on the Sino-Soviet Bloc - Address unknown since 2002.
Res. Inst. for Small and Emerging Bus. [3624], 722 12th St. NW, Washington, DC 20005, (202)628-8382
Res. Inst. for Small and Engg. Bus. [★3624]
Res; Inst. for Social [7650]
Res. Inst; Social Psychiatry [16094]
Res. Inst; Solution Mining [2755]
Res. Inst; Spring [399]

Res. Inst. - Subtropical Forestry [IO], Fuyang, People's Republic of China
Res. Inst. of the Wood Indus. [IO], Beijing, People's Republic of China
Res. Institution/Museum of the Earth; Paleontological [7429]
Res; Inter-University Consortium for Political and Social [7525]
Res; Interactive; Aquatic [★7171]
Res; Intl. Soc. for Intercultural Educ., Training and [★8667]
Res; Intl. Soc. for Paranormal [2897]
Research; Jacob Blaustein Inst. for Desert [★8673]
Res. Lab; Columbia Natl. Fisheries [★7172]
Res. Lab; Fish Pesticide [7172]
Res. Lab; Peace [★18217]
Res. Libraries; Assn. of [10338]
Res. Libraries; Assn. of Coll. and [10331]
Res. Libraries Assn; Independent [10359]
Res. Libraries; Center for [10345]
Res. Libraries Gp. [10385], 2029 Stierlin Ct., Ste. 100, Mountain View, CA 94043-4684, (650)691-2333
Research Libraries Info. Network [★10385]
Res. Libraries in Jewish Stud; Coun. of Archives and [10351]
Res. Library for Edward Woodward - Defunct.
Res. Mgt; Forum on [★6530]
Res. and Mgt. Found; ACEC [6980]
Res; Manhattan Inst. for Policy [18408]
Res; Melpomene Inst. for Women's Hea. [★16900]
Res. on Meteorites; Soc. for [★7148]
Res; Methods Time Measurements Assn. for Standards and [★7165]
Res. in Modern History of Poland; Institute for [★10878]
Res. in Modern History of Poland; Institute for [★IO]
Res. Modernization Comm; Medical [15109]
Res; MTM Assn. for Standards and [7165]
Res; Natl. Assn. for Biomedical [13700]
Res; Natl. Center for Constr. Educ. and [17632]
Res; Natl. Center for Public Policy [18463]
Res; Natl. Coalition for Cancer [17691]
Res; Natl. Coun. for Eurasian and East European [10968]
Res; Natl. Coun. for Soviet and East European [★10968]
Res; Natl. Found. for Brain [15397]
Res; Natl. Soc. for Medical [★13700]
Res; Native Amer. Cancer [13857]
Res. in Nervous and Mental Disease; Assn. for [16082]
Res. in Neurological Disorders; Natl. Coalition for [15346]
Res. on Nonprofit Organizations and Voluntary Action; Assn. for [13387]
Res. in Ophthalmology; Assn. for [★15672]
Res. Org; Human Resources [6532]
Res. Organizations; Coun. of Amer. Survey [18369]
Res. Parks; Assn. of Univ. Related [★9054]
Res. and Planning; Natl. Coun. for [8121]
Res. to Prevent Blindness [16886], 645 Madison Ave., 21st Fl., New York, NY 10022-1010, (212)752-4333
Res. of Principles; Natl. Collegiate Assn. for [8087]
Res. Prog. at Earthwatch Inst. [7574], 3 Clock Tower Pl., Ste. 100, PO Box 75, Maynard, MA 01754, (978)461-0081
Res. Prog. at Earthwatch Inst. [IO], Maynard, MA, United States
Res. Proj; Farm Labor [23998]
Res. Proj; Labor Educ. and [★24116]
Res. Project; Women's Drug [13285]
Res. in Psychotherapy; Inst. for [★16227]
Res; Public Responsibility in Medicine and [18585]
Res; Rochester Bur. of Municipal [★18427]
Res. and Sci; Acad. of Pharmaceutical [15906]
Research; Scientific Exploratory Archeological [★6454]
Res. Sect. of the Division of Christian Educ. of the Natl. Coun. of Churches; Professors and [★19939]
Res. Security Administrators [6257], c/o Audrey Holl, Sec., 99 Cleveland Rd., Apt. 24, Pleasant Hill, CA 94523, (925)935-4064
Res. on Self-Government [★18349]

Res. Ser; Educational [7895]
Res; Soc. for the Advancement of Women's Hea. [★16910]
Res. Soc. on Alcoholism [16517], 7801 N Lamar Blvd., Ste. D-89, Austin, TX 78752-1038, (512)454-0022
Res. Soc. of Am; Sci. [★24588]
Res; Soc. for Amer. Baseball [23126]
Res. Soc; Creation [20548]
Res. Soc. of Delaware Valley; Scottish Historic and [10955]
Res. Soc; Early Sites [6444]
Res; Soc; Evaluation [★7071]
Res. Soc; Food Distribution [7093]
Res. Soc; Ghost [7475]
Res; Soc. of Insurance [2241]
Res. Soc; Materials [7283]
Res. Soc; for Menstrual Cycle [15619]
Res. Soc; Military Operations [7406]
Res. Soc; Mitochondria [14275]
Res. Soc; Neuropsychiatric [★16082]
Res. Soc; Oceanic Navigation [10444]
Res. Soc; Orthopaedic [15776]
Res; Soc. for Pediatric [15899]
Res. Soc; Philosophical [10823]
Res. Soc; Psychoanalytic [16112]
Res. Soc; for Psychophysiological [16183]
Res. Soc. for Psychotherapy [16194]
Res. Soc; Radiation [7557]
Res; Soc. for Reformation [10931]
Res. Soc; Scoliosis [16395]
Res. Soc; Scottish Historic and [★10955]
Res; Soc. for Sex Therapy and [16408]
Res. Soc; Sleep [16429]
Res. Soc. for Victorian Periodicals [11080], c/o Carol Martin, Sec., English Dept., B 307, Boise State Univ., Boise, ID 83725, (208)426-1179
Res. Soc. for Victorian Periodicals [IO], Boise, ID, United States
Res; Soc. for Women's Hea. [16910]
Res. and Statistics Assn; Justice [11876]
Res. in Stereoencephalotomy; Intl. Soc. for [★15418]
Res. Study Group on Peace Movements - Address unknown since 2007.
Res. in Substance Abuse; Assn. for Medical Educ. and [8849]
Res. Task Force for the Future of Reform Judaism - Defunct.
Res. and Technological Exchange Gp. - France [IO], Paris, France
Res. and Tech. Exchange Gp. - Vietnam [IO], Hanoi, Vietnam
Res. and Therapies; Assn. for Past Life [★16617]
Res. and Therapies; Assn. for Past-Life [★16617]
Res. and Therapy; Assn. for Past-Life [★16617]
Res. Trade Assn; Marketing [★2634]
Res. and Training Center on Independent Living [11984], Univ. of Kansas, Dole Center, Ste. 4089, 1000 Sunnyside Ave., Lawrence, KS 66045-7755, (785)864-4095
Res. and Training Center; Winrock Intl. Livestock [★16959]
Res., and Training Reactors; Natl. Org. of Test, [7388]
Res. and Treatment Corp; Addiction [13213]
Res; W. E. Upjohn Inst. for Employment [12104]
Res. Workers in Animal Diseases; Conf. of [16790]
ResearchChannel [7575], Univ. of Washington, 17 Kane Hall, Box 353090, Seattle, WA 98195-3090, (877)616-7265
Researched Medicines Indus. Assn. of New Zealand [IO], Wellington, New Zealand
Researchers Assn; Amer. Chamber of Commerce [★24272]
Researchers Assn; Professional Football [23438]
Researchers Interested In Smith-Magenis Syndrome; PRISMS: Parents and [14476]
Reseau canadien de maladies genetiques [★IO]
Reseau de radios rurales des pays en developpement [★IO]
Reseau Africain d'Institutions Scientifiques et Technologiques [★IO]
Reseau pour la resolution de conflits Canada [★IO]
Reseau Canadien d'info-traitements sida [★IO]

A star before a book entry number signifies that the name is not listed separately, but is mentioned within the entry.

Reseau Canadien de Stress Traumatique [★IO]

Reseau d'acces a la Justice [★IO]

Reseau d'action des femmes handicapees du Canada [★IO]

Reseau des aliments et des materiaux davant-garde [★IO]

Reseau d'information sur le patrimoine Canadien [★IO]

Reseau d'Information sur l'education en Europe [★IO]

Reseau euro-mediterraneen des droits de l'homme [★IO]

Reseau Europeen Des Associations de Professeurs de Geographie [★IO]

Reseau Europeen des Instituts de Sciences du Sport et pour l' Emploi [★IO]

Reseau Foi et Justice Afrique - Europe [★IO]

Reseau Intl. des Institutions de Financement Alternatif [★IO]

Reseau Intl. pour l'Analyse des Reseaux Sociaux [★IO]

Reseau Intl. pour l'Analyse des Reseaux Sociaux [★7651]

Reseau canadien des cardiopathies congenitales de l'adulte [★IO]

Reseau canadien pour le traitement de l'asthma [★IO]

Reseau canadien de l'environment [★IO]

Reseau Mondial des femmes pour les droits sur la Reproduction [★IO]

Reseau juridique canadien VIH/SIDA [★IO]

Reseaux Sociaux; Reseau Intl. pour l'Analyse des [★7651]

Reservation Off; Anguilla Tourist Info. and [★24224]

Reserve Act and the Internal Revenue Code; Natl. Org. for the Repeal of the Fed. [★17666]

Reserve Assn; Fleet [21211]

Reserve Assn; Marine Corps [6082]

Reserve Assn; Naval [6097]

Reserve Assn; Naval Enlisted [6095]

Reserve City Bankers; Assn. of [★477]

Reserve Enlisted Assn. - Defunct.

Reserve; Natl. Comm. for Employer Support of the Guard and [6087]

Reserve Officers' Assn; Marine Corps [★6082]

Reserve Officers Assn; Naval [★6103]

Reserve Officers Assn. of the U.S. [6103], 1 Constitution Ave. NE, Washington, DC 20002-5618, (202)479-2200

Reserve Officers of the Naval Services [★6103]

Reservists' Comm. - Defunct.

Resettlement

Amer. Civic Assn. [12403]

Amer. Fund for Czechoslovak Relief [12802]

Amer. Jewish Philanthropic Fund [12803]

Immigration and Refugee Services of Am. [12404]

Intl. Rescue Comm. - USA [12812]

Lutheran Immigration and Refugee Ser. [12815]

New York Assn. for New Americans [12479]

Pontifical Mission for Palestine [12816]

Rav Tov Intl. Jewish Rescue Org. [12817]

Refugees Intl. [12818]

Southeast Asia Rsrc. Action Center [12820]

Spanish Refugee Aid [12821]

Tibetan Aid Proj. [12822]

World Relief [19985]

Residency Directors; Assn. of Family Medicine [15059]

Residency Rev. Comm. for Emergency Medicine [14343], c/o Accreditation Coun. for Graduate Medical Educ., 515 N State St., Ste. 2000, Chicago, IL 60610, (312)755-5000

Resident Educ; Advisory Coun. for Orthopedic [★15752]

Resident Educ. in Obstetrics and Gynecology; Coun. on [15597]

Resident Matching Prog; Natl. [8872]

Resident Matching Prog; Natl. Intern and [★8872]

Resident Theatre Assn; University/ [9269]

Resident Theatres; League of [11022]

Resident Theatres/New York; Alliance of [10997]

Residential Appraisers Inst; Natl. [3333]

Residential Boat Owners Assn. [IO], Rickmansworth, United Kingdom

Residential Care Rights [★IO]

Residential Centers; Amer. Assn. of Children's [13467]

Residential Constr. Employers Coun. [947], 3041 Woodcreek Dr., Ste. 101, Downers Grove, IL 60515, (630)512-0552

Residential Constr. Workers' Assn. [948], 3660D Wheeler Ave., Alexandria, VA 22304, (703)212-8294

Residential Development Assn; Amer. Resort and [★3298]

Residential Energy Services Network [664], PO Box 4561, Oceanside, CA 92052-4561, (760)806-3448

Residential Facilities for the Mentally Retarded; Natl. Assn. of Private [★12560]

Residential Interior Designers; Coun. for Qualification of [2257]

Residential Property Managers; Natl. Assn. of [3189]

Residential Resources; Natl. Assn. of Private [★12560]

Residential Sales Coun. [★3307]

Residential Space Planners Intl. [2275], 20 Ardmore Dr., Minneapolis, MN 55422, (800)548-0945

Residential Space Planners Intl. [IO], Minneapolis, MN, United States

Residential Specialists; Coun. of [3307]

Residents' Assn; Emergency Medicine [14332]

Residents' Assn; Natl. MedPeds [14969]

Residents Assn; Relatives and [IO]

Residents; Comm. of Interns and [24089]

Residents and Interns; Natl. Assn. of [15175]

Residents in New York City; Comm. of Interns and [★24089]

Residents in Radiation Oncology; Assn. of [15643]

Resilient Floor Covering Inst. [665], 401 E Jefferson St., Ste. 102, Rockville, MD 20850, (301)340-8580

Resilient Tile Inst. [★665]

Resin Flooring Assn. [IO], Farnham, United Kingdom

Resist [18305], 259 Elm St., Ste. 201, Somerville, MA 02144, (617)623-5110

Resist; Refuse and [18304]

Resistance Coordinating Comm; Natl. War Tax [18715]

Resistance - Defunct.

Resistance Org; Warsaw Ghetto [20191]

Resistance Task Force - Defunct.

Resistance Welder Manufacturers Assn. [★2065]

Resistance Welding Alloy Assn. - Defunct.

Resistance Welding Mfg. Alliance [2065], 550 NW Lejeune Rd., Miami, FL 33126, (305)443-9353

Resister's Penalty Fund; Tax [★18723]

Resister's Penalty Fund; War Tax [18723]

Resisting Defamation [17150], 440 El Camino Real, Sunnyvale, CA 94087

Resistive Components Inst; Variable [★1230]

RESNA: Assn. for the Advancement of Rehabilitation Tech. [★11983]

Resolution - first for family law [IO], Orpington, United Kingdom

Resolution; Amer. Bar Assn. Sect. of Dispute [5449]

Resolution Prog; Conflict [18111]

Resolution; Soc. of Professionals in Dispute [★5450]

RESOLVE [18481], 1255 23rd St. NW, Ste. 275, Washington, DC 20037, (202)944-2300

RESOLVE [★14394]

Resolve, The Natl. Infertility Assn. [14394], 8405 Greensboro Dr., Ste. 800, McLean, VA 22102-5120, (703)556-7172

Resolve Through Sharing [★12663]

Resonance Soc; Clinical Magnetic [14024]

Resonance; Soc. of Computed Body Tomography and Magnetic [16297]

Resort and Commercial Recreation Assn. [3361], PO Box 1564, Dubuque, IA 52004

Resort Development Assn; Amer. [3298]

Resort Hotel Assn. [1963], 2100 E Cary St., Ste. 3, Richmond, VA 23223, (804)525-2020

Resort and Residential Development Assn; Amer. [★3298]

Resort Timesharing Coun. of Canada [★IO]

Resorts; Dept. of Tourism and Hea. [★24363]

Rsrc. Action Center; Indochina [★12820]

Rsrc. Center; Central Am. [★17989]

Rsrc. Center; Central Amer. [18496]

Rsrc. Center for Consumers of Legal Services [★6022]

Rsrc. Center for Consumers of Legal Services [★IO]

Rsrc. Center; Ethics [17072]

Rsrc. Center; Global Issues [18151]

Rsrc. Center; Hea. Info. [14564]

Rsrc. Center; Natl. Abandoned Infants Assistance [12412]

Rsrc. Center for Nonviolence [18122], 515 Broadway, Santa Cruz, CA 95060, (831)423-1626

Rsrc. Center for Nonviolence [IO], Santa Cruz, CA, United States

Rsrc. Center for Paraprofessionals in Educ. and Related Services; Natl. [9150]

Rsrc. Center; Single Parent [12693]

Rsrc. Center; Stud. Circles [19390]

Rsrc. Centre on Nonviolence [IO], Montreal, QC, Canada

Rsrc. Certification Inst; Human [2902]

Rsrc. Conservation and Development Councils; Natl. Assn. of [4421]

Rsrc. Coun; Electricity Consumers [1184]

Rsrc. Development; Coun. for [8347]

Resource Development Services - Address unknown since 2008.

Rsrc. Economists; Assn. of Environmental and [4359]

Rsrc. and Educ. Center; Children's Television [11686]

Rsrc. Efficient Agricultural Production - Canada [IO], Ste.-Anne-de-Bellevue, QC, Canada

Rsrc. Generation [13137], 218 E 18th St., New York, NY 10003, (646)723-2231

Rsrc. and Info. Center for individuals with Disabilities; Moss Regional [★13345]

Rsrc. Mgt; Center for [4373]

Rsrc. Mgt; Inst. for [★4373]

Rsrc. Planners; Natl. Assn. of Recreation [6156]

Rsrc. Planning Soc; Human [2496]

Resource Policy Inst. [4603]

Rsrc. Ser; Nuclear Info. and [18132]

Resourceful Women [2350]

Resources Assn; Chem. Mgt. and [★6677]

Resources Assn; Natl. Human [2905]

Resources Assn; Natl. Water [7838]

Resources; Center for Public [★11488]

Resources; Coalition of Visionary [2835]

Resources for Community Change - Defunct.

Resources Coun. - Address unknown since 1991.

Resources Coun; Geothermal [7143]

Resources Defense Coun; Natural [4432]

Resources; Earth Day [★4569]

Resources Exchange Assn. - Address unknown since 2001.

Resources Gp; Amer. [4350]

Resources in Human Nurturing Intl. - Defunct.

Resources for Independent Thinking [10827], 484 Lake Park Ave., No. 24, Oakland, CA 94610-2730, (925)228-0565

Resources and Info. on Drug Educ; Parent [★13276]

Resources; Natl. Assn. for the Exchange of Indus. [8336]

Resources; Natl. Institutes for Water [7836]

Resources Network; Black Human [2901]

Resources on Southeast Asia; Comm. on Amer. Lib. [★10349]

Resources and Tech. Services Div. - of ALA [★10333]

Resources; Universities Coun. on Water [7844]

Respiratory Care; Amer. Assn. for [16599]

Respiratory Care; Comm. on Accreditation for [16610]

Respiratory Care; Natl. Assn. for Medical Direction of [★15068]

Respiratory Care; Natl. Bd. for [16626]

Respiratory Disease Assn; Natl. Tuberculosis and [★16354]

Respiratory Disease Conf; Natl. [★16357]

Respiratory Diseases

Alberta Lung Assn. [IO]

Allergy and Asthma Network Mothers of Asthmatics [16352]

Alpha-1 Assn. [16353]

Amer. Assn. for Respiratory Care [16599]

Amer. Assn. for Thoracic Surgery [16640]

Amer. Bd. of Thoracic Surgery [16641]

Reference to "IO" in place of a book number signifies that the association may be found in the 45th edition of International Organizations.

Amer. Broncho-Esophagological Assn. [13778]
Amer. Lung Assn. [16354]
Amer. Thoracic Soc. [16642]
Asian Pacific Soc. of Respirology [IO]
Assn. of Asthma Educators [16355]
Assn. of Bulgarians with Bronchial Asthma [IO]
Asthma Soc. of Canada [IO]
Asthma Soc. of Ireland [IO]
Black Lung Assn. [13323]
Canadian Cystic Fibrosis Found. [IO]
Canadian Lung Assn. [IO]
Coalition for Pulmonary Fibrosis [16356]
Comm. on Accreditation for Respiratory Care
    [16610]
Cong. of Lung Assn. Staff [16357]
Cystic Fibrosis Australia [IO]
Cystic Fibrosis Australia - Australian Capital Terri-
    tory [IO]
Cystic Fibrosis Australia - Tasmania [IO]
Cystic Fibrosis Australia - Victoria [IO]
Cystic Fibrosis Australia - Western Australia [IO]
Cystic Fibrosis Found. [16358]
Cystic Fibrosis Trust [IO]
Cystic Fibrosis Worldwide [16359]
European Respiratory Soc. [IO]
Fundacion Alfa-1 de Puerto Rico [IO]
Fundacion Alfa-1 de Puerto Rico [16360]
Hong Kong Tuberculosis, Chest and Heart
    Diseases Assn. [IO]
Intl. Assn. of Asthmology [IO]
Intl. Bronchoesophagological Soc. [13779]
Intl. Union Against Tuberculosis and Lung Disease
    [IO]
Lung Assn. of Zurich [IO]
Lung Cancer Alliance [13839]
Mitochondrial Medicine Soc. [14078]
Natl. Bd. for Respiratory Care [16626]
Natl. Home Oxygen Patients Assn. [14404]
Natl. Jewish Medical and Res. Center [16361]
Natl. Lung Cancer Partnership [13854]
Northern Ireland Chest Heart and Stroke Assn.
    [IO]
Norwegian Cystic Fibrosis Assn. [IO]
Second Wind Lung Transplant Assn. [16362]
Soc. of Thoracic Surgeons [16644]
Spanish Alpha 1 Assn. [IO]
Stop TB Partnership [IO]
Thoracic Surgery Residents Assn. [16645]
United Mitochondrial Disease Found. [16363]
U.S. Adult Cystic Fibrosis Assn. [16364]
Respiratory Nursing Soc. [15524], c/o Casey Norris,
    Pres.-Elect, 708 Gladstone CR, Maryville, TN
    37804
Respiratory Soc; European [IO]
Respiratory Therapists; Canadian Soc. of [IO]
Respiratory Therapy; Amer. Assn. for [★16599]
Respiratory Therapy Educ; Joint Rev. Comm. for
    [★16610]
Respiratory Therapy; Natl. Bd. for [★16626]
Responders; Amer. Assn. of First [★14320]
Response-Ability [20386], 460 Shadeland Ave.,
    Drexel Hill, PA 19026, (610)626-1400
Responsibilities; Sect. of Individual Rights and
    [17153]
Responsibility; Cmpt. Professionals for Social
    [18146]
Responsibility in Medicine and Res; Public [18585]
Responsibility; Students for Social [18172]
Responsible Citizens Political League [★24180]
Responsible Fed. Budget; Comm. for a [18405]
Responsible Hospitality Inst. [11985], 740 Front St.,
    Ste. 318, Santa Cruz, CA 95060, (831)469-3396
Responsible Hospitality Inst. [IO], Santa Cruz, CA,
    United States
Responsible Housing Preservation; Inst. for [5790]
Responsible Indus. for a Sound Env. [2912], 1156
    15th St. NW, Ste. 400, Washington, DC 20005,
    (202)872-3860
Responsible Journalism; Carol Burnett Fund for
    [8707]
Responsible Nutrition; Coun. for [2841]
Responsible Wealth [★17473]
Responsive Educ; Inst. for [8408]
Responsive Law; Center for Stud. of [17315]
Responsive Politics; Center for [18347]

Restaurant
Amer. Inst. of Wine and Food [22568]
Chefs de Cuisine Assn. of Am. [792]
Confrerie de la Chaine des Rotisseurs, Bailliage
    des U.S.A. [22569]
Coun. of Independent Restaurants of Am. [1580]
Coun. of Intl. Restaurant Real Estate Brokers
    [3392]
Coun. of Intl. Restaurant Real Estate Brokers [IO]
Federation of Dining Room Professionals [IO]
Fed. of Dining Room Professionals [3393]
Green Restaurant Association [5170]
Intl. Chili Soc. [22571]
Intl. Kitchen Exhaust Cleaning Assn. [1475]
Intl. Soc. of Restaurant Assn. Executives [3394]
Intl. Soc. of Restaurant Assn. Executives [IO]
Japan Restaurant Assn. [IO]
McDonald's Collectors Club [22070]
McDonald's Hispanic Operators Assn. [3395]
Mexican Assn. of Restaurants [IO]
Natl. Restaurant Assn. Multi-Unit Architects,
    Engineers and Constr. Officers [1050]
North Amer. Assn. of Subway Franchisees [1670]
Portuguese Assn. of Restaurants and Bars [IO]
Restaurant Assn. of New Zealand [IO]
Restaurant Assn. of South Africa [IO]
Restaurants' Assn. [IO]
Soc. of Wine Educators [23029]
Terlingua Intl. Chili Championship [22574]
UNITE HERE [24095]
Women Chefs and Restaurateurs [794]
Restaurant Assn. [IO], London, United Kingdom
Restaurant Assn. Educational Found; Natl. [1960]
Restaurant Assn; Educational Found. of the Natl.
    [★1960]
Restaurant Assn. Multi-Unit Architects, Engineers
    and Constr. Officers; Natl. [1050]
Restaurant Assn; Natl. [1959]
Restaurant Assn. of New Zealand [IO], Auckland,
    New Zealand
Restaurant Assn. Quality Assurance Study Group;
    Natl. [16385]
Restaurant Assn. of South Africa [IO], Douglasdale,
    Republic of South Africa
Restaurant and Catering New South Wales [IO],
    Surry Hills, Australia
Restaurant Educ; Natl. Coun. on Hotel and [★8525]
Restaurant Employees and Bartenders Intl. Union;
    Hotel and [★24095]
Restaurant Employees Intl. Union and Union of
    Needletrades, Indus. and Textile Employees; Hotel
    Employees and [★24095]
Restaurant and Foodservices Assn; Canadian [IO]
Restaurant Inst; Amer. [★1957]
Restaurant and Institutional Educ; In Coun. on Hotel,
    [★8525]
Restaurant Meat Purveyors; Natl. Assn. of Hotel and
    [★2663]
Restaurant and Personal Services Workers Union;
    Hotel, [IO]
Restaurant Trainers; Coun. of Hotel and [1939]
Restaurant Workers
Amer. Sommelier Assn. [194]
Amer. Union of Pizza Delivery Drivers [24062]
UNITE HERE [24095]
Women Chefs and Restaurateurs [794]
Restaurants of Am; Coun. of Independent [1580]
Restaurants' Assn. [IO], Vienna, Austria
Restaurants Assn. of Ireland [IO], Dublin, Ireland
Restaurants; Natl. Coun. of Chain [1957]
Restaurateurs Assn. of Great Britain [★IO]
Restaurateurs; Women Chefs and [794]
Restitution Successor Org; Jewish [20152]
Restless Legs Syndrome Found. [16549], 1610 14th
    St. NW, Ste. 300, Rochester, MN 55901, (507)287-
    6465
Restoration Assn; Christian [19786]
Restoration Comm; Walden Pond [★4464]
Restoration Found; Newport [10052]
Restoration, Inc; Hudson River Sloop [★10038]
Restoration Indus. Assn. [2475], 9810 Patuxent
    Woods Dr., Ste. K, Columbia, MD 21046-1595,
    (443)878-1000
Restoration and Mgt; Soc. for Ecological [★4522]
Restoration Proj. Intl. [12441], 74 Trinity Pl., Ste.
    606, Wall St., New York, NY 10006, (212)566-4919

Restoration Proj. Intl. [IO], New York, NY, United
    States
Restoration Soc; Capitol Hill [10017]
Restorative Dentistry; Amer. Acad. of [14110]
Restore America's Estuaries [5278], 3801 N Fairfax
    Dr., Ste. 53, Arlington, VA 22203, (703)524-0248
Restore the Constitution; Comm. to [17290]
Restorers; Assn. of [★218]
Restorers Assn; Stearman [21480]
Restorers Club; Model "A" 21712
Restorers Club of Southern California; Model A
    [★21710]
Restorer's Club; Toyota Owner's and [21798]
Restorers and Coun. of Craftsmen and Artists; Assn.
    of [218]
Restorers Soc; Natl. Corvette [21729]
Restoring Hope through Educational and Medical Aid
    [★12881]
Restoring Hope through Educational and Medical Aid
    [★IO]
Restoring Men; Natl. Org. of [11734]
Restraints Coun; Automotive Occupant [377]
Restricted Growth Assn. [IO], Yeovil, United
    Kingdom
Restroom Assn. of Singapore [IO], Singapore, Sin-
    gapore
Restructuring Advisors; Assn. of Insolvency and [15]
Resultats [★IO]
RESULTS [IO], Washington, DC, United States
RESULTS [17797], 750 First St. NE, Ste. 1040,
    Washington, DC 20002, (202)783-7100
Results Australia [IO], Belgrave, Australia
Results - Canada [IO], Ottawa, ON, Canada
Results Educational Fund [★IO]
Results Educational Fund [★17797]
Results - United Kingdom [IO], Leamington Spa,
    United Kingdom
Resume Writers' Assn; Natl. [4063]
Resume Writers and Career Coaches; Professional
    Assn. of [12097]
Resurfacers; Natl. Assn. of Independent [642]
Retail Advt. Conf. [★118]
Retail Advt. and Marketing Assn. [118], 325 7th St.
    NW, Ste. 1100, Washington, DC 20004-2818,
    (202)661-3052
Retail Advt. and Marketing Assn., Intl. [★118]
Retail Bakers of Am. [★454]
Retail Bakers of Am; Assoc. [★454]
Retail Bakers Assn. of Am. [★454]
Retail Clerks Intl. Union [★24061]
Retail Coll. Attorneys; Natl. Assn. of [5513]
Retail Confectioners Intl. [1561], 1807 Glenview Rd.,
    Glenview, IL 60025, (847)724-6120
Retail Confectioners Intl. [IO], Glenview, IL, United
    States
Retail Confectioners of North Am; Assoc. [★1561]
Retail Confectioners of the U.S; Assoc. [★1561]
Retail Consortium [★IO]
Retail Coun. of Canada [IO], Toronto, ON, Canada
Retail Credit Inst. of Am. [★2428]
Retail Dealers Assn; North Amer. [1227]
Retail Druggists; Natl. Assn. of [★2986]
Retail Fed; Amer. [★3423]
Retail Food Indus; Joint Labor Mgt. Comm. of the
    [24059]
Retail Grocers Secretaries Assn; Natl. [★3405]
Retail Grocers of the U.S; Natl. Assn. of [★3421]
Retail Grocery, Dairy and Allied Trades Assn. [IO],
    Blackrock, Ireland
Retail Hardware Assn; Natl. [★1829]
Retail Ice Cream Manufacturers; Natl. Assn. of
    [★1137]
Retail Indus. Leaders Assn. [3427], 1700 N Moore
    St., Ste. 2250, Arlington, VA 22209, (703)841-2300
Retail Industry Trade Action Coalition - Defunct.
Retail Jewelers of Am. [★2370]
Retail Liquor Package Stores Assn; Natl. [★193]
Retail Loss Prevention Assn. - Address unknown
    since 2003.
Retail Lumber Assn; Northeastern [1655]
Retail Lumber Dealers Assn; Natl. [★1653]
Retail Lumberman's Assn; Northeastern [★1655]
Retail Lumbermen's Assn; Western [★1629]
Retail Marketing Coalition [3428]
Retail Marketing Services; Assn. of [3463]

A star before a book entry number signifies that the name is not listed separately, but is mentioned within the entry.

Retail Marketing Services; TSIA—The Assn. of [3463]
Retail Merchant Bakers of Am. [★454]
Retail Merchants Assn; Natl. [★3423]
Retail Merchants' Assn. of New Zealand [★IO]
Retail Motor Indus. Fed. [IO], London, United Kingdom
Retail Motor Indus. Org. [IO], Randburg, Republic of South Africa
Retail Nurserymen's Assn. of the U.S. - Defunct.
Retail Off. Dealer Div. [★1704]
Retail Off. Furniture Forum [★1704]
Retail Packaging Assn. [2880], PO Box 17656, Covington, KY 41017, (859)341-9623
Retail Packaging Mfrs. Assn. [★2880]
Retail Paint and Wallpaper Distributors of Am. [★2274]
Retail Paint and Wallpaper Distributors of Am. [★IO]
Retail Print Music Dealers Assn. [2823], 14070 Proton Rd., Ste. 100, Dallas, TX 75244, (972)233-9107
Retail Solutions Providers Assn. [★910]
Retail Stores Forum - Defunct.
Retail Tobacco Dealers of Am. [3429], 4 Bradley Park Ct., Ste. 2-H, Columbus, GA 31904-3637, (706)494-1143
Retail Travel Agents; Assn. of [3911]
Retail and Wholesale; Assoc. Bakers of Am. - [★454]
Retail, Wholesale and Dept. Store Union [24182], 30 E 29th St., New York, NY 10016, (212)684-5300
Retail Workers; United [★24061]
Retailers of Am; Apparel [★3423]
Retailers of Am; Footwear Distributors and [1597]
Retailers; Amer. Soc. of Dermatological [86]
Retailers of Art Glass and Supplies [1734], c/o Alice Foster Zimmerman, VP, 17414 Noakes Rd., Vernonia, OR 97064
Retailers of Art Glass and Supplies [IO], Vernonia, OR, United States
Retailers Assn; Agricultural [1363]
Retailers Assn. of Am; Marine [2580]
Retailers Assn; Independent Music [2806]
Retailers Assn; Natl. AgriChemical [★1363]
Retailers Assn; Natl. Ice Cream [1137]
Retailers Assn; Natl. Ice Cream [★1137]
Retailers Assn; Natl. Ice Cream and Yogurt [★1137]
Retailers Assn; Natl. Shoe [1598]
Retailers Assn; Natl. Ski and Snowboard [3646]
Retailers Assn; Natl. Waterbed [★1705]
Retailer's Bakery Assn. [454], 8201 Greensboro Dr., Ste. 300, McLean, VA 22102, (703)610-9035
Retailers; Coalition of Visionary [★2835]
Retailers; Natl. Assn. of Beverage [★193]
Retailers Org; Archery Range and [3657]
Retailing
    Alliance of Independent Retailers [IO]
    Amer. Booksellers Assn. [3396]
    Amer. Truck Stop Owners Assn. [3397]
    Amer. Wholesale Booksellers Assn. [3398]
    Antiquarian Booksellers Assn. [IO]
    Antiquarian Booksellers' Assn. of Canada [IO]
    Argentine Coun. of Shopping Centers [IO]
    Assn. of Coupon Professionals [3399]
    Assn. of Private Market Operators [IO]
    Assn. of Retail Marketing Services [3463]
    Assn. for Retail Tech. Standards [3400]
    Assn. of Sales Admin. Managers [3464]
    The Assn. of Shopping Centres [IO]
    Associazione Nazionale fra Aziende di Vendite per Corrispondenza [IO]
    Australasian Assn. of Convenience Stores [IO]
    Australian Booksellers Assn. [IO]
    Australian Newsagents' Fed. [IO]
    Austrian Booksellers' and Publishers' Assn. [IO]
    Black Retail Action Gp. [3401]
    Bd. Retailers Assn. [3402]
    Books for Keeps [IO]
    Booksellers Assn. of the United Kingdom and Ireland [IO]
    Booksellers New Zealand [IO]
    Brazilian Assn. of Shopping Centers [IO]
    British Coun. of Shopping Centres [IO]
    British Display Soc. [IO]
    British Retail Consortium [IO]

    British Shops and Stores Assn. [IO]
    Canadian Assn. of Chain Drug Stores [IO]
    Canadian Booksellers Assn. [IO]
    CBA [IO]
    CBA [3403]
    Christian Booksellers Assn. of New Zealand [IO]
    CIES, Food Bus. Forum [IO]
    CIES, Food Bus. Forum [3404]
    Clothing Mfrs. Assn. of the U.S.A. [229]
    Coalition of Visionary Resources [2835]
    Contemporary Design Gp. [1694]
    Cooperative Grocers' Info. Network [1072]
    Danish Antiquarian Booksellers Assn. [IO]
    Danish Booksellers Assn. [IO]
    EuroCommerce [IO]
    European Assn. of Natl. Organisations of Textile Retailers [IO]
    European Booksellers Fed. [IO]
    Fed. of the Retail Licensed Trade [IO]
    Food Indus. Assn. Executives [3405]
    Food Ingredient Distributors Assn. [1510]
    Food Marketing Inst. [3406]
    Gen. Retailers and Traders Union [IO]
    German Retailers Import Trade Assn. [IO]
    Home Center Inst. [3407]
    Hong Kong Retail Mgt. Assn. [IO]
    Independent Music Retailers Assn. [2806]
    Inst. of Store Planners [3408]
    Institute of Store Planners [IO]
    Intl. Assn. of Airport Duty Free Stores [IO]
    Intl. Assn. of Airport Duty Free Stores [3409]
    Intl. Assn. of Dept. Stores [IO]
    Intl. Assn. of Ser. Evaluators [3269]
    Intl. Booksellers Fed. [IO]
    Intl. Coun. of Shopping Centers [IO]
    Intl. Coun. of Shopping Centers [3410]
    Intl. League of Antiquarian Booksellers [3411]
    Intl. League of Antiquarian Booksellers [IO]
    Intl. Mystery Shopping Alliance [3412]
    Joint Labor Mgt. Comm. of the Retail Food Indus. [24059]
    Mail Order Traders' Assn. [IO]
    Mailorder Gardening Assn. [3413]
    Marketing Agencies Assn. Worldwide [3468]
    Middle East Coun. of Shopping Centres [IO]
    Museum Store Assn. [3414]
    NARGON, the Grocery Retailers Assn. [IO]
    Natl. Assn. of Coll. Stores [3415]
    Natl. Assn. of Convenience Stores [3416]
    National Association of Convenience Stores [IO]
    Natl. Assn. of Firearms Retailers [1479]
    Natl. Assn. of Resale and Thrift Shops [3417]
    Natl. Assn. for Retail Marketing Services [3418]
    Natl. Assn. of Tobacco Outlets [3820]
    Natl. Assn. of Visual Merchandisers [1153]
    Natl. Confectionery Sales Assn. [3419]
    Natl. Convenience Store Advisory Gp. [3420]
    Natl. Cooperative Grocers Assn. [1074]
    Natl. Fed. of Retail Newsagents [IO]
    Natl. Grocers Assn. [3421]
    Natl. Independent Concessionaires Assn. [1591]
    Natl. Market Traders' Fed. [IO]
    Natl. Org. for Diversity in Sales and Marketing [2644]
    Natl. Pawnbrokers Assn. [IO]
    Natl. Piggly Wiggly Operators Assn. [3422]
    Natl. Retail Fed. [3423]
    Natl. Retail Hobby Stores Assn. [753]
    Natl. Retail Tenants Assn. [3383]
    Natl. Specialty Gift Assn. [1724]
    NATSO [3424]
    Natural Products Assn. [3425]
    New Zealand Retailers Assn. [IO].
    North Amer. Celtic Buyers Assn. [784]
    Planning and Visual Educ. Partnership [3426]
    Portuguese Coun. of Shopping Centers [IO]
    Professional Soc. for Sales and Marketing Training [3472]
    Provincial Booksellers Fairs Assn. [IO]
    Radio, Elecl. and TV Retailers' Assn. [IO]
    Retail Grocery, Dairy and Allied Trades Assn. [IO]
    Retail Indus. Leaders Assn. [3427]
    Retail Marketing Coalition [3428]
    Retail Tobacco Dealers of Am. [3429]
    Retail, Wholesale and Dept. Store Union [24182]

    Retailers of Art Glass and Supplies [1734]
    Russian Coun. of Shopping Centers [IO]
    Self Storage Assn. of Australasia [IO]
    Singapore Retailers Assn. [IO]
    South African Coun. of Shopping Centres [IO]
    Southeastern Fabric, Notions and Crafts Assn. [3798]
    Specialty Wine Retailers Assn. [4031]
    Svenska Bokhandlareforeningen [IO]
    Swedish Shoe, Textile and Clothing Retailers' Assn. [IO]
    Swiss Booksellers and Publishers Assn. [IO]
    Swiss Retail Fed. [IO]
    Union of Groups of Independent Retailers of Europe [IO]
    United Shoe Retailers Assn. [1602]
    Verband Deutscher Antiquare [IO]
    Women Grocers of Am. [3430]
    World Fed. of Direct Selling Associations [3477]
    World Floor Covering Assn. [3431]
    World Floor Covering Assn. [IO]
Retailing Assn; Amer. Collegiate [8815]
Retailing Assn; Amer. Specialty Toy [2385]
Retailing Inst; Mass [★3427]
Retailing Inst; Natl. Mass [★3427]
Retardant Chemicals Assn; Fire [★799]
Retardation; Acad. on Mental [15238]
Retardation; Amer. Acad. on Mental [★15238]
Retardation, Mental
    Aicardi Syndrome Newsl. [14437]
    Amer. Network of Community Options and Resources [12560]
    Arc of the U.S. [12561]
    Assn. for the Advancement of Blind and Retarded [16832]
    Assn. for Children with Down Syndrome [12562]
    Assn. of Univ. Centers on Disabilities [12563]
    Center for Family Support [12566]
    CFC Intl. [14435]
    Chromosome 9P Network [14443]
    Coffin-Lowry Syndrome Found. [14447]
    Coun. on Quality and Leadership [12567]
    Developmental Delay Resources [13941]
    Intl. Rett Syndrome Assn. [15333]
    JARC [12570]
    Lifespire [12572]
    Little City Found. [12573]
    Mental Disability Rights Intl. [12574]
    Natl. Apostolate for Inclusion Ministry [20026]
    Natl. Asian Amer. Pacific Islander Mental Hea. Assn. [15215]
    Natl. Assn. of Councils on Developmental Disabilities [12575]
    Natl. Assn. of State Directors of Developmental Disabilities Services [12576]
    Natl. Benevolent Assn. of the Christian Church [13177]
    Natl. Down Syndrome Cong. [12577]
    Natl. Down Syndrome Soc. [12040]
    Natl. Fragile X Found. [14469]
    Parents of Down Syndrome [12579]
    People First Intl. [12580]
    Pilot Parents of Southern Arizona [12581]
    PRISMS: Parents and Researchers Interested In Smith-Magenis Syndrome [14476]
    Special Olympics [23362]
    Symbral Found. [12582]
    Young Adult Institute/National Inst. for People with Disabilities [12584]
Retardation; Natl. Apostolate with People with Mental [★20026]
Retarded; Accreditation Coun. for Facilities for the Mentally [★12567]
Retarded; Assn. for the Advancement of Blind and [16832]
Retarded; Assn. for Jewish [★12570]
Retarded Children; Assn. for the Help of [15240]
Retarded Children; Natl. Assn. for [★12561]
Retarded Children; Natl. Assn. of Parents and Friends of Mentally [★12561]
Retarded Citizens; Assn. for [★12561]
Retarded Citizens; Jewish Assn. for [★12570]
Retarded Citizens; Natl. Assn. for [★12561]
Retarded Infants Ser. [★12566]
Retarded Mental Development; Assn. for Children with [★12572]

Reference to "IO" in place of a book number signifies that the association may be found in the 45th edition of International Organizations.

Retarded; Natl. Apostolate for the Mentally [★20026]
Retarded; Natl. Assn. of Coordinators of State Programs for the Mentally [★12576]
Retarded; Natl. Assn. of Private Residential Facilities for the Mentally [★12560]
Retarded and Other Developmentally Disabled Persons; Accreditation Coun. for Services for Mentally [★12567]
Retarded Persons; Natl. Apostolate with Mentally [★20026]
Retarded; Voice of the [12583]
Retention Network; Natl. Rural Recruitment and [14710]
Rethink [IO], London, United Kingdom
Reticuloendothelial Soc. [★16365]
Reticuloendothelial System
   Soc. for Leukocyte Biology [16365]
Retina Hong Kong [IO], Hong Kong, People's Republic of China
Retinitis Pigmentosa
   Retinitis Pigmentosa Intl. [16887]
Retinitis Pigmentosa Intl. [16887], PO Box 900, Woodland Hills, CA 91365, (818)992-0500
Retinitis Pigmentosa Intl. [IO], Woodland Hills, CA, United States
Retinitis Pigmentosa Soc; British [IO]
Retinoblastoma Intl. [IO], Los Angeles, CA, United States
Retinoblastoma Intl. [13869], 4650 Sunset Blvd., MS No. 88, Los Angeles, CA 90027, (323)669-2299
Retinoblastoma Soc. [★IO]
Retinopathy of Prematurity and Related Diseases; Assn. for [15673]
Retired Activities Br. [6104], Navy Personnel Command, PERS-675, 5720 Integrity Dr., Millington, TN 38055-6220, (866)827-5672
Retired Affairs Officers [★6104]
Retired Affairs Sect. [★6104]
Retired Army Nurse Corps Assn. [★15262]
Retired Civil Employees; Natl. Assn. of [★5710]
Retired; Diplomatic and Consular Officers, [5745]
The Retired Enlisted Assn. [21321], 1111 S Abilene Ct., Aurora, CO 80012, (303)752-0660
Retired Executives; Ser. Corps of [★3625]
Retired Fed. Employees; Natl. Assn. of [★5710]
Retired Foreign Ser. Officers Assn. [★5745]
Retired Greyhound Trust [IO], Worcester Park, United Kingdom
Retired Greyhounds As Pets [★11473]
Retired Hispanic Police; Assn. of [6171]
Retired League Postmasters of the Natl. League of Postmasters [6180], c/o Natl. League of Postmasters, 1 Beltway Ctr., 5904 Richmond Hwy., Ste. 500, Alexandria, VA 22303-1864, (703)329-4550
Retired Military Police Assn. [21209], PO Box 25343, Fayetteville, NC 28314, (910)867-4292
The Retired Officers Assn. [★21235]
Retired Persons Services [★2983]
Retired Philosphers Assn. - Defunct.
Retired and Pioneer Rural Carriers of U.S. - Defunct.
Retired Professors Registry - Defunct.
Retired and Senior Volunteer Prog. [13403], c/o Corp. for Natl. and Community Ser., 1201 New York Ave. NW, Washington, DC 20525, (202)606-5000
Retired Teamsters Fellowship Club - Defunct.
Retired Travel Club; Special Military Active [21271]
Retired and Veteran Railway Employees; Natl. Assn. of [★3286]
Retired and Veteran Railway Employees; Natl. Assn. of [3286]
Retired Veterinarians; Amer. Assn. of [16748]
Retired Western Union Employees Assn. [496], PO Box 413, Montgomery, NY 12549
Retirees
   AARP [12895]
   Alliance for Worker Retirement Security [18544]
   Amer. Assn. of Homes and Services for the Aging [11273]
   Amer. Assn. for Intl. Aging [11274]
   Amer. Assn. of Retired Veterinarians [16748]
   Amer. Assn. of Retirement Communities [12896]
   Amer. Soc. of Retired Dentists [19330]
   Assn. of Brethren Caregivers [11276]

   Assn. of Independent Retirees [IO]
   Assn. of Jewish Aging Services [11277]
   Assn. of Mature Canadians [IO]
   Assn. of Retired Americans [12897]
   B'nai B'rith Senior Citizens Housing Comm. [12469]
   The Center for Social Gerontology [11280]
   Children of Aging Parents [11282]
   Consumer Consortium on Assisted Living [11283]
   Elder Craftsmen [11285]
   Families U.S.A. Found. [11286]
   Fed. Superannuates Natl. Assn. [IO]
   Food and Drug Admin. Alumni Assn. [17606]
   Fund for Assuring an Independent Retirement [5709]
   Gray Panthers [11287]
   Intl. Assn. of Homes and Services for the Ageing [11289]
   Jewish Assn. for Services for the Aged [11290]
   Leadership Coun. of Aging Organizations [11293]
   Legal Counsel for the Elderly [12497]
   Legal Sers. for the Elderly [12499]
   Marine Corps Intelligence Assn. [19225]
   Mature Market Rsrc. Center [11296]
   Natl. Acad. for Teaching and Learning About Aging [11297]
   Natl. Active and Retired Fed. Employees Assn. [5710]
   Natl. Adult Day Services Assn. [11298]
   Natl. Alliance of Senior Citizens [11299]
   Natl. Asian Pacific Center on Aging [11300]
   Natl. Assn. of Area Agencies on Aging [11301]
   Natl. Assn. of County Aging Programs [11302]
   Natl. Assn. of Govt. Communicators [5583]
   Natl. Assn. for Human Development [11303]
   Natl. Assn. of Retired and Veteran Railway Employees [3286]
   Natl. Assn. of Senior Companion Proj. Directors [11304]
   Natl. Assn. of State Units on Aging [11305]
   Natl. Caucus and Center on Black Aged [11306]
   Natl. Coalition on Rural Aging [11307]
   Natl. Coun. on the Aging [11309]
   Natl. Coun. on Teacher Retirement [24044]
   Natl. Inst. of Senior Housing [12328]
   Natl. Interfaith Coalition on Aging [11314]
   Natl. Meals on Wheels Found. [11315]
   Natl. Reverse Mortgage Lenders Assn. [2430]
   Natl. Senior Citizens Law Center [11316]
   North Amer. Police Work Dog Assn. [6003]
   Pension Res. Coun. [12702]
   Pension Rights Center [12703]
   Professional Pilots Fed. [24016]
   SeniorNet [13302]
   Setting Priorities for Retirement Years [12900]
   Support Our Aging Religious [11321]
   United Seniors Assn. [11322]
   U.S. Secret Ser. Uniformed Div. Retirement Assn. [6009]
Retirees Assn; Amer. [21184]
Retirees Assn; Amer. Military [21282]
Retirees; Natl. Assn. for Uniformed Services [★6086]
Retirement
   AARP [12895]
   Alliance for Retired Americans [18543]
   Alliance for Worker Retirement Security [18544]
   Amer. Assn. of Homes and Services for the Aging [11273]
   Amer. Assn. for Intl. Aging [11274]
   Amer. Assn. of Retired Veterinarians [16748]
   Amer. Assn. of Retirement Communities [12896]
   Assn. of Brethren Caregivers [11276]
   Assn. of Jewish Aging Services [11277]
   Assn. of Retired Americans [12897]
   Assn. of Retirement Housing Managers [IO]
   B'nai B'rith Senior Citizens Housing Comm. [12469]
   The Center for Social Gerontology [11280]
   Children of Aging Parents [11282]
   Consumer Consortium on Assisted Living [11283]
   Elder Craftsmen [11285]
   Families U.S.A. Found. [11286]
   Gray Panthers [11287]
   Inst. for Retired Professionals [12898]

   Intl. Assn. of Homes and Services for the Ageing [11289]
   Jewish Assn. for Services for the Aged [11290]
   Leadership Coun. of Aging Organizations [11293]
   Legal Counsel for the Elderly [12497]
   Legal Sers. for the Elderly [12499]
   Mature Market Rsrc. Center [11296]
   Mennonite Assn. of Retired Persons [12899]
   Natl. Acad. for Teaching and Learning About Aging [11297]
   Natl. Active and Retired Fed. Employees Assn. [5710]
   Natl. Alliance of Senior Citizens [11299]
   Natl. Asian Pacific Center on Aging [11300]
   Natl. Assn. of Area Agencies on Aging [11301]
   Natl. Assn. of County Aging Programs [11302]
   Natl. Assn. for Human Development [11303]
   Natl. Assn. of Senior Companion Proj. Directors [11304]
   Natl. Assn. of State Retirement Administrators [5569]
   Natl. Assn. of State Units on Aging [11305]
   Natl. Caucus and Center on Black Aged [11306]
   Natl. Coalition on Rural Aging [11307]
   Natl. Conf. on Public Employee Retirement Systems [5570]
   Natl. Coun. on the Aging [11309]
   Natl. Coun. on Teacher Retirement [24044]
   Natl. Inst. of Senior Housing [12328]
   Natl. Interfaith Coalition on Aging [11314]
   Natl. Meals on Wheels Found. [11315]
   Natl. Retired Teachers Assn., Division of AARP [9065]
   Natl. Reverse Mortgage Lenders Assn. [2430]
   Natl. Senior Citizens Law Center [11316]
   Pension Res. Coun. [12702]
   Pension Rights Center [12703]
   Professional Pilots Fed. [24016]
   Setting Priorities for Retirement Years [12900]
   Support Our Aging Religious [11321]
   TIAA-CREF [9066]
   United Methodist Assn. of Hea. and Welfare Ministries [14602]
   United Seniors Assn. [11322]
Retirement Administrators; Natl. Assn. of State [5569]
Retirement Assn; U.S. Secret Ser. Uniformed Div. [6009]
Retirement Fed. of Civil Service Employees of the U.S. Govt. - Defunct.
Retirement; Fund for Assuring an Independent [5709]
Retirement Income Assn. - Address unknown since 2004.
Retirement Indus. Trust Assn. [497], c/o Scott McCartan, Treas., Millennium Trust Company LLC, 820 Jorie Blvd., Oak Brook, IL 60523, (630)368-5600
Retirement; Natl. Coun. on Teacher [24044]
Retirement Res. Found. [11318], 8765 W Higgins Rd., Ste. 430, Chicago, IL 60631-4170, (773)714-8080
Retirement Stud; Inst. for [★8153]
Retirement Systems; Natl. Conf. on Public Employee [5570]
Retort - Defunct.
Retread Info. Bur; Tire [3815]
Retread Mfrs. Assn. [IO], Crewe, United Kingdom
Retreaders' Assn; Central States [★3813]
Retreaders Assn; Natl. Tire Dealers and [★3814]
Retreading Inst; Tire [★3814]
Retreat Assn. [IO], London, United Kingdom
Retreats Intl. [IO], Chicago, IL, United States
Retreats Intl. [19710], 10 E Pearson St., 3rd Fl., Chicago, IL 60611, (312)915-7970
Retrieval Center; UFO Info. [7486]
Retrieval Professionals; ISDA - Assn. of Storage and [2847]
Retrieval Systems; Automated Storage/ [2004]
Retriever Club of Am; Curly-Coated [22252]
Retriever Club of Am; Golden [22277]
Retriever Club de France [IO], St.-Germain-en-Laye, France
Retriever Club; Hunting [22285]
Retriever Club; Natl. [23386]

A star before a book entry number signifies that the name is not listed separately, but is mentioned within the entry.

Retriever Club; Natl. Amateur [22309]
Retriever Soc. of Am; Flat-Coated [22268]
Rett's Syndrome Assn; Intl. [★15333]
Return to Freedom [16984], PO Box 926, Lompoc, CA 93438, (805)737-9246
Return to Unity [18265], PO Box 91480, Phoenix, AZ 85066, (480)829-9223
Returned Peace Corps Volunteers Comm. on Central America - Defunct.
Returns Indus. Assn. [2981]
Reumapatientenbond [IO], Amersfoort, Netherlands
Reunification of Korea; Campaign for the Peace and [★17966]
Reunion des Amateurs de Fox Terriers [IO], Brosville, France
Reunion Internationale des Laboratoires et Experts des Materiaux, Systemes de Constructions et Ouvrages [★IO]
Reunion Managers; Natl. Assn. of [3184]
Reunion of Professional Entertainers - Address unknown since 2001.
Reunion pour la Promotion et l'Enseignement de la Musique Electroacoustique [IO], Paris, France
Reunite - Intl. Child Abduction Centre [IO], Leicester, United Kingdom
Reusable Indus. Packaging Assn. [994], 8401 Corporate Dr., Ste. 450, Landover, MD 20785, (301)577-3786
Reusable Textile Assn; Amer. [3771]
Reuters Found. [IO], London, United Kingdom
Re'uth - Address unknown since 2007.
Revenue Assn; Amer. [22788]
Revenue Code; Natl. Org. for the Repeal of the Fed. Reserve Act and the Internal [★17666]
Revenue Soc; State [22880]
Revere Soc; Paul [18301]
Rev; Amer. Coll. of Podiatric Medical [16035]
Rev. Appraisers Coun; Accredited [269]
Rev. Appraisers and Mortgage Underwriters; Natl. Assn. of [3329]
Rev. Assn; Amer. Medical Peer [★16262]
Rev. Bd; Natl. Advt. [112]
Rev. Comm. on Educ. for the Surgical Technologist; Joint [★15123]
Rev. Coordinators; Natl. Assn. of Utilization [★16264]
Rev. Coun; Natl. Advt. [★112]
Rev. Physicians; Amer. Bd. of Quality Assurance and Utilization [16260]
The Revitalization Corps [12782]
Revival Fires (Christian Evangelizers Assn.) [20031]
Revival Fires (Christian Evangelizers Association) [IO], Branson West, MO, United States
Revival Ministries; Life Action [20020]
Reviving Baseball in Inner Cities [13512], c/o MLB Advanced Media, L.P., 75 Ninth Ave., 5th Fl., New York, NY 10011, (866)800-1275
Revma Liga V Ceske Republice [★IO]
Revolution; Gen. Soc., Sons of the [20672]
Revolution; Hereditary Order of Descendants of the Loyalists and Patriots of the Amer. [20673]
Revolution; Natl. Center for the Amer. [10134]
Revolution; Natl. Soc. of the Children of the Amer. [20674]
Revolution; Natl. Soc., Daughters of the Amer. [20675]
Revolution; Natl. Soc., Sons of the Amer. [20676]
Revolution and Peace; Hoover Institution on War, [18836]
Revolution in Peru; Comm. to Support the [18341]
Revolutionaries for a New Am; League of [18299]
Revolutionary Assn. of the Women of Afghanistan [IO], Quetta, Pakistan
Revolutionary Fed. of Am; Armenian [★18086]
Revolutionary Mexican Historical Soc. - Defunct.
Revolutionary Party; All-African People's [16925]
Revolutionary Party; League for the [18655]
Revolutionary Socialist League - Address unknown since 1991.
Revolutionary War Patriots Found; Black [20669]
Revolutionary War Studies Forum - Defunct.
Revolver Assn; U.S. [23731]
Rex Allen, Jr. Fan Club - Address unknown since 1995.
Rex Breed Club; Selkirk [21917]

Rex Breeders United [21915], c/o Diane Straka, Sec., 446 Itasca Ct. NW, Rochester, MN 55901
Rex Rabbit Club; Natl. [5155]
Rex Soc; Cornish [21905]
Rex Stout
  Wolfe Pack [9727]
Rexx Language Assn. [7537], PO Box 14472, Research Triangle Park, NC 27709-4472
Reye's Syndrome
  Natl. Reye's Syndrome Found. [16366]
Reye's Syndrome Soc. [★16366]
Reye's Syndrome Soc; Amer. [★16366]
Reynolds Family Assn. [21032], c/o Marilyn J. Newton, Registrar, 2240 130th St., Winterset, IA 50273-8479
Reynolds Fan Club; Friends of Debbie [24741]
Reynolds Found; Donald W. [13903]
RGK Found. [15113], 1301 W 25th St., Ste. 300, Austin, TX 78705-4236, (512)474-9298
Rhea Assn; North Amer. [5005]
RHEMA Intl. [12881], PO Box 82085, Rochester, MI 48308-2085, (248)652-2450
RHEMA Intl. [IO], Rochester, MI, United States
Rheology
  European Soc. of Rheology [IO]
  Hellenic Soc. of Rheology [IO]
  Soc. of Rheology [7579]
Rheology; British Soc. of [IO]
Rheology; Soc. of [7579]
Rhetoric
  Alliance of Rhetoric Societies [10935]
  Intl. Soc. for the History of Rhetoric [10936]
  Intl. Soc. for the History of Rhetoric [IO]
  Philolexian Soc. [10428]
  Rhetoric Soc. of Am. [10937]
Rhetoric Soc. of Am. [10937], c/o David Henry, Exec. Dir., Univ. of Nevada, Las Vegas, 4505 Maryland Pkwy., Las Vegas, NV 89154, (801)378-3581
Rheuma Assn. of Slovenia [IO], Ljubljana, Slovenia
Rheumatic Diseases
  Albanian Soc. of Rheumatology [IO]
  American College of Rheumatology [IO]
  Amer. Coll. of Rheumatology [16367]
  Amer. Juvenile Arthritis Org. [16368]
  Armenian Rheumatological Assn. [IO]
  Arthritis Care [IO]
  Arthritis Care - Central England [IO]
  Arthritis Care - North England [IO]
  Arthritis Care - Scotland [IO]
  Arthritis Care - South England [IO]
  Arthritis Care - Southeast England [IO]
  Arthritis Care - Wales [IO]
  Arthritis Found. [16369]
  Arthritis Hea. Professions Assn. [IO]
  Arthritis Ireland [IO]
  Arthritis New Zealand [IO]
  Arthritis New Zealand - Auckland [IO]
  Arthritis New Zealand - Bay of Plenty [IO]
  Arthritis New Zealand - Gisborne [IO]
  Arthritis New Zealand - Hawkes Bay [IO]
  Arthritis New Zealand - Manawatu [IO]
  Arthritis New Zealand - Manukau [IO]
  Arthritis New Zealand - Northland [IO]
  Arthritis New Zealand - Taranaki [IO]
  Arthritis New Zealand - Tauranga/Western Bay of Plenty [IO]
  Arthritis New Zealand - Waikato [IO]
  Arthritis New Zealand - Wairarapa [IO]
  Arthritis New Zealand - Waitakere [IO]
  Arthritis New Zealand - Wanganui [IO]
  Arthritis New Zealand - Wellington [IO]
  Arthritis Res. Campaign [IO]
  Arthritis and Rheumatism Natural Therapy Res. Assn. [IO]
  The Arthritis Soc. [IO]
  Asia Pacific League of Associations for Rheumatology [IO]
  Associacao Nacional dos Doentes com Artrite Infantil [IO]
  Assn. Francaise de Lutte Anti-Rhumatismale [IO]
  Assn. of Rheumatologists of Russia [IO]
  Assn. of Rheumatology Hea. Professionals [16370]
  Associazione Nazionale Malati Reumatici [IO]

  Australian Rheumatology Assn. [IO]
  Australian Rheumatology Assn. - Australian Capital Territory [IO]
  Australian Rheumatology Assn. - New South Wales [IO]
  Australian Rheumatology Assn. - Queensland [IO]
  Australian Rheumatology Assn. - South Australia [IO]
  Australian Rheumatology Assn. - Tasmania [IO]
  Australian Rheumatology Assn. - Western Australia [IO]
  BAK - Deutsche Rheuma Liga Bundesverband e.V. [IO]
  Bath Inst. for Rheumatic Diseases [IO]
  Belarusian Sci. Rheumatological Soc. [IO]
  British Soc. for Rheumatology [IO]
  Bulgarian Soc. for Rheumatology [IO]
  Canadian Rheumatology Assn. [IO]
  Childhood Arthritis and Rheumatology Res. Alliance [16371]
  Club Artritas [IO]
  Croatian League Against Rheumatism [IO]
  Croatian Soc. for Rheumatology [IO]
  Cyprus League against Rheumatism [IO]
  Czech League Against Rheumatism [IO]
  Czech Rheumatological Soc. [IO]
  Danish Org. of Youth with Rheumatism [IO]
  Danish Rheumatism Assn. [IO]
  Danish Soc. of Rheumatology [IO]
  Deutsche Gesellschaft fur Rheumatologie [IO]
  Dutch Soc. for Rheumatology [IO]
  Estonian Assn. for Rheumatology [IO]
  Estonian Youth Rheumatism Assn. [IO]
  European League Against Rheumatism [IO]
  European Rheumatoid Arthritis Surgical Soc. [IO]
  Finnish Rheumatism Assn. [IO]
  Finnish Soc. of Rheumatology [IO]
  Hellenic League Against Rheumatism [IO]
  Hellenic Soc. for Rheumatology [IO]
  Hong Kong Soc. of Rheumatology [IO]
  Hungarian Assn. of Rheumatologists [IO]
  Icelandic League against Rheumatism - Gigtarfelag Islands [IO]
  Indian Rheumatology Assn. [IO]
  Intl. League of Associations for Rheumatology [IO]
  Irish Soc. for Rheumatology [IO]
  Italian Soc. of Reumatologia [IO]
  Latvian Assn. of Rheumatologists [IO]
  Latvian Rheumatic Assn. [IO]
  Liga Portuguesa Contra as Doencas Reumaticas [IO]
  Liga Reumatologica Espanola [IO]
  Lithuanian Arthritis Assn. [IO]
  Lithuanian Rheumatologists Assn. [IO]
  Macedonian Assn. Against Rheumatism [IO]
  Moldavian League Against Rheumatism [IO]
  Moroccan Soc. for Rheumatology [IO]
  Natl. Inst. of Arthritis and Musculoskeletal and Skin Diseases Info. CH [16372]
  Natl. Rheumatoid Arthritis Soc. [IO]
  Natl. Sjogren's Syndrome Assn. [16373]
  Nordic Rheuma Coun. [IO]
  Norsk Revmatikerforbund [IO]
  Norwegian Fibromyalgia Patients' Assn. [IO]
  Norwegian Org. for Children and Youth with Rheumatism [IO]
  Norwegian Soc. for Rheumatology [IO]
  OsteoArthritis Res. Soc. Intl. [IO]
  OsteoArthritis Res. Soc. Intl. [16374]
  Osterreichische Gesellschaft fur Rheumatologie [IO]
  Osterreichische Rheumaliga [IO]
  Portuguese Soc. of Rheumatology [IO]
  Psoriasis and Psoriatic Arthritis Alliance [IO]
  Psoriatic Arthropathy Alliance [IO]
  Reumapatientenbond [IO]
  Rheuma Assn. of Slovenia [IO]
  Rheumatism Soc. [IO]
  Rheumatology Assn. of Bosnia and Herzegovina [IO]
  Rheumatology Assn. of Georgia [IO]
  Rheumatology Soc. of Cyprus [IO]
  Roger Wyburn-Mason and Jack M. Blount Found. for the Eradication of Rheumatoid Disease [16375]

Reference to "IO" in place of a book number signifies that the association may be found in the 45th edition of International Organizations.

Romanian League Against Rheumatism [IO]
Romanian Soc. of Rheumatology [IO]
Schweizerische Gesellschaft fur Rheumatologie [IO]
Sjogren's Syndrome Found. [IO]
Sjogren's Syndrome Found. [16376]
Slovak Rheumatological Soc. [IO]
Slovenian Medical Soc. [IO]
Sociedad Perunana de Reumatologia [IO]
Societe Francaise de Rhumatologie [IO]
Societe Libanaise de Rhumatologie [IO]
Spanish Soc. of Rheumatology [IO]
Spondylitis Assn. of Am. [16377]
Stowazy Szenie Mlodych Chorych [IO]
Swedish Org. of Youth with Rheumatism [IO]
Swedish Org. of Youth with Rheumatism [IO]
Swedish Rheumatism Assn. [IO]
Swedish Soc. for Rheumatology [IO]
Turkish League Against Rheumatism [IO]
Ukrainian Assn. of Rheumatologists [IO]
Vietnam Rheumatology Assn. [IO]
Vlaamse Reumaliga Belgium [IO]
Rheumatism Assn; Amer. [★16367]
Rheumatism Found; Arthritis and [★16369]
Rheumatism Soc. [IO], Istanbul, Turkey
Rheumatoid Disease Found. [★16375]
Rheumatology; Amer. Coll. of [16367]
Rheumatology Assn. of Bosnia and Herzegovina [IO], Sarajevo, Bosnia-Hercegovina
Rheumatology Assn. of Georgia [IO], Tbilisi, Georgia
Rheumatology; Intl. League of Associations for [IO]
Rheumatology Soc. of Cyprus [IO], Nicosia, Cyprus
Rhine Res. Center - Inst. for Parapsychology [7452], 2741 Campus Walk Ave., Bldg. 500, Durham, NC 27705, (919)309-4600
Rhinelander Rabbit Club of Am. [5159], c/o Linda Carter, Sec.-Treas., 1560 Vine St., El Centro, CA 92243, (530)432-3964
Rhino Rescue U.S.A. - Address unknown since 2007.
Rhinolaryngology and Head/Neck Nurses; Soc. of Oto [15526]
Rhinologic Soc; Amer. [15823]
Rhinological and Otological Soc; Amer. Laryngological, [15821]
Rhizome [9596], 210 11th Ave., 2nd Fl., New York, NY 10001, (212)219-1288
Rhizome [IO], New York, NY, United States
Rho Chi [★24571]
Rho Chi - Alpha Beta Chap. [24571], Duquesne Univ., Mylan Scholarship of Pharmacy, 600 Forbes Ave., Pittsburgh, PA 15282, (412)396-6364
Rho Epsilon - Defunct.
Rho Psi - Defunct.
Rhode Island Red Club of America - Address unknown since 1995.
Rhode Island School-To-Career Assn. - Address unknown since 2001.
Rhodes 19 Class Assn. [23213], c/o Chuck Becker, Treas., 1100 N Lake Shore Dr., Apt. 3B, Chicago, IL 60611, (312)642-1006
Rhodes Bantam Class Assn. [23214]
Rhodes Scholars; Assn. of Amer. [19345]
Rhodesian Institution of Engineers [★IO]
Rhodesian Ridgeback Club of the U.S. [22351], c/o Ross Jones, Corresponding Sec., 2008 Dorothy St. NE, Albuquerque, NM 87112, (505)296-3611
Rhodesian Ridgeback Klubben [IO], Svendborg, Denmark
Rhodesian Veterinary Assn. [★IO]
Rhododendron Res. Found. [★22500]
Rhododendron Soc; Amer. [22500]
Rhododendron Species Botanical Garden [★6648]
Rhododendron Species Found. [6648], PO Box 3798, Federal Way, WA 98063, (253)838-4646
Rhondels Fan Club; Bill Deal and the [24848]
Rhymes for Educ; Story [10986]
Rhythm and Blues
  Florence Ballard Fan Club [24888]
  Natl. Assn. of Rhythm and Blues Dee Jay's [10659]
  Official Mary Wilson Message Bd. and Fan Club [24954]
  Rhythm and Blues Rock and Roll Soc., Inc. [10692]

United in Gp. Harmony Assn. [10715]
Rhythm and Blues Rock and Roll Soc., Inc. [10692], PO Box 1949, New Haven, CT 06510, (203)924-1079
Rhythm; Natl. Commn. on Human Life, Reproduction and [16008]
RI [★IO]
Rican Hispanic Genealogical Soc; Puerto [9975]
Rice Assn. [IO], London, United Kingdom
Rice Assn; Intl. Wild [★4307]
Rice Coun. of Am. [★4321]
Rice Coun. for Market Development [★4321]
Rice Coun; U.S.A. [4321]
Rice Design Alliance [6479], MS 51, PO Box 1892, Houston, TX 77251-1892, (713)348-5668
Rice Export Development, Assn; U.S. [★4321]
Rice Fed; U.S.A. [1754]
Rice Growers Assn; Wild [★4307]
The Rice Indus. [★4321]
Rice Millers' Assn. [2739], c/o USA Rice Fed., 4301 N Fairfax Dr., Ste. 425, Arlington, VA 22203, (703)236-2300
Ricegrowers' Assn. of Australia [IO], Leeton, Australia
Rich Family Assn. [21033], PO Box 142, Wellfleet, MA 02667, (508)432-2883
Richard Burgi Fan Club [24768], 10153 1/2 Riverside Dr., No. 494, Toluca Lake, CA 91602
Richard Eden Fan Club - Address unknown since 1989.
Richard F. Stevens Institute [★7904]
Richard Fan Club of Am; Cliff [24866]
Richard Hatch Fan Club - Defunct.
Richard the III Found. [11144], 9067 Vintage Wine Ave., Las Vegas, NV 89148
Richard III; Friends of [★11145]
Richard III Soc., Amer. Br. [11145], c/o Pamela J. Butler, 11000 Anaheim Ave. NE, Albuquerque, NM 87122
Richard III Soc. of Canada [IO], Burlington, ON, Canada
Richard Jefferies Soc. [IO], Oxford, United Kingdom
Richard "Rock" Taylor Descendants - Defunct.
Richard Wagner Verband Intl. e.V. [★IO]
Richard Wright Circle [9707], c/o James A. Miller, George Washington Univ., Dept. of English, Washington, DC 20052, (202)994-6743
Richardson Boat Owners Assn. [21884], c/o Chamber of Commerce, 15 Webster St., North Tonawanda, NY 14120
Richmond County Descendants; Soc. of [21152]
Richmond Fellowship Intl. [IO], London, United Kingdom
Richmond Grain Exchange - Defunct.
Rick Springfield Support Club: Human Touch [24966], c/o Gail Plaskiewicz, Pres., 214 Johnson St., Torrington, CT 06790, (860)482-4831
Rickenbacker Automobile Club of America [21771]
Rickenbacker Car Club of America [★21771]
Rickey Family Assn. [21034]
Rickman Owners Club Intl. [22689], 9911 Central Rd., Ste. R, Apple Valley, CA 92308, (760)247-0027
Rickman Owners Club Intl. [IO], Apple Valley, CA, United States
Rick's Loyal Supporters [24967], c/o Vivian Acinelli, Ed., 4530 E Four Ridge Rd., Imperial, MO 63052
Ricky Martin Worldwide Fan Club [22719], PO Box 5825, Fullerton, CA 92838
Ricky Martin Worldwide Fan Club [IO], Fullerton, CA, United States
Ricky Skaggs Intl. Fan Club [24968], c/o Skaggs Family Records, PO Box 2478, Hendersonville, TN 37077, (615)264-8877
Ricky "The Dragon" Steamboat Fan Club - Defunct.
Ricky Van Shelton Fan Club - Defunct.
Ricsel Orchids [IO], Porto Alegre, Brazil
Ricsel Orquideas [★IO]
RID - Capital Area [★12987]
RID - U.S.A. [12987], PO Box 520, Schenectady, NY 12301, (518)372-0034
Ridden Standardbred Assn. - Defunct.
Ride Conf; Amer. Endurance [23933]
Ride Directors' Assn. of Am; Bicycle [23308]
Ride Directors Assn; U.S. [★23308]

Ride and Tie Assn. [23849], PO Box 2436, Sequim, WA 98382
Rider Club - Address unknown since 2000.
Rider Haggard Soc. [IO], Whitley Bay, United Kingdom
Riders Assn. - Defunct.
Riders Assn; Intl. Star [22685]
Riders Assn; Scoot-Tours Touring Scooter [23627]
Riders with Disabilities; Amer. Competition Opportunities for [23330]
Riders Found; Motorcycle [22688]
Riders for Hea. [15271], 260 E Jefferson St., Rockville, MD 20850
Riders for Justice [22690], PO Box 1192, Clifton, CO 81520-1192, (970)434-4644
Riders of the Wind, The Field Events Player's Assn. [23374], PO Box 43, Wallops Island, VA 23337, (757)824-1642
Riders of the Wind, The Field Events Player's Assn. [IO], Wallops Island, VA, United States
Ridesharing Professionals; Assn. of [★13334]
Riding for the Disabled Assn. - Ireland [IO], Delgany, Ireland
Riding for the Disabled Assn. of Singapore [IO], Singapore, Singapore
Riding for the Handicapped Assn; North Amer. [23357]
Riding Instructors Assn; Amer. [22583]
Riding; Natl. Center for Therapeutic [23351]
Riding Schools; Amer. Assn. of [22582]
Rifle Assn. of Am; Natl. [23723]
Rifle Assn; Amer. Single Shot [23714]
Rifle Assn; Natl. Muzzle Loading [23722]
Rifle Collectors; Assn. of Ohio Long [22425]
Rifles
  Amer. Airgun Field Target Assn. [22976]
  Amer. Single Shot Rifle Assn. [23714]
  Assn. of Ohio Longrifle Collectors [22425]
  Browning Collectors Assn. [22426]
  Fifty Caliber Shooters Assn. [22973]
  German Gun Collectors' Assn. [22029]
  Glock Collectors Assn. [22427]
  High Standard Collectors' Assn. [22428]
  Intl. Benchrest Shooters [23717]
  Intl. Handgun Metallic Silhouette Assn. [23719]
  L.C. Smith Collectors Assn. [22429]
  Natl. Assn. of Firearms Retailers [1479]
  Natl. Assn. of Shooting Ranges [3599]
  Natl. Firearms Act Trade and Collectors Assn. [1480]
  Natl. Mossberg Collectors Assn. [22430]
  Natl. Muzzle Loading Rifle Assn. [23722]
  North-South Skirmish Assn. [23727]
  Thompson Collectors Assn. [22431]
  U.S. Airsoft Corps [23620]
  U.S. Biathlon Assn. [23756]
  U.S. Revolver Assn. [23731]
  Weatherby Collectors Assn. [22432]
Rifles; Natl. Soc. of Pershing [24547]
Riggers Assn; Natl. Parachute Jumpers- [★23648]
Riggers; Natl. Coun. of Erectors, Fabricators and [1042]
Riggs-Hall Intl. Fan Club; Carla [24855]
Right for Children, Youth and Social Development [IO], Lagos, Nigeria
Right to Keep and Bear Arms; Citizens Comm. for the [17105]
Right to Know - Address unknown since 1999.
Right to Know Comm. of Correspondence - Defunct.
Right to Life
  ACT Right to Life Assn. [IO]
  Agape: Gospel of Life Disciples [19562]
  Amer. Assn. of Pro Life Obstetricians and Gynecologists [18545]
  Amer. Assn. of Pro-Life Pediatricians [18546]
  Amer. Center for Law and Justice [12901]
  Amer. Life League [12902]
  Amer. Victims of Abortion [12903]
  Americans United for Life [12904]
  Anglicans for Life [12905]
  Assn. for Interdisciplinary Res. in Values and Social Change [12906]
  Baptists for Life [12907]
  Birthright Intl. [IO]
  Birthright U.S.A. [12908]

A star before a book entry number signifies that the name is not listed separately, but is mentioned within the entry.

Black Americans for Life [12909]
Campaign Life Coalition Canada [IO]
Care Net [17283]
Catholics United for Life [12910]
Center for Bio-Ethical Reform [18547]
Children of the Rosary [18548]
Citizens United Resisting Euthanasia [12129]
Collegians Activated to Liberate Life [12911]
Democrats for Life of Am. [18549]
Dentists for Life [18550]
Eternal Life [18551]
Feminists for Life of Am. [18552]
Healing the Culture [12788]
Heartbeat Intl. [12912]
Heartbeat Intl. [IO]
Helpers of God's Precious Infants [18553]
Holy Innocents Reparation Comm. [18554]
Human Development Rsrc. Coun. [12913]
Human Life Found. [12914]
Human Life Intl. [12915]
Human Life Intl. [IO]
Human Life Intl. - Argentina [IO]
Human Life Intl. - Austria [IO]
Human Life Intl. - Belarus [IO]
Human Life Intl. - Belgium [IO]
Human Life Intl. - Bolivia [IO]
Human Life Intl. - Brazil [IO]
Human Life Intl. - Cameroon [IO]
Human Life Intl. - Chile [IO]
Human Life Intl. - Colombia [IO]
Human Life Intl. - Costa Rica [IO]
Human Life Intl. - Croatia [IO]
Human Life Intl. - El Salvador [IO]
Human Life Intl. - Germany [IO]
Human Life Intl. - Hong Kong [IO]
Human Life Intl. - Hungary [IO]
Human Life Intl. - India [IO]
Human Life Intl. - Ireland [IO]
Human Life Intl. - Italy [IO]
Human Life Intl. - Japan [IO]
Human Life Intl. - Kenya [IO]
Human Life Intl. - Latvia [IO]
Human Life Intl. - Lithuania [IO]
Human Life Intl. - Malaysia [IO]
Human Life Intl. - Mexico [IO]
Human Life Intl. - Nicaragua [IO]
Human Life Intl. - Nigeria [IO]
Human Life Intl. - Panama [IO]
Human Life Intl. - Paraguay [IO]
Human Life Intl. - Peru [IO]
Human Life Intl. - Philippines [IO]
Human Life Intl. - Poland [IO]
Human Life Intl. - Puerto Rico [IO]
Human Life Intl. - Romania [IO]
Human Life Intl. - Russia [IO]
Human Life Intl. - Singapore [IO]
Human Life Intl. - South Africa [IO]
Human Life Intl. - South Korea [IO]
Human Life Intl. - Spain [IO]
Human Life Intl. - Switzerland [IO]
Human Life Intl. - Tanzania [IO]
Human Life Intl. - Ukraine [IO]
Human Life Intl. - Uruguay [IO]
Human Life Intl. - Venezuela [IO]
Human Life Intl. - Zimbabwe [IO]
International Life Services [IO]
Intl. Life Services [12916]
Jewish Anti-Abortion League [18555]
K-W and Area Right to Life Assn. [IO]
Last Harvest Ministries [12917]
Libertarians for Life [18017]
Liberty Godparent Home [12918]
LIFE [IO]
Life Coalition Intl. [IO]
Life Coalition Intl. [12919]
Life Decisions Intl. [12920]
Life Decisions Intl. [IO]
Lutherans For Life [12921]
Lutherans for Life - Australia [IO]
March for Life Fund [18556]
Natl. Assn. of Pro-Life Nurses [18378]
Natl. Comm. for a Human Life Amendment
  [18557]
Natl. Cops for Life [18558]
Natl. Fed. of Officers for Life [18559]

Natl. Life Center [12922]
Natl. Pro-Life Religious Coun. [18560]
Natl. Right to Life Comm. [12923]
Natl. Right to Life Educational Trust Fund [18561]
Natl. Teens for Life [12924]
NSW Right to Life Assn. [IO]
Oper. Save Am. [18562]
People for Life [12925]
Pharmacists for Life Intl. [18563]
Pharmacists for Life Intl. [IO]
Presbyterians Pro-Life [12926]
Priests for Life [18564]
Pro-Life Action League [18565]
Pro-Life Action League [IO]
Pro-Life Alliance of Gays and Lesbians [12927]
Pro-Life Movement of the Czech Republic [IO]
Prof. Dr. G. A. Lindeboom Inst. [IO]
Queensland Right To Life [IO]
Republican Natl. Coalition for Life [18566]
Rock For Life [18567]
Soc. for the Protection of Unborn Children [IO]
Soc. for the Protection of Unborn Children -
  Scotland [IO]
STOPP Intl. [18568]
Students for Life of Am. [12928]
Teachers Saving Children Natl. [18569]
U.S. Coalition for Life [12929]
Univ. Faculty for Life [9025]
Victims of Choice [12930]
Voice for Life [IO]
Women Affirming Life [12931]
Women Exploited by Abortion [12932]
World Fed. of Doctors Who Respect Human Life
  [IO]
World Fed. of Doctors Who Respect Human Life
  (U.S. Sect.) [16013]
Right to Privacy Found. - Defunct.
Right Turn, Intl. [13186], 4520 Ashland City Hwy.,
  PO Box 280735, Nashville, TN 37228-0735,
  (334)727-5372
Right of Way Assn; Amer. [★6246]
Right of Way Assn; Southern California [★6246]
Right to Work Comm; Natl. [17982]
Right to Work Found; Natl. [★17983]
Right to Work Legal Defense and Educ. Found; Natl.
  [17983]
Right to Work Legal Defense Found; Natl. [★17983]
Rights Action/Guatemala Partners [12819], PO Box
  50887, Washington, DC 20091, (202)783-1123
Rights Advocates; Equal [6222]
Rights, AFL-CIO; Dept. of Civil [★17110]
Rights, AFL-CIO; Dept. of Civil, Human and
  Women's [17110]
Rights of America; Children's [11582]
Rights; Amer. Comm. for Human [★17783]
Rights of Amer. Workers; The Org. for the [1278]
Rights Assn; Amer. Family [17508]
Rights Assn; Amer. Land [6187]
Rights Assn; Men's [★18039]
Rights Assn; Natl. Youth [18855]
Rights; Attorneys for Animal [★11351]
Rights Campaign Fund's Mobilization Proj; Human
  [★17653]
Rights Campaign; Human [17653]
Rights of Catholics in the Church; Assn. for the
  [19578]
Rights; Caucus on Children's [★11583]
Rights Caucus; Congressional Human [17755]
Rights; Center for Constitutional [17097]
Rights Center; Disability [11939]
Rights; Center to Protect Workers [★24025]
Rights of the Child; Nurses for the [11737]
Rights; Children's [17100]
Rights; Citizens' Commn. on Civil [17104]
Rights Clinical Legal Educ. Prog; Disability [★11940]
Rights Coalition; Parents [12687]
Rights; Coalition for Student and Academic [7870]
Rights; Comm. on Human [17753]
Rights Coun; Children's [12007]
Rights; Coun. for Disability [11935]
Rights Documentation Exchange; Human [17989]
Rights Educ. and Defense Fund; Disability [11940]
Rights and Equality Exchange; Fathers [★12008]
Rights of Ethnic, Religious, Linguistic and Other
  Minorities; Intl. Fed. for the Protection of the
  [17768]

Rights; Formosan Assn. for Human [18692]
Rights Found; Constitutional [17291]
Rights Fund; Native Amer. [18098]
Rights and Interests of the Elderly; Center for
  Advocacy for the [11279]
Rights; Jacob Blaustein Inst. for the Advancement of
  Human [17771]
Rights in Korea; North Amer. Coalition for Human
  [★17966]
Rights; Leadership Conf. on Civil [17124]
Rights, Literature and Development; Women's World
  Org. for [18822]
Rights of Man; Intl. League for the [★17769]
Rights; Men's [18041]
Rights; Natl. Coalition for Haitian [18499]
Rights; Natl. Org. for Mexican Amer. [17709]
Rights Org; European-American Unity and [17114]
Rights Org; Grandparents [12264]
Rights; Physicians for Human [17783]
Rights Protection and Advocacy; Natl. Assn. for
  [17132]
Rights and Responsibilities; Sect. of Individual
  [17153]
Rights; Soc. for Animal [★11419]
Rights; TeleTruth: The Alliance for Customers'
  Telecommunications [17346]
Rights Union; Prisoners' [11890]
Rights of the U.S. Natl. Acad. of Sciences, Natl.
  Acad. of Engg., and Inst. of Medicine; Comm. on
  Human [★17753]
Rights, U.S.A; Emergency Comm. to Defend
  Constitutional Welfare [18443]
Rights of Way
  Intl. Right of Way Assn. [6246]
  Intl. Right of Way Assn. [IO]
Rights of Women [IO], London, United Kingdom
Rigoberta Menchu Tum Found. [IO], New York, NY,
  United States
Rigoberta Menchu Tum Found. [17151], 8 W 40th
  St., Ste. 1610, New York, NY 10017, (718)836-
  0424
Riksfoereningen Autism [★IO]
Riksforbundet for Sexuell Upplysning [★IO]
Riksforbundet Svensk Korsang [★IO]
Riksorganisationen for Kvinnojourer Och Tjejjourer i
  Sverige [★IO]
Riksorganisationen Unga Reumatiker [★IO]
Riksorganisationen Unga Reumatiker [★IO]
Riksutstallningar [★IO]
Riley Motor Club U.S.A. - Defunct.
Rim Assn; Tire and [3816]
Rin Tin Tin Fan Club [25041], c/o Ms. Daphne Here-
  ford, VP/Founder, PO Box 27, Crockett, TX 75835,
  (936)545-0471
Ring Guild of America - Defunct.
Ring Soc; Tree- [7101]
Ring of Troth [★19460]
Ringers; North Amer. Guild of Change [10678]
Ringside Physicians; Amer. Assn. of Professional
  [15988]
Rink Operators Assn; Roller Skating [★3601]
Rioja Wine Information Bur. - Defunct.
Riot Relief Fund [19266], 1125 Park Ave., Ste. 6-A,
  New York, NY 10128, (212)427-6434
Ripon Soc. [18537], 1300 L St. NW, Ste. 900,
  Washington, DC 20005, (202)216-1008
RISE [★2912]
Rising Leaders [18005], Congressional House Bldg.,
  236 Massachusetts Ave. NE, Ste. 207,
  Washington, DC 20002, (202)675-2004
Risk Anal; Soc. for [2243]
Risk and Insurance Assn; Amer. [8574]
Risk and Insurance Mgt. Assn. of Singapore [IO],
  Singapore, Singapore
Risk and Insurance Mgt. Soc. [2235], 1065 Ave. of
  the Americas, 13th Fl., New York, NY 10018,
  (212)286-9292
Risk Mgt; Amer. Soc. for Healthcare [14869]
Risk Mgt. Assn. [498], 1801 Market St., Ste. 300,
  Philadelphia, PA 19103-1628, (215)446-4000
Risk Mgt. Assn; Public [5834]
Risk Mgt. Assn; Telecommunications [3761]
Risk Mgt. Assn; Weather [4015]
Risk Mgt. Consultants; Soc. of [2244]
Risk Mgt; Inst. of [★2244]

Reference to "IO" in place of a book number signifies that the association may be found in the 45th edition of International Organizations.

Risk Mgt. Institution of Australasia [IO], Carlton South, Australia
Risk Mgt. and Insurance Assn; Univ. [8580]
Risk Mgt. Soc. of Finland [IO], Helsinki, Finland
Risk Mgt. Soc. of Taiwan, R.O.C. [IO], Taoyuan City, Taiwan
Risk Managers Assn; Public Agency [5833]
Risk Managers and Consultants Assn. of Japan [IO], Tokyo, Japan
Risk Resources Assn; Environmental [4563]
Risk Retention Assn; Natl. [2225]
Risk Studies Found. - Defunct.
Risley Family Assn. [21035], PO Box 552, Clarkson, NY 14430, (716)637-6419
Risley Family Assn. [IO], Clarkson, NY, United States
Rita Hayworth Fan Club [24769], c/o Caren Roberts-Frenzel, 3943 York Ave. S, Minneapolis, MN 55410
Rite of Christian Initiation - Address unknown since 2002.
Rites and Reason Theatre [11041], Box 1148, Brown Univ., 155 Angell St., Providence, RI 02912, (401)863-3558
Rithofundasamband Islands [★IO]
Ritter Fan Club; Tex [24982]
Ritual Abuse; S.M.A.R.T. Secretive Societies, Mind Control and [13296]
Rivendell Resources [★13294]
River Coalition; Passaic [7840]
River Conservation Comm; Upper Mississippi [4463]
River Conservation Fund [★4351]
River Foundation; Friends of the [★4399]
River; Friends of the [4399]
River Fund [11333], 11155 Roseland Rd., No. 16, Sebastian, FL 32958, (772)589-5076
River Guides Assn; Western [★23681]
River Mgt. Soc. [4445], PO Box 9048, Missoula, MT 59807-9048, (406)549-0514
River Network [4446], 520 SW 6th Ave., No. 1130, Portland, OR 97204, (503)241-3506
River Outfitters Assn; Eastern Professional [★23681]
River Rats [★21318]
River Sloop Restoration, Inc; Hudson [★10038]
River Sports
    Am. Outdoors [23681]
    Amer. Canoe Assn. [23278]
    Amer. Whitewater [23682]
    Natl. Org. for Rivers [23683]
    Qajaq USA [23981]
    U.S. Canoe Assn. [23279]
    USA Canoe/Kayak [23280]
River Touring Assn; Amer. [936]
River Watershed Coun; Connecticut [4377]
River of Words [4186], 2547 8th St., Studio 13B, Berkeley, CA 94710, (510)548-7636
Rivera Center; Thomas [★19196]
Rivera Policy Inst; Tomas [19196]
Riverina Olive Growers Assn. [IO], Wagga Wagga, Australia
Riverine Force Assn; Mobile [21346]
Riverland and Mallee Trail Horse Riders' Club [IO], Barmera, Australia
Rivermen; Sons and Daughters of Pioneer [21258]
Rivers; Amer. [4351]
Rivers Conservation Coun; Amer. [★4351]
Rivers Ports and Terminals; Inland [2604]
Rivet Coun; Tubular and Split [★1820]
Rivet and Machine Inst; Tubular [★1820]
Rivet Mfrs; Amer. Inst. of Bolt, Nut and [★1823]
Riveted and Bolted Structural Joints; Res. Coun. on [★7712]
Riveter Assn; Amer. Rosie the [21388]
Riviera Owners Assn. [21772], PO Box 457, Altoona, IA 50009-0457, (515)957-0762
Rizal-MacArthur Memorial Found. [12541], 756 N 35th St., Ste. 201, Milwaukee, WI 53208, (414)229-4277
RLM Standards Inst. - Defunct.
R.M.S. Queen Elizabeth Historical Soc. - Address unknown since 2003.
RNA Soc. [6553], 9650 Rockville Pike, Bethesda, MD 20814-3998, (301)634-7120
Road Builders Assn; Amer. [★6313]
Road Builders Training Assn. - Defunct.
Road Emulsion Assn. Limited [IO], West Sussex, United Kingdom

Road Engg. Assn. of Malaysia [IO], Shah Alam, Malaysia
Road Freight Assn. [IO], Lynnwood Ridge, Republic of South Africa
Road Haulage Assn. [IO], Weybridge, United Kingdom
The Road Info. Prog. [3892], 1726 M St. NW, Ste. 401, Washington, DC 20036-4521, (202)466-6706
Road Makers; Amer. [★6313]
Road Map Collectors of Am. [★22111]
Road Map Collectors of Am. [★IO]
Road Map Collectors Association [IO], Channelview, TX, United States
Road Map Collectors Assn. [22111], PO Box 158, Channelview, TX 77530-0158
Road Map Found; New [12360]
Road Operators' Safety Coun. [IO], Oxford, United Kingdom
Road Race Lincoln Register [IO], Metairie, LA, United States
Road Race Lincoln Register [21773], 640 Homestead Ave., Metairie, LA 70005, (504)831-4335
Road Recovery Found. [16518], PO Box 1680, Radio City Sta., New York, NY 10101-1680, (212)489-2425
Road Runners Club of Am. [23923], 1501 Lee Hwy., Ste. 140, Arlington, VA 22209, (703)525-3890
Road Runners Club; New York [23921]
Road Surface Dressing Assn. [IO], Colchester, United Kingdom
Road and Trans. Builders Assn; Amer. [6313]
Roadracers Assn; Western Eastern [★23628]
Roadracing; WERA Motorcycle [23628]
Roads and Trans. Assn. of Canada [★IO]
Roadside Business Assn. [★85]
Roadside Safety; Citizens for [12957]
Roadside Vegetation Mgt. Assn; Natl. [4802]
Roadway Safety Found. [12988], 1101 14th St. NW, Ste. 750, Washington, DC 20005, (202)857-1200
Roark Family Org; Merier-Gourley- [21000]
Roasters; Brotherhood of the Chain of [★22569]
Robb Memorial Fund; Isabel Hampton [★15516]
Robert A. Taft Inst. of Govt. - Address unknown since 2001.
Robert Bachmann Fan Club - Defunct.
Robert Brookings Graduate School of Economics and Govt. [★18424]
Robert Bruce Bradley Family Org. [21036], 5750 Carr Factory Rd., Benton, WI 53803, (608)759-2755
Robert Burns World Fed. [IO], Kilmarnock, United Kingdom
Robert E. Lee Memorial Assn. [11146], c/o Stratford Hall Plantation, 483 Great House Rd., Stratford, VA 22558-0001, (804)493-8038
Robert E. Lee Memorial Found. [★11146]
Robert F. Kennedy Memorial [13513], 1367 Connecticut Ave. NW, Ste. 200, Washington, DC 20036, (202)463-7575
Robert Flaherty Found. [★9940]
Robert Flaherty Found. [★IO]
Robert Frost; Friends of [10860]
Robert G. Ingersoll Memorial Committee [★20085]
Robert G. Ingersoll Memorial Committee [★IO]
Robert H. Smith Intl. Center for Jefferson Stud. [9003], PO Box 316, Charlottesville, VA 22902, (434)982-7500
Robert Jordan/Wheel of Time Fan Club - Address unknown since 1999.
Robert L. Gale Fund for the Stud. of Trusteeship [★7889]
Robert Morris Associates-Association of Bank Loan and Credit Officers [★498]
Robert Morris Associates/Association of Lending and Credit Risk [★498]
Robert Redford Fan Club [24770], c/o Trudy J. Hoffman, 517 William St., Dunmore, PA 18510, (570)343-5702
Robert Roesler de Villiers Found. [★13837]
Robert Shankland Family Org. [★21038]
Robert Sterling Clark Found. [11902], 135 E 64th St., New York, NY 10021, (212)288-8900
Roberts Univ. Educational Fellowship; Oral [8089]
Robin George Fan Club - Address unknown since 1989.

Robin Right Fan Club - Address unknown since 1999.
Robinson Found; Jackie [13491]
Robinson Jeffers Assn. [11190], c/o Mr. Robert Kafka, Treas., UCLA Extension, Rm. 214, 10995 LeConte Ave., Los Angeles, CA 90024-2400
Robinson Jeffers Comm. - Defunct.
Robot Inst. of Am. [★7584]
Robotech Defense Force - Defunct.
Robotic Indus. Assn. [7584], PO Box 3724, Ann Arbor, MI 48106, (734)994-6088
Robotic Indus. Assn; Vision Gp. of the [★7581]
Robotics
    Assn. for Lab. Automation [6515]
    Assn. for Unmanned Vehicle Systems Intl. [7580]
    Association for Unmanned Vehicle Systems International [IO]
    Australian Robotics and Automation Assn. [IO]
    Automated Imaging Assn. [7581]
    BARA: The Assn. for Robotics and Automation [IO]
    Fighting Robot Assn. [IO]
    IEEE Robotics and Automation Soc. [7582]
    Intl. Fed. of Robotics [IO]
    Intl. Soc. for Adaptive Behavior [6533]
    Japan Robot Assn. [IO]
    Lifeboat Found. [18668]
    Machine Vision Assn. of the Soc. of Mfg. Engineers [7583]
    Machine Vision Assn. of the Soc. of Mfg. Engineers [IO]
    Robotic Indus. Assn. [7584]
    Robotics Tech Gp. of the Soc. of Mfg. Engineers [7585]
    Robotics Tech Gp. of the Soc. of Mfg. Engineers [IO]
Robotics Intl. of the Soc. of Mfg. Engineers [★IO]
Robotics Intl. of the Soc. of Mfg. Engineers [★7585]
Robotics Tech Gp. of the Soc. of Mfg. Engineers [7585], PO Box 930, Dearborn, MI 48121, (313)271-1500
Robotics Tech Gp. of the Soc. of Mfg. Engineers [IO], Dearborn, MI, United States
Robyn Hitchcock Fan Club - Address unknown since 1995.
A Rocha Canada [IO], Surrey, BC, Canada
A Rocha France [IO], Arles, France
A Rocha Ghana [IO], Accra, Ghana
A Rocha India [IO], Bangalore, India
A Rocha Intl. [IO], Cambridge, United Kingdom
A Rocha Kenya [IO], Nairobi, Kenya
A Rocha Lebanon [IO], Beirut, Lebanon
Rochester Bur. of Municipal Res. [★18427]
Rock Art Res. Assn; Amer. [6438]
Rock Assn; Quartzite [946]
Rock Club; Amer. Barred Plymouth [★5114]
Rock Coalition; Black [17499]
Rock Creek Park Horse Centre [★23351]
Rock the Earth [4604], 1536 Wynkoop St., Ste. B200, Denver, CO 80202, (303)454-3304
Rock For Life [18567], PO Box 1350, Stafford, VA 22555, (540)659-4171
Rock Found; Chimney [★20469]
Rock Garden Soc; Amer. [★22535]
Rock Garden Soc; North Amer. [22535]
Rock Is Stoning Kids - Defunct.
Rock Mechanics Assn; Amer. [3690]
Rock Music
    Asian Worldwide Elvis Fan Club [24805]
    Debbie Harry Collector's Soc. [24872]
    Del Shannon Appreciation Soc. [24873]
    Delbert McClinton Intl. Fan Club [24874]
    Elvis Forever TCB Fan Club [24808]
    Elvis Presley Memorial Soc. [24809]
    Elvis Teddy Bears [24810]
    Gene Summers Intl. Fan Club [24899]
    Genesis Info. [24900]
    Gram Parsons Found. [24903]
    Hearing Educ. and Awareness for Rockers [16056]
    Jimi Hendrix Info. Mgt. Inst. [24921]
    KISS Rocks Fan Club [24935]
    Lou Christie Intl. Fan Club [24941]
    Presley-ites Fan Club Intl. [24813]
    REG - The Intl. Roger Waters Fan Club [24965]

A star before a book entry number signifies that the name is not listed separately, but is mentioned within the entry.

Rick Springfield Support Club: Human Touch **[24966]**
Rock the Earth **[4604]**
The Rock Poster Soc. **[9469]**
Sparks Intl. Official Fan Club **[24976]**
TCB for Elvis Fan Club **[24814]**
Three Dog Night Fan Club **[24984]**
We Remember Elvis Fan Club **[24815]**
ZZ Top Intl. Fan Club, Inc. **[24993]**
Rock Out Censorship **[17044]**, PO Box 147, Jewett, OH 43986
The Rock Poster Soc. **[9469]**, PO Box 20309, Oakland, CA 94620-0309
Rock and Roll Hall of Fame Found. - Address unknown since 1999.
Rock and Roll Soc., Inc; Rhythm and Blues **[10692]**
Rock the Vote **[17045]**, 805 21st St., 401, Washington, DC 20052, (202)962-9710
Rockabilly Music
Gene Summers Intl. Fan Club **[24899]**
Rockafellow Family Assn. **[21037]**, 1425 Watersmeet Lake Rd., Eagle River, WI 54521-8316, (715)477-1425
Rockapella Center **[24969]**, c/o PKA Mgt., Inc., 236 Huntington Ave., 5th Fl., Boston, MA 02115, (617)861-4129
Rockapella Fan Club **[★24969]**
Rockefeller Bros. Fund **[12736]**, 437 Madison Ave., 37th Fl., New York, NY 10022-7001, (212)812-4200
Rockefeller Bros. Fund **[IO]**, New York, NY, United States
Rockefeller Family Fund **[12737]**, 437 Madison Ave., 37th Fl., New York, NY 10022, (212)812-4252
Rockers; Hearing Educ. and Awareness for **[16056]**
Rocket City Astronomical Assn. **[★6511]**
Rocket Club; Natl. **[★6377]**
Rocket Cruising Assn. - Defunct.
Rocket Fan **[★IO]**
Rocket Mail Soc. - Address unknown since 2007.
Rocket Soc; Amer. **[★6369]**
Rocket Soc; Pacific **[6381]**
Rocketry Assn; Tripoli **[9117]**
Rocketry; Natl. Assn. of **[22650]**
Rockette Alumnae Assn. **[19386]**, c/o Jennifer Jiles, 365 Cabrini Blvd., No. 3H, New York, NY 10040, (718)939-0941
Rocky Flats Civil Resistance - Defunct.
Rocky Flats/Nuclear Weapons Facilities Project - Defunct.
Rocky Horror Appreciation Soc. - Defunct.
Rocky Mountain Cichlid Assn. **[22447]**, c/o Sam Chin, Treas., 2309 Oswego St., Aurora, CO 80010, (303)364-7983
Rocky Mountain Coal Mining Inst. **[848]**, 8057 S Yukon Way, Littleton, CO 80128-5510, (303)948-3300
Rocky Mountain Elk Found. **[5374]**, 5705 Grant Creek Rd., Missoula, MT 59808, (406)523-4500
Rocky Mountain Horse Assn. **[4949]**, PO Box 129, Mount Olivet, KY 41064-0129, (606)724-2354
Rocky Mountain Inst. **[18101]**, 1739 Snowmass Creek Rd., Snowmass, CO 81654-9199, (970)927-3851
Rocky Mountain Jewelers Assn. **[2382]**, c/o Terrence J. Zebarth, Exec. Dir., PO Box 1704, Colorado Springs, CO 80901-1704, (719)632-8171
Rocky Mountain Llama and Alpaca Assn. **[4148]**; c/o Robert Hance, Membership Chm., 11818 W 52nd Ave., Wheat Ridge, CO 80033, (303)422-4681
Rocky Mountain Mineral Law Found. **[6141]**, 9191 Sheridan Blvd., Ste. 203, Westminster, CO 80031, (303)321-8100
Rocky Mountain Mineral Law Foundation **[IO]**, Westminster, CO, United States
Rocky Mountain Pole and Treating Assn. - Defunct.
Rocky Mountain Social Sci. Assn. **[★7657]**
Rod Assn; Buick St. **[22919]**
Rod and Custom Assn; Goodguys **[21649]**
Rodders of Am; Salt Water Fly **[★23417]**
Rodeo
Amer. Barrel Racing Assn. **[23492]**
Amer. Junior Rodeo Assn. **[23684]**
Canadian Girls Rodeo Assn. **[IO]**
Canadian Professional Rodeo Assn. **[IO]**

Cowboy Mounted Shooting Assn. **[23716]**
Fellowship of Christian Cowboys **[19796]**
Intl. Gay Rodeo Assn. **[23685]**
Intl. Gay Rodeo Assn. **[IO]**
Intl. Professional Rodeo Assn. **[23686]**
Natl. Bucking Bull Assn. **[23687]**
Natl. Cowboy and Western Heritage Museum **[9381]**
Natl. Fed. of Professional Bullriders **[23688]**
Natl. Finals Rodeo Comm. **[23689]**
Natl. High School Rodeo Assn. **[23690]**
Natl. Intercollegiate Rodeo Assn. **[23691]**
Natl. Little Britches Rodeo Assn. **[23692]**
Professional Armed Forces Rodeo Assn. **[23693]**
Professional Armed Forces Rodeo Assn. **[IO]**
Professional Rodeo Cowboys Assn. **[23694]**
Rodeo Historical Soc. **[9382]**
U.S. Calf Ropers Assn. **[23695]**
Women's Professional Rodeo Assn. **[23696]**
Rodeo Assn; Girls **[★23696]**
Rodeo Assn; Intl. **[★23686]**
Rodeo Assn; Interstate **[★23686]**
Rodeo Assn; Professional Women's **[★23696]**
Rodeo Commn; Natl. Finals **[★23689]**
Rodeo Cowboys Assn. **[★23694]**
Rodeo Historical Soc. **[9382]**, c/o Natl. Cowboy and Western Heritage Museum, 1700 NE 63rd St., Oklahoma City, OK 73111, (405)478-2250
Rodeo; Little Britches **[★23692]**
Rodeo Media Assn. - Defunct.
Roentgen Ray Soc; Amer. **[16277]**
Roentgen Soc. of the U.S. **[★16277]**
Roentgen Soc. of the U.S. **[★IO]**
Roentgen Soc; Western **[★16293]**
Roentgenologists; Natl. Coun. of Chiropractic **[★16288]**
Roentgenology; Amer. Acad. of Oral **[★14104]**
Roentgenology to the Amer. Chiropractic Assn; Coun. on **[★16288]**
Roentgenology; Amer. Chiropractic Coun. on **[★16288]**
Roentgenology; Amer. Coun. on Chiropractic **[★16288]**
Roesler de Villiers Found; Robert **[★13837]**
Roethke Memorial Found; Theodore **[10872]**
Roger Baldwin Found. of ACLU **[★17085]**
Roger Found; John **[★12352]**
Roger Sessions Soc. **[9815]**, c/o Dept. of Music, Univ. of North Carolina Wilmington, 601 S Coll. Rd., Wilmington, NC 28403-5975, (910)962-3890
Roger Wyburn-Mason and Jack M. Blount Found. for the Eradication of Rheumatoid Disease **[16375]**, 7376 Walker Rd., Fairview, TN 37062-8141, (615)799-1002
Rogers Clan - Address unknown since 2007.
Rogers - Dale Evans Collectors Assn; Roy **[24971]**
Rogers Found; Crane- **[★18837]**
Rogers Group **[10960]**
Rogue's Gallery - Defunct.
Role Playing Game Assn. Network **[22474]**, PO Box 707, Renton, WA 98057-0707, (800)324-6496
Role-Playing Games; Comm. for the Advancement of **[22463]**
Role of Women; Gen. Commn. on the Status and **[17535]**
Rolf Found. for Structural Integration; Ida P. **[★13652]**
Rolf Inst. **[★13652]**
Rolf Inst. of Structural Integration **[13652]**, 5055 Chaparral Ct., Ste. 103, Boulder, CO 80301, (303)449-5903
Roll Forming Inst; Custom **[2706]**
Roll Label Mfrs. Assn. - Defunct.
Roll Mfrs. Inst. - Address unknown since 1995.
Rolled Zinc Mfrs. Assn. - Defunct.
Roller Bearing Engineers Comm. **[★1991]**
Roller Canary Breeders Assn; Central States **[21844]**
Roller Canary Culturists; U.S. Assn. of **[21864]**
Roller Coasters
Amer. Coaster Enthusiasts **[22970]**
Roller Hockey Coaches Assn. - Address unknown since 2001.
Roller and Silent Chain Mfrs; Assn. of **[★1993]**
Roller Skaters; U.S. Fed. of Amateur **[★23742]**

Roller Skating Assn. Intl. **[3601]**, 6905 Corporate Dr., Indianapolis, IN 46278, (317)347-2626
Roller Skating Assn. Intl. **[IO]**, Indianapolis, IN, United States
Roller Skating Assn; U.S. Amateur **[★23742]**
Roller Skating Found. of America - Defunct.
Roller Skating Operators Assn. of Am. **[★3601]**
Roller Skating Operators Assn. of Am. **[★IO]**
Roller Skating Rink Operators Assn. **[★IO]**
Roller Skating Rink Operators Assn. **[★3601]**
Roller Skating Teachers of Am; Soc. of **[23741]**
Roller Skating; U.S. Amateur Confed. of **[23742]**
Roller Sports; USA **[23746]**
RollerSoccer Intl. Fed. **[23850]**, PO Box 423318, San Francisco, CA 94142-3318, (415)864-6879
RollerSoccer Intl. Fed. **[IO]**, San Francisco, CA, United States
Rollin' Rock Club - Address unknown since 1991.
Rolling Mill Machinery and Equipment Assn. - Defunct.
Rolling Readers **[12502]**, 4007 Camino Del Rio S, Ste. 203, San Diego, CA 92108, (619)516-4095
Rolling Stones Fan Club **[★IO]**
Rolling Stones Fan Club - Defunct.
Rolling Stones Fan Club Off. **[IO]**, Copenhagen, Denmark
Rolling Thunder **[21265]**, PO Box 216, Neshanic Station, NJ 08853, (908)369-5439
Rolls-Royce Enthusiasts' Club **[IO]**, Towcester, United Kingdom
Rolls-Royce Owners' Club **[21774]**, 191 Hempt Rd., Mechanicsburg, PA 17050, (717)697-4671
Roma Natl. Cong. **[19334]**, PO Box 822, Manchaca, TX 78652, (512)295-4858
Roma Women Assn. in Romania **[IO]**, Bucharest, Romania
Romagnola Assn; Amer. **[4244]**
Romagnola and RomAngus Assn; North Amer. **[4283]**
Roman
Intl. Catacomb Soc. **[10039]**
Italic Inst. of Am. **[10262]**
Roman Catholic Clergy; Natl. Org. for Continuing Educ. of **[19936]**
Roman Catholic Fed. of America; Lithuanian **[19214]**
Roman Catholic Organist Alliance; Amer. Lithuanian **[★10540]**
Roman Catholic Union of Am; Polish **[19314]**
Roman Catholic Women's Alliance; Lithuanian Amer. **[19211]**
Roman Catholics; Soc. of Traditional **[19726]**
Roman-Germanic Commn. of German Archaeological Inst. **[IO]**, Frankfurt, Germany
Romance Writers of Am. **[11191]**, 16000 Stuebner Airline Rd., Ste. 140, Spring, TX 77379, (832)717-5200
RomAngus Assn; North Amer. Romagnola and **[4283]**
Romani Cong. **[★19334]**
Romania
Children's Relief Network **[11581]**
Christian Aid Ministries **[18570]**
Christian Aid Ministries **[18570]**
Dracula Soc. - Great Britain **[IO]**
Heart of Romania's Children Found. **[11598]**
Hungarian Human Rights Found. **[18571]**
Hungarian Human Rights Found. **[IO]**
Romanian-American Chamber of Commerce **[24369]**
Romanian Stud. Assn. of Am. **[10938]**
Romanian-U.S. Bus. Coun. **[24370]**
Soc. for Romanian Stud. **[10939]**
Transylvania Soc. of Dracula - Italy **[IO]**
Transylvanian Soc. of Dracula **[IO]**
Romania ACM SIGCHI **[IO]**, Bucharest, Romania
Romania; Christian Aid for **[★18570]**
Romania Soc. Against Epilepsy **[IO]**, Bucharest, Romania
Romanian
Amer. Friends of Romania **[19331]**
Children's Relief Network **[11581]**
Dracula Soc. **[IO]**
Gypsy Stud. **[IO]**
Iuliu Maniu Amer. Romanian Relief Found. **[19332]**

Reference to "IO" in place of a book number signifies that the association may be found in the 45th edition of International Organizations.

Romanian Stud. Assn. of Am. [10938]
Soc. for Romanian Stud. [10939]
Soc. for Romanian Stud. [IO]
Union and League of Romanian Societies [19333]
Romanian Acad. [IO], Bucharest, Romania
Romanian Alzheimer Soc. [IO], Bucharest, Romania
Romanian-American Chamber of Commerce [24369], 2 Wisconsin Cir., Ste. 700, Chevy Chase, MD 20815, (240)235-6060
Romanian Assn. for Telework and Teleactivities [IO], Drobeta-Turnu Severin, Romania
Romanian Assn. for Transpersonal Psychology [IO], Bucharest, Romania
Romanian Badminton Fed. [IO], Bucharest, Romania
Romanian Banking Assn. [IO], Bucharest, Romania
Romanian Baptist Assn. of U.S. and Canada - Defunct.
Romanian Baseball and Softball Fed. [IO], Bucharest, Romania
Romanian Catholics of America; Assn. of [19579]
Romanian Dental Assn. of Private Practitioners [IO], Bucharest, Romania
Romanian Dermatological Soc. [IO], Bucharest, Romania
Romanian EMC Assn. [IO], Craiova, Romania
Romanian Fed. for Physiotherapy [IO], Oradea, Romania
Romanian League Against Rheumatism [IO], Bucharest, Romania
Romanian Local Press Editors Assn. [IO], Brasov, Romania
Romanian Medical Assn. [IO], Bucharest, Romania
Romanian Missionary Soc. [20387], PO Box 527, Wheaton, IL 60187, (630)665-6503
Romanian Natl. Agency for Solar and Renewable Energy [IO], Bucharest, Romania
Romanian Natl. Coun. - Defunct.
Romanian Natl. Tourist Off. [3934], 355 Lexington Ave., 19th Fl., New York, NY 10017, (212)545-8484
Romanian Natl. Tourist Off. [IO], New York, NY, United States
Romanian Olympic Comm. [★IO]
Romanian Olympic and Sports Comm. [IO], Bucharest, Romania
Romanian Orthodox
American Romanian Orthodox Youth [IO]
Amer. Romanian Orthodox Youth [20540]
Romanian Philatelic Club - Defunct.
Romanian Press Club [IO], Bucharest, Romania
Romanian Skating Fed. [IO], Bucharest, Romania
Romanian Societies of Am; Union and League of [★19333]
Romanian Societies; Union and League of [19333]
Romanian Soc. of Cardiology [IO], Bucharest, Romania
Romanian Soc. for Electron Microscopy [IO], Bucharest, Romania
Romanian Soc. of Gastrointestinal Endoscopy [IO], Cluj-Napoca, Romania
Romanian Soc. of Medical Informatics [IO], Timisoara, Romania
Romanian Soc. for Meteors and Astronomy [IO], Targoviste, Romania
Romanian Soc. of Osteoporosis [IO], Bucharest, Romania
Romanian Soc. of Photogrammetry and Remote Sensing [IO], Bucharest, Romania
Romanian Soc. of Physiological Sciences [IO], Iasi, Romania
Romanian Soc. of Rheumatology [IO], Cluj-Napoca, Romania
Romanian Soc. for the Stud. of Chemotherapeutics [IO], Iasi, Romania
Romanian Stud. Assn. of Am. [10938], c/o Dr. Nicolae Harsanyi, Ed., 6937 Bay Dr., Ste. 210, Miami Beach, FL 33141, (305)994-1419
Romanian Stud. Gp. [★10939]
Romanian Stud. Gp. [★IO]
Romanian Taekwondo Fed. [IO], Bucharest, Romania
Romanian Tourist Bd. [★IO]
Romanian Tourist Bd. [★3934]
Romanian Union of Public Transport [IO], Bucharest, Romania

Romanian-U.S. Bus. Coun. [24370], c/o Chamber of Commerce of the U.S., 1615 H St. NW, Washington, DC 20062-2000, (202)659-6000
Romanian-U.S. Economic Coun. [★24370]
Romanian-U.S. Working Group [★24370]
Romanian Visual Arts Copyright Collecting Soc. [IO], Bucharest, Romania
Romanian Welfare - Address unknown since 1995.
Romano Internacionaino Jekhethanibe [★19334]
Romantic Novelists' Assn. [IO], Reading, United Kingdom
Romany
Gypsy Lore Soc. [IO]
Gypsy Lore Soc. [10940]
Roma Natl. Cong. [19334]
Romany Soc. [IO], Macclesfield, United Kingdom
Romatizma Arastirma ve Savas Dernegi [★IO]
Romero Peace Mission; Comunidad Oscar A. [★17482]
Rometsch Registry [21775], 2510 N Larchmont Ave., Santa Ana, CA 92706
Rometsch Registry [IO], Santa Ana, CA, United States
Romisch-Germanische Kommission des Deutschen Archaeologischen Instituts [★IO]
Romney Breeders' Assn; Amer. [5193]
Rom's Bar - Defunct.
Ron Bremer Inst. [★21146]
Ron Bremer Inst. [★IO]
Ron Bremer Seminars [IO], Fredonia, AZ, United States
Ron Bremer Seminars [21146], HC 65, Box 425, Fredonia, AZ 86022, (928)875-8397
Ron Craddock Fan Club - Address unknown since 1989.
Ronald Lee Shankland Family Org. [21038], 2048 Forest Park Dr., Jackson, MI 49201, (517)783-6742
Ronald Reagan Home Preservation Found. [11147], PO Box 816, Dixon, IL 61021, (815)288-5176
Ronald Reagan Philatelic Soc. - Defunct.
Ronald Reagan Restoration and Preservation Assn. [★11147]
Ronald Stevenson Soc. [IO], Edinburgh, United Kingdom
Ronnie McDowell Fan Club - Address unknown since 1995.
Ronnie Milsap Fan Club - Address unknown since 2003.
Ronnie Prophet Intl. Fan Club - Defunct.
Ronnie Smith Fan Club - Defunct.
Ronny and the Daytonas Fan Club [24970], c/o Robert J. McKenzie, Pres., 114 Prince George Dr., Hampton, VA 23669-3604, (757)838-2059
Roo Rat Soc. [5375]
Roof Coatings Manufacturers Assn. [855], 1156 - 15th St. NW, Ste. 900, Washington, DC 20005, (202)207-0919
Roof Consultants Inst. [1063], 1500 Sunday Dr., Ste. 204, Raleigh, NC 27607, (919)859-0742
Roof Drainage Mfrs. Inst. - Defunct.
Roof Tile Inst. [★681]
Roofers, Damp and Waterproof Workers Assn; United Slate, Tile and Composition [★24033]
Roofers, Waterproofers and Allied Workers; United Union of [24033]
Roofing Assn; Single Ply [IO]
Roofing Contractors Assn; Canadian [IO]
Roofing Contractors Assn; Natl. [1051]
Roofing Educ. Found; Natl. [★8144]
Roofing Found; Natl. [8144]
Roofing Indus. Bur; Asphalt [★597]
Roofing Indus. Comm. on Weather Issues [666], c/o Patty Wood-Shields, Exec. Dir., 4721 Covenant Way, Powder Springs, GA 30127, (770)726-7194
Roofing Indus. Educational Inst. [1064], 10255 W Higgins Rd., Ste. 600, Rosemont, IL 60018-5607, (847)299-9070
Roofing Inst; Tile [681]
Roofing Manufacturers Assn; Asphalt [597]
Roofing Manufacturers Assn; Natl. Tile [★681]
Rooftops Canada [IO], Toronto, ON, Canada
ROOM, the Natl. Coun. for Housing and Planning and Royal Town Planning Inst. [★IO]
Room to Read [IO], San Francisco, CA, United States

Room to Read [12053], PO Box 29127, San Francisco, CA 94129, (415)561-3331
ROOMatRTPI [IO], London, United Kingdom
Roommate Assn; Natl. [★12305]
Roommate Services; Amer. Soc. of [12305]
Roosevelt Assn; Theodore [11152]
Roosevelt Centennial Youth Proj. [★13070]
Roosevelt Center for Amer. Policy Studies - Defunct.
Roosevelt Four Freedoms Found; Franklin D. [★11111]
Roosevelt Inst; Eleanor [★11111]
Roosevelt Inst; Franklin and Eleanor [11111]
Roosevelt Memorial Assn. [★11152]
Roosevelt Memorial Assn; Women's Theodore [★11152]
Rooster Class Yacht Racing Assn. - Defunct.
Root Beer Inst. - Defunct.
Root and Br. Assn. [IO], Jerusalem, Israel
Roots of Peace [18244], 1299 Fourth St., Ste. 200, San Rafael, CA 94901, (415)455-8008
Rope Fabricators; Assoc. Wire [2001]
Rope Jumping
Amer. Double Dutch League [23697]
U.S. Amateur Jump Rope Fed. [23698]
Rope Paper Sack Manufacturers Assn. [★991]
Roper Center [★10364]
Roper Center [★IO]
Ropers Assn; U.S. Calf [23695]
Roque Assn; Natl. [★23090]
Roque Assn; Western [★23090]
Roque and Croquet Assn; Amer. [23090]
Roque League; Amer. [★23090]
Rorschach Res. Exchange [★16176]
Rorschach Res. Exchange [★IO]
Rorschach Soc; Intl. [IO]
Rosa Klub CR [★IO]
Rosacea Soc; Natl. [14210]
Rosae Crucis; Ancient Mystical Order [★19336]
Rosanne Cash Fan Club - Address unknown since 1989.
Rosary; Children of the [18548]
Rosary Crusade; Family [★19622]
Rosary; Family [19622]
Rosary for Life Org. - Defunct.
Roscoe Pound-American Trial Lawyers Found. [★6335]
Roscoe Pound Found. [★6335]
Roscoe Pound Inst. [★6335]
Roscoe Pound-NACCA Found. [★6335]
Rose Bowl Collectors [22112], PO Box 244, Danielsville, PA 18038-0244, (610)760-8134
Rose Croix Martinist Order - Address unknown since 2000.
Rose Family Assn. [21039], 1474 Montelegre Dr., San Jose, CA 95120-4831, (408)268-2137
Rose Found; Amer. [★22501]
Rose Found; Heritage [22516]
Rose Hybridizers Assn. [22539], 21 S Wheaton Rd., Horseheads, NY 14845-1077, (607)562-8592
Rose Hybridizers Association [IO], Horseheads, NY, United States
Rose Kushner Breast Cancer Advisory Center [13870], PO Box 757, Palos Verdes Estates, CA 90274
Rose O'Neill Club; Natl. [★22399]
Rose Selections; All-America [4972]
Rose Soc. of Am; Clan [20859]
Rose Soc; Amer. [22501]
Rose Soc. of Argentina [IO], Buenos Aires, Argentina
Rosedale Mennonite Missions [IO], Irwin, OH, United States
Rosedale Mennonite Missions [20253], 9920 Rosedale-Milford Center Rd., Irwin, OH 43029, (740)857-1366
Rosenberg Case; Natl. Comm. to Reopen the [17135]
Rosenberg Fund for Children [11719], 116 Pleasant St., Ste. 348, Easthampton, MA 01027-2740, (413)529-0063
Rosenstock-Huessy Soc. - Defunct.
Roses Assn; Tournament of [19040]
Roses Gp; Heritage [22517]
Roses Incorporated [★4980]
Roses Incorporated [★IO]

A star before a book entry number signifies that the name is not listed separately, but is mentioned within the entry.

Roshei Yeshivos; Coun. of [★8683]
Rosicrucian
  Rosicrucian Fellowship [20541]
  Rosicrucian Fellowship [IO]
  Rosicrucian Fraternity [19335]
  Rosicrucian Order, AMORC English Grand Lodge [19336]
Rosicrucian Fellowship [20541], 2222 Mission Ave., Oceanside, CA 92054-2329, (760)757-6600
Rosicrucian Fellowship [IO], Oceanside, CA, United States
Rosicrucian Fraternity [19335], PO Box 220, Quakertown, PA 18951, (215)536-7048
Rosicrucian Order [★19336]
Rosicrucian Order, AMORC English Grand Lodge [19336], 1342 Naglee Ave., San Jose, CA 95126-2007, (408)947-3600
Rosie the Riveter Assn; Amer. [21388]
Ross Assn. of the U.S; Clan [20860]
Ross-Sellards Family; Bloss-Pyles- [20798]
Ross Soc; Pellien/Jaeger/Loretan/Steiner/ [21022]
Rossica [★22862]
Rossica [★IO]
Rossica Soc. of Russian Philately [IO], Los Gatos, CA, United States
Rossica Soc. of Russian Philately [22862], c/o Dr. Ed Laveroni, Sec., PO Box 320997, Los Gatos, CA 95032-0116
Rossiiskoe Mineralogicheskoe Obshchestvo [★IO]
Rossika [★IO]
Rossika [★22862]
Roster of Certified Engineers of the ASEIB [★6982]
Roswell Army-Air Field, Walker AFB Veterans Assn. - Address unknown since 2007.
Rotary Club of Grand Cayman [IO], Grand Cayman, Cayman Islands
Rotary Clubs; Intl. Assn. of [★13060]
Rotary Clubs; Natl. Assn. of [★13060]
Rotary Found. [★13060]
Rotary Found. [★IO]
Rotary Intl. [IO], Evanston, IL, United States
Rotary Intl. [13060], One Rotary Center, 1560 Sherman Ave., Evanston, IL 60201, (847)866-3000
Rotary on Stamps Fellowship [22863], c/o Gerald FitzSimmons, Sec.-Treas., 105 Calle Ricardo, Victoria, TX 77904
Rotary on Stamps Fellowship [IO], Victoria, TX, United States
Rotary on Stamps Unit [★IO]
Rotary on Stamps Unit [★22863]
Rotating Elecl. Machines Assn. [IO], London, United Kingdom
Rotational Molders Intl; Assn. of [3046]
ROTC Colleges and Universities; Assn. of Naval [★8884]
ROTH [★21200]
Rotherham Chamber of Commerce [IO], Rotherham, United Kingdom
Rotherham Chamber of Commerce, Training and Enterprise [★IO]
Rotisseurs, Bailliage des U.S.A; Confrerie de la Chaine des [22569]
Rotograph Soc. of Antique Picture Post Cards - Defunct.
Rotogravure Assn. - Address unknown since 1995.
Rotorcraft
  Helicopter Club of America [21450]
  Popular Rotorcraft Assn. [21471]
  Whirly-Girls - Intl. Women Helicopter Pilots [21487]
Rotorcraft Assn; Popular [21471]
Rotterdam Arts Coun. [IO], Rotterdam, Netherlands
Rottweiler Club of Am. [★22208]
Rottweiler Club; Amer. [22208]
Rottweiler Club; Colonial [22249]
Rottweilerklubben Danmark [★IO]
Rough Fell Sheep Breeders Assn. [IO], Ripon, United Kingdom
Rough and Smooth Collie Training Assn. [IO], Hereford, United Kingdom
Rough and Tumble Engineers' Historical Assn. [22979], PO Box 9, Kinzers, PA 17535-0009, (717)442-4249
Roumanian Jewish Fed. of America - Defunct.
Round Dance Teachers; Intl. Assn. of [★9886]

Round-Table Intl. [★13061]
Round-Table Intl. [★IO]
Round Table; Loyal Knights of the [★13061]
Round Table of Natl. Orgs. for Better Education - Defunct.
Round-Table U.S.A. [13061], MD Financial Bank, 303 E Wacker Dr., Chicago, IL 60601
Round-Table U.S.A. [IO], Chicago, IL, United States
ROUNDALAB [★IO]
ROUNDALAB [★9886]
Rounders Assn. of Ireland [★IO]
Rounders Coun. of Ireland [IO], Moneymore, United Kingdom
Roundtable Found. [★IO]
Roundtable Found. [★18196]
Roundtable for Women in Foodservice [1593]
Rousseau Assn. [9708], c/o Sally H. Campbell, Sec.-Treas., Dept. of Political Sci., Concord Univ., PO Box 1000, Athens, WV 24712
Rousseau Assn. [IO], Athens, WV, United States
Rousseau Proj. [IO], Toronto, ON, Canada
Rousseau Stud; Soc. for [★9708]
Route 66 Fed; Natl. Historic [24328]
Routes to Learning Canada [IO], Kingston, ON, Canada
Rover Owners' Assn. of North America - Defunct.
Rover P4 Drivers Guild [IO], Luton, United Kingdom
Rover Saloon Touring Club of Am. [21776], c/o Glen Wilson, 733 S Providence Rd., Wallingford, PA 19086, (484)443-5000
Roving Volunteers in Christ's Ser. [23017], 1800 SE 4th St., Smithville, TX 78957, (512)237-2446
Rowing
  Amateur Rowing Assn. [IO]
  Amer. Swan Boat Assn. [23669]
  Eastern Assn. of Rowing Colleges [23699]
  Intercollegiate Rowing Assn. [23700]
  Intl. Fed. of Rowing Associations [IO]
  Irish Amateur Rowing Union [IO]
  Melbourne Argonauts Queer Rowing Club [IO]
  Middle States Regatta Assn. [23701]
  Natl. Rowing Found. [23702]
  Rowing Canada Aviron [IO]
  Scholastic Rowing Assn. of Am. [23703]
  Swiss Rowing Fed. [IO]
  U.S. Rowing Assn. [23704]
Rowing Assn. of Am; Schoolboy [★23703]
Rowing Assn; Natl. Women's [★23704]
Rowing Canada Aviron [IO], Victoria, BC, Canada
Rowing; US [★23704]
Roy Clark Intl. Fan Club - Address unknown since 2001.
Roy Clayborne Fan Club - Address unknown since 1989.
Roy Rogers - Dale Evans Collectors Assn. [24971], PO Box 1166, Portsmouth, OH 45662, (740)353-0900
Royal Academies for Sci. and the Arts of Belgium [IO], Brussels, Belgium
Royal Acad. of Arts [IO], London, United Kingdom
Royal Acad. of Dance [IO], London, United Kingdom
Royal Acad. of Dance [9896], 1412 17th St., Ste. 259, Bakersfield, CA 93301, (661)336-0160
Royal Acad. of Dancing, U.S. Br. [★9896]
Royal Acad. of Dramatic Art [IO], London, United Kingdom
Royal Acad. of Dutch Language and Literature [IO], Gent, Belgium
Royal Acad. of Engg. [IO], London, United Kingdom
Royal Acad. of Letters, History and Antiquities [IO], Stockholm, Sweden
Royal Acad. of Medicine of Belgium [IO], Brussels, Belgium
Royal Acad. of Medicine in Ireland [IO], Dublin, Ireland
Royal Academy of Music [IO], London, United Kingdom
Royal Acad. of Overseas Sciences [IO], Brussels, Belgium
Royal Acad. of Overseas Stud. [★IO]
Royal Acad. of Sci., Humanities, and Fine Arts of Belgium [IO], Brussels, Belgium
Royal Acad. of Sciences, Humanities and Fine Arts of Belgium [IO], Brussels; Belgium
Royal Aeronautical Soc. - Australian Div. [IO], Mascot, Australia

Royal Aeronautical Soc., New Zealand Div. [IO], Wellington, New Zealand
Royal Aeronautical Soc. - United Kingdom [IO], London, United Kingdom
Royal African Soc. [IO], London, United Kingdom
Royal Agricultural and Horticultural Soc. of South Australia [IO], Goodwood, Australia
Royal Agricultural Soc. of the Commonwealth [IO], Edinburgh, United Kingdom
Royal Agricultural Soc. of England [IO], Coventry, United Kingdom
Royal Agricultural Soc. of New Zealand [IO], Woodend, New Zealand
Royal Agricultural Soc. of NSW [IO], Sydney, Australia
Royal Air Force Benevolent Fund [IO], London, United Kingdom
Royal Air Force Historical Soc. [IO], Wooton-Under-Edge, United Kingdom
Royal Air Forces Assn. [IO], Leicester, United Kingdom
Royal and Ancient Golf Club [IO], Fife, United Kingdom
Royal and Ancient Golf Club of St. Andrews [IO], Fife, United Kingdom
Royal Anthropological Inst. of Great Britain and Ireland [IO], London, United Kingdom
Royal Arcanum; Supreme Coun. of the [19140]
Royal Arch Educ. Bureau [★19235]
Royal Arch Educ. Bureau [★IO]
Royal Arch Res. Assistance Program [★IO]
Royal Arch Res. Assistance Program [19235]
Royal Archaeological Inst. [IO], London, United Kingdom
Royal Architectural Inst. of Canada [IO], Ottawa, ON, Canada
Royal Asiatic Soc. of Great Britain and Ireland [IO], London, United Kingdom
Royal Asiatic Soc. - Hong Kong Br. [IO], Hong Kong, People's Republic of China
Royal Assn. in Aid of Deaf People [★IO]
Royal Assn; Amer. [4995]
Royal Assn. of British Dairy Farmers [IO], Kenilworth, United Kingdom
Royal Assn. for Deaf People [IO], Colchester, United Kingdom
Royal Assn. for Disability and Rehabilitation [IO], London, United Kingdom
Royal Assn. of Dutch Wine Traders [IO], Amsterdam, Netherlands
Royal Assn. for the Longevity and Preservation of the Honeymooners - Address unknown since 1999.
Royal Assn. of Netherlands' Shipowners [IO], Rotterdam, Netherlands
Royal Astronomical Soc. [IO], London, United Kingdom
Royal Astronomical Soc. of Canada [IO], Toronto, ON, Canada
Royal Astronomical Soc. of New Zealand [IO], Wellington, New Zealand
Royal Australasian Coll. of Dental Surgeons [IO], Sydney, Australia
Royal Australasian Coll. of Physicians - Australia [IO], Sydney, Australia
Royal Australasian Coll. of Surgeons [IO], Melbourne, Australia
Royal Australian Chem. Inst. [IO], North Melbourne, Australia
Royal Australian Chem. Inst. - ACT Br. [IO], Canberra, Australia
Royal Australian Chem. Inst. - NSW Br. [IO], Sydney, Australia
Royal Australian Chem. Inst. - NT Br. [IO], Casuarina, Australia
Royal Australian Chem. Inst. - SA Br. [IO], Bedford Park, Australia
Royal Australian Chem. Inst. - Tasmanian Br. [IO], Hobart, Australia
Royal Australian Chem. Inst. - Victorian Br. [IO], Melbourne, Australia
Royal Australian Chem. Inst. - WA Br. [IO], Rockingham, Australia
Royal Australian Coll. of Gen. Practitioners [IO], South Melbourne, Australia
Royal Australian Coll. of Ophthalmologists [★IO]

Reference to "IO" in place of a book number signifies that the association may be found in the 45th edition of International Organizations.

Royal Australian Historical Soc. **[IO]**, Sydney, Australia

Royal Australian Inst. of Architects **[IO]**, Manuka, Australia

Royal Australian and New Zealand Coll. of Obstetricians and Gynaecologists **[IO]**, East Melbourne, Australia

Royal Australian and New Zealand Coll. of Ophthalmologists **[IO]**, Surry Hills, Australia

Royal Australian and New Zealand Coll. of Psychiatrists **[IO]**, Melbourne, Australia

Royal Australian and New Zealand Coll. of Radiologists **[IO]**, Sydney, Australia

Royal Australian Planning Inst. **[★IO]**

Royal Auto. Club Motor Sports Assn. **[IO]**, Slough, United Kingdom

Royal Bath and West of England Soc. **[IO]**, Shepton Mallet, United Kingdom

Royal Belgian Aero Club **[IO]**, Brussels, Belgium

Royal Belgian Assn. of Biscuit, Chocolate, Pralines and Confectionery **[IO]**, Brussels, Belgium

Royal Belgian Football Assn. **[IO]**, Brussels, Belgium

Royal Belgian Shipowners' Assn. **[IO]**, Antwerp, Belgium

Royal Belgian Tennis Fed. **[IO]**, Brussels, Belgium

Royal Blind Soc. **[★IO]**

Royal British Legion Women's Sect. **[IO]**, London, United Kingdom

Royal British Soc. of Sculptors **[IO]**, London, United Kingdom

Royal British Virgin Islands Yacht Club **[IO]**, Tortola, British Virgin Islands

Royal Canadian Coll. of Organists **[IO]**, Toronto, ON, Canada

Royal Canadian Geographical Soc. **[IO]**, Ottawa, ON, Canada

Royal Canadian Golf Assn. **[IO]**, Oakville, ON, Canada

Royal Canadian Legion **[IO]**, Ottawa, ON, Canada

Royal Canadian Regiment Assn. **[IO]**, London, ON, Canada

Royal Celtic Soc. **[IO]**, Edinburgh, United Kingdom

Royal Chamber of the Belgian Antique Dealers **[IO]**, Brussels, Belgium

Royal Choral Soc. **[IO]**, London, United Kingdom

Royal Clan, order of Scottish Clans **[★IO]**

Royal Cliff Wine Club **[IO]**, Pattaya, Thailand

Royal Coll. of Anaesthetists **[IO]**, London, United Kingdom

Royal Coll. of Dentists of Canada **[IO]**, Toronto, ON, Canada

Royal Coll. of Gen. Practitioners **[IO]**, London, United Kingdom

Royal Coll. of Midwives **[IO]**, London, United Kingdom

Royal Coll. of Nursing **[IO]**, London, United Kingdom

Royal Coll. of Nursing - Australia **[IO]**, Deakin West, Australia

Royal Coll. of Obstetricians and Gynaecologists - United Kingdom **[IO]**, London, United Kingdom

Royal Coll. of Ophthalmologists **[IO]**, London, United Kingdom

Royal Coll. of Organists **[IO]**, London, United Kingdom

Royal Coll. of Paediatrics and Child Hea. **[IO]**, London, United Kingdom

Royal Coll. of Pathologists of Australasia **[IO]**, Surry Hills, Australia

Royal Coll. of Pathologists - United Kingdom **[IO]**, London, United Kingdom

Royal Coll. of Physicians **[IO]**, London, United Kingdom

Royal Coll. of Physicians of Edinburgh **[IO]**, Edinburgh, United Kingdom

Royal Coll. of Physicians of Ireland **[IO]**, Dublin, Ireland

Royal Coll. of Physicians and Surgeons of Canada **[IO]**, Ottawa, ON, Canada

Royal Coll. of Physicians and Surgeons of Glasgow **[IO]**, Glasgow, United Kingdom

Royal College of Physicians and Surgeons of the United States of America **[IO]**, Detroit, MI, United States

Royal Coll. of Physicians and Surgeons of the U.S.A. **[16694]**, PO Box 24224, 485 Allard Rd., Detroit, MI 48224-0224, (313)882-0641

Royal Coll. of Psychiatrists **[IO]**, London, United Kingdom

Royal Coll. of Radiologists - United Kingdom **[IO]**, London, United Kingdom

Royal Coll. of Speech and Language Therapists **[IO]**, London, United Kingdom

Royal Coll. of Surgeons of Edinburgh **[IO]**, Edinburgh, United Kingdom

Royal Coll. of Surgeons of England **[IO]**, London, United Kingdom

Royal Coll. of Surgeons in Ireland **[IO]**, Dublin, Ireland

Royal Coll. of Veterinary Surgeons **[IO]**, London, United Kingdom

Royal Commonwealth Ex-Services League **[IO]**, London, United Kingdom

Royal Commonwealth Soc. **[IO]**, London, United Kingdom

Royal Conservatory of Music **[IO]**, Toronto, ON, Canada

Royal Crown Bottlers Assn. **[512]**

Royal Danish Acad. of Fine Arts **[IO]**, Copenhagen, Denmark

Royal Danish Acad. of Sciences and Letters **[IO]**, Copenhagen, Denmark

Royal Danish Aeroclub **[IO]**, Roskilde, Denmark

Royal Danish Agricultural Soc. **[IO]**, Copenhagen, Denmark

Royal Danish Geographical Soc. **[IO]**, Copenhagen, Denmark

Royal Dublin Soc. **[IO]**, Dublin, Ireland

Royal Dutch Cricket Assn. **[IO]**, Nieuwegein, Netherlands

Royal Dutch Geographical Soc. **[IO]**, Utrecht, Netherlands

Royal Dutch Korfball Assn. **[IO]**, Zeist, Netherlands

Royal Dutch Medical Assn. **[IO]**, Utrecht, Netherlands

Royal Economic Soc. **[IO]**, London, United Kingdom

Royal Economic Soc. of Friends of Tenerife **[IO]**, Santa Cruz de Tenerife, Spain

Royal Enfield Owners Club **[★IO]**

Royal Enfield Owners Club of North Am. **[IO]**, Oshawa, ON, Canada

Royal Entomological Soc. **[IO]**, London, United Kingdom

Royal Entomological Soc. of Antwerp, Belgium **[IO]**, Hoboken, Belgium

Royal Environmental Hea. Inst. of Scotland **[IO]**, Edinburgh, United Kingdom

Royal Fed. of Aero Clubs of Australia **[IO]**, Taree, Australia

Royal Fed. of Water and Soft Drinks Indus. **[IO]**, Brussels, Belgium

Royal Flying Dr. Ser. of Australia **[IO]**, Sydney, Australia

Royal Forest and Bird Protection Soc. of New Zealand **[IO]**, Wellington, New Zealand

Royal Forestry Soc. **[IO]**, Tring, United Kingdom

Royal Geographical Soc. with the Inst. of British Geographers **[IO]**, London, United Kingdom

Royal Geographical Soc. of Queensland **[IO]**, Milton, Australia

Royal Geological and Mining Soc. of the Netherlands **[IO]**, Utrecht, Netherlands

Royal Heraldry Soc. of Canada **[IO]**, Ottawa, ON, Canada

Royal Highland and Agricultural Soc. of Scotland **[IO]**, Edinburgh, United Kingdom

Royal Highland Educ. Trust **[IO]**, Edinburgh, United Kingdom

Royal Historical Soc. of Queensland **[IO]**, Brisbane, Australia

Royal Historical Soc. - United Kingdom **[IO]**, London, United Kingdom

Royal Historical Soc. of Victoria **[IO]**, Melbourne, Australia

Royal Horticultural Soc. **[IO]**, London, United Kingdom

Royal Horticultural Soc. of Ireland **[IO]**, Dublin, Ireland

Royal Humane Soc. **[IO]**, London, United Kingdom

Royal Incorporation of Architects in Scotland **[IO]**, Edinburgh, United Kingdom

Royal Inst. of the Architects of Ireland **[IO]**, Dublin, Ireland

Royal Inst. of British Architects **[IO]**, London, United Kingdom

Royal Inst. of Chemistry **[★IO]**

Royal Inst. for Deaf and Blind Children **[IO]**, North Rocks, Australia

Royal Inst. of Dutch Architects **[IO]**, Amsterdam, Netherlands

Royal Inst. of Hea. and Hygiene and Soc. of Public Hea. **[★IO]**

Royal Inst. of Intl. Affairs **[★IO]**

Royal Inst. of Intl. Relations **[IO]**, Brussels, Belgium

Royal Inst. of Navigation **[IO]**, London, United Kingdom

Royal Inst. of Oil Painters **[IO]**, London, United Kingdom

Royal Inst. of Painters in Water Colours **[IO]**, London, United Kingdom

Royal Inst. of Philosophy **[IO]**, London, United Kingdom

Royal Inst. of Public Hea. **[IO]**, London, United Kingdom

Royal Institution of Chartered Surveyors **[IO]**, London, United Kingdom

Royal Institution of Engineers in the Netherlands **[IO]**, The Hague, Netherlands

Royal Institution of Great Britain **[IO]**, London, United Kingdom

Royal Institution of Naval Architects **[IO]**, London, United Kingdom

Royal Intl. Lipizzan Club **[★4911]**

Royal Irish Acad. **[IO]**, Dublin, Ireland

Royal Irish Acad. of Music **[IO]**, Dublin, Ireland

Royal Irish Auto. Club **[IO]**, Dublin, Ireland

Royal Isle of Wight Agricultural Soc. **[IO]**, Newport, United Kingdom

Royal Life Saving Soc. **[IO]**, Warwick, United Kingdom

Royal Life Saving Soc. Australia **[IO]**, Broadway, Australia

Royal Medical Soc. **[IO]**, Edinburgh, United Kingdom

Royal Mencap Soc. **[IO]**, Birmingham, United Kingdom

Royal Meteorological Soc. **[IO]**, Reading, United Kingdom

Royal Microscopical Soc. **[IO]**, Oxford, United Kingdom

Royal Musical Assn. **[IO]**, Manchester, United Kingdom

Royal Natl. Inst. of the Blind - UK **[IO]**, London, United Kingdom

Royal Natl. Inst. for Deaf People **[IO]**, London, United Kingdom

Royal Natl. Lifeboat Institution - Ireland **[IO]**, Dun Laoghaire, Ireland

Royal Natl. Mission to Deep Sea Fishermen **[IO]**, Whiteley, United Kingdom

Royal Natl. Rose Soc. **[IO]**, St. Albans, United Kingdom

Royal Naval Assn., New York Br. - Defunct.

Royal Naval Officers Club - Defunct.

Royal Neighbors of Am. **[19137]**, 230 16th St., Rock Island, IL 61201, (309)788-4561

Royal Nepal Acad. of Sci. and Tech. **[IO]**, Kathmandu, Nepal

Royal Netherlands Acad. of Arts and Sciences **[IO]**, Amsterdam, Netherlands

Royal Netherlands Assn. of Musicians **[IO]**, Amsterdam, Netherlands

Royal Netherlands Chem. Soc. **[IO]**, Leidschendam, Netherlands

Royal Netherlands Soc. for Agricultural Sci. **[★IO]**

Royal Netherlands Soc. for Agricultural Sciences **[IO]**, Wageningen, Netherlands

Royal New South Wales Bowling Assn. **[IO]**, Sydney, Australia

Royal New South Wales Canine Coun. **[★IO]**

Royal New Zealand Aero Club **[IO]**, Blenheim, New Zealand

Royal New Zealand Coll. of Obstetricians and Gynaecologists **[★IO]**

Royal Norwegian Soc. of Sciences and Letters **[IO]**, Trondheim, Norway

Royal Numismatic Soc. **[IO]**, London, United Kingdom

Royal Oak Found. **[10060]**, 26 Broadway, Ste. 950, New York, NY 10004-1715, (212)480-2889

A star before a book entry number signifies that the name is not listed separately, but is mentioned within the entry.

Royal Order of Piast - Address unknown since 1995.

Royal Order of Scotland [19249], PO Box 11, Charleroi, PA 15022-0011, (724)489-0670

Royal Over-Seas League [IO], London, United Kingdom

Royal Pharmaceutical Soc. of Great Britain [IO], London, United Kingdom

Royal Philatelic Soc. [IO], London, United Kingdom

Royal Philatelic Soc. of Canada [IO], Toronto, ON, Canada

Royal Philharmonic Soc. [IO], London, United Kingdom

Royal Philosophical Soc. of Glasgow [IO], Glasgow, United Kingdom

Royal Photographic Soc. of Great Britain [IO], Bath, United Kingdom

Royal Physiographical Soc. of Lund [IO], Lund, Sweden

Royal Sailors' Rests [IO], Portsmouth, United Kingdom

Royal Scottish Acad. [IO], Edinburgh, United Kingdom

Royal Scottish Acad. of Music and Drama [IO], Glasgow, United Kingdom

Royal Scottish Acad. of Painting, Sculpture and Architecture [★IO]

Royal Scottish Country Dance Soc. [IO], Edinburgh, United Kingdom

Royal Scottish Forestry Soc. [IO], Canonbie, United Kingdom

Royal Scottish Geographical Soc. [IO], Glasgow, United Kingdom

Royal Soc. [IO], London, United Kingdom

Royal Soc. of Antiquaries of Ireland [IO], Dublin, Ireland

Royal Soc. for Asian Affairs [IO], London, United Kingdom

Royal Soc. of British Artists [IO], London, United Kingdom

Royal Soc. of Canada [IO], Ottawa, ON, Canada

Royal Soc. of Chemistry [IO], London, United Kingdom

Royal Soc. of Edinburgh [IO], Edinburgh, United Kingdom

Royal Soc. for the Encouragement of Arts, Manufactures, and Commerce [IO], London, United Kingdom

Royal Soc. of Female Musicians [★IO]

Royal Soc. of Hea. [★IO]

Royal Soc. of Literature [IO], London, United Kingdom

Royal Soc. of Marine Artists [IO], London, United Kingdom

Royal Soc. of Medicine [IO], London, United Kingdom

Royal Soc. of Medicine [★15178]

Royal Soc. of Medicine Found. [15178], c/o Dr. Richard Southby, Pres, 5325 MacArthur Blvd. NW, Washington, DC 20016, (202)966-6251

Royal Soc. for Mentally Handicapped Children and Adults [★IO]

Royal Soc. of Miniature Painters, Sculptors and Gravers [IO], Gillingham, United Kingdom

Royal Soc. for Music History of the Netherlands [IO], Utrecht, Netherlands

Royal Soc. of Musicians of Great Britain [IO], London, United Kingdom

Royal Soc. for Nature Conservation, Wildlife Trusts Partnership [★IO]

Royal Soc. of New South Wales [IO], Sydney, Australia

Royal Soc. of New Zealand [IO], Wellington, New Zealand

Royal Soc. of New Zealand, Canterbury Br. [IO], Christchurch, New Zealand

Royal Soc. of New Zealand, Manawatu Br. [IO], Palmerston North, New Zealand

Royal Soc. of New Zealand, North Shore Br. [IO], Auckland, New Zealand

Royal Soc. of New Zealand, Rotorua Br. [IO], Rotorua, New Zealand

Royal Soc. of Painter-Printmakers [IO], London, United Kingdom

Royal Soc. of Portrait Painters [IO], London, United Kingdom

Royal Soc. for the Prevention of Accidents [IO], Birmingham, United Kingdom

Royal Soc. for the Prevention of Cruelty to Animals [IO], Horsham, United Kingdom

Royal Soc. for the Promotion of Hea. [IO], London, United Kingdom

Royal Soc. for the Protection of Birds [IO], Sandy, United Kingdom

Royal Soc. for Protection of Nature [IO], Thimphu, Bhutan

Royal Soc. of South Africa [IO], Cape Town, Republic of South Africa

Royal Soc. of South Australia [IO], Adelaide, Australia

Royal Soc. of Tropical Medicine and Hygiene [IO], London, United Kingdom

Royal Soc. of Ulster Architects [IO], Belfast, United Kingdom

Royal Soc. of Western Australia [IO], Welshpool, Australia

Royal Soc. of Wildlife Trusts [IO], Newark, United Kingdom

Royal Statistical Soc. [IO], London, United Kingdom

Royal Surgical Aid Soc. [IO], London, United Kingdom

Royal Swedish Acad. of Engg. Sciences [IO], Stockholm, Sweden

Royal Swedish Acad. of Sciences [IO], Stockholm, Sweden

Royal TV Soc. [IO], London, United Kingdom

Royal Town Planning Inst. [IO], London, United Kingdom

Royal Tropical Inst. [IO], Amsterdam, Netherlands

Royal Ulster Agricultural Soc. [IO], Belfast, United Kingdom

Royal Union of Dutch Shipowners [★IO]

Royal Victorian Bowls Assn. [IO], Hawthorn, Australia

Royal Watercolour Soc. [IO], London, United Kingdom

Royal Welsh Agricultural Soc. [IO], Builth Wells, United Kingdom

Royal Western Australian Historical Soc. [IO], Nedlands, Australia

Royal Western India Turf Club [IO], Bombay, India

Royal Winnipeg Ballet Alumni Assn. [IO], Winnipeg, MB, Canada

Royal Yachting Assn. [IO], Southampton, United Kingdom

Royal Zoological Soc. of New South Wales [IO], Mosman, Australia

Royal Zoological Soc. of Scotland [IO], Edinburgh, United Kingdom

Royal Zoological Soc. of South Australia [IO], Adelaide, Australia

Royalty Owners Assn; Texas Independent Producers and [2949]

Royalty Owners; Natl. Assn. of [2935]

Royalty; Soc. of Amer. [18082]

Roycroft; Found. for the Stud. of the Arts and Crafts Movement at [21530]

Roycrofters-at-Large Assn. [9840], 21 S Grove St., Ste. 110, East Aurora, NY 14052, (716)655-7252

Roycrofters-At-Large Association/Elbert Hubbard Found. [★9840]

RP Found. Fighting Blindness [★16847]

RPO Am. [★6247]

R.S. Prussia Collectors; Intl. Assn. of [22043]

RSDHope Gp. [15848], PO Box 875, Harrison, ME 04040, (207)583-4589

RSGS [★IO]

RSNZ Wellington Br. [IO], Wellington, New Zealand

RSPA [910], 4115 Taggart Creek Rd., Charlotte, NC 28208-5479, (704)357-3124

RSVP Intl. - Address unknown since 2000.

RTCA [6308], 1828 L St. NW, Ste. 805, Washington, DC 20036, (202)833-9339

RTCM [★3753]

RTCM [★IO]

RTS Bereavement Services [★12663]

RTS Parent Gp. U.S.A. [★13759]

Rubber
All India Rubber Indus. Assn. [IO]
Assn. of the Dutch Adhesive Indus. [IO]
Assn. of the German Rubber Mfg. Indus. [IO]

Assn. of Natural Rubber Producing Countries [IO]
Associazione Nazionale fra le Industrie della Gomma, Cavi Elettricifed Affini [IO]
British Rubber Manufacturers' Assn. [IO]
Colombian Plastics Indus. Assn. [IO]
Colombo Rubber Traders' Assn. [IO]
European Tyre and Rubber Mfrs'. Assn. [IO]
Indian Rubber Mfrs. Res. Assn. [IO]
Intl. Inst. of Synthetic Rubber Producers [IO]
Intl. Inst. of Synthetic Rubber Producers [3432]
Intl. Rubber Conf. Org. [IO]
Intl. Rubber Study Group [IO]
Intl. Tire Assn. [3813]
Intl. Tyre, Rubber, and Plastics Fed. [IO]
Japan Rubber Mfrs'. Assn. [IO]
Japan Valve Mfrs'. Assn. [IO]
Japanese Rubber Workers' Union Confed. [IO]
Malaysian Rubber Bd. [IO]
Malaysian Rubber Glove Manufacturers' Assn. [IO]
Malaysian Rubber Products Manufacturers Assn. [IO]
Natl. Assn. of Hose and Accessories Distribution [2047]
Natl. Consortium of the Rubber Indus. [IO]
Natl. Plastics Indus. Assn. [IO]
Natl. Union of Rubber and Polymers [IO]
Plastics Fed. of South Africa [IO]
RAPRA Tech. [IO]
Rubber Assn. of Canada [IO]
Rubber Assn. of Indonesia [IO]
Rubber Div., Amer. Chem. Soc. [3433]
Rubber Indus'. Assn. [IO]
Rubber Mfrs. Assn. [3434]
Rubber Mfrs'. Assn. of Finland [IO]
Rubber Pavements Assn. [667]
Rubber Stamp Manufacturer's Guild [IO]
Rubber Trade Assn. of North Am. [IO]
Rubber Trade Assn. of North Am. [3435]
Soc. of Rubber Indus., Japan [IO]
Styrene Info. and Res. Center [823]
Taiwan Rubber Indus. Assn. [IO]
Tire Soc. [7798]
Tun Abdul Razak Res. Centre [IO]
United Steel Workers of Am., Rubber/Plastics Indus. Conf. [24183]
Venezuelan Assn. of the Plastics Indus. [IO]

Rubber Assn. of Am. [★3434]

Rubber Assn. of Canada [IO], Mississauga, ON, Canada

Rubber Assn. of Indonesia [IO], Jakarta, Indonesia

Rubber Assn; Intl. Tire and [★3814]

Rubber Club of Am. [★3434]

Rubber Club; New England [★3434]

Rubber Dam
Amer. Acad. of Gold Foil Operators [14099]

Rubber Div., Amer. Chem. Soc. [3433], PO Box 499, Akron, OH 44309-0499, (330)972-7814

Rubber Export Assn. - Defunct.

Rubber Heel and Sole Inst. - Defunct.

Rubber Indus'. Assn. [IO], Santiago, Chile

Rubber Mfrs. Assn. [3434], 1400 K St. NW, Ste. 900, Washington, DC 20005, (202)682-4800

Rubber Mfrs'. Assn. of Finland [IO], Helsinki, Finland

Rubber Pavements Assn. [IO], Tempe, AZ, United States

Rubber Pavements Assn. [667], 1801 S Jentilly Ln., Ste. A-2, Tempe, AZ 85281-5738, (480)517-9944

Rubber and Plastic Adhesive and Sealant Manufacturers Coun. [★56]

Rubber/Plastics Indus. Conf; United Steel Workers of Am., [24183]

Rubber and Plastics Res. Assn. [★IO]

Rubber Producers Gp; Asphalt [★667]

Rubber Shippers Assn. - Defunct.

Rubber Stamp Manufacturer's Guild [IO], High Wycombe, United Kingdom

Rubber Stamps
Intl. Marking and Identification Assn. [3683]

Rubber Trade Assn. of New York [★3435]

Rubber Trade Assn. of New York [★IO]

Rubber Trade Assn. of North Am. [IO], Rockville Centre, NY, United States

Rubber Trade Assn. of North Am. [3435], 220 Maple Ave., PO Box 196, Rockville Centre, NY 11571, (516)536-7228

Reference to "IO" in place of a book number signifies that the association may be found in the 45th edition of International Organizations.

Rubella Assn; Canadian Deafblind and [IO]
Rubicon - Defunct.
Rubin Found; Samuel [13188]
Rubinstein-Taybi Parent Gp. U.S.A. [13759], c/o Ms.
 Lorrie Baxter, Coor., PO Box 146, Smith Center,
 KS 66967, (785)697-2989
Ruch Burn Found; Alisa Ann [13780]
Ruckus Soc. [18178], 369 15th St., Oakland, CA
 94612-3303, (510)763-7078
Rudd Family Res. Assn. - Defunct.
Rudder Club - Address unknown since 2002.
Rudge Enthusiasts Club [22691], c/o Charles M.
 McReynolds, Area Rep., 3338 Barhite St.,
 Pasadena, CA 91107, (626)798-7557
Rudge Enthusiasts Club [IO], Pasadena, CA, United
 States
Rudgespares [★IO]
Rudgespares [★22691]
Rudjer Boskovic Inst. [IO], Zagreb, Croatia
Rue Family Assn; Joseph Cox and Mary [20967]
Ruff Political Action Comm. - Address unknown
 since 1999.
Ruffed Grouse Soc. [5376], 451 McCormick Rd.,
 Coraopolis, PA 15108, (412)262-4044
Ruffed Grouse Soc. of Am. [★5376]
Ruffed Grouse Soc. of North Am. [★5376]
Rug Importers Assn; Oriental [2272]
Rug Inst; Carpet and [2254]
Rug Retailers of Am; Oriental [2273]
Rug Soc. of Washington, District of Columbia
 [★9450]
Rug Soc. of Washington, District of Columbia [★IO]
Rugby
 British Amateur Rugby League Assn. [IO]
 Coolmine Rugby Football Club [IO]
 Irish Rugby Football Union [IO]
 Irish Rugby Union Players Assn. [IO]
 New Zealand Rugby Players Assn. [IO]
 Professional Rugby Players' Assn. [IO]
 Rugby Fives Assn. [IO]
 Rugby Football League [IO]
 Rugby Football Union [IO]
 Rugby Union Players' Assn. [IO]
 United States Quad Rugby Association [IO]
 U.S. Quad Rugby Assn. [23705]
 U.S. Rugby Football Union [23706]
 Welsh Rugby Union [IO]
Rugby Fives Assn. [IO], London, United Kingdom
Rugby Football League [IO], Leeds, United Kingdom
Rugby Football Union [IO], Twickenham, United
 Kingdom
Rugby Football Union; Midwest [★23706]
Rugby Union; Pacific Coast [★23706]
Rugby Union Players' Assn. [IO], Sydney, Australia
Rugby Union of the United States; Western
 [★23706]
Ruger Collectors Assn. - Address unknown since
 2001.
RUGMARK Found. [11523], 2001 S St. NW, Ste.
 430, Washington, DC 20009, (202)234-9050
RUGMARK Found. [IO], Washington, DC, United
 States
Rugs Soc; Armenian [9420]
Rule of Law Consortium - Defunct.
Ruminant Practitioners; Amer. Assn. of Small
 [16749]
Runaways
 Amer. Assn. for Lost Children [12607]
 Amer. Youth Work Center [13469]
 Children of the Night [12933]
 Girls and Boys Town [12934]
 Intl. Track and Field Coaches Assn. [23919]
 Natl. Network for Youth [12935]
 Natl. Runaway Switchboard [12936]
 Outpost for Hope [12610]
 Search Reports, Inc./Central Registry of the Miss-
 ing [12611]
 Team H.O.P.E (Help Offering Parents
 Empowerment) [12606]
 Youth Development Intl. [13520]
Runkle Family Assn. [21040], PO Box 14, Ringoes,
 NJ 08551
Runnemede; Baronial Order of [★10096]
Runners Assn; Fifty-Plus [★23920]
Runners Club of Am; Road [23923]

Runners Club; New York Road [23921]
Runners; North Amer. Network of Women [23656]
Running
 Achilles Track Club [23331]
 Amer. Running Assn. [23651]
 Natl. Intercollegiate Running Club Assn. [23707]
 North Amer. Network of Women Runners [23656]
 Ride and Tie Assn. [23849]
 Running USA [23708]
 U.S. Adventure Racing Assn. [23672]
 U.S. Running Streak Assn. [23709]
 U.S.A. Track and Field [23926]
Running Assn; Amer. [23651]
Running Strong for Amer. Indian Youth [★12623]
Running USA [23708], 638 Charleston Pl., Ventura,
 CA 93004, (805)659-0015
Runnymede Trust [IO], London, United Kingdom
Runyon Cancer Res. Found; Damon [13819]
Rural Advancement Found. Intl. - USA [4108], PO
 Box 640, Pittsboro, NC 27312, (919)542-1396
Rural Advancement Found. Intl. - USA [IO], Pitts-
 boro, NC, United States
Rural Advancement Fund Intl. [★IO]
Rural Advancement Fund Intl. [★4108]
Rural Affairs; Center for [16952]
Rural Aging; Natl. Coalition on [11307]
Rural and Agricultural Educ; Dept. of [★9069]
Rural Am., Inc. [★11772]
Rural Amer. Women - Defunct.
Rural Appraisers; Amer. Soc. of Farm Managers and
 [274]
Rural Arts and Crafts Assn. - Defunct.
Rural and Assoc. Contractors Fed. of New Zealand
 [IO], Lower Hutt, New Zealand
Rural Assn. of Paraguay [IO], Mariano Roque
 Alonso, Paraguay
Rural Centre For Human Interests [IO], Solan, India
Rural Coalition [18575], 1012 14th St. NW, Ste.
 1100, Washington, DC 20005, (202)628-7160
Rural Community Assistance Partnership [7841],
 1522 K St. NW, Ste. 400, Washington, DC 20005-
 1255, (202)408-1273
Rural Community Assistance Prog. [★7841]
Rural Crafts Assn. [IO], Godalming, United Kingdom
Rural Cultural Heritage Soc. [★19387]
Rural Culture Soc. [19387]
Rural Design and Building Assn. [★IO]
Rural Development
 Across [IO]
 African Rural and Agricultural Credit Assn. [IO]
 Afro-Asian Rural Development Org. [IO]
 Aga Khan Rural Support Programme - India [IO]
 Agriculture, Food and Human Values [4093]
 Amer. Comm. for KEEP [12418]
 Arkleton Trust [IO]
 Asian NGO Coalition for Agrarian Reform and
 Rural Development [IO]
 Asian Pacific Rural and Agricultural Credit Assn.
 [IO]
 Asian Rural Inst. [IO]
 Assn. for Intl. Agriculture and Rural Development
 [7935]
 Assn. of Rural Cooperation in Africa and Latin
 Am. - Nicaragua [IO]
 Assn. for Rural Development and Action Res. [IO]
 BAIF Development Res. Found. [IO]
 BRAC [IO]
 Caribbean Network for Integrated Rural Develop-
 ment - Trinidad and Tobago [IO]
 Centro Andino de Accion Popular [IO]
 Cooperazione Internazionale - Italia [IO]
 Countryside Alliance [IO]
 Cyriac Elias Voluntary Assn. [IO]
 Developing Countries Farm Radio Network [IO]
 Development Aid from People to People in
 Zimbabwe [IO]
 Development Promotion Gp. [IO]
 Farm Found. [4101]
 Fed. of Southern Cooperatives Land Assistance
 Fund [12937]
 Flemish Org. for Assistance in Development -
 Belgium [IO]
 Fondo Ecuatoriano Populorum Progressio [IO]
 Fundacion SARTAWI [IO]
 Global Outreach Mission [12525]

 Greener Pastures Inst. [12312]
 Hector Kobbekaduwa Agrarian Res. and Training
 Inst. [IO]
 Human Environmental League for Preservation -
 Nepal [IO]
 INADES Formation Intl. - Kenya [IO]
 India Development Ser. [IO]
 India Development Ser. [18572]
 Inter-American Found. [18573]
 Inter-American Found. [IO]
 Interlink Rural Info. Ser. [IO]
 Intl. Catholic Rural Assn. [IO]
 Intl. Centre for Integrated Mountain Development
 [IO]
 Intl. Development Enterprises - India [IO]
 Intl. Inst. of Rural Reconstruction, U.S. Chap. [IO]
 Intl. Inst. of Rural Reconstruction, U.S. Chap.
 [12938]
 Intl. Rural Sociology Assn. [7664]
 Kasturba Inst. of Rural Stud. [IO]
 Lutheran World Ser. - India [IO]
 Maulik Chahida Karmashuchi [IO]
 Mysore Resettlement and Development Agency
 [IO]
 Natl. Assn. of Development Organizations Res.
 Found. [17226]
 Natl. Assn. of Rural Hea. Clinics [16245]
 Natl. Rural Economic Developers Assn. [18574]
 Natl. Rural Educ. Advocacy Coalition [9068]
 Natl. Rural Educ. Assn. [9069]
 Natl. Rural Recruitment and Retention Network
 [14710]
 Natl. Rural Water Assn. [12939]
 Neighborhood Funders Gp. [12734]
 Nigerian Integrated Rural Accelerated Develop-
 ment Org. [IO]
 NSW Dept. of Primary Indus. Rural Women's
 Network [IO]
 Partners in Community Development Fiji [IO]
 People's Multipurpose Development Soc. [IO]
 Philippine Partnership for the Development of Hu-
 man Resources in Rural Areas [IO]
 Population and Community Development Assn.
 [IO]
 Rangpur Dinajpur Rural Ser. Bangladesh [IO]
 REAP Intl. [IO]
 REAP Intl. [12940]
 Rural Centre For Human Interests [IO]
 Rural Coalition [18575]
 Rural Planning Organizations of Am. [6247]
 Rural Reconstruction Nepal [IO]
 Rural Restoration Adopt [4658]
 Rural School and Community Trust (Rural Trust)
 [9067]
 Rural Sociological Soc. [7667]
 Rurality - Env. - Development [IO]
 Scottish Women's Rural Institutes [IO]
 South-West Univ. for Nationalities [IO]
 Southern Mutual Help Assn. [11790]
 Sulabh Intl. Social Ser. Org. [IO]
 Tokushima Intl. Cooperation [IO]
 Tools for Self Reliance [IO]
 UN Sys. Network on Rural Development and
 Food Security [IO]
 Union of the Swiss Country-Women [IO]
 Windustry [7853]
 Winrock Intl. [16959]
 World Sustainable Agriculture Assn. [12941]
 World Sustainable Agriculture Assn. [IO]
 Xavier Inst. of Development Action and Stud. [IO]
 Youth for Unity and Voluntary Action [IO]
Rural Development Off; Intl. [★17832]
Rural Doctors Assn. of Australia [IO], Kingston,
 Australia
Rural Doctors Assn. of Southern Africa [IO], Con-
 gella, Republic of South Africa
Rural Education
 Books for the Barrios [12049]
 Natl. Catholic Rural Life Conf. [19677]
 Natl. Rural Educ. Advocacy Coalition [9068]
 Natl. Rural Educ. Assn. [9069]
 Soc. for the Provision of Educ. in Rural Australia
 [IO]
Rural Educ. Assn. [★9069]
Rural Educ. Assn. [★9069]

A star before a book entry number signifies that the name is not listed separately, but is mentioned within the entry.

Rural Educ; Dept. of [★9069]
Rural Electrification; Action Comm. for [1177]
Rural Fellows; Natl. [★18775]
Rural Fellows; Natl. Urban/ [★18775]
Rural Governments Coalition - Defunct.
Rural Hea. Assn; Amer. [★16248]
Rural Hea. Assn; Natl. [16248]
Rural Hea. Care Assn; Natl. [★16248]
Rural Hea. Clinics; Natl. Assn. of [16245]
Rural Hosp. Assn; Amer. Small and [★16248]
Rural Housing Alliance [★11772]
Rural Housing Coalition; Natl. [12332]
Rural Housing; Coun. for Affordable and [12310]
Rural Housing and Development; Coun. for
   [★12310]
Rural and Indus. Design and Building Assn. [IO],
   Stowmarket, United Kingdom
Rural Innovation Network, India [IO], Chennai, India
Rural Inst. [11986], Univ. of Montana Rural Inst., 52
   Corbin Hall, Missoula, MT 59812, (406)243-5467
Rural Land Alliance - Defunct.
Rural Letter Carriers' Assn; Natl. [24172]
Rural Life Conf; Natl. Catholic [19677]
Rural Loans Program - Defunct.
Rural Mental Hea; Natl. Assn. for [15217]
Rural Ministry Education Inst. - Address unknown
   since 1995.
Rural Overseas Prog; Christian [★12842]
Rural Planning Organizations of Am. [6247], c/o
   Natl. Assn. of Development Organizations, 400 N
   Capitol St. NW, Ste. 390, Washington, DC 20001,
   (202)624-7806
Rural Practice Project - Defunct.
Rural Reconstruction Nepal [IO], Kathmandu, Nepal
Rural Recruitment and Retention Network; Natl.
   [14710]
Rural/Regional Educational Assn. [★9069]
Rural Resettlement Ireland (USA) - Address
   unknown since 2000.
Rural Restoration Adopt [4658], PO Box B,
   Sikeston, MO 63801, (573)471-7966
Rural School and Community Trust (Rural Trust)
   [9067], 1530 Wilson Blvd., Ste. 240, Arlington, VA
   22209, (703)243-1487
Rural Sect. of the Amer. Sociological Soc. [★7667]
Rural Sociological Soc. [7667], Univ. of Missouri,
   104 Gentry Hall, Columbia, MO 65211-7040,
   (573)882-9065
Rural Sociologists; International Register of [★7664]
Rural Sociologists; International Register of [★IO]
Rural Southern Voice for Peace - Address unknown
   since 2001.
Rural Special Educ; Amer. Coun. on [9137]
Rural Theology Assn. [IO], East Yorkshire, United
   Kingdom
Rural Training and Res. Center; FSC [★12937]
Rural Utilities Cooperative Finance Corp; Natl.
   [1441]
Rural Voters Educ. Proj; League of [★16955]
Rural Women Hea. Assn. [★IO]
Rural Women New Zealand [IO], Wellington, New
   Zealand
Rural Youth
   4-H Ontario [IO]
   4H [IO]
   Brecknock Fed. of Young Farmers Clubs [IO]
   Canadian 4-H Coun. [IO]
   C.FF.I. Ceredigion Y.F.C. [IO]
   Danish Young Farmers [IO]
   European Fed. of City Farms [IO]
   Finnish 4H Fed. [IO]
   Foroige, Natl. Youth Development Org. [IO]
   German Fed. of Rural Youth [IO]
   Holstein Junior Prog. [4264]
   Manitoba 4-H [IO]
   Natl. Fed. of Young Farmers' Clubs [IO]
   Natl. Rural Educ. Advocacy Coalition [9068]
   Osterreichische Landjugend [IO]
   Plattelands Jongeren Nederland [IO]
   Prince Edward Island 4-H [IO]
   Rural Youth Europe [IO]
   Saskatchewan 4-H Coun. [IO]
   Scottish Assn. of Young Farmers' Clubs [IO]
   Swedish 4H Assn. [IO]
   Wales Young Farmers' Clubs [IO]

Wales Young Farmers' Clubs - Carmarthenshire
   Fed. [IO]
Wales Young Farmers' Clubs - Clwyd Fed. [IO]
Wales Young Farmers' Clubs - Eryri Fed. [IO]
Wales Young Farmers' Clubs - Glamorgan Fed.
   [IO]
Wales Young Farmers' Clubs - Gwent Fed. [IO]
Wales Young Farmers' Clubs - Meirionnydd Fed.
   [IO]
Wales Young Farmers' Clubs - Montgomery Fed.
   [IO]
Wales Young Farmers' Clubs - Pembrokeshire
   Fed. [IO]
Wales Young Farmers' Clubs - Radnor Fed. [IO]
Wales Young Farmers' Clubs - Ynys Mon Fed.
   [IO]
Rural Youth Corps - Defunct.
Rural Youth Europe [IO], Helsinki, Finland
Rural Youth of the U.S.A. Conf. - Address unknown
   since 1995.
Ruralite - Environnement - Developpement [★IO]
Rurality - Env. - Development [IO], Attert, Belgium
RuralScotland [IO], Edinburgh, United Kingdom
Ruritan Natl. [13062], PO Box 487, Dublin, VA
   24084, (540)674-5431
Ruritan Natl. Foundation [★13062]
Rushlight Club [10396], c/o Mrs. Jane Rausch, Cor-
   responding Sec., 20132 Metzger Dr., Rockwood,
   MI 48173, (734)379-3119
Rushmore Natl. Memorial Soc; Mount [10046]
Rushmore Soc; Mount [★10046]
Russell Sage Found. [7653], 112 E 64th St., New
   York, NY 10021, (212)750-6000
Russell Soc; Bertrand [9637]
Russell Surname Org. - Address unknown since
   2006.
Russell Todd Fan Club - Defunct.
Russell's Owl Collectors Club - Address unknown
   since 2003.
Russia; North Dakota Historical Soc. of Germans
   from [★19078]
Russia, Ukraine, the Baltic States and Eurasia;
   NCSJ: Advocates on Behalf of Jews in [17448]
Russian
   Amer. Assn. for the Advancement of Slavic Stud.
      [10966]
   Amer. Bus. Assn. of Russian Professionals [3181]
   Amer. Comm. for Peace in Chechnya [18189]
   American-Russian Chamber of Commerce and
      Indus. [24261]
   Amer. Russian Theatrical Alliance [11001]
   Amer. Univ. in Moscow [8597]
   Assn. of Russian-American Scholars in the U.S.A.
      [10941]
   Baidarka Historical Soc. [9954]
   Black Russian Terrier Club of Am. [22232]
   Cong. of Russian Americans [19337]
   High School Evangelism Fellowship [20013]
   Intl. Assn. of Teachers of Russian Language and
      Literature [IO]
   Intl. Borzoi Coun. [22287]
   Intl. Comm. for the Children of Chechnya [11605]
   Intl. Comm. for the Rescue of KAL 007 Survivors
      [18541]
   Intl. Found. for Terror Act Victims [12942]
   Intl. Found. for Terror Act Victims [IO]
   Lemko Assn. of U.S. and Canada [19338]
   Natl. Coun. for Eurasian and East European Res.
      [10968]
   Orthodox Soc. of Am. [19339]
   Rossica Soc. of Russian Philately [22862]
   The Russian-American Center/Track Two Inst. for
      Citizen Diplomacy [17912]
   Russian-American Chamber of Commerce
      [24294]
   Russian-American Chamber of Commerce in the
      USA [24371]
   Russian-American Chamber of Commerce in the
      USA [IO]
   Russian Amer. Jews for Israel [18576]
   Russian Amer. Medical Assn. [16378]
   Russian Amer. Medical Assn. [IO]
   Russian Brotherhood Org. of the U.S.A. [19340]
   Russian Children's Welfare Soc. [11650]
   Russian Orthodox Catholic Mutual Aid Soc. of
      U.S.A. [19341]

Russian Zone Handoverprint Stud. and Res. Gp.
   [22864]
Tolstoy Found. [19342]
Russian Acad. of Entrepreneurship [IO], Moscow,
   Russia
Russian Acad. of Sciences [IO], Moscow, Russia
Russian Advertisers Assn. [IO], Moscow, Russia
The Russian-American Center [★IO]
Russian-American Center; The [★17912]
The Russian-American Center [★17912]
The Russian-American Center/Track Two Inst. for
   Citizen Diplomacy [17912], 2670 Leavenworth,
   San Francisco, CA 94133, (415)563-4731
The Russian-American Center/Track Two Institute for
   Citizen Diplomacy [IO], San Francisco, CA, United
   States
Russian-American Chamber of Commerce [24294],
   1552 Pennsylvania St., Denver, CO 80203,
   (303)831-0829
Russian-American Chamber of Commerce in the
   USA [24371], 970 Sidney Marcus Blvd., Ste. 1504,
   Atlanta, GA 30324, (404)667-9319
Russian-American Chamber of Commerce in the
   USA [IO], Atlanta, GA, United States
Russian/American Coun. for Collaboration and
   Language Stud; Amer. Coun. of Teachers of
   [★8226]
Russian Amer. Jews for Israel [18576]
Russian Amer. Medical Assn. [16378], 36100 Euclid
   Ave., Ste. 330-B, Willoughby, OH 44094, (440)953-
   8055
Russian Amer. Medical Assn. [IO], Willoughby, OH,
   United States
Russian Assn. of Bidders and Cost Engg. [IO],
   Moscow, Russia
Russian Assn. of Bus. Educ. [IO], Moscow, Russia
Russian Assn. for Continuing Engg. Educ. [IO],
   Moscow, Russia
Russian Assn. of Engineers for Heating, Ventilation,
   Air-Conditioning, Heat Supply and Building
   Thermal Physics [IO], Moscow, Russia
Russian Assn. of Indigenous Peoples of the North,
   Siberia and Far East [IO], Moscow, Russia
Russian Assn. of Marine and River Bunker Suppliers
   [IO], St. Petersburg, Russia
Russian Assn. of Networks and Services [IO],
   Moscow, Russia
Russian Assn. of Occupational Therapists [IO], St.
   Petersburg, Russia
Russian Assn. of Orthodontists [IO], Moscow, Rus-
   sia
Russian Assn. on Osteoporosis [IO], Moscow, Rus-
   sia
Russian Assn. of Travel Agencies [★IO]
Russian Assn. of Wind Indus. [IO], St. Petersburg,
   Russia
Russian Authors' Soc. [IO], Moscow, Russia
Russian Badminton Fed. [IO], Moscow, Russia
Russian Bird Conservation Union [IO], Moscow,
   Russia
Russian Brotherhood Org. of the U.S.A. [19340],
   1733 Spring Garden St., Philadelphia, PA 19130,
   (215)563-2537
Russian Bus. Travel Assn. [IO], Moscow, Russia
Russian Children's Welfare Soc. [IO], New York, NY,
   United States
Russian Children's Welfare Soc. [11650], 200 Park
   Ave. S, Ste. 1617, New York, NY 10003, (212)473-
   6263
Russian Corps Combatants - Address unknown
   since 1995.
Russian Coun. of Shopping Centers [IO], Moscow,
   Russia
Russian Cycle Touring Club [IO], Moscow, Russia
Russian and East European Jewry; Center for
   [17946]
Russian Family Planning Assn. [IO], Moscow, Rus-
   sia
Russian Fed. Assn. for Pattern Recognition and Im-
   age Anal. [IO], Moscow, Russia
Russian Flying Disc Fed. [IO], St. Petersburg, Rus-
   sia
Russian Gestosis Assn. [IO], Moscow, Russia
Russian Historical and Genealogical Soc. in Am.
   [★21147]

Reference to "IO" in place of a book number signifies that the association may be found in the 45th edition of International Organizations.

Russian Immigrants' Representatives Assn. in America - Address unknown since 1995.
Russian Independent Mutual Aid Soc. - Defunct.
Russian League Against Epilepsy [IO], Moscow, Russia
Russian Lib. Assn. [IO], St. Petersburg, Russia
Russian Marketing Assn. [IO], Moscow, Russia
Russian Medical Soc. [IO], Moscow, Russia
Russian Natl. Billiard Fed. [IO], St. Petersburg, Russia
Russian Nobility Assn. in Am. [21147], 971 1st Ave., New York, NY 10022, (212)755-7528
Russian Numismatic Soc. [22755], PO Box 3684, Santa Rosa, CA 95402-3684, (707)527-1007
Russian Orthodox
   Fellowship of Orthodox Christians in Am. [20542]
Russian Orthodox Catholic Mutual Aid Soc. of U.S.A. [19341], 10 Downs Dr., Wilkes-Barre, PA 18705-3802, (570)822-8591
Russian Orthodox Catholic Women's Mutual Aid Soc. - Defunct.
Russian Orthodox Clubs; Federated [★20542]
Russian Orthodox Fraternity Lubov - Defunct.
Russian Orthodox Theological Fund - Address unknown since 1999.
Russian People's Center - Address unknown since 1995.
Russian Physiological Soc. [IO], Moscow, Russia
Russian Rightholders' Soc. for Collective Mgt. of Reprographic Reproduction Rights [IO], Moscow, Russia
Russian Sci. Soc. of Pharmacology [IO], Moscow, Russia
Russian Skating Union [IO], Moscow, Russia
Russian Soc. of Aesthetic Medicine [IO], Moscow, Russia
Russian Soc. for Digestive Endoscopy [IO], Moscow, Russia
Russian Soc. for Electron Microscopy [IO], Moscow, Russia
Russian Soc. of Hypertension [IO], Moscow, Russia
Russian Soc. of Nematologists [IO], Petrozavodsk, Russia
Russian Soc. of Scanning Probe Microscopy and Nanotechnology [IO], Moscow, Russia
Russian Soc. of Sociologists [IO], Moscow, Russia
Russian Software Developers Assn. [IO], St. Petersburg, Russia
Russian Squash Fed. [IO], Moscow, Russia
Russian Student Fund - Defunct.
Russian Taekwondo Union [IO], Moscow, Russia
Russian Terriers; Amer. Assn. of Black [22185]
Russian Union of Exhibitions and Fairs [IO], Nizhny Novgorod, Russia
Russian Union of Travel Indus. [IO], St. Petersburg, Russia
Russian Venture Capital Assn. [IO], St. Petersburg, Russia
Russian Wolfhound Club of Am. [★22235]
Russian Zone Handoverprint Stud. and Res. Gp. [22864]
Russo-British Chamber of Commerce [IO], London, United Kingdom
Rustic Resources [★19387]
Rustie Blue Intl. Fan Club [24972], PO Box 582, Lancaster, OH 43130
Rusty Wallace Fan Club - Defunct.
Rutan
   Central States Assn. [21434]
Rutenberg and Everett Yiddish Film Lib. [★9943]
Ruth Baseball/Softball; Babe [23106]
Ruth Birthplace Found; Babe [★23107]
Ruth Birthplace/Sports Legends at Camden Yards; Babe [23107]
Ruth; House of [12029]
Ruth Jackson Orthopaedic Soc. [15781], 6300 N River Rd., Ste. 727, Rosemont, IL 60018-4226, (847)698-1626
Rutherford B. Hayes Lib. and Museum [★11148]
Rutherford B. Hayes Presidential Center [11148], Spiegel Grove, Fremont, OH 43420-2796, (419)332-2081
Rutherford Inst. [18513], PO Box 7482, Charlottesville, VA 22906-7482, (434)978-3888
Ruthven Assembly; Lord [★10426]

RV Aftermarket Assn; WDA: The [★3982]
RV, Boat and Travel Club; Vagabundos Del Mar [22966]
RV Mfrs'. Clubs Assn. [22961], 413 Walnut St., Green Cove Springs, FL 32043-3443, (904)529-6575
RV Owners Club; Natl. [★22960]
RV Parks and Campgrounds; Natl. Assn. of [3357]
RVing Women [22962], PO Box 1940, Apache Junction, AZ 85217-1940, (480)671-6226
RX-7 Club of America - Address unknown since 1995.
Rx&D [★IO]
Ryan White Natl. Teen Educ. Prog. [★13560]
Ryan's Reach [16550], 2953 Edinger Ave., Tustin, CA 92780, (949)733-0046
Rybarske Sdruzeni Ceske Republiky [★IO]
Ryegrass Growers Assn; Manhattan [4795]
Ryegrass Growers Seed Commn; Oregon [4798]
Ryukyu Philatelic Specialist Soc. [22865], c/o Laura Edmonds, Sec., PO Box 240177, Charlotte, NC 28224-0177
Ryukyu Philatelic Specialist Soc. [IO], Clayton, CA, United States
Ryukyu Specialty Club of New York - Defunct.

S

S. Allan Taylor Soc. - Address unknown since 2001.
S2000 Club of Am. [21777], 7808 Hardwick Ct., Plano, TX 75025, (972)527-8169
Saab Club; Chicago [★21778]
Saab Club of North Am. [21778], 30 Puritan Dr., Port Chester, NY 10573
Saab Clubs of Am. [★21778]
Saab Clubs of North Am. [★21778]
Saanen Breeders Assn; Natl. [4143]
Saanen Club; Natl. [★4143]
Saathi [IO], Bombay, India
Sabah Family Planning Assn. [IO], Sabah, Malaysia
Sabbath
   Assn. of State Baptist Papers [19475]
   Bible Sabbath Assn. [20543]
   Lord's Day Alliance of the U.S. [20544]
   Seventh Day Baptist Gen. Conf. [19494]
   Seventh Day Baptist Gen. Conf. of the U.S. and Canada [20545]
   Seventh Day Baptist Historical Soc. [19495]
   Seventh Day Baptist World Fed. [19497]
   Southern Baptist Found. [19498]
   Woman's Missionary Union, SBC [19501]
   Women Nationally Active for Christ [19502]
Sabbath Assn; Bible [20543]
Sabbath Tract and Commun. Coun; Amer. [★20545]
Sabbath Tract Soc; Amer. [★20545]
Sabin Assn. - Address unknown since 2004.
Sabot Assn; Intl. Naples [23190]
Sabot One—Design Assn; Naples [23190]
Sabra Automobile Connection [21779]
Sabra Connection [★21779]
Sabre Found. [17847], 872 Massachusetts Ave., Ste. 2-1, Cambridge, MA 02139, (617)868-3510
Sabre Found. [IO], Cambridge, MA, United States
Sabres Booster Club; Buffalo [25000]
Sabun ve Deterjan Sanayicileri Dernegi [★IO]
Sack Manufacturers' Assn; Paper Shipping [991]
Sackville Rivers Assn. [IO], Lower Sackville, NS, Canada
Sacrament; Confraternity of the Blessed [19951]
Sacrament; Congregation of the Blessed [19617]
Sacred Cat of Burma Fanciers [21916], c/o Jane Bridenstein, Sec., 945 Peachcrest Ct. NE, Grand Rapids, MI 49505-6434, (616)459-5269
Sacred Dance Guild [9897], PO Box 1046, Laurel, MD 20725-1046, (877)422-8678
Sacred Dance Guild [IO], Laurel, MD, United States
Sacred Dance Soc. [19878], PO Box 323, Middletown, CA 95461, (415)971-3573
Sacred Doctrine; Soc. of Catholic Coll. Teachers of [★9273]
Sacred Dying Found. [11910], PO Box 210328, San Francisco, CA 94121, (415)585-9455
Sacred Earth Network [4605], 93A Glasheen Rd., Petersham, MA 01366, (978)724-0120
Sacred Earth Network [IO], Petersham, MA, United States

Sacred Heart Auto League [★19711]
Sacred Heart League [19711], PO Box 300, Walls, MS 38680-0300, (601)781-1360
Sacred Heart; League of Tarcisians of the [★19651]
Sacred Heart; Men of the [19659]
Sacred Heart Southern Missions [★19711]
Sacred Journey [★19894]
Sacred Journey [★IO]
Sacred Liturgy; ADOREMUS - Soc. for the Renewal of the [19561]
Sacred Liturgy; Soc. for the Renewal of the [★19561]
Sacred Passage, NatureQuest [★12362]
Sacred Passage, NatureQuest [★IO]
Sacred Passage and the Way of Nature Fellowship [IO], Tucson, AZ, United States
Sacred Passage and the Way of Nature Fellowship [12362], PO Box 3388, Tucson, AZ 85722-3388, (877)818-1881
Sacred Places; Partners for [20505]
Sacred Space Inst. [13101], PO Box 4322, San Rafael, CA 94913, (415)507-1739
Sacro Occipital Res. Soc. [★14013]
Sacro Occipital Res. Soc. [★IO]
Sacro Occipital Res. Soc. Intl. [IO], Overland Park, KS, United States
Sacro Occipital Res. Soc. Intl. [14013], PO Box 24361, Overland Park, KS 66283, (888)245-1011
Sadat Peace Found. - Defunct.
SADC Plant Genetic Resources Centre [IO], Lusaka, Zambia
Saddle Clubs Assn; Western [4971]
Saddle, Harness and Allied Trades Assn. [2419], c/o Proleptic, Inc., PO Box 818, Harrisonburg, VA 22803, (540)434-9845
Saddle Horse Assn; Natl. Spotted [4927]
Saddle Horse Breeders Assn; Amer. [★4842]
Saddle Horse Breeders' and Exhibitors' Assn; Spotted [4955]
Saddlebred Horse Assn; Amer. [4842]
Saddlebred Pleasure Horse Assn; Amer. [★4842]
Saddlebred Pleasure Horse Assn; Intl. Amer. [★4842]
Saddlebred Registry of Am; Half [4889]
Saddlebred Sporthorse Assn; Amer. [4843]
Saddlery Hardware Mfrs. Inst. - Defunct.
SADSA [★11026]
SAE Intl. - Soc. of Automotive Engineers [6520], 400 Commonwealth Dr., Warrendale, PA 15096-0001, (724)776-4841
SAE International - Society of Automotive Engineers [IO], Warrendale, PA, United States
SAE Ser. Tech. Prog. Off. [3719], c/o Soc. of Automotive Engineers, 400 Commonwealth Dr., Warrendale, PA 15096-0001, (724)776-4841
SAF - The Center for Commercial Floriculture [★1493]
Safari Club Intl. [5377], 4800 W Gates Pass Rd., Tucson, AZ 85745-9490, (520)620-1220
Safari Club Intl. [IO], Tucson, AZ, United States
Safaris
   Assn. for the Promotion of Tourism to Africa [3826]
   Natl. Hunters Assn. [23547]
   North Amer. Hunting Club [23548]
S.A.F.E. Alternatives [12557], c/o Linden Oaks Hosp., 852 S West St., Naperville, IL 60540, (630)305-5500
SAFE Assn. [6383], PO Box 130, Creswell, OR 97426-0130, (541)895-3012
Safe Boating Comm; Natl. [★12977]
Safe Boating Week Comm; Natl. [★12977]
Safe Car Educational Inst. - Address unknown since 1995.
Safe Deposit Advisory Coun; Natl. [★460]
Safe Deposit Assn; The Amer. [460]
Safe Energy Communication Coun. - Defunct.
Safe Harbour Animal Refuge [11454], PO Box 275, London, TX 76854-0275
Safe Harbour Pig Refuge [★11454]
Safe Israel; Americans for a [18052]
Safe Kids Campaign; Natl. [★11651]
Safe Kids Canada [IO], Toronto, ON, Canada
Safe Kids Worldwide [11651], 1301 Pennsylvania Ave. NW, Ste. 1000, Washington, DC 20004-1707, (202)662-0600

A star before a book entry number signifies that the name is not listed separately, but is mentioned within the entry.

Safe Mfrs. Natl. Assn. - Defunct.
Safe Return Amnesty Comm. - Defunct.
Safe Riders Found; Amer. Medical Equestrian Association/ [16474]
Safe Schools; Natl. Alliance for [9085]
SAFE - Self Abuse Finally Ends [★12557]
Safe Sitter [11537], 8604 Allisonville Rd., Ste. 248, Indianapolis, IN 46250-1597, (317)596-5001
Safe Skies Alliance; Natl. [18748]
Safe Transit Assn; National/International [★3571]
Safe Trans. of Hazardous Articles; Conf. on [3562]
Safe Trans. of Hazardous Articles; Coun. on the [★3562]
Safe and Vault Technicians Assn. [3541], 3500 Easy St., Dallas, TX 75247, (214)819-9771
Safe Water Coalition - Defunct.
Safe Winter Driving League - Defunct.
Safely in Mothers Arms [★13011]
Safer Athletic Field Environments; Found. for [23064]
Safer Soc. Found. [11891], PO Box 340, Brandon, VT 05733-0340, (802)247-3132
Safer Soc. Prog. and Press [★11891]
SaferAfrica [IO], Pretoria, Republic of South Africa
SafeSpaces.com; Natl. Safe Workplace Institute/ [12978]
Safety
  AAA Found. for Traffic Safety [12943]
  Advocates for Highway and Auto Safety [12944]
  Aerobics and Fitness Assn. of Am. [15956]
  Aircraft Recovery Assn. [12945]
  Airport Consultants Coun. [951]
  Alliance for Healthy Homes [13320]
  Amer. Acad. of Clinical Toxicology [16657]
  Amer. Assn. of Cheerleading Coaches and Advisors [23061]
  Amer. Assn. of Food Hygiene Veterinarians [16745]
  Amer. Assn. for Horsemanship Safety [12946]
  Amer. Assn. of Pesticide Safety Educators [4627]
  Amer. Assn. of Poison Control Centers [16658]
  Amer. Assn. of Safety Councils [12947]
  Amer. Assn. of Safety Councils [IO]
  Amer. Avalanche Assn. [12948]
  Amer. Biological Safety Assn. [3436]
  Amer. Bonanza Soc. [21427]
  Amer. Canyoneering Assn. [21949]
  Amer. Coll. of Medical Toxicology [16660]
  Amer. Fire Sprinkler Assn. [3437]
  Amer. Highway Users Alliance [12949]
  Amer. Horseman Alliance [1924]
  Amer. Industrial Health Coun. [15626]
  Amer. Maritime Safety, Inc. [2570]
  Amer. Riding Instructors Assn. [22583]
  Amer. Safe Climbing Assn. [21950]
  Amer. Soc. for Amusement Park Safety and Security [3526]
  Amer. Soc. of Safety Engineers [7586]
  Amer. Traffic Safety Services Assn. [3438]
  Americans for Trans. Mobility [6315]
  Anesthesia Patient Safety Found. [13679]
  Arts, Crafts and Theatre Safety [12950]
  Assn. for the Advancement of Automotive Medicine [12951]
  Assn. for Challenge Course Tech. [2869]
  Assn. of Indus. Road Safety Officers [IO]
  Assn. of Needle-Free Injection Mfrs. [2549]
  Assn. of Public-Safety Communications Officials - Intl. [6248]
  Association of Public-Safety Communications Officials - International [IO]
  Assn. of Road Users of Pakistan [IO]
  Assn. of State Dam Safety Officials [6249]
  Assn. of Swedish Municipalities with Nuclear Reactors [IO]
  ATV Safety Institute/Division of Specialty Vehicle Inst. of Am. [12952]
  Automatic Fire Alarm Assn. [3439]
  Aviation Safety Inst. [12953]
  Basic Acrylic Monomer Mfrs. [800]
  Beyond Pesticides - Natl. Coalition Against the Misuse of Pesticides [13322]
  Bicycle Helmet Safety Inst. [12954]
  Bird Strike Comm. USA [5299]
  Black Lung Assn. [13323]

  Blue Knights Intl. Law Enforcement Motorcycle Club [22669]
  BMW Motorcycle Owners of Am. [22670]
  BMW Riders Assn. Intl. [22671]
  Bd. of Canadian Registered Safety Professionals [IO]
  Bd. of Certified Hazard Control Mgt. [3440]
  Bd. of Certified Prdt. Safety Mgt. [3441]
  Bd. of Certified Safety Professionals [7587]
  Boaters Against Drunk Driving [12955]
  British Safety Coun. [IO]
  Campaign to Label Genetically Engineered Foods [17604]
  Campus Safety, Hea. and Environmental Mgt. Assn. [4300]
  Canada Safety Coun. [IO]
  Canadian Assn. of Road Safety Professionals [IO]
  Canadian Automatic Sprinkler Assn. [IO]
  Canadian Avalanche Assn. [IO]
  Canadian Soc. of Safety Engg. [IO]
  Center for Auto Safety [12956]
  Center for Chem. Process Safety [801]
  Center for Farm Hea. and Safety [12188]
  Center for Food Safety [4675]
  Central Sta. Alarm Assn. [3442]
  CHA - Certified Horsemanship Assn. [23523]
  Cherokee Pilots' Assn. [21437]
  Choice in Personal Safety [IO]
  Christian Motorcyclists Assn. [22674]
  Christian Road Safety Assn. [IO]
  Citizens Against Drug Impaired Drivers [13230]
  Citizens Aviation Watch Assn. [11509]
  Citizens for Reliable and Safe Highways [18577]
  Citizens for Roadside Safety [12957]
  Coalition Against Bigger Trucks [13337]
  Coalition for Auto Glass Safety and Public Awareness [1727]
  Coalition for Environmentally Safe Communities [12118]
  Coalition for Fire-Safe Cigarettes [12191]
  Common Ground Alliance [12958]
  Confed. of Inspection and Certification Organisations [IO]
  CyberAngels [12452]
  DanceSafe [12041]
  Danny Found. [12959]
  The Dawkins Project [11690]
  Deutsches Motorrad Register [22677]
  Divers Alert Network [23378]
  driveAWARE [12960]
  ECRI [15136]
  Elevator Escalator Safety Found. [1232]
  Elevator Escalator Safety Found. of Canada [IO]
  Environmental Info. Assn. [620]
  European Assn. for Stud. of Safety Problems in Production and Use of Propellants [IO]
  Exercise Safety Assn. [15963]
  F-4 Phantom II Soc. [21445]
  Farm Safety 4 Just Kids [12961]
  Fed. Alliance For Safe Homes [12061]
  Fire Dept. Safety Officers Assn. [6250]
  Fire Equip. Mfrs'. Assn. [3443]
  Fire Suppression Systems Assn. [3444]
  Flight Safety Found. [148]
  Forest Products Safety Conf. [12962]
  Found. for Aquatic Injury Prevention [12963]
  Found. for Safer Athletic Field Environments [23064]
  Global Environmental Mgt. Initiative [4628]
  Governors Highway Safety Assn. [6317]
  Guild of Experienced Motorists [IO]
  Handgun Safety and Educ. Coun. [17684]
  Harley Hummer Club [22679]
  Harvard Injury Control Res. Center [16690]
  Healing Waters Intl. [13410]
  Hearth Educ. Found. [1880]
  Honda Sport Touring Assn. [22681]
  Horn and Whistle Enthusiasts Gp. [22037]
  Horsemanship Safety Assn. [23525]
  Indian Motor-Cycle Club of America [22682]
  Inst. of Road Safety Officers [IO]
  Institution of Occupational Safety and Hea. [IO]
  Insurance Inst. for Highway Safety [12964]
  Inter-Amer. Safety Coun. [12965]
  Intl. Assn. for Bridge Maintenance and Safety [538]

  Intl. Assn. of Directors of Law Enforcement Standards and Training [5973]
  Intl. Assn. of Dive Rescue Specialists [23574]
  Intl. Assn. for Healthcare Security and Safety [14887]
  Intl. Assn. of Investigative Locksmiths [3528]
  Intl. Assn. for Medicinal Compliance [15041]
  Intl. Assn. of Natural Rsrc. Pilots [4187]
  Intl. Assn. of Nitrox and Tech. Divers [23379]
  Intl. Assn. of Traffic and Safety Sciences [IO]
  Intl. Campaign to Ban Landmines [17431]
  Intl. Fed. of Competitive Eating [23822]
  Intl. Gravity Sports Assn. [23823]
  Intl. Healthcare Safety Professional Certification Bd. [16379]
  Intl. Healthcare Safety Professional Certification Bd. [IO]
  Intl. Hunter Educ. Assn. [23545]
  Intl. Inst. of Risk and Safety Mgt. [IO]
  Intl. Motor Vehicle Inspection Comm. [IO]
  Intl. Municipal Signal Assn. [IO]
  Intl. Municipal Signal Assn. [6251]
  Intl. Norton Owners' Assn. [22684]
  Intl. Play Equip. Manufacturers Assn. [3060]
  Intl. Playground Contractors Assn. [1028]
  Intl. Road Safety Org. [IO]
  Intl. Safety Equip. Assn. [IO]
  Intl. Safety Equip. Assn. [3445]
  Intl. Security, Trust and Privacy Alliance [3535]
  Intl. Sharps Injury Prevention Soc. [16380]
  Intl. Sharps Injury Prevention Soc. [IO]
  Intl. Soc. of Air Safety Investigators [IO]
  Intl. Soc. of Air Safety Investigators [12966]
  Intl. Soc. of Mine Safety Professionals [15270]
  Intl. Soc. of Regulatory Toxicology and Pharmacology [14570]
  ISSA Sect. on the Prevention of Occupational Risks Due to Electricity-Gas-Long-Distance Heating-Water [IO]
  Japan Indus. Safety and Hea. Assn. [IO]
  Joint Commn. on Sports Medicine and Sci. [16483]
  Kidpower Teenpower Fullpower Intl. [12967]
  Kidpower Teenpower Fullpower Intl. [IO]
  Kids In Danger [11612]
  Knights of Life Motorcycle Club [12968]
  Law Enforcement and Emergency Services Video Assn. [6350]
  Lightning Protection Inst. [3446]
  Limousine Indus. Mfrs. Org. [391]
  Local Authority Road Safety Officers' Assn. [IO]
  Marine Stewardship Coun. [5171]
  Missile Defense Advocacy Alliance [17382]
  Mothers Against Drunk Driving [12969]
  Mothers Against Drunk Driving - Canada [IO]
  Mothers Arms [13011]
  Motorcycle Safety Found. [3447]
  Motorist Info. and Services Assn. [13344]
  Natl. Alliance for Food Safety and Security [1537]
  Natl. Alliance for the Primary Prevention of Sharps Injuries [16381]
  Natl. Antique Tractor Pullers Assn. [23004]
  Natl. Assn. of Air Traffic Specialists [24014]
  Natl. Assn. Citizens on Patrol [12970]
  Natl. Assn. of Field Training Officers [5987]
  Natl. Assn. of Fire Equip. Distributors [3448]
  Natl. Assn. of Flight Instructors [161]
  Natl. Assn. of Professional Accident Reconstructionists [6252]
  Natl. Assn. of State Motorcycle Safety Administrators [6253]
  Natl. Assn. of Vertical Trans. Professionals [2048]
  Natl. Assn. of Women Highway Safety Leaders [12971]
  Natl. Boating Safety Advisory Coun. [5546]
  Natl. Center for Food Safety and Tech. [1543]
  Natl. Child Safety Coun. [12972]
  Natl. Commn. Against Drunk Driving [12973]
  Natl. Coordinating Coun. for Medication Error Reporting and Prevention [14653]
  Natl. Drowning Prevention Alliance [12974]
  Natl. Fire Protection Assn. [12975]
  Natl. Fire Sprinkler Assn. [3449]
  Natl. Fireproofing Contractors Assn. [1476]
  Natl. Floor Safety Inst. [3450]

Reference to "IO" in place of a book number signifies that the association may be found in the 45th edition of International Organizations.

Natl. Inst. for Farm Safety [12976]
Natl. Inst. for Farm Safety [IO]
Natl. Motorists Assn. [13340]
Natl. Operating Comm. on Standards for Athletic Equip. [3451]
Natl. Org. of Alternative Programs [16382]
Natl. Organizations for Youth Safety [13502]
Natl. Pesticide Info. Center [13327]
Natl. Prog. for Playground Safety [18578]
Natl. Rsrc. Center for Hea. and Safety in Child Care and Early Educ. [11536]
Natl. Safe Boating Coun. [12977]
Natl. Safe Skies Alliance [18748]
Natl. Safe Workplace Institute/SafeSpaces.com [12978]
Natl. Safety Coun. [12979]
Natl. Safety Coun. of Ireland [IO]
Natl. Safety Mgt. Soc. [12980]
Natl. Ski Patrol Sys. [23753]
Natl. Student Safety Prog. [18579]
Natl. Teen Anglers [22454]
Natl. Truckdrivers Safety Assn. [2843]
Natl. Water Safety Cong. [12981]
National Water Safety Congress [IO]
Natl. Whistleblower Center [12982]
Natl. Youth Sports Safety Found. [16484]
Network of Employers for Traffic Safety [18746]
North America's SuperCorridor Coalition [3887]
Oper. Lifesaver [12983]
Operation Lifesaver [IO]
Orillia Against Drunk Driving [IO]
Parents Against Tired Truckers [12984]
Partnership for Food Safety Educ. [14399]
Personal Watercraft Indus. Assn. [3369]
Photoluminescent Safety Products Assn. [IO]
Physicians for a Violence-Free Soc. [12985]
The Prdt. Liability Alliance [3452]
Prdt. Liability Prevention and Defense [3453]
Professional Airways Systems Specialists [24015]
Professional Aviation Maintenance Assn. [165]
Public Risk Mgt. Assn. [5834]
REACT Intl. [6254]
REACT Intl. [IO]
Recording Artists, Actors and Athletes Against Drink Driving - Australia [IO]
Recording Artists, Actors and Athletes Against Drunk Driving [IO]
Recording Artists, Actors and Athletes Against Drunk Driving [12986]
Rickman Owners Club Intl. [22689]
RID - U.S.A. [12987]
Road Operators' Safety Coun. [IO]
Roadway Safety Found. [12988]
Royal Soc. for the Prevention of Accidents [IO]
Rudge Enthusiasts Club [22691]
Safe Kids Worldwide [11651]
Safe Sitter [11537]
Safety Assessment Fed. [IO]
Safety Equip. Distributors Assn. [3454]
Safety Equip. Inst. [3455]
Safety Glazing Certification Coun. [668]
Safety Pharmacology Soc. [15950]
Safety Razor Collectors Guild [22113]
SafetyBeltSafe U.S.A. [18580]
School and Community Safety Soc. of Am. of the Amer. Assn. for Active Lifestyles and Fitness [12989]
Seat Belt Choice Coalition [17016]
Seatbelt Law Opposition Forum [12990]
Sectoral Roundtable Assn. for the Hea. and Safety of Metal and Elecl. Workers [IO]
SEMAA - The Safety Affiliate of NIRA [3456]
Sharing Info. and Experience for Safer Operations [IO]
Sheet Metal Occupational Hea. Inst. Trust [12991]
Soc. for Human Performance in Extreme Environments [6540]
Soc. of Professional Rope Access Technicians [2068]
Standing Up for SUV, Pickup and Van Owners of Am. [17017]
State and Territorial Injury Prevention Directors Assn. [18581]
Students Against Destructive Decisions, Students Against Drunk Driving [12992]

Sun Safety Alliance [13876]
Sys. Safety Soc. [3457]
Three Mile Island Alert [18136]
Traffic Injury Res. Found. [IO]
Traffic Records Comm. [12993]
Trans. Safety Equip. Inst. [3458]
True Food Network [4677]
Underwriters Labs. [3459]
Underwriters' Labs. of Canada [IO]
United Fire Equip. Ser. Assn. [3460]
United Lightning Protection Assn. [3461]
United Sidecar Assn. [22693]
U.S. Contract Security Assn. [3543]
U.S. Life-Saving Ser. Heritage Assn. [10072]
U.S. Marine Safety Assn. [6051]
Univ. of Iowa Injury Prevention Res. Center [7588]
Velocette Owners Club of North Am. [22695]
Veterans of Safety [12994]
Vincent Owners Club - Keystone Sect. [22697]
Vintage BMW Motorcycle Owners [22698]
Vintage Motor Bike Club [22699]
Water Safety New Zealand [IO]
Window Covering Safety Coun. [4030]
World Safety Org. [18582]
World Safety Org. [IO]
Safety Advisory Conf; Helicopter [152]
Safety Advisory Coun; Natl. Boating [5546]
Safety and Asepsis Procedures; Org. for [14182]
Safety Assessment Fed. [IO], London, United Kingdom
Safety Association; American Insurance Highway [★12964]
Safety Assn; Amer. School and Community [★12989]
Safety Assn; Exer- [★15963]
Safety Assn; Exercise [15963]
Safety Assn; Governors Highway [6317]
Safety Assn; Horsemanship [23525]
Safety Assn; Intl. Exer- [★15963]
Safety Association; National Assn. of Independent Insurers [★12964]
Safety Assn; Pulp and Paper [7436]
Safety Assn; Semiconductor [★6931]
Safety Assn; Southern Pulp and Paper [★7436]
Safety Assn; U.S. Marine [6051]
Safety; Beach Educ. Advocates for Culture, Hea., Env. and [10761]
Safety Belt Coun; Amer. [★377]
Safety Belt Inst; Auto. [★377]
Safety Bur; Corresponding Surveyors to the Yacht [★7275]
Safety; Center for Chem. Plant [★801]
Safety; Center for Chem. Process [801]
Safety; Center for Farm Hea. and [12188]
Safety Center; Natl. School [9088]
Safety Communications Officers; Assoc. Public- [★6248]
Safety Conf; Western [★12962]
Safety Conf; Western Forest Products [★12962]
Safety Conf; Western States [★12962]
Safety Consortium; Food [5031]
Safety Consulting Associates - Defunct.
Safety Control Devices Assn; Amer. Traffic [★3438]
Safety Coun; Amer. Environmental [★5694]
Safety Coun; Child [★12972]
Safety Coun; Silicones Environmental, Hea. and [821]
Safety Coun; Window Covering [4030]
Safety Education
AAA Found. for Traffic Safety [12943]
Aircraft Recovery Assn. [12945]
Alliance for Healthy Homes [13320]
Amer. Assn. for Horsemanship Safety [12946]
Amer. Assn. of Safety Councils [12947]
Amer. Bonanza Soc. [21427]
Amer. Highway Users Alliance [12949]
Amer. Safe Climbing Assn. [21950]
Assn. for the Advancement of Automotive Medicine [12951]
Aviation Safety Inst. [12953]
Bicycle Helmet Safety Inst. [12954]
Black Lung Assn. [13323]
Boaters Against Drunk Driving [12955]
Center for Auto Safety [12956]

Center for Farm Hea. and Safety [12188]
CHA - Certified Horsemanship Assn. [23523]
Coalition for Auto Glass Safety and Public Awareness [1727]
Coalition for Environmentally Safe Communities [12118]
CyberAngels [12452]
Danny Found. [12959]
Divers Alert Network [23378]
driveAWARE [12960]
Found. for Aquatic Injury Prevention [12963]
Harvard Injury Control Res. Center [16690]
Horsemanship Safety Assn. [23525]
Insurance Inst. for Highway Safety [12964]
Inter-Amer. Safety Coun. [12965]
Intl. Assn. for Healthcare Security and Safety [14887]
Intl. Assn. of Nitrox and Tech. Divers [23379]
Intl. Hunter Educ. Assn. [23545]
Intl. Soc. of Air Safety Investigators [12966]
Kidpower Teenpower Fullpower Intl. [12967]
Mothers Against Drunk Driving [12969]
Mothers Arms [13011]
Motorist Info. and Services Assn. [13344]
Natl. Air Disaster Alliance [11510]
Natl. Assn. of Women Highway Safety Leaders [12971]
Natl. Child Safety Coun. [12972]
Natl. Commn. Against Drunk Driving [12973]
Natl. Drowning Prevention Alliance [12974]
Natl. Fire Protection Assn. [12975]
Natl. Inst. for Farm Safety [12976]
Natl. Pesticide Info. Center [13327]
Natl. Rsrc. Center for Hea. and Safety in Child Care and Early Educ. [11536]
Natl. Safe Boating Coun. [12977]
Natl. Safety Coun. [12979]
Natl. Water Safety Cong. [12981]
Natl. Youth Sports Safety Found. [16484]
Oper. Lifesaver [12983]
Parents Against Tired Truckers [12984]
Partnership for Food Safety Educ. [14399]
Recording Artists, Actors and Athletes Against Drunk Driving [12986]
Refractory Ceramic Fibers Coalition [788]
Safe Kids Worldwide [11651]
School and Community Safety Soc. of Am. of the Amer. Assn. for Active Lifestyles and Fitness [12989]
Seatbelt Law Opposition Forum [12990]
Sheet Metal Occupational Hea. Inst. Trust [12991]
Students Against Destructive Decisions, Students Against Drunk Driving [12992]
Sun Safety Alliance [13876]
TIPS Prog. [11847]
Traffic Records Comm. [12993]
Veterans of Safety [12994]
Safety Educ. Assn; Amer. Driver and Traffic [8210]
Safety and Educ; CHA-Association for Horsemanship [★23523]
Safety and Educ. Found; Motorcycle Indus. Coun. [★3447]
Safety; Environmental [5694]
Safety Equip. Assn; Indus. [★3445]
Safety Equip. Distributors Assn. [3454], 2105 Laurel Bush Rd., Ste. 200, Bel Air, MD 21015, (443)640-1065
Safety Equip. Inst. [3455], 1307 Dolley Madison Blvd., Ste. 3A, McLean, VA 22101, (703)442-5732
Safety Equip. Inst; Truck [★3458]
Safety Equip. Manufacturers' Agents Assn. [★3456]
Safety and Fairness Everywhere; Natl. Org. Taunting [22599]
Safety Found; Automotive [★12988]
Safety Found; Elevator Escalator [1232]
Safety Glazing Certification Coun. [668], PO Box 730, Sackets Harbor, NY 13685-0730, (315)646-2234
Safety and Hea. Assn; Semiconductor Environmental, [6931]
Safety, Health, and Environmental Resource Center Intl. - Defunct.
Safety and Health; National Inst. of [★9101]
Safety and Hea. Training Assn; Natl. Environmental, [5097]

A star before a book entry number signifies that the name is not listed separately, but is mentioned within the entry.

Safety Helmet Coun. of America - Address unknown since 1995.
Safety, Inc; Amer. Maritime [2570]
Safety Inst. of Am; Chimney [2460]
Safety; Inst. for Bus. and Home [2171]
Safety Investigators; Canadian Soc. of Air [IO]
Safety Investigators; Soc. of Air [★12966]
Safety and Law Enforcement Officers; Natl. Assn. of School [9087]
Safety Mgt. Certification Bd; Intl. Prdt. [★3441]
Safety; Natl. Campaign for Radioactive Waste [18130]
Safety; Natl. Conf. on St. and Highway [★6309]
Safety Org; Intl. Consumer Prdt. Hea. and [3178]
Safety Pharmacology Soc. [15950], PO Box 7033, Audubon, PA 19407, (610)630-0991
Safety Razor Collectors Guild [22113]
Safety Representatives; Natl. Assn. of Governors' Highway [★6317]
Safety and Security; Amer. Soc. for Amusement Park [3526]
Safety and Security Professionals; Intl. Assn. of Home [3527]
Safety Ser; Police [★12972]
The Safety Soc. [★12989]
Safety Soc; Aerospace Sys. [★3457]
Safety Standards Commn; Nuclear [IO]
Safety and Tech; Natl. Center for Food [1543]
SafetyBeltSafe U.S.A. [18580], PO Box 553, Altadena, CA 91003
S'Affirmer Ensemble [★IO]
SAGE [★12256]
Sage Found; Russell [7653]
Sahabat Alam Malaysia [IO], Penang, Malaysia
Sahabat Alam Malaysia [★IO]
Sahara Griha [IO], Kathmandu, Nepal
Sahara and Sahel Observatory [IO], Tunis, Tunisia
Saharan People's Support Comm. [IO], Ada, OH, United States
Saharan People's Support Comm. [16933]
Sahel and West Africa Club [IO], Paris, France
Sahid Khudiram Pathagar [IO], Murshidabad, India
Sahko-ja teleurakoitsijaliitto [★IO]
Sahkoinsinooriliitto [★IO]
Sahkovaltuuskunta [★IO]
Saigon Mission Assn. [IO], San Antonio, TX, United States
Saigon Mission Assn. [18782], c/o Judy Hodges, Admin. Off., 1135 Devonshire Dr., San Diego, CA 92107, (210)558-6865
Sail Am. [527], 850 Aquidneck Ave., Unit B-4, Middletown, RI 02842-7244, (401)841-0900
Sail Assist Intl. Liaison Associates - Defunct.
Sail and Life Training Soc. [IO], Victoria, BC, Canada
Sail Training Assn; Amer. [23153]
Sailboarding
  Intl. Mistral Class Org. [23710]
Sailboat Racing Assn; Intl. MC Class [★23199]
Sailfish-Sunfish Class; Alcort [★23194]
Sailfish-Sunfish Class; AMF Alcort [★23194]
Sailing Assn; Amer. [23154]
Sailing Assn; Annapolis Naval [21867]
Sailing Assn; Catalina 22 Natl. [23162]
Sailing Assn; Flying Scot [23170]
Sailing Assn. Found; Amer. [23155]
Sailing Assn; Natl. C Scow [23203]
Sailing Assn; Natl. Women's [21879]
Sailing Assn. of North Am; Inter-Collegiate [23176]
Sailing Assn. of the Principality of Liechtenstein [IO], Schaan, Liechtenstein
Sailing Assn; U.S. [★23232]
Sailing Assn; U.S. Bd. [★23236]
Sailing Assn; U.S. Intl. [★23237]
Sailing Assn. of Zimbabwe [IO], Harare, Zimbabwe
Sailing Barge Assn. [IO], Bournemouth, United Kingdom
Sailing Class Assn; Interlake [23178]
Sailing Committee; U.S. Olympic [★23238]
Sailing and Cruising Assn. [IO], London, United Kingdom
Sailing Educ. Assn; Amer. [★8811]
Sailing Fed. of Azerbaijan [IO], Baku, Azerbaijan
Sailing Fed; French [IO]
Sailing Fed. of Peru [IO], Callao, Peru

Sailing Found; U.S. [23233]
Sailing Found; Women's [★21879]
Sailors and Airmen Assn; Escort Carrier [21185]
Sailors Assn; AE [6143]
Sailors Assn; Patrol Craft [21218]
Sailors; Council of Disabled [★23155]
Sailors; Natl. Assn. of Fleet Tug [21213]
Sailors for the Sea [4447], 56 Commercial Wharf E, Boston, MA 02110
Sailors - The Natl. Assn. of Destroyer Veterans; Tin Can [21220]
Sailors' Union of the Pacific [24131], 450 Harrison St., San Francisco, CA 94105, (415)777-3400
Sailors' Union; Steamship [★24131]
Sailplane Assn; Vintage [23045]
Sailplane Homebuilders Assn. - Address unknown since 1995.
Saint Agnes; Congregation of Sisters of [19618]
Saint Agnes; Sisters of the Congregation of [★19618]
Saint Albert's Cancer AIDS Res. Found. - Address unknown since 1994.
Saint Andrew Abbey [11192], 10510 Buckeye Rd., Cleveland, OH 44104-3725, (216)721-5300
Saint Andrew the Apostle; Order of [20073]
Saint Andrew; Brotherhood of [19946]
Saint Andrew in Japan; Amer. Comm. for the Brotherhood of [★12418]
Saint Andrew; Knights of [★20073]
St. Andrew; Soc. of [20088]
Saint Andrew's Soc. of the State of New York [19355], 150 E 55th St., Ste. 3, New York, NY 10022, (212)223-4248
Saint Andrew's Ukrainian Orthodox Soc. [18755], c/o Mr. Michael Heretz, Pres., 95 Orient Way 5B/C, Rutherford, NJ 07070
Saint Andrew's Ukrainian Orthodox Soc. [IO], Rutherford, NJ, United States
St. Ansgar's Scandinavian Catholic League [IO], New York, NY, United States
St. Ansgar's Scandinavian Catholic League [19712], 3 E 28th St., New York, NY 10016-7408, (212)876-7719
St. Anthony's Guild [20388], 4 Jersey St., East Rutherford, NJ 07073-1012, (973)778-1915
Saint Apollonia Guild - Address unknown since 1995.
Saint Bernard Club of Am. [22352], c/o Cheryl Zappala, Corresponding Sec., 1043 S 140th St., Seattle, WA 98168, (206)242-7480
St. Boniface Soc; Amer. [19568]
St. Brendan Cup Comm. in America - Defunct.
St. Catherine Coll. Alumni Assn. - Address unknown since 2000.
St. Clare's Home for Children [★13553]
St. Clare's Home Properties [★13553]
Saint Columban; Missionary Soc. of [19662]
Saint Croix Hotel and Tourism Assn. [1964], PO Box 24238, Gallows Bay, St. Croix, VI 00824, (340)773-7117
Saint Croix Hotel and Tourism Assn. [IO], St. Croix, VI, United States
St. Croix Intl. Atlantic Salmon Assn. [IO], Fredericton, NB, Canada
St. David's Cathedral; Amer. Friends of [10009]
Saint David's Soc. - Address unknown since 2007.
St. David's Soc. of the State of New York [19431]
Saint Dominic; Maryknoll Sisters of [20355]
St. Dymphna; League of [19650]
St. Elizabeth Ann Seton; Natl. Shrine of [19694]
St. Ferdinand; Friends of Old [19626]
Saint Francis Assn. for Catholic Evangelism - Defunct.
St. Francis; Bros. and Sisters of Penance of [19590]
Saint Francis Burial and Counseling Soc. [★13317]
St. Francis Center [★13317]
Saint Francis de Sales; Secular Inst. of [19716]
St. Gabriel Possenti Soc. [17597], PO Box 2844, Arlington, VA 22202-0844, (703)212-9860
Saint Gabriel's League - Address unknown since 1995.
St. George Assn. of the U.S.A. - Defunct.
Saint George; Catholic Knights of [★19144]
St. Helena, Ascension, and Tristan da Cunha Philatelic Soc. [22866], c/o Ted Cookson, VP/Sec., 3501 Keyser Ave., Villa 38, Hollywood, FL 33021-2402

St. Helens Chamber of Commerce [IO], St. Helens, United Kingdom
Saint Hubert Soc. of America - Defunct.
St. Isabel; Portuguese Soc. Queen [19322]
Saint James; Fellowship of [19800]
Saint-Jean-Baptiste; Union [19065]
St. Joan's Intl. Alliance U.S. Sect. [17570]
St. Joan's Intl. Alliance U.S. Sect. [IO], Milwaukee, WI, United States
Saint John of Damascus Assn. of Orthodox Iconographers, Iconologists, and Architects - Defunct.
St. John the Divine; Fellowship of [19882]
St. John of Jerusalem, Palestine, Rhodes; Knights of [★19325]
Saint John River Salmon Anglers Assn. [IO], Fredericton, NB, Canada
Saint John; Supreme Commandery Knights of [★19006]
Saint John; Supreme Ladies Auxiliary Knights of [19009]
St. John's Guild - The Floating Hosp. [★14882]
Saint Joseph; Capuchin-Franciscans Province of [19594]
Saint Joseph Congregation [IO], Rome, Italy
St. Joseph Grain Exchange - Defunct.
Saint Jude Children's Res. Hosp; ALSAC/ [13946]
St. Jude Express - Address unknown since 2004.
St. Jude League [19713], 205 W Monroe St., Chicago, IL 60606-5013, (312)236-7782
Saint Karl Borromaus Assn. for the Dissemination of Good Literature [IO], Bonn, Germany
St. Kitt-Nevis Chamber of Indus. and Commerce [IO], Basseterre, St. Kitts and Nevis
St. Kitts Lawn Tennis Assn. [IO], Basseterre, St. Kitts and Nevis
Saint Kitts and Nevis Amateur Athletic Assn. [IO], Basseterre, St. Kitts and Nevis
St. Kitts and Nevis Olympic Assn. [IO], Basseterre, St. Kitts and Nevis
St. Kitts and Nevis Taekwondo Fed. [IO], Basseterre, St. Kitts and Nevis
Saint Kitts-Nevis Tourist Off. [★24254]
Saint Kitts Tourism Authority [24254], 414 E 75th St., Ste. 5, New York, NY 10021, (212)535-1234
St. Laba Ladies Charity Societies; United Hasroun Men's and [19732]
St. Lawrence Shipoperators [IO], Quebec, QC, Canada
Saint Louis Blueliners [★24998]
St. Louis CL-49 Assn; USS [10450]
St. Louis Railway Historical Soc. [★10926]
Saint Lucia Athletics Assn. [IO], Castries, St. Lucia
St. Lucia Chamber of Commerce, Indus. and Agriculture [IO], Castries, St. Lucia
Saint Lucia Hotel and Tourism Assn. [IO], Castries, St. Lucia
St. Lucia Lawn Tennis Assn. [IO], Castries, St. Lucia
St. Lucia Planned Parenthood Assn. [IO], Castries, St. Lucia
Saint Lucia Sailing Assn. [IO], Castries, St. Lucia
Saint Lucia Tourist Bd. [IO], Castries, St. Lucia
Saint Lucia Tourist Bd. [24255], 800 2nd Ave., 9th Fl., New York, NY 10017, (212)867-2950
St. Maarten Hospitality and Trade Assn. [IO], Philipsburg, Netherlands Antilles
St. Maarten Tourist Information Office - Address unknown since 2001.
St. Martin De Porres Guild [20389]
Saint Mary Magdalene; Soc. of [19724]
St. Mary's Coll. of California Alumni Assn. [18922], PO Box 3400, Moraga, CA 94575-3400, (925)631-4200
Saint Nicholas Soc. of the City of New York [21148], c/o Jill Spiller, Exec. Dir., 122 E 58th St., New York, NY 10022-1909, (212)753-7175
St. Patrick in the City of New York; Soc. of the Friendly Sons of [19155]
Saint Patrick's Missionary Soc. [IO], Kiltegan, Ireland
Saint Paul the Apostle; Missionary Soc. of [19663]
Saint Paul; Company of [19614]
Saint Paul; Fellowship of [19958]
Saint Paul Guild - Address unknown since 2001.
St. Paul Soc. [IO], Islamabad, Pakistan
St. Peter the Apostle for Native Clergy; Soc. of [★19725]

Reference to "IO" in place of a book number signifies that the association may be found in the 45th edition of International Organizations.

Encyclopedia of Associations, 46th Edition   4087

Saint Peter Apostle; Soc. of [19725]
St. Peter Claver; Missionary Sisters of [20364]
Saint Photios Found. [20075], PO Box 1960, St. Augustine, FL 32085, (904)829-8205
St. Photios Greek Orthodox Natl. Shrine [★20075]
St. Scholastica Alumni Assn; Coll. of [18889]
Saint Stephen; Soc. of [20523]
St. Thomas Aquinas Found. [19714]
Saint Thomas More Soc. - Defunct.
Saint Thomas-Saint John Hotel Assn. - Address unknown since 2003.
St. Vincent and the Grenadines Natl. Olympic Comm. [IO], Kingstown, St. Vincent and the Grenadines
St. Vincent Pallotti Center for Apostolic Development [20390], 415 Michigan Ave. NE, Washington, DC 20017, (202)529-3330
St. Vincent de Paul Coun. of the U.S; Soc. of [13190]
Saint Vincent de Paul Soc. - Australia [IO], Deakin West, Australia
Saint Vincent de Paul Soc. - Lesotho [IO], Maseru, Lesotho
St. Vincent de Paul; Superior Coun. of U.S. Soc. of [★13190]
St. Vincent and The Grenadines Lawn Tennis Assn. [IO], Kingstown, St. Vincent and the Grenadines
Saintpaulia Intl. - Defunct.
Saints Alive in Jesus [20032], PO Box 1347, Issaquah, WA 98027, (800)861-9888
Saints; Genealogical Soc. of the Church of Jesus Christ of Latter-day [★21115]
Saints' Stories [19715], 520 Oliphant Ln., Middletown, RI 02842-4600, (401)849-5421
Sakhartvelos Mtsvaneta Modzraoba [★IO]
Sako Collectors Assn. - Address unknown since 2002.
Salad Dressing Inst; Mayonnaise and [★1502]
Salad Dressing Manufacturers Assn; Mayonnaise and [★1502]
Salad Manufacturers Assn. [★1560]
Salaried, Machine, and Furniture Workers; Intl. Union of Electronic, Elecl., [24049]
Salaried, Machine, and Furniture Workers; Intl. Union of Electronic, Elecl., Tech., [★24049]
Salary Assn; Ohio Wage and [★1283]
Saleeby-Saliba Family Assn. [21041], PO Box 87094, Fayetteville, NC 28304
Saleen Club of Am. [21780], 2005 Poppy Pl., Jeffersonville, IN 47130, (812)283-6543
Salem Hebrew Lutheran Mission [★20019]
Salers Assn; Amer. [4245]
Salers Assn. of Canada [IO], Carstairs, AB, Canada
Salers Cattle Soc. of the UK and Ireland [IO], Shrewsbury, United Kingdom
Salers Junior Assn; Amer. [4246]
Sales
  Amer. Assn. of Professional Sales Engineers [3462]
  Assn. of Investment Mgt. Sales Executives [2329]
  Assn. of Retail Marketing Services [3463]
  Assn. of Sales Admin. Managers [3464]
  Canadian Marketing Assn. [IO]
  Canadian Professional Sales Assn. [IO]
  CCNG Intl. [2619]
  Direct Selling Assn. [3465]
  Direct Selling Assn. of New Zealand [IO]
  Direct Selling Assn. - United Kingdom [IO]
  Direct Selling Education Foundation [IO]
  Direct Selling Educ. Found. [3466]
  Fabric Salesmen's Assn. [3782]
  Fed. of European Direct Selling Associations [IO]
  Foodservice Gp. [IO]
  Foodservice Gp. [3467]
  Foodservice Sales and Marketing Assn. [1581]
  Intl. Experiential Marketing Assn. [2631]
  Marketing Agencies Assn. Worldwide [3468]
  Marketing Agencies Assn. Worldwide [IO]
  Mountains and Plains Booksellers Assn. [741]
  Multi-Level Marketing Intl. Assn. [2638]
  Natl. Alliance of Black Salesmen and Black Saleswomen [3469]
  Natl. Assn. of Sales Professionals [3470]
  Natl. Field Selling Assn. [3471]
  Natl. Healthcare Collectors Assn. [1869]

  Natl. Org. for Diversity in Sales and Marketing [2644]
  Natl. Retail Hobby Stores Assn. [753]
  Pi Sigma Epsilon [24536]
  Professional Soc. for Sales and Marketing Training [3472]
  Promotion Marketing Assn. [2647]
  Sales and Marketing Executives Intl. [3473]
  Sales and Marketing Executives Intl. [IO]
  Sales Professionals USA [IO]
  Sales Professionals USA [3474]
  Search Engine Marketing Professional Org. [2648]
  Soc. of Pharmaceutical and Biotech Trainers [3475]
  Soc. of Sales and Marketing [IO]
  United League Toy Representatives Associations [3833]
  United Professional Sales Assn. [3476]
  World Fed. of Direct Selling Associations [3477]
  World Fed. of Direct Selling Associations [IO]
Sales Agencies; NAGMR Consumer Products [★2541]
Sales Associates Mgt. Corp. - Address unknown since 1999.
Sales Assn. of the Chem. Indus. [819]
Sales Assn. of the Graphic Arts - Defunct.
Sales Assn; Natl. Confectionery [3419]
Sales Assn. of the Paper Indus. [2894], 500 Bi-County Blvd., Ste. 200E, Farmingdale, NY 11735, (866)307-7274
Sales Automation Assn. - Address unknown since 2003.
Sales Exchange for Refugee Rehabilitation and Vocation [3846], PO Box 365, New Windsor, MD 21776-0365, (608)255-0440
Sales Exchange for Refugee Rehabilitation and Vocation [IO], New Windsor, MD, United States
Sales Found; Graphic Arts [1768]
Sales Managers; Natl. Assn. of [★2481]
Sales Manpower Found. - Defunct.
Sales and Marketing Assn. of Am; Overseas [2312]
Sales and Marketing Companies; Assn. of [★1518]
Sales and Marketing Council; National [★1035]
Sales and Marketing Executives Intl. [3473], PO Box 1390, Sumas, WA 98295-1390, (312)893-0751
Sales and Marketing Executives Intl. [IO], Sumas, WA, United States
Sales Network; Used Truck [★431]
Sales Professionals USA [3474], PO Box 149, Arvada, CO 80001, (303)433-1051
Sales Professionals USA [IO], Arvada, CO, United States
Sales Res. Bur; Life Insurance [★2195]
Salesian Lay Missioners [★20391]
Salesian Lay Missioners [★IO]
Salesian Missioners [IO], New Rochelle, NY, United States
Salesian Missioners [20391], 2 Lefevre Ln., PO Box 30, New Rochelle, NY 10802-0030, (914)633-8344
Salesian Volunteers [★20391]
Salesian Volunteers [★IO]
Salesman With a Purpose [★IO]
Salesman With a Purpose [★3474]
Salesmen's Assn. of the Amer. Chem. Indus. [★819]
Salesmen's Assn; Fabric [3782]
Salesmen's Assn; Natl. Wholesale Furniture [★1702]
Salesmen's Assn. of the Paper Indus. [★2894]
Salesmen's Assn; Piece Goods [★3782]
Salesmen's Assn. of the Textile Dyeing and Printing Industry - Address unknown since 1995.
Salesmen's Guild; Fabric [★3782]
Saliba Family Assn; Saleeby- [21041]
Salina Bd. of Trade [4334]
Salisbury Hunt Club [IO], Salisbury, Australia
Salisbury Sound Assn. [21219], c/o Capt. Marian Bruce, Sec., 813 Branding Iron St. SE, Albuquerque, NM 87123, (505)293-3841
Salk Inst. Associates - Defunct.
Salle Palasz - Address unknown since 1995.
Sallie Mae Fund [8434], 12061 Bluemont Way, Reston, VA 20190, (800)824-7044
Salmagundi Club [9597], 47 5th Ave., New York, NY 10003, (212)255-7740
Salmon Conservation Org; North Atlantic [IO]

Salmon Indus. Assn; Chilean [IO]
Salmon Inst. - Defunct.
Salmon for Peace - Defunct.
Salmon Preservation Assn. for the Waters of Newfoundland [IO], Corner Brook, NL, Canada
Salmon and Trout Assn. [IO], London, United Kingdom
Salmon Unlimited [23422], 5936 N Manton Ave., Chicago, IL 60646, (773)736-5757
Salmonid Assn. of Eastern Newfoundland [IO], St. John's, NL, Canada
Salon Chain Assn; Natl. Beauty [★1081]
Salon Litteraire, Artistique et Diplomatique - Address unknown since 1995.
Salt Distributors Assn. of America - Address unknown since 1995.
SALT Education Fund - Defunct.
Salt Inst. [2744], 700 N Fairfax St., Fairfax Plz., Ste. 600, Alexandria, VA 22314-2040, (703)549-4648
Salt Mfrs'. Assn. [IO], Kendal, United Kingdom
Salt and Pepper Shakers Club; Novelty [22097]
Salt Producers Assn. [★2744]
Salt Shaker Collectors Club [★21968]
Salt Shaker Collectors Soc; Antique and Art Glass [21968]
Salt Water Fly Rodders of Am. [★23417]
Salt Water Fly Rodders of Am. [★IO]
Salters Assn; Peanut and Nut [★1556]
Salters' Company [IO], London, United Kingdom
Salters' Inst. [IO], London, United Kingdom
Saltire Soc. [IO], Edinburgh, United Kingdom
Saluki Club of Am. [22353], c/o Wendy Duggan, Recording Sec., 11101 Early Dawn, Turlock, CA 95380, (209)635-0701
Salutation Consortium - Address unknown since 2006.
Salute Our Services [11500], 2100 Reston Pkwy., Ste. 300, Reston, VA 20191, (703)234-1773
Salvador Sailing Fed. [IO], San Salvador, El Salvador
Salvadoran Amer. Leadership and Educational Fund [17484], 1625 W Olympic Blvd., Ste. 718, Los Angeles, CA 90015, (213)480-1052
Salvadoran Amer. Medical Soc. [15092], 1631 North Loop W, No. 570, Houston, TX 77008, (713)467-1384
Salvadoran Assn. of Industrials [IO], San Salvador, El Salvador
Salvadoran Chamber of the Constr. Indus. [IO], San Salvador, El Salvador
Salvadoran Chamber of Tourism [IO], San Salvador, El Salvador
Salvadoran Demographic Assn. [IO], San Salvador, El Salvador
Salvadoran Exporters' Assn. [IO], San Salvador, El Salvador
Salvadorian Soc. of Dermatology [IO], San Salvador, El Salvador
Salvage
  Comm. for Private Offshore Rescue and Towing [2574]
  Intl. Salvage Union [IO]
Salvage Assn. [IO], London, United Kingdom
Salvage Divers Reunited; U.S. Navy [21409]
Salvage Pool Assn; Amer. [342]
Salvation Army [★13153]
Salvation Army [13187], PO Box 269, 615 Slaters Ln., Alexandria, VA 22313, (703)684-5500
Salvation Army [IO], Alexandria, VA, United States
Salvation Army; Amer. [★13153]
Salvation Army - Caribbean Territory [IO], Kingston, Jamaica
Salvation Army Home League - England [★IO]
Salvation Army Home League - Intl. [IO], London, United Kingdom
Salvation Army Intl. HQ [IO], London, United Kingdom
Salvation Army UK and Ireland [IO], London, United Kingdom
Salvation Army Women's, Adult and Family Ministries - New Zealand [IO], Wellington, New Zealand
Salvation Army Women's Ministries [IO], Wellington, New Zealand
Salvation and Laughter Together - Defunct.

A star before a book entry number signifies that the name is not listed separately, but is mentioned within the entry.

Salzburg Seminar [10229], c/o The Marble Works, 152 Maple St., Ste. 102, Box 886, Middlebury, VT 05753, (802)388-0007

Sam Adams Alliance [17673], 20 N Wacker Dr., Ste. 3330, Chicago, IL 60606, (312)920-0080

Sam Davis Memorial Assn. [11149], 1399 Sam Davis Rd., Smyrna, TN 37167, (615)459-2341

Sam Rayburn Found. - Address unknown since 1995.

SAMA Gp. of Associations [3488], c/o Lab. Products Assn., 225 Reinekers Ln., Ste. 625, Alexandria, VA 22314, (703)836-1360

Samahang Malakolohiya ng Pilipinas [★IO]

Samanbaya no Kai [★IO]

Samantha Smith Found. - Defunct.

Samarbetsnamnden for Folklig Dans [★IO]

Samarbetsorganisationen for Emballagefragor i Skandinavien [★IO]

Samaritan Befrienders [★IO]

Samaritan Lay Missioners - Defunct.

Samaritan Soc; Evangelical Lutheran Good [13168]

Samaritans [★20392]

Samaritans [★IO]

Samaritans - England [IO], Ewell, United Kingdom

Samaritans Intl. [IO], Mooresville, NC, United States

Samaritans Intl. [20392], 370 E Cedar St., Mooresville, NC 28115, (704)663-7951

Samaritan's Purse [★20245]

Samaritan's Purse [20289], PO Box 3000, Boone, NC 28607, (828)262-1980

Samaritan's Purse [★IO]

Samaritans; Vacation [★20392]

Samaritans - Western Australia [IO], Subiaco, Australia

Samband Islenskra Auglysingastofa [★IO]

Sambhav [IO], Gwalior, India

Samfundet til Udgivelse of Dansk Musik [★IO]

Samfunnsokonomenes Forening [★IO]

Sammy Kershaw Fan Club [24973], 817 18th Ave. S, Nashville, TN 37203

Samnordisk Skogforskning [★IO]

Samoa Assn. of Mfrs. and Exporters [IO], Apia, Western Samoa

Samoa Badminton Assn. [IO], Apia, Western Samoa

Samoa Family Hea. Assn. [IO], Apia, Western Samoa

Samoa Sailing Assn. [IO], Apia, Western Samoa

Samoa Squash Rackets Assn. [IO], Apia, Western Samoa

Samoa Taekwondo Assn. [IO], Apia, Western Samoa

Samoa Tourism Authority [IO], Apia, Western Samoa

Samoa Weightlifting Fed. [IO], Apia, Western Samoa

Samojedhunde Klubben i Danmark [★IO]

Samojedhunde Klubben I Danmark [★IO]

Samoyed
    Samoyed Club of Am. [22354]

Samoyed Club of Am. [22354], c/o Beverly Delaney, Membership Chair, 49 Fred Short Rd., Saugerties, NY 12477, (845)246-7509

Samtok Atvinnulifsins [★IO]

Samtok Idnadarins [★IO]

Samuel A. Fryer Educational Res. Found. - Defunct.

Samuel Butler Soc. - Defunct.

Samuel Gompers Stamp Club [22867]

Samuel H. Kress Found. [13132], 174 E 80th St., New York, NY 10021, (212)861-4993

Samuel L. Jackson Fan Club - Address unknown since 2006.

Samuel Roberts Noble Found. [4082], 2510 Sam Noble Pkwy., Ardmore, OK 73401, (580)223-5810

Samuel Rubin Found. [13188], c/o Ms. Lauranne Jones, Grants Admin., 777 United Nations Plz., New York, NY 10017-3521, (212)697-8945

San Diego County Railway Museum [★10918]

San Diego Railroad Museum [★10918]

San Diego Shrinkers Soc. - Address unknown since 2003.

San Francisco African Amer. Historical and Cultural Soc. [9362], 762 Fulton St., 2nd Fl., San Francisco, CA 94102, (415)292-6172

San Francisco AIDS Found. [13584], 995 Market St., Ste. 200, San Francisco, CA 94103, (415)487-3000

San Francisco Camerawork [9945], 657 Mission St., 2nd Fl., San Francisco, CA 94105-4104, (415)512-2020

San Francisco; Chinese Culture Found. of [9788]

San Francisco Gen. Hosp; Trauma Found. at [16691]

San Francisco Grain Exchange - Defunct.

San Francisco Maritime Natl. Park Assn. [10513], PO Box 470310, San Francisco, CA 94147-0310, (415)561-6662

San Francisco Social Psychiatry Seminar [★16089]

San Francisco Social Psychiatry Seminar [★IO]

San Joaquin Valley Wine Growers Assn. [5419]

San Jose Rescue Mission [★12844]

San Juan 21 Class Assn. [23215], c/o Ken Gurganus, Sec.-Treas., 211 Gloria St., Greenville, NC 27858-8627, (252)355-6974

San Juan 24 North Amer. Class Assn. - Address unknown since 1999.

San Marcos Alumni Assn; Cal State [18881]

San Marcos Alumni Assn; California State Univ. of [★18881]

San Marino Tennis Fed. [IO], San Marino, San Marino

San Martin Soc. of U.S.A., Washington DC [11150], 19385 Cypress Ridge Terr., Unit 601, Leesburg, VA 20176-5166, (703)883-0950

San Martin Soc. of Washington, DC [★11150]

Sanatana Dharma Found. - Defunct.

Sanatorium Assn; Amer. [★16642]

Sanatorium Assn; Evangelical Lutheran [★20233]

Sanctity Movement; Pro [19705]

Sanctuaries; The Assn. of [11367]

Sanctuary Assn; Amer. [4156]

Sanctuary; Hawk Mountain [5324]

Sanctuary; PIGS - A [4147]

Sanctuary Workers and Volunteers Assn. [11455], PO Box 637, Boyd, TX 76023-0637, (940)433-5091

Sand Assn; George [9652]

Sand Assn; Natl. Indus. [2743]

Sand Castles
    Intl. Assn. of Sand Castle Builders [22971]
    World Sand Sculptors Assn. [22972]

Sand and Gravel Assn; Natl. Stone, [3699]

Sand Soc; George [9653]

Sandicast Collectors Guild [21544], 3300 W Castor St., Santa Ana, CA 92704-3908, (714)424-0111

Sandplay Therapists of Am. [16635], PO Box 4847, Walnut Creek, CA 94596, (925)825-9277

Sandtray Network [16114], 1946 Clemens Rd., Oakland, CA 94602, (510)530-1383

Sandtray Network [IO], Oakland, CA, United States

Sandwich and Cookie Manufacturers Assn; Peanut Butter [★1556]

Sandy Croft Intl. Fan Club - Defunct.

Sandy Hook Veterans Historical Soc. - Defunct.

SANE Australia [IO], South Melbourne, Australia

SANE/FREEZE: Campaign for Global Security [★18166]

SANE/FREEZE Educ. Fund [★18167]

SANE Nuclear Policy; Comm. for a [★18166]

Sanex WTA Tour [★23910]

Sanex WTA Tour [★IO]

Sangeet Natak Akademi [★IO]

Sanitaria; Asociacao Interamericana de Engenharia [★7589]

Sanitaria; Asociacion Interamericana de Intenieria [★7589]

Sanitarians
    Amer. Acad. of Sanitarians [16383]
    Amer. Assn. of Medical Milk Commissions [16384]
    Natl. Restaurant Assn. Quality Assurance Study Group [16385]

Sanitarians; Assn. of Food Indus. [★2463]

Sanitarians; California Assn. of [★14367]

Sanitarians; Intl. Assn. of Milk [★5739]

Sanitarians; Intl. Assn. of Milk and Food [★5739]

Sanitarians; Natl. Assn. of [★14367]

Sanitarians; Natl. Assn. of Bakery [★2463]

Sanitary Assn; U.S. Livestock [★16811]

Sanitary Boards; Assn. of State [★16811]

Sanitary Brass Inst. [★3066]

Sanitary Brass Inst. [★IO]

Sanitary Engg; Amer. Soc. of [7590]

Sanitary Engg; Amer. Soc. of Inspectors of Plumbing and [★7590]

Sanitary Engg. and Env; Inter-American Assn. of [★7589]

Sanitary Engg. and Environmental Sciences; Inter-American Assn. of [★7589]

Sanitary Engg; Inter-American Assn. of [★7589]

Sanitary Engineers; Amer. Acad. of [★6982]

Sanitary Engineers; Inter-American Assn. of [★7589]

Sanitary and Environmental Engg; Inter-American Assn. of [★7589]

Sanitary·Inst. of Am. [★2066]

Sanitary Inst. of Am. [★IO]

Sanitary Standards Committees, Inc; 3-A [1125]

Sanitary Supply Assn; Natl. [★2466]

Sanitary Supply Wholesaling Assn. [2476], PO Box 98, Swanton, OH 43558, (419)825-3055

Sanitation
    AIDIS-USA Sect. [7589]
    AIDIS-USA Sect. [IO]
    Amer. Acad. of Sanitarians [16383]
    Amer. Soc. of Sanitary Engg. [7590]
    Baking Indus. Sanitation Standards Comm. [448]
    British Toilet Assn. [IO]
    Environmental Mgt. Assn. [2463]
    Global Environmental Mgt. Initiative [4628]
    Healing Waters Intl. [13410]
    Intl. Sanitary Supply Assn. [2466]
    Pan Amer. Center for Sanitary Engg. and Environmental Sciences [IO]
    Portable Sanitation Assn. Intl. [4003]
    Sanitary Supply Wholesaling Assn. [2476]
    Water Advocates [9310]
    WaterPartners Intl. [13412]
    World Toilet Org. [IO]

Sanitation Assn; Portable [★4003]

Sanitation Found; Natl. [★16249]

Sanitation Mgt. Assn; Indus. [★2463]

Sanitation Mgt; Inst. of [★2463]

Sanitation Standards Comm; Baking Indus. [448]

Sanitation Suppliers and Contractors Inst. - Defunct.

Sanity; Youth for Environmental [4625]

Sankethi Assn; North Amer. [9802]

Sanomalehtien Liitto Tidningarnas Forbund [★IO]

Sanskrit
    Intl. Assn. of Sanskrit Stud. [IO]

Santa Barbara Medical Res. Found. [★15568]

Santa Cruz Mountain Vintners [★5420]

Santa Cruz Mountains Winegrowers Assn. [5420], 7605-A Old Dominion Ct., Aptos, CA 95003, (831)685-8463

Santa Gertrudis Assn; Natl. Junior [4277]

Santa Gertrudis Breeders Intl. [4292], PO Box 1257, Kingsville, TX 78364, (361)592-9357

Santa Gertrudis Breeders Intl. [IO], Kingsville, TX, United States

Santal Mission; Amer. [★20234]

Santana 20 Class Assn. [23216], c/o Zoe Gilstrap, Sec., 1266 Napa Creek Dr., Eugene, OR 97404

Sante Fe Indian School [★10745]

Santiago Chamber of Commerce [IO], Santiago, Chile

Santini's Porpoise School [★7261]

Santo Domingo Chamber of Commerce and Production [IO], Santo Domingo, Dominican Republic

Sapp Family Assn. [21042], 712 NW 95th Terr., Gainesville, FL 32607, (352)332-2065

Saq' Be': Org. for Mayan and Indigenous Spiritual Bodies [10226], PO Box 31111, Santa Fe, NM 87594, (505)466-4044

Saq' Be': Organization for Mayan and Indigenous Spiritual Bodies [IO], Santa Fe, NM, United States

Sarah Scaife Found. [IO], Pittsburgh, PA, United States

Sarah Scaife Found. [18482], One Oxford Ctre., 301 Grant St., Ste. 3900, Pittsburgh, PA 15219-6401, (412)392-2900

Sarawak Campaign Comm. [IO], Tokyo, Japan

Sarawak Teachers' Union [IO], Kuching, Malaysia

Sarawak United People's Party [IO], Kuching, Malaysia

Sarcastics Anonymous [22600]

Sarcoma Alliance [13871], 775 E Blithedale, No. 334, Mill Valley, CA 94941, (415)381-7236

Sarcoma Res. and Educ. Found; AIDS/Kaposi's [★13854]

Sartre, Jean-Paul
    North Amer. Sartre Soc. [10819]

Sartre Soc. [★10819]

Reference to "IO" in place of a book number signifies that the association may be found in the 45th edition of International Organizations.

Sartre Soc. of Canada [★IO]

Sartre Soc; North Amer. [10819]

Sarus Group Intl. - Address unknown since 2003.

SAS Global Forum [6802], c/o SAS Inst. Inc., 100 SAS Campus Dr., Cary, NC 27513-2414, (919)531-5000

SAS Global Forum [IO], Cary, NC, United States

SAS Users Gp. Intl. [★IO]

SAS Users Gp. Intl. [★6802]

Sasakawa Peace Found. [IO], Tokyo, Japan

Sash and Door Jobbers Assn; Northern [★600]

Sash and Door Jobbers Assn; Southern [★600]

Saskatchewan 4-H Coun. [IO], Saskatoon, SK, Canada

Saskatchewan Angus Assn. [IO], Regina, SK, Canada

Saskatchewan Dental Therapists Assn. [IO], Gull Lake, SK, Canada

Saskatchewan Environmental Soc. [IO], Saskatoon, SK, Canada

Saskatchewan Horse Fed. [IO], Regina, SK, Canada

Saskatchewan Lib. Assn. [IO], Regina, SK, Canada

Saskatchewan Music Festival Assn. [IO], Regina, SK, Canada

Saskatchewan Palliative Care Assn. [IO], Saskatoon, SK, Canada

Saskatchewan Snowboard Assn. [IO], Regina, SK, Canada

Saskatchewan Wheelchair Sports Assn. [IO], Saskatoon, SK, Canada

Sasquatch
   Center for Bigfoot Stud. [7472]
   Michigan/Canadian Bigfoot Info. Center [7480]
   Sasquatch Investigations of Mid-America [7484]

Sasquatch Investigations of Mid-America [7484], 2726 NW 34, Oklahoma City, OK 73112, (405)942-5161

Satanic Crime in Am; USCCCN Natl. CH on [11848]

SATELLIFE Global Hea. Info. Network [14663], 30 California St., Watertown, MA 02472, (617)926-9400

SATELLIFE Global Health Information Network [IO], Watertown, MA, United States

Satellite Assn; Direct Broadcast [★3754]

Satellite Broadcasters Assn. - Defunct.

Satellite Broadcasting and Communications Assn. [3754], 1730 M St. NW, Ste. 600, Washington, DC 20036, (202)349-3620

Satellite Broadcasting and Communications Assn. [IO], Washington, DC, United States

Satellite Corp; Radio Amateur [7783]

Satellite, Data, and Info. Ser; Natl. Environmental [4590]

Satellite Dealers Assn. Inc. [★1214]

Satellite Dealers Assn. Inc. [★IO]

Satellite Dishes
   Mobile Satellite Users Assn. [7591]

Satellite Indus. Assn. [885], 1730 M St. NW, Ste. 600, Washington, DC 20036, (202)349-3650

Satellite Operators and Users Technical Comm. - Defunct.

Satellite Professionals; Soc. of [★3755]

Satellite TV Indus. Assn. [★3754]

Satellite TV Indus. Assn. [★IO]

Satellite Users; Intl. Assn. of [★3746]

Satellite Video Exchange Soc. [IO], Vancouver, BC, Canada

Satin Rabbit Breeders' Assn; Amer. [5140]

Satire
   Intl. Assn. of Professional Bureaucrats [22595]
   Natl. Org. Taunting Safety and Fairness Everywhere [22599]

Satoko and Franz M. Joseph Found. - Address unknown since 2007.

SATRA Tech. Centre [IO], Kettering, United Kingdom

SATS/EAF Assn. [21179], c/o Alvin Wilder, Treas., PO Box 616, Havelock, NC 28532

Saturday Evening Post Soc. [★14549]

Sauces; Assn. for Dressings and [1502]

Saudi Arabia
   Saudi British Soc. [IO]

Saudi Arabian Athletics Fed. [IO], Riyadh, Saudi Arabia

Saudi Arabian Judo and Taekwondo Fed. [IO], Riyadh, Saudi Arabia

Saudi Arabian Olympic Comm. [IO], Riyadh, Saudi Arabia

Saudi Arabian Sports Medicine Assn. [IO], Riyadh, Saudi Arabia

Saudi Arabian Tennis Fed. [IO], Riyadh, Saudi Arabia

Saudi Arabian Weightlifting and Body Building Fed. [IO], Riyadh, Saudi Arabia

Saudi Arabian Youth Hostels Assn. [IO], Riyadh, Saudi Arabia

Saudi British Soc. [IO], London, United Kingdom

Saudi Chap. of Epilepsy [IO], Riyadh, Saudi Arabia

Saudi Cricket Centre [IO], Jeddah, Saudi Arabia

Saudi Osteoporosis Soc. [IO], Riyadh, Saudi Arabia

Saudi Pediatric Assn. [IO], Riyadh, Saudi Arabia

Saudi Physical Therapy Assn. [IO], Riyadh, Saudi Arabia

Saudi Soc. of Dermatology and Venereology [IO], Riyadh, Saudi Arabia

Saudi Sports Fed. for Special Needs [IO], Riyadh, Saudi Arabia

Saudi Squash Fed. [IO], Riyadh, Saudi Arabia

Sauna Soc. of Am. [3362], PO Box 19001, Washington, DC 20036-9001, (202)331-1363

Sauve/Laplante Researchers - Defunct.

Savannah Breeders' Assn; The Intl. [4208]

Savannah Cat Club [4211], 571 Millcross Rd., Lancaster, PA 17601

Save-A-Baby [★12918]

Save America's Forests [4448], 4 Lib. Ct. SE, Washington, DC 20003, (202)544-9219

Save the Apollo Launch Tower [★9341]

Save a Baby - Defunct.

Save the Battlefield Coalition [10061], PO Box 110, Catharpin, VA 20143, (803)329-8626

Save the Boat People - Defunct.

Save Cambodia - Address unknown since 1990.

Save a Cat League - Defunct.

Save the Child [IO], Lahore, Pakistan

Save the Children [11720], 54 Wilton Rd., Westport, CT 06880, (203)221-4030

Save the Children Australia [IO], Camberwell, Australia

Save the Children Australia - New South Wales [IO], Sydney, Australia

Save the Children Australia - South Australia [IO], Glenside, Australia

Save the Children Australia - Tasmania Div. [IO], Hobart, Australia

Save the Children Australia - Victoria Div. [IO], Hawthorn, Australia

Save the Children Australia - Western Australia Div. [IO], Perth, Australia

Save the Children Canada [IO], Toronto, ON, Canada

Save the Children Denmark [IO], Copenhagen, Denmark

Save the Children Dominican Republic [IO], Santo Domingo, Dominican Republic

Save the Children Egypt [IO], Cairo, Egypt

Save the Children Finland [IO], Helsinki, Finland

Save the Children Fund - Swaziland [IO], Mbabane, Swaziland

Save the Children Honduras [IO], Tegucigalpa, Honduras

Save the Children Hong Kong [IO], Hong Kong, People's Republic of China

Save the Children Italia [IO], Rome, Italy

Save the Children - Korea [IO], Seoul, Republic of Korea

Save the Children Macedonia [IO], Skopje, Macedonia

Save the Children Netherlands [IO], The Hague, Netherlands

Save the Children New Zealand [IO], Wellington, New Zealand

Save the Children - Norway [IO], Oslo, Norway

Save the Children Spain [IO], Madrid, Spain

Save the Children - Sweden [IO], Stockholm, Sweden

Save the Children - UK [IO], London, United Kingdom

Save the Chimps [4298], PO Box 12220, Fort Pierce, FL 34979, (772)429-0403

Save the Elephants [IO], Nairobi, Kenya

Save EPA Working Group - Defunct.

Save the Family Farm Coalition; Natl. [★16956]

Save a Family Plan [12166], PO Box 611832, Port Huron, MI 48061-1832, (519)672-1115

Save a Family Plan [IO], Port Huron, MI, United States

Save the Flags of Fort Sumter - Defunct.

SAVE Intl. [7185], 136 S Keowee St., Dayton, OH 45402, (937)224-7283

SAVE Intl. [IO], Dayton, OH, United States

Save Lake Tahoe; League to [4417]

Save Lebanon - Address unknown since 2006.

Save Life On Earth - Defunct.

Save the Manatee Club [5378], 500 N Maitland Ave., Maitland, FL 32751, (407)539-0990

Save the Oppressed People Comm. - Defunct.

Save Our Barns Comm. - Defunct.

Save Our Constitution - Defunct.

Save Our Family Ties - Defunct.

Save Our Flag - Defunct.

Save Our Schools [18717], c/o Maureen P. Madden, Founder/CEO, PO Box 175, Annapolis, MD 21404, (410)552-5331

Save Our Seas [4449], PO Box 813, Hanalei, HI 96714, (808)651-3452

Save Our Seas [IO], Hanalei, HI, United States

Save Our Security Coalition - Address unknown since 1999.

Save Our Streams [★4413]

Save Pound Animals From Res. Experiments - Address unknown since 1988.

Save the Redwoods League [4450], 114 Sansome St., Rm. 1200, San Francisco, CA 94104-3823, (415)362-2352

Save the Refugees Fund [★12778]

Save the Refugees Fund [★IO]

Save the Strippers Wells - Defunct.

Save The Children India [IO], Bombay, India

Save the Theatres - Defunct.

Save U.S. Jobs [1282]

Save Us From Formaldehyde Enval. Repercussions [★13324]

Save the Whales [5379], 1192 Waring St., Seaside, CA 93955, (831)899-9957

Saved by the Belt Club - Defunct.

Savers Exchange; Seed [22540]

Savers and Investors League [18699], PO Box 210, Mirror Lake, NH 03853-0210, (603)569-8283

SavetheInternet.com Coalition [17924], c/o Free Press Action Fund, PO Box 28, Northampton, MA 01061, (413)585-1533

Savez Aeroklubova Bosne I Hercegovine [IO], Sarajevo, Bosnia-Hercegovina

Savez Klizackih Sportava Bosne I Hercegovine [★IO]

Savez Klizackih Sportova Srbije i Crne Gore [★IO]

Saving Antiquities for Everyone [9389], 123 Town Square Pl., No. 151, Jersey City, NJ 07310

Saving the Arts [9598], PO Box 4045, Nooksack, WA 98276

Saving Assn. of Am; Natl. Surf Life [★12894]

Saving Kids; Mothers and Fathers Aligned [17059]

Saving and Preserving Arts and Cultural Environments [9470], 345 White Rd., Watsonville, CA 95076, (831)684-0405

Savings and Community Bankers of Am. [★461]

Savings and Credit Co-operative League of South Africa [IO], Roggebaai, Republic of South Africa

Savings Educ. Coun; Amer. [8440]

Savings Institutions; Financial Managers Soc. for [★1418]

Savings Institutions; Natl. Coun. of [★461]

Savings Institutions; Natl. Soc. of Controllers and Financial Officers of [★1418]

Savings Institutions; U.S. League of [★461]

Savings and Loan Controllers; Soc. of [★1418]

Savings and Loan Leagues; Amer. [★459]

Savings and Loan Supervisors; Natl. Assn. of State [★458]

Savings Plans Network; Coll. [8429]

Savings Supervisors; Amer. Coun. of State [458]

Savio Club Intl. - Defunct.

Savoie Acadian Cultural and Historical Soc. [21149], c/o Alice Savoie Conklin, Treas., 4250 Cuesta Dr., Irving, TX 75038

A star before a book entry number signifies that the name is not listed separately, but is mentioned within the entry.

Savory Center for Holistic Mgt; Allan [★4408]
Saw Assn. of the World; Scroll [23032]
Saw Mfrs. Assn. of Am; Hack and Band [★1830]
Sawin Soc. - Defunct.
Sawing Assn; North Amer. [1830]
Sawing and Drilling Assn; Concrete [923]
Sawyer Brown Fan Club [★24974]
Sawyer Brown Intl. Fan Club [24974], 5200 Old Harding Rd., Franklin, TN 37064-9406, (615)799-2229
Sawyer Fan Club; Elton [25005]
Sawyer - Patty Moise Fan Club; Elton [★25005]
Sax and Soul - Defunct.
Saxifrage Publications Group - Address unknown since 2001.
Saxon Owners Registry [21781], c/o Walter H. Prichard, Jr., Ed., 5250 NW Highland Way, Corvallis, OR 97330, (541)752-6231
Saxons; Alliance of Transylvanian [19117]
Saxophone Alliance; North Amer. [10679]
SAY Soccer U.S.A. [★23781]
Say Yes to Better Sports for Kids [★23290]
Say Your Peace Project - Defunct.
SB Latex Coun. [820], 1250 Connecticut Ave. NW, Ste. 700, Washington, DC 20036, (202)419-1500
SBU El Salvador [★IO]
Scaffold Contractors Assn. [★669]
Scaffold Indus. Assn. [669], PO Box 20574, Phoenix, AZ 85036-0574, (602)257-1144
Scaffolding, Shoring and Forming Inst. [670], 1300 Sumner Ave., Cleveland, OH 44115, (216)241-7333
Scaffolding, Shoring and Forming Inst. [★670]
Scaffolding and Shoring Inst; Steel [★670]
Scale Mfrs. Assn. [4017], 6724 Lone Oak Blvd., Naples, FL 34109, (239)514-3441
Scale Mfrs; Natl. Assn. of [★4017]
Scale Masters Assn; US [22660]
Scale Racing Assn; Unlimited [22659]
Scale Ship Modelers Assn. of North Am. [22656], c/o Bruce Ray, Natl. Dir., 6780 Gleason, Kalamazoo, MI 49048
Scale Warbird Racing Assn. [22657], PO Box 328, Muncie, IN 47302
Scallop Assn; Amer. [3491]
Scalp
  Inst. of Trichologists [IO]
  Intl. Assn. of Trichologists [IO]
  Natl. Alopecia Areata Found. [16386]
SCAN America - Defunct.
Scandinavia
  Hardanger Fiddle Assn. of Am. [10606]
  St. Ansgar's Scandinavian Catholic League [19712]
  Scandinavian Collectors Club [22868]
  Scandinavian Seminar [8630]
  Scandinavian Tourist Boards [24372]
  Soc. for the Advancement of Scandinavian Stud. [9070]
  Thanks to Scandinavia [8436]
Scandinavia; Thanks to [8436]
Scandinavian
  American-Scandinavian Found. [10942]
  American-Scandinavian Found. [IO]
  Augustana Historical Soc. [19343]
  Canadian-Scandinavian Found. [IO]
  Independent Order of Svithiod [19344]
  Nordic Inst. on Aland [IO]
  St. Ansgar's Scandinavian Catholic League [19712]
  Scandinavian Amer. Lawyers Assn. [5530]
  Scandinavian Collectors Club [22868]
  Soc. for the Advancement of Scandinavian Stud. [9070]
  Thanks to Scandinavia [8436]
  Viking Soc. for Northern Res. [IO]
Scandinavian-Amer. Genealogical Soc. - Defunct.
Scandinavian Amer. Lawyers Assn. [5530], 4177 Garrick, Warren, MI 48091, (586)757-4177
Scandinavian Assn. of Agricultural Scientists [★IO]
Scandinavian Assn. for Gastrointestinal Motility [IO], Goteborg, Sweden
Scandinavian Assn. of Obstetrics and Gynecology [★IO]
Scandinavian Assn. of Res. Librarians [★IO]
Scandinavian Assn. for the Stud. of Pain [IO], Oslo, Norway

Scandinavian Assn. for Thoracic and Cardiovascular Surgery [★IO]
Scandinavian Assn. for Thoracic Surgery [IO], Turku, Finland
Scandinavian Assn. of Urology [IO], Oslo, Norway
Scandinavian-Baltic Soc. for Parasitology [IO], Copenhagen, Denmark
Scandinavian Bishops Conf. [IO], Vastra Frolunda, Sweden
Scandinavian Collectors Club [IO], El Cajon, CA, United States
Scandinavian Collectors Club [22868], c/o Donald Brent, Exec. Sec., PO Box 13196, El Cajon, CA 92020
Scandinavian Copper Development Assn. [IO], Vasteras, Sweden
Scandinavian Episcopal Conf. [★IO]
Scandinavian Fed. of Res. Librarians [★IO]
Scandinavian Fraternity of America - Defunct.
Scandinavian Herpetological Soc. [IO], Herlufmagle, Denmark
Scandinavian Inst. of African Stud. [★IO]
Scandinavian Inst. of Asian Stud. [★IO]
Scandinavian Inst. of Dental Materials [★IO]
Scandinavian Inst. of Maritime Law [IO], Oslo, Norway
Scandinavian Natl. Tourist Offices [★24372]
Scandinavian Neurosurgical Soc. [IO], Stockholm, Sweden
Scandinavian Packaging Assn. [IO], Taastrup, Denmark
Scandinavian Physiological Soc. [IO], Odense, Denmark
Scandinavian Plant Physiology Soc. [IO], Frederiksberg, Denmark
Scandinavian Res. Coun. for Criminology [IO], Stockholm, Sweden
Scandinavian Seminar [IO], Amherst, MA, United States
Scandinavian Seminar [8630], 24 Dickinson St., Amherst, MA 01002, (413)253-9736
Scandinavian Soc. of Antimicrobial Chemotherapy [IO], Skien, Norway
Scandinavian Soc. of Cataract and Refractive Surgery [IO], Karlstad, Sweden
Scandinavian Soc. for Cell Toxicology [IO], Stockholm, Sweden
Scandinavian Soc. of Clinical Physiology and Nuclear Medicine [IO], Lund, Sweden
Scandinavian Soc. for Electron Microscopy [★IO]
Scandinavian Soc. of Glass Tech. [IO], Vaxjo, Sweden
Scandinavian Soc. for Head and Neck Oncology [IO], Bergen, Norway
Scandinavian Soc. for Immunology [IO], Helsinki, Finland
Scandinavian Soc. for Lab. Animal Sci. [IO], Tyreso, Sweden
Scandinavian Soc. for Prehistoric Art [IO], Tanumshede, Sweden
Scandinavian Soc. for Prosthetic Dentistry [IO], Bergen, Norway
Scandinavian Soc. for Res. in CardioThoracic Surgery [IO], Arhus, Denmark
Scandinavian Soc. for the Stud. of Diabetes [IO], Trondheim, Norway
Scandinavian Student Exchange; Amer. [★8600]
Scandinavian Tire and Rim Org. [IO], Uppsala, Sweden
Scandinavian Tourist Boards [24372], PO Box 4649, Grand Central Sta., New York, NY 10163-4649, (212)885-9700
Scandinavian Union of Museums Danish Sect. [IO], Copenhagen, Denmark
Scanner Assn. of North America - Address unknown since 1991.
Scanning Microscopy Intl. - Address unknown since 2004.
Scarab - Address unknown.
Scarce Family Org. - Defunct.
Scarf Trailers Science Fiction Social Club - Defunct.
Scenic Am. [4606], 1634 I St. NW, Ste. 510, Washington, DC 20006, (202)638-0550
Scenic Artists; United [24160]
Scenic Beauty; Coalition for [★4606]

Scenic Beauty; Natl. Coalition to Preserve [★4606]
Scent Bottle Collectors Assn; Intl. Perfume and [★22054]
Schaarschmidt Family Assn. and Data Bank [21043], PO Box 75, Moran, WY 83013, (307)543-2420
Schechter Day School Assn; Solomon [8701]
Scheduling Assn; Intl. Production Planning and [8809]
Scherman Found. [13189], 16 E 52nd St., Ste. 601, New York, NY 10022-5306, (212)832-3086
Schiffli Embroidery Inst. [★3796]
Schiffli Embroidery Mfrs. Promotion Found. [★3796]
Schiffli Embroidery Mfrs. Promotion Fund [3796], 22 Indus. Ave., Fairview, NJ 07022, (201)943-7757
Schiffli Embroidery Mfrs. Promotion Fund [★3796]
Schiffli Embroidery Promotion Coun. [★3796]
Schiffli Lace and Embroidery Mfrs. Assn. [3797], 22 Indus. Ave., Fairview, NJ 07022, (201)943-7757
Schiffli Mfrs. Promotion Fund [★3796]
Schiller Center [8453], c/o Sherry L. Schiller, PhD, Pres., 801 Duke St., Alexandria, VA 22314, (703)684-4735
The Schiller Center: Catalysts for Managing Change [★8453]
Schipperke Club of Am. [22355], c/o Lisa Haines, Futurity Chair, 44 Mission Cir., Alamogordo, NM 88310, (505)439-1133
Schizophrenia Assn. of Great Britain [IO], Bangor, United Kingdom
Schizophrenia Intl. Res. Soc. [15232], PO Box 212, Piermont, NY 10968
Schizophrenia Ireland [IO], Dublin, Ireland
Schizophrenia; North Amer. Soc. for Childhood Onset [15229]
Schizophrenia Soc. of Canada [IO], Markham, ON, Canada
Schizophrenics Anonymous [12558], c/o Natl. Schizophrenia Found., 403 Seymour Ave., Ste. 202, Lansing, MI 48933, (517)485-7168
Schlaraffia Nordamerika [19079]
Schleswig-Holstein Heritage Soc; American/ [19066]
Schmoe Family Org. - Address unknown since 1994.
Schnauzer Club of Am; Giant [22276]
Schnauzer Club of Am; Standard [22365]
Schnauzer Club; Amer. Miniature [22205]
Scholarly Editions; Comm. on [11167]
Scholarly Publishing; Soc. for [3256]
Scholarly Publishing; Women in [3260]
Scholars Against the Escalating Danger of the Far Right - Address unknown since 1995.
Scholars Assn; Turkish Amer. Scientists and [7636]
Scholars; Assn. of Voluntary Action [★13387]
Scholars and Citizens for Freedom of Information - Defunct.
Scholars Conf. Bd. of Assoc. Res. Councils; Coun. for Intl. Exchange of [★8609]
Scholars; Fellowship of Catholic [9777]
Scholars Foundation; Evans [★23471]
Scholars; Natl. Acad. of Amer. [8356]
Scholars; Natl. Assn. of [8490]
Scholars; Natl. Coalition of Independent [8491]
Scholars for Peace in the Middle East [18070], c/o Susquehanna Indus., 624 Sandra Ave., Harrisburg, PA 17109
Scholars for Peace in the Middle East [IO], Harrisburg, PA, United States
Scholars and Scientists; U.S. Fed. of [7634]
Scholars; Senior [8153]
Scholars; Soc. of Dance History [10154]
Scholars in the U.S.A; Assn. of Russian-American [10941]
Scholars; U.S. Fed. of Scientists and [★7634]
Scholarship
  Academic Cooperation Assn. [IO]
  Alpha Chi [24498]
  Alpha Chi Sigma [24428]
  Alpha Delta Kappa [24449]
  Alpha Epsilon [24395]
  Alpha Epsilon Delta [24541]
  Alpha Gamma Rho [24396]
  Alpha Iota Sorority [24413]
  Alpha Kappa Delta [24701]
  Alpha Kappa Psi [24414]
  Alpha Mu Gamma Natl. [24525]
  Alpha Omega Alpha Honor Medical Soc. [24542]

Reference to "IO" in place of a book number signifies that the association may be found in the 45th edition of International Organizations.

Alpha Omega Intl. Dental Fraternity [24437]
Alpha Sigma Nu [24500]
Alpha Zeta [24397]
Amer. Assn. of Teachers of Arabic [7958]
Arnold Air Soc. [24546]
Assn. of African Women Scholars [9071]
Assn. of African Women Scholars [IO]
Assn. for Africanist Anthropology [6408]
Assn. for Borderlands Stud. [8653]
Assn. for Canadian Stud. in the U.S. [8043]
Assn. of Coll. Honor Societies [24501]
Assn. of Concerned African Scholars [16926]
Assn. of Marshall Scholars [9072]
Assn. of Marshall Scholars [IO]
Assn. of Nepal and Himalayan Stud. [8944]
Astronaut Scholars Honor Soc. [24584]
Beta Alpha Psi [24391]
Beta Beta Beta [24408]
Beta Gamma Sigma [24415]
Beta Gamma Sigma Alumni [24416]
Beta Phi Mu [24532]
Beta Sigma Kappa [24562]
Black Alliance for Educational Options [8322]
Catching the Dream [8427]
Center for the Stud. of the Coll. Fraternity [24476]
Central Off. Executives Assn. of Natl. Pan-
   Hellenic Conf. [24477]
Centre for Indian Scholars [IO]
Chinese Language Teachers Assn. [8076]
Coun. for Intl. Exchange of Scholars/Institute of
   Intl. Educ. [8609]
Cum Laude Soc. [24503]
Delphi Found. [24451]
Delta Epsilon Sigma [24504]
Delta Kappa Epsilon [24623]
Delta Lambda Phi Natl. Social Fraternity [24624]
Delta Mu Delta Honor Soc. [24418]
Delta Omega [24582]
Delta Omicron [24550]
Delta Phi Epsilon, Professional Foreign Ser.
   Fraternity [24472]
Delta Phi Epsilon Professional Foreign Ser. Soror-
   ity [24473]
Delta Phi Upsilon [24431]
Delta Pi Epsilon [24426]
Delta Psi Omega [24444]
Delta Sigma Delta [24438]
Delta Theta Phi [24527]
Epsilon Pi Tau [24720]
Epsilon Sigma Phi [24436]
Eta Phi Beta [24419]
Eta Sigma Alpha Natl. Home School Honor Soc.
   [8316]
Eta Sigma Phi, Natl. Classics Honorary Soc.
   [24433]
Fulbright Assn. [8613]
Gamma Iota Sigma [24520]
Gamma Sigma Delta [24398]
Gamma Theta Upsilon [24491]
Golden Key Intl. Honour Soc. [24506]
Harry S. Truman Scholarship Found. [8430]
Honors Prog. Student Assn. of the Amer.
   Sociological Assn. [24702]
Intl. Alumni Assn. of Shri Mahavir Jain Vidyalaya
   [19346]
Intl. Assn. of Genocide Scholars [17661]
Intl. Soc. for the Scholarship of Teaching and
   Learning [9073]
Intl. Soc. for the Scholarship of Teaching and
   Learning [IO]
Iota Beta Sigma [24410]
Iota Phi Lambda [24421]
Kappa Delta Epsilon [24452]
Kappa Delta Pi [24453]
Kappa Mu Epsilon [24537]
Kappa Omicron Nu [24496]
Kappa Pi Intl. Honorary Art Fraternity [24404]
Kappa Tau Alpha [24522]
Lambda Alpha Intl. [24445]
Lambda Iota Tau [24533]
Mortar Bd. [24509]
Mu Alpha Theta [24538]
Mu Beta Psi [24552]
Mu Phi Epsilon Intl. [24553]
Natl. Acad. of Amer. Scholars [8356]

Natl. Acad. of Educ. [8280]
Natl. Alpha Lambda Delta [24510]
Natl. Assn. of Fellowships Advisors [9080]
Natl. Assn. of the Knights of Scorpius, Honorary
   Leadership Soc. [24511]
Natl. Assn. of Scholars [8490]
Natl. Beta Club [24592]
Natl. Block and Bridle Club [24401]
Natl. Collegiate Honors Coun. [8290]
Natl. Honor Soc. [24512]
Natl. Junior Honor Soc. [24513]
Natl. Kappa Kappa Iota [24454]
Natl. Panhellenic Conf. [24485]
Natl. Scholarship Providers Assn. [9074]
Natl. Soc. of Collegiate Scholars [9075]
Natl. Soc. of High School Scholars [9076]
Natl. Sorority of Phi Delta Kappa [24455]
Natl. Tech. Honor Soc. [24725]
Natl. Valedictorian Honor Soc. [24514]
Natl. Valedictorian Soc. [9077]
North Amer. Interfraternal Found. [24486]
North-American Interfraternity Conf. [24487]
Omega Delta [24563]
Omicron Delta Epsilon [24446]
Omicron Delta Kappa Soc. [24515]
Omicron Kappa Upsilon [24439]
Order of the Coif [24516]
Permanent Intl. Altaistic Conf. [7989]
Phi Alpha Delta [24528]
Phi Alpha Sigma [24543]
Phi Alpha Theta [24495]
Phi Beta [24405]
Phi Beta Delta [24517]
Phi Beta Kappa [24406]
Phi Chi Medical Fraternity [24544]
Phi Delta Epsilon Medical Fraternity [24540]
Phi Delta Gamma [24577]
Phi Delta Phi Intl. Legal Fraternity [24530]
Phi Kappa Phi [24518]
Phi Mu Alpha Sinfonia Fraternity and Found. Natl.
   HQ [24555]
Phi Sigma [24409]
Phi Sigma Iota [24526]
Phi Sigma Pi Natl. Honor Fraternity [24531]
Pi Kappa Phi [24651]
Pi Omicron Natl. Sorority [24601]
Professional Fraternity Assn. [24488]
Psi Beta [24579]
Psi Omega [24440]
Royal Norwegian Soc. of Sciences and Letters
   [IO]
Sigma Alpha Iota Intl. Music Fraternity [24557]
Sigma Alpha Lambda [24519]
Sigma Delta Chi Found. [24524]
Sigma Delta Epsilon, Graduate Women in Sci.
   [24587]
Silver Wings [24549]
Soc. for Academic Achievement [9078]
Soc. for the Advancement of Scandinavian Stud.
   [9070]
Soc. of Professional Journalists [3164]
Soc. for the Stud. of Early China [8077]
Southeastern Regional Off. Natl. Scholarship Ser.
   and Fund for Negro Students [8435]
Tau Epsilon Rho Law Soc. [24529]
Theta Alpha Phi [24721]
Theta Tau [24469]
Underprivileged Students of Anthropological Voca-
   tions [9079]
Upsilon Pi Epsilon Assn. [24435]
World Commun. Assn. [8005]
Xi Psi Phi [24442]

Scholarship Alumni
   Assn. of Amer. Rhodes Scholars [19345]
   Astronaut Scholars Honor Soc. [24584]
   Intl. Alumni Assn. of Shri Mahavir Jain Vidyalaya
      [19346]
   Intl. Alumni Assn. of Shri Mahavir Jain Vidyalaya
      [IO]
   Natl. Scholarship Providers Assn. [9074]
Scholarship Am. [9081], 4960 Viking Dr., Ste. 110,
   Edina, MN 55435, (952)830-7300
Scholarship Assn; Amer. Music [★10726]
Scholarship Comm; Luso-American Fraternal Fed.
   [★10890]

Scholarship, Education and Defense Fund for Racial
   Equality - Address unknown since 1995.
Scholarship Found; Harry S. Truman [8430]
Scholarship Fund; Hispanic [8431]
Scholarship Fund; International Peace [★9325]
Scholarship Fund; International Peace [★IO]
Scholarship Fund Program; LULAC Natl. [★8275]
Scholarship Fund; Thurgood Marshall [7932]
Scholarship Program; James Monroe Freedom
   [★11128]
Scholarship Ser. and Fund for Negro Students; Natl.
   [★8435]
Scholarship Ser. and Fund for Negro Students;
   Southeastern Regional Off. Natl. [8435]
Scholarship Societies of the South [★24498]
Scholarship Societies of Texas [★24498]
Scholarship; Soc. for the Promotion of Sci. and
   [3255]
Scholarship; Soc. for Textual [10432]
Scholarships
   Alpha Chi [24498]
   Alpha Chi Sigma [24428]
   Alpha Delta Kappa [24449]
   Alpha Epsilon [24395]
   Alpha Gamma Rho [24396]
   Alpha Iota Sorority [24413]
   Alpha Kappa Delta [24701]
   Alpha Kappa Psi [24414]
   Alpha Mu Gamma Natl. [24525]
   Alpha Omega Intl. Dental Fraternity [24437]
   Alpha Sigma Nu [24500]
   Alpha Zeta [24397]
   Amer. Indian Graduate Center [8426]
   Arnold Air Soc. [24546]
   Assn. of Coll. Honor Societies [24501]
   Assn. for Textual Scholarship in Art History [9432]
   Astronaut Scholars Honor Soc. [24584]
   Beta Alpha Psi [24391]
   Beta Beta Beta [24408]
   Beta Gamma Sigma [24415]
   Beta Gamma Sigma Alumni [24416]
   Beta Phi Mu [24532]
   Beta Sigma Kappa [24562]
   Black Alliance for Educational Options [8322]
   Caribbean Stud. Assn. [8050]
   Carnegie Corp. of New York [8239]
   Catching the Dream [8427]
   Center for the Stud. of the Coll. Fraternity [24476]
   Central Off. Executives Assn. of Natl. Pan-
      Hellenic Conf. [24477]
   Cum Laude Soc. [24503]
   Delphi Found. [24451]
   Delta Epsilon Sigma [24504]
   Delta Kappa Epsilon [24623]
   Delta Lambda Phi Natl. Social Fraternity [24624]
   Delta Mu Delta Honor Soc. [24418]
   Delta Phi Epsilon, Professional Foreign Ser.
      Fraternity [24472]
   Delta Phi Epsilon Professional Foreign Ser. Soror-
      ity [24473]
   Delta Phi Upsilon [24431]
   Delta Pi Epsilon [24426]
   Delta Psi Omega [24444]
   Delta Sigma Delta [24438]
   Delta Theta Phi [24527]
   Educational Found. for the Fashion Indus. [232]
   Epsilon Pi Tau [24720]
   Epsilon Sigma Phi [24436]
   Eta Phi Beta [24419]
   Eta Sigma Alpha Natl. Home School Honor Soc.
      [8316]
   Eta Sigma Phi, Natl. Classics Honorary Soc.
      [24433]
   Gamma Iota Sigma [24520]
   Gamma Sigma Delta [24398]
   Gamma Theta Upsilon [24491]
   Golden Key Intl. Honour Soc. [24506]
   Gravure Educ. Found. [8469]
   Harry S. Truman Scholarship Found. [8430]
   Hispanic Scholarship Fund [8431]
   Honors Prog. Student Assn. of the Amer.
      Sociological Assn. [24702]
   INROADS [8749]
   Intl. Alumni Assn. of Shri Mahavir Jain Vidyalaya
      [19346]

A star before a book entry number signifies that the name is not listed separately, but is mentioned within the entry.

Intl. Soc. for the Scholarship of Teaching and Learning [9073]
Iota Beta Sigma [24410]
Iota Phi Lambda [24421]
Jefferson Educational Found. [17273]
Kappa Delta Epsilon [24452]
Kappa Delta Pi [24453]
Kappa Mu Epsilon [24537]
Kappa Omicron Nu [24496]
Kappa Pi Intl. Honorary Art Fraternity [24404]
Kappa Tau Alpha [24522]
Lambda Alpha Intl. [24445]
Lambda Iota Tau [24533]
Mortar Bd. [24509]
Mu Alpha Theta [24538]
Mu Beta Psi [24552]
Natl. Alpha Lambda Delta [24510]
Natl. Assn. of Fellowships Advisors [9080]
Natl. Assn. of the Knights of Scorpius, Honorary Leadership Soc. [24511]
Natl. Beta Club [24592]
Natl. Block and Bridle Club [24401]
Natl. Forensic Assn. [9158]
Natl. Honor Soc. [24512]
Natl. Junior Honor Soc. [24513]
Natl. Kappa Kappa Iota [24454]
Natl. Panhellenic Conf. [24485]
Natl. Pell Grant Coalition [8433]
Natl. Scholarship Providers Assn. [9074]
Natl. Sorority of Phi Delta Kappa [24455]
Natl. Tech. Honor Soc. [24725]
Natl. Valedictorian Honor Soc. [24514]
Nieman Found. [8716]
North Amer. Interfraternal Found. [24486]
North-American Interfraternity Conf. [24487]
Omega Delta [24563]
Omicron Delta Epsilon [24446]
Omicron Delta Kappa Soc. [24515]
Omicron Kappa Upsilon [24439]
Order of the Coif [24516]
PEO Intl. [9325]
Phi Alpha Delta [24528]
Phi Alpha Theta [24495]
Phi Beta [24405]
Phi Beta Delta [24517]
Phi Beta Kappa [24406]
Phi Delta Gamma [24577]
Phi Delta Phi Intl. Legal Fraternity [24530]
Phi Kappa Phi [24518]
Phi Sigma [24409]
Phi Sigma Iota [24526]
Phi Sigma Pi Natl. Honor Fraternity [24531]
Pi Kappa Phi [24651]
Pi Omicron Natl. Sorority [24601]
Professional Fraternity Assn. [24488]
Psi Beta [24579]
Psi Omega [24440]
Sallie Mae Fund [8434]
Scholarship Am. [9081]
Sigma Alpha Iota Intl. Music Fraternity [24557]
Sigma Alpha Lambda [24519]
Sigma Delta Epsilon, Graduate Women in Sci. [24587]
Sigma Kappa Found. [24697]
Silver Wings [24549]
Soc. of Professional Journalists [3164]
Southeastern Regional Off. Natl. Scholarship Ser. and Fund for Negro Students [8435]
Tau Epsilon Rho Law Soc. [24529]
Theta Alpha Phi [24721]
Theta Tau [24469]
Thunderbird Amer. Indian Dancers [10754]
United Negro Coll. Fund [8437]
Upsilon Pi Epsilon Assn. [24435]
Winston Churchill Found. [8438]
Xi Psi Phi [24442]
Scholarships; Amer. Indian [★8426]
Scholastic Athletic Administrators Assn; Natl. Inter [8989]
Scholastic Music Assn; Natl. Fed. Inter [★8928]
Scholastic Officials Assn; Natl. Fed. Inter [★23874]
Scholastic Press Advisers Assn; Columbia [9010]
Scholastic Press Assn; Columbia [9011]
Scholastic Press Assn; Natl. [9013]
Scholastic Rowing Assn. of Am. [23703], c/o Matthew Ledwith, PO Box 528, Berlin, NJ 08009, (215)641-0589

Scholastic Science Fiction Fed. - Defunct.
Scholastic Speech and Debate Assn; Natl. Fed. Inter [★9161]
Scholastic Surfing Assn; Natl. [23880]
Scholastic Swimming Coaches Assn. of Am; Natl. Inter [23887]
Schomburg Center for Res. in Black Culture [9363], 515 Malcolm X Blvd., New York, NY 10037-1801, (212)491-2200
Schomburg Center for Res. in Black Culture [IO], New York, NY, United States
School ABC Prog; Natl. Public [★8321]
School Accounting and Bus. Officials of Public Schools; Natl. Assn. of [★7892]
School Accounting Officers; Natl. Assn. of [★7892]
School Accreditation; Natl. Coun. for Private [7880]
School Administrators; Amer. Assn. of [7882]
School Administrators; Amer. Fed. of [7886]
School Administrators; Amer. Soc. of Journalism [★7893]
School Administrators; Natl. Assn. of Hebrew Day [7901]
School Administrators and Supervisors Organizing Comm. [★7886]
School-Age Care Alliance; Natl. [★11528]
School of the Americas Watch [18399], PO Box 4566, Washington, DC 20017, (202)234-3440
School Assn. of Am; Folk- [★8267]
School Assn. of the Americas; Driving [8211]
School Assn; Midwest Middle [★8881]
School Assn; Natl. After [11528]
School Assn; Natl. Swim [★23892]
School Assn; U.S. Swim [23892]
School Athletic Associations; Natl. Fed. of State High [★23841]
School Athletic Directors; Natl. Coun. of Secondary [8988]
School Attendance; Natl. League to Promote [★8326]
School Audiovisual Officers; Assn. of Chief State [★8568]
School Band Directors' Assn; Amer. [8903]
School Bd. Assn; Navajo Area [8942]
School Boards
  Acad. for Spatial Res. and Planning [IO]
  Amer. Assn. of School Administrators [7882]
  Assn. of Governing Boards of Universities and Colleges [7889]
  Canadian School Boards Assn. [IO]
  Inst. for the Transfer of Tech. to Educ. [8563]
  Natl. Assn. of Boards, Commissions, and Councils of Catholic Educ. [8056]
  Natl. Assn. of Charter School Authorizers [8281]
  Natl. Assn. of State Boards of Educ. [9082]
  Natl. School Boards Assn. [9083]
  Navajo Area School Bd. Assn. [8942]
  North Amer. Assn. of Educational Negotiators [24046]
  Urban Superintendent's Assn. of Am. [9288]
School Boards Assn; Natl. Coun. of State [★9083]
School Bookshop Assn. [★IO]
School Building Officials; Natl. Assn. of [★7892]
School Bus Mfrs. Inst. - Address unknown since 1991.
School Bus. Officials; Assn. of [★7892]
School Bus. Officials; Natl. Assn. of [★7892]
School Bus. Officials of the U.S. and Canada; Assn. of [★7892]
School Change; Center for [8242]
School and Coll. Conf. on English - Address unknown since 1995.
School, Coll. and Univ. Staffing; Assn. for [★8994]
School and Community Safety Assn; Amer. [★12989]
School and Community Safety Soc. of Am. of the Amer. Assn. for Active Lifestyles and Fitness [12989], c/o Amer. Alliance for Hea., Physical Educ., Recreation & Dance, 1900 Assn. Dr., Reston, VA 20191-1598, (703)476-3400
School Counselor Assn; Amer. [8163]
School Curriculum and Assessment Authority [★IO]
School Data Educ; Soc. of Independent and Private [★8132]
School for the Deaf; Model Secondary [14766]
School and Departments of Journalism; Assn. of Accredited [★7893]

School Development Coun; Natl. [8292]
School Educ. Assn; Natl. Community [★8126]
School Educators; Natl. Alliance of Black [9217]
School Employees; Amer. Assn. of Classified [24041]
School Evaluation; Natl. Stud. of [8410]
School Evaluation; Natl. Stud. of Secondary [★8410]
School Facilities Coun. of Architecture, Educ. and Indus. [★7892]
School Facilities Coun. of Architecture, Educ. and Indus. [★IO]
School Food Ser. Assn; Amer. [★9173]
School Food Ser. Foundation [★9173]
School Hea. Assn; Amer. [14718]
School Hea. Division of Amer. Assn. for Hea., Physical Educ. and Recreation [★16234]
School; Heart of the Earth Survival [★18090]
School and Home Off. Products Assn. [2849], 3131 Elbee Rd., Dayton, OH 45439, (937)297-2250
School Improvement; Proj. Appleseed: The Natl. Campaign for Public [8332]
School Improvement; Res. Coun. of the Great Cities Prog. for [★9289]
School Inst; Home and [8261]
School of Islamic Sufism [★20576]
School Journalism; Natl. Assn. of Supervisors and Teachers of High [★8713]
School Journey Assn. [IO], London, United Kingdom
School Legal Defense Assn; Home [8339]
School Librarians; Amer. Assn. of [10317]
School Librarians Intl; Soc. of [10388]
School Libraries Division of the Amer. Lib. Assn. [★10317]
School Lib. Assn. [IO], Swindon, United Kingdom
School Library Manpower Project - Defunct.
School Lib. Media Supervisors Assn; State [★8568]
School of Living [10178], 215 Julian Woods Ln., Julian, PA 16844, (814)353-0130
School Mgt. Study Group - Address unknown since 2006.
School of Mortgage Banking [★485]
School Music Dealers; Natl. Assn. of [2819]
School Networking; Consortium for [8555]
School; New York Correspondence [★9506]
School Nurse Achievement Prog. [15525], c/o Univ. of Colorado Hea. Sciences Center, PO Box 6508, Mail Stop F-541, Aurora, CO 80045-0508, (303)724-0644
School Nurse Consultants; Natl. Assn. of State [15502]
School Nurses; Natl. Assn. of [15501]
School Nurses/NEA; Dept. of [★15501]
School Nutrition Assn. [9173], 700 S Washington St., Ste. 300, Alexandria, VA 22314, (703)739-3900
School Officers; Coun. of Chief State [8246]
School Partnership Prog; Peace Corps [★18264]
School Photographers of Am; Professional [★3012]
School Photographers; Amer. Assn. of [★3012]
School Physicians; Amer. Assn. of [★14718]
School Press Advisers; Columbia [★9010]
School Press Specialists; Columbia [★9010]
School Principals; Natl. Assn. of Elementary [9014]
School Principals; Natl. Assn. of Secondary [9016]
School Principals, NEA; Dept. of Elementary [★9014]
School Projectionist Club of America - Defunct.
School Psychologists; Natl. Assn. of [16160]
School PTAs; Natl. Assn. of Hebrew Day [8953]
School Public Relations Assn; Natl. [9033]
School; Res. Commn. of Natl. Sunday [★8088]
School; Sante Fe Indian [★10745]
School to School Prog; Peace Corps [★18264]
School Sci. and Mathematics Assn. [9115], c/o Dr. Julie Thomas, Co-Exec. Dir., Oklahoma State Univ., College of Education, 245 Willard, Stillwater, OK 74078, (405)744-7396
School Science and Mathematics Association [IO], Lubbock, TX, United States
School Secretaries; Natl. Assn. of [★7898]
School Security
  Intl. Assn. of Campus Law Enforcement Administrators [9084]
  Intl. Assn. of Campus Law Enforcement Administrators [IO]
  Natl. Alliance for Safe Schools [9085]

Reference to "IO" in place of a book number signifies that the association may be found in the 45th edition of International Organizations.

Natl. Assn. of School Rsrc. Officers [9086]
Natl. Assn. of School Safety and Law Enforcement Officers [9087]
Natl. School Safety Center [9088]
School Security Directors; Intl. Assn. of [★9087]
School Security Directors; Natl. Assn. of [★9087]
School Ser; Inter-American [★8647]
School Services
Intl. Schools Services [8647]
Natl. Assn. of Coll. Auxiliary Services [3478]
Natl. Assn. of Pupil Services Administrators [7902]
Natl. Assn. of School Nurses [15501]
Natl. Assn. of School Rsrc. Officers [9086]
Natl. Assn. of State School Nurse Consultants [15502]
Natl. Conf. on Student Leadership [9188]
Natl. Coun. on Student Development [9170]
Natl. School Supply and Equip. Assn. [3479]
Navajo Area School Bd. Assn. [8942]
School and Home Off. Products Assn. [2849]
School Services; Arab World and Islamic Resources and [9393]
School Sisters of Notre Dame [IO], Rome, Italy
School Social Work Assn. of Am. [9134], PO Box 2072, Northlake, IL 60164, (847)289-4527
School Social Workers; Natl. Assn. of [★13206]
School Standards; Cooperative Stud. of Secondary [★8410]
School Superintendents; Natl. Alliance of Black [★9217]
School Superintendents; Natl. Assn. of [★7882]
School Superintendents of the Natl. Educ. Assn; Dept. of [★7882]
School Supplies
Amer. Textbook Coun. [9258]
Armenian Natl. Educ. Comm. [7964]
Center for Social Stud. Educ. [9127]
Coun. of the Great City Schools [9289]
E-quip Africa [12704]
Educational Equity Center [8400]
Hea. Sciences Consortium [8561]
Intl. Book Proj. [8620]
PALTEX - Expanded Textbook and Instructional Materials Prog. [9261]
Stelios M. Stelson Found. [8631]
Vocational Instructional Materials Sect. [8573]
School Teachers of Journalism; Natl. Assn. of High [★8713]
School Teachers; Natl. Assn. of Catholic [8058]
School Time; Natl. Inst. on Out-of- [11543]
School Trans. Assn; Natl. [3882]
Schoolboy Rowing Assn. of Am. [★23703]
Schoolhouse Constr; Natl. Coun. on [★8335]
Schooling for Hispanics; National Commn. on Secondary [★17704]
Schooling for Hispanics; National Commn. on Secondary [★IO]
Schools
Acad. for Educational Development [8219]
Acad. of Intl. Bus. [8011]
Alliance of Girls' Schools Australasia [IO]
Alliance for Intl. Educational and Cultural Exchange [8591]
Amer. Assn. of Classified School Employees [24041]
Amer. Assn. of Colleges of Nursing [8842]
Amer. Assn. for Collegiate Independent Stud. [7944]
Amer. Assn. of Community Colleges [8117]
Amer. Assn. of Cosmetology Schools/Cosmetology Educators of Am. [8160]
Amer. Assn. of School Administrators [7882]
Amer. Assn. of School Personnel Administrators [7883]
Amer. Assn. for Vocational Instructional Materials [9298]
Amer. Coun. on Educ. [8224]
Amer. Coun. on Schools and Colls. [8225]
Amer. Debate Assn. [9151]
Amer. Dental Educ. Assn. [8193]
Amer. Fed. of School Administrators [7886]
Amer. Fed. of Teachers [24042]
Amer. Friends of the Alliance Israelite Universelle [8675]
Amer. Friends of The Hebrew Univ. [8676]

Amer. Indian Res. and Development [8464]
Amer. Montessori Soc. [8891]
Amer. Overseas Schools Historical Soc. [10012]
Amer. School Hea. Assn. [14718]
Amer. Schools Assn. [8164]
Amer. Student Govt. Assn. [9175]
Amer. Univ. in Moscow [8597]
Armenian Educational Found. [8343]
Armenian Natl. Educ. Comm. [7964]
Asian Amer. Curriculum Proj. [8598]
Assoc. Schools of Constr. [8143]
Assn. of Accredited Naturopathic Medical Colleges [8943]
Assn. for the Advancement of Intl. Educ. [8640]
Assn. of Amer. Intl. Colleges and Universities [8641]
Assn. of Amer. Medical Colleges [8846]
Assn. of Amer. Schools in Central Am., Colombia, Caribbean and Mexico [IO]
Assn. of Amer. Universities [8099]
Assn. for Assessment in Counseling and Educ. [9247]
The Assn. of Boarding Schools [9018]
Assn. of Bus. Schools [IO]
Assn. of Catholic Colleges and Universities [8051]
Assn. of Christian Schools Intl. [8081]
Assn. of Classical and Christian Schools [9089]
Assn. of Classical and Christian Schools [IO]
Assn. of Coll. Unions Intl. [9166]
Assn. of Coll. and Univ. Housing Officers Intl. [9167]
Assn. of Collegiate Schools of Planning [9285]
Assn. for Commun. Admin. [9154]
Assn. for Community Based Education [8123]
Assn. of Community Tribal Schools [8936]
Assn. for Continuing Legal Educ. [8762]
Assn. of Episcopal Colleges [8397]
Assn. for Experiential Educ. [8411]
Assn. of Free Methodist Educational Institutions [8447]
Assn. of Jesuit Colleges and Universities [8052]
Assn. of Lutheran Secondary Schools [8801]
Assn. for Media-Based Continuing Educ. for Engineers [8367]
Assn. of Military Colleges and Schools of the U.S. [8883]
Assn. of Minority Hea. Professions Schools [8850]
Assn. of Nutrition Departments and Programs [8947]
Assn. of Schools of Journalism and Mass Commun. [7893]
Assn. of Theological Schools in the U.S. and Canada [9270]
Assn. of Univ. Programs in Hea. Admin. [8857]
Augustinian Secondary Educational Assn. [8054]
Beta Chi Theta Natl. Fraternity [24618]
Big Picture Company [8353]
Black Alliance for Educational Options [8322]
Boston Theological Inst. [9271]
British Schools and Universities Found. [8102]
British Universities North Am. Club [8606]
Canhelp, Tajikistan [IO]
Center for Commun. [8003]
Center for School Change [8242]
Central and Eastern European Schools Assn. [IO]
Chess in the Schools [21945]
Chinese School Assn. in the U.S. [9090]
Christian Schools Intl. [8083]
Coalition of Essential Schools [8180]
Coll. Parents of Am. [8485]
Coll. Summit [8486]
Comm. for Educ. Funding [8345]
Communities in Schools [8323]
Community of Caring [11588]
Community Coll. Baccalaureate Assn. [8119]
CompuMentor [7728]
Consciousness-Based Educ. Assn. [9029]
Consortium for School Networking [8555]
Cordell Hull Found. for Intl. Educ. [8656]
Coun. on Accreditation of Nurse Anesthesia Educational Programs [8835]
Coun. of Administrators of Special Educ. [9139]
Coun. for Adult and Experiential Learning [8412]
Coun. for the Advancement of Standards in Higher Educ. [9177]

Coun. for Amer. Private Educ. [9020]
Coun. of Chief State School Officers [8246]
Coun. for Christian Colleges and Universities [8084]
Coun. of Educational Fac. Planners, Intl. [8335]
Coun. of the Great City Schools [9289]
Coun. for Rsrc. Development [8347]
Coun. for Spiritual and Ethical Educ. [8536]
Dance/Drill Team Directors of Am. [9876]
Danforth Found. [8250]
Decision Sciences Inst. [8021]
Distance Educ. and Training Coun. [8517]
Driving School Assn. of the Americas [8211]
E-quip Africa [12704]
Editorial Projects in Educ. [8251]
Educating for Justice [9126]
The Educ. Coalition [8325]
Educ. Commn. of the States [8252]
Educ. Law Assn. [5676]
Educ. Pioneers [9178]
Educational Exhibitors Assn. [1336]
Educational Records Bur. [9249]
Educational Res. Ser. [7895]
EF Found. for Foreign Stud. [8611]
European Network of Hea. Promoting Schools [IO]
Family, Career and Community Leaders of Am. [8417]
Fed. Educ. Assn. [24043]
Federated Coun. of Beth Jacob Schools [8691]
Fed. for Unified Sci. Educ. [9102]
Feminist Teacher Editorial Collective [9318]
Frank Lloyd Wright Assn. [7961]
Global Learning [8658]
GreatSchools [8066]
Healthy Schools Network [4635]
HeartStrong [12232]
Hispanic Coun. for Reform and Educational Options [8260]
Home and School Inst. [8261]
Home School Legal Defense Assn. [8339]
Indian Educators Fed. [8938]
Inst. for Development of Educational Activities [8263]
Intercollegiate Broadcasting Sys. [8004]
Interlochen Center for the Arts [9571]
Intl. Accrediting Commn. for Real Estate and Appraisal Educ. and Training [3313]
Intl. Alliance for Child and Adolescent Mental Hea. and Schools [15204]
Intl. Assn. of Jesuit Bus. Schools [8026]
Intl. Assn. of Law Schools [8767]
Intl. Assn. for Truancy and Dropout Prevention [8326]
Intl. Book Proj. [8620]
Intl. Schools Services [8647]
Intl. Univ. Found. [8648]
Jesuit Secondary Educ. Assn. [8055]
Learning First Alliance [8273]
Lutheran Educational Conf. of North Am. [8804]
Metro Intl. Prog. Services of New York [8624]
Mid-Atlantic Equity Consortium [8276]
Middle States Assn. of Colleges and Schools [8277]
Natl. Accrediting Commn. of Cosmetology Arts and Sciences [7877]
Natl. Alliance for Public Charter Schools [9037]
Natl. Alliance for Safe Schools [9036]
Natl. Alliance of State Sci. and Mathematics Coalitions [9106]
Natl. Assn. for the Advancement of Caring Teachers [9218]
Natl. Assn. for Alternative Certification [8360]
Natl. Assn. for Beginning Teachers [9219]
Natl. Assn. of Boards, Commissions, and Councils of Catholic Educ. [8056]
Natl. Assn. of Charter School Authorizers [8281]
Natl. Assn. for Coll. Admission Counseling [7912]
Natl. Assn. of Educational Off. Professionals [7898]
Natl. Assn. of Episcopal Schools [8398]
Natl. Assn. for the Exchange of Indus. Resources [8336]
Natl. Assn. of Federally Impacted Schools [8349]
Natl. Assn. of Hea. Sci. Educ. Partnership [9107]

A star before a book entry number signifies that the name is not listed separately, but is mentioned within the entry.

Natl. Assn. of Independent Schools [8540]
Natl. Assn. for Legal Support of Alternative Schools [7946]
Natl. Assn. of Private Special Educ. Centers [9147]
Natl. Assn. for Professional Development Schools [9091]
Natl. Assn. of Scholars [8490]
Natl. Assn. of School Nurses [15501]
Natl. Assn. of School Psychologists [16160]
Natl. Assn. of School Rsrc. Officers [9086]
Natl. Assn. of Schools of Art and Design [7978]
Natl. Assn. of Schools, Colleges and Universities of the United Methodist Church [8879]
Natl. Assn. of Schools of Dance [8188]
Natl. Assn. of Schools of Music [8921]
Natl. Assn. of Schools of Theatre [9265]
Natl. Assn. for Single Sex Public Educ. [9038]
Natl. Assn. of St. Schools [9337]
Natl. Assn. of Student Councils [9186]
Natl. Assn. of Student Personnel Administrators [7904]
Natl. Assn. of Students Against Violence Everywhere [18117]
Natl. Assn. of Substance Abuse Trainers and Educators [9198]
Natl. Assn. for Year-Round Educ. [8282]
Natl. Bus. Educ. Assn. [8036]
Natl. Catholic Educational Assn. [8059]
Natl. Catholic Forensic League [9156]
Natl. Center for Hea. Educ. [14582]
Natl. Center for the Stud. of Corporal Punishment and Alternatives [8206]
Natl. Coalition to Abolish Corporal Punishment in Schools [8207]
Natl. Coalition of Alternative Community Schools [7948]
Natl. Coalition of Girls' Schools [8288]
Natl. Collegiate Paintball Assn. [23646]
Natl. Commn. for Cooperative Educ. [8159]
Natl. Conf. on Student Leadership [9188]
Natl. Conf. of Yeshiva Principals [9017]
Natl. Consortium of Arts and Letters for Historically Black Colls. and Universities [8111]
Natl. Coun. of Educ. Providers [8329]
Natl. Coun. of Supervisors of Mathematics [8826]
Natl. Coun. on Teacher Retirement [24044]
Natl. Dance Inst. [8190]
Natl. Educ. Assn. [24045]
Natl. Fed. of State High School Associations [23841]
Natl. Geographic Soc. Educ. Found. [8458]
Natl. Guild of Community Schools of the Arts [7979]
Natl. High School Athletic Coaches Assn. [23292]
Natl. High School Baseball Coaches Assn. [23119]
Natl. History Club [8509]
Natl. Indian Educ. Assn. [8941]
Natl. Middle Level Sci. Teachers' Assn. [9112]
Natl. Parliamentary Debate Assn. [9160]
Natl. PTA - Natl. Cong. of Parents and Teachers [8954]
Natl. Registration Center for Stud. Abroad [8626]
Natl. Rural Educ. Advocacy Coalition [9068]
Natl. Rural Educ. Assn. [9069]
Natl. School Boards Assn. [9083]
Natl. School Development Coun. [8292]
Natl. School Public Relations Assn. [9033]
Natl. Service-Learning CH [9092]
Natl. Service-Learning Partnership [9120]
Natl. Soc. of High School Scholars [9076]
Natl. Soc. of Leadership and Success [9189]
Natl. Soc. for the Stud. of Educ. [8293]
Natl. Staff Development Coun. [7908]
Natl. Student Exchange [9172]
Natl. Student Nurses' Assn. [8873]
Natl. Student Safety Prog. [18579]
Navajo Area School Bd. Assn. [8942]
NEA Found. for the Improvement of Educ. [8294]
NETWORK [8295]
New England Assn. of Schools and Colleges [8296]
New Leaders for New Schools [8755]
NFHS Coaches Assn. [23294]

North Amer. Assn. of Educational Negotiators [24046]
North Amer. Assn. of Jewish High Schools [8698]
North Central Assn. of Colleges and Schools Commn. on Accreditation and School Improvement [8297]
North Central Assn. Commn. on Accreditation and School Improvement [9093]
Northeast Conf. on the Teaching of Foreign Languages [8742]
Northwest Assn. of Accredited Schools [8298]
Org. of Amer. Kodaly Educators [8929]
Organizing Bur. of European School Student Unions [IO]
Outward Bound [9204]
PALTEX - Expanded Textbook and Instructional Materials Prog. [9261]
Parents in Control [8340]
Parents for Public Schools [12052]
Pathways to Coll. Network [8493]
Pirchei Agudath Israel [8699]
Prepare Tomorrow's Parents [13511]
Public Educ. Network [9040]
Regional Educ. Bd. of the Christian Bros. [8060]
Restoration Proj. Intl. [12441]
Saving the Arts [9598]
School Nurse Achievement Prog. [15525]
Sci. Songwriters' Assn. [10693]
Scottish Coun. of Independent Schools [IO]
Sigma Alpha Lambda [24519]
Sigma Beta Rho Fraternity [24656]
Soc. for the Advancement of Educ. [8305]
Soc. of Building Sci. Educators [8363]
Soc. for Educational Reconstruction [8306]
Solace Intl. [13439]
Solomon Schechter Day School Assn. [8701]
Southern Assn. of Colleges and Schools [8308]
StandardsWork [9094]
Teachers of English to Speakers of Other Languages [8382]
Teachers Insurance and Annuity Assn. [8579]
Tel Aviv Univ.: Amer. Coun. [8679]
United Bd. for Christian Higher Educ. in Asia [8649]
U.S. High School Tennis Assn. [23912]
U.S. Student Assn. [9195]
Univ. Coun. for Educational Admin. [7909]
Univ. Risk Mgt. and Insurance Assn. [8580]
Urban Superintendent's Assn. of Am. [9288]
Western Assn. of Schools and Colleges [8314]
Woodrow Wilson Natl. Fellowship Found. [8439]
World Heritage [8634]
Worldwide Univ. Consortium [8114]
Zangle Natl. Users' Gp. [7216]
Schools; Accrediting Bur. of Hea. Educ. [15124]
Schools; Accrediting Bur. of Medical Lab. [★15124]
Schools; Accrediting Coun. for Independent Colleges and [7874]
Schools of Allied Hea. Professions; Assn. of [8855]
Schools; Amer. Assn. of Christian [7875]
Schools of Architecture; Assn. of Collegiate [7959]
Schools of Art and Design; Natl. Assn. of [7978]
Schools of the Arts; Natl. Guild of Community [7979]
Schools of the ASCP; Bd. of [★15141]
Schools Assn; Amer. [8164]
Schools; Assn. of Amer. Law [8760]
Schools in Assn. of Amer. Universities; Assn. of Graduate [7890]
Schools; The Assn. of Boarding [9018]
Schools Assn. of the Central States; Independent [8538]
Schools; Assn. of Community Tribal [8936]
Schools; Assn. of Contract Tribal [★8936]
Schools and the Assn. of Independent Colleges and Schools; Natl. Assn. of Trade and Tech. [★9303]
Schools; Assn. of Lutheran Secondary [8801]
Schools Assn; Military Impacted [8885]
Schools; Assn. of Minority Hea. Professions [8850]
Schools; Bradley Commn. on History in [★8508]
Schools of Bus; Amer. Assn. of Collegiate [★8010]
Schools; Coalition of Essential [8180]
Schools and Colls; Amer. Coun. on [8225]
Schools and Colleges; Natl. Assn. of Private, Nontraditional [7947]
Schools and Colleges; New England Assn. of [8296]

Schools and Colleges; Northwest Assn. of [★8298]
Schools and Colleges of Optometry; Assn. of [15717]
Schools and Colleges of Tech; Accrediting Commn. of Career [7873]
Schools, Colleges and Universities of the United Methodist Church; Natl. Assn. of [8879]
Schools and Colleges; Western Assn. of [8314]
Schools Commn. on Accreditation and School Improvement; North Central Assn. of Colleges and [8297]
Schools; Commission on Elementary [★8277]
Schools; Commission on Secondary [★8277]
Schools Comm; Approval of [★8835]
Schools Comm. for Economic Educ; Natl. [8218]
Schools of Constr; Assoc. [8143]
Schools; Coun. of Graduate [8488]
Schools; Coun. of the Great City [9289]
Schools; Coun. for Religion in Independent [★8536]
Schools of Dance; Natl. Assn. of [8188]
Schools for the Deaf; Assn. of Superintendents and Principals of Amer. [★14749]
Schools for the Deaf; Conf. of Executives of Amer. [★14749]
Schools and Dept. of Journalism; Amer. Assn. of [★7893]
Schools Educ. Bd; Independent [★8540]
Schools for Exceptional Children; Natl. Assn. of Private [★9147]
Schools; Federated Coun. of Beth Jacob [8691]
Schools Found; Intl. [★8647]
Schools Fund; Friends of South African [8257]
Schools for Girls; Natl. Assn. of Principals of [9015]
Schools; Hispanic-Serving Hea. Professions [8864]
Schools and Inst; Amer. Assn. of Tech. High [★9228]
Schools Internship Program; International [★8645]
Schools Internship Program; International [★IO]
Schools of Journalism; Joint Comm. of [★8703]
Schools of Journalism and Mass Commun; Assn. of [7893]
Schools; Junior Engg. Training for [★8368]
Schools of Medical Tech; Bd. of [★15141]
Schools; Middle States Assn. of Colleges and [8277]
Schools; Middle States Assn. of Colleges and Secondary [★8277]
Schools Music Assn. [IO], London, United Kingdom
Schools of Music; Natl. Assn. of [8921]
Schools; Natl. Assn. of Corp. [★2481]
Schools; Natl. Assn. of Episcopal [8398]
Schools; Natl. Assn. of Federally Impacted [8349]
Schools; Natl. Assn. of Hispanic-Serving Hea. Professions [★8864]
Schools; Natl. Assn. of Independent [8540]
Schools; Natl. Assn. for Legal Support of Alternative [7946]
Schools; Natl. Assn. of Military [★8883]
Schools; Natl. Assn. for Neighborhood [17820]
Schools; Natl. Assn. of State Administrators and Supervisors of Private [9021]
Schools; Natl. Coalition to Abolish Corporal Punishment in [8207]
Schools; Natl. Coalition of Alternative Community [7948]
Schools; Natl. Coun. of Independent [★8540]
Schools; Network of Innovative [★8295]
Schools; North Central Assn. of Colleges and [★8297]
Schools; North Central Conf. on Summer [9201]
Schools; Northwest Assn. of Secondary and Higher [★8298]
Schools of Planning; Assn. of Collegiate [9285]
Schools Press Assn; Natl. Elementary [9012]
Schools Prog. for Adult Stud; Hebrew [★20172]
Schools and Programs; Natl. Assn. of Therapeutic [13738]
Schools of Public Affairs and Admin; Natl. Assn. of [6194]
Schools of Public Hea; Assn. of [16240]
Schools; Save Our [18717]
Schools; Sect. on Gay and Lesbian Legal Issues, Assn. of Amer. Law [★8761]
Schools in South Am; Assn. of Amer. [8642]
Schools; Southern Assn. of Colleges and [8308]
Schools Talent Search Prog; Independent [★8321]

Reference to "IO" in place of a book number signifies that the association may be found in the 45th edition of International Organizations.

Schools; Teachers' Division of Natl. Assn. of Cosmetology [★8160]

Schools; Teachers' Educational Coun. - Natl. Assn. of Accredited Cosmetology [★8160]

Schools; Teachers' Educational Coun. - Natl. Assn. of Cosmetology [★8160]

Schools of Theatre; Natl. Assn. of [9265]

Schools of Theological Schools; Amer. Assn. of [★9270]

Schools of the U.S; Assn. of Military Colleges and [8883]

Schools in the U.S; Coun. of Graduate [★8488]

Schools and Universities Club of New York; British [18984]

Schools and Universities Polo Assn. [IO], Great Missenden, United Kingdom

Schools of the U.S; Assn. of Military Colleges and [★8883]

Schooner Soc; Northwest [21882]

Schreckengost Family Exchange [21044]

Schubert Soc. of the USA [9816], c/o Dr. Janet I. Wasserman, Founder/Exec. Dir., 752 W End Ave., No. 5H, New York, NY 10025-6231, (212)222-2015

Schuhplattler Clubs in North Am; Fed. of Alpine and [9627]

Schulwerk Assn; Amer. Orff- [10547]

Schumacher Soc; E. F. [16995]

Schumann Memorial Found. - Defunct.

Schuss Ski Club [IO], Adelaide, Australia

Schutzhund Clubs of Am; United [22371]

Schwab Found. For Learning [★12496]

Schwab Found; Schwab Learning - A Prog. of the Charles [12496]

Schwab Learning - A Prog. of the Charles Schwab Found. [12496], 1650 S Amphlett Blvd., Ste. 300, San Mateo, CA 94402, (650)655-2410

Schwalm Historical Assn; Johannes [21128]

Schweitzer Fellowship; Albert [11101]

Schweiz Arbeitsgruppe fuer Kartographie [★IO]

Schweiz Basketball-Verband [IO], Fribourg, Switzerland

Schweiz Blinden- und Sehbehindertenverband [★IO]

Schweiz Chorvereinigung [★IO]

Schweizer Allianz Mission [★IO]

Schweizer Brauerei-Verband [★IO]

Schweizer Buchhaendler - und Verleger - Verband [★IO]

Schweizer Bund; North Amer. [★19399]

Schweizer Forum fur Kommunikationsrecht [★IO]

Schweizer Franchise Verband [★IO]

Schweizer Heimatwerk [★IO]

Schweizer Hochschulsport-Verband [★IO]

Schweizer Jugendherbergen [★IO]

Schweizer Milchproduzenten [★IO]

Schweizer Physiotherapie Verband [★IO]

Schweizer Tanzsportverbande [★IO]

Schweizer Verband der Journalistinnen und Journalisten [IO], Fribourg, Switzerland

Schweizer Wanderwege [★IO]

Schweizer Werbe-Auftraggeberverband [IO], Zurich, Switzerland

Schweizerische Akademie der Geistes- und Sozialwissenschaften [★IO]

Schweizerische Akademie der Medizinischen Wissenschaften [★IO]

Schweizerische Akademie der Technischen Wissenschaften [★IO]

Schweizerische Bankiervereinigung [★IO]

Schweizerische Bibelgesellschaft [★IO]

Schweizerische Chemische Gesellschaft [★IO]

Schweizerische Direktoren-Konferenz Gewerblich Industrieller Berufsund Fachschulen [★IO]

Schweizerische Fachvereinigung fur Energiewirtschaft [★IO]

Schweizerische Geomorphologische Gesellschaft [★IO]

Schweizerische Gesellschaft fur Astrophysik und Astronomie [★IO]

Schweizerische Gesellschaft fur Ernahrung [★IO]

Schweizerische Gesellschaft fur Gerontologie [★IO]

Schweizerische Gesellschaft fur Gesundheitspolitik [★IO]

Schweizerische Gesellschaft fur Kardiologie [★IO]

Schweizerische Gesellschaft fur Kartografie [★IO]

Schweizerische Gesellschaft fur Kieferorthopadie [★IO]

Schweizerische Gesellschaft fur Medizinische Informatik [★IO]

Schweizerische Gesellschaft fur Photogrammetrie Bildanalyse und Fernerkundung [★IO]

Schweizerische Gesellschaft fur Rheumatologie [IO], Zurich, Switzerland

Schweizerische Gesellschaft fur Soziologie [★IO]

Schweizerische Gesellschaft fur Strahlenbiologie und Medizinische Physik [★IO]

Schweizerische Gesellschaft zum Studium des Schmerzes [★IO]

Schweizerische Gesellschaft fur Theaterkultur [★IO]

Schweizerische Gesellschaft fur Versuchstierkunde [★IO]

Schweizerische Huntington Vereinigung [IO], Oberhasli, Switzerland

Schweizerische Hypertonie Gesellschaft [★IO]

Schweizerische Lebensrettungs-Gesellschaft [★IO]

Schweizerische Liga gegen Epilepsie [★IO]

Schweizerische Mgt. Gesellschaft [★IO]

Schweizerische Nationalkommission Justitia et Pax [IO], Bern, Switzerland

Schweizerische Normen-Vereinigung [★IO]

Schweizerische Physikalische Gesellschaft [★IO]

Schweizerische Vereinigung fur Dokumentation [★IO]

Schweizerische Vereinigung gegen die Osteoprorose [★IO]

Schweizerische Vereinigung fur Schiedsgerichtsbarkeit [★IO]

Schweizerische Vereinigung fur Sonnenenergie [★IO]

Schweizerische Zentralstelle fur Heilpadagogik [★IO]

Schweizerischen Textil- und Bekleidungsindustrie [★IO]

Schweizerischer Anwaltsverband [★IO]

Schweizerischer Arbeitgeberverband [★IO]

Schweizerischer Drogisten-Verband [★IO]

Schweizerischer Elektrotechnischer Verein [★IO]

Schweizerischer Forstverein [★IO]

Schweizerischer Friedensrat [★IO]

Schweizerischer Handels- und Industrie-Verein [★IO]

Schweizerischer Ingenieur- und Architektenverein [★IO]

Schweizerischer Kanu-Verband [★IO]

Schweizerischer Konditor-Confiseurmeister-Verband [★IO]

Schweizerischer Kosmetik- und Waschmittelverband [★IO]

Schweizerischer Landfrauenverband [★IO]

Schweizerischer Leichtathletikverband [★IO]

Schweizerischer Saatgutproduzentenverband [★IO]

Schweizerischer Spirituosenverband [★IO]

Schweizerischer Squash-Verband [★IO]

Schweizerischer Tennisverband [★IO]

Schweizerischer Unihockey Verband [★IO]

Schweizerischer Verband der Akademikerinnen [IO], Bivio, Switzerland

Schweizerischer Verband der Akademikerinnen [★IO]

Schweizerischer Verband Akademischen Volks- und Betriebswirtschafter [IO], Zurich, Switzerland

Schweizerischer Verband Diplomierter ErnahrungsberaterInnen [★IO]

Schweizerischer Verband fuer Geomatik und Landmanagement [★IO]

Schweizerischer Verband der Ingenieur-Agronominnen und der Lebensmittel-Ingenieurinnen [★IO]

Schweizerischer Verband fur interne Kommunikation [★IO]

Schweizerischer Verband fur Landtechnik [IO], Riniken, Switzerland

Schweizerischer Verband der Lebensmittel-Detaillisten [★IO]

Schweizerischer Verband alleinerziehender Muetter und Vater [★IO]

Schweizerischer Verband des Personals Oeffentlicher Dienste [IO], Zurich, Switzerland

Schweizerischer Verband fur Weiterbildung [★IO]

Schweizerischer Volleyball-Verband [★IO]

Schweizerisches Arbeiterhilfswerk [★IO]

Schweizerrisher Ruderverband [★IO]

Schwenkfeldian Exile Soc. [★21244]

Schwenkfeldian Exiles; Soc. of the Descendants of the [21244]

Schwestern von der Gottlichen Vorsehung [★IO]

Sci-Fi Soc. of Long Island - Address unknown since 1999.

SCI - Intl. Voluntary Ser. [13404], 5505 Walnut Level Rd., Crozet, VA 22932, (206)350-6585

SCI - Intl. Voluntary Ser. [IO], Crozet, VA, United States

Science

AACC Intl. [6660]

Academia Colombiana de Ciencias Exactas, Fisicas y Naturales [IO]

Academia Sinica [IO]

Academie des Sciences [IO]

Acad. of Applied Sci. [7592]

Acad. of Arts and Sciences of the Americas [18830]

Acad. of Natural Sciences [7356]

Acad. of Physical, Mathematical and Natural Sciences [IO]

Acad. of Sciences of the Czech Republic [IO]

Acad. of Sciences for the Developing World [IO]

Acad. of Sciences of Lisbon [IO]

Acad. of Sciences, Lithuania [IO]

Acad. of Sciences of Moldova [IO]

Acad. of Sciences - Uzbekistan [IO]

Accademia delle Scienze di Torino [IO]

Access Res. Network [9095]

Adhesion Soc. [6661]

Advocates for Women in Sci., Engg., and Mathematics [7593]

African Acad. of Sciences [IO]

African Network of Sci. and Technological Institutions [IO]

African Sci. Inst. [7594]

African Wind Energy Assn. [IO]

All European Academies [IO]

Alliance for Sci. and Tech. Res. in Am. [7595]

Allied Social Sci. Associations [7645]

The Amazona Soc. [7410]

Ambrose Monell Found. [13110]

Amer. Acad. of Arts and Sciences [9605]

Amer. Acad. of Microbiology [6559]

Amer. Assn. for the Advancement of Sci. [7596]

Amer. Assn. for Aerosol Res. [6662]

Amer. Assn. of Behavioral and Social Sciences [6522]

Amer. Assn. of Blacks in Energy [6936]

Amer. Assn. for Crystal Growth [6851]

Amer. Assn. for Lab. Accreditation [7234]

Amer. Assn. for Medical Chronobiology and Chronotherapeutics [13751]

Amer. Assn. of Pharmaceutical Scientists [7467]

Amer. Assn. of Physical Anthropologists [6403]

Amer. Assn. of Stratigraphic Palynologists [7434]

Amer. Bd. of Bioanalysis [7235]

Amer. Bd. of Toxicology [7799]

Amer. Carbon Soc. [6663]

Amer. Ceramic Soc. [6657]

Amer. Cetacean Soc. [7258]

Amer. Chem. Soc. [6664]

Amer. Coll. of Orgonomy [15738]

Amer. Coll. of Toxicology [7800]

Amer. Comm. for the Weizmann Inst. of Sci. [7597]

Amer. Coun. of Independent Labs. [7236]

Amer. Ecological Engg. Soc. [6864]

Amer. Filtration and Separations Soc. [7724]

Amer. Genetic Assn. [7111]

Amer. Geological Inst. [7126]

Amer. Geophysical Union [7136]

Amer. Indian Sci. and Engg. Soc. [6987]

Amer. Inst. of Aeronautics and Astronautics [6369]

Amer. Inst. of Biological Sciences [6560]

Amer. Inst. of Chem. Engineers [6665]

Amer. Inst. of Chemists [6666]

Amer. Inst. of Physics [7499]

Amer. Leather Chemists Assn. [6667]

Amer. Littoral Soc. - Northeast Region [7269]

Amer. Microchemical Soc. [6668]

Amer. Microscopical Soc. [7332]

Amer. Nature Stud. Soc. [7358]

Amer. Nuclear Soc. [7385]

A star before a book entry number signifies that the name is not listed separately, but is mentioned within the entry.

Amer. Oil Chemists' Soc. **[6669]**
Amer. Philosophical Soc. **[7598]**
Amer. Physical Soc. **[7500]**
Amer. Physiological Soc. **[7510]**
Amer. Quaternary Assn. **[7359]**
Amer. Rock Art Res. Assn. **[6438]**
Amer. Sci. Affiliation **[20546]**
Amer. Soc. for Biochemistry and Molecular Biology **[6546]**
Amer. Soc. of Brewing Chemists **[6670]**
Amer. Soc. for Cell Biology **[6562]**
Amer. Soc. for Clinical Investigation **[14020]**
Amer. Soc. for Cybernetics **[6719]**
Amer. Soc. for Human Genetics **[7113]**
Amer. Soc. of Ichthyologists and Herpetologists **[7158]**
Amer. Soc. of Inventors **[7226]**
Amer. Soc. for Mass Spectrometry **[7688]**
Amer. Soc. for Microbiology **[6565]**
Amer. Soc. for Neurochemistry **[7374]**
Amer. Soc. for Testing and Materials **[7789]**
Amer. Sociological Assn. **[7658]**
Amer. Type Culture Coll. **[6567]**
Amer. Water Resources Assn. **[7827]**
Americans to Ban Cloning **[17089]**
Analytical Lab. Managers Assn. **[7237]**
Animal Behavior Mgt. Alliance **[7860]**
Animal Behavior Soc. **[7861]**
Annals of Improbable Res. **[7599]**
Annals of Improbable Res. **[IO]**
Anthropology Film Center **[6407]**
Armenian Behavioral Sci. Assn. **[6525]**
Armenian Engineers and Scientists of Am. **[7600]**
Armenian Engineers and Scientists of Am. **[IO]**
Art and Sci. Collaborations **[9607]**
ASFE **[7137]**
Asian Inst. of Gemological Sciences, Bangkok **[IO]**
Assn. for Africanist Anthropology **[6408]**
Assn. for Arid Lands Stud. **[4498]**
Assn. for Astronomy Educ. **[IO]**
Assn. for the Behavioral Sciences and Medical Educ. **[6527]**
Assn. of Black Anthropologists **[6409]**
Assn. of Black Sociologists **[7659]**
Assn. of Chinese Scientists and Engineers - U.S.A. **[6698]**
Assn. of Clinical Scientists **[14022]**
Assn. of Consulting Chemists and Chem. Engineers **[6672]**
Assn. of Consulting Scientists **[IO]**
Assn. of Educators in Imaging and Radiologic Sciences **[9096]**
Assn. of Fertilizer and Phosphate Chemists **[6673]**
Assn. for the Foundations of Sci., Language and Cognition **[IO]**
Assn. of Ground Water Scientists and Engineers - A Division of Natl. Ground Water Assn. **[7828]**
Assn. for Humanist Sociology **[7660]**
Assn. for Lab. Automation **[6515]**
Assn. of Latina and Latino Anthropologists **[6410]**
Assn. for Mexican Cave Stud. **[7691]**
Assn. for Multicultural Sci. Educ. **[9097]**
Assn. of Muslim Scientists and Engineers **[7005]**
Assn. of Muslim Social Scientists **[7646]**
Assn. of Orthodox Jewish Scientists **[7601]**
Assn. for Res. in Personality **[7543]**
Assn. for Sci. Educ. **[IO]**
Assn. of Sci. Museum Directors **[10498]**
Assn. of Science-Technology Centers **[10499]**
Assn. for the Sci. Stud. of Consciousness **[8140]**
Assn. of South African Women in Sci. and Engg. **[IO]**
Assn. of State Energy Res. and Tech. Transfer Institutions **[6945]**
Assn. for the Stud. of Food and Soc. **[7090]**
Assn. for Symbolic Logic **[7287]**
Assn. of Thai Professionals in Am. and Canada **[19406]**
Assn. for Tropical Biology and Conservation **[6570]**
Assn. of Vision Sci. Librarians **[10341]**
Assn. for Women Geoscientists **[7139]**
Assn. for Women in Sci. **[7602]**

Assn. for Women in the Sciences **[IO]**
Assn. of Women Soil Scientists **[7672]**
Astronaut Scholars Honor Soc. **[24584]**
Australasian Sci. Educ. Res. Assn. **[IO]**
Australian Acad. of Sci. **[IO]**
Australian Coun. of Deans of Sci. **[IO]**
Australian and New Zealand Assn. for the Advancement of Sci. **[IO]**
Australian and New Zealand Soc. of Respiratory Sci. **[IO]**
Austrian Acad. of Sciences **[IO]**
Austrian Sci. Fund **[IO]**
AVS Sci. and Tech. Soc. **[7822]**
BA **[IO]**
Bangladesh Acad. of Sciences **[IO]**
Beta Beta Beta **[24408]**
Beta Kappa Chi **[24585]**
Bill and Melinda Gates Found. **[12273]**
Bioelectromagnetics Soc. **[6555]**
Bioelectromagnetics Special Interest Gp. **[6556]**
Biological Stain Commn. **[6571]**
Biomass Energy Res. Assn. **[6946]**
Biomedical Engg. Soc. **[6607]**
Biophysical Soc. **[6612]**
Biosciences Fed. **[IO]**
Botanical Soc. of Am. **[6632]**
Brazilian Acad. of Sciences **[IO]**
Brazilian Soc. for the Advancement of Sci. **[IO]**
Bulgarian Acad. of Sciences **[IO]**
Bulletin of the Atomic Scientists **[7603]**
Calorimetry Conf. **[7796]**
Canadian Soc. for the History and Philosophy of Sci. **[IO]**
Carnegie Institution of Washington **[7564]**
Cave Res. Found. **[7692]**
Cell Proliferation Soc. **[6573]**
Cell Stress Soc. Intl. **[16488]**
Center for Sci. in the Public Interest **[17314]**
Central Soc. for Clinical Res. **[14023]**
Chem. Heritage Found. **[10101]**
China Assn. for Sci. and Tech. **[IO]**
Chinese Acad. of Sciences **[IO]**
Chinese Amer. Food Soc. **[7092]**
CIIT Centers for Hea. Res. **[7801]**
Climate Inst. **[4542]**
Coalition for Educ. in the Life Sciences **[9098]**
Coalition for Genetic Fairness **[17107]**
Cognitive Neuroscience Soc. **[15407]**
Colombian Acad. of Exact, Physical, and Natural Sciences **[IO]**
Colombian Assn. for the Advancement of Sci. **[IO]**
Combustion Inst. **[6709]**
Comet Media Found. of Mumbai, India **[IO]**
Commn. on Professionals in Sci. and Tech. **[7604]**
Comm. on Capacity Building Sci. **[9099]**
Comm. on Capacity Building Sci. **[IO]**
Comm. of Concerned Scientists **[17752]**
Comm. on the Status of Women in Microbiology **[6574]**
Comparative Cognition Soc. **[6400]**
Conf. Bd. of the Mathematical Sciences **[7289]**
Consortium of Social Sci. Associations **[7649]**
Coun. for the Advancement of Sci. Writing **[3107]**
Coun. for Biotechnology Info. **[6614]**
Coun. for Chem. Res. **[6679]**
Coun. of Colleges of Arts and Sciences **[7971]**
Coun. for Elementary Sci. Intl. **[9100]**
Coun. for Elementary Sci. Intl. **[IO]**
Coun. of Engineers and Scientists Organizations **[7817]**
Coun. of Entomology Dept. Administrators **[7060]**
Coun. for Intl. Congresses of Dipterology **[IO]**
Coun. on Ionizing Radiation Measurements and Standards **[7556]**
Coun. of Sci. Soc. Presidents **[7605]**
Coun. of State Sci. Supervisors **[9101]**
Coun. on Undergraduate Res. **[9059]**
Creation Health Found. **[20547]**
Creation Res. Soc. **[20548]**
Croatian Acad. of Sciences and Arts **[IO]**
The Crustacean Soc. **[7863]**
Cushman Found. for Foraminiferal Res. **[7428]**
Daguerreian Soc. **[10848]**
Delegation of the Finnish Academies of Sci. and Letters **[IO]**

Dept. for Professional Employees, AFL-CIO **[24173]**
Digital Govt. Soc. of North Am. **[7151]**
Earthwatch Inst. **[8413]**
EISCAT Sci. Assn. **[IO]**
Electrochemical Soc. **[6680]**
Emulsion Polymers Inst. **[6681]**
Engg. and Sci. Network on Thinking **[7217]**
Engg. Soc. of Detroit **[7012]**
Environmental Mutagen Soc. **[6575]**
Estonian Acad. of Sciences **[IO]**
Estuarine Res. Fed. **[7271]**
Eugenics Special Interest Gp. **[7114]**
European Colloid and Interface Soc. **[IO]**
European Coun. of Applied Sciences and Engg. **[IO]**
European Microbeam Anal. Soc. **[IO]**
European Regional Sci. Assn. **[IO]**
Evolutionary Anthropology Soc. **[6416]**
Experiments in Art and Tech. **[9439]**
Explorers Club **[7076]**
Family, Career and Community Leaders of Am. **[8417]**
Fed. of Amer. Societies for Experimental Biology **[6576]**
Fed. of Analytical Chemistry and Spectroscopy Societies **[6682]**
Fed. of Asian Sci. Academies and Societies - Malaysia **[IO]**
Fed. of Australian Sci. and Technological Societies **[IO]**
Fed. of Behavioral, Psychological, and Cognitive Sciences **[6530]**
Fed. of Galaxy Explorers **[9136]**
Fed. of Materials Societies **[7281]**
Fed. of Sci. and Tech. Unions in Bulgaria **[IO]**
Fed. for Unified Sci. Educ. **[9102]**
Fiber Soc. **[7078]**
For Inspiration and Recognition of Sci. and Tech. **[8319]**
Found. for Sci. and Disability **[11946]**
French Acad. of Sciences **[IO]**
French Canadian Assn. for the Advancement of the Sciences **[IO]**
G. Unger Vetlesen Found. **[12719]**
GalaxyGoo **[8065]**
Gender and Sci. and Tech. Assn. **[IO]**
Genesis Inst. **[20549]**
Genetics Soc. of Am. **[7115]**
Geochemical Soc. **[7141]**
Georgian Acad. of Sciences **[IO]**
German Inst. for Polymers **[IO]**
Ghana Acad. of Arts and Sciences **[IO]**
Global Assn. for Interpersonal Neurobiology Stud. **[7375]**
Guild of Natural Sci. Illustrators **[7153]**
Hands On Sci. Outreach **[8067]**
Hawkes Bay Br. of the Royal Soc. of New Zealand **[IO]**
Histochemical Soc. **[13938]**
History of Sci. Soc. **[10119]**
History of Sci. Soc. of Japan **[IO]**
HOPOS - The Intl. Soc. for the History of Philosophy of Sci. **[9103]**
Human Behavior and Evolution Soc. **[6531]**
Human Biology Assn. **[6577]**
Hungarian Acad. of Sciences **[IO]**
IEEE Nuclear and Plasma Sciences Soc. **[7386]**
Indian Acad. of Sciences **[IO]**
Indian Assn. for the Cultivation of Sci. **[IO]**
Indian Educators Fed. **[8938]**
Indian Natl. Sci. Acad. **[IO]**
Indian Sci. Cong. Assn. **[IO]**
Institute for Axiomatic Knowledge and Education **[IO]**
Inst. for Axiomatic Knowledge and Educ. **[7606]**
Inst. for Chem. Educ. **[8062]**
Inst. for Creation Res. **[20538]**
Inst. of Elecl. and Electronics Engineers **[6926]**
Inst. of Environmental Sciences and Tech. **[7570]**
Inst. of Medicine **[7607]**
Inst. of Navigation **[7369]**
Inst. of Nuclear Materials Mgt. **[7387]**
Inst. of Nuclear Power Operations **[7392]**
Inst. on Religion in an Age of Sci. **[20550]**

Reference to "IO" in place of a book number signifies that the association may be found in the 45th edition of International Organizations.

Inst. for Sci. and Intl. Security [18583]
Inst. for Sci. and Intl. Security [IO]
Inst. of Sci. Tech. [IO]
Inst. for Social Res. [7650]
Inst. for the Stud. of Man [6418]
Inst. for Women in Trades, Tech. and Sci. [4042]
Integrated Mfg. Tech. Initiative [7264]
Intl. Acad. of Sciences [IO]
Intl. Assn. for the Advancement of Earth and
  Environmental Sciences [4511]
Intl. Assn. of Animal Behavior Consultants [7864]
Intl. Assn. of Colloid and Interface Scientists [IO]
Intl. Assn. for Cryptologic Res. [6849]
Intl. Assn. of Environmental Mutagen Societies
  [6578]
Intl. Assn. for Great Lakes Res. [7239]
Intl. Assn. for Hydrogen Energy [6957]
Intl. Assn. of Nanotechnology [7741]
Intl. Assn. for the Physical Sciences of the
  Oceans [7398]
Intl. Assn. of Sci. Parks [IO]
Intl. Assn. for Sci., Tech. and Soc. [7608]
Intl. Assn. for Soc. and Natural Resources [5039]
Intl. Assn. of Wildland Fire [4686]
Intl. Behavioral Neuroscience Soc. [15408]
Intl. Biogeography Soc. [7122]
Intl. Biometric Soc., Eastern North Amer. Region
  [7708]
Intl. Cell Death Soc. [6854]
Intl. Commn. on Physics Educ. [IO]
Intl. Comm. of Historical Sciences [IO]
Intl. Comm. on Ultra-High Intensity Lasers [7245]
Intl. Coun. of Academies of Engg. and Technologi-
  cal Sciences [9104]
Intl. Coun. of Academies of Engg. and Technologi-
  cal Sciences [IO]
Intl. Coun. of Associations for Sci. Educ. [IO]
Intl. Coun. for Sci. [IO]
Intl. Cryogenic Materials Conf. [6846]
Intl. Cytokine Soc. [6580]
Intl. Dark-Sky Assn. [6506]
Intl. Endotoxin and Innate Immunity Soc. [7803]
Intl. Experimental Aerospace Soc. [6375]
Intl. Fed. of Nonlinear Analysts [7609]
Intl. Fed. of Nonlinear Analysts [IO]
Intl. Fortean Org. [7477]
Intl. Graphic Arts Educ. Assn. [8470]
Intl. Humic Substances Soc. [7610]
Intl. Humic Substances Soc. [IO]
Intl. Inst. of Connector and Interconnection Tech.
  [6929]
Intl. Inst. of Forecasters [7106]
Intl. Life Sciences Inst., European Br. [IO]
Intl. Liquid Crystal Soc. [6853]
Intl. Maillard Reaction Soc. [6683]
Intl. Microelectronic and Packaging Soc. [6930]
Intl. Microwave Power Inst. [7338]
Intl. Org. of Plant Biosystematists [6639]
Intl. Org. for Sci. and Tech. Educ. [IO]
Intl. Precious Metals Inst. [7318]
Intl. Proteolysis Soc. [6549]
Intl. Rural Sociology Assn. [7664]
Intl. Soc. for Adaptive Behavior [6533]
Intl. Soc. of African Scientists [7611]
Intl. Soc. of African Scientists [IO]
Intl. Soc. of Artificial Life [6584]
Intl. Soc. for Bayesian Anal. [7291]
Intl. Soc. for Biological and Environmental
  Repositories [6585]
Intl. Soc. for Bioluminescence and Chemilumines-
  cence [7612]
Intl. Soc. for Bioluminescence and Chemilumines-
  cence [IO]
Intl. Soc. for Biosafety Res. [6586]
Intl. Soc. of Chem. Ecology [6550]
Intl. Soc. of Coating Sci. and Tech. [6705]
Intl. Soc. of Cryptozoology [7865]
Intl. Soc. of Difference Equations [7292]
Intl. Soc. of Environmental Forensics [7098]
Intl. Soc. for the History of the Neurosciences
  [7376]
Intl. Soc. of India Chemists and Chem. Engineers
  [6685]
Intl. Soc. of Iraqi Scientists [7613]
Intl. Soc. of Iraqi Scientists [IO]

Intl. Soc. of Lyophilization - Freeze Drying [6616]
Intl. Soc. for Molecular Plant Microbe Interactions
  [6641]
Intl. Soc. of Motor Control [7377]
Intl. Soc. for Nanoscale Sci., Computation and
  Engg. [7614]
Intl. Soc. for Nanoscale Sci., Computation and
  Engg. [IO]
Intl. Soc. for Neuroimmunomodulation [15395]
Intl. Soc. for Phylogenetic Nomenclature [7116]
Intl. Soc. for Presence Res. [7572]
Intl. Soc. for Scientometrics and Informetrics [IO]
Intl. Soc. of Soil Mechanics and Geotechnical
  Engg. [7147]
Intl. Weed Sci. Soc. [4102]
Intl. Women's Anthropology Conf. [6420]
Inventors Clubs of Am. [7229]
Iranian Chemists' Assn. of the Amer. Chem. Soc.
  [6687]
ISA - Instrumentation, Systems, and Automation
  Soc. [7220]
Islamic Acad. of Sciences [IO]
Islamic Univ. of Tech. [IO]
Israel Acad. of Sciences and Humanities [IO]
Japan Info. Access Proj. [10265]
Japan Scientists' Assn. [IO]
Japan Soc. for the Promotion of Sci. [IO]
Japanese Soc. of Applied Glycoscience [IO]
JILA [7503]
John Burroughs Assn. [7362]
Junior Engg. Tech. Soc. [8368]
Kenya Natl. Acad. of Sciences [IO]
The Keystone Center [7746]
Korean-American Scientists and Engineers Assn.
  [7024]
Kroeber Anthropological Soc. [6421]
Lambda Delta Lambda [24586]
Landau Network - Centry Volta [IO]
Laser Inst. of Am. [7247]
Latin Amer. Acad. of Sciences [IO]
Latvian Acad. of Sciences [IO]
Leonardo, The Intl. Soc. for the Arts, Sciences
  and Tech. [9610]
Lisbon Acad. of Sciences [IO]
Lithuanian Acad. of Sciences [IO]
Malaysian Sci. Assn. [IO]
Malaysian Senior Scientists' Assn. [IO]
Marine Tech. Soc. [7273]
Materials Res. Soc. [7283]
Math/Science Network [8825]
Mexican Acad. of Sciences [IO]
Mexican Org. for the History of Sci. and Tech. [IO]
Microscopy Soc. of Am. [7335]
Middle Atlantic Planetarium Soc. [9105]
Minorities in Agriculture, Natural Resources and
  Related Sciences [10486]
Minority Women In Sci. [7615]
Mongolian Acad. of Sciences [IO]
The Mountain Inst. [9960]
NanoBusiness Alliance [7750]
Natl. Acad. of Exact, Physical and Natural Sci-
  ences [IO]
Natl. Acad. of Sciences [7616]
Natl. Acad. of Sciences of Armenia [IO]
Natl. Acad. of Sciences of Belarus [IO]
Natl. Acad. of Sciences of Bolivia [IO]
Natl. Acad. of Sciences of the Republic of Korea
  [IO]
Natl. Alliance of Clean Energy Bus. Incubators
  [1287]
Natl. Alliance of State Sci. and Mathematics Coali-
  tions [9106]
Natl. Assn. of Academies of Sci. [7617]
Natl. Assn. of Hea. Sci. Educ. Partnership [9107]
Natl. Assn. for the Practice of Anthropology [6422]
Natl. Assn. for Res. in Sci. Teaching [9108]
Natl. Assn. of Sci. Writers [3133]
Natl. Center for Improving Sci. Educ. [9109]
Natl. Center for Sci. Educ. [9110]
Natl. Centre for Res. [IO]
Natl. Character Lab. [6536]
Natl. Coun. of Black Engineers and Scientists
  [7618]
Natl. Coun. on Gene Resources [7118]
Natl. Coun. for GeoCosmic Res. [6841]

Natl. Coun. of Innovation, Sci. and Tech. [IO]
Natl. Coun. for Sci. and the Env. [7067]
Natl. Coun. for Sci. Res. - Lebanon [IO]
Natl. Coun. for Scientific and Technological
  Research [IO]
Natl. Coun. of State Sociological Associations
  [7665]
Natl. Earth Sci. Teachers Assn. [9111]
Natl. Hydrogen Assn. [7619]
Natl. Inst. of Ceramic Engineers [6658]
Natl. Inst. of Packaging, Handling and Logistics
  Engineers [7427]
Natl. Middle Level Sci. Teachers' Assn. [9112]
Natl. Org. of Gay and Lesbian Scientists and
  Tech. Professionals [7620]
Natl. Org. for the Professional Advancement of
  Black Chemists and Chem. Engineers [6689]
Natl. Postdoctoral Assn. [9064]
Natl. Res. Coun. [7621]
Natl. Res. Coun. of Canada [IO]
Natl. Res. Coun. of the Philippines [IO]
Natl. Sci. Coun. [IO]
Natl. Sci. Educ. Leadership Assn. [9113]
Natl. Sci. Found. [7622]
Natl. Sci. Teachers Assn. [9114]
Natl. Soc. of Black Engineers [7034]
Natl. Soc. of Consulting Soil Scientists [5222]
Natl. Soc. of Hispanic Physicists [7505]
Natl. Speleological Soc. [7693]
Natl. Tech. Assn. [7752]
Natl. Women's Hall of Fame [20716]
Natural Dyes Intl. [8213]
Natural Sci. Collections Alliance [6590]
Neutron Scattering Soc. of Am. [7506]
New York Acad. of Sciences [7623]
New Zealand Assn. of Sci. Educators [IO]
New Zealand Assn. of Scientists [IO]
Nordic Coll. of Caring Sciences [IO]
North Am. Taiwanese Engineers' Assn. [7036]
North Amer. Alliance of Chem. Engineers [6690]
North Amer. Catalysis Soc. [7624]
North Amer. Computational Social and Org. Sci-
  ences [6740]
North Amer. Forensic Entomology Assn. [7064]
North Amer. Fuzzy Info. Processing Soc. [6741]
North Amer. Meteor Network [7328]
North Amer. Truffling Soc. [7354]
North Amer. Weed Mgt. Assn. [4106]
Norwegian Soc. of Chartered Tech. and Sci.
  Professionals [IO]
Oak Ridge Assoc. Universities [7625]
The Oceanography Soc. [7403]
Org. of Biological Field Stations [6591]
Org. for Human Brain Mapping [7379]
Org. for Professional Astrology [6495]
Overseas Chinese Physics Assn. [7507]
Pacific Sci. Assn. [7626]
Pacific Sci. Assn. [IO]
Pakistan Acad. of Sciences [IO]
Paleontological Res. Institution/Museum of the
  Earth [7429]
Paleontological Soc. [7430]
Pan-American Assn. for Biochemistry and
  Molecular Biology [6551]
Panel on World Data Centers [7210]
Pattern Recognition Soc. [7457]
PET Resin Assn. [3054]
Phi Sigma [24409]
Philosophy of Sci. Assn. [10825]
Polanyi Soc. [10826]
Polish Acad. of Sciences [IO]
Pontifical Acad. of Sciences [IO]
Poultry Sci. Assn. [5116]
Proteome Soc. [7119]
Public Responsibility in Medicine and Res.
  [18585]
Radiation and Public Hea. Proj. [16270]
Radiation Res. Soc. [7557]
Reasons to Believe [20551]
Res. Prog. at Earthwatch Inst. [7574]
Romanian Acad. [IO]
Royal Acad. of Sci., Humanities, and Fine Arts of
  Belgium [IO]
Royal Institution of Great Britain [IO]
Royal Nepal Acad. of Sci. and Tech. [IO]

A star before a book entry number signifies that the name is not listed separately, but is mentioned within the entry.

Royal Soc. of New Zealand [IO]
Royal Soc. of New Zealand, Canterbury Br. [IO]
Royal Soc. of New Zealand, Manawatu Br. [IO]
Royal Soc. of New Zealand, North Shore Br. [IO]
Royal Soc. of New Zealand, Rotorua Br. [IO]
Royal Soc. of South Africa [IO]
Royal Swedish Acad. of Sciences [IO]
RSNZ Wellington Br. [IO]
Rural Sociological Soc. [7667]
Russian Acad. of Sciences [IO]
School Science and Mathematics Association [IO]
School Sci. and Mathematics Assn. [9115]
Sci. Coun. of Asia [IO]
Sci. Coun. of Japan [IO]
Sci. Coun. of the United Kingdom [IO]
Science for the People [7627]
Sci. Res. Coun. [IO]
Sci. Ser. [IO]
Sci. Ser. [7628]
Sci. Songwriters' Assn. [10693]
Sci. Comm. on Solar Terrestrial Physics [7508]
Sci. Exploration Soc. [IO]
Sci. and Tech. Res. Coun. of Turkey [IO]
Seafloor Geosciences Div. [7404]
SEAMEO Regional Centre for Educ. in Sci. and
  Mathematics [IO]
SEAMEO Regional Centre for Tropical Biology
  [IO]
Serbian Acad. of Sciences and Arts [IO]
Sigma Delta Epsilon, Graduate Women in Sci.
  [24587]
Sigma Xi, The Sci. Res. Soc. [24588]
Sigma Zeta [24589]
Sino-American Pharmaceutical Professionals
  Assn. [15951]
Skeptics Soc. [7629]
Slovak Acad. of Sciences [IO]
Social Sci. History Assn. [7654]
Social Sci. Res. Coun. [7655]
Social Sciences Services and Resources [7656]
Sociedad de Ciencias Aranzadi [IO]
Societe de Chimie Industrielle, Amer. Sect. [6693]
Soc. for Advancement of Chicanos and Native
  Americans in Sci. [7630]
Soc. for Amateur Scientists [7631]
Soc. for the Anthropology of Europe [6423]
Soc. for the Anthropology of Food and Nutrition
  [6424]
Soc. for the Anthropology of North Am. [6425]
Soc. for Applied Anthropology [6427]
Soc. for Applied Spectroscopy [7690]
Soc. of Automotive Engineers [7632]
Soc. of Automotive Engineers [6697]
Soc. for Biological Engg. [6593]
Soc. for Canadian Women in Sci. and Tech. [IO]
Soc. of Chinese Amer. Professors and Scientists
  [9024]
Soc. for Clinical Trials [14028]
Soc. of Cosmetic Chemists [6695]
Soc. for Developmental Biology [6595]
Soc. for Economic Botany [6649]
Soc. of Engg. Sci. [7041]
Soc. of Ethnobiology [6596]
Soc. for Evolutionary Anal. in Law [6539]
Soc. for Experimental Biology and Medicine
  [6597]
Soc. for Experimental Mechanics [7713]
Soc. of Exploration Geo-physicists [7149]
Soc. of Flavor Chemists [6696]
Soc. For Biomaterials [6609]
Soc. for Free Radical Biology and Medicine
  [6613]
Soc. of Gen. Physiologists [7511]
Soc. for History Educ. [8511]
Soc. for the History of Psychology [7548]
Soc. for Human Performance in Extreme Environ-
  ments [6540]
Soc. for Imaging Sci. and Tech. [7497]
Soc. for In Vitro Biology [6598]
Soc. for Indus. Microbiology [6599]
Soc. for Info. Display [6745]
Soc. of Japanese Women Scientists [IO]
Soc. for Latin Amer. Anthropology [6431]
Soc. for Medical Anthropology [6434]
Soc. of Mexican Amer. Engineers and Scientists
  [7043]

Soc. of Mineral Analysts [7345]
Soc. for Molecular Biology and Evolution [6601]
Soc. for Molecular Imaging [15181]
Soc. for Natural Philosophy [7295]
Soc. for Neuroscience [7380]
Soc. of Petrophysicists and Well Log Analysts
  [7466]
Soc. of Physics Students [7509]
Soc. for the Promotion of Sci. and Scholarship
  [3255]
Soc. for the Protection of Old Fishes [7177]
Soc. of Psychological Hypnosis [16178]
Soc. for the Psychological Stud. of Ethnic Minority
  Issues [16179]
Soc. of Rheology [7579]
Soc. for Sci. Exploration [7485]
Soc. for Sedimentary Geology [7432]
Soc. for Social Stud. of Sci. [7633]
Soc. for Theoretical and Philosophical Psychology
  [16186]
Soc. of Toxicology [7804]
Soc. of Turkish Amer. Architects, Engineers and
  Scientists [7048]
Soc. of Vertebrate Paleontology [7433]
Soc. for Visual Anthropology [6436]
Soc. for Vocational Psychology [7551]
Soc. of Wetland Scientists [4452]
Soc. for Whole Body Autoradiography [15149]
Sociological Practice Assn. [7670]
Sociological Res. Assn. [7671]
Soil Sci. Soc. of Am. [7674]
Southern Africa Assn. for the Advancement of Sci.
  [IO]
Space Settlement Studies Program [6387]
Sri Lanka Assn. for the Advancement of Sci. [IO]
Swiss Acad. of Medical Sciences [IO]
Swiss Acad. of Sciences [IO]
Teratology Soc. [6602]
Third World Network of Sci. Organizations [IO]
Third World Org. for Women in Sci. [IO]
Thomson Sci. - Europe, Middle East, and Africa
  [IO]
Toxicological History Soc. [7805]
Triangle Coalition for Sci. and Tech. Educ. [9116]
Tripoli Rocketry Assn. [9117]
Turkish Acad. of Sciences [IO]
Turkish Amer. Scientists and Scholars Assn.
  [7636]
Ukrainian Engineers' Soc. of Am. [7050]
Union of Scientists in Bulgaria [IO]
U.S. Assn. for Computational Mechanics [7300]
U.S. Comm. on Irrigation and Drainage [7842]
U.S. Fed. for Culture Collections [6603]
U.S. Fed. of Scholars and Scientists [7634]
U.S. Human Proteome Org. [6604]
U.S. Indus. Coalition [7637]
U.S.-Israel Binational Sci. Found. [IO]
U.S. Metric Assn. [7701]
U.S. Natl. Comm. for the Intl. Union of Pure and
  Applied Chemistry [6697]
U.S. Natl. Comm. on Theoretical and Applied
  Mechanics [7301]
U.S. Permafrost Assn. [7675]
Vibration Inst. [7302]
Waksman Found. for Microbiology [6605]
Weed Sci. Soc. of Am. [4109]
Western Social Sci. Assn. [7657]
Western Soc. of Naturalists [7366]
Winston Churchill Found. [8438]
W.M. Keck Found. [15115]
Women in Bio [6618]
Women Entrepreneurs in Sci. and Tech. [4050]
Women in Physics Gp. [IO]
Women in Sci. and Engg. [7635]
Women in Sci. Enquiry Network [IO]
Women in Tech. and Sci. [IO]
World Assn. for Chinese Biomedical Engineers
  [6611]
World Fed. of Sci. Workers [IO]
World Sci. and Engg. Acad. and Soc. [7054]
World Transhumanist Assn. [7163]
YLEM: Artists Using Sci. and Tech. [9532]
Young Astronaut Coun. [7925]
Zimbabwe Sci. Assn. [IO]
Sci. Abstracting and Indexing Services; Natl. Fed. of
  [★7205]

Sci; Academie Mondiale de l'Art et de la [★9612]
Sci; Acad. of Pharmaceutical Res. and [15906]
Sci. of Am; Polish Inst. of Arts and [★10881]
Sci; Amer. Assn. for Lab. Animal [13693]
Sci; American Junior Acad. of [★7617]
Sci; Amer. Soc. of Animal [4150]
Sci; Amer. Soc. for Clinical Lab. [14992]
Sci; Amer. Soc. for Horticultural [6627]
Sci; Assn. of Academies of [★7617]
Sci. Assn; Amer. Dairy [4485]
Sci. Assn; Amer. Meat [7088]
Sci. Assn; Philosophy of [10825]
Sci. Assn; Policy Stud. Gp. of the Amer. Political
  [★18477]
Sci. Assn; Poultry [5116]
Sci. Assn; Regional [★5596]
Sci. and Automation Div; Info. [★10368]
Sci. Bus. Professionals; Consumer [★970]
Science-By-Mail - Defunct.
Sci; Center for Confucian [19879]
Sci. Center; Midwest [★7172]
Sci; Center for Unified [★9102]
Sci. Churches; Intl. Assn. of Religious [★20525]
Sci. Club; Clinical [★14022]
Science Clubs of America - Defunct.
Sci. Collections Alliance; Natural [6590]
Sci. Communications Assn; Hea. [14032]
Sci. Coun. of Asia [IO], Tokyo, Japan
Sci. Coun. of Japan [IO], Tokyo, Japan
Sci. Coun. of the United Kingdom [IO], London,
  United Kingdom
Science Courses for Baccalaureate Education - Ad-
  dress unknown since 1995.
Science Court and Res. Inst. - Address unknown
  since 1999.
Sci. and Disability; Found. for [11946]
Sci. in Economics; Intl. Soc. of Statistical [★7710]
Sci. Editors; Assn. of Earth [3093]
Sci. Editors; Coun. of [3108]
Sci. and Educ; Natl. Eczema Assn. for [★14208]
Sci. Educ; Special Interest Gp. on Cmpt. [8135]
Sci. Educators; Intl. Assn. of Medical [15090]
Science and Engineering Comm. for a Secure World
  - Address unknown since 1995.
Sci. and Engg; Natl. Consortium for Graduate
  Degrees for Minorities in [★8372]
Sci. and Engg. Soc; Amer. Indian [6987]
Science Ethic Soc. - Defunct.
Science Fiction
  Acad. of Sci. Fiction, Fantasy, and Horror Films
    [9925]
  August Derleth Soc. [9634]
  British Sci. Fiction Assn. [IO]
  Broad Universe [23034]
  Burroughs Bibliophiles [9640]
  Fan Tek [10943]
  Gaylactic Network [10944]
  Gaylactic Network [IO]
  Intl. Assn. for the Fantastic in the Arts [10945]
  Intl. Assn. of Media Tie-in Writers [11176]
  Klingon Strike Force [25015]
  Libertarian Futurist Soc. [18016]
  Lost in Space Fannish Alliance [25033]
  Natl. Fantasy Fan Fed. [10946]
  New Zealand Sci. Fiction and Fantasy Writers'
    Assn. [IO]
  Parallax Soc. [IO]
  Parallax Soc. [10947]
  Sci. Fiction Assn. Singapore [IO]
  Sci. Fiction and Fantasy Assn. of New Zealand
    [IO]
  Sci. Fiction and Fantasy Writers of Am. [11193]
  Sci. Fiction Found. [IO]
  Sci. Fiction Poetry Assn. [10948]
  Sci. Fiction Res. Assn. [IO]
  Star Trek: The Official Fan Club [25016]
  STARFLEET [25017]
  Starfleet Command [25018]
  Starships of the Third Fleet [10949]
  Trekville U.S.A./International [25019]
  United Fed. of Planets, Intl. [25020]
  World Sci. Fiction Soc. [10950]
  World Sci. Fiction Soc. [IO]
Sci. Fiction Assn. Singapore [IO], Singapore, Sin-
  gapore

Reference to "IO" in place of a book number signifies that the association may be found in the 45th edition of International Organizations.

Sci. Fiction and Fantasy Artists; Assn. of [307]
Sci. Fiction and Fantasy Assn. of New Zealand [IO], Wellington, New Zealand
Sci. Fiction, Fantasy, and Horror Films; Acad. of [9925]
Sci. Fiction and Fantasy Writers of Am. [11193], PO Box 877, Chestertown, MD 21620
Sci. Fiction Films; Acad. of Horror Films and [★9925]
Sci. Fiction Found. [IO], Harold Wood, United Kingdom
Science Fiction; Jedi Knights/ [★25021]
Sci. Fiction Poetry Assn. [10948], c/o Helena Bell, Treas., 1225 W Freeman St., Apt. 12, Carbondale, IL 62901
Sci. Fiction Res. Assn. [IO], Calgary, AB, Canada
Sci. Fiction Writers of Am. [★11193]
Sci; Found. for the Advancement of Chiropractic Tenets and [14003]
Sci; Found. for Advances in Medicine and [14025]
Sci. Found; Mind [7448]
Sci. Found; Photographic Art and [8975]
Sci. and the Handicapped; Found. for [★11946]
Sci. Illustrators; Guild of Natural [7153]
Science Information Service - Defunct.
Sci. Inst; Marketing [2635]
Sci; Intl. Assn. for Dance Medicine and [15170]
Sci; Joint Commn. on Sports Medicine and [16483]
Sci., Law and Public Policy; Natl. Inst. for [4105]
Sci. Librarians; Assn. of Vision [10341]
Sci. Librarians; East Coast Marine [★10361]
Sci. Libraries Assn; Marine [★10361]
Sci. and Mathematics Teachers; Central Assn. of [★9115]
Sci. Ministers Assn; Divine [19881]
Sci. Museum Directors; Assn. of [10498]
Sci; Natl. Consortium for Graduate Degrees for Minorities in Engg. and [8372]
Sci; Natl. Coun. for Elementary [★9100]
Sci; Natl. Inst. for Applied Behavioral [★8415]
Science Network; Math/ [8825]
Sci. Network on Thinking; Engg. and [7217]
Sci. in Nuclear Medicine; Amer. Bd. of [15420]
Sci. Park Assn. [IO], Arhus, Denmark
Science for the People [7627]
Sci. Professors; Assn. of Environmental Engg. and [9023]
Sci. in the Public Interest - Alcohol Policies Proj; Center for [18703]
Sci. in the Public Interest; Center for [17314]
Sci. and Religion; Conf. on [★17916]
Sci. Res. Coun. [IO], Kingston, Jamaica
Science Res. Inst; Inter [★13649]
Sci. and Scholarship; Soc. for the Promotion of [3255]
Sci. Ser. [7628], 1719 N St. NW, Washington, DC 20036, (202)785-2255
Sci. Ser. [IO], Washington, DC, United States
Sci. Soc. of Am; Crop [4099]
Sci. Soc. of Am; Soil [7674]
Sci. Soc. of Am; Weed [4109]
Sci. Soc; Cognitive [6484]
Sci; Soc. of Jewish [20202]
Sci. Songwriters' Assn. [10693], PO Box 3531, Vista, CA 92085-3531
Sci. Songwriters' Assn. [IO], Vista, CA, United States
Sci. Supervisors Assn; Natl. [★9113]
Sci. Teachers Assn; Business-Industry Sect. of Natl. [★8048]
Sci. and Tech; Amer. Soc. for Info. [7188]
Science and Tech. Awareness Program [★7594]
Science and Technology Branch - Address unknown since 1999.
Science-Technology Centers; Assn. of [10499]
Sci. and Tech; Coun. for Agricultural [7936]
Sci. and Tech. Found. of Japan [IO], Tokyo, Japan
Sci. and Tech; Inst. of Paper [7435]
Sci. and Tech; Inst. for Theological Encounter With [12353]
Sci. and Tech; Soc. of Wood [7100]
Sci. and Tech; YLEM: Artists Using [9532]
Sci; U.S. Natl. Comm. of the Intl. Union of Radio [7785]
Sci; Whiteruthenian Inst. of Arts and [★9734]

Sci. and World Affairs; International Pugwash Conferences on [★18842]
Sci. Writers; Natl. Assn. of [3133]
Sci. Writing; Coun. for the Advancement of [3107]
Sciences; Acad. of Motion Picture Arts and [1374]
Sciences; Acad. of Pharmaceutical [★15906]
Sciences; Acad. of TV Arts and [542]
Sciences in Am; Inst. of Islamic and Arabic [8670]
Sciences in Am; Polish Amer. Historical Commn. of the Polish Inst. of Arts and [★10880]
Sciences of Am; Polish Inst. of Arts and [10881]
Sciences; Amer. Acad. of Arts and [9605]
Sciences; Amer. Acad. of Forensic [5747]
Sciences; Amer. Inst. of Biological [6560]
Sciences; Amer. Inst. for Decision [★8021]
Sciences; Archivists and Librarians in the History of the Hea. [10326]
Sciences; Assn. for Advanced Training in the Behavioral [8878]
Sciences; Assn. for Commun. Excellence in Agriculture, Natural Resources, and Life and Human [4098]
Sciences; Assn. for Politics and the Life [7522]
Sciences; Comm. on Human Rights of the U.S. Natl. Acad. of [★17753]
Sciences; Coun. of Academies of Engg. and Technological [★9104]
Sciences; Coun. for the Advancement of Psychological Professions and [★16136]
Sciences; Coun. of Colleges of Arts and [7971]
Sciences Economiques et Commerciales; Assn. Internationale Des Etudiants en [★8012]
Sciences Educ. Assn; Family and Consumer [8418]
Sciences; Fed. of Behavioral, Psychological, and Cognitive [6530]
Sciences Found; Forensic [5761]
Sciences; Hollywood Chap. of Natl. Acad. of TV Arts and [★542]
Sciences Inst; Decision [8021]
Sciences; Inst. of Environmental [★7570]
Sciences Inst. - Nutrition Found; Intl. Life [★15561]
Sciences; Inst. of Soc., Ethics, and the Life [★12125]
Sciences; IONS - Inst. of Noetic [10976]
Sciences Libraries and Info. Centers; Intl. Assn. of Marine [★10361]
Sciences; Monroe Inst. of Applied [★7378]
Sciences; Natl. Acad. of Engg., and Inst. of Medicine; Comm. on Human Rights of the U.S. Natl. Acad. of [★17753]
Sciences; Natl. Acad. of Recording Arts and [10929]
Sciences; Natl. Accrediting Agency for Clinical Lab. [15141]
Sciences; Natl. Accrediting Commn. of Cosmetology Arts and [7877]
Sciences; NTL Inst. for Applied Behavioral [8415]
Sciences Res. Found; Borderland [7471]
Sciences Services and Resources; Social [7656]
Sciences; Soc. for Chaos Theory in Psychology and Life [7547]
Sciences Soc; IEEE Nuclear and Plasma [7386]
Sciences and Tech; Inst. of Environmental [7570]
Sciences in the U.S.A; Catholic Acad. of [19919]
Sci. Apparatus Makers Assn. [★3488]
Sci. Apparatus Makers Assn; PMC Sect. of the [★3485]
Sci. Assn. of European Talc Indus. [IO], Brussels, Belgium
Sci. Assn. for Infocommunications [IO], Budapest, Hungary
Sci. Assn. for Infocommunications Hungary [IO], Budapest, Hungary
Sci. Comm. on Antarctic Res. [IO], Cambridge, United Kingdom
Sci. Comm. on Frequency Allocations for Radio Astronomy and Space Sci. [IO], Meudon, France
Sci. Comm. for the Intl. Geosphere-Biosphere Programme [★IO]
Sci. Comm. on Problems of the Env. [IO], Paris, France
Sci. Comm. on Solar Terrestrial Physics [IO], Boulder, CO, United States
Sci. Comm. on Solar Terrestrial Physics [7508], c/o Gang Lu, Sci. Sec., HAO-NCAR, 3080 Center Green, Boulder, CO 80301, (303)497-1591

Scientific Cooperation
Intl. Soc. of Iraqi Scientists [7613]
Soc. for Amateur Scientists [7631]
Turkish Amer. Scientists and Scholars Assn. [7636]
Turkish American Scientists and Scholars Association [IO]
Sci. Coun. for Osteoporosis and Skeletal Diseases [IO], Damascus, Syrian Arab Republic
Sci. Equip. and Furniture Assn. [IO], Garden City, NY, United States
Sci. Equip. and Furniture Assn. [3489], c/o David J. Sutton, CAE, Exec. Dir., 1205 Franklin Ave., Ste. 320, Garden City, NY 11530, (516)294-5424
Scientific Evaluation and Res. of Charismatic Healing - Address unknown since 1995.
Sci. Examination of Religion; Committee for the [★20085]
Sci. Examination of Religion; Committee for the [★IO]
Sci. Exploration Soc. [IO], Shaftesbury, United Kingdom
Sci. Exploration; Soc. for [7485]
Scientific Exploratory Archeological Research [★6454]
Sci. Foundation; SFPE Educational and [★7082]
Scientific Hypnotherapy; Acad. of [14913]
Sci. and Indus. Valve Mfrs. Assn. [IO], St. Petersburg, Russia
Scientific Information and Education Coun. of Physicians - Address unknown since 1995.
Sci. Instrument Soc. [IO], Middlesex, United Kingdom
Sci. Investigation of Claims of the Paranormal; Comm. for the [7444]
Sci. Manpower Commn. [★7604]
Scientific Marriage Found. - Defunct.
Scientific Products
A.C. Gilbert Heritage Soc. [22992]
Amer. Precision Optics Mfrs. Assn. [3480]
Amer. Sci. Glassblowers Soc. [3481]
Assn. of Medical Diagnostics Mfrs. [3482]
BAREMA [IO]
Canadian Lab. Suppliers Assn. [IO]
European Ombudsman Inst. [IO]
European Surgical Trade Assn. [IO]
Independent Lab. Distributors Assn. [3483]
Lab. Products Assn. [3484]
Measurement, Control, and Automation Assn. [3485]
Medical Device Mfrs. Assn. [3486]
Natl. Assn. of Sci. Materials Managers [3487]
Optical Storage Tech. Assn. [2860]
SAMA Gp. of Associations [3488]
Sci. Equip. and Furniture Assn. [3489]
Sci. Equip. and Furniture Assn. [IO]
Ultrasonic Indus. Assn. [3490]
Worshipful Company of Sci. Instrument Makers [IO]
Sci. Res. Coordination in Organic Farming; European Network for [IO]
Sci. Res. Soc. of Am. [★24588]
Scientific Responsibility
Americans to Ban Cloning [17089]
Coun. for Responsible Genetics [18584]
Fed. of Amer. Scientists [18445]
Public Responsibility in Medicine and Res. [18585]
Sci. Soc. of Endocrinology [★IO]
Sci. Soc. Executives; Coun. of Engg. and [7010]
Sci. Soc. of Mech. Engg. [IO], Budapest, Hungary
Sci. Soc. Presidents; Comm. of [★7605]
Sci. Soc. for Telecommunications [★IO]
Sci. Stud. of Consciousness; Assn. for the [8140]
Sci. Stud. of Educ; Natl. Herbart Soc. for the [★8293]
Sci. Stud. of Religion; Soc. for the [20506]
Sci. Stud. of Sex; Soc. for the [★16407]
Sci. Stud. of Sexuality; Soc. for the [16407]
Sci. and Tech. Res. Coun. of Turkey [IO], Ankara, Turkey
Sci. Workers; Amer. Assn. of [★7634]
Scientist-Artists; Intl. Soc. of [★9610]
Scientists; Acad. of Clinical Lab. Physicians and [15981]

A star before a book entry number signifies that the name is not listed separately, but is mentioned within the entry.

Scientists in Am; Soc. of Turkish Architects, Engineers and [★7048]
Scientists; Amer. Assn. of Pharmaceutical [7467]
Scientists; Assn. of Clinical [14022]
Scientists Assn; NIH Black [6395]
Scientists; Assn. of Professional Geological [★7127]
Scientists Center for Animal Welfare [11456], 7833 Walker Dr., Ste. 410, Greenbelt, MD 20770, (301)345-3500
Scientists; Comm. of Concerned [17752]
Scientists' Comm. for Public Information - Defunct.
Scientists and Engg; Soc. of Photographic [★7497]
Scientists and Engineers - A Division of Natl. Ground Water Assn; Assn. of Ground Water [7828]
Scientists and Engineers Assn. in Am; Korean [★7024]
Scientists and Engineers; Assn. of Muslim [7005]
Scientists and Engineers for Secure Energy - Address unknown since 2001.
Scientists and Engineers for Social and Political Action; SESPA [★7627]
Scientists; Fed. of Amer. [18445]
Scientists; Fed. of Atomic [★18445]
Scientists Fund; Federation of Amer. [★18445]
Scientists' Group for Reform of Animal Experimentation - Defunct.
Scientists' Inst. for Public Information - Address unknown since 1999.
Scientists; Lesbian and Gay Assoc. Engineers and [★7620]
Scientists for Life - Defunct.
Scientists; Natl. Coun. of Black Engineers and [7618]
Scientists; Natl. Soc. of Consulting Soil [5222]
Scientists Organizations; Coun. of Engineers and [7817]
Scientists for Sakharov, Orlov and Sharansky - Defunct.
Scientists and Scholars Assn; Turkish Amer. [7636]
Scientists and Scholars; U.S. Fed. of [★7634]
Scientists; Soc. of Chinese Amer. Professors and [9024]
Scientists; Soc. of Independent Professional Earth [7135]
Scientists; Soc. of Mexican Amer. Engineers and [7043]
Scientists; Soc. of Wetland [4452]
Scientists and Technologists in Am; Assn. of Chinese Food [★7092]
Scientists and Technologists; Amer. Assn. of Radon [7108]
Scientists of Tomorrow - Defunct.
Scientists; Union of Concerned [18137]
Scientology
    Artists for a Better World Intl. [9549]
Sciots; Ancient Egyptian Order of [19228]
Scipio Soc. of Naval and Military History - Address unknown since 2006.
Scleroderma
    Intl. Scleroderma Network [16387]
    Intl. Scleroderma Network [IO]
    Juvenile Scleroderma Network [16388]
    Scleroderma Found. [16389]
    Scleroderma Res. Found. [16390]
    Scleroderma Support Gp. [16391]
Scleroderma Assn. of New England [★16389]
Scleroderma Assn; Raynaud's and [IO]
Scleroderma Fed. [★16389]
Scleroderma Found. [16389], 300 Rosewood Dr., Ste. 105, Danvers, MA 01923, (978)463-5843
Scleroderma Intl. Found. - Address unknown since 2001.
Scleroderma Res. Found. [16390], 220 Montgomery St., Ste. 1411, San Francisco, CA 94104, (415)834-9444
Scleroderma Soc; Irish Raynaud's and [IO]
Scleroderma Support Gp. [16391], 18 Talbot Manor, Cranston, RI 02905, (401)781-5013
Sclerosis Alliance; Tuberous [15371]
Sclerosis Assn; Amyotrophic Lateral [15306]
Sclerosis Assn; Natl. Tuberous [★15371]
Sclerosis Found; Multiple [15338]
Sclerosis Soc. of Am; Amyotrophic Lateral [★15306]
Sclerosis Soc; Natl. Multiple [15349]
Sclerotherapy; Amer. Acad. of [★15814]

Sclerotherapy; Amer. Coll. of Osteopathic Pain Mgt. and [★15796]
Sclerotherapy; Amer. Osteopathic Acad. of [★15814]
Scoliosis
    Adolescent Scoliosis Soc. of North Am. [16392]
    Natl. Scoliosis Found. [16393]
    Scoliosis Assn., Inc. [16394]
    Scoliosis Res. Soc. [16395]
    Scoliosis Research Society [IO]
Scoliosis Assn. [IO], London, United Kingdom
Scoliosis Assn., Inc. [16394], PO Box 811705, Boca Raton, FL 33481-1705, (561)994-4435
Scoliosis Res. Soc. [16395], 555 E Wells St., Ste. 1100, Milwaukee, WI 53202-3823, (414)289-9107
Scoliosis Research Society [IO], Milwaukee, WI, United States
Scoop Club - Defunct.
Scoot-Tours Touring Scooter Riders Assn. [23627], 532 Farm Rd. 1100, Monett, MO 65708-8316
Scooter and Allied Trades Assn; Motorcycle, [★2795]
Scooter Riders Assn; Scoot-Tours Touring [23627]
Scope [IO], London, United Kingdom
SCORE [3625], 409 3rd St. SW, 6th Fl., Washington, DC 20024, (202)205-6762
SCORE; Amer. Children of [10530]
Scores; Am. [23772]
Scorpius, Honorary Leadership Soc; Natl. Assn. of the Knights of [24511]
Scotch Highland Breeders Assn; Amer. [★4227]
Scotch-Irish Found. [21150], PO Box 181, Bryn Mawr, PA 19010, (610)527-1818
Scotch-Irish Found. [IO], Bryn Mawr, PA, United States
Scotch-Irish Soc; Pennsylvania [★21151]
Scotch-Irish Soc. of the U.S.A. [21151], PO Box 181, Bryn Mawr, PA 19010
Scotch Quality Beef and Lamb Assn. [★IO]
Scotch Whisky Assn. [IO], Edinburgh, United Kingdom
Scotia; Daughters of [19353]
Scotland House [★19347]
Scotland; Royal Order of [19249]
Scotland Software Fed. [★IO]
Scotland Touch Assn. [IO], Tranent, United Kingdom
ScotlandIS [IO], Livingston, United Kingdom
Scots Language Soc. [IO], Perth, United Kingdom
Scots Leid Associe [★IO]
Scott Fitzgerald Soc; F. [9649]
Scott Humane Soc; Carver- [11374]
Scott Joplin Commemorative Comm. [★10694]
Scott Joplin Commemorative Comm. [★IO]
Scott Joplin Found. of Sedalia [★IO]
Scott Joplin Found. of Sedalia [★10694]
Scott Joplin Intl. Ragtime Found. [10694], 321 S Ohio Ave., Sedalia, MO 65301, (660)826-2271
Scott Joplin Intl. Ragtime Found. [IO], Sedalia, MO, United States
Scott Joplin Ragtime Festival [★IO]
Scott Joplin Ragtime Festival [★10694]
Scott Joplin Ragtime Festival Comm. [★10694]
Scott Joplin Ragtime Festival Comm. [★IO]
Scott Soc. of the Americas; Clan [★20861]
Scott Soc; Clan [20861]
Scott, U.S.A; Clan [★20861]
Scottish
    Amer. Scottish Found. [19347]
    Armstrong Clan Soc. [10951]
    Armstrong Clan Soc. [IO]
    Assn. of Scottish Games and Festivals [19348]
    Bell Family Assn. of the U.S. [20793]
    Bruce Intl., USA Br. [10952]
    Clan Anderson Soc. [10953]
    Clan Arthur Assn., USA [19349]
    Clan Brown Soc. [20818]
    Clan Campbell Soc., North Am. [20819]
    Clan Carmichael U.S.A. [20820]
    Clan Colquhoun Soc. of North Am. [20822]
    Clan Craig Assn. of Am. [19350]
    Clan Cunningham Soc. of Am. [20823]
    Clan Ewing in Am. [19351]
    Clan Graham Soc. [20829]
    Clan Irwin Assn. [20833]
    Clan Leslie Soc. Intl. [20836]
    Clan MacKay Soc. [20840]

    Clan MacKinnon Soc. [19050]
    Clan MacRae Soc. of North Am. [20846]
    Clan Matheson Soc. [20848]
    Clan McLaren Assn. of North America [20850]
    Clan Menzies Soc., North Amer. Br. [20851]
    Clan Moncreiffe Soc. of North Am. [20853]
    Clan Napier in North America [20856]
    Clan Phail Soc. in North America [19052]
    Clan Scott Soc. [20861]
    Clan Shaw Soc. [20862]
    Clan Sutherland Soc. of North Am. [20864]
    Clanranald Trust for Scotland [IO]
    An Comunn Gaidhealach Am. [IO]
    An Comunn Gaidhealach Am. [10954]
    Coun. of Scottish Clans and Associations [19352]
    Daughters of Scotia [19353]
    Dobie Clan of North America [20884]
    Dunlop - Dunlap Family Soc. [20888]
    Eighteenth-Century Scottish Stud. Soc. [8505]
    Intl. Assn. for Tartan Stud. [19354]
    Intl. Assn. for Tartan Stud. [IO]
    Kerr Family Assn. of North Am. [20972]
    Paisley Family Soc. [21020]
    Robert Burns World Fed. [IO]
    Saint Andrew's Soc. of the State of New York [19355]
    Saltire Soc. [IO]
    Scots Language Soc. [IO]
    Scottish Deerhound Club of Am. [22356]
    Scottish Esperanto Assn. [IO]
    Scottish Heritage U.S.A. [19356]
    Scottish Historic and Res. Soc. of Delaware Valley [10955]
    Scottish Text Soc. [IO]
    Snodgrass Clan Soc. [21053]
    Sons of Scotland Benevolent Assn. [IO]
    Tartans of Scotland [IO]
    Ulster-Scots Soc. of Am. [21154]
    U.S. Scottish Fiddling Revival [10716]
Scottish Aeromodellers Assn. [IO], Johnstone, United Kingdom
Scottish Agricultural Org. Soc. [IO], Newbridge, United Kingdom
Scottish Aikido Fed. [IO], Innerleithen, United Kingdom
Scottish Amateur Football Assn. [IO], Glasgow, United Kingdom
Scottish Amateur Gymnastics Assn. [★IO]
Scottish Amateur Music Assn. [IO], Alva, United Kingdom
Scottish Amateur Swimming Assn. [★IO]
Scottish Anglers Natl. Assn. [IO], Kinross, United Kingdom
Scottish Arts Coun. [IO], Edinburgh, United Kingdom
Scottish Assn. Advisers of Physical Educ. [★IO]
Scottish Assn. for Disabled People [★IO]
Scottish Assn. of Family Conciliation Services [★IO]
Scottish Assn. of Family History Societies [IO], Edinburgh, United Kingdom
Scottish Assn. of Geography Teachers [IO], Tranent, United Kingdom
Scottish Assn. of Hea. Councils [IO], Edinburgh, United Kingdom
Scottish Assn. for Marine Sci. [IO], Oban, United Kingdom
Scottish Assn. of Master Bakers [IO], Edinburgh, United Kingdom
Scottish Assn. of Meat Wholesalers [IO], Perth, United Kingdom
Scottish Assn. for Mental Hea. [IO], Glasgow, United Kingdom
Scottish Assn. for Parents of Handicapped Children [★IO]
Scottish Assn. for Public Transport [IO], Glasgow, United Kingdom
Scottish Assn. of Sign Language Interpreters [IO], Edinburgh, United Kingdom
Scottish Assn. of Young Farmers' Clubs [IO], Edinburgh, United Kingdom
Scottish Athletics [IO], Edinburgh, United Kingdom
Scottish Badminton Union [★IO]
Scottish Basketball Assn. [★IO]
Scottish Beekeepers' Assn. [IO], Johnstone, United Kingdom
Scottish Bible Soc. [IO], Edinburgh, United Kingdom

Reference to "IO" in place of a book number signifies that the association may be found in the 45th edition of International Organizations.

Scottish Blackface Sheep Breeder's Assn. [5216], 1699 HH Hwy., Willow Springs, MO 65793, (417)962-5499

Scottish Bowling Assn. [IO], Ayr, United Kingdom

Scottish Br. of the British Interplanetary Soc. [★IO]

Scottish Building [IO], Stenhousemuir, United Kingdom

Scottish Building Contractors Assn. [IO], Glasgow, United Kingdom

Scottish Building Employers' Fed. [IO], Stenhousemuir, United Kingdom

Scottish Campaign for Nuclear Disarmament [IO], Glasgow, United Kingdom

Scottish Canoe Assn. [IO], Edinburgh, United Kingdom

Scottish Catholic Intl. Aid Fund [IO], Glasgow, United Kingdom

Scottish Chess Assn. [★IO]

Scottish Child and Family Alliance [★IO]

Scottish Childminding Assn. [IO], Stirling, United Kingdom

Scottish Church History Soc. [IO], Edinburgh, United Kingdom

Scottish Churches Housing Action [IO], Edinburgh, United Kingdom

Scottish Churches Housing Agency [★IO]

Scottish Clan Associations; Coun. of [★19352]

Scottish Comm. Action on Smoking and Hea. [★IO]

Scottish Comm. of Optometrists [IO], Edinburgh, United Kingdom

Scottish Community Care Forum [IO], Dumbarton, United Kingdom

Scottish Consultative Coun. on the Curriculum [★IO]

Scottish Consumer Coun. [IO], Glasgow, United Kingdom

Scottish Correspondence Chess Assn. [IO], Dundee, United Kingdom

Scottish Coun. on Alcohol [★IO]

Scottish Coun. on Deafness [IO], Glasgow, United Kingdom

Scottish Coun. for Development and Indus. [IO], Glasgow, United Kingdom

Scottish Coun. on Human Bioethics [IO], Edinburgh, United Kingdom

Scottish Coun. of Independent Schools [IO], Edinburgh, United Kingdom

Scottish Coun. for Intl. Arbitration [IO], Edinburgh, United Kingdom

Scottish Coun. of Natl. Training Organisations [★IO]

Scottish Coun. for Postgraduate Medical and Dental Educ. [IO], Edinburgh, United Kingdom

Scottish Coun. for Res. in Educ. [IO], Glasgow, United Kingdom

Scottish Coun. for Single Homeless [IO], Edinburgh, United Kingdom

Scottish Coun. for Single Parents [★IO]

Scottish Coun. for the Unmarried Mother and Her Child [★IO]

Scottish Coun. for Voluntary Organisations [IO], Edinburgh, United Kingdom

Scottish for Crop Res. Inst. [IO], Dundee, United Kingdom

Scottish Croquet Assn. [IO], Edinburgh, United Kingdom

Scottish Croquet Assn. - Defunct.

Scottish Cyclists' Union [IO], Edinburgh, United Kingdom

Scottish Daily Newspaper Soc. [IO], Edinburgh, United Kingdom

Scottish Dance Teacher's Alliance [IO], Glasgow, United Kingdom

Scottish Dancesport [IO], Glasgow, United Kingdom

Scottish Decorators Fed. [IO], Edinburgh, United Kingdom

Scottish Deerhound Club of Am. [22356], c/o Mary Varda, Membership Sec., 38 Cambridge Rd., Madison, WI 53704

Scottish Disability Sport [IO], Edinburgh, United Kingdom

Scottish Ecological Design Assn. [IO], Belford, United Kingdom

Scottish Economic Soc. [IO], Glasgow, United Kingdom

Scottish Educ. and Action for Development [IO], Edinburgh, United Kingdom

Scottish Engg. [IO], Glasgow, United Kingdom

Scottish Enterprise Energy Gp. [★IO]

Scottish Enterprise Energy Team [IO], Aberdeen, United Kingdom

Scottish Equestrian Assn. [IO], Langbank, United Kingdom

Scottish Esperanto Assn. [IO], Motherwell, United Kingdom

Scottish Farm and Countryside Educational Trust [★IO]

Scottish Fed. of Housing Associations [IO], Glasgow, United Kingdom

Scottish Fed. of Meat Traders Assn. [IO], Perth, United Kingdom

Scottish Fed. of Model Boat Clubs [IO], Glasgow, United Kingdom

Scottish Fed. of Sea Anglers [IO], Fife, United Kingdom

Scottish Fiddling Revival; U.S. [10716]

Scottish Film Coun. [★IO]

Scottish FIRE [★10716]

Scottish Fishermen's Fed. [IO], Aberdeen, United Kingdom

Scottish Food and Drink Fed. [IO], Edinburgh, United Kingdom

Scottish Football Assn. [IO], Glasgow, United Kingdom

Scottish Funding Coun. [★IO]

Scottish Further Educ. Funding Coun. [IO], Edinburgh, United Kingdom

Scottish Further Educ. Funding Coun. and Scottish Higher Educ. Funding Coun. [★IO]

Scottish Further and Higher Educ. Funding Coun. [IO], Edinburgh, United Kingdom.

Scottish Games Assn. [IO], Crieff, United Kingdom

Scottish Genealogy Soc. [IO], Edinburgh, United Kingdom

Scottish Georgian Soc. [★IO]

Scottish Golf Union [IO], St. Andrews, United Kingdom

Scottish Grocers' Fed. [IO], Edinburgh, United Kingdom

Scottish Gymnastics Assn. [IO], Falkirk, United Kingdom

Scottish Harp Soc. of Am. [10695], PO Box 250504, Plano, TX 75025-0504

Scottish Heritage Assn. - Defunct.

Scottish Heritage U.S.A. [19356], PO Box 457, Pinehurst, NC 28370, (910)295-4448

Scottish Historic and Res. Soc. [★10955]

Scottish Historic and Res. Soc. of Delaware Valley [10955], 102 St. Paul's Rd., Ardmore, PA 19003-2811, (610)649-4144

Scottish History Soc. [IO], Stirling, United Kingdom

Scottish Hockey Union [IO], Edinburgh, United Kingdom

Scottish Huntington's Assn. [IO], Elderslie, United Kingdom

Scottish Ice Skating Assn. [IO], Edinburgh, United Kingdom

Scottish Inland Waterways Assn. [IO], Johnstone, United Kingdom

Scottish Inst. of Reflexology [IO], Glasgow, United Kingdom

Scottish Joint Indus. Bd. for the Elecl. Contracting Indus. [IO], Midlothian, United Kingdom

Scottish Ju Jitsu Assn. [IO], Dundee, United Kingdom

Scottish Ladies Golfing Assn. [IO], Perth, United Kingdom

Scottish Landowners Fed. [★IO]

Scottish Language Dictionaries [IO], Edinburgh, United Kingdom

Scottish Law Agents Soc. [IO], Glasgow, United Kingdom

Scottish Lawn Tennis Assn. [★IO]

Scottish Lib. Assn. [★IO]

Scottish Licensed Trade Assn. [IO], Edinburgh, United Kingdom

Scottish Local Authority Network of Physical Educ. [IO], Fife, United Kingdom

Scottish Low Pay Unit [IO], Glasgow, United Kingdom

Scottish Marine Indus. Assn. [★IO]

Scottish Master Wrights and Builders Assn. [IO], Glasgow, United Kingdom

Scottish Microbiology Assn. [IO], Wishaw, United Kingdom

Scottish Microbiology Soc. [IO], Glasgow, United Kingdom

Scottish Military Historical Soc. [IO], Glasgow, United Kingdom

Scottish Motor Neurone Disease Assn. [IO], Glasgow, United Kingdom

Scottish Motor Trade Assn. [IO], Edinburgh, United Kingdom

Scottish Museums Coun. [IO], Edinburgh, United Kingdom

Scottish Natl. Coun. of YMCA's [IO], Edinburgh, United Kingdom

Scottish Natl. Party [IO], Edinburgh, United Kingdom

Scottish Natl. Party - Women's Forum [IO], Edinburgh, United Kingdom

Scottish Natl. Ski Coun. [★IO]

Scottish Natural Heritage [IO], Inverness, United Kingdom

Scottish Newspaper Publishers Assn. [IO], Edinburgh, United Kingdom

Scottish and Northern Ireland Plumbing Employers' Fed. [IO], Edinburgh, United Kingdom

Scottish and Northern Welsh Pony and Cob Assn. [IO], Berwick-upon-Tweed, United Kingdom

Scottish Official Bd. of Highland Dancing [IO], Edinburgh, United Kingdom

Scottish Opera; Amer. Friends of [★10570]

Scottish Ornithologists' Club [★IO]

Scottish Out of School Care Network [IO], Glasgow, United Kingdom

Scottish Parent-Teacher Coun. [IO], Edinburgh, United Kingdom

Scottish Pharmaceutical Fed. [IO], Glasgow, United Kingdom

Scottish Pharmaceutical Gen. Coun. [IO], Edinburgh, United Kingdom

Scottish Photographic Fed. [IO], Cumbernauld, United Kingdom

Scottish Plant Owners Assn. [IO], Glasgow, United Kingdom

Scottish Police Fed. [IO], Glasgow, United Kingdom

Scottish Pre-School Play Assn. [IO], Glasgow, United Kingdom

Scottish Print Employers Fed. [IO], Edinburgh, United Kingdom

Scottish Publishers Assn. [IO], Edinburgh, United Kingdom

Scottish Qualifications Authority [IO], Glasgow, United Kingdom

Scottish Railway Preservation Soc. [IO], West Lothian, United Kingdom

Scottish Refugee Coun. [IO], Glasgow, United Kingdom

Scottish Regimental Soc. - Defunct.

Scottish Retail Consortium [IO], Gullane, United Kingdom

Scottish Right of Way Soc. [★IO]

Scottish Rights of Way and Access Soc. [IO], Edinburgh, United Kingdom

Scottish Rite of Free-Masonry (Northern Masonic Jurisdiction); Supreme Coun., Ancient Accepted [19252]

Scottish Rite of Freemasonry - Southern Jurisdiction; Supreme Coun. 33rd Degree, Ancient and Accepted [19251]

Scottish Rite of Freemasonry - Southern Masonic Jurisdiction; Supreme Coun. 33rd Degree, Ancient and Accepted [★19251]

Scottish Rock Garden Club [IO], Aberdeen, United Kingdom

Scottish Rural Property and Bus. Assn. [IO], Musselburgh, United Kingdom

Scottish Screen [IO], Glasgow, United Kingdom

Scottish Secondary Teachers' Assn. [IO], Edinburgh, United Kingdom

Scottish Ski Club [IO], Fort William, United Kingdom

Scottish Soc. for Autism [IO], Alloa, United Kingdom

Scottish Soc. for Conservation and Restoration [IO], Edinburgh, United Kingdom

Scottish Soc. for Contamination Control [IO], Glasgow, United Kingdom

Scottish Soc. of the History of Medicine [IO], Edinburgh, United Kingdom

A star before a book entry number signifies that the name is not listed separately, but is mentioned within the entry.

Scottish Soc. for the Mentally Handicapped [★IO]
Scottish Soc. for Mentally Handicapped Children [★IO]
Scottish Soc. for the Prevention of Cruelty to Animals [IO], Edinburgh, United Kingdom
Scottish Soc. for Psychical Res. [IO], Fife, United Kingdom
Scottish SPCA [IO], Edinburgh, United Kingdom
Scottish Spina Bifida Assn. [IO], Cumbernauld, United Kingdom
Scottish Sports Assn. [IO], Edinburgh, United Kingdom
Scottish Sports Coun. [★IO]
Scottish Squash Assn. [IO], Edinburgh, United Kingdom
Scottish Standing Conf. of Voluntary Youth Organisations [★IO]
Scottish Storytelling Forum [IO], Edinburgh, United Kingdom
Scottish Stud. Found. [★IO]
Scottish Stud. Program/Scottish Stud. Found. [IO], Toronto, ON, Canada
Scottish Sub-Aqua Club [IO], Glasgow, United Kingdom
Scottish Swimming [IO], Stirling, United Kingdom
Scottish Tartans Soc. [★IO]
Scottish Terrier Club of Am. [22357], c/o Ms. Connie Smith, Corresponding Sec., 9103 Lanshire Dr., Dallas, TX 75238, (214)341-4655
Scottish Terriers
    Scottish Terrier Club of Am. [22357]
Scottish Text Soc. [IO], Nottingham, United Kingdom
Scottish Textiles [IO], Edinburgh, United Kingdom
Scottish Timber Trade Assn. [IO], Stirling, United Kingdom
Scottish Tourism Forum [IO], Edinburgh, United Kingdom
Scottish Tourist Bd. [★IO]
Scottish Urban Archaeological Trust [IO], Perth, United Kingdom
Scottish Vocational Educ. Coun. [★IO]
Scottish Volleyball Assn. [IO], Edinburgh, United Kingdom
Scottish War Veterans of America - Address unknown since 1995.
Scottish Welsh Pony and Cob Assn. [IO], Cupar, United Kingdom
Scottish Wild Land Gp. [IO], Edinburgh, United Kingdom
Scottish Wildlife Trust [IO], Edinburgh, United Kingdom
Scottish Women's Aid [IO], Edinburgh, United Kingdom
Scottish Women's Football Assn. [IO], Glasgow, United Kingdom
The Scottish Women's Found. [★IO]
Scottish Women's Indoor Bowling Assn. [IO], Letham, United Kingdom
Scottish Women's Rural Institutes [IO], Edinburgh, United Kingdom
Scottish Young Conservatives [IO], Edinburgh, United Kingdom
Scottish Youth Hostels Assn. [IO], Stirling, United Kingdom
ScottishCricket [★IO]
Scottsdale Inst. [14713], 1660 Hwy. 100 S, Ste. 306, Minneapolis, MN 55416, (952)545-5880
Scout Assn. [IO], London, United Kingdom
Scout Assn. of Argentina [IO], Buenos Aires, Argentina
Scout Assn. of Belize [IO], Belize City, Belize
Scout Assn. of Jamaica [IO], Kingston, Jamaica
Scout Comm. of the Synagogue Coun. of Amer; Natl. Jewish Girl [★13004]
Scout Esperanto League, U.S. Sect. - Address unknown since 1995.
Scouting
    Assn. of Baptists for Scouting [12995]
    Assn. of Girl Scout Executive Staff [12996]
    Associazione Italiana Guide e Scouts d'Europa Cattolici [IO]
    Boy Scouts of Am. [12997]
    Boy Scouts Assn. of Zimbabwe [IO]
    Boys' Brigade [IO]
    Estonian Scout Assn. [IO]

Fed. of Catholic Scouts [IO]
Girl Guides Assn. of Kiribati [IO]
Girl Guides Assn. - Malaysia [IO]
Girl Guides Assn. - South Africa [IO]
Girl Guides of Canada [IO]
Girl Guides Singapore [IO]
Girl Guiding Scotland [IO]
Girl Scouts of the U.S.A. [12998]
Girlguiding UK [IO]
Girls' Brigade Intl. Coun. [IO]
Guides Australia [IO]
Guides Australia - Queensland [IO]
Guides Australia - South Australia [IO]
Guides Australia - Tasmania [IO]
Guides Australia - Victoria [IO]
Guides Australia - Western Australia [IO]
Guides New Zealand [IO]
Guides et Scouts d'Europe - France [IO]
Hungarian Scouts Assn. [12999]
Intl. Union of Guides and Scouts of Europe [IO]
Irish Girl Guides [IO]
Kenya Scouts Assn. [IO]
Natl. Assn. of Presbyterian Scouters [13000]
Natl. Catholic Comm. on Scouting [13001]
Natl. Eagle Scout Assn. [13002]
Natl. Jewish Comm. on Scouting [13003]
Natl. Jewish Girl Scout Comm. [13004]
Natl. Scouts Assn. of Panama [IO]
Order of the Arrow [13005]
Scout Assn. [IO]
Scout Assn. of Argentina [IO]
Scout Assn. of Belize [IO]
Scout Assn. of Jamaica [IO]
Scouting Assn. of Canada [IO]
Scouting For All [13006]
Scouting Ireland CSI [IO]
Scouts Canada [IO]
Scouts on Stamps Soc. Intl. [22869]
Singapore Scout Assn. [IO]
Uganda Girl Guides Assn. [IO]
World Assn. of Girl Guides and Girl Scouts [IO]
World Scout Bur. [IO]
World Scout Found. [IO]
Zimbabwe Girl Guides Assn. [IO]
Scouting Assn. of Canada [IO], Montreal, QC, Canada
Scouting; Bishops' Comm. on [★13001]
Scouting; Catholic Comm. on [★13001]
Scouting For All [13006], PO Box 2832, Petaluma, CA 94953-2832, (707)778-0564
Scouting Ireland CSI [IO], Dublin, Ireland
Scouting Traders Assn; Amer. [★22057]
Scouts de Argentina Asociacion Civil [★IO]
Scouts Canada [IO], Ottawa, ON, Canada
Scouts on Stamps Soc. [★IO]
Scouts on Stamps Soc. [★22869]
Scouts on Stamps Soc. Intl. [22869], PO Box 6228, Kennewick, WA 99336, (509)735-3731
Scouts on Stamps Soc. Intl. [IO], Kennewick, WA, United States
Scouts of the U.S.A; Girl [12998]
Scow Assn; Natl. Class E [23204]
Scow Sailing Assn; Natl. C [23203]
Scowden Family Org; Neal Dougan-Theodorus [21010]
Scrabble Assn; Natl. [22470]
Scrabble Crossword Game Players [★22470]
Scrabble Players [★22470]
Scrambl-Gram [★22473]
Scrap Iron and Steel; Inst. of [★3995]
Scrap Recycling Indus; Inst. of [3995]
Scrap Tire Management Council - Defunct.
Screaming Eagles Users Group - Defunct.
Screen Actors Guild [24158], 5757 Wilshire Blvd., 7th Fl., Los Angeles, CA 90036-3600, (323)954-1600
Screen Advt. World Assn. [IO], London, United Kingdom
Screen Cartoonists Guild - Defunct.
Screen Composers of America - Address unknown since 2002.
Screen Directors Guild of Am. [★24055]
Screen Directors Intl. Guild [★24055]
Screen Extras Guild - Address unknown since 1999.

Screen Extras Guild; TV Audience [55]
Screen Mfrs. Assn. [1833], 2850 S Ocean Blvd., No. 114, Palm Beach, FL 33480-6205, (561)533-0991
Screen Manufacturers Association [IO], Palm Beach, FL, United States
Screen Printers' Assn. of India [IO], Thane, India
Screen Printing Assn. of Canada [★IO]
Screen Printing Assn. of Canada [★1792]
Screen Printing Assn. Intl. [★1792]
Screen Printing Assn. Intl. [★IO]
Screen Printing Assn. U.K. [★IO]
Screen Printing Technical Foundation [IO], Fairfax, VA, United States
Screen Printing Tech. Found. [1789], c/o Specialty Graphic Imaging Assn., 10015 Main St., Fairfax, VA 22031, (703)385-1335
Screen Process Printing Assn. [★1792]
Screen Process Printing Assn. [★IO]
Screen Producers Assn. of Australia [IO], Surry Hills, Australia
Screen Producers Guild [★1392]
Screen Producers Ireland [IO], Dublin, Ireland
Screen Production and Development Assn. of New Zealand [IO], Wellington, New Zealand
Screen Writers' Guild [★IO]
Screening Agencies; Natl. Assn. of [3330]
Screenprinting and Graphic Imaging Assn. Intl. [★1792]
Screenprinting and Graphic Imaging Assn. Intl. [★IO]
Screenrights [IO], Neutral Bay, Australia
Screenwriters Assn. (Singapore) [IO], Singapore, Singapore
Screw Res. Assn. - Defunct.
Scriabin Circle - Defunct.
Scriabin Soc. of Am. [10696], 44 W 62nd St., Penthouse 31D, New York, NY 10023-7014
Scribes Administrative Off. [★5584]
Scribes; Soc. of [11214]
Scribes - The Amer. Soc. of Legal Writers [5584], c/o Prof. Joseph Kimble, Exec. Dir., PO Box 13038, Lansing, MI 48901, (517)371-5140
Scripophily Trade Assn; Professional [761]
Scripps Assn. of Families [8113], Scripps Coll., 1030 Columbia Ave., Claremont, CA 91711, (909)607-1542
Scripps-Booth Register - Address unknown since 2001.
Scripps Family Assn. - Address unknown since 2003.
Scripps Howard Foundation [8717], PO Box 5380, Cincinnati, OH 45201, (513)977-3035
Scriptural Christianity; Forum for [20262]
Scripture Gift Mission/U.S.A. [★19506]
Scripture Union - Australia [IO], Chapel Hill, Australia
Scripture Union - Benin [IO], Cotonou, Benin
Scripture Union - Botswana [IO], Gaborone, Botswana
Scripture Union Burundi [IO], Bujumbura, Burundi
Scripture Union - Cambodia [IO], Phnom Penh, Cambodia
Scripture Union - Cameroon [IO], Yaounde, Cameroon
Scripture Union - Canada [IO], Pickering, ON, Canada
Scripture Union - Democratic Republic of Congo [IO], Kinshasa, Democratic Republic of the Congo
Scripture Union - Egypt [IO], Cairo, Egypt
Scripture Union England and Wales [IO], Milton Keynes, United Kingdom
Scripture Union Equatorial Guinea [IO], Malabo, Equatorial Guinea
Scripture Union in Fiji [IO], Suva, Fiji
Scripture Union - India [IO], Chennai, India
Scripture Union - Indonesia [IO], Jakarta, Indonesia
Scripture Union - Israel [IO], Netanya, Israel
Scripture Union Japan [IO], Tokyo, Japan
Scripture Union of Kenya [IO], Nairobi, Kenya
Scripture Union - Kyrgyzstan [IO], Bishkek, Kirgizstan
Scripture Union of Lesotho [IO], Maseru, Lesotho
Scripture Union - Liberia [IO], Monrovia, Liberia
Scripture Union Lithuania [IO], Vilnius, Lithuania
Scripture Union of Malawi [IO], Lilongwe, Malawi
Scripture Union - Mongolia [IO], Ulan Bator, Mongolia

Reference to "IO" in place of a book number signifies that the association may be found in the 45th edition of International Organizations.

Scripture Union - Namibia [IO], Windhoek, Namibia
Scripture Union - Nepal [IO], Kathmandu, Nepal
Scripture Union - New Caledonia [IO], Noumea, New Caledonia
Scripture Union New South Wales [IO], West Ryde, Australia
Scripture Union in New Zealand [IO], Wellington, New Zealand
Scripture Union - Niger [IO], Niamey, Niger
Scripture Union Northern Ireland [IO], Belfast, United Kingdom
Scripture Union - Pakistan [IO], Lahore, Pakistan
Scripture Union - Philippines [IO], Manila, Philippines
Scripture Union Poland [IO], Wisla, Poland
Scripture Union Romania [IO], Bucharest, Romania
Scripture Union - Russia [IO], Moscow, Russia
Scripture Union Rwanda [IO], Kigali, Rwanda
Scripture Union - Samoa [IO], Apia, Western Samoa
Scripture Union Scotland [IO], Glasgow, United Kingdom
Scripture Union of Sierra Leone [IO], Freetown, Sierra Leone
Scripture Union Singapore [IO], Singapore, Singapore
Scripture Union - Sri Lanka [IO], Colombo, Sri Lanka
Scripture Union - Sudan [IO], Juba, Sudan
Scripture Union - Swaziland [IO], Mbabane, Swaziland
Scripture Union in Taiwan [IO], Taipei, Taiwan
Scripture Union of Tanzania [IO], Dar es Salaam, United Republic of Tanzania
Scripture Union - Togo [IO], Lome, Togo
Scripture Union - Tonga [IO], Nuku'alofa, Tonga
Scripture Union - Uganda [IO], Kampala, Uganda
Scripture Union - Vanuatu [IO], Port Vila, Vanuatu
Scripture Union Victoria [IO], Northcote, Australia
Scripture Union - Zambia [IO], Kitwe, Zambia
Scriptwriters Assn. Intl. - Defunct.
Scroll Soc; Quill and [24523]
Scrollsaw Assn. of the World [23032], PO Box 340, Botkins, OH 45306, (937)693-3309
Scrollsaw Association of the World [IO], Sylvania, GA, United States
Scruggs Family Assn. [21045], c/o William N. Scruggs, Sec.-Treas., 1137 Los Serenos Dr., Fillmore, CA 93015, (805)524-1832
SCSI Trade Assn. [2110], Presidio of San Francisco, Bldg. 572B, Ruger St., PO Box 29920, San Francisco, CA 94129, (415)561-6273
Scuba Assn; Handicapped [23344]

Scuba Diving
Assn. of Commercial Diving Educators [23960]
Divers Alert Network [23378]
Handicapped Scuba Assn. [23344]
Historical Diving Soc. USA [23576]
Inst. of Diving [23961]
Natl. Assn. of Black Scuba Divers [23711]
Natl. Assn. of Underwater Instructors [23963]
Portmarnock Sub-Aqua Club [IO]
Professional Assn. of Diving Instructors [23964]
Recreational Scuba Training Coun. [23965]
Underwater Soc. of Am. [23966]
Scuba Retailers Assn. - Address unknown since 2006.
Scuba Training Coun; Recreational [23965]
Sculptors; Assn. of Women Painters and [★9514]
Sculptors; Fed. of Modern Painters and [9502]
Sculptors Guild [10961], 110 Greene St., Ste. 601, New York, NY 10012, (212)431-5669
Sculptors Soc. of Ireland [★IO]

Sculpture
Amer. Artists Professional League [9489]
Anonymous Arts Recovery Soc. [10956]
Assn. of Lifecasters Intl. [10957]
Assn. of Lifecasters Intl. [IO]
Audubon Artists [9433]
Crazy Horse Memorial Found. [10739]
Fed. of Modern Painters and Sculptors [9502]
Intl. Assn. of Sand Castle Builders [22971]
Intl. Chain Saw Wood Sculptors Assn. [9446]
Intl. Sculpture Center [10958]
Intl. Wooden Bow Tie Club [243]
Kinetic Art Org. [9453]
Natl. Polymer Clay Guild [22579]

Natl. Sculpture Soc. [10959]
Natural Figure Art Assn. [9462]
Public Monuments and Sculpture Assn. [IO]
Rogers Group [10960]
Sculptors Guild [10961]
Sculpture in the Env. [17240]
Sculpture Soc. of Canada [IO]
Statue of Liberty Club [22118]
Visual Artists Ireland [IO]
World Sand Sculptors Assn. [22972]
Sculpture Center; Intl. [10958]
Sculpture in the Env. [17240], 25 Maiden Ln., New York, NY 10038-4008, (212)285-0120
Sculpture Soc. of Canada [IO], Toronto, ON, Canada
SD Card Assn. [6743], 2400 Camino Ramon, Ste. 375, San Ramon, CA 94583, (925)275-6687
SDA; IRCDA/ [★910]
SDA Kindred [★20066]
SDA Kindred [★IO]
SDA Kinship Intl. [★IO]
SDA Kinship Intl. [★20066]
SDI; Campaign to Boycott [18143]
Sdruzeni Automobiloveho Prumyslu [★IO]
Sdruzeni zastancu detskych prav - ceska sekce DCI [★IO]
Sdruzeni Najemniku [★IO]
S.E. Asia Vets (SEA Vets) [★21295]
Sea Cadets [IO], London, United Kingdom
Sea Educ. Assn. [8811], PO Box 6, Woods Hole, MA 02543, (508)540-3954
Sea Floor Div. [★7404]
Sea-food Markets; Inst. for the Cooperative Stud. of Intl. [★1484]
Sea Grant Assn. [7276], c/o Paul S. Anderson, Pres., Univ. of Maine, 5784 York Complex, Orono, ME 04469, (207)581-1435
Sea Grant Prog. Institutions; Assn. of [★7276]
Sea Grant Program; National [★7276]
Sea Heritage Found. - Address unknown since 2002.
Sea Inst; Law of the [6054]
Sea Kayak Operators Assn. of New Zealand [IO], Picton, New Zealand
Sea Lion Marine Mammal Center; Friends of the [★5361]
Sea Otter; Friends of the [5320]
Sea to See Proj. [13760]
Sea Ser. Leadership Assn. [21238], PO Box 100356, Arlington, VA 22210, (703)732-1976
Sea Shepherd Conservation Soc. [5380], PO Box 2616, Friday Harbor, WA 98250, (360)370-5650
Sea Shepherd Conservation Soc. [IO], Friday Harbor, WA, United States
Sea to Sky Freenet Assn. [IO], Squamish, BC, Canada
Sea, and Space Club; Air, [25023]
Sea Stud. Found. [IO], Rio de Janeiro, Brazil
Sea Turtle Rescue Fund [★IO]
Sea Turtle Rescue Fund [★4435]
Sea Turtle Survival League [★5305]
Sea Turtle Survival League [★IO]
Sea Turtle Survival League; Caribbean Conservation Corp. and [5305]
Sea in the U.S.A; Apostleship of the [19570]
Seabee Club Intl. - Address unknown since 2003.
Seabee Veterans of Am. [★21217]
Seabee Veterans of Am; Navy [21217]
Seabird Gp. [IO], Aberdeen, United Kingdom
Seabird Gp; Pacific [5362]
Seacoast Anti-Pollution League [4451], PO Box 1136, Portsmouth, NH 03802-1136, (603)431-5089
The Seacoast Anti-Pollution League [★4451]
Seafarers/Harry Lundberg School of Seamanship [★24132]
Seafarers and Intl. House [20232], 123 E 15th St., New York, NY 10003, (212)677-4800
Seafarers' Intl. Union of North Am. [24132], 5201 Auth Way, Camp Springs, MD 20746, (301)899-0675
Seafarers' Rights; Center for [6053]
Seafloor Geosciences Div. [7404]

Seafood
Amer. Scallop Assn. [3491]
Australian Prawn Farmers Assn. [IO]
Bd. of Trade of the Wholesale Seafood Merchants [4323]

Maine Lobstermen's Assn. [3492]
Marine Stewardship Coun. [5171]
Meat Indus. Suppliers Assn. [2661]
Middle Atlantic Fisheries Assn. [3493]
Minneapolis Grain Exchange [4329]
Molluscan Shellfish Inst. [3494]
Natl. Blue Crab Industry Assn. [3495]
Natl. Fish Meal and Oil Assn. [2855]
Natl. Fisheries Inst. [3496]
Natl. Seafood Educators [3497]
Natl. Shrimp Indus. Assn. [3498]
New England Fisheries Development Assn. [3499]
Northwest Fisheries Assn. [3500]
Pacific Coast Shellfish Growers Assn. [3501]
Pacific Seafood Processors Assn. [3502]
Pacific Shellfish Inst. [4182]
Seafood Choices Alliance [3503]
Seafood Choices Alliance [IO]
Shrimp Coun. [5172]
Southeastern Fisheries Assn. [3504]
U.S. Freshwater Prawn and Shrimp Growers Assn. [3505]
U.S. Tuna Found. [3506]
Vietnam Assn. of Seafood Exporters and Producers [IO]
Women's Fisheries Network [4671]
Seafood Choices Alliance [3503], 8401 Colesville Rd., Ste. 500, Silver Spring, MD 20910, (301)495-9570
Seafood Choices Alliance [IO], Silver Spring, MD, United States
Seafood Education and Res. Coun. - Defunct.
Seafood Merchants; Bd. of Trade of the Wholesale [4323]
Seal Assn; Intl. Slurry [★632]
Sealant Coun; Adhesive and [56]
Sealant Manufacturers Coun; Rubber and Plastic Adhesive and [★56]
Sealant and Waterproofers Inst. [★58]
Sealant and Waterproofers Inst. [★IO]
Sealant Waterproofing and Restoration Institute [IO], Kansas City, MO, United States
Sealant Waterproofing and Restoration Inst. [58], 14 W 3rd St., Ste. 200, Kansas City, MO 64105, (816)472-7974
Sealed Insulating Glass Mfrs. Assn. - Address unknown since 2004.
Sealing Assn; Fluid [2020]
Sealing Distributors; Independent [4022]
Sealyham Terrier Club; Amer. [22209]
Seaman's Center; Lutheran [★20232]
Seaman's Church Inst. of New York [★19970]
Seamanship; Seafarers/Harry Lundberg School of [★24132]

Seamen
Finnish Seamen's Union [IO]
Intl. Comm. on Seafarer's Welfare [IO]
Mission to Seafarers [IO]
Nordic Church Coun. for Seamen [IO]
North Amer. Maritime Ministry Assn. [IO]
North Amer. Maritime Ministry Assn. [13007]
Royal Sailors' Rests [IO]
Sailors for the Sea [4447]
United Seamen's Ser. [13008]
United Seamen's Ser. [IO]
Seamen and Intl. House [★20232]
Seamen and Privateers; Brotherhood of Merchant [★21408]
Seamen of Sweden - Defunct.
Seamen's Agencies; Intl. Coun. of [★13007]
Seamen's Agencies; Natl. Coun. of [★13007]
Seamen's Center [★20232]
Seamen's Church Inst. of New York and New Jersey [19970], 241 Water St., New York, NY 10038, (212)349-9090
Seamen's Union of Australia [★IO]
Seamen's Union; Coast [★24131]
Seamen's Work; Church Assn. for [★19970]
SEAMEO Proj. in Archaeology and Fine Arts [★IO]
SEAMEO Regional Centre for Archaeology and Fine Arts [IO], Bangkok, Thailand
SEAMEO Regional Centre for Educ. in Sci. and Mathematics [IO], Penang, Malaysia
SEAMEO Regional Centre for Educational Innovation and Tech. [IO], Quezon City, Philippines

A star before a book entry number signifies that the name is not listed separately, but is mentioned within the entry.

SEAMEO Regional Centre for Medical Microbiology, Parasitology and Entomology [IO], Kuala Lumpur, Malaysia

SEAMEO Regional Centre for Public Hea. [IO], Manila, Philippines

SEAMEO Regional Centre for Tropical Biology [IO], Bogor, Indonesia

SEAMEO Regional Language Centre [IO], Singapore, Singapore

SEAMEO Southeast Asian Regional Center for Graduate Stud. and Res. in Agriculture [★IO]

Seamless Garment Network [★18200]

SEAMS [★2565]

SEAMS Assn. [2565], 4921-C Broad River Rd., Columbia, SC 29212, (803)772-5861

Seaplane Pilots Assn. [167], 3859 Laird Blvd., Lakeland, FL 33811, (863)701-7979

Seaplane Pilots Assn; U.S. [★167]

Seaport Authority; Grays Harbor Historical [8812]

Seaport Museum; South St. [10446]

Seaport; Mystic [10441]

Seaports Alliance; Natl. Safe Waterways and [18749]

Seapost Cover Club; Intl. [★22841]

Search for Common Ground [18595], 1601 Connecticut Ave. NW, Ste. 200, Washington, DC 20009-1035, (202)265-4300

Search for Common Ground [IO], Washington, DC, United States

Search Consultants; Natl. Assn. of Legal [2326]

Search Dog Found; Natl. Disaster [12892]

Search Engine Marketing Professional Org. [2648], 401 Edgewater Pl., Ste. 600, Wakefield, MA 01880, (781)876-8866

Search for Extra-Terrestrial Intelligence League [★6510]

Search Family Org. - Defunct.

SEARCH Found. [6454], PO Box 1729, Crestline, CA 92325, (909)338-2468

Search for the Great Bear - Defunct.

Search Info. Services; Organized Adoption [11259]

Search Inst. [★13515]

Search for Justice and Equality in Palestine [★18071]

Search for Justice and Equality in Palestine [★IO]

Search for Justice and Equality in Palestine/Israel [IO], Framingham, MA, United States

Search for Justice and Equality in Palestine/Israel [18071], PO Box 3452, Framingham, MA 01705-3452, (508)879-0777

SEARCH; Native Seeds/ [4429]

Search Reports, Inc./Central Registry of the Missing [12611]

Search and Rescue; Natl. Assn. for [12891]

SEARCH - The Natl. Consortium for Justice Info. and Statistics [11892], 7311 Greenhaven Dr., Ste. 145, Sacramento, CA 95831, (916)392-2550

Search for Tomorrow Fan Club - Defunct.

Searching Together Educational Ministries [19909], PO Box 377, Taylors Falls, MN 55084, (651)465-6516

Sears Family Assn. [21046], c/o L Ray Sears, III, Ed., 2028 Amber Rd., Oklahoma City, OK 73170, (405)703-0779

Seas Educ. Assn; Inland [2577]

Seas; Public Lib. of the High [★10321]

Seaside Support League - POW/MIA - Defunct.

Seasoning Mfrs. Assn; Natl. [1552]

Seasoning Mfrs; Natl. Assn. of Meat [★1552]

Seasoning Mfrs; Natl. Assn. of Meat and Food [★1552]

SEASONS: Suicide Bereavement - Defunct.

Seat Belt Choice Coalition [17016], c/o Nedd Kareiva, Dir., 6000 S Central, No. 8, Chicago, IL 60638

Seat Belt Coun; Amer. [★377]

Seat Collectors Assn; Cast Iron [22607]

Seatbelt Law Opposition Forum [12990], c/o William J. Holdorf, Dir., 5839 S Harlem Ave., No. 517, Chicago, IL 60638

Seattle Grain Exchange - Defunct.

Seattle Railway Historical Soc; Spokane, Portland and [10924]

SeaWeb [5015], 8401 Colesville Rd., Ste. 500, Silver Spring, MD 20910, (301)495-9570

Sebright Club of Am. [5117]

Sebring/Cimbria Kit Car Club - Address unknown since 2001.

Second Air Div. Assn. [21403]

Second Amendment; Academics for the [17286]

Second Amendment Comm. [5727], PO Box 1776, Hanford, CA 93232, (559)584-5209

Second Amendment Found. [17152], 12500 NE 10th Pl., James Madison Bldg., Bellevue, WA 98005, (425)454-7012

Second Amendment Sisters [17598], 900 RR 620 S, Ste. C-101, PMB 228, Lakeway, TX 78734, (877)271-6216

Second Amendment; Students for the [17602]

Second Bomb Wing Assn. [21322]

Second Bombardment Assn. [20664], c/o Richard K. Radtke, Pres., 60 Villa Heights Ct., Algoma, WI 54201-1463, (920)487-3343

Second Class Mail Publications [★2455]

Second Class Mail Publications; Assn. of [★2455]

Second Class Mail Publishers; Assn. of [★2455]

Second Harvest [★12388]

Second Harvest; America's [12388]

Second Harvest, The Natl. Food Bank Network [★12388]

Second Husbands Alliance for Fair Treatment - Defunct.

Second Marine Div. Assn. [21180], PO Box 8180, Camp Lejeune, NC 28547-8180, (910)451-3167

Second Nature [8495], 18 Tremont St., Ste. 1120, Boston, MA 02108, (617)224-1610

Second Opinion - Defunct.

Second Sight [★16849]

Second Wind Lung Transplant Assn. [16362], c/o Mary Hardy, Treas., 23609 Talbot St., St. Clair Shores, MI 48082, (586)294-3162

Second Wind Org. [★16362]

Second Wives Assn. of North America - Address unknown since 1995.

Second Wives Coalition - Defunct.

Second World War Aircraft Preservation Soc. [IO], Alton, United Kingdom

Secondary Education

Alliance for Excellent Educ. [9118]

Amer. Assn. of Physics Teachers [8993]

Amer. Classical League [8726]

Amer. Forensic Assn. [9152]

Amer. Legion Auxiliary Girls Nation [17068]

Assn. of Military Colleges and Schools of the U.S. [8883]

Augustinian Secondary Educational Assn. [8054]

Bus. Professionals of Am. [9302]

Center for Lifelong Learning [8406]

Chinese Language Assn. of Secondary-Elementary Schools [8075]

Christian Schools Intl. [8083]

The Coll. Bd. [9248]

Columbia Scholastic Press Assn. [9011]

Cmpt. Sci. Teachers Assn. [8130]

Coun. on Standards for Intl. Educational Travel [8610]

Distributive Educ. Clubs of Am. [8817]

Earthwatch Inst. [8413]

Evangelical Lutheran Educ. Assn. [8802]

INROADS [8749]

Inst. for Learning Technologies [8355]

Japanese Natl. Honor Soc. [24521]

Journalism Educ. Assn. [8713]

Junior State of Am. [8750]

Junior Statesmen Found. [8751]

Natl. Assn. of Secondary School Principals [9016]

Natl. Assn. of Student Councils [9186]

Natl. Assn. of Trade and Indus. Instructors [9233]

Natl. Bd. for Professional Teaching Standards [9225]

Natl. Chinese Honor Soc. [24432]

Natl. Commun. Assn. [9157]

Natl. Coun. for Geographic Educ. [8457]

Natl. Coun. for History Educ. [8508]

Natl. Coun. of Secondary School Athletic Directors [8988]

Natl. Coun. for the Social Stud. [9128]

Natl. Forensic League [9159]

Natl. High School Band Directors Hall of Fame [8926]

Natl. High School Baseball Coaches Assn. [23119]

Natl. History Club [8509]

Natl. History Day [8510]

Natl. Interscholastic Athletic Administrators Assn. [8989]

Natl. Scholastic Press Assn. [9013]

Natl. School Boards Assn. [9083]

Natl. Traditionalist Caucus [17276]

Natl. Tutoring Assn. [9283]

NFHS Music Assn. [8928]

North Amer. Assn. of Jewish High Schools [8698]

Oper. Enterprise [8808]

School Sci. and Mathematics Assn. [9115]

Secondary School Admission Test Bd. [9257]

Sociedad Honoraria Hispanica [8499]

Soc. for Academic Achievement [9078]

Soc. for History Educ. [8511]

Soc. for Photographic Educ. [8976]

Student Org. of North Am. [9194]

Student Press Law Center [17194]

Students for the Exploration and Development of Space [7923]

Tripoli Rocketry Assn. [9117]

U.S. High School Tennis Assn. [23912]

World Heritage [8634]

Secondary Educ. Assn; Jesuit [8055]

Secondary Educ. Union [IO], Paris, France

Secondary Educational Assn; Augustinian [8054]

Secondary Heads Assn. [★IO]

Secondary Materials and Recycled Textiles [IO], Falls Church, VA, United States

Secondary Materials and Recycled Textiles [2066], 131 E Broad St., Ste. 206, Falls Church, VA 22046, (703)538-1000

Secondary Principals Assn. of New Zealand [IO], Auckland, New Zealand

Secondary School Admission Test Bd. [9257], CN 5339, Princeton, NJ 08543, (609)683-4440

Secondary School Admissions Center - Defunct.

Secondary School Athletic Directors; Natl. Coun. of [8988]

Secondary School for the Deaf; Model [14766]

Secondary School Evaluation; Natl. Stud. of [★8410]

Secondary School Principals; Natl. Assn. of [9016]

Secondary School Standards; Cooperative Stud. of [★8410]

Secondary School Theatre Assn. - Defunct.

Secondary Schooling for Hispanics; National Commn. on [★17704]

Secondary Schooling for Hispanics; National Commn. on [★IO]

Secondary Schools; Assn. of Lutheran [8801]

Secondary Schools; Commission on [★8277]

Secours Quaker Canadien [★IO]

Secret Ser; Assn. of Former Agents of the U.S. [5877]

Secret Ser. Uniformed Div. Retirement Assn; U.S. [6009]

Secret Soc. of Happy People [10212], 1315 Riverchase Dr., Ste. 2316, Coppell, TX 75019, (972)471-1485

Secretarial Assn; Natl. [73]

Secretariat for Catholic-Jewish Relations [19910], 3121 Massachusetts Ave. NE, 4th St., Washington, DC 20017-1194, (202)541-3000

Secretariat Europeen des Fabricants d'Emballages Metalliques Legers [★IO]

Secretariat for Family, Laity, Women, and Youth [12167], 3211 4th St. NE, Washington, DC 20017-1194, (202)541-3000

Secretariat for Hispanic Affairs/National Conf. of Catholic Bishops [★12282]

Secretariat for Hispanic Affairs, U.S. Conf. of Catholic Bishops [12282], 3211 4th St. NE, Washington, DC 20017, (202)541-3150

Secretariat on Laity and Family Life [★12167]

Secretariat of the Pacific Community [IO], Noumea, New Caledonia

Secretariat for the Spanish Speaking [★12282]

Secretaries and Administrative Assistants; Natl. Assn. of Executive [72]

Secretaries and Administrative Professionals; Hong Kong Assn. of [IO]

Secretaries of Am; Beer Distributors [★204]

Reference to "IO" in place of a book number signifies that the association may be found in the 45th edition of International Organizations.

Secretaries; Amer. Soc. of Corporate [★75]
Secretaries; Assn. of Certified Professional [60]
Secretaries Assn; Coll. Fraternity [★24479]
Secretaries; Assn. of Coun. [★19902]
Secretaries; Assn. of Executive [★19902]
Secretaries Assn; Natl. Retail Grocers [★3405]
Secretaries; Central Assn. of Commercial [★24251]
Secretaries and Directors of Agriculture; Natl. Assn. of Commissioners, [★5439]
Secretaries and Governance Professionals; Soc. of Corporate [75]
Secretaries; Hong Kong Inst. of Company [IO]
Secretaries Intl. [★IO]
Secretaries Intl. [★66]
Secretaries Intl; Professional [★66]
Secretaries; Natl. Assn. of Appointment [★8961]
Secretaries; Natl. Assn. of Collegiate [★66]
Secretaries; Natl. Assn. of Commercial Org. [★24251]
Secretaries; Natl. Assn. of Educational [★7898]
Secretaries; Natl. Assn. of School [★7898]
Secretaries; Natl. Assn. of State Beer Assn. [★204]
Secretaries; Natl. Conf. of Bar [★5948]
Secretaries; Natl. Conf. of Tuberculosis [★16357]
Secretaries; Nursery Assn. [★5047]
Secretaries of State; Assn. of Amer. [★6277]
Secretaries; State Beer Wholesalers [★204]
Secretaries of State; Natl. Assn. of [6277]
Secretaries of State Teachers Associations; Natl. Assn. of [★7906]
Secretaries, Young Men's Christian Associations of North Am; Assn. of [★13460]
Secretary's Open Forum [17617], US Dept. of State, S/OF, Rm. 5312A, 2201 C St. NW, Washington, DC 20520, (202)647-0819
Secretions; Assn. for Stud. of Internal [★14355]
Secretive Societies, Mind Control and Ritual Abuse; S.M.A.R.T. [13296]
Sect. 23 Leased Housing Assn. [★12329]
Sect. of Criminal Law [★5922]
Sect. of the Division of Libraries for Children and Young People of the Amer. Lib. Assn. [★10317]
Sect. on Gay and Lesbian Legal Issues, Assn. of Amer. Law Schools [★8761]
Sect. of Individual Rights and Responsibilities [17153], c/o Amer. Bar Assn., 740 15th St. NW, Washington, DC 20005-1009, (202)662-1030
Sect. of Intl. Law and Practice - Address unknown since 1999.
Sect. for Long Term Care and Rehabilitation [14894], 1 N Franklin St., Chicago, IL 60606, (312)422-3308
Sect. for Magnetic Resonance Technologists [16594], 2030 Addison St., 7th Fl., Berkeley, CA 94704, (510)841-1899
Sect. for Metropolitan Hospitals [14895], c/o Amer. Hosp. Assn., 1 N Franklin St., Ste. 27, Chicago, IL 60606, (312)422-3000
Sect. Nationale de la CIME [IO], Moscow, Russia
Sect. of Physical Oceanography of the Intl. Union of Geodesy and Geophysics [★IO]
Sect. of Physical Oceanography of the Intl. Union of Geodesy and Geophysics [★7398]
Sect. for Psychiatric and Substance Abuse Services [16093], c/o Amer. Hosp. Assn., One N Franklin, Chicago, IL 60606-3421, (312)422-3300
Sect. on the Psychology of Black Women in the Div. of the Psychology of Women of the Amer. Psychological Assn. - Address unknown since 1995.
Sect. on Twin and Sibling Studies - Address unknown since 1995.
Sect. on Women in Legal Education of the AALS - Defunct.
Sect. for Women in Public Admin. [6198], 1120 G St. NW, Ste. 700, Washington, DC 20005-3885, (202)393-7878
Sector Skills Alliance Scotland [IO], Edinburgh, United Kingdom
Sectoral Assn. of Trans. Equip. and Machines Mfg. [IO], Montreal, QC, Canada
Sectoral Roundtable Assn. for the Hea. and Safety of Metal and Elecl. Workers [IO], Longueuil, QC, Canada
Secular Carmelite Order [★IO]

Secular Humanism; Coun. for [20085]
Secular Humanism; Coun. for Democratic and [★20085]
Secular Humanist Societies; Alliance of [10193]
Secular Humanistic Jews; Intl. Fed. of [20086]
Secular Humanistic Judaism; Intl. Fed. for [★20086]
Secular Inst; DeSales [★19716]
Secular Inst. of Saint Francis de Sales [19716], 87 Gerrish Ave. T2, East Haven, CT 06512, (203)469-3277
Secular Institute of Saint Francis de Sales [IO], East Haven, CT, United States
Secular Jewish Organizations; Cong. of [10279]
Secular Order of Discalced Carmelites [IO], Rome, Italy
Secular Organizations for Sobriety [13281], 4773 Hollywood Blvd., Hollywood, CA 90027, (323)666-4295
Secular Soc. of America - Defunct.
Secular Student Alliance [17790], 48 Howard St., Albany, NY 12207, (518)632-4139

Securities
Alliance in Support of Independent Res. [3390]
Amer. Stock Exchange [3507]
Asian Securities Analysts Fed. [IO]
Asset Managers Forum [1401]
Assn. of Securities and Exchange Commn. Alumni [3508]
Canadian Securities Inst. [IO]
CFA Singapore [IO]
Chicago Bd. Options Exchange [3509]
Chicago Stock Exchange [3510]
Consolidated Tape Assn. [3511]
Coun. of Institutional Investors [3512]
Emerging Markets Private Equity Assn. [1415]
EMTA [3513]
EMTA [IO]
Fed. of European Securities Exchanges [IO]
Financial Services Authority [IO]
Financial Services Inst. of Australasia - South Australia and Northern Territory [IO]
Finnish Found. for Share Promotion [IO]
Futures and Options Assn. [IO]
Global Equity Org. [1239]
Hong Kong Securities Inst. [IO]
Ibero-American Fed. of Exchanges [IO]
Indonesian Assn. of Investment Managers [IO]
Inst. of Chartered Financial Analysts of India [IO]
Inst. of Finance Professionals New Zealand [IO]
Intl. Capital Market Assn. [IO]
Intl. Capital Market Assn., Zurich [IO]
Intl. Org. of Securities Commissions [IO]
Intl. Security, Trust and Privacy Alliance [3535]
Investment Adviser Assn. [3514]
Investment Company Inst. [3515]
Korea Certified Investment Analysts Assn. [IO]
Mutual Fund Educ. Alliance [3516]
NASD [3517]
Natl. Assn. of Bond Lawyers [6255]
Natl. Assn. of Securities Professionals [3518]
Natl. Assn. of Steel Stockholders [IO]
Natl. Assn. of Unemployment Insurance Appellate Boards [5831]
New York Soc. of Security Analysts [3519]
New York Stock Exchange [3520]
North Amer. Securities Administrators Assn. [3521]
Pacific Stock Exchange [3522]
ProShare (United Kingdom) [IO]
Res. Inst. of Investment Analysts Malaysia [IO]
Securities Analysts Assn., Chinese Taipei [IO]
Securities Analysts Assn., Thailand [IO]
Securities Industry and Financial Markets Association [3523]
Securities and Insurance Licensing Assn. [2236]
Securities Transfer Assn. [3524]
Security Traders Assn. [3525]
Zimbabwe Stock Exchange [IO]
Securities Analysts Assn., Chinese Taipei [IO], Taipei, Taiwan
Securities Analysts Assn., Thailand [IO], Bangkok, Thailand
Securities Assn; Bank Insurance and [2151]
Securities and Commercial Law Attorneys; Natl. Assn. of [★5579]

Securities Commissioners; Natl. Assn. of [★3521]
Securities Dealers; Natl. Assn. of [★3517]
Securities and Exchange Commission [★3508]
Securities and Futures Authority [★IO]
Securities Indus. Assn. and The Bond Market Association [★3523]
Securities Industry and Financial Markets Association [3523], 120 Broadway, 35th Fl., New York, NY 10271-0080, (212)608-1500
Securities Inst. of Australia and Australasian Inst. of Banking and Finance [★IO]
Securities and Insurance Licensing Assn. [2236], c/o Beth McGuire, Exec. Dir., PO Box 68203, Indianapolis, IN 46268-0203, (800)428-8329
Securities Investors Assn. - Singapore [IO], Singapore, Singapore
Securities Transfer Assn. [3524], PO Box 5220, Hazlet, NJ 07730, (732)888-6040
Security
9/11 Families for a Secure Am. [18728]
Aircraft Carrier Indus. Base Coalition [1148]
Amer. Fed. of Security Officers [24184]
Amer. Security Coun. [18586]
Amer. Soc. for Amusement Park Safety and Security [3526]
Amer. Task Force on Palestine [17860]
Americans for Fair Electronic Commerce Transactions [17441]
Asia Am. Initiative [11762]
Asian Professional Security Assn. - Hong Kong Chap. [IO]
Asian Professional Security Assn. - Malaysia Chap. [IO]
Asian Professional Security Assn. - Singapore Chap. [IO]
Assn. of Former Intelligence Officers [5878]
Assn. of Security Consultants [IO]
Atlantic Coun. of the U.S. [17014]
British Amer. Security Info. Coun. - United Kingdom [IO]
British Security Indus. Assn. [IO]
Bus. Executives for Natl. Security [18587]
Canadian Security Assn. [IO]
Center for Natl. Security Stud. [18588]
Center for Security Policy [18589]
Centurion-6 Security Ser. Intl. Assn. [IO]
Chem. and Biological Arms Control Inst. [17023]
Coalition Opposing Signal Theft [556]
Community Food Security Coalition [12192]
Coun. for Emerging Natl. Security Affairs [18590]
Coun. of Intl. Investigators [2322]
Defense Orientation Conf. Assn. [18591]
Electronic Security Distributors Assn. [IO]
Estonian Security Assn. [IO]
GlobalSecurity.org [18208]
Henry L. Stimson Center [17824]
Inst. for Defense Analyses [6256]
Inst. for Foreign Policy Anal. [17612]
Inter-American Conf. of Ministers of Labor [17394]
Intl. Assn. for Cmpt. Systems Security [905]
Intl. Assn. for Counterterrorism and Security Professionals [18731]
Intl. Assn. for Healthcare Security and Safety [14887]
Intl. Assn. of Home Safety and Security Professionals [3527]
International Association of Home Safety and Security Professionals [IO]
Intl. Assn. of Investigative Locksmiths [IO]
Intl. Assn. of Investigative Locksmiths [3528]
Intl. Assn. of Professional Protection Specialists [13009]
International Association of Professional Protection Specialists [IO]
Intl. Assn. of Professional Security Consultants [IO]
Intl. Assn. of Professional Security Consultants [3529]
Intl. Brotherhood of Police Officers [24120]
Intl. Cargo Security Coun. [3530]
Intl. Counter-Terrorism Officers Assn. [18732]
Intl. Defensive Pistol Assn. [23718]
Intl. Found. for Protection Officers [3531]
Intl. Found. for Protection Officers [IO]
Intl. Guards Union of Am. [24185]

A star before a book entry number signifies that the name is not listed separately, but is mentioned within the entry.

Intl. Inst. of Security [IO]
Intl. Intelligence Network [IO]
Intl. Intelligence Network [3532]
Intl. Org. of Black Security Executives [3533]
Intl. Professional Security Assn. - England [IO]
Intl. Security and Detective Alliance [2323]
Intl. Security Mgt. Assn. [3534]
Intl. Security Mgt. Assn. [IO]
Intl. Security, Trust and Privacy Alliance [3535]
Intl. Systems Security Engg. Assn. [7023]
Intl. Union of Police Associations [24121]
Intl. Union of Security Officers [24186]
Intl. Union, Security, Police and Fire Professionals
   of Am. [24187]
International Union, Security, Police and Fire
   Professionals of America [IO]
Irish Security Indus. Assn. [IO]
Jewelers' Security Alliance [2372]
Master Locksmiths Assn. [IO]
Military Intelligence Corps Assn. [5862]
Mine Warfare Assn. [18592]
Minuteman Civil Defense Corps [17077]
Missile Defense Advocacy Alliance [17382]
Natl. Alarm Assn. of Am. [3536]
Natl. Alliance of Police, Security and Corrections
   Organizations [24165]
Natl. Assn. Citizens on Patrol [12970]
Natl. Assn. of Field Training Officers [5987]
Natl. Assn. of Mfrs. and Installers of Security
   Systems [IO]
Natl. Assn. of Security Companies [3537]
Natl. Assn. of Unemployment Insurance Appellate
   Boards [5831]
Natl. Burglar and Fire Alarm Assn. [3538]
Natl. Constr. Investigators Assn. [5606]
Natl. Coun. of Investigation and Security Services
   [3539]
Natl. Inst. for Public Policy [18466]
Natl. Irish Safety Org. [IO]
Natl. Major Gang Task Force [5651]
Natl. Memorial Inst. for the Prevention of Terror-
   ism [18734]
Natl. Safe Skies Alliance [18748]
Natl. Safe Waterways and Seaports Alliance
   [18749]
Natl. Safety Mgt. Soc. [12980]
Natl. Security Inspectorate [IO]
Nautilus Inst. [IO]
Nautilus Inst. [18593]
NCMS — Soc. of Indus. Security Professionals
   &lsqb2092]
Nine Lives Associates [3540]
Nine Lives Associates [IO]
Norwegian Defence and Security Indus. Assn.
   [IO]
Nuclear Threat Initiative [18164]
OPSEC Professionals Soc. [18594]
Org. for Security and Co-operation in Europe [IO]
Our Voices Together [13309]
Patriots for the Defense of Am. [18186]
Plant Protection Assn. [24188]
Proj. on Defense Alternatives [17385]
Pups for Peace [12700]
Res. Security Administrators [6257]
Safe and Vault Technicians Assn. [3541]
SaferAfrica [IO]
Search for Common Ground [IO]
Search for Common Ground [18595]
Security Assn. of South Africa [IO]
Security Indus. Assn. [3542]
Security Systems and Alarms Inspection Bd. [IO]
September's Mission [13310]
Soc. of Professional Rope Access Technicians
   [2068]
Submarine Indus. Base Coun. [1149]
Terror Free Tomorrow [18736]
Ukrainian Center for Intl. Security Stud. [IO]
United to Secure Am. [18596]
U.S. Congressional Advisory Bd. [18597]
U.S. Contract Security Assn. [3543]
U.S. Indus. Coalition [7637]
U.S. Indus. Coalition [IO]
U.S. Naval Cryptologic Veterans Assn. [21327]
UrgentCall.org [18173]
Veterans for Common Sense [21330]

Vietnam Security Police Assn. [21340]
Voices of September 11th [18737]
Women in Intl. Security [18598]
Women in Intl. Security [IO]
Workplace Benefits Assn. [1247]
World Trade Center Survivors' Network [13311]
Security Agencies; Interstate Conf. of Employment
   [★5680]
Security Alliance; Jewelers' [2372]
Security Alliance of the U.S; Jewelers [★2372]
Security; Alliance for Worker Retirement [18544]
Security Assn; Info. Systems [2090]
Security Assn. of South Africa [IO], Johannesburg,
   Republic of South Africa
Security, Audit and Control; Special Interest Gp. on
   [6752]
Security on Campus [11846], 133 Ivy Ln., Ste. 200,
   King of Prussia, PA 19406-2101, (610)768-9330
Security; Center for New Natl. [17864]
Security Certification Consortium; Intl. Info. Systems
   [6758]
Security Companies; Comm. of Natl. [★3537]
Security Container Inst. - Defunct.
Security and Corrections Organizations; Natl. Alli-
   ance of Police, [24165]
Security Coun. Educ. Found; Amer. [★16986]
Security Coun; Energy [2089]
Security Coun. Found; Amer. [16986]
Security and Data Vaults; Natl. Assn. of [★2109]
Security and Detective Assn; U.S. Private [★2323]
Security Equip. Indus. Assn. [★3542]
Security Equip. Mfrs. Assn. [★3542]
Security Hardware Distributors Assn. [1834], 100 N
   20th St., 4th Fl., Philadelphia, PA 19103-1443,
   (215)564-3484
Security Indus. Assn; Natl. [★6089]
Security Indus. Assn. [3542], 635 Slaters Ln., Ste.
   110, Alexandria, VA 22314, (703)683-2075
Security Inst; Cmpt. [2088]
Security; Intl. Assn. for Hosp. [★14887]
Security; Natl. Alliance for Food Safety and [1537]
Security Officers; Natl. Assn. of Special Police and
   [24122]
Security Org; Women in Defense, a Natl. [17386]
Security; Pacific Inst. for Stud. in Development, Env.,
   and [12120]
Security Products Assn; Financial and [476]
Security; SANE/FREEZE: Campaign for Global
   [★18166]
Security Stud; Inst. for Space and [18155]
Security Stud. at Maryland; Center for Intl. and
   [★18598]
Security Stud. at Maryland; Center for Intl. and
   [★IO]
Security Systems and Alarms Inspection Bd. [IO],
   North Shields, United Kingdom
Security Traders Assn. [3525], 420 Lexington Ave.,
   Ste. 2334, New York, NY 10170, (212)867-7002
Security Traders Assn; Natl. [★3525]
Security Training
   Acad. of Security Educators and Trainers [9119]
   Academy of Security Educators and Trainers [IO]
   Intl. Assn. of Investigative Locksmiths [3528]
   Intl. Org. of Black Security Executives [3533]
   Natl. Assn. of Field Training Officers [5987]
   Terror Free Tomorrow [18736]
   U.S. Contract Security Assn. [3543]
Sedan Deliveries Limited - Defunct.
Sedimentary Geology; Soc. for [7432]
Seed
   Abundant Life Seed Found. [4338]
   African Seed Trade Assn. [IO]
   Amer. Seed Res. Found. [5173]
   Amer. Seed Trade Assn. [5174]
   Arche Noah [IO]
   Asia and Pacific Seed Assn. [IO]
   Assn. of Amer. Seed Control Officials [5434]
   Assn. of Official Seed Analysts [5435]
   Assn. of Official Seed Certifying Agencies [5436]
   Australian Seed Fed. [IO]
   Canadian Seed Growers' Assn. [IO]
   Canadian Seed Trade Assn. [IO]
   Cereals, Pulses, Oily Seeds and Products
      Exporter Union [IO]
   Chilean Seed Producers' Assn. [IO]

The Cycad Soc. [4387]
Czech-Moravian Assn. of Plant Breeders and
   Seed Traders [IO]
Egyptian Seed Assn. [IO]
European Seed Assn. [IO]
FLEUROSELECT [IO]
Greek Seed Trade Assn. [IO]
Independent Professional Seedsmen Assn. [187]
Intl. Consultative Res. Gp. on Rapeseed [IO]
Intl. Seed Fed. [IO]
Intl. Seed Testing Assn. [IO]
Japan Seed Trade Assn. [IO]
Natl. Coun. of Commercial Plant Breeders [5175]
Natl. Garden Bur. [4982]
Native Seeds/SEARCH [4429]
Paraguayan Chamber of Cereals and Oilseed
   Exporters [IO]
Polish Seed Trade Assn. [IO]
Seed Saver's Network [IO]
Seeds of Diversity Canada [IO]
Soc. of Commercial Seed Technologists [5176]
South African Natl. Seed Org. [IO]
Swiss Seed Growers Assn. [IO]
U.S. Canola Assn. [1568]
Seed Assn. of New York; Linseed Castor [★2852]
Seed Bank; Southwest Traditional Crop
   Conservancy Garden and [★4429]
Seed Certifying Agencies; Assn. of Official [5436]
Seed Commn; Oregon Ryegrass Growers [4798]
Seed Crushers' Assn; Interstate Cotton [★2854]
Seed Crushers' and Oil Processors' Assn. [IO], Sur-
   biton, United Kingdom
Seed Distributors; Arizona Cotton Planting [★4317]
Seed Exchange; True [★22540]
Seed Found; Abundant Life [4338]
Seed Pea Inst. - Defunct.
Seed Savers Exchange [22540], 3094 N Winn Rd.,
   Decorah, IA 52101, (563)382-5990
Seed Saver's Network [IO], Byron Bay, Australia
Seedlings Braille Books for Children [9297], PO Box
   51924, Livonia, MI 48151-5924, (734)427-8552
Seeds of Diversity Canada [IO], Toronto, ON,
   Canada
Seeds of Hope; Plant [★19135]
Seeds of Peace [18245], 370 Lexington Ave., Ste.
   401, New York, NY 10017, (212)573-8040
Seeds/SEARCH; Native [4429]
Seeds/Southwestern Endangered Arid-Land Rsrc.
   Clearing House; Native [★4429]
Seedsmen; Amer. Assn. of Nurserymen, Florists and
   [★5042]
Seeing; Coun. for the Educ. of the Partially [★9145]
Seeing Eye [16888], PO Box 375, Morristown, NJ
   07963-0375, (973)539-4425
Seeing Teen Stars - Address unknown since 1999.
Seeking Common Ground [13514], PO Box 101958,
   Denver, CO 80250, (303)691-2393
Seeking Harmony in Neighborhoods Everyday
   [18857]
Seeley Genealogical Soc. [21047], PO Box 337,
   Abilene, KS 67410-0337
Sefyldliad Siartredig Llyfrgellwyr a Gweithdwr Gwy-
   bodaeth Cymru [★IO]
SEG Foundation [★7149]
Segrist Family Org; Hans/Henry [20927]
Seguridad; Consejo Interamericano de [★12965]
Seimos Planavimo Ir Seksualines Sveikatos Asoci-
   acija [★IO]
Seingalt Soc. - Defunct.
Seisho Domei [★IO]
Seismological Soc. of Am. [7642], 201 Plaza Profes-
   sional Bldg., El Cerrito, CA 94530, (510)525-5474
Seismological Soc. of Japan [IO], Tokyo, Japan
Seismology
   Australian Earthquake Engg. Soc. [IO]
   Earthquake Engg. Res. Inst. [7638]
   European Assn. for Earthquake Engg. [IO]
   European-Mediterranean Seismological Centre
      [IO]
   European Seismological Commn. [IO]
   European Volcanological Assn. [IO]
   Intl. Assn. for Earthquake Engg. [IO]
   Intl. Assn. of Seismology and Physics of the
      Earth's Interior [IO]
   Intl. Assn. of Seismology and Physics of the
      Earth's Interior [7639]

Reference to "IO" in place of a book number signifies that the association may be found in the 45th edition of International Organizations.

Intl. Assn. of Volcanology and Chemistry of the Earth's Interior [IO]
Intl. Inst. of Seismology and Earthquake Engg. [IO]
Intl. Seismological Centre [IO]
Intl. Tsunami Info. Center [IO]
Intl. Tsunami Info. Center [7640]
Natl. Info. Ser. for Earthquake Engg. [7641]
NORSAR [IO]
Regional Centre for Seismology for South Am. [IO]
Seismological Soc. of Am. [7642]
Seismological Soc. of Japan [IO]
Vibration Isolation and Seismic Control Mfrs. Assn. [7643]
SEIU, District 925, AFL-CIO [23996], 3647 Stone Way, Seattle, WA 98103, (206)322-3010
Sejours [★22580]
Sekai Boeki Center Tokyo [★IO]
Sekiyu Remmei Kohobu Shiryoka [★IO]
Selden Soc. [IO], London, United Kingdom
SELECT [IO], Midlothian, United Kingdom
Select Registry, Distinguished Inns of North Am. [1965], PO Box 150, Marshall, MI 49068, (269)789-0393
Selected Independent Funeral Homes [2791], 500 Lake Cook Rd., Ste. 205, Deerfield, IL 60015, (847)236-9401
Selective Mutism Found. [15233], c/o Carolyn Miller, Co-Founder/Co-Dir., PO Box 13133, Sissonville, WV 25360-0133
Selenology
    Amer. Lunar Soc. [6499]
Self Abuse Finally Ends; SAFE - [★12557]
Self Determination for DC - Address unknown since 1989.
Self Drilling Anchors Assn. - Defunct.
Self-Employed; Natl. Assn. for the [3617]
Self-Employed Women's Assn. [IO], Ahmedabad, India
Self Esteem; Natl. Assn. for [15218]
Self-Government; Advocates for [18012]
Self-Government Advocates [★18012]
Self-Government/National Municipal League; Citizens Forum on [★6128]
Self-Help CH; Amer. [★13013]
Self-Help CH; Natl. Mental Hea. Consumers' [12553]
Self Help Found. [★12442]
Self Help Found. [★IO]
Self-Help Found; Wives- [11832]
Self Help for Hard of Hearing People [★14759]
Self-Help Initiative for Sustainable Development [IO], Acces, Ghana
Self Help Intl. [IO], Waverly, IA, United States
Self Help Intl. [12442], 805 W Bremer Ave., Waverly, IA 50677-2927, (319)352-4040
Self-Help and Mutual Aid Assn. - Defunct.
Self-Help Soc. - Defunct.
Self-Instructional Language Programs; Natl. Assn. of [8736]
Self-Insurance Inst. of Am. [2237], PO Box 1237, Simpsonville, SC 29681, (800)851-7789
Self-Mutilators Support Gp. [★12557]
Self-Publishers' Assn. of New Zealand [IO], Auckland, New Zealand
Self-Realization Fellowship [20635], 3880 San Rafael Ave., Dept. 9W, Los Angeles, CA 90065-3298, (323)225-2471
Self Reliance Assn. of Amer. Ukrainians [19414], 108 2nd Ave., New York, NY 10003-8392, (212)473-7310
Self-Reliance; Inst. for Local [11747]
Self-Rising Flour and Corn Meal Prog. [★1520]
Self-Rising Flour Inst. [★1520]
Self-Service Storage Assn. [★3983]
Self Storage Assn. [3983], 1900 N Beauregard St., Ste. 110, Alexandria, VA 22311, (703)575-8000
Self Storage Assn. of Australasia [IO], Epping, Australia
Self Storage Assn. of the United Kingdom [IO], Nantwich, United Kingdom
Self-Sufficiency; Center for [11743]
Self Winding Clock Assn. [22991]
Self Defense
    Aikido Assn. of Am. [23046]

Aikido Assn. of North Am. [23047]
Aikido Yoshokai Assn. of North Am. [7943]
All Japan Ju-Jitsu Intl. Fed. [23577]
Alliance of Guardian Angels [11834]
Amer. Chen Style Tai Chi Assn. [23578]
Amer. Kempo-Karate Assn. [23579]
Amer. Sambo Assn. [23580]
Amer. Self-Protection Assn. [23712]
Amer. Shorin Kempo Karate Assn. [23581]
Amer. Tai Chi Assn. [16593]
Amer. Teachers Assn. of the Martial Arts [23582]
Amer. Women's Self-Defense Assn. [13010]
Amer. Women's Self-Defense Assn. [IO]
Amer. Wu Shu Soc. [23583]
Amer. Yangjia Michuan Taijiquan Assn. [23584]
Assn. of Defensive Spray Mfrs. [3544]
Assn. for Renaissance Martial Arts [8820]
Assn. of Women Martial Arts Instructors [23585]
Choy Lee Fut Martial Arts Fed. of Am. [23586]
Combat Martial Art Practitioners Assn. [23587]
Empower Prog. [8945]
Feminist Karate Union [23561]
Intl. Aikido Assn. [23048]
Intl. Chinese Boxing Assn. [23262]
Intl. Defensive Pistol Assn. [23718]
Intl. Martial Arts League [23589]
Intl. Okinawa Kobudo Assn. [23590]
Intl. Seven-Star Mantis Style Lee Kam Wing Martial Art Assn. - USA [23591]
Intl. Sungja-Do Assn. [23593]
Intl. Yang Style Tai Chi Chuan Assn. [23594]
Kidpower Teenpower Fullpower Intl. [12967]
Martial Arts Indus. Assn. [2655]
Martial Arts Intl. Fed. [23596]
Martial Arts USA [23597]
Mothers Arms [13011]
Natl. Assn. of Professional Martial Artists [23598]
Natl. Assn. of Town Watch [11841]
Natl. Coun. for Taekwondo Masters Certification [23599]
Natl. Crime Prevention Coun. [11844]
North Am. Wu(Hao) Taiji Fed. [23601]
People Against Rape [13083]
Power for Women [13436]
Shudokan Martial Arts Assn. [23603]
Traditional Tae Kwon Do Chung Do Assn. [23604]
U.S. Aikido Fed. [23049]
U.S.A. Wushu-Kungfu Fed. [23605]
U.S. Hapki Hae [23606]
U.S. Isshinryu Karate Assn. [23565]
U.S. Martial Arts Assn. [23607]
U.S. Muay Thai Assn. [23608]
U.S. Sport Jujitsu Assn. [23609]
U.S. Taekwondo Union [23610]
U.S. Yudo Assn. [23611]
Universal Martial Arts Brotherhood [23612]
US Cheng Ming Martial Arts Assn. [23613]
We Are AWARE [13442]
World Head of Family Sokeship Coun. [23614]
World Jeet Kune Do Fed. [23615]
World Martial Arts Assn. [23616]
World Modern Arnis Alliance [23617]
World Traditional Karate Org. [23567]
World Ving Tsun Athletic Assn. [23618]
Zen-do Kai Martial Arts [23619]
Selfhelp
AAMED - The Amer. Assn. of Multiple Enchondroma Diseases [15749]
ABIL - Agoraphobics Building Independent Lives [12546]
Adult Children of Alcoholics World Ser. Org. [13012]
Adult Children of Alcoholics World Service Organization [IO]
Agoraphobics in Motion [12742]
Amer. Self-Help Gp. CH [13013]
Androgen Insensitivity Syndrome Support Gp. - USA [14441]
Anxiety Disorders Assn. of Am. [12743]
Anxiety Disorders Special Interest Gp. [12744]
Anxiety and Phobia Treatment Center [12745]
A.R.T.S. Anonymous [13014]
Batterers Anonymous - Beyond Abuse [12023]
Black Women's Hea. Imperative [16895]
Clutterers Anonymous [13015]

Co-Dependents Anonymous [13016]
Coalition for Harmony of Races in the U.S. [18198]
Cocaine Anonymous World Services [13232]
Debtors Anonymous [13017]
Delancey St. Found. [13018]
Deliver the Dream [13019]
Depression and Bipolar Support Alliance [15196]
Depressives Anonymous: Recovery From Depression [12547]
Donors' Offspring [13298]
Emerge: Counseling and Educ. to Stop Domestic Violence [12026]
Emotions Anonymous Intl. Ser. Center [12549]
Families Anonymous [13240]
First Sunday [12671]
Fly Without Fear [12746]
Gainsharing Inst. [13020]
Gamblers Anonymous [12211]
Homosexuals Anonymous Fellowship Services [12236]
Intl. Found. for Stutterers [16447]
Intl. Ser. Org. - COSA [13072]
Intl. Soc. for Dialogical Sci. [7544]
Intl. Stuttering Assn. [16498]
Largesse, the Network for Size Esteem [12646]
ManKind Proj. [13021]
Marijuana Anonymous World Services [13022]
Messies Anonymous [13023]
Molesters Anonymous [13024]
Natl. Adrenal Diseases Found. [14358]
Natl. Assn. for Native Amer. Children of Alcoholics [11627]
Natl. Assn. for Shoplifting Prevention [13025]
Natl. Chronic Pain Outreach Assn. [15844]
Natl. Mental Hea. Consumers' Self-Help CH [12553]
Natl. Self-Help CH [13026]
Natl. Stuttering Assn. [16454]
Nicotine Anonymous World Services [13027]
Nicotine Anonymous World Services [IO]
Obsessive-Compulsive Anonymous [12555]
Overeaters Anonymous World Ser. Off. [12648]
Parents Anonymous [11645]
Paul and Lisa Prog. [13082]
Phoenix Soc. for Burn Survivors [13785]
Pride Prog. [13437]
Protecting Adult Welfare [13028]
Real Found. [13438]
Res. and Training Center on Independent Living [11984]
S.A.F.E. Alternatives [12557]
Schizophrenics Anonymous [12558]
Self Help Intl. [12442]
Sex Addicts Anonymous [13073]
Sex Workers Anonymous [13029]
Sexaholics Anonymous [13075]
Smokenders [16435]
Soc. for Indus. and Applied Mathematics [7294]
SOL [13030]
Speak Easy Intl. Found. [16455]
Support for People with Oral and Head and Neck Cancer [13877]
Survivors of Incest Anonymous [13085]
TOPS Club (Take Off Pounds Sensibly) [12649]
UP Micro-Loans: Unlimiting People [IO]
VOICES in Action [13086]
Weight Watchers Intl. [14603]
Women and Men Against Sexual Harassment and Other Abuses [13088]
Workaholics Anonymous [13031]
Selfhelp of Emigres from Central Europe - Address unknown since 1995.
Self-Sufficiency
Amer. Jewish World Ser. [12829]
Catholic Homesteading Movement [11742]
Center for Self-Sufficiency [11743]
Fed. of Egalitarian Communities [11746]
First Nations Development Inst. [12625]
Inst. for Local Self-Reliance [11747]
Older Women's League [13435]
Opportunities Industrialization Centers of Am. [12096]
Rockefeller Family Fund [12737]
Self Help Intl. [12442]

A star before a book entry number signifies that the name is not listed separately, but is mentioned within the entry.

World Concern [12787]

Selkirk Rex Breed Club [21917], c/o Debi Kallmeyer, PO Box 213, Aromas, CA 95004-0213

Sell Overseas America, the Assn. of Amer. Export - Defunct.

Sellards Family; Bloss-Pyles-Ross- [20798]

Selle Francais Assn; North Amer. [4935]

Sellers; Assn. of Fund Raisers and Direct [★1684]

Sellers; Natl. Assn. of Direct [★1684]

Sellin Center for Studies in Criminology and Criminal Law - Defunct.

Selling Assn; Direct [3465]

Selling Assn; Natl. Field [3471]

Selling Companies; Natl. Assn. of Direct [★3465]

Selling Educ. Found; Direct [3466]

Selous Found. [16992]

SEMA Coun; Truck Cap and Accessory Alliance - a [★390]

SEMA Found. [★6521]

SEMAA - The Safety Affiliate of NIRA [3456], 105 Eastern Ave., Ste. 104, Annapolis, MD 21403, (410)263-1014

Semantics
Inst. of Gen. Semantics [10962]
Institute of General Semantics [IO]
Intl. Soc. of Neuro-Semantics [IO]
Intl. Soc. of Neuro-Semantics [16396]

Semences du Patrimoine Canada [★IO]

SEMI Intl. [IO], San Jose, CA, United States

SEMI Intl. [1228], 3081 Zanker Rd., San Jose, CA 95134, (408)943-6900

Semi-Professional Baseball Assn; Natl. [23122]

Semiconductor Assn; Fabless [1215]

Semiconductor Assn; North Am. Chinese [1226]

Semiconductor Environmental, Safety and Hea. Assn. [6931], 1313 Dolley Madison Blvd., Ste. 402, McLean, VA 22101-3926, (703)790-1745

Semiconductor Equip. and Materials Inst. [★1228]

Semiconductor Equip. and Materials Inst. [★IO]

Semiconductor Equip. and Materials Intl. [★IO]

Semiconductor Equip. and Materials Intl. [★1228]

Semiconductor Indus. Assn. [1229], 181 Metro Dr., Ste. 450, San Jose, CA 95110-1344, (408)436-6600

Semiconductor Professional Assn; Chinese Amer. [1208]

Semiconductor Res. Corp. [★1229]

Semiconductor Safety Assn. [★6931]

Semillas - Sociedad Mexicana Pro Derechos de la Mujer, AC [IO], Mexico City, Mexico

Seminar on the Acquisition of Latin Amer. Lib. Materials [IO], New Orleans, LA, United States

Seminar on the Acquisition of Latin Amer. Lib. Materials [10386], Tulane Univ., The Latin Amer. Lib., 422 Howard-Tilton Memorial Lib., 7001 Freret St., New Orleans, LA 70118, (504)247-1366

Seminar Leaders Assn; Amer. [8147]

Seminaries of the U.S. and Canada; Conf. of Theological [★9270]

Seminars on Hypnosis Found. [★14922]

Semiotic Soc. of Am. [7644], c/o Terry J. Prewitt, Exec. Dir., Univ. of West Florida, Box 32009, Pensacola, FL 32514, (850)474-2186

Semiotics
Canadian Semiotic Assn. [IO]
Intl. Assn. for Semiotic Stud. [IO]
Intl. Pragmatics Assn. [IO]
Japanese Assn. for Semiotic Stud. [IO]
Nordic Assn. for Semiotic Stud. [IO]
Semiotic Soc. of Am. [7644]

Semisocialist Coalition of Earth [18314], PO Box 4051, Bluefield, WV 24701, (304)327-6265

Semisocialist Coalition of Earth [IO], Bluefield, WV, United States

Sempervivum Fanciers Assn. - Defunct.

Senate Children's Caucus [17258], c/o Hon. Senator Christopher J. Dodd, 448 Russell Bldg., Washington, DC 20510, (202)224-2823

Senate Coalition; Northeast-Midwest [18472]

Senate Copper Caucus - Defunct.

Senate Press Photographers Gallery; U.S. [3016]

Senate Press Secretaries Assn. - Address unknown since 1995.

Senate Rail Caucus - Address unknown since 1995.

Senate Staff Club - Defunct.

Senate Steel Caucus - Defunct.

Senate Tourism Caucus [17259], c/o Sen. Conrad Burns, Co-Chm., 187 Dirksen Senate Off. Bldg., Washington, DC 20510, (202)224-2644

Senate Wine Caucus - Address unknown since 2002.

Senatorial Campaign Comm; Democratic [17405]

Senatorial Comm; Natl. Republican [18528]

Senatorial Inner Circle; National Republican [★18528]

Senegal League Against Epilepsy [IO], Dakar, Senegal

Senepol Cattle Breeders Assn. [4293], PO Box 429, O'Fallon, IL 62269, (910)617-6355

SENEVOLU [IO], Dakar, Senegal

Senility
Alzheimer's Assn. [13659]
Dementia Advocacy and Support Network Intl. [12638]
Lewy Body Dementia Assn. [15335]

Senior Action in a Gay Env. [12256], 305 7th Ave., 16th Fl., New York, NY 10001, (212)741-2247

Senior Advocates Intl. - Defunct.

Senior Beta Club [★24592]

Senior Centers; Natl. Inst. of [11313]

Senior Citizen Ski Touring Comm. - Defunct.

Senior Citizens of America - Defunct.

Senior Citizens Housing Comm; B'nai B'rith [12469]

Senior Citizens Law Center; Natl. [11316]

Senior Citizens League - Defunct.

Senior Citizens; Natl. Alliance of [11299]

Senior Community Ser. Employment Prog. [12099], c/o Division of Older Worker Programs, U.S. Dept. of Labor, Employment and Training Admin., 200 Constitution Ave. NW, Rm. N-4641, Washington, DC 20210, (202)693-3758

Senior Companion Prog. [13405], c/o Corp. for Natl. & Community Ser., 1201 New York Ave. NW, Washington, DC 20525, (202)606-5000

Senior Companion Proj. Directors; Natl. Assn. of [11304]

Senior Conformation Judges Assn. [22358], c/o Lt. Col. Wallace H. Pede, CEO, 7200 Tanager St., Springfield, VA 22150, (703)451-5656

Senior Conformation Judges Assn. Educ. Fund [★22193]

Senior Executives Assn. [5713], PO Box 44808, Washington, DC 20026-4808, (202)927-7000

Senior Executives Assn. Professional Development League [5714], c/o SEA, PO Box 44808, Washington, DC 20026, (202)927-7000

Senior Experten Ser. [IO], Bonn, Germany

Senior Foreign Scientists Fellowship Program - Defunct.

Senior Games Assn; Natl. [23655]

Senior Gleaners [12398], 1951 Bell Ave., Sacramento, CA 95838, (916)925-3240

Senior Golf Assn; Natl. [23460]

Senior Housing; Natl. Inst. of [12328]

Senior Involvement; Environmental Alliance for [11809]

Senior Mgt. Inst. for Police [★6005]

Senior Masters - Defunct.

Senior Men's Boxing Comm. of the Amateur Athletic Union [★23267]

Senior PAC - Address unknown since 1994.

Senior Physicians; Amer. Assn. of [★15155]

Senior Roller Skaters of Am. [23739], 119 Yorkshire Ct., Elyria, OH 44035, (440)365-6843

Senior Scholars [8153], c/o Kathy Manos, Dir., Off. of Continuing Educ., 341 Sears Bldg., CWRU, 10900 Euclid Ave., Cleveland, OH 44106-7116, (216)368-2090

Senior Security Network - Address unknown since 1990.

Senior Sports Org; U.S. Natl. [★23655]

Senior Volunteer Prog; Retired and [13403]

Senior Women's Tennis Assn; Natl. [23907]

SeniorNet [13302], 900 Lafayette St., Ste. 604, Santa Clara, CA 95050, (408)615-0699

SeniorNet [IO], Santa Clara, CA, United States

Seniors Assn; Christian [19787]

Seniors Assn; United [11322]

Seniors Bowling Assn; U.S. [★23255]

The Seniors Coalition [11319], 4401 Fair Lakes Ct., Ste. 210, Fairfax, VA 22033-3848, (703)631-4211

Seniors Cooperative Alert Network - Defunct.

Seniors EyeCare Prog. [15701], c/o Eye Care Am., PO Box 429098, San Francisco, CA 94142, (415)447-0381

Senmon Toshokan Kyogikai [★IO]

Sennacieca Asocio Tutmonda [★IO]

SENSE [IO], London, United Kingdom

Sense of Smell Institute [IO], New York, NY, United States

Sense of Smell Inst. [1664], 145 E 32nd St., 8th Fl., New York, NY 10016-6002, (212)725-2755

Sensible Policy in Information Resources and Information Technology - Defunct.

Sensing Soc; IEEE Geoscience and Remote [7144]

Sensitives of America Club - Defunct.

Sensus Educational Assn. [IO], Alvsjo, Sweden

Sensus Studieforbund [★IO]

Sentencing Advocates; National Assn. of [★5645]

Sentencing Proj. [11893], 514 10th St. NW, Ste. 1000, Washington, DC 20004, (202)628-0871

Sentinel Cremation Societies [★2792]

SEORO Korean Cultural Network - Address unknown since 2003.

Seoul Bankers Club [★IO]

Sepak Takraw Assn. of Canada [IO], Regina, SK, Canada

Separated and Divorced Catholics; North Amer. Conf. of [12013]

Separated and Divorced Men; Amer. Soc. of [12005]

Separated Men; Aid to Divorced and [★18039]

Separation of Church and State; Americans United for [19836]

Separation of Church and State; Natl. League for the [19838]

Separation of Church and State; Protestants and Other Americans United for [★19836]

Separation of School and State; Alliance for the [8221]

Separator Filter Mfrs. Assn. - Defunct.

Sephardi Fed; Amer. [20117]

Sephardic Congregations; Union of [20185]

Sephardic House [★20117]

Sephardic Jewish Brotherhood of Am. [20179], 109-09 72nd Rd., Forest Hills, NY 11375, (718)685-0080

Sephardic Stud. and Culture; Found. for the Advancement of [19181]

September 11 Digital Archv. [18735], George Mason Univ., Ctr. for History and New Media, Dept. of History and Art History, MSN 1E7, 4400 Univ. Dr., Fairfax, VA 22030, (703)993-9277

September 11; Families of [18729]

September 11 Widows and Victims' Families Assn. [12002], 22 Cortlandt St., 8th Fl., Ste. 801, New York, NY 10007, (212)422-3520

September 11th Families' Assn. [13371], c/o 9-11 Widows and Victims' Families Assn., 22 Cortlandt St., 20th Fl., New York, NY 10007

September 11th Fund - Defunct.

September Club - Address unknown since 2007.

September Days Club - Address unknown since 2001.

September Eleventh Families for Peaceful Tomorrows [12701], PO Box 1818, Peter Stuyvesant Sta., New York, NY 10009, (919)608-7322

September's Mission [13310], c/o HAI, 548 Broadway, 3rd Fl., New York, NY 10012, (888)424-4685

SER [★12100]

SER - Jobs for Progress [★12100]

SER - Jobs for Progress Natl. [12100], 5215 N O'Connor Blvd., Ste. 2550, Irving, TX 75039, (972)506-7815

Serama Coun. of North Am. [4201], c/o Jerry Schexnayder, Treas., PO Box 159, Vacherie, LA 70090

Seraphic Soc. for Vocations - Defunct.

Serb Natl. Fed. [19357], One 5th Ave., 7th Fl., Pittsburgh, PA 15222, (412)642-7372

Serbia
Serbian-American Chamber of Commerce [24373]
Serbian-American Chamber of Commerce [IO]
Serbian Amer. Medical and Dental Soc. [14185]
Serbian Bar Assn. of Am. [5531]
Serbia and Montenegro Skating Assn. [IO], Belgrade, Serbia

Serbia and Montenegro Tennis Fed. [IO], Belgrade, Serbia
Serbia Study Group - Address unknown since 1990.
Serbian
    Serb Natl. Fed. [19357]
    Serbian-American Chamber of Commerce [24373]
    Serbian Amer. Medical and Dental Soc. [14185]
    Serbian Natl. Defense Coun. of Am. [19358]
Serbian Acad. of Sciences and Arts [IO], Belgrade, Serbia
Serbian-Amer. Bar Assn. - Address unknown since 2003.
Serbian-American Chamber of Commerce [24373], 448 W Barry Ave., Chicago, IL 60657, (773)388-3404
Serbian-American Chamber of Commerce [IO], Chicago, IL, United States
Serbian Amer. Medical and Dental Soc. [14185], c/o Aleksandra Koritarov, Sec.-Treas., 1615 Pennsylvania Ct., Naperville, IL 60563, (630)717-9315
Serbian Bar Assn. of Am. [5531], c/o Kelly Pavich, Exec. Dir., 260 Maple St., Beecher, IL 60401
Serbian Natl. Defense Coun. of Am. [19358], 5782 N Elston Ave., Chicago, IL 60646-5546, (773)775-7772
Serbian Physiological Soc. [IO], Belgrade, Serbia
Serendipitous Order of Beavers - Defunct.
Serendipity Assn. [14832], c/o Dr. Doug Hemstreet, Chm., 4614 Edgeware Rd., No. 4, San Diego, CA 92116-4760, (619)284-2468
Serendipity Assn. and How to Make the World Work Proj. [★14832]
Serendipity Assn. for Res. and Implementation of Holistic Hea. and World Peace [★14832]
Serendipity - The Doctor Who and Science Fiction Club - Address unknown since 2007.
Sergeants Assn; Air Force [6063]
Serial Storage Architecture Industry Assn. - Address unknown since 2001.
Serials and Book Exchange; Universal [★10392]
Serials Data Prog; Natl. [10376]
Serials Interest Gp; North Amer. [10378]
Serials Round Table - of ALA [★10333]
Series Book Collectors' Soc. - Address unknown since 1988.
Sermon Publications [★19825]
Serra Intl. [19717], 70 E Lake St., Ste. 1210, Chicago, IL 60601-5938, (312)419-7411
Serra Intl. [IO], Chicago, IL, United States
Sertoma Foundation [★IO]
Sertoma Foundation [★13063]
Sertoma Intl. [13063], 1912 E Meyer Blvd., Kansas City, MO 64132-1174, (816)333-8300
Sertoma Intl. [IO], Kansas City, MO, United States
Servants in Faith and Technology [IO], Lineville, AL, United States
Servants in Faith and Tech. [17001], 2944 County Rd. 113, Lineville, AL 36266, (256)396-2017
Servas Intl. [★17914]
Servas Intl. [★IO]
Service
    Active 20-30 Assn. of U.S./Canada [13032]
    Altrusa Intl. [13033]
    AMBUCS [13034]
    Am. Council for Trade in Services [3837]
    Amer. Assn. of Ser. Coordinators [1985]
    Amer. Coun. for Tech. [5813]
    Amer. Rescue Workers [13153]
    APQC [2482]
    Assistance League [13035]
    Assn. of Gospel Rescue Missions [13155]
    Assn. for Services Mgt. Intl. [3545]
    Assn. for Services Mgt. Intl. [IO]
    Association of Support Professionals [IO]
    Assn. of Support Professionals [3546]
    Australian Services Union [IO]
    Circle K Intl. [13037]
    Civitan Intl. [13038]
    Coalition of Ser. Indus. [3547]
    Cosmopolitan Intl. [13039]
    Custom Electronic Design Installation Assn. [3548]
    Equip. Ser. Assn. [3549]
    Evangelical Lutheran Good Samaritan Soc. [13168]

Fed. Consumer Info. Center Prog. [5817]
    Good Bears of the World [13041]
    Good Fellows (Old Newsboys) [13042]
    Gyro Intl. [13043]
    Help Desk Inst. [3550]
    Innovations in Civic Participation [17075]
    Intl. Customer Ser. Assn. [3551]
    Intl. Guild of Professional Butlers [24040]
    Intl. Guild of Professional Consultants [966]
    Intl. Saw and Knife Assn. [2390]
    Intl. Virtual Assistants Assn. [68]
    Junior Chamber Intl. [13044]
    Junior Optimist Octagon Intl. [13045]
    Key Club Intl. [13046]
    Kiwanis Intl. [13047]
    La Sertoma Intl. [13048]
    Links [13049]
    Lions Clubs Intl. [13050]
    Master Window Cleaners of Am. [2469]
    Mexican-American Opportunity Found. [12276]
    Musical Instrument Technicians Assn., Intl. [2816]
    Natl. Assn. of Baby Boomer Women [13431]
    Natl. Assn. of Colored Women's Clubs [13051]
    Natl. Assn. of Junior Auxiliaries [13052]
    Natl. Assn. of Negro Bus. and Professional Women's Clubs [13053]
    Natl. Assn. of Ser. Dealers [3389]
    Natl. Assn. of Ser. Managers [3552]
    Natl. Benevolent Assn. of the Christian Church [13177]
    Natl. Coalition for Electronics Educ. [8364]
    Natl. Exchange Club [13054]
    Natl. Independent Concessionaires Assn. [1591]
    Natl. Service-Learning Partnership [9120]
    Natl. Specialty Gift Assn. [1724]
    NGA [13056]
    Optimist Intl. [13057]
    Pilot Intl. and Pilot Intl. Found. [13058]
    Presbyterian Hea., Educ. and Welfare Assn. [13184]
    Pro Players Assn. [13402]
    Professional Ser. Assn. [3553]
    Quota Intl. [13059]
    Res. Associates of Am. [24060]
    Rotary Intl. [13060]
    Round-Table U.S.A. [13061]
    Ruritan Natl. [13062]
    Salvation Army [13187]
    Sertoma Intl. [13063]
    Ser. Contract Indus. Coun. [3554]
    Ser. Employees Intl. Union [24189]
    Ser. Employees Intl. Union [IO]
    Ser. and Food Workers' Union [IO]
    Ser. Indus. Assn. [3555]
    Ser. and Support Professionals Assn. [3556]
    Service and Support Professionals Association [IO]
    Ser. Workers United [24190]
    Sew Much Comfort [11739]
    Singles in Ser. [13064]
    Soroptimist Intl. of the Americas [13065]
    UCA Intl. Users Gp. [7820]
    U.S. Junior Chamber of Commerce [24390]
    U.S. Women of Today [13067]
    Volunteers of Am. [13192]
    Women in Show Business for Children [13069]
    Youth Ser. Am. [13070]
    Zonta Intl. [13071]
Ser. and Action; Commn. on Voluntary [★13391]
Ser. to Am; Volunteers in [★13383]
Ser. Assn. of Am; Family [★12136]
Ser. Assn; Automotive [410]
Ser. Assn. for Hea; INSA, The Intl. [★14978]
Ser. Assn; Natl. Appliance [267]
Ser. Assn; Natl. Indus. [★1180]
Ser. Assn; Special Indus. Radio [★3742]
Ser. Assn., Suspension Specialists; Spring [★427]
Ser. Bd. for Religious Objectors; Natl. [★17438]
Service Center for Teachers of History - Defunct.
Ser. Civil Intl., Austrian Br. [IO], Vienna, Austria
Ser. Civil Intl. - Germany [IO], Bonn, Germany
Ser. Civil Intl., Osterreichische Zweig [★IO]
Ser. Civil Intl. - U.S.A. [★IO]
Ser. Civil Intl. - U.S.A. [★13404]
Service Clubs
    Active 20-30 Assn. of U.S./Canada [13032]

Altrusa Intl. [13033]
Altrusa Intl. [IO]
AMBUCS [13034]
Amer. Rescue Workers [13153]
Armenian Junior Chamber [IO]
Ashburton Jaycee [IO]
Assistance League [13035]
Assn. of Club Executives [1932]
Assn. of Gospel Rescue Missions [13155]
Black Women's House of Culture [IO]
Camara Junior de Argentina [IO]
Camara Junior del Paraguay [IO]
Camara Junor de Guatemala [IO]
Carnegie Hero Fund Commn. [13036]
Circle K Intl. [13037]
Circle K Intl. [IO]
Civitan Intl. [IO]
Civitan Intl. [13038]
Cosmopolitan Intl. [13039]
Cosmopolitan Intl. [IO]
Fed. of Woman's Exchanges [13040]
Good Bears of the World [13041]
Good Bears of the World [IO]
Good Fellows (Old Newsboys) [13042]
Gyro Intl. [13043]
Gyro Intl. [IO]
Indian Jaycees [IO]
Inner Wheel New Zealand [IO]
JCI Auckland [IO]
JCI Belgium [IO]
JCI Cameroon [IO]
JCI Dublin [IO]
Jeune Chambre Economique Francaise [IO]
Jeune Chambre Economique de Madagascar [IO]
Jeune Chambre Internationale - Togo [IO]
Joves Cambres de Catalunya [IO]
Junior Chamber Austria [IO]
Junior Chamber Barcelona [IO]
Junior Chamber Belarus [IO]
Junior Chamber Cyprus [IO]
Junior Chamber Empresaris de Barcelona [IO]
Junior Chamber Germany [IO]
Junior Chamber Girona [IO]
Junior Chamber Igualada [IO]
Junior Chamber Intl. [IO]
Junior Chamber Intl. [13044]
Junior Chamber Intl. Australia [IO]
Junior Chamber Intl. - Bangladesh [IO]
Junior Chamber Intl., Benin [IO]
Junior Chamber Intl., Bolivia [IO]
Junior Chamber Intl. - Botswana [IO]
Junior Chamber Intl. Brasil [IO]
Junior Chamber Intl. - Burkina [IO]
Junior Chamber Intl. Canada [IO]
Junior Chamber Intl. Colombia [IO]
Junior Chamber Intl. Denmark [IO]
Junior Chamber Intl. of Dominican Republic [IO]
Junior Chamber Intl., Ecuador [IO]
Junior Chamber Intl. Estonia [IO]
Junior Chamber Intl. Finland [IO]
Junior Chamber Intl. - Gabon [IO]
Junior Chamber Intl. - Greece [IO]
Junior Chamber Intl. Hong Kong [IO]
Junior Chamber Intl. Hungary [IO]
Junior Chamber Intl., Indonesia [IO]
Junior Chamber Intl. Ireland [IO]
Junior Chamber Intl. Island [IO]
Junior Chamber Intl. Japan [IO]
Junior Chamber Intl. - Jordan [IO]
Junior Chamber Intl. Korea [IO]
Junior Chamber Intl. Latvia [IO]
Junior Chamber Intl. Limerick [IO]
Junior Chamber Intl. Lithuania [IO]
Junior Chamber Intl. Lleida [IO]
Junior Chamber Intl. Malaysia [IO]
Junior Chamber Intl. - Mali [IO]
Junior Chamber Intl. - Mauritius [IO]
Junior Chamber Intl., Mexico [IO]
Junior Chamber Intl. New Zealand [IO]
Junior Chamber Intl. - Nigeria [IO]
Junior Chamber Intl. Pakistan [IO]
Junior Chamber Intl., Peru [IO]
Junior Chamber Intl. Philippines [IO]
Junior Chamber Intl. South Africa [IO]
Junior Chamber Intl. Sweden [IO]

A star before a book entry number signifies that the name is not listed separately, but is mentioned within the entry.

Junior Chamber Intl. The Netherlands [IO]
Junior Chamber Intl. Tunisie [IO]
Junior Chamber Intl. Turkey [IO]
Junior Chamber Intl. Ukraine [IO]
Junior Chamber Intl. United Kingdom [IO]
Junior Chamber Intl. of Venezuela [IO]
Junior Chamber Intl. Waterford [IO]
Junior Chamber Italiana [IO]
Junior Chamber Manresa [IO]
Junior Chamber Namibia [IO]
Junior Chamber Nepal [IO]
Junior Chamber Poland [IO]
Junior Chamber Reus [IO]
Junior Chamber Romania [IO]
Junior Chamber Sabadell [IO]
Junior Chamber Serbia [IO]
Junior Chamber Singapore [IO]
Junior Chamber Switzerland [IO]
Junior Chamber Tarragona [IO]
Junior Chamber Terrassa [IO]
Junior Chamber Thailand [IO]
Junior Chamber Zimbabwe [IO]
Junior Optimist Octagon International [IO]
Junior Optimist Octagon Intl. [13045]
Kenya Junior Chamber [IO]
Key Club Intl. [IO]
Key Club Intl. [13046]
Kiwanis Intl. [13047]
Kiwanis Intl. [IO]
La Sertoma Intl. [IO]
La Sertoma Intl. [13048]
Links [13049]
Lions Clubs Intl. [13050]
Lions Clubs Intl. [IO]
Macau Junior Chamber China [IO]
Malawi Junior Chamber [IO]
Mongolian Junior Chamber [IO]
NA'AMAT Canada [IO]
NA'AMAT Pioneras [IO]
Natl. Assn. of Colored Women's Clubs [13051]
Natl. Assn. of Junior Auxiliaries [13052]
Natl. Assn. of Negro Bus. and Professional
    Women's Clubs [13053]
Natl. Assn. of Ser. and Conservation Corps
    [13497]
Natl. Benevolent Assn. of the Christian Church
    [13177]
Natl. Beta Club [24592]
Natl. Exchange Club [13054]
Natl. Fed. of Plus Areas of Great Britain [IO]
Natl. Pinochle Bugs Social and Civic Club [13055]
NGA [13056]
Niger Junior Chamber [IO]
Optimist Intl. [IO]
Optimist Intl. [13057]
Ora Gp. NA'AMAT [IO]
Pilot Intl. and Pilot Intl. Found. [IO]
Pilot Intl. and Pilot Intl. Found. [13058]
Quota Intl. [13059]
Quota Intl. [IO]
Rotary Club of Grand Cayman [IO]
Rotary Intl. [IO]
Rotary Intl. [13060]
Round-Table U.S.A. [13061]
Round-Table U.S.A. [IO]
Ruritan Natl. [13062]
Sertoma Intl. [13063]
Sertoma Intl. [IO]
Singles in Ser. [13064]
Soroptimist Found. of Canada [IO]
Soroptimist Intl. [IO]
Soroptimist Intl. of the Americas [IO]
Soroptimist Intl. of the Americas [13065]
Soroptimist Intl. of Europe [IO]
Soroptimist Intl. of Great Britain and Ireland [IO]
Soroptimist Intl. of the South West Pacific [IO]
Taiwan Junior Chamber [IO]
Theta Rho Girls' Club [13518]
Uganda Junior Chamber [IO]
Unie van Soroptimist Clubs in Nederland, Suri-
    name en de Nederlandse Antillen [IO]
United Nations Women's Guild [IO]
United Nations Women's Guild [13066]
U.S. Women of Today [13067]
Venture Clubs [13068]

Women in Show Business for Children [13069]
YMCA Earth Ser. Corps [18861]
Youth Ser. Am. [13070]
Zonta Intl. [13071]
Zonta Intl. [IO]
Zonta Intl. - District 16 New Zealand [IO]
Ser. Commissions; Amer. Assn. of State [6189]
Ser. Companies; Assn. of Energy [2918]
Service Companies; Intl. Assn. [★907]
Ser. Companies; Natl. Assn. of Sewer [★3959]
Ser. and Cmpt. Dealers Intl; Assn. of [897]
Ser. and Conservation Corps; Natl. Assn. of [13497]
Ser. Contract Indus. Coun. [3554], c/o Timothy J.
    Meenan, Gen. Counsel/Exec. Dir., 204 S Monroe
    St., Tallahassee, FL 32301, (850)681-1058
Ser. Corps; Natl. Executive [747]
Ser. Corps of Retired Executives [★3625]
Ser. Councils; Automotive [★410]
Ser. d'assistance canadienne aux organismes [★IO]
Ser. Dealers Assn; Gasoline and Automotive [414]
Ser. Dealers Assn; Natl. Electronic [★1224]
Ser. Dealers; Natl. Assn. of [3389]
Ser. d'information Antiracisme [★IO]
Ser. Employees Intl. Union [IO], Washington, DC,
    United States
Ser. Employees Intl. Union [24189], 1800 Mas-
    sachusetts Ave. NW, Washington, DC 20036,
    (202)730-7000
Ser. Employees Union Local 73; Gen. [24097]
Ser. Engineers Soc; Refrigeration [1899]
Ser. and Food Workers' Union [IO], Auckland, New
    Zealand
Ser. Food Workers' Union of Aotearoa [★IO]
Service Fraternities
    Alpha Iota Omicron [24611]
    Alpha Phi Alpha Fraternity [24590]
    Alpha Phi Omega Natl. Ser. Fraternity [24591]
    Alpha Zeta [24397]
    Beta Chi Theta Natl. Fraternity [24618]
    Gamma Beta Phi Soc. [24505]
    Iota Nu Delta Fraternity [24631]
    Mortar Bd. [24509]
    Natl. Beta Club [24592]
    Natl. Honor Soc. [24512]
    Natl. Junior Honor Soc. [24513]
    Phi Beta Sigma Fraternity [24593]
    Pi Omicron Natl. Sorority [24601]
    Psi Sigma Phi Multicultural Fraternity [24594]
    Royal Canadian Regiment Assn. [IO]
    Sigma Alpha Lambda [24519]
    Sigma Beta Rho Fraternity [24656]
Ser. Indus. Assn. [3555], c/o Claudia J. Betzner,
    Exec. Dir., 2164 Historic Decatur Rd., Villa 19, San
    Diego, CA 92106, (619)221-9200
Ser. Inst; Single [★1157]
Ser; Inter-American School [★8647]
Ser. de liaison non gouvernemental de l'ONU [★IO]
Ser. and Leadership Center; DeMolay [★IO]
Ser. and Leadership Center; DeMolay [★19375]
Ser. League; Women's Overseas [21334]
Service Mgt. Inst. [★3552]
Ser. Managers of Am. [★3552]
Ser. Managers, Intl; Assn. of Field [★3545]
Ser. Members for Equality; Ex-Partners of [17437]
Ser; Methodist Fed. for Social [★20264]
Ser. Organizations; United [★18962]
Ser. for Peace [18246], 2838 Fairfield Ave.,
    Bridgeport, CT 06605, (203)610-6745
Ser. of Peace and Justice, Chile [IO], Santiago,
    Chile
Ser. Permanent du Niveau Moyen des Mers [★IO]
Ser. Professionals; Amer. Soc. for Healthcare
    Central [14864]
Ser. Professionals in Printing; Soc. for [1790]
Ser. Projects; Commn. on Youth [★13391]
Ser. Protective Assn; Amer. Foreign [19118]
Ser. Provider Indus. Consortium; Application [3722]
Ser. Social Intl. - Secretariat Gen. [★IO]
Service Societies
    Intercollegiate Knights [24507]
Service Sororities
    Alpha Kappa Alpha [24595]
    Alpha Rho Lambda Sorority [24703]
    Alpha Zeta [24397]
    Beta Sigma Phi [24596]

Delta Gamma Pi Multicultural Sorority [24704]
Delta Phi Omega Sorority [24705]
Delta Sigma Chi Sorority [24706]
Delta Sigma Theta [24597]
Delta Tau Lambda Sorority [24707]
Delta Xi Nu Multicultural Sorority [24708]
Delta Xi Phi Multicultural Sorority [24685]
DIVAS of Lambda Fe Uson Sorority [24709]
Epsilon Sigma Alpha [24598]
Gamma Alpha Omega Sorority [24599]
Gamma Delta Pi [24710]
Gamma Gamma Chi Sorority [24711]
Gamma Sigma Sigma [24600]
Kappa Phi Gamma Sorority [24712]
Lambda Psi Delta Sorority [24713]
Mortar Bd. [24509]
Natl. Beta Club [24592]
Natl. Honor Soc. [24512]
Natl. Junior Honor Soc. [24513]
Pi Omicron Natl. Sorority [24601]
Sigma Alpha [24602]
Sigma Alpha Lambda [24519]
Sigma Gamma Rho Sorority [24603]
Sigma Lambda Alpha Sorority [24714]
Sigma Lambda Gamma Natl. Sorority [24715]
Theta Chi Omega Multicultural Sorority [24716]
Zeta Chi Phi Multicultural Sorority [24717]
Zeta Phi Beta Sorority [24604]
Ser. Specialists Assn. [427], 4015 Marks Rd., Ste.
    2B, Medina, OH 44256-8316, (330)725-7160
Ser. Sta. Dealers of Am. [★2946]
Ser. Sta. Dealers of Am. and Allied Trades [★2946]
Ser. Sta. Dealers of America/National Coalition of
    Petroleum Retailers and Allied Trades [2946], 1532
    Pointer Ridge Pl., Ste. E, Bowie, MD 20716-1883,
    (301)390-4405
Ser. Stations; New York State Assn. of [★426]
Ser. Stations and Repair Shops; New York State
    Assn. of [426]
Ser. and Support Professionals Assn. [3556], 11031
    Via Frontera, Ste. A, San Diego, CA 92127,
    (858)674-5491
Service and Support Professionals Association [IO],
    San Diego, CA, United States
Ser. Technicians Soc. [★IO]
Ser. Technicians Soc. [★3719]
Ser. Tech. Prog. Off; SAE [3719]
Ser. Telecasters; Assn. of Maximum [★549]
Ser. Textile Distributors Assn; Institutional and [3788]
Ser. Tools Inst. [★1822]
Ser. Trades Dept., AFL-CIO; Union Label and
    [24213]
Ser. Volunteer Assn; Natl. Archives and Record
    [★9402]
Ser. Workers United [24190], 275 7th Ave., 10th Fl.,
    New York, NY 10001, (212)265-7000
Servicemembers for Equality; Ex-Partners of [12009]
Servicemembers Legal Defense Network [6113], PO
    Box 65301, Washington, DC 20035-5301,
    (202)328-3244
Servicemen Fellowship; Christian [★19782]
Servicemen; Natl. Alliance of Families for the Return
    of America's Missing [21263]
Servicers of Am; Natl. Assn. of TV and Electronic
    [★1224]
Services Administrators; Natl. Assn. of Pupil [7902]
Services for the Aging; Amer. Assn. of Homes and
    [11273]
Services Assn; Airline [★129]
Services Assn. of Am; Contract [1743]
Services Assn; Young Adult Lib. [10395]
Services for Families and Children; Coun. on Ac-
    creditation of [★13164]
Services Generaux Al-Anon [★IO]
Services for the Hea. in Asian and African Regions
    [IO], Tokyo, Japan
Services, Indus. Professional and Tech. Union [IO],
    Dublin, Ireland
Services for the Missing - Address unknown since
    2001.
Services for People with Disabilities; Accreditation
    Coun. on [★12567]
Services Programs; Natl. Assn. for State Community
    [6279]
Services Retirees; Natl. Assn. for Uniformed
    [★6086]

Reference to "IO" in place of a book number signifies that the association may be found in the 45th edition of International Organizations.

Services Workers, UAW Local 2320; Natl. Org. of Legal [24079]
Servicio Colombiano de Comunicacion [IO], Bogota, Colombia
Servicio Paz y Justicia en Argentina [★IO]
Servicio Paz y Justicia, Chile [★IO]
Servizio Volontariato Giovanile [★IO]
Sesame Workshop [9782], 1 Lincoln Plz., New York, NY 10023, (212)595-3456
SESKO Standardization in Finland [IO], Helsinki, Finland
SESPA (Scientists and Engineers for Social and Political Action) [★7627]
Sessions; Natl. Assn. of Coll. and Univ. Summer [★9200]
Sessions; Natl. Assn. of Summer [★9200]
Sessions Soc; Roger [9815]
Set the Date Now - Defunct.
Set Decorators Soc. of Am. [2276], 1646 N Cherokee Ave., Hollywood, CA 90028, (323)462-3060
Seth and Della Cummings Family Assn. - Defunct.
SETI League [6510], PO Box 555, Little Ferry, NJ 07643, (201)641-1770
Seton Hill University's E-magnify [8040], Box 389F, Seton Hill Univ., Seton Hill Dr., Greensburg, PA 15601, (724)830-4625
Seton; Natl. Shrine of St. Elizabeth Ann [19694]
Seton Shrine Center [★19694]
Setter Assn. of Am; English [22260]
Setter Club of Am; Gordon [22278]
Setter Club of Am; Irish [22292]
Setting the Indus. Standards for the Rehabilitation of Underground Utilities; NASSCO - [3959]
Setting Priorities for Retirement Years [12900], 3916 Rosemary St., Chevy Chase, MD 20815, (301)656-3405
Settlement Assn; Union [12785]
Settlement Purchasers Assn; Natl. [★1439]
Settlement Studies Program; Space [6387]
Settlements; Natl. Fed. of [★11792]
Settlements and Neighborhood Centers; Natl. Fed. of [★11792]
Settlements Trade Assn; Natl. Structured [6033]
Settlers and Threshers Assn; Midwest Old [9483]
Seva Found. [IO], Berkeley, CA, United States
Seva Found. [12443], 1786 5th St., Berkeley, CA 94710, (510)845-7382
Seven Directors; Natl. Assn. of Title [★11315]
Seven Seas Cruising Assn. [23217], 2501 E Commercial Blvd., Ste. 201, Fort Lauderdale, FL 33308, (954)771-5660

Seventh Day Adventist
Adventist Community Services [20552]
Adventist-Laymen's Services and Indus. [20553]
Assn. of Adventist Forums [20554]
Association of Adventist Forums [IO]
Assn. of Seventh-Day Adventist Librarians [10339]
Christians in Crisis [20555]
Natl. Assn. of Seventh-day Adventist Dentists [14171]
Seventh-Day Adventist Dietetic Assn. [15569]
Seventh Day Adventist Kinship Intl. [20066]
Seventh-Day Adventist Church Musicians Guild - Defunct.
Seventh-day Adventist Dentists; Natl. Assn. of [14171]
Seventh-Day Adventist Dietetic Assn. [15569], PO Box 400, 6100 Leoni Rd., Grizzly Flats, CA 95636-0400
Seventh Day Adventist Kinship Intl. [20066], PO Box 69, Tillamook, OR 97141-0069
Seventh Day Adventist Kinship International [IO], Sarasota, FL, United States
Seventh-Day Adventist Librarians; Assn. of [10339]
Seventh-Day Adventist Welfare Services [★12826]
Seventh-Day Adventist Welfare Services [★IO]
Seventh-Day Adventist World Ser. [★IO]
Seventh-Day Adventist World Ser. [★12826]
Seventh Day Baptist Gen. Conf. [19494], PO Box 1678, Janesville, WI 53547-1678, (608)752-5055
Seventh Day Baptist Gen. Conf. of the U.S. and Canada [20545], PO Box 1678, Janesville, WI 53547-1678, (608)752-5055

Seventh Day Baptist Historical Soc. [19495], PO Box 1678, Janesville, WI 53547-1678, (608)752-5055
Seventh Day Baptist Missionary Soc. [19496], 119 Main St., Westerly, RI 02891-2112, (401)596-4326
Seventh Day Baptist World Fed. [19497], PO Box 515, Friendship, NY 14739-0515
Seventh Day Baptist World Fed. [IO], Friendship, NY, United States
Seventh Generation Fund for Indian Development [18099], PO Box 4569, Arcata, CA 95518, (707)825-7640
Seventh Step Soc. of Canada [IO], Calgary, AB, Canada
Seventy Plus Ski Club - Address unknown since 2002.
Severn Valley Welsh Pony and Cob Assn. [IO], Welshpool, United Kingdom
Sevier Family Assn. - Address unknown since 2002.
Sew Much Comfort [11739], c/o Michele Cuppy, 13805 Frontier Ln., Burnsville, MN 55337

Sewage
Natl. Assn. of Clean Water Agencies [6237]
Natl. Sewerage Assn. [IO]
Sump and Sewage Pump Mfrs. Assn. [678]
Water and Sewer Distributors of Am. [3968]
Sewage and Indus. Wastes Associations; Fed. of [★5101]
Sewage Pump Mfrs. Assn; Sump and [678]
Sewage Works Associations; Fed. of [★5101]
Sewage Works Mfrs. Assn; Water and [★2077]
Sewalanka Found. [IO], Boralesgamuwa, Sri Lanka
Sewer Distributors of Am; Water and [3968]
Sewer Ser. Companies; Natl. Assn. of [★3959]
Sewerage Agencies; Assn. of Metropolitan [★6237]

Sewing
Amer. Bunka Embroidery Assn. [22721]
Amer. Needlepoint Guild [22148]
Amer. Sewing Guild [22150]
Belt and Button Assn. [2836]
Canadian Quilters' Assn. [IO]
Crochet Assn. Intl. [22154]
Crochet Guild of Am. [22722]
Embroiderers' Guild of Am. [22155]
Handweavers Guild of Am. [22158]
Intl. Machine Quilters Assn. [22160]
Intl. Old Lacers, Inc. [22161]
Japan Light Machinery Info. Center of Central New York [24443]
The Natl. Needle Arts Assn. [3794]
Natl. Quilting Assn. [22170]
Sewing Educator Alliance [9121]
Smocking Arts Guild of Am. [22174]
Thimble Collectors Intl. [22122]
Toy Stitchers Intl., Inc. [22998]
Vacuum Dealers Trade Assn. [268]
Sewing Assn; Home [3784]
Sewing Assn; Natl. Home [★3784]
Sewing Coun; Amer. Home [★3784]
Sewing Educator Alliance [9121], c/o Sewing Dealers Trade Assn./Vacuum Dealers Trade Assn., 2724 2nd Ave., Des Moines, IA 50313, (800)473-9464
Sewing Guild; Amer. [22150]
Sewing Machine Assn; Intl. [★3784]
Sewing Machine Trade Assn. [★1990]
Sewn Products Equip. and Suppliers of the Americas [2067], 9650 Strickland Rd., Ste. 103-324, Raleigh, NC 27615, (919)872-8909
Sewn Products Equip. Suppliers Assn. of the Americas [★2067]

Sex Addiction
Intl. Ser. Org. - COSA [13072]
International Service Organization - COSA [IO]
Sex Addicts Anonymous [13073]
Sex and Love Addicts Anonymous [13074]
Sexaholics Anonymous [13075]
Sexaholics Anonymous [IO]
Sex Addicts Anonymous [13073], PO Box 70949, Houston, TX 77270, (713)869-4902
Sex Addicts; Co-Dependents of [★13072]
Sex Educators and Counselors; Amer. Assn. of [16398]
Sex Equity in Educ; Natl. Coalition for [★8399]
Sex Equity in Education Program - Address unknown since 2001.

Sex Forum; Natl. [★16401]
Sex Info. Coun. of Am. [★16400]
Sex Info. and Educ. Coun. of Canada [IO], Toronto, ON, Canada
Sex Info. and Educ. Coun. of the U.S. [★16406]
Sex and Love Addicts Anonymous [13074], 1550 NE Loop 410, Ste. 118, San Antonio, TX 78209, (210)828-7900
Sex and Love; Soc. for the Philosophy of [10836]
Sex; Soc. for the Sci. Stud. of [★16407]
Sex Worker Found. for Art, Culture and Educ. [★13092]
Sex Workers Anonymous [13029], 3395 S Jones Blvd., Ste. 217, Las Vegas, NV 89146-6729, (702)953-6024
Sexaholics Anonymous [13075], PO Box 3565, Brentwood, TN 37024, (615)370-6062
Sexaholics Anonymous [IO], Brentwood, TN, United States
Sexes; Org. for Equal Education of the [8402]

Sexual Abuse
Anti-Child Pornography Org. [12766]
Assaulted Women's Helpline [IO]
Assn. of Sites Advocating Child Protection [11560]
Assn. for the Treatment of Sexual Abusers [6529]
Australian and New Zealand Assn. for the Treatment of Sexual Abuse [IO]
Bilateral Safety Corridor Coalition [12368]
Child Abuse Listening and Mediation [11565]
Comm. for Children [11587]
Darkness to Light [11590]
FaithTrust Inst. [12027]
Hope After Rape [IO]
Incest Survivors Anonymous [IO]
Incest Survivors Anonymous [13076]
Innocence in Danger - USA [11601]
LifeWorks Inst. [12551]
The Linkup - Survivors of Clergy Abuse [11522]
Love146 [11620]
Male Survivor: The Natl. Org. Against Male Sexual Victimization [13077]
Men's Rsrc. Center [12357]
Mothers Against Sexual Abuse [13078]
Mothers Against Sexual Predators At Large [13079]
Natl. Exchange Club Found. [11637]
Natl. Network to End Violence Against Immigrant Women [13433]
Natl. Sexual Violence Rsrc. Center [13080]
Parents United [13081]
Paul and Lisa Prog. [13082]
People Against Rape [13083]
People for Children [11716]
Prevent Child Abuse [11647]
Rape, Abuse and Incest Natl. Network [12791]
Safer Soc. Found. [11891]
S.M.A.R.T. (Secretive Societies, Mind Control and Ritual Abuse) [13296]
STAMP - Survivors Take Action Against Abuse by Military Personnel [11507]
Stop it Now! [11653]
Survivor Connections [13084]
Survivors of Incest Anonymous [13085]
Survivorship [13377]
Village of Childhelp West [11661]
VOICES in Action [13086]
VOICES in Action [IO]
WINGS Found. [13087]
Women and Men Against Sexual Harassment and Other Abuses [13088]
Women in Transition [13447]
WomensLaw.org [18823]
Sexual Abuse Anonymous [★13085]
Sexual Abuse Treatment Program; Child [★13081]
Sexual Abusers; Assn. for the Behavioral Treatment of [★6529]
Sexual Abusers; Assn. for the Treatment of [6529]
Sexual Aggression; Assn. for the Behavioral Treatment of [★6529]
Sexual Assault Centres; Canadian Assn. of [IO]
Sexual Assault Res. Assn. [★6529]
Sexual Dysfunction Assn. [IO], London, United Kingdom

Sexual Freedom
Alliance for Full Acceptance [12213]

A star before a book entry number signifies that the name is not listed separately, but is mentioned within the entry.

Assn. for Women in Psychology [16145]
Beaumont Soc. [IO]
Center For Sex and Culture [9122]
Crossdressers Intl. [13089]
Crossdressers Intl. [IO]
Gender Educ. and Advocacy [13090]
Homosexuals Anonymous Fellowship Services [12236]
Intl. Found. for Gender Educ. [13091]
Intl. Gay and Lesbian Human Rights Commn. [12239]
Intl. Sex Worker Found. for Art, Culture and Educ. [13092]
Intersex Soc. of North Am. [13093]
Intersex Soc. of North Am. [IO]
Johns and Call Girls United Against Repression [13094]
Lifestyles Org. [13095]
Loving More [13096]
NASCA Intl. [13097]
NASCA Intl. [IO]
Natl. Assn. for Res. and Therapy of Homosexuality [14434]
Natl. Coalition for Sexual Freedom [18599]
Natl. Coming Out Day [12248]
Natl. Leather Assn. - Intl. [13098]
Natl. Org. for Men Against Sexism [17779]
North Amer. Man/Boy Love Assn. [13099]
Radical Philosophy Assn. [18273]
Renaissance Transgender Assn. [13100]
Sacred Space Inst. [13101]
Seventh Day Adventist Kinship Intl. [20066]
Soc. for the Second Self [13102]
Wives of Older Men [12509]
World Professional Assn. for Transgender Hea. [13103]
World Professional Assn. for Transgender Hea. [IO]

Sexual Harassment
9 to 5, Natl. Assn. of Working Women [17512]
Center for Human Services [13112]
Equal Rights Advocates [6222]
Gay, Lesbian, and Straight Educ. Network [8456]
Labor Notes [24116]
Male Liberation Found. [18037]
Natl. Center for Men [18042]
Natl. Coun. of Churches - Women in Ministry Gp. [20622]
Stop Prisoner Rape [11894]
Tradeswomen [12101]
Wider Opportunities for Women [12106]
Women in Crisis [13443]
Women Employed [12108]
Women Employed Inst. [12109]

Sexual Health
Abstinence CH [16397]
Alliance for Microbicide Development [13555]
Amer. Assn. of Sexuality Educators, Counselors and Therapists [16398]
Amer. Bd. of Sexology [16399]
Amer. Found. for the Prevention of Venereal Disease [16409]
American Institute for Teen AIDS Prevention [13558]
Amer. Pregnancy Assn. [15588]
Amer. Social Hea. Assn. [16410]
Asociacion Puertorriquena Pro-Bienestar de la Familia [12176]
Assn. of Reproductive Hea. Professionals [12177]
Australasian Coll. of Sexual Hea. Physicians [IO]
Campaign For Our Children [13476]
Citizens Alliance for VD Awareness [16411]
Coalition for Positive Sexuality [13480]
Coun. for Sex Info. and Educ. [16400]
European Fed. of Sexology [IO]
Exodus Trust [16401]
Family Care Intl. [16402]
Family Care Intl. [IO]
German Soc. for Social Sci. Sexuality Res. [IO]
Herpes Rsrc. Center - Amer. Social Hea. Assn. [16412]
Hysterectomy Educational Resources and Services Found. [15601]
Inst. for Female Alternative Medicine [16345]
Intl. Coalition for Genital Integrity [11731]

Intl. Dalkon Shield Victims Educ. Assn. [16898]
Intl. Partnership for Microbicides [13572]
Intl. Professional Surrogates Assn. [16403]
Intl. Professional Surrogates Assn. [IO]
Intl. Soc. for the Stud. of Women's Sexual Hea. [IO]
Intl. Soc. for the Stud. of Women's Sexual Hea. [16404]
Intl. Union Against Sexually Transmitted Infections, Regional Off. for North Am. [16414]
Life Res. Inst. [14572]
Mothers' Voices [13574]
Museum of Menstruation and Women's Hea. [15611]
Natl. Abstinence Educ. Assn. [9123]
Natl. Assn. of Nurse Practitioners in Women's Hea. [15497]
Natl. Commn. on Human Life, Reproduction and Rhythm [16008]
Natl. Coun. on Women's Hea. [16904]
Natl. Org. of Circumcision Info. Rsrc. Centers [11732]
North Amer. Menopause Soc. [15614]
Sexual Medicine Soc. of North Am. [16405]
Sexuality Info. and Educ. Coun. of the U.S. [16406]
SisterSong Women of Color Reproductive Hea. Collective [18826]
Social Policy Action Network [13138]
Soc. for Assisted Reproductive Tech. [16346]
Soc. for the Psychological Stud. of Men and Masculinity [16181]
Soc. of Reproductive Surgeons [16349]
Soc. for the Sci. Stud. of Sexuality [16407]
Soc. for Sex Therapy and Res. [16408]
Soc. for the Stud. of Male Reproduction [16344]
Treatment Action Gp. [13587]
Sexual Hea. Assn; Family Planning and [IO]
Sexual Hea. and Family Planning Australia - Intl. Prog. [IO], Canberra, Australia
Sexual Medicine Soc. of North Am. [16405], 1111 N Plaza Dr., Ste. 550, Schaumburg, IL 60173, (847)517-7225
Sexual Orientation and Gender Expression; Coun. on [9132]
Sexual Therapy; Eastern Acad. of [★16408]
Sexual Victimization; Natl. Org. on Male [★13077]
Sexual Violence; TransAct - Dutch Center for Gender Issues in Healthcare and Prevention of [IO]

Sexuality
Advocates for Youth's Media Proj. [12174]
Affirmation/Gay and Lesbian Mormons [20046]
Alliance for Full Acceptance [12213]
Amer. Assn. of Sexuality Educators, Counselors and Therapists [16398]
Assn. of Welcoming and Affirming Baptists [19476]
Assn. for Women in Psychology [16145]
Brethren/Mennonite Coun. for Lesbian, Gay, Bisexual and Transgender Interest [20050]
Campaign For Our Children [13476]
Coalition for Positive Sexuality [13480]
Coun. for Sex Info. and Educ. [16400]
Dignity/USA [20053]
Evangelicals Concerned [20054]
Exodus Trust [16401]
Friends for Lesbian, Gay, Bisexual, Transgender, and Queer Concerns [20056]
Homosexuals Anonymous Fellowship Services [12236]
Integrity [20058]
Intl. Assn. for the Stud. of Sexuality, Culture and Soc. [9124]
Intl. Assn. for the Stud. of Sexuality, Culture and Soc. [IO]
Intl. Found. for Gender Educ. [13091]
Intl. Gay and Lesbian Human Rights Commn. [12239]
Intl. Sex Worker Found. for Art, Culture and Educ. [13092]
Intl. Soc. for the Stud. of Women's Sexual Hea. [16404]
Lifestyles Org. [13095]
Lutherans Concerned/North Am. [20061]

Marriage Equality USA [12506]
Metropolitan Community Churches [20062]
More Light Presbyterians for Lesbian, Gay, Bisexual and Transgender Concerns [20063]
NASCA Intl. [13097]
Natl. Abstinence Educ. Assn. [9123]
Natl. Assn. for Res. and Therapy of Homosexuality [14434]
Natl. Assn. of Social Workers Natl. Comm. on Lesbian, Gay and Bisexual Issues [12245]
Natl. Coming Out Day [12248]
Natl. Commn. on Human Life, Reproduction and Rhythm [16008]
Natl. Gay Pilot's Assn. [439]
North Amer. Man/Boy Love Assn. [13099]
ONE, Inc. [12251]
Sacred Space Inst. [13101]
Seventh Day Adventist Kinship Intl. [20066]
Sexuality Info. and Educ. Coun. of the U.S. [16406]
Social Policy Action Network [13138]
Soc. for the Philosophy of Sex and Love [10836]
Soc. for the Psychological Stud. of Lesbian, Gay and Bisexual Issues [16180]
Soc. for the Psychological Stud. of Men and Masculinity [16181]
Soc. for Sex Therapy and Res. [16408]
Spring of Living Water Ministry [20556]
United Church of Christ Coalition for Lesbian, Gay, Bisexual and Transgender Concerns [20067]
World Cong. of Gay, Lesbian, Bisexual, and Transgender Jews [20069]
Sexuality; Coalition for Positive [13480]
Sexuality Info. and Educ. Coun. of the U.S. [16406], 130 W 42nd St., Ste. 350, New York, NY 10036-7802, (212)819-9770
Sexually Transmitted Diseases
Aid for AIDS [13547]
AIDS Empowerment and Treatment Intl. [13550]
AIDS, Medicine and Miracles [13551]
AIDS Treatment Activists Coalition [11324]
Alliance for Microbicide Development [13555]
Amer. Acad. of HIV Medicine [13556]
Amer. Found. for the Prevention of Venereal Disease [16409]
American Institute for Teen AIDS Prevention [13558]
Amer. Social Hea. Assn. [16410]
Assn. of Nurses in AIDS Care [13559]
Cable Positive [11327]
CAVDA-Citizens AIDS Proj. [13562]
CDC Natl. Prevention Info. Network [13563]
Citizens Alliance for VD Awareness [16411]
Family Res. Inst. [17688]
Global AIDS Alliance [13565]
Global Bus. Coalition on HIV/AIDS [11329]
Hea. Educ. Rsrc. Org. [13568]
Hea. Global Access Proj. [11331]
Herpes Rsrc. Center - Amer. Social Hea. Assn. [16412]
HPV Support Prog. - Amer. Social Hea. Assn. [16413]
Intl. Partnership for Microbicides [13572]
Intl. Treatment Preparedness Coalition [13573]
Intl. Union Against Sexually Transmitted Infections, Regional Off. for North Am. [16414]
Intl. Union Against Sexually Transmitted Infections, Regional Off. for North Am. [IO]
Intl. Union Against Sexually Transmitted Infections - United Kingdom [IO]
Mothers' Voices [13574]
Natl. AIDS Fund [13576]
Natl. AIDS Housing Coalition [12319]
Natl. Assn. of People With AIDS [13578]
Natl. Minority AIDS Coun. [13580]
Proj. Inform [13583]
San Francisco AIDS Found. [13584]
Soc. for Prevention of Human Infertility [16347]
Student Global AIDS Campaign [13585]
Transatlantic Partners Against AIDS [13586]
Treatment Action Gp. [13587]
Women Alive Coalition [13588]
Seychelles Amateur Athletics Fed. [IO], Victoria, Seychelles

Reference to "IO" in place of a book number signifies that the association may be found in the 45th edition of International Organizations.

Seychelles Squash Rackets Assn. [IO], Victoria, Seychelles
Seychelles Tennis Assn. [IO], Victoria, Seychelles
Seychelles Yachting Assn. [IO], Victoria, Seychelles
SFI Found. [6521], 15708 Pomerado Rd., Ste. N208, Poway, CA 92064, (858)451-8868
SFPE Educational and Sci. Foundation [★7082]
SGCI Chemie Pharma Schweiz [IO], Zurich, Switzerland
SGM International/U.S.A. [★19506]
SGML Open [★7756]
SGML Open [★IO]
Sgt. Pepper's Lonely Hearts Club - Defunct.
Sha Na Na - Defunct.
Shaare Zedek Hosp. in Jerusalem; Amer. Comm. for [12455]
Shackamaxon Soc. - Defunct.
Shadan Hojin Nihon Ryokogyo Kyokai [★IO]
Shadanhojin Nipon Yakurigakkai [★IO]
Shade Tobacco Growers Agricultural Assn. - Address unknown since 2004.
Shade Tree Conf; Intl. [★5259]
Shade Tree Evaluation; Natl. [★5259]
S.H.A.D.O. - USECC [25042], c/o Commander Helen Weber, 514 Delaware Ave., Lansdale, PA 19446-3417
SHAEF and ETOUSA Veterans Assn. [21404], c/o Alan Reeves, Natl. Commander, 2301 Broadway, San Francisco, CA 94115, (415)921-8322
SHAEF Veterans Assn. [★21404]
Shafer Family Assn. [21048], 141 Hudson Ave., Chatham, NY 12037, (518)392-4544
Shaft Contractors; Assn. of Drilled [★1000]
Shagya-Arabian Soc; North Amer. [4936]
Shagya Arabian Verband; Amer. [4844]
Shahmaghsoudi; Makatab Tarighat Oveyssi [20576]
Shake Assn; Handsplit Red Cedar [★1640]
Shake Bur; Red Cedar Shingle and Handsplit [★1640]
Shaker Collectors Club; Salt [★21968]
Shakers
  Antique and Art Glass Salt Shaker Collectors Soc. [21968]
  Friends of the Shakers [10963]
  Novelty Salt and Pepper Shakers Club [22097]
Shakespeare Assn. of America - Defunct.
Shakespeare Authorship Soc. [★9689]
Shakespeare Birthplace Trust [IO], Stratford-Upon-Avon, United Kingdom
Shakespeare Data Bank - Address unknown since 2001.
Shakespeare Oxford Soc. [9709], PO Box 808, Yorktown Heights, NY 10598, (914)962-1717
Shakespeare Oxford Soc. [IO], Yorktown Heights, NY, United States
Shakespeare Recording Soc. - Defunct.
Shakespeare Soc. [9710], 45 E 78th St., New York, NY 10021, (212)327-3399
Shakespeare Soc. of Southern Africa [IO], Grahamstown, Republic of South Africa
Shakespeare Theatre Assn. of Am. [11042], c/o Laura Cole, Sec., 499 Peachtree St. NE, Atlanta, GA 30308, (404)874-5299
Shakey's Franchised Dealers Assn. - Defunct.
Shale Clay and Slate Inst; Expanded [621]
Shale Inst; Expanded [★621]
Shalom Achshav [★17935]
Shalom Achshav [★IO]
Shalom Achshav [★IO]
Shamanic Stud; Found. for [20446]
Shamanism Network; Cross-Cultural [20444]
Shanghailanders - Address unknown since 1990.
Shankland Family Org; Ronald Lee [21038]
Shanks Family Assn. [21049]
Shannon Appreciation Soc; Del [24873]
Shanti [11831], 730 Polk St., San Francisco, CA 94109, (415)674-4700
Shanti Proj. [★11831]
Shape the Debate - Address unknown since 2004.
SHAPE Science Fiction Soc. - Defunct.
SHAPE Tech. Centre [★IO]
Shape Up Am. [15969], PO Box 149, Clyde Park, MT 59018
Shape Up for Life Campaign [★15156]
Shaping Growth in Amer. Communities [★5594]

Shar-Pei Club of Am; Chinese [22244]
SHARE [★12690]
Share-A-Ride Intl. - Address unknown since 1994.
Share and Care Cockayne Syndrome Network [14480], PO Box 570618, Dallas, TX 75357, (214)728-2679
Share Found. [★17485]
Share Found. [★IO]
SHARE Found.: Building a New El Salvador Today [IO], San Francisco, CA, United States
SHARE Found.: Building a New El Salvador Today [17485], 598 Bosworth St., No. 1, San Francisco, CA 94131, (415)239-2595
Share Our Strength [12399], 1730 M St. NW, Ste. 700, Washington, DC 20036, (202)393-2925
SHARE-Pregnancy and Infant Loss Support [12690], St. Joseph Hea. Center, 300 1st Capitol Dr., St. Charles, MO 63301-2893, (636)947-6164
Share Soc; Bond and [★22046]
Share the Work Coalition - Defunct.
Share Your Birthday Found. - Defunct.
Shared Hope Intl. [13457], PO Box 65337, Vancouver, WA 98665, (360)693-8100
Shared Hope Intl. [IO], Vancouver, WA, United States
Shared Housing Rsrc. Center [★12333]
Shared Housing Rsrc. Center; Natl. [12333]
Shared Living Rsrc. Center - Defunct.
Shareholders Assn; Utility [3967]
Shareholders Res. Alliance [3391], PO Box 750471, Forest Hills, NY 11375-0471, (718)896-5060
Shareware Professionals; Assn. of [6762]
Sharing Ideas Soc. [★10905]
Sharing Indus; Coun. of Profit [★1279]
Sharing Info. and Experience for Safer Operations [IO], Pulborough, United Kingdom
Sharing the Memory Elvis Presley Fan Club of Vermont - Defunct.
Sharing of Ministries Abroad U.S.A. [20393], 5290 Saratoga Ln., Woodbridge, VA 22193, (703)878-7667
Shark Assn; Amer. [23156]
Shark Found. Switzerland [IO], Zurich, Switzerland
Shark Res. Inst. [IO], Princeton, NJ, United States
Shark Res. Inst. [5019], PO Box 40, Princeton, NJ 08540, (609)921-3522
Sharkhunters Intl. [10480], PO Box 1539, Hernando, FL 34442, (352)637-2917
Sharkhunters Intl. [IO], Hernando, FL, United States
Sharon Gless as Cagney Fan Club [★24771]
Sharon Gless Fan Club (U.S.) [24771], c/o Gail M. Reese, Pres., PO Box 91915, Los Angeles, CA 90009
Sharon Smith Intl. Fan Club - Address unknown since 1999.
Sharps Injuries; Natl. Alliance for the Primary Prevention of [16381]
Sharq Informational-Analytical Center [IO], Dushanbe, Tajikistan
Sharsheret [13872], 1086 Teaneck Rd., Ste. 3A, Teaneck, NJ 07666, (866)474-2774
Shatner and Friends Intl. [24772], PO Box 1345, Studio City, CA 91604
Shaving Mug Collectors Assn; Natl. [22086]
Shaw Found; Lloyd [8187]
Shaw Soc. of America - Defunct.
Shaw Soc; Bernard [9636]
Shaw Soc; Clan [20862]
Shawnee Pottery Collectors Club - Defunct.
Sheclimbs [23285], c/o Lilly Feldman, 296 Country Club Rd., Avon, CT 06001
Sheep
  Amer. Border Leicester Assn. [5177]
  Amer. Cheviot Sheep Soc. [5178]
  Amer. Cormo Sheep Assn. [5179]
  Amer. Corriedale Assn. [5180]
  Amer. Cotswold Record Assn. [5181]
  Amer. Delaine and Merino Record Assn. [5182]
  Amer. Dorper Sheep Breeders' Soc. [5183]
  Amer. Finnsheep Breeders Assn. [5184]
  Amer. Hampshire Sheep Assn. [5185]
  Amer. Karakul Sheep Registry [5186]
  Amer. Lamb Coun. [5187]
  Amer. Miniature Cheviot Sheep Breeders Assn. [5188]

  Amer. North Country Cheviot Sheep Assn. [5189]
  Amer. Oxford Sheep Assn. [5190]
  Amer. Polypay Sheep Assn. [5191]
  Amer. Rambouillet Sheep Breeders' Assn. [5192]
  Amer. Romney Breeders' Assn. [5193]
  Amer. Sheep Indus. Assn. [5194]
  Amer. Shetland Sheepdog Assn. [22210]
  Amer. Shropshire Registry Assn. [5195]
  Amer. Southdown Breeders' Assn. [5196]
  ARCA: Amer. Romeldale/CVM Assn. [5197]
  Australian Corriedale Assn. [IO]
  Australian Finnsheep Breeders Assn. [IO]
  Australian Poll Dorset Assn. [IO]
  Australian Sheep Breeders Assn. [IO]
  Australian Texel Stud Breeders Assn. [IO]
  Australian White Suffolk Assn. [IO]
  Badger Face Welsh Mountain Sheep Soc. [IO]
  Barbados Blackbelly Sheep Assn. Intl. [5198]
  Belgian Sheepdog Club of Am. [22228]
  Black Top and Natl. Delaine Merino Sheep Assn. [5199]
  Bluefaced Leicester Sheep Breeders Assn. [IO]
  Bluefaced Leicester Union of North Am. [5200]
  Canadian Co-Operative Wool Growers [IO]
  Canadian Sheep Breeders' Assn. [IO]
  Canadian Sheep Fed. [IO]
  Canadian Texel Assn. [IO]
  Columbia Sheep Breeders Assn. of Am. [5201]
  Continental Dorset Club [5202]
  Dorper Sheep Breeders' Soc. of South Africa [IO]
  Dorset Horn and Poll Dorset Sheep Breeders Assn. [IO]
  Exmoor Horn Sheep Breeders Soc. [IO]
  Found. for North Amer. Wild Sheep [5318]
  Hungarian Pumi Club of Am. [22284]
  Icelandic Sheepdog Assn. of Am. [22286]
  Jacob Sheep Breeders Assn. [5203]
  Jacob Sheep Soc. [IO]
  Maremma Sheepdog Club of Am. [22304]
  Miniature and Novelty Sheep Breeders Assn. and Registry [5204]
  Montadale Sheep Breeders Assn. [5205]
  Natl. Lamb Feeders Assn. [5206]
  Natl. Lincoln Sheep Breeders' Assn. [5207]
  Natl. Tunis Sheep Registry, Inc. [5208]
  Natl. Wool Growers' Assn. of South Africa [IO]
  Natural Colored Wool Growers Association [IO]
  Natural Colored Wool Growers Assn. [5209]
  Navajo-Churro Sheep Assn. [5210]
  North Amer. Babydoll Southdown Sheep Assn. and Registry [5211]
  North Amer. Babydoll Southdown Sheep Assn. and Registry [IO]
  North Amer. Clun Forest Assn. [5212]
  North Amer. Sheep Dog Soc. [22328]
  North Amer. Shetland Sheepbreeders Assn. [5213]
  North Amer. Wensleydale Sheep Assn. [5214]
  Old English Sheepdog Club of Am. [22334]
  OPP Concerned Sheep Breeders Soc. [16803]
  Painted Desert Sheep Soc. [5215]
  Polish Tatra Sheepdog Club of Am. [22342]
  Public Lands Coun. [5127]
  Rough Fell Sheep Breeders Assn. [IO]
  Scottish Blackface Sheep Breeder's Assn. [5216]
  Sheep Indus. Development Prog. [5217]
  Soays of Am. [5218]
  Soc. for the Conservation of Bighorn Sheep [5381]
  United Suffolk Sheep Assn. [5219]
  Western Range Assn. [5220]
Sheep Assn; Amer. Cotswold [★5181]
Sheep Breeders' Assn; Amer. Tunis [★5208]
Sheep Dog Soc; North Amer. [22328]
Sheep; Found. for North Amer. Wild [5318]
Sheep and Goat Practitioners; Amer. Assn. of [★16749]
Sheep Indus. Development Prog. [5217], c/o Amer. Sheep Indus. Assn., 9785 Maroon Cir., Ste. 360, Englewood, CO 80112, (303)771-3500
Sheep Producers' Coun; Amer. [★5194]
Sheep Registry; Amer. Karakul Fur [★5186]
Sheep Registry; Karakul Fur [★5186]
Sheep; Soc. for the Conservation of Bighorn [5381]
Sheep Soc; United Suffolk [★5219]

A star before a book entry number signifies that the name is not listed separately, but is mentioned within the entry.

Sheepbreeders Assn; North Amer. Shetland [5213]
Sheepdog
  Amer. Shetland Sheepdog Assn. [22210]
  Belgian Sheepdog Club of Am. [22228]
  Hungarian Pumi Club of Am. [22284]
  Icelandic Sheepdog Assn. of Am. [22286]
  Maremma Sheepdog Club of Am. [22304]
  North Amer. Sheep Dog Soc. [22328]
  Old English Sheepdog Club of Am. [22334]
  Polish Tatra Sheepdog Club of Am. [22342]
Sheepdog Assn; Amer. Shetland [22210]
Sheepdog Club of Am; Belgian [22228]
Sheepdog Club of Am; Old English [22334]
Sheet Metal and Air Conditioning Contractors' Natl.
  Assn. [1900], 4201 Lafayette Center Dr., Chantilly,
  VA 20151-1209, (703)803-2980
Sheet Metal Contractors Assn. of Alberta [IO], Cal-
  gary, AB, Canada
Sheet Metal Contractors Natl. Assn. [★1900]
Sheet Metal Industry Promotion Plan [1065]
Sheet Metal Occupational Hea. Inst. [★12991]
Sheet Metal Occupational Hea. Inst. Trust [12991],
  601 N Fairfax St., Ste. 250, Alexandria, VA 22314,
  (703)739-7130
Sheet Metal Workers' Intl. Assn. [24136], 1750 New
  York Ave. NW, Washington, DC 20006, (202)783-
  5880
Sheet Music Soc; Natl. [10668]
Sheffield Chamber of Commerce and Indus. [IO],
  Sheffield, United Kingdom
Sheffield Conservation Volunteers [IO], Sheffield,
  United Kingdom
Shelby
  Mustang Club of Am. [21722]
Shelby Amer. Auto. Club [21782], PO Box 788,
  Sharon, CT 06069
Shelby Dodge Automobile Club - Defunct.
Shelby Owners of America - Address unknown since
  1997.
Shelby Owners Assn. - Defunct.
Shelf-Stable Food Processors Assn. [2664], 1150
  Connecticut Ave. NW, 12th Fl., Washington, DC
  20036, (202)587-4273
Shellac Export Promotion Coun. [IO], Calcutta, India
Shellee Morris Fan Club - Address unknown since
  1995.
Shellers Assn; Amer. Peanut [5051]
Shellers Assn; Natl. Pecan [5059]
Shelley Assn. of Am; Keats- [9677]
Shelley China Club; Natl. [22087]
Shellfish Assn. of Great Britain [IO], London, United
  Kingdom
Shellfish Commissioners; Natl. Assn. of [★7255]
Shellfish Growers Assn; Pacific Coast [3501]
Shellfish Inst; Molluscan [3494]
Shellfish Inst. of North Am. [★3494]
Shellfish Inst; Pacific [4182]
Shells
  Amer. Malacological Soc. [7254]
  Conchologists of Am. [21999]
Shelly Bruce Fan Club - Defunct.
Shelter
  Assn. of Shelter Veterinarians [16784]
  Chimp Haven [11729]
  CityTeam Ministries [12844]
  Natl. Domestic Violence Hotline [12036]
  Natl. Org. of African Americans in Housing
    [12331]
  Natl. Storm Shelter Assn. [2831]
  Support Our Shelters [11462]
  Women's Humane Soc. Animal Shelter [11479]
Shelter Advt. Assn. [★114]
Shelter; Comm. for Food and [★12294]
Shelter for Life Intl. [19329], PO Box 28220, Min-
  neapolis, MN 55428, (763)416-0441
Shelter; Natl. Citizens Comm. for Food and
  [★12294]
Shelter Now Intl. [★19329]
Sheltered Workshops and Homebound Programs;
  Natl. Assn. of [★16312]
Shelterforce Collective [★12326]
Sheltering and Immigrant Aid Soc; Hebrew [★12471]
Shelving Mfrs. Assn. [★2071]
Shema Yisrael [★20135]
Shema Yisrael; Congregation [20135]

SHEMESH: Jewish-Arab Friendship and Coexist-
  ence in the Galilee, Israel [IO], Misgav, Israel
Shemya WWII Veterans Assn. - Address unknown
  since 1996.
Shenandoah Natl. Park Assn. [10062], 3655 US
  Hwy. 211 E, Luray, VA 22835, (540)999-3582
Shenandoah Natural History Assn. [★10062]
Shenkar Coll; Amer. Comm. for [8674]
Shepard Family Org; Ralph [21030]
Shepaug Valley Archaeological Soc. [★6447]
Shepherd Club of Am; Australian [22222]
Shepherd Club; English [22261]
Shepherds Fold Ministries - Address unknown since
  1999.
Sheppard Intl. Fan Club; T.G. [24983]
Sheppard Peace Movement [★IO]
Sheppard Vendors of Am; Randolph- [3973]
Shepway Chamber of Commerce and Indus. [★IO]
Sheriffs' Assn; Natl. [6002]
Sherlock Holmes
  Baker St. Irregulars [10964]
  Baker St. Irregulars [IO]
  Bimetallic Question [IO]
Sherlock Holmes Societies - Address unknown since
  1997.
Sherman Family Org. - Defunct.
Sherwood Anderson Soc. - Defunct.
Shetland Aquaculture [IO], Lerwick, United Kingdom
Shetland Knitwear Trades Assn. [IO], Shetland,
  United Kingdom
Shetland Pony Club/American Miniature Horse
  Registry; Amer. [4845]
Shetland Pony Identification Bur. - Defunct.
Shetland Salmon Farmers' Assn. [★IO]
Shetland Sheepbreeders Assn; North Amer. [5213]
Shetland Sheepdog Assn; Amer. [22210]
Shevchenko Sci. Soc. [19415], 63 4th Ave., New
  York, NY 10003-5200, (212)254-5130
Shevchenko Sci. Soc. [IO], New York, NY, United
  States
SHHH [★14759]
Shiatsu Assn; Amer. [★15024]
Shiatsu Educ. Center of Am. [★15748]
Shiatsu Educ. Center of Am. [★IO]
Shiatsu Therapists Alliance [IO], Thornhill, ON,
  Canada
Shiatsu Therapy Assn. of Australia [IO], Melbourne,
  Australia
Shiba Club of Am; Natl. [22320]
Shidhulai Swanirvar Sangstha [IO], Dhaka, Bang-
  ladesh
Shields Class Assn. [★23218]
Shields Class Sailing Assn. [★23218]
Shields Natl. Class Assn. [23218], PO Box 236,
  Newport, RI 02840, (401)842-6911
Shiftung DIAKONIA Weltbund von Verbaenden und
  Gemeinsdafsen der Diakonie [★IO]
Shih Tzu Club of Am. [★22211]
Shih Tzu Club; Amer. [22211]
Shingle Bur; Red Cedar [★1640]
Shingle and Handsplit Shake Bur; Red Cedar
  [★1640]
Shingles Support Soc. [IO], London, United Kingdom
Ship Assn; Intl. Passenger [★3915]
Ship Assn; USS North Carolina Battle [21411]
Ship Brokers and Agents - U.S.A; Assn. of [2603]
Ship Builders, Blacksmiths, Forgers and Helpers;
  Intl. Brotherhood of Boilermakers, Iron [24021]
Ship Building Workers of Am; Indus. Union of Marine
  and [24125]
Ship Cancellation Soc., Savannah Chap; Universal
  [★22841]
Ship Cancellation Soc; Universal [22889]
Ship Info. Center [★10439]
Ship Modelers Assn. of North Am; Scale [22656]
Shipbuilders' Assn. of Japan [IO], Tokyo, Japan
Shipbuilders Coun. of Am. [2592], 1455 F St. NW,
  Ste. 225, Washington, DC 20005, (202)347-5462
Shipbuilders; Natl. Coun. of Amer. [★2592]
Shipbuilders and Shiprepairers Assn. [IO], Egham,
  United Kingdom
Shipbuilding Assn; Amer. [591]
Shipbuilding Assn. of Canada [IO], Ottawa, ON,
  Canada
Shipman Family Org. - Defunct.

Shipmasters Assn. of the Great Lakes; Intl. [★2579]
Shipowners' Assn. of the Pacific Coast - Defunct.
Shipowners Claims Bur. [2238], 1 Battery Park Plz.,
  31st Fl., New York, NY 10004, (212)847-4500
Shipowners Refrigerated Cargo Res. Assn. [★IO]
Shippers Advisory Boards; Natl. Assn. of [★3885]
Shippers Advisory Boards; Natl. Assn. of Rail
  [★3885]
Shippers Assn; Amer. Cotton [1089]
Shippers Assn; Fashion Accessories [★250]
Shippers Assn; Florida Express Fruit [★4731]
Shippers Assn; North Amer. Rail [3885]
Shippers Assn; Parcel [2454]
Shippers Assn; Wine and Spirits [211]
Shippers for Competitive Ocean Transportation -
  Defunct.
Shippers; Natl. Assn. of Rail [★3885]
Shippers Natl. Freight Claim Coun., Inc. [★3595]
Shippers Oil Field Traffic Assn. [★2923]
Shippers Protective League; California Growers and
  [★4716]
Shippers of Recycled Textiles [3587], 7131 E Broad
  St., Ste. 206, Falls Church, VA 22046, (703)538-
  1000
Shipping
  Amer. Alliance of Ethical Movers [13346]
  Amer. Import Shippers Assn. [3557]
  Amer. Inst. for Shippers' Associations [3558]
  Amer. Maritime Safety, Inc. [2570]
  Amer. Moving and Storage Assn. [3559]
  American Moving and Storage Association [IO]
  Armored Trans. Inst. [3560]
  Assn. of Intl. Couriers and Express Services [IO]
  Assn. of Ship Brokers and Agents - U.S.A. [2603]
  Australian Fed. of Intl. Forwarders [IO]
  Australian Furniture Removers Assn. [IO]
  Australian Logistics Coun. [IO]
  Australian Ship Repairers Gp. [IO]
  Bangkok Shipowners and Agents Assn. [IO]
  Boston Shipping Assn. [3561]
  British Assn. of Removers [IO]
  Cambridge Refrigeration Tech. [IO]
  Canadian Courier and Logistics Assn. [IO]
  Canadian Intl. Freight Forwarders Assn. [IO]
  Canadian Trucking Alliance [IO]
  Certified Claims Professional Accreditation Coun.
    [3865]
  Chamber of Shipping of Am. [6059]
  Chartered Inst. of Logistics and Transport in
    Ireland [IO]
  Community of European Shipyards' Associations
    [IO]
  Conf. on Safe Trans. of Hazardous Articles [3562]
  Dangerous Goods Advisory Coun. [3563]
  Despatch Assn. [IO]
  Distribution and LTL Carriers Assn. [3564]
  European River-Sea-Transport Union [IO]
  Express Delivery and Logistics Assn. [3565]
  Fed. of Freight Forwarders' Assn. in India [IO]
  Florida Gift Fruit Shippers Assn. [4731]
  Food Shippers Assn. of North Am. [1512]
  Freight Trans. Consultants Assn. [3566]
  French Road Union [IO]
  Hellenic Professional Yacht Owners Assn. [IO]
  Hong Kong Assn. of Freight Forwarding and
    Logistics [IO]
  Household Goods Forwarders Association of
    America [IO]
  Household Goods Forwarders Assn. of Am.
    [3567]
  ICHCA Intl. Limited [IO]
  Independent Armored Car Operators Assn. [3568]
  Inland Waterways Amenity Advisory Coun. [IO]
  Intermodal Assn. of North Am. [3872]
  Intl. Assn. of Independent Tanker Owners [IO]
  Intl. Assn. of Structural Movers [IO]
  Intl. Assn. of Structural Movers [3569]
  Intl. Fed. of Freight Forwarders Associations [IO]
  Intl. Fed. of Intl. Furniture Removers [IO]
  Intl. Furniture and Trans. Logistics Coun. [IO]
  Intl. Furniture and Trans. Logistics Coun. [3570]
  Intl. Safe Transit Assn. [3571]
  Intl. Safe Transit Assn. [IO]
  Intl. Ship Managers Assn. [IO]
  Irish Intl. Freight Assn. [IO]

Reference to "IO" in place of a book number signifies that the association may be found in the 45th edition of International Organizations.

Irish Road Haulage Assn. [IO]
Israel Shippers' Coun. [IO]
Japan Trucking Assn. [IO]
Japanese Shipowners Assn. - United Kingdom [IO]
Korea Intl. Freight Forwarders Assn. [IO]
Lake Carriers' Assn. [2606]
Liberian Shipowners' Coun. [2607]
LTD Shippers Assn. [3842]
Marine Machinery Assn. [2608]
Maritime Assn. of the Port of New York/New Jersey [3572]
Maritime Trades Dept., AFL-CIO [24129]
Messenger Courier Assn. of the Americas [3573]
Mid-West Truckers Assn. [3875]
NASSTRAC [3574]
Natl. Armored Car Assn. [3575]
Natl. Assn. of Waterfront Employers [2609]
Natl. Cargo Bur. [3576]
Natl. Courier Assn. [IO]
Natl. Indus. Trans. League [3879]
Natl. Motor Freight Traffic Assn. [3577]
Natl. Private Truck Coun. [3881]
Natl. Road Carriers [IO]
Natl. Road Transport Assn. [IO]
Natl. Shippers Strategic Trans. Coun. [3578]
Natl. Solid Wastes Mgt. Assn. [3579]
Natl. Tank Truck Carriers [3580]
Natl. Waterways Conf. [3581]
New York/New Jersey Foreign Freight Forwarders and Brokers Assn. [3582]
New York Shipping Assn. [3583]
New Zealand Shipping Fed. [IO]
North Amer. Shippers Assn. [3584]
Oceanic Navigation Res. Soc. [10444]
Pacific Maritime Assn. [3585]
Pakistan Ship's Agents Assn. [IO]
Partnership for Food Safety Educ. [14399]
Professional Trucking Services Assn. [3890]
Propeller Club of the U.S. [3586]
St. Lawrence Shipoperators [IO]
Shippers of Recycled Textiles [3587]
Shipping Assn. of Barbados [IO]
Shipping Assn. of Trinidad and Tobago [IO]
Shipping Fed. of Canada [IO]
Singapore Logistics Assn. [IO]
Singapore Natl. Shippers' Coun. [IO]
Soc. of Marine Port Engineers [3588]
South African Assn. of Freight Forwarders [IO]
Specialized Carriers and Rigging Assn. [IO]
Specialized Carriers and Rigging Assn. [3589]
Sporting Goods Shippers Assn. [3590]
Steamship Assn. of Louisiana [3591]
Tech. and Maintenance Coun. of the Amer. Trucking Associations [3895]
Thai Natl. Shippers' Coun. [IO]
Trans-Atlantic Amer. Flag Liner Operators/Trans-Pacific Amer. Flag Berth Operators [3592]
Transfrigoroute Intl. [IO]
Trans. Inst. [3593]
Trans. Intermediaries Assn. [3594]
Trans. and Logistics Coun. [3595]
Trucking Mgt., Inc. [3898]
Uganda Services Exporters' Assn. [IO]
Unishippers Assn. [3596]
West African Discussion Agreement [3597]
Western Growers Assn. [4774]
Women's Intl. Shipping and Trading Assn. [3598]
Women's Intl. Shipping and Trading Assn. [IO]
Women's Intl. Shipping and Trading Assn. Israel [IO]
Women's Intl. Shipping and Trading Assn. Italy [IO]
Women's Intl. Shipping and Trading Assn. Netherlands [IO]
Women's Intl. Shipping and Trading Assn. Norway [IO]
Women's Intl. Shipping and Trading Assn. Singapore [IO]
Women's Intl. Shipping and Trading Assn. UK [IO]
Shipping of Am; Chamber of [6059]
Shipping; Amer. Bur. of [2600]
Shipping Assn. of Barbados [IO], Bridgetown, Barbados
Shipping Assn; Jewelers [2373]

Shipping Assn. of Trinidad and Tobago [IO], Port of Spain, Trinidad and Tobago
Shipping Container Inst; Plastic [992]
Shipping Container Inst; Steel [995]
Shipping Fed. of Canada [IO], Montreal, QC, Canada
Shipping, and Off. Automation Specialists; Assn. of Mailing, [2448]
Shipping Sack Manufacturers' Assn; Paper [991]
Shipping; U.S. Chamber of [★6059]
Ships Assn; Historic Naval [10440]
Ships-in-Bottles Assn. of Am. [22658], c/o Don Hubbard, Membership Chm., PO Box 180550, Coronado, CA 92178
Ships-In-Bottles Assn; Intl. [★22658]
Ship's Literary Club [★10321]
Ships on Stamps Unit [22870], c/o Myron P. Molnau, Pres., 2117 E 6th St., Moscow, ID 83843-9709, (208)882-0257
Ships on Stamps Unit [IO], Moscow, ID, United States
Shipwrites - Defunct.
Shire Horse Assn; Amer. [4846]
Shirika la Utafiti na Maendeleo va Viwanda, Tanzania [★IO]
Shirkat Gah [★IO]
Shirley Bassey Collectors' Club - Defunct.
Shirley Family Assn. [21050], c/o Betty Shirley, Pres., 10256 Glencoe Dr., Cupertino, CA 95014
Shirley Jones Fan Club - Defunct.
Shoe and Allied Craftsmen; Brotherhood of [24063]
Shoe and Allied Res. Assn. [★IO]
Shoe Assn; World [260]
Shoe Chain Stores; Natl. Assn. of [★1597]
Shoe Crew; The One [11977]
Shoe Exchange; Natl. Odd [11974]
Shoe Finders Assn; Natl. Leather and [★1600]
Shoe Lace Mfrs. Assn. - Defunct.
Shoe Mfrs. Bd. of Trade of New York - Defunct.
Shoe Pattern Mfrs. Assn. - Defunct.
Shoe Retailer Assn; Popular Price [★1597]
Shoe Retailers Assn; Natl. [1598]
Shoe Ser. Inst. of Am. [1600], 18 School St., North Brookfield, MA 01535, (508)867-7732
Shoe Travelers Assn. of New York; Boot and [1596]
Shoes Fan Club - Address unknown since 2002.
Shoeshine Boys Found. - Defunct.
Shohem Aleichem Folk Inst. - Defunct.
Sholom; Independent Order of Brith [★19178]
Shomers/Schomers Family Org. - Address unknown since 2001.
Shomrei Adamah/Keepers of the Earth - Address unknown since 1999.
Shomrim Societies; Natl. Conf. of [12478]
Shomrim Soc. [12481], c/o Murray Ellman, Financial Sec., PO Box 598, Knickerbocker, NY 10002, (718)730-8914
Shon Branham Fan Club [24803], c/o Vondol Bailey, Pres., 206 Doel Bean, Kirbyville, TX 75956, (409)423-3319
Shooters Club of America - Defunct.

Shooting

Amateur Trapshooting Assn. [23713]
Amer. Airgun Field Target Assn. [22976]
Amer. Single Shot Rifle Assn. [23714]
American Single Shot Rifle Association [IO]
Archery Shooters Assn. [23050]
Assn. of Ohio Longrifle Collectors [22425]
Assn. of Women Shooters of Canada [IO]
Belgian Clayshooting Fed. [IO]
British Shooting Sports Coun. [IO]
Browning Collectors Assn. [22426]
Canadian Shooting Sports Assn. [IO]
Cast Bullet Assn. [23715]
Clay Pigeon Shooting Assn. [IO]
Clay Target Shooting Assn. South Africa [IO]
Cowboy Mounted Shooting Assn. [23716]
Danish Shooting Union [IO]
Fifty Caliber Shooters Assn. [IO]
Fifty Caliber Shooters Assn. [22973]
Finnish Shooting Sport Fed. [IO]
Great Britain Target Shooting Fed. [IO]
Hunter's Shooting Assn. [23543]
Intl. Benchrest Shooters [23717]
Intl. Benchrest Shooters [IO]

International Defensive Pistol Association [IO]
Intl. Defensive Pistol Assn. [23718]
Intl. Handgun Metallic Silhouette Assn. [23719]
Intl. Handgun Metallic Silhouette Assn. [IO]
Intl. Practical Shooting Confed. Australia [IO]
Intl. Shooting Sport Fed. [IO]
L.C. Smith Collectors Assn. [22429]
Masters of Foxhounds Assn. of Am. [23546]
Midwest Decoy Collectors Assn. [22071]
Natl. Archery Assn. of the U.S. [23052]
Natl. Assn. of Firearms Retailers [1479]
Natl. Assn. of Shooting Ranges [3599]
Natl. Assn. of Shooting Sports Athletes [23720]
Natl. Automatic Pistol Collectors Assn. [21539]
Natl. Bench Rest Shooters Assn. [23721]
Natl. Bowhunter Educ. Found. [23053]
The Natl. Crossbowmen of the U.S.A. [23054]
Natl. Field Archery Assn. [23055]
Natl. Firearms Act Trade and Collectors Assn. [1480]
Natl. Hunters Assn. [23547]
Natl. Mossberg Collectors Assn. [22430]
Natl. Muzzle Loading Rifle Assn. [23722]
Natl. Rifle Assn. [IO]
Natl. Rifle Assn. of Am. [23723]
Natl. Rifle and Pistol Assn. of Ireland [IO]
Natl. Shooting Sports Found. [23724]
Natl. Skeet Shooting Assn. [23725]
Natl. Small-Bore Rifle Assn. [IO]
Natl. Sporting Clays Assn. [23726]
North Amer. Bowhunting Coalition [22606]
North Amer. Hunting Club [23548]
North-South Skirmish Assn. [23727]
One-Arm Dove Hunt Assn. [23358]
Pacific Intl. Trapshooting Assn. [23728]
Pacific International Trapshooting Association [IO]
Pope and Young Club [23056]
Professional Bowhunter's Soc. [23057]
Shooting Fed. of Canada [IO]
Thompson Collectors Assn. [22431]
United Kingdom Practical Shooting Assn. [IO]
United Sportsmans Assn. of North Am. [23058]
U.S. Biathlon Assn. [23756]
U.S. Helice Assn. [23729]
U.S. Practical Shooting Assn. [23730]
U.S. Revolver Assn. [23731]
USA Shooting [23732]
Weatherby Collectors Assn. [22432]
Winchester Arms Collectors Assn. [21540]
World Fast-Draw Assn. [23733]
Shooting Fed. of Canada [IO], Nepean, ON, Canada
Shooting Preserve Assn; North Amer. Game Breeders and [★4144]
Shop and Display Equip. Assn. [IO], Caterham, United Kingdom
Shop, Distributive, and Allied Employees' Assn. [IO], Melbourne, Australia
Shoplifters Alternative [★13025]
Shoplifters Anonymous [★13025]
Shoplifters Anonymous Intl. [★13025]
Shopping Centers Inst. of America - Defunct.
Shopping Providers Assn; Mystery [2639]
Shopworkers, and Granite Cutters Intl. Union; Tile, Marble, Terrazzo, Finishers, [★24032]
Shoqata Shqiptare E Dhimbjes [★IO]
Shoqata Shqiptare e Shkencave Politike [★IO]
Shore Angling Assn; U.S. [23425]
Shore and Beach Preservation Association; American [4352]
Shore Fan Club; Dinah [24876]
Shore Fishing and Casting Club Intl. [23423], c/o Neal Krueger, Jr., Pres., 2235 Versailles, Corpus Christi, TX 78418, (361)939-7643
Shore Memorial Fan Club; Dinah [24738]
Shorin Kempo Karate Assn; Amer. [23581]
Shoring and Forming Inst; Scaffolding, [670]
Short Line and Regional Railroad Assn; Amer. [3281]
Short Snout Soc. - Defunct.
Short Stature Found. [★13105]
Short Stature Found. - Address unknown since 2004.
Short Term Volunteers - Defunct.
Short Terms Abroad [★19804]
Short Wing Piper Club [21475], c/o Mr. Cliff VanVleet, Pres., 3705 Shawnee Dr., Sierra Vista, AZ 85650, (520)378-2517

A star before a book entry number signifies that the name is not listed separately, but is mentioned within the entry.

Shortening and Edible Oils; Inst. of [2851]

Shortening Mfrs; Inst. of [★2851]

Shorthaired Pointer Club of Am; German [22274]

Shorthand Reporters Assn. of Australia [IO], Sydney, Australia

Shorthand Reporters Assn; Natl. [★5630]

Shorthand Soc; Movement [★11208]

Shorthanded Sailing Assn. of Australia [IO], McMahons Point, Australia

Shorthorn Assn; Amer. [4247]

Shorthorn Assn; Amer. Junior [4233]

Shorthorn Assn; Canadian [IO]

Shorthorn Breeders Assn; Amer. [★4247]

Shorthorn Foundation [★4247]

Shorthorn Junior Soc; Amer. Milking [4236]

Shorthorn Soc; Amer. Milking [4237]

Shortness

Billy Barty Found. [13104]

Coun. on Size and Weight Discrimination [12644]

Human Growth Found. [16020]

Little People of Am. [13105]

Shortwave Assn; North Amer. [21507]

Shortwave Listeners Club; Amer. [21495]

Shosin Soc. - Defunct.

Shotcrete Assn; Amer. [916]

Shotcrete Assn; Gunite/ [★1017]

Shotcrete Contractors Assn; Gunite/ [1017]

Shotgun Red Fan Club - Address unknown since 1994.

Shoulder and Elbow Surgeons; Amer. [16567]

Shovel Assn; Power Crane and [2058]

Show Business Assn. - Address unknown since 1995.

Show Business for Children; Women in [13069]

Show Folks of America - Address unknown since 1995.

Show Horse Alliance [4950], c/o Natl. Show Horse Registry, 10368 Bluegrass Pkwy., Louisville, KY 40299, (502)266-5100

Show Horse Registry; Natl. [4925]

Show Organizers; Soc. of Independent [1348]

Show Producers Assn; Intl. Sport [1344]

Showboat [★21411]

Showmen's Guild of Great Britain [IO], Drighlington, United Kingdom

Showmen's League of Am. [19039], 300 W Randolph St., Chicago, IL 60609, (312)332-6236

Showplace Gift and Decorative Accessories Assn. - Defunct.

Shows; Natl. Assn. of Consumer [1346]

Shrimp Breaders and Processors Assn; Natl. [★3498]

Shrimp Coun. [5172], 7918 Jones Br. Dr., Ste. 700, McLean, VA 22102, (703)524-8880

Shrimp Harvesters Coalition of the Gulf and South Atlantic States - Defunct.

Shrimp Indus. Assn; Natl. [3498]

Shrimp Processors Assn; Natl. [★3498]

Shrine; Ancient Egyptian Arabic Order Nobles of the Mystic [19227]

Shrine Center; Seton [★19694]

Shrine Directors Assn. of North America - Address unknown since 2003.

Shrine and Hall of Fame; Natl. Football [★23431]

Shrine of North Am; Ladies Oriental [19241]

Shrine Recorders Assn. of North America - Address unknown since 1995.

Shrine of St. Elizabeth Ann Seton; Natl. [19694]

Shriners [★19238]

Shriner's Burns Inst. for Children [★24605]

Shriners Hospitals for Children [13973], c/o Shriners Intl. HQ, 2900 Rocky Point Dr., Tampa, FL 33607-1460, (813)281-0300

Shriners Hospitals for Children Endowment Fund [★13973]

SHRM Foundation [★2908]

SHRM Global Forum [2907], 1800 Duke St., Alexandria, VA 22314, (703)548-3440

SHRM Global Forum [IO], Alexandria, VA, United States

Shropshire Chamber of Commerce and Enterprise [IO], Telford, United Kingdom

Shropshire Registry Assn; Amer. [5195]

Shropshire Soc. - Defunct.

Shroud Guild; Holy [19635]

Shroud of Turin Res. Project - Address unknown since 1999.

Shudokan Martial Arts Assn. [23603], PO Box 6022, Ann Arbor, MI 48106, (734)645-6441

Shuffleboard

Amer. Intl. Shuffleboard [23734]

Intl. Shuffleboard Assn. [23735]

Intl. Shuffleboard Assn. [IO]

Shuffleboard Company; Amer. [★23734]

Shut-In Day Soc; Natl. [★18651]

Shut-Ins; Natl. Soc. for [18651]

Shutdown Proj. [★6235]

Shutdown Proj. [★IO]

Shwachman Diamond Am. [14481], 931-B S Main St., No. 332, Kernersville, NC 27284, (336)423-8158

Shwachman-Diamond Syndrome Canada [IO], Mississauga, ON, Canada

Shwachman-Diamond Syndrome Found. [IO], Grand Junction, CO, United States

Shwachman-Diamond Syndrome Found. [16551], 710 Brassie Dr., Grand Junction, CO 81506, (614)939-2324

Shwachman-Diamond Syndrome Intl. [★16551]

Shwachman-Diamond Syndrome Intl. [★IO]

Shy Drager Syndrome/Multiple Sys. Atrophy Support Gp. [15364], PO Box 279, Coupland, TX 78615, (866)737-4999

Si-Sawat (Korat) Soc. - Address unknown since 2001.

Sialkot Chamber of Commerce and Indus. [IO], Sialkot, Pakistan

SIAMA - Soc. for Interests of Active Missionaries in Asia, Africa, and Am. [★IO]

SIAMA U.S.A., Inc. - Defunct.

SIAMA World Mission Travel [IO], Leiden, Netherlands

Siamese Breeders and Fanciers Assn; Traditional [★21920]

Siamese Cat Soc. of America - Defunct.

Siata/Fiat 8V Register - Address unknown since 2004.

Siberia

Siberian Husky Club of Am. [22359]

Soc. for Siberian Irises [22544]

Siberian Husky Club of Am. [22359], c/o Julia Rylander, Corresponding Sec., PO Box 319, Lake Stevens, WA 98258

Siberian Husky Eye Anomaly Res. Comm. - Defunct.

Siberian Irises; Soc. for [22544]

Sibling Information Network - Defunct.

Siblings for Significant Change [11987], Empire State Bldg., 350 5th Ave., Ste. 627, New York, NY 10118, (212)643-2663

Sicilian

Arba Sicula [19359]

Arba Sicula [IO]

Intl. Assn. of Dive Rescue Specialists [23574]

Sicilian Bioethical Inst. [IO], Acireale, Italy

Sick in Am; Catholic Union of the [★19620]

Sick Child Daycare; Natl. Assn. for [11532]

Sick and Disabled; CUSA: An Apostolate of the [19620]

Sick Kids Need Involved People - Address unknown since 1999.

Sickle Cell Anemia

Amer. Sickle Cell Anemia Assn. [16415]

Sickle Cell Disease Assn. of Am. [14797]

Sickle Cell Anemia Soc; Amer. [★16415]

Sickle Cell Disease Assn. of Am. [14797], 231 E Baltimore St., Ste. 800, Baltimore, MD 21202, (410)528-1555

Sickle Cell Disease; Natl. Assn. for [★14797]

Sickle Cell Soc; Amer. [★16415]

Side Saddle Assn. [IO], Pontypool, United Kingdom

Side Saddle Org; Intl. [23529]

Side-Saddle Org. and World Sidesaddle Fed., Inc; International [★23529]

Side by Side Lay Volunteer Prog. [20394], 5625 Isleta Blvd. SW, Albuquerque, NM 87105, (505)873-2059

Side by Side Lay Volunteer Prog. [IO], Albuquerque, NM, United States

Sidecar Assn; United [22693]

Sidelines Natl. High-Risk Pregnancy Support Network [15617], PO Box 1808, Laguna Beach, CA 92652, (888)447-4754

Sidelines Natl. Support Network [★15617]

Siding Assn; Aluminum [★588]

Siding Inst; Vinyl [685]

Sidran Found. and Press [★12559]

Sidran Inst. for Traumatic Stress Educ. [12559], 200 E Joppa Rd., Ste. 207, Baltimore, MD 21286, (410)825-8888

Sidran Traumatic Stress Found. [★12559]

SIDS Alliance; First Candle/ [16525]

SIDS Inst; Amer. [★16523]

SIDS Prog. Professionals; Assn. for [★16524]

Siemens Technologies U.S; Joint Users of [880]

Sierra Carriers and Mountaineering Group - Defunct.

Sierra Club [4520], 85 2nd St., 2nd Fl., San Francisco, CA 94105, (415)977-5500

Sierra Club of Canada [IO], Ottawa, ON, Canada

Sierra Club Legal Defense Fund [★IO]

Sierra Club Legal Defense Fund [★5690]

Sierra Foothill Winery Assn. - Address unknown since 1999.

Sierra Legal Defence Fund [IO], Vancouver, BC, Canada

Sierra Leone Amateur Athletic Assn. [IO], Freetown, Sierra Leone

Sierra Leone Lawn Tennis Assn. [IO], Freetown, Sierra Leone

Sierra Leone Red Cross Soc. [IO], Freetown, Sierra Leone

Sierra Leone Students Union of the Americas - Address unknown since 1995.

Sierra Leone Weightlifting and Body Building Assn. [IO], Freetown, Sierra Leone

Sierra Student Coalition [4521], 408 C St. NE, Washington, DC 20002, (202)548-4592

Sierra Visions [12444], PO Box 3271, Laurel, MD 20709-3271, (240)554-1555

Sierra Visions [IO], Laurel, MD, United States

SIFIDA Investment Company [IO], Geneva, Switzerland

The Sig That Taste Forgot [★22590]

SIGAPP - Special Interest Gp. on Applied Computing [6821], c/o ACM, 2 Penn Plz., Ste. 701, New York, NY 10121-0701, (212)869-7440

SIGCAPH [★6803]

SIGForth - Defunct.

SIGGRAPH; ACM [894]

SIGGRAPH Capitulo Profesional Ciudad de Mexico [★IO]

Sight Restoration; Eye-Bank for [14289]

Sight Restoration Soc. - Address unknown since 1995.

Sight Savers Intl. - England [IO], Haywards Heath, United Kingdom

Sighthound Field Assn; Amer. [22212]

Sightseeing Assn; Gray Line [3868]

Siglingasamband Islands [★IO]

Sigma Alpha [24602], 2713 Ubly Rd., Bad Axe, MI 48413

Sigma Alpha Epsilon [24654], 1856 Sheridan Rd., Evanston, IL 60201-3837, (847)475-1856

Sigma Alpha Epsilon [IO], Evanston, IL, United States

Sigma Alpha Epsilon; Kappa [★24463]

Sigma Alpha Eta [★16453]

Sigma Alpha Iota Intl. Music Fraternity [24557], 1 Tunnel Rd., Asheville, NC 28805, (828)251-0606

Sigma Alpha Lambda [24519], Five Concourse Pkwy., Ste. 3000, Atlanta, GA 30328, (770)392-3376

Sigma Alpha Mu [24655], 9245 N Meridian, Ste. 105, Indianapolis, IN 46260, (317)846-0600

Sigma Alpha Phi [★9189]

Sigma Beta Rho Fraternity [24656], PO Box 107, New York, NY 10020

Sigma Chi Intl. Corp. [★24657]

Sigma Chi Intl. Fraternity [24657], PO Box 469, Evanston, IL 60201, (847)869-3655

Sigma Delta Chi [★3164]

Sigma Delta Chi Found. [24524], 3909 N Meridian St., Indianapolis, IN 46208, (317)927-8000

Sigma Delta Epsilon [★24587]

Sigma Delta Epsilon, Graduate Women in Sci. [24587], c/o Ms. Marie Drottar, Sec., PO Box 291, Avon, MA 02322, (617)697-4947

Sigma Delta Kappa - Address unknown since 2002.

Reference to "IO" in place of a book number signifies that the association may be found in the 45th edition of International Organizations.

Sigma Delta Pi [24718], The Citadel, 171 Moultrie St., Charleston, SC 29409-6430

Sigma Delta Psi [24407], The Citadel, DEAS Hall, 171 Moultrie St., Charleston, SC 29409-6430, (843)225-3294

Sigma Delta Tau [24695], 714 Adams St., Carmel, IN 46032, (317)846-7747

Sigma Epsilon Sigma - Defunct.

Sigma Gamma Epsilon [24492], c/o Dr. Charles J. Mankin, Sec.-Treas., Univ. of Oklahoma, 100 E Boyd, Rm. N-131, Norman, OK 73019, (405)325-3031

Sigma Gamma Phi [★24614]

Sigma Gamma Rho Sorority [24603], 1000 Southill Dr., Ste. 200, Cary, NC 27513, (919)678-9720

Sigma Gamma Tau [24466], Wichita State Univ., Aerospace Engg. Dept., Wichita, KS 67260-0044, (316)978-5935

Sigma Iota Chi - Defunct.

Sigma Iota Epsilon [24534], c/o Dr. G. James Francis, Pres., Colorado State Univ., 312 Rockwell Hall - Mgt. Dept., Fort Collins, CO 80523-1275, (970)491-6265

Sigma Kappa [24696], 8733 Founders Rd., Indianapolis, IN 46268, (317)872-3275

Sigma Kappa Found. [24697], 8733 Founders Rd., Indianapolis, IN 46268, (317)872-3275

Sigma Lambda Alpha Sorority [24714], PO Box 424296, Denton, TX 76204-4296, (972)299-9890

Sigma Lambda Gamma Natl. Sorority [24715], 900 W Penn St., North Liberty, IA 52317, (319)626-7679

Sigma Mu Sigma - Address unknown since 1995.

Sigma Nu Fraternity [24658], 9 Lewis St., PO Box 1869, Lexington, VA 24450, (540)463-1869

Sigma Nu Phi [★24527]

Sigma Phi Alpha [24441], c/o Bonnie Branson, Pres., UMKC School of Dentistry, 650 E 25th St., Kansas City, MO 64108, (816)235-2053

Sigma Phi Beta Fraternity [24659], PO Box 937, Tempe, AZ 85280-0937, (888)744-2382

Sigma Phi Delta - Defunct.

Sigma Phi Educational Foundation [★24661]

Sigma Phi Epsilon [24660], 310 S Blvd., PO Box 1901, Richmond, VA 23218, (804)353-1901

Sigma Phi Epsilon Educational Found. [★24660]

Sigma Phi Gamma - Address unknown since 1989.

Sigma Phi Rho - Address unknown since 2002.

Sigma Phi Soc. [24661]

Sigma Pi [★24662]

Sigma Pi Fraternity, Intl. [24662], PO Box 1897, Brentwood, TN 37024, (800)332-1897

Sigma Pi Phi Fraternity [24663], PO Box 1897, Brentwood, TN 37024-1897, (212)477-5550

Sigma Pi Sigma [24575], 1 Physics Ellipse, College Park, MD 20740, (301)209-3007

Sigma Sigma Phi [24565], 4810 Snowdrop Dr., Garland, TX 75043

Sigma Sigma Sigma [24698], 225 N Muhlenberg St., Woodstock, VA 22664-1424, (540)459-4212

Sigma Sigma Sigma Foundation [★24698]

Sigma Tau [★24468]

Sigma Tau Delta [★24470]

Sigma Tau Delta [★IO]

Sigma Tau Delta, the Intl. English Honor Soc. [IO], DeKalb, IL, United States

Sigma Tau Delta, the Intl. English Honor Soc. [24470], c/o Dr. William C. Johnson, Exec. Dir., Northern Illinois Univ., Dept. of English, DeKalb, IL 60115, (815)753-1612

Sigma Tau Gamma [24664], Marvin Millsap HQ Bldg., PO Box 54, Warrensburg, MO 64093-0054, (660)747-2222

Sigma Theta Tau [★24561]

Sigma Theta Tau [★IO]

Sigma Theta Tau Intl. [IO], Indianapolis, IN, United States

Sigma Theta Tau Intl. [24561], 550 W North St., Indianapolis, IN 46202, (317)634-8171

Sigma Xi [★24588]

Sigma Xi, The Sci. Res. Soc. [24588], PO Box 13975, Research Triangle Park, NC 27709, (919)549-4691

Sigma Zeta [24589], c/o Dr. Harold Wilkinson, Millikin Univ., 1184 W Main St., Decatur, IL 62522, (651)638-6379

Sigma Zeta Chi - Address unknown since 1995.

Sigma Zeta Development Fund [★24589]

Sigmund Freud Archives [16115], c/o Manuscript Division of the Lib. Cong., 101 Independence Ave. SE, Washington, DC 20540-4680, (516)621-6850

Sign Associates; World [1201]

Sign Assn; Amer. Highway [★85]

Sign Assn. of Canada [IO], Toronto, ON, Canada

Sign Language Interpreters Assn. of New Zealand [IO], Auckland, New Zealand

Sign Language Teachers Assn; Amer. [14741]

Sign Supply Distributors; Natl. Assn. of [4023]

Sign Trust; Hollywood [17710]

Signage Res; Inst. of [★1189]

Signal Appliance Assn. [★3291]

Signal and Communications Suppliers Assn; Railway [★3291]

Signal Company Aircraft Warning Hawaii - Signal Aircraft Warning Regiment Hawaii Assn. - Defunct.

Signal Corps Regimental Assn. [20705], 4570 Dewey Dr., Martinez, GA 30907, (706)364-1755

Signal Processing Soc. [★6365]

Signal Ser. Assn; 829th [21384]

Signal Theft; Coalition Opposing [556]

Signalmen; Brotherhood of Railroad [24178]

Signers of the Declaration of Independence; Descendants of the [20671]

Significant Living [11320], 1559 E Howard St., Pasadena, CA 91104, (626)398-2394

Signing Exact English Center for the Advancement of Deaf Children [14779], PO Box 1181, Los Alamitos, CA 90720, (562)430-1467

SIGNIS [IO], Brussels, Belgium

SII Eastern Regional Users Group - Defunct.

Sikh

Coun. of Khalistan/International Sikh Org. [20557]

Council of Khalistan/International Sikh Organization [IO]

North Amer. Sikh Medical and Dental Assn. [IO]

North Amer. Sikh Medical and Dental Assn. [16416]

Punjabi-American Cultural Assn. [10223]

Sikh Amer. Legal Defense and Educ. Fund [18600]

Sikh Coun. on Religion and Educ. [20558]

Sikh Stud. Circle [20559]

World Sikh Org. [IO]

Sikh Amer. Legal Defense and Educ. Fund [18600], 1413 K St. NW, 5th Fl., Washington, DC 20005, (202)393-2700

Sikh Coun. of North America - Defunct.

Sikh Coun. on Religion and Educ. [20558], 2446 Reedie Dr., Ste. 14, Silver Spring, MD 20902, (301)946-2800

Sikh Stud. Circle [20559], Irving Sikh Ctr., 834 N Nursery Rd., Irving, TX 75061, (972)579-9646

Sikorski Museum [★IO]

Silent Film

Louise Brooks Soc. [24755]

Silent March: Amers. Against Violence [17599]

Silent Running Soc. - Defunct.

Silesian

Soc. of the Descendants of the Schwenkfeldian Exiles [21244]

Silica and Moulding Sands Assn. [IO], London, United Kingdom

Silica and Silicates Industry Assn; Synthetic Amorphous [826]

Silica Structure Engineers; Intl. Brotherhood of [★22971]

Silicates Industry Assn; Synthetic Amorphous Silica and [826]

Silicon Valley Chinese Engineers Assn. [7039], PO Box 612283, San Jose, CA 95161

Silicon Valley Chinese Engineers Assn. [IO], San Jose, CA, United States

Silicon Valley Network; Joint Venture: [7745]

Silicones Environmental, Hea. and Safety Coun. [821], 2325 Dulles Corner Blvd., Ste. 500, Herndon, VA 20171, (703)788-6570

Silicones Hea. Coun. [★821]

Silk

Indian Silk Export Promotion Coun. [IO]

Intl. Silk Assn. - U.S.A. [3789]

Japan Silk Assn. [IO]

Japan Silk and Rayon Weavers' Assn. [IO]

Silk Assn. of India [IO]

Silk Painters Intl. [9524]

Taiwan Silk and Filament Weaving Indus. Assn. [IO]

Thai Silk Assn. [IO]

Silk Assn. [★IO]

Silk Assn. of Great Britain [IO], London, United Kingdom

Silk Assn. of India [IO], Calcutta, India

Silk Assn. - U.S.A; Intl. [3789]

Silk Commn. Mfrs. Assn. - Defunct.

Silk Gp. of Silk and Man-Made Fibre Users Assn. [★IO]

Silk Painters Intl. [9524], 6806 Trexler Rd., Lanham, MD 20706, (301)474-7347

Silk and Rayon Mfrs. Assn. - Defunct.

Silk and Rayon Print Inst. - Defunct.

Silk and Rayon Printers and Dyers Assn. of America - Address unknown since 1995.

Silkie Bantam Club; Amer. [5109]

Silky Terrier Club of Am. [22360], c/o Shari MvNaire, Membership Chair, 4913 Greenwood Dr., Rosenberg, TX 77471

Silo Assn; Natl. [★181]

Silo Manufacturers; Natl. Assn. of [★181]

Silurians; Soc. of the [3165]

Silva Forest Found. [IO], Slocan Park, BC, Canada

Silver Bar Collectors; Intl. Assn. of [★22044]

Silver Eagles of Am. [9235], PO Box 1336, Flat Rock, NC 28731, (800)801-7090

Silver Fanciers; United [21924]

Silver Ghost Assn. [21783], c/o Jim Bannon, Membership Dir., 1115 Western Blvd., Arlington, TX 76013, (817)861-6605

Silver Info. Center - Defunct.

Silver Inst. [2727], 1200 G St. NW, Ste. 800, Washington, DC 20005, (202)835-0185

Silver, Joe

Skidrow Joe Fan Club [24773]

Silver Marten Rabbit Club [5160], c/o Leslie Tucker, Sec.-Treas., 2113 Sommer St., Napa, CA 94559, (707)255-2821

Silver and Pewter Collectors Soc. - Defunct.

Silver Plate Soc; Intl. Gold and [18977]

Silver Rabbit Club; Natl. [5156]

Silver Users Assn. [2728], 11240 Waples Mill Rd., No. 200, Fairfax, VA 22030, (703)930-7790

Silver Wings [24549], c/o Univ. of Illinois at Urbana-Champaign, AFROTC Detachment 190, 229 Armory Bldg., 505 E Armory Ave., Champaign, IL 61820

Silver Wings Fraternity [21476], PO Box 44208, Cincinnati, OH 45244, (513)732-5852

Silver Wyandotte Club of Am. [5118]

Silvermine Guild of Artists [★9471]

Silvermine Guild Arts Center [9471], 1037 Silvermine Rd., New Canaan, CT 06840-4398, (203)966-9700

Silvermine Guild Center for the Arts [★9471]

Silversmiths; Soc. of Amer. [3712]

Simcoe County Brain Injury Assn. [IO], Barrie, ON, Canada

Simian Soc. of Am. [11457], c/o Mel Orr, Sec., 6 Stephens St., Dillsburg, PA 17019, (717)432-9205

Simmental Assn; Amer. [4248]

Simmental Assn; Amer. Junior [★4248]

Simon DeMontfort Soc. - Defunct.

Simon Found. [★16711]

Simon Found. - Canada [★IO]

Simon Found. for Continence [16711], PO Box 815, Wilmette, IL 60091, (847)864-3913

Simon Found; William E. [17474]

Simon Inst; Yves R. [10841]

Simon Wiesenthal Center [17724], 1399 S Roxbury Dr., Los Angeles, CA 90035, (310)553-9036

Simon Wiesenthal Center [IO], Los Angeles, CA, United States

Simple Soc. [★18637]

Simple Soc. Alliance for Human Empowerment [18637], 379 Amherst St., No. 234, Nashua, NH 03063

Simplex Motorbike Register - Defunct.

Simplified Spelling Soc. [IO], Wellesbourne, United Kingdom

Simply Divoon - Jayne Mansfield Fan Club - Address unknown since 1999.

A star before a book entry number signifies that the name is not listed separately, but is mentioned within the entry.

Simply Love [★10191]

Simply Love Found. [10191], PO Box 8888, Albuquerque, NM 87198

Simply Simon - Official Simon MacCorkindale Fan Club - Address unknown since 1994.

SIMPUTER (USA) [13301], Hickory Grove Bus. Park, 6630-J E Harris Blvd., Charlotte, NC 28215, (704)535-4774

Simulation Alliance; Intl. Training and [6735]

Simulation Assn; Intl. Building Performance [6652]

Simulation Councils, Inc. [★6746]

Simulation Councils, Inc. [★IO]

Simulation and Experiential Learning; Assn. for Bus. [8015]

Simulation and Gaming Assn; North Amer. [8455]

Simulation Indus. Assn. of Australia [IO], Lindfield, Australia

Simulation Interoperability Standards Org. [7760], c/o Van Lowe, 3280 Progress Dr., Orlando, FL 32826, (407)882-1348

Simulation and Learning; Intl. Nursing Assn. for Clinical [15485]

Simulation; Special Interest Gp. on [6753]

Sinatra, Frank
   Intl. Sinatra Soc. [24913]
   Sinatra Soc. of Am. [24995]

Sinatra Music Soc. [IO], Burntwood, United Kingdom

Sinatra Soc. of Am. [24995], PO Box 2705, Toluca Lake, CA 91610

Sinclair Assn. U.S.A; Clan [20863]

Sinclair Soc. of the U.S; Prince Henry [9922]

Sindacato Nazionale Scuola CGIL [★IO]

Sindacato Unitario Nazionale Inquilini ed Assegnatari [IO], Rome, Italy

Sindh Journalists' Network for Children [IO], Karachi, Pakistan

Sindicato da Industria da Construcao Civil no Estado do Rio de Janeiro [★IO]

Sindicato de Industriales de Panama [★IO]

Sindicato Nacional da Industria de Componentes para Veiculos Automotores [★IO]

Sindicato del Personal de la Oficina Internacional de Trabajo [★IO]

Sindikat vzgoje izobrazevanja, znanosti in kulture Slovenije [★IO]

The Sinfonia Fraternity [★24555]

Sing No More (no war no more) - Defunct.

Sing With the Earth John Denver Fan Club - Address unknown since 1988.

Singapore
   Malaysia/Singapore/Brunei Stud. Gp. of the Southeast Asia Coun. Assn. for Asian Stud. [7987]
   Singapore Amer. Bus. Assn. [763]

Singapore ACM SIGGRAPH [IO], Singapore, Singapore

Singapore Aircargo Agents Assn. [IO], Singapore, Singapore

Singapore Amateur Athletic Assn. [IO], Singapore, Singapore

Singapore Amer. Bus. Assn. [IO], Redwood City, CA, United States

Singapore Amer. Bus. Assn. [763], 333 Twin Dolphin Dr., Ste. 145, Redwood City, CA 94065, (415)252-1150

Singapore Assn. of Administrative Professionals [IO], Singapore, Singapore

Singapore Assn. of Convention and Exhibition Organisers and Suppliers [IO], Singapore, Singapore

Singapore Assn. for the Deaf [IO], Singapore, Singapore

Singapore Assn. of the Inst. of Chartered Secretaries and Administrators [IO], Singapore, Singapore

Singapore Assn. of Occupational Therapists [IO], Singapore, Singapore

Singapore Assn. of Personal and Executive Secretaries [★IO]

Singapore Assn. of Pharmaceutical Indus. [IO], Singapore, Singapore

Singapore Assn. of Social Workers [IO], Singapore, Singapore

Singapore Assn. of the Visually Handicapped [IO], Singapore, Singapore

Singapore Badminton Assn. [IO], Singapore, Singapore

Singapore Baseball and Softball Assn. [IO], Singapore, Singapore

Singapore Bus. and Professional Women's Assn. [IO], Singapore, Singapore

Singapore Chamber of Commerce - Hong Kong [IO], Hong Kong, People's Republic of China

Singapore Chefs Assn. [IO], Raffles City, Singapore

Singapore Chinese Chamber of Commerce and Indus. [IO], Singapore, Singapore

Singapore Clock and Watch Trade Assn. [IO], Singapore, Singapore

Singapore Cmpt. Soc. [IO], Singapore, Singapore

Singapore Confed. of Indus. [★IO]

Singapore Contractors Assn. Ltd. [IO], Singapore, Singapore

Singapore Corporate Counsel Assn. [IO], Singapore, Singapore

Singapore Cricket Assn. [IO], Singapore, Singapore

Singapore Cycle and Motor Traders' Assn. [IO], Singapore, Singapore

Singapore DanceSport Fed. [IO], Singapore, Singapore

Singapore Dental Assn. [IO], Singapore, Singapore

Singapore Disability Sports Coun. [IO], Singapore, Singapore

Singapore Drama Educators Assn. [IO], Singapore, Singapore

Singapore Economic Development Bd. [IO], Singapore, Singapore

Singapore Env. Connecticut [IO], Singapore, Singapore

Singapore Floorball Assn. [IO], Singapore, Singapore

Singapore Freight Forwarders Assn. [★IO]

Singapore Fruits and Vegetables Importers and Exporters Assn. [IO], Singapore, Singapore

Singapore Furniture Assn. [IO], Singapore, Singapore

Singapore Furniture Indus. Coun. [IO], Singapore, Singapore

Singapore Girl Guides Assn. [★IO]

Singapore Hotel Assn. [IO], Singapore, Singapore

Singapore Indian Chamber of Commerce [★IO]

Singapore Indian Chamber of Commerce and Indus. [IO], Singapore, Singapore

Singapore Indian Fine Arts Soc. [IO], Singapore, Singapore

Singapore Indus. Automation Assn. [IO], Singapore, Singapore

Singapore Infocomm Tech. Fed. [IO], Singapore, Singapore

Singapore Inst. of Architects [IO], Singapore, Singapore

Singapore Inst. of Food Sci. and Tech. [IO], Singapore, Singapore

Singapore Inst. of Intl. Affairs [IO], Singapore, Singapore

Singapore Inst. of Landscape Architects [IO], Singapore, Singapore

Singapore Intl. Arbitration Centre [IO], Singapore, Singapore

Singapore Intl. Chamber of Commerce [IO], Singapore, Singapore

Singapore Intl. Franchise Assn. [★IO]

Singapore Inventors' Development Assn. [IO], Singapore, Singapore

Singapore Investment Banking Assn. [IO], Singapore, Singapore

Singapore Jewellers Assn. [IO], Singapore, Singapore

Singapore Junior Chefs Club [IO], Singapore, Singapore

Singapore Logistics Assn. [IO], Singapore, Singapore

Singapore Malay Teachers' Union [IO], Singapore, Singapore

Singapore Mfrs. Fed. [IO], Singapore, Singapore

Singapore Mathematical Soc. [IO], Singapore, Singapore

Singapore Medical Assn. [IO], Singapore, Singapore

Singapore Merchant's Bankers Assn. [★IO]

Singapore Metal and Machinery Assn. [IO], Singapore, Singapore

Singapore Microcomputer Soc. [IO], Singapore, Singapore

Singapore Natl. Comm. of the Intl. Assn. on Water Pollution Res. and Control [★IO]

Singapore Natl. Comm. of the Intl. Assn. on Water Quality [★IO]

Singapore Natl. Comm. of the Intl. Water Assn. [IO], Singapore, Singapore

Singapore Natl. Employers Fed. [IO], Singapore, Singapore

Singapore Natl. Olympic Coun. [IO], Singapore, Singapore

Singapore Natl. Shippers' Coun. [IO], Singapore, Singapore

Singapore Natl. Stroke Assn. [IO], Singapore, Singapore

Singapore Netherlands Assn. [IO], Hoofddorp, Netherlands

Singapore Penjing and Stone Appreciation Soc. [IO], Singapore, Singapore

Singapore Planned Parenthood Assn. [IO], Singapore, Singapore

Singapore Plastic Indus. Assn. [IO], Singapore, Singapore

Singapore Productivity Assn. [IO], Singapore, Singapore

Singapore Psychological Soc. [IO], Singapore, Singapore

Singapore Radiological Soc. [IO], Singapore, Singapore

Singapore Red Cross [IO], Singapore, Singapore

Singapore Reinsurers' Assn. [IO], Singapore, Singapore

Singapore Retailers Assn. [IO], Singapore, Singapore

Singapore Robotics Assn. [★IO]

Singapore Sailing Fed. [IO], Singapore, Singapore

Singapore Scout Assn. [IO], Singapore, Singapore

Singapore Soc. of Finance Analysts [★IO]

Singapore Squash Rackets Assn. [IO], Singapore, Singapore

Singapore Taekwondo Fed. [IO], Singapore, Singapore

Singapore Timber Assn. [IO], Singapore, Singapore

Singapore Tourism Bd. [IO], Singapore, Singapore

Singapore Trade Development Bd. [★IO]

Singapore Turf Club [IO], Singapore, Singapore

Singapore Venture Capital and Private Equity Assn. [IO], Singapore, Singapore

Singapore Veterinary Assn. [IO], Singapore, Singapore

Singapore Water Assn. [IO], Singapore, Singapore

Singapore Water Ski and Wakeboard Fed. [IO], Singapore, Singapore

Singaporean Soc. for Mass Spectrometry [IO], Singapore, Singapore

Singer Found; Harry [18450]

Singer Nelson Charlmers; Intersure - [2191]

Singer Owners' Club [IO], Stamford, United Kingdom

Singers Alliance of Am; Polish [10687]

Singers Assn; North Amer. [10680]

Singers Assn; Professional Women [10689]

Singers Club; Amer. [21841]

Singers; Soc. of [12621]

Singers Union; North Amer. [★10680]

Singing in Am; Soc. for the Preservation and Encouragement of Barber Shop Quartet [10704]

Singing; Amer. Acad. of Teachers of [8898]

Singing; Natl. Assn. of Teachers of [8923]

Single Adoptive Parents; Natl. Council for [11256]

Single Booklovers [22142], PO Box 1658, Andalusia, PA 19020, (215)638-9966

Single and Custodial Fathers Network [12691], 608 Hastings St., Pittsburgh, PA 15206, (412)853-9903

Single Dad's Hotline - Defunct.

Single Dog Lovers Assn. - Address unknown since 2007.

Single-Footed Horse Assn; North Amer. [★4937]

Single-footing Horse Assn; North Amer. [4937]

Single-Footing Horse Found; Morgan [4915]

Single Global Currency Assn. [17021], PO Box 390, Newcastle, ME 04553, (207)586-6078

Single Global Currency Assn. [IO], Newcastle, ME, United States

Single Gourmet [19388], 211 South St., No. 331, Philadelphia, PA 19147, (215)732-0260

Single Mothers By Choice [12692], PO Box 1642, New York, NY 10028, (212)988-0993

Reference to "IO" in place of a book number signifies that the association may be found in the 45th edition of International Organizations.

Single Parent Coalition; Natl. [★12693]
Single Parent Rsrc. Center [12693], 31 E 28th St., 2nd Fl., New York, NY 10016-7923, (212)951-7030
Single Parents Comm. [★11256]
Single Persons for Tax Equality Assn. - Address unknown since 1995.
Single Ply Roofing Assn. [IO], London, United Kingdom
Single Ser. Inst. [★1157]
Single Shot Rifle Assn; Amer. [23714]
Singles
   Amer. Singles Golf Assn. [13106]
   Inst. of Singles Dynamics [20281]
   Loners of Am. [22956]
   Natl. Assn. of Single People [13107]
   Natl. Org. of Single Mothers [13108]
   Single Booklovers [22142]
   Singles in Agriculture [22143]
   Singles Press Assn. [3251]
   Unmarried-Catholics Correspondence Club [22145]
Singles in Agriculture [22143], 118 E Front Ave., Stockton, IL 61085, (815)947-3559
Singles Dynamics; Inst. of [20281]
Singles Press Assn. [3251], PO Box 2139, Sioux Falls, SD 57101, (800)825-6632
Singles in Ser. [13064], c/o Hands on Sacramento, 909 12th St., Ste. 200, Sacramento, CA 95814, (916)447-7063
Sinistral Sig - Address unknown since 2001.
Sinkers Conf; Intl. Die [★24012]
Sinkies Intl. [★22594]
Sinkies Intl. [★IO]
Sino-American Amity [★19016]
Sino-American Amity Fund [19016], 86 Riverside Dr., New York, NY 10024, (212)787-6969
Sino-American Buddhist Assn. [★19548]
Sino-American Cooperative Org. [21405], c/o Willie Baker, 2810 Highlands Blvd., Spring Valley, CA 91977
Sino-Amer. Cultural Comm. [★9793]
Sino-Amer. Cultural Comm. [★IO]
Sino-Amer. Cultural Soc. [IO], Rockville, MD, United States
Sino-Amer. Cultural Soc. [9793]
Sino-Amer. Network for Educal. Exchange - Address unknown since 2003.
Sino-American Pharmaceutical Professionals Assn. [15951], PO Box 282, Nanuet, NY 10954
Sir Arthur Sullivan Soc. [IO], Liskeard, United Kingdom
Sir Douglas Quintet Fan Club - Address unknown since 1999.
Sir Henry Royce Memorial Found. [IO], Towcester, United Kingdom
Sir Thomas Beecham Soc. [10697], 85 Morningside Dr., Falling Waters, WV 25419-4052
Sirenian Intl. [5016], 200 Stonewall Dr., Fredericksburg, VA 22401-2110
Sirenian Intl. [IO], Fredericksburg, VA, United States
Sistema de la Integracion CentroAmericana [IO], Antiguo Cuscatlan, El Salvador
Sistema Internacional de Informacion y Documentacion de Derechos Humanos [★IO]
Sister Cities Intl. [IO], Washington, DC, United States
Sister Cities Intl. [17913], 1301 Pennsylvania Ave. NW, Ste. 850, Washington, DC 20004, (202)347-8630
Sister Formation Conf. [★19708]
Sister Island Proj. [11788], c/o Victoria Santos, Co-Dir., PO Box 1413, Langley, WA 98260, (360)321-4012
Sister Kenny Found. [★16335]
Sister Kenny Inst. [★16335]
Sister Kenny Rehabilitation Inst. [16335], 800 E 28th St., Minneapolis, MN 55407, (612)863-4466
Sister to Sister Network - Defunct.
Sisterhood for Action; Black Women in [13422]
Sisterhood Agenda [11092], 524 Ridge St., Newark, NJ 07104, (973)230-2765
Sisterhood of Am; Supreme Lodge of the Danish [19032]
Sisterhood of Black Single Mothers - Address unknown since 1991.

Sisterhood is Powerful Inst. - Address unknown since 1986.
Sisterhood of Shoers [1355], 804 Vann St., Vidalia, GA 30474
Sisterhoods; Natl. Fed. of Temple [★20192]
Sisters of Am; Big Bros. Big [11676]
Sisters; Assn. of Contemplative [20563]
Sisters of Charity - Halifax [IO], Halifax, NS, Canada
Sisters of Charity of Saint Jeanne Antide Thouret [IO], Rome, Italy
Sisters of Charity of Saint Vincent de Paul [★IO]
Sisters Concerned for the Rural Poor [★12590]
Sisters' Conf; Natl. Black [19671]
Sisters of the Congregation of Saint Agnes [★19618]
Sisters in Crime [4069], PO Box 442124, Lawrence, KS 66044, (785)842-1325
Sisters of the Cross of Chavanod [IO], Geneva, Switzerland
Sisters of Divine Providence [IO], Munster, Germany
Sisters of the Good Shepherd [★IO]
Sisters of Life [20480], St. Frances de Chantal Convent, 198 Hollywood Ave., Bronx, NY 10465, (718)863-2264
Sisters Network [13873], 8787 Woodway Dr., Ste. 4206, Houston, TX 77063, (713)781-0255
Sisters of Our Lady of Charity of the Good Shepherd [IO], Rome, Italy
Sisters of Saint Dominic; Maryknoll [20355]
Sisters of Saint Joseph of the Sacred Heart [IO], North Sydney, Australia
Sisters of Saint Louis [IO], Killiney, Ireland
Sisters of St. Peter Claver; Missionary [20364]
Sisters, Servants of the Immaculate Heart of Mary; IHM Volunteer Prog. of the [20346]
Sisters of the Soc. of Mary - Marist Missionary Sisters; Missionary [20365]
Sisters; United Order True [19437]
Sisters Vocation Conf; Natl. [★19692]
SisterSong Women of Color Reproductive Hea. Collective [18826], PO Box 311020, Atlanta, GA 31131, (404)344-9629
Sit-In for Survival - Defunct.
Site Safe New Zealand [IO], Wellington, New Zealand
Sitters; Natl. Assn. of Pet [★2961]
Sitters; Natl. Assn. of Professional Pet [2961]
Situational Mgt. and Inter-Learning Est. Soc. [IO], Calcutta, India
Six of One Club: The Prisoner Appreciation Soc. [25043], 871 Clover Dr., North Wales, PA 19454-2749, (215)699-2527
Six; Southern Assn. on Children Under [★11722]
Sixth Infantry Div; Natl. Assn. of the [★20704]
Sixth Infantry Div; Natl. Assn. of the [20704]
Sixth Infantry/Motorized Div; Natl. Assn. of the [★20704]
Sixth Marine Div. Assn. [21406], c/o Florence Doman, Membership Mgr., 704 Cooper Ct., Arlington, TX 76011-5550
Sixty Now - Defunct.
Size Acceptance Assn; Intl. [12645]
Size Standard Comm; Dredging Industry [18293]
Size and Weight Discrimination; Coun. on [12644]
Sjoessuradoererenas Foerening [★IO]
Sjogren's Syndrome Assn; Natl. [16373]
Sjogren's Syndrome Found. [16376], 6707 Democracy Blvd., Ste. 325, Bethesda, MD 20817, (301)530-4420
Sjogren's Syndrome Found. [IO], Bethesda, MD, United States
Sjoraddningssallskapet [★IO]
Skaggs Intl. Fan Club; Ricky [24968]
Skandinavisk Museumsforbund Danske Afdeling [★IO]
Skat Found. [IO], St. Gallen, Switzerland
Skate Canada [IO], Ottawa, ON, Canada
Skate Sailing Assn. of America - Address unknown since 2001.
Skaters Guild of Am; Professional [★23738]
Skaters; U.S. Fed. of Amateur Roller [★23742]
Skating
   Armenia Skating Fed. [IO]
   Australia Ice Racing Coun. [IO]
   Austrian Fed. of Roller Skating and Inline Skating [IO]

   Brazilian Ice Sports Fed. [IO]
   Bulgarian Skating Fed. [IO]
   Central Collegiate Hockey Assn. [23483]
   Chinese Figure Skating Assn. [IO]
   Croatian Skating Fed. [IO]
   Cyprus Ice Skating Fed. [IO]
   Czech Figure Skating Assn. [IO]
   Czech Speed Skating Fed. [IO]
   Danish Skating Union [IO]
   Estonian Skating Union [IO]
   Fed. of Artistic Roller Skating [IO]
   Fed. of Inline Speed Skating [IO]
   Figure Skating Fed. of the Republic of Uzbekistan [IO]
   Figure Skating Fed. of Russia [IO]
   Figure and Speed Skating Assn. of Thailand [IO]
   Georgian Figure Skating Assn. [IO]
   Hellenic Ice Sports Fed. [IO]
   Hong Kong Skating Union [IO]
   Hungarian Natl. Skating Fed. [IO]
   Ice Skating Assn. of India [IO]
   Ice Skating Australia [IO]
   Ice Skating Inst. [3600]
   Ice Speed Skating New Zealand [IO]
   Icelandic Skating Assn. [IO]
   Intl. Gay Figure Skating Union [23736]
   Intl. Inline Skating Assn. [IO]
   Intl. Skating Union [IO]
   Israel Ice Skating Fed. [IO]
   Japan Skating Fed. [IO]
   Korea Skating Union [IO]
   Latvian Skating Assn. [IO]
   Lithuanian Skating Fed. [IO]
   Lithuanian Speed Skating Assn. [IO]
   Marathon Skating Intl. [23737]
   Natl. Ice Skating Assn. of the United Kingdom [IO]
   New Zealand Ice Skating Assn. [IO]
   Philippine Skating Union [IO]
   Polish Figure Skating Assn. [IO]
   Polish Speed Skating Assn. [IO]
   Professional Skaters Assn. [23738]
   Roller Skating Assn. Intl. [3601]
   RollerSoccer Intl. Fed. [23850]
   Romanian Skating Fed. [IO]
   Russian Skating Union [IO]
   Scottish Ice Skating Assn. [IO]
   Senior Roller Skaters of Am. [23739]
   Serbia and Montenegro Skating Assn. [IO]
   Skate Canada [IO]
   Skating Assn. for the Blind and Handicapped [23740]
   Skating Assn. of The Democratic People's Republic of Korea [IO]
   Skating Fed. of Azerbaijan Republic [IO]
   Skating Fed. of Bosnia and Herzegovina [IO]
   Skating Fed. of The Republic of Kazakhstan [IO]
   Skating Union of Belarus [IO]
   Skating Union of Mongolia [IO]
   Slovak Figure Skating Assn. [IO]
   Slovak Speed Skating Union [IO]
   Slovene Skating Union [IO]
   Soc. of Roller Skating Teachers of Am. [23741]
   South African Figure Skating Assn. [IO]
   South African Speed Skating Assn. [IO]
   Speed Skating Canada [IO]
   Turkish Ice Sports Fed. [IO]
   Ukrainian Figure Skating Fed. [IO]
   United Kingdom Skateboarding Assn. [IO]
   U.S. Amateur Confed. of Roller Skating [23742]
   U.S. Barrel Jumping Assn. [23743]
   U.S. Figure Skating Assn. [23744]
   U.S. Speedskating [23745]
   USA Roller Sports [23746]
   Western Collegiate Hockey Assn. [23489]
   Women's Flat Track Derby Assn. [23747]
Skating Assn. for the Blind and Handicapped [23740], 2607 Niagara St., Buffalo, NY 14207, (716)362-9600
Skating Assn. of The Democratic People's Republic of Korea [IO], Pyongyang, Democratic People's Republic of Korea
Skating Assn; U.S. Amateur Roller [★23742]
Skating Assn; U.S. Intl. [★23745]
Skating Fed. of Azerbaijan Republic [IO], Baku, Azerbaijan

A star before a book entry number signifies that the name is not listed separately, but is mentioned within the entry.

Skating Fed. of Bosnia and Herzegovina [IO], Sarajevo, Bosnia-Herzegovina
Skating Fed. of The Republic of Kazakhstan [IO], Almaty, Kazakhstan
Skating Inst. of Am; Ice [★3600]
Skating Inst; Ice [3600]
Skating Operators Assn. of Am; Roller [★3601]
Skating Rink Operators Assn; Roller [★3601]
Skating Union of Belarus [IO], Minsk, Belarus
Skating Union of Mongolia [IO], Ulan Bator, Mongolia
Skeet Shooting Assn; Natl. [23725]
Skeletal Disorders Found; Jaw Joints and Allied Musculo- [15773]
Skeletal Radiology; Soc. of [16304]
Skeleton Fed; U.S. Bobsled and [23767]
Skeptical Stud; Soc. for [7493]
Skeptics Soc. [7629], PO Box 338, Altadena, CA 91001, (626)794-3119
Sketch Club; Etch-A- [22994]
Ski Area Management - Defunct.
Ski Areas of Am; Cross Country [★3660]
Ski Areas Assn; Cross Country [3660]
Ski Areas Assn; Natl. [1961]
Ski Assn. of Am; Natl. [★23760]
Ski Assn; Amer. Water [★23979]
Ski Assn; Eastern [★23760]
Ski Assn; Midwest Collegiate [★23760]
Ski Assn; Natl. Collegiate [★23760]
Ski Assn; Natl. Collegiate Water [23977]
Ski Assn; U.S. [★23760]
Ski Boating Assn; Intl. Jet [★23976]
Ski nautique et planche Canada [★IO]
Ski Coun. of America - Defunct.
Ski Council; Canadian [★3660]
Ski Coun. of the Federated Mountain Clubs of New Zealand [★IO]
Ski Educ. Found; Pacific Northwest [★23754]
Ski Educational Found; Amer. Water [23975]
Ski Indus. Assn. [★3671]
Ski Indus. Assn; Water [★3655]
Ski Instructors of Am. Educational Foundation; Professional [★23755]
Ski for Light [★23361]
Ski for Light [23361], 1455 W Lake St., Minneapolis, MN 55408, (612)827-3232
Ski for Light [IO], Minneapolis, MN, United States
Ski for Light [★IO]
Ski Representative Assn; Midwest Winter [★3666]
Ski Representatives Assn; Eastern [★3661]
Ski Representatives Assn; Midwest [★3666]
Ski Resort Marketing Assn. - Defunct.
Ski Retailers Coun. - Defunct.
Ski Retailers Intl. - Defunct.
Ski and Snowboard Assn; U.S. Deaf [23366]
Ski and Snowboard Retailers Assn; Natl. [3646]
Ski Touring Assn; Natl. [★23934]
Ski Touring Coun. - Defunct.
Ski Touring Operators' Assn; Natl. [★3660]
Ski; USA Water [23979]
Skidrow Joe Fan Club [24773]
Skiers Assn; Natl. Amputee [★23343]
Skiers' Training Trust - Defunct.
Skiing
   Amateur Ski Instructors Assn. [23748]
   Amer. Barefoot Club [23974]
   Amer. Birkebeiner Ski Found. [23749]
   Amer. Blind Skiing Found. [23336]
   Amer. Cross Country Skiers [23750]
   Amer. Mountain Guides Assn. [23284]
   Amer. Ski-Bike Assn. [23801]
   Amer. Volkssport Assn. [23803]
   Amer. Water Ski Educational Found. [23975]
   Assn. for Promotion of Skiing [IO]
   British Assn. of Ski Patrollers [IO]
   British Assn. of Snowsport Instructors [IO]
   Camping Women [23269]
   Canadian Masters' Cross Country Ski Assn. [IO]
   Canadian Ski Coun. [IO]
   Canadian Ski Patrol Sys. [IO]
   Canadian Ski and Snowboard Professionals [IO]
   Cross Country Ski Areas Assn. [3660]
   Cross Country Ski Nova Scotia [IO]
   Cyprus Ski Club [IO]
   Edinburgh Ski Touring Club [IO]

   German Ski Fed. [IO]
   Icelandic Ski Assn. [IO]
   Intl. Ski Dancing Assn. [23751]
   Intl. Ski Fed. [IO]
   Intl. Skiing History Assn. [IO]
   Intl. Skiing History Assn. [10965]
   Kanata Cross Country Ski Club [IO]
   Melbourne Nordic Ski Club [IO]
   Midwest Winter Sports Representatives Assn. [3666]
   Natl. Brotherhood of Skiers [23752]
   Natl. Ski Patrol Sys. [23753]
   Natl. Ski and Snowboard Retailers Assn. [3646]
   New Zealand Snowsports Coun. [IO]
   Over the Hill Gang, Intl. [23846]
   Pacific Northwest Ski Assn. [23754]
   Professional Ski Instructors of Am. [23755]
   Schuss Ski Club [IO]
   Scottish Ski Club [IO]
   Snowsport England [IO]
   Snowsport GB [IO]
   Snowsport Scotland [IO]
   SnowSports Indus. Am. [3671]
   Sydney Ski Club [IO]
   Tajikistan Ski Fed. [IO]
   U.S. Biathlon Assn. [23756]
   U.S. Collegiate Ski and Snowboard Assn. [23757]
   U.S. Hydrofoil Assn. [23978]
   U.S. Monoski Assn. [23863]
   U.S. Ski Coaches Assn. [23758]
   U.S. Ski Mountaineering Assn. [23759]
   U.S. Ski and Snowboard Assn. [23760]
   U.S. Ski Team Found. [23761]
   U.S. Telemark Ski Assn. [23762]
   USA Water Ski [23979]
   Western Winter Sports Representatives Assn. [3675]
   World Masters Cross-Country Ski Assn. [23763]
   World Masters Cross-Country Ski Assn. [IO]
   Worldloppet/American Birkebeiner [IO]
   Worldloppet/American Birkebeiner [23764]
Skiing Found; Amer. Blind [23336]
Skill Standards Coun; Mfg. [7696]
Skillshare Africa [★IO]
Skillshare Botswana [IO], Gaborone, Botswana
Skillshare Intl. [IO], Leicester, United Kingdom
SkillsUSA [8546], PO Box 3000, Leesburg, VA 20177-0300, (703)777-8810
Skin Assn; Amer. [14195]
Skin Cancer Found. [13874], 149 Madison Ave., Ste. 901, New York, NY 10016, (212)725-5176
Skin Care Assn. of Am. [★1085]
Skin Disease Inst; Inflammatory [14265]
Skin Diseases Info. CH; Natl. Inst. of Arthritis and Musculoskeletal and [16372]
Skin and Leather Assn; U.S. Hide, [2421]
Skin and Leather Merchants; Amer. Assn. of Hide, [★2421]
Skin Types; Found. for Ichthyosis and Related [14201]
Skinner Associates; Tom [★20033]
Skinner Leadership Inst. [20033], 5875 Solomons Island Rd., PO Box 190, Tracys Landing, MD 20779, (301)261-9800
Skinner Surname Org. [21051], c/o Gregg Legutki, PO Box 2594, Rancho Cucamonga, CA 91729
Skinners' Company [IO], London, United Kingdom
Skioasamband Islands [★IO]
Skirmish Assn; North-South [23727]
Skirt Contractors Assn; Greater Blouse and [★237]
Skirt Mfrs; Industrial Coun. of Cloak, Suit and [★253]
Skirt, Pajama and Sportswear Manufacturers; Natl. Assn. of [★221]
Skirt and Sportswear Assn; Natl. [★254]
Skirt and Sportswear Assn; New York [254]
Skirt and Undergarment Assn; Greater Blouse, [237]
Sko and Textilhandlarna [★IO]
Skogsindustrierna [★IO]
Skolenes Landsforbund [IO], Oslo, Norway
Skuespillerunionen [★IO]
Skull Base Soc; North Amer. [15401]
Skyaid Org. [14349], 8800 SE 45th St., Mercer Island, WA 98040, (206)498-6004
Skye Terrier Club of Am. [22361], c/o Lynne Kuczynski Veazie, Sec., 1215 Pennsylvania Ave., Emmaus, PA 18049-3515, (610)965-8619

Skyhawk Assn; Cessna [★21435]
Skylane Soc; Cessna [★21435]
Skylark Club; 1953-54 Buick [21554]
Skylight
   Natl. Fenestration Rating Coun. [648]
Skyline Hikers of the Canadian Rockies [IO], Vegreville, AB, Canada
SkyTruth [4637], PO Box 3283, Shepherdstown, WV 25443-3283, (304)876-9113
Slade Fan Club; Mark [24758]
Slag Assn; Natl. [652]
Slag Cement Assn. [935], 12926 Dairy Ashford Rd., Ste. 160, Sugar Land, TX 77478, (281)242-1258
Slant 6 Club of Am. [21784]
Slant 6 Club of Am; Dart/Valiant [★21784]
Slate Inst; Expanded Shale Clay and [621]
Slate, Tile and Composition Roofers, Damp and Waterproof Workers Assn; United [★24033]
Slavery Intl; Anti- [IO]
Slavery and Trafficking; Coalition to Abolish [12370]
Slaves; Free the [12371]
Slavic
   Amer. Assn. for the Advancement of Slavic Stud. [10966]
   Amer. Assn. of Teachers of Slavic and East European Languages [9125]
   Amer. Comm. of Slavists [10967]
   British Assn. for Slavonic and East European Stud. [IO]
   Intl. Coun. for Central and East European Stud. [IO]
   Natl. Coun. for Eurasian and East European Res. [10968]
   Natl. Slavic Convention [19360]
   Slavic and East European Folklore Assn. [9962]
   Slavic Gospel Assn. [20395]
   Slavic Heritage Coalition [10969]
   World Fellowship of Slavic Evangelical Christians [19984]
Slavic Amer. Natl. Assn. - Defunct.
Slavic Awareness - Defunct.
Slavic Bibliographic and Documentation Center - Defunct.
Slavic and East European Folklore Assn. [9962], c/o Jeanmarie Rouhier-Willoughby, Sec.-Treas., Russian and Eastern Stud. and Linguistics, 1055 Patterson Off. Tower, Univ. of Kentucky, Lexington, KY 40506-0027
Slavic and East European Folklore Assn. [IO], Lexington, KY, United States
Slavic and East European Languages; Amer. Assn. of Teachers of [9125]
Slavic Gospel Assn. [20395], 6151 Commonwealth Dr., Loves Park, IL 61111, (815)282-8900
Slavic Gospel Assn. [IO], Loves Park, IL, United States
Slavic Heritage Coalition [10969], 51 W 14th St., Ste. 4R, New York, NY 10011, (212)366-5406
Slavic Stud; Amer. Assn. for the Advancement of [10966]
Slavonic Assn; Western [★19148]
Slavonic Benevolent Order of the State of Texas [★19139]
Slavonic Catholic Union; South [★19119]
Sled Dog Club; Laconia [★23395]
Sled Dog Club; Lakes Region [23395]
Sleddog Sports; Intl. Fed. of [23393]
Sleep
   Acad. of Dental Sleep Medicine [16417]
   Amer. Acad. of Sleep Medicine [16418]
   Amer. Acad. of Somnology [16419]
   Amer. Bd. of Sleep Medicine [16420]
   Amer. Sleep Apnea Assn. [16421]
   Amer. Sudden Infant Death Syndrome Inst. [16523]
   Asian Sleep Res. Soc. [IO]
   Assoc. Professional Sleep Societies [16422]
   Assn. of Polysomnographic Technologists [16423]
   Assn. of SIDS and Infant Mortality Programs [16524]
   Australasian Sleep Assn. [IO]
   Awake In Am. [18601]
   Better Sleep Coun. [16424]
   Bd. of Registered Polysomnographic Technologists [15134]

Reference to "IO" in place of a book number signifies that the association may be found in the 45th edition of International Organizations.

British Sleep Soc. [IO]
Canadian Sleep Soc. [IO]
Community Dreamsharing Network [16425]
European Sleep Res. Soc. [IO]
German Sleep Soc. [IO]
Intl. Assn. for the Stud. of Dreams [16426]
Narcolepsy Network [16427]
Natl. Sleep Found. [16428]
Sleep Res. Soc. [16429]
Tranquilliser Recovery and New Existence [IO]
World Assn. of Sleep Medicine [IO]
World Assn. of Sleep Medicine [16430]
Sleep; Assn. for the Psychophysiological Stud. of [★16429]
Sleep Assn; Specialty [1705]
Sleep Coun. (of the Intl. Sleep Products Assn.); Better [★16424]
Sleep Coun. (of the Natl. Assn. of Bedding Mfrs.); Better [★16424]
Sleep Disorders; Amer. Assn. of [★16418]
Sleep Disorders Centers; Amer. Assn. of [★16418]
Sleep Disorders Centers; Assn. of [★16418]
Sleep Products Assn; Better Sleep Coun. of the Intl. [★16424]
Sleep Res. Soc. [16429], c/o John Slater, Coor., 1 Westbrook Corporate Center, Ste. 920, Westchester, IL 60154, (708)492-1093
Sleep Societies; Assn. of Professional [★16422]
Sleeping Car Porters; Brotherhood of [★24180]
Sleepy Eye Collectors' Club of Am; Old [21934]
Slide Fastener Assn. - Defunct.
Sliding Glass Door and Window Inst. [★588]
Sligo Chamber of Commerce and Indus. [IO], Sligo, Ireland
Slim and Steve: The Bogart and Bacall Fan Club - Defunct.
Slim Whitman Collectors Intl. - Defunct.
Sling Assn; Web [★2078]
Sling and Tie Down Assn; Web [2078]
Slo-Pitch Natl. Softball [IO], Toronto, ON, Canada
Sloan Consortium [8304], Sloan Ctr., Franklin W. Olin Coll. of Engg., Olin Way, Needham, MA 02492-1200, (781)292-2523
Sloan Found; Alfred P. [18385]
Slocum Soc. [★23197]
Slocum Soc. Intl; Joshua [23197]
Sloga Fraternal Life Insurance Soc. [★19022]
Slogan Associates; Meter- [★22844]
Sloop Restoration, Inc; Hudson River [★10038]
Slovak
Czech and Slovak Assn. of Canada [IO]
Czechoslovak Soc. of Arts and Sciences [9860]
First Catholic Slovak Ladies Assn. [19361]
First Catholic Slovak Union of the U.S.A. and Canada [19362]
Natl. Slovak Soc. of the U.S.A. [19363]
Saint Andrew Abbey [11192]
Slovak-Amer. Cultural Center [10970]
Slovak-American Cultural Center [IO]
Slovak Catholic Fed. [19364]
Slovak Catholic Sokol [19365]
Slovak League of Am. [19366]
Slovak Stud. Assn. [10971]
SOKOL U.S.A. [19367]
Slovak Acad. of Sciences [IO], Bratislava, Slovakia
Slovak Aikido Assn. - Aikikai Slovakia [IO], Trnava, Slovakia
Slovak-American Cultural Center [IO], New York, NY, United States
Slovak-Amer. Cultural Center [10970]
Slovak-Amer. Natl. Coun. - Address unknown since 2002.
Slovak Assn. for Branded Products [IO], Bratislava, Slovakia
Slovak Assn. of Frisbee [IO], Bratislava, Slovakia
Slovak Assn. of Landscape Architects [IO], Bratislava, Slovakia
Slovak Athletic Fed. [IO], Bratislava, Slovakia
Slovak Badminton Fed. [IO], Bratislava, Slovakia
Slovak Baseball Fed. [IO], Bratislava, Slovakia
Slovak Catholic Fed. [19364], c/o Rev. Philip A. Altavilla, Natl. Pres., 408 N Main St., Taylor, PA 18517-1108, (570)698-5584
Slovak Catholic Fed. of Am. [★19364]
Slovak Catholic Sokol [19365], PO Box 899, 205 Madison St., Passaic, NJ 07055, (800)886-7656

Slovak Catholic Sokol; Junior [★19365]
Slovak Chamber of Commerce and Indus. [IO], Bratislava, Slovakia
Slovak Chamber of Dentists [IO], Bratislava, Slovakia
Slovak Dance Sport Fed. [IO], Bratislava, Slovakia
Slovak Dermatovenereological Soc. [IO], Bratislava, Slovakia
Slovak Electrotechnical Comm. [IO], Bratislava, Slovakia
Slovak Evangelical Union [★19219]
Slovak Family Planning Assn. [IO], Bratislava, Slovakia
Slovak Figure Skating Assn. [IO], Bratislava, Slovakia
Slovak Floorball Assn. [IO], Bratislava, Slovakia
Slovak Gymnastic Union Sokol of the U.S.A. [★19367]
Slovak Institute [★11192]
Slovak Intl. Fed. of Automatic Control - Natl. Member Org. [IO], Bratislava, Slovakia
Slovak Ladies Assn; First Catholic [19361]
Slovak League Against Epilepsy [IO], Bratislava, Slovakia
Slovak League Against Hypertension [IO], Martin, Slovakia
Slovak League of Am. [19366], 205 Madison St., Passaic, NJ 07055, (973)472-8993
Slovak League of America Heritage Found. - Address unknown since 2001.
Slovak League against Rheumatism [★IO]
Slovak Marfan Assn. [IO], Bratislava, Slovakia
Slovak Medical Assn. [IO], Bratislava, Slovakia
Slovak Medical Soc. of Infectiology [IO], Bratislava, Slovakia
Slovak Multiple Sclerosis Soc. [IO], Trnava, Slovakia
Slovak Olympic Comm. [IO], Bratislava, Slovakia
Slovak Orienteering Assn. [IO], Bratislava, Slovakia
Slovak Orthodontic Soc. [IO], Bratislava, Slovakia
Slovak Paralympic Comm. [IO], Bratislava, Slovakia
Slovak Pharmacological Soc. [IO], Bratislava, Slovakia
Slovak Physical Soc. [IO], Bratislava, Slovakia
Slovak Physiological Soc. [IO], Bratislava, Slovakia
Slovak Printing Indus. Assn. [★IO]
Slovak Relief Fund - Address unknown since 2003.
Slovak Republic Public Relations Assn. [IO], Bratislava, Slovakia
Slovak Rheumatological Soc. [IO], Piestany, Slovakia
Slovak Schoolsport Assn. [IO], Bratislava, Slovakia
Slovak Soc. of Biomedical Engg. and Medical Informatics [IO], Bratislava, Slovakia
Slovak Soc. of Cardiology [IO], Bratislava, Slovakia
Slovak Soc. of Chemotherapy [IO], Bratislava, Slovakia
Slovak Soc. of Gerontology and Geriatrics [IO], Bratislava, Slovakia
Slovak Soc. for Operations Res. [IO], Bratislava, Slovakia
Slovak Soc. of Sports Medicine [IO], Bratislava, Slovakia
Slovak Soc. of the U.S.A; Natl. [19363]
Slovak Speed Skating Union [IO], Spisska Nova Ves, Slovakia
Slovak Squash Assn. [IO], Bratislava, Slovakia
Slovak Stud. Assn. [10971], c/o Dr. Carol Skalnik Leff, Pres., Univ. of Illinois, Dept. of Political Sci., 361 Lincoln Hall, 702 S Wright St., Urbana, IL 61801, (217)244-2270
Slovak Tennis Assn. [IO], Bratislava, Slovakia
Slovak Union of Newspaper Publishers [IO], Bratislava, Slovakia
Slovak Union against Osteoporosis [IO], Piestany, Slovakia
Slovak-U.S. Bus. Coun; Czech and [2302]
Slovak Venture Capital Assn. [IO], Bratislava, Slovakia
Slovakian Orienteering Fed. [★IO]
Slovakian Physiological Soc. [IO], Bratislava, Slovakia
Slovakian Turf Club [IO], Bratislava, Slovakia
Slovene Bone Soc. [IO], Ljubljana, Slovenia
Slovene Dance Sport Fed. [IO], Ljubljana, Slovenia
Slovene Franciscan Fathers [19718], c/o Slovenian Catholic Mission, PO Box 608, Lemont, IL 60439, (630)257-2494

Slovene Hypertension Soc. [IO], Ljubljana, Slovenia
Slovene Medical Informatics Assn. [IO], Ljubljana, Slovenia
Slovene Natl. Benefit Soc. [19369], 247 W Allegheny Rd., Imperial, PA 15126-9774, (724)695-1100
Slovene Osteoporosis Patient Soc. [IO], Ljubljana, Slovenia
Slovene Physiological Soc. [IO], Maribor, Slovenia
Slovene Skating Union [IO], Ljubljana, Slovenia
Slovene Soc. for Electron Microscopy [★IO]
Slovene Soc. for Microscopy [IO], Ljubljana, Slovenia
Slovene Tennis Assn. [IO], Ljubljana, Slovenia
Slovene Union of Univ. Women [IO], Ljubljana, Slovenia
Slovene Writers' Assn. [IO], Ljubljana, Slovenia
Slovenia Sports Medicine Soc. [IO], Ljubljana, Slovenia
Slovenian
Alpine Tourist Commn. [24223]
Amer. Mutual Life Assn. [19368]
American-Slovenian Polka Found. [10549]
Slovene Natl. Benefit Soc. [19369]
Slovenian Res. Center of Am. [10972]
Slovenian Women's Union of Am. [19370]
Soc. for Slovene Stud. [19371]
Soc. for Slovene Stud. [IO]
Slovenian Acad. of Sciences and Arts [IO], Ljubljana, Slovenia
Slovenian ACM Chap. [IO], Ljubljana, Slovenia
Slovenian Advt. Chamber [IO], Ljubljana, Slovenia
Slovenian Assn. of Landscape Architects [IO], Ljubljana, Slovenia
Slovenian Assn. of Occupational Therapists [IO], Ljubljana, Slovenia
Slovenian Assn. for Pain Mgt. [IO], Maribor, Slovenia
Slovenian Assn. of Physiotherapists [IO], Ljubljana, Slovenia
Slovenian Assn. of Pulp and Paper Engineers and Technicians [IO], Ljubljana, Slovenia
Slovenian Biochemical Soc. [IO], Ljubljana, Slovenia
Slovenian Floorball Assn. [IO], Ziri, Slovenia
Slovenian Geotechnical Soc. [IO], Ljubljana, Slovenia
Slovenian League Against Epilepsy [IO], Ljubljana, Slovenia
Slovenian Medical Assn. [IO], Ljubljana, Slovenia
Slovenian Medical Soc. [IO], Ljubljana, Slovenia
Slovenian Mutual Benefit Assn. [★19368]
Slovenian Orienteering Fed. [IO], Ljubljana, Slovenia
Slovenian Orthodontic Soc. [IO], Ljubljana, Slovenia
Slovenian Pharmaceutical Soc. [IO], Ljubljana, Slovenia
Slovenian Pharmacological Soc. [IO], Ljubljana, Slovenia
Slovenian Physical Soc. [★IO]
Slovenian Polka Found; American- [10549]
Slovenian Proj. Mgt. Assn. [IO], Ljubljana, Slovenia
Slovenian Publishers Assn. [IO], Ljubljana, Slovenia
Slovenian Res. Center of Am. [10972], 29227 Eddy Rd., Willoughby Hills, OH 44092, (440)944-7237
Slovenian Res. Proj. [★10972]
Slovenian Soc. of Cardiology [IO], Ljubljana, Slovenia
Slovenian Soc. of Chemotherapy [IO], Ljubljana, Slovenia
Slovenian Soc. for Pattern Recognition [IO], Ljubljana, Slovenia
Slovenian Squash Assn. [IO], Ljubljana, Slovenia
Slovenian Taekwondo Assn. [IO], Celje, Slovenia
Slovenian Turf Club [IO], Maribor, Slovenia
Slovenian Weightlifting Fed. [IO], Velenje, Slovenia
Slovenian Women's Union [★19370]
Slovenian Women's Union of Am. [19370], 431 N Chicago St., Joliet, IL 60432, (815)727-1926
Slovenian Writers' Assn. [IO], Ljubljana, Slovenia
Slovenska dermatovenerologicka spolocnost [★IO]
Slovenska Aikido Asociacia - Aikikai Slovakia [★IO]
Slovenska Akademia Vied [★IO]
Slovenska Akademija Znanosti in Umetnosti [★IO]
Slovenska Asociacia Skolskeho Sportu [★IO]
Slovenska Asociacia Spravcivskych spolocnosti [★IO]
Slovenska Bankova Asociacia [★IO]
Slovenska Fyzikalna Spolocnost [★IO]

A star before a book entry number signifies that the name is not listed separately, but is mentioned within the entry.

Slovenska Kardiologicka Spolocnost [★IO]
Slovenska Komora Zubnych Lekarov [★IO]
Slovenska Liga Proti Hypertenzii [★IO]
Slovenska Oglasevalska Zbornica [★IO]
Slovenska Squashova Asociacia [★IO]
Slovenske hnutie specialnych olympiad [★IO]
Slovenski nacionalni komite Svetovnega ener-
 getskega sveta [IO], Ljubljana, Slovenia
Slovensko drustvo za medicinsko informatiko [★IO]
Slovensko-Americke Kulturne Stredisko [★IO]
Slovensko-Americke Kulturne Stredisko [★10970]
Slovensko Biokemijsko Drustvo [★IO]
Slovensko Drustvo Farmakologov [★IO]
Slovensko Farmacevtsko Drustvo [★IO]
Slovensko Galopsko Drustvo [★IO]
Slovensko Zdruzenje za Projektni Mgt. [★IO]
Slovensko Zdruzenje Za Zdravljenje Bolecin [★IO]
Slovensky krasokorculiarsky zvaz [★IO]
Slovensky paralympijsky vybor [★IO]
Slovensky Atleticky Zvaz [★IO]
Slovensky Olympijsky Vybor [★IO]
Slovensky Tenisovy Zvaz [★IO]
Slovensky Zvaz Florbalu [★IO]
Slovensky Zvaz Orientacnych Sportov [★IO]
Slovensky Zvaz Sclerosis Mulitplex [★IO]
Slovensky Zvaz Tanecneho Sportu [★IO]
Slow Food Intl. [IO], Bra, Italy
Slow Food USA [IO], Brooklyn, NY, United States
Slow Food USA [9971], 20 Jay St., Ste. 313,
 Brooklyn, NY 11201, (718)260-8000
Slowlane/Stay At Home Dads [18182], c/o Jay Mas-
 sey, Admin., 1216 E Lee St., Pensacola, FL 32503,
 (850)434-2626
Slurry Seal Assn; Intl. [★632]
Slurry Tech. Assn. [★842]
Slurry Transport Assn. [★842]
S.M.A; Families of [15321]
SMA Fathers [★19719]
SMA Fathers [★IO]
SMA Lay Missionaries [20396], 256 Manor Cir.,
 Takoma Park, MD 20912, (301)891-2037
Small Brewers Assn. [★198]
Small Brewers Comm. [★198]
Small Business
 Achievers Intl. [IO]
 Amer. Bus. Women's Assn. [693]
 Amer. Franchisee Assn. [1666]
 Amer. Independent Bus. Alliance [3602]
 Amer. Small Bus. Travel Alliance [3906]
 Amer. Small Businesses Assn. [3603]
 Amer. Woman's Economic Development Corp.
  [3604]
 Asian Bus. League of San Francisco [696]
 Assn. for Enterprise Opportunity [3605]
 Assn. of Small Bus. Development Centers [3606]
 BEST Employers Assn. [3607]
 Canadian Assn. of Family Enterprise [IO]
 Center for Family Business [709]
 Coalition for Govt. Procurement [1741]
 Employers of Am. [3608]
 European Confed. of Independents [IO]
 Family Firm Inst. [IO]
 Family Firm Inst. [3609]
 FARMS Intl. [12427]
 Fed. of Small Businesses [IO]
 Independent Visually Impaired Enterprisers
  [16855]
 Indus. Development Bd. of Ceylon [IO]
 Inst. of Bus. Admin. and Mgt. [IO]
 Intl. Assn. for Bus. Organizations [IO]
 Intl. Assn. for Bus. Organizations [3610]
 Intl. Coun. for Small Bus. [3611]
 Intl. Coun. for Small Bus. [IO]
 Intl. Small Bus. Consortium [IO]
 Intl. Small Bus. Consortium [3612]
 Irish Small and Medium Enterprises Assn. [IO]
 Kauffman Center for Entrepreneurial Leadership
  [739]
 Korea Fed. of Small and Medium Bus. [IO]
 Micro Enterprise Alliance [IO]
 Micro Indus. Development Assistance and
  Services [IO]
 Natl. Alliance for Fair Competition [3613]
 Natl. Assn. of Business Leaders [3614]
 Natl. Assn. for Bus. Organizations [3615]

 Natl. Assn. of Equity Source Banks [488]
 Natl. Assn. of Home Based Businesses [1921]
 Natl. Assn. of Private Enterprise [3616]
 Natl. Assn. for the Self-Employed [3617]
 Natl. Assn. of Small Bus. Investment Companies
  [3618]
 Natl. Bus. Assn. [3619]
 Natl. Bus. Owners Assn. [3620]
 Natl. Center for Fair Competition [3621]
 Natl. Family Bus. Coun. [748]
 Natl. Fed. of Independent Bus. [3622]
 Natl. Small Bus. Assn. [3623]
 North Amer. Assn. of Subway Franchisees [1670]
 Pakistan Small Indus'. Assn. [IO]
 PUSH Commercial Div. [12098]
 Res. Inst. for Small and Emerging Bus. [3624]
 Sales Professionals USA [3474]
 SCORE [3625]
 Shareholders Res. Alliance [3391]
 Singapore Economic Development Bd. [IO]
 Small Bus. and Entrepreneurship Coun. [3626]
 Small Bus. Legislative Coun. [3627]
 Small Bus. Ser. Bur. [3628]
 Small Bus. in Telecommunications [3629]
 Small and Medium-Size Indus. Development Org.
  [IO]
 Small Publishers Assn. of North Am. [3254]
 SME Union - Small and Medium Enterprises
  Union of the EPP [IO]
 SOHO Am. [3630]
 Structured Employment Economic Development
  Corp. [12045]
 Support Services Alliance [3631]
 U.S. Assn. for Small Bus. and Entrepreneurship
  [3632]
Small Bus. Assistance Center [★3628]
Small Business Assn. of Apparel Mfrs. - Address
 unknown since 1995.
Small Bus. Assn; Natl. [★3623]
Small Business Coalition for Pollution Control -
 Defunct.
Small Bus. Coun. of Am. [17350], PO Box 2283,
 Wilmington, DE 19899, (302)691-7222
Small Business Development Corp. - Defunct.
Small Bus. and Entrepreneurship Coun. [3626],
 2944 Hunter Mill Rd., Ste. 204, Oakton, VA 22124,
 (703)242-5840
Small Bus. Exporters Assn. [★2313]
Small Bus. Exporters Assn. of the U.S. [2313], c/o
 James Morrison, Pres., 1156 15th St. NW, Ste.
 1100, Washington, DC 20005, (202)659-9320
Small Bus. Found. of Am. [★3624]
Small Bus. Intl. Trade Educators; Natl. Assn. of
 [★8031]
Small Bus. Investment Companies; Amer. Assn. of
 Minority Enterprise [★2764]
Small Bus. Legislative Coun. [3627], 1100 H St. NW,
 Ste. 540, Washington, DC 20005, (202)639-8500
Small Bus. Mgt. Development; Natl. Comm. for
 [★3611]
Small Business Network - Address unknown since
 2004.
Small Bus. Ser. Bur. [3628], 554 Main St., PO Box
 15014, Worcester, MA 01615-0014, (508)756-3513
Small Business Support Center Assn. - Address
 unknown since 1994.
Small Bus. Survival Comm. [★3626]
Small Bus. in Telecommunications [3629]
Small Business Timber Coun. - Defunct.
Small Bus. United [★3623]
Small Bus. United; Natl. [★3623]
Small Coll. Athletic Assn; Natl. [★23859]
Small Computers in the Arts Network - Defunct.
Small Craft Assn; Traditional [21885]
Small Craft Designers; Soc. of [2593]
Small Domestic Elecl. Appliance Manufacturers'
 Assn. [IO], Barcelona, Spain
Small Elecl. Appliance Marketing Assn. [IO], Cater-
 ham, United Kingdom
Small Engine Servicing Dealers Assn. - Defunct.
Small Explorers and Producers Assn. of Canada
 [IO], Calgary, AB, Canada
Small Firms Assn. [IO], Dublin, Ireland
Small Foundations; Assn. of [18267]
Small Hydro Soc. - Defunct.

Small Independent Record Mfrs. Assn. - Defunct.
Small Investor Protection Assn. [IO], Markham, ON,
 Canada
Small Landlords Assn. [★IO]
Small Luxury Hotels [★1966]
Small Luxury Hotels Assn. [★1966]
Small Luxury Hotels of the World [1966], 370
 Lexington Ave., Ste. 1506, New York, NY 10017,
 (212)953-2064
Small Luxury Hotels of the World [★1966]
Small and Medium-Size Indus. Development Org.
 [IO], Coromandel, Mauritius
Small and Mid-Size Metallurgic Indus. Assn. [IO],
 Santiago, Chile
Small Motor Mfr. Assn. [★IO]
Small Motor Mfr. Assn. [★1198]
Small Motors and Motion Assn. [★1198]
Small Motors and Motion Assn. [★IO]
Small Museum Assn. [10514], c/o Michael DiPaolo,
 Lewis Historical Soc., 110 Shipcarpenter St.,
 Lewes, DE 19958, (302)645-7670
Small Press Center for Independent Publishing
 [3252], 20 W 44th St., New York, NY 10036,
 (212)764-7021
Small Press Writers and Artists Org. - Address
 unknown since 1999.
Small Publishers, Artists and Writers Network
 [3253], PMB 123, 323 E Matilija St., Ste. 110, Ojai,
 CA 93023, (818)886-4281
Small Publishers, Artists and Writers Network [IO],
 Ojai, CA, United States
Small Publishers Assn. of North Am. [3254], 1618 W
 Colorado Ave., Colorado Springs, CO 80904,
 (719)475-1726
Small and Rural Hosp. Assn; Amer. [★16248]
Small Telecommunications Companies; Org. for the
 Promotion and Advancement of [3964]
Small Towns Inst. - Defunct.
SmallCommunity.org [★17214]
Smaller Business of America - Defunct.
Smaller Mfrs. Medical Device Assn. [★3486]
Smart Card Alliance [7761], 191 Clarksville Rd.,
 Princeton Junction, NJ 08550, (800)556-6828
Smart Card Indus. Assn. [★7761]
SMART Recovery [16519], 7537 Mentor Ave., Ste.
 306, Mentor, OH 44060, (440)951-5357
S.M.A.R.T. (Secretive Societies, Mind Control and
 Ritual Abuse) [13296], PO Box 1295, Easthamp-
 ton, MA 01027
Smart Set Intl. - Defunct.
Smartmac User Group - Address unknown since
 2005.
SMARTRISK [IO], Toronto, ON, Canada
Smartshoppers Intl. - Defunct.
SME Found. [★8373]
SME; Machining Tech. Assn. of [★7025]
SME Union - Small and Medium Enterprises Union
 of the EPP [IO], Brussels, Belgium
Smell Inst; Sense of [1664]
Smelter Workers; Intl. Union of Mine, Mill and
 [★24137]
Smile Alliance Intl. [11721], PO Box 240, Cle Elum,
 WA 98922, (509)674-2274
SMILE - Defunct.
Smile Intl; Oper. [★12534]
Smile; Oper. [★12534]
Smith Assn; Lewis J. [8274]
Smith Collectors Assn; L.C. [22429]
Smith Commemorative Soc; Kate [24930]
Smith; Friends of Kate [★24930]
Smith/God Bless Am. Found; Kate [★24930]
Smith-Hedrick Family Assn. [21052], 1164 Heber
 Springs Rd. S, Heber Springs, AR 72543-8464,
 (501)362-2180
Smith-Magenis Syndrome; PRISMS: Parents and
 Researchers Interested In [14476]
Smith Soc; Bessie [24847]
Smith Soc; Thorne [9715]
Smithsonian Science Information Exchange -
 Defunct.
SMMA - The Assn. for Elec. Motors, Their Control
 and Application [★1198]
SMMA - The Assn. for Elec. Motors, Their Control
 and Application [★IO]
SMMA - The Motor and Motion Association [IO],
 South Dartmouth, MA, United States

Reference to "IO" in place of a book number signifies that the association may be found in the 45th edition of International Organizations.

SMMA - The Motor and Motion Assn. **[1198]**, PO Box P182, South Dartmouth, MA 02748, (508)979-5935

Smocking Arts Guild of Am. **[22174]**, PO Box 2846, Grapevine, TX 76099, (800)520-3101

Smoke Control Assn. - Defunct.

Smoke Prevention Assn. of Amer. **[★5081]**

Smoke Prevention Assn. of Amer. **[★IO]**

Smoke Watchers - Defunct.

Smokefree Am. **[★16434]**

SmokeFree Educational Services **[16434]**, c/o Michael Tacelosky, Smokescreen, 1502 21st St. NW, Washington, DC 20036, (202)955-9099

Smokeless Tobacco Coun. **[3822]**

Smokenders **[16435]**, PO Box 316, Kensington, MD 20895, (800)828-HELP

Smoker's Rights Alliance - Address unknown since 1999.

Smokers; The Universal Coterie of Pipe **[22898]**

Smokey Robinson and the Miracles Fan Club - Defunct.

Smoking
   Action on Smoking and Hea. **[16431]**
   Action on Smoking and Hea. - England **[IO]**
   Action on Smoking and Hea. - Ireland **[IO]**
   Action on Smoking and Hea. - Scotland **[IO]**
   Airspace Action on Smoking and Hea. **[IO]**
   Amer. Lung Assn. **[16354]**
   Americans for Nonsmokers' Rights **[16432]**
   APPEAL: Asian Pacific Partners for Empowerment and Leadership **[11760]**
   Asia Pacific Assn. for the Control of Tobacco **[IO]**
   Assn. for the Treatment of Tobacco Use and Dependence **[16653]**
   Canadian Coun. for Tobacco Control **[IO]**
   Cigarette Pack Collectors Assn. **[21994]**
   Coalition for Fire-Safe Cigarettes **[12191]**
   Community on Youth Smoking Prevention **[IO]**
   Cong. of Lung Assn. Staff **[16357]**
   Cystic Fibrosis Found. **[16358]**
   Doctors Ought to Care **[14554]**
   European Network for Smoking Prevention **[IO]**
   European Network on Young People and Tobacco **[IO]**
   Intl. Assn. of Pipe Smokers Clubs **[22897]**
   Intl. Network of Women Against Tobacco **[18744]**
   Lifegain Inst. **[14573]**
   Lung Cancer Alliance **[13839]**
   Natl. Center for Tobacco-Free Kids **[16433]**
   Natl. Emphysema Found. **[13932]**
   Natl. Latino Coun. on Alcohol and Tobacco Prevention **[12269]**
   On the Lighter Side, Intl. Lighter Collectors **[22100]**
   Quit **[IO]**
   SmokeFree Educational Services **[16434]**
   Smokenders **[16435]**
   Tobacco Control Rsrc. Center **[13331]**
   The Universal Coterie of Pipe Smokers **[22898]**

Smoking Policy Inst. - Address unknown since 1994.

Smoking Pollution; California Gp. Against **[★16432]**

SMOLOSKYP, Ukrainian Info. Ser. **[17450]**, PO Box 8041, Bridgewater, NJ 08807, (908)725-5322

SMOLOSKYP, Ukrainian Info. Ser. **[IO]**, Bridgewater, NJ, United States

Smurf Collectors' Club Intl. - Defunct.

SMV Fan Club **[24975]**

Snack Food Assn. **[1562]**, 1600 Wilson Blvd., Ste. 650, Arlington, VA 22209, (703)836-4500

Snaffle Bit Assn; Natl. **[4926]**

Snipe Class Intl. Racing Assn. **[23219]**, c/o Jerelyn W. Biehl, Exec. Dir., 2812 Canon St., San Diego, CA 92106-2742, (619)224-6998

Snipe Class Intl. Racing Assn. **[IO]**, San Diego, CA, United States

Snodgrass Clan Soc. **[21053]**, 8221 Stonewall Dr., Vienna, VA 22180-6947.

Snow Biz - Address unknown since 2006.

Snow Conf; Western **[7845]**

Snow and Ice Mgt. Assn. **[6325]**, 2221-C Peninsula Dr., Erie, PA 16510, (814)835-3577

Snow Sports
   Alberta Snowboarding Assn. **[IO]**
   Amateur Ski Instructors Assn. **[23748]**
   Amer. Assn. of Snowboard Instructors **[23765]**

Amer. Avalanche Assn. **[12948]**
Amer. Blind Skiing Found. **[23336]**
Amer. Coun. of Snowmobile Associations **[23766]**
Amer. Mountain Guides Assn. **[23284]**
Amer. Ski-Bike Assn. **[23801]**
Antique Snowmobile Club of Am. **[22943]**
Arctic Cat Club of Am. **[22944]**
Assn. of the Intl. Olympic Winter Sports Federations **[IO]**
Assn. of Ontario Snowboarders **[IO]**
British Columbia Snowboard Assn. **[IO]**
British Snowboard Assn. **[IO]**
Canadian Assn. of Snowboard Instructors **[IO]**
Canadian Coun. of Snowmobile Organizations **[IO]**
Canadian Snowboard Fed. **[IO]**
Intl. Fed. of Sleddog Sports **[23393]**
Intl. Ski Dancing Assn. **[23751]**
Intl. Skiing History Assn. **[10965]**
Intl. Sled Dog Racing Assn. **[23394]**
Intl. Snowmobile Mfrs. Assn. **[3368]**
Lakes Region Sled Dog Club **[23395]**
Marathon Skating Intl. **[23737]**
Midwest Winter Sports Representatives Assn. **[3666]**
Natl. Ski Patrol Sys. **[23753]**
Natl. Ski and Snowboard Retailers Assn. **[3646]**
North Amer. Ski Joring Assn. **[23845]**
Nova Scotia Snowboard Assn. **[IO]**
Nova Scotia Snowboarding Assn. **[IO]**
Pacific Northwest Ski Assn. **[23754]**
Professional Ski Instructors of Am. **[23755]**
Saskatchewan Snowboard Assn. **[IO]**
Siberian Husky Club of Am. **[22359]**
Snow Sports New Zealand **[IO]**
Snowsport Wales **[IO]**
SnowSports Indus. Am. **[3671]**
Snowsports South Africa **[IO]**
U.S. Biathlon Assn. **[23756]**
U.S. Bobsled and Skeleton Fed. **[23767]**
U.S. Collegiate Ski and Snowboard Assn. **[23757]**
U.S. Cross Country Snowmobile Racing Assn. **[23768]**
U.S. Monoski Assn. **[23863]**
U.S. Ski Coaches Assn. **[23758]**
U.S. Ski and Snowboard Assn. **[23760]**
U.S. Ski Team Found. **[23761]**
U.S. Snowshoe Assn. **[23769]**
U.S. Telemark Ski Assn. **[23762]**
World Masters Cross-Country Ski Assn. **[23763]**
Worldloppet/American Birkebeiner **[23764]**

Snow Sports New Zealand **[IO]**, Wellington, New Zealand

Snowboard Assn; British **[IO]**

Snowboard Assn; U.S. Deaf Ski and **[23366]**

Snowboard Assn; U.S. Ski and **[23760]**

Snowboard Instructors; Amer. Assn. of **[23765]**

Snowboard Instructors; Canadian Assn. of **[IO]**

Snowboard Retailers Assn; Natl. Ski and **[3646]**

Snowmobile Associations; Amer. Coun. of **[23766]**

Snowmobile Club of Am; Antique **[22943]**

Snowmobiles
   Amer. Coun. of Snowmobile Associations **[23766]**
   Antique Snowmobile Club of Am. **[22943]**
   Arctic Cat Club of Am. **[22944]**
   BlueRibbon Coalition **[23680]**
   Intl. Snowmobile Mfrs. Assn. **[3368]**
   U.S. Cross Country Snowmobile Racing Assn. **[23768]**

Snowshoe Racing
   U.S. Snowshoe Assn. **[23769]**

Snowsport England **[IO]**, Halesowen, United Kingdom

Snowsport GB **[IO]**, Midlothian, United Kingdom

Snowsport Scotland **[IO]**, Midlothian, United Kingdom

Snowsport Wales **[IO]**, Cardiff, United Kingdom

SnowSports Indus. Am. **[3671]**, 8377-B Greensboro Dr., McLean, VA 22102-3587, (703)556-9020

Snowsports South Africa **[IO]**, Norkem Park, Republic of South Africa

Snuff Bottle Soc; Chinese **[★21890]**

Snuff Producers Coun. **[★3822]**

SNV/Organisation Neerlandaise de Developpement au Burkina Faso **[★IO]**

Soap Box Derby
   Intl. Soap Box Derby **[23770]**
   Natl. Derby Rallies **[23771]**

Soap and Detergent Assn. **[822]**, 1500 K St. NW, Ste. 300, Washington, DC 20005, (202)347-2900

Soap and Detergent Indus. Assn. **[★IO]**

Soap Opera Friends - Address unknown since 1999.

Soaps and Detergents Indus. Assn. **[IO]**, Istanbul, Turkey

Soaring Assn. of Canada **[IO]**, Ottawa, ON, Canada

Soaring Assn; Collegiate **[23039]**

Soaring Found; Natl. **[23042]**

Soaring Soc. of Am. **[23043]**, PO Box 2100, Hobbs, NM 88241-2100, (505)392-1177

Soays of Am. **[5218]**, PO Box 551, Gig Harbor, WA 98335

Sobriety; Secular Organizations for **[13281]**

Sobriety; Women for **[13284]**

SOC **[IO]**, East Lothian, United Kingdom

SOC; Friends of Israel Missionary and Relief **[★20010]**

Soccer
   African Football Confed. **[IO]**
   Am. Scores **[23772]**
   Amer. Amputee Soccer Assn. **[23773]**
   Amer. Youth Soccer Org. **[23774]**
   Asean Football Fed. **[IO]**
   Asian Football Confed. **[IO]**
   Assyrian Chaldean Athletics of North Am. **[23062]**
   Australian Football Assn. of North Am. **[23429]**
   Big East Conf. **[23807]**
   Big Ten Conf. **[23808]**
   Calgary United Soccer Assn. **[IO]**
   Calgary Women's Soccer Assn. **[IO]**
   Canadian Soccer Assn. **[IO]**
   Cosmopolitan Soccer League **[23775]**
   Coun. of Ivy Gp. Presidents **[23817]**
   Cyprus Football Assn. **[IO]**
   Danish Football Assn. **[IO]**
   Eastern Coll. Soccer Assn. **[23776]**
   Eastern Collegiate Hockey Assn. **[23485]**
   English Schools Football Assn. **[IO]**
   Estonian Football Assn. **[IO]**
   Football Assn. of the Czech Republic **[IO]**
   Football Assn. of England **[IO]**
   Football Assn. of Iceland **[IO]**
   Football Assn. of Ireland **[IO]**
   Football Assn. of Moldova **[IO]**
   Football Fed. of Armenia **[IO]**
   Football Fed. Australia **[IO]**
   Football Fed. of Ukraine **[IO]**
   Football Union of Russia **[IO]**
   Grassroot Soccer **[11330]**
   Indoor Soccer Coaches Assn. **[23288]**
   Intl. Fed. of Assn. Football **[IO]**
   Intl. Gay and Lesbian Football Assn. **[IO]**
   Intl. Gay and Lesbian Football Assn. **[23777]**
   Latvian Football Fed. **[IO]**
   Malta Football Assn. **[IO]**
   Natl. Assn. of Intercollegiate Athletics **[23835]**
   Natl. Collegiate Athletic Assn. **[23838]**
   Natl. Intercollegiate Soccer Officials Assn. **[23778]**
   Natl. Junior Coll. Athletic Assn. **[23843]**
   Natl. Soccer Coaches Assn. of Am. **[23779]**
   North Amer. Chinese Soccer League **[23780]**
   North Amer. Chinese Soccer League **[IO]**
   North Amer. Sports Fed. **[23065]**
   Norwegian Football Assn. **[IO]**
   Pacific 10 Conf. **[23847]**
   Polish Football Assn. **[IO]**
   Portuguese Football Fed. **[IO]**
   Professional Footballers' Assn. **[IO]**
   RollerSoccer Intl. Fed. **[23850]**
   Royal Belgian Football Assn. **[IO]**
   Scottish Football Assn. **[IO]**
   Soccer Assn. for Youth **[23781]**
   Soccer Indus. Coun. of Am. **[3651]**
   Soccer in the Streets **[11789]**
   Southeastern Conf. **[23851]**
   Southern Conf. **[23852]**
   Union of European Football Associations **[IO]**
   U.S. Adult Soccer Assn. **[23857]**
   U.S. Collegiate Athletic Assn. **[23859]**
   U.S. Collegiate Sports Coun. **[23860]**
   U.S. Futsal Fed. **[23862]**

A star before a book entry number signifies that the name is not listed separately, but is mentioned within the entry.

U.S. Indoor Soccer Assn. [23782]
U.S. Power Soccer Assn. [23783]
U.S. Youth Soccer Assn. [23784]
US Club Soccer [23785]
US Soccer [23786]
USA Sanatan Sports and Cultural Assn. [23787]
Valley Intl. Foosball Assn. [1717]
Soccer Assn. for Youth [23781], 1 N Commerce Park Dr., Ste. 306-320, Cincinnati, OH 45215, (513)769-3800
Soccer Football Assn; U.S. [★23786]
Soccer Indus. Coun. of Am. [3651], c/o Sporting Goods Mfrs. Assn., 1150 17th St. NW, Ste. 850, Washington, DC 20036, (202)775-1762
Soccer Officials Assn; Natl. Intercollegiate [23778]
Soccer Officials Bur; Eastern [★23776]
Soccer Officials Bur; Eastern Coll. [★23776]
Soccer in the Streets [11789], 2323 Perimeter Park Dr. NE, Atlanta, GA 30341, (770)452-0505
Soccer U.S.A; SAY [★23781]
Social Accountability Intl. [18828], 220 E 23rd St., Ste. 605, New York, NY 10010, (212)684-1414
Social Accountability Intl. [IO], New York, NY, United States

Social Action
AIDS Treatment Activists Coalition [11324]
All One Heart [17080]
Alliance for Southern African Progress [12417]
Amer. Decency Assn. [17281]
Amer. Soc. for Kurds [13154]
Anti-Child Pornography Org. [12766]
Anti-Racist Action-Los Angeles/People Against Racist Terror [17092]
Aouon Archv. [9418]
Applied Res. Center [18635]
Assn. of Community Organizations for Reform Now [11749]
Assyrian Aid Soc. of Am. [11508]
Bertrand Russell Soc. [9637]
Black Women United for Action [13423]
A Call to Serve Intl. [11765]
Center for Community and Org. Development [11750]
Center for the Stud. of Political Graphics [9434]
Central Bur., Catholic Central Union of Am. [19610]
Christian Community Development Assn. [20278]
Citizens for Consumer Justice [18641]
Coalition for Fire-Safe Cigarettes [12191]
The Creative Coalition [18290]
Debts AIDS Trade Africa [16928]
Democracy for Am. [18291]
Disciples Justice Action Network [19793]
Educating for Justice [9126]
Empower Prog. [8945]
Enough Is Enough [17923]
ESA [18602]
Evangelical Social Action Commn. [20005]
Free Wheelchair Mission [11947]
Fresh Lifelines for Youth [13484]
Generation Green [17054]
GeoHazards Intl. [12633]
Global AIDS Alliance [13565]
Global Bus. Coalition on HIV/AIDS [11329]
Global Youth Connect [18851]
Goree Inst. [IO]
Indicorps [12406]
Indify [13488]
Innovations in Civic Participation [17075]
Intl. Coalition for Children and the Env. [4636]
Intl. Comm. for the Rescue of KAL 007 Survivors [18541]
Interreligious Found. for Community Org. [11797]
Jesuit Volunteer Corps: Northwest [19644]
Joint Action in Community Ser. [11803]
Just Think [18852]
"Love Yourself" Stop the Violence [17250]
Mapendo Intl. [12868]
May I Speak Freely Media [18028]
Midwest Acad. [11751]
Mothers Against Sexual Predators At Large [13079]
Natl. Alliance to Nurture the Aged and the Youth [12358]
Natl. Assn. for the Advancement of Haitian Descendents [19097]

Natl. Assn. of Neighborhoods [11752]
Natl. Center for Urban Ethnic Affairs [11753]
Natl. Community Action Found. [11754]
Natl. Organizers Alliance [13136]
Natl. People's Action [11755]
Natl. Training and Info. Center [11799]
Neurosurgeons to Preserve Hea. Care Access [15414]
North Star Fund [12657]
Oper. HOPE, Inc. [11787]
Ophelia Proj. [13509]
Organize Training Center [11800]
Rapha Intl. [12539]
Rsrc. Center for Nonviolence [18122]
September 11th Families' Assn. [13371]
Sewalanka Found. [IO]
Southern Mutual Help Assn. [11790]
Starthrowers [18603]
Torture Abolition and Survivors Support Coalition Intl. [17786]
Women's Assn. for Educ. and Social Action [IO]
Youth Impact Intl. [13521]
Social Action; Behaviorists for [★18607]
Social Action Commn; Evangelical [20005]
Social Action; Evangelicals for [★18602]
Social Action; Methodist Fed. for [20264]
Social Action of Reform Judaism; Commn. on [★20177]
Social Activist Professors Defense Found. - Defunct.
Social Anthropology in Eastern Oceania; Assn. for [★6413]
Social Anxiety Australia [IO], Indooroopilly, Australia
Social and Behavioral Sci. Computing; Special Interest Gp. for [★6542]
Social Biology; Soc. for the Stud. of [6862]
Social Care Assn. [IO], Surbiton, United Kingdom
Social Change
20/20 Vision Natl. Proj. [18277]
100 Black Men of Am. [18865]
A. Philip Randolph Inst. [18604]
Adbusters Media Found. [IO]
Advocacy Inst. [12650]
Afghans for Civil Soc. [17079]
All One Heart [17080]
Alternatives for Simple Living [18605]
Amer. Leadership Forum [18001]
Aouon Archv. [9418]
Applied Res. Center [18635]
Aquarian Res. Found. [18606]
Asian Pacific Americans for Progress [17012]
Association des Chercheurs Iraniens [IO]
Behaviorists for Social Action [18607]
Black Leadership Forum [18867]
Black Women United for Action [13423]
Blue Earth Alliance [10847]
Brotherhood Org. of a New Destiny [18608]
Brotherhood Org. of a New Destiny [IO]
Canadian Centre for Policy Alternatives [IO]
Center for Religion, Ethics and Social Policy [18609]
Center on Religion and Soc. [20491]
Center for the Stud. of Political Graphics [9434]
Center on Urban Poverty and Community Development [18377]
Center for Visionary Leadership [18002]
Central Bur., Catholic Central Union of Am. [19610]
Club of Rome [IO]
Coalition for Justice in the Maquiladoras [IO]
Coalition for Justice in the Maquiladoras [18610]
Context Inst. [18611]
Creative Resources Guild [18612]
Eco-Justice Working Group [18613]
Educating for Justice [9126]
Empower Prog. [8945]
Episcopal Peace Fellowship [18614]
Equal Justice Soc. [6258]
Evangelical Social Action Commn. [20005]
Findhorn Found. [IO]
Found. on Economic Trends [18615]
Free Speech TV [18726]
Freedom of Thought Found. [18616]
Global Action Proj. [18849]
Graduation Pledge Alliance [18617]
Graduation Pledge Alliance [IO]

Green Party of the U.S. [18325]
Groundwork for a Just World [18618]
Groundwork for a Just World [IO]
Healing the Culture [12788]
Independent Progressive Politics Network [18619]
Indicorps [12406]
Indify [13488]
Innovations in Civic Participation [17075]
Interhelp [18620]
Interhelp [IO]
International Society for Panetics [IO]
Intl. Soc. for Panetics [18621]
Intl. Symbiosis Soc. [18622]
Intl. Symbiosis Soc. [IO]
Jesuit Volunteer Corps: Northwest [19644]
Just Think [18852]
Justice Stud. Assn. [13109]
May I Speak Freely Media [18028]
McLibel Support Campaign - UK [IO]
Midwest Acad. [11751]
Natl. Comm. for Responsive Philanthropy [12732]
Natl. Image [19102]
Natl. Organizers Alliance [13136]
Natl. Partnership for Social Enterprise [18623]
NETWORK, A Natl. Catholic Social Justice Lobby [18624]
North Star Fund [12657]
Oper. HOPE, Inc. [11787]
Peace Rsrc. Proj. [18625]
People's Inst. for Survival and Beyond [18626]
PolicyLink [18276]
Positive Futures Network [18839]
Praxis Proj. [17204]
Progressive Tech. Proj. [7758]
Proj. South: Inst. for the Elimination of Poverty and Genocide [17872]
Proutist Universal [18627]
Public Conversations Proj. [17189]
Public Media Center [17190]
Quaker Coun. for European Affairs [IO]
Questscope for Social Development in the Middle East - Jordan [IO]
Questscope for Social Development in the Middle East - United Kingdom [IO]
Quixote Center [IO]
Quixote Center [18628]
School of Living [10178]
Social Enterprise Alliance [3633]
Social Relief Intl. [12445]
Soc. for Socialist Stud. [IO]
Southeast Inst. for Gp. and Family Therapy [18629]
Southern Mutual Help Assn. [11790]
Tanzania Debate Assn. [IO]
Technocracy Inc. [18630]
Toronto Action for Social Change [IO]
Universal Proutist Youth Fed. [18631]
Venus Proj. [18632]
Women Proutists [18633]
Women's Intl. League for Peace and Freedom, U.S. Sect. [18256]
Women's Proj. [18634]
WorkingAbroad Projects [IO]
Social Change; Assn. for Interdisciplinary Res. in Values and [12906]
Social Change; Biblical Inst. for [20490]
Social Change; Martin Luther King, Jr. Center for [★18116]
Social Change; Martin Luther King, Jr. Center for Nonviolent [18116]
Social and Civic Club; Natl. Pinochle Bugs [13055]
Social Clubs
The Associated Clubs [19372]
Assoc. Humans [IO]
Assn. of Apex Clubs of Australia [IO]
Assn. of Canadian Clubs [IO]
Bald-Headed Men of Am. [19373]
Benevolent and Loyal Order of Pessimists [22591]
British Octopush Assn. [IO]
Chemists' Club [19374]
DeMolay Intl. [19375]
DeMolay Intl. [IO]
Girl Friends [19376]
Hard Hat Brotherhood [19257]

Reference to "IO" in place of a book number signifies that the association may be found in the 45th edition of International Organizations.

Inst. of Totally Useless Skills [22593]
Jim Smith Soc. [19377]
Jim Smith Soc. [IO]
Knife and Fork Club Intl. [19378]
Lefthanders Intl. [19379]
Lois Link Intl. - USA [19380]
Lois Link Intl. - USA [IO]
The Moles [19381]
Natl. Assn. of Ladies' Circles of Great Britain and
    Ireland [IO]
Natl. Conf. of State Societies [19382]
Natl. Fed. of Grandmother Clubs of Am. [19383]
Natl. Golf Clubs' Advisory Assn. [IO]
Natl. Women's Register [IO]
No Kidding! [IO]
Outsiders Club [IO]
Overseas Brats [19384]
Procrastinators' Club of Am. [19385]
Procrastinators' Club of Am. [IO]
Rockette Alumnae Assn. [19386]
Rural Culture Soc. [19387]
Single Gourmet [19388]
Soc. for the Second Self [13102]
Sons of the Whiskey Rebellion [19389]
Stud. Circles Rsrc. Center [19390]
Stunts Unlimited [19391]
Tall Persons Club - Great Britain and Ireland [IO]
Townswomen's Guilds [IO]
Travel Professionals Intl. [IO]
UKCMG [IO]
Social Concern; Division of Christian [★19484]
Social Concern; Unitarian Universalist Assn. -
    Washington Off. for [★13135]
Social Contract Press [12658], 445 E Mitchell St.,
    Petoskey, MI 49770, (231)347-1171
Social Cooperative Grado 16 [IO], Milan, Italy
Social Democracy
    Citizens for Consumer Justice [18641]
    Equal Justice Soc. [6258]
    Intl. People's Democratic Uhuru Movement
        [17395]
    Natl. Organizers Alliance [13136]
Social Democratic and Labour Party [IO], Belfast,
    United Kingdom
Social-Democratic Party of Am. [★18335]
Social Democratic Party of Austria [IO], Vienna,
    Austria
Social Democratic Party of Denmark [IO], Frederiks-
    berg, Denmark
Social Democratic Party of Germany [IO], Berlin,
    Germany
Social Democratic Party Wales [★IO]
Social Democratic Women of Austria [★IO]
Social Democratic Youth of Denmark [IO], Frederiks-
    berg, Denmark
Social Democrats of Denmark [★IO]
Social Democrats, U.S.A. [18306], 815 15th St. NW,
    Ste. 921, Washington, DC 20005, (202)638-1515
Social Development; Office of Domestic [★19613]
Social Development; Office of Domestic [★IO]
Social Development and World Peace; Department
    of [★IO]
Social Development and World Peace; Department
    of [★19613]
Social and Economic Stud; Coun. for [18440]
Social Economics; Assn. for [6873]
Social work Educ; Commn. on Gay/Lesbian Issues
    in [★9132]
Social, Emotional and Behavioural Difficulties Assn.
    [IO], Cumbria, United Kingdom
Social Enterprise Alliance [3633], c/o Jim McClung,
    Pres., 19341 8th Ave. NW, Shoreline, WA 98177,
    (206)407-3630
Social Enterprise; Natl. Partnership for [18623]
Social Ethics in the U.S. and Canada; Amer. Soc. of
    Christian [★12128]
Social Fraternities
    Acacia [24605]
    Alpha Chi Rho [24606]
    Alpha Delta Gamma [24607]
    Alpha Delta Phi [24608]
    Alpha Delta Pi [24609]
    Alpha Epsilon Pi [24610]
    Alpha Iota Omicron [24611]
    Alpha Kappa Lambda [24612]

Alpha Lambda Tau Intl. Social Fraternity [24613]
Alpha Lambda Tau Intl. Social Fraternity [IO]
Alpha Phi Delta [24614]
Alpha Psi Lambda Natl. [24615]
Alpha Sigma Phi [24616]
Alpha Tau Omega [24617]
Beta Chi Theta Natl. Fraternity [24618]
Beta Sigma Psi Natl. Lutheran Fraternity [24619]
Beta Theta Pi [24620]
Chi Phi [24621]
Chi Psi [24622]
Delta Kappa Epsilon [24623]
Delta Lambda Phi Natl. Social Fraternity [24624]
Delta Phi [24625]
Delta Psi [24626]
Delta Sigma Pi [24627]
Delta Upsilon [24628]
Delta Upsilon [IO]
Farmhouse [24629]
Fraternity Executives Assn. [24479]
Groove Phi Groove, Social Fellowship [24630]
Hard Hat Brotherhood [19257]
Iota Nu Delta Fraternity [24631]
Kappa Alpha Order [24632]
Kappa Alpha Psi Fraternity [24633]
Kappa Alpha Psi Fraternity [IO]
Kappa Alpha Soc. [24634]
Kappa Delta Rho [24635]
Kappa Sigma [24636]
Lambda Chi Alpha [24637]
Omega Gamma Delta [24638]
Omega Psi Phi Fraternity [24639]
Phi Delta Theta Intl. Fraternity [24640]
Phi Gamma Delta [24641]
Phi Kappa Sigma [24642]
Phi Kappa Sigma [IO]
Phi Kappa Tau [24643]
Phi Kappa Theta Natl. [24644]
Phi Mu Delta [24645]
Phi Sigma Kappa [24646]
Phi Sigma Nu Native Amer. Fraternity [24647]
Pi Beta Phi [24648]
Pi Delta Psi Fraternity [24649]
Pi Kappa Alpha [24650]
Pi Kappa Phi [24651]
Pi Lambda Phi Fraternity [24652]
Psi Sigma Phi Multicultural Fraternity [24594]
Psi Upsilon [24653]
Psi Upsilon [IO]
Sigma Alpha Epsilon [IO]
Sigma Alpha Epsilon [24654]
Sigma Alpha Mu [24655]
Sigma Beta Rho Fraternity [24656]
Sigma Chi Intl. Fraternity [24657]
Sigma Nu Fraternity [24658]
Sigma Phi Beta Fraternity [24659]
Sigma Phi Epsilon [24660]
Sigma Phi Soc. [24661]
Sigma Pi Fraternity, Intl. [24662]
Sigma Pi Phi Fraternity [24663]
Sigma Tau Gamma [24664]
Tau Epsilon Phi [24665]
Tau Kappa Epsilon [24666]
Theta Chi Fraternity [24667]
Theta Delta Chi [24668]
Theta Delta Chi [IO]
Theta Xi [24669]
Zeta Beta Tau [24670]
Zeta Psi Fraternity of North Am. [24671]
Social Gerontology; The Center for [11280]
Social Gerontology; Intl. Center for [★11280]
Social Hea. Assn.; Amer. [16410]
Social and Hea. Services of the Christian Church
    (Disciples of Christ) [★13177]
Social History Soc. [IO], Lancaster, United Kingdom
Social Housing Neighbourhood Fed. of Catalonia
    [IO], Barcelona, Spain
Social Hygiene Assn.; Amer. [★16410]
Social Ideas; Found. for the Stud. of Independent
    [18010]
Social Implications of Tech; IEEE Soc. [7737]
Social Insurance; Natl. Acad. of [18647]
Social Investment Forum [18646], 1612 K St. NW,
    Ste. 650, Washington, DC 20006, (202)872-5319
Social Investment Org. [IO], Toronto, ON, Canada

Social Issues
    Ad Coun. [18384]
    Alfred P. Sloan Found. [18385]
    All One Heart [17080]
    Ambrose Monell Found. [13110]
    Ambrose Monell Foundation [IO]
    Applied Res. Center [18635]
    Assn. of Albanian Girls and Women [18382]
    Benton Found. [11764]
    Bilateral Safety Corridor Coalition [12368]
    Blue Earth Alliance [10847]
    Brecht Forum [13111]
    Brecht Forum [IO]
    Captive Daughters [18383]
    Center for Assessment and Policy Development
        [18636]
    Center for Human Services [13112]
    Center for Human Services [IO]
    Center for New Community [17210]
    Center on Urban Poverty and Community
        Development [18377]
    Chaordic Commons [7409]
    Charles Stewart Mott Found. [13113]
    Chatlos Found. [20591]
    Coalition to Abolish Slavery and Trafficking
        [12370]
    Coalition of Immokalee Workers [13458]
    Compton Found. [13114]
    Compton Found. [IO]
    Connexions Info. Sharing Services [IO]
    Coun. on Contemporary Families [12149]
    Disciples Justice Action Network [19793]
    Do Right Found. [20492]
    Doris Duke Charitable Found. [13115]
    Dudley Found. [13116]
    Edward E. Ford Found. [13117]
    Edward E. Ford Found. [IO]
    Esther A. and Joseph Klingenstein Fund [15106]
    European Coun. of Skeptical Organizations [IO]
    Free the Slaves [12371]
    Fuller Found. [13118]
    Geraldine R. Dodge Found. [13119]
    Global Ideas Bank [IO]
    Healing the Culture [12788]
    Hearst Found. [13120]
    Heartland Inst. [13121]
    Hmong Natl. Development [17815]
    Intl. Possibilities Unlimited [18642]
    Ittleson Found. [13122]
    Jesuit Social and Intl. Ministries [13172]
    John S. and James L. Knight Found. [12484]
    Joseph Drown Found. [12051]
    Kresge Found. [13123]
    Kresge Found. [IO]
    L. Mike Assn. [13124]
    Leadership Coun. of Aging Organizations [11293]
    Lifeforce Found. [IO]
    "Love Yourself" Stop the Violence [17250]
    MAD DADS (Men Against Destruction - Defending
        Against Drugs and Social Disorder) [12043]
    May I Speak Freely Media [18028]
    Media Res. Center [12511]
    Mediascope [18031]
    Nathan Cummings Found. [13125]
    Natl. Sci. and Tech. Educ. Partnership [13126]
    Needmor Fund [13127]
    Norman Found. [13128]
    Omega Theatre and the Omega Arts Network
        [9590]
    One Earth One Justice [12437]
    Open Soc. Found. for Albania [IO]
    Open Soc. Found. - Romania [IO]
    Open Soc. Found. - Sofia (Bulgaria) [IO]
    Pacific Inst. for Stud. in Development, Env., and
        Security [12120]
    Pew Charitable Trusts [13129]
    PolicyLink [18276]
    Preservation Inst. [13130]
    Protection Proj. [12377]
    Public Conversations Proj. [17189]
    Public Welfare Found. [13131]
    The Revitalization Corps [12782]
    Robert Sterling Clark Found. [11902]
    Runnymede Trust [IO]
    Samuel H. Kress Found. [13132]

A star before a book entry number signifies that the name is not listed separately, but is mentioned within the entry.

Simple Soc. Alliance for Human Empowerment [18637]
Social Policy Action Network [13138]
Soc. for the Psychological Stud. of Ethnic Minority Issues [16179]
Soc. for the Psychological Stud. of Social Issues [16182]
Soc. for the Stud. of Social Problems [13133]
South Africa Inst. of Race Relations [IO]
Surface Trans. Policy Proj. [18750]
Training for Change [13134]
Unitarian Universalist Assn. of Congregations [13135]
U.S. Bus. and Indus. Coun. Educational Found. [18638]
U.S. Peace Govt. [18250]
What Kids Can Do [18859]
Women's Intl. Coalition for Economic Justice [17475]
Women's Learning Partnership for Rights, Development, and Peace [13452]
Yves R. Simon Inst. [10841]
Social Issues Res. Associates - Defunct.
Social Issues; Soc. for the Psychological Stud. of [16182]
Social Justice
Advocacy Inst. [12650]
Advocates Intl. [17998]
A.J. Muste Memorial Inst. [18188]
All One Heart [17080]
Alliance for Full Acceptance [12213]
Amer. Constitution Soc. for Law and Policy [5603]
Amer. Friends Ser. Comm. [13148]
And Justice for All [18639]
Assn. for Honest Attorneys [5486]
Assn. for Progressive Communications [17163]
Axis of Justice [18640]
Axis of Justice [IO]
Caritas Puerto Rico [12839]
Center for Economic and Social Justice [12046]
Central Bur., Catholic Central Union of Am. [19610]
Citizens for Consumer Justice [18641]
Community Food Security Coalition [12192]
Disciples Justice Action Network [19793]
Educating for Justice [9126]
Educating for Justice [IO]
Equal Justice Soc. [6258]
European Social Network [IO]
Frontiers Intl. [11778]
Global Alliance for Justice Educ. [8766]
Global Workers Justice Alliance [18074]
Hate Free Zone [17392]
Inst. for Global Communications [7772]
Intl. Possibilities Unlimited [18642]
Intl. Possibilities Unlimited [IO]
Intl. Senior Lawyers Proj. [5502]
Jamaicans For Justice [IO]
Jesuit Social and Intl. Ministries [13172]
Jobs With Justice [18827]
JustAct: Youth Action for Global Justice [18853]
Justice Stud. Assn. [13109]
Lawyers Without Borders [18008]
Life After Exoneration Prog. [17360]
Love146 [11620]
A Matter of Justice Coalition [6012]
May I Speak Freely Media [18028]
Middle East Children's Alliance [17774]
Mission for Est. of Human Rights in Iran [17777]
Natl. Action Network [17127]
Natl. Alliance for Family Court Justice [5904]
Natl. Black Justice Coalition [18643]
Natl. Economic and Social Rights Initiative [17778]
Natl. Legal Sanctuary for Community Advancement [6015]
Natl. Organizers Alliance [13136]
Natl. Youth Court Center [18854]
No Peace Without Justice [18227]
One Earth One Justice [12437]
Partners for Peace [18230]
Peace Rsrc. Proj. [18625]
People's Decade of Human Rights Educ. [17782]
People's Rights Fund [17144]
PolicyLink [18276]

Potters for Peace [9838]
Praxis Proj. [17204]
Preamble Center [5664]
Rsrc. Generation [13137]
Ruckus Soc. [18178]
Torture Abolition and Survivors Support Coalition Intl. [17786]
Women's Intl. Coalition for Economic Justice [17475]
Women's Learning Partnership for Rights, Development, and Peace [13452]
World Org. for Human Rights USA [12381]
Young Koreans United [12485]
Social Justice; Arkansas Inst. for [★11796]
Social Justice; Commn. for [17108]
Social Justice; Inst. for [11796]
Social Justice Lobby; NETWORK, A Natl. Catholic [18624]
Social Justice; Unitarian Universalist Assn. of Congregations- Washington Off. for [★13135]
Social Justice for Women - Address unknown since 2002.
Social Legislation Information Service - Defunct.
Social Ministries; Natl. Off. of Jesuit [★13172]
Social Ministry; Jesuit Off. of [★13172]
Social Network; European [IO]
Social Philosophy; North Amer. Soc. for [10820]
Social Planning Assn; Natl. Economic and [★5593]
Social Policy Action Network [13138]
Social Policy Assn. [IO], Bath, United Kingdom
Social Policy; Center for Law and [6220]
Social Policy; Center for Religion, Ethics and [18609]
Social Policy; Center for the Stud. of [18432]
Social Policy and Development; Natl. Assembly for [★13400]
Social Policy and Practice; Natl. Center for [★13206]
Social Problems
ABLE: Assn. for Better Living and Educ. Intl. [11756]
Amer. Inst. for Full Employment [12068]
Amer. Soc. of Victimology [13360]
Bilateral Safety Corridor Coalition [12368]
Catholic Charities USA [13158]
Center for Community Action of B'Nai B'rith Intl. [11766]
Central Bur., Catholic Central Union of Am. [19610]
Coalition to Abolish Slavery and Trafficking [12370]
Coalition of Immokalee Workers [13458]
Disciples Justice Action Network [19793]
Double Trouble in Recovery [12548]
FaithTrust Inst. [12027]
Free the Slaves [12371]
Genocide Watch [17660]
Lotus Outreach [13143]
"Love Yourself" Stop the Violence [17250]
One Earth One Justice [12437]
Protection Proj. [12377]
The Revitalization Corps [12782]
Soc. for Philosophy in the Contemporary World [18274]
Soc. for the Psychological Stud. of Social Issues [16182]
Soc. of St. Vincent de Paul Coun. of the U.S. [13190]
Soc. for the Stud. of Social Problems [13133]
Soc. for Urban, Natl. and Transnational/Global Anthropology [6435]
Torture Abolition and Survivors Support Coalition Intl. [17786]
Unitarian Universalist Assn. of Congregations [13135]
U.S. Soc. for Ecological Economics [6865]
World Org. for Human Rights USA [12381]
Social Problems; Soc. for the Stud. of [13133]
Social Progress Trust Fund [★17460]
Social Progress Trust Fund [★IO]
Social Psychiatry; Intl. Assn. for [★16099]
Social Psychiatry Res. Inst. [16094], 150 E 69th St., Ste. 2H, New York, NY 10021, (212)628-4800
Social Psychiatry Seminar; San Francisco [★16089]
Social Psychology; Soc. for Personality and [7549]

Social Rehabilitation Clinic [★16231]
Social Rehabilitation Clinic [★16231]
Social Relief Intl. [12445], PO Box 540765, Omaha, NE 68154, (402)403-0130
Social Relief Intl. [IO], Omaha, NE, United States
Social Res. Assn. [IO], London, United Kingdom
Social Res; Inter-University Consortium for Political and [7525]
Social Res; Ukrainian Center for [★11064]
Social Responsibilities Round Table of the American Library Association [10387], c/o Amer. Lib. Assn., 50 E Huron St., Chicago, IL 60611, (312)280-4294
Social Responsibility
20/20 Vision Natl. Proj. [18277]
Active 20-30 Assn. of U.S./Canada [13032]
Alliance for Southern African Progress [12417]
Altrusa Intl. [13033]
AMBUCS [13034]
Artists for a Better World Intl. [9549]
As You Sow Found. [11812]
Assistance League [13035]
Assn. of Americans for Civic Responsibility [17074]
Assn. of Gospel Rescue Missions [13155]
Assn. of Univ. Leaders for a Sustainable Future [8483]
Catholic Campaign for Human Development [12713]
Catholic Central Union of Am. [13157]
Catholic Charities USA [13158]
Catholic Relief Services (U.S. Catholic Conf.) [12807]
Circle K Intl. [13037]
Civitan Intl. [13038]
Cosmopolitan Intl. [13039]
Dudley Found. [13116]
Engineers for Social Responsibility [IO]
Essential Info. [17175]
Evangelical Lutheran Good Samaritan Soc. [13168]
Food Alliance [4676]
Found. for Ethics and Meaning [7069]
Frontiers Intl. [11778]
GeoHazards Intl. [12633]
Giraffe Heroes Proj. [10185]
Good Bears of the World [13041]
Good Fellows (Old Newsboys) [13042]
Gyro Intl. [13043]
Indicorps [12406]
INFORM [18644]
Intl. Coalition for Children and the Env. [4636]
Junior Chamber Intl. [13044]
Junior Optimist Octagon Intl. [13045]
Key Club Intl. [13046]
Kiwanis Intl. [13047]
La Sertoma Intl. [13048]
Ladies of Charity of the U.S.A. [13173]
Links [13049]
Lions Clubs Intl. [13050]
Message! Products [18645]
Mexican-American Opportunity Found. [12276]
Natl. Assn. of Colored Women's Clubs [13051]
Natl. Assn. of Junior Auxiliaries [13052]
Natl. Assn. of Negro Bus. and Professional Women's Clubs [13053]
Natl. Exchange Club [13054]
NGA [13056]
Optimist Intl. [13057]
Pilot.Intl. and Pilot Intl. Found. [13058]
Presbyterian Hea., Educ. and Welfare Assn. [13184]
Quota Intl. [13059]
Rainbow/PUSH Coalition [13185]
Rallying Points [14083]
The Revitalization Corps [12782]
Rotary Intl. [13060]
Round-Table U.S.A. [13061]
Ruritan Natl. [13062]
Salvation Army [13187]
Sertoma Intl. [13063]
Singles in Ser. [13064]
Social Accountability Intl. [18828]
Social Investment Forum [18646]
Social Venture Network [764]
Soc. of St. Vincent de Paul Coun. of the U.S. [13190]

Reference to "IO" in place of a book number signifies that the association may be found in the 45th edition of International Organizations.

Encyclopedia of Associations, 46th Edition   4127

Soroptimist Intl. of the Americas [13065]
U.S. Junior Chamber of Commerce [24390]
Vietnamese Professionals Soc. [19429]
Vision USA [15730]
Volunteers of Am. [13192]
Women in Show Business for Children [13069]
World Tech. Volunteers [13196]
Zonta Intl. [13071]
Social Responsibility; Architects/Designers/Planners
for [18142]
Social Responsibility; Behaviorists for [18607]
Social Responsibility; Bus. for [707]
Social Responsibility; Cmpt. Professionals for
[18146]
Social Responsibility; Educators for [17883]
Social Responsibility in Investments; Interfaith
Comm. on [★17353]
Social Responsibility; Psychologists for [18171]
Social Responsibility; Students for [18172]
Social Revolutionary Anarchist Fed. - Address
unknown since 1995.
Social Sci; Amer. Acad. of Political and [7520]
Social Sci. Assn; Rocky Mountain [★7657]
Social Sci. Educ. Consortium [9129], c/o Natl. Coun.
for the Social Stud., 8555 16th St., Ste. 500, Silver
Spring, MD 20910, (301)588-1800
Social Sci. History Assn. [7654], c/o Journals Dept.,
Duke Univ. Press, PO Box 90660, Durham, NC
27708
Social Sci. Honor Soc; Natl. [★24672]
Social Sci. Res. Coun. [7655], 810 7th Ave., New
York, NY 10019-5818, (212)377-2700
Social Sciences
Acad. of Learned Societies for the Social Sci-
ences [IO]
Acad. of Leisure Sciences [IO]
Acad. of the Social Sciences in Australia [IO]
Alliance for Human Res. Protection [17741]
Allied Social Sci. Associations [7645]
Amer. Acad. of Political and Social Sci. [7520]
Amer. Assn. of Behavioral and Social Sciences
[6522]
Amer. Coun. of Learned Societies [10197]
Amer. Institutes for Res. in the Behavioral Sci-
ences [6523]
Amer. Rock Art Res. Assn. [6438]
Amer. Soc. of Trial Consultants [6524]
Amer. Sociological Assn. [7658]
Anisa Found. [IO]
Assn. for Africanist Anthropology [6408]
Assn. of Asian Social Sci. Res. Councils [IO]
Assn. for Evolutionary Economics [6872]
Assn. for Humanist Sociology [7660]
Assn. of Latina and Latino Anthropologists [6410]
Assn. of Muslim Social Scientists [7646]
Assn. for Political and Legal Anthropology [6411]
Assn. for Res. in Personality [7543]
Assn. of Senior Anthropologists [6412]
Assn. for Social Economics [6873]
Assn. of Social Sci. Researchers [IO]
Assn. for the Stud. of the Cuban Economy [8214]
Assn. for the Stud. of Persianate Societies [8668]
Australian and New Zealand Assn. for Leisure
Stud. [IO]
Brazilian Center for Planning and Anal. [IO]
Canadian Fed. for the Humanities and Social Sci-
ences [IO]
Center for Pacific Northwest Stud. [7647]
Center for the Stud. of Gp. Processes [7648]
Chinese Acad. of Social Sciences [IO]
Consortium of Social Sci. Associations [7649]
Convoy of Hope [12847]
European Assn. of Work and Organizational
Psychology [IO]
European Consortium for Sociological Res. [IO]
European and Mediterranean Network of the
Social Sciences [IO]
Evolutionary Anthropology Soc. [6416]
German-Japanese Soc. for Social Sciences [IO]
Giovanni Agnelli Found. [IO]
Gp. for the Use of Psychology in History [10112]
HOPOS - The Intl. Soc. for the History of
Philosophy of Sci. [9103]
Human Resources Res. Org. [6532]
Indian Assn. of Social Sci. Institutions [IO]

Indian Coun. of Social Sci. Res. [IO]
Inst. for Social Res. [7650]
Inter-University Consortium for Political and Social
Res. [7525]
Intl. Assn. for Critical Realism [IO]
Intl. Assn. for Dialogue Anal. [7244]
Intl. Assn. for Relationship Res. [7571]
Intl. Assn. for Soc. and Natural Resources [5039]
Intl. Assn. for the Stud. of Sexuality, Culture and
Soc. [9124]
Intl. Comm. for Social Sci. Info. and Documenta-
tion [IO]
Intl. Inst. of Forecasters [7106]
Intl. Inst. of Islamic Thought [10247]
Intl. Network for Social Network Anal. [7651]
Intl. Network for Social Network Anal. [IO]
Intl. Rural Sociology Assn. [7664]
Intl. Social Sci. Coun. [IO]
Intl. Soc. for the Comparative Stud. of Civilizations
[IO]
Intl. Soc. for the Comparative Stud. of Civilizations
[7652]
Intl. Soc. for New Institutional Economics [6885]
Intl. Soc. for Self and Identity [7546]
Leisure Stud. Assn. [IO]
Natl. Coun. of State Sociological Associations
[7665]
North Amer. Computational Social and Org. Sci-
ences [6740]
Org. for Social Sci. Res. in Eastern and Southern
Africa [IO]
Philippine Social Sci. Coun. [IO]
Pi Gamma Mu [IO]
Pi Gamma Mu [24672]
Psychometric Soc. [16166]
Russell Sage Found. [7653]
Social Policy Action Network [13138]
Social Res. Assn. [IO]
Social Sci. History Assn. [7654]
Social Sci. Res. Coun. [7655]
Social Sciences and Humanities Res. Coun. of
Canada [IO]
Social Sciences Services and Resources [7656]
Soc. for the Anthropology of North Am. [6425]
Soc. for the Anthropology of Religion [6426]
Soc. for East Asian Anthropology [6429]
Soc. for Evolutionary Anal. in Law [6539]
Soc. for the History of Psychology [7548]
Soc. for Philosophy in the Contemporary World
[18274]
Soc. of Psychological Hypnosis [16178]
Soc. for the Psychological Stud. of Ethnic Minority
Issues [16179]
Soc. for Social Stud. of Sci. [7633]
Soc. for the Stud. of Symbolic Interaction [7669]
Soc. for Theoretical and Philosophical Psychology
[16186]
Soc. for Urban, Natl. and Transnational/Global
Anthropology [6435]
Soc. for Vocational Psychology [7551]
Sociological Practice Assn. [7670]
Space Settlement Studies Program [6387]
Statistical, Economic and Social Res. and Training
Centre for the Islamic Countries [IO]
Swedish Social Sci. Data Archv. [IO]
Swiss Acad. of Humanities and Social Sciences
[IO]
Turkish Amer. Scientists and Scholars Assn.
[7636]
U.S. Soc. for Ecological Economics [6865]
Western Social Sci. Assn. [7657]
World Acad. of Art and Sci. [9612]
Social Sciences and Humanities Res. Coun. of
Canada [IO], Ottawa, ON, Canada
Social Sciences Services and Resources [7656], PO
Box 153, Wasco, IL 60183, (630)897-5345
Social Sciences; Soc. for Automation in the [★8132]
Social Scientists Against Nuclear War - Address
unknown since 1999.
Social Security
Alliance for Worker Retirement Security [18544]
European Inst. of Social Security [IO]
Inter-American Conf. of Social Security [IO]
Intl. Social Security Assn. [IO]
Natl. Acad. of Social Insurance [18647]

Natl. Assn. of Disability Examiners [14034]
Natl. Assn. of Disability Representatives [18648]
Natl. Assn. of Unemployment Insurance Appellate
Boards [5831]
Natl. Comm. to Preserve Social Security and
Medicare [18649]
Natl. Conf. of State Social Security Administrators
[6259]
Natl. Coun. of Social Security Mgt. Associations
[6260]
Natl. Org. of Social Security Claimants'
Representatives [18650]
Pension Res. Coun. [12702]
Pension Rights Center [12703]
United Seniors Assn. [11322]
Social Security Administrators; Conf. of State
[★6259]
Social Security Administrators; Natl. Assn. of State
[★6259]
Social Security Claimants' Representatives; Natl.
Org. of [18650]
Social Security and Medicare; Natl. Comm. to
Preserve [18649]
Social Security; Natl. Comm. to Preserve [★18649]
Social Service
Action for Child Protection [11553]
Action by Churches Together Intl. [IO]
Active 20-30 Assn. of U.S./Canada [13032]
Actors' Fund of Am. [12112]
Adopt a Dr. [12750]
Afghan Women's Assn. Intl. [13416]
AIDS Treatment Activists Coalition [11324]
All4Israel [12454]
Alliance for Worker Freedom [24217]
Altrusa Intl. [13033]
AMBUCS [13034]
Amer. Assn. of Ser. Coordinators [1985]
Amer. Assn. of State Ser. Commissions [6189]
Amer. Bar Assn. Commn. on Homelessness and
Poverty [12286]
Amer. Humane Assn. Children's Services [11556]
Amer. Inst. for Public Ser. [13150]
Amer. Jewish Joint Distribution Comm. [12464]
Amer. Rescue Workers [13153]
Amer. Soc. on Aging [11275]
Amer. Soc. for Kurds [13154]
AmeriCorps VISTA [13383]
Ananda Marga [20633]
Andolan - Organizing South Asian Workers
[24138]
Arab Community Center for Economic and Social
Services [18952]
Architecture for Humanity [11761]
Artists for a New South Africa [11911]
Asian Americans/Pacific Islanders in Philanthropy
[12710]
Assistance League [13035]
Assoc. Blind [16830]
Assn. for the Advancement of Mexican Americans
[11763]
Assn. of Christian Institutes for Social Concern in
Asia [IO]
Assn. of Community Organizations for Reform
Now [11749]
Assn. of Gospel Rescue Missions [13155]
Assn. of Retired Americans [12897]
Assn. of Social Work Boards [13200]
Assyrian Aid Soc. of Am. [11508]
Batey Relief Alliance [12835]
Bethany Christian Services Intl. [11561]
Better World Chorus [12617]
Black Mental Hea. Alliance [15193]
Bread for the Journey Intl. [12711]
Brethren Volunteer Ser. [13388]
Catholic Campaign for Human Development
[12713]
Catholic Central Union of Am. [13157]
Catholic Charities USA [13158]
Catholic Relief Services (U.S. Catholic Conf.)
[12807]
Center for Community and Org. Development
[11750]
The Center for Social Gerontology [11280]
Chaldean Fed. of Am. [9395]
Charities Aid Found. Am. [13139]

A star before a book entry number signifies that the name is not listed separately, but is mentioned within the entry.

Children of the Americas [11574]
Children's HopeChest [11578]
Christian Forum Res. Found. [20560]
Christian Found. for Children and Aging [13159]
Christians Abroad [IO]
Christians Helping Animals and People [19456]
Circle K Intl. [13037]
CitiHope Intl. [12843]
Civitan Intl. [13038]
Clinical Social Work Fed. [13201]
Coalition on Human Needs [13161]
Coffee Kids [11769]
Comm. for Humanitarian Assistance to Iranian
    Refugees [12808]
Comm. for Missing Children [12603]
Community for Creative Non-Violence [12288]
Comprehensive Day Care Programs [11539]
Confessing Synod Ministries [20561]
Corporate Alliance to End Partner Violence
    [12025]
Corporate and Found. Relations [12075]
Cosmopolitan Intl. [13039]
Coun. on Accreditation [13164]
Coun. on Contemporary Families [12149]
Coun. for Hea. and Human Services Ministries,
    United Church of Christ [13165]
Coun. of Intl. Programs USA [13202]
Coun. of Religious Volunteer Agencies [13391]
Covenant World Relief [12848]
CrisisShield UK [IO]
CRISTA Ministries [13166]
Cuban Amer. Natl. Coun. [13167]
Damien Ministries [19866]
Doe Network [12608]
Dream Factory [11691]
Evangelical Lutheran Good Samaritan Soc.
    [13168]
Experience Works [12080]
Families U.S.A. Found. [11286]
Family and Home Network [12669]
Family Support Am. [12154]
Farm Worker Hea. Services [12586]
Fatherhood Proj. [12670]
Filipino Amer. Medical Inc. [14722]
Food for Life Global [12855]
Food Providers of Am. [12392]
Foster Care Alumni of Am. [11592]
Free Wheelchair Mission [11947]
Freelancers Union [24218]
Fresh Lifelines for Youth [13484]
Frontiers Intl. [11778]
Funders' Collaborative on Youth Organizing
    [12718]
Gay and Lesbian Adolescent Social Services
    [18847]
GeoHazards Intl. [12633]
Giraffe Heroes Proj. [10185]
Global Family [13140]
Global Family [IO]
Global Healing [12450]
Global Ser. Corps [13392]
Good Bears of the World [13041]
Good Fellows (Old Newsboys) [13042]
Gyro Intl. [13043]
Healing Hands Intl. [13141]
Healing Hands Intl. [IO]
Helping Hands for the Blind [13379]
Holiday Proj. [13395]
Hong Kong Christian Inst. [IO]
House of Ruth [12029]
Humanity United in Giving Internationally [11699]
Hunters Helping Hunters [22604]
Indian Youth of Am. [12626]
Innocence in Danger - USA [11601]
Innovations in Civic Participation [17075]
Intl. Aid Serving Kids [11603]
Intl. Alliance in Ser. and Educ. [11748]
Intl. Comm. for the Children of Chechnya [11605]
Intl. Fed. of Family Associations of Missing
    Persons from Armed Conflicts [12609]
Intl. Found. for Terror Act Victims [12942]
Intl. Relief And Development [11782]
Intl. Relief Teams [12863]
Intl. Women's Coffee Alliance [11783]
Interreligious Found. for Community Org. [11797]

Iranian Refugees' Alliance [12813]
Islamic Relief USA [12865]
Israel Humanitarian Found. [12458]
Jewish Community Centers Assn. of North Am.
    [12473]
Jewish Philanthropic Fund of 1933 [12475]
Joint Action in Community Ser. [11803]
Junior Chamber Intl. [13044]
Junior Optimist Octagon Intl. [13045]
Key Club Intl. [13046]
Kids Konnected [11706]
Kiwanis Intl. [13047]
La Sertoma Intl. [13048]
Ladies of Charity of the U.S.A. [13173]
LearnWell Resources [13142]
Liberty's Promise [5809]
Life After Exoneration Prog. [17360]
Links [13049]
Lions Clubs Intl. [13050]
Little Bros. - Friends of the Elderly [11295]
Lotus Outreach [13143]
Louis and Harold Price Found. [13174]
Luz Social Services [13255]
Makassed Found. of Am. [12730]
Maniilaq Assn. [12627]
Mapendo Intl. [12868]
Mennonite Women USA [20252]
Mercy-USA for Aid and Development [12871]
Mexican-American Opportunity Found. [12276]
Midwest Acad. [11751]
Mothers Against Violence in Am. [13375]
My Good Deed [13308]
Natl. Alliance for Direct Support Professionals
    [1986]
Natl. Alliance for Hispanic Hea. [13176]
Natl. Alliance to Nurture the Aged and the Youth
    [12358]
Natl. Alliance of Vietnamese Amer. Ser. Agencies
    [19423]
Natl. Assn. of Colored Women's Clubs [13051]
Natl. Assn. of Community Development Extension
    Professionals [11784]
Natl. Assn. of Disability Representatives [18648]
Natl. Assn. of Former Foster Care Children of Am.
    [11626]
Natl. Assn. of Junior Auxiliaries [13052]
Natl. Assn. of Negro Bus. and Professional
    Women's Clubs [13053]
Natl. Assn. of Neighborhoods [11752]
Natl. Assn. of Senior Companion Proj. Directors
    [11304]
Natl. Assn. of Social Workers [13206]
Natl. Center for Urban Ethnic Affairs [11753]
Natl. Center for Victims of Crime [13366]
Natl. Coalition Against Domestic Violence [12034]
Natl. Coalition for Asian Pacific Amer. Community
    Development [11785]
Natl. Coalition for the Homeless [12296]
Natl. Coalition of Homicide Survivors [13368]
Natl. Coalition on Rural Aging [11307]
Natl. Community Action Found. [11754]
Natl. Coun. on the Aging [11309]
Natl. Day Laborer Organizing Network [24111]
Natl. Domestic Violence Hotline [12036]
Natl. Exchange Club [13054]
Natl. Fair Housing Alliance [17733]
Natl. Foster Parent Assn. [12677]
Natl. Hispanic Coun. on Aging [11310]
Natl. Human Services Assembly [13400]
Natl. Inst. of Senior Housing [12328]
Natl. Meals on Wheels Found. [11315]
Natl. Network to End Violence Against Immigrant
    Women [13433]
Natl. Network for Social Work Managers [13207]
Natl. People's Action [11755]
Natl. Relief Network [12873]
Natl. Staff Development and Training Assn.
    [13180]
Natl. Training and Info. Center [11799]
New Eyes for the Needy [12533]
New York Assn. for New Americans [12479]
NGA [13056]
Nigerian Social Workers Assn. [24142]
North Amer. Alliance for the Advancement of Na-
    tive Peoples [12631]

North Amer. Assn. of Christians in Social Work
    [13208]
North Amer. St. Newspaper Assn. [18102]
November Coalition [18690]
Oper. Gratitude [11493]
Optimist Intl. [13057]
Org. for the Relief of Underprivileged Women and
    Children in Africa [12876]
Organize Training Center [11800]
Outpost for Hope [12610]
Pact Training [11830]
Partners in Hea. [12270]
Partnership for Quality Medical Donations [12537]
Patriotic Pets [11442]
People's Involvement Corp. [13183]
Physicians for Peace [15078]
Pilot Intl. and Pilot Intl. Found. [13058]
Planet Aid [13144]
Planet Aid [IO]
Presbyterian Hea., Educ. and Welfare Assn.
    [13184]
Pro Players Assn. [13402]
Quota Intl. [13059]
Rainbow/PUSH Coalition [13185]
Rapha Intl. [12539]
Refugee Coun. USA [18500]
Residential Constr. Workers' Assn. [948]
Retired and Senior Volunteer Prog. [13403]
The Revitalization Corps [12782]
Rotary Intl. [13060]
Round-Table U.S.A. [13061]
Ruritan Natl. [13062]
Salvation Army [13187]
School Social Work Assn. of Am. [9134]
SCI - Intl. Voluntary Ser. [13404]
Search Reports, Inc./Central Registry of the Miss-
    ing [12611]
Senior Companion Prog. [13405]
Sertoma Intl. [13063]
SIMPUTER (USA) [13301]
Single and Custodial Fathers Network [12691]
Singles in Ser. [13064]
Sister Island Proj. [11788]
Smile Alliance Intl. [11721]
Social Policy Action Network [13138]
Soc. of St. Vincent de Paul Coun. of the U.S.
    [13190]
A Soldier's Wish List [11501]
Solidarity and Action Against the HIV Infection in
    India [16969]
Somali Family Care Network [19392]
Soroptimist Intl. of the Americas [13065]
Southern Mutual Help Assn. [11790]
Student/Farmworker Alliance [24054]
Teaching-Family Assn. [12169]
Tech. Assistance Collaborative [13145]
Together, Inc. [12365]
Touching Hearts [11267]
United Black Fund [12204]
United Kesrawan Soc. [19206]
United North Lebanon Soc. [18954]
U.S. Junior Chamber of Commerce [24390]
U.S. Mine Rescue Assn. [12600]
U.S.A. Harvest [12402]
Veterans' Widows Intl. Network [21357]
Vietnamese Amer. Coun. [19427]
Vision USA [15730]
Volunteers of Am. [13192]
VOSH Intl. [12543]
Watchlist on Children and Armed Conflict [11664]
Welfare Res., Inc. [13193]
Welfare to Work Partnership [13146]
Winant and Clayton Volunteers [13409]
A Wish With Wings [11728]
Women in Show Business for Children [13069]
World Orphans [11667]
Youth Advocate Prog. Intl. [11668]
Zarrow Families Found. [13197]
Zonta Intl. [13071]
Social Ser., Amer. Br; Intl. [★12595]
Social Services Commn. of the Amer. Ethical Union -
    Defunct.
Social Services; Luz [13255]
Social Sororities
    Alpha Chi Omega [24673]

Reference to "IO" in place of a book number signifies that the association may be found in the 45th edition of International Organizations.

Alpha Epsilon Phi [24674]
Alpha Gamma Delta [24675]
Alpha Omicron Pi [24676]
Alpha Phi Intl. Fraternity [24677]
Alpha Phi Intl. Fraternity [IO]
Alpha Rho Lambda Sorority [24703]
Alpha Sigma Alpha [24678]
Alpha Sigma Tau [24679]
Alpha Xi Delta Women's Fraternity [24680]
Chi Omega [24681]
Delta Delta Delta [24682]
Delta Gamma [24683]
Delta Gamma [IO]
Delta Gamma Pi Multicultural Sorority [24704]
Delta Lambda Phi Natl. Social Fraternity [24624]
Delta Phi Epsilon [24684]
Delta Phi Omega Sorority [24705]
Delta Sigma Chi Sorority [24706]
Delta Xi Nu Multicultural Sorority [24708]
Delta Xi Phi Multicultural Sorority [24685]
Delta Zeta [24686]
DIVAS of Lambda Fe Uson Sorority [24709]
Gamma Alpha Omega Sorority [24599]
Gamma Delta Pi [24710]
Gamma Gamma Chi Sorority [24711]
Gamma Phi Beta [24687]
Gamma Phi Beta [IO]
Kappa Alpha Theta [24688]
Kappa Delta [24689]
Kappa Kappa Gamma [24690]
Kappa Phi Gamma Sorority [24712]
Lambda Psi Delta Sorority [24713]
Phi Beta Chi [24691]
Phi Epsilon Phi [24692]
Phi Mu Fraternity [24693]
Phi Sigma Sigma [24694]
Sigma Delta Tau [24695]
Sigma Kappa [24696]
Sigma Kappa Found. [24697]
Sigma Lambda Alpha Sorority [24714]
Sigma Lambda Gamma Natl. Sorority [24715]
Sigma Sigma Sigma [24698]
Theta Chi Omega Multicultural Sorority [24716]
Theta Phi Alpha [24699]
Zeta Chi Phi Multicultural Sorority [24717]
Zeta Phi Beta Sorority [24604]
Zeta Tau Alpha [24700]
Social Studies
Assn. for Clinical Psychosocial Res. [16139]
Assn. for Political and Legal Anthropology [6411]
Assn. of Senior Anthropologists [6412]
Assn. for the Stud. of Free Institutions [8481]
Assn. for the Stud. of Persianate Societies [8668]
Center for Social Stud. Educ. [9127]
Intl. Assn. for Citizenship Social and Economics
  Educ. [IO]
Intl. Assn. for the Stud. of Sexuality, Culture and
  Soc. [9124]
Intl. Soc. for the History, Philosophy, and Social
  Stud. of Biology [8507]
Labor and Working Class History Assn. [8723]
Modernist Stud. Assn. [8780]
Natl. Coun. for the Social Stud. [9128]
Polanyi Soc. [10826]
Social Sci. Educ. Consortium [9129]
Soc. for the Anthropology of Religion [6426]
Soc. for East Asian Anthropology [6429]
Soc. for Urban, Natl. and Transnational/Global
  Anthropology [6435]
Social Stud. at the Louis Stein Center; Louis Finkel-
  stein Inst. for Religious and [19931]
Social Stud. of Sci; Soc. for [7633]
Social Stud; Soc. For Iranian Cultural and [★10238]
Social Venture Network [764], PO Box 29221, San
  Francisco, CA 94129-0221, (415)561-6501
Social/Vocational Rehabilitation Clinic [16231]
Social Welfare
9/11 Families for a Secure Am. [18728]
Action for Child Protection [11553]
ActionAid Intl. USA [11758]
Active 20-30 Assn. of U.S./Canada [13032]
Actors' Fund of Am. [12112]
Adopt a Dr. [12750]
Advocating Change Together [11914]
Afghan Community Org. of London [IO]

Afghans for Civil Soc. [17079]
Airline Ambassadors Intl. [13147]
Airline Ambassadors International [IO]
Ali Somon Cultural and Intellectual Found. [IO]
All4Israel [12454]
Alliance for Human Res. Protection [17741]
Altrusa Intl. [13033]
AMBUCS [13034]
Amer. Assn. of Food Stamp Directors [6261]
Amer. Avalanche Assn. [12948]
Amer. Bar Assn. Commn. on Homelessness and
  Poverty [12286]
Amer. Belarussian Relief Org. [12828]
Amer. Friends of ALYN Hosp. [12825]
Amer. Friends Ser. Comm. [13148]
Amer. Friends Ser. Comm. [IO]
Amer. Humane Assn. [13149]
Amer. Inst. for Public Ser. [13150]
Amer. Jewish Joint Distribution Comm. [12464]
Amer. Public Human Services Assn. [13151]
Amer. Public Human Services Assn. - Info.
  Systems Mgt. [13152]
Amer. Rescue Workers [13153]
Amer. Soc. for Kurds [13154]
Amer. Soc. for Kurds [IO]
Americans Caring for Children Worldwide [IO]
America's Children Hunger Network [11558]
AmeriCorps VISTA [13383]
AMURT [IO]
Architecture for Humanity [11761]
Arcus Found. [18266]
The Arts We Need [13710]
Asian Americans/Pacific Islanders in Philanthropy
  [12710]
Asian Regional Exchange for New Alternatives
  [IO]
Assistance League [13035]
Assisted Living Fed. of Am. [12306]
Assn. for the Accreditation of Human Res. Protec-
  tion Programs [11225]
Assn. of Clinicians for the Underserved [14616]
Assn. of Community Organizations for Reform
  Now [11749]
Assn. of Gospel Rescue Missions [13155]
Assn. of Gospel Rescue Missions [IO]
Assn. of Retired Americans [12897]
Assn. of Social Work Boards [13200]
Assyrian Aid Soc. of Am. [11508]
Batey Relief Alliance [12835]
Be and See Inspirations [IO]
Black Women of Essence [11269]
Black Women in Sisterhood for Action [13422]
Blankets for Canada Soc. [IO]
BoardSource [12651]
Books for the Barrios [12049]
Box Proj. [12836]
Brethren Volunteer Ser. [13388]
British Assn. of Settlements and Social Action
  Centres [IO]
Builders Without Borders [12307]
A Call to Serve Intl. [11765]
Canadian Coun. on Social Development [IO]
Career Gear [12705]
Carrie Estelle Doheny Found. [13156]
Catholic Campaign for Human Development
  [12713]
Catholic Central Union of Am. [13157]
Catholic Charities USA [13158]
Catholic Relief Services (U.S. Catholic Conf.)
  [12807]
Center for Community Action of B'Nai B'rith Intl.
  [11766]
Center for Community and Org. Development
  [11750]
The Center for Social Gerontology [11280]
Central Bur., Catholic Central Union of Am.
  [19610]
Centre for Development Alternatives [IO]
Children of the Americas [11574]
Children of Persia [11576]
Children's HopeChest [11578]
Children's Network Intl. [11579]
Christian Found. for Children and Aging [13159]
Christian Found. for Children and Aging [IO]
Circle of Hea. Intl. [12268]

Circle K Intl. [13037]
Citizens Network for Sustainable Development
  [11767]
Civitan Intl. [13038]
Civitas Found. for the Civil Soc. [IO]
Clowns Without Borders - USA [11768]
Coalition for Economic Survival [13160]
Coalition on Human Needs [13161]
Coleman Found. [13162]
Comic Relief [IO]
Comm. for Humanitarian Assistance to Iranian
  Refugees [12808]
Community for Creative Non-Violence [12288]
Community Info. and Epidemiological Technolo-
  gies [12121]
Comprehensive Day Care Programs [11539]
Conrad N. Hilton Found. [13163]
Convoy of Hope [12847]
Corporate and Found. Relations [12075]
Cosmopolitan Intl. [13039]
Coun. on Accreditation [13164]
Coun. on Contemporary Families [12149]
Coun. for Disability Rights [11935]
Coun. for Hea. and Human Services Ministries,
  United Church of Christ [13165]
Coun. for Nongovernmental Organisations in
  Malawi [IO]
Coun. of Religious Volunteer Agencies [13391]
Coun. for Standards in Human Ser. Educ. [9130]
CRISTA Ministries [13166]
Cuban Amer. Natl. Coun. [13167]
Curatio Intl. Found. [IO]
Dalit Liberation Educ. Trust [IO]
Danish Assn. for Intl. Cooperation - Denmark [IO]
Debts AIDS Trade Africa [16928]
Deep Griha Soc. of Pune, India [IO]
Direct Aid Intl. [12849]
Direct Care Alliance [1868]
Double Trouble in Recovery [12548]
Downed Bikers Assn. [12612]
Dream Factory [11691]
Dress for Success Worldwide [13424]
E-quip Africa [12704]
Edge-ucate [12057]
Emergency Relief Response Fund [20562]
Empowerment Soc. Intl. [11775]
Entertainment Indus. Found. [12114]
Esperanca [14628]
European Centre for Social Welfare Policy and
  Res. [IO]
European Social Action Network [IO]
Evangelical Lutheran Good Samaritan Soc.
  [13168]
FaithWorks Intl. [11777]
Families U.S.A. Found. [11286]
Feeding Hungry Children Intl. [12390]
Filipino Amer. Medical Inc. [14722]
Finance Proj. [17583]
First Foundations [13169]
Free Wheelchair Mission [11947]
Fresh Lifelines for Youth [13484]
Friedrich Ebert Found. - Jordan [IO]
Friends for Youth [13485]
FSU - Investing in Families [IO]
Fundacion para el Desarrollo en Justicia y Paz
  [IO]
Fundacion Eugenio Espejo [IO]
Gaddafi Intl. Found. for Charity Associations [IO]
Generations United [13170]
Giraffe Heroes Proj. [10185]
Giving Children Hope [11596]
Global Economic Outreach [20341]
Global Healing [12450]
Global MissionAir [20487]
GOAL [IO]
Gonja Assn. of North Am. [11779]
Good Fellows (Old Newsboys) [13042]
Gyro Intl. [13043]
Healing Waters Intl. [13410]
Hea. Global Access Proj. [11331]
Help the Helpless [12405]
Hilfswerk der Evangelischen Kirchen Schweiz [IO]
Hmong Natl. Development [17815]
Holiday Proj. [13395]
Hong Kong Christian Ser. [IO]

A star before a book entry number signifies that the name is not listed separately, but is mentioned within the entry.

Hong Kong Coun. of Social Ser. **[IO]**
House of Ruth **[12029]**
Human Rights and Race Relations Centre **[IO]**
Humanitarian Assistance for the Women and
  Children of Afghanistan **[IO]**
Humanitarian Medical Relief **[12527]**
Hunters Helping Hunters **[22604]**
Ijaw Natl. Alliance of the Americas **[12639]**
In Kind Canada **[IO]**
Innocence in Danger - USA **[11601]**
Inter Pares **[IO]**
Intl. Aid Serving Kids **[11603]**
Intl. Comm. for the Children of Chechnya **[11605]**
Intl. Coun. on Social Welfare - Canada **[IO]**
Intl. Fed. of Family Associations of Missing
  Persons from Armed Conflicts **[12609]**
Intl. Found. for Terror Act Victims **[12942]**
Intl. Medical Equip. Collaborative **[14569]**
Intl. Relief Friendship Found. **[13171]**
Intl. Relief Friendship Found. **[IO]**
Intl. Social Ser. Canada **[IO]**
Intl. Social Ser. - Gen. Secretariat **[IO]**
Intl. Social Ser. - Japan **[IO]**
Interreligious Found. for Community Org. **[11797]**
Iranian Refugees' Alliance **[12813]**
Jesuit Centre for Social Faith and Justice **[IO]**
Jesuit Social and Intl. Ministries **[IO]**
Jesuit Social and Intl. Ministries **[13172]**
Jesuit Volunteer Corps: Northwest **[19644]**
Jewish Assn. for Services for the Aged **[11290]**
Jewish Community Centers Assn. of North Am.
  [12473]
Joni and Friends **[11956]**
Jubilee Action - UK **[IO]**
Junior Chamber Intl. **[13044]**
Junior Optimist Octagon Intl. **[13045]**
Karuna Trust **[IO]**
Key Club Intl. **[13046]**
Kids Konnected **[11706]**
Kindness in Suffering **[11616]**
Kiwanis Intl. **[13047]**
La Sertoma Intl. **[13048]**
Ladies of Charity of the U.S.A. **[13173]**
A Leg To Stand On **[12659]**
Links **[13049]**
Lions Clubs Intl. **[13050]**
Little Bros. - Friends of the Elderly **[11295]**
Louis and Harold Price Found. **[13174]**
Machne Israel **[12476]**
Magic Johnson Found. **[13175]**
Magicians Without Borders **[12503]**
Makassed Philanthropic Islamic Assn. **[IO]**
Malay for Natl. Consciousness Movement **[IO]**
Maniilaq Assn. **[12627]**
Manpower Demonstration Res. Corp. **[12777]**
Mapendo Intl. **[12868]**
Meals4Israel **[12459]**
Medical Benevolence Found. **[14725]**
Medical Wings Intl. **[14645]**
Meds and Food for Kids **[11622]**
Mercy-USA for Aid and Development **[12871]**
Midwest Acad. **[11751]**
Mir Pace Intl. **[12872]**
Miracles of Hope Network **[11623]**
Missing Pet Partnership **[12707]**
Mission Builders Intl. **[19814]**
Missions Intl. **[20037]**
Motion Picture and TV Fund **[12115]**
My Good Deed **[13308]**
Natl. AIDS Housing Coalition **[12319]**
Natl. Alliance for Hispanic Hea. **[13176]**
Natl. Alliance to Nurture the Aged and the Youth
  [12358]
Natl. Assn. of Black Social Workers **[13204]**
Natl. Assn. of Citizens Advice Bureaux **[IO]**
Natl. Assn. of Colored Women's Clubs **[13051]**
Natl. Assn. for Direct Care Workers of Color
  [14709]
Natl. Assn. of Junior Auxiliaries **[13052]**
Natl. Assn. of Negro Bus. and Professional
  Women's Clubs **[13053]**
Natl. Assn. of Neighborhoods **[11752]**
Natl. Assn. of Senior Companion Proj. Directors
  [11304]
Natl. Benevolent Assn. of the Christian Church
  [13177]

Natl. Center for Urban Ethnic Affairs **[11753]**
Natl. Chaplains Assn. **[19855]**
Natl. Chap. of Canada IODE **[IO]**
Natl. Coalition Against Domestic Violence **[12034]**
Natl. Coalition for the Homeless **[12296]**
Natl. Coalition of Homicide Survivors **[13368]**
Natl. Coalition on Rural Aging **[11307]**
Natl. Community Action Found. **[11754]**
Natl. Coun. on the Aging **[11309]**
Natl. Coun. of Local Public Human Ser.
  Administrators **[13178]**
Natl. Coun. of Social Ser. **[IO]**
Natl. Coun. of State Human Ser. Administrators
  [13179]
Natl. Exchange Club **[13054]**
Natl. Haitian Soc. **[17817]**
Natl. Hispanic Coun. on Aging **[11310]**
Natl. Human Services Assembly **[13400]**
Natl. Inst. of Senior Housing **[12328]**
Natl. Meals on Wheels Found. **[11315]**
Natl. Network for Social Work Managers **[13207]**
Natl. Org. for Human Services **[9131]**
Natl. People's Action **[11755]**
Natl. Relief Network **[12873]**
Natl. Soc. of Saint Vincent de Paul - Malaysia **[IO]**
Natl. Soc. for Shut-Ins **[18651]**
Natl. Staff Development and Training Assn.
  [13180]
Natl. Training and Info. Center **[11799]**
Natl. WIC Assn. **[6262]**
Native Amer. Church of North Am. of the Cowlitz
  Indians **[19447]**
NeighborWorks Am. **[12335]**
Nepal Reliance Org. **[IO]**
Network of Iranian Amer. Soc. **[13507]**
Neurosurgeons to Preserve Hea. Care Access
  [15414]
New Eyes for the Needy **[12533]**
New Horizon World Center **[19527]**
New York Assn. for New Americans **[12479]**
NGA **[13056]**
Nigerian Women Leadership Coun. Intl. **[12640]**
North Amer. Alliance for the Advancement of Na-
  tive Peoples **[12631]**
North Amer. Reggio Emilia Alliance **[11641]**
Ogwashi-Uku Assn., USA **[19291]**
Only a Child **[11643]**
Oper. Gratitude **[11493]**
Opportunities Industrialization Centers Intl.
  [13181]
Opportunities Industrialization Centers
  International **[IO]**
Optimist Intl. **[13057]**
Org. for the Relief of Underprivileged Women and
  Children in Africa **[12876]**
Organize Training Center **[11800]**
Orphan Resources Intl. **[11644]**
Outpost for Hope **[12610]**
Pakistan Welfare Org. **[13182]**
Pakistan Welfare Org. **[IO]**
Paraprofessional Healthcare Inst. **[1853]**
Parents' Action For Children **[12682]**
Parents Against Tired Truckers **[12984]**
Partners in Hea. **[12270]**
Partnership for Quality Medical Donations **[12537]**
People's Involvement Corp. **[13183]**
Physicians for Peace **[15078]**
Physicians for Social Responsibility - Finland **[IO]**
Physiotherapy and Rehabilitation Support for
  Afghanistan **[IO]**
Pilot Intl. and Pilot Intl. Found. **[13058]**
Pravah **[IO]**
Presbyterian Hea., Educ. and Welfare Assn.
  [13184]
Quota Intl. **[13059]**
Rainbow/PUSH Coalition **[13185]**
Rallying Points **[14083]**
Rapha Intl. **[12539]**
Refugee Coun. USA **[18500]**
Restoration Proj. Intl. **[12441]**
Retired and Senior Volunteer Prog. **[13403]**
The Revitalization Corps **[12782]**
Riders for Hea. **[15271]**
Right Turn, Intl. **[13186]**
River Fund **[11333]**

Rotary Intl. **[13060]**
Round-Table U.S.A. **[13061]**
Ruritan Natl. **[13062]**
Saint Vincent de Paul Soc. - Australia **[IO]**
Saint Vincent de Paul Soc. - Lesotho **[IO]**
Salvation Army **[IO]**
Salvation Army **[13187]**
Salvation Army Home League - Intl. **[IO]**
Salvation Army Intl. HQ **[IO]**
Salvation Army Women's, Adult and Family
  Ministries - New Zealand **[IO]**
Salvation Army Women's Ministries **[IO]**
Samaritan's Purse **[20289]**
Samuel Rubin Found. **[13188]**
Scherman Found. **[13189]**
SCI - Intl. Voluntary Ser. **[13404]**
Senior Companion Prog. **[13405]**
September 11th Families' Assn. **[13371]**
Sertoma Intl. **[13063]**
SIMPUTER (USA) **[13301]**
Singles in Ser. **[13064]**
Sister Island Proj. **[11788]**
Smile Alliance Intl. **[11721]**
Social Relief Intl. **[12445]**
Social Welfare History Gp. **[10149]**
Sociedad de San Vicente de Paul - Colombia **[IO]**
Sociedad de San Vicente de Paul - Costa Rica
  [IO]
Sociedad de San Vicente de Paul - Ecuador **[IO]**
Sociedad de San Vicente de Paul - Guatemala
  [IO]
Sociedad de San Vicente de Paul - Nicaragua
  [IO]
Sociedad de San Vicente de Paul - Republica Do-
  minicana **[IO]**
Sociedad de San Vicente de Paul - Uruguay-
  Mixed Br. **[IO]**
Societe de Saint-Vincent de Paul - Algeria **[IO]**
Societe de Saint Vincent de Paul du Burundi **[IO]**
Societe de Saint-Vincent de Paul - Cote d' Ivoire
  [IO]
Soc. of Afghan Professionals **[9343]**
Soc. for Participatory Res. in Asia **[IO]**
Soc. of Saint Vincent de Paul - Bangladesh **[IO]**
Soc. of Saint Vincent de Paul - Botswana **[IO]**
Soc. of Saint Vincent de Paul - Burkina Faso **[IO]**
Soc. of Saint Vincent de Paul - Cameroon **[IO]**
Soc. of Saint Vincent de Paul - Canada **[IO]**
Soc. of Saint Vincent de Paul - Central African
  Republic **[IO]**
Soc. of Saint Vincent de Paul Central Coun. -
  Hong Kong **[IO]**
Soc. of St. Vincent de Paul Coun. of the U.S.
  [13190]
Soc. of Saint Vincent de Paul - Egypt **[IO]**
Soc. of Saint Vincent de Paul - El Salvador **[IO]**
Soc. of Saint Vincent de Paul - Ethiopia **[IO]**
Soc. of Saint Vincent de Paul - Guyana **[IO]**
Soc. of Saint Vincent de Paul - India **[IO]**
Soc. of Saint Vincent de Paul - Intl. **[IO]**
Soc. of Saint Vincent de Paul - Ireland **[IO]**
Soc. of Saint Vincent de Paul - Jamaica **[IO]**
Soc. of Saint Vincent de Paul - Korea **[IO]**
Soc. of Saint Vincent de Paul - Liberia **[IO]**
Soc. of Saint Vincent de Paul - Lithuania **[IO]**
Soc. of Saint Vincent de Paul - Mozambique **[IO]**
Soc. of Saint Vincent de Paul - Namibia **[IO]**
Soc. of Saint Vincent de Paul - New Zealand **[IO]**
Soc. of Saint Vincent de Paul - Nigeria **[IO]**
Soc. of Saint Vincent de Paul - Pakistan **[IO]**
Soc. of Saint Vincent de Paul - Peru **[IO]**
Soc. of Saint Vincent de Paul - Philippines **[IO]**
Soc. of Saint Vincent de Paul - Rwanda **[IO]**
Soc. of Saint Vincent de Paul - Scotland **[IO]**
Soc. of Saint Vincent de Paul - Slovenia **[IO]**
Soc. of Saint Vincent de Paul - South Africa **[IO]**
Soc. of Saint Vincent de Paul - Sri Lanka **[IO]**
Soc. of Saint Vincent de Paul - Sudan **[IO]**
Soc. of Saint Vincent de Paul - Taiwan **[IO]**
Soc. of Saint Vincent de Paul - Trinidad and
  Tobago **[IO]**
Soc. of Saint Vincent de Paul - Uruguay-Female
  Br. **[IO]**
Soc. of Saint Vincent de Paul - Zimbabwe **[IO]**
Soc. for Social Work and Res. **[9135]**

Reference to "IO" in place of a book number signifies that the association may be found in the 45th edition of International Organizations.

Sociologists Without Borders [18664]
Soroptimist Intl. of the Americas [13065]
Southern Mutual Help Assn. [11790]
SustainUS [13517]
Tile Partners for Humanity [12338]
Together, Inc. [12365]
Touching Hearts [11267]
Travelers Aid Intl. [13191]
Travelers Aid Intl. [IO]
Trinity Hea. Intl. [14731]
United Black Fund [12204]
U.S. Conf. of City Human Services Officials [6263]
U.S. Junior Chamber of Commerce [24390]
United We Serve [21203]
Uplift Internationale [15737]
Veterans' Widows Intl. Network [21357]
Vietnamese Professionals Soc. [19429]
Voices in the Wilderness [18253]
Volunteers of Am. [13192]
VOSH Intl. [12543]
Watchlist on Children and Armed Conflict [11664]
Water Advocates [9310]
Water Missions Intl. [13411]
We Care Am. [13210]
Welfare Res., Inc. [13193]
Wheat Ridge Ministries [20233]
William and Flora Hewlett Found. [13194]
Winant and Clayton Volunteers [13409]
Windward Found. [13195]
WishKids Intl. [11665]
Women in Show Business for Children [13069]
Women's Royal Voluntary Ser. [IO]
World Ability Fed. [11995]
World Orphans [11667]
World Tech. Volunteers [13196]
World Technical Volunteers [IO]
Young Koreans United [12485]
Youth Advocate Prog. Intl. [11668]
Zarrow Families Found. [13197]
Zonta Intl. [13071]
Social Welfare Assembly; Natl. [★13400]
Social Welfare Assembly; Natl. Comm. on Aging of Natl. [★11309]
Social Welfare; Comm. on the History of [★10149]
Social Welfare History Gp. [10149], c/o Iris Carlton-LaNey, Pres., Univ. of North Carolina at Chapel Hill, School of Social Work, CB No. 3550, 301 Pittsboro St., Chapel Hill, NC 27516, (919)962-6536
Social Welfare Organizations; Natl. Assembly of Natl. Hea. and [★13400]
Social Welfare Policy and Law; Center on [★6232]
Social Work
ActionAid Intl. USA [11758]
Adopt a Dr. [12750]
Advocacy Inst. [12650]
Airline Ambassadors Intl. [13147]
ALMA Soc. - Adoptees' Liberty Movement Assn. [11232]
Amer. Adoption Cong. [11234]
Amer. Bar Assn. Commn. on Homelessness and Poverty [12286]
Amer. Bd. of Vocational Experts [9299]
Amer. Humane Assn. Children's Services [11556]
Amer. Public Human Services Assn. - Info. Systems Mgt. [13152]
America's Children Hunger Network [11558]
The Arts We Need [13710]
Asian and Pacific Assn. for Social Work Educ. [IO]
Assn. for Advanced Training in the Behavioral Sciences [8878]
Assn. for Community Org. and Social Admin. [13198]
Assn. of Directors of Social Services [IO]
Assn. of Directors of Social Work [IO]
Assn. For Educ. Welfare Mgt. [IO]
Assn. for Gerontology Educ. in Social Work [8461]
Assn. for Humanistic Psychology [16140]
Assn. of Jewish Center Professionals [12466]
Assn. of Oncology Social Work [13199]
Assn. for Schools of Social Work in Africa [IO]
Assn. of Social Work Boards [13200]

Assyrian Aid Soc. of Am. [11508]
Australian Assn. of Social Workers [IO]
Australian Assn. of Social Workers - Hunter Valley Br. [IO]
Australian Assn. of Social Workers - New South Wales Br. [IO]
Australian Assn. of Social Workers - North Queensland Br. [IO]
Australian Assn. of Social Workers - Northern Territory Br. [IO]
Australian Assn. of Social Workers - South Australian Br. [IO]
Australian Assn. of Social Workers - Tasmanian Br. [IO]
Australian Assn. of Social Workers - Victorian Br. [IO]
Batey Relief Alliance [12835]
BC Assn. of Social Workers [IO]
Better World Chorus [12617]
Big Bros. Big Sisters of Am. [11676]
Black Mental Hea. Alliance [15193]
British Assn. of Social Workers [IO]
Canadian Assn. of Schools of Social Work [IO]
Canadian Assn. of Social Workers [IO]
The Center for Social Gerontology [11280]
Children of the Night [12933]
Children of Persia [11576]
Children's Cross Connection Intl. [11552]
Children's Network Intl. [11579]
Circle of Hea. Intl. [12268]
CitiHope Intl. [12843]
Clinical Social Work Fed. [13201]
Concerned Persons for Adoption [11240]
Concerned United Birthparents [11241]
Coun. of Intl. Programs USA [13202]
Coun. of Intl. Programs USA [IO]
Coun. on Sexual Orientation and Gender Expression [9132]
Coun. on Social Work Educ. [9133]
Danish Assn. of Social Workers [IO]
Direct Aid Intl. [12849]
Downed Bikers Assn. [12612]
Employee Assistance Professionals Assn. [13203]
European Assn. of Schools of Social Work [IO]
European Consortium of Social Professions with Educational and Social Stud. [IO]
FaithWorks Intl. [11777]
Families Adopting Children Everywhere [11242]
Families for Private Adoption [11244]
Feeding Hungry Children Intl. [12390]
Food Providers of Am. [12392]
Foster Care Alumni of Am. [11592]
Free Wheelchair Mission [11947]
Giraffe Heroes Proj. [10185]
Giving Children Hope [11596]
Global MissionAir [20487]
Healing Waters Intl. [13410]
House of Ruth [12029]
Human Resources Social Welfare Soc. [IO]
Hunters Helping Hunters [22604]
Ijaw Natl. Alliance of the Americas [12639]
Inst. of Welfare [IO]
Intl. Aid Serving Kids [11603]
Intl. Assn. of Schools of Social Work [IO]
Intl. Comm. for the Children of Chechnya [11605]
Intl. Fed. of Social Workers [IO]
Intl. Medical Equip. Collaborative [14569]
Intl. Medical Volunteers Assn. [15075]
Intl. Soc. for Adolescent Psychiatry and Psychology [16087]
Intl. Soundex Reunion Registry [11248]
Jewish Assn. for Services for the Aged [11290]
Kids 4 Afghan Kids [11610]
Kindness in Suffering [11616]
Latin Am. Parents Assn. [11252]
A Leg To Stand On [12659]
Liberal Educ. for Adoptive Families [11253]
Mapendo Intl. [12868]
Meds and Food for Kids [11622]
Mercy-USA for Aid and Development [12871]
Mir Pace Intl. [12872]
Miracles of Hope Network [11623]
Mission Builders Intl. [19814]
Missions Intl. [20037]
My Good Deed [13308]

Natl. Adoption Center [11254]
Natl. AIDS Housing Coalition [12319]
Natl. Alliance to Nurture the Aged and the Youth [12358]
Natl. Assn. of Black Social Workers [13204]
Natl. Assn. of Former Foster Care Children of Am. [11626]
Natl. Assn. of Puerto Rican Hispanic Social Workers [13205]
Natl. Assn. of Social Workers [13206]
Natl. Assn. of Social Workers Natl. Comm. on Lesbian, Gay and Bisexual Issues [12245]
Natl. Coalition Against Domestic Violence [12034]
Natl. Coun. for Adoption [11255]
Natl. Council for Single Adoptive Parents [11256]
Natl. Foster Parent Assn. [12677]
Natl. Haitian Soc. [17817]
Natl. Network for Social Work Managers [13207]
Natl. Network for Youth [12935]
Natl. Org. of Forensic Social Work [8446]
Natl. Runaway Switchboard [12936]
Natl. Staff Development and Training Assn. [13180]
NATOPSS - Learn to Care [IO]
Network of Iranian Amer. Soc. [13507]
Newfoundland and Labrador Assn. of Social Workers [IO]
Nigerian Social Workers Assn. [24142]
Nordic Comm. of Schools of Social Work [IO]
North Amer. Assn. of Christians in Social Work [13208]
North Amer. Coun. on Adoptable Children [11257]
Only a Child [11643]
Ontario Assn. of Social Workers [IO]
Ontario Assn. of Social Workers - Eastern Br. [IO]
Ontario Assn. of Social Workers - Hamilton Area and District Br. [IO]
Organized Adoption Search Info. Services [11259]
ORIGINS [11260]
Orphan Resources Intl. [11644]
Orphan Voyage [11261]
Outpost for Hope [12610]
Pact Training [11830]
Pakistan Welfare Org. [13182]
Paraprofessional Healthcare Inst. [1853]
Prince Edward Island Assn. of Social Workers [IO]
Rapha Intl. [12539]
Reach the Children [11649]
REAP Intl. [12940]
Rebuilding Alliance [12336]
Riders for Hea. [15271]
School Social Work Assn. of Am. [9134]
SIMPUTER (USA) [13301]
Singapore Assn. of Social Workers [IO]
Smile Alliance Intl. [11721]
Social Care Assn. [IO]
Soc. for Social Work Leadership in Hea. Care [13209]
Soc. for Social Work and Res. [9135]
Soc. for Social Work and Res. [IO]
Teaching-Family Assn. [12169]
Tech. Assistance Collaborative [13145]
United We Serve [21203]
Water Advocates [9310]
Water Missions Intl. [13411]
We Care Am. [13210]
Winant and Clayton Volunteers [13409]
WishKids Intl. [11665]
Social Work Admin. in Hea. Care; Soc. for [★13209]
Social Work Boards; Amer. Assn. of State [★13200]
Social Work Conf; Evangelical [★13208]
Social Work Coun; Natl. [★13400]
Social Work; Natl. Assn. of Christians in [★13208]
Social Work; Natl. Fed. of Societies for Clinical [★13201]
Social Work Regulation; American Found. for Res. and Consumer Educ. in [★13200]
Social Work Res. Gp. [★13206]
Social Workers
ALMA Soc. - Adoptees' Liberty Movement Assn. [11232]
Amer. Adoption Cong. [11234]
Amer. Assn. of Psychiatric Technicians [16069]
Amer. Bar Assn. Commn. on Homelessness and Poverty [12286]

A star before a book entry number signifies that the name is not listed separately, but is mentioned within the entry.

Amer. Humane Assn. Children's Services [11556]
Amer. Public Human Services Assn. - Info. Systems Mgt. [13152]
Assn. for Community Org. and Social Admin. [13198]
Assn. for Gerontology Educ. in Social Work [8461]
Assn. for Humanist Sociology [7660]
Assn. for Humanistic Psychology [16140]
Assn. of Oncology Social Work [13199]
Assn. of Social Work Boards [13200]
Big Bros. Big Sisters of Am. [11676]
Black Mental Hea. Alliance [15193]
Children of the Night [12933]
Clinical Social Work Fed. [13201]
Concerned Persons for Adoption [11240]
Concerned United Birthparents [11241]
Coun. of Intl. Programs USA [13202]
Families Adopting Children Everywhere [11242]
Families for Private Adoption [11244]
Feeding Hungry Children Intl. [12390]
House of Ruth [12029]
Intl. Soc. for Adolescent Psychiatry and Psychology [16087]
Intl. Soundex Reunion Registry [11248]
Irish Assn. of Social Workers [IO]
Jewish Assn. for Services for the Aged [11290]
Latin Am. Parents Assn. [11252]
Liberal Educ. for Adoptive Families [11253]
Mothers Against Violence in Am. [13375]
Natl. Adoption Center [11254]
Natl. Alliance to Nurture the Aged and the Youth [12358]
Natl. Assn. of Disability Representatives [18648]
Natl. Assn. of Social Workers [13206]
Natl. Assn. of Social Workers Natl. Comm. on Lesbian, Gay and Bisexual Issues [12245]
Natl. Coalition Against Domestic Violence [12034]
Natl. Coun. for Adoption [11255]
Natl. Council for Single Adoptive Parents [11256]
Natl. Foster Parent Assn. [12677]
Natl. Network of Social Work Managers [13207]
Natl. Org. of Forensic Social Work [8446]
Natl. Runaway Switchboard [12936]
Natl. Staff Development and Training Assn. [13180]
Nigerian Social Workers Assn. [24142]
North Amer. Assn. of Christians in Social Work [13208]
North Amer. Coun. on Adoptable Children [11257]
Organized Adoption Search Info. Services [11259]
ORIGINS [11260]
Orphan Resources Intl. [11644]
Orphan Voyage [11261]
Pact Training [11830]
School Social Work Assn. of Am. [9134]
Soc. for Social Work Leadership in Hea. Care [13209]
Soc. for Social Work and Res. [9135]
Teaching-Family Assn. [12169]
UNISON [IO]
Winant and Clayton Volunteers [13409]
Social Workers; Amer. Assn. of Medical [★13206]
Social Workers; Amer. Assn. of Psychiatric [★13206]
Social Workers; Amer. Assn. of Spinal Cord Injury Psychologists and [16459]
Social Workers; Assn. of Pediatric Oncology [15885]
Social Workers in the Field of Learning Disability [IO], Dublin, Ireland
Social Workers; Natl. Assn. of Oncology [★13199]
Social Workers; Natl. Assn. of School [★13206]
Social Workers Natl. Comm. on Lesbian, Gay and Bisexual Issues; Natl. Assn. of [12245]
Social Workers- Natl. Comm. on Lesbian and Gay Issues; Natl. Assn. of [★12245]
Social Workers; Natl. Fed. of Clinical [★13201]
Socialdemokraterne [★IO]
Socialism
  Caucus for a New Political Sci. [7523]
  Center for Socialist History [10099]
  Democratic Socialists of Am. [18652]
  Economic Affairs Bureau/Dollars and Sense [6879]
  Freedom Road Socialist Org. [6264]
  Freedom Socialist Party [18653]

Intl. People's Democratic Uhuru Movement [17395]
Intl. Socialist Org. [18654]
Intl. Socialist Org. [IO]
Intl. Socialist Org. Australia [IO]
League for the Revolutionary Party [18655]
News and Letters Comm. [18656]
Peace and Freedom Party [18330]
Religion and Socialism Commn. of the Democratic Socialists of Am. [18657]
Social Democratic Youth of Denmark [IO]
Social Democrats, U.S.A. [18306]
Socialist Action [18658]
Socialist Alternative [6265]
Spartacist League [18659]
Workers World Party [18660]
Workers World Party [IO]
Young Communist League of the U.S.A. [18661]
Young Democratic Socialists [18662]
Youth for Intl. Socialism [18663]
Youth for Intl. Socialism [IO]
Socialism Comm. of DSA; Religion and [★18657]
Socialist Action [18658], 298 Valencia St., San Francisco, CA 94103, (415)255-1080
Socialist Alliance [IO], Canberra, Australia
Socialist Alternative [6265], PO Box 45343, Seattle, WA 98145, (206)842-9487
Socialist Amer. Workers Freedom Movement; Natl. [★18802]
Socialist Educational Soc. [★18339]
Socialist Fed; Democratic [★18335]
Socialist Fed; Democratic [★18306]
Socialist Gp. in the European Parliament [★IO]
Socialist Gp. in the European Parliament [IO], Brussels, Belgium
Socialist History; Center for [10099]
Socialist Intl. [IO], London, United Kingdom
Socialist Intl. Women [IO], London, United Kingdom
Socialist Labor Party [★18335]
Socialist Labor Party of Am. [18334], PO Box 218, Mountain View, CA 94042-0218, (408)280-7266
Socialist League; Young Peoples [★18306]
Socialist Movement; Natl. [18802]
Socialist Organizing Comm; Democratic [★18652]
Socialist Organizing Comm. Youth Sect; Democratic [★18662]
Socialist Party [IO], London, United Kingdom
Socialist Party of Australia [★IO]
Socialist Party of Austria [★IO]
Socialist Party of Canada [IO], Victoria, BC, Canada
Socialist Party-Democratic Socialist Fed. [★18335]
Socialist Party-Democratic Socialist Fed. [★18306]
Socialist Party - France [IO], Paris, France
Socialist Party of the U.S; World [18339]
Socialist Party, U.S.A. [★18306]
Socialist Party U.S.A. [18335], 339 Lafayette St., Ste. 303, New York, NY 10012, (212)982-4586
Socialist Party; Worker's [★18339]
Socialist Scholars Conf. - Address unknown since 1995.
Socialist Vanguard; Natl. [18803]
Socialist White Americans Party; Natl. [★18798]
Socialist White People's Party; Natl. [★18805]
Socialist Worker Party - Address unknown since 1999.
Socialist Workers Party [18336], 306 W 37th St., 10th Fl., New York, NY 10018, (212)736-2540
Socialist Zionist Youth Movement; Hashomer Hatzair [★20140]
Socialistic Labor Party [★18334]
Socially and Ecologically Responsible Geographers - Defunct.
Sociedad Anatomica Espanola [★IO]
Sociedad de Anestesiologia de Chile [IO], Santiago, Chile
Sociedad Anglo-Chilena [★IO]
Sociedad Argentina de Biofisica [★IO]
Sociedad Argentina de Bioingeniera [★IO]
Sociedad Argentina de Biologia [★IO]
Sociedad Argentina de Botanica [★IO]
Sociedad Argentina de Cardiologia [★IO]
Sociedad Argentina De Informatica E Investigacion Operativa [IO], Buenos Aires, Argentina
Sociedad Argentina de Dermatologia [★IO]
Sociedad Argentina de Endocrinologia y Metabolismo [★IO]

Sociedad Argentina de Estudios Geograficos [★IO]
Sociedad Argentina de Fisiologica [IO], Buenos Aires, Argentina
Sociedad Argentina de Gastroenterologia [★IO]
Sociedad Argentina de Genetica [★IO]
Sociedad Argentina de Hematologia [★IO]
Sociedad Argentina de Oftalmologia [★IO]
Sociedad Argentina de Osteoporosis [IO], Buenos Aires, Argentina
Sociedad Argentina de Patologia [IO], Buenos Aires, Argentina
Sociedad Argentina de Pediatria [★IO]
Sociedad Argentina de Psicotrauma [★IO]
Sociedad de Arquitectos Paisajistas, Ecologia y Medio Ambiente [IO], La Paz, Bolivia
Sociedad Biblica Chilena [★IO]
Sociedad Biblica Colombiana [★IO]
Sociedad Biblica de Costa Rica [★IO]
Sociedad Biblica de Honduras [★IO]
Sociedad Biblica de Mexico [★IO]
Sociedad Biblica de Nicaragua [★IO]
Sociedad Biblica Peruana [★IO]
Sociedad Biblica de el Salvador [★IO]
Sociedad de Biologia de Chile [IO], Santiago, Chile
Sociedad Boliviana de Gastroenterologia y Endoscopia [IO], Cochabamba, Bolivia
Sociedad Boliviana de Osteologia y Metabolismo Mineral [IO], Santa Cruz, Bolivia
Sociedad Boliviana de Terapia Fisica [IO], Santa Cruz, Bolivia
Sociedad Chilena de Cardiologia y Cirugia Cardiovascular [★IO]
Sociedad Chilena de Ciencia de la Computacion [★IO]
Sociedad Chilena De Fertilidad [IO], Santiago, Chile
Sociedad Chilena del Derecho de Autor [IO], Santiago, Chile
Sociedad Chilena de Dermatologia y Venereologia [★IO]
Sociedad Chilena de Endocrinologia y Diabetes [IO], Santiago, Chile
Sociedad Chilena de Fotogrametria y Percepcion Remota [IO], Santiago, Chile
Sociedad Chilena de Gastroenterologia [IO], Santiago, Chile
Sociedad Chilena de Geotecnica [IO], Santiago, Chile
Sociedad Chilena de Infectologia [★IO]
Sociedad Chilena de Medicina del Deporte [IO], Santiago, Chile
Sociedad Chilena de Obstetricia y Ginecologia [★IO]
Sociedad Chilena de Urologia [IO], Santiago, Chile
Sociedad de Ciencias Aranzadi [IO], Donostia-San Sebastian, Spain
Sociedad Colombiana de Arquitectos Paisajistas [★IO]
Sociedad Colombiana de Cardiologia [★IO]
Sociedad Colombiana de Fisica [★IO]
Sociedad Colombiana de Ingenieros [★IO]
Sociedad Colombiana de Matematicas [IO], Bogota, Colombia
Sociedad Colombiana de Ortodoncia [IO], Medellin, Colombia
Sociedad Colombiana de Percepcion Remota y Sistemas de Informacion Geografica [IO], Santa Fe de Bogota, Colombia
Sociedad Cubana de Endoscopia Digestiva [IO], Havana, Cuba
Sociedad Dominicana de Cardiologia [★IO]
Sociedad Dominicana de Menopausia [IO], Santiago, Dominican Republic
Sociedad Dominicane de Medicina del Deporte [IO], Santo Domingo, Dominican Republic
Sociedad Ecuatoriana De Medicina Reproductiva [IO], Guayaquil, Ecuador
Sociedad Ecuatoriana de Dermatologia [★IO]
Sociedad Ecuatoriana de Gastroenterologia [IO], Guayaquil, Ecuador
Sociedad de Epigraphia [★10130]
Sociedad Espanola de Agroingenieria [IO], Valencia, Spain
Sociedad Espanola de Bioquimica y Biologia Molecular [IO], Madrid, Spain
Sociedad Espanola de Cardiologia [★IO]

Reference to "IO" in place of a book number signifies that the association may be found in the 45th edition of International Organizations.

Sociedad Espanola de Ceramica y Vidrio [★IO]
Sociedad Espanola de Ciencias Fisiologicas [★IO]
Sociedad Espanola de Cirugia Plastica, Reparadora y Estetica [★IO]
Sociedad Espanola para el Estudio de la Obesidad [IO], Madrid, Spain
Sociedad Espanola de Etologia [★IO]
Sociedad Espanola de Farmacologia [★IO]
Sociedad Espanola de Geomorfologia [IO], Coruna, Spain
Sociedad Espanola de Geriatria y Gerontologia [IO], Madrid, Spain
Sociedad Espanola de Gravitacion y Relatividad [★IO]
Sociedad Espanola de Informatica de la Salud [★IO]
Sociedad Espanola de Ingenieria Biomedica [★IO]
Sociedad Espanola de Investigaciones Oseas y Metabolismo Mineral [IO], Oviedo, Spain
Sociedad Espanola de Ortodoncia [IO], Madrid, Spain
Sociedad Espanola de Proteomica [★IO]
Sociedad Espanola de Quimicos Cosmeticos [★IO]
Sociedad Espanola de Reumatologia [★IO]
Sociedad de Estadistica e Investigacion Operativa [★IO]
Sociedad Europea de Educacion Comparada [★IO]
Sociedad de Farmacologia de Chile [★IO]
Sociedad de Fomento Fabril [★IO]
Sociedad de Gastroenterologia del Peru [IO], Lima, Peru
Sociedad de Genetica de Chile [IO], Santiago, Chile
Sociedad Geografica de Lima [★IO]
Sociedad Geologica de Espana [★IO]
Sociedad Geologica Mexicana [IO], Mexico City, Mexico
Sociedad de Gestion de Derechos Literarios [IO], Santiago, Chile
Sociedad Honoraria Hispanica [8499], PO Box 5318, Buffalo Grove, IL 60089-5318, (847)550-0455
Sociedad Interamericana de Cardiologia [★IO]
Sociedad Internacional de Bioetica [★IO]
Sociedad Internacional Brecht [★IO]
Sociedad Internacional Brecht [★9661]
Sociedad Latinoamericana de Cardiologia Intervencionista [★IO]
Sociedad Latinoamericana de Nefrologia e Hipertension [★IO]
Sociedad de Linguistica del Caribe [★IO]
Sociedad de Matematica de Chile [IO], Santiago, Chile
Sociedad Matematica Mexicana [IO], Mexico City, Mexico
Sociedad Mexicana de Ciencias Fisiologicas, A.C. [IO], Mexico City, Mexico
Sociedad Mexicana de Dermatologia [★IO]
Sociedad Mexicana de Entomologia [IO], Tlalnepantla, Mexico
Sociedad Mexicana de Geomorfologia [IO], Coyoacan, Mexico
Sociedad Mexicana de Historia de la Ciencia y de la Tecnologia [★IO]
Sociedad Mexicana de Historia Natural [IO], Mexico City, Mexico
Sociedad Mexicana de Ingenieria Biomedica [IO], Mexico City, Mexico
Sociedad Mexicana de Ingenieria Economica, Financiera y de Costos [★IO]
Sociedad Mexicana de Instrumentacion [★IO]
Sociedad Mexicana de Pediatria [IO], Mexico City, Mexico
Sociedad Mexicana de Psicologia [★IO]
Sociedad de Microscopia de Espana [★IO]
Sociedad Nacional de Mineria, Petroleo y Energia [★IO]
Sociedad de Obstetricia y Ginecologia de Venezuela [IO], Caracas, Venezuela
Sociedad Paraguaya De Fertilidad [IO], Asuncion, Paraguay
Sociedad Paraguaya de Dermatologia [★IO]
Sociedad Paraguaya de Medicina del Deporte [IO], Asuncion, Paraguay
Sociedad Paraguayana de Gastroenterologia [IO], Asuncion, Paraguay
Sociedad Peruana de Cardiologia [★IO]
Sociedad Peruana De Fertilidad [IO], Lima, Peru

Sociedad Peruana de Geotecnia [IO], Lima, Peru
Sociedad Peruana de Medicina y Ciencias Aplicadas al Deporte [IO], Lima, Peru
Sociedad Perunana de Reumatologia [IO], Lima, Peru
Sociedad de Psiquiatria del Uruguay [IO], Montevideo, Uruguay
Sociedad Quimica de Mexico [★IO]
Sociedad Rural Argentina [★IO]
Sociedad Salvadorena De Endoscopia Ginecologica Y Medicina [IO], San Salvador, El Salvador
Sociedad de San Vicente de Paul - Colombia [IO], Bucaramanga, Colombia
Sociedad de San Vicente de Paul - Costa Rica [IO], San Jose, Costa Rica
Sociedad de San Vicente de Paul - Ecuador [IO], Quito, Ecuador
Sociedad de San Vicente de Paul - Guatemala [IO], Quetzaltenango, Guatemala
Sociedad de San Vicente de Paul - Nicaragua [IO], Leon, Nicaragua
Sociedad de San Vicente de Paul - Republica Dominicana [IO], Santo Domingo, Dominican Republic
Sociedad de San Vicente de Paul - Uruguay-Mixed Br. [IO], Montevideo, Uruguay
Sociedad Uruguaya de Cardiologia [★IO]
Sociedad Uruguaya de Endoscopia Digestiva [IO], Montevideo, Uruguay
Sociedad Uruguaya de Informatica en la Salud [★IO]
Sociedad Uruguaya de Musica Contemporanea [★IO]
Sociedad Venezolana de Arquitectos Paisajistas [★IO]
Sociedad Venezolana de Cirugia [IO], Caracas, Venezuela
Sociedad Venezolana de Dermatologia [IO], Caracas, Venezuela
Sociedad Venezolana de Farmacologia [★IO]
Sociedad Venezolana de Medicina Deportiva [IO], Caracas, Venezuela
Sociedad Venezolana de Menopausia y Osteoporosis [IO], Maracaibo, Venezuela
Sociedad Venezolana de Oftalmologia [IO], Caracas, Venezuela
Sociedad Venezolana de Puericultura y Pediatria [IO], Chacao, Venezuela
Sociedade de Aeroporto Internacional de Macau [IO], Macau, Macao
Sociedade Biblica do Brasil [★IO]
Sociedade Biblica de Portugal [★IO]
Sociedade Brasileira de Automatica [★IO]
Sociedade Brasileira de Automatica [IO], Natal, Brazil
Sociedade Brasileira de Bioquimica e Biologia Molecular [★IO]
Sociedade Brasileira de Cardiologia [★IO]
Sociedade Brasileira de Dermatologia [★IO]
Sociedade Brasileira de Engenharia Biomedica [★IO]
Sociedade Brasileira de Entomologia [★IO]
Sociedade Brasileira de Farmacologia e Terapeutica Experimental [★IO]
Sociedade Brasileira de Fisiologica [★IO]
Sociedade Brasileira de Genetica [★IO]
Sociedade Brasileira de Geofisica [★IO]
Sociedade Brasileira de Geologia Nucleo de Minas Gerais [IO], Belo Horizonte, Brazil
Sociedade Brasileira de Hipertensao [★IO]
Sociedade Brasileira de Informatica em Saude [★IO]
Sociedade Brasileira de Medicina do Esporte [IO], Porto Alegre, Brazil
Sociedade Brasileira de Medicina Estetica [★IO]
Sociedade Brasileira de Metrologia [★IO]
Sociedade Brasileira de Microscopia e Microanalise [★IO]
Sociedade Brasileira de Odontologia Estetica [★IO]
Sociedade Brasileira de Osteoporose [★IO]
Sociedade Brasileira de Pesquisa Operacional [★IO]
Sociedade Brasileira para o Progresso da Ciencia [★IO]
Sociedade de Geografia de Lisboa [IO], Lisbon, Portugal

Sociedade Internacional de Trilogia Analitica [★IO]
Sociedade Portuguesa de Autores [IO], Lisbon, Portugal
Sociedade Portuguesa de Cardiologia [★IO]
Sociedade Portuguesa de Doencas Infecciosas [★IO]
Sociedade Portuguesa de Endoscopia Digestiva [★IO]
Sociedade Portuguesa de Esclerose Multipla [★IO]
Sociedade Portuguesa de Estomatologia E Medicina Dentaria [★IO]
Sociedade Portuguesa de Farmacologia [★IO]
Sociedade Portuguesa de Medicina Desportiva [IO], Lisbon, Portugal
Sociedade Portuguesa de Ortopedia Dento Facial [IO], Porto, Portugal
Sociedade Potuguesa de Dermatologia e Venereologia [★IO]
Sociedade Rural Brasileira [★IO]
Sociedades Biblicas Unidas [★IO]
Socieded de Epileptologia de Chile [★IO]
Societa di Bioinformatica Italiana [★IO]
Societa Chimica Italiana [★IO]
Societa Europea di Cultura [★IO]
Societa Geologica Italiana [★IO]
Societa Italiana di Anatomia [★IO]
Societa Italiana di Biofisica [★IO]
Societa Italiana di Chirurgia Endoscopica e Nuove Tecnologie [★IO]
Societa Italiana di Dermatologia Chirurgica ed Oncologica [★IO]
Societa Italiana di Dermatologia Medica, Mhirurgica, Estetica e di Malattie Sessualmente Tramesse [★IO]
Societa Italiana Di Endoscopia Digestiva [★IO]
Societa Italiana di Ecologia [★IO]
Societa Italiana di Endocrinologia [IO], Florence, Italy
Societa Italiana di Endocrinologia e Diabetologia Pediatrica [IO], Modena, Italy
Societa Italiana di Farmacia Ospedaliera [★IO]
Societa Italiana di Farmacologia [★IO]
Societa Italiana di Fertilita e Sterilita e Medicina della Riproduzione [★IO]
Societa Italiana di Fisica [★IO]
Societa Italiana di Fisiologia [★IO]
Societa Italiana di Fotogrammetria e Topografia [IO], Turin, Italy
Societa Italiana di Genetica Agraria [★IO]
Societa Italiana di Geologia Ambientale [★IO]
Societa Italiana di Gerontologia e Geriatria [★IO]
Societa Italiana di Ginecologia ed Ostetricia [IO], Rome, Italy
Societa Italiana per l'Organizzazione Internazionale [★IO]
Societa Italiana di Mgt. dello Sport [★IO]
Societa Italiana di Medicina Generale [IO], Florence, Italy
Societa Italiana di Medicina Interna [★IO]
Societa Italiana di Mineralogia e Petrologia [IO], Pisa, Italy
Societa Italiana di Neurofisiologia Clinica [IO], Naples, Italy
Societa Italiana di Neuroscienze [★IO]
Societa Italiana di Patologia Vegetale [★IO]
Societa Italiana di Pediatria [IO], Milan, Italy
Societa Italiana di Psicologia [IO], Rome, Italy
Societa Italiana Psicosintesi Terapeutica [★IO]
Societa Italiana per la Psicosomatica in Ginecologia e Ostetroicia [★IO]
Societa Italiana di Radiologia Medica [★IO]
Societa Italiana di Reumatologia [★IO]
Societa Italiana di Scienze Microscopiche [★IO]
Societa Italiana di Tossicologia [★IO]
Societa Medica Italiana di Paraplegia [IO], Turin, Italy
Societa Meteorologica Italiana [★IO]
Societa per lo Studio dei Problemi Fiscali [★IO]
Societadi Scienze Farmacologiche Applicate [★IO]
Societas Biochemica, Biophysica et Microbiologica Fenniae [★IO]
Societas Biochemica, Biophysica et Microbiological Fenniae [★IO]
Societas Biologica Fennica Vanamo [★IO]
Societas Campanariorum - Defunct.

A star before a book entry number signifies that the name is not listed separately, but is mentioned within the entry.

Societas Docta - Address unknown since 2001.
Societas Europaea Anatomorum Veterinariorum [★IO]
Societas Europaea Herpetologica [★IO]
Societas Heraldica Scandinavica [IO], Farum, Denmark
Societas Internationalis Aerosolibus in Medicina [★IO]
Societas Internationalis pro Diagnostica Ultrasonica in Ophthalmologia [★IO]
Societas Internationalis Studiis NeoLatinis Provehendis [★IO]
Societas Linguistica Europaea [★IO]
Societas Liturgica [IO], Louisville, KY, United States
Societas Liturgica [19911], c/o Alan Barthel, Sec., 100 Witherspoon St., Louisville, KY 40202, (502)569-5759
Societas Neurologica Japonica [★IO]
Societas Physiologia Plantarum Scandinavica [★IO]
Societate de Gestiune Colectiva a Dreptunior de Autor [IO], Bucharest, Romania
Societatea Astronomica Romana de Meteori [★IO]
Societatea de Educatie Contraceptiva si Sexuala [IO], Horezu, Romania
Societatea de Gestiune Colectiva a Drepturilor de Autor in Domeniul Artelor Vizuale [★IO]
Societatea de Mgt., Consulting si Tehnologie in Constructii [★IO]
Societatea Romana Alzheimer [★IO]
Societatea Romana de Cardiologie [★IO]
Societatea Romana De Stiinte Fiziologice [★IO]
Societatea Romana de Endoscopie Digestiva [★IO]
Societatea Romana de Informatica Medicala [★IO]
Societatea Romana de Medicina Sportiva [IO], Bucharest, Romania
Societe canadienne de recherches cliniques [★IO]
Societe canadienne de medecine interne [★IO]
Societe canadienne de medecine nucleaire [★IO]
Societe canadienne du sida [★IO]
Societe canadienne de biomecanique [★IO]
Societe canadienne de chimie [★IO]
Societe quebecoise de gestion collective des droits de reproduction [IO], Montreal, QC, Canada
Societe canadienne de technologie chimique [★IO]
Societe Africaine de Reassurance [★IO]
Societe des Africanistes [★IO]
Societe Alzheimer du Canada [★IO]
Societe Americaine pour l'Etude de la Numismatique Francaise - Address unknown since 2001.
Societe des Amis d'Alexandre Dumas [IO], Le Port-Marly, France
Societe Anatomique de Paris [★IO]
Societe des Architectes Diplomes par le Gouvernement Francais, Groupe Americain - Defunct.
Societe Astronomique de France [★IO]
Societe Astronomique de France [IO], Paris, France
Societe Astronomique de Suisse [★IO]
Societe du droit de reproduction des auteurs, compositeurs et editeurs au Canada [★IO]
Societe des Auteurs et Compositeurs Dramatiques [★IO]
Societe des Auteurs, Compositeurs et Editeurs de Musique [IO], Neuilly-sur-Seine, France
Societe Belge des Auteurs Compositeurs et Editeurs [IO], Brussels, Belgium
Societe Belge de Cardiologie/Belgische Vereniging Voor Cardiologie [★IO]
Societe Belge de Geologie, Piqleon-Tologie and Hydrologie [★IO]
Societe Belge de Microscopie [★IO]
Societe Belge de Photogrammetrie, de Teledetection et de Cartographie [IO], Brussels, Belgium
Societe Belge de Physiologie et de Pharmacologie Fondamentales et Cliniques [★IO]
Societe Bernoulli pour la Statistique Mathematique et la Probabilite [★IO]
Societe Bibliographique du Canada [★IO]
Societe Biblique Canadienne [★IO]
Societe de Biologie Experimentale [★IO]
Societe de Biophysique du Canada [★IO]
Societe Botanique Suisse [★IO]
Societe des designers graphiques du Canada [★IO]
Societe de la medecine rurale du Canada [★IO]
Societe statistique du Canada [★IO]
Societe pour la nature et les parcs du Canada [★IO]

Societe historique du Canada [★IO]
Societe Canadienne des Anesthesiologistes [★IO]
Societe Canadienne des Auteurs, Illustrateurs, et Artistes pour Enfants [★IO]
Societe Canadienne des Biologistes l'Environnement [★IO]
Societe Canadienne du Cancer [★IO]
Societe Canadienne de Cardiologie [★IO]
Societe Canadienne des Chirurgiens Plasticiens [★IO]
Societe Canadienne des Clinico-Chimistes [★IO]
Societe Canadienne d'Agronomie [★IO]
Societe Canadienne d'Apprentissage Psychomoteur et de Psychologie du Sport [★IO]
Societe Canadienne d'Astronomie [★IO]
Societe Canadienne d'Atherosclerose, de Thrombose et de Biologie Vasculaire [★IO]
Societe Canadienne d'Education par l'Art [★IO]
Societe Canadienne D'endocrinologie et metabolisme [★IO]
Societe Canadienne d'Esthetique [★IO]
Societe Canadienne d'Hematologie [★IO]
Societe Canadienne d'Histoire de l'Eglise Catholique - Sect. Francaise [★IO]
Societe Canadienne d'Histoire Orale [★IO]
Societe Canadienne d'Histoire et Philosophie des Sciences [★IO]
Societe Canadienne d'historie de l'Eglise [★IO]
Societe Canadienne des pharmaciens d'Hopitaux [★IO]
Societe Canadienne d'Hypertension Arterielle [★IO]
Societe Canadienne du Dialogue Humaine Machine [★IO]
Societe Canadienne d'Immunologie [★IO]
Societe Canadienne d'Ingenierie des Services de Sante [★IO]
Societe Canadienne des Directeurs de Clubs [★IO]
Societe Canadienne des Directeurs d'Association [★IO]
Societe Canadienne d'Ophthalmologie [★IO]
Societe Canadienne de Droit Canonique [★IO]
Societe Canadienne des Etudes Bibliques [★IO]
Societe Canadienne pour les Etudes Italiennes [★IO]
Societe Canadienne de Fertilite et d'Andrologie [★IO]
Societe Canadienne pour la Formation et le Perfectionnement [★IO]
Societe Canadienne de Genie Biomedical [★IO]
Societe Canadienne de Genie Chimique [★IO]
Societe Canadienne de Genie Civil [★IO]
Societe Canadienne de Genie Mecanique [★IO]
Societe Canadienne de Geotechnique [★IO]
Societe Canadienne de Geriatrie [★IO]
Societe Canadienne des Infirmieres en Sante Respiratoire [★IO]
Societe Canadienne pour l'Analyse de Documents [★IO]
Societe Canadienne de l'Autisme [★IO]
Societe Canadienne pour l'Etude de la Religion [★IO]
Societe Canadienne de l'Hemophilie [★IO]
Societe Canadienne de Mfrs. de Chaudieres [★IO]
Societe Canadienne de Meteorologie et d'Oceanographique [★IO]
Societe Canadienne des Microbiologistes [★IO]
Societe Canadienne de Musique Folklorique [★IO]
Societe Canadienne de Navigation [★IO]
Societe Canadienne de Neurochirurgie [★IO]
Societe Canadienne de Pediatrie [★IO]
Societe Canadienne de Peintres en Aquarelle [★IO]
Societe Canadienne de Pharmacologie Clinique [★IO]
Societe Canadienne de Physiologie Vegetale [★IO]
Societe Canadienne de Phytopathologie [★IO]
Societe Canadienne pour la Prevention de la Cruaute les Enfants [★IO]
Societe Canadienne des Professeurs de la Technique Alexander [★IO]
Societe Canadienne de Psychanalyse [★IO]
Societe Canadienne de Psychologie [★IO]
Societe Canadienne pour la Recherche Nautique [★IO]
Societe Canadienne de Recherche Operationnelle [★IO]

Societe Canadienne des Relations Publiques [★IO]
Societe Canadienne de Rhumatologie [★IO]
Societe Canadienne de la Sante et de la Securite au Travail [★IO]
Societe Canadienne de la Schizophrenie [★IO]
Societe Canadienne de Sci. animale [★IO]
Societe Canadienne de Sci. de Laboratoire Medical [★IO]
Societe Canadienne de la Sci. du Sol [★IO]
Societe Canadienne des Sciences du Cerveau, du Comportement et de la Cognition [★IO]
Societe Canadienne des Sciences Judiciaires [★IO]
Societe Canadienne de la Sclerose Laterale Amyotrophique [★IO]
Societe Canadienne de la Sclerose en Plaques [★IO]
Societe Canadienne de Sociologie et d'Anthropologie [★IO]
Societe Canadienne de Soins Intensifs [★IO]
Societe Canadienne du Sommeil [★IO]
Societe Canadienne de la Surete Industrielle [★IO]
Societe Canadienne pour la Technologie du Coussin d'Air [★IO]
Societe Canadienne des Technologistes en Cardiologie [★IO]
Societe Canadienne des Technologistes en Orthopedie [★IO]
Societe Canadienne de Teledetection [★IO]
Societe Canadienne des Therapeutes Respiratoires [★IO]
Societe Canadienne de Thoracologie [★IO]
Societe Canadienne pour les Traditions Musicales [★IO]
Societe Canadienne de Zoologie [★IO]
Societe des Canadiennes dans la Sci. et la Technologies [★IO]
Societe de Chimie Industrielle, Amer. Sect. [IO], Hillsborough, NJ, United States
Societe de Chimie Industrielle, Amer. Sect. [6693], 44 Deanna Dr., Ste. 128, Hillsborough, NJ 08844, (212)725-9539
Societe de Chimie Industrielle - French Sect. [IO], Paris, France
Societe de Chimie Therapeutique [IO], Chatenay-Malabry, France
Societe Civile des Auteurs Multimedia [★IO]
Societe Collective de Retransmission du Canada [★IO]
Societe Congolaise d'Osteoporose [IO], Kinshasa, Democratic Republic of the Congo
Societe Culinaire Philanthropique [19138], 305 E 47th St., Ste. 11B, New York, NY 10017, (212)308-0628
Societe Culturelle Canadienne des Sourds [★IO]
Societe canadienne d'agroeconomie [★IO]
Societe canadienne d'allergie et d'immunologie clinique [★IO]
Societe de genealogie et d'archives de Rimouski [IO], Rimouski, QC, Canada
Societe d'arthrite [★IO]
Societe educative de visites et d'echanges au Canada [★IO]
Societe d'Entomologie du Canada [★IO]
Societe d'Ethologie Veterinaire [★IO]
Societe canadienne d'etude du dix-huiteme siecle [★IO]
Societe d'etudes socialistes [★IO]
Societe canadienne d'evaluation [★IO]
Societe Ecossaise d'Heraldique [★IO]
Societe des Editeurs et Auteurs de Musique [IO], Paris, France
Societe des Editeurs de la Presse Privee [IO], Ouagadougou, Burkina Faso
Societe des Etudes Cauvssiennes [★7488]
Societe Europeene d'Ichthyologie [★IO]
Societe Europeene de Psychiatrie de l'Enfant et de l'Adolescent [★IO]
Societe Europeenne de Chirurgie Cardiovasculaire [★IO]
Societe Europeenne pour la Formation des Ingenieurs [★IO]
Societe Europeenne de Gynecologie [★IO]
Societe Europeenne des Ophtalmologistes Contactologues [★IO]
Societe des Exportateurs de Vins Suisses [★IO]

Reference to "IO" in place of a book number signifies that the association may be found in the 45th edition of International Organizations.

Societe Finno-Ougrienne [★IO]

Societe Francaise de Cardiologie [★IO]

Societe Francaise de Ceramique [★IO]

Societe Francaise de Chimie [★IO]

Societe Francaise d'Acoustique [IO], Paris, France

Societe Francaise d'Anesthesie et de Reanimation [★IO]

Societe Francaise d'Angeiologie [IO], Paris, France

Societe Francaise d'Ecologie [★IO]

Societe Francaise d'Economie Rurale [★IO]

Societe Francaise d'Endoscopie Digestive [★IO]

Societe Francaise de Dermatologie [★IO]

Societe Francaise d'Histoire Outre-Mer [★IO]

Societe Francaise d'Orchidophilie [★IO]

Societe Francaise d'Osteodensitometrie Clinic [IO], Narbonne, France

Societe Francaise de Genetique [★IO]

Societe Francaise de Geriatrie et Gerontologie [★IO]

Societe Francaise de Gynecologie et Obstetique Psychosomatique [★IO]

Societe Francaise de Medecine Manuelle Orthopedique et Osteopathique [★IO]

Societe Francaise de Medecine du Sport [IO], Caen, France

Societe Francaise de Metallurgie et de Materiaux [★IO]

Societe Francaise des Microscopies [IO], Paris, France

Societe Francaise de Musicologie [★IO]

Societe Francaise de Pharmacologie [★IO]

Societe Francaise de Physique [★IO]

Societe Francaise de Rhumatologie [IO], Paris, France

Societe Francaise des Roses 'Les Amis des Roses' [IO], Lyon, France

Societe Francaise du Vide [★IO]

Societe Francophone Vitamines et Biofacteurs [★IO]

Societe Genealogique Canadienne-Francaise [★IO]

Societe des Gens de Lettres [IO], Paris, France

Societe de Geologie Appliquee aux Gites Mineraux [★IO]

Societe Geologique de France [★IO]

Societe des Gynecologues Oncologues du Canada [★IO]

Societe H.G. Wells [★IO]

Societe Historique et Folklorique Francaise - Defunct.

Societe Historique Franco-Americaine - Address unknown since 1999.

Societe des Indexateurs [★IO]

Societe des Ingenieurs de l'Automobile [★IO]

Societe Intl. d'Ethologie Applie [★IO]

Societe Intl. d'Etudes Gemellaires [★IO]

Societe Internationale de Brecht [★IO]

Societe Internationale de Brecht [★9661]

Societe Internationale de Chimiotherapie [★IO]

Societe Internationale de Chirurgie [★IO]

Societe Internationale de Chirurgie Orthopedique et de Traumatologie [★IO]

Societe Internationale Contre la Lepre [★IO]

Societe Internationale de Criminologie [★IO]

Societe Internationale de Defense Sociale [★IO]

Societe Internationale d'Etude du XVIIIe Siecle [★IO]

Societe Internationale pour le Developpement [★IO]

Societe Internationale d'Histoire de la Medecine [★IO]

Societe Internationale d'Hydrologie et de Climatologie Medicale [★IO]

Societe Internationale de Dialectologie et Geolinguistique [★IO]

Societe Internationale d'Oncologie Pediatrique [★IO]

Societe Internationale de Droit Militaire et de Droit de la Guerre [★IO]

Societe Internationale de Droit du Travail et de la Securite Sociale [★IO]

Societe Internationale d'Urologie [IO], Montreal, QC, Canada

Societe Internationale pour l Equite en Sante [★IO]

Societe Internationale Financiere pour les Investissements et le Developpement en Afrique [★IO]

Societe Internationale Kodaly [★IO]

Societe Internationale pour l'Etude de la Philosophie Medievale [★IO]

Societe Internationale de Mecanique des Roches [★IO]

Societe Internationale de Mecanique des Sols et de la Geotechnique [★IO]

Societe Internationale de Medecine Interne [★IO]

Societe Internationale des Morphologistes de la Vie Vegetale [★IO]

Societe Internationale de Mycologie Humaine et Animales [★IO]

Societe Internationale de Neurochimie [★IO]

Societe Internationale de Neuropathologie [★IO]

Societe Internationale de Psychopathologie de l'Expression d'Art Therapie [★IO]

Societe Internationale des Radiographes et Techniciens de Radiologie [★IO]

Societe Internationale de Recherche sur le Folklore Oral [★IO]

Societe Internationale du Rorschach et des Methodes Projectives [★IO]

Societe Internationale Salzedo [★IO]

Societe Internationale de la Sci. Horticole [★IO]

Societe Internationale Scientifique des Champignons Comestibles [★IO]

Societe Internationale de Sociologie des Religions [★IO]

Societe Internationale pour la Stereologie [★IO]

Societe Internationale de Transfusion Sanguine [★IO]

Societe Internationale de Traumatologie du Ski et de Medecine des Sports d'Hiver [★IO]

Societe Jean-Jacques Rousseau [IO], Geneva, Switzerland

Societe Jersiaise [IO], Jersey, United Kingdom

Societe Kipling [★IO]

Societe de Legislation Comparee [★IO]

Societe canadienne de l'energie du sol [★IO]

Societe pour l'Etude de la Coherence [★IO]

Societe canadienne pour l'etude de l'education [★IO]

Societe pour l'Etude de l'Egypte Ancienne [★IO]

Societe canadienne pour l'etude de l'enseignement superieur [★IO]

Societe de l'Hepatite C du Canada [★IO]

Societe Libanaise de Gastroenterologie [★IO]

Societe Libanaise de Rhumatologie [IO], Beirut, Lebanon

Societe Litteraire de Bruxelles [★IO]

Societe Luxembourgeoise d'Orthodontie [IO], Luxembourg, Luxembourg

Societe Marocaine De Fertilite Et De Contraception [IO], Casablanca, Morocco

Societe Marocaine de Rhumatologie [★IO]

Societe Mathematique du Canada [★IO]

Societe de Microscopie du Canada [★IO]

Societe Mondiale pour la Protection des Animaux [IO]

Societe de Musique des Universites Canadiennes [★IO]

Societe Nationale Canadienne des Sourds-Aveugles [★IO]

Societe des Naturalistes Luxembourgeois [★IO]

Societe de Neuroendocrinologie [IO], Bordeaux, France

Societe Nucleaire Canadienne [★IO]

Societe de Numismatique Orientale [★IO]

Societe des Obstetriciens et Gynecologues du Canada [★IO]

Societe des Ornithologistes du Canada [★IO]

Societe Pan-Africaine de Cardiologie [★IO]

Societe Parkinson Canada [★IO]

Societe Parkinson d'Ottawa [★IO]

Societe Parkinson du Quebec [★IO]

Societe de Pastel de L'est du Canada [★IO]

Societe de Pathologie Exotique [★IO]

Societe de Pathologie Exotique [IO], Paris, France

Societe de Pharmacologie du Canada [★IO]

Societe de Physiologie [★IO]

Societe Planetaire pour l'Assainissement de l'Energie [★IO]

Societe des Professeurs Francais en Amerique [★8450]

Societe des Professeurs Francais et Francophones d'Amerique [8450], PO Box 6026, FDR Sta., New York, NY 10150-6026

Societe pour la Protection de la Nature en Israel [★IO]

Societe de Recherche sur le Cancer [★IO]

Societe Royale Belge des Electriciens [IO], Brussels, Belgium

Societe Royale de Chimie [IO], Brussels, Belgium

Societe Royale D'Economie Politique De Belgique [IO], Charleroi, Belgium

Societe Royale Du Canada [★IO]

Societe Royale Heraldique du Canada [★IO]

Societe Royale de Numismatique de Belgique [IO], Brussels, Belgium

Societe Royale des Sciences de Liege [IO], Liege, Belgium

Societe de Saint Vincent de Paul [★IO]

Societe de Saint-Vincent de Paul - Algeria [IO], Algiers, Algeria

Societe de Saint Vincent de Paul du Burundi [IO], Bujumbura, Burundi

Societe de Saint-Vincent de Paul - Canada [★IO]

Societe de Saint-Vincent de Paul - Cote d' Ivoire [IO], Abidjan, Cote d'Ivoire

Societe Suisse de Biochimie [★IO]

Societe Suisse d'Ethique Biomedicale [★IO]

Societe Suisse d'Heraldique [★IO]

Societe Suisse d'Hydrogeologie [★IO]

Societe Suisse pour l'Optique et l'Optometrie [★IO]

Societe Suisse de Pharmacologie et de Toxicologie [★IO]

Societe Swisse de Medecine du Sport [IO], Bern, Switzerland

Societe des Textes Anglais Anciens [★IO]

Societe de Theorie et Culture Existentialiste et Phenomenologique [★IO]

Societe Tunisien de Medecine du Sport [IO], Tunis, Tunisia

Societe Tunisienne de Cardiologie et de Chirurgie Cardiovasculaire [★IO]

Societe Tunisienne de Codification [★IO]

Societe Universitaire Europeenne de Recherches Financieres [★IO]

Societes des Auters dans les Arts Graphiques et Plastiques [IO], Paris, France

Societas Internationales Limnologiae Theoreticae et Applicatae [★IO]

Societas Internationales Limnologiae Theoreticae et Applicatae [★7240]

Societies; Amer. Coun. of Learned [10197]

Societies; Natl. Conf. of State [19382]

Societies for the Stud. of Religion; Coun. of [9274]

Soc. of the 3rd Infantry Div. [21186], c/o Raymond C. Anderson, Sec.-Treas., 10 Paddington Ct., Hockessin, DE 19707-9766, (302)239-1525

Soc. for Academic Achievement [9078]

Soc. for Academic Continuing Medical Educ. [8875], c/o Prime Mgt. Services, 3416 Primm Ln., Birmingham, AL 35216, (205)978-7990

Society for Academic Continuing Medical Education [IO], Birmingham, AL, United States

Soc. for Academic Emergency Medicine [14344], 901 N Washington Ave., Lansing, MI 48906-5137, (517)485-5484

Soc. of Academic and Res. Surgery [IO], London, United Kingdom

Soc. for Accessible Travel for the Handicapped [★17420]

Soc. for Accessible Travel and Hospitality [17420], 347 5th Ave., Ste. 605, New York, NY 10016, (212)447-7284

Soc. of Accredited Marine Surveyors [7720], 4605 Cardinal Blvd., Jacksonville, FL 32210, (904)384-1494

Society of Accredited Marine Surveyors [IO], Jacksonville, FL, United States

Soc. of Actuaries [2239], 475 N Martingale Rd., No. 600, Schaumburg, IL 60173, (847)706-3500

Soc. for Acupuncture Res. [13537], c/o Richard Harris, PhD, PO Box 385, Ann Arbor, MI 48106

Soc. for Acupuncture Res. [IO], Ann Arbor, MI, United States

Soc. for Adolescent Medicine [13974], 1916 Copper Oaks Cir., Blue Springs, MO 64015, (816)224-8010

Soc. to Advance Foreclosure Education - Defunct.

Soc. for Advanced Legal Stud. [IO], London, United Kingdom

Soc. for the Advancement of Ambulatory Care - Defunct.

A star before a book entry number signifies that the name is not listed separately, but is mentioned within the entry.

Soc. for the Advancement of Amer. Philosophy [**10828**], c/o Dr. Thomas Alexander, Pres., Dept. of Philosophy, Southern Illinois Univ., Faner Hall, Rm. 3065, Mailcode 4505, Carbondale, IL 62901, (618)536-6641

Soc. for the Advancement of Anaesthesia in Dentistry [**IO**], London, United Kingdom

Soc. for the Advancement of Architecture [★**IO**]

Soc. for the Advancement of Behavior Anal. [**6538**], 1219 S Park St., Kalamazoo, MI 49001-5607, (269)492-9310

Soc. for the Advancement of Blood Mgt. [**14798**], 555 E Wells St., Ste. 1100, Milwaukee, WI 53202-3800, (414)276-9339

Soc. for the Advancement of Blood Mgt. [**IO**], Milwaukee, WI, United States

Soc. for the Advancement of Botany - Address unknown since 1995.

Soc. for Advancement of Chicanos and Native Americans in Sci. [**7630**], PO Box 8526, Santa Cruz, CA 95061-8526, (831)459-0170

Soc. for the Advancement of Continuing Education for Ministry - Address unknown since 1994.

Soc. for the Advancement of Criminology [★**11899**]

Soc. for the Advancement of Economic Theory [**6893**], Univ. of Illinois, Dept. of Economics, 330 Wohlers Hall, 1206 S 6th St., Champaign, IL 61820, (217)333-0120

Soc. for the Advancement of Educ. [**8305**], 500 Bi-County Blvd., Ste. 203, Farmingdale, NY 11735, (631)293-4343

Soc. for the Advancement of Excellence in Educ. [**IO**], Kelowna, BC, Canada

Soc. for the Advancement of the Field Theory - Address unknown since 2000.

Soc. for the Advancement of Fission Energy - Defunct.

Soc. for the Advancement of Food Service Res. - Address unknown since 2004.

Soc. for the Advancement of Freestanding Ambulatory Surgical Care [★**16582**]

Soc. for Advancement of Games and Simulation in Educ. and Training [**IO**], Ryton, United Kingdom

Soc. for the Advancement of Games and Simulations in Educ. and Training [**IO**], Ryton, United Kingdom

Soc. for the Advancement of Gastroenterology [★**14405**]

Soc. for the Advancement of Gen. Systems Theory [★**IO**]

Soc. for the Advancement of the George Economy - Defunct.

Soc. for the Advancement of Good English - Defunct.

Soc. for the Advancement of Judaism [**20180**], 15 W 86th St., New York, NY 10024, (212)724-7000

Soc. for Advancement of Mgt. [**2515**], 6300 Ocean Dr. - FC 111, Corpus Christi, TX 78412, (361)825-6045

Soc. for the Advancement of Material and Process Engg. [**7285**], 1161 Park View Dr., Ste. 200, Covina, CA 91724, (626)331-0616

Soc. for Advancement in Nursing - Address unknown since 1999.

Soc. for the Advancement of Scandinavian Stud. [**9070**], Brigham Young Univ., Box 26118, Provo, UT 84602-6118, (801)422-5598

Soc. for the Advancement of Social Psychology - Defunct.

Soc. for the Advancement of Socio-Economics [**17472**], PO Box 39008, Baltimore, MD 21212, (410)435-6617

Soc. for the Advancement of Space Travel - Defunct.

Soc. for the Advancement of Women's Hea. Res. [★**16910**]

Soc. for the Advancement of Women's Imaging [**16294**], PO Box 885, Schererville, IN 46375, (219)864-3065

Soc. of Aeronautical Weight Engineers, Inc. [★**7699**]

Soc. of Aerospace Material and Process Engineers [★**7285**]

Soc. of Afghan Professionals [**9343**], 39155 Liberty St., Ste. D460, Fremont, CA 94538, (510)574-2183

Soc. of African Missions [**19719**], 23 Bliss Ave., Tenafly, NJ 07670-3001, (201)567-0450

Soc. of African Missions [★**20396**]

Soc. of African Missions [**IO**], Tenafly, NJ, United States

Soc. of Africanists [**IO**], Paris, France

Soc. Against Elephant Exploitation - Address unknown since 1995.

Soc. Against Governmental Abuse - Address unknown since 1999.

Soc. Against Vivisection [**11458**]

Soc. for Agricultural Bacteriology [★**IO**]

Soc. of Agricultural Meteorology of Japan [**IO**], Tokyo, Japan

Soc. for Agricultural Training through Integrated Voluntary Activities - Address unknown since 1999.

Soc. of Air Force Anesthesiologists [★**13683**]

Soc. of Air Force Clinical Surgeons [**16587**], 5350 Dunlay Dr., Unit 214, Sacramento, CA 95835-1563, (916)924-0352

Soc. of Air Force Physician Assistants [**20665**], PO Box 340838, San Antonio, TX 78234-0838

Soc. of Air Force Physicians [**15264**], PO Box 64, Devine, TX 78016-0064, (830)665-4048

Soc. of Air Line Meteorologists - Address unknown since 1995.

Soc. of Air Safety Investigators [★**12966**]

Soc. of Air Safety Investigators [★**IO**]

Soc. of Aircraft Material and Process Engineers [★**7285**]

Soc. of Alexandria - Defunct.

Soc. for All Artists [**IO**], Newark, United Kingdom

Soc. Alliance for Human Empowerment; Simple [**18637**]

Soc. of Allied Weight Engineers [**7699**], c/o Mr. Ronald L. Fox, Exec. Dir., 2131 Tevis Ave., Long Beach, CA 90815-3352, (562)596-2873

Soc. for Amateur Radio in The Netherlands [**IO**], Arnhem, Netherlands

Soc. for Amateur Scientists [**7631**], 5600 Post Rd., Ste. 114-341, East Greenwich, RI 02818, (401)398-7001

Soc. for Ambulatory Anesthesia [**13688**], 520 N Northwest Hwy., Park Ridge, IL 60068-2573, (847)825-5586

Soc. for Ambulatory Care Professionals - Address unknown since 2003.

Soc. for Amer. Archaeology [**6455**], 900 2nd St. NE, No. 12, Washington, DC 20002-3560, (202)789-8200

Soc. of Amer. Archivists [**9403**], 527 S Wells St., 5th Fl., Chicago, IL 60607, (312)922-0140

Society of Amer. Artists [★**9496**]

Soc. of Amer. Bacteriologists [★**6565**]

Soc. for Amer. Baseball Res. [**23126**], 812 Huron Rd., No. 719, Cleveland, OH 44115, (216)575-0500

Soc. of Amer. Bus. and Economic Writers [★**3161**]

Soc. of Amer. Bus. Editors and Writers [**3161**], c/o Missouri Scholarship of Journalism, 385 McReynolds, Columbia, MO 65211-1200, (573)882-7862

Soc. of Amer. Bus. Writers [★**3161**]

Soc. of Amer. Etchers [★**9992**]

Soc. of Amer. Etchers, Gravers, Lithographers and Woodcutters [★**9992**]

Soc. of Amer. Fight Directors [**9268**], 1350 E Flamingo Rd., No. 25, Las Vegas, NV 89119, (800)659-6579

Soc. of Amer. Florists [**1493**], 1601 Duke St., Alexandria, VA 22314-3406, (703)836-8700

Soc. of Amer. Florists and Ornamental Horticulturists [★**1493**]

Soc. of Amer. Foresters [**4695**], 5400 Grosvenor Ln., Bethesda, MD 20814-2198, (301)897-8720

Soc. of Amer. Gastrointestinal and Endoscopic Surgeons [**14428**], 11300 W Olympic Blvd., Ste. 600, Los Angeles, CA 90064, (310)437-0544

Society of American Gastrointestinal and Endoscopic Surgeons [**IO**], Los Angeles, CA, United States

Soc. of Amer. Graphic Artists [**9992**], 32 Union Sq., Rm. 1214, New York, NY 10003

Soc. of Amer. Historians - Defunct.

Soc. of Amer. Historical Artists - Defunct.

Soc. for Amer. Indian Studies and Res. - Defunct.

Soc. of Amer. Inventors - Address unknown since 1991.

Soc. of Amer. Law Teachers - Defunct.

Soc. of Amer. Legion Founders - Defunct.

Soc. of Amer. Magicians [**22623**], PO Box 510260, St. Louis, MO 63151, (314)846-5659

Soc. of Amer. Mosaic Artists [**9525**], PO Box 624, Ligonier, PA 15658, (724)238-3087

Soc. for Amer. Music [**10698**], Univ. of Pittsburgh, Stephen Foster Memorial, Pittsburgh, PA 15260, (412)624-3031

Soc. of Amer. Period Furniture Makers [**9970**], c/o Brian Coe, Ed., 2865 Friendship-Ledford Rd., Winston-Salem, NC 27107

Soc. for Amer. Philosophy - Defunct.

Soc. of Amer. Registered Architects [**6480**], 14 E 38th St., 11th Fl., New York, NY 10016, (218)724-5568

Soc. of Amer. Royalty [**18082**], PO Box 190313, Dallas, TX 75219, (972)224-6881

Soc. of Amer. Silversmiths [**3712**], PO Box 72839, Providence, RI 02907, (401)461-6840

Soc. of Amer. Travel Writers [**3162**], 7044 S 13th St., Oak Creek, WI 53154, (414)908-4949

Soc. of Amer. Value Engineers [★**7185**]

Soc. of Amer. Value Engineers [★**IO**]

Soc. of Amer. Ventriloquists - Defunct.

Soc. of Amer. Wood Preservers - Defunct.

Soc. of Amer. Woodworkers - Defunct.

Soc. of Amers. of Colonial Descent - Defunct.

Soc. of Americans for Vashchenko Emigration - Defunct.

Soc. for Anaerobic Microbiology [**IO**], London, United Kingdom

Soc. for the Anal. of African-American Public Hea. Issues [**16253**], PO Box 360350, Decatur, GA 30036

Soc. for Analytical Chemistry [★**IO**]

Soc. for Analytical Cytology [★**IO**]

Soc. for Analytical Cytology [★**6583**]

Soc. for Analytical Feminism [**10829**], c/o Sharon Crasnow, Pres., 925 Archer St., San Diego, CA 92109

Soc. for Ancient Greek Philosophy [**10830**], c/o Anthony Preus, Sec.-Treas., Binghamton Univ., Dept. of Philosophy, Binghamton, NY 13902-6000, (607)777-2886

Soc. for Ancient Hellenic Stud. [**IO**], Port Melbourne, Australia

Soc. of Ancient Military Historians [**10481**], c/o Dr. Lee L. Brice, Pres., Morgan Hall 445, Dept. of History, Western Illinois Univ., Macomb, IL 61455-1390, (309)298-1053

Soc. for Ancient Numismatics - Address unknown since 1995.

Soc. of Andrology - India [**IO**], Hyderabad, India

Soc. for Anglo-Chinese Understanding [**IO**], Cheltenham, United Kingdom

Soc. of Animal Artists [**9526**], 47 5th Ave., New York, NY 10003, (212)741-2880

Soc. for Animal Protective Legislation [**11459**], PO Box 3719, Washington, DC 20027, (703)836-4300

Soc. for Animal Rights [★**11419**]

Soc. for Animal Rights [★**IO**]

Soc. and Animals Forum [**11460**], PO Box 1297, Washington Grove, MD 20880-1297, (301)963-4751

Soc. for Anthropology in Community Colleges [**7954**], c/o Laura Gonzalez, VP for Membership and Development, Miramar Coll., Dept. of Anthropology, 10440 Black Mountain Rd., San Diego, CA 92126, (619)388-7534

Soc. for the Anthropology of Consciousness [**7955**], c/o Amer. Anthropological Assn., 2200 Wilson Blvd., Ste. 600, Arlington, VA 22201, (703)528-1902

Soc. for the Anthropology of Europe [**6423**], c/o Amer. Anthropological Assn., 2200 Wilson Blvd., Ste. 600, Arlington, VA 22201, (703)528-1902

Soc. for the Anthropology of Europe [**IO**], Arlington, VA, United States

Soc. for the Anthropology of Food and Nutrition [**6424**], c/o Craig Hadley, Sec.-Treas., Univ. of Michigan, Center for Social Epidemiology and Population Hea., 1214 S Univ. Ave., 2nd Fl., Ann Arbor, MI 48104-2592, (734)615-9215

Soc. for the Anthropology of North Am. [**6425**], c/o Amer. Anthropological Assn., 2200 Wilson Blvd., Ste. 600, Arlington, VA 22201, (703)528-1902

Reference to "IO" in place of a book number signifies that the association may be found in the 45th edition of International Organizations.

Soc. for the Anthropology of Religion [6426], c/o Andrew Buckser, Purdue Univ., Dept. of Sociology and Anthropology, 700 W State St., West Lafayette, IN 47907-1365

Soc. for the Anthropology of Visual Commun. [★6436]

Soc. of Antiquaries of London [IO], London, United Kingdom

Soc. of Antiquaries of Newcastle-upon-Tyne [IO], Newcastle upon Tyne, United Kingdom

Soc. of Antiquaries of Scotland [IO], Edinburgh, United Kingdom

Soc. of Antique Label Collectors - Address unknown since 1999.

Soc. of Antique Modelers [21477], c/o Mike Myers, Pres./Legal Counsel, 911 Kilmary Dr., Glendale, CA 91207-1105, (818)241-9154

Soc. of Apothecaries of London [★IO]

Soc. for the Application of Free Energy - Address unknown since 2003.

Soc. for Applied Anthropology [6427], PO Box 2436, Oklahoma City, OK 73101-2436, (405)843-5113

Soc. for Applied Anthropology [IO], Oklahoma City, OK, United States

Soc. for Applied Bacteriology [★IO]

Soc. of Applied Botany [IO], Braunschweig, Germany

Soc. for Applied Immunohistochemistry [15873], c/o Richard W. Cartun, PhD, Sec.-Treas., Dept. of Pathology, Hartford Hosp., 80 Seymour St., Hartford, CT 06102, (860)545-1596

Soc. for Applied Learning Tech. [8571], 50 Culpeper St., Warrenton, VA 20186, (540)347-0055

Soc. for Applied Microbiology [IO], Bedford, United Kingdom

Soc. for Applied Pharmacological Sciences [IO], Milan, Italy

Soc. for Applied Philosophy [IO], Lancaster, United Kingdom

Soc. for Applied Psychological Res. in the Performing Arts [16170], 3 E Wilson St., Batavia, IL 60510, (877)761-8230

Soc. for Applied Sociology [7668], c/o Assn. for Applied and Clinical Sociology, 712 Pray-Harrold, Dept. of Sociology, Eastern Michigan Univ., Ypsilanti, MI 48197, (734)487-0012

Soc. for Applied Spectroscopy [7690], 201B Broadway St., Frederick, MD 21701-6501, (301)694-8122

Soc. of Archer-Antiquaries [IO], South Gloucestershire, United Kingdom

Soc. of Architectural and Assoc. Technicians [★IO]

Soc. of Architectural Historians [10150], 1365 N Astor St., Chicago, IL 60610-2144, (312)573-1365

Soc. of Architectural Historians of Great Britain [IO], Edinburgh, United Kingdom

Soc. of Archivists - Ireland [IO], Dublin, Ireland

Soc. of Archivists - United Kingdom [IO], Taunton, United Kingdom

Soc. of the Ark and the Dove [20758], PO Box 16374, Baltimore, MD 21201

Soc. for Armenian Stud. [9407], c/o Armenian Stud. Prog., California State Univ., 5245 N Backer Ave., PB4, Fresno, CA 93740-8001, (559)278-2669

Soc. for Armenian Stud. [IO], Fresno, CA, United States

Soc. of Army Historical Res. [IO], London, United Kingdom

Soc. of Army Physician Assistants [15977], PO Box 07490, Fort Myers, FL 33919, (239)482-2162

Soc. for the Arts in Healthcare [13714], 2437 15th St. NW, Washington, DC 20009, (202)299-9770

Soc. for the Arts in Healthcare [IO], Washington, DC, United States

Soc. for the Arts, Religion and Contemporary Culture [9599], c/o Nelvin Vos, Exec. Dir., 15811 Kutztown Rd., Box 15, Maxatawny, PA 19538, (610)683-7581

Soc. for Asian Art [9472], Asian Art Museum, 200 Larkin St., San Francisco, CA 94102, (415)581-3701

Soc. for Asian and Comparative Philosophy [10831], c/o Michiko Yusa, Pres., 516 High St., Dept. of Modern And Classical Languages and Literatures, Western Washington Univ., Bellingham, WA 98225-9057, (360)650-4851

Soc. for Asian Music [10699], PO Box 7819, Austin, TX 78713-7819, (512)232-7621

Soc. for Asian Music [IO], Austin, TX, United States

Soc. of Assistants Teaching in Preparatory Schools [IO], Great Dunmow, United Kingdom

Soc. of Assistants Teaching in Preparatory Schools [★IO]

Soc. for Assisted Reproductive Tech. [16346], c/o Amer. Soc. for Reproductive Medicine, 1209 Montgomery Hwy., Birmingham, AL 35216-2809, (205)978-5000

Soc. of Assn. Executives [★IO]

Soc. of Assn. Optometric Executives [★IO]

Soc. of Assn. Optometric Executives [★15720]

Soc. of Australasian Specialists [★22871]

Soc. of Australasian Specialists [★IO]

Soc. of Australasian Specialists/Oceania [IO], San Jose, CA, United States

Soc. of Australasian Specialists/Oceania [22871], PO Box 24764, San Jose, CA 95154-4764, (408)978-0193

Soc. of Australian Genealogists [IO], Sydney, Australia

Society for Austrian and Habsburg History [IO], Minneapolis, MN, United States

Soc. for Austrian and Habsburg History [9628], c/o Gary B. Cohen, Center for Austrian Stud., Univ. of Minnesota, 314 Social Sci. Bldg., 267 19th Ave. S, Minneapolis, MN 55455, (612)624-9811

Soc. of Authors - England [IO], London, United Kingdom

Soc. of Authors' Representatives [★171]

Soc. of the Autistically Handicapped [★IO]

Soc. for Automation in Bus. Educ. [★IO]

Soc. for Automation in Bus. Educ. [★8132]

Soc. for Automation in English and the Humanities [★8132]

Soc. for Automation in English and the Humanities [★IO]

Soc. for Automation in Fine Arts [★IO]

Soc. for Automation in Fine Arts [★8132]

Soc. for Automation in Professional Educ. [★8132]

Soc. for Automation in Professional Educ. [★IO]

Soc. for Automation in the Sciences and Mathematics - Address unknown since 1995.

Soc. for Automation in the Social Sciences [★8132]

Soc. for Automation in the Social Sciences [★IO]

Soc. of Auto. Engineers [★IO]

Soc. of Auto. Engineers [★6520]

Soc. of Automotive and Aerospace Engineers - Defunct.

Soc. of Automotive Analysts [365], 3300 Washtenaw Ave., Ste. 220, Ann Arbor, MI 48104-4200, (734)677-3518

Soc. of Automotive Engineers [7632], 400 Commonwealth Dr., Warrendale, PA 15096-0001, (724)776-4970

Soc. of Automotive Engineers [IO], Warrendale, PA, United States

Soc. of Automotive Engineers (Australasia) [IO], North Melbourne, Australia

Soc. of Automotive Engineers of China [IO], Beijing, People's Republic of China

Soc. of Automotive Engineers (Japan) [IO], Tokyo, Japan

Soc. of Automotive Engineers; SAE Intl. - [6520]

Soc. of Automotive Engineers - Thailand [IO], Bangkok, Thailand

Society of Automotive Historians [IO], Gales Ferry, CT, United States

Soc. of Automotive Historians [21785], 1102 Long Cove Rd., Gales Ferry, CT 06335-1812

Soc. for Basic Urologic Res. [16712], 1111 N Plaza Dr., Ste. 550, Schaumburg, IL 60173, (847)517-7225

Soc. of Basque Stud. in Am. [9733], 19 Colonial Gardens, Brooklyn, NY 11209

Soc. of Basque Stud. in Am. [IO], Brooklyn, NY, United States

Soc. of Batik Artists - Defunct.

Soc. of Bead Researchers [6456], c/o Alice Scherer, Sec.-Treas., PO Box 13719, Portland, OR 97213

Soc. of Bead Researchers [IO], Parkin, AR, United States

Soc. of Bead Researchers - Canada [IO], Ottawa, ON, Canada

Soc. of Beaux-Arts Architects [★7963]

Soc. of Behavioral Medicine [13740], 555 E Wells St., Ste. 1100, Milwaukee, WI 53202-3823, (414)918-3156

Soc. for Behavioral Neuroendocrinology [13741], c/o Geert De Vries, Pres., Univ. of Massachusetts, Center for Neuroendocrine Stud., Amherst, MA 01003-7720

Soc. for Behavioral Pediatrics [★15898]

Soc. of Bell Ringers - Defunct.

Soc. of the Bible in the Hands of Its Creators - Defunct.

Soc. of Biblical Literature [19530], Luce Center, 825 Houston Mill Rd., Atlanta, GA 30329, (404)727-3100

Soc. of Biblical Literature and Exegesis [★19530]

Soc. for the Bibliography of Natural History [★IO]

Soc. for Bioethics Consultation [★8845]

Soc. for Bioethics Consultation [★8845]

Soc. of Biological Chemists, India [IO], Bangalore, India

Soc. for Biological Engg. [6593], c/o Amer. Inst. of Chem. Engineers, 3 Park Ave., 19th Fl., New York, NY 10016

Soc. of Biological Psychiatry [16095], c/o Mayo Clinic of Jacksonville, Research-Birdsall 310, 4500 San Pablo Rd., Jacksonville, FL 32224, (904)953-2842

Soc. of Biological Psychiatry [IO], Jacksonville, FL, United States

Soc. for Biological Therapy [★IO]

Soc. for Biological Therapy [★13835]

Soc. for Biomedical Engg. [IO], Wetzlar, Germany

Soc. for Biomedical Equipment Technicians - Defunct.

Soc. for Biomolecular Sciences [6694], 36 Tamarack Ave., No. 348, Danbury, CT 06811, (203)743-1336

Society for Biomolecular Sciences [IO], Danbury, CT, United States

Soc. for Biomolecular Screening [★IO]

Soc. for Biomolecular Screening [★6694]

Soc. for Biotechnology, Japan [IO], Osaka, Japan

Soc. of Blessed Gianna Beretta Molla [IO], Warminster, PA, United States

Soc. of Blessed Gianna Beretta Molla [20038], PO Box 2946, Warminster, PA 18974, (215)672-3551

Soc. of Boat and Yacht Designers [1154], 117 E Louisa St., No. 268, Seattle, WA 98102-3203, (801)225-6060

Soc. of Bookbinders [IO], Farnham, United Kingdom

Soc. of Border Leicester Sheep Breeders [IO], Alnwick, United Kingdom

Soc. of Breast Imaging [16295], 1891 Preston White Dr., Reston, VA 20191-4397, (703)715-4390

Soc. of British Aerospace Companies [IO], London, United Kingdom

Soc. of British Fight Directors [★IO]

Soc. of British Gas Indus. [IO], Leamington Spa, United Kingdom

Soc. of British Neurological Surgeons [IO], London, United Kingdom

Soc. of British Printing Ink Mfrs. [★IO]

Soc. of British Water Indus. [IO]

Soc. of British Water and Wastewater Indus. [IO], Leamington Spa, United Kingdom

Society of Broadcast Engineers [IO], Indianapolis, IN, United States

Soc. of Broadcast Engineers [582], 9102 N Meridian St., Ste. 150, Indianapolis, IN 46260, (317)846-9000

Soc. of Brooklyn Etchers [★9992]

Soc. of Bros. [★20481]

Soc. of Building Sci. Educators [8363], c/o Judy Theodorson, Sec.-Treas., PO Box 1495, Spokane, WA 99210

Soc. of Business Advisory Professions - Defunct.

Soc. of Bus. Economists [IO], Andover, United Kingdom

Society for Business Ethics [IO], St. Joseph, MN, United States

Soc. for Bus. Ethics [12127], c/o Joe DesJardins, Exec. Dir., Dept. of Philosophy, Coll. of St. Benedict, St. John's Univ., Coll. Ave., St. Joseph, MN 56374, (320)363-5915

Soc. of Business Folk - Defunct.

A star before a book entry number signifies that the name is not listed separately, but is mentioned within the entry.

Soc. of Bus. Magazine Editors [★3084]

Soc. of Cable Telecommunication Engineers [IO], Watford, United Kingdom

Soc. of Cable Telecommunications Engineers [7040], 140 Philips Rd., Exton, PA 19341-1318, (610)363-6888

Soc. of Cable TV Engineers [★7040]

Soc. of Cable TV Engineers [★IO]

Soc. of Caddy-Spoon Collectors - Address unknown since 1995.

Soc. of California Pioneers [21255], 300 4th St., San Francisco, CA 94107-1272, (415)957-1849

Soc. for Calligraphy [11213], PO Box 64174, Los Angeles, CA 90064-0174

Soc. of Canadian Ornithologists [IO], Montreal, QC, Canada

Soc. for Canadian Women in Sci. and Tech. [IO], Vancouver, BC, Canada

Soc. of Carbide Engineers [★7322]

Soc. of Carbide and Tool Engineers [7322], c/o Pittsburgh Chap. No. 10, PO Box 77, McKeesport, PA 15135, (724)352-5151

Soc. for Cardiac Angiography and Interventions [13924], 2400 N St. NW, Washington, DC 20037-1153, (202)375-6195

Soc. for Cardiological Sci. and Tech. [IO], Sutton Coldfield, United Kingdom

Soc. of Cardiology [★IO]

Soc. of Cardiothoracic Surgeons of Great Britain and Ireland [IO], London, United Kingdom

Soc. of Cardiovascular Anesthesiologists [IO], Richmond, VA, United States

Soc. of Cardiovascular Anesthesiologists [13689], 2209 Dickens Rd., Richmond, VA 23230-2005, (804)282-0084

Soc. of Cardiovascular and Interventional Radiology [★16300]

Soc. for Cardiovascular Magnetic Resonance [15147], 19 Mantua Rd., Mount Royal, NJ 08061, (856)423-8955

Soc. for Cardiovascular Magnetic Resonance [IO], Mount Royal, NJ, United States

Soc. for Cardiovascular Mgt. [★13885]

Soc. for Cardiovascular Pathology [13925], c/o Dr. Peter G. Anderson, Treas., UAB Pathology, UH 213, 1670 Univ. Blvd., Birmingham, AL 35294-0019, (205)934-2414

Society for Cardiovascular Pathology [IO], Birmingham, AL, United States

Soc. for Caribbean Linguistics [IO], St. Augustine, Trinidad and Tobago

Soc. of Carnival Glass Collectors - Defunct.

Soc. of Cartographers [IO], Glasgow, United Kingdom

Soc. of Catholic Coll. Teachers of Sacred Doctrine [★9273]

Soc. of Certified Credit Executives [1447], PO Box 390106, Minneapolis, MN 55439, (952)926-6547

Soc. of Certified Data Pros [★8129]

Soc. of Certified Insurance Counselors [8577], 3630 N Hills Dr., Austin, TX 78731-3028, (512)345-7932

Soc. of Certified Kitchen Designers [2277], c/o Sean Ruck, 687 Willow Grove St., Hackettstown, NJ 07840, (908)813-3792

Soc. of Chairmen of Academic Radiology Departments [16296], c/o Lise Steg Thorsby, Account Exec., 820 Jorie Blvd., Oak Brook, IL 60523, (630)368-3731

Soc. for Chaos Theory in Psychology and Life Sciences [7547], PO Box 484, Pewaukee, WI 53072

Soc. of Chartered Property and Casualty Underwriters [★2160]

Soc. of Chartered Surveyors in the Republic of Ireland [IO], Dublin, Ireland

Soc. for Chem. Engg. and Biotechnology [IO], Frankfurt am Main, Germany

Soc. of Chem. Indus. [IO], London, United Kingdom

Soc. of Chemists and Technologists of Macedonia [IO], Skopje, Macedonia

Soc. of Chemotherapeutists in Bulgaria [IO], Varna, Bulgaria

Soc. of Chest Pain Centers and Providers [15849], 770 Jasonway Ave., Ste. 1B, Columbus, OH 43214, (614)442-5950

Soc. of Chief Quantity Surveyors [★IO]

Soc. for Children with Craniosynostosis - Address unknown since 1999.

Soc. of Children with Mucopolysaccharidosis and Diseases Related [IO], Warsaw, Poland

Soc. of Children's Book Writers [★11194]

Soc. of Children's Book Writers and Illustrators [11194], 8271 Beverly Blvd., Los Angeles, CA 90048, (323)782-1010

Soc. of Chinese Amer. Professors and Scientists [9024], c/o Dr. Zuotao Zeng, Treas., PO Box 5735, Woodridge, IL 60517

Soc. for Ch'ing Studies - Address unknown since 2007.

Soc. of Chiropodists and Podiatrists [IO], London, United Kingdom

Soc. of Chiropractic Orthospinology [14014], c/o Dr. Kirk Eriksen, Pres., 2500 Flowers Chapel Rd., Dothan, AL 36305, (334)793-7992

Soc. of Christian Engineers - Address unknown since 1994.

Soc. of Christian Ethics [12128], PO Box 5126, St. Cloud, MN 56302-5126, (320)253-5407

Soc. of Christian Philosophers [10832], c/o Kelly James Clark, Sec.-Treas., Calvin Coll., Dept. of Philosophy, 3201 Burton St. SE, Grand Rapids, MI 49546-4388, (616)526-6421

Society of Christian Philosophers [IO], Grand Rapids, MI, United States

Soc. for Church Archaeology [IO], York, United Kingdom

Soc. of the Cincinnati [IO], Washington, DC, United States

Soc. of the Cincinnati [20677], 2118 Massachusetts Ave. NW, Washington, DC 20008-2810, (202)785-2040

Soc. of Cinema Collectors and Historians - Address unknown since 1995.

Soc. for Cinema and Media Stud. [9946], 729 Elm Ave., Hester Hall, Rm. 170, Norman, OK 73019, (405)325-8075

Soc. for Cinema Stud. [★9946]

Soc. for Cinematologists [★9946]

Soc. for Cinephiles/Cinecon [9947], 3727 W Magnolia Blvd., No. 760, Burbank, CA 91505, (800)411-0455

Soc. of Civil Engg. Technicians [★IO]

Soc. of Civil War Historians [10151], Dept. of History, Florida Atlantic Univ., Boca Raton, FL 33431, (561)297-2621

Soc. of Cleaning and Restoration Technicians [2477], 200 Vantage Way, Franklin, TN 37067, (615)591-9610

Soc. of Cleaning Technicians [★2477]

Soc. of Clinical Child and Adolescent Psychology [16171], c/o Richard Abidin, EdD, Treas., PO Box 170231, Atlanta, GA 30317, (770)493-7880

Soc. for Clinical Ecology [★14360]

Soc. for Clinical Ecology [★IO]

Soc. for Clinical and Experimental Hypnosis [14927], 221 Rivermoor St., Boston, MA 02132, (617)469-1981

Soc. of Clinical and Medical Electrologists [★14310]

Soc. for Clinical and Medical Hair Removal [14310], 2810 Crossroads Dr., Ste. 3800, Madison, WI 53718, (608)443-2470

Soc. of Clinical Res. Associates [14027], 530 W Butler Ave., Ste. 109, Chalfont, PA 18914, (215)822-8644

Soc. of Clinical Res. Associates [IO], Chalfont, PA, United States

Soc. of Clinical Surgery - Defunct.

Soc. for Clinical Trials [14028], 600 Wyndhurst Ave., Ste. 112, Baltimore, MD 21210, (410)433-4722

Soc. for Clinical Vascular Surgery [13926], 900 Cummings Ctr., No. 221-U, Beverly, MA 01915, (978)927-8330

Soc. for the Collection of Brand-Name Pencils - Defunct.

Soc. of Coll., Natl. and Univ. Libraries [IO], London, United Kingdom

Soc. for Coll. and Univ. Planning [9000], 339 E Liberty, Ste. 300, Ann Arbor, MI 48104-2205, (734)998-7832

Soc. for Collegiate Journalists - Address unknown since 1999.

Soc. of Collision Repair Specialists [428], PO Box 909, Prosser, WA 99350, (708)598-3384

Soc. for Colonial History - Defunct.

Soc. for Colposcopy and Cervical Pathology of Singapore [IO], Singapore, Singapore

Soc. for Comic Art Res. and Preservation - Address unknown since 1995.

Soc. of Commercial Archeology [9485], PO Box 45828, Madison, WI 53744-5828

Soc. of Commercial Seed Technologists [5176], 101 E State St., No. 214, Ithaca, NY 14850, (607)256-3313

Society Commn. for Heart Disease Resources; Inter. [★13890]

Soc. of Commissioned Officers - Defunct.

Soc. for Commissioning New Music - Defunct.

Soc. for Community Development [★IO]

Soc. of Community Medicine [★IO]

Soc. for Companion Animal Stud. [IO], Burford, United Kingdom

Soc. of the Companions of the Holy Cross [19971], Adelynrood Retreat and Community Center, 46 Elm St., Byfield, MA 01922-2812, (978)462-6721

Soc. of Comparative Legislation [IO], Paris, France

Soc. for the Comparative Stud. of Soc. and History [10152], c/o Dr. David Akin, Managing Ed., Univ. of Michigan, 1007 E Huron, Ann Arbor, MI 48109-1690, (734)764-6362

Soc. of the Compassionate Friends [★12666]

Soc. of Competitive Intelligence Professionals [7211], 1700 Diagonal Rd., Ste. 600, Alexandria, VA 22314, (703)739-0696

Society of Competitive Intelligence Professionals [IO], Alexandria, VA, United States

Soc. of Competitor Intelligence Professionals [★IO]

Soc. of Competitor Intelligence Professionals [★7211]

Soc. of Composers, Authors and Music Publishers of Canada [IO], Toronto, ON, Canada

Soc. of Composers, Inc. [9817], Box 450, New York, NY 10013-0450

Soc. of Computed Body Tomography [★16297]

Soc. of Computed Body Tomography and Magnetic Resonance [16297], 1891 Preston White Dr., Reston, VA 20191, (703)476-1117

Soc. for Computer-Aided Engineering/FMA - Defunct.

Soc. for Cmpt. Applications in Radiology [★16299]

Soc. for Computer Science in Biology and Medicine - Defunct.

Soc. for Cmpt. Simulation [★6746]

Soc. for Cmpt. Simulation [★IO]

Soc. for Computerized Tomography and Neuroimaging [★16281]

Soc. for Computers and Law [IO], Bristol, United Kingdom

Soc. for Computers in Psychology [6744], c/o Kay Livesay, Sec.-Treas., Dept. of Psychology, Linfield Coll., 900 SE Baker St., McMinnville, OR 97128, (503)883-2708

Soc. for Computing and Tech. in Anaesthesia [IO], London, United Kingdom

Soc. for Conceptual and Content Analysis by Computer - Address unknown since 2001.

Soc. of Connoisseurs in Murder - Defunct.

Soc. to Conquer Mental Illness - Defunct.

Soc. for the Conservation of Bighorn Sheep [5381], PO Box 94182, Pasadena, CA 91109-4182, (310)679-2102

Soc. for Conservation Biology [6594], 4245 N Fairfax Dr., Ste. 400, Arlington, VA 22203-1651, (703)276-2384

Soc. for Conservation Biology [IO], Arlington, VA, United States

Soc. for Conservation GIS [6831], PO Box 7183, Redlands, CA 92375

Soc. of Constr. Law [IO], Wantage, United Kingdom

Soc. of Constr. and Quantity Surveyors [IO], Huddersfield, United Kingdom

Soc. of Construction Superintendents - Address unknown since 1995.

Soc. of Consulting Marine Engineers and Ship Surveyors [IO], London, United Kingdom

Soc. of Consulting Psychology [16172], 750 1st St. NE, Washington, DC 20002-4242, (202)336-6013

Reference to "IO" in place of a book number signifies that the association may be found in the 45th edition of International Organizations.

Soc. of Consumer Affairs Professionals in Bus. **[3196]**, 675 N Washington St., Ste. 200, Alexandria, VA 22314, (703)519-3700

Soc. of Consumer Psychology **[17344]**, c/o Larry D. Compeau, Exec. Off., Box 5795, Potsdam, NY 13699, (315)268-6605

Soc. for Cooperation in Russian and Soviet Stud. **[IO]**, London, United Kingdom

Soc. for Coptic Archaeology (North Am.) **[10153]**, 914 E Lemon St., Ste. 108, Tempe, AZ 85281, (480)731-3201

Soc. for Corporate Environmental and Social Responsibility **[IO]**, Halifax, NS, Canada

Soc. of Corporate Meeting Professionals - Defunct.

Soc. of Corporate Secretaries and Governance Professionals **[75]**, 521 5th Ave., New York, NY 10175, (212)681-2000

Soc. of Correctional Physicians **[16011]**, 1145 W Diversey Pkwy., Chicago, IL 60614, (800)229-7380

Soc. of Cosmetic Chemists **[6695]**, 120 Wall St., Ste. 2400, New York, NY 10005-4088, (212)668-1500

Soc. of Cosmetic Chemists of South Africa **[IO]**, Johannesburg, Republic of South Africa

Soc. of Cosmetic Scientists **[IO]**, Luton, United Kingdom

Soc. of Cosmetic Scientists (Singapore) **[IO]**, Singapore, Singapore

Soc. of Cost Estimating and Anal. **[1448]**, 527 Maple Ave. E, Ste. 301, Vienna, VA 22180, (703)938-5090

Soc. for Costa Rica Collectors **[22872]**, 4832 SW Lake Grove Cir., Palm City, FL 34990

Soc. of Cotton Products Analysts **[★6669]**

Soc. of Cotton Products Analysts **[★IO]**

Soc. of Counselling and Psychotherapy Educators **[IO]**, Melbourne, Australia

Soc. of County Secretaries **[★IO]**

Soc. of County Treasurers **[IO]**, Taunton, United Kingdom

Soc. for Court Stud. **[IO]**, London, United Kingdom

Soc. of Craft Designers **[1915]**

Soc. for Craniofacial Morphometry **[14066]**, c/o Dr. Curtis K. Deutsch, Shriver Center, Harvard Medical School, 200 Trapelo Rd., Waltham, MA 02452-6332, (781)642-0163

Soc. for Creative Anachronism **[10463]**, PO Box 360789, Milpitas, CA 95036-0789, (408)263-9305

Soc. for Creative Anachronism, New Zealand **[IO]**, Wellington, New Zealand

Soc. for Creative Ethics **[★10793]**

Soc. of Critical Care Medicine **[14071]**, 701 Lee St., Ste. 200, Des Plaines, IL 60016, (847)827-6869

Soc. of Critical Care Medicine **[IO]**, Des Plaines, IL, United States

Soc. for Cross-Cultural Res. **[10230]**, c/o David Cournoyer, Sec.-Treas., 43 O'Connell Rd., Colchester, CT 06415, (860)570-9155

Soc. for Cryo-Ophthalmology **[★15666]**

Soc. for Cryobiology **[6847]**, c/o Wendell Q. Sun, Treas., 1 Millennium Way, Branchburg, NJ 08876, (908)947-1176

Soc. of Crystallographers in Australia and New Zealand **[IO]**, Palmerston North, New Zealand

Soc. for Cuisine in America - Defunct.

Soc. for Cultural Anthropology **[6428]**, c/o Judith Farquhar, Pres., Univ. of Chicago, Dept. of Anthropology, 1126 E 59th St., Chicago, IL 60637

Soc. for Curriculum Development **[★8178]**

Soc. to Curriculum Development **[★IO]**

Soc. to Curtail Ridiculous, Outrageous and Ostentatious Gift Exchanges - Address unknown since 2002.

Soc. of Czech Architects **[IO]**, Prague, Czech Republic

Soc. for Czechoslovak Philately - Address unknown since 1999.

Soc. of Daily Communicants - Defunct.

Soc. of Dairy Tech. **[IO]**, Appleby-in-Westmorland, United Kingdom

Soc. of Dance History Scholars **[10154]**, 3416 Primm Ln., Birmingham, AL 35216, (205)978-1404

Soc. of Danish Authors **[★IO]**

Soc. of Danish Poets **[★IO]**

Soc. for Data Educators **[★IO]**

Soc. for Data Educators **[★8132]**

Soc. of Data Processing Consultants - Address unknown since 1995.

Soc. of Daughters of Holland Dames **[20759]**, c/o Barbara Brinkley, Dir. Gen., PO Box 82, Jay, NY 12941-0082, (518)946-2501

Soc. of Decorative Painters **[22175]**, 393 N McLean Blvd., Wichita, KS 67203-5968, (316)269-9300

Soc. of Depreciation Professionals **[52]**, 8100-M4 Wyoming Blvd. NE, No. 228, Albuquerque, NM 87113, (505)867-9513

Soc. of Dermatologists, Venereologists and Leprologists of Nepal **[IO]**, Kathmandu, Nepal

Soc. of Dermatology Physician Assistants **[15978]**, PO Box 701461, San Antonio, TX 78270, (800)380-3992

Soc. of the Descendants of the Colonial Clergy **[20760]**, 17 Lowell Mason Rd., Medfield, MA 02052-1709

Soc. of the Descendants of the Schwenkfeldian Exiles **[21244]**, 105 Seminary St., Pennsburg, PA 18073-1898, (215)679-3103

Soc. of the Descendants of Washington's Army at Valley Forge **[20678]**, c/o Timothy E. Massey, Commander-in-Chief, 319 Pine Ridge Dr., Afton, TN 37616-5156, (423)798-0525

Soc. for Design Admin. **[6481]**, 5020 Clark Rd., No. 134, Sarasota, FL 34233-3231, (941)925-8402

Soc. of Designer Craftsmen **[IO]**, London, United Kingdom

Soc. of Designers in Ireland **[★IO]**

Soc. for the Development of Austrian Economics **[6894]**, c/o Joe Salerno, Pres.-Elect, 725 Garibaldi Ave., South Plainfield, NJ 07080

Soc. for Developmental and Behavioral Pediatrics **[15898]**, 6728 Old McLean Village Dr., McLean, VA 22101, (703)556-9222

Soc. for Developmental Biology **[6595]**, 9650 Rockville Pike, Bethesda, MD 20814-3998, (301)634-7815

Society for Developmental Biology **[IO]**, Bethesda, MD, United States

Soc. of the Devotees of Jerusalem **[★20156]**

Soc. of Diagnostic Medical Sonography **[16438]**, 2745 N Dallas Pkwy., Ste. 350, Plano, TX 75093-8730, (214)473-8057

Soc. of Die Casting Engineers **[★2054]**

Soc. of Dirty Old Men - Defunct.

Soc. for Disability Stud. **[11988]**, c/o Joy Hammel, PhD, Exec. Off., Univ. of Illinois at Chicago, MC626, Dept. of Disability and Human Development, 1640 W Roosevelt Rd., No. 236, Chicago, IL 60608-1316, (312)996-4664

Soc. of Dismas - Defunct.

Soc. of Dramatic Authors and Composers **[IO]**, Paris, France

Soc. for Drug Res. **[★IO]**

Soc. of Dyers and Colourists - England **[IO]**, Bradford, United Kingdom

Soc. for Ear, Nose, and Throat Advances in Children **[15827]**, c/o Anthony E. Magit, MD, Sec., Children's Hosp. of San Diego, 3030 Children's Way, Ste. 402, San Diego, CA 92123, (858)576-4085

Soc. of Early Amer. Decoration **[★9482]**

Soc. of Early Recorded Music - Address unknown since 1995.

Soc. of Earthbound Extraterrestrials - Address unknown since 2007.

Soc. for Earthquake and Civil Engg. Dynamics **[IO]**, London, United Kingdom

Soc. for East Asian Anthropology **[6429]**, c/o Prof. Lisa Hoffman, Sec., Dept. of Urban Stud., Univ. of Washington - Tacoma, 1900 Commerce St., Tacoma, WA 98402-3100, (253)692-5895

Soc. for Ecological Restoration **[★4522]**

Soc. for Ecological Restoration Intl. **[4522]**, 285 W 18th St., Ste. 1, Tucson, AZ 85701, (520)622-5485

Soc. for Ecological Restoration and Mgt. **[★4522]**

Soc. for Economic Anthropology **[6430]**, c/o Judith E. Marti, Sec.-Treas., Dept. of Anthropology, California State Univ. - Northridge, 18111 Nordhoff St., Northridge, CA 91330-8244

Soc. for Economic Botany **[6649]**, PO Box 61788, Honolulu, HI 96839

Soc. of Economic Geologists **[7134]**, 7811 Shaffer Pkwy., Littleton, CO 80127, (720)981-7882

Soc. of Economic Paleontologists and Mineralogists **[★7432]**

Soc. of Editors **[IO]**, Cambridge, United Kingdom

Soc. for Editors and Proofreaders **[IO]**, London, United Kingdom

Soc. for Educ. in Anesthesia **[13690]**, 520 N Northwest Hwy., Park Ridge, IL 60068-2573, (847)825-5586

Soc. for Educ. through Art **[★IO]**

Soc. for Educ., Music and Psychology Res. **[IO]**, London, United Kingdom

Soc. for Educational Data Systems **[★IO]**

Soc. for Educational Data Systems **[★8132]**

Soc. of Educational Programmers and Systems Analysts **[★8132]**

Soc. of Educational Programmers and Systems Analysts **[★IO]**

Soc. for Educational Reconstruction **[8306]**, c/o Dr. David Conrad, Sec., 35 Wilson St., Burlington, VT 05401, (802)658-1047

Soc. for Educational Visits and Exchanges in Canada **[IO]**, Ottawa, ON, Canada

Soc. for Educative Communication - Address unknown since 1995.

Soc. of Educators and Scholars **[10231]**, c/o Prof. Sounny Slitine, Dir., 1801 MLK, San Antonio, TX 78203, (210)531-3396

Soc. of Educators and Scholars **[IO]**, San Antonio, TX, United States

Soc. of Elecl. and Mech. Engineers Serving Local Govt. **[IO]**, Maidstone, United Kingdom

Soc. for Electro-Acoustic Music in the U.S. **[10700]**, c/o Mark Zaki, VP for Membership, PO Box 272, Milltown, NJ 08850, (408)924-4632

Soc. of Emergency Medicine Physician Assistants **[15979]**, 222 S Westmonte Dr., No. 101, Altamonte Springs, FL 32714, (407)774-7880

Soc. of Employers; Amer. **[1251]**

Soc. for the Encouragement of Res. and Invention - Defunct.

Soc. for Endangered Languages **[IO]**, Cologne, Germany

Soc. for Endocrinology **[IO]**, Bristol, United Kingdom

Soc. for Endocrinology, Metabolism and Diabetes of South Africa **[IO]**, Johannesburg, Republic of South Africa

Soc. for Endocrinology, Metabolism and Diabetes of Southern Africa **[IO]**, Sandton, Republic of South Africa

Soc. of Endocrinology and Metabolism of Turkey **[IO]**, Ankara, Turkey

Soc. for Energy Educ. **[6972]**, 2526 Van Hise Ave., Madison, WI 53705, (608)246-6487

Soc. of Energy Professionals Intl. - Defunct.

Soc. for Engg. in Agriculture **[IO]**, Barton, Australia

The Soc. for Engg. in Agriculture, Food and Biological Systems **[★IO]**

The Soc. for Engg. in Agriculture, Food and Biological Systems **[★6990]**

Soc. of Engineering Illustrators - Defunct.

Soc. of Engg. Sci. **[7041]**, c/o Prof. Judith A. Todd, Sec., Pennsylvania State Univ., Dept. of Engineering Science and Mechanics, 212 EES Bldg., University Park, PA 16802

Soc. for Entrepreneurship Res. and Application - Defunct.

Soc. for Env. and Human Development **[IO]**, Dhaka, Bangladesh

Soc. of Environmental Engineers **[IO]**, Buntingford, United Kingdom

Soc. of Environmental Engineers **[★IO]**

Soc. of Environmental Engineers **[★7570]**

Soc. for Environmental Exploration **[IO]**, London, United Kingdom

Soc. for Environmental Graphic Design **[1809]**, 1000 Vermont Ave. NW, Ste. 400, Washington, DC 20005, (202)638-5555

Soc. of Environmental Graphic Designers **[★1809]**

Soc. of Environmental Journalists **[8718]**, PO Box 2492, Jenkintown, PA 19046, (215)884-8174

Soc. for Environmental Stabilization - Defunct.

Soc. of Environmental Toxicology and Chemistry **[14370]**, 1010 N 12th Ave., Pensacola, FL 32501-3370, (850)469-1500

A star before a book entry number signifies that the name is not listed separately, but is mentioned within the entry.

Soc. for Environmental Truth - Defunct.

Soc. of Environmental Understanding and Sustainability **[5274]**, c/o Mr. Kenneth Davis, Pres., 716 Kent Rd., Kenilworth, IL 60043, (847)251-2079

Soc. for Epidemiologic Res. **[14377]**, PO Box 990, Clearfield, UT 84089, (801)525-0231

Soc. of Epileptologists of Lithuania **[IO]**, Kaunas, Lithuania

Soc. of Equestrian Artists **[IO]**, Faldingworth, United Kingdom

Soc. for the Eradication of TV **[17193]**, Box 10491, Oakland, CA 94610-0491

Soc., Ethics, and the Life Sciences; Inst. of **[★12125]**

Soc. of Ethnic and Special Studies - Address unknown since 2001.

Soc. of Ethnobiology **[6596]**, c/o Margaret Scarry, Sec.-Treas., Univ. of North Carolina, Dept. of Anthropology, CB 3115, Alumni Bldg., Chapel Hill, NC 27599-3155, (919)962-3841

Society of Ethnobiology **[IO]**, Chapel Hill, NC, United States

Soc. for Ethnomusicology **[10701]**, Morrison Hall 005, 1165 E 3rd St., Bloomington, IN 47405-3700, (812)855-6672

Soc. of European Nematologists **[★IO]**

Society of European Stage Authors and Composers **[★9817]**

Soc. of Evangelical Agnostics - Defunct.

Soc. for Evolutionary Anal. in Law **[6539]**, c/o Janelle Steele, Admin. Asst., Vanderbilt Univ. Law School, 131 21st Ave. S, Nashville, TN 37203-1181, (615)343-2034

Soc. for Evolutionary Anal. in Law **[IO]**, Nashville, TN, United States

Soc. for Exact Philosophy **[IO]**, Gainesville, FL, United States

Soc. for Exact Philosophy **[10833]**, Univ. of Florida, Dept. of Philosophy, 300 Griffin-Floyd Hall, Gainesville, FL 32611-8545, (352)392-2084

Soc. for Excellence in Eyecare **[15702]**, PO Box 6677, Aurora, IL 60598-0677, (630)699-1929

Soc. of Exchange Counselors - Address unknown since 1989.

Soc. for Executive Leadership in Academic Medicine Intl. **[15179]**, PO Box 72, Jenkintown, PA 19046, (215)842-6473

Soc. for Executive Leadership in Academic Medicine Intl. **[IO]**, Jenkintown, PA, United States

Soc. for Existential Anal. **[IO]**, London, United Kingdom

Soc. for Existential and Phenomenological Theory and Culture **[IO]**, St. Catharines, ON, Canada

Soc. for Experimental Biology **[IO]**, Southampton, United Kingdom

Soc. for Experimental Biology and Medicine **[6597]**, 197 W Spring Valley Ave., Maywood, NJ 07607-1727, (201)291-9080

Soc. for Experimental and Descriptive Malacology **[7256]**

Soc. for Experimental Mechanics **[7713]**, 7 School St., Bethel, CT 06801, (203)790-6373

Soc. of Experimental Psychologists - Defunct.

Soc. of Experimental Social Psychology - Defunct.

Soc. for Experimental Stress Anal. **[★7713]**

Soc. of Experimental Test Pilots **[6384]**, PO Box 986, Lancaster, CA 93584-0986, (661)942-9574

Soc. of Exploration Geo-physicists **[7149]**, PO Box 702740, Tulsa, OK 74170-2740, (918)497-5500

Soc. of Exploration Geophysicists of Japan **[IO]**, Tokyo, Japan

Soc. for the Exploration of Psychotherapy Integration **[IO]**, Silver Spring, MD, United States

Soc. for the Exploration of Psychotherapy Integration **[16232]**, 3100 N Leisure World Blvd., No. 1021, Silver Spring, MD 20906, (301)598-0969

Soc. of Explorers **[★10826]**

Soc. of Explosives Engineers **[★7020]**

Soc. of Explosives Engineers **[★IO]**

Soc. of Extracorporeal Circulation Technicians; Amer. **[★15129]**

Soc. of Eye Surgeons **[15703]**, c/o Intl. Eye Found., 10801 Connecticut Ave., Kensington, MD 20895, (240)290-0263

Soc. for the Family of Man - Defunct.

Soc. Farsarotul **[18971]**, PO Box 753, Trumbull, CT 06611, (203)375-0600

Soc. of Fed. Labor and Employee Relations Professionals **[5919]**, PO Box 25112, Arlington, VA 22202, (703)685-4130

Soc. of Fed. Labor Relations Professionals **[★5919]**

Soc. of Federal Linguists - Defunct.

Soc. of Feed Technologists **[IO]**, Reading, United Kingdom

Soc. for Fermentation and Bioengineering Japan **[★IO]**

Soc. for Fetal Urology **[16713]**, c/o Ms. Kris Greiner, Admin. Coor., Dept. of Urology, Univ. of Iowa, 200 Hawkins Dr., 3 RCP, Iowa City, IA 52242-1089, (319)353-7871

Soc. for Field Experience Educ. **[★8414]**

Soc. of the Fifth Div. **[21187]**, c/o Warner Smith, Sec., PO Box 1422, Bridgeview, IL 60455, (708)839-0608

Soc. of Film Distribution **[★IO]**

Soc. for Film History Res. - Defunct.

Soc. of Financial Examiners **[6209]**, 174 Grace Blvd., Altamonte Springs, FL 32714, (407)682-4930

Soc. of Financial Ser. Professionals **[2240]**, 17 Campus Blvd., Ste. 201, Newtown Square, PA 19073-3230, (215)321-9662

Society of Financial Service Professionals **[IO]**, Newtown Square, PA, United States

Soc. of Fine Art Auctioneers and Valuers **[IO]**, Woking, United Kingdom

Soc. of Finnish Composers **[IO]**, Helsinki, Finland

Soc. of Fire Protection Engineers **[7082]**, 7315 Wisconsin Ave., Ste. 620E, Bethesda, MD 20814, (301)718-2910

Soc. of Fire Protection Technicians - Address unknown since 1995.

Soc. of the First Infantry Div. **[20706]**, 1933 Morris Rd., Blue Bell, PA 19422-1422, (888)324-4733

Soc. of Flavor Chemists **[6696]**, 3301 Rte. 66, Bldg. C, Ste. 205, Neptune, NJ 07753, (732)922-3393

Soc. of Flight Test Engineers **[6385]**, 44814 N Elm Ave., Lancaster, CA 93534, (661)949-2095

Soc. of Floristry **[IO]**, Chichester, United Kingdom

Soc. for Folk Arts Preservation **[9963]**, 75 Timberhill Ln., South Fallsburg, NY 12779, (845)436-7314

Soc. for Folk Life Stud. **[IO]**, Cardiff, United Kingdom

Soc. of Food Hygiene Tech. **[IO]**, Middleton, United Kingdom

Soc. for Foodservice Mgt. **[1594]**, 304 W Liberty St., Ste. 201, Louisville, KY 40202, (502)583-3783

Soc. For Biomaterials **[6609]**, 15000 Commerce Pkwy., Ste. C, Mount Laurel, NJ 08054, (856)439-0826

Soc. For Clinical Data Mgt. **[2982]**, 555 E Wells St., Ste. 1100, Milwaukee, WI 53202-3823, (414)226-0362

Soc. For Iranian Cultural and Social Stud. **[★10238]**

Soc. of Forensic Toxicologists **[5767]**, One MacDonald Center, 1 N MacDonald St., Ste. 15, Mesa, AZ 85201, (480)839-9106

Soc. of Former Special Agents of the Fed. Bur. of Investigation **[19202]**, PO Box 1027, Quantico, VA 22134, (703)640-6469

Soc. of the Founders and Friends of Norwich, Connecticut **[10063]**, PO Box 13, Norwich, CT 06360-0013, (860)889-9440

Soc. of the Founders of Norwich, Connecticut **[★10063]**

Soc. for Free Radical Biology and Medicine **[6613]**, 8365 Keystone Crossing, Ste. 107, Indianapolis, IN 46240, (317)205-9482

Society for Free Radical Biology and Medicine **[IO]**, Indianapolis, IN, United States

Soc. of Freelance Editors and Proofreaders **[★IO]**

Soc. of Freight Car Historians **[10922]**, PO Box 2480, Monrovia, CA 91017

Soc. for French-Amer. Affairs - Defunct.

Soc. for French Amer. Cultural Services and Educational Aid **[★8560]**

Soc. for French Historical Stud. **[10155]**, c/o Jeremy D. Popkin, Exec. Dir., Univ. of Kentucky, Dept. of History, 1725 POT, Lexington, KY 40506-0027, (859)335-6254

Soc. for French Stud. **[IO]**, London, United Kingdom

Soc. of the Friendly Sons of St. Patrick in the City of New York **[19155]**, 80 Wall St., Rm. 712, New York, NY 10005, (212)269-1770

Soc. of Friends of Puerto Rico - Address unknown since 1995.

Soc. of Friends of Touro Synagogue **[★10070]**

Soc. for the Furtherance and Study of Fantasy and Science Fiction - Address unknown since 1999.

Soc. of Garden Designers **[IO]**, Ross-On-Wye, United Kingdom

Soc. of Gastroenterology Nurses and Associates **[14429]**, 401 N Michigan Ave., Chicago, IL 60611, (312)321-5165

Soc. of Gastrointestinal Assistants **[★14429]**

Soc. of Gastrointestinal Radiologists **[16298]**, c/o Intl. Meeting Managers, Inc., 4550 Post Oak Pl., Ste. 342, Houston, TX 77027, (713)965-0566

Soc. of Genealogists **[IO]**, London, United Kingdom

Soc. of Gen. Internal Medicine **[14970]**, 2501 M St. NW, Ste. 575, Washington, DC 20037, (202)887-5150

Soc. for Gen. Microbiology **[IO]**, Reading, United Kingdom

Soc. for Gen. Music **[8930]**, c/o MENC: The Natl. Assn. for Music Educ., 1806 Robert Fulton Dr., Reston, VA 20191, (703)860-4000

Soc. of Gen. Physiologists **[7511]**, PO Box 257, Woods Hole, MA 02543-0257, (508)540-6719

Soc. for Gen. Systems Res. **[★IO]**

Soc. of Geniuses of Distinction - Defunct.

Soc. for Geology Applied to Mineral Deposits **[IO]**, Prague, Czech Republic

Soc. of Geomagnetism and Earth, Planetary and Space Sci. **[IO]**, Tokyo, Japan

Soc. of Geriatric Cardiology **[13927]**, Heart House, 7910 Woodmont Ave., Ste. 1050, Bethesda, MD 20814, (301)656-1802

Soc. of Geriatric Ophthalmology - Defunct.

Soc. for German-American Stud. **[9979]**, c/o Dr. LaVern J. Rippley, Newsl. Ed., St. Olaf Coll., German Dept., Northfield, MN 55057-1098, (507)786-3233

Soc. of German Cooks **[IO]**, Frankfurt, Germany

Soc. of Ghana Philatelists - Defunct.

Soc. of Glass and Ceramic Decorators **[1735]**, PO Box 2489, Zanesville, OH 43702, (740)588-9882

Soc. of Glass Decorators **[★1735]**

Soc. for Glass Science and Practices - Address unknown since 1994.

Soc. of Glass Tech. **[IO]**, Sheffield, United Kingdom

Soc. of the Golden Sect. - Defunct.

Soc. of Govt. Economists **[5674]**, PO Box 77082, Washington, DC 20013, (410)963-0134

Soc. of Govt. Meeting Professionals **[2691]**, 908 King St., Lower Level, Alexandria, VA 22314, (703)549-0892

Soc. of Govt. Ser. Urologists **[16714]**, PO Box 681965, San Antonio, TX 78268-1965, (210)681-5800

Soc. of Govt. Travel Professionals **[6327]**, 6935 Wisconsin Ave., No. 200, Bethesda, MD 20815, (301)654-8595

Soc. of Graduate Surgeons - Address unknown since 2006.

Soc. of Grain Elevator Superintendents **[★1750]**

Soc. of Graphic Designers of Canada **[IO]**, Ottawa, ON, Canada

Soc. of Grasslands Naturalists **[IO]**, Medicine Hat, AB, Canada

Soc. for Gynecologic Investigation **[15618]**, 409 12th St. SW, Washington, DC 20024-2125, (202)863-2544

Soc. of Gynecologic Oncologists **[15654]**, 230 W Monroe St., Ste. 710, Chicago, IL 60606, (312)235-4060

Soc. of Gynecologic Oncologists of Canada **[IO]**, Ottawa, ON, Canada

Soc. of H2S Safety Contractors - Defunct.

Soc. of the Hawley Family **[21054]**, PO Box 964, Southeastern, PA 19399-0964

Soc. of Head and Neck Surgeons **[★15819]**

Soc. of Headmasters and Headmistresses of Independent Schools **[IO]**, Market Harborough, United Kingdom

Soc. for Hea. Educ. **[IO]**, Male, Maldives

Soc. of Hea. Educ. and Hea. Promotion Specialists **[IO]**, Sheffield, United Kingdom

Reference to "IO" in place of a book number signifies that the association may be found in the 45th edition of International Organizations.

Soc. of Hea. Educ. and Promotion Specialists [★IO]

Soc. for Hea. and Human Values [★8845]

Soc. for Healthcare Consumer Advocacy of the Amer. Hosp. Assn. [15005], 1 N Franklin St., Chicago, IL 60606, (312)422-3700

Soc. of Healthcare Epidemiologists of Am. [★14378]

Soc. for Healthcare Epidemiology of Am. [14378], 1300 Wilson Blvd., Ste. 300, Arlington, VA 22209, (703)684-1006

Soc. of Healthcare Executive Assistants - Defunct.

Soc. for Healthcare Planning and Marketing of the Amer. Hosp. Assn. [★14896]

Soc. for Healthcare Strategy and Market Development of the Amer. Hosp. Assn. [14896], 1 N Franklin, 31st Fl., Chicago, IL 60606, (312)422-3888

Soc. of Hearing Aid Audiologists [★14763]

Soc. of Hearing Aid Audiologists [★IO]

Soc. of Heating, Airconditioning and Sanitary Engineers of Japan [IO], Tokyo, Japan

Soc. for Helping People with Autism [IO], Bratislava, Slovakia

Soc. for Hematopathology [15874], 3643 Walton Way Extension, Augusta, GA 30909, (706)733-7550

Soc. for Heraldic Arts [IO], Devon, United Kingdom

Soc. for Hindu-Christian Stud. [20528], c/o Bradley J. Malkovsky, Treas./Ed., Univ. of Notre Dame, 232 Malloy Hall, Notre Dame, IN 46556, (574)631-7128

Soc. of Hispanic Professional Engineers [7042], 5400 E Olympic Blvd., Ste. 210, Los Angeles, CA 90022, (323)725-3970

Soc. of Historians of Amer. Foreign Relations [10156], Dept. of History, Ohio State Univ., 106 Dulles Hall, 230 W 17th Ave., Columbus, OH 43210, (614)292-1951

Soc. for Historians of the Early Amer. Republic [10157], 3355 Woodland Walk, Philadelphia, PA 19104-4531, (215)746-5393

Soc. for Historical Archaeology [6457], 15245 Shady Grove Rd., Ste. 130, Rockville, MD 20850, (301)990-2454

Soc. for Historical Archaeology [IO], Rockville, MD, United States

Soc. for Historical Res. - Address unknown.

Soc. for the History of Alchemy and Chemistry [IO], Sutton, United Kingdom

Society for the History of Authorship, Reading and Publishing [IO], Wilmington, NC, United States

Soc. for the History of Authorship, Reading and Publishing [9754], PO Box 30, Wilmington, NC 28402-0030, (910)254-0308

Soc. for the History of Czechoslovak Jews [10289]

Soc. for the History of Discoveries [10158], c/o George Chalou, Treas., 3348 Sheffield Ct., Falls Church, VA 22042, (612)788-6570

Soc. for the History of Discoveries [IO], Arlington, TX, United States

Soc. for History Educ. [8511], California State Univ., Long Beach, 1250 Bellflower Blvd., Long Beach, CA 90840, (562)985-2573

Soc. for History in the Fed. Govt. [10159], Box 14139, Benjamin Franklin Sta., Washington, DC 20044, (301)451-4344

Soc. for the History of the Germans in Maryland [9980], c/o German-American Citizens Assn. of Maryland, PO Box 22367, Baltimore, MD 21203, (410)522-4144

Soc. for the History of Natural History [IO], London, United Kingdom

Soc. for the History of Psychology [7548], c/o Deborah F. Johnson, Pres.-Elect, PO Box 9300, Portland, ME 04104-9300

Soc. for History, Res. and Preservation - Address unknown since 1999.

Soc. and History; Soc. for the Comparative Stud. of [10152]

Soc. for the History of Tech. [10160], 618 Ross Hall, Dept. of History, Iowa State Univ., Ames, IA 50011, (515)294-8469

Soc. of Homeopaths [IO], Northampton, United Kingdom

Soc. of Hosp. Attorneys [★5782]

Soc. of Hosp. Epidemiologists of Am. [★14378]

Soc. of Hosp. Linen Ser. and Laundry Managers [IO], Bolton, United Kingdom

Soc. of Hosp. Medicine [14897], 190 N Independence Mall W, Philadelphia, PA 19106-1508, (215)351-2742

Soc. for Human Ecology [14371], c/o Ms. Barbara Carter, Exec. Asst., Coll. of the Atlantic, 105 Eden St., Bar Harbor, ME 04609, (207)288-5015

Soc. for Human Ecology [IO], Bar Harbor, ME, United States

Soc. for Human Performance in Extreme Environments [6540], 2652 Corbyton Ct., Orlando, FL 32828, (407)381-7762

Soc. for Human Rsrc. Mgt. [2908], 1800 Duke St., Alexandria, VA 22314-3499, (703)548-3440

Soc. for Humane Abortion - Address unknown since 1995.

Soc. for Humanistic Judaism [20181], 28611 W 12 Mile Rd., Farmington Hills, MI 48334, (248)478-7610

Soc. for Humanistic Judaism [IO], Farmington Hills, MI, United States

Soc. for the Humanities [10203], Andrew D. White House, 27 East Ave., Cornell Univ., Ithaca, NY 14853-1101, (607)255-9274

Soc. for Hungarian Philately [22873], 1920 Fawn Ln., Hellertown, PA 18055-2117

Society for Hungarian Philately [IO], Hellertown, PA, United States

Soc. for Iberian and Latin Amer. Thought - Address unknown since 2002.

Soc. of Icelandic Advt. Agencies [IO], Reykjavik, Iceland

Society of Illustrators [IO], New York, NY, United States

Soc. of Illustrators [9527], 128 E 63rd St., New York, NY 10021-7303, (212)838-2560

Soc. for Imaging Informatics in Medicine [16299], 19440 Golf Vista Plz., Ste. 330, Leesburg, VA 20176, (703)723-0432

Soc. for Imaging Sci. and Tech. [7497], 7003 Kilworth Ln., Springfield, VA 22151, (703)642-9090

Soc. for In Vitro Biology [6598], 514 Daniels St., Ste. 411, Raleigh, NC 27605, (919)420-7940

Soc. of Incentive and Travel Executives [3935], 401 N Michigan Ave., Chicago, IL 60611, (312)321-5148

Soc. of Incentive Travel Executives [★3935]

Soc. of Incentive Travel Executives [★IO]

Soc. of Incentive and Travel Executives [IO], Chicago, IL, United States

Soc. for the Increase of the Ministry [20290], 924 Farmington Ave., No. 100, West Hartford, CT 06107, (860)233-1732

Soc. of Independent Brewers [IO], Thirsk, United Kingdom

Soc. of Independent Financial Advisors - Defunct.

Soc. of Independent Gasoline Marketers of Am. [2947], 11495 Sunset Hills Rd., Ste. 215, Reston, VA 20190-5213, (703)709-7000

Soc. of Independent and Private School Data Educ. [★8132]

Soc. of Independent and Private School Data Educ. [★IO]

Soc. of Independent Producers - Address unknown since 1995.

Soc. of Independent Professional Earth Scientists [7135], 4925 Greenville Ave., Ste. 1106, Dallas, TX 75206, (214)363-1780

Soc. of Independent Roundabout Proprietors [IO], Retford, United Kingdom

Soc. of Independent Show Organizers [★1339]

Soc. of Independent Show Organizers [1348], 7000 W Southwest Hwy., Chicago Ridge, IL 60415, (708)361-0900

Soc. of Indexers [IO], Sheffield, United Kingdom

Soc. of Indian Auto. Mfrs. [IO], New Delhi, India

Soc. of Indiana Pioneers [21256], 140 N Senate Ave., Indianapolis, IN 46204-2207, (317)233-6588

Soc. for Individual Liberty [★18015]

Soc. for Individual Liberty [★IO]

Soc. for Individual Responsibility - Defunct.

Soc. of Indochina Philatelists - Defunct.

Soc. for Indonesian-Americans [19116], PO Box 9486, Washington, DC 20016, (202)234-6392

Soc. for Indus. and Applied Mathematics [7294], 3600 Market St., 6th Fl., Philadelphia, PA 19104-2688, (215)382-9800

Soc. for Indus. Archeology [6458], c/o Don Durfee, Coor., Social Sciences Dept., Michigan Technological Univ., 1400 Townsend Dr., Houghton, MI 49931-1295, (906)487-1889

Soc. of Indus. Artists and Designers [★IO]

Soc. of Indus. Engineers [★2515]

Soc. for Indus. Microbiology [6599], 3929 Old Lee Hwy., Ste. 92A, Fairfax, VA 22030-2421, (703)691-3357

Soc. of Indus. and Off. Realtors [3343], 1201 New York Ave. NW, Ste. 350, Washington, DC 20005, (202)449-8200

Soc. for Indus. and Organizational Psychology [16173], 440 E Poe Rd., Ste. 101, Bowling Green, OH 43402-0087, (419)353-0032

Society for Industrial and Organizational Psychology [IO], Bowling Green, OH, United States

Soc. of Indus. Realtors [★3343]

Soc. of Infectious Diseases Pharmacists [15952], 823 Cong. Ave., Ste. 230, Austin, TX 78701, (512)479-0425

Soc. of Infectious Diseases (Singapore) [IO], Singapore, Singapore

Society for Information Display [IO], San Jose, CA, United States

Soc. for Info. Display [6745], 610 S 2nd St., San Jose, CA 95112-5710, (408)977-1013

Soc. for Information and Documentation - Defunct.

Soc. for Info. Mgt. [2516], 401 N Michigan Ave., Chicago, IL 60611-4267, (312)527-6734

Soc. for Info. Tech. Mgt. [IO], Northampton, United Kingdom

Soc. for Info. Tech. and Teacher Educ. [9243], PO Box 1545, Chesapeake, VA 23327-1545, (757)366-5606

Soc. of Inkwell Collectors [22114], 562 Sanderling Dr., Indialantic, FL 32903, (309)579-3040

Society of Inkwell Collectors [IO], Mossville, IL, United States

Soc. for Insect Stud. [IO], Roseville, Australia

Soc. of Instrument and Control Engineers [IO], Tokyo, Japan

Soc. of Insurance Accountants [★53]

Soc. of Insurance Financial Mgt. [53], PO Box 9001, Mount Vernon, NY 10552, (914)966-3180

Soc. of Insurance Res. [2241], c/o Ed Budd, Exec. Dir., 631 Eastpointe Dr., Shelbyville, IN 46176, (317)398-3684

Soc. of Insurance Trainers and Educators [8578], 6635 W Happy Valley Rd., Ste. A104-444, Glendale, AZ 85310, (623)547-6401

Soc. of Integral Psychoanalysis [★IO]

Soc. for Integrative and Comparative Biology [7867], 1313 Dolley Madison Blvd., Ste. 402, McLean, VA 22101-3926, (703)790-1745

Soc. for Integrative Graphology - Defunct.

Soc. for Interactive Learning [★IO]

Soc. for Intercultural Educ., Training and Res. [★IO]

Soc. for Intercultural Educ., Training and Res. [★8667]

Soc. for Intercultural Educ., Training and Res. U.S.A. [8667], 603 Stewart St., Ste. 610, Seattle, WA 98101, (206)859-4351

Soc. for Intercultural Educ., Training and Res. U.S.A. [IO], Seattle, WA, United States

Soc. for Interests of Active Missionaries Abroad [★IO]

Soc. of Internal Medicine; Amer. Coll. of Physicians-American [14966]

Soc. of Intl. Bus. Fellows [2291], One Georgia Ctr., 600 W Peachtree St., Ste. 490, Atlanta, GA 30308, (404)525-7423

Soc. of Intl. Bus. Fellows [IO], Atlanta, GA, United States

Soc. of Intl. Chinese in Educational Tech. [IO], Prescott Valley, AZ, United States

Soc. of Intl. Chinese in Educational Tech. [9236], c/o Hong Zhan, Sec.-Treas., 7200 E Pioneer Ln., Prescott Valley, AZ 86314, (928)523-0408

Soc. of Intl. Cultural Exchange - Address unknown since 2001.

Soc. for Intl. Development [IO], Rome, Italy

Soc. for Intl. Development - Italy [IO], Rome, Italy

Soc. for Intl. Development - USA [IO], Washington, DC, United States

A star before a book entry number signifies that the name is not listed separately, but is mentioned within the entry.

Soc. for Intl. Development - USA [17848], 1875 Connecticut Ave. NW, Ste. 720, Washington, DC 20009-5728, (202)884-8590

Soc. of Intl. Gas Tanker and Terminal Operators [IO], United Kingdom

Soc. for Intl. Hockey Res. [IO], Toronto, ON, Canada

Soc. for Intl. Numismatics - Address unknown since 2001.

Soc. of Intl. Treasurers [IO], London, United Kingdom

Soc. of Internet Professionals [IO], Richmond Hill, ON, Canada

Soc. of Interventional Pain Mgt. Surgery Centers [16588], 81 Lakeview Dr., Paducah, KY 42001, (270)554-9412

Soc. of Interventional Radiology [16300], 3975 Fair Ridge Dr., Ste. 400 N, Fairfax, VA 22033, (703)691-1805

Soc. of Invasive Cardiovascular Professionals [13928], 1500 Sunday Dr., Ste. 102, Raleigh, NC 27607-5151, (919)861-4546

Soc. for Invertebrate Pathology - Defunct.

Soc. for the Investigation of Recurring Events - Address unknown since 2002.

Soc. for the Investigation of the Unexplained - Address unknown since 2007.

Soc. for Investigative Dermatology [14214], 820 W Superior Ave., 7th Fl., Cleveland, OH 44113-1807, (216)579-9300

Soc. for Iranian Stud. [★10238]

Soc. of the Irish Motor Indus. [IO], Dublin, Ireland

Soc. of Israel Philatelists [22874], c/o Mr. Michael Bass, Pres., PO Box 507, Northfield, OH 44067, (330)467-7446

Soc. for Italian-Amer. Scientists and Physicians - Defunct.

Soc. for Italian Historical Stud. [8681], c/o Prof. Alan J. Reinerman, Exec. Sec.-Treas., Boston Coll., Dept. of History, Chestnut Hill, MA 02467, (617)552-3814

Soc. for Italic Handwriting [IO], Birmingham, United Kingdom

Soc. for Italic Stud. [★10262]

Society of Japanese Aerospace Companies [★154]

Soc. of Japanese Aerospace Companies [IO], Tokyo, Japan

Society of Japanese Aerospace Companies [★IO]

Soc. for Japanese Arts [IO], Bergeijk, Netherlands

Soc. for Japanese Irises [22541], c/o Dennis Hager, Pres., PO Box 390, Millington, MD 21651, (410)928-3147

Soc. of Japanese Women Scientists [IO], Hiratsuka, Japan

Soc. of Jewish Bibliophiles - Defunct.

Soc. of Jewish Composers, Publishers and Songwriters - Defunct.

Soc. of Jewish Sci. [20202], 109 E 39th St., New York, NY 10016, (212)682-2626

Soc. for Jewish Youth Educ. in the Middle East and North Africa [★20171]

Soc. for Judgement and Decision Making [8041], c/o Bud Fennema, Sec.-Treas., Florida State Univ., Colorado of Bus., PO Box 3061110, Tallahassee, FL 32306-1110, (850)644-8231

Society for Judgement and Decision Making [IO], Tallahassee, FL, United States

Soc. of Kabalarians of Canada [IO], Vancouver, BC, Canada

Soc. of Kastorians "Omonoia" [19092], 150-28 14th Ave., Whitestone, NY 11357, (718)746-4505

Soc. of King Charles the Martyr [19455], c/o Dr. Mark A. Wuonola, American Rep., 291 Bacon St., Piety Corner, Waltham, MA 02451

Soc. for Lab. Animal Sci. [IO], Hannover, Germany

Soc. of Laparoendoscopic Surgeons [16589], 7330 SW 62nd Pl., Ste. 410, Miami, FL 33143-4825, (305)665-9959

Soc. for Latin Amer. Anthropology [6431], c/o AAA Membership Services, 4350 N Fairfax Dr., Ste. 640, Arlington, VA 22203-1620, (703)528-1902

Soc. for Latin Amer. Anthropology [IO], Arlington, VA, United States

Soc. for Latin Amer. Stud. [IO], Oxford, United Kingdom

Soc. of Laundry Engineers and Allied Trades [IO], Kingston Upon Thames, United Kingdom

Soc. of Leather Technologists and Chemists [IO], Northampton, United Kingdom

Soc. of Leather Technologists and Chemists (South African Sect.) [IO], Pietermaritzburg, Republic of South Africa

Soc. of Legal Scholars in the United Kingdom and Ireland [IO], Southampton, United Kingdom

Soc. of Lesbian and Gay Anthropologists [6432], 4350 N Fairfax Dr., Ste. 640, Arlington, VA 22203-1620, (703)528-1902

Soc. for Leukocyte Biology [16365], 9650 Rockville Pike, Bethesda, MD 20814, (301)634-7810

Soc. for Libertarian Life - Defunct.

Soc. for Libyan Stud. [IO], London, United Kingdom

Soc. of Licensed Aircraft Engineers and Technologists [★IO]

Soc. for Life History Res. - Address unknown since 2003.

Soc. of Life with Osteoporosis [IO], Ankara, Turkey

Society for Light Treatment and Biological Rhythms [IO], Chincoteague Island, VA, United States

Soc. for Light Treatment and Biological Rhythms [16636], 4648 Main St., Chincoteague Island, VA 23336

Soc. of Limerents - Defunct.

Soc. of Lincoln Cent Collectors [22756], c/o Dr. Sol Taylor, Pres., 13515 Magnolia Blvd., Sherman Oaks, CA 91423-1417, (818)789-7805

Soc. for Lincolnshire History and Archaeology [IO], Lincoln, United Kingdom

Soc. for Linguistic Anthropology [6433], c/o Joel C. Kuipers, Pres., George Washington Univ., Dept. of Anthropology, 2112 G St. NW, Rm. 201, Washington, DC 20052, (202)994-6545

Soc. of the Little Flower [19720], 1313 Frontage Rd., Darien, IL 60561-5340, (630)968-9400

Soc. of Local Authority Chief Executives and Senior Managers [IO], London, United Kingdom

Soc. of Local Coun. Clerks [IO], Taunton, United Kingdom

Soc. of Logistics Engineers [★IO]

Soc. of Logistics Engineers [★7186]

Soc. of London Art Dealers [IO], London, United Kingdom

Soc. of London Theatre [IO], London, United Kingdom

Soc. for Louisiana Irises [22542], c/o Richard J. Sloan, Treas., 118 E Walnut St., Alma, AR 72921-3608, (479)632-4962

Soc. for Low Temperature Biology [IO], Dunbeg, United Kingdom

Soc. of Loyalist Descendants - Address unknown since 2002.

Soc. for Luminescence Microscopy and Spectroscopy - Defunct.

Soc. for Machine Intelligence - Defunct.

Soc. of Magazine Photographers [★2992]

Soc. of Magazine Writers [★11158]

Soc. for Magnetic Resonance [★16290]

Soc. for Magnetic Resonance [★IO]

Soc. for Magnetic Resonance Imaging - Defunct.

Soc. for Maintenance and Reliability Professionals [2478], 8201 Greensboro Dr., Ste. 300, McLean, VA 22102, (703)245-8011

Soc. for Male Reproduction and Urology [16343], 1209 Montgomery Hwy., Birmingham, AL 35216-2809, (205)978-5000

Soc. of Mgt. Accountants of Canada [IO], Mississauga, ON, Canada

Soc. for Mgt. Info. Systems [★2516]

Soc. of Mfg. Engineers [7268], PO Box 930, Dearborn, MI 48121, (313)271-1500

Soc. of Mfg. Engineers; Assn. for Electronics Mfg. of the [6907]

Soc. of Mfg. Engineers Educ. Found. [8373], 1 SME Dr., PO Box 930, Dearborn, MI 48121-0930, (313)425-3300

Soc. of Mfg. Engineers; Machining and Material Removal Community of the [7747]

Soc. of Mareen Duvall Descendants [21055], c/o Barrett L. McKown, Registrar, 3580 S River Terr., Edgewater, MD 21037, (410)798-4531

Soc. of Marine Consultants - Defunct.

Soc. for Marine Mammalogy [5017], c/o Heather Koopman, Sec., Univ. of North Carolina at Wilmington, 601 S Coll. Rd., Wilmington, NC 28403, (910)962-7199

Soc. for Marine Mammalogy [IO], Wilmington, NC, United States

Soc. of Marine Port Engineers [3588], PO Box 369, Eatontown, NJ 07724, (732)389-2009

Soc. of Maritime Arbitrators [5463], 30 Broad St., 7th Fl., New York, NY 10004-2304, (212)344-2400

Soc. of Maritime Indus. [IO], London, United Kingdom

Soc. for Marketing Professional Services [2649], 99 Canal Center Plz., Ste. 330, Alexandria, VA 22314, (703)549-6117

Soc. of Master Printers of Scotland [★IO]

Soc. of Master Shoe Repairers [★IO]

Soc. for Maternal-Fetal Medicine [15902], 409 12th St. SW, Washington, DC 20024-2125, (202)863-2476

Soc. for Mathematical Biology [6600], PO Box 11283, Boulder, CO 80301, (303)661-9942

Soc. of Mathematicians, Physicists and Astronomers of Slovenia [IO], Ljubljana, Slovenia

Soc. of Medalists - Defunct.

Soc. for Medical Anthropology [6434], c/o Marcia Inhorn, Pres., Health Behavior and Health Education, School of Public Health, Univ. of Michigan, 1420 Washington Heights, Ann Arbor, MI 48109-2029

Soc. of Medical Banking Excellence [1449], c/o The Medical Banking Proj., 320 Main St., Ste. 230, Franklin, TN 37064, (615)794-2009

Soc. of Medical Consultants to the Armed Forces [15265], 5 Southern Way, Fredericksburg, VA 22406, (540)548-2019

Soc. for Medical Decision Making [15180], 100 N 20th St., 4th Fl., Philadelphia, PA 19103, (215)545-7697

Soc. of Medical Friends of Wine [23028], c/o Susan Guerguy, Exec. Sec., 511 Jones Pl., Walnut Creek, CA 94597-3141, (925)933-9691

Soc. for Medical Informatics of Bosnia and Herzegovina [IO], Sarajevo, Bosnia-Hercegovina

Soc. of Medical Jurisprudence [15006]

Soc. of Medical Jurisprudence and State Medicine [★15006]

Soc. of Medical Lab. Technologists of the Cape [★IO]

Soc. of Medical Lab. Technologists of Natal [★IO]

Soc. of Medical Lab. Technologists of South Africa [IO], Roggebaai, Republic of South Africa

Soc. of Medical Lab. Technologists of Southern Transvaal [★IO]

Soc. of Medical Officers of Hea. [★IO]

Soc. of Medicinal Plant Res. [IO], Emmering, Germany

Soc. for Medicines Res. [IO], Leicester, United Kingdom

Soc. for Medieval Archaeology [IO], Leeds, United Kingdom

Soc. for Medieval and Renaissance Philosophy [10464], c/o Prof. Jeremiah Hackett, Sec.-Treas., Univ. of South Carolina, Dept. of Philosophy, Columbia, SC 29208

Soc. for Melanoma Res. [13875], 305 Hermosa Dr. SE, Albuquerque, NM 87108-2613, (505)272-6513

Soc. for Menstrual Cycle Res. [15619], c/o Mary Anna Friederich, MD, Sec.-Treas., 10559 N 104th Pl., Scottsdale, AZ 85258, (480)451-9731

Soc. of Metaphysicians [IO], Hastings, United Kingdom

Soc. of Mexican Amer. Engineers and Scientists [7043], 11500 Northwest Fwy., Ste. 200V, Houston, TX 77092, (281)557-3677

Soc. of Midland Authors [4070], PO Box 10419, Chicago, IL 60610

Soc. for Military History [10482], c/o Jour. of Military History, George C. Marshall Lib., Virginia Military Inst., Lexington, VA 24450, (540)464-7468

Soc. of Military Ophthalmologists - Address unknown since 1999.

Soc. of Military Orthopaedic Surgeons [15266], c/o T.R.U.E. Res. Found., 8610 N New Braunfels Ave., Ste. 705, San Antonio, TX 78217, (210)829-1239

Soc. of Military Otolaryngologists [★15267]

Soc. of Military Otolaryngologists - Head and Neck Surgeons [15267], c/o Sue Pearce, Admin. Sec., 9231 Shadow Lawn Cir., Converse, TX 78109, (210)945-9006

Reference to "IO" in place of a book number signifies that the association may be found in the 45th edition of International Organizations.

Soc. of Military Widows **[21200]**, c/o Dorinda Ruelas, Pres., 2486 N Camino Valle Verde, Tucson, AZ 85715, (800)842-3451

Soc. of Mineral Analysts **[7345]**, PO Box 404, Lewiston, ID 83501, (208)799-3286

Soc. of Mining Engineers **[★7349]**

Soc. for Mining, Metallurgy, and Exploration **[7349]**, 8307 Shaffer Pkwy., Littleton, CO 80127-4102, (303)973-9550

Soc. for Mining, Metallurgy, Rsrc. and Environmental Tech. **[IO]**, Clausthal-Zellerfeld, Germany

Soc. of Missionaries of Africa **[19721]**, 1624 21st St. NW, Washington, DC 20009-1003, (202)232-5154

Soc. for Modeling and Simulation Intl. **[6746]**, PO Box 17900, San Diego, CA 92177-7900, (858)277-3888

Soc. for Modeling and Simulation Intl. **[IO]**, San Diego, CA, United States

Soc. of Modern Grammar **[IO]**, Taegu City, Republic of Korea

Soc. for Molecular Biology and Evolution **[6601]**, c/o Jianzhi George Zhang, Sec., Univ. of Michigan, Dept. of Ecology and Evolutionary Biology, 1075 Natural Sci. Bldg., 830 N Univ. Ave., Ann Arbor, MI 48109-1048, (734)763-0527

Soc. for Molecular Imaging **[15181]**, PO Box 293878, Kerrville, TX 78029-3878, (830)257-0112

Soc. for Molecular Imaging **[IO]**, Kerrville, TX, United States

Soc. of Mortgage Consultants **[★489]**

Soc. of Motion Picture Art Directors **[★9929]**

Soc. of Motion Picture and TV Art Directors **[★9929]**

Soc. of Motion Picture and TV Engineers **[7044]**, 3 Barker Ave., White Plains, NY 10601, (914)761-1100

Soc. of Motor Mfrs. and Traders **[IO]**, London, United Kingdom

Soc. for Mucopolysaccharide Diseases (The MPS Soc.) **[IO]**, Amersham, United Kingdom

Society for Mucosal Immunology **[IO]**, Bethesda, MD, United States

Soc. for Mucosal Immunology **[14943]**, 5272 River Rd., Ste. 630, Bethesda, MD 20816, (301)718-6516

Soc. for Multivariate Experimental Psychology **[16174]**, c/o Prof. Patrick Shrout, Sec.-Treas., New York Univ., Dept. of Psychology, 6 Washington Pl., New York, NY 10003, (212)998-7895

Soc. of Municipal Arborists **[6121]**, PO Box 641, Watkinsville, GA 30677, (706)769-7412

Soc. for Muscular Dystrophy Info. Intl. **[IO]**, Bridgewater, NS, Canada

Soc. of Museum Archaeologists **[IO]**, Colchester, United Kingdom

Soc. for Music Anal. **[IO]**, Tonbridge, United Kingdom

Soc. for Music Teacher Educ. **[8931]**, c/o MENC: Natl. Assn. for Music Educ., 1806 Robert Fulton Dr., Reston, VA 20191, (703)860-4000

Soc. for Music Theory **[10702]**, Dept. of Music, Univ. of Chicago, 1010 E 59th St., Chicago, IL 60637, (773)834-3821

Soc. for Music Theory **[IO]**, Chicago, IL, United States

Soc. for Musteline Arts and Literature - Address unknown since 1999.

Soc. for Name Stud. in Britain and Ireland **[IO]**, Bristol, United Kingdom

Soc. for Natal Effects on Hea. in Adult Life **[IO]**, Bombay, India

Soc. of Natl. Assn. Publications **[321]**, 8405 Greensboro Dr., No. 800, McLean, VA 22102, (703)506-3285

Soc. for Natural Philosophy **[7295]**, c/o Prof. Anna Vainchtein, Treas., Dept. of Mathematics, Univ. of Pittsburgh, 301 Thackeray Hall, Pittsburgh, PA 15260

Soc. for the Nature Protection of Croatia **[IO]**, Zagreb, Croatia

Soc. for Nautical Res. **[IO]**, Hailsham, United Kingdom

Soc. of Naval Architects and Marine Engineers **[7368]**, 601 Pavonia Ave., Jersey City, NJ 07306, (201)798-4800

Soc. of Nematologists **[7371]**, PO Box 311, Marceline, MO 64658, (660)256-3331

Soc. for Neonatology and Paediatric Intensive Care **[IO]**, Tuebingen, Germany

Soc. of Netherlands Literature **[IO]**, Leiden, Netherlands

Society of Neuro-Linguistic Programming **[IO]**, Snohomish, WA, United States

Soc. of Neuro-Linguistic Programming **[15012]**, c/o Bennett/Stellar Univ., 6930 132nd St. SE, Snohomish, WA 98296, (206)729-8658

Soc. of Neurological Surgeons **[15416]**, c/o Dennis D. Spencer, MD, Pres., PO Box 208082, New Haven, CT 06520-8082, (203)785-2285

Soc. for Neuronal Regulation **[★15394]**

Soc. for Neuronal Regulation **[★IO]**

Soc. for Neuroscience **[7380]**, 1121 14th St. NW, Ste. 1010, Washington, DC 20005, (202)962-4000

Soc. of Neurosurgical Anesthesia and Critical Care **[15417]**, 520 N Northwest Hwy., Park Ridge, IL 60068-2573, (847)825-5586

Soc. for New Language Stud. **[10307]**, c/o Dr. Peter J. Fields, Sec./Ed., English Dept., Midwestern State Univ., 3410 Taft Blvd., Wichita Falls, TX 76308, (940)397-4246

Soc. for New Testament Stud. **[IO]**, Amsterdam, Netherlands

Society for News Design **[IO]**, North Kingstown, RI, United States

Soc. for News Design **[3163]**, 1130 Ten Rod Rd., Ste. D 202, North Kingstown, RI 02852-4180, (401)294-5233

Soc. of Newspaper Design **[★3163]**

Soc. of Newspaper Design **[★IO]**

Soc. on Non-Destructive Examination **[★IO]**

Soc. of Non-Invasive Vascular Tech. **[★16731]**

Soc. for Nondestructive Testing **[★7787]**

Soc. for Nonprofit Organizations **[322]**, 5820 Canton Center Rd., Ste. 165, Canton, MI 48187-2683, (734)451-3582

Soc. for North Amer. Goldsmiths **[9841]**, 540 Oak St., Ste. A, Eugene, OR 97401, (541)345-5689

Soc. for North Amer. Union - Address unknown since 2001.

Soc. for Northwestern Vertebrate Biology **[7364]**, c/o Julie Grialou, Treas., 18304 Hwy. 20, Winthrop, WA 98862, (509)996-2402

Soc. of Nuclear Medical Technologists - Defunct.

Soc. of Nuclear Medicine **[15424]**, 1850 Samuel Morse Dr., Reston, VA 20190-5316, (703)708-9000

Soc. of Nuclear Medicine; Technologist Sect. of the **[★15425]**

Soc. of Nuclear Medicine Technologist Sect. **[15425]**, 1850 Samuel Morse Dr., Reston, VA 20190, (703)708-9000

Soc. for Nursing History - Defunct.

Soc. for Nutrition Educ. **[15570]**, 7150 Winton Dr., Ste. 300, Indianapolis, IN 46268, (317)328-4627

Soc. for Obstetric Anesthesia and Perinatology **[15903]**, 2 Summit Park Dr., No. 140, Cleveland, OH 44131-2571, (216)447-7863

Soc. of Obstetricians and Gynaecologists of Canada **[IO]**, Ottawa, ON, Canada

Soc. for Occlusal Studies - Address unknown since 2004.

Soc. for Occupational and Environmental Hea. **[15633]**, 6728 Old McLean Village Dr., McLean, VA 22101, (703)556-9222

Soc. of Occupational Medicine **[IO]**, London, United Kingdom

Soc. for Office-Based Surgery **[★16558]**

Soc. for Old Testament Stud. **[IO]**, Cambridge, United Kingdom

Soc. of Operations Engineers **[IO]**, London, United Kingdom

Soc. in Opposition to Human-Animal Hybridization - Address unknown since 2001.

Soc. of Oral Physiology and Occlusion - Defunct.

The Soc. for Organic Petrology **[7463]**, c/o Paul Hackley, U.S. Geological Survey, 956 Natl. Ctr., Reston, VA 20192, (703)648-6458

The Soc. for Organic Petrology **[IO]**, Reston, VA, United States

Society for Organizational Learning **[IO]**, Cambridge, MA, United States

Soc. for Organizational Learning **[2868]**, 25 First St., Ste. 414, Cambridge, MA 02141-1802, (617)300-9500

Soc. of Ornamental Turners **[IO]**, London, United Kingdom

Society of Ortho-Bionomy International **[IO]**, Indianapolis, IN, United States

Soc. of Ortho-Bionomy Intl. **[13767]**, 5335 N Tacoma St., Ste. 21G, Indianapolis, IN 46220, (317)536-0064

Soc. of Orthodox Youth Organizations **[★19882]**

Soc. of Otorhinolaryngology and Head/Neck Nurses **[15526]**, 202 Julia St., Ste. A, New Smyrna Beach, FL 32168, (386)428-1695

Soc. of Our Lady of the Most Holy Trinity **[19722]**, 109 W Ave. F, Robstown, TX 78380, (361)387-2754

Soc. of Our Lady of the Way - Address unknown since 2003.

Soc. for Pacific Coast Native Iris **[22543]**, c/o Terri Hudson, Sec.-Treas., 33450 Little Valley Rd., Fort Bragg, CA 95437, (707)964-3907

Society for Pacific Coast Native Iris **[IO]**, Fort Bragg, CA, United States

Soc. of Packaging Professionals; SPHE - The **[★7426]**

Soc. of Paper Money Collectors **[22757]**, c/o Frank Clark, Membership Dir., PO Box 117060, Carrollton, TX 75011

Soc. of Park and Recreation Educators **[6163]**, c/o Gallaudet Univ., 22377 Belmont Ridge Rd., U.S. Department of of Physical Educ. and Recreation, 800 Florida Ave. NE, Washington, DC 20002, (202)651-5591

Soc. of Parrot Breeders and Exhibitors **[21860]**, c/o Dr. Al Decoteau, CEO, PO Box 546, Hollis, NH 03049, (603)672-4568

Soc. for Participatory Res. in Asia **[IO]**, New Delhi, India

Soc. of Patient Representatives **[★15005]**

Soc. for Pediatric Anesthesia **[13691]**, 2209 Dickens Rd., Richmond, VA 23230-2005, (804)282-9780

Soc. for Pediatric Dermatology **[14215]**, 8365 Keystone Crossing, Ste. 107, Indianapolis, IN 46240, (317)202-0224

Soc. for Pediatric Nurses **[15527]**, 7794 Grow Dr., Pensacola, FL 32514, (850)494-9467

Soc. for Pediatric Pathology **[15875]**, c/o U.S. and Canada Acad. of Pathology (USCAP), 3643 Walton Way Extension, Augusta, GA 30909, (706)364-3375

Soc. for Pediatric Psychology **[16175]**, PO Box 170231, Atlanta, GA 30317, (404)373-1099

Society for Pediatric Psychology **[IO]**, Atlanta, GA, United States

Soc. for Pediatric Radiology **[16301]**, 1891 Preston White Dr., Reston, VA 20191, (703)648-0680

Soc. for Pediatric Res. **[15899]**, 3400 Res. Forest Dr., Ste. B-7, The Woodlands, TX 77381, (281)419-0052

Soc. for Pediatric Urology **[16715]**, 900 Cummings Ctr., Ste. 221-U, Beverly, MA 01915, (978)927-8330

Soc. of Pelvic Surgeons - Defunct.

Soc. of Pension Consultants **[IO]**, London, United Kingdom

Soc. for Pentecostal Stud. **[20465]**, PO Box 3802, Cleveland, TN 37320-3802, (423)614-8577

Soc. of the Performing Arts - Defunct.

Soc. of Perinatal Obstetricians **[★15902]**

Soc. for Peripheral Vascular Nursing **[★15530]**

Soc. of Permanent Cosmetic Professionals **[1087]**, 69 N Broadway, Des Plaines, IL 60016, (847)635-1330

Soc. for Personal Growth **[IO]**, Edmonton, AB, Canada

Society for Personality Assessment **[IO]**, Falls Church, VA, United States

Soc. for Personality Assessment **[16176]**, 6109H Arlington Blvd., Falls Church, VA 22044, (703)534-4772

Soc. for Personality and Social Psychology **[7549]**, c/o Christie Marvin, Off. Mgr., Dept. of Psychology, Cornell Univ., 239 Uris Hall, Ithaca, NY 14853, (607)254-5416

Soc. for Personnel Admin. **[★1267]**

Soc. for Personnel Admin. **[★IO]**

Soc. of Petroleum Engineers **[IO]**, Richardson, TX, United States

---

A star before a book entry number signifies that the name is not listed separately, but is mentioned within the entry.

Soc. of Petroleum Engineers [7464], 222 Palisades Creek Dr., PO Box 833836, Richardson, TX 75083-3836, (972)952-9393

Soc. of Petroleum Engineers - London Off. [IO], London, United Kingdom

Soc. of Petroleum Evaluation Engineers [7465], 1001 McKinney, Ste. 801, Houston, TX 77002, (713)651-1639

Soc. of Petroleum Geophysicists [★7149]

Soc. of Petrophysicists and Well Log Analysts [7466], 8866 Gulf Fwy., Ste. 320, Houston, TX 77017, (713)947-8727

Soc. of Phantom Friends [9739], c/o Kate Emburg, 4100 Cornelia Way, North Highlands, CA 95660

Society of Phantom Friends [IO], Antelope, CA, United States

Soc. of Pharmaceutical and Biotech Trainers [3475], 4423 Pheasant Ridge Rd., Ste. 100, Roanoke, VA 24014-5274, (540)725-3859

Soc. of Pharmaceutical Medicine [IO], London, United Kingdom

Soc. for Phenomenology and Existential Philosophy [10834], c/o John M. Rose, Sec.-Treas., Philosophy Dept., Goucher Coll., 1021 Dulany Valley Rd., Baltimore, MD 21204, (410)337-6258

Soc. of Philatelic Americans - Defunct.

Soc. of Philatelists and Numismatists - Defunct.

Soc. of Philaticians - Defunct.

Soc. of Philippine Surgeons in America - Defunct.

Soc. of Philosophers in America - Address unknown since 2001.

Soc. for the Philosophical Stud. of Genocide and the Holocaust [10835], c/o Prof. James R. Watson, PhD, Pres., Loyola Univ. - New Orleans, Dept. of Philosophy, New Orleans, LA 70118, (504)865-3940

Soc. for the Philosophical Stud. of Genocide and the Holocaust [IO], New Orleans, LA, United States

Soc. for the Philosophical Stud. of Marxism [10452], c/o Peter Amato, Coor., Drexel Univ., 3141 Chestnut St., Dept. of English and Philosophy, 5030 MacAlister Hall, Philadelphia, PA 19104, (215)382-1448

Soc. for Philosophy in the Contemporary World [18274], PO Box 7147, Charlottesville, VA 22906-7147, (434)220-3300

Society for Philosophy in the Contemporary World [IO], Charlottesville, VA, United States

Soc. for Philosophy of Creativity [★10793]

Soc. for Philosophy and Psychology [7492], c/o Thomas W. Polger, Sec.-Treas., Univ. of Cincinnati, Dept. of Philosophy, 206 McMicken Hall, Cincinnati, OH 45221, (513)556-6328

Soc. for Philosophy and Public Affairs - Address unknown since 2006.

Soc. for Philosophy of Religion [8970], c/o Frank R. Harrison, III, Sec.-Treas., Univ. of Georgia, Dept. of Philosophy, Peabody Hall, Athens, GA 30602, (706)542-2823

Soc. for the Philosophy of Sex and Love [10836], c/o Dr. Carol Caraway, Dept. of Philosophy, Indiana Univ. of Pennsylvania, 452 Sutton Hall, Indiana, PA 15705-0001, (724)357-2310

Soc. for Philosophy and Tech. [10837], c/o Philosophy Documentation Center, PO Box 7147, Charlottesville, VA 22906-7147, (434)220-3300

Society for Philosophy and Technology [IO], Charlottesville, VA, United States

Soc. of Photo-Optical Instrumentation Engineers [★IO]

Soc. of Photo-Optical Instrumentation Engineers [★7408]

Soc. of Photo-Technologists [3014], 11112 S Spotted Rd., Cheney, WA 99004-9038, (509)624-9621

Soc. of Photo-Technologists [IO], Cheney, WA, United States

Soc. of Photographer and Artist Representatives - Address unknown since 2004.

Soc. for Photographic Educ. [8976], Art Crat Bldg., No. 403, 2530 Superior Ave., Cleveland, OH 44114, (513)529-8328

Soc. of Photographic Engg. [★7497]

Soc. of Photographic Illustrators - Address unknown since 1995.

Soc. of Photographic Instrumentation Engineers [★7408]

Soc. of Photographic Instrumentation Engineers [★IO]

Soc. of Photographic Sci. and Tech. of Japan [IO], Tokyo, Japan

Soc. of Photographic Scientists and Engg. [★7497]

Soc. for Physical Regulation in Biology and Medicine [6554], c/o Gloria L. Parsley, Exec. Dir., 2412 Cobblestone Way, Frederick, MD 21702-2626, (301)663-4556

Soc. for Physical Regulation in Biology and Medicine [IO], Frederick, MD, United States

Soc. for Physician Assistants in Pediatrics [15980], 950 N Washington St., Alexandria, VA 22314-1552

Soc. of Physicists of the Republic of Macedonia [IO], Skopje, Macedonia

Soc. of Physics Students [7509], c/o Amer. Inst. of Physics, One Physics Ellipse, College Park, MD 20740-3843, (301)209-3007

Soc. of Piping Engineers and Designers [7045], 9105 W Sam Houston Pkwy. N, Ste. 700-193, Houston, TX 77064, (832)286-3404

Soc. for Plant Morphology and Physiology [★6632]

Soc. of Plastics Engineers [7514], 14 Fairfield Dr., PO Box 403, Brookfield, CT 06804-0403, (203)775-0471

Society of Plastics Engineers [IO], Brookfield, CT, United States

Soc. of the Plastics Indus. [3059], 1667 K St. NW, Ste. 1000, Washington, DC 20006, (202)974-5200

Soc. of Ploughmen [IO], Doncaster, United Kingdom

Soc. for Police and Criminal Psychology [16177], c/o Gary S. Aumiller, PhD, Exec. Dir., 750 Veterans Memorial Hwy., Hauppauge, NY 11788, (631)724-5522

Soc. for Policy Modeling - Address unknown since 2003.

Soc. of Polish-American Travel Agents [3936], 74 Nassau Ave., Brooklyn, NY 11222, (718)383-7211

Soc. for Polish Philately [IO], London, United Kingdom

Soc. of Polish Town Planners [IO], Warsaw, Poland

Soc. of Political Item Enthusiasts - Defunct.

Soc. for Popular Astronomy [IO], Nottingham, United Kingdom

Soc. of Population Ecology [IO], Kyoto, Japan

Soc. for Post-Medieval Archaeology [IO], York, United Kingdom

Soc. of the Postal History of Eretz Israel [IO], Jerusalem, Israel

Soc. of Practising Veterinary Surgeons [IO], Warwick, United Kingdom

Soc. of Practitioners of Insolvency [★IO]

Soc. of Pragmatic Mysticism [IO], Pawlet, VT, United States

Soc. of Pragmatic Mysticism [20448], c/o Leonebel Connaway, Dir., 23501 Vermont Rte. 30, Pawlet, VT 05761, (802)325-3107

Soc. of Prayer for World Peace [★18258]

Soc. of Prayer for World Peace [★IO]

Society for the Preservation and Advancement of the Harmonica [IO], Troy, MI, United States

Soc. for the Preservation and Advancement of the Harmonica [10703], Dept. W, PO Box 865, Troy, MI 48099-0865, (586)771-4866

Soc. for the Preservation of Amer. Business History - Defunct.

Soc. for the Preservation and Appreciation of Antique Motor Fire Apparatus in Am. [22423], PO Box 2005, Syracuse, NY 13220-2005, (734)632-0350

Soc. for the Preservation and Appreciation of Old Time Music and Dancing [★IO]

Soc. for the Preservation of Birds of Prey [5382], 12335 Santa Monica Blvd., PMB 345, West Los Angeles, CA 90025, (310)840-2322

Soc. for the Preservation and Encouragement of Barber Shop Quartet Singing in Am. [10704], 110 Seventh Ave. N, Nashville, TN 37203-3704, (615)823-3993

Soc. for the Preservation of English Language and Literature [8381], PO Box 321, Braselton, GA 30517, (770)586-0184

Soc. for the Preservation and Enhancement of the Recognition of Millard Fillmore, Last of the Whigs [22601], 37 Hillside Rd., Stratford, NJ 08084, (856)627-5118

Soc. for the Preservation and Enjoyment of Carriages in America - Defunct.

Soc. for the Preservation of Film Music [★10595]

Soc. for the Preservation of the Greek Heritage [9997], 5125 MacArthur Blvd. NW, Ste. 11B, Washington, DC 20016, (202)363-4337

Soc. for the Preservation of Jewish Holy Sites; Athra Kadisha: The [10274]

Soc. for the Preservation of Natural History Collections [10064], c/o Barbara Brown, Treas., PO Box 797, Washington, DC 20044-0797, (212)769-5864

Soc. for the Preservation of New England Antiquities [★10035]

Soc. for the Preservation of Old Mills [10065], 5667 Leisure South Dr. SE, Kentwood, MI 49548-6851, (616)455-0609

Soc. for the Preservation of Poultry Antiquities [5119], c/o Dr. Charles Everett, Sec.-Treas., 1057 Nick Watts Rd., Lugoff, SC 29078, (803)408-9846

Soc. for the Preservation and Propagation of Barber Shop Quartet Singing in the U.S. [★10704]

Soc. for the Preservation of Variety Arts - Defunct.

Soc. to Preserve and Encourage Radio Drama, Variety and Comedy [22930], PO Box 7177, Van Nuys, CA 91409-7177, (310)219-0053

Soc. to Preserve the Engrossing Enjoyment of DXing - Defunct.

Soc. of the President Street Fellows - Defunct.

Soc. for the Prevention of Asbestosis and Indus. Diseases [★IO]

Soc. for the Prevention of Crime - Defunct.

Soc. for Prevention of Human Infertility [16347], 877 Park Ave., New York, NY 10021, (212)744-5500

Soc. for Prevention of Human Infertility [IO], New York, NY, United States

Society for Prevention Research [IO], Fairfax, VA, United States

Soc. for Prevention Res. [16520], 11240 Waples Mill Rd., Ste. 200, Fairfax, VA 22030, (703)934-4850

Soc. for the Prevention of World War III - Defunct.

Soc. of Priests for a Free Ministry - Address unknown since 1995.

Soc. of Primary Care Policy Fellows [14664], 1522 K St. NW, Ste. 702, Washington, DC 20005, (202)289-7735

Soc. of Private and Pioneer Numismatists [22758], 98 Main St., Ste. 201, Tiburon, CA 94920, (415)435-2601

Soc. of Procurement Officers in Local Govt. [IO], Leicester, United Kingdom

Soc. of Producers of Advt. Music, Soc. of Producers of Applied Music [★IO]

Soc. for Producers and Composers of Applied Music [★IO]

Soc. of Professional Accountants [IO], Great Missenden, United Kingdom

Soc. of Professional Accountants of Canada [IO], Toronto, ON, Canada

Soc. of Professional Archaeologists [★6453]

Soc. of Professional Assessors - Address unknown since 1995.

Soc. of Professional Audio Recording Services [3351], 9 Music Sq. S, Ste. 222, Nashville, TN 37203, (800)771-7727

Soc. of Professional Audio Recording Studios [★3351]

Soc. of Professional Benefit Administrators [1245], Two Wisconsin Cir., Ste. 670, Chevy Chase, MD 20815, (301)718-7722

Soc. of Professional Business Consultants - Defunct.

Soc. of Professional Drivers [3893], 5235 Mission Oaks Blvd., Ste. 200, Camarillo, CA 93012, (818)774-3889

Soc. of Professional Engineers [IO], Northampton, United Kingdom

Soc. of Professional Investigators [5890], PO Box 1128, Bellmore, NY 11710, (516)781-5100

Soc. of Professional Journalists [3164], 3909 N Meridian St., Indianapolis, IN 46208-4011, (317)927-8000

Soc. of Professional Journalists, Sigma Delta Chi [★3164]

Soc. of Professional Mgt. Consultants [★2499]

Soc. of Professional Pilots - Address unknown since 1995.

Reference to "IO" in place of a book number signifies that the association may be found in the 45th edition of International Organizations.

Soc. of Professional Rope Access Technicians [2068], 994 Old Eagle School Rd., Ste. 1019, Wayne, PA 19087-1802, (610)971-4850

Soc. of Professional Well Log Analysts [★7466]

Soc. of Professional Wireless Pioneers [★3757]

Soc. of Professional Women in Petroleum [2948], PO Box 550788, Houston, TX 77255-0788, (713)939-2263

Soc. of Professional Women in Petroleum [IO], Houston, TX, United States

Soc. of Professionals in Dispute Resolution [★5450]

Soc. of Professors of Child and Adolescent Psychiatry [16096], 3615 Wisconsin Ave. NW, Washington, DC 20016, (202)966-7300

Soc. of Professors of Child Psychiatry [★16096]

Soc. of Professors of Educ. [8307], c/o Robert C. Morris, Sec.-Treas., Univ. of West Georgia, Coll. of Educ., Dept. of Educational Leadership and Professional Stud., 1600 Maple St., Carrollton, GA 30118-5160, (770)836-4426

Soc. for Progressive Supranuclear Palsy [14286], Executive Plz. III, 11350 McCormick Rd., Ste. 906, Hunt Valley, MD 21031, (410)785-7004

Soc. for Projective Techniques and Personality Assessment [★16176]

Soc. for Projective Techniques and Personality Assessment [★IO]

Soc. for Projective Techniques and Rorschach Inst. [★IO]

Soc. for Projective Techniques and Rorschach Inst. [★16176]

Soc. for Promoting Christian Knowledge [IO], London, United Kingdom

Soc. for Promoting and Encouraging Arts and Knowledge of the Church [19972], 805 County Rd. 102, Eureka Springs, AR 72632, (479)253-9701

Soc. Promoting Environmental Conservation [IO], Vancouver, BC, Canada

Soc. for the Promotion of African, Asian, and Latin Amer. Literature [IO], Frankfurt, Germany

Soc. for the Promotion of Byzantine Stud. [IO], Oxford, United Kingdom

Soc. for the Promotion of Educ. and Awareness [IO], Multan, Pakistan

Soc. for the Promotion of Educ. and Res. [IO], Belize City, Belize

Soc. for the Promotion of Hellenic Stud. [IO], London, United Kingdom

Soc. for the Promotion of Japanese Animation [9473], 1733 S Douglass Rd., Ste. G, Anaheim, CA 92806, (714)937-2994

Soc. for the Promotion of Mohammedan Missions - Defunct.

Soc. for the Promotion of Nature Conservation [★IO]

Soc. for the Promotion of Nature Reserves [★IO]

Soc. for the Promotion of New Music [IO], London, United Kingdom

Soc. for the Promotion of Roman Stud. [IO], London, United Kingdom

Soc. for the Promotion of Sci. and Scholarship [3255], 4139 El Camino Way, PO Box 10139, Palo Alto, CA 94303-0139, (650)853-0111

Soc. for Promotion of Youth and Masses [IO], New Delhi, India

Soc. for the Propagation of the Faith [IO], Scarborough, ON, Canada

Soc. for the Propagation of the Faith [19723], 366 5th Ave., New York, NY 10001-2211, (212)563-8700

Soc. for the Propagation of the Gospel in Foreign Parts [★IO]

Soc. of Prospective Medicine - Defunct.

Soc. for Protecting Individual Rights and Liberty - Defunct.

Soc. for Protecting the Rights of the Child [IO], Tehran, Iran

Soc. for the Protection of Ancient Buildings [IO], London, United Kingdom

Soc. for the Protection of Animals Abroad [IO], London, United Kingdom

Soc. for the Protection of Animals in North Africa [★IO]

Soc. for the Protection of East Asians' Human Rights - Address unknown since 2001.

Soc. for the Protection of Nature in Israel [IO], Tel Aviv, Israel

Soc. for Protection of Nature in Lebanon [IO], Beirut, Lebanon

Society for the Protection of Old Fishes [IO], Edmonds, WA, United States

Soc. for the Protection of Old Fishes [7177], c/o Dr. Alan J. Mearns, Pres., 20315 92nd Ave. W, Edmonds, WA 98020, (425)774-9069

Soc. for the Protection of the Unborn Child - New Zealand [★IO]

Soc. for the Protection of Unborn Children [IO], London, United Kingdom

Soc. for the Protection of Unborn Children - Scotland [IO], Glasgow, United Kingdom

Soc. for the Protection of the Unborn Through Nutrition - Defunct.

Soc. for Protective Coatings; SSPC: The [2885]

Soc. of Protozoologists [★7866]

Soc. of Protozoologists [★IO]

Soc. for the Provision of Educ. in Rural Australia [IO], Osborne Park, Australia

Soc. for Psychical Res. [IO], London, United Kingdom

Soc. for Psychological Anthropology [7550], c/o Thomas Weisner, Pres., Departments of Psychiatry and Anthropology, Univ. of California, 760 Westwood Blvd., Los Angeles, CA 90024-1759, (310)794-3632

Soc. for Psychological Assistance - Croatia [IO], Zagreb, Croatia

Soc. of Psychological Hypnosis [16178], c/o Jen Tuzikow, Membership Chair, 120 Bent Tree Dr., West Chester, PA 19380

Soc. for the Psychological Stud. of Ethnic Minority Issues [16179], c/o Beth Boyd, PhD, Pres.-Elect, Univ. of South Dakota, Psychology Dept., 414 E Clark St., Vermillion, SD 57069, (605)677-5363

Soc. for the Psychological Stud. of Lesbian, Gay and Bisexual Issues [16180], c/o Amer. Psychological Assn., 750 First St. NE, Washington, DC 20002

Soc. for the Psychological Stud. of Lesbian and Gay Issues [★16180]

Soc. for the Psychological Stud. of Men and Masculinity [16181], c/o Mark Stevens, Pres., Univ. Counseling Services, CSUN 18111 Nordhoff St., Northridge, CA 91330-8217, (818)677-2364

Soc. for the Psychological Stud. of Social Issues [16182], 208 I St. NE, Washington, DC 20002-4340, (202)675-6956

Soc. of Psychologists in Addictive Behaviors - Address unknown since 1995.

Soc. for Psychophysiological Res. [16183], 2810 Crossroads Dr., Ste. 3800, Madison, WI 53718, (608)443-2472

Society for Psychophysiological Research [IO], Madison, WI, United States

Soc. of Psychosomatic Obstetrics and Gynaecology, Brazil [IO], Sao Paulo, Brazil

Soc. for Psychotherapy Res. [16194], c/o Jacques P. Barber, PhD, Pres.-Elect, Center for Psychotherapy Res., Dept. of Psychiatry, Univ. of Pennsylvania School of Medicine, 3535 Market St., Rm. 648, Philadelphia, PA 19104-3309

Soc. of Public Hea. [★IO]

Society for Public Health Education [IO], Washington, DC, United States

Soc. for Public Hea. Educ. [16254], 750 First St. NE, Ste. 910, Washington, DC 20002-4241, (202)408-9804

Soc. of Public Hea. Educators [★16254]

Soc. of Public Hea. Educators [★IO]

Soc. of Public Info. Networks [IO], Loughborough, United Kingdom

Soc. of Public Teachers of Law [★IO]

Soc. for the Publication of Danish Music [IO], Copenhagen, Denmark

Soc. of Publication Designers [1810], 17 E 47th St., 6th Fl., New York, NY 10017, (212)223-3332

Soc. of Publication Designers [★1810]

Soc. of Publishers in Asia [IO], Hong Kong, People's Republic of China

Soc. for the Punishment of War Criminals - Address unknown since 1995.

Soc. of Purchasing Officers in Local Govt. [★IO]

Soc. of Quality Assurance [IO], Charlottesville, VA, United States

Soc. of Quality Assurance [3270], 2365 Hunters Way, Charlottesville, VA 22911, (434)297-4772

Soc. for Quantitative Analyses of Behavior [6541], c/o Dr. Michael Lamport Commons, Co-Pres., 234 Huron Ave., Cambridge, MA 02138-1328, (617)497-5270

Soc. of Quantitative Analysts [1450], PO Box 539, Webster, NY 14580-0539, (800)918-7930

Soc. for Radiation Oncology Administrators [16302], 5272 River Rd., Ste. 630, Bethesda, MD 20816, (301)718-6510

Soc. of Radio Personalities and Programmers - Defunct.

Soc. of Radiographers of South Africa [IO], Cape Town, Republic of South Africa

Soc. for Radiological Protection [IO], London, United Kingdom

Soc. of Radiologists in Ultrasound [16303], 44211 Slatestone Ct., Leesburg, VA 20176-5109, (703)858-9210

Soc. of Radiotherapists [★IO]

Soc. for Range Mgt. [5166], 10030 W 27th Ave., Wheat Ridge, CO 80215-6601, (303)986-3309

Soc. of Ration Token Collectors [22759], c/o Samuel M. Hevener, Dir., 3583 Everett Rd., Richfield, OH 44286-9723

Soc. of Real Estate Appraisers [★275]

Soc. of Recorder Players [IO], London, United Kingdom

Soc. of Recreation Executives [3363], Box 520, Gonzalez, FL 32560-0520, (850)937-8354

Soc. for Reformation Res. [10931], c/o Jeffery Tyler, Treas., Hope Coll., PO Box 9000, Holland, MI 49422-9000

Soc. of Registered Professional Adjusters [2242], PO Box 3810, Napa, CA 94558, (707)226-5762

Soc. of Registered Professional Adjusters [IO], Napa, CA, United States

Soc. of Rehabilitation and Crime Prevention [IO], Hong Kong, People's Republic of China

Soc. for the Rehabilitation of the Facially Disfigured [★14065]

Soc. of Reliability Engineers [7046], c/o Mr. Russell Chicoine, PO Box 2, Bloomfield, CT 06002-0002, (860)243-7473

Soc. for Religion in Higher Educ. [★19940]

Soc. for Renaissance Stud. [IO], Nottingham, United Kingdom

Soc. for the Renewal of the Sacred Liturgy [★IO]

Soc. for the Renewal of the Sacred Liturgy [★19561]

Soc. for the Renewal of the Sacred Liturgy; ADORE-MUS - [19561]

Soc. for Reproduction Rights of Authors, Composers and Publishers in Canada [IO], Montreal, QC, Canada

Soc. for Reproductive Biology [IO], Balnarring, Australia

Soc. for Reproductive Endocrinology and Infertility [16348], c/o Amer. Soc. for Reproductive Medicine, 1209 Montgomery Hwy., Birmingham, AL 35216-2809, (205)978-5000

Soc. of Reproductive Surgeons [16349], 1209 Montgomery Hwy., Birmingham, AL 35216-2809, (205)978-5000

Soc. of Res. Administrators [7576], 1901 N Moore St., Ste. 1004, Arlington, VA 22209, (703)741-0140

Soc. for Res. on Adolescence [13515], 2950 S South St., Ste. 401, Ann Arbor, MI 48104, (734)926-0700

Soc. for Res. in Child Development [11546], 2950 S State St., Ste. 401, Ann Arbor, MI 48104, (734)926-0600

Society for Research in Child Development [IO], Ann Arbor, MI, United States

Soc. for Res. and Educ. in Primary Care Internal Medicine [★14970]

Soc. for Res. into Higher Educ. [IO], London, United Kingdom

Soc. for Res. into Hydrocephalus and Spina Bifida [IO], Bicester, United Kingdom

Society for Research on Identity Formation [IO], Miami, FL, United States

Soc. for Res. on Identity Formation [8960], c/o William M. Kurtines, PhD, Treas., Florida Intl. Univ., Dept. of Psychology, 11200 SW 8th St., Univ. Park, DM 269-F, Miami, FL 33199, (305)348-3941

A star before a book entry number signifies that the name is not listed separately, but is mentioned within the entry.

Soc. for Res. and Initiatives for Sustainable Technologies and Institution [IO], Ahmedabad, India

Soc. for Res. on Meteorites [★7148]

Soc. for Res. on Nicotine and Tobacco [5249], 2810 Crossroads Dr., Ste. 3800, Madison, WI 53718, (608)443-2462

Soc. for Res. in Psychology of Music and Music Educ. [★IO]

Soc. for Res. on Rapport and Telekinesis - Defunct.

Soc. for the Responsible Use of Resources in Agriculture and on the Land [IO], Fordingbridge, United Kingdom

Soc. for the Restoration and Preservation of Red M & M's - Defunct.

Soc. of Rheology [7579], c/o A. Jeffrey Giacomin, Sec., Rheology Res. Center, Univ. of Wisconsin, Madison, WI 53706, (608)262-7473

Soc. of Richmond County Descendants [21152], PO Box 848, Rockingham, NC 28380, (910)997-6641

Soc. for Risk Anal. [2243], 1313 Dolley Madison Blvd., Ste. 402, McLean, VA 22101, (703)790-1745

Soc. of Risk Mgt. Consultants [2244], 330 S Executive Dr., Ste. 301, Brookfield, WI 53005-4275, (800)765-SRMC

Soc. of Roller Skating Teachers of Am. [23741], 6905 Corporate Dr., Indianapolis, IN 46278, (317)347-2626

Soc. for Romanian Stud. [10939], c/o Paul E. Michelson, Pres., Huntington Coll., Dept. of History, Huntington, IN 46750, (260)359-4242

Soc. for Romanian Stud. [IO], Huntington, IN, United States

Soc. of Rosicrucians in America - Address unknown since 2003.

Soc. for Rousseau Stud. [★9708]

Soc. for Rousseau Stud. [★IO]

Soc. of Rubber Indus., Japan [IO], Tokyo, Japan

Soc. of Rural Physicians of Canada [IO], Shawville, QC, Canada

Soc. of Russian Veterans of the World War - Address unknown since 1995.

Soc. of St. Andrew [20088], 3383 Sweet Hollow Rd., Big Island, VA 24526, (434)299-5956

Soc. of Saint Gregory of Am. [★20428]

Soc. of Saint Mary Magdalene [19724], PO Box 1309, Issaquah, WA 98027, (727)548-9173

Soc. of St. Monica - Defunct.

Soc. of Saint Peter Apostle [19725], 366 5th Ave., 12th Fl., New York, NY 10001-2211, (212)563-8700

Soc. of St. Peter the Apostle [★IO]

Soc. of St. Peter the Apostle for Native Clergy [★19725]

Soc. of Saint Pius X [IO], Menzingen, Switzerland

Soc. of Saint Stephen [20523], c/o Martha Ann Fox, 12805 St. Charles, Little Rock, AR 72211, (501)954-7916

Soc. of Saint Vincent de Paul - Bangladesh [IO], Dhaka, Bangladesh

Soc. of Saint Vincent de Paul - Botswana [IO], Serowe, Botswana

Soc. of Saint Vincent de Paul - Burkina Faso [IO], Ouagadougou, Burkina Faso

Soc. of Saint Vincent de Paul - Cameroon [IO], Limbe, Cameroon

Soc. of Saint Vincent de Paul - Canada [IO], Halifax, NS, Canada

Soc. of Saint Vincent de Paul - Central African Republic [IO], Bangui, Central African Republic

Soc. of Saint Vincent de Paul Central Coun. - Hong Kong [IO], Hong Kong, People's Republic of China

Soc. of St. Vincent de Paul Coun. of the U.S. [13190], 58 Progress Pkwy., Maryland Heights, MO 63043-3706, (314)576-3993

Soc. of Saint Vincent de Paul - Egypt [IO], Cairo, Egypt

Soc. of Saint Vincent de Paul - El Salvador [IO], San Salvador, El Salvador

Soc. of Saint Vincent de Paul - Ethiopia [IO], Addis Ababa, Ethiopia

Soc. of Saint Vincent de Paul - Guyana [IO], Demerara, Guyana

Soc. of Saint Vincent de Paul - India [IO], Bombay, India

Soc. of Saint Vincent de Paul - Intl. [IO], Paris, France

Soc. of Saint Vincent de Paul - Ireland [IO], Dublin, Ireland

Soc. of Saint Vincent de Paul - Jamaica [IO], Kingston, Jamaica

Soc. of Saint Vincent de Paul - Korea [IO], Seoul, Republic of Korea

Soc. of Saint Vincent de Paul - Liberia [IO], Monrovia, Liberia

Soc. of Saint Vincent de Paul - Lithuania [IO], Vilnius, Lithuania

Soc. of Saint Vincent de Paul - Mozambique [IO], Maputo, Mozambique

Soc. of Saint Vincent de Paul - Namibia [IO], Windhoek, Namibia

Soc. of Saint Vincent de Paul - New Zealand [IO], Wellington, New Zealand

Soc. of Saint Vincent de Paul - Nigeria [IO], Ibadan, Nigeria

Soc. of Saint Vincent de Paul - Pakistan [IO], Karachi, Pakistan

Soc. of Saint Vincent de Paul - Peru [IO], Lima, Peru

Soc. of Saint Vincent de Paul - Philippines [IO], Manila, Philippines

Soc. of Saint Vincent de Paul - Rwanda [IO], Kigali, Rwanda

Soc. of Saint Vincent de Paul - Scotland [IO], Glasgow, United Kingdom

Soc. of Saint Vincent de Paul - Slovenia [IO], Ljubljana, Slovenia

Soc. of Saint Vincent de Paul - South Africa [IO], Overport, Republic of South Africa

Soc. of Saint Vincent de Paul - Sri Lanka [IO], Colombo, Sri Lanka

Soc. of Saint Vincent de Paul - Sudan [IO], Khartoum, Sudan

Soc. of Saint Vincent de Paul - Taiwan [IO], Taichung, Taiwan

Soc. of Saint Vincent de Paul - Trinidad and Tobago [IO], Port of Spain, Trinidad and Tobago

Soc. of Saint Vincent de Paul - Uruguay-Female Br. [IO], Montevideo, Uruguay

Soc. of Saint Vincent de Paul - Zimbabwe [IO], Harare, Zimbabwe

Soc. of Sales Mgt. Administrators [★IO]

Soc. of Sales and Marketing [IO], London, United Kingdom

Soc. of Satellite Professionals [★IO]

Soc. of Satellite Professionals [★3755]

Soc. of Satellite Professionals Intl. [3755], The New York Info. Tech. Center, 55 Broad St., 14th Fl., New York, NY 10004, (212)809-5199

Soc. of Satellite Professionals Intl. [IO], New York, NY, United States

Soc. of Saunterers, Intl. - Defunct.

Soc. of Savings and Loan Controllers [★1418]

Soc. for Scholarly Publishing [3256], 10200 W 44th Ave., Ste. 304, Wheat Ridge, CO 80033-2840, (303)422-3914

Soc. of School Librarians Intl. [10388], 19 Savage St., Charleston, SC 29401, (843)577-5351

Society of School Librarians International [IO], Charleston, SC, United States

Soc. of Schoolmasters [★IO]

Soc. of Schoolmasters and Schoolmistresses [IO], Kent, United Kingdom

Soc. for a Sci. of Clinical Psychology [16184], c/o Denise M. Sloan, PhD, Temple Univ., Dept. of Psychology, Weiss Hall, Philadelphia, PA 19122

Soc. for Sci. Exploration [7485], PO Box 7065, Lawrence, KS 66044, (800)627-0326

Soc. for the Sci. Investigation of Para-Sciences [IO], Rossdorf, Germany

Society for the Scientific Study of Religion [IO], Indianapolis, IN, United States

Soc. for the Sci. Stud. of Religion [20506], c/o Arthur E. Farnsley, II, Exec. Off., Indiana Univ. - Purdue Univ. Indianapolis, Cavanaugh Hall 341, 425 Univ. Blvd., Indianapolis, IN 46202

Soc. for the Sci. Stud. of Sex [★16407]

Soc. for the Sci. Stud. of Sexuality [16407], c/o David L. Fleming, Exec. Dir., PO Box 416, Allentown, PA 18105-0416, (610)530-2483

Soc. of Scottish Artists [IO], Glasgow, United Kingdom

Soc. of Scribes [11214], PO Box 933, New York, NY 10150, (212)452-0139

Soc. of Scribes and Illuminators [IO], London, United Kingdom

Soc. for the Second Self [13102], c/o Jane Ellen Fairfax, Chair, PO Box 980638, Houston, TX 77098-0638, (713)349-8969

Soc. for Sedimentary Geology [7432], 6128 E 38th St., Ste. 308, Tulsa, OK 74135-5814, (918)610-3361

Soc. for Self-Playing Musical Instruments [IO], Essen, Germany

Soc. of Senior Aerospace Executives - Address unknown since 2003.

Soc. for Sensible Gun Control - Defunct.

Soc. of Separationists - Address unknown since 2000.

Soc. for Ser. Professionals in Printing [1790], 433 E Monroe Ave., Alexandria, VA 22301, (703)684-0044

Soc. for Seventeenth-Century Music [10705], c/o Prof. Stefanie Tcharos, Treas., Dept. of Music, Univ. of California, Santa Barbara, CA 93106-6070, (805)893-4027

Soc. for Sex Therapy and Res. [16408], PO Box 96920, Washington, DC 20090-6920, (202)863-1644

Soc. for Shoe Fitters [IO], Hingham, United Kingdom

Soc. for Siberian Irises [22544], c/o Judy Hollingworth, Pres., 124 Sherwood Rd. E, Williamston, MI 48895, (517)349-8121

Soc. of Signalmen - Address unknown since 1995.

Soc. of the Silurians [3165], PO Box 1195, Madison Square Sta., New York, NY 10159, (212)532-0887

Soc; Simple [★18637]

Soc. for Simulation in Healthcare [15148], 223 N Guadalupe St., PMB 300, Santa Fe, NM 87501, (505)983-4923

Soc. for Simulation in Healthcare [IO], Santa Fe, NM, United States

Soc. of Singers [12621], 15456 Ventura Blvd., Ste. 304, Sherman Oaks, CA 91403, (818)995-7100

Soc. of Skeletal Radiology [16304], 1111 N Plaza Dr., Ste. 550, Schaumburg, IL 60173, (847)517-3302

Soc. for Skeptical Stud. [7493], c/o Dr. Richard Greene, Exec. Dir., Weber State Univ., Dept. of Political Sci. and Philosophy, 1203 Univ. Cir., Ogden, UT 84408-1203

Soc. for Slovene Stud. [19371], c/o Michael Biggins, Sec., Univ. of Washington, Suzzallo Lib., Box 352900, Seattle, WA 98195, (315)472-0538

Soc. for Slovene Stud. [IO], Syracuse, NY, United States

Soc. of Small Craft Designers [2593]

Soc. for the Social History of Medicine [IO], Manchester, United Kingdom

Soc. for Social Medicine [IO], Leeds, United Kingdom

Soc. for Social Responsibility in Science - Defunct.

Soc. for Social Stud. of Sci. [7633], c/o Dr. Wesley Shrum, Sec., Louisiana State Univ., Dept. of Sociology, 126 Stubbs Hall, Baton Rouge, LA 70803, (225)578-5311

Soc. for Social Work Admin. in Hea. Care [★13209]

Soc. for Social Work Leadership in Hea. Care [13209], 100 N 20th St., 4th Fl., Philadelphia, PA 19103, (215)599-6134

Soc. for Social Work and Res. [9135], 11240 Waples Mill Rd., Ste. 200, Fairfax, VA 22030, (703)352-7797

Soc. for Social Work and Res. [IO], Fairfax, VA, United States

Soc. for Socialist Stud. [IO], Red Deer, AB, Canada

Soc. of Soft Drink Technologists [★IO]

Soc. of Soft Drink Technologists [★6543]

Soc. for Software Quality [6775], PO Box 86958, San Diego, CA 92138-6958

Soc. of South African Geographers [IO], Bloemfontein, Republic of South Africa

Soc. for South Asian Stud. [IO], London, United Kingdom

Soc. for South India Studies - Defunct.

Reference to "IO" in place of a book number signifies that the association may be found in the 45th edition of International Organizations.

Soc. of Spanish Engineers, Planners and Architects - Defunct.

Soc. of Spanish and Spanish-American Stud. **[10974]**, Univ. of Colorado, Dept. of Spanish and Portuguese, 134 McKenna Languages Bldg., 278 UCB, Boulder, CO 80309-0278, (303)492-5900

Soc. of Spanish and Spanish-American Stud. **[IO]**, Boulder, CO, United States

Soc. of Special Needs Adoptive Parents **[IO]**, Vancouver, BC, Canada

Soc. for Spinal Res. **[IO]**, Cuxhaven, Germany

Soc. for Spiritual Mind - Defunct.

Soc. of Sponsors of the U.S. Navy - Address unknown since 2001.

Soc. of Sport and Event Photographers **[3015]**, 229 Peachtree St. NE, Ste. 2200, Atlanta, GA 30303-1608, (877)427-3778

Soc. of Sport and Event Photographers **[IO]**, Atlanta, GA, United States

Soc. of Sports Therapists **[IO]**, Glasgow, United Kingdom

Soc. of the SR - Defunct.

Soc. of Stage Directors and Choreographers **[24159]**, 1501 Broadway, Ste. 1701, New York, NY 10036-5653, (212)391-1070

Soc. of State Directors of Hea., Physical Educ. and Recreation **[8992]**, 1900 Assn. Dr., Ste. 100, Reston, VA 20191-1599, (703)390-4599

Soc. of State Directors of Physical and Hea. Educ. **[★8992]**

Soc. for Storytelling **[IO]**, Reading, United Kingdom

Soc. for Strings **[10706]**, c/o Mary McGowan-Welp, Admissions Dir., Meadowmount School of Music, 1424 County Rte. 10, Westport, NY 12993, (518)962-2400

Soc. for the Stud. of Addiction to Alcohol and Other Drugs **[IO]**, Leeds, United Kingdom

Soc. for the Stud. of Alternative Lifestyles **[★13095]**

Soc. for the Stud. of Amer. Women Writers **[11195]**, c/o Prof. Melissa J. Homestead, Membership and Finances Off., PO Box 88033, Lincoln, NE 68588-0333

Soc. for the Stud. of Amer. Women Writers **[IO]**, Lincoln, NE, United States

Soc. for the Stud. of Amphibians and Reptiles **[7160]**, c/o Roy McDiarmid, Pres., PO Box 37012, Washington, DC 20013, (540)231-5728

Soc. for the Stud. of Architecture in Canada **[IO]**, Ottawa, ON, Canada

Soc. for the Stud. of Biological Rhythms **[★IO]**

Soc. for the Stud. of Biological Rhythms **[★6587]**

Soc. for the Study of Blood - Address unknown since 1994.

Soc. for the Stud. of Breast Disease **[★13772]**

Soc. for the Stud. of Christian Spirituality **[19826]**, c/o The Johns Hopkins Univ. Press, PO Box 19966, Baltimore, MD 21211-0966, (800)548-1784

Soc. for the Stud. of Coherence **[IO]**, Paris, France

Soc. for the Stud. of Development and Growth **[★IO]**

Soc. for the Stud. of Development and Growth **[★6595]**

Soc. for the Stud. of Dictionaries and Lexicography **[★9747]**

Soc. for the Stud. of Early China **[8077]**, c/o Inst. of East Asian Stud., Univ. of California, Publications Off., 2223 Fulton St., 6th Fl., Berkeley, CA 94720-2318, (510)643-6325

Soc. for the Stud. of Early China **[IO]**, Berkeley, CA, United States

Soc. for the Stud. of Early Modern Women **[9331]**, c/o Nancy A. Guttierez, Treas., Coll. of Arts and Sciences, Univ. of North Carolina at Charlotte, 9201 Univ. City Blvd., Charlotte, NC 28223, (704)687-3388

Soc. for the Stud. of Egyptian Antiquities **[IO]**, Toronto, ON, Canada

Soc. for the Stud. of Evolution **[7073]**, c/o Dale Clayton, Sec., Univ. of Utah, 257 S 1400 E, Salt Lake City, UT 84112, (781)388-8599

Soc. for the Stud. of German Art **[IO]**, Berlin, Germany

Soc. for the Stud. of Human Biology **[IO]**, Hull, United Kingdom

Soc. for the Stud. of Hypertension in Pregnancy; North Amer. **[16342]**

Soc. for the Stud. of Inborn Errors of Metabolism **[IO]**, London, United Kingdom

Soc. for the Stud. of Indigenous Languages of the Americas **[IO]**, Arcata, CA, United States

Soc. for the Stud. of Indigenous Languages of the Americas **[10308]**, PO Box 555, Arcata, CA 95518

Soc. for the Stud. of Ingestive Behavior **[13742]**, c/o Marianne Van Wagner, Exec. Coor., 8181 Tezel Rd., No. 10269, San Antonio, TX 78250, (830)796-9393

Soc. for the Stud. of Internationalism **[★10143]**

Soc. for the Stud. of Japanese Religions **[20529]**, c/o Dr. Barbara Ambros, Exec. Sec., Univ. of North Carolina, Dept. of Religious Studies, 125 Saunders Hall, CB No. 3225, Chapel Hill, NC 27599-3225

Soc. for the Stud. of Labour History **[IO]**, Leeds, United Kingdom

Soc. for the Study of Male Psychology and Physiology - Defunct.

Soc. for the Stud. of Male Reproduction **[16344]**, 1111 N Plaza Dr., Ste. 550, Schaumburg, IL 60173, (847)517-7225

Soc. for the Stud. of Medieval Languages and Literature **[IO]**, Oxford, United Kingdom

Soc. for the Stud. of Midwestern Literature **[10430]**, c/o Mr. Roger J. Bresnahan, PhD, Sec.-Treas., Michigan State Univ., Dept. of Writing, Rhetoric and Amer. Cultures, 235 Bessey Hall, East Lansing, MI 48824-1033

Soc. for the Study of the Multi-Ethnic Literature of the U.S. - Address unknown since 1999.

Soc. for the Stud. of Myth and Tradition **[10729]**, 135 E 15 St., New York, NY 10003, (212)505-6200

Soc. for the Stud. of Neuronal Regulation **[★15394]**

Soc. for the Stud. of Neuronal Regulation **[★IO]**

Soc. for the Stud. of Normal Psychology **[IO]**, London, United Kingdom

Soc. for the Stud. of Pain, Nigeria **[IO]**, Ibadan, Nigeria

Soc. for the Stud. of Peace, Conflict, and Violence: Peace Psychology Div. of the Amer. Psychological Assn. **[16185]**, c/o John Gruszkos, Treas., Glen Forest Associates Ltd., 7301 Forest Ave., Ste. 201, Richmond, VA 23226

Soc. for the Stud. of Pre-Han China **[★8077]**

Soc. for the Stud. of Pre-Han China **[★IO]**

Soc. for the Stud. of Process Philosophies **[10838]**, c/o Dr. Jude Jones, Dir., Fordham Univ., Dept. of Philosophy, Collins Hall, 441 E Fordham Rd., Bronx, NY 10458, (718)817-4721

Soc. for the Stud. of Reproduction **[16350]**, 1619 Monroe St., Madison, WI 53711-2063, (608)256-2777

Soc. for the Stud. of Social Biology **[6862]**, c/o Eileen M. Crimmins, Sec.-Treas., Univ. of Southern California, Andrus Gerontology Ctr., Los Angeles, CA 90089-0191

Soc. for the Stud. of Social Problems **[13133]**, 901 McClung Tower, Univ. of Tennessee, Knoxville, TN 37996-0490, (865)974-7026

Soc. for the Stud. of Southern Literature **[10431]**, c/o Jeff Abernathy, Dean/Sec.-Treas., Augustana Coll., 639 38th St., Rock Island, IL 61201

Soc. for the Stud. of Speciation **[★7073]**

Soc. for the Stud. of Symbolic Interaction **[7669]**, c/o Leslie Wasson, Treas., Social Sciences, Chapman Univ., 530 Kings County Dr., Ste. 102, Hanford, CA 93230, (559)587-3445

Soc. for the Study of Women in Legal History - Defunct.

Soc. of Stukely Westcott Descendants of Am. **[21056]**, c/o Lewis O. Westcott, Registrar, 8121 Beverly Dr., Prairie Village, KS 66208

Soc. for Surgery of the Alimentary Tract **[16590]**, 900 Cummings Ctr., Ste. 221-U, Beverly, MA 01915, (978)927-8330

Soc. of Surgical Oncology **[15655]**, 85 W Algonquin Rd., Ste. 550, Arlington Heights, IL 60005, (847)427-1400

Soc. of Swedish Authors in Finland **[IO]**, Helsinki, Finland

Soc. of Systematic Biologists **[7868]**, c/o Keith A. Crandall, Exec. VP, Brigham Young Univ., Dept. of Zoology, 574 Widtsoe Bldg., Provo, UT 84602-5555

Soc. for the Systematic Documentation of Paranormal Experiments - Address unknown since 2003.

Soc. of Systematic Zoology **[★7868]**

Soc. of Taiwanese Americans, Chicago Chap. **[19403]**, c/o Frank Huang, 2645 N Forrest Rd., Arlington Heights, IL 60004

Soc. of Taiwanese Americans, Chicago Chap. **[IO]**, Arlington Heights, IL, United States

Soc. of Teachers of the Alexander Technique **[IO]**, London, United Kingdom

Soc. of Teachers in Education of Professional Photography - Address unknown since 2004.

Soc. of Teachers of Emergency Medicine **[★14344]**

Soc. of Teachers of Family Medicine **[14387]**, 11400 Tomahawk Creek Pkwy., Ste. 540, Leawood, KS 66211, (913)906-6000

Soc. of Teachers of Speech and Drama **[IO]**, Mansfield, United Kingdom

Soc. of Tech. Analysts **[IO]**, Vernham Dean, United Kingdom

Society for Technical Communication **[IO]**, Arlington, VA, United States

Soc. for Tech. Commun. **[IO]**, Nepean, ON, Canada

Soc. for Tech. Commun. **[886]**, 901 N Stuart St., Ste. 904, Arlington, VA 22203-1822, (703)522-4114

Soc. of Tech. Writers and Editors **[★886]**

Soc. of Tech. Writers and Editors **[★IO]**

Soc. of Tech. Writers and Publishers **[★IO]**

Soc. of Tech. Writers and Publishers **[★886]**

Soc. for the Technological Advancement of Reporting **[5631]**, 222 S Westmonte Dr., Ste. 101, Altamonte Springs, FL 32714, (407)774-7880

Soc. for Tech. in Anesthesia **[13692]**, 2 Summit Park Dr., Ste. 140, Cleveland, OH 44131, (216)447-7864

Soc. for Tech. in Anesthesia **[IO]**, Cleveland, OH, United States

Soc. of Telecom Executives **[★IO]**

Soc. of Telecommunications Consultants **[3756]**, PO Box 70, Old Station, CA 96071-0070, (530)335-7313

Soc. of TV Lighting Directors **[IO]**, High Wycombe, United Kingdom

Soc. of TV Pioneers - Address unknown since 1995.

Soc. of Tempera Painters **[9528]**, c/o Michael Bergt, Pres., PO Box 30766, Santa Fe, NM 87592-0766, (505)473-9654

Soc. for Textual Scholarship **[10432]**, c/o Prof. Robin G. Schulze, Exec. Dir., Penn State Univ., Dept. of English, 117 Burrowes Bldg., State College, PA 16802-6200, (814)863-0258

Soc. for Thai Philately **[22875]**, c/o Peter K. Iber, 9379 W Escuda Dr., Peoria, AZ 85382

Soc. for Theatre Res. **[IO]**, London, United Kingdom

Soc. for Theological Discussion - Defunct.

Soc. for Theoretical and Philosophical Psychology **[16186]**, c/o Louis Sass, Pres., 152 Frelinghuysen Rd., Piscataway, NJ 08854

Soc. for Theriogenology **[16806]**, PO Box 3007, Montgomery, AL 36109, (334)395-4666

Soc. for Thermal Medicine **[16639]**, 10105 Cottesmore Ct., Great Falls, VA 22066-3540, (703)757-0044

Soc. of Thoracic Radiology **[16305]**, PO Box 7169, Rochester, MN 55903-7169, (507)288-5620

Soc. of Thoracic Surgeons **[16644]**, 633 N St. Clair St., No. 2320, Chicago, IL 60611, (312)202-5800

Soc. for Threatened Peoples **[IO]**, Gottingen, Germany

Soc. of Tobacco Jar Collectors **[21936]**, 1705 Chanticleer Dr., Cherry Hill, NJ 08003, (856)489-8363

Soc. of Token, Medal and Obsolete Paper Money Collectors **[★22763]**

Soc. of Tool and Die Craftsmen - Address unknown since 1995.

Soc. of Toxicologic Pathologists **[★15876]**

Soc. of Toxicologic Pathology **[15876]**, 1821 Michael Faraday Dr., Ste. 300, Reston, VA 20190, (703)438-7508

Soc. of Toxicology **[7804]**, 1821 Michael Faraday Dr., Ste. 300, Reston, VA 20190, (703)438-3115

Soc. of Tractor Engineers **[★6520]**

Soc. of Tractor Engineers **[★IO]**

Soc. for Traditional Music - Defunct.

A star before a book entry number signifies that the name is not listed separately, but is mentioned within the entry.

Soc. for Traditional Music in Switzerland [IO], Pfaffikon, Switzerland

Soc. of Traditional Roman Catholics [19726], PO Box 130, Mead, WA 99021-0130

Soc. of Translators and Interpreters of Canada [★IO]

Soc. of Trauma Nurses [15528], 1926 Waukegan Rd., Ste. 1, Glenview, IL 60025, (847)657-6745

Soc. for Traumatic Stress Stud. [★16489]

Soc. for Traumatic Stress Stud. [★IO]

Soc. of Travel Agents in Govt. [★6327]

Soc. of Travel and Tourism Educators [★3925]

Soc. of Travel and Tourism Educators [★IO]

Soc. for Treatment of Autism [IO], Calgary, AB, Canada

Soc. of Tribologists and Lubrication Engineers [IO], Park Ridge, IL, United States

Soc. of Tribologists and Lubrication Engineers [7047], 840 Busse Hwy., Park Ridge, IL 60068, (847)825-5536

Soc. for Tropical Horticulture; InterAmerican [4979]

Soc. for Tropical Veterinary Medicine [16807], c/o Dr. Thomas E. Walton, Sec.-Treas., 555 S Howes, Fort Collins, CO 80521, (970)490-8100

Soc. for Tropical Veterinary Medicine [IO], Fort Collins, CO, United States

Soc. of Trust and Estate Practitioners [IO], London, United Kingdom

Soc. of Trust and Estate Practitioners Ireland [IO], Dublin, Ireland

Soc. of Trust and Estate Practitioners USA [1332], 7 Times Sq., New York, NY 10036-7311, (914)636-2531

Soc. of Turkish Amer. Architects, Engineers and Scientists [7048], 821 United Nations Plz., Turkish Ctr., 2nd Fl., New York, NY 10017, (646)312-3366

Soc. of Turkish Amer. Architects, Engineers and Scientists [IO], New York, NY, United States

Soc. of Turkish Architects, Engineers and Scientists in Am. [★IO]

Soc. of Turkish Architects, Engineers and Scientists in Am. [★7048]

Soc. of Turnaround Professionals [IO], London, United Kingdom

Soc. of Tympanuchus Cupido Pinnatus [5383]

Soc. of Typographic Aficionados [1791], c/o Tamye Riggs, Dir., 3025 Alta Vista, Alameda, CA 94502, (510)748-0784

Soc. of Ukrainian Engineers in Am. [★7050]

Soc. of Ukrainian Philatelists [★22883]

Soc. of Ukrainian Philatelists [★IO]

Soc. for Ultrastructural Pathology [15877], c/o Dr. John Shelburne, Sec.-Treas., Box 3712, Dept. of Pathology, Duke Univ. Medical Center, Durham, NC 27710-3712, (919)286-6907

Soc. for Underwater Exploration [★IO]

Soc. for Underwater Tech. [IO], London, United Kingdom

Soc. of U.S. Air Force Flight Surgeons [13543], PO Box 35387, Brooks City Base, TX 78235, (210)975-2109

Soc. for U.S. Commemorative Coins [22760], PO Box 2335, Huntington Beach, CA 92647

Soc. of U.S. Medical Consultants in World War II [★15265]

Soc. of U.S. Naval Flight Surgeons [13544], PO Box 33008, Pensacola, FL 32508-3008, (850)452-2257

Soc. of U.S. Pattern Collectors [22761], c/o Andy Lustig, R.M. Smythe, Inc., 2 Rector St., 12th Fl., New York, NY 10006, (800)622-1880

Soc. of Univ. Olodaryngologists [★15828]

Soc. of Univ. Otolaryngologists - Head and Neck Surgeons [15828], c/o Donna Hoffman, MA, Exec. Admin., USC School of Medicine, Dept. of Otolaryngology, 1200 N State St., Box 795, Los Angeles, CA 90033, (323)226-7315

Soc. of Univ. Patent Administrators [★5838]

Soc. of Univ. Surgeons [16591], 341 N Maitland Ave., Ste. 130, Maitland, FL 32751, (407)647-7714

Soc. of Univ. Urologists [16716], 1100 E Woodfield Rd., Ste. 520, Schaumburg, IL 60173, (847)517-7225

Soc. for Upgrading the Built Env. [IO], Giza, Egypt

Soc. for Urban Anthropology - Address unknown since 1994.

Soc. for Urban, Natl. and Transnational/Global Anthropology [6435], c/o Deborah Pellow, Pres.-Elect, Syracuse Univ., The Maxwell School, 209 Maxwell Hall, Syracuse, NY 13244

Soc. of Urologic Nurses and Associates [15529], E Holly Ave., Box 56, Pitman, NJ 08071-0056, (856)256-2335

Soc. of Uroradiology [16717], 4550 Post Oak Pl., Ste. 342, Houston, TX 77027, (713)965-0566

Soc. for the Use of On-Line Computers in Psychology [★6744]

Soc. for Utopian Stud. [10839], c/o Dr. Carrie Hintz, Pres., Queens/CUNY, 65-30 Kissena Blvd., Flushing, NY 11367, (718)997-4677

Soc. for Utopian Stud. [IO], Flushing, NY, United States

Soc. of Vacuum Coaters [856], 71 Pinon Hill Pl. NE, Albuquerque, NM 87122, (505)856-7188

Soc. for Values in Higher Educ. [19940], c/o Portland State Univ., PO Box 751, Portland, OR 97207-0751, (503)725-2575

Soc. for Vascular Medicine and Biology [16729], 60 Revere Dr., Ste. 500, Northbrook, IL 60062, (847)480-2961

Soc. for Vascular Nursing [15530], 203 Washington St., Salem, MA 01970, (978)744-5005

Soc. for Vascular Surgery [16730], 633 N St. Clair, 24th Fl., Chicago, IL 60611, (312)202-5600

Soc. for Vascular Tech. [★16731]

Soc. for Vascular Ultrasound [16731], 4601 Presidents Dr.,Ste. 260, Lanham, MD 20706-4831, (301)459-7550

Soc. for Vector Ecologists [★5079]

Soc. for Vector Ecology [5079], 1966 Compton Ave., Corona, CA 92881-3318, (951)340-9792

Soc. of Vertebrate Paleontology [7433], 60 Revere Dr., Ste. 500, Northbrook, IL 60062, (847)480-9095

Society of Vertebrate Paleontology [IO], Northbrook, IL, United States

Soc. for Veterinary Ethology [★IO]

Soc. for Veterinary Medical Ethics [16808], c/o John S. Wright, DVM, Treas., Coll. of Veterinary Medicine, Univ. of Minnesota, Dept. of Small Animal Clinical Sciences, C339 Veterinary Teaching Hosp., 1352 Boyd Ave., St. Paul, MN 55108, (509)335-2956

Soc. of Vietnamese Rangers - Address unknown since 1995.

Soc. for Visual Anthropology [6436], c/o Mary Strong, Sec., 1708 11th Ave., Brooklyn, NY 11218

Soc. for Vocational Psychology [7551], c/o Rasheed Ali, Communications Off., Univ. of Iowa, Div. of Psychological and Quantitative Foundations, 361 Lindquist Ctr., Iowa City, IA 52242, (319)335-5495

Soc. for Voluntary Control of Trade Fair and Exhibition Statistics [IO], Berlin, Germany

Soc. of the War of 1812 in the Commonwealth of Pennsylvania - Address unknown since 2002.

Soc. of the War of 1812 in Connecticut [★21354]

Soc. of the War of 1812 in Pennsylvania [★21354]

Soc. for Welfare Awakening Training and Hea. Implementation [IO], Warangal, India

Soc. of Wetland Scientists [4452], 1313 Dolley Madison Blvd., Ste. 402, McLean, VA 22101, (703)790-1745

Soc. of the Whiskey Rebellion of 1794 - Defunct.

Soc. for Whole Body Autoradiography [15149], c/o Alfred Lordi, Sec., QPS, Quest Pharmaceutical Services, 110 Executive Dr., Ste. 7, Newark, DE 19702, (302)369-5204

Soc. of Wildlife Artists [IO], London, United Kingdom

Soc. of Wildlife Specialists [★5401]

Soc. of Wine Educators [23029], 1212 New York Ave. NW, Ste. 425, Washington, DC 20005, (202)408-8777

Society of Wine Educators [IO], Washington, DC, United States

Soc. of Wireless Pioneers [3757], PO Box 86, Geyserville, CA 95441-0086

Soc. of Woman Geographers [7124], 415 E Capitol St. SE, Washington, DC 20003, (202)546-9228

Soc. of Woman Geographers [IO], Washington, DC, United States

Soc. for Women and AIDS in Africa [IO], Dakar, Senegal

Soc. of Women Artists [IO], Gillingham, United Kingdom

Soc. of Women Engineers [7049], 230 E Ohio St., Ste. 400, Chicago, IL 60611-3265, (312)596-5223

Soc. of Women in Military Aviation - Address unknown since 1986.

Soc. for Women in Philosophy, Eastern Div. - Defunct.

Soc. for Women in Philosophy, Midwest Div. - Address unknown since 1990.

Soc. for Women in Philosophy, Southwestern Div. - Address unknown since 1994.

Soc. for Women in Plastics - Address unknown since 2000.

Soc. of Women in Urology [16718], c/o Ann Marie Bray, CMP, 1110 E Woodfield Rd., Ste. 520, Schaumburg, IL 60173, (847)517-7225

Soc. of Women Writers and Journalists [IO], Walton-On-Thames, United Kingdom

Soc. of Women Writers - Victoria [IO], Carrum, Australia

Soc. for Women's Hea. Res. [16910], 1025 Connecticut Ave. NW, Ste. 701, Washington, DC 20036, (202)223-8224

Soc. of Wood Engravers [IO], Oundle, United Kingdom

Soc. of Wood Sci. and Tech. [7100], 1 Gifford Pinchot Dr., Madison, WI 53726-2398, (608)231-9347

Soc. for a World Service Fed. - Defunct.

Soc. of World War One Aero Historians - Defunct.

Soc. of Writers to Her Majesty's Signet [IO], Edinburgh, United Kingdom

Soc. of Young Publishers [IO], London, United Kingdom

Soc. for Young Victims, Missing Children Center - Address unknown since 2000.

Soc. of Zoologists; Amer. [★7867]

Society's League Against Molestation - Address unknown since 2002.

Socio-Ecological Union [IO], Moscow, Russia

Socio Economics of Allergy; Joint Coun. of [★13602]

Socio-Economics; Soc. for the Advancement of [17472]

Socio-Legal Stud. Assn. [IO], Belfast, United Kingdom

Sociocyberneering, Inc; Assn. [★18632]

SocioEconomic Stud; Inst. for [18458]

Sociological Assn. of Australia and New Zealand [IO], Brisbane, Australia

Sociological Assn. of Ireland [IO], Cork, Ireland

Sociological Practice Assn. [7670], c/o Ross Koppel, PhD, Pres., Social Res. Corp., PO Box 15, Wyncote, PA 19005, (215)576-8221

Sociological Res. Assn. [7671], c/o Amer. Sociological Assn., 1307 New York Ave. NW, Ste. 700, Washington, DC 20005, (202)383-9005

Sociological Soc; Amer. [★7658]

Sociological Soc; Amer. Catholic [★7661]

Sociological Soc; Rural Sect. of the Amer. [★7667]

Sociological Stud. of Jewry; Assn. of the [★8685]

Sociologists in Business - Address unknown since 2004.

Sociologists; Caucus of Black [★7659]

Sociologists; International Register of Rural [★7664]

Sociologists; International Register of Rural [★IO]

Sociologists Without Borders [IO], Chapel Hill, NC, United States

Sociologists Without Borders [18664], 7019 Old NC Hwy. 86, Chapel Hill, NC 27516

Sociologists for Women in Soc. [9924], c/o Jessica Holden Sherwood, PhD, Exec. Off., Univ. of Akron, Chafee Social Sci. Center, Kingston, RI 02881, (401)874-9510

Sociologists for Women in Soc. [IO], Kingston, RI, United States

Sociology

Alpha Kappa Delta [IO]

Alpha Kappa Delta [24701]

Amer. Sociological Assn. [7658]

Anabaptist Sociology and Anthropology Assn. [7559]

Asia Pacific Sociological Assn. [IO]

Assn. for Africanist Anthropology [6408]

Assn. of Black Sociologists [7659]

Assn. for Humanist Sociology [7660]

Reference to "IO" in place of a book number signifies that the association may be found in the 45th edition of International Organizations.

Assn. of Latina and Latino Anthropologists [6410]
Assn. of Senior Anthropologists [6412]
Assn. for the Sociology of Religion [7661]
The Assn. for the Stud. of Play [10858]
Australian Sociological Assn. [IO]
British Sociological Assn. [IO]
Bulgarian Sociological Assn. [IO]
Canadian Sociology and Anthropology Assn. [IO]
Center for Res. in Faith and Moral Development [20534]
Christian Sociological Soc. [7662]
Comm. on the Status of Women in Sociology [9923]
Cuban Amer. Natl. Coun. [13167]
ERIS Roundtable for Independent Study [10792]
European Soc. for Rural Sociology [IO]
European Sociological Assn. [IO]
Evolutionary Anthropology Soc. [6416]
Honors Prog. Student Assn. of the Amer. Sociological Assn. [24702]
Intl. Assn. of French Language Sociologists [IO]
Intl. Inst. of Sociology [IO]
Intl. Inst. of Sociology [7663]
Intl. Org. for the Stud. of Gp. Tensions [10189]
Intl. Rural Sociology Assn. [7664]
Intl. Rural Sociology Assn. [IO]
Intl. Soc. for Human Ethology [6534]
Intl. Sociological Assn. [IO]
Intl. Time Capsule Soc. [10041]
Intl. Women's Anthropology Conf. [6420]
Japanese Sociological Soc. [IO]
Natl. Coun. of State Sociological Associations [7665]
North Amer. Soc. for the Sociology of Sport [7666]
Polish Sociological Assn. [IO]
Rural Sociological Soc. [7667]
Russian Soc. of Sociologists [IO]
Soc. for Applied Anthropology [6427]
Soc. for Applied Sociology [7668]
Soc. for Cross-Cultural Res. [10230]
Soc. for Res. in Child Development [11546]
Soc. for the Stud. of Social Biology [6862]
Soc. for the Stud. of Symbolic Interaction [7669]
Sociological Assn. of Australia and New Zealand [IO]
Sociological Assn. of Ireland [IO]
Sociological Practice Assn. [7670]
Sociological Res. Assn. [7671]
Sociologists Without Borders [18664]
Sociologists Without Borders [IO]
Sociologists for Women in Soc. [9924]
Space Settlement Studies Program [6387]
Swiss Sociological Assn. [IO]
Western Social Sci. Assn. [7657]
World Soc. for Ekistics [IO]
Sociology Assn; Clinical [★7670]
Sociology; Comm. on the Status of Women in [9923]
Sociology of Education Assn. - Address unknown since 1995.
Sociometry, and Gp. Psychotherapy; Amer. Bd. of Examiners of Psychodrama, [16201]
Socket Screw Products Bur. - Defunct.
Sod Growers Assn. of Mid-America - Address unknown since 2002.
Sod House Soc. - Address unknown since 2000.
Sod Producers Assn; Amer. [★4799]
Soda Ash Corp; Amer. Natural [1725]
Soda Ash Export Assn; U.S. [★1725]
Soda Dispensing Equip. Assn; Natl. [★507]
Soda Pulp Mfrs. Assn. - Defunct.
Sodality Movement and Queens Work [★19680]
Soeurs du Bon Pasteur [★IO]
Soeurs de la Charite de Sainte Jeanne Antide Thouret [★IO]
Soeurs de la Croix de Chavanod [★IO]
Soeurs Missionnaires du Coeur Immacule de Marie [★IO]
Soeurs de Saint Louis [★IO]
Soft Drink Assn; Natl. [★503]
Soft Drink and Distillery Workers of Am. (AFL-CIO); Intl. Union of United Brewery, Flour, Cereal, [★24020]
Soft Drink and Fruit Juice Producers' Assn. [IO], Lisbon, Portugal

Soft Drink Technologists; Soc. of [★6543]
Soft Drink Workers Conf. - U.S.A. and Canada; Brewery and [24020]
Soft Fibre Mfrs. Inst. - Defunct.
Soft Furnishing Indus. Assn. of Australia [IO], Reservoir, Australia
Soft Furnishing Indus. Assn. of Australia - New South Wales [IO], Mortdale, Australia
Soft Furnishing Indus. Assn. of Australia - Queensland [IO], Brisbane, Australia
Soft Furnishing Indus. Assn. of Australia - South Australia [IO], Adelaide, Australia
Soft Furnishing Indus. Assn. of Australia - Tasmania [IO], Reservoir, Australia
Soft Furnishing Indus. Assn. of Australia - Victoria [IO], Reservoir, Australia
Soft Furnishing Indus. Assn. of Australia - Western Australia [IO], Joondalup, Australia
Soft Serve and Fast Food Association; National [★1958]
Soft Serve and Fast Food Association; United [★1958]
Softball
Alberta Amateur Softball Assn. [IO]
Amateur Softball Assn. of Am. [23788]
Babe Ruth Baseball/Softball [23106]
Cinderella Softball Leagues [23789]
Hong Kong Softball Assn. [IO]
Intl. Senior Softball Assn. [IO]
Intl. Senior Softball Assn. [23790]
Intl. Softball Fed. [23791]
Intl. Softball Fed. [IO]
Natl. Fastpitch Coaches Assn. [23840]
Natl. Softball Assn. [23792]
Natl. Wheelchair Softball Assn. [23356]
North Amer. Fastpitch Assn. [23793]
North American Fastpitch Association [IO]
North Amer. Sports Fed. [23065]
Pony Baseball and Softball [23124]
Professional Assn. of Volleyball Officials [23875]
Slo-Pitch Natl. Softball [IO]
Softball Canada [IO]
U.S. Fastpitch Assn. [23794]
U.S. Specialty Sports Assn. [23795]
Softball Alberta [★IO]
Softball Assn; Natl. Wheelchair [23356]
Softball Assn; U.S.A. Slo-Pitch [★23795]
Softball; Babe Ruth Baseball/ [23106]
Softball Canada [IO], Ottawa, ON, Canada
Softball; Little League Baseball and [23111]
Softball; Pony Baseball and [23124]
Softbll Soc; Natl. Finch and [21854]
Software Alliance; Bus. [5840]
Software Assn. - of ADAPSO; Microcomputer [★6768]
Software Assn; Bus. [★5840]
Software Assn; Entertainment [6766]
Software Assn; Hearing Instrument Manufacturers' [14758]
Software Assn; Interactive Digital [★6766]
Software Contractors' Guild [1143], 3 Country Club Dr., No. 303, Manchester, NH 03102
Software Cooperative; Educational [6765]
Software Dealers Assn; Video [333]
Software Defined Radio Forum [6776], 1616 17th St., Ste. 264, Denver, CO 80202, (303)628-5461
Software Distributors' Assn. [IO], Santiago, Chile
Software Engg; Special Interest Gp. on [6779]
Software Found; Free [6767]
Software Human Rsrc. Coun. [★IO]
Software Indus. Division of ADAPSO [★6768]
Software and Info. Indus. Assn. [5858], 1090 Vermont Ave. NW, 6th Fl., Washington, DC 20005-4930, (202)289-7442
Software Management Assn. - Defunct.
Software New Zealand [IO], Milford, New Zealand
Software Productivity Consortium [★6780]
Software in the Public Interest [6777], PO Box 501248, Indianapolis, IN 46250-6248
Software Publishers Assn. and Info. Indus. Assn. [★5858]
Software Quality; Soc. for [6775]
Software Testing Inst. [6778], PO Box 831056, Richardson, TX 75083-1056, (972)680-8507
Software Theft; Canadian Alliance Against [IO]

Softwood Export Coun. [IO], Portland, OR, United States
Softwood Export Coun. [1619], 520 SW 6th Ave., Ste. 810, Portland, OR 97204-1514, (503)248-0406
SOHO Am. [3630], PO Box 941, Hurst, TX 76053-0941, (800)495-SOHO
Soil
Asia Soil Conservation Network for the Humid Tropics [IO]
Assn. for the Environmental Hea. of Soils [5221]
Assn. of Women Soil Scientists [7672]
Australian Collaborative Land Evaluation Prog. [IO]
Australian Stabilisation Indus. Assn. [IO]
British Soc. of Soil Sci. [IO]
Canadian Soc. of Soil Sci. [IO]
Compost Tea Indus. Assn. [186]
Indian Soc. of Soil Sci. [IO]
Inst. of Professional Soil Scientists [IO]
Intl. Humic Substances Soc. [7610]
Intl. Sand Collectors Soc. [22056]
Intl. Soc. for Soil Mechanics and Geotechnical Engg. [IO]
Intl. Soil Reference and Info. Centre [IO]
Intl. Union of Soil Sciences [IO]
Japanese Soc. of Soil Sci. and Plant Nutrition [IO]
Korean Soc. of Soil Sci. and Fertilizer [IO]
Mulch and Soil Coun. [1651]
Natl. Soc. of Consulting Soil Scientists [5222]
New Zealand Soc. of Soil Sci. [IO]
Soil and Plant Anal. Coun. [7673]
Soil Sci. Soc. of Am. [7674]
Soil Sci. Soc. of South Africa [IO]
Swedish Geotechnical Soc. [IO]
U.S. Consortium of Soil Sci. Associations [5223]
U.S. Permafrost Assn. [7675]
World Assn. of Soil and Water Conservation [4473]
Soil Assn. [IO], Bristol, United Kingdom
Soil Conservation
Australian Soc. of Soil Sci. [IO]
Erosion Control Tech. Coun. [IO]
Erosion Control Tech. Coun. [5224]
Natl. Mitigation Banking Assn. [4425]
Natl. Soc. of Consulting Soil Scientists [5222]
New Zealand Assn. of Rsrc. Mgt. [IO]
U.S. Consortium of Soil Sci. Associations [5223]
Soil Conservation Districts; Natl. Assn. of [★4420]
Soil Conservation Soc. of Am. [★4453]
Soil Coun; Mulch and [1651]
Soil and Found. Engineers; Assoc. [★7137]
Soil and Found. Engineers; Assn. of [★7137]
Soil and Hea. Assn. of New Zealand [IO], Auckland, New Zealand
Soil Mechanics and Found. Engg; U.S. Natl. Soc. for the Intl. Soc. of [★7147]
Soil Pipe Inst; Cast Iron [3027]
Soil and Plant Anal. Coun. [7673], 300 Speedway Cir., Ste. 2, Lincoln, NE 68502, (402)476-0300
Soil Producers Assn; Natl. Bark and [★1651]
Soil Sci. Soc. of Am. [7674], 677 S Segoe Rd., Madison, WI 53711, (608)273-8080
Soil Sci. Soc. of South Africa [IO], Erasmusrand, Republic of South Africa
Soil Survey Assn; Amer. [★7674]
Soil Testing and Plant Anal; Coun. on [★7673]
Soil and Water Conservation Districts; Natl. Assn. of [★4420]
Soil and Water Conservation Soc. [4453], 945 SW Ankeny Rd., Ankeny, IA 50023-9723, (515)289-2331
Soiland Irrigation Res. Inst. [★IO]
Soils Sect. of Amer. Soc. of Agronomy [★7674]
Sojourner Truth Org. - Address unknown since 1985.
Sojourners [19827], 3333 14th St. NW, Ste. 200, Washington, DC 20010, (202)328-8842
Sojourners Club [★19246]
Sojourners; Natl. [19246]
Sojuzpushnina [IO], Moscow, Russia
Sojuzupak [★IO]
Soka Gakkai International-United States of Am. [IO], Santa Monica, CA, United States
Soka Gakkai International-United States of Am. [19556], 606 Wilshire Blvd., Santa Monica, CA 90401, (310)260-8900

A star before a book entry number signifies that the name is not listed separately, but is mentioned within the entry.

Sokol [★19025]
Sokol Educational and Physical Culture Org; Amer. [19025]
SOKOL U.S.A. [19367], PO Box 189, East Orange, NJ 07019-0189, (973)676-0280
SOL [13030], PO Box 2276, North Canton, OH 44720, (330)497-9645
Solace Intl. [13439], 408 E Camino Limon Verde, Sahuarita, AZ 85629-8748, (520)393-8776
Solace Intl. [IO], Sahuarita, AZ, United States
Solanaceae Enthusiasts - Defunct.
Solano Silver Round Club [22762], c/o Jan D. Henke, PO Box 3518, Fairfield, CA 94533-0518, (707)427-0482
Solar
  Amer. Solar Energy Soc. [7676]
  North Amer. Bd. of Certified Energy Practitioners [6967]
  Solar Cookers Intl. [5100]
  Solar Elec. Power Assn. [7678]
  Solar Energy Indus. Assn. [7679]
  Solar Rating and Certification Corp. [7681]
  Sustainable Buildings Indus. Coun. [7682]
Solar Action - Defunct.
Solar Box Cookers Intl. [★5100]
Solar Box Cookers Intl. [★IO]
Solar Cookers Intl. [IO], Sacramento, CA, United States
Solar Cookers Intl. [5100], 1919 21st St., Ste. 101, Sacramento, CA 95814, (916)455-4499
Solar Elec. Power Assn. [7678], 805 15th St. NW, Ste. 510, Washington, DC 20005, (202)857-0898
Solar Energy
  Amer. Coun. on Renewable Energy [6939]
  Amer. Solar Energy Soc. [7676]
  Australian and New Zealand Solar Energy Soc. [IO]
  Enersol Associates [18665]
  European Assn. for Renewable Energy [IO]
  European Solar Indus. Fed. [IO]
  European Solar Thermal Indus. Fed. [IO]
  Intl. Solar Energy Soc. [IO]
  North Amer. Bd. of Certified Energy Practitioners [6967]
  Northeast Sustainable Energy Assn. [6968]
  Renew the Earth [7677]
  Renew the Earth [IO]
  Romanian Natl. Agency for Solar and Renewable Energy [IO]
  Sci. Comm. on Solar Terrestrial Physics [7508]
  Solar Cookers Intl. [5100]
  Solar Elec. Power Assn. [7678]
  Solar Energy Indus. Assn. [7679]
  Solar Energy Intl. [7680]
  Solar Energy Intl. [IO]
  Solar Energy Soc. [IO]
  Solar Energy Soc. of Canada [IO]
  Solar Rating and Certification Corp. [7681]
  Solar Trade Assn. [IO]
  SunDance [IO]
  Sustainable Buildings Indus. Coun. [7682]
  Swiss Solar Energy Soc. [IO]
Solar Energy Assn; Amer. [★7676]
Solar Energy Construction Assn. - Defunct.
Solar Energy Indus. Assn. [7679], 805 15th St. NW, Ste. 510, Washington, DC 20005, (202)682-0556
Solar Energy Inst. of North America - Defunct.
Solar Energy Intl. [7680], PO Box 715, Carbondale, CO 81623, (970)963-8855
Solar Energy Intl. [IO], Carbondale, CO, United States
Solar Energy Res. and Educ. Foundation [★7679]
Solar Energy Soc. [IO], Abingdon, United Kingdom
Solar Energy Soc. of America - Address unknown since 1995.
Solar Energy Soc; Amer. [7676]
Solar Energy Soc; Amer. Sect. of the Intl. [★7676]
Solar Energy Soc. of Canada [IO], Kingston, ON, Canada
Solar Heating and Cooling; Natl. [★6951]
Solar Lobby [★7677]
Solar Lobby [★IO]
Solar Projects - Defunct.
Solar Rating and Certification Corp. [7681], c/o FSEC, 1679 Clearlake Rd., Cocoa, FL 32922-5703, (321)638-1537

Solar Terrestrial Physics; Inter-Union Commn. on [★7508]
Solar Trade Assn. [IO], Milton Keynes, United Kingdom
Solartherm - Address unknown since 2003.
Solbrekken Evangelistic Assn. of Canada [IO], Edmonton, AB, Canada
Soldier; Any [11490]
Soldier of Fortune
  Omega First Amendment Legal Fund [17140]
Soldier to the Movies; Oper.: Take a [11498]
Soldier Org; Vietnam Veterans Against the War/ Winter [★18784]
Soldier Support; Oper. [11497]
Soldiers Am; Support Our [11502]
Soldiers' Angels [19259], PO Box 20431, Colorado City, CO 81019-2431, (615)676-0239
Soldiers; Books For [11491]
Soldiers of Freedom - Address unknown since 1999.
Soldiers League; U.S. Maimed [★21320]
Soldiers Overseas Family Gateway [12598], 503 Regency Cir., Vacaville, CA 95696
Soldiers for Peace - Defunct.
Soldiers, Sailors, Airmen and Families Assn. Forces Help [IO], London, United Kingdom
Soldiers for the Truth [20683], PO Box 54365, Irvine, CA 92619-4365
Soldiers of the War of 1812; New England Assn. of [★21354]
A Soldier's Wish List [11501], c/o Mrs. Julieann Najar, Founder, 11143 Larimore Rd., St. Louis, MO 63138, (314)868-2264
SOLE - The Intl. Soc. of Logistics [7186], 8100 Professional Pl., Ste. 111, Hyattsville, MD 20785-2229, (301)459-8446
SOLE - The Intl. Soc. of Logistics [IO], Hyattsville, MD, United States
Solent Skiers Assn. [IO], Fareham, United Kingdom
Solicitors Family Law Assn. [★IO]
Solid Axle Corvette Club [IO], North Highlands, CA, United States
Solid Axle Corvette Club [21786], PO Box 1134, El Dorado, CA 95623
Solid Carbide Tool Inst. - Address unknown since 1995.
Solid Fibre Box Group - Defunct.
Solid Fuel Advisory Coun. of America - Defunct.
Solid Fuel Assn. [IO], Alfreton, United Kingdom
Solid-State Circuits Coun; IEEE [★6904]
Solid-State Circuits Soc; IEEE [6904]
Solid Waste Assn. of North Am. [6355], 1100 Wayne Ave., Ste. 700, Silver Spring, MD 20910, (301)585-2898
Solid Waste Composting Coun. [★6356]
Solid Waste Coun. of the Paper Industry - Defunct.
Solid Waste Mgt. Officials; Assn. of State and Territorial [6353]
Solid Wastes Mgt. Assn; Natl. [3579]
Solidaridad Internacional [IO], Madrid, Spain
Solidaritat mit Frauen in Not [★IO]
Solidarity: A Socialist-Feminist Network - Defunct.
Solidarity and Action Against the HIV Infection in India [16969], 900 W 190th St., No. 15B, New York, NY 10040, (212)532-0189
Solidarity and Action Against the HIV Infection in India [IO], Chicago, IL, United States
Solidarity Alliance; Workers [16982]
Solidarity for Children in Africa and the World [IO], Cotonou, Benin
Solidarity; Comm. in Support of [★17446]
Solidarity Philippines Australia Network [IO], Brisbane, Australia
Solidarity, U.S.A; Christian [★20521]
Solidarity With the People of Guatemala; Network in [17681]
Solidarity with Women in Distress [IO], Boppard, Germany
Solids Handling and Processing Assn. [IO], Leicester, United Kingdom
Soling Assn; U.S. [23234]
Solomon Island Graduate Women's Assn. [IO], Honiara, Solomon Islands
Solomon Islands Taekwondo Union [IO], Honiara, Solomon Islands
Solomon Islands Tennis Assn. [IO], Honiara, Solomon Islands

Solomon Islands Weightlifting Fed. [IO], Honiara, Solomon Islands
Solomon Islands Yachting Assn. [IO], Honiara, Solomon Islands
Solomon Schechter Day School Assn. [8701], 155 5th Ave., 5th Fl., New York, NY 10010-6802, (212)533-7800
Soluis; Irish Arts Center - An Claidheamh [10243]
Solution Mining Res. Inst. [2755], 105 Apple Valley Cir., Clarks Summit, PA 18411, (570)585-8092
Solutions Assn; Natl. Nitrogen [★1363]
Solutions to Tragedies of Police Pursuits - Address unknown since 2004.
Solvent Abuse Found. for Education - Address unknown since 2002.
Solvent Extractors' Assn. of India [IO], Bombay, India
Solvents Indus. Alliance; Halogenated [809]
Solvents Indus. Assn. [IO], Harwich, United Kingdom
SOMA U.S.A. [★20393]
Somali Athletics Fed. [IO], Sharjah, United Arab Emirates
Somali Badminton Fed. [IO], Mogadishu, Somalia
Somali Cat Club of Am. [21918], 5027 Armstrong, Wichita, KS 67204
Somali Environmental Protection and Anti-Desertification Org. [IO], Abu Dhabi, United Arab Emirates
Somali Family Care Network [19392], 2724 Dorr Ave., Ste. 102, Fairfax, VA 22031, (703)560-0005
Somali Intl. Cat Club [21919], c/o George Hilton, Treas., 2210 21st St., Lake Charles, LA 70601
Somali Weightlifting Fed. [IO], Mogadishu, Somalia
Somalia
  Somali Family Care Network [19392]
Somalia Squash Fed. [IO], Mogadishu, Somalia
Somatics Assn. [12363], 1516 Grant Ave., Ste. 212, Novato, CA 94945, (415)892-0617
Somerset Chamber of Commerce and Indus. [IO], Taunton, United Kingdom
Sommelier Soc. of Am. [209], PO Box 20080, West Village Sta., New York, NY 10014, (212)679-4190
Somnology; Amer. Acad. of [16419]
Somnology; American Bd. of [★16419]
Son of a Witch - Address unknown since 1999.
Sonar Class Assn. [23220], c/o Sarah Sheldon, Sec., 43 Cottage Farm Rd., Brookline, MA 02446, (617)738-1021
Song Soc. of Am; Country Dance and [★9873]
Song Soc; Country Dance and [9873]
Songsmith Soc. - Defunct.
Songwriters Assn. of Canada [IO], Toronto, ON, Canada
Songwriters Assn; Nashville [★10654]
Songwriters, Composers And Lyricists Assn. [IO], Kensington Park, Australia
Songwriters and Composers; Guild of Intl. [IO]
Songwriters Guild [★5859]
Songwriters Guild of Am. [5859], 209 Tenth Ave. S, Ste. 321, Nashville, TN 37203, (615)742-9945
Songwriters Guild; Intl. [2828]
Songwriters Guild; Southern [2824]
Songwriters and Lyricists Club - Defunct.
Songwriters; Natl. Acad. of [★5859]
Songwriters Protective Assn. [★5859]
Songwriters of Wisconsin Intl. [9818], PO Box 1027, Neenah, WI 54957-1027, (920)725-5129
Songwriting/Musician Networking Org; Just Plain Folks [2829]
Sonic Arts Network [IO], London, United Kingdom
Sonics and Ultrasonics Soc; IEEE [★6366]
Sonneck Soc. [★10698]
Sonny James and Friends - Defunct.
Sonographers; Canadian Soc. of Diagnostic Medical [IO]
Sonography
  Amer. Inst. of Ultrasound in Medicine [16436]
  Amer. Registry of Diagnostic Medical Sonography [16437]
  Amer. Soc. of Echocardiography [13891]
  Amer. Soc. for Ophthalmic Ultrasonography [15667]
  Australasian Soc. for Ultrasound in Medicine [IO]
  Australian Sonographers Assn. [IO]
  British Medical Ultrasound Soc. [IO]

Reference to "IO" in place of a book number signifies that the association may be found in the 45th edition of International Organizations.

Canadian Soc. of Diagnostic Medical Sonographers [IO]

European Fed. of Societies for Ultrasound in Medicine and Biology [IO]

Intl. Veterinary Ultrasound Soc. [16797]

Joint Rev. Comm. on Educ. in Diagnostic Medical Sonography [8837]

Musculoskeletal Ultrasound Soc. [16696]

Soc. of Diagnostic Medical Sonography [16438]

Sonography; Joint Rev. Comm. on Educ. in Diagnostic Medical [8837]

Sonoma County Grape Growers Assn. [5421], PO Box 1959, Sebastopol, CA 95473, (707)829-3963

Sonoma County Vintners [5422], 420 Aviation Blvd., Ste. 106, Santa Rosa, CA 95403, (707)522-5840

Sonoma County Wine Growers Assn. [★5422]

Sonoma County Wineries Assn. [★5422]

Sonoran Desert Alliance; Intl. [4582]

Sons of Am; Patriotic Order [21242]

Sons of the Amer. Colonists; Natl. Soc., [20748]

Sons of the Amer. Legion [21201], PO Box 1055, Indianapolis, IN 46206, (317)630-1200

Sons of the Amer. Revolution; Natl. Soc., [20676]

Sons of Bosses Intl. [★748]

Sons of Charity [IO], Paris, France

Sons of Colonial New England Natl. Soc. [20761], 300 N Hill Rd., Sutton, WV 26601, (304)765-0321

Sons of Confederate Veterans [20730], c/o Ben C. Sewell, III, Exec. Dir., PO Box 59, Columbia, TN 38402-0059, (931)380-1844

Sons and Daughters of the First Settlers of Newbury, Massachusetts - Address unknown since 2001.

Sons and Daughters In Touch [12599], PO Box 100366, Arlington, VA 22210, (800)984-9994

Sons and Daughters of Malta - Address unknown since 1995.

Sons and Daughters of Oregon Pioneers [21257], PO Box 6685, Portland, OR 97228

Sons and Daughters of Pioneer Rivermen [21258], c/o Richard Prater, Sec., 602 Country Club Ave. NE, Fort Walton Beach, FL 32547, (850)864-5590

Sons and Daughters of the Soddies - Address unknown since 2001.

Sons and Daughters of the U.S.A; Children, [★11335]

Sons of the Desert [24828], c/o Laurel and Hardy Museum, PO Box 99, Harlem, GA 30814, (706)556-3448

Sons of the Desert [IO], Harlem, GA, United States

Sons of the Golden West; Native [18987]

Sons of Hermann in Texas; Grand Lodge Order of the [19125]

Sons of Israel; United [20187]

Sons of Light [★13030]

Sons of Norway [19293], 1455 W Lake St., Minneapolis, MN 55408-2666, (612)827-3611

Sons of Norway [IO], Minneapolis, MN, United States

Sons of Pericles [19093], 1909 Q St. NW, Ste. 500, Washington, DC 20009-1007, (202)232-6300

Sons of Poland; Assn. of the [19303]

Sons of the Revolution; Gen. Soc., [20672]

Sons of St. Patrick in the City of New York; Soc. of the Friendly [19155]

Sons of Scotland Benevolent Assn. [IO], Toronto, ON, Canada

Sons of Sherman's March to the Sea/Civil War Sons - Address unknown since 2006.

Sons of Spanish Amer. War Veterans [21268], c/o Alexander Loo, PNP, Natl. Treas., 1213 Eisenhower Dr., Augusta, GA 30904-5915

Sons of Union Veterans of the Civil War [20731], PO Box 1865, Harrisburg, PA 17105-1865, (717)232-7000

Sons of Union Veterans of the Civil War; Auxiliary to [20723]

Sons of Utah Pioneers [★21254]

Sons of Utah Pioneers; Natl. Soc. of the [21254]

Sons of Veterans, USA [★20731]

Sons of the Whiskey Rebellion [19389], c/o John H. Norris, Adjutant, PO Box 509, 38525 Woodward Ave., Bloomfield Hills, MI 48304, (248)646-4300

Sony Ericsson WTA Tour [23910], 1 Progress Plz., Ste. 1500, St. Petersburg, FL 33701, (727)895-5000

Sony Ericsson WTA Tour [IO], St. Petersburg, FL, United States

Soo Line Historical and Tech. Soc. [10923], c/o C. David Pulse, Treas., 39105 Fishermans Ln., Chassell, MI 49916

Soong Ching Ling Found. [IO], Beijing, People's Republic of China

SOPAR [IO], Gatineau, QC, Canada

Sophus Frederick Hansen Family Org. - Defunct.

Sorbo's Official Fan Club; Kevin [24820]

Sorghum Producers; Natl. Grain [★4311]

Soroptimist Clubs; Amer. Fed. of [★13065]

Soroptimist Fed. of the Americas [★13065]

Soroptimist Fed. of the Americas [★IO]

Soroptimist Fed. of Great Britain and Ireland [★IO]

Soroptimist Found. of Canada [IO], Peterborough, ON, Canada

Soroptimist Intl. [IO], Cambridge, United Kingdom

Soroptimist Intl. of the Americas [IO], Philadelphia, PA, United States

Soroptimist Intl. of the Americas [13065], 1709 Spruce St., Philadelphia, PA 19103-6103, (215)893-9000

Soroptimist Intl. d'Europe [★IO]

Soroptimist Intl. of Europe [IO], Geneva, Switzerland

Soroptimist Intl. of Great Britain and Ireland [IO], Stockport, United Kingdom

Soroptimist Intl. of the South West Pacific [IO], Sydney, Australia

Sororities

Alpha Rho Lambda Sorority [24703]

Delta Gamma Pi Multicultural Sorority [24704]

Delta Phi Omega Sorority [24705]

Delta Sigma Chi Sorority [24706]

Delta Tau Lambda Sorority [24707]

Delta Xi Nu Multicultural Sorority [24708]

Delta Xi Phi Multicultural Sorority [24685]

DIVAS of Lambda Fe Uson Sorority [24709]

Gamma Alpha Omega Sorority [24599]

Gamma Delta Pi [24710]

Gamma Gamma Chi Sorority [24711]

Kappa Phi Gamma Sorority [24712]

Lambda Psi Delta Sorority [24713]

Sigma Lambda Alpha Sorority [24714]

Sigma Lambda Gamma Natl. Sorority [24715]

Theta Chi Omega Multicultural Sorority [24716]

Zeta Chi Phi Multicultural Sorority [24717]

Sororities, Service

Alpha Kappa Alpha [24595]

Alpha Rho Lambda Sorority [24703]

Beta Sigma Phi [24596]

Delta Gamma Pi Multicultural Sorority [24704]

Delta Phi Omega Sorority [24705]

Delta Sigma Chi Sorority [24706]

Delta Sigma Theta [24597]

Delta Tau Lambda Sorority [24707]

Delta Xi Nu Multicultural Sorority [24708]

Delta Xi Phi Multicultural Sorority [24685]

DIVAS of Lambda Fe Uson Sorority [24709]

Epsilon Sigma Alpha [24598]

Gamma Alpha Omega Sorority [24599]

Gamma Delta Pi [24710]

Gamma Gamma Chi Sorority [24711]

Gamma Sigma Sigma [24600]

Kappa Phi Gamma Sorority [24712]

Lambda Psi Delta Sorority [24713]

Sigma Alpha [24602]

Sigma Gamma Rho Sorority [24603]

Sigma Lambda Alpha Sorority [24714]

Sigma Lambda Gamma Natl. Sorority [24715]

Sigma Sigma Sigma [24698]

Theta Chi Omega Multicultural Sorority [24716]

Zeta Chi Phi Multicultural Sorority [24717]

Zeta Phi Beta Sorority [24604]

Sororities, Social

Alpha Chi Omega [24673]

Alpha Epsilon Phi [24674]

Alpha Gamma Delta [24675]

Alpha Omicron Pi [24676]

Alpha Phi Intl. Fraternity [24677]

Alpha Rho Lambda Sorority [24703]

Alpha Sigma Alpha [24678]

Alpha Sigma Tau [24679]

Alpha Xi Delta Women's Fraternity [24680]

Chi Omega [24681]

Delta Delta Delta [24682]

Delta Gamma [24683]

Delta Gamma Pi Multicultural Sorority [24704]

Delta Phi Epsilon [24684]

Delta Phi Omega Sorority [24705]

Delta Sigma Chi Sorority [24706]

Delta Xi Nu Multicultural Sorority [24708]

Delta Xi Phi Multicultural Sorority [24685]

Delta Zeta [24686]

DIVAS of Lambda Fe Uson Sorority [24709]

Gamma Alpha Omega Sorority [24599]

Gamma Delta Pi [24710]

Gamma Gamma Chi Sorority [24711]

Gamma Phi Beta [24687]

Kappa Alpha Theta [24688]

Kappa Delta [24689]

Kappa Kappa Gamma [24690]

Kappa Phi Gamma Sorority [24712]

Lambda Psi Delta Sorority [24713]

Phi Beta Chi [24691]

Phi Epsilon Phi [24692]

Phi Mu Fraternity [24693]

Phi Sigma Sigma [24694]

Sigma Delta Tau [24695]

Sigma Kappa [24696]

Sigma Lambda Alpha Sorority [24714]

Sigma Lambda Gamma Natl. Sorority [24715]

Theta Chi Omega Multicultural Sorority [24716]

Theta Phi Alpha [24699]

Zeta Chi Phi Multicultural Sorority [24717]

Zeta Tau Alpha [24700]

Sorority; Beta Pi Sigma [24417]

Sorority; Delta Phi Epsilon Professional Foreign Ser. [24473]

Sorority Editors Conf. [★24448]

Sorority; Pi Omicron Natl. [24601]

SOROS Found. for an Open Soc. [★IO]

Sorptive Minerals Inst. [2745], 1155 15th St. NW, Ste. 500, Washington, DC 20005, (202)289-2760

Sorting It Out - Defunct.

Sortir du Nucleaire [★IO]

SOS Children's Villages of India [IO], New Delhi, India

SOS Children's Villages - Jamaica [IO], Montego Bay, Jamaica

SOS Children's Villages - Kenya [IO], Nairobi, Kenya

SOS Femmes [IO], St. Dizier, France

SOS: Human Rights for Guyana - Address unknown since 1990.

SOS Sahel Intl. - UK [IO], Oxford, United Kingdom

SOS Sexisme [IO], Meudon, France

SOSA Gliding Club [IO], Rockton, ON, Canada

Sosiaa-ja terveydenhuollon titojenkasittelyyhdistys ry [★IO]

Sotos Syndrome Support Assn. [IO], Wheaton, IL, United States

Sotos Syndrome Support Assn. [14482], PO Box 4626, Wheaton, IL 60189, (630)682-8815

Sotsialno-Ekologicheskiy Soyuz [★IO]

Soul Friends [16637], 401 Center St., Wallingford, CT 06492, (203)679-0849

Soulforce [17657], PO Box 3195, Lynchburg, VA 24503-0195, (434)384-7696

Soumen kielitieteellinen yhdistys [★IO]

Soumen Sulkapalloliitto [★IO]

Sound Challenge Assn; Intl. Auto [1219]

Sound Collections; Assn. for Recorded [10337]

Sound and Communications Assn; Natl. [★1225]

Sound Editors; Motion Picture [1371]

Sound Healers Assn. [13653], PO Box 2240, Boulder, CO 80306, (303)443-8181

Sound Recordings and Multimedia Assn. [IO], Riyadh, Saudi Arabia

Sound Seekers [★IO]

SoundAid [★IO]

SoundAid [★14746]

Soundex Reunion Registry; Intl. [11248]

Soundness; Amer. Veterinary Soc. for the Stud. of Breeding [★16806]

Source Banks; Natl. Assn. of Equity [488]

Source - Defunct.

South Africa

Africa Network [17740]

Amer. Dorper Sheep Breeders' Soc. [5183]

A star before a book entry number signifies that the name is not listed separately, but is mentioned within the entry.

Amer.-Southern Africa Chamber of Trade and Indus. **[24375]**
Artists for a New South Africa **[11911]**
South Africa Partners **[18666]**
South Africa Partners **[IO]**
South African Tourism **[24374]**
South African USA Chamber of Commerce **[24295]**
South Africa ACM SIGCHI **[IO]**, Port Elizabeth, Republic of South Africa
South Africa Assn. of Tourism Professionals **[IO]**, Johannesburg, Republic of South Africa
South Africa Club of North America - Defunct.
South Africa Found. **[★IO]**
South Africa Found. - Address unknown since 2001.
South Africa Inst. of Race Relations **[IO]**, Johannesburg, Republic of South Africa
South Africa Partners **[IO]**, Boston, MA, United States
South Africa Partners **[18666]**, 89 S St., Ste. 401, Boston, MA 02111, (617)443-1072
South Africa Stainless Steel Development Assn. **[IO]**, Rivonia, Republic of South Africa
South African Acad. for Sci. and Arts **[IO]**, Arcadia, Republic of South Africa
South African Aerospace Maritime and Defence Indus. Assn. **[IO]**, Centurion, Republic of South Africa
South African Aloe and Succulent Soc. **[★IO]**
South African Antique Dealers Assn. **[IO]**, Fontainebleau, Republic of South Africa
South African Archaeological Soc. **[IO]**, Vlaeberg, Republic of South Africa
South African Article Numbering Assn. **[★IO]**
South African Assn. of Botanists **[IO]**, Matieland, Republic of South Africa
South African Assn. of Competitive Intelligence Professionals **[IO]**, Pretoria, Republic of South Africa
South African Assn. of Consulting Engineers **[IO]**, Johannesburg, Republic of South Africa
South African Assn. for Food Sci. and Tech. **[IO]**, Ferndale, Republic of South Africa
South African Assn. of Freight Forwarders **[IO]**, Parktown, Republic of South Africa
South African Assn. for Geotechnology **[IO]**, Arcadia, Republic of South Africa
South African Assn. for Learning and Educational Difficulties **[IO]**, Johannesburg, Republic of South Africa
South African Assn. for Marine Biological Res. **[IO]**, Durban, Republic of South Africa
South African Assn. of Paediatric Surgeons **[IO]**, Tygerberg, Republic of South Africa
South African Assn. of Physicists in Medicine and Biology **[IO]**, Bloemfontein, Republic of South Africa
South African Assn. of Univ. Women for Graduate Women **[★IO]**
South African Assn. of Women Graduates **[IO]**, Gauteng, Republic of South Africa
South African Avocado Growers' Assn. **[IO]**, Tzaneen, Republic of South Africa
South African Bird Ringing Unit **[IO]**, Rondebosch, Republic of South Africa
South African Broadcasting Corp. **[IO]**, Auckland Park, Republic of South Africa
South African Chamber of Bus. **[IO]**, Saxonwold, Republic of South Africa
South African Chefs Assn. **[IO]**, Melville, Republic of South Africa
South African Chem. Inst. **[IO]**, Wits, Republic of South Africa
South African Chiropractic Assn. **[★IO]**
South African Coal Processing Soc. **[IO]**, Johannesburg, Republic of South Africa
South African Comm. **[★IO]**
South African Cong. for Early Childhood Development **[IO]**, Pretoria, Republic of South Africa
South African Coun. of Churches **[IO]**, Marshalltown, Republic of South Africa
South African Coun. for the Proj. and Constr. Mgt. Professions **[IO]**, Halfway House, Republic of South Africa
South African Coun. for the Quantity Surveying Profession **[IO]**, Halfway House, Republic of South Africa

South African Coun. of Shopping Centres **[IO]**, Bracken Gardens, Republic of South Africa
South African Dental Assn. **[IO]**, Gauteng, Republic of South Africa
South African Depression and Anxiety Gp. **[IO]**, Benmore, Republic of South Africa
South African Electrotechnical Export Coun. **[IO]**, Halfway House, Republic of South Africa
South African Fed. of Civil Engg. Contractors **[IO]**, Bedfordview, Republic of South Africa
South African Figure Skating Assn. **[IO]**, Cape Town, Republic of South Africa
South African Fiscal Assn. **[IO]**, Cape Town, Republic of South Africa
South African Freelancer's Assn. **[IO]**, Sun Valley, Republic of South Africa
South African Geophysical Assn. **[IO]**, Bryanston, Republic of South Africa
South African Hea. Informatics Assn. **[IO]**, Cape Town, Republic of South Africa
South African Holstein Breeders' Assn. **[IO]**, Bloemfontein, Republic of South Africa
South African Inst. of Architects **[IO]**, Randburg, Republic of South Africa
South African Inst. of Chartered Accountants **[IO]**, Johannesburg, Republic of South Africa
South African Inst. of Elecl. Engineers **[IO]**, Gardenview, Republic of South Africa
South African Inst. of Forestry **[IO]**, Menlo Park, Republic of South Africa
South African Inst. of Intl. Affairs **[IO]**, Braamfontein, Republic of South Africa
South African Inst. of Mining and Metallurgy **[IO]**, Marshalltown, Republic of South Africa
South African Insurance Assn. **[IO]**, Braamfontein, Republic of South Africa
South African Jewish Bd. of Deputies **[★IO]**
South African Jewish Bd. of Deputies **[★20124]**
South African Marfan Syndrome Org. **[IO]**, Pretoria, Republic of South Africa
South African Masters Sports Assn. **[IO]**, Johannesburg, Republic of South Africa
South African Mathematical Soc. **[IO]**, Durban, Republic of South Africa
South African Medical Assn. **[IO]**, Pretoria, Republic of South Africa
South African Medical Physics Soc. **[IO]**, Cape Town, Republic of South Africa
South African Medical Res. Coun. **[IO]**, Cape Town, Republic of South Africa
South African Military Refugee Aid Fund - Defunct.
South African Museums Assn. **[IO]**, Port Elizabeth, Republic of South Africa
South African Music Rights Org. **[IO]**, Braamfontein, Republic of South Africa
South African Nasionale Verbruikerunie **[★IO]**
South African Natl. Biodiversity Inst. **[IO]**, Pretoria, Republic of South Africa
South African Natl. Consumer Union **[IO]**, Pretoria, Republic of South Africa
South African Natl. Coun. for the Blind **[IO]**, Pretoria, Republic of South Africa
South African Natl. Seed Org. **[IO]**, Lynnwood Ridge, Republic of South Africa
South African Natl. Tuberculosis Assn. **[IO]**, Edenvale, Republic of South Africa
South African Nursing Assn. **[★IO]**
South African Optometric Assn. **[IO]**, Halfway House, Republic of South Africa
South African Orchid Coun. **[IO]**, Noorder Paarl, Republic of South Africa
South African Org. of Music Teachers **[★IO]**
South African Orthopaedic Assn. **[IO]**, Brandhof, Republic of South Africa
South African Paint Mfrs. Assn. **[IO]**, Johannesburg, Republic of South Africa
South African Petroleum Indus. Assn. **[IO]**, Roggebaai, Republic of South Africa
South African Pharmacology Soc. **[IO]**, Potchefstroom, Republic of South Africa
South African Protea Producers and Exporters Assn. **[IO]**, Paarl, Republic of South Africa
South African Red Cross Soc. **[IO]**, Cape Town, Republic of South Africa
South African Reinforced Concrete Engineers' Assn. **[IO]**, Bedfordview, Republic of South Africa

South African Rock Lobster Assn. - Defunct.
South African Scout Assn. **[IO]**, Clareinch, Republic of South Africa
South African Soc. of Biochemistry and Molecular Biology **[IO]**, Cape Town, Republic of South Africa
South African Soc. for Enology and Viticulture **[IO]**, Dennesig, Republic of South Africa
South African Soc. of Music Teachers **[IO]**, Noordbrug, Republic of South Africa
South African Soc. of Occupational Hea. Nursing Practitioners **[IO]**, Boksburg, Republic of South Africa
South African Soc. of Physiotherapy **[IO]**, Norwood, Republic of South Africa
South African Soc. for the Prevention of Child Abuse and Neglect **[IO]**, Parkview, Republic of South Africa
South African Soc. for Professional Engineers **[IO]**, Sandton, Republic of South Africa
South African Soc. of Psychiatrists **[IO]**, Naboomspruit, Republic of South Africa
South African Soc. of Teachers of the Alexander Technique **[IO]**, Cape Town, Republic of South Africa
South African Soc. of Travel Medicine **[IO]**, Johannesburg, Republic of South Africa
South African Speed Skating Assn. **[IO]**, Gauteng, Republic of South Africa
South African Sports Confed. and Olympic Comm. **[IO]**, Houghton, Republic of South Africa
South African Sports Medicine Assn. **[IO]**, Bedfordview, Republic of South Africa
South African Statistical Assn. **[IO]**, Pretoria, Republic of South Africa
South African Sugar Assn. **[★IO]**
South African Sugar Indus. Agronomists' Assn. **[IO]**, Durban, Republic of South Africa
South African Sugar Technologists' Assn. **[IO]**, Mount Edgecombe, Republic of South Africa
South African Sugarcane Res. Inst. **[IO]**, Mount Edgecombe, Republic of South Africa
South African Taekwondo Fed. **[IO]**, Rivonia, Republic of South Africa
South African Tennis Assn. **[IO]**, Saxonwold, Republic of South Africa
South African Textile Indus. Export Coun. **[IO]**, Bellville, Republic of South Africa
South African Tourism **[24374]**, 500 Fifth Ave., 20th Fl., Ste. 2040, New York, NY 10110, (212)730-2929
South African Tourism Bd. **[★24374]**
South African Tourist Corp. **[★24374]**
South African Translators' Inst. **[IO]**, Johannesburg, Republic of South Africa
South African USA Chamber of Commerce **[24295]**, 515 E Las Olas Blvd., Ste. 950, Fort Lauderdale, FL 33301-2278, (954)776-8158
South African Venture Capital Assn. **[IO]**, Houghton, Republic of South Africa
South African Veterinary Assn. **[IO]**, Pretoria, Republic of South Africa
South African Water Ski Fed. **[IO]**, Centurion, Republic of South Africa
South African Wind Energy Assn. **[IO]**, Cape Town, Republic of South Africa
South African Wine and Spirit Exporters Assn. **[★IO]**
South African Women's Agricultural Union **[IO]**, Centurion, Republic of South Africa
South African Youth Hostels Assn. **[IO]**, Muizenberg, Republic of South Africa
South Am; Assn. of Amer. Schools in **[8642]**
South Am. Mission **[20397]**, 1021 Maxwell Mill Rd., Ste. B, Fort Mill, SC 29708, (803)802-8580
South Amer. Athletic Confed. **[IO]**, Manaus, Brazil
South Amer. Commn. for the Control of Foot-and-Mouth Disease **[IO]**, Sao Bento, Brazil
South Amer. Explorers **[IO]**, Ithaca, NY, United States
South Amer. Explorers **[3937]**, 126 Indian Creek Rd., Ithaca, NY 14850, (607)277-0488
South Amer. Explorers Club **[★3937]**
South Amer. Explorers Club **[★IO]**
South Amer. Indian Info. Center **[★IO]**
South Amer. Indian Info. Center **[★17818]**
South Amer. Indian Mission **[★20397]**

Reference to "IO" in place of a book number signifies that the association may be found in the 45th edition of International Organizations.

South Amer. Mission Prayer League [★20234]
South Amer. Mission Prayer League [★IO]
South Amer. Missionary Soc. - USA [20398], PO Box 399, Ambridge, PA 15003, (724)266-0669
South Amer. Travel Org. - Address unknown since 1995.
South Asia; Comm. on Amer. Lib. Resources on [★10349]
South Asia Partnership Canada [IO], Ottawa, ON, Canada
South Asian Amer. Leaders of Tomorrow [18667], 6930 Carroll Ave., Ste. 400 L, Takoma Park, MD 20912, (301)270-1855
South Asian Amer. Voting Youth [18366], 1718 M St. NW, Ste. 290, Washington, DC 20036
South Asian Assn. for Regional Cooperation [IO], Kathmandu, Nepal
South Asian Journalists Assn. [IO], New York, NY, United States
South Asian Journalists Assn. [3166], c/o Prof. Sreenath Sreenivasan, Columbia Graduate School of Journalism, 2950 Broadway, New York, NY 10027, (212)854-5979
South Asian Language Teachers Assn. [7991], Univ. of Pennsylvania, 820 Williams Hall, Philadelphia, PA 19104-6305, (215)898-7475
South Asian Women's Centre [IO], Toronto, ON, Canada
South Australia Arts and Industry Development [IO], Adelaide, Australia
South Australia Dental Therapists' Assn. [IO], Torrensville, Australia
South Australian Croquet Assn. [IO], Adelaide, Australia
South Australian Employers Chamber of Commerce [IO], Unley, Australia
South Australian English Teachers Assn. [IO], Kensington Gardens, Australia
South Australian Photographic Fed. [IO], Kent Town, Australia
South Carolina Hugo Relief Fund - Defunct.
South Carolina Therapeutic Assn. [★11852]
South and Central Amer. Indian Info. Center [★17818]
South and Central Amer. Indian Info. Center [★IO]
South Centre [IO], Geneva, Switzerland
South Chesire Chamber [IO], Crewe, United Kingdom
South Dakota Alumni Assn; Univ. of [18937]
South Development Partnership; Katalysis North/ [★17048]
South Devon Assn; North Amer. [4284]
South Dublin Chamber of Commerce [IO], Dublin, Ireland
South-East Asia Center [IO], Chicago, IL, United States
South-East Asia Center [18502], 5120 N Broadway, Chicago, IL 60640, (773)989-6927
South East Asia Iron and Steel Inst. [IO], Shah Alam, Malaysia
South East Asian Assn. for Institutional Res. [IO], Hawthorn, Australia
South East Folk Arts Network [IO], Brighton, United Kingdom
South East Queensland ACM SIGGRAPH [IO], Brisbane, Australia
South East Queensland Olive Assn. [IO], Tabragalba, Australia
South and Eastern Tribes; United [12632]
South Eastern Welsh Pony and Cob Assn. [IO], Godalming, United Kingdom
South India ACM SIGCHI [IO], Chennai, India
South Korea
 Physicians for Human Rights [17783]
South; League of the [17125]
South and Meso-American Indian Info. Center [★17818]
South and Meso-American Indian Info. Center [★IO]
South and Meso-American Indian Rights Center [IO], Oakland, CA, United States
South and Meso-American Indian Rights Center [17818], PO Box 7829, Oakland, CA 94601, (510)534-4882
South Okanagan Similkameen Brain Injury Soc. [IO], Penticton, BC, Canada

South Pacific Applied Geoscience Commn. [IO], Suva, Fiji
South Pacific Commn. [★IO]
South Pacific; Found. for the Peoples of the [★12426]
South Pacific Islands Fisheries Development Agency [★IO]
South Pacific Regional Env. Programme [★IO]
South Pacific Underwater Medicine Soc. [IO], Melbourne, Australia
South Rugby Union [★23706]
South Skirmish Assn; North- [23727]
South Slavic Philatelic Soc. - Defunct.
South Slavonian Socialist Labor Fed. - Defunct.
South Slavonic Catholic Union [★19119]
South St. Seaport Museum [10446], 12 Fulton St., New York, NY 10038, (212)748-8600
South West Fed. of Croquet Clubs [IO], Rhoose Point, United Kingdom
South-West Inst. for Nationalities [★IO]
South West Olive Assn. [IO], Perth, Australia
South West Region Campaign for Nuclear Disarmament [IO], Exeter, United Kingdom
South-West Univ. for Nationalities [IO], Chengdu, People's Republic of China
South Western Assn. of WPCS [IO], Sherborne, United Kingdom
Southampton Coll. Alumni Assn; Long Island Univ. - [18907]
Southampton and Fareham Chamber of Commerce and Indus. [IO], Southampton, United Kingdom
Southdown Breeders' Assn; Amer. [5196]
Southeast Asia
 Champa Cultural Preservation Assn. of USA [11082]
 Japan Soc. for Southeast Asian History [IO]
 North Amer. South Asian Bar Assn. [5527]
 Southeast Asia Rsrc. Action Center [12820]
Southeast Asia; Comm. on Amer. Lib. Resources on [★10349]
Southeast Asia Found. - Address unknown since 1999.
Southeast Asia Rsrc. Action Center [12820], 1628 16th St. NW, 3rd Fl., Washington, DC 20009-3099, (202)667-4690
Southeast Asia Women's Assn. of the U.S.A; Pan-Pacific and [17907]
Southeast Asian Geotechnical Soc. [IO], Pathumthani, Thailand
Southeast Asian Languages; Coun. of Teachers of [7990]
Southeast Asian Ministers of Educ. Org. [IO], Bangkok, Thailand
Southeast Asian Regional Center for Graduate Stud. and Res. in Agriculture [IO], Laguna, Philippines
Southeast Desalting Assn. [5283], 2409 SE Dixie Hwy., Stuart, FL 34996, (772)781-7698
Southeast Inst. [★18629]
Southeast Inst. for Gp. and Family Therapy [18629], 103 Edwards Ridge Rd., Chapel Hill, NC 27517-9201, (919)929-1171
Southeast Singles Assn. - Defunct.
Southeast Waterfowl Comm. [★5295]
Southeastern Assn. of Fish and Wildlife Agencies [5734], c/o Robert M. Brantly, Exec. Sec., 8005 Freshwater Farms Rd., Tallahassee, FL 32308, (850)893-1204
Southeastern Assn. of Game and Fish Commissioners [★5734]
Southeastern Community Development Assn. - Defunct.
Southeastern Composers' League [10707], c/o Betty Wishart, Pres., 209 Maple Dr., Erwin, NC 28339
Southeastern Conf. [23851], 2201 Richard Arrington Blvd. N, Birmingham, AL 35203, (205)458-3000
Southeastern Cottonseed Crushers Assn. - Address unknown since 1995.
Southeastern Fabric, Notions and Crafts Assn. [3798], 2724 2nd Ave., Des Moines, IA 50313, (515)282-9101
Southeastern Fabric Show [★3798]
Southeastern Fisheries Assn. [3504], 1118-B Thomasville Rd., Tallahassee, FL 32303, (850)224-0612
Southeastern Florida Holocaust Memorial Center [★17717]

Southeastern Historical Keyboard Soc. [22720], c/o Martha Clinkscale, Treas., PO Box 670282, Dallas, TX 75367-0282
Southeastern Legal Found. [5954], 6100 Lake Forrest Dr. NW, Ste. 520, Atlanta, GA 30328, (404)257-9667
Southeastern Lumber Mfrs. Assn. [1620], PO Box 1788, Forest Park, GA 30298, (404)361-1445
Southeastern Manufactured Housing Inst. [★2527]
Southeastern Peanut Assn. [★5051]
Southeastern Pecan Growers Assn. - Address unknown since 1999.
Southeastern Poultry and Egg Assn. [★5122]
Southeastern Regional Off. Natl. Scholarship Ser. and Fund for Negro Students [8435], 230 Peachtree St., Ste. 530, Atlanta, GA 30303, (404)522-7260
Southeastern Resource Policy Assn. - Address unknown since 1985.
Southeastern Theatre Conf. [11043], PO Box 9868, Greensboro, NC 27429, (336)272-3645
Southeastern Tribes; United [★12632]
Southern
 Assn. of Southern Baptist Campus Ministers [19474]
 Inst. for Southern Stud. [9377]
 Jessie Ball duPont Fund [12727]
 Soc. for the Stud. of Southern Literature [10431]
 Southern Baptist Found. [19498]
 Southern Baptist Historical Lib. and Archives [19499]
 Southern Christian Leadership Conf. [17154]
 Southern Educ. Found. [8309]
 Southern Historical Assn. [9378]
 Southern Poverty Law Center [17155]
 Southern Regional Coun. [17156]
 Southern States Commun. Assn. [9162]
 Woman's Missionary Union, SBC [19501]
Southern Africa
 Alliance for Southern African Progress [12417]
 Amer.-Southern Africa Chamber of Trade and Indus. [24375]
 Friends of Malawi [9851]
 South African Scout Assn. [IO]
Southern Africa AIDS Info. Dissemination Ser. [★IO]
Southern Africa Assn. for the Advancement of Sci. [IO], Irene, Republic of South Africa
Southern Africa Bus. Assn. [★IO]
Southern Africa Bus. Forum [IO], London, United Kingdom
Southern Africa Cat Coun. [IO], Kensington, Republic of South Africa
Southern Africa; Church Proj. on U.S. Investments in [★17353]
Southern Africa Comm. - Defunct.
Southern Africa Development Community - Botswana [IO], Gaborone, Botswana
Southern Africa Fed. for AIDS [★IO]
Southern Africa Fed. of the Disabled [IO], Bulawayo, Zimbabwe
Southern Africa HIV and AIDS Info. Dissemination Ser. [IO], Harare, Zimbabwe
Southern Africa Inst. for Mgt. Services [IO], Pretoria, Republic of South Africa
Southern Africa Network - Defunct.
Southern Africa Political Economy Series Trust [IO], Harare, Zimbabwe
Southern Africa Project - Defunct.
Southern Africa Res. and Documentation Centre [IO], Harare, Zimbabwe
Southern African Acoustics Inst. [IO], Lynnwood Ridge, Republic of South Africa
Southern African Assn. for Early Childhood Educare [★IO]
Southern African Assn. of Geomorphologists [IO], Bloemfontein, Republic of South Africa
Southern African Assn. for Learning and Educational Difficulties [IO], Johannesburg, Republic of South Africa
Southern African Assn. for Learning and Educational Disabilities [★IO]
Southern African Biofuels Assn. [IO], Houghton, Republic of South Africa
Southern African Catholic Bishops' Conf. [IO], Pretoria, Republic of South Africa

A star before a book entry number signifies that the name is not listed separately, but is mentioned within the entry.

Southern African Catholic Bishops' Conf. - Justice and Peace [IO], Pretoria, Republic of South Africa

Southern African Center for Cooperation in Agricultural and Natural Resources Res. and Training [IO], Gaborone, Botswana

Southern African Cong. for Early Childhood Development [★IO]

Southern African Digital Broadcasting Assn. [IO], Cresta, Republic of South Africa

Southern African Hypertension Soc. [IO], River Club, Republic of South Africa

Southern African Inst. of Ecologists and Environmental Scientists [IO], Cape Town, Republic of South Africa

Southern African Inst. of Forestry [IO], Menlo Park, Republic of South Africa

Southern African Marketing Res. Assn. [IO], Randburg, Republic of South Africa

Southern African Museums Assn. [★IO]

Southern African Network of AIDS Ser. Organizations [IO], Harare, Zimbabwe

Southern African Non-Governmental Org. Network [IO], Braamfontein, Republic of South Africa

Southern African Soc. of Aquatic Scientists [IO], Auckland Park, Republic of South Africa

Southern African Soc. of Human Genetics [IO], Mowbray, Republic of South Africa

Southern African Soc. for Plant Pathology [IO], Stellenbosch, Republic of South Africa

Southern Alberta Brain Injury Soc. [IO], Calgary, AB, Canada

Southern Alberta Curling Assn. [IO], Calgary, AB, Canada

Southern Alberta Epilepsy Assn. [IO], Lethbridge, AB, Canada

Southern Alternative Agriculture Network [IO], Satun, Thailand

Southern Appalachian Coal Operators Assn. - Defunct.

Southern Appalachian Dulcimer Assn. [10708]

Southern Appalachian Studies - Defunct.

Southern Apparel Contractors Assn. [★222]

Southern Apparel Contractors Assn. [★IO]

Southern Arizona Vehicle Enthusiast - Address unknown since 2001.

Southern Ash Assn. - Defunct.

Southern Asian Art; Amer. Coun. for [9413]

Southern Asians

Alpha Iota Omicron [24611]

Andolan - Organizing South Asian Workers [24138]

Beta Chi Theta Natl. Fraternity [24618]

Delta Phi Omega Sorority [24705]

Indus Women Leaders [18003]

Kappa Phi Gamma Sorority [24712]

Natl. South Asian Bar Assn. [6018]

Network of Indian Professionals [19115]

North Amer. South Asian Law Student Assn. [8773]

Sigma Beta Rho Fraternity [24656]

South Asian Amer. Leaders of Tomorrow [18667]

Trikone [12258]

Southern Assn. of Agricultural Scientists - Address unknown since 1990.

Southern Assn. of Baptist Colleges and Schools [★9276]

Southern Assn. on Children Under Six [★11722]

Southern Assn. of Colleges and Schools [8308], 1866 Southern Ln., Decatur, GA 30033-4033, (404)679-4500

Southern Assn. of Independent Fastener Distributors [★1828]

Southern Assn. of Science and Industry - Address unknown since 1995.

Southern Assn. of Sculptors - Defunct.

Southern Automobile Racing Assn. - Address unknown since 2008.

Southern Baptist Campus Ministers; Assn. of [19474]

Southern Baptist Convention Flyers - Defunct.

Southern Baptist Found. [19498], 901 Commerce St., Ste. 600, Nashville, TN 37203, (615)254-8823

Southern Baptist Historical Lib. and Archives [19499], 901 Commerce St., Ste. 400, Nashville, TN 37203-3630, (615)244-0344

Southern Baptist Press Assn. [★19475]

Southern Bean Assn. [21057], c/o Dianna B. Hokanson, Ed., 4010 Longherridge Dr., Pearland, TX 77581, (281)482-0304

Southern Building Code Cong. Intl. [5555], c/o Intl. Code Coun., 500 New Jersey Ave. NW, 6th Fl., Washington, DC 20001-2070, (888)422-7233

Southern Building Code Cong. Intl. [IO], Falls Church, VA, United States

Southern California Advt. Agencies Assn. [★107]

Southern California Hang Glider Assn. [★23044]

Southern California Right of Way Assn. [★6246]

Southern California Right of Way Assn. [★IO]

Southern California Souvenir Spoon Collectors Soc. [★IO]

Southern California Souvenir Spoon Collectors Soc. [★21966]

Southern California Timing Assn. - Address unknown since 1995.

Southern Case Writers [★4065]

Southern Casualty and Surety Conf. [★2194]

Southern Center for Human Rights [17036], 83 Poplar St. NW, Atlanta, GA 30303-2122, (404)688-1202

Southern Christian Leadership Conf. [17154], PO Box 89128, Atlanta, GA 30312, (404)522-1420

Southern Classified Advt. Managers Assn. [119], c/o Hugh J. Rushing, Exec. Off., PO Box 531335, Mountain Brook, AL 35253-1335, (205)823-3448

Southern Coal Producers' Assn. - Defunct.

Southern Coalition for Educational Equity - Address unknown since 2003.

Southern Conf. [23852], 702 N Pine St., Spartanburg, SC 29303, (864)591-5100

Southern Conf. of Black Mayors [★6129]

Southern Conf. Educational Fund - Defunct.

Southern Connecticut State Univ. Alumni Assn. [18923], 501 Crescent St., New Haven, CT 06515, (203)392-6501

Southern Cooperative Development Fund [★12783]

Southern Cooperatives; Fed. of [★12937]

Southern Cooperatives Land Assistance Fund; Fed. of [12937]

Southern Cotton Assn. [1097], 88 Union Ave., Ste. 1204, Memphis, TN 38103, (901)525-2272

Southern Cotton Ginners Assn. [1098], 874 Cotton Gin Pl., Memphis, TN 38106, (901)947-3104

Southern Counties Folk Fed. [IO], Southampton, United Kingdom

Southern Counties Welsh Pony and Cob Assn. [IO], Petersfield, United Kingdom

Southern Cypress Mfrs. Assn. [1621], 400 Penn Center Blvd., Ste. 530, Pittsburgh, PA 15235, (877)607-SCMA

Southern Dental Assn. [★14131]

Southern Development Found. [12783]

Southern Early Childhood Assn. [11722], PO Box 55930, Little Rock, AR 72215-5930, (501)221-1648

Southern and Eastern African Mineral Centre [IO], Dar es Salaam, United Republic of Tanzania

Southern Economic Assn. [6895], Univ. of Tennessee at Chattanooga, 313 Fletcher Hall, Dept. 6106, 615 McCallie Ave., Chattanooga, TN 37403-2598, (423)425-4118

Southern Educ. Found. [8309], 135 Auburn Ave. NE, 2nd Fl., Atlanta, GA 30303, (404)523-0001

Southern Education Program - Defunct.

Southern Flinders Olive Growers Assn. [IO], Laura, Australia

Southern Folklore; Center for [9376]

Southern Forest Inst. - Defunct.

Southern Forest Products Assn. [1622], 2900 Indiana Ave., Kenner, LA 70065, (504)443-4464

Southern Furniture Mfrs. Assn. [★1690]

Southern Furniture Market [★1701]

Southern Garment Manufacturers Assn. [★221]

Southern Governors' Assn. [6287], 444 N Capitol St. NW, Ste. 200, Hall of the States, Washington, DC 20001, (202)624-5897

Southern Governors' Conf. [★6287]

Southern Hardwood Lumber Mfrs. Assn. [★1648]

Southern Hardwood Producers [★1648]

Southern Hardwood Square Assn. - Defunct.

Southern Historical Assn. [9378], Univ. of Georgia, Dept. of History, Rm. 111A, LeConte Hall, Athens, GA 30602-1602, (706)542-8848

Southern Humanities Conf. [★10204]

Southern Humanities Coun. [10204], c/o Mark Ledbetter, Exec. Dir., 1204 Jackson Springs Rd., Macon, GA 31211, (478)992-9110

Southern Indus. Insurers' Conf. [★2194]

Southern Inst. for Appropriate Tech. [★17001]

Southern Inst. for Appropriate Tech. [★IO]

Southern Interagency Conf. - Defunct.

Southern Jurisdiction; Supreme Coun. 33rd Degree, Ancient and Accepted Scottish Rite of Freemasonry - [19251]

Southern Literature; Soc. for the Stud. of [10431]

Southern Masonic Jurisdiction; Supreme Coun. 33rd Degree, Ancient and Accepted Scottish Rite of Freemasonry - [★19251]

Southern Missions; Sacred Heart [★19711]

Southern Mutual Help Assn. [11790], 3602 Old Jeanerette Rd., New Iberia, LA 70563, (337)367-3277

Southern Newspaper Publishers Assn. [3257], 3680 N Peachtree Rd., Ste. 300, Atlanta, GA 30341, (404)256-0444

Southern Oak Flooring Indus. [★656]

Southern Pacific Intl. Fan Club - Defunct.

Southern Paint and Wallcovering Dealers Assn. [★2274]

Southern Paint and Wallcovering Dealers Assn. [★IO]

Southern Paper Trade Assn. - Defunct.

Southern Peanut Warehousemen's Assn. [★5057]

Southern Pine Coun. [4057], c/o SFPA, 2900 Indiana Ave., Kenner, LA 70065-4605, (504)443-4464

Southern Pine Inspection Bur. [1623], c/o Bob Browder, Dir., PO Box 10915, Pensacola, FL 32524-0915, (850)434-2611

Southern Pine Lumber Manufacturers [★1623]

Southern Planning Consultants [★5655]

Southern Plywood Mfrs. Assn. [★1649]

Southern Poverty Law Center [17155], 400 Washington Ave., Montgomery, AL 36104, (334)956-8200

Southern Poverty Law Center [IO], Montgomery, AL, United States

Southern Presbyterian Peace Fellowship [★18241]

Southern Pressure Treaters' Assn. [1624], PO Box 3219, Pineville, LA 71361-3219, (318)619-8589

Southern Public Admin. Educ. Found. [6199], 2103 Fairway Ln., Harrisburg, PA 17112, (717)540-5477

Southern Pulp and Paper Safety Assn. [★7436]

Southern Purchasing Inst. [★3266]

Southern Region Campaign for Nuclear Disarmament [IO], Southampton, United Kingdom

Southern Regional Coun. [17156], 1201 W Peachtree St. NE, Ste. 2000, Atlanta, GA 30309, (404)522-8764

Southern Rice Export Corp. - Defunct.

Southern-Rock Music

Alabama Fan Club [24838]

Southern Sash and Door Jobbers Assn. [★600]

Southern Scale Warbirds Assn. [★22644]

Southern Scale Warbirds Assn. [★IO]

Southern Soc. of Genealogists - Address unknown since 2002.

Southern Soc. for Philosophy and Psychology [7494], c/o Hajime Otani, Pres.-Elect, Central Michigan Univ., Dept. of Psychology, Mount Pleasant, MI 48859, (517)774-6494

Southern Songwriters Guild [2824], PO Box 52656, Shreveport, LA 71135-2656

Southern Speech Assn. [★9162]

Southern Speech Commun. Assn. [★9162]

Southern States Commun. Assn. [9162], c/o J. Emmett Winn, Exec. Dir., Auburn Univ., Commun. and Journalism, 217 Tichenor Hall, Auburn University, AL 36849-5211, (334)844-2853

Southern States Indus. Coun. [★17639]

Southern Strawberry Packers Assn. - Address unknown since 1995.

Southern Student Organizing Comm. - Defunct.

Southern Stud; Inst. for [9377]

Southern Textile Assn. [3799], PO Box 66, Gastonia, NC 28053, (704)824-3522

Southern U.S. Trade Assn. [4083], 2 Canal St., Ste. 2515, New Orleans, LA 70130, (504)568-5986

Southern Wood Seasoning Assn. - Defunct.

Reference to "IO" in place of a book number signifies that the association may be found in the 45th edition of International Organizations.

Southern Woodwork Assn. - Defunct.

The Southerners - Defunct.

Southface Energy Inst. [6973], 241 Pine St. NE, Atlanta, GA 30308, (404)872-3549

Southland Head Injury Soc. [IO], Invercargill, New Zealand

Southmost Coll. Alumni Assn; Univ. of Texas at Brownsville and Texas [18938]

Southpaw's Intl. - Defunct.

Southwark Habitat for Humanity [IO], London, United Kingdom

Southwest Alliance for Latin America - Defunct.

Southwest Assn. of Petroleum Geologists [★7125]

Southwest Athletic Conf. [23853], A.G. Gaston Bldg., 1527 5th Ave. N, Birmingham, AL 35204, (205)251-7573

Southwest Athletic Conference [IO], Birmingham, AL, United States

Southwest Bluegrass Assn. [10709], 5206 Calle de Ricardo, Torrance, CA 90505

Southwest Case Res. Inst. [8042], c/o Joseph Kavanaugh, PhD, Pres., Management/Marketing Dept., Sam Houston State Univ., Huntsville, TX 77341, (936)294-1236

Southwest Celtic Music Assn. [9779], 833 Exposition Ave., Ste. 101, Dallas, TX 75226-2490

Southwest Coun. of La Raza [★12278]

Southwest Coun. of La Raza [★IO]

Southwest Developmental Vision Soc. [★15718]

Southwest; Mining Club of the [★2752]

Southwest; Mining Found. of the [2752]

Southwest Parks and Monuments Assn. [★7365]

Southwest Railway Museum; Pacific [10918]

Southwest Res. and Info. Center [17345], PO Box 4524, Albuquerque, NM 87106, (505)262-1862

Southwest Spanish Mustang Assn. [4951], PO Box 948, Antlers, OK 74523, (580)326-6005

Southwest Traditional Crop Conservancy Garden and Seed Bank [★4429]

Southwest Vintage Radio and Phonograph Soc. [★22931]

Southwest Voter Registration Educ. Proj. [18367], Kelly USA, Bldg. 1670, 206 Lombard St., 2nd Fl., San Antonio, TX 78226, (210)922-0225

Southwestern Bigfoot Res. Team [★7472]

Southwestern Donkey and Mule Soc. [21521], c/o Judy Shulter, Treas., 13390 County Rd. 4016, Kemp, TX 75143, (903)498-3377

Southwestern Endangered Arid-Land Rsrc. Clearing House; Native Seeds/ [★4429]

Southwestern Legal Found. [★5931]

Southwestern Legal Found. [★IO]

Southwestern Monuments Assn. [★7365]

Southwestern Peanut Growers Assn. [5062], PO Box 338, 304 SE Lubbock, Gorman, TX 76454, (254)734-2222

Southwestern Pioneer Cowboys Assn. - Address unknown since 1995.

Southwestern Union for the Study of Great Religions - Defunct.

Souvenir Building Collectors Soc. [22115], c/o Bob Kneisel, Treas., 1278 Mar Vista Ave., Pasadena, CA 91104-2951

Souvenir Card Collectors Soc. - Address unknown since 2007.

Souvenir Distributors Assn; Post Card and [3074]

Souvenir and Gift Novelty Trade Assn. [★861]

Souvenir Napoleonien [IO], Paris, France

Souvenir and Novelty Trade Assn. [★861]

Souvenir Spoon Collectors of Am. [★21966]

Souvenir Spoon Collectors of Am. [★IO]

Souvenir Spoon Collectors Soc; Southern California [★21966]

Sovereign Byzantine Order Lascaris Comnenus of Saints Constantine the Great and Helen, A.D. 312 - Address unknown since 1995.

Sovereign Hospitaller Order of Saint John - Defunct.

Sovereignty Intl. [17873], PO Box 191, Hollow Rock, TN 38342, (731)986-0099

Sovereignty Intl. [IO], Hollow Rock, TN, United States

Sovereignty Prog; Tribal [★18099]

Sovereignty Soc; Stockholders [★17351]

Sovereignty Task Force; Amer. [17859]

Sovereignty; Walter Bagehot Res. Coun. on Natl. [7528]

Soviet Amer. Relations; Inst. for [★17899]

Soviet and East European Law; Committee on [★5475]

Soviet and East European Res; Natl. Coun. for [★10968]

Soviet Exchanges; Org. for Amer.- [★17905]

Soviet Jewry; Amer. Jewish Conf. on [★17448]

Soviet Jewry Legal Advocacy Center - Defunct.

Soviet Jewry; Natl. Conf. on [★17448]

Soviet Jewry Res. Bur. - Address unknown since 2000.

Soviet Jewry; Student Struggle for [17451]

Soviet Jews; Union of Councils for [★17452]

Soviet Political Prisoners; Amer. Assn. of Former [★17766]

Soviet-Type Economies; Assn. for the Stud. of [★6870]

Soviet Union

Amer. Comm. for Peace in Chechnya [18189]

Ashburn Inst. for Global Stud. in Federalism and Democracy [18308]

Center for Russian and East European Jewry [17946]

Counterpart Intl. [12426]

Inst. for Intl. Entrepreneurship [727]

Intl. Comm. for the Children of Chechnya [11605]

Rossica Soc. of Russian Philately [22862]

Russian Zone Handoverprint Stud. and Res. Gp. [22864]

Soc. for Cooperation in Russian and Soviet Stud. [IO]

U.S. Assn. of Former Members of Cong. [17253]

Soy Protein Coun. [1563], 1255 23rd St. NW, Washington, DC 20037-1174, (202)467-6610

Soybean Assn; Amer. [4304]

Soybean Bd; United [4767]

Soybean Coun. of America - Defunct.

Soybean Growers of America - Address unknown since 1995.

Soybean Processors Assn; Natl. [★2857]

Soybeans

Amer. Soybean Assn. [4304]

Soyfoods Assn. of North Am. [4316]

Soycrafters Assn. of North Am. [★4316]

Soyfoods Assn. of North Am. [4316], 1050 17th St. NW, Ste. 600, Washington, DC 20036, (202)659-3520

Soyuz Arkhitektorov Rossii [★IO]

Sozial Demokratische Partei Osterreichs [★IO]

Sozialdemokratische Partei Deutschlands [★IO]

Sozialdienst Katholischer Frauen [IO], Dortmund, Germany

Sozialverband Vdk Deutschland [IO], Bonn, Germany

SP 250 Register [IO], Dorking, United Kingdom

Spa Assn. Singapore [IO], Singapore, Singapore

Spa Bus. Assn. [IO], Bagshot, United Kingdom

Spa and Hea. Resort Assn; Amer. [3352]

Spa and Pool Inst; Natl. [★3353]

Spa Professionals; Assn. of Pool and [3353]

Space

Aerospace Medical Assn. [13538]

Amer. Inst. of Aeronautics and Astronautics [6369]

Amer. Soc. for Gravitational and Space Biology Student Assn. [6563]

Assn. of U.S. Members of the Intl. Inst. of Space Law [6372]

Chinese Acad. of Space Tech. [IO]

Fed. of Galaxy Explorers [9136]

Global Network Against Weapons and Nuclear Power in Space [18152]

High Frontier [6374]

Indian Space Res. Org. [IO]

Intl. Assn. of Military Flight Surgeon-Pilots [13541]

Intl. Assn. of Space Entrepreneurs [3634]

Intl. Assn. of Space Entrepreneurs [IO]

Intl. Cryogenic Materials Conf. [6846]

Intl. Experimental Aerospace Soc. [6375]

Intl. Meteorite Collectors Assn. [22981]

Intl. Space Sci. Inst. [IO]

Lifeboat Found. [18668]

Mars Soc. [7683]

Mars Soc. [IO]

Moon Soc. [7684]

Natl. Assn. of Rocketry [22650]

Natl. Coalition for Aviation Educ. [7995]

Natl. Space Club [6377]

Natl. Space Soc. [6378]

Natl. Space Soc. of Australia [IO]

The Planetary Soc. [6382]

The Planetary Soc. of Youth [IO]

Space Access Soc. [7685]

Space Assn. of Australia [IO]

Space Found. [7922]

Space Frontier Found. [7686]

Space Frontier Found. [IO]

Space Stud. Bd. [7687]

Space Stud. Inst. [6388]

Space Topic Stud. Unit [22876]

Starships of the Third Fleet [10949]

Student Experimental Payload Prog. [6390]

Students for the Exploration and Development of Space [7923]

United Kingdom Rocketry Assn. [IO]

Universities Space Res. Assn. [6392]

Space: 1999 Fan Activity Network - Defunct.

Space Access Soc. [7685], 5515 N 7th St., No. 134-348, Phoenix, AZ 85014, (602)431-9283

Space Assn. of Australia [IO], Mulgrave, Australia

Space Biology Student Assn; Amer. Soc. for Gravitational and [6563]

Space; Center for the Studies of Human Communities in [★6387]

Space Club; Air, Sea, and [25023]

Space Club; Natl. [6377]

Space Coast Writers Conf; Florida [★11196]

Space Coast Writers' Guild [11196], PO Box 262, Melbourne, FL 32902-0262

Space Companies; Society of Japanese Aero [★154]

Space Companies; Society of Japanese Aero [★IO]

Space Energy Assn. [6386], PO Box 1136, Clearwater, FL 33757-1136, (954)749-6553

Space Fannish Alliance; Lost in [25033]

Space and Flight Equip. Assn. [★6383]

Space Found. [7922], 310 S 14th St., Colorado Springs, CO 80904, (719)576-8000

Space Found; U.S. [★7922]

Space Frontier Found. [7686], 16 1st Ave., Nyack, NY 10960, (818)985-7367

Space Frontier Found. [IO], Nyack, NY, United States

Space Indus. Assn. of Canada; Aero [★IO]

Space Indus. Assn. of Canada; Aero [★154]

Space Indus. Associations; Coun. of Defense and [147]

Space Inst; Natl. [★6378]

Space Law; Assn. of U.S. Members of the Intl. Inst. of [6372]

Space Philatelists Intl. Soc. - Address unknown since 2001.

Space Res. Assn; Universities [6392]

Space Res. Inst. - Defunct.

Space Res. Org. Netherlands [IO], Utrecht, Netherlands

Space and Security Stud; Inst. for [18155]

Space Settlement Studies Program [6387]

Space Soc; Natl. [6378]

Space; Students for the Exploration and Development of [7923]

Space Stud. Bd. [7687], c/o Natl. Res. Coun., 500 Fifth St. NW, 10th Fl., Washington, DC 20001, (202)334-3477

Space Stud. Inst. [6388], PO Box 82, Princeton, NJ 08542, (609)921-0377

Space Topic Educ. Program [★7923]

Space Topic Stud. Unit [22876], c/o Carmine Torrisi, Sec., PO Box 780241, Maspeth, NY 11378

Space Topic Stud. Unit [IO], Maspeth, NY, United States

Space Topics Study Group [★IO]

Space Topics Study Group [★22876]

Space Toy Information Center - Defunct.

Space Trans. Assn. [6389], c/o Richard Coleman, Pres., 4305 Underwood St., University Park, MD 20782, (703)855-3917

Space and Unexplained Celestial Events Res. Soc. - Defunct.

Space Unit [★22876]

Space Unit [★IO]

A star before a book entry number signifies that the name is not listed separately, but is mentioned within the entry.

Spacecraft Res. Found. - Defunct.

Spain
  Commercial Off. of Spain [24376]
  Spanish Refugee Aid [12821]
  Spanish Water Dog Assn. of Am. [22362]

Spain; Amer. Acad. of Res. Historians of Medieval [10081]

Spain-United States Chamber of Commerce [24296], Empire State Bldg., 350 5th Ave., Ste. 2600, New York, NY 10118, (212)967-2170

Spain-United States Chamber of Commerce [IO], New York, NY, United States

Spalding Univ. Alumni Assn. [18924], 851 S 4th St., Louisville, KY 40203-2188, (502)585-9911

SpamCon Found. [6822], 829 14th St., San Francisco, CA 94114, (415)552-2557

SpamCon Found. [IO], San Francisco, CA, United States

Spaniel Breeders Soc. - Address unknown since 1991.

Spaniel Club of Am; Brittany [★22190]
Spaniel Club of Am; Cavalier King Charles [22242]
Spaniel Club of Am; Clumber [22246]
Spaniel Club of Am; English Cocker [22259]
Spaniel Club of Am; English Toy [22263]
Spaniel Club of Am; Irish Water [22294]
Spaniel Club of Am; Japanese [★22299]
Spaniel Club of Am; Tibetan [22366]
Spaniel Club of Am; Welsh Springer [22380]
Spaniel Club; Amer. Cavalier King Charles [22194]
Spaniel Club Francais [IO], Aubigny-sur-Nere, France

Spaniel Field Trial Assn; English Springer [22262]

Spaniel Soc. of Am; Field [22266]

Spanish
  Amer. Assn. of Teachers of Spanish and Portuguese [8725]
  Amer. Spanish Comm. [17088]
  Assn. of Hispanists of Great Britain and Ireland [IO]
  Basque Educational Org. [9732]
  Commercial Off. of Spain [24376]
  Conquistadores 1492 [18669]
  Queen Sofia Spanish Inst. [10973]
  Queen Sofia Spanish Inst. [IO]
  Sigma Delta Pi [24718]
  Sociedad Honoraria Hispanica [8499]
  Soc. of Spanish and Spanish-American Stud. [10974]
  Soc. of Spanish and Spanish-American Stud. [IO]
  Spain-United States Chamber of Commerce [24296]
  Spanish Refugee Aid [12821]
  Spanish Water Dog Assn. of Am. [22362]
  Twentieth Century Spanish Assn. of Am. [10975]
  Twentieth Century Spanish Assn. of Am. [IO]
  World Spanish Cong. [IO]
  World Spanish Cong. [19393]

Spanish Advt. Agencies' Assn. [IO], Madrid, Spain
Spanish Aerosols Assn. [IO], Barcelona, Spain
Spanish Alpha 1 Assn. [IO], Cadiz, Spain
Spanish ALS Assn. [IO], Madrid, Spain

Spanish American War
  Independence Seaport Museum [21266]
  Natl. Fort Daughters of '98, Auxiliary United Spanish War Veterans [21267]
  Sons of Spanish Amer. War Veterans [21268]

Spanish Article Numbering Assn. [IO], Barcelona, Spain
Spanish Assn. Against Osteoporosis [IO], Madrid, Spain
Spanish Assn. of Beer and Malt Technicians [IO], Madrid, Spain
Spanish Assn. of Bioenterprises [IO], Madrid, Spain
Spanish Assn. of Dance Sport and Competition Dancing [IO], Barcelona, Spain
Spanish Assn. of Digestive Endoscopy [IO], Pamplona, Spain
Spanish Assn. of Egg Producers [IO], Madrid, Spain
Spanish Assn. of Flour and Semolina Mfrs. [IO], Madrid, Spain
Spanish Assn. of Mfrs. of Irrigation Equip. [IO], Madrid, Spain
Spanish Assn. of the Meat Indus. [IO], Madrid, Spain
Spanish Assn. of Multiple Sclerosis [IO], Madrid, Spain

Spanish Assn. for Parents with Autistic Children [IO], Madrid, Spain
Spanish Assn. for Pattern Recognition and Image Anal. [IO], Granada, Spain
Spanish Assn. of Petroleum Products Operators [IO], Madrid, Spain
Spanish Assn. of Sugar Confectionery and Chewing Gum Manufacturers [IO], Barcelona, Spain
Spanish Assn. of Toy Mfrs. [IO], Ibi, Spain
Spanish-Barb Breeders Assn. [4952], PO Box 1628, Silver City, NM 88062
Spanish Benevolent Soc. "La Nacional" - Address unknown since 2002.
Spanish Bottled Water Assn. [IO], Madrid, Spain
Spanish Ceramic Tile Mfrs'. Assn. [★IO]
Spanish Chamber of Commerce in Great Britain [IO], London, United Kingdom

Spanish Civil War
  Spanish Refugee Aid [12821]
  Veterans of the Abraham Lincoln Brigade [21269]

Spanish Colonial Arts Soc. [10005], PO Box 5378, Santa Fe, NM 87502-5378, (505)982-2226
Spanish Comm; Amer. [17088]
Spanish Confed. of Animal Feed Manufacturers [IO], Madrid, Spain
Spanish Confed. of Bakery Organisations [IO], Madrid, Spain
Spanish Confed. of Bus. Organisations [IO], Madrid, Spain
Spanish Confed. of Family Alzheimer Associations [IO], Pamplona, Spain
Spanish Confed. of Medical and Tech. Advisers Associations [IO], Ourense, Spain
Spanish Confed. of Plastics Indus. [IO], Madrid, Spain
Spanish Confed. of Small and Medium-Sized Companies [IO], Madrid, Spain
Spanish Cotton Spinners and Weavers Assn. [IO], Barcelona, Spain
Spanish Cricket Assn. [IO], Murcia, Spain
Spanish Dairy Fed. [IO], Madrid, Spain
Spanish Economic Assn. [IO], Bilbao, Spain
Spanish Entomological Assn. [IO], Alicante, Spain
Spanish Ethological Soc. [IO], Barcelona, Spain
Spanish Evangelical Publishers Assn. - Address unknown since 2004.
Spanish Exporters and Mfrs. of Table Olives Assn. [IO], Seville, Spain
Spanish Fed. of Clothing Companies [IO], Madrid, Spain
Spanish Fed. of Confectionery Mfrs. [IO], Barcelona, Spain
Spanish Fed. of Elecl. Appliances Retailers [IO], Madrid, Spain
Spanish Food and Drink Indus. Fed. [IO], Madrid, Spain
Spanish Gas Assn. [IO], Barcelona, Spain
Spanish Heritage Assn. [★IO]
Spanish Heritage Assn. [★8634]
Spanish Heritage-Herencia Espanola [★8634]
Spanish Heritage-Herencia Espanola [★IO]
Spanish Hotel Fed. [IO], Madrid, Spain
Spanish Inventors Club [IO], Barcelona, Spain
Spanish Jewelry, Silverware and Watches Assn. [IO], Madrid, Spain
Spanish Knitting Assn. [IO], Barcelona, Spain
Spanish League Against Epilepsy [IO], Madrid, Spain
Spanish Microscopy Soc. [IO], Madrid, Spain
Spanish Motor Vehicle Manufactures' Assn. [IO], Madrid, Spain
Spanish Mustang Assn; Southwest [4951]
Spanish Mustang Registry [4953], c/o Carol Dildine, Sec., 323 County Rd. 419, Chilton, TX 76632, (254)546-2177
Spanish Natl. Honor Soc. [★8499]
Spanish Neuromodulation Soc. [IO], Las Palmas de Gran Canaria, Spain
Spanish-Norman Horse Registry [4954], c/o Linda Osterman-Hamid, Registrar, PO Box 985, Woodbury, CT 06798, (203)266-4048
Spanish Olive Oil Exporters Assn. [IO], Madrid, Spain
Spanish Paint and Printing Inks Manufactures' Assn. [IO], Madrid, Spain

Spanish Paper Inst. [IO], Madrid, Spain
Spanish Paprika Inst. - Address unknown since 1995.
Spanish Paralympic Comm. [IO], Madrid, Spain
Spanish Philatelic Soc. Spanish Civil War Study Group - Defunct.
Spanish Refugee Aid [12821], c/o Intl. Rescue Comm., 122 E 42nd St., New York, NY 10168-1289, (212)551-3000
Spanish Reproduction Rights Centre [IO], Madrid, Spain
Spanish Royal Soc. of Physics [IO], Madrid, Spain
Spanish Soc. of Anatomy [IO], Leioa, Spain
Spanish Soc. of Biomedical Engg. [IO], Madrid, Spain
Spanish Soc. of Cardiology [IO], Madrid, Spain
Spanish Soc. of Cartography, Photogrammetry and Remote Sensing [IO], Madrid, Spain
Spanish Soc. of Ceramic and Glass [IO], Madrid, Spain
Spanish Soc. of Cosmetic Chemists [IO], Barcelona, Spain
Spanish Soc. for Electron Microscopy [★IO]
Spanish Soc. of Gravitation and Relativity [IO], Lejona, Spain
Spanish Soc. of Hea. Informatics [IO], Madrid, Spain
Spanish Soc. and League of Hypertension [IO], Madrid, Spain
Spanish Soc. of Pharmacology [IO], Barcelona, Spain
Spanish Soc. of Plastic, Reconstructive and Aesthetic Surgery [IO], Madrid, Spain
Spanish Soc. of Proteomics [IO], Cordoba, Spain
Spanish Soc. of Psychosomatic Obstetrics and Gynaecology [IO], Granada, Spain
Spanish Soc. of Real Chemistry [IO], Madrid, Spain
Spanish Soc. of Rheumatology [IO], Madrid, Spain

Spanish-Speaking
  Hispanic Dental Assn. [14155]
  Inter-Amer. Safety Coun. [12965]
  Mexican-American Opportunity Found. [12276]
  Natl. Assn. of Hispanic Nurses [15494]
  Natl. Veterans Outreach Prog. [13355]
  Queen Sofia Spanish Inst. [10973]
  REFORMA: Natl. Assn. to Promote Lib. Services to the Spanish-Speaking [10384]
  Seminar on the Acquisition of Latin Amer. Lib. Materials [10386]
  SER - Jobs for Progress Natl. [12100]
  U.S. Hispanic Chamber of Commerce [24327]

Spanish Speaking; Bishops' Comm. for the [★12282]
Spanish Speaking CPA's; Amer. Associations of [★16]
Spanish Speaking; Div. for the [★12282]
Spanish Speaking Elected Officials; Natl. League of [★6122]
Spanish-Speaking Librarians; REFORMA: Natl. Assn. of [★10384]
Spanish Speaking Mental Hea. Organizations; Coalition of [★13176]
Spanish Speaking Officials; Elected [★6122]
Spanish-Speaking; REFORMA: Natl. Assn. of Lib. Services to the [★10384]
Spanish-Speaking; REFORMA: Natl. Assn. to Promote Lib. Services to the [10384]
Spanish Speaking; Secretariat for the [★12282]
Spanish Speaking-Spanish Surnamed Nurses; Natl. Assn. of [★15494]
Spanish Stainless Steel Development Assn. [IO], Madrid, Spain
Spanish Statistical and Operations Res. Soc. [IO], Madrid, Spain
Spanish Textile Machinery Mfrs. Assn. [IO], Barcelona, Spain
Spanish Timbrado Breeders; Amer. Assn. of [21834]
Spanish Unihockey and Floorball Assn. [IO], Madrid, Spain
Spanish War Veterans; Natl. Fort Daughters of '98, Auxiliary United [21267]
Spanish Water Dog Assn. of Am. [22362], c/o David R. Sang, Treas., 2409 Longfellow Ave., Scotch Plains, NJ 07076
Spanish Wine Fed. [IO], Madrid, Spain
Spanish; Women in [★10000]

Reference to "IO" in place of a book number signifies that the association may be found in the 45th edition of International Organizations.

Spanish World Gospel Broadcasting [★20399]
Spanish World Gospel Broadcasting [★IO]
Spanish World Gospel Mission [★IO]
Spanish World Gospel Mission [★20399]
Spanish World Ministries [20399], PO Box 542, Wi-
nona Lake, IN 46590, (574)267-8821
Spanish World Ministries [IO], Winona Lake, IN,
United States
Spanish Youth Hostels [IO], Madrid, Spain
Spark Plug Collectors of Am. [22116], PO Box 2229,
Ann Arbor, MI 48106, (734)646-7735
Sparks Family Assn. [21058], c/o James A. Hopper,
27909 83rd Dr. NW, Stanwood, WA 98292-9513
Sparks Intl. Official Fan Club [24976], PO Box
25038, Los Angeles, CA 90025
Sparks Intl. Official Fan Club [IO], Los Angeles, CA,
United States
Spartacist League [18659], PO Box 1377, New York,
NY 10116, (212)732-7860
Spartacus Youth Club - Address unknown since
2002.
Spartan Intl. - Defunct.
Spasete Gi Decata [★IO]
Spasmodic Dysphonia Assn; Natl. [15352]
Spasmodic Torticollis
    Natl. Infant Torticollis Assn. [14945]
    Natl. Spasmodic Torticollis Assn. [15353]
Spasmodic Torticollis Assn; Natl. [15353]
The Spastic Centre of New South Wales [IO], Syd-
ney, Australia
Spatial; Association Europeenne des Constructeurs
de Material Aero [★IO]
Spatial; Association Europeenne des Constructeurs
de Material Aero [★154]
SPCA of Illinois [★11364]
Speak Easy [IO], St. John, NB, Canada
Speak Easy Intl. Found. [16455], 233 Concord Dr.,
Paramus, NJ 07652, (201)262-0895
Speak Out! [★11482]
Speakability [IO], London, United Kingdom
Speakers Assn; Natl. [10903]
Speakers Assn; Natl. Capital [10902]
Speakers' Bur; Asian [17607]
Speakers Res. Comm. for the United Nations
[★18763]
Speakers Res. Comm. for the United Nations [★IO]
Speakers and Writers; Amer. Soc. of Contrarian
[5601]
SpeakersOnAsianTopics.org [★17607]
Spearfishing Assn; Intl. Underwater [23418]
Special Agents of the Fed. Bur. of Investigation; Soc.
of Former [19202]
Special Approaches to Juvenile Assistance -
Defunct.
Special Arts Services Div. [★9491]
Special Care Dentistry [14186], 401 N Michigan
Ave., Ste. 2200, Chicago, IL 60611, (312)527-6764
Special Care Organizations in Dentistry; Fed. of
[★14186]
Special Citizens Futures Unlimited [★11987]
Special Comm. of 24 [★17157]
Special Comm. of 24 [★IO]
Special Comm. on Care for the Indigent - Defunct.
Special Comm. on Decolonization [★17157]
Special Comm. on Decolonization [★IO]
Special Comm. on the Situation with Regard to the
Implementation of the Declaration on the Granting
of Independence to Colonial Countries and
Peoples [IO], New York, NY, United States
Special Comm. on the Situation with Regard to the
Implementation of the Declaration on the Granting
of Independence to Colonial Countries and
Peoples [17157], UN HQ, Rm. S-2977, First Ave.
at 46th St., New York, NY 10017, (212)963-3051
Special Comm. for U.S. Exports - Defunct.
Special Comm. for Workplace Product Liability
Reform - Address unknown since 1999.
Special Constituency Sect. for Mental Hea. and
Psychiatric Services [★16093]
Special Constituency Sect. for Psychiatric and
Substance Abuse Services [★16093]
Special Days
    African Amer. Holiday Assn. [22974]
    Comm. for Natl. Arbor Day [18670]
    Father's Day/Mother's Day Coun. [18671]

    Golden Glow of Christmas Past [22975]
    Golden Glow of Christmas Past [IO]
    Holiday Inst. of Yonkers [18672]
    Natl. Arbor Day Found. [18673]
    Natl. Father's Day Comm. [18674]
    Natl. Mother's Day Comm. [18675]
    Natl. Soc. for Shut-Ins [18651]
    Thanks-Giving Found. [18676]
    Thanks-Giving Found. [IO]
Special Education
    Amer. Coun. on Rural Special Educ. [9137]
    Australian Fed. of SPELD Associations [IO]
    AVKO Dyslexia Res. Found. [9138]
    Coun. of Administrators of Special Educ. [9139]
    Coun. for Children with Behavioral Disorders
    [9140]
    Coun. for Exceptional Children [9141]
    Coun. of Parent Attorneys and Advocates [9142]
    Div. on Career Development and Transition [9143]
    Div. for Early Childhood of the Coun. for
    Exceptional Children [9144]
    Div. on Visual Impairments [9145]
    Education-A-Must [12056]
    Friends of LADDERS [12491]
    Inter-American Conductive Educ. Assn. [9146]
    Inter-American Conductive Educ. Assn. [IO]
    Irish Assn. of Teachers in Special Educ. [IO]
    MOVE Intl.: Mobility Opportunities Via Educ. -
    USA [11962]
    Natl. Assn. for Adults with Special Learning Needs
    [8204]
    Natl. Assn. for the Educ. of African Amer. Children
    with Learning Disabilities [12493]
    Natl. Assn. of Private Special Educ. Centers
    [9147]
    Natl. Assn. of Special Educ. Teachers [9148]
    Natl. Assn. of State Directors of Special Educ.
    [9149]
    Natl. Educational Assn. of Disabled Students [IO]
    Natl. Rsrc. Center for Paraprofessionals in Educ.
    and Related Services [9150]
    Nonverbal Learning Disorders Assn. [14998]
    PACER Center - Parent Advocacy Coalition for
    Educational Rights [14246]
    Swiss Inst. of Special Educ. [IO]
    Yes I Can! Found. for Exceptional Children
    [11998]
Special Educ; Coun. of Administrators of [9139]
Special Elite Forces Soc. - Address unknown since
1995.
Special Events Soc; Intl. [1311]
Special Forces
    Special Forces Assn. [21270]
    Women of Naval Special Warfare [6145]
Special Forces Assn. [21270], PO Box 41436, Fay-
etteville, NC 28309-1436, (910)485-5433
Special Friends of Dottie West - Address unknown
since 1999.
Special Indus. Radio Ser. Assn. [★3742]
Special Interest Auto Club - Defunct.
Special Interest Comm. for Computers and the
Physically Handicapped [★6803]
Special Interest Gp. on Accessible Computing
[6803], c/o Vicki Hanson, Chair, IBM T.J. Watson
Res. Center, 19 Skyline Dr., Hawthorne, NY
10532, (914)784-6603
Special Interest Gp. on Ada [7538], c/o Dr. John W.
McCormick, Chm., Univ. of Northern Iowa, Cmpt.
Sci. Dept., Cedar Falls, IA 50614-0507, (319)273-
6056
Special Interest Gp. on Algorithms Computability
Theory [★7539]
Special Interest Gp. on Algorithms and Computation
Theory [7539], c/o Richard Ladner, Chm., Univ. of
Washington, Dept. of Cmpt. Sci. and Engg., Box
352350, Seattle, WA 98195, (206)543-9347
Special Interest Gp. on the APL and J Languages
[7540], c/o Assn. for Computing Machinery, 1515
Broadway, New York, NY 10036, (212)869-7440
Special Interest Gp. on Applied Computing; SIGAPP
- [6821]
Special Interest Gp. for Architecture of Cmpt.
Systems [6747], c/o Doug Burger, Info. Dir., Univ.
of Texas at Austin, Dept. of Cmpt. Sci., 1 Univ. Sta.
C0500, Austin, TX 78712-0233, (512)471-9795

Special Interest Gp. on Artificial Intelligence [6487],
c/o Irene Frawley, Assn. for Computing Machinery,
2 Penn Plz., Ste. 701, New York, NY 10121-0701,
(212)869-7440
Special Interest Gp. on Automata and Computability
Theory [★7539]
Special Interest Gp. on Biomedical Computing
[★6783]
Special Interest Gp. for Biomedical Info. Processing
[★6783]
Special Interest Group for Business Data Processing
and Mgt. [76]
Special Interest Gp. on Cmpt. and Human Interac-
tion [6542], 1515 Broadway, New York, NY 10036,
(212)626-0500
Special Interest Gp. for Cmpt. Personnel Res.
[★6824]
Special Interest Group for Computer Personnel Res.
- Defunct.
Special Interest Gp. on Cmpt. Sci. Educ. [8135], c/o
Assn. for Computing Machinery, 2 Penn Plz., Ste.
701, New York, NY 10121-0701, (212)869-7440
Special Interest Group for Computer Uses in Educa-
tion - Defunct.
Special Interest Gp. for Computers and the Physi-
cally Handicapped [★6803]
Special Interest Gp. for Computers and Soc. [6748],
c/o Assn. for Computing Machinery, PO Box
30777, New York, NY 10087-0777, (212)626-0500
Special Interest Gp; Consultant Dieticians [★15554]
Special Interest Gp. on Data Commun. [★6750]
Special Interest Gp. on Data Communications of the
Assn. for Computing Machinery [6804], c/o Mark
Crovella, Chm., Boston Univ., U.S. Department of
Cmpt. Sci., 111 Cummington St., Boston, MA
02215, (617)353-8923
Special Interest Gp. for Design Automation [6749],
c/o Prof. Diana Marculescu, Chair, Carnegie Mel-
lon Univ., Dept. of Elecl. and Cmpt. Engg.,
Pittsburgh, PA 15213-3890, (412)268-1167
Special Interest Gp. on Design of Commun. [6823],
c/o Assn. for Computing Machinery, 2 Penn Plz.,
Ste. 701, New York, NY 10121-0701, (212)626-
0605
Special Interest Gp. for Documentation [★6823]
Special Interest Gp. on Info. Retrieval [7212], c/o
Elizabeth D. Liddy, Chair, Syracuse Univ., School
of Info. Stud., Center for Natural Language
Processing, 335 Hinds Hall, Syracuse, NY 13210,
(315)443-5484
Special Interest Gp. on Mgt. of Data [6750], c/o
Mary Fernandez, Sec.-Treas., 180 Park Ave., Bldg.
103, E277, Florham Park, NJ 07932-0971,
(973)360-8679
Special Interest Gp. on Mgt. Info. Systems [6824],
c/o Janice C. Sipior, Chair, Coll. of Commerce and
Finance, Villanova Univ., 800 Lancaster Ave., Vill-
anova, PA 19085, (610)519-4347
Special Interest Group for Mathematical Program-
ming - Defunct.
Special Interest Gp. on Measurement and Evaluation
[6751], c/o Vishal Misra, 512 CSC, 1214 Amster-
dam Ave., MC 0401, New York, NY 10027-7003,
(212)939-7061
Special Interest Gp. of Mensa; Irish [10244]
Special Interest Group on Microprogramming and
Microarchitecture - Address unknown since 2003.
Special Interest Gp. on Mobility of Systems Users,
Data, and Computing [6825], c/o Fran Spinola,
Prog. Coor., 2 Penn Plz., Ste. 701, New York, NY
10121-0701, (212)626-0603
Special Interest Gp. on Multimedia [6826], c/o Assn.
for Computing Machinery, 2 Penn Plz., Ste. 701,
New York, NY 10121-0701, (212)869-4770
Special Interest Group on Numerical Mathematics -
Defunct.
Special Interest Gp. on Programming Languages
[7541], c/o Kathleen S. Fisher, Chair, 1 River Oaks
Pl., San Jose, CA 95134
Special Interest Gp. on Security, Audit and Control
[6752], c/o Prof. Virgil D. Gligor, Chm., Univ. of
Maryland, Dept. of Elecl. and Cmpt. Engg., 2405
A.V. Williams Bldg., College Park, MD 20742,
(301)405-3647
Special Interest Gp. on Simulation [6753], c/o Assn.
for Computing Machinery, 2 Penn Plz., Ste. 701,
New York, NY 10036-5701, (212)626-0500

A star before a book entry number signifies that the name is not listed separately, but is mentioned within the entry.

Special Interest Gp. for Social and Behavioral Sci. Computing [★6542]

Special Interest Gp. on Software Engg. [6779], c/o Assn. for Computing Machinery, 2 Penn Plz., Ste. 701, New York, NY 10121-0701, (212)626-0613

Special Interest Gp. on Supporting Work Gp. - Defunct.

Special Interest Gp. for Symbolic and Algebraic Manipulation [7296], c/o Daniel Lichtblau, Treas., Kernel Technology Gp., Wolfram Research, Inc., 100 Trade Center Dr., Champaign, IL 61820

Special Interest Group for Systems Documentation - Address unknown since 2003.

Special Interest Group for Univ. and Coll. Computing Services - Defunct.

Special Interest Groupware and Groupwork - Address unknown since 2002.

Special Investigation Units; Intl. Assn. of [2188]

Special Libraries Assn. [10389], 331 S Patrick St., Alexandria, VA 22314-3501, (703)647-4900

Special Libraries Assn. [IO], Alexandria, VA, United States

Special Military Active Retired Travel Club [IO], Pensacola, FL, United States

Special Military Active Retired Travel Club [21271], 600 Univ. Off. Blvd., Ste. 1A, Pensacola, FL 32504, (850)478-1986

Special Needs Advocate for Parents [11652], 3029 Wilshire Blvd., Ste. 200, Santa Monica, CA 90403, (310)452-3759

Special Needs; Fed. for Children with [12569]

Special Needs Network Found; Natl. [14232]

Special Needs Network; Natl. [★14232]

Special Olympics [23362], 1133 19th St. NW, Washington, DC 20036, (202)628-3630

Special Olympics [IO], Washington, DC, United States

Special Olympics Albania [IO], Tirana, Albania

Special Olympics Andorra [IO], Andorra la Vella, Andorra

Special Olympics Armenia [IO], Yerevan, Armenia

Special Olympics Australia [IO], Concord, Australia

Special Olympics Austria [IO], Schladming, Austria

Special Olympics Bangladesh [IO], Dhaka, Bangladesh

Special Olympics Belarus [IO], Minsk, Belarus

Special Olympics Benin [IO], Cotonou, Benin

Special Olympics Bolivia [IO], La Paz, Bolivia

Special Olympics Bosnia and Herzegovina [IO], Brussels, Belgium

Special Olympics Botswana [IO], Gaborone, Botswana

Special Olympics Bulgaria [IO], Sofia, Bulgaria

Special Olympics Burkina Faso [IO], Ouagadougou, Burkina Faso

Special Olympics Cameroon [IO], Yaounde, Cameroon

Special Olympics Canada [IO], Toronto, ON, Canada

Special Olympics Chad [IO], N'Djamena, Chad

Special Olympics Costa Rica [IO], San Jose, Costa Rica

Special Olympics Croatia [IO], Zagreb, Croatia

Special Olympics Cuba [IO], Havana, Cuba

Special Olympics Cyprus [IO], Nicosia, Cyprus

Special Olympics Czech Republic [IO], Prague, Czech Republic

Special Olympics East Asia [IO], Beijing, People's Republic of China

Special Olympics Ecuador [IO], Quito, Ecuador

Special Olympics El Salvador [IO], San Salvador, El Salvador

Special Olympics Finland [IO], Slu, Finland

Special Olympics Gambia [IO], Serrekunda, Gambia

Special Olympics Germany [IO], Berlin, Germany

Special Olympics Ghana [IO], Accra, Ghana

Special Olympics Greece [IO], Athens, Greece

Special Olympics Honduras [IO], Tegucigalpa, Honduras

Special Olympics Iceland [IO], Reykjavik, Iceland

Special Olympics Ireland [IO], Dublin, Ireland

Special Olympics Italy [IO], Rome, Italy

Special Olympics Japan [IO], Tokyo, Japan

Special Olympics Kenya [IO], Nairobi, Kenya

Special Olympics Latvia [IO], Riga, Latvia

Special Olympics Lesotho [IO], Maseru, Lesotho

Special Olympics Malaysia [IO], Selangor, Malaysia

Special Olympics Moldova [IO], Chisinau, Moldova

Special Olympics Netherlands [IO], Bunnik, Netherlands

Special Olympics Norway [IO], Oslo, Norway

Special Olympics Paraguay [IO], Asuncion, Paraguay

Special Olympics Philippines [IO], Quezon City, Philippines

Special Olympics Poland [IO], Warsaw, Poland

Special Olympics Portugal [IO], Lisbon, Portugal

Special Olympics Russia [IO], Moscow, Russia

Special Olympics Slovakia [IO], Bratislava, Slovakia

Special Olympics Slovenia [IO], Ljubljana, Slovenia

Special Olympics Spain [IO], Barcelona, Spain

Special Olympics Sweden [IO], Stockholm, Sweden

Special Olympics Switzerland [IO], Fribourg, Switzerland

Special Olympics Thailand [IO], Bangkok, Thailand

Special Olympics Uganda [IO], Kampala, Uganda

Special Olympics Uruguay [IO], Montevideo, Uruguay

Special Olympics Uzbekistan [IO], Tashkent, Uzbekistan

Special Police and Security Officers; Natl. Assn. of [24122]

Special Project on the Forgotten Woman - Defunct.

Special Recreation for Disabled [★11989]

Special Recreation for Disabled [★IO]

Special Recreation for disABLED Intl. [IO], Iowa City, IA, United States

Special Recreation for disABLED Intl. [11989], 701 Oaknoll Dr., Iowa City, IA 52246-5168, (319)466-3192

Special Refractories Assn. - Defunct.

The Special Relief League - Defunct.

Special Study Group on Sonic Boom in Relation to Man - Defunct.

A Special Wish Found. [11723], 1250 Memory Ln., Columbus, OH 43209, (614)258-3186

Specialist Access Engg. and Maintenance Assn. [IO], London, United Kingdom

Specialist Anglers' Alliance [IO], Hemel Hempstead, United Kingdom

Specialist Ceilings and Interiors Assn. [★IO]

Specialists in Gp. Work; Assn. for [11820]

Specialists; Intl. Assn. of Concrete Repair [★927]

Specialists; Natl. Assn. of Investigative [2325]

Speciality Automotive Mfrs. Assn. [★396]

Specialized Carriers and Rigging Assn. [3589], 2750 Prosperity Ave., Ste. 620, Fairfax, VA 22031-4312, (703)698-0291

Specialized Carriers and Rigging Assn. [IO], Fairfax, VA, United States

Specialized and Cooperative Lib. Agencies; Assn. of [10340]

Specialized Info. Publishers Assn. [3258], 8201 Greensboro Dr., Ste. 300, McLean, VA 22102, (703)610-0260

Specialized Info. Publishers Assn. [IO], Surrey, United Kingdom

Specialty Advt. Assn. [★IO]

Specialty Advt. Assn. [★116]

Specialty Advt. Assn. of Canada [★IO]

Specialty Advt. Assn. Intl. [★IO]

Specialty Advt. Assn. Intl. [★116]

Specialty Advt. Guild Intl. [★116]

Specialty Advt. Guild Intl. [★IO]

Specialty Advt. Natl. Assn. [★IO]

Specialty Advt. Natl. Assn. [★116]

Specialty Bakery Owners of America - Address unknown since 1994.

Specialty Coffee Assn. of Am. [513], 330 Golden Shore, Ste. 50, Long Beach, CA 90802, (562)624-4100

Specialty Coffee Assn. of Europe [IO], Chelmsford, United Kingdom

Specialty Contracting Indus; Coun. of Mech. [★1006]

Specialty Contractors; Assoc. [1006]

Specialty Crop Trade Coun. [4761], 710 Striker Ave., Sacramento, CA 95834, (916)561-5900

Specialty Equip. Manufacturers Assn. [★397]

Specialty Equip. Market Assn. [397], PO Box 4910, Diamond Bar, CA 91765-0910, (909)396-0289

Specialty Food Trade; Natl. Assn. for the [1541]

Specialty Graphic Imaging Assn. [1792], 10015 Main St., Fairfax, VA 22031-3489, (703)385-1335

Specialty Graphic Imaging Assn. [IO], Fairfax, VA, United States

Specialty Sleep Assn. [1705], c/o Tambra Jones, Exec. Dir., 46639 Jones Ranch Rd., Friant, CA 93626, (559)868-4187

Specialty Sports Assn; U.S. [23795]

Specialty Steel Indus. of North Am. [2729], 3050 K St. NW, Washington, DC 20007, (202)342-8630

Specialty Steel Indus. of the U.S. [★2729]

Specialty Tools and Fasteners Distributors Assn. [2069], PO Box 44, Elm Grove, WI 53122, (262)784-4774

Specialty Toy Retailing Assn; Amer. [2385]

Specialty Vehicle Inst. of Am. [398], 2 Jenner St., Ste. 150, Irvine, CA 92618-3812, (949)727-3727

Specialty Wine Retailers Assn. [4031], 915 L St., Ste. 1000, Sacramento, CA 95814, (916)446-4708

Specialty Wire Assn. [★1999]

Species Iris Gp. of North Am. [22545], c/o Rodney Barton, 3 Wolters St., Hickory Creek, TX 75065

Specifications Inst; Constr. [6836]

Spectromatic Associates of America - Defunct.

Spectrometry; Amer. Soc. for Mass [7688]

Spectroscopy

Amer. Soc. for Mass Spectrometry [7688]

Canadian Soc. for Analytical Sciences and Spectroscopy [IO]

Coblentz Soc. [7689]

European Soc. for Mass Spectrometry [IO]

Singaporean Soc. for Mass Spectrometry [IO]

Soc. for Applied Spectroscopy [7690]

Spectroscopy Societies; Fed. of Analytical Chemistry and [6682]

Spectroscopy Soc. of Canada [★IO]

Speech

Abilities! [11913]

Acad. of Aphasia [13704]

Acad. of Rehabilitative Audiology [14734]

Acoustical Soc. of Am. [6364]

ADARA: Professionals Networking for Excellence in Ser. Delivery with Individuals who are Deaf or Hard of Hearing [14735]

Alexander Graham Bell Assn. for the Deaf and Hard of Hearing [14736]

Alliance of Rhetoric Societies [10935]

Amer. Assn. of Phonetic Sciences [10842]

Amer. Debate Assn. [9151]

Amer. Forensic Assn. [9152]

Amer. Hearing Res. Found. [14740]

Amer. Hyperlexia Assn. [13940]

Amer. Neurotology Soc. [16441]

Amer. Parliamentary Debate Assn. [9153]

Amer. Soc. for Deaf Children [14742]

Amer. Soc. of Professional Communicators [873]

Amer. Speech Language Hearing Assn. [16442]

Assn. for Commun. Admin. [9154]

Assn. of Pediatric Therapists [16606]

Australian Speech Sci. and Tech. Assn. [IO]

Better Hearing Inst. [14745]

Conf. of Educational Administrators of Schools and Programs for the Deaf [14749]

Coun. of Amer. Instructors of the Deaf [14750]

Coun. on Educ. of the Deaf [14751]

Deafness Res. Found. [14753]

Delta Sigma Rho - Tau Kappa Alpha [24719]

Dogs for the Deaf [14754]

Genealogical Speakers Guild [10899]

HEAR Center [14756]

Hearing Loss Assn. of Am. [14759]

Helen Keller Natl. Center for Deaf-Blind Youths and Adults [14760]

House Ear Inst. [16446]

IDEA: The Intl. Debate Educ. Assn. [18677]

Intl. Assn. of Laryngectomees [11953]

Intl. Assn. of Orofacial Myology [15869]

Intl. Assn. of Speakers Bureaus [10900]

Intl. Found. for Stutterers [16447]

Intl. Hearing Dog, Inc. [14762]

Intl. Hearing Soc. [14763]

Intl. Platform Assn. [10901]

Intl. Speech Commun. Assn. [IO]

Intl. Stuttering Assn. [16498]

Reference to "IO" in place of a book number signifies that the association may be found in the 45th edition of International Organizations.

Judson Welliver Soc. [10127]
Mend Our Tongues Soc. [10407]
Model Secondary School for the Deaf [14766]
Natl. Assn. of the Deaf [14767]
Natl. Assn. of Professionals with Language
  Impairment in Children [IO]
Natl. Assn. of Rehabilitation Providers and Agen-
  cies [16326]
Natl. Assn. of Urban Debate Leagues [9155]
Natl. Capital Speakers Assn. [10902]
Natl. Captioning Inst. [14769]
Natl. Catholic Forensic League [9156]
Natl. Center for Stuttering [16450]
Natl. Christian Forensics and Communications
  Assn. [8521]
Natl. Commun. Assn. [9157]
Natl. Fed. of State High School Associations
  [23841]
Natl. Forensic Assn. [9158]
Natl. Forensic League [9159]
Natl. Parliamentary Debate Assn. [9160]
Natl. Ser. Dog Center [14774]
Natl. Spasmodic Dysphonia Assn. [15352]
Natl. Speakers Assn. [10903]
Natl. Student Speech Language Hearing Assn.
  [16453]
NFHS Speech, Debate and Theatre Assn. [9161]
Open Debates [17488]
Oral Hearing-Impaired Sect. [14775]
Parents' Sect. of the Alexander Graham Bell
  Assn. for the Deaf and Hard of Hearing [14776]
Polish Phonetic Assn. [IO]
Private Practice Section/American Physical
  Therapy Assn. [16633]
Public Conversations Proj. [17189]
Registry of Interpreters for the Deaf [14778]
Rhetoric Soc. of Am. [10937]
Selective Mutism Found. [15233]
Southern States Commun. Assn. [9162]
Spellbinders [10984]
Telecommunications for the Deaf and Hard of
  Hearing, Inc. [14780]
Toastmasters Intl. [10904]
Toastmasters New Zealand [IO]
U.S. Soc. for Augmentative and Alternative
  Commun. [17198]
Voice Found. [16457]
VoiceCare Network [9163]
Speech Action; Natl. Assn. for Hearing and
  [★16442]
Speech Agencies; Natl. Assn. of Hearing and
  [★16442]
Speech Arts; Natl. Assn. of Dramatic and [11026]
Speech Assn. of Am. [★9157]
Speech Association/Deaf Children's Literacy Proj;
  Natl. Cued [16452]
Speech Assn. for the Deaf; Volta [★14736]
Speech Assn; Southern [★9162]
Speech Commun. Assn. [★9157]
Speech Commun; Assn. of Departments and
  Administrators in [★9154]
Speech Commun. Assn; Religious [★8116]
Speech Commun. Assn; Southern [★9162]
Speech to the Deaf; Amer. Assn. to Promote the
  Teaching of [★14736]
Speech and Debate Assn; Natl. Fed. Interscholastic
  [★9161]
Speech Division of Speech Commun. Assn;
  Religious [★8116]
Speech Found. of Am. [★16456]
Speech and Hearing
  Abilities! [11913]
  Acad. of Rehabilitative Audiology [14734]
  ADARA: Professionals Networking for Excellence
    in Ser. Delivery with Individuals who are Deaf
    or Hard of Hearing [14735]
  AFASIC - Unlocking Speech and Language [IO]
  Alexander Graham Bell Assn. for the Deaf and
    Hard of Hearing [14736]
  Amer. Acad. of Audiology [16439]
  Amer. Auditory Soc. [14738]
  Amer. Hearing Res. Found. [14740]
  Amer. Inst. for Stuttering Treatment and Profes-
    sional Training [16440]
  Amer. Neurotology Soc. [16441]

Amer. Soc. for Deaf Children [14742]
Amer. Speech Language Hearing Assn. [16442]
Amer. Tinnitus Assn. [16443]
Assn. of Late-Deafened Adults [14743]
Assn. of Pediatric Therapists [16606]
Audiology Awareness Campaign [13716]
Balearic Assn. of Stutterers [IO]
Better Hearing Inst. [14745]
British Stammering Assn. [IO]
British Stammering Assn. - Scotland [IO]
British Tinnitus Assn. [IO]
Canadian Assn. of Speech-Language Pathologists
  and Audiologists [IO]
Canadian Stuttering Assn. [IO]
Childhood Apraxia of Speech Assn. [16444]
Conf. of Educational Administrators of Schools
  and Programs for the Deaf [14749]
Coun. of Amer. Instructors of the Deaf [14750]
Coun. on Educ. of the Deaf [14751]
Deaf History Intl. [14081]
Deafness Res. Found. [14753]
European Assn. for Speech Signal and Image
  Processing [IO]
European League of Stuttering Associations [IO]
Friends: The Natl. Assn. of Young People Who
  Stutter [16445]
HEAR Center [14756]
Hearing Loss Assn. of Am. [14759]
Helen Keller Natl. Center for Deaf-Blind Youths
  and Adults [14760]
Hong Kong Assn. of Speech Therapists [IO]
House Ear Inst. [16446]
Intl. Assn. of Logopedics and Phoniatrics [IO]
Intl. Assn. of Orofacial Myology [15869]
Intl. Assn. of Physicians in Audiology [IO]
Intl. Catholic Deaf Assn. - U.S. Sect. [19641]
Intl. Found. for Stutterers [16447]
Intl. Hearing Dog, Inc. [14762]
Intl. Hearing Soc. [14763]
Intl. Stuttering Assn. [16498]
Irish Stammering Assn. [IO]
Japanese Assn. of Speech-Language-Hearing
  Therapists [IO]
Lithuanian Stuttering Problem Club [IO]
Malaysian Assn. of Speech Language and Hear-
  ing [IO]
Model Secondary School for the Deaf [14766]
Natl. Assn. of the Deaf [14767]
Natl. Assn. of Rehabilitation Providers and Agen-
  cies [16326]
Natl. Assn. of School Nurses for the Deaf [14768]
Natl. Black Assn. for Speech-Language and Hear-
  ing [16448]
Natl. Captioning Inst. [14769]
Natl. Catholic Off. for the Deaf [19675]
Natl. Center for Neurogenic Commun. Disorders
  [16449]
Natl. Center for Stuttering [16450]
Natl. Center for Voice and Speech [16451]
Natl. Cued Speech Association/Deaf Children's
  Literacy Proj. [16452]
Natl. Inst. on Deafness and Other Commun.
  Disorders Info. CH [14773]
Natl. Ser. Dog Center [14774]
Natl. Student Speech Language Hearing Assn.
  [16453]
Natl. Stuttering Assn. [16454]
Oral Hearing-Impaired Sect. [14775]
Parents' Sect. of the Alexander Graham Bell
  Assn. for the Deaf and Hard of Hearing [14776]
Private Practice Section/American Physical
  Therapy Assn. [16633]
Registry of Interpreters for the Deaf [14778]
Royal Coll. of Speech and Language Therapists
  [IO]
Selective Mutism Found. [15233]
Soc. of Teachers of Speech and Drama [IO]
Speak Easy [IO]
Speak Easy Intl. Found. [16455]
Speakability [IO]
Speech Language Hearing Assn. Singapore [IO]
Speech Pathology Australia [IO]
Standing Liaison Comm. of EU Speech and
  Language Therapists and Logopedists [IO]
Stuttering Found. of Am. [16456]

Swiss Assn. of Logopedics [IO]
Telecommunications for the Deaf and Hard of
  Hearing, Inc. [14780]
Voice Found. [16457]
VOICES [13211]
Speech and Hearing Assn; Natl. Student [★16453]
Speech and Hearing Assn; Student Jour. Gp. of the
  Amer. [★16453]
Speech and Hearing Center - Defunct.
Speech Language Hearing Assn. Singapore [IO],
  Singapore, Singapore
Speech-Language and Hearing; Natl. Black Assn. for
  [16448]
Speech Pathology Australia [IO], Melbourne,
  Australia
Speed Assn; Amer. [23072]
Speed Coaches Assn. - Address unknown since
  2001.
Speed Equip. Manufacturers Assn. [★397]
Speed Skating Canada [IO], Ottawa, ON, Canada
Speedskating Assn; U.S. Intl. [★23745]
SpeedSkating Union of the U.S; Amateur [★23745]
Speedskating; U.S. [23745]
SPEEDUP Soc.: Swiss Forum for GRID and High
  Performance Computing [IO], Fribourg,
  Switzerland
Speedways of North Am; United [23671]
Spelean Historical Assn; Amer. [10091]
Speleological Fed. of Latin Am. and the Caribbean
  [IO], Mendoza, Argentina
Speleological Soc; Natl. [7693]
Speleology
  Amer. Spelean Historical Assn. [10091]
  Assn. for Mexican Cave Stud. [7691]
  Assn. for Mexican Cave Stud. [IO]
  British Cave Res. Assn. [IO]
  British Caving Assn. [IO]
  British Caving Assn. [IO]
  Bulgarian Fed. of Speleology [IO]
  Cave Res. Found. [7692]
  Intl. Soc. for Spelaeological Art [IO]
  Intl. Union of Speleology [IO]
  Natl. Speleological Soc. [7693]
  Speleological Fed. of Latin Am. and the Carib-
    bean [IO]
Spellbinders [10984], PO Box 128, Woody Creek,
  CO 81656, (970)922-1444
Spelling
  Academic Language Therapy Assn. [12488]
  Amer. Literacy Coun. [8785]
Spelling Coun; Phonemic [★8785]
Spencer Family Assn. [★21153]
Spencer Found. [12054], 625 N Michigan Ave., Ste.
  1600, Chicago, IL 60611, (312)337-7000
Spencer Historical and Genealogical Soc. [21153],
  c/o Marion G. Spencer, Pres., 3214 Wintergreen
  Terr., Grapevine, TX 76051
SpenderMenders Intl. - Defunct.
Spenser Soc; Intl. [9663]
Sphagnum Peat Moss Assn. - Address unknown
  since 1995.
SPHE - The Soc. of Packaging Professionals
  [★7426]
Sphere Proj. [IO], Geneva, Switzerland
Sphinx Org. [10710], 400 Renaissance Ctr., Ste.
  2550, Detroit, MI 48243, (313)877-9100
SPI Composites Inst. - Defunct.
Spice Indus. Assn. [IO], Bonn, Germany
Spice Trade Assn; Amer. [1498]
Spices Bd. India [IO], Cochin, India
Spidshundeklubben [★IO]
SPIE - The Intl. Soc. for Optical Engg. [IO], Belling-
  ham, WA, United States
SPIE - The Intl. Soc. for Optical Engg. [7408], PO
  Box 10, Bellingham, WA 98227-0010, (360)676-
  3290
Spike Jones Intl. Fan Club - Address unknown since
  1999.
Spill Control Assn. of Am. [3073], 2105 Laurel Bush
  Rd., Ste. 200, Bel Air, MD 21015, (443)640-1085
Spill Control Inst., Tech. Services Division [★3073]
Spin Fishing Assn; Intl. [★23417]
Spina Bifida
  Spina Bifida Assn. of Am. [16458]
Spina Bifida Assn. of Am. [16458], 4590 MacArthur
  Blvd. NW, Ste. 250, Washington, DC 20007-4226,
  (202)944-3285

A star before a book entry number signifies that the name is not listed separately, but is mentioned within the entry.

Spina Bifida Assn. of Japan **[IO]**, Tokyo, Japan
Spina Bifida and Hydrocephalus; Assn. for **[IO]**
Spina Bifida and Hydrocephalus Assn. of Canada
 [IO], Winnipeg, MB, Canada
Spina Bifida and Hydrocephalus; Irish Assn. for **[IO]**
Spina Bifida und Hydrocephalus Osterreich **[IO]**, Vi-
 enna, Austria
Spina Bifida; Soc. for Res. into Hydrocephalus and
 [IO]
Spinach Assn; Natl. **[★4738]**
Spinal Cord Injuries Australia **[IO]**, Matraville,
 Australia
Spinal Cord Injury Assn; Natl. **[16468]**
Spinal Cord Injury Found; Natl. **[★16468]**
Spinal Cord Injury Nurses; Amer. Assn. of **[15441]**
Spinal Cord Res. Found. **[★20768]**
Spinal Cord Res. Found; Kent Waldrep Intl.
 [★16463]
Spinal Cord Soc. **[16469]**, 19051 County Hwy. 1,
 Fergus Falls, MN 56537-7609, (218)739-5252
Spinal Injuries Action Assn. **[IO]**, Dublin, Ireland
Spinal Injuries Assn. **[IO]**, Milton Keynes, United
 Kingdom
Spinal Injury
 Adolescent Scoliosis Soc. of North Am. **[16392]**
 Amer. Assn. of Spinal Cord Injury Nurses **[15441]**
 Amer. Assn. of Spinal Cord Injury Psychologists
  and Social Workers **[16459]**
 Amer. Paraplegia Soc. **[16460]**
 Amer. Spinal Injury Assn. **[16461]**
 Amer. Syringomyelia Alliance Proj. **[15305]**
 Arbeitsgemeinschaft Spina Bifida und Hydroceph-
  alus **[IO]**
 Asociacion Guatemalteca de Espina Bifida **[IO]**
 Associacao Spina Bifida e Hidrocefalia de
  Portugal **[IO]**
 Assn. for Spina Bifida and Hydrocephalus **[IO]**
 Australian Spina Bifida and Hydrocephalus Assn.
  [IO]
 Cervical Spine Res. Soc. **[IO]**
 Cervical Spine Res. Soc. **[16462]**
 Christopher and Dana Reeve Found. **[16463]**
 Federacion Espanola de Asociaciones de Espina
  Bifida e Hidrocefalia **[IO]**
 Federazione Associazioni Italiane Spina Bifida e
  Idrocefalo **[IO]**
 Indian Spina Bifida Assn. **[IO]**
 Intl. Intradiscal Therapy Soc. **[IO]**
 Intl. Intradiscal Therapy Soc. **[16464]**
 Intl. Spinal Cord Soc. **[IO]**
 Intl. Spinal Development and Res. Found. **[IO]**
 Intl. Spinal Development and Res. Found. **[16465]**
 Intl. Spine Intervention Soc. **[16466]**
 Jennifer Trust for Spinal Muscular Atrophy **[IO]**
 Kent Waldrep Natl. Paralysis Found. **[16467]**
 Natl. Spinal Cord Injury Assn. **[16468]**
 Polish Assn. for Spina Bifida and Hydrocephalus
  [IO]
 Scoliosis Assn. **[IO]**
 Scoliosis Assn., Inc. **[16394]**
 Scoliosis Res. Soc. **[16395]**
 Soc. for Res. into Hydrocephalus and Spina Bifida
  [IO]
 Soc. for Spinal Res. **[IO]**
 Spina Bifida Assn. of Am. **[16458]**
 Spina Bifida Assn. of Japan **[IO]**
 Spina Bifida and Hydrocephalus Assn. of Canada
  [IO]
 Spina Bifida und Hydrocephalus Osterreich **[IO]**
 Spinal Cord Soc. **[16469]**
 Spinal Injuries Action Assn. **[IO]**
 Spinal Injuries Assn. **[IO]**
 Spine Soc. of Europe **[IO]**
 Think First Natl. Injury Prevention Found. **[16470]**
 Vlaamse Vereniging voor Spina Bifida en Hydro-
  cephalus vzw **[IO]**
 World Spine Soc. **[15405]**
Spinal Injury Assn; Amer. **[16461]**
Spinal Res. **[★IO]**
Spindrift Assn; Starwind/ **[★23207]**
Spine Assn; North Amer. Lumbar **[★15402]**
Spine Radiology; Amer. Soc. of **[16284]**
Spine Soc. of Europe **[IO]**, Uster, Switzerland
Spine Soc; North Amer. **[15402]**
Spinners Assn; Amer. Yarn **[3774]**

Spinners' Assn; Northwest Regional **[22172]**
Spinners and Weavers Assn. of Korea **[IO]**, Seoul,
 Republic of Korea
Spinners and Weavers Assn. of Korea - Defunct.
Spinone Club of Am. **[22363]**, PO Box 307, Warsaw,
 VA 22572, (804)333-0309
Spirit of Adventure - Address unknown since 1995.
Spirit of Am. **[18488]**, 12021 Wilshire Blvd., Ste. 558,
 Los Angeles, CA 90025, (800)691-2209
Spirit Association; National Fed. Interscholastic
 [★23841]
Spirit and Breath **[★13788]**
Spirit of Drum Corps Alumni Assn. **[IO]**, Calgary, AB,
 Canada
Spirit of the Future Creative Inst. - Address unknown
 since 1990.
Spirit, John Denver Fan Club - Address unknown
 since 1989.
Spirit of Women Hosp. Network **[14898]**, 1100
 Republic Bldg., 25 W Prospect Ave., Cleveland,
 OH 44115, (216)523-1300
Spirited People of the 1st Nations **[★IO]**
Spirits Coun. of the U.S; Distilled **[199]**
Spirits Indus. Fed. **[IO]**, Buenos Aires, Argentina
Spirits Inst; Distilled **[★199]**
Spirits Shippers Assn; Wine and **[211]**
Spirits Wholesalers of Am; Wine and **[212]**
Spiritual Advisory Coun. - Address unknown since
 1999.
Spiritual Alliance; The Natl. **[20452]**
Spiritual Assembly of the Baha'is of Malaysia **[IO]**,
 Kuala Lumpur, Malaysia
Spiritual Assembly of the Baha'is of New Zealand;
 Natl. **[IO]**
Spiritual Assembly of the Baha'is of the U.S. and
 Canada; Natl. **[★19467]**
Spiritual Assembly of the Baha'is of the U.S; Natl.
 [19467]
Spiritual Counterfeits Proj. **[19876]**, PO Box 4308,
 Berkeley, CA 94704-0308, (510)540-0300
Spiritual Directors Intl. **[20507]**, PO Box 3584, Belle-
 vue, WA 98009-3584, (425)455-1565
Spiritual Directors Intl. **[IO]**, Bellevue, WA, United
 States
Spiritual Emergence Network **[★15194]**
Spiritual and Environmental Awareness; Inst. for
 [20572]
Spiritual and Ethical Educ; Coun. for **[8536]**
Spiritual, Ethical and Religious Values in Counseling;
 Assn. for **[8166]**
Spiritual Frontiers Fellowship Intl. **[20579]**, PO Box
 7868, Philadelphia, PA 19101-7868, (215)222-1991
Spiritual Frontiers Fellowship Intl. **[IO]**, Philadelphia,
 PA, United States
Spiritual Hea; Center for Psychological and **[15194]**
Spiritual Life
 Advocate Hea. Care **[14821]**
 Aetherius Soc. **[20568]**
 Aloha Intl. **[12340]**
 Amer. Hindu Assn. **[20077]**
 Anthroposophical Soc. in Am. **[19457]**
 Assn. of Contemplative Sisters **[20563]**
 Assn. of Life-Giving Churches **[19843]**
 Assn. for the Restoration of the Church and Home
  [19844]
 Astara **[20443]**
 Bear Butte Intl. Alliance **[19446]**
 Center for Psychological and Spiritual Hea.
  [15194]
 Center for Respect of Life and Env. **[4620]**
 Church of Spiritual Discovery **[20569]**
 Church Universal and Triumphant **[19462]**
 Community Ser. **[17214]**
 Conf. for Catholic Lesbians **[20051]**
 Coun. on Spiritual Practices **[20564]**
 Cross-Cultural Shamanism Network **[20444]**
 Feathered Pipe Found. **[12345]**
 Fellowship of Saint Paul **[19958]**
 Flower Essence Soc. **[14818]**
 Found. for a Course in Miracles **[20571]**
 Found. of Human Understanding **[10465]**
 Found. for the Preservation of the Mahayana
  Tradition **[19550]**
 Hanuman Found. **[12347]**
 Healers League of the Natl. Spiritualist Assn. of
  Churches **[20449]**

Hea. Ministries Assn. **[16339]**
HUNA Res. **[12349]**
Inst. for the Development of the Harmonious Hu-
 man Being **[12351]**
Inst. on Religious Life **[19639]**
Inst. for Spiritual and Environmental Awareness
 [20572]
Inst. for Theological Encounter With Sci. and
 Tech. **[12353]**
Interfaith Church of Metaphysics **[20573]**
Intl. Anchoritic Soc. **[10460]**
Intl. Assn. of Sufism **[20101]**
Intl. Assn. of Transpersonal Therapists and Physi-
 cians **[15205]**
Intl. Center for Spirit at Work **[20575]**
IONS - Inst. of Noetic Sciences **[10976]**
Islamic Correctional Reunion Assn. **[20105]**
Jagannath Org. for Global Awareness **[20527]**
Krishnamurti Found. of Am. **[12355]**
Makatab Tarighat Oveyssi Shahmaghsoudi
 [20576]
Mooncircles **[20577]**
Morris Pratt Inst. Assn. **[20451]**
Muhyiddin Ibn Arabi Soc. **[20578]**
Natl. Interfaith Coalition on Aging **[11314]**
Natl. Marriage Encounter **[12507]**
Natl. Spiritualist Assn. of Churches **[20453]**
Natl. Spiritualist Teachers Club **[20454]**
Neighborhood Bible Stud. **[19526]**
ORACLE Religious Assn. **[20070]**
Pathwork Helpers Assn. of North Am. **[20565]**
Promise Keepers **[19834]**
Quartus Found. for Spiritual Res. **[12361]**
The Radiance Technique Intl. Assn. **[13648]**
Sacred Dance Soc. **[19878]**
Sacred Passage and the Way of Nature Fellow-
 ship **[12362]**
Serendipity Assn. **[14832]**
Slovene Franciscan Fathers **[19718]**
Soc. of the Companions of the Holy Cross
 [19971]
Soc. of Jewish Sci. **[20202]**
Soc. of Pragmatic Mysticism **[20448]**
Soc. for the Stud. of Christian Spirituality **[19826]**
Spiritual Life Inst. **[20566]**
Spiritual Life Inst. **[IO]**
Spiritual Unity of Nations **[20580]**
Sri Aurobindo Assn. **[20636]**
Subud U.S.A. **[20589]**
Tayu Center **[20581]**
Teleos Inst. **[12364]**
Thanks-Giving Square **[20584]**
Theosophical Book Assn. for the Blind **[20592]**
Theosophical Soc. in Am. **[20593]**
Truth Missionaries Chap. of Positive Accord
 [20585]
United Lodge of Theosophists **[20594]**
United Religions Initiative **[20518]**
U.S. Assn. of Consecrated Virgins **[19733]**
Urantia Found. **[20587]**
Vedic Friends Assn. **[10977]**
Wainwright House **[20588]**
Well-Springs Found. **[10179]**
Wheels for the World **[11994]**
White Mountain Educ. Assn. **[20567]**
Women In Conscious Creative Action **[20625]**
Women's Alliance for Theology, Ethics and Ritual
 [20626]
Women's Division of the Gen. Bd. of Global
 Ministries of the United Methodist Church
 [20269]
Women's Spirituality Forum **[20628]**
World Coun. of Religious Leaders **[20519]**
World Literature Ministries **[19832]**
World Union of Deists **[20531]**
Yoga Alliance **[11220]**
Yoga Res. Found. **[20637]**
Zarathushtrian Assembly **[20510]**
Spiritual Life Inst. **[20566]**, c/o NADA Hermitage, PO
 Box 219, Crestone, CO 81131, (719)256-4778
Spiritual Life Inst. **[IO]**, Crestone, CO, United States
Spiritual Life Inst. of Am. **[★IO]**
Spiritual Life Inst. of Am. **[★20566]**
Spiritual Ministry - Defunct.
Spiritual Res; Quartus Found. for **[12361]**

Reference to "IO" in place of a book number signifies that the association may be found in the 45th edition of International Organizations.

Spiritual Sci. Fellowship [IO], Montreal, QC, Canada
Spiritual Sci. Fellowship [★IO]
Spiritual Understanding
  Aetherius Soc. [IO]
  Aetherius Soc. [20568]
  Aloha Intl. [12340]
  Amer. Hindu Assn. [20077]
  Anthroposophical Soc. in Am. [19457]
  Assn. of Contemplative Sisters [20563]
  Assn. for the Restoration of the Church and Home [19844]
  Assn. for Spirit at Work [IO]
  Astara [20443]
  Bear Butte Intl. Alliance [19446]
  Black Holocaust Soc. [16938]
  Care Ministries [19532]
  Center for Psychological and Spiritual Hea. [15194]
  Center for Visionary Leadership [18002]
  Church of Spiritual Discovery [20569]
  Church Universal and Triumphant [19462]
  Circle Sanctuary [20570]
  Circle Sanctuary [IO]
  Conf. for Catholic Lesbians [20051]
  Coun. on Spiritual Practices [20564]
  Cross-Cultural Shamanism Network [20444]
  East-West Cultural Center [9619]
  Feathered Pipe Found. [12345]
  Fellowship of Saint Paul [19958]
  Found. for a Course in Miracles [20571]
  Found. for the Preservation of the Mahayana Tradition [19550]
  Friends of Falun Gong [17061]
  Hanuman Found. [12347]
  Healers League of the Natl. Spiritualist Assn. of Churches [20449]
  HUNA Res. [12349]
  Inst. for the Development of the Harmonious Human Being [12351]
  Inst. on Religious Life [19639]
  Inst. for Spiritual and Environmental Awareness [20572]
  Inst. for Theological Encounter With Sci. and Tech. [12353]
  Interfaith Church of Metaphysics [20573]
  Intl. Assn. for Spiritual Consciousness [20574]
  Intl. Assn. for Spiritual Consciousness [IO]
  Intl. Assn. of Sufism [20101]
  Intl. Center for Spirit at Work [20575]
  Intl. Thomas Merton Soc. [9665]
  IONS - Inst. of Noetic Sciences [10976]
  Islamic Correctional Reunion Assn. [20105]
  Jagannath Org. for Global Awareness [20527]
  Jewel Heart [19552]
  Jews for Judaism [20500]
  Krishnamurti Found. of Am. [12355]
  Makatab Tarighat Oveyssi Shahmaghsoudi [20576]
  Mooncircles [20577]
  Morris Pratt Inst. Assn. [20451]
  Muhyiddin Ibn Arabi Soc. [20578]
  Natl. Marriage Encounter [12507]
  Natl. Spiritualist Assn. of Churches [20453]
  Natl. Spiritualist Teachers Club [20454]
  Neighborhood Bible Stud. [19526]
  Pediatric Chaplains Network [19755]
  Prison-Ashram Proj. [11886]
  Quartus Found. for Spiritual Res. [12361]
  The Radiance Technique Intl. Assn. [13648]
  Re-Formed Congregation of the Goddess - Intl. [20623]
  Sacred Dance Soc. [19878]
  Sacred Passage and the Way of Nature Fellowship [12362]
  Saq' Be': Org. for Mayan and Indigenous Spiritual Bodies [10226]
  Slovene Franciscan Fathers [19718]
  Soc. of the Companions of the Holy Cross [19971]
  Soc. of Jewish Sci. [20202]
  Soc. of Pragmatic Mysticism [20448]
  Soc. for the Stud. of Christian Spirituality [19826]
  Spiritual Frontiers Fellowship Intl. [20579]
  Spiritual Frontiers Fellowship Intl. [IO]
  Spiritual Life Inst. [20566]

Spiritual Unity of Nations [20580]
Sri Aurobindo Assn. [20636]
Subud U.S.A. [20589]
Swedenborg Assn. [9164]
Tayu Center [20581]
Teleos Inst. [12364]
Temple of Man [20582]
Temple of Understanding [20583]
Thanks-Giving Square [20584]
Thanks-Giving Square [IO]
Theosophical Book Assn. for the Blind [20592]
Theosophical Soc. in Am. [20593]
Truth Missionaries Chap. of Positive Accord [20585]
Unarius Acad. of Sci. [12366]
United Lodge of Theosophists [20594]
United Religions Initiative [20518]
Universal Pantheist Soc. [20586]
Urantia Found. [20587]
Urantia Found. [IO]
Wainwright House [20588]
Wisdom of the Heart Found. [IO]
Women In Conscious Creative Action [20625]
Women's Alliance for Theology, Ethics and Ritual [20626]
Women's Division of the Gen. Bd. of Global Ministries of the United Methodist Church [20269]
Women's Spirituality Forum [20628]
World Coun. of Elders [9855]
World Coun. of Religious Leaders [20519]
World Literature Ministries [19832]
World Union of Deists [20531]
Yoga Res. Found. [20637]
Zarathushtrian Assembly [20510]
Spiritual Unity of Nations [20580], PO Box 9553, Wyoming, MI 49509, (616)531-1339
Spiritualist
  Astara [20443]
  Coun. on Spiritual Practices [20564]
  Intl. Center for Spirit at Work [20575]
  Saq' Be': Org. for Mayan and Indigenous Spiritual Bodies [10226]
  Soc. of Pragmatic Mysticism [20448]
  Spiritual Sci. Fellowship [IO]
Spiritualist Assn. of Churches; Healers League of the Natl. [20449]
Spiritualist Assn. of Churches; Natl. [20453]
Spiritualist Teachers Club; Natl. [20454]
Spiritualist Yoga Fellowship [IO], Montreal, QC, Canada
Spirituality Educ. Forum; Susan B. Anthony Women's [★20628]
Spirituality Forum; Women's [20628]
Spitz Club of Am; Finnish [22267]
Spitz Dog Club [IO], Vejle, Denmark
SPJST [19139], PO Box 100, Temple, TX 76503, (254)773-1575
Spohr Soc. of Great Britain [IO], Sheffield, United Kingdom
Spokane, Portland and Seattle Railway Historical Soc. [10924], c/o Duane Cramer, Treas., 2618 NW 113th St., Vancouver, WA 98685
The Spokespeople [★13336]
The Spokespeople [★IO]
Spolecnost pro Elektroakustickou Hudbu [IO], Prague, Czech Republic
Spolecnost pro Projektove Rizeni [★IO]
Spolecnost pro Vedy a Umeni [★IO]
Spolecnost pro Vedy a Umeni [★9860]
Spolocnost na pomoc osobam s autizmom [★IO]
Spolocnost biomedicinskeho inzinierstva a medicinskej informatiky [★IO]
Spolocnost pre Planovane Rodicovstvo [★IO]
Spolocnost pre Projektove Riadenie [★IO]
Spondylitis Assn. of Am. [16377], PO Box 5872, Sherman Oaks, CA 91413, (818)981-1616
Spondylitis Assn; Ankylosing [★16377]
Sponge and Chamois Inst. [2420], c/o Jules Schwimmer, Exec. Sec., 117 Wilmot Cir., No. 2, Scarsdale, NY 10583-6761, (914)725-4646
Spongetones Fan Club - Defunct.
Sponsors of Open Housing Investment [★17819]
Spoon Collectors of Am; Souvenir [★21966]
Spoon Collectors Guild; Northeastern [22096]

Spoon Collectors Soc; Southern California Souvenir [★21966]
Spooner - Defunct.
Sport Aircraft Assn. of Australia - Chap. 1 Sydney North [IO], Frenchs Forest, Australia
Sport Aircraft Assn. of Australia - Chap. 2 Camden [IO], Picton, Australia
Sport Aircraft Assn. of Australia - Chap. 4 South Coast [IO], Figtree, Australia
Sport Aircraft Assn. of Australia - Chap. 5 Central Coast [IO], Gorokan, Australia
Sport Aircraft Assn. of Australia - Chap. 6 Coffs Harbour [IO], Nambucca Heads, Australia
Sport Aircraft Assn. of Australia - Chap. 7 Mid North Coast [IO], Port Macquarie, Australia
Sport Aircraft Assn. of Australia - Chap. 8 Mangalore [IO], Melbourne, Australia
Sport Aircraft Assn. of Australia - Chap. 10 South West, Western Australia [IO], Bunbury, Australia
Sport Aircraft Assn. of Australia - Chap. 11 Hills District, New South Wales [IO], Castle Hill, Australia
Sport Aircraft Assn. of Australia - Chap. 12 Sydney Southern [IO], Sydney, Australia
Sport Aircraft Assn. of Australia - Chap. 13 Albany District, Western Australia [IO], Wellstead, Australia
Sport Aircraft Assn. of Australia - Chap. 14 Latrobe Valley [IO], Hernes Oak, Australia
Sport Aircraft Assn. of Australia - Chap. 15 Queensland [IO], Mount Cotton, Australia
Sport Aircraft Assn. of Australia - Chap. 17 Pallamana-Murray Bridge [IO], Norwood, Australia
Sport Aircraft Assn. of Australia - Chap. 18 Melbourne [IO], Melbourne, Australia
Sport Aircraft Assn. of Australia - Chap. 19 Gold Coast [IO], Paradise Point, Australia
Sport Aircraft Assn. of Australia - Chap. 20 Kyneton District [IO], Bendigo, Australia
Sport Aircraft Assn. of Australia - Chap. 21 Moorabbin [IO], Moorabbin, Australia
Sport Aircraft Assn. of Australia - Chap. 22 Sunshine Coast, Queensland [IO], Beerwah, Australia
Sport Aircraft Assn. of Australia - Chap. 23 Frogs Hollow, New South Wales [IO], Merimbula, Australia
Sport Aircraft Assn. of Australia - Chap. 24 Jandakot, Western Australia [IO], Maida Vale, Australia
Sport Aircraft Assn. of Australia - Chap. 25 Port Lincoln [IO], Port Lincoln, Australia
Sport Balloon Soc. of the U.S.A. - Defunct.
Sport Canada [IO], Gatineau, QC, Canada
Sport Climbing Australia [IO], St. Peters, Australia
Sport Dance Fed. of the Republic of Kazakhstan [IO], Karaganda, Kazakhstan
Sport Fishery Res. Found. [★23408]
Sport Fishing Assn; Amer. [★23408]
Sport Fishing Coun; Great Lakes [23416]
Sport Fishing Inst. - Address unknown since 2001.
Sport History; North Amer. Soc. for [10139]
Sport Horse Guild; Amer. Warmblood and [4853]
Sport Horse Owners and Breeders Assn. [23539]
Sport Horse and Warmblood Registry; Iberian [4892]
Sport Horses of Color; Intl. [4905]
Sport Hunting; Comm. to Abolish [11380]
Sport Interuniversitaire Canadien [★IO]
Sport of Kings Soc. - Address unknown since 1999.
Sport Mgt. Art and Science Soc. - Defunct.
Sport Mgt. Assn. of Australia and New Zealand [IO], Bundall, Australia
Sport Marketing Assn. [3672], The Univ. of Memphis, Bur. of Sport and Leisure Commerce, Dept. of Human and Sport Sciences, 101 Wilder Tower, Memphis, TN 38152
Sport; Natl. Art Museum of [9457]
Sport; Natl. Assn. for Girls and Women in [8983]
Sport; Natl. Assn. of Governor's Councils on Physical Fitness and [★15967]
Sport; North Amer. Soc. for the Sociology of [7666]
Sport Nova Scotia [IO], Halifax, NS, Canada
Sport Org. for the Deaf in Israel [★IO]
Sport and Physical Activity; North Amer. Soc. for the Psychology of [23666]
Sport and Physical Educ; Natl. Assn. for [8986]
Sport Physiotherapy Canada [IO], Gloucester, ON, Canada

A star before a book entry number signifies that the name is not listed separately, but is mentioned within the entry.

Sport Psychology; Assn. for the Advancement of Applied [16479]
Sport and Recreation Law Assn. [23870], c/o Lori K. Miller, Exec. Dir., Campus Box 16, Wichita, KS 67260-0016, (316)978-3340
Sport Show Producers Assn; Intl. [1344]
Sport Touring Assn; Honda [22681]
Sportfishing Assn; Amer. [23408]
Sporthorse Assn; Amer. Saddlebred [4843]
Sporthorse Intl; Curly [4874]
Sporthorse Registry of Am; Akhal-Teke [★4808]
Sporting Arms and Ammunitions Mfrs. Inst. [1482], c/o Flintlock Ridge Off. Center, 11 Mile Hill Rd., Newtown, CT 06470-2359, (203)426-4358
Sporting Clays Assn; Natl. [23726]

Sporting Goods
    Amer. Cuemakers Assn. [518]
    Amer. Fly-Fishing Trade Assn. [3635]
    Amer. Recreational Golf Assn. [3636]
    Amer. Recreational Racket Sports Assn. [3637]
    Archery Trade Assn. [3638]
    Archery Trade Assn. [IO]
    Assn. of Cycle Traders [IO]
    Assn. of European Mfrs. of Sporting Ammunition [IO]
    Assn. of Golf Merchandisers [3639]
    Athletic Equip. Managers Assn. [23805]
    Bicycle Assn. of Great Britain [IO]
    Bicycle Prdt. Suppliers Assn. [3640]
    Billiard and Bowling Inst. of Am. [3641]
    Bd. Retailers Assn. [3402]
    Canadian Sporting Goods Assn. [IO]
    China Bicycle Assn. [IO]
    Diving Equip. and Marketing Assn. [IO]
    Diving Equip. and Marketing Assn. [3642]
    European Fishing Tackle Trade Assn. [IO]
    Fed. of the European Sporting Goods Indus. [IO]
    Fed. of Sports and Play Associations [IO]
    Fletchers' Company [IO]
    French Fed. of the Sporting Goods Indus. [IO]
    Golf Collectors Soc. [22031]
    Intl. Cuemakers Assn. [519]
    Italian Assn. of Sporting Goods Mfrs. [IO]
    Japan Golf Goods Assn. [IO]
    Kite Trade Association International [IO]
    Kite Trade Assn. Intl. [3643]
    Natl. Assn. of Bicycle and Sports Retailers [IO]
    Natl. Assn. of Sporting Goods Wholesalers [3644]
    Natl. Bicycle Dealers Assn. [3645]
    Natl. Fishing Lure Collectors Club [22082]
    Natl. Ski and Snowboard Retailers Assn. [3646]
    Natl. Snow Indus. Assn. [IO]
    Natl. Sporting Goods Assn. [3647]
    NSGA Team Dealer Div. [3648]
    Outdoor Indus. Assn. [IO]
    Professional Clubmakers' Soc. [3649]
    Professional Paddlesports Assn. [3650]
    SnowSports Indus. Am. [3671]
    Soccer Indus. Coun. of Am. [3651]
    Sport Marketing Assn. [3672]
    Sporting Arms and Ammunitions Mfrs. Inst. [1482]
    Sporting Goods Manufacturers Assn. Intl. [3652]
    Sporting Goods Manufacturers Assn. Intl. [IO]
    Sporting Goods Shippers Assn. [3590]
    Sports Goods Export Promotion Coun. [IO]
    Taiwan Bicycle Exporters' Assn. [IO]
    Taiwan Sporting Goods Manufacturers Assn. [IO]
    Tennis Indus. Assn. [3653]
    Trade Assn. of Paddlesports [3654]
    Trade Assn. of Paddlesports [IO]
    U.S. Racquet Stringers Assn. [3674]
    Water Sports Indus. Assn. [3655]
    World Fed. of the Sporting Goods Indus. [IO]
Sporting Goods Agents Assn. [IO], Morton Grove, IL, United States
Sporting Goods Agents Assn. [176], PO Box 998, Morton Grove, IL 60053, (847)296-3670
Sporting Goods Manufacturers Assn. [★3652]
Sporting Goods Manufacturers Assn. [★IO]
Sporting Goods Manufacturers Assn. Intl. [IO], Washington, DC, United States
Sporting Goods Manufacturers Assn. Intl. [3652], 1150 17th St. NW, Ste. 850, Washington, DC 20036, (202)775-1762
Sporting Goods Mfrs. Credit Interchange - Defunct.

Sporting Goods; Non Profit Assn. for [★3648]
Sporting Goods Representatives Assn. [★176]
Sporting Goods Representatives Assn. [★IO]
Sporting Goods Shippers Assn. [3590], 9237 Dove Ct., Gilroy, CA 95020, (408)846-9592
Sporting Wheelies and Disabled Sport and Recreation Assn. of Queensland [IO], Bowen Hills, Australia

Sports
    Access Fund [23796]
    Achilles Track Club [23331]
    Adirondack Forty-Sixers [23930]
    Adirondack Mountain Club [23931]
    Adirondack Trail Improvement Soc. [23932]
    Adventure Cycling Assn. [23304]
    Adventure Found. Pakistan [IO]
    Aeronaut Soc. [23097]
    af2 Natl. Fan Club [24829]
    Afghanistan Athletic Fed. [IO]
    Aikido Assn. of Am. [23046]
    Aikido Assn. of North Am. [23047]
    Aikido Yoshokai Assn. of North Am. [7943]
    All-Amer. Collegiate Golf Found. [23443]
    All Japan Ju-Jitsu Intl. Fed. [23577]
    All-Russia Athletic Fed. [IO]
    Amateur Athletic Assn. of Barbados [IO]
    Amateur Athletic Assn. of Cyprus [IO]
    Amateur Athletic Assn. of England [IO]
    Amateur Athletic Fed. of Iran [IO]
    Amateur Athletic Fed. Turkmenistan [IO]
    Amateur Athletic Union [23797]
    Amateur Baseball Umpires' Assn. [23798]
    Amateur Ski Instructors Assn. [23748]
    Amateur Softball Assn. of Am. [23788]
    Amateur Trapshooting Assn. [23713]
    Amaury Sport Org. [IO]
    Am. Outdoors [23681]
    Amer. Acad. of Podiatric Sports Medicine [16471]
    Amer. Acad. of Sports Physicians [16472]
    Amer. Airgun Field Target Assn. [22976]
    Amer. Amateur Baseball Cong. [23100]
    Amer. Amateur Karate Fed. [23559]
    Amer. Amputee Hockey Assn. [23799]
    Amer. Amputee Soccer Assn. [23773]
    Amer. Armsport Assn. [23059]
    Amer. Assn. of adaptedSPORTS Programs [23333]
    Amer. Assn. of Cheerleading Coaches and Advisors [23061]
    Amer. Assn. for Horsemanship Safety [12946]
    Amer. Assn. for the Improvement of Boxing [23259]
    Amer. Assn. of Snowboard Instructors [23765]
    Amer. Athletic Trainers Assn. and Certification Bd. [23953]
    Amer. Auto Racing Writers and Broadcasters Assn. [23069]
    Amer. Barefoot Club [23974]
    Amer. Barrel Racing Assn. [23492]
    Amer. Bicycle Assn. [23305]
    Amer. Bicycle Polo Assn. [23658]
    Amer. Bicycle Racing [23667]
    Amer. Blind Golf Assn. [23335]
    Amer. Canoe Assn. [23278]
    Amer. Casting Assn. [23406]
    Amer. Chen Style Tai Chi Assn. [23578]
    Amer. Coll. of Sports Medicine [16473]
    Amer. Competition Opportunities for Riders with Disabilities [23330]
    Amer. Cmpt. Barrel Racing Assn. [23493]
    Amer. Coon Hunters Assn. [23541]
    Amer. Crappie Assn. [22449]
    Amer. CueSports Alliance [23144]
    Amer. Darters Assn. [23327]
    Amer. Darts Org. [23328]
    Amer. Double Dutch League [23697]
    Amer. Endurance Ride Conf. [23933]
    Amer. Funny Car Series [23070]
    Amer. Greyhound Track Operators Assn. [23391]
    Amer. Gp. Gymnastics Assn. [23473]
    Amer. Hiking Soc. [23934]
    Amer. Hockey Coaches Assn. [23481]
    Amer. Hockey League [23482]
    Amer. Horseman Alliance [1924]
    Amer. Hot Rod Assn. [23071]

    Amer. Intl. Shuffleboard [23734]
    Amer. Judo Assn. [23552]
    Amer. Junior Golf Assn. [23444]
    Amer. Junior Rodeo Assn. [23684]
    Amer. Kempo-Karate Assn. [23579]
    Amer. Kenpo Karate Intl. [23560]
    Amer. Legion Baseball [23103]
    Amer. Lumberjack Assn. [23800]
    Amer. Medical Athletic Assn. [23650]
    Amer. Medical Tennis Assn. [23898]
    Amer. Motorcycle Heritage Found. [23621]
    Amer. Mountain Guides Assn. [23284]
    Amer. Orthopaedic Soc. for Sports Medicine [16476]
    Amer. Osteopathic Acad. of Sports Medicine [16477]
    Amer. Platform Tennis Assn. [23899]
    Amer. Power Boat Assn. [23152]
    Amer. Roque and Croquet Assn. [23090]
    Amer. Running Assn. [23651]
    Amer. Sail Training Assn. [23153]
    Amer. Sailing Assn. [23154]
    Amer. Sambo Assn. [23580]
    Amer. Self-Protection Assn. [23712]
    Amer. Shark Assn. [23156]
    Amer. Single Shot Rifle Assn. [23714]
    Amer. Ski-Bike Assn. [23801]
    Amer. Sports Assn. [3656]
    Amer. Sports Org. [23993]
    Amer. Swan Boat Assn. [23669]
    Amer. Swimming Coaches Assn. [23882]
    Amer. Tai Chi Assn. [16593]
    Amer. Teachers Assn. of the Martial Arts [23582]
    Amer. Tennis Assn. [23900]
    Amer. Track Racing Assn. [23306]
    Amer. Trails [23935]
    Amer. Trans. Bowling Assn. [23249]
    Amer. Turners [23802]
    Amer. Vaulting Assn. [23967]
    Amer. Volkssport Assn. [23803]
    Amer. Volleyball Coaches Assn. [23969]
    Amer. Water Ski Educational Found. [23975]
    Amer. Wheelchair Bowling Assn. [23339]
    Amer. Whitewater [23682]
    Amer. Wu Shu Soc. [23583]
    Amer. Yangjia Michuan Taijiquan Assn. [23584]
    Amer. Youth Soccer Org. [23774]
    America's Athletes with Disabilities [23340]
    AMOA Natl. Dart Assn. [23329]
    Anguilla Amateur Athletic Fed. [IO]
    Appalachian Mountain Club [23936]
    Appalachian Trail Conservancy [23937]
    Aquatic Exercise Assn. [23652]
    Arabian Jockey Club [23494]
    Arabian Professional and Amateur Horseman's Assn. [4862]
    Archery Range and Retailers Org. [3657]
    Archery Shooters Assn. [23050]
    Arctic Winter Games Intl. Comm. [IO]
    Asia, Pacific and Oceania Sports Assembly [IO]
    Associacao de Atletismo de Macau [IO]
    Assn. for Adventure Sports [IO]
    Assn. of Canadian Mountain Guides [IO]
    Assn. for Challenge Course Tech. [2869]
    Assn. of Commercial Diving Educators [23960]
    Assn. of Disabled Amer. Golfers [23341]
    Assn. of Dive Prog. Administrators [23377]
    Assn. for Historical Fencing [23399]
    Assn. of Luxury Suite Directors [3676]
    Assn. of Minor League Umpires [23104]
    Assn. of Northwest Steelheaders [23409]
    Assn. of Professional Ball Players of Am. [23105]
    Assn. of Recognized IOC Intl. Sports Federations [23804]
    Assn. of Recognized IOC Intl. Sports Federations [IO]
    Assn. for Renaissance Martial Arts [8820]
    Assn. of Schoolsports Clubs Czech Republic [IO]
    Assn. of Surfing Professionals [23877]
    Assn. of Volleyball Professionals [24191]
    Assn. for Women in Sports Media [3097]
    Assyrian Chaldean Athletics of North Am. [23062]
    Athletes in Action [19990]
    Athletic Assn. of Antigua and Barbuda [IO]
    Athletic Assn. of Ireland [IO]

Reference to "IO" in place of a book number signifies that the association may be found in the 45th edition of International Organizations.

Athletic Assn. of Sri Lanka [IO]
Athletic Assn. of Thailand [IO]
Athletic Equip. Managers Assn. [23805]
Athletic Fed. of Bosnia and Herzegovina [IO]
Athletic Fed. of Georgia [IO]
Athletic Fed. of Kyrgyz Republic [IO]
Athletic Fed. of Nigeria [IO]
Athletic Fed. of Republic of Armenia [IO]
Athletic Fed. of Republic of Kazakhstan [IO]
Athletic Fed. of Tajikistan [IO]
Athletic Fed. of Uzbekistan [IO]
Athletic Inst. [3658]
Athletic Solomons [IO]
Athletic Success Inst. [23665]
Athletics Assn. of Malawi [IO]
Athletics Assn. of Maldives [IO]
Athletics Associations of Guyana [IO]
Athletics Canada [IO]
Athletics Cook Islands [IO]
Athletics Fed. of India [IO]
Athletics Fed. of Pakistan [IO]
Athletics Fiji [IO]
Athletics Kenya [IO]
Athletics Namibia [IO]
Athletics New Zealand [IO]
Athletics Samoa [IO]
Atlanta Flames Fan Club [24996]
Atlantic Coast Conf. [23806]
Atletska Zveza Slovenije [IO]
Australian Football Assn. of North Am. [23429]
Australian Sports Commn. [IO]
Austrian Sports Fed. [IO]
Auto. Competition Comm. for the U.S. FIA [23073]
Azerbaijan Athletics Fed. [IO]
Babe Ruth Birthplace/Sports Legends at Camden Yards [23107]
Badminton Pan Amer. Confed. [23088]
Bahrain Athletics Assn. [IO]
Balloon Fed. of Am. [23098]
Bangladesh Amateur Athletic Assn. [IO]
Barrel Futurities of Am. [23495]
Bass Anglers Sportsman Soc. [23410]
Belarus Athletic Fed. [IO]
Belize Amateur Athletic Assn. [IO]
Bhutan Amateur Athletic Assn. [IO]
Bicycle Parking Proj. [23307]
Bicycle Ride Directors' Assn. of Am. [23308]
Big East Conf. [23807]
Big Ten Conf. [23808]
Big West Conf. [23809]
Billiard Cong. of Am. [23145]
Blackhawk Standbys, Inc. [24997]
Blind Sailing Intl. [23151]
Blueliners [24998]
BlueRibbon Coalition [23680]
Boat Owners Assn. of the U.S. [23160]
Bobby Labonte Fan Club [24999]
Botswana Athletics Assn. [IO]
Bowfishing Assn. of Am. [23411]
Bowlers to Veterans Link [23250]
Bowling Inc. [23810]
Bowling Proprietors' Assn. of Am. [3659]
Bowling Proprietors' Assn. of Canada [IO]
British Assn. of Sport and Exercise Sciences [IO]
British Virgin Islands Amateur Athletic Fed. [IO]
Brotherhood of the Jungle Cock [23412]
Brunei Amateur Athletic Assn. [IO]
Buffalo Sabres Booster Club [25000]
Bulgarian Athletics Fed. [IO]
Bullseye Assn. [23161]
Calgary Ultimate Assn. [IO]
Camanachd Assn. [IO]
Canada Games Coun. [IO]
Canadian Assn. for the Advancement of Women and Sport and Physical Activity [IO]
Canadian Colleges Athletic Assn. [IO]
Canadian Football League Players Assn. [IO]
Canadian Golf Superintendents Assn. [IO]
Canadian Interuniversity Sport [IO]
Canadian School Sport Fed. [IO]
Canadian Ski Instructors' Alliance [IO]
Caribbean Amer. Netball Assn. [23633]
Catalina 22 Natl. Sailing Assn. [23162]
Catboat Assn. [23163]

Cayman Islands Amateur Athletic Assn. [IO]
Central Collegiate Hockey Assn. [23483]
Central Coun. of Physical Recreation [IO]
Central Intercollegiate Athletic Assn. [23811]
CHA - Certified Horsemanship Assn. [23523]
Challenge Aspen at Snowmass [23342]
Championship Assn. of Mechanics [23075]
Championship Auto Racing Teams [23076]
China School Sport Fed. [IO]
Chinese-American Golf Assn. [23445]
Chinese Athletic Assn. [IO]
Chinese Radio Sports Assn. [IO]
Choy Lee Fut Martial Arts Fed. of Am. [23586]
Christian Fencers Assn. [23400]
Christian Golfers' Assn. [23283]
Christian Sports Intl. [23298]
Cinderella Softball Leagues [23789]
Citizenship Through Sports Alliance [23812]
Cleveland Hockey Booster Club [25001]
Club E: The Dale Earnhardt Fan Club [25002]
Coll. Athletic Bus. Mgt. Assn. [23813]
Coll. Gymnastics Assn. [23474]
Coll. Sports Info. Directors of Am. [23814]
Coll. Swimming Coaches Assn. of Am. [23883]
Collegiate Commissioners Assn. [23815]
Collegiate Soaring Assn. [23039]
Combat Martial Art Practitioners Assn. [23587]
Commonwealth Games Fed. [IO]
Confederacao Brasileira do Desporto Escolar [IO]
Confederacion Atletica del Uruguay [IO]
Consolidated Athletic Commn. [23816]
Continental Basketball Assn. [23129]
Continental Divide Trail Soc. [23938]
Cosmopolitan Soccer League [23775]
Coun. of Ivy Gp. Presidents [23817]
Coun. of Sailing Associations [23165]
Court of Arbitration for Sport [IO]
Cowboy Mounted Shooting Assn. [23716]
Croatian Athletic Fed. [IO]
Croquet Found. of Am. [23300]
Cross Country Ski Areas Assn. [3660]
Cyprus Sport Org. [IO]
Dale Jarrett Fan Club [25003]
Danish Athletic Fed. [IO]
Danish Schoolsport [IO]
Day Sailer Assn. [23167]
Derrike Cope Fan Club [24783]
Devils Fan Club [25004]
Divers Alert Network [23378]
Dominica Amateur Athletic Assn. [IO]
Dwarf Athletic Assn. of Am. [23063]
Eastern Assn. of Rowing Colleges [23699]
Eastern Coll. Athletic Conf. [23484]
Eastern Coll. Soccer Assn. [23776]
Eastern Intercollegiate Gymnastic League [23475]
Eastern Surfing Assn. [23878]
Eastern Winter Sports Representatives Assn. [3661]
Egyptian Athletic Fed. [IO]
El Toro Intl. Yacht Racing Assn. [23168]
Elton Sawyer Fan Club [25005]
Eritrean Natl. Athletics Fed. [IO]
Esport Escolar [IO]
Estonian Athletic Assn. [IO]
Estonian Schoolsport Union [IO]
Ethiopian Athletic Fed. [IO]
European Arenas Assn. [IO]
European Assn. for Sport Mgt. [IO]
European Athletic Assn. [IO]
European Coll. of Sport Sci. [IO]
European Gay and Lesbian Sports Fed. [IO]
European Network of Sport Sci., Educ. and Employment [IO]
European Non-Governmental Sports Org. [IO]
Federacao Angolana de Atletismo [IO]
Federacao de Atletismo da Guinea-Bissau [IO]
Federacao Mocambicana de Atletismo [IO]
Federacao Portuguesa de Atletismo [IO]
Federacion Atletica de Chile [IO]
Federacion Mexicana de Atletismo [IO]
Federacion Nicaraguense de Atletismo [IO]
Federacion Panamena de Atletismo [IO]
Federacion Paraguaya de Atletismo [IO]
Federacion Peruana de Atletismo [IO]
Federacion Venezolana de Atletismo [IO]

Federated States of Micronesia Athletic Assn. [IO]
Federatia de Atletism din Republica Moldova [IO]
Federatia Romana de Atletism [IO]
Fed. Algerienne du Sport Scolaire [IO]
Fed. Beninoise d'Athletisme Amateur [IO]
Fed. Congolaise d'Athletisme [IO]
Fed. d'Athletisme du Burundi [IO]
Fed. d'Athletisme Mauritanie [IO]
Fed. of Fly Fishers [23413]
Fed. Gabonaise d'Athletisme [IO]
Fed. Gabonaise du Sport Scolaire [IO]
Fed. of Gay Games [IO]
Fed. of Gay Games [23818]
Fed. of Intl. Polo [23819]
Fed. of Intl. Polo [IO]
Fed. Ivoirienne d'Athletisme [IO]
Fed. Libanaise d'Athletisme [IO]
Fed. Luxembourgeoise d'Athletisme [IO]
Fed. Malagasy d'Athletisme [IO]
Fed. Malienne d'Athletisme Amateur [IO]
Fed. Monegasque d'Athletisme [IO]
Fed. Nigerienne d'Athletisme [IO]
Fed. Royale Marocaine d'Athletisme [IO]
Fed. Royale Marocaine du Sport Scolaire [IO]
Fed. Rwandaise d'Athletisme [IO]
Fed. Senegalaise d'Athletisme [IO]
Fed. Togolaise d'Athletisme [IO]
Fed. Tunisienne d'Athletisme [IO]
Federazione Italiana di Atletica Leggera [IO]
Federazione Sammarinese Atletica Leggera [IO]
Fellowship of Christian Athletes [20008]
Fifty Caliber Shooters Assn. [22973]
Finnish School Sport Fed. [IO]
Finnish Sports Fed. [IO]
FJ U.S. [23169]
Florida Trail Assn. [23939]
Flying Scot Sailing Assn. [23170]
Football Writers Assn. of Am. [23430]
Force 5 Class Assn. [23171]
Free Throwers Boomerang Soc. [23247]
Future Fisherman Found. [23415]
Gaelic Athletic Assn. [IO]
Gambia Athletics Assn. [IO]
Gartlan USA's Collectors' League [22028]
Geary 18 Intl. Yacht Racing Assn. [23172]
Gen. Assn. of Intl. Sports Federations [IO]
George Khoury Assn. of Baseball Leagues [23109]
German Sports Confed. [IO]
Ghana Athletic Assn. [IO]
Global Alliance of Natl. Baton Twirling and Majorette Associations [23141]
Golf Coaches Assn. of Am. [23448]
Golf Collectors Soc. [22031]
Golf Course Builders Assn. of Am. [3662]
Golf Course Superintendents Assn. of Am. [3663]
Golf Range Assn. of Am. [3664]
Golf Tournament Assn. of Am. [23449]
Golf Writers Assn. of Am. [23450]
Grand Amer. Road Racing Assn. [23068]
Great Lakes Sport Fishing Coun. [23416]
Grenada Athletic Assn. [IO]
Gp. Fore Golf Found. [23451]
Guam Natl. Olympic Comm. [23636]
Hampton One-Design Class Racing Assn. [23173]
Handicapped Scuba Assn. [23344]
Harness Horse Youth Found. [23496]
Harness Horsemen Intl. [23497]
Harness Racing Museum and Hall of Fame [23498]
Harness Tracks of Am. [23499]
Hartford Whalers Booster Club [25006]
Heritage Trails Fund [23940]
Highamerica Balloon Club [23099]
Highlander Class Intl. Assn. [23174]
Historical Diving Soc. USA [23576]
Hockey North Am. [23486]
Hong Kong Amateur Athletic Assn. [IO]
Hong Kong Wushu Union [IO]
Horsemanship Safety Assn. [23525]
Hungarian Schoolsport Fed. [IO]
Ice Skating Institute [IO]
Icelandic Athletic Fed. [IO]
Inland Lake Yachting Assn. [23175]
Inst. of Diving [23961]

A star before a book entry number signifies that the name is not listed separately, but is mentioned within the entry.

Inter-Collegiate Sailing Assn. of North Am. [23176]
Inter-Lake Yachting Assn. [23177]
Intercollegiate Assn. of Amateur Athletes of Am. [23820]
Intercollegiate Fencing Assn. [23401]
Intercollegiate Horse Show Assn. [23526]
Intercollegiate Outing Club Assn. [23941]
Intercollegiate Rowing Assn. [23700]
Intercollegiate Tennis Assn. [23902]
Intl. 210 Assn. [23179]
Intl. 505 Yacht Racing Assn., Amer. Sect. [23180]
Intl. Acad. of Aquatic Art [23884]
Intl. Acad. for Sports Dentistry [16481]
Intl. Aerobatic Club [23040]
Intl. Aikido Assn. [23048]
Intl. Alliance for Youth Sports [23994]
Intl. Assn. of Athletics Federations [IO]
Intl. Assn. of Gay and Lesbian Martial Artists [23588]
Intl. Assn. of Sport Kinetics [IO]
Intl. Assn. for Sports Info. [IO]
Intl. Assn. for Sports Surface Sciences [IO]
Intl. Barrel Racing Assn. [23500]
Intl. Benchrest Shooters [23717]
Intl. Biathlon Union [IO]
Intl. Blue Jay Class Assn. [23181]
Intl. Bonefishing Soc. [22452]
Intl. Boxing Fed. [23260]
Intl. Boxing Hall of Fame Museum [23261]
Intl. Centre for Sports History and Culture [IO]
Intl. Chinese Boxing Assn. [23262]
Intl. Coun. for Hea., Physical Educ., Recreation, Sport, and Dance [8981]
Intl. Coun. of Sport Sci. and Physical Educ. [IO]
Intl. Cuemakers Assn. [519]
Intl. D.N. Ice Yacht Racing Assn. [23183]
Intl. Dodge Ball Fed. [23821]
International Dodge Ball Federation [IO]
Intl. Equestrian Drill Team Alliance [23527]
Intl. Etchells Class Assn. [23184]
Intl. Fed. of Bodybuilders and Fitness [IO]
Intl. Fed. of Competitive Eating [IO]
Intl. Fed. of Competitive Eating [23822]
Intl. Fed. of Sleddog Sports [23393]
Intl. Female Boxers Assn. [23263]
Intl. Flying Dutchman Class Assn. of the U.S. [23185]
Intl. Game Fish Assn. [23417]
Intl. Gay Figure Skating Union [23736]
Intl. Golf Associates [23452]
Intl. Golf Fed. [23453]
Intl. Gravity Sports Assn. [23823]
International Gravity Sports Association [IO]
Intl. Guild of Knot Tyers [IO]
Intl. Handgun Metallic Silhouette Assn. [23719]
Intl. Hobie Class Assn. [23186]
Intl. Hot Rod Assn. [23077]
Intl. Hunter Educ. Assn. [23545]
Intl. J/22 Class Assn. [23187]
Intl. Jet Sports Boating Assn. and Amer. Watercraft Assn. [23976]
Intl. Kart Fed. [23568]
Intl. Lacrosse Fed. [23570]
Intl. League of Professional Baseball Clubs [23110]
Intl. Lightning Class Assn. [23188]
Intl. Log Rolling Assn. [23824]
Intl. Log Rolling Assn. [IO]
Intl. Martial Arts League [23589]
Intl. Medalist Assn. [23825]
Intl. Medalist Assn. [IO]
Intl. Mental Game Coaching Assn. [23289]
Intl. Military Sports Coun. [IO]
Intl. Motor Contest Assn. [23078]
Intl. Motor Sports Assn. [23079]
Intl. Mountain Bicycling Assn. [23310]
Intl. Naples Sabot Assn. [23190]
Intl. Natural Bodybuilding and Fitness Fed. [23243]
Intl. Okinawa Kobudo Assn. [23590]
Intl. Penguin Class Dinghy Assn. [23191]
Intl. Physical Fitness Assn. [3665]
International Physical Fitness Association [IO]
Intl. Prindle Class Racing Assn. [23192]

Intl. Professional Rodeo Assn. [23686]
Intl. Racquetball Fed. [23677]
Intl. Senior Softball Assn. [23790]
Intl. Seven-Star Mantis Style Lee Kam Wing Martial Art Assn. - USA [23591]
Intl. Shuffleboard Assn. [23735]
Intl. Side Saddle Org. [23529]
Intl. Ski Dancing Assn. [23751]
Intl. Skiing History Assn. [10965]
Intl. Sled Dog Racing Assn. [23394]
Intl. Soap Box Derby [23770]
Intl. Soc. of Sports Nutrition [15562]
Intl. Soc. of Sports Psychology [16155]
Intl. Softball Fed. [23791]
Intl. Sport Show Producers Assn. [1344]
Intl. Sports Engg. Assn. [IO]
Intl. Sports Exchange [IO]
Intl. Sports Exchange [23826]
Intl. Sports Heritage Assn. [23827]
Intl. Sports Massage Fed. [16482]
Intl. Sunfish Class Assn. [23194]
Intl. Sungja-Do Assn. [23593]
Intl. Swimming Hall of Fame [23886]
Intl. Tennis Hall of Fame [23903]
Intl. Thunderbird Class Assn. [23195]
Intl. Track and Field Coaches Assn. [23919]
Intl. Traditional Karate Fed. [23562]
Intl. Trotting and Pacing Assn. [23501]
Intl. Unicycling Fed. [23311]
Intl. Univ. Sports Fed. [IO]
Intl. Vaulting Club [23968]
Intl. Veteran Boxers Assn. [23264]
Intl. Weight Pull Assn. [23384]
Intl. Wheelchair Road Racers Club [23346]
Intl. Women's Fishing Assn. [23419]
Intl. World Games Assn. [IO]
Intl. Yang Style Tai Chi Chuan Assn. [23594]
IOCALUM [23942]
Iran School Sport Fed. [IO]
Iraqi Amateur Athletic Fed. [IO]
Irish Schoolsport Fed. [IO]
Irish Sports Coun. [IO]
Israeli Athletic Assn. [IO]
Jamaica Amateur Athletic Assn. [IO]
Japan Aikido Assn. U.S.A. [23595]
Japan Assn. of Athletics Federations [IO]
Japanese Assn. for Women in Sport [IO]
Jet 14 Class Assn. [23196]
The Jockey Club [23502]
Jockeys' Guild [23503]
Johnny Benson Fan Club [24784]
Joint Commn. on Sports Medicine and Sci. [16483]
Jordan Amateur Athletic Fed. [IO]
Keith Bulluck Fan Club [24830]
Khmer Amateur Athletic Assn. [IO]
Kiribati Athletics Assn. [IO]
Knights Boxing Team - Intl. [23265]
Koninklijke Nederlandse Atletiek Unie [IO]
Korean Amer. Professional Tennis Assn. [23904]
Korean Athletics Fed. [IO]
Kuwait Assn. of Athletic Fed. [IO]
Ladies Professional Golf Assn. [23454]
Lakes Region Sled Dog Club [23395]
Landslaget Fysisk Fostring I Skolen [IO]
Lao Amateur Athletic Assn. [IO]
Latvian Athletic Fed. [IO]
Latvian Schoolsport Fed. [IO]
League Against Cruel Sports [IO]
League of Amer. Bicyclists [23312]
Lesotho Amateur Athletics Assn. [IO]
Liberia Track and Field Fed. [IO]
Libya Amateur Athletic Fed. [IO]
Lido 14 Intl. Class Assn. [23198]
Light Living Library [23272]
Ligue des Associations Sportives Estudiantes Lux-embourgeoises [IO]
Lincoln Heritage Trail Found. [23943]
Lithuanian Athletic Fed. [IO]
Little League Baseball and Softball [23111]
Little League Found. [23112]
Los Angeles Kings Booster Club [25007]
Maccabi USA/Sports for Israel [23828]
Macedonian School Sport Fed. [IO]
Major League Baseball [23113]

Major Wingfield Historical Soc. [23905]
Malaysia Amateur Athletic Union [IO]
Malta Amateur Athletic Assn. [IO]
Marathon Skating Intl. [23737]
Marshall Islands Athletics [IO]
Martial Arts Intl. Fed. [23596]
Martial Arts USA [23597]
Masters of Foxhounds Assn. of Am. [23546]
MC Sailing Assn. [23199]
Melpomene Inst. [16900]
Metropolitan Intercollegiate Basketball Assn. [23131]
Middle States Regatta Assn. [23701]
Midwest Winter Sports Representatives Assn. [3666]
Miniature Golf Assn. of the U.S. [23829]
Ministero de Deporte y Juventud [IO]
Mongolian Athletic Fed. [IO]
Montana Outfitters and Guides Assn. [23944]
Mountaineering Coun. of Ireland [IO]
Mountaineers [23945]
Mounted Games Across Am. [23830]
Multicultural Golf Assn. of Am. [23455]
Multisport Assn. of Russia [IO]
Musical Dog Sport Assn. [23385]
Myanmar Track and Field Fed. [IO]
Naismith Memorial Basketball Hall of Fame [23132]
Natl. Ability Center [23347]
Natl. Acad. of Sports [23831]
Natl. Advt. Golf Assn. [23456]
Natl. Air-Racing Gp. [23041]
Natl. Alliance for Accessible Golf [23348]
Natl. Alliance for Youth Sports [23290]
Natl. Amateur Athletic Assn. of Trinidad and Tobago [IO]
Natl. Amateur Baseball Fed. [23115]
Natl. Amateur Body Builders Assn. USA [23244]
Natl. Amer. Motors Drivers and Racers Assn. [23080]
Natl. Amputee Golf Assn. [23349]
Natl. Archery Assn. of the U.S. [23052]
Natl. Art Museum of Sport [9457]
Natl. Assn. of Athletic Development Directors [23832]
Natl. Assn. of Bankshot Operators [3667]
Natl. Assn. of Basketball Coaches [23133]
Natl. Assn. of Collegiate Directors of Athletics [23833]
Natl. Assn. of Collegiate Gymnastics Coaches/ Women [23476]
Natl. Assn. of Collegiate Marketing Administrators [23834]
Natl. Assn. for Girls and Women in Sport [8983]
Natl. Assn. for Hea. and Fitness [15967]
Natl. Assn. of Intercollegiate Athletics [23835]
Natl. Assn. of Left-Handed Golfers [23458]
Natl. Assn. of Off-Track Betting [23505]
Natl. Assn. for Physical Educ. in Higher Educ. [8985]
Natl. Assn. of Professional Baseball Leagues [23116]
Natl. Assn. for Recreational Equality [23836]
Natl. Assn. of Shooting Ranges [3599]
Natl. Assn. of Shooting Sports Athletes [23720]
Natl. Assn. for Sport and Physical Educ. [8986]
Natl. Assn. of Sports Commissions [23871]
Natl. Assn. of Sports Officials [23872]
Natl. Assn. of Sports Officials - Organizations Network [23873]
Natl. Assn. for Stock Car Auto Racing [23081]
Natl. Assn. of Underwater Instructors [23963]
Natl. Assn. of Women's Gymnastic's Judges [23477]
Natl. Athletic and Cultural Assn. of Ireland [IO]
Natl. Athletic Trainers' Assn. [23954]
Natl. Athletics Assn. of Zimbabwe [IO]
Natl. Auto Racing Historical Soc. [23082]
Natl. Baseball Cong. [23117]
Natl. Baseball Hall of Fame and Museum [23118]
Natl. Basketball Assn. [23134]
Natl. Basketball Athletic Trainers Assn. [23135]
Natl. Basketball Players Assn. [24192]
Natl. Baton Twirling Assn. Intl. [23142]
Natl. Bicycle League [23313]

Reference to "IO" in place of a book number signifies that the association may be found in the 45th edition of International Organizations.

Natl. Bicycle Tour Directors Assn. [23314]
Natl. Boating Fed. [23201]
Natl. Bowhunter Educ. Found. [23053]
The Natl. Bowling Assn. [23252]
Natl. Bucking Bull Assn. [23687]
Natl. Butterfly Assn. [23202]
Natl. C Scow Sailing Assn. [23203]
Natl. Camp Assn. [23277]
Natl. Center for Bicycling and Walking [23315]
Natl. Christian Barrel Racers Assn. [23507]
Natl. Christian Coll. Athletic Assn. [23837]
Natl. Class E Scow Assn. [23204]
Natl. Coalition for Promoting Physical Activity [23653]
Natl. Collegiate Athletic Assn. [23838]
Natl. Collegiate Paintball Assn. [23646]
Natl. Collegiate Roller Hockey Assn. [23487]
Natl. Collegiate Table Tennis Assn. [23895]
Natl. Coun. of Athletic Training [8987]
Natl. Coun. for School Sport [IO]
Natl. Coun. of Secondary School Athletic Directors [8988]
Natl. Coun. for Taekwondo Masters Certification [23599]
Natl. Coun. of Youth Sports [23839]
The Natl. Crossbowmen of the U.S.A. [23054]
Natl. Derby Rallies [23771]
Natl. Disability Sports Alliance [23353]
Natl. Duckpin Bowling Cong. [23253]
Natl. Elec. Drag Racing Assn. [23396]
Natl. Fastpitch Coaches Assn. [23840]
Natl. Fed. of Professional Bullriders [23688]
Natl. Fed. of Professional Trainers [23956]
Natl. Fed. of State High School Associations [23841]
Natl. Field Archery Assn. [23055]
Natl. Field Hockey Coaches Assn. [23404]
Natl. Finals Rodeo Comm. [23689]
Natl. Fishing Lure Collectors Club [22082]
Natl. Football Found. and Coll. Hall of Fame [23431]
Natl. Football League [23432]
Natl. Football League Alumni [23433]
Natl. Football League Players Assn. [23434]
Natl. Golf Course Owners Assn. [3668]
Natl. Golf Found. [3669]
Natl. Gym Assn. [23654]
Natl. Hea. Club Assn. [3670]
Natl. High School Athletic Coaches Assn. [23292]
Natl. High School Baseball Coaches Assn. [23119]
Natl. High School Rodeo Assn. [23690]
Natl. Hockey League Booster Clubs Assn. [25008]
Natl. Hockey League Players' Assn. [IO]
Natl. Horseshoe Pitchers Assn. of Am. [23540]
Natl. Hot Rod Assn. [23083]
Natl. Hunter Jumper Assn. [23530]
Natl. Hunters Assn. [23547]
Natl. Intercollegiate Rodeo Assn. [23691]
Natl. Intercollegiate Running Club Assn. [23707]
Natl. Intercollegiate Soccer Officials Assn. [23778]
Natl. Interscholastic Athletic Administrators Assn. [8989]
Natl. Interscholastic Swimming Coaches Assn. of Am. [23887]
Natl. Intramural-Recreational Sports Assn. [23842]
Natl. Jousting Assn. [23551]
Natl. Junior Baseball League [23120]
Natl. Junior Coll. Athletic Assn. [23843]
Natl. Little Britches Rodeo Assn. [23692]
Natl. Museum of Racing and Hall of Fame [23508]
Natl. Muzzle Loading Rifle Assn. [23722]
Natl. Offshore Dept. [23205]
Natl. One Design Racing Assn. [23206]
Natl. Org. for Rivers [23683]
Natl. Org. of I Walkers [23971]
Natl. Paddleball Assn. [23092]
Natl. Pitching Assn. [23121]
Natl. Public Parks Tennis Assn. [23906]
Natl. Scholastic Surfing Assn. [23880]
Natl. Semi-Professional Baseball Assn. [23122]
Natl. Senior Games Assn. [23655]
Natl. Ski Patrol Sys. [23753]
Natl. Soccer Coaches Assn. of Am. [23779]

Natl. Softball Assn. [23792]
Natl. Sporting Clays Assn. [23726]
Natl. Sportscasters and Sportswriters Assn. [3144]
Natl. Starwind/Spindrift Class Assn. [23207]
Natl. Steeplechase Assn. [23509]
Natl. Strength and Conditioning Assn. [23957]
Natl. Thoroughbred Racing Assn. [23510]
Natl. Throws Coaches Assn. [23293]
Natl. Tractor Pullers Assn. [23928]
Natl. Trail Ride Assn. [23946]
Natl. Wheelchair Basketball Assn. [23354]
Natl. Wheelchair Poolplayer Assn. [23355]
Natl. Wheelchair Softball Assn. [23356]
Natl. Women's Martial Arts Fed. [23600]
Natl. Wrestling Coaches Assn. [23987]
Natl. Youth Sports Safety Found. [16484]
Native Amer. Recreation and Sport Inst. [23631]
Native Amer. Sports Coun. [23632]
Nederlands Antilliaanse Atletiek Unie [IO]
Nepal Athletics Assn. [IO]
NETA - Natl. Exercise Trainers Assn. [23037]
New England Trails Conf. [23948]
New York Islanders Booster Club [25009]
New York Rangers Fan Club [25010]
New York Triathlon Club [23922]
New Zealand Secondary Schools Sports Coun. [IO]
NFHS Coaches Assn. [23294]
NFHS Officials Assn. [23874]
Nigerian School Sports Fed. [IO]
North Am. Wu(Hao) Taiji Fed. [23601]
North Amer. Bowhunting Coalition [22606]
North Amer. Boxing Fed. [23266]
North Amer. Bungee Assn. [23844]
North Amer. Bungee Assn. [IO]
North Amer. Chinese Soccer League [23780]
North Amer. Dog Agility Coun. [23387]
North Amer. Fastpitch Assn. [23793]
North Amer. Fishing Club [23421]
North Amer. Football League [23435]
North Amer. Formula 18 Assn. [23208]
North Amer. Hunting Club [23548]
North Amer. Kettlebell Fed. [23984]
North Amer. Natural Bodybuilding Fed. [23245]
North Amer. Network of Women Runners [23656]
North Amer. Powerlifting Fed. [23662]
North Amer. Pt-to-Pt Assn. [23511]
North Amer. Riding for the Handicapped Assn. [23357]
North Amer. Ski Joring Assn. [23845]
North Amer. Soc. for Sport History [10139]
North Amer. Sports Fed. [23065]
North Amer. Strongman [23246]
North Amer. Thoroughbred Soc. [23538]
North Amer. Tornado Assn. [23209]
North Amer. Trail Ride Conf. [23949]
North Country Trail Assn. [23950]
North-South Skirmish Assn. [23727]
Northern Marianas Islands Track and Field Fed. [IO]
Norwegian Athletics Fed. [IO]
Olson 30 Class Assn. [23210]
Oman Athletic Assn. [IO]
One-Arm Dove Hunt Assn. [23358]
One-Design Class Coun. [23211]
Oregon Horsemen's Benevolent Protective Assn. [23512]
Outfitters Assn. of Am. [23642]
Over the Hill Gang, Intl. [23846]
Over the Hill Gang, Intl. [IO]
Pacific 10 Conf. [23847]
Pacific Northwest Ski Assn. [23754]
Pakistan School Sports Assn. [IO]
Pan-American Union of Karatedo Organizations [23564]
Papua New Guinea Athletic Union [IO]
Paralympic Sports Assn. [IO]
Patience T'ai Chi Assn. [23897]
PGA TOUR Tournaments Assn. [23461]
Philadelphia Flyers Fan Club [25011]
Philippine Amateur Track and Field Assn. [IO]
Physically Challenged Golf Assn. [23359]
Pittsburgh Penguins Booster Club [25012]
Polish Amer. Golf Assn. [23462]

Polski Zwiazek Lekkiej Atletyki [IO]
Pony Baseball and Softball [23124]
Pope and Young Club [23056]
Positive Coaching Alliance [23296]
Prindle Class Assn. [23212]
Pro Athletes Outreach [20029]
Pro Players Assn. [13402]
Professional Assn. of Diving Instructors [23964]
Professional Assn. of Volleyball Officials [23875]
Professional Baseball Athletic Trainers Soc. [23125]
Professional Bowhunter's Soc. [23057]
Professional Bowlers Assn. of Am. [23254]
Professional Football Researchers Assn. [23438]
Professional Golf Teachers Assn. of Am. [23463]
Professional Golfers' Assn. of Am. [23464]
Professional Lacrosse Players Assn. [24193]
Professional Putters Assn. [23465]
Professional Rodeo Cowboys Assn. [23694]
Professional Skaters Assn. [23738]
Professional Ski Instructors of Am. [23755]
Professional Tennis Registry [23909]
Protection Sports Assn. [23848]
Qajaq USA [23981]
Qatar Assn. of Athletics Fed. [IO]
Rails-to-Trails Conservancy [23952]
Randonneurs USA [23316]
Recreational Scuba Training Coun. [23965]
Red Wing For'em Club [25013]
Reel Recovery [11519]
Referees' Assn. [IO]
Rhodes 19 Class Assn. [23213]
Rhodes Bantam Class Assn. [23214]
Ride and Tie Assn. [23849]
Roller Skating Assn. Intl. [IO]
RollerSoccer Intl. Fed. [IO]
RollerSoccer Intl. Fed. [23850]
Royal Auto. Club Motor Sports Assn. [IO]
Running USA [23708]
Saint Kitts and Nevis Amateur Athletic Assn. [IO]
Saint Lucia Athletics Assn. [IO]
Salmon Unlimited [23422]
San Juan 21 Class Assn. [23215]
Santana 20 Class Assn. [23216]
Saudi Arabian Athletics Fed. [IO]
Scoot-Tours Touring Scooter Riders Assn. [23627]
Scottish Games Assn. [IO]
Scottish Sports Assn. [IO]
Senior Roller Skaters of Am. [23739]
Sepak Takraw Assn. of Canada [IO]
Seven Seas Cruising Assn. [23217]
Seychelles Amateur Athletics Fed. [IO]
Sheclimbs [23285]
Shore Fishing and Casting Club Intl. [23423]
Shudokan Martial Arts Assn. [23603]
Sierra Leone Amateur Athletic Assn. [IO]
Singapore Amateur Athletic Assn. [IO]
Slovak Athletic Fed. [IO]
Slovak Schoolsport Assn. [IO]
Snipe Class Intl. Racing Assn. [23219]
SnowSports Indus. Am. [3671]
Soccer Assn. for Youth [23781]
Soccer Indus. Coun. of Am. [3651]
Soccer in the Streets [11789]
Soc. for Amer. Baseball Res. [23126]
Soc. of Roller Skating Teachers of Am. [23741]
Soc. of Sport and Event Photographers [3015]
Soc. of State Directors of Hea., Physical Educ. and Recreation [8992]
Somali Athletics Fed. [IO]
Sony Ericsson WTA Tour [23910]
South Amer. Athletic Confed. [IO]
Southeastern Conf. [23851]
Southern Conf. [23852]
Southwest Athletic Conf. [23853]
Southwest Athletic Conference [IO]
Special Olympics [23362]
Sport Canada [IO]
Sport Mgt. Assn. of Australia and New Zealand [IO]
Sport Marketing Assn. [3672]
Sport Nova Scotia [IO]
Sport and Recreation Law Assn. [23870]
Sports Charities USA [23854]
Sports Coun. for Northern Ireland [IO]

A star before a book entry number signifies that the name is not listed separately, but is mentioned within the entry.

Sports Coun. for Wales [IO]
Sports Hall of Oblivion [23855]
Sports Leaders UK [IO]
Sportscar Vintage Racing Assn. [23085]
SportScotland [IO]
Sportsmen's Assn. for Firearms Educ. [17600]
Sportsplex Operators and Developers Assn. [23856]
Standardbred Owners Assn. [23513]
St. Sled Sports Racers Intl. [IO]
STRIDE: Sports and Therapeutic Recreation Instruction/Developmental Educ. [8205]
Sudan Athletic Assn. [IO]
Surfrider Found. [23881]
Surinaamse Athletiek Bond [IO]
Svenska Skolidrottsforbundet [IO]
Swan Owners Assn. of Am. [23221]
Swaziland Athletics Assn. [IO]
Swaziland School Sports Assn. [IO]
Swedish Athletic Assn. [IO]
Swiss Athletic Fed. [IO]
Swiss Univ. Sports Fed. [IO]
Synchro Swimming U.S.A. [23889]
Syrian Arab Amateur Athletic Fed. [IO]
Szkolny Zwiazek Sportowy [IO]
Tandem Club of Am. [23317]
Tanzania Amateur Athletic Assn. [IO]
Thoroughbred Club of Am. [23514]
Thoroughbred Owners and Breeders Assn. [23515]
Thoroughbred Racing Associations [23516]
Thoroughbred Racing Protective Bur. [23517]
Tonga Amateur Athletic Assn. [IO]
Traditional Tae Kwon Do Chung Do Assn. [23604]
Turkish Athletic Fed. [IO]
Turks and Caicos Islands Amateur Athletic Assn. [IO]
Uganda Amateur Athletics Fed. [IO]
UK Athletics [IO]
Ukraine School Sport Fed. [IO]
Ukrainian Athletic Fed. [IO]
Ultimate Players Assn. [23375]
Underwater Soc. of Am. [23966]
Unicycling Soc. of Am. [23319]
Union Nationale du Sport Scolaire [IO]
United Arab Emirates Athletics Assn. [IO]
United Arab Emirates Interschool Sports Assn. [IO]
United Black Drag Racers Assn. [23397]
United Fly Tyers [23424]
United School Sport Assn. South Africa [IO]
United Sportsmans Assn. of North Am. [23058]
U.S. A-Class Catamaran Assn. [23225]
U.S. Adult Soccer Assn. [23857]
U.S. Adventure Racing Assn. [23672]
U.S. Aikido Fed. [23049]
U.S. Airsoft Corps [23620]
U.S. Albacore Assn. [23226]
U.S. Amateur Confed. of Roller Skating [23742]
U.S. Amateur Tug of War Assn. [23959]
U.S.A. Cricket Assn. [23299]
U.S.A. Deaf Basketball [23136]
U.S.A. Netball Assn. [23634]
U.S.A. Wushu-Kungfu Fed. [23605]
U.S. Apnea Assn. [23380]
U.S. Aquatic Sports [23890]
U.S. ArmSports [23991]
U.S. Assn. of Independent Gymnastic Clubs [3673]
U.S. Auto Club [23086]
U.S. Barrel Jumping Assn. [23743]
U.S. BASE Assn. [23647]
U.S. Basketball Writers Assn. [23137]
U.S. Biathlon Assn. [23756]
U.S. Bicycle Polo Assn. [23660]
U.S. Blind Golf Assn. [23364]
U.S. Bobsled and Skeleton Fed. [23767]
U.S. Bocce Fed. [23241]
U.S. Boomerang Assn. [23248]
U.S. Bowling Cong. [23255]
U.S. Broomball Assn. [23858]
U.S. Calf Ropers Assn. [23695]
U.S. Canoe Assn. [23279]
U.S. Classic Racing Assn. [22694]
U.S. Collegiate Athletic Assn. [23859]

U.S. Collegiate Ski and Snowboard Assn. [23757]
U.S. Collegiate Sports Coun. [23860]
U.S. Competitive Aerobics Fed. [23038]
U.S. Croquet Assn. [23301]
U.S. Cross Country Snowmobile Racing Assn. [23768]
U.S. Cultural Exchange and Sports Soc. [23861]
U.S. Curling Assn. [23302]
U.S. Cycling Fed. [23320]
U.S. Dental Tennis Assn. [23911]
U.S. Disc Sports [23376]
U.S. Dog Agility Assn. [23388]
U.S. Dressage Fed. [23533]
U.S. Equestrian Fed. [23534]
U.S. Eventing Assn. [23535]
U.S. Fastpitch Assn. [23794]
U.S. Fencing Assn. [23402]
U.S. Fencing Coaches Assn. [23403]
U.S. Field Hockey Assn. [23405]
U.S. Figure Skating Assn. [23744]
U.S. Flag Football League [23440]
U.S. Flag and Touch Football League [23441]
U.S. Floorball Assn. [23093]
U.S. Football Alliance [23442]
U.S. Futsal Fed. [23862]
U.S. Girls' Wrestling Assn. [23988]
U.S. Golf Assn. [23467]
U.S. Handball Assn. [23480]
U.S. Handcycling Fed. [23321]
U.S. Hang Gliding and Paragliding Assn. [23044]
U.S. Helice Assn. [23729]
U.S. High School Tennis Assn. [23912]
U.S. Hunter Jumper Assn. [23536]
U.S. Hydrofoil Assn. [23978]
U.S. Indoor Soccer Assn. [23782]
U.S. Intercollegiate Lacrosse Assn. [23571]
U.S. Isshinryu Karate Assn. [23565]
U.S. J/24 Class Assn. [23227]
U.S. Judo [23554]
U.S. Judo Assn. [23555]
U.S. Lacrosse [23572]
U.S. Lacrosse Assn., Women's Div. [23573]
U.S. Late Model Assn. [23087]
U.S. Lawn Bowls Assn. [23256]
U.S. Lawn Mower Racing Assn. [23673]
U.S. Luge Assn. [23575]
U.S. Mariner Class Assn. [23228]
U.S. Martial Arts Assn. [23607]
U.S. Masters Swimming [23891]
U.S. Mirror Class Assn. [23229]
U.S. Modern Pentathlon Assn. [23925]
U.S. Mondioring Assn. [23389]
U.S. Monoski Assn. [23863]
U.S. Muay Thai Assn. [23608]
U.S. Natl. Tennis Acad. [23913]
U.S. Olympic Comm. [23637]
U.S. Orienteering Fed. [23641]
U.S. Parachute Assn. [23648]
U.S. Polo Assn. [23661]
U.S. Pony Clubs [23537]
U.S. Power Soccer Assn. [23783]
U.S. Power Squadrons [23231]
U.S. Powered Paragliding Assn. [23643]
U.S. Professional Diving Coaches Assn. [23381]
U.S. Professional Poolplayers Assn. [23147]
U.S. Professional Tennis Assn. [23914]
U.S. ProMiniGolf Assn. [23469]
U.S. Quad Rugby Assn. [23705]
U.S. Racquet Stringers Assn. [3674]
U.S. Racquetball Assn. [23678]
U.S. Revolver Assn. [23731]
U.S. Rowing Assn. [23704]
U.S. Rugby Football Union [23706]
U.S. Running Streak Assn. [23709]
U.S. Sailing Assn. [23232]
U.S. Sailing Found. [23233]
U.S. Shore Angling Assn. [23425]
U.S. Ski Coaches Assn. [23758]
U.S. Ski Mountaineering Assn. [23759]
U.S. Ski and Snowboard Assn. [23760]
U.S. Ski Team Found. [23761]
U.S. Snooker Assn. [23148]
U.S. Snowshoe Assn. [23769]
U.S. Soling Assn. [23234]
U.S. Specialty Sports Assn. [23795]

U.S. Speedskating [23745]
U.S. Sport Jujitsu Assn. [23609]
U.S. Sports Acad. [23864]
U.S. Sports Acrobatics [23035]
U.S. Sports Massage Fed. [16485]
U.S. Sportsmen's Alliance [23550]
U.S. Squash Racquets Assn. [23876]
U.S. Swim School Assn. [23892]
U.S. Taekwondo Union [23610]
U.S. Tchoukball Assn. [23094]
U.S. Team Penning Assn. [23518]
U.S. Telemark Ski Assn. [23762]
U.S. Tennis Assn. [23915]
U.S. Trotting Assn. [23519]
U.S. Twirling Assn. [23143]
U.S. Volleyball Association/USA Volleyball [23970]
U.S. Water Fitness Assn. [23657]
U.S. Water Polo [23973]
U.S. Wayfarer Assn. [23235]
U.S. Windsurfing Assn. [23236]
U.S. Women's Curling Assn. [23303]
U.S. Yngling Assn. [23237]
U.S. Youth Soccer Assn. [23784]
U.S. Yudo Assn. [23611]
Universal Martial Arts Brotherhood [23612]
Universal Wheelchair Football Assn. [23368]
Univ. Athletic Assn. [23865]
US Cheng Ming Martial Arts Assn. [23613]
US Club Soccer [23785]
US Log Rolling Assn. [23982]
US Soccer [23786]
USA Badminton [23089]
U.S.A. Baseball [23127]
U.S.A. Basketball [23138]
USA Boxing [23267]
USA Broomball [23095]
USA Canoe/Kayak [23280]
USA Climbing [23286]
USA Deaf Sports Fed. [23369]
USA Diving [23382]
U.S.A. Finn Assn. [23238]
USA Gymnastics [23479]
USA Hockey [23488]
U.S.A. Karate Fed. [23566]
USA Powerlifting [23664]
USA Pulling [23929]
USA Sanatan Sports and Cultural Assn. [23787]
USA Shooting [23732]
USA Swimming [23893]
U.S.A. Table Tennis [23896]
USA Tennis - NJTL [23916]
U.S.A. Track and Field [23926]
USA Triathlon [23927]
USA Water Ski [23979]
USA Weightlifting [23985]
U.S.A. Wrestling [23989]
USGA Green Sect. [23470]
Vanuatu Athletics Assn. [IO]
Vietnam Athletic Fed. [IO]
Vintage Base Ball Assn. [23128]
Virgin Islands Olympic Comm. [23638]
Washington Capitals Fan Club [25014]
Western Athletic Conf. [23866]
Western Collegiate Hockey Assn. [23489]
Western Golf Assn. [23471]
Western Winter Sports Representatives Assn. [3675]
Western Women Premier Bowlers [23257]
Windmill Class Assn. [23239]
Women Involved in Sports Evolution [23067]
Women Outdoors [23644]
Women's All-Star Assn. [23258]
Women's Basketball Coaches Assn. [23139]
Women's Flat Track Derby Assn. [23747]
Women's Lacrosse Australia [IO]
Women's Natl. Basketball Players Assn. [23140]
Women's Professional Rodeo Assn. [23696]
Women's Sports Found. [23867]
Women's Sports Found. [IO]
World Aquatic Babies and Children [23894]
World Armsport Fed. [23060]
World Assn. of Benchers and Dead Lifters [23986]
World Atlatl Assn. [22611]
World Canine Freestyle Org. [23390]

Reference to "IO" in place of a book number signifies that the association may be found in the 45th edition of International Organizations.

World Confed. of Billiard Sports [23150]
World Darts Fed. [IO]
World Diving Coaches Assn. [23383]
World Fast-Draw Assn. [23733]
World Freestyle Watercraft Alliance [23983]
World Head of Family Sokeship Coun. [23614]
World Jeet Kune Do Fed. [23615]
World Juggling Fed. [23558]
World Martial Arts Assn. [23616]
World Masters Cross-Country Ski Assn. [23763]
World Modern Arnis Alliance [23617]
World Olympians Assn. [23639]
World Senior Golf Fed. [23472]
World Sport Stacking Assn. [23868]
World Sport Stacking Association [IO]
World Sports Medicine Assn. of Registered
    Therapists [16486]
World Traditional Karate Org. [23567]
World Ving Tsun Athletic Assn. [23618]
Worldloppet/American Birkebeiner [23764]
Wrestlers WithOut Borders [23990]
WTA Tour Players Assn. [23917]
Yachting Club of Am. [23240]
Yemen Amateur Athletic Fed. [IO]
Young Racers of Am. [23674]
Zambia Amateur Athletic Assn. [IO]
Zen-do Kai Martial Arts [23619]
Sports Acrobatic Fed; U.S. [★23035]
Sports Acrobatics; U.S. [23035]
Sports Alliance; Natl. Disability [23353]
Sports Ambassadors [20400], Dwight D. Eisenhower
    Bldg., 1956 Ambassador Way, Spokane, WA
    99224, (509)534-0431
Sports of the Amer. Assn. of Hea., Physical Educ.,
    and Recreation; Division of Girl's and Women's
    [★8983]
Sports; Armed Forces [6069]
Sports Assn; Adaptive [23332]
Sports Assn; Diabetes Exercise and [14222]
Sports Assn; Historic Motor [21657]
Sports Assn; U.S. Specialty [23795]
Sports Car Club of Am. [21787], PO Box 19400,
    Topeka, KS 66619-0400, (785)357-7222
Sports Car Club of Am; Vintage [21811]
Sports Car Collectors Soc. of America - Defunct.
Sports Car Racing; Professional [★23079]
Sports for Cerebral Palsy; Natl. Assn. of [★23353]
Sports Charities USA [23854], 1100 Larkspur Land-
    ing Cir., Ste. 340, Larkspur, CA 94939, (800)874-
    0740
Sports Club; Indoor [11951]
Sports Club; Opel Motor [21752]
Sports Coach UK [IO], Leeds, United Kingdom
Sports Coaches Assn; Natl. Youth [★23290]
Sports Comm; Armed Forces [★6069]
Sports Comm; Interservice [★6069]
Sports Coun; Interservice [★6069]
Sports Coun. for Northern Ireland [IO], Belfast,
    United Kingdom
Sports Coun. for Wales [IO], Cardiff, United
    Kingdom
Sports Dentistry; Acad. for [★16481]
Sports Dietitians Australia [IO], Richmond, Australia
Sports; Direction [13482]
Sports Evolution; Women Involved in [23067]
Sports Facilities
    Achilles Track Club [23331]
    Adirondack Forty-Sixers [23930]
    Adirondack Mountain Club [23931]
    Adirondack Trail Improvement Soc. [23932]
    Am. Outdoors [23681]
    Amer. Armsport Assn. [23059]
    Amer. Athletic Trainers Assn. and Certification Bd.
        [23953]
    Amer. Barefoot Club [23974]
    Amer. Bicycle Assn. [23305]
    Amer. Blind Bowling Assn. [23334]
    Amer. Cuemakers Assn. [518]
    Amer. Hiking Soc. [23934]
    Amer. Hot Rod Assn. [23071]
    Amer. Junior Rodeo Assn. [23684]
    Amer. Kenpo Karate Intl. [23560]
    Amer. Medical Tennis Assn. [23898]
    Amer. Motorcycle Heritage Found. [23621]
    Amer. Platform Tennis Assn. [23899]

Amer. Swimming Coaches Assn. [23882]
Amer. Tennis Assn. [23900]
Amer. Trails [23935]
Amer. Turners [23802]
Amer. Vaulting Assn. [23967]
Amer. Volleyball Coaches Assn. [23969]
Amer. Water Ski Educational Found. [23975]
Amer. Whitewater [23682]
AMOA Natl. Dart Assn. [23329]
Appalachian Mountain Club [23936]
Appalachian Trail Conservancy [23937]
Aquatic Exercise Assn. [23652]
Arabian Jockey Club [23494]
Assn. of Commercial Diving Educators [23960]
Assn. of Luxury Suite Directors [3676]
Assn. of Northwest Steelheaders [23409]
Assn. of Surfing Professionals [23877]
Athletic Equip. Managers Assn. [23805]
Babe Ruth Birthplace/Sports Legends at Camden
    Yards [23107]
Bicycle Parking Proj. [23307]
Bicycle Ride Directors' Assn. of Am. [23308]
Big West Conf. [23809]
BlueRibbon Coalition [23680]
Catalina 22 Natl. Sailing Assn. [23162]
Central Collegiate Hockey Assn. [23483]
Championship Assn. of Mechanics [23075]
Cinderella Softball Leagues [23789]
Coll. Gymnastics Assn. [23474]
Coll. Swimming Coaches Assn. of Am. [23883]
Collegiate Soaring Assn. [23039]
Continental Divide Trail Soc. [23938]
Divers Alert Network [23378]
Eastern Surfing Assn. [23878]
Field in Trust [IO]
Florida Trail Assn. [23939]
Free Throwers Boomerang Soc. [23247]
Future Fisherman Found. [23415]
Golf Tournament Assn. of Am. [23449]
Great Lakes Sport Fishing Coun. [23416]
Hampton One-Design Class Racing Assn. [23173]
Harness Horse Youth Found. [23496]
Heritage Trails Fund [23940]
Inland Lake Yachting Assn. [23175]
Inst. of Diving [23961]
Intercollegiate Outing Club Assn. [23941]
Intercollegiate Tennis Assn. [23902]
Intl. 210 Assn. [23179]
Intl. 505 Yacht Racing Assn., Amer. Sect. [23180]
Intl. Acad. of Aquatic Art [23884]
Intl. Assn. of Gay and Lesbian Martial Artists
    [23588]
Intl. Assn. for Sports and Leisure Facilities [IO]
Intl. Boxing Fed. [23260]
Intl. Boxing Hall of Fame Museum [23261]
Intl. Fed. of Sleddog Sports [23393]
Intl. Hunter Educ. Assn. [23545]
Intl. J/22 Class Assn. [23187]
Intl. Lacrosse Fed. [23570]
Intl. Mountain Bicycling Assn. [23310]
Intl. Naples Sabot Assn. [23190]
Intl. Racquetball Fed. [23677]
Intl. Sports Exchange [23826]
Intl. Sports Heritage Assn. [23827]
Intl. Swimming Hall of Fame [23886]
Intl. Tennis Hall of Fame [23903]
Intl. Thunderbird Class Assn. [23195]
Intl. Track and Field Coaches Assn. [23919]
Intl. Weight Pull Assn. [23384]
IOCALUM [23942]
Light Living Library [23272]
Lincoln Heritage Trail Found. [23943]
Maccabi USA/Sports for Israel [23828]
Major Wingfield Historical Soc. [23905]
Montana Outfitters and Guides Assn. [23944]
Mountaineers [23945]
Multicultural Golf Assn. of Am. [23455]
Natl. Ability Center [23347]
Natl. Acad. of Sports [23831]
Natl. Assn. of Athletic Development Directors
    [23832]
Natl. Assn. of Collegiate Marketing Administrators
    [23834]
Natl. Assn. of Shooting Ranges [3599]
Natl. Assn. of Sports Commissions [23871]

Natl. Assn. of Sports Officials [23872]
Natl. Assn. of Sports Officials - Organizations
    Network [23873]
Natl. Assn. of Underwater Instructors [23963]
Natl. Athletic Trainers' Assn. [23954]
Natl. Baseball Hall of Fame and Museum [23118]
Natl. Basketball Athletic Trainers Assn. [23135]
Natl. Camp Assn. [23277]
Natl. Disability Sports Alliance [23353]
Natl. Fed. of Professional Trainers [23956]
Natl. Football League Players Assn. [23434]
Natl. Interscholastic Swimming Coaches Assn. of
    Am. [23887]
Natl. Junior Baseball League [23120]
Natl. Org. for Rivers [23683]
Natl. Org. of I Walkers [23971]
Natl. Public Parks Tennis Assn. [23906]
Natl. Scholastic Surfing Assn. [23880]
Natl. Senior Games Assn. [23655]
Natl. Softball Assn. [23792]
Natl. Sporting Clays Assn. [23726]
Natl. Starwind/Spindrift Class Assn. [23207]
Natl. Strength and Conditioning Assn. [23957]
Natl. Thoroughbred Racing Assn. [23510]
Natl. Tractor Pullers Assn. [23928]
Natl. Women's Martial Arts Fed. [23600]
Natl. Wrestling Coaches Assn. [23987]
NETA - Natl. Exercise Trainers Assn. [23037]
New England Trails Conf. [23948]
New York Triathlon Club [23922]
NFHS Officials Assn. [23874]
North Amer. Fishing Club [23421]
North Amer. Network of Women Runners [23656]
North Country Trail Assn. [23950]
Olson 30 Class Assn. [23210]
Over the Hill Gang, Intl. [23846]
Pan-American Union of Karatedo Organizations
    [23564]
Patience T'ai Chi Assn. [23897]
Professional Assn. of Diving Instructors [23964]
Professional Assn. of Volleyball Officials [23875]
Professional Baseball Athletic Trainers Soc.
    [23125]
Professional Tennis Registry [23909]
Rails-to-Trails Conservancy [23952]
Recreational Scuba Training Coun. [23965]
San Juan 21 Class Assn. [23215]
Scoot-Tours Touring Scooter Riders Assn. [23627]
Sony Ericsson WTA Tour [23910]
Sport Marketing Assn. [3672]
Sports Hall of Oblivion [23855]
Sports Turf Res. Inst. [IO]
Sportscar Vintage Racing Assn. [23085]
Sportsplex Operators and Developers Assn.
    [23856]
Stadium Managers Assn. [23869]
Surfrider Found. [23881]
Synchro Swimming U.S.A. [23889]
Tandem Club of Am. [23317]
Ultimate Players Assn. [23375]
Underwater Soc. of Am. [23966]
United Fly Tyers [23424]
U.S. Amateur Tug of War Assn. [23959]
U.S. Aquatic Sports [23890]
U.S. ArmSports [23991]
U.S. Blind Golf Assn. [23364]
U.S. Bobsled and Skeleton Fed. [23767]
U.S. Bocce Fed. [23241]
U.S. Competitive Aerobics Fed. [23038]
U.S. Cultural Exchange and Sports Soc. [23861]
U.S. Dental Tennis Assn. [23911]
U.S. Disc Sports [23376]
U.S. Flag and Touch Football League [23441]
U.S. Judo [23554]
U.S. Judo Assn. [23555]
U.S. Masters Swimming [23891]
U.S. Mirror Class Assn. [23229]
U.S. Natl. Tennis Acad. [23913]
U.S. Professional Diving Coaches Assn. [23381]
U.S. Professional Tennis Assn. [23914]
U.S. Ski and Snowboard Assn. [23760]
U.S. Soling Assn. [23234]
U.S. Sports Acad. [23864]
U.S. Squash Racquets Assn. [23876]
U.S. Swim School Assn. [23892]

A star before a book entry number signifies that the name is not listed separately, but is mentioned within the entry.

U.S. Tennis Assn. [23915]
U.S. Volleyball Association/USA Volleyball [23970]
U.S. Water Fitness Assn. [23657]
U.S. Yngling Assn. [23237]
Univ. Athletic Assn. [23865]
USA Canoe/Kayak [23280]
USA Diving [23382]
U.S.A. Karate Fed. [23566]
USA Roller Sports [23746]
USA Shooting [23732]
USA Swimming [23893]
U.S.A. Table Tennis [23896]
USA Tennis - NJTL [23916]
U.S.A. Track and Field [23926]
USA Triathlon [23927]
USA Water Ski [23979]
USA Weightlifting [23985]
U.S.A. Wrestling [23989]
USGA Green Sect. [23470]
Western Athletic Conf. [23866]
Western Collegiate Hockey Assn. [23489]
Western Women Premier Bowlers [23257]
Women Outdoors [23644]
Women's All-Star Assn. [23258]
Women's Sports Found. [23867]
World Aquatic Babies and Children [23894]
World Armsport Fed. [23060]
World Diving Coaches Assn. [23383]
World Fast-Draw Assn. [23733]
World Masters Cross-Country Ski Assn. [23763]
WTA Tour Players Assn. [23917]
Sports Fed. and Olympic Comm. of Hong Kong,
China [IO], Hong Kong, People's Republic of
China
Sports Fed; U.S.A. [★23637]
Sports Fed; USA Deaf [23369]
Sports Field Contractors Association - Defunct.
Sports Found; Natl. Shooting [23724]
Sports Goods Export Promotion Coun. [IO], New
Delhi, India
Sports Hall of Oblivion [23855], PO Box 69025,
Pleasant Ridge, MI 48069, (248)543-9412
Sports Hall of SHAME - Defunct.
The Sports Indus. Fed. [★IO]
Sports Indus. Assn; Water [3655]
Sports Injuries and Physical Fitness; Amer. Chiro-
practic Assn. Coun. on [13989]
Sports; Intl. Fed. of Sleddog [23393]
Sports for Israel; Maccabi USA/ [23828]
Sports in Israel; U.S. Comm. for [★23828]
Sports for Israel; U.S. Comm. [★23828]
Sports; Joint Commn. on Competitive Safeguards
and the Medical Aspects of [★16483]
Sports Journalists' Assn. of Great Britain [IO], South
Croydon, United Kingdom
Sports for Kids; Say Yes to Better [★23290]
Sports Law
Australian and New Zealand Sports Law Assn.
[IO]
Black Entertainment and Sports Lawyers Assn.
[5687]
Sport and Recreation Law Assn. [23870]
Sports Lawyers Assn. [6266]
U.S. Sportsmen's Alliance [23550]
Sports Lawyers Assn. [6266], 12100 Sunset Hills
Rd., Ste. 130, Reston, VA 20190, (703)437-4377
Sports Lawyers Assn; Black Entertainment and
[5687]
Sports Leaders UK [IO], Milton Keynes, United
Kingdom
Sports Legends at Camden Yards; Babe Ruth
Birthplace/ [23107]
Sports Media; Assn. for Women in [3097]
Sports Medical Comm. of Ethiopia [IO], Addis
Ababa, Ethiopia
Sports Medicine
Amer. Acad. of Podiatric Sports Medicine [16471]
Amer. Acad. of Sports Physicians [16472]
Amer. Athletic Trainers Assn. and Certification Bd.
[23953]
Amer. Chiropractic Assn. Coun. on Sports Injuries
and Physical Fitness [13989]
Amer. Coll. of Sports Medicine [16473]
Amer. Medical Equestrian Association/Safe Riders
Found. [16474]

Amer. Medical Soc. for Sports Medicine [16475]
Amer. Nordic Walking Assn. [15960]
Amer. Orthopaedic Soc. for Sports Medicine
[16476]
Amer. Osteopathic Acad. of Sports Medicine
[16477]
Amer. Running Assn. [23651]
Amer. Sports Medicine Inst. [16478]
Asociacion Guatemalteca de Medicina Deportiva
[IO]
Asociation Ivorienne de Medicine Sportive [IO]
Associacion Nicaraguense de Medicina del De-
porte [IO]
Association for the Advancement of Applied Sport
Psychology [IO]
Assn. for the Advancement of Applied Sport
Psychology [16479]
Assn. Gabonaise de Medecine du Sport [IO]
Assn. Marocaine de Medecine du Sport [IO]
Assn. Mauritaninne de Medecine du Sport [IO]
Assn. of Sports Medicine of the Balkans [IO]
Assn. of Sports Medicine of Ghana [IO]
Assn. Tchadienne de Medecine du Sport [IO]
Austrian Soc. of Sports Medicine [IO]
Bangladesh Assn. of Sports Medicine [IO]
Barbados Sport Medicine Assn. [IO]
Big Picture Alliance [16480]
Bosnia and Herzegovina Sports Medicine Assn.
[IO]
British Assn. of Sport Rehabilitators and Trainers
[IO]
Canadian Acad. of Sport Medicine [IO]
Canadian Soc. for Psychomotor Learning and
Sport Psychology [IO]
Caribbean Assn. of Sports Medicine [IO]
Center for Sports and Osteopathic Medicine
[16055]
Croatian Sports Medicine Soc. [IO]
Cyprus Assn. of Sports Medicine [IO]
Czech Soc. of Sports Medicine [IO]
Danish Assn. of Sports Medicine [IO]
Estonian Sports Medicine Fed. [IO]
European Soc. of Sports Traumatology, Knee
Surgery and Arthroscopy 2000 [IO]
Exercise Safety Assn. [15963]
Federacion Argentina de Medicina del Deporte
[IO]
Federacion Boliviana de Medicina Deportiva [IO]
Federacion Cubana de Medicina del Deporte [IO]
Federacion Ecuatoriana de Medicina Deportiva
[IO]
Federacion Espanola de Medicina del Deporte
[IO]
Finnish Soc. of Sports Medicine [IO]
Georgian Assn. of Sports Medicine [IO]
German Fed. of Sports Medicine and Prevention
[IO]
Hong Kong Assn. of Sports Medicine and Sports
Sci. [IO]
Hungarian Soc. of Sports Medicine [IO]
Indian Assn. of Sports Medicine [IO]
Indonesian Assn. for Sports Hea. [IO]
Instituto di Medicina Pa Deporte di Aruba [IO]
Intl. Acad. of Olympic Chiropractic Officers
[14006]
Intl. Acad. for Sports Dentistry [16481]
Intl. Acad. for Sports Dentistry [IO]
Intl. Fed. of Sports Chiropractic [IO]
Intl. Fed. of Sports Medicine [IO]
Intl. Mental Game Coaching Assn. [23289]
Intl. Soc. of Arthroscopy, Knee Surgery and Ortho-
paedic Sports Medicine [15771]
Intl. Soc. for Ski Traumatology and Medicine of
Winter Sports [IO]
Intl. Sports Massage Fed. [16482]
Israel Soc. of Sports Medicine [IO]
Italian Sports Medicine Fed. [IO]
Joint Commn. on Sports Medicine and Sci.
[16483]
Kazakhistanian Assn. of Sports Medicine [IO]
Kuwait Sports Medicine Assn. [IO]
Latvia Sports Medicine Assn. [IO]
Lithuanian Sports Medicine Assn. [IO]
Macau Sports Medicine Assn. [IO]
Natl. Athletic Trainers' Assn. [23954]

Natl. Fed. of Professional Trainers [23956]
Natl. Strength and Conditioning Assn. [23957]
Natl. Youth Sports Safety Found. [16484]
Netherlands Assn. of Sports Medicine [IO]
Nigerian Assn. of Sports Medicine [IO]
Pakistan Sports Medicine Assn. [IO]
Poland Sports Medicine Assn. [IO]
Saudi Arabian Sports Medicine Assn. [IO]
Slovak Soc. of Sports Medicine [IO]
Slovenia Sports Medicine Soc. [IO]
Sociedad Chilena de Medicina del Deporte [IO]
Sociedad Dominicane de Medicina del Deporte
[IO]
Sociedad Paraguaya de Medicina del Deporte
[IO]
Sociedad Peruana de Medicina y Ciencias Aplica-
das al Deporte [IO]
Sociedad Venezolana de Medicina Deportiva [IO]
Sociedade Brasileira de Medicina do Esporte [IO]
Sociedade Portuguesa de Medicina Desportiva
[IO]
Societatea Romana de Medicina Sportiva [IO]
Societe Francaise de Medecine du Sport [IO]
Societe Swisse de Medecine du Sport [IO]
Societe Tunisien de Medecine du Sport [IO]
South African Sports Medicine Assn. [IO]
Sports Medical Comm. of Ethiopia [IO]
Sports Medicine Assn. of Belgium [IO]
Sports Medicine Assn. of Greece [IO]
Sports Medicine Assn. of the Philippines [IO]
Sports Medicine Australia [IO]
Sports Medicine Australia - New South Wales Br.
[IO]
Sports Medicine Australia - Northern Territory Br.
[IO]
Sports Medicine Australia - Queensland Br. [IO]
Sports Medicine Australia - Victoria Br. [IO]
Sports Medicine Australia - Western Australia Br.
[IO]
Sports Medicine Fed. of Iran [IO]
Sri Lanka Sports Medicine Assn. [IO]
Tanzania Sports Medicine Assn. [IO]
Turkish Assn. of Sports Medicine [IO]
Uganda Games and Sports Medicine Assn. [IO]
United Arab Emirates Sports Medicine Comm.
[IO]
U.S. Running Streak Assn. [23709]
U.S. Sports Chiropractic Fed. [23282]
U.S. Sports Massage Fed. [16485]
World Sports Medicine Assn. of Registered
Therapists [16486]
World Sports Medicine Assn. of Registered
Therapists [IO]
Zimbabwe Sports Medicine Assn. [IO]
Sports Medicine Assn; Amer. Canine [16761]
Sports Medicine Assn. of Belgium [IO], Leuven,
Belgium
Sports Medicine Assn. of Greece [IO], Thessaloniki,
Greece
Sports Medicine Assn. of the Philippines [IO],
Manila, Philippines
Sports Medicine Australia [IO], Canberra, Australia
Sports Medicine Australia - New South Wales Br.
[IO], Rhodes, Australia
Sports Medicine Australia - Northern Territory Br.
[IO], Darwin, Australia
Sports Medicine Australia - Queensland Br. [IO], Mil-
ton, Australia
Sports Medicine Australia - Victoria Br. [IO], South
Melbourne, Australia
Sports Medicine Australia - Western Australia Br.
[IO], Claremont, Australia
Sports Medicine Fed. of Iran [IO], Tehran, Iran
Sports; Natl. Alliance for Youth [23290]
Sports Officials
Achilles Track Club [23331]
Amateur Baseball Umpires' Assn. [23798]
Am. Outdoors [23681]
Amer. Armsport Assn. [23059]
Amer. Barefoot Club [23974]
Amer. Baseball Coaches Assn. [23101]
Amer. Bicycle Assn. [23305]
Amer. Hiking Soc. [23934]
Amer. Hot Rod Assn. [23071]
Amer. Junior Rodeo Assn. [23684]

Reference to "IO" in place of a book number signifies that the association may be found in the 45th edition of International Organizations.

Amer. Kenpo Karate Intl. [23560]
Amer. Motorcycle Heritage Found. [23621]
Amer. Platform Tennis Assn. [23899]
Amer. Swimming Coaches Assn. [23882]
Amer. Tennis Assn. [23900]
Amer. Trails [23935]
Amer. Turners [23802]
Amer. Vaulting Assn. [23967]
Amer. Volleyball Coaches Assn. [23969]
Amer. Water Ski Educational Found. [23975]
Amer. Whitewater [23682]
AMOA Natl. Dart Assn. [23329]
Aquatic Exercise Assn. [23652]
Arabian Jockey Club [23494]
Assn. of Commercial Diving Educators [23960]
Assn. of Dive Prog. Administrators [23377]
Assn. of Minor League Umpires [23104]
Assn. of Northwest Steelheaders [23409]
Assn. of Professional Ball Players of Am. [23105]
Assn. of Surfing Professionals [23877]
Athletic Equip. Managers Assn. [23805]
Babe Ruth Birthplace/Sports Legends at Camden
  Yards [23107]
Bicycle Parking Proj. [23307]
Bicycle Ride Directors' Assn. of Am. [23308]
Big West Conf. [23809]
Catalina 22 Natl. Sailing Assn. [23162]
Central Collegiate Hockey Assn. [23483]
Championship Assn. of Mechanics [23075]
Cinderella Softball Leagues [23789]
Coll. Gymnastics Assn. [23474]
Coll. Swimming Coaches Assn. of Am. [23883]
Collegiate Soaring Assn. [23039]
Continental Divide Trail Soc. [23938]
Divers Alert Network [23378]
Eastern Surfing Assn. [23878]
Florida Trail Assn. [23939]
Free Throwers Boomerang Soc. [23247]
Future Fisherman Found. [23415]
Golf Tournament Assn. of Am. [23449]
Great Lakes Sport Fishing Coun. [23416]
Hampton One-Design Class Racing Assn. [23173]
Harness Horse Youth Found. [23496]
Heritage Trails Fund [23940]
Inland Lake Yachting Assn. [23175]
Inst. of Diving [23961]
Intercollegiate Tennis Assn. [23902]
Intl. 210 Assn. [23179]
Intl. 505 Yacht Racing Assn., Amer. Sect. [23180]
Intl. Acad. of Aquatic Art [23884]
Intl. Assn. of Gay and Lesbian Martial Artists
  [23588]
Intl. Boxing Fed. [23260]
Intl. Boxing Hall of Fame Museum [23261]
Intl. Fed. of Sleddog Sports [23393]
Intl. Hunter Educ. Assn. [23545]
Intl. J/22 Class Assn. [23187]
Intl. Lacrosse Fed. [23570]
Intl. Mental Game Coaching Assn. [23289]
Intl. Mountain Bicycling Assn. [23310]
Intl. Naples Sabot Assn. [23190]
Intl. Racquetball Fed. [23677]
Intl. Sports Exchange [23826]
Intl. Sports Heritage Assn. [23827]
Intl. Swimming Hall of Fame [23886]
Intl. Tennis Hall of Fame [23903]
Intl. Thunderbird Class Assn. [23195]
Intl. Track and Field Coaches Assn. [23919]
Intl. Veteran Boxers Assn. [23264]
Intl. Weight Pull Assn. [23384]
Light Living Library [23272]
Lincoln Heritage Trail Found. [23943]
Maccabi USA/Sports for Israel [23828]
Major Wingfield Historical Soc. [23905]
Montana Outfitters and Guides Assn. [23944]
Mountaineers [23945]
Multicultural Golf Assn. of Am. [23455]
Naismith Memorial Basketball Hall of Fame
  [23132]
Natl. Ability Center [23347]
Natl. Acad. of Sports [23831]
Natl. Assn. of Athletic Development Directors
  [23832]
Natl. Assn. of Basketball Coaches [23133]
Natl. Assn. of Collegiate Marketing Administrators
  [23834]

Natl. Assn. of Sports Commissions [23871]
Natl. Assn. of Sports Officials [23872]
Natl. Assn. of Sports Officials - Organizations
  Network [23873]
Natl. Assn. of Underwater Instructors [23963]
Natl. Assn. of Women's Gymnastic's Judges
  [23477]
Natl. Baseball Hall of Fame and Museum [23118]
Natl. Basketball Athletic Trainers Assn. [23135]
Natl. Bicycle Tour Directors Assn. [23314]
Natl. Camp Assn. [23277]
Natl. Disability Sports Alliance [23353]
Natl. Fastpitch Coaches Assn. [23840]
Natl. Fed. of Professional Trainers [23956]
Natl. Football Found. and Coll. Hall of Fame
  [23431]
Natl. Football League Players Assn. [23434]
Natl. High School Athletic Coaches Assn. [23292]
Natl. High School Baseball Coaches Assn.
  [23119]
Natl. Intercollegiate Soccer Officials Assn. [23778]
Natl. Interscholastic Swimming Coaches Assn. of
  Am. [23887]
Natl. Junior Baseball League [23120]
Natl. Org. for Rivers [23683]
Natl. Org. of I Walkers [23971]
Natl. Public Parks Tennis Assn. [23906]
Natl. Scholastic Surfing Assn. [23880]
Natl. Senior Games Assn. [23655]
Natl. Softball Assn. [23792]
Natl. Sporting Clays Assn. [23726]
Natl. Starwind/Spindrift Class Assn. [23207]
Natl. Thoroughbred Racing Assn. [23510]
Natl. Throws Coaches Assn. [23293]
Natl. Tractor Pullers Assn. [23928]
Natl. Women's Martial Arts Fed. [23600]
Natl. Wrestling Coaches Assn. [23987]
NETA - Natl. Exercise Trainers Assn. [23037]
New England Trails Conf. [23948]
New York Triathlon Club [23922]
NFHS Officials Assn. [23874]
North Amer. Fishing Club [23421]
North Amer. Network of Women Runners [23656]
North Amer. Sports Fed. [23065]
North Country Trail Assn. [23950]
Olson 30 Class Assn. [23210]
Over the Hill Gang, Intl. [23846]
Pan-American Union of Karatedo Organizations
  [23564]
Positive Coaching Alliance [23296]
Professional Assn. of Diving Instructors [23964]
Professional Assn. of Volleyball Officials [23875]
Professional Baseball Athletic Trainers Soc.
  [23125]
Professional Tennis Registry [23909]
Recreational Scuba Training Coun. [23965]
San Juan 21 Class Assn. [23215]
Scoot-Tours Touring Scooter Riders Assn. [23627]
Sony Ericsson WTA Tour [23910]
Sports Hall of Oblivion [23855]
Sportscar Vintage Racing Assn. [23085]
Surfrider Found. [23881]
Synchro Swimming U.S.A. [23889]
Tandem Club of Am. [23317]
Ultimate Players Assn. [23375]
Underwater Soc. of Am. [23966]
United Fly Tyers [23424]
U.S. Adventure Racing Assn. [23672]
U.S. Amateur Tug of War Assn. [23959]
U.S. Aquatic Sports [23890]
U.S. ArmSports [23890]
U.S. Bobsled and Skeleton Fed. [23767]
U.S. Bocce Fed. [23241]
U.S. Competitive Aerobics Fed. [23038]
U.S. Cultural Exchange and Sports Soc. [23861]
U.S. Disc Sports [23376]
U.S. Flag and Touch Football League [23441]
U.S. High School Tennis Assn. [23912]
U.S. Judo [23554]
U.S. Judo Assn. [23555]
U.S. Masters Swimming [23891]
U.S. Mirror Class Assn. [23229]
U.S. Natl. Tennis Acad. [23913]
U.S. Professional Diving Coaches Assn. [23381]
U.S. Professional Tennis Assn. [23914]

U.S. Ski and Snowboard Assn. [23760]
U.S. Soling Assn. [23234]
U.S. Specialty Sports Assn. [23795]
U.S. Sports Acad. [23864]
U.S. Squash Racquets Assn. [23876]
U.S. Swim School Assn. [23892]
U.S. Tennis Assn. [23915]
U.S. Volleyball Association/USA Volleyball [23970]
U.S. Water Fitness Assn. [23657]
U.S. Water Polo [23973]
U.S. Yngling Assn. [23237]
Univ. Athletic Assn. [23865]
USA Boxing [23267]
USA Canoe/Kayak [23280]
USA Diving [23382]
U.S.A. Karate Fed. [23566]
USA Swimming [23893]
U.S.A. Table Tennis [23896]
USA Tennis - NJTL [23916]
U.S.A. Track and Field [23926]
USA Triathlon [23927]
USA Water Ski [23979]
USA Weightlifting [23985]
U.S.A. Wrestling [23989]
USGA Green Sect. [23470]
Western Athletic Conf. [23866]
Western Collegiate Hockey Assn. [23489]
Western Women Premier Bowlers [23257]
Women Outdoors [23644]
Women's All-Star Assn. [23258]
Women's Basketball Coaches Assn. [23139]
Women's Sports Found. [23867]
World Aquatic Babies and Children [23894]
World Armsport Fed. [23060]
World Diving Coaches Assn. [23383]
World Fast-Draw Assn. [23733]
World Masters Cross-Country Ski Assn. [23763]
WTA Tour Players Assn. [23917]
Sports Officials' Development Prog. and Media
  Center [★23842]
Sports Org; U.S. Natl. Senior [★23655]
Sports and Osteopathic Medicine; Center for [16055]
Sports Owners Assn; Triumph [★21813]
Sports for the People - Defunct.
Sports Philatelists Intl. [22877], c/o Margaret A.
  Jones, Membership Chair, 5310 Lindenwood Ave.,
  St. Louis, MO 63109-1758
Sports Philatelists International [IO], St. Louis, MO,
  United States
Sports Potential; Assn. for the Advancement of
  [★16480]
Sports Program; Youth [★23353]
Sports and Recreation Assn; Natl. Handicapped
  [★23343]
Sports Sect., Amer. Coll. Public Relations Assn.
  [★23814]
Sports and Therapeutic Recreation Instruction/
  Developmental Educ; STRIDE: [8205]
Sports Turf Managers Assn. [2399], 805 New
  Hampshire St., Ste. E, Lawrence, KS 66044,
  (800)323-3875
Sports Turf Managers Association [IO], Lawrence,
  KS, United States
Sports Turf Res. Inst. [IO], Bingley, United Kingdom
Sports; U.S. Assn. of Cerebral Palsy [★23353]
Sports; U.S. Disc [23376]
Sports USA; Disabled [23343]
Sports - U.S.A; Intl. People's [★23803]
Sports, USA; Wheelchair [23371]
Sportscar Vintage Racing Assn. [23085], 257 Dekalb
  Indus. Way, Decatur, GA 30030, (404)298-3323
Sportscasters Assn; Amer. [544]
Sportscasters and Sportswriters Assn; Natl. [3144]
SportScotland [IO], Edinburgh, United Kingdom
Sportsman Soc; Bass Anglers [23410]
Sportsmans Assn. of North Am; United [23058]
Sportsmanship Brotherhood - Defunct.
Sportsmen's Alliance; U.S. [23550]
Sportsmen's Assn. for Firearms Educ. [17600], PO
  Box 343, Commack, NY 11725, (631)475-8125
Sportsmen's Assn; Natl. Inconvenienced [★23343]
Sportsmen's Clubs; Boys of Woodcraft Sportsmen's
  Clubs/Girl of Woodcraft [★19440]
Sportsmen's Clubs/Girl of Woodcraft Sportsmen's
  Clubs; Boys of Woodcraft [★19440]

A star before a book entry number signifies that the name is not listed separately, but is mentioned within the entry.

Sportsmen's Ser. Bur. [★23724]
Sportsplex Operators and Developers of Am. [★23856]
Sportsplex Operators and Developers Assn. [23856], PO Box 24263, Westgate Sta., Rochester, NY 14624-0263, (585)426-2215
Sportsplex Owners and Directors of Am. [★23856]
Sportswear Assn; Natl. Knitwear and [251]
Sportswear Assn; Natl. Outerwear and [★221]
Sportswear Assn; Natl. Skirt and [★254]
Sportswear Assn; New York Skirt and [254]
Sportswear Buyers; Natl. Assn. of Men's [247]
Sportswear Manufacturers; Natl. Assn. of Skirt, Pajama and [★221]
Sportswear Salesman's Assn. - Address unknown since 1994.
Sportswriters Assn; Natl. Sportscasters and [3144]
Spot Rabbit Club; Amer. English [5134]
Spotted Asses; Amer. Coun. of [4125]
Spotted Draft Horse Assn; North Amer. [4938]
Spotted Horse Registry Assn; Intl. [4907]
Spotted Poland China Record; Amer. [★5239]
Spotted Poland China Record; Natl. [★5239]
Spotted Saddle Horse Assn; Natl. [4927]
Spotted Saddle Horse Breeders' and Exhibitors' Assn. [4955], PO Box 1046, Shelbyville, TN 37162, (931)684-7496
Spotted Swine Record [★5239]
Spotted Swine Record; Natl. [5239]
Spouse Found; Well [★16553]
Spouse Network; Straight [12508]
Spouses of Gays Assn. - Defunct.
Spray Mfrs; Assn. of Defensive [3544]
Sprayberry/Spraberry/Sprabary Family Assn. - Defunct.
Sprayed Concrete Assn. [IO], Aldershot, United Kingdom
Sprayed Mineral Fiber Mfrs; Assn. - Defunct.
SPRI [949], 77 Rumford Ave., Ste. 3B, Waltham, MA 02453, (781)647-7026
Spring of Living Water Ministry [20556], Hope Outreach, PO Box 1067, Enid, OK 73702-1067, (580)237-4673
Spring Mfrs. Assn. [★1835]
Spring Mfrs. Inst. [1835], 2001 Midwest Rd., Ste. 106, Oak Brook, IL 60523-1335, (630)495-8588
Spring Res. Assn. [★IO]
Spring Res. Inst. [399], 3034 N Fleming Cir., Shelbyville, IN 46176, (317)398-3822
Spring Res. and Mfrs. Assn. [★IO]
Spring Ser. Assn., Suspension Specialists [★427]
Springboard Enterprises [4046], 2100 Foxhall Rd. NW, Washington, DC 20007, (202)242-6282
Springer Rescue Am; English [11390]
Springer Spaniel Club of Am; Welsh [22380]
Springer Spaniel Field Trial Assn; English [22262]
Springfield Support Club: Human Touch; Rick [24966]
Sprinkler Assn; Amer. Fire [3437]
Sprinkler Assn; Canadian Automatic [IO]
Sprinkler Assn; Natl. Automatic [★3449]
Sprinkler Assn; Natl. Fire [3449]
Sprinkler and Fire Control Assn; Natl. Automatic [★3449]
Sprinkler Irrigation Assn. [★182]
Sprinkler Irrigation Assn. [★IO]
Sprit and Vinleverantorsforeningen [★IO]
Sprite-Midget Owners Group - Address unknown since 1999.
Sprocket Chain Mfrs. Assn; Amer. [★1993]
Sprue Assn; Midwestern Celiac [★14413]
Sprue; Whoo Who [★15543]
Spuria Iris Soc. [22546], c/o Keith Smith, Pres., 6008 Wonder Dr., Fort Worth, TX 76133, (817)292-5804
Spuria Iris Society [IO], Gower, MO, United States
Spurlock Family Assn. [21059], c/o Bill Spurlock, 5950 Western Hills Dr., Norcross, GA 30071
Spurlock/Scurlock Family [★21059]
SQL Server; Professional Assn. for [909]
Squadron Headhunters' Assn; 80th Fighter [5442]
Squadrons; U.S. Power [23231]
Square Dance
   Callerlab - Intl. Assn. of Square Dance Callers [9869]

Country Dance and Song Soc. [9873]
Jimmy Kish "The Flying Cowboy" Fan Club [24922]
   Natl. Square Dance Convention [9895]
   United Square Dancers of Am. [9898]
Square Dance Convention; Natl. [9895]
Square Dancers of Am; United [9898]
Square Dancing; Foundation for the Promotion and Preservation of [★9869]
Square Dancing; Foundation for the Promotion and Preservation of [★IO]
Squash
   Algerian Tennis Fed. [IO]
   Andorra Squash Rackets Assn. [IO]
   Antigua Squash Rackets Assn. [IO]
   Armenian Squash Fed. [IO]
   Aruba Squash Assn. [IO]
   Asociacion Argentina de Squash Rackets [IO]
   Asociacion Nacional de Squash de Guatemala [IO]
   Assn. Marocaine De Squash [IO]
   Bahamas Squash Raquets Assn. [IO]
   Bahrain Badminton and Squash Assn. [IO]
   Bangladesh Squash Rackets Fed. [IO]
   Barbados Squash Rackets Assn. [IO]
   Belgium Squash Fed. [IO]
   Bermuda Squash Racquets Assn. [IO]
   Botswana Squash Rackets Assn. [IO]
   Brunei Squash Rackets Assn. [IO]
   Bulgaria Squash Fed. [IO]
   Chinese Squash Assn. [IO]
   Confederacao Brasiliera de Squash [IO]
   Confederacion Nacional de Squash de Panama [IO]
   Cook Islands Squash Racquets Assn. [IO]
   Croatian Squash Fed. [IO]
   Cyprus Squash Rackets Assn. [IO]
   Czech Squash Assn. [IO]
   Danish Squash Assn. [IO]
   Deutscher Squash Rackets Verband E.V. [IO]
   Estonian Squash Fed. [IO]
   European Squash Fed. [IO]
   Federacion Colombiana de Squash [IO]
   Federacion Dominicana Republica de Squash [IO]
   Federacion Ecuatoriana De Squash [IO]
   Federacion Peruana de Squash [IO]
   Federacion Salvadorena De Squash [IO]
   Federacion de Squash de Mexico, A.C. [IO]
   Federacion Uruguaya de Squash [IO]
   Federacion Venezolana de Squash [IO]
   Fed. Francaise de Squash [IO]
   Fed. Monegasque De Squash Rackets [IO]
   Fed. de Squash Luxembourgeoise [IO]
   Finnish Squash Assn. [IO]
   Ghana Squash Assn. [IO]
   Gibraltar Squash Assn. [IO]
   Greek Squash Rackets Fed. [IO]
   Guyana Squash Assn. [IO]
   Honduras Squash Assn. [IO]
   Iceland Squash Comm. [IO]
   Iran Squash Fed. [IO]
   Irish Squash [IO]
   Israel Squash Rackets Assn. [IO]
   Italian Squash Fed. [IO]
   Jamaica Squash Assn. [IO]
   Japan Squash Assn. [IO]
   Jordan Squash Assn. [IO]
   Kenya Squash Rackets Assn. [IO]
   Korea Squash Fed. [IO]
   Kuwait Squash Fed. [IO]
   Latvian Squash Fed. [IO]
   Lebanese Squash Fed. [IO]
   Lesotho Squash Fed. [IO]
   Liechtenstein Squash Rackets Assn. [IO]
   Lithuanian Squash Fed. [IO]
   Magyar Fallabda (Squash) Szovetseg [IO]
   Mauritius Squash Rackets Assn. [IO]
   Moldavian Squash Fed. [IO]
   Mongolian Squash Fed. [IO]
   Namibian Squash Assn. [IO]
   Nepal Squash Rackets Assn. [IO]
   Nigerian Squash Rackets Assn. [IO]
   Norwegian Squash Assn. [IO]
   Osterreichischer Squash Rackets Verband [IO]
   Pakistan Squash Fed. [IO]
   Papua New Guinea Squash Rackets Fed. [IO]

Paraguay Squash Assn. [IO]
Persatuan Squash Indonesia [IO]
Polska Federacja Squasha [IO]
Portuguese Squash Assn. [IO]
Professional Squash Assn. [IO]
Qatar Squash Fed. [IO]
Real Federacion Espanola de Squash [IO]
Russian Squash Fed. [IO]
Samoa Squash Rackets Assn. [IO]
Saudi Squash Fed. [IO]
Scottish Squash Assn. [IO]
Seychelles Squash Rackets Assn. [IO]
Singapore Squash Rackets Assn. [IO]
Slovak Squash Assn. [IO]
Slovenian Squash Assn. [IO]
Somalia Squash Fed. [IO]
Squash Australia [IO]
Squash Bond Nederland [IO]
Squash Canada [IO]
Squash Fed. of Chile [IO]
Squash Fed. of Oman [IO]
Squash Fiji [IO]
Squash Malawi [IO]
Squash New Zealand [IO]
Squash Rackets Assn. of Chinese Taipei [IO]
Squash Rackets Assn. of Malta [IO]
Squash Rackets Assn. of the Philippines [IO]
Squash Rackets Fed. of India [IO]
Squash South Africa [IO]
Sri Lanka Squash Fed. [IO]
Sudan Squash Fed. [IO]
Svenska Squash Forbundet [IO]
Swaziland Squash Assn. [IO]
Swiss Squash [IO]
Tanzania Squash Rackets Assn. [IO]
Thailand Squash Rackets Assn. [IO]
Tonga Squash Rackets Assn. [IO]
Turkish Squash Fed. [IO]
Uganda Squash Rackets Assn. [IO]
Ukraine Squash Fed. [IO]
United Arab Emirates Squash Rackets Assn. [IO]
U.S. Squash Racquets Assn. [23876]
Vanuatu Squash Rackets Assn. [IO]
World Squash Fed. [IO]
Zambia Squash Assn. [IO]
Zimbabwe Squash Rackets Assn. [IO]
Squash Australia [IO], Milton, Australia
Squash Bond Nederland [IO], Zoetermeer, Netherlands
Squash Canada [IO], Ottawa, ON, Canada
Squash Fed. of Chile [IO], Santiago, Chile
Squash Fed. of Oman [IO], Muscat, Oman
Squash Fiji [IO], Suva, Fiji
Squash Malawi [IO], Blantyre, Malawi
Squash New Zealand [IO], Henderson, New Zealand
Squash Rackets Assn. of Chinese Taipei [IO], Taipei, Taiwan
Squash Rackets Assn. of Malta [IO], Marsa, Malta
Squash Rackets Assn. of the Philippines [IO], Makati City, Philippines
Squash Rackets Fed. of India [IO], Chennai, India
Squash South Africa [IO], Northlands, Republic of South Africa
Squash Zveza Slovenije [★IO]
Squire SS-100 Club [★21788]
Squire SS-100 Registry [21788], c/o Arthur R. Stahl, 11826 S 51st St., Phoenix, AZ 85044-2313, (480)893-9451
Sri Aurobindo Assn. [20636], PO Box 163237, Sacramento, CA 95816, (209)339-3710
Sri Aurobindo Center; Matagiri [★20636]
Sri Aurobindo Soc. [IO], Pondicherry, India
Sri Lanka
   Ceylon (Sri Lanka) Tourist Dept. [24377]
Sri Lanka Amateur Baseball and Softball Assn. [IO], Colombo, Sri Lanka
Sri Lanka Assn. of Administrative and Professional Secretaries [IO], Colombo, Sri Lanka
Sri Lanka Assn. for the Advancement of Sci. [IO], Colombo, Sri Lanka
Sri Lanka Assn. of Dermatologists [IO], Colombo, Sri Lanka
Sri Lanka Badminton Assn. [IO], Colombo, Sri Lanka
Sri Lanka Cricket [IO], Colombo, Sri Lanka
Sri Lanka Heart Assn. [IO], Colombo, Sri Lanka

Reference to "IO" in place of a book number signifies that the association may be found in the 45th edition of International Organizations.

Sri Lanka Lib. Assn. [IO], Colombo, Sri Lanka
Sri Lanka Natl. Lib. Services Bd. [★IO]
Sri Lanka Prajanthantravadi Samajavadi Janarajaye Eksath Jatheenge Sangamaya [★IO]
Sri Lanka Proj. [IO], London, United Kingdom
Sri Lanka Soc. of Occupational Therapists [IO], Panadura, Sri Lanka
Sri Lanka Soc. of Physiotherapy [IO], Colombo, Sri Lanka
Sri Lanka Sports Medicine Assn. [IO], Colombo, Sri Lanka
Sri Lanka Squash Fed. [IO], Colombo, Sri Lanka
Sri Lanka Tea Bd. [IO], Colombo, Sri Lanka
Sri Lanka Tennis Assn. [IO], Colombo, Sri Lanka
Sri Lankan
    Assn. of Sri-Lankans in Am. [19394]
    Ceylon (Sri Lanka) Tourist Dept. [24377]
Sri Lankan Geotechnical Soc. [IO], Colombo, Sri Lanka
SRL, A Free Religious Fellowship - Defunct.
SSA Global Users - North Am. [3728], 401 N Michigan Ave., Chicago, IL 60611, (312)527-6651
SSA Marketing - Address unknown since 2002.
SSPC: The Soc. for Protective Coatings [2885], 40 24th St., 6th Fl., Pittsburgh, PA 15222-4656, (412)281-2331
SSPC: The Society for Protective Coatings [IO], Pittsburgh, PA, United States
Stability Res. Coun; Structural [7714]
Stable Value Assn. [★2351]
Stable Value Investment Assn. [2351], 1025 Connecticut Ave. NW, Ste. 1000, Washington, DC 20036, (202)580-7620
Stablemen and Helpers of Am; Intl. Brotherhood of Teamsters, Chauffeurs, [★24198]
Stacking Assn; World Sport [23868]
Stadium Managers Assn. [23869], 525 SW 5th St., Ste. A, Des Moines, IA 50309-4501, (515)282-8192
Staff Association; National Head Start [★9006]
Staff Assn. of the Org. of Amer. States [★24144]
Staff Development Coun; Natl. [7908]
Staff Development Org; Natl. Nursing [15511]
Staff Development and Training Assn; Natl. [13180]
Staff and Educational Development Assn. [IO], London, United Kingdom
Staff Leasing Assn; Natl. [★1273]
Staff Officers Assn. of America - Address unknown since 1995.
Staff Physician Recruiters; Assn. of [15995]
Staff Union of the Intl. Labour Org. [IO], Geneva, Switzerland
Staffing; Assn. for School, Coll. and Univ. [★8994]
Staffing; Natl. Assn. for Alternative [1268]
Staffing Services; Natl. Assn. of Temporary and [★1254]
Stafford Canary Club of Am. [21861], c/o Carl Biers, VP, 851 Neptune St., Port Charlotte, FL 33948
Stafford Canary Club of America [IO], Glendale, CA, United States
Staffordshire Terrier Club of Am. [22364], c/o Stephen Cabral, Recording Sec., 3033 Gardi St., Duarte, CA 91010, (626)358-2891
STAG [★6327]
Stage Authors and Composers; Society of European [★9817]
Stage Directors and Choreographers Found. [11044], 1501 Broadway, Ste. 1701, New York, NY 10036-5600, (212)302-5359
Stage Directors and Choreographers; Soc. of [24159]
Stage Employees, Motion Picture Technicians, Artists and Allied Crafts of the U.S., U.S. Territories and Canada; Intl. Alliance of Theatrical [★24156]
Stage Mgt. Assn. [IO], London, United Kingdom
Staggerwing Club [21478]
Stain Commn; Biological [6571]
Stained Glass Assn. of Am. [1736], 10009 E 62nd St., Raytown, MO 64133, (816)737-2090
Stained Glass Club - Defunct.
Stained Glass Lamp Artists; Assn. of [2392]
Stained Glass Professionals Assn. - Defunct.
Stainless Steel Indus. Comm; Tool and [★2729]
Stainless Steel Plumbing Fixture Coun. - Defunct.
Stainless Steel Sink Coun. - Defunct.
Stains; Commn. on Standardization of Biological [★6571]

Stair Soc. [IO], Edinburgh, United Kingdom
Stamp Advisory Comm; Citizens' [22806]
Stamp Alliance; Confederate [22811]
Stamp Club; Humor [22827]
Stamp Club; Samuel Gompers [22867]
Stamp Dealers Assn; Amer. [1910]
Stamp Exchange Club; Armed Forces [22793]
Stamp Mfrs. Assn; Intl. [★3683]
Stamp Out AIDS - Defunct.
Stamp Out Regulatory Excesses - Defunct.
Stamp Soc; Meter [22844]
Stamp Soc; Precancel [22861]
Stamp Soc; Swiss Amer. [★22782]
Stamp Soc; U.S. [22888]
STAMP - Survivors Take Action Against Abuse by Military Personnel [11507], 500 Greene Tree Pl., Fairborn, OH 45324, (937)879-9304
Stampe Club Intl. [21479], 2940 Falcon Way, Midlothian, TX 76065, (214)723-1504
Stampe Club Intl. [IO], Midlothian, TX, United States
Stamping Assn; Amer. Metal [★2726]
Stamping and Embossing Assn; Foil [2707]
Stamps Club; Bicycle [22796]
Stamps; Collectors of Religion on [22809]
Stamps Fellowship; Rotary on [22863]
Stamps Soc; Scouts on [★22869]
Stamps on Stamps - Centenary Unit [★22878]
Stamps on Stamps - Centenary Unit [★6937]
Stamps on Stamps - Centenary Unit [★IO]
Stamps on Stamps Collectors Club [IO], Mendham, NJ, United States
Stamps on Stamps Collectors Club [22878], c/o Michael Merritt, Sec.-Treas., 73 Mountainside Rd., Mendham, NJ 07945
Stamps on Stamps Unit [★22878]
Stamps on Stamps Unit [★IO]
Stamps Stud. Unit; Cats on [22801]
Stamps Stud. Unit; Chemistry and Physics on [22802]
Stamps Stud. Unit; Dogs on [22815]
Stamps Stud. Unit; Journalists, Authors and Poets on [10778]
Stamps Unit; Rotary on [★22863]
Stamps Unit; Ships on [22870]
Stamps for the Wounded [22879], c/o Don Montlack, 8784 Thames River Dr., Boca Raton, FL 33433-6274
Stamps; Youth Org. on [★22869]
Stan Mikita Hockey School for the Hearing Impaired [★23337]
Stand Up For Africa [IO], London, United Kingdom
Standard Comm; Amer. Lumber [1634]
Standard Comm; Dredging Industry Size [18293]
Standard Independent Data Format Assn. - Defunct.
Standard Jack and Jennet Registry of Am. [★4130]
Standard Plumbing Code Comm; Natl. [5553]
Standard Quarter Horse Assn. - Address unknown since 1995.
Standard Schnauzer Club of Am. [22365], c/o Judy Houskeeper, Publications Mgr., 7907 S 44th West Ave., Tulsa, OK 74132-3466, (918)446-6761
Standard Schnauzer Club of America [IO], Tulsa, OK, United States
Standardbred Owners Assn. [23513], 733 Yonkers Ave., Ste. 102, Yonkers, NY 10704-2659, (914)968-3599
Standardbred Retirement Found. [4956], 108F Old York Rd., Hamilton, NJ 08620, (609)324-1500
Standardization of Biological Stains; Commn. on [★6571]
Standardized Yiddish Orthography; Comm. for the Implementation of the [10276]
Standards
    1394 High Performance Serial Bus Trade Assn. [3720]
    African Regional Org. for Standardization - Kenya [IO]
    Agile Mfg. Benchmarking Consortium [2545]
    Amer. CueSports Alliance [23144]
    Amer. Measuring Tool Mfrs. Assn. [7694]
    Amer. Natl. Metric Coun. [18678]
    Amer. Natl. Standards Inst. [6267]
    Americans for Customary Weight and Measure [18679]
    Article Numbering Assn. of Bosnia and Herzegovina [IO]

Article Numbering Assn. of Mauritius [IO]
Asia-Pacific Legal Metrology Forum [IO]
Assn. for Automatic Identification and Mobility North Am. [336]
Assn. for Challenge Course Tech. [2869]
Assn. of Fruit and Vegetable Inspection and Standardization Agencies [1674]
Assn. of Natl. Numbering Agencies [IO]
Assn. for Retail Tech. Standards [3400]
Automatic Identification Assn. [IO]
BBM Canada [IO]
Brazilian Soc. for Metrology [IO]
British Measurement and Testing Assn. [IO]
British Standards Institution [IO]
Canadian Gen. Standards Bd. [IO]
Coalition for Fire-Safe Cigarettes [12191]
Coalition for Healthcare eStandards [14623]
CompactFlash Assn. [6723]
Consumer Products Codification Assn. [IO]
Coun. on Ionizing Radiation Measurements and Standards [7556]
Croatian Soc. for Communications, Computing, Electronics, Measurement and Control [IO]
Cyprus Org. for Promotion of Quality [IO]
Danish Standards Assn. [IO]
Data Interchange Standards Assn. [18680]
Dozenal Soc. of Am. [7695]
EAN Czech Republic [IO]
EAN Iceland [IO]
EAN Lithuania [IO]
EAN Malta [IO]
Egyptian Article Numbering Assn. [IO]
Ente Nazionale Italiano di Unificazione [IO]
Equip. Appraisers Assn. of North Am. [279]
European Comm. for Standardization [IO]
European Cooperation in Legal Metrology [IO]
The European Gp. of Valuers' Associations [IO]
European Telecommunications Standards Inst. [IO]
European Training and Simulation Assn. [IO]
Food Ingredient Distributors Assn. [1510]
French Article Numbering Assn. [IO]
French Assn. for Standardization [IO]
Global Org. for Multi-Vendor Integration Protocol [18681]
GS1 Chile [IO]
GS1 Macedonia [IO]
GS1 Nederland [IO]
GS1 Philippines [IO]
GS1 Republica Dominicana [IO]
GS1 South Africa [IO]
GS1 Tunisia [IO]
GS1 Ukraine [IO]
GS1 Uruguay [IO]
Healthcare Laundry Accreditation Coun. [2403]
Inst. of Measurement and Control [IO]
Insurance Marketplace Standards Assn. [2180]
Intl. Alliance for Interoperability [7018]
Intl. Assn. for Prdt. Development [3177]
Intl. Assn. for the Properties of Water and Steam [6268]
Intl. Assn. for the Properties of Water and Steam [IO]
Intl. Assn. of Protocol Consultants [965]
Intl. Bur. of Weights and Measures [IO]
Intl. Electrotechnical Commn. [IO]
Intl. Fed. of Standards Users [IO]
Intl. Info. Centre for Terminology [IO]
Intl. Measurement Confed. [IO]
Intl. Org. of Legal Metrology [IO]
Intl. Org. for Standardization [IO]
Intl. Play Equip. Manufacturers Assn. [3060]
Intl. Soc. of Agile Mfg. [2558]
Intl. Soc. of Six Sigma Professionals [7534]
Intl. Soc. for the Systems Sciences [IO]
Israeli Metrological Soc. [IO]
Japanese Standards Assn. [IO]
Kenya Bur. of Standards [IO]
Localization Indus. Standards Assn. [IO]
Mfg. Skill Standards Coun. [7696]
Metric Opposition Forum [18682]
Metrology Soc. of Australia [IO]
Metrology Soc. of Thailand [IO]
Mexican Article Numbering Assn. [IO]
MultiMediaCard Assn. [7305]

A star before a book entry number signifies that the name is not listed separately, but is mentioned within the entry.

Natl. Assn. for Proficiency Testing [7792]
Natl. Comm. for Certifying Agencies [16916]
Natl. Conf. on Weights and Measures [6269]
Natl. Fireproofing Contractors Assn. [1476]
Natl. Inst. of Metrology, Standardization and Indus. Quality [IO]
Natl. Inst. of Prdt. Coding [IO]
Natl. Standards Authority of Ireland [IO]
Natl. Standards Educators Assn. [7697]
Natl. Storm Shelter Assn. [2831]
NCSL Intl. [7698]
NCSL Intl. [IO]
Netherlands Standardization Inst. [IO]
North Amer. Bd. of Certified Energy Practitioners [6967]
Pan Amer. Standards Commn. [IO]
Postsecondary Electronic Standards Coun. [9165]
Roofing Indus. Comm. on Weather Issues [666]
SD Card Assn. [6743]
SESKO Standardization in Finland [IO]
Social Accountability Intl. [18828]
Soc. of Allied Weight Engineers [7699]
Spanish Article Numbering Assn. [IO]
Standards Assn. of Zimbabwe [IO]
Standards Coun. of Canada [IO]
Standards Engg. Soc. [7700]
Standards New Zealand [IO]
StandardsWork [9094]
Swiss Assn. for Standardization [IO]
Thai Indus. Standards Inst. [IO]
UCA Intl. Users Gp. [7820]
UK Metric Assn. [IO]
Unicode Consortium [18683]
U.S. Metric Assn. [7701]
U.S. Prdt. Data Assn. [2112]
Wi-Fi Alliance [6829]
World Sport Stacking Assn. [23868]
Standards Assn; Amer. [★6267]
Standards Assn; Intl. Radiator [★19897]
Standards Assn; Materials and Methods [636]
Standards Assn; Mortar Mfrs. [★636]
Standards Assn. of New Zealand [★IO]
Standards; Assn. for Retail Tech. [3400]
Standards Assn; Video Electronics [6932]
Standards Assn. of Zimbabwe [IO], Harare, Zimbabwe
Standards for Athletic Equip; Natl. Operating Comm. on [3451]
Standards Bd; Financial Accounting [29]
Standards Bd; Governmental Accounting [5427]
Standards Comm; Amer. Engg. [★6267]
Standards Comm; Baking Indus. Sanitation [448]
Standards Comm. - Z39; Amer. Natl. [★7206]
Standards Committees, Inc; 3-A Sanitary [1125]
Standards Coun. of Canada [IO], Ottawa, ON, Canada
Standards Engg. Soc. [7700], 13340 SW 96th Ave., Miami, FL 33176, (305)971-4798
Standards Engineers Soc. [★7700]
Standards in Higher Educ; Coun. for the Advancement of [9177]
Standards in Human Ser. Educ; Coun. for [9130]
Standards Inst; Friction Materials [385]
Standards Inst; U.S.A. [★6267]
Standards; Natl. Bd. for Professional Teaching [9225]
Standards; Natl. Conf. of States on Building Codes and [5552]
Standards New Zealand [IO], Wellington, New Zealand
Standards Org; Natl. Info. [7206]
Standards Org. - Z39; Natl. Info. [★7206]
Standards, Productivity and Innovation Bd. of Singapore [IO], Singapore, Singapore
Standards and Res; Methods Time Measurements Assn. for [★7165]
Standards and Res; MTM Assn. for [7165]
Standards for Student Services/Development Programs; Coun. for the Advancement of [★9177]
Standards, and Student Testing; Natl. Center for Res. on Evaluation, [8285]
StandardsWork [9094], 1001 Connecticut Ave. NW, Ste. 840, Washington, DC 20036, (202)835-2000
Standbys, Inc; Blackhawk [24997]
Standing Commn. on Church Music [19973]

Standing Commn. on Ecumenical Relations of the Episcopal Church [19974], 815 2nd Ave., New York, NY 10017, (212)716-6220
Standing Comm. of the European Glass Indus. [IO], Brussels, Belgium
Standing Comm. of the Hospitals of the European Union [★IO]
Standing Comm. for Nobel Prize Winners' Congresses [IO], Lindau, Germany
Standing Conf. of the Canonical Orthodox Bishops in the Americas [IO], New York, NY, United States
Standing Conf. of the Canonical Orthodox Bishops in the Americas [19886], 10 E 79th St., New York, NY 10021-0106, (212)774-0526
Standing Conf. on Lib. Materials on Africa [IO], London, United Kingdom
Standing Conf. of Natl. and Univ. Libraries [★IO]
Standing Conf. of Principals [★IO]
Standing Conferences on Drug Abuse [★IO]
Standing Liaison Comm. of EU Speech and Language Therapists and Logopedists [IO], Paris, France
Standing Up for SUV, Pickup and Van Owners of Am. [17017], PO Box 34076, Washington, DC 20043, (202)289-4370
StandWithUs [17941], PO Box 341069, Los Angeles, CA 90034-1069, (310)836-6140
Stanford Chicano/Latino Alumni Assn. [18925], PO Box 86204, Los Angeles, CA 90086-0204, (213)473-7528
Stangl Fulper Collectors Club [22117]
Stanislaus Alumni Assn; California State Univ. - [18884]
Stanley Badminton Club [IO], Stanley, United Kingdom
Stanton Found. - Address unknown since 2002.
Staple and Stapling Machine Mfrs. Assn. - Defunct.
Staples Family History Assn. - Defunct.
Stapling Mfrs. Inst; Indus. [★1825]
Stapling and Nailing Tech. Assn; Indus. [★1825]
Star Alliance Found. - Address unknown since 1991.
Star Class Yacht Racing Assn; Intl. [23193]
Star Mothers of Am; Blue [21193]
Star Observers; Amer. Assn. of Variable [6497]
Star Riders Assn; Intl. [22685]
Star Route Mail Contractors Assn; Natl. [2453]
Star-Spangled Banner Flag House Assn. [21095], 844 E Pratt St., Baltimore, MD 21202, (410)837-1793

Star Trek
Fans of Leonard Nimoy and DeForest Kelley [24739]
Klingon Strike Force [25015]
Shatner and Friends Intl. [24772]
Star Trek: The Official Fan Club [25016]
STARFLEET [25017]
Starfleet Command [25018]
Starfleet Command [IO]
Trekville U.S.A./International [25019]
United Fed. of Planets, Intl. [25020]
Star Trek III: the Official Fan Club [★25016]
Star Trek: The Official Fan Club [25016], 253 Granby St., Norfolk, VA 23510-1813, (866)375-TREK
Star Trek Welcommittee - Defunct.

Star Wars
Campaign to Boycott SDI [18143]
Jedi Knights of Orange County [25021]
Starblazers Fan Club - Defunct.
Starcraft Campers Club - Address unknown since 2002.
STARFLEET [25017], PO Box 94288, Lubbock, TX 79493-4288
Starfleet Command [25018], PO Box 33565, Indianapolis, IN 46203-0565, (317)508-9351
Starfleet Command [IO], Indianapolis, IN, United States
Starfleet Marine Brigade - Address unknown since 1999.
Stargazers Fan Club - Defunct.
Starlight Children's Found. [★11724]
Starlight Found. [★11724]
Starlight Starbright Children's Found. [11724], 5757 Wilshire Blvd., Ste. M-100, Los Angeles, CA 90036, (310)479-1212

Starptautiskas Apmainas Centrs [★IO]
Stars and Bars; Military Order of the [20729]
Stars and Bars; Order of the [★20729]
Stars of David [★11262]
Stars of David [★IO]
Stars of David Intl. [IO], Northbrook, IL, United States
Stars of David Intl. [11262], 3175 Commercial Ave., Ste. 100, Northbrook, IL 60062-1915, (847)509-9929
Stars for Stripes [20770], 109 Rivers Edge Ct., Nashville, TN 37214, (615)872-2122
Stars and Stripes Assn. - Address unknown since 2001.
Starships of the Third Fleet [10949], 10358 Aquilla Dr., Lakeside, CA 92040-2236
Starthrowers [18603], PO Box 192, Franklin, LA 70538, (337)828-2375
Starwind/Spindrift 19 Assn. [★23207]
Starwind/Spindrift Assn. [★23207]
STASH - Defunct.
State Administrators for Family Consumer Sciences; Natl. Assn. of [8514]
State Administrators of Hea. Occupations Educ; Natl. Assn. for [★8870]
State Administrators and Supervisors of Private Schools; Natl. Assn. of [9021]
State Administrators of Vocational Rehabilitation; Coun. of [16320]
State Agencies for Surplus Property; Natl. Assn. [6185]
State Alcohol and Drug Abuse Directors; Natl. Assn. of [13264]
State of Am; Junior [8750]
State; Americans United for Separation of Church and [19836]
State Approving Agencies; Natl. Assn. of [6345]
State Aquaculture Coordinators; Natl. Assn. of [4180]
State Archaeologists; Natl. Assn. of [6450]
State Archives and Records Administrators; Natl. Assn. of [★5820]
State Arts Agencies; Natl. Assembly of [9583]
State; Assn. of Amer. Secretaries of [★6277]
State Assn. Presidents; Natl. Coun. of [★7906]
State Associations of Counties; Conf. of Executives of [★5624]
State Auditors, Comptrollers, and Treasurers; Natl. Assn. of [6206]
State Auditors Coordinating Comm. - Defunct.
State Aviation Officials Center for Aviation Res. and Educ; Natl. Assn. of [★5537]
State Aviation Officials; Natl. Assn. of [5540]
State Bank Supervisors; Conf. of [5544]
State Banks; Natl. Assn. of Supervisors of [★5544]
State-Based Child Advocacy Organizations; Natl. Assn. of [★11662]
State Beer Assn. of Executives of Am. [★204]
State Beer Assn. Secretaries; Natl. Assn. of [★204]
State Beer Wholesalers Secretaries [★204]
State Boards of Accountancy; Natl. Assn. of [5428]
State Boards of Cosmetology; Natl. - Interstate Coun. of [5616]
State Boards of Educ; Natl. Assn. of [9082]
State Boards of Geology; Natl. Assn. of [7133]
State Boards of Nursing; Natl. Coun. of [15508]
State Boards, Veterinary; Amer. Assn. of [16755]
State Boating Law Administrators; Natl. Assn. of [5545]
State Budget Officers; Natl. Assn. of [6207]
State Capital Global Law Firm Gp. [324], 1747 Pennsylvania Ave. NW, Ste. 1200, Washington, DC 20006, (202)659-6601
State Capital Global Law Firm Group [IO], Washington, DC, United States
State Capital Law Firm Gp. [★IO]
State Capital Law Firm Gp. [★IO]
State Capital Law Firm Gp. [★324]
State Catholic Conf. Directors; Natl. Assn. of [19668]
State Chamber of Commerce (New South Wales) [IO], Sydney, Australia
State Charity Officials; Natl. Assn. of [5769]
State Chief Info. Officers; Natl. Assn. of [5821]
State Civil Defense Directors; Natl. Assn. of [★5565]
State Climatologists; Amer. Assn. of [7324]

Reference to "IO" in place of a book number signifies that the association may be found in the 45th edition of International Organizations.

State Colleges and Universities; Amer. Assn. of [8096]
State Colleges and Universities; Assn. of [★8096]
State Contractors Licensing Agencies; Natl. Assn. of [1040]
State Controlled Substances Authorities; Natl. Assn. of [5672]
State Correctional Administrators; Assn. of [11858]
State Counseling Boards; Amer. Assn. of [14054]
State, County and Municipal Employees; Amer. Fed. of [24069]
State Court Administrators; Conf. of [5625]
State Court Administrators; Natl. Conf. of [★5625]
State Courts; Natl. Center for [5908]
State Credit Union Examination; Natl. Inst. for [★5633]
State Credit Union Supervisors; Natl. Assn. of [5633]
State Criminal Justice Planning Administrators; Natl. Conf. of [★11881]
State Dam Safety Officials; Assn. of [6249]
State Debt Mgt. Network [6288], c/o Natl. Assn. of State Treasurers, 2760 Res. Park Dr., PO Box 11910, Lexington, KY 40578-1910, (859)244-8175
State Defense Force Assn. of the U.S. [★6105]
State Democratic Chairmen; Assn. of [★17399]
State Democratic Chairs; Assn. of [17399]
State Dept. Watch [17618], PO Box 65398, Washington, DC 20035-5398
State Departments of Agriculture; Natl. Assn. of [5439]
State Development Agencies; Natl. Assn. of [5592]
State Directors of Community Colleges; Natl. Coun. of [8122]
State Directors of Developmental Disabilities Services; Natl. Assn. of [12576]
State Directors for Disaster Preparedness; Natl. Assn. of [★5565]
State Directors of Hea., Physical Educ. and Recreation; Soc. of [8992]
State Directors of Migrant Educ; Natl. Assn. of [12592]
State Directors of Physical and Hea. Educ; Soc. of [★8992]
State Directors of Special Educ; Natl. Assn. of [9149]
State Directors of Teacher Educ. and Certification; Natl. Assn. of [9224]
State Directors of Veterans Affairs; Natl. Assn. of [6346]
State Directors of Vocational Tech. Educ. Consortium; Natl. Assn. of [9307]
State Drinking Water Administrators; Assn. of [6211]
State Economic Development Agencies; Natl. Assn. of [★5592]
State Economic Opportunity Off. Directors; Natl. Assn. for [★6279]
State Educ. Associations; Natl. Coun. of [7906]
State Educational Media Professionals; Natl. Assn. of [8568]
State Educational Tech. Directors Assn. [9244], c/o Mary Ann Wolf, Exec. Dir., PO Box 10, Glen Burnie, MD 21060, (410)647-6965
State Election Directors; Natl. Assn. of [1176]
State EMS Training Coordinators Coun. of NASEMSO [14345], c/o Natl. Assn. of State EMS Officials, 201 Park Washington Ct., Falls Church, VA 22046-4513, (703)538-1794
State Energy Officials; Natl. Assn. of [5685]
State Environmental Education Coordinators Assn. - Defunct.
State Facilities Administrators; Natl. Assn. of [6195]
State Farm Agents; Natl. Assn. of [2218]
State-Federal Relations; Office of [★6283]
State Fleet Administrators; Natl. Conf. of [6322]
State Foresters; Natl. Assn. of [4689]
State Game and Fish Commissioners; Western Assn. of [★5735]
State Garden Clubs; Natl. Coun. of [★22528]
State Gen. Ser. Officers; Natl. Conf. of [★6278]
State Geologists; Assn. of Amer. [7129]
State Government
  Amer. Coun. on Alcohol Problems [13220]
  Amer. Fed. of State, County and Municipal Employees [24069]
  Assn. of Capitol Reporters and Editors [6181]

  Civil Ser. Employees Assn. [24073]
  Conf. of State Bank Supervisors [5544]
  Conf. of State Court Administrators [5625]
  Coun. on Governmental Ethics Laws [6270]
  Coun. on Licensure, Enforcement and Regulation [6271]
  Coun. of State Community Development Agencies [6272]
  Coun. of State Governments [6273]
  Democratic Governors Assn. [6274]
  Fed. of Tax Administrators [6292]
  Fiscal Stud. Prog. [6275]
  Intl. Assn. of Clerks, Recorders, Election Officials and Treasurers [5775]
  Intl. Conf. of Funeral Ser. Examining Boards of the U.S. [6120]
  Multistate Tax Commn. [6297]
  Natl. Acad. for State Hea. Policy [14649]
  Natl. Assn. of Attorneys Gen. [6276]
  Natl. Assn. of Govt. Employees [24075]
  Natl. Assn. of Insurance Commissioners [5830]
  Natl. Assn. of Secretaries of State [6277]
  Natl. Assn. of State Auditors, Comptrollers, and Treasurers [6206]
  Natl. Assn. of State Budget Officers [6207]
  Natl. Assn. of State Chief Administrators [6278]
  Natl. Assn. for State Community Services Programs [6279]
  Natl. Assn. of State Credit Union Supervisors [5633]
  Natl. Assn. of State Development Agencies [5592]
  Natl. Assn. of State Facilities Administrators [6195]
  Natl. Assn. of State Personnel Executives [6280]
  Natl. Assn. of State Procurement Officials [6238]
  Natl. Assn. of State Treasurers [6208]
  Natl. Assn. of State Units on Aging [11305]
  Natl. Black Caucus of State Legislators [6281]
  Natl. Conf. of Commissioners on Uniform State Laws [6282]
  Natl. Conf. of Insurance Legislators [5832]
  Natl. Conf. of State Legislatures [6283]
  Natl. Conf. of State Trans. Specialists [6323]
  Natl. Coun. of County Assn. Executives [5624]
  Natl. Coun. of State Housing Agencies [5795]
  Natl. Fed. of Fed. Employees [24077]
  Natl. Governors Assn. [6284]
  Natl. Lieutenant Governors Assn. [6285]
  Reason Public Policy Inst. [6131]
  Republican Governors Assn. [6286]
  Southern Governors' Assn. [6287]
  State Debt Mgt. Network [6288]
  State Guard Assn. of the U.S. [6105]
State Govt. Affairs Coun. [1746], 515 King St., Ste. 325, Alexandria, VA 22314, (703)684-0967
State Govt. Affairs Coun. Found. [★1746]
State Governmental Affairs Coun. [★1746]
State Guard Assn. of the U.S. [6105], PO Box 1416, Fayetteville, GA 30214-1416, (770)460-1215
State Hea. Policy Leadership; Forum for [17689]
State High School Associations; Natl. Fed. of [23841]
State High School Athletic Associations; Natl. Fed. of [★23841]
State Higher Educ. Executive Officers [9001], 3035 Center Green Dr., Ste. 100, Boulder, CO 80301-2251, (303)541-1600
State Highway Officials; Amer. Assn. of [★6312]
State Highway and Trans. Officials; Amer. Assn. of [6312]
State Historic Preservation Officers; Natl. Conf. of [5787]
State Housing Agencies; Coun. of [★5795]
State Housing Agencies; Natl. Coun. of [5795]
State Human Ser. Administrators; Natl. Coun. of [13179]
State Humanities Councils; Fed. of [10198]
State Info. Rsrc. Executives; Natl. Assn. of [★5821]
State and Interstate Water Pollution Control Administrators; Assn. of [5688]
State Land Reclamationists; Natl. Assn. of [6118]
State Legislative Leaders; Natl. Conf. of [★6283]
State Legislators; Natl. Soc. of [★6283]
State Lib. Agencies; Chief Officers of [10346]
State Liquor Administrators; Natl. Conf. of [5447]

State and Local Govt; Acad. for [18417]
State and Local History; Amer. Assn. for [10084]
State and Local Policies; Conf. on Alternative [★18429]
State and Local Public Policies; Conf. on Alternative [★18429]
State Medical Boards of the U.S; Fed. of [15165]
State Medical Examining Boards; Amer. Confed. of [★15165]
State Mental Hea. Prog. Directors; Natl. Assn. of [15219]
State Motorcycle Safety Administrators; Natl. Assn. of [6253]
State; Natl. League for the Separation of Church and [19838]
State Outdoor Recreation Liaison Officers; Natl. Assn. of [6157]
State Park Directors; Natl. Assn. of [6158]
State Parks; Natl. Conf. on [★6161]
State Pharmaceutical Assn; Natl. Coun. of [★15943]
State Pharmaceutical Assn. Secretaries; Natl. Conf. of [★15943]
State Pharmacy Assn. Executives; Natl. Coun. of [★15943]
State Planning and Development Agencies; Assn. of [★5592]
State Poetry Societies; Natl. Fed. of [10865]
State Procurement Officials; Natl. Assn. of [6238]
State Programs for the Mentally Retarded; Natl. Assn. of Coordinators of [★12576]
State; Protestants and Other Americans United for Separation of Church and [★19836]
State Public Hea. Veterinarians; Assn. of [★16747]
State Public Hea. Veterinarians; Natl. Assn. of [★16747]
State Public Interest Res. Groups' Campaign on Genetically Engineered Foods [4779], c/o U.S. PIRG Educ. Fund, 218 D St. SE, Washington, DC 20003-1900, (202)546-9707
State Public Welfare Administrators; Natl. Coun. of [★13179]
State Purchasing Officials; Natl. Assn. of [★6238]
State Racing Commissioners; Natl. Assn. of [★6240]
State Recreation Planners; Natl. Assn. of [★6156]
State Retirement Administrators; Natl. Assn. of [5569]
State Revenue Soc. [22880], c/o Kent Gray, Sec., PO Box 67842, Albuquerque, NM 87193
State Sanitary Boards; Assn. of [★16811]
State Savings Supervisors; Amer. Coun. of [458]
State School Audiovisual Officers; Assn. of Chief [★8568]
State School Boards Assn; Natl. Coun. of [★9083]
State School Lib. Media Supervisors Assn. [★8568]
State School Nurse Consultants; Natl. Assn. of [15502]
State School Officers; Coun. of Chief [8246]
State Sci. Supervisors; Coun. of [9101]
State Ser. Commissions; Amer. Assn. of [6189]
State Social Security Administrators; Natl. Conf. of [6259]
State Social Work Boards; Amer. Assn. of [★13200]
State Societies; Conf. of [★19382]
State Societies; Natl. Conf. of [19382]
State Supervisors of Distributive Educ; Natl. Assn. of [★8818]
State Supervisors of Foreign Languages; Natl. Coun. of [8738]
State Supervisors of Mathematics; Assn. of [8822]
State Supervisors of Vocational Home Economics; Natl. Assn. of [★8514]
State Tax Commn; Multi [6297]
State Taxation; Comm. On [★18709]
State Taxation; Coun. On [18709]
State Teachers Associations; Natl. Assn. of Secretaries of [★7906]
State Telecommunications Directors; Natl. Assn. of [6306]
State and Territorial AIDS Directors; Natl. Alliance of [16967]
State and Territorial Air Pollution Prog. Administrators and Assn. of Local Air Pollution Control Officials [★5696]
State and Territorial Dental Directors; Assn. of [14146]

A star before a book entry number signifies that the name is not listed separately, but is mentioned within the entry.

State and Territorial Directors of Hea. Promotion and Public Hea. Educ; Assn. of [★6215]

State and Territorial Directors of Public Hea. Educ; Assn. of [★6215]

State and Territorial Epidemiologists; Conf. of [★14374]

State and Territorial Epidemiologists; Coun. of [14374]

State and Territorial Hea. Officers; Assn. of [★6212]

State and Territorial Hea. Officials; Assn. of [6212]

State and Territorial Injury Prevention Directors Assn. [18581], 2965 Flowers Rd. S, Ste. 105, Atlanta, GA 30341, (770)690-9000

State and Territorial Public Hea. Veterinarians; Assn. of [★16747]

State and Territorial Public Hea. Veterinarians; Natl. Assn. of [★16747]

State and Territorial Solid Waste Mgt. Officials; Assn. of [6353]

State Textbook Administrators; Natl. Assn. of [9260]

State Textbook Administrators; Natl. Assn. of [★9261]

State Textbook Directors; Natl. Assn. of [★9261]

State Tourism Directors; Natl. Coun. of [24385]

State Trans. Specialists; Natl. Conf. of [6323]

State Treasurers; Natl. Assn. of [6208]

State Troopers; Amer. Assn. of [5960]

State Troopers Coalition; Natl. Black [5430]

State Units on Aging; Natl. Assn. of [11305]

State Universities and Allied Institutions; Assn. of Governing Boards of [★7889]

State Universities; Assn. of Land-Grant Colleges and [★8110]

State Universities and Land-Grant Colleges; Natl. Assn. of [8110]

State Universities and Land-Grant Colleges; Off. for the Advancement of Public Black Colleges of the Natl. Assn. of [8112]

State Universities and Land-Grant Colleges; Off. for Advancement of Public Negro Colleges - of the Natl. Assn. of [★8112]

State Utility Commn. Engineers; Conf. of [★6341]

State Utility Consumer Advocates; Natl. Assn. of [6340]

State Veterans Homes; Natl. Assn. of [13354]

State VOCAL Orgs; Natl. Assn. of [13365]

State of the World Forum [18841], PO Box 29434, San Francisco, CA 94129, (415)561-2345

State of the World Forum [IO], San Francisco, CA, United States

Statens Kulturrad [★IO]

States Assn. of Motion Picture Exhibitors; Allied [★1315]

States on Building Codes and Standards; Natl. Conf. of [5552]

States; Center for the Stud. of [★6275]

States; Educ. Commn. of the [8252]

States; Environmental Coun. of the [4632]

States of Malaysia Chamber of Mines [★IO]

States Org. for Boating Access [528], 200 E Randolph Dr., Ste. 5100, Chicago, IL 60601, (312)946-6283

States Rights
Coun. of Conservative Citizens [18684]
Public Advocate of the U.S. [18685]

Statesmen Found; Junior [8751]

Statewide Steering Comm. [★5785]

Sta. David's Benefit and Benevolent Soc. of the City of New York [★19431]

Sta. David's Benevolent Soc. [★19431]

Sta. David's Benevolent Soc. of the Cities of New York and Brooklyn [★19431]

Sta. Employees; Brotherhood of Railway, Airline and Steamship Clerks, Freight Handlers, Express and [★24180]

Sta. Employees; Brotherhood of Railway and Steamship Clerks, Freight Handlers, Express and [★24180]

Sta. Helena and Dependencies Philatelic Soc. [★22866]

Sta. Peter Claver; Knights and Ladies of [★19005]

Station Representatives Assn. - Defunct.

Stationary Engine Res. Gp; British [★22977]

Stationary Engine Soc. [★22977]

Stationary Engine Soc. [★IO]

Stationary Firemen; Intl. Brotherhood of [★24058]

Stationers Assn; Bank [★3678]

Stationers Forum; Contract [★3685]

Stationers Guild of America - Defunct.

Stationers' and Newspaper Makers' Company [IO], London, United Kingdom

Stationery
Argentine Chamber of Stationers, Bookshops and Related Businesses [IO]
British Engraved Stationery Assn. [IO]
Bus. Forms Mgt. Assn. [3677]
Check Payment Systems Assn. [3678]
Document Mgt. Indus. Assn. [3679]
Engraved Stationery Mfrs. Assn. [3680]
Envelope Makers' and Mfg. Stationers' Assn. [IO]
Envelope Mfrs. Assn. [3681]
European Writing Instrument Mfrs. Assn. [IO]
Greeting Card Assn. [IO]
Greeting Card Assn. [3682]
Intl. Marking and Identification Assn. [3683]
Intl. Marking and Identification Assn. [IO]
Korea Stationery Indus. Cooperative [IO]
Label Printing Indus. of Am. [3684]
Natl. Assn. of Stationery Manufacturers [IO]
Natl. Off. Products Alliance [3685]
Nepal Stationery and Educational Materials Indus. Assn. [IO]
Off. Products Wholesalers Assn. [3686]
Stationers' and Newspaper Makers' Company [IO]
Tag and Label Mfrs. Inst. [3687]
Taiwan Assn. of Stationery Indus. [IO]
United Postal Stationery Soc. [22885]
Writing Instrument Mfrs. Assn. [3688]

Stationery Mfrs. Res. Institute; Engraved [★3680]

Stationery Soc; United Postal [22885]

Stations; New York State Assn. of Ser. [★426]

Stations and Repair Shops; New York State Assn. of Ser. [426]

Statistical Assn; Hardware Mfrs. [★1819]

Statistical Assn; Insurance Accounting and [★2172]

Statistical, Economic and Social Res. and Training Centre for the Islamic Countries [IO], Ankara, Turkey

Statistical Inst. for Asia and the Pacific [IO], Chiba, Japan

Statistical Off. of the European Communities [IO], Luxembourg, Luxembourg

Statistical Process Control Soc. [★IO]

Statistical Process Control Soc. [★7554]

Statistical Process Controls [7554], 5908 Toole Dr., Ste. C, Knoxville, TN 37919, (865)584-5005

Statistical Process Controls [IO], Knoxville, TN, United States

Statistical Sci. in Economics; Intl. Soc. of [★7710]

Statistical and Social Inquiry Soc. of Ireland [IO], Dublin, Ireland

Statistical Soc. of Australia [IO], Canberra, Australia

Statistical Soc. of Canada [IO], Ottawa, ON, Canada

Statisticians; Assn. of Football [★IO]

Statisticians and Insurance Accountants Assn; Assn. of Casualty Accountants and [★53]

Statistics
Amer. Lib. Assn. - Off. for Res. and Statistics [10934]
Amer. Statistical Assn. [7702]
Assn. of Football Statisticians [IO]
Austrian Statistical Soc. [IO]
Bernoulli Soc. for Mathematical Statistics and Probability [IO]
Biometric Application Programming Interface Consortium [6572]
Caucus for Women in Statistics [7703]
Caucus for Women in Statistics [IO]
Comm. of Presidents of Statistical Societies [7704]
Coun. of Professional Associations on Fed. Statistics [5816]
Econometric Soc. [7705]
Econometric Soc. [IO]
German Statistical Soc. [IO]
Housing Statistics Users Gp. [5789]
Indian Soc. for Medical Statistics [IO]
Inst. of Mathematical Statistics [7706]
Inter-American Statistical Inst. [IO]
Intl. Assn. of Black Actuaries [2186]

Intl. Assn. for Official Statistics [IO]
Intl. Assn. for Res. in Income and Wealth [18407]
Intl. Assn. for Statistical Computing [IO]
Intl. Assn. of Survey Statisticians [IO]
Intl. Biometric Soc. [IO]
Intl. Biometric Soc. [7707]
Intl. Biometric Soc., Eastern North Amer. Region [7708]
Intl. Biometric Soc., Western North Amer. Region [7709]
Intl. Biometric Soc., Western North Amer. Region [IO]
Intl. Soc. for Bayesian Anal. [7291]
Intl. Soc. for Clinical Biostatistics [IO]
Intl. Soc. for Computational Biology [2094]
Intl. Soc. of Statistical Sci. [7710]
Intl. Soc. of Statistical Sci. [IO]
Intl. Statistical Inst. [IO]
Japan Statistical Soc. [IO]
Japanese Soc. of Computational Statistics [IO]
Natl. Inst. of Statistical Sciences [7711]
Netherlands Soc. for Statistics and Operations Res. [IO]
New Zealand Statistical Assn. [IO]
Org. of Professional Users of Statistics [IO]
Professional Football Researchers Assn. [23438]
Royal Statistical Soc. [IO]
Soc. for Amer. Baseball Res. [23126]
South African Statistical Assn. [IO]
Spanish Statistical and Operations Res. Soc. [IO]
Statistical Inst. for Asia and the Pacific [IO]
Statistical Off. of the European Communities [IO]
Statistical and Social Inquiry Soc. of Ireland [IO]
Statistical Soc. of Australia [IO]
Statistical Soc. of Canada [IO]
Statistiek en Economische Informatie - Statistique et Info. Economique [IO]

Statistics; Amer. Assn. for Vital Records and Public Hea. [★6218]

Statistics; Amer. Bur. of Metal [7309]

Statistics Assn; Criminal Justice [★11876]

Statistics Assn; Justice Res. and [11876]

Statistics Belgium [★IO]

Statistics; Center for [★8284]

Statistics; Coun. of Professional Associations on Fed. [5816]

Statistics; Natl. Center for Charitable [12731]

Statistics; Natl. Center for Educ. [8284]

Statistics; Natl. Center for Educ. [★8284]

Statistics Users Gp; Housing [5789]

Statistiek en Economische Informatie - Statistique et Info. Economique [IO], Brussels, Belgium

Statstjanstemannaforbundet [★IO]

Statue of Liberty Club [22118], c/o Dick Izsak, Treas., 3665 Orchard Way, Powell, OH 43065

Statue of Liberty - Ellis Island Found. [10066], c/o History Center, 17 Battery Pl., No. 210, New York, NY 10004-3507, (212)561-4588

Status and Role of Women; Gen. Commn. on the [17535]

Status of Women in the Economics Profession; Comm. on the [5673]

Status of Women in Microbiology; Comm. on the [6574]

Status of Women in Sociology; Comm. on the [9923]

Stay At Home Dads; Slowlane/ [18182]

Stealth Club of America - Defunct.

Steam Auto. Club of Am. [21789], c/o Tom Kimmel, Pres., PO Box 8, Berrien Springs, MI 49103, (269)471-7408

Steam Engines
Indian Steam Railway Soc. [IO]
Intl. Stationary Steam Engine Soc. [IO]
Intl. Stationary Steam Engine Soc. [22977]
Natl. Threshers Assn. [9484]
Newcomen Soc. of the U.S. [10138]
North Amer. Steam Boat Assn. [21881]
Northwest Steam Soc. [22978]
Rough and Tumble Engineers' Historical Assn. [22979]
Steam Auto. Club of Am. [21789]
Steamship Historical Soc. of Am. [22980]

Steam and Fluid Specialty Mfrs; Natl. Assn. of [★2018]

Steam Heating Equipment Mfrs. Assn. - Defunct.

Reference to "IO" in place of a book number signifies that the association may be found in the 45th edition of International Organizations.

Steam and Hot Water Fitters; Natl. Assn. of Master [★1033]

Steam Plough Club [IO], Reading, United Kingdom

Steam Specialty Club; Natl. [★2018]

Steam Trains - Address unknown since 1995.

Steam Whistle Enthusiasts; Air Horn and [★22037]

Steamboat Assn. of Sweden [IO], Akersberga, Sweden

The Steamboaters [4454], c/o Steamboat Inn, 42705 N Umpqua Hwy., Idleyld Park, OR 97447-9729, (541)498-2230

Steamfitting Indus. Promotion Fund [1901], 44 W 28th St., New York, NY 10001, (212)481-1493

Steamship Assn. of Louisiana [3591], 2217 World Trade Center, 2 Canal St., New Orleans, LA 70130-1407, (504)522-9392

Steamship Assn; New Orleans [★3591]

Steamship Assn; Pacific Amer. [★6059]

Steamship Clerks, Freight Handlers, Express and Sta. Employees; Brotherhood of Railway and [★24180]

Steamship Clerks, Freight Handlers, Express and Sta. Employees; Brotherhood of Railway, Airline and [★24180]

Steamship Clerks, Freight Handlers, Express and Sta. Employees; Carmen Division of the Brotherhood of Railway, Airline and [★24179]

Steamship Historical Soc. of Am. [22980], 1029 Waterman Ave., East Providence, RI 02914, (401)274-0805

Steamship Historical Soc; Amer. [★22980]

Steamship Lines; Comm. of Amer. [★6059]

Steamship Sailors' Union [★24131]

Steamship and Tourist Agents Assn; Amer. [★3907]

Steamtown Museum Assn. - Defunct.

Stearman Restorers Assn. [21480], Chino Airport, 7000 Merrill Ave., Box 90, Chino, CA 91710-8800

Steel Alliance [2730]

Steel Alliance; North Amer. [2724]

Steel Assn; Amer. Iron and [★2697]

Steel Bar Inst; Cold Finished [2703]

Steel Bar Mills [★2732]

Steel Boiler Inst. - Defunct.

Steel Can Recycling Inst. [★4004]

Steel Carriers Group - Defunct.

Steel Castings Assn. [★IO]

Steel Constr; Amer. Inst. of [6834]

Steel Constr; Canadian Inst. of [IO]

Steel Constr. Inst. [IO], Ascot, United Kingdom

Steel Contractors; Natl. Assn. of Reinforcing [1039]

Steel and Copper Plate Engravers; Natl. Assn. of [★3680]

Steel Deck Inst. [671], PO Box 25, Fox River Grove, IL 60021, (847)458-4647

Steel Detailing; Natl. Inst. of [2721]

Steel Distributors; Assn. of [2700]

Steel Division of the Metallurgical Soc. of AIME; Iron and [★7312]

Steel Door and Frame Assn; Natl. [★2719]

Steel Door Inst. [672], c/o Wherry Associates, 30200 Detroit Rd., Cleveland, OH 44145-1967, (440)899-0010

Steel Door Inst; Insulated [628]

Steel Erectors Assn. of Am. [6839], 2216 W Meadowview Dr., Ste. 115, Greensboro, NC 27407, (336)294-8880

Steel Forms Assn. [★IO]

Steel Founders' Soc. of Am. [IO], Crystal Lake, IL, United States

Steel Founders' Soc. of Am. [2070], 780 McArdle Dr., Unit G, Crystal Lake, IL 60014-8155, (815)455-8240

Steel Framing Alliance [2731], 1201 15th St. NW, Ste. 320, Washington, DC 20005, (202)785-2022

Steel Framing Alliance [IO], Washington, DC, United States

Steel Guitar Assn; Pedal [10685]

Steel Guitar Convention; Annual [★10629]

Steel Indus. Assn; All India Stainless [IO]

Steel Indus; Assn. of Hungarian [IO]

Steel Indus. Comm; Tool and Stainless [★2729]

Steel Indus. of North Am; Specialty [2729]

Steel Indus. of the U.S; Specialty [★2729]

Steel Inst; Amer. Iron and [2697]

Steel Inst; Concrete Reinforcing [612]

Steel; Inst. of Scrap Iron and [★3995]

Steel Joist Inst. [673], 3127 Mr. Joe White Ave., Myrtle Beach, SC 29577-6760, (843)626-1995

Steel Kitchen Cabinet Mfrs. Assn. - Address unknown since 1995.

Steel Lintel Manufacturers Assn. [IO], Newport, United Kingdom

Steel Mfrs. Assn. [2732], 1150 Connecticut Ave. NW, Ste. 715, Washington, DC 20036-4131, (202)296-1515

Steel Pipe Assn; Natl. Corrugated [3035]

Steel Pipe Distributors; Natl. Assn. of [3032]

Steel Producers Assn; Canadian [IO]

Steel Producers Assn; Natl. [2732]

Steel Producers' Assn; Swedish [IO]

Steel Recycling Inst. [4004], 680 Andersen Dr., Pittsburgh, PA 15220-2700, (412)922-2772

Steel Scaffolding and Shoring Inst. [★670]

Steel Ser. Center Inst. [★2718]

Steel Shipping Container Inst. [995], 1101 14th St. NW, Ste. S-1001, Washington, DC 20005, (202)408-1900

Steel Soc; Iron and [★7312]

Steel Structures Painting Coun. [★2885]

Steel Structures Painting Coun. [★IO]

Steel Tank Inst. and Steel Plate Fabricators Assn. [996], 570 Oakwood Rd., Lake Zurich, IL 60047, (847)438-8265

Steel Treaters' Soc; Amer. [★7311]

Steel Treating; Amer. Soc. for [★7311]

Steel Treating Res. Soc. [★7311]

Steel Treating Res. Soc. [★IO]

Steel Truss and Component Assn. [2733], 6300 Enterprise Ln., Ste. 300, Madison, WI 53719, (608)217-3712

Steel Tube Inst; Formed [★997]

Steel Tube Inst. of North Am. [997], 2000 Ponce de Leon, Ste. 600, Coral Gables, FL 33134, (305)421-6326

Steel Tube Inst. of North Am. [IO], Coral Gables, FL, United States

Steel Tube Inst; Welded [★997]

Steel Window Assn. [IO], London, United Kingdom

Steel Window Inst. [674], 1300 Sumner Ave., Cleveland, OH 44115-2851, (216)241-7333

Steel Workers of Am., Rubber/Plastics Indus. Conf; United [24183]

Steel Workers Organizing Comm. [★24137]

Steelworkers of Am; United [24137]

Steeplechase Assn; Natl. [23509]

Steeplechase and Hunt Assn; Natl. [★23509]

STEER [20401], PO Box 1236, Bismarck, ND 58502, (701)258-4911

STEER [IO], Bismarck, ND, United States

Steere Family Assn. [21060], 82 Waltham St., No. 8, Boston, MA 02118

Steering Comm. for Sustainable Agriculture [★4100]

Stefan Batory Found. [IO], Warsaw, Poland

Stefanie Powers' Official Fan Club [24774], PO Box 5087, Sherman Oaks, CA 91403

Steiff Club [22119], PO Box 460, Raynham Center, MA 02768-0460, (508)828-2377

Steiff Collectors Club; Toy Stores [22999]

Stein Collectors Intl. [22120], PO Box 222076, Newhall, CA 91322

Stein Collectors Intl. [IO], Newhall, CA, United States

Stein Guild; Edith [19621]

Steinbeck Center Found. [★9695]

Steinbeck Center; Natl. [9695]

Steiner/Ross Soc; Pellien/Jaeger/Loretan/ [21022]

Stelios M. Stelson Found. [8631]

The Stelle Gp. - Defunct.

Stelson Found; Stelios M. [8631]

Stem Cell Res; Comm. for the Advancement of [18542]

Stem Cell Res; Intl. Soc. for [14503]

Stem Cell Res; Student Soc. for [15114]

Stencil Artisans League, Inc. [9474]; PO Box 3109, Los Lunas, NM 87031, (505)865-9119

Stencil Artisans League, Inc. [IO], Los Lunas, NM, United States

Stenotypists of Am; Assoc. [★5630]

Step-Up Found. [★16711]

Step Up Women's Network [13440], 3540 Wilshire Blvd., Ste. 502, Los Angeles, CA 90010, (213)382-9161

Stepfamily Assn. of Am. - Defunct.

Stepfamily Found. [12168], 333 W End Ave., New York, NY 10023, (212)877-3244

Stephen Leacock Assn. [IO], Orillia, ON, Canada

Stephen; Soc. of Saint [20523]

Stephens Owners Registry - Defunct.

Stephenson Locomotive Soc. [IO], Northampton, United Kingdom

STEPS: Assn. for People with Lower Limb Abnormalities [★IO]

Steps Charity Worldwide [IO], Lymm, United Kingdom

Stereo Photographers, Collectors and Enthusiasts Club [★10853]

Stereoencephalotomy; Intl. Soc. for Res. in [★15418]

Stereoscopic Assn; Natl. [10853]

Stereoscopic Soc. [IO], Greenford, United Kingdom

Stereoscopic Soc. of America - Defunct.

Stereotactic Soc; World [★15418]

Sterile Disposable Device Comm. - Defunct.

Sterile Processing and Distribution Personnel; Natl. Inst. for the Certification of Healthcare [★15119]

Sterility; Amer. Soc. for the Stud. of [★14389]

Sterilization Assn; Ethylene Oxide [808]

Sterling Silversmiths Guild of America - Defunct.

Steuben Soc. of Am. [19080], 6705 Fresh Pond Rd., Ridgewood, NY 11385-4505, (718)381-0900

Steve Cochran Fan Club - Address unknown since 1989.

Steve Earle Fan Org. - Address unknown since 1991.

Steve Long Fan Club - Defunct.

Steven Spielberg Film Soc. - Defunct.

Stevengraph Collectors' Assn. - Address unknown since 1991.

Stevens Brazer Guild; Esther [★9482]

Stevens-Duryea Associates - Defunct.

Stevens Fan Club; Connie [24868]

Stevens Institute; Richard F. [★7904]

Steward/Stewardess Div., Air Line Pilots Assn. [★24009]

Steward/Stewardess Div., Air Line Pilots Assn. [★IO]

Stewardess Div., Air Line Pilots Assn; Steward/ [★24009]

Stewardesses for Women's Rights - Address unknown since 1995.

Stewards and Caterers Assn; Executive [★1584]

Stewards and Caterers Assn; Intl. [★1584]

Stewards of the Range [18381], PO Box 490, Meridian, ID 83680-0490, (208)855-0707

Stewards Union; Marine Cooks and [★24132]

Stewardship Assn; Christian [20512]

Stewardship Coun; Christian [★20512]

Stewardship Coun; Marine [5171]

Stewardship Coun; Natl. Catholic [★19642]

Stewardship; Natl. Catholic Conf. for Total [19673]

Stewart Family Assn. - Address unknown since 2004.

Stichting Agromisa [★IO]

Stichting ALS Onderzoekfonds [★IO]

Stichting Eurodata [★IO]

Stichting voor Fundamenteel Onderzoek der Materie [★IO]

Stichting Gaudeamus [★IO]

Stichting Gilles de la Tourette [★IO]

Stichting Lobi [IO], Paramaribo, Suriname

Stichting Natuur en Milieu [★IO]

Stichting Nederlandse Industriele Inschakeling Defensieopdrachten [★IO]

Stichting Nederlandse Vrienden van Jose Carreras [★IO]

Stichting Platform Bio-Energie [★IO]

Stichting Ruimteonderzoek Nederland [★IO]

Stichting Transnational Inst. [★IO]

Stichting VONK Projecten [★IO]

Stichting tegen Vrouwenhandel [★IO]

Stichting Werkgroep Urgenta [★IO]

Stickler Involved People [IO], Augusta, KS, United States

Stickler Involved People [14483], 15 Angelina Dr., Augusta, KS 67010, (316)259-5194

Stiftelsen IMTEC [★IO]

Stiftelsen for Industriell og Teknisk Forskning ved Norges Tekniske Hogskole [★IO]

A star before a book entry number signifies that the name is not listed separately, but is mentioned within the entry.

Stiftelsen Skogsbrukets Forskningsinstitut [★IO]
Stiftung DIAKONIA Weltbund von Verbaenden und Gemeinschaften der DIAKONIE [★IO]
Stiftung fur Europaische Sprach- und Bildungszentren [★IO]
Stiftung Europaisches Naturerbe [★IO]
Stiftung Frauen-Literatur-Forschung e.V. [★IO]
Stiftung Global Harmony [★IO]
Stiftung Wissenschaft und Politik [★IO]
Stigma CH; Natl. [15228]
Still Bank Collectors Club of Am. [21827], c/o Mr. Elliotte Harold, Membership Chm., 440 Homestead Ave., Metairie, LA 70005, (504)833-2715
Still Waters Found. - Address unknown since 1999.
Stillbirth and Neonatal Death Soc. [IO], London, United Kingdom
Stillbirth Support Gp; Miscarriage Infant Death and [16540]
Stillborns; Assn. for Recognizing the Life of [12661]
Stilton Cheese Makers' Assn. [IO], Surbiton, United Kingdom
Stimson Center; Henry L. [17824]
Stinson Club; Natl. [21467]
Stires Family Assn. [21061]
Stock Car Auto Racing; Natl. Assn. for [23081]
Stock Company Assn. - Defunct.
Stock Exchange; Amer. [3507]
Stock Exchange; Chicago [3510]
Stock Exchange Firms; Assn. of [★3523]
Stock Exchange; Midwest [★3510]
Stock Exchange; New York [3520]
Stock Exchange; Pacific [3522]
Stock Exchange; Pacific Coast [★3522]
Stock Horse Assn; Amer. Paint [★4834]
Stock Inst. of Am; PSI Chap; Paper [★4002]
Stock Option Writers Assn. - Defunct.
Stock Plan Professionals; Natl. Assn. of [1469]
Stock Registry; Amer. Mammoth Jack [★4130]
Stock Transfer Assn. [★3524]
Stock Transfer Assn; New York [★3524]
Stockbridge Family of New England - Defunct.
Stockbrokers; Assn. of Private Client Investment Managers and [IO]
Stockholder Relations Soc. of New York - Address unknown since 1995.
Stockholders Against the Govt. Burden [★17351]
Stockholders of America - Address unknown since 1994.
Stockholders Sovereignty Soc. [★17351]
Stockholders for World Freedom [★17351]
Stockholm Chamber of Commerce [IO], Stockholm, Sweden
Stockholm Env. Inst. - Sweden [IO], Stockholm, Sweden
Stockholm Environmental Inst. - Tallinn [IO], Tallinn, Estonia
Stockholm Herpetological Soc. [IO], Stockholm, Sweden
Stockholmi Keskkonnainstituudi Tallinna Keskus [★IO]
Stockholms Herpetologiska Forening [★IO]
Stockowners Rights; Fund for [17351]
Stockpile; Comm. to Release [★2694]
Stoker, Bram
  Vampire Pen Pal Network [25022]
Stoker Mfrs. Assn. - Address unknown since 1995.
Stoker Memorial Assn; Bram [9639]
Stokowski Soc. of Am; Leopold [★9812]
Stolen Children Information Exchange - Address unknown since 1995.
Stolen Horse Intl. [11461], PO Box 1341, Shelby, NC 28151, (704)484-2165
Stolen Horse Intl. [IO], Shelby, NC, United States
Stoma Care Soc. [IO], Kuala Lumpur, Malaysia
Stomatological Soc. of Greece [IO], Athens, Greece
Stone
  Allied Stone Indus. [3689]
  Amer. Rock Mechanics Assn. [3690]
  Barre Granite Assn. [3691]
  Building Stone Inst. [3692]
  Elberton Granite Assn. [3693]
  Finnish Natural Stone Assn. [IO]
  Indiana Limestone Inst. of Am. [3694]
  Inst. of Quarrying - Australia [IO]
  Inst. of Quarrying - England [IO]

Inst. of Quarrying - Hong Kong Br. [IO]
  Inst. of Quarrying - Southern Africa [IO]
  International Colored Gemstone Association [IO]
  Intl. Colored Gemstone Assn. [3695]
  Intl. Meteorite Collectors Assn. [22981]
  International Meteorite Collectors Association [IO]
  Jeweler's Advisory Gp. [2369]
  Leading Jewelers of the World [2377]
  Marble Inst. of Am. [3696]
  Marble Inst. of Am. [IO]
  Master Carvers Assn. [IO]
  Natl. Assn. of the German Gravel and Sand Indus. [IO]
  Natl. Building Granite Quarries Assn. [3697]
  Natl. Fed. of Terrazzo, Marble and Mosaic Specialists [IO]
  Natl. Graniteware Soc. [22083]
  Natl. Quartz Producers Coun. [3698]
  Natl. Stone, Sand and Gravel Assn. [3699]
  North Amer. Rock Garden Soc. [22535]
  North Amer. Stone Skipping Assn. [22939]
  United Kingdom Cast Stone Assn. [IO]
Stone and Allied Products Workers of Am; United [★24137]
Stone Assn; Natl. [★3699]
Stone Assn; Natl. Crushed [★3699]
Stone, Glass and Clay Coordinating Comm. - Defunct.
Stone Inst; Cast [919]
Stone Quarrymen's Assn; Intl. Cut [★3692]
Stonehenge Study Group [6459]
Stonewall Day Prog. [★18847]
Stooges Fan Club; Three [24800]
Stop Abuse by Counselors - Defunct.
Stop Abuse for Everyone [12039], 16869 SW 65th Ave., PMB 212, Lake Oswego, OR 97035-7865, (503)853-8686
Stop the Deployment of the Cruise and Pershing II Missles in Europe - Defunct.
Stop Domestic Violence; Emerge: Counseling and Educ. to [12026]
Stop Equal Rights Amendment - Defunct.
STOP Forced Busing - Defunct.
Stop Net Abusers [17241]
Stop it Now! [11653], 351 Pleasant St., Ste. B319, Northampton, MA 01060, (413)585-3500
Stop the Olympic Prison - Defunct.
Stop OSHA Project - Defunct.
Stop Parental Kidnapping - Defunct.
Stop Planned Parenthood [★18568]
Stop Prisoner Rape [11894], 3325 Wilshire Blvd., Ste. 340, Los Angeles, CA 90010, (213)384-1400
Stop Project ELF - Defunct.
Stop TB Partnership [IO], Geneva, Switzerland
Stop Teen-Age Addiction to Tobacco - Address unknown since 2007.
Stop the Violence, Face The Music [13376], 723 Casino Center Blvd., 2nd Fl., Las Vegas, NV 89101-6716, (800)732-6366
Stop the Violence, Face The Music [IO], Las Vegas, NV, United States
Stop the War Coalition [IO], London, United Kingdom
Stop War Toys Campaign - Defunct.
STOPP Intl. [18568], PO Box 1350, Stafford, VA 22555, (540)659-4171
Stoppers U.S.A; Crime [★11836]
StopSIDS.org [16527], 1673 Rte. 9, Ste. 2, Clifton Park, NY 12065, (888)521-9499
Storage Assn; Amer. Moving and [3559]
Storage Assn; Self [3983]
Storage Assn; Self-Service [★3983]
Storage Coun. [★3980]
Storage Coun. of the Material Handling Indus. of Am; Order Selection, Staging and [3980]
Storage Equip. Mfrs. Assn. [2071], 8720 Red Oak Blvd., Ste. 201, Charlotte, NC 28217, (704)676-1190
Storage and Handling Equip. Distributors' Assn. [IO], Birmingham, United Kingdom
Storage Indus. Consortium; Natl. [★903]
Storage Networking Indus. Assn. [6754], 500 Sansome St., Ste. 504, San Francisco, CA 94111, (415)402-0006
Storage and Retrieval Professionals; ISDA - Assn. of [2847]

Storage/Retrieval Systems; Automated [2004]
Storage Systems; Controlled Mech. [★2004]
Store Assn; Museum [3414]
Store Fixture Manufacturers; Natl. Assn. of [644]
Store, Oper. Pass-Along; Anglican Book [★19972]
Store Planners; Inst. of [3408]
Stores Assn; Natl. Retail Liquor Package [★193]
Stores; Intl. Assn. of Chain [★3404]
Stores; Natl. Assn. of Chain Drug [2985]
Stores; Natl. Assn. of Coll. [3415]
Stores; Natl. Assn. of Convenience [3416]
Stores; Natl. Assn. of Shoe Chain [★1597]
Stores Res. and Educational Found; College [★3415]
Storm Appreciation Soc; Gale [24744]
Storm Chasers and Spotters; Natl. Assn. of [13413]
Storm Shelter Assn; Natl. [2831]
Storm Water Mgt. Agencies; Natl. Assn. of Flood and [6140]
Story Circle Network [10985], PO Box 500127, Austin, TX 78750-0127, (512)454-9833
Story Circle Network [IO], Austin, TX, United States
Story League; Natl. [10982]
Story Rhymes for Educ. [10986], PO Box 416, Denver, CO 80201-0416, (303)575-5676
Story Tellers' League [★10982]
Storytellers; Assn. of Black [★10981]
Storytelling
  By Word of Mouth Storytelling Guild [10978]
  Intl. Order of E.A.R.S. [10979]
  Intl. Order of E.A.R.S. [IO]
  Jewish Storytelling Coalition [10980]
  Natl. Assn. of Black Storytellers [10981]
  Natl. Story League [10982]
  Natl. Storytelling Network [10983]
  New Zealand Guild of Storytellers [IO]
  Scottish Storytelling Forum [IO]
  Soc. for Storytelling [IO]
  Spellbinders [10984]
  Story Circle Network [10985]
  Story Circle Network [IO]
  Story Rhymes for Educ. [10986]
  Storytelling Assn. - Singapore [IO]
  Wordcraft Circle of Native Writers and Storytellers [9859]
Storytelling Assn; Natl. [★10983]
Storytelling Assn. - Singapore [IO], Singapore, Singapore
Storytelling; Natl. Assn. for the Preservation and Perpetuation of [★10983]
Stout, Rex
  Wolfe Pack [9727]
Stoval, Stoveal, Stoball [★21062]
Stovall Family Assn. [21062], c/o Thomas Stovall, Jour. Ed., 3345 Tibey Ct., Dubuque, IA 52002, (563)557-9227
Stove Assn; Antique [21524]
Stove, Furnace and Allied Appliance Workers Intl. Union of North Am. [★24001]
Stove, Furnace, Energy, and Allied Appliance Workers Division of the Intl. Brotherhood of Boilermakers [24001], 5016 Spedale Ct., No. 399, Spring Hill, TN 37174, (615)791-3861
Stove Info. CH; Antique [21525]
Stowarsysenie Bibliotekarzy Polskich [★IO]
Stowarszyszeine Miedzynarodowe Triennale Grafiki [★IO]
Stowarzyszenie Antywariuszy Polskich [★IO]
Stowarzyszenie Chorych z Przepuklina Oponowo-Rdzeniowa R.P. [★IO]
Stowarzyszenie Dziennikarzy Polskich [★IO]
Stowarzyszenie Filmowcow Polskich [★IO]
Stowarzyszenie Gazet Lokalnych [★IO]
Stowarzyszenie Geomorfologow Polskich [★IO]
Stowarzyszenie Inzynierow i Technikow Lesnictwa i Drzewnictwa [★IO]
Stowarzyszenie Papiernikow Polskich [★IO]
Stowarzyszenie na Rzecz Osob z Choroba Huntingtona w Polsce [IO], Paslek, Poland
Stowazy Szenie Mlodych Chorych [IO], Poznan, Poland
Stowe Center; Harriet Beecher [9655]
Stowe-Day Found. [★9655]
Strabismus
  Amer. Assn. of Certified Orthoptists [15657]

Reference to "IO" in place of a book number signifies that the association may be found in the 45th edition of International Organizations.

Strabismus; Amer. Assn. for Pediatric Ophthalmology and [15660]
Straight Chiropractic Academic Standards Assn. - Defunct.
Straight Chiropractors and Organizations; Fed. of [14001]
STRAIGHT, Inc. - Address unknown since 1999.
Straight Partners - Defunct.
Straight Spouse Network [12508], c/o Kathryn Callori, Exec. Dir., PO Box 507, Mahwah, NJ 07430, (201)825-7763
Straight Spouse Support Network [★12508]
Strait Fan Club; George [24901]
Strangers Club [★10946]
Strategic Account Mgt. Assn. [2650], 150 N Wacker Dr., Ste. 2222, Chicago, IL 60606, (312)251-3131
Strategic Account Management Association [IO], Chicago, IL, United States
Strategic Air Command Judo Assn. [★23555]
Strategic Defense Initiative
High Frontier Org. [18686]
Strategic Industries Assn. - Defunct.
Strategic Leadership Forum - Address unknown since 2003.
Strategic Planning Soc. [IO], London, United Kingdom
Strategic Services on Unemployment and Workers' Compensation and the Natl. Found. for UC & WC [★13348]
Strategic Services on Unemployment and Workers' Compensation; UWC - [13348]
Strategies for Media Literacy - Address unknown since 2001.
Strategy Gaming Soc. [22475], c/o Prof. George Phillies, Treas., 87-6 Park Ave., Worcester, MA 01605, (508)831-5334
Strategy Info. Center; Natl. [17383]
Strategy; Inst. for Amer. [★16986]
Strategy and Marketing; Alliance for Healthcare [2612]
Stratis Hea. [14600], 2901 Metro Dr., Ste. 400, Bloomington, MN 55425-1525, (952)854-3306
Stratman Assn. - Defunct.
Stratton Porter Memorial Soc; Gene [9651]
Strawberry Advisory Bd; California [★4720]
Strawberry Commn; California [4720]
Strawberry Growers Assn; North Amer. [4750]
Strawberry Shortcake Chat Gp. [22406], c/o Jennifer Bowles, Ed., 138 E Main Cross, Greenville, KY 42345, (270)338-4318
Strawberry Shortcake Doll Club [★22406]
Stream Improvement; Natl. Coun. for Air and [4690]
Streams; Save Our [★4413]
Street Acad. Program - Defunct.
St. Child Rescue Ghana [IO], Accra, Ghana
Street and Highway Safety Lighting Bur. - Defunct.
St. and Highway Safety; Natl. Conf. on [★6309]
St. Kids Intl; Students Helping [11725]
St. Law [6035], 1010 Wayne Ave., Ste. 870, Silver Spring, MD 20910, (301)589-1130
St. Law Inst; Natl. [★6035]
St. Machine Assn; United [21807]
St. Rod Assn; Buick [22919]
St. Rod Assn; Natl. [21738]
Street Sharks Fan Club - Address unknown since 1999.
St. Sled Sports Racers Intl. [IO], Oxford, United Kingdom
Streeter Family Assn. [21063], c/o Ms. Erma Hosmer, PO Box 1071, Ceres, CA 95307
Strength Coaches Assn; Natl. [★23957]
Strength and Conditioning Assn; Natl. [23957]
Strength and Fitness; Natl. Coun. on [23955]
Strep Assn; Gp. B [13962]
Stress
Amer. Inst. of Stress [16487]
Amer. Psychological Assn. - Div. of Trauma Psychology [16128]
Argentine Soc. for Psychotrauma [IO]
Armenian Amer. Soc. for Stud. on Stress and Genocide [15190]
Assn. de Langue Francaise pour l'Etude du Stress et du Traumatisme [IO]
Assn. of Stress Consultants [IO]
Australasian Critical Incident Stress Assn. [IO]

Australasian Critical Incident Stress Assn. - New South Wales [IO]
Australasian Critical Incident Stress Assn. - Queensland [IO]
Australasian Critical Incident Stress Assn. - Tasmania [IO]
Australasian Critical Incident Stress Assn. - Victoria [IO]
Australasian Soc. for Traumatic Stress Stud. [IO]
Body Stress Release Assn. - UK [IO]
Canadian Centre for Stress and Well-Being/Stress Mgt. Center [IO]
Canadian Inst. of Stress [IO]
Canadian Traumatic Stress Network [IO]
Cell Stress Soc. Intl. [IO]
Cell Stress Soc. Intl. [16488]
Deutschsprachige Gesellschaft Fur Psychotraumatologie [IO]
EMDR - Humanitarian Assistance Programs [12767]
EMDR Intl. Assn. [16215]
European Soc. for Traumatic Stress Stud. [IO]
Gift From Within [12768]
Himalayan Intl. Inst. of Yoga Sci. and Philosophy of the U.S.A. [12348]
Inst. of HeartMath [10174]
Inst. for Labor and Mental Health [15202]
Intl. Critical Incident Stress Found. [16491]
Intl. Laughter Soc. [10188]
Intl. REST Investigators Soc. [16220]
Intl. Soc. for Traumatic Stress Stud. [16489]
International Society for Traumatic Stress Studies [IO]
Intl. Stress Mgt. Assn. [IO]
Intl. Stress Mgt. Assn. - India [IO]
Kuwaiti Soc. for Traumatic Stress Stud. [IO]
Natl. Center for Post Traumatic Stress Disorder [16490]
North Amer. Yoga Fed. [11219]
Sci. and Tech. Found. of Japan [IO]
SOL [13030]
Stress and Anxiety Res. Soc. [IO]
VietNow Natl. [13359]
Stress Analysis
Amer. Inst. of Stress [16487]
Armenian Amer. Soc. for Stud. on Stress and Genocide [15190]
Cell Stress Soc. Intl. [16488]
EMDR Intl. Assn. [16215]
International Critical Incident Stress Foundation [IO]
Intl. Soc. of Stress Analysts [5764]
Intl. Soc. for Traumatic Stress Stud. [16489]
Res. Coun. on Structural Connections [7712]
Soc. for Experimental Mechanics [7713]
Structural Stability Res. Coun. [7714]
Stress Anal; Soc. for Experimental [★7713]
Stress Analysts; Natl. Soc. of [★5764]
Stress and Anxiety Res. Soc. [IO], Dusseldorf, Germany
Stress Management
Amer. Inst. of Stress [16487]
Gift From Within [12768]
Intl. Critical Incident Stress Found. [16491]
Intl. Soc. for Traumatic Stress Stud. [16489]
Natl. Center for Post Traumatic Stress Disorder [16490]
Stress Stud; Soc. for Traumatic [★16489]
Stretch Glass Soc. - Address unknown since 1994.
Strict Baptist Historical Soc. [IO], Caterham, United Kingdom
STRIDE: Sports and Therapeutic Recreation Instruction/Developmental Educ. [8205], PO Box 778, Rensselaer, NY 12144, (518)598-1279
Strike Ten Entertainment [★23810]
String Bass; Intl. Inst. for the [★10625]
String Teachers Assn; Amer. [8904]
Stringers Assn; U.S. Racquet [3674]
Strings; Soc. for [10706]
Striped Bass Growers Assn. [4670], 111 W Washington St., Ste. 1, Charles Town, WV 25414, (304)728-2167
Stripers Unlimited - Defunct.
Stripper Well Assn; Natl. [2940]
Stroke
Amer. Stroke Assn. [16492]

British Assn. of Stroke Physicians [IO]
Children's Hemiplegia and Stroke Assn. [16493]
Intl. Stroke Soc. [IO]
Natl. Stroke Assn. [16494]
Natl. Stroke Assn. of Malaysia [IO]
Singapore Natl. Stroke Assn. [IO]
Soc. for Women's Hea. Res. [16910]
Stroke Assn. [IO]
Stroke Awareness for Everyone [IO]
Stroke Awareness for Everyone [16495]
Stroke Clubs, Intl. [16496]
Stroke Network [16497]
Stroke Network [IO]
Stroke Soc. of Australasia [IO]
Stroke Assn. [IO], London, United Kingdom
Stroke Awareness for Everyone [IO], Los Angeles, CA, United States
Stroke Awareness for Everyone [16495], c/o Bernadette Manion, Treas., PO Box 36186, Los Angeles, CA 90036
Stroke Club; The [★16496]
The Stroke Club [★16496]
Stroke Club of America [★16496]
Stroke Clubs, Intl. [16496]
Stroke Info. and Referral Center [★16494]
Stroke Network [16497], PO Box 492, Abingdon, MD 21009
Stroke Network [IO], Abingdon, MD, United States
Stroke Network; Courage [★13890]
Stroke Soc. of Australasia [IO], Crows Nest, Australia
Strong Family Assn. of Am. [21064], PO Box 546, Kendallville, IN 46755-0546, (260)347-2030
Structural Bd. Assn. [IO], Markham, ON, Canada
Structural Cement-Fiber Products Assn. - Defunct.
Structural Clay Products Inst. [★604]
Structural Clay Products Res. Found. [★604]
Structural Clay Tile Assn. [★604]
Structural Connections; Res. Coun. on [7712]
Structural Engineers Associations; Natl. Coun. of [7032]
Structural Insulated Panel Assn. [675], PO Box 1699, Gig Harbor, WA 98335, (253)858-7472
Structural Integration; Ida P. Rolf Found. for [★13652]
Structural Joints; Res. Coun. on Riveted and Bolted [★7712]
Structural, Ornamental and Reinforcing Iron Workers; Intl. Assn. of Bridge, [24134]
Structural Stability Res. Coun. [7714], 301 Butler Carlton Hall, Rolla, MO 65409-0030, (573)341-6610
Structured Employment Economic Development Corp. [12045], 915 Broadway, 17th Fl., New York, NY 10010, (212)473-0255
Struggle to Save Ethiopian Jewry [20182], 459 Columbus Ave., Ste. 316, New York, NY 10024, (212)687-6200
Struggle to Save Ethiopian Jewry [IO], New York, NY, United States
Stuart, Charles
Soc. of King Charles the Martyr [19455]
Stuart Fan Club; Marty [24945]
Stuart Found; Jesse [9674]
Stucco Manufacturers Assn. [676], 2402 Vista Nobleza, Newport Beach, CA 92660, (949)640-9902
Studbook in North America; Dutch Warmblood [★4931]
Studebaker
Avanti Owners Assn. Intl. [21589]
School Nutrition Assn. [9173]
Studebaker Automobile Club of America - Address unknown since 1985.
Studebaker Club; Antique [21580]
Studebaker Driver's Club [21790], PO Box 1715, Maple Grove, MN 55311-6715, (763)420-7829
Studebaker Family Natl. Assn. [21065], 6555 S State Rte. 202, Tipp City, OH 45371-9444, (937)667-7013
Studebaker Owners Club [★21790]
Student and Academic Rights; Coalition for [7870]
Student Action Corps for Animals - Address unknown since 1999.
Student Action for Education - Defunct.

A star before a book entry number signifies that the name is not listed separately, but is mentioned within the entry.

Student Ad Hoc Comm. to Support the President's Policy in Vietnam - Defunct.
Student Advisors; Natl. Assn. of Foreign [★8445]
Student Advisory Comm. on Intl. Affairs - Defunct.
Student Affairs; Natl. Assn. for Foreign [★8445]
Student Affairs Professionals; Natl. Assn. of [7903]
Student Affl. Gp. [9191], Univ. of Akron, Dept. of Psychology, Arts and Sciences Bldg., Akron, OH 44325-4301, (330)972-7280
Student African Amer. Brotherhood [19444], PO Box 350842, Toledo, OH 43635, (419)530-3221
Student Aid Funds; United [★8434]
Student Alliance [★9193]
Student Alliance; Lakota [19275]
Student Alternatives to Violence - Defunct.
Student Amer. Dental Assn. [★8194]
Student Amer. Medical Assn. [★8844]
Student Amer. Pharmaceutical Assn. [★15919]
Student Amer. Veterinary Medical Assn. [16809], c/o AVMA, 1931 N Meacham Rd., Ste. 100, Schaumburg, IL 60173, (847)925-8070
Student American Veterinary Medical Association [IO], Schaumburg, IL, United States
Student Animal Rights Alliance [11337], 275 Seventh Ave., 23rd Fl., New York, NY 10001, (212)696-7911
Student Anthropologists; Natl. Assn. of [7953]
Student Assn; Amer. Law [★8769]
Student Assn; Amer. Medical [8844]
Student Assn; Amer. Optometric [15714]
Student Assn. of the Amer. Sociological Assn; Honors Prog. [24702]
Student Association; Christian Honor [★8089]
Student Assn; Tech. [8547]
Student Assn; U.S. Natl. [★9195]
Student Assn. for Voter Empowerment [17490], 1615 L St. NW, Ste. 400, Washington, DC 20036, (847)502-5012
Student Campaign Against Hunger and Homelessness; Natl. [12396]
Student Campaign Against Hunger; Natl. [★12396]
Student Campaign for Voter Registration; Natl. [18360]
Student Christian Movement of Hong Kong [IO], Hong Kong, People's Republic of China
Student Christian Movement in New York State - Defunct.
Student Coalition for Relevant Sex Education - Defunct.
Student Coalition for the Right to Drink - Defunct.
Student Coalition; Sierra [4521]
Student Comm. for the Right to Bear Arms - Defunct.
Student Commun; Found. for [8023]
Student Conf; Japan-America [8622]
Student Conservation Assn. [4455], PO Box 550, Charlestown, NH 03603-0550, (603)543-1700
Student Cooperative Org; North Amer. [★9190]
Student Dental Assn; Amer. [8194]
Student Div; Law [8769]
Student Educ. Fund; Women's Leadership Network, Natl. [★9195]
Student Educational Fund; Natl. [★9196]
Student Employment Administrators; Natl. Assn. of [★8996]
Student Employment Assn; Natl. [8996]
Student Empowerment Training Proj. [9192], c/o Abe Scarr, Proj. Dir., 407 S Dearborn, Ste. 701, Chicago, IL 60605, (312)291-0395
Student Environmental Action Coalition [4607], PO Box 31909, Philadelphia, PA 19104-0609, (215)222-4711
Student Exchange; Amer. Intercultural [8596]
Student Exchange; Amer. Scandinavian [★8600]
Student Experimental Payload Prog. [6390]
Student/Farmworker Alliance [24054], PO Box 603, Immokalee, FL 34143, (239)657-8311
Student Financial Aid Administrators; Natl. Assn. of [8350]
Student Foreign Missions Fellowship [★20347]
Student Foreign Missions Fellowship [★20347]
Student Global AIDS Campaign [13585], c/o Global Justice, 1225 Connecticut Ave. NW, Ste. 401, Washington, DC 20036, (202)296-6727
Student Hea. Assn; Amer. [★14714]

Student Health Orgs. - Defunct.
Student Homophile League [★12224]
Student Insurance Producers Assn. - Defunct.
Student Intl. Law Societies; Assn. of [★5868]
Student Interracial Ministry - Defunct.
Student Jour. Gp. of the Amer. Speech and Hearing Assn. [★16453]
Student Leadership Network [9193]
Student Legal Action Orgs. - Defunct.
Student Letter Exchange [22144], 211 Broadway, Ste. 201, Lynbrook, NY 11563, (516)887-8628
Student Loan Administrators; Natl. Assn. of [8432]
Student Lobby; Natl. [★9195]
Student Missions Fellowship [★20347]
Student Mobilization Comm. to End the War in Vietnam - Defunct.
Student Movement - U.S.A; Lutheran [20227]
Student Musicians; Natl. Fraternity of [8924]
Student; Natl. Assn. on Work and the Coll. [★8996]
Student Natl. Coordinating Comm. - Address unknown since 1995.
Student Natl. Dental Assn. [8198], c/o Calysta Beatty, Treas., 1022 Exchange Pl., Durham, NC 27713
Student Natl. Educ. Assn. [★24045]
Student Natl. Medical Assn. [8876], 5113 Georgia Ave. NW, Washington, DC 20011, (202)882-2881
Student Natl. Podiatric Medical Assn. - Address unknown since 1999.
Student Nurses' Assn. in memory of Frances Tompkins; Foundation of the Natl. [★8873]
Student Nurses' Assn; Natl. [8873]
Student Org; Natl. Postsecondary Agricultural [7941]
Student Org. of North Am. [9194], c/o Jose Manuel Castellon, Co-Chm., PO Box 210300, Tucson, AZ 85721-0300, (520)626-4392
Student Orgs; Intl. Islamic Fed. of [10248]
Student Osteopathic Medical Assn. [15815], 142 E Ontario St., Chicago, IL 60611, (312)202-8193
Student Osteopathic Medical Assn. - Address unknown since 1995.
Student Peace Coalition; Natl. Youth and [18226]
Student Peace Union - Defunct.
Student Personnel Administrators; Conf. on Jesuit [★7896]
Student Personnel Administrators; Jesuit Assn. of [7896]
Student Personnel Administrators; Natl. Assn. of [7904]
Student Personnel Assn. for Teacher Educ. [★8527]
Student Pharmacists; Amer. Pharmacists Assn. Acad. of [15919]
Student Photographic Soc. [10857], 229 Peachtree St. NE, Ste. 2200, Atlanta, GA 30303, (866)886-5325
Student Pledge Against Gun Violence [17601], 112 Nevada St., Northfield, MN 55057, (507)645-5378
Student Press Law Center [17194], 1101 Wilson Blvd., Ste. 1100, Arlington, VA 22209, (703)807-1904
Student Press Ser; Jewish [8694]
Student and Professional Italian-Americans; Assn. of [19160]
Student Program; Ella Baker [★17097]
Student Programs Division [★19012]
Student Pugwash; Intl. [★18842]
Student Pugwash U.S.A. [18842], 1015 18th St. NW, Ste. 704, Washington, DC 20036, (202)429-8900
Student Safety Prog; Natl. [18579]
Student Science Training Program - Defunct.
Student Sect; Amer. Pharmaceutical Assn. [★15919]
Student Services
  Amer. Coll. Personnel Assn. [8961]
  Assn. of Coll. Unions Intl. [9166]
  Assn. of Coll. Unions Intl. [IO]
  Assn. of Coll. and Univ. Housing Officers Intl. [IO]
  Assn. of Coll. and Univ. Housing Officers Intl. [9167]
  Assn. of Coll. and Univ. Religious Affairs [9168]
  Canadian Assn. of Coll. and Univ. Student Services [IO]
  Canadian Assn. of Student Activity Advisors [IO]
  Natl. Assn. for Campus Activities [9169]
  Natl. Assn. of Coll. and Univ. Food Services [1588]

Natl. Assn. of Fellowships Advisors [9080]
Natl. Assn. of Student Affairs Professionals [7903]
Natl. Assn. of Student Employment Services [IO]
Natl. Assn. of Student Loan Administrators [8432]
Natl. Coun. on Student Development [9170]
Natl. Coun. for Support of Disability Issues [13212]
Natl. Scholarship Providers Assn. [9074]
Natl. Student Assistance Assn. [9171]
Natl. Student Exchange [9172]
Pan-American Assn. of Educational Credit Institutions [IO]
Prog. of Academic Exchange [8628]
School Nutrition Assn. [9173]
Student Services West [★8608]
Student Services West [★IO]
Student Services; YMCA Intl. [★13462]
Student Soc. of Am; Public Relations [9034]
Student Soc. for Stem Cell Res. [15114], 303 Bannockburn Ave., Tampa, FL 33617, (813)368-8937
Student Society for Stem Cell Research [IO], Tampa, FL, United States
Student Speech Language Hearing Assn; Natl. [16453]
Student Struggle for Soviet Jewry [17451]
Student Struggle for Soviet Jewry [IO], New York, NY, United States
Student/Teacher Org. to Prevent Nuclear War - Defunct.
Student Teaching; Assn. for [★9212]
Student Testing; Natl. Center for Res. on Evaluation, Standards, and [8285]
Student Training; Natl. Assn. of Supervisors of [★9212]
Student Travel Ser; U.S. [★8617]
Student Union of Latvia [IO], Riga, Latvia
Student Veterinary Emergency and Critical Care Soc. [IO], Athens, GA, United States
Student Veterinary Emergency and Critical Care Soc. [16810], c/o Desiree Broach, Externship Coor., 14 Chrisaren Ln., Athens, GA 30601
Student Visitors Ser; Intl. [★8617]
Student Volunteers for Amer. Indians - Defunct.
Student and Youth Travel Assn. [3938], 3048 Clarkston Rd., Lake Orion, MI 48362, (248)814-7982
Student and Youth Travel Assn. [IO], Lake Orion, MI, United States
Student Zionist Org. - Defunct.
Studentrad Haskola Islands [IO], Reykjavik, Iceland
Studentravel Assn. - Defunct.
Students
  ACT [9246]
  Adult Higher Educ. Alliance [7915]
  AFS Intercultural Programs [8589]
  AIESEC - Canada [IO]
  AIESEC - U.S. [8012]
  Alliance for Excellent Educ. [9118]
  Alpha Lambda Tau Intl. Social Fraternity [24613]
  Amer. Alliance for Hea., Physical Educ., Recreation and Dance [8979]
  Amer. Assn. of adaptedSPORTS Programs [23333]
  Amer. Assn. of Behavioral and Social Sciences [6522]
  Amer. Assn. for Collegiate Independent Stud. [7944]
  Amer. Assn. of Human Design Practitioners [1151]
  Amer. Assn. of Teachers of Arabic [7958]
  Amer. Assn. for Women in Community Colleges [9313]
  Amer. Catholic Philosophical Assn. [8965]
  Amer. Collegiate Horsemen's Assn. [4814]
  Amer. Debate Assn. [9151]
  Amer. Indian Bus. Leaders [2830]
  Amer. Indian Res. and Development [8464]
  Amer. Inst. for Foreign Stud. [8652]
  Amer. Inst. for Foreign Stud. Found. [8595]
  Amer. Medical Student Assn. [8844]
  Amer. Mock Trial Assn. [9281]
  Amer. Overseas Schools Historical Soc. [10012]
  Amer. Pre-Veterinary Medical Assn. [16774]
  Amer. Psychological Assn. of Graduate Students [16129]
  Amer. Soc. for Gravitational and Space Biology Student Assn. [6563]

Reference to "IO" in place of a book number signifies that the association may be found in the 45th edition of International Organizations.

Amer. Student Assn. of Community Colleges [9174]
Amer. Student Govt. Assn. [9175]
Asian Medical Student's Assn. - Philippines [IO]
ASPECT Found. [8599]
ASSE Intl. Student Exchange Programs [8600]
Assn. for Asian Stud. [7983]
Assn. for Borderlands Stud. [8653]
Assn. for Career and Tech. Educ. Res. [9301]
Assn. of Coll. Unions Intl. [9166]
Assn. des Etats Genereaux des Etudiants de l'Europe [IO]
Assn. of Governing Boards of Universities and Colleges [7889]
Assn. Internationale des Etudiants en Siences Economiques et Commerciales [IO]
Assn. of Native Amer. Medical Students [15087]
Assn. for Non-Traditional Students in Higher Educ. [7916]
Assn. of Nutrition Departments and Programs [8947]
Assn. of Teachers of Tech. Writing [9332]
Assn. for World Travel Exchange [8602]
Astronaut Scholars Honor Soc. [24584]
Australian Medical Students' Assn. [IO]
Austrian Medical Students Assn. [IO]
Austrian Natl. Union of Students [IO]
Belarusian Students Assn. [IO]
Beta Chi Theta Natl. Fraternity [24618]
Big Picture Company [8353]
Break Away: The Alternative Break Connection [12795]
Breakthroughs Abroad [9176]
Breakthroughs Abroad [IO]
British Universities North Am. Club [8606]
Broadcast Found. of College/University Students [8002]
Bus. Professionals of Am. [9302]
Canadian Alliance of Student Associations [IO]
Canadian Assn. for Internship Programs [IO]
Canadian Assn. of Pharmacy Students and Interns [IO]
Canadian Fed. of Medical Students [IO]
Canadian Fed. of Students [IO]
Carol Burnett Fund for Responsible Journalism [8707]
Catching the Dream [8427]
Center for Commercial-Free Public Educ. [8241]
Center for Commun. [8003]
Chinese Law Soc. of Am. [5933]
Clinical Legal Educ. Assn. [8763]
Close Up Found. [17071]
Coalition of Essential Schools [8180]
Coll. Parents of Am. [8485]
Coll. Summit [8486]
Collegiate Assn. of Table Top Gamers [22462]
Collegiate Broadcasters, Inc. [540]
Community of Caring [11588]
Compete Am. [8365]
Coun. for the Advancement of Standards in Higher Educ. [9177]
Coun. of Australian Postgraduate Associations [IO]
Coun. on Career for Minorities [8047]
Coun. for Children with Behavioral Disorders [9140]
Coun. for Elementary Sci. Intl. [9100]
Coun. for Intl. Exchange of Scholars/Institute of Intl. Educ. [8609]
Coun. of Latin-American Students of Architecture [292]
Coun. on Medical Student Educ. in Pediatrics [8861]
Coun. on Sexual Orientation and Gender Expression [9132]
Dance/Drill Team Directors of Am. [9876]
Div. on Career Development and Transition [9143]
Div. for Early Childhood of the Coun. for Exceptional Children [9144]
Educating for Justice [9126]
Educ. Pioneers [9178]
Educators Serving the Community [8318]
EF Found. for Foreign Stud. [8611]
Egyptian Student Assn. in North Am. [9179]
Egyptian Student Assn. in North Am. [IO]

Empower Prog. [8945]
ESIB - Natl. Unions of Students in Europe [IO]
Eta Sigma Alpha Natl. Home School Honor Soc. [8316]
European Pharmaceutical Students' Assn. [IO]
Fed. of Estonian Student Unions [IO]
Fed. des Etudiant(e)s Francophones [IO]
Feminist Teacher Editorial Collective [9318]
Financial Mgt. Assn. Intl. [8441]
Finnish Medical Students' Intl. Comm. [IO]
Found. for European Language and Educational Centres U.S.A. [8731]
Found. for Intl. Cooperation [8612]
Found. for Student Commun. [8023]
Francena Purchase Applied Liberal Stud. Soc. [9180]
Francena Purchase Applied Liberal Stud. Soc. [IO]
The Fund for Amer. Stud. [8747]
Future Bus. Leaders of Am. - Phi Beta Lambda [24622]
Gay, Lesbian, and Straight Educ. Network [8456]
Girlstart [8468]
Global Alliance for Justice Educ. [8766]
Global Nomads Gp. [9336]
GreatSchools [8066]
Green Leaf Natl. Honor Soc. [24471]
Hallgatoi Onkormanyzatok Orszagos Konferenciaja [IO]
Harry S. Truman Scholarship Found. [8430]
Hea. Occupations Students of Am. [8863]
Help Darfur Now [12259]
Hispanic Scholarship Fund [8431]
IES, Inst. for the Intl. Educ. of Students [8405]
INROADS [8749]
Intercollegiate Stud. Inst. [17271]
InterExchange [8617]
Intl. Alumni Assn. of Shri Mahavir Jain Vidyalaya [19346]
Intl. Assn. for the Exchange of Students for Tech. Experience [9181]
Intl. Assn. for the Exchange of Students for Tech. Experience [IO]
Intl. Assn. for Intelligence Educ. [8581]
Intl. Assn. for Learning Alternatives [7945]
Intl. Assn. of Students in Economics and Mgt. - Hong Kong Natl. Comm. [IO]
Intl. Assn. for Truancy and Dropout Prevention [8326]
Intl. Fed. of Medical Students' Associations [IO]
Intl. Medical Cooperation Comm. [IO]
Intl. Pharmaceutical Students' Fed. [IO]
Intl. Public Debate Assn. [9041]
Intl. Soc. of Anglo-Saxonists [8379]
Intl. Soc. for the Scholarship of Teaching and Learning [9073]
Intl. Student Week Ilmenau [IO]
Intl. Student/Young Pugwash - Norway [IO]
Intl. Union of Students [IO]
Intl. Veterinary Students' Assn. [IO]
InterVarsity Link [IO]
InterVarsity Link [9182]
Iranian Amer. Tech. Coun. [2352]
Japanese Natl. Honor Soc. [24521]
Jesuit Assn. of Student Personnel Administrators [7896]
Jewish Student Press Ser. [8694]
Junior State of Am. [8750]
Junior Statesmen Found. [8751]
Just Think [18852]
Labor and Working Class History Assn. [8723]
Law Student Div. [8769]
Law Students for Choice [18517]
Leadership Enterprise for a Diverse Am. [9183]
Lisle Intercultural [8623]
Mgt. Educ. Alliance [8029]
Metro Intl. Prog. Services of New York [8624]
Mid-American Greek Coun. Assn. [24483]
Military Child Educ. Coalition [8886]
Minority Student Achievement Network [8401]
Muslim Students Assn. of the U.S. and Canada [9184]
Muslim Students Assn. of the U.S. and Canada [IO]
NACEL Open Door [8625]

Natl. Abstinence Educ. Assn. [9123]
Natl. Adult Educ. Honor Soc. [24392]
Natl. Alliance of Blind Students [16871]
Natl. Alliance of State Sci. and Mathematics Coalitions [9106]
Natl. Assn. for the Advancement of Caring Teachers [9218]
Natl. Assn. for Community Coll. Entrepreneurship [8033]
Natl. Assn. of Community Coll. Teacher Educ. Programs [9221]
Natl. Assn. of Engg. Student Councils [7030]
Natl. Assn. of Fellowships Advisors [9080]
Natl. Assn. of Graduate-Professional Students [9185]
Natl. Assn. of Hea. Sci. Educ. Partnership [9107]
Natl. Assn. for Industry-Education Cooperation [8048]
Natl. Assn. of Private Special Educ. Centers [9147]
Natl. Assn. of Pupil Services Administrators [7902]
Natl. Assn. of School Nurses for the Deaf [14768]
Natl. Assn. of Special Educ. Teachers [9148]
Natl. Assn. of Student Councils [9186]
Natl. Assn. of Student Personnel Administrators [7904]
Natl. Assn. of Students Against Violence Everywhere [18117]
Natl. Assn. of Univ. Women [9320]
Natl. Black Graduate Student Assn. [18869]
Natl. Chinese Honor Soc. [24432]
Natl. Christian Forensics and Communications Assn. [8521]
Natl. Circus Proj. [8286]
Natl. CH for Commuter Programs [9187]
Natl. Coalition of Advocates for Students [8328]
Natl. Collegiate Paintball Assn. [23646]
Natl. Commun. Assn. [9157]
Natl. Conf. on Student Leadership [9188]
Natl. Coun. of Educ. Providers [8329]
Natl. Coun. On Bible Curriculum In Public Schools [9052]
Natl. Coun. on Student Development [9170]
Natl. Dance Inst. [8190]
Natl. Dropout Prevention Center/Network [8330]
Natl. FFA Org. [7940]
Natl. Forensic Assn. [9158]
Natl. Fraternity of Student Musicians [8924]
Natl. Geographic Soc. Educ. Found. [8458]
Natl. Hispanic Bus. Assn. [8039]
Natl. History Club [8509]
Natl. Intercollegiate Flying Assn. [21466]
Natl. Intercollegiate Running Club Assn. [23707]
Natl. Latina/Latino Law Student Assn. [17996]
Natl. Middle Level Sci. Teachers' Assn. [9112]
Natl. Org. for Human Services [9131]
Natl. Parliamentary Debate Assn. [9160]
Natl. Pell Grant Coalition [8433]
Natl. PTA - Natl. Cong. of Parents and Teachers [8954]
Natl. Scholarship Providers Assn. [9074]
Natl. Sci. Teachers Assn. [9114]
Natl. Soc. of Leadership and Success [9189]
Natl. Student Employment Assn. [8996]
Natl. Student Exchange [9172]
Natl. Student Nurses' Assn. [8873]
Natl. Student Safety Prog. [18579]
Natl. Student Union of Macedonia [IO]
Natl. Traditionalist Caucus [17276]
Natl. Tutoring Assn. [9283]
Natl. Union of Israel Students [IO]
Natl. Union of Students - Australia [IO]
Natl. Union of Students - United Kingdom [IO]
Natl. Valedictorian Soc. [9077]
Natl. Women's Stud. Assn. [9323]
Nieman Found. [8716]
North Amer. Assn. of Commencement Officers [8492]
North Amer. Coordinating Coun. on Japanese Lib. Resources [8781]
North Amer. South Asian Law Student Assn. [8773]
North Amer. Students of Cooperation [9190]
Oper. Enterprise [8808]
Org. of Amer. Kodaly Educators [8929]

A star before a book entry number signifies that the name is not listed separately, but is mentioned within the entry.

Outward Bound [9204]
Parents for Public Schools [12052]
Pathways to Coll. Network [8493]
Peer Hea. Exchange [9338]
People to People Intl. [17909]
Philosophy of Educ. Soc. [8969]
Photo Imaging Educ. Assn. [8974]
Plan of Action for Challenging Times [8331]
Prepare Tomorrow's Parents [13511]
Prog. of Academic Exchange [8628]
Public Relations Student Soc. of Am. [9034]
Religious Commun. Assn. [8116]
River of Words [4186]
Sallie Mae Fund [8434]
Sci. Songwriters' Assn. [10693]
Scripps Assn. of Families [8113]
Security on Campus [11846]
Sierra Student Coalition [4521]
Sigma Alpha Lambda [24519]
Sigma Beta Rho Fraternity [24656]
Soc. for the Advancement of Scandinavian Stud. [9070]
Soc. of Building Sci. Educators [8363]
Southeastern Regional Off. Natl. Scholarship Ser. and Fund for Negro Students [8435]
StandardsWork [9094]
Student Affl. Gp. [9191]
Student African Amer. Brotherhood [19444]
Student Amer. Veterinary Medical Assn. [16809]
Student Animal Rights Alliance [11337]
Student Christian Movement of Hong Kong [IO]
Student Conservation Assn. [4455]
Student Empowerment Training Proj. [9192]
Student Environmental Action Coalition [4607]
Student/Farmworker Alliance [24054]
Student Global AIDS Campaign [13585]
Student Leadership Network [9193]
Student Org. of North Am. [9194]
Student Osteopathic Medical Assn. [15815]
Student Photographic Soc. [10857]
Student Soc. for Stem Cell Res. [15114]
Student Union of Latvia [IO]
Student Veterinary Emergency and Critical Care Soc. [16810]
Student and Youth Travel Assn. [3938]
Studentrad Haskola Islands [IO]
Students for America [17277]
Students for the Exploration and Development of Space [7923]
Students in Free Enterprise [17637]
Students Helping St. Kids Intl. [11725]
Students Partnership Worldwide - UK [IO]
Students for the Second Amendment [17602]
Suzuki Assn. of the Americas [8932]
Swedish Natl. Union of Students [IO]
Taiwanese Collegian [19405]
Tech. Student Assn. [8547]
Tripoli Rocketry Assn. [9117]
Undergraduate Philosophy Assn. [8971]
Underprivileged Students of Anthropological Vocations [9079]
Union of North Am. Vietnamese Students Assn. [19426]
Union of Students in Ireland [IO]
U.S. Assn. of Former Members of Cong. [17253]
U.S. Collegiate Ski and Snowboard Assn. [23757]
U.S. Student Assn. [9195]
USSA Found. [9196]
Visitor Stud. Assn. [9280]
Washington Workshops Found. [8093]
What Kids Can Do [18859]
Wilderness Classroom Org. [8951]
World Commun. Assn. [8005]
World Heritage [8634]
Youth For Understanding USA [8639]
Zangle Natl. Users' Gp. [7216]
Students Against Destructive Decisions, Students Against Drunk Driving [12992], 255 Main St., Marlborough, MA 01752, (877)SADD-INC
Students Against Drunk Driving [★12992]
Students Against Drunk Driving; Students Against Destructive Decisions, [12992]
Students Against Famine Everywhere - Defunct.
Students Against Nuclear Suicide - Defunct.
Students for America [17277]

Students of Am; Hea. Occupations [8863]
Students of Anthropological Vocations; Underprivileged [9079]
Students' Assn. of Am; Armenian [18967]
Students Assn; Amer. Indian Law [★8772]
Students Assn; Amer. Podiatric [★16038]
Students' Assn; Amer. Podiatric Medical [16038]
Students Assn; Angelo State Univ. Ex- [★18874]
Students Assn; Black Amer. Law [★8771]
Students Assn; Dawn Bible [19517]
Students Assn; Intercollegiate Taiwanese Amer. [19401]
Students Assn; Natl. Black Law [8771]
Students Assn; Natl. Native Amer. Law [8772]
Students Assn; Natl. Women Law [9322]
Students Assn; Native Amer. Law [★8772]
Students; Broadcast Found. of College/University [8002]
Students for Change - Defunct.
Students Concerned With Public Health - Defunct.
Students for a Democratic Soc. - Defunct.
Students with Disabilities; Natl. Coalition for [★13212]
Students -English in Action; Greater New York Coun. for Foreign [★17885]
Students for the Exploration and Development of Space [7923], 77 Massachusetts Ave., MIT Rm. W20-401, Cambridge, MA 02139, (847)987-3879
Students in Free Enterprise [17637], The Jack Shewmaker SIFE World HQ, 1959 E Kerr St., Springfield, MO 65803-4775, (417)831-9505
Students Helping St. Kids Intl. [11725], PO Box 24117, Baltimore, MD 21227, (410)525-1051
Students Helping Street Kids International [IO], Baltimore, MD, United States
Students for a Libertarian Soc. - Defunct.
Students for Life of Am. [12928], 4141 N Henderson Rd., Ste. 4, Arlington, VA 22203, (703)351-6280
Students; Natl. Alliance of Blind [16871]
Students; Natl. Assn. of Graduate-Professional [9185]
Students; Natl. Coalition of Advocates for [8328]
Students; Natl. Fund for Minority Engg. [★8369]
Students; Natl. Scholarship Ser. and Fund for Negro [★8435]
Students' Org. in the U.S.A. and Canada; Israeli [19158]
Students Partnership Worldwide - UK [IO], London, United Kingdom
Students of Pharmacy; Acad. of [★15919]
Students of Pharmacy; Amer. Pharmaceutical Assn. Acad. of [★15919]
Students to Save Baltic and Mediterranean Avenues - Defunct.
Students for the Second Amendment [17602], 9624 Braun Run, San Antonio, TX 78254, (210)674-5559
Students for Social Responsibility [18172], c/o Student Center, PO Box 3010, Brooklyn, NY 11203-2098, (718)270-3160
Students; Soc. of Physics [7509]
Students; Southeastern Regional Off. Natl. Scholarship Ser. and Fund for Negro [8435]
Students for Tech. Experience (U.S.); Intl. Assn. for the Exchange of [★8601]
Students Together Ending Poverty - Address unknown since 2002.
Students Travel; Coun. on [★8608]
Students; Wayland Baptist Univ. Assn. of Former [18943]
Studiengesellschaft fur Unterirdische Verkehrsanlagen [★IO]
Stud. in Amer. Music; Inst. for [8911]
Stud; Assn. for the Advancement of Dutch-American [9908]
Stud. Assn; Amer. [9367]
Stud. Assn; Puerto Rican [19326]
Stud; Natl. Assn. for Ethnic [9919]
Stud; Natl. Assn. of Hispanic and Latino [9920]
Stud; Natl. Coun. on Foreign Language and Intl. [★8593]
Stud. in Tunis; Center for Maghrib [★7927]
Stud. in Tunis; Center for Maghrib [★IO]
Studio Art Quilt Associates [21547], PO Box 572, Storrs, CT 06268-0572, (860)487-4199

Studio Collector's Club - Address unknown since 1999.
Studio Publicity Directors' Comm. - Defunct.
Studio Suppliers Assn. - Address unknown since 1988.
Studiorum Novi Testamenti Societas [★IO]
Studium: North Amer. Study Center for Polish Affairs - Address unknown since 1999.
Studium Polski Podziemnej [★IO]
Stud. of African-American Life and History; Assn. for the [9356]
Stud. of Aging of Albany; Center for the [11281]
Stud. Circles Rsrc. Center [19390], PO Box 203, Pomfret, CT 06258, (860)928-2616
Stud. of the Coll. Fraternity; Center for the [24476]
Stud. of Democratic Societies; Center for the [17388]
Stud. and Documentation Centre on Appropriate Tech. in Developing Countries [★IO]
Study of Employment Policy; Natl. Found. for the [★12077]
Study; ERIS Roundtable for Independent [10792]
Stud. of Ethnoviolence; Prejudice Institute/Center for the Applied [17146]
Stud. of the Feebleminded; Amer. Assn. for the [★15239]
Study Group for Conservation of Clean Air and Water in Western Europe [★IO]
Study Group for Mathematical Learning - Address unknown since 2001.
Study Group on Social Security - Defunct.
Study Group; Stonehenge [6459]
Stud. of Human Knowledge; Inst. for the [10175]
Stud. of Islam Sect. [20108], c/o Omid Safi, Colgate Univ., Dept. of Philosophy and Religion, 13 Oak Dr., Hamilton, NY 13346
Stud. of Midwestern Literature; Soc. for the [10430]
Stud. of Play; The Assn. for the [10858]
Stud. of Prejudice and Ethnoviolence; Center for the Applied [★17146]
Stud. for the Promotion of Byzantine Stud. [IO], Oxford, United Kingdom
Stud. of Religion; Coun. of Societies for the [9274]
Stud. Soc. [★IO]
Stud. of Soc. and History; Soc. for the Comparative [10152]
Stud. of Southern Literature; Soc. for the [10431]
Stud. of Soviet-Type Economies; Assn. for the [★6870]
Stud. of States; Center for the [★6275]
Stud. Unit; Chemistry and Physics [★22802]
Stud. of Welfare Policy; Center for the [★18432]
Studying Hea. Sys. Change; Center for [14621]
Stukely Westcott Descendants of Am; Soc. of [21056]
Stumpwork Soc. - Address unknown since 2001.
Stuntmen's Assn; Black [1379]
Stuntmen's Assn. of Motion Pictures [1393], 10660 Riverside Dr., 2nd Fl., Ste. E, Toluca Lake, CA 91602, (818)766-4334
Stunts Unlimited [19391], 7551 W Sunset Blvd., Ste. 203, Los Angeles, CA 90046-3442, (323)851-1970
Stuntwomen's Assn. of Motion Pictures [1394], 12457 Ventura Blvd., No. 208, Studio City, CA 91604-2411, (818)762-0907
Sturge-Weber Found. [15365], PO Box 418, Mount Freedom, NJ 07970-0418, (973)895-4445
Sturvil Corp. - Address unknown since 2004.
Stutter; Friends: The Natl. Assn. of Young People Who [16445]
Stutterers; Intl. Found. for [16447]
Stuttering
　Intl. Found. for Stutterers [16447]
　Intl. Stuttering Assn. [16498]
　Intl. Stuttering Assn. [IO]
　Speak Easy Intl. Found. [16455]
Stuttering Assn; Natl. [16454]
Stuttering Found. of Am. [16456], 3100 Walnut Grove Rd., Ste. 603, PO Box 11749, Memphis, TN 38111-0749, (901)452-7343
Stuttering; Natl. Center for [16450]
Stuttering Treatment and Professional Training; Amer. Inst. for [16440]
Stutz Club [21791], PO Box 86, Greenford, OH 44422, (330)730-9498

Reference to "IO" in place of a book number signifies that the association may be found in the 45th edition of International Organizations.

Stvaralacka omladina Novog Sada [★IO]
Styrene Butadiene Latex Mfrs. Coun. (SBLMC) [★820]
Styrene and Ethylbenzene Assn. - Defunct.
Styrene Info. and Res. Center [823], 1300 Wilson Blvd., Ste. 1200, Arlington, VA 22209, (703)741-5010
Sub-Aqua Assn. [IO], Liverpool, United Kingdom
Subacute Care Assn; Natl. [★14728]
Subacute and Post-Acute Care; Natl. Assn. of [14728]
Subaru 360 Drivers' Club [21792], 2341 S Circle X Pl., Tucson, AZ 85713, (520)290-6492
Subcommn. for Catholic-Jewish Relations [★19910]
Subcontractors Assn; Amer. [1003]
Subcontractors Assn. (FASA); Foundation of the Amer. [★1003]
Submarine Indus. Base Coun. [1149], 1399 New York Ave. NW, Ste. 550, Washington, DC 20005, (202)207-3633
Submarine League; Naval [17384]
Submarine Veterans of World War II; U.S. [21410]
Submersible Wastewater Pump Assn. [677], 1866 Sheridan Rd., Ste. 201, Highland Park, IL 60035-2545, (847)681-1868
Submetering and Utility Allocation Assn; Natl. [3961]
Subrogation Professionals; Natl. Assn. of [3185]
Subscription Fulfillment Managers Assn. [★3224]
Subscription TV Assn. - Defunct.
Substance Abuse
    ABLE: Assn. for Better Living and Educ. Intl. [11756]
    Addiction Res. and Treatment Corp. [13213]
    Addictions Ontario [IO]
    Adult Children of Alcoholics World Ser. Org. [13012]
    Al-Anon Family Gp. HQ, World Ser. Off. [13214]
    Al-Anon Family Gp. HQ, World Ser. Off. [IO]
    Al-Anon Family Groups - United Kingdom and Eire [IO]
    Alateen [IO]
    Alateen [13215]
    Alcohol Concern [IO]
    Alcohol and Drug Problems Assn. of North Am. [13216]
    Alcohol Focus Scotland [IO]
    Alcohol and Other Drugs Coun. of Australia [IO]
    Alcohol Res. Info. Ser. [13217]
    Alcoholics Anonymous - Australia [IO]
    Alcoholics Anonymous - Brazil [IO]
    Alcoholics Anonymous - England [IO]
    Alcoholics Anonymous - French Gen. Services Off. [IO]
    Alcoholics Anonymous World Services [IO]
    Alcoholics Anonymous World Services [13218]
    Alcoholics Anonymous World Services - Gen. Ser. Bd. for French-Speaking Belgium [IO]
    Alcoholics Anonymous World Services - New Zealand Gen. Services Off. [IO]
    Alcoholics Anonymous World Services - Swedish Gen. Services Off. [IO]
    Amer. Acad. of Addiction Psychiatry [16062]
    Amer. Assn. for the Treatment of Opioid Dependence [16499]
    Amer. Coll. of Addiction Treatment Administrators [13219]
    Amer. Coun. on Alcohol Problems [13220]
    Amer. Coun. on Alcoholism [13221]
    Amer. Coun. for Drug Educ. [13222]
    Amer. Hea. and Temperance Assn. [13303]
    Amer. Osteopathic Acad. of Addiction Medicine [16500]
    Amer. Outreach Assn. [13223]
    Amer. Psychological Assn. - Addictions Div. [16123]
    Amer. Soc. of Addiction Medicine [16501]
    Assn. of Halfway House Alcoholism Programs of North Am. [13224]
    Assn. for Medical Educ. and Res. in Substance Abuse [8849]
    Assn. of Recovering Motorcyclists [13225]
    Assn. for the Treatment of Tobacco Use and Dependence [16653]
    Australian Drug Found. [IO]
    BACCHUS Network [IO]

BACCHUS Network [13226]
Black Mental Hea. Alliance [15193]
Calix Soc. [13227]
Calix Soc. [IO]
Canada Atlantic Region of Narcotics Anonymous [IO]
Canadian Centre on Substance Abuse [IO]
Center for Substance Abuse Prevention [16502]
Children of Alcoholics Found. [13228]
Chinook Area of Narcotics Anonymous [IO]
Christian Addiction Rehabilitation Assn. [13229]
Citizens Against Drug Impaired Drivers [13230]
Co-Anon Family Groups [13231]
Cocaine Anonymous World Services [13232]
Cocaine Anonymous World Services [IO]
Common Sense for Drug Policy [18436]
Community Anti-Drug Coalitions of Am. [13233]
Consortium of Behavioral Hea. Nurses and Associates [15474]
Corporate and Found. Relations [12075]
DanceSafe [12041]
D.A.R.E. Am. [13234]
Do It Now Found. [13235]
Drug and Alcohol Testing Indus. Assn. [13236]
Drug Free Kids: America's Challenge [18687]
Drug Strategies [16503]
DrugScope [IO]
Dual Disorders Anonymous [13237]
Edmonton Area Narcotics Anonymous [IO]
Employee Assistance Professionals Assn. [13203]
Entertainment Indus. Coun. [13238]
Entertainment Indus. Found. [12114]
Ethos Found. [13239]
European Assn. for the Treatment of Addiction - U.K. [IO]
European Blue Cross Youth Assn. [IO]
Faces and Voices of Recovery [18688]
Families Anonymous [13240]
Families Anonymous [IO]
Families Worldwide [IO]
Families Worldwide [13241]
Family Coun. on Drug Awareness [13242]
Family Coun. on Drug Awareness [IO]
Family Res. Inst. [17688]
Friendly Hand Found. [13243]
Friends of Temperance [IO]
Fundacion Antidrogas de El Salvador [IO]
Harm Reduction Coalition [12042]
Hazelden Found. [13244]
Hea. Connection [13245]
Impaired Physician Prog. [13246]
Inst. for a Drug-Free Workplace [13247]
Inst. on Global Drug Policy [13248]
Inst. on Global Drug Policy [IO]
Inst. for Integral Development [13249]
Inter-Association Task Force on Alcohol and Other Substance Abuse Issues [13250]
Intl. Assn. of Addictions and Offender Counselors [11824]
Intl. Assn. for Educ. to a Life Without Drugs - Norway [IO]
Intl. Coalition for Addiction Stud. Educ. [9197]
Intl. Commn. for the Prevention of Alcoholism and Drug Dependency [13251]
Intl. Commn. for the Prevention of Alcoholism and Drug Dependency [IO]
Intl. Coun. on Alcohol and Addictions [IO]
Intl. Coun. on Alcohol, Drugs and Traffic Safety [IO]
Intl. Coun. on Alcohol, Drugs and Traffic Safety [16504]
Intl. Doctors in Alcoholics Anonymous [13252]
Intl. Doctors in Alcoholics Anonymous [IO]
Intl. Fed. of the Blue Cross [IO]
Intl. Hea. and Temperance Assn. [13304]
Intl. Lawyers in Alcoholics Anonymous [13253]
Intl. Narcotics Interdiction Assn. [5742]
Intl. Nurses Anonymous [16505]
International Nurses Anonymous [IO]
Intl. Nurses Soc. on Addictions [15484]
Intl. Soc. for Biomedical Res. on Alcoholism [16506]
Intl. Soc. for Biomedical Res. on Alcoholism [IO]
Intl. Substance Abuse and Addiction Coalition [IO]
Jewish Alcoholics, Chemically Dependent Persons and Significant Others [IO]

Jewish Alcoholics, Chemically Dependent Persons and Significant Others [13254]
Join Together [18689]
Lifegain Inst. [14573]
Luz Social Services [13255]
MAD DADS (Men Against Destruction - Defending Against Drugs and Social Disorder) [12043]
Moderation Mgt. [16507]
Mothers Against Drunk Driving [12969]
Mothers Against Misuse and Abuse [16508]
Motion Picture and TV Fund [12115]
NAADAC The Assn. for Addiction Professionals [16509]
Narcotic Educational Found. of Am. [13256]
Narcoticos Anonimos de Argentina [IO]
Narcotics Anonymous [13257]
Narcotics Anonymous Berlin [IO]
Narcotics Anonymous Bombay, India [IO]
Narcotics Anonymous British Columbia Region [IO]
Narcotics Anonymous - Hamilton Area [IO]
Narcotics Anonymous Ireland [IO]
Narcotics Anonymous Malta [IO]
Narcotics Anonymous Mexico Region [IO]
Narcotics Anonymous Polish Region [IO]
Narcotics Anonymous Southern Area Ser. Comm. [IO]
Narcotics Anonymous UK Region [IO]
Narcotics Anonymous - Victoria Area [IO]
National Acupuncture Detoxification Association [IO]
Natl. Acupuncture Detoxification Assn. [16510]
Natl. African Amer. Drug Policy Coalition [17440]
Natl. Alliance of Advocates for Buprenorphine Treatment [16511]
Natl. Alliance of Methadone Advocates [14293]
Natl. Asian Pacific Amer. Families Against Substance Abuse [13258]
Natl. Assn. of Addiction Treatment Providers [13259]
Natl. Assn. on Alcohol, Drugs and Disability [16512]
Natl. Assn. of Athletes Against Drugs [13260]
Natl. Assn. for Children of Alcoholics [13261]
Natl. Assn. on Drug Abuse Problems [13262]
Natl. Assn. of Drug Court Professionals [6289]
National Association of Drug Court Professionals [IO]
Natl. Assn. of Drug Diversion Investigators [5986]
Natl. Assn. of Lesbian/Gay Addiction Professionals [13263]
Natl. Assn. of Psychiatric Hea. Systems [16091]
Natl. Assn. of State Alcohol and Drug Abuse Directors [13264]
Natl. Assn. of Substance Abuse Trainers and Educators [9198]
Natl. Black Alcoholism and Addiction Coun. [13265]
Natl. Catholic Coun. on Alcoholism and Related Drug Problems [13266]
National Catholic Council on Alcoholism and Related Drug Problems [IO]
Natl. CH for Alcohol and Drug Info. [16513]
Natl. Commn. Against Drunk Driving [12973]
Natl. Comm. for the Prevention of Alcoholism and Drug Dependency [13267]
National Committee for the Prevention of Alcoholism and Drug Dependency [IO]
Natl. Coun. on Alcoholism and Drug Dependence [13268]
Natl. Families in Action [13269]
Natl. Family Partnership [13270]
Natl. Gym Assn. [23654]
Natl. Inhalant Prevention Coalition [16514]
Natl. Org. on Fetal Alcohol Syndrome [16515]
Natl. Temperance and Prohibition Coun. [13305]
Natl. Woman's Christian Temperance Union [13306]
New Hope Found. [13271]
Nordic Coun. for Alcohol and Drug Res. [IO]
North West England and North Wales Narcotics Anonymous [IO]
November Coalition [18690]
Our Youths Found. [IO]

A star before a book entry number signifies that the name is not listed separately, but is mentioned within the entry.

Partnership for a Drug-Free Am. [13272]
People Against Impaired Driving [IO]
People Against Rape [13083]
Phoenix House [13273]
Pill Addicts Anonymous [13274]
Pills Anonymous [13275]
Pioneer Total Abstinence Assn. [IO]
PRIDE Youth Programs [13276]
Proj. Renewal [13277]
Rational Recovery Systems [16516]
Re-Solv, the Soc. for the Prevention of Solvent
 and Volatile Substance Abuse [IO]
Recovered Alcoholic Clergy Assn. [13278]
Recovery Ministries [13279]
Remembering ADAM [13280]
Res. Soc. on Alcoholism [16517]
Road Recovery Found. [16518]
Sect. for Psychiatric and Substance Abuse
 Services [16093]
Secular Organizations for Sobriety [13281]
SMART Recovery [16519]
SmokeFree Educational Services [16434]
Soc. for Prevention Res. [16520]
Society for Prevention Research [IO]
Soc. for the Stud. of Addiction to Alcohol and
 Other Drugs [IO]
Students Against Destructive Decisions, Students
 Against Drunk Driving [12992]
Substance Abuse Prog. Administrators Assn.
 [16521]
Substance Abuse Prog. Administrators Assn. [IO]
Therapeutic Communities of Am. [13282]
Toronto Area of Narcotics Anonymous [IO]
Triangle Club [13283]
VietNow Natl. [13359]
Vocational Found., Inc. [12103]
Women for Sobriety [13284]
Women in Transition [13447]
Women's Drug Res. Project [13285]
Youth Organizations U.S.A. [13523]
Substance Abuse; Assn. for Medical Educ. and Res.
 in [8849]
Substance Abuse Intl; Consolidated Assn. of Nurses
 in [★15484]
Substance Abuse Issues; Inter-Association Task
 Force on Campus Alcohol and Other [★13250]
Substance Abuse Librarians and Info. Specialists
 [10390], PO Box 9513, Berkeley, CA 94709-0513,
 (510)597-3440
Substance Abuse Librarians and Information
 Specialists [IO], Berkeley, CA, United States
Substance Abuse Prog. Administrators Assn. [IO],
 Germantown, MD, United States
Substance Abuse Prog. Administrators Assn.
 [16521], 1014 Whispering Oak Dr., Bardstown, KY
 40004, (800)672-7229
Substance Abuse Services; Sect. for Psychiatric and
 [16093]
Substances Authorities; Natl. Assn. of State
 Controlled [5672]
Substituted Anilines Task Force - Address unknown
 since 1994.
Subterranean Construction
 Amer. Underground Constr. Assn. [7715]
 Common Ground Alliance [12958]
 London Subterranean Survey Assn. [IO]
Subterranean Sociological Assn. - Address unknown
 since 2000.
Subud
 Subud Intl. Cultural Assn. - U.S.A. [9600]
 Subud U.S.A. [20589]
Subud Intl. Cultural Assn. [★9600]
Subud Intl. Cultural Assn. - U.S.A. [9600], 14019 NE
 8th St., Ste. A, Bellevue, WA 98007, (425)643-
 1904
Subud North Am. [★20589]
Subud U.S.A. [20589], 14019 NE 8th St., Ste. A,
 Bellevue, WA 98007, (425)643-1904
Subud Youth Assn. [13516], 14019 NE 8th St., Ste.
 A, Bellevue, WA 98007, (425)643-1904
Suburban Newspapers of Am. [3259], 116 Cass St.,
 Traverse City, MI 49684, (843)390-1531
Suburban Sect. of the Natl. Newspaper Assn.
 [★3259]
Successful Magazine Publishers Group - Defunct.

Succulent Res; Arizona Cactus and [6631]
Succulent Soc. of Am; Cactus and [22506]
Succulent Soc. of South Africa [IO], Pretoria,
 Republic of South Africa
Sucro-Sac-Ologists Soc. Intl. - Defunct.
Sudan-American Found. for Educ. [8073], 4141 N
 Henderson Rd., Ste. 1205, Arlington, VA 22203,
 (703)525-9045
Sudan Athletic Assn. [IO], Khartoum, Sudan
Sudan Development Assn. - Defunct.
Sudan Lawn Tennis Assn. [IO], Khartoum, Sudan
Sudan Squash Fed. [IO], Khartoum, Sudan
Sudan Stud. Assn. [IO], Providence, RI, United
 States
Sudan Stud. Assn. [7930], c/o Dr. Richard Lobban,
 Exec. Dir., Rhode Island Coll., Dept. of Anthropol-
 ogy, 600 Mt. Pleasant Ave., Providence, RI 02908,
 (401)456-8784
Sudan Stud. Soc. of the United Kingdom [IO],
 Grange-Over-Sands, United Kingdom
SUDANAID - Caritas Sudan [IO], Khartoum, Sudan
Sudanese Standard and Metrology Org. [IO], Khar-
 toum, Sudan
Sudanese Taekwondo Fed. [IO], Khartoum, Sudan
Sudden Arrhythmia Death Syndromes Found.
 [14484], 508 E South Temple, Ste. 20, Salt Lake
 City, UT 84102-1013, (801)531-0937
Sudden Cardiac Arrest Assn. [13933], 1133 Con-
 necticut Ave. NW, 11th Fl., Washington, DC 20036,
 (202)719-8909
Sudden Infant Death Syndrome
 Amer. Guild for Infant Survival [16522]
 Amer. Sudden Infant Death Syndrome Inst.
  [16523]
 Assn. of SIDS and Infant Mortality Programs
  [16524]
 First Candle/SIDS Alliance [16525]
 Irish Sudden Infant Death Assn. [IO]
 Natl. SIDS/Infant Death Rsrc. Center [16526]
 StopSIDS.org [16527]
 Sudden Infant Death Syndrome Awareness for
  Africa [IO]
Sudden Infant Death Syndrome Alliance [★16525]
Sudden Infant Death Syndrome Awareness for Africa
 [IO], Lagos, Nigeria
Sudden Infant Death Syndrome CH; Natl. [★16526]
Sudden Infant Death Syndrome (SIDS) Alliance
 [★16525]
Suede and Leather Refinishers of America - Defunct.
Sueriges Skeppsmaklareforening [★IO]
SUFFER [★13324]
Suffolk Chamber of Commerce [IO], Ipswich, United
 Kingdom
Suffolk County Comm. for a World Peace Tax Fund
 [★18716]
Suffolk Horse Assn; Amer. [4847]
Suffolk Sheep Assn; United [5219]
Suffolk Sheep Soc; United [★5219]
Suffrage Assn; Natl. Woman's [★18459]
Sufi Psychology Assn. [16187], 9985 Horn Rd., Ste.
 C, Sacramento, CA 95827, (916)368-5530
Sufism
 Intl. Sufi Movement [IO]
Sufism; Intl. Assn. of [20101]
Sufism; School of Islamic [★20576]
Sugar
 All Trinidad Sugar and Gen. Workers' Trade Union
  [IO]
 Amer. Soc. of Sugar Cane Technologists [3700]
 Amer. Sugar Alliance [1499]
 Amer. Sugar Cane League of the U.S.A. [5225]
 Amer. Sugarbeet Growers Assn. [5226]
 Argentine Sugar Center [IO]
 Australian Cane Farmers Assn. [IO]
 Australian Soc. of Sugar Cane Technologists [IO]
 Beet Sugar Development Found. [5227]
 Canadian Sugar Inst. [IO]
 Canegrowers [IO]
 Chamber of Sugar Producers [IO]
 European Comm. for Sugar Manufacturers [IO]
 Global Alliance for Sugar Trade Reform and Liber-
  alisation [IO]
 Hawaii Agriculture Res. Center [5228]
 Honduran Assn. of Sugar Producers [IO]
 Indian Sugar Mills Assn. [IO]

 Intl. Confed. of European Sugar-Beet Growers
  [IO]
 Intl. Soc. of Sugar Cane Technologists [IO]
 Intl. Sugar Org. [IO]
 Intl. Sweeteners Assn. [IO]
 Natl. Assn. of Sugar, Alcohol and Yeast
  Manufacturers [IO]
 Natl. Chamber of the Sugar and Alcohol Indus.
  [IO]
 Natl. Sugar Ingredient Marketing Assn. [1553]
 Natl. Sweet Sorghum Producers and Processors
  Assn. [871]
 Pakistan Sugar Mills Assn. [IO]
 Philippine Sugar Millers Assn. [IO]
 Red River Valley Sugarbeet Growers Assn. [5229]
 Refined Sugar Assn. [IO]
 South African Sugar Indus. Agronomists' Assn.
  [IO]
 South African Sugar Technologists' Assn. [IO]
 South African Sugarcane Res. Inst. [IO]
 Spanish Assn. of Sugar Confectionary and Chew-
  ing Gum Manufacturers [IO]
 Sugar Assn. [1564]
 Sugar Assn. of London [IO]
 Sugar Bur. [IO]
 Sugar Indus. Technologists [7097]
 Sugar Technologists' Assn. of India [IO]
 Sugar Traders Assn. of the United Kingdom [IO]
 Swaziland Sugar Assn. [IO]
 U.S. Beet Sugar Assn. [1567]
 World Assn. of Beet and Cane Growers [IO]
 World Sugar Res. Org. [IO]
Sugar Alliance; Amer. [1499]
Sugar Assn. [1564], 1300 L St. NW, Ste. 1001,
 Washington, DC 20005, (202)785-1122
Sugar Assn. of London [IO], London, United
 Kingdom
Sugar Assn; U.S. Beet [1567]
Sugar Beet Technologists; Amer. Soc. of [7089]
Sugar Bur. [IO], London, United Kingdom
Sugar Glider Assn; Intl. [11483]
Sugar Indus. Technologists [7097], 164 N Hall Dr.,
 Sugar Land, TX 77478, (281)494-2046
Sugar Indus. Technologists [IO], Sugar Land, TX,
 United States
Sugar Indus; U.S. Beet [★1567]
Sugar Information Bur. - Defunct.
Sugar Ingredient Marketing Assn; Natl. [1553]
Sugar Mfrs. Assn; U.S. [★1567]
Sugar Milling Res. Inst. [IO], Durban, Republic of
 South Africa
Sugar Packet Collectors Club - Defunct.
Sugar Planters Assn., Amer. Cane Growers Assn.
 and; Louisiana [★5225]
Sugar Planters' Assn; Hawaiian [★5228]
Sugar Technologists' Assn. of India [IO], New Delhi,
 India
Sugar Traders Assn. of the United Kingdom [IO],
 London, United Kingdom
Suicide
 Amer. Assn. of Suicidology [13286]
 Amer. Found. for Suicide Prevention [13287]
 Befrienders Worldwide [IO]
 Canadian Assn. for Suicide Prevention [IO]
 Communities Against Violence Network [13374]
 Compassion in Dying Fed. [12130]
 Euthanasia Res. and Guidance Org. [12132]
 Girls and Boys Town [12934]
 Heartbeat [13288]
 Intl. Assn. for Suicide Prevention [IO]
 Irish Assn. of Suicidology [IO]
 Natl. Org. for People of Color Against Suicide
  [13289]
 Org. for Attempters and Survivors of Suicide in
  Interfaith Services [13290]
 Proj. YES [9339]
 Ray of Hope [13291]
 Samaritans - England [IO]
 Samaritans - Western Australia [IO]
 Suicide Info. and Educ. Coll. [IO]
 Suicide and Mental Hea. Assn. Intl. [15234]
 Suicide Prevention Action Network USA [13292]
 William Wendt Center for Loss and Healing
  [13317]
Suicide Found; Maryland [★13287]

Reference to "IO" in place of a book number signifies that the association may be found in the 45th edition of International Organizations.

Suicide Info. and Educ. Coll. [IO], Calgary, AB, Canada

Suicide; Intl. Task Force on Euthanasia and Assisted [12133]

Suicide and Mental Hea. Assn. Intl. [15234], PO Box 702, Sioux Falls, SD 57101-0702

Suicide and Mental Hea. Assn. Intl. [IO], Sioux Falls, SD, United States

Suicide Prevention Action Network USA [13292], 1025 Vermont Ave. NW, Ste. 1066, Washington, DC 20005, (202)449-3600

Suicide Prevention; Amer. Found. for [13287]

Suid-Afrikaanse Avokadokwekersverening [★IO]

Suid-Afrikaanse Chemiese Instituut [★IO]

Suid-Afrikaanse Federasie van Druknywerhede [★IO]

Suid-Afrikaanse Marfansindroom Ondersteunings-groep [★IO]

Suid-Afrikaanse Mediese Fisika Vereniging [★IO]

Suid-Afrikaanse Orgideeraad [★IO]

Suid-Afrikaanse Ortopediese Vereniging [★IO]

Suid-Afrikaanse Vereniging van Kinderchirurge [★IO]

Suid-Afrikaanse Vertalersinstituut [★IO]

Suid Afrikaanse Wingerd en Wynkundevereniging [★IO]

Suid-Afrikaanse Wiskundevereniging [★IO]

Suider-Afrika Genootskap vir die Bevordering van die Wetenskap [★IO]

Suider Afrikaanse Akoestiekinstituut [★IO]

Suider Afrikaanse Museumvereniging [★IO]

Suit Assn; New York Coat and [253]

Suit Mfrs. Assn; Amer. Cloak and [223]

Suit and Skirt Mfrs; Industrial Coun. of Cloak, [★253]

Suite Assn; Executive [★74]

Suite Directors; Assn. of Luxury [3676]

Sulabh Intl. Org. [★IO]

Sulabh Intl. Social Ser. Org. [IO], New Delhi, India

Sulfate of Potash Magnesia Export Assn. - Defunct.

Sulfonated Oils Mfrs. Assn. - Defunct.

Sullivan Soc; Gilbert and [9809]

Sullivan Soc; Midwestern Gilbert and [9813]

Sullivant Moss Soc. [★6621]

Sullivant Moss Soc. [★IO]

Sulphur Export Corp. - Defunct.

Sulphur Horse Assn; Amer. [22585]

The Sulphur Inst. [824], 1140 Connecticut Ave. NW, Ste. 612, Washington, DC 20036, (202)331-9660

The Sulphur Inst. [IO], Washington, DC, United States

Sultan Qaboos bin Said Res. Center [★IO]

Sultan Qaboos bin Said Res. Center [★18062]

Sumatran Orangutan Soc. - UK [IO], Oxford, United Kingdom

Sumatran Orangutan Soc. USA [5384], 7017 High-view Terr., Apt. No. 102, Hyattsville, MD 20782, (301)648-3855

Sumi-e Soc. of Am. [9475], c/o Ms. Karen Kurka Jensen, Membership Sec., 2523 Zika Ave. NW, Cedar Rapids, IA 52405, (703)812-8175

Summer and Casual Furniture Mfrs. Assn. [1706], c/o Joseph P. Logan, Exec. Dir., 317 W High Ave., 10th Fl., High Point, NC 27260, (336)884-5000

Summer Flight Acad. for Youth [★164]

Summer Institutes for Secondary School Teachers - Defunct.

Summer School

Assn. of Univ. Summer Sessions [9199]

Natl. Assn. of Women Bus. Owners [744]

North Amer. Assn. of Summer Sessions [9200]

North Amer. Assn. of Summer Sessions [IO]

North Central Conf. on Summer Schools [9201]

Summer Sessions Deans and Directors; Assn. of [★9199]

Summer Sessions; Natl. Assn. of [★9200]

Summer Sessions; Natl. Assn. of Coll. and Univ. [★9200]

Summer Vocal Institute [★8900]

Summer Vocal Institute [★IO]

Summerbridge Natl. [★8236]

Summerhill Collective - Address unknown since 1995.

Summerhill Soc. - Address unknown since 1995.

Summerland Olives [IO], Casino, Australia

The Summit Lighthouse [★19462]

Sumner Family Assn. [21066], 7540 Rolling River Pkwy., Nashville, TN 37221-3322, (615)646-9946

Sumner Family Assn. [IO], Nashville, TN, United States

Sump Pump Mfrs. Assn. [★IO]

Sump Pump Mfrs. Assn. [★678]

Sump and Sewage Pump Mfrs. Assn. [678], PO Box 647, Northbrook, IL 60065-0647, (847)559-9233

Sump and Sewage Pump Manufacturers Association [IO], Northbrook, IL, United States

Sun Bay Recovery - Intl. Missing Children's Div. - Address unknown since 1995.

Sun Do Mountain Taoist Breathing Meditation Center [★10294]

Sun Do Mountain Taoist Breathing Meditation Center [★IO]

Sun Glass Inst. of America - Defunct.

Sun Growers of California - Defunct.

Sun-Maid Growers of California [4762], 13525 S Be-thel Ave., Kingsburg, CA 93631, (559)896-8000

Sun Marine Employees Assn. - Defunct.

Sun Mountain Res. Center [★4656]

Sun Safety Alliance [13876], c/o Phil Schneider, Exec. Dir., 413 N Lee St., Alexandria, VA 22314, (703)837-4202

SUN Symphony Soc. Inc. [★9601]

SUN Symphony Soc. Inc. [★IO]

Sun User Group - Address unknown since 2002.

Sunbathing Assn; Amer. [★10760]

Sunbeam

California Assn. of Tiger-Owners [21603]

Tigers East/Alpines East [21796]

Sunbeam Alpine Club - Defunct.

Sunbeam Car Club - Defunct.

Sunbeam Rapier Registry [21793], c/o James Ma-zour, Founder, 3212 Orchard Cir., West Des Moines, IA 50266, (515)226-9475

Sunbeam Rapier Registry of North Am. [★21793]

Sunbeam Registry; Midwest [21706]

SunBelt Inst. - Address unknown since 2000.

SunCoast Fundogs Agility Club [IO], Brisbane, Australia

SunDance [IO], Sissach, Switzerland

Sundance Inst. [9948], PO Box 684426, Park City, UT 84068, (801)328-3456

Sunday and Feature Editors; Amer. Assn. of [3079]

Sunday School; Res. Commn. of Natl. [★8088]

Sunday School Union; Amer. [★20296]

Sunfish Class; Alcort Sailfish- [★23194]

Sunfish Class; AMF Alcort Sailfish- [★23194]

Sunfish Class Assn; Intl. [★23194]

Sunfish Racing Class Assn; AMF [★23194]

Sunflower Alliance - Defunct.

Sunflower Assn. of Am. [★4312]

Sunflower Assn; Natl. [4312]

Sunflowers Processors Assn. - Defunct.

Sunglass Assn. of Am. [257], 390 N Bridge St., La-Belle, FL 33935, (863)612-0085

Sunkist Growers [4763], PO Box 7888, Van Nuys, CA 91409-7888, (818)986-4800

Sunny Von Bulow Natl. Victim Advocacy Center [★13366]

SunnyTravelers [22963], PO Box 169, Osceola, IN 46561, (574)258-0571

Sunroom Assn; Natl. [653]

Sunshine Found. [11726], 1041 Mill Creek Dr., Feasterville, PA 19053, (215)396-4770

Sunshine Proj. [IO], Hamburg, Germany

Sunsweet Growers [4764], 901 N Walton Ave., Yuba City, CA 95993, (530)674-5010

Suntanning Assn. for Educ. [3364], PO Box 1181, Gulf Breeze, FL 32562, (800)536-8255

SUNY Biomedical Communication Network - Defunct.

Suomen hahmontunnistustutkimusken seura ry [★IO]

Suomen 4H-liitto [★IO]

Suomen Aikidoliitto [★IO]

Suomen Akateemisten Naisten Liitto - Finlands Kvinnliga Akademikers Forbund ry [★IO]

Suomen Ammattilittojen Solidaarissuskeskus [★IO]

Suomen Ampumahiihtoliito [★IO]

Suomen Ampumaurheiluliitto [★IO]

Suomen Anaetesiologiyhdistys [★IO]

Suomen Apteekkariliitto [★IO]

Suomen Autokoululiitto [★IO]

Suomen Automaatioseura [★IO]

Suomen Autoteknillinen Liitto ry [★IO]

Suomen Avaruustutkimusseura [★IO]

Suomen Bensiinikauppiaitten Liitto ry [★IO]

Suomen Biljardiliitto [★IO]

Suomen Biologian Seura Vanamo [IO], Helsinki, Finland

Suomen Curlingliitto [★IO]

Suomen Egyptologinen Seura [★IO]

Suomen Elintarviketyoelaeisten Liitto [★IO]

Suomen Farmakologiyhdistys [★IO]

Suomen Franchising-Yhdistys [★IO]

Suomen Fyysikkoseura Finlands Fysikerforening r.y. [★IO]

Suomen Gynekologiyhdistys Ry [★IO]

Suomen Historiallinen Seura [★IO]

Suomen Journalistiliitto [★IO]

Suomen Kalankasvattajaliitto [★IO]

Suomen Kansanopistoyhdistys [★IO]

Suomen Kardiologinen Seura [★IO]

Suomen Kehitysvammaisten Liikunta ja Urheilu Ty [★IO]

Suomen Kelloseppaliitto ry [★IO]

Suomen Kirjailijaliitto [★IO]

Suomen Kirjastoseura [★IO]

Suomen Krikettiliitto RY [★IO]

Suomen Kulttuurirahasto [★IO]

Suomen Kuntatekniikan Yhdistys [★IO]

Suomen Kustannusyhdistys [★IO]

Suomen Laakariliitto [★IO]

Suomen Laulajain ja Soittajain Liitto [★IO]

Suomen Leipuriliitto ry [★IO]

Suomen Liikennelentajaliitto [★IO]

Suomen Liikunta ja Urheilu [★IO]

Suomen Liitokiekkoliitto ry [★IO]

Suomen Maalarimestariliitto [★IO]

Suomen Maarakentajien Keskusliitto ry [★IO]

Suomen Maisema-arkkitehtiliitto [★IO]

Suomen Merimies-Unioni [★IO]

Suomen Mielenterveysseura [★IO]

Suomen MS-Liitto [★IO]

Suomen Museoliitto [★IO]

Suomen Musiikkikustantajat ry [★IO]

Suomen Musiikkioppilaitosten Liitto [★IO]

Suomen Muusikkojen Liitto [★IO]

Suomen Naytelmakirjailijaliitto [★IO]

Suomen Nuorisoyhteistyo Allianssi [★IO]

Suomen Nuorkauppakamarit ry [★IO]

Suomen Olympiakomitea [★IO]

Suomen Pakolaisapu [★IO]

Suomen Pankkiyhdistys [★IO]

Suomen Paralympiakomitea [★IO]

Suomen Parkinson- liitto ry Finlands Parkinson for-bund rf [★IO]

Suomen Perhostutkijain Seura ry [★IO]

Suomen Radioamatooriliitto ry [★IO]

Suomen Rakennusinsinoeoerien Liitto RIL [★IO]

Suomen Retkeilymajajarjesto [★IO]

Suomen Ruususeura r.y. - Finska Rosensallskapet r.f. [★IO]

Suomen Sadankomitealiitto [★IO]

Suomen Sahkotukkuliikkeiden Liitto ry [★IO]

Suomen Salibandyliitto [★IO]

Suomen Satamaliitto [★IO]

Suomen Saveltajat [★IO]

Suomen Sinfoniaorkesterit [★IO]

Suomen Sosialidemokraattinen Puolue [★IO]

Suomen Suoramarkkinointiliitto [★IO]

Suomen Sydanliitto ry [★IO]

Suomen Taekwondoliitto [★IO]

Suomen Taideyhdistys [★IO]

Suomen Taiteilijaseura [★IO]

Suomen Tanssiurheiluliitto Ry [★IO]

Suomen Tennisliitto [★IO]

Suomen Tiedeakatemiain Valtuuskunta [★IO]

Suomen Turkiselainten Kasvattajain Liitto ry [★IO]

Suomen Tuulivoimayhdistys ry [★IO]

Suomen Uimaliitto [★IO]

Suomen Vakuutusyhtioeiden Keskusliitto [★IO]

Suomen Valkonauhaliitto [★IO]

Suomen Varustamoyhdistys Ry [★IO]

Suomen Vesihiihtourheilu ry [★IO]

Suomen YK-Liitto [★IO]

A star before a book entry number signifies that the name is not listed separately, but is mentioned within the entry.

Suomi-Amerikka Yhdistysten Liitto [★IO]
Suore Missionarie dell'Apostolato Cattolico [★IO]
Suore Missionarie del Preziosissimo Sangue [★IO]
Suore Missionarie di San Pietro Claver [★IO]
Super Chevys Limited - Defunct.
Super Coupe Club of Am. [21794], c/o George Davenport, Interim Coor., 4322 Hamilton Rd., Medina, OH 44256, (330)242-1122
Super Heroes
Interlac [22042]
Super Sunfish Class Assn. - Defunct.
Supercat Race Assn. Intl. - Address unknown since 1999.
Superconductor Applications Assn. - Defunct.
Superintendents; Amer. Assn. of Railroad [3277]
Superintendents; Amer. Assn. of Wardens and [★11884]
Superintendents of Amer. Institutions for Insane; Assn. of Medical [★16076]
Superintendents Assn. of Am; Golf Course [3663]
Superintendent's Assn. of Am; Urban [9288]
Superintendents Assn; Amer. Pulp and Paper Mill [★2893]
Superintendents Assn; Natl. Greenkeeping [★3663]
Superintendents of Buildings and Grounds of Universities and Colleges; Assn. of [★8333]
Superintendents of Mental Hospitals; Assn. of Medical [★14861]
Superintendents; Natl. Alliance of Black School [★9217]
Superintendents; Natl. Assn. of School [★7882]
Superintendents of the Natl. Educ. Assn; Dept. of [★7882]
Superintendents of the Natl. Educ. Assn; Dept. of School [★7882]
Superintendents (of NEA); County Intermediate Unit [★7882]
Superintendents and Principals of Amer. Schools for the Deaf; Assn. of [★14749]
Superintendents of U.S. and Canada; Assn. of Hosp. [★14863]
Superintendents of U.S. Naval Shore Establishments; Natl. Assn. of [6085]
Superior Coun. of U.S. Soc. of St. Vincent de Paul [★13190]
Superior Iron Ore Assn; Lake [★2696]
Superior Shore Systems - Address unknown since 1994.
Supermarket Inst. [★3406]
Supersonic Tunnel Assn. - Address unknown since 1989.
Superstition Mountain Historical Soc. [9383], PO Box 3845, Apache Junction, AZ 85217-3845, (480)983-4888
Superstition Mountain/Lost Dutchman Museum [★9383]
Supervised Visitation Network [11654], 2804 Paran Pointe Dr., Cookeville, TN 38506, (931)537-3414
Supervised Visitation Network [IO], Cookeville, TN, United States
Supervision; Assn. for Counselor Educ. and [8165]
Supervision and Curriculum Development (of NEA); Dept. of [★8178]
Supervisors and Administrators; Amer. Assn. of Clinical Lab. [★14993]
Supervisors and Administrators of Hea. Occupations Educ; Natl. Assn. of [8870]
Supervisors of Agricultural Educ; Natl. Assn. of [7939]
Supervisors; Amer. Coun. of Indus. Arts [★9232]
Supervisors; Amer. Coun. of State Savings [458]
Supervisors Assn; Amer. Railway and Airline [★24180]
Supervisors Assn; Natl. Sci. [★9113]
Supervisors Assn; Western Railway [★24180]
Supervisors of Bus. Educ; Natl. Assn. of [8034]
Supervisors of Bus. and Off. Educ; Natl. Assn. of [★8034]
Supervisors; Conf. of State Bank [5544]
Supervisors, Dept. of Defense; Natl. Assn. of [★5708]
Supervisors and Directors of Instruction (of NEA); Dept. of [★8178]
Supervisors of Distributive Educ; Natl. Assn. of State [★8818]

Supervisors, Fed. Govt; Natl. Assn. of [★5708]
Supervisors of Foreign Languages; Natl. Coun. of State [8738]
Supervisors of Mathematics; Assn. of State [8822]
Supervisors of Mathematics; Natl. Coun. of [8826]
Supervisors; Natl. Assn. of [★5708]
Supervisors; Natl. Assn. of Distributive Educ. Local [★8818]
Supervisors; Natl. Assn. of Home Economics [★8514]
Supervisors; Natl. Assn. of Small Loan [★5610]
Supervisors; Natl. Assn. of State Credit Union [5633]
Supervisors Natl. Conf; Music [★8913]
Supervisors Organizing Comm; School Administrators and [★7886]
Supervisors of Private Schools; Natl. Assn. of State Administrators and [9021]
Supervisors of State Banks; Natl. Assn. of [★5544]
Supervisors of Student Training; Natl. Assn. of. [★9212]
Supervisors of Vocational Home Economics; Natl. Assn. of State [★8514]
Supervisory Professionals; Assn. of Tech. and [5737]
Supima [4317], 4141 E Broadway Rd., Phoenix, AZ 85040, (602)437-1364
Supima Assn. of Am. [★4317]
Supplemental Air Carrier Conf. - Defunct.
Supplier Development Coun; Natl. Minority [2769]
Supplier Inst; Amer. [7725]
Suppliers of Advanced Composite Materials Assn. [★589]
Suppliers of Advanced Composite Materials Assn. - Defunct.
Suppliers of Am; Mfg. Jewelers and [2378]
Suppliers of the Americas; Sewn Products Equip. and [2067]
Suppliers Assn; Airline [★2550]
Suppliers Assn. of the Americas; Sewn Products Equip. [★2067]
Suppliers Assn; Aviation [2550]
Suppliers Assn; Car Wash Mfrs. and [★411]
Suppliers Assn; Casting Indus. [2009]
Suppliers Assn; Financial [★2623]
Suppliers; Assn. of Fund-Raising Distributors and [1684]
Suppliers; Assn. of Independent Medical Equip. [★14670]
Suppliers Assn; Meat Indus. [2661]
Suppliers' Assn., Natl. Assn. of Metal Finishers and Amer. Electroplaters and Surface Finishers Soc; Metal Finishing [★1474]
Suppliers Assn. for Professional Audio, Video and Lighting Equip. in Sweden [IO], Stockholm, Sweden
Suppliers Assn; U.S. Aquaculture [4026]
Suppliers Assn; U.S. Telecommunications [★3759]
Suppliers Assn; Wire and Cable Indus. [1231]
Suppliers Benchmarking Assn; Auto [703]
Suppliers Benchmarking Consortium; Auto [★703]
Suppliers; Cosmetic Indus. Buyers and [1843]
Suppliers to the Paper Indus; Assn. of [2003]
Suppliers of Printing, Publishing and Converting Technologies; NPES - The Assn. for [1782]
Supplies Assn; Dairy and Ice Cream Machinery and [★1133]
Supply Assn; Amer. [3061]
Supply Assn; Central [★3061]
Supply Assn; Natl. Sanitary [★2466]
Supply Assn; North Amer. Horticultural [4984]
Supply Assn; Western Wholesale Pet [★2968]
Supply Assn; Western World Pet [★2968]
Supply Associations; Amer. Inst. of [★3061]
Supply Chain Benchmarking Assn; Procurement and [760]
Supply-Chain Coun. [2111], 1400 Eye St. NW, Ste. 1050, Washington, DC 20005, (202)962-0440
Supply-Chain Coun. [IO], Washington, DC, United States
Supply-Chain Coun. - Brazil Chap. [IO], Barueri, Brazil
Supply-Chain Coun. - Europe Chap. [IO], Brussels, Belgium
Supply-Chain Coun. - Greater China Chap. [IO], Shanghai, People's Republic of China
Supply-Chain Coun. - South East Asia Chap. [IO], Singapore, Singapore

Supply-Chain Coun. - Southern African Chap. [IO], Cape Town, Republic of South Africa
Supply Chain and Logistics Canada [IO], Richmond Hill, ON, Canada
Supply Comm; Natural Gas [★1682]
Supply Improvement Assn; Natl. Water [★7824]
Supply and Machinery Mfrs. Assn; Amer. [★2027]
Supply Mgt; Inst. for [3263]
Supply Ser. Assn; Communications [3954]
Support A Child Intl. [11655], 1130 S Wabash, Ste. 304, Chicago, IL 60605, (312)922-8421
Support A Child Intl. [IO], Chicago, IL, United States
Support; Amer. Assn. for Klinefelter Syndrome Info. and [14538]
Support; Assn. for Children for Enforcement of [11673]
Support Assn. for the Women of Afghanistan - Australia [IO], Bedford Park, Australia
Support; Center for Family [12566]
Support Coalition Intl. [★17776]
Support Dogs for the Handicapped [★11990]
Support Dogs for the Handicapped [★IO]
Support Dogs, Inc. [IO], St. Louis, MO, United States
Support Dogs, Inc. [11990], 11645 Lilburn Park Rd., St. Louis, MO 63146, (314)997-2325
Support of Educ; Coun. for Advancement and [8245]
Support Gp; Chronic Pain [15839]
Support Gp; Evans Syndrome Res. and [14934]
Support Gp; Freeman-Sheldon Parent [14063]
Support Gp. Intl; Twinless Twins [12615]
Support Gp; Klippel-Trenaunay [13755]
Support Groups
AAMED - The Amer. Assn. of Multiple Enchondroma Diseases [15749]
AARP Grief and Loss Prog. [13414]
Addison's Disease Self Help Gp. [IO]
Adolescent Scoliosis Soc. of North Am. [16392]
Adult Children of Alcoholics World Ser. Org. [13012]
African Amer. Breast Cancer Alliance [13786]
Agoraphobics in Motion [12742]
Aicardi Syndrome Newsl. [14437]
Al-Anon Family Gp. HQ, World Ser. Off. [13214]
Albinism World Alliance [15242]
Alcohol Res. Info. Ser. [13217]
Alcoholics Anonymous World Services [13218]
Alive Alone [11511]
Alliance for Childhood Cancer [13787]
Amer. Coun. on Alcohol Problems [13220]
Amer. Coun. on Alcoholism [13221]
Amer. Found. for Suicide Prevention [13287]
Amer. Hea. and Temperance Assn. [13303]
Amer. Hemochromatosis Soc. [14543]
Amer. Partnership for Eosinophilic Disorders [14408]
Amer. Porphyria Found. [15243]
Amer. Self-Help Gp. CH [13013]
Amyloidosis Support Groups [14250]
Amyloidosis Support Network [14251]
Androgen Insensitivity Syndrome Support Gp. - USA [14441]
Anesthesia Awareness Campaign [13677]
Angelman Syndrome Found. [16528]
Angioma Alliance [15307]
Anxiety Disorders Assn. of Am. [12743]
Anxiety Disorders Special Interest Gp. [12744]
Anxiety and Phobia Treatment Center [12745]
AppleWorks Users Gp. [6760]
Assn. for the Bladder Exstrophy Community [14252]
Assn. of Halfway House Alcoholism Programs of North Am. [13224]
Assn. of Nutrition Services Agencies [14720]
Assn. for Repetitive Motion Syndromes [15631]
Attachment Parenting Intl. [12662]
Audiology Awareness Campaign [13716]
Australasian Tuberous Sclerosis Soc. [IO]
Autism Network Intl. [13719]
Autism Soc. of British Columbia [IO]
Avenues, Natl. Support Gp. for Arthrogryposis Multiplex Congenita [15309]
BACCHUS Network [13226]
Batterers Anonymous - Beyond Abuse [12023]
Because I Love You: The Parent Support Gp. [13293]

Reference to "IO" in place of a book number signifies that the association may be found in the 45th edition of International Organizations.

Biliary Atresia and Liver Transplant Network [16529]
Billy Barty Found. [13104]
Bladder Cancer Advocacy Network [13799]
Bonus Families [12143]
Brave Kids [13949]
Burns United Support Groups [13782]
Cancer Care [13803]
Cancer Hope Network [13806]
Cancer Quality Alliance [13809]
Candlelighters Childhood Cancer Found. [13810]
Care4Dystonia [15312]
Catholic Parents Network [12664]
CCHS Family Network [14255]
CDG Family Network Found. [16530]
Center for Loss in Multiple Birth [12665]
Charles Ray III Diabetes Assn. [14220]
Chem. Injury Info. Network [16656]
CHERUBS - Assn. of Congenital Diaphragmatic Hernia Res., Advocacy and Support [13753]
Children and Adults With Attention Deficit/ Hyperactivity Disorder [15314]
Children of Alcoholics Found. [13228]
Children of Deaf Adults [14747]
Children's Hemiplegia and Stroke Assn. [16493]
Children's Liver Assn. for Support Services [14804]
Children's PKU Network [15245]
Children's Tumor Found. [15315]
Chromosome 9P Network [14443]
Chromosome 18 Registry and Res. Soc. [14444]
Chromosome Deletion Outreach [14445]
Chronic Syndrome Support Assn. [14259]
Co-Anon Family Groups [13231]
Co-Dependents Anonymous [13016]
Coalition of Cancer Cooperative Groups [13814]
Coffin-Lowry Syndrome Found. [14447]
COLAGE [12223]
Columbia Queer Alliance [12224]
Coma Recovery Assn. [14029]
The Compassionate Friends [12666]
Congenital Heart Defects Awareness [13900]
Congenital Heart Info. Network [13901]
Cri du Chat Syndrome Mutual Help Gp. [14448]
Crigler-Najjar Assn. [14805]
Cuba Support Gp. - Ireland [IO]
CUSA: An Apostolate of the Sick and Disabled [19620]
Cyclic Vomiting Syndrome Assn. [14415]
Cystic Fibrosis Worldwide [16359]
Cystinosis Found. [15246]
Cystinosis Res. Network [15247]
Darkness to Light [11590]
DateAble [11936]
DEBRA European [IO]
Debtors Anonymous [13017]
Dementia Advocacy and Support Network Intl. [12638]
Depression and Related Affective Disorders Assn. [15197]
Donors' Offspring [13298]
Downed Bikers Assn. [12612]
Dual Disorders Anonymous [13237]
Dysautonomia Youth Network of Am. [15318]
Dystonia Medical Res. Found. [15319]
Education-A-Must [12056]
Ehlers Danlos Natl. Found. [16651]
Esophageal Cancer Awareness Assn. [13822]
Fabry Support and Info. Gp. [14262]
Facing Our Risk of Cancer Empowered [13823]
Fairview Pregnancy and Newborn Loss Information [12668]
Families of Adults Afflicted with Asperger's Syndrome [16531]
Families for Natural Living [8416]
Family Pride Coalition [12227]
Fanconi Anemia Res. Fund [14450]
Fatty Oxidation Disorders (FOD) Family Support Gp. [16532]
FG Syndrome Family Alliance [16533]
FG Syndrome Family Alliance [IO]
Filipinos for Affirmative Action [18270]
FireFlag/EMS [5773]
First Candle/SIDS Alliance [16525]
Five P Minus Soc. [16534]

Floating Harbor Syndrome Support Gp. of North Am. [14451]
FRAXA Res. Found. [16535]
Friendly Hand Found. [13243]
Gam-Anon Intl. Ser. Off. [12210]
Gamers Intl. [22478]
Genetic Alliance [16536]
Gift From Within [12768]
Global Autism Proj. [13725]
Grandparents United for Children's Rights [17058]
GriefNet [13294]
Hartlepool Special Needs Support Gp. [IO]
Hazelden Found. [13244]
Heartbeat [13288]
Hydrocephalus Assn. [15330]
Hypoparathyroidism Assn. [14356]
Incest Survivors Anonymous [13076]
Incontinentia Pigmenti Intl. Found. [14455]
Indoor Sports Club [11951]
Inter-Association Task Force on Alcohol and Other Substance Abuse Issues [13250]
Intl. Center for Fabry Disease [16537]
International Center for Fabry Disease [IO]
Intl. Children's Anophthalmia Network [16857]
Intl. Commn. for the Prevention of Alcoholism and Drug Dependency [13251]
Intl. Doctors in Alcoholics Anonymous [13252]
Intl. Fed. of Black Prides [12238]
Intl. Hea. and Temperance Assn. [13304]
Intl. Post Polio Support Org. [16048]
Intl. Rett Syndrome Assn. [15333]
Intl. Size Acceptance Assn. [12645]
Intl. Stillbirth Alliance [13982]
Intl. Treatment Preparedness Coalition [13573]
Interstitial Cystitis Assn. [16708]
Just One Break [11957]
Kids With Food Allergies [13603]
KIDSCOPE [11518]
Klinefelter Syndrome and Associates [16538]
Klippel-Trenaunay Support Gp. [13755]
Kythe [IO]
Lewy Body Dementia Assn. [15335]
Life Raft Gp. [13838]
The Linkup - Survivors of Clergy Abuse [11522]
Little People of Am. [13105]
LMBS Network [16539]
Loved Ones and Drivers Support [13347]
Lung Cancer Alliance [13839]
Lyme Disease Found. [14272]
Make a Child Smile [11708]
Make Today Count [13841]
ManKind Proj. [13021]
Meniere's Network [15826]
Miscarriage Infant Death and Stillbirth Support Gp. [16540]
Mobility Intl. USA [11961]
MUMS Natl. Parent-to-Parent Network [16541]
Myasthenia Gravis Found. of Am. [15340]
Myotubular Myopathy Rsrc. Gp. [16542]
Nail Patella Syndrome Worldwide [14467]
Natl. Adrenal Diseases Found. [14358]
Natl. Alliance for Direct Support Professionals [1986]
Natl. Assn. of Blind Merchants [525]
Natl. Assn. for Children of Alcoholics [13261]
Natl. Assn. of Hepatitis Task Forces [14812]
Natl. Assn. of Lesbian/Gay Addiction Professionals [13263]
Natl. Assn. for Native Amer. Children of Alcoholics [11627]
Natl. Assn. of Non-Custodial Moms [11538]
Natl. Assn. for Pseudoxanthoma Elasticum [14207]
Natl. Assn. to Stop Guardian Abuse [12059]
Natl. Attention Deficit Disorder Assn. [15343]
Natl. Catholic Coun. on Alcoholism and Related Drug Problems [13266]
Natl. Center for Stuttering [16450]
Natl. Chronic Fatigue Syndrome and Fibromyalgia Assn. [14278]
Natl. Chronic Pain Soc. [15845]
Natl. Coalition of Homicide Survivors [13368]
Natl. Comm. for the Prevention of Alcoholism and Drug Dependency [13267]
Natl. Coun. on Alcoholism and Drug Dependence [13268]

Natl. Coun. on Problem Gambling [12212]
Natl. Eosinophilia-Myalgia Syndrome Network [16662]
Natl. Heartburn Alliance [14423]
Natl. Hepatitis C Advocacy Coun. [14813]
Natl. Hydrocephalus Found. [14280]
Natl. Incontinentia Pigmenti Found. [14470]
Natl. Infertility Network Exchange [12678]
Natl. Marfan Found. [16652]
Natl. Multiple Sclerosis Soc. [15349]
Natl. Necrotizing Fasciitis Found. [16543]
Natl. Org. for Albinism and Hypopigmentation [15255]
Natl. Org. For Empowering Caregivers [13295]
National Organization For Empowering Caregivers [IO]
Natl. Osteoporosis Found. [15775]
Natl. Potter Syndrome Support Gp. [16544]
Natl. Self-Help CH [13026]
Natl. SIDS/Infant Death Rsrc. Center [16526]
Natl. Tay-Sachs and Allied Diseases Assn. [15354]
Natl. Temperance and Prohibition Coun. [13305]
Natl. Woman's Christian Temperance Union [13306]
Networking Proj. for Young Adults with Disabilities [11975]
Nevus Network [16545]
Nevus Network [IO]
Nevus Outreach [14284]
No Greater Love [13370]
Nurses' House [15518]
Obsessive-Compulsive Anonymous [12555]
Oper. Gratitude [11493]
Oper. Soldier Support [11497]
Organic Acidemia Assn. [14472]
Org. for Attempters and Survivors of Suicide in Interfaith Services [13290]
Oxalosis and Hyperoxaluria Found. [15296]
Pacific Post Partum Support Soc. [IO]
Parent Support Assn. of Calgary [IO]
Parents Against Childhood Epilepsy [14382]
Parents, Families, and Friends of Lesbians and Gays [12253]
Parents of Infants and Children with Kernicterus [15358]
Parents of Murdered Children [12685]
Parents Network for the Post Institutionalized Child [16546]
Parkinson's Disease Found. [15360]
Paul and Lisa Prog. [13082]
PBCers Org. [14816]
Pediatric Chaplains Network [19755]
Pediatric Neurotransmitter Disease Assn. [15361]
Pierre Robin Network [14473]
Platelet Disorder Support Assn. [13730]
Polio Soc. [15362]
Prader-Willi Found. [14474]
Prevent Blindness in Premature Babies [16883]
PRISMS: Parents and Researchers Interested In Smith-Magenis Syndrome [14476]
Progeria Res. Found. [16547]
Progeria Res. Found. [IO]
Prune Belly Syndrome Network [14478]
Pull-thru Network [14427]
R.A. Bloch Cancer Found. [13867]
Ray of Hope [13291]
Reach Out for Youth with Ileitis and Colitis [16548]
Reclamation Inc. [12556]
Renal Support Network [15299]
Res. and Training Center on Independent Living [11984]
Restless Legs Syndrome Found. [16549]
Rubinstein-Taybi Parent Gp. U.S.A. [13759]
Ryan's Reach [16550]
Scleroderma Support Gp. [16391]
Senior Action in a Gay Env. [12256]
Sex and Love Addicts Anonymous [13074]
SHARE-Pregnancy and Infant Loss Support [12690]
Sharsheret [13872]
Shwachman-Diamond Syndrome Found. [IO]
Shwachman-Diamond Syndrome Found. [16551]
Shy Drager Syndrome/Multiple Sys. Atrophy Support Gp. [15364]

A star before a book entry number signifies that the name is not listed separately, but is mentioned within the entry.

Siblings for Significant Change [11987]
Single and Custodial Fathers Network [12691]
SMART Recovery [16519]
S.M.A.R.T. (Secretive Societies, Mind Control and Ritual Abuse) [13296]
A Soldier's Wish List [11501]
Sons and Daughters In Touch [12599]
Sotos Syndrome Support Assn. [14482]
The Spastic Centre of New South Wales [IO]
Speak Easy Intl. Found. [16455]
Special Recreation for disABLED Intl. [11989]
Stickler Involved People [14483]
Stroke Awareness for Everyone [16495]
Stroke Clubs, Intl. [16496]
Survivor Connections [13084]
Survivors of Incest Anonymous [13085]
Take Charge! Cure Parkinson's [15366]
Take Root [12605]
Taking Control of Your Diabetes [14231]
Tall Clubs Intl. [13300]
Thyroid Found. of Am. [16649]
Toughlove Intl. [12694]
Tourette Syndrome Assn. [15367]
Transverse Myelitis Assn. [15368]
Tremor Action Network [15369]
Trichotillomania Learning Center [15236]
Trigeminal Neuralgia Assn. [15370]
Tuberous Sclerosis Alliance [15371]
Turner Syndrome Assn. of Australia [IO]
Turner Syndrome Soc. of the U.S. [14486]
Uglies Unlimited [12102]
UNITE [12695]
United Amputee Services Assn. [15080]
United Brachial Plexus Network [15403]
United Mitochondrial Disease Found. [16363]
United Spouses Assn. [21202]
U.S. Adult Cystic Fibrosis Assn. [16364]
U.S. Hereditary Angioedema Assn. [14487]
Us TOO Intl. [13879]
Vasculitis Found. [IO]
Vasculitis Found. [16552]
Velo-Cardio-Facial Syndrome [14488]
VOICES in Action [13086]
Well Spouse Assn. [16553]
Wide Smiles [16554]
Woman to Woman Support Network [16555]
Women Alive Coalition [13588]
Women and Men Against Sexual Harassment and Other Abuses [13088]
Women of Naval Special Warfare [6145]
Women for Sobriety [13284]
Workaholics Anonymous [13031]
World Ability Fed. [11995]
World Arnold Chiari Malformation Association [IO]
World Arnold Chiari Malformation Assn. [16556]
Young Onset Parkinson's Assn. [15374]
Young Survival Coalition [13883]
Support Groups; Alliance of Genetic [★16536]
Support Groups; Burns United [13782]
Support Groups for Monosomy 9P [★14443]
Support Groups for Monosomy 9P [★IO]
The Support-In [★17776]
Support; Natl. Conf. on Uniform Reciprocal Enforcement of [★5701]
Support Network; Adoptee-Birthparent [11228]
Support Network; Beckwith-Wiedemann [14442]
Support Org. For Trisomy 13/18 and Related Disorders - UK [IO], Sutton Coldfield, United Kingdom
Support Org. for Trisomy 13/18 Ireland [IO], Ballinlough, Ireland
Support Org. for Trisomy 18, 13, and Related Disorders [14485], c/o Barb VanHerreweghe, Pres., 2982 S Union St., Rochester, NY 14624, (585)594-4621
Support Our Aging Religious [11321], 900 Varnum St. NE, Washington, DC 20017, (202)529-7627
Support Our Shelters [11462], c/o Judith White, 100 Walsh Rd., Lansdowne, PA 19050, (610)626-6647
Support Our Soldiers Am. [11502], 55 Bergen St., Brooklyn, NY 11201, (718)237-1097
Support for People with Oral and Head and Neck Cancer [13877], PO Box 53, Locust Valley, NY 11560-0053, (800)377-0928
Support Professionals; Assn. of [3546]

Support Professionals Assn; Ser. and [3556]
Support Proj; Death Row [11863]
Support Services Alliance [3631], PO Box 130, Schoharie, NY 12157, (800)836-4772
Support; SHARE-Pregnancy and Infant Loss [12690]
Support of Solidarity; Comm. in [★17446]
Support Staff; Natl. Assn. of Rehabilitation [16327]
Support and Training in Preparatory Schools [★IO]
Support; Y-Me Natl. Org. for Breast Cancer Info. and [★13882]
Supporters of Silkwood - Defunct.
Supporting Our Sons [11547], 555 Bryant St., No. 527, Palo Alto, CA 94301, (866)687-7667
Suppression Systems Assn; Fire [3444]
Supranuclear Palsy; Soc. for Progressive [14286]
Supreme Assembly, Intl. Order of Rainbow for Girls [19250], PO Box 1868, McAlester, OK 74502, (918)423-1328
Supreme Assembly, Intl. Order of Rainbow for Girls [IO], McAlester, OK, United States
Supreme Camp of the Amer. Woodmen [★19441]
Supreme Camp of the Amer. Woodmen - Defunct.
Supreme Cauldron, Daughters of Mokanna [★19231]
Supreme Commandery Knights of Saint John [★19006]
Supreme Commandery Knights of Saint John [★IO]
Supreme Comm. for the Liberation of Lithuania - Defunct.
Supreme Cossack Representation in Exile - Address unknown since 1995.
Supreme Coun. 33rd Degree, Ancient and Accepted Scottish Rite of Freemasonry - Southern Jurisdiction [19251], 1733 16th St. NW, Washington, DC 20009-3103, (202)232-3579
Supreme Coun. 33rd Degree, Ancient and Accepted Scottish Rite of Freemasonry - Southern Masonic Jurisdiction [★19251]
Supreme Coun., Ancient Accepted Scottish Rite of Free-Masonry (Northern Masonic Jurisdiction) [19252], PO Box 519, Lexington, MA 02420-0519, (781)862-4410
Supreme Coun. Catholic Benevolent Legion [★19004]
Supreme Coun. Catholic Benevolent Legion [★IO]
Supreme Coun. of the Independent Associated Spiritualists - Defunct.
Supreme Coun., Mystic Order of Veiled Prophets of the Enchanted Realm [19253], 430 Beecher Rd., Gahanna, OH 43230, (614)933-9193
Supreme Coun. Order of the Amaranth [19254], PO Box 557579, Chicago, IL 60655-7579, (708)499-5939
Supreme Coun. of the Royal Arcanum [19140], 61 Batterymarch St., Boston, MA 02110-3208, (617)426-4135
Supreme Coun. of the Western Catholic Union [★19010]
Supreme Court Historical Soc. [10161], Opperman House, 224 E Capitol St. NE, Washington, DC 20003, (202)543-0400
Supreme Emblem Club of the U.S.A. [19037], c/o Shirley Brigham, Supreme Corresponding Sec., 3608 Redwood Ave., Los Angeles, CA 90066, (802)365-7292
Supreme Forest Woodmen Circle [★19441]
Supreme Grove, United Ancient Order of Druids - Address unknown since 2007.
Supreme Ladies Auxiliary Knights of Saint John [19009], c/o Mrs. Ann Friday, Supreme Sec., 2330 Kirby Dr., Hillcrest Heights, MD 20748-3265, (301)423-6516
Supreme Lodge of the Danish Sisterhood of Am. [19032], c/o Sindy Poremba, Natl. Pres./Ed., 622 Palm Ave., Penngrove, CA 94951, (707)794-8430
Supreme Lodge Knights of Pythias [19188], 59 Coddington St., Ste. 202, Quincy, MA 02169-4510, (617)472-8800
Supreme Lodge of the World, Loyal Order of Moose [★19058]
Supreme Lodge of the World, Loyal Order of Moose [★IO]
Supreme Master Ching Hai Meditation Association [IO], San Jose, CA, United States
Supreme Master Ching Hai Meditation Assn. [19557], PO Box 730247, San Jose, CA 95173-0247, (408)998-2342

Supreme Pup Tent, Military Order of the Cootie [21323], 604 Braddock Ave., Turtle Creek, PA 15145-2068, (412)824-2240
Supreme Royal Zuanna, Ladies of the Orient - Defunct.
Supreme Shrine of the Order of the White Shrine of Jerusalem - Address unknown since 1999.
Supreme Temple Order Pythian Sisters [19189], PO Box 40713, Portland, OR 97240-0713
Supreme Travel Club [22964], PO Box 191, Osceola, IN 46561, (574)258-0571
Supremes
    Florence Ballard Fan Club [24888]
    Official Mary Wilson Message Bd. and Fan Club [24954]
Supremes Intl. Fan Club [★24954]
Supremes, Marvellettes, and Martha and the Vandellas Fan Club [★24975]
Surdna Found. [12738], 330 Madison Ave., 30th Fl., New York, NY 10017, (212)557-0010
Surefire Fan Club - Defunct.
Surety Agents; Natl. Assn. of Casualty and [★2159]
Surety Agents Promotional Soc. - Defunct.
Surety Assn. of Am. [★2245]
Surety Bond Producers; Natl. Assn. of [2219]
Surety Companies; Assn. of Casualty and [★2139]
Surety Conf; Southern Casualty and [★2194]
Surety and Fidelity Assn. of Am. [2245], 1101 Connecticut Ave. NW, Ste. 800, Washington, DC 20036, (202)463-0600
Surf Life Saving Assn. of Am; Natl. [★12894]
Surf Life Saving Assn. of Great Britain [IO], Exeter, United Kingdom
Surf Life Saving Australia [IO], Bondi Beach, Australia
Surface Coatings Assn. Australia [IO], Toorak, Australia
Surface Coatings Assn. New Zealand [IO], Auckland, New Zealand
Surface Design Assn. [3800], PO Box 360, Sebastopol, CA 95473-0360, (707)829-3110
Surface Engg. Assn. [IO], Birmingham, United Kingdom
Surface Engg. Coating Assn. [6706], Univ. of Buffalo Tech. Center, 1576 Sweet Home Rd., Ste. 102, Amherst, NY 14228, (716)791-8100
Surface Finishers Soc; Metal Finishing Suppliers' Assn., Natl. Assn. of Metal Finishers and Amer. Electroplaters and [★1474]
Surface Mining and Reclamation; Amer. Soc. for [★6114]
Surface Mount Equipment Mfrs. Assn. - Address unknown since 2002.
Surface Mount Tech. Assn. [2072], 5200 Willson Rd., Ste. 215, Edina, MN 55424, (952)920-7682
Surface Transport Nurses Assn; Air and [★15427]
Surface Trans. Policy Proj. [18750], 1100 17th St. NW, 10th Fl., Washington, DC 20036, (202)466-2636
Surfaces in Biomaterials Found. [6617], 1000 Westgate Dr., Ste. 252, St. Paul, MN 55114, (651)290-6267
SurfAid Intl. [11791], 191 Calle Magdalena, Ste. 290b, Encinitas, CA 92024, (760)753-1103
SurfAid Intl. [IO], Encinitas, CA, United States
Surfers Against Sewage [IO], Cornwall, United Kingdom
Surfer's Medical Assn. [15096], PO Box 1210, Aptos, CA 95001, (831)684-0916
Surfing
    Assn. of Surfing Professionals [23877]
    Bd. Retailers Assn. [3402]
    British Surfing Assn. [IO]
    Eastern Surfing Assn. [23878]
    European Surf Indus. Mfrs. Assn. [IO]
    European Surfing Fed. [IO]
    Intl. Surfing Assn. [IO]
    Intl. Surfing Assn. [23879]
    Natl. Scholastic Surfing Assn. [23880]
    North Amer. Formula 18 Assn. [23208]
    SurfAid Intl. [11791]
    Surfer's Medical Assn. [15096]
    Surfing South Africa [IO]
    Surfrider Found. [IO]
    Surfrider Found. [23881]

Reference to "IO" in place of a book number signifies that the association may be found in the 45th edition of International Organizations.

UK Windsurfing Assn. [IO]
U.S. Windsurfing Assn. [23236]
Surfing Assn; U.S. Wind [23236]
Surfing South Africa [IO], Rondebosch, Republic of South Africa
Surfrider Found. [IO], San Clemente, CA, United States
Surfrider Found. [23881], PO Box 6010, San Clemente, CA 92674-6010, (949)492-8170
Surfun: The Official Jan and Dean Fan Club [24977], 328 Sumner Ave., Sumner, WA 98390
Surgeon; Amer. Soc. of Cosmetic [★14037]
Surgeon Assistants; Amer. Assn. of [★16560]
Surgeons; Amer. Acad. of Neurological and Orthopaedic [15409]
Surgeons; Amer. Acad. of Orthopaedic [15752]
Surgeons; Amer. Acad. of Osteopathic [★15792]
Surgeons; Amer. Assn. of Cosmetic [★14037]
Surgeons; Amer. Assn. of Genito-Urinary [16699]
Surgeons; Amer. Assn. of Hip and Knee [16559]
Surgeons; Amer. Assn. of Neurological [15410]
Surgeons; Amer. Assn. of Oral and Maxillofacial [15732]
Surgeons; Amer. Assn. of Oral and Plastic [★14040]
Surgeons; Amer. Assn. of Plastic [14040]
Surgeons; Amer. Coll. of Eye [16564]
Surgeons; Amer. Coll. of Foot [★16034]
Surgeons; Amer. Coll. of Foot and Ankle [16034]
Surgeons; Amer. Coll. of Oral and Maxillofacial [15734]
Surgeons; Amer. Coll. of Osteopathic [15797]
Surgeons; Amer. Coll. of Veterinary [16771]
Surgeons; Amer. Shoulder and Elbow [16567]
Surgeons; Amer. Soc. of Abdominal [16568]
Surgeons; Amer. Soc. of Colon and Rectal [16060]
Surgeons; Amer. Soc. of Gen. [16571]
Surgeons; Amer. Soc. of Head and Neck [★15819]
Surgeons; Amer. Soc. of Maxillofacial [15735]
Surgeons; Amer. Soc. of Oral [★15732]
Surgeons; Amer. Soc. of Plastic [14044]
Surgeons; Amer. Soc. of Transplant [16667]
Surgeons; Asian - Australasian Soc. of Neurological [IO]
Surgeons; Assn. of Amer. Physicians and [15990]
Surgeons; Assn. of Bone and Joint [15763]
Surgeons; Assn. of Military Osteopathic Physicians and [15807]
Surgeons; Educ. Found. of Amer. Soc. of Plastic and Reconstructive [★14051]
Surgeons of England; British Assn. of Paediatric [IO]
Surgeons; Natl. Bd. of Examiners for Osteopathic Physicians and [★15812]
Surgeons; Puerto Rico Assn. of Pediatric [15897]
Surgeons; Soc. of Air Force Clinical [16587]
Surgeons; Soc. of Amer. Gastrointestinal and Endoscopic [14428]
Surgeons; Soc. of Eye [15703]
Surgeons; Soc. of Laparoendoscopic [16589]
Surgeons; Soc. of Military Orthopaedic [15266]
Surgeons; Soc. of Military Otolaryngologists - Head and Neck [15267]
Surgeons; Soc. of Neurological [15416]
Surgeons; Soc. of Reproductive [16349]
Surgeons; Soc. of Thoracic [16644]
Surgeons; Soc. of U.S. Air Force Flight [13543]
Surgeons; Soc. of Univ. [16591]
Surgeons; Soc. of Univ. Otolaryngologists - Head and Neck [15828]
Surgeons; South African Assn. of Paediatric [IO]
Surgeons of the U.S.A; Royal Coll. of Physicians and [16694]
Surgeons of the U.S; Assn. of Military [15263]
Surgery
Acad. of Ambulatory Foot and Ankle Surgery [16023]
Acoustic Neuroma Assn. [15816]
African Fed. of Gastroenterology [IO]
Amer. Acad. of Cosmetic Surgery [14037]
Amer. Acad. of Facial Plastic and Reconstructive Surgery [14038]
Amer. Acad. of Implant Prosthodontics [14102]
Amer. Acad. of Orthopaedic Surgeons [15752]
Amer. Acad. of Otolaryngology - Head and Neck Surgery [15817]
Amer. Assn. for Accreditation of Ambulatory Surgery Facilities [16557]

Amer. Assn. of Ambulatory Surgery Centers [16558]
Amer. Assn. of Colleges of Podiatric Medicine [16025]
Amer. Assn. of Genito-Urinary Surgeons [16699]
Amer. Assn. for Hand Surgery [14522]
Amer. Assn. of Hip and Knee Surgeons [16559]
Amer. Assn. of Hosp. Podiatrists [16026]
Amer. Assn. of Plastic Surgeons [14040]
Amer. Assn. for the Surgery of Trauma [16687]
Amer. Assn. of Surgical Physician Assistants [16560]
Amer. Assn. for Thoracic Surgery [16640]
Amer. Bd. of Abdominal Surgery [16561]
Amer. Bd. of Cardiovascular Perfusion [13887]
American Bd. of Clinical Metal Toxicology [16659]
Amer. Bd. of Colon and Rectal Surgery [16059]
Amer. Bd. of Facial Plastic and Reconstructive Surgery [16562]
Amer. Bd. of Hair Restoration Surgery [14518]
Amer. Bd. of Orthopaedic Surgery [15755]
Amer. Bd. of Otolaryngology [15818]
Amer. Bd. of Plastic Surgery [14041]
Amer. Bd. of Podiatric Orthopedics and Primary Podiatric Medicine [16030]
Amer. Bd. of Podiatric Surgery [16031]
Amer. Bd. of Surgery [16563]
Amer. Bd. of Thoracic Surgery [16641]
Amer. Bd. of Urology [16700]
Amer. Coll. of Angiology [16719]
Amer. Coll. of Cardiology [13888]
Amer. Coll. of Chest Physicians [13889]
Amer. Coll. of Eye Surgeons [16564]
Amer. Coll. of Foot and Ankle Orthopedics and Medicine [16032]
Amer. Coll. of Foot and Ankle Pediatrics [16033]
Amer. Coll. of Foot and Ankle Surgeons [16034]
Amer. Coll. of Intl. Physicians [14973]
Amer. Coll. of Oral and Maxillofacial Surgeons [15734]
Amer. Coll. of Osteopathic Surgeons [15797]
Amer. Coll. of Surgeons [16565]
Amer. Coll. of Surgeons [IO]
Amer. Coll. of Veterinary Surgeons [16771]
Amer. Fracture Assn. [15756]
Amer. Hernia Soc. [16566]
American Hernia Society [IO]
Amer. Organ Transplant Assn. [16664]
Amer. Orthopaedic Soc. for Sports Medicine [16476]
Amer. Osteopathic Acad. of Orthopedics [15759]
Amer. Osteopathic Assn. [15798]
Amer. Otological Soc. [15822]
Amer. Podiatric Medical Assn. [16037]
Amer. Rhinologic Soc. [15823]
Amer. Shoulder and Elbow Surgeons [16567]
Amer. Soc. of Abdominal Surgeons [16568]
Amer. Soc. for Aesthetic Plastic Surgery [14042]
Amer. Soc. for Bariatric Surgery [16569]
Amer. Soc. of Breast Surgeons [16570]
Amer. Soc. of Cataract and Refractive Surgery [15665]
Amer. Soc. of Colon and Rectal Surgeons [16060]
Amer. Soc. for Dermatologic Surgery [14196]
Amer. Soc. of Gen. Surgeons [16571]
Amer. Soc. for Laser Medicine and Surgery [14997]
Amer. Soc. of Lipo-Suction Surgery [16572]
Amer. Soc. of Maxillofacial Surgeons [15735]
Amer. Soc. for Mohs Surgery [15641]
Amer. Soc. of Plastic Surgeons [14044]
Amer. Soc. of Plastic Surgeons and Plastic Surgery Educ. Found. [14045]
Amer. Soc. of Plastic Surgical Nurses [15461]
Amer. Soc. of Podiatric Medical Assistants [16040]
Amer. Soc. for Reconstructive Microsurgery [16573]
American Society for Reconstructive Microsurgery [IO]
Amer. Soc. for Reconstructive Surgery [16574]
Amer. Soc. for Surgery of the Hand [14525]
Amer. Soc. of Transplant Surgeons [16667]
Amer. Surgical Assn. [16575]
Amer. Thoracic Soc. [16642]

Amer. Trauma Soc. [16689]
Amer. Urological Assn. [16704]
Anesthesia Patient Safety Found. [13679]
Arab African Soc. of GE and Endoscopy [IO]
Arthroscopy Assn. of North Am. [15762]
Asian-Pacific Soc. of Digestive Endoscopy [IO]
Asian Soc. for Cardiovascular Surgery [IO]
Asian Surgical Assn. [IO]
Asociation Colombiana de Endoscopia Digestiva [IO]
Associacion Mexicana de Endoscopia Gastrointestinal [IO]
Assn. for Academic Surgery [16576]
Assn. of Amer. Physicians and Surgeons [15990]
Assn. of Bone and Joint Surgeons [15763]
Assn. of Gastroenterologists of Bosnia and Herzegovina [IO]
Assn. of Laparoscopic Surgeons of Great Britain and Ireland [IO]
Assn. of Military Osteopathic Physicians and Surgeons [15807]
Assn. of Nurses Endorsing Transplantation [15670]
Assn. of Organ Procurement Organizations [14287]
Assn. of PeriOperative Registered Nurses [15468]
Assn. of Physician Assistants in Cardiovascular Surgery [13895]
Assn. of Prog. Directors in Surgery [16577]
Assn. of Prog. Directors in Vascular Surgery [16578]
Assn. of Rural Surgeons of India [IO]
Assn. for Surgical Educ. [8856]
Assn. of Surgical Technologists [15133]
Assn. of Women Surgeons [16579]
Assn. of Women Surgeons [IO]
Australian Assn. of Vaginal and Incontinence Surgeons [IO]
Belgian Soc. of Digestive Endoscopy [IO]
BeNeLux Assn. of Bariatric Surgeons [IO]
Bones Soc. [15764]
British Assn. of Day Surgery [IO]
Bulgarian Soc. of Gastroenterology [IO]
Canadian Assn. of Gen. Surgeons [IO]
Canadian Assn. of Paediatric Surgeons [IO]
Canadian Neurosurgical Soc. [IO]
Center for Organ Recovery and Educ. [16670]
Children's Corrective Surgery Soc. [16580]
Children's Craniofacial Assn. [14057]
Chinese Soc. of Digestive Endoscopy [IO]
Chinese Taiwan Soc. of Digestive Endoscopy [IO]
Christian Orthopaedic Partners [15765]
Contact Lens Assn. of Ophthalmologists [15680]
Coun. on Podiatric Medical Educ. [16042]
CTSNet: Cardiothoracic Surgery Network [16643]
CyberKnife Soc. [16581]
Ear Found. [15825]
Egyptian Soc. of Gastrointestinal Endoscopy [IO]
Endoscopic Sect. of the Gastroenterological Assn. of Thailand [IO]
Esperanca [14628]
Estonian Soc. of Gastrointestinal Endoscopy [IO]
European Assn. for Endoscopic Surgery and Other Interventional Techniques [IO]
European Assn. for Osseointegration [IO]
European Bd. of Plastic, Reconstructive and Aesthetic Surgery [IO]
European Foot and Ankle Soc. [IO]
European Soc. for Surgery of Shoulder and Elbow [IO]
European Soc. for Surgical Res. [IO]
European Soc. for Vascular Surgery [IO]
Eye Bank Assn. of Am. [14288]
Eye-Bank for Sight Restoration [14289]
Federated Ambulatory Surgery Assn. [16582]
Fed. of European Societies for Surgery of the Hand [IO]
Finnish Soc. of Gastroenterology [IO]
Focus [15681]
Found. for Hand Res. and Educ. [14526]
French Soc. of Digestive Endoscopy [IO]
Gastroenterological and Digestive Endoscopy Soc. of Sri Lanka [IO]
Gastroenterological Soc. of Singapore [IO]
German Soc. of Plastic and Reconstructive Surgery [IO]

A star before a book entry number signifies that the name is not listed separately, but is mentioned within the entry.

German Soc. of Visceral Surgery [IO]
Gift of Life Intl. [12524]
Global Perioperative Res. Org. [14026]
Gynecologic Surgery Soc. [15600]
Heart Care Intl. [13904]
Hong Kong Soc. of Digestive Endoscopy [IO]
Hong Kong Soc. of Minimal Access Surgery [IO]
Ibero-Latin Amer. Fed. of Plastic Surgery [IO]
Indonesian Soc. of Digestive Endoscopy [IO]
Interamerican Coll. of Physicians and Surgeons [16000]
Intl. Assn. of Military Flight Surgeon-Pilots [13541]
Intl. Assn. of Ocular Surgeons [15684]
Intl. Assn. of Oral and Maxillofacial Surgeons [15736]
Intl. Assn. for Organ Donation [16671]
Intl. Coll. of Angiology [16724]
Intl. Coll. of Surgeons [16583]
Intl. Coll. of Surgeons [IO]
Intl. Cytokine Soc. [6580]
Intl. Dental Hea. Found. [14166]
Intl. Eye Found. [15685]
Intl. Fed. of Foot and Ankle Societies [16045]
Intl. Fed. of Surgical Colleges [IO]
Intl. Liver Transplantation Soc. [16672]
Intl. RadioSurgery Assn. [16269]
Intl. Refractive Surgery Club [15689]
Intl. Soc. of Arthroscopy, Knee Surgery and Ortho-paedic Sports Medicine [15771]
Intl. Soc. for Cmpt. Assisted Orthopaedic Surgery [15772]
Intl. Soc. of Cosmetic and Laser Surgeons [14048]
Intl. Soc. of Cryosurgery [IO]
Intl. Soc. for Dermatologic Surgery [14204]
Intl. Soc. for Digestive Surgery [14420]
Intl. Soc. for Hair Restoration Surgery [14521]
Intl. Soc. for Heart and Lung Transplantation [16674]
Intl. Soc. of Surgery [IO]
Intl. Soc. for Vascular Surgery [IO]
Intl. Soc. for Vascular Surgery [16584]
Intl. Trachoma Initiative [16858]
Israeli Assn. of Gastroenterology and Hepatology [IO]
Italian Soc. of Digestive Endoscopy [IO]
Italian Soc. for Endoscopic Surgery and New Technologies [IO]
Japan Surgical Soc. [IO]
Jordanian Soc. of Gastroenterology [IO]
Korean Soc. of Gastrointestinal Endoscopy [IO]
Latvian Assn. of Gastroenterology [IO]
Lebanese Soc. of Gastroenterology [IO]
Lithuanian Soc. of Gastrointestinal Endoscopy [IO]
Luxembourg Soc. of Gastroenterology and Diges-tive Endoscopy [IO]
Malaysian Soc. of Gastroenterology and Hepatol-ogy [IO]
Michael E. DeBakey Intl. Surgical Soc. [13917]
Natl. Acad. of Surgery [IO]
Natl. Bd. of Podiatric Medical Examiners [16046]
Natl. Coun. on Minority Educ. in Transplantation [16677]
Natl. Found. for Facial Reconstruction [14065]
Natl. Found. for Transplants [16678]
Natl. Podiatric Medical Assn. [16047]
Natl. Surgical Asst. Assn. [16585]
Neurosurgeons to Preserve Hea. Care Access [15414]
Neurosurgery Intl. [15415]
Neurosurgical Assn. of Thailand [IO]
New Zealand Soc. of Gastroenterology [IO]
North Amer. Soc. for Dialysis and Transplantation [15295]
North Amer. Transplant Coordinators Org. [16681]
Norwegian Gastroenterological Assn. [IO]
Oper. Smile [12534]
Orthopaedic Res. Soc. [15776]
Orthopedic Surgical Mfrs. Assn. [1865]
Outpatient Ophthalmic Surgery Soc. [15698]
Pakistan Soc. of Gastroenterology and G.I. Endo-scopy [IO]
Pan-African Assn. of Plastic and Reconstructive Surgeons [IO]

Pediatric Keratoplasty Assn. [15700]
Pediatric Orthopedic Soc. of North Am. [15780]
Philippine Soc. of Gastrointestinal Endoscopy [IO]
Plastic Surgery Educational Found. [14051]
Plastic Surgery Res. Coun. [14052]
Plastica Infantil con Excelencia en el Logro [IO]
Portuguese Soc. of Digestive Endoscopy [IO]
Preoperative Assn. [IO]
Prosthetics Outreach Found. [16586]
Pull-thru Network [14427]
Romanian Soc. of Gastrointestinal Endoscopy [IO]
Royal Coll. of Surgeons of England [IO]
Royal Coll. of Surgeons in Ireland [IO]
Royal Surgical Aid Soc. [IO]
Russian Soc. for Digestive Endoscopy [IO]
Simon Found. for Continence [16711]
Sociedad Boliviana de Gastroenterologia y Endo-scopia [IO]
Sociedad Cubana de Endoscopia Digestiva [IO]
Sociedad Ecuatoriana de Gastroenterologia [IO]
Sociedad de Gastroenterologia del Peru [IO]
Sociedad Paraguayana de Gastroenterologia [IO]
Sociedad Uruguaya de Endoscopia Digestiva [IO]
Sociedad Venezolana de Cirugia [IO]
Soc. of Academic and Res. Surgery [IO]
Soc. of Air Force Clinical Surgeons [16587]
Soc. of Amer. Gastrointestinal and Endoscopic Surgeons [14428]
Soc. of Cardiothoracic Surgeons of Great Britain and Ireland [IO]
Soc. of Cardiovascular Anesthesiologists [13689]
Soc. for Ear, Nose, and Throat Advances in Children [15827]
Soc. of Eye Surgeons [15703]
Soc. For Biomaterials [6609]
Soc. of Interventional Pain Mgt. Surgery Centers [16588]
Soc. of Laparoendoscopic Surgeons [16589]
Soc. of Medical Friends of Wine [23028]
Soc. of Military Orthopaedic Surgeons [15266]
Soc. for Pediatric Urology [16715]
Soc. of Reproductive Surgeons [16349]
Soc. for Surgery of the Alimentary Tract [16590]
Soc. of Thoracic Surgeons [16644]
Soc. of U.S. Naval Flight Surgeons [13544]
Soc. of Univ. Otolaryngologists - Head and Neck Surgeons [15828]
Soc. of Univ. Surgeons [16591]
Soc. of Univ. Urologists [16716]
Soc. for Vascular Surgery [16730]
Soc. for Vascular Ultrasound [16731]
Spanish Assn. of Digestive Endoscopy [IO]
Spanish Soc. of Plastic, Reconstructive and Aesthetic Surgery [IO]
Swedish Soc. of Gastroenterology [IO]
Swedish Surgical Soc. [IO]
Thoracic Surgery Residents Assn. [16645]
Transplant Recipients Intl. Org. [16682]
Transplant Speakers Intl. [16683]
Ukrainian Medical Assn. of North Am. [15182]
Ukrainian Soc. of Gastrointestinal Endoscopy [IO]
Uplift Internationale [15737]
Veterinary Orthopedic Soc. [16816]
Vietnam Gastroenterology Assn. [IO]
West African Coll. of Surgeons [IO]
Western Surgical Assn. [16592]
World Org. for Digestive Endoscopy [IO]
Yugoslav Soc. of Plastic, Reconstructive and Aesthetic Surgery [IO]
Surgery Administrative Assn; Plastic [14050]
Surgery; Amer. Acad. of Cosmetic [14037]
Surgery; Amer. Acad. of Facial Plastic and Reconstructive [14038]
Surgery; Amer. Acad. of Otolaryngology - Head and Neck [15817]
Surgery; Amer. Assn. for Hand [14522]
Surgery; Amer. Assn. for Thoracic [16640]
Surgery; Amer. Bd. of Colon and Rectal [16059]
Surgery; Amer. Bd. of Neurological [15411]
Surgery; Amer. Bd. of Oral [★15733]
Surgery; Amer. Bd. of Oral and Maxillofacial [15733]
Surgery; Amer. Bd. of Orthopaedic [15755]
Surgery; Amer. Bd. of Plastic [14041]
Surgery; Amer. Bd. of Podiatric [16031]

Surgery; Amer. Bd. of Thoracic [16641]
Surgery; Amer. Coll. of Chemo [★15636]
Surgery; Amer. Coll. of Gen. Practitioners in Osteopathic Medicine and [★15793]
Surgery; Amer. Otorhinologic Soc. for Plastic [★14038]
Surgery; Amer. Soc. for Aesthetic Plastic [14042]
Surgery; Amer. Soc. of Cataract and Refractive [15665]
Surgery; Amer. Soc. for Dermatologic [14196]
Surgery; Amer. Soc. of Facial Plastic [★14038]
Surgery; Amer. Soc. for Head and Neck [★15819]
Surgery; Amer. Soc. for Laser Medicine and [14997]
Surgery; Amer. Soc. of Ophthalmic Plastic and Reconstructive [14043]
Surgery; Amer. Soc. for Stereotactic and Functional Neuro [15412]
Surgery Assistants; Hong Kong Assn. of Dental [IO]
Surgery; Assn. of Academic Chairmen of Plastic [14046]
Surgery; Assn. of Diplomates of the Amer. Bd. of Oral [★15734]
Surgery Assn; Freestanding Ambulatory [★16582]
Surgery; Assn. of Physician Assistants in Cardiovascular [13895]
Surgery and Cutaneous Oncology; Amer. Coll. of Mohs Micrographic [15636]
Surgery Educ. Found; Amer. Soc. of Plastic Surgeons and Plastic [14045]
Surgery Educational Found; Plastic [14051]
Surgery; European Acad. of Facial Plastic [IO]
Surgery; European Soc. of Ophthalmic Plastic and Reconstructive [IO]
Surgery Facilities; Amer. Assn. for Accreditation of Ambulatory Plastic [★16557]
Surgery of the Hand; Amer. Found. for [14523]
Surgery of the Hand; Amer. Soc. for [14525]
Surgery; Intl. Soc. of Hair Restoration [14521]
Surgery; Intl. Soc. for Minimally Invasive Cardiac [★13914]
Surgery; Intl. Soc. for Minimally Invasive Cardiotho-racic [13914]
Surgery Res. Coun; Plastic [14052]
Surgery Soc; Gynecologic [15600]
Surgery; Soc. for Office-Based [★16558]
Surgery Soc; Outpatient Ophthalmic [15698]
Surgery; Soc. for Vascular [16730]
Surgery of Trauma; Amer. Assn. for the [16687]
Surgical Anesthesia and Critical Care; Soc. of Neuro [15417]
Surgical Asst. Assn; Natl. [16585]
Surgical Assn; Amer. [16575]
Surgical Assn; Amer. Pediatric [15883]
Surgical Assn; Asian [IO]
Surgical Assn; Western [16592]
Surgical Care; Soc. for the Advancement of Freestanding Ambulatory [★16582]
Surgical Dressing Manufacturers Assn. [IO], Roch-dale, United Kingdom
Surgical Eye Expeditions Intl. [IO], Goleta, CA, United States
Surgical Eye Expeditions Intl. [16889], 7200 Hollister Ave., Unit A, Goleta, CA 93117-2807, (805)963-3303
Surgical Instrument Manufacturers Assn. of Pakistan [IO], Sialkot, Pakistan
Surgical Mfrs. Assn; Medical- [★14669]
Surgical Mfrs. Assn; Orthopedic [1865]
Surgical Nurses; Acad. of Medical [15426]
Surgical Nurses; Amer. Soc. of Plastic [15461]
Surgical Nurses; Amer. Soc. of Plastic and Reconstructive [★15461]
Surgical Oncology; Soc. of [15655]
Surgical Physician Assistants; Amer. Assn. of [16560]
Surgical Res; Acad. of [15099]
Surgical Res; Indiana Found. for Hand [★14526]
Surgical Technologist; Joint Rev. Comm. on Educ. for the [★15123]
Surgical Technologist; Liaison Coun. on Certification for the [★13534]
Surgical Technologists; Assn. of [15133]
Surgical Tech; Accreditation Rev. Comm. on Educ. in [15123]
Surgical Tech; Accreditation Rev. Comm. for Educational Programs in [★15123]

Reference to "IO" in place of a book number signifies that the association may be found in the 45th edition of International Organizations.

Surgical Trade Assn; Amer. [★1860]
Surgical Trade Found. [★1860]
Surinaams Olympisch Comite [★IO]
Surinaamse Athletiek Bond [IO], Paramaribo, Suriname
Surinaamse Badminton Bond [IO], Paramaribo, Suriname
Surinaamse Tennisbond [IO], Paramaribo, Suriname
Surinaamse Vereniging voor Fysiotherapie [IO], Paramaribo, Suriname
Suriname Freedom Union - Address unknown since 1985.
Suriname Olympic Comm. [IO], Paramaribo, Suriname
Suriname Taekwondo Associatie [IO], Paramaribo, Suriname
Surinamese Weightlifting and Bodybuilding Fed. [IO], Paramaribo, Suriname
Surname Org; Britenburg [20809]
Surplus
    Assoc. Surplus Dealers [3701]
    Investment Recovery Assn. [3702]
Surplus Lines Offices; Natl. Assn. of Professional [2216]
Surplus Property; Natl. Assn. State Agencies for [6185]
Surratt Soc. [10067], c/o Laurie Verge, Dir., 9118 Brandywine Rd., Box 427, Clinton, MD 20735, (301)868-1121
Surrey Chambers of Commerce [IO], Woking, United Kingdom
Surrogate Mothers
    Center for Surrogate Parenting [13297]
    Donors' Offspring [13298]
    Org. of Parents Through Surrogacy [13299]
Surrogate Parent Found. [★13297]
Surrogate Parenthood
    Center for Surrogate Parenting [13297]
    Donors' Offspring [13298]
    Org. of Parents Through Surrogacy [13299]
Surrogates by Choice - Defunct.
Sursawera [IO], New Delhi, India
Surtees Soc. [IO], Durham, United Kingdom
Surtsey Res. Soc. [IO], Reykjavik, Iceland
Surtseyjarfelagid [★IO]
Surveillance Proj. of the Amer. Friends Ser. Comm; Mississippi [★17093]
Survey Agencies; Assn. of Hea. Fac. [6210]
The Survey Assn. [IO], Newark, United Kingdom
Survey Res. Organizations; Coun. of Amer. [18369]
Surveying
    Amer. Assn. for Geodetic Surveying [7716]
    Amer. Cong. on Surveying and Mapping [7717]
    Assn. of Canada Lands Surveyors [IO]
    Assn. of Certified Marine Surveyors [2572]
    Australian Inst. of Quantity Surveyors [IO]
    Canadian Coun. of Land Surveying [IO]
    Canadian Hydrographic Assn. [IO]
    Canadian Hydrographic Assn. - Ottawa Br. [IO]
    Canadian Hydrographic Assn. - Prairie Schooner Br. [IO]
    Commonwealth Assn. of Surveying and Land Economy [IO]
    Coun. of Professional Surveyors [3703]
    German Assn. of Land Surveyors [IO]
    German Assn. of Surveying [IO]
    Guild of Incorporated Surveyors [IO]
    Hong Kong Inst. of Surveyors [IO]
    The Hydrographic Soc. of Am. [7718]
    Institution of Civil Engg. Surveyors [IO]
    Institution of Surveyors, Australia [IO]
    Intl. Fed. of Hydrographic Societies [IO]
    Intl. Fed. of Surveyors [IO]
    Intl. Hydrographic Bur. [IO]
    Natl. Assn. of Marine Surveyors [7275]
    Natl. Coun. of Examiners for Engg. and Surveying [7031]
    Natl. Soc. of Professional Surveyors [7719]
    New Zealand Inst. of Quantity Surveyors [IO]
    Pacific Assn. of Quantity Surveyors [IO]
    Rating Surveyors' Assn. [IO]
    Royal Institution of Chartered Surveyors [IO]
    Society of Accredited Marine Surveyors [IO]
    Soc. of Accredited Marine Surveyors [7720]
    Soc. of Chartered Surveyors in the Republic of Ireland [IO]

    Soc. of Constr. and Quantity Surveyors [IO]
South African Coun. for the Quantity Surveying Profession [IO]
The Survey Assn. [IO]
Surveyors Historical Soc. [10162]
Swiss Assn. of Geomatics and Landmanagement [IO]
U.S. Surveyors Assn. [7721]
Surveying and Mapping; Cartography Division of the Amer. Cong. on [★6654]
Surveying and Mapping; Control Surveys Division of the Amer. Cong. on [★7716]
Surveying; Natl. Coun. of Examiners for Engg. and [7031]
Surveyors Historical Soc. [10162], 300 W High St., Lawrenceburg, IN 47025-1912, (812)537-2000
Surveyors; Mgt. Assn. for Private Photogrammetric [7496]
Surveyors; Natl. Assn. of County [5623]
Surveyors; Natl. Assn. of Marine [7275]
Surveyors; Natl. Soc. of Professional [7719]
Surveyors to the Yacht Safety Bur; Corresponding [★7275]
SURVIVAL [IO], London, United Kingdom
Survival
    California Wilderness Survival League [9202]
    Live-Free, USA [9203]
    Live-Free, USA [IO]
    Natl. Assn. of Storm Chasers and Spotters [13413]
    Outward Bound [9204]
Survival of Amer. Indians Assn. - Address unknown since 1999.
Survival and Beyond; People's Inst. for [18626]
Survival Consciousness - Address unknown since 2003.
Survival Deutschland [IO], Berlin, Germany
Survival Education Assn. - Defunct.
Survival and Flight Equip. Assn. [★6383]
Survival of a Free Cong; Comm. for the [★17268]
Survival Fund; Natl. Black [12780]
Survival Intl. - Espana [IO], Madrid, Spain
Survival Intl. - France [★IO]
Survival Intl. - France [IO], Paris, France
Survival Intl. - Italia [IO], Milan, Italy
Survival Intl., U.S.A. - Defunct.
Survival Prog; Food for [★12780]
Survival Program; Health Care for [★12780]
Survival Program; Jobs for [★12780]
Survival and Res. Center; Wild Canid [5393]
Survival Res. Found. [7453], 1000 Island Blvd., No. 512, Aventura, FL 33160, (305)936-1408
Survival School; Heart of the Earth [★18090]
Survivalists
    California Wilderness Survival League [9202]
Survive; Hug-A-Tree and [11600]
Survivor Connections [13084], 52 Lyndon Rd., Cranston, RI 02905-1121, (401)941-2548
Survivors And Victims Empowered [11656], 1725 Oregon Pike, Ste. 106, Lancaster, PA 17601, (717)569-0550
Survivors Anonymous; Incest [13076]
Survivors Assn; Pearl Harbor [21399]
Survivors' Assn; Thyroid Cancer [16648]
Survivors of Clergy Abuse; The Linkup - [11522]
Survivors; Concerns of Police [12752]
Survivors and Friends in Pursuit of Justice; Holocaust [17719]
Survivors of Incest Anonymous [13085], c/o World Ser. Off., PO Box 190, Benson, MD 21018-0190, (410)893-3322
Survivors; Natl. Assn. of Radiation [18129]
Survivors Network; Landmine [11959]
Survivors Network of Those Abused by Priests [13372], PO Box 6416, Chicago, IL 60680, (312)409-2720
Survivors of Sacrifice - Defunct.
Survivors Take Action Against Abuse by Military Personnel; STAMP - [11507]
Survivors; Tragedy Assistance Prog. for [11503]
Survivors in the U.S; Comm. of Atomic Bomb [18144]
Survivorship [13377], PMB 139, 3181 Mission St., San Francisco, CA 94110
Survivorship; Natl. Coalition for Cancer [13852]

Susan B. Anthony Women's Spirituality Educ. Forum [★20628]
Susan G. Komen Breast Cancer Found. [13878], 5005 LBJ Fwy., Ste. 250, Dallas, TX 75244, (972)855-1600
Susan G. Komen Found. [★13878]
Susan Glaspell Soc. [11197], c/o Martha C. Carpentier, VP, Dept. of English, Seton Hall Univ., 400 S Orange Ave., South Orange, NJ 07079
Susan Hayward Collectors Club - Address unknown since 1999.
Susanne Severeid Fan Club - Address unknown since 1995.
Susila Dharma Intl. [IO], Vancouver, BC, Canada
Susivienijimas Lietuviu Amerikoje [★19208]
Suspended Access Equip. Mfrs'. Assn. [★IO]
Suspended Ceiling Mfrs. Assn. - Defunct.
Suspension Specialists Assn. [★427]
Sussex Cattle Assn. of America - Defunct.
Sussex Chamber of Commerce and Enterprise [IO], Burgess Hill, United Kingdom
Sussex Peace Alliance [IO], Hailsham, United Kingdom
Sustain: The Alliance for Better Food and Farming [IO], London, United Kingdom
Sustainability Educ. Project [★4413]
Sustainable Agriculture
    Assn. of Natural Biocontrol Producers [5074]
    Center for Respect of Life and Env. [4620]
    Community Food Security Coalition [12192]
    Food Alliance [4676]
    The Land Inst. [4647]
    Natl. Assn. for Sustainable Agriculture Australia [IO]
    Natl. Inst. for Sci., Law and Public Policy [4105]
    Positive Futures Network [18839]
    Sustainable Development Network [IO]
    Wild Farm Alliance [4661]
Sustainable Agriculture; Comm. for [★4100]
Sustainable Agriculture; Steering Comm. for [★4100]
Sustainable Agriculture and Wetlands [★4413]
Sustainable Buildings Indus. Coun. [7682], 1112 16th St. NW, Ste. 240, Washington, DC 20036, (202)628-7400
Sustainable Desert Occupancy; Inst. for [4510]
Sustainable Development Network [IO], Bristol, United Kingdom
Sustainable Development Tech. Canada [IO], Ottawa, ON, Canada
Sustainable Energy Assn; Northeast [6968]
Sustainable Energy; Bus. Coun. for [1285]
Sustainable Harvest Intl. [4115], 779 N Bend Rd., Surry, ME 04684, (207)669-8254
Sustainable Hospitals Proj. [14899], Kitson 200, 1 Univ. Ave., Lowell, MA 01854, (978)934-3386
Sustainable Obtainable Solutions [5129], PO Box 1424, Helena, MT 59624, (406)495-0738
Sustainable Population Australia [IO], Weston Creek, Australia
Sustainable Tech; Renewable Energy Policy Proj. - Center For Renewable Energy and [6970]
Sustainable Travel Intl. [5252], PO Box 1313, Boulder, CO 80306, (720)273-2975
Sustainable Travel Intl. [IO], Boulder, CO, United States
Sustainable Village-Based Development; Consortium for [★11793]
Sustainable World; Engineers for a [11776]
Sustainably Yours - Defunct.
SustainUS [13517], 1414 E 59th St., No. 624, Chicago, IL 60637-2916
Sut Soc. - Defunct.
Sutherland Soc. of North Am; Clan [20864]
Sutton Movement Writing; Center for [11208]
Suunnittelu- ja konsulttitoimistojen liitto [★IO]
Suzuki
    LeMans Am. [22686]
    Suzuki Assn. of the Americas [8932]
Suzuki Assn. of the Americas [8932], PO Box 17310, Boulder, CO 80308, (303)444-0948
Suzy Bogguss Fan Club [24978], c/o Suzy Bogguss Concerts, Suzy Fan Mail, PMB 186, 8161 Hwy. 100, Nashville, TN 37220
Svaz knihovniku a informacnich pracovniku Ceske republiky [★IO]

A star before a book entry number signifies that the name is not listed separately, but is mentioned within the entry.

Svaz prumyslu a dopravy CR [★IO]
Svaz Obchodu A Cestovniho Ruchu Cr [★IO]
Svaz Prumyslu Papiru a Celulozy [★IO]
Svensk forening for informationsspecialister [★IO]
Svensk Armaturindustri [★IO]
Svensk Beteendemedicinsk Forening [★IO]
Svensk Biblioteksforening [★IO]
Svensk-Botswanska Vanskapsforeningen [★IO]
Svensk Flyghistorisk Forening [★IO]
Svensk Flyktinghjalp [★IO]
Svensk Forening for Geriatrik and Gerontologi [★IO]
Svensk Form [★IO]
Svensk Gastroenterologisk Forening [★IO]
Svensk Handel [★IO]
Svensk-Irlandska Foreningen [★IO]
Svensk Kirurgisk Forening [★IO]
Svensk Mjoelk [★IO]
Svensk Samhallsvetenskaplig Datatjanst [★IO]
Svensk Snickeriindustri [★IO]
Svensk Teaterunion - Svenska ITI [★IO]
Svensk Teknik och Design [★IO]
Svensk Ungdom - Svenska Folkpartiets Ungdomsorganisation [★IO]
Svenska lantbruksproducenternas centralforbund [★IO]
Svenska Arkeologiska Samfundet [★IO]
Svenska Arkivsamfundet [★IO]
Svenska Astronomiska Sallskapet [★IO]
Svenska Bankforeningen [★IO]
Svenska Baseboll och Softboll Forbundet [★IO]
Svenska Betongforeningen [★IO]
Svenska Bokhandlareforeningen [IO], Stockholm, Sweden
Svenska Bryggareforeningen [★IO]
Svenska Budoforbundet Aikidosektionen [IO], Stockholm, Sweden
Svenska Cardiologforeningen [★IO]
Svenska Central Forbundet [★19397]
Svenska Danssportforbundet [★IO]
Svenska Filminstitutet [★IO]
Svenska Folkhogskolans Lararforbund [IO], Sundbyberg, Sweden
Svenska Folkpartiet [★IO]
Svenska Foreningen OIKOS [★IO]
Svenska Fornminnesforeningen [★IO]
Svenska Forsakringsforeningen [★IO]
Svenska Forskningsgruppen i Geomorfologi [★IO]
Svenska Fotografers Forbund [IO], Stockholm, Sweden
Svenska Franchise Foereningen [★IO]
Svenska Freds och Skiljedomsforeningen [★IO]
Svenska Friidrottsforbundet [★IO]
Svenska Frisbeesport Forbundet [★IO]
Svenska Fysikersamfundet [★IO]
Svenska Gasforeningen [★IO]
Svenska Geotekniska Foreningen [★IO]
Svenska Gjuteriforeningen [★IO]
Svenska Glasbruksforeningen [★IO]
Svenska Innebandyforbundet [★IO]
Svenska Kanot Forbundet [★IO]
Svenska Kvinnoforbundet [★IO]
Svenska Kyltekniska Foreningen [★IO]
Svenska Kyrkans Mission [★IO]
Svenska Lakaresallskapet [★IO]
Svenska Ljussattare Foreningen [★IO]
Svenska Marfanforeningen [★IO]
Svenska Matematikersamfundet [★IO]
Svenska Mineralogiska Sallskapet [★IO]
Svenska Museiforeningen [★IO]
Svenska Musikerforbundet [★IO]
Svenska Naturskyddsforeningen [★IO]
Svenska OptikSallskapet [★IO]
Svenska Orienteringsforbundet [★IO]
Svenska Ortodontiforeningen [★IO]
Svenska PEN [★IO]
Svenska Petroleum Institutet [★IO]
Svenska Psykoanalytiska Foreningen [★IO]
Svenska Reumatikerforbundet [★IO]
Svenska Sallskapet for Antropologi och Geografi [★IO]
Svenska Sallskapet for Automatiserad Bildanalys [★IO]
Svenska Samfundet for Musikforskning [★IO]
Svenska Skolidrottsforbundet [IO], Stockholm, Sweden

Svenska Squash Forbundet [IO], Malmo, Sweden
Svenska Tennisforbundet [★IO]
Svenska Tidningsutgivarefoereningen [★IO]
Svenska Tidningsutgivareforeningen [★IO]
Svenska Unescoradet [★IO]
Svenska Uppfinnare Foreningen [★IO]
Svenska Vattenskidforbundet [★IO]
Svenska Vegetariska Foreningen [★IO]
Svenska Yngling Forbundet [IO], Helsingborg, Sweden
Svenskt Naringsliv [★IO]
Svenskt ProjektForum [★IO]
Sveriges advokatsamfund [★IO]
Sveriges 4H [★IO]
Sveriges Angbats Forening [★IO]
Sveriges Annonsorer [★IO]
Sveriges Bageriforbund [★IO]
Sveriges Begravningsbyraers Forbund [IO], Stockholm, Sweden
Sveriges Civilingenjorsforbund [★IO]
Sveriges Dovas Riksforbund [★IO]
Sveriges Fackoversattarforening [★IO]
Sveriges Faerghandlares Riksfoerbund [★IO]
Sveriges Film- och Videofoerbund [★IO]
Sveriges Forenade Studentkarer [★IO]
Sveriges Forfattarforbund [★IO]
Sveriges Gerontologiska Sallskap [★IO]
Sveriges Hotell-och Restaurangforetagare [★IO]
Sveriges Koepmannafoerbund [★IO]
Sveriges Konst Och Antikhandlarforening [IO], Stockholm, Sweden
Sveriges Kristna Rad [★IO]
Sveriges Lakarforbund [★IO]
Sveriges Lakarforbund [★IO]
Sveriges Moebelhandlare [★IO]
Sveriges Olympiska Kommitte [★IO]
Sveriges Psykologforbund [★IO]
Sveriges Redare-Forening [★IO]
Sveriges Redovisningskonsulters Forbund [★IO]
Sveriges Reklamfoerbund [★IO]
Sveriges Skolledarforbund [★IO]
Sveriges Skorstensfejaremaestares Riksfoerbund [★IO]
Sveriges Tandlakarforbund [★IO]
Sveriges Tidskrifter [★IO]
Sveriges Universitetslararforbund [★IO]
Sveriges Verkstadsindustrier [★IO]
Sveriges Veterinarforbund [★IO]
Svithiod; Independent Order of [19344]
SW5 [IO], London, United Kingdom
Swadhina [IO], Calcutta, India
Swan-Avon Olive Assn. [IO], Midland, Australia
Swan Boat Assn; Amer. [23669]
Swan Owners Assn. of Am. [23221], 17 Oyster Point, Warren, RI 02885
Swan Soc; The Trumpeter [5388]
Swankyswig Club - Defunct.
Swaziland Athletics Assn. [IO], Mbabane, Swaziland
Swaziland Natl. Badminton Assn. [IO], Mbabane, Swaziland
Swaziland Natl. Tennis Union [IO], Manzini, Swaziland
Swaziland Olympic and Commonwealth Games Assn. [IO], Mbabane, Swaziland
Swaziland School Sports Assn. [IO], Manzini, Swaziland
Swaziland Squash Assn. [IO], Mbabane, Swaziland
Swaziland Sugar Assn. [IO], Mbabane, Swaziland
SWCA Lib. [★22991]
SweatFree Communities [24106], c/o Bjorn Claeson, Exec. Dir., 30 Blackstone St., Bangor, ME 04401, (207)262-7277
Sweatshop Watch [17977], 1250 S Los Angeles St., Ste. 212, Los Angeles, CA 90015, (213)748-5945

Sweden
Amer. Soc. of Swedish Engineers [6998]
Amer. Swedish Historical Museum [10987]
Intl. Assn. of Speakers Bureaus [10900]
Saab Club of North Am. [21778]
Scandinavian Tourist Boards [24372]
Swedish-American Historical Soc. [10989]
Swedish Amer. Museum Assn. of Chicago [10990]
Swedish Colonial Soc. [10991]
Swedish Translators in North Am. [11059]
Swedenborg Assn. [9164], PO Box 9111, Lutherville, MD 21093, (410)504-1949

Swedenborg Found. [9711], 320 N Church St., West Chester, PA 19380, (610)430-3222
Swedenborg Soc. [IO], London, United Kingdom
Swedish
Amer. Nyckelharpa Assn. [10546]
Amer. Soc. of Swedish Engineers [6998]
Amer. Swedish Historical Museum [10987]
Amer. Swedish Inst. [10988]
Amer. Swedish Inst. [IO]
Intl. Order of Runeberg [9952]
John Ericsson Soc. [11130]
Jussi Bjorling Soc. - USA [9508]
Saab Club of North Am. [21778]
Swedenborg Found. [9711]
Swedish-American Bar Assn. [5532]
Swedish-American Chambers of Commerce, USA [24297]
Swedish-American Historical Soc. [10989]
Swedish Amer. Museum Assn. of Chicago [10990]
Swedish Amer. Museum Assn. of Chicago [IO]
Swedish Colonial Society [IO]
Swedish Colonial Soc. [10991]
Swedish Coun. of Am. [19395]
Swedish Trade Coun. [3847]
Swedish Translators in North Am. [11059]
Swedish Women's Educational Assn. Intl. [19396]
Swedish Women's Educational Assn. Intl. [IO]
United Swedish Societies [19397]
Swedish 4H Assn. [IO], Katrineholm, Sweden
Swedish Acad. of Pharmaceutical Sciences [IO], Stockholm, Sweden
Swedish Advertisers' Assn. [IO], Stockholm, Sweden
Swedish Advt. Assn. [IO], Stockholm, Sweden
Swedish Amateur Theatre Coun. [IO], Fagersta, Sweden
Swedish-American Bar Assn. [5532], c/o Mikael Koltai, Esq., Founder, 5020 Campus Dr., Newport Beach, CA 92660, (949)706-9111
Swedish-American Chamber of Commerce [★24297]
Swedish-American Chamber of Commerce [★IO]
Swedish-American Chambers of Commerce, USA [IO], Alexandria, VA, United States
Swedish-American Chambers of Commerce, USA [24297], 1403 King St., Alexandria, VA 22314, (703)836-6560
Swedish-American Historical Soc. [10989], 3225 W Foster Ave., Box 48, Chicago, IL 60625, (773)583-5722
Swedish Amer. Museum Assn. of Chicago [10990], 5211 N Clark St., Chicago, IL 60640, (773)728-8111
Swedish Amer. Museum Assn. of Chicago [IO], Chicago, IL, United States
Swedish Anti-Nuclear Movement [IO], Stockholm, Sweden
Swedish Archaeological Soc. [IO], Stockholm, Sweden
Swedish Archival Assn. [IO], Lund, Sweden
Swedish Assn. of Accounting Consultants [IO], Falun, Sweden
Swedish Assn. of Agents [IO], Stockholm, Sweden
Swedish Assn. for Amer. Stud. [IO], Harnosand, Sweden
Swedish Assn. of Dietitians [IO], Stockholm, Sweden
Swedish Assn. of Door and Shutter Suppliers [IO], Stockholm, Sweden
Swedish Assn. for the Electrically and VDT Injured [★IO]
Swedish Assn. for the Electrosensitive [IO], Stockholm, Sweden
Swedish Assn. of Engineers [IO], Stockholm, Sweden
Swedish Assn. of Graduate Engineers [IO], Stockholm, Sweden
Swedish Assn. of Graduates in Documentation, Info. and Culture [★IO]
Swedish Assn. of Head Teachers and Principals [★IO]
Swedish Assn. for Info. Specialists [IO], Stockholm, Sweden
Swedish Assn. of Marine Underwriters [IO], Stockholm, Sweden
Swedish Assn. of Mines, Minerals and Metal Producers [IO], Stockholm, Sweden

Reference to "IO" in place of a book number signifies that the association may be found in the 45th edition of International Organizations.

Swedish Assn. of Neurologically Disabled **[IO]**, Stockholm, Sweden

Swedish Assn. of Occupational Therapists **[IO]**, Nacka, Sweden

Swedish Assn. of Orthodontists **[IO]**, Linkoping, Sweden

Swedish Assn. of the Pharmaceutical Indus. **[IO]**, Stockholm, Sweden

Swedish Assn. of Physicians for the Env. **[★IO]**

Swedish Assn. of Preschool Teachers **[★IO]**

Swedish Assn. for the Protection of Ancient Monuments **[IO]**, Stockholm, Sweden

Swedish Assn. of Registered Physiotherapists **[IO]**, Stockholm, Sweden

Swedish Assn. of School Leaders **[★IO]**

Swedish Assn. of School Principals and Directors of Educ. **[IO]**, Stockholm, Sweden

Swedish Assn. for Sexuality Educ. **[IO]**, Stockholm, Sweden

Swedish Assn. of Suppliers of Effluent and Water Treatment Equip. **[IO]**, Stockholm, Sweden

Swedish Assn. of Suppliers of Elecl. Household Appliances **[IO]**, Stockholm, Sweden

Swedish Assn. of Translators **[IO]**, Bastad, Sweden

Swedish Assn. of Univ. Teachers **[IO]**, Stockholm, Sweden

Swedish Assn. of Univ. Women **[IO]**, Stockholm, Sweden

Swedish Astronomical Soc. **[IO]**, Stockholm, Sweden

Swedish Athletic Assn. **[IO]**, Solna, Sweden

Swedish Aviation Historical Soc. **[IO]**, Stockholm, Sweden

Swedish Bankers' Assn. **[IO]**, Stockholm, Sweden

Swedish Bar Assn. **[IO]**, Stockholm, Sweden

Swedish Baseball and Softball Fed. **[IO]**, Farsta, Sweden

Swedish Brewers' Assn. **[IO]**, Stockholm, Sweden

Swedish Bus. Assn. of Singapore **[IO]**, Singapore, Singapore

Swedish-Canadian Chamber of Commerce **[IO]**, Toronto, ON, Canada

Swedish Canadian Chamber of Commerce - Canadian Swedish Bus. Assn. **[★IO]**

Swedish Canoe Fed. **[IO]**, Nykoping, Sweden

Swedish Cartographic Soc. **[IO]**, Gavle, Sweden

Swedish Chimney Sweep Masters Assn. **[IO]**, Stockholm, Sweden

Swedish Choral Assn. **[IO]**, Stockholm, Sweden

Swedish Christian Educational Assn. **[★IO]**

Swedish Clothing and Textile Retailers' Assn. **[★IO]**

Swedish Colonial Society **[IO]**, West Chester, PA, United States

Swedish Colonial Soc. **[10991]**, c/o Doriney Seagers, Registrar, 371 Devon Way, West Chester, PA 19380, (215)389-1513

Swedish Concrete Assn. **[IO]**, Danderyd, Sweden

Swedish Confed. of Professional Associations **[IO]**, Stockholm, Sweden

Swedish Confed. of Professional Employees **[IO]**, Stockholm, Sweden

Swedish Cosmetic, Toiletry and Household Products Suppliers' Assn. **[IO]**, Stockholm, Sweden

Swedish Coun. of Am. **[19395]**, 2600 Park Ave., Minneapolis, MN 55407, (612)871-0593

Swedish Crystal Mfrs. Assn. **[IO]**, Stockholm, Sweden

Swedish Dairy Assn. **[IO]**, Stockholm, Sweden

Swedish Dance Sport Fed. **[IO]**, Marbackagatan, Sweden

Swedish Dance Sport Org. **[★IO]**

Swedish Dental Assn. **[IO]**, Stockholm, Sweden

Swedish Dental Trade Assn. **[IO]**, Stockholm, Sweden

Swedish Direct Marketing Assn. **[IO]**, Stockholm, Sweden

Swedish Doctors for the Env. **[IO]**, Stockholm, Sweden

Swedish Electronics Retailers' Assn. **[IO]**, Stockholm, Sweden

Swedish Engineers; Amer. Soc. of **[6998]**

Swedish-English Literary Translators' Assn. **[IO]**, Welwyn Garden City, United Kingdom

Swedish Epilepsy Soc. **[IO]**, Goteborg, Sweden

Swedish Farmers Safety and Preventive Hea. Assn. **[IO]**, Stockholm, Sweden

Swedish Fed. of Architects and Consulting Engineers **[★IO]**

Swedish Fed. of Consulting Engineers and Architects **[IO]**, Stockholm, Sweden

Swedish Fed. of Film and Video Amateurs **[IO]**, Stockholm, Sweden

Swedish Fed. of Govt. Affairs **[★IO]**

Swedish Fellowship of Reconciliation **[IO]**, Sundbyberg, Sweden

Swedish Film Inst. **[IO]**, Stockholm, Sweden

Swedish Finn Assn. **[IO]**, Sandviken, Sweden

Swedish-Finnish Benevolent and Aid Assn. of Am. and Swedish-Finnish Temperance Assn. **[★IO]**

Swedish-Finnish Benevolent and Aid Assn. of Am. and Swedish-Finnish Temperance Assn. **[★9952]**

Swedish Floorball Fed. **[IO]**, Solna, Sweden

Swedish Flooring Trade Assn. **[IO]**, Stockholm, Sweden

Swedish Forensic Sci. Assn. **[IO]**, Goteborg, Sweden

Swedish Forest Indus. Fed. **[IO]**, Stockholm, Sweden

Swedish Foundry Assn. **[IO]**, Jonkoping, Sweden

Swedish Franchise Assn. **[IO]**, Goteborg, Sweden

Swedish Frisbeesport Fed. **[IO]**, Goteborg, Sweden

Swedish Frozen Food Assn. **[IO]**, Stockholm, Sweden

Swedish Fur Breeders Assn. **[IO]**, Solvesborg, Sweden

Swedish Furniture Indus. Assn. **[IO]**, Stockholm, Sweden

Swedish Furniture Retailers' Assn. **[IO]**, Stockholm, Sweden

Swedish Gas Assn. **[IO]**, Stockholm, Sweden

Swedish Geotechnical Soc. **[IO]**, Linkoping, Sweden

Swedish Gerontological Soc. **[IO]**, Uppsala, Sweden

Swedish Glass Mfrs'. Assn. **[★IO]**

Swedish Gotland Breeder's Assn. **[★4957]**

Swedish Gotland Breeders' Soc. **[4957]**, 3240 Hinton-Webber Rd., Corinth, KY 41010-8952, (859)234-5707

Swedish Heating Boilers Assn. **[★IO]**

Swedish Heating Boilers and Burners Assn. **[IO]**, Stockholm, Sweden

Swedish Hemophilia Soc. **[IO]**, Sundbyberg, Sweden

Swedish Hotel and Restaurant Assn. **[IO]**, Stockholm, Sweden

Swedish Hypertension Soc. **[IO]**, Goteborg, Sweden

Swedish Inst; Augustana **[★19343]**

Swedish Inst. for Fibre and Polymer Res. **[IO]**, Molndal, Sweden

Swedish Inst. of Intl. Affairs **[IO]**, Stockholm, Sweden

Swedish Insurance Soc. **[IO]**, Stockholm, Sweden

Swedish Inventors Assn. **[IO]**, Stockholm, Sweden

Swedish-Irish Soc. **[IO]**, Spanga, Sweden

Swedish Journalists Assn. of America - Address unknown since 1995.

Swedish Lib. Assn. **[IO]**, Stockholm, Sweden

Swedish Machine Tool and Cutting Tool Mfrs. Assn. **[IO]**, Stockholm, Sweden

Swedish Magazine Publishers' Assn. **[IO]**, Stockholm, Sweden

Swedish Marfan Assn. **[IO]**, Stockholm, Sweden

Swedish Mathematical Soc. **[IO]**, Goteborg, Sweden

Swedish Meat Indus. Assn. **[IO]**, Stockholm, Sweden

Swedish Medical Assn. **[IO]**, Stockholm, Sweden

Swedish Mineralogical Soc. **[IO]**, Stockholm, Sweden

Swedish Museum and Cultural Center **[★IO]**

Swedish Museum and Cultural Center **[★10990]**

Swedish Museums Assn. **[IO]**, Stockholm, Sweden

Swedish Musicians' Union **[IO]**, Stockholm, Sweden

Swedish Natl. Assn. of the Deaf **[IO]**, Stockholm, Sweden

Swedish Natl. Commn. for UNESCO **[IO]**, Stockholm, Sweden

Swedish Natl. Comm. on Physiology **[IO]**, Uppsala, Sweden

Swedish Natl. Coun. of Adult Educ. **[IO]**, Stockholm, Sweden

Swedish Natl. Coun. for Cultural Affairs **[IO]**, Stockholm, Sweden

Swedish Natl. Union of Students **[IO]**, Stockholm, Sweden

Swedish Newspaper Publishers Assn. **[IO]**, Stockholm, Sweden

Swedish Newspapers' Assn. **[IO]**, Stockholm, Sweden

Swedish NGO Secretariat on Acid Rain **[IO]**, Goteborg, Sweden

Swedish Olympic Comm. **[IO]**, Stockholm, Sweden

Swedish Operations Res. Soc. **[IO]**, Stockholm, Sweden

Swedish Optical Soc. **[IO]**, Stockholm, Sweden

Swedish Org. of Emergency Shelters for Battered Women **[★IO]**

Swedish Org. of Youth with Rheumatism **[IO]**, Farsta, Sweden

Swedish Org. of Youth with Rheumatism **[IO]**, Stockholm, Sweden

Swedish Orienteering Fed. **[IO]**, Solna, Sweden

Swedish Osteoporosis Soc. **[IO]**, Goteborg, Sweden

Swedish Paint Trade Fed. **[IO]**, Stockholm, Sweden

Swedish Peace and Arbitration Soc. **[IO]**, Stockholm, Sweden

Swedish PEN Centre **[IO]**, Stockholm, Sweden

Swedish People's Party of Finland **[IO]**, Helsinki, Finland

Swedish Petroleum Inst. **[IO]**, Stockholm, Sweden

Swedish Physical Soc. **[IO]**, Uppsala, Sweden

Swedish Pioneer Centennial Comm. **[★10989]**

Swedish Pioneer Historical Soc. **[★10989]**

Swedish Plastics and Chem. Fed. **[IO]**, Stockholm, Sweden

Swedish Plastics Fed. **[★IO]**

Swedish Precast Concrete Fed. **[IO]**, Stockholm, Sweden

Swedish Proj. Mgt. Soc. **[IO]**, Stockholm, Sweden

Swedish Psoriasis Assn. **[IO]**, Johanneshov, Sweden

Swedish Psychoanalytical Soc. **[IO]**, Stockholm, Sweden

Swedish Psychological Assn. **[IO]**, Stockholm, Sweden

Swedish Refugee Aid **[IO]**, Stockholm, Sweden

Swedish Res. Coun. for Env., Agricultural Sciences and Spatial Planning **[IO]**, Stockholm, Sweden

Swedish Res. Gp. in Geomorphology **[IO]**, Uppsala, Sweden

Swedish Rheumatism Assn. **[IO]**, Stockholm, Sweden

Swedish Sea Rescue Soc. **[IO]**, Vastra Frolunda, Sweden

Swedish Shipbrokers' Assn. **[IO]**, Goteborg, Sweden

Swedish Shipowners' Assn. **[IO]**, Goteborg, Sweden

Swedish Shoe Retailers' Assn. **[★IO]**

Swedish Shoe, Textile and Clothing Retailers' Assn. **[IO]**, Stockholm, Sweden

Swedish Social Sci. Data Archv. **[IO]**, Goteborg, Sweden

Swedish Social Sci. Data Ser. **[★IO]**

Swedish Soc. of Aeronautics and Astronautics **[IO]**, Solna, Sweden

Swedish Soc. Against Painful Experiments on Animals **[★IO]**

Swedish Soc. Against Painful Experiments on Animals **[IO]**, Alvsjo, Sweden

Swedish Soc. of Agricultural Engineers **[IO]**, Uppsala, Sweden

Swedish Soc. for Anthropology and Geography **[IO]**, Stockholm, Sweden

Swedish Soc. for Automated Image Anal. **[IO]**, Linkoping, Sweden

Swedish Soc. of Behavioral Medicine **[IO]**, Goteborg, Sweden

Swedish Soc. of Cardiology **[IO]**, Stockholm, Sweden

Swedish Soc. of Coll. Engineers **[★IO]**

Swedish Soc. of Crafts and Design **[IO]**, Stockholm, Sweden

Swedish Soc. of Engineers **[★IO]**

Swedish Soc. of Gastroenterology **[IO]**, Lund, Sweden

Swedish Soc. for Geriatric Medicine and Gerontology **[IO]**, Solna, Sweden

Swedish Soc. of Medicine **[IO]**, Stockholm, Sweden

Swedish Soc. for Musicology **[IO]**, Stockholm, Sweden

Swedish Soc. for Nature Conservation **[IO]**, Stockholm, Sweden

Swedish Soc. OIKOS **[IO]**, Lund, Sweden

Swedish Soc. of Organbuilding **[IO]**, Stockholm, Sweden

A star before a book entry number signifies that the name is not listed separately, but is mentioned within the entry.

Swedish Soc. of Popular Music Composers [IO], Stockholm, Sweden

Swedish Soc. of Psychosomatic Obstetrics and Gynaecology [IO], Linkoping, Sweden

Swedish Soc. of Refrigeration [IO], Helsingborg, Sweden

Swedish Soc. for Rheumatology [IO], Stockholm, Sweden

Swedish Special Tooling Assn. [IO], Stockholm, Sweden

Swedish Spirits and Wine Suppliers [IO], Stockholm, Sweden

Swedish Steel Producers' Assn. [IO], Stockholm, Sweden

Swedish Surgical Soc. [IO], Stockholm, Sweden

Swedish Teachers' Union [IO], Stockholm, Sweden

Swedish Tennis Assn. [IO], Stockholm, Sweden

Swedish Textile and Clothing Indus'. Assn. [IO], Stockholm, Sweden

Swedish Theater Union - Swedish ITI [IO], Stockholm, Sweden

Swedish Trade Commn. [★IO]

Swedish Trade Commn. [★3847]

Swedish Trade Coun. [3847], 150 N Michigan Ave., Ste. 1950, Chicago, IL 60601, (312)781-6222

Swedish Trade Coun. [IO], Stockholm, Sweden

Swedish Trade Coun. [IO], Chicago, IL, United States

Swedish Trade Coun.- North Am. [★IO]

Swedish Trade Coun.- North Am. [★3847]

Swedish Trade Coun. - U.S. [★3847]

Swedish Trade Coun. - U.S. [★IO]

Swedish Trade Fed. [IO], Stockholm, Sweden

Swedish Translators in North Am. [IO], Seattle, WA, United States

Swedish Translators in North Am. [11059], c/o Laura A. Wideburg, Sec.-Treas., 6008 Corliss Ave. N, Seattle, WA 98103

Swedish Travel and Tourism Coun. [3939], PO Box 4649, Grand Central Sta., New York, NY 10163-4649, (212)885-9700

Swedish Travel and Tourism Coun. [IO], New York, NY, United States

Swedish Travelling Exhibitions [IO], Stockholm, Sweden

Swedish Union of Social Workers, Personnel, and Public Administrators [★IO]

Swedish Union of Specialist Teachers [★IO]

Swedish Union of Teachers [★IO]

Swedish Union of Tenants [IO], Stockholm, Sweden

Swedish Vegetarian Fed. [IO], Stockholm, Sweden

Swedish Veterinary Assn. [IO], Stockholm, Sweden

Swedish Warm Blood Assn. of North Am. [★4958]

Swedish Warmblood Assn. of North Am. [4958], PO Box 788, Socorro, NM 87801, (505)835-1318

Swedish Water Ski Fed. [IO], Falun, Sweden

Swedish Women's Educational Assn. Intl. [IO], Carlsbad, CA, United States

Swedish Women's Educational Assn. Intl. [19396], 5928 Balfour Ct., Ste. B, Carlsbad, CA 92008, (760)918-9653

Swedish Writers' Union [IO], Stockholm, Sweden

Swedish Youth of Finland - Youth Org. of the Swedish People's Party [IO], Helsinki, Finland

Sweeping Assn; North Amer. Power [2473]

Sweet Adelines, Inc. [★10711]

Sweet Adelines, Inc. [★IO]

Sweet Adelines Intl. [IO], Tulsa, OK, United States

Sweet Adelines Intl. [10711], PO Box 470168, Tulsa, OK 74147-0168, (918)622-1444

Sweet Dreams and Toast [★1936]

Sweet Dreams and Toast; Bed and Breakfast League/ [1936]

Sweet Family Org. - Defunct.

Sweet Hearts [★13243]

Sweet Mother Intl. [IO], Gawler, Australia

Sweet Potato Coun; U.S. [4771]

Sweet Valley High Fan Club - Address unknown since 1999.

Sweet Wine Producers Assn. [★5419]

Sweetener Producers Gp; U.S. [★1499]

Sweetener Users Assn. - Address unknown since 2004.

Sweets Global Network [IO], Munich, Germany

Swift Assn; Intl. [★21481]

Swift Boat Veterans for Truth [21324], c/o Weymouth D. Symmes, Treas., PO Box 26184, Alexandria, VA 22313

Swift Museum Found. [21481], PO Box 644, McMinn County Airport, Hangar 4, Athens, TN 37371-0644, (423)745-9547

Swim America [★23882]

Swim Ireland [IO], Dublin, Ireland

Swimmers; Polar Bear Club - Winter [★23888]

Swimming

Amateur Swimming Assn. [IO]

Amer. Swimming Coaches Assn. [23882]

Amer. Volkssport Assn. [23803]

Aquatic Exercise Assn. [23652]

Assn. of Pool and Spa Professionals [3353]

British Long Distance Swimming Assn. [IO]

Channel Crossing Assn. [IO]

Channel Swimming Assn. [IO]

Coll. Swimming Coaches Assn. of Am. [23883]

Fed. Internationale de Natation Amateur [IO]

International Academy of Aquatic Art [IO]

Intl. Acad. of Aquatic Art [23884]

Intl. Amateur Swimming Fed. [IO]

Intl. Gay and Lesbian Aquatics [IO]

Intl. Gay and Lesbian Aquatics [23885]

Intl. Swimming Hall of Fame [23886]

Intl. Swimming Hall of Fame [IO]

Natl. Drowning Prevention Alliance [12974]

Natl. Interscholastic Swimming Coaches Assn. of Am. [23887]

Natl. Swimming Pool Found. [3360]

Nordic Swimming Federations Assn. [IO]

Northern Mariana Islands Swimming Fed. [IO]

Out to Swim London [IO]

Polar Bear Club - U.S.A. [23888]

Scottish Swimming [IO]

Swim Ireland [IO]

Swimming Pool Water Treatment Professionals [825]

Swimming Teachers' Assn. [IO]

Synchro Swimming U.S.A. [23889]

U.S. Aquatic Sports [23890]

U.S. Masters Swimming [23891]

U.S. Swim School Assn. [23892]

U.S. Water Fitness Assn. [23657]

USA Swimming [23893]

World Aquatic Babies and Children [23894]

World Aquatic Babies and Children [IO]

Swimming Comm. of the AAU; Masters [★23891]

Swimming Comm. of the Amateur Athletic Union; Competitive [★23893]

Swimming Division of the Amateur Athletic Union; Synchronized [★23889]

Swimming Fed; Intl. Amateur [IO]

Swimming Found; U.S. [★23894]

Swimming/Natation Canada [IO], Ottawa, ON, Canada

Swimming Pool and Allied Trades Assn. [IO], Andover, United Kingdom

Swimming Pool Found; Natl. [3360]

Swimming Pool Inst; Natl. [★3353]

Swimming Pool Water Treatment Professionals [825], 21939 Camille Dr., Nuevo, CA 92567, (949)364-1990

Swimming Teachers of America - Address unknown since 2007.

Swimming Teachers' Assn. [IO], Walsall, United Kingdom

Swimming; U.S. Synchronized [★23889]

Swimming U.S.A; Synchro [23889]

Swine

Amer. Assn. of Swine Veterinarians [16750]

Amer. Berkshire Assn. [5230]

Amer. Guinea Hog Assn. [5231]

Amer. Landrace Assn. [5232]

Amer. Yorkshire Club [5233]

Chester White Swine Record Assn. [5234]

Natl. Assn. of Swine Records [5235]

Natl. Hereford Hog Record Assn. [5236]

Natl. Junior Swine Assn. [5237]

Natl. Pig Carvers Assn. [22169]

Natl. Pork Producers Coun. [5238]

Natl. Show Pig Assn. [22982]

Natl. Spotted Swine Record [5239]

Natl. Swine Improvement Fed. [5240]

Natl. Swine Registry [5241]

Poland China Record Assn. [5242]

Safe Harbour Animal Refuge [11454]

United Duroc Swine Registry [5243]

Swine Growers Coun; Natl. [★5238]

Swine Record; Spotted [★5239]

Swine Registry; Hampshire [★5241]

Swine Registry; United Duroc [★5241]

Swine Veterinarians; Amer. Assn. of [16750]

Swiss

Amer. Helvetia Philatelic Soc. [22782]

American-Swiss Found. [19398]

American-Swiss Found. [IO]

Euler Soc. [10453]

North Amer. Swiss Alliance [19399]

Pennsylvania German Soc. [21243]

Pro Helvetia Arts Coun. of Switzerland [IO]

Swiss-American Bus. Coun. [2314]

Swiss-American Coun. of Women [18815]

Swiss Amer. Historical Soc. [10992]

Swiss Amer. Historical Soc. [IO]

Swiss Benevolent Soc. of New York [19400]

Switzerland Convention and Incentive Bur. [24379]

Swiss Acad. of Engg. Sciences [IO], Zurich, Switzerland

Swiss Acad. of Humanities and Social Sciences [IO], Bern, Switzerland

Swiss Acad. of Medical Sciences [IO], Basel, Switzerland

Swiss Acad. of Sciences [IO], Bern, Switzerland

Swiss ACM SIGCHI [IO], Zurich, Switzerland

Swiss Alliance of Development Organisations [IO], Bern, Switzerland

Swiss Alliance Mission [IO], Winterthur, Switzerland

Swiss Aluminium Assn. [IO], Zurich, Switzerland

Swiss Aluminum Assn. [★IO]

Swiss-American Bus. Coun. [2314], PO Box 641724, Chicago, IL 60601, (312)498-7285

Swiss-American Chamber of Commerce [24378], c/o Mrs. Annemarie Gilman, Admin., New York Chap., 500 5th Ave., Rm. 1800, New York, NY 10110, (212)246-7789

Swiss - Amer. Chamber of Commerce [IO], Zurich, Switzerland

Swiss-American Coun. of Women [18815], 100 Park Ave., Ste. 1600, New York, NY 10017, (212)351-5005

Swiss Amer. Historical Soc. [10992], c/o Marianne Burkhard, 5521 Rosalie Dr., Peoria, IL 61614

Swiss Amer. Historical Soc. [IO], Peoria, IL, United States

Swiss-American Soc. for Cultural Relations [IO], Zurich, Switzerland

Swiss Amer. Stamp Soc. [★IO]

Swiss Amer. Stamp Soc. [★22782]

Swiss Arbitration Assn. [IO], Basel, Switzerland

Swiss-Argentine Chamber of Commerce [IO], Buenos Aires, Argentina

Swiss Army Knife Soc. - Defunct.

Swiss Assn. of Agricultural and Food Stuff Engineers [IO], Zollikofen, Switzerland

Swiss Assn; American- [★19398]

Swiss Assn. of Chemists [★IO]

Swiss Assn. of Consulting Engineers [IO], Bern, Switzerland

Swiss Assn. of Dealers in Antiques and Arts [IO], Zurich, Switzerland

Swiss Assn. for Development and Cooperation - Vietnam [★IO]

Swiss Assn. for Documentation [IO], Zug, Switzerland

Swiss Assn. for Energy Economics [IO], Zurich, Switzerland

Swiss Assn. of Geodesy and Rural Engg. [★IO]

Swiss Assn. of Geomatics and Landmanagement [IO], Solothurn, Switzerland

Swiss Assn. of High School Principals [IO], St. Gallen, Switzerland

Swiss Assn. of Insurance and Risk Managers [IO], Fribourg, Switzerland

Swiss Assn. for Internal Commun. [IO], Bern, Switzerland

Swiss Assn. for Intl. Cooperation - Helvetas Vietnam [IO], Hanoi, Vietnam

Reference to "IO" in place of a book number signifies that the association may be found in the 45th edition of International Organizations.

Encyclopedia of Associations, 46th Edition   4193

Swiss Assn. of Inventors and Researchers [IO], Fribourg, Switzerland
Swiss Assn. of Logopedics [IO], Zurich, Switzerland
Swiss Assn. for Nutrition [IO], Bern, Switzerland
Swiss Assn. against Osteoporosis [IO], Geneva, Switzerland
Swiss Assn. for Pattern Recognition [IO], Bern, Switzerland
Swiss Assn. of Physiotherapy [IO], Sursee, Switzerland
Swiss Assn. for Standardization [IO], Winterthur, Switzerland
Swiss Assn. for the Stud. of Pain [IO], Aeugstertal, Switzerland
Swiss Assn. of Tenants [IO], Geneva, Switzerland
Swiss Assn. for Theatre Stud. [IO], Basel, Switzerland
Swiss Astronomical Soc. [IO], Neukirch, Switzerland
Swiss Athletic Fed. [IO], Bern, Switzerland
Swiss-Australian Chamber of Commerce and Indus. [IO], Sydney, Australia
Swiss Bankers Assn. [IO], Basel, Switzerland
Swiss Bar Assn. [IO], Bern, Switzerland
Swiss Benevolent Soc. of New York [19400], 500 5th Ave., Rm. 1800, New York, NY 10110-1804, (212)246-0655
Swiss Bible Soc. [IO], Bienne, Switzerland
Swiss Biochemical Soc. [IO], Epalinges, Switzerland
Swiss Bone and Mineral Soc. [IO], Zurich, Switzerland
Swiss Booksellers and Publishers Assn. [IO], Zurich, Switzerland
Swiss Botanical Soc. [IO], Basel, Switzerland
Swiss Br. of the Intl. Fiscal Assn. [IO], Basel, Switzerland
Swiss Brewers' Assn. [IO], Zurich, Switzerland
Swiss Bus. Assn. Singapore [IO], Singapore, Singapore
Swiss Bus. Fed. [IO], Zurich, Switzerland
Swiss Canoe Fed. [IO], Moehlin, Switzerland
Swiss Cattle Breeders Assn. of the U.S.A; Brown [4258]
Swiss Chem. Soc. [IO], Bern, Switzerland
Swiss Chocolate Manufacturers' Assn. [★IO]
Swiss Christian Democratic Party [IO], Bern, Switzerland
Swiss Coalition of Development Organisations [★IO]
Swiss Comm. Against Torture [★IO]
Swiss Comm. for the Jews in the Former Soviet Union [IO], Bottmingen, Switzerland
Swiss Confectionery and Pastry Bakers' Assn. [IO], Bern, Switzerland
Swiss Conf. of Directors of Professional and Indus. Schools [IO], Raterschen, Switzerland
Swiss Cosmetic and Detergent Assn. [IO], Zurich, Switzerland
Swiss Craft Found. [IO], Zurich, Switzerland
Swiss Cricket Assn. [IO], Geneva, Switzerland
Swiss DanceSport Assn. [IO], Glattbrugg, Switzerland
Swiss Dietetic Assn. [IO], Sursee, Switzerland
Swiss Egg Producers' Assn. [IO], Zurich, Switzerland
Swiss Electrotechnical Assn. [IO], Fehraltorf, Switzerland
Swiss Fed. for Adult Educ. [★IO]
Swiss Fed. for Adult Learning [IO], Zurich, Switzerland
Swiss Fed. of the Blind and Visually Impaired [IO], Bern, Switzerland
Swiss Fed. of Cricket Umpires and Scorers [IO], Winterthur, Switzerland
Swiss Fed. of Trade Unions [IO], Bern, Switzerland
Swiss Floorball Assn. [IO], Bern, Switzerland
Swiss Food Retailers' Assn. [IO], Bern, Switzerland
Swiss Footpaths Fed. [★IO]
Swiss Forestry Soc. [IO], Zurich, Switzerland
Swiss Forum for Communications Law [IO], Zurich, Switzerland
Swiss Forum for GRID and High Performance Computing; SPEEDUP Soc.: [IO]
Swiss Found. for Sexual and Reproductive Hea. [IO], Lausanne, Switzerland
Swiss Franchise Assn. [IO], Zurich, Switzerland
Swiss Genealogical Soc; Orangeburgh German [21139]

Swiss Geomorphological Soc. [IO], Lausanne, Switzerland
Swiss Golf Assn. [IO], Epalinges, Switzerland
Swiss Graphic Designers [IO], Zurich, Switzerland
Swiss Heraldry Soc. [IO], Salavaux, Switzerland
Swiss Hiking Fed. [IO], Bern, Switzerland
Swiss Hosp. Assn. [IO], Bern, Switzerland
Swiss Hydrogeological Soc. [IO], Lausanne, Switzerland
Swiss Inst. for Experimental Cancer Res. [IO], Epalinges, Switzerland
Swiss Inst. of Special Educ. [IO], Lucerne, Switzerland
Swiss Interchurch Aid [★IO]
Swiss Lab. Animal Sci. Assn. [IO], Reinach, Switzerland
Swiss Labour Assistance [IO], Zurich, Switzerland
Swiss League Against Epilepsy [IO], Zurich, Switzerland
Swiss Lifesaving Assn. [IO], Nottwil, Switzerland
Swiss Malaysian Bus. Assn. [IO], Kuala Lumpur, Malaysia
Swiss Mgt. Assn. [IO], Zurich, Switzerland
Swiss Medical Assn. [IO], Bern, Switzerland
Swiss Mineral Water and Soft Drink Producers' Assn. [IO], Zurich, Switzerland
Swiss Museums Assn. [IO], Zurich, Switzerland
Swiss Musicians' Assn. [IO], Lausanne, Switzerland
Swiss Natl. Coun. for CIS Jewry [★IO]
Swiss Natl. Tourist Off. [★24379]
Swiss Olympic Assn. [IO], Bern, Switzerland
Swiss Org. for Geographic Info. [IO], Basel, Switzerland
Swiss Orthodontic Soc. [IO], Gumligen-Bern, Switzerland
Swiss Paralympic Comm. [IO], Spiez, Switzerland
Swiss Peace Coun. [IO], Zurich, Switzerland
Swiss Physical Soc. [IO], Basel, Switzerland
Swiss Physiological Soc. [IO], Bern, Switzerland
Swiss Private Bankers Assn. [IO], Geneva, Switzerland
Swiss Pulp, Paper and Cardboard Indus. Assn. [IO], Zurich, Switzerland
Swiss Radio and TV Retailers' Assn. [IO], Grenchen, Switzerland
Swiss Retail Chemists' Assn. [IO], Biel, Switzerland
Swiss Retail Fed. [IO], Bern, Switzerland
Swiss Rowing Fed. [IO], Sarnen, Switzerland
Swiss Seed Growers Assn. [IO], Delley, Switzerland
Swiss Soc. of Astrophysics and Astronomy [IO], Bern, Switzerland
Swiss Soc. for Biochemistry [IO], Epalinges, Switzerland
Swiss Soc. for Biomedical Ethics [IO], Basel, Switzerland
Swiss Soc. of Cardiology [IO], Bern, Switzerland
Swiss Soc. of Cartography [IO], Wabern, Switzerland
Swiss Soc. of Chem. Indus. [★IO]
Swiss Soc. of Engineers and Architects [IO], Zurich, Switzerland
Swiss Soc. of Gerontology [IO], Bern, Switzerland
Swiss Soc. for Hea. Policy [IO], Zurich, Switzerland
Swiss Soc. of Hypertension [IO], Bern, Switzerland
Swiss Soc. for Infectious Diseases [IO], Zurich, Switzerland
Swiss Soc. for Medical Informatics [IO], Bern, Switzerland
Swiss Soc. for Microbiology [IO], Schwarzenburg, Switzerland
Swiss Soc. for Optics and Microscopy [IO], Basel, Switzerland
Swiss Soc. of Optometry [IO], Adligenswil, Switzerland
Swiss Soc. of Pharmacology and Toxicology [IO], Lausanne, Switzerland
Swiss Soc. of Photogrammetry Image Anal. and Remote Sensing [IO], Wabern, Switzerland
Swiss Soc. of Radiobiology and Medical Physics [IO], Bern, Switzerland
Swiss Sociological Assn. [IO], Kreuzlingen, Switzerland
Swiss Solar Energy Soc. [IO], Bern, Switzerland
Swiss Spirits Producers' Assn. [IO], Bern, Switzerland

Swiss Sports Fed. [★IO]
Swiss Squash [IO], Steffisburg, Switzerland
Swiss Squash Rackets Assn. [★IO]
Swiss Teachers Fed. [IO], Zurich, Switzerland
Swiss Tech. Distributors' Assn. [IO], Zurich, Switzerland
Swiss Tennis [IO], Bienne, Switzerland
Swiss Tennis Assn. [★IO]
Swiss Textile Fed. [IO], Zurich, Switzerland
Swiss Textiles Fed. (Clothing and Textile Indus.) [IO], Zurich, Switzerland
Swiss Tropical Inst. [IO], Basel, Switzerland
Swiss Union of Liberal Trade Unions [★IO]
Swiss Universities Sports Assn. [★IO]
Swiss Univ. Sports Fed. [IO], St. Gallen, Switzerland
Swiss Volleyball Fed. [IO], Bern, Switzerland
Swiss Wine Exporters Assn. [IO], Lausanne, Switzerland
Swiss Youth Hostels [IO], Zurich, Switzerland
Swissmem L'Industrie Suisse de Machines, des Equipements Electriques et des Metaux [★IO]
Swissmem - Swiss Mech. and Elecl. Engg. Indus. [IO], Zurich, Switzerland
Switchboard; Natl. Runaway [12936]
Switching Forum; Multiservice [★881]
Switchmen's Union of North Am. [★24181]

Switzerland
Alpine Tourist Commn. [24223]
Amer. Helvetia Philatelic Soc. [22782]
Swiss-American Bus. Coun. [2314]
Swiss-American Chamber of Commerce [24378]
Swiss Amer. Historical Soc. [10992]
Switzerland Convention and Incentive Bur. [24379]
Switzerland; Amer. Chamber of Commerce in [★24378]
Switzerland; Amer. Friends of [★19398]
Switzerland; Amer. Soc. for Friendship with [★19398]
Switzerland Cheese Assn. - Defunct.
Switzerland Convention and Incentive Bur. [24379], c/o Switzerland Tourism, 608 5th Ave., New York, NY 10020, (212)757-5944
Switzerland Convention and Incentive Bur. [IO], Zurich, Switzerland
Switzerland Tourism [★24379]
Sword of the Spirit [★IO]
Sword Swallowers Assn. Intl. [10776], 3729 Belle Oaks Dr., Antioch, TN 37013
Swords Debaillon Louisiana Iris Soc; Mary [★22542]
Swordsmen and Sorcerers' Guild of America - Address unknown since 1995.
Sybil Jason Fan Club; Intl. [24746]
Sydney ACM SIGGRAPH Chap. [IO], West Pymble, Australia
Sydney SIGMOBILE ACM Chap. [IO], Broadway, Australia
Sydney Ski Club [IO], Sydney, Australia
Sydney Underwater Buddies [IO], Sydney, Australia
Sylvia Fan Club - Address unknown since 1989.
Symbionese Liberation Army - Defunct.
Symbolic and Algebraic Manipulation; Special Interest Gp. for [7296]
Symbolic Interaction; Soc. for the Stud. of [7669]
Symbolic Logic; Assn. for [7287]
Symbral Found. [12582]
Sympathetic Dystrophy Syndrome Assn. of Am; Reflex [15363]

Symphonic Music
Amer. Beethoven Soc. [9803]
Amer. Symphony Orchestra League [10552]
Asiatic Philharmonia Soc. [10557]
Charles Ives Soc. [10574]
Classical Music Lovers' Exchange [10578]
Cobbett Assn. for Chamber Music Res. [10579]
Early Music Network [10591]
Ernst Bacon Soc. [10593]
Intl. Conf. of Symphony and Opera Musicians [10618]
Jana Jae Fan Club [24916]
Jussi Bjorling Soc. - USA [9508]
Kurt Weill Found. for Music [10635]
Mozart Soc. of Am. [9814]
Natl. Symphony Orchestra Assn. [10669]
New Violin Family Assn. [10672]

A star before a book entry number signifies that the name is not listed separately, but is mentioned within the entry.

Schubert Soc. of the USA [9816]
Sphinx Org. [10710]
World Fed. of Amateur Orchestras [10766]
Symphony Found. of America - Address unknown
since 1995.
Symphony, Opera and Ballet Musicians; Intl. Guild of
[24157]
Symphony Orchestra Assn; Natl. [10669]
Symphony Orchestra League; Amer. [10552]
Symphony Soc; Guam [10603]
Symphony for United Nations [9601], 3240 NE 11
St., Pompano Beach, FL 33062, (954)782-9703
Symphony for United Nations [IO], Pompano Beach,
FL, United States
Symposium on Cmpt. Applications in Medical Care
[★14079]
Syna die Gewerkschaft [IO], Zurich, Switzerland
Synagogue of Am; Natl. Women's League of the
United [★20193]
Synagogue of Am; United [★20188]
Synagogue of Am; Women's League of the United
[★20193]
Synagogue Commn. on Jewish Educ; United
[★8702]
Synagogue of Conservative Judaism Commn. on
Jewish Educ; United [8702]
Synagogue Coun. of America - Address unknown
since 1999.
Synagogue Executives; North Amer. Assn. of
[20517]
Synagogue Lib. Assn; Church and [10348]
Synagogue Youth; Natl. Conf. of [20165]
Synagogue Youth; United [20189]
Synanon Comm. for a Responsible Amer. Press -
Address unknown since 1999.
Synchro Canada [IO], Gloucester, ON, Canada
Synchro Swimming U.S.A. [23889], 201 S Capitol,
Ste. 901, Indianapolis, IN 46225, (317)237-5700
Synchronized Swimming
  Intl. Swimming Hall of Fame [23886]
  Synchro Canada [IO]
  Synchro Swimming U.S.A. [23889]
  U.S. Aquatic Sports [23890]
Synchronized Swimming Division of the Amateur
Athletic Union [★23889]
Synchronized Swimming; U.S. [★23889]
Syndesmos [IO], Holargos, Greece
Syndesmos Epistimonon Michanikon Kyprou [★IO]
Syndicat Canadien des Communications, de
l'Energie et du Papier [★IO]
Syndicat Canadien des Officiers de Marine March-
ande [★IO]
Syndicat Canadien des Techniciens de Chaufferies
et des Manoeuvres [★IO]
Syndicat Canadien des Telecommunications Trans-
marines [★IO]
Syndicat Educ. et Sciences [★IO]
Syndicat des Enseignants [IO], Paris, France
Syndicat des Enseignants de Hongrie [★IO]
Syndicat des Entreprises de Commerce Intl. de
Material Audio/Video et Info. Grand Public [★IO]
Syndicat Europeen de l'Industrie des Futs Fibre
[★IO]
Syndicat Gen. de l'Education Nationale [IO], Paris,
France
Syndicat de l'Eclairage [★IO]
Syndicat de l'emploi et de l'immigration du Canada
[★IO]
Syndicat des Locataires - Huurdersbond [IO], Brus-
sels, Belgium
Syndicat Natl. de la Biscotterie et de la Panification
Fine [★IO]
Syndicat Natl. du Caoutchouc et des Polymeres
[★IO]
Syndicat Natl. des Employees et Employes Gener-
aux et du Secteur Public [★IO]
Syndicat Natl. des Enseignants [★IO]
Syndicat Natl. des Enseignements de Second Degre
[★IO]
Syndicat Natl. des Fabricants de Boites, Emballages
et Bouchages Metalliques [★IO]
Syndicat Natl. des Fabricants de Bouillons et Po-
tages [IO], Paris, France
Syndicat Natl. de l'Edition [★IO]
Syndicat Natl. de l'Edition Phonographique [★IO]

Syndicat Natl. de l'Edition Phonographique [IO],
Paris, France
Syndicat Natl. des Residences de Tourisme [★IO]
Syndicat de la Presse Parisienne [★IO]
Syndicat de la Presse Quotidienne Nationale [IO],
Paris, France
Syndicat de la Presse Quotidienne Regionale [IO],
Paris, France
Syndicat Suisse des Antiquares et Commercants
d'Art [★IO]
Syndicat des Travailleurs et Travailleuses des
Postes [★IO]
Syndicate of Journalists of the Czech Republic [IO],
Prague, Czech Republic
Syndicated Network TV Assn. [120], 630 Fifth Ave.,
Ste. 2320, New York, NY 10111, (212)259-3740
Syndikat novinaru Ceske republiky [★IO]
Syndrome Assn. U.S.A; Prader-Willi [★14475]
Syndrome Found; False Memory [16150]
Syndrome Found; Restless Legs [16549]
Syndrome Info. and Support; Amer. Assn. for
Klinefelter [14538]
Syndrome X Assn. [15259], PO Box 331, Munroe
Falls, OH 44262
Synergetic Soc. - Address unknown since 2004.
Synergos Inst. [12784], 51 Madison Ave., 21st Fl.,
New York, NY 10010, (212)447-8111
Synergos Inst. [IO], New York, NY, United States
Synergy Power Inst. - Defunct.
Synfoam Inst. - Defunct.
Synod Ministries; Confessing [20561]
Syntbetic Amorphous Silica and Silicates Industry
Assn. [826]
Synthetic Flooring Inst; Wood and [★635]
Synthetic Fuels; Coun. on [★1677]
Synthetic Fuels Production; Natl. Coun. of [★1677]
Synthetic Organic Chem. Manufacturers Assn. [827],
1850 M St. NW, Ste. 700, Washington, DC 20036-
5810, (202)721-4100
Synthetic and Rayon Textiles Export Promotion
Coun. [IO], Bombay, India
Synthetic Turf Coun. - Defunct.
Synthetic Yarn and Fiber Assn. [3801], PO Box 66,
Gastonia, NC 28053-0066, (704)824-3522
Synthetic Yarn Mfrs; Assn. of [★3774]
Synthetics Soc; Intl. Geo [6700]
Synthetics Soc; North Amer. Geo [6701]
Syphilology; Amer. Acad. of Dermatology and
[★14189]
Syrian Arab Amateur Athletic Fed. [IO], Damascus,
Syrian Arab Republic
Syrian Arab Badminton Fed. [IO], Damascus, Syrian
Arab Republic
Syrian Arab Soc. of Dermatology [IO], Aleppo, Syr-
ian Arab Republic
Syrian Arab Taekwondo Fed. [IO], Damascus, Syrian
Arab Republic
Syrian Arab Tennis Fed. [IO], Damascus, Syrian
Arab Republic
Syrian Cardiovascular Assn. [IO], Damascus, Syrian
Arab Republic
Syrian Chap. of Epilepsy [IO], Damascus, Syrian
Arab Republic
Syrian Family Planning Assn. [IO], Damascus, Syr-
ian Arab Republic
Syrian Orthodox Youth Org. [★19882]
Syrian Physical Therapy Assn. [IO], Damascus, Syr-
ian Arab Republic
Syrian Stud. Assn. [8880], c/o Prof. Peter Sluglett,
Pres., Carlson Hall, 214 C Hall History, 380 S
1400 E, Rm. 211, Salt Lake City, UT 84112
Syringomyelia Alliance Proj; Amer. [15305]
Syrup Urine Disease; Families with Maple [★15250]
Syrups; Natl. Assn. of Fruits, Flavors and [★1539]
Sys. Administrators Guild [★6806]
System Independent Data Format Assn. - Defunct.
Sys. Safety Soc. [3457], PO Box 70, Unionville, VA
22567-0070, (540)854-8630
Sys. Safety Soc; Aerospace [★3457]
Systematic and Applied Acarology Soc. [IO], Can-
berra, Australia
Systematic Biologists; Soc. of [7868]
Systematic Zoology; Soc. of [★7868]
Systematics Assn. [IO], Egham, United Kingdom
Systematics Assn. of New Zealand [IO], Auckland,
New Zealand

Systematics Collections; Assn. of [★6590]
Systeme Economique Latinoamericain et Caribeen
[★IO]
Systems Analysts; Soc. of Educational Programmers
and [★8132]
Systems Assn; Insurance Accounting and [2172]
Systems Assn; Natl. Independent Bank Equip. and
[★476]
Systems, and Automation Soc; ISA - Instrumenta-
tion, [7220]
Systems Builders Assn. [★2528]
Systems Contractors Assn; Natl. [1225]
Systems Dealers Assn; Intl. [★2847]
Systems Engg. Soc. of China [IO], Beijing, People's
Republic of China
Systems Integrators
  Control and Info. Systems Integrators Assn.
  [3704]
  LonMark Intl. [3705]
  Mfg. Enterprise Solutions Assn. Intl. [7722]
  NASBA - The Assn. of Sys. Builders and Integra-
  tors [3706]
  Natl. Assn. of Campus Card Users [3707]
  UCA Intl. Users Gp. [7820]
Systems, Man, and Cybernetics Soc; IEEE [6728]
Systems Mgt. Benchmarking Consortium; Info. [725]
Systems Programmers Assn; Natl. [★6799]
Systems Security Certification Consortium; Intl. Info.
[6758]
Systems Soc; IEEE Circuits and [6914]
Systems and Software Consortium, Inc. [6780],
2214 Rock Hill Rd., Herndon, VA 20170-4227,
(703)742-8877
Systems; Special Interest Gp. for Architecture of
Cmpt. [6747]
Szabad Demokratak Szovetsege [★IO]
Szkolny Zwiazek Sportowy [IO], Warsaw, Poland
Szyk Soc; Arthur [9497]
Szyk Soc; Historic Art's Arthur [★9497]

T

T-18 Builders and Owners Assn. - Defunct.
T. J.'s Fans of Soul - Defunct.
T. Rextasy Japanese Fan Club [IO], Saitama, Japan
T. Rextasy UK Fan Club [IO], Epping, United
Kingdom
T-Ten Class Assn. [23222], c/o Stan Mehaffey, Exec.
Sec., 360 E Randolph St., Apt. 803, Chicago, IL
60601, (312)861-0766
Table and Art Glassware Mfrs. - Defunct.
Table ronde Des Hommes D'Affaires d'Afrique [★IO]
Table Fashion Inst. - Address unknown since 1995.
Table Grape Commn; California [4721]
Table; Loyal Knights of the Round [★13061]
Table Tennis
  Alberta Table Tennis Assn. [IO]
  Canadian Table Tennis Assn. [IO]
  English Schools' Table Tennis Assn. [IO]
  English Table Tennis Assn. [IO]
  European Table Tennis Union [IO]
  Intl. Table Tennis Fed. [IO]
  Japan Table Tennis Assn. [IO]
  Natl. Collegiate Table Tennis Assn. [23895]
  Table Tennis Assn. of Wales [IO]
  U.S.A. Table Tennis [23896]
  Veterans English Table Tennis Soc. [IO]
Table Tennis Assn; U.S. [★23896]
Table Tennis Assn. of Wales [IO], Bristol, United
Kingdom
Table Tennis; U.S.A. [23896]
Tabletop Assn; Natl. [★3711]
Tableware
  Amer. Edged Products Manufacturers Assn.
  [3708]
  Assoc. Glass and Pottery Mfrs. [3709]
  Butter Pat Patter Assn. [21981]
  Canadian Gift and Tableware Assn. [IO]
  Cutlery and Allied Trades Res. Assn. [IO]
  European Fed. for Table and Ornamental Ware
  [IO]
  Fed. of the European Cutlery, Flatware, Hol-
  loware, and Cookware Indus. [IO]
  FoodService Packaging Assn. [IO]
  Foodservice and Packaging Inst. [1157]

Reference to "IO" in place of a book number signifies that the association may be found in the 45th edition of International Organizations.

Gift Associates Interchange Network [3710]
Giftware Assn. [IO]
Homer Laughlin China Collectors Assn. [22036]
Intl. Assn. of Dinnerware Matchers [1971]
Natl. Tabletop and Giftware Assn. [3711]
Soc. of Amer. Silversmiths [3712]
Tackett Family Assn. [21067], c/o Jim W. Tackitt, Pres., 260 Bella Vista Way, Rio Vista, CA 94571
Tackle/Shooting Sports Agents Assn. - Defunct.
Tactical Officers Assn; Natl. [6175]
Tacy Soc; Betsy- [9638]
Taekwon-Do Zveza Slovenije [★IO]
Taekwondo Assn. of Thailand [IO], Bangkok, Thailand
Taekwondo Australia [IO], Sydney, Australia
Taekwondo Bond Nederland [IO], Arnhem, Netherlands
Taekwondo Comm; U.S. Natl. Amateur Athletic Union [★23610]
Taekwondo Fed. of Armenia [IO], Yerevan, Armenia
Taekwondo Fed. of Bosnia and Herzegovina [IO], Sarajevo, Bosnia-Hercegovina
Taekwondo Fed. of India [IO], New Delhi, India
Taekwondo Fed. of Islamic Republic of Iran [IO], Te-hran, Iran
Taekwondo Fed. of the Republic of Kazakhstan [IO], Almaty, Kazakhstan
Taekwondo Fed. of the Republic of Tajikistan [IO], Dushanbe, Tajikistan
Taekwondo Fed. of Turkey [IO], Ankara, Turkey
Taekwondo Fed; World [IO]
Taekwondo Papua New Guinea [IO], Boroko, Papua New Guinea
Taekwondo Samband Islands [★IO]
Taekwondo Union; U.S. [23610]
Taekwondo Union of the U.S.A; Natl. AAU [★23610]
Taeria Found. - Address unknown since 1988.
Taft Family Assn. [21068], c/o Berneta M. DeVries, Sec.-Treas., PO Box 406, Mendon, MA 01756
Tag and Chaffeur's Badge Collectors Newsl; Disabled Veterans Keychain [22011]
TAG Intl. [★5]
Tag and Label Mfrs. Inst. [3687], 40 Shuman Blvd., Ste. 295, Naperville, IL 60563-8251, (630)357-9222
Tag Mfrs. Inst. [★3687]
Tahi Flores Exoticas [IO], Yautepec, Mexico
Tahiti Jet Club [IO], Tahiti, French Polynesia
Tahoe Improvement and Conservation Assn. [★4417]
Tahoe; League to Save Lake [4417]
Tahtitieteellinen yhdistys Ursa [★IO]
T'ai Chi
    Amer. Tai Chi Assn. [16593]
    Intl. Yang Style Tai Chi Chuan Assn. [23594]
    Patience T'ai Chi Assn. [23897]
Tai Chi Assn; Amer. Chen Style [23578]
Tai Chi Assn. of Australia [IO], Jannali, Australia
Tai Chi Chuan/Shaolin Chuan Assn. - Defunct.
Tai Hei Yo Bashi - Address unknown since 2001.
Taidemaalariliitto [★IO]
Taiga Rescue Network [IO], Jokkmokk, Sweden
Taiheiyo Hoso Kyokai [★IO]
Taildragger Pilots Assn. - Address unknown since 1995.
Tailhook Assn. [6106], 9696 Businesspark Ave., San Diego, CA 92131, (858)689-9223
Tailors and Designers Assn. of Am; Custom [231]
Tailors and Designers Assn. of Am; Merchant [★231]
Taino People; United Confed. of [18989]
Taipei Amer. Chamber of Commerce [★IO]
Taipei Assn. of Advt. Agencies [IO], Taipei, Taiwan
Taipei Bus. Assn. in Singapore [IO], Singapore, Sin-gapore
Taipei Economic and Cultural Off. in New York; Info. Div., [★9792]
Taipei Economic and Cultural Off. in New York; Press Div., [9792]
Taipei Soc. of Infectious Diseases [IO], Taipei, Taiwan
Taipei/Taiwan ACM Chap. [IO], Taipei, Taiwan
Taipei World Trade Center and China External Trade Development Coun. [IO], Taipei, Taiwan
An Taisce [★IO]
Taiwan
    Center for Taiwan Intl. Relations [IO]

Center for Taiwan Intl. Relations [18691]
Formosan Assn. for Human Rights [18692]
Formosan Assn. for Public Affairs [18693]
Formosan Assn. for Public Affairs [IO]
Inst. of Chinese Culture [9791]
Natl. Comm. on United States-China Relations [17064]
North Am. Taiwanese Engineers' Assn. [7036]
North Amer. Taiwan Stud. Assn. [9205]
North Amer. Taiwan Stud. Assn. [IO]
Press Div., Taipei Economic and Cultural Off. in New York [9792]
Professor Chen Wen-Chen Memorial Found. [18694]
Taiwanese Amer. Lawyers Assn. [5533]
US-Taiwan Bus. Coun. [2294]
Taiwan Assn. of Iron Indus. [★IO]
Taiwan Assn. of Machinery Indus. [IO], Taipei, Taiwan
Taiwan Assn. of Stationery Indus. [IO], Taipei, Taiwan
Taiwan Bags Assn. [IO], Taipei, Taiwan
Taiwan Bicycle Exporters' Assn. [IO], Taipei, Taiwan
Taiwan Chain Store and Franchise Assn. [IO], Taipei, Taiwan
Taiwan Cotton Spinners' Assn. [IO], Taipei, Taiwan
Taiwan Elec. and Electronic Mfrs'. Assn. [IO], Taipei, Taiwan
Taiwan Elec. Wire and Cable Indus'. Assn. [IO], Taipei, Taiwan
Taiwan Epilepsy Soc. [IO], Taipei, Taiwan
Taiwan External Trade Development Coun. [IO], Taipei, Taiwan
Taiwan Footwear Mfrs. Assn. [IO], Taipei, Taiwan
Taiwan Foundry Soc. [IO], Kaohsiung, Taiwan
Taiwan Frozen Seafood Indus. Assn. [IO], Kaohsi-ung, Taiwan
Taiwan Garment Indus. Assn. [IO], Taipei, Taiwan
Taiwan Gas Appliance Manufacturers' Assn. [IO], Taipei, Taiwan
Taiwan Gift and Houseware Exporters Assn. [IO], Taipei, Taiwan
Taiwan Hand Tool Mfrs'. Assn. [IO], Taipei, Taiwan
Taiwan Handicraft Promotion Center [IO], Taipei, Taiwan
Taiwan Jewelry Indus. Assn. [IO], Taipei, Taiwan
Taiwan Junior Chamber [IO], Taipei, Taiwan
Taiwan Knitting Indus. Assn. [IO], Taipei, Taiwan
Taiwan Man-Made Fiber Indus. Assn. [IO], Taipei, Taiwan
Taiwan Margarine Indus. Assn. [IO], Taipei, Taiwan
Taiwan Medical Assn. [IO], Taipei, Taiwan
Taiwan Mold and Die Indus. Assn. [IO], Taipei, Taiwan
Taiwan Non-Woven Fabrics Indus. Assn. [IO], Taipei, Taiwan
Taiwan Occupational Therapy Assn. [IO], Taipei, Taiwan
Taiwan Pediatric Assn. [IO], Taipei, Taiwan
Taiwan Plastics Indus. Assn. [IO], Taipei, Taiwan
Taiwan Provincial Assn. of Iron Indus. [★IO]
Taiwan Provincial Confed. of the Machinery Indus. [★IO]
Taiwan Regional Assn. of Adhesive Tape Mfrs. [IO], Taipei, Taiwan
Taiwan Regional Assn. of Educational Material Indus. [★IO]
Taiwan Regional Assn. of Filament Fabrics Printing, Dyeing and Finishing Indus. [IO], Taipei, Taiwan
Taiwan Regional Assn. of Synthetic Leather Indus. [IO], Taipei, Taiwan
Taiwan Rubber Indus. Assn. [IO], Taipei, Taiwan
Taiwan Silk and Filament Weaving Indus. Assn. [IO], Taipei, Taiwan
Taiwan Soc. of Cardiology [IO], Taipei, Taiwan
Taiwan Soc. of Clinical Neurophysiology [IO], Taipei, Taiwan
Taiwan Sporting Goods Manufacturers Assn. [IO], Taipei, Taiwan
Taiwan Textile Fed. [IO], Taipei, Taiwan
Taiwan Toy Mfrs'. Assn. [IO], Taipei, Taiwan
Taiwan Venture Capital Assn. [IO], Taipei, Taiwan
Taiwan Visitors Assn. [IO], New York, NY, United States
Taiwan Visitors Assn. [3940], c/o Taipei Economic and Cultural Off. in New York, 1 E 42 St., 9th Fl., New York, NY 10017, (212)867-1632

Taiwan Visitors Assn. - Taipei [IO], Taipei, Taiwan
Taiwan Watch and Clock Indus. Assn. [IO], Taipei, Taiwan
Taiwan Zippers Mfrs. Assn. [IO], Taipei, Taiwan
Taiwanese
    Intercollegiate Taiwanese Amer. Students Assn. [19401]
    North Am. Taiwanese Engineers' Assn. [7036]
    North Am. Taiwanese Professors' Assn. [19402]
    North Am. Taiwanese Professors' Assn. [IO]
    North Amer. Taiwan Stud. Assn. [9205]
    Press Div., Taipei Economic and Cultural Off. in New York [9792]
    Soc. of Taiwanese Americans, Chicago Chap. [19403]
    Soc. of Taiwanese Americans, Chicago Chap. [IO]
    Taiwanese Amer. Citizens League [19404]
    Taiwanese Amer. Lawyers Assn. [5533]
    Taiwanese Collegian [19405]
Taiwanese Amer. Citizens League [19404], 3001 Walnut Grove Ave., No. 7, Rosemead, CA 91770, (626)202-0170
Taiwanese Amer. Lawyers Assn. [5533], c/o June J. Hsieh, Pres., 17800 Castleton St., Ste. 383, City of Industry, CA 91748, (626)810-0685
Taiwanese-Amer. Soc. - Address unknown since 1989.
Taiwanese Assn. of America - Address unknown since 1995.
Taiwanese Assn. for Artificial Intelligence [IO], Taipei, Taiwan
Taiwanese Coalition for Self-Determination - Defunct.
Taiwanese Collegian [19405], PO Box 1685, Tempe, AZ 85285-1685
Tajikistan Ski Fed. [IO], Dushanbe, Tajikistan
Take Charge! Cure Parkinson's [15366], 1489 W Palmetto Park Rd., Ste. 442, Boca Raton, FL 33486, (561)620-1970
Take a Look Found. - Defunct.
Take Off Pounds Sensibly [★12649]
Take Root [12605], PO Box 930, Kalama, WA 98625, (360)673-3720
Take a Soldier to the Movies; Oper.: [11498]
Takemusu Aiki Assn. of Australia [IO], Sydney, Australia
Taking Control of Your Diabetes [14231], 1110 Camino Del Mar, Ste. B, Del Mar, CA 92014, (858)755-5683
Takoma Urban Farm [★4105]
Talent Agents; Assn. of [172]
Talent Managers Assn. [1325], 4804 Laurel Canyon Blvd., No. 611, Valley Village, CA 91607, (310)205-8495
Talent Search Prog; Independent Schools [★8321]
Talk Show Hosts.com [IO], Las Vegas, NV, United States
Talking Newspaper Assn. of the United Kingdom [IO], Heathfield, United Kingdom
Tall Bearded Iris Soc. [IO], McKinney, TX, United States
Tall Bearded Iris Soc. [22547], PO Box 303, McKin-ney, TX 75070, (806)792-1878
Tall Buildings and Urban Habitat; Coun. on [6474]
Tall Cedar Foundation [★19255]
Tall Cedars of Lebanon of North Am. [19255], 2609 N Front St., Harrisburg, PA 17110, (717)232-5991
Tall Cedars of Lebanon of the U.S.A. [★19255]
Tall Clubs Intl. [13300], PMB 400 W 3 St. D156, Santa Rosa, CA 95401, (888)468-2552
Tall Clubs Intl. [IO], Santa Rosa, CA, United States
Tall Grass Writers Guild [11198], c/o Outrider Press, 2036 N Winds Dr., Dyer, IN 46311, (219)322-7270
Tall Oil Assn. [★818]
Tall Persons Club - Great Britain and Ireland [IO], Redbourn, United Kingdom
Tall Timbers [★4457]
Tall Timbers Land Conservancy [4456], c/o Tall Timbers Res. Sta., 13093 Henry Beadel Dr., Tal-lahassee, FL 32312, (850)893-4153
Tall Timbers Res. [★4457]
Tall Timbers Res. Sta. [4457], 13093 Henry Beadel Dr., Tallahassee, FL 32312-0918, (850)893-4153
Tall Timbers Res. Station [★4457]
Taller Ecologista [★IO]
Tallgrass Prairie Found. [★4404]

A star before a book entry number signifies that the name is not listed separately, but is mentioned within the entry.

Tallinn Frisbee Club **[IO]**, Tallinn, Estonia
Tallness
   Coun. on Size and Weight Discrimination **[12644]**
   Human Growth Found. **[16020]**
      Tall Clubs Intl. **[13300]**
      Tall Clubs Intl. **[IO]**
Talmadge Family Org. - Address unknown since 1994.
Talmudic Schools; Assn. of Advanced Rabbinical and **[8683]**
Talyllyn Railway Preservation Soc. **[IO]**, Tywyn, United Kingdom
Tam Tam Femme **[IO]**, Zanzibar, United Republic of Tanzania
TAMAR Proj. **[★IO]**
Tamarin Conservation Program; Golden Lion **[★5321]**
Tamarind Inst. **[8471]**, 108-110 Cornell Dr. SE, Albuquerque, NM 87106, (505)277-3901
Tamarind Lithography Workshop **[★8471]**
Tamburitza
   CFU Junior Cultural Fed. **[9844]**
Tamburitza Assn. of Am. **[10712]**, c/o Joseph R. Novosel, Esq., Pres., 3894 Spartan Dr., Fort Gratiot, MI 48059, (810)385-9667
Tamiment Inst. - Address unknown since 2001.
Tamizdat **[9853]**, PO Box 20618, New York, NY 10009, (212)260-8444
Tammy Graham Fan Club - Address unknown since 1989.
Tammy Wynette Intl. Fan Club **[24979]**
Tamworth and District Olive Growers Assn. **[IO]**, Tamworth, Australia
Tamworth Swine Assn. - Address unknown since 2002.
Tan Son Nhut Assn. **[21336]**, PO Box 236, Penryn, PA 17564-0236
Tandem Club of Am. **[23317]**, c/o Smith Doss, 10708 Cambium Ct., Raleigh, NC 27613-6304, (919)847-8437
Tang Center for Herbal Medicine Res. **[14986]**, Univ. of Chicago, Pritzer Scholarship of Medicine, Dept. of Anesthesia and Critical Care, 5841 S Maryland Ave., MC 4028, Chicago, IL 60637, (773)834-2399
Tang Center for Herbal Medicine Research **[IO]**, Chicago, IL, United States
Tanganyika Wildlife Soc. **[★IO]**
Tangent Gp. **[12257]**, PO Box 310, Bell, CA 90201, (585)880-0831
Tangents **[★12257]**
Tangible Assets
   Indus. Coun. for Tangible Assets **[3713]**
Tangier Amer. Legation Museum Soc. **[10068]**, c/o Stephan Eastman, Treas., PO Box 43, Merrimac, MA 01860, (978)346-9078
Tangier; Voice of **[★20403]**
Tank Assn; Natl. Truck **[★998]**
Tank Battalion Assn. Friends; 749th **[20698]**
Tank Conf. of the Truck Trailer Mfrs. Assn. **[998]**, 1020 Princess St., Alexandria, VA 22314, (703)549-3010
Tank Destroyer Battalion Assn; 704th **[21383]**
Tank Inst; Natl. Wood **[988]**
Tank Mfrs. Assn; Wood **[3366]**
Tank and Pipe Inst; Fiberglass **[979]**
Tank and Trailer Tank Inst; Natl. Truck **[★998]**
Tank Truck Carriers; Natl. **[3580]**
Tanka Soc. of Am. **[10871]**, c/o Carole MacRury, Sec.-Treas., 1636 Edwards Dr., Point Roberts, WA 98281
Tanker Assn; Airlift/ **[20646]**
Tanners' Coun. of Am. **[★2416]**
Tanners' Coun. of Japan **[IO]**, Hyogo, Japan
Tanners; Natl. Assn. of **[★2416]**
Tannu Tuva Collectors' Soc. **[22881]**, c/o Kenneth R. Simon, Pres., 513 6th Ave. S, Lake Worth, FL 33460
Tannu Tuva Collectors' Soc. **[IO]**, Lake Worth, FL, United States
Tantalum Intl. Stud. Center **[★IO]**
Tantalum-Niobium Intl. Stud. Center **[IO]**, Brussels, Belgium
Tantalum Producers Assn. - Defunct.
Tantalum Producers Intl. Stud. Center **[★IO]**
Tantur Ecumenical Inst. **[IO]**, Jerusalem, Israel

Tanya Roberts Fan Club - Address unknown since 1999.
Tanya Tucker Fan Club **[24980]**, PO Box 158, Arrington, TN 37014, (615)395-0117
Tanya Tucker Fan Club **[IO]**, Arrington, TN, United States
Tanygnathus Soc. **[4202]**, 4510 Buckingham Rd., Fort Myers, FL 33905
Tanzania Amateur Athletic Assn. **[IO]**, Dar es Salaam, United Republic of Tanzania
Tanzania Amateur Radio Club **[IO]**, Dar es Salaam, United Republic of Tanzania
Tanzania Assn. of Non Governmental Organizations **[IO]**, Dar es Salaam, United Republic of Tanzania
Tanzania Assn. of Tour Operators **[IO]**, Arusha, United Republic of Tanzania
Tanzania Badminton Assn. **[IO]**, Morogoro, United Republic of Tanzania
Tanzania Consumers Protection Assn. **[IO]**, Dar es Salaam, United Republic of Tanzania
Tanzania Cricket Assn. **[IO]**, Dar es Salaam, United Republic of Tanzania
Tanzania Debate Assn. **[IO]**, Dar es Salaam, United Republic of Tanzania
Tanzania Fed. of Cooperatives **[IO]**, Dar es Salaam, United Republic of Tanzania
Tanzania Gender Networking Prog. **[IO]**, Dar es Salaam, United Republic of Tanzania
Tanzania Indus. Res. and Development Org. **[IO]**, Dar es Salaam, United Republic of Tanzania
Tanzania Lawn Tennis Assn. **[IO]**, Dar es Salaam, United Republic of Tanzania
Tanzania Lib. Assn. **[IO]**, Dar es Salaam, United Republic of Tanzania
Tanzania Professional Teachers Assn. **[★IO]**
Tanzania Sports Medicine Assn. **[IO]**, Dar Es Salaam, United Republic of Tanzania
Tanzania Squash Rackets Assn. **[IO]**, Dar es Salaam, United Republic of Tanzania
Tanzania Teachers' Union **[IO]**, Dar es Salaam, United Republic of Tanzania
Tanzania eco Volunteerism **[IO]**, Tanga, United Republic of Tanzania
Tanzania Weightlifting Fed. **[IO]**, Dar es Salaam, United Republic of Tanzania
Tanzania Women Graduates Fed. **[IO]**, Dar es Salaam, United Republic of Tanzania
Tanzania Youth in Action for Development **[IO]**, Dar es Salaam, United Republic of Tanzania
Tanzer 16 Assn; Canadian **[★23223]**
Tanzer 16 Class Assn. **[23223]**, 104 Dynasty Dr., Cary, NC 27513
Tanzer 16 Class Assn; U.S. **[★23223]**
Tanzer 22 Class Assn. **[IO]**, Nepean, ON, Canada
Taoist Tai Chi Soc. of Australia **[IO]**, Bayswater, Australia
Taos Natl. Soc. of Watercolorists **[9476]**, PO Box 2943, Taos, NM 87571
Tap Assn; Intl. **[9888]**
Tape Assn; Consolidated **[3511]**
Tape Assn; Intl. **[★1370]**
Tape Coun; Pressure Sensitive **[57]**
Tape/Disc Assn; Intl. **[★1370]**
Tapered Steel Transmission Pole Inst. - Defunct.
Tapes for the Blind - Defunct.
Tapestry Alliance; Amer. **[9416]**
Taphorn Family Soc. - Defunct.
TAPOL/USA - Campaign for the Release of Indonesian Political Prisoners - Defunct.
Tapori Intl. ATD Fourth World **[IO]**, Geneva, Switzerland
Tapori Intl. ATD Quart Monde **[★IO]**
TAPPI - Tech. Assn. of the Pulp and Paper Indus. **[2895]**, 15 Tech. Pkwy. S, Norcross, GA 30092, (770)446-1400
Tapping Screw Service Bur. - Defunct.
Tara Collectors Club - Defunct.
Taralye **[★IO]**
Tarcisians; League of **[19651]**
Tarcisians of the Sacred Heart; League of **[★19651]**
Tardive Dyskinesia/Tardive Dystonia Natl. Assn. - Address unknown since 2001.
Tarentaise Assn; Amer. **[4249]**
Target Assn; Amer. Airgun Field **[22976]**
Targeted Jobs Tax Credit Coalition - Address unknown since 1989.

Tarlton Inst. for Marine Education - Defunct.
Tarot
   Amer. Tarot Assn. **[22983]**
   Amer. Tarot Assn. **[IO]**
   Tarot Guild of Australia **[IO]**
Tarot Guild of Australia **[IO]**, Melbourne, Australia
Tarpon Springs Sponge Exchange - Defunct.
Tarpon Unlimited; Bonefish and **[4987]**
Tartan Educational and Cultural Assn., Inc. **[★19354]**
Tartan Educational and Cultural Assn., Inc. **[★IO]**
Tartans of Scotland **[IO]**, Dunkeld, United Kingdom
Tarten Ten
   T-Ten Class Assn. **[23222]**
Tartu Uurnike Uhing Estonian **[★IO]**
TASH **[11991]**, 1025 Vermont Ave., 7th Fl., Washington, DC 20005, (202)263-5600
Task Force Against Nuclear Pollution **[18135]**, PO Box 564, Greenbelt, MD 20768, (301)474-8311
Task Force on Alternatives in Print **[★10315]**
Task Force for Child Survival and Development **[12542]**, 750 Commerce Dr., Ste. 400, Decatur, GA 30030, (404)371-0466
Task Force on Creative Finance for Manufactured Housing - Defunct.
Task Force; Environmental **[★4558]**
Task Force on Equality of Women in Judaism - Defunct.
Task Force on Families in Crisis - Address unknown since 1991.
Task Force on Gay Liberation **[★12214]**
Task Force on Intl. Developmental Assistance and Intl. Education - Defunct.
Task Force for Lebanon; Amer. **[19204]**
Task Force on Lesbian/Gay Issues **[★9132]**
Task Force (SRRT); Ethnic Materials Info. Exchange **[★10354]**
Task Force on Teaching as a Profession - Defunct.
Task Force on Using Mass Media **[★8565]**
Task Force on Using Mass Media **[★IO]**
Task Force on Women and Judaism - Defunct.
Task Force on Women and Minorities - Defunct.
Task Force for Women in Public Admin. **[★6198]**
Task Force on World Hunger/Presbyterian Church in the U.S. **[★12397]**
Tasmania Dental Therapists' Assn. **[IO]**, Ulverstone, Australia
Tasmanian Canine Assn. **[IO]**, Glenorchy, Australia
Tasmanian Chamber of Commerce and Indus. **[IO]**, Hobart, Australia
Tasmanian History Teachers Assn. **[IO]**, Bellerive, Australia
Tasmanian Infection Control Assn. **[IO]**, Hobart, Australia
Tasmanian Olive Coun. **[IO]**, Hadspen, Australia
Tasmanian Secondary Principals Assn. **[IO]**, Devonport, Australia
Tasseraluk Inst. - Defunct.
Tasters Guild Intl. **[210]**, c/o Joe Borrello, Pres./CEO, 1515 Michigan NE, Grand Rapids, MI 49503, (616)454-7815
Tatry Housing Org. **[12300]**, 603 S Ann St., Baltimore, MD 21231, (410)342-7200
Tatry Housing Org. **[IO]**, Baltimore, MD, United States
Tattoo-a-Pet **[11463]**, 6571 SW 20th Ct., Fort Lauderdale, FL 33317, (954)581-5834
Tattoo Club of America - Address unknown since 2006.
Tattoo Club of Great Britain **[IO]**, Oxford, United Kingdom
Tattoo Club of the World; Natl. **[★10994]**
Tattooing
   Alliance of Professional Tattooists **[3714]**
   Amer. Acad. of Micropigmentation **[14039]**
   Assn. of Professional Piercers **[3715]**
   Christian Tattoo Assn. **[20590]**
   Empire State Tattoo Club of Am. **[10993]**
   Natl. Tattoo Assn. **[10994]**
   Natl. Tattoo Assn. **[IO]**
   Professional Tattoo Artists Guild **[3716]**
   Tattoo-a-Pet **[11463]**
Tau Alpha Pi **[24467]**, 1818 N St. NW, Ste. 600, Washington, DC 20036, (202)350-5762
Tau Beta Pi Assn. **[24468]**, PO Box 2697, Knoxville, TN 37901-2697, (865)546-4578

Reference to "IO" in place of a book number signifies that the association may be found in the 45th edition of International Organizations.

Tau Beta Sigma **[24558]**, PO Box 849, Stillwater, OK 74076-0849, (800)543-6505

Tau Delta Phi - Address unknown since 1995.

Tau Epsilon Phi **[24665]**, 1000 White Horse Rd., Ste. 512, Voorhees, NJ 08043, (856)782-9837

Tau Epsilon Phi Found. **[★24665]**

Tau Epsilon Rho Law Fraternity **[★24529]**

Tau Epsilon Rho Law Soc. **[24529]**, c/o Alan M. Tepper, Natl. Treas./Exec. Dir., 1951 Old Cuthbert Rd., Ste. 413, Cherry Hill, NJ 08034; (856)429-3901

Tau Gamma Delta - Address unknown since 2001.

Tau Kappa Alpha **[★24719]**

Tau Kappa Alpha; Delta Sigma Rho - **[24719]**

Tau Kappa Epsilon **[24666]**, 8645 Founders Rd., Indianapolis, IN 46268, (317)872-6533

Tau Omega **[★24466]**

Tau Phi Lambda - Address unknown since 1995.

Tau Sigma Delta **[24403]**, c/o Elizabeth I. Louden, Pres., Coll. of Architecture, PO Box 42091, Texas Tech Univ., Lubbock, TX 79409-2091, (806)742-3136

Taunting Safety and Fairness Everywhere; Natl. Org. **[22599]**

Taurine Bibliophiles of Am. **[9755]**, c/o Gil Arruda, 59 Pearl Ave., North Providence, RI 02904, (401)353-6326

Tavern Keepers; Flagon and Trencher - Descendants of Colonial **[20737]**

Tavern Owners; Natl. Assn. of Bar and **[205]**

Tavistock Inst. **[IO]**, London, United Kingdom

Tax Administrators; Commonwealth Assn. of **[IO]**

Tax Administrators; Natl. Assn. of **[★6292]**

Tax Analysts **[18718]**, 400 S Maple Ave., Ste. 400, Falls Church, VA 22046, (703)533-4400

Tax Analysts and Advocates **[★18718]**

Tax Assn; FSC/DISC **[★2281]**

Tax Assn; Natl. **[★6302]**

Tax Campaign- U.S; Conscience and Military **[★18716]**

Tax Club; FSC/DISC **[★2281]**

Tax Coalition; Natl. Alcohol **[★18703]**

Tax Coun. **[6303]**, 1301 K St. NW, Ste. 800W, Washington, DC 20005-3317, (202)822-8062

Tax Council-Alcoholic Beverage Indus. **[★199]**

Tax Counsel; Amer. Coll. of **[5924]**

Tax Credit Coalition; Affordable Housing **[586]**

Tax Executives Inst. **[6304]**, 1200 G St. NW, Ste. 300, Washington, DC 20005-3814, (202)638-5601

Tax-Exempt Sons of Italy Foundation **[★19168]**

Tax Found. **[6305]**, 2001 L St. NW, Ste. 1050, Washington, DC 20036, (202)464-6200

Tax Free America - Defunct.

Tax Fund; Natl. Campaign for a World Peace **[★18712]**

Tax Fund; Natl. Coun. for a World Peace **[★18712]**

Tax Fund Steering Comm; World Peace **[★18712]**

Tax Fund; Suffolk County Comm. for a World Peace **[★18716]**

Tax History Center **[★10079]**

Tax Inst. of Am. **[★6302]**

Tax Inst. of Am; Natl. Tax Assn. - **[6302]**

Tax Limitation/Balanced Budget Coalition - Defunct.

Tax-Me-Not - Defunct.

Tax Planning Assn; Intl. **[IO]**

Tax Practitioners; Natl. Assn. of **[★6301]**

Tax Professionals; Amer. Soc. of **[10]**

Tax Reform

Howard Jarvis Taxpayers Assn. **[18695]**

Invest to Compete Alliance **[738]**

Liberty Services **[17766]**

Natl. Retail Sales Tax Alliance **[18696]**

Policy and Taxation Gp. **[18697]**

ReformAMT **[18698]**

Savers and Investors League **[18699]**

Taxpayers for Common Sense **[18700]**

Tax Reform Action Coalition - Defunct.

Tax Reform Immediately **[★18721]**

Tax Reform Res. Group - Defunct.

Tax Res; Center for Local **[★18704]**

Tax Resister's Penalty Fund **[★18723]**

Tax Token Soc; Amer. **[22727]**

Taxation

Accreditation Coun. for Accountancy and Taxation **[3]**

Amer. Civil Liberties Union Found. **[17085]**

Amer. Revenue Assn. **[22788]**

Amer. Soc. of Tax Problem Solvers **[6290]**

Amer. Soc. of Tax Professionals **[10]**

Amer. Tax Policy Inst. **[18701]**

Amer. Tax Token Soc. **[22727]**

Amer. Taxation Assn. **[6291]**

Americans for Tax Reform **[18702]**

Canadian Property Tax Assn. **[IO]**

Canadian Tax Found. **[IO]**

Canadian Taxpayers' Fed. **[IO]**

Center for Public Dialogue **[18430]**

Center for Sci. in the Public Interest - Alcohol Policies Proj. **[18703]**

Center for the Stud. of Economics **[18704]**

Citizens for an Alternative Tax Sys. **[18705]**

Citizens for Tax Justice **[18706]**

Common Ground - U.S.A. **[18707]**

Commonwealth Assn. of Tax Administrators **[IO]**

Confed. Fiscale Europeenne **[IO]**

Coun. for Electronic Revenue Commun. Advancement **[3740]**

Coun. of Georgist Organizations **[18708]**

Coun. On State Taxation **[18709]**

Dutch Intl. Fiscal Assn. Br. **[IO]**

Fed. of Exchange Accommodators **[3717]**

Fed. of Tax Administrators **[6292]**

Forest Landowners Tax Coun. **[6293]**

German Assn. of Tax Advisers **[IO]**

Henry George Inst. - New York **[18710]**

Inst. for Fiscal Stud. **[IO]**

Inst. for Professionals in Taxation **[6294]**

Inst. of Revenues, Rating and Valuation **[IO]**

Inst. of Tax Consultants **[6295]**

Inst. on Taxation and Economic Policy **[17470]**

Intl. Assn. of Assessing Officers **[6296]**

Intl. Assn. of Assessing Officers **[IO]**

Intl. Bur. of Fiscal Documentation **[IO]**

Intl. Fiscal Assn. **[IO]**

Intl. Fiscal Assn. - Belgium **[IO]**

Intl. Fiscal Assn. - Brazil **[IO]**

Intl. Fiscal Assn. - Canada Br. **[IO]**

Intl. Fiscal Assn. - China **[IO]**

Intl. Fiscal Assn. - Colombia **[IO]**

Intl. Fiscal Assn. - Cyprus **[IO]**

Intl. Fiscal Assn. - Czech Republic **[IO]**

Intl. Fiscal Assn. - Egypt **[IO]**

Intl. Fiscal Assn. - Estonia **[IO]**

Intl. Fiscal Assn. - Finland **[IO]**

Intl. Fiscal Assn. - France **[IO]**

Intl. Fiscal Assn. - Germany **[IO]**

Intl. Fiscal Assn. - Greece **[IO]**

Intl. Fiscal Assn. - Hong Kong **[IO]**

Intl. Fiscal Assn. - Hungary **[IO]**

Intl. Fiscal Assn. - Indonesia **[IO]**

Intl. Fiscal Assn. - Ireland **[IO]**

Intl. Fiscal Assn. - Israel **[IO]**

Intl. Fiscal Assn. - Italy **[IO]**

Intl. Fiscal Assn. - Japan **[IO]**

Intl. Fiscal Assn. - Luxembourg **[IO]**

Intl. Fiscal Assn. - Malaysia **[IO]**

Intl. Fiscal Assn. - Malta **[IO]**

Intl. Fiscal Assn. - Mauritius **[IO]**

Intl. Fiscal Assn. - Poland **[IO]**

Intl. Fiscal Assn. - Russia **[IO]**

Intl. Fiscal Assn. - Singapore **[IO]**

Intl. Fiscal Assn. - Spain **[IO]**

Intl. Fiscal Assn. - Sri Lanka **[IO]**

Intl. Fiscal Assn. - Uruguay **[IO]**

Intl. Fiscal Intl. - Australia **[IO]**

Intl. Tax Planning Assn. **[IO]**

Intl. Union for Land Value Taxation and Free Trade **[IO]**

Irish Taxation Inst. **[IO]**

Latin Amer. Tax Law Inst. **[IO]**

Leadership Conf. on Civil Rights **[17124]**

Moore Stephens North Am. **[41]**

Multistate Tax Commn. **[6297]**

Natl. Assn. of Computerized Tax Processors **[6298]**

Natl. Assn. of Enrolled Agents **[6299]**

Natl. Assn. of Form 1099 Filers **[18711]**

Natl. Assn. of Indus. and Off. Properties **[3320]**

Natl. Assn. of Tax Advisors **[IO]**

Natl. Assn. of Tax Consultants **[6300]**

Natl. Assn. of Tax Professionals **[6301]**

Natl. Campaign for a Peace Tax Fund **[18712]**

Natl. Justice Found. of Am. **[17298]**

Natl. Tax Assn. - Tax Inst. of Am. **[6302]**

Natl. Tax-Limitation Comm. **[18713]**

Natl. Taxpayers Union **[18714]**

Natl. War Tax Resistance Coordinating Comm. **[18715]**

Non-Violent Action Community of Cascadia and the CMTC Escrow Fund **[18716]**

Nordic Coun. for Tax Res. **[IO]**

Portuguese Fiscal Assn. **[IO]**

Save Our Schools **[18717]**

South African Fiscal Assn. **[IO]**

Swiss Br. of the Intl. Fiscal Assn. **[IO]**

Tax Analysts **[18718]**

Tax Coun. **[6303]**

Tax Executives Inst. **[6304]**

Tax Found. **[6305]**

Taxation Inst. of Australia **[IO]**

Taxpayers Against Fraud, The False Claims Act Legal Center **[18719]**

Taxpayers Assn. of Europe **[IO]**

Thomas Jefferson Equal Tax Soc. **[18720]**

TRIM **[18721]**

Urban-Brookings Tax Policy Center **[18722]**

War Tax Resister's Penalty Fund **[18723]**

Taxation; Accreditation Coun. for Accountancy and **[3]**

Taxation; Amer. Coun. on Capital Gains and Estate **[★17347]**

Taxation Inst. of Australia **[IO]**, Sydney, Australia

Taxation With Representation **[★18718]**

Taxation With Representation Fund **[★18718]**

Taxi

Canadian Taxicab Assn. **[IO]**

Checker Car Club of Am. **[21606]**

Gibraltar Taxi Assn. **[IO]**

London Vintage Taxi Assn. **[IO]**

London Vintage Taxi Assn. - Amer. Sect. **[21690]**

New Zealand Taxi Fed. **[IO]**

Taxi Assn. - Amer. Sect; London Vintage **[21690]**

Taxi Drivers; Guild of **[★24180]**

Taxi-Stop **[★22580]**

Taxicab Assn; Amer. **[★3894]**

Taxicab Industry Group - Address unknown since 2001.

Taxicab, Limousine and Paratransit Assn. **[3894]**, 3849 Farragut Ave., Kensington, MD 20895-2004, (301)946-5701

Taxicab, Limousine and Paratransit Association **[IO]**, Kensington, MD, United States

Taxicab and Livery Assn; Intl. **[★3894]**

Taxicab Owners; Natl. Assn. of **[★3894]**

Taxidermists; Guild of **[IO]**

Taxidermy

Natl. Taxidermists Assn. **[3718]**

Taxonomists; Amer. Soc. of Plant **[6629]**

Taxpayers - Address unknown since 1995.

Taxpayers Against Fraud, The False Claims Act Legal Center **[18719]**, 1220 19th St. NW, Ste. 501, Washington, DC 20036, (202)296-4826

Taxpayers Assn. of Europe **[IO]**, Munich, Germany

Taxpayers Assn; Howard Jarvis **[18695]**

Taxpayers Campaign for Urban Priorities - Defunct.

Taxpayers' Comm. - Defunct.

Taxpayers for Common Sense **[18700]**, 651 Pennsylvania Ave. SE, Washington, DC 20003, (202)546-8500

Taxpayers Educ. Lobby **[★18717]**

Tay-Sachs and Allied Diseases Assn; Natl. **[15354]**

Tay-Sachs Assn; Natl. **[★15354]**

Tay-Sachs Found; Late-Onset **[14460]**

Taybi Parent Gp. U.S.A; Rubinstein- **[13759]**

Taylor Soc. **[★2515]**

Tayu Center **[20581]**, PO Box 11554, Santa Rosa, CA 95406, (707)829-9579

Tayu Fellowship **[★20581]**

Tayu Inst. **[★20581]**

TB Vaccine Found; Aeras Global **[14372]**

TCB for Elvis Fan Club **[24814]**

TCB Fan Club; Elvis Forever **[24808]**

TDI- **[★14780]**

Te Deum Intl. - Address unknown since 1995.

Te Kaunihera O Nga Neehi Maori O Aotearoa **[★IO]**

Te Kaunihera Wahine O Aotearoa **[★IO]**

A star before a book entry number signifies that the name is not listed separately, but is mentioned within the entry.

TE Lawrence Soc. [IO], Oxford, United Kingdom
Te Pouhere Whakaako o Te Reo Pakeha o Aotearoa [★IO]
Te Roopu Turi o Aoearoa [★IO]
Te Roopu Whaka Waihanga Iwi O Aotearoa [★IO]
Te Roopu Whakaritenga o nga Ture [★IO]
Te Ropu Kairangahau Tikanga-a-iwi o Aotearoa [★IO]
Te Ropu Kaiwhakamaori a-waha, a tuhi o Aotearoa [★IO]
Te Tari Puna Ora o Aotearoa [★IO]
Tea
  Austrian Coffee and Tea Bd. [IO]
  Bangladesh Tea Bd. [IO]
  Caffeine Awareness Alliance [13747]
  Indian Tea Assn. [IO]
  Intl. Compost Tea Coun. [5244]
  Sri Lanka Tea Bd. [IO]
  Tea Assn. of Canada [IO]
  Tea Bd. of India [515]
  Urasenke Tea Ceremony Soc. [10269]
Tea Assn. of Canada [IO], Toronto, ON, Canada
Tea Assn. of the U.S.A. [514], 420 Lexington Ave., Ste. 825, New York, NY 10170, (212)986-9415
Tea Bd. of India [515]
Tea Bd. of Kenya [IO], Nairobi, Kenya
Tea Ceremony Soc; Urasenke [10269]
Tea Coun. [IO], London, United Kingdom
Tea Coun. of Canada [★IO]
Tea Coun. of the U.S.A. [IO], New York, NY, United States
Tea Coun. of the U.S.A. [516], 420 Lexington Ave., Ste. 825, New York, NY 10170, (212)986-9415
Tea Family Org. - Defunct.
Tea Leaf Club Intl. [21937], PO Box 377, Belton, MO 64012, (614)258-5258
Tea Soc; Women's Mountain Bike and [23323]
TEACH (Teaching Each Other About Conquering Handicaps) - Defunct.
Teach; World [8315]
Teacher Author League of America - Defunct.
Teacher Editorial Collective; Feminist [9318]
Teacher Education
  Amer. Assn. for Agricultural Educ. [7933]
  Amer. Assn. of Colleges for Teacher Educ. [9208]
  Amer. Assn. of Teaching and Curriculum [9209]
  Amer. Tech. Educ. Assn. [9228]
  Assn. for the Advancement of Intl. Educ. [8640]
  Assn. for Direct Instruction [8232]
  Assn. Montessori Intl.-U.S.A. [8892]
  Assn. of Teacher Educators [9212]
  Carnegie Found. for the Advancement of Teaching [9214]
  Coun. on Tech. Teacher Educ. [8543]
  High/Scope Educational Res. Found. [8181]
  Intl. Coun. on Educ. for Teaching [9216]
  Intl. Tech. Educ. Assn. [9231]
  Joseph Campbell Found. [9206]
  Montessori Accreditation Coun. for Teacher Educ. [8278]
  Natl. Assn. for Alternative Certification [8360]
  Natl. Assn. for Beginning Teachers [9219]
  Natl. Assn. of Community Coll. Teacher Educ. Programs [9221]
  Natl. Assn. of Indus. and Tech. Teacher Educators [8544]
  Natl. Assn. for Res. in Sci. Teaching [9108]
  Natl. Assn. of State Directors of Teacher Educ. and Certification [9224]
  Natl. Center for Community Educ. [8125]
  Natl. Coun. of Teachers of English [8380]
  Natl. Urban Alliance for Effective Educ. [9291]
  NETWORK [8295]
  ProLiteracy Worldwide [8797]
  Soc. for Info. Tech. and Teacher Educ. [9243]
  Woodrow Wilson Natl. Fellowship Found. [8439]
Teacher Educ; Amer. Coun. on Indus. Arts [★8543]
Teacher Educ; Coun. for Distributive [★8818]
Teacher Educ; Coun. on Music [★8931]
Teacher Educ. Institutions of Metropolitan Districts; Natl. Assn. of [★9208]
Teacher Educ; Natl. Assn. for Bus. [8032]
Teacher Educ; Natl. Coun. for Accreditation of [7879]
Teacher Educ; Soc. for Music [8931]
Teacher Educ; Student Personnel Assn. for [★8527]

Teacher Educators in Agriculture; Amer. Assn. of [★7933]
Teacher Educators for Family and Consumer Sciences; Natl. Assn. of [8515]
Teacher Educators for Home Economics; Natl. Assn. of [★8515]
Teacher Educators; Natl. Assn. of Indus. [★8544]
Teacher Educators; Natl. Assn. of Indus. and Tech. [8544]
Teacher Educators for Vocational Home Economics; Natl. Assn. of [★8515]
Teacher Information Center - Defunct.
Teacher-Mom Program - Address unknown since 1995.
Teacher Organizations; Natl. Coun. of Dance [★8189]
Teacher Organizing Project - Address unknown since 1995.
Teacher Placement Assn; Natl. Institutional [★8994]
Teacher Retirement; Natl. Coun. on [24044]
Teacher Trainers; Natl. Assn. of Indus. [★8544]
Teacher Trainers Sect. of the Agricultural Division of the Assn. for Career and Tech. Educ. [★7933]
Teacher Training Assn; Evangelical [★19925]
Teachers
  Accordionists and Teachers Guild, Intl. [8897]
  African Language Teachers Assn. [9207]
  Alberta Teachers' Assn. [IO]
  Amateur Ski Instructors Assn. [23748]
  Amer. Acad. of Advt. [7919]
  Amer. Acad. of Teachers of Singing [8898]
  Amer. Assn. for Agricultural Educ. [7933]
  Amer. Assn. of Christian Schools [7875]
  Amer. Assn. of Classified School Employees [24041]
  Amer. Assn. of Colleges for Teacher Educ. [9208]
  Amer. Assn. for Employment in Educ. [8994]
  Amer. Assn. of Physics Teachers [8993]
  Amer. Assn. of Snowboard Instructors [23765]
  Amer. Assn. of Teachers of Arabic [7958]
  Amer. Assn. of Teachers of French [8448]
  Amer. Assn. of Teachers of German [8460]
  Amer. Assn. of Teachers of Slavic and East European Languages [9125]
  Amer. Assn. of Teachers of Spanish and Portuguese [8725]
  Amer. Assn. of Teachers of Turkic Languages [9282]
  Amer. Assn. of Teaching and Curriculum [9209]
  Amer. Assn. of Univ. Professors [9022]
  Amer. Assn. for Vocational Instructional Materials [9298]
  Amer. Assn. for Women in Community Colleges [9313]
  Amer. Bridge Teachers' Assn. [21892]
  Amer. Catholic Philosophical Assn. [8965]
  Amer. Classical League [8726]
  Amer. Coun. on Rural Special Educ. [9137]
  Amer. Coun. on the Teaching of Foreign Languages [8727]
  Amer. Educ. Finance Assn. [8342]
  Amer. Educational Stud. Assn. [8228]
  Amer. Fed. of Teachers [24042]
  Amer. Inst. for Foreign Stud. [8652]
  Amer. Mathematical Assn. of Two-Year Colleges [8821]
  Amer. Real Estate Soc. [9049]
  Amer. Recorder Teachers Assn. [8902]
  Amer. Sign Language Teachers Assn. [14741]
  Amer. Soc. for Bioethics and Humanities [8845]
  Amer. Teachers Assn. of the Martial Arts [23582]
  Amer. Tech. Educ. Assn. [9228]
  Amer. Textbook Coun. [9258]
  Art Teachers' Assn. [IO]
  Assn. for the Advancement of Intl. Educ. [8640]
  Assn. of Arts Admin. Educators [7967]
  Assn. of British Columbia Drama Educators [IO]
  Assn. of Canadian Coll. and Univ. Teachers of English [IO]
  Assn. for Canadian Stud. in the U.S. [8043]
  Assn. of Canadian Univ. and Coll. Teachers of French [IO]
  Assn. for Career and Tech. Educ. [9300]
  Assn. for Career and Tech. Educ. Res. [9301]
  Assn. for Childhood Educ. Intl. [8064]

  Assn. of Christian Teachers [IO]
  Assn. for Direct Instruction [8232]
  Assn. Montessori International-U.S.A. [8892]
  Assn. of Optometric Educators [8851]
  Assn. of Orthodox Jewish Teachers [9210]
  Assn. for Sci. Teacher Educ. [9211]
  Assn. for Teacher Educ. in Europe [IO]
  Assn. of Teacher Educators [9212]
  Assn. of Teachers of Japanese [8682]
  Assn. of Teachers and Lecturers [IO]
  Assn. of Teachers of Tech. Writing [9332]
  Assn. for the Teaching of the Social Sciences [IO]
  Assn. for Tech. in Music Instruction [8905]
  Assn. of Univ. Teachers - Scotland [IO]
  Assn. of WORKSHOP WAY Consultants [9213]
  Australian Assn. of Mathematics Teachers [IO]
  Australian Fed. of Modern Language Teachers Associations [IO]
  Australian Sci. Teachers Assn. [IO]
  Australian Teachers of Media [IO]
  Belgian Assn. of Teachers of the Alexander Technique [IO]
  Black Educators Assn. of Nova Scotia [IO]
  British Columbia Art Teachers' Assn. [IO]
  British Columbia Assn. of Teachers of Modern Languages [IO]
  British Columbia Primary Teachers' Assn. [IO]
  British Columbia Teachers' Fed. [IO]
  Canadian Alliance of French-Language Teachers and Administrators [IO]
  Canadian Assn. of Immersion Teachers [IO]
  Canadian Assn. of Second Language Teachers [IO]
  Canadian Assn. of Teachers of Tech. Writing [IO]
  Canadian Assn. of Univ. Teachers of German [IO]
  Canadian Coll. of Teachers [IO]
  Canadian Coun. of Teachers of English Language Arts [IO]
  Canadian Soc. of Teachers of the Alexander Technique [IO]
  Canadian Teachers' Fed. [IO]
  Carnegie Found. for the Advancement of Teaching [9214]
  Carol Burnett Fund for Responsible Journalism [8707]
  Catholic Negro-Amer. Mission Bd. [19601]
  Cecchetti Coun. of Am. [8183]
  Center for Commercial-Free Public Educ. [8241]
  Center for Lifelong Learning [8406]
  CHA - Certified Horsemanship Assn. [23523]
  Chinese Language Teachers Assn. [8076]
  Christian Home Educators Assn. of California [8516]
  Clinical Legal Educ. Assn. [8763]
  Club Francais d'Amerique [8449]
  Coalition of Essential Schools [8180]
  Coll. Music Soc. [8907]
  Coll. of Teachers [IO]
  Columbia Scholastic Press Advisers Assn. [9010]
  Comm. on Capacity Building Sci. [9099]
  Comm. on Public Doublespeak [17173]
  Commonwealth Assn. of Sci., Tech. and Mathematics Educators [IO]
  Community of Caring [11588]
  Cmpt. Sci. Teachers Assn. [8130]
  Conf. on Coll. Composition and Commun. [8376]
  Conf. on English Educ. [8377]
  Conf. on English Leadership [1175]
  Conf. of Univ. Teachers of German in Great Britain and Ireland [IO]
  Cordell Hull Found. for Intl. Educ. [8656]
  Coun. for the Advancement of Standards in Higher Educ. [9177]
  Coun. of Amer. Instructors of the Deaf [14750]
  Coun. of Chief State School Officers [8246]
  Coun. for Elementary Sci. Intl. [9100]
  Coun. on Tech. Teacher Educ. [8543]
  Dance Educators of Am. [8184]
  Dance Masters of Am. [8186]
  Danforth Found. [8250]
  Designs for Change [9035]
  Earth Sci. Teachers' Assn. [IO]
  Earthwatch Inst. [8413]
  Educ. Development Center [8253]
  Educ. Indus. Assn. [9215]

Reference to "IO" in place of a book number signifies that the association may be found in the 45th edition of International Organizations.

Educ. Intl. **[IO]**
Educ. Intl., Africa Regional Off. **[IO]**
Educ. Intl., Asia-Pacific Regional Off. **[IO]**
Educ. Intl., Latin Am. Regional Off. **[IO]**
Educ. Intl., North America-Caribbean Regional Off. **[IO]**
Educational Development Assn. **[IO]**
Educational Planning Inst. **[8998]**
Educational Testing Ser. **[9250]**
Educational Theatre Assn. **[9264]**
Elderhostel, Inc. **[8149]**
English Inst. **[8378]**
European Acad. of Teachers in Gen. Practice **[IO]**
European Assn. of Teachers - UK Sect. **[IO]**
Fed. Assn. of Teachers of Dancing **[IO]**
Fed. Educ. Assn. **[24043]**
Fed. for Unified Sci. Educ. **[9102]**
Feminist Teacher Editorial Collective **[9318]**
Gen. Teaching Coun. for Scotland **[IO]**
Girlstart **[8468]**
Headteachers' Assn. of Scotland **[IO]**
High/Scope Educational Res. Found. **[8181]**
Horace Mann League of the U.S.A. **[9036]**
Horsemanship Safety Assn. **[23525]**
Human Anatomy and Physiology Soc. **[7951]**
Icelandic Teachers' Union **[IO]**
Inst. for Chem. Educ. **[8062]**
Inst. of Training Professionals **[IO]**
Intl. Assn. for Cmpt. Info. Systems **[8132]**
Intl. Assn. of Duncan Certified Ceramic Teachers **[21928]**
Intl. Assn. for Jazz Educ. **[8912]**
Intl. Assn. for Learning Alternatives **[7945]**
Intl. Assn. for Truancy and Dropout Prevention **[8326]**
Intl. Center of Photography **[8972]**
Intl. Coalition for Addiction Stud. Educ. **[9197]**
Intl. Coun. on Educ. for Teaching **[9216]**
Intl. Coun. on Educ. for Teaching **[IO]**
Intl. Educator's Inst. **[8645]**
Intl. Reading Assn. **[9043]**
Intl. Soc. for Educational Planning **[8999]**
Intl. Soc. for the Scholarship of Teaching and Learning **[9073]**
Intl. Soc. for Teacher Educ. **[IO]**
Intl. Soc. for Tech. in Educ. **[8134]**
Intl. Stud. Assn. for Teachers and Teaching **[IO]**
Intl. Tech. Educ. Assn. **[9231]**
Intl. Textile and Apparel Assn. **[3791]**
Japan Assn. of Coll. English Teachers **[IO]**
Joint Assn. of Classical Teachers **[IO]**
Labor and Working Class History Assn. **[8723]**
Latvian Assn. of Language Teachers **[IO]**
Learning Resources Network **[8151]**
Lutheran Educ. Assn. **[8803]**
Marketing Educ. Assn. **[8818]**
Medau Movement **[IO]**
MENC: The Natl. Assn. for Music Educ. **[8913]**
Middle Atlantic Planetarium Soc. **[9105]**
Modern Language Assn. of Am. **[8735]**
Music Teachers Natl. Assn. **[8918]**
NAFSA/Association of Intl. Educators **[8445]**
Natl. Alliance of Black School Educators **[9217]**
Natl. Art Educ. Assn. **[7977]**
Natl. Assn. for the Advancement of Caring Teachers **[9218]**
Natl. Assn. of Agricultural Educators **[7938]**
Natl. Assn. for Alternative Certification **[8360]**
Natl. Assn. of Baptist Professors of Religion **[9277]**
Natl. Assn. for Beginning Teachers **[9219]**
Natl. Assn. of Biology Teachers **[8000]**
Natl. Assn. of Blind Teachers **[9220]**
Natl. Assn. for Bus. Teacher Educ. **[8032]**
Natl. Assn. of Catholic School Teachers **[8058]**
Natl. Assn. for Chicana and Chicano Stud. **[8498]**
Natl. Assn. of Coll. Wind and Percussion Instructors **[8919]**
Natl. Assn. of Community Coll. Teacher Educ. Programs **[9221]**
Natl. Assn. for Developmental Educ. **[8200]**
Natl. Assn. of Early Childhood Teacher Educators **[9222]**
Natl. Assn. for the Educ. of Young Children **[8069]**
Natl. Assn. of Geoscience Teachers **[8459]**

Natl. Assn. for Girls and Women in Sport **[8983]**
Natl. Assn. of Hea. Sci. Educ. Partnership **[9107]**
Natl. Assn. of Hebrew Day School PTAs **[8953]**
Natl. Assn. for Humanities Educ. **[8531]**
Natl. Assn. of Indus. and Tech. Teacher Educators **[8544]**
Natl. Assn. for Legal Support of Alternative Schools **[7946]**
Natl. Assn. of Maritime Educators **[8813]**
Natl. Assn. of Pastoral Musicians **[8920]**
Natl. Assn. of Percussion Teachers **[IO]**
Natl. Assn. for Physical Educ. in Higher Educ. **[8985]**
Natl. Assn. for Professional Development Schools **[9091]**
Natl. Assn. of Professional Educators **[9223]**
Natl. Assn. for Res. in Sci. Teaching **[9108]**
Natl. Assn. of Scholars **[8490]**
Natl. Assn. of Special Educ. Teachers **[9148]**
Natl. Assn. of State Directors of Teacher Educ. and Certification **[9224]**
Natl. Assn. of Students Against Violence Everywhere **[18117]**
Natl. Assn. for the Stud. and Performance of African-American Music **[8922]**
Natl. Assn. of Teacher Educators for Family and Consumer Sciences **[8515]**
Natl. Assn. of Teachers of Singing **[8923]**
Natl. Assn. of Trade and Indus. Instructors **[9233]**
Natl. Bd. for Professional Teaching Standards **[9225]**
Natl. Bus. Educ. Assn. **[8036]**
Natl. Center for Community Educ. **[8125]**
Natl. Commun. Assn. **[9157]**
Natl. Community Educ. Assn. **[8126]**
Natl. Coun. of Educ. Providers **[8329]**
Natl. Coun. for Geographic Educ. **[8457]**
Natl. Coun. for History Educ. **[8508]**
Natl. Coun. of Japanese Language Teachers **[9226]**
Natl. Coun. for the Social Stud. **[9128]**
Natl. Coun. of Supervisors of Mathematics **[8826]**
Natl. Coun. on Teacher Retirement **[24044]**
Natl. Coun. of Teachers of English **[8380]**
Natl. Coun. of Teachers of Mathematics **[8827]**
Natl. Dance Teacher's Assn. **[23325]**
Natl. Earth Sci. Teachers Assn. **[9111]**
Natl. Educ. Assn. **[24045]**
Natl. Fed. of Modern Language Teachers Associations **[8739]**
Natl. Fraternity of Student Musicians **[8924]**
Natl. Guild of Piano Teachers **[8925]**
Natl. History Club **[8509]**
Natl. Home Educ. Res. Inst. **[8522]**
Natl. Kindergarten Alliance **[9007]**
Natl. Marine Educators Assn. **[8810]**
Natl. Middle Level Sci. Teachers' Assn. **[9112]**
Natl. Middle School Assn. **[8881]**
Natl. Photography Instructors Assn. **[8973]**
Natl. Piano Found. **[8927]**
Natl. PTA - Natl. Cong. of Parents and Teachers **[8954]**
Natl. Reading Conf. **[9044]**
Natl. Retired Teachers Assn., Division of AARP **[9065]**
Natl. Rural Educ. Assn. **[9069]**
Natl. Schools Comm. for Economic Educ. **[8218]**
Natl. Sci. Teachers Assn. **[9114]**
Natl. Service-Learning Partnership **[9120]**
Natl. Soc. for the Stud. of Educ. **[8293]**
Natl. Urban Alliance for Effective Educ. **[9291]**
Natl. Women's Stud. Assn. **[9323]**
Natl. Writing Proj. **[9334]**
NEA Found. for the Improvement of Educ. **[8294]**
NETWORK **[8295]**
New Zealand Educational Inst. **[IO]**
Noah Webster House **[10053]**
North Amer. Assn. of Educational Negotiators **[24046]**
North Amer. Colleges and Teachers of Agriculture **[7942]**
North Amer. Coun. of Automotive Teachers **[7993]**
North Amer. Professors of Christian Educ. **[8088]**
Northeast Conf. on the Teaching of Foreign Languages **[8742]**

Org. of Amer. Kodaly Educators **[8929]**
Org. of Professional Acting Coaches and Teachers **[9267]**
Organizational Behavior Teaching Soc. **[6537]**
People to People Intl. **[17909]**
Philosophy of Educ. Soc. **[8969]**
Photo Imaging Educ. Assn. **[8974]**
Photographic Art and Sci. Found. **[8975]**
Post Primary Teachers Assn. **[IO]**
Probe Ministries Intl. **[8090]**
Professional Assn. of Alexander Teachers **[IO]**
Professional Assn. of Teachers - UK **[IO]**
Professional Dance Teachers Assn. **[8191]**
Professional Golf Teachers Assn. of Am. **[23463]**
Professional Ski Instructors of Am. **[23755]**
Reading Is Fundamental **[9047]**
Reading Recovery Coun. of North Am. **[9048]**
Religious Commun. Assn. **[8116]**
Sci. Songwriters' Assn. **[10693]**
Scottish Assn. of Geography Teachers **[IO]**
Sewing Educator Alliance **[9121]**
Social Sci. Educ. Consortium **[9129]**
Soc. for the Advancement of Scandinavian Stud. **[9070]**
Soc. for Anthropology in Community Colleges **[7954]**
Soc. of Building Sci. Educators **[8363]**
Soc. for Gen. Music **[8930]**
Soc. for Music Teacher Educ. **[8931]**
Soc. for Philosophy of Religion **[8970]**
Soc. for Photographic Educ. **[8976]**
Soc. of Professors of Educ. **[8307]**
Soc. of Roller Skating Teachers of Am. **[23741]**
Soong Ching Ling Found. **[IO]**
Suzuki Assn. of the Americas **[8932]**
Swiss Assn. of High School Principals **[IO]**
Teachers of English to Speakers of Other Languages **[8382]**
Teachers Insurance and Annuity Assn. **[8579]**
Teachers Resisting Unhealthy Children's Entertainment **[11657]**
Teachers Union Norway **[IO]**
Tech. Inst. for Music Educators **[8933]**
U.S. Ski Coaches Assn. **[23758]**
U.S. Ski Team Found. **[23761]**
U.S. Soc. for Educ. Through Art **[7980]**
Universities Coun. for the Educ. of Teachers **[IO]**
Univ. and Coll. Union **[IO]**
Univ. Professors for Academic Order **[9026]**
Urban Affairs Assn. **[9287]**
Values and Visions **[8155]**
Volunteers in Asia **[13407]**
Wilderness Classroom Org. **[8951]**
Women Band Directors Intl. **[8934]**
Women Educators **[9328]**
Woodrow Wilson Natl. Fellowship Found. **[8439]**
World Commun. Assn. **[8005]**
World Cong. of Teachers of Dancing **[8192]**
Worldloppet/American Birkebeiner **[23764]**
WorldTeach **[8315]**
Teachers: A Community Teacher Training and Support Org. - Address unknown since 1995.
Teachers Against Violence in Educ; Parents and **[8208]**
Teachers' Agencies; Natl. Assn. of **[1275]**
Teachers Agencies of the South; Assn. of **[★1275]**
Teachers of Agriculture; Natl. Assn. of Colleges and **[★7942]**
Teachers of Agriculture; North Amer. Colleges and **[7942]**
Teachers of Am; Soc. of Roller Skating **[23741]**
Teachers; Amer. Assn. of Philosophy **[8964]**
Teachers; Amer. Assn. of Physics **[8993]**
Teachers; Amer. Fed. of **[24042]**
Teachers of Arabic; Amer. Assn. of **[7958]**
Teachers Assn; Amer. **[★24045]**
Teachers' Assn; Amer. Bridge **[21892]**
Teachers Assn; Amer. String **[8904]**
Teachers Assn; Business-Industry Sect. of Natl. Sci. **[★8048]**
Teachers Assn; Chinese Language **[8076]**
Teachers Assn; Assn. of Coll. Geology **[★8459]**
Teachers Assn., Division of AARP; Natl. Retired **[9065]**
Teachers; Assn. of Geology **[★8459]**

A star before a book entry number signifies that the name is not listed separately, but is mentioned within the entry.

Teachers' Assn; History [★8511]
Teachers Assn; Natl. [★24045]
Teachers Assn; Natl. Bus. [★8036]
Teachers Assn; Natl. Earth Sci. [9111]
Teachers Assn; Natl. Sci. [9114]
Teachers Assn; Natl. Visiting [8955]
Teachers Assn; Overseas [★24043]
Teachers Assn; Professional Dance [8191]
Teachers Assn; South Asian Language [7991]
Teachers Associations; Natl. Assn. of Secretaries of State [★7906]
Teachers Associations; Natl. Cong. of Mothers and Parent- [★8954]
Teachers Associations; Natl. Fed. of Modern Language [8739]
Teachers' Centers Exchange - Defunct.
Teachers; Central Assn. of Sci. and Mathematics [★9115]
Teachers of Chinese Language and Culture; Amer. Assn. of [★8074]
Teachers Club; Natl. Spiritualist [20454]
Teachers Colleges; Amer. Assn. of [★9208]
Teachers' Comm. on Central America - Address unknown since 1999.
Teachers Comm. for Peace in Vietnam - Defunct.
Teachers; Cooperative Bur. for [★1263]
Teachers of Czech; North Amer. Assn. of [★9861]
Teachers' Division of Natl. Assn. of Cosmetology Schools [★8160]
Teachers of Educ. Institutions; Assn. of [★8096]
Teachers of Educ; Natl. Soc. of Coll. [★8307]
Teachers' Educational Coun. - Natl. Assn. of Accredited Cosmetology Schools [★8160]
Teachers' Educational Coun. - Natl. Assn. of Cosmetology Schools [★8160]
Teachers of Emergency Medicine; Soc. of [★14344]
Teachers of English; Natl. Coun. of [8380]
Teachers of English to Speakers of Other Languages [8382], 700 S Washington St., Ste. 200, Alexandria, VA 22314-4287, (703)836-0774
Teachers of English to Speakers of Other Languages Aotearoa New Zealand [IO], Wellington, New Zealand
Teachers of English to Speakers of Other Languages - Arabia [IO], Dubai, United Arab Emirates
Teachers of English to Speakers of Other Languages - France [IO], Paris, France
Teachers of Family Medicine; Soc. of [14387]
Teachers Freedom Party - Address unknown since 1995.
Teachers of German; Amer. Assn. of [8460]
Teachers Guild; Dance [★9866]
Teachers Guild; Natl. Dance [★9866]
Teachers of High School Journalism; Natl. Assn. of Supervisors and [★8713]
Teachers of Insurance; Amer. Assn. of Univ. [★8574]
Teachers Insurance and Annuity Assn. [8579], 730 3rd Ave., New York, NY 10017-3206, (212)490-9000
Teachers; Intl. Assn. of Duncan Certified Ceramic [21928]
Teachers of Japanese; Assn. of [8682]
Teachers of Journalism; Amer. Assn. of [★8706]
Teachers of Journalism; Natl. Assn. of High School [★8713]
Teachers of Mathematics; Natl. Coun. of [8827]
Teachers; Natl. Assn. of Biology [8000]
Teachers; Natl. Assn. of Catholic School [8058]
Teachers; Natl. Assn. of Coll. Automotive [★7993]
Teachers; Natl. Assn. for Distributive Educ. [★8818]
Teachers; Natl. Assn. of Geoscience [8459]
Teachers; Natl. Assn. of Marketing [★2613]
Teachers Natl. Assn; Music [8918]
Teachers; Natl. Assn. for Remedial [★9043]
Teachers; Natl. Cong. of Colored Parents and [★8954]
Teachers; Natl. Cong. of Parents and [★8954]
Teachers; Natl. Coun. of Geography [★8457]
Teachers; Natl. Guild of Piano [8925]
Teachers; Natl. PTA - Natl. Cong. of Parents and [8954]
Teachers Network; Gay/Lesbian Straight [★8456]
Teachers; North Amer. Assn. for Celtic Language [8741]

Teachers; North Amer. Coun. of Automotive [7993]
Teachers of Oral Diagnosis; Org. of [8197]
Teachers; Org. of Professional Acting Coaches and [9267]
Teachers of Peace; Children as [★18196]
Teachers of Preventive Medicine; Assn. of [★16054]
Teachers Resisting Unhealthy Children's Entertainment [11657], PO Box 441261, Somerville, MA 02144
Teachers of Russian/American Coun. for Collaboration and Language Stud; Amer. Coun. of [★8226]
Teachers of Sacred Doctrine; Soc. of Catholic Coll. [★9273]
Teachers Saving Children Natl. [18569], PO Box 125, Damascus, OH 44619-0125, (330)821-2747
Teachers of Singing; Amer. Acad. of [8898]
Teachers of Singing; Natl. Assn. of [8923]
Teachers of Slavic and East European Languages; Amer. Assn. of [9125]
Teachers of Southeast Asian Languages; Coun. of [7990]
Teachers of Tech. Writing; Assn. of [9332]
Teachers of Turkic Languages; Amer. Assn. of [9282]
Teachers of Turkish; Amer. Assn. of [★9282]
Teachers' Union of Hungary [IO], Budapest, Hungary
Teachers' Union of Ireland [IO], Dublin, Ireland
Teachers Union Norway [IO], Oslo, Norway
Teachers and Writers Collaborative [9335], 520 8th Ave., Ste. 2020, New York, NY 10018, (212)691-6590
Teaching About China; Center for [8552]
Teaching Aids at Low Cost [IO], St. Albans, United Kingdom
Teaching; Assn. for Student [★9212]
Teaching; Center for the Ministry of [19920]
Teaching for Change [8359], PO Box 73038, Washington, DC 20056, (202)588-7204
Teaching Economics; Found. for [8216]
Teaching Entrepreneurship; Natl. Found. for [8038]
Teaching-Family Assn. [12169], PO Box 2007, Midlothian, VA 23113, (804)632-0155
Teaching of Foreign Languages; Amer. Coun. on the [8727]
Teaching of Foreign Languages; Northeast Conf. on the [8742]
Teaching Hospitals; Coun. of [14879]
Teaching Individual Protective Strategies [★11847]
Teaching Individuals Positive Solutions [★11847]
Teaching and Learning About Aging; Natl. Acad. for [11297]
Teaching and Learning About Aging Proj. [★11297]
Teaching, Learning and Tech. Gp. [6898], 1 Columbia Ave., Takoma Park, MD 20912, (301)270-8312
Teaching, Learning and Technology Group [IO], Takoma Park, MD, United States
Teaching; Medieval Acad. Reprints for [★10458]
Teaching; Natl. Assn. for Res. in Sci. [9108]
Teaching; Natl. Univ. Consortium for Telecommunications in [★8566]
Teaching Resources Center; ASA [★7658]
Teaching Soc; Organizational Behavior [6537]
Teaching of Speech to the Deaf; Amer. Assn. to Promote the [★14736]
Team 16 Fire Safety Exchange - Address unknown since 2003.
Team Drivers Intl. Union [★24198]
Team H.O.P.E (Help Offering Parents Empowerment) [12606], 310 Pensdale St., Philadelphia, PA 19128, (866)305-4653
Team Ironclad [★23309]
Team Ironclad [★IO]
Team Penning Assn; U.S. [23518]
Team and Workplace Excellence Forum [7555], PO Box 3005, Milwaukee, WI 53201-3005, (414)272-1734
Teamsters, Chauffeurs, Stablemen and Helpers of Am; Intl. Brotherhood of [★24198]
Teamsters for a Democratic Union [24199], PO Box 10128, Detroit, MI 48210, (313)842-2600
Teamsters; Graphic Communications Conf. of the Intl. Brotherhood of [24083]
Teamsters; Intl. Brotherhood of [24198]
Teamsters; Intl. Brotherhood of [★24083]

Teamsters Natl. Union [★24198]
Tear Australia [IO], Blackburn, Australia
Tear Film and Ocular Surface Soc. [IO], Boston, MA, United States
Tear Film and Ocular Surface Soc. [15729], PO Box 130146, Boston, MA 02113
Tearfund [IO], Teddington, United Kingdom
TECH CORPS [13406], 199 Forest St., Marlborough, MA 01752, (703)357-3055
TECH, Tech. Exchange for Christian Healthcare [20244], PO Box 1912, Midland, MI 48641-1912, (989)837-5515
TechHome Div; Consumer Electronics Assn. [1178]
TechLaw Gp. [5955], c/o Robert Cathey, Ackermann Pr., 1111 Northshore Dr., Ste. N-400, Knoxville, TN 37919, (865)588-7456
Tech. Advisors Gp. [IO], Plymouth, United Kingdom
Tech. Analysts Soc. (Singapore) [IO], Singapore, Singapore
Tech. Appraisers; Amer. Soc. of [★272]
Tech. Assistance Centers; Natl. Assn. of Mgt. and [★9309]
Tech. Assistance Collaborative [13145], 535 Boylston St., Ste. 1301, Boston, MA 02116, (617)266-5657
Technical Assistance Consortium to Improve Coll. Services - Defunct.
Tech. Assistance Gp. [★9593]
Tech. Assistance Network; Peer [★11968]
Tech. Assistance Program/American Dance Guild [★9593]
Tech. Assistance Project/American Dance Festival [★9593]
Tech. Assistance; Volunteers in [12448]
Tech. Assistance; Volunteers for Intl. [★12448]
Technical-Assistants; Coun. on Lib. [★8783]
Tech. Assn; Flexographic [1766]
Tech. Assn. of the Graphic Arts [7155], 200 Deer Run Rd., Sewickley, PA 15143, (412)259-1706
Tech. Assn. of the Graphic Arts [IO], Sewickley, PA, United States
Tech. Assn. of the Lithographic Indus. [★IO]
Tech. Assn. of the Lithographic Indus. [★7155]
Tech. Assn; Natl. [7752]
Tech. Assn. of the Pulp and Paper Indus; TAPPI - [2895]
Tech. Assn; Recycled Paperboard [993]
Tech. Assn. for Solid Wastes Mgt. [IO], Bilbao, Spain
Tech. Center for Clay, Tiles, and Bricks [IO], Clamart, France
Technical Ceramics Mfrs. Assn. - Defunct.
Tech. Commn. for Oceanography and Marine Meteorology [IO], Geneva, Switzerland
Tech. Comm; Intl. Glutamate [1528]
Tech. Commun; Soc. for [886]
Tech. Communicators Assn. of New Zealand [IO], Auckland, New Zealand
Tech. Consultants Assn; Professional and [969]

Technical Consulting
  Amer. Sportfishing Assn. [23408]
  Mfg. Enterprise Solutions Assn. Intl. [7722]
  Manufacturing Enterprise Solutions Association International [IO]
  Musical Instrument Technicians Assn., Intl. [2816]
  SAE Ser. Tech. Prog. Off. [3719]
  Volunteers in Tech. Assistance [12448]

Technical Education
  Amer. Foundry Soc. [9227]
  Amer. Tech. Educ. Assn. [9228]
  Amer. Tech. Educ. Assn. [IO]
  Australasian Soc. for Computers in Learning in Tertiary Educ. [IO]
  Caribbean Engg. and Tech. Professionals [IO]
  Gen. Soc. of Mechanics and Tradesmen of the City of New York [9229]
  Inst. of Tech. and Polytechnics of New Zealand [IO]
  Intl. Coun. for Machinery Lubrication [7253]
  Intl. Fire Ser. Training Assn. [9230]
  Intl. Fire Ser. Training Assn. [IO]
  Intl. Org. on Shape Memory and Superelastic Technologies [7317]
  Intl. Tech. Educ. Assn. [9231]
  Intl. Tech. Educ. Assn. [IO]
  Intl. Tech. Educ. Assn. - Coun. for Supervisors [IO]

Reference to "IO" in place of a book number signifies that the association may be found in the 45th edition of International Organizations.

Intl. Tech. Educ. Assn. - Coun. for Supervisors [9232]
Natl. Assn. of PreCollege Directors [8371]
Natl. Assn. of Trade and Indus. Instructors [9233]
Natl. Tech Prep Network [8358]
Organizational Systems Res. Assn. [9234]
ORT Am. [12480]
Sewing Educator Alliance [9121]
Silver Eagles of Am. [9235]
Volunteers in Tech. Assistance [12448]
World Coun. of Associations for Tech. Educ. [IO]
World Tech. Volunteers [13196]
Tech. Educ; Assn. for Career and [9300]
Technical Education Found; Natl. Vocational [9308]
Tech. Employees; Assn. of [★24024]
Tech., Engg. and Elecl. Union [IO], Dublin, Ireland
Tech. Engineers; Amer. Fed. of [★24052]
Technical Engineers Assn. - Address unknown since 2002.
Tech. Engineers; Intl. Fed. of Professional and [24052]
Tech. Exchange for Christian Healthcare; TECH, [20244]
Tech. Experience (U.S.); Intl. Assn. for the Exchange of Students for [★8601]
Tech. Found. of Am. - Address unknown since 2004.
Tech. Found; Graphic Arts [1769]
Tech. Found; Screen Printing [1789]
Tech. High Schools and Inst; Amer. Assn. of [★9228]
Technical Honor Soc; Natl. Vocational- [★24725]
Technical Info. Center [★9227]
Tech. Interchange Between East and West; Center for Cultural and [★17882]
Technical Intl. Administrative Coun. - Defunct.
Technical Marketing Soc. of America - Address unknown since 1994.
Tech. Professionals; Natl. Org. of Gay and Lesbian Scientists and [7620]
Tech. Publishing Soc. [★886]
Tech. Publishing Soc. [★IO]
Tech., Salaried, Machine, and Furniture Workers; Intl. Union of Electronic, Elecl., [★24049]
Tech. Schools and the Assn. of Independent Colleges and Schools; Natl. Assn. of Trade and [★9303]
Tech. Ser. Assn. [★6677]
Tech. Ser. Indus; Natl. Coun. of [★1743]
Tech. Services; Assn. for Lib. Collections and [10333]
Technical Services Assn; Natl. [7753]
Technical Services Industry Assn. [★7753]
Tech. Soc; Soo Line Historical and [10923]
Tech. Soc; Terminal Railroad Assn. Historical and [10925]
Tech. and Supervisory Professionals; Assn. of [5737]
Tech. Teacher Educators; Natl. Assn. of Indus. and [8544]
Tech. Textile and Nonwoven Assn. [IO], Melbourne, Australia
Tech. Valuation Soc. [★272]
Tech. Writers and Editors; Soc. of [★886]
Tech. Writing; Assn. of Teachers of [9332]
Technician Educ. Coun; Aviation [7921]
Technician Excellence; North Amer. [1897]
Technicians; Acad. of Veterinary Emergency and Critical Care [16734]
Technicians; Amer. Assn. of Nephrology Nurses and [★15286]
Technicians; Amer. Assn. of Orthopic [★15657]
Technicians; Amer. Registry of Radiological [★15128]
Technicians; Amer. Registry of X-Ray [★15128]
Technicians; Amer. Soc. of Clinical Lab. [★14992]
Technicians; Amer. Soc. of Extracorporeal Circulation [★15129]
Technicians; Amer. Soc. of Piano [★2822]
Technicians; Amer. Soc. of X-Ray [★15131]
Technicians; Apprenticeship Training Prog. for Balancing [★598]
Technicians; Assn. of Marine [2573]
Technicians; Assn. of Operating Room [★15133]
Technicians Assn; Safe and Vault [3541]
Technicians; Assn. of Zoo Veterinary [16787]

Technicians - Communications Workers of Am; Natl. Assn. Broadcast Employees and [24024]
Technicians; Coun. on Library-Media [8783]
Technicians Educ. Found; Natl. Automotive [7992]
Technicians Guild; Piano [2822]
Technicians; Intl. Soc. of Cleaning [★2477]
Technicians Labor-Mgt. Cooperation Fund; Instrument [1021]
Technicians; Natl. Assn. of Bus. and Educational Radio and Assn. of Communications [★3752]
Technicians; Natl. Assn. of Emergency Medical [14335]
Technicians; Natl. Assn. of Photographic Equip. [3004]
Technicians; Natl. Registry of Emergency Medical [14342]
Technicians Soc; Ser. [★3719]
Technion Soc; Amer. [★8677]
Technische Org. der Europaischen Reifen- und Felgenhersteller [★IO]
Techno Found. - Defunct.
Technocracy Inc. [18630], c/o Continental HQ, 2475 Harksell Rd., Ferndale, WA 98248-9764, (360)366-1012
Technological Advancement of Reporting; Soc. for the [5631]
Technological Amer. Party - Address unknown since 1978.
Technological Sciences; Coun. of Academies of Engg. and [★9104]
Technologies; Center for Energy Efficiency and Renewable [4526]
Technologies Coun; Gasification [1722]
Technologies du Developpement Durable du Canada [★IO]
Technologies Gp. of Electronic Indus. Assn; Info. and Telecommunications [★3759]
Technologies; Inst. for Learning [8355]
Technologies; NPES - The Assn. for Suppliers of Printing, Publishing and Converting [1782]
Technologies Users Assn., OCR/Scanner/Fax Assn; Recognition [★6787]
Technologist; Joint Rev. Comm. on Educ. for the Surgical [★15123]
Technologist Sect; Soc. of Nuclear Medicine [15425]
Technologist Sect. of the Soc. of Nuclear Medicine [★15425]
Technologists; Amer. Bd. of Registration of EEG [★14305]
Technologists; Amer. Bd. of Registration of EEG and EP [14305]
Technologists; Amer. Chiropractic Registry of Radiologic [16273]
Technologists; Amer. Medical [15127]
Technologists; Amer. Registry of Radiologic [15128]
Technologists; Amer. Soc. of Electroencephalographic [★14307]
Technologists; Amer. Soc. of Master Dental [14143]
Technologists; Amer. Soc. of Medical [★14992]
Technologists; Amer. Soc. of Radiologic [15131]
Technologists Assn; Amer. Cardiology [★13885]
Technologists; Assn. of Polysomnographic [16423]
Technologists; Inst. of Food [7094]
Technologists; Natl. Alliance of Cardiovascular [★13885]
Technologists; Natl. Assn. of Nephrology [★15293]
Technologists; Natl. Assn. of Nephrology Technicians/ [15293]
Technologists; Natl. Assn. of Orthopaedic [15144]
Technologists; Natl. Bd. for Certification of Orthopaedic [15774]
Technologists; Natl. Soc. of Cardiopulmonary [★13885]
Technologists and Technicians; Amer. Soc. of Anesthesia [15083]
Technology
10 Gigabit Ethernet Alliance [7372]
1394 High Performance Serial Bus Trade Assn. [3720]
ABET [6979]
Acad. of Applied Sci. [7592]
Acad. of Arts and Sciences of the Americas [18830]
Advanced Card Tech. Assn. of Canada [IO]
Advanced Media Workflow Assn. [3721]

Affiliated Inventors Found. [7224]
African-American Women in Tech. [6394]
Agency for Instructional Tech. [8549]
Alfred P. Sloan Found. [18385]
Alliance for Public Tech. [7723]
Alliance for Sci. and Tech. Res. in Am. [7595]
Alliance for Tech. Access [11915]
Alternative Tech. Assn. [IO]
Amer. Assn. of Electronic Reporters and Transcribers [3180]
Amer. Assn. of Paging Carriers [872]
Amer. Assn. for Tech. in Psychiatry [16070]
Amer. Commun. Assn. [6710]
Amer. Cooperative Coun. on Compensation Tech. [4059]
Amer. Decentralized Wastewater Assn. [4006]
Amer. Engg. Alliance [6985]
Amer. Filtration and Separations Soc. [7724]
Amer. Indian Sci. and Engg. Soc. [6987]
Amer. Indus. Extension Alliance [2546]
Amer. Medical Informatics Assn. [14079]
Amer. Rainwater Catchment Systems Assn. [7825]
Amer. Soc. of Certified Engg. Technicians [6991]
Amer. Soc. for Mohs Histotechnology [15130]
Amer. Soc. of Sugar Cane Technologists [3700]
Amer. Supplier Inst. [7725]
Amer. TeleEdCommunications Alliance [7766]
Americans for Fair Electronic Commerce Transactions [17441]
Antique Wireless Assn. [22923]
Application Ser. Provider Indus. Consortium [3722]
Applied Tech. Coun. [7000]
Aprovecho Res. Center [16993]
Art and Sci. Collaborations [9607]
Asian Inst. of Tech. [IO]
Assn. for Automatic Identification and Mobility North Am. [336]
Assn. for Challenge Course Tech. [2869]
Assn. of Chinese Scientists and Engineers - U.S.A. [6698]
Assn. for Community Networking [8124]
Assn. for Competitive Tech. [3723]
Assn. for Educational Communications and Tech. [8551]
Assn. for Elecl., Electronic and Info. Technologies [IO]
Assn. for Electronic Hea. Care Transactions [14618]
Assn. for Enterprise Integration [700]
Assn. of European Sci. and Tech. Transfer Professionals [IO]
Assn. Global View [8017]
Assn. for Lab. Automation [6515]
Assn. for Machine Translation in the Americas [7807]
Assn. of Macintosh Trainers [6810]
Assn. for Mfg. Tech. [7262]
Assn. of Medical Directors of Info. Systems [14957]
Assn. of North Amer. Radio Clubs [21498]
Assn. of Science-Technology Centers [10499]
Assn. for Software Testing [6763]
Assn. of State Energy Res. and Tech. Transfer Institutions [6945]
Assn. of Teachers of Tech. Writing [9332]
Assn. of Thai Professionals in Am. and Canada [19406]
Assn. of Univ. Tech. Managers [5838]
ATOL [IO]
Australian Spatial Info. Bus. Assn. [IO]
Bill and Melinda Gates Found. [12273]
BioIndustry Assn. [IO]
Biometric Application Programming Interface Consortium [6572]
Broadband Services Forum [3737]
Calgary Coun. for Advanced Tech. [IO]
California Engg. Found. [7007]
Canadian Advanced Tech. Alliance [IO]
Canadian Coun. of Technicians and Technologists [IO]
CDMA Development Gp. [7726]
Center for Democracy and Tech. [17167]
Center for Sci. in the Public Interest [17314]

A star before a book entry number signifies that the name is not listed separately, but is mentioned within the entry.

Charles A. and Anne Morrow Lindbergh Found. [4539]
Chinese Amer. Semiconductor Professional Assn. [1208]
Clean Energy Gp. [6948]
Clean Energy States Alliance [6949]
Coalition to Keep Am. Connected [18724]
CommerceNet [7727]
Commn. on Professionals in Sci. and Tech. [7604]
Commonwealth Partnership for Tech. Mgt. [IO]
CompactFlash Assn. [6723]
CompuMentor [7728]
Cmpt. Sci. Teachers Assn. [8130]
Computers for Children [8137]
ControlNet Intl. [7729]
Corporate Event Marketing Assn. [2621]
Corrections Tech. Assn. [1076]
Coun. for Biotechnology Info. [6614]
Coun. on Ionizing Radiation Measurements and Standards [7556]
Coun. of Regional Info. Tech. Associations [7192]
Coun. on Tech. Teacher Educ. [8543]
CrossRef [3220]
Dalmo Giacometti Found. [IO]
Digital Cinema Soc. [1380]
Digital Govt. Soc. of North Am. [7151]
Digital Media Device Assn. [7303]
Distributed Computing Indus. Assn. [899]
Domestic Technologies [16994]
Ebix Users Assn. [340]
The Educ. Coalition [8325]
Electricity Storage Assn. [3957]
Electrocoat Assn. [7730]
Electronic Frontier Found. [7731]
Embedded Linux Consortium [6726]
Engg. Soc. of Detroit [7012]
EnterpriseWorks/VITA [16996]
Epsilon Pi Tau [24720]
Epsilon Pi Tau [IO]
European Assn. of Res. and Tech. Organisations [IO]
European Coastal Assn. for Sci. and Tech. [IO]
European Sealing Assn. [IO]
Experiments in Art and Tech. [9439]
Fabless Semiconductor Assn. [1215]
Fed. of Galaxy Explorers [9136]
Fed. of Tech. and Sci. Societies, Hungary [IO]
Fiber Optic Assn. [9238]
Financial Services Tech. Consortium [7732]
Finnish Academies of Tech. [IO]
For Inspiration and Recognition of Sci. and Tech. [8319]
Foresight Inst. [7733]
French Assn. for Info. Commun. Tech. Development [IO]
Future of Music Coalition [10598]
GALA: Globalization and Localization Assn. [1168]
Game Audio Network Guild [1715]
Geekcorps [3724]
Geeks Without Borders [11806]
Global Bus. and Tech. Assn. [778]
Global Envision [12194]
Global Nomads Gp. [9336]
Global Spatial Data Infrastructure Assn. [7734]
Global Spatial Data Infrastructure Assn. [IO]
GlobalPlatform [7735]
HAVi [6513]
Hi-Ethics - Hea. Internet Ethics [14676]
Higher Educ. Info. Tech. Alliance [8489]
HomePlug Powerline Alliance [1216]
IDB Forum [7736]
IEEE Soc. Social Implications of Tech. [7737]
IMS Forum [7771]
INCITS - InterNational Comm. for Info. Tech. Standards [7738]
Indigenous Peoples Coun. on Biocolonialism [12407]
Info. Tech. Solution Provider Alliance [2102]
Inst. for Prospective Technological Stud. [IO]
Inst. for the Transfer of Tech. to Educ. [8563]
Inst. for Women in Trades, Tech. and Sci. [4042]
Integrated Mfg. Tech. Initiative [7264]
Interaction Design Assn. [6863]
Interactive Travel Services Assn. [3946]
Intermediate Tech. Development Gp. of North Am. [16997]

Intl. Alliance of Avaya Users [3745]
Intl. Assn. for Biometrics [IO]
Intl. Assn. of Cmpt. Investigative Specialists [8133]
Intl. Assn. for Contract and Commercial Mgt. [772]
Intl. Assn. for Impact Assessment [7739]
Intl. Assn. for Impact Assessment [IO]
Intl. Assn. for the Mgt. of Tech. [7740]
Intl. Assn. of Messaging Professionals [6711]
Intl. Assn. of Nanotechnology [7741]
Intl. Assn. of Nanotechnology [IO]
Intl. Assn. for the Plant Protection Sciences [6397]
Intl. Assn. for Sci., Tech. and Soc. [7608]
Intl. Assn. of Software Architects [6770]
Intl. Assn. of Space Entrepreneurs [3634]
Intl. Assn. for Structural Mechanics in Reactor Tech. [7742]
Intl. Assn. for Structural Mechanics in Reactor Tech. [IO]
Intl. Biometric Indus. Assn. [7743]
Intl. Building Performance Simulation Assn. [6652]
Intl. Christian Technologists Assn. [20282]
Intl. Comm. on Ultra-High Intensity Lasers [7245]
Intl. Coun. for Machinery Lubrication [7253]
Intl. DB2 Users Gp. [6856]
Intl. Experimental Aerospace Soc. [6375]
Intl. Geosynthetics Soc. [6700]
Intl. Maillard Reaction Soc. [6683]
Intl. Multimedia Telecommunications Consortium [7775]
Intl. Nanocasting Assn. [562]
Intl. .NET Assn. [6771]
Intl. Network for Terminology [IO]
Intl. Nursing Assn. for Clinical Simulation and Learning [15485]
Intl. Org. on Shape Memory and Superelastic Technologies [7317]
Intl. Photonics Commercialization Alliance [2862]
Intl. Radio Club of Am. [21503]
Intl. Rainwater Catchment Systems Assn. [7832]
Intl. Security, Trust and Privacy Alliance [3535]
Intl. Ser. for the Acquisition of Agri-biotech Applications [6398]
Intl. Soc. of Agile Mfg. [2558]
Intl. Soc. of Artificial Life [6584]
Intl. Soc. for Bioluminescence and Chemiluminescence [7612]
Intl. Soc. for Biosafety Res. [6586]
Intl. Soc. of Coating Sci. and Tech. [6705]
Intl. Soc. for Cmpt. Assisted Orthopaedic Surgery [15772]
Intl. Soc. for Ethics and Info. Tech. [7198]
Intl. Soc. for Law and Tech. [5945]
Intl. Soc. of Lyophilization - Freeze Drying [6616]
Intl. Soc. for Nanoscale Sci., Computation and Engg. [7614]
Intl. Soc. of Parametric Analysts [6734]
Intl. Soc. for Phylogenetic Nomenclature [7116]
Intl. Soc. for Presence Res. [7572]
Intl. Soc. for Tech. in Educ. [8134]
Intl. Tech. Educ. Assn. [9231]
Intl. Tech. Educ. Assn. - Coun. for Supervisors [9232]
Intl. Tech. Inst. [7744]
Intl. Tech. Inst. [IO]
Intl. Training and Simulation Alliance [6735]
Intl. Union of Tech. Associations and Organizations [IO]
Intervention and Coiled Tubing Assn. [7512]
Ithaka [7200]
Japan Info. Access Proj. [10265]
Japan Sci. and Tech. Corp. [IO]
Joint Venture: Silicon Valley Network [7745]
The Keystone Center [7746]
Kids Universe, Inc. [8320]
Knowbility [11958]
Korea Info. Tech. Network [6736]
Laser and Electro-Optics Mfrs. Assn. [7246]
Latinos in Info. Sciences and Tech. Assn. [7201]
League of Professional Sys. Administrators [6815]
Longwave Club of Am. [21505]
Machining and Material Removal Community of the Soc. of Mfg. Engineers [7747]
Malayalee Engineers Assn. in North Am. [7026]

Markle Found. [6713]
Medical Equip. and Tech. Assn. [7306]
Metro Ethernet Forum [7748]
Metro Ethernet Forum [IO]
Mobile Marketing Assn. [110]
Mobile Voter [18032]
Monte Jade Sci. and Tech. Assn. [7749]
MPLS and Frame Relay Alliance [6714]
MultiMediaCard Assn. [7305]
Musculoskeletal Ultrasound Soc. [16696]
NanoBusiness Alliance [7750]
Natl. Alliance of Clean Energy Bus. Incubators [1287]
Natl. Alliance for Hea. Info. Tech. [15142]
Natl. Alliance of Medical Researchers and Teaching Physicians [15143]
Natl. Alliance of Primary Care Informatics [14956]
Natl. Alliance of State Sci. and Mathematics Coalitions [9106]
Natl. Assn. of Commun. Systems Engineers [6715]
Natl. Assn. of Emergency Vehicle Technicians [418]
Natl. Assn. of Indus. Tech. [8545]
Natl. Assn. for Justice Info. Systems [5648]
Natl. Assn. for Public Hea. Info. Tech. [7203]
Natl. Assn. for Tech Prep Leadership [9239]
Natl. Center for Food Safety and Tech. [1543]
Natl. Center For Advanced Technologies [7751]
Natl. Clean Cities [6399]
Natl. Coalition for Tech. in Educ. and Training [9241]
Natl. Collegiate Inventors and Innovators Alliance [7218]
Natl. Coun. of Sci. and Technological Development [IO]
Natl. Energy Marketers Assn. [1288]
Natl. Indus. Coalition [IO]
Natl. InStar Users Gp. [7221]
Natl. Inst. for Certification in Engg. Technologies [7033]
Natl. MIS User Gp. [7207]
Natl. Org. of Gay and Lesbian Scientists and Tech. Professionals [7620]
Natl. Tech. Assn. [7752]
Natl. Technical Services Assn. [7753]
Natl. Urban Tech. Center [7754]
NetAction [17242]
Netherlands Soc. of Technological Sciences and Engg. [IO]
Network of Alternative Tech. and Tech. Assessment [IO]
NextGen Energy Coun. [6966]
NiUG Intl. [7208]
North Am. Chinese Semiconductor Assn. [1226]
North Am. Taiwanese Engineers' Assn. [7036]
North Amer. Chap. of the Assn. for Computational Linguistics [10408]
North Amer. Computational Social and Org. Sciences [6740]
North Amer. Confed. of the Red Dragon [22479]
North Amer. Coun. for Online Learning [7949]
North Amer. Geosynthetics Soc. [6701]
North Amer. Radio Archives [22926]
North Amer. Shortwave Assn. [21507]
North Amer. Soc. for Trenchless Tech. [7819]
Northwest Steam Soc. [22978]
Norwegian Acad. of Technological Sciences [IO]
Norwegian Geotechnical Inst. [IO]
Norwegian Geotechnical Soc. [IO]
Novell Users Intl. [3725]
OASIS PKI Member Sect. [7780]
ODF Alliance [7209]
One Economy [7755]
The Open Gp. [2108]
Optical Internetworking Forum [3726]
Optical Storage Tech. Assn. [2860]
Optoelectronics Indus. Development Assn. [2861]
Org. for the Advancement of Structured Info. Standards [7756]
PACON Intl. [5011]
PC/104 Consortium [3727]
Peace X Peace [18237]
Phone-TTY [14777]
Plastic Optical Fiber Trade Org. [2863]

Reference to "IO" in place of a book number signifies that the association may be found in the 45th edition of International Organizations.

Prog. for Appropriate Tech. in Hea. [17000]
Programmers Guild [7757]
Progressive Tech. Proj. [7758]
Proteome Soc. [7119]
Public Tech. Inst. [6197]
Quarter Century Wireless Assn. [21509]
Radio Club of Am. [22928]
Radio Collectors of Am. [22929]
RDMA Consortium [7759]
Rehabilitation Tech. Assn. [16334]
ResearchChannel [7575]
Residential Energy Services Network [664]
Rough and Tumble Engineers' Historical Assn.
    [22979]
Science for the People [7627]
SD Card Assn. [6743]
Search Engine Marketing Professional Org.
    [2648]
Sect. for Magnetic Resonance Technologists
    [16594]
SeniorNet [13302]
SIGAPP - Special Interest Gp. on Applied
    Computing [6821]
SIMPUTER (USA) [13301]
Simulation Interoperability Standards Org. [7760]
Sino-American Pharmaceutical Professionals
    Assn. [15951]
SkyTruth [4637]
Smart Card Alliance [7761]
Soc. for Amateur Scientists [7631]
Soc. for Applied Learning Tech. [8571]
Soc. of Building Sci. Educators [8363]
Soc. for the History of Tech. [10160]
Soc. for Info. Tech. and Teacher Educ. [9243]
Soc. of Instrument and Control Engineers [IO]
Soc. of Intl. Chinese in Educational Tech. [IO]
Soc. of Intl. Chinese in Educational Tech. [9236]
Soc. of Internet Professionals [IO]
Soc. for Philosophy and Tech. [10837]
Soc. for Simulation in Healthcare [15148]
Software in the Public Interest [6777]
Special Interest Gp. on Data Communications of
    the Assn. for Computing Machinery [6804]
SSA Global Users - North Am. [3728]
State Educational Tech. Directors Assn. [9244]
Steamship Historical Soc. of Am. [22980]
Swedish Assn. for Info. Specialists [IO]
Teaching, Learning and Tech. Gp. [6898]
TECH CORPS [13406]
TechLaw Gp. [5955]
Tech. Inst. for Music Educators [8933]
Tech. Mgt. Educ. Assn. [9245]
Tech. New Zealand [IO]
Tech. Student Assn. [8547]
Tech. Transfer Soc. [7762]
Tech. Without Borders [7763]
Technopreneurs Assn. of Malaysia [IO]
Triangle Coalition for Sci. and Tech. Educ. [9116]
True Food Network [4677]
UCA Intl. Users Gp. [7820]
Unicorn Users Gp. Intl. [7214]
U.S. Combined Heat and Power Assn. [7821]
U.S. Connected Communities Assn. [6716]
U.S. Display Consortium [3729]
U.S. Human Proteome Org. [6604]
U.S. Indus. Coalition [7637]
U.S. Microscopic Welding Assn. [7849]
U.S. Permafrost Assn. [7675]
U.S. Prdt. Data Assn. [2112]
Vintage Radio and Phonograph Soc. [22931]
Volunteers in Tech. Assistance [12448]
VON Coalition [2321]
VXIbus Consortium [7793]
Web Analytics Assn. [7222]
Web3D Consortium [6828]
WECAI Network [1167]
Welders Without Borders [7850]
Wi-Fi Alliance [6829]
Windustry [7853]
Winrock Intl. [16959]
Wire and Cable Indus. Suppliers Assn. [1231]
Wired Woman [IO]
Women in Bio [6618]
Women Entrepreneurs in Sci. and Tech. [4050]
Women in Tech. Intl. [7764]

Women in Tech. Intl. [IO]
Women of Wind Energy [7854]
World Bamboo Org. [5041]
World Energy Efficiency Assn. [6978]
World Fed. of Tech. Organizations [IO]
World Internet Numismatic Soc. [22768]
World Neighbors [17921]
World Sci. and Engg. Acad. and Soc. [7054]
World Transhumanist Assn. [7163]
World Wide Web Consortium [6756]
Worldwide Television-FM DX Assn. [21510]
XML.org [6757]
Zangle Natl. Users' Gp. [7216]
Tech. - ABET; Accreditation Bd. for Engg. and
    [★6979]
Tech; Accreditation Rev. Comm. on Educ. in Surgical
    [15123]
Tech; Accrediting Commn. of Career Schools and
    Colleges of [7873]
Tech; African-American Women in [6394]
Tech; Agency for Instructional [8549]
Tech; Alliance for Environmental [1632]
Tech; Amer. Soc. of Extra-Corporeal [15129]
Tech; Amer. Soc. for Info. Sci. and [7188]
Tech; Amer. Soc. for Medical [★14992]
Tech; Amer. Soc. of Milling and Baking [★6660]
Tech. Applications Prog., Intl. City Mgt. Assn.
    [★6197]
Tech. Assistance Ser; Natl. Appropriate [★6951]
Tech. Assn; Advanced Medical [14669]
Technology Assn; Asian Amer. Multi [1204]
Tech. Assn. of the Automotive Indus. [IO], Orbas-
    sano, Italy
Tech. Assn; Bus. [2844]
Tech. Assn; Coal [842]
Tech; Assn. for Educ. in Healthcare Info. [15132]
Tech; Assn. for Educational Communications and
    [8551]
Tech. Assn; Entertainment Services and [2556]
Tech. Assn; Geospatial Info. and [900]
Tech. Assn; Hospitality Info. [6717]
Tech; Assn; Lib. and Info. [10368]
Tech; Assn. for Mfg. [7262]
Tech; Assn. for Preservation [★10016]
Tech. Assn. of SME; Machining [★7025]
Tech. Assn; Surface Mount [2072]
Tech. Assn; Waste Equip. [4005]
Tech; Bd. of Nephrology Examiners Nursing and
    [15290]
Tech; Bd. of Nephrology Examiners - Nursing and
    [★15290]
Tech; Center for Neighborhood [17209]
Technology Centers; Assn. of Science- [10499]
Tech. Certification Bd; Nuclear Medicine [15423]
Tech; Commn. on Professionals in Sci. and [7604]
Tech; Consumer Proj. on [7542]
Tech; Coun. for Agricultural Sci. and [7936]
Tech. Coun; Applied [7000]
Tech. Coun; Environmental [3993]
Tech. Coun; Instructional [8565]
Tech; Coun. on Lib. [★8783]
Tech. Development Gp. of North Am; Intermediate
    [16997]

Technology Education
Amer. TeleEdCommunications Alliance [7766]
Assn. for the Advancement of Computing in Educ.
    [9237]
Assn. for Community Networking [8124]
Assn. of Macintosh Trainers [6810]
CompuMentor [7728]
Cmpt. Sci. Teachers Assn. [8130]
The Educ. Coalition [8325]
Fiber Optic Assn. [9238]
Fiber Optic Assn. [IO]
For Inspiration and Recognition of Sci. and Tech.
    [8319]
Geeks Without Borders [11806]
Higher Educ. Info. Tech. Alliance [8489]
Intl. Assn. for the Exchange of Students for Tech.
    Experience [9181]
Intl. Assn. for the Mgt. of Tech. [7740]
Intl. Assn. of Messaging Professionals [6711]
Intl. Org. on Shape Memory and Superelastic
    Technologies [7317]
Internet Bus. Alliance [3730]

Ithaka [7200]
Link Found. [7765]
Natl. Alliance of State Sci. and Mathematics Coali-
    tions [9106]
Natl. Assn. for Tech Prep Leadership [9239]
Natl. Coalition of Advanced Tech. Centers [9240]
Natl. Coalition of Advanced Tech. Centers [IO]
Natl. Coalition for Tech. in Educ. and Training
    [9241]
Natl. Tech Prep Network [8358]
North Amer. Coun. for Online Learning [7949]
Open Door Educ. Found. [9242]
SeniorNet [13302]
SeniorNet [IO]
Soc. for the History of Tech. [10160]
Soc. for Info. Tech. and Teacher Educ. [9243]
State Educational Tech. Directors Assn. [9244]
Teaching, Learning and Tech. Gp. [6898]
Tech. Mgt. Educ. Assn. [9245]
Volunteers in Tech. Assistance [12448]
Welders Without Borders [7850]
Technology Education for Children Coun. - Address
    unknown since 1991.
Tech. to Educ; Inst. for the Transfer of [8563]
Tech. Educ. Partnership; Natl. Sci. and [13126]
Tech; Experiments in Art and [9439]
Tech; Fashion Inst. of [★232]
Tech. and Graduate Stud; Maritime Inst. of [★24128]
Tech; Hea. Division of Prog. for the Introduction and
    Adaptation of Contraceptive [★17000]
Tech., Inc; Public [★6197]
Tech. Indus. of Finland [IO], Helsinki, Finland
Tech. Indus. Assn; Computing [898]
Tech. Indus. Coun; Info. [904]
Tech. Info. Center; Conservation [4384]
Tech. Inst; Cooling [616]
Tech; Inst. of Environmental Sciences and [7570]
Tech. Inst; Gas [1678]
Tech; Inst. of Gas [★1678]
Tech. Inst. for Music Educators [8933], 305 Maple
    Ave., Wyncote, PA 19095, (617)747-2816
Tech; Inst. of Paper Sci. and [7435]
Tech; Inst. for Theological Encounter With Sci. and
    [12353]
Tech; Inst. on Women and [★12754]
Tech; Intl. Network of Women in [★7764]
Tech; Joint Rev. Comm. on Educ. in Radiologic
    [8838]
Tech. Laboratories; Construction [★933]
Tech. and Maintenance Coun. of the Amer. Trucking
    Associations [3895], 950 N Glebe Rd., Ste. 210,
    Arlington, VA 22203-4181, (703)838-1763
Tech. and Mgt; DEMA, The Assn. for Input [★6787]
Tech. Mgt. Educ. Assn. [9245], c/o Chuck Rutledge,
    71 James Way, Eatontown, NJ 07724, (973)285-
    3850
Tech. and Mgt; Hospitality Inst. of [1943]
Tech. Managers; Assn. of Univ. [5838]
Tech. in Music Instruction; Assn. for [8905]
Tech; Natl. Assn. of Indus. [8545]
Tech; Natl. Bd. for Certification in Dental [14173]
Tech; Natl. Center for Appropriate [16998]
Tech; Natl. Soc. for Cardiopulmonary [★13885]
Technology; Natl. Soc. for Histo [15146]
Tech. Network; Financial Services [1461]
Tech. New Zealand [IO], Wellington, New Zealand
Tech; North Amer. Soc. for Trenchless [7819]
Tech. Professionals in Higher Educ; ACUTA: The
    Assn. for Communications [8548]
Tech; Prog. for the Introduction and Adaptation of
    Contraceptive [★17000]
Tech. Representatives Assn; Power-Motion [2059]
Technology Resource Consortium [7213]
Tech; Servants in Faith and [17001]
Technology Services [★6089]
Tech; Soc. for Applied Learning [8571]
Tech; Soc. for the History of [10160]
Tech. and Soc; Intl. Assn. for Sci., [7608]
Tech. Soc; Marine [7273]
Tech. and Soc; Natl. Assn. for Sci., [★7608]
Tech; Soc. for Philosophy and [10837]
Tech; Soc. of Wood Sci. and [7100]
Tech. Student Assn. [8547], 1914 Assn. Dr., Reston,
    VA 20191-1540, (703)860-9000
Tech; Trans-National Network of Appropriate/Alterna-
    tive [★17002]

A star before a book entry number signifies that the name is not listed separately, but is mentioned within the entry.

Tech. Transfer Coun; Petroleum [2944]
Technology Transfer; Industry Coalition on [1217]
Tech. Transfer Soc. [7762], 2005 Arthur Ln., Austin, TX 78704, (512)447-4409
Tech; U.S. - ASEAN Coun. for Bus. and [★3848]
Tech; U.S. Inst. for Theatre [11052]
Technology Utilization Program - Defunct.
Tech. Without Borders [7763], PO Box 445, The Plains, VA 20198, (703)220-7327
Tech., Work and Character; Proj. on [7168]
Tech; YLEM: Artists Using Sci. and [9532]
Technonet Asia [IO], Singapore, Singapore
Technopreneurs Assn. of Malaysia [IO], Petaling Jaya, Malaysia
TechnoServe [IO], Washington, DC, United States
TechnoServe [17849], 1800 M St. NW, Ste. 1066, South Tower, Washington, DC 20036, (202)785-4515
TechnoServe - Tanzania [IO], Arusha, United Republic of Tanzania
Tecnica - Address unknown since 1995.
Ted McGinley Fan Club - Defunct.
Teddy Bear Org; Heather's [22035]
Teddy Bears; Elvis [24810]
Tee it up for the Troops [13357], 2422 E 117th St., No. 102, Burnsville, MN 55337, (952)646-2490
Teen-Age Assembly of America - Defunct.
Teen Age Republican HQ; Natl. [18529]
Teen Anglers; Natl. [22454]
Teen Assn. of Model Railroaders [22637], c/o Mr. Tim Vermande, 6100 Ohio Dr., Apt. 1611, Plano, TX 75024
Teen Assn. of Model Railroading [★22637]
Teen Challenge Intl. [20643], PO Box 1015, Springfield, MO 65801, (417)862-6969
Teen Challenge Intl. [IO], Springfield, MO, United States
Teen Challenge Intl., USA [★IO]
Teen Challenge Intl., USA [★20643]
Teen Challenge; Natl. [★20643]
Teen Challenge Natl. [★20643]
Teen Challenge Natl. [★IO]
Teen Challenge World Wide Network [★IO]
Teen Challenge World Wide Network [★20643]
Teen Educ. Prog; Ryan White Natl. [★13560]
Teen Intl. Entomology Gp. [★7066]
Teen-Lift; Delta [13341]
Teen Mission [★20402]
Teen Mission [★IO]
Teen Missions Intl. [IO], Merritt Island, FL, United States
Teen Missions Intl. [20402], 885 E Hall Rd., Merritt Island, FL 32953, (321)453-0350
TEEN-PAC - Defunct.
Teen Pregnancy; Natl. Campaign to Prevent [13499]
Teens for Life; Natl. [12924]
Teens; Natl. Tots and [13503]
Teens Teaching AIDS Prevention - Defunct.
Teeth In the Neck Gang [★9702]
Teeth In the Neck Gang [★IO]
Tehran/Iran ACM Chap. [IO], Tehran, Iran
TEI Educ. Fund [★6304]
Teilhard Assn; Amer. [9632]
Teilhard Assn. for the Future of Man; Amer. [★9632]
Teilhard de Chardin Assn; Amer. [★9632]
Tekakwitha Conf. Natl. Center [19727], PO Box 6768, Great Falls, MT 59406-6768, (406)727-0147
Tekakwitha League; Blessed Kateri [★19727]
Tekijanoikeuden tiedotus- ja valvontakeskus [★IO]
Tekniikan Akateemisten Liito Tek [★IO]
Teknillistieteellisten Akatemioiden [★IO]
Teknisk-naturvitenskapelig forening [★IO]
Teknokemian Yhdistys [★IO]
Teknologiateollisuus [★IO]
Teknologisk Institut [★IO]
Tekstiili - ja vaatetusteollisuus ry [★IO]
Tekstiili- Ja Jalkinetoimittajat ry [★IO]
Tel Aviv Univ.: Amer. Coun. [8679], 39 Broadway, Ste. 1510, New York, NY 10006, (212)742-9070
Tel Aviv Univ; Amer. Friends of the [★8679]
Tel-Med [14601]
Telapak [IO], Bogor, Indonesia
Telecasters; Assn. of Maximum Ser. [★549]
Telecom Assn. of Hong Kong [★IO]
Telecom Assn; U.S. [3965]

Telecom Coun; United [3762]
Telecommunication Professionals in Higher Educ; ACUTA: The Assn. for [★8548]
Telecommunication Soc. of Australia [IO], Melbourne, Australia
Telecommunication Standardization Bur. [IO], Geneva, Switzerland

Telecommunications

1-800 Amer. Free Trade Assn. [3950]
Alliance Against Fraud in Telemarketing and Electronic Commerce [17302]
Alliance for Telecommunications Indus. Solutions [3731]
Amer. Assn. of Paging Carriers [872]
Amer. Facsimile Assn. [3732]
Amer. Medical Informatics Assn. [14079]
Amer. Public Communications Coun. [3733]
Amer. TeleEdCommunications Alliance [7766]
Amer. Telemedicine Assn. [16595]
Antique Telephone Collectors Assn. [22985]
Antique Wireless Assn. [22923]
Application Ser. Provider Indus. Consortium [3722]
Arab Satellite Communications Org. [IO]
Argentine Chamber of Informatics and Communications [IO]
Asia Pacific Telecommunity [IO]
Assn. of Call Center Managers [2520]
Assn. for Community Networking [8124]
Assn. of Fed. Communications Consulting Engineers [7767]
Assn. for Interactive Marketing [3734]
Assn. of North Amer. Radio Clubs [21498]
Assn. of TeleServices Intl. [3735]
Assn. of TeleServices Intl. [IO]
Assn. of Wireless Tech. [IO]
Australian Mobile Telecommunications Assn. [IO]
BICSI [IO]
BICSI [3736]
British Approvals Bd. for Telecommunications [IO]
British Cables Assn. [IO]
Broadband Services Forum [3737]
Broadband Wireless Assn. [IO]
Cable Positive [11327]
Cable and Telecommunications Human Resources Assn. [1980]
Call Centre Assn. of India [IO]
Call Centre Mgt. Assn., Ireland [IO]
Canadian Assn. of Internet Providers [IO]
Canadian Call Mgt. Assn. [IO]
Canadian Independent Telephone Assn. [IO]
Canadian Overseas Telecommunications Union [IO]
Canadian Satellite Users Assn. [IO]
Canadian Telecommunications Employees' Assn. [IO]
Canadian Wireless Telecommunications Assn. [IO]
Caribbean Assn. of Natl. Telecommunication Organizations [IO]
Catholic Acad. for Commun. Arts Professionals [9761]
CDMA Development Gp. [7726]
Cellular Operators Assn. of India [IO]
Chamber of Telecommunications Businesses [IO]
Coalition to Keep Am. Connected [18724]
Commonwealth Telecommunications Org. [IO]
Communications Assn. of Hong Kong [IO]
Communications Fraud Control Assn. [2087]
Communications and Info. Tech. Assn. [IO]
Communications Mgt. Assn. [IO]
Communications Marketing Assn. [3738]
Communications Users Assn. of South Africa [IO]
Cmpt. and Communications Indus. Assn. [3739]
Confed. of Aerial Indus. [IO]
CONNECT: The Union for Professionals in Communications [IO]
Contact Centre Assn. of Singapore [IO]
CONTACT USA [19865]
Coun. for Electronic Revenue Commun. Advancement [3740]
Coun. for Responsible Telemedicine [16596]
CTIA - The Wireless Assn. [3741]
Customer Contact Mgt. Assn. [IO]
DICOM Standards Comm. [7178]

Digital Media Device Assn. [7303]
EEMA [IO]
Energy Telecommunications and Elecl. Assn. [1185]
Enterprise Wireless Alliance [3742]
European Competitive Telecommunications Assn. [IO]
European Info., Communications and Consumer Electronics Tech. Indus. Assn. [IO]
European Inst. for Res. and Strategic Stud. in Telecommunications GmbH [IO]
European Internet Services Providers Assn. [IO]
European Satellite Operators Assn. [IO]
European Telecommunications Network Operators' Assn. [IO]
European Telecommunications Satellite Org. [IO]
Fibre Channel Indus. Assn. [3743]
Fibreoptic Indus. Assn. [IO]
Forest Indus. Telecommunications [1606]
GALA: Globalization and Localization Assn. [1168]
Hi-Ethics - Hea. Internet Ethics [14676]
Hong Kong Call Centre Assn. [IO]
IEEE Broadcast Tech. Soc. [7768]
IEEE Communications Soc. [7769]
IEEE Info. Theory Gp. [7770]
IMS Forum [7771]
IMS Forum [IO]
Indonesian Telecommunications Soc. [IO]
Inst. for Global Communications [IO]
Inst. for Global Communications [7772]
Inter-American Telecommunication Commn. [3744]
Inter-American Telecommunication Commn. [IO]
Intl. Alliance of Avaya Users [3745]
Intl. Assn. for Radio, Telecommunications and Electromagnetics [7773]
Intl. Assn. of Satellite Users and Suppliers [3746]
Intl. BBSing and Electronic Communications Corp. [3747]
Intl. Cable Protection Comm. [IO]
Intl. Call Center Benchmarking Consortium [731]
Intl. Commun. Assn. [3748]
Intl. Commun. Assn. [IO]
Intl. Disaster Recovery Assn. [7774]
Intl. Maritime Satellite Org. [IO]
Intl. Mobile Satellite Org. [IO]
International Multimedia Telecommunications Consortium [IO]
Intl. Multimedia Telecommunications Consortium [7775]
Intl. Nortel Networks Users Assn. [7776]
Intl. Org. of Space Communications [IO]
Intl. Radio Club of Am. [21503]
Intl. Telecommunication Union [IO]
Intl. (Telecommunications) Disaster Recovery Assn. [IO]
Intl. Telecommunications Satellite Org. [IO]
Intl. Telecommunications Satellite Org. [7777]
Intl. Telecommunications Soc. [3749]
Intl. Telecommunications Soc. [IO]
Intl. Telecommunications Users Gp. [IO]
Intl. Telework Assn. and Coun. [IO]
Intl. Telework Assn. and Coun. [3750]
Intl. Union of Radio Sci. [IO]
Japan Fed. of Telecommunications, Electronic Info. and Allied Workers [IO]
Joint Radio Co. [IO]
Land Mobile Communications Coun. [3751]
Lib. and Info. Tech. Assn. [10368]
Longwave Club of Am. [21505]
Mobile Marketing Assn. [110]
Mobile Voter [18032]
MPLS and Frame Relay Alliance [6714]
Natl. Assn. of Black Telecommunications Professionals [7778]
Natl. Assn. of Commun. Systems Engineers [6715]
Natl. Assn. for Multi-Ethnicity in Communications [2757]
Natl. Assn. of State Telecommunications Directors [6306]
Natl. Assn. of Telecommunications Officers and Advisors [6307]
Natl. Dental EDI Coun. [14176]
Native Amer. Public Telecommunications [9767]

Reference to "IO" in place of a book number signifies that the association may be found in the 45th edition of International Organizations.

NetAction [17242]
No-Code Intl. [21506]
North Amer. Assn. of Telecommunications Dealers [7779]
North Amer. Radio Archives [22926]
North Amer. Shortwave Assn. [21507]
OASIS PKI Member Sect. [7780]
Open Mobile Alliance [7781]
Pacific Telecommunications Coun. [7782]
Pacific Telecommunications Coun. [IO]
PCIA - The Wireless Infrastructure Association [IO]
PCIA - The Wireless Infrastructure Assn. [3752]
Phone-TTY [14777]
Plastic Optical Fiber Trade Org. [2863]
Private Citizen, Inc. [17147]
Progress and Freedom Found. [17188]
Quarter Century Wireless Assn. [21509]
Radio Amateur Satellite Corp. [7783]
Radio Club of Am. [22928]
Radio Collectors of Am. [22929]
Radio Tech. Commn. for Maritime Services [3753]
Radio Tech. Commn. for Maritime Services [IO]
Radio and TV Res. Coun. [7784]
Radiocommunication Bur. [IO]
Regional African Satellite Communications Org. [IO]
RTCA [6308]
Russian Assn. of Networks and Services [IO]
Satellite Broadcasting and Communications Assn. [IO]
Satellite Broadcasting and Communications Assn. [3754]
Sci. Assn. for Infocommunications [IO]
Sci. Assn. for Infocommunications Hungary [IO]
SeniorNet [13302]
Small Bus. in Telecommunications [3629]
Soc. of Cable Telecommunications Engineers [7040]
Soc. of Satellite Professionals Intl. [3755]
Soc. of Satellite Professionals Intl. [IO]
Soc. of Telecommunications Consultants [3756]
Soc. of Wireless Pioneers [3757]
Tel-Med [14601]
Telecommunication Soc. of Australia [IO]
Telecommunication Standardization Bur. [IO]
Telecommunications Benchmarking Intl. Gp. [3758]
Telecommunications for the Deaf and Hard of Hearing, Inc. [14780]
Telecommunications Indus. Assn. [3759]
Telecommunications Indus. Forum [3760]
Telecommunications Risk Mgt. Assn. [3761]
Telecommunications Users Assn. of New Zealand [IO]
TelecomPioneers [12203]
Teleflora [1494]
Telephone Collectors Intl. [22986]
TeleTruth: The Alliance for Customers' Telecommunications Rights [17346]
Teligen [IO]
U.S. Natl. Comm. of the Intl. Union of Radio Sci. [7785]
United Telecom Coun. [3762]
Veteran Wireless Operators Assn. [3763]
Vintage Radio and Phonograph Soc. [22931]
VON Coalition [2321]
West Africa Telecommunication Regulators Assn. [IO]
Wi-Fi Alliance [6829]
Wireless Communications Assn. Intl. [3764]
Wireless Communications Assn. Intl. [IO]
Wireless Dealers Assn. [3765]
World Teleport Assn. [3766]
World Teleport Assn. [IO]
Worldwide Television-FM DX Assn. [21510]
Telecommunications; Amer. Coun. for Competitive [★3955]
Telecommunications Assn; Competitive [★3955]
Telecommunications Assn. for Marketing; CTAM - Cable and [558]
Telecommunications Assn; Natl. Asian Amer. [★17166]
Telecommunications Assn; Natl. Cable and [573]
Telecommunications Assn; Natl. Educational [8337]

Telecommunications Benchmarking Intl. Gp. [3758], 4606 FM 1960 W, Ste. 250, Houston, TX 77069, (281)440-5044
Telecommunications Companies; Org. for the Promotion and Advancement of Small [3964]
Telecommunications Consortium; Instructional [★8565]
Telecommunications Consultants Assn; Canadian [IO]
Telecommunications Consumer Coalition - Defunct.
Telecommunications Cooperative Network - Address unknown since 2008.
Telecommunications Coun; Instructional [★8565]
Telecommunications Coun; Utilities [★3762]
Telecommunications for the Deaf and Hard of Hearing, Inc. [14780], 8630 Fenton St., Ste. 604, Silver Spring, MD 20910, (301)589-3786
Telecommunications for the Deaf, Inc. [★14780]
Telecommunications and Elecl. Assn; Energy [1185]
Telecommunications Engineers; Soc. of Cable [7040]
Telecommunications Financial Mgt. Assn; Public [★578]
Telecommunications; Forest Indus. [1606]
Telecommunications Heritage Gp. [IO], South Croydon, United Kingdom
Telecommunications Indus. Assn. [★IO]
Telecommunications Indus. Assn. [3759], 2500 Wilson Blvd., Ste. 300, Arlington, VA 22201-3834, (703)907-7700
Telecommunications Indus; CTAM, The Marketing Soc. for the Cable and [★558]
Telecommunications Indus. Forum [3760], c/o Alliance for Telecommunications Indus. Solutions, 1200 G St. NW, Ste. 500, Washington, DC 20005, (202)628-6380
Telecommunications Intl. Union - Defunct.
Telecommunications in Learning; Intl. Univ. Consortium for [★8566]
Telecommunications Marketing/Sales Assn. - Defunct.
Telecommunications; Native Amer. Public [9767]
Telecommunications Res. and Action Center [17195], PO Box 27279, Washington, DC 20005
Telecommunications Risk Mgt. Assn. [3761], 4 Becker Farm Rd., Roseland, NJ 07068, (973)871-4080
Telecommunications Standards Inst; European [IO]
Telecommunications Study Unit - Defunct.
Telecommunications Suppliers Assn; U.S. [★3759]
Telecommunications in Teaching; Natl. Univ. Consortium for [★8566]
Telecommunications Technologies Gp. of Electronic Indus. Assn; Info. and [★3759]
Telecommunications and Telephone Assn. - Address unknown since 2001.
Telecommunications Users Assn. of New Zealand [IO], Auckland, New Zealand
Telecommunications Users Coalition - Defunct.
Telecommuting Advisory Council/International Telework Assn. [★3750]
Telecommuting Advisory Council/International Telework Assn. [★IO]
TelecomPioneers [12203], 930 15th St., 12th Fl., Denver, CO 80202, (303)571-1200
Teleflora [1494], PO Box 60910, Los Angeles, CA 90060-0910, (800)835-3356
Telegift Network [★1724]
Telegrams; Central Bur. for Astronomical [6504]
Telegraph Delivery Ser. [★1494]
Telegraphy
  Morse Telegraph Club [22984]
  Morse Telegraph Club [IO]
  Morse Telegraph Club [IO]
  Morse Telegraph Club, Edmonton Chap. [IO]
  No-Code Intl. [21506]
  Veteran Wireless Operators Assn. [3763]
Telehealth Ser. Providers; Assn. of [15160]
Telemark Technological Res. and Development Centre, Dept. of Powder Sci. and Tech. [IO], Porsgrunn, Norway
Telemarketing Assn; Amer. [★2614]
Telemarketing and Electronic Commerce; Alliance Against Fraud in [17302]
Telemarketing Managers Assn. [★2619]

Telematica Transporti Sicurezza [★IO]
Telemedia Coun; Natl. [9766]
Telemedicine Assn; Amer. [16595]
Telemedicine; Coun. for Responsible [16596]
Telemedicine Ser. Providers; Assn. of [★15160]
Telemessaging Services Intl; Assn. of [★3735]
Telemetry
  Intl. Found. for Telemetering [7786]
  Intl. Found. for Telemetering [IO]
Teleministries U.S.A; CONTACT [★19865]
Teleministry, Inc; CONTACT [★19865]
Teleos Inst. [12364], 7119 E Shea Blvd., Ste. 109, PMB 418, Scottsdale, AZ 85254, (480)948-1800
Telephone Answering Exchanges; Assoc. [★3735]
Telephone Assn. of Am; Independent [★3965]
Telephone Assn; Natl. Independent [★3965]
Telephone Assn; U.S. [★3965]
Telephone Assn; U.S. Independent [★3965]
Telephone Collectors Intl. [22986], 3805 Spurr Cir., Brea, CA 92823, (801)849-6520
Telephone Collectors Intl. [IO], Brea, CA, United States
Telephone Companies; Assn. of Long Distance [★3955]
Telephone Companies; Org. for the Protection and Advancement of Small [★3964]
Telephone Credit Union Assn; Intl. [★1110]
Telephone Exchanges; Assoc. [★3735]
Telephone Ministries; Natl. Coun. for [★19865]
Telephone Museum - Address unknown since 1999.
Telephone Pioneers of Am. [★12203]
Telephone Service
  1-800 Amer. Free Trade Assn. [3950]
  Amer. Public Communications Coun. [3733]
  Assn. of Call Center Managers [2520]
  Broadband Services Forum [3737]
  Coalition to Keep Am. Connected [18724]
  Communications Supply Ser. Assn. [3954]
  CompTel/ALTS [3955]
  CONTACT USA [19865]
  CTIA - The Wireless Assn. [3741]
  Intl. Prepaid Communications Assn. [3767]
  Intl. Telecommunications Soc. [3749]
  Lesbian, Bisexual, Gay and Transgendered United Employees at AT&T [12242]
  Natl. Exchange Carrier Assn. [3960]
  Org. for the Promotion and Advancement of Small Telecommunications Companies [3964]
  Telecommunications Res. and Action Center [17195]
  TeleTruth: The Alliance for Customers' Telecommunications Rights [17346]
  U.S. Telecom Assn. [3965]
  VON Coalition [2321]
Telephone Systems; Natl. Assn. of Radio [★3752]
Telephones
  1-800 Amer. Free Trade Assn. [3950]
  Amer. Public Communications Coun. [3733]
  Amer. Teleservices Assn. [2614]
  Antique Telephone Collectors Assn. [22985]
  Assn. of TeleServices Intl. [3735]
  Coalition to Keep Am. Connected [18724]
  Communications Supply Ser. Assn. [3954]
  CONTACT USA [19865]
  CTIA - The Wireless Assn. [3741]
  Info. Technologies Credit Union Assn. [1110]
  Intl. Alliance of Avaya Users [3745]
  Intl. Telecommunications Soc. [3749]
  Lesbian, Bisexual, Gay and Transgendered United Employees at AT&T [12242]
  Natl. Exchange Carrier Assn. [3960]
  Natl. Fraud Info. Center/Internet Fraud Watch [17339]
  Tel-Med [14601]
  Telephone Collectors Intl. [22986]
  Telephone Collectors Intl. [IO]
  U.S. Telecom Assn. [3965]
  VON Coalition [2321]
Telephony Forum; Enterprise Cmpt. [878]
Telephony; Museum of Independent [★22985]
Teleprofessional Managers Assn. [★2619]
Teleram Users Group - Defunct.
Telescope Soc; Antique [21526]
Teleservices Assn; Amer. [2614]
TeleTruth: The Alliance for Customers' Telecommunications Rights [17346], 568 Broadway, Ste. 404, New York, NY 10012, (800)870-1939

A star before a book entry number signifies that the name is not listed separately, but is mentioned within the entry.

Teletypewriters for the Deaf [★14780]
Television
Acad. of TV Arts and Sciences [542]
Advanced Media Workflow Assn. [3721]
Air, Sea, and Space Club [25023]
Alliance for Community Media [17161]
Alliance for Inclusion in the Arts [10996]
Alliance of Motion Picture and TV Producers [1375]
Amer. Bandstand Fan Club [25024]
Amer. Cable Assn. [779]
Amer. Cinema Editors [1376]
Amer. Family Assn. [17162]
Amer. Fed. of TV and Radio Artists [24022]
Amer. Lib. Assn. - Public Info. Off. [10897]
Amer. Psychological Assn. - Media Psychology Div. [16131]
Amer. Screenwriters Assn. [4060]
The Andy Griffith Show Rerun Watchers Club [25025]
Argentine TV and Radio Assn. [IO]
Asian TV Australia Assn. [IO]
Assoc. Press Broadcasters [546]
Assn. of America's Public TV Stations [547]
Assn. of Film Commissioners Intl. [1368]
Assn. of Independent Commercial Producers [90]
Assn. for Interactive Marketing [3734]
Audio Engg. Soc. [6909]
Barbara Eden's Official Fan Club [24731]
Betty White Fan Club [24732]
Black Awareness in TV [17164]
Blue-ray Disc Assn. [1207]
Boating Writers Intl. [3100]
British TV Shopping Assn. [IO]
Broadband Services Forum [3737]
Broadcast Cable Financial Mgt. Assn. [553]
Cabletelevision Advt. Bur. [95]
Catholic Acad. for Commun. Arts Professionals [9761]
Catweazle Fan Club [IO]
Caucus for TV Producers, Writers, and Directors [17165]
Children's Television Rsrc. and Educ. Center [11686]
Corp. for Public Broadcasting [9762]
CTAM - Cable and Telecommunications Assn. for Marketing [558]
Dark Shadows Official Fan Club [25026]
Dark Shadows Official Fan Club [IO]
David Birney Intl. Fan Club [24737]
Digital TV Gp. [IO]
Dr. Who Info. Network [IO]
Educational Broadcasting Corp. [9763]
Elvira Fan Club [24817]
Fed. Without TV [18725]
FilmAid Intl. [12811]
Flight Patrol Fan Club [25027]
Free Speech TV [18726]
Free TV Australia [IO]
F.U.G.I.T.I.V.E.S. [25028]
Galaxy Patrol Fan Club [25029]
Gale Storm Appreciation Soc. [24744]
Garden Writers Assn. [22512]
Gilligan's Island Fan Club [25030]
Guiding Light Fan Club [25031]
Hispanic Org. of Latin Actors [10001]
Hollywood Foreign Press Assn. [3115]
Hollywood Radio and TV Soc. [559]
Howdy Doody Memorabilia Collectors Club [22038]
Independent TV Assn. [IO]
Intl. Acad. of TV Arts and Sciences [560]
Intl. Assn. of Media Tie-in Writers [11176]
Intl. Assn. for Radio, Telecommunications and Electromagnetics [7773]
Intl. Radio and TV Soc. Found. [563]
Intl. Soc. of Certified Electronics Technicians [1220]
Jon-Erik Hexum Fan Club [24749]
Junior Hollywood Radio and TV Soc. [564]
Klingon Strike Force [25015]
The Lambs [11019]
Laura Hendler Fan Club [24751]
Linda Gray's Official Fan Club [24753]
Lindsay Wagner's Official Fan Club [24754]

Location Managers Guild of Am. [2522]
Lone Ranger Fan Club [25032]
Lost in Space Fannish Alliance [25033]
Magic of Bewitched Fan Club [25034]
Magnum Memorabilia [25035]
Magnum Memorabilia [IO]
Man from U.N.C.L.E. Fan Club [25036]
Mark Slade Fan Club [24758]
Media Access Proj. [17182]
Media Action Network for Asian Americans [18029]
Media Communications Assn. Intl. [1388]
Media Fellowship Intl. [20024]
Michael Crawford Intl. Fan Assn. [24760]
Michele Lee Fan Club/Michele Lee Online [24761]
Motion Picture and TV Fund [12115]
Natl. Acad. of TV Arts and Sciences [567]
Natl. Assn. of Black Journalists [3129]
Natl. Assn. of Black Owned Broadcasters [568]
Natl. Assn. Broadcast Employees and Technicians - Communications Workers of Am. [24024]
Natl. Assn. of Broadcasters [569]
Natl. Assn. of Farm Broadcasting [570]
Natl. Assn. of Latino Independent Producers [1390]
Natl. Assn. of Public Affairs Networks [17026]
Natl. Assn. of TV Prog. Executives [571]
Natl. Black Programming Consortium [9764]
Natl. Black Public Relations Soc. [3194]
Natl. Broadcast Assn. for Community Affairs [572]
Natl. Cable and Telecommunications Assn. [573]
Natl. Cable TV Inst. [574]
Natl. Center for Film and Video Preservation [9942]
Natl. Conf. of Editorial Writers [3136]
Natl. Press Club [3141]
New Jetsons Fan Club [25037]
Newswomen's Club of New York [3150]
Official Gilligan's Island Fan Club [25038]
Official Red Dwarf Fan Club [25039]
Official Robert Newman Fan Club [24765]
Oh Ji Ho Intl. Fan Club [24781]
Once Upon A Time (The Prisoner Fan Club) [25040]
Org. of Black Screenwriters [1323]
Outdoor Writers Assn. of Am. [3153]
Pacific Islanders in Communications [10455]
Peter Breck Fan Club [24766]
PlanetRead [8796]
Popular Culture Assn. [10888]
PROMAX [577]
Public Broadcasting Ser. [9768]
Radio-Television Correspondents Assn. [580]
Radio and TV Fed. [IO]
Radio-Television News Directors Assn. [581]
Radio and TV Res. Coun. [7784]
Richard Burgi Fan Club [24768]
Rin Tin Tin Fan Club [25041]
Screen Production and Development Assn. of New Zealand [IO]
Sesame Workshop [9782]
Set Decorators Soc. of Am. [2276]
S.H.A.D.O. - USECC [25042]
Six of One Club: The Prisoner Appreciation Soc. [25043]
Soc. for the Eradication of TV [17193]
Soc. of Motion Picture and TV Engineers [7044]
Star Trek: The Official Fan Club [25016]
STARFLEET [25017]
Starfleet Command [25018]
Stop the Violence, Face The Music [13376]
Syndicated Network TV Assn. [120]
Telecommunications Res. and Action Center [17195]
TV Audience Screen Extras Guild [55]
TV Bur. of Advt. [121]
TV Operators Caucus [583]
Traffic Directors Guild of Am. [584]
Trekville U.S.A./International [25019]
U.N.C.L.E. HQ [25044]
United Fed. of Planets, Intl. [25020]
United Nations Correspondents Assn. [3168]
United Network Command [25045]
United Network Command [IO]
U.S. Marine Corps Combat Correspondents Assn. [3171]

We Love Lucy/International Lucille Ball Fan Club [24776]
White House Correspondents' Assn. [3173]
Women in Cable Telecommunications [585]
The World of Dark Shadows [25046]
Writers Guild of Am., East [24220]
Writers Guild of Am., West [24221]
Young and the Restless Fan Club [25047]
TV Accessory Mfrs. Inst. - Defunct.
TV Action Comm. for Today and Tomorrow [★9766]
TV Admin. and Marketing Soc; Cable [★558]
Television Advt. Bur; Cable [95]
TV; Agency for Instructional [★8549]
TV Alliance; Independent Film and [1382]
TV Allocations Study Org. - Defunct.
TV; Amer. Women in Radio and [545]
TV Archives Advisory Comm; Film and [★9932]
TV Arts and Sciences; Acad. of [542]
TV Arts and Sciences; Hollywood Chap. of Natl. Acad. of [★542]
TV Arts and Sciences; Natl. Acad. of [567]
Television Assn; Assoc. Press Radio- [546]
TV Assn; Interactive [★3734]
TV Assn; Intl. [★1388]
TV; Assn. for Maximum Ser. [549]
TV Assn; Natl. Cable [★573]
TV Assn; Natl. Community [★573]
TV Assn; Natl. Indus. [★1388]
TV Audience Screen Extras Guild [55], Guild Penthouse, LaFong Tower, 8311 54th Ave. S, Seattle, WA 98118-4702, (206)725-0873
TV; Black Awareness in [17164]
TV Broadcasters Assn. [★569]
TV Broadcasters; Natl. Assn. of Radio and [★569]
TV Bur. of Advt. [121], 3 E 54th St., 10th Fl., New York, NY 10022-3108, (212)486-1111
TV Commn; Protestant Radio and [★19537]
TV Cooperative; Natl. Cable [781]
Television Correspondents Assn; Radio- [580]
TV Credit Assn; Motion Picture and [1434]
TV Credit Managers Assn; Motion Picture and [★1434]
TV Critics Assn. - Defunct.
TV Directors Guild; Radio and [★24055]
TV and Electronic Servicers of Am; Natl. Assn. of [★1224]
TV Engineers; Soc. of Cable [★7040]
TV Engineers; Soc. of Motion Picture and [7044]
TV Executive Soc; Radio and [★563]
TV Fund; Motion Picture and [12115]
TV Guild; Veterans Hosp. Radio and [★12116]
TV Indus. Assn; Satellite [★3754]
TV Information Office - Defunct.
TV Inst; Natl. Cable [574]
TV Journalists; Natl. Acad. of [3128]
TV Labs; Cable [780]
TV Lib; Natl. Instructional [★8549]
TV Licensing Center - Defunct.
TV Manufacturers Assn; Radio [★1212]
TV Manufacturers Assn; Radio Electronics [★1212]
TV Mission; Christian [19536]
TV; Natl. Coun. for Children and [★17186]
TV; Natl. Coun. for Families and [17186]
TV; Natl. Educational [★9763]
Television News Directors Assn; Radio- [581]
TV Operators Caucus [583], c/o Mary Jo Manning, Coor., 1776 K St. NW, Washington, DC 20006, (202)719-7090
TV Producers; Alliance of Motion Picture and [1375]
TV Prog. Executives; Natl. Assn. of [571]
TV Program Export Assn. - Address unknown since 1995.
TV Public Affairs Assn; Cable [★5556]
TV and Radio Artists; Amer. Fed. of [24022]
Television-Radio Farm Directors; Natl. Assn. of [★570]
TV Recording Artists; Amer. Fed. of [★17981]
TV Res. Coun; Radio and [7784]
Television Rsrc. and Educ. Center; Children's [11686]
TV Soc; Amer. [★563]
TV; Soc. for the Eradication of [17193]
TV Soc. Found; Intl. Radio and [563]
TV Soc; Hollywood Radio and [559]
TV Soc; Indus. [★1388]

Reference to "IO" in place of a book number signifies that the association may be found in the 45th edition of International Organizations.

TV Soc; Intl. Radio and [★563]
TV Stations; Assn. of America's Public [547]
TV Stations; Natl. Assn. of Public [★547]
TV Unions; New York Coun. of Motion Picture and [24056]
TV Workshop; Children's [★9782]
Telework Assn. [IO], Warwick, United Kingdom
Telework Assn; Telecommuting Advisory Council/ International [★3750]
Telework New Zealand [IO], Waitakere, New Zealand
Teligen [IO], Brentford, United Kingdom
Telluride Assn. [8310], 217 West Ave., Ithaca, NY 14850, (607)273-5011
Telluride Institute [★8310]
Telocator Network of Am. [★3752]
Telocator Network of Am. [★IO]
Telocator, The Personal Communications Indus. [★IO]
Telocator, The Personal Communications Indus. [★3752]
Telophase Soc. [2792], c/o Stewart Enterprises, Inc., 1333 S Clearview Pkwy., Jefferson, LA 70121, (619)299-0805
Telugu Assn; Amer. [9848]
Temas Atuais na Promocao da Saude [IO], Florianopolis, Brazil
Tembeza Kenya [IO], Nairobi, Kenya
Temperance
Al-Anon Family Gp. HQ, World Ser. Off. [13214]
Alcoholics Anonymous World Services [13218]
Amer. Coun. on Alcohol Problems [13220]
Amer. Coun. on Alcoholism [13221]
Amer. Hea. and Temperance Assn. [13303]
Assn. of Halfway House Alcoholism Programs of North Am. [13224]
BACCHUS Network [13226]
Children of Alcoholics Found. [13228]
Finnish White Ribbon Union [IO]
Friendly Hand Found. [13243]
Hazelden Found. [13244]
Inter-Association Task Force on Alcohol and Other Substance Abuse Issues [13250]
Intl. Commn. for the Prevention of Alcoholism and Drug Dependency [13251]
Intl. Doctors in Alcoholics Anonymous [13252]
Intl. Hea. and Temperance Assn. [13304]
Intl. Hea. and Temperance Assn. [IO]
Natl. Assn. for Children of Alcoholics [13261]
Natl. Assn. of Lesbian/Gay Addiction Professionals [13263]
Natl. Catholic Coun. on Alcoholism and Related Drug Problems [13266]
Natl. Comm. for the Prevention of Alcoholism and Drug Dependency [13267]
Natl. Coun. on Alcoholism and Drug Dependence [13268]
Natl. Temperance and Prohibition Coun. [13305]
Natl. Woman's Christian Temperance Union [13306]
Nordic Alcohol and Drug Policy Network [IO]
Partisan Prohibition Historical Soc. [22103]
Temperance Assn; Swedish-Finnish Benevolent and Aid Assn. of Am. and Swedish-Finnish [★9952]
Temperance Coun; Youth [★13306]
Temperance Education Found. - Defunct.
Temperance League of Am. [★13220]
Temperance League; Natl. [★13220]
Temperance Legion; Loyal [★13306]
Temperance Soc; Amer. [★13303]
Temperance Soc; Amer. Hea. and [★13303]
Temperance and Tolerance Assn. of America - Defunct.
Temperature Calorimetry Conf; Low [★7796]
Tempering Assn; Glass [★1728]
Templars; Natl. Coun. of the U.S., Intl. Org. of Good [19081]
Templars; Natl. Grand Lodge, Intl. Order of Good [★19081]
Temple Administrators; Natl. Assn. of [20163]
Temple Brotherhoods; Natl. Fed. of [★20160]
Temple Brotherhoods; North Amer. Fed. of [★20160]
Temple Educators; Natl. Assn. of [20164]
Temple Hill Assn; Natl. [10050]
Temple Inst. [IO], Jerusalem, Israel

Temple of Man [20582]
Temple Musicians; Guild of [20431]
Temple de la Renomme et la Musee de Football Canadien [★IO]
Temple Sisterhoods; Natl. Fed. of [★20192]
Temple Sisterhoods; Women of Reform Judaism, The Fed. of [20192]
Temple of Understanding [20583], 211 E 43rd St., Ste. 1600, New York, NY 10017, (212)573-9224
Temple Youth; North Amer. Fed. of [19185]
Templeton Found; John [20501]
Templin Family Assn. [21069], c/o Marvin T. Templin, Genealogist, 107 County Rd. 60, Athens, TN 37303-6656
Temporal Bone Banks Prog. of The DRF; Natl. [★15121]
Temporal Bone, Hearing and Balance Pathology Rsrc. Registry; Natl. [★15121]
Temporal Bone, Hearing and Balance Pathology Rsrc. Registry; NIDCD - Natl. [15121]
Temporary Employees; Natl. Assn. of Part-Time and [1271]
Temporary Services; Inst. of [★1254]
Temporary Services; Natl. Assn. of [★1254]
Temporary and Staffing Services; Natl. Assn. of [★1254]
Ten-4 Intl. - Defunct.
Ten Class Assn. - Address unknown since 1991.
Tenant Assn. in Bergen [IO], Bergen, Norway
Tenant Farmers' Assn. [IO], Reading, United Kingdom
Tenant Participation Advisory Ser. [IO], Manchester, United Kingdom
Tenants Advice Ser. [IO], East Perth, Australia
Tenants Natl. Energy Assn. - Defunct.
Tenants Org. of Denmark [IO], Copenhagen, Denmark
Tenants Org. - Norway [IO], Oslo, Norway
Tenants and Residents Org. of England [IO], Huddersfield, United Kingdom
Tenants Union of Australia Capital Territory [IO], Civic Square, Australia
Tenants Union of New South Wales [IO], Surry Hills, Australia
Tenants' Union of Queensland [IO], Fortitude Valley, Australia
Tenants Union of Victoria [IO], Fitzroy, Australia
Tender Hearts [★12614]
Teniska Zveza Slovenije [★IO]
Tennessee Assn. of Economics Educators - Defunct.
Tennessee, CSA and U.S.A; Armies of [20722]
Tennessee Fainting Goat Assn; Amer. [4781]
Tennessee Folklore Soc. [9964], PO Box 201, Middle Tennessee State Univ., Murfreesboro, TN 37132, (615)898-2573
Tennessee Regulatory Authority [6341], 460 James Robertson Pkwy., Nashville, TN 37243-0505, (615)741-4648
Tennessee Walking Horse Breeders' Assn. of Am. [★4959]
Tennessee Walking Horse Breeders' Assn. of Am. [★IO]
Tennessee Walking Horse Breeders' and Exhibitors' Association [IO], Lewisburg, TN, United States
Tennessee Walking Horse Breeders' and Exhibitors' Assn. [4959], PO Box 286, Lewisburg, TN 37091, (931)359-1574
Tennis
Afghanistan Tennis Fed. [IO]
Albanian Tennis Fed. [IO]
All India Tennis Assn. [IO]
All Nepal Tennis Assn. [IO]
Amer. Medical Tennis Assn. [23898]
Amer. Platform Tennis Assn. [23899]
Amer. Recreational Racket Sports Assn. [3637]
Amer. Sports Builders Assn. [1002]
Amer. Tennis Assn. [23900]
Antigua and Barbuda Tennis Assn. [IO]
Armenian Tennis Fed. [IO]
Aruba Lawn Tennis Bond [IO]
Asian Tennis Fed. [IO]
Asociacion Argentina de Tenis [IO]
Asociacion Paraguaya de Tenis [IO]
Asociacion Uruguaya de Tenis [IO]
Azerbaijan Tennis Fed. [IO]

Bahamas Lawn Tennis Assn. [IO]
Bahrain Tennis Fed. [IO]
Bangladesh Tennis Fed. [IO]
Barbados Tennis Assn. [IO]
Belarus Tennis Assn. [IO]
Belize Tennis Assn. [IO]
Bermuda Lawn Tennis Assn. [IO]
Bhutan Tennis Fed. [IO]
Botswana Tennis Assn. [IO]
British Virgin Islands Lawn Tennis Assn. [IO]
Brunei Darussalam Tennis Assn. [IO]
Bulgarian Tennis Fed. [IO]
Cambodia Tennis Fed. [IO]
Chinese Taipei Tennis Assn. [IO]
Confederacao Brasileira de Tenis [IO]
Confederacion Sudamericana de Tenis [IO]
Confed. of African Tennis [IO]
COTECC [IO]
Croatian Tennis Assn. [IO]
Cyprus Tennis Fed. [IO]
Czech Tenisova Asociace [IO]
Dansk Tennis Forbund [IO]
Deutscher Tennis Bund [IO]
Dominica Lawn Tennis Assn. [IO]
Equatorial Guinea Tennis Fed. [IO]
Eritrean Tennis Fed. [IO]
Estonian Tennis Assn. [IO]
Ethiopian Tennis Fed. [IO]
European Tennis Fed. - Tennis Europe [IO]
Fed Andorrana de Tennis St. Antoni [IO]
Federacao Angolana de Tenis [IO]
Federacao Cabo Verdiana de Tenis [IO]
Federacao Mocambicana de Tenis [IO]
Federacao Portuguesa de Tenis [IO]
Federacion Boliviana De Tenis [IO]
Federacion Colombiana de Tenis [IO]
Federacion Costarricense de Tenis [IO]
Federacion Cubana de Tenis De Ocampo [IO]
Federacion Dominicana de Tenis [IO]
Federacion Ecuatoriana de Tenis [IO]
Federacion Hondurena de Tenis [IO]
Federacion Mexicana de Tenis [IO]
Federacion Nicaraguense de Tenis [IO]
Federacion Panamena de Tenis [IO]
Federacion Salvadorena de Tenis [IO]
Federacion de Tenis de Chile [IO]
Federacion de Tenis de Peru [IO]
Federacion Venezolana de Tenis [IO]
Federated States of Micronesia Lawn Tennis Assn. [IO]
Federatia Romana de Tennis [IO]
Fed. Beninoise de Lawn Tennis [IO]
Fed. Burkinabe De Tennis [IO]
Fed. Camerounaise de Tennis [IO]
Fed. Centrafricaine de Tennis [IO]
Fed. Congolaise Democratique de Lawn Tennis [IO]
Fed. Congolaise de Lawn Tennis [IO]
Fed. Djiboutienne de Tennis [IO]
Fed. Francaise de Tennis [IO]
Fed. Gabonaise de Tennis [IO]
Fed. Haitienne de Tennis [IO]
Fed. Ivoirienne de Tennis [IO]
Fed. Libanaise de Tennis [IO]
Fed. Luxembourgeoise de Tennis [IO]
Fed. Malgache de Tennis [IO]
Fed. Malienne de Tennis [IO]
Fed. Mauritanienne de Tennis [IO]
Fed. Nigerienne de Tennis [IO]
Fed. Royale Marocaine de Tennis [IO]
Fed. Rwandaise de Tennis [IO]
Fed. Senegalaise de Tennis [IO]
Fed. de Tennis du Burundi [IO]
Fed. de Tennis de la Guinee-Bissau [IO]
Fed. de Tennis de Vanuatu [IO]
Federazione Italiana Tennis [IO]
Fiji Tennis Assn. [IO]
Finnish Tennis Assn. [IO]
Gambia Lawn Tennis Assn. [IO]
Gay and Lesbian Tennis Alliance [IO]
Gay and Lesbian Tennis Alliance [23901]
Georgian Tennis Fed. [IO]
Ghana Tennis Assn. [IO]
Grenada Tennis Assn. [IO]
Guyana Lawn Tennis Assn. [IO]

A star before a book entry number signifies that the name is not listed separately, but is mentioned within the entry.

Hellenic Tennis Fed. [IO]
Hong Kong Tennis Assn. [IO]
Icelandic Tennis Assn. [IO]
Indonesian Tennis Assn. [IO]
Intercollegiate Tennis Assn. [23902]
Intl. Tennis Fed. [IO]
Intl. Tennis Hall of Fame [IO]
Intl. Tennis Hall of Fame [23903]
Iraqi Tennis Fed. [IO]
Israel Tennis Assn. [IO]
Jordan Tennis Fed. [IO]
Kazakhstan Tennis Fed. [IO]
Kenya Lawn Tennis Assn. [IO]
Kiribati Tennis Assn. [IO]
Koninklijke Nederlandse Lawn Tennis Bond [IO]
Korea Tennis Assn. [IO]
Korean Amer. Professional Tennis Assn. [23904]
Kuwait Tennis Fed. [IO]
Kyrgyzstan Tennis Fed. [IO]
Lao Tennis Fed. [IO]
Latvian Tennis Union [IO]
Lawn Tennis Assn. [IO]
Lawn Tennis Assn. of Malawi [IO]
Lawn Tennis Assn. of Thailand [IO]
Lesotho Lawn Tennis Assn. [IO]
Liberia Tennis Fed. [IO]
Libyan Arab Tennis and Squash Fed. [IO]
Liechtensteiner Tennisverband [IO]
Lithuanian Tennis Assn. [IO]
Macedonian Tennis Fed. [IO]
Magyar Tenisz Szovetseg [IO]
Major Wingfield Historical Soc. [23905]
Malta Tennis Fed. [IO]
Marshall Islands Tennis Fed. [IO]
Mauritius Tennis Fed. [IO]
Moldova Republic Tennis Fed. [IO]
Monegasque Tennis Fed. [IO]
Mongolian Tennis Assn. [IO]
Namibia Tennis Assn. [IO]
Natl. Collegiate Table Tennis Assn. [23895]
Natl. Paddleball Assn. [23092]
Natl. Public Parks Tennis Assn. [23906]
Natl. Senior Women's Tennis Assn. [23907]
Natl. Tennis Fed. of Republic of Tajikistan [IO]
Nauru Tennis Assn. [IO]
Netherlands Antilles Tennis Fed. [IO]
Nigeria Tennis Fed. [IO]
Northern Mariana Islands Tennis Assn. [IO]
Norwegian Tennis Assn. [IO]
Oceania Tennis Fed. [IO]
Oman Tennis Assn. [IO]
Osterreichischer Tennisverband [IO]
Pakistan Tennis Fed. [IO]
Palau Tennis Fed. [IO]
Palestinian Tennis Assn. [IO]
Papua New Guinea Lawn Tennis Assn. [IO]
Peter Burwash Intl. Special Tennis Programs [IO]
Peter Burwash Intl. Special Tennis Programs
   [23908]
Philippine Tennis Assn. [IO]
Professional Tennis Registry [23909]
Qatar Tennis Fed. [IO]
Real Federacion Espanola de Tenis [IO]
Royal Belgian Tennis Fed. [IO]
St. Kitts Lawn Tennis Assn. [IO]
St. Lucia Lawn Tennis Assn. [IO]
St. Vincent and The Grenadines Lawn Tennis
   Assn. [IO]
San Marino Tennis Fed. [IO]
Saudi Arabian Tennis Fed. [IO]
Serbia and Montenegro Tennis Fed. [IO]
Seychelles Tennis Assn. [IO]
Sierra Leone Lawn Tennis Assn. [IO]
Slovak Tennis Assn. [IO]
Slovene Tennis Assn. [IO]
Solomon Islands Tennis Assn. [IO]
Sony Ericsson WTA Tour [IO]
Sony Ericsson WTA Tour [23910]
South African Tennis Assn. [IO]
Sri Lanka Tennis Assn. [IO]
Sudan Lawn Tennis Assn. [IO]
Surinaamse Tennisbond [IO]
Swaziland Natl. Tennis Union [IO]
Swedish Tennis Assn. [IO]
Swiss Tennis [IO]

Syrian Arab Tennis Fed. [IO]
Tanzania Lawn Tennis Assn. [IO]
Tennis Assn. of Austria [IO]
Tennis Assn. of Bosnia and Herzegovina [IO]
Tennis Assn. of Democratic People's Republic of
   Korea [IO]
Tennis Assn. of the Maldives [IO]
Tennis Assn. of Trinidad and Tobago [IO]
Tennis Canada [IO]
Tennis Cook Islands [IO]
Tennis Fed. of the Cayman Islands [IO]
Tennis Fed. of Islamic Republic of Iran [IO]
Tennis Fed. of Myanmar [IO]
Tennis Indus. Assn. [3653]
Tennis Ireland [IO]
Tennis Jamaica [IO]
Tennis Samoa [IO]
Tennis Scotland [IO]
Tennis Wales [IO]
Tennis Zimbabwe [IO]
Tonga Tennis Assn. [IO]
Turkish Tennis Fed. [IO]
Turkmenistan Tennis Assn. [IO]
Turks and Caicos Tennis Assn. [IO]
Tuvalu Tennis Assn. [IO]
Uganda Tennis Assn. [IO]
Ukrainian Tennis Fed. [IO]
United Arab Emirates Tennis Assn. [IO]
U.S. Dental Tennis Assn. [23911]
U.S. High School Tennis Assn. [23912]
U.S. Natl. Tennis Acad. [23913]
U.S. Professional Tennis Assn. [23914]
U.S. Professional Tennis Assn. [IO]
U.S. Tennis Assn. [23915]
USA Tennis - NJTL [23916]
Uzbekistan Tennis Fed. [IO]
Vietnam Tennis Fed. [IO]
WTA Tour Players Assn. [23917]
Yemen Tennis Fed. [IO]
Zambia Lawn Tennis Assn. [IO]
Tennis Acad; Natl. [★23913]
Tennis Acad; U.S. Natl. [23913]
Tennis Assn; Amer. Platform [23899]
Tennis Assn. of Austria [IO], Vosendorf, Austria
Tennis Assn. of Bosnia and Herzegovina [IO], Sara-
   jevo, Boshia-Hercegovina
Tennis Assn. of Democratic People's Republic of
   Korea [IO], Pyongyang, Democratic People's
   Republic of Korea
Tennis Assn; Indoor [★3021]
Tennis Assn. of the Maldives [IO], Male, Maldives
Tennis Assn; Natl. [★3021]
Tennis Assn; Natl. Indoor [★3021]
Tennis Assn; Natl. Senior Women's [23907]
Tennis Assn. of Trinidad and Tobago [IO], Port of
   Spain, Trinidad and Tobago
Tennis Assn; U.S. Lawn [★23915]
Tennis Assn. of U.S; Professional Lawn [★23914]
Tennis Assn; U.S. Professional Lawn [★23914]
Tennis Assn; U.S. Table [★23896]
Tennis Assn; Women's [★23917]
Tennis Assn; Women's Intl. [★23917]
Tennis Canada [IO], Toronto, ON, Canada
Tennis Coaches Assn; Natl. Collegiate [★23902]
Tennis Cook Islands [IO], Rarotonga, Cook Islands
Tennis Coun; Women's [★23910]
Tennis Coun; Women's Intl. Professional [★23910]
Tennis Educational Found. [★23903]
Tennis Educational Found. [★IO]
Tennis Educational Found; Natl. [★23903]
Tennis Fed. of the Cayman Islands [IO], George
   Town, Cayman Islands
Tennis Fed. of Islamic Republic of Iran [IO], Tehran,
   Iran
Tennis Fed. of Myanmar [IO], Yangon, Myanmar
Tennis Found. and Hall of Fame; Natl. [★23903]
Tennis Found. of North Am. [★3653]
Tennis Indus. Assn. [3653], 117 Executive Ctr., Hil-
   ton Head Island, SC 29928, (843)686-3036
Tennis Indus. Fed; Amer. [★3653]
Tennis Ireland [IO], Dublin, Ireland
Tennis Jamaica [IO], Kingston, Jamaica
Tennis League; USTA/National Junior [★23916]
Tennis Manufacturers Assn. [★3653]
Tennis Registry; U.S. Professional [★23909]

Tennis Registry - U.S.A; Professional [★23909]
Tennis Samoa [IO], Apia, Western Samoa
Tennis Scotland [IO], Edinburgh, United Kingdom
Tennis; U.S.A. Table [23896]
Tennis Wales [IO], Cardiff, United Kingdom
Tennis Zimbabwe [IO], Harare, Zimbabwe
Tennissamband Island [★IO]
Tennyson Soc. [IO], Lincoln, United Kingdom
Tenovus Scotland [IO], Glasgow, United Kingdom
Tension Centre; Relax [★10179]
Tensioning Inst; Post- [663]
Teollisuustaiteen Liitto Ornamo [★IO]
Teratology Info. Services; Org. of [13758]
Teratology Societies; Intl. Fed. of [IO]
Teratology Soc. [6602], 1821 Michael Faraday Dr.,
   Ste. 300, Reston, VA 20190, (703)438-3104
Teratology Soc; Neurobehavioral [15356]
Teresa Brewer Fan Club - Address unknown since
   1999.
Teresian Inst. - Address unknown since 2004.
Terlingua Intl. Chili Championship [22574], c/o Alan
   Dean, Exec. Dir., 112 Leaning Oak Cir., Johnson
   City, TX 78636, (512)567-2835
Terlingua Intl. Chili Championship [IO], Johnson City,
   TX, United States
Term Limits Found; U.S. [18316]
Terman Soc; Lewis M. [9985]
Terminal Elevator Grain Assn. [★1753]
Terminal Grain - Defunct.
Terminal Operators Assn; Independent [2929]
Terminal Railroad Assn. Historical and Tech. Soc.
   [10925], c/o Larry Thomas, Sec.-Treas./Ed., PO
   Box 1688, St. Louis, MO 63188-1688, (314)535-
   3101
Terminally Ill
   ALSAC/Saint Jude Children's Res. Hosp. [13946]
   Amer. Assn. of Critical-Care Nurses [15433]
   Amer. Inst. of Life Threatening Illness and Loss
      (Division of Found. of Thanatology) [11908]
   Assistance Dogs of Am., Inc. [11922]
   Assn. of Oncology Social Work [13199]
   Believe In Tomorrow Natl. Children's Found.
      [11674]
   Children's Wish Found. Intl. [11687]
   Compassion in Dying Fed. [12130]
   Cystic Fibrosis Found. [16358]
   Dream Catchers, USA [11943]
   Dream Factory [11691]
   End-of-Life Choices [12131]
   Euthanasia Res. and Guidance Org. [12132]
   Famous Fone Friends [11692]
   Fed. for Children with Special Needs [12569]
   Friends of Karen [11694]
   Hospice Educ. Inst. [14854]
   Hospice and Palliative Nurses Assn. [15482]
   Living/Dying Proj. [13316]
   Make-A-Wish Found. of Am. [11707]
   Natl. Alliance of Senior Citizens [11299]
   Natl. Assn. for Home Care and Hospice [14840]
   Natl. Hospice and Palliative Care Org. [14856]
   Natl. Inst. for Jewish Hospice [14857]
   Natl. Prison Hospice Assn. [14858]
   Natl. Reye's Syndrome Found. [16366]
   Sacred Dying Found. [11910]
   Soc. of Critical Care Medicine [14071]
   A Special Wish Found. [11723]
   Starlight Starbright Children's Found. [11724]
   Sunshine Found. [11726]
   William Wendt Center for Loss and Healing
      [13317]
   World Homecare and Hospice Org. [14844]
Terminals Assn; Independent Liquid [3977]
Terminals; Inland Rivers Ports and [2604]
Terra Cotta; Friends of [10029]
Terra Soc. - Address unknown since 1995.
TERRAP [★12748]
TERRAP Programs [12748], c/o LaFrance and As-
   sociates Counseling Services, PO Box 19, Her-
   shey, PA 17033, (717)832-3347
Terraplane Historical Soc; Hudson Essex [21660]
Terrarium Assn. [22548]
Terrazzo, Finishers, Shopworkers, and Granite Cut-
   ters Intl. Union; Tile, Marble, [★24032]
Terrazzo, Marble Contractors and Affiliates; Assn. of
   Tile, [★1053]

Reference to "IO" in place of a book number signifies that the association may be found in the 45th edition of International Organizations.

Terrazzo and Mosaic Assn; Natl. [1052]
Terrazzo Tile and Marble Assn. of Canada [IO], Concord, ON, Canada
terre des homes Deutschland e.V. [★IO]
Terre des Femmes [★IO]
Terre des Hommes [IO], Basel, Switzerland
Terre des Hommes Germany [IO], Osnabruck, Germany
Terre des Hommes Germany - Cambodia [IO], Phnom Penh, Cambodia
Terre des Hommes Germany - India [IO], Pune, India
Terre des Hommes Germany - Indonesia [IO], Jakarta, Indonesia
Terre des Hommes Germany - Philippines [IO], Davao City, Philippines
Terre des Hommes Germany - Southeast Asia [IO], Bangkok, Thailand
Terre des Hommes Germany - Vietnam [IO], Ho Chi Minh City, Vietnam
Terre des Hommes Germany - Zimbabwe and Zambia [IO], Harare, Zimbabwe
Terrestrial Physics; Inter-Union Commn. on Solar [★7508]
Terri Clark Fan Club [24981], c/o Spalding Entertainment, 1025 16th Ave. S, Ste. 303, Nashville, TN 37212
Terri Gibbs Fan Club - Address unknown since 1995.
Terri LaVelle Fan Club - Address unknown since 1995.
Terrier Assn. of Am; Jack Russell [★22337]
Terrier Assn. of Am; Parson Russell [22337]
Terrier Assn; Natl. Amer. Pit Bull [22311]
Terrier Assn; Natl. Toy Fox [22321]
Terrier Club of Am; Airedale [22180]
Terrier Club of Am; Australian [22223]
Terrier Club of Am; Border [22234]
Terrier Club of Am; Boston [22236]
Terrier Club of Am; Bull [22237]
Terrier Club of Am; Cairn [22238]
Terrier Club of Am; Dandie Dinmont [22255]
Terrier Club of Am; Irish [22293]
Terrier Club of Am; Jack Russell [22297]
Terrier Club of Am; Miniature Bull [22307]
Terrier Club of Am. Rescue Ser; Welsh [★22389]
Terrier Club of Am; Scottish [22357]
Terrier Club of Am; Silky [22360]
Terrier Club of Am; Skye [22361]
Terrier Club of Am; Staffordshire [22364]
Terrier Club of Am; Tibetan [22367]
Terrier Club of Am; West Highland White [22381]
Terrier Club of Am; Yorkshire [22390]
Terrier Club; Amer. Fox [22200]
Terrier Club; Amer. Manchester [22204]
Terrier Club; Amer. Sealyham [22209]
Terrier Club; Amer. Toy Fox [22214]
Terrier Club; Amer. Toy Manchester [★22204]
Terrier Club; Norwich [★22333]
Terrier Club; Norwich and Norfolk [22333]
Terrier Club; U.S. Kerry Blue [22374]
Terrier Club; U.S. Lakeland [22375]
Terrier Welfare; North Amer. Border [12019]
Terriers; Amer. Assn. of Black Russian [22185]
Terris Humane Educ. Center; Norma [★11433]
Territorial AIDS Directors; Natl. Alliance of State and [16967]
Territorial Air Pollution Prog. Administrators and Assn. of Local Air Pollution Control Officials; State and [★5696]
Territorial Apprehensiveness [★12748]
Territorial Dental Directors; Assn. of State and [14146]
Territorial Directors of Hea. Promotion and Public Hea. Educ; Assn. of State and [★6215]
Territorial Directors of Public Hea. Educ; Assn. of State and [★6215]
Territorial Epidemiologists; Conf. of State and [★14374]
Territorial Epidemiologists; Coun. of State and [14374]
Territorial Hea. Officials; Assn. of State and [6212]
Territorial Solid Waste Mgt. Officials; Assn. of State and [6353]
Territory Alliance; Northwest [9374]
Territory, Canadian and French Heritage Center; Northwest [★20720]

Territory of Ely-Chatelaine; Free [18351]
Terror Free Tomorrow [18736], 5335 Wisconsin Ave. NW, Ste. 440, Washington, DC 20015-2052, (202)274-1800
Terror Free Tomorrow [IO], Washington, DC, United States
Terrorism
    9/11 CitizensWatch [18727]
    9/11 Families for a Secure Am. [18728]
    All4Israel [12454]
    Amer. Friends of ALYN Hosp. [12825]
    Americans United for Israel [19157]
    Anti-Repression Rsrc. Team [17093]
    Coalition of 9/11 Families [13307]
    Families of September 11 [18729]
    Free Muslims Coalition [18084]
    Hearts and Minds Network [18730]
    Homefront Hugs USA [13352]
    Inst. for Counter-Terrorism [IO]
    Inst. for Regional and Intl. Stud. [17047]
    Inst. for Victims of Trauma [13362]
    Intl. Assn. for Counterterrorism and Security Professionals [18731]
    International Association for Counterterrorism and Security Professionals [IO]
    International Counter-Terrorism Officers Association [IO]
    Intl. Counter-Terrorism Officers Assn. [18732]
    Intl. Found. for Terror Act Victims [12942]
    Lifeboat Found. [18668]
    Move Am. Forward [18733]
    My Good Deed [13308]
    Natl. Legal Sanctuary for Community Advancement [6015]
    Natl. Memorial Inst. for the Prevention of Terrorism [18734]
    Natl. Safe Skies Alliance [18748]
    Natl. Safe Waterways and Seaports Alliance [18749]
    Natl. Youth and Student Peace Coalition [18226]
    No Greater Love [13370]
    Our Voices Together [13309]
    Patriots for the Defense of Am. [18186]
    Pups for Peace [12700]
    Russian Amer. Jews for Israel [18576]
    September 11 Digital Archv. [18735]
    September 11th Families' Assn. [13371]
    September Eleventh Families for Peaceful Tomorrows [12701]
    September's Mission [13310]
    Terror Free Tomorrow [18736]
    Terror Free Tomorrow [IO]
    Tuesday's Children [12003]
    U.S. Contract Security Assn. [3543]
    Voices of September 11th [18737]
    Win Without War [18124]
    World Trade Center Survivors' Network [13311]
    WTC Families For Proper Burial [13312]
Terry Fox Found. [IO], Chilliwack, BC, Canada
Terry and the Pirates Fan Club - Defunct.
Tertiary Capuchins of Our Lady of Sorrows [IO], Rome, Italy
Tesla Coil Builders Assn. - Defunct.
Tesla Engine Builders Assn. [679], 5464 N Port Washington Rd., No. 293, Milwaukee, WI 53217-4925
Tesla Memorial Soc. [11151], c/o William H. Terbo, Exec. Sec., Southwyck Village, 21 Maddaket, Scotch Plains, NJ 07076-3136, (732)396-8852
Tesla Memorial Soc. [IO], Scotch Plains, NJ, United States
Tesla Soc. - Defunct.
Test Boring Assn. - Address unknown since 2001.
Test Engineers; Soc. of Flight [6385]
Test; Fair [★9255]
Test Pilots; Soc. of Experimental [6384]
Test Publishers; Assn. of [3210]
Test Res. Service - Defunct.
Test, Res., and Training Reactors; Natl. Org. of [7388]
Testing
    ACT [9246]
    Amer. Soc. for Nondestructive Testing [7787]
    Amer. Soc. of Test Engineers [7788]
    Amer. Soc. for Testing and Materials [7789]

    Argentine Assn. of Non-Destructive and Structural Evaluation [IO]
    Assn. for Assessment in Counseling and Educ. [9247]
    Assn. for Software Testing [6763]
    British Inst. of Non-Destructive Testing [IO]
    Canadian Evaluation Soc. [IO]
    Canadian Inst. for NDE [IO]
    Canadian Testing Assn. [IO]
    Caribbean Examinations Coun. [IO]
    The Coll. Bd. [9248]
    Controlled Env. Testing Assn. [7790]
    Drug and Alcohol Testing Indus. Assn. [13236]
    Educational Records Bur. [9249]
    Educational Records Bur. [IO]
    Educational Testing Ser. [9250]
    German Soc. for Non-Destructive Testing [IO]
    Graduate Record Examinations Bd. [9251]
    Intl. Soc. for Performance Improvement [9252]
    Intl. Soc. for Performance Improvement [IO]
    Intl. Soc. for Performance Improvement - Arabia [IO]
    Intl. Soc. for Performance Improvement - Argentina [IO]
    Intl. Soc. for Performance Improvement - Cameroon [IO]
    Intl. Soc. for Performance Improvement - Europe [IO]
    Intl. Soc. for Performance Improvement - India [IO]
    Intl. Soc. for Performance Improvement - Israel [IO]
    Intl. Soc. for Performance Improvement - Italy [IO]
    Intl. Soc. for Performance Improvement - Japan [IO]
    Intl. Soc. for Performance Improvement - Kurachi, Pakistan [IO]
    Intl. Soc. for Performance Improvement - Melbourne [IO]
    Intl. Soc. for Performance Improvement - Mexico [IO]
    Intl. Soc. for Performance Improvement - Montreal [IO]
    Intl. Soc. for Performance Improvement - Nigeria [IO]
    Intl. Soc. for Performance Improvement - South Africa [IO]
    Intl. Soc. for Performance Improvement - Sydney [IO]
    Intl. Soc. for Performance Improvement - United Kingdom [IO]
    Intl. Soc. for Performance Improvement - Vancouver [IO]
    Intl. Test and Evaluation Assn. [IO]
    Intl. Test and Evaluation Assn. [7791]
    Natl. Assessment of Educational Progress [9253]
    Natl. Assn. for Proficiency Testing [7792]
    Natl. Assn. of Test Directors [9254]
    Natl. Center for Fair and Open Testing [9255]
    Natl. Coun. on Measurement in Educ. [9256]
    Natl. Safe Skies Alliance [18748]
    NORDTEST [IO]
    North Amer. Specialized Coagulation Lab. Assn. [14996]
    Secondary School Admission Test Bd. [9257]
    Software Testing Inst. [6778]
    VXIbus Consortium [7793]
    West African Examinations Coun. [IO]
    XML.org [6757]
Testing Assn; Natl. Elecl. [★1187]
Testing Inst; Reliability Engg. and Mgt. Institute/Reliability [7038]
Testing Inst; Software [6778]
Testing Professionals; Alliance of Deep Found. [6650]
Testing; Soc. for Nondestructive [★7787]
Teton Club Intl. [22632], 3700 S Westport Ave., No. 2590, Sioux Falls, SD 57106-6360
Teton Club Intl. [IO], Sanbornville, NH, United States
Teverbaugh - Teverbaugh Surname Org. [21070]
Teverbaugh Surname Org; Teverbaugh - [21070]
Tex Jones Fan Club - Defunct.
Tex Ritter Fan Club [24982], c/o Sharon L. Richards-Sweeting, Pres., 828 Wandering Creek Dr., Bothell, WA 98021

A star before a book entry number signifies that the name is not listed separately, but is mentioned within the entry.

Tex Ritter Fan Club [IO], Bothell, WA, United States
Texaco Consignees; Natl. Assn. of [★2936]
Texans for Educational Excellence [★7998]
Texans for Educational Excellence [★IO]
Texas A&M Univ. - Commerce Alumni Assn. [18926], c/o Derryle Peace, Dir., PO Box 3011, Commerce, TX 75429-3011, (903)886-5765
Texas Armadillo Assn. - Address unknown since 2000.
Texas Brigade Assn; Hood's [20726]
Texas at Brownsville and Texas Southmost Coll. Alumni Assn; Univ. of [18938]
Texas Centennial Soc. - Address unknown since 1995.
Texas Date Nail Collectors Assn. [22121], c/o Jerry Waits, Sec., 501 W Horton, Brenham, TX 77833, (979)830-1495
Texas; Daughters of the Republic of [21114]
Texas; Grand Lodge Order of the Sons of Hermann in [19125]
Texas Independent Producers and Royalty Owners Assn. [2949], 919 Cong. Ave., Ste. 1000, Austin, TX 78701, (512)477-4452
Texas Intl. Theatrical Arts Soc. [11045], 3625 N Hall St., Ste. 740, Dallas, TX 75219, (214)528-6112
Texas Intl. Theatrical Arts Soc. [IO], Dallas, TX, United States
Texas Longhorn Assn; Intl. [4269]
Texas Longhorn Breeders Assn. of Am. [4294], 2315 N Main St., Ste. 402, PO Box 4430, Fort Worth, TX 76164, (817)625-6241
Texas - Pan-American Alumni Assn; Univ. of [18939]
Texas; Slavonic Benevolent Order of the State of [★19139]
Texas Southmost Coll. Alumni Assn; Univ. of Texas at Brownsville and [18938]
Text and Academic Authors Assn. [11199], PO Box 76477, St. Petersburg, FL 33734-6477, (727)563-0020
Text Soc; Renaissance English [10932]
Text Translation Soc; Buddhist [19544]
Textbook Administrators; Natl. Assn. of State [★9261]
Textbook Authors Assn. [★11199]
Textbook Directors; Natl. Assn. of State [★9261]
Textbook Prog; Internal Admin. [★9261]
Textbook Review
  Educational Res. Analysts [9259]
Textbooks
  Amer. Textbook Coun. [9258]
  British Educational Suppliers Assn. [IO]
  Educational Res. Analysts [9259]
  Independent Online Booksellers Assn. [530]
  Natl. Assn. of State Textbook Administrators [9260]
  PALTEX - Expanded Textbook and Instructional Materials Prog. [9261]
  Teaching Aids at Low Cost [IO]
  Text and Academic Authors Assn. [11199]
  Worlddidac [IO]
Textielvereniging KRL [★IO]
Textile and Apparel Indus; Gen. Arbitration Coun. of the [5453]
Textile Assn; Knitted [★3795]
Textile Assn; Northern [★3795]
Textile Bag Mfrs. Assn. - Defunct.
Textile Bag and Packaging Assn. [999], c/o Maxine Shapiro, Sec., 3181-306 Charlevoix SE, Grand Rapids, MI 49546, (616)942-9654
Textile Bag Processors Assn. [★999]
Textile Care Allied Trades Assn. [2407], 271 Rte. 46 W, No. D203, Fairfield, NJ 07004, (973)244-1790
Textile Chemical Mfrs. Assn. - Defunct.
Textile Clothing and Footwear Coun. of Australia [★IO]
Textile Clothing and Footwear Union of Australia [IO], Campsie, Australia
The Textile Color Card Assn. of Am. [★866]
Textile Converters Assn. [24195]
Textile Coun. of Hong Kong [IO], Hong Kong, People's Republic of China
Textile Data Processing Assn. [★3772]
Textile Dealers Assn. of America - Defunct.
Textile Distributors Assn. [3802], 980 Ave. of the Americas, New York, NY 10018-3617, (212)868-2210

Textile Distributors Inst. [★3802]
Textile Fabric Distributors Assn. [★3802]
Textile Fabrics; Natl. Assn. of Finishers of [★3772]
Textile and Fashion Fed. (Singapore) [IO], Singapore, Singapore
Textile Fed. [IO], Bruma, Republic of South Africa
Textile Fibers and By-Products Assn. [3803], PO Box D, 1531 Indus. Dr., Griffin, GA 30224, (770)412-2325
Textile History Soc. - Defunct.
Textile Importers' Assn. in Sweden [IO], Stockholm, Sweden
Textile Indus; Gen. Arbitration Coun. of the [★5453]
Textile Info. Users Coun. [3804], c/o Philadelphia Coll. of Textiles and Sci., 4201 Henry Ave., Philadelphia, PA 19144, (215)951-2842
Textile Inst. [IO], Manchester, United Kingdom
Textile Inst; Cotton [★3772]
Textile Laundry Coun. - Defunct.
Textile Machinery Assn. [IO], Frankfurt, Germany
Textile Machinery Assn; Amer. [1997]
Textile Machinery Assn; Japan [IO]
Textile Machinery Assn. of Sweden [IO], Stockholm, Sweden
Textile Machinery Mfrs; Natl. Assn. of [★1997]
Textile Mfrs. Assn; Tufted [★2254]
Textile Merchants and Assoc. Indus. of Chicago [★221]
Textile Merchants and Assoc. Indus. of St. Louis [★221]
Textile Merchants of New York; Assn. of Cotton [★3772]
Textile Printers and Dyers Labor Relations Inst. - Address unknown since 1995.
Textile Processors, Service Trades, Health Care, Professional and Technical Employees Intl. Union - Address unknown since 2004.
Textile Quality Control Assn. - Address unknown since 2002.
Textile Recycling Assn. [IO], Maidstone, United Kingdom
Textile Recycling; Coun. for [3991]
Textile Refinishers Assn. - Address unknown since 1995.
Textile Rental Services Assn. of Am. [3386], 1800 Diagonal Rd., Ste. 200, Alexandria, VA 22314, (703)519-0029
Textile Res. Inst. [★3806]
Textile Res. Inst. [★IO]
Textile Res; U.S. Inst. for [★3806]
Textile Rsrc. and Res. Center; Natl. [★22165]
Textile Salesmen's Assn. - Defunct.
Textile Ser. Assn; Uniform and [2408]
Textile Services Assn. [IO], Harrow, United Kingdom
Textile Soc. of Am. [IO], Earleville, MD, United States
Textile Soc. of Am. [3805], PO Box 70, Earleville, MD 21919-0070, (410)275-2329
Textile Soc. for the Stud. of Art, Design and History [IO], London, United Kingdom
Textile Supplies and Credit Assn. - Address unknown since 1995.
Textile Veterans Assn. Hospitalized Veterans Fund - Defunct.
Textile Waste Assn. [★3803]
Textile Waste Exchange [★3803]
Textiles
  Acrylic Coun. [3768]
  All Nippon Nonwovens Assn. [IO]
  All Pakistan Textile Mills Assn. [IO]
  American Association of Textile Chemists and Colorists [IO]
  Amer. Assn. of Textile Chemists and Colorists [7794]
  Amer. Fiber Mfrs. Assn. [3769]
  Amer. Flock Assn. [3770]
  Amer. Quilt Study Group [9828]
  Amer. Reusable Textile Assn. [3771]
  Amer. Soc. of Knitting Technologists [7795]
  Amer. Textile Mfrs. Inst. [3772]
  Amer. Wool Coun. [3773]
  Amer. Yarn Spinners Assn. [3774]
  Armenian Rugs Soc. [9420]
  Assn. of Austrian Textile Indus. [IO]
  Assn. of Chemists of the Textile Indus. [IO]

Assn. for Contract Textiles [3775]
Assn. of Guilds of Weavers, Spinners and Dyers [IO]
Assn. of Knitwear Designers [228]
Assn. of Textile and Footwear Importers and Wholesalers [IO]
Assn. of Textile Retailers - Netherlands [IO]
Assn. of Thai Textile Bleaching, Dyeing, Printing and Finishing Indus. [IO]
Assn. of Yarn Distributors [3776]
Bangladesh Jute Spinners Assn. [IO]
Boston Wool Trade Assn. [3777]
Brazilian Assn. of the Nonwoven and Tech. Textiles Indus. [IO]
Brazilian Dimensional Embroidery Intl. Guild [IO]
Brazilian Dimensional Embroidery Intl. Guild [22987]
Brazilian Textile and Apparel Indus. Assn. [IO]
British Hand Knitting Confed. [IO]
British Interior Textiles Assn. [IO]
British Wool Marketing Bd. [IO]
Burlap and Jute Assn. [3778]
Bus. Alliance for Commerce in Hemp [18283]
Canadian Textiles Inst. [IO]
Carpet Export Promotion Coun. [IO]
Carpet Inst. of Australia [IO]
Cashmere and Camel Hair Mfrs. Inst. [3779]
Central Confed. of the Textile Indus. in Germany [IO]
Chilean Textile Inst. [IO]
Colonial Coverlet Guild of Am. [21998]
Comm. of the Wool Textile Indus. in the European Economic Community [IO]
Confed. of British Wool Textiles [IO]
Costa Rican Textile Chamber [IO]
Cotton Textiles Export Promotion Coun. [IO]
Coun. of the United Textile Workers of Am. [24194]
Danish Technological Inst. [IO]
Danish Textile Union [IO]
Dutch Textile-Employers Assn. [IO]
Dutch Textile Inst. [IO]
Elastic Fabric Mfrs. Coun. of the Natl. Textile Assn. [3780]
Embroidery Trade Assn. [3781]
EURATEX: European Apparel and Textile Org. [IO]
European Assn. for Textile Polyolefins [IO]
European Glass Weavers Assn. [IO]
European Textile Finishers' Org. [IO]
European Textile Network [IO]
European Textile Services Assn. [IO]
Fabric Salesmen's Assn. [3782]
Fed. Assn. of the Textile Trade [IO]
Fed. of Argentine Textile Indus. [IO]
Fed. of the Belgian Textile Indus. [IO]
Fed. of Danish Textile and Clothing [IO]
Fiber Economics Bur. [1366]
Handloom Export Promotion Coun. [IO]
Handweavers Guild of Am. [22158]
Harris Tweed Authority [IO]
Healthcare Laundry Accreditation Coun. [2403]
Hemp Indus. Assn. [3783]
Hemp Indus. Assn. [IO]
Home Sewing Assn. [3784]
Hong Kong Assn. of Textile Bleachers, Dyers, Printers and Finishers [IO]
Hong Kong Chinese Textile Mills Assn. [IO]
Hungarian Soc. of Textile Tech. and Sci. [IO]
INDA, Assn. of the Nonwoven Fabrics Indus. [3785]
Independent Textile Rental Assn. [3786]
Independent Textile Rental Assn. [IO]
Indian Jute Mills Assn. [IO]
Indian Textile Accessories and Machinery Mfrs'. Assn. [IO]
Indus. Fabrics Assn. Intl. [IO]
Indus. Fabrics Assn. Intl. [3787]
Inst. of Textiles and Clothing [IO]
Institutional and Ser. Textile Distributors Assn. [3788]
Intl. Assn. for Textile Care Labelling [IO]
Intl. Assn. of Wool Textile Labs. [IO]
Intl. Bur. for the Standardisation of Man-Made Fibres [IO]

Reference to "IO" in place of a book number signifies that the association may be found in the 45th edition of International Organizations.

Intl. Geosynthetics Soc. [6700]
Intl. Hajji Baba Soc. [9450]
Intl. Rayon and Synthetic Fibres Comm. [IO]
Intl. Silk Assn. - U.S.A. [3789]
Intl. Soc. of Industrial Fabric Mfrs. [3790]
Intl. Textile and Apparel Assn. [3791]
Intl. Textile and Apparel Assn. [IO]
Intl. Textile, Garment and Leather Workers' Fed.
    [IO]
Intl. Textile Mfrs. Fed. [IO]
Intl. Wool Textile Org. [IO]
Irish Linen Guild [IO]
Japan Chem. Fibers Assn. [IO]
Japan Linen, Ramie and Jute Spinners' Assn. [IO]
Japan Spinners' Assn. [IO]
Japan Textile Finishers' Assn. [IO]
Jute Manufacturers Development Coun. [IO]
Knitting Indus'. Fed. [IO]
Korea Fed. of Textile Indus. [IO]
Korea Textile Trade Assn. [IO]
Malaysian Textile Mfrs'. Assn. [IO]
Mercers' Company [IO]
Narrow Fabrics Institute [IO]
Narrow Fabrics Inst. [3792]
Natl. Assn. of Decorative Fabric Distributors
    [3793]
The Natl. Needle Arts Assn. [3794]
Natl. Quilting Assn. [22170]
Natl. Textile Assn. [3795]
Natl. Union of Small and Medium-Sized Textile
    and Clothing Companies [IO]
Needleloom Underlay Mfrs. Assn. [IO]
Nepal Carpet Exporters' Assn. [IO]
Nippon Interior Fabrics Assn. [IO]
North Amer. Geosynthetics Soc. [6701]
Org. of Black Designers [9907]
Performance Textiles Assn. [IO]
Schiffli Embroidery Mfrs. Promotion Fund [3796]
Schiffli Lace and Embroidery Mfrs. Assn. [3797]
Scottish Textiles [IO]
Secondary Materials and Recycled Textiles [2066]
Silk Assn. of Great Britain [IO]
Silk Painters Intl. [9524]
South African Textile Indus. Export Coun. [IO]
Southeastern Fabric, Notions and Crafts Assn.
    [3798]
Southern Textile Assn. [3799]
Spanish Cotton Spinners and Weavers Assn. [IO]
Spinners and Weavers Assn. of Korea [IO]
Surface Design Assn. [3800]
Swedish Inst. for Fibre and Polymer Res. [IO]
Swedish Textile and Clothing Indus'. Assn. [IO]
Swiss Textile Fed. [IO]
Swiss Textiles Fed. (Clothing and Textile Indus.)
    [IO]
Synthetic and Rayon Textiles Export Promotion
    Coun. [IO]
Synthetic Yarn and Fiber Assn. [3801]
Taiwan Knitting Indus. Assn. [IO]
Taiwan Man-Made Fiber Indus. Assn. [IO]
Taiwan Non-Woven Fabrics Indus. Assn. [IO]
Taiwan Regional Assn. of Filament Fabrics Print-
    ing, Dyeing and Finishing Indus. [IO]
Taiwan Textile Fed. [IO]
Tech. Textile and Nonwoven Assn. [IO]
Textile Bag and Packaging Assn. [999]
Textile Care Allied Trades Assn. [2407]
Textile Converters Assn. [24195]
Textile Coun. of Hong Kong [IO]
Textile Distributors Assn. [3802]
Textile and Fashion Fed. (Singapore) [IO]
Textile Fibers and By-Products Assn. [3803]
Textile Importers' Assn. in Sweden [IO]
Textile Info. Users Coun. [3804]
Textile Inst. [IO]
Textile Machinery Assn. [IO]
Textile Machinery Assn. of Sweden [IO]
Textile Recycling Assn. [IO]
Textile Rental Services Assn. of Am. [3386]
Textile Services Assn. [IO]
Textile Soc. of Am. [IO]
Textile Soc. of Am. [3805]
Thai Synthetic Fiber Manufacturers' Assn. [IO]
Thai Textile Mfg. Assn. [IO]
Thai Weaving Indus. Assn. [IO]

Thailand Textile Inst. [IO]
TRI/Princeton [IO]
TRI/Princeton [3806]
Union Textile Merchants' Assn. [IO]
U.S. Assn. of Importers of Textiles and Apparel
    [3807]
U.S. Indus. Fabrics Inst. [3808]
Verein Deutscher Textilveredlungsfachleute e.V
    [IO]
Weave a Real Peace [11505]
Wool Mfrs. Coun. [3809]
Woolmark Company [3810]
Woolmens' Company [IO]
Worshipful Company of Framework Knitters [IO]
Textiles and Clothing; Assn. of Coll. Professors of
    [★3791]
Textiles, Clothing and Leather Processing Assn. [IO],
    Ljubljana, Slovenia
Textiles; Natl. Fed. of [★3772]
Textiles; Shippers of Recycled [3587]
Textilimportoererna [★IO]
Textilipari Muszaki es Tudomanyos Egyesulet [★IO]
Textilverband Schweiz [★IO]
Textual Scholarship; Soc. for [10432]
Textured Yarn Assn. of Am. [★3801]
Tezkoatletska Zveza Slovenije [★IO]
T.G. Sheppard Intl. Fan Club [24983], 5123 Secor
    Rd., No. 6, Toledo, OH 43623-2326
Thai
    Assn. of Thai Professionals in Am. and Canada
        [19406]
    Soc. for Thai Philately [22875]
    U.S. Muay Thai Assn. [23608]
Thai Assn. - Address unknown since 1995.
Thai Assn. of Conf. Interpreters [IO], Bangkok,
    Thailand
Thai Assn. of Landscape Architects [IO], Bangkok,
    Thailand
Thai Assn. of Orthodontists [IO], Bangkok, Thailand
Thai Assn. for the Stud. of Pain [IO], Bangkok,
    Thailand
Thai Assn. of Univ. Women [IO], Bangkok, Thailand
Thai Bankers' Assn. [IO], Bangkok, Thailand
Thai Broiler Processing Exporters Assn. [IO],
    Bangkok, Thailand
Thai Chamber of Commerce [IO], Bangkok, Thailand
Thai Coffee Exporters Assn. [IO], Bangkok, Thailand
Thai Entertainment Content Trade Assn. [IO],
    Bangkok, Thailand
Thai Environmental Engineers Assn. [★IO]
Thai Food Processors' Assn. [IO], Bangkok,
    Thailand
Thai Frozen Foods Assn. [IO], Bangkok, Thailand
Thai Furniture Indus. Assn. [IO], Bangkok, Thailand
Thai Garment Manufacturers Assn. [IO], Bangkok,
    Thailand
Thai Gem and Jewelry Traders' Assn. [IO], Bangkok,
    Thailand
Thai Hypertension League [IO], Bangkok, Thailand
Thai Indus. Standards Inst. [IO], Bangkok, Thailand
Thai Information Center - Address unknown since
    1995.
Thai Jet Sports Boating Assn. [IO], Bangkok,
    Thailand
Thai Life Assurance Assn. [IO], Bangkok, Thailand
Thai Natl. Comm. of the Intl. Assn. on Water Pollu-
    tion Res. and Control [★IO]
Thai Natl. Comm. of the Intl. Assn. on Water Quality
    [IO], Bangkok, Thailand
Thai Natl. Shippers' Coun. [IO], Bangkok, Thailand
Thai Packaging Assn. [IO], Bangkok, Thailand
Thai Philately; Soc. for [22875]
Thai Physicians Assn. of Am. [16012], 1350 Coving-
    ton Ct., Crown Point, IN 46307, (219)757-6077
Thai Population Assn. [IO], Nakhon Pathom,
    Thailand
Thai Red Cross Soc. [IO], Bangkok, Thailand
Thai Silk Assn. [IO], Bangkok, Thailand
Thai Soc. of Clinical Neurophysiology [IO], Bangkok,
    Thailand
Thai Soc. for the Prevention of Cruelty to Animals
    [IO], Bangkok, Thailand
Thai Spa Assn. [IO], Bangkok, Thailand
Thai Spa Operators Assn. [IO], Bangkok, Thailand
Thai Synthetic Fiber Manufacturers' Assn. [IO],
    Bangkok, Thailand

Thai Tapioca Trade Assn. [IO], Bangkok, Thailand
Thai Textile Mfg. Assn. [IO], Bangkok, Thailand
Thai Toy Indus. Assn. [IO], Bangkok, Thailand
Thai Vacation Ownership Assn. [IO], Bangkok,
    Thailand
Thai Venture Capital Assn. [IO], Bangkok, Thailand
Thai Weaving Indus. Assn. [IO], Bangkok, Thailand
Thai Wine Assn. [IO], Bangkok, Thailand
Thai Youth Hostels Assn. [IO], Bangkok, Thailand
Thailand
    Amer. Refugee Comm. [12805]
    Assn. of Thai Professionals in Am. and Canada
        [19406]
    Soc. for Thai Philately [22875]
    U.S. Muay Thai Assn. [23608]
Thailand ACM Chap. [IO], Samut Prakan, Thailand
Thailand Bus. Coun. for Sustainable Development
    [IO], Nonthaburi, Thailand
Thailand Chap. of the Internet Soc. [IO], Samut Pra-
    kan, Thailand
Thailand Dance Sport Assn. [IO], Bangkok, Thailand
Thailand Golf Assn. [IO], Bangkok, Thailand
Thailand Incentive and Convention Assn. [IO],
    Bangkok, Thailand
Thailand Squash Rackets Assn. [IO], Bangkok,
    Thailand
Thailand Textile Inst. [IO], Bangkok, Thailand
Thalassemia
    Cooley's Anemia Found. [14788]
Thalassemia Action Group [★14788]
Thalidomide Soc. [IO], Pinner, United Kingdom
Thames Valley Chamber of Commerce [IO], Slough,
    United Kingdom
ThanaCAP [★17330]
Thanatology
    Americans for Better Care of the Dying [13313]
    Assn. for Recognizing the Life of Stillborns
        [12661]
    Center for Death Educ. and Bioethics [13314]
    Dying with Dignity [IO]
    First Sunday [12671]
    Intl. Inst. for the Stud. of Death [13315]
    Intl. Inst. for the Stud. of Death [IO]
    Japanese Assn. for Death Stud. and Bereavement
        Support [IO]
    Living/Dying Proj. [13316]
    RAINBOWS [11718]
    Violent Death Bereavement Soc. [11513]
    William Wendt Center for Loss and Healing
        [13317]
Thanatology; Found. of [★11908]
Thanet and East Kent Chamber [IO], Broadstairs,
    United Kingdom
Thanet and East Kent Chamber of Commerce [★IO]
Thank-You Research - Address unknown since
    1999.
Thanks-Giving Foundation [★20584]
Thanks-Giving Found. [18676], PO Box 131770,
    Dallas, TX 75313-1770, (214)969-1977
Thanks-Giving Foundation [★IO]
Thanks-Giving Found. [IO], Dallas, TX, United
    States
Thanks-Giving Square [IO], Dallas, TX, United
    States
Thanks-Giving Square [20584], PO Box 131770,
    Dallas, TX 75313-1770, (214)969-1977
Thanks to Scandinavia [8436], 165 E 56th St., New
    York, NY 10022, (212)891-1403
Thanks to Scandinavia [IO], New York, NY, United
    States
Thanksgiving; Center for World [★20584]
Thanksgiving Commn; Natl. [★18676]
THAW - Address unknown since 1994.
THE NETWORK [★9324]
Theater
    Actors' Equity Assn. [24148]
    Alliance of Resident Theatres/New York [10997]
    Amer. Alliance for Theatre and Educ. [10998]
    Amer. Assn. of Community Theatre [10999]
    Amer. Dinner Theatre Inst. [1297]
    Amer. Guild of Variety Artists [24151]
    Amer. Russian Theatrical Alliance [11001]
    Amer. Soc. for Aesthetics [9545]
    Amer. Theatre Arts for Youth [11003]
    Amer. Theatre and Drama Soc. [11005]

A star before a book entry number signifies that the name is not listed separately, but is mentioned within the entry.

Arthur Miller Soc. [11159]
Assoc. Actors and Artistes of Am. [24153]
Assn. for Theatre in Higher Educ. [9262]
Audience Development Comm. [11006]
Black Awareness in TV [17164]
Burlesque Historical Soc. [11009]
Costume Soc. of Am. [9822]
Dance Theater Workshop [9566]
Dancers Without Borders [9880]
Delta Psi Omega [24444]
Drama Desk [11010]
Dramatists Guild of Am. [11012]
Educational Theatre Assn. [9264]
Episcopal Actors' Guild of Am. [11013]
Ford's Theatre Soc. [11015]
Friars Club [11016]
Hosp. Audiences [11017]
Inst. of the Amer. Musical [10610]
Inst. of Outdoor Drama [11018]
Interlochen Center for the Arts [9571]
The Lambs [11019]
Large Format Cinema Assn. [1387]
League of Amer. Theatres and Producers [11020]
League of Historic Amer. Theatres [11021]
League of Resident Theatres [11022]
Movement Theatre Intl. [11025]
Natl. Assn. of Schools of Theatre [9265]
Natl. Center of Afro-American Artists [9361]
Natl. Corporate Theatre Fund [11027]
Natl. Found. for Advancement in the Arts [9587]
Natl. Movement Theatre Assn. [11028]
Natl. New Play Network [11030]
Natl. Theatre Conf. [11032]
Natl. Theatre Workshop of the Handicapped
    [11033]
New Dramatists [11034]
New England Theatre Conf. [11035]
Omega Theatre and the Omega Arts Network
    [9590]
O'Neill Critics Inst. [11036]
O'Neill Natl. Theater Inst. [9266]
Org. of Professional Acting Coaches and Teach-
    ers [9267]
Outer Critics Circle [11037]
The Players [11038]
Playwrights Conf. [11039]
Shakespeare Oxford Soc. [9709]
Shakespeare Soc. [9710]
Shakespeare Theatre Assn. of Am. [11042]
Southeastern Theatre Conf. [11043]
Texas Intl. Theatrical Arts Soc. [11045]
Theatre Authority [11046]
Theatre Communications Gp. [11047]
Theatre Development Fund [11048]
Theatre Guild [11049]
Theatre Historical Soc. of Am. [11050]
Theatre Lib. Assn. [10391]
Theatre for Young Audiences/USA [11051]
Theta Alpha Phi [24721]
U.S. Inst. for Theatre Tech. [11052]
University/Resident Theatre Assn. [9269]
Wolf Trap Found. for the Performing Arts [9602]
Yiddish Theatrical Alliance [11053]
Young Audiences [9603]
Ziegfeld Club [11054]
Theater Assn; Univ. and Coll. [★9262]
Theater Center; O'Neill [★11014]
Theater of Dreams [IO], Culemborg, Netherlands
Theater Found; Eugene O'Neill Memorial [★11014]
Theater; Illusion [12030]
Theater Workshop Boston [★9590]
Theater Workshop; Dance [9566]
Theatre
    Actors Studio [10995]
    Alliance for Inclusion in the Arts [10996]
    Alliance of Resident Theatres/New York [10997]
    Amer. Alliance for Theatre and Educ. [10998]
    Amer. Assn. of Community Theatre [10999]
    Amer. Conservatory Theater Found. [11000]
    Amer. Guild of Variety Artists [24151]
    Amer. Russian Theatrical Alliance [11001]
    Amer. Soc. for Theatre Res. [11002]
    Amer. Theatre Arts for Youth [11003]
    Amer. Theatre Critics Assn. [11004]
    Amer. Theatre and Drama Soc. [11005]

Amer. Theatre and Drama Soc. [IO]
Andrea McArdle Fan Club [24728]
Assn. of British Theatre Technicians [IO]
Assn. for Canadian Theatre Res. [IO]
Assn. of Lighting Designers [IO]
Assn. of Swedish Lighting Designers [IO]
Assn. for Theatre in Higher Educ. [9262]
Assn. of Theatre Movement Educators [9263]
Association of Theatre Movement Educators [IO]
Audience Development Comm. [11006]
Bilingual Found. of the Arts [11007]
Black Theatre Network [11008]
British Acad. of Dramatic Combat [IO]
British Centre of the Intl. Theatre Inst. [IO]
British Puppet and Model Theatre Guild [IO]
Burlesque Historical Soc. [11009]
Canadian Theatre Critics Assn. [IO]
Caravan Farm Theatre [IO]
Carousel Theatre Soc. [IO]
Centre for Indigenous Theatre [IO]
Cinema Theatre Assn. [IO]
Costume Soc. of Am. [9822]
Dance Theater Workshop [9566]
Danish Amateur Theatre Coun. [IO]
David Birney Intl. Fan Club [24737]
Delta Psi Omega [24444]
Drama Desk [11010]
Drama League [11011]
Dramatists Guild of Am. [11012]
Educational Theatre Assn. [9264]
Episcopal Actors' Guild of Am. [11013]
Eugene O'Neill Memorial Theater Center [11014]
Faroe Islands Amateur Theatre Coun. [IO]
Finnish Centre of AITA/IATA [IO]
Finnish Dramatists' Union [IO]
Ford's Theatre Soc. [11015]
Fractured Atlas [9503]
Friars Club [11016]
Greater Vancouver Professional Theatre Alliance
    [IO]
Guild of Drama Adjudicators [IO]
Hosp. Audiences [11017]
Icelandic Amateur Theatre Assn. [IO]
Independent Theatre Coun. [IO]
Inst. of the Amer. Musical [10610]
Inst. of Outdoor Drama [11018]
Intl. Amateur Theatre Assn. [IO]
Intl. Assn. of Theatre for Children and Young
    People [IO]
Intl. Assn. of Theatre Critics [IO]
Intl. Cinema Tech. Assn. [IO]
Intl. Cinema Tech. Assn. [3811]
Intl. Fed. for Theatre Res. [IO]
Intl. Theatre Inst. - France [IO]
Intl. Theatre Inst. - Switzerland [IO]
Jack Point Preservation Soc. [9811]
Japanese Soc. for Theatre Res. [IO]
Kaleidoscope Theatre Productions Soc. [IO]
The Lambs [11019]
League of Amer. Theatres and Producers [11020]
League of Historic Amer. Theatres [11021]
League of Resident Theatres [11022]
Literary Managers and Dramaturgs of the
    Americas [11023]
Little Theatre Guild of Great Britain [IO]
The Masquers [11024]
Movement Theatre Intl. [11025]
Movement Theatre Intl. [IO]
Natl. Assn. of Drama Educ. [IO]
Natl. Assn. of Dramatic and Speech Arts [11026]
Natl. Assn. of Schools of Theatre [9265]
Natl. Assn. of Youth Theatres [IO]
Natl. Center of Afro-American Artists [9361]
Natl. Commun. Assn. [9157]
Natl. Corporate Theatre Fund [11027]
Natl. Coun. for Drama Training [IO]
Natl. Movement Theatre Assn. [11028]
Natl. Music Theater Network [11029]
Natl. New Play Network [11030]
Natl. Operatic and Dramatic Assn. [IO]
Natl. Performance Network [11031]
Natl. Theatre Conf. [11032]
Natl. Theatre of the Deaf [IO]
Natl. Theatre Workshop of the Handicapped
    [11033]

New Dramatists [11034]
New England Theatre Conf. [11035]
New Zealand Theatre Fed. [IO]
Nordic Amateur Theatre Coun. [IO]
Omega Theatre and the Omega Arts Network
    [9590]
O'Neill Critics Inst. [11036]
O'Neill Natl. Theater Inst. [9266]
Org. of Professional Acting Coaches and Teach-
    ers [9267]
Outer Critics Circle [11037]
The Players [11038]
Playwrights Conf. [11039]
Professional Assn. of Canadian Theatres [IO]
Puerto Rican Traveling Theatre Company [11040]
Rites and Reason Theatre [11041]
Shakespeare Oxford Soc. [9709]
Shakespeare Soc. [9710]
Shakespeare Theatre Assn. of Am. [11042]
Soc. of Amer. Fight Directors [9268]
Soc. of London Theatre [IO]
Soc. for Theatre Res. [IO]
Southeastern Theatre Conf. [11043]
Stage Directors and Choreographers Found.
    [11044]
Stage Mgt. Assn. [IO]
Swedish Amateur Theatre Coun. [IO]
Swiss Assn. for Theatre Stud. [IO]
Texas Intl. Theatrical Arts Soc. [IO]
Texas Intl. Theatrical Arts Soc. [11045]
Theatre Authority [11046]
Theatre Communications Gp. [11047]
Theatre Development Fund [11048]
Theatre Guild [11049]
Theatre Historical Soc. of Am. [11050]
Theatre Lib. Assn. [10391]
Theatre for Young Audiences/USA [11051]
Theta Alpha Phi [24721]
United Drive-In Theatre Owners Assn. [2794]
U.S. Inst. for Theatre Tech. [11052]
University/Resident Theatre Assn. [9269]
Up With People [8311]
Yiddish Theatrical Alliance [11053]
Young Audiences [9603]
Ziegfeld Club [11054]
Theatre Alliance; Intl. Museum [10507]
Theatre; American Ballet [★9868]
Theatre Assn; Amer. [★9262]
Theatre Assn; Amer. Community [★10999]
Theatre Assn; NFHS Speech, Debate and [9161]
Theatre Authority [11046]
Theatre Comm. for Eugene O'Neill - Defunct.
Theatre Communications Gp. [11047], 520 8th Ave.,
    24th Fl., New York, NY 10018-4156, (212)609-
    5900
Theatre Consultants; Amer. Soc. of [955]
Theatre Development Fund [11048], 1501
    Broadway, 21st Fl., New York, NY 10036-5652,
    (212)221-0885
Theatre Education Assn. - Defunct.
Theatre in Education - Defunct.
Theatre Equip. Assn. [★3811]
Theatre Equip. Assn. [★IO]
Theatre Found; Ballet [9868]
Theatre Fund; Corporate [★11027]
Theatre Guild [11049], 135 Central Park W, Ste. 4S,
    New York, NY 10023, (212)873-0676
Theatre Guild Abroad [★11049]
Theatre Historical Soc. of Am. [11050], York Theatre
    Bldg., 152 N York, 2nd Fl., Elmhurst, IL 60126-
    2889, (630)782-1800
Theatre Historical Soc. of Am. [★11050]
Theatre for Ideas - Defunct.
Theatre Inst. [IO], Prague, Czech Republic
Theatre Inst; Amer. Dinner [1297]
Theatre Inst; Natl. [★9266]
Theatre of Latin America - Defunct.
Theatre Lib. Assn. [10391], c/o The New York Public
    Lib. for the Performing Arts, 40 Lincoln Center Plz.,
    New York, NY 10023
Theatre and Literary Agency [★IO]
Theatre; Natl. Alliance for Musical [10656]
Theatre Organ Enthusiasts; Amer. [★10553]
Theatre Organ Enthusiasts; Amer. Assn. of
    [★10553]

Reference to "IO" in place of a book number signifies that the association may be found in the 45th edition of International Organizations.

Theatre Organ Soc; Amer. [10553]
Theatre Owners of Am. [★1315]
Theatre Owners of Am. [★IO]
Theatre Owners Assn; United Drive-In [2794]
Theatre Owners; Natl. Assn. of [1315]
Theatre Recording Soc. - Defunct.
Theatre Safety; Arts, Crafts and [12950]
Theatre Society; American [★11049]
Theatre TV Authority - Address unknown since 1995.
Theatre Writers Union [★IO]
Theatre for Young Audiences/USA [11051], 1602 Belle View Blvd., No. 810, Alexandria, VA 22307, (202)416-8837
Theatres Assn; Musical Arena [★9594]
Theatres; League of New York [★11020]
Theatres and Producers; League of New York [★11020]
Theatrical Alliance; Yiddish [11053]
Theatrical Dealers Assn. [★2556]
Theatrical Dealers Assn. [★IO]
Theatrical, Literary and Audiovisual Agency [IO], Prague, Czech Republic
Theatrical Mutual Assn. - Address unknown since 2001.
Theatrical Press Agents and Managers; Assn. of [24154]
Theatrical Stage Employees, Motion Picture Technicians, Artists and Allied Crafts of the U.S., U.S. Territories and Canada; Intl. Alliance of [★24156]
Theft Bur; Intl. Aviation [★433]
Theft Bur; Natl. Auto. [★2224]
Theft; Coalition Opposing Signal [556]
Theft Conf; Intl. Livestock Brand and [★4998]
Theft Investigators Assn; Intl. Livestock Identification and [★4998]
Theme Party Operators; Natl. Assn. of Casino and [★1313]
Themed Entertainment Assn. [1326], 175 E Olive Ave., Ste. 100, Burbank, CA 91502, (818)843-8497
Themed Entertainment Assn. [IO], Burbank, CA, United States
THEO BC [IO], Vancouver, BC, Canada
Theodor Herzl Inst. - Address unknown since 2001.
Theodore von Karman Memorial Found. - Defunct.
Theodore Roethke Memorial Found. [10872], c/o John Shek, 11 W Hannum Blvd., Saginaw, MI 48602, (989)792-5567
Theodore Roosevelt Assn. [11152], PO Box 719, Oyster Bay, NY 11771, (516)921-6319
Theodore Roosevelt Conservation Partnership [4458], 555 Eleventh St. NW, 6th Fl., Washington, DC 20004, (202)654-4600
Theodore Roosevelt Memorial Assn; Women's [★11152]
Theodorus Scowden Family Org; Neal Dougan- [21010]
Theological Encounter With Sci. and Tech; Inst. for [12353]
Theological Lib. Assn; Amer. [10323]
Theological Schools; Amer. Assn. of [★9270]
Theological Schools; Amer. Assn. of Schools of [★9270]
Theological Seminaries of the U.S. and Canada; Conf. of [★9270]
Theological Seminary; Ecumenical [19924]
Theological Soc. of Am; Catholic [9776]
Theological Soc. in Am; Orthodox [19885]
Theological Soc; Evangelical [19980]
Theological Students Fellowship - Defunct.
Theology
   Acad. of Homiletics [20081]
   Accrediting Coun. for Theological Educ. in Africa [IO]
   Amer. Baptist Historical Soc. [19470]
   Amer. Bible Soc. [19504]
   Amer. Humanist Assn. [20084]
   Amer. Inst. for Patristic and Byzantine Stud. [9770]
   Amer. Sci. Affiliation [20546]
   Amer. Teilhard Assn. [9632]
   Amer. Theological Lib. Assn. [10323]
   Anglican Assn. of Biblical Scholars [19449]
   Arthur Vining Davis Foundations [12048]
   ASGM [19506]
   Asian Women's Rsrc. Centre for Culture and Theology [IO]

Assn. of Classical and Christian Schools [9089]
Assn. for Clinical Pastoral Educ. [19915]
Assn. for the Development of Religious Info. Systems [20091]
Assn. for Theological Educ. in South East Asia [IO]
Assn. of Theological Schools in the U.S. and Canada [IO]
Assn. of Theological Schools in the U.S. and Canada [9270]
Baptist Bible Fellowship Intl. [19477]
Berean Bible Soc. [19509]
Bible League [19510]
Bishops' Comm. for Ecumenical and Interreligious Affairs [19584]
Black Women in Church and Soc. [20617]
Boston Theological Inst. [9271]
Campus Ministry Women [19918]
Caribbean Assn. of Theological Schools [IO]
Catholic Biblical Assn. of Am. [9272]
Catholic Theological Soc. of Am. [9776]
Catholic Traditionalist Movement [19604]
Center for Res. in Faith and Moral Development [20534]
Chatlos Found. [20591]
Chatlos Found. [IO]
Coll. Theology Soc. [9273]
Coun. for Secular Humanism [20085]
Coun. of Societies for the Stud. of Religion [9274]
Covenant of Unitarian Universalist Pagans [20459]
Division of Higher Educ., Christian Church-Disciples of Christ [19854]
Ecumenical Theological Seminary [19924]
European Soc. of Women in Theological Res. [IO]
Evangelical Theological Soc. [19980]
Found. for Christian Theology [19960]
Gabriel Marcel Soc. [10794]
Hartford Seminary [20100]
Henry Luce Found. [12050]
Inst. for Advanced Stud. of World Religions [9275]
Inst. for Advanced Stud. of World Religions [IO]
Inst. for Biblical Res. [19519]
Inst. on Religious Life [19639]
Interdisciplinary Biblical Res. Inst. [19928]
Intl. Assn. of Baptist Colleges and Universities [9276]
Intl. Assn. of Biblical Counselors [19867]
Intl. Bible Soc. [19520]
Intl. Bible Students Assn. [19521]
Intl. Coun. for Evangelical Theological Educ. [IO]
Intl. Fed. of Secular Humanistic Jews [20086]
Intl. Org. for Septuagint and Cognate Stud. [19522]
Intl. Soc. for Hildegard Von Bingen Stud. [11124]
Jews for Judaism [20500]
Lessing Soc. [9680]
Life Understanding Found. [20484]
Louis Finkelstein Inst. for Religious and Social Stud. at the Louis Stein Center [19931]
Mariological Soc. of Am. [19656]
Natl. Assn. of Baptist Professors of Religion [9277]
Natl. Baptist Convention, U.S.A. [19493]
Orthodox Theological Soc. in Am. [19885]
Progressive, Radically Inclusive Student Ministry [19938]
Rosicrucian Fellowship [20541]
Rural Theology Assn. [IO]
St. Thomas Aquinas Found. [19714]
Searching Together Educational Ministries [19909]
Soc. of Biblical Literature [19530]
Soc. of Christian Philosophers [10832]
Soc. of Jewish Sci. [20202]
Soc. for the Sci. Stud. of Religion [20506]
Soc. for the Stud. of Christian Spirituality [19826]
Soc. for the Stud. of Japanese Religions [20529]
Swedenborg Assn. [9164]
Swedenborg Found. [9711]
Theosophical Soc. in Am. [20593]
Tyndale Soc. [20530]
United Lodge of Theosophists [20594]
Washington Ethical Soc. [20087]
Westar Inst. [20509]
Women's Alliance for Theology, Ethics and Ritual [20626]

World Union of Deists [20531]
   Wycliffe Bible Translators [19531]
Theology; European Soc. for the Stud. of Sci. and [IO]
Theology; Found. for Christian [19960]
Theology and Public Policy; Churches' Center for [18434]
Theology Soc; Coll. [9273]
Theory Gp; IEEE Info. [7770]
Theory in Psychology and Life Sciences; Soc. for Chaos [7547]
Theory Soc; IEEE Info. [★7770]
Theory and Techniques Soc; IEEE Microwave [7337]
THEOS Found. - Address unknown since 2003.
Theosophical
   Theosophical Book Assn. for the Blind [20592]
   Theosophical Soc. [IO]
   Theosophical Soc. in Am. [20593]
   United Lodge of Theosophists [20594]
   United Lodge of Theosophists [IO]
   United Lodge of Theosophists - Belgium [IO]
   United Lodge of Theosophists - India [IO]
   United Lodge of Theosophists - Ottawa [IO]
   United Lodge of Theosophists - United Kingdom [IO]
Theosophical Book Assn. for the Blind [20592], 54 Krotona Hill, Ojai, CA 93023, (805)614-4977
Theosophical Publishing House [★20593]
Theosophical Soc. [IO], Chennai, India
Theosophical Soc. in Am. [20593], PO Box 270, Wheaton, IL 60189-0270, (630)668-1571
Theosophical Soc. in England [IO], London, United Kingdom
Therapeutic Assn; Amer. Women's Physical [★16603]
Therapeutic Assn; South Carolina [★11852]
Therapeutic and Clinical Res. Assn; Osteopathic Manipulative [★15790]
Therapeutic Communities of Am. [13282], 1601 Connecticut Ave. NW, Ste. 803, Washington, DC 20009, (202)296-3503
Therapeutic Humor; Amer. Assn. for [★16605]
Therapeutic Info; Drug and [★15940]
Therapeutic Massage and Bodywork; Natl. Certification Bd. for [15032]
Therapeutic Neuroradiology; Amer. Soc. of Interventional and [16280]
Therapeutic Radiologists; Amer. Soc. of [★16285]
Therapeutic Radiology and Oncology; Amer. Soc. for [16285]
Therapeutic Recreation Assn; Amer. [16315]
Therapeutic Recreation Certification; Natl. Coun. for [16627]
Therapeutic Recreation Soc; Natl. [16628]
Therapeutic Riding; Natl. Center for [23351]
Therapeutic Schools and Programs; Natl. Assn. of [13738]
Therapeutics; Amer. Acad. of Veterinary Pharmacology and [16738]
Therapeutics; Amer. Soc. for Clinical Pharmacology and [15920]
Therapeutics; Amer. Soc. for Experimental Neuro [15379]
Therapeutics; Amer. Soc. for Pharmacology and Experimental [15925]
Therapeutics Assn; Plasma Protein [13765]
Therapeutics and Rehabilitation; Coun. of Chiropractic Physiological [13999]
Therapies of Asia; Amer. Org. for Bodywork [15024]
Therapies; Assn. for Past Life Res. and [★16617]
Therapies; Assn. for Past-Life Res. and [★16617]
Therapies Associations; Natl. Coalition of Creative Arts [16224]
Therapies; Found. for Alternative Cancer [★13824]
Therapies; Intl. Assn. for Regression Res. and [16617]
Therapists and Allied Hea. Practitioners Intl; Assoc. Professional Massage [★15025]
Therapists of Am; Sandplay [16635]
Therapists; Amer. Assn. of Behavioral [13744]
Therapists; Amer. Assn. of Inhalation [★16599]
Therapists; Amer. Assn. of Professional Hypno [14915]
Therapists; Amer. Assn. of Sexuality Educators, Counselors and [16398]

A star before a book entry number signifies that the name is not listed separately, but is mentioned within the entry.

Therapists; Amer. Guild of Hypno [14919]
Therapists; Amer. Registry of Inhalation [★16626]
Therapists; Amer. Soc. of Alternative [13624]
Therapists; Amer. Soc. of Hand [14524]
Therapists; Assn. of Christian [19765]
Therapists; Assn. of Pediatric [16606]
Therapists and Bodyworkers; Assoc. Professional Massage [★15025]
Therapists; Certification Bd. for Music [16213]
Therapists; Natl. Acad. of Counselors and Family [★12137]
Therapists; Natl. Assn. of Cognitive-Behavioral [16193]
Therapists; Natl. Assn. of Recreation [★16628]
Therapists and Psychodiagnosticians; Amer. Bd. of Medical Psycho [16202]
Therapy
Acad. of Organizational and Occupational Psychiatry [15621]
Acad. of Psychosomatic Medicine [16195]
Acad. of Scientific Hypnotherapy [14913]
Adventures in Movement for the Handicapped [16597]
All India Occupational Therapists Assn. [IO]
AMEND [12020]
Amer. Acad. of Hea. Physics [16598]
Amer. Acad. of Psychoanalysis and Dynamic Psychiatry [16101]
Amer. Acad. of Psychotherapists [16198]
Amer. Assn. of Anger Mgt. Providers [15185]
Amer. Assn. of Christian Counselors [19862]
Amer. Assn. for Respiratory Care [16599]
Amer. Assn. of Sexuality Educators, Counselors and Therapists [16398]
Amer. Assn. for Tech. in Psychiatry [16070]
Amer. Bd. of Examiners of Psychodrama, Sociometry, and Gp. Psychotherapy [16201]
Amer. Bd. of Psychiatry and Neurology [16071]
Amer. Counseling Assn. [11815]
Amer. Family Therapy Acad. [11816]
Amer. Gp. Psychotherapy Assn. [16204]
Amer. Hippotherapy Assn. [16600]
American Hippotherapy Association [IO]
Amer. Horticultural Therapy Assn. [16601]
Amer. Hypnosis Assn. [14920]
Amer. Manual Medicine Assn. [13618]
Amer. Massage Therapy Assn. [15022]
Amer. Occupational Therapy Assn. [16602]
Amer. Physical Therapy Assn. [16603]
Amer. Psychiatric Assn. [16076]
Amer. Psychiatric Assn. Alliance [16077]
Amer. Psychoanalytic Assn. [16102]
Amer. Psychopathological Assn. [16190]
Amer. Psychosomatic Soc. [16196]
Amer. Psychotherapy Assn. [16207]
Amer. Soc. for Adolescent Psychiatry [16078]
Amer. Soc. of Alternative Therapists [13624]
Amer. Soc. of Psychoanalytic Physicians [16104]
AMHS [11817]
Animal Assisted Therapy Found. [16604]
Anxiety Disorders Assn. of Am. [12743]
Anxiety Disorders Special Interest Gp. [12744]
Anxiety and Phobia Treatment Center [12745]
Arts in Therapy Network [13709]
Asccoaciacion Peruana de Terapistas Fisicos [IO]
Asocacion Colombiana de Terapia Ocupacional [IO]
Asociacion Argentina de Terapistas Ocupacionales [IO]
Asociacion Espanola de Fisioterapeutas [IO]
Asociacion de Fisioterapeutas del Uruguay [IO]
Asociacion Nacional de Fisioterapistas de Guatemala [IO]
Asociacion Panamena de Fisioterapia Kinesiologia [IO]
Associacion Colombiana de Fisioterapia [IO]
Associacion Costarricense de Terapeutas Fisicos de Costa Rica [IO]
Associacion Mexicana de Fisioterapia [IO]
Assn. for Advanced Training in the Behavioral Sciences [8878]
Assn. for Advancement of Psychoanalysis (of the Karen Horney Psychoanalytic Inst. and Center) [16105]
Assn. for the Advancement of Psychotherapy [16210]

Assn. for Applied and Therapeutic Humor [16605]
Assn. for Behavioral and Cognitive Therapies [13733]
Assn. of Christian Therapists [19765]
Assn. for Convulsive Therapy [15192]
Assn. for Dance Movement Therapy - United Kingdom [IO]
Assn. of Hungarian Physiotherapists [IO]
Assn. of Icelandic Physiotherapists [IO] .
Assn. of Independent Physical Therapists [IO]
Assn. Luxembourgeoise Des Kinesitherapeutes [IO]
Assn. for Multicultural Counseling and Development [11819]
Assn. of Occupational Therapists of Ireland [IO]
Assn. Of Danish Physiotherapists [IO]
Assn. of Pediatric Therapists [16606]
Assn. of Personal Counsellors [IO]
Assn. of Physiotherapists of Swaziland [IO]
Assn. of Physiotherapists in Tanzania [IO]
Assn. for Play Therapy [16607]
Assn. of Professional Music Therapists [IO]
Assn. for Psychoanalytic Medicine [16107]
Assn. of Solution Oriented Counsellors and Hypnotherapists of Australia [IO]
Assn. for Specialists in Gp. Work [11820]
Assn. of Therapeutic Communities [IO]
Assn. for Therapeutic Eurythmy in North Am. [IO]
Assn. for Therapeutic Eurythmy in North Am. [16608]
Assn. of Vision Educators [15677]
Associazione Italiana Fisioterapisti [IO]
Associazione Italiana di Terapia Occupazionale [IO]
Athletic Success Inst. [23665]
Australian Hand Therapy Assn. [IO]
Australian Music Therapy Assn. [IO]
Australian Physiotherapy Assn. [IO]
Austrian Physiotherapy Assn. [IO]
Barbados Physical Therapy Assn. [IO]
B.C. Assn. of Clinical Counsellors [IO]
Bermuda Occupational Therapy Assn. [IO]
Bermuda Physiotherapy Assn. [IO]
Biomagnetic Therapy Assn. [16609]
Botswana Physiotherapy Assn. [IO]
British Assn. of Art Therapists [IO]
British Assn. and Coll. of Occupational Therapists [IO]
British Assn. for Counselling and Psychotherapy [IO]
British Assn. of Dramatherapists [IO]
British Assn. of Occupational Therapists [IO]
British Assn. of Play Therapists [IO]
British Assn. for Sexual and Relationship Therapy [IO]
British Columbia Assn. for Play Therapy [IO]
British Reflexology Assn. [IO]
British Soc. for Music Therapy [IO]
Bulgarian Assn. of Kinesitherapists and Rehabilitators [IO]
Cameroon Soc. of Physiotherapy [IO]
Canadian Assn. for Child and Play Therapy [IO]
Canadian Assn. for Music Therapy [IO]
Canadian Assn. of Occupational Therapists [IO]
Canadian Athletic Therapists Assn. [IO]
Canadian Orthopractic Manual Therapy Assn. [IO]
Canadian Physiotherapy Assn. [IO]
Canadian Soc. of Respiratory Therapists [IO]
Canadian Sport Massage Therapists Assn. [IO]
Certification Bd. for Music Therapists [16213]
Chartered Soc. of Physiotherapy [IO]
Commn. on Accreditation for Marriage and Family Therapy Educ. [8819]
Commn. on Rehabilitation Counselor Certification [11822]
Commn. on Religious Counseling and Healing [19445]
Comm. on Accreditation for Respiratory Care [16610]
Community Guidance Ser. [16214]
Confederacion de Kinesiologos y Fisioterapeutas de la Republica Argentina [IO]
Coun. of Chiropractic Physiological Therapeutics and Rehabilitation [13999]
Coun. on Compulsive Gambling of New Jersey [12209]

Coun. of Occupational Therapists for the European Countries [IO]
Coun. for Sex Info. and Educ. [16400]
Counsellors and Psychotherapists Assn. of New South Wales [IO]
Counsellors' and Psychotherapists' Assn. of Victoria [IO]
Create A Smile Dental Found. [13318]
Croatian Assn. of Physiotherapists [IO]
Cyprus Assn. of Physiotherapists [IO]
Czech Assn. of Occupational Therapists [IO]
Dance-Movement Therapy Assn. of Australia [IO]
Delta Soc. [16611]
Early Childhood Music and Movement Assn. [12618]
Emirates Physiotherapy Soc. [IO]
Epilepsy Therapy Development Proj. [14381]
Equine Assisted Growth and Learning Assn. [16216]
Estonian Physiotherapists Assn. [IO]
European Fed. of Therapeutic Communities [IO]
European Music Therapy Confed. [IO]
Family Therapy Sect. of the Natl. Coun. on Family Relations [16612]
Federacion Ecuatoriana De Fisoterepia [IO]
Federacion Venezolana de Terapeutas Ocupacionales [IO]
Fed. Francaise des Masseurs Kinesitherapeutes Reeducateurs [IO]
Fiji Physiotherapy Assn. [IO]
Finnish Assn. of Physiotherapists [IO]
Found. for Physical Therapy [16613]
German Assn. for Music Therapy [IO]
German Assn. for Physiotherapy [IO]
Ghana Assn. of Physiotherapists [IO]
Gp. for the Advancement of Psychiatry [16084]
Hong Kong Occupational Therapy Assn. [IO]
Indian Assn. of Physiotherapists [IO]
Indonesian Physiotherapists Assn. [IO]
Infusion Nurses Soc. [16614]
Inst. on Psychiatric Services/American Psychiatric Assn. [16085]
Inst. of Transactional Anal. [IO]
Intl. Alliance for Animal Therapy and Healing [13703]
Intl. Assn. for Cognitive Psychotherapy [16218]
Intl. Assn. for Colon Hydrotherapy [14567]
Intl. Assn. of Human-Animal Interaction Organizations [16615]
Intl. Assn. of Human-Animal Interaction Organizations [IO]
Intl. Assn. for Marriage and Family Counselors [11825]
Intl. Assn. for Oxygen Therapy [16616]
Intl. Assn. for Oxygen Therapy [IO]
Intl. Assn. of Pastoral Psychologists [16151]
Intl. Assn. for Regression Res. and Therapies [16617]
Intl. Assn. for Relational Psychoanalysis and Psychotherapy [16108]
Intl. Assn. of Structural Integrators [13638]
Intl. Assn. of Transpersonal Therapists and Physicians [15205]
Intl. Assn. for Voice Movement Therapy [13711]
Intl. Bd. for Regression Therapy [16618]
Intl. Bd. for Regression Therapy [IO]
Intl. EECP Therapists Assn. [IO]
Intl. EECP Therapists Assn. [16619]
Intl. Expressive Arts Therapy Assn. [13712]
Intl. Fed. for Psychoanalytic Educ. [9028]
Intl. Fed. of Societies for Hand Therapy [IO]
International Institute of Reflexology [IO]
Intl. Inst. of Reflexology [16620]
Intl. Medical Soc. for Bio-Physical Info. - Therapy Assn. [IO]
Intl. Medical Spa Assn. [1870]
Intl. Palmtherapy Assn. [16621]
International Palmtherapy Association [IO]
Intl. Professional Surrogates Assn. [16403]
Intl. RadioSurgery Assn. [16269]
Intl. REST Investigators Soc. [16220]
Intl. Soc. for Biological Therapy of Cancer [13835]
Intl. Soc. for Dialogical Sci. [7544]
Intl. Soc. for Music in Medicine [IO]
Intl. Transactional Anal. Assn. [16089]

Reference to "IO" in place of a book number signifies that the association may be found in the 45th edition of International Organizations.

Encyclopedia of Associations, 46th Edition

4215

Iranian Physiotherapy Assn. [IO]
Irish Soc. of Chartered Physiotherapists [IO]
Israeli Assn. of Creative and Expressive
  Therapies [IO]
Israeli Assn. of Physiotherapists [IO]
Israeli Org. of Occupational Therapy [IO]
Jamaica Physiotherapy Assn. [IO]
Japanese Assn. of Occupational Therapists [IO]
Japanese Physical Therapy Assn. [IO]
Jordanian Physiotherapy Soc. [IO]
Jordanian Soc. for Occupational Therapy [IO]
Kenya Occupational Therapists Assn. [IO]
Kenya Soc. of Physiotherapists [IO]
Korean Physical Therapy Assn. [IO]
Latvian Assn. of Occupational Therapists [IO]
Latvian Physiotherapists Assn. [IO]
Laughter Therapy [16622]
Lithuanian Kinezitherapy Assn. [IO]
Love on a Leash - The Found. for Pet Provided
  Therapy [16623]
Malaysia Occupational Therapists Assn. [IO]
Malaysian Physiotherapy Assn. [IO]
Malta Assn. of Occupational Therapists [IO]
Malta Assn. of Physiotherapists [IO]
Medical Spa Soc. [1871]
Mental Res. Inst. [13737]
Metamorphic Assn. [IO]
Music Therapy Assn. of British Columbia [IO]
Namibia Assn. of Occupational Therapists [IO]
Namibian Soc. of Physiotherapy [IO]
Natl. Alliance for Infusion Therapy [14839]
Natl. Assn. for the Advancement of
  Psychoanalysis [16110]
Natl. Assn. of Counsellors, Hypnotherapists and
  Psychotherapists [IO]
Natl. Assn. of Myofascial Trigger Point Therapists
  [16624]
Natl. Assn. for Proton Therapy [15649]
Natl. Assn. of Psychiatric Hea. Systems [16091]
Natl. Assn. of Rehabilitation Providers and Agen-
  cies [16326]
Natl. Assn. for Res. and Therapy of Homosexual-
  ity [14434]
Natl. Assn. of Therapeutic Schools and Programs
  [13738]
Natl. Assn. of Therapeutic Wilderness Camps
  [23276]
Natl. Bd. for Certification in Occupational Therapy
  [16625]
Natl. Bd. for Respiratory Care [16626]
Natl. Coalition of Creative Arts Therapies Associa-
  tions [16224]
Natl. Coun. for Therapeutic Recreation Certifica-
  tion [16627]
Natl. Fed. for Biblio/Poetry Therapy [16225]
Natl. Fitness Therapy Assn. [15968]
Natl. Guild of Hypnotists [14926]
Natl. Home Oxygen Patients Assn. [14404]
Natl. Psychological Assn. for Psychoanalysis
  [16111]
Natl. Remotivation Therapy Org. [16226]
Natl. Therapeutic Recreation Soc. [16628]
Nepal Physiotherapy Assn. [IO]
Neuro-Developmental Treatment Assn. [15399]
New Zealand Soc. of Diversional Therapists [IO]
New Zealand Soc. for Music Therapy [IO]
New Zealand Soc. of Physiotherapists [IO]
Nigerian Assn. of Occupational Therapists [IO]
North Amer. Vodder Assn. of Lymphatic Therapy
  [15019]
Norwegian Assn. of Occupational Therapists [IO]
Occupational Therapists Assn. Mauritius [IO]
Occupational Therapists Assn., Tanzania [IO]
Occupational Therapists Assn. of Thailand [IO]
Occupational Therapy Assn. of the Philippines
  [IO]
Option Inst. Intl. Learning and Training Center [IO]
Option Inst. Intl. Learning and Training Center
  [16629]
Orthopaedic Sect., Amer. Physical Therapy Assn.
  [16630]
Outpatient Intravenous Infusion Therapy Assn.
  [16631]
Pakistan Occupational Therapy Assn. [IO]
Panhellenic Physiotherapists Assn. [IO]

Parrots and People [11516]
People-Animals-Love [16632]
People, Animals, Nature [13319]
Philippine Physical Therapy Assn. [IO]
Physical Therapy Assn. of Thailand [IO]
Physiotherapeuten Verband Furstentum Liechten-
  stein [IO]
Physiotherapy Assn. of Malawi [IO]
Physiotherapy Assn. of Trinidad and Tobago [IO]
Polish Soc. of Physiotherapy [IO]
Praying Hands Ranches [23360]
Private Practice Section/American Physical
  Therapy Assn. [16633]
Proj. Magic [16634]
Psychohistory Forum [16113]
Psychotherapists and Counsellors Assn. of
  Western Australia [IO]
Psychotherapy and Counselling Fed. of Australia
  [IO]
Quebec Assn. of Marriage and Family Therapy
  [IO]
Queensland Counsellors Assn. [IO]
Radical Caucus in Psychiatry [16092]
Recovery, Inc. [16230]
Romanian Fed. for Physiotherapy [IO]
Russian Assn. of Occupational Therapists [IO]
Sandplay Therapists of Am. [16635]
Sandtray Network [16114]
Saudi Physical Therapy Assn. [IO]
Sigmund Freud Archives [16115]
Slovenian Assn. of Occupational Therapists [IO]
Slovenian Assn. of Physiotherapists [IO]
Social Psychiatry Res. Inst. [16094]
Social/Vocational Rehabilitation Clinic [16231]
Sociedad Boliviana de Terapia Fisica [IO]
Soc. of Biological Psychiatry [16095]
Soc. for Companion Animal Stud. [IO]
Society for Light Treatment and Biological
  Rhythms [IO]
Soc. for Light Treatment and Biological Rhythms
  [16636]
Soc. of Ortho-Bionomy Intl. [13767]
Soc. of Sports Therapists [IO]
Soul Friends [16637]
South African Soc. of Physiotherapy [IO]
Southeast Inst. for Gp. and Family Therapy
  [18629]
Sri Lanka Soc. of Occupational Therapists [IO]
Sri Lanka Soc. of Physiotherapists [IO]
Stamps for the Wounded [22879]
Story Rhymes for Educ. [10986]
STRIDE: Sports and Therapeutic Recreation
  Instruction/Developmental Educ. [8205]
Surinaamse Vereniging voor Fysiotherapie [IO]
Swedish Assn. of Occupational Therapists [IO]
Swiss Assn. of Physiotherapy [IO]
Syrian Physical Therapy Assn. [IO]
Taiwan Occupational Therapy Assn. [IO]
Therapy Dogs Intl. [IO]
Therapy Dogs Intl. [16638]
Uganda Assn. of Physiotherapy [IO]
U.S. Assn. for Body Psychotherapy [16188]
U.S. Hereditary Angioedema Assn. [14487]
U.S. Medical Massage Assn. [15033]
U.S. Trager Assn. [13656]
Upledger Inst. [13657]
William Glasser Inst. [16233]
World Assn. for Social Psychiatry [16099]
World Confed. for Physical Therapy [IO]
World Fed. of Occupational Therapists [IO]
World Sports Medicine Assn. of Registered
  Therapists [16486]
World Wide Essence Soc. [14833]
Zambia Soc. of Physiotherapy [IO]
Zimbabwe Assn. of Occupational Therapists [IO]
Zimbabwe Physiotherapy Assn. [IO]
Therapy Acad; Amer. Family [11816]
Therapy; Acad. of Scientific Hypno [14913]
Therapy; Ackerman Inst. for Family [★12134]
Therapy; Amer. Assn. for Inhalation [★16599]
Therapy; Amer. Assn. for Marriage and Family
  [16200]
Therapy; Amer. Assn. for Music [★16205]
Therapy; Amer. Assn. for Respiratory [★16599]
Therapy; Amer. Bd. of Chelation [★16659]

Therapy; Amer. Psychological Assn. - Division of
  Psycho [16206]
Therapy; Amer. Soc. of Gene [14495]
Therapy Assn; Academic Language [12488]
Therapy; Assn. for the Advancement of Gestalt
  [16135]
Therapy; Assn. for the Advancement of Psycho
  [16210]
Therapy Assn; Amer. Art [16199]
Therapy Assn; Amer. Colon [★16061]
Therapy Assn; Amer. Corrective [★16311]
Therapy Assn; Amer. Dance [16203]
Therapy Assn; Amer. Family [★11816]
Therapy Assn; Amer. Gp. Psycho [16204]
Therapy Assn; Amer. Kinesio [16311]
Therapy Assn; Amer. Massage [15022]
Therapy Assn; Amer. Oriental Bodywork [★15024]
Therapy Assn; Amer. Polarity [13619]
Therapy Assn; Amer. Psycho [16207]
Therapy; Assn. for Comprehensive Neuro [15383]
Therapy Assn; Inhalation [★16599]
Therapy; Assn. for Poetry [★16223]
Therapy Assn; Prolo [★15753]
Therapy Assn; World Poetry [★16223]
Therapy Associations; Natl. Coalition of Arts
  [★16224]
Therapy; Bd. of Schools of Inhalation [★16610]
Therapy Dogs Intl. [16638], 88 Bartley Rd.,
  Flanders, NJ 07836, (973)252-9800
Therapy Dogs Intl. [IO], Flanders, NJ, United States
Therapy; Eastern Acad. of Sexual [★16408]
Therapy; Found. for Advancement in Cancer [13824]
Therapy Found; Amer. Occupational [15628]
Therapy of Homosexuality; Natl. Assn. for Res. and
  [14434]
Therapy; Inst. for Reality [★16233]
Therapy; Intl. Assn. for Enterostomal [★15533]
Therapy; Natl. Assn. for Drama [16222]
Therapy; Natl. Assn. for Poetry [16223]
Therapy; Natl. Assn. for Proton [15649]
Therapy; Natl. Bd. for Respiratory [★16626]
Therapy; Natl. Fed. for Biblio/Poetry [16225]
Therapy; Natl. Soc. for the Promotion of Oc-
  cupational [★16602]
Therapy Network; Family [★16228]
Therapy Oncology Gp; Radiation [15653]
Therapy Org; Natl. Remotivation [16226]
Therapy and Psychodrama; Amer. Soc. of Gp. Psy-
  cho [16208]
Therapy Res; Soc. for Psycho [16194]
Therapy and Res; Soc. for Sex [16408]
Therapy Soc; Amer. Api [13614]
Therapy; Southeast Inst. for Gp. and Family [18629]
Theriogenologists; Amer. Coll. of [16763]
Theriogenology; Soc. for [16806]

Thermal Analysis
  Calorimetry Conf. [7796]
  European Comm. for the Advancement of
    Thermal Sciences and Heat Transfer [IO]
  Intl. Confed. for Thermal Anal. and Calorimetry
    [IO]
  North Amer. Thermal Anal. Soc. [7797]
  Soc. for Thermal Medicine [16639]
Thermal Insulation Contractors Assn. [IO], Darling-
  ton, United Kingdom
Thermal Insulation Mfrs. Assn. - Defunct.
Thermal Insulation Mfrs. and Suppliers Assn. [IO],
  Aldershot, United Kingdom
Thermal and Nuclear Power Engg. Soc. [IO], Tokyo,
  Japan
Thermal Spraying and Surface Engg. Assn. [IO],
  Rugby, United Kingdom
Thermographers Assn; Intl. [2889]
Thermographers' Assn; Law Enforcement [5982]

Thermology
  Geothermal Resources Coun. [7143]
  Intl. Thermoelectric Soc. [IO]
Thermometer Collectors Club of Am. - Defunct.
Thermoplastic Exterior Building Division of the Soc.
  of the Plastics Indus. [★685]
Thermoplastic Pavement Marking Manufacturers
  Assn. - Address unknown since 2007.
Thermoplastic Pipe Division of the Soc. of the
  Plastics Indus. [★3038]
Thermoset Resin Formulators Assn. [857], c/o Jeri-
  lyn J. Church, CAE, Exec. Dir., 800 Roosevelt Rd.,
  Bldg. C, Ste. 312, Glen Ellyn, IL 60137, (630)942-
  6596

A star before a book entry number signifies that the name is not listed separately, but is mentioned within the entry.

Thespian Soc; Natl. [★9264]

Thespian Talent Club - Defunct,

Thessalonikian Soc. of America "Saint Demetrios" - Address unknown since 1995.

Theta Alpha Phi [24721], PO Box 14773, Columbus, OH 43214, (614)447-8045

Theta Chi Beta [24583], Syracuse Univ., Dept. of Religion, 501 Hall of Languages, Syracuse, NY 13244-1170, (315)443-3861

Theta Chi Fraternity [24667], 3330 Founders Rd., Indianapolis, IN 46268-1333, (317)824-1881

Theta Chi Omega Multicultural Sorority [24716], PO Box 190837, Arlington, TX 76019

Theta Delta Chi [24668], 214 Lewis Wharf, Boston, MA 02110, (617)742-8886

Theta Delta Chi [IO], Boston, MA, United States

Theta Delta Chi Educational Found. [★IO]

Theta Delta Chi Educational Found. [★24668]

Theta Delta Chi Founder's Corporation [★24668]

Theta Delta Chi Founder's Corporation [★IO]

Theta Intl. - Defunct.

Theta Kappa Nu [★24516]

Theta Kappa Nu [★24637]

Theta Kappa Omega - Address unknown since 1986.

Theta Kappa Phi [★24644]

Theta Lambda Phi [★24527]

Theta Nu Epsilon Soc. - Address unknown since 2005.

Theta Phi Alpha [24699], 27025 Knickerbocker Rd., Bay Village, OH 44140-2300, (440)899-9282

Theta Phi Fraternity - Address unknown since 1999.

Theta Psi [24566], c/o KCOM, A.T. Still Univ. of Hea. Sciences, Dept. of Student and Alumni Services, 800 W Jefferson St., Kirksville, MO 63501, (660)626-2121

Theta Rho Girls' Club [13518], 422 Trade St., Winston-Salem, NC 27101-2830, (336)725-5955

Theta Sigma Phi [★874]

Theta Sigma Upsilon - Address unknown since 1995.

Theta Tau [24469], 1011 San Jacinto, Ste. 205, Austin, TX 78701, (512)472-1904

Theta Upsilon [★24686]

Theta Xi [24669], PO Box 411134, St. Louis, MO 63141-3134, (314)993-6294

They Might Be Giants Information Club - Address unknown since 1999.

Thimble Collectors Intl. [22122], 1039 Hill Rd., No. 121, Pickerington, OH 43147

Thimble Collectors Intl. [IO], Pickerington, OH, United States

Thimble Guild [22123]

Thimbles
  Thimble Collectors Intl. [22122]
  Thimble Guild [22123]

Think First Found.: Natl. Injury Prevention Programs [★16470]

Think First Natl. Injury Prevention Found. [16470], 29W120 Butterfield Rd., Ste. 105, La Grange, IL 60525, (630)393-1400

Think Ink - Defunct.

Think Tank; Independence [★17219]

Think Twice Global Vaccine Inst. [14944], PO Box 9638, Santa Fe, NM 87504, (505)983-1856

Thinking; Center for Critical [8179]

Thinking; Engg. and Sci. Network on [7217]

Thinking and Moral Critique; Center for Critical [★8179]

Third Class Mail Assn. [★2449]

Third Continental Cong. [17299]

Third Generation [17278], c/o Heritage Found., 214 Massachusetts Ave. NE, Washington, DC 20002-4999, (202)546-4400

Third Millennium: Advocates for the Future [17674]

Third Order of Carmel [IO], Rome, Italy

Third Order Carmelites [★19647]

Third Order of Mary/Marists [19728], c/o Fr. Albert Dianni, Dir., 27 Isabella St., Boston, MA 02116-5216, (617)426-4448

Third Order Secular of Our Blessed Lady of Mount Carmel and St. Theresa of Jesus [★IO]

Third Reich Study Group [IO], Natick, MA, United States

Third Reich Study Group [22882], c/o Robert Dunn, 3318 Running Cedar Way, Williamsburg, VA 23188

Third World
  Action for World Solidarity [IO]
  Adopt a Dr. [12750]
  Adventist Development and Relief Agency Intl. [12826]
  Amer. Assn. for Intl. Aging [11274]
  Amer. Jewish World Ser. [12829]
  AMG Intl. [20298]
  Angelcare [11672]
  Ashoka: Innovators for the Public [12419]
  Assn. for the Advancement of Policy, Res. and Development in the Third World [17828]
  Assn. on Third World Affairs [17829]
  BIO Ventures for Global Hea. [14975]
  Center for Third World Organizing [17099]
  Christian Found. for Children and Aging [13159]
  Christian Medical and Dental Associations [20238]
  Comm. on Missionary Evangelism [20001]
  Consultative Gp. on Intl. Agricultural Res. [12425]
  CRISTA Ministries [13166]
  Development Gp. for Alternative Policies [17835]
  Edge-ucate [12057]
  Educational Concerns for Hunger Org. [12389]
  Feeding Hungry Children Intl. [12390]
  Flying Doctors of Am. [12523]
  Food for the Hungry [12391]
  Found. for the Support of Intl. Medical Training [14977]
  Freedom from Hunger [12394]
  Futures for Children [11695]
  Global Healing [12450]
  Global Hea. Coun. [14979]
  Global Outreach Mission [12525]
  Global Ser. Corps [13392]
  Healing the Children [11697]
  Hea. Volunteers Overseas [12526]
  Heifer Proj. Intl. [12429]
  Hermandad [17046]
  Hesperian Found. [14980]
  Holt Intl. Children's Services [11698]
  Humanity Intl. [12859]
  Intl. Acad. of Health Care Professionals [14705]
  Intl. Fed. of Ophthalmological Societies [15686]
  The Intl. Found. [12434]
  Intl. Inst. of Rural Reconstruction, U.S. Chap. [12938]
  Intl. Relief And Development [11782]
  Just Act: Youth Action for Global Justice [12435]
  MAP Intl. [20243]
  Media Associates Intl. [19981]
  Mission Doctors Assn. [12532]
  Need [12875]
  Open Voting Consortium [17489]
  Oper. Smile [12534]
  OXFAM Am. [12438]
  Presbyterian Hunger Prog. [12397]
  Self Help Intl. [12442]
  Sister Island Proj. [11788]
  Trickle Up Prog. [12446]
  United Methodist Comm. on Relief [20267]
  Volunteers in Tech. Assistance [12448]
  Winrock Intl. [16959]
  World Medical Mission [20245]

Third World Acad. of Sciences [★IO]

Third World Conf. Found. [IO], Chicago, IL, United States

Third World Conf. Found. [17850], 1525 E 53rd St., Ste. 437, Chicago, IL 60615-4509, (773)241-6688

Third World Feminist Collective - Defunct.

Third World Forum - African Off. [IO], Dakar, Senegal

Third World Forum - Middle East Off. [IO], Cairo, Egypt

Third World Info. Network [★IO]

Third World Moving Images Project - Defunct.

Third World Network - Malaysia [IO], Penang, Malaysia

Third World Network of Sci. Organizations [IO], Trieste, Italy

Third World Org. for Women in Sci. [IO], Trieste, Italy

Third World Rpts. - Defunct.

Third World Women's Project - Defunct.

Thirdworld Education Outreach - Defunct.

Thirkell Soc; Angela [9633]

Thirst for Learning Found. - Address unknown since 1999.

Thistle Class Assn. [23224], c/o Patty Lawrence, Sec.-Treas., 6758 Little River Ln., Loveland, OH 45140, (513)583-5080

Thom Bierdz Intl. Fan Club - Defunct.

Thom Christopher Fan Club - Address unknown since 1995.

Thomas A. Dooley Found. [★14982]

Thomas A. Dooley Found. [★IO]

Thomas A. Dooley Foundation/INTERMED U.S.A. [★IO]

Thomas A. Dooley Foundation/INTERMED U.S.A. [★14982]

Thomas Aquinas Found; St. [19714]

Thomas B. Fordham Found. [17477], 1701 K St. NW, Ste. 1000, Washington, DC 20006, (202)223-5452

Thomas Blair Family Org. - Defunct.

Thomas Borland Family Org. - Defunct.

Thomas Fellowship Program; Julius A. [★8047]

Thomas Glisson Family Org. - Address unknown since 2006.

Thomas Guthrie Family Org. - Defunct.

Thomas Hall Family Org. - Address unknown since 2007.

The Thomas Hardy Assn. [9712], c/o Rosemarie Morgan, Pres./Ed., 124 Bishop St., New Haven, CT 06511

Thomas Hardy Festival Soc. [★IO]

Thomas Hardy Soc. [IO], Dorchester, United Kingdom

Thomas Hardy Soc. of America - Defunct.

Thomas Jefferson Equal Tax Soc. [18720]

Thomas Jefferson Inst. for the Study of Religious Freedom - Address unknown since 1994.

Thomas Jefferson Soc. of the U.S.A. - Address unknown since 1995.

Thomas Jefferson's Poplar Forest [10069], PO Box 419, Forest, VA 24551-0419, (434)525-1806

Thomas Kinkade Collectors' Soc. [21545], c/o Members Ser. Dept., 900 Lightpost Way, Morgan Hill, CA 95037

Thomas Legal Defense Fund - Defunct.

Thomas Lovell Beddoes Soc. [IO], Belper, United Kingdom

Thomas McDonough Family Org. - Address unknown since 2006.

Thomas Minor Family Soc. [★21071]

Thomas Minor Soc. [21071], c/o Ray Howell, Sec., 38 W 1600 S, Orem, UT 84058, (801)377-8294

Thomas More Assn. [19729]

Thomas More Soc. of Am. - Address unknown since 1999.

Thomas Nast Soc. [9477], c/o Morristown-Morris Township Lib., 1 Miller Rd., Morristown, NJ 07960, (973)538-3473

Thomas Paine Natl. Historical Assn. [11153], 983 North Ave., New Rochelle, NY 10804-3609, (914)434-7270

Thomas Rivera Center [★19196]

Thomas Thorn and Mary Ann Downman Family Org. - Defunct.

Thomas Wolfe Soc. [9713], c/o David Strange, Membership Coor., PO Box 1146, Bloomington, IN 47402-1146

Thomist Assn. - Defunct.

Thompson Collectors Assn. [22431], PO Box 1675, Ellicott City, MD 21041-1675

Thompson Collectors Assn. [IO], Ellicott City, MD, United States

Thomson Found. [IO], Cardiff, United Kingdom

Thomson Sci. - Europe, Middle East, and Africa [IO], London, United Kingdom

Thoracic Medicine
  Amer. Assn. for Thoracic Surgery [16640]
  Amer. Bd. of Thoracic Surgery [16641]
  Amer. Thoracic Soc. [16642]
  Amer. Thoracic Soc. [16642]
  CTSNet: Cardiothoracic Surgery Network [16643]
  European Assn. for Cardio-Thoracic Surgery [IO]
  European Soc. of Thoracic Surgeons [IO]
  Hong Kong Thoracic Soc. [IO]
  Latin Amer. Thoracic Soc. [IO]
  Scandinavian Assn. for Thoracic Surgery [IO]

Reference to "IO" in place of a book number signifies that the association may be found in the 45th edition of International Organizations.

Scandinavian Soc. for Res. in CardioThoracic Surgery [IO]
Soc. of Thoracic Surgeons [16644]
Thoracic Surgery Residents Assn. [16645]
Thoracic Radiology; Soc. of [16305]
Thoracic Soc; Hong Kong [IO]
Thoracic Surgery
Amer. Assn. for Thoracic Surgery [16640]
Amer. Bd. of Thoracic Surgery [16641]
Amer. Thoracic Soc. [16642]
CTSNet: Cardiothoracic Surgery Network [16643]
Soc. of Thoracic Surgeons [16644]
Thoracic Surgery Residents Assn. [16645]
Thoracic Surgery; Amer. Bd. of [16641]
Thoracic Surgery; Bd. of [★16641]
Thoracic Surgery Residents Assn. [16645], c/o Daniel J. Boffa, MD, Pres., 9500 Euclid Ave., H-35, Cleveland, OH 44195-5108, (216)445-6816
Thorcheron Hunter Assn. - Defunct.
Thoreau Fellowship - Defunct.
Thoreau Found. - Defunct.
Thoreau, Henry David
Thoreau Soc. [9714]
Walden Pond Advisory Comm. [4464]
Walden Woods Proj. [10076]
Thoreau Inst. [4696], PO Box 1590, Bandon, OR 97411, (541)347-1517
Thoreau Lyceum - Defunct.
Thoreau Quiet Desperation Soc. - Address unknown since 1995.
Thoreau Soc. [9714], 55 Old Bedford Rd., Concord, MA 01742, (978)369-5310
Thorne Ecological Found. [★4523]
Thorne Ecological Inst. [4523], PO Box 19107, Boulder, CO 80308-2107, (303)499-3647
Thorne Smith Soc. [9715]
Thornton W. Burgess Soc. [4608], 6 Discovery Hill Rd., East Sandwich, MA 02537, (508)888-6870
Thornton Wilder Soc. [11200], Coll. of New Jersey, PO Box 7718, Ewing, NJ 08628-0718, (609)771-2346
Thornton Wilder Soc. [IO], Ewing, NJ, United States
Thoroughbred Adoption and Retirement Assn. [12302]
Thoroughbred Breeders' Assn. [IO], Newmarket, United Kingdom
Thoroughbred Breeders Assn; Amer. [★23515]
Thoroughbred Club of Am. [23514], PO Box 8098, Lexington, KY 40533-8098, (859)254-4282
Thoroughbred Owners Assn; Amer. [★23515]
Thoroughbred Owners and Breeders Assn. [23515], PO Box 910668, Lexington, KY 40591, (859)276-2291
Thoroughbred Racing Associations [23516], 420 Fair Hill Dr., Ste. 1, Elkton, MD 21921-2573, (410)392-9200
Thoroughbred Racing Protective Bur. [23517], 420 Fair Hill Dr., Ste. 2, Elkton, MD 21921, (410)398-2261
Thoroughbred Retirement Found. [16985], PO Box 3387, Saratoga Springs, NY 12866, (518)226-0028
Thoroughbred Soc; North Amer. [23538]
Thoroughbred United Retirement Fund - Defunct.
Thorpe, Jr. Found; Merle [★18058]
Thought and Educ. Club [7957]
Thought Found; Freedom of [18616]
Thousand [★9983]
Thousand [★IO]
Thread Inst. - Defunct.
The Three Cent 1851-57 Unit [★22887]
Three Dog Night Fan Club [24984], c/o Madonna Nuckolls, Pres./Ed., PO Box 1975, Rowlett, TX 75030
Three Hundred Third BGA Membership [★21373]
Three Mile Island Alert [18136], 4100 Hillsdale Rd., Harrisburg, PA 17112-1419, (717)541-1101
Three Rivers Narrow Gauge Historical Soc. - Address unknown since 1994.
Three Stooges Fan Club [24800], PO Box 747, Gwynedd Valley, PA 19437, (267)468-0810
Three-Wheeler Club - USA Gp; Morgan [21719]
Threefold Educational Found. and School [8529], 260 Hungry Hollow Rd., Spring Valley, NY 10977, (845)352-5020
Threshers Assn; Midwest Old Settlers and [9483]

Threshers Assn; Natl. [9484]
Threshold [4609], c/o Sacred Passage and The Way of Nature, PO Box 3388, Tucson, AZ 85722-3388, (877)818-1881
Thrift Shops; Natl. Assn. of Resale and [3417]
Thrive [IO], Reading, United Kingdom
Thrivent Financial for Lutherans [19218], 4321 N Ballard Rd., Appleton, WI 54919-0001, (800)847-4836
Throat Advances in Children; Soc. for Ear, Nose, and [15827]
Thrombosis and Haemostasis; Intl. Soc. on [★14793]
Thrombosis and Vascular Biology of the Amer. Heart Assn; Coun. on Arteriosclerosis, [13902]
Through the Looking Glass - Defunct.
Throw the Hypocritical Rascals Out - Defunct.
Thunderbird Amer. Indian Dancers [10754], c/o Louis Mofsie, Dir., 204 W Central Ave., Maywood, NJ 07607, (201)587-9633
Thunderbird Assn; Intl. [★23195]
Thunderbird Class Assn. [★23195]
Thunderbird Class Assn; Intl. [23195]
Thunderbird Club of Am; Heartland Vintage [21654]
Thunderbird Club of Am; Vintage [★21812]
Thunderbird and Cougar Club of Am. [21795], 422 Cooper St., Mountain Home, AR 72653
Thunderbirds of America - Defunct.
Thunderbolt Pilots Assn; P-47 [21397]
Thunderhead Alliance [18751], PO Box 3309, Prescott, AZ 86302, (928)541-9841
Thurgood Marshall Scholarship Fund [7932], 80 Maiden Ln., Ste. 2204, New York, NY 10038, (212)573-8888
Thyroid
Amer. Assn. of Clinical Endocrinologists [14350]
Amer. Thyroid Assn. [16646]
Hypoparathyroidism Assn. [14356]
Latin Amer. Thyroid Soc. [IO]
Natl. Graves' Disease Found. [16647]
Thyroid Cancer Survivors' Assn. [16648]
Thyroid Found. of Am. [16649]
Thyroid Soc. for Educ. and Res. [16650]
Thyroid Assn; Asia and Oceania [IO]
Thyroid Cancer Survivors' Assn. [16648], PO Box 1545, New York, NY 10159-1545, (877)588-7904
Thyroid Eye Disease Assn. [IO], Calne, United Kingdom
Thyroid Found. of Am. [16649], One Longfellow Pl., Ste. 1518, Boston, MA 02114, (617)534-1500
Thyroid Soc. for Educ. and Res. [16650]
TI Personal Programmable Calculator Club - Defunct.
TIAA-CREF [9066], PO Box 1259, Charlotte, NC 28201, (800)842-2252
Tiberias Institutions Relief Soc; United [12463]
Tibet
Found. for the Preservation of the Mahayana Tradition [19550]
Intl. Campaign for Tibet [18738]
Intl. Campaign for Tibet [IO]
Jewel Heart [19552]
Kunzang Palyul Choling [19553]
Nepal and Tibet Philatelic Stud. Circle [22852]
Proj. Tibet [18739]
Proj. Tibet [IO]
Tibet Fund [11055]
Tibet Justice Center [18740]
Tibet Justice Center [IO]
Tibetan Aid Proj. [12822]
U.S.-Tibet Comm. [18741]
U.S.-Tibet Comm. [IO]
Tibet AID - Japan [IO], Kyoto, Japan
Tibet Culture Centre [IO], Tokyo, Japan
Tibet Fund [11055], 241 E 32nd St., New York, NY 10016, (212)213-5011
Tibet Justice Center [18740], 2288 Fulton St., Ste. 312, Berkeley, CA 94704, (510)486-0588
Tibet Justice Center [IO], Berkeley, CA, United States
Tibet Philatelic Stud. Circle; Nepal and [22852]
Tibet Relief Fund of the United Kingdom [★IO]
Tibet Soc. - Defunct.
Tibet Soc. and Relief Fund of the United Kingdom [★IO]

Tibet Soc. of the United Kingdom [IO], London, United Kingdom
Tibetan
Found. for the Preservation of the Mahayana Tradition [19550]
Jewel Heart [19552]
Kunzang Palyul Choling [19553]
Nepal and Tibet Philatelic Stud. Circle [22852]
Tibet Fund [11055]
Tibetan Aid Proj. [12822]
Tibetan Spaniel Club of Am. [22366]
Tibetan Aid Proj. [12822], 2910 San Pablo Ave., Berkeley, CA 94702, (510)848-4238
Tibetan Aid Proj. [IO], Berkeley, CA, United States
Tibetan Found. [★11055]
Tibetan Inst. of Performing Arts [★11055]
Tibetan Medical Institute [★11055]
Tibetan Nyingma Relief Foundation [★12822]
Tibetan Nyingma Relief Foundation [★IO]
Tibetan Refugee Youth Sponsorship Programs - Defunct.
Tibetan Spaniel Club of Am. [22366], c/o Cindie Swaim, Membership Chair, 23374 Kingsbury Rd., Middleton, ID 83644
Tibetan Studies; Institute of Higher [★11055]
Tibetan Terrier Club of Am. [22367], c/o Robert Kreis, Pres., PO Box 6243, Denver, CO 80206
Tibetan Women's Assn. [IO], Dharamsala, India
Tibetan Youth Cong. [IO], Dharamsala, India
Tibetian
Uniform and Textile Ser. Assn. [2408]
Tic Douloureux
Trigeminal Neuralgia Assn. [15370]
Ticket Brokers; Natl. Assn. of [1316]
Tiddlywinks Assn; North Amer. [22472]
Tidewater Guild for Infant Survival, Inc. [★16522]
Tidewater Nicaragua Project Found. - Address unknown since 2001.
Tie Down Assn; Web Sling and [2078]
Tie Fabrics Assn. - Defunct.
Tie Found; Men's [★252]
Tie Line - Defunct.
Tie Producers; Natl. Assn. of Railroad [★3292]
Tiers Ordre Carmelitaine [★IO]
Tietotekniikan liitto ry [★IO]
Tiffany Club [★13091]
Tiffin Glass Collectors Club [22567], PO Box 554, Tiffin, OH 44883, (419)448-0200
TIGA Sailboard Class Assn. - Defunct.
Tiger Cat Assn. - Defunct.
Tiger Horse Assn. [4960], 1604 Fescue Cir., Huddleston, VA 24104, (540)297-2276
Tiger-Owners; California Assn. of [21603]
Tigers of the 14th Air Force Assn; Flying [21393]
Tigers East/Alpines East [21796], PO Box 1260, Kulpsville, PA 19443-1260, (610)913-7872
Tigers East/Alpines East [IO], Kulpsville, PA, United States
Tilapia Assn; Amer. [4666]
Tilapia Intl. Found. [IO], Utrecht, Netherlands
The Tile Assn. [IO], Beckenham, United Kingdom
Tile Assn; Structural Clay [★604]
Tile and Composition Roofers, Damp and Waterproof Workers Assn; United Slate, [★24033]
Tile Contractors Assn. of Am. [1066], 4 E 113th Terr., Kansas City, MO 64114, (800)655-8453
Tile Contractors Assn; Natl. [1053]
Tile Coun. of Am. [★680]
Tile Coun. of North Am. [680], 100 Clemson Res. Blvd., Anderson, SC 29625, (864)646-8453
Tile Distributors of Am; Ceramic [★611]
Tile Distributors Assn; Ceramic [611]
Tile Industry Credit Assn. - Defunct.
Tile Inst. of Am; Ceramic [1009]
Tile Inst; Asphalt [★665]
Tile Inst; Asphalt and Vinyl Asbestos [★665]
Tile Inst; Resilient [★665]
Tile Inst; Roof [★681]
Tile and Mantel Contractors Assn. of Am. [★1066]
Tile Manufacturers Assn; Concrete [924]
Tile, Marble, Terrazzo, Finishers, Shopworkers, and Granite Cutters Intl. Union [★24032]
Tile Partners for Humanity [12338], 3845 Holcomb Bridge Rd., Ste. 400, Norcross, GA 30092, (770)416-0200

A star before a book entry number signifies that the name is not listed separately, but is mentioned within the entry.

Tile Partners for Humanity [IO], Norcross, GA, United States
Tile Roofing Inst. [681], 230 E Ohio St., Ste. 400, Chicago, IL 60611-3265, (312)670-4177
Tile Roofing Manufacturers Assn; Natl. [★681]
Tile, Terrazzo, Marble Contractors and Affiliates; Assn. of [★1053]
Tiles and Architectural Ceramics Soc. [IO], Stoke-On-Trent, United Kingdom
Tillage Info. Center; Conservation [★4384]
Tilling Soc. [IO], Hastings, United Kingdom
Tillis Fan Club; Mel [24946]
Tillis Fan Club; Pam [24956]
Tilt-Up Concrete Assn. [1067], PO Box 204, Mount Vernon, IA 52314, (319)895-6911
Tilt-Up Concrete Association [IO], Mount Vernon, IA, United States
Tim Daniels Fan Club - Defunct.
Tim Fedewa Fan Club - Address unknown since 2000.
Timber Assn. of California [★1605]
Timber Assn; Western [★1605]
Timber Constr; Amer. Inst. of [1633]
Timber Decking Assn. [IO], Castleford, United Kingdom
Timber Development Assn. [★IO]
Timber Frame Bus. Coun. [682], 217 Main St., Hamilton, MT 59840, (406)375-0713
Timber Frame Indus. Assn. [★IO]
Timber Framers Guild [IO], Becket, MA, United States
Timber Framers Guild [1625], PO Box 60, Becket, MA 01223, (413)623-9926
Timber Importers Assn. of America - Defunct.
Timber Mgt. Policy Reform and Sustainable Forestry Prog. [★4354]
Timber Packaging and Pallet Confed. [IO], Leicester, United Kingdom
Timber Preservers Assn. of Australia [IO], Brighton, Australia
Timber Products Mfrs. [1626], 951 E 3rd Ave., Spokane, WA 99202-2215, (509)535-4646
Timber Products Mfrs. Assn. [★1626]
Timber Res. and Development Assn. [IO], High Wycombe, United Kingdom
Timber Res. and Development Assn. [★IO]
Timber Trade Fed. [IO], London, United Kingdom
Timbers Res. Sta; Tall [4457]
Timbers Res; Tall [★4457]
Timberwolf Assn; 104th Infantry Div. Natl. [20695]
Timbrado Breeders; Amer. Assn. of Spanish [21834]
Time
   Antiquarian Horological Soc. [IO]
   British Horological Inst. [IO]
   Intl. Soc. for the Stud. of Time [IO]
   Intl. Soc. for the Stud. of Time [11056]
   Intl. Watch Collectors Soc. [22988]
   Natl. Assn. of Timetable Collectors [23008]
   Natl. Assn. of Watch and Clock Collectors [22990]
   North Amer. Sundial Soc. [9278]
Time Capsule Soc; Intl. [10041]
Time-Critical Shipment Comm. - Defunct.
Time Equipment
   Intl. Watch Collectors Soc. [22988]
   Natl. Assn. of Watch and Clock Collectors [22990]
   Natl. Time Equip. Assn. [3812]
   North Amer. Sundial Soc. [9278]
Time Keeping
   Intl. Watch Collectors Soc. [22988]
   Natl. Assn. of Timetable Collectors [23008]
   Natl. Assn. of Watch and Clock Collectors [22990]
   North Amer. Sundial Soc. [9278]
Time Measurements Assn. for Standards and Res; Methods [★7165]
Time Out to Enjoy - Defunct.
Timepieces
   Fed. of the Swiss Watch Indus. [IO]
   Finnish Watchmaker Assn. [IO]
   Intl. Watch Collectors Soc. [22988]
   Intl. Watch Fob Assn. [22989]
   Intl. Watch Fob Assn. [IO]
   Japan Watch Importers' Assn. [IO]
   Natl. Assn. of Watch and Clock Collectors [22990]
   North Amer. Sundial Soc. [9278]
   North Amer. Sundial Soc. [IO]

Self Winding Clock Assn. [22991]
Singapore Clock and Watch Trade Assn. [IO]
Taiwan Watch and Clock Indus. Assn. [IO]
Timeshare Consumers Assn. [IO], Blyth, United Kingdom
Timetable Collectors; Natl. Assn. of [23008]
TimeWarp - The Official UK Rocky Horror Fan Club [IO], Tonbridge, United Kingdom
Timing Assn; East Coast [22920]
Timor Action Network/US; East [★17442]
Timor and Indonesia Action Network/US; East [17442]
Timothy Demonbreun Soc. [★20741]
Tin Can Sailors - The Natl. Assn. of Destroyer Veterans [21220], PO Box 100, Somerset, MA 02726, (508)677-0515
Tin Can Tourists of the World - Address unknown since 1995.
Tin Mill Prdt. Producers; Comm. of [★977]
Tin Res. Inst. [★IO]
Tin Res. Inst. - Defunct.
Tin Tech. [IO], St. Albans, United Kingdom
Tin Trade Assn; Amer. [2698]
Tinker Found. [10313], 55 E 59th St., New York, NY 10022, (212)421-6858
Tinker Found. [IO], New York, NY, United States
Tinnitus Assn; Amer. [16443]
Tinnitus Assn; British [IO]
Tinnitus Intl. Service Assn. - Defunct.
Tippers Anonymous - Defunct.
Tippers Intl. - Address unknown since 2004.
TIPS Prog. [11847], 1101 Wilson Blvd., Ste. 1700, Arlington, VA 22209, (800)GET-TIPS
Tire Assn. of North Am. [★3814]
Tire Dealers; Natl. Assn. of Independent [★3814]
Tire Dealers and Retreaders Assn; Natl. [★3814]
Tire Indus. Assn. [3814], 1532 Pointer Ridge Pl., Ste. G, Bowie, MD 20716-1883, (301)430-7280
Tire Retread Info. Bur. [3815], 900 Weldon Grove Pl., Pacific Grove, CA 93950, (831)372-1917
Tire Retread Information Bureau [IO], Pacific Grove, CA, United States
Tire Retreading Inst. [★3814]
Tire and Rim Assn. [3816], 175 Montrose W Ave., Ste. 150, Copley, OH 44321, (330)666-8121
Tire and Rubber Assn; Intl. [★3814]
Tire Soc. [7798], PO Box 1502, Akron, OH 44309-1502, (330)929-5238
Tire Soc. [IO], Akron, OH, United States
Tires
   European Tyre and Rim Tech. Org. [IO]
   Imported Tyre Mfrs'. Assn. [IO]
   Intl. Tire Assn. [IO]
   Intl. Tire Assn. [3813]
   Japan Auto. Tyre Mfrs. Assn. [IO]
   Malaysia Automotive Tyre Mfrs. Indus. Gp. [IO]
   Natl. Assn. of Tire and Renovating Plants Distributors [IO]
   Natl. Assn. of Tire Specialists [IO]
   Natl. Fed. of Tire Retailers [IO]
   Natl. Tyre Distributors Assn. [IO]
   Retread Mfrs. Assn. [IO]
   Scandinavian Tire and Rim Org. [IO]
   Tire Indus. Assn. [3814]
   Tire Retread Info. Bur. [3815]
   Tire Retread Information Bureau [IO]
   Tire and Rim Assn. [3816]
   Tire Soc. [7798]
   Tire Soc. [IO]
Tirisanyo Catholic Commn. - Caritas Botswana [IO], Gaborone, Botswana
Tissue
   Amer. Assn. of Tissue Banks [16663]
   Amer. Soc. for Histocompatibility and Immunogenetics [14931]
   Amer. Soc. of Transplant Surgeons [16667]
   Angioma Alliance [15307]
   Assn. of Organ Procurement Organizations [14287]
   Center for Organ Recovery and Educ. [16670]
   Connective Tissue Oncology Soc. [15645]
   Ehlers Danlos Natl. Found. [16651]
   Intl. MYOPAIN Soc. [15842]
   Intl. Soc. for Heart and Lung Transplantation [16674]

Lupus Info. Network [15015]
Natl. Assn. of Myofascial Trigger Point Therapists [16624]
Natl. Marfan Found. [16652]
North Amer. Transplant Coordinators Org. [16681]
Stickler Involved People [14483]
Tissue Engg. Soc. Intl. [6610]
USBloodDonors.org [13766]
World Assn. of Sarcoidosis and Other Granulomatous Disorders [IO]
Tissue Banks; Amer. Assn. of [16663]
Tissue Banks Intl. [13713], 815 Park Ave., Baltimore, MD 21201, (410)752-3800
Tissue Banks Intl. [IO], Baltimore, MD, United States
Tissue Culture Assn. [★6598]
Tissue Culture Commn. [★6598]
Tissue Engg. Soc. Intl. [6610]
Tissue Engg. Soc. Intl. [IO], Baltimore, MD, United States
Tissue Reactions to Drugs; Registry of [★15867]
Tissue Sector [IO], Swindon, United Kingdom
Tissue Viability Nurses Assn. [IO], Plymouth, United Kingdom
Titan Soc. [★9987]
Titanic Enthusiasts of Am. [★10447]
Titanic Enthusiasts of Am. [★IO]
Titanic Historical Society [IO], Indian Orchard, MA, United States
Titanic Historical Soc. [10447], 208 Main St., PO Box 51053, Indian Orchard, MA 01151-0053, (413)543-4770
Titanic Intl. [★10448]
Titanic Intl. [★IO]
Titanic Intl. Soc. [IO], Freehold, NJ, United States
Titanic Intl. Soc. [10448], c/o Robert Bracken, Treas., 47 Van Blarcom Ave., Midland Park, NJ 07432, (814)899-5438
Titanium Development Assn. [★2712]
Titanium Development Assn. [★IO]
Titanium Dioxide Mfrs. Sector Gp. [IO], Brussels, Belgium
Tithing
   NewTithing Gp. [18742]
   Tithing Found. [20595]
Tithing Found. [20595], c/o Book Center, 1100 E 55th St., Chicago, IL 60615, (773)256-0681
Tithing Found; Layman [★20595]
Title Assn; Amer. [★3297]
Title Assn; Amer. Land [3297]
Title Insurers; Natl. Assn. of Bar-Related [2204]
Title Insurers; Natl. Conf. of Bar-Related [★2204]
Title Seven Directors; Natl. Assn. of [★11315]
Tiyospaya Amer. Indian Student Org. - Address unknown since 2001.
Tjanstemannens Centralorganisation [★IO]
The TLT Gp. [★IO]
The TLT Gp. [★6898]
TMJ Assn. [15850], PO Box 26770, Milwaukee, WI 53226-0770, (262)432-0350
Tmmob Jeoloji Muhendisleri Odasi [★IO]
TNG Canada/CWA [IO], Ottawa, ON, Canada
To the Best of You - Address unknown since 1990.
Toastmasters Intl. [10904], PO Box 9052, Mission Viejo, CA 92690-9052, (949)858-8255
Toastmasters Intl. [IO], Mission Viejo, CA, United States
Toastmasters New Zealand [IO], Christchurch, New Zealand
Tobacco
   Action on Smoking and Hea. [16431]
   Amer. Hea. and Temperance Assn. [13303]
   Amer. Legacy Found. [18743]
   APPEAL: Asian Pacific Partners for Empowerment and Leadership [11760]
   Assn. of Dark Leaf Tobacco Dealers and Exporters [3817]
   Assn. of the German Smoking Tobacco Indus. [IO]
   Assn. of Spanish Tobacconists [IO]
   Assn. for the Treatment of Tobacco Use and Dependence [16653]
   Bakery, Confectionery, Tobacco Workers and Grain Millers Intl. Union [24017]
   Brazilian Tobacco Indus. Assn. [IO]
   Burley Marketing Assn. [3818]

Reference to "IO" in place of a book number signifies that the association may be found in the 45th edition of International Organizations.

Encyclopedia of Associations, 46th Edition   4219

Burley Stabilization Corp. [5245]
Burley Tobacco Growers Cooperative Assn. [5246]
Cigar Assn. of America [3819]
Cigarette Indus. Assn. [IO]
Cigarette Pack Collectors Assn. [21994]
Coalition for Fire-Safe Cigarettes [12191]
Cooperation Centre for Sci. Res. Relative to Tobacco [IO]
Doctors Ought to Care [14554]
Eastern Dark-Fired Tobacco Growers Assn. [5247]
European Tobacco Wholesalers Assn. [IO]
Flue-Cured Tobacco Cooperative Stabilization Corp. [5248]
Intl. Assn. of Pipe Smokers Clubs [22897]
Intl. Hea. and Temperance Assn. [13304]
Intl. Network of Women Against Tobacco [18744]
Intl. Tobacco Growers Assn. [IO]
Italian Tobacconists' Fed. [IO]
Japan Smoking Articles Corporate Assn. [IO]
Lung Cancer Alliance [13839]
Natl. Assn. of the Cigar Indus. [IO]
Natl. Assn. of German Tobacco Wholesalers and Vending Machine Installers [IO]
Natl. Assn. of Tobacco Outlets [3820]
Natl. Latino Coun. on Alcohol and Tobacco Prevention [12269]
North Amer. Soc. of Pipe Collectors [22093]
Pipe Tobacco Coun. [3821]
Retail Tobacco Dealers of Am. [3429]
SmokeFree Educational Services [16434]
Smokeless Tobacco Coun. [3822]
Smokenders [16435]
Soc. for Res. on Nicotine and Tobacco [5249]
Soc. of Tobacco Jar Collectors [21936]
Tobacco Associates [3823]
Tobacco Assn. of Malawi [IO]
Tobacco Experts Assn. [IO]
Tobacco Growers' Assn. of Brazil [IO]
Tobacco Indus. and Marketing Bd. [IO]
Tobacco Mfrs. Assn. [IO]
Tobacco Merchants Assn. [3824]
Tobacconists' Assn. of Am. [3825]
Union of French Tobacco Growers' Co-operatives [IO]
The Universal Coterie of Pipe Smokers [22898]
Wholesale Confectionery and Tobacco Alliance [IO]
Zimbabwe Tobacco Assn. [IO]
Tobacco; Asia Pacific Assn. for the Control of [IO]
Tobacco Associates [3823], 8452 Holly Leaf Dr., McLean, VA 22102, (703)821-1255
Tobacco Assn. of Malawi [IO], Lilongwe, Malawi
Tobacco Assn. of the U.S. - Defunct.
Tobacco Control; Canadian Coun. for [IO]
Tobacco Control Rsrc. Center [13331], 102 The Fenway, Cushing Hall, Ste. 117, Boston, MA 02115, (617)373-2026
Tobacco Dealers of Am; Retail [3429]
Tobacco Distributors; Natl. Assn. of [★1500]
Tobacco Educ. Clearinghouse; California [★8556]
Tobacco Experts Assn. [IO], Izmir, Turkey
Tobacco-Free Kids; Natl. Center for [16433]
Tobacco; Freedom Org. for the Right to Enjoy Smoking [IO]
Tobacco Growers' Assn. of Brazil [IO], Santa Cruz do Sul, Brazil
Tobacco Industry Labor/Mgt. Comm. - Address unknown since 2002.
Tobacco Indus. and Marketing Bd. [IO], Harare, Zimbabwe
Tobacco Inst. - Defunct.
Tobacco Jar Collectors; Soc. of [21936]
Tobacco Mfrs. Assn. [IO], London, United Kingdom
Tobacco Merchants Assn. [3824], PO Box 8019, Princeton, NJ 08543-8019, (609)275-4900
Tobacco Salesmen's Assn. of America - Address unknown since 1995.
Tobacco Workers and Grain Millers Intl. Union; Bakery, Confectionery, [24017]
Tobacco Workers Intl. Union [★24017]
Tobacco Workers Intl. Union; Bakery, Confectionery and [★24017]
Tobacconists' Assn. of Am. [3825], 1211 N Tutor Ln., Evansville, IN 47715-9115, (812)479-8070

Toby Keith Intl. Fan Club [24985], c/o MusicCityNet, 54 Music-Sq. W, Nashville, TN 37203, (615)250-2130
TOC H [IO], Aylesbury, United Kingdom
TOCA - Defunct.
Tochi Seidoshi Gakkai [★IO]
Toddlers and Families; Zero to Three: Natl. Center for Infants, [13944]
Todos Santos Ambulance Fund - Address unknown since 1999.
Together [IO], London, United Kingdom
Together Found. for Global Unity - Address unknown since 2007.
Together, Inc. [12365], c/o The Pin Man, PO Box 52817, Tulsa, OK 74152, (918)587-2405
Together Intl./Anti-Soviet Res. Center - Defunct.
Toggenburg Club; Natl. [4787]
Toho Gakkai [★IO]
Toilet Articles; Amer. Manufacturers of [★1845]
Toilet Articles; Assoc. Manufacturers of [★1845]
Toilet Goods Assn. [★1845]
Toilet Seat Mfrs. Assn. - Defunct.
Toiletry and Fragrance Assn; Cosmetic, [1845]
Toimihenkilokeskusjarjesto [★IO]
Token Collectors Assn; Natl. [21954]
Token Collectors Club; Casino Chip and Gaming [21989]
Token Collectors; Soc. of Ration [22759]
Token Kenkyu Kai - Defunct.
Token and Medal Soc. [22763], c/o Rachel Irish, Sec., 101 W Prairie Ctr., No. 323, Hayden, ID 83835
Token Soc; Amer. Tax [22727]
Token Soc; Civil War [22732]
Token Soc; Love [22744]
Tokushima Intl. Cooperation [IO], Tokushima, Japan
Tokyo ACM SIGGRAPH [IO], Tokyo, Japan
Tokyo Bar Assn. [IO], Tokyo, Japan
Tokyo Bengoshikai Toshokan [★IO]
Tokyo Chigaku Kyokai [★IO]
Tokyo Foreign Trade Assn. [★IO]
Tokyo Geographical Soc. [IO], Tokyo, Japan
Tokyo Inst. of Psychiatry [IO], Tokyo, Japan
Tokyo Sangyo Boeki Kyokai [★IO]
Tokyo Trade and Indus. Assn. [IO], Tokyo, Japan
Toledo Bird Assn., Zebra Finch Club of America [21862]
Tolerant Majority - Defunct.
Tolerants - Defunct.
Tolkien Fellowships - Defunct.
Tolkien, J.R.R.
  Amer. Hobbit Assn. [9631]
  Elvish Linguistic Fellowship [10402]
Tolkien Soc. [IO], Oxford, United Kingdom
Tolstoy Found. [19342], PO Box 578, Valley Cottage, NY 10989, (845)268-6722
Tom Dooley Youth League - Defunct.
Tom Jones Fan Club - Address unknown since 1995.
Tom Jones Gadabouts - Defunct.
Tom Jones "Tom Terrific" Fan Club [24986], c/o Margaret Mariotti, Pres., 411 Coram Ave., Shelton, CT 06484-3134, (203)924-1553
Tom Lee Music Found. [IO], Hong Kong, People's Republic of China
Tom Mix Intl. Fan Club [24775]
Tom Skinner Associates [★20033]
Tom Sneva Fan Club - Defunct.
Tom T. Hall Fan Club - Defunct.
Tom Wopat Fan Club - Address unknown since 1995.
Tomas Rivera Policy Inst. [19196], Univ. of Southern California, School of Policy, Planning, and Development, Ralph and Goldie Lewis Hall, 650 Childs Way, Ste. 102, Los Angeles, CA 90089-0626, (213)821-5615
Tomato Comm; Florida [4733]
Tomato Exchange; Florida [★4733]
Tomato Genetics Cooperative [4765], c/o J.W. Scott, PhD, Managing Ed., Univ. of Florida, Gulf Coast Res. and Educ. Center, 14625 County Rd. 672, Wimauma, FL 33598-6101, (813)634-0000
Tomato Genetics Cooperative [IO], Wimauma, FL, United States
Tommy Cash Fan Club - Defunct.
Tommy Roe Intl. Fan Club - Defunct.

Tomography and Magnetic Resonance; Soc. of Computed Body [16297]
Tomography and Neuroimaging; Soc. for Computerized [★16281]
Tomography; Soc. of Computed Body [★16297]
Tomography Soc; Computerized [★16287]
Tompkins; Foundation of the Natl. Student Nurses' Assn. in memory of Frances [★8873]
Tom's Look of Love - Address unknown since 1995.
Tom's Love Connection - Address unknown since 2006.
Tomy Jennings Fan Club - Address unknown since 1988.
Tonal Music; Amer. Festival of Micro [10533]
Toncan Culvert Mfrs. Assn. - Defunct.
Toned Coin Collectors Soc. [22764], 703 E Court St., Flint, MI 48503
Tonga Amateur Athletic Assn. [IO], Nuku'alofa, Tonga
Tonga Amateur Sports Assn. and Natl. Olympic Comm. [IO], Nuku'alofa, Tonga
Tonga Chamber of Commerce and Indus. [IO], Nuku'alofa, Tonga
Tonga Cricket Assn. [IO], Nuku'alofa, Tonga
Tonga Family Hea. Assn. [IO], Nuku'alofa, Tonga
Tonga Sports Assn. and Natl. Olympic Comm. [★IO]
Tonga Squash Rackets Assn. [IO], Nuku'alofa, Tonga
Tonga Tennis Assn. [IO], Nuku'alofa, Tonga
Tonga and Tin Can Mail Study Circle - Defunct.
Tonga Visitors Bur. [IO], Nuku'alofa, Tonga
Tony Booth Fan Club - Defunct.
Tony Orlando Fan Club - Defunct.
Tool Collector's Assn; Antique Reloading [22424]
Tool Collectors Assn; Mid-West [22608]
Tool and Die Mfrs. Assn; Natl. [★2031]
Tool, Die and Mold Makers Guild [★24100]
Tool, Die and Mold Makers; Intl. Union of [24100]
Tool, Die and Precision Machining Assn; Natl. [★2031]
Tool Distributors' Assn; Amer. Machine [1995]
Tool Engineers; Amer. Soc. of [★7268]
Tool Engineers; Soc. of Carbide and [7322]
Tool and Gauge Manufacturers Assn. of India [IO], Bombay, India
Tool Inst; Elec. [★1831]
Tool Inst; Equip. and [383]
Tool Inst; Metal Cutting [★2076]
Tool Inst; Power [1831]
Tool Inst; U.S. Cutting [2076]
Tool Mfrs. of Am; Cutting [★2076]
Tool Mfrs. Assn; Amer. Measuring [7694]
Tool Mfrs. Assn; Cutting [★2076]
Tool Mfrs. Assn; Hydraulic [2025]
Tool Mfrs'. Inst; Powder Actuated [2057]
Tool and Mfg. Engineers; Amer. Soc. of [★7268]
Tool Mark Examiners; Assn. of Firearm and [7083]
Tool and Stainless Steel Indus. Comm. [★2729]
Tool and Trades History Soc. [IO], Devon, United Kingdom
Tooling Assn; Michigan [★2073]
Tooling Component Mfrs. Assn. Intl. - Address unknown since 2004.
Tooling Indus. Forum of Australia [IO], Wantirna South, Australia
Tooling and Mfg. Assn. [2566], 1177 S Dee Rd., Park Ridge, IL 60068, (847)825-1120
Tooling, Mfg. and Technologies Assn. [2073], PO Box 9151, Farmington Hills, MI 48333-9151, (248)488-0300
Tools and Fasteners Distributors Assn; Specialty [2069]
Tools and Indus. Assn; Potomac Antique [22610]
Tools Inst; Hand [1822]
Tools Inst; Ser. [★1822]
Tools for Self Reliance [IO], Southampton, United Kingdom
Toonan Ajia Shigakkai [★IO]
Toothpick Holder Collectors' Soc. [★22089]
Toothpick Holder Collectors' Soc; Natl. [22089]
Top End Assn. for Mental Hea. [IO], Darwin, Australia
Top Farmers of America Assn. - Defunct.
Top One Percent Soc. [★9985]
Topical Assn; Fine Arts Unit of Amer. [★22819]

A star before a book entry number signifies that the name is not listed separately, but is mentioned within the entry.

Topical Numismatics Soc. - Defunct.
Toplumsal Saydamlik Hareketi Dernegi [★IO]
Topographic Engineers of World War II [IO], Olathe, KS, United States
Topographic Engineers of World War II [21407]
Topolino Register of North Am. [21797], 3301 Shetland Rd., Beavercreek, OH 45434, (937)426-0098
TOPS [★12649]
TOPS Club (Take Off Pounds Sensibly) [12649], 4575 S 5th St., Milwaukee, WI 53207, (414)482-4620
Torah Educ; Amer. Comm. for the Advancement of [★8678]
Torah Fund - a Campaign [★20193]
Torah Institutions of Israel; Ohr [8678]
Torah Movement; Iranian B'nei [20145]
Torah Observance; Comm. for the Furtherance of [★20169]
Torah Registry; Universal [20190]
Torah Sedaka Fund; B'nei [★20145]
Torah Umesorah - Natl. Soc. for Hebrew Day Schools - Defunct.
Torch Clubs; Intl. Assn. of [10894]
Torino Montego Registry; Cyclone [★21626]
Torino Registry; Cyclone Montego [21626]
Tornado Assn; North Amer. [23209]
Tornado Assn; U.S. [★23209]
Tornado and Storm Res. Org. [IO], Oxford, United Kingdom
Toro Intl. Yacht Racing Assn; El [23168]
Toronto Action for Social Change [IO], Toronto, ON, Canada
Toronto Anti-Draft Programme - Defunct.
Toronto Area of Narcotics Anonymous [IO], Toronto, ON, Canada
Toronto Hard of Hearing Br. [IO], North York, ON, Canada
Torquay Pottery Collectors' Soc. [IO], Torquay, United Kingdom
Torrey Botanical Club - Address unknown since 2001.
Tort Reform Assn; Amer. [5926]
Torticollis Assn; Natl. Spasmodic [15353]
Tortilla Indus. Assn. [1565], 8201 Greensboro Dr., Ste. 300, McLean, VA 22102, (703)610-9036
Tortilla Indus. Assn. [IO], McLean, VA, United States
Tortoise Coun; Desert [5309]
Tortoise Preserve Comm; Desert [4390]
Tortoise Soc; New York Turtle and [5348]
TortoiseAid Intl. [5385], PO Box 260, Apple Valley, CA 92307-0005
TortoiseAid Intl. [IO], Apple Valley, CA, United States
Torture Abolition and Survivors Support Coalition Intl. [IO], Washington, DC, United States
Torture Abolition and Survivors Support Coalition Intl. [17786], 4121 Harewood Rd. NE, Ste. B, Washington, DC 20017, (202)529-2991
Torture; Assn. for the Prevention of [IO]
Torture; Canadian Centre for Victims of [IO]
Torture; Center for Victims of [13361]
Torture Victims; Medical Rehabilitation Center for [IO]
Torture; World Org. Against [IO]
Total Educ. in the Total Env. [★4602]
Total Energy Mgt. Professionals [★6942]
Total Energy Mgt. Professionals [★IO]
Total Environmental Action Found. - Defunct.
Total Immersion Fluency Training [★16440]
Tots Found; Marine Corps Toys for [★11709]
Tots Found; Marine Toys for [11709]
Tots and Teens; Natl. [13503]
A Touch of Days - Defunct.
Touch Football Australia [IO], Deakin, Australia
Touch Football League; U.S. Flag and [23441]
Touch-Healing
   Amer. Qigong Assn. [13620]
   Amer. Reiki Master Assn. [13622]
   Commn. on Religious Counseling and Healing [19445]
   Hospital-Based Massage Network [15027]
   Intl. Assn. of Reiki Professionals [13637]
   Intl. Found. of Bio-Magnetics [16654]
   International Foundation of Bio-Magnetics [IO]
   Intl. Thai Therapists Assn. [15031]
   Intl. Yan Xin Qigong Assn. [13640]

Natl. Qigong (Chi Kung) Assn. [13644]
   QiGong Res. Soc. [13647]
   Reflexology Assn. of Am. [13650]
   U.S. Medical Massage Assn. [15033]
   U.S. Trager Assn. [13656]
Touch for Hea. Assn. [★13654]
Touch for Hea. Assn. of Am. [★13654]
Touch for Hea. Found. [★13654]
Touch for Hea. Kinesiology Assn. [13654], PO Box 392, New Carlisle, OH 45344-0392, (937)845-3404
Touch Rugby Assn. of Thailand [IO], Bangkok, Thailand
Touching Hearts [11267], PO Box 761, Novi, MI 48376
Toughlove [★12694]
Toughlove [★IO]
Toughlove Intl. [IO], Los Angeles, CA, United States
Toughlove Intl. [12694], PO Box 491670, Los Angeles, CA 90049-1670
Toughlove for Kids Program [★12694]
Toughlove for Kids Program [★IO]
Tour Assn; Natl. [3930]
Tour Brokers Assn; Natl. [★3930]
Tour Operators; Intl. Assn. of Antarctica [3921]
Tour Players Assn; WTA [23917]
Tourette Syndrome Assn. [15367], 42-40 Bell Blvd., Ste. 205, Bayside, NY 11361-2820, (718)224-2999
Tourette Syndrome Assn. of Australia [IO], Maroubra, Australia
Tourette Syndrome Assn; Gilles de la [★15367]
Tourette Syndrome (UK) Assn. [IO], London, United Kingdom
Touring
   Alpine Tourist Commn. [24223]
   Amer. Indonesian Chamber of Commerce [24332]
   Amer. Small Bus. Travel Alliance [3906]
   Anguilla Tourist Bd. [24224]
   Assn. for the Promotion of Tourism to Africa [3826]
   Austrian Tourist Off. [24231]
   Barbados Tourism Authority [24234]
   Belgian Tourist Off. [24236]
   Bermuda Dept. of Tourism [24237]
   Bonaire Govt. Tourist Off. [24361]
   Caribbean Tourism Org., Amer. Br. [24252]
   Cayman Islands Dept. of Tourism [24256]
   Center for Cuban Studies/Cuban Art Space [9845]
   Ceylon (Sri Lanka) Tourist Dept. [24377]
   Cruise Club of Am. [3914]
   Curacao Convention Bureau/Tourist Bd. [24362]
   Cyprus Tourism Org. [24315]
   Delta Teen-Lift [13341]
   European Travel Commn. [3916]
   German Convention Bur. [24324]
   Greek Natl. Tourist Org. [3869]
   Grenada Bd. of Tourism [24253]
   Interactive Travel Services Assn. [3946]
   Intl. Family Recreation Assn. [12798]
   Jamaica Tourist Bd. [24340]
   Japan Convention Bur. [24341]
   Japan Natl. Tourist Org. [24344]
   Jordan Info. Bur. [24349]
   Malaysia Tourism Promotion Bd. [24355]
   Mexico Tourism Bd. [24356]
   Netherlands Bd. of Tourism and Conventions [24359]
   New Zealand Tourism Bd. [24363]
   Oceanic Soc. Expeditions [23016]
   Pacific Asia Travel Assn. [3933]
   Portuguese Natl. Tourist Off. [24367]
   Portuguese Trade Commn. [24368]
   Romanian Natl. Tourist Off. [3934]
   Rover Saloon Touring Club of Am. [21776]
   Saint Kitts Tourism Authority [24254]
   Saint Lucia Tourist Bd. [24255]
   Scandinavian Tourist Boards [24372]
   South African Tourism [24374]
   Student and Youth Travel Assn. [3938]
   Sustainable Travel Intl. [5252]
   Switzerland Convention and Incentive Bur. [24379]
   Tourism Ireland [24335]
   Travel Info. Service/MossRehab ResourceNet [13345]
   U.S. Tourist Coun. [4462]

VisitBritain [24242]
   World Heritage Alliance [10077]
   World Ocean and Cruise Liner Soc. [23020]
Touring Alliance; Amer. Auto. [3905]
Touring Assn; Honda Sport [22681]
Touring Assn; Honda V-4 Sport [★22681]
Touring Club; Austin-Healey Sports and [21586]
Touring Club; Pioneer Auto. [21762]
Touring Scooter Riders Assn; Scoot-Tours [23627]
Touring Soc; Venture [★23626]
Tourism
   Aboriginal Tourism Australia [IO]
   Alliance of Tribal Tourism Advocates [19267]
   Alpine Tourist Commn. [24223]
   Amer. Indonesian Chamber of Commerce [24332]
   Amer. Small Bus. Travel Alliance [3906]
   Anguilla Tourist Bd. [24224]
   Antigua Hotels and Tourist Assn. [IO]
   Assoc. Luxury Hotels Intl. [1931]
   Assn. of Approved Tourist Guides of Ireland [IO]
   Assn. of Chilean Tourism Agencies [IO]
   Assn. of Greek Tourist Enterprises [IO]
   Assn. for the Promotion of Tourism to Africa [IO]
   Assn. for the Promotion of Tourism to Africa [3826]
   Assn. of Tour Operators and Travel Agents of the Czech Republic [IO]
   Austrian Tourist Off. [24231]
   Barbados Hotel and Tourism Assn. [IO]
   Barbados Tourism Authority [24234]
   Belgian Tourist Off. [24236]
   Bermuda Dept. of Tourism [24237]
   Bonaire Govt. Tourist Off. [24361]
   Bulgarian Assn. for Alternative Tourism [IO]
   Canadian/American Border Trade Alliance [3838]
   Caribbean-Central Amer. Action [12421]
   Caribbean Tourism Org., Amer. Br. [24252]
   Cayman Islands Dept. of Tourism [24256]
   Ceylon (Sri Lanka) Tourist Dept. [24377]
   Chilean Assn. of Tourism Wholesalers and Representatives [IO]
   Convention Indus. Coun. [3827]
   Cruise Club of Am. [3914]
   Curacao Convention Bureau/Tourist Bd. [24362]
   Cyprus Tourism Org. [24315]
   Cyprus Tourism Org. [IO]
   Ecotourism Australia [IO]
   Egyptian Gen. Company for Tourism and Hotels [IO]
   Estonian Rural Tourism Org. [IO]
   European Fed. of Farm and Village Tourism [IO]
   European Travel Commn. [3916]
   Field Guides Assn. of South Africa [IO]
   German Convention Bur. [24324]
   Greek Natl. Tourist Org. [3869]
   Green Tourism Assn. [IO]
   Grenada Bd. of Tourism [24253]
   Inst. for the Advancement of Hawaiian Affairs [10883]
   Inter-American Travel Cong. [3919]
   Interactive Travel Services Assn. [3946]
   Intl. Assn. of Antarctica Tour Operators [3921]
   Intl. Assn. of Reservation Executives [3828]
   Intl. Assn. of Reservation Executives [IO]
   Intl. Assn. of Tour Managers - Central Europe [IO]
   Intl. Assn. of Tour Managers - France [IO]
   Intl. Assn. of Tour Managers - Israel [IO]
   Intl. Assn. of Tour Managers - Italy [IO]
   Intl. Assn. of Tour Managers - North Amer. Region [3922]
   Intl. Assn. of Tour Managers - Pacific [IO]
   Intl. Assn. of Tour Managers - Spain [IO]
   Intl. Assn. of Tour Managers - Taiwan [IO]
   Intl. Centre for Res. and Stud. on Tourism [IO]
   The Intl. Ecotourism Soc. [IO]
   The Intl. Ecotourism Soc. [3829]
   Intl. Family Recreation Assn. [12798]
   Intl. Fed. of Festival Organizations [1307]
   Intl. Gay and Lesbian Travel Assn. [3924]
   Irish Tourist Indus. Confed. [IO]
   Israel Tourist and Travel Agents' Assn. [IO]
   Jamaica Tourist Bd. [24340]
   Japan Convention Bur. [24341]
   Japan Natl. Tourist Org. [24344]
   Jordan Info. Bur. [24349]

Malaysia Tourism Promotion Bd. [24355]
Mexico Tourism Bd. [24356]
Ministry of Hotels and Tourism [IO]
Motorist Info. and Services Assn. [13344]
Natl. Assn. of Black Hotel Owners, Operators and
  Developers [1950]
Natl. Coun. of State Tourism Directors [24385]
Natl. Fed. of Tourist Guide Associations-USA
  [24380]
Natl. Fed. of the Travel and Tourism Indus. [IO]
Natl. Tour Assn. [3930]
Natl. Tourism Org. of Serbia [IO]
Natl. Travel Club [3931]
Natl. Union of Tourism Hospitality [IO]
Natl. Union of Tourism and Outdoor Associations
  [IO]
Native Tourism Alliance [24381]
Netherlands Bd. of Tourism and Conventions
  [24359]
New Zealand Tourism Bd. [24363]
Northern Frontier Visitors Assn. [IO]
Northern Rockies Alaska Highway Tourism Assn.
  [IO]
Pacific Asia Travel Assn. [3933]
Pakistan Tourism Development Corp. [IO]
Papua New Guinea Tourism Promotion Authority
  [IO]
Polish Tourist Country-Lovers' Soc. [IO]
Port Douglas Daintree Tourism Assn. [IO]
Portuguese Natl. Tourist Off. [24367]
Portuguese Trade Commn. [24368]
Professional Tour Guide Assn. of Australia [IO]
Quality Tourism Services Assn. [IO]
Resort and Commercial Recreation Assn. [3361]
Romanian Natl. Tourist Off. [3934]
Saint Croix Hotel and Tourism Assn. [1964]
Saint Kitts Tourism Authority [24254]
Saint Lucia Hotel and Tourism Assn. [IO]
Saint Lucia Tourist Bd. [24255]
Salvadoran Chamber of Tourism [IO]
Scandinavian Tourist Boards [24372]
Scottish Tourism Forum [IO]
Senate Tourism Caucus [17259]
Singapore Tourism Bd. [IO]
Soc. for Accessible Travel and Hospitality [17420]
Soc. of Incentive and Travel Executives [3935]
Soc. of Polish-American Travel Agents [3936]
South Africa Assn. of Tourism Professionals [IO]
South African Tourism [24374]
Sustainable Travel Intl. [5252]
Switzerland Convention and Incentive Bur.
  [24379]
Taiwan Visitors Assn. [3940]
Tonga Visitors Bur. [IO]
Tourism Authority of Thailand [IO]
Tourism Indus. Assn. New Zealand [IO]
Tourism Indus. Assn. of the Yukon [IO]
Tourism Ireland [24335]
Tourist Assn. of Slovenia [IO]
Travel Info. Service/MossRehab ResourceNet
  [13345]
Travel and Tourism Agencies' Assn. [IO]
Travel and Tourism Res. Assn. [3942]
Trinidad Restaurants, Hotels and Tourism Assn.
  [IO]
Turkish Tourism Investors' Assn. [IO]
U.S. Air Tour Assn. [3830]
U.S. Tour Operators Assn. [3943]
U.S. Tourist Coun. [4462]
U.S. Travel Data Center [3944]
Vanuatu Tourism Off. [IO]
VisitBritain [24242]
Women in Tourism [IO]
World Heritage Alliance [10077]
World Ocean and Cruise Liner Soc. [23020]
Tourism Assn; Caribbean [★24252]
Tourism Authority; Barbados [24234]
Tourism Authority; Brazilian [★24238]
Tourism Authority; Saint Kitts [24254]
Tourism Authority of Thailand [IO], Bangkok,
  Thailand
Tourism and Automobile Clubs; Arab Intl. Assn. for
  [23009]
Tourism; Barbados Bd. of [★24234]
Tourism; Bermuda Dept. of [24237]

Tourism Bd; Mexico [24356]
Tourism Bd; New Zealand [24363]
Tourism Caucus; Senate [17259]
Tourism; Cayman Islands Dept. of [24256]
Tourism and Conventions; Netherlands Bd. of
  [24359]
Tourism Directors; Natl. Coun. of State [24385]
Tourism; Grenada Bd. of [24253]
Tourism and Hea. Resorts; Dept. of [★24363]
Tourism, Hotels and Restaurants Assn. [IO], Ljubl-
  jana, Slovenia
Tourism Indus. Assn. of Canada [IO], Ottawa, ON,
  Canada
Tourism Indus. Assn. New Zealand [IO], Wellington,
  New Zealand
Tourism Indus. Assn. of the Yukon [IO], Whitehorse,
  YT, Canada
Tourism Ireland [24335], 345 Park Ave., 17th Fl.,
  New York, NY 10154, (212)418-0800
Tourism; Netherlands Bd. of [★24359]
Tourism Off; Brazil [24238]
Tourism Off; Mexican Govt. [★24356]
Tourism Org., Amer. Br; Caribbean [24252]
Tourism Organization; Caribbean [★24252]
Tourism Org; Cyprus [24315]
Tourism Promotion Bd; Malaysia [24355]
Tourism Res. and Development Center; Caribbean
  [★24252]
Tourism Soc. [IO], Sutton, United Kingdom
Tourism; South African [24374]
Tourist Agents Assn; Amer. Steamship and [★3907]
Tourist Assn; Caribbean [★24252]
Tourist Assn; Japan Natl. [★24344]
Tourist Assn. of Slovenia [IO], Ljubljana, Slovenia
Tourist Authority; British [★24242]
Tourist Bd; Anguilla [24224]
Tourist Bd; Curacao [★24362]
Tourist Bd; Irish [★24335]
Tourist Bd; Jamaica [24340]
Tourist Bd; Romanian [★3934]
Tourist Bd; Saint Lucia [24255]
Tourist Boards; Curacao and Bonaire [★24362]
Tourist Boards; Scandinavian [24372]
Tourist Commn; Alpine [24223]
Tourist Corp; South African [★24374]
Tourist Coun; U.S. [4462]
Tourist Dept; Ceylon (Sri Lanka) [24377]
Tourist Development Corp. of Malaysia [★IO]
Tourist House Assn. of America - Address unknown
  since 2003.
Tourist Info. Off; Anguilla [★24224]
Tourist and Info. Off; Portugese [★24367]
Tourist Info. and Reservation Off; Anguilla [★24224]
Tourist Off; Austrian [24231]
Tourist Off; Austrian Natl. [★24231]
Tourist Off; Belgian [24236]
Tourist Off; Bonaire Govt. [24361]
Tourist Off; Portuguese Natl. [24367]
Tourist Off; Saint Kitts-Nevis [★24254]
Tourist Off; Swiss Natl. [★24379]
Tourist Offices; Scandinavian Natl. [★24372]
Tourist Org; Greek Natl. [★3869]
Tourist Org; Japan Natl. [24344]
Tourist and Publicity Off; New Zealand [★24363]
Tourist Railway Assn. [3293], c/o Dan Ranger, Exec.
  Dir., PO Box 1245, Chama, NM 87520-1245,
  (505)756-1240
Tourist Railway Assn. [IO], Chama, NM, United
  States
Tourist and Trade Off; Portugese Info., [★24367]
Tournament Directors; Natl. Assn. of Golf [23457]
Tournament of Roses Assn. [19040], 391 S Orange
  Grove Blvd., Pasadena, CA 91184, (626)449-4100
Touro Synagogue Found. [10070], 85 Touro St.,
  Newport, RI 02840, (401)847-4794
Touro Synagogue; Soc. of Friends of [★10070]
Toward Freedom [17645], PO Box 468, Burlington,
  VT 05402, (802)657-3733
Toward Freedom [IO], Burlington, VT, United States
Toward Tradition [20508], PO Box 58, Mercer Island,
  WA 98040, (206)236-3046
Towards Freedom [17503], 2116 Pico Blvd., No. B,
  Santa Monica, CA 90405, (310)866-6116
Towarzystwo Biblijne w Polsce [★IO]
Towarzystwo imienia Fryderyka Chopina [★IO]

Towarzystwo Przetwarzania Obrazow [★IO]
Towarzystwo Urbanistow Polskich [★IO]
Towboat and Harbor Carriers Conf./Amer.
  Waterways Operators - Address unknown since
  2001.
Tower Erectors; Natl. Assn. of [6653]
Tower Inst; Cooling [★616]
Towing; Comm. for Private Offshore Rescue and
  [2574]
Towing Operators Working to Eliminate Drunk Driv-
  ing - Address unknown since 2008.
Towing and Recovery Assn. of Am. [429], 2121
  Eisenhower Ave., Ste. 200, Alexandria, VA 22314,
  (703)684-7713
Town Affiliation Assn. of the U.S., Inc. [★17913]
Town Affiliation Assn. of the U.S., Inc. [★IO]
Town and Country Owners Registry; Chrysler
  [21612]
Town and Country Planning Assn. [IO], London,
  United Kingdom
Town and Country Religious Res. Center [★19628]
Town Creek Found. - Defunct.
Town House Intl. School [★9609]
Town House Intl. School [★IO]
Town Jerusalem; Amer. Friends of Boys [★13473]
Town Watch; Natl. Assn. of [11841]
Towner Rating Bur. [★2245]
Towns and Townships; Natl. Assn. of [6126]
Townsend Plan Natl. Lobby - Address unknown
  since 1988.
Townships; Natl. Assn. of Towns and [6126]
Townswomen's Guilds [IO], Birmingham, United
  Kingdom
Toxic Exposure
  Alliance for Healthy Homes [13320]
  Amer. Acad. of Clinical Toxicology [16657]
  Amer. Assn. of Poison Control Centers [16658]
  Amer. Coll. of Medical Toxicology [16660]
  Asbestos Disease Awareness Org. [16655]
  Asbestos Disease Awareness Org. [IO]
  Asbestos Litigation Gp. [13321]
  Assn. of Lighting and Mercury Recyclers [5168]
  Basel Action Network [18797]
  Beyond Pesticides - Natl. Coalition Against the
    Misuse of Pesticides [13322]
  Black Lung Assn. [13323]
  Chem. Injury Info. Network [16656]
  Chem. Injury Info. Network [IO]
  Children's Hea. Environmental Coalition [13953]
  CURE Formaldehyde Poisoning Assn. [13324]
  Global Village Inst. [6235]
  Hawaii Heptachlor Res. and Educ. Found.
    [13325]
  Mercury Policy Proj. [18745]
  Military Toxics Proj. [5033]
  Natl. Inst. for Chem. Stud. [13326]
  Natl. Pesticide Info. Center [13327]
  Northwest Coalition for Alternatives to Pesticides
    [13328]
  Occupational Knowledge Intl. [5099]
  Pesticide Action Network North Am. Regional
    Center [13329]
  Rachel Carson Coun. [13330]
  Soc. of Toxicologic Pathology [15876]
  Tobacco Control Rsrc. Center [13331]
  White Lung Assn. [13332]
  White Lung Association [IO]
Toxicologic Pathologists; Soc. of [★15876]
Toxicologic Pathology; Dept. of Environmental and
  [15867]
Toxicologic Pathology; Soc. of [15876]
Toxicological Assn. of Dyes and Organic Pigments
  Mfrs; ETAD North Am. - Ecological and [5089]
Toxicological History Soc. [7805], 5757 Hall St. SE,
  Grand Rapids, MI 49546-3845, (616)391-9099
Toxicological Risk Assessment; Intl. Acad. of
  [★4593]
Toxicologists; Amer. Coll. of Veterinary [★16736]
Toxicologists; Soc. of Forensic [5767]
Toxicology
  Alliance for Healthy Homes [13320]
  Amer. Acad. of Clinical Toxicology [16657]
  Amer. Assn. of Poison Control Centers [16658]
  American Bd. of Clinical Metal Toxicology [16659]
  Amer. Bd. of Toxicology [7799]

A star before a book entry number signifies that the name is not listed separately, but is mentioned within the entry.

Amer. Bd. of Toxicology [IO]
Amer. Bd. of Veterinary Toxicology [16760]
Amer. Coll. of Medical Toxicology [16660]
Amer. Coll. of Toxicology [7800]
Amer. Coll. of Toxicology [IO]
Asbestos Disease Awareness Org. [16655]
Asbestos Litigation Gp. [13321]
Assn. of European Toxicologists and European
    Societies of Toxicology [IO]
Behavioral Toxicology Soc. [16661]
British Toxicology Soc. [IO]
Canadian Network of Toxicology Centres [IO]
Chem. Injury Info. Network [16656]
Chinese Soc. of Toxicology [IO]
CIIT Centers for Hea. Res. [7801]
CURE Formaldehyde Poisoning Assn. [13324]
DES Action, U.S.A. [13821]
European Assn. of Poisons Centres and Clinical
    Toxicologists [IO]
European Soc. for Toxicology In Vitro [IO]
Genetic Toxicology Assn. [7802]
Hawaii Heptachlor Res. and Educ. Found.
    [13325]
The Intl. Assn. of Forensic Toxicologists [IO]
Intl. Assn. of Therapeutic Drug Monitoring and
    Clinical Toxicology [IO]
Intl. Endotoxin and Innate Immunity Soc. [IO]
Intl. Endotoxin and Innate Immunity Soc. [7803]
Intl. Life Sciences Inst. - North Am. [15561]
Intl. Soc. of Regulatory Toxicology and
    Pharmacology [14570]
Intl. Soc. on Toxinology [IO]
Italian Soc. of Toxicology [IO]
Natl. Eosinophilia-Myalgia Syndrome Network
    [16662]
Natl. Pesticide Info. Center [13327]
Northwest Coalition for Alternatives to Pesticides
    [13328]
Pesticide Action Network North Am. Regional
    Center [13329]
Rachel Carson Coun. [13330]
Scandinavian Soc. for Cell Toxicology [IO]
Soc. of Toxicologic Pathology [15876]
Soc. of Toxicology [7804]
Toxicological History Soc. [7805]
Toxicology Forum [7806]
Toxicology; Amer. Acad. of Veterinary and Compara-
    tive [16736]
Toxicology; American Bd. of Forensic [★5767]
Toxicology; Amer. Bd. of Medical [★16660]
Toxicology; Amer. Bd. of Veterinary [16760]
Toxicology; Australasian Soc. of Oral Medicine and
    [IO]
Toxicology Center; Reproductive [14393]
Toxicology; Chem. Indus. Inst. of [★7801]
Toxicology and Chemistry; Soc. of Environmental
    [14370]
Toxicology Forum [7806], 1300 Eye St. NW, Ste.
    1010 E, Washington, DC 20005, (202)659-0030
Toxicology; Intl. Assn. of Therapeutic Drug Monitor-
    ing and Clinical [IO]
Toxics Proj; Military [5033]
Toy
A.C. Gilbert Heritage Soc. [22992]
Amy's Doll Lover's Club [22391]
Antique Toy Collectors of Am. [22993]
Assn. of Game and Puzzle Collectors [22460]
Beyond the Pond.International Frog Collectors
    Club [21977]
Chatty Cathy Collectors Club [22393]
Cracker Jack Collectors Assn. [22003]
Diecast Exchange Club [22010]
Doll Artisan Guild [22394]
Doll Costumer's Guild [22395]
Etch-A-Sketch Club [22994]
GI Joe Collectors' Club [22996]
Heather's Teddy Bear Org. [22035]
Howdy Doody Memorabilia Collectors Club
    [22038]
Intl. Coun. of Toy Indus. [3831]
Intl. Doll Makers Assn. [22397]
Intl. Rose O'Neill Club Found. [22399]
Lionel Railroader Club [22634]
M&M's Collectors Club [22067]
Marine Toys for Tots Found. [11709]

McDonald's Collectors Club [22070]
Natl. Assn. of Rocketry [22650]
Natl. Inst. of Amer. Doll Artists [22403]
Natl. Model Railroad Assn. [22636]
Original Doll Artists Coun. of Am. [22404]
Ships-in-Bottles Assn. of Am. [22658]
Still Bank Collectors Club of Am. [21827]
Strawberry Shortcake Chat Gp. [22406]
Teachers Resisting Unhealthy Children's
    Entertainment [11657]
Teen Assn. of Model Railroaders [22637]
Toy Car Collectors Assn. [22997]
Toy Stitchers Intl., Inc. [22998]
Toy Train Collectors Soc. [22638]
Toy Train Operating Soc. [22639]
Train Collectors Assn. [22640]
Treasures for Little Children [23000]
United Fed. of Doll Clubs [22407]
United League Toy Representatives Associations
    [3833]
U.S.A. Toy Lib. Assn. [11548]
Women in Toys [3834]
Toy Assn; Antique Engine, Tractor, and [23001]
Toy Car Collectors Assn. [22997], c/o Dana Johnson
    Enterprises, PO Box 1824, Bend, OR 97709-1824,
    (541)318-7176
Toy Car Collectors Association [IO], Bend, OR,
    United States
Toy Collectors Assn; Diecast [★22997]
Toy Collectors; Natl. Doll and [★22407]
Toy Dish Collectors [★23000]
Toy Fox Terrier Assn; Natl. [22321]
Toy Fox Terrier Club; Amer. [22214]
Toy Fox Terrier Club of Canada [IO], Camrose, AB,
    Canada
Toy Guidance Coun. - Defunct.
Toy and Hobby Wholesalers Assn. of America -
    Defunct.
Toy Indus. of Europe [IO], Brussels, Belgium
Toy Indus. Assn. [3832], 1115 Broadway, Ste. 400,
    New York, NY 10010, (212)675-1141
Toy Lib. Assn; U.S.A. [11548]
Toy Mfrs. of Am. [★3832]
Toy Manufacturers' Assn. [IO], Sao Paulo, Brazil
Toy Retailers Assn. [IO], Gainsborough, United
    Kingdom
Toy Retailing Assn; Amer. Specialty [2385]
Toy Spaniel Club of Am; English [22263]
Toy Stitchers Intl., Inc. [22998], c/o Lynn Furman,
    PO Box 200, Savannah, NY 13146-0200
Toy Stores Steiff Collectors Club [22999], c/o The
    Toy Store Collectors Gallery, Westgate Village,
    3301 W Central Ave., Toledo, OH 43606,
    (419)531-2839
Toy Traders of Europe [IO], Nuremberg, Germany
Toy Train Collectors Soc. [22638], c/o Louis A.
    Bohn, Membership Chm., 109 Howedale Dr.,
    Rochester, NY 14616-1534, (585)663-4188
Toy Train Operating Soc. [22639], 136 E Santa
    Clara St., No. 2, Arcadia, CA 91006, (626)547-
    7453
Toy Workers of the U.S. and Canada; Intl. Union of
    Doll and [★24196]
Toyah Fan Club; North Amer. [24951]
Toyota Owners Assn. - Defunct.
Toyota Owner's and Restorer's Club [21798], 2849
    Long Beach Blvd., Long Beach, CA 90806
Toyota Sport Car Club - Defunct.
Toyota Territory Off-Roaders Assn. [22965], PO Box
    2323, Mont Belvieu, TX 77580, (281)414-1645
Toys
A.C. Gilbert Heritage Soc. [22992]
Amy's Doll Lover's Club [22391]
Antique Engine, Tractor, and Toy Assn. [23001]
Antique Toy Collectors of Am. [22993]
Assn. of Game and Puzzle Collectors [22460]
Beyond the Pond.International Frog Collectors
    Club [21977]
Brickish Assn. [IO]
Canadian Toy Collectors' Soc. [IO]
Chatty Cathy Collectors Club [22393]
China Toy Assn. [IO]
Cracker Jack Collectors Assn. [22003]
Diecast Exchange Club [22010]
Doll Artisan Guild [22394]

Doll Costumer's Guild [22395]
Etch-A-Sketch Club [22994]
Fisher-Price Collector's Club [22995]
Fisher-Price Collector's Club [IO]
French Fed. of Toy Indus. [IO]
GI Joe Collectors' Club [22996]
Heather's Teddy Bear Org. [22035]
Howdy Doody Memorabilia Collectors Club
    [22038]
Intl. Coun. of Toy Indus. [3831]
Intl. Coun. of Toy Indus. [IO]
Intl. Doll Makers Assn. [22397]
Intl. Rose O'Neill Club Found. [22399]
Intl. Union of Allied Novelty and Prdt.ion Workers
    [24196]
Lionel Railroader Club [22634]
Magic Lantern Soc. of the U.S. and Canada
    [21531]
M&M's Collectors Club [22067]
Marine Toys for Tots Found. [11709]
Matchbox U.S.A. [22069]
McDonald's Collectors Club [22070]
Natl. Antique Doll Dealers Assn. [22402]
Natl. Assn. of Rocketry [22650]
Natl. Inst. of Amer. Doll Artists [22403]
Natl. Model Railroad Assn. [22636]
Original Doll Artists Coun. of Am. [22404]
Original Paper Doll Artists Guild [22405]
Romanian-American Chamber of Commerce
    [24369]
Ships-in-Bottles Assn. of Am. [22658]
Spanish Assn. of Toy Mfrs. [IO]
Still Bank Collectors Club of Am. [21827]
Strawberry Shortcake Chat Gp. [22406]
Taiwan Toy Mfrs'. Assn. [IO]
Teachers Resisting Unhealthy Children's
    Entertainment [11657]
Teen Assn. of Model Railroaders [22637]
Thai Toy Indus. Assn. [IO]
Toy Car Collectors Association [IO]
Toy Car Collectors Assn. [22997]
Toy Indus. of Europe [IO]
Toy Indus. Assn. [3832]
Toy Manufacturers' Assn. [IO]
Toy Stitchers Intl., Inc. [22998]
Toy Stores Steiff Collectors Club [22999]
Toy Traders of Europe [IO]
Toy Train Collectors Soc. [22638]
Toy Train Operating Soc. [22639]
Toys Manufacturers' Assn. of Hong Kong [IO]
Train Collectors Assn. [22640]
Treasures for Little Children [23000]
United Fed. of Doll Clubs [22407]
United League Toy Representatives Associations
    [3833]
Women in Toys [3834]
Toys Manufacturers' Assn. of Hong Kong [IO], Hong
    Kong, People's Republic of China
Toys, Playthings, Novelties and Allied Prdts. of the
    U.S. and Canada; Intl. Union of Dolls, [★24196]
Toys for Tots Found. [★11709]
Toys for Tots Found; Marine [11709]
Toys for Tots Found; Marine Corps [★11709]
TQM Users Group - Address unknown since 1999.
TR8 Car Club of Am. [21799], c/o Joe Worsley,
    Membership Coor./Treas., 1591 Peoples Creek
    Rd., Advance, NC 27006-7451, (336)998-6501
Tra- och Mobelindustriforbundet [★IO]
Trac 16 Catamaran Class Assn. - Defunct.
Trachoma Initiative; Intl. [16858]
Traci Lords Fan Club - Defunct.
Track Betting; Natl. Assn. of Off- [23505]
Track Club; Achilles [23331]
Track and Field
Amer. Samoa Track and Field Assn. [IO]
Amer. Sports Builders Assn. [1002]
Aruba Athletic Fed. [IO]
Assn. of Track and Field Statisticians [IO]
Athletics Australia [IO]
Bahamas Assn. of Athletic Associations [IO]
Chinese Taipei Track and Field Assn. [IO]
DECA, The Decathlon Assn. [23918]
Hong Kong Distance Runners Club [IO]
Hong Kong Ladies Road Runners Club [IO]
Intl. Track and Field Coaches Assn. [IO]

Reference to "IO" in place of a book number signifies that the association may be found in the 45th edition of International Organizations.

Intl. Track and Field Coaches Assn. [23919]
Lifelong Fitness Alliance [23920]
New York Road Runners Club [23921]
New York Triathlon Club [23922]
Road Runners Club of Am. [23923]
U.S. Cross Country Coaches Assn. [23924]
U.S. Modern Pentathlon Assn. [23925]
United States Modern Pentathlon Association [IO]
U.S.A. Track and Field [23926]
USA Triathlon [23927]
World Masters Athletics [IO]
Track and Field Assn. of the U.S.A. - Defunct.
Track and Field Athletes of America - Defunct.
Track Operators Assn; Amer. Greyhound [23391]
Track Owners Assn. [1916], 417 Oak Pl., No. 2, Port
Orange, FL 32127, (580)237-1699
Track Owners Assn. [IO], Port Orange, FL, United
States
Track Owners Assn. of Am. [★IO]
Track Owners Assn. of Am. [★1916]
Track Two Inst. for Citizen Diplomacy; The Russian-
American Center/ [17912]
Tracks of Am; Harness [23499]
Tract and Commun. Coun; Amer. Sabbath [★20545]
Tract Soc; Amer. [19987]
Tract Soc; Canadian [19987]
Tract Soc. of New York; Watchtower Bible and
[20109]
Tractor Dealers; Cooperative Assn. of [1070]
Tractor Engineers; Soc. of [★6520]
Tractor Pulling
  Natl. Antique Tractor Pullers Assn. [23004]
  Natl. Tractor Pullers Assn. [23928]
  Professional Putters Assn. [23465]
  USA Pulling [23929]
Tractors
  Antique Engine, Tractor, and Toy Assn. [23001]
  Antique Truck Club of Am. [23022]
  Early Day Gas Engine and Tractor Assn. [22410]
  Gravely Tractor Club of Am. [23002]
  Intl. Harvester Collectors [23003]
  Intl. Harvester Collectors [IO]
  Midwest Equip. Dealers Assn. [4092]
  Natl. Antique Tractor Pullers Assn. [23004]
  Natl. Tractor Pullers Assn. [23928]
  Natl. Vintage Tractor and Engine Club [IO]
  Two-Cylinder Club [23005]
  U.S. Lawn Mower Racing Assn. [23673]
  USA Pulling [23929]
Tracy Byrd Online Fan Club [24987], PO Box
120795, Nashville, TN 37212, (615)297-7002
Tracy Clinic; John [14764]
Tracy Lawrence Fan Club - Address unknown since
2007.
Tracy Lynne Intl. Fan Club - Address unknown since
2001.
Trade
  1-800 Amer. Free Trade Assn. [3950]
  1394 High Performance Serial Bus Trade Assn.
  [3720]
  Aftermarket Coun. on Electronic Commerce
  [3835]
  Air Barrier Assn. of Am. [587]
  All India Exporters' Chamber [IO]
  All-Poland Alliance of Trade Unions [IO]
  Alliance for Responsible Trade [IO]
  Alliance for Responsible Trade [3836]
  Am. Council for Trade in Services [3837]
  America-Georgia Bus. Coun. [2296]
  America-Israel Chamber of Commerce and Indus.
  [24336]
  Amer. and African Bus. Women's Alliance [691]
  Amer. Assn. of Exporters and Importers [2297]
  Amer. Equestrian Trade Assn. [4818]
  Amer. Exploration and Production Coun. [2914]
  Amer. Hellenic Inst. [24325]
  Amer. Indonesian Chamber of Commerce [24332]
  Amer. Intl. Chamber of Commerce [24247]
  American-Kuwaiti Alliance [2299]
  Amer. Mfg. Trade Action Coalition [2547]
  Amer. Mideast Bus. Associates [24357]
  American-Russian Chamber of Commerce and
  Indus. [24261]
  Amer. Seed Trade Assn. [5174]
  Amer.-Southern Africa Chamber of Trade and
  Indus. [24375]

Amman World Trade Center [IO]
Argentine Chamber of Exporters [IO]
Armenian Amer. Chamber of Commerce [24263]
ASEAN Promotion Centre on Trade, Investment
  and Tourism [IO]
Asia-Pacific Economic Cooperation [IO]
Asia Pacific - USA Chamber of Commerce
  [24264]
Asian Indian Chamber of Commerce [24228]
Assn. of African Amer. Financial Advisors [1455]
Assn. of Amer. Chambers of Commerce in Latin
  Am. [24352]
Assn. of Commercial Stock Image Licensors
  [1378]
Assn. of Customs Brokers of Kazakhstan [IO]
Assn. of Icelandic Importers, Exporters, and
  Wholesale Merchants [IO]
Assn. of Importers and Exporters of the Republic
  of Argentina [IO]
Assn. of Manufactured Goods Exporters [IO]
Assn. of Modified Asphalt Producers [601]
Assn. of Peruvian Exporters [IO]
Assn. of Trade and Forfaiting in the Americas
  [1404]
Australian Horticultural Exporters Assn. [IO]
Australian New Zealand - Amer. Chambers of
  Commerce [24248]
Australian Trade Commn. [24229]
Austrian Press and Info. Ser. [24230]
Austrian Tourist Off. [24231]
Austrian Trade Commn. [24232]
Automotive Trade Policy Coun. [350]
Automotive Undercar Trade Org. [352]
Barbados Customs Brokers and Clerks Assn. [IO]
Belgian Fed. of Distributors [IO]
Bd. of External Trade [IO]
Bolivian Inst. of Foreign Trade [IO]
Brazil-U.S. Bus. Coun. [24266]
Brazilian-American Chamber of Commerce
  [24239]
Brazilian Govt. Trade Bur. of the Consulate Gen.
  of Brazil in New York [24240]
British Exporters Assn. [IO]
British Trade Off. at Consulate-General [24241]
BritishAmerican Bus. Inc. of New York and
  London [24267]
Bulgarian-American Chamber of Commerce
  [24243]
Bus. Alliance for Local Living Economies [887]
Bus. Assn. Italy Am. [2300]
Buying Influence [17310]
Cameroon-USA Chamber of Commerce [24249]
Canada-Singapore Bus. Assn. [IO]
Canada Taiwan Trade Assn. [IO]
Canadian/American Border Trade Alliance [IO]
Canadian/American Border Trade Alliance [3838]
Canadian Assn. of Importers and Exporters [IO]
Canadian Assn. of Regulated Importers [IO]
Canadian Comm. for Pacific Economic Coopera-
  tion [IO]
Caribbean Export Development Agency [IO]
Centre for Importers of Paraguay [IO]
Centre for the Promotion of Imports from Develop-
  ing Countries Netherlands [IO]
Chile-U.S. Chamber of Commerce [24270]
China Coun. for the Promotion of Intl. Trade [IO]
China Customs Brokers Assn. [IO]
Chinese Amer. Assn. of Commerce [24308]
Chinese Amer. Assn. of Engg. [7008]
Chinese Chamber of Commerce of Hawaii
  [24309]
Chinese Natl. Export Enterprises Assn. [IO]
CitizensLobby.com [18435]
Colombian Amer. Assn. [24312]
Colombian Govt. Trade Bur. [24271]
Colon Free Zone Users Assn. [IO]
ComexPeru Peruvian Foreign Trading Soc. [IO]
Commercial Off. of Spain [24376]
Composite Lumber Mfrs. Assn. [1642]
Cong. of South African Trade Unions [IO]
Consuming Indus. Trade Action Coalition [771]
Corporate Coun. on Africa [169]
Coun. of the Americas [24353]
Coun. on Competitiveness [3839]
Croatian-American Chamber of Commerce
  [24314]

Culligan Dealers Assn. of North Am. [1667]
Czech-North Amer. Chamber of Commerce
  [24274]
Czech and Slovak-U.S. Bus. Coun. [2302]
Danish Amer. Chamber of Commerce [24316]
Danish Import Promotion Off. for Products from
  Developing Countries [IO]
Debts AIDS Trade Africa [16928]
Delphi Intl. Prog. of World Learning [17881]
Ecuatorian Assn. of Exporters [IO]
Educational Exhibitors Assn. [1336]
Egyptian Exporters Assn. [IO]
eMarketing Assn. [1166]
Emergency Comm. for Amer. Trade [2303]
EMTA [3513]
Engg. Export Promotion Coun. [IO]
Engg. Export Promotion Coun. of India [2304]
Estonian Amer. Chamber of Commerce and
  Indus. [24318]
Euro-American Women's Coun. [17530]
European Confed. of Intl. Trading Houses As-
  sociations [IO]
European Fair Trade Assn. [IO]
Export Inst. of the U.S. [IO]
Export Inst. of the U.S. [3840]
Exporters' Assn. of Northern Greece [IO]
FCIB-NACM Corp. [2282]
Fed. of Associations of Ghanaian Exporters [IO]
Fed. of Distribution Companies [IO]
Fed. of the German Export Trade [IO]
Fed. of Icelandic Trade [IO]
Fed. of Indian Export Organisations [IO]
Fed. of Intl. Trade Associations [2283]
Fed. of Philippine Amer. Chambers of Commerce
  [24277]
Fed. of Swiss Importers and Wholesalers [IO]
Financial Markets Assn. - U.S.A. [475]
Finland-Israel Trade Assn. [IO]
Finnish Amer. Chamber of Commerce [24319]
FINPRO: Finnish Bus. Solutions Worldwide [IO]
Flag Mfrs. Assn. of Am. [1487]
GALA: Globalization and Localization Assn. [1168]
Georgia-USA Chamber of Commerce [24278]
German Amer. Chamber of Commerce [24323]
German Centre Singapore [IO]
Ghana Export Promotion Coun. [IO]
Ghana-USA Chamber of Commerce [24279]
Greek Amer. Chamber of Commerce [24280]
Greek Fed. of Customs Brokers Associations [IO]
Handcrafted Soap Makers Guild [1155]
Hellenic-American Chamber of Commerce
  [24326]
Hong Kong Exporters' Assn. [IO]
Hong Kong - New Zealand Bus. Assn. [IO]
Hong Kong Trade Development Coun. [IO]
Hong Kong Trade Development Coun. [24329]
Hong Kong Trade Development Coun. - London
  Off. [IO]
Honolulu Japanese Chamber of Commerce
  [24348]
Hungarian Assn. of Customs Affairs [IO]
Importers and Exporters Assn. of Taipei [IO]
India Pepper and Spice Trade Assn. [IO]
India Trade Promotion Org. [IO]
Indian Assn. of Ghana [IO]
Indian Oil Seeds and Produce Exporters' Assn.
  [IO]
Indian Trade Promotion Org. [IO]
Indus. Minerals Assn. - North Am. [2742]
Info. Tech. Solution Provider Alliance [2102]
Innovation Norway - U.S. [24283]
Inst. for Agriculture and Trade Policy [16955]
Inst. of Export [IO]
Intl. Assn. of Trading Organizations for a Develop-
  ing World [IO]
Intl. Economics and Finance Soc. [6884]
Intl. Enterprise Singapore [IO]
Intl. Fed. of Customs Brokers Associations [IO]
Intl. Peace Operations Assn. [18213]
Intl. Photonics Commercialization Alliance [2862]
Intl. Reciprocal Trade Assn. [3841]
Intl. Reciprocal Trade Assn. [IO]
Intl. Trade Centre [IO]
Intl. Trade Club of Chicago [2284]
Intl. Trade Coun. [2285]

A star before a book entry number signifies that the name is not listed separately, but is mentioned within the entry.

Intl. Trade Exhibitions in France [1345]
INTERPRED - World Trade Center Sofia [IO]
Iraqi Amer. Chamber of Commerce and Indus. [24285]
Irish Exporters Assn. [IO]
Islamic Centre for Development of Trade [IO]
Israel Export and Intl. Cooperation Inst. [IO]
Italian-American Chamber of Commerce [24338]
Italy-America Chamber of Commerce [24339]
Jamaica Exporters Assn. [IO]
Jamaica Tourist Bd. [24340]
Jamaica USA Chamber of Commerce [24287]
Japan Assn. for Trade with Russia and Central-Eastern Europe [IO]
Japan Customs Brokers Assn. [IO]
Japan External Trade Org. [IO]
Japan External Trade Org. [24342]
Japan Foreign Trade Coun. [IO]
Japan Machinery Center for Trade and Investment [IO]
Japan Overseas Enterprises' Assn. [IO]
Japan Paper Exporters' Assn. [IO]
Japan Paper Importers' Assn. [IO]
Jeweler's Advisory Gp. [2369]
Jewelers Bd. of Trade [2371]
Joint Indus. Gp. [2306]
Jordan Info. Bur. [24349]
The Korea Soc. [24350]
Korea Trade Promotion Center [24351]
Korea Trade Promotion Corp. [IO]
Korean Amer. Soc. of Entrepreneurs [773]
Korean Customs Brokers Assn. [IO]
Latin Chamber of Commerce of U.S.A. [24354]
Le Havre World Trade Center [IO]
Loan Syndications and Trading Assn. [484]
LTD Shippers Assn. [3842]
LTD Shippers Assn. [IO]
Lyon Commerce Intl. [IO]
Macau Importers and Exporters Assn. [IO]
Managed Funds Assn. [24334]
Manufactured Imports Promotion Org. [IO]
Mfrs. for Fair Trade [2538]
Mauritius Export Processing Zone Assn. [IO]
Middle East Assn. [IO]
Military Heraldry Soc. [IO]
Mobile Marketing Assn. [110]
Moroccan Exporters' Assn. [IO]
Morocco-U.S. Coun. on Trade and Investment [3843]
Myanmar Customs Brokers Assn. [IO]
Natl. Alliance for Fair Competition [3613]
Natl. Assn. of Condo Hotel Owners [1952]
Natl. Assn. of Dealer Counsel [361]
Natl. Assn. of Export Companies [2307]
Natl. Assn. of Foreign-Trade Zones [2308]
Natl. Assn. of Importers and Exporters [IO]
Natl. Assn. of Responsible Loan Officers [1978]
Natl. Assn. of Trade Exchanges [3844]
Natl. Confed. of Hungarian Trade Unions [IO]
Natl. Coordinating Comm. for Multiemployer Plans [1242]
Natl. Coun. of Asian Amer. Bus. Associations [774]
Natl. Customs Brokers and Forwarders Assn. of Am. [2309]
Natl. Foreign Trade Coun. [2289]
Natl. Guild of Master Craftsmen [IO]
Natl. Introducing Brokers Assn. [1714]
Natl. Org. of Trade Unions [IO]
Natl. Org. for Diversity in Sales and Marketing [2644]
Natl. United States-Arab Chamber of Commerce [24290]
Native Amer. Indian Info. and Trade Center [24358]
Native Tourism Alliance [24381]
Natural Products Assn. [3425]
Netherlands Chamber of Commerce in the U.S. [24360]
New York Bd. of Trade [3845]
New Zealand Trade and Enterprise [IO]
North America-Mongolia Bus. Coun. [2310]
North American-Bulgarian Chamber of Commerce [24291]
North Amer. Celtic Buyers Assn. [784]

North American-Chilean Chamber of Commerce [24307]
North Amer. Importers Assn. [2311]
North Amer. Steel Alliance [2724]
North America's SuperCorridor Coalition [3887]
Norwegian Amer. Chamber of Commerce - New York City [24292]
Norwegian Seafood Export Coun. [1486]
Norwegian Trade Coun. - London Br. [IO]
Organic Exchange [2864]
Org. of Women in Intl. Trade Alberta [IO]
Overseas Sales and Marketing Assn. of Am. [2312]
Pacific Basin Economic Coun. - Canadian Comm. [IO]
Pacific Economic Cooperation Coun. [IO]
Pakistani Amer. Bus. Executives Assn. [758]
Philippine-Amer. Chamber of Commerce [24365]
Philippine Assn. of Ser. Exporters [IO]
Philippine Exporters Confed. [IO]
Plastic Optical Fiber Trade Org. [2863]
Polish Amer. Chamber of Commerce [24293]
Polish Trade and Indus. Assn. [IO]
Polish-U.S. Bus. Coun. [24366]
Representative of German Indus. and Trade [762]
Romanian-U.S. Bus. Coun. [24370]
Russian-American Chamber of Commerce [24294]
Russian-American Chamber of Commerce in the USA [24371]
Sales Exchange for Refugee Rehabilitation and Vocation [3846]
Sales Exchange for Refugee Rehabilitation and Vocation [IO]
Salvadoran Exporters' Assn. [IO]
Singapore Amer. Bus. Assn. [763]
South African USA Chamber of Commerce [24295]
Spain-United States Chamber of Commerce [24296]
Sporting Goods Shippers Assn. [3590]
Steel Framing Alliance [2731]
Steel Truss and Component Assn. [2733]
Swedish-American Chambers of Commerce, USA [24297]
Swedish Trade Coun. [3847]
Swedish Trade Coun. [IO]
Swedish Trade Coun. [IO]
Swedish Trade Fed. [IO]
Swiss-American Bus. Coun. [2314]
Taipei World Trade Center and China External Trade Development Coun. [IO]
Tokyo Trade and Indus. Assn. [IO]
Trading Standards Inst. [IO]
Traidcraft [IO]
TransFair Canada [IO]
Trinidad and Tobago/USA Chamber of Commerce [24298]
Turkish-American Chamber of Commerce and Indus. [24384]
Uganda Export Promotion Bd. [IO]
Union of Exporters of Uruguay [IO]
U.S. of America-China Chamber of Commerce [24310]
U.S. - ASEAN Bus. Coun. [3848]
U.S. - ASEAN Bus. Coun. [IO]
U.S.-Bahrain Bus. Coun. [2315]
U.S.-Cuba Trade Assn. [2316]
U.S. Indian Amer. Chamber of Commerce [24331]
United States-Indonesia Soc. [775]
U.S.-Kazakhstan Bus. Assn. [2317]
United States-Mexico Chamber of Commerce [24302]
US-China Bus. Coun. [2319]
US-Ireland Alliance [776]
US-Taiwan Bus. Coun. [2294]
US-Vietnam Chamber of Commerce [24387]
Venezuelan Amer. Assn. of the U.S. [24386]
Venezuelan Exporters' Assn. [IO]
VITA [912]
Wales North Am. Bus. Chamber [24306]
WECAI Network [1167]
Western U.S. Agricultural Trade Assn. [4118]
Women's Intl. Shipping and Trading Assn. [3598]
Word of Mouth Marketing Assn. [2653]

World Alliance of Gourmet Robustas [1738]
World Economic Processing Zones Assn. [3849]
World Economic Processing Zones Assn. [IO]
World Trade Center Assn. of Brussels [IO]
World Trade Center Barcelona [IO]
World Trade Center Basel [IO]
World Trade Center Bogota [IO]
World Trade Center Budapest [IO]
World Trade Center Cairo [IO]
World Trade Center Curacao [IO]
World Trade Center Eindhoven [IO]
World Trade Center Geneva [IO]
World Trade Center Genoa [IO]
World Trade Center Grenoble [IO]
World Trade Center Hamburg [IO]
World Trade Center Israel [IO]
World Trade Center Leipzig [IO]
World Trade Center Lille [IO]
World Trade Center Madrid [IO]
World Trade Center Metro Manila [IO]
World Trade Center Metz-Sarrebruck [IO]
World Trade Center Mexico City [IO]
World Trade Center Moscow [IO]
World Trade Center of New Orleans [2295]
World Trade Center of Nigeria [IO]
World Trade Center Panama [IO]
World Trade Center Paris [IO]
World Trade Center Rotterdam [IO]
World Trade Center Ruhr Valley [IO]
World Trade Center Sao Paulo [IO]
World Trade Center Seville [IO]
World Trade Center Stockholm [IO]
World Trade Center Taichung [IO]
World Trade Center Tokyo [IO]
World Trade Center Vienna Airport [IO]
World Trade Center Zurich [IO]
World Trade Centers Assn. [IO]
World Trade Centers Assn. [3850]
World Trade Centers Assn. of Antwerp [IO]
World Trade Centre Beijing [IO]
World Trade Centre Johannesburg [IO]
World Trade Centre Montreal [IO]
World Trade Centre Ottawa-Gatineau [IO]
World Trade Centre Shanghai [IO]
World Trade Centre Vancouver [IO]
World Trade and Convention Centre Halifax [IO]
World Trade Org. [IO]
Worldwide Responsible Apparel Production [261]
Zimbabwe Cong. of Trade Unions [IO]
Trade; Allied Bd. of [2249]
Trade Assn; Amer. Surgical [★1860]
Trade Assn; Cleaning Equip. [2461]
Trade Assn; Copper and Brass Fabricators Foreign [★2704]
Trade Assn. Executives; Amer. [★315]
Trade Assn; Intl; Kite [3643]
Trade Assn; Marketing Res. [★2634]
Trade Assn; Natl. Structured Settlements [6033]
Trade Assn. of New York; Rubber [★3435]
Trade Assn. of Paddlesports [3654], PO Box 6353, Olympia, WA 98507, (360)352-0764
Trade Assn. of Paddlesports [IO], Olympia, WA, United States
Trade Assn. of Proprietary Plants - Defunct.
Trade Assn; SCSI [2110]
Trade Assn; Sewing Machine [★1990]
Trade Assn; Vacuum Dealers [268]
Trade Assn; Western U.S. Agricultural [4118]
Trade; Bankers' Assn. for Foreign [★469]
Trade Bur. of the Consulate Gen. of Brazil in New York; Brazilian Govt. [24240]
Trade Bur; PUSH Intl. [★12098]
Trade Card Collectors Assn. [22124], Box 284, Marlton, NJ 08053
Trade Center; Intl. House - World [★2295]
Trade Center; North Am. Native Amer. (Indian) Info. and [10752]
Trade Circulation Found., Inc; Natl. [3242]
Trade Club of Chicago; Intl. [★2284]
Trade Commn; Australian [24229]
Trade Commn; Austrian [24232]
Trade Commn; Italian [634]
Trade Commn. of Norway [★24283]
Trade Commn. of Norway [★IO]
Trade Commn; Portuguese [24368]

Reference to "IO" in place of a book number signifies that the association may be found in the 45th edition of International Organizations.

Trade Commn; Swedish [★3847]
Trade Commn. Trial Lawyers Assn; Intl. [★6332]
Trade Coun; Agricultural [★2285]
Trade Coun; Danish Amer. [★24316]
Trade Coun; Natl. Mech. [★1049]
Trade Coun.- North Am; Swedish [★3847]
Trade Coun; U.S.-Vietnam [17010]
Trade Development Bd; Bermuda [★24237]
Trade Development Coun; Hong Kong [24329]
Trade Development Off; British [★24241]
Trade; Emergency Comm. for Amer. [2303]
Trade Exchanges; Intl. Assn. of [★3841]
Trade Exhibition Assn. (Thai) [IO], Bangkok, Thailand
Trade Found; Surgical [★1860]
Trade and Indus. Instructors; Natl. Assn. of [9233]
Trade and Indus; Amer.-Southern Africa Chamber of [24375]
Trade and Info. Center; North Amer. Indian [★10750]
Trade and Investment Off; British [★24241]
Trade; Jewelers Bd. of [2371]
Trade Law; Inst. for Intl. and Foreign [★5867]
Trade Marks Patents and Designs Fed. [IO], London, United Kingdom
Trade Mart; Intl. [★2295]
Trade Off. at Consulate-General; British [24241]
Trade Off; Portugese Info., Tourist and [★24367]
Trade Off; Portugese Govt. [★24368]
Trade Org; Japan External [24342]
Trade Policy; Inst. for Agriculture and [16955]
Trade Press Assn. [IO], Barcelona, Spain
Trade Promotion Center; Korea [24351]
Trade Promotion Mgt. Associates [122], 1055 Parsippany Blvd., Ste. 405, Parsippany, NJ 07054, (646)442-3703
Trade Reform Action Coalition - Defunct.
Trade Relations Assn. - Address unknown since 1995.
Trade Relations Coun. of the U.S. - Address unknown since 2003.
Trade Show Bur. [★1335]
Trade Show Exhibitors Assn. [1349], 2301 S Lake Shore Dr., Ste. 1005, Chicago, IL 60616, (312)842-8732
Trade Show Exhibitors Assn; Natl. [★1349]
Trade Show Services Assn. - Defunct.
Trade Specialist Training Prog; International [★5592]
Trade and Tech. Schools and the Assn. of Independent Colleges and Schools; Natl. Assn. of [★9303]
Trade and Tourism Alliance - Defunct.
Trade Union Advisory Comm. to the OECD [IO], Paris, France
Trade Union Cong. of the Philippines [IO], Quezon City, Philippines
Trade Union of Educ. in Finland [IO], Helsinki, Finland
Trade Union of Educ. - Germany [IO], Frankfurt, Germany
Trade Union Leadership Coun. [17158], 8670 Grand River Ave., Detroit, MI 48204, (313)894-0303
Trade Union Solidarity Centre of Finland [IO], Helsinki, Finland
Trade Union Women of African Heritage - Address unknown since 1999.
Trade Unionists; Coalition of Black [24202]
Trade Unions; Natl. Org. of Indus. [24103]
Trade Zones; Natl. Assn. of Foreign- [2308]
Trademark Assn; Intl. Patent and [★5848]
Trademark Assn; U.S. [★5850]
Trademark and Copyright Bureau [★3802]
Trademark Depository Lib. Prog; Patent and [6168]
Trademark Off. Soc; Patent and [5857]
Trademark Soc. [5860], Gen. Info. Services, Patent and Trademark Off., Crystal Plz., Rm. 2002, Washington, DC 20231, (703)308-4357
Traders Assn; Amer. Scouting [★22057]
Traders Assn; Emerging Markets [★3513]
Traders Assn; Natl. Security [★3525]
Traders Assn; Security [3525]
Traders Assn; Western [★22057]
Trades Division of the Jewish Labor Comm; United Hebrew [★24214]
Trades Employers' Assn; Building [609]

Trades; Intl. Union of Painters and Allied [24146]
Trades - New York Division of the Jewish Labor Comm; United Hebrew [24214]
Trades, Tech. and Sci; Inst. for Women in [4042]
Trades Union Cong. - England [IO], London, United Kingdom
Trades Union Cong. - Women's Comm. [IO], London, United Kingdom
Tradesmen of the City of New York; Gen. Soc. of Mechanics and [9229]
Tradesmen; Gen. Soc. of Mechanics and [★9229]
Tradeswomen [12101], 1433 Webster St., Oakland, CA 94612, (510)891-8773
Tradex - Address unknown since 1995.
Trading Assn; Coal [843]
Trading Stamp Inst. of Am. [★3463]
Trading Standards Inst. [IO], Basildon, United Kingdom
Tradition, Family and Property; Amer. Soc. for the Defense of [★19763]
Tradition; Soc. for the Stud. of Myth and [10729]
Traditional Arts; Natl. Coun. for the [9961]
Traditional Boat Squadron of Australia - Australian Capital Territory [IO], Erindale Centre, Australia
Traditional Cat Assn. [21920], c/o Diana Fineran, Sec.-Treas./Founder, PO Box 178, Heisson, WA 98622-0178
Traditional and Classic Cat Intl. [21921], c/o Randi Briggs, Sec., 7615 Clyde Way, Smartville, CA 95977
Traditional and Classic Cat Intl. [IO], Smartville, CA, United States
Traditional Country Music Assn. [★10670]
Traditional Country Music Assn; Natl. [★10670]
Traditional Country Music Assn; Natl. [10670]
Traditional Irish Music, Singing and Dancing Soc. [IO], Monkstown, Ireland
Traditional Irish Singing and Dancing Soc. [★IO]
Traditional Japanese Music Soc. of the City Univ. of New York - Defunct.
Traditional Judaism; Union for [20186]
Traditional Medicine and Preventive Hea. Care; Inst. for [13635]
Traditional Music Assn; Natl. [★10670]
Traditional Roman Catholics; Soc. of [19726]
Traditional Siamese Breeders and Fanciers Assn. [★21920]
Traditional Small Craft Assn. [21885], PO Box 350, Mystic, CT 06355
Traditional Tae Kwon Do Chung Do Assn. [23604], 1209 Gilmore Ln., Louisville, KY 40213, (502)964-3800
Traditional Values; Found. for [18505]
Traditional Wooden Boat Soc. - Defunct.
Traditionalist Caucus; Natl. [17276]
Traditionalist Movement; Catholic [19604]
Traditions pour Demain [★IO]
Traditions for Tomorrow [IO], Geneva, Switzerland
Traditions for Tomorrow - Address unknown since 2003.
Traffic
AAA Found. for Traffic Safety [12943]
Amer. Driver and Traffic Safety Educ. Assn. [8210]
Amer. Highway Users Alliance [12949]
Amer. Soc. of Trans. and Logistics [3861]
Amer. Traffic Safety Services Assn. [3438]
Assn. for the Advancement of Automotive Medicine [12951]
Assn. for Commuter Trans. [13334]
Aviation Safety Inst. [12953]
Bicycle Network [13336]
Center for Auto Safety [12956]
Conf. on Safe Trans. of Hazardous Articles [3562]
driveAWARE [12960]
Insurance Inst. for Highway Safety [12964]
Inter-Amer. Safety Coun. [12965]
Intl. Soc. of Air Safety Investigators [12966]
Messenger Courier Assn. of the Americas [3573]
Mothers Against Drunk Driving [12969]
Motorcycle Safety Found. [3447]
Natl. Assn. of Air Traffic Specialists [24014]
Natl. Assn. of Professional Accident Reconstructionists [6252]
Natl. Assn. of Women Highway Safety Leaders [12971]

Natl. Commn. Against Drunk Driving [12973]
Natl. Comm. on Uniform Traffic Laws and Ordinances [6309]
Natl. Indus. Trans. League [3879]
Natl. Motor Freight Traffic Assn. [3577]
Natl. Motorists Assn. [13340]
Natl. Safety Coun. [12979]
Network of Employers for Traffic Safety [18746]
School and Community Safety Soc. of Am. of the Amer. Assn. for Active Lifestyles and Fitness [12989]
Students Against Destructive Decisions, Students Against Drunk Driving [12992]
Traffic Audit Bur. for Media Measurement [123]
Traffic Court Prog. of the Amer. Bar Assn. [6310]
Traffic Directors Guild of Am. [584]
Traffic Records Comm. [12993]
Trans. Clubs Intl. [3896]
Trans. Safety Equip. Inst. [3458]
Traffic Accident Data Comm. [★12993]
Traffic Accident Data Proj. Comm. [★12993]
Traffic Accident Reconstructionists and Investigators; Natl. Assn. of [5887]
Traffic Accident Statistics; Comm. on Uniform [★12993]
Traffic Accidents Statistics; Natl. Comm. on Uniform [★12993]
Traffic Assn; Energy [2923]
Traffic Assn; Natl. Bus [3878]
Traffic Assn; Natl. Motor Freight [3577]
Traffic Assn; Natl. Passenger [★3929]
Traffic Audit Bur. [★123]
Traffic Audit Bur. for Media Measurement [123], 212 Madison Ave., Ste. 1504, New York, NY 10016, (212)972-8075
Traffic Clubs; Assoc. [★3896]
Traffic Clubs Intl. [★3896]
Traffic Clubs Intl. [★IO]
Traffic Conf; Natl. Furniture [★3570]
Traffic Conf; Natl. Small Shipments [★3574]
Traffic Control Assn; Air [132]
Traffic Controllers Assn; Natl. Air [24013]
Traffic Court Prog. of the Amer. Bar Assn. [6310]
Traffic Directors Guild of Am. [584], 26000 Avenida Aeropuerto No. 114, San Juan Capistrano, CA 92675, (949)429-7063
Traffic Engineers; Inst. of [★7812]
Traffic Injury Res. Found. [IO], Ottawa, ON, Canada
Traffic Laws; Citizens Coalition for Rational [★13340]
Traffic Laws; Citizens for Rational [★13340]
Traffic League; Natl. Indus. [★3879]
TRAFFIC North Am. [5386], 1250 24th St. NW, Washington, DC 20037, (202)293-4800
Traffic Records Comm. [12993], c/o Natl. Safety Coun., 1121 Spring Lake Dr., Itasca, IL 60143-3201, (630)285-1121
Traffic Safety; AAA Found. for [12943]
Traffic Safety Control Devices Assn; Amer. [★3438]
Traffic Safety Educ. Assn; Amer. Driver and [8210]
Traffic Safety and Mgt; Assn. for Road [IO]
Traffic Safety Now - Defunct.
Traffic Safety Services Assn; Amer. [3438]
Traffic Services Assn; Amer. [★3438]
Traffic Specialists; Natl. Assn. of Air [24014]
Traffic System; National [★21494]
Traffic and Trans; Amer. Soc. of [★3861]
TRAFFIC - U.S.A. [★5386]
Trafficking; Coalition to Abolish Slavery and [12370]
Trafficking of Women and Children; Polaris Proj. Combating [17784]
Tragedy Assistance Prog. for Survivors [11503], 910 17th St., NW Ste. 800, Washington, DC 20006, (202)588-8277
Traidcraft [IO], Gateshead, United Kingdom
Trail Riders of the Canadian Rockies [IO], Calgary, AB, Canada
Trail Riders of Today [23532], c/o Michelle Beachley, Membership Chair, 26309 Howard Chapel Dr., Damascus, MD 20872, (301)351-6211
Trail of Tears Assn. [11057], 1100 N Univ., Ste. 143, Little Rock, AR 72207, (501)666-9032
Trailer Coach Assn. [★2527]
Trailer Coach Assn; Recreational Vehicle Division of the [★3371]

A star before a book entry number signifies that the name is not listed separately, but is mentioned within the entry.

Trailer Coach Mfrs. Assn. [★2527]
Trailer Dealers Assn; Natl. [3883]
Trailer Hitch Mfrs. Assn. - Defunct.
Trailer Indus. Assn; Recreational Park [3373]
Trailer Mfrs. Assn. [★2583]
Trailer Mfrs. Assn; Tank Conf. of the Truck [998]
Trailer Mfrs. Assn; Truck [401]
Trailer Mfrs; Natl. Assn. of [393]
Trailer Owners; Natl. Assn. of [22959]
Trailer Tank Inst; Natl. Truck Tank and [★998]

Trails
  Adirondack Forty-Sixers [23930]
  Adirondack Mountain Club [23931]
  Adirondack Trail Improvement Soc. [23932]
  Alpine Club of Canada [IO]
  Alpine Club - England [IO]
  Am. Outdoors [23681]
  Amer. Endurance Ride Conf. [23933]
  Amer. Hiking Soc. [23934]
  Amer. Mountain Guides Assn. [23284]
  Amer. Trails [23935]
  Appalachian Mountain Club [23936]
  Appalachian Trail Conservancy [23937]
  Assn. of Mountaineering Instructors [IO]
  Backpackers Club [IO]
  British Assn. Mountain Guides [IO]
  British Mountaineering Coun. [IO]
  Bruce Trail Assn. [IO]
  Continental Divide Trail Soc. [23938]
  Florida Trail Assn. [23939]
  French Alpine Club [IO]
  Friends of the Outdoors [IO]
  German Alpine Assn. [IO]
  Guild of Registered Tourist Guides [IO]
  Heritage Trails Fund [23940]
  Hiking South Africa [IO]
  Hong Kong Mountaineering Union [IO]
  Intercollegiate Outing Club Assn. [23941]
  Intl. Mountain Bicycling Assn. [23310]
  IOCALUM [23942]
  Lincoln Heritage Trail Found. [23943]
  Montana Outfitters and Guides Assn. [23944]
  Mountaineering Coun. of Scotland [IO]
  Mountaineers [23945]
  Natl. Trail Ride Assn. [23946]
  New England Trail Rider Assn. [23947]
  New England Trails Conf. [23948]
  North Amer. Trail Ride Conf. [23949]
  North Country Trail Assn. [23950]
  Nova Scotia Trails Fed. [IO]
  Outfitters Assn. of Am. [23642]
  Pacific Northwest Trail Assn. [23951]
  Philippine Airlines Mountaineering Club [IO]
  Rails-to-Trails Conservancy [23952]
  Ramblers' Assn. [IO]
  Scottish Rights of Way and Access Soc. [IO]
  Skyline Hikers of the Canadian Rockies [IO]
  Swiss Hiking Fed. [IO]
  Trail Riders of the Canadian Rockies [IO]
  Trail of Tears Assn. [11057]
  U.S. Ski Mountaineering Assn. [23759]
  Women Climbing [IO]
Trails Assn; Oregon-California [10056]
Trails Coun; Natl. [★23935]
Trails Network; Amer. [★23935]
Trailsmen - Address unknown since 1995.
Train Collectors Assn. [22640], PO Box 248, Strasburg, PA 17579-0248, (717)687-8623
Train Collectors Assn. [IO], Strasburg, PA, United States
Train Collectors Soc; Toy [22638]
Train Dispatchers Assn; Amer. [★24175]
Train Dispatchers Dept. of the BLE; Amer. [24175]
Train Heritage Soc. of Am; Orphan [21140]
Train Operating Soc; Toy [22639]
Trainees; Acad. of Security Educators and [★9119]

Trainers
  Amer. Athletic Trainers Assn. and Certification Bd. [23953]
  Amer. Collegiate Horsemen's Assn. [4814]
  Amer. Dog Trainers Network [3851]
  Amer. Horseman Alliance [1924]
  Arabian Professional and Amateur Horseman's Assn. [4862]
  Arizona Canine Acad. [22219]

  Assn. for Applied Interactive Multimedia [2666]
  Assn. of Macintosh Trainers [6810]
  Assn. of Pet Dog Trainers [1160]
  Canadian Soc. for Training and Development [IO]
  Coun. of Advanced Automotive Trainers [341]
  Equine Assisted Growth and Learning Assn. [16216]
  Fiber Optic Assn. [9238]
  Harness Racing Museum and Hall of Fame [23498]
  Innovation Network [2115]
  Intl. Assn. of Canine Professionals [1161]
  Intl. Assn. of Nitrox and Tech. Divers [23379]
  Intl. Law Enforcement Educators and Trainers Assn. [5978]
  Intl. Soc. for Fire Ser. Instructors [5720]
  Natl. Assn. of Field Training Officers [5987]
  Natl. Athletic Trainers' Assn. [23954]
  Natl. Basketball Athletic Trainers Assn. [23135]
  Natl. Coun. on Strength and Fitness [23955]
  Natl. Environmental, Safety and Hea. Training Assn. [5097]
  Natl. Fed. of Professional Trainers [23956]
  Natl. Pitching Assn. [23121]
  Natl. Reined Cow Horse Assn. [22586]
  Natl. Strength and Conditioning Assn. [23957]
  New Zealand Assn. for Training and Development [IO]
  Oregon Horsemen's Benevolent Protective Assn. [23512]
  Professional Baseball Athletic Trainers Soc. [23125]
  Professional Golf Teachers Assn. of Am. [23463]
  Protection Sports Assn. [23848]
  Sector Skills Alliance Scotland [IO]
  Standardbred Owners Assn. [23513]
  Thoroughbred Club of Am. [23514]
  Thoroughbred Owners and Breeders Assn. [23515]
  Thoroughbred Racing Associations [23516]
  Thoroughbred Racing Protective Bur. [23517]
  United Professional Horsemen's Assn. [4961]
  U.S. Trotting Assn. [23519]
  Walking Horse Trainers Assn. [4967]
Trainers; Acad. of Security Educators and [9119]
Trainers Assn; Intl. Marine Animal [6401]
Trainers Assn; Natl. Basketball Athletic [23135]
Trainers; Assn. of Pet Dog [1160]
Trainers Assn; Walking Horse [4967]
Trainers and Breeders; Natl. Cong. of Animal [11435]
Trainers; Coun. of Hotel and Restaurant [1939]
Trainers and Educators; Natl. Assn. of Substance Abuse [9198]
Trainers and Educators; Soc. of Insurance [8578]
Trainers; Natl. Soc. of Pharmaceutical Sales [★3475]
Trainers Network [★22219]
Trainers Soc; Professional Baseball Athletic [23125]
Trainers Soc; Professional Football Athletic [23437]
Training; Accrediting Coun. for Continuing Educ. and [8145]
Training Administrators; Natl. Assn. of County of Employment and [★5618]
Training, and Advocacy; Multicultural Educ., [11625]
Training Assn; Amer. Sail [23153]
Training Assn; Evangelical [19925]
Training Assn; Evangelical Teacher [★19925]
Training Assn; Intl. Vocational Educ. and [9306]
Training Assn; Natl. Environmental [★5097]
Training Assn; Natl. Environmental, Safety and Hea. [5097]
Training Assn; Natl. Staff Development and [13180]
Training Assn; U.S. Combined [★23535]
Training in the Behavioral Sciences; Assn. for Advanced [8878]
Training Center on Independent Living; Res. and [11984]
Training Center; Winrock Intl. Livestock Res. and [★16959]
Training for Change [13134], 3241 Columbus Ave. S, Minneapolis, MN 55407, (612)827-7323
Training Comm; NAGWS Athletic [★8987]
Training Comm; Natl. Joint Painting, Decorating, and Drywall Apprenticeship and [★12082]

Training Coun; Athletic [★8987]
Training Coun; Distance Educ. and [8517]
Training and Development; Amer. Soc. for [★8018]
Training and Development; Amer. Soc. for [3182]
Training and Development; Natl. Assn. for Govt. [2904]
Training Directors; Amer. Soc. of [★8018]
Training Directors' Forum - Defunct.
Training; Eiseman Center for Color Info. and [6707]
Training for Employment; Center on Educ. and [9304]
Training and Employment Inst; 70001 [★12105]
Training and Employment Professionals; Natl. Assn. of County [★5618]
Training Fund; Intl. Joint Painting, Decorating and Drywall Apprenticeship and Manpower [★12082]
Training for Indian Managers; Management Inst.: [★12628]
Training and Info. Center; Natl. [11799]
Training and Info. Proj; Parent [★12569]
Training Inst. for Conflict Resolution, Mediation, and Peacemaking [★8139]
Training; Inst. for Development [★14978]
Training Institutes; Lawyers [★8765]
Training Managers Coun; Automotive [351]
Training Media Assn. - Defunct.
Training; Natl. Coun. of Athletic [8987]
Training; Natl. Coun. for Continuing Educ. and [8152]
Training Officials; Assn. of Coll. Police [★11899]
Training; Pact [11830]
Training Personnel; Intl. Assn. of Correctional [11871]
Training and Productivity Authority of Fiji [IO], Nasinu, Fiji
Training; Professional Soc. for Sales and Marketing [3472]
Training Prog; Regional Victim Assistance [★13369]
Training Proj; Student Empowerment [9192]
Training Reactors; Natl. Org. of Test, Res., and [7388]
Training Res. Assessment Consultants [★6528]
Training Res. Assessment Consultants [★IO]
Training and Res. Associates; Educ., [8556]
Training and Res. Center; FSC Rural [★12937]
Training and Res; Intl. Soc. for Intercultural Educ., [★8667]
Training and Simulation Alliance; Intl. [6735]
Training and Simulation Assn; Natl. [6738]
Training Systems Assn; Natl. [★6089]
Trainmen; Brotherhood of Railroad [★24181]
Trakehner Assn; Amer. [4848]
Trakehner Assn; North Amer. [★4848]
Trakehner Breed Assn. and Registry of America - Defunct.
Tramway and Light Railway Soc. [IO], Brightlingsea, United Kingdom
TRANET [IO], Mason, OH, United States
TRANET [17002], 4457 Bethany Rd., Bldg. F, Mason, OH 45040, (513)459-8700
Tranquilliser Recovery and New Existence [IO], Glen Iris, Australia
Trans-Am Assn; Mopar [★21806]
Trans Am Club U.S.A. - Address unknown since 1991.
Trans-Atlantic Amer. Flag Liner Operators/Trans-Pacific Amer. Flag Berth Operators [3592], 80 Wall St., Ste. 1117, New York, NY 10005-3688, (212)269-2415
Trans-Continental Railroad Passenger Assn. - Defunct.
Trans European Policy Stud. Assn. [IO], Brussels, Belgium
TRANS IV User Group - Defunct.
Trans Lunar Res. [6391], c/o Randa Milliron, Co-Founder, PO Box 661, Mojave, CA 93502-0661, (661)824-1662
Trans-Mississippi Philatelic Soc. - Address unknown since 1999.
Trans-National Network of Appropriate/Alternative Tech. [★17002]
Trans-National Network of Appropriate/Alternative Tech. [★IO]
Trans-Pacific Amer. Flag Berth Operators; Trans-Atlantic Amer. Flag Liner Operators/ [3592]

Reference to "IO" in place of a book number signifies that the association may be found in the 45th edition of International Organizations.

Trans-Species Unlimited [★11358]

Trans World Radio [20403], PO Box 8700, Cary, NC 27512-8700, (919)460-3700

Trans World Radio [IO], Cary, NC, United States

TransAct - Dutch Center for Gender Issues in Healthcare and Prevention of Sexual Violence [IO], Utrecht, Netherlands

Transaction Processing Performance Coun. [6755], PO Box 29920, San Francisco, CA 94129-0920, (415)561-6272

Transactional Anal. Assn; U.S.A. [13743]

Transactional Anal; European Assn. of [IO]

Transactional Anal; Inst. of [IO]

TransAfrica [★IO]

TransAfrica [★16934]

TransAfrica Action Alert [★16934]

TransAfrica Action Alert [★IO]

TransAfrica Forum [IO], Washington, DC, United States

TransAfrica Forum [16934], 1629 K St. NW, Ste. 1100, Washington, DC 20006, (202)223-1960

Transamerica Student Exchange Prog. [★5868]

Transamerica Student Exchange Prog. [★IO]

Transamerican Advt. Agency Network [★IO]

Transamerican Advt. Agency Network [★124]

Transatlantic Brides and Parents Assn. - Address unknown since 1999.

Transatlantic Partners Against AIDS [13586], 165 Broadway, 36th Fl., New York, NY 10006, (212)584-1680

Transatlantic Partners Against AIDS [IO], New York, NY, United States

Transboundary Environmental Info. Agency [IO], St. Petersburg, Russia

Transcultural Nursing Soc. [IO], Livonia, MI, United States

Transcultural Nursing Soc. [15531], Madonna Univ., Coll. of Nursing and Hea., 36600 Schoolcraft Rd., Livonia, MI 48150, (888)432-5470

Transducers Res; Intl. Coordinating Comm. on Solid State [★6927]

TransFair Canada [IO], Ottawa, ON, Canada

Transfer Assn; Electronic Funds [★471]

Transfer Assn; New York Stock [★3524]

Transfer Assn; Securities [3524]

Transfer Assn; Stock [★3524]

Transfer of Tech. to Educ; Inst. for the [8563]

Transferware Collectors Club [21938], 734 Torreya Ct., Palo Alto, CA 94303

Transfiguration Prison Ministry - Defunct.

The Transformer Assn. [1836], 1300 Sumner Ave., Cleveland, OH 44115-2851, (216)241-7333

The Transformer Assn. [IO], Cleveland, OH, United States

Transformer Assn; PCPCI-The [★1836]

Transfrigoroute Intl. [IO], Brussels, Belgium

Transgender

Alliance for Full Acceptance [12213]

Alpha Lambda Tau Intl. Social Fraternity [24613]

Arcus Found. [18266]

Assn. of Welcoming and Affirming Baptists [19476]

Bi Without Borders [17024]

BiNet USA [12220]

Blind Friends of Lesbian, Gay, Transgender and Bisexual People [12221]

Brethren/Mennonite Coun. for Lesbian, Gay, Bisexual and Transgender Interest [20050]

FireFlag/EMS [5773]

Friends for Lesbian, Gay, Bisexual, Transgender, and Queer Concerns [20056]

Gay, Lesbian and Affirming Disciples Alliance [20057]

Gay, Lesbian, Bisexual, Transgender Historical Soc. [10078]

Gay, Lesbian, Bisexual, and Transgendered Disabled Veterans of Am. [20765]

HeartStrong [12232]

Interfaith Working Group [12887]

Intl. Fed. of Black Prides [12238]

Interweave Continental (Unitarian Universalists for Lesbian, Gay, Bisexual and Transgender Concerns) [20059]

Lesbian, Bisexual, Gay and Transgendered United Employees at AT&T [12242]

More Light Presbyterians for Lesbian, Gay, Bisexual and Transgender Concerns [20063]

Natl. Assn. of Lesbian, Gay, Bisexual and Trans-gender Community Centers [11804]

Natl. Black Justice Coalition [18643]

Natl. Coalition for LGBT Hea. [12247]

Natl. Gay Pilot's Assn. [439]

Natl. Transgender Advocacy Coalition [13333]

Racial Justice 911 [18493]

Scouting For All [13006]

Sigma Phi Beta Fraternity [24659]

Soulforce [17657]

Transgender Amer. Veterans Assn. [21325]

United Church of Christ Coalition for Lesbian, Gay, Bisexual and Transgender Concerns [20067]

Transgender Amer. Veterans Assn. [21325], PO Box 4513, Akron, OH 44310

Transgender Concerns; Interweave Continental Unitarian Universalists for Lesbian, Gay, Bisexual and [20059]

Transgender Concerns; More Light Presbyterians for Lesbian, Gay, Bisexual and [20063]

Transgender Concerns; United Church of Christ Coalition for Lesbian, Gay, Bisexual and [20067]

Transgender Interest; Brethren/Mennonite Coun. for Lesbian, Gay, Bisexual and [20050]

Transgender Org; Natl. Latina/o Lesbian, Gay, Bisexual, and [9972]

Transgender People in Medicine; Lesbian, Gay, Bisexual, and [12243]

Transgendered United Employees at AT0mp;T; Lesbian, Bisexual, Gay and [12242]

Transit Advertising Assn. - Defunct.

Transit Advocacy [★13339]

Transit; Amer. Disabled for Accessible Public [★17413]

Transit Assn; Advanced [7808]

Transit Assn; National/International Safe [★3571]

Transit Assn; Natl. Safe [★3571]

Transit Assn; Taxicab, Limousine and Para [3894]

Transit Benefit Assn; Natl. [6324]

Transit Comm; Natl. Safe [★3571]

Transit Consumer Orgs; Natl. Assn. of [13339]

Transit Service Coun; Amer. [6314]

Transit Union; Amalgamated [24197]

Transition; Women in [13447]

Translation

Amer. Assn. of Electronic Reporters and Transcribers [3180]

Amer. Assn. of Language Specialists [3852]

Amer. Assn. of Language Specialists [IO]

Amer. Bible Soc. [19504]

Amer. Cryptogram Assn. [22178]

Amer. Literary Translators Assn. [11058]

Amer. Translators Assn. [3853]

Asia-Pacific Assn. for Machine Translation [IO]

Assn. for Machine Translation in the Americas [IO]

Assn. for Machine Translation in the Americas [7807]

Assn. of Sci. and Tech. Translators of Slovenia [IO]

Assn. of Translation Companies [IO]

Assn. of Translators and Interpreters of Alberta [IO]

Assn. of Visual Language Interpreters of Canada [IO]

Bible League [19510]

BLI [19512]

Canadian Translators, Terminologists and Interpreters Coun. [IO]

Danish Assn. of State-Authorized Translators and Interpreters [IO]

European Assn. for Machine Translation [IO]

GALA: Globalization and Localization Assn. [1168]

Inst. for Biblical Res. [19519]

Inst. of Translation and Interpreting [IO]

Intl. Assn. of Conf. Interpreters [IO]

Intl. Assn. of Conf. Translators [IO]

Intl. Bible Soc. [19520]

Intl. Fed. of Translators [IO]

Intl. Org. for Septuagint and Cognate Stud. [19522]

Intl. Soc. of Bible Collectors [19523]

Israel Translators Assn. [IO]

Japan Assn. of Translators [IO]

Literary Translators' Assn. of Canada [IO]

Lutheran Bible Translators [19524]

Marine Corps Interrogator Translator Teams Assn. [19226]

Mexican Professional Assn. of Conf. Interpreters [IO]

Natl. Alliance of Black Interpreters [3854]

Natl. Inst. for Compilation and Translation [IO]

New Zealand Soc. of Translators and Interpreters [IO]

Norwegian Assn. of Literary Translators [IO]

Registry of Interpreters for the Deaf [14778]

Soc. of Biblical Literature [19530]

South African Translators' Inst. [IO]

Swedish Assn. of Translators [IO]

Swedish-English Literary Translators' Assn. [IO]

Swedish Translators in North Am. [IO]

Swedish Translators in North Am. [11059]

Thai Assn. of Conf. Interpreters [IO]

Translators Assn. [IO]

Translators and Interpreters Guild [3855]

Tyndale Soc. [20530]

Vietnamese Nom Preservation Found. [10433]

Wycliffe Bible Translators [19531]

Translation and Computational Linguistics; Assn. for Machine [★10400]

Translation Res. Inst. - Defunct.

Translation Soc; Buddhist Text [19544]

Translator Assn; Natl. [576]

Translator LPTV Assn; Natl. [★576]

Translators Assn. [IO], London, United Kingdom

Translators Assn; Amer. [3853]

Translators Assn; Amer. Literary [11058]

Translators Assn; Court Interpreters and [★5628]

Translators for the Deaf; Natl. Registry of Profes-sional Interpreters and [★14778]

Translators' and Interpreters' Educational Soc. - Ad-dress unknown since 2006.

Translators and Interpreters Guild [3855], 962 Wayne Ave., No. 500, Silver Spring, MD 20910, (301)563-6450

Translators; Lutheran Bible [19524]

Translators; Messengers of Christ-Lutheran Bible [★19524]

Translators; Natl. Assn. of Judiciary Interpreters and [5628]

Translators; Wycliffe Bible [19531]

Transmission Assn; Mech. Power [2045]

Transmission Assn; Multiple-V-Belt Drive and Mech. Power [★2045]

Transmission Distributors Assn; Power [2060]

Transmission Equip. Distributors Assn; Mech. Power [★2060]

Transmission Products Assn. - Defunct.

Transmission Rebuilders Assn; Automatic [373]

Transmission Representatives Assn; Power [★2059]

Transnational Diplomatic Network [17874]

Transnational Diplomatic Network [IO], Arlington, VA, United States

Transnational Found. for Peace and Future Res. [IO], Lund, Sweden

Transnational Inst. [★IO]

Transnational Inst. [IO], Amsterdam, Netherlands

Transnational Inst. [★18455]

Transocean Marine Paint Assn. [IO], Rotterdam, Netherlands

Transparence-International (France) [★IO]

Transparencia, Consciencia and Cidadania [★IO]

Transparencia Internacional Costa Rica [★IO]

Transparency, Consciousness and Citizenship [IO], Brasilia, Brazil

Transparency Intl. - Argentina [IO], Buenos Aires, Argentina

Transparency Intl. - Australia [IO], Blackburn South, Australia

Transparency Intl. - Azerbaijan [IO], Baku, Azer-baijan

Transparency Intl. - Bangladesh [IO], Dhaka, Bang-ladesh

Transparency Intl. - Benin [IO], Cotonou, Benin

Transparency Intl. - Bosnia and Herzegovina [IO], Banja Luka, Bosnia-Hercegovina

Transparency Intl. - Botswana [IO], Gaborone, Botswana

A star before a book entry number signifies that the name is not listed separately, but is mentioned within the entry.

Transparency Intl. - Brazil [★IO]
Transparency Intl. - Brazil [IO], Sao Paulo, Brazil
Transparency Intl. - Brussels [IO], Brussels, Belgium
Transparency Intl. - Bulgaria [IO], Sofia, Bulgaria
Transparency Intl. - Canada [IO], Toronto, ON, Canada
Transparency Intl. - Chile [IO], Santiago, Chile
Transparency Intl. - Colombia [IO], Bogota, Colombia
Transparency Intl. - Costa Rica [IO], San Jose, Costa Rica
Transparency Intl. - Croatia [IO], Zagreb, Croatia
Transparency Intl. - Czech Republic [IO], Prague, Czech Republic
Transparency Intl. - Denmark [IO], Copenhagen, Denmark
Transparency Intl. Deutschland e.V. [★IO]
Transparency Intl. - Fiji [IO], Suva, Fiji
Transparency Intl. - France [IO], Levallois Perret, France
Transparency Intl. - Gambia [IO], Banjul, Gambia
Transparency Intl. - Georgia [IO], Tbilisi, Georgia
Transparency Intl. - Germany [IO], Berlin, Germany
Transparency Intl. - Greece [IO], Athens, Greece
Transparency Intl. Hrvatska [★IO]
Transparency Intl. - Hungary [IO], Budapest, Hungary
Transparency Intl. - India [IO], New Delhi, India
Transparency Intl. - Indonesia [IO], Jakarta, Indonesia
Transparency Intl. - Initiative Madagascar [IO], Antananarivo, Madagascar
Transparency Intl. - Israel [IO], Tel Aviv, Israel
Transparency Intl. - Italy [IO], Milan, Italy
Transparency Intl. - Kazakhstan [IO], Almaty, Kazakhstan
Transparency Intl. - Kenya [IO], Nairobi, Kenya
Transparency Intl. - Korea [IO], Seoul, Republic of Korea
Transparency Intl. - Lithuania [IO], Vilnius, Lithuania
Transparency Intl. - Malaysia [IO], Kuala Lumpur, Malaysia
Transparency Intl. - Mauritius [IO], Curepipe, Mauritius
Transparency Intl. - Moldova [IO], Chisinau, Moldova
Transparency Intl. - Mongolia [IO], Ulan Bator, Mongolia
Transparency Intl. - Nepal [IO], Kathmandu, Nepal
Transparency Intl. - New Zealand [IO], Wellington, New Zealand
Transparency Intl. - Nigeria [IO], Abuja, Nigeria
Transparency Intl. - Philippine Chap. [IO], Manila, Philippines
Transparency Intl. - Poland [IO], Warsaw, Poland
Transparency Intl. - Romania [IO], Bucharest, Romania
Transparency Intl. - Russia [IO], Moscow, Russia
Transparency Intl. - Slovakia [IO], Bratislava, Slovakia
Transparency Intl. - South Africa [IO], Braamfontein, Republic of South Africa
Transparency Intl. - Sri Lanka [IO], Colombo, Sri Lanka
Transparency Intl. - Sweden [IO], Stockholm, Sweden
Transparency Intl. - Switzerland [★IO]
Transparency Intl. - Switzerland [IO], Bern, Switzerland
Transparency Intl. - Taiwan [IO], Taipei, Taiwan
Transparency Intl. - Tanzania [IO], Dar es Salaam, United Republic of Tanzania
Transparency Intl. - Thailand [IO], Bangkok, Thailand
Transparency Intl. - Turkey [IO], Istanbul, Turkey
Transparency Intl. - UK [IO], London, United Kingdom
Transparency Intl. - Ukraine [IO], Kiev, Ukraine
Transparency Intl. - Vanuatu [IO], Port Vila, Vanuatu
Transparency Intl. - Yemen [IO], Sana'a, Yemen
Transparency Intl. - Zambia [IO], Lusaka, Zambia
Transparency Intl. - Zimbabwe [IO], Harare, Zimbabwe
Transpersonal Institute [★10170]
Transpersonal Psychology; Assn. for [10170]
Transpersonal Therapists and Physicians; Intl. Assn. of [15205]

Transplant Assn; Children's Organ [13956]
Transplant Australia [IO], North Sydney, Australia
Transplant Found; Pittsburgh [★16670]
Transplant Fund; Organ [★16678]
Transplant Organ Procurement Org. [★16670]
Transplant Recipients Intl. Org. [16682], 2100 M St. NW, No. 170-353, Washington, DC 20037-1233, (202)293-0980
Transplant Recipients Intl. Org. [IO], Washington, DC, United States
Transplant Speakers Intl. [IO], Freehold, NJ, United States
Transplant Speakers Intl. [16683], PO Box 6395, Freehold, NJ 07728-6395, (877)609-4615
Transplantation
  Amer. Assn. of Blood Banks [13761]
  Amer. Assn. of Kidney Patients [15283]
  Amer. Assn. of Tissue Banks [16663]
  Amer. Kidney Fund [15284]
  Amer. Liver Found. [14803]
  Amer. Nephrology Nurses' Assn. [15286]
  Amer. Organ Transplant Assn. [16664]
  Amer. Soc. for Blood and Marrow Transplantation [16665]
  Amer. Soc. of Multicultural Hea. and Transplant Professionals [16666]
  Amer. Soc. of Nephrology [15288]
  Amer. Soc. for Neural Transplantation and Repair [15380]
  Amer. Soc. of Transplant Surgeons [16667]
  Amer. Soc. of Transplantation [16668]
  Amer. Transplant Assn. [16669]
  Assn. of Nurses Endorsing Transplantation [15670]
  Assn. of Organ Procurement Organizations [14287]
  Australasian and South East Asian Tissue Typing Assn. [IO]
  Belgian Transplantation Soc. [IO]
  British Soc. for Histocompatibility and Immunogenetics [IO]
  British Transplantation Soc. [IO]
  Canadian Transplant Assn. [IO]
  Center for Organ Recovery and Educ. [16670]
  Children's Liver Assn. for Support Services [14804]
  DaVita Patient Citizens [15291]
  European Heart and Lung Transplant Fed. [IO]
  European Soc. for Organ Transplantation [IO]
  European Transplant Coordinators Org. [IO]
  Eurotransplant Intl. Found. [IO]
  Eye Bank Assn. of Am. [14288]
  Eye-Bank for Sight Restoration [14289]
  Hong Kong Soc. of Transplantation [IO]
  Intl. Assn. for Organ Donation [16671]
  Intl. Liver Transplantation Soc. [16672]
  Intl. Liver Transplantation Soc. [IO]
  Intl. Pediatric Transplant Assn. [IO]
  Intl. Pediatric Transplant Assn. [16673]
  Intl. Soc. for Heart and Lung Transplantation [16674]
  Intl. Soc. for Heart and Lung Transplantation [IO]
  Intl. Transplant Coordinators Soc. [IO]
  Japan Organ Transplant Network [IO]
  Kidney Transplant/Dialysis Assn. [16675]
  LifeBanc [14290]
  The Living Bank Intl. [14291]
  Malaysian Soc. of Transplantation [IO]
  Natl. Bone Marrow Transplant Link [16676]
  Natl. Coun. on Minority Educ. in Transplantation [16677]
  Natl. Found. for Transplants [16678]
  Natl. Inst. of Transplantation [16679]
  Natl. Kidney Found. [15294]
  Natl. Marrow Donor Prog. [14292]
  Natl. Transplant Soc. [16680]
  North Amer. Soc. for Dialysis and Transplantation [15295]
  North Amer. Transplant Coordinators Org. [16681]
  Renal Physicians Assn. [15298]
  Transplant Australia [IO]
  Transplant Recipients Intl. Org. [IO]
  Transplant Recipients Intl. Org. [16682]
  Transplant Speakers Intl. [16683]
  Transplant Speakers Intl. [IO]

  The Transplantation Soc. [IO]
  UK Transplant [IO]
  United Kingdom Transplant Coordinators Assn. [IO]
  United Network for Organ Sharing [16684]
  World Marrow Donor Assn. [IO]
Transplantation; Amer. Soc. for Neural [★15380]
Transplantation; Assn. of Nurses Endorsing [15670]
Transplantation; Intl. Soc. for Heart [★16674]
Transplantation; Natl. Assn. of Patients on Hemodialysis and [★15283]
Transplantation; North Amer. Soc. for Dialysis and [15295]
Transplantation Registry; International Heart and Lung [★16674]
Transplantation Registry; International Heart and Lung [★IO]
Transplantation and Repair; Amer. Soc. for Neural [15380]
The Transplantation Soc. [IO], Montreal, QC, Canada
Transplants; Acad. for Implants and [14087]
Transport 2000 - Canada [IO], Ottawa, ON, Canada
Transport Assn. [IO], Epsom, United Kingdom
Transport Assn. of Am; Air [133]
Transport Assn; Army [★6090]
Transport Assn; Slurry [★842]
Transport for Christ [★20404]
Transport for Christ [★IO]
Transport for Christ, Intl. [IO], Marietta, PA, United States
Transport for Christ, Intl. [20404], 1525 River Rd., Marietta, PA 17547-9403, (717)426-9977
Transport for Christ; New [★20404]
Transport Coordinating Comm; Natl. Air [★140]
Transport and Gen. Workers' Union [IO], London, United Kingdom
Transport and Indus. Workers Union [IO], Laventille, Trinidad and Tobago
Transport; Museum of [★10926]
Transport Museum Assn. [10926], 2967 Barret Sta. Rd., St. Louis, MO 63122, (314)965-6885
Transport; Natl. Museum of [★10926]
Transport Planning Soc. [IO], London, United Kingdom
Transport Salaried Staffs' Assn. - Ireland [IO], Dublin, Ireland
Transport Salaried Staffs Assn. - United Kingdom [IO], London, United Kingdom
Transport Ser. Employees; United [★24180]
Transport Tech. and Historical Soc; Modern [★10922]
Transport Ticket Soc. [IO], Mansfield, United Kingdom
Transport Workers Union of Am. [24200], 1700 Broadway, 2nd Fl., New York, NY 10019, (212)259-4900
Transport Workers' Union of Australia [IO], Parramatta, Australia
Transportation
  AAA Found. for Traffic Safety [12943]
  Advanced Transit Assn. [7808]
  Adventure Travel Trade Assn. [3902]
  Agricultural and Food Transporters Conf. [3856]
  Air Brake Assn. [3274]
  Air Charity Network [14312]
  Air Courier Assn. [3857]
  Aircraft Recovery Assn. [12945]
  Airport Ground Trans. Assn. [3858]
  Airport Minority Advisory Coun. [2758]
  Alliance for a New Trans. Charter [6311]
  Alternative Energy Resources Org. [6935]
  Amalgamated Transit Union [24197]
  Am. Bikes [17022]
  Amer. Alliance of Ethical Movers [13346]
  Amer. Ambulance Assn. [14313]
  Amer. Assn. of Private Railroad Car Owners [3276]
  Amer. Assn. of Railroad Superintendents [3277]
  Amer. Assn. of State Highway and Trans. Officials [6312]
  Amer. Auto. Touring Alliance [3905]
  Amer. Bus Assn. [3859]
  Amer. Coal Ash Assn. [3986]
  Amer. Coun. of Highway Advertisers [85]

Reference to "IO" in place of a book number signifies that the association may be found in the 45th edition of International Organizations.

Amer. Highway Users Alliance [12949]
Amer. Import Shippers Assn. [3557]
Amer. Inst. for Shippers' Associations [3558]
Amer. Moving and Storage Assn. [3559]
Amer. Public Trans. Assn. [3860]
American Public Transportation Association [IO]
Amer. Railway Car Inst. [3278]
Amer. Railway Development Assn. [3279]
Amer. Railway Engg. and Maintenance of Way
    Assn. [3280]
Amer. Road and Trans. Builders Assn. [6313]
Amer. Short Line and Regional Railroad Assn.
    [3281]
Amer. Soc. of Trans. and Logistics [3861]
Amer. Traffic Safety Services Assn. [3438]
Amer. Train Dispatchers Dept. of the BLE [24175]
Amer. Transit Service Coun. [6314]
Amer. Trans. Bowling Assn. [23249]
Amer. Truck Dealers [3862]
Amer. Truck Historical Soc. [23021]
Amer. Trucking Associations [3863]
Amer. Vecturist Assn. [23006]
Amer. Voyager Assn. [22666]
Americans for Trans. Mobility [6315]
Angel Flight West [12512]
Animal Trans. Assn. [11361]
Armored Trans. Inst. [3560]
ARRB Gp. [IO]
Assoc. Soc. of Locomotive Engineers and Fire-
    men [IO]
Assn. for the Advancement of Automotive
    Medicine [12951]
Assn. of Air Medical Services [14314]
Assn. of Amer. Railroads [3282]
Assn. of British Drivers [IO]
Association for Commuter Transportation [IO]
Assn. for Commuter Trans. [13334]
Assn. for European Transport [IO]
Assn. of German Transport Undertakings [IO]
Assn. for Intelligent Transport Systems India [IO]
Assn. of Metropolitan Planning Organizations
    [17207]
Assn. of Pedestrian and Bicycle Professionals
    [18747]
Assn. for Road Traffic Safety and Mgt. [IO]
Assn. for Safe Intl. Road Travel [IO]
Assn. for Safe Intl. Road Travel [13335]
Assn. of Trans. Law Professionals [6316]
Australian Trucking Assn. [IO]
Aviation Safety Inst. [12953]
Bicycle Helmet Safety Inst. [12954]
Bicycle Network [13336]
Bicycle Network [IO]
Bikes Belong Coalition [21831]
Bridge Line Historical Soc. [22932]
British Biker Cooperative [22672]
British Intl. Freight Assn. [IO]
British Intl. Motorcycle Assn. [22673]
British Parking Assn. [IO]
British Tunnelling Soc. [IO]
Brotherhood of Locomotive Engineers and Train-
    men, A Division of the Rail Conf. of the Intl.
    Brotherhood of Teamsters [24176]
Brotherhood of Maintenance of Way Employees
    [24177]
Brotherhood of Railroad Signalmen [24178]
Brotherhood Railway Carmen Division/Transporta-
    tion Communications Union [24179]
Bus Users UK [IO]
Buses Intl. Assn. [IO]
Buses Intl. Assn. [3864]
Canadian Assn. of Token Collectors [IO]
Canadian Bus Assn. [IO]
Canadian Coun. of Motor Transport Administrators
    [IO]
Canadian Indus. Trans. Assn. [IO]
Canadian Inst. of Traffic and Trans. [IO]
Canadian Parking Assn. [IO]
Canadian Trans. Equip. Assn. [IO]
Canadian Urban Transit Assn. [IO]
Carriage Operators of North Am. [783]
Center for Auto Safety [12956]
Central Elec. Railfans' Assn. [22933]
Certified Claims Professional Accreditation Coun.
    [3865]

Chartered Inst. of Logistics Transport [IO]
Chartered Inst. of Logistics and Transport in
    Australia [IO]
Chartered Inst. of Logistics and Transport in Hong
    Kong [IO]
Chartered Inst. of Logistics and Transport in North
    America [IO]
Chartered Inst. of Logistics and Transport -
    Zimbabwe [IO]
Citizens for Roadside Safety [12957]
Coach Operators Fed. [IO]
Coal Tech. Assn. [842]
Coalition Against Bigger Trucks [13337]
Community Transport Assn. [IO]
Confed. of Passenger Transport - UK [IO]
Conf. of Minority Trans. Officials [3866]
Conf. on Safe Trans. of Hazardous Articles [3562]
Containerization and Intermodal Inst. [978]
Corporate Angel Network [13817]
Cruise Club of Am. [3914]
Dangerous Goods Advisory Coun. [3563]
Delta Nu Alpha Trans. Fraternity [24722]
Diamond T Register [23023]
Distribution and LTL Carriers Assn. [3564]
driveAWARE [12960]
Driver Employer Coun. of Am. [3867]
Eastern Asia Soc. for Trans. Stud. [IO]
Elec. Railroaders' Assn. [10911]
Eno Trans. Found. [7809]
Equip. Managers Coun. of Am. [943]
Estonian Freight Forwarders Assn. [IO]
European Chem. Transport Assn. [IO]
European Conf. of Ministers of Transport [IO]
European Express Assn. [IO]
European Fed. for Transport and Env. [IO]
European Intermodal Assn. [IO]
European Transport Safety Coun. [IO]
European Transport Workers' Fed. [IO]
Express Delivery and Logistics Assn. [3565]
Finnish Transport Workers' Union [IO]
Food Providers of Am. [12392]
Food Shippers Assn. of North Am. [1512]
Freight Carriers Assn. of Canada [IO]
Freight Transport Assn. [IO]
Freight Trans. Consultants Assn. [3566]
Governors Highway Safety Assn. [6317]
Graham Bros. Truck and Bus Club [21894]
Gray Line Sightseeing Assn. [3868]
Greek Natl. Tourist Org. [3869]
Greek Natl. Tourist Org. [IO]
High Speed Ground Trans. Assn. [7810]
Hovercraft Club of Am. [22589]
Human Powered Vehicle Assn. [7811]
Human Powered Vehicle Assn. [IO]
Independent Armored Car Operators Assn. [3568]
Independent Pet and Animal Trans. Assn. Intl.
    [2958]
Independent Truckers and Drivers Assn. [3870]
Inst. of Highway Incorporated Engineers [IO]
Inst. of Transport Admin. [IO]
Inst. of Transport Economics [IO]
Institute of Transportation Engineers [IO]
Inst. of Trans. Engineers [7812]
Institution of Highways and Trans. [IO]
Insurance Inst. for Highway Safety [12964]
Intelligent Transport Systems - Arab [IO]
Intelligent Transport Systems - Australia [IO]
Intelligent Transport Systems - Japan [IO]
Intelligent Transport Systems - Singapore [IO]
Intelligent Transport Systems - South Africa [IO]
Intelligent Transport Systems for the United
    Kingdom [IO]
Intelligent Trans. Soc. of Am. [3871]
Inter-Amer. Safety Coun. [12965]
Intermodal Assn. of North Am. [3872]
The Intl. Air Cargo Assn. [3873]
The International Air Cargo Association [IO]
Intl. Air Rail Org. [IO]
Intl. Airline Passengers Assn. [23015]
Intl. Assn. of Air Travel Couriers [153]
Intl. Assn. of Public Transport [IO]
Intl. Bicycle Fund [IO]
Intl. Bicycle Fund [13338]
Intl. Bridge, Tunnel and Turnpike Assn. [6318]
Intl. Bridge, Tunnel and Turnpike Assn. [IO]

Intl. Brotherhood of Teamsters [24198]
Intl. Bus Collectors Club [21895]
Intl. Fed. of Trade Unions of Transport Workers
    [IO]
Intl. Furniture and Trans. Logistics Coun. [3570]
Intl. Parking Inst. [2899]
Intl. Railroad and Transportation Postcard Collec-
    tors Club [22055]
Intl. Road Fed. [3874]
Intl. Road Fed. [IO]
Intl. Road Transport Union [IO]
Intl. Safe Transit Assn. [3571]
Intl. Soc. of Air Safety Investigators [12966]
Intl. Transport Workers' Fed. [IO]
International Transportation Management Associa-
    tion [IO]
Intl. Trans. Mgt. Assn. [6319]
Intl. Tunnelling Assn. [IO]
Intl. Union of Professional Drivers [IO]
Israeli Intelligent Transport Systems Assn. [IO]
Japan Road Contractors Assn. [IO]
Latin Amer. Aeronautical Assn. [438]
Lexington Gp. in Trans. History [10913]
Licensed Taxi Drivers Assn. [IO]
Light Rail Transit Assn. [IO]
Lincoln Highway Assn. [10043]
Lithuanian Roads Assn. [IO]
Locomotive Maintenance Officers' Assn. [3283]
Logistics and Transport New Zealand [IO]
London Transport Users Comm. [IO]
London Underground Railway Soc. [IO]
Loved Ones and Drivers Support [13347]
Maritime Trades Dept., AFL-CIO [24129]
Mid-Continent Railway Historical Soc. [22934]
Mid-West Truckers Assn. [3875]
The Monorail Soc. [23007]
Mothers Against Drunk Driving [12969]
Motor Bus Soc. [21896]
Motorist Info. and Services Assn. [13344]
Motorsport Indus. Assn. [IO]
Mystic Valley Railway Soc. [10914]
NASSTRAC [3574]
Natl. Accounting and Finance Coun. [3876]
Natl. African-American RV'ers Assn. [22958]
Natl. Armored Car Assn. [3575]
Natl. Assn. of Auto. Museums [10511]
Natl. Assn. of Healthcare Transport Mgt. [14579]
Natl. Assn. of Publicly Funded Truck Driving
    Schools [3877]
Natl. Assn. for Pupil Trans. [6320]
Natl. Assn. of Railroad Passengers [3284]
Natl. Assn. of Railroad Trial Counsel [6321]
Natl. Assn. of Railway Bus. Women [3285]
Natl. Assn. of Regional Councils [6244]
Natl. Assn. of Retired and Veteran Railway
    Employees [3286]
Natl. Assn. of State Motorcycle Safety Administra-
    tors [6253]
Natl. Assn. for Telematics for Transport and Safety
    [IO]
Natl. Assn. of Timetable Collectors [23008]
Natl. Assn. of Transit Consumer Orgs. [13339]
Natl. Assn. of Wastewater Transporters [3998]
Natl. Assn. of Women Highway Safety Leaders
    [12971]
Natl. Bus Traffic Assn. [3878]
Natl. Capital Historical Museum of Trans. [10133]
Natl. Clean Cities [6399]
Natl. Commn. Against Drunk Driving [12973]
Natl. Conf. of State Fleet Administrators [6322]
Natl. Conf. of State Trans. Specialists [6323]
Natl. Distribution Union [IO]
Natl. Ethanol Vehicle Coalition [4776]
Natl. Indus. Trans. League [3879]
Natl. Limousine Assn. [3880]
Natl. Motor Freight Traffic Assn. [3577]
Natl. Motorists Assn. [13340]
Natl. Motorists Assn. Australia [IO]
Natl. Parking Assn. [2900]
Natl. Private Truck Coun. [3881]
Natl. Railroad Constr. and Maintenance Assn.
    [3287]
Natl. Railway Historical Soc. [10915]
Natl. Railway Labor Conf. [3288]
Natl. Safe Boating Coun. [12977]

A star before a book entry number signifies that the name is not listed separately, but is mentioned within the entry.

Natl. Safe Skies Alliance [18748]
Natl. Safe Waterways and Seaports Alliance [18749]
Natl. Safety Coun. [12979]
Natl. School Trans. Assn. [3882]
Natl. Solid Wastes Mgt. Assn. [3579]
Natl. Tank Truck Carriers [3580]
Natl. Taxicab Assn. [IO]
Natl. Trailer Dealers Assn. [3883]
Natl. Transit Benefit Assn. [6324]
Natl. Truckers Assn. [3884]
Natl. Union of Rail, Maritime and Transport Workers [IO]
Natl. Waterways Conf. [3581]
Nautilus UK [IO]
New York/New Jersey Foreign Freight Forwarders and Brokers Assn. [3582]
Newcomen Soc. of the U.S. [10138]
North Amer. Rail Shippers Assn. [3885]
North Amer. Railcar Operators Assn. [3886]
North America's SuperCorridor Coalition [3887]
Off. Furniture Distribution Assn. [4025]
Oper. Lifesaver [12983]
Owner-Operator Independent Drivers Assn. [3888]
Pacific Railroad Soc. [10917]
Pacific Southwest Railway Museum [10918]
Partnership for Food Safety Educ. [14399]
Passenger Shipping Assn. [IO]
Passenger Vessel Assn. [2591]
Private Motor Truck Coun. of Canada [IO]
Professional Truck Driver Inst. [3889]
Professional Trucking Services Assn. [3890]
Rail, Tram and Bus Union [IO]
Railroad Enthusiasts [10919]
Railroad Sta. Historical Soc. [10920]
Railroadiana Collectors Assn. Incorporated [22936]
Railway Engineering-Maintenance Suppliers Assn. [3289]
Railway Indus. Clearance Assn. [3891]
Railway and Locomotive Historical Soc. [10921]
Railway Supply Inst. [3290]
Railway Systems Suppliers, Inc. [3291]
Railway Tie Assn. [3292]
Riders for Justice [22690]
Road Freight Assn. [IO]
Road Haulage Assn. [IO]
The Road Info. Prog. [3892]
Romanian Union of Public Transport [IO]
Rural Planning Organizations of Am. [6247]
S2000 Club of Am. [21777]
School and Community Safety Soc. of Am. of the Amer. Assn. for Active Lifestyles and Fitness [12989]
Seatbelt Law Opposition Forum [12990]
Sectoral Assn. of Trans. Equip. and Machines Mfg. [IO]
Services, Indus. Professional and Tech. Union [IO]
Snow and Ice Mgt. Assn. [6325]
Soc. of Freight Car Historians [10922]
Soc. of Operations Engineers [IO]
Soc. of Professional Drivers [3893]
Soo Line Historical and Tech. Soc. [10923]
Sporting Goods Shippers Assn. [3590]
Students Against Destructive Decisions, Students Against Drunk Driving [12992]
Surface Trans. Policy Proj. [18750]
Tank Conf. of the Truck Trailer Mfrs. Assn. [998]
Taxicab, Limousine and Paratransit Assn. [3894]
Taxicab, Limousine and Paratransit Association [IO]
Teamsters for a Democratic Union [24199]
Tech. and Maintenance Coun. of the Amer. Trucking Associations [3895]
Terminal Railroad Assn. Historical and Tech. Soc. [10925]
Thunderhead Alliance [18751]
Traffic Audit Bur. for Media Measurement [123]
Traffic Records Comm. [12993]
Transport 2000 - Canada [IO]
Transport Assn. [IO]
Transport and Gen. Workers' Union [IO]
Transport and Indus. Workers Union [IO]
Transport Museum Assn. [10926]

Transport Planning Soc. [IO]
Transport Salaried Staffs' Assn. - Ireland [IO]
Transport Salaried Staffs Assn. - United Kingdom [IO]
Transport Workers Union of Am. [24200]
Transport Workers' Union of Australia [IO]
Trans. Alternatives [7813]
Trans. Assn. of Canada [IO]
Trans. Clubs Intl. [IO]
Trans. Clubs Intl. [3896]
Trans. Communications Intl. Union [24180]
Trans. Inst. [3593]
Trans. Intermediaries Assn. [3594]
Trans. Lawyers Assn. [6326]
Trans. and Logistics Coun. [3595]
Trans. Res. Bd. [7814]
Trans. Res. Forum [7815]
Trans. Safety Equip. Inst. [3458]
TransportGroup [IO]
Triumph Intl. Owners Club [22692]
Truckers for Christ [19828]
Trucking Indus. Defense Assn. [3897]
Trucking Mgt., Inc. [3898]
Truckload Carriers Assn. [3899]
Underground Trans. Res. Assn. [IO]
Union of Bulgarian Motorists [IO]
Union of Canadian Trans. Employees [IO]
Union of Public Transport [IO]
United Motorcoach Assn. [3900]
United Road Transport Union [IO]
United Trans. Union [24181]
USMC Motor Transport Assn. [2599]
Vespa Club of Am. [22696]
Wabash, Frisco and Pacific Assn. [10927]
White Owners Register [23026]
Women's Intl. Shipping and Trading Assn. [3598]
Women's Trans. Seminar [3901]
Women's Trans. Seminar [IO]
World Ocean and Cruise Liner Soc. [23020]
World Road Assn. - France [IO]
Worshipful Company of Wheelwrights [IO]
Trans. Alternatives [7813], 127 W 26th St., Ste. 1002, New York, NY 10001, (212)629-8080
Trans; Amer. Soc. of Traffic and [★3861]
Trans; Animal Air [★11361]
Trans. Assn; Airline Ground [★3858]
Trans. Assn. of Am; Community [11772]
Transportation Assn. of America - Defunct.
Trans. Assn; Animal [11361]
Trans. Assn. of Canada [IO], Ottawa, ON, Canada
Trans. Assn; Elec. Drive [6517]
Trans. Assn. Intl; Independent Pet and Animal [2958]
Trans. Assn; Natl. Air [160]
Trans. Assn; Natl. Defense [6090]
Trans. Assn; Space [6389]
Trans. Bowling Assn; Amer. [23249]
Trans. Brokers Conf. of Am. [★3594]
Trans. Claims and Prevention Coun. [★3595]
Trans. Clubs Intl. [3896], PO Box 2223, Ocean Shores, WA 98569, (877)858-8627
Trans. Clubs Intl. [IO], Ocean Shores, WA, United States
Transportation-Communication Employees Union [★24180]
Trans. Communications Intl. Union [24180], 3 Res. Pl., Rockville, MD 20850, (301)948-4910
Transportation Communications Union; Brotherhood Railway Carmen Division/ [24179]
Trans. Conferences; Natl. Air [★160]
Trans. Consultants Assn; Freight [3566]
Trans. Consumer Protection Coun. [★3595]
Trans., Elevator and Grain Merchants Assn. [1753], 1300 L St. NW, Ste. 1020, Washington, DC 20005, (202)842-0400
Transportation Employees Union - Address unknown since 2000.
Trans. of Hazardous Articles; Conf. on Safe [3562]
Trans. of Hazardous Articles; Coun. on the Safe [★3562]
Trans. History; Lexington Gp. in [10913]
Trans. Inst. [3593], 5201 Auth Way, Camp Springs, MD 20746, (301)423-3335
Trans. Inst; Armored [3560]
Trans. Insurance Rating Bur. [★2131]

Trans. Intermediaries Assn. [3594], 1625 Prince St., Ste. 200, Alexandria, VA 22314, (703)299-5700
Transportation Law Institute [★6326]
Trans. Lawyers Assn. [6326], PO Box 15122, Lenexa, KS 66285-5122, (913)895-4615
Trans. and Logistics Coun. [3595], 120 Main St., Huntington, NY 11743, (631)549-8988
Trans. Mgt. Inst; North Amer. [8212]
Trans; Natl. Capital Historical Museum of [10133]
Trans. Practitioners; Assn. of [★6316]
Trans. Professionals; Natl. Assn. of Vertical [2048]
Trans. Res. Bd. [7814], c/o Keck Center of the Natl. Academies, 500 Fifth St. NW, Washington, DC 20001, (202)334-2934
Trans. Res. Bd; Maritime [★7272]
Trans. Res. Forum [7815], PO Box 5074, Fargo, ND 58105, (701)231-7767
Trans. Safety Equip. Inst. [3458], 10 Lab. Dr., Research Triangle Park, NC 27709, (919)406-8841
Trans. Ser. Mail Handlers, Watchmen and Messengers; Natl. Assn. of Post Off. and Postal [★24171]
Trans. Union; United [24181]
Transporters Conf; Agricultural [★3856]
Transporters; Natl. Assn. of Wastewater [3998]
TransportGroup [IO], Stockholm, Sweden
TransportGruppen [★IO]
Transportokonomis institutt [★IO]

Transsexual
Alliance for Full Acceptance [12213]
BiNet USA [12220]
Community United Against Violence [12225]
Crossdressers Intl. [13089]
Gay, Lesbian, Bisexual, Transgender Historical Soc. [10078]
Gender Educ. and Advocacy [13090]
HeartStrong [12232]
Intl. Found. for Gender Educ. [13091]
Marriage Equality USA [12506]
Natl. Black Justice Coalition [18643]
Natl. Gay Pilot's Assn. [439]
ONE, Inc. [12251]
Transverse Myelitis Assn. [15368], c/o Sanford J. Siegel, Pres./Newsletter Ed., 1787 Sutter Pkwy., Powell, OH 43065-8806, (614)766-1806
Transverse Myelitis Association [IO], Powell, OH, United States

Transvestite
Crossdressers Intl. [13089]
Intl. Found. for Gender Educ. [13091]
ONE, Inc. [12251]
Soc. for the Second Self [13102]
Transworld Advt. Agency Network [124], 7920 Summer Lake Ct., Fort Myers, FL 33907, (239)433-0669
Transworld Advt. Agency Network [IO], Fort Myers, FL, United States
Transylvania Soc. of Dracula [IO], St. John's, NL, Canada
Transylvania Soc. of Dracula - Italy [IO], Turin, Italy
Transylvanian Saxons; Alliance of [19117]
Transylvanian Soc. of Dracula [IO], Toronto, ON, Canada
Trap Collector Assn; North Amer. [22095]
Trapper Knife Collectors Club - Defunct.

Trappers
Fur Takers of Am. [5250]
Natl. Trappers Assn. [5251]
North Amer. Trap Collector Assn. [22095]
U.S. Sportsmen's Alliance [23550]

Trapping
Fur Takers of Am. [5250]
Natl. Trappers Assn. [5251]
North Amer. Trap Collector Assn. [22095]
U.S. Sportsmen's Alliance [23550]
Traprock Peace Center [18247], 103A Keets Rd., Deerfield, MA 01342, (413)773-7427
Trapshooting Assn; Amateur [23713]
Trapshooting Assn; Pacific Intl. [23728]

Trauma
Acupuncturists Without Borders [13536]
Amer. Acad. of Experts in Traumatic Stress [16685]
Amer. Acad. of Wound Mgt. [16686]
Amer. Assn. for the Surgery of Trauma [16687]

Reference to "IO" in place of a book number signifies that the association may be found in the 45th edition of International Organizations.

Amer. Professional Wound Care Assn. **[16688]**
Amer. Psychological Assn. - Div. of Trauma Psychology **[16128]**
Amer. Trauma Soc. **[16689]**
Anesthesia Awareness Campaign **[13677]**
Canadian Assn. of Wound Care **[IO]**
Coalition of 9/11 Families **[13307]**
EMDR - Humanitarian Assistance Programs **[12767]**
European Wound Mgt. Assn. **[IO]**
Families of September 11 **[18729]**
Gift From Within **[12768]**
Harvard Injury Control Res. Center **[16690]**
Intl. Cytokine Soc. **[6580]**
Intl. Soc. for Traumatic Stress Stud. **[16489]**
KIDSCOPE **[11518]**
Sidran Inst. for Traumatic Stress Educ. **[12559]**
Tragedy Assistance Prog. for Survivors **[11503]**
Trauma Found. at San Francisco Gen. Hosp. **[16691]**
Women in Neurotrauma Res. **[15404]**
Workplace Bullying Inst. **[16189]**
Trauma Action Group - Defunct.
Trauma Anesthesia and Critical Care Soc; Intl. **[13686]**
Trauma Assn; Orthopaedic **[15777]**
Trauma Care Intl. **[★13686]**
Trauma Care Intl. **[★IO]**
Trauma Counseling; Intl. Assn. of **[★11821]**
Trauma Found. at San Francisco Gen. Hosp. **[16691]**, San Francisco Gen. Hosp., Bldg. 1, Rm. 300, San Francisco, CA 94110, (415)821-8209
Trauma; Inst. for Victims of **[13362]**
Trauma Nurses; Soc. of **[15528]**
Trauma Soc; Natl. Neuro **[15398]**
Traumatic Stress Stud; Intl. Soc. for **[16489]**
Traumatic Stress Stud; Soc. for **[★16489]**
Traumatology, Knee Surgery and Arthroscopy 2000; European Soc. of Sports **[IO]**
Traumatology; Turkish Soc. of Orthopaedic Surgery and **[IO]**
Trav-L-Park Assn; Best Holiday **[3354]**
Travel
Adventure Tour Operators Assn. of India **[IO]**
Adventure Travel Trade Assn. **[3902]**
Africa Travel Assn. **[3903]**
Africa Travel Assn. **[IO]**
Air Courier Assn. **[3857]**
Airline Ambassadors Intl. **[13147]**
Alpine Coach Assn. **[22941]**
Alpine Tourist Commn. **[24223]**
Alpine Tourist Commn. **[IO]**
Amer. Accounting Assn. **[7]**
Amer. Assn. of Premium Incentive, Travel Suppliers and Agents **[3904]**
Amer. Auto. Touring Alliance **[3905]**
Amer. Clipper Owners Club **[22942]**
Amer. Friends of the Hakluyt Soc. **[10410]**
Amer. Historic Inns **[1909]**
Amer. Indonesian Chamber of Commerce **[24332]**
Amer. Sightseeing Intl. **[IO]**
Amer. Small Bus. Travel Alliance **[3906]**
Amer. Soc. of Travel Agents **[3907]**
Anguilla Tourist Bd. **[24224]**
Arab Intl. Assn. for Tourism and Automobile Clubs **[23009]**
Argentine Assn. of Travel and Tourism Agencies **[IO]**
Asia Pacific Tourism Assn. **[IO]**
Asian Inst. of Tourism **[IO]**
Assist Card Intl. **[IO]**
Assist Card Intl. **[3908]**
Assn. of British Travel Agents **[IO]**
Assn. of Bus. Travellers **[IO]**
Assn. of Canadian Travel Agencies **[IO]**
Assn. of Corporate Travel Executives **[3909]**
Assn. of Danish Travel Agents **[IO]**
Assn. of Destination Mgt. Executives **[IO]**
Assn. of Destination Mgt. Executives **[3910]**
Assn. of German Travel Agents and Tour Operators **[IO]**
Assn. of Independent Tour Operators **[IO]**
Assn. of Natl. Tourist Off. Representatives (UK) **[IO]**
Assn. for the Promotion of Tourism to Africa **[3826]**

Assn. of Retail Travel Agents **[3911]**
Assn. of Scottish Visitor Attractions **[IO]**
Assn. for the Stud. of Travel in Egypt and the Near East **[IO]**
Assn. of Travel Agencies of Czech Republic **[IO]**
Assn. of Travel Marketing Executives **[3912]**
ASTA Chap. of Greece **[IO]**
Australasian Bus. Travel Assn. **[IO]**
Australian Fed. of Travel Agents **[IO]**
Australian Tourism Export Coun. **[IO]**
Austrian Professional Travel Agents and Tour Operators Assn. **[IO]**
Austrian Tourist Off. **[24231]**
Austrian Youth Hostel Assn. **[IO]**
Avion Travelcade Club **[22945]**
Bahrain Youth Hostels Soc. **[IO]**
Barbados Tourism Authority **[24234]**
Beaver Ambassador Club **[22946]**
Belgian Tourist Off. **[24236]**
Belize Tourism Indus. Assn. **[IO]**
Bermuda Dept. of Tourism **[24237]**
Bermuda Hotel Assn. **[IO]**
Bonaire Govt. Tourist Off. **[24361]**
Bounders United **[23010]**
Brazilian Travel Agencies' Assn. **[IO]**
British Activity Holiday Assn. **[IO]**
Bulgarian Assn. of Travel Agents **[IO]**
Bus. Travel Coalition **[24382]**
Canadian Inst. of Travel Counsellors **[IO]**
Canadian Snowbird Assn. **[IO]**
Canadian Tourism Res. Inst. **[IO]**
Caribbean Hotel Assn. **[IO]**
Caribbean Hotel Assn. **[3913]**
Caribbean Tourism Org. **[IO]**
Caribbean Tourism Org., Amer. Br. **[24252]**
Carriage Travel Club **[23011]**
Cayman Islands Dept. of Tourism **[24256]**
Ceylon (Sri Lanka) Tourist Dept. **[24377]**
Chinese Taipei Youth Hostel Assn. **[IO]**
Confed. of Latin Amer. Tourism Organizations **[IO]**
Country Coach Intl. **[23012]**
Croatian Youth Hostel Assn. **[IO]**
Cross-Cultural Solutions **[11901]**
Cruise Club of Am. **[3914]**
Cruise Lines Intl. Assn. **[3915]**
Cruise Lines Intl. Assn. **[IO]**
Curacao Convention Bureau/Tourist Bd. **[24362]**
Cyprus Tourism Org. **[24315]**
Czech Youth Hostel Assn. **[IO]**
Danish Tourist Bd. **[IO]**
Danube Tourist Commn. **[IO]**
Delta Teen-Lift **[13341]**
Discovery Owners Assn., Inc. **[22947]**
Dominica Natl. Development Corp. **[IO]**
Escapees **[22948]**
Estonian Assn. of Travel Agencies **[IO]**
European Expedition Guild **[IO]**
European Tour Operators Assn. **[IO]**
European Travel Agents and Tour Operators' Associations **[IO]**
European Travel Commn. **[IO]**
European Travel Commn. **[3916]**
European Travel Commn. - Belgium **[IO]**
European Union Fed. of Youth Hostel Associations **[IO]**
European Union of Tourist Officers **[IO]**
Extra Miler Club **[23013]**
FACES: The Natl. Craniofacial Assn. **[14061]**
Family Motor Coach Assn. **[22949]**
Fed. of Amer. Consumers and Travelers **[13342]**
Fed. of Bulgarian Alpine Clubs **[IO]**
Fed. of Tour Operators **[IO]**
Fiji Visitors' Bur. **[IO]**
Finnish Tourist Bd. **[IO]**
Finnish Youth Hostel Assn. **[IO]**
French Youth Hostels Fed. **[IO]**
Frequent Bus. Travellers Club **[IO]**
Georgie Boy Owners' Club **[22950]**
German Convention Bur. **[24324]**
German Natl. Tourist Bd. **[3917]**
German Natl. Tourist Bd. **[IO]**
German Youth Hostel Assn. **[IO]**
Globe Aware **[13393]**
Globetrotters' Club **[IO]**
Good Sam Recreational Vehicle Club **[22951]**

Gray Line Sightseeing Assn. **[3868]**
Greek Natl. Tourist Org. **[3869]**
Grenada Bd. of Tourism **[24253]**
Guild of Travel Mgt. Companies **[IO]**
Handicapped Travel Club **[22952]**
Hellenic Assn. of Travel and Tourist Agencies **[IO]**
Highpointers Club **[23014]**
Homelink Intl. **[22580]**
HomeLink Intl. Canada **[IO]**
Hong Kong Assn. of Registered Tour Coordinators **[IO]**
Hong Kong Assn. of Travel Agents **[IO]**
Hong Kong Tourism Bd. **[IO]**
Hong Kong Tourism Bd. **[IO]**
Hong Kong Youth Hostels Assn. **[IO]**
Hostelling Ecuador **[IO]**
Hostelling International-American Youth Hostels **[12797]**
Hostelling Intl. Argentina **[IO]**
Hostelling Intl. Bolivia **[IO]**
Hostelling Intl. Brazil **[IO]**
Hostelling Intl. - Canada **[IO]**
Hostelling Intl. Chile **[IO]**
Hostelling Intl. Colombia **[IO]**
Hostelling Intl. Costa Rica **[IO]**
Hostelling Intl. Iceland **[IO]**
Hostelling Intl. Mexico **[IO]**
Hostelling Intl. Northern Island **[IO]**
Hostelling Intl. Norway **[IO]**
Hostelling Intl. Slovenia **[IO]**
Hungarian Natl. Tourist Off. **[IO]**
Inst. of Certified Travel Agents **[3918]**
Inst. of Travel and Tourism **[IO]**
Inter-American Travel Cong. **[IO]**
Inter-American Travel Cong. **[3919]**
Interactive Travel Services Assn. **[3946]**
InterAmerican Travel Agents Soc. **[3920]**
Interhostel **[8618]**
Intl. Airline Passengers Assn. **[23015]**
Intl. Airline Passengers Assn. **[IO]**
Intl. Airline Passengers Assn. - London **[IO]**
Intl. Airline Passengers' Assn. - United Kingdom **[IO]**
International Association of Antarctica Tour Operators **[IO]**
Intl. Assn. of Antarctica Tour Operators **[3921]**
Intl. Assn. for Medical Assistance to Travellers **[13343]**
Intl. Assn. for Medical Assistance to Travellers **[IO]**
Intl. Assn. for Medical Assistance to Travellers - Canada **[IO]**
Intl. Assn. for Medical Assistance to Travellers - New Zealand **[IO]**
Intl. Assn. for Medical Assistance to Travellers - Switzerland **[IO]**
Intl. Assn. of Sci. Experts in Tourism **[IO]**
Intl. Assn. of Tour Managers - North Amer. Region **[IO]**
Intl. Assn. of Tour Managers - North Amer. Region **[3922]**
Intl. Bur. of Social Tourism **[IO]**
Intl. Coun. of Cruise Lines **[3923]**
Intl. Family Recreation Assn. **[12798]**
Intl. Fed. of Women's Travel Organizations **[IO]**
Intl. Food, Wine and Travel Writers Assn. **[3118]**
Intl. Galapagos Tour Operators Assn. **[24383]**
Intl. Galapagos Tour Operators Assn. **[IO]**
Intl. Gay and Lesbian Travel Assn. **[3924]**
Intl. Soc. of Travel Medicine **[15172]**
Intl. Soc. of Travel and Tourism Educators **[3925]**
Intl. Soc. of Travel and Tourism Educators **[IO]**
Intl. Touring Alliance **[IO]**
Intl. Travel Writers and Editors Assn. **[IO]**
Intl. Travel Writers and Editors Assn. **[3926]**
Intl. Youth Hostel Fed. **[IO]**
Interval Intl. **[22581]**
Irish Tour Operators Assn. **[IO]**
Irish Travel Agents Assn. **[IO]**
Irish Youth Hostel Assn. **[IO]**
Israel Youth Hostels Assn. **[IO]**
Italian Fed. of Tour Operators and Travel Agencies **[IO]**
Jamaica Tourist Bd. **[24340]**
Japan Assn. of Travel Agents **[IO]**

A star before a book entry number signifies that the name is not listed separately, but is mentioned within the entry.

Japan Convention Bur. [24341]
Japan Natl. Tourist Org. [24344]
Japan Natl. Tourist Org. [IO]
Japan Youth Hostels [IO]
Jayco Travel Club [22955]
Jordan Info. Bur. [24349]
Kenya Assn. of Tour Operators [IO]
Kenya Youth Hostels Assn. [IO]
Klondike Visitors Assn. [IO]
Loners of Am. [22956]
Loners on Wheels [22957]
Luxembourg Youth Hostels Assn. [IO]
Malaysia Tourism Promotion Bd. [IO]
Malaysia Tourism Promotion Bd. [24355]
Malaysian Assn. of Tour and Travel Agents [IO]
Malta Tourism Authority [IO]
Mexico Tourism Bd. [24356]
Motorist Info. and Services Assn. [13344]
My Travel Bug [9279]
My Travel Bug [IO]
Natl. Assn. of Commissioned Travel Agents [3927]
Natl. Assn. of Cruise-Oriented Agencies [3928]
Natl. Assn. of Trailer Owners [22959]
Natl. Assn. of Travel Agents Singapore [IO]
Natl. Assn. of Traveling Nurses [15503]
Natl. Bed-and-Breakfast Assn. [1954]
Natl. Bus. Travel Assn. [3929]
Natl. Fed. of Tourism Chambers of Ecuador [IO]
Natl. Fed. of Tourist Guide Associations-USA
    [24380]
Natl. Gay/Lesbian Travel Desk [24322]
Natl. Historic Route 66 Fed. [24328]
Natl. Tour Assn. [3930]
Natl. Travel Club [3931]
Native Tourism Alliance [24381]
Nepal Assn. of Tour and Travel Agents [IO]
Netherlands Bd. of Tourism and Conventions
    [24359]
New Zealand Inst. of Travel and Tourism [IO]
New Zealand Tourism Bd. [24363]
North Amer. Truck Camper Owners Assn. [23025]
Nunavut Tourism [IO]
Oceanic Soc. Expeditions [IO]
Oceanic Soc. Expeditions [23016]
Opening Door [3932]
Order of United Commercial Travelers of Am. -
    Canadian Off. [IO]
Pacific Asia Travel Assn. [IO]
Pacific Asia Travel Assn. [IO]
Pacific Asia Travel Assn. [3933]
Pacific Asia Travel Assn. - Singapore [IO]
Passenger Vessel Assn. [2591]
Philippine Convention and Visitors Corp. [IO]
Philippine Travel Agencies Assn. [IO]
Polish Youth Hostels Assn. [IO]
Portuguese Natl. Tourist Off. [24367]
Portuguese Trade Commn. [24368]
Romanian Natl. Tourist Off. [3934]
Romanian Natl. Tourist Off. [IO]
Roving Volunteers in Christ's Ser. [23017]
Russian Bus. Travel Assn. [IO]
Russian Union of Travel Indus. [IO]
RV Mfrs'. Clubs Assn. [22961]
Saint Croix Hotel and Tourism Assn. [1964]
Saint Kitts Tourism Authority [24254]
Saint Lucia Tourist Bd. [24255]
Saint Lucia Tourist Bd. [IO]
Samoa Tourism Authority [IO]
Saudi Arabian Youth Hostels Assn. [IO]
Scandinavian Tourist Boards [24372]
School Journey Assn. [IO]
Scottish Youth Hostels Assn. [IO]
Senate Tourism Caucus [17259]
SIAMA World Mission Travel [IO]
Soc. for Accessible Travel and Hospitality [17420]
Soc. of Amer. Travel Writers [3162]
Soc. of Govt. Travel Professionals [6327]
Soc. of Incentive and Travel Executives [3935]
Soc. of Incentive and Travel Executives [IO]
Soc. of Polish-American Travel Agents [3936]
Soc. of Recreation Executives [3363]
South African Tourism [24374]
South African Youth Hostels Assn. [IO]
South Amer. Explorers [IO]
South Amer. Explorers [3937]

Spanish Youth Hostels [IO]
Special Military Active Retired Travel Club [IO]
Special Military Active Retired Travel Club [21271]
Student and Youth Travel Assn. [3938]
Student and Youth Travel Assn. [IO]
SunnyTravelers [22963]
Supreme Travel Club [22964]
Sustainable Travel Intl. [5252]
Sustainable Travel Intl. [IO]
Swedish Travel and Tourism Coun. [IO]
Swedish Travel and Tourism Coun. [3939]
Swiss Youth Hostels [IO]
Switzerland Convention and Incentive Bur. [IO]
Switzerland Convention and Incentive Bur.
    [24379]
Taiwan Visitors Assn. [3940]
Taiwan Visitors Assn. [IO]
Taiwan Visitors Assn. - Taipei [IO]
Tanzania Assn. of Tour Operators [IO]
Thai Youth Hostels Assn. [IO]
Tourism Indus. Assn. of Canada [IO]
Tourism Ireland [24335]
Tourism Soc. [IO]
Travel Agencies Assn. [IO]
Travel Agents Assn. of India [IO]
Travel Agents Assn. of New Zealand [IO]
Travel Agents Assn. of Pakistan [IO]
Travel Agents Assn. of Sri Lanka [IO]
Travel Air Club [21482]
Travel Companion Exchange [23018]
Travel Goods Assn. [2441]
Travel Indus. Assn. of Am. [3941]
Travel Indus. Coun. of Hong Kong [IO]
Travel Info. Service/MossRehab ResourceNet
    [13345]
Travel Journalists Guild [3167]
Travel and Tourism Res. Assn. [3942]
Travel and Tourism Res. Assn. [IO]
Travelers Aid Intl. [13191]
Travelers' Century Club [23019]
Tread Lightly! [5167]
Trekking Agents Assn. of Nepal [IO]
Ukrainian Youth Hostels Assn. [IO]
United Fed. of Travel Agents' Associations [IO]
U.S. Tour Operators Assn. [IO]
U.S. Tour Operators Assn. [3943]
U.S. Tourist Coun. [4462]
U.S. Travel Data Center [3944]
Venezuelan Tourism Assn. [3945]
Venezuelan Tourism Assn. [IO]
VisitBritain [24242]
Visitor Stud. Assn. [9280]
Visitor Stud. Assn. [IO]
VisitScotland [IO]
Wally Byam Caravan Club Intl. [22967]
Wilderness Classroom Org. [8951]
Wilderness Volunteers [22774]
Winnebago-Itasca Travelers [22968]
Women Outdoors [23644]
World Assn. of Travel Agencies [IO]
World Expeditionary Assn. Intl. [IO]
World Heritage Alliance [10077]
World Ocean and Cruise Liner Soc. [23020]
World Ocean and Cruise Liner Soc. [IO]
World Tourism Org. [IO]
World Travel and Tourism Coun. [IO]
Youth Hostel Associations of China [IO]
Youth Hostel Romania [IO]
Youth Hostels Assn. - England and Wales [IO]
Youth Hostels Assn. of India [IO]
Youth Hostels Assn. of New Zealand [IO]
Youth Hostels Assn. of Russia [IO]
Youth and Student Hostel Found. of the Philip-
    pines [IO]

Travel Abroad; Academic [8588]
Travel Abroad; Association for Academic [★8588]
Travel Agencies Assn. [IO], Madrid, Spain
Travel Agents Assn. of India [IO], Bombay, India
Travel Agents Assn. of New Zealand [IO], Welling-
    ton, New Zealand
Travel Agents Assn. of Pakistan [IO], Karachi,
    Pakistan
Travel Agents Assn. of Sri Lanka [IO], Colombo, Sri
    Lanka
Travel Agents Computer Soc. - Defunct.

Travel Agents in Govt; Soc. of [★6327]
Travel Agents Guild of America - Address unknown
    since 1995.
Travel Agents Soc; Inter-America [★3920]
Travel Air Club [21482], PO Box 127, Blakesburg, IA
    52536, (641)938-2773
Travel Assn; Amer. [★1929]
Travel Assn; Bikecentennial: The Bicycle [★23304]
Travel Assn; British [★24242]
Travel Assn; Caribbean Hotel Coun. of the Carib-
    bean [★3913]
Travel Assn; Pacific Area [★3933]
Travel China Roads [8078], 1719 E Feemster Ct.,
    Visalia, CA 93292, (559)562-3409
Travel Club; Alpenlite [22940]
Travel Club; Handicapped [22952]
Travel Club; Jayco [22955]
Travel Club; Jayco Jafari Intl. [★22955]
Travel Club; Supreme [22964]
Travel Club; Vagabundos Del Mar RV, Boat and
    [22966]
Travel Companion Exchange [23018], PO Box 833,
    Amityville, NY 11701, (631)454-0880
Travel; Coun. on Students [★8608]
Travel Desk; Natl. Gay/Lesbian [24322]
Travel Directors; Natl. Coun. of State [★24385]
Travel Executives; Soc. of Incentive [★3935]
Travel and Fly Without Fear [★12746]
Travel Goods Assn. [2441], 5 Vaughn Dr., Ste. 105,
    Princeton, NJ 08540, (609)720-1200
Travel and Holiday Assn; British [★24242]
Travel Indus. Assn. of Am. [3941], 1100 New York
    Ave. NW, Ste. 450, Washington, DC 20005-3934,
    (202)408-8422
Travel Indus. Coun. of Hong Kong [IO], Hong Kong,
    People's Republic of China
Travel Industry and Disabled Exchange - Defunct.
Travel Info. Service/MossRehab ResourceNet
    [13345], c/o MossRehab Hosp., 1200 W Tabor
    Rd., Philadelphia, PA 19141-3019, (215)456-9900
Travel Inns; Amer. [1929]
The Travel Inst. [★3918]
Travel Journalists Guild [3167], PO Box 10643,
    Chicago, IL 60610, (312)664-9279
Travel Managers Intl. - Defunct.
Travel Network; PADI [★23964]
Travel Network; PADI [★IO]
Travel Plaza and Truckstop Indus; NATSO,
    Representing the [★3424]
Travel Professionals Assn. - Defunct.
Travel Professionals Intl. [IO], Winnipeg, MB,
    Canada
Travel Ser; U.S. Student [★8617]
Travel Services
    Air Courier Assn. [3857]
    Alpine Tourist Commn. [24223]
    Amer. Auto. Assn. [403]
    Amer. Indonesian Chamber of Commerce [24332]
    Anguilla Tourist Bd. [24224]
    Barbados Tourism Authority [24234]
    Belgian Tourist Off. [24236]
    Bermuda Dept. of Tourism [24237]
    Bonaire Govt. Tourist Off. [24361]
    Caribbean Tourism Org., Amer. Br. [24252]
    Cruise Club of Am. [3914]
    Curacao Convention Bureau/Tourist Bd. [24362]
    Cyprus Tourism Org. [24315]
    FACES: The Natl. Craniofacial Assn. [14061]
    Fed. of Amer. Consumers and Travelers [13342]
    German Convention Bur. [24324]
    Greek Natl. Tourist Org. [3869]
    Homelink Intl. [22580]
    Interactive Travel Services Assn. [3946]
    Intl. Airline Passengers Assn. [23015]
    Intl. Assn. of Antarctica Tour Operators [3921]
    Intl. Assn. for Medical Assistance to Travellers
        [13343]
    Interval Intl. [22581]
    Jamaica Tourist Bd. [24340]
    Japan Natl. Tourist Org. [24344]
    Jordan Info. Bur. [24349]
    Mexico Tourism Bd. [24356]
    Motorist Info. and Services Assn. [13344]
    Natl. Gay/Lesbian Travel Desk [24322]
    Pacific Asia Travel Assn. [3933]

Reference to "IO" in place of a book number signifies that the association may be found in the 45th edition of International Organizations.

Portuguese Natl. Tourist Off. **[24367]**
Portuguese Trade Commn. **[24368]**
Romanian Natl. Tourist Off. **[3934]**
Scandinavian Tourist Boards **[24372]**
South African Tourism **[24374]**
Student and Youth Travel Assn. **[3938]**
Sustainable Travel Intl. **[5252]**
Travel Info. Service/MossRehab ResourceNet **[13345]**
Travelers Aid Intl. **[13191]**
VisitBritain **[24242]**
World Ocean and Cruise Liner Soc. **[23020]**
Travel for Tomorrow Coun. - Address unknown since 2001.
Travel and Tourism Agencies' Assn. **[IO]**, Lisbon, Portugal
Travel and Tourism Government Affairs Coun. - Defunct.
Travel and Tourism Res. Assn. **[3942]**, PO Box 2133, Boise, ID 83701, (208)429-9511
Travel and Tourism Res. Assn. **[IO]**, Boise, ID, United States
Travel Trust Assn. **[IO]**, Woking, United Kingdom
Travel Writers; Soc. of Amer. **[3162]**
Travelcade Club; Avion **[22945]**
Travelcraft Ambassadors Club - Defunct.
Travelers Aid Assn. of America - Defunct.
Travelers Aid Intl. **[13191]**, 1612 K St. NW, Ste. 206, Washington, DC 20006, (202)546-1127
Travelers Aid Intl. **[IO]**, Washington, DC, United States
Travelers Aid Societies; Natl. Org. of **[★13191]**
Travelers of Am; Order of United Commercial **[19135]**
Travelers Assn. of New York; Boot and Shoe **[1596]**
Travelers' Century Club **[23019]**, PO Box 7050, Santa Monica, CA 90406-7050, (310)458-3454
Travelers' Information Exchange **[★1936]**
Travelers; Natl. Assn. of Consumers and **[★3931]**
Travelers Protective Assn. of Am. **[19141]**, 3755 Lindell Blvd., St. Louis, MO 63108-3476, (314)371-0533
Travelers; Winnebago Intl. **[★22968]**
Travelers; Winnebago-Itasca **[22968]**
Traveling Businesswomen's Network - Defunct.
Traveling Hat Salesmen's Assn. - Defunct.
Traveling Nurses; Natl. Assn. of **[15503]**
Travelmaster Travel Club - Defunct.
Travelogues by IMPALA (Intl. Motion Picture and Lecturers Assn.) **[★1386]**
Travelogues by IMPALA (Intl. Motion Picture and Lecturers Assn.) **[★IO]**
Trax Programme Support of West Africa **[IO]**, Hebden Bridge, United Kingdom
Treacher Collins Family Network **[★14067]**
Treacher Collins Found. **[14067]**
Tread Lightly! **[5167]**, 298 24th St., Ste. 325, Ogden, UT 84401, (801)627-0077
Tread Rubber Mfrs. Group - Address unknown since 2001.
Treasure Hunting Res. and Information Center - Address unknown since 2008.
Treasure State Outfitters **[★23944]**
Treasure Trove Club - Defunct.
Treasurers Assn. of the U.S. and Canada; Municipal **[★6203]**
Treasurers and Finance Officers; Natl. Assn. of County **[6205]**
Treasurers; Natl. Assn. of Corporate **[1435]**
Treasurers; Natl. Assn. of State **[6208]**
Treasurers; Natl. Assn. of State Auditors, Comptrollers, and **[6206]**
Treasurers of Religious Institutes; Natl. Assn. for **[20516]**
Treasurers of the U.S. and Canada; Assn. of Public **[6203]**
Treasures for Little Children **[23000]**, c/o Marion Steinbrunner, Treas., PO Box 118, Chardon, OH 44024
Treasury Agents Assn; U.S. **[★5653]**
Treasury Employees Union; Natl. **[24080]**
Treasury Historical Assn. **[10163]**, PO Box 28118, Washington, DC 20038-8118, (202)298-0550
Treasury Mgt. Assn. **[★1403]**
Treasury Mgt. Assn. of Canada **[IO]**, Toronto, ON, Canada

Treatment Action Gp. **[13587]**, 611 Broadway, Ste. 308, New York, NY 10012-2608, (212)253-7922
Treatment of Animals; Psychologists for the Ethical **[★11460]**
Treatment Assn; Foster Family-Based **[11593]**
Treatment Assn; Neuro-Developmental **[15399]**
Treatment and Biological Rhythms; Soc. for Light **[16636]**
Treatment Centers for Children; Natl. Assn. of Psychiatric **[★16090]**
Treatment Corp; Addiction Res. and **[13213]**
Treatment and Res. Advancements Assn. for Personality Disorder **[15235]**, 23 Greene St., 3rd Fl., New York, NY 10013, (212)966-6514
Treatment of Sexual Abusers; Assn. for the **[6529]**
Treatment of Sexual Abusers; Assn. for the Behavioral **[★6529]**
Treatment of Sexual Aggression; Assn. for the Behavioral **[★6529]**
Treaty Network; Midwest **[19276]**
Tree Assn; Dwarf Fruit **[★5257]**
Tree Care Indus. Assn. **[5262]**, 3 Perimeter Rd., Unit 1, Manchester, NH 03103, (603)314-5380
Tree Care Indus. Assn. **[IO]**, Manchester, NH, United States
Tree Conf; Intl. Shade **[★5259]**
Tree; Conserva **[4386]**
Tree Coun. **[IO]**, London, United Kingdom
Tree Evaluation; Natl. Shade **[★5259]**
Tree Fruit Assn; California Grape and **[★4716]**
Tree Fruit League; California Grape and **[4716]**
Tree House Animal Found. **[11464]**, 1212 W Carmen Ave., Chicago, IL 60640-2999, (773)784-5488
Tree Musketeers **[4459]**, 136 Main St., Ste. A, El Segundo, CA 90245, (310)322-0263
Tree of Peace Soc. **[9913]**, 326 Cook Rd., Hogansburg, NY 13655, (518)358-2641
Tree-Ring Soc. **[7101]**, Univ. of Arizona, Lab. of Tree-Ring Res., Bldg. 58, Tucson, AZ 85721, (520)621-1608
Tree Soc; Natl. **[4594]**
Tree and Survive; Hug-A- **[11600]**
Treeing Walker Breeders and Fanciers Assn. **[22368]**, c/o Larry Hawke, Sec., 520 B County Rd. 2575, Loudonville, OH 44842, (419)994-4563
TreePeople **[4460]**, 12601 Mulholland Dr., Beverly Hills, CA 90210, (818)753-4600
Trees
African Blackwood Conservation Proj. **[4342]**
Alliance for Community Trees **[4678]**
Alliance for Intl. Reforestation **[4344]**
Amer. Bonsai Soc. **[22483]**
Amer. Conifer Soc. **[5253]**
Amer. Soc. of Consulting Arborists **[5254]**
Assn. of Consulting Foresters of Am. **[4680]**
Bonsai Clubs Intl. **[22504]**
Conservatree **[4386]**
Elm Res. Inst. **[4682]**
Forest Landowners Assn. **[4683]**
Forest Products Soc. **[7099]**
Forest Resources Assn. **[1607]**
Forest Stewardship Coun. - U.S. **[4684]**
Friends of the Natl. Arboretum **[6634]**
Intl. Assn. of Machinists and Aerospace Workers, Woodworkers District Lodge W1 **[24026]**
Intl. Chain Saw Wood Sculptors Assn. **[9446]**
Intl. Fruit Tree Assn. **[5257]**
Intl. Soc. of Arboriculture **[5259]**
Intl. Soc. of Tropical Foresters **[4687]**
Intl. Wood Collectors Soc. **[23031]**
Metropolitan Tree Improvement Alliance **[5260]**
Natl. Assn. of Plant Patent Owners **[5046]**
Natl. Assn. of State Foresters **[4689]**
Natl. Christmas Tree Assn. **[5261]**
Natl. Forest Protection Alliance **[4592]**
Natl. Tree Soc. **[4594]**
North Amer. Fruit Explorers **[22531]**
Northern Nut Growers Assn. **[2842]**
Pacific Northwest Christmas Tree Assn. **[3947]**
Redwood Region Logging Conf. **[4694]**
Seed Savers Exchange **[22540]**
Soc. of Amer. Foresters **[4695]**
Soc. of Wood Sci. and Tech. **[7100]**
Tree Care Indus. Assn. **[5262]**
Tree of Peace Soc. **[9913]**

Trees for the Future **[5263]**
Trees for Tomorrow **[4697]**
Trees, Water and People **[4610]**
Tropical Flowering Tree Soc. **[4986]**
U.S. Dept. of Agriculture - Forest Ser. Volunteers Prog. **[4699]**
Washington Forest Protection Assn. **[1627]**
Western Forestry and Conservation Assn. **[4700]**
Trees for the Future **[5263]**, PO Box 7027, Silver Spring, MD 20907, (800)643-0001
Trees for Life **[12400]**, 3006 W St. Louis St., Wichita, KS 67203-5129, (316)945-6929
Trees for Life **[IO]**, Wichita, KS, United States
Trees and Shrubs
Addington Bush Soc. **[IO]**
Amer. Bonsai Soc. **[22483]**
Amer. Conifer Soc. **[5253]**
Amer. Soc. of Consulting Arborists **[5254]**
Amer. Willow Growers Network **[5255]**
Assn. of Consulting Foresters of Am. **[4680]**
Bonsai Clubs Intl. **[22504]**
European Arboricultural Coun. **[IO]**
European Palm Soc. **[IO]**
Holly Soc. of Am. **[5256]**
Intl. Dendrology Soc. **[IO]**
International Dwarf Fruit Tree Association **[IO]**
Intl. Fruit Tree Assn. **[5257]**
Intl. Oak Soc. **[5258]**
International Oak Society **[IO]**
Intl. Soc. of Arboriculture **[IO]**
Intl. Soc. of Arboriculture **[5259]**
Intl. Soc. of Arboriculture - United Kingdom and Ireland **[IO]**
Intl. Soc. for Mangrove Ecosystems **[IO]**
Intl. Wood Collectors Soc. **[23031]**
Irish Christmas Tree Growers **[IO]**
Metropolitan Tree Improvement Alliance **[5260]**
Natl. Assn. of Plant Patent Owners **[5046]**
Natl. Christmas Tree Assn. **[5261]**
Natl. Tree Soc. **[4594]**
North Amer. Fruit Explorers **[22531]**
Poplar Coun. of Canada **[IO]**
Poplar and Fast Growing Forest Trees Res. Inst. **[IO]**
Seed Savers Exchange **[22540]**
Silva Forest Found. **[IO]**
Soc. of Amer. Foresters **[4695]**
Tree Care Indus. Assn. **[5262]**
Tree Care Indus. Assn. **[IO]**
Trees for the Future **[5263]**
Trees for Tomorrow **[4697]**
Tropical Flowering Tree Soc. **[4986]**
Western Forestry and Conservation Assn. **[4700]**
Trees Soc; Friends of the **[4400]**
Trees for Tomorrow **[4697]**, PO Box 609, 519 Sheridan St., Eagle River, WI 54521, (715)479-6456
Trees, Water and People **[4610]**, 633 Remington St., Fort Collins, CO 80524, (970)484-3678
Trees, Water and People **[IO]**, Fort Collins, CO, United States
Treforedlingsindustriens Bransjeforening **[★IO]**
Trek: The Official Fan Club; Star **[25016]**
Trek and TV Talk - Address unknown since 2007.
Trekking Agents Assn. of Nepal **[IO]**, Kathmandu, Nepal
Trekville U.S.A. **[★25019]**
Trekville U.S.A./International **[25019]**, c/o Jay S. Hastings, Pres., 1021 S 9th Ave., Scranton, PA 18504, (570)343-7806
Tremor Action Network **[15369]**, PO Box 5013, Pleasanton, CA 94566, (925)462-0111
Tremor Action Network **[IO]**, Pleasanton, CA, United States
Tremor Found; Intl. **[★15331]**
Tremor Found; Intl. Essential **[15331]**
Trenaunay Support Gp; Klippel- **[13755]**
Trench Rats; Natl. Order of **[20766]**
Trencher - Descendants of Colonial Tavern Keepers; Flagon and **[20737]**
Trenchless Tech; North Amer. Soc. for **[7819]**
Tri-College Coun. **[★15120]**
Tri-County Citrus Label Collectors **[★21995]**
Tri-Ess Sorority **[★13102]**
TRI-M Music Honor Soc. **[10713]**, 1806 Robert Fulton Dr., Reston, VA 20191, (703)860-4000

A star before a book entry number signifies that the name is not listed separately, but is mentioned within the entry.

Tri-Pacer Owners Club [★21475]
TRI/Princeton [3806], PO Box 625, Princeton, NJ 08542, (609)430-4820
TRI/Princeton [IO], Princeton, NJ, United States
Tri-State Dental Assn. [★14175]
Triad - Address unknown since 1995.
Trial Acad; Defense Counsel [★5499]
Trial Acad; Defense Counsel [★IO]
Trial Advocacy
   Amer. Assn. for Justice [6328]
   Amer. Bd. of Trial Advocates [6329]
   Amer. Coll. of Trial Lawyers [6330]
   Amer. Mock Trial Assn. [9281]
   Found. of the Amer. Bd. of Trial Advocates [5495]
   Intl. Soc. of Barristers [6331]
   Intl. Soc. of Barristers [IO]
   ITC Trial Lawyers Assn. [6332]
   Natl. Bd. of Trial Advocacy [6333]
   Natl. Inst. for Trial Advocacy [6334]
   Network of Trial Law Firms [5525]
   Pound Civil Justice Inst. [6335]
Trial Advocacy Competition; National Student [★6328]
Trial Advocates; Found. of the Amer. Bd. of [5495]
Trial Attorneys; Assn. of Defense [5825]
Trial Behavior Consultants; Assn. of [★6524]
Trial Consultants; Amer. Soc. of [6524]
Trial Counsel; Natl. Assn. of Railroad [6321]
Trial Court Administrators; Natl. Assn. of [★5627]
Trial Examiners Conf; Fed. [★5899]
Trial Judges; Natl. Coll. of State [★5914]
Trial Judges; Natl. Conf. of Fed. [5910]
Trial Lawyer Marketing Assn. [★2651]
Trial Lawyers; Assn. of Amer. [★6328]
Trial Lawyers Assn; Amer. [★6328]
Trial Lawyers Assn; Intl. Trade Commn. [★6332]
Trial Lawyers Marketing [2651]
Trial Lawyers for Public Justice [★6227]
Trial Services Rsrc. Center; Pre [★6034]
Triangle - Address unknown since 2001.
Triangle Club [13283], 2030 P St. NW, Washington, DC 20036, (202)659-8641
Triangle Coalition for Sci. and Tech. Educ. [9116], 1840 Wilson Blvd., Ste. 201, Arlington, VA 22201, (703)516-5960
Triangles [IO], London, United Kingdom
Triathlon
   British Triathlon Assn. [IO]
   China Triathlon Sports Assn. [IO]
   Intl. Triathlon Union [IO]
   Nederlandse Triathlon Bond [IO]
   Triathlon Assn. of Singapore [IO]
Triathlon Assn. of Singapore [IO], Singapore, Singapore
Triathlon Assn; U.S. [★23927]
Triathlon Club; Big Apple [★23922]
Triathlon Club; New York [23922]
Triathlon; USA [23927]
Tribal Art Dealers Assn; Antique [296]
Tribal Bison Cooperative; Inter [5036]
Tribal Child Support Assn; Natl. [11713]
Tribal Court CH [5956], The Tribal Law & Policy Inst., 8235 Santa Monica Blvd., Ste. 211, West Hollywood, CA 90046, (323)650-5467
Tribal Development Assn; Natl. [19280]
Tribal Environmental Coun; Natl. [18097]
Tribal Environmental Professionals; Inst. for [19274]
Tribal Indian Ceremonial Assn; Inter- [10747]
Tribal Indian Land Rights Assn. - Address unknown since 1995.
Tribal Preservation Prog. [10755], c/o Heritage Preservation Services, Natl. Park Ser., 1201 Eye St. NW, 2255, Washington, DC 20005, (202)354-1837
Tribal Schools; Assn. of Community [8936]
Tribal Schools; Assn. of Contract [★8936]
Tribal Sovereignty Prog. [★18099]
Tribal Tourism Advocates; Alliance of [19267]
Tribes; Coun. of Energy Rsrc. [18093]
Tribes Found; United Indians of All [18100]
Tribes of Northwest Indians; Affiliated [18948]
Tribes; United South and Eastern [12632]
Tribes; United Southeastern [★12632]
TriBeta [★24408]
Tribunal Arbitral du Sport [★IO]

Tributyl Phosphate Task Force [828], c/o SOCMA VISIONS, 1850 M St. NW, Ste. 700, Washington, DC 20036-5810, (202)721-4154
Trichotillomania Learning Center [15236], 207 McPherson St., Ste. H, Santa Cruz, CA 95060-5863, (831)457-1004
Trickle Up Prog. [12446], 104 W 27th St., 12th Fl., New York, NY 10001-6210, (212)255-9980
Tricot Inst. of America - Defunct.
Tricycle Assn. [IO], Newark, United Kingdom
Tricycle Racing Club of America - Address unknown since 1995.
Triduum - Address unknown since 1994.
The Tried and True Warriors [★24919]
Trigeminal Neuralgia Assn. [15370], 925 NW 56th Terr., Ste. C, Gainesville, FL 32605-6402, (352)331-7009
Trikon [★12258]
Trikone [12258], PO Box 14161, San Francisco, CA 94114, (415)487-8778
Trilateral Commn. [17875], 1156 15th St. NW, Washington, DC 20005, (202)467-5410
Trilateral Commn. [IO], Washington, DC, United States
Trilly Cole Fan Club - Defunct.
TRIM [18721], PO Box 8040, Appleton, WI 54912, (920)749-3780
Trimming Mfrs. Assn; Braided [★3780]
Trinidad Restaurants, Hotels and Tourism Assn. [IO], Chaguaramas, Trinidad and Tobago
Trinidad and Tobago
   Trinidad and Tobago/USA Chamber of Commerce [24298]
Trinidad and Tobago Amateur Radio Soc. [IO], Port of Spain, Trinidad and Tobago
Trinidad and Tobago Badminton Assn. [IO], Port of Spain, Trinidad and Tobago
Trinidad and Tobago Chamber of Indus. and Commerce [IO], Port of Spain, Trinidad and Tobago
Trinidad and Tobago Coalition Against Domestic Violence [IO], Port of Spain, Trinidad and Tobago
Trinidad and Tobago Draughts Assn. [IO], Carapichaima, Trinidad and Tobago
Trinidad and Tobago Inst. of Architects [IO], Port of Spain, Trinidad and Tobago
Trinidad and Tobago Mfrs. Assn. [IO], Barataria, Trinidad and Tobago
Trinidad and Tobago Olympic Comm. [IO], Port of Spain, Trinidad and Tobago
Trinidad and Tobago Reproduction Rights Org. [IO], El Socorro, Trinidad and Tobago
Trinidad and Tobago Tourism Development Authority - Defunct.
Trinidad and Tobago/USA Chamber of Commerce [24298], 111 NW 183rd St., Ste. 108, Miami, FL 33169, (305)652-2478
Trinity Hea. Intl. [14731], 34605 12 Mile Rd., Farmington Hills, MI 48331
Trinity Medical Center [14900], 4343 N Josey Ln., Carrollton, TX 75010-4603, (972)492-1010
Triological Soc. [★15821]
Triple Nine Soc. [9988], c/o Ed Schreiber, Membership Off., 4046 S Magnolia Way, Denver, CO 80237
The Triplet Connection [12614], PO Box 429, Spring City, UT 84662, (435)851-1105
TRIPOD [14781]
Tripoli Rocketry Assn. [9117], PO Box 87, Bellevue, NE 68005, (402)884-9530
Tripoli Sci. Assn. [★9117]
Tripp Family Assn. [21072]
Trips for Kids [8396], 138 Sunnyside Ave., Mill Valley, CA 94941, (415)458-2986
Trireme Trust U.S.A. [10483], c/o Ed Weiskittel, Pres., 803 S Main St., Geneva, NY 14456
Trisha Yearwood Fan Club [24988], PO Box 120895, Nashville, TN 37212
Triskaidekaphobia Illuminatus Soc. - Address unknown since 1990.
Trisomy 18, 13, and Related Disorders; Support Org. for [14485]
Tristan da Cunha Philatelic Soc; St. Helena, Ascension, and [22866]
Tristan Rogers Fan Club - Defunct.
TRITON Corp. - Address unknown since 2004.

Triumph
   TR8 Car Club of Am. [21799]
   Yamaha 650 Soc. [22703]
Triumph Intl. Owners Assn. [★22692]
Triumph Intl. Owners Assn. [★IO]
Triumph Intl. Owners Club [IO], Plympton, MA, United States
Triumph Intl. Owners Club [22692], PO Box 158, Plympton, MA 02367-0158, (508)946-1144
Triumph Intl. Owners Club - Address unknown since 1988.
Triumph Over Phobia [IO], Bath, United Kingdom
Triumph Register of Am. [21800], c/o John Warfield, Pres., 934 Coachway, Annapolis, MD 21401, (410)974-6707
Triumph Register; Vintage [21813]
Triumph Sports Owners Assn. [★21813]
Triumphant; Church Universal and [19462]
Trolley Club of New York; Interstate [★10915]
Trolley Museum; National Capital [★10133]
Trollope Soc. [9716], c/o Mercantile Lib., 17 E 47th St., New York, NY 10017, (212)758-1355
Troop Carrier Squadron Found; 27th [21365]
Troops; Homes for Our [21302]
Tropenbos Found. [★IO]
Tropenbos Intl. [IO], Wageningen, Netherlands
Trophy Dealers of Am. [★441]
Trophy Dealers and Manufacturers Assn. [★441]
Tropic Lightning Assn. [★20687]
Tropical Agricultural Res. and Higher Educ. Centre [IO], Turrialba, Costa Rica
Tropical Agricultural Res. and Training Centre [★IO]
Tropical Biology Assn. [IO], Cambridge, United Kingdom
Tropical Biology and Conservation; Assn. for [6570]
Tropical Conservation; RARE Center for [★5373]
Tropical Fish Farms Assn; Florida [4172]
Tropical Flowering Tree Soc. [4986], c/o Fairchild Tropical Botanical Garden, 10901 Old Cutler Rd., Coral Gables, FL 33156
Tropical Flowering Tree Soc. [IO], Coral Gables, FL, United States
Tropical Forest Found. [4698], c/o Keister Evans, Exec. Dir., 2121 Eisenhower Ave., Ste. 200, Alexandria, VA 22314, (703)518-8834
Tropical Forest Rsrc. Gp. [IO], Shrewsbury, United Kingdom
Tropical, Geographic, and Ecologic; Intl. Soc. of Dermatology: [★14205]
Tropical Grassland Soc. of Australia [IO], St. Lucia, Australia
Tropical Growers' Assn. [IO], Bishop's Stortford, United Kingdom
Tropical Hea. and Educ. Trust [IO], London, United Kingdom
Tropical Horticulture; InterAmerican Soc. for [4979]
Tropical Medicine
   Amer. Acad. of Tropical Medicine [16692]
   Amer. Soc. of Tropical Medicine and Hygiene [16693]
   Assn. for Tropical Biology and Conservation [6570]
   Australasian Coll. of Tropical Medicine [IO]
   Exotic Pathology Soc. [IO]
   Fed. of European Societies for Tropical Medicine and Intl. Hea. [IO]
   Intl. Fed. for Tropical Medicine [IO]
   Japanese Soc. of Tropical Medicine [IO]
   Royal College of Physicians and Surgeons of the United States of America [IO]
   Royal Coll. of Physicians and Surgeons of the U.S.A. [16694]
   Royal Soc. of Tropical Medicine and Hygiene [IO]
   Soc. for Tropical Veterinary Medicine [16807]
Tropical Medicine; Amer. Soc. of [★16693]
Tropical Sci. Center [IO], San Jose, Costa Rica
Tropical Studies
   Amer. Killifish Assn. [22434]
   Amer. Soc. of Tropical Medicine and Hygiene [16693]
   Assn. for Tropical Biology and Conservation [6570]
   European Consortium for Agricultural Res. in the Tropics [IO]
   Heliconia Soc. Intl. [4978]

Reference to "IO" in place of a book number signifies that the association may be found in the 45th edition of International Organizations.

Intl. Centre for Tropical Agriculture [IO]
Intl. Inst. of Tropical Agriculture - United Kingdom [IO]
Intl. Soc. of Tropical Foresters [4687]
Intl. Soc. for Tropical Root Crops [IO]
Org. for Tropical Stud. [IO]
Org. for Tropical Stud. [7816]
Plumeria Soc. of Am. [22537]
Rainforest Alliance [4442]
RARE [5373]
Rare Fruit Coun. Intl. [4760]
Royal Tropical Inst. [IO]
Trees for the Future [5263]
Tropical Sci. Center [IO]
Troth; Ring of [★19460]
Trotskyist League of Canada [IO], Toronto, ON, Canada
Trotting Assn; Amer. [★23519]
Trotting Assn; Natl. [★23519]
Trotting Assn; United [★23519]
Trotting Assn; U.S. [23519]
Trotting Horse Museum [★23498]
Troubles d'Apprentissage - Assn. Canadienne [★IO]
Troubles d'apprentissage - Assn. Nouveau-Brunswick [★IO]
The Troupers - Address unknown since 1990.
Trout Farmers Assn; U.S. [4184]
Trout Unlimited [5387], 1300 N 17th St., Ste. 500, Arlington, VA 22209, (703)522-0200
Trout Unlimited Canada [IO], Calgary, AB, Canada
Troy Hess Fan Club - Address unknown since 1999.
TRRA Historical Soc. [★10925]
Tru-Flyte Knife Throwers of America - Defunct.
Truck Assn; Elec. Indus. [★387]
Truck Assn; Indus. [387]
Truck Assn; Used [431]
Truck Associations of Am; Fed. [★3863]
Truck Body and Equipment Assn. - Defunct.
Truck and Bus Club; Graham Bros. [21894]
Truck Cap and Accessory Alliance - a SEMA Coun. [★390]
Truck Cap and Accessory Assn. [★390]
Truck Cap Indus. Assn. [★390]
Truck Carriers; Natl. Tank [3580]
Truck Club; Chevy GMC Intl. [21609]
Truck Coun. of Am; Private [★3881]
Truck Coun; Natl. Private [3881]
Truck Dealers; Amer. [3862]
Truck Driver Inst. of Am; Professional [★3889]
Truck Driver Inst; Professional [3889]
Truck Driving Schools; Natl. Assn. of Publicly Funded [3877]
Truck Equip. Assn; Natl. [395]
Truck-Frame and Axle Repair Assn. [430], c/o Wayne G. Reich, Admin./Consultant, 3741 Enterprise Dr. SW, Rochester, MN 55902, (800)232-8272
Truck and Heavy Equip. Claims Coun. [★2228]
Truck and Heavy Equip. Claims Coun; Natl. [2228]
Truck Historical Soc; U.S. [★23021]
Truck Leasing Sys; Natl. [3384]
Truck Mfrs. Assn. [366], 1225 New York Ave. NW, Ste. 300, Washington, DC 20005-6156, (202)638-7825
Truck Manufacturers Assn. [IO], Washington, DC, United States
Truck Manufacturers Assn; Caster and Floor [★2028]
Truck Mixer Mfrs. Bur. [400], 900 Spring St., Silver Spring, MD 20910, (301)587-1400
Truck Museum of U.S; Natl. Automotive and [10512]
Truck Recyclers; Assn. of Auto and [★3988]
Truck Rental Independents and Franchisees; Assn. for Car and [★3376]
Truck Renting and Leasing Assn. [3387], 675 N Washington St., Ste. 410, Alexandria, VA 22314-1939, (703)299-9120
Truck Safety Equip. Inst. [★3458]
Truck Sales Network; Used [★431]
Truck Stop Operators; Natl. Assn. of [★3424]
Truck Stop Owners Assn; Amer. [3397]
Truck Tank Assn; Natl. [★998]
Truck Tank and Trailer Tank Inst; Natl. [★998]
Truck Trailer Mfrs. Assn. [401], 1020 Princess St., Alexandria, VA 22314-2247, (703)549-3010

Truck Trailer Manufacturers Association [IO], Alexandria, VA, United States
Truck Trailer Mfrs. Assn; Tank Conf. of the [998]
Truck Wreckers Assn; Natl. Auto and [★3988]
Truckers Against Drunk Drivers - Defunct.
Truckers Assn; Mid-West [3875]
Truckers for Christ [19828], PO Box 48, Haysville, KS 67060, (316)633-4075
Truckers and Drivers Assn; Independent [3870]
Truckers and Drivers Assn; Maryland Independent [★3870]
Trucking
  Amer. Alliance of Ethical Movers [13346]
  Amer. Truck Historical Soc. [23021]
  Amer. Trucking Associations [3863]
  Assn. of Christian Truckers [20596]
  Commercial Vehicle Solutions Network [382]
  Diamond T Register [23023]
  Distribution and LTL Carriers Assn. [3564]
  HMI Ministries [20597]
  Independent Truckers and Drivers Assn. [3870]
  Intermodal Assn. of North Am. [3872]
  Intl. Truck Parts Assn. [388]
  Loved Ones and Drivers Support [13347]
  Mid-West Truckers Assn. [3875]
  Mobile Air Conditioning Soc. Worldwide [1893]
  Monster Truck Racing Assn. [23958]
  Natl. Assn. of Publicly Funded Truck Driving Schools [3877]
  Natl. Private Truck Coun. [3881]
  Natl. Tank Truck Carriers [3580]
  Natl. Truck Equip. Assn. [395]
  Natl. Truck Leasing Sys. [3384]
  Natl. Truckdrivers Safety Assn. [2843]
  Natl. Truckers Assn. [3884]
  NATSO [3424]
  North Amer. Trans. Mgt. Inst. [8212]
  North Amer. Truck Camper Owners Assn. [23025]
  North Amer. Trucking Industrial Relations Assn. [2906]
  Owner-Operator Independent Drivers Assn. [3888]
  Professional Truck Driver Inst. [3889]
  Professional Trucking Services Assn. [3890]
  Ser. Specialists Assn. [427]
  Soc. of Professional Drivers [3893]
  Tech. and Maintenance Coun. of the Amer. Trucking Associations [3895]
  Towing and Recovery Assn. of Am. [429]
  Trans. Clubs Intl. [3896]
  Truck-Frame and Axle Repair Assn. [430]
  Truck Mixer Mfrs. Bur. [400]
  Truck Trailer Mfrs. Assn. [401]
  Truckers for Christ [19828]
  Trucking Mgt., Inc. [3898]
  Truckload Carriers Assn. [3899]
  White Owners Register [23026]
Trucking Assn; Natl. Private [★3881]
Trucking Associations; Amer. [3863]
Trucking Associations Foundation; American [★3863]
Trucking Associations; The Maintenance Coun. of the Amer. [★3895]
Trucking Associations; Tech. and Maintenance Coun. of the Amer. [3895]
Trucking Employers [★3898]
Trucking Indus. Defense Assn. [3897], 6201 W Howard St., Ste. 201, Niles, IL 60714, (847)647-7226
Trucking Mgt., Inc. [★3898]
Trucking Mgt., Inc. [3898], 566 El Dorado St., Ste. 101, Pasadena, CA 91101, (626)792-9621
Trucking Services Assn; Professional [3890]
Truckload Carriers Assn. [3899], 555 E Braddock Rd., Alexandria, VA 22314-2182, (703)838-1950
Truckload Carriers Conf; Interstate [★3899]
Trucks
  1/87 Vehicle Club [22641]
  Airflow Club of Am. [21563]
  Alliance of Auto. Mfrs. [368]
  Amer. Truck Historical Soc. [23021]
  Amer. Truck Stop Owners Assn. [3397]
  Amer. Trucking Associations [3863]
  Amtralease [3378]
  Antique Truck Club of Am. [23022]
  Automotive Parts Remanufacturers Assn. [409]

  Automotive Recyclers Assn. [3988]
  Chevy GMC Intl. Truck Club [21609]
  Citizens for Reliable and Safe Highways [18577]
  Commercial Vehicle Solutions Network [382]
  Convoy For Kids [IO]
  Diamond T Register [IO]
  Diamond T Register [23023]
  Distribution and LTL Carriers Assn. [3564]
  Divco Club of Am. [22012]
  Dodge Pilothouse Era Truck Club of Am. [23024]
  Graham Bros. Truck and Bus Club [21894]
  Gravely Tractor Club of Am. [23002]
  Heavy Duty Representatives Assn. [386]
  Independent Truckers and Drivers Assn. [3870]
  Indus. Truck Assn. [387]
  Intl. Bus Collectors Club [21895]
  Intl. Truck Parts Assn. [388]
  Kustom Kemps of Am. [21683]
  Light Truck Accessory Alliance [390]
  Mid-West Truckers Assn. [3875]
  Model "A" Restorers Club [21712]
  Monster Truck Racing Assn. [23958]
  Monster Truck Racing Association [IO]
  Motor Bus Soc. [21896]
  Natl. Auto. Dealers Assn. [420]
  Natl. Automotive and Truck Museum of U.S. [10512]
  Natl. Private Truck Coun. [3881]
  Natl. Tank Truck Carriers [3580]
  Natl. Tractor Pullers Assn. [23928]
  Natl. Truck Equip. Assn. [395]
  Natl. Truckdrivers Safety Assn. [2843]
  North Amer. Truck Camper Owners Assn. [23025]
  North Amer. Trucking Industrial Relations Assn. [2906]
  Parents Against Tired Truckers [12984]
  Professional Truck Driver Inst. [3889]
  Professional Trucking Services Assn. [3890]
  REO Club of Am. [21770]
  Ser. Specialists Assn. [427]
  Soc. of Professional Drivers [3893]
  Spring Res. Inst. [399]
  Standing Up for SUV, Pickup and Van Owners of Am. [17017]
  Studebaker Driver's Club [21790]
  Tank Conf. of the Truck Trailer Mfrs. Assn. [998]
  Tech. and Maintenance Coun. of the Amer. Trucking Associations [3895]
  Towing and Recovery Assn. of Am. [429]
  Trans. Clubs Intl. [3896]
  Truck-Frame and Axle Repair Assn. [430]
  Truck Mfrs. Assn. [366]
  Truck Mixer Mfrs. Bur. [400]
  Truck Renting and Leasing Assn. [3387]
  Truck Trailer Mfrs. Assn. [401]
  Truckers for Christ [19828]
  Trucking Mgt., Inc. [3898]
  Truckload Carriers Assn. [3899]
  United St. Machine Assn. [21807]
  USA Pulling [23929]
  Used Truck Assn. [431]
  White Owners Register [23026]
  White Owners Register [IO]
Trucks; Coalition Against Bigger [13337]
Truckstop Indus; NATSO, Representing the Travel Plaza and [★3424]
Trudeau Soc; Amer. [★16642]
True Family Assn. - Defunct.
True Food Network [4677], 2601 Mission St., Ste. 803, San Francisco, CA 94110, (415)826-2770
True Life Inst. - Address unknown since 1999.
The True Nature Network [11465], PO Box 20672, Colombus Circle Sta., New York, NY 10023-1487, (212)581-1120
True Seed Exchange [★22540]
True Sisters; United Order [19437]
Truffling Soc; North Amer. [7354]
Truk Stop Found; Maryland [★8948]
Trull Found. [12739], 404 4th St., Palacios, TX 77465, (361)972-5241
Truman Philatelic and Historical Assn. - Defunct.
Truman Scholarship Found; Harry S. [8430]
The Trumpeter Swan Soc. [5388], 12615 County Rd. 9, Ste. No. 100, Plymouth, MN 55441-1248, (763)694-7851

A star before a book entry number signifies that the name is not listed separately, but is mentioned within the entry.

Truss Coun. of Am; Wood [689]
Truss Plate Inst. [683], 218 N Lee St., Ste. 312, Alexandria, VA 22314, (703)683-1010
Truss Plate Inst; Component Manufacturers Coun. of the [★683]
Trussed Rafter Assn. [IO], Chesterfield, United Kingdom
The Trust [★16946]
Trust Alliance; Land [4416]
Trust for America's Hea. [16255], 1707 H St. NW, 7th Fl., Washington, DC 20006, (202)223-9870
Trust Assn; Retirement Indus. [497]
Trust Center; Natl. Community Land [★17221]
Trust Companies; Assn. of Independent [1457]
Trust Companies' Assn. of Japan [IO], Tokyo, Japan
Trust for Education on the United Nations - Address unknown since 1995.
Trust and Estate Counsel; Amer. Coll. of [6183]
Trust Fund; Social Progress [★17460]
Trust Fund; Social Progress [★IO]
Trust Fund; Venezuelan [★IO]
Trust Fund; Venezuelan [★17460]
Trust for Mutual Understanding [10232], 6 W 48th St., 12th Fl., New York, NY 10036, (212)843-0404
Trust for Mutual Understanding [IO], New York, NY, United States
Trust for Philanthropy; AAFRC [★12721]
Trust for Public Land [4461], 116 New Montgomery St., 4th Fl., San Francisco, CA 94105, (415)495-4014
Trustee Assn; Museum [10510]
Trustee Companies Officers' Assn. [★IO]
Trustee Div. (of ALA) [★10335]
Trustees for Conservation - Defunct.
Trustees and Directors of Missions; Bd. of [★19496]
Trustees; Natl. Assn. of Chap. 13 [★5578]
Trustees of Not-for-Profit Hospitals; Volunteer [14902]
Trusteeship Inst. [18011], 61 Baker Rd., Shutesbury, MA 01072, (413)584-8191
Trusteeship; National Conf. on [★7889]
Trusteeship; Robert L. Gale Fund for the Stud. of [★7889]
Truth About Civil Turmoil - Defunct.
Truth in Advertising - Defunct.
Truth in Fitness [15970], 204 E 204th St., Costa Mesa, CA 92627
Truth Missionaries Chap. of Positive Accord [20585], PO Box 42772, Evergreen Park, IL 60805-0772, (773)342-0159
Truth in Press - Defunct.
Truth in Psychiatry; Comm. for [15195]
Try Us Resources [★2761]
T.S.H.I.R.T.S.: The Soc. Handling the Interchange of Remarkable T-Shirts - Defunct.
TSIA—The Assn. of Retail Marketing Services [3463]
TTS Inst. [IO], Helsinki, Finland
TTS Work Efficiency Inst. [★IO]
Tube Assn; Collapsible Metal [★2881]
Tube Assn; Natl. Fibre Can and [★976]
Tube Assn. and Tube and Pipe Fabricators Assn., Intl; Amer. [★3040]
Tube Coun. of North Am. [2881], 87 West St., Ste. 101, Walpole, MA 02081, (508)850-5179
Tube Engineering Panel Advisory Coun. - Defunct.
Tube Inst; Composite Can and [976]
Tube Inst; Formed Steel [★997]
Tube Inst; Welded Steel [★997]
Tube Packaging Coun. of North Am; Metal [★2881]
Tube and Pipe Assn., Intl. [3040], 833 Featherstone Rd., Rockford, IL 61107-6301, (815)399-8775
Tube and Pipe Assn., Intl. [IO], Rockford, IL, United States
Tuberculosis Assn; Natl. [★16354]
Tuberculosis, Chest and Heart Diseases Assn; Hong Kong [IO]
Tuberculosis Controllers Assn; Natl. [14283]
Tuberculosis and Lung Disease; Intl. Union Against [IO]
Tuberculosis; Natl. Assn. for the Stud. and Prevention of [★16354]
Tuberculosis and Respiratory Disease Assn; Natl. [★16354]
Tuberculosis Secretaries; Natl. Conf. of [★16357]

Tuberculosis Welfare League - Defunct.
Tuberculosis Workers; Natl. Conf. of [★16357]
Tuberous Sclerosis Alliance [15371], 801 Roeder Rd., Ste. 750, Silver Spring, MD 20910, (301)562-9890
Tuberous Sclerosis Assn. [IO], Birmingham, United Kingdom
Tuberous Sclerosis Assn. of America - Address unknown since 1995.
Tuberous Sclerosis Assn; Natl. [★15371]
Tubers - Defunct.
Tubists Universal Brotherhood Assn. [★10631]
Tubists Universal Brotherhood Assn. [★IO]
Tubular Brass Inst. [★IO]
Tubular Brass Inst. [★3066]
Tubular Exchanger Mfrs. Assn. [1902], 25 N Broadway, Tarrytown, NY 10591, (914)332-0040
Tubular Finishers and Processors Assn. - Defunct.
Tubular Rivet and Machine Inst. [★1820]
Tubular and Split Rivet Coun. [★1820]
Tucker Auto. Club of Am. [21801], 9509 Hinton Dr., Santee, CA 92071-2760
Tucker Fan Club; Tanya [24980]
Tucker's Orchid Nursery [IO], Auckland, New Zealand
Tuerkiye Isci Sendikalari Konfederasyonu [★IO]
Tuerkiye Kimya Sanayicileri Dernegi [★IO]
Tuesday's Children [12003], 390 Plandome Rd., Ste. 217, Manhasset, NY 11030, (516)562-9000
Tuetuen Eksperleri Dernegi [★IO]
Tufted Textile Mfrs. Assn. [★2254]
Tufts Center for Animals and Public Policy [11466], Tufts Univ., 200 Westboro Rd., North Grafton, MA 01536, (508)839-7991
Tufts Univ. Alumni Assn. [18927], Office Of Alumni Relations, 80 George St., Ste. 100-3, Medford, MA 02155, (617)627-3532
Tug of War
U.S. Amateur Tug of War Assn. [23959]
Tug of War Fed; North Amer. [★23959]
Tugboat Enthusiasts Soc. of the Americas [21886], 38 Kimball Ave., Unit No. 2, Ipswich, MA 01938
Tugboat Underwriting Syndicate - Defunct.
Tuli Assn; North Amer. [4285]
Tum Gida Ithalatcilari Dernegi [★IO]
Tum Gida Ithalatcilari Dernegi [IO]
Tumblehome Recreational Canoe Club [IO], St. John's, NL, Canada
Tumor Assn; Amer. Brain [13791]
Tumor Found. for Children; Brain [13948]
Tumor Found. of the U.S; Pediatric Brain [13863]
Tumor Network Assn; Pituitary [★16022]
Tumor Registrars Assn; Natl. [★15651]
Tumor Soc; Brain [14254]
Tumor Soc; Musculoskeletal [15274]
Tun Abdul Razak Res. Centre [IO], Hertford, United Kingdom
Tuna Found; U.S. [3506]
Tuna Res. Found. [★3506]
Tuna Boat Owners' Assn. - Defunct.
Tunas Harapan Found. [IO], Pati, Indonesia
Tune-Up Manufacturers Coun. [402], 10 Lab. Dr., PO Box 13966, Research Triangle Park, NC 27709-3966, (919)549-4800
Tune-up Manufacturers Inst. [★402]
Tuneful Viewer's Soc. for the Preservation of T.V. Theme Songs - Defunct.
Tuners; Natl. Assn. of Piano [★2822]
Tung Res. and Development League - Defunct.
Tungsten Inst. - Defunct.
Tunis; Center for Maghrib Stud. in [★7927]
Tunis; Center for Maghrib Stud. in [★IO]
Tunis Sheep Breeders' Assn; Amer. [★5208]
Tunis Sheep Registry, Inc; Natl. [5208]
Tunisia
Amer. Inst. for Maghrib Stud. [7927]
Tunisian Assn. Against Epilepsy [IO], Sfax, Tunisia
Tunisian Chap. of IASP [IO], Tunis, Tunisia
Tunisian Economic Assn. [IO], Tunis, Tunisia
Tunisian Red Crescent [IO], Tunis, Tunisia
Tunisian Soc. of Cardiology and Cardiovascular Surgery [IO], Tunis, Tunisia
Tunisian Soc. of Dermatology and Venereology [IO], Tunis, Tunisia
Turbine Div; Gas [★7001]

Turbine Inlet Cooling Assn. [7055], 427 Prairie Knoll Dr., Ste. 102, Naperville, IL 60565, (630)357-3960
Turbine Inst; Intl. Gas [★7001]
Turf Direktorium fur die Slowakei [★IO]
Turf Institute/American Sod Producers Assn; Better Lawn and [★4794]
Turf and Landscape Assn; New York State [2397]
Turf and Landscape Conf; Professional [★2397]
Turf Managers Assn; Sports [2399]
Turf and Ornamental Communicators Assn. [2400], PO Box 156, New Prague, MN 56071, (952)758-6340
Turf and Ornamental Distributors Assn; Independent [2394]
Turf Res. Found. - Defunct.
Turf Writers Assn; Natl. [3145]
Turfgrass Producers Intl. [4799], 2 E Main St., East Dundee, IL 60118, (847)649-5555
Turfgrass Producers Intl. [IO], East Dundee, IL, United States
Turfgrass Visiting Ser. [★23467]
Turisticka Organizacija Srbije [★IO]
Turk Dishekimleri Birligi [★IO]
Turk Elektron Mikroskopi Dernegi [★IO]
Turk Elektronik Sanayicileri Dernegi [★IO]
Turk Farmakoloji Dernegi [★IO]
Turk Kardiyoloji Dernegi [★IO]
Turk Musavir Muhendisler ve Mimarlar Birligi [★IO]
Turk Ortodonti Dernegi [★IO]
Turk Ortopedi ve Travmatoloji Dernegi [★IO]
Turk Tabipleri Birligi [★IO]
Turk Universiteli Kadinlar Dernegi [★IO]
Turkey
Amer. Friends of Turkey [IO]
Amer. Friends of Turkey [18752]
Amer. Poultry Intl. [5108]
Amer. Res. Inst. in Turkey [11060]
American-Turkish Coun. [18753]
American-Turkish Coun. [IO]
Found. for the Advancement of Sephardic Stud. and Culture [19181]
Inst. of Turkish Stud. [11061]
Natl. Turkey Fed. [5113]
Turkish-American Chamber of Commerce and Indus. [24384]
Turkish-American Chamber of Commerce and Indus. [IO]
Turkish Coalition of Am. [18754]
Turkey Center; Wild [★5343]
Turkey Fed; Natl. [5113]
Turkey Fed; Natl. Wild [5343]
Turkey Vulture Soc. [5389], 6622 Wise Ave., St. Louis, MO 63139
Turkhana Desert Fund [★12883]
Turkhana Desert Fund [★IO]
Turkic Languages; Amer. Assn. of Teachers of [9282]
Turkish
Amer. Assn. of Teachers of Turkic Languages [9282]
Amer. Res. Inst. in Turkey [11060]
Amer. Res. Inst. in Turkey [IO]
Amer. Turkish Soc. [IO]
Amer. Turkish Soc. [19407]
Assembly of Turkish Amer. Associations [19408]
European Assembly of Turkish Academics [IO]
European Assn. of Turkish Academics - Belgium [IO]
Fed. of Turkish Amer. Associations [19409]
Inst. of Turkish Stud. [11061]
Soc. of Turkish Amer. Architects, Engineers and Scientists [7048]
Turkish Amer. Alliance for Fairness [19410]
Turkish Coalition of Am. [18754]
Turkish Stud. Assn. [11062]
Turkish Stud. Assn. [IO]
Turkish Acad. of Sciences [IO], Ankara, Turkey
Turkish Amer. Alliance for Fairness [19410], PO Box 6151, San Rafael, CA 94903, (641)715-3900
Turkish-Amer. Assn. - Address unknown since 2003.
Turkish; Amer. Assn. of Teachers of [★9282]
Turkish-American Chamber of Commerce and Indus. [24384], c/o Ipek Ozuak, Dir., 28 W 44th St., Ste. 1630, New York, NY 10001, (646)429-1530
Turkish-American Chamber of Commerce and Indus. [IO], New York, NY, United States

Reference to "IO" in place of a book number signifies that the association may be found in the 45th edition of International Organizations.

Turkish Amer. Friendship Soc. of the U.S. - Address unknown since 1995.

Turkish Amer. Physicians Assn. - Address unknown since 2001.

Turkish Amer. Scientists and Scholars Assn. [7636], 1526 18th St. NW, Washington, DC 20036, (800)620-4120

Turkish American Scientists and Scholars Association [IO], Washington, DC, United States

Turkish-American Societies; Fed. of [★19409]

Turkish Architects, Engineers and Scientists in Am; Soc. of [★7048]

Turkish Assn. for Hypertension Control [IO], Ismir, Turkey

Turkish Assn. of Marketing and Public Opinion Researchers [IO], Istanbul, Turkey

Turkish Assn. of Sports Medicine [IO], Izmir, Turkey

Turkish Assn. of Trauma and Emergency Surgery [IO], Istanbul, Turkey

Turkish Assn. of Univ. Women [IO], Istanbul, Turkey

Turkish Athletic Fed. [IO], Ankara, Turkey

Turkish Badminton Fed. [IO], Ankara, Turkey

Turkish Banking Assn. [★IO]

Turkish British Chamber of Commerce and Indus. [IO], London, United Kingdom

Turkish Chem. Mfrs'. Assn. [IO], Istanbul, Turkey

Turkish Children Foster Care - Address unknown since 2002.

Turkish Clothing Manufacturers Assn. [IO], Istanbul, Turkey

Turkish Coalition of Am. [18754], 1025 Connecticut Ave. NW, Ste. 1000, Washington, DC 20036, (202)370-1399

Turkish Confed. of Employer Associations [IO], Ankara, Turkey

Turkish Contractors Assn. [IO], Ankara, Turkey

Turkish Contractors Assn. [★IO]

Turkish Cultural Center [★19409]

Turkish Cypriot Assn. of Univ. Women [IO], Mersin, Turkey

Turkish Dental Assn. [IO], Ankara, Turkey

Turkish Electronics and Info. Indus. Assn. [IO], Istanbul, Turkey

Turkish Fine Arts Ensemble - Address unknown since 2004.

Turkish Food Importers Assn. [★IO]

Turkish Foundrymen's Assn. [IO], Istanbul, Turkey

Turkish Gymnastic and DanceSport Fed. [IO], Ankara, Turkey

Turkish Ice Sports Fed. [IO], Ankara, Turkey

Turkish Iron and Steel Producers Assn. [IO], Ankara, Turkey

Turkish League Against Epilepsy [IO], Istanbul, Turkey

Turkish League Against Rheumatism [IO], Ankara, Turkey

Turkish Medical Informatics Assn. [IO], Ankara, Turkey

Turkish Orthodontic Soc. [IO], Ankara, Turkey

Turkish Osteoporosis Soc. [IO], Istanbul, Turkey

Turkish Pharmacological Soc. [IO], Ankara, Turkey

Turkish Physical Soc. [IO], Istanbul, Turkey

Turkish Physiotherapy Assn. [IO], Ankara, Turkey

Turkish Psychological Assn. [IO], Ankara, Turkey

Turkish Red Crescent Soc. [IO], Ankara, Turkey

Turkish Retired Officers Assn. [IO], Ankara, Turkey

Turkish Rheumatism Soc. [★IO]

Turkish Soc. of Antimicrobial Chemotherapy [IO], Istanbul, Turkey

Turkish Soc. of Cardiology [IO], Istanbul, Turkey

Turkish Soc. of Chemotherapy [IO], Istanbul, Turkey

Turkish Soc. of Dermatology [IO], Ankara, Turkey

Turkish Soc. of Dermatopathology [IO], Ankara, Turkey

Turkish Soc. for Electron Microscopy [IO], Istanbul, Turkey

Turkish Soc. for Image Anal. and Pattern Recognition [IO], Istanbul, Turkey

Turkish Soc. of Orthopaedic Surgery and Traumatology [IO], Ankara, Turkey

Turkish Soc. of Physiological Sciences [IO], Konya, Turkey

Turkish Squash Fed. [IO], Ankara, Turkey

Turkish Stud. Assn. [IO], Cambridge, MA, United States

Turkish Stud. Assn. [11062], c/o Andras Riedlmayer, Pres., Fine Arts Lib., Harvard Univ., 32 Quincy St., Cambridge, MA 02138, (617)495-3372

Turkish Stud; Inst. of [11061]

Turkish Tennis Fed. [IO], Ankara, Turkey

Turkish Tourism Investors' Assn. [IO], Istanbul, Turkey

Turkish Underwater Sports, Life-Saving, Water Ski and Fin Swimming Fed. [IO], Ankara, Turkey

Turkish Women's League of America - Address unknown since 2002.

Turkiskaupan Liitto ry [★IO]

Turkiye Atletizm Federasyonu [★IO]

Turkiye Badminton Federasyonu [★IO]

Turkiye Bankalar Birligi [★IO]

Turkiye Bilimler Akademisi [★IO]

Turkiye Bilimsel ve Teknolojik Arastirma Kurumu [★IO]

Turkiye Dokum Sanayicileri Dernegi [★IO]

Turkiye Emekli Subaylar Dernegi [★IO]

Turkiye Endokrinoloji Ve Metabolizma Dernegi [★IO]

Turkiye Esnaf ve Sanatkarlari Konfederasyonu [★IO]

Turkiye Fizyoterapistler Dernegi [★IO]

Turkiye Giyim Sanayicileri Dernigi [★IO]

Turkiye Isveren Sendikalari Konfederasyonu [★IO]

Turkiye Jokey Kulubu [★IO]

Turkiye Kizilay Dernegi [★IO]

Turkiye Milli Olimpiyat Komitesi [★IO]

Turkiye Muteahhitler Birligi [★IO]

Turkiye Osteoporoz Dernegi [★IO]

Turkiye Sigorta ve Reasurans Sirketleri Birligi [★IO]

Turkiye Sualti Sporlari Federasyonu [★IO]

Turkiye Tenis Federasyonu [★IO]

Turkiye Turizm Dernegi [★IO]

Turkmenistan Badminton Fed. [IO], Ashgabat, Turkmenistan

Turkmenistan Tennis Assn. [IO], Ashgabat, Turkmenistan

Turks and Caicos Assn. of Off. Professionals [IO], Providenciales, Turks and Caicos Islands

Turks and Caicos Islands Amateur Athletic Assn. [IO], Grand Turk, Turks and Caicos Islands

Turks and Caicos Tennis Assn. [IO], Providenciales, Turks and Caicos Islands

Turn Toward Peace [★18259]

Turnaround Mgt. Assn. [2517], 150 S Wacker Dr., Ste. 900, Chicago, IL 60606, (312)578-6900

Turnaround Professionals; Assn. of Certified [956]

Turnbull Clan Assn. [21073], c/o Wally R. Turnbull, Pres., 5216 Tahoe Dr., Durham, NC 27713, (919)361-5041

Turnbull Clan Assn. of North Am. [★21073]

Turner Found. [4611], 133 Luckie St. NW, 2nd Fl., Atlanta, GA 30303, (404)681-9900

Turner Soc. [IO], London, United Kingdom

Turner Syndrome Assn. of Australia [IO], Frenchs Forest, Australia

Turner Syndrome Soc. of the U.S. [14486], 10960 Millridge North Dr., No. 214A, Houston, TX 77014, (832)365-9944

Turnerbund; Amer. [★23802]

Turners; Amer. [23802]

Turners Ser. Bur; Wood- [★1657]

Turners and Shapers Assn; Wood [★1657]

Turner's Syndrome Soc. [IO], Ottawa, ON, Canada

Turners Syndrome Support Soc. (UK) [IO], Clydebank, United Kingdom

Turnkey Inst; Educ. [8557]

Turnkey Systems; Educ. [★8557]

Turtle Assn; Cowboys [★23694]

Turtle Force - The Official Fan Club of the Teenage Mutant Ninja Turtles - Address unknown since 2000.

Turtle Rescue Fund; Sea [★4435]

Turtle Survival League; Caribbean Conservation Corp. and Sea [5305]

Turtle and Tortoise Soc; New York [5348]

Turtles - Greece; MEDASSET: Mediterranean Assn. to Save the Sea [IO]

Tuskegee Airmen, Inc. [20651], PO Box 9166, Arlington, VA 22219-1166, (703)286-7653

Tutmonda Esperantista Junulara Organizo [★IO]

Tutoring

Natl. Tutoring Assn. [9283]

Tutoring and Mentoring Centers; Natl. Org. of [★9283]

Tutoring; Natl. Assn. of [★9283]

Tuvalu and Kiribati Philatelic Soc. - Address unknown since 1995.

Tuvalu Tennis Assn. [IO], Funafuti, Tuvalu

TV-Free Am. [★12170]

TV-Turnoff Network [12170], c/o Center for Screen-Time Awareness, 1200 29th St. NW, Lower Level No. 1, Washington, DC 20007, (202)333-9220

T.V. Writers Guild [★24221]

TVR Car Club [★21802]

TVR Car Club of England, U.S. Area [★21802]

TVR Car Club North Am. [21802], c/o Marshall Moore, Pres., 3559 Overbrook Dr., Roanoke, VA 24018, (540)772-0952

Twain Assn. of New York; Mark [★9685]

Twain Boyhood Home Associates; Mark [9684]

Twain Circle of New York; Mark [9685]

Twain Home Found; Mark [9686]

Twain House and Museum; Mark [9687]

Twain Memorial; Mark [★9687]

Twain Res. Found; Mark [9688]

Twentieth Anniversary Mobilization - Address unknown since 1985.

Twentieth Century Fund [★18433]

Twentieth Century Soc. [IO], London, United Kingdom

Twentieth Century Spanish Assn. of Am. [IO], Boulder, CO, United States

Twentieth Century Spanish Assn. of Am. [10975], Univ. of Colorado at Boulder, Dept. of Spanish and Portuguese, Boulder, CO 80309-0278, (303)492-5900

Twenty-First Century Found. [12740], 132 W 112th St., Ground Level, New York, NY 10026, (212)662-3700

Twenty-Four Karat Club of the City of New York [2383], c/o John J. Kennedy, Sec., Jewelers Security Alliance of the U.S., 6 E 45th St., No. 1005, New York, NY 10017, (212)687-0328

Twenty Year Club [★555]

TWIN [IO], London, United Kingdom

Twin Bonanza Assn. [21483], 19684 Lakeshore Dr., Three Rivers, MI 49093, (269)279-2540

Twin Towers Fund - Defunct.

Twinless Twins Support Gp. [★12615]

Twinless Twins Support Gp. [★IO]

Twinless Twins Support Group International [IO], Ypsilanti, MI, United States

Twinless Twins Support Gp. Intl. [12615], PO Box 980481, Ypsilanti, MI 48198-0481, (888)205-8962

Twins

Center for the Stud. of Multiple Birth [15272]

Conjoined Twins Intl. [16695]

Conjoined Twins Intl. [IO]

Intl. Soc. for Twin Stud. [IO]

Natl. Org. of Mothers of Twins Clubs [12613]

The Triplet Connection [12614]

Twins Found. [12616]

Twins Clubs; Natl. Org. of Mothers of [12613]

Twins Found. [12616], PO Box 6043, Providence, RI 02940-6043, (401)751-8946

Twins and Multiple Births Assn. [IO], Guildford, United Kingdom

Twins Support Gp. Intl; Twinless [12615]

Twins Support Gp; Twinless [★12615]

Twins, Triplets, and More Assn. of Calgary [IO], Calgary, AB, Canada

Twirling Assn. Intl; Natl. Baton [23142]

Twirling Assn; U.S. [23143]

Twirling and Majorette Associations; Global Alliance of Natl. Baton [23141]

Twirling and Majorette Associations; World Fed. of Baton [★23141]

Twirly Birds [21484], c/o Jim Hamilton, Pres., 7140 Rolling Acres Trail, Fair Oaks Ranch, TX 78015-4021, (830)755-4566

Twisted Jute Packing and Oakum Inst. - Defunct.

Twisted Sister Fan Club - Address unknown since 1989.

Two-Cylinder Club [23005], PO Box 430, Grundy Center, IA 50638-0430, (319)824-6060

Two-Cylinder Ford Register - Defunct.

Two-Cylinder Worldwide [★23005]

Two Spirited People of the First Nations [IO], Toronto, ON, Canada

A star before a book entry number signifies that the name is not listed separately, but is mentioned within the entry.

Two/Ten Associates [★1601]

Two/Ten Footwear Found. [1601], 1466 Main St., Waltham, MA 02451, (781)736-1500

Two/Ten Found. [★1601]

Two/Ten Natl. Found. [★1601]

Two-Year Colleges; Amer. Mathematical Assn. of [8821]

Ty Herndon Fan Club - Defunct.

Tylers' and Bricklayers' Company [IO], Thames Ditton, United Kingdom

Tympanuchus Cupido Pinnatus; Soc. of [5383]

Tyndale Soc. [20530], c/o Jennifer Bekemeier, Regent Univ., ADM 154, 1000 Regent Univ. Dr., Virginia Beach, VA 23464, (757)226-4347

Tyne and Wear Campaign for Nuclear Disarmament [IO], Newcastle upon Tyne, United Kingdom

Type Culture Coll; Amer. [6567]

Type Directors Club [7156], 127 W 25th St., 8th Fl., New York, NY 10001, (212)633-8943

Typecasting Fellowship; Amer. [9990]

Typewriter Collectors Assn; Early [22015]

Typewriter Mfrs. Export Assn. - Defunct.

Typewriter and Off. Machine Dealers Assn; Natl. [★2844]

Typographic Aficionados; Soc. of [1791]

Typographic Communications Assn. - Defunct.

Typographic Designers of Canada [★IO]

Typographical Union; Intl. [★24086]

Typophiles [9993], 30 E 23rd St., 8th Fl., New York, NY 10010

Typothetae of Am; United [★1788]

Tyrolean and Bavarian Zither Club - Address unknown since 1995.

Tyrone Guthrie Centre [IO], Newbliss, Ireland

Tzeghagrons; ARF [★18087]

Tzeirai Etr Tzion [★20140]

Tzivos Hashem [10290], 792 Eastern Pkwy., Brooklyn, NY 11213, (718)467-6630

Tzivos Hashem Book Club [★10290]

U

UAE Golf Assn. [IO], Dubai, United Arab Emirates

UCA Intl. Users Gp. [7820], 10604 Candler Falls Ct., Raleigh, NC 27614, (919)847-2241

UCD Alumni Assn. [IO], Dublin, Ireland

UCJG de Cameroon [★IO]

Udruzenje kardiologa Bosne i Hercegovine [★IO]

Udruzenje Jugoslovenskih Jevreja u U.S.A. [★19175]

Udruzenje Poslovnih Zena [★IO]

Udruzenje Stanara Hrvatske [★IO]

Udruzenje-Udruga Stanjara BIHUSS-Saravejo [★IO]

Udruzenje Za Gas Srbije [★IO]

Udruzenjeza Numericiju Artikala Bosne I Hercegovine [★IO]

UERMMMC Nursing Alumni Assn. U.S.A. [18928], 9 Mimosa Ln., Piscataway, NJ 08854, (732)463-0504

UFM Intl. [★20326]

UFM Intl. [★IO]

UFO Contact Center Intl. - Defunct.

UFO Info. Retrieval Center [7486], 3131 W Cochise Dr., No. 158, Phoenix, AZ 85051-9511, (602)284-5427

UFO Information Retrieval Center [IO], Phoenix, AZ, United States

UFO Network; Midwest [★7481]

UFO Network; Mutual [7481]

UFO Res; Fund for [7474]

UFO Secrecy; Citizens Against [7473]

UFO Stud; Center for [★7479]

UFO Stud; J. Allen Hynek Center for [7479]

Uganda Amateur Athletics Fed. [IO], Kampala, Uganda

Uganda Amateur Draughts Assn. [IO], Kampala, Uganda

Uganda Assn. of Consulting Engineers [IO], Kampala, Uganda

Uganda Assn. of Physiotherapy [IO], Kampala, Uganda

Uganda Assn. of Univ. Women [IO], Kampala, Uganda

Uganda Baseball and Softball Assn. [IO], Kampala, Uganda

Uganda Dance Sport Assn. [IO], Kampala, Uganda

Uganda Diabetic Assn. [IO], Kampala, Uganda

Uganda Export Promotion Bd. [IO], Kampala, Uganda

Uganda Games and Sports Medicine Assn. [IO], Kampala, Uganda

Uganda Girl Guides Assn. [IO], Kampala, Uganda

Uganda IDEA Proj. [IO], Kampala, Uganda

Uganda Junior Chamber [IO], Kampala, Uganda

Uganda Medical Assn. [IO], Kampala, Uganda

Uganda Newspaper Editors and Proprietors Assn. [IO], Kampala, Uganda

Uganda Services Exporters' Assn. [IO], Kampala, Uganda

Uganda Soc. [IO], Kampala, Uganda

Uganda Squash Rackets Assn. [IO], Kampala, Uganda

Uganda Tennis Assn. [IO], Kampala, Uganda

Uganda Weightlifting Fed. [IO], Kampala, Uganda

Uganda Women's Effort to Save Orphans [IO], Kampala, Uganda

Uganda Women's Effort to Save Orphans - U.S.A. - Address unknown since 2001.

Ugandan AIDS Project - Address unknown since 1999.

Ugbajo Itsekiri USA [19260], PO Box 11465, Washington, DC 20008

Ughdarras a Chlo Hearaich [★IO]

Uglies Unlimited [12102], 1906 Juniper Ln., Lufkin, TX 75904, (936)634-1429

UHL Collectors Soc. [22125], c/o Amy Busler, Sec.-Treas., 398 S Star, Santa Claus, IN 47579, (812)544-2987

Uhuru Movement; Intl. People's Democratic [17395]

UIL-Scuola [IO], Rome, Italy

UIM Intl. [★IO]

UIM Intl. [★20405]

UJA Fed. - Jewish Info. Ser. of Greater Toronto [IO], Toronto, ON, Canada

UK Apitherapy Soc. [IO], Cheshunt, United Kingdom

UK Assn. of Online Publishers [IO], London, United Kingdom

UK Athletics [IO], Solihull, United Kingdom

UK Cleaning Products Indus. Assn. [IO], Chester, United Kingdom

UK Coalition of People Living with HIV and AIDS [IO], London, United Kingdom

UK Comm. for UNICEF [IO], London, United Kingdom

UK Coun. on Deafness [IO], Colchester, United Kingdom

UK eHealth Assn. [IO], Camberley, United Kingdom

UK Fashion Exports [IO], London, United Kingdom

UK Forest Products Assn. [IO], Stirling, United Kingdom

UK Inbound [IO], London, United Kingdom

UK Indus. Vision Assn. [IO], Royston, United Kingdom

U.K. Irrigation Assn. [IO], Lincoln, United Kingdom

UK Metric Assn. [IO], Glasgow, United Kingdom

UK Paruresis Assn. [★IO]

UK Paruresis Trust [IO], Kendal, United Kingdom

UK Public Hea. Assn. [IO], London, United Kingdom

UK Pyrotechnics Soc. [IO], Mirfield, United Kingdom

U.K. Sailing Acad. [IO], Isle of Wight, United Kingdom

UK Soc. of Investment Professionals [IO], London, United Kingdom

UK Soc. for Modelling and Simulation [IO], Nottingham, United Kingdom

UK Soc. for the Stud. of Dissociation [IO], Norwich, United Kingdom

UK Sports Assn. for People with Learning Disability [IO], London, United Kingdom

U.K. Spring Mfrs'. Assn. [★IO]

UK Steel [IO], London, United Kingdom

UK Steel Assn. [IO], London, United Kingdom

UK Steel Assn. [★IO]

UK Timber Frame Assn. [IO], Alloa, United Kingdom

UK Transplant [IO], Bristol, United Kingdom

UK Ultimate Assn. [IO], Leicester, United Kingdom

UK Web Design Assn. [IO], Fareham, United Kingdom

UK Windsurfing Assn. [IO], Haywards Heath, United Kingdom

UKCMG [IO], Watford, United Kingdom

Ukiyo-e Soc. of America - Address unknown since 2001.

UKOLUG - the UK Online User Gp. [★IO]

Ukraine

All-Ukrainian Evangelical Baptist Fellowship [19469]

Amer. Assn. for Ukrainian Stud. [8650]

Amers. for Human Rights in Ukraine [17744]

Ukrainian Acad. of Arts and Sciences in the U.S. [11063]

Ukrainian Educational Coun. [11064]

Ukrainian Engineers' Soc. of Am. [7050]

Ukrainian Inst. of Am. [11065]

Ukrainian Medical Assn. of North Am. [15182]

Ukrainian Philatelic and Numismatic Soc. [22883]

Ukraine Assn. of Cartoonists [IO], Kiev, Ukraine

Ukraine, the Baltic States and Eurasia; NCSJ: Advocates on Behalf of Jews in Russia, [17448]

Ukraine Floorball Fed. [IO], Kiev, Ukraine

Ukraine/Kiev Chap. of the Assn. of Energy Engineers [IO], Kiev, Ukraine

Ukraine Physiological Soc. [IO], Kiev, Ukraine

Ukraine School Sport Fed. [IO], Kiev, Ukraine

Ukraine Squash Fed. [IO], Kiev, Ukraine

Ukrainian

All-Ukrainian Evangelical Baptist Fellowship [19469]

Amer. Assn. for Ukrainian Stud. [8650]

Amers. for Human Rights in Ukraine [17744]

Assn. of United Ukrainian Canadians [IO]

League of Ukrainian Catholics of Am. [19411]

League of Ukrainian Canadian Women [IO]

Plast, Ukrainian Scouting Org. - U.S.A. [19412]

Providence Assn. of Ukrainian Catholics in Am. [19413]

Saint Andrew's Ukrainian Orthodox Soc. [18755]

Saint Andrew's Ukrainian Orthodox Soc. [IO]

Self Reliance Assn. of Amer. Ukrainians [19414]

Shevchenko Sci. Soc. [19415]

Shevchenko Sci. Soc. [IO]

Ukrainian Acad. of Arts and Sciences in the U.S. [IO]

Ukrainian Acad. of Arts and Sciences in the U.S. [11063]

Ukrainian Cong. Comm. of Am. [18756]

Ukrainian Cong. Comm. of Am. [IO]

Ukrainian Educational Coun. [IO]

Ukrainian Educational Coun. [11064]

Ukrainian Engineers' Soc. of Am. [7050]

Ukrainian Fraternal Assn. [19416]

Ukrainian Fraternal Assn. [IO]

Ukrainian Gold Cross [19417]

Ukrainian Inst. of Am. [11065]

Ukrainian Inst. of Am. [IO]

Ukrainian Medical Assn. of North Am. [15182]

Ukrainian Natl. Assn. [19418]

Ukrainian Natl. Info. Ser. [18757]

Ukrainian Natl. Info. Ser. [IO]

Ukrainian Natl. Women's League of Am. [19419]

Ukrainian Philatelic and Numismatic Soc. [22883]

U.S. - Ukraine Found. [18758]

U.S. - Ukraine Found. [IO]

United Ukrainian Amer. Relief Comm. [19420]

The Washington Gp. [19421]

Women's Assn. for the Defense of Four Freedoms for Ukraine [18759]

World Fed. of Ukrainian Women's Organizations [IO]

Ukrainian Acad. of Arts and Sciences in the U.S. [IO], New York, NY, United States

Ukrainian Acad. of Arts and Sciences in the U.S. [11063], 206 W 100 St., New York, NY 10021-1018, (212)222-1866

Ukrainian Amer. League - Address unknown since 2004.

Ukrainian Amer. Veterans [21326], PO Box 172, Holmdel, NJ 07733-0172, (732)888-0494

Ukrainian Amer. War Veterans [★21326]

Ukrainian Artists Assn. in U.S.A. - Address unknown since 1994.

Ukrainian Assn. of Automatic Control [IO], Kiev, Ukraine

Ukrainian Assn. of Dermatologists, Venereologists and Cosmetologists [IO], Kiev, Ukraine

Ukrainian Assn. of Furriers [IO], Kiev, Ukraine

Reference to "IO" in place of a book number signifies that the association may be found in the 45th edition of International Organizations.

Ukrainian Assn. of Orthodontists [IO], Lviv, Ukraine
Ukrainian Assn. on Osteoporosis [IO], Kiev, Ukraine
Ukrainian Assn. of Rheumatologists [IO], Kiev, Ukraine
Ukrainian Assn. of Software Developers [IO], Kiev, Ukraine
Ukrainian Athletic Fed. [IO], Kiev, Ukraine
Ukrainian Badminton Fed. [IO], Kiev, Ukraine
Ukrainian Catholic Students of the U.S. - Defunct.
Ukrainian Catholic Youth League [★19411]
Ukrainian Center for Independent Political Res. [IO], Kiev, Ukraine
Ukrainian Center for Intl. Security Stud. [IO], Kiev, Ukraine
Ukrainian Center for Social Res. [★IO]
Ukrainian Center for Social Res. [★11064]
Ukrainian Cong. Comm. of Am. [18756], 203 2nd Ave., New York, NY 10003, (212)228-6840
Ukrainian Cong. Comm. of Am. [IO], New York, NY, United States
Ukrainian Dance Sport Assn. [IO], Kiev, Ukraine
Ukrainian Democratic Club - Defunct.
Ukrainian Draughts Fed. [IO], Kiev, Ukraine
Ukrainian Economic Advisory Assn. - Defunct.
Ukrainian Educational Coun. [11064], PO Box 391, Cooper Sta., New York, NY 10276-0391, (212)477-1200
Ukrainian Educational Coun. [IO], New York, NY, United States
Ukrainian Energy Brigades [IO], Rivne, Ukraine
Ukrainian Engineers in Am; Soc. of [★7050]
Ukrainian Engineers' Soc. of Am. [7050], 2 E 79th St., New York, NY 10021
Ukrainian Evangelical Baptist Fellowship; All- [19469]
Ukrainian Figure Skating Fed. [IO], Kiev, Ukraine
Ukrainian Fraternal Assn. [IO], Scranton, PA, United States
Ukrainian Fraternal Assn. [19416], 371 N 9th Ave., Scranton, PA 18504-2005, (570)342-0937
Ukrainian Free Soc. of America - Address unknown since 1995.
Ukrainian Gerontology and Geriatrics Soc. [IO], Kiev, Ukraine
Ukrainian Gold Cross [19417]
Ukrainian Guild of Agri-journalists [IO], Kiev, Ukraine
Ukrainian Inst. of Am. [IO], New York, NY, United States
Ukrainian Inst. of Am. [11065], 2 E 79th St., New York, NY 10021, (212)288-8660
Ukrainian Internet Assn. [IO], Kiev, Ukraine
Ukrainian League Against Epilepsy [IO], Kiev, Ukraine
Ukrainian Legal Found. [IO], Kiev, Ukraine
Ukrainian Library Assn. of Am. - Address unknown since 2008.
Ukrainian Life Cooperative Assn. - Defunct.
Ukrainian Marketing Assn. [IO], Kiev, Ukraine
Ukrainian Medical Assn. of North Am. [15182], 2247 W Chicago Ave., Chicago, IL 60622, (888)RXU-MANA
Ukrainian Medical Soc; Amer. [★15182]
Ukrainian Mineralogical Soc. [IO], Kiev, Ukraine
Ukrainian Natl. Aid Assn. of America - Address unknown since 2004.
Ukrainian Natl. Assn. [19418], 2200 Rte. 10 W, Parsippany, NJ 07054, (973)292-9800
Ukrainian Natl. Info. Ser. [18757], 311 Massachusetts Ave. NE, Washington, DC 20002, (202)547-0018
Ukrainian Natl. Info. Ser. [IO], Washington, DC, United States
Ukrainian Natl. Sportive Billiard Fed. [IO], Kiev, Ukraine
Ukrainian Natl. Women's League of Am. [19419], 203 2nd Ave., New York, NY 10003, (212)533-4646
Ukrainian Patriarchal World Fed. [19730]
Ukrainian Philatelic and Numismatic Soc. [22883], PO Box 3, Springfield, VA 22150-0003
Ukrainian Philatelic and Numismatic Soc. [IO], Springfield, VA, United States
Ukrainian Philatelists; Soc. of [★22883]
Ukrainian Physical Soc. [IO], Kiev, Ukraine
Ukrainian Political Science Assn. in the U.S. - Address unknown since 1999.

Ukrainian Res. and Documentation Center [★11065]
Ukrainian Res. and Documentation Center [★IO]
Ukrainian Res. Found. - Defunct.
Ukrainian Res. and Information Inst. - Defunct.
Ukrainian Soc. of Cardiology [IO], Kiev, Ukraine
Ukrainian Soc. of Gastrointestinal Endoscopy [IO], Kiev, Ukraine
Ukrainian Soc. of Photogrammetry and Remote Sensing [IO], Lviv, Ukraine
Ukrainian Taekwondo Fed. [IO], Kharkov, Ukraine
Ukrainian Tennis Fed. [IO], Kiev, Ukraine
Ukrainian Weightlifting Fed. [IO], Kiev, Ukraine
Ukrainian Workingmen's Assn. [★IO]
Ukrainian Workingmen's Assn. [★19416]
Ukrainian Youth Assn. of America - Defunct.
Ukrainian Youth Hostels Assn. [IO], Kiev, Ukraine
Ukrainian Youth League of America - Defunct.
Ukrains'ke Mineralogichne Tovarystvo [★IO]
Ulcer Advisory Panel; Natl. Pressure [14657]
ULI Found. [18777], 1025 Thomas Jefferson St. NW, Ste. 500 W, Washington, DC 20007, (202)624-7000
Ulster Archaeological Soc. [IO], Belfast, United Kingdom
Ulster Architectural Heritage Soc. [IO], Belfast, United Kingdom
Ulster Cancer Found. [IO], Belfast, United Kingdom
Ulster Farmers' Union [IO], Belfast, United Kingdom
Ulster Folk Life Soc. [★IO]
Ulster Folk and Transport Museum [IO], Holywood, United Kingdom
Ulster Historical Found. [IO], Belfast, United Kingdom
Ulster-Irish Soc. - Address unknown since 1995.
Ulster-Scot Historical Soc. [★IO]
Ulster-Scots Language Soc. [IO], Belfast, United Kingdom
Ulster-Scots Soc. of Am. [21154], c/o Glen Pratt, Pres., PO Box 3969, Amarillo, TX 79116
Ulster Soc. of Organists and Choirmasters [IO], Belfast, United Kingdom
Ulster Teachers' Union [IO], Belfast, United Kingdom
Ultimate Players Assn. [23375], 4730 Table Mesa Dr., Ste. J-200, Boulder, CO 80305, (303)447-3472
Ultimatism
  Ultimatist Religious Bodies on Earth [20598]
  Ultimatist Religious Bodies on Earth [IO]
Ultimatist Life Society [★IO]
Ultimatist Life Society [★20598]
Ultimatist Life Soc. - Address unknown since 1989.
Ultimatist Religious Bodies on Earth [20598]
Ultimatist Religious Bodies on Earth [IO], Erie, PA, United States
Ultra Marathon Cycling Association [IO], Boulder, CO, United States
Ultra Marathon Cycling Assn. [23318], PO Box 18028, Boulder, CO 80308-1028
Ultralight Assn; EAA [21441]
Ultralight Assn; U.S. [21486]
Ultralight Flight Org. - Address unknown since 1995.
Ultrasonic Indus. Assn. [3490], PO Box 2307, Dayton, OH 45401-2307, (937)586-3725
Ultrasonic Indus. Coun. [★3490]
Ultrasonic Mfrs. Assn. [★3490]
Ultrasonics, Ferroelectrics, and Frequency Control Soc; IEEE [6366]
Ultrasonics Soc; IEEE Sonics and [★6366]
Ultrasound
  Amer. Assn. for Ophthalmic Standardized Echography [15659]
  Amer. Inst. of Ultrasound in Medicine [16436]
  Amer. Registry of Diagnostic Medical Sonography [16437]
  European Soc. of Sonochemistry [IO]
  Intl. Veterinary Ultrasound Soc. [16797]
  Joint Rev. Comm. on Educ. in Diagnostic Medical Sonography [8837]
  Musculoskeletal Ultrasound Soc. [16696]
  Musculoskeletal Ultrasound Soc. [IO]
  Soc. of Diagnostic Medical Sonography [16438]
  Soc. of Radiologists in Ultrasound [16303]
  Ultrasonic Indus. Assn. [3490]
Ultrasound in Medicine; Amer. Inst. of [16436]
Ultrasound in Medicine; Australasian Soc. for [IO]
Ultrasound in Medicine and Biology; European Fed. of Societies for [IO]

Ultrasound in Obstetrics and Gynecology; Intl. Soc. of [IO]
Ultrasound Soc; British Medical [IO]
Ultrasound; Soc. for Vascular [16731]
Ultrasound Tech. Specialists; Amer. Soc. of [★16438]
Ultrastructural Pathology; Soc. for [15877]
Ulusal Travma ve Acil Cerrahi Dernegi [★IO]
Uluslararasi Mavi Hilal [★IO]
Ulysses S. Grant Assn. [11154], Southern Illinois Univ., Morris Lib., Carbondale, IL 62901, (618)453-2773
Umanotera, Slovenian Found. for Sustainable Development [IO], Ljubljana, Slovenia
Umanotera, Slovenska fundacija za trajnostni razvoj, ustanova [★IO]
Umbrella Assn. of German Pig Production [IO], Bonn, Germany
Umpires' Assn; Amateur Baseball [23798]
Umpires Assn; World [24019]
Umuleri Progressive Assn. of North Am. - Address unknown since 2004.
Umuryango w'Abasoma Bibiliya [★IO]
Umuryango w'Abasoma Bibliya mu Rwanda [★IO]
Un-Jap Two-Stroke Club - Defunct.
U.N. Office for Emergency Operations in Africa - Defunct.
U.N. Reform Electoral Campaign Comm. [★18762]
UN Sys. Network on Rural Development and Food Security [IO], Rome, Italy
UNA Intl. Ser. [IO], York, United Kingdom
Una Voce in the U.S. - Defunct.
UNAIDS - Joint United Nations Programme on HIV/AIDS [IO], Geneva, Switzerland
Unarius Acad. of Sci. [IO], El Cajon, CA, United States
Unarius Acad. of Sci. [12366], 145 S Magnolia Ave., El Cajon, CA 92020-4522, (619)444-7062
Unarius Educational Found. [★12366]
Unarius Educational Found. [★IO]
Unclaimed Property Administrators; Assn. of [★6186]
Unclaimed Property Administrators; Natl. Assn. of [6186]
U.N.C.L.E. HQ Inc. [★25036]
U.N.C.L.E. HQ [25044], c/o Brian Collins, 1903 60th Pl. E, Ste. M4391, Bradenton, FL 34203
Uncle Remus Museum [9717], PO Box 184, Eaton-ton, GA 31024, (706)485-6856
An Uncommon Legacy Found. [17658], c/o Kim Hoover, Mgr., PO Box 33727, Washington, DC 20033, (202)309-5209
Unconscious; Assn. for Philosophy of the [10786]
The Unconservatory [10714], 8035 SW 26th St., Miami, FL 33155, (305)266-9673
UNDA U.S.A. Natl. Catholic Assn. for Communicators [★9761]
Undeb Badminton Cymru [★IO]
Undeb Rygbi Cymru [★IO]
Under Thirty Group for Transit - Defunct.
Undercover Officers; Intl. Assn. of [5976]
Underfashion Club [258], 326 Field Rd., Clinton Corners, NY 12514, (845)758-6405
Undergarment Accessories Assn. - Defunct.
Undergarment Assn; Greater Blouse, Skirt and [237]
Undergraduate Philosophy Assn. [8971], 313 Waggener Hall, Dept. of Philosophy, Univ. of Texas, Austin, TX 78712, (512)475-9185
Undergraduate Res; Coun. on [9059]
Undergraduate Res; Natl. Conferences on [9062]
Undergraduate Res. Participation Program - Defunct.
Underground Constr. Assn; Amer. [7715]
Underground Engg. Contractors' Assn. [★1015]
Underground Evangelism Intl. - Address unknown since 2000.
Underground Injection Practices Coun. [★3994]
Underground Security Storage Assn. - Defunct.
Underground Technology Res. Coun. Education Comm. - Address unknown since 1994.
Underground Trans. Res. Assn. [IO], Cologne, Germany
Underground Utilities; NASSCO - Setting the Indus. Standards for the Rehabilitation of [3959]
Underprivileged Students of Anthropological Vocations [9079]

A star before a book entry number signifies that the name is not listed separately, but is mentioned within the entry.

Undersea and Hyperbaric Medical Soc. [16697], 21 W Colony Pl., Ste. 280, Durham, NC 27705, (919)490-5140

Undersea Medical Soc. [★16697]

Undersea Medicine
European Underwater and BaroMedical Soc. [IO]
South Pacific Underwater Medicine Soc. [IO]
Undersea and Hyperbaric Medical Soc. [16697]

Underserved; Assn. of Clinicians for the [14616]

Understanding Aging; Center for [★11297]

Underwater Photography Instruction Assn. - Defunct.

Underwater Soc. of Am. [23966], PO Box 628, Daly City, CA 94017, (650)583-8492

Underwater Spearfishing Assn; Intl. [23418]

Underwater Sports
Assn. of Commercial Diving Educators [23960]
Assn. of Dive Prog. Administrators [23377]
Historical Diving Soc. USA [23576]
Hong Kong Underwater Assn. [IO]
Inst. of Diving [23961]
Intl. Swimming Hall of Fame [23886]
Natl. Assn. for Cave Diving [23962]
Natl. Assn. of Underwater Instructors [23963]
Professional Assn. of Diving Instructors [23964]
Professional Assn. of Diving Instructors [IO]
Recreational Scuba Training Coun. [23965]
Underwater Soc. of Am. [23966]
U.S. Apnea Assn. [23380]

Underwear-Negligee Associates - Address unknown since 1994.

Underwriter Soc; Chartered Property Casualty [★2160]

Underwriter Training Coun; Life [8576]

Underwriters
Amer. Inst. of Marine Underwriters [2138]
Amer. Nuclear Insurers [3948]
Assn. for Advanced Life Underwriting [2144]
Consumer Credit Industry Association [2158]
CPCU Soc. [2160]
Environmental Risk Resources Assn. [4563]
Gp. Underwriters Assn. of Am. [2167]
Inland Marine Underwriters Assn. [2170]
Natl. Assn. of Hea. Underwriters [2208]
Natl. Assn. of Insurance and Financial Advisors [2212]
Natl. Assn. of Rev. Appraisers and Mortgage Underwriters [3329]
Surety and Fidelity Assn. of Am. [2245]
Underwriters Labs. [3459]
Women in Insurance and Financial Services [2247]

Underwriters; Amer. Inst. for Chartered Property Casualty [★2137]

Underwriters; Amer. Inst. of Marine [2138]

Underwriters; Amer. Inst. for Property and Liability [★2137]

Underwriters; Assn. of Home Off. [2148]

Underwriters Assn; Home Off. Life [★2148]

Underwriters Assn; Inland Marine [2170]

Underwriters Assn; Intermediaries and Reinsurance [2185]

Underwriters Confed; Women Life [★2247]

Underwriters Conf. of the Natl. Assn. of Life Underwriters; Women Life [★2247]

Underwriters Grain Assn. - Address unknown since 1995.

Underwriters; Intl. Assn. of Accident and Hea. [★2208]

Underwriters; Intl. Assn. of Hea. [★2208]

Underwriters Labs. [3459], 333 Pfingsten Rd., Northbrook, IL 60062-2096, (847)272-8800

Underwriters' Labs. of Canada [IO], Toronto, ON, Canada

Underwriters; Mutual Atomic Energy Liability [2201]

Underwriters; Natl. Assn. of Accident and Hea. [★2208]

Underwriters; Natl. Assn. of Hea. [2208]

Underwriters; Natl. Assn. of Life [★2212]

Underwriters; Natl. Assn. of Rev. Appraisers and Mortgage [3329]

Underwriters; Natl. Bd. of Fire [★2139]

Underwriters of New York; Bur. of Inspection of Bd. of [★3576]

Underwriters of San Francisco; Bd. of Marine [★3576]

Underwriters; Soc. of Chartered Property and Casualty [★2160]

Underwriting; Academy Life [★2148]

Underwriting; Academy Life [★IO]

Underwriting; Assn. for Advanced Life [2144]

Unemployment
AARP [12895]
ACCION Intl. [17205]
Intl. Assn. of Workforce Professionals [5679]
A Job is a Right Campaign [12083]
Milton S. Eisenhower Found. [11839]
Natl. Assn. of State Workforce Agencies [5680]
Natl. Assn. of Unemployment Insurance Appellate Boards [5831]
Natl. Employment Law Proj. [12092]
UWC - Strategic Services on Unemployment and Workers' Compensation [13348]
W. E. Upjohn Inst. for Employment Res. [12104]
Welfare to Work Partnership [13146]
Wildcat Ser. Corp. [12107]
Work Fairness [12110]

Unemployment Compensation Agencies; Interstate Conf. of [★5680]

Unemployment Compensation and Workers Compensation; Natl. Found. for [5681]

Unemployment and Poverty Action Comm. - Address unknown since 1991.

Unemployment and Workers' Compensation and the Natl. Found. for UC & WC; Strategic Services on [★13348]

Unemployment and Workers' Compensation; UWC - Strategic Services on [13348]

UNESCO; Americans for [18760]

UNESCO; Americans for the Universality of [★18760]

UNESCO-ASCHBERG Bursaries for Artists Programme [IO], Paris, France

UNESCO Association/U.S.A. [IO], Oakland, CA, United States

UNESCO Association/U.S.A. [18768], 5815 Lawton Ave., Oakland, CA 94618-1510, (510)654-4638

UNESCO Club - Malta [IO], Hamrun, Malta

UNESCO Co-Action Programme [IO], Paris, France

UNESCO Co-Operative Action Programme [★IO]

UNESCO-IHE Inst. for Water Educ. [IO], Delft, Netherlands

UNESCO Inst. for Educ. [★IO]

UNESCO Inst. for Lifelong Learning [IO], Hamburg, Germany

UNESCO Regional Bur. for Sci. in Europe [IO], Venice, Italy

UNESCO Regional Off. for Sci. and Tech. for Europe [★IO]

Unevangelized Fields Missions [★IO]

Unevangelized Fields Missions [★20326]

Unexpected Wildlife Refuge [11467], c/o The New Beaver Defenders, PO Box 765, Newfield, NJ 08344-0765, (856)697-3541

Unfinished Furniture Assn. [1707], 15000 Commerce Pkwy., Ste. C, Mount Laurel, NJ 08054, (800)487-8321

Unger Vetlesen Found; G. [12719]

Uni-Bell Plastic Pipe Assn. [★3041]

Uni-Bell Plastic Pipe Assn. [★IO]

Uni-Bell PVC Pipe Association [IO], Dallas, TX, United States

Uni-Bell PVC Pipe Assn. [3041], 2711 LBJ Fwy., Ste. 1000, Dallas, TX 75234, (972)243-3902

Uni-Ops - Defunct.

Unia Wolnosci [★IO]

Uniao Biblica Mocambique [IO], Maputo, Mozambique

Uniao Brasileira de Compositores [★IO]

Uniao Cultural Brasil Estados Unidos [★IO]

Uniao da Geomorfologia Brasileira [★IO]

Uniao Portuguesa Continental do Estado da California [★19131]

UNICEF - Afghanistan [IO], Herat, Afghanistan

UNICEF - Albania [IO], Tirana, Albania

UNICEF - Algeria [IO], Algiers, Algeria

UNICEF - Angola [IO], Luanda, Angola

UNICEF - Antigua and Barbuda [IO], Bridgetown, Barbados

UNICEF - Argentina [IO], Buenos Aires, Argentina

UNICEF Austria [IO], Vienna, Austria

UNICEF - Azerbaijan [IO], Baku, Azerbaijan

UNICEF - Bahrain [IO], Riyadh, Saudi Arabia

UNICEF - Bangladesh [IO], Dhaka, Bangladesh

UNICEF - Barbados [IO], Bridgetown, Barbados

UNICEF - Belarus [IO], Minsk, Belarus

UNICEF Belgium [IO], Brussels, Belgium

UNICEF - Belize [IO], Belize City, Belize

UNICEF - Benin [IO], Cotonou, Benin

UNICEF - Bhutan [IO], Thimphu, Bhutan

UNICEF - Bolivia [IO], La Paz, Bolivia

UNICEF Bolivia [IO], Cochabamba, Bolivia

UNICEF - Bosnia and Herzegovina [IO], Sarajevo, Bosnia-Hercegovina

UNICEF, Brazil-Brasilia [IO], Brasilia, Brazil

UNICEF - Brazil-Fortaleza [IO], Fortaleza, Brazil

UNICEF - Brazil-Recife [IO], Recife, Brazil

UNICEF - Brazil-Rio de Janeiro [IO], Rio de Janeiro, Brazil

UNICEF, Brazil-Salvador [IO], Salvador, Brazil

UNICEF - Brazil-Sao Luis [IO], Sao Luis, Brazil

UNICEF - Bulgaria [IO], Sofia, Bulgaria

UNICEF - Burkina Faso [IO], Ouagadougou, Burkina Faso

UNICEF - Burundi [IO], Bujumbura, Burundi

UNICEF - Cambodia [IO], Phnom Penh, Cambodia

UNICEF - Cameroon [IO], Yaounde, Cameroon

UNICEF Canada [IO], Toronto, ON, Canada

UNICEF - Cape Verde [IO], Praia, Cape Verde

UNICEF - Central African Republic [IO], Bangui, Central African Republic

UNICEF - Chad [IO], N'Djamena, Chad

UNICEF - Chile [IO], Santiago, Chile

UNICEF - China [IO], Beijing, People's Republic of China

UNICEF; Citizens Comm. for [★11658]

UNICEF - Colombia [IO], Bogota, Colombia

UNICEF - Comoros [IO], Moroni, Comoros

UNICEF - Costa Rica [IO], San Jose, Costa Rica

UNICEF - Cote d'Ivoire [IO], Abidjan, Cote d'Ivoire

UNICEF - Croatia [IO], Zagreb, Croatia

UNICEF - Cuba [IO], Havana, Cuba

UNICEF - Czech Republic [IO], Prague, Czech Republic

UNICEF Denmark [IO], Copenhagen, Denmark

UNICEF - Djibouti [IO], Djibouti, Djibouti

UNICEF - Dominican Republic [IO], Santo Domingo, Dominican Republic

UNICEF - Ecuador [IO], Quito, Ecuador

UNICEF - Egypt [IO], Cairo, Egypt

UNICEF - El Salvador [IO], San Salvador, El Salvador

UNICEF - Equatorial Guinea [IO], Malabo, Equatorial Guinea

UNICEF - Estonia [IO], Tallinn, Estonia

UNICEF - Ethiopia [IO], Addis Ababa, Ethiopia

UNICEF - Fiji [IO], Suva, Fiji

UNICEF - Finland [IO], Helsinki, Finland

UNICEF - France [IO], Paris, France

UNICEF - Gabon [IO], Libreville, Gabon

UNICEF - Gambia [IO], Banjul, Gambia

UNICEF - Georgia [IO], Tbilisi, Georgia

UNICEF Germany [IO], Cologne, Germany

UNICEF - Ghana [IO], Accra, Ghana

UNICEF - Greece [IO], Athens, Greece

UNICEF - Grenada [IO], Bridgetown, Barbados

UNICEF - Guatemala [IO], Guatemala City, Guatemala

UNICEF - Guinea [IO], Conakry, Guinea

UNICEF - Guinea-Bissau [IO], Bissau, Guinea-Bissau

UNICEF - Guyana [IO], Georgetown, Guyana

UNICEF Hungary [IO], Budapest, Hungary

UNICEF - Iceland [IO], Reykjavik, Iceland

UNICEF Ireland [IO], Dublin, Ireland

UNICEF - Israel [IO], Jerusalem, Israel

UNICEF Japan [IO], Tokyo, Japan

UNICEF Jordan [IO], Amman, Jordan

UNICEF Latvia [IO], Riga, Latvia

UNICEF Lithuania [IO], Vilnius, Lithuania

UNICEF Luxembourg [IO], Luxembourg, Luxembourg

UNICEF - Madagascar [IO], Antananarivo, Madagascar

UNICEF - Malawi [IO], Lilongwe, Malawi

UNICEF - Malaysia [IO], Kuala Lumpur, Malaysia

Reference to "IO" in place of a book number signifies that the association may be found in the 45th edition of International Organizations.

UNICEF - Mali **[IO]**, Bamako, Mali
UNICEF - Mauritania **[IO]**, Nouakchott, Mauritania
UNICEF Mauritius **[IO]**, Port Louis, Mauritius
UNICEF - Mexico **[IO]**, Mexico City, Mexico
UNICEF - Mongolian **[IO]**, Ulan Bator, Mongolia
UNICEF - Mozambique **[IO]**, Maputo, Mozambique
UNICEF - Myanmar **[IO]**, Yangon, Myanmar
UNICEF - Nepal **[IO]**, Kathmandu, Nepal
UNICEF - Netherlands **[IO]**, The Hague, Netherlands
UNICEF New Zealand **[IO]**, Wellington, New Zealand
UNICEF - Nicaragua **[IO]**, Managua, Nicaragua
UNICEF - Niger **[IO]**, Niamey, Niger
UNICEF - Nigeria **[IO]**, Abuja, Nigeria
UNICEF; Non-Governmental Organizations Comm. on **[18766]**
UNICEF Norway **[IO]**, Oslo, Norway
UNICEF - Oman **[IO]**, Muscat, Oman
UNICEF - Pakistan **[IO]**, Islamabad, Pakistan
UNICEF - Panama **[IO]**, Panama City, Panama
UNICEF - Papua New Guinea **[IO]**, Port Moresby, Papua New Guinea
UNICEF - Paraguay **[IO]**, Asuncion, Paraguay
UNICEF - Peru **[IO]**, Lima, Peru
UNICEF - Philippines **[IO]**, Makati City, Philippines
UNICEF - Poland **[IO]**, Warsaw, Poland
UNICEF - Portugal **[IO]**, Lisbon, Portugal
UNICEF - Republic of the Congo **[IO]**, Brazzaville, Republic of the Congo
UNICEF Republic of Korea **[IO]**, Seoul, Republic of Korea
UNICEF - Republic of Moldova **[IO]**, Chisinau, Moldova
UNICEF - Romania **[IO]**, Bucharest, Romania
UNICEF - Russia **[IO]**, Moscow, Russia
UNICEF - Rwanda **[IO]**, Kigali, Rwanda
UNICEF San Marino **[IO]**, San Marino, San Marino
UNICEF - Saudi Arabia **[IO]**, Riyadh, Saudi Arabia
UNICEF - Senegal **[IO]**, Dakar, Senegal
UNICEF Slovakia **[IO]**, Bratislava, Slovakia
UNICEF Somalia **[IO]**, Nairobi, Kenya
UNICEF - South Africa **[IO]**, Pretoria, Republic of South Africa
UNICEF - Spain **[IO]**, Madrid, Spain
UNICEF - Sri Lanka **[IO]**, Colombo, Sri Lanka
UNICEF - Sudan **[IO]**, Khartoum, Sudan
UNICEF Sverige **[★IO]**
UNICEF - Swaziland **[IO]**, Mbabane, Swaziland
UNICEF - Sweden **[IO]**, Stockholm, Sweden
UNICEF - Switzerland **[IO]**, Zurich, Switzerland
UNICEF - Syria **[IO]**, Damascus, Syrian Arab Republic
UNICEF - Tajikistan **[IO]**, Dushanbe, Tajikistan
UNICEF - Thailand **[IO]**, Bangkok, Thailand
UNICEF - Togo **[IO]**, Lome, Togo
UNICEF - Tunisia **[IO]**, Tunis, Tunisia
UNICEF Tunisie **[★IO]**
UNICEF - Turkey **[IO]**, Ankara, Turkey
UNICEF Turkey Natl. Comm. **[IO]**, Ankara, Turkey
UNICEF - Uganda **[IO]**, Kampala, Uganda
UNICEF - Ukraine **[IO]**, Kiev, Ukraine
UNICEF United Kingdom **[IO]**, London, United Kingdom
UNICEF - United Republic of Tanzania **[IO]**, Dar es Salaam, United Republic of Tanzania
UNICEF - Uruguay **[IO]**, Montevideo, Uruguay
UNICEF - Uzbekistan **[IO]**, Tashkent, Uzbekistan
UNICEF - Vanuatu **[IO]**, Port Vila, Vanuatu
UNICEF - Venezuela **[IO]**, Caracas, Venezuela
UNICEF - Vietnam **[IO]**, Hanoi, Vietnam
UNICEF - Yemen **[IO]**, Sana'a, Yemen
UNICEF - Zambia **[IO]**, Lusaka, Zambia
UNICEF - Zimbabwe **[IO]**, Harare, Zimbabwe
Unico **[★19169]**
Unico Foundation **[★19169]**
Unico Natl. **[19169]**, 271 US Hwy. 46 W, Ste. A-108, Fairfield, NJ 07004, (973)808-0035
Unicode Consortium **[18683]**, c/o Magda Danish, Sr. Admin. Dir., Microsoft Bldg. 5, 1065 L'Avenida St., Mountain View, CA 94043, (650)693-3921
Unicorn Users Gp. Intl. **[7214]**, c/o Old Colony Lib. Network, 220 Forbes Rd., Ste. 401, Braintree, MA 02184
Unicorns Unanimous - Defunct.
Unicycling Soc. of Am. **[23319]**, PO Box 21487, Minneapolis, MN 55421-0487

Unicyclist's Assn. of Am. **[★23319]**
Unidentified Flying Objects; Natl. Investigations Comm. on **[7482]**
Unidentified Spheres of Light - Address unknown since 2004.
UNIDO Center for Regional Cooperation in Turkey **[IO]**, Ankara, Turkey
Unie der Belgische Adverteerders **[★IO]**
Unie der Designers in Belgie **[★IO]**
Unie van Soroptimist Clubs in Nederland, Suriname en de Nederlandse Antillen **[IO]**, Amsterdam, Netherlands
Unie van de Uitgevers van de Periodieke Pers **[★IO]**
Unie Vydavatelu **[★IO]**
UNIFEM Natl. Comm. Japan **[IO]**, Kanagawa, Japan
UNIFEM New Zealand **[IO]**, Wellington, New Zealand
Unified Abrasives Mfrs'. Assn. **[2567]**, 30200 Detroit Rd., Cleveland, OH 44145-1967, (440)899-0010
Unified Abrasives Mfrs'. Assn. - Grain Div. **[2074]**, 30200 Detroit Rd., Cleveland, OH 44145-1967, (440)899-0010
Unified Abrasives Mfrs'. Assn. - Superabrasives Div. **[2075]**, 30200 Detroit Rd., Cleveland, OH 44145-1967, (440)899-0010
Unified Independent Party; Comm. for a **[18321]**
Unified Sci; Center for **[★9102]**
Unified Sci. Educ; Fed. for **[9102]**
Uniform Boiler and Pressure Vessel Laws Soc. - Address unknown since 2006.
Uniform Code Coun. **[★337]**
Uniform Collectors; Assn. of Amer. Military **[22628]**
Uniform Grocery Prdt. Code Coun. **[★337]**
Uniform Law Commissioners **[★6282]**
Uniform Manufacturers and Distributors; Natl. Assn. of **[248]**
Uniform Manufacturers Exchange **[★248]**
Uniform Prdt. Code Coun. **[★337]**
Uniform Reciprocal Enforcement of Support; Natl. Conf. on **[★5701]**
Uniform State Laws; Natl. Conf. of Commissioners on **[6282]**
Uniform and Textile Ser. Assn. **[2408]**, 1501 Lee Hwy., Ste. 304, Arlington, VA 22209, (703)247-2600
Uniform Traffic Accident Statistics; Comm. on **[★12993]**
Uniform Traffic Accidents Statistics; Natl. Comm. on **[★12993]**
Uniform Traffic Laws and Ordinances; Natl. Comm. on **[6309]**
Uniformed Div. Retirement Assn; U.S. Secret Ser. **[6009]**
Uniformed Services Acad. of Family Physicians **[15268]**, 1503 Santa Rosa Rd., Richmond, VA 23229, (804)968-4436
Uniformed Services Former Spouses Protection Act (USFSPA) Law; Alliance Against the **[6112]**
Uniformed Services; Natl. Assn. for **[6086]**
Uniformed Services Retirees; Natl. Assn. for **[★6086]**
Uniformology Soc. - Defunct.
UniForum Assn. **[6805]**, PO Box 3177, Annapolis, MD 21403, (410)715-9500
UniForum Assn. **[IO]**, Annapolis, MD, United States
UniForum New Zealand **[IO]**, Wellington, New Zealand
Uniions Chretiennes Feminines du Cameroun **[★IO]**
UNIMA **[IO]**, Charleville-Mezieres, France
UNIMA-U.S.A., American Center of the Union Internationale de la Marionnette **[IO]**, Atlanta, GA, United States
UNIMA-U.S.A., Amer. Center of the Union Internationale de la Marionnette **[22916]**, c/o Vincent Anthony, Gen. Sec., 1404 Spring St. NW, Atlanta, GA 30309-2820, (404)873-3089
Uninsured; Cover the **[14960]**
Unio de Radioaficionats Andorrans **[★IO]**
Union mondiale des societes catholiques de philosophie **[★IO]**
Union europeenne de et des petites et moyennes enterprises **[★IO]**
Union europeenne des veterinaires praticiens **[★IO]**
Union Africaine des Aveugles **[★IO]**
Union for African Population Stud. **[IO]**, Accra, Ghana

Union de Agencias de Viajes **[★IO]**
Union of Agrarian Cooperators of Albania **[IO]**, Tirana, Albania
Union Aid Abroad - Australian People for Hea., Educ. and Development Abroad **[IO]**, Sydney, Australia
Union of Amer. Biological Societies - Defunct.
Union of Amer. Hebrew Congregations; Religious Action Center of the **[★17954]**
Union of Amer. Physicians and Dentists **[★24092]**
Union of Amer. Physicians and Dentists **[24092]**, 180 Grand Ave., Ste. 1380, Oakland, CA 94612, (510)839-0193
Union des Annnonceurs **[IO]**, Paris, France
Union Arabe de Ciment et des Materiaux de Constr. **[★IO]**
Union of Architects in Bulgaria **[IO]**, Sofia, Bulgaria
Union of Architects of Romania **[IO]**, Bucharest, Romania
Union of Architects of Russia **[IO]**, Moscow, Russia
Union of Armenians of Anteb in America - Defunct.
Union Army of Commemoration - Defunct.
Union des Artistes de la Reunion **[IO]**, St.-Denis, France
Union de Asociaciones de Estanqueros de Espana **[★IO]**
Union Assn; Intl. Telephone Credit **[★1110]**
Union des Associations de Boissons des Pays Membres de l' UE **[★IO]**
Union des Associations Europeennes de Football **[★IO]**
Union of Associations of Slovene Librarians **[IO]**, Ljubljana, Slovenia
Union des Assurances du Burkina **[★IO]**
Union Astronomique Internationale **[★IO]**
Union; Atlantic Independent **[24161]**
Union of Australian Women **[IO]**, Melbourne, Australia
Union des Avocats Europeens **[★IO]**
Union Belge des Annonceurs **[IO]**, Brussels, Belgium
Union of Belgian Brewers **[IO]**, Brussels, Belgium
Union Biblica Argentina **[IO]**, Buenos Aires, Argentina
Union Biblica Chilena **[IO]**, Santiago, Chile
Union Biblica de Colombia **[IO]**, Barranquilla, Colombia
Union Biblica Ecuatorina **[IO]**, Quito, Ecuador
Union of Black Episcopalians - Defunct.
Union Bouddhique d'Europe **[★IO]**
Union of Brazilian Composers **[IO]**, Rio de Janeiro, Brazil
Union of Bulgarian Artists **[IO]**, Sofia, Bulgaria
Union of Bulgarian Composers **[IO]**, Sofia, Bulgaria
Union of Bulgarian Motorists **[IO]**, Sofia, Bulgaria
Union of Canadian Trans. Employees **[IO]**, Ottawa, ON, Canada
Union of Catholic Asian News **[IO]**, Hong Kong, People's Republic of China
Union Catholique Internationale de la Presse **[★IO]**
Union of Chemists in Bulgaria **[IO]**, Sofia, Bulgaria
Union Chretienne Feminine **[★IO]**
Union Chretienne de Jeunes Gens du Senegal **[★IO]**
Union Chretienne des Pensionnes **[IO]**, Brussels, Belgium
Union of Civil Servants **[IO]**, Stockholm, Sweden
Union; Coast Seamen's **[★24131]**
Union of Concerned Scientists **[18137]**, 2 Brattle Sq., Cambridge, MA 02238-9105, (617)547-5552
Union of Constr., Allied Trades and Technicians - United Kingdom **[IO]**, London, United Kingdom
Union Constructors; NEA - The Assn. of **[1056]**
Union Control of Govt; Americans Against **[17979]**
Union des Cooperatives des Planteurs de Tabac de France **[★IO]**
Union for the Coordination of Transmission of Electricity **[IO]**, Brussels, Belgium
Union pour la Coordination du Transport de l'Electricite **[★IO]**
Union Costarricense de Camaras y Asociaciones de la Empresa Privada **[★IO]**
Union Coun; Natl. Independent **[★24210]**
Union of Councils **[★17452]**
Union of Councils **[★IO]**
Union of Councils for Jews in the Former Soviet Union **[IO]**, Washington, DC, United States

A star before a book entry number signifies that the name is not listed separately, but is mentioned within the entry.

Union of Councils for Jews in the Former Soviet Union [17452], PO Box 11676, Cleveland Park, Washington, DC 20008, (202)237-8262
Union of Councils for Soviet Jews [★17452]
Union of Councils for Soviet Jews [IO]
Union Cycliste Internationale [★IO]
Union of Czech Mathematicians and Physicists [IO], Prague, Czech Republic
Union of Czech and Moravian Producer Co-Operatives [IO], Prague, Czech Republic
Union of the Deaf in Bulgaria [IO], Sofia, Bulgaria
Union Democracy; Assn. for [24113]
Union for Democratic Communications [17196], c/o Jennifer Proffitt, Dept. of Commun., Florida State Univ., Univ. Ctr., Bldg. C, Ste. 3100, Tallahassee, FL 32306-2664, (850)644-8748
Union for Democratic Communications [IO], Tallahassee, FL, United States
Union of Democratic Thais in the U.S. - Address unknown since 1995.
Union Democratique Bretonne [★IO]
Union of Denturists in Finland [IO], Helsinki, Finland
Union Des Artistes [★IO]
Union of Designers in Belgium [IO], Brussels, Belgium
Union of Economists of Slovenia [IO], Ljubljana, Slovenia
Union des Editeurs de la Presse Periodique [IO], Brussels, Belgium
Union of EEC Soft Drinks Assn. [★IO]
Union of the Elec. Indus. - EURELECTRIC [IO], Brussels, Belgium
Union of Estonian Breweries [IO], Viljandi, Estonia
Union of Estonian Emergency Medical Services [IO], Tartu, Estonia
Union of Estonian Psychologists [IO], Tartu, Estonia
Union of EU Soft Drinks Associations [★IO]
Union of European Beverages Assn. [IO], Brussels, Belgium
Union of European Chambers of Commerce and Indus. of the Rhine, Rhone, Danube and the Alps [IO], Basel, Switzerland
Union of European Football Associations [IO], Nyon, Switzerland
Union of European Historic Houses Associations [IO], Brussels, Belgium
Union of European Mfrs. of Gas Meters [★IO]
Union of European Non-Alcoholic Beverages Assn. [★IO]
Union of European Railway Indus. [IO], Brussels, Belgium
Union of European Tax Advisor Associations [★IO]
Union Europeene de Judo [★IO]
Union Europeenne des Associations Nationales de Services d'Eau [★IO]
Union Europeenne des Aveugles [★IO]
Union Europeenne des Cadres du Tourisme [★IO]
Union Europeenne de la Carrosserie [★IO]
Union Europeenne du Commerce du Betail et de la Viande [★IO]
Union Europeenne du Commerce des Produits Laitiers et Derives [★IO]
Union Europeenne Des Medecins Specialistes [★IO]
Union Europeenne des Entrepeneurs du Paysage [★IO]
Union Europeenne pour l'Agrement technique dans la construction [★IO]
Union Europeenne de l'Ameublement [★IO]
Union Europeenne de l'Hopitalisation Privee [★IO]
Union Europeenne des Miroitiers Vitriers [★IO]
Union Europeenne de la Navigation Fluviale [★IO]
Union Europeenne de la Presse Sportive [★IO]
Union Europeenne des Producteurs de Granulats [★IO]
Union Europeenne des Promoteurs Constructeurs [★IO]
Union Europeenne de Radio-Television [★IO]
Union Evangelica Bautista Espanola [IO], Valencia, Spain
Union of Exhibitions and Fairs [★IO]
Union de Exportadores del Uruguay [★IO]
Union of Exporters of Uruguay [IO], Montevideo, Uruguay
Union of Finance Personnel in Europe [IO], Berlin, Germany

Union des Finanzpersonals in Europa [★IO]
Union of Finnish Writers [IO], Helsinki, Finland
Union of Flight Attendants [★IO]
Union of Flight Attendants [★24011]
Union des Foires Internationales [★IO]
Union Francaise des Indus. Petrolieres [★IO]
Union of French Aerospace and Space Indus. [IO], Paris, France
Union of French Tobacco Growers' Co-operatives [IO], Paris, France
Union Gen. de Trabajadores [★IO]
Union Geophysique Canadienne [★IO]
Union of German Catholic Women [IO], Cologne, Germany
Union of Groups of Independent Retailers of Europe [IO], Brussels, Belgium
Union Haddiema Maghqudin [★IO]
Union; Hotel and Restaurant Employees and Bartenders Intl. [★24095]
Union Indus. Argentina [★IO]
Union of Indus. and Employers' Confederations of Europe [★IO]
Union Indus. Paraguaya [★IO]
Union europaischer industrie- und Handelskammern Rhein, Rhone, Donau, Alpen [★IO]
Union des Indus. et de la Distribution des Plastiques et du Caoutchouc [★IO]
Union of Indus. of the European Community [★IO]
Union des Indus. Ferroviaires Europeenes [★IO]
Union Information Center; Natl. Employee [24076]
Union of Info. Tech. Enterprises [IO], Yerevan, Armenia
Union Internacional de Tecnicos de la Industria del Calzado [★IO]
Union of Intl. Contractors, Turkey [★IO]
Union of Intl. Fairs [IO], Paris, France
Union for the Intl. Language Ido [IO], Heemskerk, Netherlands
Union Intl. des Transports Routiers [★IO]
Union Internationale pour les livres de jeunesse [★IO]
Union Internationale des Architectes [★IO]
Union Internationale des Associations et Organismes Techniques [★IO]
Union Internationale des Assureurs Aviation [★IO]
Union Internationale des Avocats [★IO]
Union Internationale des Centres du Batiment [★IO]
Union Internationale des Chauffeurs Routiers [★IO]
Union Internationale des Chemins de Fer [★IO]
Union Internationale Chretienne des Dirigeants d'Entreprise [★IO]
Union Internationale du Cinema Non Professionnel [★IO]
Union Internationale Contre le Cancer [★IO]
Union Internationale Contre la Tuberculose et les Maladies Respiratoires [★IO]
Union Internationale de Cristallographie [★IO]
Union Internationale d'Angiologie [★IO]
Union Internationale Des Magistrats [★IO]
Union Internationale d'Histoire et de Philosophie des Sciences [★IO]
Union Internationale des Editeurs [★IO]
Union Internationale des Etudiants [★IO]
Union Internationale des Guides et Scouts d'Europe [★IO]
Union Internationale Humaniste et Laique [★IO]
Union Internationale des Instituts de Recherches Forestieres [★IO]
Union Internationale pour les applications d l'electricite [★IO]
Union Internationale pour l'Etude du Quarternaire [★IO]
Union Internationale pour l'Etude Scientifique de la Population [★IO]
Union Internationale de l'Industrie du Gaz [★IO]
Union Internationale des Magistrats [★IO]
Union Internationale de la Marionnette; UNIMA-U.S.A., Amer. Center of the [22916]
Union Internationale Motonautique [IO], Monaco, Monaco
Union Internationale de Physique Pure et Appliquee [★IO]
Union Internationale de la Presse Electronique [IO], Tettnang, Germany
Union Internationale de Promotion de la Sante et d'Education pour la Sante [★IO]

Union Internationale pour la Protection des Obtentions Vegetales [★IO]
Union Internationale de Radioecologie [★IO]
Union Internationale pour la Sci., la Technique et les Applications du Vide [★IO]
Union Internationale de Sci. et de Technologie Alimentaires [★IO]
Union Internationale des Sciences Anthropologiques et Ethnologiques [★IO]
Union Internationale des Sciences Biologiques [★IO]
Union Internationale des Sciences Geologiques [★IO]
Union Internationale des Sciences Prehistoriques et Protohistoriques [★IO]
Union Internationale des Societes de Microbiologie [★IO]
Union Internationale de Speleologie [★IO]
L'Union Internationale pour la Taxatione sur la Valeur de la Terre et le Libre-Echange [★IO]
Union Internationale des Telecommunications [★IO]
Union Internationale des Transports Publics [★IO]
Union Internationale Vegetarienne [★IO]
Union Internationale des Wagons Prives [★IO]
Union Interparlementaire [★IO]
Union of Inventors of Bulgaria [IO], Sofia, Bulgaria
Union of Japanese Scientists and Engineers [IO], Tokyo, Japan
Union of Jewish Women [★IO]
Union des Journalistes de l'Afrique de l'Ouest [★IO]
Union of Journalists in Finland [IO], Helsinki, Finland
Union Label and Ser. Trades Dept., AFL-CIO [24213], 815 16th St. NW, Washington, DC 20006, (202)508-3700
Union of Latin Amer. Universities [IO], Mexico City, Mexico
Union Latinoamericana de Ciegos [★IO]
Union and League of Romanian Societies [19333], 7805 Brookpark Rd., Parma, OH 44129-1111, (216)351-2094
Union and League of Romanian Societies of Am. [★19333]
Union de l'Europe Occidentale [★IO]
Union of Librarians and Info. Services Officers [IO], Sofia, Bulgaria
Union Local 73; Gen. Ser. Employees [24097]
Union Luxembourgeoise de Ski Nautique [★IO]
Union of Macedonian Political Organizations [★IO]
Union of Macedonian Political Organizations [★19221]
Union du Mahgreb Arabe [★IO]
Union des Maisons de Bordeaux [IO], Bordeaux, France
Union des Maisons de Bordeaux [★IO]
Union des Maisons de Champagne [★IO]
Union of the Mfrs. and Consumers of Packages and Packaging Products [IO], Moscow, Russia
Union Matematica Argentina [★IO]
Union Mauritanienne des Femmes d'Entreprise et de Commerce [IO], Nouakchott, Mauritania
Union Medica Nacional [IO], San Jose, Costa Rica
Union Mondiale des Organisations Feminines Catholiques [★IO]
Union Mundial pro Interlingua [IO], De Bilt, Netherlands
Union Mundial para la Naturaleza Oficina Regional para Mesoamerica [IO], San Jose, Costa Rica
Union Mundial pour la Nature - Mauritanie [★IO]
Union Nationale des Associations Diocesaines de Secours et de Developpement - Caritas Tchad [IO], N'Djamena, Chad
Union Nationale des Associations de Tourisme et de Plein Air [★IO]
Union Nationale des Entrepreneurs du Paysage [★IO]
Union Nationale de la Femme Tunisienne [★IO]
Union Nationale des Pharmacies de France [★IO]
Union Nationale du Sport Scolaire [IO], Paris, France
Union Network Intl. - Asian and Pacific Regional Off. [IO], Singapore, Singapore
Union of Nordic Pharmacists [★IO]
Union of North Amer. Vietnamese Students Assn. [IO], Westminster, CA, United States
Union of North Amer. Vietnamese Students Assn. [19426], PO Box 433, Westminster, CA 92684, (504)931-5878

Reference to "IO" in place of a book number signifies that the association may be found in the 45th edition of International Organizations.

Union; Off. Employees Intl. [★23995]
Union Oil Company Cooperative [★4482]
Union of Orthodox Jewish Congregations of Am;
Orthodox Union - [20170]
Union of Orthodox Rabbis of the U.S. and Canada
[20183], 235 E Broadway, New York, NY 10002,
(212)964-6337
Union of the Pacific; Inlandboatman's [2605]
Union of Painters and Allied Trades; Intl. [24146]
Union of Palestinian Women's Assn. in North
America - Address unknown since 2001.
Union Panafricaine des Postes [★IO]
Union Petroliere Europeenne Independante [IO],
Hamburg, Germany
Union of the Physicists in Bulgaria [IO], Sofia,
Bulgaria
Union of the Plastics and Rubber Indus. [IO], Paris,
France
Union of Poles in Am. [19318], 9999 Granger Rd.,
Garfield Heights, OH 44125, (216)478-0120
Union of Polish Philatelists [★IO]
Union of Polish Women in Am. [19319], 2636-38 E
Allegheny Ave., Philadelphia, PA 19134-5185,
(215)425-3807
Union Postal De Las Americas, Espana, y Portugal
[★IO]
Union Postale Universelle [★IO]
Union Presidents; Natl. Assn. of Credit [★1112]
Union de la Presse Francophone [★IO]
Union des Producteurs Agricoles [★IO]
Union of Professional Airmen [★IO]
Union of Professional Airmen [★24005]
Union of Professionals [★IO]
Union Professionnelle des Entreprises d'Assurances
[★IO]
Union Professionnelle du Secteur Immobilier [★IO]
Union for the Protection of the Human Person by
Intl., Social and Economic Cooperation - Defunct.
Union for Protection of Tenants MakeDom [IO], Sko-
pje, Macedonia
Union of Public Transport [IO], Paris, France
Union for Radical Political Economics [6896], URPE
Gordon Hall, Univ. of Massachusetts, 418 N Pleas-
ant St., Amherst, MA 01002-1735, (413)577-0806
Union Radio Scientifique Internationale [★IO]
Union for Reform Judaism [20184], 633 3rd Ave.,
New York, NY 10017-6778, (212)650-4000
Union Routiere de France [★IO]
Union Royale des Armateurs Belges [★IO]
Union Royale Belge des Societes de Football-
Association [★IO]
Union of Russian Jews - Address unknown since
1995.
Union Saint-Jean-Baptiste [19065], c/o Saint-Jean-
Baptiste Educ. Found., Box F, Woonsocket, RI
02895, (401)769-0520
Union of Sci. and Educ. [IO], Luxembourg,
Luxembourg
Union of Sci. Workers in Bulgaria [★IO]
Union of Scientists in Bulgaria [IO], Sofia, Bulgaria
Union of Sephardic Congregations [20185], 8 W
70th St., New York, NY 10023, (212)873-0300
Union Settlement Assn. [12785], 237 E 104th St.,
New York, NY 10029, (212)828-6000
Union of Shop, Distributive and Allied Workers [IO],
Manchester, United Kingdom
Union Sindical Obrera [★IO]
Union of Slovak Mathematicians and Physicists
[★IO]
Union; Steamship Sailors' [★24131]
Union of Students in Ireland [IO], Dublin, Ireland
Union Suisse des Chorales [IO], Aarau, Switzerland
Union Suisse des Societes d'Ingenieurs-Conseils
[★IO]
Union of Swiss Chocolate Manufacturers [IO], Bern,
Switzerland
Union of the Swiss Country-Women [IO], Brugg,
Switzerland
Union Syndicale Suisse [★IO]
Union Syndicat Veterinaire Belge [★IO]
Union des Syndicats de Monaco [★IO]
Union of Taekwondo Tanzania [IO], Dar es Salaam,
United Republic of Tanzania
Union Textile Merchants' Assn. [IO], Bangkok,
Thailand

Union for Traditional Judaism [20186], 811 Palisade
Ave., Teaneck, NJ 07666, (201)801-0707
Union des Transports Publics [★IO]
Union des Travailleurs Esperantistes des Pays de
Langue Francaise/Esperanto-Informations [IO],
Paris, France
Union de Universidades de Am. Latina y El Caribe
[★IO]
Union Veterans of the Civil War, 1861-1865;
Daughters of [20725]
Union Veterans of the Civil War; Auxiliary to Sons of
[20723]
Union Veterans of the Civil War; Sons of [20731]
Union WAGE - Defunct.
Union of Western European Chambers of Com-
merce and Indus. of the Rhine, Rhone and
Danube [★IO]
Union of Women Teachers [★IO]
Union Women's Alliance to Gain Equality - Defunct.
Union of YMCA's in Bulgaria YMCA-YWCA [IO], So-
fia, Bulgaria
Unione Costruttori Italiani Stampi E Attrezzature di
Precisione [★IO]
Unione Cristiana Delle Giovani [★IO]
Unione Industriali Pastai Italiani [★IO]
Unione Italiana Ciechi [★IO]
Unione Matematica Italiana [★IO]
Unione Nazionale dell'Avicoltura [★IO]
Unione Nazionale Industria Conciaria [★IO]
Unione Nazionale Industrie Dentarie Italiane [★IO]
Unione Nazionale Piccola e Media Industria Tessile
Abbigliamento [★IO]
Unione Nazionale Rappresentanti Autoveicoli Esteri
[★IO]
Unione Petrolifera [IO], Rome, Italy
Unione Produttori Italiani Viteria e Bulloneria [★IO]
Unionism - A Special Proj. of the Natl. Right to Work
Legal Defense Found; Concerned Educators
Against Forced [17971]
Uniono por la Linguo Internaciona Ido [★IO]
Unions
AFL-CIO [24096]
African Regional Labour Admin. Centre -
Zimbabwe [IO]
AFT Healthcare [24087]
Air Line Pilots Assn., Intl. [24005]
Aircraft Mechanics Fraternal Assn. [24006]
Algemeen Christelijk Vakverbond van Belgie [IO]
All China Fed. of Trade Unions [IO]
Amalgamated Transit Union [24197]
Amer. Assn. of Classified School Employees
[24041]
Amer. Fed. of Govt. Employees [24068]
Amer. Fed. of Security Officers [24184]
Amer. Fed. of State, County and Municipal
Employees [24069]
Amer. Fed. of Teachers [24042]
Amer. Foreign Ser. Assn. [24070]
Amer. Guild of Variety Artists [24151]
Amer. Independent Cockpit Alliance [24008]
Amer. Musicians Union [24152]
Amer. Postal Workers Union [24166]
Amer. Radio Assn. [24023]
Amer. Rights at Work [17968]
Amer. Train Dispatchers Dept. of the BLE [24175]
Amer. Union of Pizza Delivery Drivers [24062]
Asia Monitor Rsrc. Center [IO]
Associates of the Amer. Foreign Ser. Worldwide
[24071]
Assn. for Behavioral Hea. and Wellness [24088]
Assn. of Flight Attendants - CWA [24009]
Assn. of Labor Relations Agencies [24112]
Assn. of Minor League Umpires [23104]
Assn. for Union Democracy [24113]
Assn. of Volleyball Professionals [24191]
Assn. of Western Pulp and Paper Workers
[24064]
Australian Coun. of Trade Unions [IO]
Australian Workers' Union [IO]
Austrian Trade Union Fed. - Christian Fraction
[IO]
Bakery, Confectionery, Tobacco Workers and
Grain Millers Intl. Union [24017]
Brewery and Soft Drink Workers Conf. - U.S.A.
and Canada [24020]

Brotherhood of Locomotive Engineers and Train-
men, A Division of the Rail Conf. of the Intl.
Brotherhood of Teamsters [24176]
Brotherhood of Maintenance of Way Employees
[24177]
Brotherhood of Railroad Signalmen [24178]
Brotherhood Railway Carmen Division/Transporta-
tion Communications Union [24179]
Brotherhood of Shoe and Allied Craftsmen
[24063]
Brotherhood of Utility Workers of New England
[24215]
Building and Constr. Trades Dept. - AFL-CIO
[24025]
BusinessEurope [IO]
Canadian Natl. Fed. of Independent Unions [IO]
Cement, Lime, Gypsum, and Allied Workers Div.
[24038]
Central Org. of Trade Unions (Kenya) [IO]
Centre of Indian Trade Unions [IO]
Centro Uruguayo de Tecnologias Apropiadas [IO]
Change to Win [IO]
Change to Win [24201]
Civil Ser. Employees Assn. [24073]
Coalition of Black Trade Unionists [24202]
Coalition of Labor Union Women [24203]
Coalition of Labor Union Women Center for Educ.
and Res. [24204]
Comm. for Asian Women [IO]
Comm. of Interns and Residents [24089]
Confed. of Independent Trade Unions in Bulgaria
[IO]
Confed. of Natl. Trade Unions [IO]
Confed. of Trade Unions of Monaco [IO]
Confed. of Turkish Trade Unions [IO]
Cong. of Independent Unions [24205]
Coun. of Engineers and Scientists Organizations
[7817]
Coun. of Nordic Trade Unions [IO]
Coun. on Union-Free Env. [3949]
Coun. of the United Textile Workers of Am.
[24194]
Danish Confed. of Trade Unions [IO]
Dept. for Professional Employees, AFL-CIO
[24173]
Directors Guild of Am. [24055]
Distribution Contractors Assn. [24162]
Employers and Industrialists Fed. [IO]
European Confed. of Independent Trade Unions
[IO]
European Trade Union Inst. for Res., Educ. and
Hea. and Safety [IO]
Farm Labor Organizing Comm. [23997]
Fed. Educ. Assn. [24043]
Fed. of Korean Trade Unions [IO]
Fed. of Natl. Educ. and Res. Unions [IO]
Fed. of Westinghouse Independent Salaried
Unions [24047]
Freelancers Union [24218]
Gen. Fed. of Trade Unions [IO]
Gen. Ser. Employees Union Local 73 [24097]
Glass Molders, Pottery, Plastics, and Allied Work-
ers Intl. Union [24066]
Graphic Arts Employers of Am. [24082]
Graphic Communications Conf. of the Intl.
Brotherhood of Teamsters [24083]
Hong Kong Confed. of Trade Unions [IO]
Hong Kong Fed. of Trade Unions [IO]
Indian Natl. Trade Union Cong. [IO]
Indus. Union of Marine and Ship Building Workers
of Am. [24125]
Indus. Workers of the World [24098]
Indus. Workers of the World Starbucks Workers
Union [24206]
Inst. of the Ironworking Indus. [24133]
Inst. of Labor and Indus. Relations [24114]
Intl. Allied Printing Trades Assn. [24084]
Intl. Assn. of Bridge, Structural, Ornamental and
Reinforcing Iron Workers [24134]
Intl. Assn. of Fire Fighters [24057]
Intl. Assn. of Machinists [24011]
Intl. Assn. of Machinists and Aerospace Workers
[24012]
Intl. Assn. of Machinists and Aerospace Workers,
Woodworkers District Lodge W1 [24026]

A star before a book entry number signifies that the name is not listed separately, but is mentioned within the entry.

Intl. Brotherhood of Boilermakers, Iron Ship Builders, Blacksmiths, Forgers and Helpers [24021]
Intl. Brotherhood of DuPont Workers [24034]
Intl. Brotherhood of Elecl. Workers [24048]
Intl. Brotherhood of Police Officers [24120]
Intl. Civil Ser. Commn. [24143]
Intl. Confed. of Free Trade Unions [IO]
Intl. Confed. of Free Trade Unions - African Regional Org. [IO]
Intl. Fed. of Professional and Tech. Engineers [24052]
Intl. Guards Union of Am. [24185]
Intl. Labor Org. - U.S. [24207]
Intl. Labor Org. - U.S. [IO]
Intl. Labour Off. - Switzerland [IO]
Intl. Labour Org. [IO]
Intl. Labour Org. Ankara [IO]
Intl. Labour Org. Beijing Off. [IO]
Intl. Labour Org. Cairo Off. [IO]
Intl. Labour Org. Caribbean Off. [IO]
Intl. Labour Org. Jakarta Off. [IO]
Intl. Labour Org. Off. for the European Union and the Benelux countries [IO]
Intl. Labour Org. Off. in Germany: ILO-Berlin [IO]
Intl. Labour Org. Off. for Italy and San Marino [IO]
Intl. Labour Org. Off. for the United Kingdom and Republic of Ireland [IO]
Intl. Labour Org. Regional Off. for Africa [IO]
Intl. Labour Org. Regional Off. for the Arab States [IO]
Intl. Labour Org. Regional Off. for Asia and the Pacific [IO]
Intl. Labour Org. Subregional Off. - Budapest Off. [IO]
Intl. Labour Org. Subregional Off. for East Asia [IO]
Intl. Labour Org. Subregional Off. for Eastern Europe and Central Asia [IO]
Intl. Labour Org. Subregional Off. for South Asia [IO]
Intl. Labour Org. Subregional Off. for South-East Asia and the Pacific [IO]
Intl. Labour Org. Subregional Off. for Southern Africa [IO]
Intl. Labour Org. Suva Off. [IO]
Intl. Longshore and Warehouse Union [24126]
Intl. Longshoremen's Assn. [24127]
Intl. Org. of Masters, Mates and Pilots, ILA, AFL-CIO [24128]
Intl. Plate Printers, Die Stampers, and Engravers' Union of North Am. [24085]
Intl. Union of Allied Novelty and Prdt.ion Workers [24196]
Intl. Union of Bricklayers and Allied Craftworkers [24027]
Intl. Union of Electronic, Elecl., Salaried, Machine, and Furniture Workers [24049]
Intl. Union of Elevator Constructors [24099]
Intl. Union of Indus. and Independent Workers [24208]
Intl. Union of Indus. and Independent Workers [IO]
Intl. Union of Operating Engineers [24028]
Intl. Union of Petroleum and Indus. Workers [24163]
Intl. Union of Police Associations [24121]
Intl. Union of Security Officers [24186]
Intl. Union, Security, Police and Fire Professionals of Am. [24187]
Intl. Union of Tool, Die and Mold Makers [24100]
Intl. Union, United Auto., Aerospace and Agricultural Implement Workers of Am. [24004]
Irish Cong. of Trade Unions [IO]
Japan Fed. of Ser. and Distributive Workers Unions [IO]
Japan Railway Trade Unions Confed. [IO]
Japanese Confed. of Port and Transport Workers' Unions [IO]
Japanese Fed. of Pulp and Paper Workers' Unions [IO]
Joint Labor Mgt. Comm. of the Retail Food Indus. [24059]
Kalabaw-No-Kai [IO]
Labor Coun. for Latin Amer. Advancement [24094]
Labor and Employment Relations Assn. [24115]

Labor Proj. for Working Families [24117]
Labor Res. Assn. [24118]
Laborers' Intl. Union of North Am. [24029]
Labour Women's Coun. [IO]
LO/TCO Secretariat of Intl. Trade Union Development [IO]
Luxembourg Confed. of Christian Trade Unions [IO]
Machinists Non-Partisan Political League [24101]
Major League Baseball Players Assn. [24018]
Maritime Trades Dept., AFL-CIO [24129]
Metal Trades Dept., AFL-CIO [24135]
Millwright Gp. [24102]
Natl. Air Traffic Controllers Assn. [24013]
Natl. Alliance for Fair Contracting [24030]
Natl. Alliance of Postal and Fed. Employees [24167]
Natl. Assn. of Air Traffic Specialists [24014]
Natl. Assn. of Govt. Employees [24075]
Natl. Assn. of Letter Carriers of the U.S.A. [24168]
Natl. Assn. of Postal Supervisors [24169]
Natl. Assn. of Professional Educators [9223]
Natl. Basketball Players Assn. [24192]
Natl. Center for the Stud. of Collective Bargaining in Higher Educ. and the Professions [24036]
Natl. Conf. of Firemen and Oilers [24058]
Natl. Conservation District Employees Assn. [24209]
Natl. Coordinating Comm. for Multiemployer Plans [1242]
Natl. Coun. on Teacher Retirement [24044]
Natl. Day Laborer Organizing Network [24111]
Natl. Educ. Assn. [24045]
Natl. Employee Union Information Center [24076]
Natl. Fed. of Fed. Employees [24077]
Natl. Fed. of Independent Unions [24210]
Natl. Forest Workers' Union of Japan [IO]
Natl. League of Postmasters of the U.S. [24170]
Natl. Org. of Indus. Trade Unions [24103]
Natl. Org. of Legal Services Workers, UAW Local 2320 [24079]
Natl. Postal Mail Handlers Union [24171]
Natl. Rural Letter Carriers' Assn. [24172]
Natl. Trades Union Cong. [IO]
Natl. Treasury Employees Union [24080]
Natl. Union of Law Enforcement Associations [24124]
Natl. Union of Workers [IO]
Natl. Women's Coun. of the New Zealand Coun. of Trade Unions [IO]
New York Coun. of Motion Picture and TV Unions [24056]
New Zealand Coun. of Trade Unions [IO]
The Newspaper Guild [24140]
North Amer. Assn. of Educational Negotiators [24046]
OAS Staff Assn. [24144]
Off. and Professional Employees Intl. Union [23995]
Operative Plasterers and Cement Masons Intl. Assn. of U.S. and Canada [24031]
Pacific Coast Marine Firemen, Oilers, Watertenders and Wipers Assn. [24130]
Pancyprian Fed. of Labor [IO]
Paper, Allied-Indus., Chem. and Energy Workers Intl. Union [24211]
Philippine Workers Support Comm. [24212]
Philippine Workers Support Comm. [IO]
Plant Protection Assn. [24188]
Printing, Publishing and Media Workers Sector of the CWA [24086]
Professional Airways Systems Specialists [24015]
Res. Associates of Am. [24060]
Retail, Wholesale and Dept. Store Union [24182]
Sailors' Union of the Pacific [24131]
Samuel Gompers Stamp Club [22867]
Seafarers' Intl. Union of North Am. [24132]
SEIU, District 925, AFL-CIO [23996]
Self-Employed Women's Assn. [IO]
Ser. Employees Intl. Union [24189]
Ser. Workers United [24190]
Sheet Metal Workers' Intl. Assn. [24136]
Stove, Furnace, Energy, and Allied Appliance Workers Division of the Intl. Brotherhood of Boilermakers [24001]

Student/Farmworker Alliance [24054]
SweatFree Communities [24106]
Swiss Fed. of Trade Unions [IO]
Swiss Labour Assistance [IO]
Syna die Gewerkschaft [IO]
Teamsters for a Democratic Union [24199]
Textile Converters Assn. [24195]
Trade Union Advisory Comm. to the OECD [IO]
Trade Union Cong. of the Philippines [IO]
Trade Union Solidarity Centre of Finland [IO]
Trades Union Cong. - England [IO]
Trades Union Cong. - Women's Comm. [IO]
Transport Workers Union of Am. [24200]
Trans. Communications Intl. Union [24180]
Turkish Confed. of Employer Associations [IO]
Union Aid Abroad - Australian People for Hea., Educ. and Development Abroad [IO]
Union Label and Ser. Trades Dept., AFL-CIO [24213]
UNITE HERE [24095]
United Assn. of Journeymen and Apprentices of the Plumbing, Pipe Fitting, Sprinkler Fitting Indus. of the U.S. and Canada [24164]
United Brotherhood of Carpenters and Joiners of Am. [24032]
United Food and Commercial Workers Intl. Union [24061]
United Furniture Workers Insurance Fund [24065]
United Hebrew Trades - New York Division of the Jewish Labor Comm. [24214]
United Mine Workers of Am. [24139]
United Nations Staff Union [24145]
United Steel Workers of Am., Rubber/Plastics Indus. Conf. [24183]
United Steelworkers of Am. [24137]
United Trans. Union [24181]
United Union of Roofers, Waterproofers and Allied Workers [24033]
USWA Flint/Glass Workers Conf. [24067]
Utility Workers Union of Am., AFL-CIO [24216]
Wire Ser. Guild [24141]
Women's Natl. Basketball Players Assn. [23140]
Workers Solidarity Alliance [16982]
World Confed. of Labour [IO]
World Fed. of Trade Unions [IO]
Writers Guild of Am., East [24220]
Writers Guild of Am., West [24221]
Unions of Am; Confederated [★24210]
Unions; Assn. of Coll. [★9166]
Unions' Nation-Wide Coordinating Coun. for Oil and Allied Industries - Defunct.
Unions for Professional Employees; Coun. of AFL-CIO [★24173]
UniPro Foodservice [1566], 2500 Cumberland Pkwy., Ste. 600, Atlanta, GA 30339, (770)952-0871
Unishippers Assn. [3596], 746 E Winchester St., Ste. 200, Salt Lake City, UT 84107, (801)487-0600
UNISON [IO], London, United Kingdom
Unison Inst. [17197], 1742 Connecticut Ave. NW, Washington, DC 20009, (202)797-7200
Unit; Coun. on the Continuing Educ. [★8150]
Unit Production Managers Guild of Hollywood [★24055]
Unitarian Christian Advance [★20600]
Unitarian Christian Comm. [★20600]
Unitarian Christian Fellowship [★20600]
Unitarian Educational Directors Assn. [★20599]
Unitarian Historical Soc. [★20601]
Unitarian Historical Soc. [IO], Edinburgh, United Kingdom
Unitarian Ser. Comm. [★IO]
Unitarian Ser. Comm. [★20603]
Unitarian Ser. Comm. of Canada [★IO]
Unitarian Universalist
Canadian Unitarian Coun. [IO]
Covenant of Unitarian Universalist Pagans [20459]
Interweave Continental (Unitarian Universalists for Lesbian, Gay, Bisexual and Transgender Concerns) [20059]
Liberal Religious Educators Assn. [20599]
Unitarian Historical Soc. [IO]
Unitarian Universalist Christian Fellowship [20600]
Unitarian Universalist Historical Soc. [20601]
Unitarian Universalist Ministers Assn. [20602]

Reference to "IO" in place of a book number signifies that the association may be found in the 45th edition of International Organizations.

Unitarian Universalist Ministers Association [IO]
Unitarian Universalist Musicians' Network [20436]
Unitarian Universalist Ser. Comm. [20603]
Unitarian Universalist Ser. Comm. [IO]
Unitarian Universalist Women's Fed. [20604]
Young Religious Unitarian Universalists [20605]
Unitarian Universalist Association [★20600]
Unitarian Universalist Assn. of Congregations [13135], 25 Beacon St., Boston, MA 02108, (617)742-2100
Unitarian Universalist Assn. of Congregations - Washington Off. for Faith in Action [★13135]
Unitarian Universalist Assn. of Congregations- Washington Off. for Social Justice [★13135]
Unitarian Universalist Assn. Jubilee Working Group for Anti-Racism - Defunct.
Unitarian Universalist Assn. - Washington Off. for Social Concern [★13135]
Unitarian Universalist Christian Fellowship [20600], PO Box 6702, Tulsa, OK 74156, (918)794-4637
Unitarian Universalist Genealogical Soc. - Defunct.
Unitarian Universalist Historical Soc. [20601], PO Box 38, Duxbury, MA 02331-0038, (781)934-2781
Unitarian Universalist Ministers Assn. [20602], 25 Beacon St., Boston, MA 02108, (617)848-0498
Unitarian Universalist Ministers Association [IO], Boston, MA, United States
Unitarian Universalist Ministers' Partners Soc. - Address unknown since 2003.
Unitarian Universalist Musicians' Network [20436], c/o Donna Fisher, Admin., 2208 Henery Tuckers Ct., Charlotte, NC 28270, (800)969-8866
Unitarian Universalist Ser. Comm. [20603], 130 Prospect St., Cambridge, MA 02139-1845, (617)868-6600
Unitarian Universalist Ser. Comm. [IO], Cambridge, MA, United States
Unitarian Universalist Soc. for Alcohol and Drug Education - Address unknown since 2001.
Unitarian Universalist Women's Fed. [20604], 25 Beacon St., Boston, MA 02108, (617)948-4692
Unitarian Universalists for Black and White Action - Defunct.
Unitarian Universalists for Lesbian, Gay, Bisexual and Transgender Concerns; Interweave Continental [20059]
Unitarian Universalists for Lesbian and Gay Concerns [★20059]
Unitarian Women; Alliance of [★20604]
UNITE [12695], PO Box 65, Drexel Hill, PA 19026, (215)728-3777
UNITE HERE [24095], 275 7th Ave., New York, NY 10001-6708, (212)265-7000
Unite for Sight [13381], 31 Brookwood Dr., Newtown, CT 06470
Unite for Sight [IO], Newtown, CT, United States
United 510 Owners - Defunct.
United Abrasives Mfrs'. Assn. - Superabrasives Div. [★2075]
United Action for Animals [11468], PO Box 635, New York, NY 10021, (212)249-9178
United Activists for Animal Rights [11469], PO Box 2448, Riverside, CA 92516, (951)776-4040
United African Appeal - Address unknown since 1995.
United African Nationalist Movement - Address unknown since 1995.
United Agribusiness League [4084], 54 Corporate Park, Irvine, CA 92606-5105, (949)975-1424
United Amateur Press [★22912]
United Amateur Press Assn. [★22912]
United Amateur Press Assn. of Am. [22912], c/o Deborah Beachboard, Sec.-Treas., 343 SW Pacific Ave., Chehalis, WA 98532-2925
United Amateur Press Assn. of Am. [★22912]
United Amer.-Arab Cong. - Address unknown since 1995.
United Amer. and Captive Nations Patriotic Movement - Address unknown since 1995.
United Amer. Contractors Assn. - Address unknown since 2002.
United Amer. Croats - Address unknown since 1995.
United Amer. Muslim Assn. [20441], 59-11 8th Ave., Brooklyn, NY 11220, (718)438-6919
United Amer. Progress Assn. - Address unknown since 2002.

United Amputee Services Assn. [15080], PO Box 4277, Winter Park, FL 32793-4277, (407)359-5500
United Ancient Order of Druids - Address unknown since 2001.
United Animal Nations [11470], PO Box 188890, Sacramento, CA 95818, (916)429-2457
United Animal Nations U.S.A. [★11470]
United Arab Emirates Athletics Assn. [IO], Dubai, United Arab Emirates
United Arab Emirates Cricket Bd. [IO], Sharjah, United Arab Emirates
United Arab Emirates Interschool Sports Assn. [IO], Dubai, United Arab Emirates
United Arab Emirates Sports Medicine Comm. [IO], Dubai, United Arab Emirates
United Arab Emirates Squash Rackets Assn. [IO], Dubai, United Arab Emirates
United Arab Emirates Tennis Assn. [IO], Dubai, United Arab Emirates
United Assn. of Christian Counselors Intl. - Address unknown since 2002.
United Assn. of Equip. Leasing [3388], 78120 Calle Estado, Ste. 201, La Quinta, CA 92253, (760)564-2227
United Assn. of Journeymen and Apprentices of the Plumbing and Pipe Fitting Indus. of the U.S. and Canada [★24164]
United Assn. of Journeymen and Apprentices of the Plumbing, Pipe Fitting, Sprinkler Fitting Indus. of the U.S. and Canada [24164], United Assn. Bldg., 901 Massachusetts Ave. NW, Washington, DC 20001-4397, (202)628-5823
United Assn. for Labor Educ. [8722], c/o Dennis Serrette, Pres., 501 Third St. NW, Washington, DC 20001, (202)434-9503
United Assn. Mfrs. Representatives [2544], PO Box 986, Dana Point, CA 92629, (949)240-4966
United Assn. of Oil Services - Defunct.
United Assn. of Railroad Veterans - Defunct.
United Auto Workers [★24004]
United Auto Workers Community Action Prog. [★18298]
United Auto Workers - Work and Family Unit - Address unknown since 2006.
United Baltic Appeal [18980], 115 W 183 St., Bronx, NY 10453-1103, (718)367-8802
United Baltic Appeal [IO], Bronx, NY, United States
United Beauty Assn. [★1086]
United Better Dress Mfrs. Assn. - Defunct.
United Bible Societies [IO], Reading, United Kingdom
United Bible Societies in Venezuela [IO], Caracas, Venezuela
United Black Christians - Address unknown since 1999.
United Black Church Appeal [16947]
United Black Drag Racers Assn. [23397], 17 Santa Fe Dr., St. Louis, MO 63119, (314)968-1720
United Black Fund [12204], 2500 Martin Luther King, Jr. Ave. SE, Washington, DC 20020, (202)783-9300
United Black Fund of Am. [★12204]
United Black Republican Coalition [18538], PO Box 4585, Wichita, KS 67204, (316)265-5209
United Bd. for Christian Colleges in China [★8649]
United Bd. for Christian Colleges in China [★IO]
United Bd. for Christian Higher Educ. in Asia [IO], New York, NY, United States
United Bd. for Christian Higher Educ. in Asia [8649], 475 Riverside Dr., Ste. 1221, New York, NY 10115, (212)870-2600
United Brachial Plexus Network [15403], 1610 Kent St., Kent, OH 44240, (866)877-7004
United Braford Breeders [4295], 422 E Main, No. 218, Nacogdoches, TX 75961, (936)569-8200
United Brethren Church; Historical Soc. of the Evangelical [★10467]
United Breweries of America - Address unknown since 1995.
United Brotherhood of Carpenters and Joiners of Am. [24032], c/o Carpenters Union Warehouse, 14110-D Sullyfield Cir., Chantilly, VA 20151, (703)378-9000
United Burmese Cat Fanciers [21922], 4116 Pine Cone Terr., North Port, FL 34286, (941)426-4691

United Bus Owners of Am. [★3900]
United Bus. Educ. Assn. [★8036]
United Calvinist Youth [★19831]
United Campus Christian Fellowship - Defunct.
United Campuses to Prevent Nuclear War - Defunct.
United Cancer Coun. - Defunct.
United Caribbean Youth - Defunct.
United Cat Fed. [21923], c/o Georgann Chambers, Recorder, 5510 Ptolemy Way, Mira Loma, CA 91752, (951)685-3252
United Catholic Music and Video Assn. [19731], PO Box 230, Donnellson, IA 52625, (319)835-9340
United Cerebral Palsy Associations [13935], 1660 L St. NW, Ste. 700, Washington, DC 20036, (202)776-0406
United Cerebral Palsy Res. and Educational Found. [★13935]
United Chainsaw Carvers Guild [9842], PO Box 255, Ridgway, PA 15853-0255
United Chambers of Commerce [★IO]
United Charity Institutions of Jerusalem [IO], Brooklyn, NY, United States
United Charity Institutions of Jerusalem [12462]
United Choral Conductors Club of America - Defunct.
United Christian Missionary Soc. [19856], PO Box 1986, Indianapolis, IN 46206, (317)635-3100
United Christian Youth Movement - Defunct.
United Church Bd. for World Ministries - Defunct.
United Church of Christ
  Biblical Witness Fellowship [20606]
  Evangelical and Reformed Historical Soc. [20607]
  United Church of Christ Justice and Witness Ministries [20608]
United Church of Christ Coalition for Lesbian, Gay, Bisexual and Transgender Concerns [20067], 2592 W 14th St., Cleveland, OH 44113, (216)861-0799
United Church of Christ Commn. for Racial Justice [★20608]
United Church of Christ Coordinating Center for Women in Church and Soc. - Defunct.
United Church of Christ Gay Caucus [★20067]
United Church of Christ Justice and Witness Ministries [20608], c/o United Church of Christ, 700 Prospect Ave., Cleveland, OH 44115-1110, (216)736-3704
United Church of Christ Ministers for Racial and Social Justice [★20608]
United Church Coalition for Lesbian/Gay Concerns [★20067]
United Church Peace Fellowship - Defunct.
United Church People for Biblical Witness [★20606]
United Church Women [IO], Toronto, ON, Canada
United Church Women of the Natl. Coun. of Churches; Dept. of [★20618]
United Citizens Coastal Protection League - Defunct.
United Civil Party [IO], Minsk, Belarus
United Commercial Travelers of Am; Order of [19135]
United Community Funds and Councils of Am. [★12205]
United Concerned Students - Address unknown since 1989.
United Confederate Veterans [★20730]
United Confed. of Taino People [18989], US Regional Coordinating Off., PO Box 4515, New York, NY 10163, (212)604-4186
United Congressional Appeal - Defunct.
United Cooperatives [★4484]
United Coun. of Church Women [★20618]
United Coun. of Corvette Clubs [21803], 1861 Springfield, Flint, MI 48503, (412)444-5555
United Cricket Bd. of South Africa [IO], Northlands, Republic of South Africa
United Dairy [★1127]
United Dairy Industry Assn. [1140]
United Dance Merchants of Am. [1142], 376 Main Rd., Granville, MA 01034, (413)357-8500
United Daughters of the Confederacy [20732], UDC Bus. Off., 328 North Blvd., Richmond, VA 23220-4009, (804)355-1636
United Designers Assn. [★6464]
United Developers Council [★3323]
United Dirt Track Racing Assn. - Address unknown since 2006.

A star before a book entry number signifies that the name is not listed separately, but is mentioned within the entry.

United Doberman Club [22369], PO Box 58455, Renton, WA 98058-1455, (425)226-4810

United Drag Racers Assn. [★23070]

United Drive-In Theatre Owners Assn. [2794], PO Box 24771, Middle River, MD 21220

United Duroc Record Assn. [★5241]

United Duroc Swine Registry [5243], PO Box 2417, West Lafayette, IN 47996-2417, (765)463-3594

United Duroc Swine Registry [★5241]

United Egg Assn. [★5121]

United Egg Assn. Further Processors [5120], 1720 Windwind Concourse, Ste. 230, Alpharetta, GA 30005, (770)360-9220

United Egg Producers [5121], 1720 Windward Concourse, Ste. 230, Alpharetta, GA 30005, (770)360-9220

United Elecl., Radio and Machine Workers of Am. [24050], 1 Gateway Ctr., Ste. 1400, Pittsburgh, PA 15222-1416, (412)471-8919

United Engg. Found. [7051], PO Box 70, Mount Vernon, VA 22121-0070, (973)244-2328

United Engg. Soc. [★7051]

United Engg. Trustees [★7051]

United English Breeders and Fanciers - Address unknown since 1995.

United European Gastroenterology Fed. [IO], Vienna, Austria

United for a Fair Economy [17473], 29 Winter St., Boston, MA 02108, (617)423-2148

United Families of America - Address unknown since 1989.

United Farm Workers of Am. [23999], PO Box 62, Keene, CA 93531, (818)565-5603

United Farm Workers Organizing Comm. [★23999]

United Fascist Union [18315], PO Box 2209, Elkton, MD 21922

United Fathers of Am. [12014], 1651 E Fourth St., Ste. 122, Santa Ana, CA 92701, (714)558-7949

United Fed. of CFS/CFIDS/CEBV Orgs. - Defunct.

United Fed. of Charities; Natl. Black [16943]

United Fed. of Doll Clubs [22407], 10900 N Pomona Ave., Kansas City, MO 64153, (816)891-7040

United Fed. of Planets, Intl. [25020], PO Box 3157, Chula Vista, CA 91909-3157

United Fed. of Police [★5995]

United Fed. of Postal Clerks [★24166]

United Fed. of Russian Workers' Orgs. of U.S.A. and Canada - Address unknown since 1995.

United Fed. of Travel Agents' Associations [IO], Monaco, Monaco

United Fellowship for Christian Ser. [★IO]

United Fellowship for Christian Ser. [★20351]

United Film Carriers Assn. - Defunct.

United Fire Equip. Ser. Assn. [3460], 500 Telcer Rd., Lake Zurich, IL 60047, (847)438-2343

United Firefighters' Union of Australia, Queensland Br. [IO], West End, Australia

United Fly Tyers [IO], Woburn, MA, United States

United Fly Tyers [23424], PO Box 2478, Woburn, MA 01888

United Flying Octogenarians [21485], PO Box 11114, Montgomery, AL 36111-0114, (334)832-2413

United Focus [★8299]

United Food Animal Assn. - Defunct.

United Food and Commercial Workers Intl. Union [24061], 1775 K St. NW, Washington, DC 20006, (202)223-3111

United Ford Owners [21804], PO Box 32419, Columbus, OH 43232, (614)265-9095

United Four-Wheel Drive Associations [21805], 14525 SW Milikan Way 22622, Beaverton, OR 97005-2343, (920)667-4940

United Four-Wheel Drive Associations [IO], Beaverton, OR, United States

United Franchise Benefits Assn. [3365]

United Freedom Front - Defunct.

United Fresh Fruit and Vegetable Assn. and International Fresh-Cut Produce Assn. [★4766]

United Fresh Produce Assn. [4766], 1901 Pennsylvania Ave. NW, Ste. 1100, Washington, DC 20006, (202)303-3400

United Friends of Needy and Displaced People of Yugoslavia - Address unknown since 1995.

United Fund for Federal Employee Rights - Defunct.

United Fund for Jewish Culture - Defunct.

United Fund; Natl. Black [12656]

United Fur Mfrs. Assn. - Address unknown since 1990.

United Furniture Workers of Am. [★24065]

United Furniture Workers Insurance Fund [24065], 1910 Air Lane Dr., Nashville, TN 37210, (615)889-8860

United Future New Zealand [IO], Wellington, New Zealand

United Galician Jews of America - Defunct.

United Garment Workers of Am. [★24061]

United; Generations [13170]

United Gloster Breeders [21863], c/o Barbara Rosario, Sec.-Treas., 715 Avocado Ct., Del Mar, CA 92014-3911

United Gloster Breeders [IO], Del Mar, CA, United States

United Golfers' Assn. - Address unknown since 2001.

United Grand Imperial Coun; Red Cross of Constantine - [19248]

United Greek Orthodox Charities - Defunct.

United Grief Support [★12695]

United in Gp. Harmony Assn. [10715], PO Box 185, Clifton, NJ 07015-0185, (973)365-0049

United Halsingian Soc. of America - Defunct.

United Hasroun Men's and St. Laba Ladies Charity Societies [19732]

United Health Founds. - Defunct.

United Healthcare Systems [★14597]

United Hebrew Trades Division of the Jewish Labor Comm. [★24214]

United Hebrew Trades Division of the Labor Comm. [★24214]

United Hebrew Trades - New York Division of the Jewish Labor Comm. [24214]

United Hebrew Trades of the State of New York [★24214]

United Hellenic Amer. Cong. [19094], 980 N Michigan Ave., Ste. 1210, Chicago, IL 60611, (312)640-1055

United Hellenic Voters of Am. [19095], 525 W Lake St., Addison, IL 60101, (630)628-0820

United Hellenic Voters of Illinois [★19095]

United HIAS Ser. [★12471]

United HIAS Ser. [★IO]

United Homeowners' Assn. - Address unknown since 2004.

United Horological Assn. of Amer. [★2359]

United Humanitarians [11471]

United Hungarian Jews of America - Address unknown since 1995.

United Hunts Racing Assn. [★23509]

United Indian Development Assn. [★12628]

United Indian Missions, Intl. [20405], PO Box 336010, 800 8th Ave., Ste. 201, Greeley, CO 80633-0601, (970)330-7788

United Indian Missions, Intl. [IO], Greeley, CO, United States

United Indian Planners Assn. - Defunct.

United Indian War Veterans, U.S.A. - Address unknown since 1995.

United Indians of All Tribes Found. [18100], Discovery Park, PO Box 99100, Seattle, WA 98199, (206)285-4425

United Infants' and Children's Wear Assn. - Defunct.

United Infertility Org. - Address unknown since 1995.

United Inventors Assn. of the U.S.A. [7232], c/o Carol Oldenburg, Admin., 999 Lehigh Sta. Rd., Henrietta, NY 14467, (585)359-9310

United Inventors and Scientists of America - Defunct.

United Israel Appeal - Address unknown since 2002.

United Israel World Union [20424], PO Box 561476, Charlotte, NC 28256

United Israel World Union [IO], Charlotte, NC, United States

United Italian Amer. Labor Coun. - Address unknown since 1995.

United Italian Amer. League - Address unknown since 2004.

United Jewish Appeal [★12483]

United Jewish Appeal - Fed. of Jewish Philanthropies of New York [12482], 130 E 59th St., New York, NY 10022, (212)980-1000

United Jewish Appeal - Fed. of Jewish Philanthropies of New York Task Force on Compulsive Gambling - Defunct.

United Jewish Appeal of Greater New York [★12482]

United Jewish Communities [12483], PO Box 30, New York, NY 10113, (212)284-6500

United Karate Fed. - Address unknown since 1995.

United Kennel Club [22370], 100 E Kilgore Rd., Kalamazoo, MI 49002-5584, (269)343-9020

United Kesrawan Soc. [19206]

United Kingdom

British Schools and Universities Found. [8102]

British Trade Off. at Consulate-General [24241]

BritishAmerican Bus. Inc. of New York and London [24267]

Cambridge in Am. [9284]

Intl. Assn. of Speakers Bureaus [10900]

Intl. Friends of the London Lib. [10363]

Scottish Historic and Res. Soc. of Delaware Valley [10955]

VisitBritain [24242]

Wales North Am. Bus. Chamber [24306]

Winant and Clayton Volunteers [13409]

United Kingdom Assn. for European Law [IO], London, United Kingdom

United Kingdom Assn. for Milk Banking [IO], London, United Kingdom

United Kingdom Assn. of Professional Engineers [IO], Bromley, United Kingdom

United Kingdom Automatic Control Coun. [IO], Stevenage, United Kingdom

United Kingdom Bartenders Guild [IO], Linlithgow, United Kingdom

United Kingdom Cast Stone Assn. [IO], Northampton, United Kingdom

United Kingdom Comm. of Intl. Water Assn. [IO], London, United Kingdom

United Kingdom Coun. for Psychotherapy [IO], London, United Kingdom

United Kingdom Dance and Drama Fed. [IO], Stoke-On-Trent, United Kingdom

United Kingdom Educ. and Res. Networking Assn. [IO], Didcot, United Kingdom

United Kingdom eInformation Gp. [IO], Leyburn, United Kingdom

United Kingdom Environmental Law Assn. [IO], London, United Kingdom

United Kingdom Environmental Mutagen Soc. [IO], Ware, United Kingdom

United Kingdom Forum for Organisational Hea. [IO], East Molesey, United Kingdom

United Kingdom Home Care Assn. [IO], Sutton, United Kingdom

United Kingdom Housekeepers Assn. [IO], London, United Kingdom

United Kingdom Hydrogen Assn. [IO], Gateshead, United Kingdom

United Kingdom Immigrants' Advisory Ser. [★IO]

United Kingdom Indus. Vision Assn. [IO], Royston, United Kingdom

United Kingdom Inst. for Conservation of Historic and Artistic Works [IO], London, United Kingdom

United Kingdom-Ireland Controlled Release Soc. [IO], Birmingham, United Kingdom

United Kingdom Ju-Jitsu Intl. Martial Arts Assn. [★IO]

United Kingdom Jujitsu Assn. Intl. [IO], Rochdale, United Kingdom

United Kingdom Literacy Assn. [IO], Leicester, United Kingdom

United Kingdom Major Ports Gp. [IO], London, United Kingdom

United Kingdom Maritime Pilots' Assn. [IO], London, United Kingdom

United Kingdom Multiple Sclerosis Specialist Nurse Assn. [IO], Ledbury, United Kingdom

United Kingdom Natl. Comm. of the Intl. Assn. on Water Pollution Res. and Control [★IO]

United Kingdom Offshore Operators' Assn. [IO], London, United Kingdom

United Kingdom Onshore Operators Gp. [IO], Cranbrook, United Kingdom

United Kingdom Paintball Sports Fed. [IO], Rochdale, United Kingdom

United Kingdom Petroleum Indus. Assn. [IO], London, United Kingdom

United Kingdom Pilots Assn. [★IO]

Reference to "IO" in place of a book number signifies that the association may be found in the 45th edition of International Organizations.

United Kingdom Polocrosse Assn. [IO], Sheffield, United Kingdom
United Kingdom Practical Shooting Assn. [IO], Harlow, United Kingdom
United Kingdom Provision Trade Fed. [★IO]
United Kingdom Reading Assn. [★IO]
United Kingdom Remote Sensing and Photogrammetry Soc. [IO], Nottingham, United Kingdom
United Kingdom Rocketry Assn. [IO], Sheffield, United Kingdom
United Kingdom Sci. Park Assn. [IO], Cambridge, United Kingdom
United Kingdom Skateboarding Assn. [IO], Waltham Abbey, United Kingdom
United Kingdom Soc. for Trenchless Tech. [IO], Leamington Spa, United Kingdom
United Kingdom Spring Mfrs. Assn. [IO], Sheffield, United Kingdom
United Kingdom Tang Soo (Soo Bahk) Do Fed. [IO], Watford, United Kingdom
United Kingdom Tea Assn. [IO], London, United Kingdom
United Kingdom Transplant Coordinators Assn. [IO], Kingsbridge, United Kingdom
United Kingdom Vineyards Assn. [IO], Cambridge, United Kingdom
United Kingdom Warehousing Assn. [IO], London, United Kingdom
United Kingdom Wayfarer Assn. [IO], Colchester, United Kingdom
United Kingdom Weighing Fed. [IO], Northampton, United Kingdom
United Kingdom's Disabled People's Coun. [IO], Derby, United Kingdom
United Knitwear Mfrs. League - Defunct.
United Lao Congress for Democracy - Address unknown since 2006.
United Laser Toner Recyclers Assn. - Address unknown since 1999.
United Latin Americans of America - Address unknown since 1995.
United League Toy Representatives Associations [3833], 1107 Broadway, Rm. 1204, New York, NY 10010, (212)691-3030
United Lesbian and Gay Christian Scientists - Address unknown since 2003.
United Leukodystrophy Found. [15372], 2304 Highland Dr., Sycamore, IL 60178, (815)895-3211
United Leukodystrophy Foundation [IO], Sycamore, IL, United States
United Liberal Democrats [IO], Seoul, Republic of Korea
United Lightning Protection Assn. [3461], 426 North Ave., Libertyville, IL 60048, (800)668-8572
United Lithuanian Relief Fund of Am. [19216], 1913 Wallace St., Philadelphia, PA 19130-3219, (215)765-2322
United Lodge of Theosophists [20594], 245 W 33rd St., Los Angeles, CA 90007, (213)748-7244
United Lodge of Theosophists [IO], Los Angeles, CA, United States
United Lodge of Theosophists - Belgium [IO], Antwerp, Belgium
United Lodge of Theosophists - India [IO], Bombay, India
United Lodge of Theosophists - Ottawa [IO], Ottawa, ON, Canada
United Lodge of Theosophists - United Kingdom [IO], London, United Kingdom
United Lutheran Church Found. - Defunct.
United Lutheran Soc. [19219], PO Box 947, Ligonier, PA 15658-0947, (724)238-9505
United Martial Arts Assn. - Address unknown since 1995.
United Methodist Assn. of Hea. and Welfare Ministries [14602], 407 Corporate Center Dr., Ste. B, Vandalia, OH 45377, (937)415-3624
United Methodist Church; Gen. Bd. of Church and Soc. of the [20263]
United Methodist Church; Gen. Commn. on Archives and History of the [10467]
United Methodist Church; Historical Soc. of the [10113]
United Methodist Church; Natl. Assn. of Schools, Colleges and Universities of the [8879]

United Methodist Church; Women's Division of the Gen. Bd. of Global Ministries of the [20269]
United Methodist Comm. on Overseas Relief [★20267]
United Methodist Comm. on Overseas Relief [★IO]
United Methodist Comm. on Relief [IO], New York, NY, United States
United Methodist Comm. on Relief [20267], 475 Riverside Dr., Rm. 330, New York, NY 10115, (212)870-3552
United Methodist Coun. on Youth Ministry [★20268]
United Methodist Youth Org. [20268], PO Box 340003, Nashville, TN 37203-0003, (615)340-7184
United Methodists for Lesbian, Gay and Bisexual Concerns; Affirmation: [20047]
United Methodists in Music and Worship Arts; Fellowship of [20261]
United Methodists; Natl. Fed. of Asian-Amer. [20266]
United Methodists in Worship, and Other Arts; Fellowship of [★20261]
United Mine Workers of Am. [24139], 8315 Lee Hwy., Fairfax, VA 22031, (703)208-7200
United Mine Workers of Am; Intl. Union [★24139]
United Mining Couns. of America - Address unknown since 1995.
United Ministries in Educ. [★19938]
United Ministries in Higher Educ. [★19938]
United Ministries in Higher Educ. [★19938]
United Missionary Church [★20362]
United Missionary Church [★IO]
United Missionary Fellowship [★IO]
United Missionary Fellowship [★19991]
United Mitochondrial Disease Found. [16363], 8085 Saltsburg Rd., Ste. 201, Pittsburgh, PA 15239, (412)793-8077
United Mopar Club [21806]
United Mortgage Bankers of America - Address unknown since 1994.
United Motor Courts of America - Defunct.
United Motorcoach Assn. [3900], 113 S West St., 4th Fl., Alexandria, VA 22314-2824, (703)838-2929
United Movement for Democracy and Unification in Korea - Defunct.
United Movement of Iranian Natl. Forces - Defunct.
United Natl. Indian Tribal Youth [10756], PO Box 800, Oklahoma City, OK 73101, (405)236-2800
United Natl. Life Insurance Soc. [★19131]
United Nations [18769], First Ave., 46th St., New York, NY 10017, (212)963-4475
United Nations [IO], New York, NY, United States

United Nations
Academic Coun. on the United Nations Sys. [IO]
Americans for UNESCO [18760]
Arab Gulf Programme for United Nations Development Organizations [IO]
Asian Pacific Fed. of UNESCO Clubs and Associations [IO]
Center for U.N. Reform Educ. [18761]
Citizens for Global Solutions [18762]
Communications Coordination Comm. for the United Nations [18763]
Communications Coordination Comm. for the United Nations [IO]
Conf. of Intl. Non-Governmental Organizations [IO]
Coun. for a Community of Democracies [5661]
Danish United Nations Assn. [IO]
Economic and Social Coun. [17459]
Emergency Coalition for U.S. Financial Support of the United Nations [18764]
Finnish United Nations Assn. [IO]
Friends of the United Nations [18765]
Global Policy Forum [17839]
Global Vision for Peace [18207]
Intl. Bank for Reconstruction and Development [17841]
Intl. Finance Corp. [17461]
Korean Natl. Commn. for UNESCO [IO]
Natl. Model United Nations [8661]
NGO Comm. on Disarmament, Peace and Security [17432]
Non-Governmental Organizations Comm. on UNICEF [18766]
Non-Governmental Organizations Committee on UNICEF [IO]

Peoples Assembly for the United Nations [18767]
Quaker United Nations Off. - Switzerland [IO]
UNESCO Association/U.S.A. [IO]
UNESCO Association/U.S.A. [18768]
UNICEF Canada [IO]
United Nations [IO]
United Nations [18769]
United Nations Assn. of Australia [IO]
United Nations Assn. of Australia - Australian Capital Territory [IO]
United Nations Assn. of Australia - New South Wales [IO]
United Nations Assn. of Australia - South Australia [IO]
United Nations Assn. of Australia - Victoria [IO]
United Nations Assn. of Australia - Western Australia [IO]
United Nations Assn. in Canada [IO]
United Nations Assn. in Canada Calgary Br. [IO]
United Nations Assn. in Canada Edmonton Br. [IO]
United Nations Assn. in Canada Hamilton Br. [IO]
United Nations Assn. in Canada Kootenay Region Br. [IO]
United Nations Assn. in Canada - Montreal [IO]
United Nations Assn. in Canada - Natl. Capital Region Br. [IO]
United Nations Assn. in Canada Quebec Br. [IO]
United Nations Assn. in Canada Quinte and District Br. [IO]
United Nations Assn. in Canada - Saguenay Lac-Saint-Jean Br. [IO]
United Nations Assn. in Canada - St. John's Br. [IO]
United Nations Assn. in Canada Toronto Region Br. [IO]
United Nations Assn. in Canada Vancouver Br. [IO]
United Nations Assn. in Canada Victoria Br. [IO]
United Nations Assn. in Canada Winnipeg Br. [IO]
United Nations Assn. in the Democratic Socialist Republic of Sri Lanka [IO]
United Nations Assn. of Great Britain and Northern Ireland [IO]
United Nations Assn. of Hungary [IO]
United Nations Assn. of Iran [IO]
United Nations Assn. of the U.S.A. [18770]
United Nations Assn. of the U.S.A. Coun. of Organizations [18771]
United Nations Commn. on the Status of Women [18772]
United Nations Commn. on the Status of Women [IO]
United Nations Non-Governmental Liaison Ser. [IO]
United Nations Staff Union [24145]
World Bank Gp. [17856]
World Coun. of Religious Leaders [20519]
World Federalist Movement [18773]
World Federalist Movement [IO]
United Nations; Amer. Assn. for the [★18770]
United Nations Asia and Far East Inst. for the Prevention of Crime and the Treatment of Offenders [IO], Tokyo, Japan
United Nations Assn. of Australia [IO], Canberra, Australia
United Nations Assn. of Australia - Australian Capital Territory [IO], Canberra, Australia
United Nations Assn. of Australia - New South Wales [IO], Sydney, Australia
United Nations Assn. of Australia - South Australia [IO], Adelaide, Australia
United Nations Assn. of Australia - Victoria [IO], Melbourne, Australia
United Nations Assn. of Australia - Western Australia [IO], East Perth, Australia
United Nations Assn. in Canada [IO], Ottawa, ON, Canada
United Nations Assn. in Canada Calgary Br. [IO], Calgary, AB, Canada
United Nations Assn. in Canada Edmonton Br. [IO], Edmonton, AB, Canada
United Nations Assn. in Canada Hamilton Br. [IO], Dundas, ON, Canada
United Nations Assn. in Canada Kootenay Region Br. [IO], Grand Forks, BC, Canada

A star before a book entry number signifies that the name is not listed separately, but is mentioned within the entry.

United Nations Assn. in Canada - Montreal [IO], Montreal, QC, Canada

United Nations Assn. in Canada - Natl. Capital Region Br. [IO], Ottawa, ON, Canada

United Nations Assn. in Canada Quebec Br. [IO], Quebec, QC, Canada

United Nations Assn. in Canada Quinte and District Br. [IO], Belleville, ON, Canada

United Nations Assn. in Canada - Saguenay Lac-Saint-Jean Br. [IO], Chicoutimi, QC, Canada

United Nations Assn. in Canada - St. John's Br. [IO], St. John's, NL, Canada

United Nations Assn. in Canada Toronto Region Br. [IO], Ottawa, ON, Canada

United Nations Assn. in Canada Vancouver Br. [IO], Vancouver, BC, Canada

United Nations Assn. in Canada Victoria Br. [IO], Victoria, BC, Canada

United Nations Assn. in Canada Winnipeg Br. [IO], Winnipeg, MB, Canada

United Nations Assn. in the Democratic Socialist Republic of Sri Lanka [IO], Panadura, Sri Lanka

United Nations Assn. of Great Britain and Northern Ireland [IO], London, United Kingdom

United Nations Assn. of Hungary [IO], Budapest, Hungary

United Nations Assn. of Iran [IO], Tehran, Iran

United Nations Assn. of Sri Lanka [★IO]

United Nations Assn. of the U.S.A. [18770], 801 2nd Ave., 2nd Fl., New York, NY 10017, (212)907-1300

United Nations Assn. of the U.S.A. Coun. of Organizations [18771], 801 2nd Ave., 2nd Fl., New York, NY 10017, (212)907-1300

United Nations Centre Against Apartheid - Defunct.

United Nations Centre for Human Rights [★IO]

United Nations Children's Fund - Armenia [IO], Yerevan, Armenia

United Nations Children's Fund - Botswana [IO], Gaborone, Botswana

United Nations Children's Fund - Namibia [IO], Windhoek, Namibia

United Nations Children's Fund - USA [★IO]

United Nations Children's Fund - USA [★11658]

United Nations Commn. on the Status of Women [18772], c/o Div. for the Advancement of Women, 2 United Nations Plz., Rm. DC2, 12th Fl., New York, NY 10017

United Nations Commn. on the Status of Women [IO], New York, NY, United States

United Nations Comm. on the Peaceful Uses of Outer Space [IO], Vienna, Austria

United Nations; Conf. Gp. of U.S. Natl. Organizations on the [★18770]

United Nations Conf. on Trade and Development [IO], Geneva, Switzerland

United Nations Correspondents Assn. [IO], New York, NY, United States

United Nations Correspondents Assn. [3168], United Nations, 405 E 42nd St., Rm. S-326, New York, NY 10017, (212)963-7137

United Nations Decade for Women; Voluntary Fund for the [★17571]

United Nations Delegations; Hospitality Comm. for [17895]

United Nations Development Fund for Women [17571], 304 E 45th St., 15th Fl., New York, NY 10017, (212)906-6400

United Nations Development Fund for Women [IO], New York, NY, United States

United Nations Development Prog. - Armenia [IO], Yerevan, Armenia

United Nations Development Prog. - Mali [IO], Bamako, Mali

United Nations Development Prog. - Mauritania [IO], Nouakchott, Mauritania

United Nations Development Prog. - Mauritius and Seychelles [IO], Port Louis, Mauritius

United Nations Development Prog. - Nigeria [IO], Abuja, Nigeria

United Nations Development Prog. - Rwanda [IO], Kigali, Rwanda

United Nations Development Prog. - Togo [IO], Lome, Togo

United Nations Development Programme [IO], New York, NY, United States

United Nations Development Programme [17851], 1 United Nations Plz., New York, NY 10017, (212)906-5000

United Nations Development Programme - Cameroon [IO], Yaounde, Cameroon

United Nations Development Programme - Cote d'Ivoire [IO], Abidjan, Cote d'Ivoire

United Nations Development Programme - Djibouti [IO], Djibouti, Djibouti

United Nations Development Programme - Ethiopia [IO], Addis Ababa, Ethiopia

United Nations Development Programme - Gambia [IO], Cape Point, Gambia

United Nations Development Programme - Ghana [IO], Accra, Ghana

United Nations Development Programme - Malawi [IO], Lilongwe, Malawi

United Nations Development Programme - Mozambique [IO], Maputo, Mozambique

United Nations Development Programme - Namibia [IO], Windhoek, Namibia

United Nations Development Programme - Regional Bur. for Asia and the Pacific [IO], New York, NY, United States

United Nations Development Programme - Regional Bur. for Asia and the Pacific [17852], c/o United Nations Development Programme, One United Nations Plz., New York, NY 10017, (212)906-5800

United Nations Development Programme - South Africa [IO], Pretoria, Republic of South Africa

United Nations Development Programme - Tanzania [IO], Dar es Salaam, United Republic of Tanzania

United Nations Development Programme - Uganda [IO], Kampala, Uganda

United Nations Div. for the Advancement of Women [IO], New York, NY, United States

United Nations Div. for the Advancement of Women [13441], 2 United Nations Plz., DC2-12th Fl., New York, NY 10017

United Nations Economic Commn. for Africa [IO], Addis Ababa, Ethiopia

United Nations Economic Commn. for Europe [IO], Geneva, Switzerland

United Nations Economic and Social Commn. for Asia and the Pacific [IO], Bangkok, Thailand

United Nations Educational, Sci. and Cultural Org. [IO], Paris, France

United Nations Env. Prog; Friends of the [★4613]

United Nations Env. Prog; U.S. Comm. for the [4613]

United Nations Env. Programme - Kenya [IO], Nairobi, Kenya

United Nations Env. Programme - Regional Off. for Asia and the Pacific [IO], Bangkok, Thailand

United Nations Env. Programme - Regional Off. for Europe [IO], Geneva, Switzerland

United Nations Env. Programme - Regional Off. for Latin Amer. and the Caribbean [★IO]

United Nations Framework Convention on Climate Change [IO], Bonn, Germany

United Nations HQ Nongovernmental Organizations Comm. on Youth [★13508]

United Nations High Commissioner for Refugees - Regional Off. Mexico [IO], Polanco, Mexico

United Nations High Commissioner for Refugees - Switzerland [IO], Geneva, Switzerland

United Nations High Commissioner for Refugees; USA for the [12824]

United Nations Indus. Development Org. [IO], Vienna, Austria

United Nations Indus. Development Org. - Algeria [IO], Algiers, Algeria

United Nations Indus. Development Org. - Bolivia [IO], La Paz, Bolivia

United Nations Indus. Development Org. - Cameroon [IO], Yaounde, Cameroon

United Nations Indus. Development Org. - China [IO], Beijing, People's Republic of China

United Nations Indus. Development Org. - Colombia [IO], Bogota, Colombia

United Nations Indus. Development Org. - Cote d'Ivoire [IO], Abidjan, Cote d'Ivoire

United Nations Indus. Development Org. - Egypt [IO], Cairo, Egypt

United Nations Indus. Development Org. - Eritrea [IO], Asmara, Eritrea

United Nations Indus. Development Org. - Ethiopia [IO], Addis Ababa, Ethiopia

United Nations Indus. Development Org. - Ghana [IO], Accra, Ghana

United Nations Indus. Development Org. - Guinea [IO], Conakry, Guinea

United Nations Indus. Development Org. - India [IO], New Delhi, India

United Nations Indus. Development Org. - Indonesia [IO], Jakarta, Indonesia

United Nations Indus. Development Org. - Iran [IO], Tehran, Iran

United Nations Indus. Development Org. - Kenya [IO], Nairobi, Kenya

United Nations Indus. Development Org. - Lebanon [IO], Beirut, Lebanon

United Nations Indus. Development Org. - Madagascar [IO], Antananarivo, Madagascar

United Nations Indus. Development Org. - Mexico [IO], Mexico City, Mexico

United Nations Indus. Development Org. - Morocco [IO], Rabat, Morocco

United Nations Indus. Development Org. - Mozambique [IO], Maputo, Mozambique

United Nations Indus. Development Org. - Nigeria [IO], Abuja, Nigeria

United Nations Indus. Development Org. - Pakistan [IO], Islamabad, Pakistan

United Nations Indus. Development Org. - Philippines [IO], Makati City, Philippines

United Nations Indus. Development Org. - Senegal [IO], Dakar, Senegal

United Nations Indus. Development Org. - Sudan [IO], Khartoum, Sudan

United Nations Indus. Development Org. - Thailand [IO], Bangkok, Thailand

United Nations Indus. Development Org. - Tunisia [IO], Tunis, Tunisia

United Nations Indus. Development Org. - Uruguay [IO], Montevideo, Uruguay

United Nations Indus. Development Org. - Vietnam [IO], Hanoi, Vietnam

United Nations Indus. Development Org. - Zimbabwe [IO], Harare, Zimbabwe

United Nations Info. Centre - Nigeria [IO], Lagos, Nigeria

United Nations Inst. for Training and Res. [IO], Geneva, Switzerland

United Nations Intl. Children's Emergency Fund [★IO]

United Nations Intl. Children's Emergency Fund [★11658]

United Nations League of Lawyers - Address unknown since 1995.

United Nations; Natl. Model [★8661]

United Nations; Natl. Model [8661]

United Nations Non-Governmental Liaison Ser. [IO], Geneva, Switzerland

United Nations Philatelic Soc. - Defunct.

United Nations Philatelists, Inc. [22884], PO Box 146, Morrisville, PA 19067-0146, (215)295-3143

United Nations Population Fund - Afghanistan [IO], Kabul, Afghanistan

United Nations Population Fund - Albania [IO], Tirana, Albania

United Nations Population Fund - Algeria [IO], Algiers, Algeria

United Nations Population Fund - Angola [IO], Luanda, Angola

United Nations Population Fund - Argentina [IO], Buenos Aires, Argentina

United Nations Population Fund - Armenia [IO], Yerevan, Armenia

United Nations Population Fund - Azerbaijan [IO], Baku, Azerbaijan

United Nations Population Fund - Bahrain [IO], Manama, Bahrain

United Nations Population Fund - Bangladesh [IO], Dhaka, Bangladesh

United Nations Population Fund - Barbados [IO], Bridgetown, Barbados

United Nations Population Fund - Belarus [IO], Minsk, Belarus

United Nations Population Fund - Belgium [IO], Brussels, Belgium

Reference to "IO" in place of a book number signifies that the association may be found in the 45th edition of International Organizations.

United Nations Population Fund - Benin [IO], Cotonou, Benin

United Nations Population Fund - Bhutan [IO], Thimphu, Bhutan

United Nations Population Fund - Bolivia [IO], La Paz, Bolivia

United Nations Population Fund - Bosnia and Herzegovina [IO], Sarajevo, Bosnia-Hercegovina

United Nations Population Fund - Brazil [IO], Brasilia, Brazil

United Nations Population Fund - Bulgaria [IO], Sofia, Bulgaria

United Nations Population Fund - Burkina Faso [IO], Ouagadougou, Burkina Faso

United Nations Population Fund - Burundi [IO], Bujumbura, Burundi

United Nations Population Fund - Cambodia [IO], Phnom Penh, Cambodia

United Nations Population Fund - Cameroon [IO], Yaounde, Cameroon

United Nations Population Fund - Cape Verde [IO], Praia, Cape Verde

United Nations Population Fund - Central African Republic [IO], Bangui, Central African Republic

United Nations Population Fund - Chad [IO], N'Djamena, Chad

United Nations Population Fund - Chile [IO], Santiago, Chile

United Nations Population Fund - China [IO], Beijing, People's Republic of China

United Nations Population Fund - Colombia [IO], Bogota, Colombia

United Nations Population Fund - Comoros [IO], Moroni, Comoros

United Nations Population Fund - Costa Rica [IO], San Jose, Costa Rica

United Nations Population Fund - Cote d'Ivoire [IO], Abidjan, Cote d'Ivoire

United Nations Population Fund - Cuba [IO], Havana, Cuba

United Nations Population Fund - Cyprus [IO], Nicosia, Cyprus

United Nations Population Fund - Democratic People's Republic of Korea [IO], Pyongyang, Democratic People's Republic of Korea

United Nations Population Fund - Democratic Republic of Congo [IO], Kinshasa, Democratic Republic of the Congo

United Nations Population Fund - Djibouti [IO], Djibouti, Djibouti

United Nations Population Fund - Dominican Republic [IO], Santo Domingo, Dominican Republic

United Nations Population Fund - Ecuador [IO], Quito, Ecuador

United Nations Population Fund - Egypt [IO], Cairo, Egypt

United Nations Population Fund - El Salvador [IO], San Salvador, El Salvador

United Nations Population Fund - Estonia [IO], Tallinn, Estonia

United Nations Population Fund - Ethiopia [IO], Addis Ababa, Ethiopia

United Nations Population Fund - Fiji [IO], Suva, Fiji

United Nations Population Fund - Gabon [IO], Libreville, Gabon

United Nations Population Fund - Gambia [IO], Banjul, Gambia

United Nations Population Fund - Georgia [IO], Tbilisi, Georgia

United Nations Population Fund - Ghana [IO], Accra, Ghana

United Nations Population Fund - Guatemala [IO], Guatemala City, Guatemala

United Nations Population Fund - Guinea [IO], Conakry, Guinea

United Nations Population Fund - Guyana [IO], Georgetown, Guyana

United Nations Population Fund - Haiti [IO], Port-au-Prince, Haiti

United Nations Population Fund - Honduras [IO], Tegucigalpa, Honduras

United Nations Population Fund - India [IO], New Delhi, India

United Nations Population Fund - Indonesia [IO], Jakarta, Indonesia

United Nations Population Fund - Iran [IO], Tehran, Iran

United Nations Population Fund - Iraq [IO], Baghdad, Iraq

United Nations Population Fund - Jamaica [IO], Kingston, Jamaica

United Nations Population Fund - Japan [IO], Tokyo, Japan

United Nations Population Fund - Jordan [IO], Amman, Jordan

United Nations Population Fund - Kazakhstan [IO], Almaty, Kazakhstan

United Nations Population Fund - Kenya [IO], Nairobi, Kenya

United Nations Population Fund - Kuwait [IO], Safat, Kuwait

United Nations Population Fund - Kyrgyzstan [IO], Bishkek, Kirgizstan

United Nations Population Fund - Latvia [IO], Riga, Latvia

United Nations Population Fund - Lebanon [IO], Beirut, Lebanon

United Nations Population Fund - Lesotho [IO], Maseru, Lesotho

United Nations Population Fund - Liberia [IO], Monrovia, Liberia

United Nations Population Fund - Lithuania [IO], Vilnius, Lithuania

United Nations Population Fund - Madagascar [IO], Antananarivo, Madagascar

United Nations Population Fund - Malawi [IO], Lilongwe, Malawi

United Nations Population Fund - Malaysia [IO], Kuala Lumpur, Malaysia

United Nations Population Fund - Maldives [IO], Male, Maldives

United Nations Population Fund - Mali [IO], Bamako, Mali

United Nations Population Fund - Mauritania [IO], Nouakchott, Mauritania

United Nations Population Fund - Mauritius [IO], Port Louis, Mauritius

United Nations Population Fund - Mexico [IO], Mexico City, Mexico

United Nations Population Fund - Mongolia [IO], Ulan Bator, Mongolia

United Nations Population Fund - Morocco [IO], Rabat, Morocco

United Nations Population Fund - Mozambique [IO], Maputo, Mozambique

United Nations Population Fund - Myanmar [IO], Yangon, Myanmar

United Nations Population Fund - Namibia [IO], Windhoek, Namibia

United Nations Population Fund - Nepal [IO], Kathmandu, Nepal

United Nations Population Fund - Nicaragua [IO], Managua, Nicaragua

United Nations Population Fund - Niger [IO], Niamey, Niger

United Nations Population Fund - Nigeria [IO], Abuja, Nigeria

United Nations Population Fund - Pakistan [IO], Islamabad, Pakistan

United Nations Population Fund - Palestine [IO], Jerusalem, Israel

United Nations Population Fund - Panama [IO], Panama City, Panama

United Nations Population Fund - Papua New Guinea [IO], Port Moresby, Papua New Guinea

United Nations Population Fund - Paraguay [IO], Asuncion, Paraguay

United Nations Population Fund - Peru [IO], Lima, Peru

United Nations Population Fund - Philippines [IO], Makati City, Philippines

United Nations Population Fund - Poland [IO], Warsaw, Poland

United Nations Population Fund - Republic of Korea [IO], Seoul, Republic of Korea

United Nations Population Fund - Republic of Moldova [IO], Chisinau, Moldova

United Nations Population Fund - Romania [IO], Bucharest, Romania

United Nations Population Fund - Rwanda [IO], Kigali, Rwanda

United Nations Population Fund - Samoa [IO], Apia, Western Samoa

United Nations Population Fund - Sao Tome and Principe [IO], Sao Tome, Sao Tome and Principe

United Nations Population Fund - Saudi Arabia [IO], Riyadh, Saudi Arabia

United Nations Population Fund - Senegal [IO], Dakar, Senegal

United Nations Population Fund - Sierra Leone [IO], Freetown, Sierra Leone

United Nations Population Fund - South Africa [IO], Pretoria, Republic of South Africa

United Nations Population Fund - Sri Lanka [IO], Colombo, Sri Lanka

United Nations Population Fund - Sudan [IO], Khartoum, Sudan

United Nations Population Fund - Swaziland [IO], Mbabane, Swaziland

United Nations Population Fund - Syrian Arab Republic [IO], Damascus, Syrian Arab Republic

United Nations Population Fund - Tajikistan [IO], Dushanbe, Tajikistan

United Nations Population Fund - Tanzania [IO], Dar es Salaam, United Republic of Tanzania

United Nations Population Fund - Thailand [IO], Bangkok, Thailand

United Nations Population Fund - Togo [IO], Lome, Togo

United Nations Population Fund - Trinidad and Tobago [IO], Port of Spain, Trinidad and Tobago

United Nations Population Fund - Tunisia [IO], Tunis, Tunisia

United Nations Population Fund - Turkey [IO], Ankara, Turkey

United Nations Population Fund - Turkmenistan [IO], Ashgabat, Turkmenistan

United Nations Population Fund - Uganda [IO], Kampala, Uganda

United Nations Population Fund - Ukraine [IO], Kiev, Ukraine

United Nations Population Fund - United Arab Emirates [IO], Abu Dhabi, United Arab Emirates

United Nations Population Fund - Uruguay [IO], Montevideo, Uruguay

United Nations Population Fund - Uzbekistan [IO], Tashkent, Uzbekistan

United Nations Population Fund - Venezuela [IO], Caracas, Venezuela

United Nations Population Fund - Yemen [IO], Sana'a, Yemen

United Nations Res. Inst. for Social Development [IO], Geneva, Switzerland

United Nations Soc. of Mohicans - Address unknown since 1995.

United Nations; Speakers Res. Comm. for the [★18763]

United Nations Special Comm. Against Apartheid - Defunct.

United Nations Staff Assn. [★24145]

United Nations Staff Assn. [★IO]

United Nations Staff Union [IO], New York, NY, United States

United Nations Staff Union [24145], Secretariat Bldg., Rm. S-0525, New York, NY 10017, (212)963-7075

United Nations Study Unit - Defunct.

United Nations Sys. Standing Comm. on Nutrition [IO], Geneva, Switzerland

United Nations Theatre Group - Address unknown since 1994.

United Nations; U.S. Comm. for the [★18770]

United Nations Volunteers [IO], Bonn, Germany

United Nations Women's Guild [IO], New York, NY, United States

United Nations Women's Guild [13066], 1 UN Plz., DC-1, Rm. 0775, New York, NY 10017, (212)963-8279

United Native Amers. - Address unknown since 1995.

United Negro Coll. Fund [8437], 8260 Willow Oaks Corporate Dr., PO Box 10444, Fairfax, VA 22031-8044, (703)205-3404

United Negro Coll. Fund; Natl. Alumni Coun. of the [18910]

United Neighborhood Centers of Am. [11792], 11700 W Lake Park Dr., Milwaukee, WI 53224, (414)359-1040

A star before a book entry number signifies that the name is not listed separately, but is mentioned within the entry.

United Network Command [25045], c/o Stan Warpechowski, Pres., 231 Niagara St., Buffalo, NY 14201-2336
United Network Command [IO], Buffalo, NY, United States
United Network for Organ Sharing [16684], PO Box 2484, Richmond, VA 23218-2484, (804)782-4800
United New Conservationists - Defunct.
United North Lebanon Soc. [18954]
United Order of the Golden Cross [★19441]
United Order True Sisters [19437], Linton Intl. Plz., 660 Linton Blvd., Ste. 6, Delray Beach, FL 33444, (561)265-1557
United Orpington Club - Address unknown since 1995.
United Orthodox Ministers and Cantors Assn. of America and Canada - Address unknown since 1995.
United Orthodox Rabbinate - Defunct.
United Ostomy Assn. of Canada [IO], Toronto, ON, Canada
United Ostomy Assn. - Defunct.
United Pants and Novelties Contractors Assn. - Defunct.
United Paperworkers Intl. Union [24104], 3340 Perimeter Hill Dr., Nashville, TN 37202, (615)834-8590
United Paperworkers Intl. Union [IO], Nashville, TN, United States
United Parents of Absconded Children - Defunct.
United Parents and Teachers Assn. of Jewish Schools - Defunct.
United Parkinson Found. [★15360]
United Patients Assn. for Pulmonary Hypertension [★14911]
United Patriotic Front - Defunct.
United Patriots for Constitutional Act - Defunct.
United for Peace [★18248]
United for Peace [★IO]
United for Peace and Justice [IO], New York, NY, United States
United for Peace and Justice [18248], PO Box 607, Times Square Sta., New York, NY 10108, (212)868-5545
United Pegasus Found. [17732], 120 S 1st Ave., Arcadia, CA 91006, (626)279-1306
United Peregrine Soc. - Defunct.
United Plant Savers [13655], PO Box 400, East Barre, VT 05649, (802)476-6467
United Plant Savers [IO], East Barre, VT, United States
United Plastics Distributors Assn. [★IO]
United Plastics Distributors Assn. [★3051]
United Poets Laureate Intl. - Address unknown since 1988.
United Polish Women of Am. [★19311]
United Popular Dress Mfrs. Assn. [★244]
United Postal Stationery Soc. [22885], PO Box 3982, Chester, VA 23831
United Poultry Concerns [11472], PO Box 150, Machipongo, VA 23405-0150, (757)678-7875
United Presbyterian Hea., Educ. and Welfare Assn. [★13184]
United Presbyterian Peace Fellowship [★18241]
United Presbyterian Women [★20475]
United Press Associations [★3169]
United Press Associations [★IO]
United Press Intl. [IO], Washington, DC, United States
United Press Intl. [3169], 1510 H St. NW, Washington, DC 20005, (202)898-8188
United Press Intl. - Chile [IO], Santiago, Chile
United Press Intl. - Hong Kong [IO], Hong Kong, People's Republic of China
United Press Intl. - Japan [IO], Tokyo, Japan
United Press Intl. - Korea [IO], Seoul, Republic of Korea
United Press Intl. - Middle East [IO], Beirut, Lebanon
United Press Intl. - UK [IO], Middlesex, United Kingdom
United Pro-Life Coun. - Defunct.
United Producers [5030], PO Box 29800, Columbus, OH 43229, (614)890-6666
United Products Formulators and Distributors Assn. - Address unknown since 2002.

United Professional Horsemen's Assn. [4961], 4059 Iron Works Pkwy., Ste. 2, Lexington, KY 40511, (859)231-5070
United Professional Sales Assn. [3476], 1700 Pennsylvania Ave. NW, Ste. 400, Washington, DC 20006, (877)694-8262
United Professional Softball League - Defunct.
United Racquetsports for Women - Address unknown since 1995.
United Railroad Operating Crafts - Defunct.
United Religions Initiative [20518], PO Box 29242, San Francisco, CA 94129, (415)561-2300
United Religions Initiative [IO], San Francisco, CA, United States
United Republicans for Equality and Privacy [★18523]
United Retail Fish Dealers Assn. of New York - Address unknown since 1995.
United Retail Workers [★24061]
United Rink Operators - Defunct.
United Road Transport Union [IO], Manchester, United Kingdom
United Roumanian Jews of America - Defunct.
United Russian Orthodox Brotherhood of Am. [★19339]
United to Save America - Defunct.
United Savers Assn. [17638]
United Scenic Artists [24160], 29 W 38th St., New York, NY 10018, (212)581-0300
United School Sport Assn. South Africa [IO], Kempton Park, Republic of South Africa
United Schutzhund Clubs of Am. [22371], 3810 Paule Ave., St. Louis, MO 63125-1718, (314)638-9686
United Scleroderma Found. - Defunct.
United Seamen's Ser. [13008], 635 Fourth Ave., Ground Fl., Brooklyn, NY 11232, (718)369-3818
United Seamen's Ser. [IO], Brooklyn, NY, United States
United Secularists of America - Address unknown since 1988.
United to Secure Am. [18596], 1301 Pennsylvania Ave. NW, Ste. 500, Washington, DC 20004, (202)742-4251
United Self-Help Success Clubs [★13020]
United Seniors Assn. [11322], PO Box 2038, Purcellville, VA 20132, (703)359-6500
United Serpents - Address unknown since 1999.
United Ser. Organizations [★18962]
United Ser. Organizations [★IO]
United Services for New Americans [★IO]
United Services for New Americans [★12471]
United Shareholders Assn. - Address unknown since 1994.
United Shareowners of America - Defunct.
United Shipowners of America - Defunct.
United Shoe Retailers Assn. [1602], c/o Linda Hauss, Exec. Dir., PO Box 4931, West Hills, CA 91308, (818)703-6062
United Sidecar Assn. [22693], c/o Al Roach, Sec., 130 S Michigan Ave., Villa Park, IL 60181, (630)833-6732
United Silver Fanciers [21924], c/o Vicki Blandford, Sec./Membership Chair, 1535 Northwold Dr., Atlanta, GA 30350, (770)671-1121
United Sisters of Charity [20406]
United Sisters - Defunct.
United Slate, Tile and Composition Roofers, Damp and Waterproof Workers Assn. [★24033]
United Soccer League - Defunct.
United Societies of Physiotherapists - Address unknown since 2001.
United Societies of the U.S.A. - Address unknown since 2004.
United Soc. for the Propagation of the Gospel [IO], London, United Kingdom
United Soft Serve and Fast Food Association [★1958]
United Sons of Israel [20187]
United South and Eastern Tribes [12632], 711 Stewarts Ferry Pike, Ste. 100, Nashville, TN 37214, (615)872-7900
United Southeastern Tribes [★12632]
United Soybean Bd. [4767], 16640 Chesterfield Grove Rd., Ste. 130, Chesterfield, MO 63005, (636)530-1777

United Spanish War Veterans - Address unknown since 2000.
United Spanish War Veterans; Natl. Fort Daughters of '98, Auxiliary [21267]
United Specialty Agents Alliance - Address unknown since 2003.
United Speedways of North Am. [23671]
United Sports Fans of America - Address unknown since 2004.
United Sportsman Racers Assn. - Defunct.
United Sportsmans Assn. of North Am. [23058], 224 Sandbridge Rd., Pittsgrove, NJ 08318, (856)358-4891
United Spouses Assn. [21202], c/o Chanda VanDuser, 12542 Armada Pl., Woodbridge, VA 22192
United Sprint Assn. - Address unknown since 1991.
United Square Dancers of Am. [9898], c/o Si Kittle, Co-Pres., 320 Maynard Dr., Sun Prairie, WI 53590, (608)837-6958
United Stamp Soc. for Shut-Ins - Address unknown since 1995.
U.S. [★12658]

United States
Africa Action [16918]
Africa-America Inst. [16919]
Africa Faith and Justice Network [16920]
Africa News Ser. [16921]
Alpha-66 [17363]
Amer. Assembly [18418]
Amer. Civil Liberties Union [17084]
Amer. Coun. on Consumer Interests [17305]
Amer. Defense Inst. [17373]
Americans for Informed Democracy [5660]
America's Future [17624]
Arms Control Association/Arms Control Today [17422]
Asia Pacific - USA Chamber of Commerce [24264]
Assn. of Concerned African Scholars [16926]
Assn. of Thai Professionals in Am. and Canada [19406]
Atlantic Coun. of the U.S. [17014]
Bulgarian Natl. Front [17027]
Bus. Coun. for Intl. Understanding [17862]
Bus. Executives for Natl. Security [18587]
Bus. Roundtable [18402]
Center for Constitutional Rights [17097]
Center for the Defense of Free Enterprise [17625]
Center for Intl. Policy [17748]
Citizens for Governmental Restraint [17288]
Close Up Found. [17071]
Comm. to Restore the Constitution [17290]
Comm. on US/Latin Amer. Relations [19194]
Congressional Arts Caucus [17254]
Congressional Automotive Caucus [17255]
Constitutional Rights Found. [17291]
Coun. on Foreign Relations [17608]
Coun. for a Livable World [17425]
Coun. for a Livable World Educ. Fund [17426]
Croatian Amer. Assn. [17868]
East-West Center [17882]
Eisenhower Fellowships [17884]
Emergency Coalition for U.S. Financial Support of the United Nations [18764]
Extra Miler Club [23013]
Filipino Amer. Coalition for Environmental Solidarity [4634]
Flag Mfrs. Assn. of Am. [1487]
Freedom of Expression Found. [17116]
French-American Found. [17886]
Friendship Force Intl. [17889]
Fund for Constitutional Govt. [17669]
Ghana-USA Chamber of Commerce [24279]
Independent Americans [17294]
Intl. Center [17613]
Jewish Inst. for Natl. Security Affairs [17380]
John Birch Soc. [17274]
Leuva Patidar Samaj of USA [10221]
Liberty Amendment Comm. of the U.S.A. [17296]
Lincoln Inst. for Res. and Educ. [16940]
Natl. Center for Constitutional Stud. [17297]
Natl. Comm. for an Effective Cong. [17252]
Natl. Comm. on United States-China Relations [17064]

Reference to "IO" in place of a book number signifies that the association may be found in the 45th edition of International Organizations.

Encyclopedia of Associations, 46th Edition

4251

Natl. Coun. of State Tourism Directors [24385]
Natl. Coun. on U.S.-Arab Relations [18066]
Natl. Justice Found. of Am. [17298]
Natl. Lawyers Assn. [5521]
Natl. Strategy Info. Center [17383]
Oper. Crossroads Africa [16932]
Org. of Chinese Americans [17065]
Palestine Liberation Org. [18069]
Panamerican/PanAfrican Assn. [17371]
People for the Amer. Way [17143]
The Russian-American Center/Track Two Inst. for Citizen Diplomacy [17912]
Secretary's Open Forum [17617]
Senate Tourism Caucus [17259]
Serbian Bar Assn. of Am. [5531]
Sister Cities Intl. [17913]
TransAfrica Forum [16934]
Trinidad and Tobago/USA Chamber of Commerce [24298]
U.S.-Asia Inst. [17009]
U.S.-China Peoples Friendship Assn. [17066]
U.S.-Cuba Trade Assn. [2316]
United States-Indonesia Soc. [775]
U.S.-Vietnam Trade Coun. [17010]
US-Ireland Alliance [776]
Washington Off. on Africa [16935]
Winrock Intl. [16959]
World Policy Inst. [17620]
U.S. 1 Class Assn. - Address unknown since 2003.
U.S. 6 Metre Assn. - Defunct.
U.S. 420 Assn. - Address unknown since 1995.
U.S. 470 Assn. - Address unknown since 2007.
U.S. 1869 Pictoral Res. Associates [★22887]
U.S. A-Class Catamaran Assn. [23225], c/o Hall Spars, 33 Broadcommon Rd., Bristol, RI 02809
U.S. A-Div. Catamaran Assn. - Address unknown since 1990.
U.S. Acad. of Arms - Defunct.
U.S. Acad. of European Fencing [22414]
U.S. Adult Cystic Fibrosis Assn. [16364], PO Box 1618, Gresham, OR 97030-0519, (503)669-3561
U.S. Adult Soccer Assn. [23857], 9152 Kent Ave., Ste. C-50, Indianapolis, IN 46216, (317)541-8564
U.S. Advanced Ceramics Assn. - Address unknown since 1994.
U.S. Adventure Racing Assn. [23672], 12403 Bluestone Cir., Austin, TX 78758, (512)873-1205
U.S. African Development Found. [17853], 1400 I St. NW, Ste. 1000, Washington, DC 20005, (202)673-3916
U.S. Aikido Fed. [23049], c/o Susan McKenzie Wolk, Sec., 98 State St., Northampton, MA 01060, (413)586-7122
U.S. Air Force Acad; Assn. of Graduates of the [18875]
U.S. Air Force Judo Assn. [★23555]
U.S. Air Racing Assn. [★23041]
U.S. Air Tour Assn. [3830], c/o Steve Bassett, Pres., 9626 Hadleigh Ct., Ste. 101, Laurel, MD 20723, (301)483-0158
U.S. Air Traffic Controllers Org. - Defunct.
U.S. Airsoft Corps [23620], PO Box 8825, Columbia, SC 29202-8825, (803)622-7932
U.S. Albacore Assn. [23226], c/o Kay Marsh, Membership Sec./Ed., 1031 Graham St., Bethlehem, PA 18015-2520
U.S.-Albania Friendship Assn. - Address unknown since 1986.
U.S. Alpine Club - Defunct.
U.S. Amateur Ballroom Dancers Assn. [★9900]
U.S. Amateur Confed. of Roller Skating [★23746]
U.S. Amateur Confed. of Roller Skating [23742], c/o USA Roller Sports, 4730 South St., Lincoln, NE 68506, (402)483-7551
U.S. Amateur Dancers Assn. - Address unknown since 2002.
U.S. Amateur Jai Alai Players Assn. - Defunct.
U.S. Amateur Jump Rope Fed. [23698], PO Box 569, Huntsville, TX 77342-0569, (936)295-3332
U.S. Amateur Racquetball Assn. [★23678]
U.S. Amateur Roller Skating Assn. [★23742]
U.S. Amateur Tug of War Assn. [23959], 1855 Hwy. 69, Verona, WI 53593, (800)TUGOWAR
U.S. Amateur Wrestling Found. - Defunct.
U.S.A. Amateur Boxing Fed. [★23267]

U.S.A. Chap. of AIDA [★5829]
U.S.A. Chap. of AIDA [★IO]
U.S. of America-China Chamber of Commerce [IO], Chicago, IL, United States
U.S. of America-China Chamber of Commerce [24310], 55 W Monroe St., Ste. 630, Chicago, IL 60603, (312)368-9911
U.S.A. Confed. [★23742]
U.S.A. Cricket Assn. [23299], PO Box 589, Yonkers, NY 10702, (301)646-0383
U.S.A. Deaf Basketball [23136], c/o Lad Baird, Treas., 104 W Rose St., Sioux Falls, SD 57105
U.S.A. Field Hockey [★23405]
U.S.A. Natl. Comm. of the Intl. Dairy Fed. [★4487]
U.S.A. Natl. Comm. of the Intl. Dairy Fed. [★IO]
U.S.A. Netball Assn. [23634], PO Box 1105, New York, NY 10274-1105
U.S.A. Rugby Fives Assn. - Address unknown since 2004.
U.S.A. Slo-Pitch Softball Assn. [★23795]
U.S.A. Sports Fed. [★23637]
U.S.A. Standards Inst. [★6267]
U.S.A. Transactional Anal. Assn. [13743], 4810 Sutcliff Ave., San Jose, CA 95118-2341, (408)723-8231
U.S.A; Udruzenje Jugoslovenskih Jevreja u [★19175]
U.S.A. Underwater Fed. - Defunct.
U.S.A. Wushu-Kungfu Fed. [23605], 6313 Harford Rd., Baltimore, MD 21214, (410)444-6666
U.S. of Amer. Amateur Boxing Fed. [★23267]
U.S. Amputee Athletic Assn. [★23343]
U.S. - Angola Chamber of Commerce [24299], 1100 17th St., NW Ste. 1100A, Washington, DC 20036, (202)223-0540
U.S. - Angola Chamber of Commerce [IO], Washington, DC, United States
U.S. Animal Bank - Defunct.
U.S. Animal Hea. Assn. [16811], PO Box 8805, St. Joseph, MO 64508, (816)671-1144
U.S. Antarctic Prog. [7518], Off. of Polar Programs, Natl. Sci. Found., 4201 Wilson Blvd., Rm. 755, Arlington, VA 22203, (703)292-5111
U.S. Antiaircraft Assn. [★6071]
U.S. Apnea Assn. [23380], 87-3184 EA Rd., Captain Cook, HI 96704
U.S. Apnea Assn. [IO], Captain Cook, HI, United States
U.S. Apparel Coun. - Defunct.
U.S. Apple Assn. [4768], 8233 Old Courthouse Rd., Ste. 200, Vienna, VA 22182, (703)442-8850
U.S. Apple Association [IO], Vienna, VA, United States
U.S. Aquaculture Coun. - Defunct.
U.S. Aquaculture Fed. - Defunct.
U.S. Aquaculture Soc. [4183], Louisiana State Univ., 143 J.M. Parker Coliseum, Baton Rouge, LA 70803, (225)578-3137
U.S. Aquaculture Suppliers Assn. [4026]
U.S. Aquatic Sports [23890], c/o Debra Turner, Marketing Coor., 7565 Oceanline Dr., Indianapolis, IN 46214-4118, (317)829-5787
U.S.-Arab Chamber of Commerce - Defunct.
United States-Arab Chamber of Commerce; Natl. [24290]
U.S. Archery Cong. - Defunct.
U.S. Armbrust Assn. [★23058]
U.S. Armor Assn. [6107], PO Box 607, Fort Knox, KY 40121-0607, (502)942-8624
U.S. Armored Cavalry Assn. [★6107]
U.S. ArmSports [23991], 423 E Washington St., Petaluma, CA 94952, (707)537-7373
U.S. Army Ambulance Service Assn. - Defunct.
U.S. Army; Assn. of the [6071]
U.S. Army Mothers, Natl. - Defunct.
U.S. Army, Navy and Air Force Bandsmen's Assn. - Defunct.
U.S. Army Ranger Assn. [20707], PO Box 52126, Fort Benning, GA 31995-2126, (703)830-2484
U.S. Army Special Forces Decade Assn. [★21270]
U.S. Army Special Forces Decade Club [★21270]
U.S. Army Warrant Officers Assn. [6108], 462 Herndon Pkwy., Ste. 207, Herndon, VA 20170-5235, (703)742-7727
U.S. - ASEAN Bus. Coun. [3848], 1101 17th St. NW, Ste. 411, Washington, DC 20036, (202)289-1911

U.S. - ASEAN Bus. Coun. [IO], Washington, DC, United States
U.S. - ASEAN Coun. for Bus. and Tech. [★IO]
U.S. - ASEAN Coun. for Bus. and Tech. [★3848]
United States-Asia Environmental Partnership [4612], 709 Potomac St., Alexandria, VA 22314-3859, (202)835-0333
U.S.-Asia Inst. [17009], 232 E Capitol St. NE, Washington, DC 20003, (202)544-3181
U.S.-Asia Inst. [IO], Washington, DC, United States
U.S.-Asian Relations; Commn. on [★17010]
U.S. Associates of the Intl. Chamber of Commerce [★766]
U.S. Associates of the Intl. Chamber of Commerce [★IO]
U.S. Assn. for Blind Athletes [23363], 33 N Indus. St., Colorado Springs, CO 80903, (719)630-0422
U.S. Assn. for Body Psychotherapy [16188], PMB 294, 7831 Woodmont Ave., Bethesda, MD 20814, (202)466-1619
U.S. Assn. of Cerebral Palsy Sports [★23353]
U.S. Assn. for the Club of Rome - Address unknown since 2002.
U.S. Assn. for Computational Mechanics [7300], PO Box 8137, Austin, TX 78713, (512)529-7333
U.S. Assn. of Consecrated Virgins [19733], 300 W Ottawa St., Lansing, MI 48933-1577
U.S. Assn. for Energy Economics [6974], 28790 Chagrin Blvd., Ste. 350, Cleveland, OH 44122, (216)464-2785
U.S. Assn. of Evening Students - Address unknown since 1995.
U.S. Assn. of Former Members of Cong. [17253], 1401 K St. NW, Ste. 503, Washington, DC 20005, (202)222-0972
U.S. Assn. of Importers of Textiles and Apparel [3807], 13 E 16th St., 6th Fl., New York, NY 10003, (212)463-0089
U.S. Assn. of Independent Gymnastic Clubs [3673], c/o Paul Spadaro, VP, 450 N End Ave., Ste. 20F, New York, NY 10282, (212)227-9792
U.S. Assn. of Museum Volunteers [★10489]
U.S. Assn. of Roller Canary Culturists [21864]
U.S. Assn. for Small Bus. and Entrepreneurship [3632], c/o Joan Gillman, Exec. Dir., 975 Univ. Ave., No. 3260, Madison, WI 53706, (608)262-9982
U.S. Athletes Assn. - Defunct.
U.S. Atlantic and Gulf Ports/Eastern Mediterranean and North African Freight Conf. - Address unknown since 2000.
U.S. Austrian Chamber of Commerce [24233], 165 W 46th St., New York, NY 10036, (212)819-0117
U.S. Auto Club [23086], 4910 W 16th St., Speedway, IN 46224, (317)247-5151
U.S. - Azerbaijan Chamber of Commerce [24300], 1212 Potomac St. NW, Washington, DC 20007, (202)333-8702
U.S. - Azerbaijan Chamber of Commerce [IO], Washington, DC, United States
U.S. Badminton Assn. [★23089]
U.S.-Bahrain Bus. Coun. [2315], c/o Selma Habib, Exec. Dir., 1615 H St. NW, Washington, DC 20062, (202)463-5401
U.S. Ballroom Br. of the Imperial Soc. of Teachers of Dancing - Address unknown since 2006.
U.S. Barrel Jumping Assn. [23743]
U.S. Bartenders Assn. - Address unknown since 1989.
U.S. BASE Assn. [23647]
U.S. Baseball Fed. [★23127]
U.S. Basketball Writers Assn. [23137], 1818 Chouteau Ave., St. Louis, MO 63103, (314)421-0339
U.S. Bass - Defunct.
U.S. Bean Marketing Assn. - Defunct.
U.S. Beef Breeds Coun. - Address unknown since 2003.
U.S. Beet Sugar Assn. [1567], 1156 15th St. NW, Ste. 1019, Washington, DC 20005, (202)296-4820
U.S. Beet Sugar Indus. [★1567]
United States Bi-Rak-It Assn. [★23676]
U.S. Biathlon Assn. [23756], 49 Pineland Dr., Ste. 301A, New Gloucester, ME 04260, (207)688-6500
U.S. Bicycle Assn. [★23305]
U.S. Bicycle Polo Assn. [23660], PO Box 19424, Sacramento, CA 95819-0424, (916)487-1670

A star before a book entry number signifies that the name is not listed separately, but is mentioned within the entry.

U.S. Billiard Assn. **[23146]**, 1000 Kiely Blvd., No. 86, Santa Clara, CA 95051-4831, (408)615-7479

U.S. Blind Golf Assn. **[23364]**, 3094 Shamrock St. N, Tallahassee, FL 32309, (850)893-4511

U.S. Bd. on Books for Young People **[9756]**, 800 Barksdale Rd., Newark, DE 19714-8139, (302)731-1600

U.S. Bd. Sailing Assn. **[★23236]**

U.S. Bobsled and Skeleton Fed. **[23767]**, 196 Old Military Rd., Lake Placid, NY 12946, (518)523-1842

U.S. Bocce Fed. **[23241]**, 16090 Mays Ave., Monte Sereno, CA 95030-4213, (480)354-0625

U.S. Boer Goat Assn. **[4789]**, PO Box 663, Spicewood, TX 78669, (866)668-7242

U.S. Book Exchange **[10392]**, 2969 W 25th St., Cleveland, OH 44113, (216)241-6960

U.S. Book Exchange **[★10392]**

U.S. Boomerang Assn. **[23248]**, 3351 236th St. SW, Brier, WA 98036-8421, (425)485-1672

U.S. Border Collie Club **[22372]**, c/o Laura Carson, Treas., 1712 Hertford St., Greensboro, NC 27403

U.S. Border Control **[17810]**, 8180 Greensboro Dr., No. 1070, McLean, VA 22102, (703)356-6567

U.S. Bowling Cong. **[23255]**, 5301 S 76th St., Greendale, WI 53129-1128, (414)421-6400

U.S. Bowling Cong. **[IO]**, Greendale, WI, United States

U.S. Bowling Instructors Assn. - Address unknown since 2004.

U.S. Boxer Assn. **[22373]**, c/o Renee Basye, Sec., 1601 Prairie Ave., Beloit, WI 53511-3838, (989)469-3236

U.S. Braille Chess Assn. **[21947]**, c/o Jay Leventhal, Sec., 111-20 76th Rd., Apt. 5L, Forest Hills, NY 11375-6451, (718)275-2209

U.S. Br. of the Intl. Comm. for the Defense of the Breton Language **[9758]**, c/o Lois Kuter, Sec.-Treas./Ed., 169 Greenwood Ave., B-4, Jenkintown, PA 19046, (215)886-6361

U.S. Br. of the Intl. Comm. for the Defense of the Breton Language **[IO]**, Jenkintown, PA, United States

U.S. Brewers Assn. - Defunct.

U.S. Bridge Assn. **[★21893]**

U.S. Bridge Assn. **[★IO]**

U.S. Broomball Assn. **[23858]**, PO Box 13369, Salem, OR 97309

United States Bus. Assn.; Canada- **[2301]**

U.S. Business Comm. on Jamaica - Address unknown since 2000.

U.S. Bus. Coun; Czech and Slovak- **[2302]**

U.S. Bus. Coun. for Southeastern Europe **[2292]**

U.S. Bus. and Indus. Coun. **[★17639]**

U.S. Bus. and Indus. Coun. **[17639]**, 910 16th St. NW, Ste. 300, Washington, DC 20006, (202)728-1990

U.S. Bus. and Indus. Coun. Educational Found: **[18638]**, 910 16th St. NW, Ste. 300, Washington, DC 20006, (202)728-1990

U.S. Calf Ropers Assn. **[23695]**, PO Box 690, Giddings, TX 78942, (979)542-1239

U.S. Camaro Club **[★21821]**

U.S. Canada Peace Anniversary Assn. **[19299]**, PO Box 4564, Blaine, WA 98231-4564, (360)332-7165

United States Canada Peace Anniversary Association **[IO]**, Blaine, WA, United States

U.S. and Canadian Acad. of Pathology **[IO]**, Augusta, GA, United States

U.S. and Canadian Acad. of Pathology **[15878]**, 3643 Walton Way Extension, Augusta, GA 30909, (706)733-7550

U.S. Cancellation Club **[22886]**, c/o Roger Rhoads, Sec.-Treas., 6160 Brownstone Ct., Mentor, OH 44060

U.S. Cane Sugar Refiners' Assn. - Defunct.

U.S. Canoe Assn. **[23279]**, c/o Paula Thiel, Membership Chair, 53 Ross Rd., Preston, CT 06365

U.S. Canoe and Kayak Team **[★23280]**

U.S. Canola Assn. **[1568]**, 600 Pennsylvania Ave. SE, Ste. 320, Washington, DC 20003, (202)969-8113

U.S. Capitol Historical Soc. **[10164]**, 200 Maryland Ave. NE, Washington, DC 20002, (202)543-8919

U.S. Carrom Assn. **[22476]**, 25 S Michael St., Fords, NJ 08863, (973)801-9032

U.S. Catholic Bishops' Natl. Advisory Coun. - Defunct.

U.S. Catholic Conf. **[★19735]**

U.S. Catholic Conf. **[★12282]**

U.S. Catholic Conf. Migration and Refugee Services **[★12823]**

U.S. Catholic Conference/Migration and Refugee Services **[12823]**, 3211 4th St. NE, Washington, DC 20017-1194, (202)541-3065

U.S. Catholic Conference/Migration and Refugee Services **[★12823]**

U.S. Catholic Historical Soc. - Address unknown since 1995.

U.S. Catholic Mission Assn. **[19734]**, 3029 4th St. NE, Washington, DC 20017-1102, (202)832-3112

U.S. Catholic Mission Coun. **[★19734]**

U.S. Cavalry Assn. **[★6107]**

U.S. Cavalry Assn. and Memorial Res. Lib. **[10484]**, PO Box 2325, Fort Riley, KS 66442-0325, (785)784-5797

U.S. Cavalry Memorial Assn. - Defunct.

U.S. CB Radio Assn. - Defunct.

U.S. Cerebral Palsy Athletic Assn. **[★23353]**

U.S. Chamber of Commerce **[24301]**, 1615 H St. NW, Washington, DC 20062-2000, (202)659-6000

U.S. Chamber of Shipping **[★6059]**

U.S. Chess Fed. **[21948]**, PO Box 3967, Crossville, TN 38557, (931)787-1234

United States-China Arts Exchange; Center for **[9784]**

U.S.-China Educ. Found. **[8632]**, 4140 Oceanside Blvd., Ste. 159 - No. 112, Oceanside, CA 92056-6005, (760)644-0977

U.S.-China Educ. Found. **[IO]**, Oceanside, CA, United States

United States-China Educational Inst. **[★IO]**

United States-China Educational Inst. **[★9794]**

U.S. China Exchange Center - Address unknown since 1999.

U.S.-China Peoples Friendship Assn. **[17066]**, c/o Robert Sanborn, Pres., 402 E 43rd St., Indianapolis, IN 46205, (317)283-7735

U.S.-China Peoples Friendship Association **[IO]**, Indianapolis, IN, United States

United States-China Relations; Natl. Comm. on **[17064]**

U.S. Churchill Found. **[★8438]**

U.S. Citizens Comm. for a Free Cuba - Defunct.

U.S. Citizens' Cong. - Defunct.

U.S. Citizens' Rights Assn. - Address unknown since 1995.

U.S. Civil Defense Coun. **[★5563]**

U.S. Civil Defense Coun. **[★IO]**

U.S. Classic Racing Assn. **[22694]**, c/o Bob Coy, Dir., 441 Athol Rd., Richmond, NH 03470, (603)239-6778

U.S. Club Lacrosse Assn. - Address unknown since 1999.

U.S. Coalition for Life **[12929]**, Box 315, Export, PA 15632, (412)327-7379

U.S. Coast Guard Chief Petty Officers Assn. **[20734]**, 5520-G Hempstead Way, Springfield, VA 22151-4009, (703)941-0395

U.S. Coast Guards

All Navy Women's Natl. Alliance **[6144]**

U.S. Life-Saving Ser. Heritage Assn. **[10072]**

U.S. Collegiate Athletic Assn. **[23859]**, c/o Mr. William Casto, Commissioner, 4101 Washington Ave., Bldg. 601, Newport News, VA 23607, (757)688-5944

U.S. Collegiate Ski and Snowboard Assn. **[23757]**, PO Box 180, Cummington, MA 01026, (413)634-0110

U.S. Collegiate Sports Coun. **[23860]**, c/o Dr. Stanley Brassie, Exec. Dir., 305 Walton St., Monroe, GA 30655, (707)267-2681

U.S. Combined Heat and Power Assn. **[7821]**, Natl. HQ, 218 D St. SE, Washington, DC 20003, (202)544-4565

U.S. Combined Training Assn. **[★23535]**

U.S. Comm. Against Nuclear War - Defunct.

U.S. Comm. for Democracy in Greece - Address unknown since 1995.

U.S. Comm. for a Free Lebanon **[18006]**, 445 Park Ave., 9th Fl., New York, NY 10022

U.S. Comm. for the Global Atmospheric Res. Program - Defunct.

U.S. Comm. of the Intl. Assn. of Art - Address unknown since 2003.

U.S. Comm. on Irrigation and Drainage **[7842]**, 1616 17th St., No. 483, Denver, CO 80202, (303)628-5430

U.S. Comm. on Irrigation, Drainage and Flood Control **[★7842]**

U.S. Comm. for Justice to Latin Amer. Political Prisoners - Defunct.

U.S. Comm. on Large Dams **[★7843]**

U.S. Comm. for the Oceans - Defunct.

U.S. Comm. to Promote Stud. of the History of the Hapsburg Monarchy **[★9628]**

U.S. Comm. to Promote Stud. of the History of the Hapsburg Monarchy **[★IO]**

U.S. Comm. for Public Liberties in Tunisia - Defunct.

United States Comm. for Refugees **[★18503]**

United States Comm. for Refugees **[★IO]**

U.S. Comm. for Refugees and Immigrants **[IO]**, Washington, DC, United States

U.S. Comm. for Refugees and Immigrants **[18503]**, 1717 Massachusetts Ave. NW, Ste. 200, Washington, DC 20036-2003, (202)347-3507

U.S. Comm. for Sci. Cooperation With Vietnam **[8633]**, 1095 Medical Sci. Ctr., 1300 Univ. Ave., Madison, WI 53706, (608)263-4150

U.S. Comm. for Sci. Cooperation With Vietnam **[IO]**, Madison, WI, United States

U.S. Comm. in Solidarity With the People of El Salvador **[★IO]**

U.S. Comm. in Solidarity With the People of El Salvador **[★17483]**

U.S. Comm. for Sports in Israel **[★23828]**

U.S. Comm. Sports for Israel **[★23828]**

U.S. Comm. for the United Nations **[★18770]**

U.S. Comm. for the United Nations Env. Prog. **[4613]**, 47914 252nd St., Sioux Falls, SD 57198-0002, (605)594-6117

U.S. Competitive Aerobics Fed. **[23038]**, 8033 Sunset Blvd., No. 920, Los Angeles, CA 90046, (323)850-3777

U.S. Composting Coun. **[6356]**, 4250 Veterans Memorial Hwy., Ste. 275, Holbrook, NY 11741, (631)737-4931

U.S. Conf. of Catholic Bishops **[19735]**, 3211 4th St. NE, Washington, DC 20017-1194, (202)541-3000

U.S. Conf. of Catholic Bishops; Secretariat for Hispanic Affairs, **[12282]**

U.S. Conf. of City Human Services Officials **[6263]**, c/o U.S. Conf. of Mayors, 1620 Eye St. NW, Washington, DC 20006, (202)293-7330

U.S. Conf. of Local Health Officers - Defunct.

U.S. Conf. of Mayors **[6132]**, 1620 Eye St. NW, Washington, DC 20006, (202)293-7330

U.S. Conf. of Secular Insts. - Address unknown since 1994.

U.S. Conf. for the World Coun. of Churches **[19912]**, 475 Riverside Dr., Rm. 1371, New York, NY 10115-0031, (212)870-2533

U.S. Congressional Advisory Bd. **[18597]**, 201A N Main St., Culpeper, VA 22701-2619, (540)829-8005

U.S. Connected Communities Assn. **[6716]**, 1901 Pennsylvania Ave. NW, 5th Fl., Washington, DC 20006

U.S. Consortium of Soil Sci. Associations **[5223]**, c/o Mr. Jim Culver, Coor., 611 Jeffrey Dr., Lincoln, NE 68505, (402)483-0604

U.S. Constitution

Americans for Religious Liberty **[17090]**

America's Future **[17624]**

Center for Constitutional Rights **[17097]**

Citizens for Governmental Restraint **[17288]**

Comm. on the Constitutional Sys. **[17289]**

Comm. to Restore the Constitution **[17290]**

Congressional Automotive Caucus **[17255]**

Constitutional Rights Found. **[17291]**

Freedom of Expression Found. **[17116]**

Fund for Constitutional Govt. **[17669]**

Independent Americans **[17294]**

John Birch Soc. **[17274]**

Liberty Amendment Comm. of the U.S.A. **[17296]**

Natl. Center for Constitutional Stud. **[17297]**

Natl. Comm. for an Effective Cong. **[17252]**

Reference to "IO" in place of a book number signifies that the association may be found in the 45th edition of International Organizations.

People for the Amer. Way **[17143]**
Senate Tourism Caucus **[17259]**
U.S. Assn. of Former Members of Cong. **[17253]**
U.S. Contract Security Assn. **[3543]**, PO Box 54244, Atlanta, GA 30308, (770)486-3425
U.S. Copper Assn. **[★7309]**
U.S. Copts Assn. **[10192]**, 529 14th St. NW, Ste. 1081, Washington, DC 20045, (202)737-3660
U.S. Copts Association **[IO]**, Washington, DC, United States
U.S. Corporate Athletics Assn. - Address unknown since 1990.
U.S. Corporate Coun. on South Africa - Address unknown since 1991.
U.S. Coun. of Better Bus. Bureaus **[765]**, 4200 Wilson Blvd., Ste. 800, Arlington, VA 22203-1838, (703)276-0100
U.S. Coun. for Energy Awareness **[★6969]**
U.S. Coun. for Human Rights in the Balkans **[17787]**
U.S. Coun. on Intl. Banking **[★483]**
U.S. Coun. for Intl. Bus. **[766]**, 1212 Ave. of the Americas, New York, NY 10036, (212)354-4480
U.S. Coun. for Intl. Bus. **[IO]**, New York, NY, United States
U.S. Coun. of the Intl. Chamber of Commerce **[★IO]**
U.S. Coun. of the Intl. Chamber of Commerce **[★766]**
U.S. Coun. for Intl. Friendship - Defunct.
U.S. Coun. for an Open World Economy - Defunct.
U.S. Coun. for World Affairs - Defunct.
U.S. Coun. for World Freedom - Address unknown since 1991.
U.S. Coun., World Veterans Fed. - Address unknown since 1999.
U.S. Court Reporters Assn. **[5632]**, 4731 N Western Ave., Chicago, IL 60625-2012, (816)512-5608
U.S. Croquet Assn. **[23301]**, 700 Florida Mango Rd., West Palm Beach, FL 33406-4461, (561)478-0760
U.S. Cross Country Coaches Assn. **[23924]**, c/o Walt Drenth, Pres., Michigan State Univ., Jenison Fieldhouse, East Lansing, MI 48824, (517)355-1640
U.S. Cross Country Snowmobile Racing Assn. **[23768]**, PO Box 273, Minto, ND 58261, (701)248-2029
U.S. Crutch Mfrs. Assn. - Defunct.
U.S.-Cuba Bus. Coun. - Address unknown since 2006.
U.S.-Cuba Trade Assn. **[2316]**, 2300 M St. NW, Ste. 800, Washington, DC 20037, (202)530-5236
U.S. Cuban Sugar Coun. - Defunct.
U.S. Cultural Exchange Soc. **[★23861]**
U.S. Cultural Exchange and Sports Soc. **[23861]**
U.S. Curling Assn. **[23302]**, 1100 Center Point Dr., PO Box 866, Stevens Point, WI 54481-2849, (715)344-1199
U.S. Customs Inspectors' Assn. Port of New York - Address unknown since 1995.
U.S. Cutting Tool Inst. **[2076]**, 1300 Sumner Ave., Cleveland, OH 44115-2851, (216)241-7333
U.S. Cycling Fed. **[23320]**, c/o USA Cycling, 1 Olympic Plz., Colorado Springs, CO 80909, (719)866-4581
U.S. Dairy Export Coun. **[4491]**, 2101 Wilson Blvd., Ste. 400, Arlington, VA 22201-3061, (703)528-3049
U.S. Darting Assn. - Address unknown since 2003.
U.S. Deaf Cycling Assn. **[23365]**, c/o Bobby Skedsmo, Sec.-Treas., 247 Jack London Ct., Pittsburg, CA 94565-3661, (888)210-4213
U.S. Deaf Ski and Snowboard Assn. **[23366]**, c/o Rachel Loftus, Acting Pres., PO Box 513, Bondville, VT 05340
U.S. Defense Comm. - Address unknown since 1999.
U.S. Dental Tennis Assn. **[23911]**, c/o Iris Kenworthy, Exec. Dir., 1414 Rhorer Rd., Bloomington, IN 47401, (800)445-2524
U.S. Dept. of Agriculture - Forest Ser. Volunteers Prog. **[4699]**, 1400 Independence Ave. SW, Washington, DC 20250-0003, (703)605-4851
U.S. Dept. of Agriculture; Org. of Professional Employees of the **[5441]**
U.S. Disc Sports **[23376]**, c/o World Flying Disc Fed., 8550 Tujunga Valley St., Sunland, CA 91040, (818)353-6339

U.S. Display Consortium **[3729]**, 84 W Santa Clara St., Ste. 790, San Jose, CA 95113, (408)993-8111
U.S. Distance Learning Assn. **[8523]**, 8 Winter St., Ste. 508, Boston, MA 02108, (800)275-5162
U.S. Divorce Reform - Defunct.
U.S. Dog Agility Assn. **[23388]**, PO Box 850955, Richardson, TX 75085, (972)487-2200
U.S. Dressage Fed. **[23533]**, 4051 Iron Works Pkwy., Lexington, KY 40511, (859)971-2277
U.S. Dry Bean Coun. **[4769]**, PO Box 550, Grapeview, WA 98546, (360)277-0112
U.S. Duffers' Assn. - Defunct.
U.S. Durum Growers Assn. **[4318]**, 2409 Jackson Ave., Bismarck, ND 58501, (701)214-3203
U.S. Dye Mfrs. Operating Comm. of ETAD **[★5089]**
U.S. Economic Coun; Czechoslovak- **[★2302]**
U.S. Egg Marketers - Address unknown since 2004.
U.S. Electronic Mail Assn. - Defunct.
U.S. Elite Coaches' Assn. for Women's Gymnastics **[23297]**, c/o Natalie Duke, Sec.-Treas., 10 Quail Point Pl., Carmichael, CA 95608, (916)487-3559
U.S. Energy Assn. **[6975]**; 1300 Pennsylvania Ave. NW, Ste. 550, Mailbox 142, Washington, DC 20004-3022, (202)312-1230
U.S. Energy Assn. **[IO]**, Washington, DC, United States
U.S. Environment and Resources Coun. - Defunct.
U.S. Equal Employment Opportunity Commn. **[5682]**, 1801 L St. NW, Ste. 100, Washington, DC 20507, (202)663-4900
U.S. Equestrian Fed. **[23534]**, 4047 Iron Works Pkwy., Lexington, KY 40511-8483, (859)258-2472
U.S. Equestrian Team **[★23534]**
U.S. Equestrian Team - Defunct.
U.S. Eventing Assn. **[23535]**, 525 Old Waterford Rd. NW, Leesburg, VA 20176, (703)779-0440
U.S. Faceters Guild **[1121]**, c/o Jeff Ford, Treas., 2410 N 2nd St., Kalamazoo, MI 49009
U.S. Farm Raised Catfish Marketing Assn. - Defunct.
U.S. Farmers Assn. **[16958]**
U.S. Fastpitch Assn. **[23794]**, 22912 Ann Miller Rd., Panama City, FL 32412, (850)234-2839
U.S. Fed. of Amateur Roller Skaters **[★23742]**
U.S. Fed. for Culture Collections **[6603]**, c/o Darrell Jay Grimes, Pres., PO Box 7000, Ocean Springs, MS 39566-7000, (228)872-4211
U.S. Fed. of Intl. Moving Target Shooters - Defunct.
U.S. Fed. of Pelota - Address unknown since 1994.
U.S. Fed. of Police **[★5962]**
U.S. Fed. of Scholars and Scientists **[7634]**, c/o Prof. Roger Dittmann, PhD, Pres., California State Univ. at Fullerton, Dept. of Physics, Fullerton, CA 92834-6866, (714)278-3421
U.S. Fed. of Scientists and Scholars **[★7634]**
U.S. Feed Grains Coun. **[★4664]**
U.S. Feed Grains Coun. **[★IO]**
U.S. Fencing Assn. **[23402]**, 1 Olympic Plz., Colorado Springs, CO 80909-5780, (719)866-4511
U.S. Fencing Coaches Assn. **[23403]**, c/o Dirk Goldgar, Sec., 9 Titus Mill Rd., Pennington, NJ 08534, (609)737-1432
U.S. Field Artillery Assn. **[★6071]**
U.S. Field Hockey Assn. **[23405]**, 1 Olympic Plz., Colorado Springs, CO 80909, (719)866-4567
U.S. Figure Skating Assn. **[23744]**, 20 1st St., Colorado Springs, CO 80906, (719)635-5200
U.S. Financial Support of the United Nations; Emergency Coalition for **[18764]**
U.S. Fire Companies Conf. - Defunct.
U.S. Fishmeal Importers Assn. - Defunct.
U.S. Flag Assn. **[★21094]**
U.S. Flag Football Assn. **[★23440]**
U.S. Flag Football for the Deaf **[23367]**, PO Box 1453, Silver Spring, MD 20915
U.S. Flag Football League **[23440]**, c/o John D. Carrigan, Commissioner, 117 St. Gallen Ct., New Bern, NC 28562, (252)633-1014
U.S. Flag Found. **[11078]**, Flag Plz., 1275 Bedford Ave., Pittsburgh, PA 15219, (412)261-1776
U.S. Flag and Touch Football League **[23441]**, 7709 Ohio St., Mentor, OH 44060, (440)974-8735
U.S. Floor Tennis Assn. - Defunct.
U.S. Floorball Assn. **[23093]**, 4301 Fathom Ct., Raleigh, NC 27606, (919)233-7274

U.S. Football Alliance **[23442]**, PO Box 127, Sharon, PA 16146, (724)866-1714
U.S. Football League - Defunct.
U.S. Found. for Intl. Scouting - Defunct.
U.S. Freshwater Prawn and Shrimp Growers Assn. **[3505]**, 655 Napanee Rd., Leland, MS 38756, (662)686-2894
U.S. Fund for UNICEF **[11658]**, 333 E 38th St., New York, NY 10016, (212)686-5522
U.S. Fund for UNICEF **[IO]**, New York, NY, United States
U.S. Futsal Fed. **[23862]**, PO Box 40077, Berkeley, CA 94704-4077, (510)836-8733
U.S. Geodynamics Comm. - Defunct.
U.S.-German Comm. on Learning and Remembrance - Defunct.
U.S. Girls' Wrestling Assn. **[23988]**, c/o Kent Bailo, Dir., 3105 Hickory Ridge Ln., Ortonville, MI 48462, (248)627-8066
U.S. Global Strategy Coun. - Defunct.
U.S. Golf Assn. **[23467]**, PO Box 708, Far Hills, NJ 07931, (908)234-2300
U.S. Golf Teachers Fed. **[23468]**, 1295 SE Port St. Lucie Blvd., Port St. Lucie, FL 34952, (772)335-3216
U.S. Grains Coun. **[4664]**, 1400 K St. NW, Ste. 1200, Washington, DC 20005, (202)789-0789
U.S. Grains Coun. **[IO]**, Washington, DC, United States
U.S. Green Alliance - Address unknown since 1985.
U.S. Green Network **[★18325]**
U.S. Group of the Inter-Parliamentary Union - Defunct.
U.S./Guatemala Labor Educ. Proj. **[★17978]**
U.S./Guatemala Labor Educ. Proj. **[★IO]**
U.S. Gymnastics Fed. **[★23479]**
U.S. Gymnastics Safety Assn. - Defunct.
U.S. Handball Assn. **[23480]**, 2333 N Tucson Blvd., Tucson, AZ 85716, (520)795-0434
U.S. Handcycling Fed. **[23321]**, PO Box 3538, Evergreen, CO 80437, (303)459-4159
U.S. Hang Gliding Assn. **[★23044]**
U.S. Hang Gliding and Paragliding Assn. **[23044]**, PO Box 1330, Colorado Springs, CO 80901-1330, (719)632-8300
U.S. Hapki Hae **[23606]**, 4826 Old Natl. Hwy., College Park, GA 30337, (404)768-0507
U.S. Hardware Indus. Assn. **[1837]**, 7115 W North Ave., No. 272, Oak Park, IL 60302, (708)453-0080
U.S. Harness Writers' Assn. **[3170]**, c/o Jerry Connors, Sec., Box 1314, Mechanicsburg, PA 17055, (717)766-3219
U.S. Helice Assn. **[23729]**, 10701 CR 1200, Malakoff, TX 75148, (817)233-1025
U.S. Helsinki Watch **[★17763]**
U.S. Helsinki Watch **[★IO]**
U.S. Hereditary Angioedema Assn. **[14487]**, c/o Dennis DeMarinis, Jr., 1149 Victoria St., New Bedford, MA 02745
U.S. Hide, Skin and Leather Assn. **[2421]**, 1150 Connecticut Ave. NW, 12th Fl., Washington, DC 20036, (202)587-4261
U.S. High School Tennis Assn. **[23912]**, 110 Roswell Farms Ln., Roswell, GA 30075, (404)685-3133
U.S. Highland Dancing Assn. - Address unknown since 1995.
U.S. Hispanic Chamber of Commerce **[24327]**, 2175 K St. NW, Ste. 100, Washington, DC 20037, (202)842-1212
U.S. Historical Documents Inst. - Address unknown since 1995.
U.S. Historical Soc. **[10071]**, 7433 Whitepine Rd., Richmond, VA 23237, (804)648-4736
U.S. Holocaust Memorial Coun. **[17725]**, 100 Raoul Wallenberg Pl. SW, Washington, DC 20024-2126, (202)488-0400
U.S. Homeland Emergency Response Org. **[12893]**, PO Box 90453, Austin, TX 78709-0453, (512)567-8196
U.S. Homeopathic Assn. - Defunct.
U.S. Horse Cavalry Assn. **[★10484]**
U.S. Human Proteome Org. **[6604]**, 2019 Galisteo St., Bldg. I-1, Santa Fe, NM 87505, (505)989-4876
United States Human Proteome Organization **[IO]**, Santa Fe, NM, United States

A star before a book entry number signifies that the name is not listed separately, but is mentioned within the entry.

U.S. Hunter Jumper Assn. [23536], 4047 Iron Works Pkwy., Lexington, KY 40511, (859)225-2055

U.S. Hydrofoil Assn. [23978], 320 Starlight Pl., Lutherville, MD 21093

U.S. Icelandic Horse Cong. [4962], 6800 E 99th Ave., Anchorage, AK 99507, (907)346-2223

U.S. Immigration and Naturalization Officers' Assn. - Address unknown since 1990.

U.S. Independent Telephone Assn. [★3965]

U.S. Indian Amer. Chamber of Commerce [24331], c/o Ron Mutch, Exec. Dir., 1725 I St. NW, Ste. No. 300, Washington, DC 20006, (202)349-1111

U.S. Indian Amer. Chamber of Commerce [IO], Washington, DC, United States

United States-Indonesia Soc. [775], 1625 Massachusetts Ave. NW, Ste. 550, Washington, DC 20036-2260, (202)232-1400

U.S. Indoor Soccer Assn. [23782], PO Box 6569, Arlington, VA 22206, (703)820-2810

U.S. Indus. Coun. [★17639]

U.S. Indus. Fabrics Inst. [3808], 1801 County Rd. B.W., Roseville, MN 55113-4061, (651)222-2508

U.S. Indus. Coalition [7637], 1525 Wilson Blvd., Ste. 150, Arlington, VA 22209, (703)526-9447

U.S. Indus. Coalition [IO], Arlington, VA, United States

U.S. Infantry Assn. [★6071]

U.S. Info. Center for Amer. Music [★10541]

U.S. Information Center for the Universal Decimal Classification - Defunct.

U.S. Inst. of Human Rights - Address unknown since 1989.

U.S. Inst. of Peace [18249], 1200 17th St. NW, Washington, DC 20036, (202)457-1700

U.S. Inst. of Peace [IO], Washington, DC, United States

U.S. Inst. for Textile Res. [★IO]

U.S. Inst. for Textile Res. [★3806]

U.S. Inst. for Theatre Tech. [11052], 6443 Ridings Rd., Syracuse, NY 13206-1111, (315)463-6463

U.S. Intercollegiate Lacrosse Assn. [23571], c/o John Spring, Exec. Dir., 3738 W Lake Rd., Perry, NY 14530, (585)237-5886

U.S. Intl. Coun. on Disabilities [11992], c/o Tapan Banerjee, PhD, Exec. Dir., 1710 Rhode Island Ave. NW, 5th Fl., Washington, DC 20036, (202)207-0338

U.S. Intl. Coun. on Disabilities [IO], Washington, DC, United States

U.S. Intl. Fireball Assn. - Defunct.

U.S. Intl. Sailing Assn. [★23233]

U.S. Intl. Skating Assn. [★23745]

U.S. Intl. Space Year Assn. - Address unknown since 1999.

U.S. Intl. Speedskating Assn. [★23745]

U.S. Intl. Tempest Assn. - Address unknown since 1995.

U.S. Internet Coun. [6827]

U.S. Internet Indus. Assn. [893], 1800 Diagonal Rd., Ste. 600, Alexandria, VA 22314, (703)647-7440

U.S. Internet Ser. Provider Assn. [911], c/o Kate Dean, 700 12th St. NW, Ste. 700E, Washington, DC 20005, (202)904-2351

U.S. Interreligious Comm. on Peace [★18257]

U.S. Interreligious Comm. on Peace [★IO]

U.S. Investments in Southern Africa; Church Proj. on [★17353]

U.S. Islands 17 Class Assn. - Defunct.

U.S.-Israel Binational Sci. Found. [IO], Jerusalem, Israel

U.S. Isshinryu Karate Assn. [23565], 2202 Surfside Dr., Anderson, SC 29625, (864)225-8610

U.S. ISSN Center [★10376]

U.S. J/24 Class Assn. [23227], 7793 Burnet Rd., No. 15, Austin, TX 78757, (512)266-0033

United States J/24 Class Association [IO], Austin, TX, United States

U.S.-Japan Bus. Coun. [24347], 2000 L St. NW, Ste. 515, Washington, DC 20036, (202)728-0068

U.S.-Japan Culture Center [10268], 2600 Virginia Ave. NW, Ste. 512, Washington, DC 20037, (202)342-5800

U.S.-Japan Culture Center [IO], Washington, DC, United States

United States-Japan Found. [IO], New York, NY, United States

United States-Japan Found. [19024], 145 E 32nd St., New York, NY 10016, (212)481-8753

U.S. Jaycee Women - Defunct.

U.S. Jaycees [★24390]

U.S. Jobs; Save [1282]

U.S. Judo [23554], 1 Olympic Plz., Ste. 505, Colorado Springs, CO 80909, (719)866-4730

U.S. Judo Assn. [23555], 21 N Union Blvd., Colorado Springs, CO 80909-5784, (719)633-7750

U.S. Judo Fed. [23556], PO Box 338, Ontario, OR 97914, (541)889-8753

U.S. Junior Chamber of Commerce [★24390]

U.S. Junior Chamber of Commerce [24390], PO Box 7, Tulsa, OK 74102-0007, (918)584-2481

U.S. Justice Found. [6228], c/o Gary G. Kreep, Exec. Dir., 932 D St., Ste. 2, Ramona, CA 92065-2355, (760)788-6624

U.S. K-9 Assn. [★6008]

U.S. Karate Assn. - Defunct.

U.S. Kart Assn. - Defunct.

U.S.-Kazakhstan Bus. Assn. [2317], 1200 G St. NW, Ste. 827, Washington, DC 20005, (202)434-8791

U.S. Kerry Blue Terrier Club [22374], c/o Bob Nazak, Membership Chm., 842 Oak Grove Dr., Mineral, VA 23117, (540)894-9331

U.S.-Korea Economic Coun. [★24350]

U.S.-Korea Soc. [★24350]

U.S. Korfball Fed. - Address unknown since 1994.

U.S./Labor Educ. in the Americas Proj. [17978], PO Box 268-290, Chicago, IL 60626, (773)262-6502

U.S./Labor Educ. in the Americas Proj. [IO], Chicago, IL, United States

U.S. Labor Party - Defunct.

U.S. Lacrosse [23572], 113 W Univ. Pkwy., Baltimore, MD 21210, (410)235-6882

U.S. Lacrosse Assn., Women's Div. [23573], 113 W Univ. Pkwy., Baltimore, MD 21210, (410)235-6882

U.S. Lakeland Terrier Club [22375], c/o Harold Tatro, Treas., 10301 Brangus Dr., Crowley, TX 76036, (817)297-2398

U.S. Lanolin and Derivatives Mfrs. Assn. - Defunct.

U.S. Late Model Assn. [23087], c/o Jeff Larsen, Pres., 701 W 4th St., Pueblo, CO 81003, (719)543-0218

U.S. Law Firm Gp. [5534], c/o John F. McClatchey, Exec. Dir., 3900 Key Ctr., 127 Public Sq., Cleveland, OH 44114-1216, (216)566-5500

U.S. Lawn Bowls Assn. [23256], c/o Lawn Balls USA, 10639 Lindamere Dr., Los Angeles, CA 90077

U.S. Lawn Mower Racing Assn. [23673], 1812 Glenview Rd., Glenview, IL 60025, (847)729-7363

U.S. Lawn Tennis Assn. [★23915]

U.S. League of Savings Institutions [★461]

U.S. Les Autres Sports Assn. - Defunct.

U.S. Letter Carriers Mutual Benefit Assn. [19142], 100 Indiana Ave. NW, Ste. 510, Washington, DC 20001-2144, (202)638-4318

U.S. Life-Saving Ser. Heritage Assn. [10072], c/o John Galluzzo, Exec. Dir., PO Box 213, Hull, MA 02045-0213, (781)724-7131

U.S. Lifesaving Assn. [12894], PO Box 322, Avon-by-the-Sea, NJ 07717, (866)FOR-USLA

U.S. Lighthouse Soc. [10073], 244 Kearny St., 5th Fl., San Francisco, CA 94108, (415)362-7255

U.S. Lipizzan Registry [4963], 707 13th St. SE, Ste. 275, Salem, OR 97301, (503)589-3172

U.S. Livestock Sanitary Assn. [★16811]

U.S. Locals Collectors - Defunct.

U.S. Log Rolling Assn. [★23982]

U.S. Luge Assn. [23575], 57 Church St., Lake Placid, NY 12946, (518)523-2071

U.S. Machine Screw Service Bur. - Defunct.

U.S. Maimed Soldiers League [★21320]

U.S. Marine Corps Combat Correspondents Assn. [3171], 110 Fox Ct., Wildwood, FL 34785-9081, (352)748-4698

U.S. Marine Corps Drill Instructors Assn. [6109], PO Box 5401, Parris Island, SC 29905, (912)632-4557

U.S. Marine Corps Scout/Sniper Assn. [21181], PO Box 762, Quantico, VA 22134

U.S. Marine Safety Assn. [6651], 5050 Indus. Rd., Farmingdale, NJ 07727, (732)751-0102

U.S. Mariner Class Assn. [23228], c/o Tom Bayer, Sec.-Treas., PO Box 775, Princeton Junction, NJ 08550, (609)655-7623

U.S. Maritime Alliance [2594], 485 Rte. 1 S, Bldg. C, Ste. 100, Iselin, NJ 08830, (732)404-2960

U.S. Maritime Comm. - Defunct.

U.S. Marshals and Peace Officers of America Assn. - Address unknown since 1999.

U.S. Martial Arts Assn. [23607], 8011 Mariposa Ave., Citrus Heights, CA 95610-1514, (916)727-1486

U.S. Martial Arts Assn. [IO], Citrus Heights, CA, United States

U.S. Masters Intl. Track Team - Defunct.

U.S. Masters Swimming [23891], PO Box 185, Londonderry, NH 03053-0185, (603)537-0203

U.S. Meat Export Fed. [2665], 1050 17th St., Ste. 2200, Denver, CO 80265, (303)623-6328

U.S. Meat Export Fed. [IO], Denver, CO, United States

U.S. Medical Massage Assn. [15033], PO Box 2394, Surf City, NC 28445, (910)328-3323

U.S. Men's Curling Assn. [★23302]

U.S. Merchant Marine Veterans of World War II [21408], SS Lane Victory, WWII Cruises, 455 WWII Cargo Ship, Berth 94, PO Box 629, San Pedro, CA 90733-0629, (310)519-9545

U.S. Metric Assn. [7701], 10245 Andasol Ave., Northridge, CA 91325-1504, (818)363-5606

U.S. Mexican Numismatic Assn. [22765], c/o Don Bailey, Interim Exec. Dir., 250 D S Lyon Ave., PMB No. 139, Hemet, CA 92543, (909)652-7875

United States-Mexico Border Hea. Assn. [★16256]

U.S.-Mexico Border Hea. Assn. [16256], 5400 Suncrest Dr., Ste. C-5, El Paso, TX 79912-5615, (915)833-6450

U.S.-Mexico Border Hea. Assn. [IO], El Paso, TX, United States

United States-Mexico Border Hea. Assn. [★IO]

United States-Mexico Chamber of Commerce [IO], Washington, DC, United States

United States-Mexico Chamber of Commerce [24302], 1300 Pennsylvania Ave. NW, Ste. G-0003, Washington, DC 20004-3021, (202)312-1520

U.S./Mexico Sister Cities Assn. - Address unknown since 1991.

U.S. Microscopic Welding Assn. [7849], c/o Lee R. Gilbert, 145 Sabin St., Pawtucket, RI 02860, (401)722-6942

U.S. Mine Rescue Assn. [12600], PO Box 1010, Uniontown, PA 15401, (724)366-5272

U.S. Mine Rescue Assn. [IO], Uniontown, PA, United States

U.S. Minutemen - Defunct.

U.S. Mirror Class Assn. [23229], c/o John M. Borthwick, Sec., 5305 Marian Dr., Lyndhurst, OH 44124, (440)461-7231

U.S. Modern Pentathlon Assn. [23925], 1 Olympic Plz., Colorado Springs, CO 80909-5780, (719)866-4608

United States Modern Pentathlon Association [IO], Colorado Springs, CO, United States

U.S. Modern Pentathlon and Biathlon Assn. [★IO]

U.S. Modern Pentathlon and Biathlon Assn. [★23925]

U.S. Mondioring Assn. [23389], c/o Ann Putegnat, Sec.-Treas., 400 Hidden Oak, Bulverde, TX 78163, (830)438-3327

U.S. Monoski Assn. [23863], 5286 Apennines Cir., San Jose, CA 95138, (408)603-9632

U.S. Muay Thai Assn. [23608], 6535 Broadway, Ste. 1K, Riverdale, NY 10471

U.S. Museum Librarian Soc. - Defunct.

U.S.-Namibia (South West Africa) Trade and Cultural Coun. - Defunct.

U.S. Natl. Amateur Athletic Union Taekwondo Comm. [★23610]

U.S. Natl. Comm. for the United Nations Education Scientific and Cultural Org. - Defunct.

U.S. Natl. Comm. for Byzantine Stud. [9771], 214 St. Mark's Sq., Philadelphia, PA 19104, (215)387-1447

U.S. Natl. Comm. on the History of Geology - Defunct.

U.S. Natl. Comm. for the Intl. Biological Program - Defunct.

U.S. Natl. Comm. of the Intl. Cargo Handling Coordination Assn. - Address unknown since 1995.

Reference to "IO" in place of a book number signifies that the association may be found in the 45th edition of International Organizations.

U.S. Natl. Comm. of the Intl. Commn. on Illumination [7252], c/o James Sultan, Treas., 11410 NE 124th St., PMB 325, Kirkland, WA 98034-4305, (206)284-3417

U.S. Natl. Comm., Intl. Commn. on Irrigation and Drainage [★7842]

U.S. Natl. Comm. of the Intl. Coun. on Monuments and Sites [10074], 401 F St. NW, Ste. 331, Washington, DC 20001-2728, (202)842-1866

U.S. Natl. Comm. of the Intl. Coun. on Monuments and Sites [IO], Washington, DC, United States

U.S. Natl. Comm. of the Intl. Coun. of Museums [10515], 1575 Eye St. NW, Ste. 400, Washington, DC 20005, (202)289-9115

U.S. Natl. Comm. of the Intl. Peat Soc. [7459], c/o Mr. Donald N. Grubich, Sec.-Treas., 10105 White City Rd., Britt, MN 55710, (218)741-2813

U.S. Natl. Comm. for the Intl. Union of Pure and Applied Chemistry [6697], The Natl. Academies, Keck Center, 500 5th St. NW, Washington, DC 20001, (202)334-2807

U.S. Natl. Comm. for the Intl. Union of Pure and Applied Chemistry [IO], Washington, DC, United States

U.S. Natl. Comm. of the Intl. Union of Radio Sci. [7785], c/o Piergiorgio L.E. Uslenghi, Chm., Univ. of Illinois at Chicago, 1120 Sci. and Engg. Offices, 851 S Morgan St., Chicago, IL 60607-7053, (312)996-6059

U.S. Natl. Comm. for Pacific Economic Cooperation [17465], 1819 L St. NW, 2nd Fl., Washington, DC 20036, (202)293-3995

U.S. Natl. Comm. for Pacific Economic Cooperation [IO], Washington, DC, United States

U.S. Natl. Comm. for the Preservation of Nubian Monuments - Defunct.

U.S. Natl. Comm. on Theoretical and Applied Mechanics [7301], Bd. on Intl. Sci. Organizations, The Natl. Academies, 500 Fifth St. NW, W541, Washington, DC 20001, (202)334-2807

U.S. Natl. Comm. for World Food Day [12401], 2175 K St. NW, Washington, DC 20437, (202)653-2404

U.S. Natl. Comm. for World Food Day [IO], Washington, DC, United States

U.S. Natl. Fed. of Christian Life Communities [★19680]

U.S. Natl. Fruit Export Coun. - Defunct.

U.S. Natl. Inst. of Dance [9899], 38 S Arlington Ave., PO Box 245, East Orange, NJ 07019, (973)673-9225

U.S. Natl. Sect. of IBBY [★9756]

U.S. Natl. Senior Sports Org. [★23655]

U.S. Natl. Seniors' Open Golf Assn. - Address unknown since 1995.

U.S. Natl. Soc. for the Intl. Soc. of Soil Mechanics and Found. Engg. [★7147]

U.S. Natl. Soc. for the Intl. Soc. of Soil Mechanics and Found. Engg. [★IO]

U.S. Natl. Soc. for the Intl. Soc. of Soil Mechanics and Geotechnical Engg. [★IO]

U.S. Natl. Soc. for the Intl. Soc. of Soil Mechanics and Geotechnical Engg. [★7147]

U.S. Natl. Student Assn. [★9195]

U.S. Natl. Student Travel Assn. - Defunct.

U.S. Natl. Tennis Acad. [23913], 3523 McKinney Ave., Ste. 208, Dallas, TX 75204, (214)887-5999

U.S. Naturalized Citizen Assn. - Address unknown since 1994.

U.S. Naval Cryptologic Veterans Assn. [21327], PO Box 16009, Pensacola, FL 32507-6009, (850)455-6026

U.S. Naval Inst. [6110], 291 Wood Rd., Annapolis, MD 21402, (410)268-6110

U.S. Navy Field Training Supervisors Assn. - Defunct.

U.S. Navy Memorial Found. [21221], c/o Nanci Watkins, 701 Pennsylvania Ave. NW, Ste. 123, Washington, DC 20004, (202)737-2300

U.S. Navy Salvage Divers Reunited [21409]

U.S. Navy TACAMO Survivors [21222], c/o Michael A. Vos, Exec. Dir., 5144 Waterloo Rd., Burlington, KY 41005, (606)586-6016

U.S. Neapolitan Mastiff Club [22376], PO Box 66, Vienna, NJ 07880-0066, (908)637-8957

United States-New Zealand Coun. [2318], DACOR Bacon House, 1801 F St. NW, Washington, DC 20006, (202)842-0772

U.S. Norton Owners' Assn. [★22684]

U.S. Norton Owners' Assn. [★IO]

U.S. Oil and Gas Assn. [2950], 217 W Capitol St., Ste. 201, Jackson, MS 39201, (601)948-8903

U.S. Olympians - Address unknown since 1995.

U.S. Olympic Assn. [★23637]

U.S. Olympic Comm. [23637], 1 Olympic Plz., Colorado Springs, CO 80909-5780, (719)632-5551

U.S. Olympic Sailing Committee [★23238]

U.S. Online Disc Jockey Assn. [2825], 209 S 4th St., West Branch, MI 48661

U.S. Operating Comm. of ETAD [★5089]

U.S. Optimist Dinghy Assn. [23230], PO Box 1301, Beach Haven, NJ 08008, (609)492-9000

U.S. Ordnance Producers Assn. - Defunct.

U.S. Org. for Disabled Athletes - Address unknown since 2003.

U.S. Org. for Medical and Educational Needs - Address unknown since 1995.

U.S. Orienteering Fed. [23641], c/o Robin Shannonhouse, Exec. Dir., PO Box 1444, Forest Park, GA 30298-1444, (404)363-2110

U.S. Othello Assn. [22477], c/o Rusty Horner, 4111 Whitford Cir., Apt. 911, Glen Allen, VA 23060

U.S. Out of Central America - Defunct.

U.S. Out of Southern Africa Network - Address unknown since 2001.

U.S. Outdoor Volleyball Assn. - Defunct.

U.S. Overseas Cooperative Development Coun. - Address unknown since 1999.

U.S. Overseas Tax Fairness Comm. - Defunct.

U.S. Pacific Issues Network - Defunct.

U.S. Pacifist Party [18337], 5729 S Dorchester Ave., Chicago, IL 60637, (773)324-0654

U.S. Paddle Tennis Assn. - Address unknown since 2003.

U.S.-Pakistan Economic Coun. - Defunct.

U.S. Pan Asian Amer. Chamber of Commerce [24303], 1329 18th St. NW, Washington, DC 20036, (202)296-5221

U.S. Pan Asian Amer. Chamber of Commerce [IO], Washington, DC, United States

U.S. Paper Exporters Coun. - Defunct.

U.S. Parachute Assn. [23648], 5401 Southpoint Centre Blvd., Fredericksburg, VA 22407, (540)604-9740

U.S. Patent Model Found. [★7227]

U.S. Peace Corps [★18263]

U.S. Peace Corps - Zambia [IO], Lusaka, Zambia

U.S. Peace Coun. - Address unknown since 1994.

U.S. Peace Govt. [18250], 2000 Capital Blvd., Fairfield, IA 52556, (877)424-3546

U.S. People for the United Nations - Defunct.

U.S. Permafrost Assn. [7675], PO Box 750141, Fairbanks, AK 99775-0141, (302)831-0852

U.S. Personal Chef Assn. [793], 610 Quantum Rd. NE, Rio Rancho, NM 87124, (505)994-6372

U.S. Peruvian Horse Assn. [4964], PO Box 9074, Pahrump, NV 89060, (775)727-1099

U.S. Pharmacopeia [15953], 12601 Twinbrook Pkwy., Rockville, MD 20852-1790, (301)881-0666

United States Pharmacopeia [IO], Rockville, MD, United States

U.S. Pharmacopeial Convention [★IO]

U.S. Pharmacopeial Convention [★15953]

U.S. Philatelic Classics Soc. [22887], 102 Old Pawling Rd., Pawling, NY 12564-2121, (845)855-1616

U.S. Physical Therapy Assn. - Defunct.

U.S. Pigeon Shooting Fed. - Defunct.

U.S. Pilots Assn. [168], 483 S Kirkwood Rd., No. 10, St. Louis, MO 63122, (314)849-8772

U.S. Poker Assn. [22901], 4100 W El Dorado Pkwy., Ste. 100 No. 405, McKinney, TX 75070, (888)FOR-USPA

U.S. Police Canine Assn. [6008], PO Box 80, Springboro, OH 45066-0080, (800)531-1614

U.S. Polo Assn. [23661], 4037 Iron Works Pkwy., Ste. 110, Lexington, KY 40511, (859)219-1000

U.S. Pony Clubs [23537], 4041 Iron Works Pkwy., Lexington, KY 40511-8483, (859)254-7669

U.S. Pony Trotting Assn. - Defunct.

U.S. Possessions Philatelic Soc. - Address unknown since 2003.

U.S. Postal Chess Union - Defunct.

U.S. Postal History Soc. - Defunct.

U.S. Potato Bd. [4770], 7555 E Hampden Ave., Ste. 412, Denver, CO 80231-4835, (303)369-7783

U.S. Potters' Assn. - Address unknown since 1999.

U.S. Poultry and Egg Assn. [5122], 1530 Cooledge Rd., Tucker, GA 30084-7303, (770)493-9401

U.S. Poultry and Egg Producers Assn. - Address unknown since 1995.

U.S. Power Soccer Assn. [23783], c/o Dominic Russo, Pres., PO Box 1181, Carmel, IN 46032

U.S. Power Squadrons [23231], 1504 Blue Ridge Rd., Raleigh, NC 27607, (888)367-8777

U.S. Powered Paragliding Assn. [23643], 931 W 75th St., Ste. 137-150, Naperville, IL 60565, (866)378-7772

U.S. Powerlifting Fed. [23663], c/o David Jeffrey, Pres., PO Box 231, Parkersburg, WV 26102, (304)489-2428

U.S. Powerlifting Fed. of the AAU [★23663]

U.S. Practical Shooting Assn. [23730], PO Box 811, Sedro Woolley, WA 98284, (360)855-2245

U.S. Privacy Coun. - Address unknown since 2003.

U.S. Private Security and Detective Assn. [★2323]

U.S. Prdt. Data Assn. [2112], 5300 Intl. Blvd., Ste. 204, North Charleston, SC 29418, (843)760-3293

U.S. Professional Cycling Fed. - Address unknown since 2001.

U.S. Professional Diving Coaches Assn. [23381], PO Box 268, Milford, OH 45150

U.S. Professional Lawn Tennis Assn. [★23914]

U.S. Professional Lawn Tennis Assn. [★IO]

U.S. Professional Poolplayers Assn. [23147], PO Box 21671, Phoenix, AZ 85036, (602)653-9974

U.S. Professional Tennis Assn. [23914], 3535 Briarpark Dr., Ste. 1, Houston, TX 77042, (713)978-7782

U.S. Professional Tennis Assn. [IO], Houston, TX, United States

U.S. Professional Tennis Registry [★23909]

U.S. ProMiniGolf Assn. [23469], c/o Hawaiian Rumble, 3210 Hwy. 17 S, North Myrtle Beach, SC 29582, (843)458-2585

U.S. Province of Congregation of Marianhill Missionaries [★19655]

U.S. Psi Squad; Mind Development Association/ [7447]

U.S. Psychiatric Rehabilitation Assn. [16336], 601 Global Way, Ste. 106, Linthicum, MD 21090, (410)789-7054

U.S. Psychiatric Rehabilitation Assn. [IO], Linthicum, MD, United States

U.S. Psychotronics Assn. [7454], 409 Marquette Dr., Louisville, KY 40222, (502)429-6600

U.S. Public Hea. Ser. Clinical Soc. [★6214]

U.S. Public Hea. Ser; Commissioned Officers Assn. of the [6214]

U.S. Public Interest Res. Gp. [18483], 218 D St. SE, Washington, DC 20003-1900, (202)546-9707

United States-Qatar Bus. Coun. [24304], 1341 Connecticut Ave. NW, Ste. 4A, Washington, DC 20036, (202)457-8555

United States-Qatar Bus. Coun. [IO], Washington, DC, United States

United States Quad Rugby Association [IO], Lake Worth, FL, United States

U.S. Quad Rugby Assn. [23705], c/o Ed Hooper, Pres., 5593 Cedar Oak Blvd., Sarasota, FL 34233, (941)924-1804

U.S. Racing Pigeon Assn. - Defunct.

U.S. Racquet Stringers Assn. [3674], 330 Main St., Vista, CA 92084, (760)536-1177

U.S. Racquetball Assn. [23678], 1685 W Uintah St., Colorado Springs, CO 80904-2969, (719)635-5396

U.S. Racquetball Assn. - Defunct.

U.S. Radionics Assn. [★7454]

U.S. Recreational Tennis Assn. - Address unknown since 1999.

U.S. Red Cedar Shingle Industry - Defunct.

U.S. Region of Congregation of Marianhill Missionaries [★19655]

U.S. Relations Office of CLAT - Address unknown since 1999.

U.S. Revolver Assn. [23731], RR No. 1, Box 548, Scotrun, PA 18355, (570)839-6363

U.S. Rice Export Development, Assn. [★4321]

U.S. Rice Producers Assn. [4790], 2825 Wilcrest Dr., Ste. 505, Houston, TX 77042-6041, (713)974-7423

A star before a book entry number signifies that the name is not listed separately, but is mentioned within the entry.

U.S. Rice Producers' Group [★1754]

U.S. Ride Directors Assn. [★23308]

U.S.-ROC (Taiwan) Bus. Coun. [★2294]

U.S.-ROC (Taiwan) Bus. Coun. [★IO]

U.S. Rocket Soc. - Defunct.

U.S. Rottweiler Club [22377], c/o Liz Crawley, Membership Off., 6060 Keller Dr., Sun Prairie, WI 53590

U.S. Route 66 Assn. - Address unknown since 2006.

U.S. Rowing Assn. [23704], 2 Wall St., Princeton, NJ 08540, (609)751-0700

U.S. Rowing Soc. - Address unknown since 2001.

U.S. Rugby Football Union [23706], 2500 Arapahoe Ave., Ste. 200, Boulder, CO 80302, (303)539-0300

U.S. Running Streak Assn. [23709], c/o Mrs. Dawn N. Strumsky, Admin., 294 Chalet Dr., Millersville, MD 21108-1118, (410)987-5215

U.S.-Russia Bus. Coun. [2293], 1701 Pennsylvania Ave. NW, Ste. 520, Washington, DC 20006, (202)739-9180

U.S.-Russia Bus. Coun. [IO], Washington, DC, United States

U.S. Sailing Assn. [★23232]

U.S. Sailing Assn. [23232], PO Box 1260, Portsmouth, RI 02871-0907, (401)683-0800

U.S. Sailing Found. [23233], c/o U.S. Sailing Assn., PO Box 1260, 15 Maritime Dr., Portsmouth, RI 02871-0907, (401)683-0800

U.S. Salvage Assn. - Defunct.

U.S. Scientific Export Assn. - Defunct.

U.S. Scottish Fiddling Revival [10716], c/o Jan Tappan, VP, 1938 Rose Villa St., Pasadena, CA 91107, (626)793-3716

U.S. Seaplane Pilots Assn. [★167]

U.S. Secret Ser; Assn. of Former Agents of the [5877]

U.S. Secret Ser. Uniformed Div. Retirement Assn. [6009]

U.S. Senate Press Photographers Gallery [3016], U.S. Capitol, S-317, Washington, DC 20510, (202)224-6548

U.S. Seniors Bowling Assn. [★23255]

U.S. Seniors Bowling Assn. [★IO]

U.S. Seniors Golf Assn. - Defunct.

U.S. Servas [17914], 1125 16th St., Ste. 201, Arcata, CA 95521-5585, (707)825-1714

U.S. Servas [IO], Arcata, CA, United States

U.S. Ser. Command [★12000]

U.S. Shake and Shingle Mfrs. Assn. - Defunct.

U.S. Shellac Importers Assn. - Defunct.

U.S. Shore Angling Assn. [23425], 7208 Wisteria Way, Carlsbad, CA 92009, (760)438-7908

U.S. Sidewinder Assn. - Defunct.

U.S. Ski Assn. [★23760]

U.S. Ski Assn. Coaches System - Defunct.

U.S. Ski Coaches Assn. [23758], PO Box 100, Park City, UT 84060, (435)649-9090

U.S. Ski Mountaineering Assn. [23759], PO Box 495, Wilson, WY 83014

U.S. Ski and Snowboard Assn. [23760], Box 100, 1500 Kearns Blvd., Park City, UT 84060, (435)649-9090

U.S. Ski Team Found. [23761], 1500 Kearns Blvd., PO Box 100, Park City, UT 84060, (435)649-9090

U.S. Ski Writers Assn. [★IO]

U.S. Skibob Fed. - Defunct.

U.S. Skiing [★23760]

U.S. Snooker Assn. [23148], 220B S San Gabriel Blvd., San Gabriel, CA 91776-1623

U.S. Snowshoe Assn. [23769], 678 County Rte. 25, Corinth, NY 12822, (518)654-7648

U.S. Soccer Football Assn. [★23786]

U.S. Soc. for Augmentative and Alternative Commun. [17198], PO Box 10906, Baltimore, MD 21234, (877)887-7222

U.S. Soc. on Dams [7843], 1616 17th St., No. 483, Denver, CO 80202-1277, (303)628-5430

U.S. Soc. for Ecological Economics [6865], PO Box 44326, West Allis, WI 53214, (414)453-0030

U.S. Soc. for Ecological Economics [IO], West Allis, WI, United States

U.S. Soc. for Educ. Through Art [7980], c/o Dr. Nanyoung Kim, Treas./Chair, East Carolina Univ., Jenkins Fine Arts Ctr., Greenville, NC 27858-4353, (252)328-1298

U.S. Soc. for Educ. Through Art [★7980]

U.S. Soc. of Esperanto Instructors [★8403]

U.S. Soda Ash Export Assn. [★1725]

U.S. Soling Assn. [23234], c/o Jude Kujanson, Admin. Sec., 3915 N Troy St., Chicago, IL 60618, (773)463-4740

U.S. South Africa Leader Exchange Program - Address unknown since 2003.

U.S.-South Africa Leadership Development Program - Address unknown since 2007.

U.S. Space Education Assn. - Defunct.

U.S. Space Found. [★7922]

U.S. Spanish Merchants Assn. - Address unknown since 1986.

U.S. Specialty Sports Assn. [23795], c/o Don DeDonatis, Exec. Dir./CEO, 611 Line Dr., Kissimmee, FL 34744, (321)697-3641

U.S. Speedskating [23745], PO Box 18370, Kearns, UT 84118, (801)417-5360

U.S. Sport Jujitsu Assn. [23609], c/o Ernie Boggs, Pres., PO Box 566, Nitro, WV 25143, (304)206-5843

U.S. Sports Acad. [23864], 1 Acad. Dr., Daphne, AL 36526-7055, (251)626-3303

U.S. Sports Acrobatic Fed. [★23035]

U.S. Sports Acrobatics [23035], 201 S Capitol Ave., Indianapolis, IN 46225, (317)829-5667

U.S. Sports Chiropractic Fed. [23282], 1035 Robertson St., Fort Collins, CO 80524, (970)224-2282

U.S. Sports Massage Fed. [16485], 3556 Kenwood Dr., Spring Valley, CA 91977-2021, (619)464-0999

U.S. Sportsmen's Alliance [23550], 801 Kingsmill Pkwy., Columbus, OH 43229, (614)888-4868

U.S. Squash Racquets Assn. [23876], 555 8th Ave., Ste. 1102, New York, NY 10018, (212)268-4090

U.S. Stamp Soc. [22888], c/o Larry Ballantyne, Exec. Sec., PO Box 6634, Katy, TX 77491-6634

U.S. Stickball League - Defunct.

U.S. Stone and Bead Importers Assn. - Defunct.

U.S. Strategic Inst. - Defunct.

U.S. Student Assn. [9195], 815 16th St. NW, 4th Fl., Washington, DC 20006, (202)637-3924

U.S. Student Travel Ser. [★8617]

U.S. Student Travel Ser. [★IO]

U.S. Submarine Veterans of World War II [21410], c/o U.S. Submarine Veterans, Inc., PO Box 3870, Silverdale, WA 98383-3870, (360)337-2978

U.S. Sugar Mfrs. Assn. [★1567]

U.S. Surfing Fed. - Address unknown since 2008.

U.S. Surveyors Assn. [7721], 13430 McGregor Blvd., Fort Myers, FL 33919, (800)245-4425

U.S. Sweet Potato Coun. [4771], 12 Nicklaus Ln., Ste. 101, Columbia, SC 29229-3363, (803)788-7101

U.S. Sweetener Producers Gp. [★1499]

U.S. Swim School Assn. [23892], PO Box 17208, Fountain Hills, AZ 85269, (480)837-5525

U.S. Swimming Assn. - Defunct.

U.S. Swimming Found. [★23894]

U.S. Swimming Found. [★IO]

U.S. Synchronized Swimming [★23889]

U.S. Systems Corp. - Address unknown since 1989.

U.S. Table Tennis Assn. [★23896]

U.S. Taekwondo Union [23610], 1 Olympic Plz., Ste. 104C, Colorado Springs, CO 80909, (719)866-4632

U.S. Tanzer 16 Class Assn. [★23223]

U.S. Targhee Sheep Assn. - Address unknown since 2008.

U.S. Tchoukball Assn. [23094], 2501 Glenallan Ave., No. 3, Silver Spring, MD 20906, (301)962-5076

U.S. Team Handball Fed. [★23096]

U.S. Team Penning Assn. [23518], PO Box 4170, Fort Worth, TX 76164-0170, (817)378-8082

United States Team Penning Association [IO], Fort Worth, TX, United States

U.S. Telecom Assn. [3965], 607 14th St. NW, Ste. 400, Washington, DC 20005, (202)326-7300

U.S. Telecommunications Suppliers Assn. [★3759]

U.S. Telemark Ski Assn. [23762], PO Box 520338, Salt Lake City, UT 84152

U.S. Telephone Assn. [★3965]

U.S. Tennis Assn. [23915], 70 W Red Oak Ln., White Plains, NY 10604, (914)696-7000

U.S. Tennis Writers Assn. - Address unknown since 2001.

U.S. Tenpin Bowling Fed. - Address unknown since 1994.

U.S. Term Limits Found. [18316], 9900 Main St., Ste. 303, Fairfax, VA 22031

U.S. Terpsichore Assn. - Address unknown since 1995.

U.S.-Tibet Comm. [18741], 241 E 32nd St., New York, NY 10016, (212)481-3569

U.S.-Tibet Comm. [IO], New York, NY, United States

U.S. Tornado Assn. [★23209]

U.S. Tour Operators Assn. [3943], 275 Madison Ave., Ste. 2014, New York, NY 10016-1101, (212)599-6599

U.S. Tour Operators Assn. [IO], New York, NY, United States

U.S. Touring Riders Assn. - Defunct.

U.S. Tourist Coun. [4462]

U.S. Trademark Assn. [★5850]

U.S. Trademark Assn. [★IO]

U.S. Trager Assn. [13656], PO Box 1009, Burton, OH 44021, (440)834-0308

U.S. Travel Data Center [3944], c/o Travel Indus. Assn. of Am., 1100 New York Ave. NW, Ste. 450, Washington, DC 20005-3934, (202)408-8422

U.S. Treasury Agents Assn. [★5653]

U.S. Triathlon Assn. [★23927]

U.S. Trivia Assn. - Defunct.

U.S. Trotting Assn. [23519], 750 Michigan Ave., Columbus, OH 43215, (614)224-2291

U.S. Trout Farmers Assn. [4184], 111 W Washington St., Ste. 1, Charles Town, WV 25414-1529, (304)728-2189

U.S. Truck Historical Soc. [★23021]

U.S. Tuna Found. [3506], c/o Natl. Fisheries Inst., 7918 Jones Br. Dr., Ste. 700, McLean, VA 22102, (703)752-8880

U.S. Twirling Assn. [23143], c/o Ms. Karen Cammer, Exec. Dir., 44 Drexel Dr., Bay Shore, NY 11706, (631)961-0499

U.S. - Ukraine Found. [18758], 1701 K St. NW, Ste. 903, Washington, DC 20006, (202)223-2228

U.S. - Ukraine Found. [IO], Washington, DC, United States

U.S. Ultralight Assn. [21486], 104 Carlisle St., Gettysburg, PA 17325, (717)339-0200

U.S. Umpires Assn. - Defunct.

U.S. - U.S. Chamber; Chamber of Commerce of the [★24301]

United States-USSR

Perhaps Kids Meeting Kids Can Make a Difference [17910]

U.S.-USSR Trade and Economic Coun. - Address unknown since 1994.

U.S.-USSR Youth Exchange Program - Defunct.

U.S. Venetian Blind Assn. [★2279]

U.S. Veterinary Medical Assn. [★16779]

U.S.-Vietnam Trade Coun. [17010], 1025 Vermont Ave. NW, Ste. 727, Washington, DC 20005, (202)263-5630

U.S.-Vietnam Trade Council [IO], Washington, DC, United States

U.S. Volleyball Association/USA Volleyball [23970], 715 S Circle Dr., Colorado Springs, CO 80910-2368, (719)228-6800

U.S. War Dogs Assn. [20769], 1313 Mt. Holly Rd., Burlington, NJ 08016, (609)747-9340

U.S. Water Fitness Assn. [23657], PO Box 243279, Boynton Beach, FL 33424-3279, (561)732-9908

U.S. Water Polo [23973], 2124 Maine St., Ste. 210, Huntington Beach, CA 92648, (714)500-5445

U.S. Wayfarer Assn. [23235], c/o Paul McVey, Treas., 42914 Brookstone Dr., Novi, MI 48377, (248)283-2259

U.S. Wheat Associates [4319], 1620 I St. NW, Ste. 801, Washington, DC 20006-4005, (202)463-0999

U.S. Wheat Associates [IO], Washington, DC, United States

U.S. Windsurfing Assn. [23236], c/o Nat Sidall, Exec. Dir., PO Box 99, Chelsea, MI 48118, (734)678-5625

U.S. Women of Today [13067], 728 Prospect St., York, PA 17403-2426

U.S. Women's Chamber of Commerce [24389], 1200 G St. NW, Ste. 800, Washington, DC 20005, (888)418-7922

Reference to "IO" in place of a book number signifies that the association may be found in the 45th edition of International Organizations.

U.S. Women's Club of Fyn [IO], Odense, Denmark

U.S. Women's Curling Assn. [23303], c/o Star Pfiffner, Pres., North Shore Curling Club, 1340 Glenview Rd., Glenview, IL 60025-3199, (847)729-7105

U.S. Women's Health Coalition - Defunct.

U.S. Women's Squash Racquets Assn. - Address unknown since 1995.

U.S. Women's Track Coaches Assn. - Defunct.

U.S. Wood Screw Service Bur. - Defunct.

U.S. Wrestling Fed. [★23989]

U.S. Yacht Racing Union [★23232]

U.S. Yngling Assn. [23237], c/o Bruce Chafee, Pres., 79 Marlborough St., Boston, MA 02116, (617)424-6107

U.S. Young Esperantists Org. - Address unknown since 1999.

U.S. Youth Coun. - Defunct.

U.S. Youth Soccer Assn. [23784], 9220 World Cup Way, Frisco, TX 75034, (972)334-9300

U.S. Yudo Assn. [23611], c/o R.M. Carver, 15959 Tiger Bend Rd., No. 116, Baton Rouge, LA 70817

U.S. Yugoslav Economic Coun. [★2292]

United Steel Workers of Am., Rubber/Plastics Indus. Conf. [24183], c/o Ron Hoover, Exec. VP, 5 Gateway Center, Pittsburgh, PA 15222, (412)562-2400

United Steelworkers of Am. [24137], 5 Gateway Ctr., Pittsburgh, PA 15222, (412)562-2400

United Steelworkers of Am. - Canadian Br. [IO], Toronto, ON, Canada

United Stockgrowers of Am; Ranchers-Cattlemen Action Legal Fund, [4290]

United Stone and Allied Products Workers of Am. [★24137]

United Strasser Club - Address unknown since 1995.

United St. Machine Assn. [21807], 430 N Batchewana, Clawson, MI 48017, (248)280-0342

United Street Rod Assn. - Defunct.

United Student Aid Funds [★8434]

United Student Assn. - Defunct.

United Students for America - Defunct.

United Students of America Found. - Defunct.

United Suffolk Sheep Assn. [5219], PO Box 256, Newton, UT 84327-0256, (435)563-6105

United Suffolk Sheep Soc. [★5219]

United Sugar Samplers' Assn. - Defunct.

United Support of Artists for Africa [★12882]

United Support of Artists for Africa [★IO]

United Survival Clubs - Address unknown since 1995.

United Swedish Societies [19397]

United Synagogue of Am. [★20188]

United Synagogue of Am. [★IO]

United Synagogue Commn. on Jewish Educ. [★8702]

United Synagogue of Conservative Judaism [20188], 155 5th Ave., New York, NY 10010-6802, (212)533-7800

United Synagogue of Conservative Judaism [IO], New York, NY, United States

United Synagogue of Conservative Judaism Commn. on Jewish Educ. [8702], c/o United Synagogue of Conservative Judaism, 155 5th Ave., New York, NY 10010-6802

United Synagogue Youth [20189], Rapaport House, 155 5th Ave., New York, NY 10010, (212)533-7800

United Telecom Coun. [3762], 1901 Pennsylvania Ave. NW, 5th Fl., Washington, DC 20006-3405, (202)872-0030

United Thoroughbred Trainers of America - Address unknown since 2007.

United Tiberias Institutions Relief Soc. [12463]

United Tobacco Growers Assn. - Defunct.

United Together - Defunct.

United Transport Ser. Employees [★24180]

United Trans. Union [24181], 14600 Detroit Ave., Cleveland, OH 44107-4250, (216)228-9400

United Trekkers - Defunct.

United Trekkers of Planet Earth - Defunct.

United Trotting Assn. [★23519]

United Truck Owners of America - Defunct.

United TVRO Owners Assn. - Defunct.

United Typothetae of Am. [★1788]

United Ukrainian Amer. Relief Comm. [19420], 1206 Cottman Ave., Philadelphia, PA 19111, (215)728-1630

United Underwear Contractors Assn. - Defunct.

United Union of Roofers, Waterproofers and Allied Workers [24033], 1660 L St. NW, Ste. 800, Washington, DC 20036-5646, (202)463-7663

United Voluntary Motor Corps - Address unknown since 1995.

United Voluntary Services - Address unknown since 1995.

United Way of Am. [12205], 701 N Fairfax St., Alexandria, VA 22314, (703)836-7100

United Way of Canada - Centraide Canada [IO], Ottawa, ON, Canada

United Way; Greater New York Fund/ [★12479]

United Way Intl. [12206], 701 N Fairfax St., Alexandria, VA 22314-2045, (703)519-0092

United Way Intl. [IO], Alexandria, VA, United States

United We Serve [21203], 1616 Cayman Cir., Plano, TX 75025, (972)398-2327

United Weighers Assn. [4320]

United Whiteruthenian Byelorussian-Amer. Relief Comm. - Address unknown since 1995.

United Women of the Americas - Address unknown since 1995.

United World Atheists/Amer. Atheists - Defunct.

United World Mission [20407], 9401-B Southern Pine Blvd., Ste. 3, Charlotte, NC 28273-5554, (704)357-3355

United World Mission [IO], Charlotte, NC, United States

United World Powerlifting Fed. [IO], Cobourg, ON, Canada

Uniterra Found. [17915], 16 Gowell Ln., Weston, MA 02493, (781)647-5295

Units and Measurements; Intl. Commn. on Radiological [★5161]

Unity-and-Diversity World Coun. [17916], c/o Leland P. Stewart, BSE, Founder/Coor., PO Box 661401, Los Angeles, CA 90066-9201, (310)391-5735

Unity-and-Diversity World Coun. [IO], Los Angeles, CA, United States

Unity Churches; Assn. of [19845]

Unity Coalition for Israel [8672], 3965 W 83rd St., No. 292, Shawnee Mission, KS 66208, (913)648-0022

Unity Coalition for Israel [IO], Shawnee Mission, KS, United States

Unity; Common Comm. for Amer. [★12404]

Unity Corps [19017], PO Box 29219, Los Angeles, CA 90029-0219, (323)850-8700

Unity Coun; Mexican Amer. [12277]

Unity of Czech Ladies and Men [★19026]

Unity in Diversity Coun. [★17916]

Unity in Diversity Coun. [★IO]

Unity and Diversity World Org. [★IO]

Unity and Diversity World Org. [★17916]

Unity Fellowship Church Movement [20068], 5148 W Jefferson Blvd., Los Angeles, CA 90016, (323)938-8322

Unity House - Defunct.

UNITY: Journalists of Color [3172], 7950 Jones Br. Dr., McLean, VA 22107, (703)854-3585

Unity Network [★10756]

Uniunea Arhitectilor din Romania [★IO]

Uniunea Generala a Industriasilor din Romania [★IO]

Uniunea Romana De Transport Public [★IO]

Universal African Nationalist Movement - Address unknown since 1995.

Universal Articulate Interdimensional Understanding of Sci. [★12366]

Universal Articulate Interdimensional Understanding of Sci. [★IO]

Universal Autograph Collectors Club [22126], c/o Michael Hecht, Pres., 1489 W Cypress Ave., San Dimas, CA 91773

Universal Buddhist Fellowship - Address unknown since 1995.

Universal Cooperatives [4484], 1300 Corporate Center Curve, Eagan, MN 55121, (651)239-1000

The Universal Coterie of Pipe Smokers [22898]

Universal Craftsmen Coun. of Engineers - Address unknown since 1995.

Universal Detective Assn. - Defunct.

Universal Esperanto Assn. [IO], Rotterdam, Netherlands

Universal Fellowship of Metropolitan Community Churches [★20062]

Universal Gym Affiliates [★3665]

Universal Gym Affiliates [★IO]

Universal Helping Hand Soc. - Defunct.

Universal Islamic Found. - Address unknown since 2000.

Universal Life Trust - Address unknown since 2000.

Universal Martial Arts Brotherhood [23612], c/o Grandmaster Eugene A. Humesky, PhD, Founder/CEO/Chm., 2427 Buckingham Rd., Ann Arbor, MI 48104, (734)971-7040

Universal Martial Arts Brotherhood [IO], Ann Arbor, MI, United States

Universal Masonic Brotherhood [19256], PO Box 6410, Seffner, FL 33583-6410, (813)662-3597

Universal Masonic Brotherhood and Order of the Eastern Star - Address unknown since 2006.

Universal Movement Theatre Repertory - Defunct.

Universal Muslim Assn. of Am. [20442], PO Box 414, Burtonsville, MD 20866, (646)932-8622

Universal Negro Improvement Assn. and African Communities League of the World - Address unknown since 1994.

Universal Pantheist Soc. [20586], PO Box 3499, Visalia, CA 93278

Universal Party - Address unknown since 1995.

Universal Peace Fed. [18251], 155 White Plains Rd., Ste. 222, Tarrytown, NY 10591, (914)631-1331

Universal Perkehner Soc. [22602]

Universal Philatelic Cover Soc. - Defunct.

Universal Postal Union [IO], Bern, Switzerland

Universal Postal Union Collectors - Defunct.

Universal Proutist Farmers Fed. [4659], 6810 Tilden Ln., Rockville, MD 20852, (301)231-0110

Universal Proutist Intellectual Fed. [★18627]

Universal Proutist Labour Fed. - Address unknown since 2006.

Universal Proutist Student Fed. - Address unknown since 2005.

Universal Proutist Youth Fed. [18631], PO Box 56533, Washington, DC 20040, (301)231-0110

Universal Proutists Women [★18633]

Universal Serials and Book Exchange [★10392]

Universal Ship Cancellation Soc. [22889], 747 Shard Ct., Fremont, CA 94539-7419

Universal Ship Cancellation Society [IO], Fremont, CA, United States

Universal Ship Cancellation Soc., Savannah Chap. [★IO]

Universal Ship Cancellation Soc., Savannah Chap. [★22841]

Universal Torah Registry [20190], 70 W 36th St., Ste. 700, New York, NY 10018-8070, (212)983-4800

Universal and Triumphant; Church [19462]

Universal Wheelchair Football Assn. [23368], c/o John Kraimer, Univ. of Cincinnati, Raymond Walters Coll., 9555 Plainfield Rd., Cincinnati, OH 45236-1096, (513)792-8625

Universal White Brotherhood [IO], Sevres, France

Universal Zetetic Soc. of America and Great Britain [★7145]

Universala Esperanto-Asocio [★IO]

Universalist Assn. of Congregations; Unitarian [13135]

Universalist Assn. of Congregations - Washington Off. for Faith in Action; Unitarian [★13135]

Universalist Assn. - Washington Off. for Social Concern; Unitarian [★13135]

Universalist Christian Fellowship; Unitarian [20600]

Universalist Historical Soc. [★20601]

Universalist Historical Soc; Unitarian [20601]

Universalist Ministers Assn; Unitarian [20602]

Universalist Musicians' Network; Unitarian [20436]

Universalist Ser. Comm. [★20603]

Universalist Ser. Comm. [★IO]

Universalist Women; Assn. of [★20604]

Universalist Women's Fed; Unitarian [20604]

Universalists for Lesbian, Gay, Bisexual and Transgender Concerns; Interweave Continental Unitarian [20059]

Universalists for Lesbian and Gay Concerns; Unitarian [★20059]

A star before a book entry number signifies that the name is not listed separately, but is mentioned within the entry.

Universality of UNESCO; Americans for the [★18760]

Universite ve Arastirma Kutuphanecileri Dernegi [★IO]

Universities for the Advancement of Vietnamese Abroad; Gp. of [9296]

Universities and Allied Institutions; Assn. of Governing Boards of State [★7889]

Universities; Amer. Assn. of Presidents of Independent Colleges and [8534]

Universities; Amer. Assn. of State Colleges and [8096]

Universities Associated for Res. and Education in Pathology - Defunct.

Universities; Assn. of Amer. [8099]

Universities; Assn. of Amer. Colleges and [8098]

Universities; Assn. of Catholic Colleges and [8051]

Universities Assn. for Continuing Educ. [★IO]

Universities; Assn. of Departments of English in Amer. Colleges and [★8374]

Universities; Assn. of Graduate Schools in Assn. of Amer. [7890]

Universities; Assn. of Intl. Colleges and [★8641]

Universities; Assn. of Jesuit Colleges and [8052]

Universities; Assn. of Land-Grant Colleges and State [★8110]

Universities Assn. for Lifelong Learning [IO], Middlesborough, United Kingdom

Universities; Assn. of NROTC Colleges and [8884]

Universities; Assn. of Presbyterian Colleges and [9005]

Universities; Assn. of State Colleges and [★8096]

Universities; Assn. of Upper Level Colleges and [★8096]

Universities Australia [IO], Canberra, Australia

Universities Bur. of the British Empire [★IO]

Universities Club of New York; British Schools and [18984]

Universities and Colleges; Assn. of Governing Boards of [7889]

Universities and Colleges; Assn. of Physical Plant Administrators of [★8333]

Universities and Colleges; Assn. of Superintendents of Buildings and Grounds of [★8333]

Universities and Colleges; Natl. Assn. of Physical Administrators of [★8333]

Universities; Coun. for Christian Colleges and [8084]

Universities Coun. for the Educ. of Teachers [IO], London, United Kingdom

Universities Coun. on Hydrology [★7844]

Universities Coun. on Water Resources [7844], c/o Southern Illinois Univ. Carbondale, 1000 Faner Dr., Rm. 4543, Carbondale, IL 62901-4526, (618)536-7571

Universities Fed. for Animal Welfare [IO], Wheathampstead, United Kingdom

Universities; Fed. of State Associations of Independent Colleges and [★8539]

Universities Field Staff -Institute of World Affairs; Amer. [★8663]

Universities Field Staff Intl. -Inst. of World Affairs [★8663]

Universities Field Staff Intl. -Inst. of World Affairs [★IO]

Universities and Land-Grant Colleges; Natl. Assn. of State [8110]

Universities and Land-Grant Colleges; Off. for the Advancement of Public Black Colleges of the Natl. Assn. of State [8112]

Universities and Land-Grant Colleges; Off. for Advancement of Public Negro Colleges - of the Natl. Assn. of State [★8112]

Universities Mission to Central Africa [★IO]

Universities; Natl. Assn. of Colls. and [★8225]

Universities; Natl. Assn. of Independent Colleges and [8539]

Universities; Natl. Consortium of Arts and Letters for Historically Black Colls. and [8111]

Universities; Natl. Coun. of Independent Colleges and [★8539]

Universities; Natl. Inst. of Independent Colleges and [★8539]

Universities North Am. Club; British [8606]

Universities; Oak Ridge Assoc. [7625]

Universities and the Quest for Peace - Defunct.

Universities Res. Assn. [7577], 1111 19th St. NW, Ste. 400, Washington, DC 20036, (202)293-1382

Universities Res. Assn. [IO], Washington, DC, United States

Universities for Res. in Astronomy; Assn. of [6501]

Universities Space Res. Assn. [6392], 10211 Wincopin Cir., Ste. 500, Columbia, MD 21044-3432, (410)730-2656

Universities UK [IO], London, United Kingdom

Univ. Administrators; Amer. Assn. of [7884]

Univ. Administrators; Inst. for Coll. and [★8745]

Univ. of Advancing Cmpt. Tech. Alumni Assn. [18929], c/o Univ. of Advancing Tech., 2625 W Baseline Rd., Tempe, AZ 85283-1056, (602)383-8228

Univ. Affiliated Facilities; Assn. of [★12563]

Univ. Affiliated Programs for the Developmentally Disabled; Amer. Assn. of [★12563]

Univ. Affiliated Programs for Persons With Developmental Disabilities; Amer. Assn. of [★12563]

Univ. of Alaska Fairbanks Alumni Assn. [18930], PO Box 750126, Fairbanks, AK 99775, (907)474-7081

Univ; Amer. Friends of The Hebrew [8676]

Univ. Anesthesiologists; Assn. of [13680]

Univ. Anesthetists; Assn. of [★13680]

Univ. Assn. for Contemporary European Stud. [IO], London, United Kingdom

Univ. Assn. for Emergency Medicine [★14344]

Univ. Athletic Assn. [23865], 151 Sully's Trail, Ste. 4, Pittsford, NY 14534, (585)419-0575

Univ. Attorneys; Natl. Assn. of Coll. and [5677]

Univ. Auditors; Assn. of Coll. and [7888]

Univ. Aviation Assn. [7924], 3410 Skyway Dr., Auburn, AL 36830, (334)844-2434

Univ. of Bremen, Res. Gp. on African Development Perspectives [IO], Bremen, Germany

Univ. Bus. Officers; Amer. Assn. of Coll. and [★7897]

Univ. Bus. Officers Associations; Natl. Fed. of Coll. and [★7897]

Univ. Bus. Officers; Natl. Assn. of Coll. and [7897]

Univ. of Calcutta Medical Assn. of America - Address unknown since 1999.

Univ. of Calgary Ballroom Dance Club [IO], Calgary, AB, Canada

Univ. Centers on Disabilities; Assn. of [12563]

Univ. Chaplains and Directors of Religious Life; National Assn. of Coll. and [★9168]

Univ. Christian Movement - Defunct.

Univ. and Coll. Designers Assn. [8572], 199 W Enon Spring Rd., Ste. 300, Smyrna, TN 37167, (615)459-4559

University and College Designers Association [IO], Smyrna, TN, United States

Univ. and Coll. Labor Educ. Assn. [★8722]

Univ. and Coll. Lecturers' Union [IO], London, United Kingdom

Univ. and Coll. Ombuds Assn. [★736]

Univ. Coll. Professional Publishers Coun. [★IO]

Univ. and Coll. Theater Assn. [★9262]

Univ. and Coll. Union [IO], London, United Kingdom

Univ. and Coll. Union Scotland [★IO]

Univ. Colleges Consortium; World [★8114]

Univ. Colleges Consortium; Worldwide [★8114]

Univ. of Colorado Hea. Sciences Center Alumni Assn. [24494], 4200 E 9th Ave., Box A-080, Denver, CO 80262, (303)315-8832

Univ. of Colorado Medical Alumni Assn. [18931], 4200 E 9th Ave., Box A-080, Denver, CO 80262, (303)315-8832

Univ. of Colorado School of Dentistry Alumni Assn. [18932], c/o UCHSC Alumni Assn., 4200 E 9th Ave., A-080, Denver, CO 80262, (303)315-8832

Univ. Composers; Amer. Soc. of [★9817]

Univ. Cmpt. Users Assn; Coll. and [7894]

Univ. Cmpt. Users Conf; Coll. and [★7894]

Univ. Consortium for Instructional Development and Technology - Defunct.

University Consortium for Political and Social Res; Inter- [7525]

Univ. Consortium for Telecommunications in Learning; Intl. [★8566]

Univ. Consortium for Telecommunications in Teaching; Natl. [★8566]

Univ. Continuing Educ. Assn. [8154], 1 Dupont Cir., Ste. 615, Washington, DC 20036, (202)659-3130

University Continuing Education Association [IO], Washington, DC, United States

Univ. Corp. for Atmospheric Res. [7329], PO Box 3000, Boulder, CO 80307-3000, (303)497-1000

Univ. Coun. for Educational Admin. [7909], 1 Univ. Sta. D5400, Dept. of Educational Admin., Univ. of Texas at Austin, Austin, TX 78712-0374, (512)475-8592

Univ. Dept. of the Natl. Catholic Educ. Assn; Coll. and [★8051]

Univ. Economic Development Assn. [9309], HFR-WCU, Ste. 440, Cullowhee, NC 28723, (828)227-7059

Univ. Educational Fellowship; Oral Roberts [8089]

Univ. Educators; Nature and Environmental Writers - Coll. and [8362]

Univ. Extension Assn; Natl. [★8154]

Univ. Faculty for Life [9025], 120 New North Bldg., Georgetown Univ., Washington, DC 20057, (202)687-6101

Univ. Faculty for Life [IO], Washington, DC, United States

Univ. Film Assn. [★8420]

Univ. Film Found. [★8421]

Univ. Film Producers Assn. [★8420]

Univ. Film and Video Assn. [8420], c/o Cheryl Jestis, Univ. of Illinois Press, 1325 S Oak St., Champaign, IL 61820-6903, (217)244-0626

Univ. Film and Video Found. [8421], c/o William O. Huie, Jr., Pres., Texas A&M Univ. - Corpus Christi, 6300 Ocean Dr., Unit 5722, Corpus Christi, TX 78412-5503, (361)825-5750

Univ. Fisheries and Wildlife Programs; Natl. Assn. of [8391]

Univ. Food Services; Natl. Assn. of Coll. and [1588]

Univ. Graduates; Assn. of Arab-American [18953]

Univ. Group Diabetes Program - Defunct.

Univ. Instructors in Accounting; Amer. Assn. of [★7]

Univ. Insurance Managers Assn. [★8580]

Univ. Interior Designers; Assn. of [2252]

Univ. of Iowa Alumni Assn. [18933], 100 Levitt Center for Univ. Advancement, Iowa City, IA 52242-1797, (319)335-3294

Univ. of Iowa Injury Prevention Res. Center [7588], c/o John A. Lundell, MA, Deputy Dir., 158 IREH Oakdale Res. Campus, Iowa City, IA 52242-5000, (319)335-4458

Univ. Labor Educ. Assn. [★8722]

Univ. Lab. Managers Assn. [★7237]

Univ. of London Examinations and Assessment Coun., 1838 [★IO]

Univ. of Louisville Alumni Assn. [18934], Alumni Off., Malcolm B. Chancey Ctr., Univ. of Louisville, Louisville, KY 40292, (502)852-6186

Univ. Machine Records Conf; Coll. and [★7894]

Univ. of Mary Alumni Assn. [18935], 7500 Univ. Dr., Bismarck, ND 58504, (701)255-7500

Univ. Media Centers; Consortium of Coll. and [8554]

Univ. of Michigan; Alumni Assn. of the [18873]

Univ. of Minnesota - Crookston Alumni Assn. [18936], 2900 Univ. Ave., Crookston, MN 56716-5000, (218)281-8434

Univ. of Minnesota Human Rights Center [★17760]

Univ. Museums and Galleries; Assn. of Coll. and [10496]

Univ. of the Negev; Amer. Associates, Ben-Gurion [8673]

Univ. of the Negev; Amer. Friends of the [★8673]

Univ. Network; Free [★8151]

Univ. Offices; Assn. for Affiliated Coll. and [★8341]

Univ. Offices; Assn. of Coll. and [★8341]

Univ. of Oklahoma Assn. [★18919]

Univ. Otolaryngologists - Head and Neck Surgeons; Soc. of [15828]

Univ. Pastors and Campus Ministry Assn; Assn. of Presbyterian [★19933]

Univ. Peace Studies Network - Defunct.

Univ. of Pennsylvania; Philomathean Soc. of the [10429]

Univ. Personnel Assn; Coll. and [★8962]

Univ. Philosophical Soc. [IO], Dublin, Ireland

Univ. Photographers Assn. of Am. [8977], c/o Jim Dusen, Pres., SUNY Brockport, 350 New Campus Dr., Brockport, NY 14420-2931, (585)395-2133

Reference to "IO" in place of a book number signifies that the association may be found in the 45th edition of International Organizations.

Univ. Planning; Soc. for Coll. and **[9000]**
Univ. Presses; Assn. of Amer. **[8550]**
Univ. Professional Assn. for Human Resources; Coll. and **[8962]**
Univ. Professors for Academic Order **[9026]**
Univ. Professors; Amer. Assn. of **[9022]**
Univ. Professors of Ophthalmology; Assn. of **[15675]**
University Prog. for Latino Res; Inter- **[19045]**
Univ. Programs in Hea. Admin; Assn. of **[8857]**
Univ. Programs in Hosp. Admin; Assn. of **[★8857]**
Univ. Radiologists; Assn. of **[16286]**
Univ. Related Res. Parks; Assn. of **[★9054]**
Univ. Religious Affairs; Assn. of Coll. and **[9168]**
Univ. Res. Administrators; Natl. Coun. of **[9063]**
University Res. Comm. **[★7851]**
Univ. and Res. Librarians Assn. **[IO]**, Ankara, Turkey
Univ. Res. Parks; Assn. of **[9054]**
University/Resident Theatre Assn. **[9269]**, 1560 Broadway, Ste. 712, New York, NY 10036, (212)221-1130
University Rsrc. Inst; College- **[9055]**
Univ. Risk and Insurance Managers Assn. **[★8580]**
Univ. Risk Mgt. and Insurance Assn. **[8580]**, PO Box 1027, Bloomington, IN 47402-1027, (812)855-6683
University Services Institute **[★709]**
Univ.-Small Business Technology Consortium - Defunct.
Univ. of South Dakota Alumni Assn. **[18937]**, PO Box 5555, Vermillion, SD 57069-2390, (605)677-6734
University Students; Broadcast Found. of College/ **[8002]**
Univ. Summer Sessions; Assn. of **[9199]**
Univ. Summer Sessions; Natl. Assn. of Coll. and **[★9200]**
Univ. Surgeons; Soc. of **[16591]**
Univ. Tech. Managers; Assn. of **[5838]**
Univ. of Texas at Brownsville and Texas Southmost Coll. Alumni Assn. **[18938]**, 80 Ft. Brown, Browns-ville, TX 78520, (956)982-0106
Univ. of Texas - Pan-American Alumni Assn. **[18939]**, 1201 W Univ. Dr., UC108, Edinburg, TX 78541, (956)381-2500
Univ. Urologists; Soc. of **[16716]**
Univ. of Virginia; Bibliographical Soc. of the **[9742]**
University of Wisconsin
    U.S. Comm. for Sci. Cooperation With Vietnam **[8633]**
Univ. of Wisconsin - Eau Claire Alumni Assn. **[18940]**, 216 Schofield Hall, 105 Garfield Ave., PO Box 4004, Eau Claire, WI 54702-4004, (715)836-3266
Univ. of Wisconsin-Milwaukee; Center for Consumer Affairs, **[17313]**
Univ. of Wisconsin - Platteville Alumni Assn. **[18941]**, Royce Hall, 1 Univ. Plz., Platteville, WI 53818-3099, (608)342-1181
Univ. Women; Amer. Assn. of **[9311]**
Univ. Women Educational Found; Amer. Assn. of **[9312]**
Univ. Women of Europe **[IO]**, Heusy, Belgium
Univ. Women; Natl. Assn. of **[9320]**
Univ. Women's Assn. - Singapore **[IO]**, Singapore, Singapore
Univ. Year for Action - Defunct.
UNIX Systems
    League of Professional Sys. Administrators **[6815]**
    USENIX Assn. **[6806]**
Unix Systems Assn. - Defunct.
Unlimited Scale Racing Assn. **[22659]**, PO Box 819, Brea, CA 92822
Unmanned Vehicle Systems Intl; Assn. for **[7580]**
Unmarried-Catholics Correspondence Club **[22145]**
UNOS **[★16684]**
Unplug **[★8241]**
Unreached Peoples Mission - Address unknown since 1989.
Unrecognised States Numismatic Soc. **[22766]**, PO Box 534, Castaic, CA 91310-0534
Unregistered Churches; Amer. Coalition of **[20520]**
Unrepresented Nations and Peoples Org. **[IO]**, Washington, DC, United States
Unwed Parents Anonymous - Defunct.
UOTS, Inc. **[★19437]**
UP Micro-Loans: Unlimiting People **[IO]**, Berlin, Germany

Up With People **[8311]**, 1600 Broadway, Ste. 1460, Denver, CO 80202, (303)460-7100
Upholstered Furniture Action Coun. **[1708]**, Box 2436, High Point, NC 27261, (336)885-5065
Upholsterers' Intl. Union of North Am. **[★24137]**
Upholstery and Decorative Fabrics Assn. of America - Defunct.
Upholstery Fabric Distributors; Natl. Assn. of **[★3793]**
Upholstery Fabric Mfrs. Assn. - Defunct.
Upjohn Inst. for Community Res; W. E. **[★12104]**
Upjohn Inst. for Employment Res; W. E. **[12104]**
UPL-AOPA Luxembourg **[★IO]**
Upledger Inst. **[13657]**, 11211 Prosperity Farms Rd., Ste. D-325, Palm Beach Gardens, FL 33410, (561)622-4334
Upledger's Intl. Assn. of Healthcare Practitioners **[★14639]**
Upledger's Intl. Assn. of Healthcare Practitioners **[★IO]**
Uplift Internationale **[IO]**, Wheat Ridge, CO, United States
Uplift Internationale **[15737]**, PO Box 582, Wheat Ridge, CO 80034, (303)707-1361
Upper Cervical Chiropractic Assn; Natl. **[14012]**
Upper Cervical Chiropractic Organizations; Acad. of **[13986]**
Upper Level Colleges and Universities; Assn. of **[★8096]**
Upper Mississippi River Conservation Comm. **[4463]**, 555 Lester Ave., Onalaska, WI 54650, (608)783-8432
Uppity Women - Address unknown since 1995.
Upsilon Alpha - Defunct.
Upsilon Pi Epsilon Assn. **[24435]**, c/o Orlando S. Madrigal, PhD, Sec., 158 Wetlands Edge Rd., American Canyon, CA 94503, (530)518-8488
Upsilon Pi Epsilon Assn. **[IO]**, American Canyon, CA, United States
Upwardly Global **[3186]**, San Francisco Off., 582 Market St., Ste. 1207, San Francisco, CA 94104, (415)834-9901
Urania Trust **[IO]**, Old Windsor, United Kingdom
Uranium Inst. of America - Address unknown since 1995.
URANTIA Assn. of the U.S. **[9051]**, c/o URANTIA Found., 533 Diversey Pkwy., Chicago, IL 60614, (773)525-3319
Urantia Found. **[20587]**, 533 Diversey Pkwy., Chicago, IL 60614, (773)525-3319
Urantia Found. **[IO]**, Chicago, IL, United States
Urasenke Tea Ceremony Soc. **[10269]**
Urbain Baudreau Graveline Genealogical Assn. **[21074]**, PO Box 905, Palmer, MA 01069, (413)283-8378
Urban Affairs
    Assn. of Collegiate Schools of Planning **[9285]**
    Assn. of Town Centre Mgt. **[IO]**
    British Urban Regeneration Assn. **[IO]**
    Center on Urban Poverty and Community Development **[18377]**
    Center for Urban and Regional Stud. **[11066]**
    Center for Urban and Regional Studies **[IO]**
    Coalition on Urban Renewal and Educ. **[18774]**
    Coun. on Tall Buildings and Urban Habitat **[6474]**
    EUROCITIES Mobility Forum - ACCESS **[IO]**
    European Acad. of the Urban Env. **[IO]**
    European Forum for Urban Safety **[IO]**
    Experimental Cities, Inc. **[17236]**
    Greener Pastures Inst. **[12312]**
    Higher Educ. Consortium for Urban Affairs **[9286]**
    Higher Educ. Consortium for Urban Affairs **[IO]**
    Inst. for SocioEconomic Stud. **[18458]**
    Intergovernmental Comm. on Urban and Regional Res. **[IO]**
    International Healthy Cities Foundation **[IO]**
    Intl. Healthy Cities Found. **[13349]**
    Legambiente Ecopolis, Turin **[IO]**
    London Soc. **[IO]**
    Natl. Assn. of Urban Hospitals **[14893]**
    Natl. Neighborhood Coalition **[17230]**
    Natl. Urban Fellows **[18775]**
    Neighborhood Funders Gp. **[12734]**
    Planning and Development Collaborative Intl. **[18776]**

Planning and Development Collaborative Intl. **[IO]**
Planning Inst. Australia **[IO]**
Public Housing Authorities Directors Assn. **[5798]**
Soc. for Upgrading the Built Env. **[IO]**
Soc. for Urban, Natl. and Transnational/Global Anthropology **[6435]**
Town and Country Planning Assn. **[IO]**
ULI Found. **[18777]**
Urban Affairs Assn. **[9287]**
Urban Inst. **[18778]**
Urban Libraries Coun. **[10393]**
Urban Superintendent's Assn. of Am. **[9288]**
Vera Inst. of Justice **[11895]**
Urban Affairs Assn. **[9287]**, c/o Univ. of Delaware, 298 Graham Hall, Newark, DE 19716, (302)831-1681
Urban Affairs; Coun. of Univ. Institutes for **[★9287]**
Urban Affairs Inst. - Address unknown since 1995.
Urban Agriculture Coun; Natl. **[4113]**
Urban Alliance on Race Relations **[IO]**, Toronto, ON, Canada
Urban Art Intl. **[IO]**, Tiburon, CA, United States
Urban Art Intl. **[1811]**, PO Box 868, Tiburon, CA 94920, (415)435-5767
Urban Bankers; Natl. Assn. of **[★499]**
Urban-Brookings Tax Policy Center **[18722]**, 2100 M St. NW, Washington, DC 20037, (202)833-7200
Urban Coalition Action Coun. **[★18287]**
Urban Crime Prevention Program - Defunct.
Urban Design; Inst. for **[6475]**
Urban Ecology Australia **[IO]**, Adelaide, Australia
Urban Economic Development; Coun. for **[★5812]**
Urban Economics Assn; Amer. Real Estate and **[9050]**
Urban Education
    Assn. of Collegiate Schools of Planning **[9285]**
    Australian Inst. of Urban Stud. **[IO]**
    Coun. of the Great City Schools **[9289]**
    Higher Educ. Consortium for Urban Affairs **[9286]**
    Jackie Robinson Found. **[13491]**
    Literacy USA **[8792]**
    Natl. Coun. of Urban Educ. Associations **[9290]**
    Natl. Urban Alliance for Effective Educ. **[9291]**
    New Leaders for New Schools **[8755]**
    Urban Affairs Assn. **[9287]**
    Urban Libraries Coun. **[10393]**
Urban Elderly Coalition - Defunct.
Urban Environment Conf. - Defunct.
Urban Ethnic Affairs; Natl. Center for **[11753]**
Urban Farm; Takoma **[★4105]**
Urban Fellows; Natl. **[★18775]**
Urban Financial Services Coalition **[499]**, 1212 New York Ave. NW, Ste. 950, Washington, DC 20005, (202)289-8335
Urban Flood Mgt. Agencies; Natl. Assn. of **[★6140]**
Urban Foresters Soc; Municipal Arborists and **[★6121]**
Urban Habitat; Coun. on Tall Buildings and **[6474]**
Urban History Group - Defunct.
Urban Homesteading Assistance Bd. **[12339]**, 120 Wall St., 20th Fl., New York, NY 10005, (212)479-3300
Urban Hospitals; Center for **[★14895]**
Urban Hospitals; Natl. Assn. of **[14893]**
Urban Initiatives - Address unknown since 2004.
Urban Inst. **[18778]**, 2100 M St. NW, Washington, DC 20037, (202)833-7200
Urban Land Found. **[★18777]**
Urban Land Institute **[★18777]**
Urban Land Inst. **[5597]**, 1025 Thomas Jefferson St. NW, Ste. 500 W, Washington, DC 20007-5230, (202)624-7000
Urban Land Inst. Found. **[★18777]**
Urban Land Res. Found. **[★18777]**
Urban Law Inst. of Antioch School of Law - Defunct.
Urban League; Natl. **[17138]**
Urban Libraries Coun. **[10393]**, 125 S Wacker Dr., Ste. 1050, Chicago, IL 60606, (312)676-0999
Urban Lib. Trustees Coun. **[★10393]**
Urban and Regional Info. Systems Assn. **[7215]**, 1460 Renaissance Dr., Ste. 305, Park Ridge, IL 60068, (847)824-6300
Urban Resources; Inst. for Art and **[★9595]**
Urban/Rural Fellows; Natl. **[★18775]**
Urban Scientific and Educational Res., Inc. - Defunct.

A star before a book entry number signifies that the name is not listed separately, but is mentioned within the entry.

Urban Superintendent's Assn. of Am. **[9288]**, c/o C. Fred Bateman, Exec. Dir., PO Box 1248, Chesapeake, VA 23327-1248, (757)436-1032

Urban Training Center for Christian Mission - Defunct.

Urbanturban **[IO]**, Trondheim, Norway

Urdd Cerddoriaeth Cymru **[★IO]**

Urethane; Bur. of **[★3057]**

Urethane Foam Contractors Assn; Canadian **[IO]**

Urethane Foam Contractors Assn. - Defunct.

Urethane Inst., Soc. of the Plastics Indus. Polyurethane Div. **[★3047]**

Urgent Action Network **[★17988]**

Urgent Action Network **[★IO]**

Urgent Care Assn. of Am. **[13665]**, 4320 Winfield Rd., Warrenville, IL 60555, (630)836-8514

Urgent Care Medicine; North Amer. Assn. of **[★13663]**

Urgent Care; North Amer. Assn. for Ambulatory **[13663]**

Urgent Treatment; Natl. Assn. of Centers for **[★13663]**

Urgenta Found. **[IO]**, Utrecht, Netherlands

UrgentCall.org **[18173]**, c/o Inst. for Defense and Disarmament Stud., 675 Massachusetts Ave., Cambridge, MA 02139, (617)354-4337

Urinary Surgeons; Amer. Assn. of Genito- **[16699]**

Urine Disease; Families with Maple Syrup **[★15250]**

Urine Family Support Gp; Maple Syrup **[15250]**

Urogynecologic Soc; Amer. **[16703]**

Urologic Allied Hea. Professionals; Amer. Bd. of **[★16706]**

Urologic Nurses and Associates; Soc. of **[15529]**

Urological Soc. of Australasia **[IO]**, Edgecliff, Australia

Urological Soc. of India **[IO]**, Patna, India

Urology

Amer. Assn. of Clinical Urologists **[16698]**

Amer. Assn. of Genito-Urinary Surgeons **[16699]**

Amer. Assn. of Kidney Patients **[15283]**

Amer. Bd. of Urology **[16700]**

Amer. Kidney Fund **[15284]**

Amer. Prostate Soc. **[16701]**

Amer. Soc. of Andrology **[16702]**

Amer. Soc. of Nephrology **[15288]**

Amer. Urogynecologic Soc. **[16703]**

Amer. Urological Assn. **[16704]**

Amer. Urological Assn. Found. **[16705]**

Asia Pacific Assn. of Paediatric Urologists **[IO]**

Assn. for Continence Advice **[IO]**

Assn. of German Urologists **[IO]**

Bladder Cancer Advocacy Network **[13799]**

British Assn. of Urological Surgeons **[IO]**

Canadian Continence Found. **[IO]**

Canadian Urological Assn. **[IO]**

Certification Bd. for Urologic Nurses and Associates **[16706]**

Continence Restored, Inc. **[16707]**

European Assn. of Urology **[IO]**

European Bd. of Urology **[IO]**

European Soc. for Paediatric Urology **[IO]**

European Soc. of Residents in Urology **[IO]**

Hong Kong Urological Assn. **[IO]**

Interstitial Cystitis Assn. **[16708]**

Japanese Urological Assn. **[IO]**

National Association for Continence **[IO]**

Natl. Assn. for Continence **[16709]**

Natl. Kidney Found. **[15294]**

Natl. Kidney and Urologic Diseases Info. CH **[16710]**

Philippine Urological Assn. **[IO]**

Renal Physicians Assn. **[15298]**

Scandinavian Assn. of Urology **[IO]**

Simon Found. for Continence **[16711]**

Sociedad Chilena de Urologia **[IO]**

Societe Internationale d'Urologie **[IO]**

Soc. for Basic Urologic Res. **[16712]**

Soc. for Fetal Urology **[16713]**

Soc. of Govt. Ser. Urologists **[16714]**

Soc. for Male Reproduction and Urology **[16343]**

Soc. for Pediatric Urology **[16715]**

Soc. for the Stud. of Male Reproduction **[16344]**

Soc. for Univ. Urologists **[16716]**

Soc. of Urologic Nurses and Associates **[15529]**

Soc. of Uroradiology **[16717]**

Soc. of Women in Urology **[16718]**

Urological Soc. of Australasia **[IO]**

Urological Soc. of India **[IO]**

Urostomy Assn. **[IO]**

Urostomy Assn. **[IO]**, Uttoxeter, United Kingdom

Urostomy Assn. of Great Britain and Ireland **[★IO]**

Ursa Astronomical Assn. **[IO]**, Helsinki, Finland

Ursuline Companions in Mission **[20408]**, c/o Diane Fulgenzi, Coor., 210 Glennon Heights Rd., Crystal City, MO 63019, (636)937-6206

Uruguay Collectors Club - Defunct.

Uruguayan Assn. of the Analytical Psychotherapy **[IO]**, Montevideo, Uruguay

Uruguayan Circle of Advt. Agencies **[IO]**, Montevideo, Uruguay

Uruguayan Dermatological Soc. **[IO]**, Montevideo, Uruguay

Uruguayan Family Planning Assn. **[IO]**, Montevideo, Uruguay

Uruguayan Found. of Joint Cooperation and Development **[IO]**, Montevideo, Uruguay

Uruguayan Hypertension Comm. **[IO]**, Montevideo, Uruguay

Uruguayan League Against Arterial Hypertension **[IO]**, Montevideo, Uruguay

Uruguayan League Against Epilepsy **[IO]**, Montevideo, Uruguay

Uruguayan Rose Assn. **[IO]**, Montevideo, Uruguay

Uruguayan Soc. of Cardiology **[IO]**, Montevideo, Uruguay

Uruguayan Soc. of Clinical Neurophysiology **[IO]**, Montevideo, Uruguay

Uruguayan Soc. of Hea. Informatics **[IO]**, Montevideo, Uruguay

US-Azerbaijan Coun. **[17876]**, 1010 Vermont Ave. NW, Ste. 814, Washington, DC 20005, (202)662-1343

US Cheng Ming Martial Arts Assn. **[23613]**, 2220 Coit Rd., Ste. 200K, Plano, TX 75075, (972)740-8458

US-China Bus. Coun. **[2319]**, 1818 N St. NW, Ste. 200, Washington, DC 20036-2470, (202)429-0340

US-China Peoples Friendship Assn. **[★8552]**

US Club Soccer **[23785]**, 716 8th Ave. N, Myrtle Beach, SC 29577, (843)429-0006

US-Cuba Reconciliation Initiative **[17675]**, c/o Fund for Reconciliation & Development, 355 W 39th St., New York, NY 10118, (212)760-9903

US-Cuba Reconciliation Initiative **[IO]**, New York, NY, United States

US Flag Football League **[★23441]**

US Foreclosure Network **[★325]**

US Fuel Cell Coun. **[6976]**, 1100 H St. NW, Ste. 800, Washington, DC 20005, (202)293-5500

US Green Building Coun. **[684]**, 1800 Massachusetts Ave. NW, Ste. 300, Washington, DC 20036, (202)742-3792

U.S., Inc. **[★12658]**

US-Ireland Alliance **[776]**, 2800 Clarendon Blvd., No. 502 W, Arlington, VA 22201, (703)841-5843

US Log Rolling Assn. **[23982]**, 711 Glenna Dr., Hudson, WI 54016

US Natl. and Olympic Teams **[★23788]**

US Scale Masters Assn. **[22660]**, 9151 Larkspur Dr., Westminster, CA 92683, (714)894-2747

US Soccer **[23786]**, 1801 S Prairie Ave., Chicago, IL 60616, (312)808-1300

US-Taiwan Bus. Coun. **[2294]**, 1700 N Moore St., Ste. 1703, Arlington, VA 22209, (703)465-2930

US-Taiwan Bus. Coun. **[IO]**, Arlington, VA, United States

Us TOO Intl. **[IO]**, Downers Grove, IL, United States

Us TOO Intl. **[13879]**, 5003 Fairview Ave., Downers Grove, IL 60515, (630)795-1002

US-Vietnam Chamber of Commerce **[24387]**, PO Box 71274, Oakland, CA 94612, (510)219-0637

U.S.A. for Africa **[12882]**, 5670 Wilshire Blvd., Ste. 1450, Los Angeles, CA 90036, (323)954-3124

U.S.A. for Africa **[IO]**, Los Angeles, CA, United States

USA Badminton **[23089]**, 1 Olympic Plz., Colorado Springs, CO 80909, (719)866-4808

U.S.A. Baseball **[23127]**, PO Box 1131, Durham, NC 27702, (919)474-8721

U.S.A. Basketball **[23138]**, 5465 Mark Dabling Blvd., Colorado Springs, CO 80918-3842, (719)590-4800

USA-BIAC **[★766]**

USA-BIAC **[★IO]**

USA Boxing **[23267]**, 1 Olympic Plz., Colorado Springs, CO 80909, (719)866-4506

USA Broomball **[23095]**, PO Box 20201, Bloomington, MN 55420, (763)241-1789

U.S.A. - Bus. and Indus. Advisory Comm. to the OECD **[17466]**, c/o U.S. Coun. for Intl. Bus., 1212 Ave. of the Americas, New York, NY 10036, (212)354-4480

USA Canoe/Kayak **[23280]**, 301 S Tryon St., Ste. 1750, Charlotte, NC 28282, (704)348-4330

USA Climbing **[23286]**, PO Box 3405, Boulder, CO 80307, (888)944-4244

U.S.A. Convertible Club - Defunct.

USA Dance **[9900]**, PO Box 152988, Cape Coral, FL 33915-2988, (239)242-0805

USA Deaf Sports Fed. **[23369]**, 102 N Krohn Pl., Sioux Falls, SD 57103-1800, (605)367-5760

U.S.A. Defenders of Greyhounds **[11473]**, PO Box 1256, Carmel, IN 46082, (317)244-0113

USA Diving **[23382]**, 201 S Capitol Ave., Ste. 430, Indianapolis, IN 46225, (317)237-5252

USA Dry Pea and Lentil Coun. **[4116]**, 2780 W Pullman Rd., Moscow, ID 83843-4024, (208)882-3023

USA Engage **[17467]**, c/o Jake Colvin, Dir., 1625 K St. NW, Ste. 200, Washington, DC 20006, (202)464-2025

U.S.A. Equestrian Assn. **[★23534]**

U.S.A. Fed. of Bocce **[★23241]**

USA Fed. of Pankration Athlima **[23066]**, 1935 S Plum Grove Rd., No. 321, Palatine, IL 60067, (847)971-2343

USA Fibromyalgia Assn. - Address unknown since 2006.

U.S.A. Field Hockey Assn. **[★23405]**

U.S.A. Film Festival **[9949]**, 6116 N Central Expy., Ste. 105, Dallas, TX 75206, (214)821-6300

U.S.A. Finn Assn. **[23238]**, 319 Monroe Dr., West Palm Beach, FL 33405, (828)251-1886

U.S.A. Found. for Research and Education - Address unknown since 1994.

USA Gp. **[★8434]**

USA Gymnastics **[23479]**, Pan Amer. Plz., Ste. 300, 201 S Capitol Ave., Indianapolis, IN 46225, (317)237-5050

U.S.A. Harvest **[12402]**, PO Box 1628, Louisville, KY 40201-1628, (502)895-3924

USA Hockey **[23488]**, 1775 Bob Johnson Dr., Colorado Springs, CO 80906-4090, (719)576-8724

U.S.A. Karate Fed. **[23566]**, 1300 Kenmore Blvd., Akron, OH 44314, (330)753-3114

U.S.A.-Korean Karate Assn. - Defunct.

USA Natl. Host - Defunct.

U.S.A; Oper. **[12535]**

U.S.A. Out of the Middle East Now Coalition - Defunct.

USA Pentathlon **[★23925]**

USA Pentathlon **[★IO]**

U.S.A. Plowing Org. **[4660]**, c/o Roger Neate, Sec.-Treas., 14837 Greenville Rd., Van Wert, OH 45891, (419)965-2284

U.S.A. Poultry and Egg Export Coun. **[5123]**, 2300 W Park Pl. Blvd., Ste. 100, Stone Mountain, GA 30087, (770)413-0006

USA Powerlifting **[23664]**, c/o Dr. Larry J. Maile, PhD, Pres., PO Box 668, Columbia City, IN 46725, (260)248-4889

USA Pulling **[23929]**, 15501 WCR 13, Platteville, CO 80651, (800)750-7048

USA Racquetball **[★23678]**

U.S.A.-Republic of China Economic Coun. **[★2294]**

U.S.A.-Republic of China Economic Coun. **[★IO]**

U.S.A. Rice Coun. **[4321]**, 4301 N Fairfax Dr., Ste. 425, Arlington, VA 22203, (703)236-2300

U.S.A. Rice Fed. **[1754]**, 4301 N Fairfax Dr., Ste. 425, Arlington, VA 22203, (703)236-2300

U.S.A.-ROC Economic Coun. **[★2294]**

U.S.A.-ROC Economic Coun. **[★IO]**

U.S.A. Roller Skating **[★23746]**

USA Roller Sports **[23746]**, PO Box 6579, Lincoln, NE 68506-0579, (402)483-7551

USA Sanatan Sports and Cultural Assn. **[23787]**, PO Box 5050, Elk Grove, CA 95758, (916)396-6072

USA Shooting **[23732]**, 1 Olympic Plz., Colorado Springs, CO 80909, (719)866-4670

Reference to "IO" in place of a book number signifies that the association may be found in the 45th edition of International Organizations.

USA Softball [★23788]
USA Swimming [23893], 1 Olympic Plz., Colorado Springs, CO 80909, (719)866-4578
U.S.A. Table Tennis [23896], 1 Olympic Plz., Colorado Springs, CO 80909-5769, (719)866-4583
U.S.A Team Handball [23096], One Olympic Plz., Colorado Springs, CO 80909, (719)632-5551
USA Tennis - NJTL [23916], 70 W Red Oak Ln., White Plains, NY 10604-3602, (914)696-7000
U.S.A. Toy Lib. Assn. [11548], 1326 Wilmette Ave., Wilmette, IL 60091, (847)920-9030
U.S.A. Track and Field [23926], 1 RCA Dome, Ste. 140, Indianapolis, IN 46225, (317)261-0500
USA Triathlon [23927], 1365 Garden of the Gods Rd., Ste. 250, Colorado Springs, CO 80907-3425, (719)597-9090
USA for the United Nations High Commissioner for Refugees [12824], 1775 K St. NW, Ste. 290, Washington, DC 20006, (202)296-1115
USA for the United Nations High Commissioner for Refugees [IO], Washington, DC, United States
U.S.A.-USSR Citizens' Dialogue - Defunct.
U.S.A. Victory Alliance - Address unknown since 1989.
USA Volleyball; U.S. Volleyball Association/ [23970]
USA Water Ski [23979], 1251 Holy Cow Rd., Polk City, FL 33868, (863)324-4341
USA Weightlifting [23985], 1 Olympic Plz., Colorado Springs, CO 80909, (719)866-4508
U.S.A. Wrestling [23989], 6155 Lehman Dr., Colorado Springs, CO 80918, (719)598-8181
Usability Professionals' Assn. [2113], 140 N Bloom-ingdale Rd., Bloomingdale, IL 60108-1017, (630)980-4997
Usability Professionals' Assn. [IO], Bloomingdale, IL, United States
USAF Medical Ser. Corps Assn. [13590], 1006 Rosemary St., Denver, CO 80230-7089, (866)818-2110
USASPCA - U.S. Animal Soc. for the Prevention of Cruelty to Animals [★11360]
USASPCA - U.S. Animal Soc. for the Prevention of Cruelty to Animals [★IO]
USBE [★10392]
USBloodDonors.org [13766], c/o Pat Boone Found., 9220 Sunset Blvd., Ste. 310, Los Angeles, CA 90069
USC Canada [IO], Ottawa, ON, Canada
USCCCN Natl. CH on Satanic Crime in Am. [11848], c/o USCCCN Intl., PO Box 663, South Plainfield, NJ 07080-0663, (908)226-8715
USE, Inc. - Defunct.
Used Building Materials Assn. [★608]
Used Car Dealers Assn; Natl. [★423]
Used Cars
   Natl. Assn. of Fleet Resale Dealers [419]
Used Clothing Exporters Assn. of America - Address unknown since 1995.
Used Construction Equipment Res. Corp. - Defunct.
Used Equip. Dealers; Intl. Assn. of [3052]
Used Oil Mgt. Assn. [1903], c/o Mary Beth Bosco, 2550 M St. NW, Washington, DC 20037, (202)457-6420
Used Truck Assn. [431], 909 Eagles Landing Pkwy., Ste. 140-216, Stockbridge, GA 30281, (877)438-7882
Used Truck Sales Network [★431]
Useless Skills; Inst. of Totally [22593]
U.S.English [18307], 1747 Pennsylvania Ave. NW, Ste. 1050, Washington, DC 20006, (202)833-0100
USENIX Assn. [6806], 2560 9th St., Ste. 215, Berkeley, CA 94710, (510)528-8649
User Gp; Christian Macintosh [6790]
User Gp; Xy [6808]
User Services Assn. of Amer. Lib. Assn; Reference and [10383]
Users Assn; Coll. and Univ. Cmpt. [7894]
Users of Automatic Information Display Equipment - Address unknown since 1995.
Users Gp; Arizona Macintosh [6782]
Users Gp; Housing Statistics [5789]
Users' Gp; Regis Sys. [6801]
Users Gp; XyVision [★6808]
Users Network; International Ventilator [★11981]
Users Network; International Ventilator [★IO]

Uses Coun; New [4080]
USF Constellation Found. [★10449]
USFN-America's Mortgage Banking Attorneys [325], c/o Ms. Alberta E. Hultman, CAE, Exec. Dir./CEO, 14471 Chambers Rd., Ste. 260, Tustin, CA 92780, (714)838-7167
USGA Green Sect. [23470], PO Box 708, Far Hills, NJ 07931, (908)234-2300
USGA Junior Golf Found. - Defunct.
Usher Syndrome Self-Help Network - Defunct.
Ushers
   Natl. United Church Ushers Assn. of Am. [20609]
Ushers Assn; Natl. United Church [★20609]
USMA - Address unknown since 2007.
USMC Motor Transport Assn. [2599], PO Box 1372, Jacksonville, NC 28541-1372
USMC Vietnam Tankers Assn. [21337], 5537 Lower Mountain Rd., New Hope, PA 18938
USO-All Ser. Postal Chess Club [★21941]
USO World HQ [18962], 2111 Wilson Blvd., Ste. 1200, Arlington, VA 22201, (703)908-6400
USO World HQ [IO], Arlington, VA, United States
USRowing [★23704]
USS Antares - Defunct.
USS (BB-42) Idaho Assn. [21223], PO Box 711247, San Diego, CA 92171, (858)271-6106
USS Chilton Assn. [21224], c/o H. Edward Ritterhoff, 1000 SW 6th St., Lee's Summit, MO 64081-2616, (816)358-8624
USS Constellation Museum [10449], 301 E Pratt St., Pier 1, Baltimore, MD 21202-3134, (410)539-1797
USS Intrepid Assn. of Former Crew Members [21225], Intrepid Sq., 86 N River Pier, New York, NY 10036-1012, (631)261-1568
USS Iowa; Veteran's Assn. of the [21233]
U.S.S. LCI Natl. Assn. [21328], 101 Rice Bent Way, No. 6, Columbia, SC 29229, (803)865-5665
USS Leyte CV32 Assn. [21226], c/o William A. Crawford, 170 NW Silver Glen, Lake City, FL 32055-4899, (904)737-4673
USS Liberty Veterans Assn. [21227], c/o James M. Ennes, Jr., PO Box 789, Woodinville, WA 98072
USS LSM-LSMR Assn. [21228], c/o Larry Glaser, Sr., 3727 Kingston Blvd., Sarasota, FL 34238
USS Natoma Bay Assn. - Address unknown since 2006.
USS Nevada Assn. (BB-36/SSBN-733) [21229]
USS Nimitz (CVN-68) Assn. [21230], c/o John Wilder, Treas., 54 Jackson Rd., Medford, MA 02155
USS Nitro (AE-2/AE-23) Assn. [5468], c/o Robert F. Eberlein, VP/Founder, 12215 Ashland St., Granger, IN 46530-9654, (574)277-3128
USS North Carolina Battleship Assn. [21411], PO Box 480, Wilmington, NC 28402-0480, (910)251-5797
USS Oklahoma Assn. - Defunct.
USS Pioneer - Address unknown since 2002.
USS Pyro AE-1 and AE-24 Assn. [21231], c/o Jared S. Cameron, Pres., 3808 Brighton Ct., Alexandria, VA 22305-1571, (703)837-1977
USS St. Louis CL-49 Assn. [10450], c/o Jack R. Jones, Ed., 1112 N 18th St., Cambridge, OH 43725, (740)432-5305
USS Wainwright Veterans Assn. [21329], 114 S Oakland Ave., Rock Hill, SC 29730-4522, (901)388-3049
USS Wisconsin Assn. [21232], c/o Dom Menta, HC 1 Box 1021, Tannersville, PA 18372, (570)620-1446
USSA Found. [9196], c/o U.S. Student Assn., 815 16th St. NW, 4th Fl., Washington, DC 20006, (202)637-3924
USSR
   CEC ArtsLink [17370]
   Natl. Coun. for Eurasian and East European Res. [10968]
   Russian-American Chamber of Commerce in the USA [24371]
USSR Football Fed. [★IO]
USSR Initiatives; Center for U.S. - [★17879]
USTA/National Junior Tennis League [★23916]
Ustav Mezinarodnich Vztahu Praha [★IO]
USWA Flint/Glass Workers Conf. [24067]
Utah Pioneers; Natl. Soc. Daughters of [★21252]

Utah Pioneers; Natl. Soc. of the Sons of [21254]
Utah Pioneers; Sons of [★21254]
Utdanningsforbundet [★IO]
Utenti Pubblicita Associati [IO], Milan, Italy
Utilities
   1-800 Amer. Free Trade Assn. [3950]
   Amer. Backflow Prevention Assn. [7818]
   American Backflow Prevention Association [IO]
   Amer. Decentralized Wastewater Assn. [4006]
   Amer. Public Gas Assn. [3951]
   Amer. Public Power Assn. [6336]
   Amer. Water Works Assn. [4008]
   Americans for Balanced Energy Choices [17495]
   Arab Union of Producers, Transporters and Distributors of Electricity [IO]
   Assn. of Boards of Certification [6337]
   Assn. for the Conservation of Energy [IO]
   Assn. of Edison Illuminating Companies [3952]
   Assn. of Electricity Producers [IO]
   Australasian Soc. for Trenchless Tech. [IO]
   Automatic Meter Reading Assn. [3953]
   Brotherhood of Utility Workers of New England [24215]
   Canadian Assn. of Members of Public Utility Tribunals [IO]
   Canadian Electricity Assn. [IO]
   Center for Energy Efficiency and Renewable Technologies [4526]
   China Soc. for Trenchless Tech. [IO]
   Combined Heat and Power Assn. [IO]
   Communications Supply Ser. Assn. [3954]
   CompTel/ALTS [3955]
   Distribution Contractors Assn. [24162]
   Edison Elec. Inst. [3956]
   Edison Elec. Inst. [IO]
   Electricity Storage Assn. [IO]
   Electricity Storage Assn. [3957]
   Energy Assn. [IO]
   Energy Supply Assn. of Australia [IO]
   EPRI [6953]
   Equip. Managers Coun. of Am. [943]
   European Coal Combustion Products Assn. [IO]
   European Fed. of Local Public Energy Distribution Companies [IO]
   European Small Hydropower Assn. [IO]
   French Soc. for Trenchless Tech. [IO]
   Indian Soc. for Trenchless Tech. [IO]
   Inst. of Nuclear Power Operations [7392]
   Inst. of Public Utilities [3958]
   Intl. Soc. for Trenchless Tech. [IO]
   Intl. Utilities Revenue Protection Assn. [IO]
   Intl. Utilities Revenue Protection Assn. [6338]
   Investment Recovery Assn. [3702]
   Lesbian, Bisexual, Gay and Transgendered United Employees at AT&T [12242]
   NASSCO - Setting the Indus. Standards for the Rehabilitation of Underground Utilities [3959]
   Natl. Assn. of Regulatory Utility Commissioners [6339]
   Natl. Assn. of State Utility Consumer Advocates [6340]
   Natl. Assn. of Water Companies [4010]
   Natl. Exchange Carrier Assn. [3960]
   Natl. Ground Water Assn. [4011]
   Natl. Rural Utilities Cooperative Finance Corp. [1441]
   Natl. Rural Water Assn. [12939]
   Natl. Submetering and Utility Allocation Assn. [3961]
   Natl. Telecommunications Cooperative Assn. [3962]
   Natl. Utility Locating Contractors Assn. [1055]
   Natl. Utility Training and Safety Educ. Assn. [3963]
   Native Amer. Water Assn. [4012]
   New Water Supply Coalition [7839]
   North Amer. Soc. for Trenchless Tech. [7819]
   Nuclear Energy Inst. [6969]
   Nuclear Info. and Records Mgt. Assn. [7389]
   Org. for the Promotion and Advancement of Small Telecommunications Companies [3964]
   Power Generation Contractors Assn. [IO]
   Residential Energy Services Network [664]
   Solar Elec. Power Assn. [7678]
   Tennessee Regulatory Authority [6341]

A star before a book entry number signifies that the name is not listed separately, but is mentioned within the entry.

UCA Intl. Users Gp. [7820]
United Kingdom Soc. for Trenchless Tech. [IO]
U.S. Combined Heat and Power Assn. [7821]
U.S. Telecom Assn. [3965]
United Telecom Coun. [3762]
Utilities Ser. Alliance [3966]
Utility Shareholders Assn. [3967]
Utility Workers Union of Am., AFL-CIO [24216]
Water Quality Assn. [4013]
Water and Sewer Distributors of Am. [3968]
Water and Wastewater Equip. Mfrs. Assn. [2077]
World Energy Efficiency Assn. [6978]
Utilities; Assn. of Boards of Certification for Operating Personnel in Water and Wastewater [★6337]
Utilities Commissioners; Natl. Assn. of Railway and [★6339]
Utilities Cooperative Finance Corp; Natl. Rural [1441]
Utilities Radio; Natl. Comm. for [★3762]
Utilities Ser. Alliance [3966], 9200 Indian Creek Pkwy., Ste. 201, Overland Park, KS 66210, (913)451-5641
Utilities Telecommunications Coun. [★3762]
Utility Airplane Coun. - Defunct.
Utility Arborist Assn. - Address unknown since 2002.
Utility Commn. Engineers; Conf. of [★6341]
Utility Commn. Engineers; Conf. of State [★6341]
Utility Communicators Intl. [125], c/o Elliot Boardman, Exec. Dir., 1818 Country Creek Ct., Magnolia, TX 77354, (936)271-5005
Utility Communicators Intl. [IO], Georgetown, TX, United States
Utility Contractors Assn; Natl. [1054]
Utility Nuclear Waste and Transportation Program - Address unknown since 1995.
Utility Professionals; Women's Intl. Network of [1200]
Utility Shareholders Assn. [3967], 52 Woods Rd., Little Falls, NJ 07424-2051, (973)785-1609
Utility Workers Union of Am., AFL-CIO [24216], 815 16th St. NW, Washington, DC 20006, (202)974-8200
Utilization Rev. Coordinators; Natl. Assn. of [★16264]
Utilization Rev. Physicians; Amer. Bd. of Quality Assurance and [16260]
Utopia - Address unknown since 1995.
Utopian Stud; Conf. on [★10839]
Utrikespolitiska Institutet [★IO]
Uttaranchal Assn. of North Am. [10219], 10560 Main St., Ste. LL-1, Fairfax, VA 22030, (703)273-7982
Uveitis Soc; Amer. [15668]
UWC - Strategic Services on Unemployment and Workers' Compensation [13348], 910 17th St. NW, Ste. 315, Washington, DC 20006, (202)223-8902
Uyghur Amer. Assn. [17788], 1700 Pennsylvania Ave. NW, Ste. 400, Washington, DC 20006, (202)349-1496
Uyghur Amer. Assn. [IO], Washington, DC, United States
Uzbek Assn. on Reproductive Hea. [IO], Tashkent, Uzbekistan
Uzbekistan Badminton Fed. [IO], Tashkent, Uzbekistan
Uzbekistan Baseball Fed. [IO], Tashkent, Uzbekistan
Uzbekistan Taekwondo Assn. [IO], Tashkent, Uzbekistan
Uzbekistan Tennis Fed. [IO], Tashkent, Uzbekistan

V

V Fan Club - Defunct.
VA Physicians and Dentists; Natl. Assn. of [16007]
Vaad Harabonim of Am; Amer. Bd. of Rabbis - [20111]
Vaad Hatzala Rehabilitation Comm. - Address unknown since 1995.
Vacation Assn; Jewish [★23275]
Vacation Bible Schools [★19483]
Vacation Bible Schools [★IO]
Vacation Exchange Club [★22580]
Vacation Home Rental Managers; Assn. of [★3344]
Vacation Ownership Coun. - Defunct.
Vacation Rental Managers Assn. [3344], PO Box 1202, Santa Cruz, CA 95061-1202, (831)426-8762

Vacation Samaritans [★20392]
Vacation Samaritans [★IO]
Vaccine Awareness League; Global [14559]
Vaccine Found; Aeras Global TB [14372]
Vaccine and Infectious Disease Org. [IO], Saskatoon, SK, Canada
Vaccine Info. Center; Natl. [13972]
Vaccine Inst; Think Twice Global [14944]
Vachel Lindsay Assn. [9718], 603 S Fifth St., PO Box 9357, Springfield, IL 62791, (217)528-9254
Vacuum Bag Mfrs. Assn. - Defunct.
Vacuum Cleaner Manufacturers Assn. [★264]
Vacuum Cleaner Mfrs. Assn. - Defunct.
Vacuum Cleaners
  Hoover Historical Center [21534]
  Vacuum Dealers Trade Assn. [268]
Vacuum Coaters; Soc. of [856]
Vacuum Dealers Trade Assn. [268], 2724 2nd Ave., Des Moines, IA 50313-4933, (515)282-9101
Vacuum Equip. Mfrs. Intl; Assn. of [★2006]
Vacuum Metallizers Assn. [★851]
Vacuum Soc. of Australia [IO], Callaghan, Australia
Vacuum Technology
  AVS Sci. and Tech. Soc. [7822]
  French Vacuum Soc. [IO]
  Hoover Historical Center [21534]
  Intl. Union for Vacuum Sci., Technique and Applications [IO]
  Israel Vacuum Soc. [IO]
  Italian Vacuum Assn. [IO]
  Vacuum Soc. of Australia [IO]
Vacuum Tech; Comm. on [★7822]
Vacuum Wood Preservers Inst. - Address unknown since 1995.
Vaestoliitto [★IO]
Vagabundos Del Mar RV, Boat and Travel Club [IO], Rio Vista, CA, United States
Vagabundos Del Mar RV, Boat and Travel Club [22966], 190 Main St., Rio Vista, CA 94571, (707)374-5511
Vahey Family Assn. - Defunct.
Vakuutusvaeen Liitto ry [★IO]
Valedictorian Honor Soc; Natl. [24514]
Valedictorian Soc; Natl. [9077]
Valentine Collectors' Assn; Natl. [22090]
Valiant
  Slant 6 Club of Am. [21784]
Valium Anonymous - Defunct.
Valkommen Till Tekoindustrierna [★IO]
Valley Camera and Movie Collectors [★10844]
Valley Fig Growers [4772], 2028 S 3rd St., Fresno, CA 93702, (559)237-3893
Valley Forge; Freedoms Found. at [17644]
Valley Forge Historical Soc. [9375]
Valley Forge; Soc. of the Descendants of Washington's Army at [20678]
Valley Intl. Foosball Assn. [1717], 201 S Henry St., Bay City, MI 48706, (989)893-1800
Valley International Foosball Association [IO], Bay City, MI, United States
Valley of the Kings Found. [IO], Kent, United Kingdom
Valley Migrant League - Address unknown since 1995.
Valorisation de Innovation dans l'Ameublement [★IO]
Valuation Analysts; Natl. Assn. of Certified [45]
Valuation Soc; Tech. [★272]
Valuation Specialists; Amer. Assn. of Bus. [692]
Value Engg. Soc. Intl. [7052], PO Box 930, Ligonier, PA 15658
Value Engg. Soc. Intl. [IO], Ligonier, PA, United States
Value Engineers; Soc. of Amer. [★7185]
Value Found. [★7184]
Value Inquiry; Amer. Soc. for [10784]
Value of Life Comm. - Address unknown since 2001.
Values; Found. for Traditional [18505]
Values in Higher Educ; Soc. for [19940]
Values and Social Change; Assn. for Interdisciplinary Res. in [12906]
Values and Visions [8155], 15 W 24th St., 10th Fl., New York, NY 10010
Valve and Fittings Indus; Mfrs. Standardization Soc. of the [2040]

Valve Mfrs. Assn. [★1838]
Valve Mfrs. Assn. of Am. [1838], 1050 17th St. NW, Ste. 280, Washington, DC 20036, (202)331-8105
Valve Remanufacturers Coun. [★1839]
Valve Repair Coun. [1839], 1050 17th St. NW, Ste. 280, Washington, DC 20036, (202)331-0104
Valves and Fittings Sweden [IO], Stockholm, Sweden
Vampire - Defunct.
The Vampire Empire [24824], 29 Washington Sq. W, Penthouse N, New York, NY 10011-9180
Vampire Info. Exchange [7455], PO Box 290328, Brooklyn, NY 11229-0328
Vampire Pen Pal Network [25022], PO Box 290328, Brooklyn, NY 11229-0328
Vampire Pen Pal Network - Defunct.
Vampire Res. Center - Defunct.
Vampire Studies Soc. - Defunct.
Vampire's Vault - Defunct.
Van Alen Inst.: Projects in Public Architecture [7963], 30 W 22nd St., New York, NY 10010, (212)924-7000
Van Andel Educ. Inst. [8312], 333 Bostwick Ave. NE, Grand Rapids, MI 49503, (616)234-5528
Van Buren Fan Club; Martin [11136]
Van Buren, Martin
  Friends of Lindenwald [10027]
Van Doren Fan Club; Mamie [24757]
Van Halen Fan Club - Address unknown since 1995.
Van Pool Operators; Natl. Assn. of [★13334]
Van Valkenburg Family; Natl. Assn. of the [21008]
Van Voorhees Assn. [21075], c/o Mr. Albert T. Van Voorhies, 9 Purdy Ave., East Northport, NY 11731-4501
Vanadium Producers and Reclaimers Assn. [2734], 900 2nd St. NE, Ste. 201, Washington, DC 20002, (202)842-0219
Vance Family Assn. - Address unknown since 1995.
Vancouver ACM SIGGRAPH [IO], Vancouver, BC, Canada
Vancouver Chinese Choir Assn. [IO], Vancouver, BC, Canada
Vancouver Island Head Injury Soc. [IO], Victoria, BC, Canada
Vancouver Univ. Worldwide [★IO]
Vancouver Univ. Worldwide [★8114]
Vandelay Indus. - A Seinfeld Fan Club - Address unknown since 2001.
Vandellas Fan Club; Supremes, Marvellettes, and Martha and the [★24975]
The Vanguard Found. [★883]
Vanilla Bean Assn. of America - Address unknown since 1999.
Vanilla Information Bur. - Defunct.
Vanished Children's Alliance [11659], 991 W Hedding St., Ste. 101, San Jose, CA 95126, (408)296-1113
Vantage - Defunct.
Vanuatu Athletics Assn. [IO], Port Vila, Vanuatu
Vanuatu Cricket Assn. [IO], Port Vila, Vanuatu
Vanuatu Family Hea. Assn. [IO], Port Vila, Vanuatu
Vanuatu Natl. Olympic Comm. [IO], Port Vila, Vanuatu
Vanuatu Red Cross Soc. [IO], Port Vila, Vanuatu
Vanuatu Sport Fed. Blind Disabled [IO], Port Vila, Vanuatu
Vanuatu Squash Rackets Assn. [IO], Port Vila, Vanuatu
Vanuatu Taekwondo Assn. [IO], Port Vila, Vanuatu
Vanuatu Tourism Off. [IO], Port Vila, Vanuatu
Vanuatu Weightlifting Fed. [IO], Port Vila, Vanuatu
Variable Annuities; Natl. Assn. for [2220]
Variable Electronic Components Inst. [1230], PO Box 1070, Vista, CA 92085-1070, (760)631-0178
Variable Resistive Components Inst. [★1230]
Variable Resistive Components Inst. - Defunct.
Variable Star Observers; Amer. Assn. of [6497]
Variety Artists; Amer. Guild of [24151]
Variety Clubs Intl. [★11660]
Variety Clubs Intl. [★IO]
Variety and Comedy; Soc. to Preserve and Encourage Radio Drama [22930]
Variety Intl. - The Children's Charity [11660], 350 5th Ave., Ste. 1233, New York, NY 10118, (212)695-3818

Reference to "IO" in place of a book number signifies that the association may be found in the 45th edition of International Organizations.

Variety International - The Children's Charity [IO], New York, NY, United States
Various Ventures - Defunct.
Varnish Assn; Natl. Paint, Oil and [★2884]
Varnish and Lacquer Assn; Natl. Paint, [★2884]
Varnish Production Clubs; Fed. of Paint and [★6704]
Varsity Christian Fellowship; Inter [20347]
Vasa Order of Am. [19143], c/o Tore Kellgren, Membership Chm., 5971 W Walbrook Dr., San Jose, CA 95129
Vasa Order of Am. [IO], Richmond, CA, United States
Vascular Access Networks; Natl. Assn. of [★16722]
Vascular Biology of the Amer. Heart Assn; Coun. on Arteriosclerosis, Thrombosis and [13902]
Vascular Credentialing Intl; Cardio [★13898]
Vascular Labs; Intersocietal Commn. for the Accreditation of [★16726]
Vascular Nursing; Soc. for [15530]
Vascular Nursing; Soc. for Peripheral [★15530]
Vascular Perfusion; Amer. Bd. of Cardio [13887]
Vascular and Pulmonary Rehabilitation; Amer. Assn. of Cardio [13886]
Vascular Res. Found. - Defunct.
Vascular Soc; Michael E. DeBakey Intl. Cardio [★13917]
Vascular Surgery; European Soc. for [IO]
Vascular Surgery; Soc. for [16730]
Vascular Surgery; Soc. for Clinical [13926]
Vascular System
    Amer. Coll. of Angiology [16719]
    Amer. Coll. of Phlebology [16720]
    Amer. Venous Forum [16721]
    Assn. of Prog. Directors in Vascular Surgery [16578]
    Assn. for Vascular Access [16722]
    Assn. of Vascular and Interventional Radiographers [16723]
    Australian Vascular Biology Soc. [IO]
    British Microcirculation Soc. [IO]
    Canadian Soc. of Atherosclerosis, Thrombosis and Vascular Biology [IO]
    Ehlers Danlos Natl. Found. [16651]
    European Atherosclerosis Soc. [IO]
    European Soc. for Microcirculation [IO]
    Intl. Coll. of Angiology [IO]
    Intl. Coll. of Angiology [16724]
    Intl. Soc. of Endovascular Specialists [16725]
    Intl. Soc. of Endovascular Specialists [IO]
    Intl. Soc. for Vascular Surgery [16584]
    Intersocietal Commn. for the Accreditation of Vascular Labs. [16726]
    Japan Atherosclerosis Soc. [IO]
    Microcirculatory Soc. [16727]
    Natl. Alliance for Thrombosis and Thrombophilia [13931]
    North Amer. Vascular Biology Org. [16728]
    Peripheral Arterial Disease Coalition [13922]
    Raynaud's and Scleroderma Assn. [IO]
    Societe Francaise d'Angeiologie [IO]
    Soc. for Vascular Medicine and Biology [16729]
    Soc. for Vascular Nursing [15530]
    Soc. for Vascular Surgery [16730]
    Soc. for Vascular Ultrasound [16731]
    Venous Soc. of Am. [16732]
Vascular Technologists; Natl. Alliance of Cardio [★13885]
Vascular Tech; Natl. Bd. of Cardio [★13898]
Vascular Tech; Soc. of [★16731]
Vascular Tech; Soc. of Non-Invasive [★16731]
Vascular Ultrasound; Soc. for [16731]
Vasculitis Found. [16552], PO Box 28660, Kansas City, MO 64188-8660, (816)436-8211
Vasculitis Found. [IO], Kansas City, MO, United States
Vaseline Glass Collectors, Inc. [22127], 14560 Schleisman, Corona, CA 92880
Vatican Lib; Amer. Friends of the [10318]
Vaudeville
    Intl. Al Jolson Soc. [24911]
Vaughter(s) Family Assn; Vawter - Vauter - [21076]
Vault Assn; Natl. Concrete Burial [2787]
Vault Technicians Assn; Safe and [3541]
Vaulting
    Amer. Vaulting Assn. [23967]

Intl. Vaulting Club [23968]
Intl. Vaulting Club [IO]
Vaulting Assn; Amer. [23967]
Vaults; Natl. Assn. of Security and Data [★2109]
Vauter - Vaughter(s) Family Assn; Vawter - [21076]
Vawter - Vauter - Vaughter(s) Family Assn. [21076], c/o Patricia Vawter Renton, 2372 Bear Creek Rd., Pipe Creek, TX 78063, (936)560-5254
VD Alliance Comm; Chicago [★16411]
VD Awareness; Chicago Alliance for [★16411]
VD Awareness; Citizens Alliance for [16411]
VDI-Commission on Air Pollution Prevention [★IO]
Vector Ecologists; Soc. of [★5079]
Vector Ecology; Soc. for [5079]
Vector Intl. - Address unknown since 1995.
Vecturist Assn; Amer. [23006]
Vedanta
    Ramakrishna - Vivekananda Center [20610]
Vedic Astrology; Amer. Coun. of [★21548]
Vedic Astrology; Coun. of [21548]
Vedic Friends Assn. [10977], PO Box 15082, Detroit, MI 48215
Vegaaniliitto [★IO]
Vegan Action [11071], PO Box 4288, Richmond, VA 23220, (804)502-8736
Vegan Awareness Found. [★11071]
Vegan Soc; Amer. [11067]
Vegan Soc. of Australia [IO], Seaford, Australia
Vegan Soc. - England [IO], Birmingham, United Kingdom
Vegan Soc. of Finland [IO], Helsinki, Finland
Vegetable Assn; Florida Fruit and [4730]
Vegetable Assn. and International Fresh-Cut Produce Assn; United Fresh Fruit and [★4766]
Vegetable Distributors; Natl. League of Wholesale Fresh Fruit and [★4766]
Vegetable Growers Assn. of America - Defunct.
Vegetable Growers Assn; Natl. Junior [★22530]
Vegetable Oil Export Corp. - Defunct.
Vegetable Res. and Development Center; Asian [IO]
Vegetable Shippers Assn; Amer. Fruit and [★4766]
Vegetables
    Amer. Gourd Soc. [22489]
    Amer. Vegan Soc. [11067]
    Canned Vegetable Coun. [3969]
    Food for Life Global [12855]
    Intl. Connoisseurs of Green and Red Chile [22572]
    Vegan Action [11071]
    Vegetarian Awareness Network [11072]
Vegetarian Action - Defunct.
Vegetarian Assn. of America - Defunct.
Vegetarian Awareness Network [11072], PO Box 321, Knoxville, TN 37901, (800)280-8343
Vegetarian Brotherhood of America - Defunct.
Vegetarian Gourmet Society [★15745]
Vegetarian Info. Ser. [★11394]
Vegetarian Rsrc. Gp. [11073], PO Box 1463, Baltimore, MD 21203, (410)366-8343
Vegetarian Soc. - Am; Jewish [★11068]
Vegetarian Soc; Amer. Jewish [★11068]
Vegetarian Soc; Intl. Jewish [IO]
Vegetarian Soc. of Ireland [IO], Ballsbridge, Ireland
Vegetarian Soc. of New York - Defunct.
Vegetarian Soc. Singapore [IO], Singapore, Singapore
Vegetarian Soc. of the United Kingdom [IO], Altrincham, United Kingdom
Vegetarian Union; Intl. [IO]
Vegetarian Youth Network - Defunct.
Vegetarianism
    Amer. Vegan Soc. [11067]
    Animal Rights Intl. [11357]
    Australian Vegetarian Soc. [IO]
    Christian Vegetarian Assn. [IO]
    Christian Vegetarian Assn. [20611]
    Coalition for Non-Violent Food [11377]
    Compassion Over Killing [11382]
    Compassionate Cooks [13350]
    European Vegetarian Union [IO]
    FARM (Farm Animal Reform Movement) [11394]
    Fed. of Jain Associations in North America [20495]
    Feminists for Animal Rights [11396]
    Food for Life Global [12855]

Fruitarian Worldwide Network [IO]
Intl. Jewish Vegetarian Soc. [IO]
Intl. Vegetarian Union [IO]
Intervega - Movement for Compassionate Living (the Vegan Way) [IO]
Jewish Vegetarian Soc. - North Am. [11068]
Jewish Vegetarians of North Am. [11069]
New Zealand Vegetarian Soc. [IO]
North Amer. Vegetarian Soc. [11070]
Seventh-Day Adventist Dietetic Assn. [15569]
Swedish Vegetarian Fed. [IO]
United Poultry Concerns [11472]
Vegan Action [11071]
Vegan Soc. of Australia [IO]
Vegan Soc. - England [IO]
Vegan Soc. of Finland [IO]
Vegetarian Awareness Network [11072]
Vegetarian Rsrc. Gp. [11073]
Vegetarian Soc. of Ireland [IO]
Vegetarian Soc. Singapore [IO]
Vegetarian Soc. of the United Kingdom [IO]
Viva! USA [11484]
Vegetarians; Baltimore [★11073]
Vegetarians Intl. Voice for Animals [★11484]
Vegetarians Intl. Voice for Animals [★IO]
Vegetation Mgt. Assn; Natl. Roadside [4802]
Vehicle Administrators; Amer. Assn. of Motor [5535]
Vehicle Assn. of America; Missionary [★20367]
Vehicle Assn. of the Americas; Elec. [★6517]
Vehicle Assn; Contemporary Historical [21620]
Vehicle Assn; Intl. Human Powered [★7811]
Vehicle Assn; Missionary [20367]
Vehicle Builders and Repairers Assn. [IO], Leeds, United Kingdom
Vehicle Choice; Coalition for [17015]
Vehicle Club; 1/87 [22641]
Vehicle Club Directors Assn; Recreational [★22961]
Vehicle Club; Good Sam Recreational [22951]
Vehicle Club; Holiday Rambler Recreational [22954]
Vehicle Dealers Assn. of Am; Recreation [3370]
Vehicle Division of the Trailer Coach Assn; Recreational [★3371]
Vehicle Equipment Safety Commn. - Defunct.
Vehicle Indus. Assn; Recreation [3371]
Vehicle Inst. of Am; ATV Safety Institute/Division of Specialty [12952]
Vehicle Inst. of Am; Specialty [398]
Vehicle Inst; Recreational [★3371]
Vehicle Leasing Assn; California [★3385]
Vehicle Leasing Assn; Natl. [3385]
Vehicle Leasing Assn; Western [★3385]
Vehicle Preservation Assn; Military [22630]
Vehicle Rental Assn; Recreation [3372]
Vehicle Systems; Automatic Guided [★2005]
Vehicle Systems Intl; Assn. for Unmanned [7580]
Vehicle Systems Sect. of the Material Handling Inst; Automatic Guided [2005]
Vehicles; Natl. Assn. for Remotely Piloted [★7580]
Vehicular Tech. Soc; IEEE [6925]
Veidt Soc; Conrad [24735]
Veiled Prophets of the Enchanted Realm; Supreme Coun., Mystic Order of [19253]
Veitch Historical Soc. [21077], c/o Patricia A. McConnell, VP, Membership, 134 Rhonda Dr., Universal City, TX 78148-3420, (210)659-6813
Velasquez Inst; William C. [19197]
Velo-Cardio-Facial Syndrome [14488], PO Box 874, Milltown, NJ 08850, (732)238-8803
Velo-Cardio-Facial Syndrome [IO], Milltown, NJ, United States
Velocette Owners Club of North Am. [22695], c/o Tom Ross, 11830 Ridgecrest Dr., Riverside, CA 92505, (951)354-6444
Velocette Owners Club; West Coast [★22695]
Venceremos Brigade [17917], PO Box 5202, Englewood, NJ 07631-5202, (212)560-4360
Vending
    Automatic Vending Assn. [IO]
    Canadian Automatic Merchandising Assn. [IO]
    European Gaming and Amusement Fed. [IO]
    International Association of Ice Cream Vendors [IO]
    Intl. Assn. of Ice Cream Vendors [3970]
    Italian Vending Machines' Assn. [IO]
    Japan Vending Machine Mfrs. Assn. [IO]

A star before a book entry number signifies that the name is not listed separately, but is mentioned within the entry.

Natl. Automatic Merchandising Assn. [**3971**]
Natl. Bulk Vendors Assn. [**3972**]
Natl. Vending Machine Assn. [**IO**]
Randolph-Sheppard Vendors of Am. [**3973**]
Vendor Assn; Open DeviceNet [**892**]
Vendors Assn; Natl. [★**3972**]
Veneer Association/American Walnut Manufacturers Assn; Fine Hardwood [★**1635**]
Veneer Assn; Hardwood Plywood and [**1649**]
Venereal Disease; Amer. Found. for the Prevention of [**16409**]
Venereal Diseases and the Treponematoses, Regional Off. for North Am; Intl. Union Against the [★**16414**]
Venereology; Hellenic Assn. of Dermatology and [**IO**]
Venereology; Hong Kong Soc. of Dermatology and [**IO**]
Venetian Blind Assn; U.S. [★**2279**]
Venetian Blind Coun. - Defunct.
Venetian and Vertical Blind Assn. of America - Defunct.
Venezolano Americana de Comercio e Industria; Camara [★**24305**]
Venezuela
  Peace Villages Found. Venezuela [**IO**]
  Venezuelan Amer. Assn. of the U.S. [**24386**]
Venezuelan Amer. Assn. of the U.S. [**24386**], 30 Vesey St., Ste. 506, New York, NY 10007, (212)233-7776
Venezuelan-American Chamber of Commerce [**24305**], c/o Hilda Guinand, 2332 Galiano St., Coral Gables, FL 33134, (305)728-7042
Venezuelan-American Chamber of Commerce [★**IO**]
Venezuelan-American Chamber of Commerce and Indus. [**IO**], Caracas, Venezuela
Venezuelan Assn. of the Chem. and Petrochemical Indus. [**IO**], Caracas, Venezuela
Venezuelan Assn. of Concentrated Animal Food Mfrs. [**IO**], Caracas, Venezuela
Venezuelan Assn. of Mining and Metallurgical Indus. [**IO**], Caracas, Venezuela
Venezuelan Assn. of Paper, Pulp and Carton Producers [**IO**], Caracas, Venezuela
Venezuelan Assn. of Pasta Mfrs. [**IO**], Caracas, Venezuela
Venezuelan Assn. of the Plastics Indus. [**IO**], Caracas, Venezuela
Venezuelan Chamber of the Automotive Indus. [**IO**], Caracas, Venezuela
Venezuelan Chamber of Commerce of the U.S. [★**24386**]
Venezuelan Chamber of Info. Tech. Businesses [**IO**], Caracas, Venezuela
Venezuelan Chamber of Insurance Companies [**IO**], Caracas, Venezuela
Venezuelan Chamber of Petroleum Indus. [**IO**], Caracas, Venezuela
Venezuelan Confed. of Indus. [**IO**], Caracas, Venezuela
Venezuelan Exporters' Assn. [**IO**], Caracas, Venezuela
Venezuelan Food Indus. Assn. [**IO**], Caracas, Venezuela
Venezuelan Inst. of Genealogy [**IO**], Caracas, Venezuela
Venezuelan Physiological Soc. [**IO**], Caracas, Venezuela
Venezuelan Soc. of Landscape Architects [**IO**], Caracas, Venezuela
Venezuelan Soc. of Pharmacology [**IO**], Caracas, Venezuela
Venezuelan Tourism Assn. [**IO**], Sausalito, CA, United States
Venezuelan Tourism Assn. [**3945**], PO Box 3010, Sausalito, CA 94966-3010, (415)331-0100
Venezuelan Trust Fund [★**17460**]
Venezuelan Trust Fund [★**IO**]
Venezuelean League Against Epilepsy [**IO**], Caracas, Venezuela
Venomological Artifact Soc. [★**7805**]
Venous Soc. of Am. [**16732**], c/o Denise M. Rossignol, Exec. Dir., 5 Daremy Ct., Nesconset, NY 11767-1547, (631)366-1429
Venstre [★**IO**]
Ventana - Cultural Workers for Nicaragua - Address unknown since 1995.

Ventilating Inst. Division of the Air Movement Control Assn; Home [★**1883**]
Ventilating Inst; Home [**1883**]
Ventilating Inst; Home [★**1883**]
Ventilator Users Network; International [★**11981**]
Ventilator Users Network; International [★**IO**]
Ventriloquists; North Amer. Assn. of [**1322**]
Ventura Publisher User's Group - Address unknown since 2003.
Venture Capital Alliance; Community Development [**11771**]
Venture Capital Assn; Natl. [**2348**]
Venture Club Coun. of the Americas [★**13068**]
Venture Clubs [**13068**], c/o Soroptimist Intl. of the Americas, 1709 Spruce St., Philadelphia, PA 19103-6103, (215)893-9000
Venture Clubs; Amer. Coun. of [★**13068**]
Venture Clubs of the Americas [★**13068**]
Venture Res; Center for [**2330**]
Venture Scotland [**IO**], Edinburgh, United Kingdom
Venture Touring Soc. [★**23626**]
Venue Mgt. Assn. - Asia Pacific [**IO**], Toowong, Australia
Venue Mgt; World Coun. for [**1350**]
Venus Proj. [**18632**], 21 Valley Ln., Venus, FL 33960, (863)465-0321
Vera Found. [★**11895**]
Vera Found. [★**24037**]
Vera Inst. of Justice [**11895**], 233 Broadway, 12th Fl., New York, NY 10279, (212)334-1300
Verband der Akademikerinnen Osterreichs [★**IO**]
Verband deutscher Archivarinnen und Archivare [★**IO**]
Verband der Auslandsbanken in der Schweiz [★**IO**]
Verband der Automobilindustrie [★**IO**]
Verband Beratender Ingenieure [★**IO**]
Verband Bildung und Erziehung [★**IO**]
Verband der Brauereien Oesterreichs [★**IO**]
Verband der Chemischen Industrie [★**IO**]
Verband der Cigarettenindustrie [★**IO**]
Verband der Deutschen Dental-Industrie [★**IO**]
Verband der Deutschen Heimtextilien-Industrie [★**IO**]
Verband der Deutschen Lederindustrie [★**IO**]
Verband der Deutschen Margarineindustrie [★**IO**]
Verband der Deutschen Milchwirtschaft [★**IO**]
Verband Deutscher Antiquare [**IO**], Elbingen, Germany
Verband Deutscher Grossbackereien [★**IO**]
Verband Deutscher Konzert Choere [★**IO**]
Verband Deutscher Maschinen- und Anlagenbau [**IO**], Frankfurt am Main, Germany
Verband Deutscher Metallhaendler e.v. [★**IO**]
Verband Deutscher Oelmuhlen e.v. [**IO**], Berlin, Germany
Verband Deutscher Papierfabriken [★**IO**]
Verband Deutscher Pfandbriefbanken [★**IO**]
Verband Deutscher Reeder [★**IO**]
Verband Deutscher Schiffsausruester e.v. [★**IO**]
Verband Deutscher Schulmusiker [★**IO**]
Verband Deutscher Verkehrsunternehmen [★**IO**]
Verband Deutscher Vermessungsingenieure [★**IO**]
Verband Deutscher Wirtschaftsingenieure [★**IO**]
Verband Deutscher Zeitschriftenverleger [**IO**], Berlin, Germany
Verband der Diatassistenten - Deutscher Bundesverband [★**IO**]
Verband der Donauschwaben in Kanada [★**IO**]
Verband der Elektrotechnik Elektronik und Informationstechnik [★**IO**]
Verband der Europaischen Angelgeratehersteller [★**IO**]
Verband der Europaischen Bettfedern- und Bettwarenindustrie [★**IO**]
Verband der Europaischen Elektrowerkzeug-Hersteller [★**IO**]
Verband der Fleischwirtschaft e.V. [★**IO**]
Verband der Fluglinien Europaischer Regionen [★**IO**]
Verband der deutschen Fruchtsaft-Industrie e.V. [★**IO**]
Verband Hannoverscher Warmblutzuechter [**IO**], Verden, Germany
Verband der Internationalen Kraftfahrzeughersteller [★**IO**]
Verband der Internationalen Lyceum Clubs in Deutschland [**IO**], Hamburg, Germany

Verband der Koche Deutschlands [★**IO**]
Verband der Landesarchaologen in der Bundesrepublik Deutschland [★**IO**]
Verband der Museen der Schweiz [★**IO**]
Verband Oesterreichischer Verkehrspiloten [★**IO**]
Verband der Osterreichischen Musikwirtschaft [**IO**], Vienna, Austria
Verband Osterreichischer Banken und Bankiers [★**IO**]
Verband Osterreichischer Ingenieure [**IO**], Vienna, Austria
Verband Osterreichischer Zeitungen [★**IO**]
Verband der Polyurethan-Weichschaum Industrie [**IO**], Frankfurt, Germany
Verband der deutschen Rauchtabakindustrie [★**IO**]
Verband der Reformwaren-Hersteller [★**IO**]
Verband fur Schiffbau und Meerestechnik [★**IO**]
Verband Schweizer Galerien [★**IO**]
Verband der Schweizer Unternehmen [★**IO**]
Verband der Schweizerischen Uhrenindustrie [★**IO**]
Verband der Schweizerischen Zellstoff-, Papier- und Kartonindustrie [★**IO**]
Verband Schweizerischer Mineralquellen und Soft Drink-Produzenten [★**IO**]
Verband Schweizerischer Radio- und Televisions-Fachgeschaefte [★**IO**]
Verband Schweizerischer Technischer Haendler [★**IO**]
Verband Selbstandiger Ingenieure und Architekten [**IO**], Ettlingen, Germany
Verbindung der Schweizer Arztinnen und Arzte [★**IO**]
Verbond der Vlaamse Tandartsen [**IO**], Brussels, Belgium
Verdi Stud; Amer. Inst. for [**10539**]
Verdun-Meuse-Argonne Veterans Assn. - Address unknown since 1995.
Vereeniging van Handelaren in Oude Kunst in Nederland [★**IO**]
Verein of Am; Catholic Central [★**13157**]
Verein Demokratischer Pharmazeutinnen und Pharmazeuten [★**IO**]
Verein Deutscher Bibliothekare [★**IO**]
Verein Deutscher Ingenieure [★**IO**]
Verein Deutscher Ingenieure - Landesgruppe Brasilien [★**IO**]
Verein Deutscher Textilveredlungsfachleute e.V [**IO**], Leimen, Germany
Verein Deutscher Werkzeugmaschinenfabriken [★**IO**]
Verein Deutscher Zementwerke [★**IO**]
Verein zur Forderung des Offentlichen Bewegten und Unbewegten Datenverkehrs [**IO**], Bielefeld, Germany
Verein Fur Socialpolitik [**IO**], Frankfurt, Germany
Verein vom Heiligen Karl Borromaeus zur Verbreitung Guter Literatur [★**IO**]
Verein ICC - Schweiz [**IO**], Nyon, Switzerland
Verein fur Internationale Jugendarbeit - Arbeitsgemeinschaft Christlicher Frauen Bundesverein [★**IO**]
Verein der Kohlenimporteure e.V. [★**IO**]
Verein Ungarischer Chemiker [★**IO**]
Verein der Zellstoff-und Papier-Chemiker und-Ingenieure [★**IO**]
Vereinigung fur Angewandte Botanik e.V. [★**IO**]
Vereinigung zur Erforschung der Neueren Geschichte [★**IO**]
Vereinigung der Ernahrungsindustriens der EWG [★**IO**]
Vereinigung der Freunde Antiker Kunst [★**IO**]
Vereinigung Osterreichischer Bibliothekarinnen und Bibliothekare [★**IO**]
Vereinigung der Schmelzkaseindustrie in der EU [★**IO**]
Vereinigung des Schweizerischen Import- und Grosshandels [★**IO**]
Vereniging van kinderverpleegkundigen [★**IO**]
Vereniging voor de Bakkerij- en Zoetwarenindustrie [★**IO**]
Vereniging voor de Bakkerij en Zoetwarenindustrie [★**IO**]
Vereniging van Communicatie-adviesbureaus [★**IO**]
Vereniging voor Experimenteel Radio Onderzoek In Nederland [★**IO**]

Reference to "IO" in place of a book number signifies that the association may be found in the 45th edition of International Organizations.

Vereniging van Geneeskundige Laboratorium Tegnoloe van Suid-Afrika [★IO]
Vereniging van Huntington [IO], The Hague, Netherlands
Vereniging voor Infectieziekten [★IO]
Vereniging voor Japanse Kunst [★IO]
Vereniging Leveranciers van Huishoudelijke Apparaten in Nederland [★IO]
Vereniging voor Mededingingsrecht [IO], The Hague, Netherlands
Vereniging Milieudefensie [★IO]
Vereniging Mitex [★IO]
Vereniging van Nederlandse Agenten, Commissionairs, Makelaars en Taxateurs in Wijn en Gedistilleerd [★IO]
Vereniging van de Nederlandse Chemische Industrie [★IO]
Vereniging van Nederlandse Fabrikanten van Eetbare Olien en Vetten [IO], The Hague, Netherlands
Vereniging Nederlandse Lijmindustrie [★IO]
Vereniging van de Nederlandse Pluimveeverwerkende Industrie [★IO]
Vereniging Nederlandse Scheepsbouw Industrie [★IO]
Vereniging van Openbare Bibliotheken [★IO]
Vereniging van Radiograwe van Suid-Afrika [★IO]
Vereniging Spierziekten Nederland [IO], Baarn, Netherlands
Vereniging Spierziekten Nederland [★IO]
Vereniging voor Statistiek en Operationele Res. [★IO]
Vereniging van Verfgroothandelaren in Nederland [★IO]
Vereniging van Vrouwen met Hogere Opleiding [IO], Utrecht, Netherlands
Vereniging voor Zorgadministratie en Informatie [★IO]

Vergil
Vergilian Soc. [9719]
Vergilian Soc. [9719], c/o Bee English, Sec., Lake Travis High Scholarship, 3324 Ranch Rd., 620 S, Lakeway, TX 78738, (210)685-0157
Veriniging van Bloemenveilingen [★IO]
Veris Res. Info. Ser. - Defunct.
Verite [12063], 44 Belchertown Rd., Amherst, MA 01002, (413)253-9227
Verite [IO], Amherst, MA, United States
Verkefnastjornunarfelag Islands [★IO]
Vermazen/Vermason Family Org. - Defunct.
The Vermiculite Assn. [IO], Lincoln, United Kingdom
Vermiculite Inst. - Defunct.
Vermont Maple Indus. Coun. [1569], c/o Timothy Perkins, Proctor Maple Res. Center, PO Box 233, Underhill, VT 05489, (802)899-9926
Vernacular Architecture Forum [6482], c/o Gabrielle M. Lanier, Sec., PO Box 1511, Harrisonburg, VA 22803-1511
Vernacular Soc. - Address unknown since 2008.
Vertebrate Biology; Soc. for Northwestern [7364]
Vertebrate Paleontology; Soc. of [7433]
Vertical Trans. Professionals; Natl. Assn. of [2048]
Vertical Turbine Pump Assn. - Defunct.
Very Special Arts [★11993]
Very Special Arts [★IO]
Very Special Arts Bahamas [IO], Nassau, Bahamas
Very Special Arts do Brasil [★IO]
Vesalius Trust [8472], c/o Lisa Warren, Exec. Dir., 20751 W Chartwell Dr., Kildeer, IL 60047, (847)540-8671
Vespa Club of Am. [22696], PO Box 54825, Oklahoma City, OK 73154-4825, (719)473-4692
Vessel Assn; Passenger [2591]
Vessel Inspectors; Natl. Bd. of Boiler and Pressure [5824]
Vessel Mfrs. Assn; Pressure [2061]
Vessel Owners Assn; Cleveland [★2606]
Vessel Owners; Natl. Assn. of Passenger [★2591]
Vesterheim Genealogical Center [★21155]
Vesterheim Genealogical Center and Naeseth Lib. [21155], 415 W Main St., Madison, WI 53703-3316, (608)255-2224
Vestibular Disorders Assn. [15829], PO Box 13305, Portland, OR 97213, (503)229-7705
Vestibular Disorders Assn. [IO], Portland, OR, United States

Vestigia - Defunct.
Veteran Corps of Artillery, State of New York, Constituting the Military Soc. of the War of 1812 [21204], 7th Regiment Armory, 643 Park Ave., New York, NY 10021, (212)249-3919
Veteran-Cycle Club [IO], Hitchin, United Kingdom
Veteran Feminists of Am. [17572], c/o Jacqui Ceballos, Pres., Gateway Terr., 1942 NE 6th Ct., E-203, Fort Lauderdale, FL 33304, (954)805-1559
Veteran Motor Car Club of Am. [21808], c/o Mike Welsh, Sec., 7501 Manchester Ave., Kansas City, MO 64138, (816)298-6412
Veteran Railway Employees; Natl. Assn. of Retired and [3286]
Veteran Ser; Community and [★11766]
Veteran Vespa Club, U.S. - Defunct.
Veteran Wireless Operators Assn. [3763], PO Box 1003, Peck Slip, New York, NY 10272-1003
Veterans
2nd Infantry Div. (2id), Korean War Veterans Alliance [21167]
11th Armored Cavalry's Veterans of Vietnam and Cambodia [21341]
25th Infantry Div. Assn. [20687]
63rd Infantry Div. Assn. [20690]
77th Artillery Assn. [21342]
78th Div. Veterans Assn. [21272]
82nd Airborne Div. Assn. [21273]
90th Div. Assn. [21274]
187th Airborne Regimental Combat Team Assn. [20697]
303rd Bomb Gp. (H) Assn. [21373]
369th Veterans' Assn. [21275]
461st Bombardment Gp. Assn. [20657]
494th Bombardment Gp. (H) Assn. 7th Air Force [20658]
508th Parachute Infantry Regiment Assn. [21379]
African Amer. Post Traumatic Stress Disorder Assn. [21276]
Air Commando Assn. [21277]
Air Force Navigators Observer Assn. [20659]
Air Weather Assn. [21278]
Air Weather Reconnaissance Assn. [21279]
Airlift/Tanker Assn. [20646]
Amer. Fighter Aces Assn. [20647]
Amer. GI Forum of U.S. [21280]
Amer. Gulf War Veterans Assn. [21281]
Amer. Legion [20666]
Amer. Legion Auxiliary [21189]
Amer. Military Retirees Assn. [21282]
Amer. Military Soc. [6065]
Amer. Patriots Assn. [21239]
Amer. Veterans Alliance [21283]
Amer. Veterans Assn. - Natl. HQ [21284]
Amer. Veterans for Equal Rights [12215]
Amer. Veterans Medical Airlift Ser. [6342]
Amer. War Mothers [21190]
AMVETS - Amer. Veterans [21285]
Army Distaff Foundation/Knollwood [21192]
Army, Navy, and Air Force Veterans in Canada [IO]
Army and Navy Union, U.S.A. [21286]
Assn. for Counselors and Educators in Govt. [11818]
Assn. of Jewish Ex-Servicemen and Women [IO]
Assn. of Psychology Postdoctoral and Internship Centers [8854]
Assn. of Veterans Affairs Anesthesiologists [13681]
Assn. of Veterans Affairs Ophthalmologists [15676]
Auxiliary to Sons of Union Veterans of the Civil War [20723]
Bay of Pigs Veterans Assn. [20717]
Beirut Veterans of Am. [21287]
Berlin Veterans Assn. [21288]
Black Veterans for Social Justice [21289]
Blinded Veterans Assn. [16837]
Bowlers to Veterans Link [23250]
Canadian Peacekeeping Veterans Assn. [IO]
Catholic War Veterans Auxiliary of the U.S.A. [21194]
Catholic War Veterans of the U.S.A. [21290]
Centennial Legion of Historic Military Commands [21240]

Center for Veterans Issues [21291]
Center for Women Veterans [21292]
Children of the Confederacy [20724]
Chosin Few [21169]
Circle of Friends for Amer. Veterans [21293]
Citizen Soldier [6073]
Coalition to Salute America's Heroes [21294]
Coast Guard Combat Veterans Assn. [21295]
Cold War Veterans Assn. [21296]
Colonial Order of the Acorn [20735]
Combat Helicopter Pilots Assn. [20648]
Combat Veterans Motorcycle Assn. [22675]
Congressional Medal of Honor Soc. [20710]
Cuban Amer. Veterans Assn. [21297]
Cyprus Veterans Assn. World War II [IO]
Daedalian Found. [20649]
Daughters of the Cincinnati [20670]
Daughters of Union Veterans of the Civil War, 1861-1865 [20725]
Descendants of the Signers of the Declaration of Independence [20671]
Desert Storm Veterans Assn. [21298]
Disabled Amer. Veterans [20763]
Disabled Amer. Veterans Auxiliary [20764]
Disabled Veterans Keychain Tag and Chauffeur's Badge Collectors Newsl. [22011]
Distinguished Flying Cross Soc. [20711]
Fed. Employees Veterans Assn. [6343]
Fed. of French War Veterans [21416]
Flagon and Trencher - Descendants of Colonial Tavern Keepers [20737]
Forty and Eight [20667]
Friends and Buddies of the Hour Glass Assn. [21299]
Gen. Soc. of Colonial Wars [20738]
Gen. Soc., Sons of the Revolution [20672]
Gen. Soc. of the War of 1812 [21354]
Grosse Pointe War Memorial Assn. [21300]
Help Hospitalized Veterans [13351]
Hereditary Order of Descendants of the Loyalists and Patriots of the Amer. Revolution [20673]
Hispanic Amer. Veterans Assn. [21301]
Hof Reunion Assn. [20682]
Homefront Hugs USA [13352]
Homes for Our Troops [21302]
Homosexual Info. Center [12235]
Hood's Texas Brigade Assn. [20726]
Intl. Assn. of Airborne Veterans [21303]
Iraq and Afghanistan Veterans of Am. [21335]
Iraq War Veterans Org. [21304]
Iraq War Veterans Org. [IO]
Irish United Nations Veterans Assn. [IO]
Japanese Amer. Veterans Assn. [21305]
Jewish War Veterans of Canada [IO]
Jewish War Veterans of the U.S.A. [21306]
Jewish War Veterans of the U.S.A. - Natl. Ladies Auxiliary [21196]
Korea Veterans Assn. of Canada [IO]
Korean War Proj. [6344]
Ladies Auxiliary, Military Order of the Purple Heart, U.S.A. [20713]
Ladies Auxiliary to the Veterans of Foreign Wars of the U.S. [21307]
Legion of Valor of the U.S.A. [20714]
Marine Corps Cryptologic Assn. [21174]
Marine Corps Interrogator Translator Teams Assn. [19226]
Marine Embassy Guard Assn. [21177]
Military Officers Assn. of Am. [21235]
Military Order of the Loyal Legion of the U.S. [20728]
Military Order of the Purple Heart of the U.S.A. [20715]
Military Order of the Stars and Bars [20729]
Military, Veterans and Patriotic Ser. Organizations of Am. [21245]
Mobile Riverine Force Assn. [21346]
Montford Point Marine Assn. [6084]
Natl. Amputation Found. [11965]
Natl. Assn. of Atomic Veterans [13353]
Natl. Assn. for Black Veterans [21308]
Natl. Assn. of County Veterans Ser. Officers [21309]
Natl. Assn. of State Approving Agencies [6345]
Natl. Assn. of State Directors of Veterans Affairs [6346]

A star before a book entry number signifies that the name is not listed separately, but is mentioned within the entry.

Natl. Assn. of State Veterans Homes [13354]
Natl. Assn. of VA Physicians and Dentists [16007]
Natl. Assn. of Veterans Prog. Administrators [9292]
Natl. Assn. of Veterans' Res. and Educ. Foundations [6347]
Natl. Assn. of Widows - England [IO]
Natl. Coalition for Homeless Veterans [21310]
Natl. Counter Intelligence Corps Assn. [21164]
Natl. Gulf War Rsrc. Center [21311]
National Gulf War Resource Center [IO]
Natl. Museum of Amer. Jewish Military History [21312]
Natl. Native Amer. Veterans Assn. [21313]
Natl. Order of Trench Rats [20766]
Natl. Org. of Veterans' Advocates [6348]
Natl. Soc. of the Children of the Amer. Revolution [20674]
Natl. Soc., Daughters of the Amer. Colonists [20746]
Natl. Soc., Daughters of the Amer. Revolution [20675]
Natl. Soc., Sons of the Amer. Revolution [20676]
Natl. Soc., U.S. Daughters of 1812 [21355]
Natl. Soc. Women Descendants of the Ancient and Honorable Artillery Company [20749]
Natl. Veterans Legal Services Prog. [21314]
Natl. Veterans Org. of Am. [21315]
Natl. Veterans Outreach Prog. [13355]
Natl. Veterans Services Fund [13356]
Natl. War Dog Memorial Fund [21347]
Navy Seabee Veterans of Am. [21217]
Navy Wifeline Assn. [21199]
New Zealand Ex-Wrens Assn. [IO]
Non Commissioned Officers Assn. [21316]
Not Forgotten Assn. [IO]
Nurses Org. of Veterans Affairs [15519]
Oper. Truth [21317]
Order of Daedalians [20650]
Order of the Founders and Patriots of Am. [20755]
Paralyzed Veterans of Am. [20768]
PBR Forces Veterans Assn. [21348]
Proj.: Hearts and Minds [12538]
Red River Valley Fighter Pilots Assn. [21318]
Regular Amer. Veterans [21319]
Regular Veterans Assn. [21320]
The Retired Enlisted Assn. [21321]
Rolling Thunder [21265]
Royal Canadian Legion [IO]
SATS/EAF Assn. [21179]
Second Bomb Wing Assn. [21322]
Soc. of the Ark and the Dove [20758]
Soc. of the Cincinnati [20677]
Soc. of Daughters of Holland Dames [20759]
Soc. of the Descendants of the Colonial Clergy [20760]
Soc. of the Descendants of Washington's Army at Valley Forge [20678]
Soldiers, Sailors, Airmen and Families Assn. Forces Help [IO]
Soldiers for the Truth [20683]
Sons of the Amer. Legion [21201]
Sons of Confederate Veterans [20730]
Sons of Union Veterans of the Civil War [20731]
Special Forces Assn. [21270]
Stamps for the Wounded [22879]
Star-Spangled Banner Flag House Assn. [21095]
Stars for Stripes [20770]
Supreme Pup Tent, Military Order of the Cootie [21323]
Swift Boat Veterans for Truth [21324]
Tan Son Nhut Assn. [21336]
Tee it up for the Troops [13357]
Tin Can Sailors - The Natl. Assn. of Destroyer Veterans [21220]
Tragedy Assistance Prog. for Survivors [11503]
Transgender Amer. Veterans Assn. [21325]
Turkish Retired Officers Assn. [IO]
Ukrainian Amer. Veterans [21326]
United Daughters of the Confederacy [20732]
U.S. Armor Assn. [6107]
U.S. Coast Guard Chief Petty Officers Assn. [20734]
U.S. Marine Corps Drill Instructors Assn. [6109]

U.S. Marine Corps Scout/Sniper Assn. [21181]
U.S. Naval Cryptologic Veterans Assn. [21327]
U.S. War Dogs Assn. [20769]
United We Serve [21203]
USMC Vietnam Tankers Assn. [21337]
U.S.S. LCI Natl. Assn. [21328]
USS Leyte CV32 Assn. [21226]
USS LSM-LSMR Assn. [21228]
USS North Carolina Battleship Assn. [21411]
USS Wainwright Veterans Assn. [21329]
Veteran Wireless Operators Assn. [3763]
Veterans Bedside Network [12116]
Veterans for Common Sense [21330]
Veterans Educ. Proj. [13358]
Veterans of Foreign Wars of the U.S. [21331]
Veterans' Widows Intl. Network [21357]
Vietnam Dog Handler Assn. [21338]
Vietnam Era Seabees [21339]
Vietnam Security Police Assn. [21340]
Vietnam Veteran Wives [21332]
VietNow Natl. [13359]
Visually Impaired Veterans of Am. [16891]
War Widows' Assn. of Great Britain [IO]
Women Veterans of Am. [21333]
Women's Army Corps Veterans' Assn. [20708]
Women's Overseas Ser. League [21334]
World Veterans Fed. [IO]
Veterans of the Abraham Lincoln Brigade [21269], 799 Broadway, Rm. 227, New York, NY 10003, (212)674-5398
Veterans Admin; Nurses Org. of the [★15519]
Veterans of AEF Siberia - Defunct.
Veterans Affairs; Nurses Org. of [15519]
Veterans Against the War Anti-Imperialist; Vietnam [18785]
Veterans Against the War; Vietnam [18784]
Veterans Against the War/Winter Soldier Org; Vietnam [★18784]
Veterans for Am. [17918], 1025 Vermont Ave. NW, 7th Fl., Washington, DC 20005, (202)483-9222
Veterans of Am; Gay, Lesbian, and Bisexual [★12215]
Veterans of Am; Gay, Lesbian, Bisexual, and Transgendered Disabled [20765]
Veterans of Am; Navy Seabee [21217]
Veterans of Am; Paralyzed [20768]
Veterans of Am; Seabee [★21217]
Veterans of Am; Vietnam [18786]
Veterans of Am; Visually Impaired [16891]
Veterans; Amer. Merchant Marine [21387]
Veterans Assn; 1/77 Artillery [★21342]
Veterans Assn; 1/77th Artillery Vietnam [★21342]
Veterans Assn; 32nd Infantry Div. [20688]
Veterans Assn; 43rd Infantry Div. [20689]
Veterans Assn; 147th Engineers [21372]
Veterans Assn. of Am; Polish Army [21259]
Veterans Assn; Americal Div. [21385]
Veterans Assn; Bay of Pigs [20717]
Veterans Assn; Blinded [16837]
Veterans Assn; Fed. Employees [★24075]
Veterans Assn; First Marine Aviation Force [★6080]
Veterans Assn; Natl. [★21315]
Veterans Assn; Navy Mail Ser. [21216]
Veterans Assn; Regular [★21320]
Veterans Assn; SHAEF [★21404]
Veterans Assn; SHAEF and ETOUSA [21404]
Veterans Assn. of the U.S; Regular [★21320]
Veteran's Assn. of the USS Iowa [21233], c/o Gerald E. Gneckow, Pres., 8314 W Promenade Dr., Homosassa, FL 34448, (352)621-0675
Veterans Assn; USS Liberty [21227]
Veterans' Assn; Women's Army Corps [20708]
Veterans Auxiliary; Disabled Amer. [20764]
Veterans Auxiliary of the U.S.A; Catholic War [21194]
Veterans of the Battle of the Bulge [21412], PO Box 101418, Arlington, VA 22210-4418, (703)528-4058
Veterans Bedside Network [12116], 10 Fiske Pl., Rm. 301, Mount Vernon, NY 10550-3205, (914)699-6069
Veterans; Black [★21289]
Veterans of the Central City; Interested [★21308]
Veterans of the Civil War, 1861-1865; Daughters of Union [20725]
Veterans of the Civil War; Auxiliary to Sons of Union [20723]

Veterans of the Civil War; Sons of Union [20731]
Veterans Coalition; Natl. Vietnam [★18781]
Veterans Coalition; Natl. Vietnam and Gulf War [18781]
Veterans for Common Sense [21330], 1101 Pennsylvania Ave. SE, Ste. 203, Washington, DC 20003-2229, (202)558-4553
Veterans in Cong; Vietnam Era [18783]
Veterans Corps of Artillery, State of New York [★21204]
Veterans Coun. for Amer. Rights and Equality - Address unknown since 1989.
Veterans; Coun. of Vietnam [★18786]
Veterans; Descendants of Mexican War [21183]
Veterans; Disabled Amer. [20763]
Veterans Educ. Proj. [13358], PO Box 416, Amherst, MA 01004, (413)253-4947
Veterans English Table Tennis Soc. [IO], Letchworth, United Kingdom
Veterans for Equal Rights; Amer. [12215]
Veterans; Fed. of French War [21416]
Veterans of Foreign Ser; Amer. [★21331]
Veterans of Foreign Wars
   Amer. Gulf War Veterans Assn. [21281]
   Coalition to Salute America's Heroes [21294]
   Desert Storm Veterans Assn. [21298]
   Homefront Hugs USA [13352]
   Iraq and Afghanistan Veterans of Am. [21335]
   Iraq War Veterans Org. [21304]
   Japanese Amer. Veterans Assn. [21305]
   Supreme Pup Tent, Military Order of the Cootie [21323]
   Tan Son Nhut Assn. [21336]
   Vietnam Dog Handler Assn. [21338]
   Vietnam Security Police Assn. [21340]
Veterans of Foreign Wars of the U.S. [21331], 406 W 34th St., Kansas City, MO 64111, (816)756-3390
Veterans Found; Blinded Amer. [20762]
Veterans; Friends of Israel Disabled [21166]
Veterans of Hiroshima and Nagasaki; Comm. for U.S. [★13353]
Veterans Hosp. Radio and TV Guild [★12116]
Veterans Intl. [★17918]
Veterans of Israel; Amer. [21165]
Veterans Keychain Tag and Chaffeur's Badge Collectors Newsl; Disabled [22011]
Veterans Link; Bowlers to [★23250]
Veterans Memorial Found; Rainbow Div. [21419]
Veterans Memorial Fund; Vietnam [21352]
Veterans; Natl. Alliance Daughters of [★20725]
Veterans; Natl. Assn. Rainbow Div. [★21419]
Veterans; Natl. Fort Daughters of '98, Auxiliary United Spanish War [21267]
Veterans for Peace [18252], 216 S Meramec Ave., St. Louis, MO 63105, (314)725-6005
Veterans for Peace [IO], St. Louis, MO, United States
Veterans of Pearl Harbor Soc. - Defunct.
Veterans of Safety [12994], c/o Lyle M. Rice, Pres., 97141 Kapalama Dr., Diamondhead, MS 39525, (228)586-9954
Veterans Ser; Metropolitan [★21308]
Veterans; Sons of Confederate [20730]
Veterans; Sons of Spanish Amer. War [21268]
Veterans; Ukrainian Amer. War [★21326]
Veterans; United Confederate [★20730]
Veterans of the U.S. Posse Comitatus - Address unknown since 1989.
Veterans, U.S.A., Ladies Auxiliary; Polish Legion of Amer. [21260]
Veterans of the U.S.A. - Natl. Ladies Auxiliary; Jewish War [21196]
Veterans, U.S.A. Natl. Memorial; Jewish War [★21312]
Veterans; Vietnam Combat [21350]
Veterans of the Vietnam War [21349], 805 S Township Blvd., Pittston, PA 18640-3327, (570)603-9740
Veterans Vigil of Honor - Address unknown since 1987.
Veterans' Widows Intl. Network [21357], c/o Edmee J. Hills, Natl. Chair, 3657E S Laredo St., Aurora, CO 80013, (303)693-4745
Veterans' Widows Intl. Network [IO], Aurora, CO, United States

Reference to "IO" in place of a book number signifies that the association may be found in the 45th edition of International Organizations.

Veterans of World War I of U.S.A. [21360], PO Box 8027, Alexandria, VA 22306-8027, (703)780-5660
Veterans of World War I of the U.S.A; Natl. Ladies Auxiliary to [21359]
Veterans of World War II; U.S. Merchant Marine [21408]
Veterans of World War II; U.S. Submarine [21410]
Veterans Writing Proj; Hospitalized [16321]
Veterinaire; Assn. Mondiale pour l'Advancement de Parasitologie [★16818]
Veterinarian Assn. [★16776]
Veterinarian Assn. for the Attention of Exotic and Wild Animals [IO], Bellaterra, Spain
Veterinarians; Amer. Assn. of Food Hygiene [16745]
Veterinarians for Animal Rights; Assn. of [11368]
Veterinarians; Assn. of State Public Hea. [★16747]
Veterinarians; Assn. of State and Territorial Public Hea. [★16747]
Veterinarians; Bur. of Animal Indus. [★16799]
Veterinarians; Natl. Assn. of Bur. of Animal Indus. [★16799]
Veterinarians; Natl. Assn. of State Public Hea. [★16747]
Veterinarians; Natl. Assn. of State and Territorial Public Hea. [★16747]
Veterinary; Amer. Assn. State Boards, [★16755]
Veterinary Assn. for Arbitration and Jurisprudence [IO], Carlisle, United Kingdom
Veterinary Assn. of Malaysia [IO], Ipoh, Malaysia
Veterinary Botanical Medicine Assn. [16812], c/o Jasmine C. Lyon, Exec. Dir., 1785 Poplar Dr., Kennesaw, GA 30144
Veterinary Cancer Soc. [16813], PO Box 1763, Spring Valley, CA 91979-1763, (619)474-8929
Veterinary Coun. of Ireland [IO], Dublin, Ireland
Veterinary Distributors Assn; Amer. [2957]

Veterinary Education
Amer. Assn. of Equine Veterinary Technicians [16743]
Amer. Assn. of Human-Animal Bond Veterinarians [13702]
Amer. Coll. of Veterinary Emergency and Critical Care [16766]
Amer. Pre-Veterinary Medical Assn. [16774]
Assn. of Amer. Veterinary Medical Colleges [9293]
Assn. of Veterinary Technician Educators [9294]
Computer-Aided Learning in Veterinary Educ. [IO]
European Coll. of Veterinary Anaesthesia [IO]
Intl. Assn. of Fly Fishing Veterinarians [22451]
Natl. Animal Control Assn. [11430]
Natl. Assn. of Veterinary Technicians in Am. [16800]
Soc. for Tropical Veterinary Medicine [16807]
Soc. for Veterinary Medical Ethics [16808]
Student Amer. Veterinary Medical Assn. [16809]
Student Veterinary Emergency and Critical Care Soc. [16810]
World Assn. of Veterinary Educators [9295]
World Assn. of Veterinary Educators [IO]
Veterinary Ethology; Amer. Soc. of [★16780]
Veterinary Exhibitors Assn; Amer. [1334]
Veterinary Graduates; Educational Commn. for Foreign [★16779]
Veterinary History Soc. [IO], Solihull, United Kingdom
Veterinary Holistic Medical Assn; Amer. [★16773]
Veterinary Hosp. Managers Assn. [16814], PO Box 2280, Alachua, FL 32616-2280, (518)433-8911
Veterinary Infectious Disease Org. [★IO]
Veterinary Inst. of Integrative Medicine [16815], c/o Julie Andrus, Educational Consultant, PO Box 740053, Arvada, CO 80006, (303)277-8227
Veterinary Medical Assn. Found; American [★16779]
Veterinary Medical Assn; Intermountain [★16817]
Veterinary Medical Assn; U.S. [★16779]
Veterinary Medical Assn; Women's [★16786]

Veterinary Medicine
Academia Nacional de Agronomia y Veterinaria [IO]
Acad. of Veterinary Allergy and Clinical Immunology [16733]
Acad. of Veterinary Emergency and Critical Care Technicians [16734]
Acad. of Veterinary Homeopathy [16735]
Alliance of Veterinarians for the Env. [4626]

Amer. Acad. of Veterinary and Comparative Toxicology [16736]
Amer. Acad. of Veterinary Nutrition [16737]
Amer. Acad. of Veterinary Pharmacology and Therapeutics [16738]
Amer. Animal Hosp. Assn. [16739]
Amer. Assn. of Avian Pathologists [16740]
Amer. Assn. of Bovine Practitioners [16741]
Amer. Assn. of Equine Practitioners [16742]
Amer. Assn. of Equine Veterinary Technicians [16743]
Amer. Assn. of Equine Veterinary Technicians [IO]
Amer. Assn. of Feline Practitioners [16744]
Amer. Assn. of Food Hygiene Veterinarians [16745]
Amer. Assn. of Housecall Veterinarians [16746]
Amer. Assn. of Human-Animal Bond Veterinarians [13702]
Amer. Assn. of Public Hea. Veterinarians [16747]
Amer. Assn. of Retired Veterinarians [16748]
Amer. Assn. of Small Ruminant Practitioners [16749]
Amer. Assn. of Swine Veterinarians [16750]
American Association of Swine Veterinarians [IO]
Amer. Assn. of Veterinary Clinicians [16751]
Amer. Assn. of Veterinary Immunologists [16752]
Amer. Assn. of Veterinary Lab. Diagnosticians [16753]
Amer. Assn. of Veterinary Parasitologists [16754]
Amer. Assn. of Veterinary State Boards [16755]
Amer. Assn. of Wildlife Veterinarians [16756]
Amer. Assn. of Zoo Veterinarians [16757]
Amer. Bd. of Veterinary Practitioners [16758]
Amer. Bd. of Veterinary Specialties [16759]
Amer. Bd. of Veterinary Toxicology [16760]
Amer. Canine Sports Medicine Assn. [16761]
Amer. Coll. of Lab. Animal Medicine [16762]
Amer. Coll. of Theriogenologists [16763]
Amer. Coll. of Veterinary Anesthesiologists [16764]
Amer. Coll. of Veterinary Dermatology [16765]
Amer. Coll. of Veterinary Emergency and Critical Care [16766]
Amer. Coll. of Veterinary Internal Medicine [16767]
Amer. Coll. of Veterinary Ophthalmologists [16768]
Amer. Coll. of Veterinary Pathologists [16769]
Amer. Coll. of Veterinary Radiology [16770]
Amer. Coll. of Veterinary Surgeons [16771]
Amer. Heartworm Soc. [16772]
Amer. Holistic Veterinary Medical Assn. [16773]
Amer. Medical Equestrian Association/Safe Riders Found. [16474]
Amer. Pre-Veterinary Medical Assn. [16774]
Amer. Soc. of Veterinary Ophthalmology [16775]
Amer. Veterinarian Ser. Assn. [16776]
Amer. Veterinary Chiropractic Assn. [16777]
Amer. Veterinary Dental Soc. [16778]
Amer. Veterinary Exhibitors Assn. [1334]
Amer. Veterinary Medical Assn. [16779]
Amer. Veterinary Medical Law Assn. [5927]
Amer. Veterinary Soc. of Animal Behavior [16780]
Animal Care Coll. [IO]
Animal Hea. Distributors Assn. [IO]
Animal Hea. Found. [16781]
Animal Hea. Info. Specialists [IO]
Animal Hea. Trust [IO]
Animal Medical Center [11353]
Assn. of Avian Veterinarians - USA [16782]
Assn. of Avian Veterinarians - USA [IO]
Association of Reptilian and Amphibian Veterinarians [IO]
Assn. of Reptilian and Amphibian Veterinarians [16783]
Assn. of Shelter Veterinarians [16784]
Assn. of Shelter Veterinarians [IO]
Assn. of Veterinarians for Animal Rights [11368]
Assn. of Veterinary Anaesthetists [IO]
Assn. of Veterinary Hematology and Transfusion Medicine [16785]
Assn. for Veterinary Teaching and Res. Work [IO]
Assn. for Women Veterinarians [16786]
Assn. of Zoo Veterinary Technicians [16787]
Australian Small Animal Veterinary Assn. [IO]

Australian Veterinary Assn. [IO]
Belgian Veterinary Cmpt. Assn. [IO]
British Assn. of Veterinary Ophthalmologists [IO]
British Cattle Veterinary Assn. [IO]
British Equine Veterinary Assn. [IO]
British Small Animal Veterinary Assn. [IO]
British Veterinary Assn. [IO]
British Veterinary Dental Assn. [IO]
British Veterinary Nursing Assn. [IO]
Canadian Animal Hea. Inst. [IO]
Canadian Veterinary Medical Assn. [IO]
Canine Cancer Awareness [16788]
Center for Veterinary Medicine [16789]
Christian Veterinary Missions of Canada [IO]
Commonwealth Veterinary Assn. [IO]
Conference of Research Workers in Animal Diseases [IO]
Conf. of Res. Workers in Animal Diseases [16790]
Controlled Release Soc. [6678]
Cornell Feline Hea. Center [16791]
European Assn. of Establishments for Veterinary Educ. [IO]
European Assn. of Veterinary Anatomists [IO]
European Assn. of Veterinary Diagnostic Imaging [IO]
European Bd. of Veterinary Specialization [IO]
European Coll. of Lab. Animal Medicine [IO]
European Coll. of Veterinary Diagnostic Imaging [IO]
European Coll. of Veterinary Internal Medicine - Companion Animals [IO]
European Coll. of Veterinary Pathologists [IO]
European Coll. of Veterinary Surgeons [IO]
European Soc. of Feline Medicine [IO]
European Soc. for Lab. Animal Veterinarians [IO]
European Soc. of Veterinary Cardiology [IO]
European Soc. of Veterinary Clinical Ethology [IO]
European Soc. of Veterinary Dermatology [IO]
European Soc. of Veterinary Neurology [IO]
European Soc. of Veterinary Ophthalmology [IO]
European Soc. of Veterinary Orthopaedics and Traumatology [IO]
European Soc. of Veterinary Pathology [IO]
European Soc. of Veterinary Virology [IO]
European Union of Veterinary Practitioners [IO]
European Veterinary Dental Coll. [IO]
European Veterinary Dental Soc. [IO]
European Veterinary Soc. for Small Animal Reproduction [IO]
Fed. of European Companion Animal Veterinary Associations [IO]
Fed. of Veterinarians of Europe [IO]
Feline Advisory Bur. [IO]
Ferret Fanciers Club [22416]
Finnish Veterinary Assn. [IO]
Goat Veterinary Soc. [IO]
Hong Kong Veterinary Assn. [IO]
Intl. Alliance for Animal Therapy and Healing [13703]
Intl. Assn. for Aquatic Animal Medicine [16792]
Intl. Assn. for Aquatic Animal Medicine [IO]
Intl. Assn. of Fly Fishing Veterinarians [22451]
Intl. Assn. for Paratuberculosis [16793]
Intl. Embryo Transfer Soc. [16794]
Intl. Embryo Transfer Soc. [IO]
Intl. Soc. for Adaptive Behavior [6533]
Intl. Soc. for Applied Ethology [IO]
Intl. Soc. of Veterinary Dermatopathology [IO]
Intl. Soc. of Veterinary Dermatopathology [16795]
Intl. Standing Comm. of the Intl. Cong. on Animal Reproduction [IO]
Intl. Veterinary Acupuncture Soc. [IO]
Intl. Veterinary Acupuncture Soc. [16796]
Intl. Veterinary Assistance [11420]
Intl. Veterinary Ultrasound Soc. [16797]
Intl. Veterinary Ultrasound Soc. [IO]
Israel Veterinary Medical Assn. [IO]
Japanese Soc. of Veterinary Sci. [IO]
Malta Veterinary Assn. [IO]
Mid-Atlantic States Assn. of Avian Veterinarians [16798]
Natl. Animal Control Assn. [11430]
Natl. Assn. of Fed. Veterinarians [16799]
Natl. Assn. of Gen. Practitioner Veterinarians [IO]

A star before a book entry number signifies that the name is not listed separately, but is mentioned within the entry.

Natl. Assn. of Veterinary Technicians in Am. [16800]
Natl. Humane Educ. Soc. [11440]
Natl. Veterinarian Ser. Assn. [16801]
New Zealand Veterinary Assn. [IO]
NMC [16802]
Norwegian Veterinary Assn. [IO]
OPP Concerned Sheep Breeders Soc. [16803]
Options for Animals Intl. [16804]
Orthopedic Found. for Animals [16805]
Pancyprian Veterinary Assn. [IO]
Phi Zeta [24723]
Polish Soc. of Veterinary Sci. [IO]
Royal Coll. of Veterinary Surgeons [IO]
Singapore Veterinary Assn. [IO]
Soc. of Practising Veterinary Surgeons [IO]
Soc. for the Stud. of Reproduction [16350]
Soc. for Theriogenology [16806]
Soc. for Tropical Veterinary Medicine [16807]
Soc. for Tropical Veterinary Medicine [IO]
Soc. for Veterinary Medical Ethics [16808]
South African Veterinary Assn. [IO]
Student American Veterinary Medical Association [IO]
Student Amer. Veterinary Medical Assn. [16809]
Student Veterinary Emergency and Critical Care Soc. [16810]
Student Veterinary Emergency and Critical Care Soc. [IO]
Swedish Veterinary Assn. [IO]
United Action for Animals [11468]
U.S. Animal Hea. Assn. [16811]
Vaccine and Infectious Disease Org. [IO]
Veterinarian Assn. for the Attention of Exotic and Wild Animals [IO]
Veterinary Assn. of Malaysia [IO]
Veterinary Botanical Medicine Assn. [16812]
Veterinary Cancer Soc. [16813]
Veterinary Coun. of Ireland [IO]
Veterinary History Soc. [IO]
Veterinary Hosp. Managers Assn. [16814]
Veterinary Inst. of Integrative Medicine [16815]
Veterinary Orthopedic Soc. [16816]
Western Veterinary Conf. [16817]
World Assn. for the Advancement of Veterinary Parasitology [16818]
World Assn. for the Advancement of Veterinary Parasitology [IO]
World Assn. for Buiatrics [IO]
World Assn. for the History of Veterinary Medicine [IO]
World Assn. of Veterinary Anatomists [IO]
World Assn. of Veterinary Educators [9295]
World Assn. of Veterinary Lab. Diagnosticians [16819]
World Assn. of Veterinary Lab. Diagnosticians [IO]
World Org. for Animal Hea. [IO]
World Small Animal Veterinary Assn. [IO]
World Veterinary Assn. [IO]
World Veterinary Poultry Assn. [IO]
Zimbabwe Veterinary Assn. [IO]
Veterinary Medicine; Assn. of Amer. Bd. of Examiners in [★16755]
Veterinary Medicine; Assn. of Deans of Amer. Colleges of [★9293]
Veterinary Nutritionists; Amer. Assn. of [★16737]
Veterinary Orthopedic Soc. [16816], PO Box 705, Okemos, MI 48805-0705, (517)381-2468
Veterinary Radiology; Amer. Bd. of [★16770]
Veterinary Soc. for the Stud. of Breeding Soundness; Amer. [★16806]
Veterinary Specialties; Advisory Bd. on [★16759]
Veterinary Toxicologists; Amer. Coll. of [★16736]
Vetlesen Found; G. Unger [12719]
Vetplantvereniging van Suid-Afika [★IO]
Vets With a Mission [IO], Newberry, SC, United States
Vets With a Mission [17011], PO Box 202, Newberry, SC 29108, (803)405-9926

Vexillology
Burgee Data Archives [IO]
Canadian Flag Assn. [IO]
Flag Inst. [IO]
Flag Res. Center [11074]
Intl. Fed. of Vexillological Associations [11075]

Intl. Fed. of Vexillological Associations [IO]
Natl. Flag Day Found. [21094]
Natl. Flag Found. [11076]
North Amer. Vexillological Assn. [11077]
U.S. Flag Found. [11078]
VHA [14901], PO Box 140909, Irving, TX 75014-0909, (972)830-0000
VHL Family Alliance [14489], 2001 Beacon St., Ste. 208, Boston, MA 02135-7787, (617)277-5667
Vi Hjaelper Hinanden [★IO]
Viatical Assn. of Am. [★1472]
Viatical and Life Settlement Assn. of Am. [1472]
Vibrating Screen Mfrs. Assn. - Address unknown since 1994.
Vibration Found. [★7302]
Vibration Inst. [7302], 6262 S Kingery Hwy., Ste. 212, Willowbrook, IL 60527, (630)654-2254
Vibration Isolation and Seismic Control Mfrs. Assn. [7643], 994 Old Eagle School Rd., Ste. 1019, Wayne, PA 19087-1866, (610)971-4850
Victim Advocacy Center; Sunny Von Bulow Natl. [★13366]
Victim Assistance Training Prog; Regional [★13369]
Victim Found; Natl. Burn [13784]
Victim Offender Mediation Assn. [18780], c/o Doreene Langason, Admin., Center for Policy, Planning and Performance, 2233 Univ. Ave. W, Ste. 300, St. Paul, MN 55114, (612)874-0570
Victim Offender Mediation Assn. [IO], St. Paul, MN, United States
Victim Support [IO], London, United Kingdom
Victimization; Male Survivor: The Natl. Org. Against Male Sexual [13077]
Victimization; Natl. Org. on Male Sexual [★13077]

Victims
9/11 Families for a Secure Am. [18728]
All4Israel [12454]
Amer. Friends of ALYN Hosp. [12825]
Amer. Soc. of Victimology [13360]
Amer. Victims of Abortion [12903]
Assn. of Albanian Girls and Women [18382]
Captive Daughters [18383]
Center for Victims of Torture [13361]
European Fed. of Road Traffic Victims [IO]
European Forum for Victim Services [IO]
Gift From Within [12768]
Inst. for Victims of Trauma [13362]
Intl. Comm. for the Children of Chechnya [11605]
Intl. Comm. for the Rescue of KAL 007 Survivors [18541]
Intl. Found. for Terror Act Victims [12942]
Life After Assault League [13363]
LifeWorks Inst. [12551]
Male Survivor: The Natl. Org. Against Male Sexual Victimization [13077]
Murder Victims' Families for Reconciliation [17032]
My Good Deed [13308]
Natl. Assn. of Crime Victim Compensation Boards [13364]
Natl. Assn. of State VOCAL Orgs. [13365]
Natl. Assn. to Stop Guardian Abuse [12059]
Natl. Center for Victims of Crime [13366]
Natl. Child Abuse Defense and Rsrc. Center [13367]
Natl. Coalition of Homicide Survivors [13368]
Natl. Crime Victim Bar Assn. [6349]
Natl. Org. for Victim Assistance [13369]
Natl. Victims' Constitutional Amendment Network [18779]
No Greater Love [13370]
Our Voices Together [13309]
P.U.L.S.E. [14662]
Rape, Abuse and Incest Natl. Network [12791]
September 11th Families' Assn. [13371]
September's Mission [13310]
Stop it Now! [11653]
Survivors of Incest Anonymous [13085]
Survivors Network of Those Abused by Priests [13372]
Torture Abolition and Survivors Support Coalition Intl. [17786]
Tuesday's Children [12003]
Victim Offender Mediation Assn. [18780]
Victim Offender Mediation Assn. [IO]

Victims' Assistance Legal Org. [5639]
Victims of Chiropractic [14015]
Victims of Crime and Leniency [13373]
Witness Justice [18790]
Women and Men Against Sexual Harassment and Other Abuses [13088]
World Soc. of Victimology [IO]
World Trade Center Survivors' Network [13311]
WTC Families For Proper Burial [13312]
Victims Anonymous - Address unknown since 1989.
Victims' Assistance Legal Org. [5639], 8180 Greensboro Dr., Ste. 1070, McLean, VA 22102-3823, (703)748-0811
Victims of Child Abuse Laws [★13365]
Victims of Chiropractic [14015], 10049 San Juan Ct., Fountain Valley, CA 92708, (714)962-8683
Victims of Choice [12930], PO Box 815, Naperville, IL 60566-0815, (630)378-1680
Victims of Crime and Leniency [13373], 111 N St. Andrews St., Dothan, AL 36303, (334)242-7197
Victims Educ. Assn; Intl. Dalkon Shield [16898]
Victims Empowered; Survivors And [11656]
Victims' Families Assn; September 11 Widows and [12002]
Victims of Incest Can Emerge [★13086]
Victims of Incest Can Emerge [★IO]
Victims of Incest Can Emerge Survivors [★IO]
Victims of Incest Can Emerge Survivors [★13086]
Victims of Incest Concerned Effort [★13086]
Victims of Incest Concerned Effort [★IO]
Victims Intl; Agent Orange [★13356]
Victims for Victims - Defunct.
Victims of Violence [IO], Ottawa, ON, Canada
Victoria Dental Therapists' Assn. [IO], Parkville, Australia
Victoria Habitat for Humanity [IO], Victoria, BC, Canada
Victoria League for Commonwealth Friendship [IO], London, United Kingdom

Victorian
Antique and Art Glass Salt Shaker Collectors Soc. [21968]
Australasian Victorian Stud. Assn. [IO]
Fairy Lamp Club [22019]
Majolica Intl. Soc. [21931]
North Amer. Victorian Stud. Assn. [11079]
Res. Soc. for Victorian Periodicals [11080]
Res. Soc. for Victorian Periodicals [IO]
Victorian Homeowner's Assn. and Old House Lovers [10075]
Victorian Soc. in Am. [11081]
Victorian Artists Soc. [IO], East Melbourne, Australia
Victorian Assn. for the Teaching of English [IO], Melbourne, Australia
Victorian Employers' Chamber of Commerce and Indus. [IO], Melbourne, Australia
Victorian Farmers Fed. [IO], Melbourne, Australia
Victorian Hairwork Soc. [22176], c/o Leila Cohoon, 1333 S Noland Rd., Independence, MO 64055, (816)833-2955
Victorian Homeowner's Assn. and Old House Lovers [10075]
Victorian Infection Control Professionals Assn. [IO], Carlton, Australia
Victorian Ladies' Bowling Assn. [IO], Hawthorn, Australia
Victorian Military History Inst. - Defunct.
Victorian Military Soc. [IO], Newbury, United Kingdom
Victorian Model Aeronautical Assn. [IO], Cranbourne, Australia
Victorian Olive Coun. [IO], Lara, Australia
Victorian Soc. [IO], London, United Kingdom
Victorian Soc. in Am. [11081], 205 S Camac St., Philadelphia, PA 19107, (215)545-8340
Victory Force; America's [21343]
Victory League; Bowlers' [★23250]
Vida Humana Internacional [★IO]

Video
Amer. Guild of Court Videographers [6019]
Asian CineVision [9930]
Assn. of Cinema and Video Labs. [1367]
Assn. of Commercial Stock Image Licensors [1378]
Assn. of Independent Video and Filmmakers [9931]

Reference to "IO" in place of a book number signifies that the association may be found in the 45th edition of International Organizations.

Assn. for Info. Media and Equip. [328]
Assn. of Moving Image Archivists [9932]
Assn. Quebecoise de L'Industrie du Disque, du Spectacle et de la Video [IO]
Black Awareness in TV [17164]
Christian Media Assn. [20237]
Coun. on Intl. Nontheatrical Events [9935]
Film Advisory Bd. [9936]
Film Arts Found. [9937]
Film/Video Arts [9938]
Found. for Informed Medical Decision Making [15137]
Global Action Proj. [18849]
Intl. Documentary Assn. [1385]
Intl. Film Seminars [9940]
Intl. Soc. of Certified Electronics Technicians [1220]
Law Enforcement and Emergency Services Video Assn. [6350]
Natl. Alliance for Media Arts and Culture [9580]
Natl. Assn. of Video Distributors [1391]
Natl. Center for Film and Video Preservation [9942]
Natl. Legal Video Assn. [6016]
Outfest [9944]
Pacific Islanders in Communications [10455]
PMA - Independent Book Publishers Assn. [3248]
ResearchChannel [7575]
Soc. of Professional Audio Recording Services [3351]
United Catholic Music and Video Assn. [19731]
Video Software Dealers Assn. [333]
Video Alliance for the Performing Arts - Address unknown since 1989.
Video Arts; Film/ [9938]
Video Assn; Adult [17037]
Video Assn; United Catholic Music and [19731]
Video Assn; Univ. Film and [8420]
Video Bible Inst. - Defunct.
Video Communicators; IFPA Film and [★1384]
Video Distributors; Natl. Assn. of [1391]
Video-Documentary Clearinghouse - Address unknown since 2002.
Video Electronics Standards Assn. [6932], 860 Hill-view Ct., Ste. 150, Milpitas, CA 95035, (408)957-9270
Video and Film Distributors Coun. - Defunct.
Video and Filmmakers; Assn. of Independent [9931]
Video Labs; Assn. of Cinema and [1367]
Video Preservation; Natl. Center for Film and [9942]
Video Retailers Assn. - Defunct.
Video Retailers Assn; Professional Audio [★1209]
Video Software Dealers Assn. [333], 16530 Ventura Blvd., Ste. 400, Encino, CA 91436-4551, (818)385-1500
Video Tape Network - Defunct.
Video; Women in Film and [1373]
Videotape
Found. for Informed Medical Decision Making [15137]
Videotex Indus. Assn. [★737]
Videotex Indus. Assn. [★IO]
VIDION/Intl. Assn. of Video - Address unknown since 2004.
Vidskiptarad Islands [★IO]
Vieilles Maisons Francaises; Friends of [★10024]
Vienna Inst. for Development and Cooperation [IO], Vienna, Austria
Viers/Veirs Family Org. - Defunct.
Vietnam
Amer. Fighter Aces Assn. [20647]
Amer. Legion Auxiliary [21189]
Center for Social Stud. Educ. [9127]
Champa Cultural Preservation Assn. of USA [11082]
Counterpart Intl. [12426]
EAA Warbirds of Am. [21443]
Indochina Center [10122]
Natl. Alliance of Vietnamese Amer. Ser. Agencies [19423]
Special Forces Assn. [21270]
Swift Boat Veterans for Truth [21324]
Tan Son Nhut Assn. [21336]
US-Vietnam Chamber of Commerce [24387]

USMC Vietnam Tankers Assn. [21337]
Vietnam Era Seabees [21339]
Vietnam Security Police Assn. [21340]
Vietnam Veteran Wives [21332]
Vietnamese Nom Preservation Found. [10433]
Vietnamese Professionals Soc. [19429]
Volunteers in Asia [13407]
Waifs of War Found. [IO]
Vietnam Assistance for the Handicapped - Ho Chi Minh City [IO], Ho Chi Minh City, Vietnam
Vietnam Assn. of Certified Public Accountants [IO], Hanoi, Vietnam
Vietnam Assn. of Seafood Exporters and Producers [IO], Hanoi, Vietnam
Vietnam Athletic Fed. [IO], Hanoi, Vietnam
Vietnam Badminton Fed. [IO], Hanoi, Vietnam
Vietnam and Cambodia; 11th Armored Cavalry's Veterans of [21341]
Vietnam Charities - Defunct.
Vietnam Christian Service - Defunct.
Vietnam Combat Veterans [21350], PO Box 715, White Pine, MI 49971, (906)885-5599
Vietnam Dog Handler Assn. [21338], c/o Robert L. Palochik, Treas., 8203 Parting Clouds Ct., Las Vegas, NV 89117-7614
Vietnam Engg. Consultant Assn. [IO], Hanoi, Vietnam
Vietnam Era Seabees [21339], PO Box 5177, Mid-lothian, VA 23112-0020
Vietnam Era Veterans in Cong. [18783], 2211 Ray-burn, Washington, DC 20515, (202)225-5905
Vietnam Era Veterans Inter-Tribal Assn. - Address unknown since 1995.
Vietnam Found. - Defunct.
Vietnam Gastroenterology Assn. [IO], Hanoi, Vietnam
Vietnam Gen. Assn. of Medicine and Pharmacy [IO], Hanoi, Vietnam
Vietnam Generation; Proj. on the [★10122]
Vietnam Gift Pac - Defunct.
Vietnam Helicopter Pilots Assn. [21351], 5530 Birdcage St., Ste. 105, Citrus Heights, CA 95610-7698, (800)505-VHPA
Vietnam Human Rights Network [12378], 14550 Magnolia St., Ste. 203, Westminster, CA 92683, (714)897-1950
Vietnam Human Rights Network [IO], Westminster, CA, United States
Vietnam Medical Assn. [IO], Hanoi, Vietnam
Vietnam Moratorium Comm. - Defunct.
Vietnam Natl. Heart Assn. [IO], Hanoi, Vietnam
Vietnam Olympic Comm. [IO], Hanoi, Vietnam
Vietnam Proj. [★17918]
Vietnam Red Cross Soc. [IO], Hanoi, Vietnam
Vietnam Rheumatology Assn. [IO], Hanoi, Vietnam
Vietnam Security Police Assn. [21340], c/o Phil Car-roll, Membership Chm., PO Box 8, Gladstone, OR 97027
Vietnam Software Assn. [IO], Hanoi, Vietnam
Vietnam Taekwondo Assn. [IO], Ho Chi Minh City, Vietnam
Vietnam Tennis Fed. [IO], Hanoi, Vietnam
Vietnam Trade Coun; U.S.- [17010]
Vietnam Veteran Wives [21332], PO Box 396, Republic, WA 99166, (509)775-8893
Vietnam Veterans
Amer. Fighter Aces Assn. [20647]
Amer. Legion Auxiliary [21189]
Natl. Vietnam and Gulf War Veterans Coalition [18781]
Private Agencies Collaborating Together [6351]
Private Agencies Collaborating Together [IO]
Saigon Mission Assn. [IO]
Saigon Mission Assn. [18782]
Special Forces Assn. [21270]
Tan Son Nhut Assn. [21336]
USMC Vietnam Tankers Assn. [21337]
Vietnam Dog Handler Assn. [21338]
Vietnam Era Seabees [21339]
Vietnam Era Veterans in Cong. [18783]
Vietnam Security Police Assn. [21340]
Vietnam Veteran Wives [21332]
Vietnam Veterans Against the War [18784]
Vietnam Veterans Against the War Anti-Imperialist [18785]

Vietnam Veterans of Am. [18786]
Vietnam Veterans Assn. of Australia - Natl. Coun. [IO]
Vietnam Veterans Against the War [18784], PO Box 408594, Chicago, IL 60640, (773)276-4189
Vietnam Veterans Against the War Anti-Imperialist [18785], PO Box 21604, Seattle, WA 98111-3604, (206)374-2215
Vietnam Veterans Against the War/Winter Soldier Org. [★18784]
Vietnam Veterans of Am. [18786], 8605 Cameron St., No. 400, Silver Spring, MD 20910, (301)585-4000
Vietnam Veterans of Amer. Found. [★17918]
Vietnam Veterans Assn; 1/77th Artillery [★21342]
Vietnam Veterans Assn. of Australia - Natl. Coun. [IO], Warnbro, Australia
Vietnam Veterans Coalition; Natl. [★18781]
Vietnam Veterans in Cong. Caucus [★18783]
Vietnam Veterans; Coun. of [★18786]
Vietnam Veterans, Inc. - Defunct.
Vietnam Veterans Memorial Fund [21352], 1023 15th St. NW, 2nd Fl., Washington, DC 20005, (202)393-0090
Vietnam War
11th Armored Cavalry's Veterans of Vietnam and Cambodia [21341]
77th Artillery Assn. [21342]
America's Victory Force [21343]
Associates of Vietnam Veterans of Am. [21344]
Gamewardens of Vietnam Assn. [21345]
Indochina Center [10122]
Mobile Riverine Force Assn. [21346]
Natl. Alliance of Families for the Return of America's Missing Servicemen [21263]
Natl. War Dog Memorial Fund [21347]
PBR Forces Veterans Assn. [21348]
Sons and Daughters In Touch [12599]
Tan Son Nhut Assn. [21336]
USMC Vietnam Tankers Assn. [21337]
Veterans of the Vietnam War [21349]
Vietnam Combat Veterans [21350]
Vietnam Dog Handler Assn. [21338]
Vietnam Era Seabees [21339]
Vietnam Helicopter Pilots Assn. [21351]
Vietnam Security Police Assn. [21340]
Vietnam Veteran Wives [21332]
Vietnam Veterans Memorial Fund [21352]
Vietnam Women's Memorial Found. [21353]
Vietnam War; Veterans of the [21349]
Vietnam Women's Memorial Found. [21353], 1735 Connecticut Ave. NW, 3rd Fl., Washington, DC 20009, (866)822-8963
Vietnam Women's Memorial Proj. [★21353]
Vietnamese
Cambodian Mutual Assistance Assn. [19422]
Champa Cultural Preservation Assn. of USA [11082]
Gp. of Universities for the Advancement of Vietnamese Abroad [9296]
Intl. Assn. for Res. in Vietnamese Music [10614]
Natl. Alliance of Vietnamese Amer. Ser. Agencies [19423]
Natl. Assn. for the Educ. and Advancement of Cambodian, Laotian, and Vietnamese Americans [19424]
Natl. Assn. of Vietnamese Nurses [15504]
Natl. Center for Victims of Crime [13366]
Natl. Cong. of Vietnamese Americans [19425]
Union of North Amer. Vietnamese Students Assn. [19426]
Union of North Amer. Vietnamese Students Assn. [IO]
US-Vietnam Chamber of Commerce [24387]
Vietnamese Amer. Coun. [19427]
Vietnamese-Amer. Professionals Alliance [19428]
Vietnamese-Amer. Professionals Alliance [IO]
Vietnamese Nom Preservation Found. [10433]
Vietnamese Professionals Soc. [19429]
Vietnamese Professionals Soc. [IO]
Vietnamese Amer. Assn. - Defunct.
Vietnamese-Amer. Children's Fund - Defunct.
Vietnamese Amer. Coun. [19427], 780 S 1st St., San Jose, CA 95113, (408)315-8472
Vietnamese Amer. Educ; Natl. Assn. for [★19424]

A star before a book entry number signifies that the name is not listed separately, but is mentioned within the entry.

Vietnamese Amer. Medical Assn. [★15183]
Vietnamese Amer. Medical Assn. [★IO]
Vietnamese-Amer. Professionals Alliance [IO], Sunnyvale, CA, United States
Vietnamese-Amer. Professionals Alliance [19428]
Vietnamese Amer. Soc. - Defunct.
Vietnamese Buddhist Mutual Aid Assn. in North America - Defunct.
Vietnamese Canadian Fed. [IO], Ottawa, ON, Canada
Vietnamese Catholic Fed. in the U.S.A. - Defunct.
Vietnamese Chamber of Commerce in Orange County - Address unknown since 2002.
Vietnamese Cultural Assn. of North America - Address unknown since 1989.
Vietnamese Geotechnical Soc. [IO], Hanoi, Vietnam
Vietnamese Medical Assn. of the U.S.A. [IO], San Diego, CA, United States
Vietnamese Medical Assn. of the U.S.A. [15183], 6255 Univ. Ave., Ste. A-2, San Diego, CA 92115, (619)583-0553
Vietnamese Nom Preservation Found. [10433], 229 Beachers Brook Ln., Cary, NC 27511
Vietnamese Nom Preservation Found. [IO], Cary, NC, United States
Vietnamese Org. to Exterminate Communists and Restore the Nation - Address unknown since 1997.
Vietnamese Professionals Soc. [19429], 5150 Fair Oaks Blvd., Ste. 101-128, Carmichael, CA 95608-5758, (916)484-3519
Vietnamese Professionals Soc. [IO], Carmichael, CA, United States
Vietnamese Senior Citizens Assn. - Address unknown since 2001.
VietNow [★13359]
VietNow Natl. [13359], 1835 Broadway, Rockford, IL 61104, (815)227-5100
VIEW Clubs of Australia [IO], Sydney, Australia
Viewers for Quality TV - Defunct.
Viewpoint; Amer. [★17072]
Viewpoint Soc; Amer. [★17072]
Vihara; Buddhist [19545]
Vik Chandler Fan Club - Address unknown since 1989.
Viking, Anglo-Saxon, Anglo-Norman, and Angevin History; Haskins Soc. for [★10459]
Viking Brotherhood [★19461]
Viking Club [★IO]
Viking Ship; Leif Ericson [11134]
Viking Soc. for Northern Res. [IO], London, United Kingdom
Vikings; Independent Order of [19127]
Vikki's Special People - Defunct.
Villa-Lobos Music Soc. [10717], 153 E 92nd St., No. 4R, New York, NY 10128-2479, (212)427-5103
Villa-Lobos Music Soc. [IO], New York, NY, United States
Village Assn; Czech [★19028]
Village-Based Development; Consortium for Sustainable [★11793]
Village Bee Breeders Assn. [★IO]
Village of Childhelp [★11661]
Village of Childhelp West [11661], PO Box 247, Beaumont, CA 92223, (909)845-3155
Village Earth: CSVBD [11793], PO Box 797, Fort Collins, CO 80522, (970)491-5754
Village Earth: CSVBD [IO], Fort Collins, CO, United States
Village Educ. Rsrc. Center [IO], Dhaka, Bangladesh
Villers Advocacy Associates - Defunct.
Villers Found. [★11286]
Villiers Found; Robert Roesler de [★13837]
Vilnius Chamber of Commerce, Indus., and Crafts [IO], Vilnius, Lithuania
VIM, Inc. - Defunct.
Vin og Spiritus Organisationen i Danmark [★IO]
Vince Gill Fan Club [24989], PO Box 700, Grover, MO 63040
Vince Smith and Carol Redo Fan Club - Address unknown since 2004.
Vincent Owners Club - Keystone Sect. [22697]
Vincent Pallotti Center for Apostolic Development; St. [20390]
Vincent de Paul Coun. of the U.S; Soc. of St. [13190]

Vindmolleindustrien [★IO]
Vinegar Connoisseurs Intl. [IO], Roslyn, SD, United States
Vinegar Connoisseurs Intl. [22575], c/o Lawrence Diggs, PO Box 41, Roslyn, SD 57261, (800)342-4519
Vinegar Inst. [1570], 1100 Johnson Ferry Rd., Ste. 300, Atlanta, GA 30342, (404)252-3663
Vineyard Found; Amer. [5408]
Vinifera Wine Growers Assn. [5423], PO Box 10045, Alexandria, VA 22310, (703)922-7049
Vining Davis Foundations; Arthur [12048]
Vinland Alliance [★19460]
Vinland Assn; Amer. [19460]
Vintage Alfa Romeo Intl. - Defunct.
Vintage Arms Assn. [IO], Harleston, United Kingdom
Vintage Austin Register [IO], Alfreton, United Kingdom
Vintage Base Ball Assn. [23128], c/o Rich Arpi, Treas., 2445 Londin Ln. E, Unit 410, Maplewood, MN 55119, (651)739-6986
Vintage BMW [★22698]
Vintage BMW [★IO]
The Vintage BMW Club [★IO]
The Vintage BMW Club [★22698]
Vintage BMW Motorcycle Owners [22698], c/o Roland Slabon, Ed.-in-Chief, PO Box 67, Exeter, NH 03833, (603)772-9799
Vintage BMW Motorcycle Owners [IO], Exeter, NH, United States
Vintage Car Club of Am; BMW [21593]
Vintage Chevrolet Club of Am. [21809], PO Box 5387, Orange, CA 92863-5387, (626)963-2438
Vintage Corvette Club of America - Defunct.
Vintage Drivers Club of Am. [21810], 13505 Running Water Rd., Palm Beach Gardens, FL 33418-7933, (561)622-7554
Vintage Fashion and Costume Jewelry Club [22128], PO Box 265, Glen Oaks, NY 11004
Vintage Fashion/Costume Jewelry Club [IO], Glen Oaks, NY, United States
Vintage Locomotive Soc. [IO], Winnipeg, MB, Canada
Vintage Motor Bike Club [22699], c/o Joyce Lee, 537 W Huntington St., Montpelier, IN 47359, (417)881-7411
Vintage Poster Dealers Assn; Intl. [106]
Vintage Racers of Old Motorcycles - Address unknown since 2005.
Vintage Racing Assn; Sportscar [23085]
Vintage Radio and Phonograph Soc. [22931], PO Box 165345, Irving, TX 75016, (972)353-4862
Vintage Sailplane Assn. [23045], 4673 Sapphire Dr., Hoffman Estates, IL 60195
Vintage Sports Car Club of Am. [21811], c/o John J. Schieffelin, Pres., PO Box 60425, Florence, MA 01062, (413)584-4210
Vintage Taxi Assn. - Amer. Sect; London [21690]
Vintage Thunderbird Club of Am. [★21812]
Vintage Thunderbird Club of Am. [★IO]
Vintage Thunderbird Club of Am; Heartland [21654]
Vintage Thunderbird Club Intl. [21812], c/o Marilyn Paliani, Exec. Sec., 1304 Greenwood, Schertz, TX 78154-2808, (210)566-2118
Vintage Thunderbird Club Intl. [IO], Schertz, TX, United States
Vintage Triumph Register [21813], PO Box 655, Howell, MI 48844
Vintage Volkswagen Club of Am. [21814], c/o Sherri Corrao, VP, 516 Bruce St., New London, WI 54961
Vintage White Truck Assn. - Defunct.
Vintage Wooden Boat Assn. [IO], Potton, United Kingdom
Vintners; Assn. of African Amer. [195]
Vintners Assn; Napa Valley [5416]
Vintners' Fed. of Ireland [IO], Dublin, Ireland
Vintners and Growers Assn; Monterey County [5414]
Vintners; Santa Cruz Mountain [★5420]
Vinyl Asbestos Tile Inst; Asphalt and [★665]
Vinyl Coun. of Australia [IO], Altona, Australia
Vinyl Fabrics Inst. [★IO]
Vinyl Fabrics Inst. [★3048]
Vinyl Metal Industry Assn. - Defunct.
Vinyl and Rubber Flooring Div., Rubber Mfrs. Assn. - Defunct.

Vinyl Siding Inst. [685], 1201 15th St. NW, Ste. 220, Washington, DC 20005, (202)587-5100
Vinyl Window and Door Inst. - Address unknown since 2001.
Viola d'Amore Soc. of Am. [10718], 10917 Pickford Way, Culver City, CA 90230, (310)838-5509
Viola da Gamba Soc. of Am. [10719], c/o Mr. Ken Perlow, Treas., 131 S Humphrey Ave., Oak Park, IL 60302, (708)383-4608
Viola Res. Soc. [★10554]
Viola Soc; Amer. [10554]
Viola Soc; Canadian [IO]

Violence

All4Israel [12454]
AMEND [12020]
Amer. Decency Assn. [17281]
Amer. Family Assn. [17162]
Anti-Repression Rsrc. Team [17093]
ASARian [11521]
Assassination Archives and Res. Center [18787]
Batterers Anonymous - Beyond Abuse [12023]
Canadians Concerned About Violence in Entertainment [IO]
Center for Neighborhood Enterprise [17208]
Coalition to Stop Gun Violence [17590]
Communities Against Violence Network [13374]
Community United Against Violence [12225]
Corporate Alliance to End Partner Violence [12025]
Drums No Guns [17591]
Ending Relationship Abuse Soc. of British Columbia [IO]
Historians Against the War [18795]
INCITE! Women of Color Against Violence [18788]
Inst. for Victims of Trauma [13362]
Intl. Org. for the Stud. of Gp. Tensions [10189]
"Love Yourself" Stop the Violence [17250]
Love146 [11620]
MAD DADS (Men Against Destruction - Defending Against Drugs and Social Disorder) [12043]
Men Stopping Violence [12643]
Million Mom March [17596]
Mothers Against Violence in Am. [13375]
Murder Victims' Families for Reconciliation [17032]
My Good Deed [13308]
Natl. Alliance of Gang Investigators Associations [5638]
Natl. Assn. of Professional Accident Reconstructionists [6252]
Natl. Assn. to Stop Guardian Abuse [12059]
Natl. Latino Alliance for the Elimination of Domestic Violence [12037]
Natl. Network to End Violence Against Immigrant Women [13433]
Natl. Sexual Violence Rsrc. Center [13080]
Our Voices Together [13309]
Parents of Murdered Children [12685]
Partners for Peace [18230]
Peace X Peace [18237]
Physicians for Social Responsibility [18169]
Pups for Peace [12700]
Racial Justice 911 [18493]
Refugee Coun. USA [18500]
September's Mission [13310]
Silent March: Amers. Against Violence [17599]
S.M.A.R.T. (Secretive Societies, Mind Control and Ritual Abuse) [13296]
Stop the Violence, Face The Music [13376]
Stop the Violence, Face The Music [IO]
Student Pledge Against Gun Violence [17601]
Survivorship [13377]
Violence Policy Center [18789]
Witness Justice [18790]
Women Against Gun Violence [18791]
Women in Black [18255]
Women and Men Against Sexual Harassment and Other Abuses [13088]
Workplace Bullying Inst. [16189]
World Connections for Women [18824]
World Trade Center Survivors' Network [13311]
Violence Against Women; Natl. Communications Network for the Elimination of [★12034]
Violence; Amer. Alliance Against [★17589]

Reference to "IO" in place of a book number signifies that the association may be found in the 45th edition of International Organizations.

Violence; Brady Campaign to Prevent Gun [17588]
Violence; Brady Center to Prevent Gun [17589]
Violence; Center to Prevent Handgun [★17589]
Violence; Coalition to Stop Gun [17590]
Violence; Comm. Against Anti-Asian [17006]
Violence in Educ; Parents and Teachers Against [8208]
Violence; Educational Fund to End Handgun [★17592]
Violence; Educational Fund to Stop Gun [17592]
Violence; Eisenhower Found. for the Prevention of [★11839]
Violence; Emerge: A Men's Counseling Ser. on Domestic [★12026]
Violence; Emerge: Counseling and Educ. to Stop Domestic [12026]
Violence Everywhere; Natl. Assn. of Students Against [18117]
Violence and Extremism; Inst. for Prevention and Control of [★17146]
Violence-Free Soc; Physicians for a [12985]
Violence Hotline; Natl. Domestic [12036]
Violence; Natl. Coalition Against Domestic [12034]
Violence; Natl. Coun. on Child Abuse and Family [12035]
Violence; Natl. Inst. Against Prejudice and [★17146]
Violence Policy Center [18789], 1730 Rhode Island Ave. NW, Ste. 1014, Washington, DC 20036, (202)822-8200
Violence; Prejudice Institute/Center for the Applied Stud. of Ethno [17146]
Violence Prevention Fund; Family [12028]
Violence; Victims of [IO]
Violent Death Bereavement Soc. [11513], c/o Laura Jeffs, Prog. Coor., PO Box 1930, Seattle, WA 98199, (206)223-6398
Violet Soc. [IO], Market Drayton, United Kingdom
Violet Soc. of Am; African [22480]
Violin and Bow Makers; Amer. Fed. of [2797]
Violin Making; Amer. Soc. for the Advancement of [★10720]
Violin Soc. of Am. [10720], 48 Acad. St., Poughkeepsie, NY 12601, (845)452-7557
Violoncello Soc. [10721]
VIP Div. [★11896]
Virago Owners Club [22700], c/o Paul Boyd, Treas., 1386 Reynolds Cir., Binghamton, NY 13903, (607)669-4352
Virchow-Pirquet Medical Soc. - Address unknown since 1999.
Virgin Islands
  Conf. of Chief Justices [5896]
  Conf. of State Bank Supervisors [5544]
  Conf. of State Court Administrators [5625]
  Fed. of State Humanities Councils [10198]
  Friends of Virgin Islands Natl. Park [5264]
  Natl. Assn. State Agencies for Surplus Property [6185]
  Natl. Coun. of Architectural Registration Boards [5466]
  Natl. Coun. of State Housing Agencies [5795]
  Southeastern Assn. of Fish and Wildlife Agencies [5734]
  Virgin Islands Olympic Comm. [23638]
Virgin Islands Dept. of Economic Development and Agriculture - Defunct.
Virgin Islands Olympic Comm. [23638], PO Box 1578, Frederiksted, VI 00841, (340)778-2229
Virgin Islands Olympic Comm. [IO], Frederiksted, VI, United States
Virgin Mary
  Ambassadors of Mary [19565]
  Assn. of Marian Helpers [19576]
  Blue Army of Our Lady of Fatima, U.S.A. [19589]
  Central Assn. of the Miraculous Medal [19609]
  Church Universal and Triumphant [19462]
  Pro Maria Comm. [19704]
  Reparation Soc. of the Immaculate Heart of Mary [19709]
  Third Order of Mary/Marists [19728]
Virginia Antiquities; Assn. for the Preservation of [★10013]
Virginia-Carolina Peanut Assn. [5063], PO Box 8, Nashville, NC 27856-0088, (252)459-9977
Virginia-Carolina Peanut Promotions [5064], 103 Triangle Ct., Nashville, NC 27856-0008, (252)459-9977

Virginia Community Development Org. [★11798]
Virginia Country Civil War Soc. [★10103]
Virginia Crab Packers Assn. - Defunct.
Virginia Dark-Fired and Sun Cured Tobacco Export Assn. - Defunct.
Virginia Functional Jaw Stud. Club; Northern [★14115]
Virginia; Huguenot Soc. of the Founders of Manakin in the Colony of [21162]
Virginia Poultry Breeders Assn. [5124], c/o Judy Sanderlin, Sec., 3816 Wayside Rd., Charles City, VA 23030
Virginia Poultry Breeders Club [★5124]
Virginia Woolf Soc. [★9666]
Virginia Woolf Soc. [★IO]
Virology; Amer. Soc. for [6547]
Virtual Assistants Assn; Intl. [68]
Virtual Private Network Consortium [2320], 127 Segre Pl., Santa Cruz, CA 95060, (831)426-9827
Virtual Private Network Consortium [IO], Santa Cruz, CA, United States
Visao Mundial - Brazil [★IO]
Vise Assn; Machinists [★1822]
Vision; Amer. Medical Assn. for the Conservation of [★16882]
Vision Assn; Automated [★7581]
Vision Australia [IO], Enfield, Australia
Vision Australia Found. [IO], Kooyong, Australia
Vision Care; Natl. Optometric Soc. for Developmental [★15718]
Vision Community Services [★16868]
Vision Community Services - A Division of the Massachusetts Assn. for the Blind [★16868]
Vision Coun. of Am. [1866], 1700 Diagonal Rd., Ste. 500, Alexandria, VA 22314, (703)548-4560
Vision; Coun. of Citizens With Low [★11934]
Vision Development; Coll. of Optometrists in [15718]
Vision Educ; Parents Active for [16880]
Vision Educational Found. - Defunct.
Vision Found. for Blind Youth [★15724]
Vision Gp. of the Robotic Indus. Assn. [★7581]
Vision Indus. Coun. of Am. [★1866]
Vision Inst; Better [15678]
Vision Intl; Coun. of Citizens With Low [11934]
Vision Mondiale Canada [★IO]
Vision Mundial Colombia [★IO]
Vision and Ophthalmology; Assn. for Res. in [15672]
Vision and Perception Training; Natl. Soc. for [★15718]
Vision Professionals; Natl. Assn. of [15693]
Vision Prog. Consultants; Natl. Assn. of [★15693]
Vision Sci. Librarians; Assn. of [10341]
Vision Service Plan Natl. - Defunct.
Vision Soc; Southwest Developmental [★15718]
Vision USA [15730], 243 N Lindbergh Blvd., St. Louis, MO 63141-7881, (800)766-4466
Vision U.S.A. [★15712]
Vision World Wide [16890], 5707 Brockton Dr., Ste. 302, Indianapolis, IN 46220-5481, (317)254-1332
Vision World Wide [IO], Indianapolis, IN, United States
Visionaries In Action - Across Africa [IO], Johannesburg, Republic of South Africa
Visionary Resources; Coalition of [2835]
Visionary Retailers; Coalition of [★2835]
Visions in Action [12447], 2710 Ontario Rd. NW, Washington, DC 20009, (202)625-7402
Visions in Action [IO], Washington, DC, United States
Visions Found. - Address unknown since 2004.
VisitBritain [24242], 551 5th Ave., 7th Fl., No. 701, New York, NY 10176-0799, (212)850-0330
VisitBritain [IO], New York, NY, United States
Visiting Friends - Defunct.
Visiting Geographical Scientist Prog. [★24491]
Visiting Nurse Associations of Am. [15532], Admin. Off., 99 Summer St., Ste. 1700, Boston, MA 02110, (617)737-3200
Visiting Nurses Associations and Services; Amer. Affiliation of [★15532]
Visiting Teachers Assn; Natl. [8955]
Visiting Women Scientists - Defunct.
Visitor Information Publications - Defunct.
Visitor Prog. Ser. of Meridian House Intl. [★17902]
Visitor Stud. Assn. [9280], PO Box 14375, Columbus, OH 43214-4375, (614)670-7379

Visitor Stud. Assn. [IO], Columbus, OH, United States
Visitors Program; International [★17902]
VisitScotland [IO], Edinburgh, United Kingdom
VISTA Citizens Corporations - Defunct.
Visual Anthropology; Soc. for [6436]
Visual Artists and Galleries Assn. [5861]
Visual Artists Ireland [IO], Dublin, Ireland
Visual Arts Assn; African Amer. [9409]
Visual Arts; Lesbians in the [9454]
Visual Arts Ontario [IO], Toronto, ON, Canada
Visual Commun; Soc. for the Anthropology of [★6436]
Visual Communicators; Assn. of [★1384]
Visual Educ. Dealers; Natl. Assn. of [★331]
Visual Impairments; Div. on [9145]
Visual Indicators Coun. [7053], 188 Rte. 10, Ste. 307, East Hanover, NJ 07936, (973)884-1668
Visual Instruction; Dept. of [★8551]
Visual Instruction; Natl. Acad. of [★8551]
Visual Literacy; Conf. on [★8271]
Visual Lunacy Soc. - Address unknown since 1999.
Visual Merchandise Representatives; Assn. of [2535]
Visual Merchandisers; Natl. Assn. of [1153]
Visual Packaging Assn. - Defunct.
Visual Resources Assn. [334], c/o Liz Edgar Hernandez, Membership Services Coor., 4201 Wilson Blvd., No. 110-331, Box 331, Arlington, VA 22203-1859, (202)422-4876
Visual Resources Assn. [IO], Arlington, VA, United States
Visual Sci. Librarians; Assn. of [★10341]
Visual Stud. Workshop [9950], 31 Prince St., Rochester, NY 14607, (585)442-8676
Visually Handicapped; Assn. for Educ. of the [★16833]
Visually Handicapped; Bibles for the Blind and [19511]
Visually Handicapped; Div. for the [★9145]
Visually Handicapped; Natl. Accreditation Coun. for Agencies Serving the Blind and [★16870]
Visually Handicapped; Natl. Aid to [★16874]
Visually Impaired
  ACB Radio Amateurs [21492]
  Achromatopsia Network [16820]
  Action for Blind People [IO]
  ADARA: Professionals Networking for Excellence in Ser. Delivery with Individuals who are Deaf or Hard of Hearing [14735]
  African Union of the Blind - Kenya [IO]
  Aicardi Syndrome Newsl. [14437]
  Albinism World Alliance [15242]
  All Russia Assn. of the Blind [IO]
  Amer. Acad. of Ophthalmology [15656]
  Amer. Action Fund for Blind Children and Adults [16821]
  Amer. Assn. of the Deaf-Blind [14737]
  Amer. Blind Bowling Assn. [23334]
  Amer. Blind Golf Assn. [23335]
  Amer. Blind Skiing Found. [23336]
  Amer. Bd. of Ophthalmology [15661]
  Amer. Coun. of the Blind [16822]
  Amer. Coun. of the Blind Enterprises and Services [16823]
  Amer. Coun. of Blind Govt. Employees [16824]
  Amer. Coun. of the Blind Lions [16825]
  Amer. Found. for the Blind [16826]
  Amer. Israeli Lighthouse [16827]
  Amer. Israeli Lighthouse [IO]
  Amer. Nystagmus Network [16828]
  Amer. Ophthalmological Soc. [15662]
  Amer. Orthoptic Coun. [15663]
  Amer. Printing House for the Blind [16829]
  Amer. Soc. of Contemporary Medicine, Surgery, and Ophthalmology [15666]
  Amer. Soc. of Ophthalmic Registered Nurses [15458]
  Amer. Uveitis Soc. [15668]
  Assoc. Blind [16830]
  Assoc. Services for the Blind [16831]
  Assn. for the Advancement of Blind and Retarded [16832]
  Assn. of Blind and Partially Sighted Teachers and Students [IO]
  Assn. of Blind Piano Tuners [IO]

A star before a book entry number signifies that the name is not listed separately, but is mentioned within the entry.

Assn. for Educ. and Rehabilitation of the Blind and Visually Impaired [16833]
Assn. for Macular Diseases [15669]
Assn. of Nurses Endorsing Transplantation [15670]
Assn. for Retinopathy of Prematurity and Related Diseases [15673]
Assn. of Tech. Personnel in Ophthalmology [15674]
Assn. of Univ. Professors of Ophthalmology [15675]
Assn. of Vision Educators [15677]
Better Vision Inst. [15678]
Bibles for the Blind and Visually Handicapped [19511]
BiOptic Driving Network - USA [15705]
Blind Children's Fund [16834]
Blind Citizens Australia [IO]
Blind Friends of Lesbian, Gay, Transgender and Bisexual People [12221]
Blind Info. Tech. Specialists [16835]
Blind Info. Tech. Specialists [IO]
Blind Sailing Intl. [23151]
Blind Ser. Assn. [16836]
Blinded Veterans Assn. [16837]
Braille Authority of North Am. [16838]
Braille Authority of North Am. [IO]
Braille Bible Found. [19513]
Braille Found. of Uruguay [IO]
Braille Revival League [16839]
British Cmpt. Assn. of the Blind [IO]
Canadian Coun. of the Blind [IO]
Canadian Guide Dogs for the Blind [IO]
Canadian Natl. Inst. for the Blind [IO]
Carroll Center for the Blind [16840]
Challenge Aspen at Snowmass [23342]
Christian Blind Mission [IO]
Christian Blind Mission Intl. [IO]
Christian Blind Mission Intl. [16841]
Christian Record Services [16842]
Christian Services for the Blind [16843]
Clearer Vision Ministries [13378]
Clearer Vision Ministries [IO]
Cornea Res. Found. of Am. [15105]
Coun. of Citizens With Low Vision Intl. [11934]
Coun. of Families with Visual Impairment [16844]
Croatian Assn. of the Blind [IO]
DB-Link: The Natl. Info. CH On Children Who Are Deaf-Blind [16845]
Div. on Visual Impairments [9145]
European Assn. for Vision and Eye Res. [IO]
European Blind Union [IO]
European Eye Bank Assn. [IO]
Eye Bank Assn. of Am. [14288]
Eye-Bank for Sight Restoration [14289]
Fidelco Guide Dog Found. [16846]
Finnish Fed. of the Visually Impaired [IO]
Focus [15681]
Found. Fighting Blindness [16847]
Friends-in-Art of Amer. Coun. of the Blind [9504]
Friends of Libraries for Blind and Physically Handicapped Individuals in North America [10357]
The Glaucoma Found. [15682]
Glaucoma Res. Found. [15683]
Gospel Assn. for the Blind [16848]
Guide Dog Found. for the Blind [16849]
Guide Dog Users, Inc. [16850]
Guide Dogs of Am. [16851]
Guide Dogs for the Blind [16852]
Guide Dogs for the Blind [IO]
Guide Dogs for the Blind Assn. [IO]
Guiding Eyes for the Blind [IO]
Guiding Eyes for the Blind [16853]
Helen Keller Intl. [16854]
Helen Keller Intl. [IO]
Helen Keller Intl. - Asia-Pacific Regional Off. [IO]
Helen Keller Intl. - Indonesia [IO]
Helen Keller Intl. - Morocco [IO]
Helen Keller Intl. - Nepal [IO]
Help Hospitalized Veterans [13351]
Helping Hands for the Blind [13379]
Independent Soc. of the Blind [IO]
Independent Visually Impaired Enterprisers [16855]

Intercontinental Fed. of Behavioral Optometry [15719]
Intl. Agency for the Prevention of Blindness [IO]
Intl. Assn. of Audio Info. Services [IO]
Intl. Assn. of Audio Info. Services [16856]
Intl. Assn. of Optometric Executives [15720]
Intl. Children's Anophthalmia Network [16857]
Intl. Children's Anophthalmia Network [IO]
Intl. Ocular Inflammation Soc. [IO]
Intl. Perimetric Soc. [15688]
Intl. Trachoma Initiative [16858]
International Trachoma Initiative [IO]
Interprofessional Fostering of Ophthalmic Care for Underserved Sectors [16859]
InTouch Networks [16860]
Irish Guide Dogs for the Blind [IO]
Italian Union of the Blind [IO]
JBI Intl. - Jewish Braille Inst. of Am. [IO]
JBI Intl. - Jewish Braille Inst. of Am. [16861]
Jewish Guild for the Blind [16862]
John Milton Soc. for the Blind in Canada [IO]
Joint Commn. on Allied Hea. Personnel in Ophthalmology [15692]
Keren Or [16863]
Keren Or [IO]
Latin Amer. Blind Union - Uruguay [IO]
Leader Dogs for the Blind [IO]
Leader Dogs for the Blind [16864]
Lib. Users of Am. [10370]
Lighthouse Intl. [16865]
Lighthouse Intl. [IO]
Lutheran Braille Evangelism Association [IO]
Lutheran Braille Evangelism Assn. [16866]
Lutheran Braille Workers [16867]
Lutheran Braille Workers [IO]
MAB Community Services [16868]
Macular Degeneration Found. [16869]
Natl. Accreditation Coun. for Agencies Serving the Blind and Visually Impaired [16870]
Natl. Alliance of Blind Students [16871]
Natl. Alliance for Eye and Vision Res. [16872]
Natl. Assn. for the Blind, India [IO]
Natl. Assn. of Blind Merchants [525]
Natl. Assn. for Parents of Children With Visual Impairments [16873]
Natl. Assn. of State Veterans Homes [13354]
Natl. Assn. of Vision Professionals [15693]
Natl. Assn. for Visually Handicapped [16874]
Natl. Beep Baseball Assn. [23350]
Natl. Blind Children's Soc. [IO]
Natl. Braille Assn. [16875]
Natl. Braille Press [16876]
Natl. Church Conf. of the Blind [13380]
Natl. Contact Lens Examiners [15723]
Natl. Coun. for the Blind of Ireland [IO]
Natl. Examining Bd. of Ocularists [15694]
Natl. Eye Res. Found. [15724]
Natl. Fed. of the Blind [16877]
Natl. Indus. for the Blind [16878]
Natl. Org. of Parents of Blind Children [16879]
Natl. Veterans Services Fund [13356]
New Eyes for the Needy [12533]
Oper. Eyesight Universal [IO]
Parents Active for Vision Educ. [16880]
Partially Sighted Soc. [IO]
Pilot Dogs [16881]
Prevent Blindness Am. [16882]
Prevent Blindness in Premature Babies [16883]
Protestant Guild for Human Services [16884]
Recording for the Blind and Dyslexic [16885]
Res. to Prevent Blindness [16886]
Retina Hong Kong [IO]
Retinitis Pigmentosa Intl. [IO]
Retinitis Pigmentosa Intl. [16887]
Retinoblastoma Intl. [13869]
Royal Natl. Inst. of the Blind - UK [IO]
Sea to See Proj. [13760]
Seedlings Braille Books for Children [9297]
Seeing Eye [16888]
Sight Savers Intl. - England [IO]
Singapore Assn. of the Visually Handicapped [IO]
South African Natl. Coun. for the Blind [IO]
Surgical Eye Expeditions Intl. [IO]
Surgical Eye Expeditions Intl. [16889]
Swiss Fed. of the Blind and Visually Impaired [IO]

Talking Newspaper Assn. of the United Kingdom [IO]
Unite for Sight [IO]
Unite for Sight [13381]
Veterans Educ. Proj. [13358]
Vision Australia Found. [IO]
Vision World Wide [IO]
Vision World Wide [16890]
Visually Impaired Veterans of Am. [16891]
Vitamin Angel Alliance [15571]
VOSH Intl. [12543]
World Blind Union [IO]
Xavier Soc. for the Blind [16892]
Visually Impaired Attorneys; Amer. Assn. of [5474]
Visually Impaired; Carroll Rehabilitation Center for the [★16840]
Visually Impaired Data Processors Intl. [★16835]
Visually Impaired Data Processors Intl. [★IO]
Visually Impaired Information Specialists - Defunct.
Visually Impaired; Natl. Assn. for Parents of the [★16873]
Visually Impaired Piano Tuners Intl. - Defunct.
Visually Impaired Veterans of Am. [16891], c/o Amer. Coun. of the Blind, 1155 15th St. NW, Ste. 1004, Washington, DC 20005, (202)467-5081
VITA [912], PO Box 19658, Fountain Hills, AZ 85269, (480)837-7486
Vital, Elan
  Eureka Soc. [20634]
Vital Records and Hea. Statistics; Assn. for [★6218]
Vital Records and Public Hea. Statistics; Amer. Assn. for [★6218]
Vitalise [IO], London, United Kingdom
Vitamin Angel Alliance [IO], Santa Barbara, CA, United States
Vitamin Angel Alliance [15571], 1450 Orange Grove Ave., Santa Barbara, CA 93105, (805)565-9919
Vitamin Information Bur. - Defunct.
Vitamin Soc. of Japan [IO], Kyoto, Japan
Viticulture; Amer. Soc. for Enology and [5407]
Vitiligo Found; Natl. [14211]
Vitreous Enamel Services [IO], St. Helens, United Kingdom
Vitrified China Assn. - Defunct.
Vitro Biology; Soc. for In [6598]
Viva! USA [11484], 1123 Broadway, Ste. 912, New York, NY 10010, (212)989-8482
Viva! USA [IO], New York, NY, United States
Vivekananda Center; Ramakrishna - [20610]
Vivien Leigh Soc. Intl. - Address unknown since 2006.
Vivisection, Anti-
  Irish Anti-Vivisection Soc. [IO]
  Soc. Against Vivisection [11458]
Vivisection Investigation League [11474]
Vivisection; Soc. Against [11458]
Vivisection Soc; Amer. Anti- [11345]
Vivisection Soc; Natl. Anti- [11432]
Vivisection Soc. of New York; Anti- [★11474]
Vivit [6807], PO Box 18510, Boulder, CO 80308, (646)414-9895
Vizsla
  Vizsla Club of Am. [22378]
Vizsla Club of Am. [22378], c/o Shella A. Fuhrman, 185 Golden Ln., Friendsville, TN 37737-3141, (865)995-1385
Vizsla Club of France [IO], Walincourt, France
Vlaamse Reumaliga Belgium [IO], Mechelen, Belgium
Vlaamse Squash Federatie [★IO]
Vlaamse Vereniging voor Spina Bifida en Hydro-cephalus vzw [IO], Oosterzele, Belgium
Vlaamse Vereniging voor Watersport [★IO]
Vlaamse Vereinigung voor Ontwikkelings Samen-werking [★IO]
Vladimir Nabokov Soc. [★IO]
Vladimir Nabokov Soc. [★9667]
VMM [★IO]
VNFTP [★IO]
VNO-NCW Confed. of Netherlands Indus. and Employers [IO], The Hague, Netherlands
VOCAL [★13365]
Vocal Ensembles; Assn. of Professional [★10577]
Vocal Ensembles; Chorus Am.: Assn. of Professional [★10577]

Reference to "IO" in place of a book number signifies that the association may be found in the 45th edition of International Organizations.

Vocal Institute; Summer [★8900]
Vocal Institute; Summer [★IO]
VOCAL Orgs; Natl. Assn. of State [13365]
Vocation Conf; Natl. Religious [19692]
Vocation Conf; Natl. Sisters [★19692]
Vocation Directors; Natl. Conf. of Diocesan [19682]
Vocation Directors; Natl. Conf. of Religious [★19692]
Vocation; Sales Exchange for Refugee Rehabilitation and [3846]
Vocational Agricultural Teachers Assn; Natl. [★7938]
Vocational Agriculture; Amer. Assn. for Agricultural Engg. and [★9298]
Vocational Assn; Amer. [★9300]
Vocational Assn. of the Middle West [★9300]
Vocational Counseling; Amer. Bd. on Professional Standards in [★8169]
Vocational Education
Amer. Assn. for Vocational Instructional Materials [9298]
Amer. Bd. of Vocational Experts [9299]
Amer. Rescue Team Intl. [12287]
Arctic Region Found. of Vocational Training [IO]
ASEAN Network for Women in Skills Training [IO]
Asian and Pacific Skill Development Programme [IO]
Assn. for Career and Tech. Educ. [9300]
Assn. for Career and Tech. Educ. Res. [9301]
Bus. Professionals of Am. [9302]
Canadian Vocational Assn. [IO]
Career Coll. Assn. [9303]
Cedefop - European Centre for the Development of Vocational Training [IO]
Center on Educ. and Training for Employment [9304]
European Training Found. [IO]
Inter-American Res. and Documentation Centre on Vocational Training [IO]
Intl. Assn. of Jewish Vocational Services [IO]
Intl. Assn. of Jewish Vocational Services [9305]
Intl. Vocational Educ. and Training Assn. [9306]
International Vocational Education and Training Association [IO]
Iota Lambda Sigma [24724]
Irish Vocational Educ. Assn. [IO]
Israel Humanitarian Found. [12458]
MS-Training Center for Development Co-operation [IO]
Natl. Assn. of Agricultural Educators [7938]
Natl. Assn. of State Directors of Vocational Tech. Educ. Consortium [9307]
Natl. Assn. of Supervisors of Agricultural Educ. [7939]
Natl. Tech. Honor Soc. [24725]
Natl. Vocational Technical Education Found. [9308]
ORT Am. [12480]
Scottish Qualifications Authority [IO]
Skillshare Botswana [IO]
Skillshare Intl. [IO]
SkillsUSA [8546]
Swiss Conf. of Directors of Professional and Indus. Schools [IO]
Training and Productivity Authority of Fiji [IO]
Underprivileged Students of Anthropological Vocations [9079]
Univ. Economic Development Assn. [9309]
Vocational Instructional Materials Sect. [8573]
Vocational Educ; Center for [★9304]
Vocational Educ; Natl. Center for Res. in [★9304]
Vocational Educ; Natl. Soc. for [★9300]
Vocational Educ. Res. Assn; Amer. [★9301]
Vocational Educ. and Training Assn; Intl. [9306]
Vocational Educational Found; Natl. [★9308]
Vocational Educational Professional Development Found; Natl. [★9308]
Vocational Evaluation and Career Assessment Professionals [16337], PO Box 2958, Salina, KS 67402-2958, (785)404-2105
Vocational Evaluation and Career Assessment Professionals [IO], Salina, KS, United States
Vocational Evaluation and Work Adjustment Assn. [★IO]
Vocational Evaluation and Work Adjustment Assn. [★16337]

Vocational Experts; Amer. Bd. of [9299]
Vocational Found. Bur. of the Assn. for the Prevention of Crime [★12103]
Vocational Found., Inc. [12103], 52 Broadway, 6th Fl., New York, NY 10004, (212)823-1001
Vocational Guidance Assn; Natl. [★12090]
Vocational Guidance and Workshop Center [★24603]
Vocational Home Economics; Natl. Assn. of State Supervisors of [★8514]
Vocational Indus. Clubs of Am. [★8546]
Vocational Instructional Materials Sect. [8573], c/o Dr. Dana Tannehill, Dir., Univ. of Missouri, Instructional Materials Lab., 1400 Rock Quarry Center, Columbia, MO 65211, (573)882-2883
Vocational Rehabilitation Clinic; Social/ [16231]
Vocational Rehabilitation; Coun. of State Administrators of [16320]
Vocational Services; Natl. Assn. of Jewish [★9305]
Vocational Tech. Educ. Consortium; Natl. Assn. of State Directors of [9307]
Vocational Technical Education Found; Natl. [9308]
Vocational-Technical Honor Soc; Natl. [★24725]
Vocations; Bishops' Comm. on [19586]
Vocations for Social Change - Defunct.
Vocations; Underprivileged Students of Anthropological [9079]
Vodka Trade Assn. [★IO]
Voetslaan Suid-Afrika [★IO]
VOICE [IO], Bombay, India
Voice of Amer. Dissidents - Defunct.
Voice for Animals [11475], PO Box 120095, San Antonio, TX 78212, (210)737-3138
Voice of China and Asia Missionary Soc. [20409], PO Box 15, Pasadena, CA 91102, (626)441-0640
Voice of China and Asia Missionary Soc. [IO], Pasadena, CA, United States
Voice Found. [16457], 1721 Pine St., Philadelphia, PA 19103, (215)735-7999
Voice of Healing [★20314]
Voice of Healing [★IO]
Voice Identification; Intl. Assn. of [★5763]
Voice Input/Output Soc; Applied [6720]
Voice of Liberty Assn. - Defunct.
Voice for Life [IO], Wellington, New Zealand
Voice of the Listener [★IO]
Voice of the Listener and Viewer [IO], Gravesend, United Kingdom
Voice of the Martyrs [20410], PO Box 443, Bartlesville, OK 74005, (918)337-8015
Voice Phenomena; Amer. Assn. - Electronic [★7469]
Voice Phenomena; Amer. Assn. of Electronic [7469]
Voice of Reason [★17090]
Voice Rehabilitation Inst. [★11953]
Voice Rehabilitation Inst. [★IO]
Voice of the Retarded [12583], 5005 Newport Dr., Ste. 108, Rolling Meadows, IL 60008, (847)253-6020
Voice and Speech; Natl. Center for [16451]
Voice of Tangier [★20403]
Voice of Tangier [★IO]
Voice and Vision Intl. - Address unknown since 2007.
Voice of Women for Guatamala - Defunct.
VoiceCare Network [9163], c/o Dept. of Music, St. John's Univ., Collegeville, MN 56321, (320)363-3374
VOICES in Action [13086], 8041 Hosbrook Rd., Ste. 236, Cincinnati, OH 45236, (513)745-9555
VOICES in Action [IO], Cincinnati, OH, United States
Voices for America's Children [11662], 1000 Vermont Ave. NW, Ste. 700, Washington, DC 20005, (202)289-0777
VOICES Assn. [13211], 11132 S Freeman Ave., Ste. C, Inglewood, CA 90304, (310)910-3555
Voices of September 11th [18737], 93 Cherry St., New Canaan, CT 06840, (203)966-3911
Voices in the Wilderness [18253], 1460 W Carmen Ave., Chicago, IL 60640, (773)784-8065
Voices in the Wilderness [IO], Chicago, IL, United States
Voicespondence Club - Defunct.
Voix des Femmes Canadiennes pour la Paix [★IO]
Volcanological Soc. of Japan [IO], Tokyo, Japan
Volcanology
Pele Defense Fund [4440]

Volcanology and Chemistry of the Earth's Interior; Intl. Assn. of [IO]
Volks-wagen Amer. Dealers Assn. [★IO]
Volks-wagen Amer. Dealers Assn. [★404]
Volkssport Assn; Amer. [23803]
Volkswagen Club of Am. [21815], PO Box 154, North Aurora, IL 60542, (630)896-2803
Volkswagen Club of Am; Vintage [21814]
Volkswagen Convertible Owners of America - Defunct.
Volkswagen Split Window Club of America - Address unknown since 1994.
Volkswagen Toy Collectors of America - Defunct.
Volleyball
Aer Lingus Volleyball Club [IO]
Amer. Volleyball Coaches Assn. [23969]
Assn. of Volleyball Professionals [24191]
Bulgarian Volleyball Fed. [IO]
Calgary Beach Volleyball Assn. [IO]
Intl. Volleyball Fed. - Switzerland [IO]
North Amer. Sports Fed. [23065]
Professional Assn. of Volleyball Officials [23875]
Scottish Volleyball Assn. [IO]
Swiss Volleyball Fed. [IO]
U.S. Volleyball Association/USA Volleyball [23970]
Volleyball Assn. of Ireland [IO]
Volleyball Assn. of Ireland [IO], Dublin, Ireland
Volleyball Officials; Professional Assn. of [23875]
Volleyball Professionals; Assn. of [24191]
Volontariato Internazionale per lo Sviluppo [★IO]
Volta Speech Assn. for the Deaf [★IO]
Volta Speech Assn. for the Deaf [★14736]
Voltaire Soc. - Address unknown since 1995.
Volume Footwear Retailers of Am. [★1597]
Volume Footwear Retailers Assn. [★1597]
Voluntarios de las Naciones Unidas [★IO]
Voluntarism
ACDI/VOCA [4481]
Air Charity Network [14312]
Alliance of European Voluntary Ser. Organizations [IO]
Amer. Assn. for Museum Volunteers [10489]
Amer. Assn. of State Ser. Commissions [6189]
Amer. Inst. for Public Ser. [13150]
Amer. Jewish Soc. for Ser. [12465]
Amer. Soc. of Directors of Volunteer Services [13382]
AmeriCorps VISTA [13383]
Amigos de las Americas [13384]
Amigos de las Americas [IO]
Amizade Global Service-Learning and Volunteer Programs [IO]
Amizade Global Service-Learning and Volunteer Programs [13385]
Assn. of Air Medical Services [14314]
Assn. for Intl. Medical Study [12834]
Assn. of Junior Leagues Intl. [13386]
Assn. of Junior Leagues Intl. [IO]
Association for Research on Nonprofit Organizations and Voluntary Action [IO]
Assn. for Res. on Nonprofit Organizations and Voluntary Action [13387]
Assn. for Res. in the Voluntary and Community Sector [IO]
Assn. of Voluntary Ser. Organisations [IO]
Attend [IO]
Awaiting Angels [IO]
Better World Chorus [12617]
Big Bros. Big Sisters of Am. [11676]
Brethren Volunteer Ser. [13388]
Brethren Volunteer Ser. [IO]
Bridges to Community [13389]
Brother's Brother Found. [12837]
Bus. Volunteers Unlimited [13390]
Catholic Medical Mission Bd. [12515]
Catholic Network of Volunteer Ser. [19602]
Challenges Worldwide [IO]
Child Relief and You Am. [11569]
Christian Children's Fund [11688]
Community Built Assn. [11770]
Cooperative Off. for Voluntary Organizations [18792]
Coun. of Religious Volunteer Agencies [13391]
Earthwise Living Found. New Zealand [IO]
Ecuador Volunteer [IO]

A star before a book entry number signifies that the name is not listed separately, but is mentioned within the entry.

Educational Concerns for Hunger Org. [12389]
European Coun. for Non-Profit Organisations [IO]
Flying Doctors of Am. [12523]
Global Ser. Corps [13392]
Global Ser. Corps [IO]
Globe Aware [IO]
Globe Aware [13393]
Good Shepherd Volunteers [13394]
Gp. of Volunteers of Italian Switzerland [IO]
Holiday Proj. [13395]
Independent Sector [12725]
Intl. Assn. of Building Companions [IO]
Intl. Assn. of Charities [IO]
Intl. Assn. for Volunteer Effort [IO]
Intl. Assn. for Volunteer Effort [13396]
Intl. Coun. of Voluntary Agencies [IO]
Intl. Medical Volunteers Assn. [15075]
Intl. Voluntary Ser. [IO]
Intl. Volunteer Prog. [IO]
Intl. Volunteer Prog. [13397]
Intl. Volunteer Programs Assn. [13398]
Intl. Volunteer Programs Assn. [IO]
Intl. Volunteers for Development [IO]
Intl. Workcamp Org. [IO]
Join Hands Day [17203]
Kids Korps USA [13399]
Minuteman Civil Defense Corps [17077]
Mission Doctors Assn. [12532]
Mission to Haiti [12267]
Natl. Assn. of Volunteer Programs in Local Govt.
  [6352]
Natl. Center for Charitable Statistics [12731]
Natl. Coalition of Concerned Legal Professionals
  [12501]
Natl. Comm. for Responsive Philanthropy [12732]
Natl. Coun. for Voluntary Organisations [IO]
Natl. Human Services Assembly [13400]
Natl. Relief Network [12873]
Natl. Voluntary Organizations Active in Disaster
  [12874]
Pillar Voluntary Sector Network [IO]
Points of Light Found. [13401]
Preservation Volunteers [10059]
Pro Players Assn. [13402]
Proj. Trust [IO]
Retired and Senior Volunteer Prog. [13403]
The Revitalization Corps [12782]
Sanctuary Workers and Volunteers Assn. [11455]
SCI - Intl. Voluntary Ser. [13404]
SCI - Intl. Voluntary Ser. [IO]
Senior Companion Prog. [13405]
Senior Experten Ser. [IO]
Ser. Civil Intl., Austrian Br. [IO]
Ser. for Peace [18246]
Student Conservation Assn. [4455]
TECH CORPS [13406]
U.S. Dept. of Agriculture - Forest Ser. Volunteers
  Prog. [4699]
Urbanturban [IO]
Visionaries In Action - Across Africa [IO]
Visions in Action [12447]
VOICES Assn. [13211]
Voluntary Action Network India [IO]
Voluntary Ser. Intl. [IO]
Voluntary Ser. Overseas - England [IO]
Voluntary Workcamps Assn. of Uganda [IO]
Volunteer Canada [IO]
Volunteer Committees of Art Museums of Canada
  and the U.S. [10516]
Volunteer Development - Scotland [IO]
Volunteer Gp. Khoop Khun Maak [IO]
Volunteer Missionary Movement - U.S. Off.
  [19736]
Volunteer Ser. Abroad - New Zealand [IO]
Volunteer Ser. Abroad - Vietnam [IO]
VolunteerMatch [18793]
Volunteers in Asia [13407]
Volunteers in Asia [IO]
Volunteers in Hea. Care [14665]
Volunteers in Overseas Cooperative Assistance -
  USA [13408]
Volunteers in Overseas Cooperative Assistance -
  USA [IO]
We Care Am. [13210]
Wilderness Volunteers [22774]

Winant and Clayton Volunteers [13409]
Winant and Clayton Volunteers [IO]
WorldTeach [8315]
Youth Voluntary Ser. of Italy [IO]
Voluntarism; National Acad. for [★12205]
Voluntary Action Network India [IO], New Delhi, India
Voluntary Action Scholars; Assn. of [★13387]
Voluntary Adviser Corps - Defunct.
Voluntary Census Comm. - Address unknown since
  1999.
Voluntary Cooperation Movement [16981], c/o Ed
  Stamm, PO Box 1402, Lawrence, KS 66044-8402
Voluntary Cooperation Movement [IO], Lawrence,
  KS, United States
Voluntary Effort to Contain Health Care Costs -
  Defunct.
Voluntary Eugenics and Surrogate Parentage Euro-
  Group - Address unknown since 2003.
Voluntary Euthanasia Soc. [★IO]
Voluntary Euthanasia Soc. of New Zealand [IO],
  Auckland, New Zealand
Voluntary Euthanasia Soc. of Scotland [★IO]
Voluntary Euthanasia Soc. of Victoria [★IO]
Voluntary Fund for the United Nations Decade for
  Women [★IO]
Voluntary Fund for the United Nations Decade for
  Women [★17571]
Voluntary Hospitals of Am. [★14901]
Voluntary Organisations in Cooperation in Emergen-
  cies [IO], Brussels, Belgium
Voluntary Organizations Active in Disaster; Natl.
  [12874]
Voluntary Organizations; Coalition of Natl. [★12725]
Voluntary Protection Programs Participants' Assn.
  [15634], 7600-E Leesburg Pike, Ste. 440, Falls
  Church, VA 22043, (703)761-1146
Voluntary Ser. and Action; Commn. on [★13391]
Voluntary Ser; Intl. [★13404]
Voluntary Ser. Intl. [IO], Dublin, Ireland
Voluntary Ser; Mennonite [20251]
Voluntary Ser. Overseas - England [IO], London,
  United Kingdom
Voluntary Surgical Contraception; Assn. for
  [★12180]
Voluntary Workcamps Assn. of Uganda [IO], Kam-
  pala, Uganda
The Voluntaryists [18018], PO Box 275-D, Gramling,
  SC 29348, (864)472-2750
Volunteer Accounting Services; CH for [19]
Volunteer Agencies; Coun. of Religious [13391]
Volunteer Americans; Coun. of [18309]
Volunteer Assn; Natl. Archives and Record Ser.
  [★9402]
Volunteer Assn; Natl. Archives and Records Admin.
  [9402]
Volunteer Assn; Parents [★12578]
Volunteer Benevoles [★IO]
Volunteer Bureaus; Assn. of [★13401]
Volunteer Canada [IO], Ottawa, ON, Canada
Volunteer Center; Natl. [★13401]
Volunteer; Christian Bros. [★20352]
Volunteer Committees of Art Museums of Canada
  and the U.S. [10516], c/o Nancy Rosenbloom,
  Pres., 400 Loring Ave., Los Angeles, CA 90024
Volunteer Corps; Lutheran [20228]
Volunteer Corps: Northwest; Jesuit [19644]
Volunteer Development - Scotland [IO], Stirling,
  United Kingdom
Volunteer Fire Coun; Natl. [5723]
Volunteer Firefighters' Associations; Federation of
  [★5723]
Volunteer Gp. Khoop Khun Maak [IO], Chiba, Japan
Volunteer Info., Tech. Assistance, and Leadership;
  Project [★13580]
Volunteer Lawyers for the Arts [6036], 1 E 53rd St.,
  6th Fl., New York, NY 10022, (212)319-2787
Volunteer Ministries; Intl. Liaison, U.S. Catholic
  Coordinating Center for Lay [★19602]
Volunteer Missionary Movement - Europe [IO], Dub-
  lin, Ireland
Volunteer Missionary Movement - U.S. Off. [19736],
  5980 W Loomis Rd., Greendale, WI 53129-1824,
  (414)423-8660
Volunteer Optometric Services to Humanity/
  International [★12543]

Volunteer Optometric Services to Humanity/
  International [★IO]
Volunteer Prison League - Defunct.
Volunteer Prog. of the Sisters, Servants of the Im-
  maculate Heart of Mary; IHM [20346]
Volunteer Ser. Abroad - New Zealand [IO], Welling-
  ton, New Zealand
Volunteer Ser. Abroad - Vietnam [IO], Wellington,
  New Zealand
Volunteer Ser; Catholic Network of [19602]
Volunteer Ser; Intl. Liaison for [★19602]
Volunteer Ser. Overseas - United Kingdom [IO],
  London, United Kingdom
Volunteer Services; Amer. Soc. of Directors of
  [13382]
Volunteer Services for the Blind [★16831]
Volunteer Services Commn. of B'Nai Birth Intl; Com-
  munity [★11766]
Volunteer Services; Goodwill Indus. [11950]
Volunteer Services of the Sisters, Servants of the
  Immaculate Heart of Mary; We Care - IHM
  [★20346]
Volunteer Soc. Nepal [IO], Kathmandu, Nepal
Volunteer Trustees of Not-for-Profit Hospitals
  [14902], 818 18th St. NW, Ste. 410, Washington,
  DC 20006, (202)659-0338
Volunteering Ecuador Org. [IO], Quito, Ecuador
Volunteering Ireland [IO], Dublin, Ireland
Volunteering New Zealand [IO], Wellington, New
  Zealand
Volunteerism; Natl. Info. Center on [★13401]
VolunteerMatch [18793], 717 California St., 2nd Fl.,
  San Francisco, CA 94108, (415)241-6868
Volunteers in Action - Defunct.
Volunteers of Am. [13192], 1660 Duke St.,
  Alexandria, VA 22314, (703)341-5000
Volunteers of Am; Literacy [★8797]
Volunteers; Amer. Assn. for Museum [10489]
Volunteers in Asia [13407], 965 Mission St., Ste.
  751, San Francisco, CA 94103, (415)904-8033
Volunteers in Asia [IO], San Francisco, CA, United
  States
Volunteers in Christ's Ser; Roving [23017]
Volunteers' Circle of the Natl. Gallery of Canada
  [IO], Ottawa, ON, Canada
Volunteers in Cooperative Assistance; Agricultural
  Cooperative Development Intl. and [★4481]
Volunteers in Hea. Care [14665], 111 Brewster St.,
  Pawtucket, RI 02860, (401)729-3284
Volunteers for Intl. Development [★18239]
Volunteers for Intl. Development [★IO]
Volunteers for Intl. Tech. Assistance [★12448]
Volunteers and Interns for Balinese Educ. Found.
  [IO], Bali, Indonesia
Volunteers for Israel [IO], New York, NY, United
  States
Volunteers for Israel [17942], 330 W 42nd St., Ste.
  1618, New York, NY 10036, (212)643-4848
Volunteers; Lasallian [20352]
Volunteers and Lay Missionaries; Claretian [19612]
Volunteers; League of Winant [★13409]
Volunteers; Lesbian, Gay and Bisexual Returned
  Peace Corps [★18260]
Volunteers; Literacy [★8797]
Volunteers in Mission - Congregation of the Sisters
  of Charity of the Incarnate Word; CCVI [★19607]
Volunteers in Mission (U.S. Catholic Network of Lay
  Mission Programs); Intl. Liaison of Lay [★19602]
Volunteers in Overseas Assistance [★4481]
Volunteers in Overseas Assistance [★IO]
Volunteers in Overseas Cooperative Assistance -
  USA [IO], Washington, DC, United States
Volunteers in Overseas Cooperative Assistance -
  USA [13408], 50 F St. NW, Ste. 1075,
  Washington, DC 20001, (202)638-4661
Volunteers for Peace [17919], 1034 Tiffany Rd., Bel-
  mont, VT 05730, (802)259-2759
Volunteers for Peace [IO], Belmont, VT, United
  States
Volunteers for Peaceful Change - Address unknown
  since 1987.
Volunteers in Prevention, Probation, Prisons
  [11896], Grand Park Ctre., 28 W Adams, Ste.
  1310, Detroit, MI 48226, (313)964-1110
Volunteers for Prison Inmates [IO], Kumba, Cam-
  eroon

Reference to "IO" in place of a book number signifies that the association may be found in the 45th edition of International Organizations.

Volunteers in Probation [★11896]
Volunteers in Ser. to Am. [★13383]
Volunteers in Service to India's Oppressed and Neglected - Address unknown since 2001.
Volunteers for TAU - Defunct.
Volunteers in Tech. Assistance [12448], 1825 Connecticut Ave. NW, Ste. 630, Washington, DC 20009, (202)293-4600
Volunteers; U.S. Assn. of Museum [★10489]
Volunteers for Vision - Defunct.
Volunteers; World Tech. [13196]
Volvo Car Club - Defunct.
Volvo Club of Am. [21816], Box 16, Afton, NY 13730, (607)639-2279
Volvo Sports America 1800 Registry - Defunct.
Vomiting Syndrome Assn; Cyclic [★14415]
Von Braun Astronomical Soc. [6511], PO Box 1142, Huntsville, AL 35807, (256)539-0316
Von Bulow Natl. Victim Advocacy Center; Sunny [★13366]
VON Coalition [2321], c/o Beverly Orr, Exec. Admin., 1718 M St. NW, PMB No. 336, Washington, DC 20036, (202)387-5282
von Gierke's Disease
 Assn. for Glycogen Storage Disease [15244]
Von Hippel-Lindau Family Alliance [★14489]
von Hohnheim, Theophrastus
 League of Conservation Voters [18312]
VooDoo Child [★24921]
Voorhees Assn; Van [21075]
Voorlichtingsbureau Vlees [★IO]
VOSH Intl. [IO], Lake Mary, FL, United States
VOSH Intl. [12543], c/o Charles H. Covington, Sr., Sec.-Treas., 111 Linda Ln., Lake Mary, FL 32746-4208, (407)328-5825
Vote America Found. - Address unknown since 1999.
Vote; Oper. Big [18362]
Vote!; Proj. [18364]
Vote Rap; Operation Big [★18362]
Voter Education Project - Address unknown since 2002.
Voter Participation; Black Women's Roundtable on [18346]
Voter Participation; Natl. Coalition on Black [★18358]
Voter Registration
 Coun. for a Community of Democracies [5661]
 Honest Ballot Assn. [17486]
 Mobile Voter [18032]
 Natl. Voice [17076]
 Open Voting Consortium [17489]
 Special Interest Gp. on Mgt. Info. Systems [6824]
Voter Registration Educ. Proj; Southwest [18367]
Voter Registration; Natl. Student Campaign for [18360]
Voter Rights March [17491], PO Box 3275, New York, NY 10167
Voters of Am; United Hellenic [19095]
Voters; Amer. Assn. of Women [★18419]
Voters for Choice [★18521]
Voters for Choice/Friends of Family Planning [18521]
Voters Educ. Fund; League of Women [18459]
Voters Educ. Proj; League of Rural [★16955]
Voters of Illinois; United Hellenic [★19095]
Voters; League of Conservation [18312]
Voters; League of Private Property [17985]
Voters; Natl. League of Women [★18355]
Voters Telecomm Watch - Defunct.
Voters Telecommunication Watch Center for Internet Education - Address unknown since 2006.
Voters of the U.S; League of Women [18355]
VoterWatch [5600], 695 Arkansas St., San Francisco, CA 94107
Votes Natl. Comm. - Address unknown since 1995.
Voting Consortium; Open [17489]
Voting and Democracy; Center for [18348]
Voting Integrity Project - Address unknown since 2006.
Voting Rights Service Corp. - Defunct.
Voyager Mission Soc. - Defunct.
Voyageur Coun; North Amer. [10055]
Voyaging Soc; Polynesian [22775]
The VP Found. [★15620]

The VP Found. [★IO]
VPP: Assn. of Intellectual Property Rights [IO], Duisburg, Germany
Vrouwen Overleg Komitee [IO], Brussels, Belgium
Vrouwen in de Volkspartij voor Vrijheid en Democratie [IO], The Hague, Netherlands
VSA arts [IO], Washington, DC, United States
VSA arts [11993], 818 Connecticut Ave. NW, Ste. 600, Washington, DC 20006, (202)628-2800
VSA arts of Albania [IO], Tirana, Albania
VSA arts of Argentina [IO], Buenos Aires, Argentina
VSA arts of Brazil [IO], Rio de Janeiro, Brazil
VSA arts of Cyprus [IO], Nicosia, Cyprus
Vserossiiskoe Obschestvo Slepykh [★IO]
VUFO-NGO Rsrc. Centre [IO], Hanoi, Vietnam
Vultee Owners and Pilots Assn. - Address unknown since 1999.
Vulture Study Group [★IO]
Vulval Pain Soc. [IO], Nottingham, United Kingdom
Vulvar Pain Foundation [IO], Graham, NC, United States
Vulvar Pain Found. [15620], 203 1/2 N Main St., Ste. 203, Graham, NC 27253, (336)226-0704
Vulvodynia Assn; Natl. [16905]
Vuokralaisten Keskusliito [★IO]
VW-Audi Frontdriver - Defunct.
VXIbus Consortium [7793], c/o Bob Helsel, Exec. Dir., PO Box 1016, Niwot, CO 80544-1016, (303)652-2585

W

W. E. Upjohn Inst. for Community Res. [★12104]
W. E. Upjohn Inst. for Employment Res. [12104], 300 S Westnedge Ave., Kalamazoo, MI 49007-4686, (269)343-5541
W. K. Lypynsky East European Res. Inst. - Address unknown since 2006.
W. Maurice Young Centre for Applied Ethics [IO], Vancouver, BC, Canada
W. T. Bandy Center for Baudelaire and Modern French Stud. [9720], c/o Central Lib., Vanderbilt Univ., Jean and Alexander Heard Lib., Box 6325, Sta. B, Nashville, TN 37235, (615)343-0372
W. T. Bandy Center for Baudelaire Stud. [★9720]
WA Horse Trekkers Club [IO], Perth, Australia
WAAG Agility Dog Club [IO], Wongawallan, Australia
Wabash, Frisco and Pacific Assn. [10927], c/o Mr. Michael Lorance, Treas., 17238 Hilltop Ridge Dr., Eureka, MO 63025, (636)587-3538
WAC Theatre Unlimited [★IO]
WACS - Address unknown since 2001.
Wade Hayes Fan Network [24990], PO Box 128546, Nashville, TN 37212
Wage and Salary Assn; Ohio [★1283]
Wages for Housework Campaign [★13428]
Wages for Housework Campaign [★IO]
Wages for Housework; Intl. Black Women for [18811]
Wages and Not Tips - Address unknown since 1999.
Wagner Soc. of America - Address unknown since 1990.
Wagner Soc. of New York [10722], PO Box 230949, Ansonia Sta., New York, NY 10023-0949, (212)749-4561
Wagner's Official Fan Club; Lindsay [24754]
WAGRO Res. Foundation [★20191]
Wagyu Assn; Amer. [4250]
Wahana Lingkungan Hidup Indonesia [★IO]
WAIF - Address unknown since 2008.
Waifs of War Found. [IO], Ho Chi Minh City, Vietnam
Waikato Head Injury Soc. [IO], Hamilton, New Zealand
Wain Fan Club; Malcolm [24756]
Wainwright House [20588], 260 Stuyvesant Ave., Rye, NY 10580-3115, (914)967-6080
Wainwright House Center for Development of Human Potential [★20588]
Wainwright Veterans Assn; USS [21329]
Waitakere Junior Chamber [★IO]
Waiters Assn. [1967], c/o Vivienne J. Wildes, PhD, Founder, 1100 W Beaver Ave., State College, PA 16801, (814)238-3447
Wakeboarding New Zealand [IO], Auckland, New Zealand

Waksman Found. for Microbiology [6605], c/o Amy Cheng Vollmer, Pres., Dept. of Biology, Swarthmore Coll., 500 Coll. Ave., Swarthmore, PA 19081-1390, (610)328-8044
Wal-Mart Alliance for Reform Now [24107], 1344 W Cass St., Ste. A, Tampa, FL 33606, (813)258-4030
Wal-Mart Workers of Am. [24108], 1775 K St. NW, Ste. 320, Washington, DC 20006, (866)587-2299
Wal-Mart Workers Assn. [24109], 1344 W Cass St., Ste. A, Tampa, FL 33606, (813)258-4030
Walden Forever Wild - Address unknown since 2003.
Walden Pond Advisory Comm. [4464]
Walden Pond Restoration Comm. [★4464]
Walden Woods Proj. [10076], 44 Baker Farm Rd., Lincoln, MA 01773-3004, (781)259-4700
Waldensian
 Amer. Waldensian Soc. [20612]
Waldensian Aid Soc; Amer. [★20612]
Waldorf Early Childhood Assn. of North Am. [9008], 285 Hungry Hollow Rd., Chestnut Ridge, NY 10977, (845)352-1690
Waldorf Kindergarten Assn. of North Am. [★9008]
Waldrep Intl. Spinal Cord Res. Found; Kent [★16463]
Waldrep Natl. Paralysis Found; Kent [16467]
Wales Craft Coun. [IO], Welshpool, United Kingdom
Wales North Am. Bus. Chamber [24306], c/o Chris Jones, Pres., 69 Closter Rd., Palisades, NY 10964, (845)398-0619
Wales Young Farmers' Clubs [IO], Builth Wells, United Kingdom
Wales Young Farmers' Clubs - Carmarthenshire Fed. [IO], Carmarthen, United Kingdom
Wales Young Farmers' Clubs - Clwyd Fed. [IO], Ruthin, United Kingdom
Wales Young Farmers' Clubs - Eryri Fed. [IO], Caernarfon, United Kingdom
Wales Young Farmers' Clubs - Glamorgan Fed. [IO], Pencoed, United Kingdom
Wales Young Farmers' Clubs - Gwent Fed. [IO], Usk, United Kingdom
Wales Young Farmers' Clubs - Meirionnydd Fed. [IO], Dolgellau, United Kingdom
Wales Young Farmers' Clubs - Montgomery Fed. [IO], Newtown, United Kingdom
Wales Young Farmers' Clubs - Pembrokeshire Fed. [IO], Haverfordwest, United Kingdom
Wales Young Farmers' Clubs - Radnor Fed. [IO], Llandrindod Wells, United Kingdom
Wales Young Farmers' Clubs - Ynys Mon Fed. [IO], Caergybi, United Kingdom
WALHI [IO], Jakarta, Indonesia
Walk Across Am. and Europe [★17813]
Walkaloosa Horse Assn. [4965], PO Box 3170, Carefree, AZ 85377, (480)488-7169
Walkaloosa Horse Assn. [IO], Carefree, AZ, United States
Walker Breeders and Fanciers Assn; Treeing [22368]
Walker Fan Club; Jerry Jeff [24919]
Walking
 Am. on the Move Found. [14537]
 Amer. Nordic Walking Assn. [15960]
 Amer. Volkssport Assn. [23803]
 Assn. of Pedestrian and Bicycle Professionals [18747]
 Friends of Peace Pilgrim [11116]
 Long Distance Walkers Assn. [IO]
 Natl. Org. of I Walkers [23971]
 Thunderhead Alliance [18751]
Walking Assn. - Defunct.
Walking Horse Assn; Natl. [4928]
Walking Horse Breeders' and Exhibitors' Assn; Tennessee [4959]
Walking Horse Owners' Assn. [4966], PO Box 4007, Murfreesboro, TN 37129, (615)494-8822
Walking Horse Trainers Assn. [4967], PO Box 61, Shelbyville, TN 37162, (931)684-5866
Walking Horse Trainers Assn. [★4967]
Walking Impaired Golfers of Am. - Address unknown since 2007.
Walking; Natl. Center for Bicycling and [23315]
Walking Pony Assn; Amer. [4850]
Walkways Center - Defunct.

A star before a book entry number signifies that the name is not listed separately, but is mentioned within the entry.

Wall and Ceiling Indus; Found. of the [624]
Wall Street Action - Defunct.
Wall Street Planning Group - Address unknown since 1999.
Wallace Genetic Found. [4117], 4910 Massachusetts Ave. NW, Ste. 221, Washington, DC 20016, (202)966-2932
Wallace Nutting Collectors Club - Defunct.
Wallace-Reader's Digest Funds [12055], 5 Penn Plz., 7th Fl., New York, NY 10001, (212)251-9700
Wallcovering Dealers Assn; Southern Paint and [★2274]
Wallcovering Distributors Assn. [★2278]
Wallcovering Mfrs. Assn. [★2278]
Wallcoverings Assn. [2278], 401 N Michigan Ave., Ste. 2200, Chicago, IL 60611, (312)644-6610
Wallenberg Comm. of the U.S; Raoul [17449]
Wallenberg Working Group; Raoul [★17449]
Walleye Anglers Assn. of America - Defunct.
Wallpaper Assn. of Am; Paint and [★2274]
Wallpaper Distributors of Am; Retail Paint and [★2274]
Wallpaper Wholesalers Assn. [★2278]
Wallpaper Wholesalers Assn; Natl. [★2278]
Wally Byam Caravan Club Intl. [22967], PO Box 612, Jackson Center, OH 45334, (937)596-5211
Walmsley Soc. [IO], Eastbourne, United Kingdom
Walnut Assn; Fine Hardwoods Amer. [★1635]
Walnut Coun. [5065], c/o Wright Forestry Center, 1011 N 725 W, West Lafayette, IN 47906-9431, (765)583-3501
Walnut Export Sales Company - Defunct.
Walnut Growers; Diamond [5055]
Walnut Manufacturers Assn; Amer. [1635]
Walnut Marketing Bd. [5066], 101 Parkshore Dr., Ste. 250, Folsom, CA 95630, (916)932-7070
Walpole Soc. [IO], London, United Kingdom
Walsh Family Assn. - Defunct.
Walt Disney Collectors Soc. [22129], PO Box 6220, Burbank, CA 91510-6220, (800)932-5749
Walt Kelly Soc; Pogo Fan Club and [24794]
Walt Whitman Birthplace Assn. [9721], 246 Old Walt Whitman Rd., Huntington Station, NY 11746-4148, (631)427-5240
Walt Whitman Soc. of America - Defunct.
Walter Bagehot Res. Coun. on Natl. Sovereignty [7528]
Walter Burley Griffin Soc. of Am. [9398], 1152 Center Dr., St. Louis, MO 63117, (314)644-4546
Walter Koenig Intl. - Address unknown since 1999.
Walter R. Brooks Memorial Fund [★24821]
Walter Reed Soc. - Address unknown since 1995.
Waltermire Family Assn. [21078], 141 Hudson Ave., Chatham, NY 12037, (518)392-4544
Walters Intl. Speakers Bur. [10905], PO Box 398, Glendora, CA 91740, (626)335-8069
Walther League - Address unknown since 1995.
Walton League of Am. Endowment; Izaak [4414]
Walton League of Am; Izaak [4413]
WAND Educ. Fund [18174], 691 Massachusetts Ave., Arlington, MA 02476, (781)643-6740
Wanderer Forum Found. [19737], PO Box 542, Hudson, WI 54016-0542, (651)276-1429
Wang Software Vendors' Assn. - Defunct.
WAP Forum [★7781]
War of 1812 in Connecticut; Soc. of the [★21354]
War of 1812; Military Soc. [★21204]
War of 1812; New England Assn. of Soldiers of the [★21354]
War of 1812 in Pennsylvania; Soc. of the [★21354]
War of 1812; Veteran Corps of Artillery, State of New York, Constituting the Military Soc. of the [21204]
War Agencies Employee Protection Agency [★5776]
War Agencies Employee Protection Agency [★IO]
War; Amer. Comm. on the History of the Second World [★10167]
War; Amer. Ex-Prisoners of [21262]
War Anti-Imperialist; Vietnam Veterans Against the [18785]
War Assn; Amer. Civil [10087]
War Child USA [11663], PO Box 212, Peterborough, NH 03458, (603)924-4318
War Child USA [IO], Peterborough, NH, United States
War and Civilian Blind; Amer. Braille Press for [★16854]

War on Community Ugliness - Defunct.
War Control Planners - Address unknown since 1999.
War Coun; World Without [18259]
War Criminals to Justice; Ad Hoc Comm. to Bring Nazi [★17719]
War Dead; Natl. Shrine to the Jewish [★21312]
War Devastated Libraries; Amer. Book Center for [★10392]
War Dog Memorial Fund; Natl. [21347]
War Dogs Assn; U.S. [20769]
War on Drugs - Defunct.
War Educ. Fund; World Without [★18259]
War of 1812
    Gen. Soc. of the War of 1812 [21354]
    Natl. Soc., U.S. Daughters of 1812 [21355]
    Patriots of Fort McHenry-Living Classrooms [10057]
    Star-Spangled Banner Flag House Assn. [21095]
War Fund; Permanent Blind Relief [★16854]
War Historians; Soc. of Civil [10151]
War Info. Sharing Proj; Intl. Accidental [★18229]
War; Intl. Comm. for the History of the Second World [IO]
War Memorial Assn; Grosse Pointe [21300]
War Mothers; Amer. [21190]
War Patriots Found; Black Revolutionary [20669]
War and Peace Found. [18254], 20 E 9th St., No. 23E, New York, NY 10003, (212)228-5836
War and Peace Found. [IO], New York, NY, United States
War/Peace Stud; Center for [17865]
War; Poets Against the [11189]
War Prevention Proj; Accidental Nuclear [★18229]
War Prevention Proj; Accidental Nuclear [18140]
War Proj; Korean [6344]
War Relief Services - Natl. Catholic Welfare Conf. [★12807]
War Relief Services - Natl. Catholic Welfare Conf. [★IO]
War Resistance
    Americans Against World Empire/Americans Against Bombing [18794]
    Center on Conscience and War [17438]
    Central Comm. for Conscientious Objectors [17439]
    Galway Alliance Against War [IO]
    Historians Against the War [18795]
    Iraq Action Coalition [17928]
    Iraq Veterans Against the War [21356]
    Military Families Speak Out [18796]
    Mothers Against War [18221]
    Natl. Youth and Student Peace Coalition [18226]
    Physicians for Social Responsibility [18169]
    Poets Against the War [11189]
    Reaching Critical Will [17436]
    Seeds of Peace [18245]
    Voices in the Wilderness [18253]
War Resisters' Intl. [IO], London, United Kingdom
War Resisters League [18123], 339 Lafayette St., New York, NY 10012, (212)228-0450
War, Revolution and Peace; Hoover Institution on [18836]
War Soc; Civil [10103]
War Soc; Virginia Country Civil [★10103]
War Sufferers; Joint Distribution Comm. for Relief of Jewish [★12464]
War Tax Resistance Coordinating Comm; Natl. [18715]
War Tax Resistance - Defunct.
War Tax Resister's Penalty Fund [18723], c/o Cliff Kindy, PO Box 25, North Manchester, IN 46962
War Veterans Auxiliary of the U.S.A; Catholic [21194]
War Veterans (Beit Halochem); Friends of Israel Disabled [★21166]
War Veterans; Descendants of Mexican [21183]
War Veterans; Fed. of French [21416]
War Veterans; Sons of Spanish Amer. [21268]
War Veterans; Ukrainian Amer. [★21326]
War Veterans of the U.S.A. Auxiliary; Catholic [★21194]
War Veterans of the U.S.A; Jewish [21306]
War Veterans of the U.S.A. - Natl. Ladies Auxiliary; Jewish [21196]

War Veterans, U.S.A. Natl. Memorial; Jewish [★21312]
War; Veterans of the Vietnam [21349]
War; Vietnam Veterans Against the [18784]
War on Want [IO], London, United Kingdom
WAR/WATCH Found. - Address unknown since 2002.
War Widows' Assn. of Great Britain [IO], London, United Kingdom
War; Win Without [18124]
War/Winter Soldier Org; Vietnam Veterans Against the [★18784]
Warbird Assn; World Miniature [22662]
Warbird Racing Assn; Scale [22657]
Warbirds of Am; EAA [21443]
Warbirds Assn; Giant Scale [22644]
Ward Found. [★9529]
Ward Museum of Wildfowl Art, Salisbury Univ. [9529], 909 S Schumaker Dr., Salisbury, MD 21804, (410)742-4988
Wardens Assn. of Am. [★11884]
Wardens Assn. of Am. [★IO]
Wardens; Natl. Assn. of Game Commissioners and [★4360]
Wardens and Superintendents; Amer. Assn. of [★11884]
Wardner Family Historical Assn. [21079], c/o Jon Wardner, Chm., 2921 Override Dr., Ann Arbor, MI 48104, (734)973-8039
Wardrups in Amer. - Defunct.
Warehouse Assn. of Am; Cotton [1093]
Warehouse Assn; Burley Auction [★3818]
Warehouse Distributors Assn. [★3982]
Warehouse Distributors Assn; Automotive [379]
Warehouse Distributors Assn. for Leisure and Mobile Products - Defunct.
Warehouse Union; Intl. Longshore and [24126]
Warehousemen's Assn; Amer. [★3979]
Warehousing
    Affiliated Warehouse Companies [3974]
    Allied Distribution, Inc. [3975]
    Amer. Chain of Warehouses [3976]
    Independent Liquid Terminals Assn. [3977]
    Intl. Assn. of Refrigerated Warehouses [3978]
    Intl. Assn. of Refrigerated Warehouses [IO]
    Intl. Warehouse Logistics Assn. [IO]
    Intl. Warehouse Logistics Assn. [3979]
    Logistics Officer Assn. [2736]
    Order Selection, Staging and Storage Coun. of the Material Handling Indus. of Am. [3980]
    Performance Warehouse Assn. [3981]
    Recreational Vehicle Aftermarket Assn. [3982]
    Self Storage Assn. [3983]
    Warehousing Educ. and Res. Coun. [3984]
    World Food Logistics Org. [3985]
    World Food Logistics Org. [IO]
Warehousing Educ. and Res. Coun. [3984], 1100 Jorie Blvd., Ste. 170, Oak Brook, IL 60523-4423, (630)990-0001
Wares Assn; Aluminum [★1970]
Warfare Assn; Mine [18592]
Wargaming Alliance; Natl. [★22475]
Wargaming Assn; Amer. [★22475]
Warlander Soc. and Registry; Intl. [4908]
Warm Blankets Orphan Care Intl. [11727], 5105 Tollview Dr., Ste. 155, Rolling Meadows, IL 60008, (847)577-1070
Warmblood Assn. of North Am; Swedish [4958]
Warmblood Assn; North Amer. [★4852]
Warmblood Breeders of North Am. [4968], PO Box 2221, Vashon, WA 98070, (206)567-4346
Warmblood Registry; Amer. [4851]
Warmblood Registry; Iberian Sport Horse and [4892]
Warmblood Soc; Amer. [4852]
Warmblood and Sport Horse Guild; Amer. [4853]
Warmblood Studbook of the Netherlands; North Amer. Dept. of the Royal [4931]
Warner Junior League Football; Pop [★23436]
Warrant Officers Assn. of the U.S.A. - Defunct.
Warrant Officers Assn; U.S. Army [6108]
Warrant Officers Assn., U.S. Coast Guard; Chief Warrant and [6072]
Warren Legal Training Prog; Earl [8765]
Warrington Anglers Assn. [IO], Warrington, United Kingdom

Reference to "IO" in place of a book number signifies that the association may be found in the 45th edition of International Organizations.

Warrington Chamber of Commerce and Indus. [IO], Warrington, United Kingdom
Wars; Gen. Soc. of Colonial [20738]
Wars; Order of the Indian [10479]
Wars of the U.S; Ladies Auxiliary to the Veterans of Foreign [21307]
Wars of the U.S; Military Order of Foreign [21236]
Wars of the U.S; Order of Indian [★10482]
Wars of the U.S; Veterans of Foreign [21331]
Warsaw Ghetto Resistance Org. [20191], 122 W 30th St., Ste. 205, New York, NY 10001, (212)564-1065
Warwick China Collectors Club - Defunct.
Washable Suits, Novelties and Sportswear Contractors Assn. - Address unknown since 1990.
Washburn Alumni Assn. [18942], 1700 SW Coll. Ave., Topeka, KS 66621, (785)670-1641
Washer Mfrs. Assn; Pressure [2062]
Washfrock Salesmen's Assn. - Address unknown since 1995.
Washington Area Bicyclist Association [★12954]
Washington Calligraphers Guild [11215], PO Box 3688, Merrifield, VA 22116-3688
Washington Capitals Fan Club [25014], PO Box 4671, Capitol Heights, MD 20791-4671
Washington Chinese Business Assn. - Address unknown since 2004.
Washington, DC; Gridiron Club of [3114]
Washington Ethical Soc. [20087], 7750 16th St. NW, Washington, DC 20012-1462, (202)882-6650
Washington Feed Assn. [★4314]
Washington Forest Protection Assn. [1627], 724 Columbia St. NW, Ste. 250, Olympia, WA 98501, (360)352-1500
Washington Friends Seminar Prog. [★17619]
The Washington Gp. [19421], PO Box 11248, Washington, DC 20008, (202)586-7227
Washington HQ Assn. [★11137]
Washington Home Center for Palliative Care Stud. [★14082]
Washington Inst. of Foreign Affairs [17877], 2121 Massachusetts Ave. NW, Washington, DC 20008, (202)332-1616
Washington Inst. of Foreign Affairs [IO], Washington, DC, United States
Washington Irving Soc. - Defunct.
Washington Journalism Center [8719], c/o Boston Univ., 2807 Connecticut Ave. NW, Washington, DC 20008, (202)756-7800
Washington Legal Found. [6229], 2009 Massachusetts Ave. NW, Washington, DC 20036-1004, (202)588-0302
Washington Natl. Monument Assn. - Defunct.
Washington Off. on Africa [16935], 212 E Capitol St., Washington, DC 20003, (202)547-7503
Washington Office on Haiti - Address unknown since 1999.
Washington Off. on Latin Am. [17995], 1630 Connecticut Ave. NW, Ste. 200, Washington, DC 20009, (202)797-2171
Washington Off. on Latin Am. [IO], Washington, DC, United States
Washington Off. for Social Concern; Unitarian Universalist Assn. - [★13135]
Washington-Paris-Moscow; Independent Univ., [★8597]
Washington Press Club [★3141]
Washington Reef Net Owners Assn. - Address unknown since 1995.
Washington Res. Proj; Children's Defense Fund of the [★11685]
Washington State Apple Commn. [4773], PO Box 18, Wenatchee, WA 98807-0018, (509)663-9600
Washington State Holly Growers Assn. - Defunct.
Washington Strategy Seminar - Address unknown since 2001.
Washington Task Force on African Affairs - Defunct.
Washington Women's Network - Defunct.
Washington Workshops Found. [8093], 3222 N St. NW, Ste. 340, Washington, DC 20007, (202)965-3434
Washington's Army at Valley Forge [★20678]
Washington's Army at Valley Forge; Soc. of the Descendants of [20678]
Waste
Air and Waste Mgt. Assn. [5081]

Alliance of Foam Packaging Recyclers [5265]
Aluminium Packaging Recycling Org. [IO]
Amer. Coal Ash Assn. [3986]
Amer. Decentralized Wastewater Assn. [4006]
Asphalt Recycling and Reclaiming Assn. [3987]
Assn. of Boards of Certification [6337]
Assn. of Cities and Regions for Recycling and Sustainable Rsrc. Mgt. [IO]
Assn. of Lighting and Mercury Recyclers [5168]
Assn. of Municipal Recycling Coordinators [IO]
Assn. of State and Territorial Solid Waste Mgt. Officials [6353]
Assn. for the Sustainable Use and Recovery of Resources in Europe [IO]
Automotive Recyclers Assn. [3988]
Basel Action Network [18797]
Basel Action Network [IO]
British Recovered Paper Assn. [IO]
Bur. of Intl. Recycling [IO]
Canadian Assn. of Recycling Indus. [IO]
Canadian Polystyrene Recycling Assn. [IO]
Cement Kiln Recycling Coalition [4337]
Center for Alternative Mining Development Policy [4536]
Center For Hea., Env. and Justice [5266]
Center for Waste Reduction Technologies [3989]
Chartered Institution of Wastes Mgt. [IO]
Coalition for Responsible Waste Incineration [3990]
Community Environmental Coun. [5267]
Container Recycling Alliance [4479]
Container Recycling Inst. [4480]
Coun. for Textile Recycling [3991]
Environmental Action Found. [4558]
Environmental Contractors Mgt. Assn. [IO]
Environmental Indus. Associations [3992]
Environmental Res. and Educ. Found. [4633]
Environmental Services Assn. [IO]
Environmental Tech. Coun. [3993]
Equip. Managers Coun. of Am. [943]
European Fed. of Waste Mgt. and Environmental Services [IO]
European Union for Responsible Incineration and Treatment of Special Waste [IO]
Global Alliance for Incinerator Alternatives [5268]
Ground Water Protection Coun. [3994]
Household Hazardous Waste Proj. [5269]
Indus. Coun. for Electronic Equip. Recycling [IO]
Institute of Scrap Recycling Industries [IO]
Inst. of Scrap Recycling Indus. [3995]
Integrated Waste Services Assn. [5270]
Intl. Cartridge Recycling Assn. [3996]
Intl. Solid Wastes Assn. [IO]
Keep Am. Beautiful [4584]
Local Authority Recycling Advisory Comm. [IO]
Municipal Waste Mgt. Assn. [6354]
Natl. Assn. of Clean Water Agencies [6237]
Natl. Assn. for PET Container Resources [3997]
Natl. Assn. of Wastewater Transporters [3998]
Natl. Biosolids Partnership [5096]
Natl. Household Hazardous Waste Forum [IO]
Natl. Off. Paper Recycling Proj. [3999]
Natl. Onsite Wastewater Recycling Assn. [5271]
Natl. Recycling Coalition [4000]
Natl. Rural Water Assn. [12939]
Natl. Solid Waste Assn. of India [IO]
Natl. Waste Prevention Coalition [4001]
Native Am. Water Assn. [4012]
North Amer. Hazardous Materials Mgt. Assn. [4806]
OSPAR Commn. [IO]
Paper Stock Indus. Chap. of ISRI [4002]
Portable Sanitation Assn. Intl. [4003]
Portable Sanitation Assn. Intl. [IO]
Radioactive Waste Mgt. Advisory Comm. [IO]
Recycling Coun. of Alberta [IO]
Resource Policy Inst. [4603]
Solid Waste Assn. of North Am. [6355]
Steel Recycling Inst. [4004]
Tech. Assn. for Solid Wastes Mgt. [IO]
U.S. Composting Coun. [6356]
Waste Equip. Tech. Assn. [4005]
Waste Mgt. Assn. of Australia [IO]
Waste Watch [IO]
Zero Waste Alliance [IO]

Zero Waste Alliance [5272]
Waste Assn; Textile [★3803]
Waste Care [IO], Leeds, United Kingdom
Waste; Citizens Against Govt. [17668]
Waste Composting Coun; Solid [★6356]
Waste Contractors; Natl. Assn. of Ordnance and Explosive [1038]
Waste Equip. Mfrs. Inst. [★4005]
Waste Equip. Tech. Assn. [4005], c/o Gary T. Satterfield, Exec. VP, 4301 Connecticut Ave. NW, Ste. 300, Washington, DC 20008-2304, (202)244-4700
Waste Exchange; Textile [★3803]
Waste Mgt. Assn. of Australia [IO], Burwood, Australia
Waste Mgt. and Recycling Assn. of Singapore [IO], Singapore, Singapore
Waste Oil Heating Mfrs. Assn. [★1903]
Waste Paper Utilization Coun. - Defunct.
Waste Safety; Natl. Campaign for Radioactive [18130]
Waste Watch [IO], London, United Kingdom
Waste Watch - Defunct.
Wastes Associations; Fed. of Sewage and Indus. [★5101]
Wastes Mgt. Assn; Natl. Solid [3579]
Wastewater Equip. Mfrs. Assn; Water and [2077]
Wastewater Instrumentation Testing Assn. of North Am; Water and [★2124]
Wastewater Pump Assn; Submersible [677]
Wastewater Utilities; Assn. of Boards of Certification for Operating Personnel in Water and [★6337]
Watch Assn; Amer. [2358]
Watch and Clock Collectors; Natl. Assn. of [22990]
Watch Mark Identification Bureau; National [★2359]
Watch Material Distributors Assn. of Am. [★2375]
Watch Material and Jewelry Distributors Assn. [★2375]
Watchable Wildlife [5286], PO Box 319, Marine on St. Croix, MN 55047, (651)433-4100
Watchdog; Project [★24524]
Watchlist on Children and Armed Conflict [11664], c/o Women's Commn. for Refugee Women and Children, 122 E 42nd St., 12th Fl., New York, NY 10168-1289, (212)551-3111
Watchlist on Children and Armed Conflict [IO], New York, NY, United States
Watchmaker Inst; Amer. [★2359]
Watchmakers-Clockmakers Inst; Amer. [2359]
Watchmakers Inst; Amer. [★2359]
Watchmakers of Switzerland Info. Center [★IO]
Watchmakers of Switzerland Marketing Inst. of America - Defunct.
Watchman Fellowship [19877], 913 Huffman Rd., Birmingham, AL 35215, (205)833-2858
Watchmen; Intl. Union of Guards and [★24186]
Watchmen, Messengers, and Gp. Leaders; Natl. Post Off. Mail Handlers, [★24171]
Watchmen and Messengers; Natl. Assn. of Post Off. and Postal Trans. Ser. Mail Handlers, [★24171]
Watchtower Bible and Tract Soc. of New York [20109], 25 Columbia Heights, Brooklyn, NY 11201-2483, (718)560-5000
Water
Africare [16924]
Amer. Backflow Prevention Assn. [7818]
Amer. Canal Soc. [9772]
Amer. Cave Conservation Assn. [4345]
Amer. Decentralized Wastewater Assn. [4006]
Amer. Fire Sprinkler Assn. [3437]
Amer. Ground Water Trust [4007]
Amer. Inst. of Hydrology [7823]
Amer. Membrane Tech. Assn. [7824]
Amer. Rivers [4351]
American Shore and Beach Preservation Association [4352]
Amer. Soc. of Irrigation Consultants [7826]
Amer. Water Resources Assn. [7827]
Amer. Water Works Assn. [4008]
Amer. Water Works Assn. [IO]
Asia Bottled Water Assn. [IO]
Associacao Brasileira da Industria de Aguas Minerais [IO]
Assn. of Environmental and Rsrc. Economists [4359]
Assn. of European Water Meter Mfrs. [IO]

A star before a book entry number signifies that the name is not listed separately, but is mentioned within the entry.

Assn. of Water Technologies [4009]
Australasian Bottled Water Inst. [IO]
Australian Soc. for Limnology [IO]
Australian Water Assn. [IO]
British Columbia Water and Wastewater Assn.
   [IO]
Canadian Bottled Water Assn. [IO]
Canadian Ground Water Assn. [IO]
Canadian Water Quality Assn. [IO]
Canadian Water and Wastewater Assn. [IO]
Canal Soc. of New York State [9773]
The Coastal Soc. [7395]
Coastal States Org. [7396]
Columbia Basin Trust [IO]
Culligan Dealers Assn. of North Am. [1667]
EarthEcho Intl. [4391]
Environmental and Contamination Res. Center
   [7172]
Environmental and Energy Stud. Inst. [4507]
European Water Resources Assn. [IO]
FishAmerica Found. [4393]
Floodplain Mgt. Assn. [5038]
Found. for Aquatic Injury Prevention [12963]
Freshwater Soc. [5091]
Friends of the River [4399]
Green Empowerment [4335]
Ground Water Protection Coun. [3994]
Groundwater Mgt. Caucus [7829]
Groundwater Mgt. Districts Assn. [5276]
Healing Waters Intl. [13410]
Healing Waters Intl. [IO]
Hudson River Sloop Clearwater [10038]
Inst. of Public Utilities [3958]
Intl. Assn. for Colon Hydrotherapy [14567]
Intl. Assn. of Dive Rescue Specialists [23574]
Intl. Assn. for the Properties of Water and Steam
   [6268]
Intl. Assn. of Theoretical and Applied Limnology
   [7240]
Intl. Bottled Water Assn. [509]
Intl. Coun. of Bottled Water Associations [IO]
Intl. Desalination Assn. [7831]
Intl. Humic Substances Soc. [7610]
Intl. Joint Commn. [5040]
Intl. Off. for Water [IO]
Intl. SeaKeepers Soc. [5010]
Intl. Water Resources Assn. [7834]
Interstate Coun. on Water Policy [6138]
Keepers of the Waters [5273]
League to Save Lake Tahoe [4417]
Marine Fish Conservation Network [4419]
Natl. Assn. of Water Companies [4010]
Natl. Coalition for Marine Conservation [4423]
Natl. Ground Water Assn. [4011]
National Ground Water Association [IO]
Natl. Hydropower Assn. [6964]
Natl. Institutes for Water Resources [7836]
Natl. Rural Water Assn. [12939]
Natl. Safe Boating Coun. [12977]
Natl. Safe Waterways and Seaports Alliance
   [18749]
Natl. Water Center [7837]
Natl. Water Resources Assn. [7838]
Natl. Water Safety Cong. [12981]
Native Amer. Water Assn. [4012]
New Water Supply Coalition [7839]
North Amer. Benthological Soc. [4516]
North Amer. Steam Boat Assn. [21881]
Ocean Conservancy [4435]
Ocean Res. and Conservation Assn. [4436]
Oz GREEN - Global Rivers Environmental Educ.
   Network - Australia [IO]
Ozark Soc. [4438]
People Food and Land Found. [4656]
Resource Policy Inst. [4603]
River of Words [4186]
Rural Community Assistance Partnership [7841]
Sailors for the Sea [4447]
Save Our Seas [4449]
Scottish Inland Waterways Assn. [IO]
Singapore Water Assn. [IO]
Soc. of Environmental Understanding and Sus-
   tainability [5274]
Soil and Water Conservation Soc. [4453]
Southeast Desalting Assn. [5283]

Submersible Wastewater Pump Assn. [677]
Trees, Water and People [4610]
Trout Unlimited [5387]
U.S. Comm. on Irrigation and Drainage [7842]
U.S. Water Polo [23973]
United Telecom Coun. [3762]
Universities Coun. on Water Resources [7844]
Upper Mississippi River Conservation Comm.
   [4463]
US Log Rolling Assn. [23982]
Walden Pond Advisory Comm. [4464]
Water Advocates [9310]
Water Advocates [IO]
Water Inst. of Southern Africa [IO]
Water Missions Intl. [IO]
Water Missions Intl. [13411]
Water for People [17854]
Water Planet USA [5018]
Water Quality Assn. [4013]
Water Quality Insurance Syndicate [2246]
Water Services Assn. of Australia [IO]
Water and Sewer Distributors of Am. [3968]
Water Systems Coun. [4014]
WaterPartners Intl. [13412]
WaterPartners Intl. [IO]
World Assn. of Soil and Water Conservation
   [4473]
World Water Coun. [IO]
Worldwide Aquatic Bodywork Assn. [13658]
Water Action; Clean [5087]
Water Action Proj; Clean [★5087]
Water Action Proj; Fisherman's Clean [★5087]
Water Administrators; Assn. of State Drinking [6211]
Water Advocates [9310], 1506 21st St. NW,
   Washington, DC 20036, (202)293-4002
Water Advocates [IO], Washington, DC, United
   States
Water Agencies; Assn. of Metropolitan [6135]
Water Assn; Amer. Bottled [★509]
Water Assn; Natl. Rural [12939]
Water Buffalo Assn; Amer. [4996]
Water Center [★7837]
Water Center; Natl. [★7837]
Water Center; Natl. [7837]
Water Color and Craft Inst; Crayon, [★1799]
Water Colour Soc. of Ireland [IO], Limerick, Ireland
Water Companies Assn. [★IO]
Water Company Conf; Natl. [★4010]
Water Conditioning Assn. Intl. [★4013]
Water Conditioning Found. [★4013]
Water Conservation
   Cooling Tech. Inst. [616]
   Environmental and Energy Stud. Inst. [4507]
   Friends of the River [4399]
   Groundwater Found. [5275]
   Groundwater Mgt. Districts Assn. [5276]
   Intl. SeaKeepers Soc. [5010]
   Keepers of the Waters [5273]
   Natl. Org. for Water Awareness [5277]
   Natl. Rural Water Assn. [12939]
   New Zealand Coastal Soc. [IO]
   People Food and Land Found. [4656]
   Resource Policy Inst. [4603]
   Restore America's Estuaries [5278]
   Soc. of Environmental Understanding and Sus-
     tainability [5274]
   Soil and Water Conservation Soc. [4453]
   Southeast Desalting Assn. [5283]
   WateReuse Assn. [5279]
Water Conservation Districts; Natl. Assn. of Soil and
   [★4420]
Water Conservation Soc; Soil and [4453]
Water Dog Club of Am; Portuguese [22345]
Water Env. Fed. [5101], 601 Wythe St., Alexandria,
   VA 22314-1994, (703)684-2400
Water Env. Fed. [IO], Alexandria, VA, United States
Water Facts Consortium - Defunct.
Water Fitness Assn; U.S. [23657]
Water Fitters; Natl. Assn. of Master Steam and Hot
   [★1033]
Water Fly Rodders of Am; Salt [★23417]
Water; Food and [17328]
Water Fund; Clean [5088]
Water Inst. Directors; Natl. Assn. of [★7836]
Water Inst. of Southern Africa [IO], Johannesburg,
   Republic of South Africa

Water Irradiation; Natl. Coalition to Stop Food and
   [★17328]
Water Jetting Assn. [IO], Sawtry, United Kingdom
Water Lily Soc. [★IO]
Water Lily Soc. [★22524]
Water Mgt. Agencies; Natl. Assn. of Flood and Storm
   [6140]
Water Mgt. Districts Assn; Ground [★7829]
Water Ministry; Spring of Living [20556]
Water Missions Intl. [13411], PO Box 31258,
   Charleston, SC 29417, (843)769-7395
Water Missions Intl. [IO], Charleston, SC, United
   States
Water for People [17854], 6666 W Quincy Ave.,
   Denver, CO 80235-3098, (303)734-3490
Water Planet USA [5018], 203 Greenwood Dr.,
   Panama City Beach, FL 32407, (850)230-6030
Water Planet USA [IO], Panama City Beach, FL,
   United States
Water Policy; Interstate Conf. on [★6138]
Water Policy; Interstate Coun. on [6138]
Water Pollution
   Africa Rainforest and River Conservation [4341]
   Amer. Backflow Prevention Assn. [7818]
   Amer. Decentralized Wastewater Assn. [4006]
   European Water Assn. [IO]
   European Water Assn. [IO]
   Hudson River Sloop Clearwater [10038]
   Ocean Futures Soc. [5280]
   Ocean Futures Soc. [IO]
Water Pollution; Centre for Documentation, Res. and
   Experimentation on Accidental [IO]
Water Pollution Control Administrators; Assn. of
   State and Interstate [5688]
Water Pollution Control Fed. [★5101]
Water Pollution Control Fed. [★IO]
Water Polo
   Collegiate Water Polo Assn. [23972]
   U.S. Aquatic Sports [23890]
   U.S. Water Polo [23973]
Water Polo Assn; Collegiate [23972]
Water Polo Canada [IO], Gloucester, ON, Canada
Water Polo Comm. of the Amateur Athletic Union
   [★23973]
Water Proj; Natl. Demonstration [★7841]
Water Project; Natl. Environmental Development
   Assn./Ground [★7835]
Water Protection Coun; Ground [3994]
Water Pump Assn; Submersible Waste [677]
Water Quality Assn. [4013], 4151 Naperville Rd.,
   Lisle, IL 60532-1088, (630)505-0160
Water Quality Insurance Syndicate [2246], 80 Broad
   St., 21st Fl., New York, NY 10004, (212)292-8700
Water Res. Inst. - Address unknown since 2001.
Water Resources
   Amer. Backflow Prevention Assn. [7818]
   Amer. Inst. of Hydrology [7823]
   Amer. Membrane Tech. Assn. [7824]
   American Membrane Technology Association [IO]
   Amer. Rainwater Catchment Systems Assn.
     [7825]
   Amer. Soc. of Irrigation Consultants [7826]
   Amer. Water Resources Assn. [7827]
   Amer. Water Resources Assn. [IO]
   Assn. of Ground Water Scientists and Engineers -
     A Division of Natl. Ground Water Assn. [7828]
   Assn. of State Dam Safety Officials [6249]
   Assn. of State and Interstate Water Pollution
     Control Administrators [5688]
   BHR Gp. [IO]
   British Dam Soc. [IO]
   British Hydrological Soc. [IO]
   Canadian Dam Assn. [IO]
   Canadian Water Resources Assn. [IO]
   Chartered Institution of Water and Environmental
     Mgt. [IO]
   Clay Pipe Development Assn. [IO]
   Clean Water Action [5087]
   Clean Water Coun. [5281]
   EarthEcho Intl. [4391]
   Environmental Working Group [4564]
   European Desalination Soc. [IO]
   European Union of Natl. Associations of Water
     Suppliers and Waste Water Services [IO]
   Friends of the River [4399]

Reference to "IO" in place of a book number signifies that the association may be found in the 45th edition of International Organizations.

Groundwater Mgt. Caucus [7829]
Groundwater Mgt. Districts Assn. [5276]
Healing Waters Intl. [13410]
Inst. for Soil, Climate and Water [IO]
Institution of Water Officers [IO]
Intl. Assn. of Hydrogeologists [IO]
Intl. Assn. of Hydrogeologists [7830]
Intl. Assn. of Hydrogeologists - Argentina [IO]
Intl. Assn. of Hydrogeologists - Australia [IO]
Intl. Assn. of Hydrogeologists - Australian Capital
    Territory [IO]
Intl. Assn. of Hydrogeologists - Belgium [IO]
Intl. Assn. of Hydrogeologists - Bulgaria [IO]
Intl. Assn. of Hydrogeologists - Canadian Natl.
    Chap. [IO]
Intl. Assn. of Hydrogeologists - Chile [IO]
Intl. Assn. of Hydrogeologists - China [IO]
Intl. Assn. of Hydrogeologists - Columbia [IO]
Intl. Assn. of Hydrogeologists - Croatia [IO]
Intl. Assn. of Hydrogeologists - Czech Republic
    [IO]
Intl. Assn. of Hydrogeologists - Egypt [IO]
Intl. Assn. of Hydrogeologists - France [IO]
Intl. Assn. of Hydrogeologists - Georgia [IO]
Intl. Assn. of Hydrogeologists - Germany [IO]
Intl. Assn. of Hydrogeologists - Hungary [IO]
Intl. Assn. of Hydrogeologists - Irish Gp. [IO]
Intl. Assn. of Hydrogeologists - Italy [IO]
Intl. Assn. of Hydrogeologists - Japan [IO]
Intl. Assn. of Hydrogeologists - Mexico [IO]
Intl. Assn. of Hydrogeologists - Morocco [IO]
Intl. Assn. of Hydrogeologists - Netherlands [IO]
Intl. Assn. of Hydrogeologists - Northern Territory
    [IO]
Intl. Assn. of Hydrogeologists - Norway [IO]
Intl. Assn. of Hydrogeologists - Peru [IO]
Intl. Assn. of Hydrogeologists - Poland [IO]
Intl. Assn. of Hydrogeologists - Queensland [IO]
Intl. Assn. of Hydrogeologists - Republic of Korea
    [IO]
Intl. Assn. of Hydrogeologists - Romania [IO]
Intl. Assn. of Hydrogeologists - Russia [IO]
Intl. Assn. of Hydrogeologists - Slovakia [IO]
Intl. Assn. of Hydrogeologists - Slovenia [IO]
Intl. Assn. of Hydrogeologists - Spain [IO]
Intl. Assn. of Hydrogeologists - United Kingdom
    [IO]
Intl. Assn. of Hydrogeologists - Western Australia
    [IO]
Intl. Assn. of Hydrological Sciences [IO]
Intl. Commn. on Irrigation and Drainage - England
    [IO]
Intl. Commn. on Irrigation and Drainage - India
    [IO]
Intl. Commn. on Large Dams [IO]
Intl. Desalination Assn. [IO]
Intl. Desalination Assn. [7831]
Intl. Network on Participatory Irrigation Mgt.
    [7233]
Intl. Rainwater Catchment Systems Assn. [7832]
International Rainwater Catchment Systems As-
    sociation [IO]
Intl. Rivers Network [IO]
Intl. Rivers Network [7833]
Intl. Water History Assn. [IO]
Intl. Water Mgt. Inst. [IO]
Intl. Water Resources Assn. [IO]
Intl. Water Resources Assn. [7834]
IRC Intl. Water and Sanitation Centre [IO]
Keepers of the Waters [5273]
Marine Fish Conservation Network [4419]
Mekong River Commn. [IO]
Natl. Assn. of Flood and Storm Water Mgt. Agen-
    cies [6140]
Natl. Coalition for Marine Conservation [4423]
Natl. Environmental Development Assn./Resource
    Conservation and Recovery Act Project [7835]
Natl. Institutes for Water Resources [7836]
Natl. Rural Water Assn. [12939]
Natl. Water Center [7837]
Natl. Water Resources Assn. [7838]
Native Amer. Water Assn. [4012]
New Water Supply Coalition [7839]
New Zealand Hydrological Soc. [IO]
Nordic Assn. for Hydrology [IO]

North Amer. Lake Mgt. Soc. [7241]
Palestinian Hydrology Gp. for Water and
    Environmental Resources Development [IO]
Passaic River Coalition [7840]
Portuguese Gp. of the Intl. Assn. of Hydrogeolo-
    gists [IO]
Puerto Rico Water and Env. Assn. [5282]
Restore America's Estuaries [5278]
River Mgt. Soc. [4445]
River Network [4446]
Rural Community Assistance Partnership [7841]
Soc. of British Water and Wastewater Indus. [IO]
Soc. of Environmental Understanding and Sus-
    tainability [5274]
Southeast Desalting Assn. [5283]
Swiss Hydrogeological Soc. [IO]
U.S. Comm. on Irrigation and Drainage [7842]
U.S. Soc. on Dams [7843]
Universities Coun. on Water Resources [7844]
Upper Mississippi River Conservation Comm.
    [4463]
Walden Pond Advisory Comm. [4464]
Water Env. Fed. [5101]
Water Missions Intl. [13411]
Water Sciences and Tech. Assn. [IO]
Water UK [IO]
WaterPartners Intl. [13412]
Western Snow Conf. [7845]
Water Resources Cong. - Address unknown since
    1999.
Water Safety Cong; Natl. [12981]
Water Safety New Zealand [IO], Wellington, New
    Zealand
Water Sciences and Tech. Assn. [IO], Manama,
    Bahrain
Water Services Assn. of Australia [IO], Melbourne,
    Australia
Water and Sewage Works Mfrs. Assn. [★2077]
Water and Sewer Distributors of Am. [3968], 100 N
    20th St., 4th Fl., Philadelphia, PA 19103-1443,
    (215)564-3484
Water Ski Assn. [★IO]
Water Ski Assn; Amer. [★23979]
Water Ski Educational Found; Amer. [23975]
Water Ski Indus. Assn. [★3655]
Water Ski Museum Hall of Fame [★23975]
Water Ski and Wakeboard Canada [IO], Ottawa,
    ON, Canada
Water Skiing
    Amer. Barefoot Club [23974]
    Amer. Water Ski Educational Found. [23975]
    Australian Water Ski Fed. [IO]
    Austrian Water Ski Fed. [IO]
    Austrian Waterski Fed. [IO]
    Brazilian Water Ski Confed. [IO]
    Brisbane Water Ski Club [IO]
    British Water Ski [IO]
    Chinese Taipei Water Ski Assn. [IO]
    Cyprus Water Ski Fed. [IO]
    Czech Water Ski Fed. [IO]
    Danish Water Ski Fed. [IO]
    Finnish Water Ski Sports Fed. [IO]
    Geelong Waterski Club [IO]
    Hong Kong Water Ski Assn. [IO]
    Hungarian Water Ski and Wakeboard Fed. [IO]
    Intl. Jet Sports Boating Assn. and Amer.
        Watercraft Assn. [IO]
    Intl. Jet Sports Boating Assn. and Amer.
        Watercraft Assn. [23976]
    Intl. Water Ski Fed. [IO]
    Irish Waterski Fed. [IO]
    Korea Water Ski Assn. [IO]
    Luxembourg Water Ski Fed. [IO]
    Natl. Collegiate Water Ski Assn. [23977]
    New Zealand Water Ski Racing Assn. [IO]
    Singapore Water Ski and Wakeboard Fed. [IO]
    South African Water Ski Fed. [IO]
    Swedish Water Ski Fed. [IO]
    Turkish Underwater Sports, Life-Saving, Water Ski
        and Fin Swimming Fed. [IO]
    U.S. Hydrofoil Assn. [23978]
    USA Water Ski [23979]
    Water Ski and Wakeboard Canada [IO]
    Waterski Assn. Zimbabwe [IO]
    World Freestyle Watercraft Alliance [23983]

Water Soluble Gum Assn. - Address unknown since
    1995.
Water Spaniel Club of Am; Irish [22294]
Water Sports
    Amer. Barefoot Club [23974]
    Amer. Canoe Assn. [23278]
    Amer. Power Boat Assn. [23152]
    Amer. Sail Training Assn. [23153]
    Amer. Sailing Assn. [23154]
    Amer. Shark Assn. [23156]
    Amer. Swan Boat Assn. [23669]
    Amer. Water Ski Educational Found. [23975]
    Amer. Watercraft Assn. [23980]
    Amer. Whitewater [23682]
    Antique and Classic Boat Soc. [21868]
    Aquatic Exercise Assn. [23652]
    Assn. of Commercial Diving Educators [23960]
    Assn. of Dive Prog. Administrators [23377]
    Assn. of Surfing Professionals [23877]
    Australian Kitesurfing Assn. [IO]
    Blind Sailing Intl. [23151]
    Boat Owners Assn. of the U.S. [23160]
    British Kite Surfing Assn. [IO]
    Bulgarian Water Polo Fed. [IO]
    Bullseye Assn. [23161]
    Catalina 22 Natl. Sailing Assn. [23162]
    Catboat Assn. [23163]
    Classic Yacht Assn. [21871]
    A Contre-Courant [IO]
    Coun. of Sailing Associations [23165]
    Day Sailer Assn. [23167]
    Eastern Assn. of Rowing Colleges [23699]
    El Toro Intl. Yacht Racing Assn. [23168]
    FJ U.S. [23169]
    Flemish Watersports Assn. [IO]
    Flying Scot Sailing Assn. [23170]
    Force 5 Class Assn. [23171]
    Found. for Aquatic Injury Prevention [12963]
    Gar Wood Soc. [21873]
    Geary 18 Intl. Yacht Racing Assn. [23172]
    Hampton One-Design Class Racing Assn. [23173]
    Highlander Class Intl. Assn. [23174]
    Inland Lake Yachting Assn. [23175]
    Inst. of Diving [23961]
    Inter-Collegiate Sailing Assn. of North Am.
        [23176]
    Inter-Lake Yachting Assn. [23177]
    Intercollegiate Rowing Assn. [23700]
    Intl. 210 Assn. [23179]
    Intl. 505 Yacht Racing Assn., Amer. Sect. [23180]
    Intl. Assn. of Water Polo Referees [IO]
    Intl. Blue Jay Class Assn. [23181]
    Intl. Canoe Fed. [IO]
    Intl. D.N. Ice Yacht Racing Assn. [23183]
    Intl. Etchells Class Assn. [23184]
    Intl. Flying Dutchman Class Assn. of the U.S.
        [23185]
    Intl. Hobie Class Assn. [23186]
    Intl. J/22 Class Assn. [23187]
    Intl. Jet Sports Boating Assn. and Amer.
        Watercraft Assn. [23976]
    Intl. Lightning Class Assn. [23188]
    Intl. Naples Sabot Assn. [23190]
    Intl. Penguin Class Dinghy Assn. [23191]
    Intl. Prindle Class Racing Assn. [23192]
    Intl. Sunfish Class Assn. [23194]
    Intl. Thunderbird Class Assn. [23195]
    Intl. Underwater Spearfishing Assn. [23418]
    Jet 14 Class Assn. [23196]
    Jet Sports Racing Assn. of Great Britain [IO]
    Lido 14 Intl. Class Assn. [23198]
    MC Sailing Assn. [23199]
    Middle States Regatta Assn. [23701]
    Natl. Assn. of Black Scuba Divers [23711]
    Natl. Assn. of Underwater Instructors [23963]
    Natl. Boating Fed. [23201]
    Natl. Butterfly Assn. [23202]
    Natl. C Scow Sailing Assn. [23203]
    Natl. Class E Scow Assn. [23204]
    Natl. Offshore Dept. [23205]
    Natl. One Design Racing Assn. [23206]
    Natl. Safe Boating Coun. [12977]
    Natl. Starwind/Spindrift Class Assn. [23207]
    Natl. Water Safety Cong. [12981]
    Nautical Res. Guild [21880]

A star before a book entry number signifies that the name is not listed separately, but is mentioned within the entry.

North Amer. Formula 18 Assn. [23208]
North Amer. Model Boat Assn. [22654]
North Amer. Stone Skipping Assn. [22939]
North Amer. Tornado Assn. [23209]
Olson 30 Class Assn. [23210]
One-Design Class Coun. [23211]
Polish Jet Sports Boating Assn. [IO]
Prindle Class Assn. [23212]
Professional Assn. of Diving Instructors [23964]
Professional Paddlesports Assn. [3650]
Qajaq USA [23981]
Recreational Scuba Training Coun. [23965]
Rhodes 19 Class Assn. [23213]
Rhodes Bantam Class Assn. [23214]
Richardson Boat Owners Assn. [21884]
San Juan 21 Class Assn. [23215]
Santana 20 Class Assn. [23216]
Scale Ship Modelers Assn. of North Am. [22656]
Seven Seas Cruising Assn. [23217]
Ships on Stamps Unit [22870]
Snipe Class Intl. Racing Assn. [23219]
Solent Skiers Assn. [IO]
Surfrider Found. [23881]
Swan Owners Assn. of Am. [23221]
Tahiti Jet Club [IO]
Traditional Small Craft Assn. [21885]
Underwater Soc. of Am. [23966]
U.S. A-Class Catamaran Assn. [23225]
U.S. Albacore Assn. [23226]
U.S. Apnea Assn. [23380]
U.S. Canoe Assn. [23279]
U.S. Hydrofoil Assn. [23978]
U.S. J/24 Class Assn. [23227]
U.S. Mariner Class Assn. [23228]
U.S. Masters Swimming [23891]
U.S. Mirror Class Assn. [23229]
U.S. Power Squadrons [23231]
U.S. Professional Diving Coaches Assn. [23381]
U.S. Rowing Assn. [23704]
U.S. Sailing Assn. [23232]
U.S. Sailing Found. [23233]
U.S. Soling Assn. [23234]
U.S. Swim School Assn. [23892]
U.S. Water Fitness Assn. [23657]
U.S. Water Polo [23973]
U.S. Wayfarer Assn. [23235]
U.S. Windsurfing Assn. [23236]
U.S. Yngling Assn. [23237]
US Log Rolling Assn. [23982]
USA Diving [23382]
U.S.A. Finn Assn. [23238]
USA Water Ski [23979]
Wakeboarding New Zealand [IO]
Water Polo Canada [IO]
Western Canadian Watercross Assn. [IO]
Wild Water Kayak Club [IO]
Windmill Class Assn. [23239]
Women in Film [1396]
World Diving Coaches Assn. [23383]
World Freestyle Watercraft Alliance [23983]
World Freestyle Watercraft Alliance [IO]
World Masters Cross-Country Ski Assn. [23763]
World Underwater Fed. [IO]
World Waterpark Assn. [1329]
Yachting Club of Am. [23240]
Water Sports Indus. Assn. [3655], PO Box 568512,
   Orlando, FL 32856-8512, (407)251-9039
Water Supply Improvement Assn. [★7831]
Water Supply Improvement Assn. [★IO]
Water Supply Improvement Assn; Natl. [★7824]
Water Systems Coun. [4014], 1101 30th St. NW,
   Ste. 500, Washington, DC 20007, (202)625-4387
Water Systems Coun; Pitless Adapter Division of
   [★4014]
Water Tech. Division of the Natl. Water Well Assn;
   Ground [★7828]
Water Transport Assn. - Defunct.
Water UK [IO], London, United Kingdom
Water and Wastewater Equip. Mfrs. Assn. [2077],
   PO Box 17402, Washington, DC 20041, (703)444-
   1777
Water and Wastewater Instrumentation Testing Assn.
   of North Am. [★2124]
Water and Wastewater Instrumentation Testing Assn.
   of North Am. [★IO]

Water and Wastewater Utilities; Assn. of Boards of
   Certification for Operating Personnel in [★6337]
Water Well Assn; Natl. [★4011]
Water Works Mfrs. Assn. [★2077]
Waterbed Coun. [★1705]
Waterbed Mfrs. Assn. [★1705]
Waterbed Retailers Assn; Natl. [★1705]
The Waterbird Soc. - Address unknown since 2002.
Waterbirth Intl. [13984], PO Box 1400, Wilsonville,
   OR 97070, (503)673-0026
Waterbirth International [IO], Wilsonville, OR, United
   States
Watercolor Soc; Amer. [9417]
Watercolor Soc; California Natl. [★9461]
Watercolor Soc; Natl. [9461]
Watercraft Indus. Assn; Personal [3369]
WateReuse Assn. [5279], 1199 N Fairfax St., Ste.
   410, Alexandria, VA 22314, (703)548-0880
Waterford Chamber [IO], Waterford, Ireland
Waterfowl Advisory Comm. - Defunct.
Waterfowl Alliance, Waterfowl U.S.A; Natl. [★4465]
Waterfowl Comm; Northeast [★5295]
Waterfowl Comm; Southeast [★5295]
Waterfowl Coun; Atlantic [★5295]
Waterfowl Found; Delta [5308]
Waterfowl Soc; Amer. Pheasant and [5292]
Waterfowl U.S.A; Natl. Waterfowl Alliance, [★4465]
Waterfowl U.S.A. [4465], Box 50, Waterfowl Bldg.,
   Edgefield, SC 29824, (803)637-5767
Waterfront and Allied Workers' Union [IO], Roseau,
   Dominica
The Waterfront Center [11794], PO Box 32129,
   Washington, DC 20007, (202)337-0356
Waterfront Employers; Natl. Assn. of [2609]
WaterJet Tech. Assn. [7086], 906 Olive St., Ste.
   1200, St. Louis, MO 63101-1448, (314)241-1445
Waterless Printing Assn. [1793], PO Box 1252,
   Woodstock, IL 60098, (815)337-7681
Waterlily and Water Gardening Soc; Intl. [22524]
Watermark Assn. of Artisans [303], 150 US Hwy.
   158 E, Camden, NC 27921, (252)338-0853
Watermelon Assn; Natl. [4747]
Waterpark Assn; Amer. [★1329]
WaterPartners Intl. [13412], 2405 Grand Blvd., Ste.
   860, Box 12, Kansas City, MO 64108, (913)312-
   8600
WaterPartners Intl. [IO], Kansas City, MO, United
   States
Waterproof Workers Assn; United Slate, Tile and
   Composition Roofers, Damp and [★24033]
Waterproofers and Allied Workers; United Union of
   Roofers, [24033]
Waterproofing and Restoration Inst; Sealant [58]
Waterproofing and Structural Repair Contractors;
   Natl. Assn. of [645]
Waters; Coun. of Natural [★509]
Waters Found. [8313], 6085 N Kolb Rd., Tucson, AZ
   85750, (503)679-5309
Watershed Coun; Connecticut River [4377]
Watershed Found. - Address unknown since 2000.
Waterside Workers' Fed. of Australia [★IO]
Waterski Assn. Zimbabwe [IO], Bulawayo,
   Zimbabwe
Waterslager Soc; Amer. [21842]
Watertenders of the Pacific; Marine Firemen, Oilers
   and [★24130]
Watertenders and Wipers Assn; Pacific Coast
   Marine Firemen, Oilers, [24130]
Waterways Bulk Transportation Coun. - Address
   unknown since 1995.
Waterways Conf; Natl. [3581]
Waterways Freight Bur. - Defunct.
Waterways Operators; Amer. [2601]
Watson's Collectors' Club - Defunct.
Wattle Res. Inst. [★IO]
Watusi Intl. Assn. [★IO]
Watusi Intl. Assn. [★4297]
WAVE [12105], 525 School St. SW, Ste. 500,
   Washington, DC 20024-2795, (202)484-0103
WAVES Natl. [21234], c/o Ms. Sharon Woods, Pres.,
   16547 S Red Rock Dr., Strongsville, OH 44136,
   (440)655-0100
Waves Natl. Corp. [★21234]
Wax Chandlers' Company [IO], London, United
   Kingdom

Waxed Paper Inst. [★2875]
Waxed Paper Merchandising Coun. - Defunct.
The Way [★20411]
The Way [★IO]
Way of Christ: Peace Pilgrimage Partners - Defunct.
The Way Intl. [20411], PO Box 328, New Knoxville,
   OH 45871-0328, (419)753-2523
The Way Intl. [IO], New Knoxville, OH, United States
Way of Mountain Learning Center - Address
   unknown since 2002.
Wayfarer Assn; U.S. [23235]
Wayfarers Club - Defunct.
Wayland Baptist Univ. Assn. of Former Students
   [18943], 1900 W 7th St., No. 437, Plainview, TX
   79072, (806)291-3600
Wayne Hann Band Fan Club - Address unknown
   since 1989.
Wayside Club [★10863]
W.C. Fields Fan Club [24801], c/o Ted Wioncek,
   Pres., Dept. EOA, PO Box 506, Stratford, NJ
   08084-0506
WCRLA Computer Technology SIG - Defunct.
WDA: The RV Aftermarket Assn. [★3982]
We Are AWARE [13442], PO Box 242, Bedford, MA
   01730-0242, (781)893-0500
We Are Family [17659], PO Box 21806, Charleston,
   SC 29413, (843)762-3275
We Believe! [19738], PO Box 100045, Cudahy, WI
   53110-6100
We Can Do! - Address unknown since 1999.
We Care Am. [13210], 44180 Riverside Pkwy., Ste.
   201, Lansdowne, VA 20176, (703)554-8600
We Care - IHM Volunteer Services of the Sisters,
   Servants of the Immaculate Heart of Mary
   [★20346]
We Care Prog. [11897], 3493 Hwy. 21, Atmore, AL
   36502, (251)368-8818
We Interrupt This Message [18034], 1215 York St.,
   San Francisco, CA 94110, (415)621-3302
We Love Lucy/International Lucille Ball Fan Club
   [24776], PO Box 56234, Sherman Oaks, CA
   91413-1234
We Love Lucy/International Lucille Ball Fan Club
   [IO], Sherman Oaks, CA, United States
We the People [18138], 200 Harrison St., Oakland,
   CA 94607-4114, (510)836-3273
We the People, United - Address unknown since
   1999.
We Remember Dean Intl. - Address unknown since
   1999.
We Remember Elvis Fan Club [24815]
WEA Intl. [★6897]
WEA Intl. [★IO]
WEA Scottish Assn. [IO], Edinburgh, United
   Kingdom
Weapons Freeze Campaign; Nuclear [★18166]
Weapons and Nuclear Power in Space; Global
   Network Against [18152]
Weather
   Inst. of Global Env. and Soc. [4574]
   Intl. SeaKeepers Soc. [5010]
   Japanese Soc. of Snow and Ice [IO]
   Minor Found. for Major Challenges [IO]
   Natl. Assn. of Storm Chasers and Spotters
      [13413]
   Natl. Storm Shelter Assn. [2831]
   Roofing Indus. Comm. on Weather Issues [666]
   Weather Risk Mgt. Assn. [4015]
   Weather Risk Management Association [IO]
Weather Assn; Air [21278]
Weather Assn; Natl. [7327]
Weather Control Res. Assn. [★7330]
Weather Modification Assn. [7330], PO Box 26926,
   Fresno, CA 93729-6926, (559)434-3486
Weather Reconnaissance Assn; Air [21279]
Weather Related Companies; Assn. of Private
   [★7326]
Weather Risk Mgt. Assn. [4015], 1156 15th St. NW,
   Ste. 900, Washington, DC 20005, (202)289-3800
Weather Risk Management Association [IO],
   Washington, DC, United States
Weather Services
   Natl. Weather Ser. Employees Org. [6357]
Weather Services Assn; Commercial [7326]
Weather Underground - Address unknown since
   1997.

Reference to "IO" in place of a book number signifies that the association may be found in the 45th edition of International Organizations.

Weatherby Collectors Assn. [**22432**], PO Box 478, Pacific, MO 63069, (636)239-0348

Weatherford Family Assn. - Defunct.

Weatherhead Center for Intl. Affairs [**17878**], Harvard Univ., 1737 Cambridge St., Cambridge, MA 02138, (617)495-4420

Weatherhead Center for Intl. Affairs [**IO**], Cambridge, MA, United States

Weave a Real Peace [**11505**], 3102 N Classen Blvd., Oklahoma City, OK 73118-3899

Weavers; Complex [**308**]

Weavers Guild of Am; Hand [**22158**]

Weavers; Natl. Assn. of Wheat [**22166**]

WEB [★**1246**]

WEB [★**IO**]

Web Analytics Assn. [**7222**], 2300 M St., Ste. 800, Washington, DC 20037, (800)349-1070

Web Consortium; World Wide [**6756**]

Web Host Guild - Defunct.

Web Network of Employee Benefits [★**1246**]

Web Network of Employee Benefits [★**IO**]

Web Network of Professional Benefits [★**IO**]

Web Network of Professional Benefits [★**1246**]

Web Offset Assn. [**1794**], c/o Graphic Arts Info. Network, PIA/GATF, 200 Deer Run Rd., Sewickley, PA 15143, (412)741-6860

Web Printing Assn. [**1795**], c/o PIA/GATF, 200 Deer Run Rd., Sewickley, PA 15143, (412)741-6860

Web Sect; Non-Heatset [★**1795**]

Web Sling Assn. [★**2078**]

Web Sling and Tie Down Assn. [**2078**], 2105 Laurel Bush Rd., Ste. 200, Bel Air, MD 21015, (443)640-1070

Web Watch; Consumer [**17322**]

WEB - Worldwide Employee Benefits Network [**1246**], 1700 Pennsylvania Ave. NW, Ste. 400, Washington, DC 20006-4707, (888)795-6862

WEB - Worldwide Employee Benefits Network [**IO**], Washington, DC, United States

Web3D Consortium [**6828**], 325 Sharon Park Dr., Ste. 623, Menlo Park, CA 94025, (248)342-7662

Webb/DeGrass Family Org. - Defunct.

Webb Soc. [**6512**], c/o John Isles, North Amer. Sec.-Treas., 10575 Darrel Dr., Hanover, MI 49241

Webb Soc. [**IO**], Hanover, MI, United States

Webcasting Assn; Intl. [**2667**]

Weber Found; Sturge- [**15365**]

Webmasters and Designers; Intl. Assn. of [**888**]

Webmasters; Natl. Assn. of [★**2114**]

Webster Found; Noah [★**10053**]

Webster House; Noah [**10053**]

WEC Intl. [**20034**], PO Box 1707, Fort Washington, PA 19034, (215)646-2322

WEC Intl. [**IO**], Fort Washington, PA, United States

WECAI Network [**1167**], 7100 Pembroke Rd., Miramar, FL 33023, (954)625-6606

Wedding and Event Videographers Assn. Intl. [**1395**], 8499 S Tamiami Trail, PMB 208, Sarasota, FL 34238, (941)923-5334

Wedding and Event Videographers Assn. Intl. [**IO**], Sarasota, FL, United States

Wedding Photographers of Am. [★**IO**]

Wedding Photographers of Am. [★**3017**]

Wedding Photographers Intl. [★**3017**]

Wedding Photographers Intl. [★**IO**]

Wedding Planners; Amer. Assn. of [**2654**]

Wedding and Portrait Photographers Intl. [**3017**], 1312 Lincoln Blvd., PO Box 2003, Santa Monica, CA 90406-2003, (310)451-0090

Wedding and Portrait Photographers Intl. [**IO**], Santa Monica, CA, United States

Wedding Professionals; Amer. Soc. of [**532**]

Wedding Professionals Intl; Assn. for [**1935**]

Weddings Beautiful Worldwide [**537**], 1004 N Thompson St., Ste. 205, Richmond, VA 23230, (804)342-6061

Weddings Beautiful Worldwide [**IO**], Richmond, VA, United States

Wedgwood Collectors Soc. - Defunct.

Wedgwood Intl. Seminar [**21939**], c/o Mr. Michael Smith, Treas., PO Box 674, Ontario, CA 91762-8674

Wedgwood Intl. Seminar [**IO**], Ontario, CA, United States

Wedgwood Soc. - Defunct.

Wedgwood Soc. of Great Britain [**IO**], London, United Kingdom

Wee Scots - Address unknown since 1989.

Weed Control Conferences; Assn. of Regional [★**4109**]

Weed Mgt. Assn; North Amer. [**4106**]

Weed Sci. Soc. of Am. [**4109**], PO Box 7050, Lawrence, KS 66044-8897, (800)627-0629

Weed Sci. Soc; Northeastern [**4990**]

Weed Soc. of Am. [★**4109**]

Weed Soc. of Victoria [**IO**], Frankston, Australia

Weedman Family Genealogy - Defunct.

WEF Ministries [★**19991**]

WEF Ministries [★**IO**]

Wefel Family Assn. [**21080**]

Wegeners Found. - Address unknown since 2001.

Wegener's Granulomatosis Assn. [★**16552**]

Wegener's Granulomatosis Assn. [★**IO**]

Wegener's Granulomatosis Support Gp. [★**IO**]

Wegener's Granulomatosis Support Gp. [★**16552**]

Wegener's Granulomatosis Support Gp. Intl. [★**16552**]

Wegener's Granulomatosis Support Gp. Intl. [★**IO**]

Weighers Assn; United [**4320**]

Weighing

   Amer. Assn. of Grain Inspection and Weighing Agencies [**1747**]

   Intl. Soc. of Antique Scale Collectors [**22059**]

   Intl. Soc. of Weighing and Measurement [**4016**]

   Intl. Soc. of Weighing and Measurement [**IO**]

   Natl. Conf. on Weights and Measures [**6269**]

   Scale Mfrs. Assn. [**4017**]

Weighing Agencies; Amer. Assn. of Grain Inspection and [**1747**]

Weight-Control Info. Network [**15578**], 1 WIN Way, Bethesda, MD 20892-3665, (202)828-1025

Weight Discrimination; Coun. on Size and [**12644**]

Weight Engineers; Soc. of Allied [**7699**]

Weight and Measure; Americans for Customary [**18679**]

Weight Pull Assn; Intl. [**23384**]

Weight Watchers Intl. [**14603**], 11 Madison Ave., New York, NY 10010, (212)589-2700

Weight Watchers Intl. [**IO**], New York, NY, United States

Weightlifting

   Afghanistan Weightlifting Fed. [**IO**]

   Antilliaanse Gewichthef Bond [**IO**]

   Bahrain Weightlifting and Bodybuilding Assn. [**IO**]

   Bangladesh Weightlifting Fed. [**IO**]

   Barbados Amateur Weightlifting Assn. [**IO**]

   British Weight Lifters' Assn. [**IO**]

   Canadian Powerlifting Union [**IO**]

   Chinese Taipei Weightlifting Assn. [**IO**]

   Cyprus Weightlifting Fed. [**IO**]

   Emirates Body Building and Weightlifting Fed. [**IO**]

   Ethiopian Weightlifting Fed. [**IO**]

   European Powerlifting Fed. [**IO**]

   European Weightlifting Fed. [**IO**]

   Federacion Paraguaya de Halterofilia [**IO**]

   Federacion Uruguaya de Pesas [**IO**]

   Federated States of Micronesia Weightlifting Assn. [**IO**]

   Fed. Comorienne d'Halterophilie [**IO**]

   Federazione Sammarinese [**IO**]

   Fiji Weightlifting Fed. [**IO**]

   Hellenic Weightlifting Fed. [**IO**]

   Icelandic Weightlifting Fed. [**IO**]

   Intl. Natural Bodybuilding and Fitness Fed. [**23243**]

   Jntl. Weightlifting Fed. [**IO**]

   Irish Amateur Weightlifting Assn. [**IO**]

   Khmer Weightlifting Fed. [**IO**]

   Kiribati Weightlifting Fed. [**IO**]

   Kuwait Boxing and Weightlifting Assn. [**IO**]

   Lesotho Weightlifting Fed. [**IO**]

   Lithuanian Weightlifting Fed. [**IO**]

   Macau Amateur Weightlifting Fed. [**IO**]

   Malta Amateur Weightlifting Assn. [**IO**]

   Marshall Islands Weightlifting Fed. [**IO**]

   Myanmar Weightlifting Fed. [**IO**]

   Natl. Amateur Body Builders Assn. USA [**23244**]

   Natl. Weightlifting Fed. of Georgia [**IO**]

   Nepal Weight Lifting Assn. [**IO**]

   Nigerian Weightlifting Fed. [**IO**]

   North Amer. Kettlebell Fed. [**IO**]

   North Amer. Kettlebell Fed. [**23984**]

   North Amer. Natural Bodybuilding Fed. [**23245**]

   North Amer. Powerlifting Fed. [**23662**]

   North Amer. Strongman [**23246**]

   Oceania Weightlifting Fed. [**IO**]

   Palau Weightlifting Assn. [**IO**]

   Qatar Weightlifting Fed. [**IO**]

   Queensland Weightlifting Assn. [**IO**]

   Samoa Weightlifting Fed. [**IO**]

   Saudi Arabian Weightlifting and Body Building Fed. [**IO**]

   Sierra Leone Weightlifting and Body Building Assn. [**IO**]

   Slovenian Weightlifting Fed. [**IO**]

   Solomon Islands Weightlifting Fed. [**IO**]

   Somali Weightlifting Fed. [**IO**]

   Surinamese Weightlifting and Bodybuilding Fed. [**IO**]

   Tanzania Weightlifting Fed. [**IO**]

   Uganda Weightlifting Fed. [**IO**]

   Ukrainian Weightlifting Fed. [**IO**]

   USA Weightlifting [**23985**]

   Vanuatu Weightlifting Fed. [**IO**]

   Weightlifting Assn. of Amer. Samoa [**IO**]

   Weightlifting and Body Building Assn. of Swaziland [**IO**]

   Weightlifting and Body Building Fed. of Sudan [**IO**]

   Weightlifting Fed. of Azerbaijan [**IO**]

   Weightlifting Fed. of Kyrgyzstan [**IO**]

   Weightlifting Fed. of Republic of Kazakhstan [**IO**]

   Weightlifting Fed. of Tonga [**IO**]

   Weightlifting Fed. of Turkmenistan [**IO**]

   Weightlifting Fed. of Vietnam [**IO**]

   World Association of Benchers and Dead Lifters [**IO**]

   World Assn. of Benchers and Dead Lifters [**23986**]

   Yemen Weightlifting Fed. [**IO**]

   Zambia Amateur Weightlifting Assn. [**IO**]

   Zimbabwe Weightlifting Assn. [**IO**]

Weightlifting Assn. of Amer. Samoa [**IO**], Pago Pago, American Samoa

Weightlifting and Body Building Assn. of Swaziland [**IO**], Mbabane, Swaziland

Weightlifting and Body Building Fed. of Sudan [**IO**], Khartoum, Sudan

Weightlifting and Body Building Fed. of Tanzania [★**IO**]

Weightlifting Fed. of Azerbaijan [**IO**], Baku, Azerbaijan

Weightlifting Fed. of Kyrgyzstan [**IO**], Bishkek, Kirgizstan

Weightlifting Fed. of Republic of Kazakhstan [**IO**], Almaty, Kazakhstan

Weightlifting Fed. of Tonga [**IO**], Nuku'alofa, Tonga

Weightlifting Fed. of Turkmenistan [**IO**], Ashgabat, Turkmenistan

Weightlifting Fed. of Vietnam [**IO**], Hanoi, Vietnam

Weights and Measures; Natl. Conf. on [**6269**]

Weill Found. for Music; Kurt [**10635**]

Weill/Lenya Res. Center [★**10635**]

Weill/Lenya Res. Center [★**IO**]

Weimaraner Club of Am. [**22379**], c/o Ellen Dodge, Exec. Sec., PO Box 489, Wakefield, RI 02880-0489, (401)782-3725

Weimaraners

   Weimaraner Club of Am. [**22379**]

Weiss, Ehrich

   Houdini Historical Center/Outagamie County Historical Soc. [**11123**]

Weizmann Inst. of Sci; Amer. Comm. for the [**7597**]

Welara Pony Soc; Amer. [**4854**]

Welcome to Our Elvis World - Defunct.

Welded Ring Mfrs. Assn. - Defunct.

Welded Steel Tube Inst. [★**997**]

Welded Steel Tube Inst. [★**IO**]

Welders; Intl. Union, United [★**24028**]

Welders Without Borders [**7850**], c/o Arizona Western Coll., PO Box 929, Yuma, AZ 85366-0929, (928)344-7699

Welders Without Borders [**IO**], Yuma, AZ, United States

Welding

   Amer. Coun. of the Intl. Inst. of Welding [**7846**]

A star before a book entry number signifies that the name is not listed separately, but is mentioned within the entry.

Amer. Welding Soc. [7847]
Amer. Welding Soc. [IO]
Canadian Welding Bur. [IO]
Edison Welding Inst. [7848]
European Fed. for Welding, Joining and Cutting [IO]
Gases and Welding Distributors Assn. [2021]
German Welding Soc. [IO]
Intl. Inst. of Welding [IO]
Italian Inst. of Welding [IO]
Natl. Blacksmiths and Weldors Assn. [524]
Plastics and Bd. Indus. Fed. [IO]
Resistance Welding Mfg. Alliance [2065]
U.S. Microscopic Welding Assn. [7849]
Welders Without Borders [7850]
Welders Without Borders [IO]
Welding Res. Coun. [7851]
Welding Tech. Inst. of Australia [IO]
Welding Bur; Natl. Certified Pipe [3033]
Welding Distributors; Assn. of [IO]
Welding Distributors Assn; Gases and [2021]
The Welding Inst. [IO], Cambridge, United Kingdom
Welding Mfrs. Assn. [IO], London, United Kingdom
Welding Res. Coun. [7851], PO Box 1942, New York, NY 10156, (216)658-3847
Welding Supply Assn; Natl. [★2021]
Welding Tech. Inst. of Australia [IO], Silverwater, Australia
Weldors Assn; Natl. Blacksmiths and [524]
Welfare Administrators; Natl. Assn. of Public Child [11629]
Welfare Administrators; Natl. Coun. of Local Public [★13178]
Welfare Administrators; Natl. Coun. of State Public [★13179]
Welfare Agencies; Fed. of Protestant [20482]
Welfare Assembly; Natl. Comm. on Aging of Natl. Social [★11309]
Welfare Assembly; Natl. Social [★13400]
Welfare Assn. of Am; Family [★12136]
Welfare Assn; Amer. Public [★13151]
Welfare Assn; Armenian Women's [18968]
Welfare Assn; Natl. Indian Child [19277]
Welfare Assn; Natl. Presbyterian Hea. and [★13184]
Welfare Association; Phi Chi [★24544]
Welfare Assn; Presbyterian Hea., Educ. and [13184]
Welfare Assn; United Presbyterian Hea., Educ. and [★13184]
Welfare of the Blind - Defunct.
Welfare Bd; Natl. Jewish [★12473]
Welfare Center; Italian Charity and [★19164]
Welfare Conf; Catholic Relief Services - Natl. Catholic [★12807]
Welfare Conf; War Relief Services - Natl. Catholic [★12807]
Welfare of Cripples; Intl. Soc. for the [★16333]
Welfare Directors; Natl. Assn. of County [★5618]
Welfare Found; Public [13131]
Welfare Info. Network [★12771]
Welfare Info. Systems Mgt; Amer. Assn. of Public [★13152]
Welfare Inst; Child [11571]
Welfare Law Center [★6232]
Welfare League of Am; Child [11572]
Welfare League Assn. of New York [★11885]
Welfare Made a Difference Natl. Campaign - Address unknown since 2008.
Welfare Ministries; United Methodist Assn. of Hea. and [14602]
Welfare; Natl. Catholic Soc. for Animal [★11419]
Welfare; Natl. Comm. on Foundations and Trusts for Community [★12652]
Welfare Organizations; Natl. Assembly of Natl. Hea. and Social [★13400]
Welfare and Pension Plans; Natl. Found. of Hea., [★1240]
Welfare Plans; Assn. of Private Pension and [★6169]
Welfare Policy; Center for the Stud. of [★18432]
Welfare; Protecting Adult [13028]
Welfare Res., Inc. [13193], 112 State St., Albany, NY 12207, (518)432-2563
Welfare Rights, U.S.A; Emergency Comm. to Defend Constitutional [18443]
Welfare Services; Seventh-Day Adventist [★12826]

Welfare Services, United Church of Christ; Coun. for Hea. and [★13165]
Welfare Warriors [18183], 2711 W Michigan Ave., Milwaukee, WI 53208, (414)342-6662
Welfare to Work Partnership [13146]
Well Assn; Natl. Stripper [2940]
Well Assn; Natl. Water [★4011]
Well-Being; Center for Professional [14700]
Well-Being of Hea. Professionals; Center for the [★14700]
Well Drillers Assn. [IO], Nuneaton, United Kingdom
Well Log Analysts; Soc. of Petrophysicists and [7466]
Well Log Analysts; Soc. of Professional [★7466]
Well Services Contractors Assn. [IO], Aberdeen, United Kingdom
Well Spouse Assn. [16553], 63 W Main St., Ste. H, Freehold, NJ 07728, (732)577-8899
Well Spouse Found. [★16553]
Well-Springs Found. [10179], c/o Pat Kinnamon, Exec. Dir., 550 W Butternut Rd., Summerville, SC 29483, (843)873-1960
Wellesley Centers for Women [9327], Wellesley Coll., 106 Central St., Wellesley, MA 02481, (781)283-2500
Wellesley Coll. Alumnae Assn. [24400], Green Hall, Rm. 246, 106 Central St., Wellesley, MA 02481, (781)283-2331
Welliver Soc; Judson [10127]
Wellness Associates [16058], PO Box 8422, Asheville, NC 28814, (206)984-0948
Wellness Center - Defunct.
Wellness Councils of Am. [14732], 9802 Nicholas St., Ste. 315, Omaha, NE 68114, (402)827-3590
Wellness and Health Activation Networks - Address unknown since 2001.
Wellness Inst; Natl. [16057]
Wellness; Nature of [13701]
Wellness Rsrc. Center [★16058]
Wells Appreciation Soc; Kitty [★24936]
Wells Family Res. Assn. [21081], PO Box 5427, Kent, WA 98064-5427
Wells Family Res. Assn. [IO], Kent, WA, United States
Wells-Johnny Wright-Bobby Wright Intl. Fan Club; Kitty [24936]
Wells/Johnny Wright Fan Club; Kitty [★24936]
Wellstart Intl. [14666], PO Box 80877, San Diego, CA 92138-0877, (619)295-5192

Welsh
Cardigan Welsh Corgi Club of Am. [22240]
Natl. Welsh-American Found. [19430]
North Amer. Assn. for the Stud. of Welsh Culture and History [11083]
North Amer. Assn. for the Stud. of Welsh Culture and History [IO]
Pembroke Welsh Corgi Club of Am. [22340]
St. David's Soc. of the State of New York [19431]
Underfashion Club [258]
Welsh-American Genealogical Soc. [21156]
Welsh Natl. Gymanfa Ganu Assn. [19432]
Welsh Natl. Gymanfa Ganu Assn. [IO]
WTCARES [22389]
Welsh Amateur Dance Sport Assn. [IO], Cardiff, United Kingdom
Welsh Amateur Music Fed. [IO], Cardiff, United Kingdom
Welsh-American Found; Natl. [19430]
Welsh-American Genealogical Soc. [21156], 60 Norton Ave., Poultney, VT 05764-1029
Welsh Badminton Union [IO], Cardiff, United Kingdom
Welsh Black Cattle Assn. - Defunct.
Welsh Black Cattle Soc. [IO], Caernarfon, United Kingdom
Welsh Books Coun. [IO], Aberystwyth, United Kingdom
Welsh Centre for Intl. Affairs [IO], Cardiff, United Kingdom
Welsh Corgi Club of Am; Cardigan [22240]
Welsh Corgi Club of Am; Pembroke [22340]
Welsh Croquet Assn. [IO], Caldicot, United Kingdom
Welsh Harp Soc. of North America - Address unknown since 1999.
Welsh Judo Assn. [IO], Abertillery, United Kingdom

Welsh Liberal Democrats [IO], Cardiff, United Kingdom
Welsh Liberal Party [★IO]
Welsh Music Guild [IO], Llanelli, United Kingdom
Welsh Natl. Gymanfa Ganu Assn. [IO], Hartland, MI, United States
Welsh Natl. Gymanfa Ganu Assn. [19432], c/o Dr. John Ellis, Exec. Dir., PO Box 215, Hartland, MI 48353-0215, (810)632-7850
Welsh Natl. Party [★IO]
Welsh Pony and Cob Soc. [IO], Aberystwyth, United Kingdom
Welsh Pony and Cob Soc. of Am. [4969], 720 Green St., Stephens City, VA 22655, (540)868-7669
Welsh Pony and Cob Soc. of Am. [★4969]
Welsh Pony Soc. of Am. [★4969]
Welsh Propriety Soc. - Defunct.
Welsh Rugby Union [IO], Cardiff, United Kingdom
Welsh Secondary Schools Assn. [IO], Swansea, United Kingdom
Welsh Springer Spaniel Club of Am. [22380], c/o Carla Vooris, Corresponding Sec., 783 Ellington Farm Rd., Manson, NC 27553, (252)456-3645
Welsh Terrier Club of America - Address unknown since 2001.
Welsh Terrier Club of Am. Rescue Ser. [★22389]
Welsh Women's Aid - Cardiff Natl. Off. [IO], Cardiff, United Kingdom
Welt-Gesellschaft fur Buiatrik [★IO]
Welt-Tierarztegesellschaft [★IO]
Welthaus Bielefeld [★IO]
Weltorganisation fur Schiffsmodellbau und Schiffs-modellsport [★IO]
Weltrat fur Erneuerbare Energien [★IO]
Welttierschutzgesellschaft e.V. [★IO]
Weltverband der Sportartikel-Industrie [★IO]
Weltverband fur Technische Bildung [★IO]
Wemos [IO], Amsterdam, Netherlands
Wen-Chen Memorial Found; Professor Chen [18694]
Wendel Adkins Fan Club - Defunct.
Wendt Center for Loss and Healing; William [13317]
Wensleydale Longwool Sheep Breeders' Assn. [IO], Heighington, United Kingdom
WEP Intl. [IO], The Hague, Netherlands
WERA Motorcycle Roadracing [23628], 2555 Mari-etta Hwy., Ste. 104, Canton, GA 30114, (770)720-5010
Wereldsolidariteit [★IO]
Werewolf Res. Center - Defunct.
Werkstatt 3 [★IO]
Wernicke-Korsakoff Syndrome Assn. - Defunct.
Wert Family History Assn. [21082], PO Box 240, Port Royal, PA 17082-0240, (717)527-4399
Wescosa Lumber Assn. - Defunct.
Wesleyan/Holiness Women Clergy [20291], c/o Rev. Carla Sunberg, Treas., 8611 Mayhew Rd., Fort Wayne, IN 46835, (260)241-2993
Wesleyan/Holiness Women Clergy [IO], Grantham, PA, United States
Wesleyan Service Guild - Defunct.
West Africa
African Heritage Center for African Dance and Music [9347]
Egbe Omo Yoruba: Natl. Assn. of Yoruba Descendants in North America [19289]
Sierra Visions [12444]
West Africa Bus. Assn. [IO], London, United Kingdom
West Africa Network for Peacebuilding [IO], Accra, Ghana
West Africa Rice Development Assn. [★IO]
West Africa Telecommunication Regulators Assn. [IO], Abuja, Nigeria
West African Coll. of Surgeons [IO], Lagos, Nigeria
West African Discussion Agreement [3597]
West African Examinations Coun. [IO], Accra, Ghana
West African Journalists Assn. [IO], Dakar, Senegal
West Australian Croquet Assn. [IO], Mount Lawley, Australia
West Australian Olive Coun. [IO], Claremont, Australia
West; Center for Cultural and Tech. Interchange Between East and [★17882]
West Coast Crossarm Assn. - Defunct.
West Coast Electronics Manufacturers Assn. [★1203]

Reference to "IO" in place of a book number signifies that the association may be found in the 45th edition of International Organizations.

West Coast Electronics Manufacturers Assn. [★IO]
West Coast Environmental Law [IO], Vancouver, BC, Canada
West Coast Lumber Inspection Bur. [1628], PO Box 23145, Tigard, OR 97281, (503)639-0651
West Coast Lumbermen's Assn. [★1631]
West Coast Mineral Assn. - Address unknown since 1995.
West Coast Shrimp Producers Assn. - Defunct.
West Coast Velocette Owners Club [★22695]
West Cultural Center; East- [9619]
West-Europaisches Institut fur Holzimpragnierung [★IO]
West Gulf Maritime Assn. [2595], 1717 E Loop, Portway Plz., Ste. 200, Houston, TX 77029, (713)678-7655
West Highland White Terrier Club of Am. [22381], c/o Cheryl Stinson, Membership Chair, 10613 Elder Ln., Prospect, KY 40059, (502)423-1668
West Indian
  Anguilla Tourist Bd. [24224]
  Grenada Bd. of Tourism [24253]
  Montserrat Progressive Soc. of New York [19433]
  Saint Lucia Tourist Bd. [24255]
West Indian Students Assn. - Address unknown since 1995.
West Indies Mission [★20417]
West Indies Mission [★IO]
West Kent Chamber of Commerce and Indus. [IO], Tonbridge, United Kingdom
West Kootenay Brain Injury Assn. [IO], Castlegar, BC, Canada
West Midlands Campaign for Nuclear Disarmament [IO], Birmingham, United Kingdom
West; Native Daughters of the Golden [18986]
West; Native Sons of the Golden [18987]
West Point
  Assn. of Graduates [8882]
West Point Societies [★8882]
West Soc; Zane Grey's [9728]
West Wales Chamber of Commerce [IO], Swansea, United Kingdom
West World Holiday Exchange [★22580]
Westar Inst. [20509], PO Box 7268, Santa Rosa, CA 95407, (707)523-1323
Westbeth Corp. [9530], 463 West St., New York, NY 10014, (212)691-1500
Westbeth Playwrights Feminist Collective - Defunct.
Westcott Descendants of Am; Soc. of Stukely [21056]
Western Amateur Astronomers - Address unknown since 2001.
Western Ancient Forest Campaign - Address unknown since 2001.
Western Apicultural Soc. of North America - Address unknown since 2003.
Western Apparel and Equip. Manufacturers Assn. [★259]
Western Armenian Athletic Assn. - Address unknown since 2001.
Western Assoc. Modelers [22661], c/o Doug Barton, Pres., 160 Park Ave., Woodland, CA 95695, (530)662-6469
Western Assn. of Architects [★6463]
Western Assn. for Art Conservation [304], c/o Alexis Miller, Sec., Balboa Art Conservation Center, PO Box 3755, San Diego, CA 92163-1755, (619)236-9702
Western Assn. of Art Conservators [★304]
Western Assn. of Christian Schools [★8081]
Western Assn. of Christian Schools [★IO]
Western Assn. of Fish and Wildlife Agencies [5735], c/o Larry L. Kruckenberg, Sec., Wyoming Game and Fish Dept., 5400 Bishop Blvd., Cheyenne, WY 82009, (307)777-4569
Western Assn. of Map Libraries [10394], c/o Mary Douglass, Pres., Seattle Public Lib., History, Travel, Maps Dept., 1000 4th Ave., Seattle, WA 98104, (206)386-4627
Western Assn. of Schools and Colleges [8314], c/o Accrediting Commn. for Senior Colleges and Universities, 985 Atlantic Ave., Ste. 100, Alameda, CA 94501, (510)748-9001
Western Assn. of State Game and Fish Commissioners [★5735]

Western Athletic Conf. [23866], 9250 E Costilla Ave., Ste. 300, Englewood, CO 80112, (303)799-9221
Western Australia Scripture Union [IO], Mount Hawthorn, Australia
Western Australian Assn. for Mental Hea. [IO], Perth, Australia
Western Australian Farmers Fed. [IO], East Perth, Australia
Western Australian Secondary School Executives Assn. [IO], West Leederville, Australia
Western Beet Sugar Producers - Defunct.
Western Behavioral Sciences Inst. - Defunct.
Western Bird Banding Assn. - Address unknown since 1995.
Western Bohemian Catholic Union [★18998]
Western Bohemian Fraternal Assn. [★19030]
Western Buddhist Order; Friends of the [19551]
Western Building Material Assn. [1629], PO Box 1699, Olympia, WA 98507, (360)943-3054
Western Canada Conservation and Reclamation Assn. [★IO]
Western Canada Psychoanalytic Psychotherapy Assn. [IO], Vancouver, BC, Canada
Western Canada Wilderness Comm. [IO], Vancouver, BC, Canada
Western Canadian Watercross Assn. [IO], Saskatoon, SK, Canada
Western Catholic Union [19010], 510 Maine St., Quincy, IL 62301, (217)223-9721
Western Center on Law and Poverty [6037], 3701 Wilshire Blvd., Ste. 208, Los Angeles, CA 90010-2809, (213)487-7211
Western Central Atlantic Fishery Commn. [IO], Christ Church, Barbados
Western Civilization; The Comm. for [8243]
Western Coal Coun. Mission [★6702]
Western Coal Trans. Assn. [★844]
Western Coll. Assn. - Defunct.
Western Coll. Reading Assn. [★9042]
Western Coll. Reading and Learning Assn. [★9042]
Western Collegiate Hockey Assn. [23489], 2211 S Josephine, Rm. 302, Denver, CO 80210, (303)871-4223
Western Coun. of Constr. Consumers [950], 31320 Via Colinas, Ste. 120, Westlake Village, CA 91362, (818)735-4733
Western Coun. on Intl. Banking [★483]
Western Coun. of Model Boating [★22654]
Western Coun. of Model Boating [★IO]
Western Cover Soc. [22890], c/o John Drew, Sec., 15370 Skyview Terr., San Jose, CA 95132-3042, (408)258-6922
Western Crop Protection Assn. - Address unknown since 2004.
Western Dredging Assn. [2596], c/o Lawrence M. Patella, Exec. Dir., PO Box 5797, Vancouver, WA 98668-5797, (360)750-0209
Western Eastern Roadracers Assn. [★23628]
Western Eastern Roadracer's Assn., Inc. [★23628]
Western Economic Assn. Intl. [6897], 7400 Center Ave., Ste. 109, Huntington Beach, CA 92647-3039, (714)898-3222
Western Economic Assn. Intl. [IO], Huntington Beach, CA, United States
Western Educational Soc. for Telecommunications - Defunct.
Western Electronics Manufacturers Assn. [★1203]
Western Electronics Manufacturers Assn. [★IO]
Western Engine Rebuilders Assn. [★1295]
Western and English Manufacturers Assn. [★259]
Western/English Retailers of America - Defunct.
Western-English Trade Assn. [259], 451 E 58th Ave., No. 4323, Denver, CO 80216-8468, (303)295-2001
Western European Inst. for Wood Preservation [IO], Brussels, Belgium
Western European Metal Trades Employers' Org. [★IO]
Western European Union [IO], Brussels, Belgium
Western Fairs Assn. [1327], 1776 Tribute Rd., Ste. 210, Sacramento, CA 95815-4495, (916)927-3100
Western Falconry Assn. - Defunct.
Western Fast-Draw Assn. [★23733]
Western Film Club; Old Time [24827]
Western Floor Covering Assn. [★3431]
Western Floor Covering Assn. [★IO]

Western Forest Products Safety Conf. [★12962]
Western Forestry Center [★4701]
Western Forestry Center [★IO]
Western Forestry and Conservation Assn. [IO], Portland, OR, United States
Western Forestry and Conservation Assn. [4700], 4033 SW Canyon Rd., Portland, OR 97221, (503)226-4562
Western Found. of Dualism - Defunct.
Western Found. for Raptor Conservation [★7419]
Western Found. for Raptor Conservation [★IO]
Western Fraternal Life Assn. [19030], 1900 1st Ave. NE, Cedar Rapids, IA 52402-5372, (319)363-2653
Western Front Assn. - U.S. Br. [10485], 96 Coll. Ave., Poughkeepsie, NY 12603, (845)486-6189
Western Fruit Jobbers Assn. [★4766]
Western Gamebird Alliance [4466], PO Box 14152, Tucson, AZ 85732, (520)241-3534
Western Gerontological Soc. [★11275]
Western Goals Found. - Address unknown since 1989.
Western Golf Assn. [23471], 1 Briar Rd., Golf, IL 60029, (847)724-4600
Western Growers Assn. [4774], PO Box 2130, Newport Beach, CA 92658, (949)863-1000
Western Growers Protective Assn. [★4774]
Western Hardwood Assn. [1630], PO Box 1095, Camas, WA 98607, (360)835-1600
Western Hemisphere Assn. of Meat Marketers - Address unknown since 2002.
Western Hemisphere Friendship Assn. - Address unknown since 1988.
Western Heraldry Org. - Address unknown since 2004.
Western Heritage Center; Natl. Cowboy Hall of Fame and [★9381]
Western Heroes Appreciation Soc. - Defunct.
Western Highway Inst. - Address unknown since 2003.
Western Historical Res. Associates - Defunct.
Western History Assn. [9384], Univ. of Missouri - St. Louis, 152C Univ. Center, 1 Univ. Blvd., St. Louis, MO 63121, (314)516-7282
Western Hockey League - Address unknown since 1995.
Western Home Furnishings Assn. [1709], 500 Giuseppe Ct., Ste. 6, Roseville, CA 95678, (916)784-7677
Western Humor and Irony Membership [★10210]
Western Humor and Irony Membership [★IO]
Western Independent Bankers [500], 600 Montgomery St., Ste. 1200, San Francisco, CA 94111, (415)352-2323
Western Intl. Trade Group - Defunct.
Western Intl. Walking Horse Assn. [4970], c/o Kim Swingley, Sec., PO Box 872228, Vancouver, WA 98687-2228, (503)570-0108
Western Intl. Walking Horse Assn. [IO], Vancouver, WA, United States
Western Interpreters Assn. [★7363]
Western Interstate Energy Board/WINB [18139], c/o Douglas C. Larson, Exec. Dir., 1600 Broadway, Ste. 1700, Denver, CO 80202, (303)573-8910
Western Interstate Nuclear Compact [★18139]
Western Iron Ore Assn. [★2696]
Western Iron Ore Assn. [★IO]
Western Literature Assn. [10434], Utah State Univ., English Dept., 3200 Old Main Hill, Logan, UT 84322-3200, (435)797-1603
Western Manufactured Housing Communities Assn. [2532], 455 Capitol Mall, Ste. 800, Sacramento, CA 95814, (916)448-7002
Western Mobilehome Parkowners Assn. [★2532]
Western Music; Acad. of Country and [★10518]
Western Music Assn. [10723], c/o Roger S. Banks, Exec. Dir., 3342 Cedarhill Dr., San Angelo, TX 76904, (325)234-4306
Western Music Assn. [★10723]
Western Music Assn; Intl. [★10723]
Western Natl. Parks Assn. [7365], 12880 N Vistoso Village Dr., Tucson, AZ 85755, (520)622-1999
Western New Mexico Univ. Alumni Assn. [18944], PO Box 680, Silver City, NM 88062, (505)538-6675
Western Oil and Gas Assn. [★2951]

A star before a book entry number signifies that the name is not listed separately, but is mentioned within the entry.

Western Olive Assn. [IO], Dubbo, Australia

Western Pacific Assn. of Transactional Analysts [IO], Mosman, Australia

Western Payments Alliance [1451], 685 Market St., Ste. 540, San Francisco, CA 94105, (415)433-1230

Western Petroleum Refiners Assn. [★2939]

Western Pine Assn. [★1631]

Western Plumbing Officials Assn. [★5549]

Western Plumbing Officials Assn. [★IO]

Western Public Radio [3273], Fort Mason Center, Bldg. D, San Francisco, CA 94123, (415)771-1160

Western Pulp and Paper Workers; Assn. of [24064]

Western Railroad Assn. - Address unknown since 1999.

Western Railroad Traffic Assn. - Address unknown since 1999.

Western Railway Historical Soc; Ontario and [10916]

Western Railway Supervisors Assn. [★24180]

Western Range Assn. [5220]

Western Red Cedar Assn. - Address unknown since 2001.

Western Red Cedar Lumber Assn. [IO], Vancouver, BC, Canada

Western Retail Lumbermen's Assn. [★1629]

Western River Guides Assn. [★23681]

Western Roentgen Soc. [★16293]

Western Roque Assn. [★23090]

Western Rugby Union of the United States [★23706]

Western Saddle Clubs Assn. [4971], c/o Teri Spence, Sec., 47009 Company Rd. 13, St. Peter, MN 56082, (507)345-5856

Western Safety Conf. [★12962]

Western Sahara Campaign for Human Rights and Humanitarian Relief - Defunct.

Western Shoe Retailers Assn. [★1602]

Western Single Side Band Assn. - Defunct.

Western Slavonic Assn. [★19148]

Western Snow Conf. [7845], c/o Randall Osterhuber, Documents Mgr., PO Box 810, Soda Springs, CA 95728, (530)426-0318

Western Social Sci. Assn. [7657], c/o Larry Gould, Exec. Dir., Northern Arizona Univ., Coll. of Social and Behavioral Sciences, Box 15700, Flagstaff, AZ 86011, (928)523-9508

Western Soc. of Business Publications - Defunct.

Western Soc. of Malacologists [7257], c/o Victor Smith, Sec.-Treas., 53 Woodbine Dr., Mill Valley, CA 94941

Western Soc. of Naturalists [7366], Dept. of Biology, San Diego State Univ., 5500 Campanile Dr., San Diego, CA 92182

Western Soc. of Periodontology [14187], PO Box 458, Artesia, CA 90702, (562)493-4080

Western Society of Periodontology [IO], Artesia, CA, United States

Western States Advt. Agencies Assn. [★107]

Western States Angus Assn. - Address unknown since 1999.

Western States Legal Found. [6148], 1204 Preservation Pkwy., Oakland, CA 94612, (510)839-5877

Western States Meat Assn. [★2662]

Western States Meat Packers Assn. [★2662]

Western States Petroleum Assn. [2951], 1415 L St., Ste. 600, Sacramento, CA 95814-3964, (916)498-7750

Western States Safety Conf. [★12962]

Western Surfing Assn. - Address unknown since 1990.

Western Surgical Assn. [16592], c/o Gregory J. Jurkovich, MD, Sec., UW Harborview Medical Center, 325 Ninth Ave., Seattle, WA 98104-2420, (206)731-8485

Western Timber Assn. [★1605]

Western Traders Assn. [★22057]

Western Traders Assn. [★IO]

Western Union Employees Assn; Retired [496]

Western U.S. Agricultural Trade Assn. [4118], 4601 NE 77th Ave., Ste. 120, Vancouver, WA 98662-4730, (360)693-3373

Western Vehicle Leasing Assn. [★3385]

Western Veterinary Conf. [16817], 2425 E Oquendo Rd., Las Vegas, NV 89120, (702)739-6698

Western Victorian Olive Assn. [IO], Armstrong, Australia

Western Wheat Assn. [★IO]

Western Wheat Assn. [★4319]

Western Wholesale Druggists [★2984]

Western Wholesale Pet Supply Assn. [★2968]

Western Wholesale Pet Supply Assn. [★IO]

Western Winter Sports Representatives Assn. [3675], 726 Tenacity Dr., Unit B, Longmont, CO 80504, (303)532-4002

Western Women Bowlers [★23257]

Western Women Premier Bowlers [23257], c/o Mrs. Laura Hardeman, Sec., 938 Redbud Rd., Chula Vista, CA 91910

Western Women Professional Bowlers [★23257]

Western Wood Heel Mfrs. Assn. - Defunct.

Western Wood Moulding Producers [★688]

Western Wood Moulding Producers [★IO]

Western Wood Products Assn. [1631], 522 SW 5th Ave., Ste. 500, Portland, OR 97204-2122, (503)224-3930

Western Wooden Box Assn. - Address unknown since 1994.

Western World Avon Club - Defunct.

Western World Haiku Soc. - Defunct.

Western World Pet Supply Assn. [★2968]

Western World Pet Supply Assn. [★IO]

Western Writers of Am. [11201], c/o Rod Miller, 1665 E Julio St., Sandy, UT 84093

Western Young Buddhist League [19558], c/o Buddhist Churches of Am., 1710 Octavia St., San Francisco, CA 94109

Westerners Found. [★9385]

Westerners Found. [★IO]

Westerners Intl. [IO], Oklahoma City, OK, United States

Westerners Intl. [9385], 1700 NE 63rd St., Oklahoma City, OK 73111, (800)541-4650

Westfalen Warmblood Assn. of Am. - Address unknown since 2001.

Westinghouse Engineers Assn. Natl. - Defunct.

Westinghouse Independent Salaried Unions; Fed. of [24047]

Westland Training - Defunct.

Westminster Kennel Club [22382], 149 Madison Ave., Ste. 402, New York, NY 10016-6713, (212)213-3165

Weston A. Price Found. [15572], PMB 106-380, 4200 Wisconsin Ave. NW, Washington, DC 20016, (202)363-4394

Weston A. Price Memorial Found. [★15568]

Wet Ground Mica Assn. - Defunct.

WeTip [11849], PO Box 1296, Rancho Cucamonga, CA 91729-1296, (909)987-5005

Wetland Managers; Assn. of State [4363]

Wetland Scientists; Soc. of [4452]

Wetlands
  Amer. Wildlands [4354]
  Assn. of State Wetland Managers [4363]
  Izaak Walton League of Am. [4413]
  Izaak Walton League of Am. Endowment [4414]
  Natl. Mitigation Banking Assn. [4425]
  Natl. Wetlands Coalition [5284]
  Soc. of Wetland Scientists [4452]
  Wetlands Intl. [IO]
  Wilderness Classroom Org. [8951]

Wetlands Intl. [IO], Wageningen, Netherlands

Wetlands Intl. Asia Pacific-Indonesia Programme [IO], Jawa Barat, Indonesia

Wetlands for Wildlife - Defunct.

Wett Ones [IO], Newtown, Australia

Wetterling Found; Jacob [11608]

Wexford Chamber of Indus. and Commerce [IO], Wexford, Ireland

Whale Adoption Proj. [5390], 7 Nelson St., Plymouth, MA 02360, (508)746-2522

Whale and Dolphin Conservation Soc. [IO], Chippenham, United Kingdom

Whale Found; Pacific [5363]

Whale Program; Adopt-A- [★5363]

Whale Protection Fund [★4435]

Whale Protection Fund [★IO]

Whale Res; Center for [7260]

Whale Res. and Conservation Fund - Defunct.

Whalers Booster Club; Hartford [25006]

Whales
  Blue Dolphin Alliance [5008]
  Greenpeace U.S.A. [4571]
  Interspecies [7223]
  Japan Whaling Assn. [IO]
  Ocean Soc. [7401]
  Oceanic Soc. Expeditions [23016]
  Pacific Whale Found. [5363]
  Save the Whales [5379]
  Whale Adoption Proj. [5390]
  Whale and Dolphin Conservation Soc. [IO]
  Whaling Museum Soc. [10451]
  World Whale Police [5285]

Whales; Save the [5379]

Whaling Commn; Intl. [IO]

Whaling Museum; Cold Spring Harbor [★10451]

Whaling Museum Soc. [10451], PO Box 25, Cold Spring Harbor, NY 11724, (631)367-3418

What If Org. [18858]

What Kids Can Do [18859], PO Box 603252, Providence, RI 02906, (401)247-7665

Wheat Assn; Natl. Soft [★2738]

Wheat Assn; Western [★4319]

Wheat Export Trade Educ. Comm. [4791], 415 2nd St. NE, Ste. 300, Washington, DC 20002, (202)547-2004

Wheat Flour Inst. [★2738]

Wheat Foods Coun. [1755], 10841 S Crossroads Dr., Ste. 105, Parker, CO 80138, (303)840-8787

Wheat Gluten Industry Coun. - Defunct.

Wheat; Great Plains [★4319]

Wheat Growers; Natl. Assn. of [4309]

Wheat Improvement Assn. Hard Winter Wheat Quality Coun; Kansas [★4322]

Wheat Industry Coun. - Defunct.

Wheat Inst; Durum [★2738]

Wheat Quality Coun. [4322], c/o Ben Handcock, Exec. VP, 106 W Capitol, Ste. 2, PO Box 966, Pierre, SD 57501-0966, (605)224-5187

Wheat Quality Coun; Kansas Wheat Improvement Assn. Hard Winter [★4322]

Wheat Ridge Found. [★20233]

Wheat Ridge Ministries [20233], 1 Pierce Pl., Ste. 250E, Itasca, IL 60143-2634, (630)766-9066

Wheat Weavers; Natl. Assn. of [22166]

Wheat and Wheat Foods Found. - Defunct.

Wheatland; James Buchanan Found. for the Preservation of [11126]

Wheel of Progress - Address unknown since 1995.

Wheelchair Assn; Irish [IO]

Wheelchair Athletic Assn; Natl. [★23371]

Wheelchair Aviators; California [★21457]

Wheelchair Basketball Assn; Natl. [23354]

Wheelchair Bowling Assn; Amer. [23339]

Wheelchair Football Assn; Universal [23368]

Wheelchair Motorcycle Assn. [23370]

Wheelchair Pilots Assn. - Defunct.

Wheelchair Poolplayer Assn; Natl. [23355]

Wheelchair Softball Assn; Natl. [23356]

Wheelchair Sports Alberta [IO], Edmonton, AB, Canada

Wheelchair Sports Assn; BC [IO]

Wheelchair Sports Assn. of Newfoundland and Labrador [IO], Paradise, NL, Canada

Wheelchair Sports Assn. of South Australia [IO], Northfield, Australia

Wheelchair Sports, USA [23371], PO Box 5266, Kendall Park, NJ 08824, (732)422-4546

Wheelchair Sports Victoria [IO], Abbotsford, Australia

Wheelchair Tennis Players Assn. - Address unknown since 2000.

Wheeler Club - USA Gp; Morgan Three- [21719]

The Wheelmen [23322], c/o Paul Brekus, Treas., 4485 Utica St., Denver, CO 80212-2436

Wheelmen/Bicycle U.S.A; League of Amer. [★23312]

WheelPower - British Wheelchair Sport [IO], Stoke Mandeville, United Kingdom

Wheels; Women on [★23630]

Wheels for the World [11994], c/o Joni and Friends Intl. Disability Center, PO Box 3333, Agoura Hills, CA 91376-3333, (818)707-5664

Wheels for the World [IO], Agoura Hills, CA, United States

Whey Products Inst. [★1130]

Which [IO], London, United Kingdom
Whiggamores - Defunct.
Whigs; Soc. for the Preservation and Enhancement of the Recognition of Millard Fillmore, Last of the [22601]
Whimsical Alternative Political Action Comm. - Defunct.
Whippet Club; Amer. [22216]
Whirlpool Bath Mfrs. Assn. - Defunct.
Whirly-Girls - Intl. Women Helicopter Pilots [21487], c/o Teen Corey, PO Box 265, Pinehurst, TX 77362
Whirly-Girls - Intl. Women Helicopter Pilots [IO], Pinehurst, TX, United States
Whiskey Painters of America - Defunct.
Whiskey Rebellion; Sons of the [19389]
Whisky Pitcher Collectors Assn. of Am. [22130], 22862 Bluejay Ave., Mattawan, MI 49071, (269)668-4169
Whisky Pitcher Collectors Association of America [IO], Mattawan, MI, United States
Whisper - Defunct.
Whistle Collectors Assn; Call and [21983]
Whistle Enthusiasts; Air Horn and Steam [★22037]
Whistle Enthusiasts Gp; Horn and [22037]
Whistleblower Center; Natl. [12982]
White Americans Party; Natl. Socialist [★18798]
White Aryan Resistance - Address unknown since 1994.
White Bison [10757], 6145 Lehman Dr., Ste. 200, Colorado Springs, CO 80918, (719)548-1000
White Confederacy [18807], c/o Natl. Socialist Movement, PO Box 580669, Minneapolis, MN 55458-0669, (651)659-6307
White Cross; Knights of the [★19293]
White Fan Club; Betty [24732]
White Found; William Allen [9723]
White Front Drapery Concessionaires [★2256]
White German Shepherd Dog Club of Am. [22383], c/o Tracie Karsjens, Natl. Show and Trial Coor./Ed./Webmaster, 22761 Claire Ct., Rogers, MN 55374
White German Shepherd Dog Club of Am. [IO], Rogers, MN, United States
White Goods Suppliers' Assn. [IO], Istanbul, Turkey
White Horse and Amer. Creme Horse Registry; Amer. [4855]
White House Correspondents' Assn. [3173], 1920 N St. NW, Ste. 300, Washington, DC 20036, (202)452-4836
White House Historical Assn. [10165], PO Box 27624, Washington, DC 20038-7624, (202)737-8292
White House News Photographers Assn. [3018], 7119 Ben Franklin Sta., Washington, DC 20044-7119, (202)785-5230
White Ironstone China Assn. [21940], c/o Diane Dorman, PO Box 855, Fairport, NY 14450-0855, (212)715-9246
White Lung Assn. [13332], PO Box 1483, Baltimore, MD 21203-1483, (410)243-5864
White Lung Association [IO], Baltimore, MD, United States
White Mountain Educ. Assn. [20567], PO Box 11975, Prescott, AZ 86304, (928)778-0638
White Owners Register [23026], 1624 Perkins Dr., Arcadia, CA 91006, (626)355-7679
White Owners Register [IO], Arcadia, CA, United States
White Park Cattle Assn. of Am. [★4218]
White People's Party; Natl. Socialist [★18805]
White Plate Flat Trackers Assn. [23629], PO Box 897, Sturgis, SD 57785

White Supremacy
Center for Democratic Renewal [17098]
The Creativity Movement [18798]
The Creativity Movement [IO]
Intelligence Proj. [17121]
Knights of the Ku Klux Klan [18799]
Natl. Alliance [18800]
Natl. Assn. for the Advancement of White People Natl. [18801]
Natl. Socialist Movement [18802]
National Socialist Movement [IO]
Natl. Socialist Vanguard [18803]
The Nationalist Movement [18804]

New Order [18805]
New Order [IO]
New Order Legion [18806]
White Confederacy [18807]
White Swine Record Assn; Chester [5234]
White Terrier Club of Am; West Highland [22381]
Whitebred Shorthorn Assn. [IO], Brampton, United Kingdom
Whitehall Found. [7381], PO Box 3423, Palm Beach, FL 33480, (561)655-4474
Whiteruthenian Amer. Relief - Defunct.
Whiteruthenian Inst. of Arts and Sci. [★9734]
Whiteruthenian Inst. of Arts and Sci. [★IO]
Whitetails Unlimited [5391], PO Box 720, Sturgeon Bay, WI 54235, (920)743-6777
Whiteware Res. Assn. - Defunct.
Whitewater Affiliation; Amer. [★23682]
Whitewater; Amer. [23682]
Whitman Birthplace Assn; Walt [9721]
Whitman-Radclyffe Found. - Defunct.
Whitman, Walt
Walt Whitman Birthplace Assn. [9721]
Whitney Houston's Official Fan Club - Address unknown since 2002.
Who is Colin Baker Fan Club of America - Defunct.
WHO Intl. Reference Centre for Community Water Supply [★IO]
Wholesale
Natl. Assn. of Tobacco Outlets [3820]
Natl. Specialty Gift Assn. [1724]
Retail, Wholesale and Dept. Store Union [24182]
Wholesale; Assoc. Bakers of Am. - Retail and [★454]
Wholesale Beer Assn. Executives of Am. [★204]
Wholesale Booksellers Assn; Amer. [3398]
Wholesale Commn. Florists of Am. [★1495]
Wholesale Confectionery and Tobacco Alliance [IO], Farnham, United Kingdom
Wholesale and Dept. Store Union; Retail, [24182]
Wholesale Distribution
Canadian Assn. of Wholesale Sales Representatives [IO]
Comite Royal Belge de la Distribution [IO]
Coun. of Supply Chain Mgt. Professionals [4018]
Distribution Bus. Mgt. Assn. [4019]
Distribution Res. and Educ. Found. [4020]
European Assn. of Pharmaceutical Full-Line Wholesalers [IO]
Fed. of Finnish Commerce and Trade [IO]
Gen. Merchandise Distributors Coun. [4021]
Independent Sealing Distributors [4022]
Natl. Assn. of Plumbing Specialty Distributors [3063]
Natl. Assn. of Sign Supply Distributors [4023]
Natl. Assn. of Wholesaler-Distributors [4024]
Natl. Convenience Store Distributors Assn. [IO]
Netherlands Wholesale and Intl. Trade Fed. [IO]
Off. Furniture Distribution Assn. [4025]
U.S. Aquaculture Suppliers Assn. [4026]
Wholesale Markets Brokers' Assn. [IO]
World Union of Wholesale Markets [IO]
Wholesale Distributors Assn. [3067], 10935 Estate Ln., Ste. 110, Dallas, TX 75238, (972)513-1134
Wholesale Distributors Assn. Educational Foundation [★3067]
Wholesale Druggists' Assn; Natl. [★2984]
Wholesale Druggists Merchandising Assn. - Address unknown since 1995.
Wholesale Druggists; Western [★2984]
Wholesale Florist and Florist Supplier Assn. [1495], 147 Old Solomons Island Rd., Ste. 302, Annapolis, MD 21401, (410)573-0400
Wholesale Florists and Florist Suppliers of Am. [★1495]
Wholesale Fresh Fruit and Vegetable Distributors; Natl. League of [★4766]
Wholesale Frozen Food Distributors Assn; Natl. [★1547]
Wholesale Furniture Assn; Natl. [★1700]
Wholesale Furniture Salesmen's Assn; Natl. [★1702]
Wholesale Lumber Assn; North Amer. [1611]
Wholesale Marketers Assn; Amer. [1500]
Wholesale Markets Brokers' Assn. [IO], London, United Kingdom
Wholesale Seafood Merchants; Bd. of Trade of the [4323]

Wholesale Stationers Assn. - Address unknown since 2003.
Wholesale Variety Bakers Assn. [455], c/o Steve Baldinger, Pres., 215 Eva St., St. Paul, MN 55107, (651)224-5761
Wholesalers of Am; Wine and Spirits [212]
Wholesalers Assn; Central [3064]
Wholesalers Assn; Drug [★2984]
Wholesalers Assn; Farm Equip. [180]
Wholesalers; Assn. of Independent Optical [★1864]
Wholesalers Assn; Natl. Beer [207]
Wholesalers Assn; Natl. Candy [★1500]
Wholesalers Assn; Natl. Elec. [★1190]
Wholesalers Assn; Natl. Wallpaper [★2278]
Wholesalers Assn; North Central [3064]
Wholesalers Assn; Northamerican Heating, Refrigeration, and Airconditioning [★1882]
Wholesalers Assn; Optical [★1864]
Wholesalers Assn; Wallpaper [★2278]
Wholesalers Intl; Air-Conditioning and Refrigeration [★1882]
Wholesalers; Intl. Fed. of Pharmaceutical [2976]
Wholesalers; Natl. Assn. of Musical Merchandise [★2814]
Wholesalers Natl. Assn; Optical [★1864]
Wholesalers; Natl. Assn. of Sporting Goods [3644]
Wholesalers Secretaries; State Beer [★204]
Wholesaling Assn; Sanitary Supply [2476]
Whoo Who Sprue [★15543]
Whooping Crane Conservation Assn. [5392], c/o Keith Durham, Web Admin., 715 Earl Dr., Lawrenceburg, TN 38464
Whooping Crane Conservation Gp. [★5392]
WHTour [IO], Brussels, Belgium
Wi-Fi Alliance [6829], 3925 W Braker Ln., Austin, TX 78759, (512)305-0790
WIC Assn; Natl. [6262]
WIC Directors; Natl. Assn. of [★6262]
Wiccan
Alternative Religions Educational Network [20457]
Church and School of Wicca [20613]
Church and School of Wicca [IO]
Circle Sanctuary [20570]
Pagan/Occult/Witchcraft Special Interest Gp. [10768]
The Witches' Voice [20614]
Wichita Bd. of Trade - Defunct.
Wide Smiles [16554], PO Box 5153, Stockton, CA 95205-0153, (209)942-2812
Wider Opportunities for Women [12106], 1001 Connecticut Ave. NW, Ste. 930, Washington, DC 20036, (202)464-1596
Wider Quaker Fellowship [20045], 1506 Race St., Philadelphia, PA 19102-1406, (215)241-7250
Widowed Persons Ser. [★13414]
Widowhood
AARP Grief and Loss Prog. [13414]
Natl. Assn. of Military Widows [21197]
Parents Without Partners [12688]
People-Animals-Love [16632]
Single Booklovers [22142]
Single Mothers By Choice [12692]
Veterans' Widows Intl. Network [21357]
Veterans' Widows Intl. Network [IO]
Widows Consultation Center - Defunct.
Widows; Natl. Assn. of Military [21197]
Widows; Natl. Assn. of Ministers Wives and Ministers' [★19897]
Widows; Soc. of Military [21200]
Widows and Victims' Families Assn; September 11 [12002]
Widows of World War I - Defunct.
Widows of World War II; Amer. [★21195]
Wiedemann Support Network; Beckwith- [14442]
Wielkopolska Izba Przemystowo-Hnadlowa [★IO]
Wiener Institut fur Entwicklungsfragen und Zusammenarbeit [★IO]
Wiesenthal Center; Simon [17724]
Wifeline Assn; Navy [21199]
Wilbur Found. [10205], PO Box 3370, Santa Barbara, CA 93130-3370
Wilbur Hot Springs Hea. Sanctuary [10180], 3375 Wilbur Springs Rd., Williams, CA 95987-9709, (530)473-2306
Wild Animal Orphanage [11476], PO Box 690422, San Antonio, TX 78269, (210)688-9038

A star before a book entry number signifies that the name is not listed separately, but is mentioned within the entry.

Wild Animal Propagation Trust - Defunct.
Wild Bird Feeding Indus. [1361], 1305 N Tahoe Trail, Sioux Falls, SD 57110-6410, (888)839-1237
Wild Bird Rehabilitation Center; Florida Keys [5317]
Wild Bird Soc. of Japan [IO], Tokyo, Japan
Wild Blueberry Association of North America [IO], Old Town, ME, United States
Wild Blueberry Assn. of North Am. [4775], PO Box 100, Old Town, ME 04468, (207)570-3535
Wild Burro Rescue and Preservation Proj. [11517], PO Box 10, Olancha, CA 93549-0010, (760)384-8523
Wild Canid Survival and Res. Center [5393], PO Box 760, Eureka, MO 63025, (636)938-5900
Wild Earth [4467], PO Box 455, Richmond, VT 05477, (802)434-4077
Wild Earth [IO], Richmond, VT, United States
Wild Farm Alliance [4661], PO Box 2570, Watsonville, CA 95077, (831)761-8408
Wild Flower Preservation Soc; New England [★4434]
Wild Flower Soc; New England [4434]
Wild Goose Assn. [★7370]
Wild Goose Assn. [★IO]
Wild Horse and Burro Prog; Bur. of Land Mgt. Natl. [4868]
Wild Horse Organized Assistance [5394], PO Box 555, Reno, NV 89504
Wild Horse Sanctuary [11477], PO Box 30, Shingletown, CA 96088-0030, (530)335-2241
Wild Horse Spirit [11478], 25 Lewers Creek Rd., Carson City, NV 89704, (775)883-5488
Wild Horses of Am. Registry [★5330]
Wild Horses of Am. Registry [5395], c/o Karen A. Sussman, Registrar, PO Box 55, Lantry, SD 57636-0055, (605)964-6866
Wild Horses of Am. Registry [★IO]
Wild Rice Growers Assn. [★IO]
Wild Rice Growers Assn. [★4307]
Wild Sheep; Found. for North Amer. [5318]
Wild Turkey Center [★5343]
Wild Turkey Fed; Natl. [5343]
Wild Water Kayak Club [IO], Swords, Ireland
WildAid [IO], San Francisco, CA, United States
WildAid [5396], 450 Pacific Ave., Ste. 201, San Francisco, CA 94133, (415)834-3174
Wildcat Ser. Corp. [12107], 17 Battery Pl., New York, NY 10004, (212)209-6000
Wilder Memorial Soc; Laura Ingalls [9679]
Wilderness Alliance; Amer. [★4354]
Wilderness Classroom Org. [8951], 4605 Grand Ave., Western Springs, IL 60558, (312)505-9973
Wilderness Educ. Assn. [8952], 900 E 7th St., Bloomington, IN 47405, (812)855-4095
Wilderness Educ. Assn. [★8952]
Wilderness Inquiry [23274], 808 14th Ave. SE, Minneapolis, MN 55414-1516, (612)676-9400
Wilderness Leadership Intl. - Address unknown since 2006.
Wilderness Medical Soc. [15184], PO Box 7065, Lawrence, KS 66044, (800)627-0629
The Wilderness Soc. [4468], 1615 M St. NW, Washington, DC 20036, (202)833-2300
The Wilderness Soc. [IO], Washington, DC, United States
The Wilderness Soc. - Australia [IO], Hobart, Australia
Wilderness Survival League; California [9202]
Wilderness Volunteers [22774], PO Box 22292, Flagstaff, AZ 86002-2292, (928)556-0038
Wilderness Watch - Defunct.
Wildflower Center; Lady Bird Johnson [6642]
Wildflower Preservation Soc. - Defunct.
Wildflowers Inst. [9794], 354 Pine St., 7th Fl., San Francisco, CA 94104, (415)399-1199
Wildflowers Inst. [IO], San Francisco, CA, United States
Wildfowl Art, Salisbury Univ; Ward Museum of [9529]
Wildfowl Found. - Defunct.
The Wildfowl Trust [★IO]
Wildfowl Trust of North Am. [5397], 600 Discovery Ln., PO Box 519, Grasonville, MD 21638, (410)827-6694
Wildfowl and Wetlands Trust [IO], Gloucester, United Kingdom

Wildlands; Amer. [4354]
Wildlands Proj. [4614], PO Box 5284, Titusville, FL 32783, (877)554-5234

Wildlife
Activists for Protective Animal Legislation [11338]
Actors and Others for Animals [11339]
African Wild Dog Conservancy [5288]
African Wildlife Found. [5289]
Alliance of Marine Mammal Parks and Aquariums [5006]
Amer. Anti-Vivisection Soc. [11345]
Amer. Assn. of Wildlife Veterinarians [16756]
Amer. Assn. of Zoo Veterinarians [16757]
Amer. Bird Conservancy [5290]
Amer. Fed. of Aviculture [21840]
Amer. Land Conservancy [4348]
Amer. Lands Alliance [4533]
Amer. Mookee Assn. [4191]
Amer. Sanctuary Assn. [4156]
Amer. Soc. for the Prevention of Cruelty to Animals [11350]
Amer. Wildlands [4354]
Animal Legal Defense Fund [11351]
Animal Medical Center [11353]
Animal Protection Inst. of Am. [11355]
Animal Rights Network/Institute for Animals and Soc. [11359]
Animal Welfare Inst. [11362]
Aquarium and Zoo Facilities Assn. [7856]
Asiatic Breeders Assn. [4192]
Assoc. Humane Societies [11366]
Assn. of Fish and Wildlife Agencies [4360]
Atlantic Flyway Coun. [5295]
Audubon Naturalist Soc. of the Central Atlantic States [4364]
Bear Trust Intl. [5297]
Bide-A-Wee Home Assn. [11371]
The Billfish Found. [5298]
Birds of Prey Found. [5300]
Blue Dolphin Alliance [5008]
Bonefish and Tarpon Unlimited [4987]
Boone and Crockett Club [5301]
Boreal Songbird Initiative [5302]
Bounty Wildlife Info. Ser. [5303]
Brotogeris Soc. Intl. [4194]
Camp Fire Club of Am. [4369]
Camp Fire Conservation Fund [4370]
Children of the Earth United [4621]
Chimp Haven [11729]
Comm. to Abolish Sport Hunting [11380]
Concern for Helping Animals in Israel [11383]
Conservation Treaty Support Fund [4385]
Defenders of Wildlife [5307]
Desert Tortoise Preserve Comm. [4390]
Ducks Unlimited [5311]
Earth Island Inst. [4550]
Earthtrust [5312]
EarthWave Soc. [4556]
Ecological Soc. of Am. [4506]
Elephant Care Intl. [5313]
Elephant Managers Assn. [4158]
Elephant Sanctuary in Tennessee [11389]
Endangered Species Coalition [5315]
Exotic Wildlife Assn. [5316]
FARM (Farm Animal Reform Movement) [11394]
Florida Keys Wild Bird Rehabilitation Center [5317]
ForestEthics [4685]
Found. for North Amer. Wild Sheep [5318]
Friends of Animals [11397]
Friends of the Australian Koala Found. [5319]
Friends of the Sea Otter [5320]
Fund for Animals [11398]
Fund for Horses [4159]
Fur Free Alliance [4153]
Global Gecko Assn. [5169]
Golden Lion Tamarin Mgt. Comm. [5321]
Great Ape Proj. [11400]
Great Bear Found. [5322]
Greater Yellowstone Coalition [4406]
Hawk Mountain Sanctuary [5324]
Humane Soc. of the U.S. [11412]
Intl. Assn. for Bear Res. and Mgt. [5325]
Intl. Bird Rescue Res. Center [5326]
Intl. Crane Found. [5327]

Intl. Defenders of Animals [11414]
Intl. Fund for Animal Welfare [11416]
Intl. Game Fish Assn. [23417]
Intl. League of Conservation Photographers [5080]
Intl. Primate Protection League [11418]
Intl. Soc. for Animal Rights [11419]
Intl. Soc. for Endangered Cats [4209]
Intl. Veterinary Assistance [11420]
Intl. Wild Waterfowl Assn. [5331]
Intl. Wildlife Coalition - USA [5332]
Intl. Wildlife Rehabilitation Coun. [5333]
Izaak Walton League of Am. Endowment [4414]
Johns Hopkins Center for Alternatives to Animal Testing [11423]
Keeping Track [5335]
Lewa Wildlife Conservancy (USA) [5337]
Marine Mammal Stranding Center [5338]
Midwest Assn. of Fish and Wildlife Agencies [5339]
Mission: Wolf [5340]
Morris Animal Found. [11428]
Natl. Animal Control Assn. [11430]
Natl. Anti-Vivisection Soc. [11432]
Natl. Aquarium Soc. [10442]
Natl. Assn. for Humane and Environmental Educ. [11433]
Natl. Cat Protection Soc. [11434]
Natl. Cong. of Animal Trainers and Breeders [11435]
Natl. Humane Educ. Soc. [11440]
Natl. Military Fish and Wildlife Assn. [5342]
Natl. Opossum Soc. [4160]
Natl. Wild Turkey Fed. [5343]
Natl. Wildlife Control Operators Assn. [4027]
Natl. Wildlife Fed. [4426]
Natl. Wildlife Refuge Assn. [5345]
Natl. Wildlife Rehabilitators Assn. [5346]
Native Amer. Fish and Wildlife Soc. [4595]
Natural Resources Defense Coun. [4432]
New York Turtle and Tortoise Soc. [5348]
North Amer. Bear Soc. [5351]
North Amer. Bluebird Soc. [5352]
North Amer. Crane Working Group [5353]
North Amer. Elk Breeders Assn. [4028]
North Amer. Grouse Partnership [5354]
North Amer. Wildlife Park Found. [5358]
North Amer. Wolf Assn. [5359]
Oceanic Soc. Expeditions [23016]
Org. of Wildlife Planners [5360]
Pacific Seabird Gp. [5362]
Pacific Whale Found. [5363]
Pelican Man's Bird Sanctuary [5364]
People Protecting Animals and Their Habitats [11445]
The Peregrine Fund [5365]
Pheasants Forever [5366]
Predator Conservation Alliance [5368]
Primarily Primates, Inc. [11452]
Purple Martin Conservation Assn. [5369]
Quaker Parakeet Soc. [4200]
Raptor Educ. Found. [5371]
Return to Freedom [16984]
Roo Rat Soc. [5375]
Ruffed Grouse Soc. [5376]
Sanctuary Workers and Volunteers Assn. [11455]
Save the Chimps [4298]
Save the Manatee Club [5378]
Save the Whales [5379]
Scientists Center for Animal Welfare [11456]
Sirenian Intl. [5016]
Soc. for Animal Protective Legislation [11459]
Soc. and Animals Forum [11460]
Soc. for the Conservation of Bighorn Sheep [5381]
Soc. for the Preservation of Birds of Prey [5382]
Soc. of Tympanuchus Cupido Pinnatus [5383]
Student Conservation Assn. [4455]
Sumatran Orangutan Soc. USA [5384]
Theodore Roosevelt Conservation Partnership [4458]
Thornton W. Burgess Soc. [4608]
TortoiseAid Intl. [5385]
TRAFFIC North Am. [5386]
Trout Unlimited [5387]

Reference to "IO" in place of a book number signifies that the association may be found in the 45th edition of International Organizations.

The Trumpeter Swan Soc. [5388]
Turkey Vulture Soc. [5389]
Unexpected Wildlife Refuge [11467]
United Action for Animals [11468]
United Humanitarians [11471]
Ward Museum of Wildfowl Art, Salisbury Univ. [9529]
Watchable Wildlife [5286]
Water Planet USA [5018]
Waterfowl U.S.A. [4465]
Western Assn. of Fish and Wildlife Agencies [5735]
Whale Adoption Proj. [5390]
Whooping Crane Conservation Assn. [5392]
Wild Canid Survival and Res. Center [5393]
Wild Horse Organized Assistance [5394]
Wild Horses of Am. Registry [5395]
WildAid [5396]
Wilderness Classroom Org. [8951]
Wilderness Medical Soc. [15184]
The Wilderness Soc. [4468]
Wilderness Volunteers [22774]
Wildlife Conservation Soc. [4469]
Wildlife Disease Assn. [5398]
Wildlife Forever [5399]
Wildlife Habitat Coun. [4470]
Wildlife Info. Center [5400]
Wildlife Mgt. Inst. [4471]
The Wildlife Soc. [5401]
Wildlife Trust [5402]
Wolf Haven Intl. [4472]
World Environmental Org. [4475]
World Parks [4617]
World Whale Police [5285]
Wildlife Agencies; Assn. of Midwest Fish and [★5339]
Wildlife Agencies; Southeastern Assn. of Fish and [5734]
Wildlife Agencies; Western Assn. of Fish and [5735]
Wildlife Aid [IO], Leatherhead, United Kingdom
Wildlife Clubs of Kenya [IO], Nairobi, Kenya
Wildlife Commissioners; Assn. of Midwest Fish and [★5339]
Wildlife Conservation
Abundant Wildlife Soc. of North Am. [5287]
Activists for Protective Animal Legislation [11338]
African Wild Dog Conservancy [5288]
African Wild Dog Conservancy [IO]
African Wildlife Found. [IO]
African Wildlife Found. [5289]
Alberta Wilderness Assn. [IO]
Alliance for Am. [11807]
Alliance of Marine Mammal Parks and Aquariums [5006]
Amer. Anti-Vivisection Soc. [11345]
Amer. Assn. of Wildlife Veterinarians [16756]
Amer. Assn. of Zoo Veterinarians [16757]
Amer. Bird Conservancy [5290]
Amer. Fed. of Aviculture [21840]
Amer. Horse Protection Assn. [5291]
Amer. Lands Alliance [4533]
Amer. Mookee Assn. [4191]
Amer. Pheasant and Waterfowl Soc. [5292]
Amer. Sanctuary Assn. [4156]
Amer. Soc. for the Prevention of Cruelty to Animals [11350]
Amer. Wildlands [4354]
Animal Legal Defense Fund [11351]
Animal Medical Center [11353]
Animal Protection Inst. of Am. [11355]
Animal Rights Network/Institute for Animals and Soc. [11359]
Animal Welfare Inst. [11362]
Appalachian Bear Rescue [5293]
Aquarium and Zoo Facilities Assn. [7856]
Asiatic Breeders Assn. [4192]
Assoc. Humane Societies [11366]
Assn. of Fish and Wildlife Agencies [4360]
Assn. Promoting Educ. and Conservation in Amazonia [5294]
Assn. Promoting Educ. and Conservation in Amazonia [IO]
Atlantic Flyway Coun. [5295]
Audubon Naturalist Soc. of the Central Atlantic States [4364]

Australian Koala Found. [IO]
Australian Wildlife Protection Coun. [IO]
Bat Conservation Intl. [IO]
Bat Conservation Intl. [5296]
Bat Conservation Trust - UK [IO]
Bear Trust Intl. [IO]
Bear Trust Intl. [5297]
Bide-A-Wee Home Assn. [11371]
Big Thicket Natural Heritage Trust [4368]
The Billfish Found. [5298]
Bird Life Intl. - United Kingdom [IO]
Bird Strike Comm. USA [5299]
Birds of Prey Found. [5300]
Birds of Prey Working Group [IO]
Blue Dolphin Alliance [5008]
Bonefish and Tarpon Unlimited [4987]
Boone and Crockett Club [5301]
Boreal Songbird Initiative [5302]
Boreal Songbird Initiative [IO]
Bounty Wildlife Info. Ser. [5303]
British Deer Soc. [IO]
British Hedgehog Preservation Soc. [IO]
Brooks Bird Club [5304]
Brotogeris Soc. Intl. [4194]
Butterfly Conservation [IO]
Camp Fire Club of Am. [4369]
Camp Fire Conservation Fund [4370]
Canadian Wildlife Fed. [IO]
Care for the Wild Germany [IO]
Care for the Wild India [IO]
Care for the Wild Intl. [IO]
Care for the Wild Kenya [IO]
Caribbean Conservation Corporation and Sea Turtle Survival League [IO]
Caribbean Conservation Corp. and Sea Turtle Survival League [5305]
Ceta-Research [IO]
Cetacean Soc. Intl. [IO]
Cetacean Soc. Intl. [5306]
Children of the Earth United [4621]
Chimp Haven [11729]
Comm. to Abolish Sport Hunting [11380]
Concern for Helping Animals in Israel [11383]
Conservation Treaty Support Fund [4385]
Defenders of Wildlife [5307]
Delta Waterfowl Found. [5308]
Desert Protective Coun. [4389]
Desert Tortoise Coun. [5309]
Desert Tortoise Preserve Comm. [4390]
Dian Fossey Gorilla Fund Intl. [5310]
Dian Fossey Gorilla Fund International [IO]
Ducks Unlimited [5311]
Durrell Wildlife Conservation Trust [IO]
Earth Island Inst. [4550]
Earthroots [IO]
Earthtrust [IO]
Earthtrust [5312]
EarthWave Soc. [4556]
East African Wild Life Soc. [IO]
Ecological Soc. of Am. [4506]
Elephant Care Intl. [5313]
Elephant Care Intl. [IO]
Elephant Mgt. and Owners Assn. [IO]
Elephant Managers Assn. [4158]
Elephant Res. Found. [5314]
Endangered Species Coalition [5315]
Endangered Wildlife Trust [IO]
Enkosini Wildlife Sanctuary [IO]
Exotic Wildlife Assn. [5316]
FARM (Farm Animal Reform Movement) [11394]
Florida Keys Wild Bird Rehabilitation Center [5317]
ForestEthics [4685]
Found. for North Amer. Wild Sheep [5318]
Found. for Wild Life Argentina [IO]
Freshwater Mollusk Conservation Soc. [5034]
Friends of Animals [11397]
Friends of Asian Elephants [IO]
Friends of the Australian Koala Found. [5319]
Friends of the Sea Otter [5320]
Fund for Animals [11398]
Fund for Horses [4159]
Fur Free Alliance [4153]
Galapagos Conservancy [4401]
Game Conservancy Trust [IO]

German-Namibian Soc. [IO]
Global Gecko Assn. [5169]
Golden Lion Tamarin Mgt. Comm. [5321]
Great Ape Proj. [11400]
Great Bear Found. [5322]
Great Lakes Indian Fish and Wildlife Commn. [5323]
Greater Yellowstone Coalition [4406]
Hawk Mountain Sanctuary [5324]
Humane Soc. of the U.S. [11412]
Interfaith Coun. for the Protection of Animals and Nature [4409]
Intl. Assn. for Bear Res. and Mgt. [5325]
International Association for Bear Research and Management [IO]
Intl. Bird Rescue Res. Center [IO]
Intl. Bird Rescue Res. Center [5326]
Intl. Crane Found. [5327]
International Crane Foundation [IO]
Intl. Defenders of Animals [11414]
Intl. Fund for Animal Welfare [11416]
Intl. Game Fish Assn. [23417]
Intl. Inst. of Central Asia Biodiversity [IO]
Intl. League of Conservation Photographers [5080]
The Intl. Osprey Found. [5328]
The International Osprey Foundation [IO]
Intl. Primate Protection League [11418]
Intl. Snow Leopard Trust [5329]
Intl. Snow Leopard Trust [IO]
Intl. Soc. for Animal Rights [11419]
Intl. Soc. for Endangered Cats [4209]
Intl. Soc. for Endangered Cats [IO]
Intl. Soc. for the Protection of Mustangs and Burros [IO]
Intl. Soc. for the Protection of Mustangs and Burros [5330]
Intl. Sonoran Desert Alliance [4582]
Intl. Veterinary Assistance [11420]
Intl. Whaling Commn. [IO]
Intl. Wild Waterfowl Assn. [IO]
Intl. Wild Waterfowl Assn. [5331]
Intl. Wildlife Coalition - USA [5332]
Intl. Wildlife Coalition - USA [IO]
Intl. Wildlife Rehabilitation Coun. [IO]
Intl. Wildlife Rehabilitation Coun. [5333]
Izaak Walton League of Am. Endowment [4414]
Jane Goodall Inst. for Wildlife Res., Educ., and Conservation [5334]
Johns Hopkins Center for Alternatives to Animal Testing [11423]
Keeping Track [5335]
Last Chance Forever [5336]
Lewa Wildlife Conservancy (USA) [5337]
Marine Aquarium Coun. [4175]
Marine Connection [IO]
Marine Fish Conservation Network [4419]
Marine Mammal Stranding Center [5338]
MEDASSET: Mediterranean Assn. to Save the Sea Turtles - Greece [IO]
MEDASSET: Mediterranean Assn. to Save the Sea Turtles - United Kingdom [IO]
Midwest Assn. of Fish and Wildlife Agencies [5339]
Mission: Wolf [5340]
Morris Animal Found. [11428]
Mountain Lion Found. [5341]
Natl. Animal Control Assn. [11430]
Natl. Anti-Vivisection Soc. [11432]
Natl. Assn. for Humane and Environmental Educ. [11433]
Natl. Assn. of Rsrc. Conservation and Development Councils [4421]
Natl. Cat Protection Soc. [11434]
Natl. Cong. of Animal Trainers and Breeders [11435]
Natl. Elephant Collectors Soc. [22081]
Natl. Endangered Species Act Reform Coalition [17504]
Natl. Endowment for the Animals [11437]
Natl. Horse Protection Coalition [11439]
Natl. Humane Educ. Soc. [11440]
Natl. Military Fish and Wildlife Assn. [5342]
Natl. Opossum Soc. [4160]
Natl. Wild Turkey Fed. [5343]

A star before a book entry number signifies that the name is not listed separately, but is mentioned within the entry.

Natl. Wilderness Inst. [5344]
Natl. Wildlife Fed. [4426]
Natl. Wildlife Refuge Assn. [5345]
Natl. Wildlife Rehabilitators Assn. [5346]
Native Amer. Fish and Wildlife Soc. [4595]
Native Fish Soc. [5347]
Natural Resources Defense Coun. [4432]
New York Turtle and Tortoise Soc. [5348]
Norcross Wildlife Found. [5349]
North Amer. Bear Center [5350]
North Amer. Bear Soc. [5351]
North Amer. Bluebird Soc. [5352]
North American Bluebird Society [IO]
North Amer. Crane Working Group [5353]
North Amer. Grouse Partnership [5354]
North Amer. Loon Fund [5355]
North Amer. Plant Preservation Coun. [5356]
North Amer. Wildlife Enforcement Officers Assn. [5357]
North Amer. Wildlife Park Found. [5358]
North Amer. Wolf Assn. [5359]
Northern Ireland Bat Gp. [IO]
Ocean Soc. [7401]
Org. of Wildlife Planners [5360]
Pacific Marine Mammal Center [5361]
Pacific Seabird Gp. [5362]
Pacific Whale Found. [5363]
Pelican Man's Bird Sanctuary [5364]
People Protecting Animals and Their Habitats [11445]
People's Trust for Endangered Species [IO]
The Peregrine Fund [IO]
The Peregrine Fund [5365]
Pheasants Forever [5366]
Polar Bears Intl. [5367]
Polar Bears International [IO]
Predator Conservation Alliance [5368]
Primarily Primates, Inc. [11452]
Purple Martin Conservation Assn. [5369]
Quail Unlimited [5370]
Quaker Parakeet Soc. [4200]
Rabbits Unlimited Inc. [4161]
Raptor Educ. Found. [5371]
Raptor Res. Found. [5372]
RARE [5373]
Return to Freedom [16984]
Rocky Mountain Elk Found. [5374]
Roo Rat Soc. [5375]
Royal Soc. for the Protection of Birds [IO]
Royal Soc. of Wildlife Trusts [IO]
Ruffed Grouse Soc. [5376]
Safari Club Intl. [5377]
Safari Club Intl. [IO]
Sanctuary Workers and Volunteers Assn. [11455]
Save the Chimps [4298]
Save the Elephants [IO]
Save the Manatee Club [5378]
Save Our Seas [4449]
Save the Whales [5379]
Scientists Center for Animal Welfare [11456]
Scottish Wildlife Trust [IO]
Sea Shepherd Conservation Soc. [IO]
Sea Shepherd Conservation Soc. [5380]
Shark Found. Switzerland [IO]
Shark Res. Inst. [5019]
Sirenian Intl. [5016]
Soc. for Animal Protective Legislation [11459]
Soc. and Animals Forum [11460]
Soc. for the Conservation of Bighorn Sheep [5381]
Soc. for the Preservation of Birds of Prey [5382]
Soc. of Tympanuchus Cupido Pinnatus [5383]
Southeastern Assn. of Fish and Wildlife Agencies [5734]
Student Conservation Assn. [4455]
Sumatran Orangutan Soc. USA [5384]
Tall Timbers Land Conservancy [4456]
Tall Timbers Res. Sta. [4457]
Tattoo-a-Pet [11463]
Theodore Roosevelt Conservation Partnership [4458]
Thornton W. Burgess Soc. [4608]
TortoiseAid Intl. [5385]
TortoiseAid Intl. [IO]
TRAFFIC North Am. [5386]

Trout Unlimited [5387]
Trout Unlimited Canada [IO]
The Trumpeter Swan Soc. [5388]
Turkey Vulture Soc. [5389]
Unexpected Wildlife Refuge [11467]
United Action for Animals [11468]
United Humanitarians [11471]
Watchable Wildlife [5286]
Waterfowl U.S.A. [4465]
Western Assn. of Fish and Wildlife Agencies [5735]
Whale Adoption Proj. [5390]
Whitetails Unlimited [5391]
Whooping Crane Conservation Assn. [5392]
Wild Bird Soc. of Japan [IO]
Wild Canid Survival and Res. Center [5393]
Wild Horse Organized Assistance [5394]
Wild Horses of Am. Registry [5395]
WildAid [5396]
WildAid [IO]
The Wilderness Soc. [4468]
Wilderness Volunteers [22774]
Wildfowl Trust of North Am. [5397]
Wildlands Proj. [4614]
Wildlife Clubs of Kenya [IO]
Wildlife Conservation Soc. [4469]
Wildlife Conservation Soc. of Tanzania [IO]
Wildlife Disease Association [IO]
Wildlife Disease Assn. [5398]
Wildlife and Env. Soc. of South Africa [IO]
Wildlife and Env. Zimbabwe [IO]
Wildlife and Environmental Conservation Soc. of Zambia [IO]
Wildlife Forever [5399]
Wildlife Habitat Coun. [4470]
Wildlife Info. Center [5400]
Wildlife Mgt. Inst. [4471]
Wildlife Preservation Soc. of Australia [IO]
Wildlife Protection Soc. of India [IO]
The Wildlife Soc. [5401]
Wildlife Soc. of Namibia [IO]
Wildlife Trust [5402]
Wolf Haven Intl. [4472]
World Bird Sanctuary [5403]
World Bird Sanctuary [IO]
World Coun. of Whalers [IO]
World Environmental Org. [4475]
World Parks [4617]
World Pheasant Assn. [IO]
World Whale Police [5285]
World Wide Fund for Nature Japan [IO]
World Wildlife Fund - Canada [IO]
World Wildlife Fund - Denmark [IO]
World Wildlife Preservation Soc. [IO]
World Wildlife Preservation Soc. [5404]
WWF Intl. [IO]
Xerces Soc. [IO]
Xerces Soc. [5405]
Yellowstone Grizzly Found. [5406]
Wildlife Conservation Intl. [★4469]
Wildlife Conservation Soc. [4469], 2300 Southern Blvd., Bronx, NY 10460, (718)220-5100
Wildlife Conservation Soc; NYZS/The [★4469]
Wildlife Conservation Soc. of Tanzania [IO], Arusha, United Republic of Tanzania
Wildlife Coordinating Committee - Defunct.
Wildlife Disease Assn. [5398], PO Box 1897, Lawrence, KS 66044-8897, (785)843-1221
Wildlife Disease Association [IO], Lawrence, KS, United States
Wildlife and Env. Soc. of Malawi [IO], Limbe, Malawi
Wildlife and Env. Soc. of South Africa [IO], Howick, Republic of South Africa
Wildlife and Env. Soc. of Southern Africa [IO], Howick, Republic of South Africa
Wildlife and Env. Zimbabwe [IO], Harare, Zimbabwe
Wildlife and Environmental Conservation Soc. of Zambia [IO], Lusaka, Zambia
Wildlife Fed; Natl. [4426]
Wildlife Forever [5399], 2700 Freeway Blvd., No. 1000, Brooklyn Center, MN 55430, (763)253-0222
Wildlife Found; Amer. [★5308]
Wildlife Found; North Amer. [★5308]
Wildlife Fund - U.S; World [★4478]
Wildlife Habitat Canada [IO], Ottawa, ON, Canada

Wildlife Habitat Coun. [4470], 8737 Colesville Rd., Ste. 800, Silver Spring, MD 20910, (301)588-8994
Wildlife Habitat Enhancement Coun. [★4470]
Wildlife Info. Center [5400], PO Box 198, Slatington, PA 18080-0198, (610)760-8889
Wildlife Inst; Amer. [★4471]
Wildlife Inst; Amer. [★5308]
Wildlife Leadership Found; African [★5289]
Wildlife Legislative Fund of Am. [★23550]
Wildlife Mgt. Inst. [4471], 1146 19th St. NW, Ste. 700, Washington, DC 20036, (202)371-1808
Wildlife Preservation Soc. of Australia [IO], Brighton-Le-Sands, Australia
Wildlife Preservation Trust Intl. [★5402]
Wildlife Prog. Administrators; Assn. of Univ. Fisheries and [★8391]
Wildlife Programs; Natl. Assn. of Univ. Fisheries and [8391]
Wildlife Protection Soc. of India [IO], New Delhi, India
Wildlife Refuge Reform Coalition - Defunct.
Wildlife Refuge; Unexpected [11467]
Wildlife Rehabilitation Coun. [★5333]
Wildlife Rehabilitation Coun. [★IO]
Wildlife Restoration Found. - Defunct.
The Wildlife Soc. [5401], 5410 Grosvenor Ln., Ste. 200, Bethesda, MD 20814-2144, (301)897-9770
Wildlife Soc. [★IO]
Wildlife Soc. of Namibia [IO], Windhoek, Namibia
Wildlife Soc. of Zimbabwe [★IO]
Wildlife Sound Recording Soc. - Address unknown since 1995.
Wildlife Specialists; Soc. of [★5401]
Wildlife Trust [5402], 460 W 34th St., 17th Fl., New York, NY 10001, (212)380-4460
Wildlife Trusts [IO], Newark, United Kingdom
Wildlife Veterinarians; Amer. Assn. of [16756]
Wilhelm Furtwangler Soc. of Am. [9819], PO Box 620702, Woodside, CA 94062-0702
Wilkerson/Wilkinson Clearinghouse [21083]
Wilkes Veterans Home; Alston [11852]
Wilkie Collins Soc. [IO], London, United Kingdom
Wilkinson Clearinghouse; Wilkerson/ [21083]
Wilkinson Fan Club; June [24750]
Willa Cather Found. [★9722]
Willa Cather Pioneer Memorial and Educational Found. [9722], 413 N Webster St., Red Cloud, NE 68970-2466, (402)746-2653
Willa Cather Soc. [★9722]
Willcox, Toyah
    North Amer. Toyah Fan Club [24951]
Willem Mengelberg Soc. - Defunct.
William Allen and Nancy Stone Family Assn. - Defunct.
William Allen White Found. [9723], c/o William Allen White Lib., Emporia State Univ., 1200 Commercial St., Emporia, KS 66801-5092, (316)341-5038
William Armstrong and Mary Kirk Family Org. - Defunct.
William Barnes Soc. [IO], Dorchester, United Kingdom
William Bradford Compact; Governor [21248]
William Burrup Family Org. [21084], c/o Jay G. Burrup, Genealogist, 6602 W King Valley Rd., West Valley City, UT 84128-4217, (801)250-9017
William C. Velasquez Inst. [19197], Kelly USA Bldg. 1670, 206 Lombard St., 1st Fl., San Antonio, TX 78226, (210)922-3118
William Cobbett Soc. [IO], Petersfield, United Kingdom
William Dean Howells Soc. [9724], c/o Prof. Elsa Nettels, Treas., 211 Indian Springs Rd., Williamsburg, VA 23185
William E. Simon Found. [17474], 310 S St., PO Box 1913, Morristown, NJ 07962-1913, (212)661-8366
William Faulkner Found. - Defunct.
William and Flora Hewlett Found. [13194], 2121 Sand Hill Rd., Menlo Park, CA 94025, (650)234-4500
William Geddes Family Org. [21085], c/o Jay G. Burrup, Genealogist, 6602 W King Valley Rd., West Valley City, UT 84128-4217, (801)250-9017
William Glasser Inst. [16233], 22024 Lassen St., Ste. 118, Chatsworth, CA 91311, (818)700-8000

Reference to "IO" in place of a book number signifies that the association may be found in the 45th edition of International Organizations.

William H. Donner Found. **[13880]**, 60 E 42nd St., Ste. 1560, New York, NY 10165, (212)949-0404

William H. Whitsitt Baptist Heritage Soc. **[19500]**, 1028 S Haven Dr., Hewitt, TX 76643

William Herschel Soc. **[IO]**, Bath, United Kingdom

William Hunter Soc. - Defunct.

William Hutchinson and Jane Penman Family Org. - Defunct.

William J. Clinton Found. **[17855]**, 1200 Pres. Clinton Ave., Little Rock, AR 72201, (501)370-8000

William J. Kerby Found. - Address unknown since 1995.

William J. Murray Evangelistic Assn. **[★12880]**

William J. Murray Faith Found. **[★12880]**

William Jacob Heckman Family Org. **[21086]**, 200 Los Robles Way, Woodland, CA 95695, (530)666-5493

William Kindel Family Org. **[21087]**

William L. Patterson Found. - Defunct.

William and Mary Greve Found. - Address unknown since 2007.

William McFarland Family Org. - Address unknown since 2006.

William McNamara Fan Club - Address unknown since 2006.

William Morris Soc. **[IO]**, London, United Kingdom

William Morris Soc., Amer. Br. **[★9725]**

William Morris Soc., North Amer. Br. **[★9725]**

William Morris Soc. in the U.S. **[9725]**, c/o Florence Boos, Pres., PO Box 53263, Washington, DC 20009

William Penn Assn. **[19144]**, 709 Brighton Rd., Pittsburgh, PA 15233-1821, (412)231-2979

William Penn Coll. Alumni Assn. **[★18945]**

William Penn Fraternal Assn. **[★19144]**

William Penn House **[17619]**, 515 E Capitol St. SE, Washington, DC 20003, (202)543-5560

William Penn Univ. Alumni Assn. **[18945]**, 201 Trueblood Ave., Oskaloosa, IA 52577-1799, (641)673-1046

William Perry Fan Club - Defunct.

William Shatner Connection **[★24772]**

William Shatner Fellowship - Defunct.

William Synett Family Org. - Defunct.

William T. Grant Found. **[11549]**, 570 Lexington Ave., 18th Fl., New York, NY 10022-6837, (212)752-0071

William T. Grant Foundation **[IO]**, New York, NY, United States

William Wendt Center for Loss and Healing **[13317]**, 4201 Connecticut Ave. NW, Ste. 300, Washington, DC 20008, (202)624-0010

Williams Family Assn. - Defunct.

Williams Family Org; James Leonard **[20957]**

Williams Grove Old Timers **[★21634]**

Williams Intl. Fan Club; Hank **[24905]**

Williams Jr. Fan Club; Hank **[24906]**

Williams, Sr. Intl. Fan Club; Hank **[★24905]**

Williams Syndrome Assn. **[14490]**, PO Box 297, Clawson, MI 48017-0297, (248)244-2229

Willing Workers on Organic Farms **[IO]**, Seoul, Republic of Korea

Willing Workers on Organic Farms **[★IO]**

Willing Workers on Organic Farms - Australia **[IO]**, Buchan, Australia

Willing Workers on Organic Farms - Austria **[IO]**, Graz, Austria

Willing Workers on Organic Farms - Denmark **[IO]**, Bindslev, Denmark

Willing Workers on Organic Farms - Ghana **[IO]**, Accra, Ghana

Willing Workers on Organic Farms - Japan **[IO]**, Sapporo, Japan

Willing Workers on Organic Farms - New Zealand **[IO]**, Nelson, New Zealand

Willing Workers on Organic Farms - Norway **[IO]**, Oslo, Norway

Willing Workers on Organic Farms - Switzerland **[★IO]**

Willkie Political Items Collectors - Defunct.

Willkommen im Curling Club Hamburg e.V. **[★IO]**

Willow Growers Network; Amer. **[5255]**

Willow Mixed Media **[17199]**, PO Box 194, Glenford, NY 12433, (845)657-2914

Wills Club **[★21817]**

Wills Sainte Claire Museum **[21817]**, 2408 Wills St., Marysville, MI 48040, (810)987-2854

Wills Sainte Claire Owners Club **[★21817]**

Willson Family Org; Brough/Nielsen/Wilson/ **[★20810]**

Willson Family Org; Brough/Wilson/ **[20810]**

Willys Club - Address unknown since 2001.

Willys - Knight Automobiles; Natl. Registry of **[★21819]**

Willys Overland Jeepster Club **[21818]**, 255 Thompsonville Rd., McMurray, PA 15317

Willys-Overland-Knight Registry **[21819]**, c/o Duane A. Perrin, Registrar, 1749 Chain Bridge Rd., McLean, VA 22102-2934

Willys-Overland-Knight Registry **[IO]**, McLean, VA, United States

Wilshire Club - Defunct.

Wilson Birthplace Found; Woodrow **[★11155]**

Wilson Fan Club; Mary **[★24954]**

Wilson; Friends of Dennis **[24892]**

Wilson Knight Interdiscipline Soc. and Found. - Defunct.

Wilson Message Bd. and Fan Club; Official Mary **[24954]**

Wilson Natl. Fellowship Found; Woodrow **[8439]**

Wilson Ornithological Soc. **[7424]**, c/o OSNA Bus. Off., 5400 Bosque Blvd., Ste. 680, Waco, TX 76710, (254)399-9636

Wilson Orthological Club **[★7424]**

Wilson Presidential Lib. Found; Woodrow **[11155]**

Wilson/Willson Family Org; Brough/ **[20810]**

Wilson/Willson Family Org; Brough/Nielsen/ **[★20810]**

Wilson's Disease Assn. Intl. **[15260]**, 1802 Brookside Dr., Wooster, OH 44691, (330)264-1450

Wilson's Disease; Found. for the Study of **[★15251]**

Wilson's Disease; Natl. Center for the Study of **[15251]**

Wimachtendienk, Wingolauchsik, Witahemui; WWW. **[★13005]**

Wimbum Cultural and Development Assn. in the U.S.A. **[9344]**, PO Box 3108, Bellaire, TX 77402

WIN - Defunct.

Win Without War **[18124]**, 1320 18th St. NW, 5th Fl., Washington, DC 20036, (202)822-2075

Winant and Clayton Volunteers **[13409]**, 109 E 50th St., New York, NY 10022, (212)378-0271

Winant and Clayton Volunteers **[IO]**, New York, NY, United States

Winant Volunteers; League of **[★13409]**

WINB; Western Interstate Energy Board/ **[18139]**

Winchell Cancer Fund; Damon Runyon - Walter **[★13819]**

Winchell Cancer Res. Fund; Damon Runyon - Walter **[★13819]**

Winchester Arms Collectors Assn. **[21540]**, PO Box 367, Silsbee, TX 77656, (409)385-5768

Wind Energy

Amer. Coun. on Renewable Energy **[6939]**

Amer. Wind Energy Assn. **[7852]**

Australian Wind Energy Assn. **[IO]**

British Wind Energy Assn. **[IO]**

Canadian Wind Energy Assn. **[IO]**

Danish Wind Indus. Assn. **[IO]**

Estonian Wind Power Assn. **[IO]**

European Wind Energy Assn. **[IO]**

Finnish Wind Power Assn. **[IO]**

German WindEnergy Assn. **[IO]**

Global Wind Energy Coun. **[IO]**

Indian Wind Energy Assn. **[IO]**

Irish Wind Energy Assn. **[IO]**

Lithuanian Wind Energy Assn. **[IO]**

New Zealand Wind Energy Assn. **[IO]**

Russian Assn. of Wind Indus. **[IO]**

South African Wind Energy Assn. **[IO]**

Windustry **[7853]**

Women of Wind Energy **[7854]**

World Wind Energy Assn. **[IO]**

Wind Energy Soc. of America - Defunct.

Wind and Percussion Arts; Academy of **[★10660]**

Wind and Percussion Instructors; Natl. Assn. of Coll. **[8919]**

Wind; Women in the **[22701]**

Winding Assn; Intl. Coil **[★1183]**

Windmill Class Assn. **[23239]**, 1856 Runneymeade Rd., Winston-Salem, NC 27104-3110

Windmill Stud. Unit **[IO]**, Sittingbourne, United Kingdom

Window

Amer. Architectural Manufacturers Assn. **[588]**

Assn. of Millwork Distributors **[600]**

Efficient Windows Collaborative **[4029]**

Intl. Window Film Assn. **[633]**

Master Window Cleaners of Am. **[2469]**

Natl. Fenestration Rating Coun. **[648]**

Steel Window Inst. **[674]**

Window Covering Mfrs. Assn. **[2279]**

Window Covering Safety Coun. **[4030]**

Window Coverings Assn. of Am. **[2280]**

Window and Door Manufacturers Assn. **[686]**

Window Covering Mfrs. Assn. **[2279]**, 355 Lexington Ave., 17th Fl., New York, NY 10017, (212)297-2122

Window Covering Mfrs. Assn; Amer. **[★2279]**

Window Covering Safety Coun. **[4030]**, 355 Lexington Ave., Ste. 1500, New York, NY 10017, (212)297-2109

Window Coverings Assn. of Am. **[2280]**, 2646 Hwy. 109, Ste. 205, Wildwood, MO 63040, (636)273-4090

Window and Door Assn; Natl. Wood **[★686]**

Window and Door Manufacturers Assn. **[686]**, 1400 E Touhy Ave., Ste. 470, Des Plaines, IL 60018, (847)299-5200

Window Film Assn; Intl. **[633]**

Window Film Mfrs. Assn. - Address unknown since 1995.

Window Inst; Sliding Glass Door and **[★588]**

Window Inst; Steel **[674]**

Window Manufacturers Assn; Aluminum **[★588]**

Window Shade Mfrs. Assn. - Defunct.

Windows of Hope Family Relief Fund **[12004]**, c/o Bloomberg LP, 731 Lexington Ave., New York, NY 10022, (212)617-3710

Windows of Hope Family Relief Fund **[IO]**, New York, NY, United States

Windows/Presentation Manager Assn. - Address unknown since 1995.

Windshield Repair Assn; Natl. **[425]**

Windsor Family Historical Assn. - Defunct.

Windstar Found. **[4615]**, PO Box 656, Snowmass, CO 81654-0656, (970)927-5430

Windsurfing Assn; U.S. **[23236]**

Windustry **[7853]**, 2105 1st Ave. S, Minneapolis, MN 55404, (612)870-3461

Windward Found. **[13195]**, 55 Windward Ln., Klickitat, WA 98628, (509)369-2000

Wine

African Amer. Wine Tasting Soc. **[190]**

Amer. Bartenders' Assn. **[192]**

Amer. Inst. of Wine and Food **[22568]**

Amer. Soc. for Enology and Viticulture **[5407]**

Amer. Sommelier Assn. **[194]**

Amer. Vineyard Found. **[5408]**

Amer. Wine Alliance for Res. and Educ. **[5409]**

Amer. Wine Soc. **[5410]**

Assembly of Wine Producing European Regions **[IO]**

Assn. of African Amer. Vintners **[195]**

Assn. of Australian Boutique Winemakers **[IO]**

Assn. of Champagne Producers **[IO]**

Assn. of the Cider and Fruit Wine Indus. of the European Union **[IO]**

Assn. of Producers and Exporters of Fine Wines **[IO]**

Assn. of Traders and Bottlers of Wines and Spirits from Northern Portugal **[IO]**

Assn. of Winery Suppliers **[196]**

Australian Soc. of Viticulture and Oenology **[IO]**

Australian Wine and Brandy Corp. **[IO]**

Australian Wine Consumers' Co-operative Soc. **[IO]**

Bourgogne Wine Producers' Assn. **[IO]**

Brotherhood of the Knights of the Vine **[5411]**

California Assn. of Winegrape Growers **[5412]**

Canadian Corkscrew Collectors Club **[21985]**

Confrerie de la Chaine des Rotisseurs, Bailliage des U.S.A. **[22569]**

Confrerie des Chevaliers du Tastevin **[IO]**

Cork Quality Coun. **[1645]**

Danish Wine and Spirits' Assn. **[IO]**

A star before a book entry number signifies that the name is not listed separately, but is mentioned within the entry.

El Dorado Winery Assn. [200]
Finger Lakes Wine Growers Assn. [5413]
Flair Bartenders' Assn. [201]
Free the Grapes! [16971]
Hong Kong Wine Soc. [IO]
Intl. Correspondence of Corkscrew Addicts [22052]
Italian Assn. of Indus. Producers, Exporters and Importers of Wine, Spirits, Syrups and Vinegars [IO]
Japan Wines and Spirits Importers' Assn. [IO]
Les Amis d'Escoffier Soc. of New York [1535]
Licensed Vintners' Assn. [IO]
Market Development Advisory Comm. [IO]
Monterey County Vintners and Growers Assn. [5414]
Napa Valley Grapegrowers [5415]
Napa Valley Vintners Assn. [5416]
Napa Valley Wine Lib. Assn. [23027]
Natl. Interprofessional Off. of Wine [IO]
Natl. Viticulture Inst. [IO]
Natl. Wine Trade Fed. [IO]
New York Wine/Grape Found. [5417]
North Amer. Brewers' Assn. [208]
Opimian, the Wine Soc. of Canada [IO]
Organic Grapes Into Wine Alliance [5418]
Port and Douro Wines Inst. [IO]
Royal Cliff Wine Club [IO]
San Joaquin Valley Wine Growers Assn. [5419]
Santa Cruz Mountains Winegrowers Assn. [5420]
Soc. of Medical Friends of Wine [23028]
Soc. of Wine Educators [23029]
Society of Wine Educators [IO]
Sonoma County Grape Growers Assn. [5421]
Sonoma County Vintners [5422]
Spanish Wine Fed. [IO]
Specialty Wine Retailers Assn. [4031]
Tasters Guild Intl. [210]
Thai Wine Assn. [IO]
Vinifera Wine Growers Assn. [5423]
Vintners' Fed. of Ireland [IO]
Wine Appreciation Guild [5424]
Wine Development Bd. of Ireland [IO]
Wine Indus. Suppliers Australia [IO]
Wine Inst. [5425]
Wine Soc. [IO]
Wine and Vineyards Inst. [IO]
WineAmerica Natl. Assn. of Amer. Wineries [4032]
Winemakers' Fed. of Australia [IO]
Wines of South Africa [IO]
Women for Winesense [23030]
Wine Advisory Bd. [★5424]
Wine Alliance for Res. and Educ; Amer. [5409]
Wine and Allied Workers Intl. Union; Distillery, [★24061]
Wine Appreciation Guild [5424], 360 Swift Ave., Unit 30-40, South San Francisco, CA 94080, (650)866-3020
Wine and Beer Trade Assn; Home [202]
Wine Conf. of America - Defunct.
Wine Coun; New York [★5417]
Wine Country Assn; Monterey [★5414]
Wine Development Bd. of Ireland [IO], Dublin, Ireland
Wine Exporters Assn; Swiss [IO]
Wine and Food; Amer. Inst. of [22568]
Wine and Food Inst; Italian [1534]
Wine and Food Soc. - London; Intl. [IO]
Wine and Foreign Spirits; Assn. of Agents, Brokers and Valuers of [IO]
Wine Futures Exchange - Defunct.
Wine Grape Growers; New York State [★5417]
Wine Growers Assn; Sonoma County [★5422]
Wine Indus. Suppliers Australia [IO], Adelaide, Australia
Wine Inst. [5425], 425 Market St., Ste. 1000, San Francisco, CA 94105, (415)512-0151
Wine Inst. of New Zealand [IO], Auckland, New Zealand
Wine Producers Assn; Sweet [★5419]
Wine Producers; New York Assn. of [★5417]
Wine Soc. [IO], Stevenage, United Kingdom
Wine and Spirit Assn. [★IO]
Wine and Spirit Assn. of Great Britain and Northern Ireland [★IO]

Wine and Spirit Trade Assn. [IO], London, United Kingdom
Wine and Spirits Guild of America - Address unknown since 2003.
Wine and Spirits Shippers Assn. [211], 11800 Sunrise Valley Dr., Ste. 332, Reston, VA 20191, (703)860-2300
Wine and Spirits Wholesalers of Am. [212], 805 15th St. NW, Ste. 430, Washington, DC 20005, (202)371-9792
Wine Traders; Royal Assn. of Dutch [IO]
Wine and Vineyards Inst. [IO], Lisbon, Portugal
WineAmerica Natl. Assn. of Amer. Wineries [4032], 1212 New York Ave., Ste. 425, Washington, DC 20005, (202)783-2756
Winemakers' Fed. of Australia [IO], Manuka, Australia
Winery Assn; El Dorado [200]
Winery Suppliers; Assn. of [196]
Wines of South Africa [IO], Stellenbosch, Republic of South Africa
Wines; Women for New York State [★5417]
Wing For'em Club; Red [25013]
Wingate Inst. for Physical Educ. in Israel [★23828]
Winged Fellowship Trust [★IO]
Winged Warriors/National B-Body Owners Assn. [21820], 216 12th St., Boone, IA 50036-2019, (515)432-3001
Wingfield Family Soc. [21088], c/o Robert Wingfield, Membership Chm./Treas., 90 Woodstone, Buffalo Grove, IL 60089
Wingfield Family Soc. [IO], Buffalo Grove, IL, United States
Wingfield Historical Soc; Major [23905]
Wingfoot Lighter-Than-Air Soc. [★21460]
Wingfoot Lighter-Than-Air Soc. [★IO]
Wingolauchsik, Witahemui; WWW Wimachtendienk, [★13005]
Wings Club - Defunct.
WINGS Found. [13087], 8725 W 14th Ave., Ste. 150, Lakewood, CO 80215, (303)238-8660
Wings of Hope [12883], 18370 Wings of Hope Blvd., Chesterfield, MO 63005, (636)537-1302
Wings of Hope [IO], Chesterfield, MO, United States
Wingspread Conf. of Intl. Voluntary Agencies - Defunct.
Winne Family Assn; Woenne/Wonne/ [21089]
Winnebago Intl. Travelers [★22968]
Winnebago/Itasca Travelers [★22968]
Winnebago-Itasca Travelers [22968], PO Box 268, Forest City, IA 50436-0268, (641)585-6874
Winrock Intl. [16959], 2101 Riverfront Dr., Little Rock, AR 72202, (501)280-3000
Winrock Intl. [IO], Little Rock, AR, United States
Winrock Intl. Inst. for Agricultural Development [★IO]
Winrock Intl. Inst. for Agricultural Development [★16959]
Winrock Intl. Livestock Res. and Training Center [★16959]
Winrock Intl. Livestock Res. and Training Center [★IO]
Winston Churchill Found. [8438], 600 Madison Ave., 16th Fl., New York, NY 10022-1615, (212)752-3200
Winston Family Assn. - Address unknown since 2003.
Winston S. Churchill Assn. - Defunct.
Winston S. Churchill Stud. Unit [★11109]
Winter Soldier Archive - Defunct.
Winter Soldier Org; Vietnam Veterans Against the War/ [★18784]
Winter Sports Representatives Assn; Eastern [3661]
Winter Sports Representatives Assn; Western [3675]
Winter Swimmers; Polar Bear Club - [★23888]
Wipers Assn; Pacific Coast Marine Firemen, Oilers, Watertenders and [24130]
Wiping Cloth Mfrs; Intl. Assn. of [★2066]
Wire Assn. [★7323]
Wire Assn. [★IO]
Wire Assn. Intl. [IO], Guilford, CT, United States
Wire Assn. Intl. [7323], PO Box 578, Guilford, CT 06437, (203)453-2777
Wire Assn; Specialty [★1999]
Wire and Cable Indus. Suppliers Assn. [1231], 1867 W Market St., Akron, OH 44313, (330)864-2122

Wire Cloth Inst; Amer. [1998]
Wire Cloth Inst; Indus. [★1998]
Wire Cloth Mfrs. Assn; Paper Mill Fourdrinier [★2056]
Wire Collectors Assn; New Mexico Barbed [22091]
Wire Coun; Fourdrinier [★2056]
Wire Fabricators Assn. [1840], PO Box 304, Montgomery, IL 60538, (630)896-1469
Wire Fabricators Association [IO], Montgomery, IL, United States
Wire Industry Suppliers Assn. [2079]
Wire Machinery Builders Assn. [★2079]
Wire and Metal Lathers' Intl. Union; Wood, [★24032]
Wire Producers Assn; Amer. [1999]
Wire Producers Assn; Independent [★1999]
Wire Products Assn; Woven [2082]
Wire Reinforcement Inst. [687], 942 Main St., Ste. 300, Hartford, CT 06103, (800)552-4974
Wire Rope Fabricators; Assoc. [2001]
Wire Rope Technical Bd. - Address unknown since 2002.
Wire Ser. Guild [24141], c/o Local 31222 The Newspaper Guild/Communications Workers of Am., 424 W 33rd St., Ste. 260, New York, NY 10001, (212)869-9290
Wire Soc; Antique Barbed [21969]
Wirebound Box Mfrs. Assn. - Defunct.
Wired Woman [IO], Vancouver, BC, Canada
Wirehaired Pointer Club of Am; German [22275]
Wirehaired Vizsla Club of Am. [22384], 7709 Delhi Rd., Woodway, TX 76712
Wireless Assn; Antique [22923]
Wireless Assn; Quarter Century [21509]
Wireless Club, Limited; Junior [★22928]
Wireless Communications Assn. Intl. [3764], 1333 H St. NW, Ste. 700 W, Washington, DC 20005-4754, (202)452-7823
Wireless Communications Assn. Intl. [IO], Washington, DC, United States
Wireless Dealers Assn. [3765], 9746 Tappenbeck Dr., Houston, TX 77055-4102, (713)467-0077
Wireless Information Networks Forum - Address unknown since 2003.
Wireless Infrastructure Assn; PCIA - The [3752]
Wireless Inst. of Australia [IO], Caulfield Junction, Australia
Wireless Operators Assn; Veteran [3763]
Wireless Pioneers of the Seven Seas; Amer. Soc. of [★3757]
Wireless Pioneers; Soc. of [3757]
Wireless Pioneers; Soc. of Professional [★3757]
Wiring Harness Manufacturer's Assn. [1199], 7500 Flying Cloud Dr., Ste. 900, Eden Prairie, MN 55344, (952)253-6225
Wirral Chamber of Commerce and Indus. [IO], Wirral, United Kingdom
Wirtschafts Junioren Deutschland [★IO]
Wirtschaftskammer Osterreich [★IO]
Wirtschaftsverband der Deutschen Kautschukindustrie [★IO]
Wirtschaftsverband Erdol- und Erdgasgewinnung [★IO]
Wirtschaftsverband Grosshandel Metallhalbzeug [IO], Berlin, Germany
Wirtschaftsverband der deutschen Kautschukindustrie [★IO]
Wirtschaftsverband Stahl - und Metallverarbeitung [★IO]
Wirtschaftsvereinigung Alkoholfreie Getranke e.V. [★IO]
Wirtschaftsvereinigung Bergbau E.v. [★IO]
Wisconsin Cheese Makers' Assn. [1141], 8030 Excelsior Dr., Ste. 305, Madison, WI 53717-1950, (608)828-4550
Wisconsin Cheese and Sausage Promotions - Defunct.
Wisconsin Cheese Seminar [★1522]
Wisconsin Cheese Seminar [★IO]
Wisconsin Cheese and Specialty Food Merchants Assn. - Defunct.
Wisconsin Coordinating Coun. on Nicaragua [17920], PO Box 1534, Madison, WI 53701, (608)257-7230
Wisconsin Coordinating Coun. on Nicaragua [IO], Madison, WI, United States

Reference to "IO" in place of a book number signifies that the association may be found in the 45th edition of International Organizations.

Wisconsin Creameries Assn. [★4495]
Wisconsin Dairy Foods Assn. [★4495]
Wisconsin Dairy Products Assn. [4495], 8383 Greenway Blvd., Middleton, WI 53562, (608)836-3336
Wisconsin - Eau Claire Alumni Assn; Univ. of [18940]
Wisconsin-Milwaukee; Center for Consumer Affairs, Univ. of [17313]
Wisconsin - Platteville Alumni Assn; Univ. of [18941]
Wisdom of the Heart Found. [IO], Tijuana, Mexico
Wise Family Assn; Adam [20773]
Wise Owl Prog. [★16882]
WISH [★5770]
Wish Found. of Am; Make-A- [11707]
Wish Found; Children's [★11687]
Wish Found; A Special [11723]
WISH List [5770], 333 N Fairfax St., Ste. 302, Alexandria, VA 22314, (703)778-5550
A Wish With Wings [11728], 917 W Sanford St., Arlington, TX 76012, (817)469-9474
Wishing Well [22146], PO Box 178440, San Diego, CA 92177-8440, (858)695-3139
Wishing Well [IO], San Diego, CA, United States
WishKids Intl. [11665], 10903 Muddy River Rd., Indianapolis, IN 46234, (317)295-9441
WISTA Singapore [★IO]
Witahemui; WWW Wimachtendienk, Wingolauchsik, [★13005]
Witch Doctors Club - Defunct.
Witchcraft
    Alternative Religions Educational Network [20457]
    Pagan/Occult/Witchcraft Special Interest Gp. [10768]
    The Witches' Voice [20614]
Witchcraft Special Interest Gp; Pagan/Occult/ [10768]
Witches
    Alternative Religions Educational Network [20457]
    Assoc. Daughters of Early Amer. Witches [21358]
Witches Anti-Discrimination Lobby - Defunct.
The Witches' Voice [20614], PO Box 341018, Tampa, FL 33694-1018
With A Little Help From My Friends - Address unknown since 1989.
WITH/Curam, parent and carer NGO in Ireland [IO], Dun Laoghaire, Ireland
With Umbrella, Charm and Bowler - Defunct.
Within You, Inc./Just Say No Clubs - Defunct.
WITNESS [17789], 80 Hanson Pl., 5th Fl., Brooklyn, NY 11217, (718)783-2000
Witness Anonymous Program [★11849]
Witness Assn; Forensic Expert [5760]
Witness Fellowship; Biblical [20606]
Witness Justice [18790], PO Box 475, Frederick, MD 21705-0475, (301)898-1009
Witness Ministries; United Church of Christ Justice and [20608]
Witness for Peace [18107], 3628 12th St. NE, 1st Fl., Washington, DC 20017, (202)547-6112
Witness for Peace [IO], Washington, DC, United States
Wives of Am; Gold Star [21195]
Wives of the Armed Forces, Emeritus - Defunct.
Wives Assn; Natl. Military [★21198]
Wives and Ministers' Widows; Natl. Assn. of Ministers [★19897]
Wives; Natl. Action for Former Military [12012]
Wives; Natl. Assn. of Ministers' [★19897]
Wives of Older Men [12509], c/o Beliza Ann Furman, Founder, 1029 Sycamore Ave., Tinton Falls, NJ 07724, (732)747-5586
Wives-Self-Help Found. [11832], Smylie Times Bldg., Ste. 205, 8001 Roosevelt Blvd., Philadelphia, PA 19152, (215)332-2311
Wives of World War II; Gold Star [★21195]
W.K. Kellogg Found. [18400], 1 Michigan Ave. E, Battle Creek, MI 49017-4012, (269)968-1611
W.M. Keck Found. [15115], 550 S Hope St., Ste. 2500, Los Angeles, CA 90071, (213)680-3833
Wobblies [★24098]
Wobblies [★IO]
Wobbly Parrot Rescue [IO], Reading, United Kingdom
The Wodehouse Soc. [9726], c/o Amy Plofker, Corresponding Sec., 111 Rice Ave., Fl. 1, Sleepy Hollow, NY 10591-1937, (914)631-2554

Woenne/Wonne/Winne Family Assn. [21089], 12800 Briar Forest Dr., Ste. 83, Houston, TX 77077-2206, (281)531-1956
Wofford Coll. Natl. Alumni Assn. [18946], 429 N Church St., Spartanburg, SC 29303-3663, (864)597-4000
Wolf Assn; North Amer. [5359]
Wolf Fund - Address unknown since 2001.
Wolf Haven Intl. [4472], 3111 Offut Lake Rd., Tenino, WA 98589, (360)264-4695
Wolf Haven Intl. [IO], Tenino, WA, United States
Wolf; Mission: [5340]
Wolf for Natl. Mammal Campaign - Defunct.
Wolf Trap Found. for the Performing Arts [9602], 1645 Trap Rd., Vienna, VA 22182, (703)255-1900
Wolf Trap Opera Company [★9602]
Wolfe Angel Comm. - Defunct.
Wolfe Pack [9727], PO Box 230822, New York, NY 10023
Wolfe Soc; Thomas [9713]
Wolfensberger Family Assn. [21090], c/o David E. Wolfenbarger, Treas., 768 Chain Ridge Rd., St. Louis, MO 63122, (314)961-5032
Wolfhound
    Intl. Borzoi Coun. [22287]
Wolfhound Club of Am; Irish [22295]
Wolfhound Club of Am; Russian [★22235]
Wolfpack Fan Club [24991], PO Box 292797, Nashville, TN 37229-2797, (615)780-3579
Wolseley Register [IO], Roade, United Kingdom
The Woman Activist [17573]
The Woman Activist Fund [17574], PO Box 6530, Alexandria, VA 22306-6530, (571)216-4107
Woman and Family [IO], Minsk, Belarus
Woman Health Intl. - Defunct.
Woman To Woman - Address unknown since 2007.
Woman to Woman Support Network [16555], Unit 5, Airport Plz., 1341 W Main Rd., Middletown, RI 02842, (401)841-9211
Womanhood; Natl. Inst. of [13432]
Womankind Worldwide [IO], London, United Kingdom
Womanquest - Defunct.
Woman's Amer. Baptist Foreign Mission Soc. [★19483]
Woman's Amer. Baptist Foreign Mission Soc. [★IO]
Woman's Amer. Baptist Home Mission Soc. [★19484]
Woman's Auxiliary to the Amer. Soc. of Mech. Engineers [★7299]
Woman's Benefit Assn. [★19145]
Woman's Bd. of Missions; Christian [★19856]
Woman's Christian Temperance Union; Natl. [13306]
Woman's Economic Development Corp; Amer. [3604]
Woman's Foreign Missionary Soc. [★20371]
Woman's Foreign Missionary Soc. [★IO]
Woman's Home and Foreign Mission Soc. [19443], PO Box 23152, Charlotte, NC 28227, (704)545-6161
Woman's Life Insurance Soc. [19145], PO Box 5020, Port Huron, MI 48061-5020, (800)521-9292
Woman's Missionary Soc. [★20371]
Woman's Missionary Soc. [★IO]
Woman's Missionary Soc. of the Church of God; Natl. [★19835]
Woman's Missionary Union, SBC [19501], PO Box 830010, Birmingham, AL 35283-0010, (205)991-8100
Woman's Natl. Auxiliary Convention of Free Will Baptists [★19502]
Woman's Natl. Democratic Club [17410], 1526 New Hampshire Ave. NW, Washington, DC 20036, (202)232-7363
Woman's Natl. Sabbath Alliance - Defunct.
Woman's Party; Natl. [17562]
Woman's Soc. of Certified Public Accountants; Amer. [12]
Woman's Suffrage Assn; Natl. [★18459]
Woman's Trust - Address unknown since 1990.
Woman's Workshop - Defunct.
Womelsdorf Family Assn. - Address unknown since 2004.
Women
    AACR-Women in Cancer Res. [16893]

About-Face [13415]
ABW Ministries [19468]
Act Together [IO]
Advt. Women of New York [81]
Afghan Women's Assn. Intl. [13416]
Afghan Women's Assn. Intl. [IO]
African-American Female Entrepreneurs Alliance [4033]
African-American Women in Tech. [6394]
African-Amer. Women's Clergy Assn. [20615]
African Asian Latina Lesbians United [17649]
African Women Global Network [18808]
African Women Global Network [IO]
African Women's Development and Commun. Network [IO]
AGENDA Feminist Media [IO]
Aglow Intl. [IO]
Aglow Intl. [20616]
Aid to Incarcerated Mothers [11851]
All India Women's Conf. [IO]
All India Women's Conf. - North Am. [IO]
All India Women's Conf. - North Am. [13417]
All Navy Women's Natl. Alliance [6144]
Alliance of Amer. and Russian Women [13418]
Alliance for Microbicide Development [13555]
Alliance for Women's Equality [13455]
Alpha Rho Lambda Sorority [24703]
ALTISA Intl. Network [IO]
Amazone [IO]
AMEND [12020]
Amer. and African Bus. Women's Alliance [691]
Amer. Agri-Women [16948]
Amer. Agri-Women Rsrc. Center [16949]
Amer. Assn. of Univ. Women [9311]
Amer. Assn. of Univ. Women Educational Found. [9312]
Amer. Assn. of Univ. Women Legal Advocacy Fund [6358]
Amer. Assn. for Women in Community Colleges [9313]
Amer. Assn. of Women Dentists [14119]
Amer. Bus. Women's Assn. [693]
Amer. Cloak and Suit Mfrs. Assn. [223]
Amer. Found. for Maternal and Child Health [15586]
Amer. Jewish World Ser. [12829]
Amer. Legion Auxiliary Girls Nation [17068]
Amer. Medical Women's Assn. [14696]
Amer. Menopause Found. [16894]
Amer. Mothers, Inc. [12139]
Amer. News Women's Club [3083]
Amer. Rosie the Riveter Assn. [21388]
Amer. Soc. of Women Accountants [11]
Amer. Woman's Economic Development Corp. [3604]
Amer. Woman's Soc. of Certified Public Accountants [12]
Amer. Women's Assn. of Hong Kong [IO]
Amer. Women's Assn. of Vienna [IO]
Amer. Women's Club Antwerp [IO]
Amer. Women's Club of London [IO]
Amer. Women's Club of Madrid [IO]
Amer. Women's Club of Thailand [IO]
Amer. Women's Self-Defense Assn. [13010]
Arab Amer. Women's Coun. [18951]
Arab Women Connect - Arab States Regional Off. [IO]
Arab Women's Solidarity Assn. [IO]
Arab Women's Solidarity Assn. [13419]
Archconfraternity of Christian Mothers [19572]
Arias Found. for Peace and Human Progress [IO]
Armed Females of Am. [17587]
Armenian Assn. of Women with Univ. Educ. [IO]
Asian Women in Bus. [697]
Asmita Women's Publishing House, Media and Rsrc. Org. [IO]
Asociacion de Mujeres Universitarias de El Salvador [IO]
Asociacion de Mujeres Universitarias de Vizcaya [IO]
Asociatiei Nationale A Femeilor Cu Diploma Universitara Din Romania [IO]
Associacao Brasileira de Mulheres Universitarias [IO]
Associated Corset and Brassiere Mfrs. [227]

A star before a book entry number signifies that the name is not listed separately, but is mentioned within the entry.

Associates of the Amer. Foreign Ser. Worldwide [24071]
Assn. Albanaise Des Femmes Diplomees Des Universites [IO]
Assn. of Albanian Girls and Women [18382]
Assn. of Amer. Wives of Europeans [IO]
Assn. of Atlantic Women Bus. Owners [IO]
Assn. of Black Women in Higher Educ. [9314]
Assn. Burkinabe des Femmes Diplomees des Universites [IO]
Assn. Burundaise des Femmes Diplomees des Universites [IO]
Assn. of Contemplative Sisters [20563]
Assn. of Cooperation in Tunisia [IO]
Assn. Francaise des Femmes Diplomees des Universites [IO]
Assn. of Full Gospel Women Clergy [20275]
Assn. for Improvement in the Maternity Services [IO]
Assn. of Institutions for Feminist Educ. and Res. in Europe [IO]
Assn. of Labor Assistants and Childbirth Educators [13977]
Assn. of Nurse Advocates for Childbirth Solutions [13978]
Assn. on Programs for Female Offenders [11857]
Assn. of Real Estate Women [3300]
Assn. for Social Advancement [IO]
Assn. pour le Soutien et l'Appui a la Femme Entrepreneur [IO]
Assn. Suisse Des Remmes Diplomees Des Universites [IO]
Assn. of Tongan Univ. Women [IO]
Assn. for Women in Architecture [291]
Assn. for Women in Aviation Maintenance [4034]
Assn. for Women in Computing [6786]
Assn. of Women Educators [IO]
Assn. of Women in Environmental Professions [4619]
Assn. for Women Geoscientists [7139]
Assn. of Women Indus. Designers [7179]
Assn. of Women Martial Arts Instructors [23585]
Assn. for Women in Mathematics [7288]
Assn. of Women in the Metal Indus. [4035]
Assn. for Women in Psychology [16145]
Assn. for Women in Sci. [7602]
Assn. of Women Soil Scientists [7672]
Assn. for Women in Sports Media [3097]
Assn. for Women Veterinarians [16786]
Atira Women's Rsrc. Soc. [IO]
Australian Businesswomen's Network [IO]
Australian Coun. of Women and Policing [IO]
Australian Fed. of Univ. Women [IO]
Australian Fed. of Univ. Women - Tasmania [IO]
Austrian Fed. of Univ. Women [IO]
Automotive Women's Alliance [353]
Auxiliaries of Our Lady of the Cenacle [19581]
Auxiliary to Sons of Union Veterans of the Civil War [20723]
Azerbaijan Women and Development Center [IO]
Azerbaijan Women's Assn. [IO]
Bangladesh Fed. of Univ. Women [IO]
Baptist Women in Ministry/Folio [19481]
Batterers Anonymous - Beyond Abuse [12023]
Be Active, Be Emancipated [IO]
Belgian Fed. of Univ. Graduate Women [IO]
Bilateral Safety Corridor Coalition [12368]
Black, Indian, Hispanic, and Asian Women in Action [13420]
Black Women in Church and Soc. [20617]
Black Women of Essence [11269]
Black Women Organized for Educational Development [13421]
Black Women in Sisterhood for Action [13422]
Black Women United for Action [13423]
Black Women United for Action [IO]
Black Women's Hea. Imperative [16895]
Breast Cancer Action [13801]
British Fed. of Women Graduates [IO]
British Housewives' League [IO]
British Menopause Soc. [IO]
Broad Universe [23034]
Buddhist Churches of Am. Fed. of Buddhist Women's Associations [19543]
Bulgarian Assn. of Univ. Women [IO]

Bus. and Professional Women's Found. [11084]
Bus. Women's Network [4036]
Cameroon Assn. of Univ. Women [IO]
Camping Women [23269]
Canadian Fed. of Univ. Women [IO]
Canadian Res. Inst. for the Advancement of Women [IO]
Canadian Soc. for Women in Philosophy [IO]
Canadian Women's Hea. Network [IO]
Canadian Women's Stud. Assn. [IO]
Caribbean Amer. Netball Assn. [23633]
Catalyst [11085]
Caucus for Women in Statistics [7703]
Center for the Educ. of Women [9315]
Center for Women Veterans [21292]
Center for Women's Bus. Res. [4037]
Centre for Hea. Educ., Training and Nutrition Awareness [IO]
Centre for Women's Development Stud. [IO]
Centre for Women's Hea. [IO]
Centro de Estudios para el Desarrollo de la Mujer [IO]
Charlotte W. Newcombe Found. [12749]
Childbirth and Postpartum Professional Assn. [13980]
Church Women United [20618]
Cinderella Softball Leagues [23789]
Circle of Hea. Intl. [12268]
Co-operative Women's Guild [IO]
Coalition for Improving Maternity Services [15596]
Coalition of Labor Union Women [24203]
Coalition of Labor Union Women Center for Educ. and Res. [24204]
Coalition for Women's Appointments [17520]
Cojolya Assn. of Maya Women Weavers [IO]
Command Trust Network [16896]
A Commitment to Training and Employment for Women [IO]
Comm. of 200 [713]
Comm. on the Status of Women in the Economics Profession [5673]
Comm. on the Status of Women in Microbiology [6574]
Comm. on the Status of Women in Sociology [9923]
Communaute Francaise de Belgique [IO]
Comunicacion Intercambio y Desarrollo Humano en Am. Latina, A.C. [IO]
Conf. for Catholic Lesbians [20051]
Congregation of Sisters of Saint Agnes [19618]
Congressional Club [19434]
Consortium of Doctors [12074]
Cosmetic Executive Women [1842]
Coun. of Women's and Infants' Specialty Hospitals [14880]
Country Women's Assn. of Australia [IO]
Croatian Assn. of Univ. Women [IO]
Danish Assn. of Univ. Women [IO]
Deaf Women United [11905]
Defense Advisory Comm. on Women in the Services [6075]
Delta Gamma Pi Multicultural Sorority [24704]
Delta Phi Omega Sorority [24705]
Delta Sigma Chi Sorority [24706]
Delta Tau Lambda Sorority [24707]
Delta Xi Nu Multicultural Sorority [24708]
Delta Xi Phi Multicultural Sorority [24685]
DES Action Canada [IO]
Deutscher Akademikerinnen Bund [IO]
Deutscher Hausfrauen-Bund [IO]
DidiBahini [IO]
Diplomas Nok Magyarorszagi Szovetsege [IO]
DIVAS of Lambda Fe Uson Sorority [24709]
Dress for Success Worldwide [13424]
Dress for Success Worldwide [IO]
Educ. Centre for Women in Democracy [IO]
Educational Equity Center [8400]
Educational Found. for Women in Accounting [9316]
Educational Inst. of Scotland [IO]
Egyptian Assn. of Univ. Women [IO]
Eleanor Leff Jewish Women's Rsrc. Center [10280]
EMILY's List [18294]
Empowerment Soc. of the U.S.A. [13425]

Emunah Women of Am. [20136]
Episcopal Women's Caucus [19956]
Equality Now [18809]
Equality Now [IO]
Estonian Assn. of Univ. Women [IO]
Ethiopian North Amer. Hea. Professionals Assn. [14629]
European Assn. Against Violence Against Women at Work [IO]
Evangelical and Ecumenical Women's Caucus [19978]
Every Mother is a Working Mother Network [18810]
Executive Women Intl. [63]
Executive Women's Coun. [4038]
Executive Women's Golf Assn. [23447]
Facing Our Risk of Cancer Empowered [13823]
Faith at Work [19893]
FaithTrust Inst. [12027]
Federated Women's Institutes of Canada [IO]
Fed. of Univ. Women (Russia) [IO]
Felag Islenzkra Haskolakvenna [IO]
Feminist Center for Human Growth and Development [13426]
The Feminist Press at the City Univ. of New York [9317]
Feminist Teacher Editorial Collective [9318]
Feminists for Animal Rights [11396]
Femme Developpement Entreprise en Afrique [IO]
Fianna Fail [IO]
Fiji Women's Crisis Centre [IO]
Financial Women's Assn. of New York [1421]
Finnish and Amer. Women's Network [17586]
Finnish Fed. of Univ. Women [IO]
Foreign Executive Women [IO]
Found. for Stud. and Res. on Women [IO]
Found. for Women's Equality [IO]
Found. for Women's Hea. Res. and Development [IO]
Found. for Women's Resources [9319]
Freedom Socialist Party [18653]
Friendly Hand Found. [13243]
Friends of Lulu [22134]
Fundacion Boliviana para el Desarrollo de la Mujer [IO]
Gambia Women's Finance Assn. [IO]
Gamma Alpha Omega Sorority [24599]
Gamma Delta Pi [24710]
Gamma Gamma Chi Sorority [24711]
Gender Action [18825]
Gen. Fed. of Women's Clubs [19435]
Gen. Fed. of Women's Clubs [IO]
German Assn. of Women and Men Working in the Home [IO]
German Professional Women's Assn. [4039]
Girls Inc. [13486]
Global Alliance for Women's Hea. [16897]
Global Alliance for Women's Hea. [IO]
Good Tidings [19629]
Grailville [19630]
Greater Blouse, Skirt and Undergarment Assn. [237]
Greek Orthodox Ladies Philoptochos Soc. [20071]
Gp. of Samanway - Japan [IO]
Hadassah, The Women's Zionist Org. of Am. [20139]
Hard Hatted Women [4040]
Help-One Women's Org. [IO]
Helping Our Teen Girls in Real Life Situations [12261]
Hispanas Organized for Political Equality [17703]
Hispanic Professional Women's Assn. [4041]
Hispanic Women's Corp. [10003]
Holistic Moms Network [12673]
Hong Kong Assn. of Univ. Women [IO]
Hope Intl. [IO]
Hope Intl. [13427]
The Hosiery Assn. [239]
Hysterectomy Educational Resources and Services Found. [15601]
IDB Family Assn. [19436]
Ikatan Sarjana Wanita Indonesia [IO]
Impuls - Vorming, Training en Procesbeheer [IO]
INCITE! Women of Color Against Violence [18788]

Reference to "IO" in place of a book number signifies that the association may be found in the 45th edition of International Organizations.

Indian Women's Assn. [IO]
Indus Women Leaders [18003]
Informed Homebirth/Informed Birth and Parenting [15602]
Inst. of Apostolic Oblates [19638]
Inst. for Female Alternative Medicine [16345]
Inst. of Social Stud. Trust [IO]
Inst. for Women in Trades, Tech. and Sci. [4042]
Inst. for Women's Policy Res. [17539]
Instituto Ecuatoriano de Investigaciones y Capacitacion de la Mujer [IO]
Instituto Nacional de las Mujeres [IO]
Inter-American Parliamentary Gp. on Population and Development [12432]
The Intl. Alliance for Women [728]
Intl. Assn. of Physical Educ. and Sport for Girls and Women [8980]
Intl. Assn. of Professional and Bus. Women in Bulgaria [IO]
Intl. Assn. of Women Ministers [IO]
Intl. Assn. of Women Ministers [20619]
Intl. Black Women for Wages for Housework [18811]
Intl. Consortium for Emergency Contraception [12183]
Intl. Dalkon Shield Victims Educ. Assn. [16898]
International Dalkon Shield Victims Education Association [IO]
Intl. Disciples Women's Ministries [IO]
Intl. Disciples Women's Ministries [20620]
Intl. Fed. for Res. in Women's History [IO]
Intl. Fed. of Univ. Women - Switzerland [IO]
Intl. Female Boxers Assn. [23263]
Intl. Network of Women Against Tobacco [18744]
Intl. Partnership for Microbicides [13572]
Intl. Premature Ovarian Failure Assn. [15606]
Intl. Rebecca West Soc. [11178]
Intl. Side Saddle Org. [23529]
Intl. Soc. Daughters of Utah Pioneers [21252]
Intl. Soc. for the Stud. of Women's Sexual Hea. [16404]
Intl. Wages for Housework Campaign [13428]
Intl. Wages for Housework Campaign [IO]
Intl. Women's Anthropology Conf. [6420]
Intl. Women's Coffee Alliance [11783]
Intl. Women's Fishing Assn. [23419]
Intl. Women's Forum [13429]
Intl. Women's Forum [IO]
Intl. Women's Hea. Coalition [IO]
Intl. Women's Hea. Coalition [16899]
Intl. Women's Media Found. [4043]
International Women's Media Foundation [IO]
Intl. Women's Writing Guild [11180]
Intimate Apparel Square Club [12201]
Iraqi Widows Org. [IO]
Iris Films/Iris Feminist Collective [11086]
Irish Fed. of Univ. Women [IO]
Isis Internacional [IO]
Israel Assn. of Univ. Women [IO]
Italian Fed. of Univ. Women [IO]
IUD Claims Info. Source [6216]
Japanese Assn. of Univ. Women [IO]
Jewish War Veterans of the U.S.A. - Natl. Ladies Auxiliary [21196]
Jewish Women Intl. [20153]
Jewish Women's Coalition [13430]
Jordanian Natl. Comm. for Women [IO]
Justice, Economic Dignity and Independence for Women [18812]
Kahayag Found. [IO]
Kappa Phi Gamma Sorority [24712]
Kenya Female Advisory Org. [IO]
Knowledge for Iraqi Woman Soc. [IO]
Korean Assn. of Univ. Women [IO]
Korean Inst. for Women and Politics [IO]
Korean Women's Inst. [IO]
KVINFO - Danish Centre for Info. on Women and Gender [IO]
Ladies Apparel Contractors Assn. [244]
Ladies Auxiliary, Military Order of the Purple Heart, U.S.A. [20713]
Ladies Professional Golf Assn. [23454]
Ladyslipper [11087]
Lambda Psi Delta Sorority [24713]
Largesse, the Network for Size Esteem [12646]

Latin Amer. and Caribbean Women's Hea. Network [IO]
Latvian Assn. of Univ. Women [IO]
Laura Ingalls Wilder Memorial Soc. [9679]
Leadership Conf. of Women Religious [19649]
Lebanese Coun. to Resist Violence Against Women [IO]
Lesbian Herstory Educational Found. [IO]
Lesbian Herstory Educational Found. [11088]
Lietuvos Universitetu Moteru Asociacija [IO]
Links [13049]
Lutheran Deaconess Assn. [20219]
Lutheran Women's Missionary League [20229]
Makeni Ecumenical Centre [IO]
Martha Org. [IO]
Maternal Life Intl. [16341]
Matrix Found. [18813]
Media Watch [17185]
Medical Women's Intl. Assn. [IO]
Meet A Mum Assn. [IO]
Melpomene Inst. [16900]
Men Stopping Violence [12643]
Midmarch Associates [9510]
Minority Women In Sci. [7615]
Miss Am. Org. [22135]
MOMS in Touch Intl. [20621]
MOMS in Touch Infl. [IO]
Mongolian Assn. of Univ. Women [IO]
Mooncircles [20577]
Mothers Against Sexual Predators At Large [13079]
Mothers Against Violence in Am. [13375]
Mothers Against War [18221]
Mothers And More [12086]
Mothers Arms [13011]
Mothers' Home Bus. Network [1920]
Motor Maids [23625]
Mujeres Activas en Letras Y Cambio Social [8497]
Museum of Menstruation and Women's Hea. [15611]
Na'amat U.S.A. [20162]
NARAL Pro-Choice Am. [18518]
Natl. Advisory Coun. on the Employment of Women [IO]
Natl. Asian Women's Hea. Org. [IO]
Natl. Asian Women's Hea. Org. [16901]
Natl. Assn. for the Advancement of Colored People Legal Defense and Educational Fund [17130]
Natl. Assn. of Baby Boomer Women [13431]
Natl. Assn. of Black Female Executives in Music and Entertainment [12117]
Natl. Assn. of Blouse Mfrs. [245]
Natl. Assn. of Colored Women's Clubs [13051]
Natl. Assn. for Female Executives [742]
Natl. Assn. for Girls and Women in Sport [8983]
Natl. Assn. of Insurance Women Intl. [2213]
Natl. Assn. of Junior Auxiliaries [13052]
Natl. Assn. of Military Widows [21197]
Natl. Assn. of Minority Women in Business [2766]
Natl. Assn. of Negro Bus. and Professional Women's Clubs [13053]
Natl. Assn. of Non-Custodial Moms [11538]
Natl. Assn. of Postpartum Care Services [16902]
Natl. Assn. of Railway Bus. Women [3285]
Natl. Assn. of Univ. Women [9320]
Natl. Assn. of Univ. Women (Moldova) [IO]
Natl. Assn. of Women Artists [9514]
Natl. Assn. of Women Highway Safety Leaders [12971]
Natl. Assn. of Women Law Enforcement Executives [5989]
Natl. Assn. of Women Lawyers [5514]
Natl. Assn. of Women Organizations in Uganda [IO]
Natl. Assn. of Women Writers [11183]
Natl. Assn. for Women's Hea. [16903]
Natl. Black Herstory Task Force [11089]
Natl. Black Police Assn. [5990]
Natl. Black Sisters' Conf. [19671]
Natl. Catholic Women's Union [19678]
Natl. Chamber of Commerce for Women [24388]
Natl. Coalition for Women and Girls in Educ. [9321]

Natl. Conf. of Women's Bar Associations [5518]
Natl. Coun. of Athletic Training [8987]
Natl. Coun. of Catholic Women [19684]
Natl. Coun. of Churches - Women in Ministry Gp. [20622]
Natl. Coun. of Jewish Women [20166]
Natl. Coun. of Woman of Malta [IO]
Natl. Coun. of Women of Kenya [IO]
Natl. Coun. on Women's Hea. [16904]
Natl. Fed. of Press Women [3137]
Natl. Fed. of Women's Institutes [IO]
Natl. Found. for Women Legislators [6359]
Natl. Inst. of Womanhood [13432]
Natl. Latina Hea. Network [14589]
Natl. League of Amer. Pen Women [9588]
Natl. Lung Cancer Partnership [13854]
Natl. Network to End Violence Against Immigrant Women [13433]
Natl. Order of Women Legislators [6038]
Natl. Org. of Immigrants and Visible Minority Women of Canada [IO]
Natl. Peach Partners [4745]
Natl. Pinochle Bugs Social and Civic Club [13055]
Natl. Rsrc. and Info. Center [18814]
Natl. Soc. of the Colonial Dames of Am. [20743]
Natl. Soc. Colonial Dames XVII Century [20744]
Natl. Soc., Daughters of the Amer. Colonists [20746]
Natl. Soc., U.S. Daughters of 1812 [21355]
Natl. Soc. Women Descendants of the Ancient and Honorable Artillery Company [20749]
Natl. Vulvodynia Assn. [16905]
Natl. Woman's Christian Temperance Union [13306]
Natl. Women Law Students Assn. [9322]
Natl. Women's Bus. Coun. [4044]
Natl. Women's Conf. Center [17564]
Natl. Women's Coun. of Ireland [IO]
Natl. Women's Hall of Fame [20716]
Natl. Women's Hea. Network [16906]
Natl. Women's Hea. Rsrc. Center [16907]
Natl. Women's History Proj. [11090]
Natl. Women's Justice Coalition [IO]
Natl. Women's Martial Arts Fed. [23600]
Natl. Women's Sailing Assn. [21879]
Natl. Women's Stud. Assn. [9323]
Natl. Work at Home Mom Assn. [1922]
Native Amer. Women's Hea. Educ. Rsrc. Center [16908]
Native Amer. Women's Hea. Educ. Rsrc. Center [IO]
Navy Club of the U.S.A. Auxiliary [6100]
Nepal Assn. of Univ. Women [IO]
New Brunswick Women's Inst. [IO]
New Dawn [22140]
New York Skirt and Sportswear Assn. [254]
New York Women in Communications, Inc. Found. [883]
New Zealand Educational Inst. - Women's Network [IO]
New Zealand Fed. of Graduate Women [IO]
News Brunswick Advisory Coun. on the Status of Women [IO]
Newswomen's Club of New York [3150]
Niger Delta Women for Justice [IO]
Nigeria Assn. of Univ. Women [IO]
Nirnaya [IO]
Nisaa Inst. for Women's Development [IO]
Nordic Assn. for Women's Stud. and Gender Res. [IO]
Nordic Inst. for Women's Stud. and Gender Res. [IO]
North Amer. Menopause Soc. [15614]
North Amer. Network of Women Runners [23656]
Norwegian Women and Family Assn. [IO]
The Nurturing Network [13434]
Off. of Women in Higher Educ., Amer. Coun. on Educ. [9324]
Older Women's League [13435]
Older Women's Network NSW [IO]
Org. for the Relief of Underprivileged Women and Children in Africa [12876]
Our Bodies, Ourselves [16909]
Pacific Soc. for Women in Philosophy [10822]
Pacific Women's Rsrc. Bur. [IO]

A star before a book entry number signifies that the name is not listed separately, but is mentioned within the entry.

Pakistan Fed. of Univ. Women [IO]
Peace X Peace [18237]
Pen and Brush [9521]
PEO Intl. [9325]
PEO Intl. [IO]
Philippine Assn. of Univ. Women [IO]
Post and Antenatal Depression Assn. [IO]
Post Natal Depression Support Assn. South Africa
   [IO]
Power for Women [13436]
Presbyterian Women [20475]
Pride Prog. [13437]
Professional Assn. of Volleyball Officials [23875]
Professional Women in Constr. [1062]
Professional Women in Healthcare [4045]
Professional Women Photographers [3013]
Professional Women's Appraisal Assn. [287]
Public Leadership Educ. Network [9326]
Public Media Found. [18033]
Radiology Mammography Intl. [13774]
Re-Formed Congregation of the Goddess - Intl.
   [20623]
Reach Out [IO]
Real Found. [13438]
REAL Women of Canada [IO]
Red Hat Soc. [11091]
Religious Coalition for Reproductive Choice
   [18519]
Revolutionary Assn. of the Women of Afghanistan
   [IO]
Rose Kushner Breast Cancer Advisory Center
   [13870]
Roundtable for Women in Foodservice [1593]
Ruth Jackson Orthopaedic Soc. [15781]
RVing Women [22962]
Schweizerischer Verband der Akademikerinnen
   [IO]
Secretariat for Family, Laity, Women, and Youth
   [12167]
Sect. for Women in Public Admin. [6198]
Secular Inst. of Saint Francis de Sales [19716]
Seton Hill University's E-magnify [8040]
Shared Hope Intl. [IO]
Sharsheret [13872]
Sheclimbs [23285]
Shidhulai Swanirvar Sangstha [IO]
Sigma Delta Epsilon, Graduate Women in Sci.
   [24587]
Sigma Lambda Alpha Sorority [24714]
Sigma Lambda Gamma Natl. Sorority [24715]
Singapore Bus. and Professional Women's Assn.
   [IO]
Single Mothers By Choice [12692]
Sisterhood Agenda [11092]
Sisterhood of Shoers [1355]
Sisters in Crime [4069]
SisterSong Women of Color Reproductive Hea.
   Collective [18826]
Slovene Union of Univ. Women [IO]
Soc. for the Advancement of Women's Imaging
   [16294]
Soc. of the Companions of the Holy Cross
   [19971]
Soc. of Daughters of Holland Dames [20759]
Soc. for Executive Leadership in Academic
   Medicine Intl. [15179]
Soc. of Professional Women in Petroleum [2948]
Soc. for the Stud. of Amer. Women Writers
   [11195]
Soc. for the Stud. of Early Modern Women [9331]
Soc. of Woman Geographers [7124]
Soc. of Women Artists [IO]
Soc. of Women Engineers [7049]
Soc. for Women's Hea. Res. [16910]
Sociologists for Women in Soc. [9924]
Solace Intl. [13439]
Solace Intl. [IO]
Solidarity with Women in Distress [IO]
Solomon Island Graduate Women's Assn. [IO]
Sony Ericsson WTA Tour [23910]
SOS Femmes [IO]
South African Assn. of Women Graduates [IO]
Spirit of Women Hosp. Network [14898]
Springboard Enterprises [4046]
Step Up Women's Network [13440]

Story Circle Network [10985]
Stuntwomen's Assn. of Motion Pictures [1394]
Support Assn. for the Women of Afghanistan -
   Australia [IO]
Swedish Assn. of Univ. Women [IO]
Swiss-American Coun. of Women [18815]
Tam Tam Femme [IO]
Tanzania Gender Networking Prog. [IO]
Tanzania Women Graduates Fed. [IO]
Theta Chi Omega Multicultural Sorority [24716]
TOC H [IO]
Turkish Assn. of Univ. Women [IO]
Turkish Cypriot Assn. of Univ. Women [IO]
Turners Syndrome Support Soc. (UK) [IO]
Uganda Assn. of Univ. Women [IO]
Union of Australian Women [IO]
Unitarian Universalist Women's Fed. [20604]
United Daughters of the Confederacy [20732]
United Nations Div. for the Advancement of
   Women [13441]
United Nations Div. for the Advancement of
   Women [IO]
United Order True Sisters [19437]
U.S.A. Netball Assn. [23634]
U.S. Assn. of Consecrated Virgins [19733]
U.S. Girls' Wrestling Assn. [23988]
U.S. Women of Today [13067]
U.S. Women's Chamber of Commerce [24389]
U.S. Women's Curling Assn. [23303]
Univ. Women of Europe [IO]
Vereniging van Vrouwen met Hogere Opleiding
   [IO]
Veteran Feminists of Am. [17572]
Veterans' Widows Intl. Network [21357]
WAND Educ. Fund [18174]
WAVES Natl. [21234]
We Are AWARE [13442]
WECAI Network [1167]
Welfare Warriors [18183]
Wellesley Centers for Women [9327]
Wellstart Intl. [14666]
WEP Intl. [IO]
Western Women Premier Bowlers [23257]
Whirly-Girls - Intl. Women Helicopter Pilots
   [21487]
Wider Opportunities for Women [12106]
WISH List [5770]
Wishing Well [22146]
WITH/Curam, parent and carer NGO in Ireland
   [IO]
Wives-Self-Help Found. [11832]
Womankind Worldwide [IO]
Woman's Home and Foreign Mission Soc.
   [19443]
Woman's Missionary Union, SBC [19501]
Women in Aerospace [6393]
Women in Agribusiness [4085]
Women Alive Coalition [13588]
Women as Allies [18816]
Women in the Arts [11093]
Women in Aviation Intl. [4047]
Women in Aviation Intl. [IO]
Women Band Directors Intl. [8934]
Women in Bio [6618]
Women in Cable Telecommunications [585]
Women Chefs and Restaurateurs [794]
Women, Children and Family Ser. Charities of
   Am. [12207]
Women Church Convergence [20624]
Women of Color Rsrc. Center [19438]
Women Contractors Assn. [4048]
Women in Crisis [13443]
Women in Defense, a Natl. Security Org. [17386]
Women in Direct Marketing Intl. [2652]
Women Educators [9328]
Women Employed [12108]
Women Employed Inst. [12109]
Women in Engg. ProActive Network [4049]
Women Entrepreneurs of Saskatchewan [IO]
Women Entrepreneurs in Sci. and Tech. [4050]
Women Executives in Public Relations [3197]
Women for Faith and Family [19739]
Women in Fed. Law Enforcement [6010]
Women in Film [1396]
Women in the Fire Ser. [5724]

Women in Flavor and Fragrance Commerce
   [4051]
Women in Food Indus. Mgt. [IO]
Women in Govt. [6133]
Women in Govt. Relations [17676]
Women in Govt. Relations LEADER Found.
   [17677]
Women Grocers of Am. [3430]
Women in Hea. Care Mgt. [14667]
Women In Conscious Creative Action [20625]
Women in Informal Employment: Globalizing and
   Organizing [13444]
Women, Ink [13445]
Women, Ink [IO]
Women Inst. [IO]
Women in Insurance and Financial Services
   [2247]
Women Involved in Farm Economics [16960]
Women Involved in Sports Evolution [23067]
Women Leaders Online [18817]
Women Leaders Online/Women Organizing For
   Change [18818]
Women Living Under Muslim Laws [IO]
Women Make Movies [11094]
Women in Mgt. [2518]
Women Marines Assn. [21182]
Women and Mathematics Educ. [8828]
Women in Military Ser. for Am. Memorial Found.
   [6360]
Women in Mining [2756]
Women in Municipal Govt. [6134]
Women of Naval Special Warfare [6145]
Women in Neurotrauma Res. [15404]
Women in Numismatics [22767]
Women On Wheels Motorcycle Assn. [23630]
Women Organized to Respond to Life-
   Threatening Diseases [13589]
Women Outdoors [23644]
Women in Packaging [2882]
Women in Philanthropy [18269]
Women in Photography Intl. [3019]
Women in Production [1796]
Women in Progress [13446]
Women in Progress [IO]
Women in Real Estate [9329]
Women of Reform Judaism, The Fed. of Temple
   Sisterhoods [20192]
Women Refugees Community in Zambia [IO]
Women in Scholarly Publishing [3260]
Women in Tech. Intl. [7764]
Women in Toys [3834]
Women in Transition [13447]
Women Veterans of Am. [21333]
Women in the Wind [22701]
Women of Wind Energy [7854]
Women for Winesense [23030]
Women With Disabilities Australia [IO]
Women for Women [12792]
Women for Women's Human Rights/New Ways
   [IO]
Women Work! The Natl. Network for Women's
   Employment [18819]
Women Working Worldwide [IO]
Women of the World [IO]
Women of the World [13448]
Women Writing the West [4071]
WomenHeart: Natl. Coalition for Women with
   Heart Disease [13929]
Women's Action for Change [IO]
Women's Action for New Directions [18175]
Women's Aid - Ireland [IO]
Women's Aid Org. [IO]
Women's All-Star Assn. [23258]
Women's Alliance for Theology, Ethics and Ritual
   [20626]
Women's Alliance for Theology, Ethics and Ritual
   [IO]
Women's Aquatic Network [7277]
Women's Army Corps Veterans' Assn. [20708]
Women's Automotive Assn. Intl. [367]
Women's Auxiliary of the ICA [14016]
Women's Basketball Coaches Assn. [23139]
Women's Bur. of the U.S. Department of Labor
   [6361]
Women's Bus. Enterprise Natl. Coun. [4052]

Women's Caucus for Art [9531]
Women's Caucus for Political Sci. [7529]
Women's Classical Caucus [9801]
Women's Coll. Coalition [9330]
Women's Corona Soc. - Hong Kong Br. [IO]
Women's Coun. on Energy and the Env. [6977]
Women's Division of the Gen. Bd. of Global Ministries of the United Methodist Church [20269]
Women's Documentation Center [IO]
Women's Drug Res. Project [13285]
Women's Economic Round Table [18484]
Women's Flat Track Derby Assn. [23747]
Women's Foreign Policy Gp. [18820]
Women's Foreign Policy Gp. [IO]
Women's Freedom Network [13449]
Women's Funding Network [13450]
Women's Hea. [IO]
Women's Hea. and Economic Development Assn. [IO]
Women's History Network [11095]
Women's Initiatives for Gender Justice [IO]
Women's Inter-Church Coun. of Canada [IO]
Women's Interart Center [11096]
Women's Intl. Center [13451]
Women's Intl. Center [IO]
Women's Intl. Coalition for Economic Justice [17475]
Women's Intl. Network of Utility Professionals [1200]
Women's Intl. News Gathering Ser. [IO]
Women's Intl. Public Hea. Network [16257]
Women's Intl. Shipping and Trading Assn. [3598]
Women's Intl. Stud. Europe [IO]
Women's Jewelry Assn. [2384]
Women's Leadership Forum [17411]
Women's League for Conservative Judaism [20193]
Women's Learning Partnership for Rights, Development, and Peace [13452]
Women's Learning Partnership for Rights, Development, and Peace [IO]
Women's Missionary Society, AME Church [IO]
Women's Missionary Soc., AME Church [20627]
Women's Motorcyclist Found. [22702]
Women's Natl. Basketball Players Assn. [23140]
Women's Natl. Book Assn. [3174]
Women's Network Australia [IO]
Women's Ordination Conf. [19740]
Women's Philanthropy Inst. [12741]
Women's Policy, Inc. [18821]
Women's Prison Assn. [11898]
Women's Professional Billiard Assn. [23149]
Women's Professional Rodeo Assn. [23696]
Women's Proj. [18634]
Women's Regional Publications of Am. [4053]
Women's Rsrc. Centre [IO]
Women's Services Worldwide [IO]
Women's Services Worldwide [13453]
Women's Soc. of Christian Ser. Gen. Conf. [IO]
Women's Spirituality Forum [20628]
Women's Sports Found. [23867]
Women's Stud. Assn. [IO]
Women's Trans. Seminar [3901]
Women's Voices for the Earth [4616]
Women's World Banking - USA [13454]
Women's World Banking - USA [IO]
Women's World Organization for Rights, Literature and Development [IO]
Women's World Org. for Rights, Literature and Development [18822]
Women's World Summit Found. [IO]
WomensLaw.org [18823]
Working Women's Forum [IO]
World Connections for Women [IO]
World Connections for Women [18824]
World Day of Prayer Intl. Comm. [20629]
World Day of Prayer Intl. Comm. [IO]
World War II War Brides [21205]
World Wide Opportunity for Women [IO]
WorldWIDE Network, Women in Development and Environment [4618]
WTA Tour Players Assn. [23917]
Young Judaea [20198]
Young Survival Coalition [13883]

Young Women Social Entrepreneurs [770]
Young Women's Christian Association - Puerto Rico [IO]
Zambia Natl. Women's Lobby Gp. [IO]
Zeta Chi Phi Multicultural Sorority [24717]
Women; 9 to 5, Natl. Assn. of Working [17512]
Women Accountants; Amer. Soc. of [11]
Women Achieving Greater Economic Status - Defunct.
Women in Adult and Vocational Educ. [IO], Carlton, Australia
Women in Advt. and Marketing [★874]
Women in Aerospace [6393], 2200 Wilson Blvd., No. 102-248, Arlington, VA 22201, (703)522-7745
Women Affirming Life [12931], PO Box 35532, Brighton, MA 02135, (617)254-2277
Women for Afghan Women [12379], 32-17 Coll. Point Blvd., Rm. 206, Flushing, NY 11354, (718)321-2434
Women for Afghan Women [IO], Flushing, NY, United States
Women Against Gun Control [IO], South Jordan, UT, United States
Women Against Gun Control [17685], PO Box 95357, South Jordan, UT 84095, (801)328-9660
Women Against Gun Violence [18791], PO Box 1501, Culver City, CA 90232-1501, (310)204-2348
Women Against Lung Cancer [★13854]
Women Against Military Madness [18078], 310 E 38th St., Ste. 222, Minneapolis, MN 55409-1337, (612)827-5364
Women Against Pornography - Address unknown since 1999.
Women Against Rape - Address unknown since 1999.
Women Against Tobacco; Intl. Network of [18744]
Women Against Violence Against Women - Address unknown since 1991.
Women Against Violence in Pornography and Media - Defunct.
Women in Agribusiness [4085]
Women Airforce Ser. Pilots WWII [21413], Texas Woman's Univ., TWU Libraries, PO Box 425528, Denton, TX 76204-5528, (940)898-3701
Women in Alcoholics Anonymous; Intl. Advisory Coun. for Homosexual Men and [★13283]
Women Alive Coalition [13588], 1566 Burnside Ave., Los Angeles, CA 90019, (323)965-1564
Women of All Red Nations - Address unknown since 2003.
Women; Alliance of Unitarian [★20604]
Women as Allies [18816], PO Box 2193, Los Banos, CA 93635, (209)826-8710
Women in Am; Assn. of Polish [★19311]
Women for Am; Concerned [19791]
Women in Am; Union of Polish [19319]
Women of Am; United Polish [★19311]
Women; Amer. Agri- [16948]
Women; Amer. Assn. of [18419]
Women; Amer. Baptist [★19468]
Women; Amer. Mizrachi [★20119]
Women in Animation [1372], PO Box 17706, Encino, CA 91416, (818)759-9596
Women Artists; Natl. Assn. of [9514]
Women in the Arts [11093], PO Box 1427, Indianapolis, IN 46206-1427, (317)713-1144
Women in the Arts - Defunct.
Women; Assn. of Professional Insurance [★2142]
Women; Assn. for the Promotion of the Mathematics Educ. of Girls and [★8828]
Women; Assn. of Universalist [★20604]
Women Athletics Administrators; Natl. Assn. of Collegiate [8982]
Women Attorneys; Assn. of Black [5484]
Women in Aviation Intl. [4047], Morningstar Airport, 3647 State Rte. 503 S, West Alexandria, OH 45381, (937)839-4647
Women in Aviation Intl. [IO], West Alexandria, OH, United States
Women Band Directors Intl. [IO], Palos Park, IL, United States
Women Band Directors Intl. [8934], 10611 Ridgewood Dr., Palos Park, IL 60464-2589, (765)463-1738
Women Band Directors Natl. Assn. [★8934]

Women Band Directors Natl. Assn. [★IO]
Women in Banking [★IO]
Women in Banking and Finance [IO], West Wickham, United Kingdom
Women in Bio [6618], PO Box 34043, Bethesda, MD 20827, (703)819-7647
Women in Black [18255], PO Box 20554, New York, NY 10021, (212)560-0905
Women; Black Career [19323]
Women Bowlers; Western [★23257]
Women Bowling Writers Assn; Bowling Writers Assn. of Am. and Natl. [★3101]
Women in Broadcast Technology - Address unknown since 1999.
Women in Bus; Graduate [★745]
Women in Business; Natl. Assn. of Minority [2766]
Women in Bus; Natl. Educ. Center for [★8040]
Women Bus. Owners; Assn. of [★744]
Women Bus. Owners; Natl. Assn. of [744]
Women Bus. Owners; Natl. Found. for [★4037]
Women for Bus. and Political Development; Alliance of Minority [2759]
Women in Cable [★585]
Women in Cable Telecommunications [585], PO Box 791305, Baltimore, MD 21279-1305, (703)234-9810
Women; Camping [23269]
Women; Campus Ministry [19918]
Women in Cancer Res. [★16893]
Women in Cancer Res; AACR- [16893]
Women Center for Educ. and Res; Coalition of Labor Union [24204]
Women for Change [IO], Lusaka, Zambia
Women Chefs and Restaurateurs [794], 455 S Fourth St., Ste. 650, Louisville, KY 40202, (502)581-0300
Women Chefs and Restaurateurs; Intl. Assn. of [★794]
Women Chiefs of Enterprises Intl. [IO], Toowong, Australia
Women and Children; Comm. on Christian Literature for [★12376]
Women, Children and Family Ser. Charities of Am. [12207], 1100 Larkspur Cir., Ste. 340, Larkspur, CA 94939, (800)626-6481
Women of the Church [★20475]
Women in the Church Coalition [★20624]
Women Church Convergence [20624], c/o Bridget Mary Meehan, 5856 Glen Forest Dr., Falls Church, VA 22041, (703)671-6712
Women of the Church of God [19835], 1201 E 5th St., Anderson, IN 46018-2328, (765)648-2102
Women of the Church of Jesus Christ of Latter-Day Saints; Young [20209]
Women Clergy; Assn. of Full Gospel [20275]
Women Climbing [IO], Wellington, New Zealand
Women; Coalition of Labor Union [24203]
Women of Color; Natl. Inst. for [★17541]
Women of Color Partnership Program - Defunct.
Women of Color Rsrc. Center [19438], 1611 Telegraph Ave., No. 303, Oakland, CA 94612, (510)444-2700
Women in Communications [★874]
Women in Communications; Assn. for [874]
Women in Communications Found. [★883]
Women in Community Ser. [12786], 1900 N Beauregard St., Ste. 103, Alexandria, VA 22311, (703)671-0500
Women in Computing; Assn. for [6786]
Women Constr. Owners and Executives, U.S.A. [1068], 4401A Connecticut Ave. NW, Washington, DC 20008, (800)788-3548
Women in Constr; Professional [1062]
Women Contractors Assn. [4048], PO Box 6757, Houston, TX 77265, (713)807-9977
Women; Cosmetic Career [★1842]
Women; Cosmetic Executive [1842]
Women in Crisis [13443], 360 W 125th St., No. 11, New York, NY 10027, (212)665-2020
Women Dedicated to the Environment; World [★4618]
Women in Defense [★17386]
Women in Defense, a Natl. Security Org. [17386], 2111 Wilson Blvd., Ste. 400, Arlington, VA 22201-3061, (703)247-2552

A star before a book entry number signifies that the name is not listed separately, but is mentioned within the entry.

Women; Delegation for Friendship Among [17528]

Women Dentists; Amer. Assn. of [14119]

Women Dentists; Assn. of Amer. [★14119]

Women Descendants of the Ancient and Honorable Artillery Company; Natl. Soc. [20749]

Women in Design Intl. [★1811]

Women in Design Intl. [★IO]

Women in Direct Marketing Intl. [IO], New York, NY, United States

Women in Direct Marketing Intl. [2652], c/o Berenice Ladden, Pres., 200 Circle Dr. N, Piscataway, NJ 08854, (732)469-8414

Women in the Economics Profession; Comm. on the Status of [5673]

Women Educ. Fund; 9 to 5 Working [17513]

Women Educators [9328], c/o Paula Lane, Treas., Sonoma State Univ., School of Educ., 1801 E Co-tati, Rohnert Park, CA 94928, (805)893-5356

Women Emergency Physicians; Amer. Assn. of [14324]

Women Employed [12108], 111 N Wabash, Ste. 1300, Chicago, IL 60602, (312)782-3902

Women Employed Inst. [12109], 111 N Wabash, Ste. 1300, Chicago, IL 60602, (312)782-3902

Women and Employment [★12073]

Women in Endocrinology [14359], c/o Carolyn L. Smith, PhD, Communications Comm. Chair, Dept. of Molecular and Cellular Biology, Baylor Coll. of Medicine, One Baylor Plz., Houston, TX 77030-3411, (713)798-6235

Women in Energy - Defunct.

Women in Engg. ProActive Network [4049], c/o C. Diane Matt, CAE, Exec. Dir., 1901 E Asbury Ave., Denver, CO 80208, (303)871-4643

Women Engineers; Soc. of [7049]

Women Entrepreneurs of Canada [IO], Toronto, ON, Canada

Women Entrepreneurs - Defunct.

Women Entrepreneurs of Saskatchewan [IO], Saskatoon, SK, Canada

Women Entrepreneurs in Sci. and Tech. [4050], 155 Seaport Blvd., 11th Fl., Boston, MA 02210, (617)988-6120

Women and Env. Proj. [★IO]

Women in the Environment; World [★4618]

Women and Environments and Development Found. [★IO]

Women Executives Intl. Tourism Assn. - Defunct.

Women Executives in Public Relations [3197], PO Box 7657, FDR Sta., New York, NY 10150-7657, (212)859-7375

Women Executives in State Govt. - Address unknown since 2006.

Women Exploited by Abortion [12932]

Women for Faith and Family [19739], PO Box 300411, St. Louis, MO 63130-0261, (314)863-8385

Women and Families; Natl. Partnership for [17561]

Women in Fed. Law Enforcement [6010], 2200 Wilson Blvd., Ste. 102, PMB-204, Arlington, VA 22201, (703)548-9211

Women; Federally Employed [17531]

Women; Fed. of French Amer. [19063]

Women in Film [1396], 8857 W Olympic Blvd., Ste. 201, Beverly Hills, CA 90211, (310)657-5144

Women in Film Foundation [★1396]

Women in Film and TV - United Kingdom [IO], London, United Kingdom

Women in Film and Video [1373], 3628 12th St. NE, Washington, DC 20017, (202)429-9438

Women in the Fire Ser. [5724], PO Box 5446, Madison, WI 53705, (608)233-4768

Women in Fire Suppression [★5724]

Women in Flavor and Fragrance Commerce [4051], 3301 Rte. 66, Ste. 205, Bldg. C, Neptune, NJ 07753, (732)922-0500

Women in Food Indus. Mgt. [IO], Richmond Hill, ON, Canada

Women and Food Information Network - Defunct.

Women in Foodservice; Roundtable for [1593]

Women and Foundations/Corporate Philanthropy [★17575]

Women in Franchising [1671], 53 W Jackson Blvd., Ste. 1157, Chicago, IL 60604, (312)431-1467

Women; Gen. Commn. on the Status and Role of [17535]

Women Geoscientists; Assn. of [★7139]

Women Geoscientists; Assn. for [7139]

Women in Govt. [6133], 2600 Virginia Ave. NW, Ste. 709, Washington, DC 20037-1925, (202)333-0825

Women in Govt. [IO], Washington, DC, United States

Women in Govt; Executive [5706]

Women in Govt. Relations [17676], 801 N Fairfax St., Ste. 211, Alexandria, VA 22314-1757, (703)299-8546

Women in Govt. Relations LEADER Found. [17677], c/o Women in Government Relations, 801 N Fair-fax St., Ste. 211, Alexandria, VA 22314-1757, (703)299-8546

Women Grocers of Am. [3430], c/o Natl. Grocers Assn., 1005 N Glebe Rd., Ste. 250, Arlington, VA 22201-5758, (703)516-0700

Women for Guatemala - Defunct.

Women; Handicapped Organized [★11978]

Women in Hea. Care Mgt. [14667], 84 Fenwick Rd., Newton, MA 02468

Women Hea. Educ. Rsrc. Center; Native Amer. [★12630]

Women and Health Roundtable - Address unknown since 1995.

Women at the Helm: Intl. Women's Sailing - Defunct.

Women Helping Women - Defunct.

Women Highway Safety Leaders; Natl. Assn. of [12971]

Women in History; Coordinating Coun. for [17526]

Women in the Home [★IO]

Women in Housing and Finance [1452], 717 Princess St., Alexandria, VA 22314, (703)683-4742

Women in ICT [IO], Sandton, Republic of South Africa

Women In Conscious Creative Action [20625], PO Box 5296, Eugene, OR 97405, (541)485-3654

Women In Constant Creative Action [★20625]

Women Incorporated - Address unknown since 2006.

Women in Informal Employment: Globalizing and Organizing [13444], Harvard Univ., 79 John F. Kennedy St., Cambridge, MA 02138, (617)496-1310

Women in Information Processing - Address unknown since 2002.

Women, Ink [13445], 777 United Nations Plz., New York, NY 10017, (212)687-8633

Women, Ink [IO], New York, NY, United States

Women Inst. [IO], Santiago, Chile

Women in Insurance and Financial Services [IO], Larkspur, CO, United States

Women in Insurance and Financial Services [2247], 6748 Wauconda Dr., Larkspur, CO 80118, (303)681-9777

Women and Intl. Affairs CH [★17578]

Women and Intl. Affairs CH [★IO]

Women; The Intl. Alliance, An Assn. of Executive and Professional [★728]

Women; Intl. Assn. for Personnel [★2905]

Women - Intl; Credit [★1411]

Women Intl; Natl. Assn. of Insurance [2213]

Women in Intl. Security [18598], Georgetown Univ., Center for Peace and Security Stud., Edmund A. Walsh School of Foreign Ser., 3600 N St. NW, Washington, DC 20007, (202)687-3366

Women in Intl. Security [IO], Washington, DC, United States

Women in Intl. Trade [★2290]

Women Involved in Farm Economics [16960], c/o Alice Fairfax, Membership Chair, 27248 Goodwill Chapel Rd., Sedalia, MO 65301, (660)826-0220

Women Involved in Sports Evolution [23067], c/o Pierpont Racquet Club, 500 Sanjon Rd., Ventura, CA 93001, (805)648-5161

Women Judges; Found. for [★5907]

Women Judges' Fund for Justice [★5907]

Women Judges; Natl. Assn. of [5907]

Women, Law, and Development [★IO]

Women in Law and Development in Africa [IO], Harare, Zimbabwe

Women, Law, and Development Intl. - Address unknown since 2008.

Women Lawyers' Club [★5514]

Women Lawyers; Natl. Assn. of [5514]

Women Leaders Online [18817], PO Box 721066, Jackson Heights, NY 11372

Women Leaders Online/Women Organizing For Change [18818], PO Box 721066, Jackson Heights, NY 11372

Women; Legal Action for [16912]

Women of the Legion of Valor U.S.A. - Address unknown since 1995.

Women; Legion of Young Polish [19304]

Women Legislators; Natl. Order of [6038]

Women Library Workers - Defunct.

Women for Life - Address unknown since 1995.

Women; Life and Liberty for [11222]

Women Life Underwriters Confed. [★2247]

Women Life Underwriters Confed. [★IO]

Women Life Underwriters Conf. of the Natl. Assn. of Life Underwriters [★IO]

Women Life Underwriters Conf. of the Natl. Assn. of Life Underwriters [★2247]

Women in Livestock Development [4296], c/o Heifer Proj. Intl., PO Box 8058, Little Rock, AR 72203, (800)422-0474

Women in Livestock Development [IO], Little Rock, AR, United States

Women Living Under Muslim Laws [IO], London, United Kingdom

Women in the Mainstream - Defunct.

Women Make Movies [11094], 462 Broadway, Ste. 500WS, New York, NY 10013, (212)925-0606

Women in Managed Care [14693], 4435 Waterfront Dr., Ste. 101, PO Box 6026, Glen Allen, VA 23058-6026, (804)527-1905

Women in Managed Care [IO], Glen Allen, VA, United States

Women in Mgt. [2518], PO Box 1032, Dundee, IL 60118-7032, (708)386-0496

Women and Manual Trades [IO], London, United Kingdom

Women Marines Assn. [21182], PO Box 8405, Falls Church, VA 22041-8405, (888)525-1943

Women Mathematicians; Assn. of [★7288]

Women in Mathematics; Assn. for [7288]

Women and Mathematics Educ. [8828], c/o Pat Frey, Treas., PO Box 922, Buffalo, NY 14201

Women for Meaningful Summits - Address unknown since 2001.

Women in Medicine Prog; Assn. of Amer. Medical Colleges- [8847]

Women Members Network of the Royal Soc. of Chemistry [IO], Cambridge, United Kingdom

Women and Men Against Sexual Harassment and Other Abuses [13088], 4309 Sandy Spring Rd., Burtonsville, MD 20866-1139, (301)384-3727

Women in Microbiology; Comm. on the Status of [6574]

Women Military Aviators - Defunct.

Women and the Military Project - Defunct.

Women in Military Ser. for Am. Memorial Found. [6360], Dept. 560, Washington, DC 20042-0560, (703)533-1155

Women in Mining [2756], PO Box 260246, Lakewood, CO 80226-0246, (303)298-1535

Women in Mining [★2756]

Women in Ministry/Folio; Baptist [19481]

Women in Ministry Gp; Natl. Coun. of Churches - [20622]

Women in Ministry; Natl. Coun. of Churches Commn. on [★20622]

Women of the Motion Picture Industry, Intl. - Address unknown since 1999.

Women; Ms. Found. for [17549]

Women in Multimedia - Address unknown since 2006.

Women in Municipal Govt. [6134], c/o Natl. League of Cities, 1301 Pennsylvania Ave. NW, Ste. 550, Washington, DC 20004, (202)626-3000

Women of Music-Music of Women - Address unknown since 2007.

Women in Music Natl. Network [10724], 1450 Odds-tad Dr., Redwood City, CA 94063, (866)305-7963

Women/Na'amat, the Women's Labor Zionist Org. of Am; Pioneer [★20162]

Women of the Natl. Agricultural Aviation Assn. [4189], 1005 E St. SE, Washington, DC 20003-2847, (202)546-5722

Reference to "IO" in place of a book number signifies that the association may be found in the 45th edition of International Organizations.

Women; Natl. Assn. of Bank [★478]
Women; Natl. Assn. of Coll. [★9320]
Women; Natl. Assn. of Commissions for [17550]
Women; Natl. Assn. of Insurance [★2213]
Women; Natl. Assn. for Physical Educ. of Coll. [★8985]
Women; Natl. Assn. of Professional Asian Amer. [743]
Women; Natl. Assn. of Professional Mortgage [491]
Women; Natl. Assn. of Railway Bus. [3285]
Women; Natl. Coalition of 100 Black [17552]
Women; Natl. Communications Network for the Elimination of Violence Against [★12034]
Women; Natl. Conf. of Puerto Rican [17554]
Women; Natl. Coun. of Amer. Baptist [★19468]
Women; Natl. Coun. of Catholic [19684]
Women of the Natl. Coun. of Churches; Dept. of United Church [★20618]
Women; Natl. Coun. of Jewish [20166]
Women; Natl. Coun. of Negro [17555]
Women; Natl. Coun. for Res. on [17556]
Women; Natl. Fed. of Afro-American [★13051]
Women; Natl. Fed. of Democratic [17408]
Women; Natl. Fed. of Press [3137]
Women; Natl. Fed. of Republican [18525]
Women; Natl. Hook-Up of Black [17559]
Women; Natl. League of Amer. Pen [9588]
Women; Natl. Network of Commercial Real Estate [★3309]
Women; Natl. Org. for [17560]
Women; Natl. Org. of Italian-American [19167]
Women; Natl. Pork Coun. [★5238]
Women Nationally Active for Christ [19502], PO Box 5002, Antioch, TN 37011-5002, (877)767-7662
Women of Naval Special Warfare [6145]
Women in Neurotrauma Res. [15404], c/o Courtney L. Robertson, MD, Univ. of Maryland, Pediatric Critical Care, 22 S Greene St., No. N5E13, Baltimore, MD 21201
Women of New York; Advt. [81]
Women for New York State Wines [★5417]
Women in Nuclear Global [IO], London, United Kingdom
Women in Nuclear Korea [IO], Daejeon, Republic of Korea
Women in Numismatics [22767], 5175 Gloria St., Wayne, MI 48184, (734)721-4991
Women Officers Professional Assn. [★21238]
Women On Wheels Motorcycle Assn. [23630], PO Box 83076, Lincoln, NE 68501, (402)477-1280
Women; Org. of Chinese Amer. [17567]
Women Organized to Respond to Life-Threatening Diseases [13589], 414 13th St., 2nd Fl., Oakland, CA 94612-2603, (510)986-0340
Women Organized to Respond to Life-Threatening Diseases [IO], Oakland, CA, United States
Women Organizing For Change; Women Leaders Online/ [18818]
Women Organizing Proj; Working [★17512]
Women Outdoors [23644], 55 Talbot Ave., Medford, MA 02155
Women in Packaging [2882], 4290 Bells Ferry Rd., Ste. 106-17, Kennesaw, GA 30144-1300, (770)924-3563
Women Painters and Sculptors; Assn. of [★9514]
Women for Peace - Switzerland [IO], Volketswil, Switzerland
Women and Philanthropy [17575], 1828 L St. NW, Ste. 300, Washington, DC 20036, (202)466-6512
Women in Philanthropy [18269], c/o Univ. of Michigan, Off. of Development, 3003 S State St., Ste. 9000, Ann Arbor, MI 48109-1288, (734)647-6000
Women in Philosophy; Pacific Soc. for [10822]
Women Photographers; Professional [3013]
Women in Photography Intl. [3019], 569 N Rossmore Ave., No. 604, Los Angeles, CA 90004, (303)462-1444
Women Physician's Assn; Natl. Osteopathic [24564]
Women in Physics [★IO]
Women in Physics Gp. [IO], London, United Kingdom
Women Podiatrists; Amer. Assn. for [16027]
Women and Policing; Natl. Center for [5991]
Women Policy Stud; Center for [17518]

Women and Politics; Center for Amer. [17516]
Women; Presbyterian [20475]
Women and Priests Involved [★19629]
Women in Production [1796], 276 Bowery, New York, NY 10012, (212)334-2108
Women Professional Bowlers; Worldwide [★23257]
Women in Progress [13446], PO Box 18323, Minneapolis, MN 55418, (800)338-3032
Women in Progress [IO], Minneapolis, MN, United States
Women Proutists [18633], 6810 Tilden Ln., Rockville, MD 20852, (301)231-0110
Women Psychologists; Assn. for [★16145]
Women in Psychology; Assn. for [16145]
Women in Public Admin; Natl. Comm. for [★6198]
Women in Public Admin; Sect. for [6198]
Women in Public Admin; Task Force for [★6198]
Women in Public Relations; Comm. on [★3197]
Women in Public Service - Address unknown since 1995.
Women in Publishing [IO], London, United Kingdom
Women for Racial and Economic Equality - Address unknown since 2003.
Women; Radical [17569]
Women in Radio and TV; Amer. [545]
Women Radiologists; Amer. Assn. for [16271]
Women in Real Estate [9329], c/o Tracy Wood, VP, Architectural Resources Gp., Pier 9, San Francisco, CA 94111, (650)365-9226
Women of Reform Judaism, The Fed. of Temple Sisterhoods [20192], 633 3rd Ave., New York, NY. 10017, (212)650-4050
Women Refugees Community in Zambia [IO], Lusaka, Zambia
Women Refusing to Accept Tenant Harassment - Address unknown since 2003.
Women Religious; Leadership Conf. of [19649]
Women Religious of the U.S.A; Leadership Conf. of [★19649]
Women Rsrc. Center; Amer. Agri- [16949]
Women Riding For Res. [★22702]
Women Runners; North Amer. Network of [23656]
Women; RVing [22962]
Women in Sales Assn. - Address unknown since 2006.
Women in Scholarly Publishing [3260], c/o Susan Worst, Treas., 1070 Beacon St., Apt. 6D, Brookline, MA 02446-3951
Women in Sci. and Engg. [7635], c/o Natl. Acad. of Sci., 500 5th St. NW, Washington, DC 20001, (202)334-2063
Women into Sci. and Engg. [IO], London, United Kingdom
Women in Sci. Enquiry Network [IO], Melbourne, Australia
Women Secretaries' Assn. of Thailand [IO], Bangkok, Thailand
Women in the Services; Defense Advisory Comm. on [6075]
Women in Show Business for Children [13069]
Women Singers Assn; Professional [10689]
Women for Sobriety [13284], PO Box 618, Quakertown, PA 18951-0618, (215)536-8026
Women in Soccer - Address unknown since 2006.
Women Societies; Amer. Fed. of Reformed Young [★19831]
Women in Sociology; Comm. on the Status of [9923]
Women in Spanish [★10000]
Women in Sport; Natl. Assn. for Girls and [8983]
Women in Sports Media; Assn. for [3097]
Women on Stamps Study Unit - Defunct.
Women Strike for Peace - Defunct.
Women and Tech; Inst. on [★12754]
Women in Tech. Intl. [7764], 13351-D Riverside Dr., No. 441, Sherman Oaks, CA 91423, (818)788-9484
Women in Tech. Intl. [IO], Sherman Oaks, CA, United States
Women in Tech; Intl. Network of [★7764]
Women in Tech. and Sci. [IO], Dublin, Ireland
Women in Telecommunications - Defunct.
Women on Their Own - Address unknown since 2001.
Women Today; Inst. of [17538]
Women of Today; U.S. [13067]

Women in Tourism [IO], Milos Island, Greece
Women in Toys [3834], c/o Toy Indus. Assn., 1115 Broadway, Ste. 1000, New York, NY 10010
Women; Trades [12101]
Women in Transition [13447], 21 S 12th St., 6th Fl., Philadelphia, PA 19107, (215)564-5301
Women; United Coun. of Church [★20618]
Women United; Deaf [11905]
Women United - Defunct.
Women; United Presbyterian [★20475]
Women of the U.S; Natl. Coun. of [17557]
Women United for United Nations - Address unknown since 1995.
Women United in the U.S.A; Church [★20618]
Women; Universal Proutists [★18633]
Women in Urology; Soc. of [16718]
Women/USA; Bus. and Professional [17515]
Women USA; Mennonite [20252]
Women Veterans of Am. [21333], c/o Colleen Mussolino, Natl. Commander, PO Box 72, Bushkill, PA 18324, (570)588-4674
Women Veterans; Center for [21292]
Women Veterinarians; Assn. for [16786]
Women; Voluntary Fund for the United Nations Decade for [★17571]
Women Voters; Amer. Assn. of [★18419]
Women Voters Educ. Fund; League of [18459]
Women Voters; Natl. League of [★18355]
Women Voters of the U.S; League of [18355]
Women Welcome Women World Wide [IO], High Wycombe, United Kingdom
Women on Wheels [★23630]
Women; Wider Opportunities for [12106]
Women in the Wind [22701], c/o Becky Brown, Founder/Treas., PO Box 8392, Toledo, OH 43605
Women of Wind Energy [7854], c/o Windustry, 2105 First Ave. S, Minneapolis, MN 55404, (612)870-3461
Women on Wine - Address unknown since 1994.
Women for Winesense [23030], PO Box 10549, Napa, CA 94581, (800)204-1616
Women With Disabilities Australia [IO], Rosny Park, Australia
Women Without Osteoporosis [IO], Sofia, Bulgaria
Women for Women [12792], 4455 Connecticut Ave., Ste. 200, Washington, DC 20008, (202)737-7705
Women for Women in Bosnia [★12792]
Women for Women's Human Rights/New Ways [IO], Istanbul, Turkey
Women on Words and Images - Defunct.
Women Work! The Natl. Network for Women's Employment [18819], 1625 K St. NW, Ste. 300, Washington, DC 20006, (202)467-6346
Women Working Worldwide [IO], Manchester, United Kingdom
Women of the World [IO], Kansas City, MO, United States
Women of the World [13448], 7908 NW Pleasant Ford, Kansas City, MO 64152, (816)746-6869
Women to the World - Defunct.
Women World War Veterans - Address unknown since 2001.
Women Writing the West [4071], 8547 E Arapahoe Rd., Greenwood Village, CO 80112-1436, (303)773-8349
Women, and Youth; Secretariat for Family, Laity, [12167]
WomenHeart: Natl. Coalition for Women with Heart Disease [13929], 818 18th St. NW, Ste. 930, Washington, DC 20006, (202)728-7199
Womenpause - Defunct.
Women's Action Alliance [IO], Camberwell, Australia
Women's Action Alliance - Address unknown since 1997.
Women's Action for Change [IO], Suva, Fiji
Women's Action Gp. [IO], Harare, Zimbabwe
Women's Action for New Directions [18175], 691 Massachusetts Ave., Arlington, MA 02476, (781)643-6740
Women's Action for Nuclear Disarmament [★18175]
Women's Advocacy Office - Defunct.
Women's Africa Comm. of the African-American Inst. [18864], c/o African-American Inst., Graybar Bldg., 420 Lexington Ave., Ste. 1706, New York, NY 10170-0002, (212)949-5666

A star before a book entry number signifies that the name is not listed separately, but is mentioned within the entry.

Women's Aglow Fellowship [★IO]
Women's Aglow Fellowship Intl. [★IO]
Women's Aglow Fellowship Intl. [★20616]
Women's Aid - Ireland [IO], Dublin, Ireland
Women's Aid Org. [IO], Petaling Jaya, Malaysia
Women's All-Star Assn. [23258], c/o Sharon Nasta, Exec. Dir., 16 Ward Ave., Toms River, NJ 08755, (732)367-0257
Women's Alliance of Am; Polish [19317]
Women's Alliance; Gay [★12244]
Women's Alliance for Job Equity - Address unknown since 2002.
Women's Alliance; Lithuanian Amer. Roman Catholic [19211]
Women's Alliance for Peace and Human Rights in Afghanistan [12380], PO Box 77057, Washington, DC 20013-7057
Women's Alliance for Peace and Human Rights in Afghanistan [IO], Washington, DC, United States
Women's Alliance for Theology, Ethics and Ritual [IO], Silver Spring, MD, United States
Women's Alliance for Theology, Ethics and Ritual [20626], 8121 Georgia Ave., Ste. 310, Silver Spring, MD 20910, (301)589-2509
Women's Amer. Basketball Assn. - Defunct.
Women's Apparel Chains Assns. - Defunct.
Women's Appointments; Coalition for [17520]
Women's Appraisal Assn; Professional [287]
Women's Aquatic Network [7277], PO Box 4993, Washington, DC 20008
Women's Army Corps Veterans' Assn. [20708], PO Box 5577, Fort McClellan, AL 36205-0577, (256)820-6824
Women's Art Club of the City of New York [★9514]
Women's Assn. of Allied Beverage Indus; Natl. [★213]
Women's Assn; Amer. Bus. [693]
Women's Assn; Amer. Medical [14696]
Women's Assn. for the Defense of Four Freedoms for Ukraine [18759]
Women's Assn. for Educ. and Social Action [IO], Montreal, QC, Canada
Womens Assn; Intl. Aviation [437]
Women's Assn. of the Mining Indus. of Canada Found. [IO], Toronto, ON, Canada
Women's Assn. of Motion Pictures; Stunt [1394]
Women's Assn. of New York; Financial [1421]
Women's Assn; Railway Bus. [★3285]
Women's Assn. for Res. in Menopause - Address unknown since 1991.
Women's Assn. of Romania [IO], Bucharest, Romania
Women's Assn. of the U.S.A; Pan-Pacific and Southeast Asia [17907]
Women's Associations; Buddhist Churches of Am. Fed. of Buddhist [19543]
Women's Athletic Administrators; Coun. of Collegiate [★8982]
Women's Automotive Assn. Intl. [367], PO Box 2535, Birmingham, MI 48012, (248)646-5250
Women's Automotive Assn. Intl. [IO], Birmingham, MI, United States
Women's Auxiliary to the Amer. Dental Assn. [★14092]
Women's Auxiliary to the Amer. Medical Assn. [★15156]
Women's Auxiliary to the Goodwill Indus; Natl. [★11950]
Women's Auxiliary of the ICA [14016], c/o Intl. Chiropractors Assn., 1110 N Glebe Rd., Ste. 650, Arlington, VA 22201, (703)528-5000
Women's Auxiliary to the Military Order of the Cootie - Address unknown since 2002.
Women's Auxiliary to the Natl. Medical Assn. [★15161]
Women's Bar Associations; Natl. Conf. of [5518]
Women's Basketball Coaches Assn. [23139], 4646 Lawrenceville Hwy., Lilburn, GA 30047, (770)279-8027
Women's Bowling Assn; Natl. Deaf [23352]
Women's Breakfast Clubs of North Am; Credit [★1411]
Women's Breast Cancer Advisory Center [★13870]
Women's Breast Cancer Advisory Center [★13870]
Women's Bur. CH [★18814]

Women's Bur. of the U.S. Department of Labor [6361], 200 Constitution Ave. NW, Rm. S-3002, Washington, DC 20210, (202)693-6710
Women's Bus. Enterprise Natl. Coun. [4052], 1120 Connecticut Ave. NW, Ste. 1000, Washington, DC 20036, (202)872-5515
Women's Campaign Fund [17576], 734 15th St. NW, Ste. 500, Washington, DC 20005, (202)393-8164
Women's Canadian ORT [★IO]
Women's Cancer Network [13881], c/o Gynecologic Cancer Found., 230 W Monroe, Ste. 2528, Chicago, IL 60606, (312)578-1439
Women's Catholic Order of Foresters [★19007]
Women's Caucus; Amer. Educational Res. Assn. [★9328]
Women's Caucus for Art [9531], Canal St. Sta., PO Box 1498, New York, NY 10013, (212)634-0007
Women's Caucus of the Coll. Art Assn. [★9531]
Women's Caucus of the Endocrine Soc. - Address unknown since 2002.
Women's Caucus; Episcopal [19956]
Women's Caucus; Evangelical and Ecumenical [19978]
Women's Caucus for the Modern Languages - Address unknown since 2002.
Women's Caucus for Political Sci. [7529], c/o Ronnee Schreiber, Treas., SDSU Dept. of Political Sci., 5500 Campanile Dr., San Diego, CA 92182, (803)777-7442
Women's Caucus: Religious Studies - Defunct.
Women's Caucuses and Committees in the Disciplinary and Professional Associations; National Network of [★17556]
Women's Christian Assn. of the U.S.A; Young [13527]
Women's Classical Caucus [9801], c/o Prof. Maryline Parca, Sec.-Treas., Univ. of Illinois, Dept. of the Classics, 4080 Languages Bldg., 707 S Matthews Ave., Urbana, IL 61801
Women's Club; Amer. News [3083]
Women's Club; Amer. Newspaper [★3083]
Women's Club; Corset and Brassiere [★258]
Women's Club; New York Newspaper [★3150]
Women's Club of New York; Newspaper [★3150]
Women's Clubs; Federated Estonian [★18981]
Women's Clubs; Natl. Assn. of Colored [13051]
Women's Clubs; Natl. Assn. of Negro Bus. and Professional [13053]
Women's Clubs; Natl. Fed. of Bus. and Professional [★17515]
Women's Coalition to Stop U.S. Intervention in Central America and the Caribbean - Defunct.
Women's Coll. Coalition [9330], 1678 Asylum Ave., West Hartford, CT 06117, (860)231-5596
Women's Commn. of the Iranian Students Assn. - Address unknown since 1991.
Women's Committees of Art Museums; Assn. of [★10516]
Women's Computer Literacy Center - Address unknown since 1994.
Women's Conf. Center; Natl. [17564]
Women's Conf; Continuing Comm. of the Natl. [★17563]
Women's Conf; Natl. [17563]
Women's Conf. of the Socialist Intl. [★IO]
Women's Cong; Intl. Black [17542]
Women's Consciousness Raising Assn; Natl. Black [17551]
Women's Corona Soc. - Hong Kong Br. [IO], Hong Kong, People's Republic of China
Women's Corp; Hispanic [10003]
Women's Correctional Assn. [★11857]
Women's Coun; Baltic [18978]
Women's Coun. on Energy and the Env. [6977], PO Box 33211, Washington, DC 20033, (703)351-7850
Women's Coun. for the Histadrut in Israel - Defunct.
Women's Coun. of Realtors [3345], 430 N Michigan Ave., Chicago, IL 60611, (312)329-8481
Women's Coun. of Realtors of the Natl. Assn. of Realtors [★3345]
Women's Creative Network [IO], Victoria, BC, Canada
Women's Crisis Centre [★IO]
Women's Cultural Alliance; Bi [12219]
Women's Curling Assn; U.S. [23303]

Women's Dept. [★IO]
Women's Dermatologic Soc. [IO], San Francisco, CA, United States
Women's Dermatologic Soc. [14216], 575 Market St., Ste. 2125, San Francisco, CA 94105, (415)927-5727
Women's Direct Marketing Intl. [★2652]
Women's Direct Marketing Intl. [★IO]
Women's Distance Comm. - Defunct.
Women's Division of the Gen. Bd. of Global Ministries of the United Methodist Church [20269], 475 Riverside Dr., New York, NY 10115, (212)870-3660
Women's Div; U.S. Lacrosse Assn. [23573]
Women's Documentation Center [IO], Lima, Peru
Women's Drug Res. Project [13285]
Women's Economic Rights Project - Defunct.
Women's Economic Round Table [18484], c/o Dr. Amelia Augustus, Pres./Co-Founder, Knight-Bagehot Fellowship Prog., School of Journalism, Columbia Univ., 2950 Broadway, Mail Code 3850, New York, NY 10027, (914)922-1747
Women's Educational Equity Communications Network - Defunct.
Women's Electoral Lobby - Australia [IO], Civic Square, Australia
Women's Employment Proj; Natl. [★17512]
Women's Engg. Soc. [IO], Stevenage, United Kingdom
Women's Env. and Development Org. [IO], New York, NY, United States
Women's Env. and Development Org. [17577], 355 Lexington Ave., 3rd Fl., New York, NY 10017, (212)973-0325
Women's Environmental Network [IO], London, United Kingdom
Women's Equality; Commn. for [17522]
Women's Equality; Natl. Commn. for [★17522]
Women's Equity Action League - Defunct.
Women's Equity Program - Defunct.
Women's Fashion Fabrics Assn. - Defunct.
Women's Fed; Unitarian Universalist [20604]
Women's Fisheries Network [4671], 2442 NW Market St., No. 199, Seattle, WA 98107, (206)789-1987
Women's Flat Track Derby Assn. [23747], PO Box 300266, St. Louis, MO 63130
Women's Food and Farming Union [IO], Kenilworth, United Kingdom
Women's Foodservice Forum [1595], Southpoint Off. Ctr., 1650 W 82nd St., Ste. 650, Bloomington, MN 55431, (952)358-2100
Women's Foreign Policy Gp. [18820], 1875 Connecticut Ave. NW, Ste. 720, Washington, DC 20009-5728, (202)884-8597
Women's Foreign Policy Gp. [IO], Washington, DC, United States
Women's Forum; Independent [18311]
Women's Forum; Natl. [★13429]
Women's Forum on Natl. Security - Defunct.
Women's Found; Eleanor [★17529]
Women's Freedom Network [13449], 4410 Massachusetts Ave. NW, Ste. 179, Washington, DC 20016, (202)885-6245
Women's Funding Network [13450], 1375 Sutter St., Ste. 406, San Francisco, CA 94109, (415)441-0706
Women's Global Network for Reproductive Rights - Netherlands [IO], Amsterdam, Netherlands
Women's Golf Assn; Executive [23447]
Womens Golf New Zealand [IO], Wellington, New Zealand
Women's Gp. for the Abolition of Sexual Mutilation [IO], Paris, France
Women's Gymnastics; U.S. Elite Coaches' Assn. for [23297]
Women's Hall of Fame [★20716]
Women's Hall of Fame; Natl. [20716]
Women's Hea. [IO], London, United Kingdom
Women's Health and Abortion Project - Address unknown since 1995.
Women's Health Action and Mobilization - Defunct.
Women's Hea. Book Collective; Boston [★16909]
Women's Hea. Coalition; Natl. [★16899]
Women's Hea. and Economic Development Assn. [IO], Uyo, Nigeria

Reference to "IO" in place of a book number signifies that the association may be found in the 45th edition of International Organizations.

Women's Hea. and Educ. Found; Alternatives to Abortion/ [★12912]

Women's Hea; Jacobs Inst. of [14641]

Women's Hea; Museum of Menstruation and [15611]

Women's Hea; Natl. Assn. of Nurse Practitioners in [15497]

Women's Hea; Natl. Assn. of Professionals in [★16903]

Women's Hea., Obstetric and Neonatal Nurses; Assn. of [15470]

Women's Hea. Proj; Black [★16895]

Women's Hea. Res; Melpomene Inst. for [★16900]

Women's Hea. Res; Soc. for the Advancement of [★16910]

Women's Health Work Group - Defunct.

Women's Healthcare Educational Network - Address unknown since 2007.

Women's Healthy Environments Network [IO], Toronto, ON, Canada

Women's History Network [11095], c/o Natl. Women's History Proj., 3343 Indus. Dr., Ste. 4, Santa Rosa, CA 95403-2060, (707)636-2888

Women's History Res. Center [★12790]

Women's Home and Foreign Missionary Soc. [★20627]

Women's Home and Foreign Missionary Soc. [★IO]

Women's Hospitals Ser. Comm. of AMWA; Amer. [14870]

Women's Humane Soc. Animal Shelter [11479], PO Box 1470, Bensalem, PA 19020, (215)750-3100

Women's Independent Film Exchange - Defunct.

Women's Independent Label Distribution Network - Defunct.

Women's Information Bank - Address unknown since 2002.

Women's Information Exchange - Defunct.

Women's Infoteka [IO], Zagreb, Croatia

Women's Initiatives for Gender Justice [IO], The Hague, Netherlands

Women's Innovation Projects East-West [IO], Moscow, Russia

Women's Inst. for Advancement of Psychotherapy - Defunct.

Women's Inst. for Freedom of the Press [17200], 1940 Calvert St. NW, Washington, DC 20009-1502, (202)265-6707

The Women's Inst. Press - Defunct.

Women's Institutes of the United States of Am; Conf. of Major Religious Superiors of [★19649]

Women's Inter-Church Coun. of Canada [IO], Toronto, ON, Canada

Women's Interart Center [11096], 549 W 52nd St., New York, NY 10019, (212)246-1050

Women's Intl. Center [13451], PO Box 880736, San Diego, CA 92168-0736, (619)295-6446

Women's Intl. Center [IO], San Diego, CA, United States

Women's Intl. Coalition for Economic Justice [IO], New York, NY, United States

Women's Intl. Coalition for Economic Justice [17475], 12 Dongan Pl., No. 206, New York, NY 10040

Women's Intl. League for Peace and Freedom - Albania [IO], Tirana, Albania

Women's Intl. League for Peace and Freedom - Australia [IO], Adelaide, Australia

Women's Intl. League for Peace and Freedom - Belarus [IO], Minsk, Belarus

Women's Intl. League for Peace and Freedom - Bolivia [IO], Santa Cruz, Bolivia

Women's Intl. League for Peace and Freedom - Burundi [IO], Bujumbura, Burundi

Women's Intl. League for Peace and Freedom - Canada [IO], Burnaby, BC, Canada

Women's Intl. League for Peace and Freedom - Chile [IO], Las Condes, Chile

Women's Intl. League for Peace and Freedom - Colombia [IO], Bogota, Colombia

Women's Intl. League for Peace and Freedom - Costa Rica [IO], San Jose, Costa Rica

Women's Intl. League for Peace and Freedom - Denmark [IO], Copenhagen, Denmark

Women's Intl. League for Peace and Freedom - Finland [IO], Helsinki, Finland

Women's Intl. League for Peace and Freedom - France [IO], Paris, France

Women's Intl. League for Peace and Freedom - French Polynesia [IO], Papeete, French Polynesia

Women's Intl. League for Peace and Freedom - Germany [IO], Nuremberg, Germany

Women's Intl. League for Peace and Freedom - India [IO], Ahmedabad, India

Women's Intl. League for Peace and Freedom - Ireland [IO], Carrick-On-Suir, Ireland

Women's Intl. League for Peace and Freedom - Israel [IO], Bat Yam, Israel

Women's Intl. League for Peace and Freedom - Italy [IO], Rome, Italy

Women's Intl. League for Peace and Freedom - Japan [IO], Tokyo, Japan

Women's Intl. League for Peace and Freedom - Lebanon [IO], Beirut, Lebanon

Women's Intl. League for Peace and Freedom - Nepal [IO], Kathmandu, Nepal

Women's Intl. League for Peace and Freedom - Netherlands [IO], Utrecht, Netherlands

Women's Intl. League for Peace and Freedom - New Zealand [IO], Auckland, New Zealand

Women's Intl. League for Peace and Freedom - Norway [IO], Oslo, Norway

Women's Intl. League for Peace and Freedom - Peru [IO], Lima, Peru

Women's Intl. League for Peace and Freedom - Philippines [IO], Quezon City, Philippines

Women's Intl. League for Peace and Freedom - Russia [IO], Moscow, Russia

Women's Intl. League for Peace and Freedom - Sierra Lone [IO], Freetown, Sierra Leone

Women's Intl. League for Peace and Freedom - Sri Lanka [IO], Colombo, Sri Lanka

Women's Intl. League for Peace and Freedom - Sweden [IO], Stockholm, Sweden

Women's Intl. League for Peace and Freedom - Switzerland [IO], Geneva, Switzerland

Women's Intl. League for Peace and Freedom - United Kingdom [IO], Kent, United Kingdom

Women's Intl. League for Peace and Freedom, U.S. Sect. [IO], Philadelphia, PA, United States

Women's Intl. League for Peace and Freedom, U.S. Sect. [18256], 1213 Race St., Philadelphia, PA 19107-1617, (215)563-7110

Women's Intl. League for Peace and Freedom - Venezuela [IO], Caracas, Venezuela

Women's Intl. Motorcycle Assn. [IO], Bradford, United Kingdom

Women's Intl. Motorcycle Assn. - Australia [IO], Jamison, Australia

Women's Intl. Motorcycle Assn. - New South Wales [IO], St. Peters, Australia

Women's Intl. Motorcycle Assn. - Queensland [IO], Fortitude Valley, Australia

Women's Intl. Motorcycle Assn. - South Australia [IO], Ingle Farm, Australia

Women's Intl. Motorcycle Assn. - Tasmania [IO], Carnegie, Australia

Women's Intl. Motorcycle Assn. - Victoria [IO], Carnegie, Australia

Women's Intl. Motorcycle Assn. - Western Australia [IO], Victoria Park, Australia

Women's Intl. Motorcycling Assn. - New Zealand [IO], Wellington, New Zealand

Women's Intl. Network [IO], Lexington, MA, United States

Women's Intl. Network [17578], c/o WIN News, 187 Grant St., Lexington, MA 02420-2126, (781)862-9431

Women's Intl. Network of Utility Professionals [1200], PO Box 817, Fergus Falls, MN 56538-0817, (218)731-1651

Women's Intl. News Gathering Ser. [IO], Vancouver, BC, Canada

Women's Intl. Professional Tennis Coun. [★IO]

Women's Intl. Professional Tennis Coun. [★23910]

Women's Intl. Public Hea. Network [16257], 7100 Oak Forest Ln., Bethesda, MD 20817, (301)469-9210

Women's Intl. Public Hea. Network [IO], Bethesda, MD, United States

Women's Intl. Religious Fellowship - Address unknown since 1991.

Women's Intl. Resource Exchange - Address unknown since 2001.

Women's Intl. Shipping and Trading Assn. [3598], c/o Jeanne M. Grasso, Recording Sec., Blank Rome, LLP, 600 New Hampshire Ave. NW, Washington, DC 20037

Women's Intl. Shipping and Trading Assn. [IO], New Orleans, LA, United States

Women's Intl. Shipping and Trading Assn. Hellas [IO], Piraeus, Greece

Women's Intl. Shipping and Trading Assn. Israel [IO], Haifa, Israel

Women's Intl. Shipping and Trading Assn. Italy [IO], Genoa, Italy

Women's Intl. Shipping and Trading Assn. Netherlands [IO], Hellevoetsluis, Netherlands

Women's Intl. Shipping and Trading Assn. Norway [IO], Oslo, Norway

Women's Intl. Shipping and Trading Assn. Singapore [IO], Singapore, Singapore

Women's Intl. Shipping and Trading Assn. UK [IO], London, United Kingdom

Women's Intl. Stud. Europe [IO], Utrecht, Netherlands

Women's Intl. Tennis Assn. [★23917]

Women's Intl. Zionist Org. - Israel [IO], Tel Aviv, Israel

Women's Intl. Zionist Org. - Netherlands [IO], Amsterdam, Netherlands

Women's Issues; CH on [17519]

Women's Issues; Congressional Caucus for [17525]

Women's Issues, Status, and Education - Defunct.

Women's Jazz Festival - Defunct.

Women's Jewelry Assn. [2384], 19 Mantua Rd., Mount Royal, NJ 08061-1006, (856)423-3156

Women's Joint Congressional Comm. - Address unknown since 1995.

Women's Joint Legislative Comm. for Equal Rights - Defunct.

Women's Labor History Film Project - Address unknown since 1989.

Women's Labor Zionist Org. of Am; Pioneer Women/ Na'amat, the [★20162]

Women's Labor Zionist Org. of Am; Pioneer Women, The [★20162]

Women's Lacrosse Australia [IO], Melbourne, Australia

Women's Law Center - Defunct.

Women's Law Center; Natl. [17565]

Women's Law Fund - Address unknown since 1999.

Women's Law Initiative [★18823]

Women's Law Proj. [17579], 125 S 9th St., No. 300, Philadelphia, PA 19107, (215)928-9801

Women's Leadership Forum [17411], c/o The Democratic Party HQ, 430 S Capitol St. SE, Washington, DC 20003, (202)479-5103

Women's Leadership Network, Natl. Student Educ. Fund [★9195]

Women's League of Am; Ukrainian Natl. [19419]

Women's League for Animals; New York [★11353]

Women's League for Conservative Judaism [20193], 475 Riverside Dr., Ste. 820, New York, NY 10115, (212)870-1260

Women's League of Hea. and Beauty [★IO]

Women's League for Israel [20194]

Women's League; Natl. Colored [★13051]

Women's League for Palestine [★20194]

Women's League of the United Synagogue of Am. [★20193]

Women's League of the United Synagogue of Am; Natl. [★20193]

Women's Learning Partnership for Rights, Development, and Peace [13452], 4343 Montgomery Ave., Ste. 201, Bethesda, MD 20814, (301)654-2774

Women's Learning Partnership for Rights, Development, and Peace [IO], Bethesda, MD, United States

Women's Legal Defense Fund [★17561]

Women's Legal Educ. and Action Fund [IO], Toronto, ON, Canada

Women's Lobby - Defunct.

Women's Marine Assn. [★21173]

Women's Martial Arts Fed; Natl. [23600]

Women's Martial Arts Union - Defunct.

Women's Media Project - Address unknown since 1995.

Women's Media Workshop - Defunct.

A star before a book entry number signifies that the name is not listed separately, but is mentioned within the entry.

Women's Memorial Found; Vietnam [21353]

Women's Memorial Proj; Vietnam [★21353]

Women's Missionary Coun. of the Christian Methodist Episcopal Church [20270], c/o Dr. Elnora P. Hamb, Pres., 11321 S Aberdeen St., Chicago, IL 60643, (773)264-2273.

Women's Missionary League; Intl. Lutheran [★20229]

Women's Missionary League; Lutheran [★20229]

Women's Missionary League; Lutheran [20229]

Women's Missionary and Ser. Commn. of the Mennonite Church [★20252]

Women's Missionary Soc., AME Church [20627], 1134 11th St. NW, Washington, DC 20001, (202)371-8887

Women's Missionary Society, AME Church [IO], Washington, DC, United States

Women's Motorcyclist Found. [22702], 7 Lent Ave., Le Roy, NY 14482-1009, (585)768-6054

Women's Mountain Bike and Tea Soc. [23323], PO Box 757, Fairfax, CA 94978, (415)459-0980

Women's Mutual Improvement Assn; Young [★20209]

Women's Natl. Abortion Act Coalition - Defunct.

Women's Natl. Basketball Assn. - Defunct.

Women's Natl. Basketball Players Assn. [23140], 310 Lenox Ave., New York, NY 10027, (212)655-0880

Women's Natl. Book Assn. [3174], c/o Susannah Greenberg, Public Relations Mgr., PO Box 237, New York, NY 10150, (212)208-4629

Women's Natl. Commn. [IO], London, United Kingdom

Women's Natl. Inst. - Defunct.

Women's Natl. Republican Club [18539], 3 W 51st St., New York, NY 10019, (212)582-5454

Women's Network in Aquatic and Marine Affairs [★7277]

Women's Network Australia [IO], Sunnybank Hills, Australia

Women's Network of the Methodist Church [IO], London, United Kingdom

Women's Networks; Natl. Alliance of Professional and Executive [★728]

Women's Ordination Conf. [19740], PO Box 2693, Fairfax, VA 22031-0693, (703)352-1006

Women's Org. for Amer. Merchant Marine - Defunct.

Women's Org. of Amer; Mizrachi [★20119]

Women's Org; Hapoel Hamizrachi [★20136]

Women's Org. of Hapoel Hamizrachi [★20136]

Women's Org. of Hapoel Hamizrachi [★IO]

Women's Org. for Political Prisoners [IO], Tel Aviv, Israel

Women's Org. of the Social Democratic Party of Austria [IO], Vienna, Austria

Women's Org. of the Swedish People's Party in Finland [IO], Helsinki, Finland

Women's Organizations; Natl. Coun. of [17558]

Women's Outdoor Challenges - Address unknown since 2002.

Women's Overseas Ser. League [21334], PO Box 7124, Washington, DC 20044-7124

Women's Parent Mite Missionary Soc. [★20627]

Women's Parent Mite Missionary Soc. [★IO]

Women's Party for Survival [★18175]

Women's Patriotic Assn. - Defunct.

Women's Patriotic Conf. on Natl. Defense - Address unknown since 1995.

Women's Peace Initiative - Address unknown since 1995.

Women's Peace Party [★18256]

Women's Peace Party [★IO]

Women's Philanthropy Inst. [12741], 550 W North St., Ste. 301, Indianapolis, IN 46202-3272, (317)274-4200

Women's Philatelic Soc. of New York - Defunct.

Women's Physical Therapeutic Assn; Amer. [★16603]

Women's Policy, Inc. [18821], 409 12th St. SW, Ste. 310, Washington, DC 20024, (202)554-2323

Women's Policy Res; Inst. for [17539]

Women's Political Caucus; Natl. [17566]

Women's Pre-Emptive Strike for Peace; Code Pink [18199]

Women's Prison Assn. [11898], 110 2nd Ave., New York, NY 10003, (646)336-6100

Women's Professional Basketball League - Defunct.

Women's Professional Billiard Assn. [23149], PO Box 546, Goodlettsville, TN 37070-0908, (704)344-8664

Women's Professional Billiards Alliance - Address unknown since 1995.

Women's Professional Golf Assn. [★23454]

Women's Professional Golf Tour [★23451]

Women's Professional Racquetball Assn. - Address unknown since 1999.

Women's Professional Rodeo Assn. [23696], 3840 Cheyenne, Kingman, AZ 86401, (928)753-0053

Women's Proj. [18634], 55 W End Ave., New York, NY 10023, (212)765-1706

Women's Regional Publications of Am. [4053], c/o Jill Duval, VP/Membership Chair, PO Box 12955, Albuquerque, NM 87195, (505)247-9195

Women's Republican Clubs; Natl. Fed. of [★18525]

Women's Res. and Educ. Inst. [17580], 3300 N Fairfax Dr., Ste. 218, Arlington, VA 22201, (703)812-7990

Women's Rsrc. Center; Eleanor Leff Jewish [10280]

Women's Rsrc. Center; Jewish [10280]

Women's Rsrc. Centre [IO], Karachi, Pakistan

Women's Resources; Pacific [★12244]

Women's Rights

Afghan Women's Assn. Intl. [13416]

Alliance for Women's Equality [13455]

AMEND [12020]

Amer. Women's Self-Defense Assn. [13010]

Black Women's Agenda [13456]

Catalyst [11085]

Finnish and Amer. Women's Network [17586]

Gender Action [18825]

Girls Inc. [13486]

Grailville [19630]

INCITE! Women of Color Against Violence [18788]

Inter-American Parliamentary Gp. on Population and Development [12432]

Intl. Wages for Housework Campaign [13428]

Men Stopping Violence [12643]

Mothers Arms [13011]

NARAL Pro-Choice Am. [18518]

Natl. Assn. of Baby Boomer Women [13431]

Natl. Assn. of Non-Custodial Moms [11538]

Natl. Inst. of Womanhood [13432]

Natl. Network to End Violence Against Immigrant Women [13433]

Natl. Women's Conf. Center [17564]

Natl. Women's History Proj. [11090]

Polaris Proj. Combating Trafficking of Women and Children [17784]

Religious Coalition for Reproductive Choice [18519]

Rockefeller Family Fund [12737]

Second Amendment Sisters [17598]

Shared Hope Intl. [13457]

SisterSong Women of Color Reproductive Hea. Collective [18826]

Sociologists for Women in Soc. [9924]

Step Up Women's Network [13440]

Veteran Feminists of Am. [17572]

Wider Opportunities for Women [12106]

Women Employed [12108]

Women Employed Inst. [12109]

Women's Alliance for Peace and Human Rights in Afghanistan [12380]

Women's Intl. Coalition for Economic Justice [17475]

Women's Learning Partnership for Rights, Development, and Peace [13452]

Women's Services Worldwide [13453]

Women's World Org. for Rights, Literature and Development [18822]

World Connections for Women [18824]

Women's Rights, AFL-CIO; Dept. of Civil, Human and [17110]

Women's Rights Comm. [17581], c/o Amer. Fed. of Teachers, Human Rights Dept., 555 New Jersey Ave. NW, Washington, DC 20001, (202)879-4400

Women's Rights Proj. [17582], c/o Amer. Civil Liberties Union, 125 Broad St., 18th Fl., New York, NY 10004, (212)549-2644

Women's Rights Proj. of the Center for Law and Social Policy [★17565]

Women's Rodeo Assn; Professional [★23696]

Women's Roundtable on Voter Participation; Black [18346]

Women's Rowing Assn; Natl. [★23704]

Women's Royal Voluntary Ser. [IO], Abingdon, United Kingdom

Women's Sailing Found. [★21879]

Women's Services Worldwide [13453], PO Box 136, Frazier Park, CA 93225, (661)361-1177

Women's Services Worldwide [IO], Frazier Park, CA, United States

Women's Soc. of Christian Ser. Gen. Conf. [IO], Singapore, Singapore

Women's Spirituality Educ. Forum; Susan B. Anthony [★20628]

Women's Spirituality Forum [20628], PO Box 11363, Oakland, CA 94611, (510)444-7724

Women's Sports of the Amer. Assn. of Hea., Physical Educ., and Recreation; Division of Girl's and [★8983]

Women's Sports Broadcasting - Address unknown since 2004.

Women's Sports Found. [23867], Eisenhower Park, East Meadow, NY 11554, (516)542-4700

Women's Sports Found. [IO], London, United Kingdom

Women's Student Assn. - Address unknown since 2001.

Women's Studies

Assn. of Amer. Medical Colleges-Women in Medicine Prog. [8847]

Hispanic Women's Corp. [10003]

Midmarch Associates [9510]

Natl. Women Law Students Assn. [9322]

Natl. Women's Conf. Center [17564]

Natl. Women's History Proj. [11090]

Soc. for the Stud. of Amer. Women Writers [11195]

Soc. for the Stud. of Early Modern Women [9331]

Step Up Women's Network [13440]

Women's History Network [11095]

Women's Services Worldwide [13453]

Women's Stud. Assn. [IO], Wellington, New Zealand

Women's Stud. International [★9317]

Women's Stud. and Services; Center for [★17517]

Women's Support Proj. [IO], Glasgow, United Kingdom

Women's Supreme Coun. [★IO]

Women's Supreme Coun. [★20153]

Women's Tennis Assn. [★23917]

Women's Tennis Assn. [★23917]

Women's Tennis Assn; Natl. Senior [23907]

Women's Tennis Coun. [★23910]

Women's Tennis Coun. [★IO]

Women's Theodore Roosevelt Memorial Assn. [★11152]

Women's Trans. Seminar [3901], 1701 K St. NW, Ste. 800, Washington, DC 20006, (202)955-5085

Women's Trans. Seminar [IO], Washington, DC, United States

Women's Union of Am; Slovenian [19370]

Women's Union; Natl. Catholic [19678]

Women's Union of Russia [IO], Moscow, Russia

Women's Union; Slovenian [★19370]

Women's Universal Movement - Defunct.

Women's Veterinary Medical Assn. [★16786]

Women's Voices for the Earth [4616], PO Box 1067, Bozeman, MT 59771, (406)585-5549

Women's Vote Project - Defunct.

Women's War on War Conf. - Defunct.

Women's Welfare Assn; Armenian [18968]

Women's Welfare Service - Defunct.

Women's Wellness; Center for Black [★16895]

Women's Work Force Network [★12106]

Women's Work and Women's Fellowship [★IO]

Women's WORLD [★IO]

Women's WORLD [★18822]

Women's World Banking - USA [13454], 8 W 40th St., 9th Fl., New York, NY 10018, (212)768-8513

Women's World Banking - USA [IO], New York, NY, United States

Women's World Organization for Rights, Literature and Development [IO], New York, NY, United States

Women's World Org. for Rights, Literature and Development [18822], PO Box 250 891, New York, NY 10025, (212)947-2915

Reference to "IO" in place of a book number signifies that the association may be found in the 45th edition of International Organizations.

Women's World Summit Found. [IO], Geneva, Switzerland
Women's Year/Tribune Proj; Intl. [★17544]
Women's Yellow Pages; Natl. Assn. of [★4053]
WomensLaw.org [18823], 150 Court St., 2nd Fl., Brooklyn, NY 11201, (718)923-1400
Womenswear Retailers of America - Defunct.
Womyn's Educational Proj; Disabled [11942]
Wonder Woman Found. - Defunct.
Wonderland Collectors Network; Alice in [21957]
Wonne/Winne Family Assn; Woenne/ [21089]

Wood
Affiliated Woodcarvers [9533]
Amer. Assn. of Woodturners [9825]
Amer. Hardwood Export Coun. [1603]
Amer. Hardwood Info. Center [4054]
Amer. Inst. of Timber Constr. [1633]
Amer. Loggers Coun. [1604]
Amer. Lumber Standard Comm. [1634]
Amer. Walnut Manufacturers Assn. [1635]
Amer. Wood-Preservers' Assn. [1636]
Amer. Wooden Money Guild [22728]
APA: The Engineered Wood Assn. [1637]
Appalachian Hardwood Manufacturers, Inc. [1638]
Architectural Woodwork Inst. [593]
Assoc. Cooperage Indus. of Am. [972]
Assn. of Suppliers to the Paper Indus. [2003]
California Forestry Assn. [1605]
California Redwood Assn. [1639]
Caricature Carvers of Am. [9829]
Cedar Shake and Shingle Bur. [1640]
Center for Wooden Boats [21869]
Chilean Wood Corp. [IO]
Composite Lumber Mfrs. Assn. [1642]
Composite Panel Assn. [1643]
Composite Wood Coun. [4055]
Cork Inst. of Am. [1644]
Cork Quality Coun. [1645]
Dedicated Wooden Money Collectors [22736]
Engineered Wood Tech. Assn. [1646]
European Fed. of the Parquet Indus. [IO]
Forest Indus. Telecommunications [1606]
Forest Products Soc. [7099]
Forest Resources Assn. [1607]
Gar Wood Soc. [21873]
Ghana Timber Export Development Bd. [IO]
Hardwood Coun. [IO]
Hardwood Coun. [4056]
Hardwood Mfrs. Assn. [1648]
Hardwood Plywood and Veneer Assn. [1649]
Honduran Wood Indus. Assn. [IO]
Intermountain Forest Assn. [1608]
Intl. Assn. of Machinists and Aerospace Workers, Woodworkers District Lodge W1 [24026]
Intl. Chain Saw Wood Sculptors Assn. [9446]
Intl. Wood Collectors Soc. [23031]
Intl. Wood Collectors Soc. [IO]
Intl. Wood Products Assn. [1609]
Intl. Wooden Bow Tie Club [243]
Lignin Inst. [1650]
Log Homes Coun. [2525]
Malaysian Timber Indus. Bd. [IO]
Maple Flooring Manufacturers Assn. [635]
Midwest Decoy Collectors Assn. [22071]
Mulch and Soil Coun. [1651]
Natl. Assn. of Woodworkers New Zealand [IO]
Natl. Coun. for Air and Stream Improvement [4690]
Natl. Guild of Decoupeurs [22168]
Natl. Hardwood Lumber Assn. [1652]
Natl. Lumber and Building Material Dealers Assn. [1653]
Natl. Pig Carvers Assn. [22169]
Natl. Wood Carvers Assn. [22171]
Natl. Wood Flooring Assn. [655]
Natl. Wood Tank Inst. [988]
Natl. Woodland Owners Assn. [4693]
New England Kiln Drying Assn. [1610]
NOFMA: The Wood Flooring Manufacturers Assn. [656]
North Amer. Laminate Flooring Assn. [660]
North Amer. Wholesale Lumber Assn. [1611]
Northeastern Loggers Assn. [1612]
Northeastern Lumber Mfrs. Assn. [1654]
Northwest Forestry Assn. [1613]

Northwestern Lumber Assn. [1614]
Pacific Logging Cong. [1615]
Pacific Lumber Exporters Assn. [1616]
Pacific Lumber Inspection Bur. [1617]
Railway Tie Assn. [3292]
Redwood Inspection Ser. [1618]
Sales Assn. of the Paper Indus. [2894]
Scrollsaw Assn. of the World [23032]
Scrollsaw Association of the World [IO]
Singapore Timber Assn. [IO]
Soc. of Wood Sci. and Tech. [7100]
Southeastern Lumber Mfrs. Assn. [1620]
Southern Cypress Mfrs. Assn. [1621]
Southern Forest Products Assn. [1622]
Southern Pine Coun. [4057]
Southern Pine Inspection Bur. [1623]
Southern Pressure Treaters' Assn. [1624]
Swedish Forest Indus. Fed. [IO]
TAPPI - Tech. Assn. of the Pulp and Paper Indus. [2895]
Timber Preservers Assn. of Australia [IO]
Timber Products Mfrs. [1626]
United Chainsaw Carvers Guild [9842]
Ward Museum of Wildfowl Art, Salisbury Univ. [9529]
West Coast Lumber Inspection Bur. [1628]
Western Building Material Assn. [1629]
Western Hardwood Assn. [1630]
Western Wood Products Assn. [1631]
Window and Door Manufacturers Assn. [686]
Wood Component Mfrs. Assn. [1656]
Wood Engravers Network [9843]
Wood and Forestry Products Exporters Union [IO]
Wood Machinery Mfrs. of Am. [2080]
Wood Moulding and Millwork Producers Assn. [688]
Wood Products Mfrs. Assn. [1657]
Wood Truss Coun. of Am. [689]
Wooden Canoe Heritage Assn. [21887]
Woodworking Machinery Indus. Assn. [2081]
Wooton Desk Owners Soc. [22131]
Wood Assn; APA: The Engineered [1637]
Wood Carvers Assn; Natl. [22171]
Wood Collectors Soc. [★23031]
Wood Collectors Soc. [★IO]
Wood Coll. Alumni Assn. - Defunct.
Wood Component Mfrs. Assn. [1656], 741 Butlers Gate, Ste. 100, Marietta, GA 30068, (770)565-6660
Wood Energy Inst. [★1679]
Wood Engg; Amer. Inst. of [★7100]
Wood Engravers Network [9843], c/o James Horton, 3999 Waters Rd., Ann Arbor, MI 48103
Wood Engravers Network [IO], Ann Arbor, MI, United States
Wood Fibre Blanket Inst. - Defunct.
Wood Flooring Assn; Natl. [655]
Wood Flooring Manufacturers Assn; NOFMA: The [656]
Wood and Forestry Products Exporters Union [IO], Istanbul, Turkey
Wood Found. Inst. - Defunct.
Wood Hat Block Mfrs. Assn. - Defunct.
Wood Heating Alliance [★1679]
Wood Heating Educ. and Res. Found. [★1880]
Wood Kitchen Cabinets; Natl. Inst. of [★2267]
Wood Machinery Mfrs. of Am. [2080], 100 N 20th St., 4th Fl., Philadelphia, PA 19103-1443, (215)564-3484
Wood Memorial for the Eradication of Leprosy; Leonard [★15010]
Wood Moulding and Millwork Producers [★688]
Wood Moulding and Millwork Producers [★IO]
Wood Moulding and Millwork Producers Association [IO], Woodland, CA, United States
Wood Moulding and Millwork Producers Assn. [688], 507 1st St., Woodland, CA 95695, (530)661-9591
Wood Moulding Producers; Western [★688]
Wood-Preservers' Assn; Amer. [1636]
Wood Products Assn; Western [1631]
Wood Products Mfrs. Assn. [1657], PO Box 761, Westminster, MA 01473-0761, (978)874-5445
Wood Sci. and Tech; Soc. of [7100]
Wood and Synthetic Flooring Inst. [★635]
Wood and Synthetic Flooring Inst. [★IO]

Wood Tank Inst; Natl. [988]
Wood Tank Mfrs. Assn. [3366]
Wood Trades
Amer. Assn. of Woodturners [9825]
Amer. Forest and Paper Assn. [4679]
Amer. Loggers Coun. [1604]
Assn. of Woodworking and Furnishings Suppliers [4058]
Center for Wooden Boats [21869]
Composite Lumber Mfrs. Assn. [1642]
Hardwood Coun. [4056]
Intl. Assn. of Used Equip. Dealers [3052]
Intl. Wood Collectors Soc. [23031]
Midwest Decoy Collectors Assn. [22071]
Natl. Wood Carvers Assn. [22171]
Natl. Woodland Owners Assn. [4693]
Peninsula Woodturners Guild [IO]
Soc. of Amer. Period Furniture Makers [9970]
Wooden Canoe Heritage Assn. [21887]
Wood Truss Coun. of Am. [689], 6300 Enterprise Ln., Madison, WI 53719, (608)274-4849
Wood-Turners Ser. Bur. [★1657]
Wood Turners and Shapers Assn. [★1657]
Wood Utilization Coun; Northeastern [★1612]
Wood Window and Door Assn; Natl. [★686]
Wood, Wire and Metal Lathers' Intl. Union [★24032]
Woodcarvers; Affiliated [9533]
Woodcarvings
Affiliated Woodcarvers [9533]
Amer. Assn. of Woodturners [9825]
Caricature Carvers of Am. [9829]
Center for Wooden Boats [21869]
Intl. Chain Saw Wood Sculptors Assn. [9446]
Intl. Wood Collectors Soc. [23031]
Midwest Decoy Collectors Assn. [22071]
Natl. Pig Carvers Assn. [22169]
Natl. Wood Carvers Assn. [22171]
Soc. of Amer. Period Furniture Makers [9970]
United Chainsaw Carvers Guild [9842]
Ward Museum of Wildfowl Art, Salisbury Univ. [9529]
Wooden Canoe Heritage Assn. [21887]
Woodcraft Auxiliary of the Woodmen of the World; Boys of [★19440]
Woodcraft; Neighbors of [★19441]
Woodcraft Sportsmen's Clubs; Boys of Woodcraft Sportsmen's Clubs/Girl of [★19440]
Woodcraft Sportsmen's Clubs/Girl of Woodcraft Sportsmen's Clubs; Boys of [★19440]
Woodcutters; Soc. of Amer. Etchers, Gravers, Lithographers and [★9992]
Wooden Boat Assn. of New South Wales [IO], Forestville, Australia
Wooden Boat Assn. - Queensland [IO], Brisbane, Australia
Wooden Boat Assn. - Victoria [IO], Glen Huntly, Australia
Wooden Boat Guild of Tasmania [IO], Battery Point, Australia
Wooden Boats; Center for [21869]
Wooden Box Assn; Natl. [★989]
Wooden Box Inst. - Defunct.
Wooden Canoe Heritage Assn. [21887], PO Box 117, Tamworth, NH 03886, (603)323-8992
Wooden Money Collectors; Dedicated [22736]
Wooden Money Guild; Amer. [22728]
Wooden Pail and Tub Assn. - Defunct.
Wooden Pallet and Container Assn; Natl. [989]
Wooden Pallet Manufacturers Assn; Natl. [★989]
Woodie Club; Natl. [21739]
Woodill Wildfire Registry - Defunct.
Woodland Owners Assn; Natl. [4693]
Woodlands Inst. [★9960]
Woodlands Mountain Inst. [★9960]
Woodmen
Intl. Wood Collectors Soc. [23031]
Modern Woodmen of Am. [19439]
Woodmen Rangers [19440]
Woodmen of the World/Omaha Woodmen Life Insurance Soc. [19441]
Woodmen Rangers [19440], c/o Woodmen of the World/Omaha Woodmen Life Insurance Soc., Woodmen Tower, 1700 Farnam St., Omaha, NE 68102, (800)225-3108
Woodmen; Supreme Camp of the Amer. [★19441]

A star before a book entry number signifies that the name is not listed separately, but is mentioned within the entry.

Woodmen Teens - Defunct.
Woodmen of the World; Boys of Woodcraft Auxiliary of the [★19440]
Woodmen of the World/Omaha Woodmen Life Insurance Soc. [19441], Woodmen Tower, 1700 Farnam St., Omaha, NE 68102-2002, (800)225-3108
Woodrow Wilson Birthplace Found. [★11155]
Woodrow Wilson Intl. Center for Scholars [10206], 1 Woodrow Wilson Plz., 1300 Pennsylvania Ave. NW, Washington, DC 20004-3027, (202)691-4000
Woodrow Wilson Intl. Center for Scholars [IO], Washington, DC, United States
Woodrow Wilson Memorial Commn. - Defunct.
Woodrow Wilson Natl. Fellowship Found. [8439], PO Box 5281, Princeton, NJ 08543-5281, (609)452-7007
Woodrow Wilson Presidential Lib. Found. [11155], 18-24 N Coalter St., PO Box 24, Staunton, VA 24402-0024, (540)885-0897
Woodswomen - Address unknown since 2000.
Woodturners; Amer. Assn. of [9825]
Woodwork Assn; Ponderosa Pine [★686]
Woodwork Inst; Architectural [593]
Woodwork Manufacturers Assn; Natl. [★686]
Woodworkers of Am; Intl. [★24026]
Woodworkers of Am., U.S. AFL-CIO; Intl. [★24026]
Woodworking Assn. of North America - Address unknown since 2008.
Woodworking and Furnishings Suppliers; Assn. of [4058]
Woodworking Machinery; Assn. of Mfrs. of [★2080]
Woodworking Machinery Distributors Assn. - Defunct.
Woodworking Machinery Importers Assn. of Am. [★2081]
Woodworking Machinery Indus. Assn. [2081], 3313 Paper Mill Rd., Ste. 202, Phoenix, MD 21131, (410)628-1970
Woodworking Machinery Mfrs. of Am. [★2080]
Woodworking Machinery Mfrs. Assn. [★2080]
Woodworking Machinery Suppliers Assn. [IO], Cromford, United Kingdom
Wool
  Alpaca Owners and Breeders Assn. [4120]
  Amer. Cormo Sheep Assn. [5179]
  Amer. Sheep Indus. Assn. [5194]
  Amer. Wool Coun. [3773]
  Australian Superfine Wool Growers' Assn. [IO]
  Australian Wool Growers Assn. [IO]
  Boston Wool Trade Assn. [3777]
  Natl. Assn. of Wool Producers [IO]
  Natl. Textile Assn. [3795]
  Natural Colored Wool Growers Assn. [5209]
  Sheep Indus. Development Prog. [5217]
  Western Range Assn. [5220]
  Wool Mfrs. Coun. [3809]
  Woolmark Company [3810]
Wool Associates of the New York Cotton Exchange - Defunct.
Wool Bur. [★3810]
Wool Coun; Amer. [3773]
Wool Growers Assn; Natl. [★5194]
Wool Growers Assn; Natural Colored [5209]
Wool Growers; Canadian Co-Operative [IO]
Wool Hat Mfrs. Assn. of America - Defunct.
Wool Mfrs. Coun. [3809], c/o Northern Textile Assn., 6 Beacon St., Ste. 1125, Boston, MA 02108-3812, (617)542-8220
Wool Mfrs; Natl. Assn. of [★3772]
Wool Pullers Coun. of America - Defunct.
Wool Trade Assn; Boston [3777]
Wool Yarn Jobbers Credit Assn. - Defunct.
Woolen Hosiery Inst. of America - Defunct.
Woolen Jobbers Assn. - Address unknown since 1995.
Woolen and Worsteds of America - Defunct.
Woolknit Associates - Address unknown since 1999.
Woolmark Company [3810], 1230 Ave. of the Americas, 7th Fl., New York, NY 10020, (646)756-2535
Woolmens' Company [IO], London, United Kingdom
WOOMB Philippines [IO], Manila, Philippines
WOOMB Tanzania [IO], Mtwara, United Republic of Tanzania
Wooton Desk Owners Soc. [22131], 9-20 166th St., Whitestone, NY 11357, (718)767-9758

Worcester Polytechnic Inst. Alumni [★18947]
Worcester Polytechnic Inst. Alumni Assn. [18947], 100 Inst. Rd., Worcester, MA 01609-2280, (508)831-5600
Word of God Inst. [★19690]
Word of God; Natl. Inst. for the [19690]
Word Guild - Defunct.
Word of Life Fellowship [20035], PO Box 600, Schroon Lake, NY 12870, (518)494-6000
Word of Mouth Marketing Assn. [2653], 333 W North Ave., No. 500, Chicago, IL 60610, (312)853-4400
Word of Mouth Storytelling Guild; By [10978]
Wordcraft Circle of Native Writers and Storytellers [9859], 2801 Cabernet St. SW, Albuquerque, NM 87121, (505)259-3682
Wordcraft Circle of Native Writers and Storytellers [IO], Albuquerque, NM, United States
Words: A Fan Club for Barry Gibb - Defunct.
Wordsworth-Coleridge Assn. - Address unknown since 2001.
Work Adjustment Assn; Vocational Evaluation and [★16337]
Work in America Inst. - Defunct.
Work Center; Amer. Youth [13469]
Work and Character; Proj. on Tech., [7168]
Work and the Coll. Student; Natl. Assn. on [★8996]
Work Dog Assn; North Amer. Police [6003]
Work Efficiency Assn. for Agriculture [★IO]
Work Fairness [12110]
Work and the Family; Center for [12144]
Work Force Network; Women's [★12106]
Work Found. [IO], London, United Kingdom
Work Glove Inst. [★IO]
Work Glove Inst. [★2030]
Work Glove Mfrs. Assn. [★2030]
Work Glove Mfrs. Assn. [★IO]
Work at Home Moms [★722]
Work for Human Development [IO], Dhaka, Bangladesh
Work Inst; Families and [12152]
Work and Learning; Natl. Inst. for [17974]
Work; New Ways to [12094]
Work Process Improvement; The Assn. for [6787]
Work Prog; Global [★5875]
Work Prog; Global [★IO]
Workaholics Anonymous [13031], World Ser. Org., PO Box 289, Menlo Park, CA 94026-0289, (510)273-9253
Worker and Human Rights in Central Am; Natl. Labor Comm. in Support of [★17049]
Worker and Human Rights; Natl. Labor Comm. for [17049]
Worker Justice; Natl. Interfaith Comm. for [★20092]
Worker Movement; Catholic [18109]
Workers
  AFL-CIO Community Action Field Mobilization Dept. [11801]
  Alliance for Sustainable Jobs and the Env. [24053]
  Alliance for Worker Freedom [24217]
  Alliance for Worker Retirement Security [18544]
  Amer. Assn. of State Compensation Insurance Funds [2134]
  Amer. Assn. of Working People [12067]
  Amer. Inst. for Full Employment [12068]
  Amer. Rights at Work [17968]
  Amer. Union of Pizza Delivery Drivers [24062]
  Andolan - Organizing South Asian Workers [24138]
  Australian People for Hea., Educ. and Development Abroad [IO]
  Barbados Workers' Union [IO]
  Canadian Labour Cong. [IO]
  Change to Win [24201]
  Coalition to Abolish Slavery and Trafficking [12370]
  Coalition of Immokalee Workers [13458]
  Compete Am. [8365]
  European Confed. of Workers' Cooperatives, Social Cooperatives and Social and Participative Enterprises [IO]
  European Trade Union Confed. [IO]
  FACE Intel - Former and Current Employees of Intel [1262]
  Families and Work Inst. [12152]

  Finnish Wood and Allied Workers' Union [IO]
  Freelancers Union [24218]
  Gen. Workers' Union [IO]
  Global Workers Justice Alliance [18074]
  Guild of Master Craftsmen [IO]
  Indus. Workers of the World Starbucks Workers Union [24206]
  Interfaith Worker Justice [20092]
  Intl. Assn. of Employment Web Sites [1266]
  Intl. Assn. of EMTs and Paramedics [24051]
  Intl. Assn. of Heat and Frost Insulators and Asbestos Workers [24093]
  Intl. Union of Indus. and Independent Workers [24208]
  Jobs With Justice [18827]
  Just Transition Alliance [24105]
  Koepel van Christelijke Werknemersorganisaties [IO]
  Korean Women Workers Associations United [IO]
  Kristelijke Werknemersbeweging [IO]
  Legal Immigrant Assn. [5808]
  Lightmongers' Company [IO]
  Nationaal Verbond der Kristelijke Arbeidersvrouwenbeweging [IO]
  Natl. Alliance for Migrant and Seasonal Farmworker Vocational Rehabilitation [12591]
  Natl. Alliance for Worker and Employer Rights [24110]
  Natl. Assn. of Disability Examiners [14034]
  Natl. Conservation District Employees Assn. [24209]
  Natl. Day Laborer Organizing Network [24111]
  Natl. Job Corps Alumni Assn. [24093]
  Natl. Labor Alliance of Hea. Care Coalitions [24091]
  Natl. Mobilization Against Sweatshops [17975]
  Natl. Union of Law Enforcement Associations [24124]
  Natl. Workforce Assn. [1739]
  Nigerian Social Workers Assn. [24142]
  Norwegian Assn. of Res. Workers [IO]
  Peggy Browning Fund [6362]
  Privacy Rights CH [3176]
  Rescue Amer. Jobs [17984]
  Residential Constr. Workers' Assn. [948]
  Sanctuary Workers and Volunteers Assn. [11455]
  Social Accountability Intl. [18828]
  Social Accountability Intl. [IO]
  Student/Farmworker Alliance [24054]
  SweatFree Communities [24106]
  Verite [12063]
  VNO-NCW Confed. of Netherlands Indus. and Employers [IO]
  Wal-Mart Alliance for Reform Now [24107]
  Wal-Mart Workers of Am. [24108]
  Wal-Mart Workers Assn. [24109]
  Waterfront and Allied Workers' Union [IO]
  Welfare to Work Partnership [13146]
  Workers Compensation Insurance Organizations [2248]
  Workers' Educational Assn. [IO]
  Workers' Trade Union [IO]
  Workplace Bullying Inst. [16189]
  World Movement of Christian Workers [IO]
  World Solidarity [IO]
  Youth for Intl. Socialism [18663]
Workers Assn; Natl. Farm [★23999]
Workers; Bishops' Comm. for Migrant [★12282]
Workers; Christian Jail [★19745]
Workers Compensation Insurance Organizations [2248], Pennsylvania Compensation Rating Bur., Widener Bldg., 6th Fl., One S Penn Sq., Philadelphia, PA 19107-3577, (215)568-2371
Workers' Compensation and the Natl. Found. for UC & WC; Strategic Services on Unemployment and [★13348]
Workers Compensation; Natl. Found. for Unemployment Compensation and [5681]
Workers' Compensation; UWC - Strategic Services on Unemployment and [13348]
Workers' Defense League [17159]
Workers with Disabilities; Center for [11929]
Workers' Educational Assn. [IO], Stockholm, Sweden
Workers' Educational Assn. - East Midlands Region [IO], Nottingham, United Kingdom

---

Reference to "IO" in place of a book number signifies that the association may be found in the 45th edition of International Organizations.

Workers' Educational Assn. - Eastern Region [IO], Cambridge, United Kingdom

Workers' Educational Assn. - London Region [IO], London, United Kingdom

Workers' Educational Assn. - North East Region [IO], Gateshead, United Kingdom

Workers' Educational Assn. - North West Region [IO], Liverpool, United Kingdom

Workers' Educational Assn. - Northern Ireland [IO], Belfast, United Kingdom

Workers' Educational Assn. - South Wales [IO], Cardiff, United Kingdom

Workers' Educational Assn. - South Western Region [IO], Exeter, United Kingdom

Workers' Educational Assn. - Southern Region [IO], Rochester, United Kingdom

Workers' Educational Assn. - United Kingdom [IO], London, United Kingdom

Workers' Educational Assn. - West Midlands Region [IO], Birmingham, United Kingdom

Workers' Educational Assn. - Yorkshire and Humber [IO], Leeds, United Kingdom

Workers Freedom Movement; Natl. Socialist Amer. [★18802]

Workers; Intl. Brotherhood of DuPont [24034]

Workers' Intl. Liaison Comm. - Address unknown since 2006.

Workers; Intl. Union of Elecl., Radio and Machine [★24049]

Workers; Intl. Union of Electronic, Elecl., Tech., Salaried, Machine, and Furniture [★24049]

Workers Intl. Union; Paper, Allied-Indus., Chem. and Energy [24211]

Workers' Music Assn. [IO], London, United Kingdom

Workers Organizing Comm; United Farm [★23999]

Workers Party; Amer. [★18802]

Workers Party; Socialist [18336]

Workers' Rights; Center to Protect [24039]

Workers Rights; Center to Protect [★24025]

Worker's Socialist Party [★18339]

Workers Solidarity Alliance [16982], 339 Lafayette St., Rm. 202, New York, NY 10012, (212)979-8353

Workers' Trade Union [IO], Madrid, Spain

Workers, UAW Local 2320; Natl. Org. of Legal Services [24079]

Workers; United Auto [★24004]

Workers World Party [18660], 55 W 17th St., New York, NY 10011, (212)627-2994

Workers World Party [IO], New York, NY, United States

Workflow and Reengineering Intl. Assn. [IO], Lighthouse Point, FL, United States

Workflow and Reengineering Intl. Assn. [767], 2436 N Fed. Hwy., No. 374, Lighthouse Point, FL 33064, (954)782-3376

Workforce Development Professionals; Natl. Assn. of [12088]

Workgroup for Electronic Data Interchange [1854], 12020 Sunrise Valley Dr., Ste. 100, Reston, VA 20191, (703)391-2716

Working for Am. Inst; AFL-CIO [12065]

Working Class Hero Beatles Club [24788]

Working Dog Assn; German Shepherd Dog Club of Am. - [22273]

Working in Employee Benefits [★1246]

Working in Employee Benefits [★IO]

Working community of the European Gypsum Indus. [★IO]

Working Families [IO], London, United Kingdom

Working Families; Campaign for [18286]

Working Families; Labor Proj. for [24117]

Working Families Party [18338], 2-4 Nevins St., 3rd Fl., Brooklyn, NY 11217, (718)222-3796

Working Group of Alpine Regions [IO], Innsbruck, Austria

Working Group on Applied Physical Geography [IO], Amsterdam, Netherlands

Working Group for Community Development Reform - Defunct.

Working Group for Democracy in Chile - Address unknown since 1991.

Working Group on Domestic Hunger and Poverty - Defunct.

Working Group on Extraterrestrial Resources - Defunct.

Working Group on Hea. and Development Issues [★IO]

Working Group on Refugee Resettlement [IO], Toronto, ON, Canada

Working Group of U.S. Overseas Educational Advisers in South America - Defunct.

Working Group on Untouchables - Defunct.

Working Gp. on Youth Ser. Policy [★13070]

Working Kelpie Coun. of Australia [IO], Castle Hill, Australia

Working Mother Network; Every Mother is a [18810]

Working Mothers Assn. [★IO]

Working People; Amer. Assn. of [12067]

Working Pit Bull Terrier Club of Am. [22385], c/o Aja Harris, Sec., 2608 Kentucky Ave., Baltimore, MD 21213

Working Ranch Cowboys Assn. [3294], PO Box 7765, Amarillo, TX 79114, (806)374-9722

Working Riesenschnauzer Fed. [22386], c/o Martha Galuszka, Membership Dir., 324 Oakwood Ave., West Hartford, CT 06110, (860)233-2286

Working Riesenschnauzer Fed. [IO], West Hartford, CT, United States

Working Today [1672], 45 Main St., Ste. 710, Brooklyn, NY 11201, (718)222-1099

Working Women; 9 to 5, Natl. Assn. of [17512]

Working Women Educ. Fund [★17513]

Working Women Educ. Fund; 9 to 5 [17513]

Working Women, Natl. Assn. of Off. Workers [★17512]

Working Women Organizing Proj. [★17512]

Working Women's Forum [IO], Chennai, India

Working Women's Forum (India) [IO], Chennai, India

Working Women's Inst. - Defunct.

WorkingAbroad Projects [IO], Brighton, United Kingdom

Workingmen's Party [★18334]

Workman; Catholic [18998]

Workmen of Navy Yards and Naval Stations; Natl. Assn. of Master [★6085]

Workmen's Benefit Fund of the U.S.A. [19146], 399 Conklin St., Ste. 310, Farmingdale, NY 11735-2614, (516)938-6060

Workmen's Circle [19147], 45 E 33rd St., New York, NY 10016, (212)889-6800

Workmen's Compensation

Amer. Assn. of State Compensation Insurance Funds [2134]

Amer. Cooperative Coun. on Compensation Tech. [4059]

Canadian Injured Workers Alliance [IO]

Employers Coun. on Flexible Compensation [1237]

Natl. Assn. of Disability Examiners [14034]

Natl. Coun. of Self-Insurers [2222]

Natl. Found. for Unemployment Compensation and Workers Compensation [5681]

Natl. Truckdrivers Safety Assn. [2843]

Social Accountability Intl. [18828]

UWC - Strategic Services on Unemployment and Workers' Compensation [13348]

Workers Compensation Insurance Organizations [2248]

Workmen's Compensation Insurance; Natl. Coun. on [★2221]

Workplace Benefits Assn. [1247], 9221 Ravenna Rd., Ste. No. D8, Twinsburg, OH 44087, (330)425-8399

Workplace Bullying Inst. [16189], PO Box 29915, Bellingham, WA 98228, (360)656-6630

Workplace Bullying and Trauma Inst. [★16189]

Workplace Fairness [12064], 2031 Florida Ave. NW, Ste. 500, Washington, DC 20009, (202)243-7660

Workplace; Inst. for a Drug-Free [13247]

Workplace Institute/SafeSpaces.com; Natl. Safe [12978]

Works Officials; Intl. Assn. of Public [★6233]

Workshop 3 [IO], Hamburg, Germany

Workshop Center; Vocational Guidance and [★24603]

Workshop for Cultural Democracy - Address unknown since 1995.

Workshop Inst. for Living-Learning - Address unknown since 1989.

Workshop Library on World Humour - Defunct.

WORKSHOP WAY Consultants; Assn. of [9213]

Workshop Writers; Natl. Assn. of Home and [3131]

Worksite Hea. Promotion; Assn. for [★16473]

WORLD [★13589]

WORLD [★IO]

World Ability Fed. [IO], Chicago, IL, United States

World Ability Fed. [11995], 120 S Riverside Plz., Ste. 1050, Chicago, IL 60606, (312)207-0000

World Acad. of Art and Sci. [9612], 301 19th Ave. S, Minneapolis, MN 55455, (612)624-5592

World Acad. of Art and Sci. [IO], Minneapolis, MN, United States

World Affairs

50 Years is Enough: U.S. Network for Global Economic Justice [IO]

50 Years is Enough: U.S. Network for Global Economic Justice [18829]

Acad. of Arts and Sciences of the Americas [18830]

Acad. of Arts and Sciences of the Americas [IO]

Assn. of World Citizens [IO]

Assn. of World Citizens [18831]

Chem. and Biological Arms Control Inst. [17023]

Coun. on Intl. and Public Affairs [18832]

Coun. on Intl. and Public Affairs [IO]

Essential Info. [17175]

Forum Intl.: Intl. Ecosystems Univ. [18833]

Forum Intl.: Intl. Ecosystems Univ. [IO]

Fund for Peace [18834]

Global Interdependence Center [18835]

Hoover Institution on War, Revolution and Peace [18836]

Inst. of Current World Affairs [18837]

Inst. of Current World Affairs [IO]

Natl. Soc. of High School Scholars [9076]

Planetary Citizens [18838]

Planetary Citizens [IO]

Positive Futures Network [18839]

Pugwash Conferences on Sci. and World Affairs [17247]

Renaissance Universal [18840]

Rocky Mountain Inst. [18101]

State of the World Forum [18841]

State of the World Forum [IO]

Student Pugwash U.S.A. [18842]

World Affairs Councils of Am. [18843]

World Affairs Councils of Am. [IO]

World History Assn. [10166]

Worldwatch Inst. [18844]

Worldwatch Inst. [IO]

World Affairs; Amer. Universities Field Staff -Institute of [★8663]

World Affairs Center for the U.S. [★17610]

World Affairs Center for the U.S. [★IO]

World Affairs Councils of Am. [IO], Washington, DC, United States

World Affairs Councils of Am. [18843], 1800 K St. NW, Ste. 1014, Washington, DC 20006, (202)833-4557

World Affairs; Inst. of [★8663]

World Affairs; International Pugwash Conferences on Sci. and [★18842]

World Affairs Organizations; Natl. Coun. of Community [★18843]

World Affairs; Universities Field Staff Intl. -Inst. of [★8663]

World Africa Chamber of Commerce - Address unknown since 1995.

World Agroforestry Centre [IO], Nairobi, Kenya

World Airline Entertainment Association [IO], McLean, VA, United States

World Airline Entertainment Assn. [440], 8201 Greensboro Dr., Ste. 300, McLean, VA 22102, (703)610-9021

World Airline Historical Soc. [21488], PO Box 489, Ocoee, FL 34761

World Airline Historical Soc. [IO], Ocoee, FL, United States

World Airline Hobby Club [★IO]

World Airline Hobby Club [★21488]

World Airlines Clubs Assn. [IO], Montreal, QC, Canada

World Allergy Org. [IO], Milwaukee, WI, United States

World Allergy Org. [13605], 555 E Wells St., Ste. 1100, Milwaukee, WI 53202-3823, (414)276-1791

A star before a book entry number signifies that the name is not listed separately, but is mentioned within the entry.

World Alliance for Breastfeeding Action [IO], Penang, Malaysia
World Alliance of Gourmet Robustas [IO], New York, NY, United States
World Alliance of Gourmet Robustas [1738], 360 E 72nd St., Ste. C 3000, New York, NY 10021, (212)737-2548
World Alliance of Reformed Churches [IO], Geneva, Switzerland
World Amateur Golf Coun. [★IO]
World Amateur Golf Coun. [★23453]
World Antique Dealers Assn. [219]
World Apheresis Assn. [IO], Paris, France
World Apostolate of Fatima [★19589]
World Apple and Pear Assn. [IO], Brussels, Belgium
World Aquaculture Soc. [IO], Baton Rouge, LA, United States
World Aquaculture Soc. [4185], Louisiana State Univ., 143 J.M. Parker Coliseum, Baton Rouge, LA 70803, (225)578-3137
World Aquatic Babies and Children [23894], PO Box 10596, St. Petersburg, FL 33733, (727)804-3399
World Aquatic Babies and Children [IO], St. Petersburg, FL, United States
World Aquatic Babies Cong. [★IO]
World Aquatic Babies Cong. [★23894]
World Aquatic Coalition, Inc. [★23652]
World Arabian Horse Org. [IO], Gloucester, United Kingdom
World Archaeological Soc. [IO], Hollister, MO, United States
World Archaeological Soc. [6460], c/o Ron Miller, Dir., 120 Lakewood Dr., Hollister, MO 65672, (417)334-2377
World Armsport Fed. [23060], 176 Dean Rd., Mooresburg, TN 37811, (423)272-6162
World Armsport Fed. [IO], Mooresburg, TN, United States
World Armwrestling Fed. [★IO]
World Armwrestling Fed. [★23060]
World Arnold Chiari Malformation Assn. [16556], c/o Bernie Meyer, 31 Newtown Woods Rd., Newtown Square, PA 19073, (610)353-4737
World Arnold Chiari Malformation Association [IO], Newtown Square, PA, United States
World Assembly of Muslim Youth [IO], Riyadh, Saudi Arabia
World Assistance [★IO]
World Assistance [★17921]
World Assn. for the Advancement of Veterinary Parasitology [16818], c/o Dr. Ann Donoghue, Sec.-Treas., PR Pharmaceuticals, Inc., 1716 Hea. Pkwy., Fort Collins, CO 80524, (970)494-2342
World Assn. for the Advancement of Veterinary Parasitology [IO], North Aurora, IL, United States
World Assn. of the Alcohol Beverage Indus. [IO], Mason, OH, United States
World Assn. of the Alcohol Beverage Indus. [213], PO Box 191, Mason, OH 45040-0191, (513)675-3443
World Assn. for Allied Disciplines and Infant Psychiatry [★16098]
World Assn. for Allied Disciplines and Infant Psychiatry [★IO]
World Assn. for Animal Production [IO], Rome, Italy
World Assn. of Beet and Cane Growers [IO], Paris, France
World Association of Benchers and Dead Lifters [IO], Golden Valley, MN, United States
World Assn. of Benchers and Dead Lifters [23986], PO Box 27499, Golden Valley, MN 55427, (763)545-8654
World Assn. for Buiatrics [IO], Budapest, Hungary
World Assn. for Case Method Res. and Application [IO], Needham, MA, United States
World Assn. for Case Method Res. and Application [7578], 23 Mackintosh Ave., Needham, MA 02492-1218, (781)444-8982
World Assn. of Center Associates [★5874]
World Assn. of Center Associates [★IO]
World Assn. for Children and Parents [IO], Seattle, WA, United States
World Assn. for Children and Parents [11666], 315 S Second St., Renton, WA 98057, (206)575-4550
World Assn. for Chinese Biomedical Engineers [6611], c/o Savio L-Y. Woo, PhD, Chm., Univ. of Pittsburgh, Musculoskeletal Res. Ctr., 405 Center for Bioengineering, 300 Tech. Dr., Pittsburgh, PA 15219, (412)427-2000

World Assn. for Chinese Biomedical Engineers [IO], Pittsburgh, PA, United States
World Assn. for Christian Commun. [IO], London, United Kingdom
World Assn. of Christian Radio Amateurs and Listeners [IO], Pontefract, United Kingdom
World Assn. of Community Radio Broadcasters [IO], Montreal, QC, Canada
World Assn. of Cultural Psychiatry [IO], Honolulu, HI, United States
World Assn. of Cultural Psychiatry [16097], c/o Wen-Shing Tseng, MD, Pres., 1356 Lusitana St., Honolulu, HI 96813-2421
World Assn. of Detectives [IO], Blackpool, United Kingdom
World Assn. of Detectives [★IO]
World Assn. of Document Examiners - Address unknown since 2006.
World Assn. of Estonians - Defunct.
World Assn. of Girl Guides and Girl Scouts [IO], London, United Kingdom
World Assn. of Girl Guides and Girl Scouts Western Hemisphere Subcommittee - Defunct.
World Assn. for the History of Veterinary Medicine [IO], Vienna, Austria
World Assn. of Indus. and Technological Res. Organizations [IO], Shah Alam, Malaysia
World Assn. for Infant Mental Hea. [IO], East Lansing, MI, United States
World Assn. for Infant Mental Hea. [16098], Michigan State Univ., Univ. Outreach and Engagement, Kellogg Center, Garden Level No. 24, East Lansing, MI 48824, (517)432-3793
World Assn. of Judges [5870], c/o World Jurist Assn., 1000 Connecticut Ave. NW, Ste. 202, Washington, DC 20036, (202)466-5428
World Assn. of Judges [IO], Washington, DC, United States
World Assn. of Law Professors [IO], Washington, DC, United States
World Assn. of Law Professors [5871], c/o World Jurist Assn., 1000 Connecticut Ave. NW, Ste. 202, Washington, DC 20036, (202)466-5428
World Assn. of Law Students and Young Jurists [5872], 1000 Connecticut Ave. NW, Ste. 202, Washington, DC 20036, (202)466-5428
World Assn. of Law Students and Young Jurists [IO], Washington, DC, United States
World Assn. of Lawyers [IO], Washington, DC, United States
World Assn. of Lawyers [5873], 1000 Connecticut Ave. NW, Ste. 202, Washington, DC 20036, (202)466-5428
World Assn. of Marching Show Bands [IO], Calgary, AB, Canada
World Assn. of Medical Editors [IO], Chicago, IL, United States
World Assn. of Medical Editors [14303], c/o Margaret A. Winker, MD, VP, 515 N State St., Chicago, IL 60610, (312)464-2486
World Assn. of Methodist Radio Amateurs and Listeners [★IO]
World Assn. of Newspapers [IO], Paris, France
World Association of Persons with disAbilities [IO], Oklahoma City, OK, United States
World Assn. of Persons with disAbilities [14247], 5016 Alan Ln., Oklahoma City, OK 73135, (405)672-4440
World Assn. of Professional Investigators [IO], London, United Kingdom
World Association for Psychosocial Rehabilitation - U.S. Branch [IO], New York, NY, United States
World Assn. for Psychosocial Rehabilitation - U.S. Br. [16338]
World Assn. for Public Opinion Res. [18371], c/o Dr. Allan L. McCutcheon, Gen. Sec., Univ. of Nebraska-Lincoln, UNL Gallup Res. Ctr., 200 N 11th St., Lincoln, NE 68588-0242, (402)458-2030
World Assn. for Public Opinion Res. [IO], Lincoln, NE, United States
World Assn. of Publishers, Mfrs. and Distributors of Educational Materials [★IO]
World Assn. to Remove Prejudice Against the Handicapped - Address unknown since 1995.
World Assn. of Res. Professionals [IO], Amsterdam, Netherlands

World Assn. of Sarcoidosis and Other Granulomatous Disorders [IO], Milan, Italy
World Assn. for the School as an Instrument of Peace [IO], Geneva, Switzerland
World Assn. for Sexology - Address unknown since 1990.
World Assn. of Sleep Medicine [16430], c/o Allan O'Bryan, 2358 68th St. NW, Rochester, MN 55901, (507)206-1235
World Assn. of Sleep Medicine [IO], Edison, NJ, United States
World Assn. for Small and Medium Enterprises [IO], Noida, India
World Assn. for Social Psychiatry [IO], Santa Barbara, CA, United States
World Assn. for Social Psychiatry [16099], 656 Romero Canyon Rd., Santa Barbara, CA 93108, (805)969-1376
World Assn. of Societies of Pathology and Lab. Medicine [IO], Tokyo, Japan
World Assn. of Soil and Water Conservation [IO], Buffalo Center, IA, United States
World Assn. of Soil and Water Conservation [4473], c/o John M. Laflen, Treas., 5784 Hwy. 9, Buffalo Center, IA 50424
World Assn. of Theoretically Oriented Chemists [IO], Marburg, Germany
World Assn. of Travel Agencies [IO], Gland, Switzerland
World Assn. of Upper Silesians - Address unknown since 1999.
World Assn. of Valuation Organizations [IO], Singapore, Singapore
World Assn. for Vedic Stud. [IO], Atlanta, GA, United States
World Assn. for Vedic Stud. [9854], c/o Prof. BhuDev Sharma, Pres., Clark Atlanta Univ., CAU Box 764, 223 James P. Brawley Dr. SW, Atlanta, GA 30314, (404)880-6912
World Assn. of Veteran Athletes [★IO]
World Assn. of Veterinary Anatomists [IO], Bern, Switzerland
World Assn. of Veterinary Educators [IO], Tuskegee, AL, United States
World Assn. of Veterinary Educators [9295], c/o I.H. Siddique, Pres., School of Veterinary Medicine, Tuskegee Univ., Tuskegee, AL 36083, (334)727-8478
World Assn. of Veterinary Lab. Diagnosticians [16819], c/o Dr. Craig N. Carter, Sec.-Treas., PO Box 14125, Lexington, KY 40512-4125, (859)253-0571
World Assn. of Veterinary Lab. Diagnosticians [IO], Lexington, KY, United States
World Atlatl Assn. [IO], Jeffersonville, IN, United States
World Atlatl Assn. [22611], c/o Richard Lyons, Treas., 5024 King Rd., Jeffersonville, IN 47130, (812)246-9987
World Bamboo Org. [5041], c/o Ms. Susanne Lucas, Chair, 9 Bloody Pond Rd., Plymouth, MA 02360
World Bamboo Org. [IO], Plymouth, MA, United States
The World Bank [★IO]
The World Bank [★17841]
World Bank Gp. [17856], 1818 H St. NW, Washington, DC 20433, (202)473-1000
World Bank Gp. [IO], Washington, DC, United States
World Beechcraft Soc. [IO], Kent, WA, United States
World Beechcraft Soc. [21489], 8609 S 212th St., Kent, WA 98031, (866)732-3927
World Beefalo Assn. [★4123]
World Beefalo Assn. [★IO]
World Bicycle Polo Fed. - Defunct.
World Bird Sanctuary [5403], 125 Bald Eagle Ridge Rd., Valley Park, MO 63088, (636)861-3225
World Bird Sanctuary [IO], Valley Park, MO, United States
World Blind Union [IO], Madrid, Spain
World Blue Chain: For the Protection of Animals and Nature [IO], Brussels, Belgium
World Bocce Assn. [★IO]
World Bocce Assn. [★23242]
World Bocce League [23242], PO Box 286, Bensenville, IL 60106, (630)834-8349

Reference to "IO" in place of a book number signifies that the association may be found in the 45th edition of International Organizations.

World Bocce League [IO], Elmhurst, IL, United States

World Bowling Writers [IO], Chicago, IL, United States

World Bowling Writers [3175], 122 S Michigan Ave., Ste. 1506, Chicago, IL 60603, (312)341-1110

World Boxing Coun. [IO], Mexico City, Mexico

World Boxing - Defunct.

World Boxing Historians Assn. - Defunct.

World Buffalo Assn., Limited Agricultural Assn. - Address unknown since 1999.

World Bulldog Alliance [22387], c/o Ray Giacobbe, Pres., 1700 Ridgewood Ave., Ste. D, Holly Hill, FL 32117, (386)437-4762

World Bur. of Metal Statistics [IO], Ware, United Kingdom

World Bus. Associates [IO], Washington, DC, United States

World Bus. Associates [5874], 1000 Connecticut Ave. NW, Ste. 202, Washington, DC 20036, (202)466-5428

World Bus. Coun. [★768]

World Bus. Coun. [★IO]

World Cancer Res. Fund [IO], London, United Kingdom

World Canine Freestyle Org. [23390], PO Box 350122, Brooklyn, NY 11235-2525, (718)332-8336

World Care [17478], 3538 E Ellington Pl., Tucson, AZ 85713, (520)514-1588

World Care [IO], Tucson, AZ, United States

World Center for Birds of Prey [★IO]

World Center for Birds of Prey [★5365]

World Chamber of Commerce Service - Address unknown since 1995.

World Chamberlain Genealogical Soc. [21157], c/o Karen Chamberlin, Corresponding Sec., 343 W Lake Faith Dr., Maitland, FL 32751

World Championship Cutter and Chariot Racing Assn. [23281], c/o J. Victor Adams, Sec./Mgr., 2632 S 4300 W, Ogden, UT 84401, (801)731-8021

World Chap. of Disneyana Enthusiasts [22132], PO Box 470116, Celebration, FL 34747-0116, (407)275-2756

World Chap. of Disneyana Enthusiasts [IO], Celebration, FL, United States

World Chess Fed. [IO], Athens, Greece

World Children's Day Found. - Address unknown since 2001.

World Chiropractic Alliance [14017], 2950 N Dobson Rd., Ste. 1, Chandler, AZ 85224, (480)786-9235

World Chiropractic Alliance [IO], Chandler, AZ, United States

World for Christ Crusade [IO], West Milford, NJ, United States

World for Christ Crusade [20412], 1005 Union Valley Rd., West Milford, NJ 07480, (973)728-3267

World Christian Life Community [★IO]

World Church of the Creator [★IO]

World Church of the Creator [★18798]

World Citizens [★18831]

World Citizens [★IO]

World Citizens Assembly [★IO]

World Citizens Assembly [★18831]

World Citizens U.S.A. - Defunct.

World Clown Assn. [21953], c/o Pat Lay Wilson, Admin., PO Box 77236, Corona, CA 92877-0107, (951)273-0117

World Clown Association [IO], Corona, CA, United States

World Coal Inst. [IO], London, United Kingdom

World Cocoa Found. [6545], 8320 Old Courthouse Rd., Ste. 300, Vienna, VA 22182, (703)790-5012

World Commn. on Protected Areas [IO], Gland, Switzerland

World Comm. on Disability [IO], Washington, DC, United States

World Comm. on Disability [14248], c/o Natl. Org. on Disability, 910 16th St. NW, Ste. 600, Washington, DC 20006, (202)293-5960

World Comm. for a World Constitutional Convention [★18317]

World Comm. for a World Constitutional Convention [★IO]

World Commun. Assn. [IO], Whitewater, WI, United States

World Commun. Assn. [8005], c/o Barbara S. Monfils, Pres., Univ. of Wisconsin-Whitewater, 800 W Main St., Hyer 428, Whitewater, WI 53190-1790, (262)472-1055

World Community [★12376]

World Community [★12884]

World Community [★IO]

World Community [★IO]

World Community Chaplains [IO], West Hills, CA, United States

World Community Chaplains [12884], 24303 Woolsey Canyon Rd., No. 142, West Hills, CA 91304-1130, (818)884-6568

World Community Projects [★12884]

World Community Projects [★IO]

World Computer Graphics Assn. - Defunct.

World Concern [12787], 19303 Fremont Ave. N, Seattle, WA 98133, (206)546-7201

World Concern [IO], Seattle, WA, United States

World Confed. of Billiard Sports [IO], Colorado Springs, CO, United States

World Confed. of Billiard Sports [23150], c/o Stephen D. Ducoff, 4345 Beverly St., Ste. D, Colorado Springs, CO 80918, (719)264-8300

World Confed. of Gen. Zionists [★20195]

World Confed. of Gen. Zionists [★IO]

World Confed. of Jewish Community Centers [IO], Jerusalem, Israel

World Confed. of Labour [IO], Brussels, Belgium

World Confed. of Organizations of the Teaching Profession [★IO]

World Confed. for Physical Therapy [IO], London, United Kingdom

World Confed. of Productivity Sci. [IO], Montreal, QC, Canada

World Confed. of United Zionists [IO], New York, NY, United States

World Confed. of United Zionists [20195], c/o Dor Zion, 136 E 39th St., New York, NY 10016, (212)725-1211

World Conf. of Jewish Communal Service - Address unknown since 2001.

World Conf. of Jewish Orgs. - Defunct.

World Conf. of Religions for Peace [18257], 777 UN Plz., New York, NY 10017, (212)687-2163

World Conf. of Religions for Peace [IO], New York, NY, United States

World Cong. of Faiths [IO], London, United Kingdom

World Cong. of Gay, Lesbian, Bisexual, and Transgender Jews [IO], Washington, DC, United States

World Cong. of Gay, Lesbian, Bisexual, and Transgender Jews [20069], PO Box 23379, Washington, DC 20026-3379

World Congress of Poets [10873], c/o Michelle Wang, Treas., 4423 Pitch Pine Court, San Jose, CA 95136, (408)281-8041

World Cong. of Poets [IO], Taipei, People's Republic of China

World Cong. of Teachers of Dancing [8192]

World Connections for Women [18824], c/o Amelia Stinson-Wesley, 203 Shady Rest Rd., Morganton, NC 28655, (828)437-3697

World Connections for Women [IO], Morganton, NC, United States

World Conservation Union [IO], Gland, Switzerland

World Constitution and Parliament Assn. [IO], Lakewood, CO, United States

World Constitution and Parliament Assn. [18317], 8800 W 14th Ave., Lakewood, CO 80215, (303)233-3548

World Constitutional Convention; World Comm. for a [★18317]

World Convention of Churches of Christ [19857], PO Box 41487, Nashville, TN 37204-1487, (615)331-1824

World Convention of Churches of Christ [IO], Nashville, TN, United States

World Correctional Service Center - Address unknown since 1987.

World Coun. of Associations for Tech. Educ. [IO], Erfurt, Germany

World Coun. of Blind Lions [★16825]

World Coun. for Cardiovascular and Pulmonary Rehabilitation [13930], c/o Susan Rees, Off. Staff, 2810 Crossroads Dr., Ste. 3800, Madison, WI 53718, (608)443-2468

World Coun. for Cardiovascular and Pulmonary Rehabilitation [IO], Madison, WI, United States

World Coun. of Christians - Defunct.

World Coun. of Churches [IO], Geneva, Switzerland

World Coun. of Churches; U.S. Conf. for the [19912]

World Coun. of Clergy - Defunct.

World Coun. of Comparative Educ. Societies [IO], Hong Kong, People's Republic of China

World Coun. of Conservative/Masorti Synagogues [IO], New York, NY, United States

World Coun. of Conservative/Masorti Synagogues [20196], 3080 Broadway, New York, NY 10027, (212)678-5319

World Coun. of Credit Unions [1119], PO Box 2982, Madison, WI 53705, (608)395-2000

World Coun. of Credit Unions [IO], Madison, WI, United States

World Coun. for Curriculum and Instruction [IO], San Diego, CA, United States

World Coun. for Curriculum and Instruction [8182], c/o Dr. Estela C. Matriano, Exec. Dir., Alliant Intl. Univ., Graduate School of Educ., 10455 Pomerado Rd., San Diego, CA 92131, (858)635-4718

World Coun. of Elders [9855], PO Box 7915, Boulder, CO 80306, (303)444-9263

World Council of Elders [IO], Boulder, CO, United States

World Coun. of Enterostomal Therapists [IO], Mississauga, ON, Canada

World Coun. for Gifted and Talented Children [IO], Pasadena, CA, United States

World Coun. for Gifted and Talented Children [8467], c/o Sandra Kaplan, Univ. of Southern California, School of Educ., Waite, Phillips Hall 1004, Los Angeles, CA 90089-0031

World Coun. of Hellenes Abroad [19096], 980 N Michigan Ave., Ste. 1210, Chicago, IL 60611, (312)337-7243

World Council of Hellenes Abroad [IO], Chicago, IL, United States

World Coun. of Jewish Archives - Defunct.

World Coun. on Jewish Education - Address unknown since 1995.

World Coun. of Optometry [15731], 8360 Old York Rd., 4th Fl. W, Elkins Park, PA 19027, (215)780-1320

World Coun. of Optometry [IO], Elkins Park, PA, United States

World Coun. of Religious Leaders [IO], New York, NY, United States

World Coun. of Religious Leaders [20519], Empire State Bldg., 350 Fifth Ave., Ste. 5403, New York, NY 10118, (212)967-2891

World Coun. for Renewable Energy [IO], Bonn, Germany

World Coun. of Synagogues [★IO]

World Coun. of Synagogues [★20196]

World Coun. for Venue Mgt. [1350]

World Council for Venue Management [IO], Coppell, TX, United States

World Coun. for the Welfare of the Blind [★IO]

World Coun. of Whalers [IO], Qualicum Beach, BC, Canada

World Court Clubs Assn. - Defunct.

World Craniofacial Found. [14068], PO Box 515838, Dallas, TX 75251-5838, (972)566-6669

World Cultural Coun. [IO], Mexico City, Mexico

World Curling Fed. [IO], Perth, United Kingdom

World Customs Org. [IO], Brussels, Belgium

World Dance Alliance [IO], New York, NY, United States

World Dance Alliance [9901], 433 W 34th St., Apt. No. 8L, New York, NY 10001-1524, (212)695-3925

World Dance Coun. [IO], Bremen, Germany

World Dance Coun. - Germany [IO], Hamburg, Germany

World Dance and Dance Sport Coun. [★IO]

World Dance and Dance Sport Coun. - Germany [★IO]

The World of Dark Shadows [25046], PO Box 17666, Temple City, CA 91780

World Darts Fed. [IO], London, United Kingdom

World Data Center for Collections of Microorganisms [★IO]

World Day for Peace - Defunct.

A star before a book entry number signifies that the name is not listed separately, but is mentioned within the entry.

World Day of Prayer Intl. Comm. **[20629]**, 475 Riverside Dr., Rm. 729, New York, NY 10115, (212)870-3049

World Day of Prayer; Intl. Comm. for **[★20629]**

World Day of Prayer Intl. Comm. **[IO]**, New York, NY, United States

World Deist Soc. - Address unknown since 2002.

World Development Fed. **[12449]**, 6625 The Corners Pkwy., Ste. 200, Norcross, GA 30092-2901, (770)446-6996

World Development Fed. **[IO]**, Norcross, GA, United States

World Development Movement **[IO]**, London, United Kingdom

A World of Difference Inst. **[IO]**, New York, NY, United States

A World of Difference Inst. **[11487]**, 823 United Nations Plz., New York, NY 10017, (212)885-7811

World Diving Coaches Assn. **[23383]**

World Div. CUNA Intl. **[★1119]**

World Div. CUNA Intl. **[★IO]**

World Draughts - Checkers - Fed. **[IO]**, Amsterdam, Netherlands

World of Dreams Found. Canada **[IO]**, Montreal, QC, Canada

World Dredging Assn. **[★IO]**

World Dredging Assn. **[★2597]**

World Druze Cong. - Address unknown since 1987.

World Economic Forum **[IO]**, Geneva, Switzerland

World Economic Processing Zones Assn. **[IO]**, Evergreen, CO, United States

World Economic Processing Zones Assn. **[3849]**, PO Box 3808, Evergreen, CO 80437-3808, (303)679-0980

World Educ. **[7918]**, 44 Farnsworth St., Boston, MA 02210, (617)482-9485

World Educ. **[IO]**, Boston, MA, United States

World Education Fellowship, U.S. Sect. - Address unknown since 2004.

World Electroless Nickel Soc. - Defunct.

World Emergency Relief **[12885]**, PO Box 131570, Carlsbad, CA 92013, (760)930-8001

World Emergency Relief **[IO]**, Carlsbad, CA, United States

World Energy Conf. **[★IO]**

World Energy Coun. Argentina Comm. **[IO]**, Cordoba, Argentina

World Energy Coun. - England **[IO]**, London, United Kingdom

World Energy Coun. Indian Member Comm. **[IO]**, New Delhi, India

World Energy Coun. Italian Natl. Comm. **[IO]**, Rome, Italy

World Energy Coun. Polish Member Comm. **[IO]**, Warsaw, Poland

World Energy Coun. Turkish Natl. Comm. **[IO]**, Ankara, Turkey

World Energy Efficiency Association **[IO]**, Washington, DC, United States

World Energy Efficiency Assn. **[6978]**, 1101 15th St. NW, Ste. 1100, Washington, DC 20005, (202)778-4942

World Env. Center **[4474]**, 1300 Pennsylvania Ave. NW, Ste. 550, Mailbox 142, Washington, DC 20004, (202)312-1210

World Env. Center **[IO]**, Washington, DC, United States

World Environmental Org. **[4475]**, 2020 Pennsylvania Ave. NW, No. 2001, Washington, DC 20006, (800)800-2SUN

World Evangelical Alliance **[19983]**, 644 Strander Blvd., No. 154, Seattle, WA 98188, (202)223-7556

World Evangelical Alliance **[IO]**, Seattle, WA, United States

World Evangelical Fellowship **[★IO]**

World Evangelical Fellowship **[★19983]**

World Evangelical Fellowship Commun. Commn. **[★19538]**

World Evangelical Fellowship Commun. Commn. **[★IO]**

World Evangelism **[★IO]**

World Evangelism **[★20025]**

World Expeditionary Assn. **[★IO]**

World Expeditionary Assn. Intl. **[IO]**, London, United Kingdom

World Export Processing Zones Assn. **[★IO]**

World Export Processing Zones Assn. **[★3849]**

World Farriers Assn. **[1356]**, PO Box 1102, Albuquerque, NM 87103, (505)345-7550

World Farriers Assn. **[IO]**, Albuquerque, NM, United States

World Fast-Draw Assn. **[23733]**, c/o Cheryl Short, Sec., 749 9th St., Calhan, CO 80808

World Federalist Assn. **[★18762]**

World Federalist Movement **[18773]**, 708 Third Ave., 24th Fl., New York, NY 10017, (212)599-1320

World Federalist Movement **[IO]**, New York, NY, United States

World Fed. of Advertisers **[IO]**, Brussels, Belgium

World Fed. of Agricultural Workers **[★IO]**

World Fed. of Agriculture, Food, Hotel and Allied Workers **[IO]**, Brussels, Belgium

World Fed. of Amateur Orchestras **[IO]**, Grayslake, IL, United States

World Fed. of Amateur Orchestras **[10766]**, c/o Steve Hobson, 811 Essex Cir., Grayslake, IL 60030, (847)548-6443

World Fed. of Baton Twirling and Majorette Associations **[★23141]**

World Fed. of Bergen-Belsen Associations **[17726]**, PO Box 288, New York, NY 10021, (212)339-6022

World Fed. of Bergen-Belsen Associations **[IO]**, New York, NY, United States

World Fed. of Building Ser. Contractors **[IO]**, Fairfax, VA, United States

World Fed. of Building Ser. Contractors **[2479]**, 10201 Lee Hwy., Ste. 225, Fairfax, VA 22030, (703)359-7090

World Fed. of Catholic Medical Associations **[IO]**, Vatican City, Italy

World Fed. of Chiropractic **[IO]**, Toronto, ON, Canada

World Fed. of Clerical Workers **[IO]**, Brussels, Belgium

World Fed. of the Cossack Natl. Liberation Movement of Cossackia - Defunct.

World Fed. for Culture Collections **[IO]**, Surrey, United Kingdom

World Fed. of Dark Shadows Clubs **[★IO]**

World Fed. of Dark Shadows Clubs **[★25026]**

World Fed. of the Deaf **[IO]**, Helsinki, Finland

World Fed. of Diaconal Associations and Sisterhoods **[★IO]**

World Fed. of Direct Selling Associations **[IO]**, Washington, DC, United States

World Fed. of Direct Selling Associations **[3477]**, 1667 K St. NW, Ste. 1100, Washington, DC 20006, (202)452-8866

World Fed. of Doctors Who Respect Human Life **[IO]**, Ostend, Belgium

World Fed. of Doctors Who Respect Human Life (U.S. Sect.) **[IO]**, Pittsburgh, PA, United States

World Fed. of Doctors Who Respect Human Life (U.S. Sect.) **[16013]**, PO Box 101501, Pittsburgh, PA 15237, (724)444-8045

World Fed. of Engg. Organisations **[IO]**, Paris, France

World Fed. of Estonian Women's Clubs **[IO]**, Forest Hills, NY, United States

World Fed. of Estonian Women's Clubs **[18981]**, c/o Mrs. Juta Kurman, Pres., 68-50 Juno St., Forest Hills, NY 11375, (718)261-9618

World Fed. of Estonian Women's Clubs in Exile **[★18981]**

World Fed. of Estonian Women's Clubs in Exile **[★IO]**

World Fed. of Europeans (By Birth or Descent) - Address unknown since 1995.

World Fed. of Free Latvians **[17997]**, 400 Hurley Ave., Rockville, MD 20850, (301)340-7646

World Fed. of Free Latvians **[IO]**, Rockville, MD, United States

World Fed. of Great Towers **[IO]**, Melbourne, Australia

World Fed. of Hemophilia **[IO]**, Montreal, QC, Canada

World Fed. of Hungarian Artists - Address unknown since 1995.

World Fed. of Hungarian Jews - Address unknown since 2002.

World Fed. of Intl. Music Competitions **[IO]**, Geneva, Switzerland

World Fed. of Investors Corp. **[IO]**, Copenhagen, Denmark

World Fed. of Islamic Missions **[IO]**, Karachi, Pakistan

World Fed. of Jewish Community Centers **[★IO]**

World Fed. of Journalists and Travel Writers **[IO]**, St. Maximin la Sainte Saume, France

World Fed. of Liberal and Radical Youth **[★IO]**

World Fed. for Medical Educ. **[IO]**, Copenhagen, Denmark

World Fed. for Mental Hea. **[IO]**, Springfield, VA, United States

World Fed. for Mental Hea. **[15237]**, 6564 Loisdale Ct., Ste. 301, Springfield, VA 22150-1812, (703)313-8680

World Fed. of Methodist and Uniting Church Women - USA **[20271]**, c/o Mrs. Thelma Johnson, 5915 Desmond St., Cincinnati, OH 45227, (513)271-7557

World Fed. of Methodist and Uniting Church Women - USA **[IO]**, Cincinnati, OH, United States

World Fed. of Methodist Women **[★IO]**

World Fed. of Methodist Women **[★20271]**

World Fed. of Methodist Women, North America Area - Address unknown since 2002.

World Fed. of Neurology **[IO]**, London, United Kingdom

World Fed. of Neurology Res. Gp. on Motor Neuron Diseases **[IO]**, San Francisco, CA, United States

World Fed. of Neurology Res. Gp. on Motor Neuron Diseases **[15373]**, c/o Robert G. Miller, MD, Chm., Dept. of Neurology, 2324 Sacramento St., No. 150, San Francisco, CA 94115, (415)563-4321

World Fed. of Neuroradiological Societies **[16306]**, 2210 Midwest Rd., Ste. 207, Oak Brook, IL 60523-8205, (630)574-0220

World Fed. of Neuroradiological Societies **[IO]**, Oak Brook, IL, United States

World Fed. of Neurosurgical Societies **[IO]**, Stanford, CA, United States

World Fed. of Occupational Therapists **[IO]**, Forrestfield, Australia

World Fed. of Orthodontists **[IO]**, St. Louis, MO, United States

World Fed. of Orthodontists **[14188]**, 401 N Lindbergh Blvd., St. Louis, MO 63141-7816, (314)993-1700

World Fed. of Pipe Line Contractors Associations **[2952]**, c/o Pipe Line Contractors Assn., 1700 Pacific Ave., Ste. 4100, Dallas, TX 75201-4675, (214)969-2700

World Fed. of Pipe Line Contractors Associations **[IO]**, Dallas, TX, United States

World Fed. of Polish Jews, Amer. Sect. **[★19302]**

World Fed. for the Protection of Animals **[★IO]**

World Fed. of Public Hea. Associations **[IO]**, Washington, DC, United States

World Fed. of Public Hea. Associations **[16258]**, c/o Amer. Public Hea. Assn., 800 I St. NW, Washington, DC 20001-3710, (202)777-2490

World Fed. of Sci. Workers **[IO]**, Montreuil, France

World Fed. of Sisterhoods and Deaconals Associations **[★IO]**

World Fed. of Societies of Anaesthesiologists **[IO]**, London, United Kingdom

World Fed. of the Sporting Goods Indus. **[IO]**, Lausanne, Switzerland

World Fed. of Surgical Oncology Societies **[IO]**, Rio de Janeiro, Brazil

World Fed. of Taiwanese Assns. - Address unknown since 1994.

World Fed. of Tech. Organizations **[IO]**, Surrey, BC, Canada

World Fed. of Trade Unions **[IO]**, Athens, Greece

World Fed. of Ukrainian Student Orgs. of Michnowsky - Address unknown since 1995.

World Fed. of Ukrainian Women's Organizations **[IO]**, Toronto, ON, Canada

World Fed. for Ultrasound in Medicine and Biology **[IO]**, Sao Paulo, Brazil

World Fed. of Workers in Food, Tobacco and Hotel Indus. **[★IO]**

World Fed. of YMHAs and Jewish Community Centers **[★IO]**

Reference to "IO" in place of a book number signifies that the association may be found in the 45th edition of International Organizations.

World Fellowship of Buddhists [IO], Bangkok, Thailand

World Fellowship of Slavic Evangelical Christians [IO], River Grove, IL, United States

World Fellowship of Slavic Evangelical Christians [19984], PO Box 59, River Grove, IL 60171, (708)453-7997

World Floor Covering Assn. [3431], 2211 E Howell Ave., Anaheim, CA 92806, (714)978-6440

World Floor Covering Assn. [IO], Anaheim, CA, United States

World Folk Music Assn. [IO], Washington, DC, United States

World Folk Music Assn. [10725], PO Box 40553, Washington, DC 20016, (202)362-2225

World Food Logistics Org. [3985], 1500 King St., Ste. 201, Alexandria, VA 22314, (703)373-4300

World Food Logistics Org. [IO], Alexandria, VA, United States

World Food and Population Crisis Comm. - Defunct.

World Food Programme - Afghanistan [IO], Kabul, Afghanistan

World Food Programme - Algeria [IO], Algiers, Algeria

World Food Programme - Angola [IO], Luanda, Angola

World Food Programme - Armenia [IO], Yerevan, Armenia

World Food Programme - Azerbaijan [IO], Baku, Azerbaijan

World Food Programme - Bangladesh [IO], Dhaka, Bangladesh

World Food Programme - Benin [IO], Cotonou, Benin

World Food Programme - Bhutan [IO], Thimphu, Bhutan

World Food Programme - Bolivia [IO], La Paz, Bolivia

World Food Programme - Burkina Faso [IO], Ouagadougou, Burkina Faso

World Food Programme - Burundi [IO], Bujumbura, Burundi

World Food Programme - Cambodia [IO], Phnom Penh, Cambodia

World Food Programme - Cameroon [IO], Yaounde, Cameroon

World Food Programme - Cape Verde [IO], Praia, Cape Verde

World Food Programme - Central African Republic [IO], Bangui, Central African Republic

World Food Programme - Chad [IO], N'Djamena, Chad

World Food Programme - China [IO], Beijing, People's Republic of China

World Food Programme - Colombia [IO], Bogota, Colombia

World Food Programme - Congo [IO], Brazzaville, Republic of the Congo

World Food Programme - Cote d'Ivoire [IO], Abidjan, Cote d'Ivoire

World Food Programme - Cuba [IO], Havana, Cuba

World Food Programme - Djibouti [IO], Djibouti, Djibouti

World Food Programme - Dominican Republic [IO], Santo Domingo, Dominican Republic

World Food Programme - Ecuador [IO], Quito, Ecuador

World Food Programme - Egypt [IO], Cairo, Egypt

World Food Programme - El Salvador [IO], San Salvador, El Salvador

World Food Programme - Eritrea [IO], Asmara, Eritrea

World Food Programme - Ethiopia [IO], Addis Ababa, Ethiopia

World Food Programme - Gambia [IO], Banjul, Gambia

World Food Programme - Georgia [IO], Tbilisi, Georgia

World Food Programme - Ghana [IO], Accra, Ghana

World Food Programme - Guatemala [IO], Guatemala City, Guatemala

World Food Programme - Guinea [IO], Conakry, Guinea

World Food Programme - Guinea Bissau [IO], Bissau, Guinea-Bissau

World Food Programme - Haiti [IO], Port-au-Prince, Haiti

World Food Programme - Honduras [IO], Tegucigalpa, Honduras

World Food Programme - India [IO], New Delhi, India

World Food Programme - Indonesia [IO], Jakarta, Indonesia

World Food Programme - Iran [IO], Tehran, Iran

World Food Programme - Israel [★IO]

World Food Programme - Italy [IO], Rome, Italy

World Food Programme - Jordan [IO], Amman, Jordan

World Food Programme - Kenya [IO], Nairobi, Kenya

World Food Programme - Korea (DPR) [IO], Pyongyang, Democratic People's Republic of Korea

World Food Programme - Laos [IO], Vientiane, Lao People's Democratic Republic

World Food Programme - Lesotho [IO], Maseru, Lesotho

World Food Programme - Liberia [IO], Monrovia, Liberia

World Food Programme - Madagascar [IO], Antananarivo, Madagascar

World Food Programme - Malawi [IO], Lilongwe, Malawi

World Food Programme - Mali [IO], Bamako, Mali

World Food Programme - Mauritania [IO], Nouakchott, Mauritania

World Food Programme - Mozambique [IO], Maputo, Mozambique

World Food Programme - Myanmar [IO], Yangon, Myanmar

World Food Programme - Nepal [IO], Kathmandu, Nepal

World Food Programme - Nicaragua [IO], Managua, Nicaragua

World Food Programme - Niger [IO], Niamey, Niger

World Food Programme - Occupied Palestinian Territories [IO], Jerusalem, Israel

World Food Programme - Pakistan [IO], Islamabad, Pakistan

World Food Programme - Peru [IO], Lima, Peru

World Food Programme - Russia [IO], Moscow, Russia

World Food Programme - Rwanda [IO], Kigali, Rwanda

World Food Programme - Sao Tome and Principe [IO], Sao Tome, Sao Tome and Principe

World Food Programme - Senegal [IO], Dakar, Senegal

World Food Programme - Sierra Leone [IO], Freetown, Sierra Leone

World Food Programme - Sri Lanka [IO], Colombo, Sri Lanka

World Food Programme - Sudan [IO], Khartoum, Sudan

World Food Programme - Swaziland [IO], Mbabane, Swaziland

World Food Programme - Syria [IO], Damascus, Syrian Arab Republic

World Food Programme - Tajikistan [IO], Dushanbe, Tajikistan

World Food Programme - Tanzania [IO], Dar es Salaam, United Republic of Tanzania

World Food Programme - Thailand [IO], Bangkok, Thailand

World Food Programme - Uganda [IO], Kampala, Uganda

World Food Programme - United Arab Emirates [IO], Dubai, United Arab Emirates

World Food Programme - Yemen [IO], Sana'a, Yemen

World Food Programme - Zambia [IO], Lusaka, Zambia

World Food Programme - Zimbabwe [IO], Harare, Zimbabwe

World Footbag Assn. [IO], Steamboat Springs, CO, United States

World Footbag Assn. [23426], PO Box 775208, Steamboat Springs, CO 80477, (970)870-9898

World Forest Inst. [1658], c/o World Forestry Center, 4033 SW Canyon Rd., Portland, OR 97221, (503)488-2130

World Forest Institute [IO], Portland, OR, United States

World Forestry Center [IO], Portland, OR, United States

World Forestry Center [4701], 4033 SW Canyon Rd., Portland, OR 97221, (503)228-1367

World Found; Pax [★17845]

World Foundrymen Org. [IO], Zurich, Switzerland

World Foundrymen Org. - United Kingdom [IO], West Bromwich, United Kingdom

World Franchise Coun. [IO], Paris, France

World Freestyle Watercraft Alliance [IO], Duncansville, PA, United States

World Freestyle Watercraft Alliance [23983], 1060 Old Rte. 220 S, Duncansville, PA 16635, (734)652-1481

World Friendship Assn. - Address unknown since 1995.

World Future Soc. [7107], 7910 Woodmont Ave., Ste. 450, Bethesda, MD 20814, (301)656-8274

World Future Soc. [IO], Bethesda, MD, United States

World Gastroenterology Org. [IO], Munich, Germany

World Gathering of Jewish Holocaust Survivors [★17712]

World Glacier Monitoring Ser. [IO], Zurich, Switzerland

World Gold Coun. [IO], New York, NY, United States

World Gold Coun. [2746], 444 Madison Ave., New York, NY 10022, (212)317-3800

World Goodwill - Commonwealth [IO], Geneva, Switzerland

World Goodwill - USA [IO], New York, NY, United States

World Goodwill - USA [17739], 120 Wall St., 24th Fl., New York, NY 10005, (212)292-0707

World Gospel Mission [20413], PO Box 948, Marion, IN 46952-0948, (765)664-7331

World Gospel Mission [IO], Marion, IN, United States

World Govt. of the Age of Enlightenment - U.S. - Address unknown since 2004.

World Govt; Assn. for Educ. in [★17620]

World Govt. of World Citizens [★18318]

World Govt. of World Citizens [★IO]

World GRID Assn. - Address unknown since 1994.

World Head of Family Sokeship Coun. [23614], 6035 Ft. Caroline Rd., Ste. 22, Jacksonville, FL 32277

World Health Found., U.S.A. - Defunct.

World Hea. Org. [IO], Geneva, Switzerland

World Health Organization
  Natl. Woodie Club [21739]
  Pan Amer. Sanitary Bur. [14593]

World Health Org. Collaborating Centre on AIDS - Defunct.

World Hea. Org. - Regional Off. for the Eastern Mediterranean [IO], Cairo, Egypt

World Hea. Org. - Regional Off. for Europe [IO], Copenhagen, Denmark

World Hea. Org. - Regional Off. for South-East Asia [IO], New Delhi, India

World Hea. Org. - Regional Off. for the Western Pacific [IO], Manila, Philippines

World Hea. Org. - Zimbabwe [IO], Harare, Zimbabwe

World Heart Fed. [IO], Geneva, Switzerland

World Hemophilia AIDS Center - Address unknown since 1999.

World Heritage [8634], 10725 Boston St., Henderson, CO 80640, (303)252-8215

World Heritage [IO], Henderson, CO, United States

World Heritage Alliance [IO], Washington, DC, United States

World Heritage Alliance [10077], c/o United Nations Found., 1225 Connecticut Ave., 4th Fl., Washington, DC 20036, (202)887-9040

World Heritage Centre [IO], Paris, France

World History Assn. [IO], Honolulu, HI, United States

World History Assn. [10166], Univ. of Hawaii at Manoa, Sakamaki Hall A-203, 2530 Dole St., Honolulu, HI 96822, (808)956-7688

World Holstein-Friesian Fed. [IO], Leuven, Belgium

World Home Bible League [★IO]

World Home Bible League [★19510]

A star before a book entry number signifies that the name is not listed separately, but is mentioned within the entry.

World Homecare and Hospice Org. [14844], PO Box 91486, Washington, DC 20090, (202)547-7424

World Homecare and Hospice Org. [IO], Washington, DC, United States

World Hope Intl. [IO], Alexandria, VA, United States

World Hope Intl. [20292], 625 Slaters Ln., Ste. 200, Alexandria, VA 22314, (703)923-9414

World House [IO], Bielefeld, Germany

World Humor and Irony Membership [★IO]

World Humor and Irony Membership [★10210]

World Humor and Irony Movement [★10210]

World Humor and Irony Movement [★IO]

World Hunger Educ. Ser. [IO], Washington, DC, United States

World Hunger Educ. Ser. [17798], PO Box 29056, Washington, DC 20017, (202)269-6322

World Hunger/Global Development Program - Defunct.

World Hunger Year [17799], 505 8th Ave., Ste. 2100, New York, NY 10018, (212)629-8850

World Hunger Year [IO], New York, NY, United States

World Hypertension League [IO], Gaithersburg, MD, United States

World Hypertension League [14912], c/o Claude Lenfant, MD, Pres., PO Box 83027, Gaithersburg, MD 20883-3027, (301)926-1938

World Impact [20414], 2001 S Vermont Ave., Los Angeles, CA 90007, (323)735-1137

World Impact [IO], Los Angeles, CA, United States

World Info. Ser. on Energy [IO], Amsterdam, Netherlands

World Information Service on Energy - Washington - Address unknown since 1991.

World Information Systems Exchange - Defunct.

World Inst. for Advanced Phenomenological Res. and Learning [10840], 1 Ivy Pointe Way, Hanover, NH 03755, (802)295-3487

World Inst. for Advanced Phenomenological Res. and Learning [IO], Hanover, NH, United States

World Inst. of Black Communications/CEBA Awards - Defunct.

World Inst. Coun. - Defunct.

World Inst. for Development Economics Res. of the United Nations Univ. [IO], Helsinki, Finland

World Inst. on Disability [IO], Oakland, CA, United States

World Inst. on Disability [11996], 510 16th St., Ste. 100, Oakland, CA 94612, (510)763-4100

World Inst. of Holistic Therapies [★14829]

World Inst. for Scientific Humanism - Defunct.

World Inst. for World Peace - Defunct.

World Intellectual Property Org. [IO], Geneva, Switzerland

World Interfaith Relations Comm. - Defunct.

World Intl. Medical Assn. - Address unknown since 1995.

World Intl. Nail and Beauty Assn. [1088], 1221 N Lake View Ave., Anaheim, CA 92807, (714)779-9892

World Intl. Nail and Beauty Assn. [IO], Anaheim, CA, United States

World Internet Numismatic Soc. [IO], St. Louis, MO, United States

World Internet Numismatic Soc. [22768], PO Box 220904, St. Louis, MO 63122

World Investigators Network [2327], c/o Mrs. Carolyn Ward, Exec. Dir., 7501 Sparrows Point Blvd., Baltimore, MD 21219, (410)477-8879

World Investigators Network [IO], Baltimore, MD, United States

World Jazz Assn. - Defunct.

World Jeet Kune Do Fed. [23615], PO Box 52820, Tulsa, OK 74152-0820

World Jersey Cattle Bur. [IO], Jersey, United Kingdom

World Jewish Cong., Amer. Sect. [IO], New York, NY, United States

World Jewish Cong., Amer. Sect. [17955], 501 Madison Ave., 17th Fl., New York, NY 10022, (212)755-5770

World Jewish Genealogy Org. [21158], PO Box 420, Brooklyn, NY 11219, (718)435-4400

World Jewish Genealogy Org. [IO], Brooklyn, NY, United States

World Jewish Relief [IO], London, United Kingdom

World Juggling Fed. [23558], 8370 W Cheyenne Ave., No. 109-286, Las Vegas, NV 89129, (702)866-9516

World Jurist Assn. [5875], 7910 Woodmont Ave., Ste. 1440, Bethesda, MD 20814, (202)466-5428

World Jurist Assn. [IO], Washington, DC, United States

World Karate Fed. [IO], Athens, Greece

World Kouk Sun Do Soc. [IO], West Hartford, CT, United States

World Kouk Sun Do Soc. [10294], 45 S Main St., Ste. 90, West Hartford, CT 06107-2402, (860)523-5260

World Law; Pierce Butler, Jr. Found. for Educ. in [★18834]

World Learning [8635], PO Box 676, Brattleboro, VT 05302-0676, (802)257-7751

World Learning [IO], Brattleboro, VT, United States

World Libertarian Order [18019], PO Box 1911, Las Vegas, NV 89125

World Life Saving [★IO]

World Listening Service - Defunct.

World Literacy of Canada [IO], Toronto, ON, Canada

World Literacy, Inc. [★IO]

World Literacy, Inc. [★7918]

World Literature Ministries [19832], c/o CRC Publications, 2850 Kalamazoo Ave. SE, Grand Rapids, MI 49560, (616)224-0819

World Literature Ministries [IO], Grand Rapids, MI, United States

World Literature Ministries; Christian Reformed Church [★19832]

World Lottery Assn. - Canada [IO], Montreal, QC, Canada

World LP Gas Assn. [IO], Paris, France

World Magnetic Survey - Defunct.

World Mgt. Coun. - Address unknown since 1999.

World Manx Association [★19223]

World Manx Association [★IO]

World Mariculture Soc. [★IO]

World Mariculture Soc. [★4185]

World Marrow Donor Assn. [IO], Leiden, Netherlands

World Martial Arts Assn. [IO], Santa Barbara, CA, United States

World Martial Arts Assn. [23616], PO Box 1568, Santa Barbara, CA 93102, (805)569-1389

World Masters Athletics [IO], Hemel Hempstead, United Kingdom

World Masters Cross-Country Ski Assn. [IO], Bend, OR, United States

World Masters Cross-Country Ski Assn. [23763], c/o John Downing, Founder, PO Box 604, Bend, OR 97709, (541)317-0217

World Media Assn. [18035], 3600 New York Ave. NE, 3rd Fl., Washington, DC 20002, (202)636-3124

World Media Assn. [IO], Washington, DC, United States

World Medical Assn. [IO], Ferney-Voltaire, France

World Medical Corps [★IO]

World Medical Corps [★12862]

World Medical Mission [20245], c/o Samaritan's Purse, PO Box 3000, Boone, NC 28607, (828)262-1980

World Medical Mission [IO], Boone, NC, United States

World Medical Relief [IO], Detroit, MI, United States

World Medical Relief [12544], 11745 Rosa Park Blvd., Detroit, MI 48206-1270, (313)866-5333

World Meeting Planners Cong. and Exposition - Defunct.

World Mercy Fund [12886], PO Box 227, Waterford, VA 20197-0227, (540)882-3226

World Mercy Fund [IO], Waterford, VA, United States

World Meteorological Org. [IO], Geneva, Switzerland

World Methodist Coun. [IO], Lake Junaluska, NC, United States

World Methodist Coun. [20272], PO Box 518, Lake Junaluska, NC 28745, (828)456-9432

World Methodist Historical Soc. [20273], PO Box 127, Madison, NJ 07940, (973)408-3189

World Methodist Historical Soc. [IO], Madison, NJ, United States

World of Michael Jackson - Address unknown since 1995.

World Miniature Warbird Assn. [22662], c/o Ed Irons, Sec./Ed., 7100 Cottonwood Dr., Grant, FL 32949, (321)724-0584

World Miniature Warbird Association [IO], Grant, FL, United States

World Mission Fellowship - Address unknown since 2006.

World Mission Prayer League [20234], 232 Clifton Ave., Minneapolis, MN 55403-3497, (612)871-6843

World Mission Prayer League [IO], Minneapolis, MN, United States

World Modeling Assn. - Address unknown since 2002.

World Modern Arnis Alliance [23617], PO Box 5, West Seneca, NY 14224, (716)675-0899

World Movement of Christian Workers [IO], Brussels, Belgium

World Movement of Mothers [IO], Paris, France

World Muscle Soc. [IO], Ankara, Turkey

World Music Contest Found., Kerkrade [IO], Kerkrade, Netherlands

World Nature Assn. - Defunct.

World Needs Committee; Chemical Res. Applied to [★6697]

World Needs Committee; Chemical Res. Applied to [★IO]

World Neighbors [IO], Oklahoma City, OK, United States

World Neighbors [17921], 4127 NW 122nd St., Oklahoma City, OK 73120-9933, (405)752-9700

World Neighbors - Southeast Asia [IO], Bali, Indonesia

World Ninepin Bowling Assn. [IO], Hagen, Germany

World Notables

Aaron Burr Accord [11097]

Aaron Burr Assn. [11098]

Abigail Adams Historical Soc. Inc. [11099]

Abraham Lincoln Assn. [11100]

Albert Schweitzer Fellowship [11101]

Amer. Beethoven Soc. [9803]

Amer. Friends of Lafayette [11102]

Bolivarian Soc. of the U.S. [11103]

Buckminster Fuller Inst. [11104]

Buffalo Bill Historical Center [11105]

C.A.L./N-X-211 Collectors Soc. [11106]

Calvin Coolidge Memorial Found. [11107]

Captain Eddie Premier Gala [11108]

Churchill Centre [11109]

Edison Birthplace Assn. [11110]

Franklin and Eleanor Roosevelt Inst. [11111]

Frederick A. Cook Soc. [11112]

Friends of the Abraham Lincoln Museum [11113]

Friends of Franklin [11114]

Friends of Patrick Henry [11115]

Friends of Peace Pilgrim [11116]

Friends of Peace Pilgrim [IO]

Gabriel Garcia Moreno Memorial Association [IO]

Gabriel Garcia Moreno Memorial Assn. [11117]

George C. Marshall Found. [11118]

Hall of Fame for Great Americans [11119]

Harry S. Truman Lib. Inst. for Natl. and Intl. Affairs [11120]

Harry S. Truman Lib. Inst. for Natl. and Intl. Affairs [IO]

Henry Clay Memorial Found. [11121]

Herbert Hoover Presidential Lib. Assn. [11122]

Horatio Alger Assn. of Distinguished Americans [20712]

Houdini Historical Center/Outagamie County Historical Soc. [11123]

Intl. Soc. for Hildegard Von Bingen Stud. [11124]

Intl. Soc. for Hildegard Von Bingen Stud. [IO]

James Beard Found. [11125]

James Buchanan Found. for the Preservation of Wheatland [11126]

James K. Polk Memorial Assn. [11127]

James Monroe Memorial Found. [11128]

Jefferson Davis Assn. [11129]

John Ericsson Soc. [11130]

John Pelham Historical Assn. [11131]

Kahlil Gibran Memorial Found. [11132]

Ladies' Hermitage Assn. [11133]

Leif Ericson Viking Ship [11134]

Reference to "IO" in place of a book number signifies that the association may be found in the 45th edition of International Organizations.

Little Bighorn History Alliance [11135]
Maria Mitchell Assn. [6509]
Mark Twain Home Found. [9686]
Martin Van Buren Fan Club [11136]
Morris-Jumel Mansion [11137]
Mount Vernon Ladies' Assn. [11138]
Napoleonic Historical Soc. [11139]
Natl. Register of Prominent Americans and Intl. Notables [11140]
Natl. Register of Prominent Americans and Intl. Notables [IO]
Patton Soc. [11141]
Pres. Benjamin Harrison Found. [11142]
Rachel Carson Homestead Assn. [11143]
Richard the III Found. [11144]
Richard III Soc., Amer. Br. [11145]
Robert E. Lee Memorial Assn. [11146]
Ronald Reagan Home Preservation Found. [11147]
Rutherford B. Hayes Presidential Center [11148]
Sam Davis Memorial Assn. [11149]
San Martin Soc. of U.S.A., Washington DC [11150]
Societe Jean-Jacques Rousseau [IO]
Tesla Memorial Soc. [IO]
Tesla Memorial Soc. [11151]
Theodore Roosevelt Assn. [11152]
Thomas Jefferson's Poplar Forest [10069]
Thomas Paine Natl. Historical Assn. [11153]
Ulysses S. Grant Assn. [11154]
William Cobbett Soc. [IO]
Woodrow Wilson Presidential Lib. Found. [11155]
World Nuclear Assn. [IO], London, United Kingdom
World Ocean and Cruise Liner Soc. [IO], Northport, NY, United States
World Ocean and Cruise Liner Soc. [23020], PO Box 329, Northport, NY 11768, (631)261-5556
World Olympians Assn. [23639], 1750 E Boulder St., Colorado Springs, CO 80909-5724, (719)866-4989
World Olympians Assn. [IO], Miami, FL, United States
World Opportunities [IO], Century City, CA, United States
World Opportunities [20415]
World Order; Fund for Educ. in [★18834]
World Order; Inst. for [★17620]
World Order Models Project - Address unknown since 2003.
World Order; Parliamentarians for [★17433]
World Org. Against Torture [IO], Geneva, Switzerland
World Org. for Animal Hea. [IO], Paris, France
World Org. of Gen. Systems and Cybernetics [★IO]
World Org. Ovulation Method Billings [IO], North Fitzroy, Australia
World Org. Ovulation Method Billings, Argentina [IO], Buenos Aires, Argentina
World Org. Ovulation Method Billings, Canada [IO], Coquitlam, BC, Canada
World Org. Ovulation Method Billings, Italy [IO], Rome, Italy
World Org. of Systems and Cybernetics [IO], Reading, United Kingdom
World Org. Against Torture USA [★IO]
World Org. Against Torture USA [★12381]
World Org. of Bnei Akiva [★20178]
World Org. of China Painters [22177], 2641 NW 10th St., Oklahoma City, OK 73107-5400, (405)521-1234
World Org. of China Painters [IO], Oklahoma City, OK, United States
World Org. for Digestive Endoscopy [IO], Munich, Germany
World Org. of Dredging Associations [IO], Vancouver, WA, United States
World Org. of Dredging Associations [2597], c/o Western Dredging Assn., PO Box 5797, Vancouver, WA 98668-5797, (360)750-0209
World Org. for Early Childhood Educ. [IO], Quebec, QC, Canada
World Org. for Early Childhood Educ. U.S. Natl. Comm. [8071], c/o Dr. Cathy Mogharreban, Treas., PO Box 1436, Fairhope, AL 36533, (618)453-4246
World Org. of Family Doctors [IO], Singapore, Singapore

World Org. for Human Potential [IO], Wyndmoor, PA, United States
World Org. for Human Potential [11550], 8801 Stenton Ave., Wyndmoor, PA 19038, (215)233-2050
World Org. for Human Rights USA [12381], 2029 P St. NW, Ste. 301, Washington, DC 20036, (202)296-5702
World Org. for Human Rights USA [IO], Washington, DC, United States
World Org. for Jews From Arab Countries - Defunct.
World Org. for Modelship Building and Modelship Sport [IO], Vienna, Austria
World Org. of Natl. Colleges, Academies, and Academic Associations of Gen. Practitioners/Family Physicians [★IO]
World Org. of the Ovulation Method-Billings, U.S.A. [★12637]
World Org. and Public Educ. Corp. of the Natl. Assn. for the Advancement of Psychoanalysis [16116], 80 8th Ave., Ste. 1501, New York, NY 10011-5126, (212)741-0515
World Org. and Public Educ. Corp. of the Natl. Assn. for the Advancement of Psychoanalysis [IO], New York, NY, United States
World Org. for Rights, Literature and Development; Women's [18822]
World Org. of the Scout Movement [IO], Geneva, Switzerland
World Org. for Specialized Stud. on Diseases of the Esophagus [IO], Paris, France
World Org. of Webmasters [IO], Folsom, CA, United States
World Org. of Webmasters [2114], PO Box 143, Folsom, CA 95630, (916)989-2933
World Org. of Young Esperantists [IO], Rotterdam, Netherlands
World Orphans [IO], Colorado Springs, CO, United States
World Orphans [11667], 1880 Off. Club Pointe, Ste. 2100, Colorado Springs, CO 80920, (719)487-1700
World ORT [IO], Geneva, Switzerland
World Paper Currency Collectors - Address unknown since 2001.
World Parkinson Disease Assn. [IO], Milan, Italy
World Parks [IO], Washington, DC, United States
World Parks [4617], 2806 P St. NW, Washington, DC 20007, (202)333-1044
World Partners Adoption [11263], c/o Cindy Harding, Exec. Dir., 2205 Summit Oaks Ct., Lawrenceville, GA 30043, (770)962-7860
World Partners Adoption [IO], Lawrenceville, GA, United States
World Peace Bell Assn. U.S.A. - Address unknown since 2006.
World Peace Brigade, North Amer. Regional Coun. - Defunct.
World Peace; Department of Social Development and [★19613]
World Peace; Department of Social Development and [★IO]
World Peace Found. [IO], Cambridge, MA, United States
World Peace Found. [17922], PO Box 382144, Cambridge, MA 02238, (617)496-9812
World Peace Inst. - Defunct.
World Peace One [12367], 5100 Penn Ave., 3rd Fl., Pittsburgh, PA 15224, (412)661-0805
World Peace One [IO], Pittsburgh, PA, United States
World Peace Prayer Soc. [IO], Wassaic, NY, United States
World Peace Prayer Soc. [18258], c/o The World Peace Sanctuary, 26 Benton Rd., Wassaic, NY 12592, (845)877-6093
World Peace; Serendipity Assn. for Res. and Implementation of Holistic Hea. and [★14832]
World Peace; Soc. of Prayer for [★18258]
World Peace Tax Fund Steering Comm. [★18712]
World Peace Tax Fund; Suffolk County Comm. for a [★18716]
World Peace Through Law Center [★5875]
World Peace Through Law Center [★IO]
World Peace Through Tech. Org. [IO], San Francisco, CA, United States
World Peace Through Tech. Org. [7458], 150 Folsom St., San Francisco, CA 94105, (415)371-8706

World Peacemakers [18176], 11427 Scottsbury Terr. Germantown, MD 20876-6010, (301)972-4041
World Peacemakers [IO], Germantown, MD, United States
World Peacemakers - A Division of Every Church A Peace Church [★IO]
World Peacemakers - A Division of Every Church A Peace Church [★18176]
World Pen Pals [8636], PO Box 337, Saugerties, NY 12477, (845)246-7828
World Pen Pals [IO], Saugerties, NY, United States
World Petroleum Cong. - A Forum for Petroleum Sci., Tech., Economics and Mgt. [★IO]
World Petroleum Coun. - The Global Forum for Oil and Gas Sci., Tech., Economics and Mgt. [IO], London, United Kingdom
World Pets Soc. [★IO]
World Pets Soc. [★5404]
World Pheasant Assn. [IO], Fordingbridge, United Kingdom
World Pheasant Assn. of the U.S.A. - Address unknown since 1994.
World Phenomenology Inst. [★10840]
World Phenomenology Inst. [★IO]
World Photography Soc. - Address unknown since 1994.
World Piano Competition [10726], 441 Vine St., Ste. 1030, Cincinnati, OH 45202, (513)421-5342
World Ploughing Org. [IO], Hall, Netherlands
World Plumbing Coun. [IO], Hornchurch, United Kingdom
World Poetry Therapy Assn. [★16223]
World Poker Assn. [22902], 848 N Rainbow Blvd., Ste. 1000, Las Vegas, NV 89107, (702)952-2460
World Policy Inst. [17620], 66 5th Ave., 9th Fl., New York, NY 10011, (212)229-5808
World Policy Inst. [IO], New York, NY, United States
World Population Emergency Campaign [★12187]
World Population Soc. - Address unknown since 2003.
World Power Conf. [★IO]
World Prayer Center [★19553]
World Presbyterian Missions [★20468]
World Presbyterian Missions [★IO]
World Preserve [IO], Clermont, FL, United States
World Preserve [4476], 782 S Grand Hwy., Clermont, FL 34711, (352)406-7128
World Presidents' Org. [768], 110 S Union St., Ste. 200, Alexandria, VA 22314-3351, (703)684-4900
World Presidents' Org. [IO], Alexandria, VA, United States
World Press Freedom Comm. [IO], Reston, VA, United States
World Press Freedom Comm. [17201], 11690-C Sunrise Valley Dr., Reston, VA 20191, (703)715-9811
World Press Inst. [17202], Macalester Coll., 1576 Summit Ave., St. Paul, MN 55105, (651)696-6360
World Press Inst. [IO], St. Paul, MN, United States
World Print Coun. - Defunct.
World Priorities [18485], c/o Mr. James Sivard, Asst. Dir., 38664 Mt. Gilead Rd., Leesburg, VA 20175, (703)777-4352
World Priorities [IO], Washington, DC, United States
World Pro Skiing-Racers Assn. - Defunct.
World Processing Tomato Coun. [IO], Avignon, France
World Professional Armwrestling Assn. - Defunct.
World Professional Assn. for Transgender Hea. [13103], c/o Tara L. Tieso, Exec. Admin., 1300 S Second St., Ste. 180, Minneapolis, MN 55454, (612)624-9397
World Professional Assn. for Transgender Hea. [IO], Minneapolis, MN, United States
World Professional Squash Assn. [★IO]
World Proof Numismatic Assn. [IO], Pittsburgh, PA, United States
World Proof Numismatic Assn. [22769], PO Box 4094, Pittsburgh, PA 15201-0094
World Psychiatric Assn. [16100], c/o Prof. Juan E. Mezzich, Jr., Pres., Intl. Center for Mental Hea., Mt. Sinai School of Medicine of New York Univ., Fifth Ave. & 100th St., Box 1093, New York, NY 10029-6574, (718)334-5094
World Psychiatric Assn. [IO], New York, NY, United States

A star before a book entry number signifies that the name is not listed separately, but is mentioned within the entry.

World Pumpkin Confed. - Address unknown since 2004.

World Rabbinic Comm. for the Preservation of Ancient Tombs in Tiberias - Address unknown since 1988.

World Rabbit Sci. Assn. [IO], Corrosnac, France

World Radio Missionary Fellowship [★IO]

World Radio Missionary Fellowship [★20344]

World Rainforest Movement [★IO]

World Reform; Parliamentarians Global Action for Disarmament, Development, and [★17433]

World Refugee Fund [★18318]

World Refugee Fund [★IO]

World Rehabilitation Fund [IO], New York, NY, United States

World Rehabilitation Fund [11997], 16 E 40th St., Ste. 704, New York, NY 10016, (212)532-6000

World Relief [19985], 7 E Baltimore St., Baltimore, MD 21202, (443)451-1900

World Relief [IO], Baltimore, MD, United States

World Relief Commn. [★IO]

World Relief Commn. [★19985]

World Relief Commn; NAE [★19985]

World Relief Commn. of the Natl. Assn. of Evangelicals [★19985]

World Relief Commn. of the Natl. Assn. of Evangelicals [★IO]

World Relief; Episcopal Church's Presiding Bishop's Fund for [★12852]

World Relief Friendship Found. [★13171]

World Relief Friendship Found. [★IO]

World Res. Found. [IO], Sedona, AZ, United States

World Res. Found. [14604], 41 Bell Rock Plz., Sedona, AZ 86351, (928)284-3300

World Res., Inc. - Address unknown since 2003.

World Resources Inst. [4477], 10 G St. NE, Ste. 800, Washington, DC 20002, (202)729-7600

World Resources Inst. [IO], Washington, DC, United States

World Road Assn. - France [IO], Paris, France

World Robotic Boxing Assn. [1328]

World Rock 'n' Roll Confed. [IO], Ljubljana, Slovenia

World Rock Paper Scissors Soc. [IO], Toronto, ON, Canada

World Safety Org. [IO], Warrensburg, MO, United States

World Safety Org. [18582], 106 W Young Ave., Ste. G, PO Box 518, Warrensburg, MO 64093, (660)747-3132

World Safety Res. Inst. - Defunct.

World Salt Found. [20416], 6810 Lee St., Hollywood, FL 33024, (954)964-2799

World Salt Found. [IO], Hollywood, FL, United States

World Sand Sculptors Assn. [22972]

World Sci. Fiction Soc. [10950], PO Box 426159, Cambridge, MA 02142

World Sci. Fiction Soc. [IO], Cambridge, MA, United States

World Sci. and Engg. Acad. and Soc. [IO], Dallas, TX, United States

World Sci. and Engg. Acad. and Soc. [7054], c/o Yodvadee Hudak, 10650 N Central Expy., Dallas, TX 75231

World Scout Bur. [IO], Geneva, Switzerland

World Scout Found. [IO], Geneva, Switzerland

World Scout Organization [★9914]

World Secret Ser. Assn. [★IO]

World Seed Indus. Org. [★IO]

World Self-Medication Indus. [IO], Ferney-Voltaire, France

World Senior Golf Fed. [IO], Westminster, CO, United States

World Senior Golf Fed. [23472], c/o Sherry Clark, Exec. Dir., PO Box 350667, Westminster, CO 80035-0667, (303)920-4206

World Ser. Authority [18318], World Off., 1012 14th St. NW, Ste. 205, Washington, DC 20005, (202)638-2662

World Ser. Authority [IO], Washington, DC, United States

World Ser. Authority of the World Govt. of World Citizens [★IO]

World Ser. Authority of the World Govt. of World Citizens [★18318]

World Ser; Seventh-Day Adventist [★12826]

World SHARE - Address unknown since 2006.

World Ship Soc. [IO], Gravesend, United Kingdom

World Ship Trust - United Kingdom [IO], London, United Kingdom

World Shoe Association [IO], Encino, CA, United States

World Shoe Assn. [260], 15821 Ventura Blvd., Ste. 415, Encino, CA 91436, (818)379-9400

World Shortwave Listeners Club - Defunct.

World Sidereal Res. Found. - Defunct.

World Sign Associates [1201]

World Sign Associates [IO], Westminster, CO, United States

World Sikh Org. [IO], Ottawa, ON, Canada

World Ski Assn. - Address unknown since 2004.

World Small Animal Veterinary Assn. [IO], Copenhagen, Denmark

World Smart [★IO]

World Smart [★16486]

World Snooker [IO], Bristol, United Kingdom

World Socialist Party - Ireland [★IO]

World Socialist Party - New Zealand [IO], Auckland, New Zealand

World Socialist Party of the U.S. [18339], PO Box 440247, West Somerville, MA 02144, (617)628-9096

World Soc. of the Abdominal Compartment Syndrome [IO], Antwerp, Belgium

World Soc. for Ekistics [IO], Athens, Greece

World Soc. of Mixed Jurisdiction Jurists [IO], New Orleans, LA, United States

World Soc. of Mixed Jurisdiction Jurists [5957], c/o Prof. Vernon Palmer, Pres., Tulane Law School, 6329 Freret St., New Orleans, LA 70118, (504)865-5978

World Soc. for the Protection of Animals [11480], 34 Deloss St., Framingham, MA 01702, (508)879-8350

World Soc. for the Protection of Animals [IO], Framingham, MA, United States

World Soc. for the Protection of Animals - Australia [IO], St. Leonards, Australia

World Soc. for the Protection of Animals - Brazil [IO], Rio de Janeiro, Brazil

World Soc. for the Protection of Animals - Canada [IO], Toronto, ON, Canada

World Soc. for the Protection of Animals - Colombia [IO], Bogota, Colombia

World Soc. for the Protection of Animals - Costa Rica [IO], Heredia, Costa Rica

World Soc. for the Protection of Animals - Denmark [IO], Copenhagen, Denmark

World Soc. for the Protection of Animals - England [IO], London, United Kingdom

World Soc. for the Protection of Animals - Germany [IO], Bonn, Germany

World Soc. for the Protection of Animals - Netherlands [IO], Utrecht, Netherlands

World Soc. for the Protection of Animals - New Zealand [IO], Auckland, New Zealand

World Soc. for Stereotactic and Functional Neurosurgery [IO], Newark, NJ, United States

World Soc. for Stereotactic and Functional Neurosurgery [15418], c/o Michael Schulder, MD, Asst. Sec.-Treas., UMDNJ-New Jersey Medical School, 90 Bergen St., Ste. 8100, Newark, NJ 07103, (973)972-2907

World Soc. for Stereotactic and Functional Neurosurgery - Canada [IO], Toronto, ON, Canada

World Soc. of Victimology [IO], Ibaraki, Japan

World Solidarity [IO], Brussels, Belgium

World Spanish Cong. [IO], Leonia, NJ, United States

World Spanish Cong. [19393], PO Box 42, Leonia, NJ 07605, (201)567-7417

World Spine Soc. [15405], 22 Calendar Ct., 2nd Fl., La Grange, IL 60525

World Spine Soc. [IO], La Grange, IL, United States

World Spiritual Assembly - Address unknown since 2001.

World Spiritual Coun. - Address unknown since 1995.

World Sport Stacking Assn. [23868], PO Box 260526, Highlands Ranch, CO 80163-0526, (303)917-4171

World Sport Stacking Association [IO], Highlands Ranch, CO, United States

World Sports Medicine Assn. of Registered Therapists [IO], Newport Beach, CA, United States

World Sports Medicine Assn. of Registered Therapists [16486], 206 Marine Ave., PO Box 5642, Newport Beach, CA 92662, (626)445-1978

World Squash Fed. [IO], Hastings, United Kingdom

World Stereotactic Soc. [★IO]

World Stereotactic Soc. [★15418]

World Sugar Res. Org. [IO], London, United Kingdom

World Summit for Children [★IO]

World Summit for Children [★11658]

World Sustainable Agriculture Assn. [12941], 8554 Melrose Ave., West Hollywood, CA 90069, (310)657-7202

World Sustainable Agriculture Assn. [IO], West Hollywood, CA, United States

World Swing Dance Coun. [IO], Phoenix, AZ, United States

World Swing Dance Coun. [9902], c/o Cathy Tigges, 4401 E Janice Way, Phoenix, AZ 85032, (602)482-2828

World Taekwondo Fed. [IO], Seoul, Republic of Korea

World Tapes for Education - Defunct.

World Team [20417], 1431 Stuckert Rd., Warrington, PA 18976, (215)491-4900

World Team [IO], Warrington, PA, United States

World Technical Volunteers [IO], Dumfries, VA, United States

World Tech. Volunteers [13196], 12522 Sherwood Forest Dr., Culpeper, VA 22701, (571)435-2657

World Teleport Assn. [3766], 55 Broad St., 14th Fl., New York, NY 10004, (212)825-0218

World Teleport Assn. [IO], New York, NY, United States

World Through My Eyes [IO], Gaza, Mozambique

World Timecapsule Fund - Defunct.

World Toilet Org. [IO], Singapore, Singapore

World Tourism Org. [IO], Madrid, Spain

World Trade Center Assn. of Brussels [IO], Brussels, Belgium

World Trade Center Barcelona [IO], Barcelona, Spain

World Trade Center Basel [IO], Basel, Switzerland

World Trade Center Bogota [IO], Bogota, Colombia

World Trade Center Budapest [IO], Budapest, Hungary

World Trade Center Cairo [IO], Cairo, Egypt

World Trade Center Curacao [IO], Curacao, Netherlands Antilles

World Trade Center Eindhoven [IO], Eindhoven, Netherlands

World Trade Center Geneva [IO], Geneva, Switzerland

World Trade Center Genoa [IO], Genoa, Italy

World Trade Center Grenoble [IO], Grenoble, France

World Trade Center Halifax [★IO]

World Trade Center Hamburg [IO], Cologne, Germany

World Trade Center Israel [IO], Tel Aviv, Israel

World Trade Center of Japan [★IO]

World Trade Center Leipzig [IO], Leipzig, Germany

World Trade Center Lille [IO], Lille, France

World Trade Center Madrid [IO], Madrid, Spain

World Trade Center Metro Manila [IO], Pasay City, Philippines

World Trade Center Metz-Sarrebruck [IO], Metz, France

World Trade Center Mexico City [IO], Mexico City, Mexico

World Trade Center Moscow [IO], Moscow, Russia

World Trade Center of New Orleans [IO], New Orleans, LA, United States

World Trade Center of New Orleans [2295], 2 Canal St., Ste. 2900, New Orleans, LA 70130, (504)529-1601

World Trade Center of Nigeria [IO], Lagos, Nigeria

World Trade Center Panama [IO], Panama City, Panama

World Trade Center Paris [IO], Paris, France

World Trade Center Rotterdam [IO], Rotterdam, Netherlands

Reference to "IO" in place of a book number signifies that the association may be found in the 45th edition of International Organizations.

World Trade Center Ruhr Valley [IO], Gelsenkirchen, Germany

World Trade Center Sao Paulo [IO], Sao Paulo, Brazil

World Trade Center Seville [IO], Seville, Spain

World Trade Center Sofia [★IO]

World Trade Center Stockholm [IO], Stockholm, Sweden

World Trade Center Survivors' Network [13311], 22 Cortland St., 20th Fl., New York, NY 10007

World Trade Center Taichung [IO], Taichung, Taiwan

World Trade Center Tokyo [IO], Tokyo, Japan

World Trade Center Tripoli [IO], Tripoli, Libyan Arab Jamahiriya

World Trade Center Vienna Airport [IO], Vienna, Austria

World Trade Center Zurich [IO], Zurich, Switzerland

World Trade Centers Assn. [IO], New York, NY, United States

World Trade Centers Assn. [3850], 420 Lexington Ave., Ste. 518, New York, NY 10170, (212)432-2626

World Trade Centers Assn. of Antwerp [IO], Antwerp, Belgium

World Trade Centre Beijing [IO], Beijing, People's Republic of China

World Trade Centre Johannesburg [IO], Sandton, Republic of South Africa

World Trade Centre Montreal [IO], Montreal, QC, Canada

World Trade Centre Ottawa-Gatineau [IO], Ottawa, ON, Canada

World Trade Centre Shanghai [IO], Shanghai, People's Republic of China

World Trade Centre Shanghai [★IO]

World Trade Centre Vancouver [IO], Vancouver, BC, Canada

World Trade and Convention Centre Halifax [IO], Halifax, NS, Canada

World Trade Org. [IO], Geneva, Switzerland

World Trade Writers Assn. - Address unknown since 1993.

World Traditional Karate Org. [23567], c/o Mr. John J. Mullin, Exec. Chm., 138 Bradley Ave., Staten Island, NY 10314

World Traditional Karate Org. [IO], Staten Island, NY, United States

World Transhumanist Assn. [IO], Willington, CT, United States

World Transhumanist Assn. [7163], PO Box 128, Willington, CT 06279, (860)297-2376

World Travel and Tourism Coun. [IO], London, United Kingdom

World Umpires Association [IO], Neenah, WI, United States

World Umpires Assn. [24019], PO Box 394, Neenah, WI 54957

World Underwater Fed. [IO], Rome, Italy

World Union of Catholic Philosophical Societies [IO], Antigonish, NS, Canada

World Union of Catholic Women's Organisations [IO], Paris, France

World Union of Deists [20531], PO Box 47026, St. Petersburg, FL 33743, (727)239-0933

World Union of Jewish Students [IO], Jerusalem, Israel

World Union of Karatedo Organizations [★IO]

World Union of Nigerians - Address unknown since 1999.

World Union for Progressive Judaism North Am; AZRA/ [20122]

World Union for the Safeguard of Youth - Defunct.

World Union for a Universal Alphabet - Address unknown since 2003.

World Union of Wholesale Markets [IO], The Hague, Netherlands

World Univ. Colleges [★IO]

World Univ. Colleges [★8114]

World Univ. Colleges Consortium [★8114]

World Univ. Colleges Consortium [★IO]

World Univ. Ser. [★IO]

World Univ. Service/U.S.A. - Address unknown since 1999.

World Veterans Fed. [IO], Paris, France

World Veterans Fund - Defunct.

World Veterinary Assn. [IO], Copenhagen, Denmark

World Veterinary Poultry Assn. [IO], Giessen, Germany

World Ving Tsun Athletic Assn. [23618], PO Box 4091, Winter Park, FL 32793, (407)496-0113

World Vision [20418], PO Box 9716, Federal Way, WA 98063-9716, (253)815-1000

World Vision [20488], 800 W Chestnut Ave., Monrovia, CA 91016-3198, (626)303-8811

World Vision [IO], Monrovia, CA, United States

World Vision Armenia [IO], Yerevan, Armenia

World Vision Asia Pacific Region [IO], Bangkok, Thailand

World Vision Australia [IO], Melbourne, Australia

World Vision - Canada [IO], Mississauga, ON, Canada

World Vision Colombia [IO], Bogota, Colombia

World Vision Found. of Thailand [IO], Bangkok, Thailand

World Vision Hong Kong [IO], Hong Kong, People's Republic of China

World Vision India [IO], Chennai, India

World Vision Intl. [★20358]

World Vision Intl. - Azerbaijan [IO], Baku, Azerbaijan

World Vision Intl. - Brazil [IO], Sao Paulo, Brazil

World Vision Intl. - Romania [IO], Bucharest, Romania

World Vision Intl. - Vietnam [IO], Hanoi, Vietnam

World Vision Ireland [IO], Dublin, Ireland

World Vision Japan [IO], Tokyo, Japan

World Vision Malaysia [IO], Petaling Jaya, Malaysia

World Vision Middle East/Eastern Europe [IO], Nicosia, Cyprus

World Vision - New Zealand [IO], Auckland, New Zealand

World Vision Singapore [IO], Singapore, Singapore

World Vision Taiwan [IO], Taipei, Taiwan

World Vision - United Kingdom [IO], Milton Keynes, United Kingdom

World Volunteers [IO], Milan, Italy

World War; Amer. Comm. on the History of the Second [★10167]

World War I Aeroplanes [21490], 15 Crescent Rd., Poughkeepsie, NY 12601, (845)473-3679

World War I Aeroplanes [IO], Poughkeepsie, NY, United States

World War I Overseas Flyers - Defunct.

World War II; Amer. Widows of [★21195]

World War II; Gold Star Wives of [★21195]

World War II Ranger Battalions Assn. - Address unknown since 1999.

World War II War Brides [21205], c/o Ms. Erin Craig, Membership Chair, PO Box 1812, El Centro, CA 92244, (760)352-4191

World War II War Brides [IO], El Centro, CA, United States

World War I

Fed. of French War Veterans [21416]

Great War Assn. [10475]

Natl. Ladies Auxiliary to Veterans of World War I of the U.S.A. [21359]

National Ladies Auxiliary to Veterans of World War I of the U.S.A. [IO]

Veterans of World War I of U.S.A. [21360]

World War I Aeroplanes [21490]

World War Tank Corps Assn. - Address unknown since 1995.

World War II

4th Marine Div. Assn. WWII [21361]

6th Bomb Gp. Assn. [21362]

17th Airborne Div. Assn. [21363]

22nd Bomb Gp. Assn. [21364]

27th Troop Carrier Squadron Found. [21365]

70th Infantry Div. Assn. [21366]

84th Infantry Div., Railsplitter Soc. [21367]

86th Chem. Mortar Battalion Assn. [21368]

94th Infantry Div. Assn. [21369]

99th Infantry Div. Assn. [21370]

106th Infantry Div. Assn. [21371]

106th Infantry Division Association [IO]

147th Engineers Veterans Assn. [21372]

303rd Bomb Gp. (H) Assn. [21373]

325th Glider Infantry Assn. [21374]

369th Fighter Squadron Assn., 359th Fighter Gp. [20654]

397th Bomb Gp. Assn. [21375]

401st Bombardment Gp. (Heavy) Assn. [20656]

452nd Bomb Wing/Group Assn. [21376]

483rd Bombardment Gp. (H) Assn. [21377]

494th Bombardment Gp. (H) Assn. 7th Air Force [20658]

504th Parachute Infantry Regiment Assn. [21378]

508th Parachute Infantry Regiment Assn. [21379]

509th Parachute Infantry Assn. [21380]

517th Parachute Regimental Combat Team Assn. [21381]

526th Armored Infantry Battalion Assn. [21382]

704th Tank Destroyer Battalion Assn. [21383]

829th Signal Ser. Assn. [21384]

Americal Div. Veterans Assn. [21385]

Amer. Defenders of Bataan and Corregidor [21386]

Amer. Merchant Marine Veterans [21387]

Amer. Navion Soc. [21428]

Amer. Rosie the Riveter Assn. [21388]

American Rosie the Riveter Association [IO]

B-26 Marauder Historical Society [IO]

B-26 Marauder Historical Soc. [21389]

Battle of Ormoc Bay Assn. [21390]

Canadian Battlefields Found. [IO]

China-Burma-India Hump Pilot Assn. [21391]

Commemorative Air Force [21438]

Cushman Club of Am. [22676]

Eighth Air Force Historical Soc. [21392]

Fed. of French War Veterans [21416]

First Special Service Force Association [IO]

Flying Tigers of the 14th Air Force Assn. [21393]

George C. Marshall Found. [11118]

Global Alliance for Preserving the History of WWII in Asia [13459]

Global Alliance for Preserving the History of WWII in Asia [IO]

Grosse Pointe War Memorial Assn. [21300]

Intl. B-24 Liberator Club [21394]

Intl. B-24 Liberator Club [IO]

Merrill's Marauders Assn. [21395]

Natl. Alliance of Families for the Return of America's Missing Servicemen [21263]

Natl. World War II Glider Pilots Assn. [21468]

Navajo Code Talkers Assn. [21396]

P-47 Thunderbolt Pilots Assn. [21397]

P-51 Mustang Pilots Assn. [21398]

P-51 Mustang Pilots Assn. [IO]

Patton Soc. [11141]

Pearl Harbor History Associates [10144]

Pearl Harbor Survivors Assn. [21399]

Pilot Class 43-D Assn. [21400]

Polar Bear Assn. of World War II [21401]

PT Boats, Inc. [21402]

PT Boats, Inc. [IO]

Second Air Div. Assn. [21403]

Second World War Aircraft Preservation Soc. [IO]

SHAEF and ETOUSA Veterans Assn. [21404]

Sino-American Cooperative Org. [21405]

Sixth Marine Div. Assn. [21406]

Thanks to Scandinavia [8436]

Topographic Engineers of World War II [21407]

Topographic Engineers of World War II [IO]

U.S. Merchant Marine Veterans of World War II [21408]

U.S. Navy Salvage Divers Reunited [21409]

U.S. Submarine Veterans of World War II [21410]

USS North Carolina Battleship Assn. [21411]

Veterans of the Battle of the Bulge [21412]

Women Airforce Ser. Pilots WWII [21413]

World War Two Stud. Assn. [10167]

World War Two Railway Study Group [IO], Leamington Spa, United Kingdom

World War Two Stud. Assn. [IO], Manhattan, KS, United States

World War Two Stud. Assn. [10167], c/o Prof. Mark Parillo, Dept. of History, Kansas State Univ., Eisenhower Hall, Manhattan, KS 66506-1002, (913)532-0374

World Wars

1st Fighter Assn. [21414]

30th Infantry Div. Assn. [21415]

Fed. of French War Veterans [21416]

Great War Assn. [10475]

Military Order of the World Wars [21417]

A star before a book entry number signifies that the name is not listed separately, but is mentioned within the entry.

Military Order of the World Wars **[IO]**
Military Postal History Soc. **[22847]**
Order of Lafayette **[21418]**
Rainbow Div. Veterans Memorial Found. **[21419]**
Soc. of the 3rd Infantry Div. **[21186]**
World Water Coun. **[IO]**, Marseille, France
World Waterpark Assn. **[IO]**, Overland Park, KS, United States
World Waterpark Assn. **[1329]**, 8826 Santa Fe Dr., Ste. 310, Overland Park, KS 66212, (913)599-0300
World Watusi Assn. **[4297]**, PO Box 14, Crawford, NE 69339-0014, (308)665-3919
World Watusi Assn. **[IO]**, Crawford, NE, United States
World Whale Police **[IO]**, Olympia, WA, United States
World Whale Police **[5285]**, PO Box 814, Olympia, WA 98506, (360)561-7492
World-Wide Acad. of Scholars - Defunct.
World Wide Avon Bottle Collectors Club - Address unknown since 1995.
World Wide Baraca-Philathea Union - Address unknown since 2003.
World Wide Essence Soc. **[14833]**, PO Box 285, Concord, MA 01742, (978)369-8454
World Wide Essence Soc. **[IO]**, Concord, MA, United States
World Wide Fund for Nature - Australia **[★IO]**
World Wide Fund for Nature - India **[IO]**, New Delhi, India
World Wide Fund for Nature Japan **[IO]**, Tokyo, Japan
World Wide Fund for Nature - Malaysia **[IO]**, Selangor, Malaysia
World Wide Fund for Nature - Sweden **[IO]**, Stockholm, Sweden
World Wide Fund for Nature - UK **[★IO]**
World Wide Fund for Nature - WWF Intl. **[IO]**, Gland, Switzerland
World Wide Kennel Club **[IO]**, Mount Vernon, NY, United States
World Wide Kennel Club **[22388]**, PO Box 62, Mount Vernon, NY 10552, (914)771-5219
World-Wide Missions **[20419]**, PO Box 2300, Redlands, CA 92373-0761, (909)793-2009
World-Wide Missions **[IO]**, Redlands, CA, United States
World Wide Opportunities on Organic Farms - Canada **[IO]**, Nelson, BC, Canada
World Wide Opportunities on Organic Farms - Czech Republic **[IO]**, Knezice, Czech Republic
World Wide Opportunities on Organic Farms - Italia **[IO]**, Castagneto Carducci, Italy
World Wide Opportunities on Organic Farms - Korea **[IO]**, Seoul, Republic of Korea
World Wide Opportunities on Organic Farms - Nepal **[IO]**, Kathmandu, Nepal
World Wide Opportunities on Organic Farms - Slovenia **[IO]**, Sencur, Slovenia
World Wide Opportunities on Organic Farms - Sweden **[IO]**, Goteborg, Sweden
World Wide Opportunities on Organic Farms - Switzerland **[IO]**, Maur, Switzerland
World Wide Opportunities on Organic Farms - Uganda **[IO]**, Kampala, Uganda
World Wide Opportunity for Women **[IO]**, Kitchener, ON, Canada
World Wide Pet Indus. Assn. **[IO]**, Monrovia, CA, United States
World Wide Pet Indus. Assn. **[2968]**, 135 W Lemon Ave., Monrovia, CA 91016-2809, (626)447-2222
World Wide Pet Lovers Soc. - Address unknown since 1991.
World Wide Pet Supply Assn. **[★2968]**
World Wide Pet Supply Assn. **[★IO]**
World-Wide Plantation Walker Registry - Address unknown since 1999.
World-Wide Prayer and Missionary Union - Defunct.
World-Wide Stroke Found. - Address unknown since 1988.
World Wide Vermiculture - Defunct.
World Wide Web
   Amer. Assn. of Webmasters **[896]**
   Anti-Child Pornography Org. **[12766]**

Assn. of Sites Advocating Child Protection **[11560]**
eMarketing Assn. **[1166]**
Info. Resources Mgt. Assn. **[2101]**
Intl. Assn. of Employment Web Sites **[1266]**
Intl. Assn. of Webmasters and Designers **[888]**
Intl. Nanocasting Assn. **[562]**
Intl. .NET Assn. **[6771]**
Intl. Webcasting Assn. **[2667]**
Mobile Voter **[18032]**
Search Engine Marketing Professional Org. **[2648]**
Web Analytics Assn. **[7222]**
WECAI Network **[1167]**
World Internet Numismatic Soc. **[22768]**
World Wide Web Consortium **[6756]**, c/o Massachusetts Inst. of Tech., Lab. for Cmpt. Sci. and Artificial Intelligence, 32 Vassar St., Rm. 32-G515, Cambridge, MA 02139, (617)253-2613
World Wide Web Consortium **[IO]**, Cambridge, MA, United States
World-Wide White and Creme Horse Registry **[★4855]**
World Wildlife Fund **[4478]**, PO Box 97180, Washington, DC 20090-7180, (202)293-4800
World Wildlife Fund **[★IO]**
World Wildlife Fund **[★IO]**
World Wildlife Fund **[IO]**, Washington, DC, United States
World Wildlife Fund - Australia **[★IO]**
World Wildlife Fund - Canada **[IO]**, Toronto, ON, Canada
World Wildlife Fund - Denmark **[IO]**, Copenhagen, Denmark
World Wildlife Fund-Japan **[★IO]**
World Wildlife Fund - U.S. **[★IO]**
World Wildlife Fund - U.S. **[★4478]**
World Wildlife Preservation Soc. **[5404]**, 19400 Santa Rita St., Tarzana, CA 91356-3021, (818)345-5140
World Wildlife Preservation Soc. **[IO]**, Tarzana, CA, United States
A World to Win - Defunct.
World Wind Energy Assn. **[IO]**, Bonn, Germany
World Without War Coun. **[18259]**, 1730 Martin Luther King, Jr. Way, Berkeley, CA 94709, (510)845-1992
World Without War Educ. Fund **[★18259]**
World Witness, Foreign Bd. of the Associate Reformed Presbyterian Church **[20420]**, 1 Cleveland St., Ste. 220, Greenville, SC 29601, (864)233-5226
World Witness, Foreign Bd. of the Associate Reformed Presbyterian Church **[IO]**, Greenville, SC, United States
World Woman's Party - Defunct.
World Women Dedicated to the Environment **[★4618]**
World Women in the Environment **[★4618]**
World Work Proj; Serendipity Assn. and How to Make the **[★14832]**
World Young Women's Christian Association **[IO]**, Geneva, Switzerland
World Youth Alliance **[IO]**, New York, NY, United States
World Youth Alliance **[18860]**, 228 E 71st St., New York, NY 10021, (212)585-0757
World Youth Coun. **[★19855]**
World Youth Crusade for Freedom - Address unknown since 1999.
World Youth Forum - Defunct.
World Youth Found. **[IO]**, Melaka, Malaysia
WorldatWork **[IO]**, Scottsdale, AZ, United States
WorldatWork **[1283]**, 14040 N Northsight Blvd., Scottsdale, AZ 85260, (480)951-9191
Worlddidac **[IO]**, Bern, Switzerland
WorldFish Center **[IO]**, Penang, Malaysia
WorldHomes Holiday Exchange **[★IO]**
Worldloppet **[★IO]**
Worldloppet **[★23764]**
Worldloppet/American Birkebeiner **[23764]**, PO Box 911, Hayward, WI 54843, (715)634-5025
Worldloppet/American Birkebeiner **[IO]**, Hayward, WI, United States
World's Christian Endeavor Union **[IO]**, Liberty Corner, NJ, United States

World's Christian Endeavor Union **[19829]**, PO Box 326, Liberty Corner, NJ 07938-0326, (908)604-9440
World's Fair Collectors Soc. **[IO]**, Sarasota, FL, United States
World's Fair Collectors Soc. - Defunct.
World's Fairs
   1904 World's Fair Soc. **[23033]**
World's Poultry Sci. Assn. **[IO]**, Ipswich, United Kingdom
World's Poultry Sci. Assn. - The Netherlands **[IO]**, Beekbergen, Netherlands
World's Poultry Sci. Assn. - UK **[IO]**, Bury St. Edmunds, United Kingdom
World's Poultry Sci. Assn., U.S.A. Br. **[5125]**, c/o Dr. Paul Aho, Sec., Poultry Perspective, 20 Eastwood Rd., Storrs, CT 06268, (860)429-3053
World's Wristwrestling Championship **[★23991]**
WorldServe - Address unknown since 2003.
WorldTeach **[8315]**, c/o Center for Intl. Development, Harvard Univ., 79 John F. Kennedy St., Cambridge, MA 02138, (617)495-5527
WorldVenture **[19503]**, 1501 W Mineral Ave., Littleton, CO 80120-5612, (720)283-2000
WorldVenture **[IO]**, Littleton, CO, United States
WorldViews - Defunct.
Worldwatch Inst. **[18844]**, 1776 Massachusetts Ave. NW, Washington, DC 20036-1904, (202)452-1999
Worldwatch Inst. **[IO]**, Washington, DC, United States
WorldWIDE **[★4618]**
Worldwide Aquatic Bodywork Assn. **[13658]**, PO Box 1817, Middletown, CA 95461, (707)928-5860
Worldwide Assn. of Self-Adhesive Labels and Related Products **[IO]**, The Hague, Netherlands
Worldwide Assurance for Employees of Public Agencies **[IO]**, Falls Church, VA, United States
Worldwide Assurance for Employees of Public Agencies **[5776]**, 7651 Leesburg Pike, Falls Church, VA 22043, (703)790-8010
Worldwide Camaro Assn. **[★21821]**
Worldwide Camaro Club **[21821]**, c/o Eckler's Camaro, 5140 S Washington Ave., Titusville, FL 32780-7318, (800)283-0691
Worldwide Coalition for the Spiritual Development of African Churches - Address unknown since 2003.
Worldwide Collectors Club **[★22831]**
Worldwide Collectors Club **[★IO]**
Worldwide Dental Hea. Ser. **[★IO]**
Worldwide Dental Hea. Ser. **[★12525]**
Worldwide Dragonfly Assn. **[IO]**, Kidderminster, United Kingdom
Worldwide ERC; Employee Relocation Council/ **[1261]**
Worldwide Fair Play for Frogs Comm. - Defunct.
Worldwide Fast for Peace - Defunct.
Worldwide Fiero Club - Address unknown since 1994.
Worldwide Forgiveness Alliance **[8959]**, 20 Sunnyside Ave., Ste. A268, Mill Valley, CA 94941, (415)381-3372
Worldwide Forgiveness Alliance **[IO]**, Mill Valley, CA, United States
Worldwide Friendship Intl. **[IO]**, Randallstown, MD, United States
Worldwide Friendship Intl. **[22147]**, PO Box 562, Randallstown, MD 21133, (410)922-2795
Worldwide Marriage Encounter **[12510]**, 2210 E Highland Ave., Ste. 106, San Bernardino, CA 92404-4666, (909)863-9963
Worldwide Marriage Encounter **[IO]**, San Bernardino, CA, United States
Worldwide Monitors Radio Club **[★IO]**
Worldwide Monitors Radio Club **[★21510]**
Worldwide Network **[★4618]**
WorldWIDE Network, Women in Development and Environment **[4618]**
Worldwide Opportunities on Organic Farms - Germany **[IO]**, Dresden, Germany
Worldwide Opportunities on Organic Farms - UK **[IO]**, Brampton, United Kingdom
Worldwide Pen Friends - Address unknown since 1995.
Worldwide Printing Thermographers Assn. **[1797]**, 305 Plus Park Blvd., Nashville, TN 37217, (800)821-3138

Reference to "IO" in place of a book number signifies that the association may be found in the 45th edition of International Organizations.

Worldwide Printing Thermographers Assn. **[IO]**, Nashville, TN, United States

Worldwide Responsible Apparel Production **[IO]**, Arlington, VA, United States

Worldwide Responsible Apparel Production **[261]**, 2200 Wilson Blvd., Ste. 601, Arlington, VA 22201, (703)243-0970

Worldwide Television-FM DX Assn. **[21510]**, PO Box 501, Somersville, CT 06072

Worldwide Television-FM DX Assn. **[IO]**, Somersville, CT, United States

Worldwide Univ. Colleges Consortium **[★IO]**

Worldwide Univ. Colleges Consortium **[★8114]**

Worldwide Univ. Consortium **[8114]**, c/o Intl. House Bellingham, 505 N Forest, Bellingham, WA 98227, (604)689-0905

Worldwide Univ. Consortium **[IO]**, Bellingham, WA, United States

Worldwide Women Professional Bowlers **[★23257]**

WorldWise - Address unknown since 2002.

Worship Arts; Fellowship of United Methodists in Music and **[20261]**

Worship, Music and the Arts; Lutheran Soc. for **[★19900]**

Worship, and Other Arts; Fellowship of United Methodists in **[★20261]**

Worship Resources Office - Defunct.

Worshipful Company of Bakers **[IO]**, London, United Kingdom

Worshipful Company of Farriers **[IO]**, Kings Langley, United Kingdom

Worshipful Company of Framework Knitters **[IO]**, Upminster, United Kingdom

Worshipful Company of Glaziers' and Painters of Glass **[IO]**, London, United Kingdom

Worshipful Company of Grocers **[IO]**, London, United Kingdom

Worshipful Company of Info. Technologists **[IO]**, London, United Kingdom

Worshipful Company of Musicians **[IO]**, London, United Kingdom

Worshipful Company of Pattenmakers **[IO]**, Maidstone, United Kingdom

Worshipful Company of Pewterers **[IO]**, London, United Kingdom

Worshipful Company of Sci. Instrument Makers **[IO]**, London, United Kingdom

Worshipful Company of Scriveners of the City of London **[IO]**, London, United Kingdom

Worshipful Company of Shipwrights **[IO]**, London, United Kingdom

Worshipful Company of Tin Plate Workers **[IO]**, Norfolk, United Kingdom

Worshipful Company of Vintners **[IO]**, London, United Kingdom

Worshipful Company of Wheelwrights **[IO]**, Bexleyheath, United Kingdom

Worshipful Soc. of Apothecaries of London **[IO]**, London, United Kingdom

Worthington Register - Defunct.

Wound Care; Assn. for the Advancement of **[14547]**

Wound Care Assn; Amer. Professional **[16688]**

Wound Healing Soc. **[14668]**, 341 N Maitland Ave., Ste. 130, Maitland, FL 32751, (407)647-8839

Wound Mgt; Amer. Acad. of **[16686]**

Wound, Ostomy and Continence Nurses Soc.: An Assn. of E.T. Nurses **[15533]**, 15000 Commerce Pkwy., Ste. C, Mount Laurel, NJ 08054, (888)224-9626

Wound, Ostomy and Continence Nurses Soc., An Assn. of E.T. Nurses **[★15533]**

Wound, Ostomy and Continence Nurses Soc.: An Assn. of E.T. Nurses **[IO]**, Mount Laurel, NJ, United States

Wound, Ostomy and Continence Nurses Soc., An Assn. of E.T. Nurses **[★IO]**

Wound, Ostomy and Continence Nursing Certification Bd. **[15534]**, 555 E Wells St., Ste. 1100, Milwaukee, WI 53202-3823, (414)289-8721

Wounded Knee Memorial Assn. - Address unknown since 1995.

Wounded; Stamps for the **[22879]**

Woven Elastic Mfrs. Assn. **[★3780]**

Woven Fabric Belting Mfrs. Assn. **[★3792]**

Woven Fabric Belting Mfrs. Assn. **[★IO]**

Woven Wire Products Assn. **[2082]**, PO Box 610280, Birmingham, AL 35261-0280, (517)542-2501

WPC Club **[21822]**, PO Box 3504, Kalamazoo, MI 49003-3504, (269)375-5535

Wreckers Assn; Natl. Auto **[★3988]**

Wreckers Assn; Natl. Auto and Truck **[★3988]**

Wren Family Assn. - Defunct.

Wrestlers WithOut Borders **[23990]**, 63 Whitney St., San Francisco, CA 94131

Wrestlers WithOut Borders **[IO]**, San Francisco, CA, United States

Wrestling

Amer. Armsport Assn. **[23059]**

British Wrestling Assn. **[IO]**

Canadian Amateur Wrestling Assn. **[IO]**

European Sumo Union **[IO]**

Intl. Fed. of Assoc. Wrestling Styles **[IO]**

Intl. Sumo Fed. **[IO]**

Natl. Wrestling Coaches Assn. **[23987]**

U.S. ArmSports **[23991]**

U.S. Girls' Wrestling Assn. **[23988]**

U.S.A. Wrestling **[23989]**

World Armsport Fed. **[23060]**

Wrestlers WithOut Borders **[23990]**

Wrestlers WithOut Borders **[IO]**

Wrestling Championship; World's Wrist **[★23991]**

Wrestling Coaches and Officials Assn; Amer. **[★23987]**

Wrestling Coaches and Officials; Natl. Collegiate Athletic Assn. of **[★23987]**

Wrestling Fed; U.S. **[★23989]**

Wright Assn; Frank Lloyd **[7961]**

Wright-Bobby Wright Intl. Fan Club; Kitty Wells-Johnny **[24936]**

Wright Circle; Richard **[9707]**

Wright Fan Club; Kitty Wells/Johnny **[★24936]**

Wright Found; Frank Lloyd **[★7961]**

Wright Preservation Trust; Frank Lloyd **[10023]**

Wright Soc; George **[4565]**

Wristwrestling

U.S. ArmSports **[23991]**

Wristwrestling Championship; World's **[★23991]**

Write Your Congressman Club; Natl. **[★18361]**

Write Your Congressman; Natl. **[18361]**

Writers

About Books, Inc. **[3198]**

Acad. of Arts and Sciences of the Americas **[18830]**

Alexandra Writers' Centre Soc. **[IO]**

Alice in Wonderland Collectors Network **[21957]**

Amer. Amateur Press Assn. **[22910]**

Amer. Assn. of Dental Editors **[3077]**

Amer. Assn. of Language Specialists **[3852]**

Amer. Auto Racing Writers and Broadcasters Assn. **[23069]**

Amer. Boccaccio Assn. **[9629]**

Amer. Christian Fiction Writers **[11156]**

Amer. Friends of the Shakespeare Birthplace Trust **[11157]**

Amer. Friends of the Shakespeare Birthplace Trust **[IO]**

Amer. Medical Writers Assn. **[3082]**

Amer. Philatelic Soc. Writers Unit **[22786]**

Amer. Podiatric Medical Writers Assn. **[16039]**

Amer. Screenwriters Assn. **[4060]**

Amer. Screenwriters Assn. **[IO]**

Amer. Soc. of Contrarian Speakers and Writers **[5601]**

Amer. Soc. of Journalists and Authors **[11158]**

Amer. Teilhard Soc. **[9632]**

Arthur Miller Soc. **[11159]**

Asian Amer. Journalists Assn. **[3088]**

Asian Amer. Writers' Workshop **[4061]**

Assoc. Church Press **[3205]**

Assn. of Art Editors **[3207]**

Assn. of British Sci. Writers **[IO]**

Assn. of Earth Sci. Editors **[3093]**

Assn. of Italian Canadian Writers **[IO]**

Assn. of Literary Scholars and Critics **[10413]**

Assn. of Music Writers and Photographers **[10562]**

Assn. for the Stud. of Australian Literature **[IO]**

Assn. for Women in Sports Media **[3097]**

Assn. of Writers and Writing Programs **[11160]**

August Derleth Soc. **[9634]**

Australasian Medical Writers Assn. **[IO]**

Australian Soc. of Authors **[IO]**

Australian Writers' Guild **[IO]**

Austrian P.E.N. Centre **[IO]**

Authors Guild **[11161]**

Authors League of Am. **[11162]**

Ayn Rand Soc. **[10788]**

Barbara Pym Soc. **[9635]**

Baseball Writers Assn. of Am. **[3099]**

Bay Area Independent Publishers Assn. **[3212]**

Bernard Shaw Soc. **[9636]**

Bertrand Russell Soc. **[9637]**

Beyond Baroque Literary/Arts Center **[9559]**

Boating Writers Intl. **[3100]**

Bowling Writers Assn. of Am. **[3101]**

Brazilian Acad. of Letters **[IO]**

Bread Loaf Writers Conf. **[11163]**

Broad Universe **[23034]**

Burroughs Bibliophiles **[9640]**

Camus Stud. Assn. **[7488]**

Canadian Authors Assn. **[IO]**

Canadian Farm Writers' Fed. **[IO]**

Canadian Sci. Writers' Assn. **[IO]**

Canadian Soc. of Children's Authors, Illustrators and Performers **[IO]**

Canadian Writers Found. **[IO]**

Carson McCullers Soc. **[11164]**

Cassie Edwards Intl. Fan Club **[24782]**

Catharine Maria Sedgwick Soc. **[11165]**

Caucus for TV Producers, Writers, and Directors **[17165]**

Charles Lamb Soc. **[IO]**

Charles W. Chesnutt Assn. **[11166]**

Christopher Morley Knothole Assn. **[9643]**

Civil Soc. of Multimedia Authors **[IO]**

Comm. on Scholarly Editions **[11167]**

Constr. Writers Assn. **[3106]**

Cormac McCarthy Soc. **[11168]**

Coun. for the Advancement of Sci. Writing **[3107]**

Crime Writers' Assn. **[IO]**

Crime Writers of Canada **[IO]**

Danish Writers Assn. **[IO]**

Dante Soc. of Am. **[9644]**

D.H. Lawrence Soc. of North Am. **[9645]**

Dickens Soc. **[9646]**

Dog Writers' Assn. of Am. **[3110]**

Don DeLillo Soc. **[11169]**

Dramatists Centre **[IO]**

Edgar Allan Poe Soc. of Baltimore **[9647]**

Editorial Freelancers Assn. **[3111]**

Educ. Writers Assn. **[3112]**

English Assn. Sydney **[IO]**

English Centre of Intl. PEN (Poets, Playwrights, Editors, Essayists, Novelists and their Translators) **[IO]**

EPIC - Electronically Published Internet Connection **[22914]**

Eugene O'Neill Soc. **[9648]**

European Assn. for the Promotion of Poetry **[IO]**

European Writers' Cong. **[IO]**

Evelyn Scott Soc. **[11170]**

Fans of Oz **[25048]**

Fed. of BC Writers **[IO]**

Fed. of Worker Writers and Community Publishers **[IO]**

Fellowship of Australian Writers NSW **[IO]**

Ferenc Liszt Soc., Budapest **[IO]**

Football Writers Assn. of Am. **[23430]**

Ford Madox Ford Soc. **[IO]**

Francis Bacon Found. **[9650]**

Friends of Amer. Writers **[11171]**

Gene Stratton Porter Memorial Soc. **[9651]**

George Sand Assn. **[9652]**

Georgia Writers Assn. and Young Georgia Writers **[11172]**

Golf Writers Assn. of Am. **[23450]**

Gridiron Club of Washington, DC **[3114]**

Harriet Beecher Stowe Center **[9655]**

Harriet Beecher Stowe Soc. **[11173]**

Harry Stephen Keeler Soc. **[9656]**

Hebrew Writers Assn. in Israel **[IO]**

Hegel Soc. of Am. **[9657]**

Hemingway Found. and Soc. **[9658]**

Horatio Alger Soc. **[9659]**

A star before a book entry number signifies that the name is not listed separately, but is mentioned within the entry.

Horror Writers Assn. [11174]
Indian Heritage Coun. [10744]
Intl. Assn. of Bus. Communicators [879]
Intl. Assn. of Crime Writers [IO]
Intl. Assn. of Crime Writers, North Amer. Br. [IO]
Intl. Assn. of Crime Writers, North Amer. Br. [11175]
Intl. Assn. of Media Tie-in Writers [11176]
Intl. Assn. of Media Tie-in Writers [IO]
Intl. Assn. of Obituarists [IO]
Intl. Assn. of Obituarists [4062]
Intl. Black Writers and Artists [11177]
Intl. Black Writers and Artists [IO]
Intl. Brecht Soc. [9661]
Intl. Center for Journalists [3117]
Intl. Food, Wine and Travel Writers Assn. [3118]
Intl. Freedom to Publish Comm. [17041]
Intl. Labor Communications Assn., AFL-CIO/CLC [3229]
Intl. P.E.N. - England [IO]
Intl. P.E.N. - Scottish Centre [IO]
Intl. P.E.N. Women Writers' Comm. [IO]
Intl. PEN Writers Assn. [IO]
Intl. Poetry Forum [10862]
Intl. Rebecca West Soc. [11178]
Intl. Romani Writers' Assn. [IO]
Intl. Sci. Writers Assn. [3124]
Intl. Security and Detective Alliance [2323]
Intl. Soc. of Weekly Newspaper Editors [3125]
Intl. Spenser Soc. [9663]
Intl. Theodore Dreiser Soc. [9664]
Intl. Thriller Writers [11179]
Intl. Thriller Writers [IO]
Intl. Travel Writers and Editors Assn. [3926]
Intl. Virginia Woolf Soc. [9666]
Intl. Vladimir Nabokov Soc. [9667]
Intl. Women's Writing Guild [11180]
Intl. Women's Writing Guild [IO]
Irish Playwrights and Screenwriters Guild [IO]
Italian PEN Club [IO]
Jack London Res. Center [9669]
James Dickey Soc. [10875]
James Joyce Soc. [9671]
James Joyce Soc. of Southern Colorado [9672]
Jerry B. Jenkins Christian Writers Guild [20630]
Jesse Stuart Found. [9674]
John Burroughs Assn. [7362]
Jokewriters Guild [10211]
Joseph Conrad Soc. of Am. [9675]
Kafka Soc. of Am. and Jour. [9676]
Keats-Shelley Assn. of Am. [9677]
Langston Hughes Soc. [9678]
Laura Ingalls Wilder Memorial Soc. [9679]
Lessing Soc. [9680]
Literary Source [3232]
Louisa May Alcott Memorial Assn. [9682]
Lowell Celebrates Kerouac! [9683]
Manuscript Soc. [22068]
Marlowe Lives! Assn. [9689]
Melville Soc. [9691]
Mencken Soc. [9692]
Milton Soc. of Am. [9693]
Mirage Gp. [10864]
Montenegrin P.E.N. Centre [IO]
Mystery Readers Intl. [24823]
Mystery Writers of Am. [11181]
Nathaniel Hawthorne Soc. [9694]
Natl. Alliance of Short Fiction Authors [11182]
Natl. Amateur Press Assn. [22911]
Natl. Assn. of Home and Workshop Writers [3131]
Natl. Assn. of Sci. Writers [3133]
Natl. Assn. of Women Writers [11183]
Natl. Fantasy Fan Fed. [10946]
Natl. New Play Network [11030]
Natl. Press Club [3141]
Natl. Resume Writers' Assn. [4063]
National Resume Writers' Association [IO]
Natl. Sportscasters and Sportswriters Assn. [3144]
Natl. Steinbeck Center [9695]
Natl. Verbatim Reporters Assn. [4064]
Natl. Writers Union [24219]
Native Writers' Circle of the Americas [19283]
Nature and Environmental Writers - Coll. and Univ. Educators [8362]

New Dramatists [11034]
New York Coun. of Motion Picture and TV Unions [24056]
New York C.S. Lewis Soc. [9696]
New York Financial Writers' Assn. [3148]
New Zealand Soc. of Authors [IO]
New Zealand Writers Guild [IO]
North Amer. Case Res. Assn. [4065]
North Amer. Jules Verne Soc. [11184]
North Amer. Jules Verne Soc. [IO]
North Amer. Travel Journalist Assn. [4066]
Norwegian Authors' Union [IO]
Norwegian Non-Fiction Writers and Translators Assn. [IO]
Norwegian Playwrights' Assn. [IO]
Norwegian Writers for Children [IO]
Novelists, Inc. [4067]
Org. of Black Screenwriters [1323]
Outdoor Writers Assn. of Am. [3153]
Outdoor Writers of Canada [IO]
Outdoor Writers' Guild [IO]
Outer Critics Circle [11037]
Overseas Press Club of Am. [3154]
Pearl S. Buck Birthplace Found. [9699]
PEN Amer. Center [11185]
PEN Canada [IO]
PEN Center U.S.A. [11186]
PEN Club Liechtenstein [IO]
P.E.N. Club - Poland [IO]
People's News Agency [3155]
Philip Roth Soc. [11187]
Philippine Amer. Writers and Artists [11188]
Pirandello Soc. of Am. [9701]
Playwrights Conf. [11039]
P.N. Elrod Fan Club [9702]
Poe Found. [9703]
Poe Stud. Assn. [9704]
Poets Against the War [11189]
Poets and Writers [10870]
Powys Soc. of North Am. [9705]
Professional Hockey Writers' Assn. [3156]
Public Media Found. [18033]
Public Safety Writers Assn. [4068]
Quebec Writers' Fed. [IO]
Rachel Carson Homestead Assn. [11143]
Ralph Waldo Emerson Memorial Assn. [9706]
Religion News Ser. [3158]
Religion Newswriters Assn. [3159]
Renaissance Artists and Writers Assn. [10202]
Robinson Jeffers Assn. [11190]
Romance Writers of Am. [11191]
Romanian Stud. Assn. of Am. [10938]
Romantic Novelists' Assn. [IO]
Saint Andrew Abbey [11192]
Sci. Fiction and Fantasy Writers of Am. [11193]
Sci. Songwriters' Assn. [10693]
Screenwriters Assn. (Singapore) [IO]
Sculpture in the Env. [17240]
Shakespeare Oxford Soc. [9709]
Shakespeare Soc. [9710]
Sisters in Crime [4069]
Slovene Writers' Assn. [IO]
Slovenian Writers' Assn. [IO]
Sociedad Chilena del Derecho de Autor [IO]
Sociedade Portuguesa de Autores [IO]
Soc. of Amer. Bus. Editors and Writers [3161]
Soc. of Amer. Travel Writers [3162]
Soc. of Authors - England [IO]
Soc. of Children's Book Writers and Illustrators [11194]
Soc. of Dramatic Authors and Composers [IO]
Soc. of Midland Authors [4070]
Soc. for the Stud. of Amer. Women Writers [11195]
Soc. for the Stud. of Amer. Women Writers [IO]
Soc. for the Stud. of Midwestern Literature [10430]
Soc. of Swedish Authors in Finland [IO]
Soc. for Tech. Commun. [886]
Soc. of Women Writers - Victoria [IO]
Soc. of Writers to Her Majesty's Signet [IO]
Southern Songwriters Guild [2824]
Space Coast Writers' Guild [11196]
Story Circle Network [10985]
Susan Glaspell Soc. [11197]

Swedenborg Found. [9711]
Swedenborg Soc. [IO]
Swedish PEN Centre [IO]
Swedish Writers' Union [IO]
Tall Grass Writers Guild [11198]
Tanka Soc. of Am. [10871]
Text and Academic Authors Assn. [11199]
Theodore Roethke Memorial Found. [10872]
The Thomas Hardy Assn. [9712]
Thomas Wolfe Soc. [9713]
Thornton Wilder Soc. [11200]
Thornton Wilder Soc. [IO]
Travel Journalists Guild [3167]
United Amateur Press Assn. of Am. [22912]
U.S. Basketball Writers Assn. [23137]
Vachel Lindsay Assn. [9718]
W. T. Bandy Center for Baudelaire and Modern French Stud. [9720]
Walden Pond Advisory Comm. [4464]
Walmsley Soc. [IO]
Walt Whitman Birthplace Assn. [9721]
Western Writers of Am. [11201]
Willa Cather Pioneer Memorial and Educational Found. [9722]
William Allen White Found. [9723]
William Dean Howells Soc. [9724]
William Morris Soc. in the U.S. [9725]
The Wodehouse Soc. [9726]
Women in Scholarly Publishing [3260]
Women Writing the West [4071]
Women's Interart Center [11096]
Women's World Org. for Rights, Literature and Development [18822]
Wordcraft Circle of Native Writers and Storytellers [9859]
World Bowling Writers [3175]
World Fed. of Journalists and Travel Writers [IO]
Writers Guild of Alberta [IO]
Writers Guild of Am., East [24220]
Writers Guild of Am., West [24221]
Writers Guild of Canada [IO]
Writers-in-Exile Center, Amer. Br., Intl. PEN Club [IO]
Writers-in-Exile Center, Amer. Br., Intl. PEN Club [11202]
Writers in Prison Comm. of Intl. P.E.N. [IO]
Writers and Scholars Educational Trust [IO]
Writers' Trust of Canada [IO]
Writers' Union of Canada [IO]
Writers' Union of Iceland [IO]
Writers Workshop [11203]
Writing Acad. [11204]
Yeats Soc. Sligo [IO]
Zane Grey's West Soc. [9728]
Writers Alliance - Defunct.
Writers of Am; Professional Football [23439]
Writers of Am; Sci. Fiction [★11193]
Writers; Amer. Soc. of Contrarian Speakers and [5601]
Writers for Animal Rights - Defunct.
Writers and Artists for Peace in the Middle East [18072]
Writers Assn. of Am; Baseball [3099]
Writers Assn. of Am; Bowling [3101]
Writers' Assn. of Am; Dog [3110]
Writers Assn. of Am; Football [23430]
Writers Assn. of Am; Garden [★22512]
Writers Assn. of Am; Golf [23450]
Writers Assn. of Am. and Natl. Women Bowling Writers Assn; Bowling [★3101]
Writers Assn. of Am; Outdoor [3153]
Writers Assn; Amer. Medical [3082]
Writers Assn; Amer. Podiatric Medical [16039]
Writers Assn; Bowling Writers Assn. of Am. and Natl. Women Bowling [★3101]
Writers Assn; Constr. [3106]
Writers Assn; Educ. [3112]
Writers Assn; Garden [22512]
Writers; Assn. of Golf [IO]
Writers Assn; Natl. [3146]
Writers Assn; Natl. Collegiate Baseball [3135]
Writers Assn; Natl. Sportscasters and Sports [3144]
Writers Assn; Natl. Turf [3145]
Writers' Assn; New York Financial [3148]
Writers Assn; Newspaper Food Editors and [★3094]

Reference to "IO" in place of a book number signifies that the association may be found in the 45th edition of International Organizations.

Encyclopedia of Associations, 46th Edition

4315

Writers' Assn; Professional Hockey [3156]
Writers Assn; Religion News [3159]
Writers Assn; Religious News [★3159]
Writers Assn; Renaissance Artists and [10202]
Writers Assn; U.S. Basketball [23137]
Writers' Assn; U.S. Harness [3170]
Writers and Broadcasters Assn; Amer. Auto Racing [23069]
Writers and Career Coaches; Professional Assn. of Resume [12097]
Writers' Circle of the Americas; Native [19283]
Writers - Coll. and Univ. Educators; Nature and Environmental [8362]
Writers Conf; Florida Space Coast [★11196]
Writers Conf; Intl. Black [★11177]
Writer's Coun. of Am; Copy [875]
Writers' Development Trust [★IO]
Writers, and Directors; Caucus for TV Producers, [17165]
Writers and Editors; Soc. of Tech. [★886]
Writers; Freedom [★17746]
Writers; Freedom [★IO]
Writers Guild of Alberta [IO], Edmonton, AB, Canada
Writers Guild of Am., East [24220], 555 W 57th St., Ste. 1230, New York, NY 10019, (212)767-7800
Writers Guild of Am., West [24221], 7000 W Third St., Los Angeles, CA 90048, (323)951-4000
Writers Guild of Canada [IO], Toronto, ON, Canada
Writers Guild; Christian [★20630]
Writers Guild Found. [★24221]
Writers' Guild of Great Britain [IO], London, United Kingdom
Writers Guild; Radio [★24221]
Writers Guild; Southern Song [2824]
Writers Guild; T.V. [★24221]
Writers-in-Exile Center, Amer. Br., Intl. PEN Club [11202], c/o Clara Gyorgyey, Pres., 42 Derby Ave., Orange, CT 06477, (203)397-1479
Writers-in-Exile Center, Amer. Br., Intl. PEN Club [IO], Orange, CT, United States
Writers League; Armed Forces [★5583]
Writers on Legal Subjects; Amer. Soc. of [★5584]
Writers; Natl. Assn. of Home and Workshop [3131]
Writers; Natl. Assn. of Sci. [3133]
Writers; Natl. Conf. of Editorial [3136]
Writers for Peace - Defunct.
Writers and Performers Assn; Comedy [★10211]
Writers; Poets and [10870]
Writers in Prison Comm. of Intl. P.E.N. [IO], London, United Kingdom
Writers and Publishers; Soc. of Tech. [★886]
Writers and Scholars Educational Trust [IO], London, United Kingdom
Writers; Soc. of Amer. Bus. [★3161]
Writers; Soc. of Amer. Bus. and Economic [★3161]
Writers; Soc. of Amer. Bus. Editors and [3161]
Writers; Soc. of Amer. Travel [3162]
Writers; Soc. of Children's Book [★11194]
Writers; Soc. of Magazine [★11158]
Writers' Sodality of America - Defunct.
Writers Theatre - Defunct.
Writers' Trust of Canada [IO], Toronto, ON, Canada
Writers' Union of Canada [IO], Toronto, ON, Canada
Writers' Union of Iceland [IO], Reykjavik, Iceland
Writers Unit; Amer. Philatelic Soc. [22786]
Writers Unit; Amer. Philatelic Soc; Junior [★22837]
Writers Workshop [11203], c/o Univ. of Illinois at Urbana-Champaign, 608 S Wright St., 208 English Bldg., Urbana, IL 61801, (217)333-8796
Writers Workshop; Amer. Film Inst. Alumni Assn. [★11203]
Writing
Academic Language Therapy Assn. [12488]
Acad. of Arts and Sciences of the Americas [18830]
Amer. Assn. of Handwriting Analysts [11205]
Amer. Christian Fiction Writers [11156]
Amer. Handwriting Anal. Found. [11206]
Amer. Pencil Collectors Soc. [21964]
Amer. Screenwriters Assn. [4060]
Amer. Soc. of Contrarian Speakers and Writers [5601]
Amer. Soc. of Greek and Latin Epigraphy [11207]
Assn. of Art Editors [3207]
Assn. for Bus. Commun. [8014]

Assn. of Departments of English [8374]
Assn. of Teachers of Tech. Writing [9332]
Assn. of Writers and Writing Programs [11160]
Australian Soc. of Calligraphers [IO]
Barbara Pym Soc. [9635]
Beyond Baroque Literary/Arts Center [9559]
Broad Universe [23034]
Calligraphy and Lettering Arts Soc. [IO]
Carson McCullers Soc. [11164]
Cassie Edwards Intl. Fan Club [24782]
Catharine Maria Sedgwick Soc. [11165]
Center for Sutton Movement Writing [11208]
Columbia Scholastic Press Assn. [9011]
Conf. on Coll. Composition and Commun. [8376]
Constr. Writers Assn. [3106]
Cormac McCarthy Soc. [11168]
Coun. of Graphological Societies [11209]
Coun. of Writing Prog. Administrators [9333]
Early Typewriter Collectors Assn. [22015]
Edinburgh Bibliographical Soc. [IO]
English Inst. [8378]
Evelyn Scott Soc. [11170]
Fan Tek [10943]
Friends of Amer. Writers [11171]
Gene Stratton Porter Memorial Soc. [9651]
Georgia Writers Assn. and Young Georgia Writers [11172]
Hagiography Soc. [20526]
Harriet Beecher Stowe Soc. [11173]
Harry Stephen Keeler Soc. [9656]
Horror Writers Assn. [11174]
Indian Heritage Coun. [10744]
Interlochen Center for the Arts [9571]
Intl. Assn. of Crime Writers, North Amer. Br. [11175]
Intl. Assn. of Media Tie-in Writers [11176]
Intl. Assn. of Obituarists [4062]
Intl. Black Writers and Artists [11177]
Intl. Graphoanalysis Soc. [11210]
Intl. Graphoanalysis Soc. [IO]
Intl. Graphological Soc. [11211]
Intl. Graphonomics Soc. [IO]
Intl. Pentecostal Press Assn. [3122]
Intl. Poetry Forum [10862]
Intl. Rebecca West Soc. [11178]
Intl. Spenser Soc. [9663]
Intl. Thriller Writers [11179]
Intl. Women's Writing Guild [11180]
James Dickey Soc. [10875]
James Joyce Soc. of Southern Colorado [9672]
Laura Ingalls Wilder Memorial Soc. [9679]
Lowell Celebrates Kerouac! [9683]
Manuscript Soc. [22068]
Marlowe Lives! Assn. [9689]
Mirage Gp. [10864]
Mystery Writers of Am. [11181]
Natl. Acad. of TV Arts and Sciences [567]
Natl. Alliance of Short Fiction Authors [11182]
Natl. Assn. of Women Writers [11183]
Natl. Coun. of Teachers of English [8380]
Natl. Found. for Advancement in the Arts [9587]
Natl. New Play Network [11030]
Natl. Postal Arts Assn. [22139]
Natl. Soc. for Graphology [11212]
Natl. Writers Assn. [3146]
Natl. Writing Proj. [9334]
North Amer. Jules Verne Soc. [11184]
Novelists, Inc. [4067]
Org. of Black Screenwriters [1323]
PEN Amer. Center [11185]
PEN Center U.S.A. [11186]
Pen Collectors of Am. [22105]
Philip Roth Soc. [11187]
Philippine Amer. Writers and Artists [11188]
Powys Soc. of North Am. [9705]
Public Safety Writers Assn. [4068]
Romance Writers of Am. [11191]
Saint Andrew Abbey [11192]
Sci. Fiction and Fantasy Writers of Am. [11193]
Sisters in Crime [4069]
Soc. for Calligraphy [11213]
Soc. for Inkwell Collectors [22114]
Soc. for Italic Handwriting [IO]
Soc. of Scribes [11214]
Soc. of Scribes and Illuminators [IO]

Soc. for the Stud. of Amer. Women Writers [11195]
Soc. for the Stud. of Midwestern Literature [10430]
Soc. of Typographic Aficionados [1791]
Space Coast Writers' Guild [11196]
Story Circle Network [10985]
Student Letter Exchange [22144]
Susan Glaspell Soc. [11197]
Tanka Soc. of Am. [10871]
Teachers and Writers Collaborative [9335]
Text and Academic Authors Assn. [11199]
The Thomas Hardy Assn. [9712]
Thornton Wilder Soc. [11200]
Unmarried-Catholics Correspondence Club [22145]
Vietnamese Nom Preservation Found. [10433]
Washington Calligraphers Guild [11215]
William Dean Howells Soc. [9724]
Wordcraft Circle of Native Writers and Storytellers [9859]
Worldwide Friendship Intl. [22147]
Writers-in-Exile Center, Amer. Br., Intl. PEN Club [11202]
Writers Workshop [11203]
Zane Grey's West Soc. [9728]
Writing Acad. [11204], c/o Inez Schneider, New Member Coor., 4010 Singleton Rd., Rockford, IL 61114, (815)877-9675
Writing Assn; Amer. Bus. [★8014]
Writing; Coun. for the Advancement of Sci. [3107]
Writing Equip. Soc. [IO], Ipswich, United Kingdom
Writing Instrument Distributors; Natl. Assn. of [★3686]
Writing Instrument Mfrs. Assn. [3688], 15000 Commerce Pkwy., Ste. C, Mount Laurel, NJ 08054-2212, (856)638-0426
Writing; Natl. Coun. for the Advancement of Educ. [★3112]
Writing Prog. Administrators; Coun. of [9333]
Writing Prog. Administrators; Natl. Coun. of [★9333]
Writing Programs; Assoc. [★11160]
Writing Proj; Hospitalized Veterans [16321]
WSA Fraternal Life [19148], 11265 Decatur St., Ste. 100, Westminster, CO 80234, (303)451-1494
WSSFN [★15418]
WSSFN [★IO]
WTA Tour Players Assn. [23917], 1 Progress Plz., Ste. 1500, St. Petersburg, FL 33701, (727)895-5000
WTA Tout [★23910]
WTA Tout [★IO]
WTC Families For Proper Burial [13312], PO Box 236, Fanwood, NJ 07023
WTCARES [22389], c/o Lyn Hollis, Comm. Chair, 164 N Forrest Ave., Camden, TN 38320-1217, (731)584-6530
WTF Taekwondo Assn. of Canada [IO], Ottawa, ON, Canada
Wushu-Kungfu Fed; U.S.A. [23605]
WWF - Australia [IO], Sydney, Australia
WWF - Brasil [IO], Brasilia, Brazil
WWF Intl. [IO], Gland, Switzerland
WWF - Piemonte e Valle d'Aosta [IO], Turin, Italy
WWF-UK [IO], Godalming, United Kingdom
WWF Verdensnaturfonden [★IO]
WWII; 4th Marine Div. Assn. [21361]
WWII PT Boats, Tenders and Bases [★21402]
WWII PT Boats, Tenders and Bases [★IO]
WWW Wimachtendienk, Wingolauchsik, Witahemui [★13005]
Wyandotte Bantam Club of America - Address unknown since 1995.
Wyandotte Club of Am; Silver [5118]
Wyburn-Mason and Jack M. Blount Found. for the Eradication of Rheumatoid Disease; Roger [16375]
Wyckoff House and Assn. [10517], 5816 Clarendon Rd., Brooklyn, NY 11203, (718)629-5400
Wycliffe Bible Translators [19531], PO Box 628200, Orlando, FL 32862-8200, (407)852-3600
Wynette Intl. Fan Club; Tammy [24979]
Wynonna Intl. Fan Club [24992], PO Box 128229, Nashville, TN 37212, (615)234-2889
Wynonna Intl. Fan Club [IO], Nashville, TN, United States

A star before a book entry number signifies that the name is not listed separately, but is mentioned within the entry.

X

X-Ray and Electron Diffraction; Amer. Soc. for [★6852]
X-Ray and Radium Protection; Advisory Comm. on [★6242]
X-Ray Soc; Amer. Indus. Radium and [★7787]
X-Ray Technicians; Amer. Registry of [★15128]
X-Ray Technicians; Amer. Soc. of [★15131]
X-Ray Unit Comm; Intl. [★5161]
X1/9 Car Club - Defunct.
X.400 Application Program Interface Assn. - Defunct.
Xaverian Missionaries [★IO]
Xaverian Missionaries [★20421]
Xaverian Missionaries of the U.S. [IO], Wayne, NJ, United States
Xaverian Missionaries of the U.S. [20421], 12 Helene Ct., Wayne, NJ 07470, (973)942-2975
Xaverian Missionary Fathers [★IO]
Xaverian Missionary Fathers [★20421]
Xaverian Missioners of the U.S. [★IO]
Xaverian Missioners of the U.S. [★20421]
Xavier Inst. of Development Action and Stud. [IO], Jabalpur, India
Xavier Soc. for the Blind [16892]
Xenophon Soc. [★9987]
Xerces Soc. [IO], Portland, OR, United States
Xerces Soc. [5405], 4828 SE Hawthorne Blvd., Portland, OR 97215, (503)232-6639
Xeroderma Pigmentosum Soc. [14491], 437 Snyder-town Rd., Craryville, NY 12521, (518)851-2612
Xerostomia
  Sjogren's Syndrome Found. [16376]
Xi Psi Phi [24442], c/o Dr. Keith W. Dickey, Supreme Sec.-Treas., 160 S Bellwood Dr., Ste. Z, East Alton, IL 62024-2086, (618)307-5433
Xi Sigma Pi - Address unknown since 2001.
XML.org [6757], c/o OASIS, PO Box 455, Billerica, MA 01821, (978)667-5115
X.Org [★IO]
X.Org [★6830]
X.Org Found. [IO], Santa Clara, CA, United States
X.Org Found. [6830], c/o Steve Swales, Chm., SUN Microsystems, 4150 Network Cir., Santa Clara, CA 95054, (800)555-9SUN
Xplor Intl. [IO], Lutz, FL, United States
Xplor Intl. [1798], 1900 Land O'Lakes Blvd., Ste. 103, Lutz, FL 33549, (813)948-3171
XyUser Gp. [6808], c/o Bob Carr, Exec. Dir., 12310 129th St. N, Largo, FL 33774, (727)595-9240
XyVision Users Gp. [★6808]

Y

Y-Flyer Yacht Racing Assn; Amer. [23157]
Y-Me Breast Cancer Support [★13882]
Y-ME Natl. Breast Cancer Org. [13882], 212 W Van Buren St., Ste. 1000, Chicago, IL 60607-3909, (312)986-8338
Y-Me Natl. Org. for Breast Cancer Info. and Support [★13882]
Yacht Architects and Brokers Assn. [★2598]
Yacht Assn; Classic [21871]
Yacht Brokers Assn. of Am. [2598], 105 Eastern Ave., Ste. 104, Annapolis, MD 21403-3366, (410)263-1014
Yacht Brokers, Designers and Surveyors Assn. [IO], Petersfield, United Kingdom
Yacht Brokers, Designers and Surveyors Assn. [★IO]
Yacht Club Uruguayo [IO], Montevideo, Uruguay
Yacht Coun; Amer. Boat and [2569]
Yacht Designers; Soc. of Boat and [1154]
Yacht Harbour Assn. [IO], Ashford, United Kingdom
Yacht Racing Assn., Amer. Sect; Intl. 505 [23180]
Yacht Racing Assn; Amer. Y-Flyer [23157]
Yacht Racing Association; Chesapeake Bay [★23173]
Yacht Racing Assn; El Toro Intl. [23168]
Yacht Racing Assn; Geary 18 Intl. [23172]
Yacht Racing Assn; Inter-Collegiate [★23176]
Yacht Racing Assn; Intl. Flattie [★23172]
Yacht Racing Assn; Intl. Star Class [23193]
Yacht Racing Assn. of North Am; Inter-Collegiate [★23176]

Yacht Racing Assn. of Thailand Under Royal Patron-age [IO], Bangkok, Thailand
Yacht Racing Associations Coun. [★23165]
Yacht Racing Union; North Amer. [★23232]
Yacht Racing Union; U.S. [★23232]
Yacht Safety Bur; Corresponding Surveyors to the [★7275]
Yachting Assn; Amer. Model [22642]
Yachting Assn; Canadian [IO]
Yachting Assn; Gulf [21874]
Yachting Assn. of India [IO], New Delhi, India
Yachting Assn; Inland Lake [23175]
Yachting Assn; Inter-Lake [23177]
Yachting Assn. of Sri Lanka [IO], Colombo, Sri Lanka
Yachting Club of Am. [23240], Box 1040, Marco Island, FL 34146, (239)642-4448
Yachting Journalists' Assn. [IO], Faversham, United Kingdom
Yachting New Zealand [IO], Auckland, New Zealand
Yachting Professionals; Assn. of [23159]
Yachting Union of Latvia [IO], Riga, Latvia
Yachtmen's Assn. of America - Defunct.
Yachtmen's Assn; Amer. [★23160]
Yad Sarah [IO], Jerusalem, Israel
Yad Tikvah Found. - Address unknown since 1999.
Yad Vashem, The Holocaust Martyrs' and Heroes' Remembrance Authority [IO], Jerusalem, Israel
Yad V'Kidush Hashem, House of Martyrs - Address unknown since 2008.
Yale-China Assn. [8637], 442 Temple St., Box 208223, New Haven, CT 06520-8223, (203)432-0880
Yale-in-China Assn. [★8637]
Yale Univ; Elizabethan Club of [10421]
Yamaha
  Motorcycle Touring Assn. [23626]
  Virago Owners Club [22700]
Yamaha 650 Soc. [22703], 27 Green Acres Dr., Rolla, MO 65401-3910, (573)368-5852
Yamaha 650 Soc. [IO], Rolla, MO, United States
Yamaha "T" Register - Defunct.
Yang Style Tai Chi Chuan Assn; Intl. [23594]
Yankee Assn; Amer. [21429]
Yardmasters of Am; Railroad [★24181]
Yarn Assn. of Am; Textured [★3801]
Yarn Assn; Carded [★3774]
Yarn Assn; Carpet [★3774]
Yarn Assn; Long Staple [★3774]
Yarn Coun. of Am; Craft [22153]
Yarn Distributors; Assn. of [3776]
Yarn Distributors; Assn. of Cotton [★3776]
Yarn Dyers Assn. [★3774]
Yarn Mfrs; Assn. of Synthetic [★3774]
Yarn Merchants Assn. - Defunct.
Yarn Spinners Assn; Amer. [3774]
Yarn Spinners Assn; Combed [★3774]
Yarns Mfrs; Intl. Soc. of Industrial [★3790]
Yarns of Yesteryear Project - Defunct.
Yas Meyve-Sebze Iahracatcilari Birligi [★IO]
Yasodhara Ashram Soc. [IO], Kootenay Bay, BC, Canada
Yavneh - The Natl. Religious Jewish Students Assn. - Defunct.
Yaw Family Soc. - Defunct.
Yayasan Indonesia Aikikai [IO], Jakarta, Indonesia
Yayasan Lembaga Konsumen Indonesia [★IO]
Year 2000 Comm. - Defunct.
Year-Round Educ; Natl. Assn. for [8282]
Yearbook Printers Assn. - Defunct.
Yearwood Fan Club; Trisha [24988]
Yeats Soc. [★IO]
Yeats Soc. Sligo [IO], Dublin, Ireland
Yeladim Coun. for the Child in Placement [IO], Tel Aviv, Israel
Yellow Pages Assn. [3261], 200 Connell Dr., Ste. 1700, Berkeley Heights, NJ 07922-2747, (908)286-2380
Yellow Pages Integrated Media Assn. [★3261]
Yellow Pages Publishers; Amer. Assn. of [★3261]
Yellow Pages Publishers Assn. [★3261]
Yellow Pages Ser. Assn; Natl. [★3261]
Yellow Springs Inst. for Contemporary Studies and the Arts - Address unknown since 2003.
Yellowstone-Bighorn Res. Assn. - Address unknown since 2002.

Yellowstone Coalition; Greater [4406]
Yellowstone Grizzly Found. [5406]
Yemen Amateur Athletic Fed. [IO], Sana'a, Yemen
Yemen Taekwondo Fed. [IO], Sana'a, Yemen
Yemen Tennis Fed. [IO], Sana'a, Yemen
Yemen Weightlifting Fed. [IO], Sana'a, Yemen
Yes I Can! Foundation for Exceptional Children [IO], Arlington, VA, United States
Yes I Can! Found. for Exceptional Children [11998], 1110 N Glebe Rd., Ste. 300, Arlington, VA 22201-5704, (703)264-3660
Yeshiva Principals; Natl. Conf. of [9017]
Yeshivath Torath Hayim in Jerusalem - Address unknown since 1995.
Yeshivos; Coun. of Roshei [★8683]
Yesterday's Children - Address unknown since 1994.
Yevreiskaya obshtshina Estonii [★IO]
Yiddish Book Center; Natl. [10288]
Yiddish Book Exchange; Natl. [★10288]
Yiddish Culture Org; Central [10275]
Yiddish Dictionary Comm. - Defunct.
Yiddish, Inc; League for [20157]
Yiddish Orthography; Comm. for the Implementation of the Standardized [10276]
Yiddish Theatrical Alliance [11053], c/o Yablokoff Chapels, 31 E 7th St., New York, NY 10003, (212)674-3437
Yiddish Writers Union - Defunct.
Yiddisher Kultur Farband [10291]
Yisrael; Congregation Shema [20135]
YIVO Inst. for Jewish Res. [10292], 15 W 16th St., New York, NY 10011-6301, (212)246-6080
YIVO Inst. for Jewish Res. [IO], New York, NY, United States
YLEM: Artists Using Sci. and Tech. [9532], PO Box 31923, San Francisco, CA 94131-0923, (415)445-0196
YMCA
  ACJ-YMCA Guatemala [IO]
  ACM - YMCA of Kuanza Sul [IO]
  Africa Alliance of YMCAs [IO]
  Asia and Pacific Alliance of YMCAs [IO]
  Assn. of YMCA Professionals [13460]
  Barisal Young Men's Christian Association [IO]
  Bogra Young Men's Christian Association [IO]
  Chittagong Young Men's Christian Association [IO]
  Colombian Federations of YMCAs [IO]
  CVJM - Gesamtverband [IO]
  Dhaka Young Men's Christian Association [IO]
  Dinajpur Young Men's Christian Association [IO]
  Direction Sports [13482]
  East Jerusalem YMCA [IO]
  Fed. Francaise des Mouvements et Services Feminins [IO]
  French Young Men's Christian Association [IO]
  Gambia YMCAs [IO]
  Italian Fed. of the YMCA [IO]
  Jerusalem Intl. YMCA [IO]
  Korean YMCA [IO]
  Metropolitan YMCA Singapore [IO]
  Natl. Comm. of YMCAs of China [IO]
  Natl. Coun. of Tanzania YMCA [IO]
  Natl. Coun. of the YMCAs of Australia [IO]
  Natl. Coun. of YMCA's of Bangladesh [IO]
  Natl. Coun. of YMCA's of Ghana [IO]
  Natl. Coun. of YMCA's of Greece [IO]
  Natl. Coun. of YMCA's of Ireland [IO]
  Natl. Coun. of YMCA's of Jamaica [IO]
  Natl. Coun. of YMCAs of Japan [IO]
  Natl. Coun. of YMCA's of Liberia [IO]
  Natl. Coun. of YMCA's of Malaysia [IO]
  Natl. Coun. of YMCA's of Myanmar [IO]
  Natl. Coun. of YMCA's of New Zealand [IO]
  Natl. Coun. of YMCA's of Pakistan [IO]
  Natl. Coun. of YMCA's of Sri Lanka [IO]
  Natl. Coun. of YMCA's of Sudan [IO]
  Natl. Coun. of YMCA's - Zambia [IO]
  Natl. Coun. of YMCA's of Zimbabwe [IO]
  North American YMCA Development Organization [IO]
  North Amer. YMCA Development Org. [13461]
  Scottish Natl. Coun. of YMCA's [IO]
  Union of YMCA's in Bulgaria YMCA-YWCA [IO]
  World Young Women's Christian Association [IO]

Reference to "IO" in place of a book number signifies that the association may be found in the 45th edition of International Organizations.

Encyclopedia of Associations, 46th Edition

4317

YMCA Intl. Br. [IO]
YMCA Intl. Br. [13462]
YMCA Intl. Camp Counselor Prog. [8638]
YMCA Romania Fed. [IO]
YMCA Slovakia [IO]
YMCA of the USA [13463]
Young Men's Christian Association - Albania [IO]
Young Men's Christian Association - Angola [IO]
Young Men's Christian Association - Antwerp, Belgium [IO]
Young Men's Christian Association of Armenia [IO]
Young Men's Christian Association - Aruba [IO]
Young Men's Christian Association - Bahamas [IO]
Young Men's Christian Association of Barbados [IO]
Young Men's Christian Association - Belize [IO]
Young Men's Christian Association - Benin [IO]
Young Men's Christian Association - Burundi [IO]
Young Men's Christian Association - Cameroon [IO]
Young Men's Christian Association of Canada [IO]
Young Men's Christian Association - Costa Rica [IO]
Young Men's Christian Association - Democratic Republic of Congo [IO]
Young Men's Christian Association - England [IO]
Young Men's Christian Association - Ethiopia [IO]
Young Men's Christian Association - Fiji [IO]
Young Men's Christian Association of Finland [IO]
Young Men's Christian Association - Gambia [IO]
Young Men's Christian Association of Georgia [IO]
Young Men's Christian Association - Guyana [IO]
Young Men's Christian Association - Haiti [IO]
Young Men's Christian Association of Hong Kong [IO]
Young Men's Christian Association - Hungary [IO]
Young Men's Christian Association of Indonesia [IO]
Young Men's Christian Association - Jordan [IO]
Young Men's Christian Association - Lebanon [IO]
Young Men's Christian Association - Mauritius [IO]
Young Men's Christian Association of Nazareth [IO]
Young Men's Christian Association of Nepal [IO]
Young Men's Christian Association - Papua New Guinea [IO]
Young Men's Christian Association - Peru [IO]
Young Men's Christian Association of the Philippines [IO]
Young Men's Christian Association - Rwanda [IO]
Young Men's Christian Association of Samoa [IO]
Young Men's Christian Association - Senegal [IO]
Young Men's Christian Association - Sierra Leone [IO]
Young Men's Christian Association - Spain [IO]
Young Men's Christian Association of Suriname [IO]
Young Men's Christian Association of Taiwan [IO]
Young Men's Christian Association - Trinidad and Tobago [IO]
Young Men's Christian Association of Ukraine [IO]
Young Men's Christian Association and Young Women's Christian Association - Denmark [IO]
Young Women's Christian Association of Albania [IO]
Young Women's Christian Association of Amer. Samoa [IO]
Young Women's Christian Assn. - Angola [IO]
Young Women's Christian Association of Antigua [IO]
Young Women's Christian Association - Aotearoa/New Zealand [IO]
Young Women's Christian Association - Argentina [IO]
Young Women's Christian Association - Australia [IO]
Young Women's Christian Association - Bahamas [IO]
Young Women's Christian Association - Bangladesh [IO]
Young Women's Christian Association of Barbados [IO]
Young Women's Christian Association - Belarus [IO]

Young Women's Christian Association - Belgium [IO]
Young Women's Christian Association - Belize [IO]
Young Women's Christian Assn. - Benin [IO]
Young Women's Christian Association - Botswana [IO]
Young Women's Christian Association - Brazil [IO]
Young Women's Christian Assn. - Bulgaria [IO]
Young Women's Christian Assn. - Cameroon [IO]
Young Women's Christian Association - Canada [IO]
Young Women's Christian Assn. - Chile [IO]
Young Women's Christian Association - China [IO]
Young Women's Christian Association - Colombia [IO]
Young Women's Christian Assn. - El Salvador [IO]
Young Women's Christian Assn. - Estonia [IO]
Young Women's Christian Association of Ethiopia [IO]
Young Women's Christian Association of Fiji [IO]
Young Women's Christian Association - Finland [IO]
Young Women's Christian Association - Gambia [IO]
Young Women's Christian Association - Germany [IO]
Young Women's Christian Association - Ghana [IO]
Young Women's Christian Association - Great Britain [IO]
Young Women's Christian Association of Greece - XEN [IO]
Young Women's Christian Association - Grenada [IO]
Young Women's Christian Association - Guyana [IO]
Young Women's Christian Association - Hong Kong [IO]
Young Women's Christian Association - Iceland [IO]
Young Women's Christian Association of India [IO]
Young Women's Christian Association - Ireland [IO]
Young Women's Christian Association - Italy [IO]
Young Women's Christian Association - Jamaica [IO]
Young Women's Christian Association of Japan [IO]
Young Women's Christian Association - Kenya [IO]
Young Women's Christian Association - Korea [IO]
Young Women's Christian Assn. - Latvia [IO]
Young Women's Christian Association - Lebanon [IO]
Young Women's Christian Assn. - Lesotho [IO]
Young Women's Christian Assn. - Lithuania [IO]
Young Women's Christian Association - Madagascar [IO]
Young Women's Christian Association - Malaysia [IO]
Young Women's Christian Assn. - Mauritius [IO]
Young Women's Christian Association - Mexico [IO]
Young Women's Christian Association - Myanmar [IO]
Young Women's Christian Association - Namibia [IO]
Young Women's Christian Assn. - Nepal [IO]
Young Women's Christian Association - Netherlands [IO]
Young Women's Christian Association - Nigeria [IO]
Young Women's Christian Association - Norway [IO]
Young Women's Christian Association - Pakistan [IO]
Young Women's Christian Association - Palestine [IO]
Young Women's Christian Association - Papua New Guinea [IO]
Young Women's Christian Association - Peru [IO]
Young Women's Christian Association - Philippines [IO]

Young Women's Christian Association - Romania [IO]
Young Women's Christian Assn. - Russia [IO]
Young Women's Christian Assn. - Rwanda [IO]
Young Women's Christian Association of Samoa [IO]
Young Women's Christian Association of Sierra Leone [IO]
Young Women's Christian Association - Singapore [IO]
Young Women's Christian Association - Solomon Islands [IO]
Young Women's Christian Association - South Africa [IO]
Young Women's Christian Association - Sri Lanka [IO]
Young Women's Christian Association - Suriname [IO]
Young Women's Christian Association - Taiwan [IO]
Young Women's Christian Association - Thailand [IO]
Young Women's Christian Assn. - Togo [IO]
Young Women's Christian Association - Trinidad and Tobago [IO]
Young Women's Christian Association - Uganda [IO]
Young Women's Christian Association - Ukraine [IO]
Young Women's Christian Association - Uruguay [IO]
Young Women's Christian Association - Zambia [IO]
Young Women's and Young Men's Christian Association - Sweden [IO]
Y's Men Intl., U.S. Area [13464]
YWCA in Czech Republic [IO]
YMCA Earth Ser. Corps [18861], YMCA of the USA, 101 N Wacker Dr., Chicago, IL 60606, (800)872-9622
YMCA Intl. [★13463]
YMCA Intl. Br. [13462], 5 W 63rd St., 2nd Fl., New York, NY 10023, (212)727-8800
YMCA Intl. Br. [IO], New York, NY, United States
YMCA Intl. Camp Counselor Prog. [IO], New York, NY, United States
YMCA Intl. Camp Counselor Prog. [8638], 5 W 63rd St., 2nd Fl., New York, NY 10023-9197, (212)727-8800
YMCA Intl. - Defunct.
YMCA Intl. Prog. Services [★13462]
YMCA Intl. Prog. Services [★IO]
YMCA Intl. Student Services [★IO]
YMCA Intl. Student Services [★13462]
YMCA Romania Fed. [IO], Baia Mare, Romania
YMCA Slovakia [IO], Bratislava, Slovakia
YMCA na Slovensku [★IO]
YMCA of the USA [13463], c/o Assn. Advancement, 101 N Wacker Dr., Chicago, IL 60606, (312)977-0031
Ymgyrch Diogelu Cymru Wledig [★IO]
Yngling Assn. of Canada [IO], Toronto, ON, Canada
Yngling Assn; U.S. [23237]
Yngling Club Holland [IO], Lathum, Netherlands
Yngling Club Osterreich [IO], Salzburg, Austria
Yochsin Inst. [★IO]
Yochsin Inst. [★21158]

Yodeling
Ethel Delaney Intl. Fan Club [24886]

Yoga
3HO Found. [20631]
Agni Yoga Soc. [20632]
Amer. Yoga Assn. [11216]
Ananda Marga [20633]
Ananda Marga [IO]
Ananda Yoga Teachers Assn. [11217]
Assn. of Himalayan Yoga Meditation Societies [11218]
Assn. of Himalayan Yoga Meditation Societies [IO]
B.K.S. Iyengar Yoga Natl. Assn. of the U.S. [23992]
Eureka Soc. [20634]
Friends of the Western Buddhist Order [19551]
Himalayan Intl. Inst. of Yoga Sci. and Philosophy of the U.S.A. [12348]

A star before a book entry number signifies that the name is not listed separately, but is mentioned within the entry.

Intl. Sivananda Yoga Vedanta Center **[IO]**
Intl. Yoga Teachers' Assn. **[IO]**
Light on Yoga Italia **[IO]**
Mentalphysics **[20503]**
North Amer. Yoga Fed. **[11219]**
North Amer. Yoga Fed. **[IO]**
Professional Assn. of German Yoga Instructors **[IO]**
Self-Realization Fellowship **[20635]**
Spiritualist Yoga Fellowship **[IO]**
Sri Aurobindo Assn. **[20636]**
Yasodhara Ashram Soc. **[IO]**
Yoga Alliance **[11220]**
Yoga Res. Found. **[20637]**
Yoga Alliance **[11220]**, PO Box 369, Clinton, MD 20735, (301)868-4700
Yoga Res. Found. **[20637]**, 569 SW 102 Ave., Miami, FL 33143, (305)666-2006
Yoga Soc; Ananda Marga **[★20633]**
Yoga Soc; Intl. **[★20637]**
Yoga Soc; Light of **[★11216]**
Yoga Teachers' Assn; Intl. **[IO]**
Yogurt Assn; Natl. **[1138]**
Yogurt Retailers Assn; Natl. Ice Cream and **[★1137]**
Yokefellowship Prison Ministry **[★11889]**
Yokefellowship Prison Ministry **[★IO]**
Yonkers; Holiday Inst. of **[18672]**
York County Genealogical Soc. **[21159]**
York and Districts Olive Assn. **[IO]**, York, Australia
York Fan Club; Official Intl. Michael **[24763]**
Yorkshire Campaign for Nuclear Disarmament **[IO]**, Bradford, United Kingdom
Yorkshire Canary Club of America - Defunct.
Yorkshire Club; Amer. **[5233]**
Yorkshire Terrier
    Yorkshire Terrier Club of Am. **[22390]**
Yorkshire Terrier Club of Am. **[22390]**, c/o Shirley Patterson, Sec., PO Box 265, St. Peters, PA 19470-0265
Yoruba: Natl. Assn. of Yoruba Descendants in North America; Egbe Omo **[19289]**
Yosemite Assn. **[7367]**, PO Box 230, El Portal, CA 95318, (209)379-2646
Yosemite Museum Assn. **[★7367]**
Yosemite Natural History Assn. **[★7367]**
Youel Care - Address unknown since 1999.
Young Adult Adjustment Center **[★12584]**
Young Adult Institute/National Inst. for People with Disabilities **[12584]**, 460 W 34th St., New York, NY 10001-2382, (212)273-6100
Young Adult Inst. and Workshop **[★12584]**
Young Adult League; Greek Orthodox **[20072]**
Young Adult Lib. Services Assn. **[10395]**, c/o Amer. Lib. Assn., 50 E Huron St., Chicago, IL 60611, (312)280-4390
Young Adults with Disabilities; Networking Proj. for **[11975]**
Young Amer. Indian Coun. - Address unknown since 1995.
Young Americans for Freedom **[17279]**, 2300 M St. NW, Ste. 800, Washington, DC 20037, (202)470-0196
Young Amers. of Polish Descent - Defunct.
Young America's Found. **[17280]**, F.M. Kirby Freedom Ctr., 110 Elden St., Herndon, VA 20170, (703)318-9608
Young Apprentice's Assn. **[IO]**, Brasilia, Brazil
Young AREN - Address unknown since 2008.
Young Astronaut Coun. **[7925]**, 5200 27th St. NW, Washington, DC 20015, (301)617-0923
Young Astronaut Program **[★7925]**
Young Audiences **[9603]**, 115 E 92nd St., New York, NY 10128-1688, (212)831-8110
Young Australians Best Book Award Coun. **[IO]**, Kew, Australia
Young Black Programmers Coalition - Address unknown since 2001.
Young; Born **[★20865]**
Young Buddhist League; Western **[19558]**
Young Calvinist Fed. **[★19831]**
Young Children; Natl. Assn. for the Educ. of **[8069]**
Young Children: Priority One **[★13047]**
Young Children: Priority One **[★IO]**
Young Choreographers and Composers in Residence Program **[★9865]**

Young Christian Movement - Defunct.
Young Circle League of Am. **[★19147]**
Young Citizens League of America - Defunct.
Young; Clan **[20865]**
Young Club; Pope and **[23056]**
Young Communist League of the U.S.A. **[18661]**, 235 W 23rd St., Ste. 254, New York, NY 10011, (212)741-2016
Young Concert Artists **[10727]**, 250 W 57th St., Ste. 1222, New York, NY 10107, (212)307-6655
Young Conservatives **[IO]**, Frederiksberg, Denmark
Young Democratic Club of Am. **[★17412]**
Young Democratic Socialists **[18662]**, 75 Maiden Ln., Ste. 505, New York, NY 10038, (212)727-8610
Young Democrats of Am. **[17412]**, PO Box 77496, Washington, DC 20013-8496, (202)639-8585
Young Democrats of Am; Coll. **[★17400]**
Young Entomologists' Soc. **[7066]**, 6907 W Grand River Ave., Lansing, MI 48906-9131, (517)886-0630
Young Entrepreneurs Assn. of Canada **[IO]**, Victoria, BC, Canada
Young Entrepreneurs' Org. **[★718]**
Young Executives Soc. of NAPSA **[★266]**
Young Farmer Educational Assn; Natl. **[4653]**
Young Filmmakers Found. **[★9938]**
Young Friends of North America - Defunct.
Young Georgia Writers; Georgia Writers Assn. and **[11172]**
Young Guard Soc. **[★1519]**
Young Israel Coun. of Rabbis **[20197]**, c/o Natl. Coun. of Young Israel, 111 John St., Ste. 450, New York, NY 10038, (212)929-1525
Young Israel Inst. for Jewish Studies - Defunct.
Young Israel; Natl. Coun. of **[20167]**
Young Journalists; Assn. of **[3098]**
Young Judaea **[★20198]**
Young Judaea **[20198]**, 50 W 58th St., New York, NY 10019, (212)303-8014
Young Judaea/Hashachar **[★20198]**
Young Kibbutz Movement - Defunct.
Young Koreans United **[12485]**, 2701A W Peterson Ave., Ste. 102, Chicago, IL 60659, (773)506-9299
Young Koreans United **[IO]**, Chicago, IL, United States
Young Lawyers Div; Amer. Bar Assn. **[5477]**
Young Life **[20644]**, PO Box 520, Colorado Springs, CO 80901, (877)438-9572
Young Life **[IO]**, Colorado Springs, CO, United States
Young Media Australia **[IO]**, Glenelg, Australia
Young Men Societies; Amer. Fed. of Reformed **[★19831]**
Young Men's Assn. of the Men's Apparel Indus. **[★262]**
Young Men's Auxiliary Educ. and Missionary Soc. **[★19970]**
Young Men's Christian Association - Albania **[IO]**, Tirana, Albania
Young Men's Christian Association - Angola **[IO]**, Luanda, Angola
Young Men's Christian Association - Antwerp, Belgium **[IO]**, Antwerp, Belgium
Young Men's Christian Association of Armenia **[IO]**, Yerevan, Armenia
Young Men's Christian Association - Aruba **[IO]**, San Nicolas, Aruba
Young Men's Christian Association - Bahamas **[IO]**, Freeport, Bahamas
Young Men's Christian Association of Barbados **[IO]**, Bridgetown, Barbados
Young Men's Christian Association - Belize **[IO]**, Belize City, Belize
Young Men's Christian Association - Benin **[IO]**, Cotonou, Benin
Young Men's Christian Association - Burundi **[IO]**, Bujumbura, Burundi
Young Men's Christian Association - Cameroon **[IO]**, Yaounde, Cameroon
Young Men's Christian Association of Canada **[IO]**, Toronto, ON, Canada
Young Men's Christian Association - Costa Rica **[IO]**, San Jose, Costa Rica
Young Men's Christian Association - Democratic Republic of Congo **[IO]**, Kinshasa, Democratic Republic of the Congo

Young Men's Christian Association - England **[IO]**, London, United Kingdom
Young Men's Christian Association - Ethiopia **[IO]**, Addis Ababa, Ethiopia
Young Men's Christian Association - Fiji **[IO]**, Suva, Fiji
Young Men's Christian Association of Finland **[IO]**, Helsinki, Finland
Young Men's Christian Association - Gambia **[IO]**, Banjul, Gambia
Young Men's Christian Association of Georgia **[IO]**, Tbilisi, Georgia
Young Men's Christian Association - Guyana **[IO]**, Linden, Guyana
Young Men's Christian Association - Haiti **[IO]**, Port-au-Prince, Haiti
Young Men's Christian Association of Hong Kong **[IO]**, Hong Kong, People's Republic of China
Young Men's Christian Association - Hungary **[IO]**, Budapest, Hungary
Young Men's Christian Association of Indonesia **[IO]**, Jakarta, Indonesia
Young Men's Christian Association - Jordan **[IO]**, Amman, Jordan
Young Men's Christian Association - Lebanon **[IO]**, Beirut, Lebanon
Young Men's Christian Association - Mauritius **[IO]**, Quatre Bornes, Mauritius
Young Men's Christian Association of Nazareth **[IO]**, Nazareth, Israel
Young Men's Christian Association of Nepal **[IO]**, Kathmandu, Nepal
Young Men's Christian Association - Papua New Guinea **[IO]**, Lae, Papua New Guinea
Young Men's Christian Association - Peru **[IO]**, Lima, Peru
Young Men's Christian Association of the Philippines **[IO]**, Manila, Philippines
Young Men's Christian Association - Rwanda **[IO]**, Kigali, Rwanda
Young Men's Christian Association - Samoa **[IO]**, Apia, Western Samoa
Young Men's Christian Association - Senegal **[IO]**, Dakar, Senegal
Young Men's Christian Association - Sierra Leone **[IO]**, Freetown, Sierra Leone
Young Men's Christian Association - Spain **[IO]**, Madrid, Spain
Young Men's Christian Association - Suriname **[IO]**, Paramaribo, Suriname
Young Men's Christian Association of Taiwan **[IO]**, Taipei, Taiwan
Young Men's Christian Association - Trinidad and Tobago **[IO]**, Port of Spain, Trinidad and Tobago
Young Men's Christian Association of Ukraine **[IO]**, Kiev, Ukraine
Young Men's Christian Association and Young Women's Christian Association - Denmark **[IO]**, Valby, Denmark
Young Men's Christian Associations of North Am; Assn. of Secretaries, **[★13460]**
Young Men's Christian Associations of the U.S.A. **[★13463]**
Young Men's Christian Associations in the U.S; Assn. of Professional Directors, **[★13460]**
Young Men's Division-Zeirei Agudath Israel **[20199]**, 42 Broadway, New York, NY 10004, (212)797-9000
Young Men's Hebrew and Kindred Associations; Coun. of **[★12473]**
Young Mensa Intl. Special Interest Group - Defunct.
Young Menswear Assn. **[262]**, 36 W 20th St., 3rd Fl., New York, NY 10011, (212)594-6422
Young Menswear Assn. of Men's Apparel Indus. **[★262]**
Young Messianic Jewish Alliance **[★20257]**
Young Naturalists' Circle **[IO]**, Montreal, QC, Canada
Young Numismatists of Am. **[22770]**, c/o Cameron Kiefer, PO Box 7015, Visalia, CA 93290
Young Onset Parkinson's Assn. **[15374]**, 22136 Westheimer Pkwy., No. 343, Katy, TX 77450-8296, (888)937-9672
Young People of the Amer. Lib. Assn; Sect. of the Division of Libraries for Children and **[★10317]**
Young People; U.S. Bd. on Books for **[9756]**
Young People Who Stutter; Friends: The Natl. Assn. of **[16445]**

Reference to "IO" in place of a book number signifies that the association may be found in the 45th edition of International Organizations.

Young Peoples Lobby for Jobs - Defunct.
Young Peoples Socialist League [★18306]
Young Polish Women; Legion of [19304]
Young Presidents' Org. [769], 600 E Las Colinas Blvd., Ste. 1000, Irving, TX 75039, (972)587-1500
Young Professionals Div. - Address unknown since 1994.
Young Professionals of the Soc. for Personnel Administration - Defunct.
Young Racers of Am. [23674], 1609 Pleasant Run, Keller, TX 76248, (817)431-8390
Young Religious Unitarian Universalists [20605], 25 Beacon St., Boston, MA 02108, (617)948-4350
Young Republican Natl. Fed. [18540], PO Box 15293, Washington, DC 20003, (202)608-1417
Young Republican Natl. Fed; Coll. Ser. Comm. of the [★18522]
Young and the Restless Fan Club [25047], c/o CBS TV, 7800 Beverly Blvd., Ste. 3305, Los Angeles, CA 90036
Young Scientists of America Found. - Defunct.
Young Social Democrats [★18306]
Young Soc; Clan [★20865]
Young Stamp Collectors of Am. [22891], 100 Match Factory Pl., Bellefonte, PA 16823, (814)933-3820
Young Surname Org. [21091]
Young Surname Org. [★20865]
Young Survival Coalition [13883], 61 Broadway, Ste. 2235, New York, NY 10006, (646)257-3000
Young Survival Coalition [IO], New York, NY, United States
Young Unionists [★IO]
Young Women of the Church of Jesus Christ of Latter-Day Saints [20209], 76 N Main, Salt Lake City, UT 84150-6030, (801)240-1000
Young Women Social Entrepreneurs [770], 1684 Washington St., No. 5, San Francisco, CA 94109, (415)378-4417
Young Women Societies; Amer. Fed. of Reformed [★19831]
Young Women's Christian Association of Albania [IO], Tirana, Albania
Young Women's Christian Association of Amer. Samoa [IO], Pago Pago, American Samoa
Young Women's Christian Assn. - Angola [IO], Luanda, Angola
Young Women's Christian Association of Antigua [IO], St. Johns, Antigua-Barbuda
Young Women's Christian Association - Aotearoa/ New Zealand [IO], Wellington, New Zealand
Young Women's Christian Association - Argentina [IO], Buenos Aires, Argentina
Young Women's Christian Association - Australia [IO], Dickson, Australia
Young Women's Christian Association - Bahamas [IO], Nassau, Bahamas
Young Women's Christian Association - Bangladesh [IO], Dhaka, Bangladesh
Young Women's Christian Association of Barbados [IO], Bridgetown, Barbados
Young Women's Christian Association - Belarus [IO], Minsk, Belarus
Young Women's Christian Association - Belgium [IO], Antwerp, Belgium
Young Women's Christian Association - Belize [IO], Belize City, Belize
Young Women's Christian Assn. - Benin [IO], Cotonou, Benin
Young Women's Christian Association - Botswana [IO], Gaborone, Botswana
Young Women's Christian Association - Brazil [IO], Sao Paulo, Brazil
Young Women's Christian Assn. - Bulgaria [IO], Sofia, Bulgaria
Young Women's Christian Assn. - Cameroon [IO], Douala, Cameroon
Young Women's Christian Association - Canada [IO], Toronto, ON, Canada
Young Women's Christian Assn. - Chile [IO], Valparaiso, Chile
Young Women's Christian Association - China [IO], Shanghai, People's Republic of China
Young Women's Christian Association - Colombia [IO], Bogota, Colombia
Young Women's Christian Assn. - El Salvador [IO], San Salvador, El Salvador

Young Women's Christian Assn. - Estonia [IO], Tallinn, Estonia
Young Women's Christian Association of Ethiopia [IO], Addis Ababa, Ethiopia
Young Women's Christian Association of Fiji [IO], Suva, Fiji
Young Women's Christian Association - Finland [IO], Helsinki, Finland
Young Women's Christian Association - Gambia [IO], Banjul, Gambia
Young Women's Christian Association - Germany [IO], Frankfurt am Main, Germany
Young Women's Christian Association - Ghana [IO], Accra, Ghana
Young Women's Christian Association - Great Britain [IO], Oxford, United Kingdom
Young Women's Christian Association of Greece - XEN [IO], Athens, Greece
Young Women's Christian Association - Grenada [IO], St. George's, Grenada
Young Women's Christian Association - Guyana [IO], Georgetown, Guyana
Young Women's Christian Association - Hong Kong [IO], Hong Kong, People's Republic of China
Young Women's Christian Association - Iceland [IO], Reykjavik, Iceland
Young Women's Christian Association of India [IO], New Delhi, India
Young Women's Christian Association - Ireland [IO], Dublin, Ireland
Young Women's Christian Association - Italy [IO], Torre Pellice, Italy
Young Women's Christian Association - Jamaica [IO], Kingston, Jamaica
Young Women's Christian Association of Japan [IO], Tokyo, Japan
Young Women's Christian Association - Kenya [IO], Nairobi, Kenya
Young Women's Christian Association - Korea [IO], Seoul, Republic of Korea
Young Women's Christian Assn. - Latvia [IO], Riga, Latvia
Young Women's Christian Association - Lebanon [IO], Beirut, Lebanon
Young Women's Christian Assn. - Lesotho [IO], Maseru, Lesotho
Young Women's Christian Assn. - Lithuania [IO], Vilnius, Lithuania
Young Women's Christian Association - Madagascar [IO], Antananarivo, Madagascar
Young Women's Christian Association - Malaysia [IO], Petaling Jaya, Malaysia
Young Women's Christian Assn. - Mauritius [IO], Rose Hill, Mauritius
Young Women's Christian Association - Mexico [IO], Guadalajara, Mexico
Young Women's Christian Association - Myanmar [IO], Yangon, Myanmar
Young Women's Christian Association - Namibia [IO], Windhoek, Namibia
Young Women's Christian Assn. - Nepal [IO], Kathmandu, Nepal
Young Women's Christian Association - Netherlands [IO], Utrecht, Netherlands
Young Women's Christian Association - Nigeria [IO], Lagos, Nigeria
Young Women's Christian Association - Norway [IO], Oslo, Norway
Young Women's Christian Association - Pakistan [IO], Lahore, Pakistan
Young Women's Christian Association - Palestine [IO], Jerusalem, Israel
Young Women's Christian Association - Papua New Guinea [IO], Boroko, Papua New Guinea
Young Women's Christian Association - Peru [IO], Lima, Peru
Young Women's Christian Association - Philippines [IO], Manila, Philippines
Young Women's Christian Association - Puerto Rico [IO], San Juan, PR, United States
Young Women's Christian Association - Puerto Rico [13526], PO Box 10111, San Juan, PR 00908, (787)724-1037
Young Women's Christian Association - Romania [IO], Bucharest, Romania

Young Women's Christian Assn. - Russia [IO], Moscow, Russia
Young Women's Christian Assn. - Rwanda [IO], Gitarama, Rwanda
Young Women's Christian Association of Samoa [IO], Pago Pago, American Samoa
Young Women's Christian Association of Sierra Leone [IO], Freetown, Sierra Leone
Young Women's Christian Association - Singapore [IO], Singapore, Singapore
Young Women's Christian Association - Solomon Islands [IO], Honiara, Solomon Islands
Young Women's Christian Association - South Africa [IO], Bloemfontein, Republic of South Africa
Young Women's Christian Association - Sri Lanka [IO], Colombo, Sri Lanka
Young Women's Christian Association - Suriname [IO], Paramaribo, Suriname
Young Women's Christian Association - Taiwan [IO], Taipei, Taiwan
Young Women's Christian Association - Thailand [IO], Bangkok, Thailand
Young Women's Christian Assn. - Togo [IO], Lome, Togo
Young Women's Christian Association - Trinidad and Tobago [IO], Port of Spain, Trinidad and Tobago
Young Women's Christian Association - Uganda [IO] Kampala, Uganda
Young Women's Christian Association - Ukraine [IO] Kiev, Ukraine
Young Women's Christian Assn. of the U.S.A. [13527], 1015 18th St. NW, Ste. 1100, Washington, DC 20036-5271, (202)467-0801
Young Women's Christian Association - Uruguay [IO], Montevideo, Uruguay
Young Women's Christian Association - Zambia [IO], Lusaka, Zambia
Young Women's Financial Assn. of New York [★1421]
Young Women's Investment Assn. of New York [★1421]
Young Women's and Men's Assn. - Sweden [★IO]
Young Women's Mutual Improvement Assn. [★20209]
Young Women's and Young Men's Christian Association - Sweden [IO], Stockholm, Sweden
Young Workers Liberation League [★18661]
Young World Development Regional Center [★12774]
Young World Development Regional Center [★IO]
Youngchoirs [IO], Loughborough, United Kingdom
Younger Brothers Band Fan Club - Defunct.
Your Heritage Protection Assn. - Defunct.

Youth

Action for Child Protection [11553]
Action for Healthy Kids [13945]
Action for Solidarity, Equality, Env. and Diversity - Europe [IO]
Adolescent Scoliosis Soc. of North Am. [16392]
Adoption Identity Movement [11229]
Advocates for Youth [12173]
Advocates for Youth's Media Proj. [12174]
Afghan Canadian Youth Org. [IO]
African Children's Intl. Peace Forum and Ambassadors for Global Peace Intl. [IO]
African Youth Parliament [IO]
Afterschool Alliance [11524]
AIDS Alliance for Children, Youth and Families [13548]
Alliance for Eating Disorders Awareness [14297]
Alliance for Excellent Educ. [9118]
Allied Youth and Family Counseling Center [13465]
Amateur Athletic Union [23797]
Amer. Acad. of Child and Adolescent Psychiatry [16063]
Amer. Acad. of Pediatric Dentistry [14108]
Amer. Assn. of Caregiving Youth [13466]
Amer. Assn. of Children's Residential Centers [13467]
Amer. Assn. for Lost Children [12607]
Amer. Cadet Alliance [20718]
Amer. Camp Assn. [23268]
Amer. Collegiate Horsemen's Assn. [4814]
Amer. Hindu Assn. [20077]

A star before a book entry number signifies that the name is not listed separately, but is mentioned within the entry.

Amer. Indian Youth Running Strong [12623]
Amer. Jewish Soc. for Ser. [12465]
Amer. Junior Golf Assn. [23444]
Amer. Junior Paint Horse Assn. [4828]
Amer. Legion Baseball [23103]
Amer. Quarter Horse Youth Assn. [4839]
Amer. Romanian Orthodox Youth [20540]
Amer. Salers Junior Assn. [4246]
Amer. Soc. for Adolescent Psychiatry [16078]
Amer. Sports Org. [23993]
Amer. Student Govt. Assn. [9175]
Amer. Youth Circus Org. [9795]
Amer. Youth Found. [20638]
Amer. Youth Horse Coun. [4856]
Amer. Youth Policy Forum [13468]
Amer. Youth Soccer Org. [23774]
Amer. Youth Understanding Diabetes Abroad
  [14219]
Amer. Youth Work Center [13469]
America's Promise - The Alliance for Youth
  [13470]
Armenian Church Youth Org. of Am. [19458]
Asian Youth Centre [IO]
Assn. for Arab Youth - Baladna [IO]
Assn. of Children's Museums [10495]
Assn. of Girl Scout Executive Staff [12996]
Assn. of Jewish Center Professionals [12466]
Assn. of Qualified Volunteers in Youth Services
  [IO]
Assn. of Thai Professionals in Am. and Canada
  [19406]
Assn. of YMCA Professionals [13460]
Assn. for Youth Action Development [IO]
Ataxia Telangiectasia Children's Proj. [14253]
Awana Clubs Intl. [20639]
Awana Clubs Intl. [IO]
Babe Ruth Baseball/Softball [23106]
Better Boys Found. [11675]
Big Bros. Big Sisters of Canada [IO]
Big Picture Company [8353]
Bike and Build [11514]
B'nai B'rith Youth Org. [20126]
BoardSource [12651]
Boy Scouts of Am. [12997]
Boys and Girls Clubs of Am. [13471]
Boys and Girls Clubs of Canada [IO]
Boys Hope Girls Hope [13472]
Boys Hope Girls Hope - Ireland [IO]
Boys Town Jerusalem Found. of Am. [13473]
Boys' Towns of Italy [13474]
Brave Kids [13949]
Break Away: The Alternative Break Connection
  [12795]
Brotherhood of the Jungle Cock [23412]
Burundi Youth For Christ [IO]
Camp Fire USA [13475]
Campaign For Our Children [13476]
Canadian Fed. of Junior Leagues [IO]
Carnegie Coun. on Adolescent Development
  [13477]
Casa Ananda, A.C. of Mexico [IO]
Center for Youth Development and Policy Res.
  [18845]
Character Educ. Partnership [17476]
Child Trends [11679]
Child Welfare League of Am. [11572]
Children of the Night [12933]
Children's Defense Fund [11685]
Children's Friendship Proj. for Northern Ireland
  [13478]
Children's Liver Assn. for Support Services
  [14804]
Children's Relief Network [11581]
CHOICE [12178]
Choristers Guild [20426]
Christian Commun. Centre [IO]
CityKids Found. [13479]
Clubs for Young People [IO]
Coalition for Positive Sexuality [13480]
Coll. Summit [8486]
Comm. for Children [11587]
Communities Against Violence Network [13374]
Concordia - Youth Ser. Volunteers [IO]
Conservative Future [IO]
Constitutional Rights Found. [17291]

Covenant House [13481]
Creative Youth of Novi Sad [IO]
CRISTA Ministries [13166]
Croatian Youth Coun. [IO]
CSB Ministries [20640]
DanceSafe [12041]
Danish Youth Coun. [IO]
Delta Teen-Lift [13341]
Democrat Youth Community of Europe [IO]
Direction Sports [13482]
Do Something [17215]
Duke of Edinburgh's Award Intl. Assn. [IO]
Dynamic Youth Ministries [19831]
Dysautonomia Youth Network of Am. [15318]
Earth Force [4549]
East African Youth Alliance [IO]
EcoVentures Intl. [4623]
Ecumenical Youth Coun. in Europe [IO]
Education-A-Must [12056]
Educators Serving the Community [8318]
Empower Prog. [8945]
Entertainment Indus. Coun. [13238]
European Building and Services Assn. [IO]
European Fed. of Youth Ser. Organisations [IO]
European Youth Forum [IO]
European Youth Found. [IO]
Ewing Marion Kaufman Found. [18846]
Families, 4-H, and Nutrition [13483]
Fashion Outreach [235]
Fed. of Families for Children's Mental Hea.
  [12550]
Fed. of Galaxy Explorers [9136]
Fed. of German Catholic Youth [IO]
Fed. of Pediatric Organizations [15887]
Fight Crime: Invest in Kids [17057]
Finnish Youth Co-Operation Allianssi [IO]
Focus Intl. - Kenya [IO]
Foster Care Alumni of Am. [11592]
Found. for Young Australians [IO]
French Youth Assn. [IO]
Fresh Lifelines for Youth [13484]
Friends for Youth [13485]
Fundacion Juconi [IO]
Funders' Collaborative on Youth Organizing
  [12718]
Gay and Lesbian Adolescent Social Services
  [18847]
GenerationEngage [18848]
George Khoury Assn. of Baseball Leagues
  [23109]
GesherCity [19183]
Girl Scouts of the U.S.A. [12998]
Girls' Brigade Australia [IO]
Girls' Brigade Australia - New South Wales [IO]
Girls' Brigade Australia - Queensland [IO]
Girls' Brigade Australia - South Australia [IO]
Girls' Brigade Australia - Victoria [IO]
Girls' Brigade Australia - Western Australia [IO]
Girls' Brigade - England and Wales [IO]
Girls' Brigade New Zealand [IO]
Girls' Brigade Northern Ireland [IO]
Girls' Brigade Scotland [IO]
Girls' Brigade Singapore [IO]
Girls Friendly Soc. - United Kingdom - GFS
  Platform [IO]
Girls Inc. [13486]
Girlstart [8468]
Global Action Proj. [18849]
Global Action Proj. [IO]
Global Family [13140]
Global Nomads Gp. [9336]
Global Youth Action Network [18850]
Global Youth Action Network [IO]
Global Youth Connect [IO]
Global Youth Connect [18851]
Grantmakers for Children, Youth, and Families
  [12723]
Guitars Not Guns [18114]
Hands On Sci. Outreach [8067]
Hashomer Hatzair Zionist Youth Movement
  [20140]
Hea. Jam [14674]
Hetrick-Martin Inst. [12234]
Hip-Hop Assn. [10887]
Holy Childhood Assn. [19632]

Hostelling International-American Youth Hostels
  [12797]
Human Rights Educ. Radio Listener Clubs [IO]
Human Support Services [IO]
Hungarian Scouts Assn. [12999]
I Have a Dream Found. [13487]
Indian Youth of Am. [12626]
Indify [13488]
Inst. in Basic Life Principles [13489]
Inst. for the Stud. of Antisocial Behavior in Youth
  [IO]
Intl. Alliance for Child and Adolescent Mental Hea.
  and Schools [15204]
Intl. Alliance for Youth Sports [23994]
Intl. Assn. of Pediatric Lab. Medicine [15888]
Intl. Coalition for Children and the Env. [4636]
Intl. Concert Alliance [10617]
Intl. Fed. of Liberal and Radical Youth [IO]
Intl. Medalist Assn. [23825]
Intl. Org. for Adolescents [11606]
Intl. Pediatric Hypertension Assn. [14907]
Intl. Soap Box Derby [23770]
Intl. Soc. of Active Youth [IO]
Intl. Soc. for Adolescent Psychiatry and Psychol-
  ogy [16087]
Intl. Young Christian Workers - Belgium [IO]
Intl. Youth Assn. [IO]
Intl. Youth Found. [IO]
Intl. Youth Found. [13490]
Interstate Migrant Educ. Coun. [12588]
Irish Youth Found. [IO]
Jack and Jill of Am. Found. [11703]
Jackie Robinson Found. [13491]
Jewish Bd. of Family and Children's Services/
  Youth Counseling League Div. [13492]
Jobs for America's Graduates [12084]
Join Hands Day [17203]
Junge Liberalen Bonn [IO]
Junior Optimist Octagon Intl. [13045]
Junior Shag Assn. [9890]
Just Think [18852]
JustAct: Youth Action for Global Justice [18853]
Juvenile Diabetes Res. Found. Intl. [14228]
Juvenile Justice CH [6363]
Juventude Social-Democratica [IO]
Kadima [20155]
Kidpower Teenpower Fullpower Intl. [12967]
Kids for a Clean Env. [4585]
Kids Fund [11704]
Kids Universe, Inc. [8320]
Kids With Food Allergies [13603]
Kids Without Borders [11614]
Kindness in Suffering [11616]
Knights Boxing Team - Intl. [23265]
League of Young Voters [18356]
Levitt Found. [13493]
Liberal Democrat Youth and Students - UK [IO]
Lifespan Resources [11294]
Little League Baseball and Softball [23111]
Little League Found. [23112]
Lubavitch Youth Org. [20158]
Macedonian Orthodox Youth Assn. of North Am.
  [19883]
Magic Youth Intl. [22622]
Make-A-Wish Found. of Am. [11707]
Malaysian Youth Coun. [IO]
MAR-Bulgarian Youth Alliance for Development
  [IO]
Masada/Maccabi Israel Summer Programs
  [20159]
Milpas de Oaxaca [IO]
Miss Am. Org. [22135]
Mission for Youth Rights [IO]
Mobile Voter [18032]
Moderata Ungdomsforbundet [IO]
Mothers Without Borders [11624]
Mukono Multi-Purpose Youth Org. [IO]
Multicultural Golf Assn. of Am. [23455]
Natl. 4-H Coun. [13494]
Natl. Abstinence Educ. Assn. [9123]
Natl. AfterSchool Assn. [11528]
Natl. Alliance of Gang Investigators Associations
  [5638]
Natl. Alliance to Nurture the Aged and the Youth
  [12358]

Reference to "IO" in place of a book number signifies that the association may be found in the 45th edition of International Organizations.

Natl. Alliance for Youth Sports [23290]
Natl. Assn. of Extension 4-H Agents [13495]
Natl. Assn. of Former Foster Care Children of Am. [11626]
Natl. Assn. of Peer Programs [11827]
Natl. Assn. of Police Athletic Leagues [13496]
Natl. Assn. of Ser. and Conservation Corps [13497]
Natl. Assn. of St. Schools [9337]
Natl. Assn. of Therapeutic Wilderness Camps [23276]
Natl. Assn. of Youth Clubs [13498]
Natl. Assn. for Youth Drama [IO]
Natl. Black United Fed. of Charities [16943]
Natl. Bd. for Certified Counselors and Affiliates [11828]
Natl. Campaign to Prevent Teen Pregnancy [13499]
Natl. Center for Youth Law [5700]
Natl. Chaplains Assn. [19855]
Natl. Child Labor Comm. [13500]
Natl. Collaboration for Youth [11635]
Natl. Coun. of Swedish Youth Organisations [IO]
Natl. Coun. of Youth Organizations in Korea [IO]
Natl. Coun. of Youth Sports [23839]
Natl. Derby Rallies [23771]
Natl. Dissemination Center for Children with Disabilities [11971]
Natl. Eagle Scout Assn. [13002]
Natl. Fellowship of Child Care Executives [13501]
Natl. Jewish Comm. on Scouting [13003]
Natl. Junior Horticultural Assn. [22530]
Natl. Junior Santa Gertrudis Assn. [4277]
Natl. Network of Youth Ministries [20641]
Natl. Organizations for Youth Safety [13502]
Natl. Rsrc. Center for Youth Services [11639]
Natl. Runaway Switchboard [12936]
Natl. Rural Educ. Advocacy Coalition [9068]
Natl. Service-Learning Partnership [9120]
Natl. Show Pig Assn. [22982]
Natl. Teen Age Republican HQ [18529]
Natl. Teen Anglers [22454]
Natl. Tots and Teens [13503]
Natl. Union of Eritrean Youth and Students [IO]
Natl. Young Adult Assn. [13504]
Natl. Youth Advocacy Coalition [13505]
Natl. Youth Agency [IO]
Natl. Youth Coun. of Ireland [IO]
Natl. Youth Court Center [18854]
Natl. Youth Employment Coalition [13506]
Natl. Youth Rights Assn. [18855]
Natl. Youth Sports Safety Found. [16484]
Naval Sea Cadet Corps [6098]
NetAid [11486]
Network 20/20 [18004]
Network of Iranian Amer. Soc. [13507]
Networking Proj. for Young Adults with Disabilities [11975]
New Zealand Assn. for Adolescent Hea. and Development [IO]
NFHS Officials Assn. [23874]
Nongovernmental Organizations Comm. on Youth [13508]
North Amer. Fed. of Temple Youth [19185]
North Amer. Man/Boy Love Assn. [13099]
North Amer. Sankethi Assn. [9802]
North Amer. YMCA Development Org. [13461]
Oaktree Found. [IO]
Ocean Youth Trust Scotland [IO]
One Earth One Justice [12437]
Only a Child [11643]
Ophelia Proj. [13509]
Ophelia Proj. [IO]
Optimist Intl. [13057]
ORACLE Religious Assn. [20070]
Order of the Arrow [13005]
Org. for the Relief of Underprivileged Women and Children in Africa [12876]
Org. for Social Development of Unemployed Youth [IO]
Orphan Found. of Am. [11715]
Orphan Resources Intl. [11644]
Otesha Proj. [IO]
OutProud [12252]
Ozar Hatorah [20171]

PACER Center - Parent Advocacy Coalition for Educational Rights [14246]
PAHAL [IO]
Participa [IO]
Patidar Cultural Assn. of USA [10218]
PE4life [8991]
Peckglo Org. [IO]
Peer Hea. Exchange [9338]
People Against Rape [13083]
Pioneer Clubs [20642]
Play for Peace [12699]
Polish-American-Jewish Alliance for Youth Action [13510]
Polish-American-Jewish Alliance for Youth Action [IO]
Pony Baseball and Softball [23124]
Positive Coaching Alliance [23296]
Positive Youth Found. [18856]
Prepare Tomorrow's Parents [13511]
Progressive Youth Org. [IO]
Proj. YES [9339]
Religious Zionist Youth Movement - Bnei Akiva of the U.S. and Canada [20178]
Rsrc. Generation [13137]
Restoration Proj. Intl. [12441]
Reviving Baseball in Inner Cities [13512]
River of Words [4186]
Robert F. Kennedy Memorial [13513]
Saathi [IO]
Safe Sitter [11537]
Sail and Life Training Soc. [IO]
Salvation Army UK and Ireland [IO]
Scottish Young Conservatives [IO]
Scouting For All [13006]
Sea Cadets [IO]
Secretariat for Family, Laity, Women, and Youth [12167]
Seeds of Peace [18245]
Seeking Common Ground [13514]
Seeking Harmony in Neighborhoods Everyday [18857]
Shriners Hospitals for Children [13973]
Soccer Assn. for Youth [23781]
Social Cooperative Grado 16 [IO]
Social Policy Action Network [13138]
Soc. for Promotion of Youth and Masses [IO]
Soc. for Res. on Adolescence [13515]
South Asian Amer. Voting Youth [18366]
A Special Wish Found. [11723]
Sphinx Org. [10710]
Starlight Starbright Children's Found. [11724]
Stop the Violence, Face The Music [13376]
Student Animal Rights Alliance [11337]
Student/Farmworker Alliance [24054]
Student Letter Exchange [22144]
Student Org. of North Am. [9194]
Student and Youth Travel Assn. [3938]
Subud Youth Assn. [13516]
Sudan-American Found. for Educ. [8073]
Support A Child Intl. [11655]
Supporting Our Sons [11547]
SustainUS [13517]
Swedish Youth of Finland - Youth Org. of the Swedish People's Party [IO]
Syndesmos [IO]
Tanzania Youth in Action for Development [IO]
Teaching-Family Assn. [12169]
Teen Challenge Intl. [20643]
Teen Challenge Intl. [IO]
Teen Missions Intl. [20402]
Theta Rho Girls' Club [13518]
Tibetan Youth Cong. [IO]
Tree Musketeers [4459]
Tzivos Hashem [10290]
Union of North Amer. Vietnamese Students Assn. [19426]
United Methodist Youth Org. [20268]
United Natl. Indian Tribal Youth [10756]
U.S. Cultural Exchange and Sports Soc. [23861]
U.S. Field Hockey Assn. [23405]
U.S. Junior Chamber of Commerce [24390]
U.S. Tchoukball Assn. [23094]
U.S. Youth Soccer Assn. [23784]
United Synagogue Youth [20189]
USA Tennis - NJTL [23916]

Vocational Found., Inc. [12103]
Voices for America's Children [11662]
WAVE [12105]
Western Young Buddhist League [19558]
What If Org. [18858]
What Kids Can Do [18859]
William T. Grant Found. [11549]
Wimbum Cultural and Development Assn. in the U.S.A. [9344]
WishKids Intl. [11665]
World Assembly of Muslim Youth [IO]
World Fed. of Amateur Orchestras [10766]
World Youth Alliance [IO]
World Youth Alliance [18860]
World Youth Found. [IO]
YMCA Earth Ser. Corps [18861]
YMCA Intl. Br. [13462]
Young Adult Lib. Services Assn. [10395]
Young America's Found. [17280]
Young Concert Artists [10727]
Young Conservatives [IO]
Young Democratic Socialists [18662]
Young Life [IO]
Young Life [20644]
Young Men's Division-Zeirei Agudath Israel [20199]
Young Numismatists of Am. [22770]
Young Racers of Am. [23674]
Young Religious Unitarian Universalists [20605]
Young Stamp Collectors of Am. [22891]
Youth Action Network [IO]
Youth Action for Peace - Deutschland [IO]
Youth Advocate Prog. Intl. [11668]
Youth Assisting Youth [IO]
Youth for Christ/U.S.A. [20645]
Youth Crime Watch of Am. [13519]
Youth Development Intl. [13520]
Youth Educ. in the Arts [9604]
Youth Empowerment Initiative [IO]
Youth for Environmental Sanity [4625]
Youth Evangelism Assn. [20036]
Youth for Human Rights Intl. [12382]
Youth Impact Intl. [IO]
Youth Impact Intl. [13521]
Youth for Intergenerational Justice and Sustainability - Europe [IO]
Youth for Intl. Socialism [18663]
Youth Law Center [13522]
Youth League of the Coalition Party [IO]
Youth Ministry [20235]
Youth Organizations U.S.A. [13523]
Youth Ser. Am. [13070]
Youth Venture [4072]
Youth World Travel Org. [IO]
Youth to Youth Intl. [IO]
Youth to Youth Intl. [13524]
YouthBuild USA [13525]
Youthlink Scotland [IO]
Y's Men Intl., U.S. Area [13464]
Zeirei Agudath Israel [20200]
Zonta Intl. [13071]

Youth Action for Global Justice; Just Act: [12435]
Youth Action for Global Justice; JustAct: [18853]
Youth Action Network [IO], Toronto, ON, Canada
Youth Action for Peace [IO], Brussels, Belgium
Youth Action for Peace - Deutschland [IO], Frankfurt, Germany
Youth Action for Peace - Italy [IO], Rome, Italy
Youth Adult Prog. [★8808]
Youth Advocate Prog. Intl. [11668], 4545 42nd St. NW, Ste. 209, Washington, DC 20016, (202)244-1986
Youth Advocate Prog. Intl. [IO], Washington, DC, United States
Youth Against War and Fascism - Defunct.
Youth of All Nations - Defunct.
Youth Alliance for Development [★IO]
Youth Alliance; Natl. [★18800]
Youth; Allied [★13465]
Youth Ambassadors Intl. - Address unknown since 1994.
Youth of Am; Greek Orthodox [★20072]
Youth of Am; Indian [12626]
Youth; Amer. Romanian Orthodox [20540]
Youth; Amer. Theatre Arts for [11003]

A star before a book entry number signifies that the name is not listed separately, but is mentioned within the entry.

Youth Assisting Youth [IO], Toronto, ON, Canada
Youth Assn; Amer. Quarter Horse [4839]
Youth Assn; Awana [★20639]
Youth Challenge International-Canada [IO], Toronto, ON, Canada
Youth for Christ/U.S.A. [20645], PO Box 4478, Englewood, CO 80155, (303)843-9000
Youth Citizenship Fund - Address unknown since 1995.
Youth Comm. Against Poverty - Address unknown since 1995.
Youth Comm. for Peace and Democracy in the Middle East [★18073]
Youth Conflicts; Inst. in Basic [★13489]
Youth Coun; Natl. Indian [10749]
Youth Coun; World [★19855]
Youth Councils; Natl. Fed. of Diocesan Catholic [★19688]
Youth Counseling League Div; Jewish Bd. of Family and Children's Services/ [13492]
Youth Crime Watch of Am. [13519], 9200 S Dadeland Blvd., Ste. 417, Miami, FL 33156, (305)670-2409
Youth Development; 4-H Prog. and [★13483]
Youth Development Coalition - Defunct.
Youth Development Foundation [★4834]
Youth Development Intl. [13520], PO Box 178408, San Diego, CA 92177-8408, (800)HIT-HOME
Youth with Disabilities; Natl. Info. Center for Children and [★11971]
Youth Editors Assn. of America - Defunct.
Youth Educ. in the Arts [9604], 601 W Hamilton St., Allentown, PA 18101, (610)821-0345
Youth Educ. in the Arts [IO], Allentown, PA, United States
Youth Educ. in the Middle East and North Africa; Soc. for Jewish [★20171]
Youth Employment Company; 70001—The [12105]
Youth Empowerment Initiative [IO], New Delhi, India
Youth for Environmental Sanity [4625], 420 Bronco Rd., Soquel, CA 95073-9510, (831)465-1091
Youth of the European People's Party [IO], Brussels, Belgium
Youth Evangelism Assn. [20036], 13000 U.S. 41 N, Evansville, IN 47725, (812)867-2418
Youth of Evrytania - Address unknown since 1995.
Youth, and Families; Grantmakers for Children, [12723]
Youth and Families; Hazelden Center for [★13244]
Youth Fed; Universal Proutist [18631]
Youth Fellowship; Lutheran [★20235]
Youth Film Distribution Center [★9938]
Youth Football; Amer. [23428]
Youth For Understanding Intl. Exchange [★8639]
Youth For Understanding Intl. Exchange [★IO]
Youth For Understanding USA [IO], Bethesda, MD, United States
Youth For Understanding USA [8639], 6400 Goldsboro Rd., Ste. 100, Bethesda, MD 20817, (240)235-2100
Youth Found; Conservative Leadership [★8753]
Youth Found; Harness Horse [23496]
Youth Found; Hugh O'Brian [★8748]
Youth Fund; Charles Edison [★8747]
Youth Fund; Charles Edison Memorial [★8747]
Youth; Grantmakers for Children and [★12723]
Youth; Habonim Dror Labor Zionist [★20138]
Youth Highway Safety Advisory Comm. - Defunct.
Youth Horse Coun; Amer. [4856]
Youth Hostel Associations of China [IO], Guangzhou, People's Republic of China
Youth Hostel Romania [IO], Cluj-Napoca, Romania
Youth Hostels; Amer. [★12797]
Youth Hostels Assn. - England [★IO]
Youth Hostels Assn. - England and Wales [IO], Matlock, United Kingdom
Youth Hostels Assn. of India [IO], New Delhi, India
Youth Hostels Assn. of New Zealand [IO], Christchurch, New Zealand
Youth Hostels Assn. of Russia [IO], St. Petersburg, Russia
Youth for Human Rights Intl. [IO], Los Angeles, CA, United States
Youth for Human Rights Intl. [12382], PO Box 27306, Los Angeles, CA 90029, (323)663-5799

Youth; Ichud Habonim Dror Labor Zionist [★20138]
Youth; Ichud Habonim Labor Zionist [★20138]
Youth with Ileitis and Colitis; Reach Out for [16548]
Youth Impact Intl. [13521], 124 Mt. Auburn St., Univ. Pl., Harvard Sq., Ste. 200 N, Cambridge, MA 02138-5700, (617)520-6610
Youth Impact Intl. [IO], Cambridge, MA, United States
Youth Inst. for Peace in the Middle East [18073]
Youth; Inst. for the Protection of Lesbian and Gay [★12234]
Youth for Intergenerational Justice and Sustainability - Europe [IO], Hamburg, Germany
Youth for Intl. Socialism [IO], St. Paul, MN, United States
Youth for Intl. Socialism [18663], c/o Wellred Books, PO Box 4244, St. Paul, MN 55104
Youth Law Center [13522], 200 Pine St., Ste. 300, San Francisco, CA 94104, (415)543-3379
Youth Law; Natl. Center for [5700]
Youth Leadership Coun; Natl. [8754]
Youth Leadership; Hugh O'Brian [8748]
Youth League of the Coalition Party [IO], Helsinki, Finland
Youth League; Ukrainian Catholic [★19411]
Youth Liberation Press - Defunct.
Youth Ministry [20235], c/o Lutheran Church-Missouri Synod, 1333 S Kirkwood Rd., St. Louis, MO 63122-7295, (314)965-9000
Youth Ministry; Methodist Coun. on [★20268]
Youth Ministry; Natl. Fed. for Catholic [19688]
Youth Ministry Org; Natl. [★20268]
Youth Ministry; United Methodist Coun. on [★20268]
Youth Ministry, U.S. Catholic Conf. [★12167]
Youth; Mothers of Murdered [11710]
Youth Movement - Bnei Akiva of the U.S. and Canada; Religious Zionist [20178]
Youth Movement; Hashomer Hatzair Socialist Zionist [★20140]
Youth Movement; Hashomer Hatzair Zionist [20140]
Youth Movement; Jewish Defense Org. [17949]
Youth Museums; Amer. Assn. of [★10495]
Youth Museums; Assn. of [★10495]
Youth and Music of Germany [IO], Weikersheim, Germany
Youth; Natl. Commn. on Resources for [★8408]
Youth; Natl. Conf. of Synagogue [20165]
Youth; Natl. Fed. of Parents for Drug-Free [★13270]
Youth; Natl. Network for [12935]
Youth Office, Org. of Amer. States - Defunct.
Youth Org. of Am; Armenian Church [19458]
Youth Org. of the ARF; Armenian Youth Fed. - [18087]
Youth Org; B'nai B'rith [20126]
Youth Org; Hashomer Hatzair Zionist [★20140]
Youth Org; Lubavitch [20158]
Youth Org. on Stamps [★22869]
Youth Org. on Stamps [★IO]
Youth Org; Syrian Orthodox [★19882]
Youth Org; United Methodist [20268]
Youth Organizations; Soc. of Orthodox [★19882]
Youth Organizations U.S.A. [13523]
Youth Policy Inst. [18486], 634 S Spring St., Ste. 818, Los Angeles, CA 90014, (213)688-2802
Youth Power - Address unknown since 2004.
Youth Pride - Defunct.
Youth Proj; Roosevelt Centennial [★13070]
Youth Running Strong; Amer. Indian [12623]
Youth; Secretariat for Family, Laity, Women, and [12167]
Youth Sect; Democratic Socialist Organizing Comm. [★18662]
Youth Ser. Am. [13070], 1101 15th St., Ste. 200, Washington, DC 20005, (202)296-2992
Youth Ser. Policy; Working Gp. on [★13070]
Youth Ser. Projects; Commn. on [★13391]
Youth Services; Natl. Rsrc. Center for [11639]
Youth; Soccer Assn. for [23781]
Youth Soccer Assn; U.S. [23784]
Youth Soccer Org; Amer. [23774]
Youth Soc. for Peace and Development of the Balkans [IO], Plovdiv, Bulgaria
Youth Sports; Natl. Coun. of [23839]
Youth Sports Program [★23353]
Youth Sports Safety Found; Natl. [16484]

Youth and Student Hostel Found. of the Philippines [IO], Paranaque, Philippines
Youth Suicide Natl. Center - Defunct.
Youth Suicide Prevention - Address unknown since 1999.
Youth; Summer Flight Acad. for [★164]
Youth Temperance Coun. [★13306]
Youth Tennis League - Address unknown since 1999.
Youth-to-Youth Sports Comm. Intl. - Defunct.
Youth; United Natl. Indian Tribal [10756]
Youth; United Synagogue [20189]
Youth for Unity and Voluntary Action [IO], Bombay, India
Youth Venture [4072], 1700 N Moore Ave., Ste. 2000, Arlington, VA 22209, (703)527-4126
Youth; Vision Found. for Blind [★15724]
Youth Voluntary Ser. of Italy [IO], Caserta, Italy
Youth With a Mission [20422], PO Box 7206, Ventura, CA 93006, (805)642-5327
Youth World Travel Org. [IO], Kumasi, Ghana
Youth to Youth Intl. [IO], Columbus, OH, United States
Youth to Youth Intl. [13524], 547 E 11th Ave., Columbus, OH 43221, (614)224-4506
YouthBuild USA [13525], 58 Day St., Somerville, MA 02144, (617)623-9900
Youthlink Scotland [IO], Edinburgh, United Kingdom
Youths and Adults; Helen Keller Natl. Center for Deaf-Blind [14760]
Youth's Media Proj; Advocates for [12174]
Yrittajanaisten Keskusliitto [★IO]
Yrjo Kilpinen Soc. of North Am. [IO], Madison, WI, United States
Yrjo Kilpinen Soc. of North Am. [9820], c/o Paul Rowe, PO Box 2092, Madison, WI 53701-2092
Y's Men Intl., U.S. Area [13464], c/o Rob Wilby, 1165 Concord Dr., Haddonfield, NJ 08033-3502
Yugntruf - Youth for Yiddish [10293], 45 E 33rd St., No. 203, New York, NY 10016, (212)889-0381
Yugntruf - Youth for Yiddish [IO], New York, NY, United States
Yugoslav Assn. for the Stud. of Obesity [IO], Belgrade, Serbia
Yugoslav Economic Coun; U.S. [★2292]
Yugoslav Jews in the U.S.A; Assn. of [19175]
Yugoslav MND Assn. [IO], Belgrade, Serbia
Yugoslav Natl. Tourist Office - Defunct.
Yugoslav Press and Cultural Center - Defunct.
Yugoslav Soc. of Automotive Engineers [IO], Belgrade, Serbia
Yugoslav Soc. of Cervical Pathology and Colposcopy [IO], Belgrade, Serbia
Yugoslav Soc. of Plastic, Reconstructive and Aesthetic Surgery [IO], Belgrade, Serbia
Yugoslav Wine Inst. of America - Defunct.
Yugoslavia
   Jugoslavia Study Group [22836]
   Tesla Memorial Soc. [11151]
Yuki Teikei Haiku Soc. [10874], 5135 Cribari Pl., San Jose, CA 95135
Yukon
   Alaska Yukon Pioneers [21251]
   Coun. of Yukon First Nations [IO]
   Yukon Sci. Inst. [IO]
Yukon Conservation Soc. [IO], Whitehorse, YT, Canada
Yukon Historical and Museums Assn. [IO], Whitehorse, YT, Canada
Yukon Pioneers; Alaska [21251]
Yukon Sci. Inst. [IO], Whitehorse, YT, Canada
Yukon Wheelchair Recreation Soc. [IO], Whitehorse, YT, Canada
Yukuhara Haiku Soc., English Language Div. [★10874]
Yves R. Simon Inst. [10841], 3921 Glenview Dr., South Bend, IN 46628, (574)271-1187
YWCA
   Young Women's Christian Association - Puerto Rico [13526]
   Young Women's Christian Assn. of the U.S.A. [13527]
YWCA v Ceske republice [★IO]
YWCA in Czech Republic [IO], Prague, Czech Republic

Reference to "IO" in place of a book number signifies that the association may be found in the 45th edition of International Organizations.

Z

Z Car Club Assn. [21823], 6 Jason Dr., Londonderry, NH 03053, (603)425-2270

Z Series Car Club of Am. [21824], c/o Chuck Krblich, Treas., 1119 SE Third Ave., Fort Lauderdale, FL 33316

Zacherley Fans at Large - Address unknown since 2002.

Zalman Shazar Center for Jewish History [IO], Jerusalem, Israel

Zambia Amateur Athletic Assn. [IO], Lusaka, Zambia

Zambia Amateur Weightlifting Assn. [IO], Kitwe, Zambia

Zambia Assn. of Chambers of Commerce and Indus. [IO], Lusaka, Zambia

Zambia Badminton Assn. [IO], Kitwe, Zambia

Zambia Civic Educ. Assn. [IO], Lusaka, Zambia

Zambia Confed. of Indus. and Chamber of Commerce [★IO]

Zambia Export Growers' Assn. [IO], Lusaka, Zambia

Zambia Lawn Tennis Assn. [IO], Mufulira, Zambia

Zambia Lib. Assn. [IO], Lusaka, Zambia

Zambia Natl. Farmers' Union [IO], Lusaka, Zambia

Zambia Natl. Women's Lobby Gp. [IO], Lusaka, Zambia

Zambia Soc. of Physiotherapy [IO], Lusaka, Zambia

Zambia Softball and Baseball Assn. [IO], Kitwe, Zambia

Zambia Squash Assn. [IO], Ndola, Zambia

Zambia Union of Financial Institutions and Allied Workers [IO], Lusaka, Zambia

Zambia Union of Journalists [IO], Lusaka, Zambia

Zambian Indus. and Commercial Assn. [★IO]

Zane Grey's West Soc. [9728], PO Box 34, Elizabethton, TN 37644-0034, (928)775-8960

Zang Family Org. [21092], c/o Gary P. Zang, CPIM, Chm., 15186 Kelly St., Spring Lake, MI 49456

Zangle Natl. Users' Gp. [7216], c/o John Getchell, Treas., 4653 Majestic Dr., Bellingham, WA 98226

Zarathushtrian Assembly [20510], 1814 Bayless St., Anaheim, CA 92802, (714)520-9577

"Zarevo" Ukrainian Student Assn. - Address unknown since 1995.

Zarrow Families Found. [13197], 401 S Boston Ave., Ste. 900, Tulsa, OK 74103-4012, (918)295-8004

Zartman Assn. of Am. [21093], c/o I. William Zartman, Pres., 713 Quaint Acres, Silver Spring, MD 20904, (301)622-5151

ZCenter - Address unknown since 1994.

Zdruzenie Automobiloveho Priemyslu Slovenskej Republiky [★IO]

Zdruzenie Podnikatel'ov Slovenska [★IO]

Zdruzenie na Stanari na Makedonija [★IO]

Zdruzenie Uzivatelov Bytov Slovenskej Republiky [★IO]

Zdruzenje Kardiologov Slovenije [★IO]

Zdruzenje Multiple Sklerose Slovenije [IO], Ljubljana, Slovenia

Zdruzenje Najemnikov Slovenije [★IO]

Zdruzenje za Tekstilno, Oblacilno in Usnjarsko Predelovalno Industrijo [★IO]

Zdruzenje Univerzitetnih Izobrazenk Slovenije [★IO]

Zebra Finch Club of America; Toledo Bird Assn., [21862]

The Zebras - Address unknown since 2001.

Zebu Assn.; Intl. Miniature [4268]

Zebulun Israel Seafaring Soc. - Address unknown since 1995.

Zeirei Agudath Israel [20200], 42 Broadway, 14th Fl., New York, NY 10004, (212)797-9000

Zeirei Agudath Israel; Young Men's Division- [20199]

Zeiss Historical Soc. of Am. [22133], PO Box 556, Mount Kisco, NY 10549

Zeiss Historical Society of America [IO], Glen Ridge, NJ, United States

Zelena Akcija [★IO]

Zen-do Kai Martial Arts [23619], PO Box 186, Johnstown, NY 12095, (518)762-1589

Zen-do Kai Martial Arts Assn. [★23619]

Zen Inst. of Am; First [19549]

Zen Lotus Soc. [★IO]

Zen Stud. Soc. [19559], c/o New York Zendo Shobo-Ji, 223 E 67th St., New York, NY 10021-6002, (212)861-3333

Zenkoku Nogyo Kyodo Kumiai Rengo-kai [★IO]

Zenska Infoteka [★IO]

Zentralverband der Augenoptiker [★IO]

Zentralverband der Deutschen Schweineproduktion [★IO]

Zentralverband der Deutschen Schweineproduktion e.V. [★IO]

Zentralverband Deutscher Ingenieure [IO], Munich, Germany

Zentralverband Deutsches Kraftfahrzeuggewerbe [★IO]

Zentralverband Elektrotechnik- und Elektronikindustrie [★IO]

Zentralverband Schweizerischer Milchproduzenten [★IO]

Zentrum zur Sozialmedizinischen, Rechtlichen und Kulturellen Betreuung von Auslandern und Auslanderinnen in Osterreich [★IO]

Zephyr Owner's Club; Lincoln [21689]

Zeppelin Collectors Club [22892], PO Box A3843, Chicago, IL 60690-3843

Zero Balancing Assn. [★14834]

Zero Balancing Hea. Assn. [14834], Kings Contrivance Village Ctr., 8640 Guilford Rd., Ste. 240, Columbia, MD 21046, (410)381-8956

Zero Population Growth - Seattle Chap. [★12761]

Zero to Three: Natl. Center for Infants, Toddlers and Families [13944], 2000 M St. NW, Ste. 200, Washington, DC 20036, (202)638-1144

Zero Waste Alliance [5272], One World Trade Ctr., 121 SW Salmon St., Ste. 210, Portland, OR 97204, (503)279-9383

Zero Waste Alliance [IO], Portland, OR, United States

ZESPRI Intl. [IO], Mount Maunganui, New Zealand

Zeta Beta Tau [24670], 3905 Vincennes Rd., Ste. 300, Indianapolis, IN 46268-3057, (317)334-1898

Zeta Beta Tau Fraternity [24489], 3905 Vincennes Rd., Ste. 300, Indianapolis, IN 46268, (317)334-1898

Zeta Chi Phi Multicultural Sorority [24717], PO Box 461583, San Antonio, TX 78246-1583, (210)641-7841

Zeta Phi Beta Sorority [24604], 1734 New Hampshire Ave. NW, Washington, DC 20009, (202)387-3103

Zeta Phi Eta [24434], c/o Joe Arnold, Exec. Dir., 1512 24th Ave., No. 36, Kenosha, WI 53140, (414)881-7381

Zeta Psi [★24671]

Zeta Psi Educational Found. [★24671]

Zeta Psi Found. of Canada [★24671]

Zeta Psi Fraternity of North Am. [24671], 15 S Henry St., Pearl River, NY 10965, (845)735-1847

Zeta Sigma - Defunct.

Zeta Tau Alpha [24700], 3450 Founders Rd., Indianapolis, IN 46268, (317)872-0540

Zetetic Soc. of America and Great Britain; Universal [★7145]

The Zetetics [★7145]

ZHABA Facilitators Collective [IO], Budapest, Hungary

Ziegfeld Club [11054], 593 Park Ave., New York, NY 10021, (212)751-6688

Zimbabwe AIDS Network [IO], Harare, Zimbabwe

Zimbabwe Assn. of Consulting Engineers [IO], Harare, Zimbabwe

Zimbabwe Assn. of Occupational Therapists [IO], Harare, Zimbabwe

Zimbabwe Badminton Assn. [IO], Harare, Zimbabwe

Zimbabwe Baseball and Softball Assn. [IO], Harare, Zimbabwe

Zimbabwe Cong. of Trade Unions [IO], Harare, Zimbabwe

Zimbabwe Girl Guides Assn. [IO], Harare, Zimbabwe

Zimbabwe Hypertension Soc. [IO], Gaborone, Botswana

Zimbabwe Inst. of Engineers [IO], Harare, Zimbabwe

Zimbabwe Medical Assn. [IO], Harare, Zimbabwe

Zimbabwe Music Rights Assn. [IO], Harare, Zimbabwe

Zimbabwe Physiotherapy Assn. [IO], Harare, Zimbabwe

Zimbabwe Sci. Assn. [IO], Harare, Zimbabwe

Zimbabwe Sports Medicine Assn. [IO], Harare, Zimbabwe

Zimbabwe Squash Rackets Assn. [IO], Harare, Zimbabwe

Zimbabwe Stock Exchange [IO], Harare, Zimbabwe

Zimbabwe Taekwondo Assn. [IO], Harare, Zimbabwe

Zimbabwe Tobacco Assn. [IO], Harare, Zimbabwe

Zimbabwe Veterinary Assn. [IO], Harare, Zimbabwe

Zimbabwe Weightlifting Assn. [IO], Harare, Zimbabwe

Zimbabwe Women's Rsrc. Centre and Network [IO], Harare, Zimbabwe

ZimCopy [IO], Harare, Zimbabwe

Zimmer Natl. Fan Club; Norma [24950]

Zimmerman Registry [21825], 2081 Madelaine Ct., Los Altos, CA 94024, (650)967-2908

Zimmerman Registry [IO], Los Altos, CA, United States

Zinc Assn.; Amer. [2699]

Zinc Assn. - Europe; Intl. [IO]

Zinc Inst. - Defunct.

Zinc Producers Comm; Emergency Lead- [★2723]

Zinc Producers Comm; Lead- [★2723]

Zinc Producers; Lead- [★2723]

Zinc Study Group; Intl. Lead and [IO]

Zion; Daughters of [★20139]

Zion Found; Bnai [19177]

Zionic Res. and Development Inst. - Defunct.

Zionism

Amer. Coun. for Judaism [20113]

Amer. Jewish League for Israel [20116]

Amer. Zionist Movement [20118]

AMF Intl. [19988]

Central Rabbinical Cong. of the U.S.A. and Canada [20130]

Hadassah, The Women's Zionist Org. of Am. [20139]

Hashomer Hatzair Zionist Youth Movement [20140]

Jewish Natl. Fund [20150]

Religious Zionist Youth Movement - Bnei Akiva of the U.S. and Canada [20178]

World Confed. of United Zionists [20195]

Young Judaea [20198]

Zionist Org. of Am. [20201]

Zionist Archives and Library of World Zionist Org. - Amer. Sect. - Defunct.

Zionist Comm. for Public Affairs; Amer. [★18050]

Zionist Coun; Amer. [★20118]

Zionist Emergency Coun; Amer. [★20118]

Zionist Fed; Amer. [★20118]

Zionist Fed. of Great Britain and Northern Ireland [IO], London, United Kingdom

Zionist Movement; Amer. [20118]

Zionist Order; Farbard Labor [★19174]

Zionist Org. of Am. [20201], 4 E 34th St., New York, NY 10016, (212)481-1500

Zionist Org. of Am; Pioneer Women/Na'amat, the Women's Labor [★20162]

Zionist Org. of Am; Pioneer Women, The Women's Labor [★20162]

Zionist Org. of Am; Poale Zion - United Labor [★19174]

Zionist Youth; Habonim Dror Labor [★20138]

Zionist Youth; Ichud Habonim Dror Labor [★20138]

Zionist Youth; Ichud Habonim Labor [★20138]

Zionist Youth Movement - Bnei Akiva of the U.S. and Canada; Religious [20178]

Zionist Youth Movement; Hashomer Hatzair [20140]

Zionist Youth Movement; Hashomer Hatzair Socialist [★20140]

Zionist Youth Org; Hashomer Hatzair [★20140]

Zionists of Am; Assn. of Reform [★20122]

Zionists; Fed. of Amer. [★20201]

Zionists; World Confed. of Gen. [★20195]

Zippy Collectors Club - Defunct.

Zirconium Assn. - Defunct.

Zisin Gakkai [★IO]

Zivena Beneficial Soc. - Address unknown since 1995.

ZOA Refugee Care - Netherlands [IO], Apeldoorn, Netherlands

ZOA Vluchtelingenzorg [★IO]

Zonal Electric Comfort Coun. - Defunct.

ZonMw [★IO]

Zonta Clubs; Confed. of [★13071]

Zonta Intl. [IO], Chicago, IL, United States

A star before a book entry number signifies that the name is not listed separately, but is mentioned within the entry.

onta Intl. **[13071]**, 557 W Randolph St., Chicago, IL
60661-2202, (312)930-5848
onta Intl. - District 16 New Zealand **[IO]**, Auckland,
New Zealand
oo Veterinarians; Amer. Assn. of **[16757]**
oo Veterinary Technicians; Assn. of **[16787]**
ooCheck New Zealand **[IO]**, Auckland, New
Zealand
oological Action Comm. - Defunct.
oological Action Program - Defunct.
oological Gardens
Amer. Assn. of Zoo Keepers **[7855]**
Amer. Assn. for Zoological Nomenclature **[7859]**
Aquarium and Zoo Facilities Assn. **[7856]**
Assn. of Zoological Horticulture **[4974]**
Assn. of Zoos and Aquariums **[7857]**
Friends of the Natl. Zoo **[7858]**
Natl. Assn. for Interpretation **[7363]**
oological Parks and Aquariums; Amer. Assn. of
[★7857]
oological Soc. of Ireland **[IO]**, Dublin, Ireland
oological Soc. of Japan **[IO]**, Tokyo, Japan
oological Soc. of London **[IO]**, London, United
Kingdom
oological Soc. of Montreal **[IO]**, Montreal, QC,
Canada
oological Soc; New York **[★4469]**
oological Soc. of Southern Africa **[IO]**, Scottsville,
Republic of South Africa
oologists; Amer. Soc. of **[★7867]**
Zoology
Acarological Soc. of Am. **[7056]**
African Assn. of Zoos and Aquaria **[IO]**
Amer. Assn. of Zoo Keepers **[7855]**
Amer. Assn. of Zoo Veterinarians **[16757]**
Amer. Assn. for Zoological Nomenclature **[7859]**
Amer. Birding Assn. **[7411]**
Amer. Genetic Assn. **[7111]**
Amer. Topical Assn., Biology Unit **[22792]**
Animal Behavior Mgt. Alliance **[7860]**

Animal Behavior Soc. **[7861]**
Aquarium and Zoo Facilities Assn. **[7856]**
Aquatic Animal Life Support Operators **[7279]**
Assn. of British Wild Animal Keepers **[IO]**
Assn. for the Stud. of Animal Behaviour **[IO]**
Assn. of Zoological Horticulture **[4974]**
Assn. of Zoos and Aquariums **[7857]**
Australasian Regional Assn. of Zoological Parks
and Aquaria **[IO]**
Australasian Soc. of Zoo Keeping **[IO]**
Australian Mammal Soc. **[IO]**
British Sect. of Soc. of Protozoologists **[IO]**
Canadian Assn. of Zoos and Aquariums **[IO]**
Canadian Soc. of Zoologists **[IO]**
Center for the Stud. of Natural and Historical
Anomalies **[7862]**
China Zoological Soc. **[IO]**
Coun. of Entomology Dept. Administrators **[7060]**
The Crustacean Soc. **[7863]**
European Assn. for Aquatic Mammals **[IO]**
European Assn. for Zoological Nomenclature **[IO]**
European Assn. of Zoos and Aquaria **[IO]**
Intl. Assn. of Animal Behavior Consultants **[7864]**
Intl. Commn. on Zoological Nomenclature **[IO]**
Intl. Soc. for Anthrozoology **[IO]**
Intl. Soc. of Cryptozoology **[IO]**
Intl. Soc. of Cryptozoology **[7865]**
Intl. Soc. for Human Ethology **[6534]**
Intl. Soc. of Protistologists **[7866]**
Intl. Soc. of Protozoologists **[IO]**
Mammal Soc. **[IO]**
Natl. Found. of Zoological Parks and Aquaria **[IO]**
North Amer. Forensic Entomology Assn. **[7064]**
North of England Zoological Soc. **[IO]**
Royal Zoological Soc. of New South Wales **[IO]**
Royal Zoological Soc. of Scotland **[IO]**
Royal Zoological Soc. of South Australia **[IO]**
Scandinavian Herpetological Soc. **[IO]**
Soc. for Indus. Microbiology **[6599]**
Soc. for Integrative and Comparative Biology
[7867]

Soc. of Nematologists **[7371]**
Soc. of Systematic Biologists **[7868]**
Zoological Soc. of Ireland **[IO]**
Zoological Soc. of Japan **[IO]**
Zoological Soc. of London **[IO]**
Zoological Soc. of Montreal **[IO]**
Zoological Soc. of Southern Africa **[IO]**
Zoology; Soc. of Systematic **[★7868]**
Zora Neale Hurston Soc. **[9729]**, c/o Dolan Hubbard,
Chair, Morgan State Univ., 1700 E Cold Spring Ln.,
Baltimore, MD 21251, (443)885-3435
Zortman Assn. **[★21093]**
ZR-1 Owners Registry - Address unknown since
1999.
Zugzwang! Postal Chess Assn. - Defunct.
Zurcher Handelskammer **[★IO]**
Zurich Chamber of Commerce **[IO]**, Zurich,
Switzerland
Zuzu News **[24777]**, c/o Zuzu Appearances, PO Box
145, Carnation, WA 98014
Zuzu Soc. **[★24777]**
Zvaz celulozo-papierenskeho priemyslu Slovenskej
republiky **[★IO]**
Zvaz Elektrotechnickeho Priemyslu Slovenskej Re-
publiky **[★IO]**
Zvaz polygrafie na Slovensku **[★IO]**
Zvaz Strojarskeho Priemyslu Slovenskej Republiky
[★IO]
Zveza Bibliotekarskih Drustev Slovenije **[★IO]**
Zveza Radioammaterjev Slovenije **[★IO]**
Zwiazek Artystow Scen Polskich **[★IO]**
Zwiazek Biblinjy **[★IO]**
Zwiazek Kompozytorow Polskich **[★IO]**
Zwiazek Kompozytorow Polskich **[★IO]**
Zwiazek Pracodawcow Innowacyjnych Firm Farma-
ceutycznych **[★IO]**
Zwiazek Producentow Audio Video **[★IO]**
ZZ Top Intl. Fan Club, Inc. **[24993]**, PO Box 19744,
Houston, TX 77224-9744, (713)461-9851

Reference to "IO" in place of a book number signifies that the association may be found in the 45th edition of International Organizations.